2019 Washington Manufacturers Register

Published October 2019 next update October 2020

WARNING: Purchasers and users of this directory may not use this directory to compile mailing lists, other marketing aids and other types of data, which are sold or otherwise provided to third parties. Such use is wrongful, illegal and a violation of the federal copyright laws.

CAUTION: Because of the many thousands of establishment listings contained in this directory and the possibilities of both human and mechanical error in processing this information, Mergent Inc. cannot assume liability for the correctness of the listings or information on which they are based. Hence, no information contained in this work should be relied upon in any instance where there is a possibility of any loss or damage as a consequence of any error or omission in this volume.

Publisher

Mergent Inc.
444 Madison Ave
New York, NY 11022

©Mergent Inc All Rights Reserved
2019 Mergent Business Press
ISSN 1080-2614
ISBN 978-1-64141-238-4

TABLE OF CONTENTS

Summary of Contents & Explanatory Notes 4
User's Guide to Listings 6

Geographic Section
County/City Cross-Reference Index 9
Firms Listed by Location City 11

Standard Industrial Classification (SIC) Section
SIC Alphabetical Index 525
SIC Numerical Index 527
Firms Listed by SIC 529

Alphabetic Section
Firms Listed by Firm Name 669

Product Section
Product Index 861
Firms Listed by Product Category 883

SUMMARY OF CONTENTS

Number of Companies.. 15,765
Number of Decision Makers...................................... 25,240
Minimum Number of Employees.. 2

EXPLANATORY NOTES

How to Cross-Reference in This Directory

Sequential Entry Numbers. Each establishment in the Geographic Section is numbered sequentially (G-0000). The number assigned to each establishment is referred to as its "entry number." To make cross-referencing easier, each listing in the Geographic, SIC, Alphabetic and Product Sections includes the establishment's entry number. To facilitate locating an entry in the Geographic Section, the entry numbers for the first listing on the left page and the last listing on the right page are printed at the top of the page next to the city name.

Source Suggestions Welcome

Although all known sources were used to compile this directory, it is possible that companies were inadvertently omitted. Your assistance in calling attention to such omissions would be greatly appreciated. A special form on the facing page will help you in the reporting process.

Analysis

Every effort has been made to contact all firms to verify their information. The one exception to this rule is the annual sales figure, which is considered by many companies to be confidential information. Therefore, estimated sales have been calculated by multiplying the nationwide average sales per employee for the firm's major SIC/NAICS code by the firm's number of employees. Nationwide averages for sales per employee by SIC/NAICS codes are provided by the U.S. Department of Commerce and are updated annually. All sales—sales (est)—have been estimated by this method. The exceptions are parent companies (PA), division headquarters (DH) and headquarter locations (HQ) which may include an actual corporate sales figure—sales (corporate-wide) if available.

Types of Companies

Descriptive and statistical data are included for companies in the entire state. These comprise manufacturers, machine shops, fabricators, assemblers and printers. Also identified are corporate offices in the state.

Employment Data

The employment figure shown in the Geographic Section includes male and female employees and embraces all levels of the company: administrative, clerical, sales and maintenance. This figure is for the facility listed and does not include other plants or offices. It should be recognized that these figures represent an approximate year-round average. These employment figures are broken into codes A through G and used in the Product and SIC Sections to further help you in qualifying a company. Be sure to check the footnotes on the bottom of pages for the code breakdowns.

Standard Industrial Classification (SIC)

The Standard Industrial Classification (SIC) system used in this directory was developed by the federal government for use in classifying establishments by the type of activity they are engaged in. The SIC classifications used in this directory are from the 1987 edition published by the U.S. Government's Office of Management and Budget. The SIC system separates all activities into broad industrial divisions (e.g., manufacturing, mining, retail trade). It further subdivides each division. The range of manufacturing industry classes extends from two-digit codes (major industry group) to four-digit codes (product).

For example:

Industry Breakdown	Code	Industry, Product, etc.
*Major industry group	20	Food and kindred products
Industry group	203	Canned and frozen foods
*Industry	2033	Fruits and vegetables, etc.

*Classifications used in this directory

Only two-digit and four-digit codes are used in this directory.

Arrangement

1. The **Geographic Section** contains complete in-depth corporate data. This section is sorted by cities listed in alphabetical order and companies listed alphabetically within each city. A County/City Index for referencing cities within counties precedes this section.

> IMPORTANT NOTICE: It is a violation of both federal and state law to transmit an unsolicited advertisement to a facsimile machine. Any user of this product that violates such laws may be subject to civil and criminal penalties, which may exceed $500 for each transmission of an unsolicited facsimile. Mergent Inc. provides fax numbers for lawful purposes only and expressly forbids the use of these numbers in any unlawful manner.

2. The **Standard Industrial Classification (SIC) Section** lists companies under approximately 500 four-digit SIC codes. An alphabetical and a numerical index precedes this section. A company can be listed under several codes. The codes are in numerical order with companies listed alphabetically under each code.

3. The **Alphabetic Section** lists all companies with their full physical or mailing addresses and telephone number.

4. The **Product Section** lists companies under unique Harris categories. An index preceding this section lists all product categories in alphabetical order. Companies can be listed under several categories.

USER'S GUIDE TO LISTINGS

GEOGRAPHIC SECTION

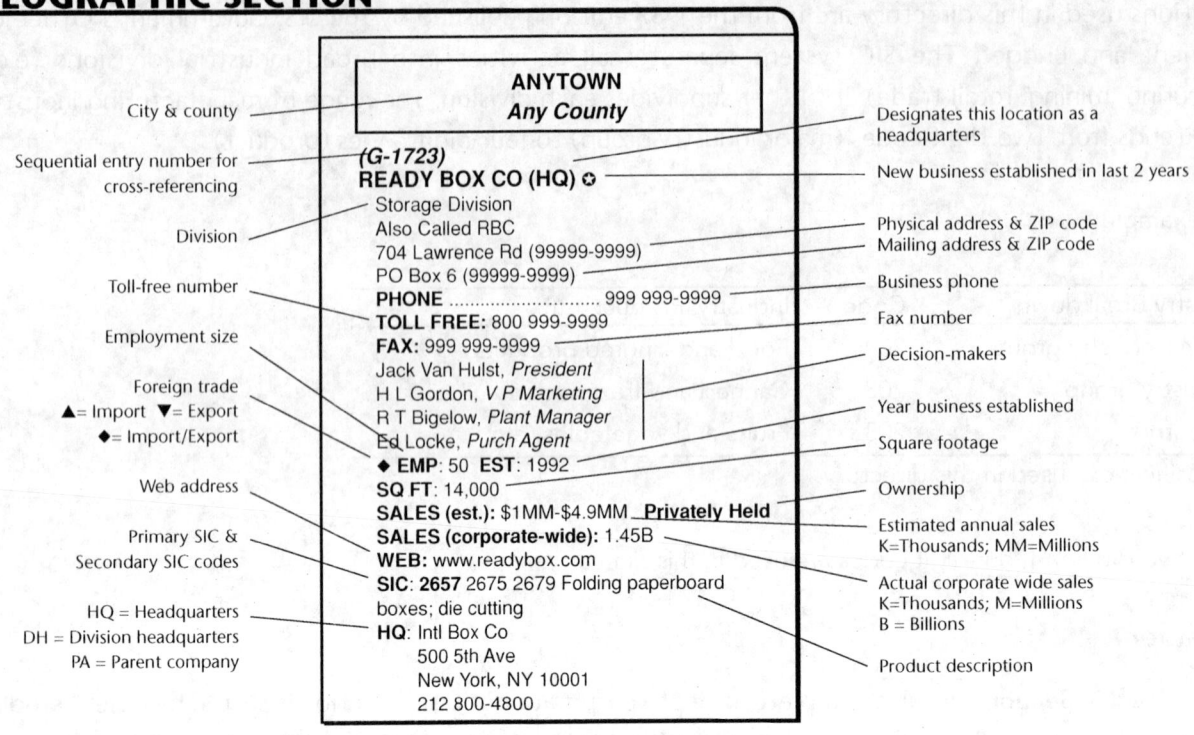

SIC SECTION

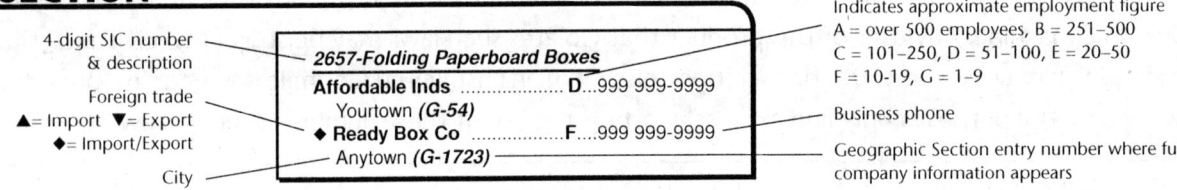

ALPHABETIC SECTION

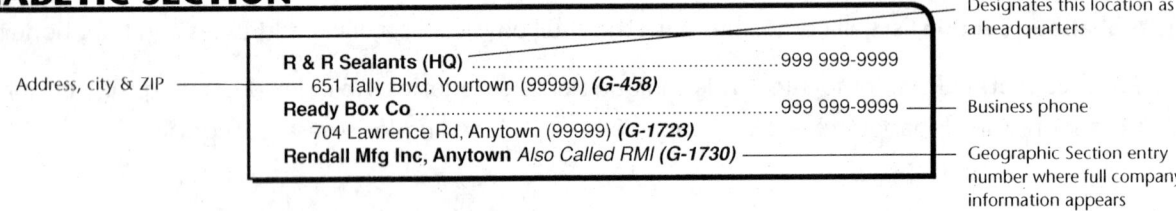

PRODUCT SECTION

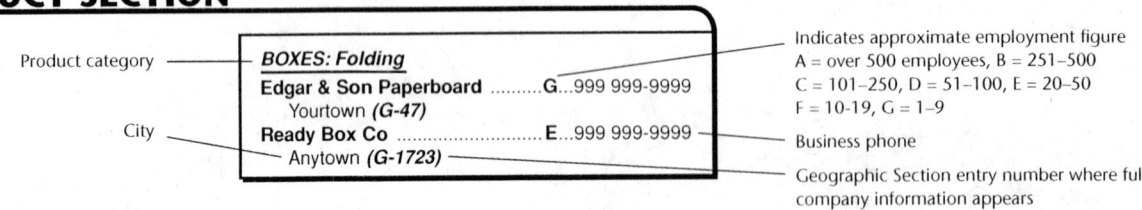

GEOGRAPHIC SECTION
Companies sorted by city in alphabetical order
In-depth company data listed

STANDARD INDUSTRIAL CLASSIFICATIONS
Alphabetical index of classifcation descriptions
Numerical index of classifcation descriptions
Companies sorted by SIC product groupings

ALPHABETIC SECTION
Company listings in alphabetical order

PRODUCT INDEX
Product categories listed in alphabetical order

PRODUCT SECTION
Companies sorted by product and manufacturing service classifications

Washington
County Map

COUNTY/CITY CROSS-REFERENCE INDEX

Adams
Hatton .... (G-4322)
Othello .... (G-7490)
Ritzville .... (G-9121)
Washtucna .... (G-15003)

Asotin
Anatone .... (G-185)
Asotin .... (G-352)
Clarkston .... (G-2619)

Benton
Benton City .... (G-1599)
Kennewick .... (G-4610)
Paterson .... (G-7658)
Prosser .... (G-8028)
Richland .... (G-8962)
West Richland .... (G-15093)

Chelan
Cashmere .... (G-2311)
Chelan .... (G-2545)
Chelan Falls .... (G-2571)
Dryden .... (G-2953)
Entiat .... (G-3267)
Leavenworth .... (G-5793)
Malaga .... (G-6230)
Manson .... (G-6238)
Peshastin .... (G-7662)
Stehekin .... (G-13003)
Wenatchee .... (G-15006)

Clallam
Beaver .... (G-756)
Clallam Bay .... (G-2618)
Forks .... (G-4008)
Port Angeles .... (G-7678)
Sekiu .... (G-11582)
Sequim .... (G-11604)

Clark
Amboy .... (G-89)
Battle Ground .... (G-686)
Brush Prairie .... (G-2027)
Camas .... (G-2227)
La Center .... (G-5502)
Ridgefield .... (G-9058)
Vancouver .... (G-14000)
Washougal .... (G-14939)
Yacolt .... (G-15481)

Columbia
Dayton .... (G-2878)
Starbuck .... (G-13001)

Cowlitz
Castle Rock .... (G-2336)
Kalama .... (G-4491)
Kelso .... (G-4515)
Longview .... (G-5881)
Silverlake .... (G-11861)
Woodland .... (G-15416)

Douglas
East Wenatchee .... (G-3004)
Orondo .... (G-7457)
Rock Island .... (G-9148)
Waterville .... (G-15004)
Wenatchee .... (G-15088)

Ferry
Curlew .... (G-2844)
Inchelium .... (G-4371)
Keller .... (G-4512)
Kettle Falls .... (G-5222)
Malo .... (G-6234)
Republic .... (G-8955)

Franklin
Connell .... (G-2791)
Eltopia .... (G-3261)
Mesa .... (G-6490)
Pasco .... (G-7551)

Garfield
Pomeroy .... (G-7671)

Grant
Coulee City .... (G-2803)
Electric City .... (G-3167)
Ephrata .... (G-3330)
Grand Coulee .... (G-4242)
Marlin .... (G-6308)
Mattawa .... (G-6404)
Moses Lake .... (G-6675)
Quincy .... (G-8288)
Royal City .... (G-9167)
Soap Lake .... (G-12036)
Warden .... (G-14929)

Grays Harbor
Aberdeen .... (G-1)
Amanda Park .... (G-86)
Cosmopolis .... (G-2797)
Elma .... (G-3240)
Grayland .... (G-4292)
Hoquiam .... (G-4327)
Humptulips .... (G-4364)
McCleary .... (G-6415)
Moclips .... (G-6539)
Montesano .... (G-6641)
Oakville .... (G-7174)
Ocean Shores .... (G-7184)
Taholah .... (G-13609)
Westport .... (G-15104)

Island
Camano Island .... (G-2205)
Clinton .... (G-2683)
Coupeville .... (G-2810)
Freeland .... (G-4027)
Greenbank .... (G-4304)
Langley .... (G-5771)
Oak Harbor .... (G-7139)
Stanwood .... (G-12952)

Jefferson
Brinnon .... (G-2023)
Chimacum .... (G-2611)
Nordland .... (G-7088)
Port Hadlock .... (G-7758)
Port Ludlow .... (G-7763)
Port Townsend ...... (G-7858)
Quilcene .... (G-8282)

King
Algona .... (G-66)
Auburn .... (G-354)
Bellevue .... (G-775)
Black Diamond ...... (G-1644)
Bothell .... (G-1744)
Burien .... (G-2087)
Carnation .... (G-2289)
Clyde Hill .... (G-2703)
Covington .... (G-2820)
Des Moines .... (G-2928)
Duvall .... (G-2978)
Enumclaw .... (G-3273)
Fall City .... (G-3698)
Federal Way .... (G-3711)
Hobart .... (G-4323)
Hunts Point .... (G-4366)
Issaquah .... (G-4378)
Kenmore .... (G-4563)
Kent .... (G-4747)
Kirkland .... (G-5267)
Lake Forest Park ... (G-5605)
Maple Valley .... (G-6252)
Medina .... (G-6446)
Mercer Island .... (G-6454)
Newcastle .... (G-7023)
Normandy Park ...... (G-7089)
North Bend .... (G-7101)
Pacific .... (G-7522)
Preston .... (G-8024)
Ravensdale .... (G-8328)
Redmond .... (G-8364)
Renton .... (G-8724)
Sammamish .... (G-9182)
Seatac .... (G-9271)
Seattle .... (G-9314)
Shoreline .... (G-11752)
Skykomish .... (G-11866)
Snoqualmie .... (G-12004)
Tukwila .... (G-13685)
Vashon .... (G-14711)
Woodinville .... (G-15168)
Yarrow Point .... (G-15722)

Kitsap
Bainbridge Island ..... (G-605)
Bremerton .... (G-1934)
Hansville .... (G-4314)
Indianola .... (G-4373)
Keyport .... (G-5244)
Kingston .... (G-5248)
Olalla .... (G-7205)
Port Gamble .... (G-7756)
Port Orchard .... (G-7780)
Poulsbo .... (G-7941)
Seabeck .... (G-9263)
Seattle .... (G-11528)
Silverdale .... (G-11826)
Southworth .... (G-12051)
Suquamish .... (G-13149)

Kittitas
Cle Elum .... (G-2661)
Ellensburg .... (G-3180)
Roslyn .... (G-9156)
Thorp .... (G-13626)

Klickitat
Appleton .... (G-187)
Bickleton .... (G-1632)
Bingen .... (G-1633)
Centerville .... (G-2378)
Dallesport .... (G-2862)
Glenwood .... (G-4178)
Goldendale .... (G-4192)
Husum .... (G-4367)
Lyle .... (G-5994)
Roosevelt .... (G-9153)
Trout Lake .... (G-13679)
White Salmon ...... (G-15109)
Wishram .... (G-15167)

Lewis
Centralia .... (G-2379)
Chehalis .... (G-2456)
Curtis .... (G-2848)
Ethel .... (G-3348)
Mineral .... (G-6538)
Morton .... (G-6667)
Mossyrock .... (G-6759)
Napavine .... (G-7011)
Onalaska .... (G-7446)
Packwood .... (G-7542)
Pe Ell .... (G-7661)
Randle .... (G-8324)
Salkum .... (G-9179)
Silver Creek .... (G-11823)
Toledo .... (G-13634)
Vader .... (G-13986)
Winlock .... (G-15145)

Lincoln
Almira .... (G-85)
Creston .... (G-2842)
Davenport .... (G-2870)
Odessa .... (G-7190)
Sprague .... (G-12948)
Wilbur .... (G-15141)

Mason
Allyn .... (G-80)
Belfair .... (G-759)
Grapeview .... (G-4288)
Hoodsport .... (G-4325)
Lilliwaup .... (G-5870)
Shelton .... (G-11672)
Tahuya .... (G-13610)
Union .... (G-13918)

Okanogan
Brewster .... (G-2015)
Coulee Dam .... (G-2806)
Loomis .... (G-5971)
Malott .... (G-6237)
Mazama .... (G-6414)
Nespelem .... (G-7022)
Okanogan .... (G-7194)
OMAK .... (G-7433)
Oroville .... (G-7461)
Pateros .... (G-7657)
Riverside .... (G-9124)
Tonasket .... (G-13645)
Twisp .... (G-13909)
Winthrop .... (G-15159)

Pacific
Bay Center .... (G-755)
Chinook .... (G-2614)
Ilwaco .... (G-4368)
Long Beach .... (G-5873)
Nahcotta .... (G-7010)
Naselle .... (G-7012)
Ocean Park .... (G-7178)
Raymond .... (G-8341)
Seaview .... (G-11529)
South Bend .... (G-12039)
Tokeland .... (G-13632)

Pend Oreille
Cusick .... (G-2850)
Ione .... (G-4375)
Metaline Falls .... (G-6497)
Newport .... (G-7053)
Usk .... (G-13984)

Pierce
Anderson Island ...... (G-186)
Bonney Lake .... (G-1716)
Buckley .... (G-2044)
Dupont .... (G-2954)
Eatonville .... (G-3049)
Edgewood .... (G-3071)
Fife .... (G-3927)
Fircrest .... (G-4000)
Fox Island .... (G-4018)
Gig Harbor .... (G-4070)
Graham .... (G-4215)
Lake Tapps .... (G-5676)
Lakebay .... (G-5688)
Lakewood .... (G-5692)
Lewis McChord ...... (G-5819)
Longbranch .... (G-5879)
Milton .... (G-6531)
Orting .... (G-7473)
Puyallup .... (G-8117)
Roy .... (G-9157)
Ruston .... (G-9178)
South Prairie .... (G-12050)
Spanaway .... (G-12052)
Steilacoom .... (G-13004)
Sumner .... (G-13053)
Tacoma .... (G-13151)
University Place .. (G-13958)
Vaughn .... (G-14747)
Wilkeson .... (G-15143)

San Juan
Blakely Island .... (G-1715)
Deer Harbor .... (G-2891)
Eastsound .... (G-3036)
Friday Harbor .... (G-4041)
Lopez Island .... (G-5978)
Olga .... (G-7213)
Orcas .... (G-7455)
Shaw Island .... (G-11671)

Skagit
Anacortes .... (G-97)
Bow .... (G-1926)
Burlington .... (G-2138)
Concrete .... (G-2784)
Conway .... (G-2796)
Hamilton .... (G-4312)
La Conner .... (G-5520)
Lyman .... (G-5997)
Marblemount .... (G-6304)
Mount Vernon .... (G-6768)
Rockport .... (G-9152)
Sedro Woolley ..... (G-11530)

COUNTY/CITY CROSS-REFERENCE

Skamania
Carson .... (G-2303)
North Bonneville .... (G-7133)
Stevenson .... (G-13008)

Snohomish
Arlington .... (G-189)
Bothell .... (G-1812)
Brier .... (G-2018)
Darrington .... (G-2866)
Edmonds .... (G-3093)
Everett .... (G-3353)
Gold Bar .... (G-4185)
Granite Falls .... (G-4265)
Index .... (G-4372)
Lake Stevens .... (G-5629)
Lynnwood .... (G-6062)
Marysville .... (G-6309)
Mill Creek .... (G-6502)
Monroe .... (G-6540)
Mountlake Terrace ...... (G-6857)
Mukilteo .... (G-6889)
Quil Ceda Village .... (G-8280)
Snohomish .... (G-11868)
Stanwood .... (G-12959)
Startup .... (G-13002)
Sultan .... (G-13021)
Tulalip .... (G-13840)

Woodway .... (G-15479)

Spokane
Airway Heights .... (G-48)
Chattaroy .... (G-2446)
Cheney .... (G-2572)
Colbert .... (G-2705)
Deer Park .... (G-2892)
Elk .... (G-3169)
Fairchild Afb .... (G-3695)
Fairfield .... (G-3696)
Greenacres .... (G-4295)
Latah .... (G-5790)
Liberty Lake .... (G-5822)
Mead .... (G-6422)
Medical Lake .... (G-6439)
Mica .... (G-6501)
Newman Lake .... (G-7043)
Nine Mile Falls .... (G-7067)
Otis Orchards .... (G-7512)
Rockford .... (G-9151)
Spangle .... (G-12083)
Spokane .... (G-12086)
Spokane Valley .... (G-12596)
Valleyford .... (G-13997)
Veradale .... (G-14748)

Stevens
Addy .... (G-46)
Chewelah .... (G-2597)
Clayton .... (G-2657)
Colville .... (G-2735)
Ford .... (G-4005)
Fruitland .... (G-4065)
Hunters .... (G-4365)
Kettle Falls .... (G-5223)
Loon Lake .... (G-5974)
Northport .... (G-7137)
Rice .... (G-8960)
Springdale .... (G-12950)
Tumtum .... (G-13847)
Valley .... (G-13987)

Thurston
Lacey .... (G-5528)
Olympia .... (G-7221)
Rainier .... (G-8312)
Rochester .... (G-9129)
Tenino .... (G-13612)
Tumwater .... (G-13848)
Yelm .... (G-15724)

Wahkiakum
Cathlamet .... (G-2359)
Skamokawa .... (G-11865)

Walla Walla
Burbank .... (G-2082)
College Place .... (G-2723)
Lowden .... (G-5990)
Prescott .... (G-8023)
Touchet .... (G-13677)
Waitsburg .... (G-14752)
Walla Walla .... (G-14759)
Wallula .... (G-14908)

Whatcom
Acme .... (G-42)
Bellingham .... (G-1236)
Blaine .... (G-1657)
Custer .... (G-2853)
Deming .... (G-2918)
Everson .... (G-3666)
Ferndale .... (G-3807)
Lummi Island .... (G-5993)
Lynden .... (G-5998)
Maple Falls .... (G-6248)
Nooksack .... (G-7086)
Point Roberts .... (G-7667)
Sumas .... (G-13041)

Whitman
Colfax .... (G-2713)
Colton .... (G-2732)

Endicott .... (G-3263)
Garfield .... (G-4066)
Lacrosse .... (G-5604)
Palouse .... (G-7544)
Pullman .... (G-8080)
Rosalia .... (G-9154)
Steptoe .... (G-13007)
Tekoa .... (G-13611)
Uniontown .... (G-13957)

Yakima
Buena .... (G-2081)
Grandview .... (G-4245)
Granger .... (G-4260)
Harrah .... (G-4320)
Mabton .... (G-6228)
Moxee .... (G-6874)
Naches .... (G-6993)
Parker .... (G-7548)
Selah .... (G-11584)
Sunnyside .... (G-13113)
Tieton .... (G-13630)
Toppenish .... (G-13663)
Union Gap .... (G-13919)
Wapato .... (G-14913)
White Swan .... (G-15136)
Yakima .... (G-15495)
Zillah .... (G-15749)

GEOGRAPHIC SECTION

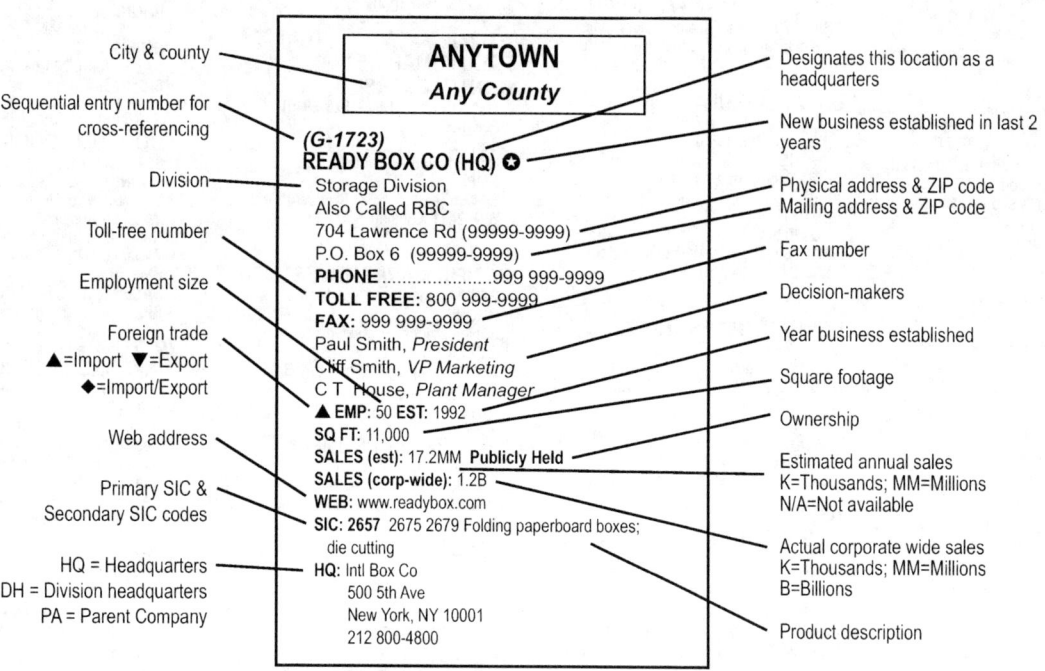

See footnotes for symbols and codes identification.
- This section is in alphabetical order by city.
- Companies are sorted alphabetically under their respective cities.
- To locate cities within a county refer to the County/City Cross Reference Index.

IMPORTANT NOTICE: It is a violation of both federal and state law to transmit an unsolicited advertisement to a facsimile machine. Any user of this product that violates such laws may be subject to civil and criminal penalties which may exceed $500 for each transmission of an unsolicited facsimile. Harris InfoSource provides fax numbers for lawful purposes only and expressly forbids the use of these numbers in any unlawful manner.

Aberdeen
Grays Harbor County

(G-1)
A & B MACHINE & HYDRAULICS
809 E Market St (98520-3431)
PHONE..................360 532-2580
Tim Kuhn, *President*
John Cady, *Admin Sec*
EMP: 15
SQ FT: 6,000
SALES (est): 1.6MM Privately Held
SIC: 3599 7692 Machine shop, jobbing & repair; welding repair

(G-2)
ARRIS KOLLMAN TRUCKING INC (PA)
2421 W 1st St (98520-4567)
PHONE..................360 532-0351
Jesse Kollman, *President*
Arris Kollman, *Shareholder*
EMP: 21 **EST:** 1987
SALES (est): 7.8MM Privately Held
SIC: 1611 1411 Highway & street construction; dimension stone

(G-3)
BARRYS STEVE POOL SERVICE LLC
1604 W Wishkah St (98520-6834)
PHONE..................360 533-0421
Christopher Judd, *Sales Mgr*
Barry Shellgren,
EMP: 5
SALES (est): 324.7K Privately Held
SIC: 3441 3444 Fabricated structural metal; sheet metalwork

(G-4)
BAY CITY SAUSAGE CO INC
2249 State Route 105 (98520-9422)
PHONE..................360 648-2344
Ronda Stroed, *President*
EMP: 3
SALES (est): 180K Privately Held
SIC: 2013 5499 5421 5451 Sausages from purchased meat; spices & herbs; seafood markets; cheese

(G-5)
BAYVIEW REDI MIX INC (PA)
100 Hagara St (98520-3126)
P.O. Box 165 (98520-0044)
PHONE..................360 533-7372
Jack L Prince, *President*
Judy D Prince, *Corp Secy*
Marvin Prince, *Vice Pres*
EMP: 25
SQ FT: 6,000
SALES (est): 4.9MM Privately Held
WEB: www.bayviewredimix.com
SIC: 5211 3273 3272 Sand & gravel; masonry materials & supplies; ready-mixed concrete; precast terrazo or concrete products

(G-6)
BERGSTROM FOUNDRY INC
316 E State St (98520-6613)
PHONE..................360 532-6981
Donald S Little, *President*
Martin Hauso, *Corp Secy*
Bill Newman, *Vice Pres*
EMP: 14 **EST:** 1945
SQ FT: 15,000
SALES: 1.5MM Privately Held
WEB: www.bergstromfoundry.com
SIC: 3369 5051 3366 3365 Nonferrous foundries; metals service centers & offices; copper foundries; aluminum foundries

(G-7)
CLARENCE H SPARGO JR
Also Called: Spargo's Printing
607 W Wishkah St (98520-6031)
P.O. Box 1006 (98520-0207)
PHONE..................360 532-1505
Clarence H Spargo Jr, *Owner*
EMP: 3 **EST:** 1964
SQ FT: 3,920
SALES (est): 22.4K Privately Held
SIC: 2752 2759 Commercial printing, offset; lithographing on metal; letterpress printing

(G-8)
DR DONS FISHFOOD LLC
320 W Market St (98520-6135)
PHONE..................360 533-6620
Don Bell, *Principal*
EMP: 2 **EST:** 2017
SALES (est): 68.6K Privately Held
SIC: 2048 Fish food

(G-9)
DUNSIRE PRINTERS INC
122 W Wishkah St (98520-6233)
P.O. Box 328 (98520-0904)
PHONE..................360 532-8791
Alex M Erwin, *President*
Susan J Erwin, *Corp Secy*
Carol A Dunsire, *Vice Pres*
EMP: 6
SQ FT: 6,500
SALES: 800K Privately Held
SIC: 2752 2741 2759 Commercial printing, offset; art copy: publishing & printing; letterpress printing

(G-10)
EMERY ENTERPRISES
Also Called: Emery's Auto Sales & Service
2004 Westport Rd (98520-6485)
PHONE..................360 532-0102
Amil Emery, *Owner*
EMP: 3
SQ FT: 6,000
SALES: 250K Privately Held
SIC: 5521 5082 2411 Automobiles, used cars only; logging equipment & supplies; logging camps & contractors

(G-11)
FRANKLIN MACHINERY
212 Fairway Dr (98520-7031)
PHONE..................360 581-5079
Bryce Patnode, *Owner*
EMP: 2 **EST:** 1975
SQ FT: 5,000
SALES: 63K Privately Held
SIC: 3559 5084 Degreasing machines, automotive & industrial; industrial machinery & equipment

(G-12)
FURFORD PICKER
283 Newskah Rd (98520-9510)
PHONE..................360 267-3303
EMP: 2 **EST:** 2011
SALES: 80K Privately Held
SIC: 3552 Picker machines, textile

Aberdeen - Grays Harbor County (G-13)   GEOGRAPHIC SECTION

(G-13)
GATEHOUSE MEDIA LLC
Also Called: Daily World
315 S Michigan St (98520-6037)
P.O. Box 269 (98520-0071)
PHONE..................360 532-4000
David Haerle, *Editor*
Emily Evans, *Advt Staff*
Ted Dickson, *Systems Mgr*
EMP: 12
SQ FT: 18,500
SALES (corp-wide): 1.5B **Publicly Held**
WEB: www.fortsmith.com
SIC: 2711 Newspapers, publishing & printing
HQ: Gatehouse Media, Llc
    175 Sullys Trl Fl 3
    Pittsford NY 14534
    585 598-0030

(G-14)
GRAYS HARBOR STAMP WORKS
110 N G St (98520-5226)
PHONE..................360 533-3830
Ronald Windell, *Partner*
David Windell, *Partner*
Kenneth Windell, *Partner*
EMP: 5 **EST:** 1916
SQ FT: 6,370
SALES: 300K **Privately Held**
WEB: www.graysharborstamp.com
SIC: 5947 5999 5099 3953 Novelties; rubber stamps; signs, except electric; marking devices

(G-15)
HARPO INVESTMENT INC
2421 Port Industrial Rd (98520-4566)
P.O. Box 773 (98520-0163)
PHONE..................360 532-5516
Robert Bell, *President*
EMP: 12
SQ FT: 25,000
SALES (est): 1.2MM **Privately Held**
SIC: 2679 Building paper, laminated: made from purchased material

(G-16)
HENSLEYS MOBILE WELDING
35 Frosty Way (98520-9635)
PHONE..................360 532-1633
Wayne Hensley, *Principal*
EMP: 2
SALES (est): 213K **Privately Held**
SIC: 3599 1799 Machine shop, jobbing & repair; special trade contractors

(G-17)
HESCO ARMOR INC
2210 Port Industrial Rd B (98520-4558)
PHONE..................360 580-1146
Stephanie Victory, *President*
Michael Hughes, *Principal*
Ryan Reed, *CTO*
EMP: 35
SALES (est): 1.7MM **Privately Held**
SIC: 3462 Armor plate, forged iron or steel

(G-18)
HESCO ARMOR LLC
2210 Port Industrial Rd B (98520-4558)
PHONE..................360 637-6867
Ryan Reed, *Mng Member*
Courtney Barclay, *Manager*
◆ **EMP:** 20 **EST:** 2012
SQ FT: 15,000
SALES (est): 5.2MM
SALES (corp-wide): 2.6MM **Privately Held**
SIC: 3083 Laminated plastics plate & sheet
HQ: Hesco Group Limited
    Unit 41 Knowsthorpe Way
    Leeds
    113 248-6633

(G-19)
INDUSTRIAL ELECTRIC SERVICE CO
2100 Industrial Rd (98520)
PHONE..................360 533-2792
Ervin Johnson, *President*
Kenneth W Johnson, *President*
Carolyn Johnson, *Corp Secy*
David Johnson, *Vice Pres*
Linda Moling, *Admin Sec*
EMP: 18
SQ FT: 19,000
SALES (est): 3.8MM **Privately Held**
SIC: 7694 5063 Electric motor repair; electrical fittings & construction materials

(G-20)
LOCAL MANUFACTURING INC
2421 Port Industrial Rd (98520-4566)
P.O. Box 1406 (98520-0279)
PHONE..................360 533-0190
Gale Dahlstrom, *President*
Kirk Dahlstrom, *Corp Secy*
EMP: 11
SQ FT: 900
SALES (est): 1.7MM **Privately Held**
SIC: 2421 Chipper mill

(G-21)
LORRAND MARKETING LLC
Also Called: Shirthouse , The
2301 Simpson Ave (98520-3515)
PHONE..................360 532-7510
Randy Beerbower,
EMP: 3
SQ FT: 3,247
SALES (est): 200K **Privately Held**
SIC: 2759 Screen printing

(G-22)
MCKAY & SON
960 Rice St (98520-1163)
PHONE..................360 532-2285
Kenneth McKay, *Partner*
EMP: 2 **EST:** 1963
SALES (est): 141.7K **Privately Held**
SIC: 2411 Logging camps & contractors

(G-23)
MNR LOGGING LLC
6918 Grange Rd (98520-7479)
PHONE..................360 532-3631
Michael Reeves, *Principal*
EMP: 2
SALES (est): 81.7K **Privately Held**
SIC: 2411 Logging

(G-24)
NORTHWEST BELT & EQUIPMENT CO
2011 W 6th St (98520-1109)
P.O. Box 1544 (98520-0267)
PHONE..................360 533-7051
Kevin H Caskey, *President*
Barbara Caskey, *Corp Secy*
EMP: 7
SQ FT: 4,200
SALES (est): 640K **Privately Held**
WEB: www.nwbelt.com
SIC: 3496 5084 Conveyor belts; conveyor systems

(G-25)
NORTHWEST ROCK INC (PA)
642 Newskah Rd (98520-9535)
PHONE..................360 533-3050
Randy Rognlin, *President*
Katie Snodgrass, *Treasurer*
Andrea Moses, *Office Mgr*
Jason Messmer, *Admin Sec*
EMP: 7 **EST:** 1941
SQ FT: 2,000
SALES (est): 8.7MM **Privately Held**
WEB: www.nwrock.com
SIC: 1442 1611 Construction sand mining; gravel mining; general contractor, highway & street construction

(G-26)
OCEAN SPRAY CRANBERRIES INC
1480 State Route 105 (98520-9524)
PHONE..................360 648-2515
John Tieder, *QC Dir*
Rick Hole, *Controller*
Rich Hoel, *Manager*
Scott Stears, *Director*
Francie Hineman, *Executive*
EMP: 72
SALES (corp-wide): 1.6B **Privately Held**
WEB: www.oceanspraycrantastics.com
SIC: 2033 2037 2035 Fruit juices: packaged in cans, jars, etc.; frozen fruits & vegetables; pickles, sauces & salad dressings
PA: Ocean Spray Cranberries, Inc.
    1 Ocean Spray Dr
    Middleboro MA 02349
    508 946-1000

(G-27)
PACIFIC MARINE CONTRACTORS
207 S Chehalis St (98520-2945)
PHONE..................360 532-2765
Steve Ziubak, *CEO*
Ron Hoffman, *President*
EMP: 8
SALES (est): 526.3K **Privately Held**
SIC: 2411 Logging

(G-28)
PACIFIC MARINE INVESTMENTS
2118 Morgan St (98520-4518)
PHONE..................360 532-2765
Steven Dziubak, *President*
EMP: 3
SALES (est): 291K **Privately Held**
SIC: 2411 Logging

(G-29)
PHOENIX SIGN COMPANY
16 Horizon Ln (98520-6900)
P.O. Box 497 (98520-0112)
PHONE..................360 612-3267
Faron Lash, *Owner*
EMP: 11
SALES (est): 1.6MM **Privately Held**
SIC: 3993 Signs & advertising specialties

(G-30)
PLASTICS WEST INC
400 W Curtis St (98520-7619)
P.O. Box 1220, Cosmopolis (98537-1220)
PHONE..................360 538-0115
Curtis Chapin, *President*
Machel Chapin, *Vice Pres*
EMP: 4
SQ FT: 3,000
SALES (est): 290K **Privately Held**
SIC: 3599 Machine shop, jobbing & repair

(G-31)
REED COMPOSITE SOLUTIONS LLC
Also Called: Hesco Armor
2210 Port Industrial Rd B (98520-4558)
PHONE..................360 637-6867
Reed P Ryan, *Administration*
EMP: 3
SALES (est): 203.9K **Privately Held**
SIC: 3089 Plastics products

(G-32)
S MAYTON CONSTRUCTION COMPANY
1417 W Huntley St (98520-6440)
PHONE..................360 532-6138
Susan Mayton, *President*
EMP: 2
SALES (est): 198K **Privately Held**
SIC: 3732 Fishing boats: lobster, crab, oyster, etc.: small

(G-33)
SCHABEN LOGGING INC
5914 Olympic Hwy (98520-8861)
PHONE..................360 589-9008
Kevin Schaben, *Administration*
EMP: 3
SALES (est): 97.7K **Privately Held**
SIC: 2411 Logging

(G-34)
SIERRA PACIFIC INDUSTRIES
Also Called: SPI
301 Hagara St (98520-3105)
PHONE..................360 532-2323
Melvin Hamilton, *Maint Spvr*
Brent Vandiver, *Accountant*
Matt Taborski, *Manager*
EMP: 220
SALES (corp-wide): 1.2B **Privately Held**
WEB: www.sierrapacificind.com
SIC: 2421 Lumber: rough, sawed or planed
PA: Sierra Pacific Industries
    19794 Riverside Ave
    Anderson CA 96007
    530 378-8000

(G-35)
SILVER LAKE PUBLISHING
1119 N Broadway St (98520-2433)
PHONE..................360 532-0308
Jim Walsh, *Owner*
EMP: 5
SALES (est): 241.5K **Privately Held**
SIC: 2731 Book publishing

(G-36)
SKOOKUM LOGGING INC
819 Shamrock Dr (98520-1552)
PHONE..................360 532-2186
Ted Mizin, *President*
William R Applin, *Vice Pres*
Robert L Thorkelsen, *Treasurer*
William C E Wilson, *Admin Sec*
EMP: 10
SALES (est): 550K **Privately Held**
SIC: 2411 Logging camps & contractors

(G-37)
T & D GRUHN TRUCKING INC
6820 Central Park Dr (98520-7465)
PHONE..................360 532-1288
Tom Gruhn, *President*
Debbie Smith, *Vice Pres*
Shirley Gruhn, *Admin Sec*
EMP: 6
SALES (est): 250K **Privately Held**
SIC: 2411 Logging

(G-38)
WASHINGTON TRACTOR INC
Also Called: John Deere Authorized Dealer
5015 Olympic Hwy (98520-6909)
P.O. Box 36 (98520-0039)
PHONE..................360 533-6393
Gary Hampton, *Branch Mgr*
EMP: 46
SALES (corp-wide): 129.6MM **Privately Held**
SIC: 3523 5083 5261 7699 Farm machinery & equipment; farm & garden machinery; lawnmowers & tractors; farm machinery repair; heavy construction equipment rental
PA: Washington Tractor, Incorporated
    2700 136th Avenue Ct E
    Sumner WA 98390
    253 863-4436

(G-39)
WEST COAST SCREEN PRINTING
323 W Market St (98520-6119)
PHONE..................360 581-6466
Christian Burgess, *Principal*
EMP: 2
SALES (est): 94K **Privately Held**
SIC: 5699 2759 Miscellaneous apparel & accessories; screen printing

(G-40)
WESTPORT WINERY INC
1 S Arbor Rd (98520-9519)
PHONE..................360 648-2224
Carrie Roberts, *Principal*
EMP: 11
SALES (est): 1.3MM **Privately Held**
SIC: 2084 Wines

(G-41)
WISHKAH RIVER DISTILLERY LLC
2210 Port Industrial Rd (98520-4558)
PHONE..................360 612-4756
Joshua Mayr, *Mng Member*
EMP: 2
SQ FT: 800
SALES (est): 220K **Privately Held**
SIC: 2085 Distilled & blended liquors

Acme
Whatcom County

(G-42)
FRANK HARKNESS TRCKG & LOG LLC (PA)
5226 Turkington Rd (98220-9600)
P.O. Box 171 (98220-0171)
PHONE..................360 826-6087

Frank Harkness Jr, *Mng Member*
Frank Harkness Sr,
EMP: 18
SQ FT: 4,000
SALES (est): 2MM Privately Held
SIC: 4731 2411 Freight transportation arrangement; logging

(G-43)
JOHN HARKNESS LOGGING
421 Valley Hwy (98220-9702)
PHONE..................................360 595-2260
John Harkness, *Owner*
EMP: 11
SALES (est): 480K Privately Held
SIC: 2411 Logging camps & contractors

(G-44)
SEA CURE TECHNOLOGY INC
1225 Bowman Rd (98220-9611)
PHONE..................................360 676-1824
Timothy Sutherland, *President*
EMP: 5
SALES (est): 592.9K Privately Held
SIC: 5088 3429 3441 Marine supplies; marine hardware; fabricated structural metal

(G-45)
SKAGIT VALLEY SIGNS
1289 Bowman Rd (98220-9611)
PHONE..................................360 755-0356
James Dahl, *Owner*
Kirk Campbell, *Broker*
EMP: 2
SALES (est): 199.9K Privately Held
WEB: www.skagitvalleysigns.com
SIC: 3993 Signs, not made in custom sign painting shops

Addy
Stevens County

(G-46)
NORTHWEST ALLOYS INC
1560a Marble Vly Basin Rd (99101-9687)
P.O. Box 115 (99101-0115)
PHONE..................................509 935-3300
Mark Stiffler, *CEO*
EMP: 3
SALES (est): 359.1K
SALES (corp-wide): 1.7B Privately Held
SIC: 3339 Magnesium refining (primary)
PA: Halco (Mining) Inc.
   323 N Shore Dr
   Pittsburgh PA 15212
   412 235-0265

(G-47)
RICHARDSON LOGGING
2229 Marble Vly Basin Rd (99101-9657)
PHONE..................................509 684-4206
Rex Richardson, *Owner*
Mary Richardson, *Partner*
EMP: 2
SALES (est): 187.9K Privately Held
SIC: 2411 Logging camps & contractors

Airway Heights
Spokane County

(G-48)
AAA CABINETS & MILLWORK INC
11403 W 21st Ave (99001-9702)
PHONE..................................509 484-7152
Tim Stewart, *President*
EMP: 12
SALES (est): 1.7MM Privately Held
SIC: 2521 Wood office filing cabinets & bookcases; cabinets, office: wood

(G-49)
BMT METAL FABRICATION INC
2700 S Hayden Rd (99001-9711)
PHONE..................................509 244-6107
Chris Batt, *President*
EMP: 8
SQ FT: 12,000
SALES (est): 1MM Privately Held
SIC: 3443 3536 3441 Tanks, standard or custom fabricated: metal plate; hoists, cranes & monorails; fabricated structural metal

(G-50)
CONTECH ENGNERED SOLUTIONS LLC
2823 S Craig Rd (99001-8786)
PHONE..................................509 244-3694
Bruce Peterson, *Manager*
EMP: 10 Privately Held
SIC: 3443 Fabricated plate work (boiler shop)
HQ: Contech Engineered Solutions Llc
   9025 Centre Pointe Dr # 400
   West Chester OH 45069
   513 645-7000

(G-51)
EXTREME INDUS COATINGS LLC
11319 W Willow Ln (99001-9756)
PHONE..................................509 991-1773
Jonathan Osborne, *Principal*
EMP: 9 EST: 2008
SALES (est): 1.7MM Privately Held
SIC: 3479 7692 7699 Etching & engraving; welding equipment repair; industrial machinery & equipment repair; agricultural equipment repair services

(G-52)
GARCO BUILDING SYSTEMS INC
2714 S Garfield Rd (99001-9595)
PHONE..................................509 244-5611
C William Savitz, *President*
David Zabinski, *General Mgr*
Paul Millar, *Corp Secy*
John Pargman, *Vice Pres*
Mark Radmaker, *Vice Pres*
EMP: 120
SQ FT: 152,000
SALES (est): 19.7MM Privately Held
SIC: 3448 Buildings, portable: prefabricated metal

(G-53)
GOLDEN HILLS BREWING CO
Also Called: Orlison Brewing Company
12921 W 17th Ave (99001)
PHONE..................................509 389-6253
Bernei Duenwald, *President*
Jim Reiha, *Vice Pres*
EMP: 2
SALES (est): 189.3K Privately Held
SIC: 2041 5084 Corn grits & flakes, for brewers' use; alcoholic beverage making equipment & supplies

(G-54)
KALISPEL TRIBE OF INDIANS
100 N Hayford Rd (99001-9465)
PHONE..................................509 242-7000
Gary Sutter, *Vice Pres*
Robert Collinge, *Purch Mgr*
Lisa Fitzgerald, *Buyer*
Tim Quinn, *Controller*
Tim Rhodes, *Sales Mgr*
EMP: 30 Privately Held
WEB: www.kalispeltribe.com
SIC: 8611 3441 Business associations; fabricated structural metal
PA: Kalispel Indian Community Of The Kalispel Reservation
   1981 Leclerc Rd N
   Cusick WA 99119
   509 445-1147

(G-55)
L & M PRCISION FABRICATION INC
13026 W Mcfarlane Rd D14 (99001-5046)
PHONE..................................509 244-5446
EMP: 25
SQ FT: 20,000
SALES (est): 6MM Privately Held
WEB: www.Lmprecfab.com
SIC: 3599 3444 Machine & other job shop work; forming machine work, sheet metal

(G-56)
METALS FABRICATION COMPANY INC
Also Called: Master Machining & Mfg
2524 S Hayford Rd (99001-9733)
P.O. Box 19266, Spokane (99219-9266)
PHONE..................................509 244-2909
Todd Weaver, *President*
Tim Mathison, *Opers Staff*
Dan Weaver, *Purch Mgr*
Sara Weaver-Lundberg, *Treasurer*
EMP: 55 EST: 1966
SQ FT: 105,000
SALES (est): 17.2MM Privately Held
WEB: www.metalsfab.com
SIC: 3599 3441 3444 Machine shop, jobbing & repair; building components, structural steel; sheet metalwork

(G-57)
NEON PIG LLC ✪
13108 W 6th Ave (99001-5042)
PHONE..................................509 244-5319
Don Mitchell, *Principal*
EMP: 3 EST: 2018
SALES (est): 123.2K Privately Held
SIC: 2813 Neon

(G-58)
OMEGA PACIFIC INC
11427 W 21st Ave (99001-9702)
PHONE..................................509 456-0170
Bert Atwater, *President*
Vince Fiattarone, *Engineer*
▲ **EMP:** 70
SQ FT: 24,000
SALES (est): 5MM Privately Held
WEB: www.omegapac.com
SIC: 3949 Golf equipment

(G-59)
ORLISON BREWING CO
12921 W 17th Ave (99001)
PHONE..................................503 894-2917
EMP: 4 EST: 2014
SALES (est): 236.8K Privately Held
SIC: 2082 Mfg Malt Beverages

(G-60)
PACIFIC MOBILE STRUCTURES INC
10920 W Sunset Hwy (99001-9719)
PHONE..................................509 244-8335
Robin Ray Tapak, *Branch Mgr*
Robin Ray, *Manager*
EMP: 3
SALES (corp-wide): 18.5MM Privately Held
SIC: 2451 1521 Mobile homes, industrial or commercial use; single-family housing construction
PA: Pacific Mobile Structures, Inc.
   1554 Bishop Rd
   Chehalis WA 98532
   360 748-0121

(G-61)
REMCON EQUIPMENT INC
2207 S Lawson St (99001)
P.O. Box 942 (99001-0942)
PHONE..................................509 244-9439
Dennis J Lux, *President*
Linda Lux, *Vice Pres*
▲ **EMP:** 10
SQ FT: 12,000
SALES (est): 1.7MM Privately Held
SIC: 3535 Conveyors & conveying equipment

(G-62)
ROBERTSON-CECO II CORPORATION
Also Called: Garco Building Systems
2714 S Garfield Rd (99001-9595)
PHONE..................................509 244-5611
Frank Fuca, *Manager*
EMP: 100
SALES (corp-wide): 2B Publicly Held
WEB: www.robertsonceco.com
SIC: 3448 2448 Prefabricated metal buildings; wood pallets & skids
HQ: Robertson-Ceco Ii Corporation
   10943 N Sam Huston Pkwy W
   Houston TX 77064

(G-63)
SHREDFAST MOBILE DATA DESTRUCT (PA)
13026 W Mcfarlane Rd (99001-5099)
P.O. Box 1180 (99001-1180)
PHONE..................................509 244-7076
David Rajewski, *President*
Stan Chesney, *General Mgr*
Teresa Rajewski, *Vice Pres*
Karl Ellwood, *Sales Staff*
Jerry Curtis, *Manager*
EMP: 40
SALES (est): 7.9MM Privately Held
WEB: www.shredfast.com
SIC: 3589 Shredders, industrial & commercial

(G-64)
SPOKANE COUNTY RACEWAY
750 N Hayford Rd (99001-5089)
PHONE..................................509 244-3333
Brycen Aaron Eugen Tarr, *Principal*
EMP: 6
SALES (est): 719.9K Privately Held
SIC: 3644 Raceways

(G-65)
SPOKANE GALVANIZING INC
2727 S Garfield Rd (99001)
P.O. Box 879 (99001-0879)
PHONE..................................509 244-4073
Randy Johnson, *President*
Marc Johnson, *Vice Pres*
Dave Lang, *Sales Staff*
EMP: 50
SQ FT: 60,000
SALES (est): 5.6MM Privately Held
WEB: www.spokanegalvanizing.com
SIC: 3479 3471 Galvanizing of iron, steel or end-formed products; plating & polishing

Algona
King County

(G-66)
AJ AEROSPACE
105 Stanley Ct (98001-4438)
PHONE..................................253 335-7775
Harpreet Jassal, *Owner*
EMP: 2
SALES: 500K Privately Held
SIC: 3728 Aircraft parts & equipment

(G-67)
BEHR PROCESS CORPORATION
840 Industry Dr N (98001-4322)
PHONE..................................253 887-8410
Jeffrey D Filley, *Branch Mgr*
EMP: 18
SALES (corp-wide): 8.3B Publicly Held
SIC: 2851 Paints & paint additives
HQ: Behr Process Corporation
   1801 E Saint Andrew Pl
   Santa Ana CA 92705

(G-68)
G E WELDING
402 Milwaukee Blvd S (98001-8515)
PHONE..................................253 653-8869
Gregory Enera, *Principal*
EMP: 2
SALES (est): 159.9K Privately Held
SIC: 7692 Welding repair

(G-69)
GCM NORTH AMERICAN AROSPC LLC
Also Called: Klune Aerospace
701 Milwaukee Ave N (98001-7404)
PHONE..................................253 872-7488
Zach Taylor, *Mng Member*
Ruth A Beyer,
Laura Delvillar,
Kenneth McNew,
EMP: 96

Algona - King County (G-70) — GEOGRAPHIC SECTION

SALES (est): 21.1MM
SALES (corp-wide): 225.3B **Publicly Held**
WEB: www.gcmfg.com
SIC: **3728** 3812 3643 3444 Aircraft assemblies, subassemblies & parts; search & navigation equipment; current-carrying wiring devices; sheet metalwork
HQ: Klune Industries, Inc.
7323 Coldwater Canyon Ave
North Hollywood CA 91605
818 503-8100

(G-70)
GREEN STORE INC
Also Called: Master Garden Products
100 10th Ave N (98001-6522)
PHONE.................253 939-5757
Jason Tan, *President*
◆ EMP: 5
SQ FT: 24,000
SALES (est): 367.9K **Privately Held**
SIC: **2519** Garden furniture, except wood, metal, stone or concrete

(G-71)
HOMECARE PRODUCTS INC (PA)
Also Called: Ez-Access
700 Milwaukee Ave N (98001-7408)
PHONE.................253 249-1108
Don Everard, *CEO*
Glenda Everard, *Owner*
Deanne Sandvold, *Owner*
Lloyd Everard, *Corp Secy*
Judson Branch, *Vice Pres*
▲ EMP: 120
SQ FT: 80,000
SALES (est): 22.5MM **Privately Held**
WEB: www.ezaccess.com
SIC: **3448** 3449 Ramps: prefabricated metal; miscellaneous metalwork

(G-72)
KENNEDY ENDEAVORS INCORPORATED (DH)
Also Called: Tim's Cascade Snacks
1150 Industry Dr N Ste C (98001-6552)
PHONE.................253 833-0255
Robert Gamgort, *President*
Jeff Leichleiter, *General Mgr*
Roger Deromedi, *Chairman*
Anthony Lobue, *Vice Pres*
Lynne Misericordia, *Treasurer*
▼ EMP: 74
SQ FT: 107,000
SALES (est): 11.7MM
SALES (corp-wide): 7.9B **Publicly Held**
SIC: **2096** Potato chips & other potato-based snacks
HQ: Birds Eye Foods, Inc.
121 Woodcrest Rd
Cherry Hill NJ 08003
585 383-1850

(G-73)
PACKAGING CORPORATION AMERICA
Also Called: PCA
501 10th Ave N (98001-6506)
PHONE.................800 223-2307
EMP: 11
SALES (corp-wide): 7B **Publicly Held**
SIC: **2653** Boxes, corrugated: made from purchased materials
PA: Packaging Corporation Of America
1 N Field Ct
Lake Forest IL 60045
847 482-3000

(G-74)
PRIMUS BUMSTEAD MANUFACTURING
4502 B St Nw (98001-1707)
PHONE.................425 688-0444
Larry Caspersen, *Principal*
▲ EMP: 3
SALES (est): 214K **Privately Held**
SIC: **3728** Aircraft parts & equipment

(G-75)
PRIMUS INTERNATIONAL INC
701 Milwaukee Ave N (98001-7404)
PHONE.................253 854-2995
Mike Royston, *Vice Pres*
EMP: 153
SALES (corp-wide): 225.3B **Publicly Held**
SIC: **3728** Aircraft body & wing assemblies & parts
HQ: Primus International Inc
610 Bllvue Way Ne Ste 200
Auburn WA 98001
425 688-0444

(G-76)
PRIMUS INTERNATIONAL INC
701 Milwaukee Ave N (98001-7404)
PHONE.................253 876-1500
Jason Wilder, *Branch Mgr*
EMP: 240
SALES (corp-wide): 225.3B **Publicly Held**
SIC: **3728** 3769 Aircraft body & wing assemblies & parts; guided missile & space vehicle parts & auxiliary equipment
HQ: Primus International Inc
610 Bllvue Way Ne Ste 200
Auburn WA 98001
425 688-0444

(G-77)
STATCODSI PROCESS SYSTEMS
901 Algona Blvd N (98001-6583)
PHONE.................253 249-7539
EMP: 3
SALES (est): 175.2K **Privately Held**
SIC: **3443** Fabricated plate work (boiler shop)

(G-78)
TNT HORSESHOE ART
121 3rd Ave N (98001-4410)
PHONE.................253 334-7653
EMP: 2
SALES (est): 140K **Privately Held**
SIC: **3462** Mfg Iron/Steel Forgings

(G-79)
WILSONART LLC
Also Called: Wilson Art
400 Boundary Blvd (98001-6523)
PHONE.................253 833-0551
Susan Stinnett, *Manager*
EMP: 24
SALES (corp-wide): 14.7B **Publicly Held**
WEB: www.wilsonart.com
SIC: **2821** 2541 Plastics materials & resins; table or counter tops, plastic laminated
HQ: Wilsonart Llc
2501 Wilsonart Dr
Temple TX 76504
254 207-7000

Allyn
Mason County

(G-80)
BAREFOOT BTNIK PBLICATIONS LLC
20 E Westlake Pl (98524-8755)
PHONE.................360 275-0798
EMP: 2
SALES (est): 59.2K **Privately Held**
SIC: **2741** Misc Publishing

(G-81)
BIGFOOT TRADING INC
140 E Olympic Ct (98524-9734)
P.O. Box 1424 (98524-1424)
PHONE.................360 340-7332
Roland Wilson, *President*
Jan Wilson, *Vice Pres*
▲ EMP: 2
SALES (est): 206.5K **Privately Held**
WEB: www.bigfoottrading.com
SIC: **2386** Coats & jackets, leather & sheep-lined

(G-82)
GEORGE KENNY SCHOOL CAINSAW
18351 E State Route 3 (98524-6672)
P.O. Box 1591 (98524-1591)
PHONE.................360 275-9570
George Kenny, *Principal*
EMP: 2
SALES (est): 137K **Privately Held**
SIC: **2499** Carved & turned wood

(G-83)
GRAPEVIEW POINT
81 E Grapeview Point Rd (98524-8765)
PHONE.................360 277-9015
Tom Regan, *Owner*
Susan Regan, *Co-Owner*
EMP: 2
SALES: 75K **Privately Held**
SIC: **3732** Boat building & repairing

(G-84)
ORNAMENTAL STONE INC
101 E North Bay Rd (98524-6706)
P.O. Box 641 (98524-0641)
PHONE.................360 275-4241
Keith Chamberlain, *President*
EMP: 3
SALES: 400K **Privately Held**
WEB: www.ornamentalstone.com
SIC: **3272** 0781 Precast terrazo or concrete products; landscape counseling & planning

Almira
Lincoln County

(G-85)
GATEWAY MILLING LLC
506 N Rail Rd (99103)
PHONE.................509 639-2431
Todd Bodeau, *Mng Member*
Marvin Clinesmith,
Anthony Marino,
Mitch Sorensen,
EMP: 4
SALES (est): 195K **Privately Held**
SIC: **2041** Flour

Amanda Park
Grays Harbor County

(G-86)
ALTA FOREST PRODUCTS LLC
7127 Us Hgwy 101 (98526)
PHONE.................360 288-2234
Leroy Morey, *Branch Mgr*
EMP: 8 **Privately Held**
WEB: www.tubafor.com
SIC: **2421** Sawmills & planing mills, general
HQ: Alta Forest Products Llc
810 Nw Alta Way
Chehalis WA 98532
360 219-0008

(G-87)
AMANDA PARK SERVICES INC
6095 Us Highway 101 (98526-9800)
P.O. Box 660 (98526-0660)
PHONE.................360 288-2230
Tom Sansom, *President*
EMP: 3 EST: 1997
SALES (est): 247K **Privately Held**
SIC: **2411** Logging

(G-88)
QUINAULT WOOD CRAFTS
454 N Shore Rd (98526-9709)
PHONE.................360 288-2848
Steve Rutledge, *Owner*
EMP: 2
SALES (est): 84K **Privately Held**
SIC: **2441** Boxes, wood

Amboy
Clark County

(G-89)
B & B LOGGING INC
43901 Ne Protzman Rd (98601-4640)
PHONE.................360 247-5237
Michael Baker, *President*
Mary Baker, *Admin Sec*
EMP: 2 EST: 1976
SALES (est): 199.1K **Privately Held**
SIC: **2411** 4959 1611 Logging camps & contractors; sanitary services; highway & street construction

(G-90)
CLEAR AND LEVEL LOGGING LLC
24319 Ne 426th St (98601-4515)
P.O. Box 462 (98601-0029)
PHONE.................360 247-5989
EMP: 2 EST: 2016
SALES (est): 81.7K **Privately Held**
SIC: **2411** Logging

(G-91)
ELITE FRAMES INC
16807 Ne Grantham Rd (98601-3149)
PHONE.................360 247-7300
Jason Carpenter, *President*
▲ EMP: 2 EST: 1996
SALES: 250K **Privately Held**
SIC: **3499** 2499 Picture frames, metal; picture & mirror frames, wood

(G-92)
EPI INC
40300 Ne 169th Ave (98601-3617)
P.O. Box 115 (98601-0115)
PHONE.................360 247-5858
John Kane, *President*
EMP: 3 EST: 2012
SALES (est): 355.5K **Privately Held**
SIC: **3812** Aircraft/aerospace flight instruments & guidance systems

(G-93)
ERIDU DESIGNS
17005 Ne Grantham Rd (98601-3203)
PHONE.................360 247-5980
Ed Barthell Jr, *Owner*
EMP: 2 EST: 1998
SALES (est): 103.9K **Privately Held**
SIC: **3441** Fabricated structural metal

(G-94)
G&L HORSE LOGGING
39815 Ne Gerber Mckee Rd (98601-3400)
PHONE.................360 247-5156
EMP: 2
SALES (est): 130K **Privately Held**
SIC: **2411** Logging

(G-95)
MODWRIGHT INSTRUMENTS INC
21919 Ne 399th St (98601-3335)
PHONE.................360 247-6688
Daniel Wright, *President*
▲ EMP: 5
SALES: 500K **Privately Held**
SIC: **3651** Household audio equipment

(G-96)
ROTSCHY TIMBER MANAGEMENT
44013 Ne Protzman Rd (98601-5002)
P.O. Box 89 (98601-0089)
PHONE.................360 247-5396
Michael Rotschy, *Owner*
EMP: 2
SALES (est): 170K **Privately Held**
SIC: **2411** Logging

Anacortes
Skagit County

(G-97)
AIRGAS USA LLC
8581 S Texas Rd (98221-9340)
PHONE.................360 293-6171
Joe Vanvoren, *Manager*
EMP: 6
SALES (corp-wide): 125.9MM **Privately Held**
WEB: www.airliquide.com
SIC: **2813** 5084 3533 4931 Industrial gases; welding machinery & equipment; oil & gas drilling rigs & equipment; electric & other services combined

▲ = Import ▼ = Export
◆ = Import/Export

HQ: Airgas Usa, Llc
259 N Radnor Chester Rd # 100
Radnor PA 19087
610 687-5253

(G-98)
ALPINE WINES
1109 29th St Apt 301 (98221-2778)
PHONE...................................208 354-9463
EMP: 4
SALES (est): 260K **Privately Held**
SIC: 2084 Mfg Wines/Brandy/Spirits

(G-99)
ALYESKA OCEAN INC
2415 T Ave Ste 208 (98221-2887)
PHONE...................................360 293-4677
Jeff Hendricks, *President*
EMP: 48 **EST:** 1980
SQ FT: 6,200
SALES (est): 4MM **Privately Held**
SIC: 8741 2092 Administrative management; fresh or frozen packaged fish

(G-100)
ANACORTES OIL VINEGAR BAR LLC
2802 17th St (98221-1332)
PHONE...................................360 293-6410
John Olsen, *Administration*
EMP: 4 **EST:** 2015
SALES (est): 138.4K **Privately Held**
SIC: 2099 Vinegar

(G-101)
ANACORTES PRINTING
1811 Commercial Ave (98221-2326)
PHONE...................................360 293-2131
Alex Larrimusic, *Owner*
EMP: 6
SALES (est): 523.9K **Privately Held**
WEB: www.anaprint.com
SIC: 2752 Commercial printing, offset

(G-102)
BAYSHORE OFFICE PRODUCTS INC
603 Commercial Ave (98221-1730)
PHONE...................................360 293-4669
Nathan Vanderpool, *President*
Duane Remmenga, *President*
Joshua Remmenga, *Vice Pres*
Doug Vanderpool, *Vice Pres*
Michele Hanson, *Graphic Designe*
EMP: 19
SQ FT: 15,000
SALES (est): 2.9MM **Privately Held**
SIC: 5712 5112 7336 2515 Office furniture; office supplies; commercial art & graphic design; mattresses & foundations

(G-103)
BLUE SEA FISHERIES
12800 Marine Dr (98221-8291)
PHONE...................................360 299-0936
Jordan Berry, *Principal*
EMP: 4 **EST:** 2008
SALES (est): 253.6K **Privately Held**
SIC: 2092 Fresh or frozen packaged fish

(G-104)
BROWN TOES LLC
2020 27th Pl (98221-3864)
P.O. Box 975 (98221-0975)
PHONE...................................360 873-8407
Anthony Young,
EMP: 3
SQ FT: 1,000
SALES (est): 160K **Privately Held**
SIC: 2844 Suntan lotions & oils

(G-105)
BUNNYBUD BOOKS
2308 24th St (98221-2486)
PHONE...................................360 293-4675
David Hall, *Principal*
EMP: 2 **EST:** 2011
SALES (est): 93K **Privately Held**
SIC: 2741 Miscellaneous publishing

(G-106)
C&J OFFSHORE SYSTEMS LLC
9117 Molly Ln Ste 110 (98221-8389)
PHONE...................................360 293-4200
Carrie McCabe,
Joan Ockerman,
EMP: 7
SQ FT: 1,500
SALES: 2MM **Privately Held**
SIC: 3678 Electronic connectors

(G-107)
CANFLEX (USA) INC
412 30th St (98221-2777)
P.O. Box 1014 (98221-1014)
PHONE...................................206 282-8233
Wesley C Udell, *President*
▲ **EMP:** 10
SQ FT: 30,000
SALES (est): 1.7MM **Privately Held**
WEB: www.canflexinc.com
SIC: 3069 Air-supported rubber structures

(G-108)
CANVAS MAN
401 34th St Ste B (98221-4606)
PHONE...................................360 293-2812
Lee Bailey, *Owner*
EMP: 3
SALES (est): 173.3K **Privately Held**
WEB: www.hoodcanvas.com
SIC: 2394 7641 5999 5091 Canvas & related products; upholstery work; canvas products; boat accessories & parts

(G-109)
CAP SANTE INTERNATIONAL INC (PA)
2915 W Ave (98221-5610)
PHONE...................................360 293-3145
Richard Wright, *President*
Shawn Dickson, *Vice Pres*
Clinch Ballew, *Sr Project Mgr*
▲ **EMP:** 20
SALES (est): 3.1MM **Privately Held**
SIC: 3732 Lifeboats, building & repairing

(G-110)
CAP SANTE MARINE LTD (PA)
2915 W Ave (98221-5610)
PHONE...................................360 293-3145
Richard Wright, *President*
Shawn Dickson, *Vice Pres*
Dave Kruse, *Facilities Mgr*
Ken Hargis, *Office Mgr*
John James, *Manager*
EMP: 26
SQ FT: 10,000
SALES (est): 5.7MM **Privately Held**
SIC: 3732 Yachts, building & repairing

(G-111)
CHEMTRADE CHEMICALS US LLC
Also Called: General Chemical
8579 N Texas Rd (98221-8360)
PHONE...................................360 299-1560
Brian J Hanson, *Manager*
EMP: 35
SALES (corp-wide): 1.2B **Privately Held**
SIC: 2819 Sulfuric acid, oleum
HQ: Chemtrade Chemicals Us Llc
90 E Halsey Rd
Parsippany NJ 07054

(G-112)
CHEMTRADE SOLUTIONS LLC
8579 N Texas Rd (98221-8360)
PHONE...................................360 293-2171
Mark Davis, *President*
EMP: 40
SALES (est): 11MM
SALES (corp-wide): 1.2B **Privately Held**
SIC: 2899 Chemical preparations
HQ: Chemtrade Chemicals Us Llc
90 E Halsey Rd
Parsippany NJ 07054

(G-113)
CIRCA 15 FABRIC STUDIO LLC
2117 18th St (98221-2059)
PHONE...................................425 309-9553
Kristen Suzuki, *Administration*
EMP: 2
SALES (est): 90.7K **Privately Held**
SIC: 2211 Broadwoven fabric mills, cotton

(G-114)
CLAM DIGGER
1811 Commercial Ave (98221-2326)
PHONE...................................360 299-3444
Richard Hill, *Owner*
EMP: 7
SALES (est): 430.8K **Privately Held**
WEB: www.clamdigger.com
SIC: 5192 2759 Magazines; commercial printing

(G-115)
CONCORDE MARINE INC
310 34th St (98221-4608)
PHONE...................................360 755-3471
Wendy Lockard, *Admin Asst*
EMP: 4
SALES (est): 192.3K **Privately Held**
SIC: 3732 Motorized boat, building & repairing; yachts, building & repairing

(G-116)
CONTRACTS COMPANY
2201 Highland Dr (98221-3145)
PHONE...................................360 299-9900
Gary Jacobson, *Principal*
EMP: 2
SALES (est): 82.2K **Privately Held**
SIC: 2731 Book publishing

(G-117)
COOKE AQUACULTURE PACIFIC LLC
Also Called: American Gold Seafoods
1201 11th St (98221-1934)
PHONE...................................360 293-9448
Dennis Guhlke, *Branch Mgr*
EMP: 7
SALES (corp-wide): 268.6MM **Privately Held**
SIC: 2092 Shellfish, frozen: prepared
HQ: Cooke Aquaculture Pacific, Llc
4019 21st Ave W Ste 300
Seattle WA 98199

(G-118)
CORTLAND COMPANY INC
Also Called: Puget Sound Rope
1012 2nd St (98221-1552)
PHONE...................................360 293-8488
John Thomas, *CEO*
Randy Longerich, *President*
Randy Arendse, *Maint Spvr*
Jeremy Tissaweerasingh, *Production*
Stephen Breen, *CFO*
◆ **EMP:** 48
SQ FT: 57,000
SALES (est): 7.9MM
SALES (corp-wide): 1.1B **Publicly Held**
WEB: www.psrope.com
SIC: 2298 Rope, except asbestos & wire
PA: Actuant Corporation
N86w12500 Westbrook Xing
Menomonee Falls WI 53051
262 293-1500

(G-119)
DAKOTA CREEK INDUSTRIES INC
820 4th St (98221-1507)
P.O. Box 218 (98221-0218)
PHONE...................................360 293-9575
Richard N Nelson, *President*
Rick Kirschman, *Vice Pres*
Mike Nelson, *Vice Pres*
Nancy Loftis, *Treasurer*
Jim Carver, *Info Tech Mgr*
◆ **EMP:** 600
SQ FT: 6,000
SALES (est): 128.9MM **Privately Held**
WEB: www.dakotacreek.com
SIC: 3732 3731 Boat building & repairing; ferryboats, building & repairing

(G-120)
DECEPTION DISTILLING LLC
9946 Padilla Heights Rd (98221-8695)
PHONE...................................360 588-1000
Harold Roy Christenson, *Administration*
EMP: 4
SALES (est): 210.3K **Privately Held**
SIC: 2085 Distilled & blended liquors

(G-121)
DENMAR INDUSTRIES INC
5314 Sunset Ave (98221-4018)
PHONE...................................206 579-9316
Dennis C Feragen, *Principal*
EMP: 3
SALES (est): 215.7K **Privately Held**
SIC: 3999 Barber & beauty shop equipment

(G-122)
DOUGLASS HEMINGWAY & CO LLC
Also Called: Friends of The Inside Passage
13589 Clayton Ln (98221-8477)
PHONE...................................360 299-0420
Donald C Douglas, *Managing Prtnr*
Reanne Hemingway,
EMP: 2
SQ FT: 3,000
SALES: 120K **Privately Held**
SIC: 2731 Books: publishing only

(G-123)
DRUG INTERV SERVICE AMER
9080 S March Point Rd A4 (98221-8603)
PHONE...................................360 299-2700
Mary Brown-Ybos, *Branch Mgr*
EMP: 2
SALES (corp-wide): 3.6MM **Privately Held**
SIC: 2899
PA: Drug Interv Service Amer
12600 Northborough Dr
Houston TX 77067
281 673-2400

(G-124)
DYNAMIC COATINGS LLC
4113 Kingsway (98221-3217)
P.O. Box 2043 (98221-7043)
PHONE...................................360 755-3649
Aaron Cervantes, *Administration*
EMP: 2
SALES (est): 115.5K **Privately Held**
SIC: 3479 Metal coating & allied service

(G-125)
EAGLE ROCK BOAT REPAIR
1315 Florida Ave (98221-1309)
PHONE...................................360 391-3219
Reinette Farsovitch, *Owner*
Dan Farsovitch, *Owner*
EMP: 2
SALES (est): 150.8K **Privately Held**
SIC: 3732 Boat building & repairing

(G-126)
EQUILON ENTERPRISES LLC
Shell Oil Products U S
8505 S Texas Rd (98221-9340)
P.O. Box 622 (98221-0622)
PHONE...................................360 293-0800
Judith Moorad, *Branch Mgr*
EMP: 360
SALES (corp-wide): 388.3B **Privately Held**
WEB: www.shellus.com
SIC: 2911 Petroleum refining
HQ: Equilon Enterprises Llc
910 Louisiana St Ste 2
Houston TX 77002
713 767-5337

(G-127)
FABRICATION TECHNOLOGIES LLC
Also Called: Fabtek
12729 Quantum Ln Unit 17 (98221-8364)
PHONE...................................360 293-3707
Carri Garrison,
Jerry Garrison,
EMP: 3
SALES (est): 328.7K **Privately Held**
SIC: 3599 3728 3769 3429 Machine shop, jobbing & repair; aircraft parts & equipment; guided missile & space vehicle parts & auxiliary equipment; aircraft hardware; welding repair

(G-128)
FASOLA TOOLS
1405 20th St (98221-3703)
PHONE...................................360 293-9231
Ken Bosworth, *Principal*

Anacortes - Skagit County (G-129)   **GEOGRAPHIC SECTION**

EMP: 2
SALES (est): 101.2K **Privately Held**
SIC: 3999 Manufacturing industries

(G-129)
FELTS SIGNS
8142 S March Point Rd (98221-8683)
PHONE 360 299-0430
EMP: 2 EST: 2009
SALES (est): 137K **Privately Held**
SIC: 3993 Signs & advertising specialties

(G-130)
FINE EDGE
14004 Biz Point Ln (98221-8416)
P.O. Box 726 (98221-0726)
PHONE 360 299-8500
Donald Douglas, *Principal*
EMP: 4
SALES (est): 14.7K **Privately Held**
SIC: 2731 Books: publishing & printing

(G-131)
FOUR-H MACHINE LLC
9056 N Texas Rd (98221-9339)
PHONE 425 471-5757
Chris Hatch,
Jimmy Hatch,
Robert Hatch,
EMP: 10
SQ FT: 10,000
SALES (est): 1.6MM **Privately Held**
SIC: 3599 Machine shop, jobbing & repair

(G-132)
GAES DRAPERIES
5048 Sharpe Rd (98221-8405)
PHONE 360 293-9732
Gae Duntom, *Partner*
Jen Duntom, *Partner*
EMP: 2
SALES: 100K **Privately Held**
WEB: www.gaesdrapery.com
SIC: 2211 5714 5719 Broadwoven fabric mills, cotton; draperies; vertical blinds

(G-133)
H F S-VITEK
301 30th St (98221-5606)
PHONE 360 293-8054
EMP: 3
SALES (est): 160K **Privately Held**
SIC: 3732 4493 Boatbuilding/Repairing Marina Operation

(G-134)
HOOK & LINE FISH
15599 Yokeko Dr (98221-8754)
PHONE 360 293-0503
Jay Gillman, *Partner*
Dawn Gillman, *Partner*
EMP: 4
SALES (est): 289K **Privately Held**
SIC: 3949 Hooks, fishing

(G-135)
INTERNATIONAL WOOD PROCESSORS
2802 17th St (98221-1332)
PHONE 360 299-9996
John Olsen, *Owner*
EMP: 60
SALES (est): 2.3MM **Privately Held**
SIC: 2599 Factory furniture & fixtures

(G-136)
ISLAND ELECTRIC
13574 Tibbles Ln (98221-8234)
PHONE 360 293-9275
John Tibbles, *President*
EMP: 2
SALES (est): 159.6K **Privately Held**
SIC: 3699 1731 Electrical equipment & supplies; electrical work

(G-137)
JASON DUNTON
Also Called: Duntons SEC Systms/Marine Wldg
13784 Redtail Ridge Ln (98221-8431)
PHONE 360 293-7256
Jason Dunton, *Owner*
Tonja Dunton, *Co-Owner*
EMP: 2
SALES: 30K **Privately Held**
SIC: 1799 7692 Welding on site; welding repair

(G-138)
JJS PRODUCTIONS LLC
12729 Quantum Ln Ste 20 (98221-8364)
PHONE 360 630-5294
EMP: 2
SALES (est): 54.1K **Privately Held**
SIC: 0139 3999 7822 ; ; motion picture & tape distribution

(G-139)
KATANA INDUSTRIES INC
12441 Bartholomew Rd (98221-9327)
PHONE 360 293-0682
Justin Rawls, *Principal*
Justin W Rawls, *Principal*
◆ EMP: 2
SALES (est): 108K **Privately Held**
SIC: 3999 Manufacturing industries

(G-140)
LENSWORK PUBLISHING
1101 8th St Ste C (98221-1800)
PHONE 360 588-1343
Brooks Jensen, *Owner*
Maureen Gallagher, *Principal*
EMP: 7 EST: 1993
SQ FT: 4,000
SALES (est): 675K **Privately Held**
WEB: www.lenswork.com
SIC: 2721 Magazines: publishing & printing

(G-141)
LGK INDUSTRIES INC
6646 Ivy St (98221-8263)
PHONE 360 299-3140
Gary King, *President*
EMP: 2
SALES (est): 60K **Privately Held**
SIC: 3999 Manufacturing industries

(G-142)
LITEAIR AVIATION PRODUCTS INC
7001 Palm Ln (98221-8652)
PHONE 360 299-6679
Terry Millard, *President*
EMP: 2
SALES (est): 158.5K **Privately Held**
SIC: 2499 Stoppers & plugs, wood

(G-143)
LONG CONSTRUCTION LLC
13760 Seaview Way (98221-8297)
PHONE 360 202-2664
Chris Long, *Owner*
EMP: 2 EST: 2017
SALES (est): 67K **Privately Held**
SIC: 2361 Girls' & children's dresses, blouses & shirts

(G-144)
LOVRICS SEA CRAFT INC
3022 Oakes Ave (98221-1323)
PHONE 360 293-2042
Florence Lovric, *President*
Bart Lovric, *Vice Pres*
John Lovric, *Vice Pres*
Anton Lovric, *Admin Sec*
EMP: 7
SQ FT: 26,200
SALES: 900K **Privately Held**
SIC: 3731 3732 Commercial cargo ships, building & repairing; boat building & repairing

(G-145)
MARINE WELDING
Also Called: Howard Security System
13784 Redtail Ridge Ln (98221-8431)
P.O. Box 2067, Petersburg AK (99833-2067)
PHONE 360 293-7256
Ken Howard, *Owner*
Laura Howard, *Co-Owner*
EMP: 2
SQ FT: 2,000
SALES: 95K **Privately Held**
SIC: 7692 3443 3442 Welding repair; industrial vessels, tanks & containers; metal doors

(G-146)
MICRO AERODYNAMICS INC
Also Called: Micro Aero Dynamics
4000 Airport Rd Ste D (98221-1171)
PHONE 360 293-8082
Charles White, *Ch of Bd*
Anni Brogan, *President*
EMP: 10
SQ FT: 10,000
SALES (est): 810K **Privately Held**
WEB: www.microaero.com
SIC: 3728 Aircraft parts & equipment

(G-147)
MITERCRAFT INC
5126 Guemes Island Rd (98221-9040)
PHONE 360 299-9979
Julie Flint, *Owner*
Ron Flint, *Co-Owner*
EMP: 7
SALES (est): 165K **Privately Held**
WEB: www.mitercraft.com
SIC: 2499 Kitchen, bathroom & household ware: wood

(G-148)
MOTOVOTANO LLC
12756 Quantum Ln 8-30 (98221-8364)
PHONE 206 363-0338
James J Mackness, *President*
EMP: 5
SALES (est): 493.1K **Privately Held**
SIC: 2393 2064 Tea bags, fabric: made from purchased materials; candy & other confectionery products

(G-149)
MUNKS LIVESTOCK SLING MFG
9578 Marchs Point Rd (98221-9332)
PHONE 360 293-6581
Donald Munks, *President*
Cathy Munks, *Corp Secy*
EMP: 6
SALES (est): 250K **Privately Held**
WEB: www.livestocksling.com
SIC: 3496 Slings, lifting: made from purchased wire

(G-150)
NEON MOON LONGHORNED CATTLE
6099 State Route 20 (98221-8331)
PHONE 360 293-2721
William T Maris, *Principal*
EMP: 2
SALES (est): 152.7K **Privately Held**
SIC: 3993 Signs & advertising specialties

(G-151)
NEXAPPEAL
4060 S Del Mar Dr (98221-8423)
PHONE 360 293-5054
Dianna Dunn, *Owner*
EMP: 2
SALES (est): 105.2K **Privately Held**
SIC: 3961 Costume jewelry

(G-152)
NORTH HARBOR PROPELLER
401 34th St Ste A (98221-4606)
PHONE 360 299-8266
Ron Kruger, *Principal*
▲ EMP: 6
SALES (est): 774.3K **Privately Held**
WEB: www.northharborpropeller.com
SIC: 3366 Propellers

(G-153)
NORTH HBR DIESL YACHT SVC INC
720 30th St (98221-2835)
PHONE 360 293-5551
Howard Bean, *President*
Pamela Bean, *Vice Pres*
▲ EMP: 43
SQ FT: 20,000
SALES (est): 5.2MM **Privately Held**
WEB: www.northharbordiesel.com
SIC: 5551 7699 3732 5088 Marine supplies & equipment; marine engine repair; boat building & repairing; marine propulsion machinery & equipment; engines & parts, diesel

(G-154)
NORTH ISLAND BOAT COMPANY INC
1910 Skyline Way (98221-2952)
PHONE 360 293-2565
Jason Graham, *President*
Mike Roff, *Principal*
Berit Schweiss, *Treasurer*
David Clark, *Manager*
EMP: 19
SALES (est): 1.2MM **Privately Held**
WEB: www.northislandboat.com
SIC: 3732 5088 5551 7699 Yachts, building & repairing; marine crafts & supplies; boat dealers; boat repair; engines & parts, diesel

(G-155)
NORTH STAR EMBROIDERY
718 Commercial Ave (98221-4111)
PHONE 360 588-0530
Joel Kifer, *Owner*
EMP: 3
SALES (est): 169.5K **Privately Held**
SIC: 2395 5699 Embroidery products, except schiffli machine; miscellaneous apparel & accessories

(G-156)
NORTHWEST YACHTS INC
2415 T Ave Ste 207 (98221-2887)
PHONE 360 299-0777
Peter S Whiting, *President*
▲ EMP: 4
SALES (est): 285.9K **Privately Held**
SIC: 3732 4489 5088 5551 Boat building & repairing; excursion boat operators; ships; outboard motors

(G-157)
OLYMPIC PROPELLER COMPANY
8142 S March Point Rd (98221-8683)
PHONE 360 299-8266
Ron Kruger, *Manager*
▲ EMP: 2
SALES (est): 366.2K **Privately Held**
SIC: 3366 Propellers

(G-158)
ORCA INFORMATION COMM SVS
715 Commercial Ave (98221-4110)
PHONE 360 588-1633
John Near,
EMP: 3
SALES (est): 275K **Privately Held**
WEB: www.orcainfo-com.com
SIC: 3669 Visual communication systems

(G-159)
PACIFIC FABRICATING
2900 T Ave Ste E (98221-2889)
PHONE 360 588-1078
Craig Beetle, *Owner*
EMP: 4
SQ FT: 4,200
SALES: 280K **Privately Held**
WEB: www.pacificfab.net
SIC: 3441 Fabricated structural metal

(G-160)
PALFINGER MARINE USA INC
2415 T Ave Ste 204 (98221-2887)
PHONE 360 299-4585
David Jones, *Branch Mgr*
EMP: 5
SALES (corp-wide): 242.1K **Privately Held**
SIC: 3732 Lifeboats, building & repairing; fishing boats: lobster, crab, oyster, etc.: small
HQ: Palfinger Marine Usa Inc
912 Highway 90 E
New Iberia LA 70560
337 365-5451

(G-161)
PIGS & ANGELS INC
Also Called: Donut House
2719 Commercial Ave (98221-2733)
PHONE 360 293-4053
Jana Pisciotta, *President*
Loraine Degroot, *Vice Pres*
EMP: 10

▲ = Import ▼ = Export
◆ = Import/Export

GEOGRAPHIC SECTION

Appleton - Klickitat County (G-188)

SALES (est): 725.2K **Privately Held**
SIC: 2051 Doughnuts, except frozen

(G-162)
PRINS ROBERT P
1213 24th St (98221-2592)
PHONE.................360 293-3101
Robert P Prins, *Principal*
EMP: 2
SALES (est): 114.2K **Privately Held**
SIC: 2752 Commercial printing, lithographic

(G-163)
R&D ENTERPRISES
1618 22nd St (98221-3710)
PHONE.................360 293-4155
Diane Monroe, *Director*
EMP: 2
SALES (est): 95.4K **Privately Held**
SIC: 7699 2221 Boat repair; fiberglass fabrics

(G-164)
SAN JUAN COMPOSITES LLC
Also Called: Sanjuanyachts
2201 Minnesota Ave (98221-4536)
PHONE.................360 299-3790
Donald Campbell,
Randy McCurdy,
▼ EMP: 45
SQ FT: 50,000
SALES (est): 6.5MM **Privately Held**
WEB: www.sanjuan38.com
SIC: 3732 5031 Yachts, building & repairing; composite board products, woodboard

(G-165)
SEABEAR COMPANY (PA)
Also Called: Made In Washington
605 30th St (98221-2884)
PHONE.................360 293-4661
Mike Mondello, *President*
Michael Mondello, *President*
Gordon Harang, *Corp Secy*
Patti Fisher, *Vice Pres*
Dan Jondal, *CFO*
EMP: 50 EST: 1957
SQ FT: 17,000
SALES (est): 20.7MM **Privately Held**
WEB: www.seabear.com
SIC: 5961 5947 2091 Food, mail order; gift items, mail order; catalog sales; gift shop; salmon, smoked

(G-166)
SHARED HEALTHCARE SYSTEMS INC
Also Called: Shs
1601 R Ave (98221-2276)
PHONE.................360 299-4000
Leo Waterson, *President*
Wayne Culmore, *Vice Pres*
EMP: 31
SQ FT: 40,000
SALES (est): 1.7MM **Privately Held**
WEB: www.shs.com
SIC: 7371 7372 Computer software development; prepackaged software

(G-167)
SHIP N SHORE
Also Called: Thomas Designs
4307 Ginnett Rd (98221-8581)
P.O. Box 124 (98221-0124)
PHONE.................360 293-8636
Thomas William Conroy, *Owner*
EMP: 3
SALES: 96K **Privately Held**
SIC: 3841 2511 Surgical & medical instruments; wood household furniture

(G-168)
SIERRA FISHERS I N C
14687 Hoxie Ln (98221-8339)
PHONE.................360 299-1469
▲ EMP: 7
SALES (est): 216.7K **Privately Held**
SIC: 7999 3732 Amusement/Recreation Services Boatbuilding/Repairing

(G-169)
SLOW LORIS INC
7238 Square Harbor Ln (98221-8906)
PHONE.................360 588-0321
EMP: 3
SALES (est): 241.1K **Privately Held**
SIC: 2759 Screen printing

(G-170)
SUGIYO USA INC
3200 T Ave (98221-3496)
P.O. Box 468 (98221-0468)
PHONE.................360 293-0180
Susan Marie, *President*
Susan Mortensen, *Vice Pres*
Brian Porche, *Natl Sales Mgr*
Cora Canaria, *Manager*
▲ EMP: 100
SQ FT: 60,000
SALES (est): 17.4MM **Privately Held**
WEB: www.sugiyo.com
SIC: 2092 Fresh or frozen packaged fish
PA: Sugiyo Co., Ltd.
   10-4-1, Nishimikaimachi
   Nanao ISH 926-0

(G-171)
SUNCATCHERS
2611 Shannon Point Rd (98221-4039)
PHONE.................360 293-6360
Pam Baughn, *Owner*
Jerry Joha, *Co-Owner*
EMP: 2
SALES (est): 104.3K **Privately Held**
SIC: 3452 Screw eyes & hooks

(G-172)
SUNLAND BARK AND TOPSOILS CO
12469 Reservation Rd (98221-9302)
PHONE.................360 293-7188
Edward Little, *President*
Jennifer Little, *Vice Pres*
EMP: 5
SALES (est): 1.2MM **Privately Held**
SIC: 2421 5261 4953 1629 Wood chips, produced at mill; top soil; fertilizer; lawn & garden supplies; recycling, waste materials; land preparation construction; compost

(G-173)
T BAILEY INC
9628 Marchs Point Rd (98221-9333)
PHONE.................360 293-0682
Gene Tanaka, *President*
Darrell Lehman, *COO*
Morris J Israel, *Vice Pres*
Christopher Parker, *Vice Pres*
Justin W Rawls, *Vice Pres*
▲ EMP: 110
SALES (est): 33MM **Privately Held**
WEB: www.tbailey.com
SIC: 3441 Fabricated structural metal

(G-174)
T-SHIRTS BY DESIGN LLC
908 31st St Unit Main (98221-3470)
PHONE.................360 293-8898
Pamela Rene' Myers,
Leslie Richards,
EMP: 3
SQ FT: 1,200
SALES: 100K **Privately Held**
SIC: 2261 Screen printing of cotton broadwoven fabrics

(G-175)
TESORO CORPORATION
10200 S March Point Rd (98221-8662)
P.O. Box 700 (98221-0700)
PHONE.................360 293-9119
Wally Groda, *Manager*
EMP: 29 **Publicly Held**
SIC: 2911 Petroleum refining
HQ: Andeavor Llc
   19100 Ridgewood Pkwy
   San Antonio TX 78259
   210 626-6000

(G-176)
TESORO MARITIME COMPANY
10200 S March Point Rd (98221-8662)
P.O. Box 700 (98221-0700)
PHONE.................360 293-3111
Dean Porter, *Manager*
EMP: 4 **Publicly Held**

HQ: Tesoro Maritime Company
   19100 Ridgewood Pkwy
   San Antonio TX 78259
   832 476-6000

(G-177)
TESORO REFINING & MKTG CO LLC
Also Called: Tesoro Refining and Mktg Co
10200 W March Point Rd (98221)
PHONE.................360 293-9119
Gregory J Goff, *CEO*
Phillip M Anderson, *President*
Keith Casey, *Exec VP*
Kim Rucker, *Exec VP*
Steven Sterin, *CFO*
EMP: 4
SALES (est): 109.8K **Publicly Held**
SIC: 2911 4491 5172 Asphalt or asphaltic materials, made in refineries; marine loading & unloading services; engine fuels & oils
HQ: Andeavor Llc
   19100 Ridgewood Pkwy
   San Antonio TX 78259
   210 626-6000

(G-178)
TRANSPAC MARINAS INC (PA)
702 R Ave (98221-4147)
P.O. Box 1169 (98221-6169)
PHONE.................360 293-8888
David Rytand, *President*
Dennis Hicks, *Regional Mgr*
Daniel Jankelson, *COO*
Kelly D Lafave, *Vice Pres*
▼ EMP: 5
SQ FT: 2,200
SALES (est): 2.3MM **Privately Held**
WEB: www.transpacmarinas.com
SIC: 2499 8711 3441 2491 Floating docks, wood; professional engineer; fabricated structural metal; wood preserving

(G-179)
TRIDENT SEAFOODS CORPORATION
1400 4th St (98221-1532)
P.O. Box 954 (98221-0954)
PHONE.................360 293-7701
Maxine Larsen, *Safety Mgr*
Cathy Schanken, *Human Res Mgr*
Ed Tostenrud, *Manager*
EMP: 125
SALES (corp-wide): 2.3B **Privately Held**
WEB: www.tridentseafoods.com
SIC: 4222 2092 7389 Warehousing, cold storage or refrigerated; fresh or frozen packaged fish; fish broker
PA: Trident Seafoods Corporation
   5303 Shilshole Ave Nw
   Seattle WA 98107
   206 783-3818

(G-180)
TRIDENT SEAFOODS CORPORATION
1400 3rd St (98221)
P.O. Box 954 (98221-0954)
PHONE.................360 293-3133
Pardeep Markanday, *Branch Mgr*
EMP: 264
SALES (corp-wide): 2.3B **Privately Held**
SIC: 2092 Fresh or frozen packaged fish
PA: Trident Seafoods Corporation
   5303 Shilshole Ave Nw
   Seattle WA 98107
   206 783-3818

(G-181)
TWOPOINTOH GARMES LLC
3420 Oakes Ave (98221-1209)
PHONE.................360 836-4266
Mike Hanson,
Heidi Hanson,
Curt Rogers,
Kristin Rogers,
EMP: 4
SALES (est): 139.8K **Privately Held**
SIC: 3944 Board games, puzzles & models, except electronic

(G-182)
UNIPAR WEST INC
619 30th St (98221-2884)
PHONE.................360 293-5332
Robert E Quinn, *President*
Allene Quinn, *Corp Secy*
EMP: 7
SQ FT: 1,600
SALES (est): 838.6K **Privately Held**
SIC: 3599 Machine shop, jobbing & repair

(G-183)
VINTAGE INVESTMENTS INC
3014 Commercial Ave Ste D (98221-2780)
P.O. Box 973 (98221-0973)
PHONE.................360 293-2596
Ron Woolworth, *President*
EMP: 5
SALES (est): 547.6K **Privately Held**
SIC: 2429 6531 6552 1522 Shakes (hand split shingles); real estate agents & managers; subdividers & developers; residential construction; single-family housing construction

(G-184)
WOOD HOUSE CUSTOM CABINETS
3111 T Ave (98221-3495)
PHONE.................360 293-2890
David Curwick, *President*
Michael Larson, *Vice Pres*
EMP: 7
SQ FT: 8,200
SALES: 550K **Privately Held**
SIC: 2434 Wood kitchen cabinets

Anatone
Asotin County

(G-185)
SNAKE RIVER FENCE
21246 Montgomery Ridge Rd (99401-9737)
PHONE.................509 758-7081
EMP: 2
SALES (est): 110K **Privately Held**
SIC: 3446 Mfg Architectural Metalwork

Anderson Island
Pierce County

(G-186)
AMERICAN TOMAHAWK COMPANY LLC
12224 Wapato Rd (98303-9722)
PHONE.................253 884-1940
Andrew Prisco, *Principal*
EMP: 3
SALES (est): 220K **Privately Held**
WEB: www.americantomahawk.com
SIC: 3423 Axes & hatchets

Appleton
Klickitat County

(G-187)
AAA TRUSS
443 Appleton Rd (98602-9798)
P.O. Box 28 (98602-0028)
PHONE.................509 365-2690
Larry M Hart, *Owner*
EMP: 5
SALES (est): 365.7K **Privately Held**
SIC: 2439 Structural wood members

(G-188)
HOG FARM CUSTOM MACHINE
12 Chuckwagon Rd (98602-9702)
PHONE.................509 365-3917
Rick Esaacson, *Partner*
Jose Mendoza, *Partner*
EMP: 2
SALES (est): 231.7K **Privately Held**
WEB: www.hogfarmcycles.com
SIC: 3599 Machine shop, jobbing & repair

Arlington
Snohomish County

(G-189)
A PATH TO AVALON
437 N Olympic Ave Ste B (98223-1299)
PHONE..................................360 403-8884
EMP: 2
SALES (est): 115.2K **Privately Held**
SIC: 3999 Candles

(G-190)
ABEL FLAMESPRAY
22627 121st Dr Ne (98223-6975)
PHONE..................................360 925-6125
Toby P Abel, *Owner*
EMP: 2
SALES: 200K **Privately Held**
SIC: 3479 Hot dip coating of metals or formed products

(G-191)
ABW TECHNOLOGIES INC
6720 191st Pl Ne (98223-4666)
PHONE..................................360 618-4400
James Anderson, *President*
Eric Anderson, *Vice Pres*
Michael Kinsley, *Vice Pres*
Betty Hanley, *CFO*
Mandy Blackwood, *Office Mgr*
EMP: 120
SQ FT: 100,000
SALES (est): 40.4MM **Privately Held**
WEB: www.abwtec.com
SIC: 3441 Fabricated structural metal

(G-192)
ACRO MACHINING INC
3817 168th St Ne (98223-8452)
PHONE..................................360 653-1492
Dan Edmonds, *President*
EMP: 2
SALES (est): 305.8K **Privately Held**
SIC: 3599 Machine shop, jobbing & repair

(G-193)
ACTION SPORTS & LOCKS INC
340 N Olympic Ave (98223-1339)
PHONE..................................360 435-9505
Richard Senff, *CEO*
Karen Senff, *Treasurer*
EMP: 3 EST: 1978
SQ FT: 2,200
SALES: 350K **Privately Held**
SIC: 5661 5699 2284 2759 Footwear, athletic; sports apparel; embroidery thread; screen printing

(G-194)
AEROFAB INDUSTRIES INC
Also Called: Excell Aerofab
19222 62nd Ave Ne (98223-7700)
PHONE..................................360 403-8994
F Allen Hoye, *President*
Sheryl L Hoye, *CFO*
EMP: 27 EST: 1998
SQ FT: 7,500
SALES (est): 4MM **Privately Held**
SIC: 3365 Aerospace castings, aluminum

(G-195)
AEROFORM INC
19421 59th Ave Ne (98223-7718)
PHONE..................................360 403-1919
Roger Kindler, *President*
EMP: 23
SALES (est): 4.2MM **Privately Held**
SIC: 3728 3724 Aircraft parts & equipment; aircraft engines & engine parts

(G-196)
AERONAUTICAL TESTING SERVICE
Also Called: A T S
18820 59th Dr Ne (98223-7833)
PHONE..................................360 363-4276
Paul Robertson, *President*
Kari Robertson, *Admin Sec*
EMP: 7
SQ FT: 5,600
SALES (est): 1.3MM **Privately Held**
WEB: www.aerotestsvc.com
SIC: 3728 3443 8711 4581 Aircraft parts & equipment; wind tunnels; consulting engineer; aircraft servicing & repairing

(G-197)
AEROSPACE DEFENSE INC
17837 59th Ave Ne 11 (98223-6303)
PHONE..................................360 548-8017
Gary Richardson, *President*
Jason Kurtz, *Manager*
EMP: 6
SALES (est): 640K **Privately Held**
SIC: 3728 Aircraft parts & equipment

(G-198)
AIRPORT PRINTS
18109 Champions Dr (98223-5080)
PHONE..................................425 760-2235
Tyler Brunkhorst, *Principal*
EMP: 2
SALES (est): 83.9K **Privately Held**
SIC: 2752 Commercial printing, lithographic

(G-199)
ALPINE PRECISION TOOLING INC
2827 Stanwood Bryant Rd (98223-7320)
PHONE..................................360 474-0547
Wayne Brem, *President*
EMP: 2
SALES: 140K **Privately Held**
SIC: 3089 Injection molding of plastics

(G-200)
ARLINGTON DRY KILNS LLC
19406 68th Dr Ne (98223-7404)
P.O. Box 487, Darrington (98241-0487)
PHONE..................................360 403-3566
Gary Davisson, *Principal*
EMP: 11
SALES (est): 2.1MM **Privately Held**
SIC: 3559 Kilns

(G-201)
ARLINGTON MACHINE & WELDING
20621 67th Ave Ne (98223-4213)
P.O. Box 65 (98223-0065)
PHONE..................................360 435-3300
Scott Taylor, *President*
Marion Taylor, *Owner*
EMP: 8
SQ FT: 8,000
SALES (est): 1.1MM **Privately Held**
SIC: 3599 7692 Machine shop, jobbing & repair; welding repair

(G-202)
ARTECH SINRUD INDUSTRIES INC
20350 71st Ave Ne Ste A (98223-7455)
PHONE..................................360 435-3520
Frances Nelson, *President*
Richard Nelson, *Treasurer*
EMP: 4
SQ FT: 3,200
SALES (est): 540K **Privately Held**
SIC: 3089 Injection molding of plastics

(G-203)
ARTISAN INDUSTRIES INC
19113 63rd Ave Ne Ste 1 (98223-4752)
PHONE..................................360 474-1282
Brad Vardy, *President*
EMP: 10
SALES (est): 1.2MM **Privately Held**
WEB: www.artisanplastics.com
SIC: 3089 Injection molded finished plastic products; injection molding of plastics

(G-204)
ATLAS COPCO COMPRESSORS LLC
18930 66th Ave Ne (98223-8702)
PHONE..................................360 530-2130
EMP: 5
SALES (corp-wide): 10.5B **Privately Held**
SIC: 3563 Air & gas compressors
HQ: Atlas Copco Compressors Llc
300 Technology
Rock Hill SC 29730
866 472-1015

(G-205)
AVIATION COVERS INC
Also Called: Aci
18712 59th Dr Ne (98223-7835)
PHONE..................................360 435-0342
Joang Shaeffer, *President*
EMP: 2
SALES (est): 301.5K **Privately Held**
SIC: 3728 Aircraft parts & equipment

(G-206)
B M G INDUSTRIES
19111 61st Ave Ne Unit 2 (98223-6305)
PHONE..................................425 415-6360
Mike Berg, *Owner*
EMP: 6
SQ FT: 4,800
SALES: 650K **Privately Held**
SIC: 3599 Machine shop, jobbing & repair

(G-207)
BAD DOG DISTILLERY LLC
19109 63rd Ave Ne Ste 1 (98223-4751)
PHONE..................................360 435-3981
Shelly McGlothern, *Manager*
EMP: 6 EST: 2014
SALES (est): 458.7K **Privately Held**
SIC: 2082 Malt beverages

(G-208)
BAIR METAL
13315 103rd Ave Ne (98223-6231)
PHONE..................................425 231-1944
EMP: 2 EST: 2015
SALES (est): 104.7K **Privately Held**
SIC: 3599 Custom machinery

(G-209)
BALLENGER INTERNATIONAL LLC
25326 133rd Ave Ne (98223-8500)
P.O. Box 478, Gunnison CO (81230-0478)
PHONE..................................970 641-9494
Mark Warren, *Vice Pres*
Carol Christenson,
EMP: 2
SALES (est): 164.7K **Privately Held**
SIC: 2399 2448 Aprons, breast (harness); wood pallets & skids; cargo containers, wood

(G-210)
BCB ENTERPRISES LLC
19220 62nd Ave Ne (98223-7700)
PHONE..................................360 435-1047
David Knutsen, *Principal*
EMP: 8
SALES (est): 1.2MM **Privately Held**
SIC: 3721 Aircraft

(G-211)
BENANDRE LLC
19405 68th Dr Ne Ste B (98223-6741)
PHONE..................................425 298-8635
Andrei Babalai, *President*
EMP: 15
SQ FT: 900
SALES (est): 748K **Privately Held**
SIC: 2434 Vanities, bathroom: wood

(G-212)
BENCHMARK BARRELS LLC
1105 Pioneer Hwy E (98223-8339)
PHONE..................................360 652-2594
Ron Sinnema,
Barry Graber,
Ronald Theodore,
EMP: 7
SALES (est): 1MM **Privately Held**
SIC: 2429 Barrels & barrel parts

(G-213)
BESTWORTH - ROMMEL INC
19818 74th Ave Ne (98223-5021)
PHONE..................................360 435-2927
Daniel Rommel, *President*
EMP: 47
SQ FT: 30,000
SALES (est): 18.8MM **Privately Held**
WEB: www.bestworth.com
SIC: 1542 1761 3444 Service station construction; architectural sheet metal work; canopies, sheet metal

(G-214)
BOULDER CREEK INDUSTRIESCOM
31124 Boulder Creek Dr (98223-9231)
PHONE..................................425 879-2322
Jack Cantrell, *Principal*
EMP: 2
SALES (est): 90.8K **Privately Held**
SIC: 3999 Manufacturing industries

(G-215)
BROOKS STEEL FABRICATION
19320 63rd Ave Ne (98223-8783)
PHONE..................................360 403-9400
Don Stoltz, *Principal*
EMP: 2
SALES (est): 195.2K **Privately Held**
SIC: 3312 Blast furnaces & steel mills

(G-216)
BUDDY SHELTERS LLC
Also Called: Buddy Building Systems
17829 59th Ave Ne Unit 13 (98223-6303)
PHONE..................................425 239-8104
Darrel Potter, *Mng Member*
EMP: 2
SALES: 131.5K **Privately Held**
SIC: 1522 3355 2611 Multi-family dwellings, new construction; aluminum rail & structural shapes; pulp produced from wood base

(G-217)
CAMERON STEEL FABRICATION
19320 63rd Ave Ne (98223-8783)
P.O. Box 952, Naches (98937-0952)
PHONE..................................360 403-9400
Janin Cameron, *Owner*
EMP: 10
SALES: 300K **Privately Held**
SIC: 3441 Fabricated structural metal

(G-218)
CEMEX CNSTR MTLS PCF LLC
23605 State Route 9 Ne (98223-8109)
PHONE..................................360 474-0173
Dana Storms, *Manager*
EMP: 2 **Privately Held**
WEB: www.rinkermaterials.com
SIC: 3271 Blocks, concrete or cinder: standard
HQ: Cemex Construction Materials Pacific, Llc
1501 Belvedere Rd
West Palm Beach FL 33406
561 833-5555

(G-219)
CHECKSUM LLC
6120 195th St Ne (98223-7714)
P.O. Box 3279 (98223-3279)
PHONE..................................360 435-5510
John Vanewkirk, *President*
Brian Nelson, *General Mgr*
Paul Norton, *Engineer*
Rachel Van Houten, *Engineer*
Jason Young, *Engineer*
▲ EMP: 30
SQ FT: 4,000
SALES (est): 7.1MM **Privately Held**
WEB: www.checksum.com
SIC: 3679 Electronic circuits

(G-220)
COMMET PRECISION PRODUCTS
15328 State Route 530 Ne (98223-5358)
P.O. Box 2570, Everett (98213-0570)
PHONE..................................360 403-7600
David Kissinger, *President*
Don Huffman, *Vice Pres*
EMP: 5
SALES (est): 75K **Privately Held**
SIC: 3721 Aircraft

(G-221)
COMPOSITE AQUATIC INNOVATIONS
20405 69th Ave Ne (98223-8236)
PHONE..................................360 403-7707
Ron Privrasky, *CEO*
Robert Stark Jr, *President*
▼ EMP: 15
SALES (est): 1.2MM **Privately Held**
SIC: 3229 Glass fiber products

GEOGRAPHIC SECTION
Arlington - Snohomish County (G-251)

(G-222)
COMPRESSED AIR SYSTEMS LLC
19009 61st Ave Ne Unit 5 (98223-4704)
PHONE 425 328-0755
Ed Graf, *Principal*
EMP: 3
SALES (est): 509.3K **Privately Held**
SIC: 3563 Air & gas compressors

(G-223)
COUNTRY SAVE PRODUCTS CORP
19704 60th Ave Ne (98223-4736)
PHONE 360 435-9868
Kris Anderson, *President*
James Brink, *Vice Pres*
EMP: 7
SQ FT: 30,000
SALES (est): 1.2MM **Privately Held**
WEB: www.countrysafe.com
SIC: 2841 2842 Detergents, synthetic organic or inorganic alkaline; dishwashing compounds; bleaches, household: dry or liquid

(G-224)
CUZ CONCRETE PRODUCTS INC (PA)
Also Called: Cuz Septice Service
19604 67th Ave Ne (98223-8769)
PHONE 360 435-5531
Wayne D Zachry, *President*
Aaron Zachry, *Vice Pres*
Brandon Zachery, *Engineer*
Cheryl Cromeenes, *Credit Mgr*
Kelli Kenney, *Manager*
▲ **EMP:** 40
SQ FT: 2,500
SALES (est): 6.1MM **Privately Held**
WEB: www.cuzconcrete.com
SIC: 3272 Septic tanks, concrete

(G-225)
CUZ CONCRETE PRODUCTS INC
19521 63rd Ave Ne (98223-6301)
PHONE 360 435-0769
Rick Mallory, *Branch Mgr*
EMP: 3
SALES (corp-wide): 6.1MM **Privately Held**
SIC: 3272 Precast terrazo or concrete products
PA: Cuz Concrete Products, Inc.
19604 67th Ave Ne
Arlington WA 98223
360 435-5531

(G-226)
D & D CEDAR STAKE
17632 Jordan Rd (98223-7967)
PHONE 360 435-2254
Rick Dills, *Partner*
Kathy Dills, *Co-Owner*
EMP: 2
SALES: 83K **Privately Held**
SIC: 2499 Surveyors' stakes, wood

(G-227)
DEER CREEK CEDAR PRODUCTS INC
22422 State Route 530 Ne (98223-9358)
PHONE 360 435-4707
EMP: 2
SALES (est): 98K **Privately Held**
SIC: 2511 Mfg Wood Household Furniture

(G-228)
DIAMOND CONCRETE PRODUCTS
19405 63rd Ave Ne (98223-7843)
PHONE 360 659-6277
Crystal Burman, *Partner*
Philip Burman, *Partner*
EMP: 5
SALES (est): 490K **Privately Held**
SIC: 3272 Concrete products, precast

(G-229)
DMM INCORPORATED
Also Called: Pioneer Manufacturing
7419 204th St Ne (98223-8204)
P.O. Box 1183, Everett (98206-1183)
PHONE 360 435-5252
EMP: 20 **EST:** 1952
SQ FT: 37,000
SALES (est): 1.9MM **Privately Held**
SIC: 3083 2435 2511 2434 Mfg Lamnatd Plstc Plates Mfg Hrdwd Veneer/Plywood Mfg Wood Household Furn Mfg Wood Kitchen Cabinet

(G-230)
DUNGENESS GEAR WORKS INC
18021 59th Ave Ne (98223-6353)
PHONE 800 548-9743
Lance Nylander, *President*
Flo Fanning, *CFO*
EMP: 35
SQ FT: 6,900
SALES: 3MM **Privately Held**
WEB: www.dungenessgearworks.com
SIC: 3429 3496 5088 Crab traps, steel; miscellaneous fabricated wire products; marine crafts & supplies

(G-231)
EAST VALLEY SAND & GRAVEL INC
5802 Cemetery Rd (98223-7781)
PHONE 360 403-7520
Glen Rengen, *Principal*
EMP: 6
SALES (est): 484.1K **Privately Held**
SIC: 1442 Construction sand & gravel

(G-232)
EAST VALLEY SAND AND GRAVEL
5802 Cemetery Rd (98223-7781)
P.O. Box 3789 (98223-0800)
PHONE 360 403-7520
Penny Gutschmidt, *President*
EMP: 26
SALES: 4.1MM **Privately Held**
WEB: www.pennyleetrucking.com
SIC: 1442 1611 1622 1795 Construction sand & gravel; highway & street construction; general contractor, highway & street construction; bridge, tunnel & elevated highway; wrecking & demolition work; local trucking, without storage; sand & gravel

(G-233)
EDWARD LAURENCE PELANCONI
24216 115th Ave Ne (98223-8560)
PHONE 360 435-2725
Edward L Pelanconi, *Owner*
EMP: 2
SALES: 110K **Privately Held**
SIC: 2411 Logging

(G-234)
ELITE AIRCRAFT DEBURRING
19221 63rd Ave Ne Ste 4 (98223-4708)
PHONE 360 435-2652
Augustine Martinez, *President*
EMP: 5
SALES: 225K **Privately Held**
SIC: 7389 3324 Finishing services; aerospace investment castings, ferrous

(G-235)
FABTEK INDUSTRIES LLC
6011 199th St Ne (98223-6381)
PHONE 360 322-7367
Dan Thomson, *Mng Member*
Dion Colinas,
Matt Nichols,
EMP: 15
SQ FT: 20,000
SALES: 2MM **Privately Held**
SIC: 3089 3442 3731 Fiberglass doors; shutters, door or window: metal; metal doors; military ships, building & repairing; commercial passenger ships, building & repairing

(G-236)
FATHEM LLC
7212 Harrow Pl (98223-4635)
PHONE 360 403-7418
Julia Goodridge, *Principal*
EMP: 2
SALES (est): 162.9K **Privately Held**
SIC: 3669 Communications equipment

(G-237)
FORGED CHAOS LLC
18530 Hawksview Dr (98223-4634)
PHONE 360 630-1947
Gordon Donaldson, *Principal*
EMP: 2
SALES (est): 118.5K **Privately Held**
SIC: 3721 Aircraft

(G-238)
G & M MANUFACTURING INC
19009 61st Ave Ne Unit 2 (98223-4704)
PHONE 206 281-4039
Gary Gaines, *President*
Mark L Gaines, *Vice Pres*
Bob Gaines, *Vice Pres*
Mark Gaines, *Vice Pres*
EMP: 5
SQ FT: 4,800
SALES (est): 570K **Privately Held**
WEB: www.gandm-mfg.com
SIC: 3599 Machine shop, jobbing & repair

(G-239)
GARDEN EXPRESSIONS
22627 State Route 530 Ne (98223-9358)
PHONE 360 403-9532
Steve Bradley, *Owner*
EMP: 2
SQ FT: 2,000
SALES (est): 159.9K **Privately Held**
WEB: www.gardenexpressions.com
SIC: 3499 2499 3423 3366 Novelties & giftware, including trophies; giftware, copper goods; garment hangers, wood; hand & edge tools; copper foundries

(G-240)
GLASAIR AVIATION LLC
18530 59th Dr Ne (98223-3723)
PHONE 360 435-8533
Chris Strachan, *Principal*
EMP: 2 **EST:** 2012
SALES (est): 139.3K **Privately Held**
SIC: 3721 Aircraft

(G-241)
GLASAIR AVIATION USA LLC (HQ)
18530 59th Dr Ne (98223-3723)
PHONE 360 435-8533
Fang Tieji, *CEO*
Ran Fang, *Finance Mgr*
Traci Abbey, *Bookkeeper*
Harry Delong, *Sales Staff*
Mikael W Via, *Mng Member*
▲ **EMP:** 30
SALES (est): 3.5MM
SALES (corp-wide): 3MM **Privately Held**
SIC: 3721 5088 Aircraft; transportation equipment & supplies
PA: Jilin Hanxing Group Co., Ltd.
No.61, Songjiang East Road, Chuanying District
Jilin 13200
432 620-4698

(G-242)
GLO TECH INC
19705 A 60th Ave Ne Ste 3 (98223)
PHONE 360 403-8928
Dave Short, *President*
Louise Short, *Vice Pres*
EMP: 6 **EST:** 1993
SALES: 125K **Privately Held**
WEB: www.glo-techinc.com
SIC: 3911 Jewelry, precious metal

(G-243)
GLOBAL MACHINE WORKS INC
19130 59th Dr Ne (98223-7821)
PHONE 360 403-8432
Bradley Stuczynski, *President*
Brent Barker, *Vice Pres*
EMP: 31
SQ FT: 14,000
SALES (est): 5.8MM **Privately Held**
WEB: www.globalmachineworks.com
SIC: 3599 Machine shop, jobbing & repair

(G-244)
GNR AEROSPACE INC
17723 3rd Ave Ne (98223-5416)
PHONE 360 652-4040
Gayle Roeber, *President*
Richard Roeber, *President*
EMP: 2 **EST:** 2016
SALES (est): 101.3K **Privately Held**
SIC: 3334 3444 Primary aluminum; sheet metal specialties, not stamped

(G-245)
GREENFIRE PRODUCTIONS
17831 59th Ave Ne (98223-6303)
PHONE 360 572-0554
EMP: 2
SALES (est): 230.4K **Privately Held**
SIC: 3999 7822 ; motion picture & tape distribution

(G-246)
HAMPTON AFFILIATES
19406 68th Dr Ne (98223-7404)
PHONE 360 403-8213
Dave Roane, *Manager*
EMP: 2
SALES (est): 86.7K **Privately Held**
SIC: 2421 Sawmills & planing mills, general

(G-247)
HAMPTON LUMBER MILLS INC
19406 68th Dr Ne A (98223-7404)
PHONE 360 474-1504
Jerry Eichner, *Manager*
EMP: 65
SALES (corp-wide): 114.6MM **Privately Held**
SIC: 2421 Lumber: rough, sawed or planed; kiln drying of lumber
PA: Hampton Lumber Mills, Inc.
9600 Sw Barnes Rd Ste 200
Portland OR 97225
503 297-7691

(G-248)
HARD INDUSTRIES HL
7226 Eaglefield Dr (98223-5984)
PHONE 360 913-2063
Harol Rosales, *Principal*
EMP: 2
SALES (est): 84.3K **Privately Held**
SIC: 3999 Manufacturing industries

(G-249)
HARD METAL SOLUTIONS INC
17837 59th Ave Ne 11 (98223-6303)
PHONE 360 548-8017
Andrey Kanarskiy, *President*
Gary Richardson, *Vice Pres*
Kevin Richardson, *Admin Sec*
EMP: 12
SALES (est): 1.2MM **Privately Held**
SIC: 3324 Aerospace investment castings, ferrous

(G-250)
HCI STEEL BUILDINGS LLC
17833 59th Ave Ne Ste C (98223-6451)
PHONE 360 403-4900
Ted Wheeler,
Ewa Wheeler,
EMP: 14
SALES (est): 1.4MM **Privately Held**
SIC: 3312 1541 1791 Structural shapes & pilings, steel; steel building construction; iron work, structural

(G-251)
HEALTH GUARD INDUSTRIES INC
25713 70th Ave Ne (98223-8148)
PHONE 360 474-9298
Becky S Richardson, *President*
Collin R Baston, *Treasurer*
EMP: 2
SQ FT: 4,000
SALES: 100K **Privately Held**
SIC: 3589 Water filters & softeners, household type

Arlington - Snohomish County (G-252) GEOGRAPHIC SECTION

(G-252)
HORIZON MANUFACTURING INDS INC
17925 59th Ave Ne (98223-6352)
PHONE..................................360 322-7368
John Cournoyer, *Principal*
Carleen Pennington, *Office Mgr*
EMP: 13
SQ FT: 10,000
SALES (est): 2.2MM **Privately Held**
WEB: www.horizonman.com
SIC: 3599 Machine shop, jobbing & repair

(G-253)
IFH GROUP WEST LLC
17301 51st Ave Ne (98223-6354)
PHONE..................................844 434-9378
James King, *Mng Member*
EMP: 6 **EST:** 2014
SALES (est): 138.4K **Privately Held**
SIC: 3444 Sheet metalwork

(G-254)
INFINITY FABRICATION INC
19225 62nd Ave Ne (98223-7700)
PHONE..................................360 435-7460
Richard P Roeber, *President*
EMP: 8
SQ FT: 30,000
SALES (est): 1MM **Privately Held**
SIC: 3599 3769 Machine shop, jobbing & repair; guided missile & space vehicle parts & auxiliary equipment

(G-255)
INSKIWRX TOOL & MACHINE LLC
12121 99th Ave Ne (98223-8852)
PHONE..................................425 238-2738
Richard Beginski,
EMP: 2
SALES (est): 68.7K **Privately Held**
SIC: 3569 Filters

(G-256)
INTEGRITY ORTHOTIC LABORATORY
Also Called: Integrity Orthotics
19113 63rd Ave Ne Ste 4 (98223-4752)
PHONE..................................360 435-0703
Peter Deluca, *President*
Mark Grumbine, *Vice Pres*
EMP: 22 **EST:** 2001
SALES: 5.2MM **Privately Held**
WEB: www.integrityortho.com
SIC: 3842 Orthopedic appliances

(G-257)
INTERSTATE ASPHALT PAVING INC
Also Called: Driveways By Interstate Paving
16821 Smokey Point Blvd (98223-8407)
PHONE..................................425 318-5008
Job W Stanley, *Principal*
EMP: 4
SALES (est): 223.7K **Privately Held**
SIC: 2951 Asphalt paving mixtures & blocks

(G-258)
ISLAND WOOD WORKS
6011 199th St Ne (98223-6381)
PHONE..................................360 403-7066
Ron Hundley, *President*
EMP: 2 **EST:** 2011
SALES (est): 162.9K **Privately Held**
SIC: 2431 Millwork

(G-259)
J L BROOKS WELDING INC
19320 63rd Ave Ne (98223-8783)
PHONE..................................360 403-9400
Don Stoltz, *President*
Karin Stoltz, *Vice Pres*
EMP: 14
SQ FT: 14,000
SALES: 5.9MM **Privately Held**
SIC: 3441 Fabricated structural metal

(G-260)
J NEWELL CORPORATION
Also Called: Newell Machine & Repair
6922 204th St Ne (98223-8278)
P.O. Box 477 (98223-0477)
PHONE..................................360 435-8955
Jeff Newell, *President*
▲ **EMP:** 50
SQ FT: 40,000
SALES (est): 7.6MM **Privately Held**
SIC: 3599 Machine shop, jobbing & repair; machine & other job shop work

(G-261)
JACKS NASTY CANDY COMPANY
19221 63rd Ave Ne Ste 1 (98223-4708)
P.O. Box 275 (98223-0275)
PHONE..................................425 418-5282
EMP: 2
SALES (est): 87K **Privately Held**
SIC: 3999

(G-262)
JL DISTRIBUTION LTD (PA)
17631 80th Dr Ne (98223-3740)
PHONE..................................206 743-1148
Pascal Jean-Louise, *President*
Stephanie Jean-Louise, *Admin Sec*
EMP: 2
SQ FT: 300
SALES (est): 150K **Privately Held**
SIC: 3432 Plumbers' brass goods: drain cocks, faucets, spigots, etc.

(G-263)
JOSEPH S HEAGNEY
Also Called: Microfoils Co.
1213 278th St Ne (98223-7041)
PHONE..................................360 631-2982
Joseph Heagney, *Owner*
Joanne Heagney, *Principal*
EMP: 2
SALES (est): 88.9K **Privately Held**
SIC: 3089 Plastic containers, except foam

(G-264)
KENT ENTERPRISES
222 N Gifford Ave (98223-1410)
PHONE..................................360 403-0242
EMP: 2 **EST:** 2010
SALES (est): 130K **Privately Held**
SIC: 3699 Mfg Electrical Equipment/Supplies

(G-265)
KETCHUM METAL POLISHING
216 E 2nd St Ste A (98223-1302)
PHONE..................................360 403-8726
Robert Ketchum, *Owner*
EMP: 2
SALES (est): 178.4K **Privately Held**
SIC: 3471 Polishing, metals or formed products

(G-266)
KGR CORPORATION
Also Called: Metal Motion
19003 59th Dr Ne (98223-7832)
PHONE..................................360 403-7330
Rob Kirkland, *President*
EMP: 5
SALES (corp-wide): 515.2K **Privately Held**
SIC: 3812 Acceleration indicators & systems components, aerospace
PA: Kgr Corporation
  8525 120th Ave Ne Ste 300
  Kirkland WA
  360 403-7330

(G-267)
KIT PLANES NORTHWEST
2359 E Mores Trail Dr (98223)
PHONE..................................360 403-0679
Brian Rossi, *President*
EMP: 5
SALES (est): 37K **Privately Held**
WEB: www.kitplanesnorthwest.com
SIC: 3721 Aircraft

(G-268)
KLEIN JOANNE KLEIN KEVIN
2121 236th St Ne (98223-7206)
PHONE..................................360 435-8615
Joanne Lynn Klein, *Owner*
Kevin Klein, *Co-Owner*
EMP: 2
SALES (est): 92.4K **Privately Held**
SIC: 3999 5947 Artificial flower arrangements; gift shop

(G-269)
KLM CUSTOM SASH LLC
19011 62nd Ave Ne Unit 1 (98223-4731)
PHONE..................................360 403-7400
Kurt Miller, *Mng Member*
Lisa Miller,
▲ **EMP:** 3
SALES (est): 350K **Privately Held**
SIC: 2431 Millwork

(G-270)
KLW MANUFACTURING & DESIGN INC
Also Called: Klw Nameplate
17739 59th Ave Ne (98223-6446)
PHONE..................................360 435-6288
Larry Weber, *President*
Paul Bartley, *Vice Pres*
EMP: 19
SQ FT: 15,000
SALES (est): 3MM **Privately Held**
SIC: 3444 Sheet metalwork

(G-271)
MACKENZIE SPCALTY CASTINGS INC
Also Called: Foundry
19430 63rd Ave Ne (98223-7843)
P.O. Box 219 (98223-0219)
PHONE..................................360 435-5539
Tony Cooper, *President*
Carol Cooper, *Corp Secy*
EMP: 32
SQ FT: 36,000
SALES (est): 7MM **Privately Held**
WEB: www.mackenziecastings.com
SIC: 3321 3325 3914 3369 Gray iron castings; ductile iron castings; steel foundries; stainless steel ware; nonferrous foundries

(G-272)
MAILBOXES DEPOT
Also Called: Mailbox Depot
3405 172nd St Ne Ste 5 (98223-7717)
PHONE..................................360 651-2651
Billy Hyung, *Owner*
EMP: 2
SALES (est): 145.2K **Privately Held**
SIC: 3444 Mail (post office) collection or storage boxes, sheet metal

(G-273)
MANY ENDEAVORS INCORPORATED
232 158th St Nw (98223-5465)
PHONE..................................360 652-1854
Mark Brower, *Principal*
EMP: 2
SALES (est): 121.3K **Privately Held**
SIC: 2499 Wood products

(G-274)
METAL FINISHING INC
18640 59th Dr Ne (98223-7836)
PHONE..................................360 659-1971
Brian Lowe, *President*
Deanna McClung, *Office Mgr*
EMP: 17
SALES: 950K **Privately Held**
WEB: www.metalfinishing.com
SIC: 3471 3479 2851 Finishing, metals or formed products; coating of metals & formed products; paints & allied products

(G-275)
MICHAEL H WOLD COMPANY INC
24325 131st Ave Ne (98223-6880)
P.O. Box 325, Silvana (98287-0325)
PHONE..................................360 435-6953
Michael H Wold, *President*
Jody Lynn Wold, *Treasurer*
EMP: 2
SALES (est): 290K **Privately Held**
SIC: 2951 1611 Asphalt paving mixtures & blocks; highway & street maintenance

(G-276)
MICROGREEN POLYMERS INC
7220 201st St Ne (98223-7477)
PHONE..................................360 435-7400
Thomas G Malone, *CEO*
Krishna V Nadella, *Admin Sec*
▲ **EMP:** 26
SQ FT: 35,000
SALES (est): 10.4MM **Privately Held**
WEB: www.microgreeninc.com
SIC: 2821 8731 Plastics materials & resins; commercial research laboratory

(G-277)
MICROGREEN POLYMERS INC
17735 59th Ave Ne (98223-6446)
PHONE..................................360 435-7400
EMP: 2 **EST:** 2014
SALES (est): 230.7K **Privately Held**
SIC: 2821 Mfg Plastic Materials/Resins

(G-278)
MID MOUNTAIN MATERIALS INC
18825 67th Ave Ne (98223-8941)
P.O. Box 80266, Seattle (98108-0266)
PHONE..................................360 435-9622
Gary Moffat, *Branch Mgr*
EMP: 26
SALES (est): 2MM
SALES (corp-wide): 11.1MM **Privately Held**
WEB: www.mid-mountain.com
SIC: 3999 7389 Barber & beauty shop equipment; textile & apparel services
PA: Mid Mountain Materials, Inc.
  5602 2nd Ave S
  Seattle WA 98108
  206 762-7600

(G-279)
MIDNITE SOLAR INC
17722 67th Ave Ne Unit C (98223-8943)
PHONE..................................360 403-7207
Roy Butler, *Sales Staff*
Robin Gudgel, *Branch Mgr*
Ryan Stankevitz, *Technical Staff*
EMP: 49
SALES (corp-wide): 10MM **Privately Held**
SIC: 3629 Electrochemical generators (fuel cells)
PA: Midnite Solar, Inc.
  14000 Burn Rd
  Arlington WA 98223
  425 374-9060

(G-280)
MILLERS WELDING
15521 Jordan Rd (98223-9453)
P.O. Box 1252, Granite Falls (98252-1252)
PHONE..................................360 435-7832
EMP: 4
SALES (est): 210K **Privately Held**
SIC: 7692 Welding Repair

(G-281)
MIXIGN INC
Also Called: Shoreline Sign & Awning
12101 Huckleberry Ln (98223-8513)
PHONE..................................206 542-8737
Michael W Richards, *President*
Brenda Richards, *Admin Sec*
EMP: 8
SQ FT: 3,600
SALES (est): 972.8K **Privately Held**
WEB: www.shorelinesign.com
SIC: 3993 Electric signs

(G-282)
MOOSE CREEK LOGGING INC
39209 State Route 530 Ne (98223-5211)
PHONE..................................360 631-3728
Steven Arthur Skaglund, *Administration*
EMP: 2
SALES (est): 89.8K **Privately Held**
SIC: 2411 Logging

(G-283)
MOREL INDUSTRIES INC
Also Called: Ballard Brass
17735 59th Ave Ne (98223-6446)
PHONE..................................360 691-9722
Stephen Morel, *President*
Mark Morel, *Vice Pres*
▼ **EMP:** 35
SQ FT: 42,500

▲ = Import ▼ = Export
◆ = Import/Export

GEOGRAPHIC SECTION

Arlington - Snohomish County (G-315)

SALES (est): 8.4MM **Privately Held**
WEB: www.ballardbrass.com
SIC: **3366** 3365 Castings (except die): brass; aluminum & aluminum-based alloy castings

(G-284)
MORGAN AEROSPACE LLC
17713 48th Dr Ne (98223-6439)
PHONE.................................360 435-9755
Tim Morgan, *CEO*
▲ EMP: 11
SALES: 1.4MM **Privately Held**
SIC: **3721** Aircraft

(G-285)
NATIONAL FOOD CORPORATION
Also Called: Pacific Egg Products
16900 51st Ave Ne (98223-6362)
PHONE.................................360 653-2904
Dwayne Paul, *Manager*
EMP: 100
SALES (corp-wide): 333.2MM **Privately Held**
WEB: www.natlfood.com
SIC: **2015** 5144 Egg processing; eggs
PA: National Food Corporation
728 134th St Sw Ste 103
Everett WA 98204
425 349-4257

(G-286)
NATIONAL FOOD CORPORATION
Also Called: National Feed
6524 180th St Ne (98223-6380)
PHONE.................................360 435-9207
George Weicker, *Manager*
EMP: 2
SALES (corp-wide): 333.2MM **Privately Held**
WEB: www.natlfood.com
SIC: **2048** Prepared feeds
PA: National Food Corporation
728 134th St Sw Ste 103
Everett WA 98204
425 349-4257

(G-287)
NEWELL CORP
6922 204th St Ne (98223-8278)
P.O. Box 477 (98223-0477)
PHONE.................................360 435-8955
Mark Newell, *Principal*
EMP: 18
SALES (est): 4.2MM **Privately Held**
SIC: **3441** Fabricated structural metal

(G-288)
NEWMATA SCREEN PRINTING
17908 11th Ave Ne (98223-5499)
PHONE.................................360 631-7860
Jonathan V Dyk, *Principal*
EMP: 2
SALES (est): 73.2K **Privately Held**
SIC: **2759** Commercial printing

(G-289)
NORTHWEST CENTER
Also Called: Metal Motion
19003 59th Dr Ne (98223-7832)
PHONE.................................360 403-7330
Mike Davidson, *Manager*
EMP: 28
SALES (corp-wide): 50.3MM **Privately Held**
WEB: www.americandataguard.com
SIC: **3599** 3544 Machine & other job shop work; industrial molds
PA: Northwest Center
7272 W Marginal Way S
Seattle WA 98108
206 285-9140

(G-290)
NORTHWEST MACHINE WORKS
20611 67th Ave Ne Ste B (98223-4239)
PHONE.................................360 435-3600
Kurt Merrifield, *Partner*
EMP: 3
SALES (est): 344.5K **Privately Held**
SIC: **3599** Machine shop, jobbing & repair

(G-291)
NORTHWEST VIDEO WALL
3011 252nd St Ne (98223-7222)
PHONE.................................360 403-7773
Mark Steneide, *Principal*
EMP: 2
SALES (est): 84.2K **Privately Held**
SIC: **5064** 1731 3861 Video camera-audio recorders (camcorders); voice, data & video wiring contractor; motion picture film

(G-292)
OBERG FILTERS LLC
17118 112th Ave Ne (98223-7442)
PHONE.................................360 403-3222
Kelly Oberg,
EMP: 2 EST: 2008
SQ FT: 1,200
SALES: 196.5K **Privately Held**
SIC: **3569** Filters

(G-293)
OBERG MANUFACTURING INC
Also Called: Oberg Race Products
17118 112th Ave Ne (98223-7442)
PHONE.................................360 435-8161
Gordon Oberg, *CEO*
Tony Wolford, *President*
EMP: 2
SALES (est): 277.3K **Privately Held**
WEB: www.obergraceproducts.com
SIC: **3599** Oil filters, internal combustion engine, except automotive

(G-294)
OLYMPIC SEC COMM SYS INC
19009 62nd Ave Ne (98223-6312)
P.O. Box 3559 (98223-3559)
PHONE.................................360 652-1088
Thomas Brown, *President*
Mitch Andrew, *Sales Staff*
EMP: 8
SQ FT: 850
SALES (est): 1.4MM **Privately Held**
SIC: **3699** 1731 Security devices; electrical work

(G-295)
OSO RAILWORKS INC (PA)
Also Called: Evergreen Hill Design
31328 N Brooks Creek Rd (98223-9390)
P.O. Box 1349, Hamilton MT (59840-1349)
PHONE.................................406 375-7555
David L Rygmyr, *President*
Lynda R Rygmyr, *Vice Pres*
Carol Petersen, *Manager*
EMP: 2
SQ FT: 2,400
SALES: 60K **Privately Held**
SIC: **3944** Railroad models: toy & hobby

(G-296)
OUTDOOR SYNERGY
17833 59th Ave Ne (98223-6450)
PHONE.................................360 435-3330
EMP: 3
SALES (est): 299.8K **Privately Held**
SIC: **3732** Boat building & repairing

(G-297)
PACIFIC AIRCRAFT MODIFICATIONS
1304 Stanwood Bryant Rd (98223-7319)
P.O. Box 2510, Stanwood (98292-2510)
PHONE.................................360 403-7282
Jim Barkhurst, *Principal*
EMP: 3
SALES (est): 207.4K **Privately Held**
SIC: **3812** Aircraft/aerospace flight instruments & guidance systems

(G-298)
PEARSON MILLWORK INC
19311 59th Ave Ne (98223-6356)
P.O. Box 3246 (98223-3246)
PHONE.................................360 435-9516
Kirsten Ingham, *President*
Carl Pearson, *Vice Pres*
Dorothy Pearson, *Treasurer*
EMP: 14
SQ FT: 17,000
SALES: 2.9MM **Privately Held**
WEB: www.pearsonmillwork.com
SIC: **2431** Millwork

(G-299)
PEDOLOGIC ORTHOTICS
6206 275th St Ne (98223-5660)
PHONE.................................360 318-3452
Joe Vasquez, *Principal*
EMP: 4 EST: 2008
SALES (est): 407.4K **Privately Held**
SIC: **3842** Orthopedic appliances

(G-300)
PENWAY LIMITED INC
18931 59th Ave Ne Unit 1 (98223-4705)
PHONE.................................360 435-6445
Penny Peters, *President*
Wayne Peters, *Vice Pres*
EMP: 2
SALES (est): 298.2K **Privately Held**
WEB: www.penway.com
SIC: **2759** Commercial printing

(G-301)
PHYSICIANS SLEEP SCORING
28830 Kunde Rd (98223-5604)
PHONE.................................360 403-7685
Reed Butterfield, *Principal*
EMP: 2
SALES (est): 188.9K **Privately Held**
SIC: **3829** Medical diagnostic systems, nuclear

(G-302)
PILCHUCK PALLETS INC
17811 25th Dr Nw (98223-8043)
PHONE.................................425 530-1857
Kevin Genty, *Principal*
EMP: 5
SALES (est): 277K **Privately Held**
SIC: **2448** Pallets, wood

(G-303)
POWDER-FAB INC
19224 62nd Ave Ne Ste 2 (98223-7700)
PHONE.................................360 435-0793
Greg Johnston, *President*
John Mathes, *General Mgr*
Steve Johnston, *Vice Pres*
Carie Kelly, *Office Mgr*
Ken Cox, *Admin Sec*
EMP: 23
SQ FT: 10,000
SALES: 1.3MM **Privately Held**
SIC: **3479** 2759 Coating of metals & formed products; screen printing

(G-304)
PRA INC
4821 226th Pl Ne (98223-7286)
PHONE.................................408 743-5300
Robert Gubser, *President*
Phyllis Gubser, *President*
EMP: 16
SQ FT: 6,000
SALES (est): 1.7MM **Privately Held**
WEB: www.prainctest.com
SIC: **7379** 3823 3829 7699 Computer related consulting services; temperature measurement instruments, industrial; anamometers; customizing services

(G-305)
PRECISION AIRMOTIVE LLC
17716 48th Dr Ne (98223-6439)
PHONE.................................360 403-4803
Scott Grafenauer, *Manager*
EMP: 6
SALES (est): 119.5K **Privately Held**
SIC: **5013** 3714 Filters, air & oil; fuel systems & parts, motor vehicle

(G-306)
PRECISION TECHNOLOGY CORP
18640 59th Dr Ne (98223-7836)
PHONE.................................360 403-0254
Michael D Ochoa, *President*
Francisco Ochoa, *Vice Pres*
EMP: 21
SQ FT: 10,000
SALES (est): 2.8MM **Privately Held**
SIC: **3369** Aerospace castings, nonferrous: except aluminum

(G-307)
PRIME BIODIESEL
16821 Smokey P (98223)
PHONE.................................360 969-3966
J Dean Jensen, *Principal*
EMP: 3
SALES (est): 120K **Privately Held**
SIC: **3999** Manufacturing industries

(G-308)
PROWSE MANUFACTURING GROUP
17617 49th Dr Ne Ste D (98223-7897)
PHONE.................................360 403-8910
Jin Prowse, *CEO*
EMP: 26
SALES (est): 628K **Privately Held**
SIC: **3999** Barber & beauty shop equipment

(G-309)
PUPPY LUNCH PRESS
10311 110th St Ne (98223-6280)
PHONE.................................360 651-9957
Marilyn Hansel, *Principal*
EMP: 2 EST: 2017
SALES (est): 59.2K **Privately Held**
SIC: **2741** Miscellaneous publishing

(G-310)
QR INDUSTRIES INC
19109 63rd Ave Ne Ste 3 (98223-4751)
PHONE.................................360 435-2840
Terry Olson, *President*
Katherine Olson, *Vice Pres*
EMP: 6
SQ FT: 144
SALES: 1.1MM **Privately Held**
SIC: **3999** Hair & hair-based products

(G-311)
R&S FORESTRY AND CNSTR LLC
39115 Sr 530 Ne (98223-5212)
P.O. Box 701, Darrington (98241-0701)
PHONE.................................360 436-1771
Shari Brewer, *CEO*
EMP: 3
SALES (est): 55.6K **Privately Held**
SIC: **0851** 1794 1795 2411 Forestry services; excavation & grading, building construction; wrecking & demolition work; logging

(G-312)
RAPID MACHINE INC
25421 57th Ave Ne (98223-7238)
PHONE.................................360 435-8135
Brad Huhta, *President*
EMP: 2
SQ FT: 1,800
SALES: 140K **Privately Held**
SIC: **3599** Machine shop, jobbing & repair

(G-313)
RECONVEYANCE PROFESSIONALS INC
3710 168th St Ne Ste B201 (98223-8465)
PHONE.................................425 257-3038
Christina Faller, *Vice Pres*
EMP: 2 EST: 2010
SALES (est): 217.1K **Privately Held**
SIC: **3535** Conveyors & conveying equipment

(G-314)
RESCOM RAILING SYSTEMS LLC (PA)
Also Called: USI Commerical
16910 59th Ave Ne # 215 (98223-3725)
PHONE.................................853 243-9841
Robert Greaves,
EMP: 4
SALES (est): 655.8K **Privately Held**
SIC: **3446** Stairs, fire escapes, balconies, railings & ladders

(G-315)
RHYTHM & BREWS
18825 67th Ave Ne (98223-8941)
PHONE.................................360 386-9509
Debra Burgess, *Principal*
EMP: 3

Arlington - Snohomish County (G-316)

SALES (est): 71.4K **Privately Held**
SIC: 2082 Malt beverages

(G-316)
ROGROC LLC
202 E Burke Ave (98223-1007)
PHONE..................................360 435-6417
Fax: 360 435-7469
EMP: 9 EST: 1995
SQ FT: 3,500
SALES (est): 910K **Privately Held**
SIC: 3599 3444 Mfg Industrial Machinery Mfg Sheet Metalwork

(G-317)
RONALD BREWER
Also Called: Rl Brewer Forestry
39115 State Route 530 Ne (98223-5212)
P.O. Box 701, Darrington (98241-0701)
PHONE..................................360 436-1771
Ronald Brewer, *Owner*
Shari Brewer, *Owner*
EMP: 4
SALES: 500K **Privately Held**
SIC: 1629 2411 Heavy construction; logging

(G-318)
RTI MANUFACTURING INC
19010 66th Ave Ne Unit 3b (98223-4701)
PHONE..................................360 435-9092
Ronald Powers, *President*
David Stoppel, *Sales Staff*
EMP: 8
SQ FT: 1,660
SALES (est): 1.3MM **Privately Held**
SIC: 3728 Aircraft parts & equipment

(G-319)
SAN JUAN SALSA CO
5919 195th St Ne Unit 5 (98223-7859)
P.O. Box 305 (98223-0305)
PHONE..................................360 435-2100
EMP: 4
SALES (est): 75.4K **Privately Held**
SIC: 2051 Bread, cake & related products

(G-320)
SCOTT GALVANIZING CO INC
6010 199th St Ne (98223-6381)
PHONE..................................206 783-3100
Hadi Mirzai, *President*
Brandon King, *Admin Sec*
EMP: 14
SQ FT: 20,000
SALES (est): 1.8MM **Privately Held**
SIC: 3479 Galvanizing of iron, steel or end-formed products

(G-321)
SDAEROSPACE
19117 63rd Ave Ne Ste B (98223-6739)
PHONE..................................425 440-9295
EMP: 2
SALES (est): 81.4K **Privately Held**
SIC: 3599 Machine shop, jobbing & repair

(G-322)
SEATTLE GALVANIZING CO INC
Also Called: Scott Galvanizing
6010 199th St Ne (98223-6381)
PHONE..................................206 783-3100
Hadi Mirzai, *President*
Brea Ann Wrzesinski, *Accountant*
EMP: 33 EST: 2005
SALES (est): 4.8MM **Privately Held**
SIC: 3479 Galvanizing of iron, steel or end-formed products

(G-323)
SENIOR OPERATIONS LLC
Also Called: Aerospace Manufacturing Tech
7305 201st St (98223)
PHONE..................................360 403-2283
EMP: 2 EST: 2017
SALES (est): 178K **Privately Held**
SIC: 3721 Aircraft

(G-324)
SENIOR OPERATIONS LLC
Absolute Manufacturing
20350 71st Ave Ne Ste C (98223-7455)
PHONE..................................360 435-1116
Albert Houde, *Branch Mgr*
EMP: 74

SALES (corp-wide): 1.3B **Privately Held**
SIC: 3795 Specialized tank components, military
HQ: Senior Operations Llc
300 E Devon Ave
Bartlett IL 60103
630 372-3500

(G-325)
SENIOR OPERATIONS LLC
Aerospace Manufacturing Tech
20100 71st Ave Ne (98223-7447)
PHONE..................................360 435-1119
Wayne Sall, *President*
Shelly McGlothern, *Project Mgr*
Matthew Boily, *Opers Staff*
Marlene Bell, *Buyer*
Jennifer Davis, *Buyer*
EMP: 290
SALES (corp-wide): 1.3B **Privately Held**
SIC: 3728 Aircraft parts & equipment
HQ: Senior Operations Llc
300 E Devon Ave
Bartlett IL 60103
630 372-3500

(G-326)
SENIOR OPERATIONS LLC
Amt
7305 201st St Ne (98223)
PHONE..................................360 435-1119
EMP: 2
SALES (corp-wide): 1.3B **Privately Held**
SIC: 3728 Aircraft parts & equipment
HQ: Senior Operations Llc
300 E Devon Ave
Bartlett IL 60103
630 372-3500

(G-327)
SENIOR OPERATIONS LLC
Also Called: Amt Division
20100 71st Ave Ne (98223-7447)
PHONE..................................360 435-1119
Jerry Goodwin, *Branch Mgr*
EMP: 450
SALES (corp-wide): 1.3B **Privately Held**
SIC: 3599 Hose, flexible metallic; tubing, flexible metallic; bellows, industrial: metal
HQ: Senior Operations Llc
300 E Devon Ave
Bartlett IL 60103
630 372-3500

(G-328)
SHORELINE POLEHOLDERS LLC
4019 178th Pl Ne (98223-8792)
PHONE..................................360 659-0826
James Barrett, *Mng Member*
EMP: 2
SALES (est): 150K **Privately Held**
SIC: 3949 Rods & rod parts, fishing

(G-329)
SKYLINE FISHERIES LLC
4018 226th Pl Ne (98223-7690)
PHONE..................................425 583-7259
Jeffrey Ludwig,
EMP: 4
SALES (est): 160.8K **Privately Held**
SIC: 3732 Fishing boats: lobster, crab, oyster, etc.: small

(G-330)
SKYVIEW FISHERIES LLC
4018 226th Pl Ne (98223-7690)
PHONE..................................425 583-7259
Jeffrey Ludwig,
EMP: 4
SALES (est): 160.8K **Privately Held**
SIC: 3732 Fishing boats: lobster, crab, oyster, etc.: small

(G-331)
SPRINGBROOK NURS & TRCKG INC
9022 84th St Ne (98223-8892)
PHONE..................................360 653-6545
Tim Little, *Owner*
Tom Little, *Owner*
EMP: 55
SQ FT: 800

SALES (est): 8.9MM **Privately Held**
SIC: 7353 5261 5193 3537 Heavy construction equipment rental; nursery stock, seeds & bulbs; nursery stock; industrial trucks & tractors; heavy hauling

(G-332)
STAR LUMBER LLC
7203 112th St Ne (98223-7567)
PHONE..................................316 942-2221
Scott Clark, *Mng Member*
EMP: 2 EST: 2011
SALES (est): 18.2K **Privately Held**
SIC: 2452 Prefabricated wood buildings

(G-333)
STEEL FAB INC
6525 188th St Ne (98223-8707)
PHONE..................................425 743-9216
Rob Matter, *President*
EMP: 50
SQ FT: 50,000
SALES (est): 12.2MM **Privately Held**
WEB: www.steel-fab.com
SIC: 3499 7692 3444 3441 Boxes for packing & shipping, metal; welding repair; sheet metalwork; fabricated structural metal

(G-334)
STELLA-JONES CORPORATION
6520 188th St Ne (98223-8707)
PHONE..................................360 435-2146
Jon D Younce, *Branch Mgr*
EMP: 70
SALES (corp-wide): 1.6B **Privately Held**
SIC: 2491 2421 3531 Wood preserving; sawmills & planing mills, general; construction machinery
HQ: Stella-Jones Corporation
1000 Cliffmine Rd Ste 500
Pittsburgh PA 15275

(G-335)
STILLAQUAMISH RESOURCES LLC
Also Called: Billy Sand and Gravel
24913 State Route 9 Ne (98223-8107)
PHONE..................................360 474-1999
Devon Bralley, *General Mgr*
EMP: 3
SALES (est): 197.7K **Privately Held**
SIC: 8742 1442 Business planning & organizing services; construction sand & gravel

(G-336)
STILLY VENOM BASEBALL CLUB
16713 Burn Rd (98223-5885)
PHONE..................................360 319-6589
Kyle Green, *Principal*
EMP: 2
SALES (est): 74.4K **Privately Held**
SIC: 2836 Venoms

(G-337)
STODDARD INTERNATIONAL LLC
18660 58th Ave Ne (98223-7722)
PHONE..................................360 435-6455
John Mascarenas, *Prdtn Mgr*
Kevin Reynolds, *Engineer*
S Mascarenas, *Mng Member*
Dave Osborn, *Mng Member*
Peggy Osborn, *Contract Mgr*
EMP: 26
SQ FT: 50,000
SALES (est): 5.5MM **Privately Held**
WEB: www.stoddardintl.com
SIC: 3728 Aircraft parts & equipment

(G-338)
THEE LEGACY WOODSHOP
2714 179th Pl Ne (98223)
PHONE..................................425 327-0208
Caroline Compise, *Owner*
EMP: 2
SALES: 98K **Privately Held**
SIC: 2421 Sawmills & planing mills, general

GEOGRAPHIC SECTION

(G-339)
TOPCUB AIRCRAFT LLC (PA)
17922 59th Ave Ne (98223)
PHONE..................................401 209-4756
Zhijun Qian, *Mng Member*
EMP: 3 EST: 2015
SQ FT: 55,000
SALES: 200K **Privately Held**
SIC: 3721 Aircraft

(G-340)
TPH INC DBA ISLAND WOOD WORKS
6011 199th St Ne (98223-6381)
P.O. Box 965, Stanwood (98292-0965)
PHONE..................................360 403-7066
EMP: 2
SALES (est): 179.7K **Privately Held**
SIC: 2431 Mfg Millwork

(G-341)
TRINITY MANUFACTURING INC
19009 61st Ave Ne Unit 3 (98223-4704)
PHONE..................................360 474-8639
Reinhard Himmel, *President*
Devon Christensen, *Marketing Mgr*
Maria Messer, *Executive Asst*
EMP: 6
SALES (est): 824.2K **Privately Held**
SIC: 3599 Machine shop, jobbing & repair

(G-342)
TRINITY MFG
19009 61st Ave Ne Unit 3 (98223-4704)
PHONE..................................360 474-8639
Ryan Hart, *Owner*
EMP: 3
SALES (est): 230K **Privately Held**
SIC: 3549 5084 Marking machines, metalworking; industrial machine parts

(G-343)
UNITED CONTACT LENS INC
19111 61st Ave Ne Unit 5 (98223-6305)
PHONE..................................360 474-9577
Neal Cook, *President*
EMP: 8
SQ FT: 2,000
SALES (est): 550K **Privately Held**
WEB: www.unitedcontactlens.com
SIC: 3851 8011 5049 Contact lenses; offices & clinics of medical doctors; optical goods

(G-344)
UNIVERSAL AEROSPACE CO INC
18640 59th Dr Ne (98223-7836)
PHONE..................................360 435-9577
Jeff Pettit, *CEO*
Sean Myers, *Vice Pres*
Sheryl Babbitt, *Prdtn Mgr*
Bobby Smith, *Purchasing*
Bill Lippert, *Director*
EMP: 120
SQ FT: 30,000
SALES (est): 35.1MM **Privately Held**
SIC: 3728 Aircraft parts & equipment

(G-345)
VANWERVEN INC
Also Called: Arcana Precision Machining
17928 59th Ave Ne (98223-6351)
P.O. Box 67 (98223-0067)
PHONE..................................360 435-2600
Eric B Van Werven, *President*
Gary A Van Werven, *Treasurer*
Gary Vanwerven, *Sales Mgr*
Bryce W Van Werven, *Admin Sec*
EMP: 2
SQ FT: 2,400
SALES (est): 250K **Privately Held**
SIC: 3545 Precision tools, machinists'

(G-346)
WEST PACIFIC RESOURCES INC
17204 Mcrae Rd Nw (98223-8090)
P.O. Box 334, Conway (98238-0334)
PHONE..................................425 210-6427
Richard W Lewis, *President*
Dan R Lewis, *Vice Pres*
Maxine Fedy, *Treasurer*
Vernitta Lewis, *Admin Sec*
EMP: 10

SALES (est): 1.1MM **Privately Held**
SIC: 2411 Logging camps & contractors

(G-347)
WESTAR MEDICAL PRODUCTS INC
18930 59th Ave Ne (98223-8763)
PHONE..............................425 290-3945
Ruth Haller, *President*
John Haller, *CFO*
▲ **EMP:** 17
SQ FT: 16,000
SALES (est): 2.5MM **Privately Held**
WEB: www.westarmed.com
SIC: 3843 Dental chairs

(G-348)
WESTERN FOREST PRODUCTS US LLC
19406 68th Dr Ne A (98223-7404)
PHONE..............................360 403-1400
EMP: 2
SALES (est): 86.7K
SALES (corp-wide): 907.2MM **Privately Held**
SIC: 2421 Sawmills & planing mills, general
HQ: Western Forest Products Us Llc
18637 Se Evergreen Hwy
Vancouver WA 98683
360 892-0770

(G-349)
WOODLAND SERVICES INC
17215 3rd Ave Ne (98223-8060)
P.O. Box 419, Silvana (98287-0419)
PHONE..............................360 652-0412
William H Knudson, *President*
Harriet L Knudson, *Corp Secy*
EMP: 4
SQ FT: 1,800
SALES (est): 18MM **Privately Held**
SIC: 2411 Logging

(G-350)
ZODIAC AEROSPACE
18825 67th Ave Ne (98223-8941)
PHONE..............................360 653-2600
Tony Quicy, *Manager*
Bryce Lavay, *Technology*
Michael Espana, *Director*
Laurel Labrum, *Director*
EMP: 2
SALES (est): 265.3K **Privately Held**
SIC: 3812 Aircraft/aerospace flight instruments & guidance systems

(G-351)
ZOMBIE TINDER
20611 67th Ave Ne (98223-4239)
PHONE..............................360 548-3132
Mike Raether, *Principal*
EMP: 2
SALES (est): 89.6K **Privately Held**
SIC: 3599 Industrial machinery

Asotin
Asotin County

(G-352)
GC SOLUTIONS LLC
Also Called: Redi Stair
110 2nd St (99402)
P.O. Box 309 (99402-0309)
PHONE..............................509 243-6030
Rich Eggleston, *Mng Member*
Guy Conversano,
EMP: 5
SALES (est): 334.2K **Privately Held**
SIC: 3446 3272 Stairs, staircases, stair treads: prefabricated metal; floor slabs & tiles, precast concrete

(G-353)
GEORGE GEHRKES GINK
Also Called: George Ghrkes Fly Fishing Pdts
16186 Snake River Rd (99402-9521)
P.O. Box 730 (99402-0730)
PHONE..............................509 243-4100
Gladys George, *Owner*
EMP: 2

SALES: 250K **Privately Held**
SIC: 3949 5199 Lures, fishing: artificial; bait, fishing

Auburn
King County

(G-354)
3 PHASE ENERGY SYSTEMS INC
3205 C St Ne (98002-1706)
PHONE..............................253 736-2248
Pete Agtuca, *Principal*
Teresa Cheam, *Pub Rel Staff*
EMP: 19 **EST:** 2007
SALES (est): 2.2MM **Privately Held**
WEB: www.3pesi.com
SIC: 3564 8711 Dust or fume collecting equipment, industrial; energy conservation engineering

(G-355)
A & B FABRICATORS INC
319 D St Nw Ste 104 (98001-3901)
PHONE..............................253 887-0442
Danette Selk, *Branch Mgr*
EMP: 2
SALES (corp-wide): 2.1MM **Privately Held**
SIC: 1799 3446 3444 3354 Ornamental metal work; architectural metalwork; sheet metalwork; aluminum extruded products
PA: A & B Fabricators, Inc.
231 D St Nw
Auburn WA
206 763-2600

(G-356)
A & G MACHINE
4132 B Pl Nw (98001-2446)
PHONE..............................253 887-8433
Guy Hall, *Principal*
EMP: 2
SALES (est): 156.6K **Privately Held**
SIC: 3599 Machine shop, jobbing & repair

(G-357)
A & G MACHINE INC
1231 37th St Nw (98001-2417)
PHONE..............................253 887-8433
Abraham Mathew, *President*
Guy Hall, *Admin Sec*
▲ **EMP:** 70
SQ FT: 18,000
SALES (est): 15.3MM **Privately Held**
WEB: www.agmachine.com
SIC: 3429 Aircraft hardware

(G-358)
A & G MACHINE INC
3520 B St Nw (98001-1731)
PHONE..............................253 887-8433
Guy Hall, *Principal*
EMP: 2
SALES (est): 202.4K **Privately Held**
SIC: 3429 Aircraft hardware

(G-359)
A B FABRICATORS
1 30th St Nw Ste 6 (98001-1711)
PHONE..............................206 763-2600
Erin Tasche, *Principal*
EMP: 4 **EST:** 2010
SALES (est): 509.6K **Privately Held**
SIC: 3441 Fabricated structural metal

(G-360)
ACME FORGE
50 37th St Ne Ste F (98002-1753)
PHONE..............................253 217-3801
EMP: 9
SALES (est): 851.4K **Privately Held**
SIC: 2421 Building & structural materials, wood

(G-361)
ACOUSTICAL SOLUTIONS
420 37th St Nw Ste D (98001-2400)
PHONE..............................253 876-0075
Greg Szwed,
▲ **EMP:** 3

SALES (est): 453.3K **Privately Held**
SIC: 3446 Acoustical suspension systems, metal

(G-362)
ADAMATIC CORPORATION
814 44th St Nw Ste 103 (98001-1754)
PHONE..............................206 322-5474
Rohin Mirza, *Principal*
▲ **EMP:** 2
SALES (est): 215.7K **Privately Held**
SIC: 3586 Measuring & dispensing pumps

(G-363)
ADVANCED SIGNS LLC
Also Called: Advanced Sign and Light
1 37th St Nw Ste C (98001-1715)
P.O. Box 1483, Sumner (98390-0310)
PHONE..............................253 987-5909
Jennifer McMahon, *Principal*
EMP: 3
SALES (est): 225.8K **Privately Held**
SIC: 3993 Signs & advertising specialties

(G-364)
AERO CONTROLS INC (PA)
1610 20th St Nw
P.O. Box 837 (98071-0837)
PHONE..............................253 269-3000
Mike Olesik, *CEO*
John Titus, *President*
Sam Thomas, *Managing Dir*
Terry Davidson, *Vice Pres*
Chris Hedien, *Vice Pres*
▲ **EMP:** 207
SQ FT: 225,000
SALES (est): 37.2MM **Privately Held**
WEB: www.aerocontrols.com
SIC: 7699 3728 5088 Aircraft & heavy equipment repair services; aircraft parts & equipment; aircraft equipment & supplies

(G-365)
AIM AEROSPACE AUBURN INC
1502 20th St Nw (98001-3428)
P.O. Box 9011, Renton (98057-3004)
PHONE..............................253 804-3355
John Feutz, *President*
Tom George, *General Mgr*
Robyn Harrell, *General Mgr*
Dan Hite, *Senior Buyer*
Robert Green, *Treasurer*
▲ **EMP:** 150
SQ FT: 80,000
SALES (est): 39.6MM
SALES (corp-wide): 168.2MM **Privately Held**
WEB: www.aim-aerospace.com
SIC: 3728 Aircraft assemblies, subassemblies & parts
PA: Aim Group Usa Inc.
705 Sw 7th St
Renton WA 98057
425 235-2750

(G-366)
AIM AEROSPACE SUMNER INC (HQ)
1502 20th St Nw (98001-3428)
PHONE..............................253 804-3355
Jeff Smith, *CEO*
John Feutz, *President*
Brian J Retzloff, *Vice Pres*
Tim Duquette, *Mfg Staff*
Hans Ulland, *CFO*
EMP: 16
SQ FT: 118,000
SALES (est): 93.3MM
SALES (corp-wide): 168.2MM **Privately Held**
WEB: www.aim-aerospace.com
SIC: 3728 3543 Aircraft assemblies, sub-assemblies & parts; industrial patterns
PA: Aim Group Usa Inc.
705 Sw 7th St
Renton WA 98057
425 235-2750

(G-367)
AJS WELDING
3320 W Valley Hwy N # 108 (98001-2457)
PHONE..............................253 333-2976
Randy Futral, *Owner*
EMP: 2
SALES (est): 154.6K **Privately Held**
SIC: 7692 Welding repair

(G-368)
ALL ABOUT SAFES AND VAULTS
1802 A St Se (98002-6617)
PHONE..............................570 839-1980
Joe Henderson, *Principal*
EMP: 3
SALES (est): 206.2K **Privately Held**
SIC: 3272 Burial vaults, concrete or precast terrazzo

(G-369)
ALL CRAFT PLASTICS
12 37th St Nw Ste 12 # 12 (98001-1738)
P.O. Box 1776, Milton (98354-1776)
PHONE..............................253 887-1768
Randy Libri, *President*
EMP: 2
SALES (est): 228.9K **Privately Held**
SIC: 3089 Injection molding of plastics; plastic processing

(G-370)
ALL METAL FAB INC
1 30th St Nw Ste 6 (98001-1711)
PHONE..............................253 737-5154
Danette Selk, *President*
Gregory Hammer, *Vice Pres*
Troy Thomas, *Treasurer*
EMP: 12
SALES (est): 522K **Privately Held**
SIC: 3446 Architectural metalwork

(G-371)
ALL PRO BLIND CLEANING REPAIR
Also Called: A All-Pro Blind Claning/Repair
3716 Auburn Way N Ste 105 (98002-1389)
PHONE..............................253 804-9497
Michael Goodwind, *Owner*
EMP: 2
SALES (est): 120K **Privately Held**
SIC: 2591 Venetian blinds

(G-372)
ALPACAS OF WINTERCREEK
3302 53rd St Se (98092-8327)
PHONE..............................253 332-4026
EMP: 2
SALES (est): 97.6K **Privately Held**
SIC: 2231 Alpacas, mohair: woven

(G-373)
ALPINE PRODUCTS INC (PA)
550 3rd St Sw Ste C (98001-5253)
PHONE..............................253 351-9828
Bart Farrar, *President*
Laurie Farrar, *Admin Sec*
EMP: 8
SQ FT: 15,000
SALES (est): 5.4MM **Privately Held**
SIC: 5198 2842 5087 5099 Paints; specialty cleaning, polishes & sanitation goods; cleaning & maintenance equipment & supplies; reflective road markers

(G-374)
AMPAC PACKAGING LLC
Ampac Flexibles
701 A St Ne (98002-4026)
P.O. Box 583 (98071-0583)
PHONE..............................253 939-8206
Mike Peasley, *Branch Mgr*
EMP: 220
SALES (corp-wide): 1.2B **Privately Held**
WEB: www.ampaconline.com
SIC: 2673 3081 Plastic bags: made from purchased materials; garment & wardrobe bags, (plastic film); garment bags (plastic film): made from purchased materials; polyethylene film
HQ: Ampac Packaging, Llc
12025 Tricon Rd
Cincinnati OH 45246
513 671-1777

(G-375)
AN-XUYEN BAKERY CO
2202 12th Ct Nw (98001-3515)
PHONE..............................253 887-7823
Quang Huynh, *Owner*
EMP: 8
SQ FT: 2,400

Auburn - King County (G-376)

SALES (est): 360K **Privately Held**
SIC: 2051 Bakery: wholesale or wholesale/retail combined

(G-376)
ARB USA
4810 D St Nw Ste 103 (98001-2466)
PHONE..................................866 293-9078
Anthony Ronald Brown, *Principal*
Casey Fivecoat, *Manager*
EMP: 4 **EST:** 2012
SALES (est): 671.1K **Privately Held**
SIC: 3714 Motor vehicle parts & accessories

(G-377)
ARMSTRONG LUMBER CO INC (PA)
Also Called: Armstrong Building Components
2709 Auburn Way N (98002-2499)
PHONE..................................253 833-6666
James Armstrong, *President*
Gayle A Kroke, *Corp Secy*
Richard C Armstrong Jr, *Vice Pres*
EMP: 30
SQ FT: 10,000
SALES (est): 8.7MM **Privately Held**
SIC: 2452 2439 5031 5211 Panels & sections, prefabricated, wood; trusses, wooden roof; millwork; millwork & lumber

(G-378)
ARROW MANUFACTURING INC
3812 B St Nw (98001-2419)
PHONE..................................253 236-4088
Alan Laford, *President*
EMP: 6
SQ FT: 9,000
SALES: 660K **Privately Held**
SIC: 3498 Tube fabricating (contract bending & shaping)

(G-379)
ASPHALT EQUIPMENT & SERVICE CO
Also Called: Aesco
1531 20th St Nw (98001-3422)
PHONE..................................253 939-4150
John Ferris, *President*
Karla Ferris, *Vice Pres*
EMP: 30 **EST:** 1980
SQ FT: 10,000
SALES (est): 10.8MM **Privately Held**
WEB: www.aescomadsen.com
SIC: 3531 3625 Asphalt plant, including gravel-mix type; electric controls & control accessories, industrial

(G-380)
ASSOCIATED MCH FABRICATION INC
1510 Boundary Blvd # 100 (98001-6579)
PHONE..................................253 395-1155
Steve Schumacher, *President*
Tom Schumacher, *Vice Pres*
EMP: 14
SQ FT: 9,000
SALES (est): 1.5MM **Privately Held**
SIC: 3599 1799 Machine shop, jobbing & repair; welding on site

(G-381)
AUBURN DAIRY PRODUCTS INC
702 W Main St (98001-5299)
PHONE..................................253 833-3400
Douglas A Smith, *President*
Jerry Dinsmore, *Vice Pres*
G Frederick Smith, *Vice Pres*
Marv Query, *Plant Mgr*
Blaine Rutledge, *Opers Mgr*
EMP: 50
SALES (est): 16.4MM **Privately Held**
SIC: 2026 Milk processing (pasteurizing, homogenizing, bottling)

(G-382)
AUBURN MARINE
5506 S 288th St (98001-2132)
PHONE..................................253 941-3046
W Weber, *Owner*
EMP: 2
SALES (est): 130K **Privately Held**
SIC: 3732 5551 Kayaks, building & repairing; kayaks

(G-383)
AUTHENTIC WOODCRAFT INC
2 37th St Nw (98001-1738)
PHONE..................................253 939-8119
Mark Michaud, *President*
Diana Michaud, *Corp Secy*
EMP: 5
SQ FT: 4,000
SALES: 450K **Privately Held**
WEB: www.authenticwoodcraft.com
SIC: 2434 1751 Wood kitchen cabinets; cabinet & finish carpentry

(G-384)
AUTOMATED CONTROLS INC
1531 14th St Nw Ste 4 (98001-3518)
P.O. Box 457 (98071-0457)
PHONE..................................206 246-6499
Glen Harter, *President*
EMP: 2
SQ FT: 3,000
SALES (est): 312.2K **Privately Held**
SIC: 3625 3621 Industrial controls: push button, selector switches, pilot; motors & generators

(G-385)
AVERY WEIGH-TRONIX LLC
1720 Pike St Nw (98001-3420)
PHONE..................................800 903-8823
Michael Spears, *Manager*
EMP: 8
SALES (corp-wide): 14.7B **Publicly Held**
SIC: 3596 Weighing machines & apparatus
HQ: Avery Weigh-Tronix, Llc
1000 Armstrong Dr
Fairmont MN 56031
507 238-4461

(G-386)
AXIS CUTPARTS LLC
226 Pike St Ne (98002-4634)
PHONE..................................253 833-5370
Chris Martin, *Principal*
EMP: 2
SALES (est): 151.6K **Privately Held**
SIC: 3599 Machine shop, jobbing & repair

(G-387)
B & S ENTERPRISES
4204 Auburn Way N Ste 3 (98002-1379)
PHONE..................................253 859-3605
Bruce Vaughn, *Owner*
EMP: 3 **EST:** 1998
SALES: 250K **Privately Held**
SIC: 3469 Machine parts, stamped or pressed metal

(G-388)
BAADER NORTH AMERICA
Also Called: Baader Food Prosessing McHy
1512 Boundary Blvd # 102 (98001-6500)
PHONE..................................253 333-0422
Michael Wulff, *Principal*
Randy Armstrong, *Manager*
▲ **EMP:** 8
SALES (est): 1.5MM **Privately Held**
SIC: 3556 Food products machinery

(G-389)
BARRONS SPECIALTY COATINGS LLC
215 Clay St Nw (98001-4213)
PHONE..................................253 939-2601
Ian Simpson, *Principal*
▲ **EMP:** 6
SALES (est): 481.9K **Privately Held**
SIC: 3479 Painting, coating & hot dipping

(G-390)
BEHR PAINT & STAIN
840 Industry Dr N Ste F (98001-4322)
PHONE..................................253 887-9337
Joe Picon, *Manager*
EMP: 4
SALES (est): 543.7K **Privately Held**
SIC: 2851 Paints & allied products

(G-391)
BELSHAW BROS INC
Also Called: Belshaw Adamatic Bakery Group
814 44th St Nw Ste 103 (98001-1754)
PHONE..................................206 322-5474
Frank Chandler, *President*
Neil McLeod, *Plant Mgr*
Josephine Ulrich, *Safety Mgr*
Chad Dycus, *Technical Mgr*
Erin Deboer, *Engineer*
◆ **EMP:** 110
SQ FT: 120,000
SALES (est): 20MM
SALES (corp-wide): 106.4K **Privately Held**
WEB: www.belshaw.com
SIC: 3586 3556 Measuring & dispensing pumps; bakery machinery; slicers, commercial, food
HQ: Ali Group North America Corporation
101 Corporate Woods Pkwy
Vernon Hills IL 60061
847 215-6565

(G-392)
BEWITCHING MOON PRESS
11 3rd St Nw Unit 1111 (98071-3251)
PHONE..................................206 380-3807
Sylvia Lawrence, *Director*
EMP: 3
SALES (est): 97.6K **Privately Held**
SIC: 2741 Miscellaneous publishing

(G-393)
BIRDS EYE FOODS INC
1150 Industry Dr N Ste C (98001-6552)
PHONE..................................253 833-0255
Search Katherine, *Branch Mgr*
EMP: 3
SALES (corp-wide): 7.9B **Publicly Held**
SIC: 2037 Frozen fruits & vegetables
HQ: Birds Eye Foods, Inc.
121 Woodcrest Rd
Cherry Hill NJ 08003
585 383-1850

(G-394)
BLACKIES GRINDING SERVICE INC
3402 C St Ne Ste 211 (98002-1737)
PHONE..................................253 735-1835
Thomas Organ, *President*
Dawne Dever, *Vice Pres*
EMP: 9
SQ FT: 3,600
SALES (est): 1.1MM **Privately Held**
SIC: 3599 7389 Grinding castings for the trade; grinding, precision: commercial or industrial

(G-395)
BOEING COMPANY
700 15th St Sw (98001-6558)
P.O. Box 3707, Seattle (98124-2207)
PHONE..................................253 931-2121
David Davis, *Project Mgr*
Michael Peila, *Project Mgr*
Douglas Brazeal, *Engineer*
Astrida Carew, *Engineer*
Trent Dubois, *Engineer*
EMP: 150
SALES (corp-wide): 101.1B **Publicly Held**
SIC: 3728 3812 Aircraft parts & equipment; search & navigation equipment
PA: The Boeing Company
100 N Riverside Plz
Chicago IL 60606
312 544-2000

(G-396)
BREAD GARDEN LTD
Also Called: Jasmine Bakery
15522 Se Lake Holm Rd (98092-5906)
PHONE..................................253 838-1639
EMP: 25
SQ FT: 12,000
SALES: 3MM **Privately Held**
SIC: 2051 Mfg Bread/Related Products

(G-397)
BREWS CUSTOMS
4515 S 362nd St (98001-9318)
PHONE..................................253 334-1694
Bruce Reed, *Principal*
EMP: 2 **EST:** 2016
SALES (est): 62.3K **Privately Held**
SIC: 2082 Malt beverages

(G-398)
BURKE GIBSON LLC (PA)
702 3rd St Sw (98001-5278)
PHONE..................................253 735-4444
Burke Gibson, *CEO*
Scott Gibson, *President*
Delores Gibson, *Corp Secy*
Bruce Gibson, *Vice Pres*
▲ **EMP:** 31
SQ FT: 5,000
SALES (est): 8.3MM **Privately Held**
WEB: www.burkegibsoninc.com
SIC: 2421 2541 3089 Wood chips, produced at mill; display fixtures, wood; cases, plastic

(G-399)
BURKE MEADOW LLC
Also Called: Meadow Burke
3416 B St Nw Ste B (98001-1759)
P.O. Box 9600 (98071-9600)
PHONE..................................253 439-6092
EMP: 2
SALES (corp-wide): 30.6B **Privately Held**
SIC: 3272 Building materials, except block or brick: concrete
HQ: Burke Meadow Llc
6467 S Falkenburg Rd
Riverview FL 33578
813 248-1945

(G-400)
CANTER-BERRY FARMS
19102 Se Green Valley Rd (98092-1590)
PHONE..................................253 939-2706
Clarissa Cross, *Partner*
EMP: 3
SALES (est): 150K **Privately Held**
WEB: www.canterberryfarms.com
SIC: 0171 2033 5947 5499 Blueberry farm; fruit pie mixes & fillings: packaged in cans, jars, etc.; gift baskets; food gift baskets

(G-401)
CARBURETORS UNLIMITED INC (PA)
Also Called: Carbs Unlimited
727 22nd St Ne (98002-2837)
P.O. Box 1617 (98071-1617)
PHONE..................................253 833-4106
Steve Pruyne, *President*
EMP: 3
SQ FT: 3,000
SALES (est): 2MM **Privately Held**
WEB: www.carbs.net
SIC: 7539 3571 3465 Carburetor repair; personal computers (microcomputers); body parts, automobile: stamped metal

(G-402)
CASCADE MANUFACTURING
Also Called: Therapedic
1124 29th St Nw (98001-2465)
PHONE..................................206 762-3750
Laurie Simpson, *Owner*
Donn Carlson, *Owner*
EMP: 8
SALES (est): 1MM **Privately Held**
SIC: 2515 Box springs, assembled

(G-403)
CENTRIC CORPORATION
Also Called: American Spray Technologies
1420 20th St Nw Ste A (98001-3413)
PHONE..................................253 833-4342
David McLeod, *President*
EMP: 16
SALES (est): 1.9MM **Privately Held**
WEB: www.cafreightfactoring.com
SIC: 3531 7699 Construction machinery; construction equipment repair

(G-404)
CERTAINTEED CORPORATION
5001 D St Nw (98001-2415)
PHONE..................................253 850-9000
Charlie Yoder, *Manager*
EMP: 300
SALES (corp-wide): 215.9MM **Privately Held**
WEB: www.certainteed.net
SIC: 3442 3089 Window & door frames; windows, plastic
HQ: Certainteed Corporation
20 Moores Rd
Malvern PA 19355
610 893-5000

GEOGRAPHIC SECTION
Auburn - King County (G-437)

(G-405)
CGT INC
1402 20th St Nw Ste 7 (98001-3441)
PHONE..................................253 833-8849
Vincent Ayers, *Principal*
EMP: 2 **EST:** 2010
SALES (est): 58K **Privately Held**
SIC: 2842 Specialty cleaning, polishes & sanitation goods

(G-406)
CHRISTINE JAMISON
403 D St Se (98002-5523)
PHONE..................................253 887-1095
Christine Jamison, *Principal*
EMP: 2
SALES (est): 90.7K **Privately Held**
SIC: 2911 Petroleum refining

(G-407)
CITY SHEET METAL HEATING & AIR
4202 Auburn Way N Ste 8 (98002-1370)
PHONE..................................253 852-2174
Patti Cunningham, *President*
Tom Cunningham, *Corp Secy*
EMP: 5 **EST:** 1974
SQ FT: 2,000
SALES (est): 1.6MM **Privately Held**
WEB: www.sondon.com
SIC: 3444 Sheet metalwork

(G-408)
CLICK IT PICKET LLC
1402 Lake Tappspkwyse 1 (98092)
PHONE..................................253 750-0182
Eddie Leach,
EMP: 2
SALES (est): 88.9K **Privately Held**
SIC: 3446 Architectural metalwork

(G-409)
CMC STEEL FABRICATORS INC
2306 B St Nw (98001-1743)
PHONE..................................253 833-9060
Randy Pulley, *Manager*
EMP: 8 **Privately Held**
SIC: 1791 3315 3449 3496 Concrete reinforcement, placing of; steel wire & related products; bars, concrete reinforcing; fabricated steel; miscellaneous fabricated wire products; concrete reinforcing bars
HQ: Cmc Steel Fabricators, Inc.
3880 Murphy Canyon Rd # 100
San Diego CA 92123

(G-410)
COMMERCIAL CRTING BOX PCKG INC
1445 R St Nw (98001-3503)
PHONE..................................253 804-8616
William Johnson, *President*
EMP: 10
SALES (est): 383.8K **Privately Held**
SIC: 2449 2653 Rectangular boxes & crates, wood; corrugated & solid fiber boxes

(G-411)
COMPLETE DEBURR INC
20 37th St Ne Ste 5 (98002-1760)
PHONE..................................253 887-0997
Darren Capps, *President*
EMP: 14
SALES (est): 1.8MM **Privately Held**
SIC: 3541 3471 Deburring machines; plating & polishing

(G-412)
COMPLEX AEROSPACE LLC
Also Called: Complex Machining
3665 C St Ne (98002-1736)
PHONE..................................253 886-1323
Anh-Huy Bui,
EMP: 5
SALES (est): 913.6K **Privately Held**
SIC: 3399 Metal fasteners

(G-413)
CONRAD MANUFACTURING CO INC
4156 B Pl Nw (98001-2446)
PHONE..................................253 852-3420
Larry Boyle, *President*
Ronald Boyle, *Vice Pres*
Bill Boyle, *Treasurer*
Linda Camp, *Admin Sec*
EMP: 12
SQ FT: 17,600
SALES: 1.4MM **Privately Held**
WEB: www.conradmfg.com
SIC: 3089 Thermoformed finished plastic products

(G-414)
CONTAINER STUFFERS LLC
Also Called: C S L
12126 Se 284th St (98092-4004)
PHONE..................................206 255-3187
Holly Williams,
Troy Williams,
EMP: 3
SALES (est): 320K **Privately Held**
SIC: 3537 Containers (metal), air cargo

(G-415)
CONTRARY DESIGN
35821 Military Rd S (98001-9158)
PHONE..................................253 653-0275
Jon Lapping, *Owner*
EMP: 2
SALES (est): 150.3K **Privately Held**
SIC: 2449 Wood containers

(G-416)
COPBONG428 LLC
3724 S 316th St (98001-3108)
PHONE..................................206 778-1436
C Nguyen, *Bd of Directors*
EMP: 2 **EST:** 2012
SALES (est): 119K **Privately Held**
SIC: 2741 Miscellaneous publishing

(G-417)
CORDSTRAP USA INC
2200 W Valley Hwy N # 110 (98001-1654)
PHONE..................................253 886-5000
Jan F Andriessen, *President*
Leslie Ll, *Finance Mgr*
Chris Raggio, *Sales Staff*
Gert Van Gammeren, *Manager*
Darren Ward, *Manager*
▲ **EMP:** 2 **EST:** 2000
SALES: 1MM **Privately Held**
SIC: 3081 Packing materials, plastic sheet

(G-418)
CREATIVE EDGE GRAPHICS
3002 B St Nw (98001-1720)
PHONE..................................253 735-5111
Matt Guthrie, *President*
Vince Miller, *Manager*
EMP: 6
SALES (est): 320K **Privately Held**
WEB: www.creativeedgegraphics.com
SIC: 2759 Screen printing

(G-419)
CUPCAKES OF AUBURN
33928 42nd Ave S (98001-9539)
PHONE..................................253 733-5547
EMP: 2
SALES (est): 82.4K **Privately Held**
SIC: 2051 Bread, cake & related products

(G-420)
CUSTOM OFFICE DESIGN INC
61 30th St Nw Ste E (98001-1703)
PHONE..................................253 735-8777
William Selvar, *President*
Bill Lakefish, *Vice Pres*
William Lakefish, *Vice Pres*
Brandon Selvar, *Receptionist*
EMP: 15
SQ FT: 15,000
SALES (est): 2.2MM **Privately Held**
SIC: 2426 8111 2521 5021 Furniture stock & parts, hardwood; legal services; wood office furniture; office furniture

(G-421)
DAHLQUIST LOGGING INC
31831 102nd Ave Se (98092-3039)
PHONE..................................253 804-9112
John Dahlquist, *President*
Delberta Dahlquist, *Treasurer*
EMP: 2
SALES (est): 155.8K **Privately Held**
SIC: 2411 1629 Logging; land preparation construction

(G-422)
DANNER CORPORATION (PA)
Also Called: Zip-Vac
307 Oravetz Pl Se (98092-8601)
PHONE..................................253 833-5333
Harold Jack Danner Jr, *CEO*
James Gautney Jr, *President*
James H Gautney Jr, *Principal*
Ted Straub, *Treasurer*
EMP: 129
SQ FT: 65,000
SALES (est): 27.3MM **Privately Held**
WEB: www.danner.net
SIC: 3728 Aircraft body assemblies & parts

(G-423)
DAVID L FLINK
19229 Se Aubrn Blck Diamn (98092-2288)
PHONE..................................253 735-5417
David Flink, *Owner*
EMP: 2
SALES (est): 170K **Privately Held**
WEB: www.ncplus.net
SIC: 3496 Cages, wire

(G-424)
DEVELOPMENTAL MACHINE
16205 Se Auburn Black Dia (98092-5923)
PHONE..................................253 631-6953
John Houghton, *Owner*
EMP: 3
SALES (est): 305.6K **Privately Held**
SIC: 3599 Machine shop, jobbing & repair

(G-425)
DEVORAH CREEK VINYARDS
37901 183rd Ave Se (98092-9519)
PHONE..................................206 579-8906
EMP: 2
SALES (est): 91.3K **Privately Held**
SIC: 2084 Brandy & brandy spirits; wines

(G-426)
DG MACHINE
3240 B St Nw Ste B (98001-1704)
PHONE..................................253 735-1373
Dale Green, *Owner*
EMP: 3
SQ FT: 1,500
SALES: 750K **Privately Held**
WEB: www.simulogics.com
SIC: 3599 7539 Machine shop, jobbing & repair; machine shop, automotive

(G-427)
DOLPHIN PRESS INC
17828 Se Lake Holm Rd (98092-9107)
PHONE..................................253 735-1856
Tim Ferrell, *President*
EMP: 3
SQ FT: 2,500
SALES (est): 260K **Privately Held**
SIC: 2752 Commercial printing, lithographic

(G-428)
DONUT STAR INC
914 Auburn Way S (98002-6101)
PHONE..................................253 833-2980
Guo Woo, *Owner*
EMP: 3
SALES (est): 101.6K **Privately Held**
SIC: 5461 2051 Doughnuts; doughnuts, except frozen

(G-429)
DRONEWORKS LLC
29832 42nd Ave S (98001-2901)
PHONE..................................253 261-3888
Michael Mann, *Principal*
EMP: 2
SALES (est): 114.7K **Privately Held**
SIC: 3721 Motorized aircraft

(G-430)
DYLAN MANUFACTURING INC
Also Called: Dylan Aerospace
1702 Pike St Nw Ste 1 (98001-3431)
PHONE..................................253 333-8260
Darrell Sutherland, *President*
EMP: 17
SQ FT: 5,500
SALES: 3.6MM **Privately Held**
WEB: www.dylanmfg.com
SIC: 3469 3499 Machine parts, stamped or pressed metal; fire- or burglary-resistive products

(G-431)
EATON CORPORATION
1604 15th St Sw Ste 114 (98001-6565)
PHONE..................................253 833-5021
Steve Bognar, *Branch Mgr*
EMP: 12 **Privately Held**
WEB: www.eaton.com
SIC: 5063 3613 Electrical apparatus & equipment; switchgear & switchboard apparatus
HQ: Eaton Corporation
1000 Eaton Blvd
Cleveland OH 44122
440 523-5000

(G-432)
ELECTRONIC IMAGING SVCS INC
Also Called: Vestcom Retail Solutions
1220 37th St Nw (98001-2433)
PHONE..................................253 887-1237
Bob Cunningham, *Branch Mgr*
EMP: 20
SALES (corp-wide): 22.7MM **Privately Held**
SIC: 8742 2759 Marketing consulting services; commercial printing; labels & seals: printing; promotional printing
HQ: Electronic Imaging Services, Inc.
2800 Cantrell Rd Ste 400
Little Rock AR 72202
501 663-0100

(G-433)
EVERGREEN CONSTRUCTION SPC INC
1410 37th St Nw Ste A (98001-2409)
PHONE..................................253 288-8455
Lance Stretch, *President*
Michael Tucker, *Vice Pres*
EMP: 18
SQ FT: 16,000
SALES (est): 7.1MM **Privately Held**
WEB: www.evconspec.com
SIC: 5072 3442 Builders' hardware; window & door frames; casements, aluminum

(G-434)
EVERGREEN TEXTILES
4226 S 280th St (98001-1168)
PHONE..................................253 852-6565
EMP: 2
SALES (est): 126.6K **Privately Held**
SIC: 5131 5023 2391 Drapery material, woven; window furnishings; curtains & draperies

(G-435)
EVIL GENIUS PUBLISHING LLC
1411 59th St Se (98092-8097)
PHONE..................................253 929-6710
Jeffery Wright, *Principal*
EMP: 2
SALES (est): 93.2K **Privately Held**
SIC: 2741 Miscellaneous publishing

(G-436)
EXACT AEROSPACE INC
3104 C St Ne Ste 200 (98002-1761)
PHONE..................................253 854-1017
Mark Evans, *President*
Jeffrey J Babb, *Pastor*
Tim Johnson, *Vice Pres*
Michael V Leibfried, *Agent*
Robert W Ackerman,
▲ **EMP:** 27
SQ FT: 3,000
SALES: 5MM **Privately Held**
WEB: www.exactaerospace.com
SIC: 3444 Sheet metalwork

(G-437)
EXAMINERCOM
14426 Se Auburn Blck Diam (98092-9211)
PHONE..................................206 459-0562
Jean Williams, *Principal*
EMP: 3

Auburn - King County (G-438) GEOGRAPHIC SECTION

SALES (est): 141.6K **Privately Held**
SIC: 2711 Newspapers, publishing & printing

(G-438)
EXCEL MANUFACTURING INC
120 37th St Ne (98002-1707)
PHONE.................................253 939-6446
Kevin Wallason, *President*
Dina Wallason, *Manager*
EMP: 4
SQ FT: 3,500
SALES: 150K **Privately Held**
SIC: 3441 Fabricated structural metal

(G-439)
EXONE COMPANY
1307 W Valley Hwy N # 104 (98001-4110)
PHONE.................................253 394-0357
EMP: 3
SALES (corp-wide): 64.6MM **Publicly Held**
SIC: 3555 Printing trades machinery
PA: The Exone Company
    127 Industry Blvd
    North Huntingdon PA 15642
    724 863-9663

(G-440)
FERGUSON
401 Lund Rd (98001-5273)
PHONE.................................206 767-7700
EMP: 2
SALES (est): 122K **Privately Held**
SIC: 5085 3494 3432 Electric tools; valves & pipe fittings; plumbing fixture fittings & trim

(G-441)
FOREST CONCEPTS LLC
3320 W Valley Hwy N # 110 (98001-2457)
PHONE.................................253 333-9663
Mike Perry, *CEO*
Jason Perry, *Prdtn Mgr*
Christopher Lanning, *Engineer*
Thomas Broderick, *Manager*
James Dooley, *CTO*
EMP: 7
SQ FT: 10,000
SALES: 1MM **Privately Held**
WEB: www.forestconcepts.com
SIC: 2499 Engraved wood products

(G-442)
FORMULA CORP
4432 C St Ne (98002-1713)
PHONE.................................253 880-0170
Charles D Werner, *President*
Alan Gangl, *Corp Secy*
▼ EMP: 21 EST: 1982
SQ FT: 34,000
SALES (est): 9.6MM **Privately Held**
WEB: www.formulacorp.com
SIC: 2842 5169 Cleaning or polishing preparations; detergents & soaps, except specialty cleaning; specialty cleaning & sanitation preparations

(G-443)
FOX BAY INDUSTRIES INC
4150 B Pl Nw Ste 101 (98001-2449)
PHONE.................................253 941-9155
Wayne Walker, *President*
Ladele Walker, *Treasurer*
EMP: 3
SQ FT: 4,500
SALES: 630K **Privately Held**
WEB: www.foxbay.com
SIC: 3842 3577 Supports: abdominal, ankle, arch, kneecap, etc.; computer peripheral equipment

(G-444)
FRISBIE COMPANY
101 F St Nw (98001-5264)
PHONE.................................253 939-0363
EMP: 2
SQ FT: 4,000
SALES (est): 126.9K **Privately Held**
SIC: 3728 Mfg Aircraft Parts/Equipment

(G-445)
FRYS WELDING INC
3240 B St Nw Ste C (98001-1704)
EMP: 2
SQ FT: 5,200
SALES: 220K **Privately Held**
SIC: 7692 3799 3537 3441 Welding Repair Mfg Transportation Equip Mfg Indstl Truck/Tractor Structural Metal Fabrctn

(G-446)
FUSION SILVER
1402 Auburn Way N (98002-3384)
PHONE.................................253 740-8117
EMP: 2
SALES (est): 142.2K **Privately Held**
SIC: 3339 Precious metals

(G-447)
GARY FLOYD & ASSOCIATES LLC
34731 14th Pl Sw (98023-7036)
PHONE.................................253 874-4582
Gary Floyd,
▲ EMP: 4
SALES (est): 316.5K **Privately Held**
SIC: 3253 Ceramic wall & floor tile

(G-448)
GENERAL ELECTRIC COMPANY
2202 Perimeter Rd Ste 107 (98001-6584)
PHONE.................................253 351-2200
Jason Pettit, *Branch Mgr*
EMP: 7
SALES (corp-wide): 121.6B **Publicly Held**
SIC: 6159 3511 3724 3632 Loan institutions, general & industrial; turbines & turbine generator sets; aircraft engines & engine parts; household refrigerators & freezers; television broadcasting stations; electromedical equipment
PA: General Electric Company
    41 Farnsworth St
    Boston MA 02210
    617 443-3000

(G-449)
GERRARD INC
Also Called: Image Craft Signs & Graphics
1320 26th St Nw Ste 1 (98001-1620)
PHONE.................................253 804-8001
Brian Gerrard, *President*
EMP: 3 EST: 2010
SALES (est): 293.1K **Privately Held**
SIC: 3993 Signs & advertising specialties

(G-450)
GLACIER WATER COMPANY LLC
Also Called: Tahoma Glacier Water
1002 15th St Sw Ste 100 (98001-6502)
PHONE.................................253 876-6500
Sungwook Choe,
Joon Choe,
Matt Owen,
EMP: 3
SQ FT: 30,000
SALES: 950K **Privately Held**
WEB: www.glacierh2o.com
SIC: 2086 Water, pasteurized: packaged in cans, bottles, etc.

(G-451)
GMS FABRICATION
1320 26th St Nw Ste 12 (98001-1620)
PHONE.................................425 677-4573
EMP: 2
SALES (est): 103.6K **Privately Held**
SIC: 3599 Machine shop, jobbing & repair

(G-452)
GMS METAL WORKS INC
1427 20th St Nw (98001-3424)
PHONE.................................253 736-2178
Chad K Christensen, *President*
Kari L Christensen, *Vice Pres*
Scott Spear, *Purchasing*
Glenda Celigoy, *Human Res Mgr*
EMP: 16
SQ FT: 6,000
SALES (est): 4.3MM **Privately Held**
WEB: www.chadchristensen.com
SIC: 3599 Machine shop, jobbing & repair

(G-453)
GMS PROCUREMENT LLC
1427 20th St Nw (98001-3424)
PHONE.................................253 852-6552
Jeffrey Scott,
EMP: 2
SALES (est): 147.2K **Privately Held**
SIC: 3568 3724 Power transmission equipment; engine mount parts, aircraft

(G-454)
GOS PRINTING CORPORATION
1433 W Valley Hwy N (98001-4124)
PHONE.................................253 939-3131
Janice Greggs, *President*
Jerry Delo, *Prdtn Mgr*
Warren Olson, *Treasurer*
EMP: 7
SQ FT: 5,000
SALES (est): 913.2K **Privately Held**
WEB: www.gosprinting.com
SIC: 2752 Commercial printing, offset

(G-455)
GRCC STUDENT CHAPTER SAF
12401 Se 320th St (98092-3622)
PHONE.................................253 288-3331
Bob Johnston, *Manager*
EMP: 11 EST: 2011
SALES (est): 1.1MM **Privately Held**
SIC: 7372 Application computer software

(G-456)
GREEN NDLE CBNETS MOLDINGS LLC
31040 133rd Ave Se (98092-3249)
PHONE.................................206 235-3061
Vadym Golovach,
Oksana Stryzheus,
Vitaliy Stryzheus,
EMP: 2 EST: 2014
SALES (est): 188.7K **Privately Held**
SIC: 2434 Wood kitchen cabinets

(G-457)
GREEN-ON-GREEN ENERGY INC
3205 C St Ne (98002-1706)
PHONE.................................206 701-7321
Lin Felton, *Ch of Bd*
Sam Felton, *Principal*
Pete Agtuca, *Vice Pres*
EMP: 4
SALES (est): 275.7K **Privately Held**
SIC: 3613 3691 Generator control & metering panels; power switching equipment; regulators, power; batteries, rechargeable

(G-458)
HAFA ADAI SIGNS & GRAPHICS LLC
Also Called: Fastsigns
1835 Auburn Way N Ste B (98002-3348)
PHONE.................................253 394-0600
Patti Worley, *Mng Member*
Frank Worley,
EMP: 2 EST: 2016
SALES (est): 50.6K **Privately Held**
SIC: 3993 Signs & advertising specialties

(G-459)
HALF LION BREWING COMPANY LLC
5123 Nathan Loop Se (98092-8711)
PHONE.................................253 561-1115
EMP: 2
SALES (est): 68.6K **Privately Held**
SIC: 2082 Malt beverages

(G-460)
HARDY ENGINEERING & MFG INC
120 37th St Ne (98002-1707)
PHONE.................................253 735-6488
Richard Hardy, *CEO*
Gay Hardy, *President*
Jonathan Hardy, *Vice Pres*
Patrice Hardy, *CFO*
EMP: 30
SQ FT: 17,000
SALES: 2.3MM **Privately Held**
WEB: www.hardyem.com
SIC: 8711 3599 Mechanical engineering; machine shop, jobbing & repair

(G-461)
HEADS UP INC
1320 26th St Nw Ste 8 (98001-1620)
PHONE.................................253 833-4546
Joanne Elston, *President*
EMP: 5
SQ FT: 6,000
SALES: 380K **Privately Held**
SIC: 3714 7539 3599 Cylinder heads, motor vehicle; machine shop, automotive; machine shop, jobbing & repair

(G-462)
HEATH GRAPHICS LLC
1720 Pike St Nw (98001-3420)
P.O. Box 1638, Kent (98035-1638)
PHONE.................................253 856-1422
Fax: 253 856-1003
EMP: 4
SALES (est): 260K **Privately Held**
SIC: 3555 Mfg Printing Trades Machinery

(G-463)
HELLY-HANSEN HOLDINGS (U S) (DH)
3703 I St Nw Unit Main (98001)
PHONE.................................425 378-8700
Ric Long, *President*
▲ EMP: 1
SQ FT: 15,000
SALES (est): 4.6MM
SALES (corp-wide): 10.6B **Privately Held**
SIC: 2339 2329 Ski jackets & pants: women's, misses' & juniors'; down-filled coats, jackets & vests: women's & misses'; ski & snow clothing: men's & boys'; men's & boys' leather, wool & down-filled outerwear
HQ: Helly Hansen As
    Munkedamsveien 35
    Oslo 0250
    692 490-00

(G-464)
HEXACOMB CORPORATION
Also Called: Auburn Hexacomb Plant
2820 B St Nw Ste 111 (98001-1760)
PHONE.................................253 288-2820
Mustafa Haziq, *Plant Mgr*
EMP: 15
SALES (corp-wide): 7B **Publicly Held**
SIC: 2671 Paper coated or laminated for packaging
HQ: Hexacomb Corporation
    1296 Barclay Blvd
    Buffalo Grove IL 60089
    847 955-7984

(G-465)
HICKS LEATHERMAKING AND WDWKG
721 19th St Se (98002-6929)
PHONE.................................253 833-8873
Amy Hicks, *Principal*
EMP: 2 EST: 2017
SALES (est): 85.2K **Privately Held**
SIC: 2431 Millwork

(G-466)
HIGH PERFORMANCE SEALS INC
3902 W Valley Hwy N # 200 (98001-2426)
PHONE.................................253 218-0123
Dave Salanan, *Branch Mgr*
EMP: 9
SALES (est): 1.8MM **Privately Held**
SIC: 2821 Thermoplastic materials

(G-467)
HILL PRINT INC
Also Called: Printco
32 G St Nw Ste A (98001-5272)
PHONE.................................425 255-7700
Matt Mewhorter, *President*
Lyle Johnson, *Vice Pres*
Lyle R Johnson, *Vice Pres*
EMP: 8 EST: 1974
SQ FT: 6,000
SALES (est): 1.4MM **Privately Held**
WEB: www.printcoinc.com
SIC: 2752 Commercial printing, offset

GEOGRAPHIC SECTION

Auburn - King County (G-499)

(G-468)
HUDSON TECHNOLOGIES INC
Also Called: Hudson Tech Company
1320 26th St Nw Ste 9 (98001-1620)
PHONE 253 887-7707
Neil James, *Branch Mgr*
EMP: 3 **Publicly Held**
SIC: 2869 Industrial organic chemicals
PA: Hudson Technologies, Inc.
    1 Blue Hill Plz Ste 1541
    Pearl River NY 10965

(G-469)
HUEBNER MANUFACTURING
30660 168th Ave Se (98092-1100)
PHONE 253 630-9600
Jack Huebner, *Owner*
EMP: 3
SALES (est): 211.6K **Privately Held**
SIC: 3599 Machine shop, jobbing & repair

(G-470)
IEG7 INC
5213 Wesley Ave Se (98092-3934)
PHONE 206 501-6193
Gary Wachowicz, *Principal*
Wendy Wachowicz,
EMP: 2 **EST:** 2015
SALES (est): 117.6K **Privately Held**
SIC: 7371 7372 Computer software systems analysis & design, custom; business oriented computer software

(G-471)
IMAGE MASTERS INC
819 14th St Ne (98002-3317)
P.O. Box 735 (98071-0735)
PHONE 253 939-5868
Ann C Stoker, *President*
Jay Hileman, *Treasurer*
Norma Hileman, *Admin Sec*
EMP: 3
SALES (est): 388.4K **Privately Held**
SIC: 3069 7389 Hard rubber & molded rubber products; engraving service

(G-472)
IMAGINETICS HOLDINGS LLC (PA)
3410 A St Se (98002-8807)
PHONE 253 735-0156
Scott Strong, *CEO*
EMP: 6
SALES (est): 58.9MM **Privately Held**
SIC: 3444 3469 3545 Sheet metalwork; metal stampings; machine tool attachments & accessories

(G-473)
IMAGINETICS LLC
3410 A St Se (98002-8807)
PHONE 253 735-0156
Dan Hiner, *Supervisor*
Scott Strong,
Michael Honey,
Robert Mazzacavallo,
Patrick Prince,
EMP: 87
SQ FT: 60,000
SALES (est): 33.1MM
SALES (corp-wide): 58.9MM **Privately Held**
WEB: www.imaginetics inc.com
SIC: 3444 3469 3545 Sheet metalwork; metal stampings; machine tool attachments & accessories
PA: Imaginetics Holdings Llc
    3410 A St Se
    Auburn WA 98002
    253 735-0156

(G-474)
IMPRESSIONS EXPRESS INC
32010 42nd Pl Sw (98023-2404)
PHONE 253 874-2923
Robert Clayton, *President*
EMP: 2
SALES (est): 176.9K **Privately Held**
WEB: www.impressions-express.com
SIC: 2741 Miscellaneous publishing

(G-475)
INCLINE CIDER COMPANY
4402 D St Nw (98001-2461)
PHONE 503 830-4414
Jordan Zehner, *Principal*
EMP: 2
SALES (est): 62.3K **Privately Held**
SIC: 2099 Cider, nonalcoholic

(G-476)
INDUSTRY SIGN & GRAPHICS INC
Also Called: Auburn Sign Company
4208 Auburn Way N Ste 1 (98002-1313)
PHONE 253 854-2333
Lorraine Henry, *President*
Salvatore Orso, *Vice Pres*
EMP: 17
SALES (est): 2.8MM **Privately Held**
WEB: www.auburnsign.com
SIC: 3993 5999 Signs, not made in custom sign painting shops; decals

(G-477)
INNOVATIVE HEARTH PRODUCTS LLC
Also Called: Lennox
1502 14th St Nw (98001-3502)
PHONE 253 735-1100
David Schaassma, *Manager*
EMP: 60
SALES (corp-wide): 113.1MM **Privately Held**
SIC: 3433 Stoves, wood & coal burning
PA: Innovative Hearth Products Llc
    2701 S Harbor Blvd
    Santa Ana CA 92704
    615 925-3417

(G-478)
JATAL INC (PA)
Also Called: Accel Plastics
4146 B Pl Nw (98001-2446)
PHONE 253 854-0034
Jack Lowrey, *President*
John Crawford, *Vice Pres*
EMP: 32
SQ FT: 20,000
SALES (est): 12.1MM **Privately Held**
WEB: www.accelplastics.com
SIC: 3089 Injection molding of plastics

(G-479)
JET CITY PARTNERS LLC (PA)
22 42nd St Nw Ste B (98001-1753)
PHONE 206 999-0047
Erik Cullen,
EMP: 3 **EST:** 2013
SQ FT: 800
SALES (est): 7.7MM **Privately Held**
SIC: 3443 3444 3412 3451 Fabricated plate work (boiler shop); sheet metalwork; metal barrels, drums & pails; screw machine products; fabricated structural metal; etching & engraving

(G-480)
JEVCO INTERNATIONAL INC
1320 26th St Nw Ste 13 (98001-1620)
P.O. Box 67, Dorset VT (05251-0067)
PHONE 253 858-2605
Eric Scheinerman, *CEO*
Kenneth Buttermore, *Treasurer*
Jennifer Kepola, *Admin Sec*
EMP: 18
SQ FT: 48,000
SALES (est): 13.6MM **Privately Held**
SIC: 3451 Screw machine products
PA: Precision Solutions, Llc
    155 Carpenter Dr
    Annville KY 40402

(G-481)
JIKOPOWER INC
3205 C St Ne At Las (98002)
PHONE 253 678-0074
EMP: 10 **EST:** 2015
SALES (est): 460.9K **Privately Held**
SIC: 3612 Power & distribution transformers

(G-482)
JIM SUZUKI
Also Called: Blackstar Industries
1 30th St Nw Ste 4 (98001-1711)
PHONE 253 804-6070
Jim Suzuki, *Owner*
EMP: 7

SALES (est): 700.6K **Privately Held**
WEB: www.blackstarindustries.com
SIC: 3089 3769 2851 Molding primary plastic; guided missile & space vehicle parts & auxiliary equipment; paints & allied products

(G-483)
KC TECHNOLOGY INC
Also Called: D3 Skis
3526 B St Nw Ste 101 (98001-5017)
PHONE 509 933-2312
Creed Kidder, *CEO*
Dennis Kidder, *President*
▲ **EMP:** 5
SALES (est): 847.3K **Privately Held**
SIC: 5091 3949 Skiing equipment; water skis

(G-484)
KING NORTHERN INC
Also Called: King Northern Publishing
32115 105th Pl Se A104 (98092-4761)
PHONE 520 604-6379
Carew Papritz, *President*
Dawnie Papritz, *Vice Pres*
EMP: 11 **EST:** 1996
SALES (est): 452.9K **Privately Held**
SIC: 2731 7389 Book publishing;

(G-485)
KOOLANCE INC
2840 W Valley Hwy N # 101 (98001-2464)
PHONE 253 249-7669
Peter Ki Oan Cheon, *President*
Issac Choi, *Controller*
▲ **EMP:** 8
SQ FT: 10,000
SALES (est): 1.5MM **Privately Held**
WEB: www.koolance.com
SIC: 3577 Computer peripheral equipment

(G-486)
L&P SCREEN PRINTING INC
1720 Pike St Nw Ste 6 (98001-3420)
PHONE 253 951-2482
Jason Palicki, *Principal*
EMP: 2
SALES (est): 134.7K **Privately Held**
SIC: 2759 Screen printing

(G-487)
LAZER TRENDS LLC
3902 W Valley Hwy N # 104 (98001-2429)
PHONE 253 886-5600
David Medina, *Mng Member*
▲ **EMP:** 3
SQ FT: 4,200
SALES: 236K **Privately Held**
WEB: www.lazertrends.com
SIC: 3479 Etching & engraving

(G-488)
LIFE ON CANVAS
4816 O Ct Ne (98002-1229)
PHONE 503 470-9474
Bonnie Harro, *Principal*
EMP: 2
SALES (est): 87.6K **Privately Held**
SIC: 2211 Canvas

(G-489)
LMI AEROSPACE INC
Also Called: Leonards Metal
101 Western Ave (98001-4209)
PHONE 253 288-9379
Ron Saks, *President*
EMP: 160
SALES (corp-wide): 355.8K **Privately Held**
WEB: www.lmiaerospace.com
SIC: 3728 3812 Aircraft parts & equipment; search & navigation equipment
HQ: Lmi Aerospace, Inc.
    411 Fountain Lakes Blvd
    Saint Charles MO 63301
    636 946-6525

(G-490)
LONE PINE PUBLISHING INC
1808 B St Nw Ste 140 (98001-1643)
PHONE 253 394-0400
Shane Kennedy, *President*
Patricia Sorensen, *Sales Staff*
Helen Ibach, *Manager*
Helen J Ibach, *Manager*

▲ **EMP:** 9
SALES (est): 812.8K **Privately Held**
WEB: www.lonepinepublishing.com
SIC: 2741 Miscellaneous publishing

(G-491)
MACHINING TECHNOLOGY INC
4340 B St Nw (98001-1709)
PHONE 253 872-0359
Robert Merkel, *President*
Sherri Hanson, *Office Mgr*
EMP: 15
SQ FT: 5,000
SALES (est): 2.7MM **Privately Held**
SIC: 3599 Machine shop, jobbing & repair

(G-492)
MAX-FIVE IMPORTING COMPANY
11001 Se 291st St (98092-1909)
PHONE 253 887-8665
EMP: 6
SALES: 500K **Privately Held**
SIC: 3089 Import/Distributes Auto Parts

(G-493)
MAYSBEAUTPRODUCTSCOM
1425 N St Ne (98002-3547)
PHONE 253 318-8772
Marilyn Brown, *Principal*
EMP: 2 **EST:** 2010
SALES (est): 109.8K **Privately Held**
SIC: 2844 Toilet preparations

(G-494)
MB PRECISION INC
328 37th St Nw Ste D (98001-2402)
PHONE 253 833-1695
Bogdan Zanadzki, *President*
Wanda Zanadzki, *Vice Pres*
EMP: 5
SQ FT: 2,500
SALES (est): 750K **Privately Held**
SIC: 3599 Machine shop, jobbing & repair

(G-495)
MCNEELEY MFG
4202 Auburn Way N (98002-1370)
PHONE 253 236-4969
EMP: 3 **EST:** 2013
SALES (est): 243.7K **Privately Held**
SIC: 3999 Manufacturing industries

(G-496)
MECHPRO INC
1320 26th St Nw Ste 4 (98001-1620)
PHONE 206 445-5230
Robert Hegge, *Principal*
EMP: 7
SALES (est): 177.5K **Privately Held**
SIC: 7349 3592 3444 Chemical cleaning services; valves; cooling towers, sheet metal

(G-497)
MILLARD TECHNICAL SERVICE
3635 C St Ne (98002-1736)
P.O. Box 88 (98071-0088)
PHONE 253 218-0115
Kris Millard, *Principal*
EMP: 3
SALES (est): 286.7K **Privately Held**
SIC: 3599 Machine shop, jobbing & repair

(G-498)
MILLER FABRICATION INC
1435 R St Nw (98001-3506)
PHONE 253 833-5400
Jerry E Miller, *President*
Beth Miller, *Corp Secy*
Janeil Hardy, *Vice Pres*
EMP: 5
SQ FT: 9,600
SALES (est): 849.2K **Privately Held**
WEB: www.millerfab.com
SIC: 3441 Fabricated structural metal

(G-499)
MISSION AFRICA
1020 30th St Ne (98002-2451)
PHONE 206 850-9155
Ndudi Chuku, *Exec Dir*
▼ **EMP:** 11
SALES: 227.1K **Privately Held**
SIC: 3366 Copper foundries

Auburn - King County (G-500) — GEOGRAPHIC SECTION

(G-500)
MITI LLC
Also Called: Mp Industrial
3902 W Valley Hwy N # 306 (98001-2426)
PHONE..................................253 833-9119
Mike Madden, *Marketing Staff*
Timothy Prather,
Michael Madden,
EMP: 5
SALES (est): 904.3K **Privately Held**
SIC: 3546 Power-driven handtools

(G-501)
MUNTERS MOISTURE CONTROL SVCS
Also Called: Auburn WA 98002
301 30th St Ne Ste 118 (98002-2353)
PHONE..................................707 863-4189
EMP: 2
SALES (est): 116.7K **Privately Held**
SIC: 3585 Mfg Refrigeration/Heating Equipment

(G-502)
MUTUAL MATERIALS COMPANY
1357 W Valley Hwy N (98001-4123)
PHONE..................................253 838-0803
Chris Houoahan, *Sales/Mktg Mgr*
EMP: 4
SQ FT: 6,892
SALES (corp-wide): 44.8MM **Privately Held**
SIC: 5032 5211 5082 3272 Masons' materials; brick; masonry equipment & supplies; concrete products, precast; retaining wall construction
PA: Mutual Materials Company
605 119th Ave Ne
Bellevue WA 98005
425 452-2300

(G-503)
NAILS ON WHEELS
5416 S 296th Ct (98001-2350)
PHONE..................................253 839-1123
Christine Osburn, *Principal*
EMP: 2
SALES (est): 116.6K **Privately Held**
SIC: 3312 Wheels

(G-504)
NATIONAL BANNER SUPPLY
4204 Auburn Way N Ste 4 (98002-1379)
PHONE..................................253 333-7443
Monty Long, *President*
EMP: 4
SALES: 200K **Privately Held**
SIC: 3949 Camping equipment & supplies

(G-505)
NELSON CONSTRUCTION INC
1 37th St Nw Ste G (98001-1715)
P.O. Box 1915 (98071-1915)
PHONE..................................253 931-6696
Lyman Frederick, *President*
Jeffrey Qualls, *Principal*
EMP: 15
SALES (est): 1.7MM **Privately Held**
SIC: 3441 Building components, structural steel

(G-506)
NEOBIOTECH GLOBAL CORPORATION
1 30th St Nw Unit 9 (98001-1711)
PHONE..................................253 732-3573
Esther Park Hwang, *President*
EMP: 3
SQ FT: 3,000
SALES: 48K **Privately Held**
SIC: 2834 Analgesics

(G-507)
NFI ENTERPRISES LLC
2536 Auburn Way N (98002-2420)
P.O. Box 58583, Seattle (98138-1583)
PHONE..................................253 245-5500
Gary Brown, *CEO*
Zach Brown, *President*
EMP: 30
SQ FT: 15,000
SALES (est): 4.6MM **Privately Held**
SIC: 1771 7389 5713 2426 Flooring contractor; interior design services; floor covering stores; flooring, hardwood

(G-508)
NOR PROP INC
3220 B St Se (98002-8832)
PHONE..................................253 939-1200
Finn Feroy, *President*
T A Feroy, *Vice Pres*
EMP: 20 **EST:** 1972
SALES (est): 1.8MM **Privately Held**
WEB: www.fishexposeattle.com
SIC: 8711 3599 Designing: ship, boat, machine & product; marine engineering; propellers, ship & boat; machined

(G-509)
NORGREN GT DEVELOPMENT CORP
425 C St Nw Ste 100 (98001-3906)
PHONE..................................206 244-1305
EMP: 110
SALES (corp-wide): 2.4B **Privately Held**
SIC: 3625 Relays & industrial controls
HQ: Norgren Gt Development Corporation
425 C St Nw Ste 100
Auburn WA 98001
206 244-1305

(G-510)
NORPLEX INC (PA)
111 3rd St Nw Bldg C (98001-4024)
P.O. Box 814 (98071-0814)
PHONE..................................253 735-3431
Ralph Schley, *President*
Gerald E Sanford, *Principal*
Lois Schley, *Vice Pres*
Adair Hendrickson, *Accounting Mgr*
Joan Thames, *Admin Sec*
▲ **EMP:** 42
SALES (est): 8.5MM **Privately Held*
WEB: www.norplex.net
SIC: 3089 Netting, plastic

(G-511)
NORTHWEST HYGIENETICS INC
Also Called: Colman's Fishing Supply
29903 43rd Ave S (98001-2906)
PHONE..................................253 529-0294
Jon Colman, *President*
▲ **EMP:** 4
SQ FT: 1,800
SALES (est): 598K **Privately Held**
SIC: 5091 3949 Fishing equipment & supplies; fishing equipment

(G-512)
NORTHWEST METAL SPINNING
5521 Duncan Ave Se (98092-8421)
P.O. Box 489 (98071-0489)
PHONE..................................253 351-8489
Martin Freelund, *Owner*
EMP: 5
SALES (est): 430.8K **Privately Held**
SIC: 3469 Spinning metal for the trade

(G-513)
NU-RAY METAL PRODUCTS INC (PA)
Also Called: Nu-Ray Metals
1234 37th St Nw (98001-2416)
PHONE..................................253 833-8637
Timothy Bankers, *President*
Michael A Bankers, *Vice Pres*
Theresa Bankers, *Treasurer*
▼ **EMP:** 17
SQ FT: 45,000
SALES (est): 7.1MM **Privately Held**
WEB: www.nuraymetals.com
SIC: 3444 Metal roofing & roof drainage equipment; metal flooring & siding

(G-514)
NW LIGHTING SOLUTIONS LLC
201 Auburn Way N Ste C (98002-5062)
PHONE..................................253 929-4657
EMP: 2
SALES (est): 119K **Privately Held**
SIC: 3648 Lighting equipment

(G-515)
NWSIGNWERXS
3414 A St Se (98002-8800)
PHONE..................................253 217-0053
Vicente Rabago, *Principal*
EMP: 3 **EST:** 2013
SQ FT: 2,900
SALES (est): 223K **Privately Held**
SIC: 3993 Signs & advertising specialties

(G-516)
OBCON INC
Also Called: AMERICAN PRODUCTS
1802 Pike St Nw (98001-3426)
P.O. Box 1744 (98071-1744)
PHONE..................................253 931-0455
Andy Oberbillig, *President*
Karen Oberbillig, *Vice Pres*
EMP: 8
SALES: 353.8K **Privately Held**
SIC: 3082 2542 5046 3089 Tubes, unsupported plastic; partitions & fixtures, except wood; store fixtures; plastic processing

(G-517)
OLDCASTLE PRECAST INC
Utility Vault
2808 A St Se (98002-7501)
P.O. Box 588 (98071-0588)
PHONE..................................253 839-3500
Gary Venn, *Manager*
EMP: 100
SALES (corp-wide): 30.6B **Privately Held**
WEB: www.oldcastle-precast.com
SIC: 3272 Concrete products
HQ: Oldcastle Infrastructure, Inc.
1002 15th St Sw Ste 110
Auburn WA 98001
253 833-2777

(G-518)
OMNIFAB INC
1316 W Main St (98001-5217)
PHONE..................................253 931-5151
Erik Cullen, *Ch of Bd*
John Shepherd, *President*
Daniel Cullen,
Tyler Mayfield,
EMP: 45
SQ FT: 50,000
SALES (est): 7.7MM **Privately Held**
WEB: www.omnifabllc.com
SIC: 3443 3444 3412 3451 Fabricated plate work (boiler shop); sheet metalwork; metal barrels, drums & pails; screw machine products; fabricated structural metal; etching & engraving
PA: Jet City Partners Llc
22 42nd St Nw Ste B
Auburn WA 98001
206 999-0047

(G-519)
OPTIMUM EXTRACTS ◆
3402 C St Ne Ste 109 (98001-1728)
PHONE..................................206 491-9617
EMP: 2 **EST:** 2018
SALES (est): 80.6K **Privately Held**
SIC: 3999 2836 ; extracts

(G-520)
ORBIS RPM LLC
2302 B St Nw Ste 102 (98001-1748)
PHONE..................................253 333-0606
Dan Jandura, *Principal*
EMP: 16
SALES (corp-wide): 1.7B **Privately Held**
SIC: 3081 Unsupported plastics film & sheet
HQ: Orbis Rpm, Llc
1055 Corporate Center Dr
Oconomowoc WI 53066
262 560-5000

(G-521)
ORION INDUSTRIES (PA)
1590 A St Ne (98002-5101)
PHONE..................................253 661-7805
Jerry Chase, *CEO*
Sean Dwyer, *General Mgr*
Kathy Powers, *Vice Pres*
Mike Barsoski, *Opers Mgr*
Rick Gilleland, *Production*
EMP: 120
SQ FT: 34,480
SALES: 28.7MM **Privately Held**
WEB: www.ori-ind.com
SIC: 3444 8331 Sheet metalwork; vocational training agency

(G-522)
PACIFIC A CRGO TRANSF SYSTEMS
Also Called: Laser Cutting Northwest
3205 C St Ne (98002-1706)
PHONE..................................253 735-5277
Peter Agtuca, *President*
Pete Agtuca, *General Mgr*
Jolene Agtuca, *Vice Pres*
EMP: 44
SQ FT: 45,000
SALES (est): 10MM **Privately Held**
WEB: www.lcnw.com
SIC: 3441 Building components, structural steel

(G-523)
PACIFIC CUSTOM CABLE INC
Also Called: Independent Commerce
4170 B Pl Nw (98001-2446)
P.O. Box 8026, Bonney Lake (98391-0999)
PHONE..................................253 373-0800
David R Maher, *President*
Kim Marie Maher, *Vice Pres*
▲ **EMP:** 10
SQ FT: 2,000
SALES (est): 1.8MM **Privately Held**
WEB: www.pacificcable.com
SIC: 5045 3679 1731 Computer peripheral equipment; harness assemblies for electronic use; wire or cable; computer installation

(G-524)
PACIFIC POWER GROUP LLC
Also Called: Pacific Power Products
1221 29th St Nw Ste D (98001-2431)
PHONE..................................253 395-9077
Jody Adesro, *Manager*
EMP: 29
SALES (corp-wide): 18.1MM **Privately Held**
SIC: 3621 5063 Motor generator sets; generators
HQ: Pacific Power Group, Llc
805 Broadway St Ste 700
Vancouver WA 98660
360 887-7400

(G-525)
PACIFIC WIRE GROUP INC
Also Called: Pacific Wire Products
2201 R St Nw (98001-1657)
PHONE..................................253 249-0249
Robin W Crist, *President*
Lynne Crist, *CFO*
Bob Brown, *VP Sales*
Andy S Domingo, *Sales Staff*
Marty Hobbs, *Sales Staff*
EMP: 14
SQ FT: 15,200
SALES (est): 3.4MM **Privately Held**
WEB: www.pacific-wire.com
SIC: 3496 5051 3315 Clips & fasteners, made from purchased wire; slings, lifting: made from purchased wire; concrete reinforcing mesh & wire; bale ties, wire; wire; steel wire & related products

(G-526)
PACTIV LLC
Also Called: PACTIV CORPORATION
2820 B St Nw Ste 109 (98001-1736)
PHONE..................................847 482-2000
Rob Williams, *Sales Mgr*
Mustafa Haziq, *Info Tech Mgr*
EMP: 60
SALES (corp-wide): 1MM **Privately Held**
WEB: www.pactiv.com
SIC: 3086 2671 Packaging & shipping materials, foamed plastic; packaging paper & plastics film, coated & laminated
HQ: Pactiv Llc
1900 W Field Ct
Lake Forest IL 60045
847 482-2000

(G-527)
PATRIOT JABEZ CONSTRUCTION JV
710 A St Nw (98001-4934)
PHONE..................................253 293-7100
Ryan Rickel, *Partner*
EMP: 2

GEOGRAPHIC SECTION

Auburn - King County (G-559)

SALES (est): 170.9K **Privately Held**
SIC: **1542** 1541 1771 3441 Commercial & office buildings, renovation & repair; industrial buildings, new construction; concrete work; fabricated structural metal

(G-528)
PATROIT FUELS LLC
13410 Se 294th Pl (98092-2115)
PHONE..................................253 507-6256
Eric Singletary, *Principal*
EMP: 4
SALES (est): 342.3K **Privately Held**
SIC: **2869** Fuels

(G-529)
PEEKAY INC
Also Called: A Touch of Romance
901 W Main St Ste A (98001-5280)
PHONE..................................818 754-1201
EMP: 10
SALES (corp-wide): 25.9MM **Privately Held**
SIC: **3993** Mfg Signs/Advertising Specialties
PA: Peekay, Inc.
901 W Main St Ste A
Auburn WA 98001
253 351-5001

(G-530)
PELL INDUSTRIAL LLC
1812 B St Nw Ste 110 (98001-1652)
PHONE..................................425 222-9672
Theresa Allegro, *Opers Mgr*
Lee Pell, *Mng Member*
EMP: 6
SALES (est): 1MM **Privately Held**
SIC: **3423** 5044 Hand & edge tools; vaults & safes

(G-531)
PERFORMANCE COATINGS INC
60 37th St Ne Ste A (98002-1766)
PHONE..................................253 735-1919
Brad Gua, *President*
EMP: 4
SQ FT: 2,000
SALES: 400K **Privately Held**
SIC: **3479** Coating of metals & formed products

(G-532)
PLANT HORMONES LLC
4272 S 290th St (98001-2836)
PHONE..................................253 332-6131
David Sturtz, *Administration*
EMP: 2
SALES (est): 81.8K **Privately Held**
SIC: **2879** Plant hormones

(G-533)
PPG INDUSTRIES
1220 37th St Nw Ste 104 (98001-2433)
PHONE..................................253 804-4350
Kurt Mensing, *Principal*
EMP: 8
SALES (est): 731.5K **Privately Held**
SIC: **2851** Paints & allied products

(G-534)
PRECISION CUSTOM CABINETS LLC
3705 Auburn Way N (98002-1321)
PHONE..................................253 397-4240
Richard Birdsong, *President*
EMP: 14
SALES: 850K **Privately Held**
SIC: **2434** Wood kitchen cabinets

(G-535)
PREMIER TORQUE CONVERTER
12561 Se Green Valley Rd (98092-8503)
P.O. Box 193 (98071-0193)
PHONE..................................253 288-2233
Jeff Deneerleer, *Principal*
EMP: 2
SALES (est): 33.3K **Privately Held**
SIC: **3566** Torque converters, except automotive

(G-536)
PRESSED IN TIME PRTG PRMTONS L
1356 32nd Pl Ne (98002-2358)
PHONE..................................253 833-1351
Criss Vefik, *Principal*
EMP: 2
SALES (est): 173K **Privately Held**
SIC: **2752** Commercial printing, lithographic

(G-537)
PRIMUS INTERNATIONAL INC (DH)
Also Called: PCC Aerostructures
610 Bllvue Way Ne Ste 200 (98001)
PHONE..................................425 688-0444
Jim Hoover, *President*
Joseph Snowden, *President*
Shawn Hagel, *Chairman*
Roger Becker, *Vice Pres*
Douglas P Fletcher, *CFO*
◆ EMP: 6 EST: 1966
SQ FT: 5,000
SALES (est): 138.7MM
SALES (corp-wide): 225.3B **Publicly Held**
WEB: www.primusint.com
SIC: **3728** Aircraft body & wing assemblies & parts
HQ: Precision Castparts Corp.
4650 Sw Mcdam Ave Ste 300
Portland OR 97239
503 946-4800

(G-538)
PRINT SERVICES NORTHWEST INC
4040 Auburn Way N Ste 3 (98002-1394)
PHONE..................................253 236-8224
EMP: 2
SALES (est): 92.3K **Privately Held**
SIC: **2752** Commercial printing, offset

(G-539)
PROFLECTIONS METAL POLISHING
Also Called: Proflections Metal Finishing
131 30th St Ne Ste 20a (98002-1700)
PHONE..................................253 735-6111
Albert Malgarin, *President*
Mike Gotowka, *Exec VP*
Christy Malgarin, *Admin Sec*
EMP: 6
SQ FT: 3,000
SALES: 385K **Privately Held**
WEB: www.proflections.com
SIC: **3471** Plating of metals or formed products

(G-540)
PUGET SOUND METAL FABRICATION
3825 S 312th St (98002-2637)
PHONE..................................253 941-7868
Richard Douvier, *Owner*
EMP: 2 EST: 1992
SALES (est): 239K **Privately Held**
SIC: **3441** Fabricated structural metal

(G-541)
QUALITY FENCE BUILDERS INC
214 21st St Se (98002-6816)
P.O. Box 854 (98071-0854)
PHONE..................................253 939-8533
Jill McCurdy, *President*
Matt McCurdy, *Vice Pres*
EMP: 44
SQ FT: 20,000
SALES: 6.1MM **Privately Held**
WEB: www.quality-fence.com
SIC: **1799** 3496 3315 3699 Fence construction; miscellaneous fabricated wire products; steel wire & related products; security devices

(G-542)
R & S ROBERTS ENTERPRISES INC
Also Called: Gosanko Chocolate Art
116 A St Se (98002-5431)
PHONE..................................253 333-7567
Ronnie Roberts, *Owner*
Susan Roberts, *Officer*
EMP: 10
SQ FT: 4,689
SALES (est): 1.2MM **Privately Held**
WEB: www.gosankochocolate.com
SIC: **2064** 2066 Candy & other confectionery products; chocolate & cocoa products

(G-543)
RAINIER DEFENSE LLC
2504 Auburn Way N (98002-2420)
PHONE..................................253 218-2999
Geoffrey Cole,
Anthony Bristol,
John Hwang,
Troy Turner,
EMP: 4
SALES (est): 191.7K **Privately Held**
SIC: **3812** Defense systems & equipment

(G-544)
RAINIER ORNA IR FBRICATION INC
19855 Se 342nd St (98092-1591)
PHONE..................................253 833-0101
Barb Sauve, *President*
EMP: 2
SALES: 260K **Privately Held**
SIC: **3446** Fences or posts, ornamental iron or steel

(G-545)
RAINIER RIGGING INC
16131 Se Green Valley Rd (98092-3926)
PHONE..................................253 833-4087
Michael Walch, *President*
EMP: 12
SALES (est): 1.2MM **Privately Held**
WEB: www.rainierrigging.com
SIC: **3532** Mining machinery

(G-546)
RBK MANUFACTURING INCORPORATED
3040 B St Nw Ste 5 (98001-1721)
PHONE..................................253 804-8636
Joseph Rohrmoser, *President*
Mike Kemler, *Vice Pres*
EMP: 15
SQ FT: 4,000
SALES (est): 2.4MM **Privately Held**
WEB: www.rbkmfg.com
SIC: **3599** Machine shop, jobbing & repair

(G-547)
RICHARDS PACKAGING INC
4103 C St Ne Ste 100 (98001-1722)
PHONE..................................253 872-2848
Josh Tarris, *Manager*
EMP: 6
SALES (corp-wide): 241.1MM **Privately Held**
WEB: www.richardspackaging.com
SIC: **3085** Plastics bottles
HQ: Richards Packaging, Inc.
2321 Ne Argyle St Ste D
Portland OR 97211
503 290-0000

(G-548)
RJM CORPORATION
Also Called: R J M
3220 C St Ne Ste G (98002-1746)
PHONE..................................253 887-9100
Gerald Minato, *President*
Ryan Minato, *Vice Pres*
EMP: 10
SQ FT: 6,000
SALES (est): 1.4MM **Privately Held**
SIC: **3599** Custom machinery

(G-549)
ROOK DEFENSE LLC
6821 Udall Pl Se Apt C104 (98092-9606)
PHONE..................................206 518-3593
Tomas Oliverez, *Principal*
EMP: 3
SALES (est): 218.5K **Privately Held**
SIC: **3812** Defense systems & equipment

(G-550)
ROY DINTELMAN
5409 S 380th St (98001-9412)
PHONE..................................253 508-9361
Roy Dintelman, *Principal*

EMP: 2
SALES (est): 86K **Privately Held**
SIC: **3721** Airplanes, fixed or rotary wing

(G-551)
RVS EXPRESS LLC
412 8th St Sw Ste A (98001-5902)
PHONE..................................253 249-7043
Roman Solovyev, *Principal*
EMP: 2
SALES (est): 189.6K **Privately Held**
SIC: **3799** Recreational vehicles

(G-552)
RWOODSII LLC
3402 C St Ne Ste 109 (98002-1728)
PHONE..................................206 491-9617
Robert Woods, *Administration*
EMP: 3
SALES (est): 60.7K **Privately Held**
SIC: **2499** Wood products

(G-553)
RYAN MACHINE INC
4164 B Pl Nw (98001-2446)
PHONE..................................253 854-9000
William J Ryan, *President*
EMP: 22
SQ FT: 8,700
SALES (est): 250K **Privately Held**
WEB: www.ryanmachine.com
SIC: **3599** Machine shop, jobbing & repair

(G-554)
RYNO ROLLERS INC (PA)
3904 B St Nw (98001-2432)
PHONE..................................253 856-0738
Jamie Rowley, *Principal*
EMP: 6
SALES (est): 934.9K **Privately Held**
SIC: **2262** Roller printing: manmade fiber & silk broadwoven fabrics

(G-555)
SAKCO PRECISION INC
3665 C St Ne (98002-1736)
PHONE..................................253 288-9702
Scott Stackle, *President*
EMP: 8
SALES (est): 990K **Privately Held**
SIC: **3812** 3728 Acceleration indicators & systems components, aerospace; aircraft parts & equipment

(G-556)
SCHILLING CIDER LLC
4402 D St Nw Ste 101 (98001-2461)
PHONE..................................408 390-8754
Colin Schilling, *CEO*
Ian Townson, *Vice Pres*
Mark Kornei, *CFO*
EMP: 12
SALES (est): 2MM **Privately Held**
SIC: **2099** Cider, nonalcoholic

(G-557)
SEAL-GUARD CORPORATION
101 F St Nw (98001-5264)
PHONE..................................253 833-7080
Robert Jones, *President*
Cary Osulbian, *Manager*
EMP: 3
SQ FT: 2,400
SALES: 300K **Privately Held**
SIC: **3053** 3599 Gaskets & sealing devices; gaskets, all materials; machine shop, jobbing & repair

(G-558)
SEATTLE EVENT PRINTING
110 42nd St Nw (98001-1730)
P.O. Box 2203 (98071-2203)
PHONE..................................253 642-6567
EMP: 2
SALES (est): 83.9K **Privately Held**
SIC: **2752** Commercial printing, lithographic

(G-559)
SEATTLE SAFETY LLC (PA)
4502 B St Nw U1 (98001-1707)
PHONE..................................253 395-4321
Matt Sikora, *General Mgr*
Michael Hughes, *Mfg Mgr*
Thomas Wittmann,
◆ EMP: 50

Auburn - King County (G-560)

SQ FT: 21,400
SALES (est): 7.8MM **Privately Held**
WEB: www.seattlesafety.com
SIC: 3825 Test equipment for electronic & electrical circuits

(G-560)
SERENA INC
202 37th St Ne (98002-1744)
P.O. Box 1532, Kent (98035-1532)
PHONE..................................253 939-6509
Tary Serena, *President*
EMP: 2
SALES (est): 210.7K **Privately Held**
SIC: 3541 3599 Machine tools, metal cutting type; machine shop, jobbing & repair

(G-561)
SERVICE HYDRAULICS INC
25 37th St Ne (98002-1715)
PHONE..................................253 351-6010
Albert E Lakin Jr, *President*
Pam Lakin, *Treasurer*
EMP: 12
SQ FT: 12,000
SALES (est): 2.5MM **Privately Held**
SIC: 7699 3594 3593 7389 Hydraulic equipment repair; motors: hydraulic, fluid power or air; fluid power cylinders & actuators; auction, appraisal & exchange services

(G-562)
SHAREWAY INDUSTRIES INC
2526 E St Ne (98002-1698)
PHONE..................................253 804-0670
Donald Shumway Jr, *President*
Roger Reiche, *Vice Pres*
Justin Shumway, *CFO*
Danny Vanlant, *Sales Mgr*
EMP: 49 EST: 1970
SQ FT: 25,000
SALES (est): 6.9MM **Privately Held**
WEB: www.shareway.com
SIC: 3599 Machine shop, jobbing & repair

(G-563)
SIGN CITY GFX
Also Called: Graphic Fx
2507 C St Sw (98001-7423)
PHONE..................................253 329-2670
Kreig Eley, *Partner*
EMP: 6
SALES (est): 490K **Privately Held**
SIC: 3993 Signs & advertising specialties

(G-564)
SK&Y INTERNATIONAL LLC
Also Called: Sky Company
1221 29th St Nw Ste C (98001-2431)
PHONE..................................253 833-9525
Susan Kim, *Mng Member*
▲ EMP: 3
SQ FT: 10,000
SALES: 2.5MM **Privately Held**
SIC: 5087 3582 Laundry equipment & supplies; commercial laundry equipment

(G-565)
SKILLS INC
425 C St Nw (98001-3906)
PHONE..................................206 782-6000
EMP: 60
SALES (corp-wide): 53.6MM **Privately Held**
SIC: 3479 Coating of metals & formed products
PA: Skills, Inc.
715 30th St Ne
Auburn WA 98002
206 782-6000

(G-566)
SLAWEK TILES
29314 45th Pl S (98001-1521)
PHONE..................................253 529-0823
EMP: 2
SALES (est): 110K **Privately Held**
SIC: 2499 Mfg Wood Products

(G-567)
SLS DEVELOPMENT INC
Also Called: Minuteman Press
3804 B St Nw (98001-2419)
PHONE..................................253 735-0322
Stephanie Christensen, *President*

Craig Christensen, *Vice Pres*
EMP: 3
SQ FT: 4,000
SALES: 410K **Privately Held**
SIC: 2752 Commercial printing, lithographic

(G-568)
SNT-GBAIN N VETROTECH AMER INC
2108 B St Nw Ste 110 (98001-1624)
PHONE..................................253 333-7592
Leonard Brunette, *Principal*
Marteen Ditty, *Principal*
▲ EMP: 7
SQ FT: 9,000
SALES (est): 1.4MM
SALES (corp-wide): 215.9MM **Privately Held**
SIC: 3211 Tempered glass
HQ: Saint-Gobain Glass Corporation
20 Moores Rd
Malvern PA 19355
484 595-9530

(G-569)
SOUTHEND MACHINE INC
1802 Pike St Nw Ste C (98001-3426)
PHONE..................................253 735-1035
EMP: 8
SQ FT: 11,000
SALES: 1MM **Privately Held**
WEB: www.southendmachine.com
SIC: 3599 Machine shop, jobbing & repair

(G-570)
SPECTRUM SIGN CO INC
301 W Main St (98001-4910)
PHONE..................................253 939-5500
Michael Harbin Jr, *President*
Jill Haner, *Office Mgr*
Karen Harbin, *Admin Sec*
Chelsea Albright, *Receptionist*
EMP: 12
SQ FT: 23,000
SALES (est): 1.5MM **Privately Held**
WEB: www.spectrumsign.com
SIC: 7389 2499 3993 2759 Lettering & sign painting services; signboards, wood; signs & advertising specialties; screen printing

(G-571)
STANS HEADERS INC
4715 Auburn Way N (98002-1312)
PHONE..................................253 854-5310
Stan Fuller, *President*
Pamela Fuller, *Vice Pres*
EMP: 10
SQ FT: 8,500
SALES (est): 888.9K **Privately Held**
WEB: www.stans-headers.com
SIC: 7533 7539 3498 Muffler shop, sale or repair & installation; brake repair, automotive; tube fabricating (contract bending & shaping)

(G-572)
STEELTEC SUPPLY INC
134 37th St Ne (98002-1707)
PHONE..................................253 333-1311
Jaroslaw Sydry, *President*
Leszek Orszulak, *Vice Pres*
EMP: 2
SQ FT: 3,000
SALES: 700K **Privately Held**
WEB: www.steeltecsupply.com
SIC: 3444 5039 5032 Sheet metalwork; prefabricated structures; drywall materials

(G-573)
STONE CASTLE FABRICATION LLC
1501 20th St Nw (98001-3422)
P.O. Box 1995 (98071-1995)
PHONE..................................253 205-8435
EMP: 3 EST: 2017
SALES (est): 202.4K **Privately Held**
SIC: 3281 Curbing, granite or stone

(G-574)
SUNSHINE SMOOTHIE INC
5607 Evergreen Loop Se (98092-8702)
PHONE..................................425 497-9211
Mary Beth Harris, *Principal*
EMP: 3

SALES (est): 189.5K **Privately Held**
SIC: 2037 Frozen fruits & vegetables

(G-575)
T & H MACHINE INC
60 37th St Ne Ste C (98002-1766)
PHONE..................................253 735-6521
Ty Wing, *President*
EMP: 2
SALES: 50K **Privately Held**
SIC: 3599 Machine shop, jobbing & repair

(G-576)
TABS TO GO INC
110 42nd St Nw (98001-1730)
PHONE..................................253 854-8227
Michael Lane, *President*
Daniel Lane, *Vice Pres*
EMP: 8
SQ FT: 4,000
SALES (est): 1.1MM **Privately Held**
WEB: www.tabstogo.com
SIC: 2679 2675 Pressed & molded pulp products, purchased material; die-cut paper & board

(G-577)
TARR ACQUISITION LLC
4510 B St Nw Ste B (98001-1744)
PHONE..................................253 859-2979
Craney Branch, *Manager*
EMP: 7
SALES (corp-wide): 58MM **Privately Held**
WEB: www.tarrllc.com
SIC: 2869 8611 Solvents, organic; business associations
PA: Tarr Acquisition, Llc
2946 Ne Columbia Blvd
Portland OR 97211
503 345-0211

(G-578)
TC MOTORSPORTS
1302 W Main St Ste 13 (98001-5216)
PHONE..................................253 887-0500
EMP: 4 EST: 2007
SALES (est): 340K **Privately Held**
SIC: 3799 Mfg Transportation Equipment

(G-579)
TEX ENTERPRISES INC
1302 W Main St Ste 13 (98001-5216)
PHONE..................................253 939-1660
Charles Pieratt, *President*
Sharon Waller, *Vice Pres*
EMP: 5
SQ FT: 12,000
SALES (est): 629.2K **Privately Held**
WEB: www.texenterprises.com
SIC: 2822 2821 Synthetic rubber; plastics materials & resins

(G-580)
THERMALINE INC
1531 14th St Nw (98001-3518)
PHONE..................................253 833-7168
Leon Sanders, *President*
Pam Giles, *Controller*
Ian Price, *Info Tech Dir*
◆ EMP: 18
SQ FT: 4,000
SALES (est): 7.2MM **Privately Held**
WEB: www.thermaline.com
SIC: 3443 Heat exchangers, condensers & components

(G-581)
THYSSENKRUPP MATERIALS LLC
Also Called: Tmx Aerospace
5002 D St Nw Ste 104 (98001-2435)
PHONE..................................253 239-6023
Jennifer Solbrack, *Administration*
EMP: 5
SALES (corp-wide): 39.8B **Privately Held**
SIC: 3721 Aircraft
HQ: Thyssenkrupp Materials, Llc
6811 S 204th St Ste 400
Kent WA 98032

(G-582)
TRI-WAY INDUSTRIES INC
506 44th St Nw (98001-1795)
PHONE..................................253 859-4585
Ken Smith, *President*

Cole Corirossi, *Principal*
Ken D Smith, *Vice Pres*
Connie L Johnson, *Admin Sec*
EMP: 90 EST: 1946
SQ FT: 80,000
SALES (est): 17.6MM **Privately Held**
WEB: www.triwayind.com
SIC: 2531 2542 2599 3444 Vehicle furniture; fixtures: display, office or store: except wood; ship furniture; sheet metalwork; manufactured hardware (general)

(G-583)
TRU SQUARE METAL PRODUCTS INC
Also Called: Tru Square Thumler's Tumbler
640 1st St Sw (98001-5262)
P.O. Box 585 (98071-0585)
PHONE..................................253 833-2310
Albert H Thumler, *President*
EMP: 9
SQ FT: 9,000
SALES: 1.6MM **Privately Held**
WEB: www.thumlerstumbler.com
SIC: 3559 3541 Stone working machinery; machine tools, metal cutting type

(G-584)
TTF AEROSPACE INC (PA)
4620 B St Nw Ste 101 (98001-1763)
PHONE..................................253 736-6300
Tim Morgan,
Janice Morgan,
Brad Wilson,
Kirsten Wilson,
EMP: 104
SQ FT: 5,000
SALES (est): 27.8MM **Privately Held**
WEB: www.ttfaero.com
SIC: 3728 8711 Aircraft parts & equipment; aviation &/or aeronautical engineering

(G-585)
TWEET PROMOTIONAL IMPRESSIONS
6646 Elizabeth Ave Se (98092-8218)
PHONE..................................206 660-6074
Timothy Tweet, *Owner*
EMP: 2
SALES (est): 92.2K **Privately Held**
SIC: 3949 Sporting & athletic goods

(G-586)
TWINTEC INC
1510 Boundary Blvd # 110 (98001-6579)
PHONE..................................253 218-0890
Chris Burrows, *President*
Steven Burrows, *Vice Pres*
EMP: 7
SQ FT: 2,900
SALES (est): 400K **Privately Held**
WEB: www.twintecinc.com
SIC: 3822 5084 Pneumatic relays, air-conditioning type; pneumatic tools & equipment

(G-587)
UNILODE AVI SOLUTION US INC (HQ)
Also Called: Chep Aerospace US Inc.
1808 B St Nw Ste 170 (98001-1640)
PHONE..................................206 824-7123
Richard Bjornholm, *President*
John Hayler, *Chairman*
Melissa L Schmidt, *Vice Pres*
Kirk Safford, *Director*
James Frye Jr, *Admin Sec*
▲ EMP: 16
SQ FT: 16,433
SALES (est): 17.8MM **Privately Held**
WEB: www.driessensvc.com
SIC: 7699 4432 2653 Industrial machinery & equipment repair; freight transportation on the Great Lakes; pallets, corrugated: made from purchased materials

(G-588)
UNITED STATES GYPSUM COMPANY
401 C St Nw (98001-3908)
PHONE..................................253 931-6600
Scott Seely, *Mfg Staff*

GEOGRAPHIC SECTION

Kevin Richardson, *Manager*
William Jarvis, *MIS Mgr*
EMP: 21
SALES (corp-wide): 8.2B **Privately Held**
WEB: www.usg.com
SIC: 3275 Gypsum products
HQ: United States Gypsum Company
550 W Adams St Ste 1300
Chicago IL 60661
312 606-4000

(G-589)
UNIVERSAL BRASS INC
131 30th St Ne Ste 25 (98002-1700)
P.O. Box 548 (98071-0548)
PHONE..................253 939-8282
Myron Lewis, *President*
Kimberly Kirkland, *Admin Sec*
▼ **EMP:** 16
SQ FT: 13,300
SALES (est): 2.3MM **Privately Held**
WEB: www.jewelryforcars.com
SIC: 3499 3471 3479 Giftware, brass goods; plating of metals or formed products; engraving jewelry silverware, or metal

(G-590)
VANATOO LLC
28838 52nd Pl S (98001-2144)
PHONE..................206 486-1002
Gary Gesellchen,
Frederick Kernen,
▲ **EMP:** 2
SQ FT: 100
SALES (est): 245K **Privately Held**
SIC: 3651 Audio electronic systems

(G-591)
VANGUARD FOODS
3416 B St Nw Ste C (98001-1759)
PHONE..................206 355-5938
EMP: 2
SALES (est): 97.1K **Privately Held**
SIC: 2741 Miscellaneous publishing

(G-592)
VISION X OFFROAD LLC
Also Called: Vision X Offroad Lighting
1601 Boundary Blvd (98001-6578)
PHONE..................888 489-9820
Anthony Georgitsis,
Joseph Biro,
George Georgitsis,
Nicholas Irwin,
EMP: 30
SALES (est): 2.6MM **Privately Held**
SIC: 3646 Commercial indusl & institutional electric lighting fixtures

(G-593)
WASHINGTON STATE HORSESHOE PIT
16010 Se 322nd St (98092-5914)
PHONE..................253 735-0213
Don Davis, *Principal*
EMP: 2
SALES (est): 147.5K **Privately Held**
SIC: 3462 Horseshoes

(G-594)
WASSER CORP
Also Called: Wasser High-Tech Coatings
4118 B Pl Nw Ste B (98001-2462)
PHONE..................360 870-3513
Rachel Maus, *Principal*
Rachel Wilson, *Office Mgr*
Ben Forde, *Technical Staff*
▼ **EMP:** 3
SQ FT: 60,000
SALES (est): 617.3K **Privately Held**
WEB: www.wassercoatings.com
SIC: 2851 Marine paints; undercoatings, paint; coating, air curing

(G-595)
WC MANUFACTURING LLC
3217 S 374th St (98001-8723)
PHONE..................425 890-9709
William Windham, *Principal*
EMP: 2 **EST:** 2014
SALES (est): 120.6K **Privately Held**
SIC: 3999 Manufacturing industries

(G-596)
WEEKS WATERJET & MFG
104 49th St Nw (98001-1742)
PHONE..................206 261-1954
EMP: 2
SALES (est): 97.9K **Privately Held**
SIC: 3999 Manufacturing industries

(G-597)
WELCOME RAMP SYSTEMS INC
3902 B St Nw Ste B (98001-2425)
PHONE..................425 754-0489
Tom Anderson, *President*
Kathleen Coyle, *Vice Pres*
Terry Garden, *Vice Pres*
EMP: 5
SQ FT: 600
SALES: 1MM **Privately Held**
SIC: 3448 Ramps: prefabricated metal

(G-598)
WEST COAST FABRICATION INC
3202 C St Ne B (98002-1705)
PHONE..................206 790-1496
Peter Agtuca, *President*
EMP: 3
SALES (est): 315.8K **Privately Held**
SIC: 3728 3499 Research & dev by manuf., aircraft parts & auxiliary equip; furniture parts, metal

(G-599)
WESTERN CABINETS
3411 C St Ne Ste 16 (98002-1749)
PHONE..................253 269-2742
Grigoriy Psarev, *Principal*
EMP: 2
SALES (est): 228.3K **Privately Held**
SIC: 2434 Wood kitchen cabinets

(G-600)
WHOLESALE NEON A DIVISION
1450 32nd St Se (98002-8134)
PHONE..................253 939-0716
John Wallsinger, *Partner*
EMP: 6
SALES (est): 442.7K **Privately Held**
SIC: 3993 Neon signs

(G-601)
WOOD WORKS BY ROB
2812 H St Se (98002-7748)
PHONE..................206 497-6345
EMP: 2
SALES (est): 124.8K **Privately Held**
SIC: 2431 Millwork

(G-602)
XTRUDX TECHNOLOGIES INC
3410 A St Se Bldg B (98002-8807)
PHONE..................206 568-3100
Thomas E Loop, *CEO*
EMP: 4
SQ FT: 2,000
SALES: 350K **Privately Held**
SIC: 2899 Chemical preparations

(G-603)
YUE FON USA INC
6840 Montevista Dr Se (98092-8223)
PHONE..................206 303-0148
Janet Lin, *President*
▼ **EMP:** 2
SALES (est): 136.4K **Privately Held**
SIC: 3961 Costume jewelry

(G-604)
ZKL PRINTING COMPANY LLC
1445 R St Nw (98001-3503)
P.O. Box 2138 (98071-2138)
PHONE..................206 369-6156
Chaoxia Liao, *Principal*
EMP: 2
SALES (est): 92.3K **Privately Held**
SIC: 2752 Commercial printing, lithographic

Bainbridge Island
Kitsap County

(G-605)
1STRATEGY LLC
7250 Ne Bay Hill Rd (98110-1280)
PHONE..................801 824-5660
Rich Uhl, *Principal*
EMP: 2
SALES (est): 83.2K **Privately Held**
SIC: 7372 Prepackaged software

(G-606)
ADAPT LABS INC
5780 Wimsey Ln Ne (98110-2155)
P.O. Box 4057, Sequim (98382-4353)
PHONE..................206 842-2040
Mark O'Brien, *Vice Pres*
EMP: 4
SALES (est): 381.9K **Privately Held**
WEB: www.adaptlabs.com
SIC: 2834 Dermatologicals

(G-607)
AGS STAINLESS INC
7873 Ne Day Rd W (98110-4207)
PHONE..................206 842-9492
Gary Giffin, *President*
Angelo Toglia, *Corp Secy*
◆ **EMP:** 16
SQ FT: 4,000
SALES (est): 4MM **Privately Held**
WEB: www.agsstainless.com
SIC: 3446 Architectural metalwork

(G-608)
AMERICAN MOLD INSPECTION
5884 Ne Eagle Harbor Dr (98110-3717)
PHONE..................425 770-4375
Dorthea Peterson, *Bd of Directors*
EMP: 2 **EST:** 2005
SALES (est): 162.5K **Privately Held**
SIC: 3544 Industrial molds

(G-609)
AQUABIOTICS CORPORATION
10750 Arrow Point Dr Ne (98110-1469)
PHONE..................206 842-1708
Mary Romeo, *President*
Sharon Romeo, *Treasurer*
Brian Almquist, *Admin Sec*
EMP: 3
SQ FT: 2,300
SALES (est): 337.3K **Privately Held**
SIC: 2836 8748 Biological products, except diagnostic; fishery consultant

(G-610)
ARBUCKLE PRESS
1863 Commodore Ln Nw (98110-2628)
PHONE..................206 409-2091
William Davis, *Principal*
EMP: 2
SALES (est): 59.2K **Privately Held**
SIC: 2741 Miscellaneous publishing

(G-611)
AUDION LABORATORY INC
12903 Manzanita Rd Ne (98110-4236)
PHONE..................206 842-5202
EMP: 5
SALES (est): 430K **Privately Held**
SIC: 3571 Mfg Digital Systems Used In Radio

(G-612)
BAINBRDGE ISLAND WNERY VNYARDS
Also Called: Bainbrdge Island Vnyrds Winery
8989 Ne Day Rd E (98110-1398)
PHONE..................206 842-9463
Gerard Bentryn, *Owner*
Joanne Bentryn, *Co-Owner*
EMP: 3
SALES: 250K **Privately Held**
WEB: www.bainbridgevineyards.com
SIC: 2084 0172 Wine cellars, bonded: engaged in blending wines; grapes

(G-613)
BAINBRIDGE BEESWAX WORKS
280 Wyatt Way Ne Apt B102 (98110-2815)
PHONE..................206 618-2569
Lucille Fox, *Administration*
EMP: 2
SALES (est): 153.6K **Privately Held**
SIC: 2842 Beeswax, processing of

(G-614)
BAINBRIDGE ORGANIC DISTILLERS
9727 Coppertop Loop Ne (98110-4633)
PHONE..................206 842-3184
Keith Barnes, *Principal*
EMP: 7 **EST:** 2009
SALES (est): 644.1K **Privately Held**
SIC: 2085 Distillers' dried grains & solubles & alcohol

(G-615)
BAINBRIDGE VINEYARDS LLC
8989 Ne Day Rd E (98110-1398)
PHONE..................206 842-9463
Elizabeth Wittick, *Co-Owner*
EMP: 2
SALES (est): 104.2K **Privately Held**
SIC: 2084 Wines

(G-616)
BARN DOOR PRODUCTIONS
9160 Fox Cove Ln Ne (98110-1433)
PHONE..................206 780-3535
Mark Shore, *President*
EMP: 2
SALES (est): 157.5K **Privately Held**
WEB: www.barndoorproductions.com
SIC: 7372 Prepackaged software

(G-617)
BERYLLIUM LLC
7869 Ne Day Rd W Ste 206 (98110-6211)
PHONE..................206 780-8900
Johan Pontin, *CEO*
Thomas Edwards, *Vice Pres*
Arturo Art J Morales, *Vice Pres*
Diana Wetmore, *Vice Pres*
Jim Fairman, *Manager*
EMP: 2
SALES (est): 270K **Privately Held**
SIC: 2899 8999 Chemical preparations; chemical consultant

(G-618)
BISCOMB FLEUDELIZA S (ARTIST)
Also Called: Biscomb, William Pl
9629 Ne Timberlane Pl (98110-1358)
PHONE..................206 842-6417
EMP: 2
SALES (est): 66.3K **Privately Held**
SIC: 7381 3952 Detective/Armored Car Services Mfg Lead Pencils/Art Goods

(G-619)
CALICO PRESS LLC
13700 Sunrise Dr Ne (98110-4159)
P.O. Box 4648, Rollingbay (98061-0648)
PHONE..................206 855-1903
John Houde, *Principal*
EMP: 2
SALES (est): 107.5K **Privately Held**
WEB: www.calicopress.com
SIC: 2731 Books: publishing only

(G-620)
CEDAR COAST PRESS
12168 Sunrise Dr Ne (98110-4304)
PHONE..................206 451-4568
Mark Doppe, *Manager*
EMP: 4
SALES (est): 196K **Privately Held**
SIC: 2741 Miscellaneous publishing

(G-621)
CHAVAL OUTDOOR
7720 Springridge Rd Ne (98110-3646)
PHONE..................206 569-0154
Mark D Boone, *President*
EMP: 2
SALES (est): 116.9K **Privately Held**
SIC: 3949 Sporting & athletic goods

(G-622)
CLASSIC CYCLE
740 Winslow Way E (98110-2410)
PHONE..................206 842-9191
Jeff Groman, *Owner*
EMP: 10

Bainbridge Island - Kitsap County (G-623)

SALES (est): 858.7K **Privately Held**
SIC: **3751** 5941 Bicycles & related parts; sporting goods & bicycle shops

(G-623)
CLAUDJA INC
11493 Blue Heron Ln Ne (98110-1292)
PHONE..................206 842-6303
Claudia Black, *Principal*
EMP: 3
SALES (est): 188.8K **Privately Held**
SIC: **2741** Miscellaneous publishing

(G-624)
CUSTOM PRINTING COMPANY
921 Hildebrand Ln Ne # 111 (98110-2879)
PHONE..................206 842-1606
Alan Dewitt, *President*
Judi Dewitt, *Admin Sec*
EMP: 4
SALES (est): 403.8K **Privately Held**
SIC: **2752** Commercial printing, offset

(G-625)
EAGLE HARBOR CABINETS LLC
9445 Ne Business Park Ln (98110-4634)
PHONE..................206 317-6942
EMP: 2
SALES (est): 91.4K **Privately Held**
SIC: **2434** Wood kitchen cabinets

(G-626)
EAGLE HARBOR EDITING
200 High School Rd Ne # 112 (98110-4619)
PHONE..................206 293-4264
Wynne Jacobson, *Principal*
EMP: 2
SALES (est): 78.7K **Privately Held**
SIC: **2741** Miscellaneous publishing

(G-627)
ECOGRAPHICS INC
Also Called: Ecographcs Envrmnt- Frindly PR
164 Grow Ave Nw (98110-1740)
PHONE..................425 825-1888
EMP: 3
SALES: 250K **Privately Held**
SIC: **2752** Offset Printing

(G-628)
ELEVEN WINERY INC
7671 Ne Day Rd W (98110-1260)
PHONE..................206 780-0905
Matt Albee, *Owner*
Talina Wood, *Manager*
EMP: 10
SALES (est): 60.5K **Privately Held**
WEB: www.elevenwinery.com
SIC: **2084** Wines

(G-629)
ELLES ISLAND SPECTACLE
4688 Lynwood Center Rd Ne # 113 (98110-2271)
PHONE..................206 715-9475
Elle Tatum, *Principal*
EMP: 2
SALES (est): 85.1K **Privately Held**
SIC: **3851** Spectacles

(G-630)
ENDPOINT LLC
7470 Ne Manual Rd (98110-3032)
PHONE..................206 780-2905
Kenneth B Klein, *Principal*
EMP: 4
SALES (est): 272.9K **Privately Held**
SIC: **2834** Pharmaceutical preparations

(G-631)
ESI DISTRIBUTION LTD
Also Called: E S I
330 Madison Ave S Ste 203 (98110-2544)
PHONE..................206 780-9623
EMP: 3
SALES (corp-wide): 556.3K **Privately Held**
SIC: **7372** Prepackaged Software Services
HQ: Esi Distribution Ltd.
428 Hemphill St
Fort Worth TX 76104
206 780-9623

(G-632)
EX OPHIDIA PRESS LLC
220 Parfitt Way Sw # 111 (98110-2560)
PHONE..................360 385-9966
Gabriel Rummonds, *Owner*
EMP: 2
SQ FT: 850
SALES (est): 99K **Privately Held**
SIC: **2731** Book publishing

(G-633)
FENWICK PUBLISHING GROUP INC
3147 Point White Dr Ne # 100 (98110-4061)
PHONE..................206 842-3981
Timothy Connolly, *Owner*
Marlen Connoly, *Owner*
EMP: 3
SALES (est): 250K **Privately Held**
WEB: www.fenwickpublishing.com
SIC: **2741** Miscellaneous publishing

(G-634)
FLETCHER BAY WINERY
8765 Battle Point Dr Ne (98110-1427)
PHONE..................206 780-9463
Jim Wilford, *Principal*
EMP: 7 EST: 2010
SALES (est): 535.8K **Privately Held**
SIC: **2084** Wines

(G-635)
FSTOPCAFE LLC
5200 Ne Forest Glade Ln (98110-1436)
PHONE..................206 842-0335
Kristine Carroll,
David Adler,
EMP: 4 EST: 2013
SQ FT: 1,500
SALES (est): 276.7K **Privately Held**
SIC: **2095** 5963 Roasted coffee; food service, coffee-cart

(G-636)
GEM CUT COMPANY
5780 Ne Crystal Ln (98110-2004)
PHONE..................206 780-0113
EMP: 2 EST: 2009
SALES (est): 99K **Privately Held**
SIC: **3915** Mfg Jewelers' Materials

(G-637)
GUIDED REALITY CORPORATION
9764 Ne Pine St (98110-2113)
PHONE..................206 856-8819
David Lashmet, *CEO*
EMP: 8 EST: 2012
SALES (est): 414.8K **Privately Held**
SIC: **3812** Navigational systems & instruments

(G-638)
HELLDYNE INC
750 Ericksen Ave Ne # 103 (98110-1881)
PHONE..................206 855-1227
Stephen Hellriegel, *President*
EMP: 3
SALES: 750K **Privately Held**
SIC: **8711** 7373 8748 7389 Electrical or electronic engineering; computer integrated systems design; systems engineering consultant, ex. computer or professional; printed circuitry graphic layout; digital test equipment, electronic & electrical circuits

(G-639)
HEMPHILL BROTHERS INC (PA)
Also Called: Northport Limestone
375 Ericksen Ave Ne (98110-1887)
P.O. Box 10190 (98110-0190)
PHONE..................206 842-0748
Thomas Hemphill, *President*
Tim Hemphill, *Admin Sec*
EMP: 4
SQ FT: 5,000
SALES (est): 6.6MM **Privately Held**
WEB: www.hemphillbrothers.net
SIC: **5032** 1422 1446 Limestone; stone, crushed or broken; crushed & broken limestone; silica mining

(G-640)
HOPE MOFFAT
Also Called: Bainbridge Procurement Svcs
407 Madison Ave N Ste 240 (98110-1807)
PHONE..................401 527-4234
Hope Maffat, *Owner*
EMP: 5
SALES (est): 196.9K **Privately Held**
SIC: **5136** 5072 2396 8711 Men's & boys' clothing; power tools & accessories; screen printing on fabric articles; building construction consultant; office & public building furniture

(G-641)
HUGH MONTGOMERY
7869 Fletcher Bay Rd Ne (98110-2654)
PHONE..................206 369-9356
Hugh N Montgomery, *Administration*
EMP: 2
SALES (est): 194.4K **Privately Held**
SIC: **2431** Millwork

(G-642)
ISLAND RIGGERS INC
8955 Woodbank Dr Ne (98110-3486)
PHONE..................206 920-3360
EMP: 2
SALES (est): 147.2K **Privately Held**
SIC: **3441** Fabricated structural metal

(G-643)
ISLAND VINTNERS
450 Winslow Way E (98110-2420)
PHONE..................206 451-4344
EMP: 2 EST: 2014
SALES (est): 83K **Privately Held**
SIC: **2084** Wines

(G-644)
JANE MARTIN
Also Called: Martin Metal
3636 Crystal Sprng Dr Ne (98110-2074)
PHONE..................206 842-4569
Jane Martin, *Owner*
EMP: 2
SALES: 50K **Privately Held**
SIC: **3961** 5094 5944 Costume jewelry, ex. precious metal & semiprecious stones; jewelry; jewelry, precious stones & precious metals

(G-645)
JUST THINK TOYS INC
13507 Chatri Pl Ne (98110-4507)
P.O. Box 10730 (98110-0730)
PHONE..................310 308-5242
Douglas Mackey, *President*
Carla Mackey, *Vice Pres*
▲ EMP: 5
SQ FT: 1,200
SALES (est): 441.3K **Privately Held**
SIC: **3944** Games, toys & children's vehicles

(G-646)
KLICKTRACK INC
9727 Coppertop Loop Ne # 202 (98110-4633)
PHONE..................206 557-3223
Brendan Hill, *Chief Mktg Ofcr*
EMP: 15
SALES (est): 307.6K **Privately Held**
SIC: **7372** Business oriented computer software

(G-647)
KRILL SYSTEMS INC
175 Parfitt Way Sw (98110-2584)
PHONE..................206 780-2901
Casey Cox, *President*
Brian Staton, *Vice Pres*
EMP: 5
SALES (est): 550.4K **Privately Held**
SIC: **7372** 3823 Application computer software; industrial process measurement equipment

(G-648)
LAVRY ENGINEERING INC
945 Hildebrand Ln Ne # 110 (98110-2877)
P.O. Box 4602, Rollingbay (98061-0602)
PHONE..................206 842-3552
EMP: 10
SALES: 1.8MM **Privately Held**
SIC: **3699** Mfg Electrical Equipment/Supplies

(G-649)
MAD APE
9720 Coppertop Loop Ne # 203 (98110-3690)
PHONE..................206 201-3275
EMP: 3 EST: 2008
SALES (est): 245.2K **Privately Held**
SIC: **3931** Guitars & parts, electric & non-electric

(G-650)
MONKEY WRENCH FABRICATION LLC
9392 Ne Wardwell Rd (98110-1594)
PHONE..................206 992-8509
Jeremy Loerch, *Principal*
EMP: 2
SALES (est): 48K **Privately Held**
SIC: **3999** Manufacturing industries

(G-651)
MUSIC EXPRESS LLC
321 High School Rd Ne D3 (98110-2647)
PHONE..................206 842-6317
Hurshel Blankenship, *Principal*
▲ EMP: 3
SALES (est): 371.9K **Privately Held**
SIC: **3161** Musical instrument cases

(G-652)
NOREASTERN TRAWL SYSTEMS INC (HQ)
Also Called: Net Systems
7910 Ne Day Rd W (98110-1254)
PHONE..................206 842-5623
Daniel Oliver, *President*
Toshio Yamamoto, *Corp Secy*
Junichi Udagawa, *Senior VP*
Craig Kitamura, *Vice Pres*
Maria Ochoa, *CFO*
▲ EMP: 49
SQ FT: 377,000
SALES: 15.1MM **Privately Held**
WEB: www.net-sys.com
SIC: **2298** Cordage & twine

(G-653)
NORTH STAR HIGH VOLTAGE CORP
5610 Rose Loop Ne (98110-3170)
PHONE..................520 780-9030
Richard Adler, *President*
Karen Adler, *Vice Pres*
EMP: 2
SALES: 500K **Privately Held**
SIC: **3825** Test equipment for electronic & electric measurement

(G-654)
NORTHWEST MILLWORK DOOR CO
611 Park Ave Ne (98110-2965)
PHONE..................360 297-0802
Mike Finnegan, *Principal*
EMP: 2
SALES (est): 271.5K **Privately Held**
SIC: **2431** Millwork

(G-655)
NORTHWEST PARENTS MEDIA
Also Called: Seattle's Child
5671 Ward Ave Ne (98110-3700)
PHONE..................206 842-8500
Linda Watson, *President*
EMP: 15
SALES (est): 509.6K **Privately Held**
WEB: www.seattleschild.com
SIC: **2711** Newspapers

(G-656)
NW WOODWORKS LLC
9636 Ne Timberlane Pl (98110-1358)
PHONE..................206 780-6753
EMP: 2
SALES (est): 123.7K **Privately Held**
SIC: **2431** Millwork

(G-657)
PETIT AND OLSON
150 Winslow Way E (98110-2426)
PHONE..................206 201-3262

GEOGRAPHIC SECTION
Battle Ground - Clark County (G-690)

Kathryn Eileen Petit, *Owner*
EMP: 4
SALES (est): 371.1K **Privately Held**
SIC: 2511 Wood household furniture

(G-658)
PHYTEC AMERICA LLC
203 Parfitt Way Sw G100 (98110-4906)
PHONE..................................206 780-9047
Karen Hooper, *General Mgr*
Craig Day, *Engineer*
Bob Disbennett, *Finance Mgr*
Rene Hack, *Manager*
Thomas L Walker,
◆ EMP: 12
SQ FT: 8,112
SALES (est): 3.7MM
SALES (corp-wide): 355.8K **Privately Held**
WEB: www.phytec.com
SIC: 3571 Electronic computers
HQ: Phytec MeBtechnik Gmbh
   Robert-Koch-Str. 39
   Mainz 55129
   613 192-210

(G-659)
PORTLAND STIRLING INCORPORATED
9208 Ne Valley Rd (98110-4343)
P.O. Box 4749, Rollingbay (98061-0749)
PHONE..................................206 855-0819
EMP: 3 EST: 2014
SALES (est): 196.8K **Privately Held**
SIC: 3621 7389 Mfg Motors/Generators

(G-660)
POSITIVE FUTURES NETWORK
Also Called: YES MAGAZINE
284 Madrona Way Ne # 116 (98110-2870)
PHONE..................................206 842-0216
David Korten, *President*
Christine Hanna, *Exec Dir*
EMP: 20
SALES: 2.2MM **Privately Held**
WEB: www.futurenet.org
SIC: 2721 Magazines: publishing & printing

(G-661)
PURPOSEFUL SOFTWARE LLC
8150 Hansen Rd Ne (98110-2677)
PHONE..................................206 855-7927
Brian Hilst, *Principal*
EMP: 2
SALES (est): 123.9K **Privately Held**
SIC: 7372 Prepackaged software

(G-662)
RACE HORSE STUDIOS
9902 Ne Monsaas Rd (98110-1103)
PHONE..................................206 451-4725
Duncan Macfarland, *Owner*
EMP: 3
SQ FT: 4,265
SALES (est): 375.7K **Privately Held**
WEB: www.racehorsestudios.com
SIC: 3663 Studio equipment, radio & television broadcasting

(G-663)
RED RIVER INDUSTRIES
12990 Phelps Rd Ne (98110-4197)
PHONE..................................206 992-2446
Dian Aversano, *Principal*
EMP: 2
SALES (est): 109.9K **Privately Held**
SIC: 3999 Manufacturing industries

(G-664)
REDSIDE CONSTRUCTION LLC
600 Winslow Way E Ste 237 (98110-4701)
PHONE..................................360 297-9557
Sam Berry,
EMP: 6
SALES (est): 1.1MM **Privately Held**
SIC: 1629 1442 Marine construction; construction sand & gravel

(G-665)
REMEOPHARMA INC
Also Called: Remeodiagnostics
9723 Coppertop Park Ste 2 (98110)
P.O. Box 11427 (98110-5247)
PHONE..................................206 805-9786
Hilary Jones, *CEO*
Sally Jones, *Director*

EMP: 10 EST: 2007
SALES (est): 1.1MM **Privately Held**
SIC: 2834 Pharmaceutical preparations

(G-666)
RIGAKU AMERICAS CORPORATION
7865 Ne Day Rd W Ste 109 (98110-6212)
PHONE..................................206 780-8927
Amy Syverson, *Manager*
EMP: 6 **Privately Held**
SIC: 3844 3826 5049 X-ray apparatus & tubes; analytical instruments; analytical instruments
HQ: Rigaku Americas Corporation
   9009 New Trails Dr
   The Woodlands TX 77381
   281 362-2300

(G-667)
RIVERSIDE SCIENTIFIC ENTPS
15708 Point Monroe Dr Ne (98110-1158)
PHONE..................................206 842-7513
Constance V Furlong, *President*
EMP: 2
SALES (est): 152.3K **Privately Held**
SIC: 5734 3826 1531 Computer & software stores; instruments measuring magnetic & electrical properties; speculative builder, single-family houses

(G-668)
RORY THURROTT
4710 Ne Eagle Harbor Dr (98110-2188)
PHONE..................................206 941-7297
Rory Thurrott, *Owner*
EMP: 2
SALES (est): 197.2K **Privately Held**
SIC: 3499 Fabricated metal products

(G-669)
SABINE F PRICE
7555 Madrona Dr Ne (98110-2901)
PHONE..................................206 780-9211
Sabine Price, *Principal*
EMP: 2
SALES (est): 108.4K **Privately Held**
SIC: 3953 Marking devices

(G-670)
SAGE MANUFACTURING CORPORATION
12715 Miller Rd Ne (98110-6217)
PHONE..................................800 952-9827
Rusty Harper, *Branch Mgr*
EMP: 10
SALES (corp-wide): 170.6MM **Privately Held**
SIC: 3949 Rods & rod parts, fishing
HQ: Sage Manufacturing Corporation
   8500 Ne Day Rd E
   Bainbridge Island WA 98110
   206 842-6608

(G-671)
SAGE MANUFACTURING CORPORATION
8500 Ne Day Rd E (98110-1395)
PHONE..................................206 842-6608
EMP: 3
SALES (corp-wide): 170.6MM **Privately Held**
SIC: 3949 Fishing equipment
HQ: Sage Manufacturing Corporation
   8500 Ne Day Rd E
   Bainbridge Island WA 98110
   206 842-6608

(G-672)
SAUNDERS INSTRUMENTS INC
1416 Elizabeth Pl Nw (98110-1603)
PHONE..................................206 842-6651
Malcolm Saunders, *President*
Richard Saunders, *Vice Pres*
EMP: 4
SQ FT: 2,200
SALES (est): 542.8K **Privately Held**
SIC: 3827 Optical instruments & apparatus

(G-673)
SMART MOVES INC
12305 Arrow Point Loop Ne (98110-1480)
PHONE..................................206 842-6575
EMP: 2
SQ FT: 1,000

SALES: 150K **Privately Held**
SIC: 3822 Mfg Electronic Actuators

(G-674)
STOURWATER PICTURES
11431 Miller Rd Ne (98110-4253)
PHONE..................................206 780-6928
Don Sellers, *Owner*
Lucy Ostrander, *Co-Owner*
EMP: 2
SALES (est): 102.8K **Privately Held**
SIC: 3861 Motion picture film

(G-675)
SWEET DAHLIA BAKING LLC
9720 Coppertop Loop Ne (98110-3690)
PHONE..................................206 201-3297
Stacey Wadkins,
EMP: 8
SALES (est): 232.9K **Privately Held**
SIC: 2051 Bread, cake & related products

(G-676)
TEAMMATES SPORTS PRODUCTS LLC
410 Robinwood Dr Ne (98110-1967)
PHONE..................................206 780-2037
EMP: 2
SALES (est): 130.1K **Privately Held**
SIC: 3949 Mfg Sporting/Athletic Goods

(G-677)
TELOS3 LLC
7563 Ne Meadowmeer Ln (98110-1223)
PHONE..................................360 536-3122
Edward Lafferty, *Principal*
EMP: 5
SALES (est): 334.3K **Privately Held**
SIC: 7372 Prepackaged software

(G-678)
THINKING INDUSTRIES INC
8465 Ne Beck Rd (98110-2251)
PHONE..................................206 201-2106
Charles Goerlitz, *Principal*
EMP: 2
SALES (est): 118.2K **Privately Held**
SIC: 3999 Manufacturing industries

(G-679)
TORRID MARINE LLC
8895 Three Tree Ln Ne (98110-5116)
P.O. Box 11742 (98110-5742)
PHONE..................................206 920-9002
Susan Anderson, *Mng Member*
Jeffrey Adams,
EMP: 3
SQ FT: 2,400
SALES: 850K **Privately Held**
SIC: 3822 5074 5064 Water heater controls; water heaters, except electric; water heaters, electric

(G-680)
VAPORPATH INC
9300 North Town Dr Ne (98110-3528)
PHONE..................................306 208-2747
Barry Goffe, *President*
Doug Fleming, *Chairman*
Cloantha Copass, *Admin Sec*
EMP: 3
SALES: 250K **Privately Held**
SIC: 3089 Caps, plastic

(G-681)
VERSATILE MACHINING INC
7873 Ne Day Rd W (98110-4207)
PHONE..................................206 855-8296
Dale Cavanaugh, *President*
▲ EMP: 5
SQ FT: 2,000
SALES: 400K **Privately Held**
WEB: www.versatilemachining.com
SIC: 3599 Machine shop, jobbing & repair

(G-682)
W H AUTOPILOTS INC
12685 Miller Rd Ne # 1400 (98110-4206)
PHONE..................................206 780-2175
Will P Hamm, *President*
▼ EMP: 10

SALES (est): 710K **Privately Held**
WEB: www.whautopilots.com
SIC: 3625 7699 Marine & navy auxiliary controls; nautical & navigational instrument repair

(G-683)
WHITE DOG PRESS
321 High School Rd Ne (98110-2647)
PHONE..................................800 257-2226
Stephanie Ager, *Principal*
EMP: 2
SALES (est): 95K **Privately Held**
SIC: 2741 Miscellaneous publishing

(G-684)
WILLIAM WALKER WOODWORKING
10115 Ne Kitsap St (98110-2391)
PHONE..................................206 780-5301
William Walker, *Owner*
EMP: 2
SALES (est): 163.5K **Privately Held**
SIC: 2511 Wood household furniture

(G-685)
ZOMBIE INC
Also Called: Zombie Studios
8477 Ne New Brooklyn Rd (98110-3611)
PHONE..................................206 623-9655
Joanna Alexander, *CEO*
Sandy Heyer, *CFO*
EMP: 30
SALES (est): 3.5MM **Privately Held**
WEB: www.zombie.com
SIC: 7371 7375 7372 Computer software development; information retrieval services; prepackaged software

Battle Ground
Clark County

(G-686)
AGRIJUANA 1 LLC
1810 Se Commerce Ave (98604-8963)
PHONE..................................360 342-8194
EMP: 2
SALES (est): 83.5K **Privately Held**
SIC: 0139 3999 ;

(G-687)
ANDERSEN DAIRY INC
305 E Main St (98604-4501)
P.O. Box 310 (98604-0310)
PHONE..................................360 687-7171
Ronald A Andersen, *Ch of Bd*
Jack Dunn, *President*
Gary Andersen, *Vice Pres*
Gladys Sinclair, *Treasurer*
EMP: 100
SQ FT: 12,000
SALES (est): 22.8MM **Privately Held**
SIC: 2026 5143 Milk processing (pasteurizing, homogenizing, bottling); dairy products, except dried or canned
PA: Green Willow Trucking, Inc.
   305 E Main St
   Battle Ground WA 98604
   360 687-7171

(G-688)
APPLIED MULTILAYERS LLC
1801 Se Commerce Ave (98604-8963)
PHONE..................................307 222-0660
Jerry Martin, *Managing Prtnr*
EMP: 5
SALES (est): 333.9K **Privately Held**
SIC: 3674 Thin film circuits

(G-689)
B TRIPLEX INC
24119 Ne 132nd Ave (98604-5520)
PHONE..................................360 904-5981
Byron Bates, *Owner*
EMP: 2
SALES (est): 60K **Privately Held**
SIC: 3599 Industrial machinery

(G-690)
BARKING ANT SOFTWARE LLC
1906 Sw 6th St (98604-3004)
PHONE..................................360 281-1118
Lawrence Wilson, *Principal*

Battle Ground - Clark County (G-691) — GEOGRAPHIC SECTION

EMP: 2
SALES (est): 121.8K **Privately Held**
SIC: 7372 Business oriented computer software

(G-691)
BATTLE GROUND AUTO LICENSE
301 W Main St (98604)
P.O. Box 814 (98604-0814)
PHONE...................................360 687-5115
Sharon Sorenson, *Owner*
EMP: 7
SALES (est): 740.1K **Privately Held**
SIC: 3469 6794 Automobile license tags, stamped metal; patent owners & lessors

(G-692)
BGS CYCLE PARTS
101 Nw 25th St (98604-2419)
PHONE...................................808 368-8122
Robert George, *President*
EMP: 2
SALES (est): 85K **Privately Held**
SIC: 3751 Motorcycles & related parts

(G-693)
BITE-A-LITE LLC
22111 Ne 182nd Ave (98604-4835)
PHONE...................................360 687-2995
George Peterson, *Principal*
EMP: 2
SALES (est): 121.6K **Privately Held**
SIC: 3449 Miscellaneous metalwork

(G-694)
CALIFORNIA COATING
1801 Se Commerce Ave (98604-8963)
PHONE...................................609 405-2683
EMP: 2
SALES (est): 69.9K **Privately Held**
SIC: 3479 Metal coating & allied service

(G-695)
CHASCO LLC
419 Sw 13th Cir (98604-2875)
PHONE...................................503 803-4675
Charles Hay,
EMP: 2
SALES: 150K **Privately Held**
SIC: 3545 7389 Machine tool accessories;

(G-696)
CREATIVE OUTLOOK
18603 Ne 85th Ave (98604-5274)
PHONE...................................360 607-4013
Linda Brown, *Partner*
Lani Brown, *Partner*
EMP: 2
SALES (est): 150K **Privately Held**
SIC: 3999 Candles

(G-697)
DETRO MANUFACTURING INC
1721 Se Grace Ave Ste E (98604-8476)
PHONE...................................360 687-9960
Larry Kopkie, *President*
Rebecca Kopkie, *Vice Pres*
▲ EMP: 5
SQ FT: 20,000
SALES: 739.5K **Privately Held**
WEB: www.detromfg.com
SIC: 2295 Coated fabrics, not rubberized

(G-698)
DOLLS BY ARLENE
19616 Ne 163rd Ave (98604-9265)
PHONE...................................360 687-4321
Arlene Martinez, *Owner*
EMP: 2
SALES: 57K **Privately Held**
SIC: 3942 Dolls, except stuffed toy animals

(G-699)
DOUBLE V DISTILLERY
1315 Se Grace Ave (98604-8487)
P.O. Box 2769 (98604-2769)
PHONE...................................360 666-0716
John Vissotzky, *Principal*
EMP: 5
SALES (est): 328.9K **Privately Held**
SIC: 2085 Distillers' dried grains & solubles & alcohol

(G-700)
EFFICIENT DRYER VENT SERVICES
25218 Ne Berlin Rd (98604-5148)
PHONE...................................360 687-7643
Alex Gaudet, *Owner*
EMP: 3
SALES (est): 445.5K **Privately Held**
SIC: 3564 Ventilating fans: industrial or commercial

(G-701)
FETHA STYX INC
6719 Ne 219th St B (98604-4038)
PHONE...................................360 687-3856
Wllliam Boyce, *CEO*
EMP: 4
SALES (est): 352.9K **Privately Held**
SIC: 3949 5091 Rods & rod parts, fishing; fishing equipment & supplies

(G-702)
FRANCIS SCIENTIFIC INC
Also Called: F S I Mechanical
22906 Ne 152nd Ave (98604-9703)
PHONE...................................360 687-7019
Kenneth E Francis, *President*
John Francis, *Treasurer*
EMP: 3 EST: 1961
SALES (est): 320K **Privately Held**
SIC: 3823 7372 3577 Industrial instrmnts msrmnt display/control process variable; prepackaged software; computer peripheral equipment

(G-703)
GAUDET SHEETMETAL INC
19207 Ne Erion Rd (98604-3945)
PHONE...................................360 892-5772
Alan Gaudet, *President*
EMP: 8 EST: 1996
SALES (est): 1MM **Privately Held**
SIC: 3444 Sheet metalwork

(G-704)
GILMOUR MACHINERY
14812 Ne 379th St (98604)
P.O. Box 1506 (98604-1506)
PHONE...................................360 263-5515
Mike Gilmour, *Owner*
EMP: 4
SQ FT: 10,000
SALES (est): 230K **Privately Held**
SIC: 3599 Machine & other job shop work

(G-705)
GREEN WILLOW TRUCKING INC (PA)
Also Called: Andy's Food Basket
305 E Main St (98604-4501)
P.O. Box 310 (98604-0310)
PHONE...................................360 687-7171
Gladys Sinclair, *President*
Jack W Dunn, *President*
Ronald Anderson, *Corp Secy*
Scott J Vangelder, *Vice Pres*
▲ EMP: 18
SALES (est): 22.8MM **Privately Held**
SIC: 3085 4212 5411 Plastics bottles; local trucking, without storage; grocery stores, independent

(G-706)
GREEN WILLOW TRUCKING INC
Also Called: Andersen's Plastics
305 E Main St (98604-4501)
P.O. Box 310 (98604-0310)
PHONE...................................360 687-7171
Ronald A Andersen, *Ch of Bd*
EMP: 34
SQ FT: 12,000
SALES (corp-wide): 22.8MM **Privately Held**
SIC: 3085 5411 Plastics bottles; grocery stores, independent
PA: Green Willow Trucking, Inc.
305 E Main St
Battle Ground WA 98604
360 687-7171

(G-707)
HARRIS METAL FAB & WELDING
19217 Ne 219th St (98604-4912)
P.O. Box 2098 (98604-2098)
PHONE...................................360 687-6273
Tom Harris, *Owner*
Lola Harris, *Co-Owner*
EMP: 2
SALES (est): 93K **Privately Held**
SIC: 7692 Welding repair

(G-708)
HARRY WIEBOLD LOGGING
7801 Ne 279th St (98604-9343)
PHONE...................................360 687-2129
Harry Wiebold, *Principal*
EMP: 6 EST: 2012
SALES (est): 437.5K **Privately Held**
SIC: 2411 Logging camps & contractors

(G-709)
INK ABILITY
717 W Main St Ste 120 (98604-4480)
PHONE...................................360 342-8174
Russell Laratta, *President*
EMP: 3 EST: 2017
SALES (est): 291.8K **Privately Held**
SIC: 2759 Commercial printing

(G-710)
J & R WOOD PRODUCTS INC
10519 Ne 314th St (98604-7649)
PHONE...................................360 687-1662
Joe Taylor, *Principal*
EMP: 2
SALES (est): 130K **Privately Held**
SIC: 2431 Millwork

(G-711)
JAMES & EILEEN KASKI
Also Called: Kaski Constuction
22011 Ne 212th Ave (98604-3713)
PHONE...................................360 687-4214
James Kaski, *Owner*
EMP: 2
SALES (est): 173.1K **Privately Held**
SIC: 2411 Logging

(G-712)
KARVONEN SAND & GRAVEL INC
21310 Ne 87th Ave (98604-9147)
P.O. Box 3130 (98604-2939)
PHONE...................................360 687-2549
Agnes Karvonen, *CEO*
Kent R Karvonen, *President*
EMP: 7 EST: 1972
SALES (est): 1.2MM **Privately Held**
SIC: 2951 1629 4212 Asphalt paving mixtures & blocks; land clearing contractor; local trucking, without storage

(G-713)
KOVA INDUSTRIES LLC
27120 Ne 220th Ave (98604-6921)
PHONE...................................360 567-5371
Hans Uskoski, *Principal*
EMP: 2 EST: 2017
SALES (est): 113K **Privately Held**
SIC: 3999 Manufacturing industries

(G-714)
KRUEGER LOGGING INC
20300 Ne 279th St (98604-7589)
P.O. Box 2218 (98604-2218)
PHONE...................................360 687-5558
Harry S Krueger, *Principal*
EMP: 6 EST: 2012
SALES (est): 186.4K **Privately Held**
SIC: 2411 Logging

(G-715)
LEVANEN INC
24209 Ne 53rd Ave (98604-5307)
PHONE...................................360 687-4314
Scott Levanen, *President*
Aila Lindberg, *Office Mgr*
EMP: 18
SALES (est): 3.1MM **Privately Held**
SIC: 2411 Logging camps & contractors

(G-716)
LEVANEN LEE JOHN
1906 Se 25th St (98604-2898)
PHONE...................................360 687-7478
Lee John Levanen, *Principal*
Debbie Levanen, *Co-Owner*
EMP: 2
SALES (est): 201.8K **Privately Held**
SIC: 2411 Logging

(G-717)
LUNAS CUSTOM PUPPETS
812 Sw 4th Ave (98604-8588)
P.O. Box 702 (98604-0702)
PHONE...................................360 721-9672
Kevin Gorby, *Principal*
EMP: 2
SALES (est): 102.2K **Privately Held**
SIC: 3999 Furs

(G-718)
MADDOX INDUSTRIAL TRANS LLC
1500 Se Commerce Ave (98604)
PHONE...................................360 512-3355
EMP: 2
SALES (est): 114.3K **Privately Held**
SIC: 3612 Transformers, except electric

(G-719)
MALONE ELECTRONICS
24702 Ne 228th Cir (98604-9641)
P.O. Box 1542 (98604-1542)
PHONE...................................360 687-1034
EMP: 2
SALES (est): 140K **Privately Held**
SIC: 3699 Mfg Electrical Equipment/Supplies

(G-720)
MEET YOUR PRICE INC
8419 Ne 154th Cir (98604-5269)
PHONE...................................360 260-2066
Wayne Chih-WEI Shu, *Principal*
EMP: 2
SALES (est): 134.5K **Privately Held**
SIC: 3571 5045 7375 Electronic computers; computers, peripherals & software; on-line data base information retrieval

(G-721)
METAL STRUCTURES LLC
8707 Ne 279th St (98604-9300)
PHONE...................................703 628-7808
Michael Bozarth,
Marina Burgstahler,
William Jonas,
EMP: 3
SALES (est): 261.8K **Privately Held**
SIC: 3448 7389 Prefabricated metal buildings;

(G-722)
MHJ WOOD WORKS
28017 Ne 132nd Ave (98604-6529)
PHONE...................................360 901-8889
Marvin Hervi, *Owner*
EMP: 2 EST: 2015
SALES (est): 78K **Privately Held**
SIC: 2421 Sawmills & planing mills, general

(G-723)
MINT VALLEY PAPER COMPANY INC
8813 Ne 244th St (98604-9507)
P.O. Box 1376 (98604-1376)
PHONE...................................360 931-9055
Alexander Mardon, *CEO*
Mark Schneider, *President*
Trina Bester, *Senior VP*
EMP: 5
SALES (est): 327.4K **Privately Held**
SIC: 2611 2621 7389 Pulp mills, chemical & semichemical processing; towels, tissues & napkins: paper & stock;

(G-724)
NIDEC AMERICA CORPORATION
318 E Main St 202 (98604-8508)
PHONE...................................360 666-2445
Karl Mattson, *Branch Mgr*
EMP: 2 **Privately Held**
WEB: www.nidec.com
SIC: 3621 3564 3679 5063 Motors, electric; blowers & fans; power supplies, all types: static; motors, electric; fans, heating & ventilation equipment
HQ: Nidec America Corporation
50 Braintree Hill Park # 110
Braintree MA 02184
781 848-0970

▲ = Import ▼ =Export
◆ =Import/Export

GEOGRAPHIC SECTION

(G-725)
OLDCASTLE BUILDINGENVELOPE INC
1611 Se Commerce Ave (98604-8951)
PHONE 360 816-7777
Greg Knight, *Manager*
EMP: 60
SALES (corp-wide): 30.6B **Privately Held**
WEB: www.oldcastleglass.com
SIC: 3231 5231 Tempered glass: made from purchased glass; insulating glass: made from purchased glass; glass
HQ: Oldcastle Buildingenvelope, Inc.
5005 Lndn B Jnsn Fwy 10
Dallas TX 75244
214 273-3400

(G-726)
ONCE UPON A PALLET
29011 Ne 164th Ave (98604-7550)
PHONE 360 798-6294
Megan Fehr, *Principal*
EMP: 4
SALES (est): 171.8K **Privately Held**
SIC: 2448 Pallets, wood

(G-727)
P & R ROCK SAND & GRAVEL
713 Nw 21st St (98604-4485)
P.O. Box 1314 (98604-1314)
PHONE 503 278-3512
Rodney Goulet, *Principal*
EMP: 3 **EST:** 2010
SALES (est): 164.4K **Privately Held**
SIC: 1442 Construction sand & gravel

(G-728)
PAT LYDON SAW MILL LLC
23907 Ne 72nd Ave (98604-5331)
PHONE 360 666-0900
EMP: 2
SALES (est): 148.5K **Privately Held**
SIC: 2421 Sawmill/Planing Mill

(G-729)
PATHFINDER PRESS
25224 Ne Jolma Rd (98604-9706)
PHONE 360 687-4319
Kent Farmer, *Owner*
Bev Farmer, *Co-Owner*
EMP: 2
SALES (est): 58K **Privately Held**
SIC: 2731 5961 Books: publishing only; books, mail order (except book clubs)

(G-730)
PC2 LLC
30748 Ne Lewisville Hwy (98604-9732)
PHONE 360 921-8066
Timothy Sarkkinen, *President*
EMP: 3
SALES (est): 254.2K **Privately Held**
SIC: 3272 7389 Concrete products, precast;

(G-731)
PENNY SAVERS
1507 Ne 17th Ave (98604-4656)
PHONE 360 723-0740
Patricia Ramirez, *Principal*
EMP: 3 **EST:** 2014
SALES (est): 75.3K **Privately Held**
SIC: 2711 Newspapers, publishing & printing

(G-732)
PRO ARC INDUSTRIES INC
23403 Ne 210th St (98604-5834)
PHONE 916 215-7269
Cindy Tripp, *Director*
EMP: 2
SALES (est): 97.7K **Privately Held**
SIC: 3999 Manufacturing industries

(G-733)
PROCESS CNTRLS INSTRUMENTATION
Also Called: Russell Automation
21211 Ne 72nd Ave (98604-5229)
PHONE 360 573-4985
Jason Russell, *President*
EMP: 5
SALES (est): 36.9K **Privately Held**
SIC: 3823 Industrial instrmnts msrmnt display/control process variable

(G-734)
R-2 MFG INC
15012 Ne 319th St (98604-9725)
PHONE 360 609-1373
Bryan Skoko, *Principal*
EMP: 2 **EST:** 2017
SALES (est): 119.9K **Privately Held**
SIC: 3999 Manufacturing industries

(G-735)
RICHARD EZETTA STUMP GRINDING
24000 Ne 101st Ct (98604-5419)
PHONE 360 687-8054
Richard Ezetta, *Principal*
EMP: 2
SALES (est): 180.9K **Privately Held**
SIC: 3599 Grinding castings for the trade

(G-736)
RIVERCREST HOLDINGS LLC
Also Called: Real Axis Machining Division
1205 Se Grace Ave (98604-8377)
PHONE 360 723-5354
Jon Reali, *President*
Charles Reali, *General Mgr*
Roger Antes, *Opers Staff*
EMP: 6
SQ FT: 7,500
SALES (est): 785.1K **Privately Held**
SIC: 3599 Machine shop, jobbing & repair

(G-737)
RUSTY GRAPE VINEYARD LLC
16712 Ne 219th St (98604-4726)
PHONE 360 513-9338
Jeremy Brown,
EMP: 7
SALES (est): 782.7K **Privately Held**
SIC: 2084 Wines

(G-738)
SAVIOR SOCKS INC
307 Sw 20th Ave (98604-3031)
P.O. Box 764, Long Beach (98631-0764)
PHONE 360 601-8036
Tammy Newbill, *Principal*
EMP: 3
SALES (est): 80.7K **Privately Held**
SIC: 2252 Socks

(G-739)
SHOOT SUIT INC
1721 Se Grace Ave Ste D (98604-8476)
PHONE 360 687-3451
Rebecca Kopkie, *President*
▲ **EMP:** 5
SQ FT: 18,000
SALES: 1.1MM **Privately Held**
WEB: www.shootsuit.com
SIC: 3465 2326 Body parts, automobile: stamped metal; work garments, except raincoats: waterproof

(G-740)
SIGNAL HOUND INC
1502 Se Commerce Ave # 101 (98604-8967)
PHONE 360 263-5006
Bruce Devine, *President*
Lori Simonds, *Buyer*
Melissa Harmon, *Controller*
EMP: 9
SQ FT: 3,000
SALES: 2.3MM **Privately Held**
WEB: www.testequipmentplus.com
SIC: 3825 7699 Test equipment for electronic & electric measurement; precision instrument repair

(G-741)
ST HELENS PRESS
25804 Ne Olson Rd (98604-3902)
PHONE 360 687-1717
James Wetherill, *Owner*
EMP: 4
SALES (est): 153.2K **Privately Held**
SIC: 2731 Book publishing

(G-742)
TACTICAL FABS INC (PA)
Also Called: Tfi Telemark
1801 Se Commerce Ave (98604-8963)
PHONE 360 723-5360
Gerald G Henderson, *Ch of Bd*
▲ **EMP:** 50
SQ FT: 30,000
SALES (est): 11.6MM **Privately Held**
SIC: 3674 3671 3559 Wafers (semiconductor devices); electron beam (beta ray) generator tubes; semiconductor manufacturing machinery

(G-743)
TARTBERRY INCORPORATED
23516 Ne 120th Ct (98604-4303)
PHONE 503 295-2700
Douglas T Schmitt, *Principal*
EMP: 5 **EST:** 2010
SALES (est): 257.2K **Privately Held**
SIC: 2024 Yogurt desserts, frozen

(G-744)
TEN TALENTS
9005 Ne 162nd St (98604-9132)
PHONE 360 256-0205
Debra Thomas, *Owner*
EMP: 2
SALES (est): 108.6K **Privately Held**
SIC: 2499 Decorative wood & woodwork

(G-745)
TFI TELEMARK
1801 Se Commerce Ave (98604-8963)
PHONE 360 723-5360
Gerald G Henderson, *President*
▲ **EMP:** 54
SQ FT: 30,000
SALES (est): 8.1MM
SALES (corp-wide): 11.6MM **Privately Held**
SIC: 3671 3674 Electron beam (beta ray) generator tubes; semiconductors & related devices
PA: Tactical Fabs, Inc.
1801 Se Commerce Ave
Battle Ground WA 98604
360 723-5360

(G-746)
TIMEZONE RACEWAY PARK (PA)
29718 Ne 132nd Ave (98604-7578)
PHONE 360 687-5100
Rick Stcyr, *Owner*
EMP: 3
SALES (est): 584.4K **Privately Held**
SIC: 3644 Raceways

(G-747)
TOP SHELF CLOSET INC
21600 Ne 72nd Ave (98604-5228)
PHONE 360 953-1690
Nora Questad, *Principal*
EMP: 6 **EST:** 2012
SALES (est): 560.2K **Privately Held**
SIC: 2673 Wardrobe bags (closet accessories): from purchased materials

(G-748)
TRAIL TECH INC
1600 Se 18th Ave (98604-4850)
PHONE 360 687-4530
Kelly L Woton, *President*
Geoff Wotton, *Design Engr*
▲ **EMP:** 5 **EST:** 2001
SALES (est): 1.4MM
SALES (corp-wide): 6B **Publicly Held**
WEB: www.trailtech.net
SIC: 3531 5531 Railway track equipment; automotive parts
PA: Polaris Industries Inc.
2100 Highway 55
Medina MN 55340
763 542-0500

(G-749)
VEVA COMPANY LLC
Also Called: Vevaco
20117 Ne 279th St (98604-7582)
PHONE 360 687-8550
Vance Wells, *Principal*
EMP: 3
SALES (est): 183.1K **Privately Held**
SIC: 3089 3993 Engraving of plastic; displays & cutouts, window & lobby

(G-750)
VIKING INDUSTRIAL GROUP INC
2118 Se 12th Ave Ste 104 (98604-5921)
P.O. Box 1074, Brush Prairie (98606-1074)
PHONE 360 666-1110
EMP: 5 **EST:** 2007
SALES (est): 660K **Privately Held**
SIC: 3826 Mfg Analytical Instruments

(G-751)
WESTERN BUSINESS FORMS & SUPS
14917 Ne 269th St (98604-9761)
PHONE 503 285-8738
Grant E Kelly, *Partner*
Brenda Kelly, *Principal*
EMP: 4
SQ FT: 3,600
SALES (est): 466.2K **Privately Held**
SIC: 2752 Commercial printing, offset

(G-752)
WESTERN STATES FIRE EQUIPMENT
1604 Nw 1st Ave (98604-6802)
P.O. Box 1173 (98604-1173)
PHONE 360 723-0032
Shane Bowman, *Owner*
EMP: 2
SALES (est): 238.2K **Privately Held**
SIC: 3569 7389 5087 Firefighting apparatus & related equipment; business services; firefighting equipment

(G-753)
WHOLESALE PRINTERS INC
10816 Ne 189th St (98604-6134)
PHONE 360 687-5500
Ronald Ermshar, *President*
Arlene Ermshar, *Admin Sec*
EMP: 22
SQ FT: 4,000
SALES (est): 3.1MM **Privately Held**
WEB: www.wholesalesignsupply.com
SIC: 2752 2791 Commercial printing, offset; typesetting

(G-754)
WOODWORK SPECIALTIES LLC
12501 Ne 308th St (98604-7738)
PHONE 360 687-5880
Michael Charlson, *Owner*
EMP: 2
SALES (est): 950K **Privately Held**
SIC: 2431 Interior & ornamental woodwork & trim

Bay Center
Pacific County

(G-755)
BAY CENTER MARICULTURE CO
Also Called: Bay Center Farms
306 Dike Rd (98527)
P.O. Box 356 (98527-0356)
PHONE 360 875-6172
Richard Wilson, *President*
Mick Pine, *Plant Mgr*
EMP: 24
SQ FT: 2,800
SALES: 1MM **Privately Held**
WEB: www.baycenterfarms.com
SIC: 0913 0273 2092 Oyster beds; mollusk farm; fresh or frozen packaged fish

---

Beaver
Clallam County

(G-756)
ENGESETH LOGGING
183 W Lake Pleasant Rd (98305-2601)
P.O. Box 55 (98305-0055)
PHONE 360 327-3391
Donald Engeseth, *Partner*
Brent Engeseth, *Partner*
EMP: 13
SALES: 2MM **Privately Held**
SIC: 2411 Logging camps & contractors

Beaver - Clallam County (G-757)

(G-757)
HILLCAR & FLETCHER INC
621 E Lake Pleasant Rd (98305)
P.O. Box 210, Forks (98331-0210)
PHONE..................................360 327-3844
Jack Hillcar, *President*
Janice Hillcar, *Corp Secy*
Barbara Fletcher, *Treasurer*
EMP: 2
SALES (est): 214.7K **Privately Held**
SIC: 1771 1429 Driveway contractor; sandstone, crushed & broken-quarrying

(G-758)
LITTLE NUT INC
Also Called: Harvest Time Fruit & Produce
11 Magnolia Rd (98305-9613)
PHONE..................................360 327-3394
EMP: 2
SALES (est): 75K **Privately Held**
SIC: 2493 Mfg Roofing Products

Belfair
Mason County

(G-759)
BELFAIR GARDEN & LIGHTING
24090 Ne State Route 3 F (98528-9665)
PHONE..................................360 275-2130
Ryan Rasmussen, *President*
EMP: 2 EST: 2011
SALES (est): 192.3K **Privately Held**
SIC: 3648 Lighting equipment

(G-760)
DELICH DISTILLERY
2590 Ne Old Belfair Hwy (98528-9611)
PHONE..................................360 552-2282
EMP: 4
SALES (est): 193.9K **Privately Held**
SIC: 2085 Distilled & blended liquors

(G-761)
ENGINEERING
Also Called: Engineering Software Appl
210 Ne Cherokee Beach Rd (98528-9488)
PHONE..................................360 275-7384
Pat Mc Cullough, *Principal*
EMP: 2
SALES (est): 161.6K **Privately Held**
SIC: 7372 Prepackaged software

(G-762)
FACTION LTD
Also Called: Faction Industries
23632 Ne State Route 3 (98528-8309)
PHONE..................................360 275-2834
Matt Cummings, *President*
Bryan Rushforth, *Vice Pres*
▲ EMP: 6
SALES (est): 1MM **Privately Held**
SIC: 2842 Waxes for wood, leather & other materials

(G-763)
HOOD CANAL LOGGING CO INC
510 Ne Alder Creek Ln (98528)
PHONE..................................360 275-4676
Eric Hurd, *President*
Amy Hurd, *Corp Secy*
EMP: 2
SALES (est): 233K **Privately Held**
SIC: 2411 Logging camps & contractors

(G-764)
JAY ONE BALL
23632 Ne State Route 3 (98528-8309)
PHONE..................................360 275-2834
◆ EMP: 2 EST: 2007
SALES (est): 66K **Privately Held**
SIC: 2842 Mfg Polish/Sanitation Goods

(G-765)
JEFFREY HEMBURY
Also Called: Tree Flelrs Contract Cutng Log
90 E Goldfinch Ln (98528-9584)
PHONE..................................360 535-3737
Jeffrey Hembury, *Owner*
EMP: 2
SALES (est): 129.4K **Privately Held**
SIC: 2411 0783 1794 Timber, cut at logging camp; removal services, bush & tree; excavation & grading, building construction

(G-766)
JKR FORKLIFT LLC
580 Ne Matthew Dr (98528-9407)
PHONE..................................360 275-4811
Donald Holmes, *Administration*
EMP: 3 EST: 2008
SALES (est): 332.4K **Privately Held**
SIC: 3537 Forklift trucks

(G-767)
LONG ROAD WINERY
550 Ne Lake Ridge Dr (98528-8720)
PHONE..................................206 859-7697
Galen Krohn, *Principal*
EMP: 4
SALES (est): 263.3K **Privately Held**
SIC: 2084 Wines

(G-768)
MOSQUITO FLEET WINERY LLC
21 Ne Old Belfair Hwy (98528)
PHONE..................................360 710-8788
EMP: 7
SALES (est): 537K **Privately Held**
SIC: 2084 Wines

(G-769)
NORTH MASON FIBER COMPANY
431 Ne Log Yard Rd (98528-8603)
P.O. Box 275 (98528-0275)
PHONE..................................360 275-0228
Robert Dressel, *President*
EMP: 9
SQ FT: 400
SALES (est): 1.7MM **Privately Held**
SIC: 2421 4789 Wood chips, produced at mill; freight car loading & unloading

(G-770)
PACIFIC NW FINE WD PDTS LLC
100 E Nahum Ln (98528-9369)
P.O. Box 935 (98528-0935)
PHONE..................................360 275-5397
Brady J Short, *Mng Member*
EMP: 4 EST: 2002
SALES (est): 230K **Privately Held**
SIC: 2499 Bakers' equipment, wood

(G-771)
QUOIZEL LIGHTING
5221 Ne North Shore Rd (98528-9758)
PHONE..................................360 275-5435
Terry Wright, *Principal*
EMP: 2
SALES (est): 121.7K **Privately Held**
SIC: 3648 Lighting equipment

(G-772)
RICHARD MEEK
Also Called: R & K Ventures
210 Ne Belfair Manor Dr (98528-9008)
P.O. Box 1196 (98528-1196)
PHONE..................................360 275-4104
Richard Meek, *Owner*
Katherine Meek, *Office Mgr*
EMP: 2
SALES: 275K **Privately Held**
SIC: 2411 Logging

(G-773)
ROCK BIZARRE
2613 Ne Old Belfair Hwy (98528-9662)
PHONE..................................360 275-9742
Jeffrey Kundinger, *Principal*
EMP: 3
SALES (est): 112.3K **Privately Held**
SIC: 3281 Marble, building; cut & shaped

(G-774)
SCHILLINGER ENTERPRISES INC
4673 E State Route 302 (98528-9384)
PHONE..................................360 275-2275
EMP: 6
SALES (est): 390K **Privately Held**
SIC: 2411 Mfg Wood Chips Produced In The Field

Bellevue
King County

(G-775)
3S PLASTICS LLC
13620 Ne 20th St Ste H (98005-4905)
PHONE..................................425 747-2827
Jocelyn Yang, *Principal*
EMP: 2
SALES (est): 81.8K **Privately Held**
SIC: 2821 Plastics materials & resins

(G-776)
7 GRAPES SOFTWARE
480 150th Pl Ne (98007-5043)
PHONE..................................425 653-2308
Samuel Menaker, *Principal*
EMP: 2
SALES (est): 178.6K **Privately Held**
SIC: 7372 Prepackaged software

(G-777)
AAA PRINTING INC
Also Called: AAA Printing and Graphics
1405 132nd Ave Ne Ste 9 (98005-2258)
PHONE..................................425 454-0156
William Reller, *President*
EMP: 21
SQ FT: 11,000
SALES: 3.3MM **Privately Held**
SIC: 2731 2732 2741 Pamphlets: publishing & printing; pamphlets: printing & binding, not published on site; business service newsletters: publishing & printing

(G-778)
AAA PRINTING & GRAPHICS INC
1405 132nd Ave Ne Ste 9 (98005-2258)
PHONE..................................425 454-0156
John D Madden, *President*
EMP: 16
SQ FT: 6,000
SALES (est): 2.8MM **Privately Held**
WEB: www.aaa-printing.com
SIC: 2759 2791 2752 7336 Commercial printing; typesetting; commercial printing, lithographic; commercial art & graphic design

(G-779)
AAV GROUP
2862 160th Pl Ne (98008-2161)
PHONE..................................972 834-2750
Ada Erzurumlu, *CEO*
EMP: 15
SALES: 15K **Privately Held**
SIC: 8699 7372 7389 Charitable organization; application computer software;

(G-780)
ADI CORPORATION
40 Lake Bellevue Dr # 310 (98005-2479)
PHONE..................................425 455-4561
Rex J Mudd, *President*
EMP: 9
SQ FT: 3,800
SALES (est): 1MM **Privately Held**
SIC: 3911 5094 5944 Jewelry, precious metal; jewelry; jewelry, precious stones & precious metals

(G-781)
ADIPRENE DIRECT INC
777 108th Ave Ne (98004-5130)
PHONE..................................425 999-3805
Christopher Jardine, *CFO*
EMP: 21
SQ FT: 10,000
SALES (est): 3.2MM **Privately Held**
SIC: 2899 Chemical preparations

(G-782)
AGRO TECHNIC LLC
10708 Main St Apt 403 (98004-5595)
PHONE..................................206 669-2446
Martin Nelson, *Mng Member*
EMP: 10
SALES (est): 1MM **Privately Held**
SIC: 2833 5122 Botanical products, medicinal: ground, graded or milled; medicinals & botanicals

(G-783)
AKAMAI TECHNOLOGIES INC
1100 112th Ave Ne Ste 150 (98004-4419)
PHONE..................................206 674-5900
Derek Chisman, *President*
Jeremiah Marett, *Engineer*
EMP: 6
SALES (corp-wide): 2.7B **Publicly Held**
SIC: 7372 Prepackaged software
PA: Akamai Technologies, Inc.
150 Broadway Ste 100
Cambridge MA 02142
617 444-3000

(G-784)
ALITHEON INC
10900 Ne 8th St Ste 613 (98004-4454)
PHONE..................................888 606-7445
Scot Land, *CEO*
Jim Beach, *CFO*
EMP: 19 EST: 2015
SALES (est): 350.4K **Privately Held**
SIC: 7371 7372 Computer software development; prepackaged software

(G-785)
ALYESKA SEAFOODS INC (DH)
3015 112th Ave Ne Ste 100 (98004-8001)
PHONE..................................206 682-5949
Rick Dutton, *President*
Mark Johahnson, *Vice Pres*
Makoto Kanezaki, *Vice Pres*
Noriaki Ito, *Treasurer*
Tim Smyer, *Admin Sec*
◆ EMP: 87
SQ FT: 60,000
SALES (est): 33.5MM **Privately Held**
SIC: 2092 Seafoods, fresh: prepared; seafoods, frozen: prepared
HQ: Maruha Capital Investment Inc
3015 112th Ave Ne Ste 100
Bellevue WA 98004
206 382-0640

(G-786)
AMERICAN GRAPHIC ARTS
Also Called: AGA Sports
1808 140th Ave Se (98005-4041)
PHONE..................................425 378-8065
Inna Opalchuke, *Owner*
EMP: 2
SALES (est): 223.1K **Privately Held**
WEB: www.agasports.com
SIC: 2759 Screen printing

(G-787)
AMPLEX BIORESOURCES LLC
12330 Ne 8th St Ste 101 (98005-3187)
PHONE..................................425 285-0628
EMP: 2
SALES (est): 74.4K **Privately Held**
SIC: 2836 Mfg Biological Products

(G-788)
ANDREW HOOVER
16803 Ne 35th St (98008-6103)
PHONE..................................425 869-1123
Andrew Hoover, *Principal*
EMP: 2
SALES (est): 73.1K **Privately Held**
SIC: 2721 Periodicals

(G-789)
APPESTEEM CORPORATION
655 156th Ave Se Ste 275 (98007-5022)
PHONE..................................240 461-5689
Dennis Batchelder, *President*
Hong Jia, *Vice Pres*
Jaimee King, *General Counsel*
EMP: 10
SQ FT: 870
SALES (est): 222.5K **Privately Held**
SIC: 8734 7372 Product certification, safety or performance; application computer software

(G-790)
APPTIO INC (HQ)
11100 Ne 8th St Ste 600 (98004-4402)
PHONE..................................866 470-0320
Thomas Bogan, *Ch of Bd*
Sunny Gupta, *President*
John Morrow, *Exec VP*
Kurt Shintaffer, *CFO*
Todd Joseph, *Ch Credit Ofcr*
EMP: 148

▲ = Import ▼=Export
◆ =Import/Export

GEOGRAPHIC SECTION
Bellevue - King County (G-819)

SQ FT: 89,000
SALES: 188.5MM **Privately Held**
SIC: 7372 Prepackaged software; application computer software; business oriented computer software
PA: Bellevue Parent, Llc
11100 Ne 8th St Ste 600
Bellevue WA 98004
866 470-0320

(G-791)
ARBITRARY SOFTWARE LLC
15135 Se 46th Way (98006-3228)
PHONE..........................425 644-7428
David Rostowsky, *Principal*
EMP: 2
SALES (est): 119.2K **Privately Held**
SIC: 7372 Prepackaged software

(G-792)
ARC DOCUMENT SOLUTIONS INC
1850 130th Ave Ne (98005-2244)
PHONE..........................425 883-1110
James Whitney, *Manager*
EMP: 3
SALES (corp-wide): 400.7MM **Publicly Held**
SIC: 2752 Commercial printing, lithographic
PA: Arc Document Solutions, Inc.
12657 Alcosta Blvd # 200
San Ramon CA 94583
925 949-5100

(G-793)
ARCBLOCK INC
3150 Richards Rd Ste 130 (98005-4466)
PHONE..........................425 442-5101
Zhihong Mao, *CEO*
EMP: 10
SALES (est): 198.7K **Privately Held**
SIC: 7374 7372 Data processing & preparation; application computer software

(G-794)
ARM INC
915 118th Ave Se 305 (98005-3819)
PHONE..........................425 602-0915
EMP: 127 **Privately Held**
SIC: 3674 Integrated circuits, semiconductor networks, etc.
HQ: Arm, Inc.
150 Rose Orchard Way
San Jose CA 95134

(G-795)
ARROW POINT MEDIA INC
2810 127th Ave Ne (98005-1628)
PHONE..........................425 885-3922
Anne Burke, *President*
Nicolle Meyers, *President*
EMP: 3
SALES (est): 289.4K **Privately Held**
SIC: 2721 Magazines: publishing only, not printed on site

(G-796)
ASCENSUS SPECIALTIES LLC (HQ)
2821 Northup Way Ste 275 (98004-1447)
PHONE..........................425 448-1679
Mike Huff, *President*
Craig Wien, *CFO*
▼ **EMP:** 82 **EST:** 2014
SQ FT: 6,000
SALES (est): 25.2MM
SALES (corp-wide): 1.8B **Privately Held**
SIC: 2869 Industrial organic chemicals
PA: Wind Point Partners, L.P.
676 N Michigan Ave # 3700
Chicago IL 60611
312 255-4800

(G-797)
ASCENTIS CORPORATION (PA)
11040 Main St Ste 101 (98004-6368)
PHONE..........................425 519-0341
Les Goldstein, *CEO*
Walter Turek, *Chairman*
David Bernstein, *Vice Pres*
Nicolas Cohen, *Vice Pres*
Michael Cross, *Vice Pres*
EMP: 28
SQ FT: 10,000
SALES (est): 14.2MM **Privately Held**
WEB: www.ascentis.com
SIC: 7372 Prepackaged software

(G-798)
ATOS IT SOLUTIONS AND SVCS INC
15400 Se 30th Pl (98007-6546)
PHONE..........................425 691-3080
Thierry Breton, *Branch Mgr*
EMP: 5
SALES (corp-wide): 166.6MM **Privately Held**
SIC: 3661 Telephones & telephone apparatus
HQ: Atos It Solutions And Services Inc.
2500 Westchester Ave Fl 3
Purchase NY 10577
914 881-3000

(G-799)
AUTOMIC SOFTWARE INC (DH)
14475 Ne 24th St Ste 210 (98007-3774)
PHONE..........................425 644-2121
Todd Delaughter, *CEO*
Jason Liu, *CEO*
Guenther Flamm, *Vice Pres*
David Min, *Opers Staff*
Nick Koopman, *Accounts Mgr*
EMP: 55
SQ FT: 20,000
SALES (est): 28.1MM
SALES (corp-wide): 20.8B **Publicly Held**
WEB: www.uc4.com
SIC: 7372 Prepackaged software
HQ: Ca Software Osterreich Gmbh
Am Europlatz 5/Gebaude C
Wien 1120
570 800-

(G-800)
AVALONPHILLY LLC
Also Called: Dia Avalon Philly
14205 Se 36th Ave Ste 100 (98006-1553)
PHONE..........................800 405-7024
Leonard C Bost, *Mng Member*
EMP: 5
SALES (est): 56.7K **Privately Held**
WEB: www.avalonphilly.com
SIC: 7929 8748 7313 2621 Entertainment service; business consulting; electronic media advertising representatives; catalog, magazine & newsprint papers; film processing, editing & titling: motion picture; trade journals: publishing & printing

(G-801)
AVANTE TECHNOLOGY LLC
17611 Se 46th Pl (98006-6531)
PHONE..........................425 273-4740
Robert Zollo, *Principal*
Ronald Aldrich, *Principal*
EMP: 5 **EST:** 2015
SALES (est): 317.2K **Privately Held**
SIC: 3089 Monofilaments, nontextile

(G-802)
AVAYA INC
2277 158th Ct Ne (98008-2123)
PHONE..........................425 881-7544
Bob Sackett-Convers, *Technical Mgr*
Dan Mason, *Manager*
EMP: 125 **Publicly Held**
WEB: www.avaya.com
SIC: 7371 3661 Custom computer programming services; telephone dialing devices, automatic
HQ: Avaya Inc.
4655 Great America Pkwy
Santa Clara CA 95054
908 953-6000

(G-803)
AVAYA INC
333 108th Ave Ne Ste 2000 (98004-5722)
PHONE..........................425 454-2715
EMP: 91
SALES (corp-wide): 5.5B **Privately Held**
SIC: 3661 Mfg Telephone/Telegraph Apparatus
HQ: Avaya Inc.
4655 Great America Pkwy
Santa Clara CA 95054
908 953-6000

(G-804)
AVIDIAN TECHNOLOGIES INC
14405 Se 36th St Ste 206 (98006-1513)
PHONE..........................800 399-8980
James Wong, *CEO*
Keith Clements, *COO*
David Archer, *Vice Pres*
Warren Stokes, *Vice Pres*
Hans Hoffmeister, *Engineer*
EMP: 22
SALES (est): 3.4MM **Privately Held**
WEB: www.avidian.com
SIC: 7372 Prepackaged software

(G-805)
BALCONY SIGNS & LAMINATING
820 102nd Ave Ne Ste 300 (98004-4117)
PHONE..........................425 454-5500
Jane Simmons, *President*
EMP: 2
SALES (est): 91.6K **Privately Held**
SIC: 3993 Signs & advertising specialties

(G-806)
BASKIN-ROBBINS
14618 Se 66th St (98006-5028)
PHONE..........................425 793-3544
James Baskin, *Principal*
EMP: 9
SALES (est): 185.3K **Privately Held**
SIC: 5812 5451 5143 2024 Ice cream stands or dairy bars; ice cream (packaged); frozen dairy desserts; ice cream & frozen desserts

(G-807)
BASTA INC
Also Called: Basta Marine
1800 Richards Rd (98005-3988)
P.O. Box 53301 (98015-3301)
PHONE..........................425 641-8911
Sam Basta, *President*
Lynette Basta, *Vice Pres*
▲ **EMP:** 23
SQ FT: 12,000
SALES (est): 2.5MM **Privately Held**
WEB: www.bastamarine.com
SIC: 3536 5088 7699 1521 Boat lifts; marine crafts & supplies; nautical repair services; patio & deck construction & repair

(G-808)
BBH SHEET METAL LLC
1414 127th Pl Ne Ste 107 (98005-2260)
PHONE..........................425 637-0360
EMP: 8
SALES (est): 1.1MM **Privately Held**
SIC: 3444 Sheet metalwork

(G-809)
BELLEVUE BREWING COMPANY LLC
1820 130th Ave Ne 2 (98005-2205)
PHONE..........................425 497-8686
John G Robertson, *Principal*
EMP: 10 **EST:** 2013
SALES (est): 959.1K **Privately Held**
SIC: 2082 Malt beverages

(G-810)
BELLEVUE DENTAL EXCELLENCE
14700 Ne 8th St Ste 210 (98007-4115)
PHONE..........................425 378-1600
Kristi Beck, *Principal*
EMP: 4
SALES (est): 383.6K **Privately Held**
SIC: 3843 Enamels, dentists'

(G-811)
BELLEVUE EMBROIDERY
4035 Factoria Sq Mall Se (98006-1286)
PHONE..........................425 646-9191
Shula Hou, *Owner*
EMP: 2 **EST:** 2000
SALES (est): 78.3K **Privately Held**
SIC: 2395 Embroidery & art needlework

(G-812)
BELLEVUE FINE ART REPRODCTN
2940 112th Ave Se (98004-7528)
PHONE..........................425 749-7396
Scott Moore, *Partner*

EMP: 3
SALES: 500K **Privately Held**
SIC: 2759 Engraving

(G-813)
BELLEVUE PARENT LLC (PA)
11100 Ne 8th St Ste 600 (98004-4402)
PHONE..........................866 470-0320
Sunny Gupta, *President*
EMP: 2
SALES (est): 188.5MM **Privately Held**
SIC: 7372 Prepackaged software; application computer software; business oriented computer software

(G-814)
BELLEVUE PRINTING LLC (PA)
Also Called: Minuteman Press
1449 130th Ave Ne (98005-2253)
PHONE..........................425 558-1862
Bruce Mezistrano,
EMP: 5
SALES (est): 1MM **Privately Held**
SIC: 7334 2752 2759 Photocopying & duplicating services; commercial printing, offset; commercial printing

(G-815)
BELLEVUE TAILORS AND FORMAL WR
13500 Ne Bel Red Rd # 14 (98005-2342)
PHONE..........................425 643-0741
Gerry Hagg, *Owner*
EMP: 4
SALES: 120K **Privately Held**
SIC: 2311 7219 Tailored suits & formal jackets; tailor shop, except custom or merchant tailor

(G-816)
BFY FOOD GROUP LLC
Also Called: Culinary Co.
1813 115th Ave Ne (98004-3002)
PHONE..........................425 298-5523
Sachin Ajith, *Mng Member*
David Israel,
EMP: 7
SALES (est): 1.2MM **Privately Held**
SIC: 2022 Cheese spreads, dips, pastes & other cheese products

(G-817)
BIOCONTROL SYSTEMS INC
12822 Se 32nd St (98005-4340)
PHONE..........................425 603-1123
Phillip Feldsine, *President*
Caroline Feldsine, *COO*
EMP: 13
SQ FT: 15,000
SALES (est): 3.9MM
SALES (corp-wide): 42.2B **Publicly Held**
WEB: www.biocontrolsys.com
SIC: 8731 2899 Biotechnical research, commercial; food contamination testing or screening kits; water treating compounds
PA: Merck & Co., Inc.
2000 Galloping Hill Rd
Kenilworth NJ 07033
908 740-4000

(G-818)
BIOZN LLC
628 140th Ct Se Apt B207 (98007-8033)
PHONE..........................206 388-7865
Chyang T Fang, *CEO*
EMP: 2
SALES (est): 147K **Privately Held**
SIC: 2844 Toilet preparations

(G-819)
BITTITAN INC (PA)
1120 112th Ave Ne Ste 300 (98004-4505)
PHONE..........................206 428-6030
Geeman Yip, *CEO*
Uzma S Burki, *Vice Pres*
Gregg Ericksonas, *Vice Pres*
Mark Kirstein, *Vice Pres*
Jenn Martin, *Vice Pres*
EMP: 53
SQ FT: 16,000
SALES: 103MM **Privately Held**
WEB: www.bittitan.com
SIC: 7372 Prepackaged software

Bellevue - King County (G-820)   GEOGRAPHIC SECTION

(G-820)
BLANKSI LLC
12748 Ne Bel Red Rd (98005-2601)
PHONE..................................425 453-1224
Alexander Domnenkov, *Administration*
EMP: 2
SALES (est): 87.9K **Privately Held**
SIC: 2752 Commercial printing, lithographic

(G-821)
BOEING COMPANY
2810 160th Ave Se (98008-5421)
P.O. Box 3707, Seattle (98124-2207)
PHONE..................................312 544-2000
Bonnie Sookik, *President*
Todd Zarfos, *Vice Pres*
Dana Jensen, *Project Mgr*
Denise Tibeau, *Project Mgr*
Scott Anderson, *Research*
EMP: 13
SALES (corp-wide): 101.1B **Publicly Held**
SIC: 3721 Aircraft
PA: The Boeing Company
   100 N Riverside Plz
   Chicago IL 60606
   312 544-2000

(G-822)
BOEING COMPANY
3365 160th Ave Se 3307 (98008)
PHONE..................................425 865-6915
Marcy McCuen, *Info Tech Mgr*
Sean Corbin, *Technology*
Jordan Bailey, *Analyst*
EMP: 26
SALES (corp-wide): 101.1B **Publicly Held**
SIC: 3721 Airplanes, fixed or rotary wing
PA: The Boeing Company
   100 N Riverside Plz
   Chicago IL 60606
   312 544-2000

(G-823)
BOEING COMPANY
3076 160th Ave Se (98008)
PHONE..................................425 865-3308
John W Prescott, *Principal*
EMP: 996
SALES (corp-wide): 101.1B **Publicly Held**
SIC: 3721 Airplanes, fixed or rotary wing
PA: The Boeing Company
   100 N Riverside Plz
   Chicago IL 60606
   312 544-2000

(G-824)
BOEING COMPANY
3265 160th Ave Se (98008)
PHONE..................................425 865-3311
Nick Warren, *Manager*
Gordon McKelvey, *Agent*
EMP: 1200
SALES (corp-wide): 101.1B **Publicly Held**
SIC: 3721 3761 3728 Airplanes, fixed or rotary wing; guided missiles & space vehicles; aircraft parts & equipment
PA: The Boeing Company
   100 N Riverside Plz
   Chicago IL 60606
   312 544-2000

(G-825)
BONFIRE PRODUCTIONS INC
2018 156th Ave Ne (98007-3825)
PHONE..................................425 748-5041
Tim C Deherrera, *President*
EMP: 11
SALES (est): 377.1K **Privately Held**
SIC: 2731 Book publishing
PA: C Money, Inc.
   Houston TX 77040

(G-826)
BOOKMARK PUBLISHING CO
15928 Se 41st Pl (98006-1807)
PHONE..................................425 562-0909
Brandon Warren, *Owner*
Carolyn Warren, *Owner*
EMP: 2

SALES (est): 217K **Privately Held**
SIC: 6162 2771 Mortgage bankers & correspondents; greeting cards

(G-827)
BOOM NOODLE
504 Bellevue Sq (98004-5017)
PHONE..................................425 453-6094
Jeremy Walcott, *Branch Mgr*
EMP: 10
SALES (corp-wide): 683.8K **Privately Held**
PA: Boom Noodle
   1411 4th Ave Ste 240
   Seattle WA 98101
   206 701-9130

(G-828)
BRAK SOFTWARE INC
15280 Ne 15th Pl Apt A (98007-4593)
PHONE..................................206 280-7157
Brian Rak, *President*
EMP: 2
SALES (est): 165K **Privately Held**
SIC: 7372 Prepackaged software

(G-829)
BROADCOM CORPORATION
2018 156th Ave Ne (98007-3825)
PHONE..................................425 748-5076
EMP: 3
SALES (corp-wide): 20.8B **Publicly Held**
SIC: 3674 Semiconductors & related devices
HQ: Broadcom Corporation
   1320 Ridder Park Dr
   San Jose CA 95131

(G-830)
BUNGIE INC (PA)
Also Called: Bungie Studios
550 106th Ave Ne Ste 207 (98004-5088)
PHONE..................................425 440-6800
Harold Ryan, *President*
Pete Parsons, *Mktg Dir*
EMP: 7
SALES (est): 2.7MM **Privately Held**
SIC: 3944 Electronic games & toys

(G-831)
BURNSTEAD CONSTRUCTION CO
Also Called: Heights of Meydenbauer, The
324 102nd Ave Se Ofc (98004-6196)
PHONE..................................425 635-1090
Joyce Pugsley, *Manager*
EMP: 16
SALES (corp-wide): 7.8MM **Privately Held**
WEB: www.burnstead.com
SIC: 1389 Construction, repair & dismantling services
PA: Burnstead Construction Co.
   11980 Ne 24th St Ste 200
   Bellevue WA 98005
   425 454-1900

(G-832)
BUSINESS COMPUTING SOLUTIONS
5832 155th Ave Se (98006-5120)
PHONE..................................425 644-6174
R Stowell, *Principal*
EMP: 2
SALES (est): 77.4K **Privately Held**
SIC: 3861 Photographic equipment & supplies

(G-833)
BYNDL AMC LLC
13555 Se 36th St Ste 270 (98006-1485)
PHONE..................................855 462-9635
Lori Marshall, *President*
EMP: 20 EST: 2015
SQ FT: 20,000
SALES (est): 668.1K **Privately Held**
SIC: 7372 Business oriented computer software

(G-834)
CA INC
14475 Ne 24th St Ste 210 (98007-3774)
PHONE..................................425 201-3500

Marvin Waschke, *Branch Mgr*
Chabree Larsen, *Manager*
EMP: 84
SALES (corp-wide): 20.8B **Publicly Held**
WEB: www.cai.com
SIC: 7372 Application computer software
HQ: Ca, Inc.
   520 Madison Ave
   New York NY 10022
   800 225-5224

(G-835)
CADENCE DESIGN SYSTEMS INC
320 120th Ave Ne Ste B103 (98005-3016)
PHONE..................................425 451-2360
Kyle Yakubu, *Branch Mgr*
EMP: 6
SALES (corp-wide): 2.1B **Publicly Held**
WEB: www.cadence.com
SIC: 7372 Application computer software
PA: Cadence Design Systems, Inc.
   2655 Seely Ave Bldg 5
   San Jose CA 95134
   408 943-1234

(G-836)
CAPE SAN LUCAS FISHING LP
10500 Ne 8th St Ste 1888 (98004-8631)
PHONE..................................425 688-1288
Chris Cook, *Partner*
EMP: 25
SALES (est): 2.1MM **Privately Held**
SIC: 3731 Fishing vessels, large: building & repairing

(G-837)
CAPITAL HOPE INNOVATIONS INC
60 Skagit Ky (98006-1031)
PHONE..................................360 480-9154
Robert Kelly, *Principal*
Shu-I Hsiao, *Principal*
Elizabeth Kelly, *Principal*
Timothy Wetzel, *Principal*
EMP: 4
SALES (est): 175.1K **Privately Held**
SIC: 3589 Water treatment equipment, industrial

(G-838)
CAPITAL INSTRUMENTS LTD
6210 Lake Wash Blvd Se (98006-6330)
PHONE..................................425 271-3756
James Dusek, *Owner*
EMP: 6
SALES: 150K **Privately Held**
SIC: 3841 5047 Surgical instruments & apparatus; hospital equipment & furniture

(G-839)
CARDIAC INSIGHT INC
2375 130th Ave Ne Ste 101 (98005-1758)
PHONE..................................206 596-2060
Brad Harlow, *CEO*
Kurt Noltensmeyer, *President*
Robert Odell, *COO*
Mike Schuh, *CFO*
EMP: 12
SALES (est): 146.4K **Privately Held**
SIC: 3841 Surgical & medical instruments

(G-840)
CARTOGRAM INC
10400 Ne 4th St Ste 500 (98004-5175)
PHONE..................................425 628-0395
Will Clausen, *President*
EMP: 20
SALES: 1.8MM **Privately Held**
SIC: 7372 Prepackaged software

(G-841)
CASSEL INC
1404 140th Pl Ne (98007-3915)
PHONE..................................206 909-9584
Percell Johnson, *President*
EMP: 150
SQ FT: 800
SALES: 2MM **Privately Held**
SIC: 2621 2671 Wrapping & packaging papers; plastic film, coated or laminated for packaging

(G-842)
CATERPILLAR INC
3535 Factoria Blvd Se # 350 (98006-1206)
PHONE..................................425 562-2060
Grant Hughes, *Sales Staff*
Kurt Norris, *Manager*
EMP: 22
SALES (corp-wide): 54.7B **Publicly Held**
WEB: www.cat.com
SIC: 3531 Construction machinery
PA: Caterpillar Inc.
   510 Lake Cook Rd Ste 100
   Deerfield IL 60015
   224 551-4000

(G-843)
CELLCYTE GENETICS CORPORATION
Also Called: (A DEVELOPMENT STAGE COMPANY)
14205 Se 36th St Ste 100 (98006-1553)
PHONE..................................425 519-3755
John M Fluke Jr, *CEO*
Douglas P Cerretti, *President*
Randy A Lieber,
EMP: 3
SALES (est): 255K **Privately Held**
WEB: www.cellcyte.com
SIC: 3841 Surgical & medical instruments

(G-844)
CELLULAR DIRECTORY CORP
1611 116th Ave Ne (98004-3045)
PHONE..................................425 646-4917
EMP: 2 EST: 2001
SALES (est): 90K **Privately Held**
SIC: 2741 Misc Publishing

(G-845)
CENTER FOR PROSTHETIC
Also Called: Cpo
1231 116th Ave Ne Ste 725 (98004-3804)
PHONE..................................425 454-4276
Larry Kirluk, *Manager*
EMP: 5
SALES (corp-wide): 2.1MM **Privately Held**
WEB: www.cpo.biz
SIC: 3842 5999 Prosthetic appliances; orthopedic & prosthesis applications
PA: Center For Prosthetics Orthotics, Inc.
   411 12th Ave Ste 200
   Seattle WA 98122
   206 328-4276

(G-846)
CENTER FOR THE DEF FREE ENTP
12500 Ne 10th Pl (98005-2532)
PHONE..................................425 455-5038
Alan Gottlieb, *President*
Ron Arnold, *Exec VP*
Samuel Slom, *Vice Pres*
Jeffery D Kane, *Treasurer*
EMP: 4 EST: 1976
SQ FT: 2,000
SALES: 577.7K **Privately Held**
WEB: www.cdfe.org
SIC: 2731 Book publishing

(G-847)
CENTRICITY PUBLISHING LLC
305 108th Ave Ne Ste 200 (98004-5706)
PHONE..................................360 692-6162
Gregory Forge, *Manager*
EMP: 2
SALES (est): 106.2K **Privately Held**
SIC: 2741 Miscellaneous publishing

(G-848)
CERTAIN SOFTWARE INC
11061 Ne 2nd St Ste 107 (98004-5810)
PHONE..................................415 353-5330
Aleks Rabrenovich, *Principal*
EMP: 2 EST: 2009
SALES (est): 129.5K **Privately Held**
SIC: 7372 Business oriented computer software

(G-849)
CHAMPLIN TECHNOLOGIES LLC
5722 155th Ave Se (98006-5118)
PHONE..................................425 736-8935
Cary Champlin, *Officer*
EMP: 2

GEOGRAPHIC SECTION
Bellevue - King County (G-879)

SALES (est): 150K **Privately Held**
SIC: 7372 Application computer software

(G-850)
CHINESE SEAFOOD NOODLE LLC
12211 Ne 5th St Apt A301 (98005-4805)
PHONE.................................425 877-8856
Hang Wang, *Principal*
EMP: 4
SALES (est): 274.5K **Privately Held**
SIC: 2098 Noodles (e.g. egg, plain & water), dry

(G-851)
CHRONUS CORPORATION
15395 Se 30th Pl Ste 140 (98007-6537)
PHONE.................................425 629-6327
Vellore Vetrivelkumaran, *CEO*
Madhan Subhas, *Vice Pres*
Alex Albuerne, *Finance Mgr*
Kira Fickenscher, *Client Mgr*
Brina Nelson, *Accounts Exec*
EMP: 18
SALES (est): 2.1MM **Privately Held**
SIC: 7372 Prepackaged software

(G-852)
CIRCUIT SERVICES WORLDWIDE
10 148th Ave Ne Ste 101 (98004-4947)
PHONE.................................425 454-7181
▲ EMP: 40
SALES (est): 4.6MM **Privately Held**
SIC: 3672 Mfg Printed Circuit Boards

(G-853)
CIRCUIT SERVICES WORLDWIDE LLC
10 148th Ave Ne Ste 101 (98004-4947)
PHONE.................................425 454-7181
Massey Zamani, *Vice Pres*
Micahel Kuo, *Mng Member*
▲ EMP: 12
SALES: 6.5MM **Privately Held**
SIC: 3672 Printed circuit boards

(G-854)
CISCO SYSTEMS INC
500 108th Ave Ne Ste 500 # 500 (98004-5588)
PHONE.................................425 468-0800
Rick Mittelstaedt, *Business Mgr*
Courtney Kullman, *Project Mgr*
Kirtis Butler, *Sales Mgr*
Paul Magnaghi, *Sales Staff*
Gary Bylund, *Branch Mgr*
EMP: 110
SALES (corp-wide): 49.3B **Publicly Held**
WEB: www.cisco.com
SIC: 3577 5045 Data conversion equipment, media-to-media: computer; computers, peripherals & software
PA: Cisco Systems, Inc.
170 W Tasman Dr
San Jose CA 95134
408 526-4000

(G-855)
CLIMATE PUBLISHING LLC
15317 Se 49th Pl (98006-3652)
PHONE.................................206 515-1795
Mark Taylor, *Principal*
EMP: 2
SALES (est): 118.6K **Privately Held**
SIC: 2741 Miscellaneous publishing

(G-856)
COAST SEAFOODS COMPANY (HQ)
1200 Robert Bush Dr (98007)
P.O. Box 166, South Bend (98586-0166)
PHONE.................................360 875-5577
John Petrie, *President*
Kay Cogan, *CFO*
▲ EMP: 83
SQ FT: 1,500
SALES (est): 28.6MM
SALES (corp-wide): 70.7MM **Privately Held**
WEB: www.coastseafoods.com
SIC: 2091 5149 0913 Oysters: packaged in cans, jars, etc.; canned goods: fruit, vegetables, seafood, meats, etc.; oyster beds

PA: Pacific Shellfish, Inc.
5040 Cass St
San Diego CA 92109
858 272-9940

(G-857)
COCA-COLA COMPANY
915 118th Ave Se Ste 300 (98005-3875)
PHONE.................................404 676-0887
George Reigelsperger, *Accountant*
Alper Aziz, *Director*
EMP: 15
SALES (corp-wide): 31.8B **Publicly Held**
WEB: www.cocacola.com
SIC: 5046 2086 Soda fountain fixtures, except refrigerated; bottled & canned soft drinks
PA: The Coca-Cola Company
1 Coca Cola Plz Nw
Atlanta GA 30313
404 676-2121

(G-858)
COINSTAR AUTOMATED RET CANADA
1800 114th Ave Se (98004-6946)
PHONE.................................425 943-8000
EMP: 4 EST: 2014
SALES (est): 142.2K
SALES (corp-wide): 2B **Privately Held**
SIC: 3578 Change making machines
HQ: Coinstar, Llc
1800 114th Ave Se
Bellevue WA 98004

(G-859)
COLBY INSTRUMENTS LLC
15375 Se 30th Pl Ste 320 (98007-6551)
PHONE.................................425 452-8889
Victor K Chinn,
▼ EMP: 5
SQ FT: 2,500
SALES (est): 500K **Privately Held**
WEB: www.colbyinstruments.com
SIC: 3825 Test equipment for electronic & electric measurement; pulse (signal) generators

(G-860)
CONCUR TECHNOLOGIES INC (DH)
601 108th Ave Ne Ste 1000 (98004-4750)
PHONE.................................425 590-5000
Mike Eberhard, *President*
Ella Cordial, *Partner*
John Gibbon, *Partner*
Geetha French, *Business Mgr*
Barry Padgett, *Exec VP*
EMP: 1488
SALES: 23.4K
SALES (corp-wide): 28.2B **Privately Held**
WEB: www.concur.com
SIC: 7371 7372 Custom computer programming services; business oriented computer software
HQ: Sap America, Inc.
3999 West Chester Pike
Newtown Square PA 19073
610 661-1000

(G-861)
CONGRUENT SOFTWARE (USA) INC
4205 148th Ave Ne Ste 100 (98007-7114)
PHONE.................................425 460-0172
Mani Krishnamurthy, *President*
EMP: 82
SQ FT: 5,000
SALES (est): 3.1MM **Privately Held**
WEB: www.congruentsoft.com
SIC: 7372 7371 Prepackaged software; custom computer programming services

(G-862)
CONTENT MASTER
14335 Ne 24th St Ste 205 (98007-3737)
PHONE.................................425 274-1970
Russell Mead, *Principal*
EMP: 2
SALES (est): 233K **Privately Held**
SIC: 7372 Prepackaged software

(G-863)
CONTINENTAL DATA GRAPHICS
3245 146th Pl Se Ste 270 (98007-6478)
PHONE.................................425 562-4050
EMP: 2 EST: 2001
SALES (est): 170K **Privately Held**
SIC: 7372 Prepackaged Software Services

(G-864)
CONVERGENT EARNED VALUE ASSOC
13606 Se 43rd Pl (98006-2230)
PHONE.................................206 293-6931
Charles Reeves, *Principal*
EMP: 4
SALES (est): 365K **Privately Held**
SIC: 3674 Semiconductors & related devices

(G-865)
COPYTONIX
14432 Se Eastgate Way # 300 (98007-6493)
PHONE.................................503 968-0364
Kyle Marvin, *Principal*
EMP: 4
SALES (est): 328.2K **Privately Held**
SIC: 3577 Computer peripheral equipment

(G-866)
COSTELLINIS LLC
14150 Ne 20th St 341 (98007-3700)
P.O. Box 300 (98009-0300)
PHONE.................................877 889-8266
Gina Costello, *CEO*
EMP: 3
SQ FT: 10,000
SALES (est): 500K **Privately Held**
WEB: www.costellini.com
SIC: 2066 Powdered cocoa

(G-867)
COUPLE POWER
2503 158th Ave Se (98008-5417)
PHONE.................................425 641-0278
Joespeh Hesketh, *Partner*
EMP: 2
SALES (est): 19.4K **Privately Held**
SIC: 3651 Speaker monitors

(G-868)
CRITICAL DELIVERY SERVICE LLC
Also Called: Cds
4957 Lakemont Blvd Se C4-104 (98006-7801)
PHONE.................................206 724-3653
Svetlana Ouzbiakova,
EMP: 5
SQ FT: 2,000
SALES: 400K **Privately Held**
SIC: 4513 3674 4225 Parcel delivery, private air; package delivery, private air; computer logic modules; general warehousing

(G-869)
CRONUS VENTURES LLC
16834 Se 58th Pl (98006-5558)
P.O. Box 3034 (98009-3034)
PHONE.................................425 641-4497
Haresh Ved, *Partner*
Vijay Vashee, *General Mgr*
EMP: 7
SALES (est): 469K **Privately Held**
WEB: www.cronusventures.com
SIC: 7372 7373 7379 8742 Business oriented computer software; computer integrated systems design; computer related consulting services; marketing consulting services

(G-870)
CROSSING BORDERS
2901 167th Ave Ne (98008-2160)
PHONE.................................425 466-7680
Mariela Stockdale, *Owner*
EMP: 3
SALES (est): 130K **Privately Held**
SIC: 3263 Tableware, household & commercial: semivitreous

(G-871)
CYTEC INDUSTRIES MATERIALS
10900 Ne 8th St (98004-4405)
PHONE.................................425 274-0485
Nancy A Klein MD, *Principal*
EMP: 2
SALES (est): 170.2K **Privately Held**
SIC: 2899 Chemical preparations

(G-872)
D E HOKANSON INC
12840 Ne 21st Pl Ste B (98005-1953)
PHONE.................................425 882-1689
Kyra Gray, *President*
Sigrid G Hokanson, *Admin Sec*
▼ EMP: 18
SQ FT: 10,000
SALES: 2.5MM **Privately Held**
WEB: www.deh-inc.com
SIC: 3841 Diagnostic apparatus, medical; blood pressure apparatus

(G-873)
D G HARD SURFACE LLC
1839 Killarney Way (98004-7049)
PHONE.................................206 718-4700
EMP: 2 EST: 2017
SALES (est): 90.1K **Privately Held**
SIC: 3471 Plating & polishing

(G-874)
DATA ENTERPRISES OF THE NW
Also Called: D E N
9 Lake Bellevue Dr # 205 (98005-2454)
PHONE.................................425 688-8805
Kalju Kaik, *Senior Engr*
D Michael Brown, *Branch Mgr*
EMP: 4
SALES (est): 274.1K
SALES (corp-wide): 196.3K **Privately Held**
WEB: www.aticts.com
SIC: 7372 Business oriented computer software
PA: Data Enterprises Of The Northwest Inc
12819 Se 38th St
Bellevue WA 98006
425 688-8805

(G-875)
DAVID G MCALEES
17425 Se 46th Pl (98006-6530)
PHONE.................................425 641-0318
David McAlees, *Principal*
EMP: 2
SALES (est): 85.9K **Privately Held**
SIC: 3577 Computer peripheral equipment

(G-876)
DE MARSS LLC
1300 114th Ave Se Ste 220 (98004-6960)
PHONE.................................425 218-3454
John De Mars,
EMP: 3
SALES (est): 115.1K **Privately Held**
SIC: 2035 Seasonings & sauces, except tomato & dry

(G-877)
DEREK ANDREW INC (PA)
6232 160th Ave Se (98006-5624)
PHONE.................................425 453-9888
Derek A Federman, *President*
Cynthia Federman, *Admin Sec*
◆ EMP: 10
SQ FT: 3,000
SALES (est): 1.1MM **Privately Held**
SIC: 2339 5621 Women's & misses' outerwear; women's sportswear

(G-878)
DINING SOLUTIONS LLC
Also Called: Meals On Wire
217 165th Ave Ne (98008-4517)
PHONE.................................425 268-6190
EMP: 2
SALES (est): 98.6K **Privately Held**
SIC: 7372 Prepackaged Software Services

(G-879)
DOMINO FASHION LLC
2042 Bellevue Sq (98004-5028)
PHONE.................................425 646-0500
George Hage, *Mng Member*
Denise Hage,
◆ EMP: 7 EST: 2010

Bellevue - King County (G-880)

SALES (est): 469.5K **Privately Held**
SIC: 3144 3171 Dress shoes, women's; women's handbags & purses

(G-880)
DORIGINAL JEWELERS
885 Bellevue Way Ne (98004-4209)
PHONE..................................425 454-5559
David W Rees Jr, *President*
EMP: 4
SQ FT: 800
SALES (est): 410.7K **Privately Held**
WEB: www.doriginaljewelers.com
SIC: 5944 7631 3911 Jewelry, precious stones & precious metals; watches; watch repair; diamond setter; jewelry repair services; necklaces, precious metal; rings, finger: precious metal; jewel settings & mountings, precious metal; mountings, gold or silver: pens, leather goods, etc.

(G-881)
DOT COM LLC
Also Called: Seattle Software Developers
4 102nd Ave Ne Ste 300 (98004-5621)
PHONE..................................425 256-2815
Julian Valentine, *Vice Pres*
Phil Fischer, *Mng Member*
EMP: 7
SALES: 4MM **Privately Held**
SIC: 7372 7389 Home entertainment computer software;

(G-882)
DOUBLEBIT SOFTWARE
3635 130th Ave Ne (98005-1351)
PHONE..................................425 503-0692
Jeff Parsons, *Principal*
EMP: 2
SALES (est): 90.1K **Privately Held**
SIC: 7372 Prepackaged software

(G-883)
DOUG PUZZLE
3620 130th Ave Ne (98005-1352)
PHONE..................................425 647-0464
Douglas Deardorff, *Principal*
EMP: 2
SALES (est): 183.7K **Privately Held**
SIC: 3944 Puzzles

(G-884)
DRESSER-RAND COMPANY
11808 Northup Way W190 (98005-1954)
PHONE..................................425 828-4919
EMP: 5
SALES (corp-wide): 95B **Privately Held**
SIC: 3563 Air & gas compressors
HQ: Dresser-Rand Company
    500 Paul Clark Dr
    Olean NY 14760
    716 375-3000

(G-885)
DS-IQ INC
3326 160th Ave Se Ste 200 (98008-6418)
P.O. Box 7178 (98008-1178)
PHONE..................................425 974-1400
Thomas Opdyke, *President*
Derek Britz, *VP Mktg*
Mark Whidby, *Asst Mgr*
William Wu, *Officer*
EMP: 100
SALES (est): 16.6MM **Privately Held**
SIC: 7372 8742 Publishers' computer software; marketing consulting services

(G-886)
EAGLE TREE SYSTEMS LLC
4957 Lakemont Blvd Se (98006-7801)
PHONE..................................425 614-0450
Marianne Parry,
EMP: 2
SALES (est): 228.7K **Privately Held**
WEB: www.eagletreesystems.com
SIC: 3944 Airplane models, toy & hobby

(G-887)
EASTSIDE SAW & SALES INC
12880 Ne Bel Red Rd Ste 1 (98005-2695)
PHONE..................................425 454-7627
Michael Lindsay, *President*
Julie Lindsay, *Vice Pres*
EMP: 30
SQ FT: 7,200
SALES: 4.3MM **Privately Held**
WEB: www.eastsidesaw.com
SIC: 7699 3425 5251 Knife, saw & tool sharpening & repair; saw blades & handsaws; tools, power

(G-888)
EASTSIDE TENT & AWNING CO
12880 Ne Bel Red Rd Ste 2 (98005-2695)
PHONE..................................425 454-7766
David Monsaas, *President*
Tony Monsaas, *Vice Pres*
Christina Monsaas, *Admin Sec*
EMP: 4
SQ FT: 2,200
SALES (est): 440.5K **Privately Held**
WEB: www.eastsideawning.com
SIC: 5999 2394 Awnings; canvas products; canvas & related products

(G-889)
EATON CORPORATION
13205 Se 30th St Ste 101 (98005-4415)
PHONE..................................425 644-5800
Ryan Hatfield, *Branch Mgr*
EMP: 40 **Privately Held**
WEB: www.eaton.com
SIC: 3674 5065 5063 3613 Semiconductors & related devices; semiconductor devices; circuit breakers; power circuit breakers
HQ: Eaton Corporation
    1000 Eaton Blvd
    Cleveland OH 44122
    440 523-5000

(G-890)
EATON CORPORATION
1300 114th Ave Se Ste 208 (98004-6960)
PHONE..................................425 451-4954
Robert Torgerson, *Branch Mgr*
EMP: 4 **Privately Held**
SIC: 3721 3812 Aircraft; aircraft/aerospace flight instruments & guidance systems
HQ: Eaton Corporation
    1000 Eaton Blvd
    Cleveland OH 44122
    440 523-5000

(G-891)
ECCO CONTRACTORS INCORPORATED
3803 138th Ave Se (98006-1429)
PHONE..................................425 957-1735
Michael Dotson, *Vice Pres*
EMP: 2
SALES: 500K **Privately Held**
SIC: 1611 3357 General contractor, highway & street construction; building wire & cable, nonferrous

(G-892)
EDUONGO INC
14205 Se 36th St Ste 100 (98006-1553)
PHONE..................................206 451-7325
Ridvan Aliu, *CEO*
Steven Yee, *COO*
Erzen Komoni, *Manager*
Durim Jusaj, *Software Dev*
EMP: 12
SQ FT: 1,500
SALES (est): 111K **Privately Held**
SIC: 8243 7371 8742 7372 Software training, computer; custom computer programming services; software programming applications; training & development consultant; educational computer software

(G-893)
ELEMENTAL CREMATION & BURIAL
2105 112th Ave Ne Ste 100 (98004-2945)
PHONE..................................206 357-1141
Jeff Jorgenson, *Principal*
EMP: 2
SALES (est): 74.4K **Privately Held**
SIC: 2819 Elements

(G-894)
EMBODI3D LLC (PA)
1010 185th Ave Ne (98008-3446)
PHONE..................................425 429-6193
Michael Itagaki, *Mng Member*
EMP: 3
SALES (est): 392K **Privately Held**
SIC: 3555 Printing trades machinery

(G-895)
EMC CORPORATION
Also Called: Emc2
15500 Se 30th Pl Ste 200 (98007-6347)
PHONE..................................425 378-9209
EMP: 10
SALES (corp-wide): 24.7B **Publicly Held**
SIC: 3572 Mfg Computer Storage Devices
PA: Emc Corporation
    176 South St
    Hopkinton MA 01748
    508 435-1000

(G-896)
EMERALD CITY ELECTRONICS
17280 Ne 8th St Apt B (98008-4144)
PHONE..................................425 649-1006
Tommy Aunan, *Executive*
EMP: 2
SALES (est): 91.8K **Privately Held**
SIC: 3679 Electronic components

(G-897)
ENDURANCE WINDOW CO
2810 131st Pl Ne (98005-1715)
PHONE..................................425 883-1345
Paul Vander Hoek Jr, *Principal*
EMP: 4
SALES (est): 370.3K **Privately Held**
SIC: 3211 Window glass, clear & colored

(G-898)
ERNIT LLC
2515 140th Ave Ne (98005-1862)
PHONE..................................425 922-3867
Reza Yasseri,
EMP: 3
SALES (est): 243.4K **Privately Held**
SIC: 3679 Electronic circuits

(G-899)
ESTERLINE CORPORATION
500 108th Ave Ne Ste 1500 (98004-5500)
PHONE..................................425 453-9400
EMP: 2
SALES (est): 105K **Privately Held**
SIC: 3728 Aircraft parts & equipment

(G-900)
ESTERLINE EUROPE COMPANY LLC
500 108th Ave Ne Ste 1500 (98004-5500)
PHONE..................................425 453-9400
Curtis C Reusser, *CEO*
EMP: 3
SALES (est): 136.6K **Privately Held**
SIC: 3812 Aircraft/aerospace flight instruments & guidance systems

(G-901)
ESTERLINE INTERNATIONAL CO
500 108th Ave Ne Ste 1500 (98004-5500)
PHONE..................................425 453-9400
Curtis C Reusser, *President*
EMP: 2 EST: 2013
SALES (est): 110.2K **Privately Held**
SIC: 3728 Aircraft assemblies, subassemblies & parts

(G-902)
ESTERLINE TECHNOLOGIES CORP (HQ)
500 108th Ave Ne Ste 1500 (98004-5500)
PHONE..................................425 453-9400
Curtis C Reusser, *Ch of Bd*
Roger A Ross, *President*
Albert S Yost, *President*
Stephen M Nolan, *CFO*
Paul P Benson, *Officer*
▼ EMP: 35
SALES: 2B
SALES (corp-wide): 3.8B **Publicly Held**
WEB: www.esterline.com
SIC: 3728 3812 3429 Aircraft assemblies, subassemblies & parts; panel assembly (hydromatic propeller test stands), aircraft; aircraft control instruments; radar systems & equipment; aircraft hardware
PA: Transdigm Group Incorporated
    1301 E 9th St Ste 3000
    Cleveland OH 44114
    216 706-2960

(G-903)
ETIOS HEALTH LLC
12701 Ne 9th Pl Apt D110 (98005-3238)
PHONE..................................585 217-1716
Jared Munir, *CEO*
Martin Chavez, *Principal*
Avadhut Joshi, *Principal*
EMP: 3
SALES (est): 83.9K **Privately Held**
SIC: 7372 Application computer software

(G-904)
EXACTTARGET INC
601 108th Ave Ne Ste 1580 (98004-8622)
PHONE..................................866 362-4538
Scott Dorsey, *CEO*
EMP: 3
SALES (corp-wide): 13.2B **Publicly Held**
SIC: 7372 Business oriented computer software
HQ: Exacttarget, Inc.
    20 N Meridian St Ste 200
    Indianapolis IN 46204
    317 423-3928

(G-905)
EXCELSIOR NANOTECH CORPORATION
2023 120th Ave Ne (98005-2108)
PHONE..................................206 898-9477
Aaron Youngbull, *CEO*
Lixin Zheng, *President*
EMP: 5 EST: 2013
SALES (est): 463.3K **Privately Held**
SIC: 2819 Industrial inorganic chemicals

(G-906)
EZION GLOBAL INC
Also Called: Jnb
16434 Se 35th St (98008-5817)
PHONE..................................206 446-9476
Jungjoon Park, *President*
EMP: 2
SALES: 800K **Privately Held**
SIC: 2273 Mats & matting

(G-907)
FANTASY CONTENT
912 142nd Ave Se (98007-5419)
PHONE..................................425 653-2207
EMP: 2
SALES (est): 85.9K **Privately Held**
SIC: 3577 Mfg Computer Peripheral Equipment

(G-908)
FASTSIGNS
13279 Ne 20th St (98005-2009)
PHONE..................................425 746-4151
Scott Juetten, *President*
Rochelle Juetten, *Vice Pres*
Summer Stumpf, *Sales Mgr*
Marcus Newman, *Graphic Designe*
EMP: 6
SALES (est): 394.2K **Privately Held**
SIC: 3993 Signs & advertising specialties

(G-909)
FEDEX OFFICE PRINT & SHIP CTR
3632 Factoria Blvd Se (98006-6128)
PHONE..................................425 641-1174
EMP: 2
SALES (est): 83.9K **Privately Held**
SIC: 2752 Commercial printing, lithographic

(G-910)
FILTRIFIC CO LLC
13280 Ne Spring Blvd # 101 (98005-5501)
PHONE..................................425 482-6777
Justin Berkey, *Sales Mgr*
Edward Berkey,
Nate Berkey,
▲ EMP: 2
SALES (est): 160K **Privately Held**
WEB: www.filtrific.com
SIC: 3589 Water treatment equipment, industrial

(G-911)
FISHING VESSEL ST JUDE LLC
11628 Se 48th St (98006-2710)
PHONE..................................425 378-0680
Joe Malley,

GEOGRAPHIC SECTION   Bellevue - King County (G-942)

EMP: 8
SALES (est): 598.9K Privately Held
SIC: 2091 Tuna fish, preserved & cured

(G-912)
FLIGHTWAYS CORPORATION
5827 167th Ave Se (98006-5566)
PHONE..................................425 747-6903
Douglas F Davis, *President*
EMP: 1
SQ FT: 2,500
SALES: 3MM Privately Held
WEB: www.flightwayscorp.com
SIC: 3721 Airplanes, fixed or rotary wing

(G-913)
FLOTBUNKER LLC
13750 Ne 34th Pl (98005-1462)
PHONE..................................206 354-5205
EMP: 3 EST: 2010
SALES (est): 255.6K Privately Held
SIC: 2911 Diesel fuels

(G-914)
FORD MOTOR CREDIT COMPANY LLC
13555 Se 36th St Ste 350 (98006-1485)
P.O. Box 1828 (98009-1828)
PHONE..................................425 643-0454
Brian Evans, *Manager*
EMP: 65
SALES (corp-wide): 160.3B Publicly Held
WEB: www.fordcredit.com
SIC: 3711 3714 6153 6141 Automobile assembly, including specialty automobiles; motor vehicle parts & accessories; financing of dealers by motor vehicle manufacturers organ.; financing: automobiles, furniture, etc., not a deposit bank; automobile insurance; credit & other financial responsibility insurance
HQ: Ford Motor Credit Company Llc
    1 American Rd
    Dearborn MI 48126
    313 322-3000

(G-915)
FORMULA WEB LLC
6745 161st Ave Se Unit B (98006-5427)
PHONE..................................425 835-3259
EMP: 4
SALES (est): 220K Privately Held
SIC: 2741 7389 Internet Publishing And Broadcasting Business Services At Non-Commercial Site

(G-916)
FOUNDATION INTERNATIONAL
15786 Ne 25th Pl (98008-2356)
PHONE..................................425 391-1281
Paul Lai, *Owner*
Margret Lai, *Owner*
EMP: 3
SALES (est): 232.2K Privately Held
SIC: 3669 Burglar alarm apparatus, electric

(G-917)
FUSION INDUSTRIES
17106 Ne 31st Pl (98008-2004)
PHONE..................................425 703-2867
EMP: 2
SALES (est): 100K Privately Held
SIC: 3999 Mfg Misc Products

(G-918)
GANNETT CO INC
Also Called: U S A Today
13810 Se Gateway 110 (98005)
PHONE..................................425 391-2530
Rick Sass, *Manager*
EMP: 24
SALES (corp-wide): 2.9B Publicly Held
WEB: www.gannett.com
SIC: 2711 2741 5192 Newspapers, publishing & printing; miscellaneous publishing; books, periodicals & newspapers
PA: Gannett Co., Inc.
    7950 Jones Branch Dr
    Mc Lean VA 22102
    703 854-6000

(G-919)
GARVEY C MAURY
15019 Ne 14th St (98007-4238)
PHONE..................................425 641-0232
Maury C Garvey, *Owner*
EMP: 3
SALES (est): 134.6K Privately Held
SIC: 2099 Food preparations

(G-920)
GATEWAY PRINTING INC
1470 127th Pl Ne (98005-2213)
PHONE..................................425 453-3272
Ken Clogston, *President*
EMP: 2
SALES (est): 288.1K Privately Held
WEB: www.gatewayprinting.net
SIC: 2752 Commercial printing, offset

(G-921)
GBC INTERNATIONAL BANK
500 108th Ave Ne Ste 1770 (98004-5532)
PHONE..................................425 214-8435
EMP: 2
SALES (est): 90.7K Privately Held
SIC: 2653 Corrugated & solid fiber boxes

(G-922)
GEKKO CORPORATION
Also Called: Pro-AM
12400 Se 38th St # 40542 (98015-5163)
PHONE..................................425 679-9188
Jeffrey Kent, *President*
EMP: 4
SALES: 15K Privately Held
SIC: 5045 7371 7372 Computer software; computer software systems analysis & design, custom; computer software development; business oriented computer software

(G-923)
GENERAL COMPUTERS INC
15613 Ne 1st Pl (98008-4307)
PHONE..................................425 405-0588
Junhua Chang, *President*
Chao Liu, *Admin Sec*
EMP: 2
SALES (est): 490K Privately Held
SIC: 3571 7371 7389 Electronic computers; computer software systems analysis & design, custom;

(G-924)
GET PLENISH INC
2020 124th Ave Ne (98005-2118)
PHONE..................................425 922-0070
Dock Leong,
EMP: 3
SALES: 40K Privately Held
SIC: 2834 Vitamin, nutrient & hematinic preparations for human use

(G-925)
GILT LLC
115 Bellevue Sq (98004-5021)
PHONE..................................425 468-4458
EMP: 2 EST: 2007
SALES (est): 93K Privately Held
SIC: 3423 Mfg Hand/Edge Tools

(G-926)
GLAXOSMITHKLINE LLC
5494 170th Pl Se (98006-5527)
PHONE..................................206 755-5725
EMP: 26
SALES (corp-wide): 39.5B Privately Held
SIC: 2834 Pharmaceutical preparations
HQ: Glaxosmithkline Llc
    5 Crescent Dr
    Philadelphia PA 19112
    215 751-4000

(G-927)
GLOBAL DISPLAY NORTH AMER LTD
Also Called: Goworld Display
14925 Se Allen Rd (98006-1643)
PHONE..................................425 698-1938
Hing WA Chan, *Principal*
Hui Zhang, *Principal*
EMP: 2

SALES (est): 145.1K
SALES (corp-wide): 711.7MM Privately Held
SIC: 3674 Light emitting diodes
HQ: Shantou Goworld Display Co., Ltd.
    No.21, Xingye Rd.
    Shantou 51504
    754 882-4566

(G-928)
GLOBAL METAL TECHNOLOGIES LLC (PA)
10500 Ne 8th St Ste 1920 (98004-8624)
PHONE..................................425 956-3506
Barney Guy, *Vice Pres*
Layne Sapp, *Mng Member*
Thomas Stephens,
EMP: 7
SQ FT: 400
SALES (est): 3.4MM Privately Held
SIC: 1081 Metal mining services

(G-929)
GLOBAL STUDIOS CONSULTING LLC
16301 Ne 8th St Ste 224 (98008-3915)
P.O. Box 343, Kellogg ID (83837-0343)
PHONE..................................425 223-5291
Darrell Jordan, *CEO*
EMP: 24
SQ FT: 1,800
SALES (est): 1.1MM Privately Held
SIC: 7371 7372 Computer software development; computer software development & applications; business oriented computer software

(G-930)
GMS INDUSTRIES INC
2000 124th Ave Ne B105 (98005-2106)
PHONE..................................425 454-9500
Mike Tong, *Principal*
▲ EMP: 8
SALES (est): 679.4K Privately Held
SIC: 3999 Manufacturing industries

(G-931)
GOOD PLANET FOODS LLC
1813 115th Ave Ne (98004-3002)
PHONE..................................425 449-8134
David Israel, *Mng Member*
Spencer Oboerg,
◆ EMP: 9
SQ FT: 500
SALES (est): 796K Privately Held
SIC: 2022 Natural cheese

(G-932)
GRACES KITCHEN INC
225 108th Ave Ne Ste 570 (98004-5789)
PHONE..................................425 635-4609
Steven Anderson, *Admin Sec*
EMP: 2
SALES (est): 62.3K Privately Held
SIC: 2037 Frozen fruits & vegetables

(G-933)
GREAT ARTISAN BEVERAGE LLC
Also Called: Wbsb
11400 Se 8th St Ste 300 (98004-6409)
PHONE..................................425 467-7952
Dave Mickelson, *President*
Nick Gagliardi,
EMP: 5
SQ FT: 1,000
SALES (est): 520.5K Privately Held
SIC: 8742 2082 Sales (including sales management) consultant; beer (alcoholic beverage)

(G-934)
H D FOWLER CO INC (PA)
13440 Se 30th St (98005-4439)
P.O. Box 160 (98009-0160)
PHONE..................................425 746-8400
Harold D Fowler, *President*
Tammi Jacobson, *Vice Pres*
David P Kirker, *Vice Pres*
David Brereton, *Project Mgr*
Doug Solis, *Project Mgr*
▼ EMP: 85 EST: 1947
SQ FT: 14,000

SALES (est): 354.3MM Privately Held
WEB: www.hdfowler.com
SIC: 5084 5083 5085 3321 Industrial machinery & equipment; landscaping equipment; industrial supplies; valves & fittings; water pipe, cast iron

(G-935)
H W IMAGE WORKS INC
811 141st Pl Se (98007-5428)
PHONE..................................760 343-3869
John Hall, *President*
Jeane Williams, *Vice Pres*
▲ EMP: 2
SQ FT: 2,000
SALES (est): 198K Privately Held
WEB: www.hwiworks.com
SIC: 2396 2395 Screen printing on fabric articles; embroidery & art needlework

(G-936)
HANGER PRSTHETCS & ORTHO INC
616 120th Ave Ne Ste 111 (98005-3078)
PHONE..................................425 451-8831
Hillary Inglehardt, *Manager*
EMP: 7
SALES (corp-wide): 1B Publicly Held
SIC: 3842 Surgical appliances & supplies
HQ: Hanger Prosthetics & Orthotics, Inc.
    10910 Domain Dr Ste 300
    Austin TX 78758
    512 777-3800

(G-937)
HASCO INC
6335 163rd Pl Se (98006-5609)
PHONE..................................425 643-2525
Chong Kim, *President*
EMP: 2
SALES (est): 85.9K Privately Held
SIC: 3575 Computer terminals

(G-938)
HAWKS PRAIRIE GOLF LLC
1416 112th Ave Ne (98004-3710)
PHONE..................................360 455-8383
Scott Oki, *Chairman*
EMP: 3
SALES (est): 320.4K Privately Held
SIC: 3949 Sporting & athletic goods

(G-939)
HELIUM ADVISORS
11820 Northup Way E101 (98005-1946)
PHONE..................................425 214-1533
Howard Morin, *Partner*
EMP: 3
SALES (est): 189.9K Privately Held
SIC: 2813 Helium

(G-940)
HER INTERACTIVE INC
325 118th Ave Se Ste 209 (98005-3539)
PHONE..................................425 460-8787
Penny Milliken, *CEO*
Rob Klee, *CFO*
Megan Gaiser, *Officer*
EMP: 25
SQ FT: 7,126
SALES: 6MM Privately Held
WEB: www.herinteractive.com
SIC: 7372 Application computer software; home entertainment computer software

(G-941)
HERITAGE HATS LLC
9518 Se 15th St (98004-6755)
PHONE..................................425 301-2887
Darren Simsek, *Principal*
EMP: 2
SALES (est): 102.6K Privately Held
SIC: 2353 Hats, caps & millinery

(G-942)
HERSHEY COMPANY
15137 Se 66th St (98006-5019)
PHONE..................................800 468-1714
EMP: 2
SALES (est): 94.8K Privately Held
SIC: 2064 2066 Mfg Candy/Confectionery Mfg Chocolate/Cocoa Prdt

---

(PA)=Parent Co (HQ)=Headquarters (DH)=Div Headquarters
✪ = New Business established in last 2 years

Bellevue - King County (G-943)

(G-943)
HI BABY SOFTWARE
16600 Se 17th St (98008-5151)
PHONE..................................206 372-8936
Scott Chamberlin, *Administration*
EMP: 2
SALES (est): 127.1K **Privately Held**
SIC: 7372 Prepackaged software

(G-944)
HIBU INC
601 108th Ave Ne Ste 1810 (98004-4625)
PHONE..................................425 454-1762
Frank Carson, *President*
Brian Nicholson, *President*
Kenneth Pizzico, *Branch Mgr*
EMP: 73
SALES (corp-wide): 431.4MM **Privately Held**
SIC: 2741 Telephone & other directory publishing
HQ: Hibu Inc.
   90 Merrick Ave Ste 530
   East Meadow NY 11554
   516 730-1900

(G-945)
HIDDEN PATH ENTERTAINMENT INC
1407 116th Ave Ne Ste 100 (98004-3819)
PHONE..................................425 452-7284
Jeff Pobst, *CEO*
Jonathan Lee, *Technology*
James Garbarini, *Officer*
Mark Terrano, *Officer*
EMP: 33
SALES (est): 2.3MM **Privately Held**
SIC: 7371 7372 Custom computer programming services; home entertainment computer software

(G-946)
HOBI INSTRUMENT SERVICES LLC
Also Called: Hobi Services
4626 143rd Ave Se (98006-2340)
PHONE..................................425 223-3438
David Dana,
EMP: 2
SALES (est): 293K **Privately Held**
SIC: 3829 7389 Geophysical & meteorological testing equipment;

(G-947)
HOLOWEAR LTD
11400 Se 8th St Ste 260 (98004-6470)
PHONE..................................408 759-4656
Chetan Desh, *CEO*
Pradnya Desh, *General Counsel*
EMP: 2 EST: 2014
SALES (est): 154.5K **Privately Held**
SIC: 3571 Computers, digital, analog or hybrid

(G-948)
HORMEL FOODS CORPORATION
320 120th Ave Ne Ste 210 (98005-3016)
PHONE..................................425 635-0109
Brian Pitzele, *Branch Mgr*
EMP: 6
SALES (corp-wide): 9.5B **Publicly Held**
WEB: www.hormel.com
SIC: 2011 Meat packing plants
PA: Hormel Foods Corporation
   1 Hormel Pl
   Austin MN 55912
   507 437-5611

(G-949)
HORVITZ NEWSPAPERS INC
500 108th Ave Ne Ste 1750 (98004-5576)
PHONE..................................425 274-4782
Peter Horvitz, *Principal*
EMP: 3
SALES (est): 177.8K **Privately Held**
SIC: 2711 Newspapers

(G-950)
HOUSE OF MATRIARCH INC
11000 Ne 10th St Apt 170 (98004-8558)
PHONE..................................425 466-7783
EMP: 2
SALES (est): 169.4K **Privately Held**
SIC: 2844 Toilet preparations

(G-951)
HUAWEI DEVICE USA INC
15375 Se 30th Pl Ste 280 (98007-6553)
PHONE..................................425 247-2700
Richard Yao, *Branch Mgr*
EMP: 10
SALES (corp-wide): 103.8B **Privately Held**
SIC: 3663 Cellular radio telephone
HQ: Huawei Device Usa Inc.
   5700 Tennyson Pkwy # 300
   Plano TX 75024
   214 919-6688

(G-952)
HULL MARIGAIL
Also Called: Applied Designs
4222 181st Ave Se Ne90th (98008-5940)
PHONE..................................425 643-3737
Marigail Hull, *Owner*
EMP: 2
SALES (est): 130K **Privately Held**
SIC: 2759 2395 Screen printing; embroidery products, except schiffli machine

(G-953)
HYDROGEN FUELED VEHICLES
118 156th Ave Se (98007-5306)
PHONE..................................425 502-7170
EMP: 3
SALES (est): 132.9K **Privately Held**
SIC: 2813 Hydrogen

(G-954)
IMPREV INC
11400 Se 8th St Ste 450 (98004-6449)
P.O. Box 53346 (98015-3346)
PHONE..................................800 809-3356
Renwick Condon, *President*
Bill Yaman, *Vice Pres*
Jon Hart, *Accounts Exec*
Charles Webb, *Accounts Exec*
Sean Smith, *Consultant*
EMP: 20
SALES (est): 2.9MM **Privately Held**
WEB: www.imprev.com
SIC: 7372 Business oriented computer software

(G-955)
IN CASCADE CONCRETE INDUSTRIES
127 Bellevue Way Se # 100 (98004-6267)
PHONE..................................425 747-0956
Rick Peterson, *Principal*
EMP: 7
SALES (est): 952.4K **Privately Held**
SIC: 3272 Concrete products

(G-956)
INCREMENTAL SYSTEMS CORP
Also Called: Incsys
3380 146th Pl Se Ste 107 (98006-6472)
PHONE..................................425 732-2377
Robin Podmore, *President*
Stella Podmore, *Corp Secy*
EMP: 6
SQ FT: 2,000
SALES (est): 800K **Privately Held**
WEB: www.incsys.com
SIC: 7372 7373 Utility computer software; computer integrated systems design

(G-957)
INCYCLE SOFTWARE CORP
Eastside Offc Ctr 1420 # 14205 (98006)
PHONE..................................425 880-9200
Barry Paquet, *Manager*
EMP: 4
SALES (corp-wide): 1.5MM **Privately Held**
SIC: 7372 Prepackaged software
PA: Incycle Software Corp.
   1120 Ave Of The Americas
   New York NY 10036
   212 626-2608

(G-958)
INNOVATION ASSOCIATES
400 112th Ave Ne (98004-5543)
PHONE..................................206 455-2332
EMP: 3 EST: 2011
SALES (est): 130K **Privately Held**
SIC: 3841 Mfg Surgical/Medical Instruments

(G-959)
INTEL CORPORATION
2700 156th Ave Ne Ste 300 (98007-6554)
PHONE..................................253 371-1052
Andy D Bryant, *Branch Mgr*
Ran Kurup, *Director*
Jon Stanton, *Technician*
EMP: 15
SALES (est): 1.8MM
SALES (corp-wide): 70.8B **Publicly Held**
SIC: 3577 Computer peripheral equipment
PA: Intel Corporation
   2200 Mission College Blvd
   Santa Clara CA 95054
   408 765-8080

(G-960)
INTERMEDIANET INC
3310 146th Pl Se (98007-6471)
PHONE..................................425 451-3393
Kwong Kim, *Manager*
EMP: 12
SALES (corp-wide): 37.1MM **Privately Held**
SIC: 5099 3695 Video & audio equipment; magnetic & optical recording media
HQ: Intermedia.Net, Inc.
   825 E Middlefield Rd
   Mountain View CA 94043
   650 641-4000

(G-961)
INTERNET MOTORS COMPANY
2018 156th Ave Ne Ste 100 (98007-3825)
PHONE..................................425 654-1154
Pawan Gupta, *President*
EMP: 2
SALES (est): 110.7K **Privately Held**
SIC: 7372 Prepackaged software

(G-962)
ISHIP INC
3545 Factoria Blvd Se # 100 (98006-6107)
PHONE..................................425 602-4848
Steve Teglovic, *President*
Steven Teglovic, *President*
Radek Migula, *Engineer*
Steve Carlson, *Manager*
Nancy Bourn, *Admin Sec*
EMP: 47 EST: 1997
SALES (est): 3.8MM
SALES (corp-wide): 71.8B **Publicly Held**
SIC: 7372 Prepackaged software
WEB: www.iship.com
PA: United Parcel Service, Inc.
   55 Glenlake Pkwy
   Atlanta GA 30328
   404 828-6000

(G-963)
ISSAQUAH SAMMAMISH REPORTER
2700 Richards Rd Ste 201 (98005-4200)
PHONE..................................425 391-0363
Jeff McDonald, *Principal*
EMP: 3 EST: 2007
SALES (est): 165.6K **Privately Held**
SIC: 2711 Commercial printing & newspaper publishing combined

(G-964)
J A RATTO COMPANY
16715 Se 14th St (98008-5109)
P.O. Box 375, Bothell (98041-0375)
PHONE..................................206 240-5601
Joseph Ratto, *President*
EMP: 2
SALES (est): 170K **Privately Held**
SIC: 7372 8748 Prepackaged software; business consulting

(G-965)
K SMITH ENTERPRISES
700 112th Ave Ne Ste 302 (98004-5106)
P.O. Box 3010 (98009-3010)
PHONE..................................425 455-0923
Lester Smith, *Owner*
Alexander M Smith, *Co-Owner*
▲ EMP: 6
SALES (est): 260.2K **Privately Held**
SIC: 2759 Commercial printing

(G-966)
K2 CARBIDE
1330 177th Ave Ne (98008-3208)
PHONE..................................425 761-2335
Don Williams, *Principal*
EMP: 4
SALES (est): 410.8K **Privately Held**
SIC: 2819 Carbides

(G-967)
KAYE-SMITH ENTERPRISES INC (PA)
700 112th Ave Ne Ste 302 (98004-5106)
P.O. Box 3010 (98009-3010)
PHONE..................................425 455-0923
Alexander M Smith, *President*
Bernice R Smith, *Vice Pres*
Lester M Smith, *Treasurer*
Joan St Marie, *Admin Sec*
EMP: 162
SQ FT: 3,000
SALES (est): 31.2MM **Privately Held**
WEB: www.kayesmith.com
SIC: 2761 Manifold business forms

(G-968)
KIMBERLY-CLARK CORPORATION
15500 Se 30th Pl Ste 202 (98007-6347)
PHONE..................................425 373-5900
Faruk Manji, *Branch Mgr*
EMP: 12
SALES (corp-wide): 18.4B **Publicly Held**
SIC: 2621 2676 Sanitary tissue paper; infant & baby paper products
PA: Kimberly-Clark Corporation
   351 Phelps Dr
   Irving TX 75038
   972 281-1200

(G-969)
KOEHLER INDUSTRIES INC
2625 166th Ave Se (98008-5438)
PHONE..................................360 793-9101
EMP: 2 EST: 2010
SALES (est): 144.1K **Privately Held**
SIC: 3999 Mfg Misc Products

(G-970)
KOGITA CUSTOM MFG & REPAIR
Also Called: Kogita Jewelry
9 Lake Bellevue Dr # 115 (98005-2454)
PHONE..................................425 453-9547
Kurt Kogita, *Owner*
Mona Kogita, *Co-Owner*
EMP: 3
SALES: 250K **Privately Held**
SIC: 3911 5944 7631 Jewelry, precious metal; jewelry, precious stones & precious metals; watch, clock & jewelry repair

(G-971)
KONNECTONE LLC
40 Lake Bellevue Dr # 350 (98005-2479)
PHONE..................................425 502-7371
Joseph Phillip, *Mng Member*
Richard Pelly, *Officer*
Horwa Wang,
EMP: 10
SQ FT: 8,000
SALES (est): 2.3MM **Privately Held**
SIC: 3663 Mobile communication equipment

(G-972)
KONO FIXED INCOME FUND 1511 LP
Also Called: American Kono Group
15566 Se 5th Ct (98007-4967)
PHONE..................................360 686-7688
EMP: 15
SALES (est): 587.5K **Privately Held**
SIC: 3721 4581 5146 5082 Mfg Aircraft Airport/Airport Services Whol Fish/Seafoods Whol Cnstn/Mining Mach

(G-973)
KOOLMASK INC
777 108th Ave Ne Ste 2000 (98004-5146)
P.O. Box 5008 (98009-5008)
PHONE..................................206 886-5248
Yang Song, *President*
EMP: 10 EST: 2016

GEOGRAPHIC SECTION

Bellevue - King County (G-1004)

SALES (est): 748.3K **Privately Held**
SIC: 3842 Gas masks

(G-974)
LA BELLE REVE LLC
Also Called: La Belle Reve Bridal
10630 Ne 8th St Ste 4 (98004-4320)
P.O. Box 214, Medina (98039-0214)
PHONE..................................425 454-7772
Olga T Earle,
EMP: 4
SALES (est): 350K **Privately Held**
SIC: 2335 Bridal & formal gowns

(G-975)
LAMBDA SOFTWARE LLC
16814 Ne 33rd St (98008-2018)
PHONE..................................425 882-3464
Alexander Frank, *Principal*
EMP: 2
SALES (est): 64.6K **Privately Held**
SIC: 7372 Prepackaged software

(G-976)
LAND OLAKES INC
3605 132nd Ave Se Ste 402 (98006-1333)
PHONE..................................425 653-4200
Jerry Breen, *Vice Pres*
EMP: 15
SALES (corp-wide): 10.4B **Privately Held**
WEB: www.landolakes.com
SIC: 2048 Stock feeds, dry; poultry feeds; feed supplements
PA: Land O'lakes, Inc.
  4001 Lexington Ave N
  Arden Hills MN 55126
  651 375-2222

(G-977)
LAPLINK SOFTWARE INC
600 108th Ave Ne Ste 610 (98004-5125)
PHONE..................................425 952-6000
Thomas Koll, *CEO*
Mike Oldham, *Vice Pres*
Dan Santos, *Vice Pres*
Jack Wilson, *Vice Pres*
Randall Clark, *CFO*
EMP: 50
SALES (est): 4.8MM **Privately Held**
WEB: www.laplinksoftware.com
SIC: 7372 Prepackaged software

(G-978)
LARRYS SCREEN PRINTING
Also Called: Larry Harvitz
3225 134th Ln Ne (98005-1457)
PHONE..................................425 885-3644
Larry Harvitz, *Owner*
EMP: 2
SALES (est): 160K **Privately Held**
SIC: 2759 Screen printing

(G-979)
LEACH INTERNATIONAL CORP
500 108th Ave Ne (98004-5580)
PHONE..................................425 519-1826
Alejandro Castro, *Engineer*
Kevin Keating, *Bd of Directors*
EMP: 4 EST: 2012
SALES (est): 310.3K
SALES (corp-wide): 3.8B **Publicly Held**
SIC: 3613 Power switching equipment
HQ: Esterline Technologies Corp
  500 108th Ave Ne Ste 1500
  Bellevue WA 98004
  425 453-9400

(G-980)
LEIGH INTERIORS
13300 Se 30th St Ste 101 (98005-4434)
PHONE..................................206 351-5158
Alex Garcia, *Manager*
EMP: 2
SALES (est): 96.2K **Privately Held**
SIC: 2599 Furniture & fixtures

(G-981)
LEISURE LOYALTY INC
2019 Killarney Way (98004-7045)
PHONE..................................425 223-5102
Paul Heath, *Principal*
Catherine Oleary, *Principal*
EMP: 2
SALES (est): 180.3K **Privately Held**
SIC: 7372 7389 Business oriented computer software;

(G-982)
LETTERING ARTS
10885 Ne 4th St Ste 1400 (98004-5579)
P.O. Box 2735, Redmond (98073-2735)
PHONE..................................206 310-6599
EMP: 2
SALES (est): 134.7K **Privately Held**
SIC: 3993 Signs & advertising specialties

(G-983)
LIGHTSPEED DESIGN INC
1611 116th Ave Ne Ste 112 (98004-3048)
PHONE..................................425 637-2818
Chris Ward, *President*
Bob Mueller, *Exec VP*
Jeff Rische, *Vice Pres*
▲ EMP: 5
SQ FT: 4,000
SALES (est): 917.9K **Privately Held**
WEB: www.lightspeeddesign.com
SIC: 7819 3861 3827 Visual effects production; motion picture apparatus & equipment; polarizers

(G-984)
LIME SOLUTIONS
11322 Se 60th St (98006-6304)
PHONE..................................425 502-7651
Lee Heung, *Principal*
EMP: 2 EST: 2010
SALES (est): 150K **Privately Held**
SIC: 3274 Lime

(G-985)
LIMITED PRODUCTIONS INC
13404 Se 32nd St (98005-4409)
PHONE..................................425 635-7489
Glenn Ryan, *President*
EMP: 5
SQ FT: 1,500
SALES (est): 699.6K **Privately Held**
SIC: 3599 Machine shop, jobbing & repair; machine & other job shop work

(G-986)
LINARE CORP
2018 156th Ave Ne (98007-3825)
PHONE..................................425 748-5099
Soma Sundaram, *Ch of Bd*
Aaron Jennings, *Vice Pres*
Dominick Paulraj, *CTO*
EMP: 50
SALES (est): 4.4MM **Privately Held**
SIC: 3575 Computer terminals, monitors & components

(G-987)
LIZZY AND ALEX ENTERPRISES LLC
10700 Ne 4th St Unit 802 (98004-5959)
PHONE..................................425 698-1439
Rhonda Beck, *Principal*
EMP: 4 EST: 2010
SALES (est): 282K **Privately Held**
SIC: 2782 Scrapbooks

(G-988)
LOGOS CHURCH
14683 Ne 16th St (98007-3945)
PHONE..................................425 378-0276
EMP: 2
SALES (est): 83.9K **Privately Held**
SIC: 2752 Commercial printing, lithographic

(G-989)
LONGWELL COMPANY
1215 120th Ave Ne Ste 204 (98005-2135)
PHONE..................................425 289-0160
Stanley Xu, *President*
Nanling Chen, *Vice Pres*
EMP: 65
SALES (est): 11MM **Privately Held**
WEB: www.longwellcompany.com
SIC: 5088 3728 6519 Aircraft & parts; aircraft parts & equipment; real property lessors

(G-990)
LUMA TECHNOLOGIES LLC
Also Called: Lumatech
13226 Se 30th St Ste B3 (98005-4448)
P.O. Box 860, Mercer Island (98040-0860)
PHONE..................................425 643-4000
Graham Maxwell, *Opers Mgr*
Bruce S Maxwell,
EMP: 11
SALES (est): 1.7MM **Privately Held**
WEB: www.lumatech.com
SIC: 3724 Aircraft engines & engine parts

(G-991)
LUMEDX CORPORATION
110 110th Ave Ne Ste 475 (98004-5884)
PHONE..................................425 450-9774
David Mc Auley, *CEO*
Jasmine Baker, *Project Mgr*
Jamie Titus, *Credit Staff*
Jennifer Muir, *HR Admin*
Tory Bos, *Sales Staff*
EMP: 59
SALES (corp-wide): 15.9MM **Privately Held**
WEB: www.lumedx.com
SIC: 7371 7372 Computer software development; prepackaged software
PA: Lumedx Corporation
  555 12th St Ste 2060
  Oakland CA 94607
  510 419-1000

(G-992)
LUMOTIVE LLC
10885 Ne 4th St Ste 250 (98004-5527)
PHONE..................................907 306-6267
William Colleran, *CEO*
EMP: 6
SALES (est): 815.2K **Privately Held**
SIC: 3674 Semiconductors & related devices

(G-993)
LYNNS FORKLIFT SERVICE
305 158th Pl Se (98008-4649)
PHONE..................................206 979-4272
EMP: 2 EST: 2010
SALES (est): 157.4K **Privately Held**
SIC: 3537 Forklift trucks

(G-994)
MABO PUBLISHERS
16053 Ne 8th St Apt 303 (98008-3930)
PHONE..................................425 746-9934
EMP: 2
SALES (est): 60.4K **Privately Held**
SIC: 2731 Books-Publishing/Printing

(G-995)
MAJESCO SOFTWARE INC
14420 Ne 35th St Apt I2 (98007-8525)
PHONE..................................425 242-0327
Soumitra Roy, *Principal*
EMP: 2
SALES (est): 116K **Privately Held**
SIC: 7372 Business oriented computer software

(G-996)
MARUHA CAPITAL INVESTMENT INC (HQ)
3015 112th Ave Ne Ste 100 (98004-8001)
PHONE..................................206 382-0640
Hiroshi Okazaki, *President*
Katsuhiko Uota, *Vice Pres*
Tatsuya Yamamoto, *Treasurer*
EMP: 14
SALES (est): 334.7MM **Privately Held**
SIC: 6799 2091 Investors; seafood products: packaged in cans, jars, etc.

(G-997)
MASTER ROLL MANUFACTURING
Also Called: Master Roll Manufacturer
14023 Ne 8th St (98007-4101)
PHONE..................................425 641-1566
Marvin Brashem, *President*
Mark Brashem, *Vice Pres*
EMP: 21
SALES (est): 1.1MM **Privately Held**
SIC: 3316 Corrugating iron & steel, cold-rolled

(G-998)
MASTERBRAND CABINETS INC
13433 Ne 20th St Ste O (98005-2024)
PHONE..................................812 482-2527
Clint Noyes, *Manager*
EMP: 11
SALES (corp-wide): 5.4B **Publicly Held**
WEB: www.mbcabinets.com
SIC: 2434 Wood kitchen cabinets
HQ: Masterbrand Cabinets, Inc.
  1 Masterbrand Cabinets Dr
  Jasper IN 47546
  812 482-2527

(G-999)
MATERIANT INC
777 108th Ave Ne Ste 1750 (98004-5139)
PHONE..................................425 209-1943
Chad Steigers, *CEO*
EMP: 50
SALES (est): 1.2MM
SALES (corp-wide): 10MM **Privately Held**
SIC: 7372 Application computer software
PA: Xenon Arc, Inc.
  777 108th Ave Ne Ste 1750
  Bellevue WA 98004
  425 646-1063

(G-1000)
MEDETECH DEVELOPMENT CORP
2023 120th Ave Ne (98005-2108)
PHONE..................................425 891-9151
Simon Johnston, *President*
Pearl Chan, *CFO*
▲ EMP: 5
SQ FT: 2,000
SALES (est): 417.3K **Privately Held**
SIC: 2842 Disinfectants, household or industrial plant

(G-1001)
MEDTRONIC USA INC
4030 Lake Wash Blvd Ste C (98006-1164)
PHONE..................................425 803-0708
Chris Lynch, *Manager*
EMP: 25 **Privately Held**
WEB: www.medtronic.com
SIC: 3845 5047 Electromedical equipment; medical & hospital equipment
HQ: Medtronic Usa, Inc.
  710 Medtronic Pkwy
  Minneapolis MN 55432
  763 514-4000

(G-1002)
MEGABESS US INC
10801 Main St Ste 100 (98004-6366)
PHONE..................................425 890-9175
Phillip Jennings, *CEO*
Henry Dean, *Chairman*
Jason Jennings, *CFO*
EMP: 3
SALES (est): 271K **Privately Held**
SIC: 3691 Storage batteries

(G-1003)
MERRIL MAIL MARKETING INC
Also Called: Merril Associates
12500 Ne 10th Pl (98005-2532)
PHONE..................................425 454-7009
Alan M Gottlieb, *President*
Julianne Versnel, *Vice Pres*
Julie H Versnel, *Vice Pres*
EMP: 6
SQ FT: 5,000
SALES (est): 595.1K **Privately Held**
WEB: www.merrilpress.com
SIC: 7331 2731 Mailing service; books: publishing only

(G-1004)
MICROSOFT CORPORATION
205 108th Ave Ne Ste 400 (98004-5770)
PHONE..................................425 705-1900
Do H Kim, *Project Mgr*
James Gagnon, *Engineer*
Amit Kumar, *Engineer*
Gouri Vaddi, *Engineer*
Adnan Alam, *Design Engr*
EMP: 100
SALES (corp-wide): 110.3B **Publicly Held**
WEB: www.microsoft.com
SIC: 7372 Application computer software
PA: Microsoft Corporation
  1 Microsoft Way
  Redmond WA 98052
  425 882-8080

Bellevue - King County (G-1005)   GEOGRAPHIC SECTION

(G-1005)
MICROSOFT CORPORATION
143 129th Ave Ne (98005-3312)
PHONE.................................770 235-8794
John Kline, *Branch Mgr*
EMP: 2
SALES (corp-wide): 110.3B **Publicly Held**
SIC: 7372 Prepackaged software
PA: Microsoft Corporation
1 Microsoft Way
Redmond WA 98052
425 882-8080

(G-1006)
MICROSOFT CORPORATION
11025 Ne 8th St (98004-4474)
PHONE.................................425 705-1900
Angus Leeming, *Software Engr*
EMP: 100
SALES (corp-wide): 110.3B **Publicly Held**
SIC: 7372 Application computer software
PA: Microsoft Corporation
1 Microsoft Way
Redmond WA 98052
425 882-8080

(G-1007)
MICROSOFT CORPORATION
11111 Ne 8th St (98004-4475)
PHONE.................................425 435-8457
Shayoni Seth, *Manager*
EMP: 50
SALES (corp-wide): 110.3B **Publicly Held**
SIC: 7372 Application computer software
PA: Microsoft Corporation
1 Microsoft Way
Redmond WA 98052
425 882-8080

(G-1008)
MIPS TECH INC
Also Called: Imagination Technologies
12737 Ne Bel Red Rd # 100 (98005-2699)
PHONE.................................408 610-5900
Steve Johnson, *Manager*
EMP: 2
SALES (corp-wide): 26.9MM **Privately Held**
SIC: 3674 6794 Microprocessors; franchises, selling or licensing
HQ: Mips Tech, Inc.
300 Orchard Cy Dr Ste 170
Campbell CA 95008

(G-1009)
MISHO GLOBAL LLC
14028 Ne Bel Red Rd (98007-3913)
PHONE.................................425 829-8881
I Jeng Lin, *Administration*
EMP: 5 EST: 2010
SALES (est): 395.2K **Privately Held**
SIC: 2329 Baseball uniforms: men's, youths' & boys'

(G-1010)
MK INDUSTRIES LLC
13336 Se 52nd St (98006-4203)
PHONE.................................425 922-0139
Megan Koontz, *Principal*
EMP: 2
SALES (est): 66.9K **Privately Held**
SIC: 3999 Manufacturing industries

(G-1011)
MNC SERVICES INC
Also Called: Winigent
13701 Ne Bel Red Rd (98005-4517)
PHONE.................................425 527-9031
Kalyani Velagapudi, *CEO*
EMP: 9
SALES (corp-wide): 6MM **Privately Held**
SIC: 7379 7372 Computer related consulting services; prepackaged software
PA: Mnc Services, Inc.
21520 Ne 144th Pl Ste 103
Woodinville WA 98077
425 527-9031

(G-1012)
MOBILE AIR APPLIED SCIENCE
14 168th Ave Ne (98008-4538)
PHONE.................................206 953-3786
H Douglas Woods, *President*
EMP: 3
SALES: 150K **Privately Held**
WEB: www.ma2si.com
SIC: 3841 3821 3564 Surgical & medical instruments; laboratory apparatus & furniture; blowers & fans

(G-1013)
MODERNCHEF INC
Also Called: Sansaire
10400 Ne 4th St Ste 500 (98004-5175)
PHONE.................................425 202-6252
Johnna Hobgood, *CEO*
Valerie Trask, *COO*
Lukas Svec, *CTO*
EMP: 8
SQ FT: 2,000
SALES: 2MM **Privately Held**
SIC: 3631 Indoor cooking equipment

(G-1014)
MONSOON SOLUTIONS INC
2405 140th Ave Ne A115 (98005-1877)
PHONE.................................425 378-8081
Jeff Reinhold, *President*
Darin Dix, *Vice Pres*
Paul Butler, *CFO*
Tyler McCurry, *Program Mgr*
EMP: 32
SQ FT: 11,050
SALES: 11.5MM **Privately Held**
WEB: www.msoon.com
SIC: 8711 3672 Electrical or electronic engineering; printed circuit boards

(G-1015)
MORUP SIGNS INC
12824 Ne 14th Pl (98005-2208)
PHONE.................................425 883-6337
Laura Gates, *President*
EMP: 4 EST: 1968
SQ FT: 1,300
SALES (est): 379.7K **Privately Held**
SIC: 7389 3993 Sign painting & lettering shop; signs & advertising specialties

(G-1016)
MOSESVUE LLC
Also Called: Pumptech
12020 Se 32nd St Ste 2 (98005-4135)
PHONE.................................425 644-8501
Laurie Beden, *Vice Pres*
Doug Davidson, *Mng Member*
EMP: 15
SALES (est): 1.8MM **Privately Held**
SIC: 3561 Pumps & pumping equipment

(G-1017)
MOUNTAIN SPRINGS BUILDING CO
Also Called: Mountain Springs Millwork
409 161st Pl Se (98008-4831)
PHONE.................................206 550-4380
Brian Hayman, *President*
EMP: 2
SALES (est): 150K **Privately Held**
SIC: 2431 Millwork

(G-1018)
MOXIE SOFTWARE CIM CORP
15 Lake Bellevue Dr # 200 (98005-2485)
PHONE.................................425 467-5000
Rebecca Ward, *President*
Alan Heitmann, *COO*
Carol Wedekind, *Opers Staff*
Patrick Maroney, *Admin Sec*
EMP: 60
SQ FT: 17,000
SALES: 35MM **Privately Held**
SIC: 7372 7371 Business oriented computer software; custom computer programming services
PA: Moxie Software, Inc.
851 Traeger Ave Ste 210
San Bruno CA 94066

(G-1019)
MSCSOFTWARE CORPORATION
150 120th Ave Ne Ste 310 (98005-3020)
PHONE.................................855 672-7638
EMP: 2
SALES (corp-wide): 4.3B **Privately Held**
SIC: 7372 Business oriented computer software
HQ: Msc.Software Corporation
4675 Macarthur Ct Ste 900
Newport Beach CA 92660
714 540-8900

(G-1020)
MUTUAL MATERIALS
605 119th Ave Ne (98005-3073)
P.O. Box 2009 (98009-2009)
PHONE.................................425 452-2300
Laura Lemke, *Director*
EMP: 80
SALES (est): 5.3MM **Privately Held**
SIC: 1741 3999 Masonry & other stonework; barber & beauty shop equipment

(G-1021)
MUTUAL-TARGET LLC (PA)
Also Called: Target Products
605 119th Ave Ne (98005-3031)
P.O. Box 2009 (98009-2009)
PHONE.................................425 452-2300
Brad Cahoon, *Principal*
EMP: 20
SALES (est): 4MM **Privately Held**
WEB: www.mutualtarget.com
SIC: 3241 Cement, hydraulic

(G-1022)
MY T-SHIRT SOURCE
13257 Ne 20th St (98005-2009)
PHONE.................................425 746-7447
EMP: 6
SALES (est): 512.7K **Privately Held**
SIC: 2253 T-shirts & tops, knit

(G-1023)
NEC CORP OF AMERICA
14335 Ne 24th St (98007-3737)
PHONE.................................425 373-4400
Ken Abramson, *Principal*
EMP: 7
SALES (est): 694.2K **Privately Held**
SIC: 3674 Photoelectric cells, solid state (electronic eye)

(G-1024)
NEETAS CREATIONS
1275 140th Pl Ne (98007-4049)
PHONE.................................585 233-1896
Neeta Mehendale, *Partner*
Teja Mehendale, *Partner*
Upendra Mehendale, *Manager*
EMP: 2
SALES (est): 135.8K **Privately Held**
SIC: 5944 2381 Jewelry stores; fabric dress & work gloves

(G-1025)
NEOCIFIC INC
1750 112th Ave Ne D161 (98004-3727)
PHONE.................................425 451-8278
Titus Lo, *Vice Pres*
EMP: 3
SALES: 500K **Privately Held**
SIC: 3663 Radio & TV communications equipment

(G-1026)
NEW CONTINENT FOOD USA INC
15320 Se 46th Way (98006-3231)
PHONE.................................425 644-6448
Xucheng Huang, *President*
Jason Huang, *Manager*
▼ EMP: 2
SALES: 100K **Privately Held**
SIC: 2092 5411 Seafoods, frozen: prepared; grocery stores

(G-1027)
NEW STANDARD COMPANY LIMITED
14670 Ne 8th St Ste 108 (98007-4127)
PHONE.................................425 641-5718
Meimei Shi, *President*
Ping Niu, *Corp Secy*
Zhiming Lu, *Vice Pres*
Kathryn Cecil,
EMP: 6
SQ FT: 2,500
SALES (est): 510K
SALES (corp-wide): 3.4MM **Privately Held**
SIC: 3612 Power & distribution transformers
PA: Beijing Xinzhige Power Technology Co., Ltd.
Room 501, Unit 1, Building 6, Jinghai No.29 Courtyard, Yizhuang
Beijing 10008
106 355-8585

(G-1028)
NEW TOP DOG LLC
5089 119th Ave Se (98006-2749)
PHONE.................................206 817-3395
Michael Migdol,
Scott Chase,
EMP: 2 EST: 2013
SALES (est): 114.6K **Privately Held**
SIC: 3089 Plastic kitchenware, tableware & houseware

(G-1029)
NEXT BIOMETRICS INC
10900 Ne 4th St (98004-5873)
PHONE.................................617 510-4086
Petter Etholm Next, *Manager*
EMP: 15
SALES (est): 2.9MM **Privately Held**
SIC: 3577 Computer peripheral equipment

(G-1030)
NEXT BIOMETRICS INC
1100 112th Ave Ne Ste 340 (98004-4419)
PHONE.................................425 406-7055
Ritu Favre, *CEO*
Campbell Kan, *Vice Pres*
Eric Jen, *Engrg Dir*
Knut Stlen, *CFO*
Charles Ng, *VP Sales*
EMP: 30
SALES: 1MM
SALES (corp-wide): 12.7MM **Privately Held**
SIC: 3577 3699 Computer peripheral equipment; security devices
HQ: Next Biometrics As
Universitetsgata 10
Oslo 0164
922 324-38

(G-1031)
NIKE INC
4026 Factoria Sq Mall Se (98006-1242)
PHONE.................................425 747-2848
EMP: 2
SALES (corp-wide): 36.4B **Publicly Held**
SIC: 3021 Rubber & plastics footwear
PA: Nike, Inc.
1 Sw Bowerman Dr
Beaverton OR 97005
503 671-6453

(G-1032)
NINTEX USA INC (DH)
10800 Ne 8th St Ste 400 (98004-4429)
PHONE.................................425 324-2400
John Burton, *CEO*
Mike Arutyunian, *Partner*
Ray Ganske, *Partner*
Brett Campbell, *Founder*
Vincent Cabral, *Vice Pres*
EMP: 84
SQ FT: 7,000
SALES (est): 28.3MM
SALES (corp-wide): 17.6MM **Privately Held**
SIC: 7372 Prepackaged software

(G-1033)
NORMAN LANGSETH
4666 172nd Pl Se (98006-6541)
PHONE.................................425 643-7751
Norman Langseth, *Principal*
EMP: 2
SALES (est): 56.5K **Privately Held**
SIC: 7372 Prepackaged software

(G-1034)
NORTH CONNECTION CORP
1400 112th Ave Se Ste 100 (98004-6901)
PHONE.................................425 637-7787
Alexey Yarmushevich, *President*
EMP: 2

GEOGRAPHIC SECTION
Bellevue - King County (G-1064)

SALES (est): 162.1K **Privately Held**
SIC: 3556 5411 Food products machinery; grocery stores

(G-1035)
NORTHWEST DESIGNS INK INC (PA)
13456 Se 27th Pl Ste 200 (98005-5208)
PHONE....................425 454-0707
German Vyacheshav, *President*
Oleg Kvasyuk, *Director*
Victor Sviridyuk, *Director*
▲ EMP: 17
SQ FT: 10,000
SALES (est): 6.7MM **Privately Held**
WEB: www.northwestdesigns.com
SIC: 5136 5137 5621 5611 Sportswear, men's & boys'; sportswear, women's & children's; women's sportswear; clothing, sportswear, men's & boys'; automotive & apparel trimmings

(G-1036)
NORTHWEST MEDIA WASHINGTON LP (PA)
Also Called: Peninsula Daily News
500 108th Ave Ne (98004-5580)
PHONE....................425 274-4782
Peter Horvitz, *General Ptnr*
EMP: 3 EST: 1937
SQ FT: 200,000
SALES (est): 14.8MM **Privately Held**
WEB: www.mi-reporter.com
SIC: 2711 Newspapers: publishing only, not printed on site; newspapers, publishing & printing

(G-1037)
NORTHWEST SATELLITE NETWORK
3400 134th Ave Ne (98005-1433)
PHONE....................425 885-5986
Keith T Riffle, *Principal*
EMP: 4
SALES (est): 179.9K **Privately Held**
SIC: 2711 Newspapers

(G-1038)
NORTN COAST LIGHTING CASH
1034 116th Ave Ne (98004-4614)
PHONE....................425 454-2122
Mistie Anderson, *Principal*
EMP: 2
SALES (est): 164.6K **Privately Held**
SIC: 3648 Strobe lighting systems

(G-1039)
NW SEXTANT LLC
4675 144th Pl Se (98006-3156)
PHONE....................425 746-6475
Aleyn Klein, *Principal*
EMP: 3 EST: 2012
SALES (est): 167.3K **Privately Held**
SIC: 3812 Sextants

(G-1040)
NWD INK INTERNATIONAL INC
1 Lake Bellevue Dr (98005-2417)
PHONE....................425 454-0707
Vyacheslav German, *Principal*
EMP: 3
SALES (est): 163.3K **Privately Held**
SIC: 2254 Shirts & t-shirts (underwear), knit

(G-1041)
NXEDGE INC
10900 Ne 8th St Ste 1525 (98004-4405)
PHONE....................425 990-0091
Jackson Chao, *President*
EMP: 5
SALES (est): 449.8K **Privately Held**
SIC: 3674 3052 Semiconductors & related devices; rubber & plastics hose & beltings

(G-1042)
OCULAR INSTRUMENTS INC
2255 116th Ave Ne (98004-3039)
PHONE....................425 455-5200
Phil J Erickson, *President*
T J Erickson, *Vice Pres*
Lisa Graham, *Purch Agent*
Staci Caldwell, *QC Mgr*
Bernard Mulcahy, *Design Engr*
EMP: 55
SQ FT: 12,000
SALES (est): 8.7MM **Privately Held**
WEB: www.ocular-instruments.com
SIC: 3827 Optical instruments & apparatus

(G-1043)
OFFERUP INC
227 Bellevue Way Ne 57 (98004-5721)
PHONE....................844 633-3787
Peter I Aeschliman, *Principal*
Rodrigo Brumana, *CFO*
EMP: 3
SALES (est): 56.6K **Privately Held**
SIC: 2389 Men's miscellaneous accessories

(G-1044)
OFFICE TIMELINE LLC
1400 112th Ave Se Ste 100 (98004-6901)
PHONE....................425 296-9002
Eddy Malik,
EMP: 40
SALES (est): 1.3MM **Privately Held**
SIC: 7372 Prepackaged software

(G-1045)
OLD & ELEGANT DISTRIBUTING
10203 Main St (98004-6195)
PHONE....................425 455-4660
Dennis True, *Owner*
EMP: 12
SQ FT: 4,200
SALES (est): 1MM **Privately Held**
WEB: www.oldandelegant.com
SIC: 3432 5072 5251 Plumbers' brass goods: drain cocks, faucets, spigots, etc.; builders' hardware; builders' hardware

(G-1046)
OLIVE GAMES CORPORATION
14205 Se 36th St Ste 100 (98006-1553)
PHONE....................425 649-1136
Yunho Jeong, *President*
EMP: 2 EST: 2012
SALES (est): 153.3K **Privately Held**
SIC: 3944 Electronic games & toys

(G-1047)
OLTIS SOFTWARE LLC
10900 Ne 4th St Ste 1450 (98004-8302)
PHONE....................800 557-1780
Oleg Tishkevich, *Branch Mgr*
EMP: 15
SALES (corp-wide): 812.3MM **Publicly Held**
WEB: www.oltis.com
SIC: 7372 Prepackaged software
HQ: Oltis Software Llc
5151 E Brdwy Blvd Ste 620
Tucson AZ 85711
520 298-5000

(G-1048)
OLYMPIC MANUFACTURING INC
12121 Northup Way Ste 107 (98005-1929)
PHONE....................425 679-6303
Gabriel Wall, *President*
Davis Hall, *Secretary*
Christina Wall, *Vice Pres*
EMP: 7
SALES (est): 470K **Privately Held**
SIC: 3999 Barber & beauty shop equipment

(G-1049)
ONEFARSTAR LLC
Also Called: Garlic It
411 165th Ave Se (98008-4727)
PHONE....................425 999-4894
Llance Kezner, *Director*
Lori Peha Kezner, *Director*
▼ EMP: 2
SALES (est): 161.2K **Privately Held**
SIC: 2035 Seasonings, seafood sauces (except tomato & dry)

(G-1050)
OODLES NOODLE BAR
437 108th Ave Ne (98004-5536)
PHONE....................425 467-7076
Malligaa Chutongkum, *Administration*
EMP: 4
SALES (est): 178.4K **Privately Held**
SIC: 2098 Noodles (e.g. egg, plain & water), dry

(G-1051)
OPEN TEXT INC
301 116th Ave Se Ste 500 (98004-6446)
PHONE....................425 455-6000
Eva Salcedo, *Vice Pres*
Damaris Estrella, *Manager*
EMP: 50
SALES (corp-wide): 2.8B **Privately Held**
SIC: 7372 Prepackaged software
HQ: Open Text Inc.
2950 S Delaware St
San Mateo CA 94403
650 645-3000

(G-1052)
OPTISTOR TECHNOLOGIES INC
11900 Ne 1st St Ste 300 (98005-3049)
P.O. Box 2702, Chelan (98816-2702)
PHONE....................425 283-5227
Ronald Studham, *CEO*
EMP: 12
SALES (est): 2.3MM **Privately Held**
WEB: www.optistor.com
SIC: 3572 Computer storage devices

(G-1053)
ORACLE CORPORATION
411 108th Ave Ne Ste 900 (98004-8419)
PHONE....................425 945-8200
John Mauricegroen, *Owner*
Lisa Hong, *Senior Partner*
Dennis Ferry, *Manager*
Alec Han, *Manager*
Joseph Lampitt, *Consultant*
EMP: 466
SALES (corp-wide): 39.5B **Publicly Held**
WEB: www.oracle.com
SIC: 7372 Business oriented computer software
PA: Oracle Corporation
500 Oracle Pkwy
Redwood City CA 94065
650 506-7000

(G-1054)
ORACLES OF GOD MINISTRIES
1810 108th Ave Se Apt 12 (98004-7354)
PHONE....................425 449-8663
Mercy W Karume, *President*
EMP: 2
SALES (est): 11.9K **Privately Held**
SIC: 7372 Prepackaged software

(G-1055)
ORDERPORT LLC
5806a 119th Ave Se 102 (98006-3717)
PHONE....................425 746-2926
Rick Belisle, *Mng Member*
Matt Payne,
Stephen Ratzlaff,
EMP: 10 EST: 2003
SALES (est): 732.7K **Privately Held**
SIC: 7372 Prepackaged software

(G-1056)
OS NEXUS INC
Also Called: Osnexus Corporation
11711 Se 8th St Ste 305 (98005-3543)
PHONE....................425 279-0172
Steven Umbehocker, *CEO*
Lauren Grob, *Sales Associate*
William Rocca, *Marketing Staff*
EMP: 12
SQ FT: 1,600
SALES: 250K **Privately Held**
SIC: 7372 Business oriented computer software

(G-1057)
P N D CORPORATION
14320 Ne 21st St Ste 6 (98007-3756)
PHONE....................425 562-7252
William Griffin, *President*
◆ EMP: 2
SQ FT: 3,000
SALES: 400K **Privately Held**
WEB: www.plugndike.com
SIC: 3822 Auto controls regulating residntl & coml environmt & applncs

(G-1058)
PACCAR INC (PA)
777 106th Ave Ne (98004-5027)
P.O. Box 1518 (98009-1518)
PHONE....................425 468-7400
Ronald E Armstrong, *CEO*
Mark C Pigott, *Ch of Bd*
Harrie C A M Schippers, *President*
R Preston Feight, *Exec VP*
Gary L Moore, *Exec VP*
EMP: 277
SALES: 23.5B **Publicly Held**
WEB: www.paccar.com
SIC: 3711 3714 3713 3537 Truck & tractor truck assembly; truck tractors for highway use, assembly of; motor vehicle parts & accessories; truck & bus bodies; industrial trucks & tractors; motor vehicle supplies & new parts; financing of dealers by motor vehicle manufacturers organ.

(G-1059)
PACCAR INC
777 106th Ave Ne (98004-5027)
P.O. Box 1518 (98009-1518)
PHONE....................425 468-7400
Claire E Hargrave, *Principal*
EMP: 49
SALES (corp-wide): 23.5B **Publicly Held**
SIC: 3711 Motor vehicles & car bodies
PA: Paccar Inc
777 106th Ave Ne
Bellevue WA 98004
425 468-7400

(G-1060)
PACIFIC RIM CON PMPG EQP CO
Also Called: Pacific Rim Equipment
3241 110th Ave Se (98004-7503)
PHONE....................425 453-8140
Edward Mantz, *President*
EMP: 1
SQ FT: 1,200
SALES: 1.3MM **Privately Held**
SIC: 5084 3561 Pumps & pumping equipment; pumps & pumping equipment

(G-1061)
PALOMAR PRODUCTS INC
500 108th Ave Ne (98004-5580)
PHONE....................425 453-9400
Curtis C Reusser, *CEO*
EMP: 2
SALES (corp-wide): 3.8B **Publicly Held**
SIC: 3728 Aircraft assemblies, subassemblies & parts
HQ: Esterline Technologies Corp
500 108th Ave Ne Ste 1500
Bellevue WA 98004
425 453-9400

(G-1062)
PANDA DENTAL SOFTWARE INC
14205 Se 36th St Ste 100 (98006-1553)
PHONE....................800 517-7716
Mike Zybutz, *President*
Anne Shields, *Vice Pres*
EMP: 2 EST: 2010
SALES (est): 142.3K **Privately Held**
SIC: 7372 Prepackaged software

(G-1063)
PASCAL COMPANY INC
Also Called: Pasco International
2929 Northup Way (98004-1430)
P.O. Box 1478 (98009-1478)
PHONE....................425 827-4694
David Watton, *President*
Ben Paschall, *Chairman*
Joe Pellicano, *Treasurer*
Carter Chang, *Accounts Mgr*
Steve Burman, *Admin Sec*
▲ EMP: 33 EST: 1933
SQ FT: 24,000
SALES (est): 6.1MM **Privately Held**
WEB: www.pascaldental.com
SIC: 3843 Dental equipment

(G-1064)
PATCEN HEALTHCARE INC
3600 136th Pl Se Ste 300 (98006-1468)
PHONE....................425 495-5143
Kshama Kumar, *President*
EMP: 2
SALES (est): 86.6K **Privately Held**
SIC: 3841 Anesthesia apparatus

Bellevue - King County (G-1065) — GEOGRAPHIC SECTION

(G-1065)
PAVEL S PUZZLES
4414 173rd Ave Se (98006-6512)
PHONE 425 643-0204
Pavel Curtis, *Principal*
EMP: 3
SALES (est): 231.3K **Privately Held**
SIC: 3944 Puzzles

(G-1066)
PB INC
Also Called: Pebblebee
1269 120th Ave Ne (98005-2121)
P.O. Box 2962, Renton (98056-0962)
PHONE 206 747-0347
Daniel Daoura, *CEO*
Nicolas Pearson-Franks, *Chief Engr*
▲ EMP: 2
SALES (est): 210.8K **Privately Held**
SIC: 3699 3651 7389 Security devices; household audio & video equipment;

(G-1067)
PEACETAGS
305 Bellevue Way Ne (98004-5719)
PHONE 206 932-8247
EMP: 2
SALES (est): 167.7K **Privately Held**
SIC: 2679 Mfg Converted Paper Products

(G-1068)
PERCO INC
24 Lopez Ky (98006-1026)
PHONE 425 373-1252
Ernie Peterson, *President*
Kristine Peterson, *Treasurer*
EMP: 2
SALES: 360K **Privately Held**
SIC: 3559 Semiconductor manufacturing machinery

(G-1069)
PERFECT BLEND LLC (PA)
10900 Ne 8th St Ste 615 (98004-4454)
PHONE 509 488-5570
Daniel T Hazen, *President*
Dan Hazen, *COO*
Reyme J Kirk, *CFO*
Reyme Kirk, *CFO*
EMP: 42
SQ FT: 30,000
SALES (est): 11.5MM **Privately Held**
WEB: www.perfect-blend.com
SIC: 2873 5191 Fertilizers: natural (organic), except compost; fertilizer & fertilizer materials

(G-1070)
PERFECT PRESS PRINTING INC
1910 132nd Ave Ne Ste 10 (98005-2233)
PHONE 425 562-0507
Don Dahl, *President*
Heather Dahl, *Vice Pres*
EMP: 3
SQ FT: 3,000
SALES (est): 426.8K **Privately Held**
WEB: www.perfectpress.com
SIC: 2752 Commercial printing, offset

(G-1071)
PETER PAN SEAFOODS INC (DH)
3015 112th Ave Ne Ste 100 (98004-8001)
PHONE 206 728-6000
Barry D Collier, *President*
Steven N Chartier, *Vice Pres*
Kirk J Koch, *Vice Pres*
Dale Schwarz Miller, *VP Prdtn*
Adrian Yonke, *Treasurer*
◆ EMP: 204 EST: 1950
SQ FT: 3,500
SALES (est): 162MM **Privately Held**
WEB: www.ppsf.com
SIC: 2092 2091 Seafoods, fresh: prepared; seafoods, frozen: prepared; fish, fresh: prepared; fish, frozen: prepared; seafood products: packaged in cans, jars, etc.; fish: packaged in cans, jars, etc.
HQ: Maruha Capital Investment Inc
  3015 112th Ave Ne Ste 100
  Bellevue WA 98004
  206 382-0640

(G-1072)
PETFORIA LLC
Also Called: Pepperdogz
4957 Lakemont Blvd Se C4271 (98006-7801)
PHONE 425 945-2300
Sean Youssefi,
▲ EMP: 2
SALES (est): 130K **Privately Held**
WEB: www.pepperdogz.com
SIC: 2047 Dog food

(G-1073)
PETRICHOR INDUSTRIES LLC (PA)
400 112th Ave Ne Ste 335 (98004-5523)
PHONE 425 454-8281
Daren Hamilton, *Mng Member*
EMP: 2
SALES (est): 1.2MM **Privately Held**
SIC: 3728 5599 4581 Aircraft body assemblies & parts; aircraft instruments, equipment or parts; aircraft maintenance & repair services

(G-1074)
PHYSWARE INC
600 108th Ave Ne Ste 1035 (98004-5129)
PHONE 562 491-1600
Vishwanath Bala, *Principal*
EMP: 7
SALES (est): 64.3K **Privately Held**
SIC: 8211 7372 Elementary & secondary schools; prepackaged software

(G-1075)
PI TECHNOLOGIES
Also Called: Payment Innovators
2018 156th Ave Ne (98007-3825)
PHONE 206 877-3720
Dariush Tari, *CEO*
EMP: 3
SALES (est): 300K **Privately Held**
SIC: 7372 Prepackaged software

(G-1076)
PIZZA BLENDS LLC (HQ)
Also Called: Pizza Blends, Inc.
400 112th Ave Ne Ste 350 (98004-5528)
PHONE 800 826-1200
Dale Tremblay, *President*
Robert Holmes, *President*
Dave Hoffman, *COO*
Mark Schuur, *CFO*
Thomas McRae, *Admin Sec*
▼ EMP: 10
SQ FT: 3,000
SALES (est): 33.5MM
SALES (corp-wide): 518MM **Privately Held**
WEB: www.pzablends.com
SIC: 2099 2045 Seasonings & spices; prepared flour mixes & doughs
PA: C.H. Guenther & Son Llc
  201 Broadway St
  San Antonio TX 78205
  210 227-1401

(G-1077)
POINT INSIDE INC
500 108th Ave Ne Ste 520 (98004-5588)
PHONE 425 590-9522
Josh Marti, *CEO*
Keane Watterson, *Partner*
Pete Coleman, *Vice Pres*
Jonathan Croy, *Vice Pres*
Michael Moricz, *VP Engrg*
EMP: 70
SALES (est): 7.6MM **Privately Held**
SIC: 7372 Business oriented computer software

(G-1078)
POWERSOFT
777 108th Ave Ne Ste 1650 (98004-5136)
PHONE 425 637-8088
EMP: 2 EST: 2003
SALES (est): 130K **Privately Held**
SIC: 7372 Prepackaged Software Services

(G-1079)
PRECISION APPLIANCE TECHNOLOGY
Also Called: Vesta
10400 Ne 4th St (98004-5174)
PHONE 206 960-2467
Bob Lamson, *CEO*
Rayman Lei, *COO*
EMP: 12
SALES (est): 664.8K **Privately Held**
SIC: 3634 Electric household cooking appliances

(G-1080)
PRECISION CASTPARTS CORP
PCC Aerostructures
915 118th Ave Se Ste 320 (98005-3878)
PHONE 425 957-6938
Joe Snowden, *COO*
EMP: 439
SALES (corp-wide): 225.3B **Publicly Held**
SIC: 3324 3369 Aerospace investment castings, ferrous; nonferrous foundries
HQ: Precision Castparts Corp.
  4650 Sw Mcdam Ave Ste 300
  Portland OR 97239
  503 946-4800

(G-1081)
PRICE JENSEN SURVEYS INC
16645 Se 16th St (98008-5117)
PHONE 425 747-4143
Lance J Jensen, *President*
Roberta Jensen, *Corp Secy*
Helen P Jensen, *Vice Pres*
EMP: 35
SQ FT: 1,600
SALES: 375K **Privately Held**
SIC: 5961 2741 Catalog & mail-order houses; miscellaneous publishing

(G-1082)
PRINTED CIRCUITS ASSEMBLY
13205 Se 30th St (98005-4401)
PHONE 425 641-7455
Chhou Taing, *Branch Mgr*
EMP: 120
SALES (corp-wide): 29.3MM **Privately Held**
SIC: 3672 Circuit boards, television & radio printed
PA: Printed Circuits Assembly Corp
  13221 Se 26th St Ste E
  Bellevue WA 98005
  425 644-7754

(G-1083)
PRINTED CIRCUITS ASSEMBLY (PA)
13221 Se 26th St Ste E (98005-4258)
PHONE 425 644-7754
Sim Taing, *President*
Chhou Taing, *Vice Pres*
EMP: 165
SQ FT: 44,442
SALES (est): 29.3MM **Privately Held**
SIC: 3672 Circuit boards, television & radio printed

(G-1084)
PRIVATEER PRESS INC
1705 136th Pl Ne Ste 220 (98005-2374)
PHONE 425 643-5900
Matt Wilson, *CEO*
Sherry Yeary, *President*
Michael Mulligan, *Project Mgr*
Michelle Horton, *Human Res Mgr*
Ron Kruzie, *Manager*
▲ EMP: 50
SALES (est): 5.6MM **Privately Held**
WEB: www.privateerpress.com
SIC: 2741 Miscellaneous publishing

(G-1085)
PROCESS INC
15600 Ne 8th St (98008-3927)
PHONE 425 401-2000
Rane Lottinville, *President*
John Loar, *COO*
Steve Skeel, *Vice Pres*
Sindy Skeel, *Admin Sec*
◆ EMP: 2
SALES (est): 413K **Privately Held**
SIC: 3559 3579 ; forms handling equipment

(G-1086)
PROVOKE SOLUTIONS INC
2010 156th Ave Ne Ste 301 (98007-3826)
PHONE 206 792-3680
Mason Pratt, *CEO*
Catherine Mikhlin, *Project Mgr*
Irene Sia, *Project Mgr*
Joshua Simmons, *Engineer*
David May, *Web Dvlpr*
EMP: 2
SALES (est): 215.5K **Privately Held**
SIC: 7372 Word processing computer software

(G-1087)
PTC INC
10900 Ne 8th St Ste 605 (98004-4454)
PHONE 425 455-1930
Fax: 425 635-7259
EMP: 30
SALES (corp-wide): 1.2B **Publicly Held**
SIC: 7372 7371 Prepackaged Software Services Custom Computer Programing
PA: Ptc Inc.
  140 Kendrick St Ste C120
  Needham MA 02210
  781 370-5000

(G-1088)
PURINA ANIMAL NUTRITION LLC
Also Called: Lol/Purina Feed
13231 Se 36th St Ste 130 (98006-7321)
PHONE 425 653-4238
Jerry Booren, *Office Mgr*
EMP: 7
SALES (corp-wide): 10.4B **Privately Held**
SIC: 2048 Prepared feeds
HQ: Purina Animal Nutrition Llc
  100 Danforth Dr
  Gray Summit MO 63039

(G-1089)
QUANTUM CORPORATION
Also Called: Quantum USA
110 110th Ave Ne Ste 200 (98004-5840)
PHONE 425 201-1400
James J Lerner, *CEO*
EMP: 90
SALES (corp-wide): 339.3MM **Privately Held**
SIC: 3572 Computer storage devices
PA: Quantum Corporation
  224 Airport Pkwy Ste 550
  San Jose CA 95110
  408 944-4000

(G-1090)
QUARTO PUBG GROUP USA INC
Also Called: BECker&mayer
11120 Ne 33rd Pl Ste 101 (98004-1444)
PHONE 425 827-7120
Marcus Leaver, *COO*
James Van Leuven, *Administration*
EMP: 50
SALES (corp-wide): 149.2MM **Privately Held**
SIC: 2732 7336 5192 Books: printing & binding; commercial art & graphic design; books, periodicals & newspapers
HQ: Quarto Publishing Group Usa Inc.
  401 2nd Ave N Ste 310
  Minneapolis MN 55401
  612 344-8100

(G-1091)
RAINMAKER SIGNS INC
2020 124th Ave Ne (98005-2118)
PHONE 425 861-7446
Michael McGinn, *President*
EMP: 5
SALES (est): 132.6K **Privately Held**
SIC: 3993 Signs, not made in custom sign painting shops

(G-1092)
RALLY SOFTWARE DEVELOPMENT
16102 Se 46th Way (98006-3279)
PHONE 206 266-8408
EMP: 2
SALES (est): 105.9K **Privately Held**
SIC: 7372 Prepackaged software

GEOGRAPHIC SECTION
Bellevue - King County (G-1123)

(G-1093)
RALPH M ERONEMO
11400 Se 66th St (98006-6408)
PHONE..................................425 985-1617
Jeff Taylor, *Principal*
EMP: 2
SALES (est): 88.3K **Privately Held**
SIC: 3691 Storage batteries

(G-1094)
RAMGEN POWER SYSTEMS LLC (PA)
11808 Northup Way W105 (98005-1936)
PHONE..................................425 828-4919
Aaron Koopman, *COO*
Jarlath Hume, *Vice Pres*
Shawn Lawlor, *Mng Member*
Steve Amsbaugh, *Manager*
Peter Baldwin,
EMP: 6
SALES (est): 2.5MM **Privately Held**
WEB: www.ramgen.com
SIC: 3441 Fabricated structural metal

(G-1095)
RAYONIER INC
3625 132nd Ave Se 200 (98006-1325)
PHONE..................................425 748-5220
Steve White, *Branch Mgr*
EMP: 20
SALES (corp-wide): 816.1MM **Publicly Held**
WEB: www.rayonier.com
SIC: 2411 5031 Logging; lumber, plywood & millwork
PA: Rayonier Inc.
1 Rayonier Way
Yulee FL 32097
904 357-9100

(G-1096)
RECORDPOINT SOFTWARE USA LLC
11711 Se 8th St Ste 310 (98005-3543)
PHONE..................................425 245-6235
EMP: 2
SALES (est): 106.3K **Privately Held**
SIC: 7372 Prepackaged software

(G-1097)
REDDEN MARINE
12505 Ne Bel Red Rd # 110 (98005-2510)
PHONE..................................206 753-0960
EMP: 2
SALES (est): 91.2K **Privately Held**
SIC: 5551 3732 Marine supplies & equipment; non-motorized boat, building & repairing

(G-1098)
RENA WARE INTERNATIONAL INC (PA)
15885 Ne 28th St (98008-2127)
PHONE..................................425 881-6171
Benjamin J Zylstra, *CEO*
Russell J Zylstra, *Ch of Bd*
Brad Rich, *President*
Michael Mossman, *Senior VP*
Jeff Roberts, *Vice Pres*
◆ EMP: 40 EST: 1938
SALES (est): 52.6MM **Privately Held**
SIC: 5963 3914 3589 5023 Houseware sales, house-to-house; stainless steel ware; water filters & softeners, household type; china; stainless steel flatware; cutlery; catalog & mail-order houses

(G-1099)
RENAISSANCE RUG CORPORATION
200 105th Ave Ne (98004-5704)
PHONE..................................425 698-1073
▲ EMP: 3
SALES (est): 340K **Privately Held**
SIC: 2273 Mfg Carpets/Rugs

(G-1100)
RENEWALLIANCE INC
1621 114th Ave Se Ste 122 (98004-6905)
PHONE..................................425 633-3368
Christina Jih, *Marketing Staff*
▲ EMP: 4
SALES (est): 275.6K **Privately Held**
SIC: 2844 Cosmetic preparations

(G-1101)
RESOLUTE MEDICAL INC
1900 112th Ave Ne Ste 102 (98004-2914)
PHONE..................................800 750-5784
Dave Marver, *CEO*
Bob Odell, *COO*
Pete McLean, *Vice Pres*
EMP: 3
SALES (est): 316.4K **Privately Held**
SIC: 3845 Electrocardiographs

(G-1102)
RH AIRPORT COMMERCE
1800 112th Ave Ne Ste 310 (98004-2993)
PHONE..................................425 454-3030
Stan Rosen, *Principal*
Karin Schoenleber, *Principal*
EMP: 27
SALES (est): 814.7K **Privately Held**
SIC: 3999 Models, general, except toy

(G-1103)
ROB SULLIVAN
2429 134th Ave Ne (98005-1811)
PHONE..................................425 882-2221
Rob Sullivan, *Principal*
EMP: 2
SALES (est): 79.9K **Privately Held**
SIC: 3585 Refrigeration & heating equipment

(G-1104)
ROBERTA PROPST
4957 Lakemont Blvd Se C4 (98006-7801)
PHONE..................................425 681-9760
Roberta Propst, *Principal*
EMP: 2
SALES (est): 115.1K **Privately Held**
SIC: 2759 Commercial printing

(G-1105)
ROBOBEAR LLC
10505 Main St Apt 654 (98004-5904)
PHONE..................................425 453-1391
EMP: 2
SALES (est): 81.4K **Privately Held**
SIC: 3599 Mfg Industrial Machinery

(G-1106)
ROCK INDUSTRIES LLC
Also Called: Rock Claims Management
4034 170th Ave Se (98008-5931)
PHONE..................................206 399-7853
Brian Rock, *Owner*
Deborah Rock, *Co-Owner*
EMP: 2
SALES (est): 99.6K **Privately Held**
WEB: www.vacationguard.com
SIC: 3999 Manufacturing industries

(G-1107)
ROCKET SOFTWARE
10900 Ne 8th St Ste 1000 (98004-4448)
PHONE..................................425 502-9684
EMP: 2
SALES (est): 139.7K **Privately Held**
SIC: 7372 Prepackaged Software Services

(G-1108)
ROCKWELL AUTOMATION INC
15375 Se 30th Pl Ste 150 (98007-6500)
PHONE..................................425 519-5109
Matt Baker, *Accounts Mgr*
Steve Humphrey, *Manager*
EMP: 13 **Publicly Held**
SIC: 3625 Relays & industrial controls
PA: Rockwell Automation, Inc.
1201 S 2nd St
Milwaukee WI 53204

(G-1109)
RSA THE SECURITY EMC
15500 Se 30th Pl Ste 200 (98007-6347)
PHONE..................................781 515-5000
Rohit Ghai, *President*
EMP: 3 EST: 2016
SALES (est): 104K **Privately Held**
SIC: 3572 Computer storage devices

(G-1110)
S & B INC
Also Called: Stead & Associates
13200 Se 30th St Ste A (98005-4490)
PHONE..................................425 746-9312
Randall T Stead, *CEO*
Valene Stead, *Corp Secy*
James E Swanson, *Vice Pres*
EMP: 11 EST: 1977
SQ FT: 8,000
SALES (est): 2.2MM **Privately Held**
SIC: 3625 3823 Relays & industrial controls; pressure measurement instruments, industrial

(G-1111)
SAFRAN
11400 Se 8th St Ste 225 (98004-6465)
PHONE..................................425 283-5031
Yves Imbert, *Principal*
▲ EMP: 4
SALES (est): 528.8K **Privately Held**
SIC: 3621 Motors, electric

(G-1112)
SAFRAN USA INC
11400 Se 8th St Ste 225 (98004-6465)
PHONE..................................425 462-8613
Fax: 425 283-5034
EMP: 25
SALES (corp-wide): 555.1MM **Privately Held**
SIC: 3643 3621 7699 3724 Mfg Conductive Wire Dvcs Mfg Motors/Generators Repair Services Mfg Aircraft Engine/Part Whol Auto Parts/Supplies
HQ: Safran Usa, Inc.
700 S Washington St Fl 3
Alexandria VA 22314
703 351-9898

(G-1113)
SALESFORCECOM INC
929 108th Ave Ne (98004-4769)
PHONE..................................206 701-1755
Michael Livingston, *Manager*
Hubert Ban, *Director*
Porwal Priyank, *Director*
Leif Clarke, *Executive*
EMP: 5
SALES (corp-wide): 13.2B **Publicly Held**
SIC: 7372 7375 Business oriented computer software; information retrieval services
PA: Salesforce.Com, Inc.
415 Mission St Fl 3
San Francisco CA 94105
415 901-7000

(G-1114)
SARANGSOFT LLC
5724 114st Pl Se St (98006)
PHONE..................................425 378-3890
Alok Chakrabarti, *CEO*
Rini Chakrabarti, *President*
EMP: 3
SALES (est): 202.1K **Privately Held**
WEB: www.sarangsoft.com
SIC: 7372 7373 7371 Prepackaged software; systems software development services; computer software development & applications

(G-1115)
SARS CORPORATION (PA)
601 108th Ave Ne Ste 1900 (98004-4376)
PHONE..................................866 276-7277
Laurence Shelver, *President*
Teresa Grote, *President*
Mark Swan, *Chairman*
Frank Bonadio, *COO*
Alan Chaffee, *CFO*
EMP: 19
SQ FT: 9,278
SALES (est): 1.1MM **Privately Held**
SIC: 7372 7373 Prepackaged software; systems software development services

(G-1116)
SCALEOUT SOFTWARE INC
600 108th Ave Ne Ste 104 (98004-5110)
PHONE..................................503 643-3422
William Bain, *Chairman*
EMP: 3
SALES (est): 287.4K **Privately Held**
SIC: 7372 Application computer software

(G-1117)
SCHOOLKITCOM INC
Also Called: Schoolkit International
4505 141st Pl Se (98006-2314)
PHONE..................................425 454-3373
Adam Smith, *CEO*
Mark Smith, *CTO*
EMP: 14
SQ FT: 1,750
SALES (est): 1.4MM **Privately Held**
WEB: www.schoolkit.com
SIC: 7372 Educational computer software

(G-1118)
SDP TECH INC
227 Bellevue Way Ne (98004-5721)
PHONE..................................206 595-3041
Bill Shannon, *President*
Chuck Doland, *Vice Pres*
Pat Mc Dermott, *Admin Sec*
EMP: 4
SALES (est): 409.8K **Privately Held**
SIC: 3555 Printing trades machinery

(G-1119)
SEA-BIRD ELECTRONICS INC
13431 Ne 20th St (98005-2010)
PHONE..................................425 643-9866
Casey Moore, *President*
Nordeen Larson, *President*
John Backes, *Vice Pres*
Richard J Baumann, *Vice Pres*
Heddy Gundersen, *Vice Pres*
◆ EMP: 105
SQ FT: 34,000
SALES (est): 25.4MM
SALES (corp-wide): 19.8B **Publicly Held**
WEB: www.seabird.com
SIC: 3829 Geophysical & meteorological testing equipment
PA: Danaher Corporation
2200 Penn Ave Nw Ste 800w
Washington DC 20037
202 828-0850

(G-1120)
SEAPORT TILE & MARBLE INC
16412 Se 9th St (98008-6014)
PHONE..................................425 644-7067
Robert Wisniewski, *President*
Teresa Wisniewski, *Vice Pres*
▲ EMP: 32
SQ FT: 9,000
SALES (est): 2.9MM **Privately Held**
WEB: www.seaporttileshop.com
SIC: 3281 1743 Table tops, marble; tile installation, ceramic

(G-1121)
SEATTLE COTTON WORKS LLC
405 114th Ave Se Ste 200 (98004-6475)
PHONE..................................425 455-8003
▲ EMP: 13
SALES (est): 1.5MM **Privately Held**
SIC: 2329 2399 Clothing Mfg
PA: Sunrise Creative Group Inc
405 114th Ave Se Ste 200
Bellevue WA 98004

(G-1122)
SECOND AMENDMENT FOUNDATION (PA)
Also Called: SECOND AMENDMENT REPORTER
12500 Ne 10th Pl (98005-2538)
PHONE..................................425 454-7012
Joe Tartaro, *President*
Jeffrey D Kane, *Vice Pres*
John Snyder, *Treasurer*
Massad Ayoob, *Director*
Allan Gottlieb, *Director*
EMP: 18 EST: 1974
SQ FT: 7,000
SALES: 3.9MM **Privately Held**
WEB: www.saf.org
SIC: 8299 2721 Educational services; magazines: publishing only, not printed on site

(G-1123)
SELAH SPRINGS LLC
Also Called: Rypyl
16552 Se 28th St (98008-5620)
PHONE..................................206 714-6068
Shawn Bigger, *Principal*
EMP: 3
SALES (est): 177.7K **Privately Held**
SIC: 7371 7372 Computer software development & applications; computer software development; business oriented computer software

Bellevue - King County (G-1124) — GEOGRAPHIC SECTION

(G-1124)
SEQUOIA SCIENTIFIC INC
2700 Richards Rd Ste 107 (98005-4200)
PHONE....................................425 641-0944
Yogesh Agrawal, *President*
Chuck Pottsmith, *President*
Henry Pottsmith, *Vice Pres*
Doug Keir, *Materials Mgr*
Thomas Leeuw, *Research*
EMP: 9
SQ FT: 5,000
SALES (est): 1.8MM **Privately Held**
SIC: 3663 3812 Biotechnical research, commercial; nautical instruments

(G-1125)
SERIOUS BIZ LLC
9628 Hilltop Rd (98004-4006)
PHONE....................................425 454-1906
Nickolas Sears, *Principal*
EMP: 2 **EST:** 2016
SALES (est): 77.3K **Privately Held**
SIC: 2741 Miscellaneous publishing

(G-1126)
SGC WORLD INC
13737 Se 26th St (98005-4099)
P.O. Box 3526 (98009-3526)
PHONE....................................425 746-6310
Bruce Wood, *President*
▲ **EMP:** 16
SQ FT: 25,000
SALES (est): 2.1MM **Privately Held**
WEB: www.sgcworld.com
SIC: 3663 Receiver-transmitter units (transceiver)

(G-1127)
SGC WORLD INC
725 172nd Pl Ne (98008-4147)
PHONE....................................425 746-6311
EMP: 2
SALES (est): 122.1K **Privately Held**
SIC: 3663 Radio & TV communications equipment

(G-1128)
SHENG MIAN NORTH AMERICA LLC
Also Called: Mein Street
76 158th Pl Se (98008-4646)
PHONE....................................215 519-5895
Fredrick Hochman,
Tzu Feng Kung,
EMP: 4
SALES (est): 116.1K **Privately Held**
SIC: 2035 2032 5149 2656 Seasonings, seafood sauces (except tomato & dry); ethnic foods: canned, jarred, etc.; dried or canned foods; sanitary food containers;

(G-1129)
SHERWIN-WILLIAMS COMPANY
3640 Factoria Blvd Se (98006-5270)
PHONE....................................425 643-8584
EMP: 8
SALES (corp-wide): 17.5B **Publicly Held**
SIC: 5231 5198 5087 3991 Wallpaper; paints, varnishes & supplies; service establishment equipment; brooms & brushes
PA: The Sherwin-Williams Company
101 W Prospect Ave # 1020
Cleveland OH 44115
216 566-2000

(G-1130)
SIEMENS
15900 Se Eastgate Way # 200 (98008-5012)
PHONE....................................425 507-4380
EMP: 2
SALES (est): 85.7K **Privately Held**
SIC: 5063 3699 Electrical apparatus & equipment; electrical equipment & supplies

(G-1131)
SIGNWORKS LLC
14205 Se 36th St Ste 100 (98006-1553)
PHONE....................................206 715-1570
Zak Haberlach, *Principal*
EMP: 2
SALES (est): 113.7K **Privately Held**
SIC: 3993 Signs & advertising specialties

(G-1132)
SIMERICS INC (PA)
1750 112th Ave Ne C250 (98005-3752)
PHONE....................................256 489-1480
Samuel A Lowry, *President*
EMP: 10
SQ FT: 1,500
SALES (est): 1.1MM **Privately Held**
SIC: 7372 7379 Prepackaged software; computer related consulting services

(G-1133)
SIMERICS INC
1750 112th Ave Ne (98005-3752)
PHONE....................................425 502-9978
Yu Jiang, *Branch Mgr*
EMP: 16
SALES (corp-wide): 1.1MM **Privately Held**
SIC: 7379 7372 Computer related consulting services; prepackaged software
PA: Simerics, Inc.
1750 112th Ave Ne C250
Bellevue WA 98004
256 489-1480

(G-1134)
SIMPLYFUN LLC
11245 Se 6th St Ste 110 (98004-6499)
PHONE....................................425 289-0858
Patty Pearcy, *President*
Glenda Peters, *Principal*
▲ **EMP:** 29
SALES (est): 5MM **Privately Held**
SIC: 3944 5092 Electronic games & toys; toys & hobby goods & supplies

(G-1135)
SKINNY PRODUCING
6617 118th Ave Se (98006-6445)
PHONE....................................425 443-4552
EMP: 2 **EST:** 2016
SALES (est): 88.2K **Privately Held**
SIC: 1311 Crude petroleum & natural gas

(G-1136)
SKOOLER INC
Also Called: Skooler US
10400 Ne 4th St (98004-5174)
PHONE....................................425 628-5000
Tor Ove Henricksen, *CEO*
EMP: 1
SALES: 3MM **Privately Held**
SIC: 3999 8299 Education aids, devices & supplies; educational services

(G-1137)
SKYLINE SOCKS
10022 Meydenbauer Way Se G3 (98004-6041)
PHONE....................................425 454-1323
EMP: 7 **EST:** 2013
SALES (est): 198K **Privately Held**
SIC: 2252 Mfg Hosiery

(G-1138)
SMART OFFICE ENVIRONMENTS LLC
4957 Lakemont Blvd Se C4 (98006-7801)
PHONE....................................206 730-8871
Casey Kelly,
EMP: 9 **EST:** 2011
SALES (est): 1MM **Privately Held**
WEB: www.smartofficeenvironments.com
SIC: 2521 Wood office furniture

(G-1139)
SMART START
13547 Se 27th Pl Ste 4b (98005-4236)
PHONE....................................425 747-4400
Marjory Dempsey, *Principal*
EMP: 3
SALES (est): 193K **Privately Held**
SIC: 3694 Engine electrical equipment

(G-1140)
SMJ INDUSTRIES LLC
1831 127th Ave Se (98005-3905)
PHONE....................................425 442-9785
EMP: 2
SALES (est): 122.7K **Privately Held**
SIC: 3999 Manufacturing industries

(G-1141)
SNIDER SOFTWARE LLC
10444 Ne 16th Pl (98004-2804)
PHONE....................................206 790-7570
EMP: 2
SALES (est): 121K **Privately Held**
SIC: 7372 Prepackaged software

(G-1142)
SNOWDEN BROTHERS LLC
1100 Bellevue Way Ne # 8 (98004-4280)
PHONE....................................206 624-1752
William L Snowden, *CEO*
Kyle Serikawa, *Manager*
Lara Fjelstad,
▲ **EMP:** 4
SALES (est): 2.7MM **Privately Held**
SIC: 3143 3144 Men's footwear, except athletic; women's footwear, except athletic

(G-1143)
SOCEDO INC
10700 Ne 4th St Unit 1202 (98004-5784)
PHONE....................................206 499-3398
Aseem Badshah, *CEO*
Bill Cogar, *Marketing Staff*
EMP: 4
SALES (est): 327.7K **Privately Held**
SIC: 7372 Business oriented computer software

(G-1144)
SOCK DOCTOR COM INC
4 168th Ave Ne (98008-4538)
PHONE....................................425 223-5173
Julia Overstreet, *President*
EMP: 4
SALES (est): 272K **Privately Held**
SIC: 2252 Socks

(G-1145)
SOHAM INC (PA)
15375 Se 30th Pl Ste 310 (98007-6500)
PHONE....................................425 445-2125
Sudheer Koneru, *CEO*
Vamshidhar Reddy, *CTO*
EMP: 100
SALES (est): 2.5MM **Privately Held**
SIC: 7372 7373 Application computer software; systems software development services

(G-1146)
SOLID MODELING SOLUTIONS INC
17708 Se 40th Pl (98008-5906)
P.O. Box 1306, Vashon (98070-1306)
PHONE....................................425 246-3943
James Presti, *President*
George Celniker, *Vice Pres*
Bill Denker, *Vice Pres*
William Denker, *Vice Pres*
Elizabeth McCalmont, *Vice Pres*
EMP: 7
SQ FT: 1,000
SALES: 850K **Privately Held**
WEB: www.smlib.com
SIC: 7372 Publishers' computer software

(G-1147)
SOS FINISHING UNLIMITED INC
825 176th Ave Ne (98008-3822)
PHONE....................................425 746-7385
James Mullen, *President*
Germaine Mullen, *Vice Pres*
Dawn Schoenleber, *Treasurer*
Michele Mullen, *Admin Sec*
EMP: 10
SQ FT: 5,000
SALES: 400K **Privately Held**
SIC: 2789 Bookbinding & related work

(G-1148)
SOUND METRICS CORP
11010 Northup Way (98004-1436)
PHONE....................................425 822-3001
Joe Burch, *President*
William Hanot, *Vice Pres*
EMP: 9
SQ FT: 3,000
SALES (est): 1.5MM **Privately Held**
WEB: www.soundmetrics.com
SIC: 3812 Sonar systems & equipment

(G-1149)
SOUND TANKS AND CNTRS L L C
227 Bellevue Way Ne # 166 (98004-5721)
PHONE....................................425 455-2668
Rick Ramsey,
EMP: 2
SALES: 250K **Privately Held**
SIC: 5084 3795 Industrial machinery & equipment; tanks & tank components

(G-1150)
SOVRANO DI RICCHEZZA GROUP
13500 Se 24th St (98005-4043)
PHONE....................................425 449-8011
Sang Y Kim, *President*
Abin B Nellams, *Shareholder*
EMP: 4
SALES (est): 99K **Privately Held**
SIC: 2869 5172 Rocket engine fuel, organic; fuel oil

(G-1151)
SPECIALTY STORES INC
Also Called: Babysakes.com
227 Bellevue Way Ne # 59 (98004-5721)
PHONE....................................206 650-0747
Jeff Walker, *President*
Kristim Walker, *Vice Pres*
EMP: 5
SQ FT: 1,000
SALES (est): 826.8K **Privately Held**
SIC: 5137 2335 Baby goods; wedding gowns & dresses

(G-1152)
SPECTACLE MAKER
1837 156th Ave Ne Ste 202 (98007-4387)
PHONE....................................425 643-5367
M Christopher Barry, *Principal*
EMP: 3 **EST:** 2012
SALES (est): 337K **Privately Held**
SIC: 3851 Spectacles

(G-1153)
SPECTRUM CONTROLS INC
1705 132nd Ave Ne (98005-2224)
P.O. Box 6489 (98008-0489)
PHONE....................................425 462-2087
Bruce Wanta, *President*
Fred Anderson, *Vice Pres*
Scott Brown, *Draft/Design*
Mike McFeters, *Engineer*
CAM Vong, *Engineer*
▼ **EMP:** 75
SQ FT: 32,000
SALES: 29.7MM **Privately Held**
WEB: www.spectrumcontrols.com
SIC: 3823 Industrial process control instruments

(G-1154)
SPOT-ON PRINT & DESIGN INC
1803 132nd Ave Ne Ste 1 (98005-2261)
PHONE....................................425 558-7768
Kris Rumpf, *President*
Bill Rumpf, *Vice Pres*
EMP: 6
SALES (est): 878K **Privately Held**
SIC: 2752 Commercial printing, offset

(G-1155)
STATESIDE BEAD SUPPLY
16830 Se 43rd St (98006-8992)
P.O. Box 1851, Issaquah (98027-0076)
PHONE....................................425 644-3448
Timothy Anthonise, *President*
Elaine Anthonise, *Vice Pres*
EMP: 2 **EST:** 2013
SALES (est): 148.8K **Privately Held**
SIC: 3915 5092 Jewel preparing: instruments, tools, watches & jewelry; arts & crafts equipment & supplies

(G-1156)
STEPHS CUSTOM SAWYERING
10648 Se 16th St (98004-7139)
PHONE....................................425 646-8783
Stephen Baxter, *Principal*
EMP: 4
SALES (est): 358.1K **Privately Held**
SIC: 3312 Tinplate

▲ = Import ▼ = Export
♦ = Import/Export

(G-1157)
STEPPIR COMM SYSTEMS INC
13406 Se 32nd St (98005-4409)
PHONE................................425 453-1910
John Mertel, *President*
Jim Thomas, *Vice Pres*
John Stanford, *CTO*
EMP: 2
SALES (est): 130.7K **Privately Held**
SIC: 3663 Antennas, transmitting & communications

(G-1158)
STEVENS WINERY
11028 Ne 18th Pl (98004-2901)
PHONE................................425 424-9463
Timothy Dstevens, *Principal*
EMP: 4 **EST:** 2013
SALES (est): 254.5K **Privately Held**
SIC: 2084 Wines

(G-1159)
STOREANYWHERECOM INC
12819 Se 38th St Ste 239 (98006-1326)
PHONE................................425 643-3268
Kefan Xu, *Owner*
EMP: 2
SALES (est): 185.9K **Privately Held**
SIC: 3571 Electronic computers

(G-1160)
STRAIGHTTHROUGH INC
10777 Main St (98004-5971)
PHONE................................425 467-1990
EMP: 2 **EST:** 2003
SALES (est): 160K **Privately Held**
SIC: 7372 Prepackaged Software Services

(G-1161)
STREAMBOX INC
1801 130th Ave Ne Ste 200 (98005-2247)
PHONE................................206 956-0544
Robert Hildeman, *President*
Brian Raine, *Vice Pres*
Dave Bolnick, *Project Mgr*
Bob Lindsey, *CFO*
Tim Heiner, *Sales Staff*
EMP: 25
SALES (est): 4.9MM **Privately Held**
WEB: www.streambox.com
SIC: 3663 Radio & TV communications equipment

(G-1162)
STS TRADING CO
6218 167th Ave Se (98006-5645)
PHONE................................425 830-6368
▼ **EMP:** 3
SALES (est): 263K **Privately Held**
SIC: 2673 Garment bags (plastic film): made from purchased materials

(G-1163)
STURTEVANTS TENNIS SHOP
1100 Bellevue Way Ne # 7 (98004-4280)
PHONE................................425 454-6465
Jeff Campbell, *Manager*
EMP: 4
SALES (est): 231.6K **Privately Held**
SIC: 3949 7997 Shafts, golf club; tennis club, membership

(G-1164)
SUBERIZER INC (PA)
2625 Northup Way Ste 100 (98004-1482)
PHONE................................425 747-8900
Robert Hesse, *President*
Chip Hesse, *Project Mgr*
Teresa Polejewski, *Purchasing*
EMP: 2 **EST:** 1977
SQ FT: 4,000
SALES (est): 1.3MM **Privately Held**
WEB: www.suberizer.com
SIC: 3523 Barn, silo, poultry, dairy & livestock machinery; crop storage bins

(G-1165)
SUEZ WTS SYSTEMS USA INC
Also Called: Suez Water Tech & Solution
3006 Northrup Way Ste 200 (98004)
PHONE................................425 828-2400
EMP: 80
SALES (corp-wide): 94.7MM **Privately Held**
SIC: 3589 Water purification equipment, household type
HQ: Suez Wts Systems Usa, Inc.
4636 Somerton Rd
Trevose PA 19053
781 359-7000

(G-1166)
SUNBIRD AEROSPACE
13854 Ne 8th St Apt D201 (98005-3473)
PHONE................................425 241-8594
EMP: 2
SALES (est): 91K **Privately Held**
SIC: 3721 Aircraft

(G-1167)
SUNRISE IDENTITY LLC
405 114th Ave Se Ste 200 (98004-6475)
PHONE................................425 214-1700
Mitchell Mounger, *CEO*
Larry Mounger, *Ch of Bd*
Mark Lynch, *COO*
Tom Economou, *Senior VP*
Becca Collins, *Warehouse Mgr*
EMP: 4
SALES (est): 271.3K **Privately Held**
SIC: 2396 2329 2339 Screen printing on fabric articles; men's & boys' sportswear & athletic clothing; women's & misses' athletic clothing & sportswear

(G-1168)
SURFTECH FINISHES CO
500 108th Ave Ne (98004-5580)
PHONE................................425 453-9400
Ron Hersh, *Principal*
EMP: 3 **EST:** 2013
SALES (est): 174.3K
SALES (corp-wide): 3.8B **Publicly Held**
SIC: 3728 Aircraft assemblies, subassemblies & parts
HQ: Esterline Technologies Corp
500 108th Ave Ne Ste 1500
Bellevue WA 98004
425 453-9400

(G-1169)
SUSSEX CLUMBER LLC
Also Called: Ross Andrew Winery
1021 92nd Ave Ne (98004-4043)
PHONE................................206 369-3615
EMP: 2
SALES (est): 90.3K **Privately Held**
SIC: 2084 Wines

(G-1170)
SUSTAIN OUTDOORS INC
16494 Se 57th Pl (98006-5536)
PHONE................................949 439-4899
Kyle Mundy, *President*
EMP: 5
SALES (est): 178.7K **Privately Held**
SIC: 3496 Miscellaneous fabricated wire products

(G-1171)
SUZIPERI
13502 Ne 12th Pl (98005-2762)
PHONE................................425 373-1954
EMP: 3
SALES (est): 17K **Privately Held**
SIC: 2353 Mfg Hats/Caps/Millinery

(G-1172)
SWIRE PACIFIC HOLDINGS INC
1150 124th Ave Ne (98005-2102)
PHONE................................425 455-2000
EMP: 4 **Privately Held**
SIC: 2086 Bottled & canned soft drinks
HQ: Swire Pacific Holdings Inc.
12634 S 265 W Bldg A
Draper UT 84020
801 816-5300

(G-1173)
SWISH
14603 Ne 20th St Ste 4c (98007-3743)
PHONE................................425 644-3545
EMP: 2 **EST:** 2013
SALES (est): 177.8K **Privately Held**
SIC: 3949 Hunting equipment

(G-1174)
SYNERGISTIC TECHNOLOGIES INC (PA)
Also Called: Syntek
11820 Northup Way E200 (98005-1946)
PHONE................................425 822-7777
Craig Howland, *President*
Don Brown, *Owner*
Dean Shipman, *Vice Pres*
▲ **EMP:** 5
SQ FT: 1,400
SALES (est): 2.9MM **Privately Held**
SIC: 5084 3829 3822 Measuring & testing equipment, electrical; machine tools & metalworking machinery; measuring & controlling devices; auto controls regulating residntl & coml environmt & applncs

(G-1175)
SYNOLOGY AMERICA CORP
3535 Factoria Blvd Se # 200 (98006-1290)
PHONE................................425 296-3177
Jane Ou, *Principal*
Mathew Fuller, *Finance*
Brendan Collins, *Sales Mgr*
Devin Santamaria, *Sales Mgr*
Billy Knowles, *Sales Staff*
◆ **EMP:** 17
SALES (est): 4.4MM
SALES (corp-wide): 75.1MM **Privately Held**
SIC: 3572 Computer tape drives & components
PA: Synology Inc.
3f-3, 106, Chang An W. Rd.,
Taipei City TAP 10351
225 521-814

(G-1176)
TACTUUM LLC
3822 131st St Ln Se L6 (98006)
PHONE................................425 941-6958
Neil Francoeur, *Managing Prtnr*
Mark Buchner, *Partner*
Graeme McClurkin, *Partner*
Vinh Tran, *Partner*
EMP: 4
SALES (est): 260.9K **Privately Held**
SIC: 7372 7389 Business oriented computer software;

(G-1177)
TANGERA TECHNOLOGIES INC
40 Lake Bellevue Dr # 100 (98005-2479)
PHONE................................425 652-7969
Jack Lee, *President*
EMP: 2
SALES (est): 109K **Privately Held**
WEB: www.tangaratech.com
SIC: 7372 Prepackaged software

(G-1178)
TANGIBLE VENTURES LLC
10710 Ne 10th St Apt 807 (98004-1059)
PHONE................................360 818-4000
Udiyan Padmanabhan,
Eman Barhoumeh,
EMP: 2 **EST:** 2010
SALES (est): 108.1K **Privately Held**
SIC: 7372 Application computer software

(G-1179)
TECPLOT INC
3535 Factoria Blvd Se # 550 (98006-1213)
P.O. Box 52708 (98015-2708)
PHONE................................425 653-1200
Tom Chan, *President*
Scott Rumage, *Partner*
Zach Oglesby, *QA Dir*
Raja Olimuthu, *Regl Sales Mgr*
Margaret Connelly, *Marketing Staff*
EMP: 43
SQ FT: 9,585
SALES: 5.5MM
SALES (corp-wide): 862.5K **Privately Held**
WEB: www.tecplot.com
SIC: 7372 8711 Application computer software; engineering services
PA: Vela Software International Inc
26 Soho St Suite 400
Toronto ON M5T 1
416 861-2279

(G-1180)
TEH INDUSTRIES LLC
1006 103rd Ave Se (98004-6701)
PHONE................................425 453-1551
EMP: 2
SALES (est): 138.4K **Privately Held**
SIC: 3999 Manufacturing industries

(G-1181)
TELLWISE INC
1750 112th Ave Ne D151 (98004-3768)
PHONE................................425 999-6935
Conrad Bayer, *CEO*
Billy Peterson, *Manager*
Claudia Bayer, *Administration*
EMP: 6
SALES (est): 633.1K **Privately Held**
SIC: 7372 Business oriented computer software

(G-1182)
TESLA INC
233 Bellevue Sq (98004-5020)
PHONE................................425 453-5021
EMP: 119
SALES (corp-wide): 21.4B **Publicly Held**
SIC: 3714 3711 Motor vehicle parts & accessories; cars, electric, assembly of
PA: Tesla, Inc.
3500 Deer Creek Rd
Palo Alto CA 94304
650 681-5000

(G-1183)
TESLA INC
Also Called: Tesla Motors
14408 Ne 20th St (98007-3711)
PHONE................................425 519-8070
EMP: 3
SALES (corp-wide): 21.4B **Publicly Held**
SIC: 3711 Motor vehicles & car bodies
PA: Tesla, Inc.
3500 Deer Creek Rd
Palo Alto CA 94304
650 681-5000

(G-1184)
TEXAS AVENUE ASSOCIATES
10500 Ne 8th St Ste 1900 (98004-4358)
PHONE................................425 889-9642
Gabe Newell, *Principal*
Erik Johnson, *Project Mgr*
Don Holden, *Engineer*
Brian Jacobson, *Engineer*
Jeff Lind, *Engineer*
EMP: 23
SALES (est): 5.2MM **Privately Held**
SIC: 3592 Valves

(G-1185)
THERMOGENESIS GROUP INC
Also Called: IMOVR
14260 Ne 21st St (98007-3720)
PHONE................................425 999-3550
Ron Wiener, *CEO*
Andy Rosenbaum, *COO*
Sondra Harris, *Cust Mgr*
Josh Leichtung, *Chief Mktg Ofcr*
EMP: 11
SQ FT: 7,600
SALES: 5.4MM **Privately Held**
SIC: 2522 5712 Office desks & tables: except wood; office furniture

(G-1186)
THOMAS DEAN & CO LLC (PA)
4957 Lakemont Blvd Se C-145 (98006-7801)
PHONE................................206 355-1009
Dean Holly, *Principal*
Thomas Bonomo,
▲ **EMP:** 3
SQ FT: 1,200
SALES (est): 1.1MM **Privately Held**
SIC: 2325 5136 Shirt & slack suits: men's, youths' & boys'; shirts, men's & boys'

(G-1187)
THREE SQUARED LLC
9638 Hilltop Rd (98004-4006)
PHONE................................206 708-5918
Marc A Lapsley, *Mng Member*
Duane Schooley,
EMP: 6
SQ FT: 6,000

Bellevue - King County (G-1188)

SALES (est): 560K **Privately Held**
SIC: 3441 Fabricated structural metal

(G-1188)
TIBA MEDICAL INC
4709 Somerset Pl Se (98006-3024)
PHONE..................................503 222-1500
Merat Bagha, *CEO*
EMP: 4
SALES (est): 280K **Privately Held**
WEB: www.tibamedical.com
SIC: 3845 Electromedical equipment

(G-1189)
TIMELINE PRESS LLC
6410 129th Pl Se (98006-4047)
PHONE..................................425 454-7447
Catherine Thorpe, *Principal*
EMP: 2 EST: 2012
SALES (est): 158.4K **Privately Held**
SIC: 2741 Miscellaneous publishing

(G-1190)
TIMEXTENDER NORTH AMERICA
411 108th Ave Ne (98004-8404)
PHONE..................................619 813-7625
EMP: 2
SALES (est): 134.8K **Privately Held**
SIC: 7372 Business oriented computer software

(G-1191)
TIPTOES SOFTWARE LLC
13330 Se 55th Pl (98006-4128)
PHONE..................................650 267-1907
Sergey Markelov, *Principal*
EMP: 2
SALES (est): 63.8K **Privately Held**
SIC: 7372 Prepackaged software

(G-1192)
TITUS TOOL COMPANY INC (HQ)
Also Called: Titus Tool Company, Inc.
2800 156th Ave Se Ste 135 (98007-6555)
PHONE..................................206 447-1489
Walter Zabriskie, *Ch of Bd*
Matthew Hurley, *President*
Ben Lee, *Treasurer*
Sidney N Mendelsohn Jr, *Admin Sec*
▲ EMP: 12
SQ FT: 1,200
SALES (est): 10.6MM
SALES (corp-wide): 2.7MM **Privately Held**
WEB: www.titusint.com
SIC: 5085 3429 Fasteners & fastening equipment; manufactured hardware (general)

(G-1193)
TOKA BOX
13908 Se 42nd Pl (98006-2255)
PHONE..................................530 505-1289
Preethi Chandrasekhar, *Principal*
EMP: 2 EST: 2017
SALES (est): 116.7K **Privately Held**
SIC: 2741 Miscellaneous publishing

(G-1194)
TOP HAT WORD & INDEX
1805 134th Ave Se Apt 21 (98005-8060)
PHONE..................................520 271-2112
Paul Sweum, *Owner*
EMP: 2
SALES (est): 1K **Privately Held**
SIC: 2741 Miscellaneous publishing

(G-1195)
TORC STAR BOLTING TOOLS LLC
1736 125th Ave Se (98005-4636)
PHONE..................................334 714-0945
Aditya Singh, *Principal*
EMP: 2
SALES (est): 93.3K **Privately Held**
SIC: 3599 Industrial machinery

(G-1196)
TRANE COMPANY
12031 Ne Northrup 106 (98005)
PHONE..................................425 455-4148
EMP: 39

SALES (corp-wide): 25.5B **Privately Held**
SIC: 3585 Mfg Refrigeration/Heating Equipment
HQ: The Trane Company
3600 Pammel Creek Rd
La Crosse WI 54601
608 787-2000

(G-1197)
TRANE US INC
2333 158th Ct Ne (98008-2100)
PHONE..................................425 643-4310
Art Smith, *President*
EMP: 100
SQ FT: 3,800 **Privately Held**
SIC: 3585 Refrigeration & heating equipment
HQ: Trane U.S. Inc.
3600 Pammel Creek Rd
La Crosse WI 54601
608 787-2000

(G-1198)
TRANS PAC ENTERPRISES INC
9839 Ne 20th St (98004-2602)
PHONE..................................425 688-0037
Raymond Chu, *President*
EMP: 12
SALES (est): 1.1MM **Privately Held**
WEB: www.transpacenterprises.com
SIC: 3942 6111 Dolls & stuffed toys; federal & federally sponsored credit agencies

(G-1199)
TRI MARINE FISHING MGT LLC
10500 Ne 8th St Ste 1888 (98004-8631)
PHONE..................................425 688-1288
Miguel De Rueda, *General Mgr*
Benny Caserma, *Prdtn Mgr*
Renato Curto,
◆ EMP: 14
SALES (est): 3.8MM **Privately Held**
SIC: 2091 Tuna fish: packaged in cans, jars, etc.

(G-1200)
TRI-MARINE INTERNATIONAL INC (PA)
Also Called: Tri Marine
10500 Ne 8th St Ste 1888 (98004-8631)
PHONE..................................425 688-1288
Renato Curto, *President*
Glenda Isiderio, *Technology*
Mike Barron, *Director*
Stephen Farno, *Admin Sec*
Dayana Trujillo, *Receptionist*
▲ EMP: 2
SALES (est): 1.1MM **Privately Held**
WEB: www.tri-marine.com
SIC: 2091 Tuna fish: packaged in cans, jars, etc.

(G-1201)
TRI-MECHANICAL INC
Also Called: TMI
1824 130th Ave Ne Ste 1 (98005-2235)
PHONE..................................425 391-6016
Bob Davy, *President*
Adra Davy, *Admin Sec*
EMP: 11
SQ FT: 1,500
SALES: 1.5MM **Privately Held**
WEB: www.trimechanical.com
SIC: 7623 3444 Refrigeration service & repair; sheet metalwork

(G-1202)
TRIADD SOFTWARE CORPORATION
13401 Ne Bel Red Rd B10 (98005-2322)
PHONE..................................425 643-3700
Morris Gorelick, *CEO*
Ken Theonnes, *President*
Jin Zhou, *CFO*
EMP: 4
SQ FT: 3,600
SALES (est): 100K **Privately Held**
SIC: 7372 7371 Prepackaged software; custom computer programming services

(G-1203)
TRICK SHOT STUDIOS LLC
122 109th Ave Se (98004-6345)
PHONE..................................858 663-7097
EMP: 2

SALES (est): 130K **Privately Held**
SIC: 7372 Prepackaged Software

(G-1204)
TUBE ART DISPLAYS INC (PA)
11715 Se 5th St Ste 200 (98005-3533)
PHONE..................................206 223-1122
Frank Dupar III, *CEO*
Jeff Hargtt, *COO*
Jeff Hargtt, *Exec VP*
Ed Becker, *Vice Pres*
William Montero, *Vice Pres*
EMP: 30
SQ FT: 25,000
SALES (est): 23.3MM **Privately Held**
SIC: 3993 Electric signs

(G-1205)
TUMBLING LEAF PRESS
12230 Ne 32nd St Ste 210 (98005-1202)
PHONE..................................425 885-6315
Linda Mackin, *Principal*
EMP: 2
SALES (est): 115.4K **Privately Held**
SIC: 2741 Miscellaneous publishing

(G-1206)
ULTRABAC SOFTWARE INC
Also Called: BEI
15015 Main St Ste 200 (98007-5229)
PHONE..................................425 644-6000
Morgan S Edwards, *President*
Paul Bunn, *Admin Sec*
EMP: 35
SQ FT: 11,000
SALES (est): 3MM **Privately Held**
SIC: 7372 Utility computer software

(G-1207)
UNIQUE ART GLASS LLC
2619 127th Ave Ne (98005-1527)
PHONE..................................425 467-5599
Mark Olson, *Mng Member*
EMP: 4
SALES: 500K **Privately Held**
WEB: www.uniqueartglass.net
SIC: 3231 Products of purchased glass

(G-1208)
UNIVERSITY SWAGING CORPORATION (DH)
610 Bellevue Way Ne # 200 (98004-5032)
PHONE..................................425 318-1965
Conrad Scheffler, *President*
Roger Becker, *Vice Pres*
Ruth Beyer, *Admin Sec*
▲ EMP: 150
SQ FT: 35,000
SALES: 40.1MM
SALES (corp-wide): 225.3B **Publicly Held**
WEB: www.u-swage.com
SIC: 3728 3731 3498 3732 Aircraft parts & equipment; marine rigging; fabricated pipe & fittings; boat building & repairing
HQ: Primus International Inc
610 Bllvue Way Ne Ste 200
Auburn WA 98001
425 688-0444

(G-1209)
US BIOPHARMA INC
4710 140th Ave Ne (98005-1145)
PHONE..................................425 242-0208
Sunil Ummat, *Principal*
EMP: 4 EST: 2012
SALES (est): 303.3K **Privately Held**
SIC: 2834 Pharmaceutical preparations

(G-1210)
US MICRO PC INC
Also Called: US Micro
13600 Ne 20th St Ste C (98005-2000)
PHONE..................................425 462-7300
John Lotzkar, *President*
Todd Marvin, *Vice Pres*
Paul Morse, *Director*
EMP: 8
SQ FT: 5,000
SALES (est): 1.3MM **Privately Held**
WEB: www.usmicro.com
SIC: 5734 5045 3577 Personal computers; computers; computer peripheral equipment; printers, computer

(G-1211)
VANITIES
1405 132nd Ave Ne (98005-2258)
PHONE..................................425 453-5353
EMP: 4
SALES (est): 330.6K **Privately Held**
SIC: 2434 Wood kitchen cabinets

(G-1212)
VAVAKO FINE CHOCOLATES
10149 Main St (98004-6023)
PHONE..................................425 453-4553
Nicholas Espinosa, *Owner*
EMP: 5
SALES (est): 230K **Privately Held**
SIC: 5947 2066 Gift shop; chocolate

(G-1213)
VECTOR BLUE SERVICES LLC
10900 Ne 4th St Ste 2300 (98004-5882)
PHONE..................................425 219-2528
James Schuster, *CEO*
John Frankovich, *President*
EMP: 12
SALES (est): 334.2K **Privately Held**
SIC: 7371 7372 7379 Computer software systems analysis & design, custom; computer software development; application computer software; business oriented computer software; computer related consulting services

(G-1214)
VERIZON COMMUNICATIONS INC
14510 Ne 20th St (98007-3715)
PHONE..................................425 641-5900
Terry Swanlund, *Manager*
EMP: 12
SALES (corp-wide): 130.8B **Publicly Held**
WEB: www.verizon.com
SIC: 4813 4812 2741 7373 Local telephone communications; voice telephone communications; data telephone communications; cellular telephone services; directories, telephone: publishing only, not printed on site; computer integrated systems design
PA: Verizon Communications Inc.
1095 Ave Of The Americas
New York NY 10036
212 395-1000

(G-1215)
VERTI TECHNOLOGY GROUP INC
3600 136th Pl Se Ste 400 (98006-1468)
PHONE..................................425 279-1200
Jessica Cobbe, *President*
Erin Laye, *Admin Sec*
EMP: 2
SALES (est): 169.2K **Privately Held**
SIC: 7372 Prepackaged software

(G-1216)
VF OUTDOOR LLC
Also Called: North Face 49, The
1001 Bellevue Sq (98004-5019)
PHONE..................................425 455-7349
Alexis Deleo, *Branch Mgr*
EMP: 22
SALES (corp-wide): 13.8B **Publicly Held**
SIC: 5651 3161 2329 Unisex clothing stores; traveling bags; men's & boys' leather, wool & down-filled outerwear; ski & snow clothing: men's & boys'
HQ: Vf Outdoor, Llc
2701 Harbor Bay Pkwy
Alameda CA 94502
510 618-3500

(G-1217)
VINEGAR & OIL
2086 Bellevue Sq (98004-5028)
PHONE..................................425 454-8497
Matt Stermer, *Principal*
EMP: 6
SALES (est): 620.4K **Privately Held**
SIC: 2099 Vinegar

(G-1218)
VINYL STATUS
10710 Ne 10th St Apt 504 (98004-1053)
PHONE..................................206 601-3598

Eli Volynsky, *Owner*
EMP: 2
SALES (est): 78.8K **Privately Held**
SIC: 2759 Screen printing

(G-1219)
VIRTUAL IMPRINTS LLC
330 102nd Ave Se (98004-8105)
PHONE.................................425 998-9994
Jessica Dwyer, *Principal*
EMP: 2
SALES (est): 137.4K **Privately Held**
SIC: 2752 Commercial printing, lithographic

(G-1220)
VOLTAIRE INC
40 Lake Bellevue Dr # 100 (98005-2479)
PHONE.................................425 274-7000
Sean Pearson, *President*
EMP: 5
SALES (est): 432.7K **Privately Held**
SIC: 3823 Temperature measurement instruments, industrial

(G-1221)
VS FOODS LLC
Also Called: Birchiq
728 177th Ln Ne (98008-4217)
PHONE.................................425 279-8089
Valeriy Goloborodko, *Vice Pres*
Solomiya Goloborodko, *Mng Member*
EMP: 3
SQ FT: 1,000
SALES: 500K **Privately Held**
SIC: 5141 2086 Food brokers; pasteurized & mineral waters, bottled & canned

(G-1222)
WAIV AEROSPACE LLC
11747 Ne 1st St Ste 201 (98005-3043)
PHONE.................................206 276-2306
Samuel Wagner,
Douglas Ives,
EMP: 2
SALES (est): 99.8K **Privately Held**
WEB: www.waivaero.com
SIC: 7389 3728 Design, commercial & industrial; ; aircraft parts & equipment

(G-1223)
WALMAN OPTICAL
1247 120th Ave Ne (98005-2121)
PHONE.................................425 462-2576
Roger Bruce, *Principal*
EMP: 2
SALES (est): 125.9K **Privately Held**
SIC: 5048 3827 Optometric equipment & supplies; optical instruments & lenses

(G-1224)
WARGAMING SEATTLE INC
500 108th Ave Ne Ste 300 (98004-5582)
PHONE.................................425 250-0209
EMP: 6
SALES (est): 567.6K **Privately Held**
SIC: 3944 Games, toys & children's vehicles

(G-1225)
WESTWARD SEAFOODS INC (DH)
Also Called: Alyeska Seafoods
3015 112th Ave Ne Ste 100 (98004-8001)
PHONE.................................206 682-5949
Rick Dutton, *President*
Johahnson Mark, *President*
Yamamoto Tatsuya, *Vice Pres*
Pj Chambers, *Receptionist*
▼ **EMP:** 204
SQ FT: 12,000
SALES (est): 66.9MM **Privately Held**
SIC: 2092 Seafoods, fresh: prepared; seafoods, frozen: prepared
HQ: Maruha Capital Investment Inc
3015 112th Ave Ne Ste 100
Bellevue WA 98004
206 382-0640

(G-1226)
WEYERHAEUSER CO ✪
1899 120th Ave Ne (98005-2120)
PHONE.................................425 455-1111
EMP: 2 **EST:** 2019
SALES (est): 90.7K **Privately Held**
SIC: 2653 Corrugated & solid fiber boxes

(G-1227)
WFM SELECT FISH INC
15 Lake Bellevue Dr # 100 (98005-2485)
PHONE.................................512 542-0676
John Mackey, *Ch of Bd*
A C Gallo, *Co-President*
Walter Robb, *Co-President*
Glenda Flanagan, *CFO*
◆ **EMP:** 18
SALES (est): 2.3MM **Publicly Held**
WEB: www.wholefoods.com
SIC: 2091 Canned & cured fish & seafoods
HQ: Whole Foods Market, Inc.
550 Bowie St
Austin TX 78703
512 477-4455

(G-1228)
WORLD DIAMONDS
1429 Bellevue Way Ne F (98004-8206)
PHONE.................................425 765-7119
Viet-An Ly, *Principal*
EMP: 2
SALES (est): 106K **Privately Held**
SIC: 3559 Special industry machinery

(G-1229)
XENON ARC INC (PA)
777 108th Ave Ne Ste 1750 (98005-5139)
PHONE.................................425 646-1063
Chad Steigers, *CEO*
Edward Lux, *Principal*
Adeline Honnas, *COO*
Chris Jardine, *CFO*
EMP: 50 **EST:** 2010
SALES (est): 10MM **Privately Held**
SIC: 3647 Vehicular lighting equipment

(G-1230)
YONG FENG AMERICA INC
11220 Se 64th St (98006-6313)
PHONE.................................425 271-8057
EMP: 3 **EST:** 1995
SQ FT: 1,640
SALES (est): 1.1MM **Privately Held**
SIC: 2221 Manmade Broadwoven Fabric Mill

(G-1231)
YOPTI LLC
Also Called: Sanesolution
227 Bellevue Way Ne # 257 (98004-5721)
PHONE.................................347 979-1735
Jonathan Bailor, *Mng Member*
Angela Bailor, *Mng Member*
EMP: 2
SALES (est): 123.6K **Privately Held**
SIC: 2741 Miscellaneous publishing

(G-1232)
ZANGO INC (PA)
3600 136th Pl Se Ste 200 (98006-1468)
PHONE.................................425 279-1200
Keith Smith, *CEO*
Daniel Todd, *President*
York Baur, *Exec VP*
Ken McGraw, *Exec VP*
Ajay Murthy, *Senior VP*
EMP: 200
SALES (est): 12.4MM **Privately Held**
SIC: 4813 7372 7311 ; application computer software; advertising agencies

(G-1233)
ZEBRA PRINTING INC
2021 130th Ave Ne Ste I (98005-2019)
PHONE.................................425 462-9775
Ejaz Yusaf, *CEO*
EMP: 10
SQ FT: 2,500
SALES: 1.2MM **Privately Held**
SIC: 2752 7334 Commercial printing, offset; photocopying & duplicating services

(G-1234)
ZEN DOG SOFTWARE LLC
3741 122nd Ave Ne (98005-1231)
PHONE.................................425 861-5777
David Johnston, *Principal*
EMP: 2
SALES (est): 167.1K **Privately Held**
SIC: 7372 Prepackaged software

(G-1235)
ZULTIMATE SELF DEFENSE STUDIOS
330 Bellevue Way Ne (98004-5718)
PHONE.................................425 688-7888
EMP: 3 **EST:** 2016
SALES (est): 190.3K **Privately Held**
SIC: 3812 Defense systems & equipment

Bellingham
Whatcom County

(G-1236)
A TO Z COMPOSITES INC
2321 E Bakerview Rd Ste E (98226-7147)
PHONE.................................435 680-3762
Darby Bradley, *President*
Charles Coffey, *Vice Pres*
EMP: 12
SQ FT: 20,000
SALES (est): 1.1MM **Privately Held**
SIC: 3624 2821 Fibers, carbon & graphite; molding compounds, plastics

(G-1237)
A-1 WELDING INC
4000 Irongate Rd (98226-8028)
PHONE.................................360 671-9414
Brad Davison, *President*
Bradley Davison, *President*
EMP: 15
SQ FT: 8,500
SALES (est): 2.5MM **Privately Held**
WEB: www.a1weldinginc.com
SIC: 7692 3535 Welding repair; unit handling conveying systems

(G-1238)
ACADEMY INFRARED TRAINING INC
Also Called: Academy Infrared Thermography
702 Kentucky St Ste 720 (98225-4200)
PHONE.................................360 676-1915
Helen Leung, *Director*
David Shaw, *Director*
EMP: 7
SALES (est): 465.5K **Privately Held**
WEB: www.infraredtraining.net
SIC: 3823 Absorption analyzers: infrared, X-ray, etc.: industrial

(G-1239)
ADVANCED COMBUSTN SYSTEMS INC
Also Called: A C S
1999 Alpine Way (98226-7604)
PHONE.................................360 676-6005
Michael Milnes, *President*
Michael Milnes Jr, *Vice Pres*
▼ **EMP:** 23
SQ FT: 10,000
SALES (est): 6.9MM **Privately Held**
WEB: www.acs-acs.com
SIC: 3567 Industrial furnaces & ovens

(G-1240)
ADVANCED POWDER COATING NW
3910 Spur Ridge Ln (98226-1227)
PHONE.................................360 398-1460
Quentin Chambers, *President*
Traci Chambers, *Admin Sec*
EMP: 5
SQ FT: 6,000
SALES (est): 783.9K **Privately Held**
SIC: 3479 Coating of metals & formed products

(G-1241)
ALAS RV
4163 Irongate Rd (98226-8186)
PHONE.................................360 676-1515
Victor Grass, *Principal*
EMP: 4 **EST:** 2012
SALES (est): 426.9K **Privately Held**
SIC: 3799 Recreational vehicles

(G-1242)
ALASKA SEAFOOD HOLDINGS INC (PA)
2825 Roeder Ave (98225)
PHONE.................................360 734-8175
Hank Baumgart, *President*
EMP: 3
SALES (est): 5.4MM **Privately Held**
SIC: 2092 Fresh or frozen packaged fish

(G-1243)
ALL AMERICAN MARINE INC
1010 Hilton Ave (98225-2909)
PHONE.................................360 647-7602
Matthew Mullett, *CEO*
Joseph Hudspeth, *Vice Pres*
Nina Mullett, *Vice Pres*
Delbert McAlpine, *Treasurer*
Nina Dee Mullett, *Admin Sec*
▲ **EMP:** 50
SQ FT: 20,000
SALES (est): 13.4MM **Privately Held**
WEB: www.allamericanmarine.com
SIC: 3732 Boat building & repairing

(G-1244)
ALLSOP INC (PA)
4201 Meridian St (98226-5532)
P.O. Box 23 (98227-0023)
PHONE.................................360 734-9090
▲ **EMP:** 82 **EST:** 1964
SQ FT: 63,000
SALES (est): 16.9MM **Privately Held**
WEB: www.allsop.com
SIC: 3572 5045 Computer storage devices; computers & accessories, personal & home entertainment

(G-1245)
ALTAIR ADVANCED INDUSTRIES
3116 Mercer Ave (98225-8446)
PHONE.................................360 756-4900
David White, *Branch Mgr*
EMP: 40
SALES (corp-wide): 34.3MM **Privately Held**
WEB: www.alpha.com
SIC: 3679 Electronic loads & power supplies
PA: Altair Advanced Industries, Inc.
3765 Alpha Way
Bellingham WA 98226
360 671-7703

(G-1246)
AMERICN-CANADIAN FISHERIES INC
2875 Roeder Ave Ste 8 (98225-2063)
P.O. Box 728 (98227-0728)
PHONE.................................360 398-1117
Andy Vitaljic, *President*
▼ **EMP:** 25
SALES (est): 5.1MM **Privately Held**
SIC: 2091 Canned & cured fish & seafoods

(G-1247)
AMJAY INC
Also Called: Amjay Screenprinting
1420 N Forest St (98225-4505)
PHONE.................................360 676-1165
Michael Green, *President*
Sharon Green, *Vice Pres*
Jessica Dorr, *Admin Sec*
EMP: 9
SQ FT: 3,000
SALES: 600K **Privately Held**
SIC: 5699 2393 T-shirts, custom printed; duffle bags, canvas: made from purchased materials

(G-1248)
ANNETTE KRAFT
1525 Electric Ave (98229-2462)
PHONE.................................501 319-5073
EMP: 2 **EST:** 2014
SALES (est): 62.3K **Privately Held**
SIC: 2022 Mfg Cheese

(G-1249)
APANA INC (PA)
4290 Pacific Hwy Unit A (98226-9319)
PHONE.................................360 746-2276
Frank Burns, *President*
Tom Doll, *Exec VP*
Matt Rose, *Vice Pres*
Matt Peterson, *Info Tech Dir*
EMP: 10
SQ FT: 2,500

Bellingham - Whatcom County (G-1250)

SALES: 1.8MM **Privately Held**
SIC: 7372 7373 Business oriented computer software; computer-aided system services

(G-1250)
APPLIED DIGITAL IMAGING INC
1803 N State St (98225-4606)
PHONE 360 671-9465
Steve Edquist, *CEO*
Donna Edquist, *President*
EMP: 35
SQ FT: 10,000
SALES (est): 4.4MM **Privately Held**
WEB: www.applieddigitalimaging.com
SIC: 2752 7334 Commercial printing, lithographic; blueprinting service

(G-1251)
AQUAMIRA TECHNOLOGIES INC
1411 Meador Ave (98229-5845)
PHONE 360 392-2730
Gary Cruikshank, *Principal*
▼ **EMP:** 3 **EST:** 2012
SALES (est): 236.9K **Privately Held**
SIC: 3559 Smelting & refining machinery & equipment

(G-1252)
ARMSTRONG MAGNETICS INC
700 Sunset Pond Ln Ste 4 (98226-7749)
PHONE 360 647-8438
Dean Ding, *CEO*
▲ **EMP:** 2
SALES (est): 279.8K **Privately Held**
SIC: 3499 Magnets, permanent: metallic

(G-1253)
ARROW MARINE SERVICES INC
2124 E Bakerview Rd (98226-8000)
PHONE 360 733-7008
Jeff Randell, *Manager*
EMP: 5
SALES (est): 294.7K **Privately Held**
SIC: 3443 Industrial vessels, tanks & containers

(G-1254)
ASLAN BREWING COMPANY LLC
1330 N Forest St (98225-4702)
PHONE 360 393-4106
Jack Lamb, *Principal*
Berit Dahl, *Mktg Dir*
Gerry Jimenez, *Marketing Staff*
Austin Martin, *Art Dir*
EMP: 5
SALES (est): 157K **Privately Held**
SIC: 2082 Malt beverages

(G-1255)
B & C FIBERGLASS INC
4823 Guide Meridian (98226)
PHONE 907 842-4767
William Henderson, *President*
Connie Henderson, *Vice Pres*
EMP: 2
SALES (est): 73.4K **Privately Held**
SIC: 2221 Glass & fiberglass broadwoven fabrics

(G-1256)
B & J FIBERGLASS LLC
1005 C St (98225-3900)
PHONE 360 398-9342
Kabith Olsen, *President*
EMP: 3
SQ FT: 6,400
SALES (est): 220K **Privately Held**
SIC: 3732 1799 5551 Boats, fiberglass: building & repairing; fiberglass work; marine supplies

(G-1257)
BARAA WOODWORKING
1428 Ellis St (98225-4904)
PHONE 360 752-0608
Vale Bates, *Principal*
EMP: 2
SALES (est): 234.5K **Privately Held**
SIC: 2431 Millwork

(G-1258)
BARCODE EQUIPMENT RECYLING CO
1135 Kelly Rd (98226-7493)
PHONE 360 393-4232
Kathy Richardson, *Owner*
EMP: 2
SQ FT: 2,800
SALES (est): 137.1K **Privately Held**
SIC: 3577 Bar code (magnetic ink) printers

(G-1259)
BATTERY RECYCLER
1 Par Ln (98229-7940)
PHONE 562 434-4502
Rebecca G Galasso, *Partner*
Frank O Galasso, *Partner*
EMP: 2
SALES (est): 149.1K **Privately Held**
SIC: 3089 8748 7389 Plastic containers, except foam; environmental consultant;

(G-1260)
BAUBLES
937 Sudden Vly (98229)
PHONE 360 647-3857
EMP: 2 **EST:** 2008
SALES (est): 76K **Privately Held**
SIC: 3961 Mfg Costume Jewelry

(G-1261)
BAY TROPHIES & ENGRAVING INC
524 Ohio St (98225-4613)
PHONE 360 676-0868
Kurt B Denedel, *President*
Betty Denadel, *Co-Owner*
EMP: 6
SQ FT: 3,000
SALES (est): 760.6K **Privately Held**
WEB: www.bayengraving.com
SIC: 3479 5999 Engraving jewelry silverware, or metal; trophies & plaques

(G-1262)
BELL CREEK CONTRACTING INC
3145 Mt Baker Hwy (98226-9598)
PHONE 360 592-3300
Thomas J Zender, *President*
EMP: 2
SALES (est): 216.3K **Privately Held**
SIC: 2411 Logging

(G-1263)
BELLINGHAM BUSINESS JOURNAL
1909 Cornwall Ave (98225-3659)
PHONE 360 647-8805
Kris Passey, *President*
Vanessa Blackburn, *Principal*
Emily Hamann, *Editor*
EMP: 6 **EST:** 1991
SALES (est): 314.3K **Privately Held**
WEB: www.thebellinghambusinessjournal.com
SIC: 2711 2741 2721 Newspapers, publishing & printing; miscellaneous publishing; periodicals

(G-1264)
BELLINGHAM BUSINESS MACHINES (PA)
205 N Commercial St (98226-4409)
PHONE 360 734-3630
Douglas D Jones, *Owner*
Rob Horgen, *Sales Mgr*
Taylor Disch, *Sales Staff*
EMP: 8
SQ FT: 5,000
SALES (est): 1.6MM **Privately Held**
WEB: www.bellinghambusinessmachines.com
SIC: 5999 7629 3661 Photocopy machines; business machines & equipment; typewriters; typewriters & business machines; business machine repair, electric; facsimile equipment

(G-1265)
BELLINGHAM ESCAPE
1417 Cornwall Ave A101 (98225-4519)
PHONE 360 519-9213
EMP: 3

SALES (est): 121.2K **Privately Held**
SIC: 2711 Newspapers, publishing & printing

(G-1266)
BELLINGHAM MARINE INDUSTRIES (PA)
1323 Lincoln St (98226-6265)
P.O. Box 8 (98227-0008)
PHONE 360 676-2800
J Everett Babbit, *President*
Phillip Greenman, *Exec VP*
Lee Bazile, *Vice Pres*
Tina Devries, *Vice Pres*
Stan Reimer, *Vice Pres*
◆ **EMP:** 75
SALES (est): 67.7MM **Privately Held**
SIC: 3448 1629 Docks: prefabricated metal; marine construction

(G-1267)
BELLINGHAM PASTA COMPANY
Also Called: Table The
3125 Mercer Ave Ste 101 (98225-8435)
PHONE 360 594-6000
Katie Hinton, *Owner*
Steve Hinton, *Co-Owner*
EMP: 19
SALES (est): 500K **Privately Held**
SIC: 5812 2099 Italian restaurant; pasta, uncooked: packaged with other ingredients

(G-1268)
BELLINGHAM PROMOTIONAL PDTS
2403 James St (98225-3835)
PHONE 360 676-5416
Michael Hahn, *President*
EMP: 3
SQ FT: 1,800
SALES (est): 309.5K **Privately Held**
WEB: www.bellinghampromotional.com
SIC: 2759 5999 2395 7389 Screen printing; banners; embroidery products, except schiffli machine; advertising, promotional & trade show services

(G-1269)
BELLINGHAM SCREEN PRINTING
4410 Northwest Dr (98226-9051)
PHONE 360 920-0114
Laura Steiger, *Principal*
EMP: 2 **EST:** 2008
SALES (est): 248K **Privately Held**
SIC: 2752 Commercial printing, lithographic

(G-1270)
BELLWETHER GATE C LLC
23 Bellwether Way (98225-2954)
PHONE 360 738-1940
EMP: 2 **EST:** 2009
SALES (est): 190K **Privately Held**
SIC: 3087 Custom Compounding-Purchased Resins

(G-1271)
BERGEN & COMPANY
4003 Irongate Rd (98226-8028)
PHONE 360 676-7503
Jan Mortensen, *Owner*
Jim Mortensen, *Owner*
EMP: 10
SQ FT: 5,800
SALES (est): 713.8K **Privately Held**
WEB: www.bergenandco.com
SIC: 5651 2395 2759 Family clothing stores; embroidery & art needlework; screen printing

(G-1272)
BIRCH EQUIPMENT COMPANY INC (PA)
Also Called: Birch Equipment Rental & Sales
1619 Kentucky St (98229-4716)
P.O. Box 30918 (98228-2918)
PHONE 360 734-5744
Sarah Rothenbuhler, *President*
Jeff Blair, *Sales Staff*
Derek Zweegman, *Sales Staff*
EMP: 44
SQ FT: 50,000

SALES (est): 28.6MM **Privately Held**
WEB: www.birchequipment.com
SIC: 5251 3599 5082 7353 Tools; machine shop, jobbing & repair; construction & mining machinery; road construction equipment; general construction machinery & equipment; earth moving equipment, rental or leasing

(G-1273)
BISON BKBINDING LETTERPRESS LP
112 Grand Ave (98225-4463)
PHONE 360 734-0481
Kevin Nelson, *Partner*
Carly James, *Partner*
David James, *Partner*
EMP: 2
SALES (est): 214K **Privately Held**
WEB: www.bisonbookbinding.com
SIC: 2759 Letterpress printing

(G-1274)
BITTER END BOATWORKS
3123 Laurelwood Ave (98225-1429)
PHONE 360 920-3862
Stuart Metler, *Partner*
Jesse Vangolen, *Partner*
EMP: 2
SALES (est): 120K **Privately Held**
SIC: 3732 Boat building & repairing

(G-1275)
BLAZING BANNERS
1780 Iowa St (98229-4702)
PHONE 360 756-9990
Andrea Evans, *President*
Andrew Evans, *Vice Pres*
EMP: 2 **EST:** 1992
SALES (est): 200K **Privately Held**
WEB: www.blazingbanners.com
SIC: 2399 3993 Banners, pennants & flags; signs & advertising specialties

(G-1276)
BLIND EYE BOOKS
1141 Grant St (98225-5210)
PHONE 360 715-9117
Dawn Kimberling, *Owner*
EMP: 3
SALES (est): 183.5K **Privately Held**
SIC: 2731 Books: publishing only

(G-1277)
BLUE HERON LAKE FARMS INC
2136 E Hemmi Rd (98226-9536)
P.O. Box 29312 (98228-1312)
PHONE 360 966-5241
J Cain, *Principal*
EMP: 2
SALES (est): 85.9K **Privately Held**
SIC: 3577 Computer peripheral equipment

(G-1278)
BLUE SEA SYSTEMS INC (DH)
4600 Ryzex Way (98226-7691)
PHONE 360 738-8230
Scott W Renne, *CEO*
David Johnson, *Senior VP*
Craig Smith, *VP Opers*
Jacob Brown, *Production*
Jim Rau, *Engineer*
◆ **EMP:** 50
SALES (est): 13.8MM
SALES (corp-wide): 30.2MM **Privately Held**
SIC: 3643 5088 Bus bars (electrical conductors); marine crafts & supplies
HQ: Power Products, Llc
N85w12545 Westbrook Xing
Menomonee Falls WI 53051
262 293-0600

(G-1279)
BLUE STAR WELDING LLC
6059 Guide Meridian (98226-9751)
PHONE 360 398-7647
Aaron Holder, *Foreman/Supr*
Frank Priebe, *Mng Member*
Jerod Priebe, *Manager*
Shawna McClelland, *Admin Asst*
EMP: 10
SALES: 1MM **Privately Held**
SIC: 7692 Welding repair

GEOGRAPHIC SECTION

Bellingham - Whatcom County (G-1306)

(G-1280)
BORNSTEIN SEAFOODS INC (PA)
1001 Hilton Ave (98225-2908)
P.O. Box 188 (98227-0188)
PHONE..................................360 734-7990
Colin Bornstein, *President*
Rich Griffith, *General Mgr*
Myer J Bornstein, *Principal*
Kevin Larsen, *Vice Pres*
Paige Johnson, *Production*
◆ **EMP:** 75
SQ FT: 30,000
SALES (est): 40.4MM **Privately Held**
WEB: www.bornstein.com
SIC: 2092 Fish, fresh: prepared; fish, frozen: prepared

(G-1281)
BOUNDARY BAY BREWING COMPANY
Also Called: Boundary Bay Brewery & Bistro
1107 Railroad Ave (98225-5007)
P.O. Box 2446 (98227-2446)
PHONE..................................360 647-5593
Edward Bennett, *Owner*
Casey Diggs, *Opers Mgr*
Brian Bendix, *Sales Staff*
Ilana Knudsen, *Sales Staff*
EMP: 30
SQ FT: 5,000
SALES (est): 4.5MM **Privately Held**
WEB: www.bbaybrewery.com
SIC: 2082 5812 5813 7299 Beer (alcoholic beverage); eating places; drinking places; banquet hall facilities; wine & beer

(G-1282)
BREEZE TREES LLC
4845 Guide Meridian (98226-8082)
PHONE..................................808 387-6167
Melissa Ambler, *Principal*
EMP: 3
SALES (est): 31K **Privately Held**
SIC: 0139 3999 0783 ; ; ornamental shrub & tree services

(G-1283)
BROOKS MANUFACTURING CO
2120 Pacific St (98229-5825)
P.O. Box 7 (98227-0007)
PHONE..................................360 733-1700
Dwayne Carter, *President*
Mary E Ferlin, *Vice Pres*
Jeff Clark, *Plant Mgr*
Nancy Garrett, *Treasurer*
EMP: 50
SQ FT: 100,000
SALES (est): 9MM **Privately Held**
WEB: www.brooksmfg.com
SIC: 2439 Trusses, wooden roof

(G-1284)
BROOKS PROPERTIES (PA)
Also Called: Melbrook Equipment
2120 Pacific St (98229-5825)
P.O. Box 7 (98227-0007)
PHONE..................................360 733-5170
John Ferlin, *President*
EMP: 9
SALES (est): 3MM **Privately Held**
SIC: 2511 6513 Wood household furniture; apartment building operators

(G-1285)
BUBBIE BIT N BUNDLE
5 Flower Ct (98229-4413)
PHONE..................................360 733-8315
Anita Bennett, *Principal*
EMP: 2 **EST:** 2013
SALES (est): 101.2K **Privately Held**
SIC: 7372 Prepackaged software

(G-1286)
CABINETS INC
2225 Old Lakeway Dr (98229-5314)
PHONE..................................360 778-1780
EMP: 4 **EST:** 2010
SALES (est): 230K **Privately Held**
SIC: 2434 Mfg Wood Kitchen Cabinets

(G-1287)
CAITAC USA CORP
205 W Smith Rd (98226-9615)
PHONE..................................360 671-1700
Masaji Kaihata, *President*
Naoyuki Ishii, *Vice Pres*
EMP: 262
SQ FT: 20,000
SALES (est): 19MM **Privately Held**
SIC: 2325 7992 Jeans: men's, youths' & boys'; public golf courses
PA: Caitac Holdings Corp.
3-12, Showacho, Kita-Ku
Okayama OKA 700-0

(G-1288)
CAMCO TOOL & PROTOTYPE INC
5395 Everson Goshen Rd (98226-9570)
PHONE..................................360 966-1106
Evan Compton, *President*
Cheryl Compton, *Corp Secy*
EMP: 4
SQ FT: 1,500
SALES (est): 290K **Privately Held**
WEB: www.stirlingeng.com
SIC: 3599 Machine shop, jobbing & repair

(G-1289)
CANFOR USA CORPORATION (DH)
4395 Curtis Rd (98226-9341)
PHONE..................................360 647-2434
Doug Martin, *Owner*
George Layton, *Principal*
Mike Thelen, *Vice Pres*
Kitti McCallum, *Controller*
Jan McGillivray, *Info Tech Dir*
EMP: 47
SQ FT: 5,180
SALES (est): 11.9MM
SALES (corp-wide): 3.8B **Privately Held**
WEB: www.canfor.com
SIC: 2421 Resawing lumber into smaller dimensions
HQ: Canadian Forest Products Ltd
1700 75th Ave W Unit 100
Vancouver BC
604 661-5241

(G-1290)
CANFOR USA CORPORATION
4395 Curtis Rd (98226-9341)
PHONE..................................360 647-2434
George Layton, *President*
EMP: 2
SALES (corp-wide): 3.8B **Privately Held**
WEB: www.canfor.com
SIC: 5031 2439 Lumber: rough, dressed & finished; structural wood members
HQ: Canfor U.S.A. Corporation
4395 Curtis Rd
Bellingham WA 98226
360 647-2434

(G-1291)
CARLSON CUSTOM
1351 Olympic Way (98225-8549)
PHONE..................................360 756-0351
James Carlson, *Principal*
EMP: 5 **EST:** 2008
SALES (est): 459.4K **Privately Held**
SIC: 2541 Counter & sink tops

(G-1292)
CASCADIA NEWSPAPER COMPANY LLC
Also Called: Cascadia Weekly
115 W Magnolia St Ste 210 (98225-4300)
P.O. Box 2833 (98227-2833)
PHONE..................................360 647-8200
Tim Johnson,
Robert Hall,
EMP: 7
SALES (est): 373.2K **Privately Held**
SIC: 2711 Newspapers, publishing & printing

(G-1293)
CAULDRON INVESTMENT GROUP LLC
Also Called: Cauldron Broths
4201 Meridian St Ste 105 (98226-5532)
PHONE..................................360 671-1098
Karl Thomas,
EMP: 8
SALES (est): 250K **Privately Held**
SIC: 2091 Broth, fish & seafood: packaged in cans, jars, etc.

(G-1294)
CDI CUSTOM DESIGN INC
2123 Grant St (98225-4203)
PHONE..................................360 650-1150
Loren J Demuth, *President*
EMP: 35
SQ FT: 10,000
SALES (est): 4.1MM **Privately Held**
WEB: www.signawn.com
SIC: 3444 3993 2431 2499 Awnings & canopies; electric signs; exterior & ornamental woodwork & trim; decorative wood & woodwork

(G-1295)
CENTER FOR EAST ASIAN STUDIES
516 High St (98225-5946)
PHONE..................................360 650-3836
Kathleen Tomlonovic, *Director*
EMP: 35
SALES (est): 1.9MM
SALES (corp-wide): 212.9MM **Privately Held**
WEB: www.wwu.edu
SIC: 2731 8221 Book publishing; colleges universities & professional schools
PA: Western Washington University
516 High St
Bellingham WA 98225
360 650-3000

(G-1296)
CHOCOLATE NECESSITY INC (PA)
Also Called: Chocolate Necessities
4600 Guide Meridian # 109 (98226-9165)
PHONE..................................360 676-0589
Kevin Buck, *President*
EMP: 4
SALES (est): 343.2K **Privately Held**
WEB: www.chocolatenecessities.com
SIC: 2066 5441 Chocolate candy, solid; candy

(G-1297)
CHUCKANUT BAY DISTILLERY INC
1115 Railroad Ave (98225-5007)
PHONE..................................360 739-0361
Matt Howell, *Principal*
▲ **EMP:** 6
SALES (est): 420.1K **Privately Held**
SIC: 2082 Malt beverages

(G-1298)
CLARUS FLUID INTELLIGENCE LLC (HQ)
3145 Mercer Ave Ste 104 (98225-8452)
P.O. Box 5020, Monroe NC (28111-5020)
PHONE..................................360 671-1514
Darryl Mayhorn, *CEO*
EMP: 44
SALES (est): 8.9MM
SALES (corp-wide): 1.1B **Publicly Held**
WEB: www.pgdcorp.com
SIC: 3731 Shipbuilding & repairing
PA: Circor International, Inc.
30 Corporate Dr Ste 200
Burlington MA 01803
781 270-1200

(G-1299)
CLARUS TECHNOLOGIES LLC (DH)
2015 Alpine Way Ste C (98226-8025)
PHONE..................................360 671-1514
Karl Thomas, *President*
Joe Koreis, *President*
▲ **EMP:** 5
SQ FT: 16,000
SALES (est): 55.5K
SALES (corp-wide): 267.4MM **Privately Held**
SIC: 3569 5084 3731 3589 Filters; petroleum industry machinery; shipbuilding & repairing; servicing machines, except dry cleaning, laundry: coin-oper.; hydraulic equipment, installation & service
HQ: Koniag Government Services, Llc
3800 Centerpoint Dr # 502
Anchorage AK 99503
907 561-2668

(G-1300)
CLYDE CURLEY
2112 J St (98225-3329)
PHONE..................................360 738-6862
Clyde Curley, *Principal*
EMP: 2 **EST:** 2012
SALES (est): 109.5K **Privately Held**
SIC: 2731 Books: publishing only

(G-1301)
COASTLINE EQUIPMENT INC
2235 E Bakerview Rd (98226-7153)
PHONE..................................360 734-8509
Kurt Lunde, *President*
Jamie Biery, *Vice Pres*
David Lunde, *Vice Pres*
Ryan Downey, *Engineer*
Andrew Dahl, *Sales Engr*
EMP: 40
SQ FT: 43,000
SALES (est): 12.1MM **Privately Held**
SIC: 3556 Fish & shellfish processing machinery

(G-1302)
CONLAN PRESS INCORPORATED
1050 Larrabee Ave Ste 104 (98225-7367)
PHONE..................................650 267-9651
Connor F Cochran, *CEO*
EMP: 2
SALES (est): 50K **Privately Held**
SIC: 2741 Miscellaneous publishing

(G-1303)
CONTEMPORARY DESIGN CO
Also Called: Shuttle Systems
4201 Meridian St Ste 101 (98226-5532)
PHONE..................................360 599-2833
Gary Graham, *President*
Heather Graham, *Vice Pres*
EMP: 14
SALES (est): 1,000K **Privately Held**
WEB: www.shuttlesystems.com
SIC: 3949 3842 Exercise equipment; surgical appliances & supplies

(G-1304)
CONTERRA INC
1600 Kentucky St Ste A3 (98229-4701)
PHONE..................................360 734-2311
Richard Allan Lipke, *President*
Todd Wagner, *COO*
EMP: 10
SQ FT: 8,000
SALES (est): 1.5MM **Privately Held**
WEB: www.conterra-inc.com
SIC: 3639 Sewing equipment

(G-1305)
CONVEYOR DYNAMICS INC
Also Called: C D I
3633 Alderwood Ave (98225-1107)
PHONE..................................360 671-2200
Lawrence K Nordell, *President*
Michael Thompson, *Treasurer*
Kimber Holkenbrink, *Bookkeeper*
Jeanluc Cornet, *Exec Dir*
EMP: 13
SQ FT: 3,200
SALES (est): 1.7MM **Privately Held**
WEB: www.conveyor-dynamics.com
SIC: 7372 8748 8711 Application computer software; systems analysis or design; engineering services

(G-1306)
CORNERSTONE PRSTHTICS ORTHTICS
3106 Northwest Ave (98225-1608)
PHONE..................................360 734-0298
Thomas Broselle, *Manager*
EMP: 3
SALES (corp-wide): 2.8MM **Privately Held**
SIC: 5999 3842 Orthopedic & prosthesis applications; limbs, artificial
PA: Cornerstone Prosthetics And Orthotics Inc
1300 44th St Se
Everett WA 98203
425 339-2559

Bellingham - Whatcom County (G-1307) — GEOGRAPHIC SECTION

(G-1307)
COUNCIL FOR EDCTL TRVL US AMER
Also Called: Cetusa
220 W Champion St Ste 260 (98225-4390)
PHONE...............................949 940-1140
Jie Chui James, *Branch Mgr*
EMP: 49
SALES (corp-wide): 4.8MM **Privately Held**
SIC: 3851 Spectacles
PA: Council For Educational Travel United States Of America
903 Calle Amanecer # 200
San Clemente CA 92673
949 940-1140

(G-1308)
COUNTERTOPS FOR LESS
4781 Guide Meridian (98226-9167)
PHONE...............................360 306-3921
Richard Bryan, *President*
EMP: 2
SALES (est): 320.7K **Privately Held**
SIC: 2541 Counter & sink tops

(G-1309)
COWDEN INC
Also Called: Cowden Gravel & Ready Mix
3463 Cedarville Rd (98226-9586)
PHONE...............................360 592-4200
Steve Cowden, *President*
Valerie Barker, *Corp Secy*
Leonard Cowden, *Vice Pres*
Jeff Van Beek, *Sales Staff*
Tom Horsmon, *Manager*
EMP: 100 **EST:** 1953
SQ FT: 2,000
SALES (est): 19.3MM **Privately Held**
WEB: www.cowdeninc.com
SIC: 3273 1442 Ready-mixed concrete; gravel mining

(G-1310)
CREATIVE DIMENSIONS
500 N State St Apt 201 (98225-5329)
P.O. Box 1393 (98227-1393)
PHONE...............................360 733-5024
Irwin Slesnick, *Partner*
Carole Slesnick, *Partner*
EMP: 2
SALES (est): 115.3K **Privately Held**
SIC: 3944 Science kits: microscopes, chemistry sets, etc.

(G-1311)
CREATIVE OPENINGS
929 N State St (98225-5071)
PHONE...............................360 671-6420
Tom D Anderson, *Owner*
EMP: 3
SQ FT: 4,000
SALES: 140K **Privately Held**
WEB: www.creativeopenings.com
SIC: 2431 Doors & door parts & trim, wood

(G-1312)
CUT TECHNOLOGIES METAL LLC
3254 Bennett Dr (98225-1114)
P.O. Box 10526, Eugene OR (97440-2526)
PHONE...............................360 733-0460
Mike Cloutier,
Shelley Macdonald, *Admin Asst*
▲ **EMP:** 10
SALES (est): 1.4MM **Privately Held**
WEB: www.cuttech.com
SIC: 3541 Machine tools, metal cutting type

(G-1313)
CUT TECHNOLOGIES USA INC (DH)
3254 Bennett Dr (98225-1114)
P.O. Box 10526, Eugene OR (97440-2526)
PHONE...............................360 733-0460
Mike Cloutier, *President*
Lauren Gaiser, *Controller*
▲ **EMP:** 25 **EST:** 2015
SQ FT: 20,000
SALES (est): 4.9MM
SALES (corp-wide): 169.6MM **Privately Held**
SIC: 3553 7699 3425 Bandsaws, woodworking; knife, saw & tool sharpening & repair; saw blades & handsaws
HQ: Burton Saw & Supply, L.L.C.
1439 W 2nd Ave
Eugene OR 97402
541 683-3337

(G-1314)
CYPRESS DESIGNS LLC
220 Mckenzie Ave (98225-7039)
P.O. Box 4341 (98227-4341)
PHONE...............................360 384-6572
Kevin Schoenmakers, *Engineer*
April Schoenmakers,
Larry Schoenmakers,
EMP: 4
SALES (est): 542.8K **Privately Held**
WEB: www.cypressdesigns.com
SIC: 2821 Molding compounds, plastics

(G-1315)
CYPRESS HOUSEWORKS LLC
511 Cypress Rd (98225-7817)
PHONE...............................360 676-9778
Michael Reeve, *Principal*
EMP: 2
SALES (est): 169.1K **Privately Held**
SIC: 3639 Household appliances

(G-1316)
D HAITRE WOODWORKS LLC
1651 Mt Baker Hwy (98226-8795)
PHONE...............................360 752-0405
EMP: 4 **EST:** 2011
SALES (est): 210K **Privately Held**
SIC: 2431 Mfg Millwork

(G-1317)
D P CLARKE
1225 E Sunset Dr Ste 727 (98226-3597)
PHONE...............................360 647-8185
David P Clarke, *Owner*
EMP: 2 **EST:** 1979
SALES (est): 227.4K **Privately Held**
SIC: 5146 2092 Fish & seafoods; fresh or frozen fish or seafood chowders, soups & stews

(G-1318)
DASHI NOODLE BAR
1900 Dakin St (98229-6011)
PHONE...............................206 595-1995
Josh Silverman, *Principal*
EMP: 8
SALES (est): 492.2K **Privately Held**
SIC: 2098 Noodles (e.g. egg, plain & water), dry

(G-1319)
DAVID WIGHT GLASS ART INC
2111 Lincoln St 102 (98225-4147)
PHONE...............................360 389-2844
David Wight, *Principal*
EMP: 2
SALES (est): 113.9K **Privately Held**
SIC: 3231 Art glass: made from purchased glass

(G-1320)
DEALER INFO SYSTEMS CORP (DH)
1315 Cornwall Ave (98225-4716)
PHONE...............................360 733-7610
Randy McIntyre, *President*
EMP: 92
SQ FT: 25,000
SALES (est): 24.1MM
SALES (corp-wide): 3B **Privately Held**
WEB: www.dis-corp.com
SIC: 7371 7372 7373 Computer software development; business oriented computer software; systems software development services
HQ: Constellation Homebuilder Systems Inc.
888 S Dsnyland Dr Ste 430
Tustin CA 92780
714 768-6100

(G-1321)
DECOMP
2205 Queen St (98229-4752)
PHONE...............................360 306-8516
Ken Manion, *Owner*
EMP: 3 **EST:** 2009
SALES (est): 345K **Privately Held**
SIC: 2657 Folding paperboard boxes

(G-1322)
DEMING LOG SHOW INC
3295 Cedarville Rd (98226-9547)
PHONE...............................360 592-3051
Sandra Bookkeeping, *Principal*
EMP: 2
SALES (est): 161.6K **Privately Held**
SIC: 2411 7389 Logging; accomodation locating services

(G-1323)
DIFFERENTIAL NETWORKS LLC
2229 Grant St (98225)
PHONE...............................360 366-8123
Matthew Bode, *Owner*
EMP: 2 **EST:** 2012
SALES (est): 276.1K **Privately Held**
SIC: 3663 7379 Digital encoders;

(G-1324)
DIVERSIFIED DEVELOPMENT CO
730 Marine Dr (98225-1530)
P.O. Box 1152 (98227-1152)
PHONE...............................360 734-1480
EMP: 5
SALES (est): 380K **Privately Held**
SIC: 1041 Development And Mining Of Gold Properties

(G-1325)
DREAM ON FUTON CO
Also Called: Custom Cusions and Foam
2020 Franklin St Ste 108 (98225-4207)
PHONE...............................360 739-2103
Nancy E Taylor, *President*
Nancy Taylor, *President*
Rachel Taylor, *Corp Secy*
Harley Taylor, *Vice Pres*
EMP: 9
SQ FT: 14,000
SALES (est): 1.1MM **Privately Held**
WEB: www.futondreams.com
SIC: 5712 2392 Beds & accessories; household furnishings

(G-1326)
DRIVE LINE SVC OF BELLINGHAM
Also Called: Drive Line Service Bellingham
2008 Humboldt St (98225-4206)
PHONE...............................360 734-7828
Toll Free:...............................888 -
Norman Bennett Sr, *Owner*
EMP: 3
SQ FT: 2,500
SALES (est): 170K **Privately Held**
SIC: 3714 7539 5531 5084 Motor vehicle parts & accessories; automotive repair shops; automotive & home supply stores; industrial machinery & equipment; speed changers, drives & gears

(G-1327)
DUCOTERRA LLC (PA)
1645 Jills Ct Ste 108 (98226-1217)
PHONE...............................360 788-4200
Patrick Beebe-Sweet, *President*
Brittany Krein, *Manager*
EMP: 4
SQ FT: 2,500
SALES: 180K **Privately Held**
SIC: 3585 3634 5075 3567 Heating equipment, complete; heating units, electric (radiant heat): baseboard or wall; electrical heating equipment; heating units & devices, industrial: electric

(G-1328)
ECHO ULTRASONICS LLC
774 Marine Dr (98225-1530)
PHONE...............................360 671-9121
Margaret Larson,
Eugene Larson,
EMP: 2
SALES: 412.5K **Privately Held**
SIC: 3829 Gauging instruments, thickness ultrasonic

(G-1329)
ECONO SIGN OF AMERICA
2006 James St (98225-4234)
PHONE...............................360 739-8480
EMP: 2 **EST:** 2007
SALES (est): 210.1K **Privately Held**
SIC: 3993 Signs & advertising specialties

(G-1330)
ED STEPHAN
523 13th St (98225-6102)
PHONE...............................360 733-4781
Ed Stephan, *Principal*
EMP: 2
SALES (est): 97.4K **Privately Held**
SIC: 2741 Miscellaneous publishing

(G-1331)
EGIS GROUP LLC
Also Called: Egis Mobile Electric
3135 Mercer Ave Ste 102 (98225-8451)
PHONE...............................360 768-1211
Eric Graham,
EMP: 5
SALES (est): 262.1K **Privately Held**
SIC: 3691 Storage batteries

(G-1332)
ELDRED BROS FARMS LLC
317 W Laurel Rd (98226-7364)
P.O. Box 2907, Ferndale (98248-2907)
PHONE...............................360 398-9757
Wes Eldred, *Mng Member*
EMP: 6
SALES (est): 823K **Privately Held**
SIC: 3523 Tractors, farm

(G-1333)
ELITE ENTERPRISE CO
1349 Lowe Ave (98229-2521)
P.O. Box 30636 (98228-2636)
PHONE...............................360 756-0205
EMP: 2 **EST:** 1974
SALES (est): 153.8K **Privately Held**
SIC: 3353 5064 Mfg Aluminum Sheet/Foil Whol Appliances/Tv/Radio

(G-1334)
EMBROIDERED EFFECTS LLC
1273 Sunset Ave (98226-9048)
PHONE...............................360 380-1928
Karl Lien, *Mng Member*
Lyn D Elton, *Mng Member*
EMP: 4
SALES: 100K **Privately Held**
SIC: 2395 Embroidery products, except schiffli machine

(G-1335)
ENNA PRODUCTS CORPORATION
1602 Carolina St Ste B3 (98229-5491)
PHONE...............................360 306-5369
Norman Bodek, *Partner*
Jun Nakamuro, *Exec Dir*
EMP: 3
SALES (est): 190K **Privately Held**
SIC: 3999 Education aids, devices & supplies

(G-1336)
ENVIRONMENTAL INSUL CONTG LLC
3003 Bennett Dr (98225-1439)
PHONE...............................360 647-2532
Rodney Holmes,
EMP: 22
SALES (est): 565.1K **Privately Held**
SIC: 1799 3296 Fiberglass work; fiberglass insulation

(G-1337)
EPIK INDUSTRIES
753 E Smith Rd (98226-9781)
PHONE...............................360 303-6488
Benjamin Fuller, *Principal*
EMP: 2
SALES (est): 138.5K **Privately Held**
SIC: 3999 Manufacturing industries

GEOGRAPHIC SECTION
Bellingham - Whatcom County (G-1367)

(G-1338)
ERSHIGS INC (HQ)
742 Marine Dr (98225-1596)
P.O. Box 1707 (98227-1707)
PHONE..................360 733-2620
Lynn Tilton, *CEO*
Thomas W Pilcher, *President*
Todd Markham, *General Mgr*
Robert B Bennett, *Vice Pres*
Rod Courtney, *Vice Pres*
EMP: 15
SQ FT: 2,000
SALES (est): 53.7MM **Privately Held**
WEB: www.ershigs.com
SIC: 3084 3089 3444 Plastics pipe; plastic & fiberglass tanks; ducting, plastic; ducts, sheet metal

(G-1339)
EVERGREEN PUBLICATIONS
1443 Lahti Dr (98226-8879)
PHONE..................360 734-4158
EMP: 2 **EST:** 2008
SALES (est): 110K **Privately Held**
SIC: 2741 Misc Publishing

(G-1340)
FABRICATED PLASTICS LIMITED
742 Marine Dr (98225-1530)
PHONE..................360 527-3430
Tom Rhone, *Branch Mgr*
EMP: 2 **Privately Held**
SIC: 3089 Plastic & fiberglass tanks
HQ: Fabricated Plastics Limited
2175 Teston Rd
Maple ON L6A 1
905 832-8161

(G-1341)
FAIRHAVEN GOLD INC
1302 12th St (98225-7153)
PHONE..................360 733-4667
William Lynch, *President*
Dan Lynch, *Corp Secy*
EMP: 2
SQ FT: 500
SALES (est): 201.5K **Privately Held**
SIC: 5944 3911 Jewelry, precious stones & precious metals; jewelry, precious metal

(G-1342)
FAITHLIFE CORPORATION
Also Called: Logos Bible Software
1313 Commercial St (98225-4307)
PHONE..................360 685-2300
Robert Pritchett, *President*
John Barry, *Publisher*
Justin Marr, *Publisher*
Abigail Stocker, *Editor*
Dale R Pritchett, *Vice Pres*
EMP: 150
SALES (est): 25MM **Privately Held**
WEB: www.logos.com
SIC: 7371 2791 Computer software development; typesetting

(G-1343)
FAT-CAT FISH LLC
6069 Hannegan Rd (98226-7433)
PHONE..................360 715-1994
Erin Vitaljic, *President*
EMP: 20 **EST:** 2008
SALES (est): 4.1MM **Privately Held**
SIC: 2048 Fish food

(G-1344)
FEDEX OFFICE & PRINT SVCS INC
501 E Holly St (98225-4708)
PHONE..................360 647-1114
EMP: 24
SALES (corp-wide): 69.6B **Publicly Held**
WEB: www.kinkos.com
SIC: 7334 7359 2789 7377 Photocopying & duplicating services; equipment rental & leasing; bookbinding & related work; computer rental & leasing
HQ: Fedex Office And Print Services, Inc.
7900 Legacy Dr
Plano TX 75024
800 463-3339

(G-1345)
FERGUSON WOODWORKING INC
5978 Guide Meridian (98226-9720)
PHONE..................360 398-1543
John Ferguson, *President*
EMP: 4
SQ FT: 4,800
SALES (est): 300K **Privately Held**
SIC: 2511 2434 Wood household furniture; wood kitchen cabinets

(G-1346)
FISHERS CHOICE WILD SALMON
1081 Sudden Vly (98229)
PHONE..................360 671-6478
Anne Mosness, *Owner*
EMP: 2
SALES (est): 68.6K **Privately Held**
SIC: 2091 Salmon, cured

(G-1347)
FIXTURE ENGINEERING INC
1600 Kentucky St A5 (98229-4701)
PHONE..................360 671-9052
Robert Johnston, *President*
EMP: 6
SQ FT: 5,000
SALES (est): 650K **Privately Held**
WEB: www.fixture-eng.com
SIC: 3441 5051 5211 Fabricated structural metal; metals service centers & offices; lumber & other building materials

(G-1348)
FIZIKL INC
114 Park Pl (98226-9414)
PHONE..................360 393-0714
Thomas Malone, *Principal*
Mark Pedro, *CFO*
EMP: 2
SALES (est): 62.1K **Privately Held**
SIC: 7372 7389 Business oriented computer software;

(G-1349)
FLAX 4 LIFE
468 W Horton Rd (98226-1205)
PHONE..................360 715-1944
William Francis, *Owner*
Kathy Francis, *Office Mgr*
Jason Shippen, *Maintence Staff*
EMP: 8
SALES (est): 642.6K **Privately Held**
WEB: www.flax4life.net
SIC: 2051 Bakery products, partially cooked (except frozen)

(G-1350)
FLOWSERVE CORPORATION
1305 Fraser St Ste 108 (98229-5840)
PHONE..................360 676-0702
Keith Stothers, *Manager*
EMP: 5
SALES (corp-wide): 3.8B **Publicly Held**
SIC: 3561 Industrial pumps & parts
PA: Flowserve Corporation
5215 N Oconnor Blvd Connor
Irving TX 75039
972 443-6500

(G-1351)
FLYING TROUT PRESS
3712 Lahti Ct (98226-6822)
PHONE..................360 647-5740
Charles W Luckmann, *Principal*
Charles Luckmann, *Principal*
EMP: 2
SALES (est): 123.5K **Privately Held**
SIC: 2741 Miscellaneous publishing

(G-1352)
FOUR U PRINTERS INC
Also Called: Printing For You
1704 N State St (98225-4605)
P.O. Box 30846 (98228-2846)
PHONE..................360 671-2032
Jude K Urich, *President*
Mark G Urich, *Vice Pres*
EMP: 4
SQ FT: 1,100
SALES (est): 275K **Privately Held**
SIC: 2752 Commercial printing, offset

(G-1353)
FOWNES BROTHERS & CO INC
Also Called: Tabar West
100 Pine St Ste 202 (98225-5463)
PHONE..................360 738-3126
Allan Martinez, *Manager*
EMP: 5
SALES (corp-wide): 76.1MM **Privately Held**
WEB: www.tabarinc.com
SIC: 3949 5137 Gloves, sport & athletic: boxing, handball, etc.; gloves, women's & children's
PA: Fownes Brothers & Co Inc
16 E 34th St Fl 5
New York NY 10016
212 683-0150

(G-1354)
FRIEDMAN SLVERSMITHS REPR PLTG
1323 Euclid Ave (98229-5104)
PHONE..................360 752-3119
David Friedman, *Principal*
EMP: 3 **EST:** 2008
SALES (est): 265.7K **Privately Held**
SIC: 3914 3471 Silversmithing; electroplating & plating

(G-1355)
FUNNY FEELING
3620 Irongate Rd (98226-8052)
P.O. Box 2806 (98227-2806)
PHONE..................360 671-7386
Jeff Galbraith, *Principal*
Jennica Lowell, *Marketing Staff*
Matt Wibby, *Marketing Staff*
EMP: 2
SALES (est): 73.1K **Privately Held**
SIC: 2721 Periodicals

(G-1356)
GAGNE INTERNATIONAL LLC
4237 Cedar Hills Ct (98229-2508)
PHONE..................360 733-9500
Michel Gagne, *Principal*
EMP: 2
SALES (est): 137.3K **Privately Held**
SIC: 2741 Miscellaneous publishing

(G-1357)
GEOCOM RESOURCES INC
114 W Magnolia St Ste 143 (98225-4478)
PHONE..................360 392-2898
John E Hiner, *President*
EMP: 2
SALES (est): 140K **Privately Held**
SIC: 1481 Nonmetallic minerals development & test boring

(G-1358)
GOODMANS SKI AND SPORTS INC
602 W Lake Samish Dr (98229-9370)
PHONE..................360 733-8937
John M Goodman, *President*
Lucy Goodman, *Corp Secy*
Ron Goodman, *Vice Pres*
Terry Goodman, *Vice Pres*
EMP: 3
SALES (est): 130K **Privately Held**
SIC: 5941 8299 3949 Water sport equipment; educational service, nondegree granting: continuing educ.; water skiing equipment & supplies, except skis

(G-1359)
GORMAN PUBLICITY
1011 Queen St (98229-2139)
PHONE..................360 676-9393
Taimi D Gorman, *Principal*
EMP: 2
SALES (est): 144.3K **Privately Held**
SIC: 2741 Miscellaneous publishing

(G-1360)
GRASSROOTS WOODWORKS LLC
5879 Milwaukee Rd (98226-7514)
PHONE..................360 836-1313
Jasmine Filley, *Principal*
EMP: 2
SALES (est): 172.9K **Privately Held**
SIC: 2426 2511 Carvings, furniture: wood; wood bedroom furniture

(G-1361)
GRAY MOLD COMPANY INC
3870 Mustang Way Ste 101 (98226-8026)
P.O. Box 30140 (98228-2140)
PHONE..................360 671-5711
Keith Gray, *President*
Susan Gray, *Admin Sec*
Susan A Gray, *Admin Sec*
EMP: 17
SALES (est): 3.4MM **Privately Held**
WEB: www.graymold.com
SIC: 3365 3544 3324 Aluminum & aluminum-based alloy castings; special dies, tools, jigs & fixtures; steel investment foundries

(G-1362)
GREG AANES FURNITURE INC
2109 Queen St (98229-4754)
PHONE..................360 733-9101
Gregory Aanes, *President*
Heather Aanes, *Admin Sec*
◆ **EMP:** 4
SQ FT: 1,000
SALES (est): 422.5K **Privately Held**
SIC: 2511 Rockers, except upholstered: wood

(G-1363)
GROWFAST SOFTWARE
2300 Taylor Ave Apt 8 (98225-6451)
PHONE..................360 224-5484
Don Harland, *President*
EMP: 2
SALES (est): 94.4K **Privately Held**
WEB: www.websolver.com
SIC: 7372 Prepackaged software

(G-1364)
GUNDIES INC (PA)
Also Called: Gundie's Auto & Truck Wrecking
1283 Mt Baker Hwy (98226-8797)
PHONE..................360 733-5036
Peter Gunderson, *President*
Don Johnson, *Corp Secy*
Harvey Gunderson, *Vice Pres*
Dion Solheim, *Sales Mgr*
Jason Weirauch, *Sales Mgr*
EMP: 26
SQ FT: 4,800
SALES (est): 6MM **Privately Held**
WEB: www.gundies.com
SIC: 5015 5093 3312 Automotive supplies, used; ferrous metal scrap & waste; blast furnaces & steel mills

(G-1365)
HARD DRIVE MARINE
3620 Irongate Rd (98226-8052)
P.O. Box 573 (98227-0573)
PHONE..................360 306-8685
Tom Day, *Principal*
EMP: 2
SALES (est): 259.8K **Privately Held**
SIC: 3732 Boat building & repairing

(G-1366)
HARRIS ACQUISITION IV LLC (HQ)
3436 Airport Dr (98226-8068)
PHONE..................360 734-3600
Gregory J Hosch, *CEO*
Michel Michno, *COO*
Gregory A Donley, *CFO*
EMP: 3
SALES (est): 334.7K **Privately Held**
SIC: 1711 3498 Plumbing contractors; pipe sections fabricated from purchased pipe

(G-1367)
HARRIS ACQUISITION IV LLC
Also Called: Diamond B Constructors
3436 Airport Dr (98226-8068)
PHONE..................360 734-3600
Pete Chapman, *Branch Mgr*
EMP: 2 **Privately Held**
SIC: 1711 3498 Plumbing contractors; pipe sections fabricated from purchased pipe
HQ: Harris Acquisition Iv, Llc
3436 Airport Dr
Bellingham WA 98226
360 734-3600

Bellingham - Whatcom County (G-1368)

(G-1368)
HEININGER HOLDINGS LLC
Also Called: Heininger Automotive
2222 Queen St (98229-4753)
PHONE..................................360 756-2411
David Dorn, *Marketing Staff*
Jeffrey V Heininger,
Jeffrey Zink,
Renee Zink,
▲ **EMP:** 8
SQ FT: 8,000
SALES (est): 1.2MM **Privately Held**
WEB: www.rackbiz.com
SIC: 5531 3429 3751 3714 Automotive accessories; bicycle racks, automotive; ski racks, automotive; motorcycles, bicycles & parts; motor vehicle parts & accessories

(G-1369)
HERITAGE GBC
3715 Irongate Rd (98226-8055)
P.O. Box 388, Everson (98247-0388)
PHONE..................................360 392-8541
EMP: 6 **EST:** 2014
SALES (est): 655.5K **Privately Held**
SIC: 2653 Corrugated & solid fiber boxes

(G-1370)
HIGHER PLANE CABINETWORKS
1905 Division St (98226-8043)
PHONE..................................360 733-4322
Kris Pflueger, *Vice Pres*
Lou Geri, *Vice Pres*
Cindy Geri, *Treasurer*
EMP: 10
SQ FT: 18,000
SALES: 931.7K **Privately Held**
SIC: 2541 2542 1751 Cabinets, lockers & shelving; cabinets: show, display or storage: except wood; cabinet & finish carpentry

(G-1371)
HOMAX GROUP INC
1835 Barkley Blvd Ste 101 (98226-3200)
PHONE..................................360 733-9029
Ross Clawson, *President*
Carolyn Resar, *Principal*
▲ **EMP:** 32
SALES (est): 29.8MM
SALES (corp-wide): 15.3B **Publicly Held**
WEB: www.homaxgroup.com
SIC: 2851 2879 5198 2813 Paint removers; insecticides & pesticides; paints, varnishes & supplies; aerosols
PA: Ppg Industries, Inc.
1 Ppg Pl
Pittsburgh PA 15272
412 434-3131

(G-1372)
HOME PORT SEAFOOD INC
2875 Roeder Ave Ste 11 (98225-2063)
PHONE..................................360 676-4707
Glen Binschus, *Owner*
Jeanne Binchus, *Co-Owner*
EMP: 80
SQ FT: 10,000
SALES (est): 4.8MM **Privately Held**
SIC: 2092 Seafoods, fresh: prepared

(G-1373)
HOT YOGA ELEMENTS
1308 Meador Ave Ste 103 (98229-5815)
PHONE..................................360 676-9642
EMP: 2
SALES (est): 74.4K **Privately Held**
SIC: 2819 Elements

(G-1374)
HOYEM PUBLICATIONS INC
229 Middlefield Rd (98225-7721)
PHONE..................................360 676-0864
Richard Koplowitz, *Principal*
EMP: 2
SALES (est): 122.8K **Privately Held**
SIC: 2741 Miscellaneous publishing

(G-1375)
HUNNICUTTS TRUCK SHOP INC
3910 Bakerview Spur (98226-8057)
PHONE..................................360 734-9859
Steve Hunnicutt, *President*
EMP: 8
SQ FT: 6,000
SALES (est): 1.4MM **Privately Held**
SIC: 3479 7532 Painting, coating & hot dipping; body shop, trucks

(G-1376)
INDEX INDUSTRIES INC
Also Called: Index Sensors & Controls
300 Harris Ave (98225-7021)
PHONE..................................360 629-5200
Steven E Anderson, *President*
Cindy Mc Graw, *Accounts Mgr*
▲ **EMP:** 55
SQ FT: 30,000
SALES (est): 13.8MM **Privately Held**
WEB: www.indexsensors.com
SIC: 3822 Switches, thermostatic

(G-1377)
INFOSOFT SOLUTIONS INC
229 Jerome St (98229-6505)
PHONE..................................360 738-3060
Robert Dentel, *President*
EMP: 5
SALES (est): 480K **Privately Held**
WEB: www.goinfosoft.com
SIC: 7372 7371 Educational computer software; computer software development

(G-1378)
INNOTECH METAL DESIGNS LLC
Also Called: Innotech Process Equipment
5971 Gide Mrdian Bllngham (98226)
PHONE..................................360 393-4108
Tracy Kaptein, *Bookkeeper*
Tim Kaptein, *Mng Member*
EMP: 10
SQ FT: 25,000
SALES (est): 1MM **Privately Held**
SIC: 3556 3462 3312 Smokers, food processing equipment; machinery forgings, ferrous; fence posts, iron & steel

(G-1379)
INNOVATIVE MANUFACTURING INC
Also Called: Whats On Tap
2118 E Hemmi Rd (98226-9536)
PHONE..................................360 966-7250
Kerry Carlson, *President*
Cathy Carlson, *Vice Pres*
EMP: 2
SALES: 150K **Privately Held**
WEB: www.inno-mfg.com
SIC: 3585 2499 Beer dispensing equipment; engraved wood products

(G-1380)
INTEGRATED SYSTEMS DESIGN
3924 Irongate Rd Ste B (98226-9190)
PHONE..................................360 746-0812
Robert Sloan, *Principal*
William Steinkamp,
EMP: 4
SALES (est): 466.2K **Privately Held**
SIC: 3799 3715 3448 3441 Trailers & trailer equipment; demountable cargo containers; prefabricated metal buildings; fabricated structural metal; bag seaming & closing machines (sewing machinery); canvas & related products

(G-1381)
INTERLUBE INTERNATIONAL INC
801 Harris Ave 1 (98225-7030)
PHONE..................................360 734-3832
Jeff H Kent, *President*
Paul Lolkema, *Vice Pres*
EMP: 22
SQ FT: 25,000
SALES (est): 2.9MM **Privately Held**
SIC: 2992 5172 Lubricating oils & greases; petroleum products

(G-1382)
INTERNATIONAL LONGLINE SUPPLY
2207 Valencia St Ste 103 (98229-4775)
PHONE..................................360 650-0412
Luhr Jensen, *President*
Eric Jensen, *President*
▲ **EMP:** 3
SQ FT: 20,000
SALES: 650K **Privately Held**
SIC: 3949 Fishing equipment; fishing tackle, general

(G-1383)
IRON STREET PRINTING LLC
1421 N Forest St (98225-4504)
PHONE..................................360 734-5809
EMP: 2
SALES (est): 83.9K **Privately Held**
SIC: 2752 Commercial printing, lithographic

(G-1384)
IRONGATE MACHINE INC
Also Called: Iron Gate Machine
4030 Irongate Rd (98226-8028)
PHONE..................................360 734-4718
Richard Rudy, *President*
Paul Berube, *Production*
Brian Reilly, *Manager*
Trudy Marino, *Office Admin*
Zack Offen, *Prgrmr*
EMP: 15
SQ FT: 23,000
SALES (est): 2.4MM **Privately Held**
WEB: www.irongatemachine.com
SIC: 3599 Machine shop, jobbing & repair

(G-1385)
ITEKENERGY LLC
Also Called: Itek Energy
3886 Hammer Dr (98226-7629)
PHONE..................................360 647-9531
John Flanagan, *CEO*
David McCarty, *COO*
Kelly Samson, *Vice Pres*
▲ **EMP:** 66
SQ FT: 40,000
SALES (est): 18.2MM **Privately Held**
SIC: 3674 Solar cells

(G-1386)
J J J FARMS INC
Also Called: Triple J Farms
777 Jorgensen Pl (98226-9794)
PHONE..................................360 398-8641
Donald Jorgensen, *President*
Jay Jorgensen, *Vice Pres*
EMP: 5
SQ FT: 4,000
SALES: 500K **Privately Held**
SIC: 2835 Veterinary diagnostic substances

(G-1387)
JARVIS SAW MILL LLC
317 Chuckanut Point Rd (98229-8926)
P.O. Box 31668 (98228-3668)
PHONE..................................360 733-7591
EMP: 2
SALES (est): 93.6K **Privately Held**
SIC: 2421 Sawmills & planing mills, general

(G-1388)
JOHN GIBB
5214 Guide Meridian (98226-8091)
P.O. Box 875, Ferndale (98248-0875)
PHONE..................................360 366-3500
John Gibb, *President*
EMP: 3
SALES (est): 156.4K **Privately Held**
WEB: www.chemco.org
SIC: 2491 Preserving (creosoting) of wood

(G-1389)
KALHOVDE BOAT WORKS
4855 N King Mountain Rd (98226-9117)
PHONE..................................360 398-1262
EMP: 2
SALES (est): 144.4K **Privately Held**
SIC: 3732 Boat building & repairing

(G-1390)
KAMAN FLUID POWER LLC
Also Called: Parker Store, The
4125 Bakerview Spur Ste C (98226-7148)
PHONE..................................360 738-1264
Chris Collins, *Manager*
EMP: 3
SALES (corp-wide): 1.8B **Publicly Held**
SIC: 5084 3492 5085 Hydraulic systems equipment & supplies; hose & tube fittings & assemblies, hydraulic/pneumatic; valves & fittings
HQ: Kaman Fluid Power, Llc
1 Vision Way
Bloomfield CT 06002
860 243-7100

(G-1391)
KASHOO CLOUD ACUNTING USA INC
1210 Lakeview St (98229-2516)
PHONE..................................888 520-5274
Jim Secord, *President*
EMP: 25
SALES (est): 972.2K **Privately Held**
SIC: 7372 7389 Business oriented computer software;

(G-1392)
KENT LABORATORIES INC
777 Jorgensen Pl (98226-9794)
PHONE..................................360 398-8641
Donald A Jorgensen, *President*
Mary Jorgensen, *Corp Secy*
Allen H Jorgensen, *Shareholder*
EMP: 10
SQ FT: 4,000
SALES (est): 1.1MM **Privately Held**
WEB: www.kentlabs.com
SIC: 3841 2835 Diagnostic apparatus, medical; in vitro & in vivo diagnostic substances

(G-1393)
KEWANNA SCREEN PRINTING INC
130 S 46th St (98229-2199)
PHONE..................................574 817-0682
Ben Fehrer, *President*
EMP: 2
SALES (est): 83.9K **Privately Held**
SIC: 2752 Commercial printing, lithographic

(G-1394)
KILN CART CONSTRUCTION
Also Called: Kiln Kart Fabrication
5590 Knight Rd (98226-9503)
PHONE..................................360 319-0414
Robert J Bertschinger, *Owner*
EMP: 2
SALES: 95K **Privately Held**
SIC: 3449 Bars, concrete reinforcing: fabricated steel

(G-1395)
KING & PRINCE SEAFOOD CORP
Also Called: Cascade Seafoods
710 Squalicum Way (98225)
P.O. Box 5221 (98227-5221)
PHONE..................................360 733-9090
Terrill Beck, *Principal*
EMP: 45 **Privately Held**
SIC: 2092 Fresh or frozen packaged fish
HQ: King & Prince Seafood Corporation
1 King And Prince Blvd
Brunswick GA 31520
912 265-5155

(G-1396)
KINGSFORD SMITH CHARLES
4312 Cordero Dr (98229-5135)
PHONE..................................360 738-6959
Helen Packer, *Principal*
EMP: 3
SALES (est): 239.7K **Privately Held**
SIC: 2861 Charcoal, except activated

(G-1397)
KOBELT MANUFACTURING
700 Coho Way (98225-2057)
PHONE..................................360 676-2774
EMP: 2
SALES (est): 68.7K **Privately Held**
SIC: 3999 Manufacturing industries

(G-1398)
KOMBUCHA TOWN
1155 N State St Ste 603 (98225-5024)
PHONE..................................360 224-2974
Kyle Petershagen, *Marketing Staff*
EMP: 5 **EST:** 2013
SALES (est): 302.1K **Privately Held**
SIC: 2086 Tea, iced: packaged in cans, bottles, etc.

GEOGRAPHIC SECTION

Bellingham - Whatcom County (G-1430)

(G-1399)
KULSHAN BREWING COMPANY (PA)
1538 Kentucky St (98229-4720)
PHONE....................360 389-5348
David Vitt, *President*
Jen Lamb, *Manager*
EMP: 2
SALES (est): 280.3K **Privately Held**
SIC: 2082 Beer (alcoholic beverage)

(G-1400)
LA BELLE ASSOCIATES INC
4100 Marblemount Ln (98226-7760)
PHONE....................360 671-5122
Galen Wiebe, *Branch Mgr*
EMP: 19
SALES (corp-wide): 30.1MM **Privately Held**
SIC: 2048 Feed concentrates
HQ: La Belle Associates, Inc.
  4040 Bakerview Spur
  Bellingham WA 98226

(G-1401)
LAKE SAMISH TERRACE PARK
921 Autumn Ln (98229-8511)
PHONE....................360 671-2741
Doug White, *Owner*
Lynn White, *Co-Owner*
EMP: 2
SALES (est): 150K **Privately Held**
SIC: 2451 Mobile homes

(G-1402)
LARSON RV PUBLISHING
1020 E Bakerview Rd (98226-9182)
PHONE....................360 733-8576
EMP: 2
SALES (est): 145.5K **Privately Held**
SIC: 2741 Misc Publishing

(G-1403)
LD FOREST INC
1964 N Springfield Ct (98229-6860)
P.O. Box 2365 (98227-2365)
PHONE....................360 733-1606
Victor Devlin, *CEO*
EMP: 4
SALES (est): 545.7K **Privately Held**
SIC: 2421 Kiln drying of lumber; box lumber; lumber stacking or sticking; lumber: rough, sawed or planed

(G-1404)
LE BEAU TAPIS
819 14th St (98225-6303)
PHONE....................360 734-9786
Drew Winbacker, *Partner*
EMP: 2
SALES (est): 168.3K **Privately Held**
WEB: www.lebeautapis.com
SIC: 2273 Carpets & rugs

(G-1405)
LEHIGH NORTHWEST CEMENT CO
Also Called: Tilbury Cement
741 Marine Dr (98225-1529)
P.O. Box 37 (98227-0037)
PHONE....................360 733-6720
Wayne Bratz, *Manager*
EMP: 11
SALES (corp-wide): 20.6B **Privately Held**
SIC: 3241 5032 Portland cement; cement
HQ: Lehigh Northwest Cement Co
  2115 N 30th St Ste 202
  Tacoma WA 98403
  800 752-6794

(G-1406)
LEISURE HOME & SPA
1813 Dakin St (98229-6012)
P.O. Box 31940 (98228-3940)
PHONE....................360 647-5529
Jerry L Hawkins, *Principal*
EMP: 2
SALES (est): 131.5K **Privately Held**
SIC: 3999 Hot tub & spa covers

(G-1407)
LEMAC MANUFACTURING CO INC
3890 Hammer Dr (98226-7629)
PHONE....................360 756-1720
Laurel McIntosh, *President*
David Bussell, *Corp Secy*
EMP: 7
SQ FT: 6,500
SALES (est): 1.2MM **Privately Held**
WEB: www.lemacmanufacturing.com
SIC: 3089 Thermoformed finished plastic products; plastic processing

(G-1408)
LFS INC
Also Called: Lfs Sports & Specialty Netting
901 Harris Ave (98225-7006)
PHONE....................360 734-6825
Dudley Nightingale, *Manager*
EMP: 40
SALES (corp-wide): 2.3B **Privately Held**
SIC: 5091 5941 3731 Fishing equipment & supplies; fishing equipment; trawlers, building & repairing
HQ: Lfs, Inc.
  851 Coho Way Ste 200
  Bellingham WA 98225
  360 734-3336

(G-1409)
LFS INC (HQ)
Also Called: Lummi Fisheries Supplies
851 Coho Way Ste 200 (98225-2070)
PHONE....................360 734-3336
Joseph Bundrant, *CEO*
◆ EMP: 30
SQ FT: 20,000
SALES (est): 32.2MM
SALES (corp-wide): 2.3B **Privately Held**
SIC: 5091 5941 3731 Fishing equipment & supplies; fishing equipment; trawlers, building & repairing
PA: Trident Seafoods Corporation
  5303 Shilshole Ave Nw
  Seattle WA 98107
  206 783-3818

(G-1410)
LIGHTHOUSE CANDLES
2114 King St (98225-4144)
PHONE....................360 671-2598
Anne Klos, *Partner*
EMP: 2
SALES (est): 99.7K **Privately Held**
SIC: 5199 3999 Candles; candles

(G-1411)
LITHTEX NORTHWEST LLC (PA)
2000 Kentucky St (98229-4730)
PHONE....................360 676-1977
Dianne Jorgenson, *President*
Scott Wheeler, *Vice Pres*
Lynelle Jones, *Project Mgr*
Karen Sheppard, *Project Mgr*
Brenda Garcia, *Human Resources*
EMP: 10
SALES (est): 3.1MM **Privately Held**
WEB: www.lithtexnw.com
SIC: 2752 Commercial printing, offset

(G-1412)
LKQ CORPORATION
Also Called: Lkq Bellingham
2020 E Bakerview Rd (98226-9100)
PHONE....................800 733-1916
EMP: 3
SALES (corp-wide): 11.8B **Publicly Held**
SIC: 5013 3592 Automotive engines & engine parts; carburetors, pistons, rings, valves
PA: Lkq Corporation
  500 W Madison St Ste 2800
  Chicago IL 60661
  312 621-1950

(G-1413)
LOKI SYSTEMS INC
119 N Coml St Ste 190 (98225)
PHONE....................800 961-5654
EMP: 2
SALES (est): 56.5K **Privately Held**
SIC: 7372 Business oriented computer software

(G-1414)
LOQU8 INC
1200 Harris Ave Ste 413 (98225-7151)
PHONE....................650 892-8901
E Timothy Uy, *President*
EMP: 2
SALES: 0 **Privately Held**
SIC: 7372 Application computer software

(G-1415)
LUMMI ISLAND WILD CO-OP L L C
3131 Mercer Ave Ste 105 (98225-8445)
PHONE....................360 366-8786
Keith Carpenter, *Principal*
EMP: 3
SALES (est): 135.6K **Privately Held**
SIC: 2399 Fishing nets

(G-1416)
M3 MACHINE INC
4290 Pacific Hwy (98229-9319)
PHONE....................360 778-1427
Steven Wynkoop, *President*
Kelly Wynkoop, *Treasurer*
EMP: 2
SALES (est): 187.2K **Privately Held**
SIC: 3599 Machine shop, jobbing & repair

(G-1417)
MAAX HYDRO SWIRL MFG CO
2150 Division St (98226-9129)
PHONE....................360 734-0616
Placide Poulin, *Ch of Bd*
EMP: 90
SQ FT: 65,000
SALES (est): 11.2MM **Privately Held**
SIC: 3088 3949 Hot tubs, plastic or fiberglass; sporting & athletic goods

(G-1418)
MAC & MAC ELECTRIC COMPANY
1410 Iowa St (98229-4710)
PHONE....................360 734-6530
Edwin Pankow, *President*
EMP: 4
SQ FT: 4,800
SALES (est): 611.8K **Privately Held**
WEB: www.macandmacelectric.com
SIC: 7694 5999 5063 Electric motor repair; rewinding services; motors, electric; motors, electric

(G-1419)
MAD CAT SALSA
1 Granite Cir (98229-7853)
PHONE....................360 647-0456
Janet Reynolds, *Owner*
EMP: 2
SQ FT: 600
SALES (est): 96.7K **Privately Held**
SIC: 2035 Pickles, sauces & salad dressings

(G-1420)
MAG LITE WARRANTY
5060 Zander Dr (98226-7407)
PHONE....................360 398-9798
EMP: 2
SALES (est): 160K **Privately Held**
SIC: 3648 Mfg Lighting Equipment

(G-1421)
MAN PIES
1215 Railroad Ave (98225-5035)
PHONE....................360 201-4294
Bryce S Sharp, *Owner*
EMP: 4
SALES (est): 16K **Privately Held**
SIC: 2038 Frozen specialties

(G-1422)
MANTHEYS COUNTRY MOBILE PARK
838 W Axton Rd Trlr 31 (98226-9687)
PHONE....................360 384-5623
John Kunz, *Principal*
EMP: 3 EST: 2007
SALES (est): 300.1K **Privately Held**
SIC: 2451 Mobile homes

(G-1423)
MARATHON N MORE
4152 Meridian St Ste 105 (98226-5589)
PHONE....................360 380-5242
Julia Creech, *Owner*
Marcus Creech, *Co-Owner*
EMP: 2
SALES (est): 89.5K **Privately Held**
WEB: www.marathonmemoriesnmore.com
SIC: 3911 7699 Medals, precious or semi-precious metal; typewriter repair, including electric

(G-1424)
MARLENE MARSHALL
Also Called: 3a Guide
1430 Mt Baker Hwy (98226-8757)
PHONE....................360 733-6479
Ron Marshall, *Owner*
EMP: 2
SALES (est): 86K **Privately Held**
SIC: 2741 Business service newsletters; publishing & printing

(G-1425)
MARTIN BOATS INC
5415 Bel West Dr (98226-9034)
PHONE....................360 380-7331
Warren Martin, *President*
Colleen Martin, *Corp Secy*
EMP: 5
SQ FT: 11,000
SALES (est): 447K **Privately Held**
SIC: 3732 0912 Boats, fiberglass: building & repairing; finfish

(G-1426)
MATH PERSPECTIVES
134 Prince Ave Ste H (98226-6703)
P.O. Box 29418 (98228-1418)
PHONE....................360 715-2782
Sheryll Russel, *Mng Member*
Kathy Richardson,
EMP: 3
SALES (est): 177.5K **Privately Held**
WEB: www.mathperspectives.com
SIC: 8999 8331 8748 2741 Writing for publication; job training & vocational rehabilitation services; educational consultant; miscellaneous publishing

(G-1427)
MATSUNAMI GLASS USA INC
1971 Midway Ln Ste K (98226-7682)
P.O. Box 32556 (98228-4556)
PHONE....................360 302-5575
Dan Cybula, *President*
▲ EMP: 2
SQ FT: 2,000
SALES: 1MM **Privately Held**
SIC: 3231 Laboratory glassware

(G-1428)
MCCLATCHY NEWSPAPERS INC
Also Called: Bellingham Herald
1155 N State St (98225-5037)
PHONE....................360 676-2600
Christine Chin, *Branch Mgr*
EMP: 150
SALES (corp-wide): 807.2MM **Publicly Held**
WEB: www.sacbee.com
SIC: 2711 Commercial printing & newspaper publishing combined
HQ: Mcclatchy Newspapers, Inc.
  2100 Q St
  Sacramento CA 95816
  916 321-1855

(G-1429)
MCLEOD MASONRY USA INC
38ab Sound Way (98227)
P.O. Box 9754 (98227-9754)
PHONE....................360 734-4427
Gordon McLeod, *CEO*
EMP: 15
SALES (est): 595.8K **Privately Held**
WEB: www.mcleodmasonry.com
SIC: 1389 Construction, repair & dismantling services

(G-1430)
MCMANN & TATE INC
831 Reveille St (98229-8804)
PHONE....................360 676-4396
Alan Crug, *Owner*
EMP: 2
SALES (est): 149.6K **Privately Held**
SIC: 2759 Commercial printing

Bellingham - Whatcom County (G-1431)

(G-1431)
MCNETT CORPORATION
1411 Meador Ave (98229-5845)
PHONE...................360 671-2227
Travis Huisman, *CEO*
Duane V McNett, *President*
Nancy B McNett, *CFO*
▲ **EMP:** 45
SQ FT: 25,000
SALES (est): 17.2MM
SALES (corp-wide): 14.5MM **Privately Held**
WEB: www.mcnett.com
SIC: 5091 3949 Sporting & recreation goods; sporting & athletic goods
PA: Coghlan's Ltd
  121 Irene St
  Winnipeg MB R3T 4
  204 284-9550

(G-1432)
MENACE INDUSTRIES LLC
3617 Illinois Ln (98226-4364)
PHONE...................360 595-4095
EMP: 2 **EST:** 2013
SALES (est): 90.1K **Privately Held**
SIC: 3999 Manufacturing industries

(G-1433)
MERMAID BAY ENTERPRISES LLC
Also Called: Aerotech Golf Shafts
1971 Midway Ln Ste J (98226-7682)
PHONE...................360 312-5522
Chris Hilleary, *Mng Member*
EMP: 2
SALES (est): 369.8K **Privately Held**
SIC: 3949 Shafts, golf club

(G-1434)
MFML PUBLISHING
1400 12th St Apt 908 (98225-7439)
PHONE...................360 603-6148
Matthew McRae, *Principal*
EMP: 2
SALES (est): 43.3K **Privately Held**
SIC: 2741 Miscellaneous publishing

(G-1435)
MILES WOODWORKING
1305 Cornwall Ave (98225-4716)
PHONE...................360 306-3048
Joe Miles, *Founder*
EMP: 2 **EST:** 2014
SALES (est): 139.6K **Privately Held**
SIC: 2431 Millwork

(G-1436)
MINUTE MAN PRESS
Also Called: Minuteman Press
1616 Cornwall Ave Ste 121 (98225-4642)
PHONE...................360 738-3539
Thomas Greg Carlslay, *Owner*
Joyce Carlslay, *Co-Owner*
EMP: 3
SQ FT: 1,400
SALES (est): 212.4K **Privately Held**
SIC: 2752 Commercial printing, lithographic

(G-1437)
MKG MFG
292 Kelly Rd (98226-9734)
PHONE...................360 398-7518
Michael Glaze, *Principal*
EMP: 2
SALES (est): 112.9K **Privately Held**
SIC: 3999 Manufacturing industries

(G-1438)
MODERN CLASSICS INC
1788 Midway Ln (98226-7603)
P.O. Box 31397 (98228-3397)
PHONE...................360 733-6400
Barry Pollack, *President*
EMP: 2 **EST:** 1999
SALES (est): 190K **Privately Held**
SIC: 2511 5712 Wood household furniture; customized furniture & cabinets

(G-1439)
MOKAJOE INC
1050 Larrabee Ave Ste 104 (98225-7367)
PHONE...................360 714-1953
Trudy Scherting, *President*
Joe Scherting, *Vice Pres*
EMP: 9
SALES: 500K **Privately Held**
WEB: www.mokajoe.com
SIC: 3634 Roasters, electric

(G-1440)
MOMENTUM INTERACTIVE LLC
Also Called: Flitelite
1201 Birch Falls Dr (98229-2427)
PHONE...................915 203-5349
David Simeur,
Wendy Simeur,
EMP: 5
SALES: 180K **Privately Held**
WEB: www.flitelite.com
SIC: 7371 3229 3674 Computer software development & applications; lenses, lantern, flashlight, headlight, etc.: glass; radiation sensors

(G-1441)
MONEYMINDERSOFTWARE
3111 Newmarket St Ste 106 (98226-8695)
PHONE...................360 255-4300
EMP: 2
SALES (est): 83.2K **Privately Held**
SIC: 7372 Prepackaged software

(G-1442)
MORAD ELECTRONICS CORPORATION
Also Called: Morad Antenna
3125 Mercer Ave Ste 106 (98226-8435)
PHONE...................206 789-2525
Ken Holland, *President*
EMP: 5
SQ FT: 7,200
SALES (est): 873.8K **Privately Held**
WEB: www.morad.com
SIC: 3663 Antennas, transmitting & communications

(G-1443)
MORRISON ART GLASS INC
2111 Lincoln St (98225-4147)
PHONE...................360 714-8732
Christopher Morrison, *President*
EMP: 2
SALES (est): 110K **Privately Held**
SIC: 3231 5231 8999 Art glass: made from purchased glass; paint, glass & wallpaper; artist

(G-1444)
MOUNT BAKER FIREPLACE SHOP
1273 Sunset Ave (98226-9048)
PHONE...................360 384-3507
Gwen Dobson, *Owner*
EMP: 2
SQ FT: 576
SALES (est): 213K **Privately Held**
SIC: 5719 3446 Fireplace equipment & accessories; railings, bannisters, guards, etc.: made from metal pipe

(G-1445)
MOUNT BAKERY
308 W Champion St Ste C (98225-4370)
PHONE...................360 715-2195
Olivier Vrambout, *President*
EMP: 3
SALES (est): 176.4K **Privately Held**
WEB: www.mountbakery.com
SIC: 2051 Bakery: wholesale or wholesale/retail combined

(G-1446)
MT BAKER CANDY CO
1 Bellis Fair Pkwy # 434 (98226-5566)
PHONE...................360 756-0661
EMP: 4
SALES: 900K **Privately Held**
SIC: 2064 Mfg Candy/Confectionery

(G-1447)
MT BAKER MINING AND MTLS LLC (PA)
5421 Guide Meridian C (98226-9771)
PHONE...................360 595-4445
Jason Gaber, *Mng Member*
Steve Gaber,
▲ **EMP:** 11 **EST:** 2010

SALES (est): 2.2MM **Privately Held**
SIC: 3325 Steel foundries

(G-1448)
MT BAKER MINING AND MTLS LLC
5421 Guide Meridian C (98226-9771)
PHONE...................360 739-7264
Jenny Chang, *Branch Mgr*
EMP: 12
SALES (corp-wide): 2.2MM **Privately Held**
SIC: 3325 Steel foundries
PA: Mt. Baker Mining And Metals Llc
  5421 Guide Meridian C
  Bellingham WA 98226
  360 595-4445

(G-1449)
MT BAKER POWDER COATING
2023 Grant St (98225-4202)
PHONE...................360 366-3233
Jason Mitchell, *President*
▲ **EMP:** 4
SQ FT: 10,000
SALES (est): 410K **Privately Held**
SIC: 3291 Diamond powder

(G-1450)
MT BAKER PRODUCTS INC
Also Called: Mt Baker Plywood
2929 Roeder Ave (98226-2065)
P.O. Box 997 (98227-0997)
PHONE...................360 733-3960
Rod Remington, *President*
Keith Swaner, *Chairman*
Steve King, *Vice Pres*
Gary Keith Swaner, *Vice Pres*
John Abts, *Purch Mgr*
▲ **EMP:** 157
SQ FT: 440,000
SALES (est): 38.7MM
SALES (corp-wide): 83MM **Privately Held**
WEB: www.mtbakerplywood.com
SIC: 2435 Plywood, hardwood or hardwood faced
PA: Swaner Hardwood Co., Inc.
  5 W Magnolia Blvd
  Burbank CA 91502
  818 953-5350

(G-1451)
MULTISONUS AUDIO INC
295 Kelly Rd (98226-9734)
PHONE...................425 241-1112
Philip Sudore, *President*
▲ **EMP:** 5 **EST:** 2014
SALES (est): 380K **Privately Held**
SIC: 3679 Headphones, radio

(G-1452)
MUSTANG SURVIVAL INC
1215 Old Fairhaven Pkwy (98225-7444)
PHONE...................360 676-1782
Warren Kanders, *Principal*
EMP: 25
SQ FT: 9,000
SALES (est): 3.4MM
SALES (corp-wide): 875.1MM **Privately Held**
SIC: 3069 Life jackets, inflatable: rubberized fabric
HQ: Safariland, Llc
  13386 International Pkwy
  Jacksonville FL 32218
  904 741-5400

(G-1453)
MUSTANG SURVIVAL HOLDINGS INC
3870 Mustang Way Ste 101 (98226-8026)
PHONE...................360 676-1782
Dwight Davies, *Chairman*
◆ **EMP:** 92
SALES (est): 1.2MM **Privately Held**
SIC: 3069 2339 2337 2311 Life jackets, inflatable: rubberized fabric; women's & misses' outerwear; women's & misses' suits & coats; men's & boys' suits & coats

(G-1454)
MYCO MOLDING INC
1650 Jills Ct (98226-7150)
PHONE...................360 676-9656
Michael Yeakel, *President*

EMP: 11
SALES: 1MM **Privately Held**
SIC: 3089 Injection molding of plastics

(G-1455)
MYRLE B FOSTER
Also Called: Circle F Enterprises
2399 Mt Baker Hwy (98226-7915)
PHONE...................360 733-2509
Guy Foster, *President*
Myrle Foster, *Admin Sec*
EMP: 4
SQ FT: 3,400
SALES: 400K **Privately Held**
SIC: 3599 Machine shop, jobbing & repair

(G-1456)
NAAN & BREW
200 E Maple St Apt 101 (98225-5169)
PHONE...................425 330-3891
EMP: 3 **EST:** 2015
SALES (est): 75.4K **Privately Held**
SIC: 2082 Malt beverages

(G-1457)
NAIMOR INC
Also Called: K&K Industries
2025 Masonry Way (98226-8011)
PHONE...................360 756-9700
Shahrokh Naieni, *President*
EMP: 24
SALES: 7.4MM **Privately Held**
SIC: 3441 3699 Fabricated structural metal; laser welding, drilling & cutting equipment

(G-1458)
NEW ADVENTURE
2511 Queen St (98226-5429)
P.O. Box 28817 (98228-0817)
PHONE...................360 961-4444
Robert Jones, *Owner*
EMP: 2
SALES (est): 102.9K **Privately Held**
SIC: 3949 Gymnasium equipment

(G-1459)
NEW WHATCOM INTERIORS
1123 Railroad Ave (98225-5007)
PHONE...................360 671-3389
John H Blethen, *Owner*
EMP: 12
SQ FT: 3,000
SALES (est): 1MM **Privately Held**
WEB: www.bellingham-real-estate.com
SIC: 5712 2431 Cabinet work, custom; millwork

(G-1460)
NON SEQUITUR MUSIC
Also Called: Non Sequitur Music Publishing
2112 Ontario St (98229-4030)
PHONE...................360 733-7145
Bruce Hamilton, *Partner*
EMP: 5
SALES (est): 321.5K **Privately Held**
WEB: www.nonsequiturmusic.com
SIC: 5199 2741 Sheet music; miscellaneous publishing

(G-1461)
NOR E FIRST RESPONSE INC
1975 Midway Ln Ste J (98226-7151)
P.O. Box 30888 (98228-2888)
PHONE...................360 738-6467
Mark McCooey, *President*
Greg Vassallo, *General Mgr*
Gary Wilson, *Vice Pres*
EMP: 4
SALES: 2.5MM **Privately Held**
WEB: www.nor-e.com
SIC: 3715 5599 Truck trailers; utility trailers

(G-1462)
NORSTAR BOATS INC
1366 Roy Rd (98229-9323)
PHONE...................360 671-3669
Gary Nordtvedt, *President*
EMP: 7
SALES: 2MM **Privately Held**
WEB: www.norstarboats.com
SIC: 3732 Boats, fiberglass: building & repairing

GEOGRAPHIC SECTION
Bellingham - Whatcom County (G-1493)

(G-1463)
NORTH AMERICAN ATK CORPORATION
Also Called: Yamato Engine Specialists 1990
2020 E Bakerview Rd (98226-9100)
PHONE.................................360 733-1916
Engines Yamato, *Branch Mgr*
EMP: 45
SALES (corp-wide): 11.8B **Publicly Held**
SIC: 3714 Motor vehicle parts & accessories
HQ: North American Atk Corporation
1102 W N Carrier
Grand Prairie TX 75050
972 647-1400

(G-1464)
NORTH COAST ELECTRIC COMPANY
1836 Racine St (98229-4738)
PHONE.................................360 671-1100
Corey Carter, *Sales/Mktg Mgr*
EMP: 18
SALES (corp-wide): 532.5MM **Privately Held**
WEB: www.ncelec.com
SIC: 5063 5065 5084 3625 Electrical supplies; electronic parts & equipment; conveyor systems; motor controls, electric
PA: North Coast Electric Company
2450 8th Ave S Ste 200
Seattle WA 98134
206 442-9898

(G-1465)
NORTH WEST BOOK OPER CO INC
782 Marine Dr (98225-1530)
PHONE.................................877 591-8608
Thomas Strohhacker, *President*
Janice Strohhacker, *Vice Pres*
▲ **EMP:** 7 **EST:** 2013
SQ FT: 17,000
SALES: 550K **Privately Held**
SIC: 2789 Bookbinding & related work

(G-1466)
NORTHWEST DESIGN & MFG
1801 Franklin St (98225-4620)
PHONE.................................360 714-8513
Jon Walters, *Owner*
EMP: 6
SALES: 600K **Privately Held**
WEB: www.designnorthwest.com
SIC: 3161 Luggage

(G-1467)
NORTHWEST HELI STRUCTURES
3911 Spur Ridge Ln (98226-1227)
PHONE.................................360 734-1073
John Wilsong, *Principal*
EMP: 6
SALES (est): 479K **Privately Held**
SIC: 2493 Insulation & roofing material, reconstituted wood

(G-1468)
NORTHWEST MARINE INDS LLC
Also Called: NW Marine Industries Nmi
809 Harris Ave Bldg 6 (98225-7030)
PHONE.................................360 389-5351
Ron A Wright,
EMP: 6
SALES (est): 999K **Privately Held**
SIC: 5091 3999 Sailboats; atomizers, toiletry

(G-1469)
NORTHWEST SFTWR PROFESSIONALS
3851 Britton Rd (98226-9436)
P.O. Box 5747 (98227-5747)
PHONE.................................360 734-5747
Gary McGill, *Owner*
EMP: 5
SALES: 300K **Privately Held**
SIC: 7372 Prepackaged software

(G-1470)
NORTHWEST SMOKING & CURING
4600 Guide Meridian # 100 (98226-9165)
P.O. Box 2976 (98227-2976)
PHONE.................................360 733-3666
Joel Kronenberg, *President*
EMP: 3
SQ FT: 1,500
SALES (est): 248.4K **Privately Held**
SIC: 2091 5146 4142 4141 Salmon, smoked; fish & seafoods; bus charter service, except local; local bus charter service; airport transportation

(G-1471)
NORTHWEST SOLUTIONS INC
5381 Waschke Rd (98226-9612)
PHONE.................................360 380-3807
Joseph Stephens, *President*
Robin Stephens, *Director*
EMP: 2
SQ FT: 2,500
SALES (est): 270K **Privately Held**
SIC: 2899 5087 5084 Chemical supplies for foundries; janitors' supplies; cleaning equipment, high pressure, sand or steam

(G-1472)
NORTHWEST TARP & CANVAS
3334 Granada Way (98225-8414)
PHONE.................................360 296-2321
EMP: 2
SALES (est): 153.9K **Privately Held**
SIC: 2211 Canvas

(G-1473)
NOVEX LLC
1313 E Maple St Ste 201 (98225-5708)
PHONE.................................360 296-3467
Ilija Miskovic, *Mng Member*
Sanja Miskovic, *Manager*
EMP: 6
SALES (est): 279.6K **Privately Held**
SIC: 3532 3823 8711 Mineral beneficiation equipment; fluidic devices, circuits & systems for process control; engineering services; pollution control engineering; petroleum, mining & chemical engineers

(G-1474)
NUCANOE INC
2125 Humboldt St (98225-4118)
PHONE.................................360 543-9019
Blake Young, *President*
◆ **EMP:** 19
SALES (est): 3.2MM **Privately Held**
SIC: 3732 0971 Canoes, building & repairing; wildlife management

(G-1475)
NUU-MUU LLC
1715 Ellis St Ste 102 (98225-4653)
P.O. Box 190 (98227-0190)
PHONE.................................360 223-7151
Christine Nienstedt, *Partner*
Ashley Fullenwider, *Partner*
EMP: 2
SALES (est): 201.3K **Privately Held**
SIC: 2339 Women's & misses' athletic clothing & sportswear

(G-1476)
NW HYDROPONICS
5655 Guide Meridian (98226-9722)
PHONE.................................360 778-3254
Ben Hassler, *Owner*
EMP: 2
SALES (est): 139.1K **Privately Held**
SIC: 3999 Hydroponic equipment

(G-1477)
OESER COMPANY
730 Marine Dr (98225-1530)
P.O. Box 156 (98227-0156)
PHONE.................................360 734-1480
Christopher M Secrist, *President*
Mark Edick, *Manager*
Sally Thomas, *Admin Sec*
EMP: 25 **EST:** 1929
SQ FT: 1,000
SALES (est): 4.1MM **Privately Held**
WEB: www.oeserco.com
SIC: 2499 5099 Poles, wood; logs, hewn ties, posts & poles

(G-1478)
OLDE ENGLISH CRACKERS INC
4071 Hannegan Rd Ste S (98226-7623)
PHONE.................................360 715-2972
Gary Stonedahl, *Partner*
Dale E Stonedahl, *Partner*
Gary Michael Stonedahl, *Partner*
◆ **EMP:** 6
SALES (est): 890.8K **Privately Held**
WEB: www.oldenglishcrackers.com
SIC: 2655 5947 Tubes, fiber or paper: made from purchased material; gifts & novelties

(G-1479)
OLIVINE CORP
928 Thomas Rd (98226-9044)
PHONE.................................360 733-3332
Corliss Smith Jr, *CEO*
Mae Smith, *Corp Secy*
EMP: 2
SQ FT: 12,000
SALES (est): 280K **Privately Held**
SIC: 3567 1429 Incinerators, metal: domestic or commercial; igneous rock, crushed & broken-quarrying

(G-1480)
ONSITE COMPUTER SERVICES
220 W Champion St Ste 260 (98225-4390)
PHONE.................................360 650-1079
Tom Scott, *Owner*
EMP: 4
SALES (est): 267.7K **Privately Held**
WEB: www.on-sitecomputer.com
SIC: 7372 7371 Prepackaged software; computer software systems analysis & design, custom

(G-1481)
ORCAS ISLAND GROWLERS
4505 Glen Meadows Pl (98226-1728)
PHONE.................................360 927-9265
Kyle Rosetta, *Principal*
EMP: 4
SALES (est): 221.3K **Privately Held**
SIC: 2711 Newspapers: publishing only, not printed on site

(G-1482)
OUR HOUSE PUBLISHING
2511 G St (98225-3405)
PHONE.................................360 676-0428
Mark Fuller, *Owner*
Barbara Fuller, *Principal*
EMP: 2
SALES (est): 120K **Privately Held**
WEB: www.ourhousepublishing.com
SIC: 2731 Books: publishing only

(G-1483)
PACE SOLUTIONS INC
3888 Sound Way (98226-9160)
P.O. Box 9754 (98227-9754)
PHONE.................................604 520-6211
William Martin, *President*
EMP: 5
SALES (est): 313.2K **Privately Held**
WEB: www.pace49.com
SIC: 3589 Water treatment equipment, industrial

(G-1484)
PACIFIC COAST BRIDE LLC
1521 Cornwall Ave (98225-4521)
PHONE.................................360 303-5047
Anna Lorenz, *Principal*
EMP: 2 **EST:** 2015
SALES (est): 115.5K **Privately Held**
SIC: 2335 Bridal & formal gowns

(G-1485)
PACIFIC INJECTION MOLDING
122 Ohio St Ste 105 (98225-4541)
PHONE.................................360 733-7466
Robert M Dyer, *President*
EMP: 4
SQ FT: 1,800
SALES (est): 684.7K **Privately Held**
WEB: www.pacificmc.com
SIC: 3089 Injection molding of plastics

(G-1486)
PACIFIC LABELS
1602 Carolina St Ste D10 (98229-5489)
PHONE.................................360 671-6507
Kent A Goto, *Owner*
Pamela Goto, *Co-Owner*
EMP: 3
SQ FT: 1,600
SALES (est): 196.9K **Privately Held**
SIC: 2759 Labels & seals: printing

(G-1487)
PACIFIC RIM PRINTING INC
Also Called: Pacific Printing
22 Southern Ct (98229-4438)
PHONE.................................360 676-4606
Carol Young, *President*
EMP: 4
SALES (est): 340.9K **Privately Held**
WEB: www.pacificrimprinting.com
SIC: 2791 Typesetting

(G-1488)
PACIFIC RIM TONEWOODS INC (PA)
619 15th St (98225-6114)
PHONE.................................360 826-6101
Stephen McMinn, *President*
▲ **EMP:** 15
SALES (est): 2.5MM **Privately Held**
SIC: 3931 5961 Musical instruments; mail order house

(G-1489)
PARAMOUNT SUPPLY CO
2230 Midway Ln (98226-1218)
P.O. Box 5764 (98227-5764)
PHONE.................................360 647-8328
Lance Dillon, *Manager*
EMP: 7
SALES (corp-wide): 48MM **Privately Held**
WEB: www.paramountsupply.com
SIC: 5074 5085 5084 5051 Pipes & fittings, plastic; gaskets; instruments & control equipment; pipe & tubing, steel; steam traps
PA: Paramount Supply Co.
816 Se Ash St
Portland OR 97214
503 232-4137

(G-1490)
PARASOL ENTERPRISES INC
3221 Cherrywood Ave (98225-1033)
PHONE.................................360 733-5579
Fax: 360 733-5078
▲ **EMP:** 2
SQ FT: 3,000
SALES (est): 170K **Privately Held**
SIC: 3999 Mfg Misc Products

(G-1491)
PARBERRY INC (PA)
Also Called: Parberry Iron & Metal
1419 C St (98225)
P.O. Box R (98227-1305)
PHONE.................................360 734-2340
Brad Parberry, *President*
Louis H Parberry Jr, *President*
Sue Parberry, *Corp Secy*
EMP: 20
SQ FT: 10,000
SALES: 0 **Privately Held**
SIC: 4953 6512 6513 3341 Recycling, waste materials; commercial & industrial building operation; apartment building operators; secondary nonferrous metals; pulp mills

(G-1492)
PAUL RAZORE
1009 Marine Dr (98225-8423)
PHONE.................................360 734-4845
Paul Razore, *Executive*
EMP: 2 **EST:** 2017
SALES (est): 62.9K **Privately Held**
SIC: 2711 Newspapers

(G-1493)
PEDERSON BROS INC
3974 Bakerview Spur (98226-8006)
P.O. Box 30437 (98228-2437)
PHONE.................................360 734-9180
Brian Pederson, *Owner*
Joe Wilson, *Principal*
Pat Zender, *Principal*
Steve Pederson, *Corp Secy*
Dan Cowan, *Controller*
EMP: 40

Bellingham - Whatcom County (G-1494)   GEOGRAPHIC SECTION

SQ FT: 41,400
SALES (est): 9.5MM **Privately Held**
SIC: **3441** Fabricated structural metal

(G-1494)
PELICAN PACKERS INC
6069 Hannegan Rd (98226-7433)
PHONE..................................360 398-8825
Lamar R Edwards Jr, *President*
Harvey Coskey, *Assistant VP*
Judy Coskey, *Assistant VP*
Mike Edwards, *Assistant VP*
EMP: 11
SALES (est): 1.7MM **Privately Held**
WEB: www.pelicanpackers.com
SIC: **2091** 5812 Canned & cured fish & seafoods; eating places

(G-1495)
PELLETS INC
1481 Island View Dr (98225-8539)
P.O. Box 5484 (98227-5484)
PHONE..................................360 733-3012
Bret Gaussoin, *President*
Kim Gaussoin, *Vice Pres*
EMP: 4
SALES (est): 466.8K **Privately Held**
WEB: www.pelletsinc.com
SIC: **2836** Veterinary biological products

(G-1496)
PERCH AND PLAY
1707 N State St (98225-4604)
PHONE..................................360 393-4925
Robert Manzanares, *Principal*
EMP: 2
SALES (est): 156.4K **Privately Held**
SIC: **3949** Playground equipment

(G-1497)
PFC INC
Also Called: Plastic Fabrication
5421 Guide Meridian (98226-9771)
PHONE..................................360 398-8889
Dan Mc Intee, *President*
Tom Mc Intee, *Treasurer*
EMP: 8
SQ FT: 6,000
SALES (est): 990K **Privately Held**
WEB: www.plasticfabrication.com
SIC: **3449** 3446 3321 3441 Miscellaneous metalwork; architectural metalwork; manhole covers, metal; fabricated structural metal; fabricated structural metal for bridges

(G-1498)
PIXELAN SOFTWARE
2950 Newmarket St Ste 101 (98226-3872)
PHONE..................................831 222-0339
Michael Feerer, *Owner*
EMP: 2
SALES (est): 159.1K **Privately Held**
WEB: www.pixelan.com
SIC: **7372** Application computer software

(G-1499)
PRAXAIR INC
4215 Britton Rd (98226-9468)
PHONE..................................360 734-3955
Stephen F Angel, *Branch Mgr*
EMP: 3 **Privately Held**
SIC: **2813** Industrial gases
HQ: Praxair, Inc.
   10 Riverview Dr
   Danbury CT 06810
   203 837-2000

(G-1500)
PRAXAIR INC
430 Ohio St Ste A (98226-4637)
PHONE..................................360 733-0971
Tate Pazaski, *Manager*
EMP: 3 **Privately Held**
SIC: **2813** Industrial gases
HQ: Praxair, Inc.
   10 Riverview Dr
   Danbury CT 06810
   203 837-2000

(G-1501)
PRAXAIR SERVICES INC
4115 Strider Loop Rd (98226-8005)
PHONE..................................360 676-8215
Larry McDevitt, *Manager*
EMP: 9 **Privately Held**

WEB: www.praxairservices.com
SIC: **7699** 1389 Tank repair & cleaning services; bailing, cleaning, swabbing & treating of wells
HQ: Praxair Services, Inc
   1585 Sawdust Rd Ste 300
   Spring TX 77380
   281 203-3600

(G-1502)
PRECISION MACHINE & MFG
733 Van Wyck Rd (98226-8789)
PHONE..................................360 734-1081
Myrna Peters, *Owner*
EMP: 5
SQ FT: 4,800
SALES: 190K **Privately Held**
SIC: **3599** 1799 Machine shop, jobbing & repair; welding on site

(G-1503)
PREMIER AGENDAS INC (HQ)
Also Called: Premier School Agendas
400 Sequoia Dr Ste 200 (98226-7634)
PHONE..................................360 734-1153
Greg Cimlik, *President*
▲ EMP: 75
SQ FT: 25,000
SALES (est): 41.8MM
SALES (corp-wide): 673.4MM **Publicly Held**
WEB: www.agendas.com
SIC: **2731** Books: publishing & printing
PA: School Specialty, Inc.
   W6316 Design Dr
   Greenville WI 54942
   920 734-5712

(G-1504)
PRICE & VISSER MILLWORK INC
2536 Valencia St (98226-3736)
PHONE..................................360 734-7700
Steven M Price, *CEO*
Robert Visser, *Vice Pres*
EMP: 11
SQ FT: 3,000
SALES (est): 1.3MM **Privately Held**
SIC: **2431** 5031 Doors, wood; lumber, plywood & millwork

(G-1505)
PRINT & COPY FACTORY LLC
4025 Irongate Rd (98226-8028)
PHONE..................................360 738-4931
Krystal Garcia, *Prdtn Mgr*
Larry Raney,
Becky Raney,
EMP: 7
SQ FT: 1,400
SALES (est): 573K **Privately Held**
WEB: www.printcopyfactory.com
SIC: **2752** Commercial printing, offset

(G-1506)
PROCON MIN & TUNNELLING US LTD
1313 E Maple St Ste 237 (98225-5750)
PHONE..................................360 685-4253
James Dales, *President*
Edward Yurkowski, *Director*
Gary Sollis, *Admin Sec*
EMP: 10 EST: 1992
SALES (est): 243.1K
SALES (corp-wide): 306.9MM **Privately Held**
SIC: **1481** 6211 1241 Nonmetallic mineral services; oil & gas lease brokers; mine preparation services
PA: Procon Mining & Tunnelling Ltd
   4664 Lougheed Hwy Unit 108
   Burnaby BC V5C 5
   604 291-8292

(G-1507)
PROLOGIC ENGINEERING INC
4041 Bakerview Spur Ste 3 (98226-8281)
PHONE..................................360 734-9625
Jerry Hohl, *President*
EMP: 59
SALES (est): 6.3MM **Privately Held**
WEB: www.prologic-eng.com
SIC: **3625** 3577 8731 Industrial controls: push button, selector switches, pilot; computer peripheral equipment; electronic research

(G-1508)
PRYOR GIGGEY CO
4206 Padden Hills Ct (98229-3377)
PHONE..................................360 647-6021
Jeff Thayer, *Principal*
EMP: 2
SALES (est): 182.2K **Privately Held**
SIC: **3297** Nonclay refractories

(G-1509)
PUGLIA ENGINEERING INC
Also Called: Fairhaven Shipyard
201 Harris Ave (98225-7018)
P.O. Box 1456, Tacoma (98401-1456)
PHONE..................................360 647-0080
Neil Turney, *President*
Rod Johnson, *Project Mgr*
Joel Underwood, *Purch Agent*
Diane Beaman, *Human Resources*
EMP: 120
SQ FT: 81,000
SALES: 34.2MM **Privately Held**
WEB: www.bbshipyard.com
SIC: **3731** 1541 Shipbuilding & repairing; prefabricated building erection, industrial

(G-1510)
PULSE PUBLICATIONS INC
Also Called: Business Pulse
2423 E Bakerview Rd (98226-7694)
PHONE..................................360 671-3933
Tony Larson, *President*
Bob Hagedorn, *Vice Pres*
EMP: 15
SQ FT: 1,700
SALES (est): 1.2MM **Privately Held**
SIC: **2721** Magazines: publishing & printing

(G-1511)
Q SEA SPECIALTY SERVICES LLC
2875 Roeder Ave Ste 8 (98225-2063)
PHONE..................................360 398-9708
Joel Harvey,
Karen Evich,
Joey Harvey,
Andy Vitaljic,
Andy J Vitaljic,
EMP: 50
SALES (est): 7.8MM **Privately Held**
SIC: **2092** Fresh or frozen packaged fish

(G-1512)
QMS 1 INC (PA)
5373 Guide Meridian E2 (98226-7418)
PHONE..................................360 201-7505
Mark Luecke, *President*
Loren Troutman, *President*
Susan Bruland, *Corp Secy*
EMP: 5
SALES (est): 280.6K **Privately Held**
SIC: **1389** Oil consultants

(G-1513)
QUANTUM PUBLISHING SERVICE
312 Highland Dr (98226-5416)
PHONE..................................360 734-2906
Lorretta L Palagi, *President*
Randel S Bilof, *Vice Pres*
EMP: 2
SALES (est): 140K **Privately Held**
WEB: www.quantumps.com
SIC: **2731** Book publishing

(G-1514)
RAISY KINDER PUBLISHING
1713 Golden Ct (98226-8770)
PHONE..................................360 752-0332
Rick Porter, *Principal*
EMP: 2
SALES (est): 109.8K **Privately Held**
SIC: **2741** Miscellaneous publishing

(G-1515)
REINKES FABRICATION INC
5825 Aldrich Rd (98226-9698)
PHONE..................................360 398-2011
Duane M Reinke, *President*
Laurice Reinke, *Vice Pres*
EMP: 10
SQ FT: 8,800
SALES (est): 800K **Privately Held**
SIC: **3441** Fabricated structural metal

(G-1516)
REVIVE A BACK INC
4200 Meridian St Ste 102 (98226-5591)
PHONE..................................360 738-6085
Gordon Cameron, *President*
Michele Cameron, *Vice Pres*
EMP: 2
SALES (est): 52K **Privately Held**
WEB: www.revive-a-back.com
SIC: **3949** 8093 Exercise equipment; rehabilitation center, outpatient treatment

(G-1517)
RISQUE INC
Also Called: Copy Source
1122 N State St (98225-5014)
PHONE..................................360 738-1280
Nadeem Israr, *President*
Alia Nadeem, *Vice Pres*
EMP: 18
SQ FT: 6,000
SALES (est): 2.5MM **Privately Held**
WEB: www.copysource.com
SIC: **7334** 2752 Blueprinting service; commercial printing, lithographic

(G-1518)
ROAD-IQ LLC
Also Called: Qualnetics
2425 E Bakerview Rd # 101 (98226-7607)
PHONE..................................360 733-4151
Mark Moeller,
EMP: 12
SALES (est): 1.8MM
SALES (corp-wide): 57.5MM **Privately Held**
SIC: **3799** 5099 3669 5045 Recreational vehicles; off-road automobiles, except recreational vehicles; safety equipment & supplies; transportation signaling devices; intercommunication systems, electric; computers, peripherals & software; computer software development & applications
PA: Velvac, Incorporated
   2405 S Calhoun Rd
   New Berlin WI 53151
   262 786-0700

(G-1519)
RODDA PAINT CO
Also Called: Rodda Paint Bellingham Bh51
747 Ohio St (98225-4625)
PHONE..................................360 738-6878
Greg Engholm, *Branch Mgr*
EMP: 5
SALES (corp-wide): 237.5MM **Privately Held**
WEB: www.roddapaint.com
SIC: **2851** 5198 5023 5231 Paints & paint additives; paints; paint brushes, rollers, sprayers; wallcoverings; window furnishings; window covering parts & accessories; paint; paint brushes, rollers, sprayers & other supplies; wallcoverings; window furnishings
HQ: Rodda Paint Co.
   6107 N Marine Dr Ste 3
   Portland OR 97203
   503 521-4300

(G-1520)
S G&C CONTRACTOR SERVICES LLC
Also Called: Berry Garage Door Company
2205 Valencia St (98229-4740)
PHONE..................................360 671-5121
Rhoda Sheri'pitzler,
Gregory Pitzler,
EMP: 7
SALES: 450K **Privately Held**
SIC: **3442** 1751 2431 Garage doors, overhead: metal; garage door, installation or erection; garage doors, overhead: wood

(G-1521)
SAFRAN CABIN BELLINGHAM INC (HQ)
3225 Woburn St (98226-5656)
PHONE..................................360 738-2005
Olivier Zarrouati, *Principal*
Yannick Assouad, *Principal*
Maurice Pinault, *Principal*
David Flemming, *Vice Pres*

▲ = Import ▼ = Export
◆ = Import/Export

GEOGRAPHIC SECTION

Warren Thomson, *Director*
◆ **EMP:** 179
SALES (est): 153.3MM
SALES (corp-wide): 833.4MM **Privately Held**
SIC: 3728 5088 Aircraft parts & equipment; aircraft & space vehicle supplies & parts
PA: Safran
2 Bd Du General Martial Valin
Paris 15e Arrondissement 75015
140 608-080

(G-1522)
SAMISH BAY SOAPS & SCENTS
1372 Del Bonita Ct (98226-8869)
PHONE..................360 752-9015
Kimberly Heinke, *Owner*
EMP: 2
SALES (est): 178K **Privately Held**
WEB: www.samishbay.net
SIC: 2841 7215 Soap: granulated, liquid, cake, flaked or chip; coin-operated laundries & cleaning

(G-1523)
SANDBOX ENTERPRISES LLC
Also Called: Sbeusa Medical
3248 Agate Heights Rd (98226-1732)
PHONE..................360 966-6677
Krista Penn,
EMP: 2
SALES (est): 45K **Privately Held**
SIC: 2399 2899 5699 5131 Pet collars, leashes, etc.: non-leather; corrosion preventive lubricant; military goods & regalia; T-shirts, custom printed; flags & banners; general merchandise, mail order; banners, flags, decals & posters

(G-1524)
SAW INDUSTRIES LLC
2009 J St (98225-5180)
PHONE..................360 306-8988
EMP: 2
SALES (est): 116.2K **Privately Held**
SIC: 3999 Manufacturing industries

(G-1525)
SAW SERVICE WASHINGTON INC
Also Called: La Cutting Products
1602 Carolina St Ste D9 (98229-5489)
PHONE..................360 738-6437
Wayne McMahon, *CEO*
Susan McMahon, *Admin Sec*
▲ **EMP:** 3
SQ FT: 1,500
SALES (est): 546.7K **Privately Held**
SIC: 3425 Saw blades & handsaws

(G-1526)
SCHOBER WOODWORKS
3962 Hoff Rd (98225-8532)
PHONE..................360 595-7519
Robert Schober, *Principal*
EMP: 2
SALES (est): 115.9K **Privately Held**
SIC: 2431 Millwork

(G-1527)
SEAFOOD PRODUCERS COOPERATIVE (PA)
2417 Meridian St Ste 105 (98225-2430)
PHONE..................360 733-0120
Thomas McLaughlin, *CEO*
◆ **EMP:** 30
SALES (est): 6.1MM **Privately Held**
WEB: www.spcsales.com
SIC: 2092 5146 Seafoods, frozen: prepared; seafoods, fresh: prepared; seafoods

(G-1528)
SEAKAMP ENGINEERING INC
3985 Hammer Dr (98226-7630)
PHONE..................360 734-2788
Kathleen Bruggenkamp, *President*
Clark A Bergman, *Vice Pres*
EMP: 15
SQ FT: 10,000
SALES (est): 1.5MM **Privately Held**
WEB: www.seakamp.com
SIC: 3443 Heat exchangers, condensers & components

(G-1529)
SEAPLANE LANDING AREA (WA13)
1622 Euclid Ave (98229-5113)
PHONE..................360 647-7839
John Sibold David Huey, *Manager*
EMP: 2
SALES (est): 145.1K **Privately Held**
SIC: 3721 Aircraft

(G-1530)
SEATTHOLE INC
Also Called: Seatthole Bellingham
126 W Holly St (98225-4344)
P.O. Box 3137 (98227-3137)
PHONE..................360 389-2154
Django R Bohren, *President*
EMP: 5
SALES (est): 280K **Privately Held**
SIC: 2253 T-shirts & tops, knit

(G-1531)
SEAVIEW BOATYARD NORTH INC
2652 N Harbor Loop Dr (98225-2022)
PHONE..................360 676-8282
Phil Riise, *President*
EMP: 26
SALES (est): 3MM **Privately Held**
SIC: 3732 Boat building & repairing

(G-1532)
SHAMROCK & SPIKE MAUL PUBG CO
2328 Yew Street Rd (98229-6800)
PHONE..................360 734-5778
Joseph Kenna, *Principal*
EMP: 2
SALES (est): 108.2K **Privately Held**
SIC: 2741 Miscellaneous publishing

(G-1533)
SIGN POST INC
2019 E Bakerview Rd (98226-9100)
PHONE..................360 671-1343
Glorene George, *President*
Ray George, *Vice Pres*
Leif Johnson, *Project Mgr*
EMP: 18
SQ FT: 5,900
SALES (est): 2.9MM **Privately Held**
WEB: www.thesignpost.com
SIC: 2431 3993 2439 Awnings, wood; signs, not made in custom sign painting shops; structural wood members

(G-1534)
SIGNS BY TOMORROW
420 Ohio St (98225-4637)
PHONE..................360 676-7117
David Koehler, *Principal*
Sarah Koehler, *Principal*
EMP: 4 **EST:** 2008
SALES (est): 414.1K **Privately Held**
SIC: 3993 Signs & advertising specialties

(G-1535)
SIGNS PLUS INC
766 Marine Dr (98225-1530)
PHONE..................360 671-7165
Dale Gravning, *President*
EMP: 19
SALES (est): 950K **Privately Held**
SIC: 3993 Signs & advertising specialties

(G-1536)
SILFAB SOLAR WA INC
800 Cornwall Ave (98225-5267)
PHONE..................360 569-4733
Hanna Ayaad,
EMP: 17
SALES (est): 3.1MM **Privately Held**
SIC: 3674 Solar cells

(G-1537)
SILHOUETTE GRAPHICS
2884 Leeward Way (98226-8610)
PHONE..................360 758-4163
Jeff Church, *President*
Karyn McKinney, *Owner*
EMP: 2 **EST:** 1994
SALES: 150K **Privately Held**
SIC: 3861 Printing frames, photographic

(G-1538)
SIR SPEEDY
810 N State St (98225-5019)
PHONE..................360 647-7565
EMP: 2 **EST:** 2001
SALES (est): 130.7K **Privately Held**
SIC: 2752 Comm Prtg Litho

(G-1539)
SIX ROBBLES
150 W Axton Rd (98225-7387)
PHONE..................360 398-7173
Neil Hendricks, *Owner*
EMP: 3
SALES (est): 207.9K **Privately Held**
SIC: 3715 Truck trailers

(G-1540)
SJE INC
Also Called: San Juan Engineering & Mfg Co
4562 Wynn Rd Ste A (98226-8314)
P.O. Box 5743 (98227-5743)
PHONE..................360 734-1910
Robert Tretwold, *President*
Bette Tretwold, *Admin Sec*
EMP: 40
SQ FT: 19,000
SALES (est): 4.3MM **Privately Held**
SIC: 3429 3714 3519 Marine hardware; motor vehicle engines & parts; internal combustion engines

(G-1541)
SKI JOURNAL
3620 Irongate Rd Ste 122 (98226-8052)
P.O. Box 2806 (98227-2806)
PHONE..................360 752-5559
Kristopher Kaiyala, *Principal*
Sakeus Bankson, *Editor*
Matt Wibby, *Director*
EMP: 3
SALES (est): 163K **Privately Held**
SIC: 2711 Newspapers, publishing & printing

(G-1542)
SKILLS FOR CREATIVE CONCEPTS
Also Called: SCC
3313 Mcalpine Rd Ste C (98225-8469)
PHONE..................360 671-1472
John McCoy, *President*
Erica McCoy, *Vice Pres*
EMP: 3
SQ FT: 460
SALES (est): 386.1K **Privately Held**
WEB: www.omnitech-engineering.com
SIC: 3089 Injection molded finished plastic products

(G-1543)
SLEEP NUMBER CORPORATION
4210 Meridian St (98225-5513)
PHONE..................360 671-1266
EMP: 4
SALES (corp-wide): 1.5B **Publicly Held**
SIC: 5712 5021 2515 Mattresses: mattresses; mattresses & bedsprings
PA: Sleep Number Corporation
1001 3rd Ave S
Minneapolis MN 55404
763 551-7000

(G-1544)
SOFTRIDE INC
913 Squalicum Way Ste 201 (98225-2078)
P.O. Box 23 (98227-0023)
PHONE..................360 647-7420
James Allsop, *President*
Ryan Allsop, *President*
Jeff Haley, *Sales Staff*
Linda Pilon, *Administration*
▲ **EMP:** 5
SALES (est): 828.5K **Privately Held**
WEB: www.softride.com
SIC: 3751 Motorcycles, bicycles & parts

(G-1545)
SOFTSOURCE LLC (PA)
3112 Maple Ridge Ct (98229-2391)
PHONE..................360 676-0999
Gary B Rohrabaugh, *President*
EMP: 6
SALES (est): 2.8MM **Privately Held**
WEB: www.softsource.com
SIC: 7373 7372 Computer-aided design (CAD) systems service; prepackaged software

(G-1546)
SOUND SERVICES
2531 Eldridge Ave (98225-2013)
PHONE..................360 920-3435
James Larrison, *Owner*
EMP: 2
SALES (est): 171.5K **Privately Held**
SIC: 3571 Electronic computers

(G-1547)
SOUNDINGS OF THE PLANET INC
1304 Meador Ave Ste 3 (98229-5847)
P.O. Box 4472 (98227-4472)
PHONE..................360 738-9368
Dean Evenson, *President*
EMP: 8
SALES (est): 983.5K **Privately Held**
SIC: 3652 7812 Magnetic tape (audio): prerecorded; compact laser discs, prerecorded; video production

(G-1548)
SOUTH BEND LATHES
1821 Valencia St (98229-4746)
PHONE..................360 734-1540
Shiraz Balolia, *President*
▲ **EMP:** 2 **EST:** 2009
SALES (est): 184.5K **Privately Held**
SIC: 3541 Lathes

(G-1549)
SPECIAL T SIGNS & GRAPHICS
Also Called: Specialty Graphics
2206 Pacific St (98229-5824)
PHONE..................360 734-7617
Tim Donnelly, *Owner*
EMP: 12
SALES (est): 1MM **Privately Held**
WEB: www.specialt.com
SIC: 3993 Signs & advertising specialties

(G-1550)
SPECIFIED FITTINGS LLC
164 W Smith Rd (98226-9616)
PHONE..................360 398-7700
Jonathan Weintraub,
EMP: 7
SALES (est): 137.9K **Privately Held**
SIC: 3494 Valves & pipe fittings

(G-1551)
SPECIFIED FITTINGS LLC
164 W Smith Rd (98226-9616)
P.O. Box 28157 (98228-0157)
PHONE..................360 398-7700
Kathleen Gundel, *President*
Greg Gundel, *Vice Pres*
Charles Michael Brewer, *Admin Sec*
◆ **EMP:** 150
SQ FT: 24,000
SALES (est): 58.3MM **Privately Held**
SIC: 3321 Cast iron pipe & fittings

(G-1552)
SPICE HUT CORPORATION
Also Called: Spice Hut, The
131 W Kellogg Rd (98226-8009)
PHONE..................360 671-2800
Tanvir Sidhu, *Principal*
Harmandir K Sidhu, *Principal*
EMP: 10
SALES (est): 1.1MM **Privately Held**
SIC: 2099 5149 5499 Seasonings & spices; spices, including grinding; spices & seasonings; coffee & tea; spices & herbs

(G-1553)
SPIRALTEC
3951 Hammer Dr (98226-7630)
PHONE..................360 734-7831
Dave Mellott, *Owner*
EMP: 6
SALES (est): 396.6K **Privately Held**
SIC: 3444 Sheet metalwork

Bellingham - Whatcom County (G-1554)

(G-1554)
SQUALICUM MARINE INC
Also Called: Squalicum Marine Upholstery
2620 N Harbor Loop Dr # 17 (98225-2072)
PHONE................................360 733-4353
Tim Mumford, *President*
EMP: 4 EST: 1968
SQ FT: 1,590
SALES (est): 280K **Privately Held**
SIC: 2394 2221 Convertible tops, canvas or boat: from purchased materials; upholstery fabrics, manmade fiber & silk

(G-1555)
STAMPADOODLE INC
Also Called: Stampadoodle Art & Paper
1825 Grant St (98225-4635)
PHONE................................360 647-9663
Steven Schwartz, *President*
Stephen Schwartz, *Owner*
Wendy Schwartz, *Owner*
EMP: 8
SQ FT: 2,300
SALES (est): 863.1K **Privately Held**
WEB: www.stampadoodle.com
SIC: 3069 5999 3953 5945 Hard rubber & molded rubber products; artists' supplies & materials; marking devices; arts & crafts supplies

(G-1556)
STARRY FIELD SERVICES
4915 Samish Way Unit 19 (98229-8938)
PHONE................................360 676-7441
Marilyn Flint, *Principal*
EMP: 2
SALES (est): 90.1K **Privately Held**
SIC: 1311 Crude petroleum & natural gas

(G-1557)
STEER STRAIGHT LLC ◆
3755 Squalicum Lake Rd (98226-8624)
PHONE................................360 398-6294
Martin Costello, *Principal*
EMP: 2 EST: 2018
SALES (est): 150.7K **Privately Held**
SIC: 3531 Construction machinery

(G-1558)
STEVE KEN BOSMAN
Also Called: A Good Sign Company
539 E Smith Rd (98226-9738)
PHONE................................360 398-7444
Steven K Bosman, *President*
Steve Bosman, *President*
Jeanie Bosman, *Admin Sec*
EMP: 4 EST: 1985
SALES: 150K **Privately Held**
WEB: www.safetyhomeaddress.com
SIC: 3993 Signs, not made in custom sign painting shops

(G-1559)
STICK IT TO VIOLENCE
400 Westerly Rd Apt 303 (98226-6410)
PHONE................................360 758-7488
Lisa Osadchuk, *Principal*
EMP: 2
SALES (est): 85.9K **Privately Held**
SIC: 3577 Computer peripheral equipment

(G-1560)
STRUCTURAL DIAGNOSTIC SERVICES
1225 E Sunset Dr Ste 640 (98226-3597)
PHONE................................360 647-6681
Thomas E Poast, *President*
James Mitchel, *Corp Secy*
David Kesler, *Vice Pres*
EMP: 2
SALES (est): 147.9K **Privately Held**
WEB: www.structuraldiagnostic.com
SIC: 7389 2819 Inspection & testing services; chemicals, high purity: refined from technical grade

(G-1561)
STRUCTURES BREWING LLC
1420 N State St (98225-4513)
PHONE................................432 770-1540
James Alexander, *Principal*
EMP: 3
SALES (est): 68.6K **Privately Held**
SIC: 2082 Beer (alcoholic beverage)

(G-1562)
SUBDUED BREWING LLC
2529 Grant St (98225-3506)
PHONE................................360 656-6611
Chris McClanahan, *Principal*
EMP: 3
SALES (est): 106.3K **Privately Held**
SIC: 2082 Beer (alcoholic beverage)

(G-1563)
SUNSHINE PRTG & QUICK COPY SVC
618 W King Tut Rd (98225-9674)
PHONE................................360 671-0191
Len Vander Stelt, *Owner*
Vicky Vander Stelt, *Principal*
EMP: 9
SQ FT: 7,000
SALES (est): 891K **Privately Held**
SIC: 2752 Commercial printing, offset

(G-1564)
SUPERIOR ENERGY SERVICES LLC
Also Called: Marine Technical Services
629 Cornwall Ave (98225-5017)
PHONE................................360 733-3030
EMP: 44 **Publicly Held**
SIC: 1389 Oil field services
HQ: Superior Energy Services, L.L.C.
203 Commission Blvd
Lafayette LA 70508
337 714-4545

(G-1565)
T SQUARED TOOLS LLC
2139 Humboldt St (98225-4118)
PHONE................................406 260-5232
Thomas Dolese, *Principal*
EMP: 2 EST: 2016
SALES (est): 98.1K **Privately Held**
SIC: 3599 Industrial machinery

(G-1566)
TAGLINE PRODUCTS LLC
309 Palm St (98225-5805)
PHONE................................360 927-2719
Amelia Black,
Rick Black,
EMP: 4 EST: 2013
SALES (est): 100K **Privately Held**
SIC: 3949 Snow skis

(G-1567)
TEST BEST INTERNATIONAL INC
Also Called: Puzzle Wise
3744 Crystal Ct Ste 33 (98225-4196)
P.O. Box 28312 (98228-0312)
PHONE................................360 650-0671
EMP: 10
SALES: 100K **Privately Held**
WEB: www.puzzlewise.com
SIC: 5999 2731 5192 Educational aids & electronic training materials; book publishing; books

(G-1568)
THEO WANNE MOUTHPIECES INSTRS
1221 Fraser St Ste 102 (98229-5844)
PHONE................................360 392-8416
Bryan Vance, *Sales Mgr*
Theo Wanne, *Manager*
EMP: 2
SALES (est): 197.9K **Privately Held**
SIC: 3931 Musical instruments

(G-1569)
THOMAS PRODUCTS LLC
4721 Spring Vista Way (98226-2232)
PHONE................................253 678-8391
EMP: 3
SALES (est): 124.5K **Privately Held**
SIC: 2048 Prepared feeds

(G-1570)
THRIFTY PAYLESS INC T/A
3227 Northwest Ave (98225-1317)
PHONE................................360 647-2175
EMP: 2
SALES (est): 94.5K **Privately Held**
SIC: 2836 Vaccines & other immunizing products

(G-1571)
TODAYS STYLE
1654 Birchwood Ave (98225-1310)
PHONE................................360 671-4922
Michael Shultz, *Owner*
EMP: 4 EST: 2007
SALES (est): 204.8K **Privately Held**
SIC: 3999 Barber & beauty shop equipment

(G-1572)
TOP TO BOTTOM INC
2620 N Harbor Loop Dr # 16 (98225-2072)
PHONE................................360 671-7022
Roger Schjelderup, *President*
EMP: 5
SQ FT: 1,000
SALES (est): 713K **Privately Held**
SIC: 3732 7999 7699 7389 Boat building & repairing; diving instruction, underwater; boat repair; divers, commercial; boat cleaning

(G-1573)
TRACK EQUIPMENT COMPANY LLC
2630 Jaeger St (98225-2122)
P.O. Box 1275 (98227-1275)
PHONE................................360 201-7881
Clayton Larkin,
EMP: 2
SALES: 250K **Privately Held**
SIC: 3531 Construction machinery

(G-1574)
TRANSITION COMPOSITES MFG INC
2321 E Bakerview Rd Ste E (98226-7147)
PHONE................................360 312-1497
Donna Blotteaux, *Vice Pres*
EMP: 5
SALES (est): 489.6K **Privately Held**
SIC: 3369 3624 Aerospace castings, nonferrous: except aluminum; brush blocks, carbon or molded graphite; electrodes, thermal & electrolytic uses: carbon, graphite; fibers, carbon & graphite

(G-1575)
TRIDENT SEAFOODS CORPORATION
2825 Roeder Ave (98225-2053)
P.O. Box 427 (98227-0427)
PHONE................................360 734-8900
William Graves, *Branch Mgr*
EMP: 150
SALES (corp-wide): 2.3B **Privately Held**
WEB: www.tridentseafoods.com
SIC: 2092 Seafoods, fresh: prepared; seafoods, frozen: prepared
PA: Trident Seafoods Corporation
5303 Shilshole Ave Nw
Seattle WA 98107
206 783-3818

(G-1576)
TRIDENT SEAFOODS CORPORATION
Also Called: Alaska Naturals Pet Products
400 W Orchard Dr (98225-1754)
PHONE................................360 671-0669
Charles Bundrant, *CEO*
EMP: 2
SALES (corp-wide): 2.3B **Privately Held**
SIC: 2092 5146 Seafoods, frozen: prepared; crabmeat, frozen; fish, frozen: prepared; seafoods
PA: Trident Seafoods Corporation
5303 Shilshole Ave Nw
Seattle WA 98107
206 783-3818

(G-1577)
TRULIFE INC
445 Sequoia Dr Ste 113 (98226-7156)
PHONE................................360 714-9000
Noel Murphy, *President*
Paul Van Metre, *President*
Mike Sumner, *Vice Pres*
Darcy Hughes, *Education*
EMP: 51
SQ FT: 14,000
SALES (est): 13.2MM **Privately Held**
WEB: www.procnc.com
SIC: 3599 Machine shop, jobbing & repair
HQ: Trulife Limited
41 Amos Road
Sheffield S9 1B
114 261-8100

(G-1578)
TRUNEK ENTERPRISES INC
Also Called: Orca Marine Cooling Systems
3883 Irongate Rd (98226-8015)
P.O. Box 5743 (98227-5743)
PHONE................................360 734-6860
Robert Trunek, *President*
Diane Trunek, *Vice Pres*
EMP: 10
SQ FT: 7,100
SALES: 720.3K **Privately Held**
WEB: www.orcamarine.com
SIC: 3443 Heat exchangers, plate type

(G-1579)
TWO HORSE LOGGING INC
165 S Garden St (98225-5817)
PHONE................................360 592-5244
EMP: 3
SALES (est): 140K **Privately Held**
SIC: 2411 Logging

(G-1580)
TYRON GLOBAL COMPANY
715 W Orchard Dr Ste 3 (98225-1767)
PHONE................................360 734-1789
Helena Ouyang, *President*
▲ EMP: 5
SQ FT: 1,000
SALES (est): 649.2K **Privately Held**
SIC: 2819 Industrial inorganic chemicals

(G-1581)
VERONICA DLNDBA GOLD STAR PUBG
4764 Corona Ct (98226-1208)
PHONE................................360 398-2446
Veronica Dolin, *Principal*
EMP: 2
SALES (est): 119.1K **Privately Held**
SIC: 2741 Miscellaneous publishing

(G-1582)
VESSEL PRINTING STUDIO
107 Grand Ave (98225-4414)
PHONE................................360 441-4622
EMP: 2
SALES (est): 92.3K **Privately Held**
SIC: 2752 Commercial printing, lithographic

(G-1583)
VISUAL COMMUNICATIONS DEV
Also Called: Visitors Guide Publications
215 W Holly St Ste H24 (98225-4357)
PHONE................................360 676-8625
Marcus Yearout, *President*
Jennifer Coleman, *Marketing Staff*
EMP: 5
SALES (est): 400.7K **Privately Held**
WEB: www.experiencewa.com
SIC: 2741 Catalogs: publishing only, not printed on site

(G-1584)
VITAL CHOICE SEAFOOD SPC
615 17th St (98225-6334)
P.O. Box 4121 (98227-4121)
PHONE................................360 325-0104
Randy L Hartnell, *President*
Jason Dean, *Opers Mgr*
David Hamburg, *CFO*
Erin Stevens, *Marketing Mgr*
Jim Nelson, *Manager*
▲ EMP: 33
SQ FT: 40,000
SALES (est): 1.4MM **Privately Held**
WEB: www.vitalchoice.com
SIC: 2091 5142 Salmon: packaged in cans, jars, etc.; frozen fish, meat & poultry

(G-1585)
VIVONET INCORPORATED (PA)
Also Called: Vivonet Halo Pos
1225 E Sunset Dr Ste 14 (98226-3597)
PHONE................................866 512-2033
Ryan Volberg, *President*
Kevin Falk, *Vice Pres*
EMP: 2 EST: 1999
SQ FT: 6,000

GEOGRAPHIC SECTION — Benton City - Benton County (G-1616)

SALES (est): 7.6MM **Privately Held**
WEB: www.autoprise.com
SIC: **7372** Application computer software

(G-1586)
VLEDS
130 W Axton Rd (98226-9659)
PHONE..................................360 543-5700
EMP: 2
SALES (est): 158.4K **Privately Held**
SIC: **3648** Lighting equipment

(G-1587)
WALFLOR INDUSTRIES
4820 Whitney St (98229-2638)
PHONE..................................425 766-4161
▲ EMP: 2 EST: 2016
SALES (est): 171.7K **Privately Held**
SIC: **3999** Manufacturing industries

(G-1588)
WALKER GOLDSMITHS
2603 Finkbonner Rd (98226-9258)
P.O. Box 665 (98227-0665)
PHONE..................................360 758-2601
Owen Walker, *Owner*
EMP: 2
SALES (est): 94.4K **Privately Held**
WEB: www.walkergoldsmiths.com
SIC: **1041** Gold ores processing

(G-1589)
WASHINGTON WIND SPORTS INC
Also Called: Wws
104 E Maple St (98225-5006)
PHONE..................................360 676-1146
Brian Gudbranson, *President*
EMP: 4
SQ FT: 1,200
SALES (est): 400K **Privately Held**
WEB: www.wws.com
SIC: **3949** Skateboards; shuffleboards & shuffleboard equipment; Indian clubs

(G-1590)
WATERLINE ENVIROTECH LTD
4301 Squalicum Lake Rd (98226-9469)
P.O. Box 28220 (98228-0220)
PHONE..................................360 676-9635
Belinda Granat, *President*
EMP: 3
SALES (est): 320K **Privately Held**
WEB: www.waterlineenvirotech.com
SIC: **3823** Water quality monitoring & control systems

(G-1591)
WESNIP
424 W Bakerview Rd # 105 (98226-8176)
PHONE..................................360 306-0345
Jon Budar, *President*
EMP: 2
SALES (est): 146.5K **Privately Held**
SIC: **3999** Pet supplies

(G-1592)
WEST COAST CUSTOM METAL DESIGN
3950 Hammer Dr Ste 104 (98226-7776)
PHONE..................................360 738-2884
Oneil Martin, *President*
▲ EMP: 4 EST: 2012
SALES (est): 665.6K **Privately Held**
SIC: **3441** 3444 3446 3449 Fabricated structural metal; sheet metalwork; architectural metalwork; miscellaneous metalwork

(G-1593)
WHATCOM WATCH NEWSPAPER
3008 Tulip Rd (98225-2246)
P.O. Box 1441 (98227-1441)
PHONE..................................360 734-6007
Bill Mc Allen, *President*
EMP: 2 EST: 1998
SALES (est): 155.4K **Privately Held**
SIC: **2711** Newspapers, publishing & printing

(G-1594)
WOMPMOBILE INC
1117 Ellis St (98225-5203)
PHONE..................................888 625-8144
Madison Miner, *CEO*

EMP: 3
SALES (est): 269.6K **Privately Held**
SIC: **7372** Application computer software

(G-1595)
WOOD STONE CORPORATION
1801 W Bakerview Rd (98226-9105)
PHONE..................................360 650-1111
Chris Trout, *President*
Tamra Nelson, *Vice Pres*
Eric Schueler, *VP Opers*
J M Miller, *Manager*
Kurt I Eickmeyer, *Risk Mgmt Dir*
◆ EMP: 130
SALES (est): 27.5MM
SALES (corp-wide): 174.4MM **Privately Held**
WEB: www.woodstone.net
SIC: **3556** Ovens, bakery
PA: Henny Penny Corporation
1219 Us Route 35
Eaton OH 45320
937 456-8400

(G-1596)
WOODSTOCK INTERNATIONAL INC (PA)
1821 Valencia St (98229-4746)
P.O. Box 2309 (98227-2309)
PHONE..................................360 734-3482
Shiraz Balolia, *President*
Andrew Cannon, *Technician*
Ethan Roe,
▲ EMP: 24
SQ FT: 35,000
SALES (est): 4.7MM **Privately Held**
WEB: www.woodstockinternational.org
SIC: **3545** 3564 5085 5075 Tools & accessories for machine tools; dust or fume collecting equipment, industrial; tools; dust collecting equipment

(G-1597)
YORKSTON OIL CO (PA)
Also Called: Yorkston Card Lock Fuels
2801 Roeder Ave (98225-2053)
P.O. Box 229111 (98229-0904)
PHONE..................................360 734-2201
Barney M Yorkston Jr, *President*
Matt Yorkston, *Corp Secy*
David L Yorkston, *Vice Pres*
J Matthew Yorkston, *Admin Sec*
EMP: 13
SQ FT: 2,500
SALES (est): 25.4MM **Privately Held**
WEB: www.yorkstonoil.com
SIC: **5172** 5411 3519 Petroleum brokers; fuel oil; convenience stores, chain; diesel, semi-diesel or duel-fuel engines, including marine

(G-1598)
ZZ INC
407 S Clarkwood Dr (98225-8702)
PHONE..................................360 734-2290
Sue Zoske, *President*
Rod Zoske, *Senior VP*
EMP: 2
SALES (est): 145.5K **Privately Held**
SIC: **2099** 5149 Sauces: gravy, dressing & dip mixes; condiments

---
Benton City
Benton County

(G-1599)
AAA PRECISE MACHINE INC
27305 E Ruppert Rd (99320-7714)
PHONE..................................509 375-3268
Albert Lemieux, *President*
EMP: 2
SQ FT: 1,800
SALES: 90K **Privately Held**
SIC: **3728** 3842 Aircraft parts & equipment; wheelchairs

(G-1600)
ALL WAVE INNOVATIONS INC
45106 N 280 Pr Ne (99320-7546)
PHONE..................................509 308-7230
Rolly Fuller, *President*
Ron Bowles, *Vice Pres*
Greg Elseth, *Vice Pres*

Gary Griffiths, *Shareholder*
EMP: 6
SALES (est): 331.9K **Privately Held**
SIC: **8748** 7371 3699 Testing services; computer software development; electrical equipment & supplies

(G-1601)
AMERICAN WINE TRADE INC
Also Called: Hedges Cellars
53511 N Sunset Rd (99320-6503)
PHONE..................................509 588-3155
Tom Hedges, *President*
Molly M Christopherson, *Controller*
EMP: 12
SALES (corp-wide): 4.4MM **Privately Held**
SIC: **0172** 2084 Grapes; wines
PA: American Wine Trade, Inc.
900 Lenora St Apt 103
Seattle WA 98121
206 357-0607

(G-1602)
BLANCA TERRA VINEYARDS INC
Also Called: Terra Blanca Vintners
34715 N Demoss Rd (99320-8797)
PHONE..................................509 588-6082
Keith Pilgrim, *President*
Renee Scott Pilgrim, *Treasurer*
Kari Schillios, *Sales Staff*
Jordan Neuhaus, *Mktg Coord*
Daryl Baker, *Manager*
EMP: 5
SALES (est): 2MM **Privately Held**
WEB: www.terrablanca.com
SIC: **0762** 2084 0172 Vineyard management & maintenance services; wines, brandy & brandy spirits; grapes

(G-1603)
CARPENTER DRILLING LLC
Also Called: Water Well Drilling
7 S Goose Gap Rd (99320-8561)
PHONE..................................509 627-6642
Jody L Carpenter,
Jody S Carpenter,
EMP: 15
SALES: 1MM **Privately Held**
SIC: **1799** 1781 1381 Core drilling & cutting; geothermal drilling; water well servicing; service well drilling

(G-1604)
CENTERLINE FABRICATION
45219 E Red Mountain Rd (99320-6729)
PHONE..................................509 948-8711
Sarah Howard, *Principal*
EMP: 2
SALES (est): 130.7K **Privately Held**
SIC: **3441** Fabricated structural metal

(G-1605)
CHANDLER REACH VINEYARD ESTATE (PA)
9506 W Chandler Rd (99320-7852)
PHONE..................................509 588-8800
Len Parris, *Principal*
Meghan Parris, *Manager*
EMP: 4
SALES (est): 384.8K **Privately Held**
SIC: **2084** Wines

(G-1606)
CHOICE WIRING LLC
Also Called: Choice Communications
55911 N Thomas Rd (99320-5614)
PHONE..................................509 588-6185
Robert Suski, *Mng Member*
Nancy B Suski,
EMP: 3
SALES (est): 336.1K **Privately Held**
WEB: www.prismcrystals.com
SIC: **7389** 3661 Telephone services; telegraph station equipment & parts, wire

(G-1607)
COL SOLARE LLP (PA)
Also Called: Col Solare Winery
50207 Antinori Rd (99320-7872)
PHONE..................................509 588-6806
Theodor Baseler, *Partner*
Sheila Newlands, *Partner*
▲ EMP: 7

SALES (est): 660.1K **Privately Held**
SIC: **2084** Wines

(G-1608)
CUSTOM BOTTLING COMPANY
8203 W Corral Creek Rd Nw (99320-9666)
PHONE..................................509 528-3196
William C Hamlin, *Principal*
EMP: 4 EST: 2011
SALES (est): 277.2K **Privately Held**
SIC: **2086** Bottled & canned soft drinks

(G-1609)
DES ETES LONGS VINEYARD LLC
34821 N 114 Pr Nw (99320-4560)
PHONE..................................509 430-5488
Delbert Long, *Principal*
EMP: 2
SALES (est): 62.3K **Privately Held**
SIC: **2084** Wines, brandy & brandy spirits

(G-1610)
EMORY VINEYARDS LLC
18809 E 583 Pr Ne (99320-7504)
PHONE..................................509 588-2988
Bruce Emory, *Principal*
EMP: 2
SALES (est): 78.4K **Privately Held**
SIC: **2084** Wines, brandy & brandy spirits

(G-1611)
FIDELITAS WINES LLC
51810 N Sunset Rd (99320-7508)
PHONE..................................509 588-3469
Loren J Hoppes, *Principal*
Stacey Hill, *Bookkeeper*
Chelsea Brophy, *Manager*
EMP: 6
SALES (est): 544.6K **Privately Held**
SIC: **2084** Wines

(G-1612)
FRICHETTE WINERY
39412 N Sunset Rd (99320-8599)
PHONE..................................509 426-3227
Greg Frichette, *Principal*
EMP: 4
SALES (est): 308.8K **Privately Held**
SIC: **2084** Wines

(G-1613)
GOOSE RIDGE LLC
Also Called: Goose Ridge Vineyards
63615 E Jacobs Rd Ne (99320-8568)
PHONE..................................509 837-4427
Bob Gates, *Officer*
Bill Monson,
▲ EMP: 15
SALES (est): 2.3MM **Privately Held**
SIC: **2084** Wines

(G-1614)
GOOSE RIDGE VINEYARDS LLC
Also Called: Goose Rdge Est Vneyards Winery
63615 E Jacobs Rd Ne (99320-8568)
PHONE..................................509 627-1618
William Monson,
Arvid Monson,
Suzanne Monson,
Valerie Monson,
Molly Stutesman,
EMP: 11 EST: 2013
SALES (est): 1.7MM **Privately Held**
SIC: **2084** Wines

(G-1615)
HALLDATA INC
Also Called: Rippedsheets.com
1580 Dale Ave (99320-8801)
P.O. Box 5290 (99320-5290)
PHONE..................................509 588-5080
Steve Hall, *President*
Leslie Ritter, *Officer*
EMP: 28
SQ FT: 20,000
SALES (est): 2.8MM **Privately Held**
SIC: **2672** Coated & laminated paper

(G-1616)
HAMILTON CELLARS LLC
55410 N Sunset Rd (99320-7502)
PHONE..................................509 628-8227
Stacie Hamilton, *Owner*

Benton City - Benton County (G-1617)

John Hamilton, *Owner*
EMP: 2
SALES (est): 171.2K **Privately Held**
SIC: 2084 Wines

(G-1617)
HIGHTOWER CELLARS
19418 E 583 Pr Ne (99320-8598)
PHONE.................................509 588-2867
Timothy Hightower, *Principal*
EMP: 7
SALES (est): 546.4K **Privately Held**
SIC: 2084 Wines

(G-1618)
KIONA VINEYARDS LLC
44612 N Sunset Rd (99320-7500)
PHONE.................................509 588-6716
Brandon Gomez, *Opers Staff*
John Williams, *Mng Member*
Ann Williams, *Mng Member*
▲ **EMP:** 12
SQ FT: 10,000
SALES: 2.4MM **Privately Held**
SIC: 5921 5182 2084 Wine; wine & distilled beverages; wines

(G-1619)
MAGDALENA VINEYARD LLC
53222 N Sunset Rd (99320-7598)
PHONE.................................509 942-4204
Magdalena Vineyard, *Principal*
EMP: 4 **EST:** 2009
SALES (est): 111.5K **Privately Held**
SIC: 2084 Wines, brandy & brandy spirits

(G-1620)
MONTE SCARLATTO ESTATE WINERY
28719 E Sr 224 Ne (99320-7542)
PHONE.................................509 531-3081
Joel Mackay, *President*
EMP: 4
SALES (est): 293.2K **Privately Held**
SIC: 2084 Wines

(G-1621)
NRG RESOURCES INC
733 9th St (99320-8813)
P.O. Box 5080 (99320-5080)
PHONE.................................509 588-4786
Kelly Edwards, *President*
Ron Morris, *General Mgr*
Jack Edwards, *Vice Pres*
EMP: 60
SQ FT: 8,000
SALES (est): 4.9MM **Privately Held**
SIC: 8742 2789 2759 2672 Marketing consulting services; bookbinding & related work; commercial printing; coated & laminated paper

(G-1622)
OAKWOOD CELLARS
12911 E Sr 224 Ne (99320-8588)
PHONE.................................509 588-1900
Evelan Skelton, *Owner*
EMP: 2
SALES: 100K **Privately Held**
WEB: www.oakwoodcellars.com
SIC: 2084 7999 0172 Wine cellars, bonded: engaged in blending wines; picnic ground operation; grapes

(G-1623)
PHEASANT BROTHERS LLC
1560 Ne 11th St (99320-6550)
PHONE.................................509 539-5899
Richard Pheasant, *President*
Anthony Pheasant,
Nathan Pheasant,
EMP: 4
SALES: 12K **Privately Held**
SIC: 5499 2033 Juices, fruit or vegetable; barbecue sauce: packaged in cans, jars, etc.

(G-1624)
PROVIDENT ELECTRIC INC
64406 N Sr 225 (99320-6618)
PHONE.................................509 588-3939
Alan Olson, *Branch Mgr*
EMP: 17

SALES (corp-wide): 7.6MM **Privately Held**
SIC: 3699 1731 Electrical equipment & supplies; electrical work
PA: Provident Electric Incorporated
17615 Se 252nd St
Kent WA
253 631-7750

(G-1625)
PURPLE STAR WINERY
56504 N East Roza Rd (99320-8895)
PHONE.................................509 628-7799
EMP: 2
SALES (est): 82.9K **Privately Held**
SIC: 2084 Wines

(G-1626)
RED MNTAIN AMRCN VNTNERS ALNCE
53511 N Sunset Rd (99320-6503)
PHONE.................................509 588-3155
Christophe Hedges, *Director*
EMP: 5
SALES (est): 351.5K **Privately Held**
SIC: 2084 Wines

(G-1627)
RIVER HOLLOW CREATIONS LLC
105b Abby Ave (99320-9703)
PHONE.................................509 497-1097
George Dale, *Principal*
EMP: 2
SALES (est): 150.3K **Privately Held**
SIC: 2431 Millwork

(G-1628)
RIVERBEND INCORPORATED
Also Called: Sleeping Dog Wines
45804 N Whitmore Pr Nw (99320-6657)
PHONE.................................509 460-2886
Laurence Oates, *President*
Joyce Oates, *Vice Pres*
EMP: 2
SQ FT: 1,200
SALES: 75K **Privately Held**
SIC: 2084 Wines

(G-1629)
SONGBIRD VINEYARD LLC
63704 N 106 Pr Ne (99320-8775)
PHONE.................................509 318-4044
Jacquie Stephens, *Administration*
EMP: 2 **EST:** 2016
SALES (est): 111.3K **Privately Held**
SIC: 2084 Wines

(G-1630)
TERRA VINUM LLC
56204 N East Roza Rd (99320-8692)
PHONE.................................509 551-0854
Kyle Joseph Johnson,
Amy Jennette Johnson,
EMP: 3
SALES: 400K **Privately Held**
SIC: 2084 8748 Wines; agricultural consultant

(G-1631)
TUCANNON CELLARS
40504 N Demoss Rd (99320-8791)
PHONE.................................509 545-9588
EMP: 2
SALES (est): 107.4K **Privately Held**
SIC: 2084 Wines

Bickleton
Klickitat County

(G-1632)
JENSEN SEED FARM INC
Also Called: Blue J Seed
255 Ferguson Rd (99322-9705)
PHONE.................................509 896-2312
Peter Jensen, *President*
Jacqueline Jensen, *Treasurer*
Marylynn Jensen, *Admin Sec*
EMP: 2
SALES (est): 183.1K **Privately Held**
SIC: 3999 Advertising curtains

Bingen
Klickitat County

(G-1633)
BLUE BUS CULTURED FOODS LLC
415 W Steuben St (98605-9184)
P.O. Box 1834, White Salmon (98672-1834)
PHONE.................................541 399-4141
Colin Franger, *Mng Member*
EMP: 3 **EST:** 2015
SALES: 100K **Privately Held**
SIC: 2035 Pickles, sauces & salad dressings

(G-1634)
CARBON CONSULTANTS LLC
Also Called: Zepher
310 S Larch St (98605-8908)
P.O. Box 2158, White Salmon (98672-2158)
PHONE.................................509 637-2520
Jason Hartmann, *Sales Staff*
Andrew Mack,
Ashley Butler,
Kirsten Dennis,
Jaime Mack,
EMP: 28
SQ FT: 24,000
SALES: 8.7MM **Privately Held**
WEB: www.zepherinc.com
SIC: 3728 Aircraft parts & equipment

(G-1635)
COMPOSITE TOOLING INNOVATIONS
1211 E Bingen Point Way (98605-8915)
P.O. Box 2142, White Salmon (98672-2142)
PHONE.................................509 637-3836
Peter Lederer,
Lindsay Lederer,
EMP: 2
SQ FT: 1,000
SALES: 60K **Privately Held**
SIC: 3949 3423 Sporting & athletic goods; tools or equipment for use with sporting arms

(G-1636)
CUSTOM INTERFACE INC
410 S Larch St (98605-8909)
P.O. Box 605 (98605-0605)
PHONE.................................509 493-8756
Nancy A White, *CEO*
Mary Rogers, *Opers Staff*
Maria Vega, *Purch Agent*
Karolynn Bruce, *Purchasing*
Cecelia Henderson, *CFO*
EMP: 46
SQ FT: 22,000
SALES (est): 11.2MM **Privately Held**
WEB: www.custominterface.net
SIC: 3679 Harness assemblies for electronic use: wire or cable

(G-1637)
INSITU INC
901 E Bingen Point Way (98605-8912)
PHONE.................................509 493-8600
EMP: 10
SALES (corp-wide): 101.1B **Publicly Held**
SIC: 8711 3999 Engineering services; atomizers, toiletry
HQ: Insitu, Inc.
118 Columbia River Way
Bingen WA 98605

(G-1638)
INSITU INC (HQ)
118 Columbia River Way (98605-9086)
PHONE.................................509 493-8600
Esina Alic, *President*
Steve Norlund, *President*
Jason Ontko, *General Mgr*
Monica Gelien, *Principal*
Heidi Capozzi, *Vice Pres*
EMP: 1200
SQ FT: 25,000

SALES (est): 118.8MM
SALES (corp-wide): 101.1B **Publicly Held**
WEB: www.insitu.com
SIC: 8711 3999 Aviation &/or aeronautical engineering; airplane models, except toy
PA: The Boeing Company
100 N Riverside Plz
Chicago IL 60606
312 544-2000

(G-1639)
LP COMPOSITES INC
314 W Steuben St (98605-9006)
P.O. Box 684 (98605-0684)
PHONE.................................509 493-4447
Stu Fisher, *President*
Peter Lederer, *Vice Pres*
EMP: 17
SQ FT: 4,000
SALES: 1MM **Privately Held**
WEB: www.lpcomposites.com
SIC: 2655 3949 Cans, composite: foil-fiber & other: from purchased fiber; sporting & athletic goods

(G-1640)
MOUNTAIN LOGGING INC
715 E Steuben St (98605-9185)
P.O. Box B, White Salmon (98672)
PHONE.................................509 493-3511
David Clark, *President*
EMP: 40
SALES (est): 1.9MM
SALES (corp-wide): 4.2MM **Privately Held**
SIC: 2411 Logging camps & contractors
PA: Mountain Logging Inc
1000 W Jewett Blvd
White Salmon WA 98672
509 493-3511

(G-1641)
RAPID READYMIX CO
900 E Steuben St (98605-9188)
P.O. Box 668 (98605-0668)
PHONE.................................509 493-3153
Matt Riley, *Manager*
EMP: 6
SALES (corp-wide): 783.3K **Privately Held**
SIC: 3273 3272 Ready-mixed concrete; septic tanks, concrete
PA: Rapid Readymix Co
740 W Railroad Ave
Goldendale WA 98620
509 773-5919

(G-1642)
SDS LUMBER CO
123 Industrial Rd (98605-9108)
P.O. Box 266 (98605-0266)
PHONE.................................509 493-1444
Jason S Spadero, *President*
Gary Collins, *General Mgr*
Harry Harvey, *Superintendent*
John L Cheney, *Vice Pres*
Katherine Stevenson, *Vice Pres*
▲ **EMP:** 250
SQ FT: 5,000
SALES (est): 57.8MM **Privately Held**
WEB: www.sdslumber.com
SIC: 2421 2436 2411 Lumber: rough, sawed or planed; sawdust, shavings & wood chips; plywood, softwood; saw logs

(G-1643)
ZEPHER INC
310 S Larch St (98605-8908)
P.O. Box 2156, White Salmon (98672-2156)
PHONE.................................509 637-2520
Andy Mack, *President*
John Brooks, *Project Mgr*
Patrick Hughes, *Project Mgr*
Kirsten Dennis, *Sales Associate*
EMP: 20 **EST:** 2004
SQ FT: 2,300
SALES: 6MM **Privately Held**
SIC: 3728 3559 Aircraft parts & equipment; semiconductor manufacturing machinery

GEOGRAPHIC SECTION   Blaine - Whatcom County (G-1675)

Black Diamond
King County

(G-1644)
ABCD VENTURES LLC
Also Called: Visual Print Solutions
22541 Se Sawyer Ridge Way
(98010-1312)
PHONE................................206 686-6089
Tracy Gaillac, *Manager*
Elizabeth Vosmeier,
EMP: 2
SALES (est): 244.1K Privately Held
SIC: 2752 Commercial printing, offset

(G-1645)
BLACK DIAMOND SMOKED MEATS
35019 257th Ave Se (98010-9701)
PHONE................................541 228-2758
EMP: 3
SALES (est): 162.9K Privately Held
SIC: 2013 Smoked meats from purchased meat

(G-1646)
C SWANSON LOGGING
29228 218th Pl Se (98010-1266)
PHONE................................360 886-0237
Cory Swanson, *Principal*
EMP: 3
SALES (est): 278.7K Privately Held
SIC: 2411 Logging camps & contractors

(G-1647)
ELDER LOGGING CO
33214 293rd Ave Se (98010-7532)
PHONE................................360 886-2779
Bob Elder, *Owner*
Mary Elder, *Vice Pres*
EMP: 2 EST: 1940
SALES (est): 100K Privately Held
SIC: 2411 Logging

(G-1648)
G DUNDAS CO INC
24301 Roberts Dr Ste A (98010-9219)
PHONE................................253 631-8008
Mario Sorci, *President*
EMP: 2 EST: 1978
SQ FT: 15,000
SALES: 400K
SALES (corp-wide): 4.8MM Privately Held
WEB: www.gdundas.com
SIC: 3841 5047 Anesthesia apparatus; medical & hospital equipment
PA: Anesthesia Equipment Supply, Inc.
    24301 Roberts Dr Ste A
    Black Diamond WA
    253 631-8008

(G-1649)
KENT D BRUCE
22543 Se 313th Pl (98010-9003)
PHONE................................360 886-9410
Kent D Bruce, *Owner*
EMP: 4
SALES (est): 549.8K Privately Held
SIC: 3647 Automotive lighting fixtures

(G-1650)
MASCOTA RESOURCES CORP
29409 232nd Ave Se (98010-1231)
PHONE................................206 818-4799
Dale Rasmussen, *President*
Mark Rodenbeck, *Admin Sec*
EMP: 2
SALES (est): 92.6K Privately Held
SIC: 1081 Metal mining services

(G-1651)
MOTION DUCKS LLC
25811 Lawson St (98010-9795)
PHONE................................253 797-0132
Tom Hardebeck, *Principal*
EMP: 4 EST: 2014
SALES (est): 343.4K Privately Held
SIC: 3949 Sporting & athletic goods

(G-1652)
PACIFIC COAST COAL COMPANY
30700 Black Diamond (98010)
P.O. Box 450 (98010-0450)
PHONE................................360 886-1060
David Morris, *General Mgr*
EMP: 3
SQ FT: 2,000
SALES (est): 340K Privately Held
SIC: 1221 Surface mining, bituminous

(G-1653)
POWELL PUBLISHING INC ✪
29103 218th Pl Se (98010-1264)
PHONE................................360 886-6650
EMP: 2 EST: 2019
SALES (est): 73.1K Privately Held
SIC: 2721 Periodicals

(G-1654)
REANO CONSTRUCTION & LOGGING
Also Called: R C & L
29726 Se 318th St (98010-7507)
P.O. Box 1035 (98010-1035)
PHONE................................360 886-1374
Kirk Reano, *President*
Heidi Reano, *Admin Sec*
EMP: 2
SALES (est): 227K Privately Held
SIC: 2411 1794 Logging camps & contractors; excavation work

(G-1655)
SHAKER INNOVATIONS LLC
22411 Se 313th Pl (98010-9004)
PHONE................................360 886-1873
Todd Larson,
EMP: 4
SALES (est): 427.2K Privately Held
SIC: 3821 Shakers & stirrers

(G-1656)
SWEET TEES
28916 218th Ave Se (98010-1260)
PHONE................................253 632-9224
Pasquel Terwillegar, *Principal*
EMP: 2
SALES (est): 94.4K Privately Held
SIC: 2759 Screen printing

Blaine
Whatcom County

(G-1657)
ADVANCED CEMENT TECH LLC
435 Martin St Ste 2040 (98230-4107)
P.O. Box 924 (98231-0924)
PHONE................................360 332-7060
Chris Kleingartner, *General Mgr*
▼ EMP: 2
SQ FT: 1,200
SALES: 3MM Privately Held
WEB: www.metakaolin.com
SIC: 3272 Concrete products

(G-1658)
ALL POLE CORPORATION
1368 4th St (98230-5020)
PHONE................................360 933-1806
Harri Rauma, *President*
EMP: 12
SALES (est): 599.4K Privately Held
SIC: 3523 8744 Loaders, farm type: manure, general utility; facilities support services

(G-1659)
ALTUS INDUSTRIES INC
435 Martin St (98230-4118)
PHONE................................360 255-7699
EMP: 5
SALES (est): 501.2K Privately Held
SIC: 3272 3647 Mfg Concrete Products Mfg Vehicle Lighting Equipment

(G-1660)
ARIA TRADING INC
8105 Birch Bay Square St # 103 (98230-9802)
PHONE................................360 525-0175
Mohamed Shouman, *CEO*
EMP: 3
SALES (est): 167.3K Privately Held
SIC: 3351 Wire, copper & copper alloy

(G-1661)
BIOPLEX NUTRITION INC
2252 Odell St (98230-9754)
PHONE................................360 332-2101
J Hugh Wiebe, *CEO*
David Mc Cleod, *CFO*
▲ EMP: 18
SQ FT: 3,000
SALES (est): 6MM Privately Held
WEB: www.bioplexnutrition.com
SIC: 5149 3556 Health foods; specialty food items; food products machinery

(G-1662)
BOUNDARY FISH COMPANY
223 Sigurdson Ave (98230-4004)
P.O. Box 2929 (98231-2929)
PHONE................................360 332-6715
Henry Yuki, *President*
Arnold Yuki, *Vice Pres*
Etsumi Yuki, *Vice Pres*
EMP: 25 EST: 1961
SQ FT: 12,000
SALES (est): 3.2MM Privately Held
SIC: 2092 Seafoods, fresh: prepared

(G-1663)
BP AMERICA INC
4519 Grandview Rd (98230-9640)
PHONE................................360 371-0373
Bill Griffith, *Chief*
Michelle Avis, *Project Mgr*
Shannon Potts, *Opers Mgr*
Jon Kornelis, *Foreman/Supr*
Amy Lu, *Engineer*
EMP: 1009
SALES (corp-wide): 298.7B Privately Held
SIC: 2911 Petroleum refining
HQ: Bp America Inc
    4101 Winfield Rd Ste 200
    Warrenville IL 60555
    630 420-5111

(G-1664)
BP CORPORATION NORTH AMER INC
Also Called: BP West Coast Products
4519 Grandview Rd (98230-9640)
PHONE................................360 371-1500
Jeff Pitzer, *Branch Mgr*
EMP: 450
SALES (corp-wide): 298.7B Privately Held
WEB: www.bpamoco.com
SIC: 2911 Petroleum refining
HQ: Bp Corporation North America Inc.
    501 Westlake Park Blvd
    Houston TX 77079
    281 366-2000

(G-1665)
BP WEST COAST PRODUCTS LLC
4519 Grandview Rd (98230-9640)
PHONE................................360 371-1500
Stacey McDaniel, *Branch Mgr*
EMP: 800
SALES (corp-wide): 298.7B Privately Held
SIC: 1311 Crude petroleum production
HQ: Bp West Coast Products Llc
    4519 Grandview Rd
    Blaine WA 98230
    310 549-6204

(G-1666)
CHUCKANUT BAY FOODS LLC
1649 Boblett St (98230-9260)
PHONE................................360 380-1908
David Loeppky, *Partner*
Matt Roth, *Partner*
Tinna Bjornsson, *Purch Mgr*
Ryan Gaylord, *Sales Staff*
Heather Chadbourne, *Mktg Dir*
EMP: 47
SALES (est): 10.5MM Privately Held
SIC: 2051 Cakes, pies & pastries

(G-1667)
DAVIS DEGRASS ENTERPRISES INC
Also Called: Lake Missuola Wine
1625 Boblett St (98230-9260)
PHONE................................360 332-2097
Tom Davis, *President*
Tracy Degrass, *Vice Pres*
EMP: 2
SALES (est): 132.5K Privately Held
SIC: 2084 Wines

(G-1668)
DESCARTES BIOMETRICS INC
9131 Great Blue Heron Ln (98230-9330)
PHONE................................650 743-4435
Katie Boczek, *Treasurer*
EMP: 2
SALES (est): 125.4K Privately Held
SIC: 7372 7389 Business oriented computer software;

(G-1669)
EVANS MFG
9606 Valley View Rd (98230-5300)
PHONE................................360 332-9505
Henry Hollander, *Owner*
EMP: 2
SALES (est): 105.6K Privately Held
SIC: 3949 Fishing tackle, general

(G-1670)
FOURTH CORNER WTR FILTERS LLC
4382 Lateener Ln (98230-9151)
PHONE................................360 296-1647
Julie Helling, *Principal*
EMP: 2
SALES (est): 207.9K Privately Held
SIC: 3569 Filters

(G-1671)
GOLDEN BOY FOODS (USA) INC
1555 Odell St (98230-9193)
PHONE................................360 332-1990
Alnasir Virani, *Principal*
Amirali Virani, *Principal*
Griffin Eric, *Opers Mgr*
EMP: 3
SALES (est): 172.3K Privately Held
SIC: 2099 Almond pastes

(G-1672)
GOLDEN CLAW VENTURES INC
810 Peace Portal Dr (98230-4042)
PHONE................................360 927-8276
Sami Vaskola, *Principal*
EMP: 2
SALES (est): 69.8K Privately Held
SIC: 1081 Metal mining services

(G-1673)
GOLDEN NUT COMPANY (USA) INC
1555 Odell St (98230-9193)
PHONE................................360 332-1990
Richard Harris, *CEO*
EMP: 22
SALES (est): 5.4MM Publicly Held
SIC: 2099 Food preparations
HQ: Golden Boy Foods Ltd
    7725 Lougheed Hwy
    Burnaby BC V5A 4
    604 433-2200

(G-1674)
GOLDMOUNTAIN EXPLORATION CORP
225 Marine Dr Ste 210 (98230-4027)
PHONE................................360 332-0905
Gregory Leigh Lyons, *CEO*
EMP: 2
SALES (est): 120K Privately Held
SIC: 1481 Mine exploration, nonmetallic minerals

(G-1675)
INTERLUBE INTERNATIONAL INC
Also Called: Opti
170 3rd St (98230-4243)
PHONE................................360 332-2132
Paige Sigston, *Principal*
▲ EMP: 7 EST: 2009

Blaine - Whatcom County (G-1676)

SALES (est): 1.3MM **Privately Held**
SIC: 2992 Lubricating oils & greases

(G-1676)
INTERNATIONAL COMANCHE SOCIETY
925 Ludwick Ave (98230-5109)
PHONE 360 332-2743
Lisa Dailey, *Director*
EMP: 2
SALES (est): 96.3K **Privately Held**
SIC: 2741 Miscellaneous publishing

(G-1677)
K B ALLOYS
8615 Semiahmoo Dr (98230-9314)
PHONE 360 371-2312
EMP: 2
SALES (est): 160K **Privately Held**
SIC: 3312 Blast Furnace-Steel Works

(G-1678)
KHANCELL CORPORATION
1685 H St (98230-5110)
PHONE 646 385-7243
Yeon Su Han, *President*
Kangil Choe, *Principal*
EMP: 2
SALES (est): 127.1K **Privately Held**
SIC: 3692 Primary batteries, dry & wet

(G-1679)
KRYSALIIS LLC
288 Martin St (98230-4045)
PHONE 888 579-7254
EMP: 2
SALES (est): 93.9K **Privately Held**
SIC: 3479 Engraving jewelry silverware, or metal

(G-1680)
LISTER CHAIN AND FORGE INC
3810 Loomis Trail Rd (98230-9106)
PHONE 360 332-4323
Michael Stobbart, *President*
EMP: 27
SALES (est): 7MM
SALES (corp-wide): 59MM **Privately Held**
WEB: www.listerchain.com
SIC: 3462 Anchors, forged
HQ: Washington Chain & Supply, Inc.
2901 Utah Ave S
Seattle WA 98134
206 623-8500

(G-1681)
LUVO USA LLC
250 H St (98230-4018)
PHONE 604 730-0387
David Negus, *Principal*
EMP: 5
SALES (est): 217.4K **Privately Held**
SIC: 2038 Frozen specialties

(G-1682)
MAGELLAN GROUP LTD
Also Called: Magellan Groul
225 Marine Dr Ste 300 (98230-4027)
PHONE 360 332-6868
EMP: 2
SALES (est): 88.3K **Privately Held**
SIC: 3634 5961 Mfg Electric Housewares/Fans Ret Mail-Order House

(G-1683)
MANTLE INDUSTRIES LLC
1100c Yew Ave (98230-9222)
PHONE 360 332-5276
Duane Bryant, *President*
EMP: 14
SQ FT: 18,426
SALES (est): 593.6K **Privately Held**
SIC: 3448 1629 Ramps: prefabricated metal; dock construction
HQ: Cmi Limited Co.
1165 Northchase Pkwy Se
Marietta GA 30067

(G-1684)
MOBETIZE CORP
8150 Birch Bay Square St # 205 (98230)
PHONE 778 588-5563
Malek Ladki, *Ch of Bd*
Peter Thornton, *Vice Pres*

Donald Duberstein, *Director*
Stephen Fowler, *Director*
Ajay Hans, *Officer*
EMP: 8
SALES: 438.2K **Privately Held**
SIC: 7372 Business oriented computer software

(G-1685)
NATURALLY NW PUBLICATIONS
Also Called: Northern Light
225 Marine Dr Ste 200 (98230-4052)
PHONE 360 332-1777
Patrick James Grubb, *President*
EMP: 2
SALES (est): 149.9K **Privately Held**
SIC: 2741 Miscellaneous publishing

(G-1686)
NATURES PATH FOODS USA INC
2220 Natures Path Way (98230-9158)
PHONE 360 332-1111
Arran Stephens, *President*
Shannon Corbett, *Vice Pres*
Dorothy Nelson, *Vice Pres*
Vijay Mani, *Prdtn Mgr*
Val Rivera, *Prdtn Mgr*
EMP: 24
SALES: 6MM **Privately Held**
SIC: 2043 Cereal breakfast foods

(G-1687)
NATURES PATH FOODS USA INC
2220 Natures Path Way (98230-9158)
PHONE 360 603-7200
Arran Stephens, *President*
Ratana Stephens, *Vice Pres*
Marcus Schramm, *Treasurer*
Shanti Schramm, *Admin Sec*
EMP: 90
SALES (est): 1.3MM **Privately Held**
SIC: 5149 2043 Groceries & related products; cereal breakfast foods
HQ: Nature's Path Foods Inc
9100 Van Horne Way
Richmond BC V6X 1
604 248-8777

(G-1688)
NORTHWEST HORSE SOURCE LLC
Also Called: Hores Source
4435 Boblett Rd (98230-9711)
P.O. Box 717 (98231-0717)
PHONE 360 332-5579
Mark Pickering, *Editor*
Karen Pickering,
EMP: 3
SALES: 250K **Privately Held**
WEB: www.nwhorsesource.com
SIC: 2721 0752 Magazines: publishing only, not printed on site; animal specialty services

(G-1689)
NORTHWEST PODIATRIC LABORATORY
1091 Fir Ave (98230-9145)
PHONE 360 332-8411
Dennis N Brown, *President*
Christopher E Smith DPM, *Vice Pres*
EMP: 70
SQ FT: 10,000
SALES (est): 9.7MM **Privately Held**
WEB: www.nwpodiatric.com
SIC: 3842 Foot appliances, orthopedic

(G-1690)
NUTRADRIED CREATIONS LLP
2252 Odell St (98230-9754)
PHONE 360 332-2101
John Gibbs, *Partner*
Jeff M Shapiro, *Partner*
J Hugh Wiebe, *Partner*
EMP: 2
SQ FT: 1,000
SALES (est): 68.6K **Privately Held**
SIC: 2064 Candy & other confectionery products

(G-1691)
OUT PEAK SERVICES INC
Also Called: Coco Mats N More
104 4th St (98230-5190)
PHONE 360 255-7282
Deepak Raghavan, *President*

Randy Regier, *Opers Mgr*
▲ **EMP:** 12 **EST:** 2013
SQ FT: 12,000
SALES: 2MM **Privately Held**
SIC: 2273 5023 Mats & matting; floor coverings

(G-1692)
PACBRAKE COMPANY
1670 Grant Ave (98230-5161)
P.O. Box 1822 (98231-1822)
PHONE 360 332-4717
Vince Meneely, *President*
▲ **EMP:** 2
SALES (est): 359.4K **Privately Held**
WEB: www.pacbrake.com
SIC: 3714 Exhaust systems & parts, motor vehicle

(G-1693)
PEACE ARCH BUSINESS CENTER
8105 Birch Bay Square St # 103 (98230-9802)
PHONE 360 366-8500
Randy Polley, *Principal*
EMP: 2
SALES (est): 136.7K **Privately Held**
SIC: 3579 Typing & word processing machines

(G-1694)
PENCHANT PRESS INTERNATIONAL
7572 Birch Bay Dr Ste 7 (98230-9647)
P.O. Box 1333 (98231-1333)
PHONE 206 687-2401
Jessica Stone, *Principal*
EMP: 3 **EST:** 2016
SALES (est): 50K **Privately Held**
SIC: 2741 Miscellaneous publishing

(G-1695)
PICS SMARTCARD INC
Also Called: ID Superstore
250 H St Ste 510 (98230-4018)
PHONE 800 667-1772
Steven Simonyi- Vindele, *President*
Chris Van Zeist, *Sales Staff*
EMP: 10
SALES (est): 870K **Privately Held**
WEB: www.idsuperstore.com
SIC: 2399 Emblems, badges & insignia

(G-1696)
POINT ROBERTS PRESS INC
Also Called: All Point Bulletin
225 Marine Dr Ste 200 (98230-4052)
PHONE 360 945-0413
Pat Grubb, *President*
Louise Mugar, *Vice Pres*
Amy Weaver, *Office Mgr*
EMP: 8 **EST:** 1991
SALES (est): 595K **Privately Held**
WEB: www.allpointbulletin.com
SIC: 2711 8611 2741 Newspapers, publishing & printing; business associations; miscellaneous publishing

(G-1697)
PRIME PALLETS AND RECYCLING
9409 Delta Line Rd (98230-9766)
P.O. Box 1969 (98231-1969)
PHONE 360 410-0238
Darrall Hofer, *President*
Tanya Hofer, *Vice Pres*
EMP: 4 **EST:** 2011
SQ FT: 500
SALES (est): 294.1K **Privately Held**
SIC: 2448 3089 Pallets, wood & wood with metal; pallets, plastic

(G-1698)
PUGET SOUND SAND AND GRAV LLC
8549 Loomis Trail Ln (98230-9403)
PHONE 360 332-3333
James Spaich, *President*
EMP: 3 **EST:** 2012
SALES (est): 145.5K **Privately Held**
SIC: 1442 Construction sand & gravel

(G-1699)
QUANTUM TECHNOLOGY CORP
250 H St Pmb 183 (98230-4018)
P.O. Box 98231 (98231)
PHONE 604 222-5539
EMP: 4
SALES (corp-wide): 2.3MM **Privately Held**
SIC: 3821 Laboratory apparatus & furniture
PA: Quantum Technology Corp
38936 Queens Way Unit 4
Squamish BC V8B 0
604 222-5539

(G-1700)
RADIAL ENERGY INC
Also Called: (A DEVELOPMENT STAGE COMPANY)
225 Marine Dr Ste 210 (98230-4027)
PHONE 360 332-0905
G Leigh Lyons, *President*
Omar Hayes, *COO*
EMP: 2
SALES (est): 207.9K **Privately Held**
SIC: 1382 Oil & gas exploration services

(G-1701)
REGAL TANKS USA INC
1733 H St Ste 330 (98230-5107)
PHONE 360 707-9948
Terry Tidy, *President*
▲ **EMP:** 4
SALES (est): 316.9K **Privately Held**
SIC: 3795 Tanks & tank components

(G-1702)
RIPTIDE CHARTERS INC
1170 Rene Ct (98230-9513)
PHONE 360 815-6568
Lloyd Dickerson, *Principal*
EMP: 3
SALES (est): 197.5K **Privately Held**
SIC: 2399 Fishing nets

(G-1703)
SIGN-O-LITE
477 Peace Portal Dr # 104 (98230-4016)
PHONE 360 746-8651
Don R Armitage, *Principal*
EMP: 2
SALES (est): 117.1K **Privately Held**
SIC: 3993 Signs & advertising specialties

(G-1704)
STEEL MAGNOLIA INC
Also Called: Miller, Kenneth D
7523 Kickerville Rd (98230-9168)
PHONE 360 366-5090
Kenneth D Miller, *President*
Debra Miller, *Vice Pres*
EMP: 2
SALES: 175K **Privately Held**
SIC: 1799 3312 Ornamental metal work; rails, steel or iron

(G-1705)
THRIFTY PAYLESS INC T/A
1733 H St Ste 500 (98230-5157)
PHONE 360 332-1616
EMP: 2 **EST:** 2010
SALES (est): 84.3K **Privately Held**
SIC: 2836 Vaccines & other immunizing products

(G-1706)
TOTALLY CHOCOLATE LLC
Also Called: Chocolate Chocolate
2025 Sweet Rd (98230-9198)
PHONE 360 332-3900
Ken Strong, *President*
▲ **EMP:** 50
SQ FT: 60,000
SALES (est): 14.3MM
SALES (corp-wide): 4.1MM **Privately Held**
WEB: www.totallychocolate.com
SIC: 2064 Candy & other confectionery products
PA: Tricor Pacific Founders Capital Inc
1111 Hastings St W Suite 200
Vancouver BC V6E 2
604 688-7669

GEOGRAPHIC SECTION

Bonney Lake - Pierce County (G-1739)

(G-1707)
TRIO MACHINERY INC
Also Called: Trio Machinery U S A
1685 H St 876 (98230-5110)
P.O. Box 8110 (98231)
PHONE.................360 671-6229
John Monroe, *Manager*
EMP: 5
SALES (corp-wide): 2.3MM **Privately Held**
WEB: www.triomachinery.com
SIC: 2092 Fresh or frozen packaged fish
PA: Trio Machinery Inc
  20252 98 Ave Unit 1
  Langley BC V1M 3
  604 888-2500

(G-1708)
TRU LINE LASER ALIGNMENT INC
8231 Blaine Rd (98230-9103)
PHONE.................360 371-0552
Lesley Cooke, *President*
Jim Zoehrer, *Vice Pres*
EMP: 8
SALES: 400K **Privately Held**
SIC: 3821 5199 5999 Laser beam alignment devices; advertising specialties; alcoholic beverage making equipment & supplies

(G-1709)
UNITED AMERICAN INC
8346 Blaine Rd (98230-9238)
PHONE.................360 371-7709
Marvin Beckwith, *President*
Viola Seibert, *Corp Secy*
Miguelina Beckwith, *Vice Pres*
EMP: 22
SQ FT: 20,000
SALES (est): 1.8MM **Privately Held**
SIC: 2899 Fire retardant chemicals

(G-1710)
WAZZBIZZ INC
1100 Yew Ave (98230-9222)
PHONE.................360 332-5276
John Wasilewski, *President*
Gail Wasilewski, *Corp Secy*
Ken Johnson, *Vice Pres*
EMP: 7
SQ FT: 10,900
SALES: 680K **Privately Held**
WEB: www.mantleramps.com
SIC: 3448 1629 Ramps: prefabricated metal; dock construction

(G-1711)
WESTMAN MARINE INC
218 Mcmillan Ave (98230)
PHONE.................360 332-5051
Jack Dawson, *President*
James Prill, *Corp Secy*
Bob Gudmundson, *Vice Pres*
Marvin Hansen, *Mng Member*
Brian Forsyth, *Manager*
EMP: 9
SQ FT: 3,600
SALES: 1MM **Privately Held**
SIC: 3731 Fishing vessels, large: building & repairing

(G-1712)
WINE ERNA A I D INC
Also Called: Wise Owl Productions
399 H St Ste 6 (98230-4100)
P.O. Box 1656 (98231-1656)
PHONE.................360 332-4888
Erna Wine, *President*
Kenneth Maurer, *Treasurer*
EMP: 3
SALES (est): 237.9K **Privately Held**
SIC: 2731 Books: publishing only

(G-1713)
WOOD WAY MFG INC
2183 Burk Rd (98230-9765)
PHONE.................360 366-4854
Lennart Franzen, *President*
Alive Farnzen, *Vice Pres*
EMP: 2
SALES (est): 194.1K **Privately Held**
SIC: 2434 2517 1751 Wood kitchen cabinets; wood television & radio cabinets; cabinet & finish carpentry

(G-1714)
ZIPPY POP INC (PA)
225 Marine Dr (98230-4027)
PHONE.................855 404-3300
Deano Cloutier, *President*
EMP: 3 **EST:** 2014
SALES (est): 581K **Privately Held**
SIC: 3634 Popcorn poppers, electric: household

Blakely Island
San Juan County

(G-1715)
SOUND SOFTWARE
1 Marina Dr (98222-5001)
PHONE.................360 375-6375
EMP: 3
SALES (est): 100K **Privately Held**
SIC: 7372 Computer Software Developer

Bonney Lake
Pierce County

(G-1716)
AQUA REC INC
Also Called: Firesite, Heart & Home
20880 State Route 410 E (98391-6301)
PHONE.................253 826-2561
Josh Champ, *Manager*
EMP: 2
SALES (corp-wide): 7.4MM **Privately Held**
WEB: www.aquarec.com
SIC: 3949 3429 7389 Swimming pools, except plastic; fireplace equipment, hardware: andirons, grates, screens; swimming pool & hot tub service & maintenance
PA: Aqua Rec, Inc.
  1407 Puyallup Ave
  Tacoma WA 98421
  253 682-1792

(G-1717)
BEARDED FELLOWS ELIXIR LLC
18408 100th Street Ct E (98391-7335)
P.O. Box 7040 (98391-0703)
PHONE.................253 750-3060
Adrian Urbina,
EMP: 2
SALES (est): 88.7K **Privately Held**
SIC: 2899 Chemical preparations

(G-1718)
BTS PARTNERS LLC
Also Called: Freedom Metal
7413 Vandermark Rd E (98391-8664)
PHONE.................253 862-4622
Stephen Byers, *Partner*
EMP: 4
SALES: 600K **Privately Held**
SIC: 3441 Fabricated structural metal

(G-1719)
CRANBERRY ROAD WINERY
19524 100th St E (98391-5957)
P.O. Box 741, Westport (98595-0741)
PHONE.................425 254-8400
Christopher D Tiffany, *President*
EMP: 4
SALES (est): 224.8K **Privately Held**
SIC: 2084 Wines

(G-1720)
CREATIVE METAL CONCEPTS LLC
Also Called: CMC
17106 116th St E (98391-8180)
PHONE.................253 230-4933
Jay Hyde,
EMP: 4
SALES (est): 300K **Privately Held**
SIC: 3446 Fences, gates, posts & flagpoles

(G-1721)
DDBD CONSTRUCTION
Also Called: Counter Stone
12421 200th Avenue Ct E (98391-5416)
PHONE.................253 576-6769
Bruce Peers, *Owner*
EMP: 9
SQ FT: 3,000
SALES (est): 621.9K **Privately Held**
SIC: 3281 Granite, cut & shaped

(G-1722)
ELEMENT
18120 85th St E (98391-7149)
PHONE.................253 335-8342
Christina Boevers, *Principal*
EMP: 3
SALES (est): 191.6K **Privately Held**
SIC: 2819 Industrial inorganic chemicals

(G-1723)
EMERALD CITY SMOOTHIE
20075 State Route 410 E (98391-8460)
PHONE.................253 826-6664
Dawn Eells, *Owner*
EMP: 4
SALES (est): 231.9K **Privately Held**
WEB: www.emeraldcitysmoothie.com
SIC: 5499 2023 Vitamin food stores; dietary supplements, dairy & non-dairy based

(G-1724)
GARJEN CORP
Also Called: Outsource Communication
19017 68th St E (98391-8828)
P.O. Box 7192 (98391-0931)
PHONE.................253 862-6140
Gary De Noble, *President*
EMP: 2
SQ FT: 315
SALES (est): 96.8K **Privately Held**
WEB: www.printsolution.com
SIC: 7336 7371 2759 7389 Graphic arts & related design; computer software development & applications; commercial printing;

(G-1725)
GEORGES CUSTOM PLASTIC INC
14607 215th Ave E (98391-7535)
PHONE.................253 939-1575
George Bendo, *President*
EMP: 2
SALES (est): 190K **Privately Held**
WEB: www.geocustomplastic.com
SIC: 3089 Plastic processing

(G-1726)
HODGE INDUSTRIES
19609 126th St E (98391-6064)
PHONE.................253 266-6921
Martha Howdd, *President*
EMP: 2 **EST:** 2009
SALES (est): 90.1K **Privately Held**
SIC: 3999 Manufacturing industries

(G-1727)
JEN GAR CORP
19017 68th St E (98391-8828)
PHONE.................253 862-6140
EMP: 2
SALES (est): 129.8K **Privately Held**
SIC: 2759 Publication printing

(G-1728)
MICHAELS MANUFACTURING
7731 184th Ave E (98391-8520)
PHONE.................253 459-4384
Michael Deshaw, *Owner*
EMP: 2 **EST:** 2017
SALES (est): 62.5K **Privately Held**
SIC: 3999 Manufacturing industries

(G-1729)
MIRACLE STUDIOS
Also Called: M S I Commerce
17120 Orting Rd N (98391-7306)
PHONE.................833 728-3233
Christopher Miller, *Owner*
EMP: 3
SALES: 350K **Privately Held**
SIC: 2844 2099 2834 Deodorants, personal; honey, strained & bottled; lip balms

(G-1730)
NOONDAY DESIGN
17813 110th Pl E (98391-7001)
PHONE.................253 517-8293
Tracey Coon, *Principal*
EMP: 2 **EST:** 2014
SALES (est): 83.7K **Privately Held**
SIC: 2741 Miscellaneous publishing

(G-1731)
OUTBOUTS LLC
11012 Canyon Rd E Ste 8p (98391)
PHONE.................253 921-0155
Gordon Herzog, *Mng Member*
Stephan Empson,
EMP: 2
SALES (est): 92.9K **Privately Held**
SIC: 7372 7389 Application computer software;

(G-1732)
PADHOLDR LLC
7518 185th Ave E (98391-7015)
PHONE.................253 447-7328
Ivory Burns, *Opers Staff*
Jim Benham, *Manager*
EMP: 7
SALES (est): 726.8K **Privately Held**
SIC: 3651 Electronic kits for home assembly: radio, TV, phonograph

(G-1733)
PLEASANT HILL CELLARS
14509 189th Avenue Ct E (98391-6152)
PHONE.................206 229-5105
EMP: 2
SALES (est): 62.3K **Privately Held**
SIC: 2084 Mfg Wines/Brandy/Spirits

(G-1734)
PLEASANT HILL WINERY LLC
14509 189th Avenue Ct E (98391-6152)
PHONE.................425 333-6770
EMP: 4
SALES (est): 340.6K **Privately Held**
SIC: 2084 Winery

(G-1735)
PRINTING CONEXIONS
7237 Vandermark Rd E (98391-8621)
PHONE.................206 383-4516
Tray Ngo, *Owner*
EMP: 4
SALES (est): 346.2K **Privately Held**
SIC: 2752 Commercial printing, offset

(G-1736)
RAINROOM ESSENTIALS
11302 205th Ave E (98391-7718)
PHONE.................253 988-5889
Frank Marshall, *Principal*
EMP: 2
SALES (est): 136.3K **Privately Held**
SIC: 2844 Toilet preparations

(G-1737)
SANDIS SIGNS INC
18317 Veterans Mem Dr E (98391-7108)
PHONE.................253 862-6885
Sandi Tolson, *Principal*
EMP: 5
SALES (est): 610.7K **Privately Held**
SIC: 3993 Signs, not made in custom sign painting shops

(G-1738)
SEATTLE WELDING INC
14622 Prairie Ridge Dr E (98391-7551)
PHONE.................206 763-0980
Lawrence M Lacock, *President*
Thomas Brucker, *Corp Secy*
Shirley Thomas, *Vice Pres*
EMP: 3
SALES (est): 299.4K **Privately Held**
WEB: www.seattlewelding.net
SIC: 7692 Welding repair

(G-1739)
SS TRAILER MANUFACTURING
9409 205th Ave E (98391-6339)
PHONE.................253 750-4724
EMP: 2
SALES (est): 106.3K **Privately Held**
SIC: 3999 3799 Manufacturing industries; trailers & trailer equipment

Bonney Lake - Pierce County (G-1740) — GEOGRAPHIC SECTION

(G-1740)
STOVER PUBLISHING
11305 208th Avenue Ct E (98391-6645)
PHONE.................................206 240-2438
Daniel Stover, *Principal*
EMP: 2 EST: 2017
SALES (est): 61.1K **Privately Held**
SIC: 2741 Miscellaneous publishing

(G-1741)
SUGARCRUSH HMMADE JAMS JELLIES
8107 183rd Ave E (98391-7060)
PHONE.................................253 830-4155
Kalee Torvik, *Principal*
EMP: 2
SALES (est): 100.2K **Privately Held**
SIC: 2033 Jams, jellies & preserves: packaged in cans, jars, etc.

(G-1742)
WATSONS WOODEN WORDS LLC
6809 183rd Ave E (98391-8831)
PHONE.................................253 348-7995
Tom Watson, *Mng Member*
EMP: 2 EST: 2017
SALES (est): 182.8K **Privately Held**
SIC: 3993 Signs & advertising specialties

(G-1743)
WESTWELD INC
9117 207th Ave E (98391-8420)
PHONE.................................253 862-1107
EMP: 2
SALES (est): 140K **Privately Held**
SIC: 7692 Welding Repair

Bothell
King County

(G-1744)
ACHIEVE LIFE SCIENCE INC
19820 North Creek Pkwy # 201 (98011-8227)
PHONE.................................425 686-1500
Richard Stewart, *CEO*
EMP: 5
SALES (est): 108.9K **Privately Held**
SIC: 2834 Pharmaceutical preparations

(G-1745)
ALDER BIOPHARMACEUTICALS INC (PA)
11804 N Creek Pkwy S (98011-8801)
PHONE.................................425 205-2900
Robert Azelby, *President*
Jeffrey T Smith, *Managing Dir*
Erin Lavelle, *COO*
Larry K Benedict, *Exec VP*
James B Bucher, *Senior VP*
EMP: 88
SQ FT: 85,000
SALES (est): 1.6MM **Publicly Held**
WEB: www.alderbio.com
SIC: 2836 2834 Biological products, except diagnostic; pharmaceutical preparations

(G-1746)
ALLIED TELESIS INC (HQ)
19800 North Creek Pkwy # 100 (98011-8206)
PHONE.................................408 519-8700
Takayoshi Oshima, *Ch of Bd*
Mike Dunbar, *President*
Justin Larkin, *Partner*
Tora Takashima, *Corp Secy*
Howard Kamerer, *COO*
▲ EMP: 170
SALES (est): 62.2MM **Privately Held**
WEB: www.alliedtelesyn.com
SIC: 3577 Computer output to microfilm units

(G-1747)
APLUS INKWORKS
19604 109th Ct Ne (98011-1700)
P.O. Box 1284 (98041-1284)
PHONE.................................206 910-9082
Paula Anderson, *Owner*
EMP: 3

SALES (est): 140K **Privately Held**
SIC: 3955 Print cartridges for laser & other computer printers

(G-1748)
AR NORTHWEST
11807 N Creek Pkwy S # 109 (98011-8804)
PHONE.................................425 485-9000
Heather Gilbert, *Principal*
EMP: 2
SALES (est): 533.1K **Privately Held**
SIC: 3721 Aircraft

(G-1749)
AVOCENT
18912 North Creek Pkwy (98011-8016)
PHONE.................................425 398-0294
EMP: 2 EST: 2014
SALES (est): 78.2K **Privately Held**
SIC: 7379 3577 Computer related services; computer peripheral equipment

(G-1750)
AVST PARENT LLC (HQ)
20000 North Creek Pkwy (98011-8228)
PHONE.................................425 951-1600
Jean Champagne, *President*
EMP: 81
SALES (est): 19.5MM **Privately Held**
PA: Xmedius Buyer, Llc
  20000 North Creek Pkwy
  Bothell WA 98011
  866 368-0400
SIC: 7372 Prepackaged software

(G-1751)
BAUSCH HEALTH AMERICAS INC
11720 N Creek Pkwy N (98011-8244)
PHONE.................................425 346-2472
EMP: 8
SALES (corp-wide): 8.3B **Privately Held**
SIC: 2834 Pharmaceutical preparations
HQ: Bausch Health Americas, Inc.
  400 Somerset Corp Blvd
  Bridgewater NJ 08807
  908 927-1400

(G-1752)
BEHRINGER USA INC
18916 North Creek Pkwy # 200 (98011-8016)
PHONE.................................425 672-0816
Raul Guevara Gerodias, *President*
Cheryl Saldana De Leon, *Admin Sec*
▲ EMP: 60 EST: 1989
SALES (est): 11.9MM **Privately Held**
WEB: www.behringer.com
SIC: 3679 3663 Recording heads, speech & musical equipment; radio & TV communications equipment

(G-1753)
CAMTRONICS INC
18230 130th Pl Ne (98011-3118)
PHONE.................................425 487-0013
Daniel Mauch, *President*
Carol Mauch, *Vice Pres*
EMP: 2
SALES (est): 300K **Privately Held**
SIC: 3625 Numerical controls

(G-1754)
CEREVAST MEDICAL INC
12100 Ne 195th St Ste 150 (98011-5763)
PHONE.................................425 748-7529
Bradford Zakes, *Chairman*
Yuquan Wang, *Director*
Xiamei Wu, *Director*
EMP: 3
SALES (est): 76.5K **Privately Held**
SIC: 8733 3845 Biotechnical research, noncommercial; medical research; ultrasonic medical equipment, except cleaning

(G-1755)
CHEMILL INC
15113 98th Ct Ne (98011-7257)
PHONE.................................425 286-5229
Raj Tejsinghani, *President*
Suchita Thakur, *Vice Pres*
Albert Garcia, *Executive*
▲ EMP: 10
SALES (est): 1.1MM **Privately Held**
SIC: 2836 Extracts

(G-1756)
COCRYSTAL PHARMA INC (PA)
19805 North Creek Pkwy (98011-8251)
PHONE.................................786 459-1831
Gary Wilcox, *Ch of Bd*
Sam Lee, *President*
James Martin, *CFO*
EMP: 10
SQ FT: 9,400
SALES (est): 6.4MM **Publicly Held**
SIC: 2834 Pharmaceutical preparations

(G-1757)
CORE CORPORATION
Also Called: Atm-Plu
8812 Ne 189th Pl (98011-2846)
PHONE.................................425 485-0574
Joel B Madrazo, *President*
Jennifer Madrazo, *Treasurer*
EMP: 5
SQ FT: 300
SALES (est): 752K **Privately Held**
SIC: 6099 3578 Automated teller machine (ATM) network; automatic teller machines (ATM)

(G-1758)
CUSTOMARRAY INC
18916 North Creek Pkwy # 115 (98011-8017)
PHONE.................................425 609-0923
Brooke Anderson, *CEO*
Hisashi Fuji, *Info Tech Mgr*
EMP: 6
SALES (est): 1.2MM **Privately Held**
SIC: 3826 Analytical instruments
HQ: Genscript Usa Holding, Inc.
  18916 North Creek Pkwy # 115
  Bothell WA 98011
  425 609-0923

(G-1759)
DOGWOOD INDUSTRIES
10037 Main St (98011-3423)
PHONE.................................425 949-7379
EMP: 2
SALES (est): 196K **Privately Held**
SIC: 3999 Manufacturing industries

(G-1760)
EKOS CORPORATION
11911 N Creek Pkwy S (98011-8809)
PHONE.................................425 415-3100
Louise Makin, *CEO*
Curtis Genstler, *Vice Pres*
Jocelyn Kersten, *Vice Pres*
Matt Stupfel, *Vice Pres*
Tina Beebe, *Project Mgr*
EMP: 250
SQ FT: 11,000
SALES (est): 66MM **Privately Held**
WEB: www.ekoscorp.com
SIC: 3841 Surgical & medical instruments
PA: Btg Plc
  5 Fleet Place
  London EC4M

(G-1761)
ESSENTIA WATER INC
18911 North Creek Pkwy # 150 (98011-8026)
PHONE.................................425 402-9555
Kenneth Uptain, *CEO*
Greg Buscher, *CFO*
Keith Huetson, *Admin Sec*
EMP: 45
SQ FT: 4,000
SALES (est): 26.8MM **Privately Held**
WEB: www.essentiawater.com
SIC: 2086 Water, pasteurized: packaged in cans, bottles, etc.

(G-1762)
EUROFINS MICROBIOLOGY LABS INC
11720 N Creek Pkwy N (98011-8244)
PHONE.................................425 686-1996
EMP: 4
SALES (est): 295K **Privately Held**
SIC: 2835 Microbiology & virology diagnostic products

(G-1763)
FENETTE CELLARS
20412 123rd Ave Ne (98011-7656)
PHONE.................................425 417-6260
Penny Johansen, *Owner*
EMP: 2
SALES (est): 62.3K **Privately Held**
SIC: 2084 Wines, brandy & brandy spirits

(G-1764)
FLUKE METAL PRODUCTS INC
10223 Woodinville Dr (98011-3298)
PHONE.................................425 485-9666
Robert E Fluke, *President*
Darrell Wells, *Opers Mgr*
Ron Savage, *Engineer*
Annette Cotton, *Manager*
Andy Heikkinen, *Manager*
EMP: 53
SQ FT: 12,500
SALES (est): 9.2MM **Privately Held**
WEB: www.flukemetal.com
SIC: 3599 Machine shop, jobbing & repair

(G-1765)
GENERAL DYNMICS OTS AROSPC INC (DH)
Also Called: General Dynamics Ots Seattle
11714 N Creek Pkwy N # 200 (98011-8250)
PHONE.................................425 420-9311
Michael S Wilson, *President*
Mark Roualet, *Chairman*
Del S Dameron, *Vice Pres*
Gregory Gallopoulos, *Vice Pres*
Firat Gezen, *Treasurer*
EMP: 809
SALES (est): 68MM
SALES (corp-wide): 36.1B **Publicly Held**
SIC: 3823 3764 3825 Industrial instrmnts msrmnt display/control process variable; guided missile & space vehicle propulsion unit parts; test equipment for electronic & electrical circuits
HQ: General Dynamics Ordnance And Tactical Systems, Inc.
  11399 16th Ct N Ste 200
  Saint Petersburg FL 33716
  727 578-8100

(G-1766)
GLACIER NORTHWEST INC
6423 Ne 175th St (98028-4808)
PHONE.................................425 486-3281
James Repman, *President*
EMP: 4
SQ FT: 27,550 **Privately Held**
WEB: www.glaciernw.com
SIC: 3273 Ready-mixed concrete
HQ: Glacier Northwest, Inc.
  5975 E Marginal Way S
  Seattle WA 98134
  206 764-3000

(G-1767)
INDUSTRIAL SOFTWARE SOLUTNS
Also Called: Wonderware Pacwest
19909 120th Ave Ne Ste 10 (98011-8242)
PHONE.................................425 368-7310
Glenn Carlson, *President*
Zofia Murczek, *Opers Staff*
Ellie Sanchez, *Accounts Mgr*
Steve Johns, *Accounts Exec*
Becky Carlson, *Mktg Coord*
EMP: 50
SQ FT: 4,500
SALES (est): 8MM **Privately Held**
WEB: www.isswonderware.com
SIC: 7372 Prepackaged software

(G-1768)
INFOMETRIX INC
11807 N Creek Pkwy S # 111 (98011-8804)
PHONE.................................425 402-1450
Brian G Rohrback, *President*
Stan Christie, *Software Dev*
Paul Bailey, *Admin Sec*
EMP: 10
SQ FT: 3,500
SALES (est): 659.4K **Privately Held**
WEB: www.infometrix.com
SIC: 8999 7372 7371 Scientific consulting; application computer software; custom computer programming services

▲ = Import ▼ = Export
◆ = Import/Export

GEOGRAPHIC SECTION
Bothell - King County (G-1797)

(G-1769)
INNERSCAN INC
17401 102nd Ave Ne (98011-3745)
PHONE.................................425 419-7718
EMP: 4 **EST:** 2015
SALES (est): 190.5K **Privately Held**
SIC: 3845 Mfg Electromedical Equipment

(G-1770)
IRON SOFTWARE DEVELOPMENT LLC
15730 116th Ave Ne 110b (98011-4184)
PHONE.................................425 892-2287
Drew Delano, *Principal*
EMP: 2 **EST:** 2016
SALES (est): 103.9K **Privately Held**
SIC: 7372 Prepackaged software

(G-1771)
JM VENTURES INC
Also Called: Inhance
10328 Ne 201st Pl (98011-2480)
PHONE.................................206 718-3355
Jeff Mourer, *President*
EMP: 2
SALES (est): 30K **Privately Held**
SIC: 2426 Flooring, hardwood

(G-1772)
LABELS & LISTS INC
18912 North Creek Pkwy # 201 (98011-8016)
PHONE.................................425 822-1984
Bruce Willsie, *President*
Linden Criddle, *Chairman*
Jamie Criddle, *Vice Pres*
Jonathan Criddle, *Vice Pres*
Frank Girolami, *Vice Pres*
EMP: 17
SQ FT: 8,000
SALES (est): 1.2MM **Privately Held**
WEB: www.lalnet.com
SIC: 7331 2759 Mailing list compilers; labels & seals; printing

(G-1773)
LEE COMPANY
19125 North Creek Pkwy # 120 (98011-8035)
PHONE.................................425 488-5842
Bill Favenesi, *Branch Mgr*
EMP: 2
SALES (corp-wide): 214.3MM **Privately Held**
WEB: www.eeco.com
SIC: 3823 Fluidic devices, circuits & systems for process control
PA: The Lee Company
2 Pettipaug Rd
Westbrook CT 06498
860 399-6281

(G-1774)
LUCKIEST LETTERPRESS
15031 93rd Pl Ne (98011-6835)
PHONE.................................425 241-8229
Catherine Wilson, *Bd of Directors*
EMP: 3
SALES (est): 205.1K **Privately Held**
SIC: 2759 Letterpress printing

(G-1775)
MA ASSOC
15519 65th Pl Ne (98028-4327)
PHONE.................................206 719-1363
Josh Warren, *Principal*
EMP: 5
SALES (est): 467.1K **Privately Held**
SIC: 2951 Asphalt paving mixtures & blocks

(G-1776)
MARTINGALE & COMPANY INC
Also Called: That Patchwork Place
19021 120th Ave Ne # 102 (98011-9511)
PHONE.................................425 483-3313
Keith Brants, *Principal*
Jennifer Keltner, *Principal*
Karen Soltys, *Principal*
Sheila Ryan, *Editor*
Tammy Malloy, *Accounting Mgr*
▲ **EMP:** 40
SALES (est): 626.3K **Privately Held**
WEB: www.martingale-pub.com
SIC: 2731 Books: publishing only

(G-1777)
MEDIAPRO HOLDINGS LLC
20021 120th Ave Ne # 102 (98011-8248)
PHONE.................................425 483-4700
Steve Conrad, *President*
EMP: 47
SQ FT: 6,000
SALES (est): 7MM **Privately Held**
WEB: www.mediapro.com
SIC: 7379 7812 8299 7374 Computer related consulting services; training motion picture production; educational services; computer processing services; educational computer software

(G-1778)
MEDICIS TECHNOLOGIES CORP
11818 N Creek Pkwy N (98011-8225)
P.O. Box 1676 (98041-1676)
PHONE.................................425 420-2100
Jonah Shacknai, *CEO*
EMP: 61
SQ FT: 25,000
SALES (est): 5.2MM
SALES (corp-wide): 8.3B **Privately Held**
WEB: www.liposonix.com
SIC: 2834 Pharmaceutical preparations
HQ: Medicis Pharmaceutical Corp
700 Us Highway 202/206
Bridgewater NJ 08807
866 246-8245

(G-1779)
NEW CINGULAR WIRELESS SVCS INC
Also Called: AT&T Wireless
18517 126th Ave Ne (98011-9347)
PHONE.................................425 288-3132
Curt Kwak, *Manager*
EMP: 19
SALES (corp-wide): 170.7B **Publicly Held**
WEB: www.attws.com
SIC: 4812 3661 Cellular telephone services; telephone station equipment & parts, wire
HQ: New Cingular Wireless Services, Inc.
7277 164th Ave Ne
Redmond WA 98052

(G-1780)
NEW CULTURE MEDIA
15515 J Woodinville Ne (98011)
PHONE.................................206 406-1934
EMP: 2
SALES (est): 74.4K **Privately Held**
SIC: 2836 Culture media

(G-1781)
NORTHWEST NATURALS LLC
11805 N Creek Pkwy S # 104 (98011-8803)
PHONE.................................425 885-5252
Tom Hurson,
Mike Marquant,
Danny Shaeffer,
◆ **EMP:** 20
SQ FT: 10,000
SALES (est): 7.3MM
SALES (corp-wide): 399.9MM **Privately Held**
WEB: www.nwnaturals.com
SIC: 2087 Extracts, flavoring
PA: Tree Top, Inc.
220 E 2nd Ave
Selah WA 98942
509 697-7251

(G-1782)
NOVA-TECH ENGINEERING LP
19909 120th Ave Ne (98011-8242)
PHONE.................................425 245-7000
Benny Teal, *CEO*
EMP: 4
SALES (corp-wide): 88.5MM **Privately Held**
SIC: 3812 Search & navigation equipment
HQ: Nova-Tech Engineering, Lp
2805 E Plano Pkwy Ste 100
Plano TX 75074
425 245-7000

(G-1783)
NOVUSON SURGICAL INC
11824 N Creek Pkwy N # 103 (98011-8204)
PHONE.................................425 481-7165
Stuart Mitchell, *CEO*
Marco Daoura, *Exec VP*
Jean Maixner, *Vice Pres*
Francesco Curra, *Chief Engr*
Riki Strough, *Office Mgr*
EMP: 3
SALES (est): 254.8K **Privately Held**
SIC: 3841 8731 Surgical & medical instruments; biological research

(G-1784)
POWERCOM INC (PA)
11824 N Creek Pkwy N S (98011-8204)
PHONE.................................425 489-8549
Ken Partridge, *President*
Daryl Ando, *Project Mgr*
Colin Thompson, *CFO*
Rodney Firth, *Sr Project Mgr*
Pete Jobe, *Manager*
EMP: 54
SALES (est): 9.6MM **Privately Held**
WEB: www.callpower.com
SIC: 3661 7622 Telephone & telegraph apparatus; radio & television repair

(G-1785)
PULSE POWER SOLUTIONS LLC
Also Called: Pulsed Power Solutions
18333 Bothell Way Ne # 510 (98011-1971)
PHONE.................................206 369-8277
Christopher Pihl, *Mng Member*
Samuel Andreason,
EMP: 2
SALES (est): 121.8K **Privately Held**
SIC: 3679 Electronic circuits; pulse forming networks; oscillators; electronic loads & power supplies

(G-1786)
QUADREP NORTHWEST INC
19125 North Creek Pkwy (98011-8035)
PHONE.................................425 201-0420
EMP: 2
SALES (est): 108.7K **Privately Held**
SIC: 3629 Electronic generation equipment

(G-1787)
RJC ENTERPRISES LLC
11711 N Creek Pkwy S # 103 (98011-8808)
PHONE.................................425 481-3281
Roger Wolthuis, *Mng Member*
James Hartl,
EMP: 18 **EST:** 1997
SQ FT: 5,000
SALES (est): 4MM **Privately Held**
WEB: www.rjcenterprises.net
SIC: 3829 Measuring & controlling devices

(G-1788)
RUNWAY LIQUIDATION LLC
Also Called: Bcbg
14050 Janita Dr Ne Ste A (98011)
PHONE.................................253 474-0610
EMP: 2
SALES (corp-wide): 645.5MM **Privately Held**
SIC: 2335 Women's, juniors' & misses' dresses
HQ: Runway Liquidation, Llc
2761 Fruitland Ave
Vernon CA 90058
323 589-2224

(G-1789)
SAYWHATCLUB
18620 89th Ave Ne (98011-2828)
PHONE.................................425 486-2667
Alan Sprague, *Principal*
EMP: 3
SALES (est): 140K **Privately Held**
SIC: 3842 Hearing aids

(G-1790)
SCOTT LUMBER PACKAGING LLC
9222 Ne 143rd Pl (98011)
PHONE.................................425 821-2075
Richard Galbraith,
▲ **EMP:** 12 **EST:** 2010
SALES (est): 2MM **Privately Held**
SIC: 2631 Container, packaging & boxboard

(G-1791)
SEATTLE TIMES COMPANY
Also Called: Seattle Times, The
19200 120th Ave Ne (98011-9506)
PHONE.................................425 489-7000
Dave Clemens, *Safety Mgr*
Doug Ranes, *Manager*
EMP: 284
SQ FT: 368,564
SALES (corp-wide): 226.3MM **Privately Held**
WEB: www.seattletimes.nwsource.com
SIC: 2711 Commercial printing & newspaper publishing combined; newspapers, publishing & printing
HQ: Seattle Times Company
1000 Denny Way Ste 501
Seattle WA 98109
206 464-2111

(G-1792)
SIGN UP SIGN CO INC
18720 Bothell Way Ne (98011-1931)
PHONE.................................425 488-9247
Lawrence Rombrec, *President*
EMP: 3
SALES (est): 250.8K **Privately Held**
SIC: 3993 7532 Signs, not made in custom sign painting shops; truck painting & lettering

(G-1793)
SOLA BOTHELL
Also Called: Sola Bothell Church
18333 Bothell Way Ne (98011-1901)
PHONE.................................501 487-7652
Scott Molvar, *President*
EMP: 2
SALES (est): 27.6K **Privately Held**
SIC: 8299 7372 Religious school; application computer software

(G-1794)
SOLTA MEDICAL INC
11720 N Creek Pkwy N # 100 (98011-8244)
PHONE.................................425 354-1857
EMP: 12
SALES (corp-wide): 8.3B **Privately Held**
SIC: 3845 Electromedical equipment
HQ: Solta Medical, Inc.
7031 Koll Center Pkwy # 260
Pleasanton CA 94566
510 786-6946

(G-1795)
SPECTECH AEROSPACE LLC
11805 N Creek Pkwy S (98011-8803)
PHONE.................................425 286-1101
EMP: 3
SALES (est): 242.8K **Privately Held**
SIC: 3721 Aircraft

(G-1796)
SPECTRUM EMBROIDERY & PRINTING
18705 Beardslee Blvd (98011-1717)
PHONE.................................206 851-9687
Traci Trygg, *Principal*
EMP: 2
SALES (est): 90.2K **Privately Held**
SIC: 2752 Commercial printing, lithographic

(G-1797)
STARCOM COMPUTER CORPORATION
19515 North Creek Pkwy # 204 (98011-8200)
PHONE.................................425 486-6464
Richard Nuss, *President*
Paul Sager, *Software Dev*
EMP: 10
SALES (est): 651.1K **Privately Held**
WEB: www.starcomsoft.com
SIC: 7371 7372 Computer software development; prepackaged software

Bothell - King County (G-1798)

(G-1798)
SYSTEM TO ASIC INC
Also Called: S T A
12100 Ne 195th St Ste 180 (98011-5762)
PHONE.................................425 488-0575
Vadim Bondarev, *President*
Matthew Hicks, *Engineer*
EMP: 11
SALES (est): 1.6MM **Privately Held**
WEB: www.systemtoasic.com
SIC: 3674 Integrated circuits, semiconductor networks, etc.; semiconductor circuit networks; solid state electronic devices

(G-1799)
TALENTWISE INC
Also Called: Talent Shield
19910 North Creek Pkwy # 200 (98011-8239)
P.O. Box 1048 (98041-1048)
PHONE.................................425 974-8863
EMP: 270 **EST:** 2006
SALES (est): 48MM
SALES (corp-wide): 89.8MM **Privately Held**
SIC: 7371 7372 Custom Computer Programming Prepackaged Software Services
PA: Sterling Infosystems, Inc.
1 State St Fl 24
New York NY 10004
800 899-2272

(G-1800)
TETHERS UNLIMITED INC
11711 N Creek Pkwy S (98011-8808)
PHONE.................................425 486-0100
Robert Hoyt, *President*
Jeffrey Slostad, *Vice Pres*
Nestor Voronka, *Vice Pres*
Lars Osborne, *Engineer*
Mathew Hicks, *Manager*
EMP: 9
SQ FT: 4,500
SALES (est): 4.2MM **Privately Held**
WEB: www.tethers.com
SIC: 3724 3769 3429 3315 Research & development on aircraft engines & parts; guided missile & space vehicle parts & auxiliary equipment; manufactured hardware (general); steel wire & related products; aviation &/or aeronautical engineering

(G-1801)
THIRD WAVE SOFTWARE CORP
14033 95th Ave Ne (98011)
PHONE.................................425 825-9082
Allison Clevenger, *Principal*
EMP: 2
SALES (est): 110.3K **Privately Held**
SIC: 7372 Prepackaged software

(G-1802)
TRANE US INC
19201 120th Ave Ne (98011-9517)
PHONE.................................425 492-2155
EMP: 2 **Privately Held**
SIC: 3585 Refrigeration & heating equipment
HQ: Trane U.S. Inc.
3600 Pammel Creek Rd
La Crosse WI 54601
608 787-2000

(G-1803)
TRANSFORMER DIAGNOSTIC TESTING
17529 93rd Ave Ne (98011-3607)
PHONE.................................425 486-4110
Robert Hickey, *Owner*
Barbara Hickey, *Co-Owner*
EMP: 2
SALES: 75K **Privately Held**
SIC: 3612 Power transformers, electric

(G-1804)
UNLIMITED POSSIBILITIES NOW
Also Called: OCG
20118 107th Ave Ne (98011-2463)
P.O. Box 1926 (98041-1926)
PHONE.................................206 930-9100
Patricia A Baccili, *President*
EMP: 5

SALES: 325K **Privately Held**
SIC: 8742 3663 Management consulting services; receiver-transmitter units (transceiver)

(G-1805)
VERATHON INC (HQ)
20001 North Creek Pkwy (98011-8218)
PHONE.................................425 867-1348
Neil Hunn, *President*
Hironobu Ito, *Managing Dir*
Daniel Estay, *Principal*
Russ Garrison, *Principal*
Gerald McMorrow, *Principal*
▲ **EMP:** 140
SQ FT: 97,000
SALES (est): 107.1MM
SALES (corp-wide): 5.1B **Publicly Held**
WEB: www.verathon.com
SIC: 3845 Electromedical apparatus; ultrasonic scanning devices, medical
PA: Roper Technologies, Inc.
6901 Prof Pkwy E Ste 200
Sarasota FL 34240
941 556-2601

(G-1806)
VIOGUARD INC
19201 120th Ave Ne # 200 (98011-9518)
PHONE.................................425 280-7735
EMP: 8
SALES (est): 1MM **Privately Held**
SIC: 3841 Surgical & medical instruments

(G-1807)
VPT INC
19909 120th Ave Ne # 102 (98011-8242)
PHONE.................................425 353-3010
Mike Bosmann, *Branch Mgr*
EMP: 6 **Publicly Held**
WEB: www.vpt-inc.com
SIC: 3679 8734 Static power supply converters for electronic applications; testing laboratories
HQ: Vpt, Inc.
1971 Kraft Dr 1000
Blacksburg VA 24060

(G-1808)
WINSHUTTLE LLC (PA)
19820 North Creek Pkwy # 200 (98011-8227)
PHONE.................................425 368-2708
John Pierson, *CEO*
Joel Chaplin, *President*
Mark Hallam, *Managing Dir*
Mary Lee, *Vice Pres*
Matthew Moore, *Vice Pres*
EMP: 110
SQ FT: 8,100
SALES (est): 43.2MM **Privately Held**
WEB: www.winshuttle.com
SIC: 7372 Business oriented computer software; application computer software

(G-1809)
WINSHUTTLE SOFTWARE CANADA INC
20021 120th Ave Ne (98011-8248)
PHONE.................................425 368-2708
Lewis Carpenter, *CEO*
Phil Landry, *Executive*
Ted Shingleton, *Executive*
EMP: 2 **EST:** 2014
SALES (est): 116.7K **Privately Held**
SIC: 7372 Prepackaged software

(G-1810)
XMEDIUS AMERICA INC (DH)
20000 North Creek Pkwy # 200 (98011-8228)
PHONE.................................425 951-1600
Brian M Wall, *Ch of Bd*
Jean Champagne, *President*
Tom Minifie, *General Mgr*
Michale Drury, *Vice Pres*
Dan Ravetto, *Vice Pres*
▲ **EMP:** 33
SALES (est): 19.5MM **Privately Held**
WEB: www.avst.com
SIC: 7372 Prepackaged software
HQ: Avst Parent, Llc
20000 North Creek Pkwy
Bothell WA 98011
425 951-1600

(G-1811)
XMEDIUS BUYER LLC (PA)
20000 North Creek Pkwy (98011-8228)
PHONE.................................866 368-0400
Jean Champagne, *President*
EMP: 1
SALES (est): 19.5MM **Privately Held**
SIC: 7372 Prepackaged software

Bothell
Snohomish County

(G-1812)
A JS CUSTOM PORTABLE SAWMILLI
19304 Filbert Rd (98012-9651)
PHONE.................................425 775-7999
EMP: 9
SALES (est): 814.8K **Privately Held**
SIC: 2421 Sawmills & planing mills, general

(G-1813)
A THRIFTY CUSTOM SCREENS
22923 Meridian Ave S (98021-8717)
PHONE.................................425 337-2211
EMP: 3
SALES (est): 177.3K **Privately Held**
SIC: 3442 Screen & storm doors & windows

(G-1814)
ACCRA MANUFACTURING INC
17703 15th Ave Se (98012-6470)
PHONE.................................425 424-1000
Keith Mehus, *President*
Roger Becker, *Vice Pres*
Steven Blackmore, *Treasurer*
Elizabeth Brane, *Manager*
Howard Murray, *Info Tech Dir*
▲ **EMP:** 95
SQ FT: 70,000
SALES (est): 36.1MM **Privately Held**
WEB: www.accramfg.com
SIC: 3728 3769 Aircraft parts & equipment; guided missile & space vehicle parts & auxiliary equipment

(G-1815)
ADEMCO INC
Also Called: ADI Global Distribution
22121 17th Ave Se Ste 103 (98021-7404)
PHONE.................................425 485-3938
Duane Westmore, *Manager*
EMP: 5
SALES (corp-wide): 4.8B **Publicly Held**
WEB: www.adilink.com
SIC: 5063 3669 3822 Electrical apparatus & equipment; emergency alarms; auto controls regulating residntl & coml environmt & applncs
HQ: Ademco Inc.
1985 Douglas Dr N
Golden Valley MN 55422
800 468-1502

(G-1816)
AGC BIOLOGICS INC
21511 23rd Dr Se (98021-3900)
P.O. Box 13858, Mill Creek (98082-1858)
PHONE.................................425 485-0280
Claes Glassell, *CEO*
Gustavo Mahler, *COO*
Paul Tsang, *Vice Pres*
Jesper Bramming, *Vice Pres*
Douglas Sanders, *CFO*
EMP: 120
SQ FT: 77,000
SALES (est): 50.3MM **Privately Held**
SIC: 2834 Pharmaceutical preparations
PA: Agc Inc.
1-5-1, Marunouchi
Chiyoda-Ku TKY 100-0

(G-1817)
AGRIACCESS INC
4714 175th St Se (98012-6730)
PHONE.................................425 806-9356
Joel F Mangalindan, *President*
Ruby Sue Mangalindan, *Shareholder*
EMP: 2 **EST:** 1994
SALES (est): 230.7K **Privately Held**
SIC: 2048 Livestock feeds

(G-1818)
ALPINE INDUSTRIES INC
Also Called: Alpine Windows
19720 Bothell Everett Hwy (98012-7120)
PHONE.................................425 481-7101
Eric Bacon, *President*
EMP: 350 **EST:** 1973
SQ FT: 160,000
SALES (est): 26.9MM **Privately Held**
SIC: 3442 3089 Casements, aluminum; windows, plastic
PA: Cfa Holding Company
1023 Reynolds Rd
Charlotte MI

(G-1819)
ANTENNA DEXTERRA INC
Also Called: Accompany Mobile Technology
21540 30th Dr Se Ste 230 (98021-7015)
PHONE.................................425 939-3100
EMP: 140
SQ FT: 15,000
SALES (est): 8.5MM
SALES (corp-wide): 590MM **Publicly Held**
SIC: 7372 Prepackaged Software Services
HQ: Antenna Software, Inc.
111 Town Square Pl # 520
Jersey City NJ 07310

(G-1820)
APOLLO VIDEO TECHNOLOGY LLC
24000 35th Ave Se (98021-8990)
PHONE.................................425 483-7100
Ying Chang, *Manager*
Rodell Nothbohm,
April Johnson,
▲ **EMP:** 110
SQ FT: 45,000
SALES (est): 38MM
SALES (corp-wide): 125MM **Privately Held**
WEB: www.apollovideotechnology.com
SIC: 3699 Security control equipment & systems
PA: Luminator Technology Group, Llc
900 Klein Rd
Plano TX 75074
972 424-6511

(G-1821)
APPLIED NAVIGATION LLC
4423 220th St Se (98021-8088)
PHONE.................................503 329-3126
Marius Niculescu, *Mng Member*
Michael Allen, *Mng Member*
EMP: 3
SALES: 100K **Privately Held**
SIC: 7379 7371 3812 Computer related consulting services; custom computer programming services; aircraft/aerospace flight instruments & guidance systems; navigational systems & instruments

(G-1822)
AR KALMUS CORP
Also Called: AR Modular Rs
21222 30th Dr Se Ste 200 (98021-7019)
PHONE.................................425 485-9000
Donald R Shepherd, *President*
Chris Heavens, *Vice Pres*
▼ **EMP:** 33 **EST:** 2001
SQ FT: 17,000
SALES (est): 8.6MM
SALES (corp-wide): 34.4MM **Privately Held**
WEB: www.ar-worldwide.com
SIC: 3663 Amplifiers, RF power & IF
PA: Amplifier Research Corp.
160 Schoolhouse Rd
Souderton PA 18964
215 723-8181

(G-1823)
AR WORLDWIDE
21222 30th Dr Se Ste 200 (98021-7019)
PHONE.................................425 485-9000
EMP: 2
SALES (est): 224.4K **Privately Held**
SIC: 3663 Radio & TV communications equipment

GEOGRAPHIC SECTION
Bothell - Snohomish County (G-1855)

(G-1824)
ASCENT ENGINEERING LLC
21540 30th Dr Se Ste 200 (98021-7304)
PHONE..............................425 686-7191
Nick Scarsella, *President*
EMP: 7
SALES (corp-wide): 386.8MM **Privately Held**
SIC: 3544 Special dies, tools, jigs & fixtures
HQ: Ascent Engineering, Llc
2374 Daniel Island Dr
Daniel Island SC 29492
586 726-0500

(G-1825)
ATL INTERNATIONAL LLC
22100 Bothell Everett Hwy (98021-8431)
PHONE..............................425 487-7000
EMP: 3
SALES (est): 187.3K
SALES (corp-wide): 20.8B **Privately Held**
SIC: 3845 Electromedical apparatus
PA: Koninklijke Philips N.V.
High Tech Campus 5
Eindhoven 5656
402 791-111

(G-1826)
ATWOOD FABRICATING
19106 43rd Ave Se (98012-7445)
P.O. Box 12765, Mill Creek (98082-0765)
PHONE..............................425 481-5388
Michael T Atwood, *Owner*
EMP: 5
SALES (est): 400K **Privately Held**
SIC: 3441 Fabricated structural metal

(G-1827)
BIOLIFE SOLUTIONS INC
3301 Monte Villa Pkwy (98021-8941)
PHONE..............................425 402-1400
Michael Rice, *Branch Mgr*
EMP: 5
SALES (corp-wide): 19.7MM **Publicly Held**
SIC: 3845 Electromedical equipment
PA: Biolife Solutions, Inc.
3303 Monte Villa Pkwy
Bothell WA 98021
425 402-1400

(G-1828)
BIOLIFE SOLUTIONS INC (PA)
3303 Monte Villa Pkwy (98021-8969)
PHONE..............................425 402-1400
Raymond W Cohen, *Ch of Bd*
Michael Rice, *President*
Aby J Mathew, *Senior VP*
Karen Foster, *Vice Pres*
Roderick De Greef, *CFO*
EMP: 36
SQ FT: 30,000
SALES: 19.7MM **Publicly Held**
WEB: www.biolifesolutions.com
SIC: 3845 8731 Electromedical equipment; biological research

(G-1829)
BITTIUM USA INC (HQ)
22722 29th Dr Se Ste 100 (98021-4420)
PHONE..............................425 780-4480
Veli-Matti Ihme, *Managing Dir*
Jani Lyrintzis, *Vice Pres*
Christoph Dietachmayr, *Engineer*
Jared Combs, *Software Engr*
Kevin Ting, *Software Engr*
EMP: 1 EST: 1996
SQ FT: 1,000
SALES: 9MM
SALES (corp-wide): 805.9K **Privately Held**
SIC: 7372 Business oriented computer software
PA: Bittium Oyj
Ritaharjuntie 1
Oulu 90590
403 442-000

(G-1830)
BJORKLUND MACHINE AND TOOL CO
18831 13th Ave Se (98012-6265)
PHONE..............................425 949-5761
EMP: 2

SALES (est): 88.5K **Privately Held**
SIC: 5084 3599 Machine tools & accessories; machine shop, jobbing & repair

(G-1831)
BOEING COMPANY
16211 40th Ave Se (98012-5047)
PHONE..............................425 359-3777
Julio Pabon, *Engineer*
EMP: 895
SALES (corp-wide): 101.1B **Publicly Held**
SIC: 3721 Airplanes, fixed or rotary wing
PA: The Boeing Company
100 N Riverside Plz
Chicago IL 60606
312 544-2000

(G-1832)
BW LIBERTY INN DUPONT
18205 3rd Dr Se (98012-4529)
PHONE..............................253 912-8777
Hyeong Song, *Principal*
EMP: 2
SALES (est): 74.4K **Privately Held**
SIC: 2879 Agricultural chemicals

(G-1833)
C E PUBLICATIONS INC
Also Called: C E Weekly
18323 Bothell Everett Hwy # 310 (98012-5246)
P.O. Box 3006 (98041-3006)
PHONE..............................425 806-5200
Jerry Erickson, *President*
Janice Erickson, *Corp Secy*
EMP: 13
SALES (est): 1.5MM **Privately Held**
WEB: www.ceweekly.com
SIC: 2721 7361 Magazines: publishing only, not printed on site; trade journals: publishing only, not printed on site; employment agencies

(G-1834)
CARDIODYNAMICS INTL CORP ✪
21919 30th Dr Se (98021-3904)
PHONE..............................208 332-2502
EMP: 2 EST: 2019
SALES (est): 86.6K **Privately Held**
SIC: 3845 Electromedical equipment

(G-1835)
CARDLOCK VENDING INC
3922 148th St Se Ste 105 (98012-4752)
PHONE..............................888 487-5040
Charles Norchrop, *President*
▼ EMP: 7
SALES (est): 762.7K **Privately Held**
WEB: www.cardlockvending.com
SIC: 5962 3581 Merchandising machine operators; automatic vending machines

(G-1836)
CARROT MEDICAL LLC
22122 20th Ave Se Ste 166 (98021-4441)
PHONE..............................425 318-8089
Jeremy Wiggins, *CEO*
Christopher Coldiron, *Opers Staff*
Clayton Eubanks, *Opers Staff*
Nicole Ressler, *CFO*
EMP: 10
SQ FT: 3,500
SALES: 3.5MM **Privately Held**
SIC: 3845 Ultrasonic medical equipment, except cleaning

(G-1837)
CASCADIA SEISMIC INC
1322 238th Pl Sw (98021-9477)
PHONE..............................206 801-5999
Dave Lane, *Owner*
EMP: 2
SALES (est): 141.4K **Privately Held**
SIC: 1382 Seismograph surveys

(G-1838)
CELEBRATION BOATWORKS
114 240th St Se (98021-8714)
PHONE..............................206 321-0794
Jared Hickman, *Principal*
EMP: 2
SALES (est): 191.8K **Privately Held**
SIC: 3732 Boat building & repairing

(G-1839)
CLINE RENTALS LLC
21424 1st Ave W (98021-7514)
PHONE..............................206 375-0705
Benjamin Cline,
EMP: 4
SALES (est): 81.8K **Privately Held**
SIC: 7519 3531 Trailer rental; excavators: cable, clamshell, crane, derrick, dragline, etc.

(G-1840)
CMC BIOLOGICS SARL CORP (HQ)
Also Called: AGC Biologics
21511 23rd Dr Se (98021-3900)
PHONE..............................425 485-1900
Gustavo Mahler, *CEO*
Tracy Kinjerski, *Director*
EMP: 39 EST: 2001
SALES (est): 1MM **Privately Held**
SIC: 2834 Solutions, pharmaceutical

(G-1841)
COMPANY 43 LLC
24016 21st Ave W (98021-9265)
PHONE..............................425 269-0430
Russell Froehlich, *President*
EMP: 2
SALES (est): 108.3K **Privately Held**
SIC: 7372 Prepackaged software

(G-1842)
CONTROLLED POWER INCORPORATED
17909 Bothell Everett Hwy # 102 (98021-6391)
PHONE..............................425 485-1778
Michael Dizard, *President*
Pat Dizard, *Vice Pres*
Mike De Rham, *Engineer*
Dennis Berkshire, *Project Engr*
Christina Dizard, *Bd of Directors*
EMP: 20 EST: 1980
SQ FT: 10,000
SALES (est): 5.5MM **Privately Held**
WEB: www.controlledpowerinc.com
SIC: 3613 Control panels, electric; switchgear & switchgear accessories

(G-1843)
COVENANT CABINETS
21819 49th Ave Se (98021-8043)
PHONE..............................425 481-4799
Tim Dilger, *Owner*
EMP: 2
SALES (est): 125K **Privately Held**
SIC: 2434 Wood kitchen cabinets

(G-1844)
COVINGTON CELLARS LLC
21219 45th Ave Se (98021-7982)
PHONE..............................253 347-9463
EMP: 4
SALES (est): 358.9K **Privately Held**
SIC: 2084 Wines

(G-1845)
DADDY DAUGHTER DINER LLC
21322 Damson Rd (98021-8123)
PHONE..............................425 442-8307
EMP: 3 EST: 2013
SALES (est): 120K **Privately Held**
SIC: 2099 Mfg Food Preparations

(G-1846)
DISTRIBUTION NORTHWEST INC
22508 31st Ave Se (98021-7813)
P.O. Box 27491, Seattle (98165-2491)
PHONE..............................206 963-6126
William E Whitmarsh, *President*
Ronald Whitmarsh, *Corp Secy*
James Whitmarsh, *Vice Pres*
EMP: 4
SQ FT: 1,500
SALES (est): 40.2K **Privately Held**
SIC: 5091 1499 Spa equipment & supplies; diatomaceous earth mining

(G-1847)
DOOLEY ENTERPRISES LLC (PA)
Also Called: Photonics-Usa
416 228th St Sw Apt G102 (98021-9792)
PHONE..............................303 619-7101
Nona Dooley, *Owner*
EMP: 2
SALES (est): 236.2K **Privately Held**
SIC: 3429 Manufactured hardware (general)

(G-1848)
DOWLING SOFTWARE CONSULTA
23311 22nd Dr Se (98021-9576)
PHONE..............................425 489-3026
Craig Dowling, *Principal*
EMP: 2
SALES (est): 83.2K **Privately Held**
SIC: 7372 Prepackaged software

(G-1849)
DREAMTONES INC
21209 40th Dr Se (98021-5405)
PHONE..............................650 265-0576
Ganesan Ramachandran, *President*
EMP: 2
SALES (est): 56.5K **Privately Held**
SIC: 7372 Application computer software

(G-1850)
DYACO COML & MED N AMER LLC
18303 Bothell Everett Hwy # 210 (98012-5232)
PHONE..............................408 966-4239
Michael Lin, *President*
Jerry Savage, *Director*
EMP: 7
SQ FT: 8,000
SALES (est): 234.4K **Privately Held**
SIC: 3949 Exercise equipment; gloves, sport & athletic: boxing, handball, etc.

(G-1851)
EMERALD ENERGY NW LLC
17505 7th Ave W (98012-9110)
PHONE..............................425 830-2757
John Barclay, *Managing Dir*
EMP: 5
SALES: 309K **Privately Held**
SIC: 1321 7389 Natural gas liquids production;

(G-1852)
ETERNITY SOFTWARE
20415 Bothell Everett Hwy (98012-7109)
PHONE..............................425 486-1622
John J Foster, *Principal*
EMP: 2
SALES (est): 119.1K **Privately Held**
SIC: 7372 Prepackaged software

(G-1853)
FISHER-ROSEMOUNT SYSTEMS INC
1916 220th St Se Ste 101 (98021-8406)
PHONE..............................425 488-4111
Don Church, *Manager*
EMP: 5
SALES (corp-wide): 17.4B **Publicly Held**
SIC: 3625 3823 Relays & industrial controls; industrial instrmnts msrmnt display/control process variable
HQ: Fisher-Rosemount Systems, Inc.
1100 W Louis Henna Blvd
Round Rock TX 78681

(G-1854)
FLAGSTONE
18123 34th Dr Se (98012-8085)
PHONE..............................425 892-9134
EMP: 2 EST: 2015
SALES (est): 62.6K **Privately Held**
SIC: 3281 Flagstones

(G-1855)
FOGGY NOGGIN BREWING
22329 53rd Ave Se (98021-8017)
PHONE..............................425 486-1070
James Jamison, *Principal*
EMP: 8

Bothell - Snohomish County (G-1856) GEOGRAPHIC SECTION

SALES (est): 599.5K **Privately Held**
SIC: 2082 Malt beverages

(G-1856)
FRED MISNER
22410 35th Ave Se (98021-7804)
PHONE 425 398-7184
Fred Misner, *Principal*
EMP: 2
SALES (est): 184.4K **Privately Held**
SIC: 2521 Cabinets, office: wood

(G-1857)
FREEDOM ADAPTIVE SYSTEMS LLC
21021 49th Ave Se (98021-7979)
PHONE 425 286-9597
James Mercier, *Mng Member*
EMP: 2 **EST:** 2012
SALES (est): 110K **Privately Held**
SIC: 3949 Fishing equipment; rods & rod parts, fishing

(G-1858)
FUJIFILM SONOSITE INC (HQ)
21919 30th Dr Se (98021-3904)
PHONE 425 951-1200
Takaaki Ueda, *CEO*
Lee D Unbar, *President*
Bob Massa, *Managing Dir*
John S Bowers Jr, *Senior VP*
Diku Mandavia MD, *Senior VP*
▲ **EMP:** 370 **EST:** 1986
SQ FT: 125,000
SALES (est): 275.3MM **Privately Held**
WEB: www.sonosite.com
SIC: 3845 Ultrasonic medical equipment, except cleaning

(G-1859)
FUJIFILM SONOSITE INC
22011 30th Dr Se (98021-4444)
PHONE 425 951-1200
John Torentino, *Manager*
EMP: 250 **Privately Held**
SIC: 3845 Ultrasonic medical equipment, except cleaning
HQ: Fujifilm Sonosite, Inc.
  21919 30th Dr Se
  Bothell WA 98021
  425 951-1200

(G-1860)
GELENE LEGAULT
21922 8th Pl W (98021-8162)
PHONE 425 481-5560
Gelene Legault, *Principal*
EMP: 2
SALES (est): 74.4K **Privately Held**
SIC: 2899 Chemical preparations

(G-1861)
GLOBAL SOFTWARE LLC
22522 29th Dr Se Ste 202 (98021-4443)
PHONE 425 822-3140
Matthew Kupferman, *Manager*
EMP: 10
SALES (corp-wide): 22MM **Privately Held**
SIC: 7372 7371 Application computer software; business oriented computer software; custom computer programming services
PA: Global Software, Llc
  3301 Benson Dr Ste 200
  Raleigh NC 27609
  919 872-7800

(G-1862)
GOEDECKE & GOEDECKE
Also Called: Market Wear
128 224th St Se (98021-8359)
PHONE 425 481-1153
Gary Goedecke, *Owner*
EMP: 4
SALES (est): 210K **Privately Held**
SIC: 2499 3911 Kitchen, bathroom & household ware: wood; decorative wood & woodwork; jewelry, precious metal

(G-1863)
GUTTERS INC
23815 23rd Ave W (98021-9207)
PHONE 425 482-2679
Brian Tyler, *President*
EMP: 3

SALES: 250K **Privately Held**
SIC: 3089 1761 Gutters (glass fiber reinforced), fiberglass or plastic; roofing contractor

(G-1864)
HAWKINS LETTERING
Also Called: Hawkins Lettering EMB Mfg
18303 Bothell Everett Hwy # 120 (98012-5232)
PHONE 425 481-1938
Don L Hawkins, *Owner*
Don Hawkins, *General Mgr*
Marian Hawkins, *Co-Owner*
Clay Hawkins, *Manager*
EMP: 16
SALES: 1.3MM **Privately Held**
SIC: 2395 Embroidery & art needlework

(G-1865)
HELIX BIOMEDIX INC
22121 17th Ave Se Ste 112 (98021-7404)
PHONE 425 402-8400
R Stephen Beatty, *President*
Robin L Carmichael, *COO*
Kelly Forsythe, *Mktg Dir*
EMP: 8
SQ FT: 5,300
SALES (est): 1.8MM **Privately Held**
WEB: www.helixbiomedix.com
SIC: 2834 Pharmaceutical preparations

(G-1866)
INFINITY INDUSTRIES LLC
16520 North Rd Apt D205 (98012-4911)
PHONE 425 418-1151
EMP: 2
SALES (est): 74.6K **Privately Held**
SIC: 3999 Manufacturing industries

(G-1867)
IRON MOUNTAIN QUARRY LLC (PA)
22121 17th Ave Se Ste 117 (98021-7404)
PHONE 425 338-0607
James Burnett,
Pat Hughes,
EMP: 5 **EST:** 1987
SQ FT: 2,500
SALES (est): 9.2MM **Privately Held**
WEB: www.rentonconcreterecyclers.com
SIC: 1081 Metal mining services

(G-1868)
ITTY BITTY BAKING COMPANY LLC
24023 4th Pl W (98021-8646)
PHONE 206 715-6134
Lea Jones, *Principal*
EMP: 4
SALES (est): 171.6K **Privately Held**
SIC: 2051 Bread, cake & related products

(G-1869)
JASPER KNOW PRINT
830 216th St Sw (98021-8182)
PHONE 425 486-7147
Courtney Bolin-Walker, *Principal*
EMP: 2
SALES (est): 101.5K **Privately Held**
SIC: 2752 Commercial printing, lithographic

(G-1870)
JIMA SOFTWARE INCORPORATED
4426 216th Pl Se (98021-7980)
PHONE 206 354-7309
EMP: 2 **EST:** 2016
SALES (est): 81.5K **Privately Held**
SIC: 7372 Prepackaged software

(G-1871)
JP TRODDEN DISTILLING LLC
3122 218th St Se (98021-7805)
PHONE 206 399-6291
Mark Nesheim, *Principal*
EMP: 2
SALES (est): 107.4K **Privately Held**
SIC: 2085 Distilled & blended liquors

(G-1872)
KAUFFMANN INDUSTRIES INC
17903 Bothell Everett Hwy (98012-6318)
PHONE 425 770-5781

Alan P Kauffmann, *President*
EMP: 3
SQ FT: 2,000
SALES (est): 292.7K **Privately Held**
SIC: 3444 5064 Sheet metalwork; water heaters, electric

(G-1873)
LASER PRINTERS PLUS INC
18029 25th Dr Se (98012-9306)
PHONE 206 786-0107
EMP: 2
SALES (est): 92.3K **Privately Held**
SIC: 2752 Commercial printing, lithographic

(G-1874)
LEVITON MANUFACTURING CO INC
2222 222nd St Se (98021-4416)
PHONE 425 486-2222
Ross Goldman, *General Mgr*
Ken Morayama, *General Mgr*
Bill McNeil, *Prdtn Mgr*
Larry Kuehl, *Buyer*
Timothy Nair, *QC Mgr*
EMP: 200
SALES (corp-wide): 1.4B **Privately Held**
WEB: www.leviton.com
SIC: 3643 Current-carrying wiring devices
PA: Leviton Manufacturing Co., Inc.
  201 N Service Rd
  Melville NY 11747
  631 812-6000

(G-1875)
LOCKHEED MARTIN ACULIGHT CORP
22121 20th Ave Se (98021-4408)
PHONE 425 482-1100
Marillyn A Hewson, *CEO*
Richard F Ambrose, *Exec VP*
Sondra L Barbour, *Exec VP*
Dale P Bennett, *Exec VP*
Robert Afzal, *Vice Pres*
EMP: 87
SQ FT: 23,000
SALES (est): 10.4MM **Publicly Held**
WEB: www.aculight.com
SIC: 8732 3845 Business research service; laser systems & equipment, medical
PA: Lockheed Martin Corporation
  6801 Rockledge Dr
  Bethesda MD 20817

(G-1876)
LOCKHEED MARTIN CORPORATION
22121 20th Ave Se (98021-4408)
PHONE 425 482-1100
Karen Klamm, *Project Mgr*
Nicholas Neuenfeld, *Engineer*
Kurt Olden, *Design Engr*
Angela Harkins, *Human Res Mgr*
Eric Honea, *Program Mgr*
EMP: 13 **Publicly Held**
WEB: www.lockheedmartin.com
SIC: 3812 Search & navigation equipment
PA: Lockheed Martin Corporation
  6801 Rockledge Dr
  Bethesda MD 20817

(G-1877)
MISIU SYSTEMS LLC
3808 209th Pl Se (98021-7005)
PHONE 425 402-8700
Todd Hodgen, *President*
Randy Boroughs, *Vice Pres*
EMP: 3
SALES (est): 416.9K **Privately Held**
SIC: 3679 Commutators, electronic

(G-1878)
NAT SEATTLE INC
22125 17th Ave Se Ste 107 (98021-7406)
PHONE 425 424-3370
Debra Sarrot, *CEO*
EMP: 23
SQ FT: 8,000
SALES (est): 3.4MM
SALES (corp-wide): 2.3B **Privately Held**
SIC: 3812 Aircraft control systems, electronic

HQ: Chelton Avionics, Inc.
  6400 Wilkinson Dr
  Prescott AZ 86301
  928 708-1500

(G-1879)
NEXTRX CORPORATION
21312 30th Dr Se 101 (98021-7010)
PHONE 425 402-3485
EMP: 13
SQ FT: 8,200
SALES (est): 1.2MM **Privately Held**
SIC: 3559 Mfg Misc Industry Machinery

(G-1880)
NION BEAUTY INC
4424 185th St Se (98012-7728)
PHONE 206 228-5988
Donny Shieh, *President*
EMP: 2
SALES (est): 68.2K **Privately Held**
SIC: 5999 5122 2844 7389 Cosmetics; cosmetic preparations;

(G-1881)
NOZZLEWORKS INC (PA)
3812 209th St Se (98021-7076)
PHONE 360 668-2548
Sanjiv Vora, *President*
EMP: 3
SALES (est): 60K **Privately Held**
WEB: www.spratronics.com
SIC: 7389 3523 Design, commercial & industrial; sprayers & spraying machines, agricultural

(G-1882)
ONE STEP AHEAD INC
1517 183rd St Se Ste 3 (98012-5235)
PHONE 425 487-1869
Tom Rigg, *President*
EMP: 6
SALES (est): 520K **Privately Held**
SIC: 2499 Ladders & stepladders, wood

(G-1883)
PACER DESIGN & MANUFACTURING
19315 Bothell Everett Hwy (98012-7196)
PHONE 425 481-5300
John E Stave, *President*
Donald M Johnson, *Corp Secy*
EMP: 10
SQ FT: 5,000
SALES (est): 1.5MM **Privately Held**
SIC: 3599 3799 5084 Machine shop, jobbing & repair; golf carts, powered; pumps & pumping equipment

(G-1884)
PERFORMANCE SOFTWARE CORP
21520 30th Dr Se (98021-7009)
PHONE 425 481-4956
Timothy Bigelow, *Branch Mgr*
EMP: 4
SALES (est): 260.3K
SALES (corp-wide): 30MM **Privately Held**
SIC: 7372 Prepackaged software
PA: Performance Software Corporation
  2095 W Pinnacle Peak Rd # 120
  Phoenix AZ 85027
  623 780-1517

(G-1885)
PERMESYS INC
18719 36th Dr Se (98012-6720)
PHONE 860 961-5367
Roger C Adami, *CEO*
EMP: 3
SALES (est): 247.2K **Privately Held**
SIC: 2834 Pharmaceutical preparations

(G-1886)
PHILIPS ORAL HEALTHCARE LLC
Also Called: Sonicare
22100 Bothell Everett Hwy (98012-8431)
P.O. Box 3003 (98041-3003)
PHONE 425 487-7000
Sinead Kwant,
Paul Cavanaugh,
David Dripchak,
Jack Gallagher,

Joseph Innamorati,
▼ **EMP**: 1800
SQ FT: 130,000
SALES (est): 200.7MM
SALES (corp-wide): 20.8B Privately Held
WEB: www.usa.philips.com
SIC: 3843 Dental equipment & supplies
HQ: Philips North America Llc
  3000 Minuteman Rd Ms1203
  Andover MA 01810
  978 659-3000

(G-1887)
PHILIPS ULTRASOUND INC (DH)
Also Called: Philips Medical Systems
22100 Bothell Everett Hwy (98021-8431)
P.O. Box 3003 (98041-3003)
PHONE..................................800 982-2011
Conrad Smits, *CEO*
David A Dripchak, *President*
James Mark Mattern II, *President*
Donald D Blem, *Senior VP*
Victor H Reddick, *Senior VP*
◆ **EMP**: 120 **EST**: 1973
SQ FT: 285,000
SALES (est): 288.7MM
SALES (corp-wide): 20.8B Privately Held
SIC: 3845 Electromedical apparatus
HQ: Philips North America Llc
  3000 Minuteman Rd Ms1203
  Andover MA 01810
  978 659-3000

(G-1888)
POSH DIGS
17326 31st Dr Se (98012-8550)
PHONE..................................425 286-6245
EMP: 2
SALES (est): 93.2K Privately Held
SIC: 3999 Candles

(G-1889)
PRIMUS INTERNATIONAL
17703 15th Ave Se (98012-6470)
PHONE..................................425 424-1085
Joseph Snowden, *President*
EMP: 3
SALES (est): 483.3K Privately Held
SIC: 3728 Aircraft parts & equipment

(G-1890)
PRINTING NGO LLC
18008 Bothell Everett Hwy E (98012-6842)
PHONE..................................206 569-8388
Tray Ngo, *CEO*
EMP: 6
SALES: 220K Privately Held
SIC: 2752 Commercial printing, offset

(G-1891)
PROMETCO INC
2201 192nd St Se Apt Y102 (98012-7957)
PHONE..................................425 486-0759
Phillip Proctor, *President*
Diane Proctor, *Corp Secy*
John Mike, *Vice Pres*
▲ **EMP**: 12 **EST**: 1944
SQ FT: 15,000
SALES (est): 2.3MM Privately Held
SIC: 3441 Fabricated structural metal

(G-1892)
PROPDOCKET LLC
3820 219th Pl Se (98021-4232)
PHONE..................................330 285-6526
Max Bressler, *Principal*
Andy Sather,
EMP: 2
SALES (est): 75.2K Privately Held
SIC: 7372 Application computer software

(G-1893)
QUINTON CARDIOLOGY SYSTEMS INC (DH)
3303 Monte Villa Pkwy # 100 (98021-8970)
PHONE..................................425 556-9761
EMP: 1
SQ FT: 34,000
SALES (est): 15.3MM Privately Held
SIC: 3841 Mfg Surgical/Medical Instruments
HQ: Cardiac Science Corporation
  N7w22025 Johnson Dr
  Waukesha WI 53186
  262 798-8282

(G-1894)
RESONANT SOLUTIONS LLC
916 219th Pl Se (98021-7647)
PHONE..................................206 619-7672
Jeremy Vargas, *Mng Member*
EMP: 5
SALES: 98K Privately Held
SIC: 7372 7389 Business oriented computer software;

(G-1895)
RMV INDUSTRIES INC
20611 Bothell Everett Hwy (98012-7146)
PHONE..................................253 297-2556
EMP: 2
SALES (est): 95.7K Privately Held
SIC: 3999 Manufacturing industries

(G-1896)
ROCKWELL COLLINS INC
Collins Air Transport Systems
3350 Monte Villa Pkwy # 200 (98021-8963)
PHONE..................................425 492-1400
Fred Sandow, *Director*
EMP: 40
SALES (corp-wide): 66.5B Publicly Held
WEB: www.keo.com
SIC: 3812 Search & navigation equipment
HQ: Rockwell Collins, Inc.
  400 Collins Rd Ne
  Cedar Rapids IA 52498

(G-1897)
ROMAC INDUSTRIES INC (PA)
Also Called: Hays Div
21919 20th Ave Se Ste 100 (98021-4446)
PHONE..................................425 951-6200
Manford R Mc Neil, *Ch of Bd*
James L Larkin, *President*
Pat Ferguson, *Area Mgr*
Keith Hutsell, *Area Mgr*
John Nelson, *Area Mgr*
◆ **EMP**: 200 **EST**: 1966
SQ FT: 57,000
SALES (est): 82MM Privately Held
WEB: www.romacindustries.com
SIC: 3494 3541 Pipe fittings; machine tools, metal cutting type; tapping machines

(G-1898)
RV COMFORT SYSTEMS LLC
24025 Bothell Everett Hwy (98021-9342)
P.O. Box 1554 (98041-1554)
PHONE..................................425 408-3140
Larry McGaugh, *Mng Member*
EMP: 2
SALES: 140K Privately Held
SIC: 3585 Heating equipment, complete

(G-1899)
SCHREIBER FOODS INC
1225 183rd St Se (98012-7495)
PHONE..................................425 286-6598
EMP: 196
SALES (corp-wide): 2.4B Privately Held
SIC: 2022 Processed cheese
PA: Schreiber Foods, Inc.
  400 N Washington St
  Green Bay WI 54301
  920 437-7601

(G-1900)
SCOTSMAN GUIDE MEDIA INC
22118 20th Ave Se Ste 129 (98021-4417)
P.O. Box 692 (98041-0692)
PHONE..................................425 485-2282
Brian Simmons, *Principal*
Brian Britton-Simmons, *Broker*
EMP: 2
SALES (est): 274.7K Privately Held
SIC: 2721 Magazines: publishing only, not printed on site

(G-1901)
SCOTSMAN PUBLISHING INC
Also Called: Scotsman Guide
22118 20th Ave Se Ste 129 (98021-4417)
P.O. Box 692 (98041-0692)
PHONE..................................425 485-2282
Geary Brittonsimmons, *Chairman*
Audrey Gagnier, *Vice Pres*
Cody Noyes, *Accounts Exec*
Julie Murphy, *Publications*
Marilyn Burns, *Office Mgr*
EMP: 20
SALES (est): 2.5MM Privately Held
WEB: www.scotsmanguide.com
SIC: 2721 Magazines: publishing only, not printed on site

(G-1902)
SEATTLE GENETICS INC (PA)
21823 30th Dr Se (98021-3907)
PHONE..................................425 527-4000
Clay B Siegall, *Ch of Bd*
Darren S Cline, *Exec VP*
Jean I Liu, *Exec VP*
Brandi Robinson, *Vice Pres*
Antonia Sanchez, *Safety Mgr*
EMP: 277
SALES: 654.7MM Publicly Held
WEB: www.seattlegenetics.com
SIC: 2836 8731 Biological products, except diagnostic; biotechnical research, commercial

(G-1903)
SEATTLE GENETICS INC
22515 29th Dr Se (98021-4437)
PHONE..................................425 483-1037
EMP: 2
SALES (est): 74.4K Privately Held
SIC: 2836 Biological products, except diagnostic

(G-1904)
SHUTTERPATED
22603 1st Pl W (98021-8322)
PHONE..................................360 607-9692
Martha Cheesebrough, *Principal*
EMP: 2 **EST**: 2010
SALES (est): 163.7K Privately Held
SIC: 3442 Shutters, door or window: metal

(G-1905)
SLOPE INDICATOR COMPANY (INC)
3450 Monte Villa Pkwy (98021-8906)
PHONE..................................425 806-2200
R E Swayne, *President*
Richard E Swayne, *President*
Robert L Martin, *Vice Pres*
Matt Lewang, *Controller*
EMP: 48
SQ FT: 37,000
SALES (est): 5.2MM Privately Held
WEB: www.dimasusa.com
SIC: 3823 Industrial instrmnts msrmnt display/control process variable
HQ: Longyear Company
  2455 S 3600 W
  West Valley City UT 84119

(G-1906)
SMILEY DOG
20224 48th Ave Se (98012-7327)
PHONE..................................206 903-9631
Craig Weindling, *Principal*
EMP: 3
SALES (est): 249.1K Privately Held
SIC: 3999 Pet supplies

(G-1907)
SOLID VISIONS INC
4604 212th St Se (98021-7960)
PHONE..................................206 949-4203
Todd Liljebeck, *President*
Bonny Liljebeck, *Corp Secy*
Roy Liljebeck, *Vice Pres*
EMP: 40
SQ FT: 40,000
SALES (est): 4.1MM Privately Held
SIC: 2521 Wood office furniture

(G-1908)
T N T ENTERPRISES
Also Called: T N T Precision Shtmtl Mfg
17121 3rd Ave Se (98012-9149)
PHONE..................................425 742-8210
Richard Twedt, *Partner*
Keith Twedt, *Partner*
EMP: 5
SQ FT: 3,000
SALES (est): 500K Privately Held
SIC: 3444 Sheet metalwork

(G-1909)
TOONHOUND STUDIOS LLC
20532 2nd Dr Se (98012-7077)
PHONE..................................214 733-9626
Scott Kurtz,
EMP: 2
SALES (est): 132K Privately Held
SIC: 2721 7389 Comic books: publishing only, not printed on site;

(G-1910)
TOWACO SCREW MCH PDTS CO LLC
Also Called: Towaco Screw Machine Pdts Co
16215 Sunset Rd (98012-6171)
PHONE..................................425 481-7100
Donald Totten, *Mng Member*
Ellen Vanderwall,
EMP: 6
SQ FT: 2,000
SALES (est): 544.5K Privately Held
SIC: 3451 Screw machine products

(G-1911)
TRANSTECH MATERIALS LLC
24023 26th Dr Se (98021-6521)
PHONE..................................425 402-3665
Miqin Zhang, *CEO*
EMP: 3 **EST**: 2011
SALES (est): 106.1K Privately Held
SIC: 3999 Manufacturing industries

(G-1912)
VALBERG MFG INC
Also Called: Agile Electrical Solutions
316 181st Pl Sw (98012-6201)
PHONE..................................206 920-1296
Merrill Valberg, *President*
Jo Anna Valberg, *Principal*
EMP: 4
SALES (est): 534.9K Privately Held
SIC: 3643 Current-carrying wiring devices

(G-1913)
VENTEC LIFE SYSTEMS INC
22002 26th Ave Se Ste 104 (98021-4903)
PHONE..................................425 686-1728
Douglas Devries, *CEO*
Chris Brooks, *Managing Dir*
Christopher Kipe, *COO*
Joseph Cipollone, *Vice Pres*
Cipollone Joe, *Vice Pres*
EMP: 30 **EST**: 2011
SALES (est): 1.3MM Privately Held
SIC: 3845 Electromedical apparatus

(G-1914)
VIAVI SOLUTIONS INC
Also Called: Jdsu
22215 26th Ave Se (98021-4450)
PHONE..................................425 398-1298
Steven W Lytle, *Branch Mgr*
EMP: 12
SALES (corp-wide): 880.4MM Publicly Held
SIC: 3826 Laser scientific & engineering instruments
PA: Viavi Solutions Inc.
  6001 America Center Dr # 6
  San Jose CA 95002
  408 404-3600

(G-1915)
WADE SUMPTER INDUSTRIES INC
17321 31st Dr Se (98012-8550)
PHONE..................................425 486-9541
Trevis Sumpter, *President*
Jeannette Sumpter, *President*
EMP: 5
SALES: 100K Privately Held
SIC: 2851 Putty, wood fillers & sealers

(G-1916)
WESCO SALES GROUP INC
24210 23rd Ave Se (98021-9579)
PHONE..................................206 227-5980
Robert Monks, *Principal*
EMP: 4
SALES (est): 441.6K Privately Held
SIC: 3824 Mechanical & electromechanical counters & devices

(G-1917)
WESTOVER SCIENTIFIC INC
Also Called: Advanced Microscopy Group
22025 20th Ave Se Ste 100 (98021-4406)
PHONE..................................425 368-0444
Gregory Lucier, *CEO*
Steven W Lytle, *CEO*

Bothell - Snohomish County (G-1918)

Mark Stevenson, *President*
Erik Bennigson, *Vice Pres*
David Hoffmeister, *CFO*
▲ **EMP:** 65
SQ FT: 57,131
SALES (est): 18.3MM
SALES (corp-wide): 24.3B **Publicly Held**
SIC: 3827 Microscopes, except electron, proton & corneal
HQ: Life Technologies Corporation
5781 Van Allen Way
Carlsbad CA 92008
760 603-7200

(G-1918)
WHITEHOUSE ANTIQUE & CANDY
Also Called: Now & Again
23712 Bothell Everett Hwy (98021-9315)
PHONE 425 486-8453
Arlene McDuffee, *Owner*
EMP: 3
SALES (est): 172.4K **Privately Held**
WEB: www.whitehouseantiqueandcandyshop.com
SIC: 5099 2064 Antiques; candy & other confectionery products

(G-1919)
WIDE FORMAT GEEKS
2929 168th St Se Ofc (98012-6007)
PHONE 509 868-2319
Shawn Bly, *Principal*
EMP: 2 **EST:** 2017
SALES (est): 101.8K **Privately Held**
SIC: 2759 Commercial printing

(G-1920)
WILD RIVER PUBLISHING INC
Also Called: Wild River Press
2315 210th St Se (98021-4206)
P.O. Box 13360, Mill Creek (98082-1360)
PHONE 425 486-3638
Thomas R Pero, *President*
EMP: 3
SALES (est): 250K **Privately Held**
SIC: 2731 Books: publishing only

(G-1921)
WINN ENTERPRISES LLC
20702 Bothell Everett Hwy (98012-7793)
PHONE 425 482-6000
Dan Winn, *Principal*
EMP: 3
SQ FT: 1,444
SALES (est): 260.7K **Privately Held**
SIC: 2992 Lubricating oils

(G-1922)
WOODWORKING UNLIMITED
21819 1st Ave W (98021-8222)
PHONE 425 481-7451
Rod Countryman, *Owner*
EMP: 2
SALES (est): 148.3K **Privately Held**
SIC: 2511 3944 Wood household furniture; games, toys & children's vehicles

(G-1923)
WRIGLEY JR CO
1522 217th Pl Se (98021-7617)
PHONE 408 528-4376
EMP: 2 **EST:** 2016
SALES (est): 61.8K **Privately Held**
SIC: 2067 Chewing gum

(G-1924)
XNRGI INC
22722 29th Dr Se Ste 100 (98021-4420)
P.O. Box 1866, Edmonds (98020-1866)
PHONE 425 272-2703
Gerard C D'Couto, *President*
Jeffrey A May, *CFO*
EMP: 3 **EST:** 2001
SQ FT: 2,000
SALES (est): 512.6K **Privately Held**
WEB: www.neahpower.com
SIC: 8731 3674 Energy research; integrated circuits, semiconductor networks, etc.

(G-1925)
ZYMOGENETICS INC
3450 Monte Villa Pkwy (98021-8906)
PHONE 425 398-9637
EMP: 2
SALES (corp-wide): 15.8B **Publicly Held**
SIC: 2834 Mfg Pharmaceutical Preparations
HQ: Zymogenetics, Inc.
1201 Eastlake Ave E
Seattle WA 98102
206 442-6600

Bow
Skagit County

(G-1926)
ARGUSEA MAR WDWKG & FINSHG LLC
17608 Samish Heights Rd (98232-9788)
PHONE 360 708-9702
Michael D Nevitt, *Administration*
EMP: 4
SALES (est): 332K **Privately Held**
SIC: 2431 Millwork

(G-1927)
BLAU OYSTER COMPANY INC
11321 Blue Heron Rd (98232-9326)
PHONE 360 766-6171
Ed Blau, *President*
EMP: 15
SALES (est): 3.3MM **Privately Held**
WEB: www.virtualseattle.com
SIC: 5146 2092 Seafoods; fresh or frozen packaged fish

(G-1928)
BLUE HERON WOODWORKS
9382 Marshall Rd (98232-9362)
PHONE 360 766-4475
Timothy Gebhard, *Principal*
EMP: 2
SALES (est): 170.1K **Privately Held**
SIC: 2431 Millwork

(G-1929)
GARY N LAMB
Also Called: Samish Island Winery
10990 Samish Island Rd (98232-9339)
PHONE 360 766-6086
Gary N Lamb, *Principal*
EMP: 2
SALES (est): 104.5K **Privately Held**
SIC: 2084 Wines

(G-1930)
LUCKY DUMPSTER
14011 Mactaggart Ave (98232-9246)
PHONE 360 766-4049
EMP: 3
SALES (est): 143.2K **Privately Held**
SIC: 3443 Dumpsters, garbage

(G-1931)
MARK S VOROBIK
6496 Bayview Edison Rd (98232-9021)
PHONE 360 766-6252
Mark Vorobik, *Principal*
EMP: 2
SALES (est): 97.6K **Privately Held**
SIC: 3499 Fabricated metal products

(G-1932)
SENSITRONICS LLC
16120 Park Pl (98232-8530)
PHONE 360 766-8800
Franklin Eventoff,
EMP: 6
SALES (est): 526.9K **Privately Held**
SIC: 5736 3571 3812 Musical instrument stores; electronic computers; electronic detection systems (aeronautical)

(G-1933)
SMITH & VALLEY GALLERY
5742 Gilkey Ave (98232-9253)
PHONE 360 766-6230
Wesley A Smith, *Owner*
Andrew Vallee, *Vice Pres*
EMP: 5 **EST:** 2009
SALES (est): 600K **Privately Held**
SIC: 8412 2431 5031 Art gallery; woodwork, interior & ornamental; lumber, plywood & millwork

Bremerton
Kitsap County

(G-1934)
ADVANCED ADHESIVE
1616 Ne Dawn Rd (98311-3123)
PHONE 360 373-1156
EMP: 3
SALES (est): 123.2K **Privately Held**
SIC: 2891 Adhesives

(G-1935)
ARIES EFD LLLP
2600 Burwell St (98312-4021)
PHONE 360 710-7093
Earnest Hughes, *Principal*
EMP: 4
SALES (est): 166.1K **Privately Held**
SIC: 3599 Machine shop, jobbing & repair

(G-1936)
B & J PRINTING INC
Also Called: Minuteman Press
187 Ne Conifer Dr (98311-8792)
PHONE 360 692-3470
Darwin Aiken, *Principal*
EMP: 3
SALES (est): 255.9K **Privately Held**
SIC: 2752 Commercial printing, lithographic

(G-1937)
BATTERY X-CHANGE & REPAIR INC
5869 W Werner Rd (98312-3244)
PHONE 360 373-2921
Dck Bond, *Branch Mgr*
EMP: 2
SALES (corp-wide): 6.8MM **Privately Held**
SIC: 3699 Electrical equipment & supplies
PA: Battery X-Change & Repair Inc
3750 Se Belmont St
Portland OR 97214
503 232-8248

(G-1938)
BENTHIC FISHING LLC
2038 Taft Ave (98312-2916)
P.O. Box 2123, Sumner (98390-0470)
PHONE 253 219-1500
Michael Ellis,
EMP: 30
SALES (est): 3.9MM **Privately Held**
SIC: 2091 7389 Canned & cured fish & seafoods;

(G-1939)
BREMERTON LETTERPRESS CO LLC
423 Pacific Ave Ste 103 (98337-1941)
PHONE 360 620-8967
EMP: 3 **EST:** 2012
SALES (est): 185.9K **Privately Held**
SIC: 2759 Letterpress printing

(G-1940)
BRICOR CERAMIC INDUSTRIES
2591 Ne Cecilia Ln (98310-8321)
PHONE 360 377-9197
Mary Crane, *President*
Michael Crane, *Vice Pres*
EMP: 2
SALES (est): 177.9K **Privately Held**
SIC: 3567 Ceramic kilns & furnaces

(G-1941)
BUTLER DID IT
3851 Ne Campus Ln (98311-9424)
PHONE 360 662-0629
Todd Butler, *Principal*
EMP: 2
SALES (est): 170.4K **Privately Held**
SIC: 2542 Cabinets: show, display or storage: except wood

(G-1942)
CHINGS EMBROIDERY
7277 Sunset Ave Ne (98311-8204)
PHONE 360 613-9861
Ching Campbell, *President*
George Campbell, *Corp Secy*
David McKay, *Vice Pres*
EMP: 5 **EST:** 1992
SALES (est): 168K **Privately Held**
SIC: 2397 2395 Schiffli machine embroideries; pleating & stitching

(G-1943)
COLLECTIBLE CREATIONS
8604 Payne Ln Nw (98311-9081)
PHONE 360 613-1799
Brenda Bynum, *Owner*
EMP: 2
SALES (est): 113K **Privately Held**
SIC: 2511 Tables, household: wood

(G-1944)
COPPERWOOD LLC
5765 Imperial Way Sw (98312-4946)
PHONE 360 674-3122
Scott Simons, *Administration*
EMP: 4
SALES (est): 324.2K **Privately Held**
SIC: 2434 Wood kitchen cabinets

(G-1945)
DEFIANCE BOATS LLC
5120 Sw Nixon Loop (98312-8934)
PHONE 360 674-7098
EMP: 2 **EST:** 2016
SALES (est): 234.6K **Privately Held**
SIC: 3732 Boat building & repairing

(G-1946)
DEFIANCE BOATS LLC
Also Called: Big Salt Bait Tanks
7510 Bree Dr (98312-4987)
PHONE 360 329-6865
Stanley Palmer,
▼ **EMP:** 30
SALES (est): 7.3MM **Privately Held**
SIC: 3732 Boat building & repairing

(G-1947)
DIGITLIS EDUCATN SOLUTIONS INC
817 Pacific Ave (98337-1921)
PHONE 360 616-8915
Robert Spearman, *President*
EMP: 10
SQ FT: 2,700
SALES (est): 1.1MM **Privately Held**
WEB: www.digitaliseducation.com
SIC: 7372 Educational computer software

(G-1948)
DIRECTED TECHNOLOGIES DRLG INC (PA)
Also Called: Dtd
3476 W Belfair Valley Rd (98312-4930)
PHONE 800 239-5950
Dan Ombalski, *President*
Jim Doesburg, *General Mgr*
James Doesburg, *Vice Pres*
Jean Doesburg, *Admin Sec*
EMP: 7
SALES (est): 3.4MM **Privately Held**
SIC: 8748 1381 Environmental consultant; directional drilling oil & gas wells

(G-1949)
DUNMIRE MANUFACTURING
8468 Kaster Dr Ne (98311-4154)
PHONE 360 241-9099
EMP: 2
SALES (est): 91.9K **Privately Held**
SIC: 3999 Manufacturing industries

(G-1950)
ECONOMY HEARTH & HOME INC
8753 State Highway 303 Ne (98311-8785)
PHONE 360 692-8709
EMP: 2
SALES (est): 95.4K **Privately Held**
SIC: 3585 Heat pumps, electric

(G-1951)
EDEN SIGN
2923 Wheaton Way (98310-3434)
PHONE 360 377-3040
Sangjean Lee, *Principal*
EMP: 2
SALES (est): 118.1K **Privately Held**
SIC: 3993 Signs & advertising specialties

▲ = Import ▼ = Export
♦ = Import/Export

GEOGRAPHIC SECTION
Bremerton - Kitsap County (G-1984)

(G-1952)
ENTENMANNS OROWEAT FOODS
5887 State Highway 303 Ne (98311-3745)
PHONE.................................360 475-8283
Mike Sullivan, *Principal*
EMP: 14
SALES (est): 1.1MM **Privately Held**
SIC: 2052 Bakery products, dry

(G-1953)
EXONE COMPANY
252 Wilkes Ave (98312-3352)
PHONE.................................360 286-0556
Sean Sutterfield, *Branch Mgr*
EMP: 3
SALES (corp-wide): 64.6MM **Publicly Held**
SIC: 2754 Job printing, gravure
PA: The Exone Company
    127 Industry Blvd
    North Huntingdon PA 15642
    724 863-9663

(G-1954)
FIRE SOLUTIONS NW LLC
1100 Wheaton Way Ste B (98310-4459)
PHONE.................................855 876-3473
Josh Fitzpatrick, *President*
Jason Mathews, *Vice Pres*
Cara Kurts, *Office Mgr*
EMP: 8 **EST:** 2016
SQ FT: 1,000
SALES (est): 191.8K **Privately Held**
SIC: 7382 3999 Fire alarm maintenance & monitoring; grenades, hand (fire extinguishers)

(G-1955)
GALE INDUSTRIES INC
4843 Auto Center Way (98312-4389)
PHONE.................................360 479-6271
Robert Manroe, *Principal*
EMP: 2
SALES (est): 85.4K **Privately Held**
SIC: 3999 Manufacturing industries

(G-1956)
GENERAL DYNAMICS NASCCO
6000 W Werner Rd (98312-3241)
PHONE.................................360 373-2845
EMP: 2
SALES (est): 248.7K **Privately Held**
SIC: 3731 Shipbuilding & repairing

(G-1957)
GEORGE G SHARP INC
2450 Wycoff Way Bldg 550 (98314-6013)
PHONE.................................360 476-8896
Ken Ahl, *Branch Mgr*
EMP: 72
SALES (corp-wide): 32.1MM **Privately Held**
WEB: www.ggsharp.com
SIC: 4225 8712 3731 General warehousing; architectural services; commercial cargo ships, building & repairing
PA: George G. Sharp, Inc.
    160 Broadway
    New York NY 10038
    212 732-2800

(G-1958)
GLOBEK LLC
130 Tweed Ln Nw Ste 2 (98312-3125)
PHONE.................................360 627-9714
Stacey Tucker,
EMP: 2
SALES: 500K **Privately Held**
SIC: 2842 Sweeping compounds, oil or water absorbent, clay or sawdust

(G-1959)
GUY CHAI INC
5885 State Highway 303 Ne (98311-3792)
PHONE.................................360 710-5962
Mark Kuehn, *CEO*
EMP: 4
SALES (est): 211K **Privately Held**
SIC: 2099 Tea blending

(G-1960)
HIGHSIDE DISTILLING LLC
7766 Chico Way Nw (98312-1046)
PHONE.................................425 417-9000
Matthew Glenn, *Manager*
EMP: 5
SQ FT: 1,700
SALES (est): 134.2K **Privately Held**
SIC: 2085 Distilled & blended liquors

(G-1961)
HOOF PRINTS KITSAP
5100 Hart St Nw (98311-2485)
PHONE.................................360 932-3992
Heather Roberts, *Principal*
EMP: 2 **EST:** 2014
SALES (est): 143.7K **Privately Held**
SIC: 2752 Commercial printing, lithographic

(G-1962)
INTEGRITY SUPPLEMENTS LLC
Also Called: Biooptimal
2620 Ne Strand Rd (98311-9385)
P.O. Box 3098, Silverdale (98383-3098)
PHONE.................................800 210-4863
Elvir Ajanovic, *Mng Member*
Autumn Ajanovic,
EMP: 3
SALES (est): 135.6K **Privately Held**
SIC: 2833 Medicinals & botanicals

(G-1963)
J & E JENSEN INC
Also Called: Novaks Continuous Met Gutters
6608 Kitsap Way Ste 4 (98312-1785)
P.O. Box 916, Silverdale (98383-0916)
PHONE.................................253 851-2282
Jim Jensen, *President*
EMP: 5
SALES (est): 769.6K **Privately Held**
SIC: 3444 1761 Gutters, sheet metal; gutter & downspout contractor

(G-1964)
J A JACK & SONS INC
Also Called: Kitsap Reclamation & Materials
5902 W Sherman Heights Rd (98312-4824)
PHONE.................................360 479-4659
EMP: 12
SALES (corp-wide): 1.4B **Publicly Held**
SIC: 4953 1442 Recycling, waste materials; construction sand & gravel
HQ: J. A. Jack & Sons, Inc.
    5427 Ohio Ave S
    Seattle WA 98134
    206 762-7622

(G-1965)
JERRY H HYMAN
Also Called: Navy Castings
3237 Birch Ave (98310-2803)
PHONE.................................360 479-1724
Jerry Hyman, *Owner*
EMP: 6
SALES: 600K **Privately Held**
SIC: 3364 3321 3325 3365 Nonferrous die-castings except aluminum; gray & ductile iron foundries; steel foundries; aluminum foundries; copper foundries; nonferrous foundries

(G-1966)
JETT INDUSTRIES INC
Also Called: True North Trading Company
4635 Marine Drive Pl (98312-2023)
P.O. Box 4144 (98312-0144)
PHONE.................................360 649-3840
Rebecca Jett, *CEO*
EMP: 2
SALES: 50K **Privately Held**
SIC: 3999 Manufacturing industries

(G-1967)
JPL HABITABILITY INC
112 Shore Dr (98310-4847)
PHONE.................................360 377-7660
Jerry Patrick Letexier, *President*
Mike Walls, *Design Engr*
EMP: 12
SQ FT: 10,000
SALES (est): 2MM **Privately Held**
SIC: 2514 2522 2542 3444 Metal household furniture; office furniture, except wood; partitions & fixtures, except wood; sheet metalwork; wood office furniture; wood household furniture

(G-1968)
KITSAP COATINGS
2501 N Wycoff Ave (98312-2711)
PHONE.................................360 550-3777
Dianne Sellers, *Principal*
EMP: 2
SALES (est): 117.8K **Privately Held**
SIC: 3479 Metal coating & allied service

(G-1969)
KITSAP CUSTOM COATINGS LLC
6801 Holland Rd Nw (98311-8903)
P.O. Box 2229, Silverdale (98383-2229)
PHONE.................................360 471-3095
Derek R Turner, *Administration*
EMP: 2
SALES (est): 106.4K **Privately Held**
SIC: 3479 Metal coating & allied service

(G-1970)
KITSAP SUN
545 5th St (98337-1413)
P.O. Box 259 (98337-0053)
PHONE.................................360 792-3350
Brent W Morris, *Publisher*
EMP: 100
SALES (est): 4.6MM **Privately Held**
SIC: 2711 Commercial printing & newspaper publishing combined

(G-1971)
KNOX CELLARS MASON BEES
7075 Corfu Blvd Ne (98311-9547)
PHONE.................................360 286-2025
EMP: 2
SALES (est): 126.4K **Privately Held**
SIC: 2084 Wines

(G-1972)
KRAIG GREEN MACHINING
5244 Minard Rd W (98312-9728)
PHONE.................................360 275-3732
Kraig Green, *Owner*
EMP: 2
SALES (est): 120.1K **Privately Held**
SIC: 3599 Machine shop, jobbing & repair

(G-1973)
LIFE SAFER
5883 State Highway 303 Ne # 202 (98311-3769)
PHONE.................................800 328-9890
EMP: 2
SALES (est): 115.3K **Privately Held**
SIC: 3694 Alternators, automotive

(G-1974)
LOCAL CHURCH PUBLISHING
1127 Poindexter Ave (98312-4336)
P.O. Box 296, Tracyton (98393-0296)
PHONE.................................360 710-8751
Scott Gregson, *Owner*
EMP: 2 **EST:** 1992
SALES: 110K **Privately Held**
WEB: www.kjv.com
SIC: 4813 2752 ; commercial printing, lithographic

(G-1975)
MACHINE DEVELOPMENT COMPANY
Also Called: Histandard
3360 Old Sawmill Pl Nw (98312-9574)
PHONE.................................360 479-4484
A Holt, *Principal*
EMP: 2
SALES (est): 130K **Privately Held**
SIC: 3531 Construction machinery

(G-1976)
MAD LABEL INDUSTRIES INC
Also Called: Mad Custom Coating
5800 W Werner Rd Ste A (98312-3245)
PHONE.................................844 623-4897
Gregory Simao, *President*
David Teves, *Vice Pres*
EMP: 6
SQ FT: 4,500
SALES: 320K **Privately Held**
SIC: 2851 Paints & allied products

(G-1977)
MC GAVINS BAKERY
619 N Callow Ave (98312-3903)
PHONE.................................360 373-2414
Billy Sheldon, *Owner*
EMP: 4
SQ FT: 5,000
SALES: 200K **Privately Held**
SIC: 2051 5461 Bread, cake & related products; bakeries

(G-1978)
METRO MACHINE CORP
Nassco Bremerton
423 Pacific Ave Ste 200 (98337-1943)
PHONE.................................360 782-5600
Jeff Brooks, *General Mgr*
EMP: 99
SQ FT: 5,000
SALES (corp-wide): 36.1B **Publicly Held**
SIC: 3731 Combat vessels, building & repairing
HQ: Metro Machine Corp.
    200 Ligon St
    Norfolk VA 23523
    757 543-6801

(G-1979)
MINUTEMAN PRESS INTL INC
187 Ne Conifer Dr (98311-3776)
PHONE.................................360 692-3470
Darwin Aiken, *Owner*
EMP: 3
SALES (est): 320.2K **Privately Held**
SIC: 2752 Commercial printing, lithographic

(G-1980)
NEW UNIFORMITY LLC
Also Called: Uniform Trading Company
330 N Callow Ave (98312-4011)
PHONE.................................360 373-2785
Malgorzata Alexander, *Mng Member*
EMP: 2
SALES: 400K **Privately Held**
SIC: 2311 Military uniforms, men's & youths': purchased materials

(G-1981)
NORTH WEST CAB & REFACING LLC
2518 E 16th St (98310-4913)
PHONE.................................360 415-9999
Julie Ullrich, *CEO*
Bill Ullrich, *President*
EMP: 2
SALES: 80K **Privately Held**
SIC: 2434 Wood kitchen cabinets

(G-1982)
OLYMPIC JANTR SUP & SVC LLC
7604 Ne Tyee Ct (98311-9316)
PHONE.................................360 692-0832
Dewayne Kalista,
EMP: 2
SALES (est): 112.3K **Privately Held**
SIC: 2842 Degreasing solvent

(G-1983)
OPTIMA CABINETS
121 N Wycoff Ave (98312-4016)
PHONE.................................509 868-5691
Cezary Nowowiejski, *Principal*
EMP: 2
SALES (est): 126.6K **Privately Held**
SIC: 2434 Wood kitchen cabinets

(G-1984)
PACIFIC PRINTING INC
3930 Burwell St (98312-3566)
PHONE.................................360 377-0844
Bradley Nelson, *President*
Gene Nelson, *Corp Secy*
Brian Nelson, *Vice Pres*
EMP: 4
SALES (est): 329.7K **Privately Held**
SIC: 7336 2752 7311 Graphic arts & related design; commercial printing, lithographic; advertising consultant

Bremerton - Kitsap County (G-1985)   GEOGRAPHIC SECTION

(G-1985)
PACIFIC SHIP REPR FBRCTION INC
8390 Sw Barney White Rd (98312-4914)
PHONE 360 674-2480
Greg Bryant, *General Mgr*
Rich Hill, *Engineer*
EMP: 114
SALES (corp-wide): 45.1MM **Privately Held**
WEB: www.pacship.com
SIC: 3731 3732 Combat vessels, building & repairing; boat building & repairing
PA: Pacific Ship Repair & Fabrication, Inc.
1625 Rigel St
San Diego CA 92113
619 232-3200

(G-1986)
PARKER LUMBER CO INC (PA)
Also Called: Do It Best
4119 Wheaton Way (98310-3624)
PHONE 425 806-7253
Toll Free: .... 888 -
Fax: 360 377-5819
EMP: 30 **EST:** 1922
SQ FT: 14,000
SALES: 37.9MM **Privately Held**
SIC: 5211 2439 Ret Lumber/Building Materials Mfg Structural Wood Members

(G-1987)
PAUL SESSIONS
13842 Kloshi Ct Nw (98312-8516)
PHONE 360 265-1658
Paul Sessions, *Principal*
EMP: 2
SALES (est): 159.2K **Privately Held**
SIC: 2221 Broadwoven fabric mills, manmade

(G-1988)
PLASMA STEEL LLC
1415 Madrona Point Dr (98312-2346)
PHONE 360 801-0444
Kristina Younger, *Principal*
EMP: 2
SALES (est): 81.8K **Privately Held**
SIC: 2836 Plasmas

(G-1989)
POWER PUNCH DISTRIBUTORS LLC (PA)
1700 W Sunn Fjord Ln L210 (98312-5947)
PHONE 360 479-0673
Peter J Morey, *Mng Member*
Gordon Mamer,
Roberta Morey,
EMP: 5
SQ FT: 1,000
SALES (est): 1.4MM **Privately Held**
SIC: 5172 2899 Lubricating oils & greases; oil treating compounds

(G-1990)
PRO ABRASIVES INC
Also Called: Pro-Grit Products
1776 3rd Ave W (98312-5300)
P.O. Box 5, Tracyton (98393-0005)
PHONE 360 509-4152
Jeff Fergusson, *President*
▲ **EMP:** 3
SQ FT: 3,800
SALES (est): 250K **Privately Held**
WEB: www.proabrasives.com
SIC: 3291 Abrasive products

(G-1991)
PYRAMID MATERIALS KITSAP QUAR
818 Archie Ave W (98312-8892)
PHONE 360 373-8708
EMP: 3
SALES (est): 130.4K **Privately Held**
SIC: 1422 Crushed & broken limestone

(G-1992)
REDS ELECTRIC MOTORS INC
2300 6th St (98312-3944)
PHONE 360 377-3903
Doug Dillon, *President*
Tim Dillon, *Vice Pres*
Joye Dillon, *Admin Sec*
EMP: 5
SQ FT: 2,000
SALES (est): 622.5K **Privately Held**
WEB: www.redselectricmotors.com
SIC: 7694 5251 5084 Electric motor repair; pumps & pumping equipment; pumps & pumping equipment

(G-1993)
REYES COCA-COLA BOTTLING LLC
5001 Auto Center Blvd (98312-3345)
PHONE 360 475-6528
Richard Arneberg, *Manager*
EMP: 52
SALES (corp-wide): 713.8MM **Privately Held**
SIC: 2086 Bottled & canned soft drinks
PA: Reyes Coca-Cola Bottling, L.L.C.
3 Park Plz Ste 600
Irvine CA 92614
213 744-8616

(G-1994)
RIES PRODUCTIONS LLC
Also Called: Ries Tripod
2600 Burwell St (98312-4021)
PHONE 360 627-8795
Deborah Hughes, *Mng Member*
E Hughes, *Bd of Directors*
Earnest M Hughes Jr,
EMP: 8
SALES (est): 670.9K **Privately Held**
SIC: 3443 3449 3479 5043 Metal parts; miscellaneous metalwork; etching & engraving; cameras & photographic equipment; scientific & engineering equipment & supplies

(G-1995)
ROCKETCAT LLC
Also Called: Rocketcat Games
7305 Chico Way Nw (98312-1035)
PHONE 360 204-4037
Anthony Auwae, *Owner*
EMP: 2
SALES (est): 68.9K **Privately Held**
SIC: 7372 Home entertainment computer software

(G-1996)
S&L FOODS LLC
6349 Juanita Cir Ne (98311-3166)
PHONE 360 627-7809
Sotero Tiburcio, *Principal*
EMP: 3
SALES (est): 141.7K **Privately Held**
SIC: 2099 Food preparations

(G-1997)
SABRE BLASTING INDUSTRIES LLC
1338 Bertha Ave Nw (98312-2607)
PHONE 360 990-2492
Stephanie Anderson, *Principal*
EMP: 2
SALES (est): 100.7K **Privately Held**
SIC: 3999 Manufacturing industries

(G-1998)
SAFE BOATS INTERNATIONAL LLC
8800 Sw Barney White Rd (98312-4921)
PHONE 360 674-7161
Dennis Morris, *CEO*
Mark Talbert, *Vice Pres*
Jim Bankson, *Project Mgr*
Gary Seibert, *Materials Mgr*
Robin Tew, *Buyer*
◆ **EMP:** 408 **EST:** 1996
SQ FT: 200,000
SALES (est): 71.8MM **Privately Held**
SIC: 5551 3732 Marine supplies & equipment; boat building & repairing

(G-1999)
SILENT VINEYARDS INC
7875 Forest Ridge Dr Ne (98311-3869)
PHONE 360 692-7497
John Adamski, *Principal*
EMP: 2 **EST:** 2016
SALES (est): 62.3K **Privately Held**
SIC: 2084 Wines, brandy & brandy spirits

(G-2000)
SILVERDALE ORTHODONTIC LAB
6102 Widgeon Ct (98312-8834)
PHONE 360 479-5536
Rudy Francisco, *Owner*
EMP: 2
SQ FT: 400
SALES (est): 110K **Privately Held**
SIC: 3843 8072 Orthodontic appliances; orthodontic appliance production

(G-2001)
SKOOKUM ENTERPRISES LLC
4525 Auto Center Way (98312-4312)
PHONE 360 475-0756
Scott Bell, *Governor*
Jeff Dolven, *Governor*
Scott Droppelman, *Governor*
Mark Heasley, *Governor*
EMP: 61
SALES (est): 2MM **Privately Held**
SIC: 3559 4119 1542 7379 Automotive maintenance equipment; local passenger transportation; nonresidential construction; computer related consulting services

(G-2002)
SP MARINE FABRICATION LLC
Also Called: Allied Boats
7510 Bree Dr (98312-4987)
PHONE 360 813-3600
Stanley B Palmer Jr, *Mng Member*
EMP: 10
SALES (est): 466.7K **Privately Held**
SIC: 3732 Fishing boats: lobster, crab, oyster, etc.: small

(G-2003)
STRIPES GLOBAL INC
245 4th St Ste 204 (98337-1801)
PHONE 800 690-8219
Tyson Schultz, *CEO*
EMP: 5
SQ FT: 800
SALES: 2.9MM **Privately Held**
SIC: 3841 Surgical & medical instruments

(G-2004)
SUN NEWSPAPER DAILY
545 5th St (98337-1476)
P.O. Box 259 (98337-0053)
PHONE 360 792-3324
Ron Muhleman, *Director*
EMP: 5
SALES (est): 297.1K **Privately Held**
SIC: 2711 Newspapers, publishing & printing

(G-2005)
SUPERCRITICAL TECHNOLOGIES
2448 Rocky Point Rd Nw (98312-2022)
P.O. Box 869 (98337-0189)
PHONE 518 225-3275
Chal Davidson, *CEO*
Brooke Macomber, *COO*
Josh Walter, *Chief Engr*
Max Effgen, *Development*
Nico Spitz, *CFO*
EMP: 6
SALES (est): 484.8K **Privately Held**
SIC: 3511 7389 Turbines & turbine generator set units, complete;

(G-2006)
TOM & CHERYL MCCALLAUM
Also Called: Samson's Inland Printing
1222 Park Ave (98337-1785)
PHONE 360 377-1606
Cheryl McCallaum, *Co-Owner*
Tom McCallaum, *Co-Owner*
EMP: 2
SQ FT: 1,500
SALES (est): 104.2K **Privately Held**
SIC: 2752 7334 Offset & photolithographic printing; photocopying & duplicating services

(G-2007)
TOUCH COLOR SCREEN PRINTING
2336 8th St (98312-3927)
PHONE 360 377-5660
Robert Caldwell, *Owner*
EMP: 2
SALES (est): 103.9K **Privately Held**
SIC: 2759 Screen printing

(G-2008)
TUCKER DISTILLERY
7501 Clover Blossom Ln Ne (98311-3945)
PHONE 360 698-7043
EMP: 3
SALES (est): 115.4K **Privately Held**
SIC: 2085 Distilled & blended liquors

(G-2009)
U2 INC
Also Called: Posh Speakers Systems
5830 W Werner Rd (98312-3245)
P.O. Box 5522 (98312-0546)
PHONE 360 627-8068
William D Benson, *President*
Steve Mc Clure, *Manager*
▲ **EMP:** 10
SQ FT: 5,000
SALES (est): 1.8MM **Privately Held**
WEB: www.nutsabouthifi.com
SIC: 3651 Home entertainment equipment, electronic; pickup heads, phonograph

(G-2010)
VILLAS JOSEY
Also Called: Midnite Sun Printing
3451 Partridge Holw Ne (98310-9747)
PHONE 360 405-1944
Josey Villas, *Owner*
EMP: 2
SALES (est): 150.7K **Privately Held**
SIC: 2752 Commercial printing, lithographic

(G-2011)
WESTBAY AUTO PARTS INC
Also Called: Westbay Industrial Sales
1550 Navy Yard Hwy (98312-4623)
PHONE 360 373-1424
Tim Olson, *General Mgr*
EMP: 13
SQ FT: 8,889
SALES (corp-wide): 71.5MM **Privately Held**
WEB: www.westbayautoparts.com
SIC: 5531 5013 3599 Automotive parts; automotive supplies & parts; machine shop, jobbing & repair
PA: Westbay Auto Parts, Inc.
2610 Se Mile Hill Dr
Port Orchard WA 98366
360 876-8008

(G-2012)
WESTERN TECHNOLOGY INC
3517 W Arsenal Way (98312-3610)
P.O. Box 5809 (98312-0593)
PHONE 360 917-0080
James Giese, *President*
▲ **EMP:** 6
SQ FT: 2,000
SALES (est): 1.4MM **Privately Held**
SIC: 3646 Commercial indusl & institutional electric lighting fixtures

(G-2013)
WOODCRAFT STUDIO
301 13th St (98337-1882)
PHONE 404 426-1229
EMP: 2
SALES (est): 131.5K **Privately Held**
SIC: 2511 Wood household furniture

(G-2014)
ZONECRO LLC
1810 Ne Rustic Ln (98310-9755)
PHONE 760 702-9290
Jasuha Parks, *Principal*
EMP: 2
SALES (est): 79K **Privately Held**
SIC: 2326 3648 Men's & boys' work clothing; flashlights

Brewster
Okanogan County

(G-2015)
BREWSTER MANUFACTURING INC
62 Bailey Way (98812-9622)
PHONE.................................509 923-2264
Chris Bailey, *President*
Mary Bailey, *Vice Pres*
EMP: 15
SALES (est): 2.5MM **Privately Held**
SIC: 3444 0175 Sheet metalwork; apple orchard

(G-2016)
GODBEY RED-E-MIX CONCRETE INC
505 Sw Ansil St (98812)
PHONE.................................509 689-2415
Wanda Godbey, *President*
EMP: 9 EST: 1949
SALES (est): 920K **Privately Held**
SIC: 3273 Ready-mixed concrete

(G-2017)
TROUT-BLUE CHELAN-MAGI INC
Also Called: Chelanmagi
410 State Way 97 (98812)
PHONE.................................509 689-2511
Jim Divis, *CEO*
EMP: 35
SALES (corp-wide): 154.9MM **Privately Held**
WEB: www.chelanfruit.com
SIC: 4222 0723 3537 Warehousing, cold storage or refrigerated; fruit (fresh) packing services; trucks: freight, baggage, etc.; industrial, except mining
PA: Trout-Blue Chelan-Magi, Inc.
8 Howser Rd
Chelan WA 98816
509 682-2591

Brier
Snohomish County

(G-2018)
BRIER BREWING LLC
3501 217th Pl Sw (98036-4201)
PHONE.................................206 258-4987
Morgan Ferry, *Principal*
EMP: 2
SALES (est): 66K **Privately Held**
SIC: 2082 Malt beverages

(G-2019)
DTG INC
Also Called: Lazerquick Printing
2805 223rd Pl Sw (98036-2727)
PHONE.................................206 622-4387
Phil Solbrig, *President*
EMP: 6
SALES (est): 699.6K **Privately Held**
SIC: 2752 Commercial printing, offset

(G-2020)
KJS HANDCRAFTED JEWELRY
22148 34th Ave W (98036-8065)
PHONE.................................425 582-8488
Michael Durfee, *Principal*
EMP: 2
SALES (est): 149.1K **Privately Held**
SIC: 3961 Costume jewelry

(G-2021)
LOKI AEROSPACE INCORPORATED
2827 232nd St Sw (98036-8333)
PHONE.................................425 361-2353
Harmony Crawford, *Principal*
EMP: 2
SALES (est): 114.1K **Privately Held**
SIC: 3721 Aircraft

(G-2022)
THEO CORAM CORPORATION
21355 Poplar Way (98036-8910)
PHONE.................................425 774-4731
Hank Choi, *President*
Eun Sim Choi, *Sales/Mktg Dir*
EMP: 2
SALES: 800K **Privately Held**
SIC: 2899 2759 Chemical supplies for foundries; screen printing

Brinnon
Jefferson County

(G-2023)
AMERICAN TIMBER RESOURCES LLC
275 Dogwood Ln (98320-9571)
P.O. Box 810 (98320-0810)
PHONE.................................360 796-4236
Michael S Boling,
EMP: 3
SALES (est): 208.3K **Privately Held**
SIC: 2411 Logging

(G-2024)
JSB LOGGING
61 Elk Ct W (98320-9658)
P.O. Box 542 (98320-0542)
PHONE.................................360 301-9675
Jason Boling, *Principal*
EMP: 2 EST: 2015
SALES (est): 88.3K **Privately Held**
SIC: 2411 Logging

(G-2025)
MCKAY SHRIMP & CRAB GEAR INC
306362 Us Highway 101 (98320-9690)
P.O. Box 370 (98320-0370)
PHONE.................................360 796-4555
Say Beck, *President*
EMP: 5
SALES (est): 407.2K **Privately Held**
SIC: 3496 3949 Traps, animal & fish; sporting & athletic goods

(G-2026)
PORTER ETUV MANUFACTURING INC
235 Salmon St (98320-9627)
PHONE.................................360 796-3172
EMP: 2
SALES (est): 110K **Privately Held**
SIC: 3999 Mfg Misc Products

Brush Prairie
Clark County

(G-2027)
ADVANCED EXTRACTS
21911 Ne 147th St (98606-5403)
PHONE.................................360 949-5325
Rod Jones, *Principal*
EMP: 2
SALES (est): 74.4K **Privately Held**
SIC: 2836 Extracts

(G-2028)
AHOLA TIMBER INC
15310 Ne Ahola Dr (98606-5413)
PHONE.................................360 892-2243
Merlin Nahola, *Principal*
EMP: 5
SALES (est): 300.3K **Privately Held**
SIC: 2411 Logging camps & contractors

(G-2029)
ARTIFACTORY
19810 Ne Davis Rd (98606-9711)
PHONE.................................360 260-2660
Connie Dees, *Principal*
EMP: 2
SALES (est): 175.8K **Privately Held**
SIC: 3944 Puzzles

(G-2030)
BETHEL LUTHERAN CHURCH
12919 Ne 159th St (98606-9507)
P.O. Box 175 (98606-0175)
PHONE.................................360 892-4231
Ron Zsehoche, *Pastor*
EMP: 6 EST: 1919
SALES (est): 272.9K **Privately Held**
SIC: 8661 2411 Lutheran Church; logging

(G-2031)
BRUSH PRAIRIE ALPACAS
19000 Ne 139th St (98606-9655)
PHONE.................................360 892-1011
Alan Espasandin, *Principal*
EMP: 2
SALES (est): 87.6K **Privately Held**
SIC: 2231 Alpacas, mohair; woven

(G-2032)
COLUMBIA SIGN
Also Called: Real Estate Sign Service
12003 Ne 121st St (98606-2105)
PHONE.................................360 696-1919
Coddie Reych, *President*
EMP: 3
SALES (est): 280.9K **Privately Held**
SIC: 3993 Electric signs

(G-2033)
DUST CONTROL TECHNOLOGIES INC
Also Called: Dct
16121 Ne 119th St (98606-7106)
PHONE.................................360 256-2479
David Goff, *President*
Try Lehner, *General Mgr*
EMP: 7
SQ FT: 2,200
SALES (est): 1MM **Privately Held**
WEB: www.dustcontroltech.com
SIC: 5075 5999 3564 Air pollution control equipment & supplies; air purification equipment; blowers & fans

(G-2034)
EVOQUA WATER TECHNOLOGIES LLC
15403 Ne Caples Rd (98606-9399)
PHONE.................................360 699-7392
EMP: 7
SALES (corp-wide): 1.3B **Publicly Held**
SIC: 3589 3569 3823 3826 Sewage & water treatment equipment; water treatment equipment, industrial; sewage treatment equipment; water purification equipment, household type; filters, general line: industrial; water quality monitoring & control systems; water testing apparatus
HQ: Evoqua Water Technologies Llc
210 6th Ave Ste 3300
Pittsburgh PA 15222
724 772-0044

(G-2035)
FIRST CHOICE MARKET INC
16105 Ne 182nd Ave (98606-9765)
PHONE.................................360 253-9149
Curt Walz, *President*
EMP: 20
SALES (est): 1.4MM **Privately Held**
SIC: 1389 Gas field services

(G-2036)
JACK E BROSSARD
16206 Ne 170th Ave (98606-7207)
PHONE.................................360 892-7538
Jack Brossard, *Principal*
EMP: 2
SALES (est): 78.8K **Privately Held**
SIC: 7692 Welding repair

(G-2037)
M R K ELECTRIC
14000 Ne 195th Ave (98606-3901)
PHONE.................................360 253-8310
Robert Kimbro, *Owner*
EMP: 3
SALES (est): 208.9K **Privately Held**
SIC: 1731 7694 General electrical contractor; electric motor repair

(G-2038)
NORTHWEST TRAFFIC CONTROL INC
16818 Ne Maddox Ct (98606-6103)
PHONE.................................360 604-5655
Patricia Marti, *Branch Mgr*
EMP: 2
SALES (est): 139.6K **Privately Held**
SIC: 3669 Traffic signals, electric
PA: Northwest Traffic Control, Inc.
4950 Ne 148th Ave
Portland OR 97230

(G-2039)
PREWITT HARDWOOD FLOORS INC
14607 Ne 170th St (98606-6019)
PHONE.................................360 666-9663
Richard Prewitt, *Owner*
EMP: 3 EST: 2016
SALES (est): 50.2K **Privately Held**
SIC: 2499 Laundry products, wood

(G-2040)
QUADRADYNE TECHNOLOGIES LLC
14200 Ne 132nd Ave (98606-3408)
PHONE.................................248 342-5977
Leslie Washko, *Principal*
EMP: 2 EST: 2015
SALES (est): 76.4K **Privately Held**
SIC: 3499 Friction material, made from powdered metal

(G-2041)
REFINER49ER LLC
24511 Ne Rawson Rd (98606-9641)
PHONE.................................360 254-0884
John Emenegger, *Warden*
EMP: 3
SALES (est): 347.8K **Privately Held**
SIC: 3827 Optical test & inspection equipment

(G-2042)
REPCON NW INC
18307 Ne 221st Ave (98606-8723)
PHONE.................................800 325-8707
Raymond Freeman, *President*
EMP: 3
SALES (est): 180K **Privately Held**
SIC: 3842 Surgical appliances & supplies

(G-2043)
WESTERN ADHESIVE SOLUTIONS
15601 Ne 194th Ct (98606-7735)
P.O. Box 265 (98606-0265)
PHONE.................................360 904-5005
Robert Lecomte, *President*
EMP: 2
SALES: 230K **Privately Held**
SIC: 2891 Adhesives

Buckley
Pierce County

(G-2044)
A & R PRINT SERVICES INC
11312 222nd Ave Ct E (98321-9147)
PHONE.................................206 321-5263
EMP: 2
SALES (est): 83.9K **Privately Held**
SIC: 2752 Commercial printing, lithographic

(G-2045)
ACTION EQUIPMENT INC
12008 238th Ave E (98321-9680)
P.O. Box 7645, Bonney Lake (98391-0961)
PHONE.................................360 897-0890
Dennis Haines Jr, *President*
Sherrilyn Askew, *Treasurer*
EMP: 4
SALES (est): 300K **Privately Held**
WEB: www.actionequipment.com
SIC: 2631 Automobile board

Buckley - Pierce County (G-2046)

(G-2046)
ARMADILLO EQUIPMENT & PARTS
28120 State Route 410 E D10 (98321-8721)
PHONE..................360 829-4107
Douglas Briese, *CEO*
Christy Briese, *Manager*
▲ **EMP:** 6
SALES (est): 1MM Privately Held
SIC: 3559 3569 3532 3531 ; filters; drills, bits & similar equipment; forestry related equipment

(G-2047)
AUDREY JOSIAS CERAMICS
23914 66th St E (98321-8702)
PHONE..................253 862-2365
Audrey Josias, *Owner*
EMP: 2
SALES (est): 102.6K Privately Held
SIC: 3269 Pottery products

(G-2048)
B & B PARROTTS WELDING INC
Also Called: B & B Welding
22021 96th St E (98321-9244)
PHONE..................253 862-4955
Bill Parrott, *President*
EMP: 4
SALES (est): 250K Privately Held
SIC: 7692 Welding repair

(G-2049)
BILT-RITE CUSTOM CABINETS
152 S River Ave (98321-8017)
P.O. Box 12 (98321-0012)
PHONE..................360 829-0663
David Dave Kooreny, *Owner*
David Kooreny, *Owner*
EMP: 2
SQ FT: 12,000
SALES (est): 217K Privately Held
SIC: 2511 2434 Wood household furniture; china closets; stands, household, wood; vanities, bathroom: wood

(G-2050)
CAMELOT TREASURES
12722 State Route 165 E (98321-9003)
PHONE..................360 829-9774
Brian McCarty, *Owner*
EMP: 2
SALES (est): 118.3K Privately Held
SIC: 2431 Ornamental woodwork: cornices, mantels, etc.

(G-2051)
CLASSIC SIGN AND GRAPHICS
8221 256th Ave E (98321-9379)
P.O. Box 1982 (98321-1982)
PHONE..................253 862-8035
Stephen Jannsen, *Principal*
EMP: 2
SALES (est): 214.5K Privately Held
SIC: 3993 Signs & advertising specialties

(G-2052)
COFFEE VAULT LLC
23220 Smner Buckley Hwy E (98321-8426)
PHONE..................253 227-5798
Kathy Emry, *Principal*
EMP: 3
SALES (est): 212K Privately Held
SIC: 3272 Burial vaults, concrete or precast terrazzo

(G-2053)
CONVEYOR WORKS INC
Also Called: Conveying Solutions
11012 254th Ave E (98321-7464)
P.O. Box 1827 (98321-1827)
PHONE..................360 829-5378
Scott Schunke, *President*
Renee Schunke, *Vice Pres*
EMP: 4
SQ FT: 4,000
SALES (est): 643.4K Privately Held
SIC: 3535 Belt conveyor systems, general industrial use

(G-2054)
COOPER SMITHING CO
12610 Mundy Loss Rd (98321-8794)
PHONE..................253 906-0425
EMP: 2
SALES (est): 157.8K Privately Held
SIC: 3441 Fabricated structural metal

(G-2055)
CW MACHINE LLC
28120 State Route 410 E B8 (98321-8717)
PHONE..................360 829-4171
Charles Johnston,
EMP: 2
SQ FT: 950
SALES (est): 200K Privately Held
SIC: 3541 Lathes, metal cutting & polishing

(G-2056)
DAILY GRIND
11017 223rd Avenue Ct E (98321-9745)
PHONE..................253 632-7992
Brianna Gottschalk, *Principal*
EMP: 3
SALES (est): 214.1K Privately Held
SIC: 3599 Grinding castings for the trade

(G-2057)
DMC SIDECARS LLC
15616 Crbnado S Pririe Rd (98321-9585)
PHONE..................360 825-4610
Tara Holtzclaw, *Office Mgr*
Donovan Giese,
EMP: 10
SQ FT: 15,000
SALES (est): 755.9K Privately Held
SIC: 3751 Motorcycle accessories

(G-2058)
F W ENTERPRISES LLC
9610 226th Avenue Ct E (98321-8484)
P.O. Box 583, South Prairie (98385-0583)
PHONE..................253 439-8090
Jason West, *Principal*
EMP: 3
SALES (est): 351.5K Privately Held
SIC: 2451 Mobile buildings: for commercial use

(G-2059)
IMPULSE MEDICAL TECH INC
Also Called: Electrode Store, The
159 W Mason Ave (98321-8532)
P.O. Box 188, Enumclaw (98022-0188)
PHONE..................360 829-0400
Steven Obey, *President*
EMP: 18 **EST:** 2015
SALES (est): 1MM Privately Held
SIC: 3841 3842 3845 5047 Surgical & medical instruments; surgical appliances & supplies; electrotherapeutic apparatus; medical & hospital equipment; ophthalmic goods

(G-2060)
INTEGRATED STAIR SYSTEMS INC
Also Called: Complete Access
1345 Ryan Rd (98321-9123)
P.O. Box 1170 (98321-1170)
PHONE..................360 829-4220
Larry Warford, *President*
Salvatore Carrera, *Sales Mgr*
Terri Leffel, *Administration*
EMP: 36
SQ FT: 3,500
SALES (est): 11.4MM Privately Held
SIC: 3446 Ladders, for permanent installation: metal

(G-2061)
LEON WICKIZER EXCAVATING
26513 112th St E (98321-8004)
P.O. Box 1069 (98321-1069)
PHONE..................253 261-2978
Leon L Wickizer, *Owner*
EMP: 2
SALES (est): 250K Privately Held
SIC: 1794 2411 Excavation work; logging

(G-2062)
LEONSDELI EXPRESS
27909 Hwy 410 E (98321-9212)
PHONE..................360 863-1998
EMP: 2 **EST:** 2006
SALES (est): 100K Privately Held
SIC: 2741 Misc Publishing

(G-2063)
MCCOY ELECTRIC
27609 96th St E (98321-9430)
PHONE..................360 829-5273
EMP: 4
SALES (est): 300K Privately Held
SIC: 3699 Mfg Electrical Equipment/Supplies

(G-2064)
MIKES HELP KEY LLC
23218 124th St E (98321-9301)
PHONE..................360 897-2880
Michael G Dempsey,
EMP: 5
SALES (est): 275K Privately Held
WEB: www.mikeshelpkey.com
SIC: 3572 7378 Disk drives, computer; computer maintenance & repair

(G-2065)
OOAK PRINTS LLC
719 Main St (98321-8509)
PHONE..................253 886-1539
Brennon Gulin, *Principal*
EMP: 2 **EST:** 2017
SALES (est): 92.3K Privately Held
SIC: 2752 Commercial printing, lithographic

(G-2066)
PARKER PACIFIC INC
27120 112th St E (98321-9260)
PHONE..................253 862-9133
Dave Parker, *President*
EMP: 40
SQ FT: 2,400
SALES (est): 5.6MM Privately Held
WEB: www.parkerpacificinc.com
SIC: 2411 1629 Logging camps & contractors; land clearing contractor

(G-2067)
PEARLS MBL WLDG & FABRICATION
12617 231st Ave E (98321-9130)
PHONE..................360 897-9288
Gary M Perreault, *Owner*
Sharla Perreault, *Co-Owner*
EMP: 4
SALES (est): 170.6K Privately Held
SIC: 7692 Welding repair

(G-2068)
RANIER WELDING & FABRICATION
28910 Smner Buckley Hwy E (98321-9248)
PHONE..................360 829-0445
Debra Lewis, *Partner*
Richard Lewis, *Partner*
EMP: 2
SALES (est): 150K Privately Held
SIC: 7692 Welding repair

(G-2069)
RAWSON LOGGING
27312 153rd St E (98321-9663)
PHONE..................360 829-0474
Gene Rawson, *Owner*
EMP: 6 **EST:** 1975
SALES (est): 1MM Privately Held
SIC: 2411 Logging camps & contractors

(G-2070)
ROGERS RUBBER MANUFACTURING
22115 108th Street Ct E (98321-9218)
PHONE..................253 845-8374
Tom Brown, *President*
Paula Kunselman, *Vice Pres*
EMP: 7
SALES (est): 880K Privately Held
SIC: 3061 Mechanical rubber goods

(G-2071)
SEY MIK CABINETS & MILLWORK
23220 Smner Buckley Hwy E (98321-8426)
PHONE..................360 829-0173
Glen Emery, *President*
Kathy Emery, *Vice Pres*
EMP: 6
SALES (est): 340K Privately Held
SIC: 2434 Wood kitchen cabinets

(G-2072)
SHELLY SHAY
Also Called: Precision Chain Saw
29022 State Route 410 E (98321-9402)
PHONE..................360 829-2350
Shelly Shay, *Owner*
EMP: 2
SQ FT: 320
SALES: 52K Privately Held
SIC: 5072 3546 Power tools & accessories; saws & sawing equipment

(G-2073)
STEELHEAD COMMUNICATIONS INC (PA)
28120 State Route 410 E A3 (98321-8721)
PHONE..................360 829-1330
David Moorehouse, *President*
Curt Cole, *Project Mgr*
Gino Luby, *Project Mgr*
Matt Nevin, *Project Mgr*
Jerry Trierweiler, *Info Tech Mgr*
▲ **EMP:** 40 **EST:** 2000
SALES (est): 7.3MM Privately Held
WEB: www.steelheadcom.com
SIC: 3441 Tower sections, radio & television transmission

(G-2074)
STENERSON & SONS
27605 96th St E (98321-9430)
PHONE..................360 829-1219
Robert Stenerson, *Owner*
EMP: 2
SQ FT: 3,400
SALES (est): 143.2K Privately Held
SIC: 3599 Machine shop, jobbing & repair

(G-2075)
STEVES HOT SMKED CHEESE SALMON
26806 166th St E (98321-9199)
PHONE..................360 829-2244
Steve Shindle, *Owner*
EMP: 5
SALES (est): 400K Privately Held
SIC: 5451 2091 Cheese; salmon, smoked

(G-2076)
STL INTERNATIONAL INCORPORATED
Also Called: Hang-UPS
9713 233rd Ave E (98321-8773)
PHONE..................253 840-5252
Roger Teeter, *President*
Rylie Teeter, *Vice Pres*
Jennifer M Teeter, *Admin Sec*
▲ **EMP:** 22
SALES (est): 13.1MM Privately Held
WEB: www.teeterhangups.com
SIC: 5091 3089 5047 Exercise equipment; injection molding of plastics; medical & hospital equipment

(G-2077)
TODD PORTER CAMPBELL
Also Called: Stick It Vinyl Sign and Banner
256 S C St (98321-8038)
PHONE..................253 230-2391
Todd Porter Campbell, *Owner*
Joanne Campbell, *Co-Owner*
EMP: 2
SALES (est): 99.4K Privately Held
SIC: 3993 Signs & advertising specialties

(G-2078)
VAN DAM WELDING INC
28421 112th St E (98321-9265)
P.O. Box 132 (98321-0132)
PHONE..................360 761-7297
Henry Dam, *President*
EMP: 6 **EST:** 2015
SALES: 500K Privately Held
SIC: 7692 Welding repair

(G-2079)
VERZITELLE LLC
13119 Fettig Rd E (98321-9644)
PHONE..................360 829-1628
Leana Lamb, *Mng Member*

Margaret Goegebuer,
EMP: 2
SALES (est): 172.8K **Privately Held**
WEB: www.verzitelle.com
SIC: 2678 Memorandum books, notebooks & looseleaf filler paper

(G-2080)
WHITE RIVER LOGGING
Also Called: Wozeniak Gordon Trucking
27115 Smner Buckley Hwy E (98321-9698)
P.O. Box 68 (98321-0068)
PHONE 360 829-1630
Gordon Wozeniak, *Owner*
Trichelle Wozeniak, *Co-Owner*
EMP: 10
SALES (est): 594K **Privately Held**
SIC: 2411 0782 Logging camps & contractors; lawn & garden services

Buena
Yakima County

(G-2081)
VALCOM INC
1111 Buena Rd (98921)
P.O. Box 267 (98921-0267)
PHONE 509 865-5511
Ward Deaton, *President*
EMP: 6
SALES (est): 664.9K **Privately Held**
SIC: 2048 Prepared feeds

Burbank
Walla Walla County

(G-2082)
B AND P ENTERPRISES
83 Reinken Blvd (99323-9509)
PHONE 509 545-9125
EMP: 2
SALES (est): 88.5K **Privately Held**
SIC: 3581 Mfg Vending Machines

(G-2083)
DESERT RAIN
304 Tuttle Ln (99323-9717)
PHONE 509 545-1900
Brent Lehman, *Principal*
EMP: 2 **EST:** 1994
SALES (est): 120K **Privately Held**
SIC: 3432 Lawn hose nozzles & sprinklers

(G-2084)
HARRIS MANUFACTURING IRRI
1257 Hanson Loop C (99323-9562)
PHONE 509 539-1725
Jerry Harris, *Owner*
EMP: 3
SALES: 180K **Privately Held**
SIC: 3999 Barber & beauty shop equipment

(G-2085)
QUALITY BACKHOE SERVICES INC
26905 Ice Harbor Dr (99323-9725)
PHONE 509 545-0242
Luis Sanchez, *President*
EMP: 2
SALES (est): 175.2K **Privately Held**
SIC: 3531 Backhoes

(G-2086)
TRIPLE A DRILLING INC
785 Tumbleweed Ln (99323-8648)
P.O. Box 278 (99323-0278)
PHONE 509 543-3331
Olin Amos, *President*
Penny Amos, *Treasurer*
EMP: 3
SALES (est): 495.3K **Privately Held**
SIC: 1381 Drilling water intake wells

Burien
King County

(G-2087)
A & J GRAPHICS & DESIGN
440 Sw 143rd St (98166-1534)
P.O. Box 48308 (98148-0308)
PHONE 206 439-1766
Jean Courter, *Co-Owner*
Rod Courter, *Co-Owner*
EMP: 2
SALES (est): 123.5K **Privately Held**
SIC: 5999 2759 Trophies & plaques; screen printing

(G-2088)
A AND M IMPRESSIONS LLC
12849 9th Ave Sw (98146-3106)
PHONE 206 595-1111
Anthony Olheiser, *Principal*
EMP: 2
SALES (est): 171.8K **Privately Held**
SIC: 2759 Commercial printing

(G-2089)
ACCURATE TOOL & DIE
15415 Ambaum Blvd Sw (98166-2422)
PHONE 206 277-0234
John Larfen, *President*
EMP: 2
SQ FT: 9,275
SALES (est): 331.7K **Privately Held**
WEB: www.accuratetoolonline.com
SIC: 3599 Machine shop, jobbing & repair

(G-2090)
ACE GALVANIZING
16019 3rd Pl S (98148-1486)
PHONE 206 687-7688
EMP: 2
SALES (est): 90.8K **Privately Held**
SIC: 3312 Ammonia & liquor, from chemical recovery coke ovens

(G-2091)
ARCH PARENT INC
158 Sw 148th St (98166-1924)
PHONE 206 664-0217
EMP: 1904
SALES (corp-wide): 3B **Privately Held**
SIC: 2752 Commercial printing, lithographic
PA: Arch Parent Inc.
9 W 57th St Fl 31
New York NY 10019
212 796-8500

(G-2092)
ARMOIRE
Also Called: Springtime Bakery
825 Sw 152nd St (98166-1841)
PHONE 206 397-4703
Mara Culhane, *Owner*
EMP: 6 **EST:** 2011
SALES (est): 312K **Privately Held**
SIC: 2066 5461 5812 Chocolate & cocoa products; bakeries; coffee shop

(G-2093)
BERNARD MANUFACTURING
13662 17th Ave Sw (98166-1043)
PHONE 206 242-4017
Kenneth Bernard, *Owner*
EMP: 10
SALES (est): 1MM **Privately Held**
SIC: 3272 2511 Concrete products; wood household furniture

(G-2094)
BURIEN SAND AND GRAVEL LLC
818 Sw 142nd St (98166-1554)
PHONE 206 244-1023
EMP: 2
SALES (est): 72.4K **Privately Held**
SIC: 1442 Construction sand & gravel

(G-2095)
CITLALI CREATIVO
14441 Ambaum Blvd Sw A (98166-1491)
PHONE 206 779-5664
EMP: 4
SALES (est): 297.1K **Privately Held**
SIC: 2754 Stationery & invitation printing, gravure

(G-2096)
CKREED DEFENSE LLC
16637 10th Ave Sw (98166-2935)
PHONE 206 297-2116
Charles Reed, *Principal*
EMP: 3
SALES (est): 200.9K **Privately Held**
SIC: 3812 Defense systems & equipment

(G-2097)
COLOR PRINTING SYSTEMS INC
15106 10th Ave Sw (98166-1820)
PHONE 206 763-7704
Ken Peterson, *President*
EMP: 13
SALES (est): 4MM **Privately Held**
WEB: www.colorprintingsystems.com
SIC: 2752 Commercial printing, offset

(G-2098)
COMPETITIVE EDGE ATHLETICS
14443 Ambaum Blvd Sw (98166-1423)
PHONE 206 246-7211
Thuat Bui, *Owner*
EMP: 2
SQ FT: 1,500
SALES (est): 112.1K **Privately Held**
SIC: 5699 2396 Sports apparel; screen printing on fabric articles

(G-2099)
CORBITZ LTD
16428 12th Ave Sw (98166-2812)
PHONE 206 241-9877
Marcus M Bing, *Owner*
EMP: 2
SALES (est): 120K **Privately Held**
WEB: www.corbitz.com
SIC: 3089 Holders: paper towel, grocery bag, etc.: plastic

(G-2100)
CUSTOM WELDING
Also Called: Al's Custom Welding
14622 9th Ave Sw (98166-1859)
PHONE 206 242-5047
Al Book, *Owner*
EMP: 2
SQ FT: 1,680
SALES: 120K **Privately Held**
SIC: 7692 7532 1799 Welding repair; customizing services, non-factory basis; welding on site

(G-2101)
D&J CUSTOM METAL FABRICATION
11615 12th Ave S (98168-2129)
PHONE 206 242-3238
David Wilcox, *Owner*
EMP: 2
SALES (est): 263K **Privately Held**
SIC: 3499 5013 1799 Metal household articles; automotive servicing equipment; welding on site

(G-2102)
DIANE M YOUNG
239 Sw 138th St (98166-1347)
PHONE 310 284-8704
Diane Young, *Principal*
EMP: 3
SALES (est): 126.9K **Privately Held**
SIC: 3554 Paper industries machinery

(G-2103)
DUX TECHNOLOGIES INC
13838 1st Ave S Ste C (98168-3414)
PHONE 206 248-0808
Brad Rice,
EMP: 2
SALES (est): 113K **Privately Held**
SIC: 2851 Paints & allied products

(G-2104)
E H P & ASSOCIATES INC
Also Called: AMS Offices Solutions
15106 10th Ave Sw (98166-1820)
PHONE 206 764-3344
Evan Hamid Padilla, *President*
EMP: 13
SQ FT: 5,400
SALES (est): 1.8MM **Privately Held**
WEB: www.amslaser.com
SIC: 7699 3555 Printing trades machinery & equipment repair; printing trades machinery

(G-2105)
ENGINEERED BLDG CONTRLS LLC
1834 Sw 152nd St (98166-1725)
PHONE 206 229-7475
EMP: 2
SALES (est): 193.4K **Privately Held**
SIC: 3822 Mfg Environmental Controls

(G-2106)
EXPRESSIONS GLASS II
648 Sw 152nd St (98166-2213)
PHONE 206 242-2860
Kathy Johnson, *Partner*
Lael Smidt, *Partner*
EMP: 2
SQ FT: 4,800
SALES (est): 160K **Privately Held**
SIC: 3231 5945 5231 Stained glass: made from purchased glass; arts & crafts supplies; glass, leaded or stained

(G-2107)
FASTSIGNS 632
922 Sw 151st St (98166-1838)
PHONE 206 577-4077
James Pike, *Exec Dir*
EMP: 3
SALES (est): 205.9K **Privately Held**
SIC: 3993 Signs & advertising specialties

(G-2108)
FOCUS GROUP INC
2201 Sw 152nd St Ste 3 (98166-2080)
PHONE 206 281-1977
Brian Thurston, *President*
EMP: 6
SALES (est): 961.7K **Privately Held**
WEB: www.huntershandbook.com
SIC: 2721 7389 Magazines: publishing only, not printed on site; advertising, promotional & trade show services

(G-2109)
GARAGE SPORTS WOODWORKING
12233 22nd Ave S (98168-2319)
PHONE 206 433-1645
EMP: 2
SALES (est): 150K **Privately Held**
SIC: 2431 Mfg Millwork

(G-2110)
GARDEN GUYS LLC
17824 1st Ave S (98148-1712)
PHONE 206 257-4024
EMP: 2 **EST:** 2010
SALES (est): 100K **Privately Held**
SIC: 3524 Mfg Lawn/Garden Equipment

(G-2111)
HAHN SOFTWARE LLC
2419 Sw 149th St (98166-1646)
PHONE 206 724-4735
August Hahn, *Principal*
EMP: 5
SALES (est): 265.9K **Privately Held**
SIC: 7372 Prepackaged software

(G-2112)
HOT SHOT EXPRESS INC
19034 7th Ave S (98148-2026)
PHONE 206 241-5516
EMP: 2 **EST:** 2010
SALES (est): 110K **Privately Held**
SIC: 1389 Oil/Gas Field Services

(G-2113)
INFORMATICA PUBG GROUP LLC
15410 Maplewild Ave Sw (98166-2061)
PHONE 480 361-6300
EMP: 2 **EST:** 2011
SALES (est): 97K **Privately Held**
SIC: 2741 Misc Publishing

Burien - King County (G-2114)

(G-2114)
JAY LAURIS & COMPANY INC
Also Called: Jay Lauris Jewelry
920 Sw 152nd St Ste 102 (98166-1884)
PHONE................................206 243-9890
Robert Simpson-Park, *President*
Juanita Simpson, *Corp Secy*
EMP: 2
SQ FT: 750
SALES: 125K **Privately Held**
SIC: 3911 5944 7631 Jewelry, precious metal; jewelry, precious stones & precious metals; jewelry repair services

(G-2115)
JURY VERDICTS NORTHWEST
13258 1st Ave S Ste B (98166-2689)
PHONE................................425 487-9848
Lynn Griesel, *President*
Donna Davidson, *Corp Secy*
Melissa McCann, *Manager*
EMP: 3
SALES (est): 252.6K **Privately Held**
SIC: 2741 8111 Miscellaneous publishing; legal services

(G-2116)
KWANG NAM HWANG
Also Called: Brim Press
446 Sw 153rd St (98166-2215)
PHONE................................206 433-8811
Kwang Nam Hwang, *Owner*
Ken Lee, *Manager*
▲ EMP: 13
SQ FT: 2,400
SALES: 1.2MM **Privately Held**
SIC: 2752 2759 Commercial printing, offset; commercial printing

(G-2117)
LAWRENSON ELECTRONICS CO INC
Also Called: Lawrence Electronic Company
14636 Ambaum Blvd Sw (98166-1810)
P.O. Box 66556, Seattle (98166-0556)
PHONE................................206 243-7310
Gary Lawrenson, *President*
▼ EMP: 5
SQ FT: 3,000
SALES (est): 829.8K **Privately Held**
SIC: 3829 8734 Measuring & controlling devices; product testing laboratory, safety or performance

(G-2118)
LK SEWING CO
Also Called: Sassy Dog Wear
15849 6th Ave Sw (98166-3005)
PHONE................................206 240-9973
Kim Nguyen, *President*
EMP: 5
SALES: 444.1K **Privately Held**
SIC: 2399 2393 Horse & pet accessories, textile; bags & containers, except sleeping bags: textile

(G-2119)
NELSON ESTATE
Also Called: Nelson Estate Vineyards
16349 Maplewild Ave Sw (98166-3129)
P.O. Box 66067, Seattle (98166-0067)
PHONE................................206 241-9463
David Nelson, *Owner*
Holly Nelson, *Partner*
EMP: 2
SALES (est): 140K **Privately Held**
SIC: 3199 Whips, leather

(G-2120)
PELLING INDUSTRIES INC
13206 3rd Ave S (98168-2646)
PHONE................................206 243-1941
EMP: 2
SALES (est): 66.1K **Privately Held**
SIC: 3999 Manufacturing industries

(G-2121)
PRINTCOM INC
1000 Sw 149th St (98166-1824)
P.O. Box 66948, Seattle (98166-0948)
PHONE................................206 763-7600
Jim Coovert, *President*
Judy Coovert, *Corp Secy*
EMP: 13
SQ FT: 13,000
SALES (est): 2.1MM **Privately Held**
WEB: www.printcominc.com
SIC: 2752 5112 5199 8748 Commercial printing, offset; business forms; manifold business forms; advertising specialties; publishing consultant; art design services

(G-2122)
PROMENADE PUBLISHING INC
16210 12th Ave Sw (98166-2810)
PHONE................................800 342-6947
James A Lemmon, *Principal*
EMP: 2
SALES (est): 135.4K **Privately Held**
SIC: 2741 Miscellaneous publishing

(G-2123)
RAINIER RANCH INC
16644 16th Ave Sw (98166-3455)
P.O. Box 301, Seahurst (98062-0301)
PHONE................................206 243-2044
Joann Bergseth, *President*
EMP: 3
SALES (est): 240K **Privately Held**
WEB: www.rainierranch.com
SIC: 2077 4214 Grease rendering, inedible; local trucking with storage

(G-2124)
RAMLYN ENGRAVING & SIGN CO
14926 Ambaum Blvd Sw (98166-1848)
PHONE................................206 439-8555
James Mullert, *President*
EMP: 3
SALES (est): 316.8K **Privately Held**
WEB: www.ramlyn.com
SIC: 3993 Signs & advertising specialties

(G-2125)
REGENCY CLEANERS LLC
12825 Des Moines Mem Dr S (98168-2843)
PHONE................................206 650-6933
Alina Garrity, *Principal*
EMP: 4
SALES (est): 600.7K **Privately Held**
SIC: 2842 Window cleaning preparations

(G-2126)
RISING MOON PRODUCTS
Also Called: Gebetto's Rising Moon Products
2017 Sw 146th St (98166-1024)
PHONE................................206 439-0338
Sharon Ray, *Owner*
George Bower, *Manager*
EMP: 2
SALES: 40K **Privately Held**
WEB: www.risingmoon.com
SIC: 2499 Decorative wood & woodwork

(G-2127)
RUST PROVED SOFTWARE
11628 30th Ave Sw (98146-2466)
PHONE................................206 244-0643
EMP: 2 EST: 2011
SALES (est): 100K **Privately Held**
SIC: 7372 Prepackaged Software Services

(G-2128)
SNAPPYDUDS
135 Sw 153rd St (98166-2311)
PHONE................................206 243-8478
Scott Guy, *Branch Mgr*
EMP: 2
SALES (corp-wide): 1.1MM **Privately Held**
SIC: 2395 Embroidery & art needlework
PA: Snappyduds
3201 Hesper Rd Ste 3
Billings MT 59102
406 656-2333

(G-2129)
SNIDER BURIEN DRAPERIES
247 Sw 153rd St (98166-2313)
PHONE................................206 243-3600
Evella Kuxhaus, *Partner*
Sharon Bixby, *Partner*
EMP: 2
SQ FT: 2,400
SALES: 61K **Privately Held**
WEB: www.sbdrapes.com
SIC: 2391 5714 Draperies, plastic & textile: from purchased materials; draperies

(G-2130)
SPIO INC
127 Sw 156th St (98166-2515)
PHONE................................253 893-0390
Brad Shatto, *General Mgr*
Janet Vamzow-Bliss, *CFO*
Ken Dilag, *Manager*
▲ EMP: 5
SQ FT: 881
SALES: 1.4MM
SALES (corp-wide): 12.6MM **Privately Held**
SIC: 3841 Surgical & medical instruments
PA: Dynamic Family Services
10811 Se Kent Kangley Rd
Kent WA 98030
253 854-5660

(G-2131)
SQUEALOCK SYSTEMS INC ◆
126 Sw 148th St (98166-1984)
PHONE................................206 519-4620
Komlan Wussinu, *Principal*
Kossi Alifa, *Principal*
EMP: 2 EST: 2018
SALES (est): 56.5K **Privately Held**
SIC: 7372 Application computer software

(G-2132)
STRAIGHT EDGE ASPHALT & MAINT
15715 13th Ave Sw (98166-2120)
PHONE................................206 949-4666
Dennon Weiler, *Owner*
EMP: 2
SALES: 60K **Privately Held**
SIC: 2951 Asphalt paving mixtures & blocks

(G-2133)
TOSTRZ LLC
3114 Sw 172nd St (98166-3162)
PHONE................................206 595-3044
Connie Davolt,
Lorraine Fitz,
EMP: 2
SALES (est): 142K **Privately Held**
WEB: www.tostrz.com
SIC: 2329 Jackets (suede, leatherette, etc.), sport: men's & boys'

(G-2134)
TRADE PRINTERY LLC
16022 Maplewild Ave Sw (98166-2624)
PHONE................................206 241-3322
Beth Snider, *Principal*
EMP: 2
SALES (est): 141.6K **Privately Held**
SIC: 2752 Commercial printing, offset

(G-2135)
UTE LTD
12622 4th Ave Sw (98146-3331)
P.O. Box 46457, Seattle (98146-0457)
PHONE................................206 510-8621
Randy Cryer, *President*
Curtis Cryer, *Vice Pres*
▲ EMP: 3 EST: 2000
SALES: 180K **Privately Held**
WEB: www.uteltd.com
SIC: 3713 Truck beds

(G-2136)
VITAMIN SHOPPE INDUSTRIES INC
Also Called: Super Supplement
15870 1st Ave S (98148-1301)
PHONE................................855 715-8530
EMP: 3 **Publicly Held**
SIC: 2834 Hormone preparations
HQ: Vitamin Shoppe Industries Inc
300 Harmon Meadow Blvd
Secaucus NJ 07094
201 868-5959

(G-2137)
WHITE HERON
15217 8th Ave S (98148-2566)
PHONE................................206 246-5080
EMP: 2 EST: 2014
SALES (est): 68.6K **Privately Held**
SIC: 2084 Brandy & brandy spirits

Burlington
Skagit County

(G-2138)
BURLINGTON SHELL
575 S Burlington Blvd (98233-2207)
PHONE................................360 755-0400
Keith Bower, *Manager*
EMP: 2
SALES (est): 123.4K **Privately Held**
SIC: 3578 Automatic teller machines (ATM)

(G-2139)
BUSHWACKER BOATS
11095 Jensen Ln (98233-3617)
PHONE................................360 969-1648
Eric J Werner, *Principal*
EMP: 4
SALES (est): 327.5K **Privately Held**
SIC: 3732 Boat building & repairing

(G-2140)
CARGILL INCORPORATED
16939 State Route 20 (98233-3582)
PHONE................................360 757-4012
Robert Bills, *Manager*
EMP: 16
SALES (corp-wide): 114.7B **Privately Held**
WEB: www.cargill.com
SIC: 2048 Prepared feeds
PA: Cargill, Incorporated
15407 Mcginty Rd W
Wayzata MN 55391
952 742-7575

(G-2141)
CASCADE CONCRETE INDUSTRIES
1912 S Burlington Blvd (98233-3228)
PHONE................................360 757-2900
Rick Peterson, *Owner*
▲ EMP: 12
SALES: 5MM **Privately Held**
WEB: www.cascadeconcreteindustries.com
SIC: 3271 5032 Concrete block & brick; concrete building products

(G-2142)
CEDAR CREEK PRINTING CO
105 Cedar St (98233-2807)
PHONE................................360 757-7588
EMP: 2
SALES (est): 73.2K **Privately Held**
SIC: 2759 Publication printing

(G-2143)
CHUCKANUT WOODWORKS
2822 Old Highway 99 N Rd (98233-8561)
PHONE................................360 724-3129
Chuck Wagoner, *Principal*
EMP: 2
SALES (est): 254.1K **Privately Held**
SIC: 2431 Millwork

(G-2144)
CITY BOOKS YELLOW PAGES INC
1415 Pacific Dr (98233-3123)
PHONE................................805 473-1686
▲ EMP: 16
SALES (est): 960K **Privately Held**
SIC: 2759 Commercial Printing

(G-2145)
CLEARSNAP HOLDING INC (PA)
15218 Josh Wilson Rd (98233-9648)
PHONE................................360 293-6634
Sterling Gardner, *President*
▲ EMP: 60
SQ FT: 38,400
SALES (est): 10.1MM **Privately Held**
WEB: www.colorbox.com
SIC: 3069 Stationers' rubber sundries

(G-2146)
COPPERHEAT
11837 Watertank Rd (98233-3631)
P.O. Box 2449, Mount Vernon (98273-7449)
PHONE................................360 757-2589
Tom Twedt, *Principal*

GEOGRAPHIC SECTION

Burlington - Skagit County (G-2175)

EMP: 3 EST: 2011
SALES (est): 303.8K **Privately Held**
SIC: 3398 Metal heat treating

(G-2147)
CORBELLS PORTABLE WELDING
2161 Old Highway 99 N Rd (98233-8554)
PHONE.................................360 724-4700
Angela Corbell, *Partner*
Phillip Corell, *Partner*
EMP: 2
SALES (est): 201.9K **Privately Held**
SIC: 7692 Welding repair

(G-2148)
CREATIVE MACHINING COMPANY
15846 Preston Pl (98233-3550)
PHONE.................................360 855-1981
Joseph Lubanski, *President*
Helen Gurno, *Vice Pres*
EMP: 10
SQ FT: 10,000
SALES: 850K **Privately Held**
SIC: 3599 Machine shop, jobbing & repair

(G-2149)
CROWN FILMS LLC
527 N Hill Blvd (98233-4615)
PHONE.................................360 757-8880
Joel M Bittner,
Richard Mathes,
Sandra Wenzel,
EMP: 4
SALES (est): 568.1K **Privately Held**
SIC: 2295 Resin or plastic coated fabrics

(G-2150)
D & R RV LLC
Also Called: Dreamchasers Rv of Burlington
1757 Walton Dr (98233-4639)
PHONE.................................360 755-3218
Philip Van Voorst, *Foreman/Supr*
Raymond Goda, *Mng Member*
Deborah Goda,
EMP: 12
SQ FT: 2,000
SALES (est): 2.5MM **Privately Held**
SIC: 5561 3792 Motor homes; camper & travel trailer dealers; truck campers (slide-in)

(G-2151)
DEBOER DAIRY LLC
8426 District Line Rd (98233-9568)
PHONE.................................360 757-2660
Sidney Deboer, *CEO*
EMP: 20
SALES (est): 671.8K **Privately Held**
SIC: 2023 Dry, condensed, evaporated dairy products

(G-2152)
DRI-EAZ PRODUCTS INC (HQ)
15180 Josh Wilson Rd (98233-9656)
PHONE.................................360 757-7776
Bill Bruders, *President*
Susan Cook, *Opers Staff*
Robert Sorakubo, *CFO*
Steven Fane, *Sales Mgr*
Anna Jaderlund, *Sales Mgr*
▲ EMP: 125 EST: 1982
SQ FT: 56,000
SALES (corp-wide): 5.3B **Publicly Held**
WEB: www.dri-eaz.com
SIC: 3589 Commercial cleaning equipment
PA: Rpm International Inc.
2628 Pearl Rd
Medina OH 44256
330 273-5090

(G-2153)
DRY AIR TECHNOLOGY INC
1387 Pacific Dr (98233-3128)
PHONE.................................360 755-9176
Grant Reuter, *President*
Trish Hatley, *Vice Pres*
▲ EMP: 12
SQ FT: 5,000
SALES (est): 2.5MM **Privately Held**
SIC: 3585 Heating equipment, complete; humidifiers & dehumidifiers

(G-2154)
DYNES FARMS INC (PA)
Also Called: Broadview Farms
1145 S Anacortes St (98233-3013)
P.O. Box 286 (98233-0286)
PHONE.................................360 757-4025
Charles G Dynes, *President*
A William Dynes, *Treasurer*
Joe Van Notriac, *Manager*
EMP: 35 EST: 1952
SQ FT: 500
SALES: 5.3MM **Privately Held**
WEB: www.dynesfarms.com
SIC: 0252 5144 2015 Chicken eggs; eggs; poultry slaughtering & processing

(G-2155)
EK PROJECTS LLC
Also Called: Eddyline Kayaks
11977 Westar Ln (98233-3620)
PHONE.................................360 757-2300
Scott Holley, *President*
EMP: 16
SQ FT: 18,000
SALES (est): 657.6K **Privately Held**
SIC: 2499 Oars & paddles, wood

(G-2156)
FAB-TECH INC
9587 Green Rd (98233-4634)
PHONE.................................360 755-0215
Randy Rockafellow, *President*
EMP: 3
SQ FT: 3,000
SALES (est): 460.9K **Privately Held**
SIC: 3441 5531 5261 1799 Fabricated structural metal; trailer hitches, automotive; lawnmowers & tractors; welding on site

(G-2157)
FARM TO MARKET FOODS LLC
11141 View Ridge Dr (98233-9657)
PHONE.................................360 708-6103
Anthony Wisdom,
EMP: 2
SALES (est): 97.8K **Privately Held**
SIC: 2099 Vegetables, peeled for the trade

(G-2158)
FIDALGO BAY COFFEE INC (PA)
Also Called: Fidalgo Bay Roasting
856 N Hill Blvd (98233-4640)
PHONE.................................360 757-8818
Gary Sawyer, *President*
Derek Evans, *Vice Pres*
David Evans, *Treasurer*
Darla Henning, *Controller*
Pat Burt, *Manager*
EMP: 20
SQ FT: 10,000
SALES (est): 2.3MM **Privately Held**
WEB: www.fidalgobaycoffee.com
SIC: 2095 5499 Coffee roasting (except by wholesale grocers); coffee

(G-2159)
GOLDEN HARVEST INC (PA)
Also Called: Gh
11944 Westar Ln (98233-3620)
P.O. Box 287 (98233-0287)
PHONE.................................360 757-4334
Kevin Buchanan, *President*
Leonard Prather, *Treasurer*
Frank Bazzano, *Sales Staff*
Charlene Griffin, *Admin Sec*
EMP: 53
SQ FT: 26,500
SALES (est): 12.5MM **Privately Held**
WEB: www.goldenharvestinc.com
SIC: 3822 Hydronic controls

(G-2160)
HANGING H COMPANIES LLC
Also Called: Hanging H Company
1912 S Burlington Blvd (98233-3228)
PHONE.................................360 899-4638
Brent Huwa,
Corey Huwa,
Tyrun Huwa,
EMP: 7
SALES (est): 1.2MM **Privately Held**
SIC: 3317 Pipes, wrought: welded, lock joint or heavy riveted

(G-2161)
HB JAEGER COMPANY LLC
1687 Port Dr (98233-3106)
PHONE.................................360 707-5958
John Gadberry, *Sales Staff*
Herb Bracus,
EMP: 5
SALES (est): 1MM **Privately Held**
WEB: www.hbjaeger.com
SIC: 5084 5051 3561 Pumps & pumping equipment; metals service centers & offices; pumps & pumping equipment

(G-2162)
HECKMAN INC
5803 Jennifer Ln (98233-5011)
P.O. Box 1298, Stanwood (98292-1298)
PHONE.................................360 724-4580
James Heckman, *Principal*
EMP: 7
SALES (est): 1MM **Privately Held**
SIC: 3823 Industrial instrmnts msrmnt display/control process variable

(G-2163)
HEXCEL CORPORATION
15062 Steele Rd (98233-3627)
PHONE.................................360 757-7212
Roy R Redmond, *QC Mgr*
James Collins, *Manager*
Adam A Schuehle, *Manager*
EMP: 120
SALES (corp-wide): 2.1B **Publicly Held**
WEB: www.hexcel.com
SIC: 3728 Aircraft parts & equipment
PA: Hexcel Corporation
281 Tresser Blvd Ste 1503
Stamford CT 06901
203 969-0666

(G-2164)
HIETT LOGGING INC
2540 Old Hwy 99n Rd (98233-8558)
PHONE.................................360 724-5505
Marian Hiett, *President*
EMP: 4
SALES (est): 106.4K **Privately Held**
SIC: 1081 Metal mining services

(G-2165)
HOSE SHOP INC
856 S Alder St (98233-2800)
PHONE.................................360 757-3776
Dennis Geissler, *CEO*
Kristine Geissler, *President*
EMP: 3
SALES (est): 363.1K **Privately Held**
SIC: 3492 Hose & tube fittings & assemblies, hydraulic/pneumatic

(G-2166)
KEMASON INC
Also Called: Fara Haven Organic Flour Mill
808 N Hill Blvd (98233-4640)
PHONE.................................360 757-9947
Kevin Christenson, *Owner*
EMP: 4 EST: 2011
SALES: 750K **Privately Held**
SIC: 2041 Flour & other grain mill products

(G-2167)
LANGES HONEY SKEP INC
Also Called: Belleville Honey Co
18898 Dahlstedt Rd (98233-9691)
PHONE.................................360 757-1073
Eric Thompson, *President*
Hank Thompson, *Vice Pres*
Heather Thompson, *Treasurer*
EMP: 8
SALES (est): 856.7K **Privately Held**
SIC: 2099 5191 0279 Honey, strained & bottled; beekeeping supplies (non-durable); apiary (bee & honey farm)

(G-2168)
LEGEND BRANDS
15180 Josh Wilson Rd (98233-9656)
PHONE.................................360 757-7776
Jason Alexander, *Principal*
EMP: 2
SALES (est): 138.9K **Privately Held**
SIC: 3589 Commercial cooking & food-warming equipment

(G-2169)
LOUWS TRUSS INC
1010 S Spruce St (98233-2836)
P.O. Box 3168, Ferndale (98248-3168)
PHONE.................................360 384-9000
John M Louws, *President*
Cindy Louws, *Admin Sec*
Jack Louws, *Admin Sec*
EMP: 80
SQ FT: 17,000
SALES (est): 11.8MM **Privately Held**
WEB: www.louwstruss.com
SIC: 2439 Trusses, wooden roof

(G-2170)
MAKO REELS INC
11777 Watertank Rd (98233-3630)
PHONE.................................360 757-7328
EMP: 4
SALES (est): 304.6K **Privately Held**
SIC: 3949 Reels, fishing

(G-2171)
MILES SAND & GRAVEL COMPANY
Also Called: Concrete Norwest Division
663 Pease Rd
P.O. Box 280, Mount Vernon (98273-0280)
PHONE.................................360 757-3121
Brad Parton, *Manager*
EMP: 115
SALES (corp-wide): 88MM **Privately Held**
SIC: 3273 5211 5032 1442 Ready-mixed concrete; sand & gravel; sand, construction; gravel; construction sand & gravel
PA: Miles Sand & Gravel Company
400 Valley Ave Ne
Puyallup WA 98372
253 833-3705

(G-2172)
NORDIC TUGS INCORPORATED
11367 Higgins Airport Way (98233-5309)
PHONE.................................360 757-8847
Wayne Basler, *President*
Dave Allen, *Cust Svc Dir*
Buddy Brown, *Manager*
Gary Miller, *Admin Sec*
EMP: 30
SQ FT: 83,000
SALES (est): 7.6MM **Privately Held**
WEB: www.nordictugsinc.com
SIC: 3732 Boats, fiberglass: building & repairing

(G-2173)
NORTH HILL RESOURCES INC
657 N Hill Blvd (98233-4600)
PHONE.................................360 757-1866
Sean McGuiness, *President*
Rhonda Twaddle, *Principal*
Eben Twaddle, *Vice Pres*
Patti Baker, *Admin Sec*
EMP: 15
SALES (est): 1.3MM **Privately Held**
SIC: 5032 1794 3531 4212 Brick, stone & related material; excavation & grading, building construction; rock crushing machinery, portable; local trucking, without storage; construction & civil engineering; tunnel construction

(G-2174)
NORTHWEST CUSTOM CABINETS INC
15609 Peterson Rd Ste C (98233-3666)
PHONE.................................360 757-8788
Derrick Slotemaker, *President*
EMP: 10
SALES (est): 1MM **Privately Held**
WEB: www.nwcustomcabinets.com
SIC: 2434 Wood kitchen cabinets

(G-2175)
NORTHWEST FARM FOOD COOP
1370 S Anacortes St (98233-3038)
PHONE.................................360 757-4225
Vern Peterson, *Manager*
EMP: 25 EST: 1947
SQ FT: 25,000
SALES (est): 7.4MM **Privately Held**
SIC: 5191 2047 Feed; dog & cat food

Burlington - Skagit County (G-2176)

(G-2176)
NORTHWEST WILDFOODS CO INC
12535 Pulver Rd (98233-9439)
PHONE.................360 757-7940
Rick Lamonte, *Principal*
▲ **EMP:** 3
SALES (est): 371.9K **Privately Held**
SIC: 3523 Harvesters, fruit, vegetable, tobacco, etc.

(G-2177)
PACIFIC WOODTECH CORPORATION
1850 Park Ln (98233-4630)
PHONE.................360 707-2200
David L Dewitte, *President*
Randall Schillinger, *Vice Pres*
Daniel Scmsak, *Vice Pres*
William Spyksma, *CFO*
JD Dombek, *Sales Mgr*
◆ **EMP:** 200
SQ FT: 8,000
SALES (est): 57.6MM **Privately Held**
WEB: www.pacificwoodtech.com
SIC: 2499 Bearings, wood
PA: Itochu Corporation
2-5-1, Kitaaoyama
Minato-Ku TKY 107-0

(G-2178)
PALLET SERVICES INC (PA)
201 E Fairhaven Ave (98233-1702)
PHONE.................360 424-8171
Jeanine Dimmick, *President*
EMP: 9
SQ FT: 6,000
SALES (est): 13.3MM **Privately Held**
SIC: 2448 Pallets, wood

(G-2179)
PALLET SERVICES INC (PA)
201 E Fairhaven Ave (98233-1702)
PHONE.................360 424-8171
Gorden Lucas, *Manager*
EMP: 8
SALES (est): 1MM **Privately Held**
SIC: 2448 Pallets, wood

(G-2180)
PEPSI COLA 7 UP BOTTLING CO
Also Called: Pepsi-Cola
1946 Park Ln (98233-4602)
PHONE.................360 757-0044
Tim Rawles, *Principal*
EMP: 3
SALES (est): 135K **Privately Held**
SIC: 2086 Soft drinks: packaged in cans, bottles, etc.

(G-2181)
PIONEER AEROFAB COMPANY INC
15259 Flightline Rd (98233-3624)
PHONE.................360 757-4780
Tim Williamson, *CEO*
EMP: 12
SQ FT: 10,000
SALES: 1.8MM **Privately Held**
WEB: www.pioneeraerofab.com
SIC: 2399 3199 Seat belts, automobile & aircraft; novelties, leather

(G-2182)
PRORESTORE PRODUCTS
15180 Josh Wilson Rd (98233-9656)
PHONE.................412 264-8340
EMP: 25
SALES (est): 740K
SALES (corp-wide): 5.3B **Publicly Held**
SIC: 2836 Biological products, except diagnostic
HQ: Skagit Northwest Holdings, Inc.
15180 Josh Wilson Rd
Burlington WA 98233

(G-2183)
ROBIN FERRIS MANUFACTURING
15254 Flightline Rd (98233-3624)
PHONE.................360 757-6804
Robin Carpenter,
EMP: 5
SALES: 150K **Privately Held**
SIC: 2399 Emblems, badges & insignia

(G-2184)
SALISH COAST ENTERPRISES LLC
Also Called: Skagit Valley Malting
11966 Westar Ln (98233-3620)
PHONE.................360 333-5280
Wane Carpenter, *CEO*
Juan Baldovinos, *Vice Pres*
R Clare Wixom, *CFO*
EMP: 9
SALES (est): 484K **Privately Held**
SIC: 2083 Malt

(G-2185)
SAPPHIRE SCIENTIFIC INC
Also Called: Legend Brands
15180 Josh Wilson Rd (98233-9656)
PHONE.................928 445-3030
EMP: 32
SALES (corp-wide): 5.3B **Publicly Held**
SIC: 3589 Commercial cleaning equipment
HQ: Sapphire Scientific Inc.
2604 Liberator
Prescott AZ 86301

(G-2186)
SCRATCH AND PECK LLC
Also Called: Scratch and Peck Feeds
872 N Hill Blvd (98233-4640)
PHONE.................360 318-7585
Diana Ambauen-Meade, *President*
Bryon Meade, *COO*
Dennis Meade, *Vice Pres*
Steve Thiele, *Opers Mgr*
EMP: 24
SALES (est): 2.7MM **Privately Held**
SIC: 5191 2048 Feed; alfalfa or alfalfa meal, prepared as animal feed

(G-2187)
SKAGIT COUNTY FIRE DST 14
18726 Parkview Ln (98233-8549)
PHONE.................360 724-3451
Marty Coble, *Principal*
Patrick Curran, *Commissioner*
Michael Nemnich, *Commissioner*
EMP: 20
SALES (est): 1.1MM **Privately Held**
SIC: 3711 Motor vehicles & car bodies

(G-2188)
SKAGIT NORTHWEST HOLDINGS INC (HQ)
Also Called: Legend Brands
15180 Josh Wilson Rd (98233-9656)
PHONE.................360 757-7776
William Bruders, *President*
Stephen Henkel, *Vice Pres*
Sheila Kenny, *VP Human Res*
Eric Bosell, *Marketing Staff*
Michael Kerner, *Consultant*
EMP: 125
SQ FT: 56,000
SALES: 44.5MM
SALES (corp-wide): 5.3B **Publicly Held**
SIC: 3589 Commercial cleaning equipment; sewer cleaning equipment, power
PA: Rpm International Inc.
2628 Pearl Rd
Medina OH 44256
330 273-5090

(G-2189)
SKAGIT TRANSMISSION INC
303 Lila Ln (98233-3318)
PHONE.................360 757-6551
Glenn Becker Jr, *President*
Francis Becker, *Corp Secy*
Steven Becker, *Vice Pres*
EMP: 6
SQ FT: 5,600
SALES (est): 834.3K **Privately Held**
SIC: 3714 Transmissions, motor vehicle

(G-2190)
SKAGIT VEHICLE LICENSING INC
Also Called: Skagit Auto Licensing
327 S Burlington Blvd (98233-1710)
PHONE.................360 755-0419
Beverly Harrington, *Owner*
Tammy Hannon, *Manager*
Tami Hofkamp, *Manager*
EMP: 3

SALES (est): 317.3K **Privately Held**
SIC: 3469 Automobile license tags, stamped metal

(G-2191)
SONOFRESCO LLC
1365 Pacific Dr (98233-3128)
PHONE.................360 757-2800
Jerry Whitfield, *Mng Member*
Rober Penrose,
Sean Robinson,
Carol Whitfield,
▼ **EMP:** 1
SQ FT: 1,000
SALES (est): 1.5MM
SALES (corp-wide): 90.6MM **Publicly Held**
WEB: www.sonofresco.com
SIC: 5149 3556 Coffee, green or roasted; roasting machinery: coffee, peanut, etc.
PA: Coffee Holding Co., Inc.
3475 Victory Blvd Ste 4
Staten Island NY 10314
718 832-0800

(G-2192)
SYCAMORE WOODWORKS
10954 Peter Anderson Rd (98233-9713)
PHONE.................360 757-4120
Jennifer Bradbury, *Principal*
EMP: 2 **EST:** 2010
SALES (est): 192.7K **Privately Held**
SIC: 2431 Millwork

(G-2193)
TEAM CORPORATION
11591 Watertank Rd (98233-3626)
PHONE.................360 757-3944
Bob Tauscher, *President*
Bruce L Huntley, *COO*
EMP: 45
SQ FT: 20,600
SALES (est): 14.2MM **Privately Held**
WEB: www.teamcorporation.com
SIC: 8711 3829 Consulting engineer; vibration meters, analyzers & calibrators
HQ: Lansmont Corporation
17 Mandeville Ct
Monterey CA 93940
831 655-6600

(G-2194)
TEAM INDUSTRIAL SERVICES
11837 Watertank Rd (98233-3631)
PHONE.................360 757-2589
Dan Sewell, *COO*
EMP: 6
SALES (est): 679.9K **Privately Held**
SIC: 3398 Metal heat treating

(G-2195)
U S PRACTICAL SHOOTING ASSN
1639 Lindamood Ln (98233-4113)
PHONE.................360 855-2245
Kimberly Williams, *Exec Dir*
EMP: 11
SQ FT: 1,500
SALES (est): 1.6MM **Privately Held**
SIC: 7997 5699 2721 Gun club, membership; sports apparel; magazines: publishing & printing

(G-2196)
UNIFORM FACTORY OUTL ARIZ LLC
Also Called: Uniform Destination
240 Fashion Way (98233-3242)
PHONE.................360 707-2608
Stacy Edmiston, *Manager*
EMP: 8 **Privately Held**
SIC: 2326 Work uniforms
PA: Uniform Factory Outlet Of Arizona, Llc
7401 N La Cholla Blvd
Tucson AZ 85741

(G-2197)
UNIVERSAL PLANT SERVICES OF NO
245 N Hill Blvd (98233-4641)
PHONE.................360 757-4646
Brandon Souza, *Branch Mgr*
EMP: 20

SALES (corp-wide): 165.4MM **Privately Held**
SIC: 3599 Custom machinery
HQ: Universal Plant Services Of Northern California, Inc.
505 Lopes Rd Ste D
Fairfield CA 94534
707 864-0100

(G-2198)
US MOWER INC
11949 Westar Ln (98233-3620)
PHONE.................360 757-7555
Al Schlemmer, *President*
Chris Schlemmer, *Treasurer*
EMP: 16 **EST:** 1996
SQ FT: 10,000
SALES (est): 3.4MM **Privately Held**
WEB: www.usmower.com
SIC: 3523 5083 3524 Turf & grounds equipment; farm & garden machinery; lawn & garden equipment

(G-2199)
VOLANT AEROSPACE HOLDINGS LLC
11817 Westar Ln (98233-3623)
PHONE.................360 757-2376
EMP: 3
SALES (est): 118.1K **Privately Held**
SIC: 3812 Aircraft/aerospace flight instruments & guidance systems

(G-2200)
WESTERN HYDRO LLC
902 S Spruce St (98233-2834)
PHONE.................360 428-4704
Tim Miller, *Principal*
EMP: 7
SALES (corp-wide): 1.3B **Publicly Held**
SIC: 3561 Pumps & pumping equipment
HQ: Western Hydro Llc
2034 Research Dr
Livermore CA 94550
559 275-3305

(G-2201)
WHIDBEY ISLAND SIGN SLTONS LLC
Also Called: Image360-Burlington, WA
789 Chrysler Dr (98233-4100)
PHONE.................360 299-0430
Anthony Asp, *Principal*
EMP: 5
SALES (est): 392.8K **Privately Held**
SIC: 7336 3993 Graphic arts & related design; signs & advertising specialties

(G-2202)
WILLIAM BOUNDS CUSTOM FRAMES
1034 S Anacortes St (98233-3012)
PHONE.................360 404-2002
Bill Bounds, *Owner*
EMP: 2
SALES (est): 99K **Privately Held**
SIC: 2512 Living room furniture: upholstered on wood frames

(G-2203)
WILLIAM E MUNSON COMPANY
Also Called: Munson Boats
15806 Preston Pl (98233-3550)
PHONE.................360 707-2752
William Munson, *Ch of Bd*
Jon Wise, *President*
Jesse Munson, *Vice Pres*
Jan Munson, *Treasurer*
▼ **EMP:** 53
SQ FT: 17,000
SALES: 1MM **Privately Held**
SIC: 3732 Boats, fiberglass: building & repairing

(G-2204)
WIMAN CORPORATION
527 N Hill Blvd (98233-4615)
PHONE.................360 757-8880
EMP: 2
SALES (corp-wide): 330.1MM **Privately Held**
SIC: 3081 Polyvinyl film & sheet

GEOGRAPHIC SECTION

Camas - Clark County (G-2237)

HQ: Wiman Corporation
180 Industrial Blvd
Sauk Rapids MN 56379
320 259-2554

Camano Island
Island County

(G-2205)
4 VALVES LLC
587 Utsalady Rd (98282-7217)
PHONE..............................360 387-2272
EMP: 2
SALES (est): 120.6K **Privately Held**
SIC: 3592 Valves

(G-2206)
ALLIED FORCES INC
Also Called: Living From Vision
1837 Cascade View Dr (98282-8483)
P.O. Box 1530, Stanwood (98292-1530)
PHONE..............................360 387-5713
Don Paris, *President*
Ilona Selke, *Vice Pres*
EMP: 3
SALES: 400K **Privately Held**
WEB: www.se-5.com
SIC: 3651 8742 Household audio equipment; business consultant

(G-2207)
ARRANTS BOAT WORKS
2681 Se Camano Dr (98282-8238)
PHONE..............................425 293-4660
EMP: 2 EST: 2010
SALES (est): 88K **Privately Held**
SIC: 3732 Boatbuilding/Repairing

(G-2208)
C & C PACKAGING SERVICES INC
1851 Se Camano Dr (98282-7638)
PHONE..............................425 673-6347
Alfredo R Curva, *President*
Katherine Curva, *Principal*
EMP: 21
SALES (est): 4MM **Privately Held**
SIC: 3565 Packaging machinery

(G-2209)
CAMANO MOLD INC
122 Ne Camano Dr (98282-5516)
PHONE..............................360 387-0961
Theresa Gilbertson, *President*
Tony Kline, *Engineer*
EMP: 40
SQ FT: 10,000
SALES (est): 2.9MM **Privately Held**
WEB: www.camanomold.com
SIC: 3599 Custom machinery

(G-2210)
COYOTE HILL PRESS
930 Cambell Dr (98282-7378)
PHONE..............................951 295-9552
Robin Hanks, *Principal*
EMP: 2
SALES (est): 66.4K **Privately Held**
SIC: 2741 Miscellaneous publishing

(G-2211)
DUSTY CELLARS WINERY
529 Michael Way (98282-8464)
PHONE..............................360 387-2171
Dusty Kramer,
Ryan Kramer,
EMP: 2
SALES: 60K **Privately Held**
SIC: 2084 Wines

(G-2212)
FINISHING TOUCH
Also Called: Elder, Daniel
1498 Arrowhead Rd (98282-7229)
PHONE..............................360 391-2108
Daniel Elder, *Owner*
EMP: 2
SALES (est): 173.7K **Privately Held**
SIC: 2819 7389 Nonmetallic compounds;

(G-2213)
FROSTY BAY SEAFOODS LLC
Also Called: Bonnies Best Bet Batter
285 Driftwood Shores Rd (98282-8486)
PHONE..............................360 387-7685
Bonnie Brindle, *Owner*
EMP: 2
SALES (est): 149.9K **Privately Held**
SIC: 2051 Bakery: wholesale or wholesale/retail combined

(G-2214)
FUSION9 DESIGN LLC
263 Grandview Ave (98282-7338)
P.O. Box 2709, Stanwood (98292-2709)
PHONE..............................360 831-0899
Robert Suryan, *Principal*
John Hubbard,
EMP: 2
SALES: 300K **Privately Held**
SIC: 1731 2591 3651 5099 Sound equipment specialization; voice, data & video wiring contractor; lighting contractor; window shade rollers & fittings; household audio & video equipment; video & audio equipment

(G-2215)
K LINE INDUSTRIES LLC
298 Echo Ridge Way (98282-6687)
PHONE..............................425 870-4228
EMP: 3 EST: 2007
SALES (est): 192.3K **Privately Held**
SIC: 3999 Manufacturing industries

(G-2216)
LITTLE BUDDIES SHANTIES
958 Haven Pl (98282-7034)
PHONE..............................360 387-0678
Pepe Lowel, *Owner*
EMP: 2
SALES (est): 63K **Privately Held**
SIC: 2499 Wood products

(G-2217)
MELANGE PUBLISHING
832 Margie Ann Dr (98282-8444)
PHONE..............................360 387-2395
Norman Wilson, *Principal*
EMP: 2
SALES (est): 116.4K **Privately Held**
SIC: 2741 Miscellaneous publishing

(G-2218)
MR RPM LLC
587 Utsalady Rd (98282-7217)
PHONE..............................360 387-2272
Richard P Maccoon,
Betty Maccoon,
EMP: 2
SALES (est): 143.4K **Privately Held**
WEB: www.mrrpm.com
SIC: 3724 7389 Research & development on aircraft engines & parts; design services

(G-2219)
NIMBUS BOARD SPORTS LLC
1551 Bonnie Ln (98282-7611)
PHONE..............................360 387-1951
Jeffery Yarter, *Owner*
EMP: 2
SALES (est): 123.7K **Privately Held**
SIC: 3949 Sporting & athletic goods

(G-2220)
NW WOOD BOX
1244 Moore Rd Ste I2 (98282-8899)
P.O. Box 1387, Stanwood (98292-1387)
PHONE..............................360 939-2434
Brian Clearman, *Owner*
EMP: 2
SALES (est): 73.2K **Privately Held**
SIC: 2759 Visiting cards (including business): printing

(G-2221)
PINCHKNITTER
880 Saratoga Way (98282-6526)
PHONE..............................360 939-0769
Sirkku Bingham, *Owner*
EMP: 2
SALES (est): 195.7K **Privately Held**
SIC: 2281 Knitting yarn, spun

(G-2222)
PUPPY STAIRS
355 Melissa St (98282-8635)
PHONE..............................360 387-4861
Jeanne Wolfington, *President*
Krystal Hanson, *Vice Pres*
EMP: 2
SALES (est): 110K **Privately Held**
WEB: www.puppystairs.com
SIC: 3999 Pet supplies

(G-2223)
RALPH A PARISE
956 Arrowhead Rd (98282-7267)
PHONE..............................360 387-1794
EMP: 2
SALES (est): 120K **Privately Held**
SIC: 3499 Mfg Misc Fabricated Metal Products

(G-2224)
RICHERT LINA
Also Called: Richert Enterprises
1886 Journeys End Ln (98282-6340)
PHONE..............................206 660-3332
Lina Richert, *Principal*
EMP: 2
SALES (est): 100.3K **Privately Held**
SIC: 3562 Ball bearings & parts

(G-2225)
T J BROOKS LOGGING
1549 Graham Dr (98282-8385)
PHONE..............................425 220-2263
Wendee Brooks, *Principal*
EMP: 2
SALES (est): 81.7K **Privately Held**
SIC: 2411 Logging

(G-2226)
VETCH CONSTRUCTION LLC
159 Chelsea Ln (98282-8505)
PHONE..............................425 387-3244
Bruce Vetch, *Mng Member*
EMP: 9
SALES: 1MM **Privately Held**
SIC: 3531 Road construction & maintenance machinery

Camas
Clark County

(G-2227)
ALMAR TLS & CUTTER GRINDERS CO
4859 Nw Lake Rd (98607-7648)
PHONE..............................503 255-2763
Luis Heredia, *Ch of Bd*
Alejandro Heredia, *President*
Marcelo Heredia, *Vice Pres*
EMP: 14 EST: 1980
SQ FT: 6,500
SALES (est): 2.5MM **Privately Held**
SIC: 3541 3545 Machine tools, metal cutting type; machine tool accessories

(G-2228)
ANALOG DEVICES INC
4200 Nw Pacific Rim Blvd (98607-8801)
PHONE..............................360 834-1900
Jim Lucy, *Branch Mgr*
EMP: 2
SALES (corp-wide): 6.2B **Publicly Held**
SIC: 3674 Semiconductors & related devices
PA: Analog Devices, Inc.
1 Technology Way
Norwood MA 02062
781 329-4700

(G-2229)
ARTISTIC HOME & GARDEN LLC
Also Called: Artistic Gardener
550 25th St (98607)
PHONE..............................360 834-7021
Tammy Ramadan, *Principal*
Farouk Ramadan, *Principal*
▲ EMP: 3

SALES (est): 326.4K **Privately Held**
WEB: www.historystones.com
SIC: 2431 Moldings & baseboards, ornamental & trim

(G-2230)
ATS
1109 Nw Klickitat Ln (98607-7940)
PHONE..............................360 260-2627
Qun Chen, *Principal*
EMP: 2
SALES (est): 117.5K **Privately Held**
SIC: 2752 Commercial printing, lithographic

(G-2231)
BC SIGNS INC
106 Se Weir St Ste 1 (98607-2454)
PHONE..............................360 835-3570
Carol Taylor, *Principal*
EMP: 2
SALES (est): 149.1K **Privately Held**
SIC: 3993 Signs & advertising specialties

(G-2232)
BIRCHWOOD ACRES LLC
3804 Nw Knapp Ln (98607-7510)
PHONE..............................360 433-8690
Andrew Wheeler, *Managing Prtnr*
EMP: 2
SALES (est): 27.9K **Privately Held**
SIC: 0752 2841 Honey straining services (on farm); soap: granulated, liquid, cake, flaked or chip

(G-2233)
BLACK LABEL SWITCHES
3510 Ne 3rd Ave (98607-2411)
PHONE..............................360 607-3559
EMP: 2
SALES (est): 109.6K **Privately Held**
SIC: 3679 Mfg Electronic Components

(G-2234)
BODYCOTE IMT INC
Also Called: Bodycote Hot Isostatic Prsg
4605 Nw Pacific Rim Blvd (98607-9401)
PHONE..............................360 833-1120
Joe Dyer, *Branch Mgr*
EMP: 35
SALES (corp-wide): 935.8MM **Privately Held**
SIC: 3398 3269 Metal heat treating; laboratory & industrial pottery
HQ: Bodycote Imt, Inc.
155 River St
Andover MA 01810
978 470-0876

(G-2235)
BRAVO MANUFACTURING INC
26401 Ne Brunner Rd (98607-7024)
PHONE..............................360 817-9124
John Aldrich, *President*
Heather Aldrich, *Vice Pres*
EMP: 2 EST: 1990
SALES (est): 171.8K **Privately Held**
WEB: www.bravomfg.com
SIC: 2394 Tents: made from purchased materials

(G-2236)
CAMAS AUTO LICENSE
3252 3rd Ave Lacamas Ctr (98607)
PHONE..............................360 835-2977
Debie, *Principal*
Jean Monahan, *Principal*
EMP: 4
SALES (est): 190.7K **Privately Held**
SIC: 7549 3469 Automotive services; automobile license tags, stamped metal

(G-2237)
CAMAS-WASHOUGAL POST-RECORD
Also Called: Circulation Department
425 Ne 4th Ave (98607-2129)
P.O. Box 180, Vancouver (98666-0180)
PHONE..............................360 834-2141
Mike Gallagher, *Principal*
EMP: 12
SALES (est): 415.7K **Privately Held**
WEB: www.camaspostrecord.com
SIC: 2711 Newspapers: publishing only, not printed on site

Camas - Clark County (G-2238)

(G-2238)
CHEVRON CORPORATION
1605 Nw 6th Ave (98607-2650)
PHONE..................360 887-8101
EMP: 2
SALES (corp-wide): 166.3B **Publicly Held**
SIC: 2911 Petroleum refining
PA: Chevron Corporation
6001 Bollinger Canyon Rd
San Ramon CA 94583
925 842-1000

(G-2239)
COLUMBIA LITHO INC
Also Called: Columbia Litho Prtg & Imaging
302 Ne 6th Ave (98607-2034)
P.O. Box 1030 (98607-0030)
PHONE..................360 834-4662
Patrick Guard, *President*
Elizabeth Ward, *Corp Secy*
Betsy Ward, *Office Mgr*
Charmane Guard, *Director*
EMP: 7 EST: 1944
SQ FT: 5,000
SALES (est): 1.1MM **Privately Held**
WEB: www.columbialitho.com
SIC: 2752 Commercial printing, offset

(G-2240)
COLUMBIA MANUFACTURING
330 Ne 5th Ave (98607-2029)
PHONE..................360 210-5124
EMP: 2
SALES (est): 62.5K **Privately Held**
SIC: 3999 Manufacturing industries

(G-2241)
COMFORT ACRYLICS INC
2103 Ne 272nd Ave (98607-9749)
PHONE..................360 834-9218
Richard Moore, *President*
Richard Boyd, *Vice Pres*
EMP: 3
SALES (est): 339.7K **Privately Held**
WEB: www.comfortacrylics.com
SIC: 3843 Dental materials

(G-2242)
CONCRETE PRODUCTS CO ORE LLC
1615 Se 6th Ave (98607-2260)
P.O. Box 1002 (98607-0002)
PHONE..................360 834-3459
Doug Phelps, *Manager*
EMP: 20
SALES (est): 1.6MM **Privately Held**
SIC: 3272 Concrete products

(G-2243)
CONTROL SYSTEMS AMERICA INC
2027 Nw Sierra Ln (98607-2535)
PHONE..................360 210-7475
Scott Gregson, *Principal*
EMP: 3
SALES (est): 260.8K **Privately Held**
SIC: 3823 Industrial instrmnts msrmnt display/control process variable

(G-2244)
DEBORAH FUNCHES JEWELRY DESIGN
19322 Se 33rd St (98607-9450)
PHONE..................503 381-4017
Deborah Funches, *Owner*
▲ EMP: 4
SQ FT: 400
SALES (est): 100K **Privately Held**
SIC: 3961 Costume jewelry

(G-2245)
EATON HYDRAULICS LLC
7780 Ne Lessard Rd (98607-9600)
PHONE..................360 834-0653
EMP: 2 **Privately Held**
SIC: 3699 Mfg Electrical Equipment/Supplies
HQ: Eaton Hydraulics Llc
14615 Lone Oak Rd
Eden Prairie MN 55344
952 294-7953

(G-2246)
ECHO-SENSE INC
2005 Se 192nd Ave (98607-7475)
PHONE..................360 833-9032
EMP: 5
SALES (est): 383.5K **Privately Held**
SIC: 3845 Electromedical equipment

(G-2247)
ECO SAFE TECHNOLOGIES LLC
Also Called: Ecosafe Lighting
4600 Nw Camas Meadows Dr (98607-7761)
PHONE..................360 567-1923
Mike Gerard,
Joseph Zarelli,
▲ EMP: 5
SALES (est): 1.2MM **Privately Held**
SIC: 3648 Lighting equipment

(G-2248)
ENCON UNITED COMPANY
1615 Se 6th Ave (98607-2260)
P.O. Box 1002 (98607-0002)
PHONE..................360 834-3459
Doug Phelps, *Principal*
EMP: 17
SALES (corp-wide): 82.4MM **Privately Held**
WEB: www.eprecast.com
SIC: 3272 Concrete products, precast
PA: Encon United Company
2140 S Ivanhoe St Ste 100
Denver CO 80222
303 298-1900

(G-2249)
ENGLISH RACING
24514 Ne Dresser Rd (98607-7184)
PHONE..................360 210-7484
Lucas English, *President*
EMP: 9 EST: 2012
SALES (est): 1.2MM **Privately Held**
SIC: 3799 All terrain vehicles (ATV)

(G-2250)
EVANS ADHESIVES CORPORATION
28303 Ne 50th St (98607-9793)
PHONE..................614 410-6027
EMP: 3
SALES (est): 123.2K **Privately Held**
SIC: 2891 Adhesives

(G-2251)
FOCUS DESIGNS INC
4032 Se 199th Ave (98607-9410)
PHONE..................360 329-2537
Daniel Wood, *President*
▲ EMP: 3
SALES (est): 298K **Privately Held**
SIC: 3751 Motorcycles, bicycles & parts

(G-2252)
FOREST PUBLICATIONS INC
1430 Nw Whitman St (98607-8401)
PHONE..................360 609-4400
Robert Mc Manus, *President*
Judy Mc Manus, *Vice Pres*
EMP: 4
SALES: 1MM **Privately Held**
SIC: 2731 Book publishing

(G-2253)
FOSTER SURVEYING INC
3517 Se 198th Ave (98607-8858)
PHONE..................503 997-1100
David Foster, *Principal*
EMP: 2
SALES (est): 134.5K **Privately Held**
SIC: 1389 Surveying wells

(G-2254)
GEORGIA-PACIFIC LLC
401 Ne Adams St (98607-2135)
PHONE..................404 652-4000
EMP: 111
SALES (corp-wide): 42.6B **Privately Held**
SIC: 2676 Sanitary paper products
HQ: Georgia-Pacific Llc
133 Peachtree St Nw
Atlanta GA 30303
404 652-4000

(G-2255)
GRAINS OF WRATH BREWERY
337 Ne 4th Ave (98607-2127)
PHONE..................847 727-5100
EMP: 2
SALES (est): 62.3K **Privately Held**
SIC: 2082 Malt beverages

(G-2256)
HAVENS WOODWORKS & REFINISHING
407 Se Everett Rd (98607-7167)
PHONE..................360 833-9446
Jeffrey Haven, *Owner*
Roberta Haven, *Co-Owner*
EMP: 2
SALES (est): 217.1K **Privately Held**
SIC: 2431 Millwork

(G-2257)
INNOVATIVE DENTAL TECH INC
Also Called: I D T
2005 Se 192nd Ave (98607-7475)
PHONE..................971 303-5659
Phillip Fraser, *CEO*
Hari Reyes, *President*
Jessica Fraser, *Principal*
EMP: 2
SALES (est): 136.2K **Privately Held**
SIC: 3843 Dental equipment & supplies

(G-2258)
INVENTIST INC
1821 Nw 8th Ave (98607-2617)
PHONE..................360 833-2357
Shane Chen, *President*
▲ EMP: 5
SALES (est): 493K **Privately Held**
WEB: www.inventist.com
SIC: 3949 Team sports equipment

(G-2259)
JAMES WILE
28201 Se 7th St (98607-7266)
PHONE..................360 606-0706
James Wile, *Principal*
EMP: 2
SALES (est): 88.3K **Privately Held**
SIC: 3669 Communications equipment

(G-2260)
KARCHER NORTH AMERICA INC
Karcher Commercial
4275 Nw Pacific Rim Blvd (98607-8801)
PHONE..................360 833-1600
Kris Cannon, *Vice Pres*
Linda Edwards, *Buyer*
Allen Hurtado, *Engineer*
Quinn Trammell, *Engineer*
Jane Smith, *Human Resources*
EMP: 11
SALES (corp-wide): 2.8B **Privately Held**
SIC: 3452 Washers
HQ: Karcher North America, Inc.
4555 Airport Way Fl 4
Denver CO 80239
303 762-1800

(G-2261)
KARCHER NORTH AMERICA INC
Also Called: Camas Division
4275 Nw Pacific Rim Blvd (98607-8801)
PHONE..................360 833-1600
Keith Price, *Manager*
EMP: 75
SALES (corp-wide): 2.8B **Privately Held**
SIC: 3589 High pressure cleaning equipment
HQ: Karcher North America, Inc.
4555 Airport Way Fl 4
Denver CO 80239
303 762-1800

(G-2262)
KEYKING INC
Also Called: Apiary Security
2005 Se 192nd Ave (98607-7475)
P.O. Box 1009 (98607-0009)
PHONE..................360 977-7870
Avigdor Daga, *CEO*
EMP: 5 EST: 2009
SALES: 500K **Privately Held**
SIC: 3699 1731 5065 7382 Security control equipment & systems; safety & security specialization; access control systems specialization; security control equipment & systems; confinement surveillance systems maintenance & monitoring

(G-2263)
LANDA INC
4275 Nw Pacific Rim Blvd (98607-8801)
PHONE..................360 833-9100
Andrew Gale, *CEO*
Matt Almond, *Marketing Staff*
▲ EMP: 85
SALES (est): 7.6MM **Privately Held**
SIC: 3589 7359 Sewage & water treatment equipment; high pressure cleaning equipment; equipment rental & leasing

(G-2264)
LINDE NORTH AMERICA INC
5509 Nw Parker St (98607-8557)
PHONE..................360 834-9519
Tim Eastland, *Manager*
EMP: 2
SALES (corp-wide): 1.4B **Privately Held**
WEB: www.bocsureflow.com
SIC: 2813 Industrial gases
HQ: Messer North America, Inc.
200 Somerset Corporate Bl
Bridgewater NJ 08807
908 464-8100

(G-2265)
LINEAR TECHNOLOGY CORPORATION
4200 Nw Pacific Rim Blvd (98607-8801)
PHONE..................360 834-1900
Bob Sullivan, *Engineer*
Victor Liang, *Manager*
Denton Hess, *Manager*
EMP: 250
SALES (corp-wide): 6.2B **Publicly Held**
SIC: 3674 Wafers (semiconductor devices)
HQ: Linear Technology Llc
1630 Mccarthy Blvd
Milpitas CA 95035
408 432-1900

(G-2266)
LOGITECH INC
Also Called: Ultimate Ears
4700 Nw Camas Meadows Dr (98607-7699)
PHONE..................360 817-1200
EMP: 18
SALES (corp-wide): 2.2B **Privately Held**
SIC: 3577 Input/output equipment, computer
HQ: Logitech Inc.
7700 Gateway Blvd
Newark CA 94560
510 795-8500

(G-2267)
MANCEPS INC
416 Ne Dallas St Ste 209 (98607-2189)
PHONE..................503 922-1164
Al Kari, *President*
EMP: 4
SALES (est): 258.8K **Privately Held**
SIC: 8748 7372 Systems engineering consultant, ex. computer or professional; prepackaged software

(G-2268)
MAXCESS INTERNATIONAL CORP
2305 Se 8th Ave (98607-2261)
PHONE..................360 834-2345
Lee Pinkerton, *Purch Mgr*
Stephanie Tuggle, *Manager*
EMP: 70
SALES (corp-wide): 2.9B **Privately Held**
WEB: www.maxcessintl.com
SIC: 2679 Pressed fiber & molded pulp products except food products
HQ: Maxcess International Corp
222 W Memorial Rd
Oklahoma City OK 73114
405 755-1600

GEOGRAPHIC SECTION

Carnation - King County (G-2302)

(G-2269)
MEDILOGIC LLC
3424 Nw Lacamas Ln (98607-8646)
PHONE.................................541 991-1006
Jason Works,
EMP: 5 **EST:** 2015
SALES (est): 225.6K **Privately Held**
SIC: 3069 Medical & laboratory rubber sundries & related products

(G-2270)
MILL CITY BREW WERKS
325 Ne Cedar St (98607-2142)
PHONE.................................360 210-4761
Jamin Pitchford, *Principal*
EMP: 6
SALES (est): 466.9K **Privately Held**
SIC: 2431 Millwork

(G-2271)
MOBIMAGING LLC
4019 Nw Jasmine St (98607-4405)
PHONE.................................859 559-5138
Miao Liao, *CEO*
EMP: 2
SALES (est): 75.6K **Privately Held**
SIC: 7372 Application computer software

(G-2272)
MR ED FLOATS
4001 Se Crown Rd (98607-9503)
PHONE.................................360 834-3986
Gaye Larm, *Owner*
EMP: 2
SALES (est): 92.7K **Privately Held**
SIC: 3086 Plastics foam products

(G-2273)
PATTERN INTEGRITY LLC
2144 Nw 22nd Ave (98607-7404)
PHONE.................................503 752-6018
Kristen Kingsbury,
EMP: 2
SALES (est): 73.2K **Privately Held**
SIC: 7812 3543 Video production; industrial patterns

(G-2274)
PEI MANUFACTURING LLC
2848 Nw 11th Ave (98607-9371)
PHONE.................................360 210-4165
Jarrod Royston, *General Mgr*
John Mohr,
EMP: 55
SALES (est): 4.4MM **Privately Held**
SIC: 3999 Manufacturing industries

(G-2275)
PLEXSYS INTERFACE PRODUCTS INC (PA)
4900 Nw Camas Meadows Dr (98607-7684)
PHONE.................................360 838-2500
Ron Wiegand, *President*
Winston Fairbrother, *General Mgr*
Scott Harris, *Project Mgr*
Michael Hawks, *Project Mgr*
Matthew Frickey, *Opers Staff*
EMP: 50
SQ FT: 20,000
SALES (est): 37.9MM **Privately Held**
WEB: www.plexsysipi.com
SIC: 3728 7373 Research & dev by manuf., aircraft parts & auxiliary equip; systems software development services

(G-2276)
PREMIUM CUSTOM CNSTR LLC
915 Ne 36th Ave (98607-1161)
PHONE.................................503 515-4119
Mikhail Linchevskiy,
EMP: 2
SALES: 50K **Privately Held**
SIC: 3253 Ceramic wall & floor tile

(G-2277)
PRUNE HILL SOFTWARE LLC
1013 Nw 36th Ct (98607-4208)
PHONE.................................360 834-3067
EMP: 2 **EST:** 2010
SALES (est): 110K **Privately Held**
SIC: 7372 Prepackaged Software Services

(G-2278)
RECROCHETIONS
1203 Nw Drake Way (98607-1562)
PHONE.................................360 450-8757
Laurinda Reddig, *Principal*
EMP: 2
SALES (est): 95.5K **Privately Held**
SIC: 2399 Hand woven & crocheted products

(G-2279)
ROBINSONS INC
1304 Se 195th Ave (98607-9579)
PHONE.................................360 834-0929
Anson Robinson, *Owner*
EMP: 2 **EST:** 1991
SALES (est): 98.5K **Privately Held**
SIC: 3952 Paints, gold or bronze: artists'

(G-2280)
SAMSON SPORTS LLC
4327 Nw Lake Rd (98607-7643)
PHONE.................................360 833-2507
Scott Parnell, *Mng Member*
EMP: 16
SQ FT: 12,000
SALES (est): 2.5MM **Privately Held**
WEB: www.samsonsports.com
SIC: 3499 Welding tips, heat resistant: metal

(G-2281)
SEALASKA TIMBER CORPORATION
532 Ne 3rd Ave Ste 250 (98607-2171)
PHONE.................................360 834-3700
Duane Woodruff, *President*
EMP: 3
SALES (corp-wide): 429.3MM **Privately Held**
SIC: 2411 Timber, cut at logging camp
HQ: Sealaska Timber Company, Llc.
1900 First Ave Ste 315
Ketchikan AK 99901
907 225-9444

(G-2282)
SIGNFACTORY
7711 Ne 317th Pl (98607-8159)
PHONE.................................360 833-1515
Don Coates, *Principal*
EMP: 2
SALES (est): 213.7K **Privately Held**
SIC: 3993 Electric signs

(G-2283)
SKT2 LLC
Also Called: KAGWERKS
3400 Se 196th Ave Ste 100 (98607-8862)
PHONE.................................775 303-3788
Garett Schwindel, *President*
Decisive Point, *Vice Pres*
EMP: 2
SALES (est): 3.1MM **Privately Held**
SIC: 3663 Radio broadcasting & communications equipment

(G-2284)
TRUEGEM LLC
Also Called: Truegem Online
4156 Nw 12th Ave (98607-7961)
PHONE.................................360 836-0310
Helen Crowell,
Jon Crowell,
EMP: 2 **EST:** 2013
SALES (est): 112.3K **Privately Held**
SIC: 7372 7389 Application computer software;

(G-2285)
TSMC DEVELOPMENT INC (DH)
Also Called: Taiwan Semicdtr Mfg Co Ltd
5509 Nw Parker St (98607-8557)
PHONE.................................360 817-3000
Sue Metzger, *Managing Dir*
Kc Shu, *Principal*
Kevin Tseng, *Vice Chairman*
Felix Tai, *COO*
Ben Anderson, *Mfg Mgr*
▲ **EMP:** 180
SALES (est): 160.1MM
SALES (corp-wide): 33.3B **Privately Held**
SIC: 3674 Semiconductor circuit networks

(G-2286)
UNIVERSAL VAULT OF WASHINGTON
1711 Se 279th Ave (98607-9564)
PHONE.................................360 834-4086
Kenneth L Bkorklund, *Principal*
Kenneth L Bjorklund, *Principal*
EMP: 3 **EST:** 2012
SALES (est): 209.7K **Privately Held**
SIC: 3272 Burial vaults, concrete or precast terrazzo

(G-2287)
WAFERTECH LLC
5509 Nw Parker St (98607-9299)
PHONE.................................360 817-3000
Kc Hsu,
Carlton Ku,
▲ **EMP:** 925
SQ FT: 20,000
SALES (est): 104.3MM
SALES (corp-wide): 33.3B **Privately Held**
WEB: www.wafertech.com
SIC: 3674 7361 Semiconductor circuit networks; employment agencies
HQ: Tsmc Development, Inc.
5509 Nw Parker St
Camas WA 98607

(G-2288)
WAVE ENGINE SOLUTIONS INC
3101 Se 197th Ct (98607-8803)
PHONE.................................317 554-7201
Brian Robards, *President*
EMP: 2
SALES (est): 123.6K **Privately Held**
SIC: 3519 Engines, diesel & semi-diesel or dual-fuel

Carnation
King County

(G-2289)
ALAIRX LLC
Also Called: Artisan Machinery
11126 318th Pl Ne (98014-9758)
PHONE.................................425 281-3180
Richard Widdle,
Alaina Pizzo,
EMP: 2 **EST:** 2013
SALES (est): 143.6K **Privately Held**
SIC: 2514 7389 Metal household furniture;

(G-2290)
BUTTONSMITH INC
31722 E Eugene St Unit 9 (98014-6010)
PHONE.................................800 789-4364
Darcy Burner, *CEO*
Jonathan Shapiro, *COO*
EMP: 5
SQ FT: 2,990
SALES (est): 527K **Privately Held**
SIC: 3965 2399 Buttons & parts; emblems, badges & insignia

(G-2291)
CASCADE ROSE ALPACAS
1826 324th Ave Ne (98014-5911)
PHONE.................................206 715-6910
Shari Hollinger, *Principal*
EMP: 2 **EST:** 2017
SALES (est): 107K **Privately Held**
SIC: 2231 Alpacas, mohair: woven

(G-2292)
CREATIVE CONCRETE CONCEPTS
8718 Ames Lake Carnation (98014-8601)
PHONE.................................425 466-4479
Artie Sandoval, *Owner*
EMP: 5 **EST:** 2011
SALES (est): 396.3K **Privately Held**
SIC: 3272 Concrete products

(G-2293)
CUSTOM CONCRETE CASTING CORP
3660 Tolt Ave (98014-7510)
PHONE.................................425 333-4737
Harold Weckworth, *President*
Peter D Jarvis, *Admin Sec*
EMP: 12 **EST:** 1972
SALES (est): 1.7MM **Privately Held**
SIC: 3272 Concrete products, precast

(G-2294)
GRAND REVE VINTNERS
404 289th Pl Ne (98014-9637)
PHONE.................................425 892-9848
EMP: 4 **EST:** 2016
SALES (est): 369.6K **Privately Held**
SIC: 2084 Wines

(G-2295)
MACAW RESCUE AND SANTUARY
34032 Ne Lake Joy Rd (98014-7121)
PHONE.................................425 788-4721
Robert Earl Dawson, *President*
EMP: 2
SALES (est): 47.1K **Privately Held**
SIC: 3999 Manufacturing industries

(G-2296)
NESTLE USA INC
Also Called: Nestle Regional Training Ctr
28901 Ne Carnation Frm Rd (98014-8800)
PHONE.................................425 844-3201
Vance Berkey, *Manager*
EMP: 139
SALES (corp-wide): 92B **Privately Held**
WEB: www.nestleusa.com
SIC: 2023 Evaporated milk
HQ: Nestle Usa, Inc.
1812 N Moore St Ste 118
Rosslyn VA 22209
818 549-6000

(G-2297)
NORTHWESTERN PRECISION TOOL &
31910 E Entwistle St (98014-5031)
P.O. Box 929 (98014-0929)
PHONE.................................425 333-5201
Mary O'Keefe, *General Mgr*
EMP: 3
SALES (est): 340.6K **Privately Held**
SIC: 3599 Machine shop, jobbing & repair

(G-2298)
SHOCKER METALSHOP LLC WELDING
5915 322nd Ave Ne (98014-6312)
PHONE.................................425 246-5825
Richard Tignor, *Principal*
EMP: 2
SALES (est): 93.9K **Privately Held**
SIC: 7692 Welding repair

(G-2299)
STRATODATA LLC
31722 Ne 111th St (98014-9757)
PHONE.................................425 623-0094
Jeffrey Miller, *CEO*
EMP: 2
SALES (est): 90.6K **Privately Held**
SIC: 3812 Aircraft/aerospace flight instruments & guidance systems

(G-2300)
TERRAMAR INSTRUMENTS LLC
7930 327th Ave Ne (98014-6711)
PHONE.................................425 306-0174
Matthew Benson, *Principal*
EMP: 2
SALES (est): 175.2K **Privately Held**
SIC: 3829 Measuring & controlling devices

(G-2301)
TRAFFIC SIGNS INC
Also Called: Vinal Letter Specialist
2204 Fall City Carnation (98014-5908)
P.O. Box 930 (98014-0930)
PHONE.................................425 333-6222
Ray Hooper, *President*
EMP: 5
SQ FT: 5,000
SALES: 500K **Privately Held**
SIC: 3993 5099 Signs & advertising specialties; signs, except electric

(G-2302)
WAYNE DAVIDSON
Also Called: Davidson's Sawmill
32405 Ne 12th Pl (98014-5902)
PHONE.................................425 333-4242
Wayne Davidson, *Owner*

EMP: 3
SALES (est): 420K **Privately Held**
SIC: 5031 2421 Lumber: rough, dressed & finished; sawmills & planing mills, general

Carson
Skamania County

(G-2303)
BOBS WELDING & AUTO REPAIR
91 Callahan Rd (98610-3332)
P.O. Box 69 (98610-0069)
PHONE.................................509 427-5094
Bob Calahan, *President*
Tim Calahan, *Vice Pres*
EMP: 2
SALES (est): 290.4K **Privately Held**
SIC: 7692 7538 7549 Welding repair; general automotive repair shops; towing service, automotive

(G-2304)
CARSON NC INC
91 Cloverdale Ave (98610-3250)
P.O. Box 740 (98610-0740)
PHONE.................................509 427-8616
Les Ellison, *President*
EMP: 3
SALES (est): 150K **Privately Held**
SIC: 3568 Joints, swivel & universal, except aircraft & automotive

(G-2305)
NORTH PACIFIC CRANE FAB HYD
1132 Old State Rd (98610-3107)
P.O. Box 1184 (98610-1184)
PHONE.................................509 427-4530
EMP: 7
SALES (est): 97.6K **Privately Held**
SIC: 7692 Welding repair

(G-2306)
RISLEY SONS WLDG FBRCATION LLC
492 Cedar Creek Rd (98610)
PHONE.................................509 427-2206
Casey Risley, *CEO*
EMP: 2
SALES (est): 118.5K **Privately Held**
SIC: 1761 1799 1791 3548 Architectural sheet metal work; ornamental metal work; storage tanks, metal: erection; arc welding generators, alternating current & direct current; gas welding equipment

(G-2307)
SHERMAN TECHNICAL INDS INC
11 Chapman Ave 2226 (98610)
P.O. Box 908, Stevenson (98648-0908)
PHONE.................................509 427-8089
Bill Sherman, *Principal*
EMP: 3
SALES (est): 155.1K **Privately Held**
SIC: 3672 Printed circuit boards

(G-2308)
SHERMAN TECHNICAL INDS INC
132 Chapman Ave (98610-1300)
PHONE.................................509 427-8089
William Sherman, *President*
Jeanie Sherman, *Vice Pres*
EMP: 4
SQ FT: 4,000
SALES (est): 475.5K **Privately Held**
WEB: www.shermantechnical.com
SIC: 3672 Printed circuit boards

(G-2309)
TWIN PEAKS
201 Josheanka Dr (98610)
PHONE.................................509 427-4759
Kelly Cummings, *Owner*
EMP: 2
SALES (est): 147.1K **Privately Held**
SIC: 3531 Construction machinery

(G-2310)
WILKINS KAISER & OLSEN INC
Also Called: W K O
2022 Wind River Hwy (98610)
P.O. Box 8 (98610-0008)
PHONE.................................509 427-5967
William T Wilkins, *President*
Bradley D Wilkins, *Vice Pres*
Mike Greenberg, *Controller*
Garret Stump, *Controller*
Deborah K Chamberlain, *Admin Sec*
EMP: 130 **EST:** 1962
SQ FT: 3,000
SALES (est): 44.5MM **Privately Held**
WEB: www.wkoinc.com
SIC: 2421 2411 Lumber: rough, sawed or planed; logging

Cashmere
Chelan County

(G-2311)
A1 ASBESTOS LLC
4113 Mission Creek Rd (98815-9629)
PHONE.................................509 881-0074
Timothy Brett Powell, *Principal*
Tim Powell, *Administration*
EMP: 7
SALES (est): 622.2K **Privately Held**
SIC: 3292 Asbestos products

(G-2312)
ALL SEASONS SWEEPING SERVICE
Also Called: Northwest Snow & Ice Equipment
5295 Sunset Hwy (98815-9558)
PHONE.................................509 782-8015
Charles Bray, *President*
Karen Hughes Bray, *Treasurer*
EMP: 3
SQ FT: 3,200
SALES (est): 250K **Privately Held**
SIC: 3531 1799 Blades for graders, scrapers, dozers & snow plows; parking facility equipment & maintenance; parking facility equipment installation

(G-2313)
ALTELS LOGGING INC
4660 Brisky Canyon Rd (98815-9466)
PHONE.................................509 782-5808
Martin Stoller, *President*
Heidi Stoller, *Admin Sec*
EMP: 6
SALES (est): 526.5K **Privately Held**
SIC: 2411 Logging

(G-2314)
ANJOU BAKERY AND CATERING
3898 Old Monitor Rd (98815-9711)
P.O. Box 255 (98815-0255)
PHONE.................................509 782-4360
Heather Knight, *Owner*
EMP: 2
SALES (est): 121.6K **Privately Held**
WEB: www.anjoubakery.com
SIC: 2051 5812 Bread, cake & related products; caterers

(G-2315)
APPLE CITY ELECTRIC LLC
4080 Mission Creek Rd (98815-9628)
PHONE.................................509 782-2334
EMP: 2
SALES (est): 138.5K **Privately Held**
SIC: 3571 Mfg Electronic Computers

(G-2316)
ARCHIBALD LOG HOMES INC
7992 Brender Canyon Rd (98815-9478)
P.O. Box 396, Leavenworth (98826-0396)
PHONE.................................509 782-3703
Keith J Archibald, *President*
Kathy Archibald, *Admin Sec*
EMP: 3
SALES (est): 500K **Privately Held**
SIC: 1521 2452 Single-family housing construction; log cabins, prefabricated, wood

(G-2317)
BETHLEHEM CONSTRUCTION INC (PA)
5505 Titchenal Rd (98815-1112)
P.O. Box 505 (98815-0505)
PHONE.................................509 782-1001
Michael J Addleman, *President*
Linda B Addleman, *Admin Sec*
EMP: 30 **EST:** 1980
SQ FT: 10,000
SALES (est): 79.5MM **Privately Held**
WEB: www.bethlehemc.com
SIC: 1541 1542 3272 Warehouse construction; commercial & office building, new construction; concrete products

(G-2318)
COLUMBIA CASCADE WINERY ASSN
301 Angier Ave 3b (98815-1301)
PHONE.................................509 782-3845
Pat Valison, *Principal*
EMP: 2
SALES (est): 126.2K **Privately Held**
WEB: www.columbiacascadewines.com
SIC: 2084 Wines

(G-2319)
CRUNCH PAK LLC (PA)
300 Sunset Hwy (98815-1327)
PHONE.................................509 782-2807
John Graden, *Human Res Dir*
Marco Gutierrez, *Sales Staff*
Alessandro De Nadai,
Jannine Waldner, *Administration*
Diane Huntsinger Carson,
▲ **EMP:** 700
SQ FT: 60,000
SALES (est): 87.4MM **Privately Held**
WEB: www.crunchpak.com
SIC: 2099 Ready-to-eat meals, salads & sandwiches

(G-2320)
GERRIS DRY BUNK
3264 Mission Creek Rd (98815-9659)
PHONE.................................509 782-2653
Gerri Dolman, *Partner*
James Dolman, *Partner*
EMP: 2
SALES (est): 252.2K **Privately Held**
SIC: 2676 5113 4225 2842 Sanitary paper products; industrial & personal service paper; general warehousing; specialty cleaning, polishes & sanitation goods

(G-2321)
GILYARD CO
Also Called: Gilyard Home Furnishings
107 Railroad Ave (98815-1128)
PHONE.................................509 782-1817
Galen Gilyard, *Partner*
Ted Gilyard, *Partner*
EMP: 2
SALES (est): 242K **Privately Held**
SIC: 5713 3544 Carpets; special dies, tools, jigs & fixtures

(G-2322)
ITS 5 LLC
Also Called: It's 5 Oclock Somewhere Dist
207 Mission Ave (98815-1008)
PHONE.................................509 679-9771
Colin Levi, *Mng Member*
EMP: 4
SALES (est): 171.9K **Privately Held**
SIC: 2085 Distilled & blended liquors

(G-2323)
JOE NESTOR
Also Called: Dog & Pony Brewing Company
5427 Binder Rd (98815-1205)
PHONE.................................509 264-0800
Joe Nestor, *Owner*
EMP: 3 **EST:** 2010
SALES (est): 68.6K **Privately Held**
SIC: 2082 Beer (alcoholic beverage)

(G-2324)
L E WILSON INC
Also Called: Wilson Tools & Gages
404 Pioneer Ave (98815-1702)
PHONE.................................509 782-1328
Jon Morrison, *CEO*
Daniel Reichert, *President*
Donetta Fries, *CFO*
EMP: 8 **EST:** 1927
SQ FT: 6,000
SALES (est): 935.1K **Privately Held**
WEB: www.lewilson.com
SIC: 3484 Pistols or pistol parts, 30 mm. & below; rifles or rifle parts, 30 mm. & below

(G-2325)
LA TOSCANA BED BRAKFAST WINERY
9020 Foster Rd (98815-9417)
PHONE.................................509 548-5448
Warren Moyles, *Owner*
Julie Moyles, *Co-Owner*
EMP: 2
SALES (est): 35K **Privately Held**
SIC: 7011 2084 Bed & breakfast inn; wine cellars, bonded: engaged in blending wines

(G-2326)
LIBERTY ORCHARDS COMPANY INC
117 Mission Ave (98815-1007)
P.O. Box C (98815-0485)
PHONE.................................509 782-4088
Gregory A Taylor, *President*
J Michael Rainey, *Vice Pres*
Brad Thomas, *Treasurer*
▲ **EMP:** 80 **EST:** 1918
SQ FT: 95,000
SALES (est): 15.8MM **Privately Held**
WEB: www.libertyorchards.com
SIC: 2064 5961 Fruit & fruit peel confections; mail order house

(G-2327)
NCW MEDIA INC
Also Called: Cashmere Valley Record
201 Cottage Ave (98815-1616)
PHONE.................................509 782-3781
Jim D Owner, *Branch Mgr*
Bill Forhan, *Manager*
EMP: 2
SALES (corp-wide): 2MM **Privately Held**
WEB: www.leavenworthecho.com
SIC: 2711 Newspapers
PA: Ncw Media Inc
215 14th St
Leavenworth WA 98826
509 548-5286

(G-2328)
OVENELL CUSTOM CABINETS
305 Mission Ave (98815-1083)
PHONE.................................509 782-3400
Steve Ovenell, *Principal*
EMP: 2
SALES (est): 256.8K **Privately Held**
SIC: 2434 Wood kitchen cabinets

(G-2329)
S&S INDUSTRIES LLC
Also Called: Leony's Cellars
6367 Unit 4 Kimber Rd (98815)
PHONE.................................360 500-9942
Sandi Grimnes Moreno,
EMP: 2
SALES (est): 143.5K **Privately Held**
SIC: 2084 Wines

(G-2330)
STEWARTS HANGER 21 INC
211 Chapel St (98815-1305)
PHONE.................................509 782-3626
Doug Stewart, *President*
EMP: 2
SALES (est): 361.7K **Privately Held**
SIC: 3721 Aircraft

(G-2331)
TREE TOP INC
200 Tichenal Rd (98815-9800)
P.O. Box O (98815-0845)
PHONE.................................509 782-6809
Joe Brooks, *Branch Mgr*
EMP: 100
SALES (corp-wide): 399.9MM **Privately Held**
SIC: 2033 2087 Fruit juices: packaged in cans, jars, etc.; flavoring extracts & syrups

PA: Tree Top, Inc.
220 E 2nd Ave
Selah WA 98942
509 697-7251

(G-2332)
WENATCHEE BUSINESS JOURNAL
201 Cottage Ave Ste 4 (98815-1616)
PHONE.................................509 663-6730
Chris Passe, *President*
EMP: 7
SALES (est): 519.3K **Privately Held**
SIC: 2721 2752 Periodicals: publishing only; commercial printing, lithographic

(G-2333)
WENATCHEE QLTY WLDG FBRICATION
5830 Sunset Hwy (98815-9532)
PHONE.................................509 782-0807
Douglas Fehrer, *Owner*
EMP: 13
SALES (est): 1.5MM **Privately Held**
SIC: 3441 3599 1799 Fabricated structural metal; industrial machinery; welding on site

(G-2334)
WESTWOOD LOGGING
9264 Foster Rd (98815-9418)
PHONE.................................509 548-7681
Raymond West, *Owner*
EMP: 3
SALES (est): 202.8K **Privately Held**
SIC: 2411 Logging camps & contractors

(G-2335)
WILDFIRE SAFE LLC
5930 Sunburst Ln (98815-9555)
PHONE.................................509 670-3816
Kyle Walter, *Principal*
EMP: 2 **EST:** 2012
SALES (est): 211.2K **Privately Held**
SIC: 3711 Fire department vehicles (motor vehicles), assembly of

Castle Rock
Cowlitz County

(G-2336)
3 X BAR INC
1512 Albert Andrson Ln Ne (98611-9000)
PHONE.................................360 274-4502
Gary Horsely, *President*
EMP: 3
SALES (est): 333.1K **Privately Held**
SIC: 2411 Logging

(G-2337)
AQUATECH
198 Newell Rd (98611-3900)
PHONE.................................360 957-5203
Calvin Bruno, *Principal*
EMP: 3 **EST:** 2013
SALES (est): 250K **Privately Held**
SIC: 5074 3561 Water purification equipment; pumps & pumping equipment

(G-2338)
BJ & BOBS FARM BUTCHERING
Also Called: Bolar's Custom Meat Cutting
381 Delameter Rd (98611-9411)
PHONE.................................360 274-4202
Fax: 360 274-4202
EMP: 5
SQ FT: 1,600
SALES (est): 260K **Privately Held**
SIC: 2011 0751 Meat Cutting/Packing & Livestock Slaughtering

(G-2339)
DIAMOND TIMBER COMPANY
450 Toutle River Rd (98611-9728)
P.O. Box 248 (98611-0248)
PHONE.................................360 274-7914
Jeff Gould, *President*
Christina Gould, *Corp Secy*
EMP: 10
SALES (est): 994.2K **Privately Held**
WEB: www.diamondtimber.com
SIC: 2411 Logging

(G-2340)
DUANE BRUNER LOGGING INC
1176 Chapman Rd (98611-9655)
P.O. Box 568 (98611-0568)
PHONE.................................360 274-7103
Duane Bruner, *President*
EMP: 23
SALES (est): 1.6MM **Privately Held**
SIC: 2411 Logging camps & contractors

(G-2341)
ECCENTRIXX LLC
2626 Hazel Dell Rd (98611-9432)
PHONE.................................360 274-4954
Mathew Schwinn, *Mng Member*
EMP: 2 **EST:** 2009
SALES (est): 193.7K **Privately Held**
SIC: 3949 Sporting & athletic goods

(G-2342)
ELECTRIC CONCEPT LABS INC
Also Called: Nevic
102 Chapman Rd (98611-9616)
P.O. Box 21 (98611-0021)
PHONE.................................503 244-3000
EMP: 3 **EST:** 2017
SQ FT: 600
SALES (est): 111.4K **Privately Held**
SIC: 3625 1542 Nonresidential Construction Mfg Relays/Industrial Controls

(G-2343)
GOULD & SONS LOGGING INC
1627 Tower Rd (98611-9742)
P.O. Box 1899 (98611-1899)
PHONE.................................360 274-9425
William Gould, *President*
Debbie Gould, *Treasurer*
EMP: 25
SALES (est): 2.6MM **Privately Held**
SIC: 2411 Logging camps & contractors

(G-2344)
GOULD-SUNRISE LOGGING INC
1036 Huntington Ave S (98611-9680)
PHONE.................................360 274-8000
Edward Gould, *President*
EMP: 16
SALES (est): 2MM **Privately Held**
SIC: 2411 Logging camps & contractors

(G-2345)
HORSLEY TIMBER & CONSTRUCTION
684 Melton Rd (98611-9418)
PHONE.................................360 274-7272
Michelle Hprsley, *Vice Pres*
EMP: 2
SALES (est): 300K **Privately Held**
SIC: 2411 Logging

(G-2346)
JEFFREY GOULD
450 Toutle River Rd (98611-9728)
P.O. Box 248 (98611-0248)
PHONE.................................360 274-7914
Jeffrey Gould, *Owner*
EMP: 10
SALES (est): 431.8K **Privately Held**
SIC: 2411 Logging

(G-2347)
KAYSER FARMS
Also Called: Kayser, Melvin L
615 Monahan Rd (98611-9512)
PHONE.................................360 274-6277
Melvin L Kayser Jr, *Partner*
EMP: 3
SALES (est): 270K **Privately Held**
SIC: 0251 2411 Broiler, fryer & roaster chickens; logging

(G-2348)
KRUME LOGGING EXCAVATION
501 Kroll Rd (98611-9341)
PHONE.................................360 274-8667
Eric Krume, *Owner*
EMP: 19
SALES (est): 1.5MM **Privately Held**
SIC: 2411 Logging camps & contractors

(G-2349)
PACIFIC ENGINEERING & MFG CO
Also Called: Pemco
317 Sandy Bend Rd (98611-9173)
PHONE.................................360 274-8323
Richard L Moss, *President*
Tricia Moss, *Office Mgr*
EMP: 4
SQ FT: 3,000
SALES (est): 482.1K **Privately Held**
SIC: 3799 3825 Towing bars & systems; instruments to measure electricity

(G-2350)
PURSLEY LOGGING CO INC
2300 Hazel Dell Rd (98611-9434)
PHONE.................................360 274-7297
Ronald Pursley, *Manager*
EMP: 6
SQ FT: 763
SALES (est): 100K **Privately Held**
SIC: 2411 Logging camps & contractors

(G-2351)
QUALITY INSTANT PRINT
742 Carnine Rd (98611-9714)
PHONE.................................360 274-0337
Tim Sedig, *Principal*
EMP: 3
SALES (est): 204.1K **Privately Held**
SIC: 2752 Commercial printing, offset

(G-2352)
QUALITY LOGGING LLC
1212 Schaffran Rd (98611-9772)
PHONE.................................360 640-1555
A Douglas, *Bd of Directors*
EMP: 3
SALES (est): 213.7K **Privately Held**
SIC: 2411 Logging

(G-2353)
TIM BROWN LOGGING INC
2970 Tower Rd (98611-9798)
PHONE.................................360 274-4422
Tim Brown, *President*
Jennifer Brown, *Corp Secy*
EMP: 20
SALES (est): 3MM **Privately Held**
SIC: 2411 Logging camps & contractors

(G-2354)
TIM EASTMAN EQP REPR WLDG LLC
112 Headquarters Rd (98611-9365)
P.O. Box 26, Kalama (98625-0100)
PHONE.................................360 274-7607
Timothy Eastman, *Mng Member*
Vicky Eastman,
EMP: 10
SQ FT: 360
SALES (est): 300K **Privately Held**
SIC: 3531 7699 Construction machinery attachments; construction equipment repair

(G-2355)
TIN CAN ALLEY
160 Huntington Ave N (98611-8912)
P.O. Box 642 (98611-0642)
PHONE.................................360 353-0773
Ronald Daley, *Principal*
EMP: 3
SALES (est): 85.6K **Privately Held**
SIC: 3411 Tin cans

(G-2356)
TRI-TEX INC
Also Called: Tri-Tex Oil Co
1140 Dougherty Dr Ne (98611-8034)
P.O. Box 70 (98611-0070)
PHONE.................................360 274-8511
Dale Mc Gee, *President*
Tom Scott, *Corp Secy*
Neil Mc Gee, *Vice Pres*
EMP: 30
SALES (est): 13.5MM **Privately Held**
SIC: 5171 2411 5172 Petroleum bulk stations; logging; petroleum products

(G-2357)
WEYERHAEUSER COMPANY
500 Burma Rd (98611)
P.O. Box 190 (98611-0190)
PHONE.................................360 274-3058
EMP: 101
SALES (corp-wide): 7.4B **Publicly Held**
SIC: 2411 Logging
PA: Weyerhaeuser Company
220 Occidental Ave S
Seattle WA 98104
206 539-3000

(G-2358)
YOUR DAILY DOSE LLC
477 Agren Rd (98611-9646)
PHONE.................................360 749-7414
Therese Wortman, *Principal*
EMP: 3 **EST:** 2016
SALES (est): 69.2K **Privately Held**
SIC: 2711 Newspapers

Cathlamet
Wahkiakum County

(G-2359)
ANDERSON SHAKE & SHINGLE MILL
256 E State Route 4 (98612-9554)
P.O. Box 1 (98612-0001)
PHONE.................................360 795-3069
James Anderson Jr, *President*
Dean Anderson, *Principal*
Cheryl Parker, *Principal*
Scott Anderson, *Vice Pres*
EMP: 4 **EST:** 1964
SQ FT: 6,000
SALES (est): 1MM **Privately Held**
SIC: 2429 Shakes (hand split shingles); shingles, wood: sawed or hand split

(G-2360)
BOB NELSON
Also Called: Wahkiakum County Eagle
77 Main St (98612)
PHONE.................................360 795-3391
Bob Nelson, *Owner*
Lois Nelson, *Co-Owner*
EMP: 3
SQ FT: 2,700
SALES (est): 185.2K **Privately Held**
SIC: 2711 2752 Newspapers: publishing only, not printed on site; commercial printing, lithographic

(G-2361)
BURNS CONSTRUCTION INC
770 Elochoman Valley Rd (98612-9603)
PHONE.................................360 957-4183
Leroy Burns, *President*
EMP: 2 **EST:** 1952
SALES (est): 500K **Privately Held**
SIC: 1442 1611 Gravel mining; highway & street construction

(G-2362)
CARLSON AND SONS LOGGING INC
1010 Beaver Creek Rd (98612-9634)
PHONE.................................360 795-3068
EMP: 4 **EST:** 2016
SALES (est): 115.1K **Privately Held**
SIC: 2411 Logging

(G-2363)
CARLSON LOGIN INC
1010 Beaver Creek Rd (98612-9634)
PHONE.................................360 795-3068
Brad Carlson, *Principal*
EMP: 6 **EST:** 2013
SALES (est): 473.8K **Privately Held**
SIC: 2411 Logging camps & contractors

(G-2364)
DANDY DIGGER AND SUPPLY INC
244 W State Route 4 (98612-9619)
PHONE.................................360 795-3617
James Mc Mahon, *President*
James McMahon, *CFO*
EMP: 19 **EST:** 1961

SALES (est): 3.8MM **Privately Held**
WEB: www.dandydigger.com
SIC: 3531 Construction machinery

(G-2365)
ELOCHOMAN MILLWORK INC
23 Boege Rd (98612-9551)
P.O. Box 183 (98612-0183)
PHONE...................................360 795-3637
Robert Jungers, *President*
Dawn Marie Jungers, *Corp Secy*
▲ **EMP:** 2
SQ FT: 12,000
SALES (est): 313.4K **Privately Held**
SIC: 2431 Doors, wood

(G-2366)
FAUBION WILLIAM J ATTY AT LAW
260 Una St (98612)
P.O. Box 153 (98612-0153)
PHONE...................................360 795-3367
William J Faubion, *Owner*
EMP: 3
SALES (est): 241.8K **Privately Held**
SIC: 8111 2411 General practice attorney, lawyer; logging

(G-2367)
FLOREK LOGGING LTD INC
911 Elochoman Valley Rd (98612-9628)
PHONE...................................360 795-8058
John Florek, *President*
EMP: 2
SALES (est): 160K **Privately Held**
SIC: 2411 Logging camps & contractors

(G-2368)
HANSON AGGREGATES LLC
273 W State Route 4 (98612-9619)
PHONE...................................360 795-3221
Mel Souvneir, *Manager*
EMP: 15
SALES (corp-wide): 20.6B **Privately Held**
WEB: www.hansonind.com
SIC: 3272 Concrete products
HQ: Hanson Aggregates Llc
8505 Freeport Pkwy Ste 500
Irving TX 75063
469 417-1200

(G-2369)
JERRY DEBRIAE LOGGING CO INC
45 Elochoman Valley Rd (98612-9602)
P.O. Box 182 (98612-0182)
PHONE...................................360 795-3309
Jerry Debriae, *President*
Linda Debriae, *Corp Secy*
EMP: 100 **EST:** 1973
SALES (est): 12MM **Privately Held**
SIC: 2411 Logging camps & contractors

(G-2370)
L ROCK INDUSTRIES INC
1902 E State Route 4 (98612-9547)
PHONE...................................360 575-8868
Lemmie Rockford, *President*
EMP: 2
SALES (est): 47.1K **Privately Held**
SIC: 3999 Manufacturing industries

(G-2371)
NOREAH/BROWNFIELD PRESS LLC
361 E Birnie Slough Rd (98612-9709)
PHONE...................................360 849-4857
Christine Towler, *Principal*
EMP: 2
SALES (est): 83.9K **Privately Held**
SIC: 2741 Miscellaneous publishing

(G-2372)
R & H LOGGING & CONTRACT CUTNG
169 Beaver Creek Rd (98612-9611)
PHONE...................................360 795-3334
Randle Hoxit, *Principal*
EMP: 2
SALES (est): 109.2K **Privately Held**
SIC: 2411 Logging

(G-2373)
REPUBLIC LOCOMOTIVE WORKS
16 Little Cape Horn Rd (98612-9544)
PHONE...................................360 577-6479
Marshall T Thomson, *Owner*
EMP: 4
SALES (est): 89K **Privately Held**
SIC: 3944 Trains & equipment, toy: electric & mechanical; railroad models: toy & hobby

(G-2374)
S & J LOGGING INC
45 Elochoman Valley Rd (98612-9602)
P.O. Box 182 (98612-0182)
PHONE...................................360 795-3309
Jerry Debriae, *President*
Linda Debriae, *Corp Secy*
EMP: 2
SALES (est): 160K **Privately Held**
SIC: 2411 Logging camps & contractors

(G-2375)
SOUTHWEST CONCRETE CO
276 E State Route 4 (98612-9554)
P.O. Box 188 (98612-0188)
PHONE...................................360 795-8211
Kevin Wirkkala, *Owner*
EMP: 2 **EST:** 1998
SALES: 300K **Privately Held**
SIC: 3273 Ready-mixed concrete

(G-2376)
STANLEYS SANITARY SERVICE
20 Hedlund Rd (98612-9710)
P.O. Box 548 (98612-0548)
PHONE...................................360 795-3369
Fred Stanley, *Owner*
Crystal Stanley, *Partner*
EMP: 5
SALES (est): 240K **Privately Held**
SIC: 3589 4212 Garbage disposers & compactors, commercial; local trucking, without storage

(G-2377)
WOODYS RELICS
223 N Welcome Slough Rd (98612-9718)
PHONE...................................360 849-4257
Lee Tischer, *Principal*
EMP: 3
SALES (est): 109.3K **Privately Held**
SIC: 2711 Newspapers

Centerville
Klickitat County

(G-2378)
VISUAL VERVE DESIGN PRINT LLC
2308 Centerville Hwy (98613-3021)
PHONE...................................509 773-4596
Kacie L Bane, *Principal*
EMP: 2
SALES (est): 110K **Privately Held**
SIC: 2752 Commercial printing, lithographic

Centralia
Lewis County

(G-2379)
ACE INTERNATIONAL INC
Wood Fibre Division
1830 Central Blvd (98531-5502)
P.O. Box 885 (98531-0885)
PHONE...................................360 736-3937
Kent Johnson, *Manager*
EMP: 27 **Privately Held**
SIC: 2421 Sawmills & planing mills, general
PA: Ace International Inc.
520 N Gold St
Centralia WA 98531

(G-2380)
ACE INTERNATIONAL INC (PA)
520 N Gold St (98531-5120)
PHONE...................................360 736-9999
Murray Hill, *President*
Arlene Hill, *Corp Secy*
▼ **EMP:** 5
SALES (est): 2MM **Privately Held**
SIC: 2421 Sawdust & shavings

(G-2381)
ACE OF SPADES INC
700 S Tower Ave (98531-2517)
PHONE...................................360 807-6442
Russ Rockwell, *President*
Ian Brown, *Vice Pres*
EMP: 2
SALES (est): 65K **Privately Held**
SIC: 3751 Motorcycle accessories

(G-2382)
ALLOY POLISHING CO
809 N Tower Ave (98531-4756)
PHONE...................................360 736-2716
David Barr, *Principal*
EMP: 3
SALES (est): 215.9K **Privately Held**
WEB: www.alloypolishing.com
SIC: 3471 Polishing, metals or formed products

(G-2383)
AMERICAN PLATING
524 N Gold St (98531-5120)
PHONE...................................360 736-0052
Keith Henderson, *Principal*
EMP: 2
SALES (est): 226.4K **Privately Held**
SIC: 3471 Plating of metals or formed products

(G-2384)
ATLAS CONCRETE PRODUCTS INC
3031 Harrison Ave (98531-9357)
PHONE...................................360 736-7642
Toll Free:...................................888 -
Rod Liseth, *President*
Gary Bishop, *Manager*
EMP: 15
SQ FT: 5,000
SALES (est): 1.4MM **Privately Held**
SIC: 3272 3273 Septic tanks, concrete; ready-mixed concrete

(G-2385)
BLANC INDUSTRIES INC
Also Called: Washington Poster Company
3639 Galvin Rd (98531-9053)
PHONE...................................360 736-8988
Barrett Blakesley, *President*
Bethel Blakesley, *Vice Pres*
Luanne Blakesley, *Controller*
▲ **EMP:** 26
SALES (est): 3MM
SALES (corp-wide): 12.3MM **Privately Held**
WEB: www.wpsignsystems.com
SIC: 3993 2396 Signs, not made in custom sign painting shops; automotive & apparel trimmings
PA: Blanc Industries Inc.
88 King St Ste 1
Dover NJ 07801
973 537-0090

(G-2386)
BUOY WEAR LLC
3833 Cooks Hill Rd (98531-9080)
PHONE...................................206 899-7926
Mike Curtright, *Principal*
EMP: 4
SALES (est): 247.7K **Privately Held**
SIC: 3949 Sporting & athletic goods

(G-2387)
C & R ELECTRIC MOTOR SERVICE
820 N Tower Ave (98531-4757)
PHONE...................................360 736-2521
Kevin Cearley, *President*
Barbara Cearley, *Admin Sec*
EMP: 2
SQ FT: 8,000
SALES: 220K **Privately Held**
SIC: 5999 5063 7694 Motors, electric; electronic parts & equipment; motors, electric; electrical supplies; electric motor repair

(G-2388)
CENTRAL GLASS WORKS
109 W Main St (98531-4205)
PHONE...................................360 623-1099
Kevin Regan, *Owner*
EMP: 3
SQ FT: 2,250
SALES (est): 206.6K **Privately Held**
SIC: 3231 Products of purchased glass

(G-2389)
CENTRALIA BOX & VAULT CO
705 State St (98531-3751)
PHONE...................................360 736-4757
Jeffrey Spencer, *Owner*
EMP: 2 **EST:** 1933
SQ FT: 2,100
SALES (est): 120K **Privately Held**
SIC: 3272 Burial vaults, concrete or precast terrazzo

(G-2390)
CENTRALIA KNITTING MILLS INC
Also Called: Skookum Sportswear
1002 W Main St (98531-2853)
P.O. Box 269 (98531-0269)
PHONE...................................360 736-3994
Dorothy Thoreson, *President*
Randy Thoreson, *Corp Secy*
Ralph E Thoreson, *Vice Pres*
EMP: 24 **EST:** 1939
SQ FT: 9,000
SALES (est): 3.2MM **Privately Held**
WEB: www.centraliaknittingmills.com
SIC: 2253 5699 Jackets, knit; cold weather knit outerwear, including ski wear; sports apparel

(G-2391)
CENTRALIA SUPPLY & FABRICATION
901 W Main St (98531-2850)
PHONE...................................360 736-7277
EMP: 2
SQ FT: 10,000
SALES: 550K **Privately Held**
SIC: 3312 5051 7699 5231 Fabrication & Sales Of Steel Miscellaneous Repair Service Ret Hardware & Welding Service

(G-2392)
CHEHALIS MINTS CO CORP
2677 Little Hanaford Rd (98531-8956)
P.O. Box 445, Chehalis (98532-0445)
PHONE...................................360 736-9899
Sue Schofield, *President*
Jeff Schofield, *Vice Pres*
EMP: 4
SALES (est): 210K **Privately Held**
WEB: www.chehalismints.com
SIC: 2064 Candy & other confectionery products

(G-2393)
CHURCHILL N MFG CO INC
Also Called: J Churchill Glove Co
544 N Pearl St (98531-4661)
P.O. Box 298 (98531-0298)
PHONE...................................360 736-9923
James Churchill, *President*
Andy Churchill, *Vice Pres*
N Churchill, *Vice Pres*
EMP: 13 **EST:** 1895
SQ FT: 16,200
SALES: 750K **Privately Held**
WEB: www.feeltheride.com
SIC: 3151 2381 Gloves, leather: work; mittens, leather; fabric dress & work gloves

(G-2394)
COALVIEW LTD LLC
1044 Big Hanaford Rd (98531-9101)
PHONE...................................360 623-7525
Michael Tzougrakis, *Ch of Bd*
Roger Fish, *President*
C David Henry, *President*
David Schwedel, *Exec Dir*
EMP: 50 **EST:** 2011
SALES (est): 4MM **Privately Held**
SIC: 1221 Bituminous coal & lignite loading & preparation

GEOGRAPHIC SECTION

Centralia - Lewis County (G-2424)

PA: Coalview Holdings, Llc
75 Valencia Ave Ste 600
Coral Gables FL 33134
305 851-8450

(G-2395)
COMPUTER CONNECTIONS
Also Called: Nelson, Carol Ea
213 E Main St (98531-4449)
PHONE.................360 736-2177
Carol J Nelson, *Owner*
EMP: 3
SALES (est): 287.1K **Privately Held**
SIC: 7372 Prepackaged software

(G-2396)
CURFMAN CUSTOM FABRICATION LLC
Also Called: Ccfab
901 W Main St (98531-2850)
PHONE.................360 736-7277
Jonathan Curfman, *Mng Member*
Jason Curfman, *Mng Member*
EMP: 2
SALES (est): 350K **Privately Held**
SIC: 3441 Fabricated structural metal

(G-2397)
D & D DIVIDERS LLC
Also Called: Kz Packaging
530 N Gold St (98531-5120)
P.O. Box 117 (98531-0117)
PHONE.................360 951-4852
Phillip Rupp, *Managing Prtnr*
EMP: 3
SALES (est): 346.4K **Privately Held**
SIC: 3399 Primary metal products

(G-2398)
D AND D TRIM AND CABINETS INC
153 Mcatee Rd (98531-8919)
PHONE.................360 736-4279
Derral Foster, *Principal*
EMP: 2 EST: 2012
SALES (est): 110.6K **Privately Held**
SIC: 2434 Wood kitchen cabinets

(G-2399)
DULIN CONSTRUCTION INC
3300 Galvin Rd (98531-9062)
P.O. Box 38 (98531-0038)
PHONE.................360 736-9225
Mark Dulin, *President*
Sara Dulin, *Vice Pres*
EMP: 16
SQ FT: 1,000
SALES (est): 2.2MM **Privately Held**
SIC: 1622 1429 Bridge construction; boulder, crushed & broken-quarrying

(G-2400)
ERNESTINAS TORTILLAS LLC
1649 Kresky Ave (98531-8912)
PHONE.................360 669-0319
EMP: 3
SALES (est): 76.2K **Privately Held**
SIC: 2099 Mfg Food Preparations

(G-2401)
EXPERT COMPUTER TECH INC
Also Called: Zebra Computers
1600 S Gold St Ste 4 (98531-7901)
PHONE.................360 736-7000
Michael Painter, *President*
Jeremy Painter, *Manager*
EMP: 5
SALES (est): 236.1K **Privately Held**
WEB: www.zebracomputers.com
SIC: 7371 1731 3823 3571 Computer software development; computer installation; computer interface equipment for industrial process control; electronic computers; personal computers (microcomputers); computer storage devices

(G-2402)
FUNERAL DIRECTORS RESEARCH
Also Called: Amra Instruments
623 N Tower Ave (98531-4666)
P.O. Box 359 (98531-0359)
PHONE.................360 736-7105
Charles Rector, *Owner*
EMP: 2
SQ FT: 700
SALES (est): 120K **Privately Held**
WEB: www.amrainstruments.com
SIC: 3841 7261 Surgical & medical instruments; funeral service & crematories

(G-2403)
GLACIER NORTHWEST INC
305 E Summa St (98531-3841)
PHONE.................360 736-1131
Larry Granger, *Branch Mgr*
EMP: 16 **Privately Held**
SIC: 3273 5211 5261 Ready-mixed concrete; cement; lawn & garden supplies
HQ: Glacier Northwest, Inc.
5975 E Marginal Way S
Seattle WA 98134
206 764-3000

(G-2404)
GREAT IMPRESSIONS RBR STAMPS
220 W Center St (98531-4642)
PHONE.................360 807-8462
Deone Mackenzie, *President*
Ken Mackenzie, *Vice Pres*
EMP: 18
SQ FT: 5,000
SALES (est): 1.7MM **Privately Held**
WEB: www.greatimpressionsstamps.com
SIC: 3953 Marking devices

(G-2405)
HALLS DRUG CENTER INC
Also Called: Halls Medical Center Pharmacy
505 S Tower Ave A (98531-3919)
PHONE.................360 736-5000
Warren Hall, *Manager*
EMP: 25
SALES (corp-wide): 6.9MM **Privately Held**
SIC: 5912 5999 5047 3999 Drug stores; telephone & communication equipment; medical equipment & supplies; wheelchair lifts
PA: Halls Drug Center, Inc
505 S Tower Ave Ste 2
Centralia WA 98531
360 736-5000

(G-2406)
HEXEN GLASS STUDIO LLC
21631 Oregon Trl (98531-9617)
PHONE.................360 807-4217
Renata Cowan, *Mng Member*
EMP: 2 EST: 2013
SALES (est): 123.1K **Privately Held**
SIC: 3231 7389 Stained glass: made from purchased glass;

(G-2407)
HI TECH SIGNS & BANNERS
1616 S Gold St Ste 10 (98531-8930)
PHONE.................360 736-6322
Thomas P Duffy, *Owner*
EMP: 5
SALES: 250K **Privately Held**
SIC: 3993 5999 Signs, not made in custom sign painting shops; banners

(G-2408)
HOW 2 PUBLISHING LLC
1634 S Scheuber Rd (98531-8818)
PHONE.................360 878-9274
Chet Womach, *Principal*
EMP: 2
SALES (est): 116.3K **Privately Held**
SIC: 2741 Miscellaneous publishing

(G-2409)
HRH DOOR CORP
Wayne - Dalton of Centralia
2001 Industrial Dr (98531-1913)
PHONE.................360 736-7651
Greg Penley, *Principal*
John Peterson, *VP Mktg*
EMP: 91
SALES (corp-wide): 600.8MM **Privately Held**
WEB: www.waynedalton.com
SIC: 2431 5031 Doors, wood; doors & windows
PA: Hrh Door Corp.
1 Door Dr
Mount Hope OH 44660
850 208-3400

(G-2410)
JANICE ARNOLD
Also Called: J Arnold Felt
20604 Grand Mound Way Sw (98531-9642)
PHONE.................360 273-8548
Janice Arnold, *Owner*
EMP: 3
SALES: 50K **Privately Held**
SIC: 2389 Costumes

(G-2411)
JAYS CUSTOM WOODWORKS
2614 Eureka Ave (98531-3618)
PHONE.................360 807-0976
Jeremiah Hinkley, *Principal*
EMP: 2
SALES (est): 138.7K **Privately Held**
SIC: 2431 Millwork

(G-2412)
JOHN DUANE KING
Also Called: Kings Quality Cabinets
1127 N Tower Ave (98531-5043)
PHONE.................360 736-6707
John Duane King, *Owner*
EMP: 3
SQ FT: 2,880
SALES (est): 219.9K **Privately Held**
SIC: 2434 5712 5031 1751 Wood kitchen cabinets; cabinet work, custom; kitchen cabinets; cabinet & finish carpentry

(G-2413)
JOSEPH GILLUM (PA)
Also Called: J & B Log Stackers
1010 W Reynolds Ave (98531-3330)
P.O. Box 1220, Forks (98331-1220)
PHONE.................800 624-4578
Joseph Gillum, *Owner*
EMP: 7
SQ FT: 3,200
SALES: 3.7MM **Privately Held**
SIC: 3531 5082 5999 7699 Logging equipment; logging & forestry machinery & equipment; alcoholic beverage making equipment & supplies; cash register repair

(G-2414)
KULIEN SHOE FACTORY
Also Called: Kulien Handmade Shoes
611 N Tower Ave (98531-4666)
PHONE.................360 736-6943
John Kohnke, *Partner*
Laurie Kohnke, *Partner*
▲ EMP: 4 EST: 1877
SQ FT: 4,000
SALES (est): 260K **Privately Held**
WEB: www.kulienshoes.com
SIC: 3143 3144 Men's footwear, except athletic; women's footwear, except athletic

(G-2415)
LAFROMBOISE NEWSPAPERS (PA)
Also Called: Nisqualley Valley News
321 N Pearl St (98531-4323)
P.O. Box 580 (98531-0580)
PHONE.................360 736-3311
J R Lafromboise, *President*
Dennis Waller, *President*
Steve Walker, *Treasurer*
EMP: 100 EST: 1885
SQ FT: 20,000
SALES (est): 13.5MM **Privately Held**
WEB: www.nisquallyvalleyonline.com
SIC: 2711 Commercial printing & newspaper publishing combined; newspapers, publishing & printing

(G-2416)
LAFROMBOISE NEWSPAPERS
Chronicle Printing Division
3802 Galvin Rd (98531-9055)
PHONE.................360 807-8716
J Lafromboise, *Principal*
EMP: 12
SALES (corp-wide): 13.5MM **Privately Held**
SIC: 2711 Commercial printing & newspaper publishing combined

PA: Lafromboise Newspapers
321 N Pearl St
Centralia WA 98531
360 736-3311

(G-2417)
LEFT COAST WOODWORKS LLC
21344 Old Highway 99 Sw (98531-9644)
PHONE.................360 790-3188
Mary Harroun, *Bd of Directors*
EMP: 2
SALES (est): 147.8K **Privately Held**
SIC: 2431 Millwork

(G-2418)
LOUIS STOFFER & SON
1410 Harrison Ave (98531-4529)
PHONE.................360 736-3820
Louis Stoffer Jr, *Owner*
Gary Stoffer, *Co-Owner*
EMP: 5
SQ FT: 3,840
SALES (est): 351.1K **Privately Held**
SIC: 1711 3444 Warm air heating & air conditioning contractor; ventilation & duct work contractor; sheet metalwork

(G-2419)
NORPLEX INC
1703 Lum Rd (98531-1963)
PHONE.................360 736-0727
Scott McCauley, *Branch Mgr*
EMP: 10
SALES (corp-wide): 8.5MM **Privately Held**
SIC: 3089 Netting, plastic
PA: Norplex, Inc.
111 3rd St Nw Bldg C
Auburn WA 98001
253 735-3431

(G-2420)
NORTH FORK TIMBER COMPANY CORP (PA)
Also Called: Pls Pole Yard
417 W Main St Ste C (98531-4263)
PHONE.................360 748-8333
EMP: 10
SQ FT: 700
SALES (est): 9.9MM **Privately Held**
SIC: 2411 1611 Logging camps & contractors; highway & street construction

(G-2421)
NORTHWEST SAUSAGE & DELI
5945 Prather Rd Sw (98531-9618)
PHONE.................360 736-7760
Richard A Young, *Owner*
EMP: 10
SQ FT: 6,200
SALES (est): 980K **Privately Held**
SIC: 5411 2013 Delicatessens; sausages from purchased meat

(G-2422)
OK TOOL & MACHINE WORKS
2122 Seminary Hill Rd (98531-8969)
PHONE.................360 736-8350
EMP: 3 EST: 1977
SALES (est): 170K **Privately Held**
SIC: 1799 3599 Trade Contractor Mfg Industrial Machinery

(G-2423)
PARADYCE INDUSTRIES INC
Also Called: Print Shop The
411 E Union St (98531-3759)
PHONE.................360 736-4474
Jamie Carey, *President*
Virgina Carey, *Corp Secy*
EMP: 5
SQ FT: 2,400
SALES: 800K **Privately Held**
WEB: www.theprint-shop.com
SIC: 2752 Commercial printing, offset

(G-2424)
PLACTIC SERVICES AND PRODUCTS
3500 Northpark Dr (98531-9049)
PHONE.................360 736-5616
Richard Reese, *Manager*
EMP: 30
SALES (est): 2.2MM **Privately Held**
SIC: 3084 Plastics pipe

Centralia - Lewis County (G-2425)

(G-2425)
PRECISION PRINTING INC
1624 Kresky Ave (98531)
PHONE..................360 736-7232
Dorothy Due, *President*
EMP: 3
SALES (est): 214.2K **Privately Held**
SIC: 2752 Commercial printing, offset

(G-2426)
PRINT PRO
3802 Galvin Rd (98531-9055)
PHONE..................360 807-8716
EMP: 2
SALES (est): 195.6K **Privately Held**
SIC: 2752 Lithographic Commercial Printing

(G-2427)
QUICK QUOTES INC
210 Northup St (98531-3836)
PHONE..................360 736-3004
Patsy Gaut, *President*
Shannon Jennings, *Vice Pres*
Andrew Millet, *Treasurer*
Stacy Millet, *Admin Sec*
▲ **EMP:** 13
SQ FT: 13,000
SALES (est): 1.2MM **Privately Held**
WEB: www.shopquickquotes.com
SIC: 2782 Scrapbooks

(G-2428)
ROCKING HORSE BARNS LLC
2205 Graf Rd (98531-9085)
PHONE..................360 736-5403
Joe Fasano, *Principal*
EMP: 3
SALES (est): 54.6K **Privately Held**
SIC: 3944 Rocking horses

(G-2429)
ROGERS MACHINERY COMPANY INC
3509 Galvin Rd (98531-9002)
P.O. Box 548 (98531-0548)
PHONE..................360 736-9356
Eric Forslund, *Branch Mgr*
EMP: 34
SQ FT: 2,000
SALES (corp-wide): 69.8MM **Privately Held**
SIC: 3561 3564 5084 7699 Industrial pumps & parts; blowers & fans; industrial machinery & equipment; compressors, except air conditioning; pumps & pumping equipment; compressor repair; pumps & pumping equipment repair; industrial machinery & equipment repair
PA: Rogers Machinery Company, Inc.
14650 Sw 72nd Ave
Portland OR 97224
503 639-0808

(G-2430)
SAYLER CUSTOM CONTROLS INC
1708 Midway Ct (98531-8842)
PHONE..................360 816-4193
Gayle Sayler, *President*
Douglas Sayler, *Vice Pres*
EMP: 4
SALES: 300K **Privately Held**
SIC: 3625 Industrial controls: push button, selector switches, pilot

(G-2431)
SCOT INDUSTRIES INC
3020 Foron Rd (98531)
PHONE..................360 623-1305
Craig Hach, *Branch Mgr*
EMP: 65
SQ FT: 73,000
SALES (corp-wide): 155.5MM **Privately Held**
SIC: 3317 5051 3412 Seamless pipes & tubes; bars, metal; metal barrels, drums & pails
PA: Scot Industries, Inc.
3756 Fm 250 N
Lone Star TX 75668
903 639-2551

(G-2432)
SHIRE MOUNTAIN LOG HOMES INC
812 Rainier Ave (98531-2940)
PHONE..................360 262-9338
Jay Robinson, *President*
EMP: 3
SALES: 120K **Privately Held**
SIC: 2452 Log cabins, prefabricated, wood

(G-2433)
SIERRA PACIFIC INDUSTRIES
3115 Kuper Rd (98531-9337)
PHONE..................360 736-5417
Scott North, *Branch Mgr*
EMP: 161
SALES (corp-wide): 1.2B **Privately Held**
SIC: 2421 Lumber: rough, sawed or planed
PA: Sierra Pacific Industries
19794 Riverside Ave
Anderson CA 96007
530 378-8000

(G-2434)
SIGN PRO INC
Also Called: Sign Pro of Lewis County
321 N Pearl St (98531-4323)
PHONE..................360 736-6322
Chris Sharp, *Manager*
EMP: 5
SALES (est): 437K **Privately Held**
WEB: www.signpro100.com
SIC: 3993 Electric signs

(G-2435)
SISSYS SPECIALTY FOODS
905 Spring Ln (98531-9021)
PHONE..................360 807-4305
Larry Deckert, *Principal*
EMP: 3 **EST:** 2011
SALES (est): 248K **Privately Held**
SIC: 2099 Food preparations

(G-2436)
STERLING BREEN CRUSHING INC
887 State Route 507 (98531-9205)
P.O. Box 1347, Chehalis (98532-0318)
PHONE..................360 736-4240
Sterling Breen, *President*
EMP: 20
SALES: 5MM **Privately Held**
WEB: www.sterlingbreencrushing.com
SIC: 1429 4212 Basalt, crushed & broken-quarrying; local trucking, without storage

(G-2437)
TAURMAN DISTRIBUTING & MFG
Also Called: Tdm
2208 Sandra Ave (98531-9382)
P.O. Box 1713 (98531-0706)
PHONE..................360 330-5886
Joe Taurman, *President*
Wayne Taurman, *Partner*
William Taurman, *Corp Secy*
EMP: 3 **EST:** 1999
SALES (est): 227K **Privately Held**
SIC: 3999 3491 Manufacturing industries; fire hydrant valves

(G-2438)
TRANSALTA CENTRALIA MINING LLC
913 Big Hanaford Rd (98531-9101)
PHONE..................360 807-8020
Steve Snyder,
Doug Jackson,
EMP: 520
SQ FT: 25,000
SALES (est): 42.8MM
SALES (corp-wide): 1.7B **Privately Held**
SIC: 1222 Underground mining, subbituminous
PA: Transalta Corporation
110 12 Ave Sw
Calgary AB T2R 0
403 267-7110

(G-2439)
TRUCK ACCESSORIES GROUP LLC
Pace-Edwards Company
2400 Commercial Rd (98531-9328)
PHONE..................360 736-9991
Doris Swalander, *Human Res Mgr*
EMP: 100
SALES (corp-wide): 1.2B **Privately Held**
WEB: www.leer.com
SIC: 3792 3713 Pickup covers, canopies or caps; truck & bus bodies
HQ: Truck Accessories Group, Llc
28858 Ventura Dr
Elkhart IN 46517
574 522-5337

(G-2440)
TWIN CITIES PRINTING
540 N Tower Ave (98531-4665)
PHONE..................360 807-1200
Gary Wells, *Owner*
EMP: 3
SALES (est): 209K **Privately Held**
SIC: 2759 Commercial printing

(G-2441)
VAN QUILL LARRY R
Also Called: Independence Printing
712 W Main St (98531-2847)
P.O. Box 577 (98531-0577)
PHONE..................360 736-1776
Andrew Van Quill, *President*
Larry Van Quill, *Vice Pres*
Barbara Van Quill, *Treasurer*
Kimberly Van Quill, *Admin Sec*
EMP: 4
SQ FT: 5,000
SALES (est): 376.5K **Privately Held**
WEB: www.independenceprinting.com
SIC: 2759 7334 2791 2789 Screen printing; photocopying & duplicating services; typesetting; bookbinding & related work; commercial printing, lithographic

(G-2442)
WEYERHAEUSER COMPANY
Also Called: Weyerhaeuser Hardwoods
3000 Galvin Rd (98531-9059)
PHONE..................360 736-2811
Doug Samtson, *Branch Mgr*
EMP: 160
SALES (corp-wide): 7.4B **Publicly Held**
SIC: 2421 2426 Sawmills & planing mills, general; hardwood dimension & flooring mills
PA: Weyerhaeuser Company
220 Occidental Ave S
Seattle WA 98104
206 539-3000

(G-2443)
WHODAT TOWERS
1708 Midway Ct (98531-8842)
PHONE..................360 786-1984
James Brinkerhoff, *Principal*
EMP: 2
SALES (est): 217.7K **Privately Held**
SIC: 3441 Fabricated structural metal

(G-2444)
WOODFORD PHOENIX AEROSPACE MFG
112 E 1st St (98531-4731)
PHONE..................360 736-9689
Trefford Woodford, *Owner*
Chuck Vanneste, *Prdtn Mgr*
EMP: 8
SQ FT: 7,000
SALES (est): 630K **Privately Held**
SIC: 3728 3599 Aircraft parts & equipment; machine shop, jobbing & repair

(G-2445)
WOODS BEE CO
919 W Reynolds Ave (98531-3327)
PHONE..................360 623-3359
EMP: 2
SALES (est): 129.6K **Privately Held**
SIC: 3999 Manufacturing industries

Chattaroy
Spokane County

(G-2446)
FLATTER HEIGHTS
30009 N Elk Chattaroy Rd (99003-8768)
PHONE..................509 238-6192
Dolores Flatter, *Partner*
EMP: 2
SALES (est): 91K **Privately Held**
SIC: 3961 Jewelry apparel, non-precious metals

(G-2447)
HYDRO-TECH GENERTR REPAIR PLUS
1004 E Owens Rd (99003-9739)
P.O. Box 279 (99003-0279)
PHONE..................509 276-2063
Loretta Roberts, *Branch Mgr*
EMP: 12
SALES (corp-wide): 2.7MM **Privately Held**
WEB: www.hydraulicsplusinc.com
SIC: 7699 3599 Hydraulic equipment repair; machine shop, jobbing & repair
PA: Hydro-Tech Generator Repair Plus, Inc.
5507 E Broadway Ave
Spokane Valley WA 99212
509 536-9464

(G-2448)
NAPALM RACING
27915 N Perry Rd (99003-8572)
PHONE..................509 991-9759
Nathan Palm, *Principal*
EMP: 2
SALES (est): 126.1K **Privately Held**
SIC: 2899 Napalm

(G-2449)
NORTHSIDE SAND & GRAVEL
32704 N Hwy 2 (99003)
P.O. Box 1617, Mead (99021-1617)
PHONE..................509 551-5830
EMP: 3
SALES (est): 131.6K **Privately Held**
SIC: 1442 Construction sand & gravel

(G-2450)
OMH INNOVATIONS USA INC
Also Called: Omh Proscreen
30627 N Hardesty Rd (99003-8820)
P.O. Box 559 (99003-0559)
PHONE..................509 264-1129
▲ **EMP:** 5
SALES (est): 570K **Privately Held**
SIC: 3532 5082 Mfg Crushing Pulverizing And Screening Equip/Whol & Ret Crushing Pulverizing And Screening Equip

(G-2451)
PRECISIONHX LLC
Also Called: Hydro Excavation / Vac Truck
11528 E Antler Rd (99003-9721)
PHONE..................509 951-1266
Larry Jenkins,
EMP: 2
SALES (est): 119.7K **Privately Held**
SIC: 1799 7699 3531 1389 Grave excavation; posthole digging; catch basin cleaning; entrenching machines; excavating slush pits & cellars

(G-2452)
SCULPTURES IN GLASS
29512 N Elk Chattaroy Rd (99003-8739)
PHONE..................509 951-3615
Rod Robinson, *Owner*
Judy Robinson, *Co-Owner*
EMP: 2
SALES: 35K **Privately Held**
SIC: 3229 Pressed & blown glass

(G-2453)
SILVER CITY LUMBER INC (PA)
Also Called: Silver City Timber Company
3916 E Chattaroy Rd (99003-9679)
P.O. Box 1383, Deer Park (99006-1383)
PHONE..................509 238-6960
H James Peterson, *President*
Linda M Peterson, *Corp Secy*
EMP: 30

SQ FT: 1,800
SALES (est): 5.1MM Privately Held
WEB: www.silvercitytimber.com
SIC: 2421 Sawmills & planing mills, general

(G-2454)
WAGGING TAILS VINEYARD
9419 E Big Meadows Rd (99003-9566)
PHONE.................................509 847-5287
Cynthia Case, *Principal*
Dominic Case,
EMP: 2
SALES (est): 42.5K Privately Held
SIC: 2084 Wine cellars, bonded: engaged in blending wines

(G-2455)
Z-MACHINE LLC
35611 N Dunn Rd (99003-7727)
PHONE.................................509 991-8628
Katherin Jensen, *Principal*
EMP: 2
SALES (est): 86.1K Privately Held
SIC: 3599 Industrial machinery

Chehalis
Lewis County

(G-2456)
A & S POWDER COATING
185 Keasling Rd (98532-8409)
PHONE.................................360 880-2487
Tammi Amman, *Principal*
EMP: 2
SALES (est): 101.9K Privately Held
SIC: 3479 Metal coating & allied service

(G-2457)
A-1 TIMBER CONSULTANTS INC (PA)
185 Hamilton Rd N (98532-8803)
P.O. Box 1001 (98532-0130)
PHONE.................................360 748-8987
Tom Loushine, *President*
Reicki Loushine, *Vice Pres*
Tina Loushine, *Admin Sec*
EMP: 18
SALES (est): 2.5MM Privately Held
SIC: 2491 Structural lumber & timber, treated wood

(G-2458)
ADVOCATE PRINTING
429 N Market Blvd (98532-2627)
PHONE.................................360 748-3335
Frank Debaul, *President*
Judy Devaul, *Vice Pres*
EMP: 5
SALES (est): 430.7K Privately Held
SIC: 2759 2711 Commercial printing; newspapers

(G-2459)
AGATE CREEK FARM
Also Called: Agatecreek Cellars
105 Agate Creek Ln (98532-9197)
PHONE.................................360 740-1692
John Petaja, *Owner*
Gayle Willis, *Co-Owner*
EMP: 2
SALES (est): 119.4K Privately Held
SIC: 2084 Wines

(G-2460)
ALASKAN CAMPERS INC
420 Alaskan Way (98532-2493)
P.O. Box 766, Winlock (98596-0766)
PHONE.................................360 748-6494
Bryan Wheat, *President*
EMP: 6
SQ FT: 10,000
SALES (est): 825K Privately Held
WEB: www.alaskancamper.com
SIC: 3792 Campers, for mounting on trucks

(G-2461)
ALLIED MINERAL PRODUCTS INC
Also Called: Pryor Giggey, The
138 Sears Rd (98532-8719)
PHONE.................................360 748-9295
Allen R Davis, *Engr R&D*
Pat Swanson-Plant, *Branch Mgr*
EMP: 9
SALES (corp-wide): 149.2MM Privately Held
WEB: www.pryorgiggey.com
SIC: 3255 3297 5085 Firebrick, clay; non-clay refractories; refractory material
PA: Allied Mineral Products, Inc.
2700 Scioto Pkwy
Columbus OH 43221
614 876-0244

(G-2462)
ALS WLDG STL FABRICATION INC
222 Downie Rd (98532-8762)
PHONE.................................360 740-8020
Alan Nieman, *Principal*
Nickolas Fagernes, *Manager*
EMP: 19
SALES (est): 1.8MM Privately Held
SIC: 7692 Welding repair

(G-2463)
ALTA FOREST PRODUCTS LLC (HQ)
810 Nw Alta Way (98532-7648)
PHONE.................................360 219-0008
Mike Pedersen, *President*
Peter Strobler, *CFO*
Todd Shipp, *Manager*
◆ EMP: 25
SALES (est): 220MM Privately Held
SIC: 2421 Lumber: rough, sawed or planed

(G-2464)
ALTA FOREST PRODUCTS LLC
810 Nw Liberty Pl (98532)
PHONE.................................360 426-9721
Mike Pedersen, *Branch Mgr*
EMP: 8 Privately Held
SIC: 2499 Fencing, wood
HQ: Alta Forest Products Llc
810 Nw Alta Way
Chehalis WA 98532
360 219-0008

(G-2465)
ALTA FOREST PRODUCTS LLC
714 W Main St Ste A (98532-1506)
PHONE.................................800 599-5596
Jeff Cook, *Branch Mgr*
EMP: 7 Privately Held
SIC: 2499 Fencing, wood
HQ: Alta Forest Products Llc
810 Nw Alta Way
Chehalis WA 98532
360 219-0008

(G-2466)
APEX MOBILE MIX LLC
1310 Nw State Ave (98532-1833)
PHONE.................................360 304-8797
Jerry Nixon, *Principal*
EMP: 4 EST: 2009
SALES (est): 312.5K Privately Held
SIC: 3273 Ready-mixed concrete

(G-2467)
ARISTOCRATIC CABINETS INC
151 Sturdevant Rd (98532-8720)
PHONE.................................360 740-0609
Larry S Walker, *President*
Wanda Walker, *Corp Secy*
EMP: 75 EST: 1975
SQ FT: 38,500
SALES (est): 7.7MM Privately Held
WEB: www.aristocraticcabinets.com
SIC: 2434 2542 Wood kitchen cabinets; cabinets: show, display or storage: except wood

(G-2468)
B & M LOGGING INC
281 Hamilton Rd N (98532-8993)
PHONE.................................360 748-6904
Brandon Smith, *President*
Matthew Smith, *Vice Pres*
EMP: 45
SQ FT: 1,700
SALES (est): 10.2MM Privately Held
SIC: 2411 Logging camps & contractors

(G-2469)
B L LOGGING
132 Newaukum Valley Rd (98532-8810)
PHONE.................................360 748-8248
Joe Balmelli, *Owner*
EMP: 2
SALES (est): 151.7K Privately Held
SIC: 2411 Logging

(G-2470)
BAYCRAFT MARINE SALES INC
554 Sw 18th St (98532-3819)
PHONE.................................253 863-8522
Robert F Pleier, *President*
Bonnie Pleier, *Admin Sec*
EMP: 2
SALES (est): 208K Privately Held
SIC: 3732 Boat building & repairing

(G-2471)
BIRCHFIELD WINERY
242 Kennicott Rd (98532-8609)
PHONE.................................360 978-6176
Gary Fox, *Principal*
EMP: 4
SALES (est): 219.3K Privately Held
SIC: 2084 Wines

(G-2472)
BOOK N BRUSH
518 N Market Blvd (98532-2110)
PHONE.................................360 748-6221
David Hartz, *Owner*
Beverly Hartz, *Owner*
Melissa Maurer, *Manager*
EMP: 4 EST: 1969
SQ FT: 3,000
SALES (est): 239.1K Privately Held
SIC: 5942 5999 2499 College book stores; artists' supplies & materials; picture & mirror frames, wood

(G-2473)
BRADKEN - ATLAS LLC
Bradken's Chehalis Foundry
109 Sears Rd (98532-8719)
PHONE.................................360 748-6645
EMP: 82
SALES (corp-wide): 1B Privately Held
SIC: 3325 Steel Foundry
HQ: Bradken - Atlas, Llc
3021 S Wilkeson St
Tacoma WA 98409
253 475-4600

(G-2474)
BRAUN NORTHWEST INC
150 Northstar Rd (98532-8799)
P.O. Box 1204 (98532-0230)
PHONE.................................800 245-6303
John E Braun, *President*
Jack Braun, *President*
Linda Braun, *Exec VP*
James Braun, *Vice Pres*
Melaina Witchey, *Manager*
EMP: 120
SQ FT: 95,000
SALES (est): 31.7MM Privately Held
WEB: www.braunnw.com
SIC: 3711 7539 5012 Ambulances (motor vehicles), assembly of; automotive repair shops; ambulances

(G-2475)
BUSINESS TO BUSINESS
433 N Market Blvd (98532-2627)
PHONE.................................360 748-6848
Judy Devaul, *Principal*
EMP: 3
SALES (est): 114.3K Privately Held
SIC: 2711 Newspapers

(G-2476)
C W NIELSEN MANUFACTURING
225 Nw Cascade Ave (98532-2115)
P.O. Box 826 (98532-0826)
PHONE.................................360 748-8835
Jeffrey T Nielsen, *President*
Dorothy Nielsen, *Admin Sec*
EMP: 20 EST: 1971
SQ FT: 3,500
SALES (est): 1.8MM Privately Held
WEB: www.cwnielsenmfg.com
SIC: 3999 Badges, metal: policemen, firemen, etc.

(G-2477)
CALLISONS INC
Also Called: I P Callison & Sons
799 N National Ave (98532-2113)
P.O. Box 120 (98532-0120)
PHONE.................................360 748-3316
Lef Toews, *VP Mfg*
Amanda Serl, *Production*
Greg Biza, *Info Tech Dir*
EMP: 30
SALES (corp-wide): 24.6MM Privately Held
WEB: www.ipcallison.com
SIC: 2087 Flavoring extracts & syrups
PA: Callisons, Inc.
2400 Callison Rd Ne
Lacey WA 98516
360 412-3340

(G-2478)
CARDINAL CORP
214 Downie Rd (98532-8762)
PHONE.................................360 242-4400
Carolyn E Kerr, *President*
Robert Fudge, *Purch Agent*
EMP: 3
SALES (est): 246.3K Privately Held
SIC: 3231 Products of purchased glass

(G-2479)
CARDINAL GLASS INDUSTRIES INC
214 Downie Rd (98532-8762)
PHONE.................................360 242-4400
Terry Eisenhower, *Facilities Mgr*
Keith Smotherman, *Purch Mgr*
Mark Reidy, *Manager*
Dennis Wright, *Technical Staff*
EMP: 100
SALES (corp-wide): 1B Privately Held
WEB: www.cardinalcorp.com
SIC: 3211 Flat glass
PA: Cardinal Glass Industries Inc
775 Pririe Ctr Dr Ste 200
Eden Prairie MN 55344
952 229-2600

(G-2480)
CARDINAL TG
214 Downie Rd (98532-8762)
PHONE.................................360 242-4352
EMP: 11
SALES (est): 1.3MM Privately Held
SIC: 3231 Products of purchased glass

(G-2481)
CARROLLS PRINTING INC
1976 S Market Blvd (98532-4124)
PHONE.................................360 345-1399
Linda Hanson, *Principal*
EMP: 2
SQ FT: 2,000
SALES: 100K Privately Held
SIC: 2752 2741 Commercial printing, offset; posters: publishing & printing

(G-2482)
CASCADE HARDWOODS LLC
158 Ribelin Rd (98532-8718)
P.O. Box 269 (98532-0269)
PHONE.................................360 748-3317
Lindsay Crawford,
Scott Janni,
▼ EMP: 130
SQ FT: 1,200
SALES: 53MM Privately Held
WEB: www.chwa.com
SIC: 2421 2426 Lumber: rough, sawed or planed; lumber, hardwood dimension

(G-2483)
CHEHALIS BREWING GROUP LLC
173 Beam Rd (98532-9303)
P.O. Box 976 (98532-0976)
PHONE.................................360 701-7873
Tim Moriarty, *Principal*
EMP: 2
SALES (est): 62.3K Privately Held
SIC: 2082 Malt beverages

Chehalis - Lewis County (G-2484)

(G-2484)
CLAQUATO FARMS INC
272 Highway 603 (98532-9035)
P.O. Box 267 (98532-0267)
PHONE................360 748-6220
Frederick L Young, *President*
Fred L Young Sr, *President*
Fred Young Jr, *Vice Pres*
Kevin L Young, *Treasurer*
June Young, *Admin Sec*
EMP: 5
SALES (est): 451.8K **Privately Held**
SIC: 0241 2411 Milk production; logging

(G-2485)
COUNTY OF LEWIS
Also Called: Department Community Services
351 Nw North St (98532-1926)
PHONE................360 748-9121
Dave Schilperoort, *Branch Mgr*
EMP: 150 **Privately Held**
SIC: 7999 8322 0752 2759 Recreation services; agricultural fair; senior citizens' center or association; shelters, animal; commercial printing
PA: County Of Lewis
351 Nw North St
Chehalis WA 98532
360 740-1192

(G-2486)
COWLITZ VALLEY MACHINE INC
Also Called: Cvm
126 Northstar Rd (98532-8799)
PHONE................360 748-0124
Gary White, *President*
Melissa White, *Vice Pres*
EMP: 4
SQ FT: 4,200
SALES (est): 550K **Privately Held**
SIC: 3599 Machine shop, jobbing & repair

(G-2487)
CRESLINE-NORTHWEST LLC
223 Maurin Rd (98532-8716)
PHONE................360 740-0700
Richard Schroeder, *President*
EMP: 38
SQ FT: 62,352
SALES (corp-wide): 7.2MM **Privately Held**
WEB: www.cresline-northwest.com
SIC: 3084 Plastics pipe
PA: Cresline-Northwest Llc
600 N Cross Pointe Blvd
Evansville IN 47715
812 428-9300

(G-2488)
DEFBOOTY LLC
127 Springbrook Dr (98532-9052)
P.O. Box 854 (98532-0854)
PHONE................800 311-5887
Bret Goss, *President*
EMP: 2
SALES (est): 74.1K **Privately Held**
SIC: 7539 5172 3519 5084 Fuel system repair, motor vehicle; engine fuels & oils; diesel, semi-diesel or duel-fuel engines, including marine; engines & parts, diesel

(G-2489)
DEVAUL PUBLISHING INC
Also Called: Guide & Classified
429 N Market Blvd (98532-2627)
PHONE................360 748-3335
Frank Devaul, *President*
Renae Justice, *Business Mgr*
Judy Devaul, *Vice Pres*
EMP: 30
SALES (est): 6MM **Privately Held**
SIC: 7311 2711 2752 Advertising agencies; newspapers; commercial printing, lithographic

(G-2490)
DWIGHT COMPANY LLC
414 Hewitt Rd (98532-8664)
PHONE................360 262-9844
Jay Dwight, *Mng Member*
Mary Jane Dwight,
EMP: 3
SQ FT: 2,000
SALES: 200K **Privately Held**
WEB: www.weldlab.com
SIC: 8734 7389 7371 7372 Metallurgical testing laboratory; design services; computer software development; application computer software

(G-2491)
DYNO NOBEL INC
1516 Bunker Creek Rd (98532-9703)
PHONE................360 740-0128
Kevin Hartley, *Branch Mgr*
EMP: 6
SQ FT: 3,120 **Privately Held**
SIC: 2892 Explosives
HQ: Dyno Nobel Inc.
2795 E Cottonwood Pkwy # 500
Salt Lake City UT 84121
801 364-4800

(G-2492)
EMU EMPRIUM HLTHY ALTERNATIVES
3512 Jackson Hwy (98532-8715)
PHONE................360 269-3459
Julie F Brown, *Partner*
Signe Backman, *Partner*
EMP: 2
SALES (est): 100K **Privately Held**
WEB: www.emu-emporium.com
SIC: 2844 5699 5999 5421 Face creams or lotions; leather garments; pet supplies; meat markets, including freezer provisioners

(G-2493)
ESCO PACIFIC SIGNS INC
627 Nw Middle St (98532-1714)
PHONE................360 748-6461
Dale Swayze, *President*
Diana Swayze, *Admin Sec*
EMP: 7
SQ FT: 6,000
SALES (est): 872.1K **Privately Held**
WEB: www.esco-pacific.com
SIC: 3993 Neon signs

(G-2494)
ESSEX LABORATORIES LLC
Also Called: Essex Labs
115 Klein Rd (98532-8426)
P.O. Box 1195, Napavine (98565-1195)
PHONE................360 740-1770
Doug Walker, *President*
Robert Frank, *Vice Pres*
Mark Morlan, *CFO*
▲ **EMP:** 8
SALES (est): 1.7MM **Privately Held**
WEB: www.essexlabs.com
SIC: 2899 Essential oils

(G-2495)
EXPERMNTAL ARCFT MET FBRCATION
693 Curtis Hill Rd (98532-9105)
PHONE................360 245-3478
Steve Furjesi, *Owner*
EMP: 3
SQ FT: 2,016
SALES (est): 230K **Privately Held**
WEB: www.eametalfab.com
SIC: 3441 Fabricated structural metal

(G-2496)
FAGERNES CUTTING INC
219 Aust Rd (98532-9248)
PHONE................360 245-3249
Conrad E Fagernes, *President*
EMP: 3
SALES (est): 327K **Privately Held**
SIC: 2411 Logging camps & contractors

(G-2497)
FLEX FUEL
79 Sw 10th St (98532-4704)
PHONE................360 520-9773
Mallory Long, *Principal*
EMP: 2
SALES (est): 74.4K **Privately Held**
SIC: 2869 Fuels

(G-2498)
GARKSE LOGGING & ROAD BLDG LLC
330a Brockway Rd (98532-9691)
PHONE................360 520-2707
Tracy Garske,
EMP: 5
SALES (est): 423K **Privately Held**
SIC: 2411 1611 Logging; highway & street construction

(G-2499)
HADLEY DOOR & TRIM INC
915 Nw State Ave (98532-1736)
PHONE................360 748-0116
Kirk D Hadley, *President*
EMP: 3
SALES: 338.8K **Privately Held**
SIC: 3442 Metal doors, sash & trim

(G-2500)
HAMILTON SPRAY
1316 Nw River St (98532-1321)
PHONE................360 748-9615
Rick Hamilton, *Owner*
EMP: 2
SALES (est): 162.4K **Privately Held**
SIC: 0721 2491 Weed control services after planting; poles & pole crossarms, treated wood

(G-2501)
HARDEL MUTUAL PLYWOOD CORP (PA)
Also Called: Hardel Builders Center
143 Maurin Rd (98532-8716)
PHONE................360 740-0232
Tuan Vo, *President*
Kha Phan, *Vice Pres*
An Lee, *Treasurer*
Long Ha, *Director*
Danny Jamieson, *Admin Sec*
EMP: 190
SQ FT: 2,000
SALES (est): 32.2MM **Privately Held**
WEB: www.hardel.com
SIC: 2435 Hardwood veneer & plywood

(G-2502)
HEYMANN WHINERY ETC
731 Sw 21st St (98532-4213)
PHONE................360 623-1106
Bob Heyman, *Owner*
Flossie Heyman, *Co-Owner*
EMP: 4
SALES (est): 160K **Privately Held**
SIC: 2084 Wines

(G-2503)
HITCHCOCK CUTTING
678 Logan Hill Rd (98532-9511)
PHONE................360 748-7480
Mike Hitchcock, *Owner*
Jane Hitchcock, *Co-Owner*
EMP: 2
SALES: 100K **Privately Held**
SIC: 2411 Timber, cut at logging camp

(G-2504)
IMPERIAL GROUP MFG INC
Also Called: Imperial Fabricating
206 Maurin Rd (98532-8716)
PHONE................360 748-4201
Joel Ball, *Manager*
EMP: 113
SALES (corp-wide): 529.1MM **Privately Held**
SIC: 3713 Truck & bus bodies
PA: Imperial Group Manufacturing, Inc.
4545 Airport Rd
Denton TX 76207
940 565-8505

(G-2505)
INDUSTRIAL FBRICATION TSTG INC
138 Chase Rd (98532-8761)
PHONE................360 345-1400
Kenneth A Lyon, *President*
EMP: 8
SQ FT: 6,000
SALES: 1.4MM **Privately Held**
SIC: 3441 Fabricated structural metal

(G-2506)
JIMBONEYS MALT MILLS & MORE
435 Nw Center St (98532-2041)
PHONE................541 571-1144
Jim Thurman, *Principal*
EMP: 4
SALES (est): 477.4K **Privately Held**
SIC: 3556 Malt mills

(G-2507)
KATIES CANDIES INC (PA)
Also Called: Emerald Sweets
26 Se Spring St (98532-4228)
PHONE................360 748-8967
Kathleen Dillon, *President*
Eileen Dillon, *Manager*
EMP: 15
SALES (est): 1.4MM **Privately Held**
SIC: 2064 5441 Candy & other confectionery products; candy, nut & confectionery stores

(G-2508)
KENNETH WALKER
Also Called: Walker Engine & Machine
249 Chilvers Rd (98532-9695)
PHONE................360 748-7519
Kenneth Walker, *Owner*
Theresa Walker, *Co-Owner*
EMP: 2
SALES (est): 190K **Privately Held**
SIC: 5531 3599 Truck equipment & parts; machine shop, jobbing & repair

(G-2509)
LEWIS CNTY WORK OPPORTUNITIES
122 Sears Rd (98532-8719)
PHONE................360 748-9921
Dennis Brown, *Exec Dir*
EMP: 24
SQ FT: 6,000
SALES: 496.9K **Privately Held**
SIC: 8331 2511 2448 2411 Sheltered workshop; wood household furniture; wood pallets & skids; logging

(G-2510)
LOGGERS WORLD PUBLICATIONS
4206 Jackson Hwy (98532-8425)
P.O. Box 1631 (98532-0400)
PHONE................360 262-3376
Michael Crouse, *Owner*
Susan Crouse, *Partner*
EMP: 5
SQ FT: 5,000
SALES: 640K **Privately Held**
WEB: www.loggersworld.com
SIC: 2721 Magazines: publishing only, not printed on site

(G-2511)
LYDENS SPECIALTY MACHINE LLC
161 Hamilton Rd N (98532-8803)
PHONE................360 345-1010
Lyden Jeffers, *Mng Member*
EMP: 9
SQ FT: 9,350
SALES: 700K **Privately Held**
SIC: 3599 Machine shop, jobbing & repair

(G-2512)
MATCHLOCK CLAMP CO
1423 Highway 603 (98532-8960)
PHONE................360 262-9942
Scott Holloway, *Principal*
EMP: 2
SQ FT: 528
SALES (est): 109.6K **Privately Held**
SIC: 3429 Clamps, metal

(G-2513)
MAYWOOD SHOPS INC
465 Nw Prindle St (98532-2030)
PHONE................360 748-9244
Larry Kerr, *Mfg Mgr*
Carlos Galarza, *Asst Mgr*
EMP: 16
SQ FT: 40,000

GEOGRAPHIC SECTION
Chehalis - Lewis County (G-2543)

SALES (corp-wide): 3.5MM **Privately Held**
WEB: www.maywoodshops.com
SIC: **2511** 2521 2512 Wood household furniture; wood office furniture; upholstered household furniture
PA: Maywood Shops Inc
3199 Arprpt Loop Dr Ste E
Costa Mesa CA 92626
951 278-0300

(G-2514)
METAL MILL CORPORATION
146 Estep Rd (98532-8705)
PHONE..................360 262-9080
Mark Bolender, *President*
EMP: 7
SQ FT: 8,400
SALES (est): 500K **Privately Held**
WEB: www.metalmill.com
SIC: **3444** 5211 5033 Roof deck, sheet metal; siding, sheet metal; roofing material; siding; roofing, asphalt & sheet metal; siding, except wood

(G-2515)
MOERKE FAMILY 3 LLC
493 Cousins Rd (98532-9057)
PHONE..................360 748-8952
Sandra Moerke, *Vice Pres*
Loren Moerke, *Mng Member*
EMP: 7
SALES (est): 475K **Privately Held**
SIC: **2411** Logging

(G-2516)
NATIONAL FROZEN FOODS CORP
Also Called: Processing Plant
436 Nw State Ave (98532-1640)
PHONE..................360 748-9963
Pat Sauter, *Branch Mgr*
Mark Fletcher, *Executive*
EMP: 172
SALES (corp-wide): 228.8MM **Privately Held**
SIC: **2037** 2038 Fruits, quick frozen & cold pack (frozen); vegetables, quick frozen & cold pack, excl. potato products; frozen specialties
PA: National Frozen Foods Corporation
1600 Frview Ave E Ste 200
Seattle WA 98102
206 322-8900

(G-2517)
NORTH FORK TIMBER COMPANY CORP
Also Called: North Fork Timber Shop
258 Hamilton Rd (98532-8824)
P.O. Box 35, Centralia (98531-0035)
PHONE..................360 748-8333
Gary Storm, *Manager*
EMP: 3
SALES (est): 626.1K
SALES (corp-wide): 9.9MM **Privately Held**
SIC: **2411** Logging camps & contractors
PA: North Fork Timber Company Corporation
417 W Main St Ste C
Centralia WA 98531
360 748-8333

(G-2518)
NORTHSIDE METAL CARPORTS LLC
110 Avery Rd E (98532-8405)
PHONE..................360 262-9354
EMP: 4
SALES (est): 336.3K **Privately Held**
SIC: **3448** Prefabricated metal buildings

(G-2519)
PACIFIC NW COOKIE CO LLC
219 Frogner Rd (98532-9142)
PHONE..................360 280-4179
Callie Carpenter, *Mng Member*
EMP: 4
SALES (est): 163.6K **Privately Held**
SIC: **2052** Bakery products, dry

(G-2520)
PACIFICORP
1813 Bishop Rd (98532-8732)
PHONE..................360 827-6467
Mark Miller, *Branch Mgr*
EMP: 5
SALES (corp-wide): 225.3B **Publicly Held**
SIC: **1311** Natural gas production
HQ: Pacificorp
825 Ne Multnomah St # 300
Portland OR 97232
888 221-7070

(G-2521)
PANESKO PUBLISHING
222 Se Spring St (98532-4242)
PHONE..................360 748-0505
John Panesko, *Principal*
EMP: 2
SALES (est): 105.6K **Privately Held**
SIC: **2741** Miscellaneous publishing

(G-2522)
PE ELL PUB
211 W Main St (98532-4819)
PHONE..................360 291-2707
EMP: 3
SALES (est): 110K **Privately Held**
SIC: **2731** Books-Publishing/Printing

(G-2523)
PERDUE FOODS LLC
Also Called: Draper Valley Farms
575 W Main St (98532-1543)
PHONE..................360 748-9466
Chuck Nye, *Manager*
EMP: 8
SQ FT: 1,920
SALES (corp-wide): 6B **Privately Held**
SIC: **2015** Poultry slaughtering & processing
HQ: Perdue Foods Llc
31149 Old Ocean City Rd
Salisbury MD 21804

(G-2524)
PHILLIPS & REICHERT SHAKE MILL
1383 Nw State Ave (98532-1832)
PHONE..................360 978-4392
Del Phillips, *Partner*
EMP: 3 EST: 1976
SALES (est): 221K **Privately Held**
SIC: **2429** 2411 Shakes (hand split shingles); logging

(G-2525)
PINE FILTER LLC
232 Middle Fork Rd (98532-8603)
PHONE..................360 262-9132
Selena Davis, *Principal*
EMP: 2 EST: 2011
SALES (est): 213.1K **Privately Held**
SIC: **3569** Filters

(G-2526)
PRICE CONTAINER AND PACKG CORP
153 Sturdevant Rd (98532-8720)
PHONE..................360 266-5598
EMP: 2
SALES (est): 90.7K **Privately Held**
SIC: **2631** Container, packaging & boxboard

(G-2527)
QUALI CAST FOUNDRY
109 Sears Rd (98532-8719)
PHONE..................360 748-6645
Fax: 360 748-3956
EMP: 2
SALES (est): 169K **Privately Held**
SIC: **3446** Mfg Architectural Metalwork

(G-2528)
QUANEX SCREENS LLC
137 Sears Rd (98532-8719)
PHONE..................360 748-9201
Brian Cummings, *Vice Pres*
Robert Zahn, *Purch Mgr*
EMP: 17 **Publicly Held**
SIC: **3272** Concrete products
HQ: Quanex Screens Llc
1800 West Loop S Ste 1500
Houston TX 77027
713 961-4600

(G-2529)
RAMSEY COMPANY INC
382 Hamilton Rd (98532-8824)
PHONE..................360 748-8918
Larry Ramsey, *President*
EMP: 6
SALES (est): 999K **Privately Held**
WEB: www.ramseycoinc.com
SIC: **3531** Forestry related equipment; scrapers, graders, rollers & similar equipment; concrete grouting equipment

(G-2530)
ROCK SERVICES INC
258 Hamilton Rd (98532-8824)
P.O. Box 35, Centralia (98531-0035)
PHONE..................360 748-8333
Derald Grose, *President*
Lloyd Peterson, *Corp Secy*
Gordon Plgorelc, *Vice Pres*
EMP: 8 EST: 1997
SALES (est): 1.1MM **Privately Held**
WEB: www.rockanddirt.com
SIC: **1429** Igneous rock, crushed & broken-quarrying

(G-2531)
ROCK SERVICES INC
258 Hamilton Rd N (98532-8993)
P.O. Box 35, Centralia (98531-0035)
PHONE..................360 748-8333
Gordon Pogorelc, *President*
Derald Grose, *Vice Pres*
Lloyd Peterson, *Treasurer*
EMP: 8
SQ FT: 1,000
SALES (est): 510.7K **Privately Held**
SIC: **1429** 1611 Boulder, crushed & broken-quarrying; gravel or dirt road construction

(G-2532)
RODDA PAINT CO
920 Nw State Ave (98532-1737)
PHONE..................253 283-6581
EMP: 2
SALES (corp-wide): 237.5MM **Privately Held**
SIC: **2851** Paints & allied products
HQ: Rodda Paint Co.
6107 N Marine Dr Ste 3
Portland OR 97203
503 521-4300

(G-2533)
RWSD LUMBERYARD
1612 Bishop Rd (98532-8733)
PHONE..................503 910-9822
EMP: 2
SALES (est): 115K **Privately Held**
SIC: **2431** Millwork

(G-2534)
S BOONE MECHANICAL CUTTING
425 N Market Blvd (98532-2627)
PHONE..................360 748-4293
Daniel L Sheets, *President*
Jennifer Lee Sheets, *Admin Sec*
EMP: 3
SALES (est): 1MM **Privately Held**
SIC: **2411** Timber, cut at logging camp

(G-2535)
SEAMLESS ATTENUATING TECH
Also Called: Satech
1769 Bishop Rd (98532-8713)
P.O. Box 1264 (98532-0260)
PHONE..................360 748-8711
Bryce Betteridge, *CEO*
Woodford Garrigus, *Vice Pres*
Valerie Sparks, *Controller*
Chad Lindstrom, *VP Mktg*
Ashley Baker, *Manager*
▲ EMP: 20
SQ FT: 12,500
SALES (est): 3.8MM **Privately Held**
WEB: www.satechinc.com
SIC: **3996** Hard surface floor coverings

(G-2536)
SEASOFT SCUBA INC
Also Called: Watermark Scuba
434 Nw Prindle St (98532-2031)
PHONE..................253 939-5510
Bruce Justinen, *President*
Janine Thompson, *Vice Pres*
Brock Justinen, *Vice Pres*
▲ EMP: 5
SALES (est): 412K **Privately Held**
SIC: **3949** Skin diving equipment, scuba type

(G-2537)
STEEL PARTNERS INC
154 Devereese Rd (98532-9048)
PHONE..................360 748-9406
Dennis Gift, *President*
EMP: 10
SQ FT: 5,000
SALES (est): 1.8MM **Privately Held**
SIC: **3645** 3648 Residential lighting fixtures; lighting equipment

(G-2538)
TAYLOR DRILLING INC
4304 Jackson Hwy (98532-8424)
P.O. Box 597 (98532-0597)
PHONE..................360 262-9274
John Taylor, *President*
Joan Borge, *Corp Secy*
Jackie Sumb, *Vice Pres*
EMP: 14 EST: 1949
SQ FT: 800
SALES (est): 1MM **Privately Held**
SIC: **1381** Directional drilling oil & gas wells

(G-2539)
TRIDENT SEAFOODS CORPORATION
112 Sears Rd (98532-8719)
PHONE..................360 740-7816
Chuck Bundrant, *Branch Mgr*
EMP: 261
SALES (corp-wide): 2.3B **Privately Held**
SIC: **2092** Fresh or frozen packaged fish
PA: Trident Seafoods Corporation
5303 Shilshole Ave Nw
Seattle WA 98107
206 783-3818

(G-2540)
ULRICH TRUCKING INCORPORATE
Also Called: Ulrich Peterson Trucking
120 Cabe Rd (98532-9005)
PHONE..................360 748-0026
Albert Paul Ulrich, *President*
EMP: 5
SALES (est): 510K **Privately Held**
SIC: **3531** Crane carriers

(G-2541)
UNDERSHIRT INC
143 Crest Ln (98532-9685)
PHONE..................360 740-8048
EMP: 3 EST: 2015
SALES (est): 169.2K **Privately Held**
SIC: **2759** Screen printing

(G-2542)
WESTLANDS RESOURCES CORP INC (PA)
2451 Ne Kresky Ave Unit J (98532-2436)
P.O. Box 1512 (98532-0430)
PHONE..................360 740-1970
Gary Holgate, *President*
Adam Dean, *Vice Pres*
EMP: 2
SALES: 2MM **Privately Held**
SIC: **2411** 0811 Logging; timber tracts

(G-2543)
WILLAPA HILLS CHEESE LLC
4680 State Route 6 (98532-9321)
P.O. Box 274, Doty (98539-0274)
PHONE..................360 291-3937
Vicki Muething, *Marketing Staff*
Stephen Hueffed,
Marilyn Hueffed,
Amy Turnbull,
EMP: 5
SQ FT: 3,000

Chehalis - Lewis County (G-2544)

SALES (est): 568.6K **Privately Held**
SIC: 2022 Natural cheese

(G-2544)
YOUNG GUN NW
2249 Jackson Hwy (98532-4411)
PHONE 360 996-4275
Brett Daugherty, *Owner*
EMP: 3
SALES (est): 148.6K **Privately Held**
SIC: 3993 Signs & advertising specialties

Chelan
Chelan County

(G-2545)
50ST SEATTLE WINERY LLC
3395 Highway 150 (98816-8023)
PHONE 206 409-0994
EMP: 2 EST: 2015
SALES (est): 93.7K **Privately Held**
SIC: 2084 Mfg Wines/Brandy/Spirits

(G-2546)
ANTOINE CREEK RANCH
75 Antoine Creek Rd (98816-9671)
PHONE 509 682-9025
Lori Ludwig, *Principal*
EMP: 2
SALES (est): 100K **Privately Held**
SIC: 0139 3999 0291 ; ; animal specialty farm, general

(G-2547)
ANTOINE CREEK VINEYARDS LLC
728 Golf Course Dr (98816-9562)
PHONE 509 682-4448
EMP: 2 EST: 2016
SALES (est): 78.4K **Privately Held**
SIC: 2084 Wines

(G-2548)
BLUE WATER INC
Also Called: All Seasons Storage & Rentals
611 E Woodin Ave (98816-9740)
P.O. Box 1717 (98816-1717)
PHONE 509 682-5544
Leo S Miller, *President*
Wade Miller, *Vice Pres*
Polly Miller, *Admin Sec*
EMP: 6
SQ FT: 6,000
SALES (est): 1MM **Privately Held**
SIC: 7359 5984 5082 3546 Equipment rental & leasing; propane gas, bottled; contractors' materials; saws & sawing equipment

(G-2549)
CHELAN CONCRETE INC
Also Called: Godbey Ready Mixed
23300 State Rte 97a (98816)
P.O. Box 966 (98816-0966)
PHONE 509 682-2915
Wanda D Godbey, *President*
Portia Pauli, *Corp Secy*
Stephen Pauli, *Vice Pres*
EMP: 10 EST: 1967
SALES (est): 1.6MM **Privately Held**
SIC: 3273 5211 3272 1442 Ready-mixed concrete; sand & gravel; concrete products; construction sand & gravel

(G-2550)
CHELAN ESTATE WINERY LLC (PA)
755 S Lakeshore Rd (98816-9323)
P.O. Box 2686 (98816-2686)
PHONE 509 682-5454
Bob Broderick, *Mng Member*
Mary Broderick,
EMP: 2
SALES (est): 273.4K **Privately Held**
SIC: 2084 Wines

(G-2551)
CHELAN PRINTING
234 Highway 150 (98816-8003)
P.O. Box 2180 (98816-2180)
PHONE 509 682-5157
Mark Strain, *Owner*
Barbara Strain, *Co-Owner*

EMP: 3
SALES (est): 260.9K **Privately Held**
SIC: 2752 2759 Commercial printing, offset; commercial printing

(G-2552)
CHELAN SAND & GRAVEL LLC
879 Howard Flats Rd (98816-4515)
P.O. Box 1027 (98816-1027)
PHONE 509 682-2569
Camisha Hughbanks, *Principal*
EMP: 6
SALES (est): 450.2K **Privately Held**
SIC: 1442 Construction sand & gravel

(G-2553)
EMPIRE CONTROLS LLC
101 Gala Ave (98816-8068)
P.O. Box 1210 (98816-1210)
PHONE 509 795-5615
Sheila Merchant, *Accounts Mgr*
Carl Lucas, *Manager*
EMP: 8
SALES (est): 607.8K **Privately Held**
SIC: 3823 Computer interface equipment for industrial process control

(G-2554)
FROYO EARTH
246 W Manson Hwy (98816-9583)
PHONE 509 888-7201
Susie Wahlquist, *General Mgr*
EMP: 8
SALES (corp-wide): 330.7K **Privately Held**
SIC: 2026 Yogurt
PA: Froyo Earth
   1415 N Standard St
   Spokane WA 99202
   509 455-8000

(G-2555)
IMS CORPORATION
Also Called: Tribasix Nutrition
104 Jacob Pl (98816-5704)
PHONE 509 687-8116
Kurtis Conrad, *Manager*
EMP: 2
SALES (est): 136.5K **Privately Held**
SIC: 2023 7389 Dietary supplements, dairy & non-dairy based;

(G-2556)
KARMA KANYON LLC
Also Called: Karma Vineyards
1681 S Lakeshore Rd (98816-9162)
PHONE 509 669-5753
EMP: 7
SALES (est): 575.3K **Privately Held**
SIC: 2084 Wines

(G-2557)
LAKE CHELAN TRADING COMPANY
Also Called: Lake Chelan Winery
3519 Highway 150 (98816-8013)
PHONE 509 687-9463
Barbara Kludt, *Owner*
Barbara Cludt, *Owner*
Rachel Evans, *Accountant*
EMP: 10
SALES (est): 1.3MM **Privately Held**
WEB: www.lakechelanwinery.com
SIC: 2084 Wines

(G-2558)
LAM-HAMMER INC
7560 Chelan Ridge Rd (98816-8776)
PHONE 509 687-2421
Jefferson Van Horne, *President*
Karen Rich, *Treasurer*
EMP: 2
SALES (est): 120K **Privately Held**
SIC: 3423 Hammers (hand tools)

(G-2559)
LILLY TIN
229 E Woodin Ave (98816-9196)
PHONE 509 888-8101
Jennifer Dalmira, *Owner*
EMP: 10
SALES (est): 252.5K **Privately Held**
SIC: 5812 3356 Eating places; tin

(G-2560)
NEFARIOUS CELLERS
495 S Lakeshore Rd (98816)
PHONE 509 682-9505
Dean Neff, *Principal*
EMP: 4
SALES (est): 167.9K **Privately Held**
SIC: 2084 Wines

(G-2561)
NORTHWING UNINSURED ULTRALIGHT
Also Called: Northwing Uum
103 Gala Ave (98816-8068)
PHONE 509 682-4359
Kamron Belvins, *President*
▲ EMP: 12
SQ FT: 8,000
SALES (est): 1.5MM **Privately Held**
WEB: www.northwing.com
SIC: 3721 Aircraft

(G-2562)
PRINTING SPECIALTIES PRESS
4560 Navarre Coulee Rd (98816-9393)
PHONE 509 687-9362
Vincent Cannasso, *Owner*
Rita Cannasso, *Co-Owner*
EMP: 2
SQ FT: 400
SALES (est): 95.7K **Privately Held**
SIC: 2752 Commercial printing, offset

(G-2563)
RJS MARINE LLC
1058 E Woodin Ave Bldg A (98816-9787)
P.O. Box 2720 (98816-2720)
PHONE 509 888-4568
Erin Mudd, *Mng Member*
Ronald Mudd,
EMP: 2
SALES: 350K **Privately Held**
SIC: 3732 Motorized boat, building & repairing

(G-2564)
STORMY MOUNTAIN RANCH INC
1325 Navarre Coulee Rd (98816-9222)
P.O. Box 1437 (98816-1437)
PHONE 509 687-3295
Gisela Fuller, *President*
Ray Fuller, *Vice Pres*
EMP: 5
SALES (est): 500K **Privately Held**
WEB: www.stormymtn.com
SIC: 0175 2411 Deciduous tree fruits; logging

(G-2565)
TAL HOLDINGS LLC
Also Called: Marson & Marson Lumber
105 S Bradley St (98816-9184)
P.O. Box 2098 (98816-2098)
PHONE 509 682-1617
Tom Boyd, *General Mgr*
Kenneth G Marson Jr, *Branch Mgr*
EMP: 8
SALES (corp-wide): 16MM **Privately Held**
SIC: 3089 5211 Windows, plastic; lumber products; roofing material
PA: Tal Holdings, Llc
   201 Ne Park Plaza Dr # 240
   Vancouver WA 98684
   541 382-0957

(G-2566)
TNT CRANE & CONSTRUCTION
4580 Navarre Coulee Rd (98816-9393)
PHONE 509 682-7711
Todd Sweeney, *Owner*
EMP: 4
SALES (est): 338.8K **Privately Held**
SIC: 3531 Cranes

(G-2567)
TRIANGLE C FARMS INC
175 Turtteman Rd (98816)
P.O. Box 507 (98816-0507)
PHONE 509 682-2189
David E Chark, *President*
EMP: 3
SALES: 300K **Privately Held**
SIC: 0762 2411 Farm management services; logging

(G-2568)
TUNNEL HILL WINERY
39 Knapps Coulee Rd (98816-9805)
PHONE 509 682-3243
Guy Evans, *Principal*
EMP: 2
SALES (est): 146K **Privately Held**
SIC: 2084 Wines

(G-2569)
VIN DU LAC WINERY
105 Highway 150 (98816-8007)
PHONE 509 682-2882
Larry Lehmbecker, *Owner*
EMP: 3 EST: 2008
SALES (est): 406.6K **Privately Held**
SIC: 5921 2084 Wine; wines

(G-2570)
WEST ISLE AIR INC
Also Called: Chelan Seaplanes
1328 W Woodin Ave (98816-9303)
PHONE 425 235-1996
Clyde Carlson, *President*
EMP: 10
SALES (corp-wide): 2.3MM **Privately Held**
SIC: 3728 Aircraft parts & equipment
PA: West Isle Air Inc
   4000 Airport Rd Ste A
   Anacortes WA 98221
   360 293-4691

Chelan Falls
Chelan County

(G-2571)
COAXSHER INC
50 Chestnut St (98817)
PHONE 509 663-5148
Kyle Cox, *President*
Kevin Cox, *Vice Pres*
Lisa Wareham, *Manager*
EMP: 25
SQ FT: 7,000
SALES: 1.5MM **Privately Held**
SIC: 3949 Camping equipment & supplies

Cheney
Spokane County

(G-2572)
A PRINTING
27711 S Cheney Spangle Rd (99004-9441)
PHONE 509 235-5160
Mike Biallas, *Owner*
EMP: 7
SALES (est): 675.1K **Privately Held**
SIC: 2752 Commercial printing, lithographic

(G-2573)
ACTION MATERIALS INC
10710 S Cheney Spokane Rd (99004-9527)
P.O. Box 19425, Spokane (99219-9425)
PHONE 509 448-9386
Wade Matson, *President*
EMP: 25
SALES (est): 6.9MM **Privately Held**
SIC: 3531 5211 Construction machinery; sand & gravel

(G-2574)
ADM MILLING CO
601 1st St (99004-1653)
PHONE 509 235-6216
Luke Burger, *Manager*
EMP: 15
SALES (corp-wide): 64.3B **Publicly Held**
WEB: www.admmilling.com
SIC: 2041 Grain mills (except rice)
HQ: Adm Milling Co.
   8000 W 110th St Ste 300
   Overland Park KS 66210
   913 491-9400

GEOGRAPHIC SECTION
Chewelah - Stevens County (G-2605)

(G-2575)
AG ENTERPRISE SUPPLY INC
(PA)
17005 W State Route 904 (99004-7983)
P.O. Box 367, Wilbur (99185-0367)
PHONE.................................509 235-2006
Gary R Farrell, *President*
EMP: 17
SQ FT: 12,200
SALES (est): 10.6MM **Privately Held**
WEB: www.agenterprise.com
SIC: 0721 3523 5083 7699 Crop planting & protection; farm machinery & equipment; farm equipment parts & supplies; agricultural equipment repair services

(G-2576)
AMX LLC
Also Called: Autopatch Group
2416 Cheney Spokane Rd (99004-9082)
PHONE.................................509 235-1464
Radmer Duane, *Electrical Engi*
Steven Anderson, *Manager*
EMP: 150 **Privately Held**
WEB: www.amx.com
SIC: 3679 Electronic switches
HQ: Amx, Llc
  3000 Research Dr
  Richardson TX 75082
  469 624-8740

(G-2577)
BLACKSTONE MANUFACTURING INC
530 W 3rd St (99004-1443)
PHONE.................................509 495-1405
Casey Barsness, *CFO*
EMP: 2
SALES (est): 90.4K **Privately Held**
SIC: 3599 Machine shop, jobbing & repair

(G-2578)
C & C ASSOCIATES TECHNOLOGIES
11112 S Spotted Rd (99004-9038)
PHONE.................................509 710-4464
Chuck A Bertone, *Owner*
EMP: 5
SALES (est): 194.4K **Privately Held**
WEB: www.cchomestudy.com
SIC: 2741 Miscellaneous publishing

(G-2579)
CABIN MILL LLC
20321 W Sterling Rd (99004-9744)
PHONE.................................509 235-1808
Kenneth Allestad, *Principal*
EMP: 2
SALES (est): 141.5K **Privately Held**
SIC: 2431 Millwork

(G-2580)
CASCADIA VIDEO PDTS CVP LLC
1321 2nd St (99004-1808)
PHONE.................................509 202-4230
Colin Campbell,
Wade Taylor,
EMP: 5
SALES (est): 1MM **Privately Held**
SIC: 3699 Security control equipment & systems; security devices

(G-2581)
COHERENT RESOURCES INC
12102 S Andrus Rd (99004-9649)
PHONE.................................509 747-3541
Bruce Tinnel, *President*
Tina Taino, *Vice Pres*
EMP: 12
SALES (est): 790K **Privately Held**
SIC: 3599 Custom machinery

(G-2582)
CRYSTALWOLFE BLENDS
1320 3rd St Apt 9 (99004-1879)
PHONE.................................509 217-2132
Rich Baker, *Principal*
EMP: 2
SALES (est): 156.3K **Privately Held**
WEB: www.crystalwolfeblends.net
SIC: 2844 Toilet preparations

(G-2583)
CULTURED ELEMENTS LLC
13120 W Meadow Lake Rd (99004-9034)
PHONE.................................425 442-4595
EMP: 2
SALES (est): 48.8K **Privately Held**
SIC: 0139 3999 2819 ; ; elements

(G-2584)
EASTERN WASHINGTON UNIVERSITY
207 Physcial Educatn Bldg (99004-2476)
PHONE.................................509 359-6047
Erik Rasnussen, *Principal*
EMP: 15
SALES (corp-wide): 148.6MM **Privately Held**
SIC: 8221 3949 University; sporting & athletic goods
PA: Eastern Washington University Inc
  307 Showalter Hall
  Cheney WA 99004
  509 359-6200

(G-2585)
FELONY PRINTS
4708 W Pinto Rd (99004-9510)
PHONE.................................509 443-6702
Crystal Giacomini, *Principal*
EMP: 2
SALES (est): 83.9K **Privately Held**
SIC: 2752 Commercial printing, lithographic

(G-2586)
GILLINGHAM SAND & GRAVEL CO
9701 W Champion Ln (99004-9605)
PHONE.................................509 456-5527
Jack Gillingham, *Principal*
EMP: 6
SALES (est): 470K **Privately Held**
SIC: 1442 Construction sand & gravel

(G-2587)
HUBBARD JOINTERS INCORPORATED
19606 S Cheney Plaza Rd (99004-9717)
PHONE.................................509 235-2148
Rick Hubbard, *President*
Carol Hubbard, *Vice Pres*
EMP: 6
SQ FT: 1,700
SALES: 300K **Privately Held**
WEB: www.hubbardjointers.com
SIC: 3544 Special dies & tools

(G-2588)
JOURNAL-NEWS PUBLISHING CO
Also Called: Cheney Free Press
1616 W 1st St (99004-8800)
P.O. Box 218 (99004-0218)
PHONE.................................509 235-6184
Harlan Schellabarger, *Manager*
EMP: 20
SALES (corp-wide): 3.3MM **Privately Held**
WEB: www.cheneyfreepress.com
SIC: 2711 Commercial printing & newspaper publishing combined
PA: Journal-News Publishing Co Inc
  29 Alder St Sw
  Ephrata WA 98823
  509 754-4636

(G-2589)
NORTHSTAR EQUIPMENT INC
1341 W 1st St (99004-8801)
PHONE.................................509 235-9200
Rhonda M Elliott, *President*
Robert Creighton, *Vice Pres*
Randy Harrison, *Office Mgr*
▲ **EMP:** 12
SQ FT: 10,000
SALES (est): 2.3MM **Privately Held**
WEB: www.northstarequipment.com
SIC: 3559 Pottery making machinery

(G-2590)
NORTHWEST PARK MODELS LLC
18607 W Williams Lake Rd (99004-9778)
PHONE.................................509 235-2522
Brent Oty,
Jerry Plank,
EMP: 2
SALES (est): 124.6K **Privately Held**
SIC: 3999 Models, general, except toy

(G-2591)
R AND M EXTERMINATORS INC
Also Called: Rat Man
24212 S D St (99004-8914)
PHONE.................................509 239-4411
Michael Jackson, *Owner*
Helen Jackson, *Admin Sec*
EMP: 33
SALES (est): 1.3MM **Privately Held**
SIC: 7342 2879 Pest control in structures; agricultural chemicals

(G-2592)
RICHARD WARRINGTON
Also Called: Warrington Studios
3907 W Washington Rd (99004-9540)
PHONE.................................509 448-8713
Richard Warrington, *Owner*
EMP: 3
SALES: 30K **Privately Held**
WEB: www.rwarrington.com
SIC: 3299 7389 Art goods: plaster of paris, papier mache & scagliola; columns, papier mache or plaster of paris;

(G-2593)
SHREDSUPPLY INC
Also Called: US Federal Shredding
406 1st St Ste D (99004-5166)
P.O. Box 30816, Spokane (99223-3013)
PHONE.................................509 235-3800
Rocky Rajewski, *President*
Lex Katich, *Admin Sec*
EMP: 9
SALES (est): 1.2MM **Privately Held**
WEB: www.shredsupply.com
SIC: 3589 Shredders, industrial & commercial

(G-2594)
TURLEY LOG & TIMBERLAND MGT
24406 S Pine Spring Rd (99004-9751)
PHONE.................................509 239-4523
Robert T Turley, *President*
Kelly Turley, *Vice Pres*
EMP: 5
SALES: 800K **Privately Held**
SIC: 2411 Logging camps & contractors

(G-2595)
VERTICAL WORKS LLC
13120 W Meadow Lake Rd (99004-9034)
PHONE.................................509 251-0513
Jeremy F Alvis, *Principal*
EMP: 4
SALES (est): 460.4K **Privately Held**
SIC: 2591 Blinds vertical

(G-2596)
XN TECHNOLOGIES INC
Also Called: Autopatch
2416 Cheney Spokane Rd (99004-9082)
PHONE.................................509 235-2672
Alan Hale, *President*
Dick Welk, *Vice Pres*
Steve Anderson, *CFO*
▲ **EMP:** 100
SQ FT: 50,000
SALES (est): 17.2MM **Privately Held**
WEB: www.autopatch.com
SIC: 3679 Electronic switches

Chewelah
Stevens County

(G-2597)
AGT INC
Smith Rd (99109)
P.O. Box 1106 (99109-1106)
PHONE.................................509 935-6140
Ervin Bezami, *Principal*
EMP: 5
SALES (est): 191K **Privately Held**
SIC: 3999 Slot machines

(G-2598)
AH LOGGING
3244 Smola Rd (99109-9662)
PHONE.................................509 935-4565
Anthony Hansen, *Owner*
Susan Hansen, *Owner*
EMP: 2
SALES (est): 120K **Privately Held**
SIC: 2411 Logging camps & contractors

(G-2599)
BURYA LOGGING AND TRUCKING INC
310 E King Ave (99109-8998)
P.O. Box 1285 (99109-1285)
PHONE.................................509 935-6816
Brett Burya, *President*
Brian Burya, *Corp Secy*
EMP: 14
SALES (est): 1.3MM **Privately Held**
SIC: 2411 Logging camps & contractors

(G-2600)
CHEWELAH INDEPENDENT INC
401 S Park St (99109-9337)
P.O. Box 5 (99109-0005)
PHONE.................................509 935-8422
Nancy C Blake, *President*
Michael Brunson, *Editor*
Pat Johnson, *Mayor*
Mario Martinez, *Mayor*
Jerry Phillips, *Mayor*
EMP: 6
SQ FT: 1,100
SALES (est): 435.3K **Privately Held**
SIC: 2711 Newspapers: publishing only, not printed on site

(G-2601)
CONNELLY COMPANY INC
Also Called: Lodi Water Co
1767 Highway 395 S (99109-9703)
PHONE.................................509 935-6755
James Connelly, *CEO*
Tammy Connely, *Vice Pres*
EMP: 5
SALES (est): 375K **Privately Held**
WEB: www.lodispring.com
SIC: 7389 5963 2086 Water softener service; beverage services, direct sales; bottled water delivery; water, pasteurized: packaged in cans, bottles, etc.

(G-2602)
HANSEN LOGGING LLC
2464 Quarry Browns Lk Rd (99109-9685)
P.O. Box 168 (99109-0168)
PHONE.................................509 935-4515
John N Hansen, *Mng Member*
Sherri L Hansen,
EMP: 50 **EST:** 1974
SQ FT: 1,400
SALES: 5.7MM **Privately Held**
SIC: 2411 4212 1611 Logging camps & contractors; lumber (log) trucking, local; highway & street maintenance

(G-2603)
KLA FUELS REDUCTIONS
206 W Franklin Ave (99109-9244)
PHONE.................................509 680-0110
Kim Allan, *Owner*
EMP: 2
SALES (est): 188.6K **Privately Held**
SIC: 3825 Instruments to measure electricity

(G-2604)
MONUMENTAL CHEWELAH
401 S Park St (99109-9337)
PHONE.................................509 935-6962
EMP: 2 **EST:** 2017
SALES (est): 109K **Privately Held**
SIC: 3272 Monuments & grave markers, except terrazo

(G-2605)
NORTHWEST APPLIED MARINE LLC
3376 Cottonwood Creek Rd (99109-9656)
PHONE.................................509 936-4316
Robert Stevens,
EMP: 4

SALES (est): 310K Privately Held
SIC: 3679 Harness assemblies for electronic use: wire or cable

(G-2606)
RICH RICHMOND LOGGING LLC
1507 N Pinebrook Dr (99109)
P.O. Box 344 (99109-0344)
PHONE..................................509 935-4833
Peggy Richmond, Mng Member
Dale E Richmond II,
EMP: 25
SQ FT: 1,500
SALES (est): 3.6MM Privately Held
SIC: 2411 Logging camps & contractors

(G-2607)
RICHART COMPANY INC
2714e Quarry Browns Lk Rd (99109-9633)
PHONE..................................509 935-8857
Jonathan Richart, President
Dan Richart, Treasurer
EMP: 8
SALES (est): 523.6K Privately Held
SIC: 2411 Timber, cut at logging camp

(G-2608)
SKYLINE LOGGING LLC
1670 W Blue Creek Rd (99109-9706)
PHONE..................................509 935-7200
Deanna Metlow,
EMP: 3
SALES (est): 222.4K Privately Held
SIC: 2411 Logging camps & contractors

(G-2609)
VIRTUAL TIMBERS INC
2126 Old Hwy Nw (99109-9510)
PHONE..................................509 935-4680
Luke McGuire, President
EMP: 3
SQ FT: 11,000
SALES: 286.7K Privately Held
WEB: www.virtualtimbers.com
SIC: 2491 Structural lumber & timber, treated wood

(G-2610)
WHITE STONE CALCIUM CORP
Also Called: White Stone Co
2432 Highway 395 S (99109-6006)
PHONE..................................509 935-0838
James F Bennett, Manager
EMP: 8 Privately Held
SIC: 1429 5032 Dolomitic marble, crushed & broken-quarrying; building stone
PA: White Stone Calcium Corporation
Rittinger Rd
Kettle Falls WA 99141

Chimacum
Jefferson County

(G-2611)
BENCHMARK WOODS
102 Dena Ln (98325-7710)
P.O. Box 344 (98325-0344)
PHONE..................................360 732-0993
William Tolf, Owner
EMP: 2
SALES: 78K Privately Held
SIC: 2431 Woodwork, interior & ornamental

(G-2612)
BREITHAUPT LOGGING INC
425 Whispering Cedars Ln (98325-8754)
PHONE..................................360 732-4225
Phillip Breithaupt, President
Dee Breithaupt, Vice Pres
EMP: 5
SALES (est): 430.3K Privately Held
SIC: 2411 Logging camps & contractors

(G-2613)
PORT TOWNSEND LCL MKTPLC LLC
Also Called: Chimacum Valley Dairy
3383 W Valley Rd (98325-9751)
PHONE..................................360 732-0696
Bruce Gleeman, Principal
Amy Rose Dubin,
EMP: 2
SALES (est): 127.5K Privately Held
SIC: 2022 Natural cheese

Chinook
Pacific County

(G-2614)
BELL BUOY CRAB CO INC
18 Valley St (98614-1343)
P.O. Box 274 (98614-0274)
PHONE..................................360 777-8272
Steve Gray, President
Dwight Eager, Corp Secy
Dean Ellsworth, Vice Pres
Jim Kemmer, Vice Pres
EMP: 40
SQ FT: 4,500
SALES (est): 5.3MM Privately Held
WEB: www.bellbuoyofseaside.com
SIC: 2092 2091 Seafoods, fresh: prepared; canned & cured fish & seafoods

(G-2615)
CHINOOK MARINE REPAIR INC
785 State Route 101 (98614-1338)
P.O. Box 61 (98614-0061)
PHONE..................................360 777-8361
Dale Hughes, President
Kathy Hughes, Corp Secy
EMP: 2
SQ FT: 4,000
SALES (est): 471.7K Privately Held
SIC: 7699 3732 Marine engine repair; boat building & repairing

(G-2616)
EDWING BOAT INC
Corner Of 4th And Hwy 101 (98614)
P.O. Box 273 (98614-0273)
PHONE..................................360 777-8771
Edwin Erola, President
EMP: 3
SQ FT: 8,100
SALES (est): 280K Privately Held
SIC: 3732 Boat building & repairing

(G-2617)
MOBILE MARINE MAINTENANCE
10a Prince St E (98614-1328)
P.O. Box 224 (98614-0224)
PHONE..................................360 777-0001
EMP: 2
SALES (est): 120K Privately Held
SIC: 3519 Internal Combustion Engines, Nec

Clallam Bay
Clallam County

(G-2618)
CORRECTIONAL INDUSTRIES
1830 Eagle Crest Way (98326-9724)
PHONE..................................360 963-3332
Fred Brown, Principal
EMP: 2
SALES (est): 75.1K Privately Held
SIC: 3999 Manufacturing industries

Clarkston
Asotin County

(G-2619)
ANTHONY ROUSSEAU
Also Called: Hot Wire Direct
1712 13th St (99403-3005)
PHONE..................................509 758-8379
Tony Rousseau, Owner
Chris Rousseau, Project Mgr
John Rousseau, Director
▼ EMP: 9
SQ FT: 18,000
SALES (est): 660K Privately Held
WEB: www.hotwiredirect.com
SIC: 3531 Construction machinery

(G-2620)
APEX CURB & TURF LLC
1280 Fair St (99403-2229)
P.O. Box 417, Asotin (99402-0417)
PHONE..................................509 758-1543
John Larson,
Molly Larson,
EMP: 10
SQ FT: 7,000
SALES (est): 1.5MM Privately Held
WEB: www.apexcurbandturf.com
SIC: 3441 8748 Fabricated structural metal; business consulting

(G-2621)
AWARDS ETC
2613 20th St (99403-1531)
PHONE..................................509 758-3537
Pamela Carman, Owner
EMP: 2
SALES (est): 96.7K Privately Held
SIC: 5999 2759 Trophies & plaques; engraving

(G-2622)
BASALT CELLARS
906 Port Dr (99403-1845)
PHONE..................................509 758-6442
Joan Standridge, Principal
EMP: 4
SALES (est): 323.7K Privately Held
SIC: 2084 Wines

(G-2623)
BENNETT LUMBER PRODUCTS INC (PA)
Also Called: Guy Bennett Lumber Co
2050 Wilma Dr (99403-9748)
P.O. Box 670 (99403-0670)
PHONE..................................509 758-5558
Frank Bennett, President
Brett Bennett, President
Janice B Dimke, Corp Secy
EMP: 150
SQ FT: 35,000
SALES (est): 13.3MM Privately Held
SIC: 2421 3731 Lumber: rough, sawed or planed; planing mills; wood chips, produced at mill; sawdust & shavings; barges, building & repairing

(G-2624)
BENNETT LUMBER PRODUCTS INC
1951 Wilma Dr (99403-8714)
PHONE..................................208 875-1321
Janice Dimke, President
EMP: 150
SALES (corp-wide): 13.3MM Privately Held
SIC: 2426 2421 Lumber, hardwood dimension; planing mills
PA: Bennett Lumber Products Inc
2050 Wilma Dr
Clarkston WA 99403
509 758-5558

(G-2625)
BLUE HORIZON CABINET CO LLC
1142 16th Ave Ste B (99403-6000)
PHONE..................................509 254-1430
Tim Rogers, Bd of Directors
EMP: 2 EST: 2016
SALES (est): 139.4K Privately Held
SIC: 2434 Wood kitchen cabinets

(G-2626)
BRUNSWICK CORPORATION
Also Called: Thunder Jet
1401 Bridge St (99403-2333)
P.O. Box 727 (99403-0727)
PHONE..................................509 769-2142
EMP: 85
SALES (corp-wide): 5.1B Publicly Held
SIC: 3732 Boat building & repairing
PA: Brunswick Corporation
26125 N Riverwoods Blvd # 500
Mettawa IL 60045
847 735-4700

(G-2627)
CONTEMPO INC
1390 Fair St (99403-2340)
PHONE..................................509 758-1694
Sandra Tuntland, Principal
EMP: 2
SALES (est): 90.4K Privately Held
SIC: 2521 Wood office furniture

(G-2628)
COUNTY OF ASOTIN
Also Called: Asotin County Jail
838 5th St (99403-2634)
P.O. Box 130, Asotin (99402-0130)
PHONE..................................509 758-1668
Ken Bankrupt, Sheriff
EMP: 15 Privately Held
SIC: 9223 3571 Jail, government; electronic computers
PA: County Of Asotin
135 2nd St
Asotin WA 99402
509 243-2014

(G-2629)
COVER ME SCREEN PRINTING
1801 13th St (99403-3006)
PHONE..................................509 552-1940
EMP: 4
SALES (est): 246.3K Privately Held
SIC: 2752 Commercial printing, offset

(G-2630)
D & L OUTDOOR SPECIALTIES
2480 19th St (99403-1413)
PHONE..................................509 758-5875
Daniel Long, Partner
EMP: 2
SALES (est): 116.7K Privately Held
SIC: 3949 Hunting equipment

(G-2631)
DESIGNCRAFT CABINETS INC
1710 13th St (99403-3005)
P.O. Box 757 (99403-0757)
PHONE..................................509 758-2160
Robert Breier, President
Kim Geist, Corp Secy
EMP: 5 EST: 1974
SQ FT: 5,000
SALES (est): 569.1K Privately Held
SIC: 2434 Wood kitchen cabinets

(G-2632)
DIAMONDCRAFT JEWELS
Also Called: Diamond Craft Jeweler's
1327 Commercial Way (99403)
PHONE..................................509 758-1449
EMP: 2 EST: 1979
SALES: 45K Privately Held
SIC: 5944 3911 Jewelry stores; jewelry, precious stones & precious metals; jewelry, precious metal

(G-2633)
DUCKWORTH BOAT WORKS INC
1061 16th Ave (99403-2808)
P.O. Box 580 (99403-0580)
PHONE..................................509 758-9831
Daniel N Larson, Ch of Bd
James Moore, President
Gerald W Wooley, Vice Pres
EMP: 50
SQ FT: 23,000
SALES: 14.3MM
SALES (corp-wide): 22.2MM Privately Held
WEB: www.duckworthboats.com
SIC: 3732 Motorboats, inboard or outboard: building & repairing
PA: Renaissance Marine Group, Inc.
1061 16th Ave
Clarkston WA 99403
509 758-9189

(G-2634)
EAGLE SCOREBOARD SYSTEMS
3871 Swallows Nest Ct (99403-1741)
PHONE..................................509 751-7228
EMP: 5
SALES (est): 307K Privately Held
SIC: 3993 Signs & advertising specialties

(G-2635)
HIHOSILVER
911 6th St (99403-2003)
PHONE..................................509 758-8419
Dorothy Heywood, Principal
EMP: 4

GEOGRAPHIC SECTION

Cle Elum - Kittitas County (G-2667)

SALES (est): 334.4K **Privately Held**
SIC: 3423 Jewelers' hand tools

(G-2636)
JETCO MCH & FABRICATION LLC
3610 Riverside Dr (99403-9715)
PHONE..................................509 243-8910
Carey Dale, *Opers Mgr*
Tony Maiorana, *Mng Member*
Kim Cole, *Admin Asst*
EMP: 16
SQ FT: 9,500
SALES: 1.5MM **Privately Held**
WEB: www.jetco-usa.com
SIC: 3441 3599 Fabricated structural metal; machine shop, jobbing & repair

(G-2637)
JODEE MAIORANA
Also Called: Sundog Digitizing & Design
704 24th Ave (99403-3240)
PHONE..................................509 758-1035
Jodee Maiorana, *Partner*
Linda Shewey, *Partner*
EMP: 4
SALES: 110K **Privately Held**
SIC: 2395 Embroidery & art needlework

(G-2638)
KZBG BIG COUNTRY 977
2470 Appleside Blvd (99403-1425)
PHONE..................................509 751-0977
Jim Nelly, *Principal*
EMP: 2
SALES (est): 160.6K **Privately Held**
SIC: 3663 Radio broadcasting & communications equipment

(G-2639)
OBENAUFS ONLINE
1440 7th St (99403-2724)
PHONE..................................509 254-3542
Bryan Hossner, *Manager*
EMP: 3 **EST:** 2010
SALES (est): 292.1K **Privately Held**
SIC: 3111 Leather tanning & finishing

(G-2640)
PCS LASER AND MEMORIAL
403 Diagonal St (99403-1938)
PHONE..................................208 746-1033
Al Peterson, *Mng Member*
EMP: 2
SALES (est): 164.2K **Privately Held**
SIC: 2759 7389 Laser printing; engraving service

(G-2641)
POWDER KEG LLC
1329 Setlow Ct (99403-1459)
PHONE..................................509 758-7300
Chris Roberts,
Kathy Roberts,
▲ **EMP:** 5 **EST:** 2008
SQ FT: 3,000
SALES (est): 530.5K **Privately Held**
SIC: 3799 Snowmobiles

(G-2642)
QUALITY CONCRETE PRODUCTS
3050 Wilma Dr (99403-9752)
PHONE..................................509 758-2655
Jim Blinzler, *Owner*
EMP: 6
SQ FT: 1,000
SALES (est): 572.1K **Privately Held**
WEB: www.qualityconcreteproducts.com
SIC: 3272 3271 Precast terrazo or concrete products; concrete block & brick

(G-2643)
QUANTUM
1524 Lydon Ct (99403-2778)
PHONE..................................509 751-6407
Kevin Tinder, *Owner*
EMP: 2
SALES (est): 210.8K **Privately Held**
SIC: 3569 Lubrication equipment, industrial

(G-2644)
RENAISSANCE MARINE GROUP INC (PA)
Also Called: Duckworth
1061 16th Ave (99403-2808)
P.O. Box 580 (99403-0580)
PHONE..................................509 758-9189
Byron Bolton, *CEO*
Daniel Larson, *President*
Bruce Larson, *CFO*
▼ **EMP:** 75
SQ FT: 23,000
SALES (est): 22.2MM **Privately Held**
SIC: 3732 Boats, fiberglass: building & repairing

(G-2645)
RIGGEL PRODUCTIONS LIMITED
417 Morrison St (99403-2234)
PHONE..................................509 758-3209
Harold Riggel, *Owner*
EMP: 2
SALES (est): 118.7K **Privately Held**
SIC: 7372 Prepackaged software

(G-2646)
RIVERPORT BREWING
150 9th St (99403-1856)
PHONE..................................509 758-8889
Karen Eveland, *Principal*
EMP: 7
SALES (est): 571.5K **Privately Held**
SIC: 2082 Beer (alcoholic beverage)

(G-2647)
ROUSSEAU COMPANY
1392 Port Dr (99403-1807)
P.O. Box 635 (99403-0635)
PHONE..................................509 758-3954
Dale Aldridge, *Owner*
▲ **EMP:** 40
SALES (est): 2.5MM **Privately Held**
SIC: 3546 Power-driven handtools

(G-2648)
SEAPORT MACHINE INC
1719 13th St (99403-3004)
P.O. Box 757 (99403-0757)
PHONE..................................509 758-2605
Kim Geist Jr, *President*
Bob Breier, *Corp Secy*
Ashley Morrison, *Office Mgr*
EMP: 14
SQ FT: 8,000
SALES: 1.4MM **Privately Held**
WEB: www.seaportmachine.com
SIC: 3553 3444 Woodworking machinery; sheet metalwork

(G-2649)
STEALTH MARINE
1268 Bridge St (99403-2219)
PHONE..................................509 758-8019
EMP: 2
SALES (est): 129.1K **Privately Held**
SIC: 3731 Shipbuilding & repairing

(G-2650)
SUNRISE W QUARTER HORSES LLC
2240 4th Ave (99403-1326)
PHONE..................................509 780-9426
Patricia M Smith, *Manager*
EMP: 3
SALES (est): 178.6K **Privately Held**
SIC: 3131 Quarters

(G-2651)
THE O-RING STORE LLC
1847 Wilma Dr (99403-9717)
PHONE..................................208 413-6377
Marty Forsed, *President*
Marty Frostad, *President*
EMP: 9
SALES (est): 1.3MM **Privately Held**
SIC: 3053 Gaskets, packing & sealing devices

(G-2652)
TIMBER SAVERS INC
2275 Pitchstone Dr (99403-8733)
PHONE..................................208 799-8748
EMP: 2

SALES (est): 66K **Privately Held**
SIC: 1442 Construction Sand And Gravel, Nsk

(G-2653)
WDK SIGNS
1249 7th St (99403-3319)
PHONE..................................509 758-0483
EMP: 2 **EST:** 2011
SALES (est): 78K **Privately Held**
SIC: 3993 Mfg Signs/Advertising Specialties

(G-2654)
WELDCRAFT MARINE INDUSTRIES
908 4th St (99403)
P.O. Box 580 (99403-0580)
PHONE..................................509 758-9831
Daniel Larson, *Ch of Bd*
Gerald Wooley, *President*
James E Moore, *Director*
EMP: 120
SQ FT: 17,500
SALES (est): 7.9MM
SALES (corp-wide): 22.2MM **Privately Held**
WEB: www.weldcraftmarine.com
SIC: 3732 Motorboats, inboard or outboard: building & repairing
PA: Renaissance Marine Group, Inc.
1061 16th Ave
Clarkston WA 99403
509 758-9189

(G-2655)
WESTECH INDUSTRIES LLC
1487 15th St (99403-2952)
PHONE..................................509 751-0401
Aj J Kasper, *Administration*
EMP: 2 **EST:** 2014
SALES (est): 210.9K **Privately Held**
SIC: 3999 Manufacturing industries

(G-2656)
XTR OFF-ROAD PRODUCTS
2014 Andreasen Dr (99403-1358)
PHONE..................................208 717-1515
Randall Fairbank, *Principal*
EMP: 2
SALES (est): 139.6K **Privately Held**
SIC: 3714 Motor vehicle parts & accessories

Clayton
Stevens County

(G-2657)
DOGFENCE OF NORTH AMERICA
4608 Williams Valley Rd (99110-9740)
PHONE..................................509 991-0385
Dennis Hogan, *Principal*
EMP: 2
SALES (est): 113.6K **Privately Held**
SIC: 3714 Motor vehicle parts & accessories

(G-2658)
HIGH MOUNTAIN TANNERY
4847 Whittier Rd (99110-9797)
PHONE..................................509 435-3478
Josh Judd, *Principal*
EMP: 2 **EST:** 2016
SALES (est): 106.6K **Privately Held**
SIC: 3111 Leather tanning & finishing

(G-2659)
PEETZ ENTERPRISES
4968 Mason Rd (99110-9622)
P.O. Box 852, Deer Park (99006-0852)
PHONE..................................509 276-2608
Robert Peetz, *Owner*
Connie Peetz, *Co-Owner*
EMP: 2
SALES (est): 91K **Privately Held**
SIC: 2759 Commercial printing

(G-2660)
WHITTIER MACHINE & TOOL CO
4632 Oregon Way (99110-9793)
PHONE..................................509 276-7855
Pearl Hopkins Hubbard, *Partner*

Everett Hopkins Hubbard, *Partner*
EMP: 2
SALES: 30K **Privately Held**
SIC: 3599 Machine shop, jobbing & repair

Cle Elum
Kittitas County

(G-2661)
CLASSIC VINYL LLC
50 Pioneer Trl (98922-8523)
PHONE..................................509 656-3011
Colette Rarden,
Daron Rarden,
Justin Rarden,
EMP: 3
SALES (est): 168.8K **Privately Held**
SIC: 3993 5999 Signs & advertising specialties; banners, flags, decals & posters

(G-2662)
COMTRONIC SYSTEMS LLC
110 E 2nd St (98922-1110)
PHONE..................................509 573-4300
Jeffrey A Dantzler, *Mng Member*
Steve Healey, *Manager*
EMP: 18
SQ FT: 12,000
SALES (est): 1.4MM **Privately Held**
WEB: www.comtronic.com
SIC: 7371 7372 Computer software development; prepackaged software

(G-2663)
CORPORATION OF THE PRESIDENT
Also Called: Ensign Ranch
3551 Hundley Rd (98922-9431)
PHONE..................................509 656-2344
Jim Todd, *Branch Mgr*
EMP: 2
SALES (corp-wide): 3.7B **Privately Held**
SIC: 8661 2411 Churches, temples & shrines; logging
PA: Corporation Of The President Of The Church Of Jesus Christ Of Latter-Day Saints
50 E North Temple
Salt Lake City UT 84150
801 240-1000

(G-2664)
COUNTY PUBLIC WORKS
Also Called: Kittitas Public Works
1009 E 3rd St (98922-1311)
PHONE..................................509 674-2502
Charles Reed, *Director*
EMP: 9
SALES (est): 574.8K **Privately Held**
SIC: 3531 Road construction & maintenance machinery

(G-2665)
DOGSTAR CABINETS INC
2040 Ley Rd (98922-9102)
PHONE..................................509 674-4229
John Brown, *President*
EMP: 6 **EST:** 1979
SALES: 450K **Privately Held**
SIC: 2434 1751 2521 Wood kitchen cabinets; cabinet building & installation; wood office furniture

(G-2666)
FOOF LLC
131 Spirea Ct (98922-3201)
PHONE..................................425 260-8897
James Becker,
Lila Becker,
EMP: 2
SALES (est): 62.1K **Privately Held**
SIC: 7372 7371 Application computer software; custom computer programming services

(G-2667)
FUNKY SCREENPRINT
205 E 1st St (98922-1103)
PHONE..................................509 674-5121
Carolyn Cameron, *Owner*
EMP: 2 **EST:** 2007
SALES (est): 139.4K **Privately Held**
SIC: 2759 Screen printing

Cle Elum - Kittitas County (G-2668)

(G-2668)
GARY G GUZZIE INSURANCE
216 N Pennsylvania Ave (98922-1129)
P.O. Box 160 (98922-0160)
PHONE..................................509 674-4433
Ray Rogalski, *Owner*
EMP: 5
SALES (est): 212.9K **Privately Held**
SIC: 6411 2411 Insurance agents; logging

(G-2669)
HALWEST TECHNOLOGIES INC
107 Owens Rd (98922-1318)
P.O. Box 759 (98922-0759)
PHONE..................................509 674-1882
Bob Haley, *President*
Ron Silverson, *Vice Pres*
EMP: 2
SQ FT: 4,000
SALES (est): 250K **Privately Held**
WEB: www.hal-west.com
SIC: 3599 Machine shop, jobbing & repair

(G-2670)
LAVINAL INC
22732 Hwy 97 (98922-8310)
PHONE..................................509 857-2224
Anton Cebe, *President*
EMP: 2
SALES (est): 146.9K **Privately Held**
SIC: 1411 Dimension stone

(G-2671)
LONGVIEW FIBRE PPR & PACKG INC
Also Called: Willis Enterprises
300 S Bullfrog Rd (98922-9688)
PHONE..................................509 674-1791
EMP: 2
SALES (corp-wide): 2.3B **Publicly Held**
SIC: 2421 2611 Sawmill/Planing Mill Pulp Mill
HQ: Longview Fibre Paper And Packaging, Inc.
300 Fibre Way
Longview WA 98632
360 425-1550

(G-2672)
MULE AND ELK BREWING CO LLC
418 E 1st St Ste 7 (98922-1243)
P.O. Box 1149 (98922-2149)
PHONE..................................206 909-9622
Adam Burtt, *Mng Member*
EMP: 7
SALES (est): 108.9K **Privately Held**
SIC: 5813 2082 Tavern (drinking places); bars & lounges; ale (alcoholic beverage)

(G-2673)
NORTHERN KITTITAS CNTY TRIBUNE
807 W Davis St (98922-1027)
PHONE..................................509 674-2511
Casey Clark, *Principal*
EMP: 2
SALES (est): 118K **Privately Held**
SIC: 2759 2711 Publication printing; newspapers

(G-2674)
OWENS MEATS INC
502 E 1st St (98922-1256)
PHONE..................................509 674-2530
Doug Owens, *President*
EMP: 4
SQ FT: 7,500
SALES (est): 454.3K **Privately Held**
WEB: www.ieztc.com
SIC: 2011 5421 Beef products from beef slaughtered on site; meat markets, including freezer provisioners

(G-2675)
PEOH POINT ALPACA FARM
Also Called: Alpaca Country Shop
691 Upper Peoh Point Rd (98922-9058)
PHONE..................................509 674-9120
Cindy Yockey, *Partner*
Linda Lindgreen, *Partner*
EMP: 2
SQ FT: 1,000
SALES (est): 6.6K **Privately Held**
WEB: www.alpacacountryshop.com
SIC: 2231 Animal fiber fabrics, except wool: woven

(G-2676)
PIONEER COFFEE ROASTING CO LLC (PA)
121 N Pennsylvania Ave (98922-1126)
PHONE..................................509 674-4100
Christopher Madsen, *President*
EMP: 7
SQ FT: 2,000
SALES (est): 821.2K **Privately Held**
WEB: www.pioneercoffeeco.com
SIC: 2095 5812 Roasted coffee; eating places

(G-2677)
RJH AEROSPACE NW
220 Thornton View Rd (98922-9047)
PHONE..................................425 394-3775
Roger Hayes, *Principal*
EMP: 2 **EST:** 2016
SALES (est): 125.3K **Privately Held**
SIC: 3721 Aircraft

(G-2678)
RUSTIK KREATIONS
486 Sunshine Way (98922)
P.O. Box 458 (98922-0458)
PHONE..................................509 674-7271
EMP: 2
SALES (est): 142K **Privately Held**
SIC: 2499 Decorative wood & woodwork

(G-2679)
SHOEMAKER MANUFACTURING CO
104 N Montgomery Ave (98922-1298)
PHONE..................................509 674-4414
Jerry Hein, *President*
Patti Hein, *Corp Secy*
Claire Nicholls, *Vice Pres*
Cody Coles, *Opers Staff*
Elaine Jamerson, *Opers Staff*
▲ **EMP:** 100
SQ FT: 40,000
SALES (est): 18.7MM **Privately Held**
WEB: www.shoemakermfg.com
SIC: 3446 3444 Grillwork, ornamental metal; louvers, ventilating; registers (air), metal; sheet metalwork

(G-2680)
TALL TIMBER CONTRACTORING INC
Also Called: Tall Timber Contractors
6740 Westside Rd (98922-9348)
PHONE..................................509 681-1275
Pavel Slach, *President*
EMP: 4
SALES (est): 220K **Privately Held**
SIC: 2411 0783 Logging; ornamental shrub & tree services

(G-2681)
TRIBUNE OFFICE SUPPLY & PRTG
221 N Pennsylvania Ave (98922-1128)
P.O. Box 308 (98922-0308)
PHONE..................................509 674-2511
Jack Stoner, *Principal*
EMP: 2
SALES (est): 134.4K **Privately Held**
SIC: 2752 Commercial printing, offset

(G-2682)
ZACKLIFT INTERNATIONAL INC
1102 E 1st St (98922-9518)
PHONE..................................509 674-4426
Stanley Zackovich, *President*
Susan Zackovich, *Admin Sec*
◆ **EMP:** 13
SQ FT: 30,000
SALES (est): 3.1MM **Privately Held**
WEB: www.zacklift.com
SIC: 3799 Towing bars & systems

Clinton
Island County

(G-2683)
ANIMAL PEOPLE INC
4357 Terra Bella Ln (98236-9424)
P.O. Box 960 (98236-0960)
PHONE..................................360 579-2505
Kim Bartlett, *Publisher*
Meritt Clifton, *Principal*
Merritt Clifton, *Manager*
Patrice Greanville, *Director*
EMP: 2
SALES (est): 190.9K **Privately Held**
SIC: 2711 Newspapers

(G-2684)
BRADLEY HEAVY CONSTRUCTION
6992 Holst Rd (98236-8730)
PHONE..................................360 341-5967
Randy Bradley, *President*
Myrna Bradley, *Corp Secy*
EMP: 2
SALES (est): 157.5K **Privately Held**
SIC: 1794 1629 2411 Excavation work; land clearing contractor; logging

(G-2685)
CADEE DISTILLERY LLC
8912 Hwy 525 (98236)
P.O. Box 857 (98236-0857)
PHONE..................................360 969-6041
EMP: 6
SALES (est): 147K **Privately Held**
SIC: 2085 Bourbon whiskey; gin (alcoholic beverage); rye whiskey; vodka (alcoholic beverage)

(G-2686)
CRAIG YAMAMOTO WOODWORKER LLC
7598 Hamilton Ln (98236-4501)
PHONE..................................206 571-5821
Craig Yamamoto, *Principal*
EMP: 2 **EST:** 2012
SALES (est): 126.2K **Privately Held**
SIC: 2431 Millwork

(G-2687)
CULTUS BAY TILES INC
7712 Hellman Rd (98236-9407)
PHONE..................................360 579-3079
Meredith Macleod, *President*
John Dewit, *Vice Pres*
EMP: 3
SQ FT: 1,000
SALES (est): 98K **Privately Held**
SIC: 3229 3253 Pressed & blown glass; mosaic tile, glazed & unglazed: ceramic

(G-2688)
D POWERS CONSULTING
Also Called: Whidbey Publishing
6513 Spencer Ln (98236-9665)
PHONE..................................360 341-1533
David Powers, *Ch of Bd*
EMP: 3 **EST:** 2011
SALES (est): 172.6K **Privately Held**
SIC: 2731 Books: publishing only

(G-2689)
HEZEL VINEYARD AND CELLARS LLC
6164 Countner Ct (98236-9109)
PHONE..................................360 321-4898
Cheryl Hezel, *Principal*
EMP: 2
SALES (est): 72.3K **Privately Held**
SIC: 2084 Wines

(G-2690)
ISLAND CUSTOM MACHINING
7206 Heggenes Rd (98236-9608)
PHONE..................................360 341-5687
Sally Mulcahy, *Principal*
EMP: 2 **EST:** 2015
SALES (est): 98.6K **Privately Held**
SIC: 3599 Industrial machinery

(G-2691)
ISLAND PROSTHETICS & ORTHOTICS
6921 High Point Dr (98236-8702)
PHONE..................................360 331-7070
Dave Mathew, *President*
Donna Estill, *Vice Pres*
EMP: 3
SALES (est): 259.8K **Privately Held**
WEB: www.island-prosthetics.com
SIC: 3842 Prosthetic appliances

(G-2692)
NORTH STAR TRADING CO LLP
11247 State Route 525 (98236-8646)
P.O. Box 933 (98236-0933)
PHONE..................................360 341-2953
Nick Van Dyke, *Owner*
Patrick L Vandyke, *Partner*
Elizabeth Vandyke, *Partner*
EMP: 3
SQ FT: 1,500
SALES (est): 170K **Privately Held**
WEB: www.sheepskingoods.com
SIC: 3143 3144 5699 Men's footwear, except athletic; women's footwear, except athletic; leather garments

(G-2693)
POSSESSION POINT WOODWORKING
7927 Blakely Ave (98236-9232)
PHONE..................................360 579-2183
Geoffrey Wirth, *Principal*
EMP: 2 **EST:** 2010
SALES (est): 207.3K **Privately Held**
SIC: 2431 Millwork

(G-2694)
RESONANT BOTANICALS LLC
7459 Maxwelton Rd (98236-9212)
PHONE..................................360 969-5065
Michael Yocco, *Principal*
EMP: 4
SALES (est): 301.6K **Privately Held**
SIC: 2844 Toilet preparations

(G-2695)
RETCO INC
Also Called: Bait Boy
6694 S Viewmont Dr (98236)
P.O. Box 590 (98236-0590)
PHONE..................................360 341-1487
Ron Maurer, *President*
Pam Gregory, *Treasurer*
EMP: 3
SQ FT: 1,400
SALES (est): 396.8K **Privately Held**
SIC: 5091 3949 Fishing equipment & supplies; fishing equipment

(G-2696)
SALISH TECHNOLOGY
7524 Maxwelton Rd (98236-9243)
PHONE..................................360 632-4522
EMP: 4
SALES (est): 219.7K **Privately Held**
SIC: 3369 Nonferrous foundries

(G-2697)
SAVAGE SCREEN
11247 State Route 525 (98236-8646)
PHONE..................................360 321-2040
EMP: 2
SALES (est): 92.3K **Privately Held**
SIC: 2759 Screen printing

(G-2698)
SHARON ROSE
Also Called: Whidbey Island Prtg & Off Sup
2838 Sunlight Dr (98236-9005)
PHONE..................................360 341-1898
EMP: 5 **EST:** 2012
SALES: 190K **Privately Held**
SIC: 2752 5943 Advertising posters, lithographed; business form & card printing, lithographic; cards, lithographed; office forms & supplies

(G-2699)
SP INDSTRIAL LUBRICATION A LLC
7190 Terrapin Ln (98236-9721)
PHONE..................................360 579-2646
Steven T Perkins, *Mng Member*

Julie Perkins,
EMP: 6 **EST:** 2011
SALES: 800K **Privately Held**
SIC: 3569 5013 Lubrication equipment, industrial; automotive supplies

(G-2700)
SUNLIGHT COTTAGE INDUSTRIES
2845 Sunlight Dr (98236-9005)
PHONE.................................360 321-8302
EMP: 2
SALES (est): 112.9K **Privately Held**
SIC: 3999 Manufacturing industries

(G-2701)
TREE-TOP BAKING
3650 Orcas Dr (98236-9213)
PHONE.................................360 720-1937
Gerry Betz, *Principal*
EMP: 8
SALES (est): 611.3K **Privately Held**
SIC: 2051 Bread, cake & related products

(G-2702)
WHIDBEY DESIGN WORKS
2715 Evening Glory Ct (98236-9114)
PHONE.................................360 321-8221
Robert Toombs, *Owner*
EMP: 2
SALES: 150K **Privately Held**
SIC: 2511 Wood household furniture

Clyde Hill
King County

(G-2703)
CLYDE HILL PUBLISHING LLC
2011 89th Ave Ne (98004-2413)
PHONE.................................425 454-8220
Gregory Shaw, *Principal*
EMP: 3
SALES (est): 118.2K **Privately Held**
SIC: 2711 Newspapers

(G-2704)
MOON DONKEY PRESS LLC
3015 92nd Pl Ne (98004-1757)
PHONE.................................425 990-8149
Patricia Rovzar, *Principal*
EMP: 2
SALES (est): 101.7K **Privately Held**
SIC: 2741 Miscellaneous publishing

Colbert
Spokane County

(G-2705)
5 SHOT LEATHER
18018 N Lidgerwood Ct (99005-9139)
PHONE.................................509 844-3969
John Ralston, *Principal*
EMP: 2
SALES (est): 137.1K **Privately Held**
SIC: 3199 Leather goods

(G-2706)
COBRA KEY SYSTEMS LLC
21912 N Saddle Mtn Ln (99005-9048)
P.O. Box 28971, Spokane (99228-8971)
PHONE.................................509 466-1918
Robert A Brown,
EMP: 7
SALES (est): 742.1K **Privately Held**
SIC: 3429 Locks or lock sets; security cable locking system

(G-2707)
HARVEST HOUSE
9919 E Greenbluff Rd (99005-9541)
PHONE.................................509 238-6970
Gordon Beck, *President*
Marilyn Beck, *Admin Sec*
EMP: 5
SALES: 300K **Privately Held**
SIC: 2026 Fluid milk

(G-2708)
HUGHES CUSTOM WOODWORKING INC
Also Called: Military Displays Online
1705 W Monroe Rd (99005-5106)
PHONE.................................509 921-8090
Larry Huges, *President*
Devin Hughes, *Treasurer*
EMP: 4
SALES: 300K **Privately Held**
SIC: 2499 Kitchen, bathroom & household ware: wood; decorative wood & woodwork

(G-2709)
J D PRECISION MFG INC
10524 E Ruff Ln (99005)
P.O. Box 523 (99005-0523)
PHONE.................................509 496-2607
John Darby, *President*
EMP: 7
SALES: 250K **Privately Held**
SIC: 3999 Barber & beauty shop equipment

(G-2710)
KINGDOM LIFE PUBLISHING
21816 Buckeye Lake Ln (99005-9147)
PHONE.................................509 465-0672
R Scott Rodin, *President*
EMP: 2
SALES (est): 108.5K **Privately Held**
SIC: 2741 Miscellaneous publishing

(G-2711)
MARIAS HAWAIIAN SNOW
507 E Cooper Ln (99005-9302)
PHONE.................................509 217-1612
Maria Crabb, *Principal*
EMP: 4 **EST:** 2001
SALES (est): 189.3K **Privately Held**
SIC: 2024 Ice cream, bulk

(G-2712)
TOWNSHEND CELLAR
8022 E Greenbluff Rd (99005-9561)
P.O. Box 4067, Spokane (99220-0067)
PHONE.................................509 481-5465
EMP: 2
SALES (est): 78.4K **Privately Held**
SIC: 2084 Wines, brandy & brandy spirits

Colfax
Whitman County

(G-2713)
DAILY BULLETIN
211 N Main St (99111-1816)
P.O. Box 770 (99111-0770)
PHONE.................................509 397-3332
Gordon Forgey, *Principal*
EMP: 9
SALES (est): 348.8K **Privately Held**
SIC: 2711 Newspapers, publishing & printing

(G-2714)
GREEN HOLLOW FARM INC
361 Roberts Rd (99111-8659)
PHONE.................................509 397-3569
Vic Roberts, *President*
Julie Roberts, *Treasurer*
EMP: 2
SALES (est): 125.4K **Privately Held**
SIC: 3523 Driers (farm): grain, hay & seed

(G-2715)
KROLL MACHINE & SUPPLY INC
Also Called: Federated Auto Parts
602 N Main St (99111-2119)
PHONE.................................509 397-4666
Michael J Kroll, *President*
James E Kroll, *Corp Secy*
EMP: 3
SQ FT: 6,730
SALES (est): 300K **Privately Held**
SIC: 5531 3599 5013 Automotive parts; machine shop, jobbing & repair; automotive engines & engine parts

(G-2716)
MCGREGOR COMPANY
Also Called: Equipment Division
28232 Endicott Rd (99111-6007)
P.O. Box 740 (99111-0740)
PHONE.................................509 397-4360
Neil Tevlin, *Branch Mgr*
EMP: 15
SALES (corp-wide): 220.7MM **Privately Held**
WEB: www.mcgregoreq.com
SIC: 5261 5084 3523 2874 Fertilizer; industrial machinery & equipment; farm machinery & equipment; phosphatic fertilizers
PA: The Mcgregor Company
401 Colfax Airport Rd
Colfax WA 99111
509 397-4355

(G-2717)
MEDICAL MICRO MACHINING INC
1115 N Clay St (99111-2149)
PHONE.................................509 397-2276
Robin C Whitmore, *President*
Katherine Whitmore, *Vice Pres*
EMP: 3
SQ FT: 4,500
SALES (est): 440K **Privately Held**
SIC: 3599 Machine shop, jobbing & repair

(G-2718)
NE WELDING AND FABRICATION
127752 State Route 26 (99111-9690)
PHONE.................................509 549-3982
Norm Pauls, *Partner*
Ed Broecker, *Partner*
EMP: 3
SALES: 200K **Privately Held**
SIC: 7692 Welding repair

(G-2719)
PALOUSE GUTTERS AND CNSTR LLC
1009 S Lake St (99111-1523)
PHONE.................................509 397-0404
Tony Allison, *Mng Member*
Kerensa Allison,
EMP: 2
SALES (est): 104K **Privately Held**
SIC: 3444 7389 Gutters, sheet metal;

(G-2720)
PALOUSE RIVER QUILTS
101 S Main St (99111-1803)
PHONE.................................509 397-2278
Margo Balzarini, *President*
EMP: 2
SALES (est): 152.5K **Privately Held**
SIC: 2395 Quilting & quilting supplies

(G-2721)
TODD IMESON
207 E Thorn St (99111-1745)
PHONE.................................509 397-6570
Todd Imeson, *Principal*
EMP: 5 **EST:** 2010
SALES (est): 293.1K **Privately Held**
SIC: 2041 Flour & other grain mill products

(G-2722)
VINCENT R TAYLOR
Also Called: Colfax Meat Packing Plant
100 E Upton St (99111)
PHONE.................................509 397-3305
Vincent R Taylor, *Owner*
EMP: 3 **EST:** 1971
SALES (est): 167.8K **Privately Held**
SIC: 2011 Meat packing plants

College Place
Walla Walla County

(G-2723)
COLUMBIA LASER CENTERS INC
108 Sw 9th St (99324-1535)
PHONE.................................509 529-7711
Ruth B Rittenbach, *Principal*
EMP: 3
SALES (est): 199.9K **Privately Held**
SIC: 3845 Laser systems & equipment, medical

(G-2724)
GRAPHIC APPAREL
860 Ne Rose St (99324-2001)
PHONE.................................509 525-7630
Lynette Gordon, *Owner*
David Gordon, *Co-Owner*
EMP: 7
SALES (est): 300K **Privately Held**
WEB: www.graphicapparel.biz
SIC: 2395 Embroidery & art needlework

(G-2725)
HORIZON IMAGING LLC
29 Sw 9th St (99324-1532)
PHONE.................................509 525-2860
Steve Wagner,
EMP: 3 **EST:** 1998
SALES (est): 177.5K **Privately Held**
WEB: www.horizonimaging.com
SIC: 7372 Publishers' computer software

(G-2726)
RACK & MAINTENANCE SOURCE LLC
400 W Whitman Dr (99324-2052)
PHONE.................................509 525-7006
Robert Smith,
EMP: 5
SALES (est): 912.4K **Privately Held**
SIC: 5021 2542 Racks; mail racks & lock boxes, postal service: except wood

(G-2727)
SCHREINER CONSTRUCTION
512 Se 6th St (99324-1351)
PHONE.................................509 525-6205
EMP: 2 **EST:** 1998
SALES (est): 110K **Privately Held**
SIC: 2514 Mfg Metal Household Furniture

(G-2728)
SOMETHING FOR EVERYBODY
1212 Se Newgate Dr (99324-1879)
PHONE.................................541 805-8495
Carolyn S Reagan, *President*
EMP: 2 **EST:** 2017
SALES (est): 147.7K **Privately Held**
SIC: 2841 5122 Soap & other detergents; cosmetics

(G-2729)
TERRY AND KATHY LONEY
704 Se Quail Run (99324-2602)
PHONE.................................509 375-4005
Terry Loney, *Principal*
EMP: 2
SALES (est): 79.5K **Privately Held**
SIC: 2721 Periodicals

(G-2730)
WALLA WALLA VALLEY MOBILE LLC
349 Ne Myra Rd (99324-9701)
PHONE.................................509 386-8549
EMP: 2
SALES (est): 128.6K **Privately Held**
SIC: 2899

(G-2731)
WEST COAST GEMSTONES INC
Also Called: West Coast Mining
360 Sw 12th St (99324-1409)
P.O. Box 133 (99324-0133)
PHONE.................................509 522-4851
Dale Huett, *President*
Susan Huett, *Vice Pres*
EMP: 2
SALES (est): 300.2K **Privately Held**
WEB: www.wcmining.com
SIC: 1499 5944 Gem stones (natural) mining; agate mining; jewelry stores

Colton
Whitman County

(G-2732)
BADGER BRACES LLC
502 Steptoe St (99113)
P.O. Box 28 (99113-0028)
PHONE 509 229-3635
Ed Robertson, *Mng Member*
EMP: 3
SALES (est): 391.3K **Privately Held**
SIC: 3842 Surgical appliances & supplies

(G-2733)
PROFESSIONAL MENTORS & PRO
1202 Lincoln St (99113-9740)
PHONE 832 216-9134
EMP: 2
SALES (est): 90K **Privately Held**
SIC: 3674 Mfg Semiconductors/Related Devices

(G-2734)
PROFESSNL MNTRS & PRO LIFE SKL
Also Called: Riser Products
1202 Lincoln St (99113-9740)
PHONE 832 216-9134
Darryl Riser,
▲ EMP: 2
SALES (est): 252.1K **Privately Held**
SIC: 3674 Semiconductors & related devices

Colville
Stevens County

(G-2735)
ALADDIN VALLEY MODULAR MFG
2211 Gold Field Mine Rd (99114-9157)
PHONE 509 732-6159
James M Quilter, *President*
EMP: 5
SALES (est): 440K **Privately Held**
SIC: 2451 Mobile buildings: for commercial use

(G-2736)
ANDREW A KROISS
Also Called: A Kroiss Logging & Farming
287 Mantz Rickey Rd (99114-9556)
PHONE 509 684-4929
EMP: 6 EST: 2001
SALES (est): 510K **Privately Held**
SIC: 2411 0191 Logging & Farming

(G-2737)
ANDREW RUSSELL POND
285 Corbett Creek Rd (99114-9690)
PHONE 509 690-8509
Andrew Pond, *Principal*
EMP: 5
SALES (est): 300.6K **Privately Held**
SIC: 2411 Logging

(G-2738)
BGI TOOLING COMPANY
806 Gillette Rd B (99114-9647)
PHONE 509 684-5556
Brian Gogarty, *President*
EMP: 2
SALES (est): 336.3K **Privately Held**
SIC: 3599 Machine shop, jobbing & repair

(G-2739)
BIO-TOPE RESEARCH INC (PA)
512 Williams Lake Rd (99114-8614)
PHONE 509 684-1512
Ilse Myren, *President*
Marlene Vyrostek, *Vice Pres*
EMP: 2
SQ FT: 2,000
SALES: 250K **Privately Held**
SIC: 2048 8731 5149 Fish food; commercial physical research; pet foods

(G-2740)
BIO-TOPE RESEARCH INC
512 Williams Lake Rd (99114-8614)
PHONE 509 684-1154
Ilse Myren, *Manager*
EMP: 2
SALES (corp-wide): 250K **Privately Held**
SIC: 2048 Fish food
PA: Bio-Tope Research Inc
512 Williams Lake Rd
Colville WA 99114
509 684-1512

(G-2741)
BOISE INC
634 Highway 395 S (99114-8621)
PHONE 509 685-9825
EMP: 3
SALES (est): 280.4K **Privately Held**
SIC: 2631 Paperboard mills

(G-2742)
C&T NORTHWEST SERVICES
1159 Orin Rice Rd (99114-9530)
PHONE 509 680-4890
Trina Foust, *Owner*
EMP: 3
SALES (est): 105.6K **Privately Held**
SIC: 7349 0782 7692 Janitorial service, contract basis; lawn care services; welding repair

(G-2743)
CLARKS ALL-SPORTS INC
557 S Main St (99114-2591)
PHONE 509 684-5069
Raymond G Clark, *President*
Julie Clark, *Corp Secy*
EMP: 23
SQ FT: 1,250
SALES (est): 3.2MM **Privately Held**
WEB: www.clarksallsports.com
SIC: 5699 5941 2395 Western apparel; sporting goods & bicycle shops; art goods for embroidering, stamped: purchased materials

(G-2744)
COLUMBIA CEDAR INC
634 Highway 395 S (99114-8621)
PHONE 509 738-4711
Ralph Schmidt, *President*
EMP: 3
SALES (corp-wide): 15.7MM **Privately Held**
SIC: 2421 Sawmills & planing mills, general
PA: Columbia Cedar, Inc.
24419 Highway 395 N
Kettle Falls WA 99141
509 738-4711

(G-2745)
COLVILLE PRINTING LLC
511 S Main St (99114-2503)
P.O. Box 88 (99114-0088)
PHONE 509 684-5869
Holly Berkeley, *Mng Member*
EMP: 3
SALES: 350K **Privately Held**
SIC: 2759 Commercial printing

(G-2746)
COLVILLE SIGN CO
153 N Wynne St (99114-2311)
PHONE 509 685-2185
Lynn Oconner, *Owner*
EMP: 3
SALES: 160K **Privately Held**
WEB: www.colvillesign.com
SIC: 3993 Signs, not made in custom sign painting shops

(G-2747)
COLVILLE VALLEY CONCRETE CORP
1175 E 3rd Ave (99114-9462)
P.O. Box 343 (99114-0343)
PHONE 509 684-2534
Steven Connelly, *President*
Geoff Mc Niven, *Treasurer*
EMP: 24
SQ FT: 10,000
SALES (est): 3.5MM **Privately Held**
SIC: 3273 5032 Ready-mixed concrete; sand, construction; gravel

(G-2748)
COLVILLE WDWKG & STAINED GL
115 S Main St (99114-2405)
PHONE 509 684-7670
Baarbara Harmon, *Owner*
EMP: 2
SALES (est): 195.4K **Privately Held**
SIC: 2431 Millwork

(G-2749)
D & E ENTERPRISES
938 Kitt Narcisse Rd (99114-9710)
P.O. Box 643 (99114-0643)
PHONE 509 684-6618
Evelyn Ann Bell, *Owner*
Dan Bell, *Co-Owner*
EMP: 2
SALES (est): 173.8K **Privately Held**
SIC: 8711 2731 7338 Electrical or electronic engineering; books: publishing only; secretarial & typing service

(G-2750)
DALE BUTLER S FURNITURE
2829 Aladdin Rd (99114-9104)
PHONE 509 732-4381
Dale Butler, *Principal*
EMP: 3
SALES (est): 267.2K **Privately Held**
SIC: 2499 Furniture inlays (veneers)

(G-2751)
DONNER LOGGING LLC
740d Arden Butte Rd (99114-8761)
PHONE 509 675-2717
Douglas Drake, *Principal*
EMP: 3 EST: 2008
SALES (est): 170.8K **Privately Held**
SIC: 2411 Logging camps & contractors

(G-2752)
FIR LINE TRANS & BRAKE
374 Gold Creek Loop Rd (99114-9671)
PHONE 509 684-5484
Paul Staeheli, *Principal*
EMP: 2
SALES (est): 53K **Privately Held**
SIC: 2842 Automobile polish

(G-2753)
FOUST FABRICATION CO
1159 Orin Rice Rd (99114-9530)
PHONE 509 684-3754
Trina Michelle Foust, *Administration*
EMP: 3
SALES (est): 373.6K **Privately Held**
SIC: 3599 Industrial machinery

(G-2754)
HANDMAIDEN BEAD & JWLY SHOPPE
162 S Main St (99114-2406)
PHONE 509 680-5785
Theresa Anderson, *Owner*
EMP: 2
SQ FT: 1,650
SALES (est): 55.4K **Privately Held**
SIC: 5944 3915 7631 Jewelry stores; jewelers' materials & lapidary work; jewelry repair services

(G-2755)
HEARTH & HOME TECHNOLOGIES LLC
1445 North Highway (99114-2008)
PHONE 509 684-3745
Jeni Forman, *Vice Pres*
Aaron Leishman, *Controller*
Shannon Tucker, *Human Res Mgr*
Michael Canciglia, *Marketing Staff*
Jason Olmstead, *Manager*
EMP: 275
SALES (corp-wide): 2.2B **Publicly Held**
WEB: www.heatnglo.com
SIC: 3433 Heating equipment, except electric
HQ: Hearth & Home Technologies, Llc
7571 215th St W
Lakeville MN 55044

(G-2756)
HEWES MARINE CO INC
Also Called: Hewescraft
2600 North Highway (99114-8554)
PHONE 509 684-5235
David Ralph Hewes, *President*
Bill Hewes, *Corp Secy*
Launa Hewes, *Vice Pres*
William Edward Hewes, *Admin Sec*
EMP: 92
SQ FT: 34,000
SALES: 27.6MM **Privately Held**
WEB: www.hewescraft.com
SIC: 3732 Motorboats, inboard or outboard: building & repairing

(G-2757)
HIGHWATER FILTERS
325 S Alder St (99114-3223)
PHONE 509 685-0933
Hilary OHM, *Principal*
EMP: 2
SALES (est): 233.1K **Privately Held**
SIC: 3569 Filters

(G-2758)
JEFFREY MARK BASHE
Also Called: Seymour Chnnel Stllite Systems
156 N Main St (99114-2306)
PHONE 509 684-6925
Jeffrey Bashe, *Owner*
EMP: 5
SALES (est): 516.5K **Privately Held**
SIC: 3663 5731 Satellites, communications; radio, television & electronic stores; antennas; antennas, satellite dish

(G-2759)
JERRY BROWN
181 E 1st Ave (99114-2801)
P.O. Box 326 (99114-0326)
PHONE 509 684-3736
Jerry Brown, *Principal*
EMP: 2
SALES (est): 153.3K **Privately Held**
SIC: 3843 Enamels, dentists'

(G-2760)
JONES LOGGING LLC
2117a Lotze Creek Rd (99114-8637)
PHONE 509 732-4511
Jason Jones, *Principal*
EMP: 3
SALES (est): 103.6K **Privately Held**
SIC: 2411 Logging

(G-2761)
K AND M FUEL LLC
370 Knapp Rd (99114-9238)
PHONE 509 675-3005
Chad Beardsley, *Bd of Directors*
EMP: 6
SALES (est): 783.9K **Privately Held**
SIC: 2869 Fuels

(G-2762)
KEITH AUSTIN LOGGING
1622 Clugston Onion Crk (99114-8652)
PHONE 509 684-8869
EMP: 2 EST: 2010
SALES (est): 97K **Privately Held**
SIC: 2411 Logging

(G-2763)
KUBESHS SITE MIXED CON INC
476 Williams Lake Rd (99114-8631)
PHONE 509 684-1381
Barbara Kubesh, *President*
Theodore Kubesh, *Vice Pres*
EMP: 5 EST: 2000
SALES (est): 580K **Privately Held**
SIC: 3273 Ready-mixed concrete

(G-2764)
MAGNA VIS GRAPHIC IMPRESSIONS
1355 Kegel Way (99114-9044)
PHONE 509 684-5659
Erne Kegel, *Owner*
EMP: 2
SALES (est): 130.5K **Privately Held**
WEB: www.magna-vis.com
SIC: 2396 7336 Screen printing on fabric articles; commercial art & graphic design

▲ = Import ▼ = Export
◆ = Import/Export

GEOGRAPHIC SECTION

(G-2765)
MASTER PRINTING INC
511 S Main St (99114-2503)
P.O. Box 88 (99114-0088)
PHONE...................................509 684-5869
Bradley Graham, *President*
EMP: 4
SQ FT: 2,400
SALES (est): 440K **Privately Held**
SIC: 7334 2752 2721 Photocopying & duplicating services; commercial printing, offset; periodicals

(G-2766)
MONTGOMERY LAW FIRM
Also Called: Montgomery, Chris
287 E Astor Ave (99114-2815)
P.O. Box 269 (99114-0269)
PHONE...................................509 684-2519
Chris A Montgomery, *Owner*
EMP: 4
SQ FT: 2,200
SALES (est): 481.5K **Privately Held**
SIC: 8111 2411 General practice attorney, lawyer; logging

(G-2767)
OLD DOMINION WOODWORKS
760 Hardenbrook Rd (99114-9771)
PHONE...................................509 684-7931
EMP: 2
SALES (est): 197.7K **Privately Held**
SIC: 2431 Millwork

(G-2768)
PETES LOGGING LLC
344 E Birch Ave Ste 102 (99114-2761)
P.O. Box 1044 (99114-5012)
PHONE...................................509 684-6231
Peter McNinch,
EMP: 3 **EST:** 2014
SALES (est): 188.2K **Privately Held**
SIC: 2411 Logging

(G-2769)
POST ALL EXPRESSIONS
Also Called: Don's Printery
166 Buena Vista Dr B (99114-9601)
PHONE...................................509 684-3723
Michael Nichols, *Owner*
EMP: 2
SQ FT: 1,200
SALES: 250K **Privately Held**
SIC: 7389 3444 Mailbox rental & related service; mail (post office) collection or storage boxes, sheet metal

(G-2770)
QUAIL MEADOW CREATIONS
615 Rocky Lake Rd (99114-9775)
PHONE...................................509 685-1429
Tom Shuhda, *Principal*
EMP: 2
SALES (est): 100.5K **Privately Held**
SIC: 2841 Soap & other detergents

(G-2771)
RAIDER BOATS INC
367 Old Dominion Rd (99114-9241)
PHONE...................................509 684-8348
George M Melby, *President*
Ryan Warner, *General Mgr*
Vicki Melby, *Vice Pres*
EMP: 16
SQ FT: 18,500
SALES (est): 3.5MM **Privately Held**
WEB: www.raiderboats.com
SIC: 3732 Boat building & repairing

(G-2772)
RAYS CUSTOM CUTTING
Also Called: Panorama Ice Company
1043 Miller Rd (99114-8723)
PHONE...................................509 684-5544
EMP: 2
SQ FT: 160
SALES: 80K **Privately Held**
SIC: 2011 5199 Meat Packing Plant

(G-2773)
RICHARD EVANS
Also Called: Evans & Assoc
565 Knapp Rd (99114-9258)
P.O. Box 254 (99114-0254)
PHONE...................................509 684-1079
Richard Evans, *Owner*
EMP: 2
SALES (est): 224.7K **Privately Held**
SIC: 3829 Polygraph devices

(G-2774)
SACKMAN ENTERPRISES
719 Old Arden Hwy (99114-9762)
PHONE...................................509 684-5547
Gene Sackman, *Owner*
EMP: 3
SALES (est): 252.2K **Privately Held**
SIC: 2499 Wood products

(G-2775)
STATESMAN-EXAMINER INC (PA)
Also Called: Tri County Tribune
220 S Main St (99114-2408)
P.O. Box 271 (99114-0271)
PHONE...................................509 684-4567
Rolan Mc Bride, *President*
Shannon Chapman, *Advt Staff*
McIlroy Chris, *Advt Staff*
EMP: 25
SQ FT: 4,500
SALES (est): 2.4MM **Privately Held**
SIC: 2711 2752 2731 Newspapers: publishing only, not printed on site; commercial printing, lithographic; book publishing

(G-2776)
STEWART LOGGING INC
177 Dubois Rd (99114-9255)
PHONE...................................509 684-6746
John Stewart, *President*
Gladys Stewart, *Corp Secy*
EMP: 3
SALES: 450K **Privately Held**
SIC: 2411 Logging camps & contractors

(G-2777)
T&B LOGGING INC
563 Finley Gulch Rd (99114-9149)
PHONE...................................509 684-4316
Lauren Tanner, *President*
Sandra Tanner, *Admin Sec*
EMP: 2
SALES: 274K **Privately Held**
SIC: 2411 Logging camps & contractors

(G-2778)
UNITED STATES BAKERY
Also Called: Franz Bakery
183 Buena Vista Dr (99114-9692)
PHONE...................................509 684-6976
Carl Todd, *Principal*
EMP: 3
SALES (corp-wide): 541.5MM **Privately Held**
SIC: 2051 4225 Bakery: wholesale or wholesale/retail combined; general warehousing
PA: United States Bakery
315 Ne 10th Ave
Portland OR 97232
503 232-2191

(G-2779)
VAAGEN BROS LUMBER INC (PA)
565 W 5th Ave (99114-2132)
PHONE...................................509 684-5071
Duanne R Vaagen, *President*
Duane Vaagen, *President*
Russell Vaagen, *President*
Josh Anderson, *Vice Pres*
Herb Janhson, *Vice Pres*
EMP: 130 **EST:** 1952
SQ FT: 4,400
SALES (est): 77.3MM **Privately Held**
SIC: 2421 Lumber: rough, sawed or planed

(G-2780)
VAAGEN TIMBERS LLC
1245 North Highway (99114-2005)
PHONE...................................509 684-5071
Alan Aldous, *CFO*
Russell Vaagen, *Administration*
EMP: 2
SALES (est): 115.4MM **Privately Held**
SIC: 2452 Panels & sections, prefabricated, wood

(G-2781)
WALDON ABEL GUIDE PINS LLC
1467 Onion Creek Rd (99114-9648)
P.O. Box 1062 (99114-5012)
PHONE...................................509 684-2009
Richard Moore, *Principal*
EMP: 5
SALES (est): 577K **Privately Held**
SIC: 3452 Pins

(G-2782)
WAYNE POND LOGGING INC
1264 Slide Creek Rd (99114-8718)
PHONE...................................509 684-8732
Wayne Pond, *President*
Susan Pond, *Corp Secy*
EMP: 6
SALES (est): 542.8K **Privately Held**
SIC: 2411 Logging

(G-2783)
WEBLEY LUMBER INC
578d Webley Mill Rd (99114-9633)
PHONE...................................509 684-3980
Darrell Webley, *President*
EMP: 2
SALES (est): 850K **Privately Held**
SIC: 2421 Sawmills & planing mills, general

Concrete
Skagit County

(G-2784)
CAPE HORN MAINTENANCE CO
7849 Fir St (98237-8493)
PHONE...................................360 826-9105
Dopnna Shaver, *Principal*
EMP: 2
SALES: 90K **Privately Held**
SIC: 3823 Water quality monitoring & control systems

(G-2785)
FRANK HARKNESS TRCKG & LOG LLC
39394 State Route 20 (98237-9241)
PHONE...................................360 595-2496
Frank R Harkness Jr, *Administration*
EMP: 2 **Privately Held**
SIC: 4731 2411 Freight transportation arrangement; logging
PA: Frank Harkness Trucking & Logging, L.L.C.
5226 Turkington Rd
Acme WA 98220

(G-2786)
GATOR DENTAL EQUIP
Also Called: Gator Dental Repair Services
7576 Skagit View Dr (98237-9363)
PHONE...................................360 770-3502
Tim Cooley, *Owner*
EMP: 2
SQ FT: 900
SALES: 160K **Privately Held**
SIC: 3843 Dental equipment

(G-2787)
JASON K MILLER
7674 Cedar Park (98237-7704)
PHONE...................................360 853-8213
Jason K Miller, *Principal*
EMP: 3 **EST:** 2010
SALES (est): 117.3K **Privately Held**
SIC: 2711 Newspapers

(G-2788)
JEFF HAUENSTEIN LOGGING
38423 State Route 20 (98237-9462)
PHONE...................................360 826-3490
Jeff Hauenstein, *Owner*
EMP: 8
SALES (est): 499.9K **Privately Held**
SIC: 2411 Logging

(G-2789)
KOMA KULSHAN ASSOCIATES
44710 Baker Lake Rd (98237-9553)
PHONE...................................360 853-8530
Convanta Energy, *Partner*
EMP: 3 **EST:** 1990
SALES (est): 349.6K **Privately Held**
SIC: 3621 Power generators

(G-2790)
PACIFIC RIM TONEWOODS INC
38511 State Route 20 (98237-9463)
PHONE...................................360 826-6101
Stephen McMinn, *President*
EMP: 15 **Privately Held**
SIC: 3931 5961 Musical instruments; mail order house
PA: Pacific Rim Tonewoods Inc
619 15th St
Bellingham WA 98225

Connell
Franklin County

(G-2791)
COLBY CREATIONS INC
449 E Edison (99326)
PHONE...................................509 234-9736
Virginia Colby, *President*
EMP: 2 **EST:** 2008
SALES (est): 150K **Privately Held**
SIC: 2211 Sheets, bedding & table cloths: cotton

(G-2792)
CONNELL SAND & GRAVEL INC
200 W Date St (99326)
P.O. Box 83, Kahlotus (99335-0083)
PHONE...................................509 234-3221
Alan Hille, *Branch Mgr*
EMP: 30
SALES (corp-wide): 5.5MM **Privately Held**
SIC: 1442 Construction sand & gravel
PA: Connell Sand & Gravel, Inc.
200 W Date St
Connell WA 99326
509 234-3221

(G-2793)
CONNELL SAND & GRAVEL INC (PA)
200 W Date St (99326)
PHONE...................................509 234-3221
Alan Hille, *President*
Toni Hille, *Vice Pres*
EMP: 18
SQ FT: 3,000
SALES: 5.5MM **Privately Held**
SIC: 1442 5032 Construction sand & gravel; sand, construction

(G-2794)
FRANKLIN COUNTY GRAPHIC
346 S Columbia St (99326)
P.O. Box 160 (99326-0160)
PHONE...................................509 234-3181
Kathy Valdez, *Owner*
EMP: 3 **EST:** 1954
SQ FT: 1,900
SALES (est): 206.3K **Privately Held**
SIC: 2711 Newspapers: publishing only, not printed on site

(G-2795)
LAMB WESTON HOLDINGS INC
811 W Gum St (99326)
P.O. Box 799 (99326-0799)
PHONE...................................509 234-5511
Del Krumm, *Branch Mgr*
EMP: 459
SALES (corp-wide): 3.4B **Publicly Held**
WEB: www.conagra.com
SIC: 2099 Food preparations
PA: Lamb Weston Holdings Inc
599 S Rivershore Ln
Eagle ID 83616
208 938-1047

Conway
Skagit County

(G-2796)
BELL LUMBER & POLE COMPANY
18488 Main St (98238-7009)
P.O. Box 748 (98238-0748)
PHONE.................360 445-5565
Frank Gribbel, *Branch Mgr*
EMP: 7
SALES (corp-wide): 2.7MM **Privately Held**
WEB: www.bellpole.com
SIC: 2421 Outdoor wood structural products
HQ: Bell Lumber & Pole Company
778 1st St Nw
New Brighton MN 55112
651 633-4334

Cosmopolis
Grays Harbor County

(G-2797)
ARTIC TIMBER
42 Lund Rd (98537-9705)
PHONE.................360 533-6490
Fax: 360 533-6014
EMP: 9
SALES (est): 610K **Privately Held**
SIC: 2421 Sawmill/Planing Mill

(G-2798)
CASKEY INDUSTRIAL SUPPLY CO
1608 1st St (98537)
PHONE.................360 533-6366
Kelly Caskey, *President*
Marie Caskey, *Corp Secy*
EMP: 5
SALES: 950K **Privately Held**
SIC: 5085 3599 Chains, power transmission; sprockets; bearings; machine shop, jobbing & repair

(G-2799)
COSMO SPECIALTY FIBERS INC
1701 1st St (98537)
PHONE.................360 500-4600
Nicholas B Dottino, *CEO*
Robert Gachan, *Vice Pres*
▼ **EMP:** 164
SALES (est): 48MM **Privately Held**
SIC: 2611 Pulp mills, dissolving pulp processing

(G-2800)
COSMOPOLIS SPECIALTY FIBER
1701 1st St (98537)
P.O. Box 539 (98537-0539)
PHONE.................360 533-7531
Sandy Corrion, *Principal*
▼ **EMP:** 8 **EST:** 2010
SALES (est): 1.9MM **Privately Held**
SIC: 3552 Fiber & yarn preparation machinery & equipment

(G-2801)
OPAL ART GLASS
1232 1st St (98537)
P.O. Box 1218 (98537-1218)
PHONE.................360 532-9268
Johnny Camp, *Owner*
Darlene Camp, *Owner*
EMP: 3
SQ FT: 2,500
SALES (est): 100K **Privately Held**
SIC: 3231 Products of purchased glass

(G-2802)
WEYERHAEUSER COMPANY
Also Called: Pulp Mill
1701 E 1st St (98537)
P.O. Box 1000 (98537-1000)
PHONE.................360 532-7110
David Walseth, *Manager*
EMP: 400
SALES (corp-wide): 7.4B **Publicly Held**
SIC: 2611 Pulp mills
PA: Weyerhaeuser Company
220 Occidental Ave S
Seattle WA 98104
206 539-3000

Coulee City
Grant County

(G-2803)
JOHN MCLEAN SEED CO
9516 State Route 17 N (99115-9644)
PHONE.................509 632-8709
John Mc Lean, *President*
EMP: 2
SALES (est): 213.6K **Privately Held**
SIC: 5261 2048 Nursery stock, seeds & bulbs; cereal-, grain-, & seed-based feeds

(G-2804)
PARSONS EQUIPMENT INC
302 N 2nd St (99115-5107)
P.O. Box 758 (99115-0758)
PHONE.................509 632-5205
Patty Parson, *Treasurer*
Patty Parsons, *Treasurer*
EMP: 2
SALES (est): 155.6K **Privately Held**
SIC: 3523 Farm machinery & equipment

(G-2805)
PRATHERS WELDING & FABRICATION
10668 Highway 2 E (99115-9626)
PHONE.................509 632-5321
Kevin Prather, *President*
Kelly Prather, *Vice Pres*
EMP: 2
SQ FT: 2,500
SALES: 200K **Privately Held**
SIC: 5999 7699 3523 Farm equipment & supplies; agricultural equipment repair services; farm machinery & equipment

Coulee Dam
Okanogan County

(G-2806)
BURKE ELECTRIC
102 Stevens Ave (99116-1503)
PHONE.................509 633-8046
EMP: 2
SALES (est): 110K **Privately Held**
SIC: 3699 Mfg Electrical Equipment/Supplies

(G-2807)
COULEE VIEW FOOD AND FUEL
2 Okanogan Ave (99116-1502)
PHONE.................509 633-2951
EMP: 3 **EST:** 2011
SALES (est): 229.3K **Privately Held**
SIC: 2869 Fuels

(G-2808)
SEATONS GROVE GREENHOUSE
Star Rte (99116)
PHONE.................509 633-0404
John Francis, *Owner*
EMP: 3
SALES (est): 124.7K **Privately Held**
SIC: 0181 3993 Bedding plants, growing of; displays & cutouts, window & lobby

(G-2809)
TILLMANS INC
Also Called: Coulee Dam Concrete
3008 Highway 155 (99116-9738)
P.O. Box 66 (99116-0066)
PHONE.................509 633-2542
Paul Tillman, *President*
EMP: 5
SALES: 733K **Privately Held**
SIC: 3273 Ready-mixed concrete

Coupeville
Island County

(G-2810)
COASTLINE WOODWORKING
926 Blockhouse Rd (98239-3508)
PHONE.................360 678-7572
Neil Anthony, *Principal*
EMP: 4
SALES (est): 431.7K **Privately Held**
SIC: 2431 Millwork

(G-2811)
COMPOST TEA BY SEANEEN
107 S Main St Ste A103 (98239-3542)
PHONE.................360 678-3288
Seaneen Hummel, *Principal*
EMP: 3
SALES (est): 89K **Privately Held**
SIC: 2875 Compost

(G-2812)
COOK ON CLAY
19762 State Route 20 (98239-9656)
PHONE.................360 678-1818
Robbie Lobell, *President*
EMP: 4
SALES (est): 305K **Privately Held**
SIC: 3269 Cookware: stoneware, coarse earthenware & pottery

(G-2813)
GANAPATI STUDIOS
2671 Libbey Rd (98239-3212)
PHONE.................206 547-2239
Phillip Brazeau, *Partner*
Sarah Brazeau, *Partner*
EMP: 2
SALES: 98K **Privately Held**
WEB: www.ganapatistudios.com
SIC: 2771 Greeting cards

(G-2814)
LIGHTHOUSE ENVMTL PROGRAMS
Also Called: Keepers Admrlty Head Lghthouse
1280 Engle Rd (98239-9805)
P.O. Box 565 (98239-0565)
PHONE.................360 579-4489
Rick Blank, *President*
Linda Crow, *Vice Pres*
Wendy Visconty, *Treasurer*
Kathy Fritts, *Admin Sec*
EMP: 4
SQ FT: 400
SALES: 203.6K **Privately Held**
SIC: 3731 5947 Lighthouse tenders, building & repairing; gift shop

(G-2815)
RAIN SHADOW CELLARS LLC
2291 Roberts Pond Ln (98239-3127)
PHONE.................360 320-3115
Sean Merrill,
EMP: 4
SALES (est): 140.5K **Privately Held**
SIC: 2084 7389 Wine cellars, bonded: engaged in blending wines;

(G-2816)
REMPEL BROS CONCRETE INC
27364 State Route 525 (98239-9698)
P.O. Box 206, Greenbank (98253-1206)
PHONE.................360 678-4622
David Walden, *CEO*
Ed Rempel, *Treasurer*
EMP: 12
SQ FT: 600
SALES (est): 1.8MM **Privately Held**
SIC: 3273 Ready-mixed concrete

(G-2817)
SAUNDERS SOLUTIONS INC
701 Ne 4th St (98239-3585)
PHONE.................360 678-4788
David Saunders, *President*
EMP: 3 **EST:** 2009
SALES (est): 194.4K **Privately Held**
SIC: 3999 Manufacturing industries

(G-2818)
SOUND PUBLISHING INC
Also Called: Whidbey News Times
107 S Main St Ste E101 (98239-3569)
PHONE.................360 675-6611
Marcia Van Dyke, *Branch Mgr*
EMP: 20 **Privately Held**
WEB: www.soundpublishing.com
SIC: 2711 2731 Newspapers: publishing only, not printed on site; book publishing
HQ: Sound Publishing, Inc.
11323 Commando Rd W Main
Everett WA 98204
360 394-5800

(G-2819)
WHIDBEY EXAMINER LLC
Also Called: Examiner The
107 S Main St Ste 101 (98239-3541)
P.O. Box 948 (98239-0948)
PHONE.................360 678-8060
Gloria Fletcher, *President*
EMP: 4
SALES (est): 270.2K **Privately Held**
SIC: 2711 Commercial printing & newspaper publishing combined; newspapers, publishing & printing

Covington
King County

(G-2820)
AVAILABLE BACKFLOW TESTERS
27732 168th Ave Se (98042-9119)
PHONE.................425 652-9970
EMP: 2
SALES (est): 141.5K **Privately Held**
SIC: 1389 Testing, measuring, surveying & analysis services

(G-2821)
BUILD-A-BRACELET
29780 214th Ave Se (98042-9245)
PHONE.................919 757-1219
Barbara Friedman, *Principal*
EMP: 2
SALES (est): 104.4K **Privately Held**
SIC: 3961 Bracelets, except precious metal

(G-2822)
CARGO EXPRESS INC
15657 Se 272nd St (98042-4234)
P.O. Box 3814, Federal Way (98063-3814)
PHONE.................253 630-7294
EMP: 2 **EST:** 2005
SALES (est): 120K **Privately Held**
SIC: 2741 Misc Publishing

(G-2823)
CHERRY DE PON
17327 Se 270th Pl Ste 101 (98042-5451)
PHONE.................253 277-1907
EMP: 4 **EST:** 2013
SALES (est): 301.2K **Privately Held**
SIC: 2024 Ice cream, bulk

(G-2824)
CULLEN BINDERY LLC
20504 Se 269th St (98042-6129)
PHONE.................206 799-6295
Dave Cullen, *Mng Member*
John Cullen,
EMP: 15
SQ FT: 15,000
SALES (est): 1.1MM **Privately Held**
SIC: 2789 Trade binding services

(G-2825)
DK9 DOG WALKING
17017 Se 263rd St (98042-8397)
PHONE.................425 922-4685
Danielle Dechant, *Principal*
EMP: 2
SALES (est): 116.9K **Privately Held**
SIC: 3999 Pet supplies

GEOGRAPHIC SECTION

Custer - Whatcom County (G-2856)

(G-2826)
DYNAMIC SOFTWARE
Also Called: Rhinestones Golor
18403 Se Wax Rd (98042-4865)
P.O. Box 404, Maple Valley (98038-0404)
PHONE..................................253 630-7026
Brett Martin, *Owner*
EMP: 4
SALES (est): 280K **Privately Held**
SIC: 7372 Prepackaged software

(G-2827)
EMS DENTAL DESIGNS INC
18529 Se 244th Pl (98042-4824)
PHONE..................................425 584-7206
Laura Emmons, *President*
Donald L Emmons III, *Vice Pres*
EMP: 2
SALES (est): 248.3K **Privately Held**
SIC: 3843 Dental hand instruments

(G-2828)
GEORGIA-PACIFIC LLC
16720 Se 271st St Ste 205 (98042-7342)
PHONE..................................253 631-3250
Cathy Cole, *Branch Mgr*
EMP: 2
SALES (corp-wide): 42.6B **Privately Held**
WEB: www.gp.com
SIC: 2621 Fine paper
HQ: Georgia-Pacific Llc
  133 Peachtree St Nw
  Atlanta GA 30303
  404 652-4000

(G-2829)
HIPPLE FAMILY LTD LIABILITY CO
Also Called: Voice of The Valley
26909 206th Ave Se (98042-6124)
P.O. Box 307, Maple Valley (98038-0307)
PHONE..................................425 432-9696
Sandy Hipple,
Donna Hayes,
EMP: 7
SALES (est): 478.8K **Privately Held**
SIC: 2711 Newspapers, publishing & printing

(G-2830)
IMAGINE FOOD
25816 163rd Ave Se (98042-8804)
PHONE..................................917 428-4173
Maxime Bilet, *Principal*
EMP: 5
SALES (est): 186.2K **Privately Held**
SIC: 2099 Food preparations

(G-2831)
KY INTERNATIONAL LLC
13330 Se 252nd St (98042-6655)
PHONE..................................253 373-9602
Rong Yan, *Principal*
◆ **EMP:** 4
SALES (est): 362.9K **Privately Held**
SIC: 3441 Fabricated structural metal

(G-2832)
MCNEELEY MFG
24634 185th Pl Se (98042-4843)
PHONE..................................206 255-7818
Joshua McNeeley, *Principal*
EMP: 3
SALES (est): 332.3K **Privately Held**
SIC: 3999 Manufacturing industries

(G-2833)
MICHAEL ENTERPRISES CO
26420 180th Ave Se (98042-4918)
PHONE..................................253 630-4259
EMP: 2
SALES (est): 130K **Privately Held**
SIC: 3446 Mfg Architectural Metalwork

(G-2834)
MOLSON RUNNER SLEDS
17515 Se 257th St (98042-8367)
PHONE..................................425 445-2975
Kellen Huebner, *Mng Member*
EMP: 2
SALES: 25K **Privately Held**
SIC: 3944 7389 Sleds, children's;

(G-2835)
NORTHWEST MODULAR SERVICE
16817 Se 264th St (98042-5814)
PHONE..................................253 631-2802
Roy Keen, *Owner*
Stella Keen, *Manager*
EMP: 4
SALES (est): 295.2K **Privately Held**
SIC: 2452 Modular homes, prefabricated, wood

(G-2836)
PROGENICA THERAPEUTICS LLC
16016 Se 249th Pl (98042-4167)
P.O. Box 703, Kent (98035-0703)
PHONE..................................253 347-7018
Helen Newman, *Mng Member*
EMP: 3
SALES (est): 142K **Privately Held**
SIC: 3842 Implants, surgical

(G-2837)
PROGENICA THERAPEUTICS LLC
16016 Se 249th Pl (98042-4167)
P.O. Box 703, Kent (98035-0703)
PHONE..................................253 347-7018
EMP: 3
SALES (est): 117.4K **Privately Held**
SIC: 3842 Implants, surgical; grafts, artificial: for surgery

(G-2838)
SIGN COMPANY
25431 161st Ave Se (98042-4178)
PHONE..................................253 630-6313
Vickie Currie, *Principal*
EMP: 2 **EST:** 2009
SALES (est): 120K **Privately Held**
SIC: 3993 Signs & advertising specialties

(G-2839)
SOOS CREEK DENTAL
17615 Se 272nd St Ste 108 (98042-4957)
PHONE..................................253 631-8241
Perindible Singh MD, *President*
Gary Clusserath, *President*
EMP: 10
SALES (est): 945.3K **Privately Held**
SIC: 3843 8021 Enamels, dentists'; offices & clinics of dentists

(G-2840)
WOODWORKERS OUTPOST
25914 193rd Pl Se (98042-6035)
PHONE..................................253 653-8607
Daniel Shaw, *Owner*
EMP: 2
SALES: 700K **Privately Held**
SIC: 2431 Millwork

(G-2841)
YANGARRA ALPACAS
25915 160th Ave Se (98042-8239)
PHONE..................................253 630-5422
Karen Higginson, *Owner*
EMP: 2 **EST:** 2017
SALES (est): 85.5K **Privately Held**
SIC: 2231 Alpacas, mohair: woven

Creston
Lincoln County

(G-2842)
LTH FARM CORP
23526 S Rd 2 E (99117)
P.O. Box 33 (99117-0257)
PHONE..................................509 636-2673
Loren Houger, *President*
Colleen Houger, *Admin Sec*
EMP: 2 **EST:** 2001
SALES (est): 177.8K **Privately Held**
SIC: 3523 Driers (farm): grain, hay & seed

(G-2843)
WHITESTONE WINERY INC
Also Called: Yurt, Vineyard & Winery
42399 Jump Canyon Rd N (99117-9739)
PHONE..................................509 636-2001
Walter J Haig II, *President*
Judy Haig, *Founder*
Judith Haig, *Admin Sec*
EMP: 3 **EST:** 2000
SALES (est): 462.6K **Privately Held**
SIC: 0721 2084 Vines, cultivation of; wines

Curlew
Ferry County

(G-2844)
BROWN LUMBER CO
983 Customs Rd (99118-9612)
PHONE..................................509 779-4738
Steve Brown, *Owner*
Bowe Brown, *Co-Owner*
June Brown, *Co-Owner*
EMP: 3
SALES: 50K **Privately Held**
SIC: 5211 2411 7389 Planing mill products & lumber; logging;

(G-2845)
CURLEW COUNTRY HERBS
Also Called: Curlew Country Body Luxuries
396 Customs Rd (99118-9633)
PHONE..................................509 779-4941
EMP: 2
SALES (est): 106.3K **Privately Held**
SIC: 2841 Manufacture Soap And Other Detergents

(G-2846)
PEOPLES SOLAR INC
787 Customs Rd (99118-9629)
P.O. Box 162 (99118-0162)
PHONE..................................530 217-6020
Rick Diamond, *President*
Jeannette Diamond, *Corp Secy*
EMP: 2
SALES (est): 136.4K **Privately Held**
SIC: 3612 Transformers, except electric

(G-2847)
STOTTS CONSTRUCTION INC
Also Called: Stotts Premix
17814 N Highway 21 (99118-9668)
PHONE..................................509 779-4987
John Lee Stotts, *President*
Leslie Stotts, *Vice Pres*
Kay Torzewski, *Treasurer*
EMP: 16 **EST:** 1956
SQ FT: 8,000
SALES (est): 2.1MM **Privately Held**
SIC: 1794 3273 Excavation work; ready-mixed concrete

Curtis
Lewis County

(G-2848)
CHRISTMAS FOREST
445 Beaver Creek Rd (98538-9737)
P.O. Box 10 (98538-0010)
PHONE..................................360 245-3202
Rodrick Holt, *Partner*
Ramona Holt, *Partner*
EMP: 50
SQ FT: 6,000
SALES: 460K **Privately Held**
WEB: www.christmasforest.com
SIC: 3999 5961 5947 Wreaths, artificial; catalog & mail-order houses; gift baskets

(G-2849)
WEYERHAEUSER COMPANY
Also Called: Curtis Pole Yard
246 Boistfort Rd (98538)
P.O. Box 40 (98538-0040)
PHONE..................................360 245-3245
Jason Hankey, *General Mgr*
EMP: 5
SALES (corp-wide): 7.4B **Publicly Held**
SIC: 2411 Pole cutting contractors
PA: Weyerhaeuser Company
  220 Occidental Ave S
  Seattle WA 98104
  206 539-3000

Cusick
Pend Oreille County

(G-2850)
LOST CREEK LOGGING
396875 Highway 20 (99119-9604)
PHONE..................................509 442-3218
Dustin Chantry, *Owner*
EMP: 2
SALES (est): 202.5K **Privately Held**
WEB: www.potc.net
SIC: 2411 Logging camps & contractors

(G-2851)
MAC ARTHUR LAND & TIMBER
398892 Highway 20 (99119-9634)
PHONE..................................509 442-3805
Ross Mac Arthur, *Owner*
Debby McArthur, *Co-Owner*
EMP: 2
SALES (est): 105.4K **Privately Held**
SIC: 2411 6552 Logging; subdividers & developers

(G-2852)
SILVER KING MINING & MILLING
Also Called: S-K Marine
411352 Highway 20 (99119-9616)
PHONE..................................509 445-1406
Roy Haikkila, *President*
Norman Haikkila, *Vice Pres*
EMP: 6 **EST:** 1965
SQ FT: 1,400
SALES (est): 556.5K **Privately Held**
SIC: 1094 1021 1031 1044 Uranium ore mining; copper ores; zinc ores mining; lead ores mining; silver ores; machine shop, jobbing & repair; pontoons, except aircraft & inflatable

Custer
Whatcom County

(G-2853)
CASCADE CNC LLC
2772 Birch Bay Lynden Rd (98240-9703)
PHONE..................................360 366-2580
EMP: 2 **EST:** 2015
SALES (est): 84.8K **Privately Held**
SIC: 3599 Industrial machinery

(G-2854)
COLUMBIA GAMES INC
3190 Haynie Rd (98240-9204)
PHONE..................................360 366-2228
Thomas Dalgliesh, *President*
Grant Dalgliesh, *Director*
Martin Doyle, *Director*
▲ **EMP:** 3
SALES: 675.2K **Privately Held**
WEB: www.columbiagames.com
SIC: 2731 Books: publishing only

(G-2855)
JAKE MABERRY PACKING INC
8143 Sunrise Rd (98240-9613)
PHONE..................................206 366-5411
Juan Martinez, *Principal*
EMP: 4
SALES (est): 177.9K **Privately Held**
SIC: 2037 Frozen fruits & vegetables

(G-2856)
LUKENS FARMS INC
Also Called: Grace Harbor Farms
2347 Birch Bay Lynden Rd (98240-9702)
PHONE..................................360 366-4151
Timothy P Lukens, *President*
David Lukens, *Vice Pres*
Grace Lukens, *Admin Sec*
EMP: 7 **EST:** 2010
SQ FT: 1,800
SALES (est): 636.2K **Privately Held**
SIC: 0241 2026 Dairy farms; milk processing (pasteurizing, homogenizing, bottling)

Custer - Whatcom County (G-2857)

(G-2857)
MALONE MANUFACTURING LLC
3023 W 75th St (98240-9535)
PHONE...................360 366-9964
Margarita Malone,
Donald E Malone,
EMP: 2
SALES (est): 151.8K **Privately Held**
SIC: 2389 2392 2676 Hospital gowns; chair covers & pads: made from purchased materials; diapers, paper (disposable): made from purchased paper

(G-2858)
OCEANUS PLASTICS INC
2445 Salashan Loop (98240)
P.O. Box 1237, Ferndale (98248-1237)
PHONE...................360 366-7474
Brent Diakaw, *President*
Dan Smith, *President*
Daniel Smith, *Vice Pres*
EMP: 7
SALES (est): 1.2MM
SALES (corp-wide): 4.1MM **Privately Held**
WEB: www.oceanusplastics.com
SIC: 3089 3732 2431 Plastic boats & other marine equipment; boat building & repairing; millwork
PA: Oceanus Reinforced Plastics Ltd
1949 Marina Way Unit 2
North Saanich BC V8L 6
250 656-7733

(G-2859)
RAY FANNS WHISPERING PINES
8746 Delta Line Rd (98240-9607)
PHONE...................360 384-4750
Hallie Fann, *Owner*
EMP: 2 **EST:** 1997
SALES (est): 185K **Privately Held**
SIC: 3441 Fabricated structural metal

(G-2860)
SIGNATURE PLASTICS LLC
7837 Custer School Rd (98240-9515)
PHONE...................360 366-5044
Bob Guenser, *President*
John Cavers, *Vice Pres*
Derek Service, *Mfg Staff*
EMP: 15
SALES (est): 2.9MM **Privately Held**
WEB: www.signatureplastics.com
SIC: 2821 3679 3089 Molding compounds, plastics; electronic circuits; plastic containers, except foam

(G-2861)
STRAIGHT LINE INDUSTRIES INC
7634 Zell Rd (98240-9700)
PHONE...................360 366-0223
Kurtis Nelson, *President*
Kathie Nelson, *Treasurer*
EMP: 6
SALES (est): 478.4K **Privately Held**
WEB: www.straightlineindustries.com
SIC: 7692 Welding repair

Dallesport
Klickitat County

(G-2862)
DALLESPORT FOUNDRY INC
102 Parallel Ave (98617)
P.O. Box 209 (98617-0209)
PHONE...................509 767-1183
Brett M Rose, *President*
EMP: 20
SQ FT: 16,000
SALES (est): 5MM **Privately Held**
SIC: 3321 Gray iron castings

(G-2863)
GREENHILL LUMBER CO INC
134 Tidyman Rd (98617-0824)
P.O. Box 22 (98617-0022)
PHONE...................509 767-0010
James Hodge, *President*
Mary Hodge, *Treasurer*
EMP: 10
SALES (est): 1.3MM **Privately Held**
SIC: 2499 Fencing, docks & other outdoor wood structural products; fencing, wood

(G-2864)
MARSHALS WINERY INC
150 Oak Creek Rd (98617-0706)
P.O. Box 306 (98617-0306)
PHONE...................509 767-4633
Ron Johnson, *President*
EMP: 7
SALES (est): 525.3K **Privately Held**
SIC: 2084 Wines

(G-2865)
SHADY GROVE WINERY LLC
2297 Dallesport Rd (98617-0672)
P.O. Box 89 (98617-0089)
PHONE...................509 767-1400
Anthony E Fuller, *Principal*
EMP: 4
SALES (est): 215.4K **Privately Held**
SIC: 2084 Wines

Darrington
Snohomish County

(G-2866)
BARRY RANKIN LOGGING INC
31710 Crawford Loop Rd (98241-9416)
PHONE...................360 436-1947
Barry A Rankin, *President*
Troy Rankin, *Principal*
Vicki Rankin, *Principal*
EMP: 3
SALES (est): 270K **Privately Held**
SIC: 2411 7389 Logging camps & contractors; log & lumber broker

(G-2867)
DIRECTEQ LLC
25207 480th Dr Ne (98241-9209)
P.O. Box 729 (98241-0729)
PHONE...................425 818-9510
Allen Searle, *CEO*
Scott Searle, *Info Tech Mgr*
EMP: 2
SALES (est): 83.8K **Privately Held**
WEB: www.directeq.com
SIC: 7372 Prepackaged software

(G-2868)
GREENHAVEN LLC
1311 Ne State Rte 530 (98241)
PHONE...................360 436-1420
Christine Hoffer,
Freelin Hummel,
EMP: 2 **EST:** 2013
SALES (est): 104.1K **Privately Held**
SIC: 0139 3999 ;

(G-2869)
SAUK SUIATTLE INDIAN TRIBE TRU
Also Called: Mountain Loop Country Store
5318 Chief Brown Ln B (98241-9420)
PHONE...................360 436-0131
Jason Joseph, *Ch of Bd*
Katie Villamena, *Treasurer*
Emma Nicolas, *Exec Dir*
Nancy Decoteau,
Ben Joseph,
EMP: 18
SALES (est): 875.7K **Privately Held**
SIC: 5541 3911 Gasoline service stations; cigar & cigarette accessories

Davenport
Lincoln County

(G-2870)
FOSTCO INC
705 Marshall St (99122-5143)
P.O. Box 456 (99122-0456)
PHONE...................509 725-3765
Merrie Foster, *President*
Shawn Foster, *VP Sales*
EMP: 4
SQ FT: 1,000
SALES (est): 856.6K **Privately Held**
WEB: www.fostco.com
SIC: 5084 3545 Drilling equipment, excluding bits; drilling machine attachments & accessories

(G-2871)
HUCKLEBERRY PRESS
38291 State Route 25 N (99122-9384)
PHONE...................844 344-8344
Val Mohney, *Principal*
EMP: 2
SALES (est): 60.5K **Privately Held**
SIC: 2741 Miscellaneous publishing

(G-2872)
JOURNAL-NEWS PUBLISHING CO
Also Called: Davenport Times
506 Morgan St (99122-5213)
P.O. Box 66 (99122-0066)
PHONE...................509 725-0101
Bill Ifft, *Owner*
EMP: 3
SALES (corp-wide): 3.3MM **Privately Held**
WEB: www.cheneyfreepress.com
SIC: 2711 2759 Commercial printing & newspaper publishing combined; commercial printing
PA: Journal-News Publishing Co Inc
29 Alder St Sw
Ephrata WA 98823
509 754-4636

(G-2873)
LIGHTNING NUGGETS INC
604 Logan St (99122)
P.O. Box 928 (99122-0928)
PHONE...................509 725-6211
Maura Doohan, *President*
EMP: 11
SALES (est): 1.7MM **Privately Held**
WEB: www.lightningnuggets.com
SIC: 2899 Fuel treating compounds

(G-2874)
LINCOLN ADVERTISER
Also Called: Lincoln Advertiser The
701 12th St (99122)
P.O. Box 1125 (99122-1125)
PHONE...................509 725-8007
Dave Hoppes, *President*
Chris Hoppes, *Vice Pres*
EMP: 3
SALES (est): 350.6K **Privately Held**
SIC: 2752 Lithographing on metal

(G-2875)
LINCOLN SAND & GRAVEL
35031 Indian Creek Rd N (99122-8856)
PHONE...................509 725-4531
Jackie Stormo, *Vice Pres*
EMP: 4
SALES (est): 375.5K **Privately Held**
SIC: 1442 Construction sand & gravel

(G-2876)
REED FARMS INC
41295 State Route 25 N (99122-9315)
PHONE...................509 725-4394
Terry Reed, *President*
Joel Reed, *Vice Pres*
EMP: 2
SALES (est): 197.9K **Privately Held**
SIC: 3523 Driers (farm): grain, hay & seed

(G-2877)
S & R SPIRAL LLC
Also Called: Spiral & Railing House, The
6747 Kieffer Rd (99122-9728)
PHONE...................509 747-4723
Robert Yeager, *President*
Sharon Lee Yeager, *Governor*
EMP: 20
SQ FT: 2,500
SALES (est): 2.4MM **Privately Held**
SIC: 3446 Stairs, staircases, stair treads: prefabricated metal

Dayton
Columbia County

(G-2878)
AZURE MOUNTAIN BOTANICALS
420 E Spring St (99328-1339)
PHONE...................425 478-3902
Brenda Hall, *Principal*
EMP: 2
SALES (est): 129.3K **Privately Held**
SIC: 2841 Soap & other detergents

(G-2879)
CHIEF SPRINGS FIRE & IRONS BRW
148 E Main St (99328-1351)
PHONE...................509 382-4677
Ann Spring, *CEO*
Mike Spring, *COO*
EMP: 8 **EST:** 2012
SALES (est): 361.9K **Privately Held**
SIC: 2082 Beer (alcoholic beverage)

(G-2880)
DANS TOOL TRUCK
108 Johnson Hollow (99328-9613)
PHONE...................509 520-4531
Daniel Harrington, *Principal*
EMP: 2
SALES (est): 89.6K **Privately Held**
SIC: 3599 Industrial machinery

(G-2881)
DESPARADO COWBOY BULLETS LLC
2 Port Way (99328-8629)
PHONE...................509 382-8926
Richard Swanson,
Ed Kemmer,
Leann Kemmer,
EMP: 3
SALES (est): 365.8K **Privately Held**
SIC: 2892 Gunpowder

(G-2882)
GEMMELLS MACHINE WORKS INC
Also Called: Gemmell's Diving Services
3 Port Way (99328-8629)
P.O. Box 25 (99328-0025)
PHONE...................509 382-4159
Robert J Gemmell, *President*
Margarett Gemmell, *Treasurer*
Carla Rowe, *Admin Sec*
EMP: 3
SQ FT: 3,500
SALES (est): 353.7K **Privately Held**
SIC: 3599 Machine shop, jobbing & repair

(G-2883)
KONEN ROCK CRUSHING INC
910 N Touchet Rd (99328-8772)
P.O. Box 3088, Walla Walla (99362-0372)
PHONE...................509 382-2768
Thomas Konen, *President*
Stephanie Konen, *Corp Secy*
EMP: 7
SALES (est): 834.9K **Privately Held**
SIC: 3295 1442 Minerals, ground or treated; gravel & pebble mining

(G-2884)
SENECA FOODS CORPORATION
301 Seneca Way (99328-2101)
P.O. Box 100 (99328-0100)
PHONE...................509 382-8323
Wayne Peterson, *Branch Mgr*
EMP: 127
SALES (corp-wide): 1.2B **Publicly Held**
SIC: 2033 2037 Vegetables: packaged in cans, jars, etc.; fruits: packaged in cans, jars, etc.; vegetables, quick frozen & cold pack, excl. potato products; fruits, quick frozen & cold pack (frozen); fruit juices, frozen
PA: Seneca Foods Corporation
3736 S Main St
Marion NY 14505
315 926-8100

(G-2885)
SKYE BOOK & BREW
503 N Willow St (99328-1059)
PHONE.....................509 382-4677
William Graham, *Principal*
EMP: 3
SALES (est): 195.4K **Privately Held**
SIC: 2082 5942 Beer (alcoholic beverage); book stores

(G-2886)
SKYLINE FLUID POWER INC
109 N Front St (99328-1297)
PHONE.....................509 382-4781
Robert Mc Keen, *President*
Jean Mc Keen, *Corp Secy*
EMP: 8
SQ FT: 4,200
SALES (est): 1MM **Privately Held**
SIC: 3714 7699 5084 Hydraulic fluid power pumps for auto steering mechanism; hydraulic equipment repair; hydraulic systems equipment & supplies

(G-2887)
TOUCHET VALLEY NEWS INC
Also Called: Dayton Chronicle
163 E Main St (99328-1350)
PHONE.....................509 382-2221
Jack Williams, *President*
EMP: 2
SALES (est): 196.6K **Privately Held**
SIC: 2711 2752 Newspapers; commercial printing, offset

(G-2888)
VERTICAL TECHNOLOGIES
609 S 5th St (99328-1524)
P.O. Box 177 (99328-0177)
PHONE.....................509 382-2119
Curtis Seiss, *Principal*
EMP: 6
SALES (est): 1MM **Privately Held**
SIC: 2591 Blinds vertical

(G-2889)
VESTAS-AMERICAN WIND TECH INC
517 Cameron St (99328-1279)
P.O. Box 63 (99328-0063)
PHONE.....................509 382-1800
Jacocb Rough, *Manager*
EMP: 15
SALES (corp-wide): 11.6B **Privately Held**
SIC: 3511 Hydraulic turbines
HQ: Vestas-American Wind Technology, Inc.
1417 Nw Everett St
Portland OR 97209

(G-2890)
WINDTOGREEN LLC
610 Patit Rd (99328-8800)
PHONE.....................509 382-4034
Peter Swearengen,
EMP: 6
SALES (est): 445.2K **Privately Held**
SIC: 2873 Nitrogenous fertilizers

Deer Harbor
San Juan County

(G-2891)
DOWN ISLAND TRADING CO
Also Called: Deer Harbor Boat Works
155 Channel Rd (98243)
P.O. Box 34 (98243-0034)
PHONE.....................360 376-4056
Michael Durland, *President*
EMP: 3
SQ FT: 4,000
SALES (est): 200K **Privately Held**
WEB: www.purrain.com
SIC: 3732 1791 5084 5999 Boat building & repairing; storage tanks, metal: erection; tanks, storage; water purification equipment

Deer Park
Spokane County

(G-2892)
A & V INVESTMENTS INC
Also Called: Evergreen Truss & Supply
2003 E Crawford St (99006-5094)
P.O. Box 1283 (99006-1283)
PHONE.....................509 276-5088
Dwight S Tipton, *President*
EMP: 38
SQ FT: 12,000
SALES: 3MM **Privately Held**
WEB: www.e-truss.net
SIC: 2439 5031 1751 Trusses, wooden roof; lumber, plywood & millwork; kitchen cabinets; cabinet building & installation

(G-2893)
AMERICAN SOLUTIONS FOR BUS
5552 S Wallbridge Rd (99006-9475)
PHONE.....................509 276-8700
Douglas Shuff, *Principal*
EMP: 2
SALES (est): 160.5K **Privately Held**
SIC: 2754 Business form & card printing, gravure

(G-2894)
BUCK SNORT INDUSTRIES
21516 N Felspar Rd (99006-8785)
PHONE.....................509 939-7777
Alex Schmauch, *Administration*
EMP: 2 **EST:** 2016
SALES (est): 86.1K **Privately Held**
SIC: 3999 Manufacturing industries

(G-2895)
CAREKS COUNTRY CUSTOM MEATS
Also Called: Rusty's Country Meats
3125 W Findley Rd (99006-8208)
PHONE.....................509 276-2237
Rusty Minnameier, *Owner*
EMP: 2
SALES (est): 81K **Privately Held**
SIC: 2011 5421 0751 Meat packing plants; meat markets, including freezer provisioners; livestock services, except veterinary

(G-2896)
CLEAN LINES LLC
4865 W Csberg Brroughs Rd (99006)
PHONE.....................509 939-2957
Theodore Simonson,
EMP: 2
SALES (est): 90.7K **Privately Held**
SIC: 2951 1721 Asphalt paving mixtures & blocks; painting & paper hanging

(G-2897)
DARREN MODE
Also Called: Western Security Systems
3711 E Deer Park Milan Rd (99006-9149)
PHONE.....................509 292-2438
Darren Mode, *Owner*
EMP: 4
SQ FT: 3,000
SALES: 500K **Privately Held**
SIC: 3699 5065 Security control equipment & systems; security control equipment & systems

(G-2898)
DEER PARK GAZETTE LLC
5011 W Dahl Rd (99006-9578)
PHONE.....................509 276-7737
Patricia Ann Barden,
EMP: 2
SALES (est): 113.8K **Privately Held**
SIC: 2711 Newspapers, publishing & printing

(G-2899)
DEER PARK PRINTING
220 N Main St (99006-5170)
PHONE.....................509 276-9712
Porter Reiter, *Owner*
EMP: 2

SALES (est): 42.5K **Privately Held**
SIC: 2752 Commercial printing, lithographic

(G-2900)
EQUITY PUBLISHING
4910 W Dahl Rd (99006-8517)
P.O. Box 410 (99006-0410)
PHONE.....................509 994-0505
Terry White, *Principal*
EMP: 2
SALES (est): 118.8K **Privately Held**
SIC: 2741 Music, sheet: publishing only, not printed on site

(G-2901)
ETS INC
Also Called: Energy Technology Systems
859 S Main St (99006-8234)
P.O. Box 317, Chattaroy (99003-0317)
PHONE.....................509 276-2015
Eric Sari, *President*
Jim Lehto, *Research*
Brian Stumm, *Engineer*
Roderick Paugh, *Manager*
EMP: 12
SQ FT: 25,000
SALES (est): 113.8K **Privately Held**
SIC: 3567 Infrared ovens, industrial

(G-2902)
FRESENIUS MED CARE HLDINGS INC
822 S Main St (99006-8234)
PHONE.....................509 276-7338
EMP: 66
SALES (corp-wide): 18.9B **Privately Held**
SIC: 3841 Surgical & medical instruments
HQ: Fresenius Medical Care Holdings, Inc.
920 Winter St
Waltham MA 02451

(G-2903)
FROG CREEK CO
4896 N Williams Valley Rd (99006-9408)
PHONE.....................509 276-6467
Richard Trent, *Principal*
EMP: 2
SALES (est): 244.3K **Privately Held**
SIC: 3523 Tractors, farm

(G-2904)
GUY SUNGLASS
39402 N Locher Rd (99006-8142)
PHONE.....................509 489-2963
EMP: 2 **EST:** 2005
SALES (est): 82K **Privately Held**
SIC: 3231 Mfg Products-Purchased Glass

(G-2905)
HORIZON PUBLICATIONS INC
Also Called: Deer Park Tribune
104 N Main St (99006-5086)
PHONE.....................509 276-5043
Cathie Babbick, *Manager*
EMP: 12
SALES (corp-wide): 71.5MM **Privately Held**
WEB: www.malvern-online.com
SIC: 2711 Newspapers, publishing & printing
PA: Horizon Publications, Inc.
1120 N Carbon St Ste 100
Marion IL 62959
618 993-1711

(G-2906)
INDUSTRIAL SUPPORT SERVICE LLC
5579 W Mcknzie Woolard Rd (99006-9499)
PHONE.....................509 276-5131
John Schmidlkofer, *Mng Member*
EMP: 8
SALES (est): 1.6MM **Privately Held**
SIC: 3629 1731 7699 Electronic generation equipment; electrical work; general electrical contractor; industrial equipment services; industrial machinery & equipment repair

(G-2907)
KANIKSU FEEDS INC
39124 N Sherman Rd (99006-8126)
PHONE.....................509 406-1995
Ben Wood, *President*

Dana Wood, *Vice Pres*
EMP: 2
SALES (est): 62.3K **Privately Held**
SIC: 2041 Flour & other grain mill products

(G-2908)
MARTIN FRANK
35414 N Findley Rd (99006-8184)
PHONE.....................509 292-2685
Frank Martin, *Principal*
EMP: 6 **EST:** 2003
SALES (est): 446.5K **Privately Held**
SIC: 2411 Logging camps & contractors

(G-2909)
MOBILE STORAGE UNITS INC
2927 W Owens Rd (99006-9367)
P.O. Box 448 (99006-0448)
PHONE.....................509 276-8220
Robert D Wishman, *President*
Ken Knight, *Vice Pres*
EMP: 6
SALES (est): 1MM **Privately Held**
SIC: 2452 7359 5211 Farm buildings, prefabricated or portable: wood; garage facility & tool rental; prefabricated buildings

(G-2910)
NEWCORE AVIATION LLC
Also Called: Newcore Aerospace
110 W Crawford St (99006-5356)
P.O. Box 607 (99006-0607)
PHONE.....................509 276-8200
Roscoe A Sharp,
EMP: 7
SQ FT: 400
SALES (est): 163.2K
SALES (corp-wide): 1.3MM **Privately Held**
SIC: 3812 1542 5083 Search & navigation equipment; nonresidential construction; farm & garden machinery
PA: Newcore Enterprises, Llc
110 W Crawford St
Deer Park WA 99006
509 276-8200

(G-2911)
NEWCORE ENTERPRISES LLC (PA)
110 W Crawford St (99006-5356)
P.O. Box 607 (99006-0607)
PHONE.....................509 276-8200
Roscoe A Sharp, *Mng Member*
EMP: 6 **EST:** 2014
SQ FT: 400
SALES (est): 1.3MM **Privately Held**
SIC: 3812 1542 5083 Search & navigation equipment; nonresidential construction; farm & garden machinery

(G-2912)
NW EVERGREEN PRODUCTS
6410 W Groove Ln (99006)
PHONE.....................509 276-7825
Marilyn Thompson, *Owner*
Steve Thompson, *Co-Owner*
EMP: 2
SALES (est): 142.2K **Privately Held**
SIC: 3545 Sockets (machine tool accessories)

(G-2913)
PRECISION WOODCRAFT
5192 S Swenson Rd (99006-8439)
PHONE.....................509 276-1362
Bethany R Shertzer, *Principal*
EMP: 2
SALES (est): 167.6K **Privately Held**
SIC: 2511 Wood household furniture

(G-2914)
SILVER CITY TIMBER
518 S Fir Ave (99006-2621)
P.O. Box 1383 (99006-1383)
PHONE.....................509 276-5126
Corey Peterson, *Principal*
EMP: 2
SALES (est): 92.2K **Privately Held**
SIC: 2411 Peeler logs

(G-2915)
SPORTS N SORTS
7911 W Ridgeway Rd (99006-9752)
PHONE.....................509 276-6170
EMP: 2

Deer Park - Spokane County (G-2916)

SALES (est): 105.6K Privately Held
SIC: 2396 Mfg Auto/Apparel Trimming

(G-2916)
STANLEY PLOWING
32413 N Cedar Rd (99006-9167)
PHONE....................509 218-2419
Jason Stanley, *Executive*
EMP: 3
SALES (est): 220K Privately Held
SIC: 2851 Removers & cleaners

(G-2917)
STATESMAN-EXAMINER INC
Also Called: Tri County Tribune
104 N Main St (99006-5086)
PHONE....................509 276-5043
Kathie Babbick, *Branch Mgr*
EMP: 6
SALES (corp-wide): 2.4MM Privately Held
SIC: 2711 Newspapers
PA: Statesman-Examiner Inc
   220 S Main St
   Colville WA 99114
   509 684-4567

Deming
Whatcom County

(G-2918)
CASCADIA STONEWARE USA IN
5651 Strand Rd (98244-9121)
PHONE....................360 595-1171
Jeffrey McDougall, *Principal*
EMP: 3
SALES (est): 274K Privately Held
SIC: 3269 Stoneware pottery products

(G-2919)
FAST SIGN MAN LLC
5131 Mosquito Lake Rd (98244-9300)
PHONE....................360 592-4599
Stephen Pile, *Principal*
EMP: 3
SALES (est): 122.4K Privately Held
SIC: 3993 Signs & advertising specialties

(G-2920)
JOE ZENDER & SONS INC
Also Called: Zender Joe & Sons Logging Shop
6272 Mt Baker Hwy (98244-9512)
P.O. Box 81 (98244-0081)
PHONE....................360 599-2064
Doug Zender, *President*
Luis Zender, *Principal*
Dean Zender, *Vice Pres*
EMP: 8
SALES (est): 886.9K Privately Held
SIC: 2411 4212 Logging camps & contractors; local trucking, without storage

(G-2921)
MOON VALLEY NATURAL PDTS LLC
Also Called: Moon Valley Organics
3288 Valley Hwy (98244-9212)
PHONE....................360 595-0500
Kim L Denend,
Aaron Otto,
EMP: 8
SALES: 800K Privately Held
WEB: www.moonvalleyhoney.com
SIC: 2844 Face creams or lotions

(G-2922)
QUINTANA CUTTING INC
Also Called: Middle Forth Temper Cutt
6375 Rutsatz Rd (98244-9403)
PHONE....................360 592-5943
Mike Quintana, *President*
EMP: 3
SALES (est): 240K Privately Held
SIC: 2411 Timber, cut at logging camp

(G-2923)
SKANDIA NORTHWEST MFG
Also Called: Twin Country Rv Service
6807 Mt Baker Hwy (98244-9549)
PHONE....................360 599-2681
Al Vatne, *Owner*
EMP: 9

SALES: 700K Privately Held
SIC: 3799 Recreational vehicles

(G-2924)
STOOTHOFF AEROSPACE INC
2485 Mosquito Lake Rd (98244-9748)
PHONE....................360 595-0314
Robert Irving Stoothoff, *Principal*
EMP: 2
SALES (est): 174.4K Privately Held
SIC: 3663

(G-2925)
VAN DYK & SON LOGGING INC
5240 Mosquito Lake Rd (98244-9308)
P.O. Box 84 (98244-0084)
PHONE....................360 592-5951
Thomas L Van Dyk, *President*
Glenda Van Dyk, *Admin Sec*
EMP: 4
SALES (est): 500K Privately Held
SIC: 2411 Logging camps & contractors

(G-2926)
WILLIAM BLOCKLEY CONTRACTING
5725 Mt Baker Hwy (98244-9530)
PHONE....................360 592-5843
William H Blockley Jr, *President*
Clyde Blockley, *Vice Pres*
Marlene Blockley, *Administration*
EMP: 5
SALES (est): 495.3K Privately Held
SIC: 2411 Logging

(G-2927)
ZENDER BROS & WILBURN LOGGING
6269 Mt Baker Hwy (98244-9512)
P.O. Box 52 (98244-0052)
PHONE....................360 599-2859
Gregory Zender, *President*
Marty Wilburn, *Corp Secy*
Scott Zender, *Vice Pres*
EMP: 8
SALES (est): 713.3K Privately Held
SIC: 2411 Logging camps & contractors

Des Moines
King County

(G-2928)
ALL SCRAPPED UP INC
23302 17th Pl S (98198-7501)
PHONE....................206 824-3762
Sherri Leonard, *President*
EMP: 3
SALES (est): 255.3K Privately Held
SIC: 2782 Scrapbooks

(G-2929)
BIBLESOFT INC
22030 7th Ave S Ste 204 (98198-6219)
PHONE....................206 824-0547
Ken Davin, *President*
Tammie Springs, *Software Dev*
Richard Krekel, *Director*
EMP: 18
SQ FT: 7,500
SALES (est): 1.5MM Privately Held
WEB: www.biblesoft.com
SIC: 7372 7371 Business oriented computer software; custom computer programming services

(G-2930)
BISON FIBER PALLET
24305 11th Ave S (98198-3871)
PHONE....................206 291-0778
Andy Hoang Ha, *Principal*
EMP: 3
SALES (est): 119.9K Privately Held
SIC: 2448 Wood pallets & skids

(G-2931)
BOEING CO
519 S 214th St (98198-3664)
PHONE....................206 351-8601
EMP: 2
SALES (est): 221.2K Privately Held
SIC: 3721 Aircraft

(G-2932)
CANOPY WORLD INC
22820 Pacific Hwy S (98198-7262)
PHONE....................206 824-3877
Shawn Shaffer, *Manager*
EMP: 4
SQ FT: 1,400
SALES (est): 254.4K
SALES (corp-wide): 4.6MM Privately Held
WEB: www.canopy-world.com
SIC: 3444 Sheet metalwork
PA: Canopy World, Inc
   10025 Pacific Ave S
   Tacoma WA 98444
   253 531-5192

(G-2933)
DESTINATION DES MOINES ○
22511 Marine View Dr S (98198-6835)
PHONE....................206 824-9462
Ric Jacobson, *Owner*
EMP: 2 EST: 2018
SALES (est): 62.3K Privately Held
SIC: 2084 Wines, brandy & brandy spirits

(G-2934)
DO OR DYE SELF DEFENSE
26431 7th Ave S (98198-9303)
PHONE....................253 653-5696
Jennifer Dye, *Principal*
EMP: 3 EST: 2017
SALES (est): 175.6K Privately Held
SIC: 3812 Defense systems & equipment

(G-2935)
FINAL STATE PRESS LLC
1913 S 262nd Pl Ste 101 (98198-9233)
PHONE....................253 237-2474
Matthew Briggs, *Principal*
EMP: 2 EST: 2013
SALES (est): 129.8K Privately Held
SIC: 2741 Miscellaneous publishing

(G-2936)
GRAKON LLC (PA)
1911 S 218th St (98198-8370)
P.O. Box 98984, Seattle (98198-0984)
PHONE....................206 824-6000
Eric Ko, *Design Engr*
Justin Graham, *Executive*
Dennis Graham,
Bryan Keeton,
◆ EMP: 155
SQ FT: 60,000
SALES (est): 80.7MM Privately Held
WEB: www.grakon.com
SIC: 3648 Lighting equipment

(G-2937)
IDK WEAR
20426 5th Ave S (98198-2812)
PHONE....................425 346-1904
Debbie Lamb, *General Ptnr*
EMP: 2
SALES (est): 178.2K Privately Held
SIC: 2759 Screen printing

(G-2938)
J C MANUFACTURING INC
22507 1/2 Mar View Dr S (98198)
P.O. Box 98488 (98198-0488)
PHONE....................206 824-7650
Jeff Cissell, *President*
EMP: 10
SQ FT: 5,500
SALES (est): 1.8MM Privately Held
SIC: 3728 Aircraft parts & equipment

(G-2939)
LAGOON CONSERVATION LLC
28200 9th Ave S (98198-8259)
P.O. Box 23893, Federal Way (98093-0893)
PHONE....................253 202-6479
Jared Adams, *Principal*
Paul Ashley, *Principal*
EMP: 3
SALES (est): 280K Privately Held
SIC: 3646 Commercial indusl & institutional electric lighting fixtures

(G-2940)
LOST CITY DIGITAL LLC
26016 11th Pl S (98198-9143)
PHONE....................206 327-4537

Justin Quinn,
EMP: 2 EST: 2014
SALES (est): 84K Privately Held
SIC: 7372 7389 Application computer software;

(G-2941)
NORTHWEST PRIME TIME
22712 10th Ave S (98198-6917)
PHONE....................206 824-8600
Michelle Roedell, *Principal*
EMP: 2
SALES (est): 69.2K Privately Held
SIC: 2711 Newspapers: publishing only, not printed on site

(G-2942)
POWERS MACHINE & FABRICATION
919 S 222nd St (98198-6306)
PHONE....................206 824-9726
Troy Powers, *Owner*
EMP: 4
SALES (est): 198K Privately Held
SIC: 3599 Machine shop, jobbing & repair

(G-2943)
PRINT PLACE
Also Called: Print Place, The
22207 7th Ave S Ste 2 (98198-6221)
PHONE....................206 878-1380
Dan Johnson, *Owner*
EMP: 8
SQ FT: 3,700
SALES (est): 436.4K Privately Held
WEB: www.danjohnson.com
SIC: 2752 Commercial printing, offset

(G-2944)
R B SALES
20714 1st Ave S (98198-2849)
P.O. Box 98844, Seattle (98198-0844)
PHONE....................206 870-0741
Rusty Brannan, *Principal*
EMP: 2
SALES (est): 165.7K Privately Held
SIC: 5136 2329 2326 Work clothing, men's & boys'; men's & boys' clothing; men's & boys' work clothing

(G-2945)
REAL TIME SCREEN PRINTINGINC
2051 S 223rd St (98198-7934)
PHONE....................206 818-6346
Sara Southichack, *Principal*
EMP: 2
SALES (est): 80.6K Privately Held
SIC: 2759 Commercial printing

(G-2946)
SOUND HYDRAULICS INC
20931 4th Ave S (98198-3604)
PHONE....................206 824-7450
Jerry Thomas, *Corp Secy*
Pavel Kozorezov, *Vice Pres*
▲ EMP: 4
SQ FT: 5,000
SALES: 311K Privately Held
SIC: 7699 3594 Hydraulic equipment repair; motors: hydraulic, fluid power or air

(G-2947)
SUNTOWER SYSTEMS
21834 12th Ave S (98198-8328)
P.O. Box 13094, Seattle (98198-1001)
PHONE....................206 878-0578
JC Harris, *Partner*
Hugh Donnelly, *Partner*
J C Harris, *Partner*
Alec Marron, *Partner*
Sean Marron, *Partner*
EMP: 17
SQ FT: 1,600
SALES (est): 799.6K Privately Held
WEB: www.suntowersystems.com
SIC: 7372 7371 Prepackaged software; custom computer programming services

(G-2948)
ULTIMATE SEAL LLC
22419 Pacific Hwy S (98198-5106)
PHONE....................866 567-9149
Dion Garnett, *Mng Member*
Alexander Lee,

GEOGRAPHIC SECTION

Duvall - King County (G-2981)

EMP: 5
SQ FT: 5,200
SALES: 1.8MM Privately Held
SIC: 2869 Industrial organic chemicals

(G-2949)
URBAN DIAMOND TOOLS
23260 25th Ave S (98198-8715)
PHONE...................................206 824-6819
Brett Paracy, President
EMP: 2 EST: 1996
SALES: 300K Privately Held
WEB: www.urbandiamondtools.com
SIC: 5094 3545 Diamonds (gems); diamond cutting tools for turning, boring, burnishing, etc.

(G-2950)
VILLAGE FRAME & GALLERY
22507 Marine View Dr S (98198-6835)
PHONE...................................206 824-3068
Tammie Martinjako, Owner
EMP: 3
SQ FT: 1,200
SALES: 70K Privately Held
SIC: 2499 5961 5947 5999 Picture & mirror frames, wood; arts & crafts equipment & supplies, mail order; gift shop; picture frames, ready made

(G-2951)
WEST COAST ELEVATOR LLC
111 S 197th St (98148-2430)
PHONE...................................206 878-9378
Sylvia Gange, Mng Member
EMP: 6
SALES (est): 600K Privately Held
SIC: 3534 Elevators & moving stairways

(G-2952)
WOODWARD & WHITE MANUFACTURING
Also Called: Woodward White Mch Manufacturi
27051 10th Ave S (98198-9315)
PHONE...................................253 839-7581
Joel Woodward, President
Bob Rowley, Principal
EMP: 2
SQ FT: 18,000
SALES (est): 381.7K Privately Held
SIC: 3553 Woodworking machinery

Dryden
Chelan County

(G-2953)
METAL WORKS INC
8611 Frontage Rd (98821)
P.O. Box 451 (98821-0451)
PHONE...................................509 782-8811
Frank Andrews, President
Diane Andrews, Corp Secy
David Andrews, Vice Pres
▲ EMP: 2
SALES (est): 257.5K Privately Held
SIC: 3441 7692 3599 Fabricated structural metal; welding repair; machine shop, jobbing & repair

Dupont
Pierce County

(G-2954)
AGCO
3895 Pioneer Ave Ste 101 (98327-9520)
PHONE...................................253 964-2313
Earl Mintz, Principal
▲ EMP: 4 EST: 2003
SALES (est): 545.9K Privately Held
SIC: 3523 Farm machinery & equipment

(G-2955)
BASALITE BUILDING PRODUCTS LLC
3299 International Pl (98327-7707)
PHONE...................................253 964-5000
Jeff Vanallen, Opers Mgr
Phil Bonnell, Manager
EMP: 50

SALES (corp-wide): 1.6B Privately Held
WEB: www.basalite.com
SIC: 3272 3271 Concrete products, precast; concrete block & brick
HQ: Basalite Building Products, Llc
    2150 Douglas Blvd Ste 260
    Roseville CA 95661
    707 678-1901

(G-2956)
CAKE TIME UNQUE TSTE SWEET LLC
Also Called: Cake Time Unique Sweet
1649 Palisade Blvd (98327-9716)
PHONE...................................253 886-9366
Nancy Johnson, Manager
EMP: 6 EST: 2014
SALES (est): 236.6K Privately Held
SIC: 5963 5149 2051 5461 Bakery goods, house-to-house; bakery products; cakes, pies & pastries; bakery, for home service delivery; cakes;

(G-2957)
CALPORTLAND COMPANY
4301 Pioneer Ave (98327-7736)
P.O. Box 509 (98327-0509)
PHONE...................................253 912-8500
Scott Nicholson, Manager
EMP: 8 Privately Held
SIC: 5261 5211 5032 3273 Lawn & garden supplies; concrete & cinder block; concrete & cinder building products; ready-mixed concrete
HQ: Calportland Company
    2025 E Financial Way
    Glendora CA 91741
    626 852-6200

(G-2958)
DUPONT DE NEMOURS INC
1495 Wilmington Dr (98327-8807)
PHONE...................................253 212-2278
Sandy Ikemeier, Branch Mgr
EMP: 3
SALES (corp-wide): 85.9B Publicly Held
SIC: 2879 Agricultural chemicals
PA: Dupont De Nemours, Inc.
    974 Centre Rd
    Wilmington DE 19805
    302 774-1000

(G-2959)
DUPONT DELIVERY LLC
707 Penniman St (98327-9024)
P.O. Box 556 (98327-0556)
PHONE...................................253 884-2824
Sarah Wilson, Principal
EMP: 2
SALES (est): 90K Privately Held
SIC: 2879 Agricultural chemicals

(G-2960)
DUPONT LIBRARY
1540 Wilmington Dr (98327-8771)
PHONE...................................253 548-3326
Susan McBride, Principal
EMP: 2
SALES (est): 74.4K Privately Held
SIC: 2879 Agricultural chemicals

(G-2961)
DUPONT PET SITTING & SERVICES
1726 Brown Ave (98327-8794)
PHONE...................................816 517-7045
Kristy Bowman, Principal
EMP: 2
SALES (est): 74.4K Privately Held
SIC: 2879 Agricultural chemicals

(G-2962)
DUPONT VETERINARY CENTER
1525 Wilmington Dr (98327-7722)
PHONE...................................253 267-5431
EMP: 2
SALES (est): 74.4K Privately Held
SIC: 2879 Agricultural chemicals

(G-2963)
FERRIS FUN FOODS
18524 190th St Sw (98327-9508)
PHONE...................................253 964-2828
Kenneth Ferris, Principal
EMP: 3

SALES (est): 282K Privately Held
SIC: 2099 Food preparations

(G-2964)
GLACIER NORTHWEST INC
Also Called: Lone Star Northwest
4301 Pioneer Ave (98327-7736)
P.O. Box 509 (98327-0509)
PHONE...................................253 912-8500
Scott Nicholson, Manager
EMP: 75 Privately Held
WEB: www.glaciernw.com
SIC: 5032 3273 1442 Brick, stone & related material; ready-mixed concrete; construction sand & gravel
HQ: Glacier Northwest, Inc.
    5975 E Marginal Way S
    Seattle WA 98134
    206 764-3000

(G-2965)
HDC FILTERS LLC
1939 Ogden Ave (98327-7701)
PHONE...................................253 964-0707
Charles Despars, Principal
EMP: 2
SALES (est): 162.5K Privately Held
SIC: 3569 Filters

(G-2966)
HOME TEAM DUPONT
2705 Macarthur St (98327-8719)
PHONE...................................253 576-1907
Dawn Smith, Broker
EMP: 2
SALES (est): 130.4K Privately Held
SIC: 2879 Agricultural chemicals

(G-2967)
HOME2 SUITES BY HILTON DUPONT
600 Station Dr (98327-8501)
PHONE...................................253 912-1000
EMP: 2
SALES (est): 74.4K Privately Held
SIC: 2879 Agricultural chemicals

(G-2968)
KOH GEN DO AMERICAS LLC
2620 Williamson Pl # 133 (98327-9518)
PHONE...................................253 267-1769
David Dunne, Mng Member
▲ EMP: 8
SQ FT: 2,000
SALES (est): 1.7MM Privately Held
SIC: 2844 Cosmetic preparations

(G-2969)
LIFE CHURCH DUPONT
1315 Rowan Ct (98327-8776)
P.O. Box 102 (98327-0102)
PHONE...................................253 279-1507
Derek Thomas, Principal
EMP: 2
SALES (est): 74.4K Privately Held
SIC: 2879 Agricultural chemicals

(G-2970)
MOMS CLUB OF DUPONT
2390 Simmons St Unit A (98327-7765)
P.O. Box 247 (98327-0247)
PHONE...................................206 209-9048
Karen Hetz, Principal
EMP: 2
SALES (est): 86.5K Privately Held
SIC: 2879 Agricultural chemicals

(G-2971)
ORACLE HYPNOSIS
3098 Mcallister St (98327-8768)
PHONE...................................859 893-8147
Kelly Bruce, Principal
EMP: 2 EST: 2016
SALES (est): 56.5K Privately Held
SIC: 7372 Prepackaged software

(G-2972)
RANGER PUBLISHING INC
1274 Oneil Ct (98327-9764)
PHONE...................................253 964-2680
Thomas H Swarner, President
EMP: 18
SALES (est): 1MM Privately Held
SIC: 2711 Newspapers: publishing only, not printed on site

(G-2973)
TRAX AT DUPONT STATION
1430 Wilmington Dr (98327-9055)
PHONE...................................253 503-0693
EMP: 2
SALES (est): 74.4K Privately Held
SIC: 2879 Agricultural chemicals

(G-2974)
TRAX AT DUPONT STATION
930 Ross Loop (98327-9044)
PHONE...................................253 912-8729
Melanie Timothy, Manager
EMP: 6
SALES (est): 644.1K Privately Held
SIC: 2879 Agricultural chemicals

(G-2975)
WASHINGTON DUPONT WA
1575 Wilmington Dr # 120 (98327-9033)
PHONE...................................253 964-3403
EMP: 2
SALES (est): 76.8K Privately Held
SIC: 2879 Agricultural chemicals

(G-2976)
WESTERN GROUP PACIFIC
3250 International Pl (98327-7707)
PHONE...................................253 964-6201
Zanley Galton, Owner
James Bennett, General Mgr
Steve Jewell, General Mgr
Lonelle Yarbrough, Accountant
EMP: 2
SALES (est): 237.4K Privately Held
SIC: 3496 7389 Fabrics, woven wire; business services

(G-2977)
WESTERN WIRE WORKS INC
Also Called: Pacific Northwest Wire Works
3250 International Pl (98327-7707)
PHONE...................................253 964-6201
James Bennett, Branch Mgr
EMP: 20
SALES (corp-wide): 33.6MM Privately Held
SIC: 3315 Wire & fabricated wire products
PA: Western Wire Works, Inc.
    3950 Nw Saint Helens Rd
    Portland OR 97210
    503 445-0319

Duvall
King County

(G-2978)
ACE ANTHONY EQUITY MGT LLC
14906 280th Pl Ne (98019-8117)
PHONE...................................425 333-6024
Ace Hill,
EMP: 14
SALES (est): 374.8K Privately Held
SIC: 3999 Manufacturing industries

(G-2979)
AMERICAN MEDICAL CONCEPTS
28126 Ne 144th St (98019-8125)
PHONE...................................425 844-2840
Bradley Mace, Principal
EMP: 2
SALES (est): 130K Privately Held
SIC: 3841 Surgical & medical instruments

(G-2980)
CHASE RACE
16809 W Snqlmie Vly Rd Ne (98019-9309)
PHONE...................................425 269-5636
Douglas Chase, Principal
EMP: 3
SALES (est): 414K Privately Held
SIC: 3799 Trailer hitches

(G-2981)
CHERRY VALLEY LOGGING COMPANY
Also Called: C V L
30002 Ne Cherry Valley Rd (98019-7801)
P.O. Box 597 (98019-0597)
PHONE...................................206 396-0002

Duvall - King County (G-2982)

Justin Vanhulle, *President*
Charles Vanhulle, *Vice Pres*
Nancy Vanhulle, *Treasurer*
Micky Vanhulle, *Admin Sec*
EMP: 10
SALES (est): 1.7MM **Privately Held**
SIC: 2411 1794 Logging camps & contractors; excavation work

(G-2982)
DETONATOR GAMES LLC
20241 296th Ave Ne (98019-8827)
PHONE..................................206 355-6682
EMP: 14
SALES (est): 940K **Privately Held**
SIC: 7372 Prepackaged Software Services

(G-2983)
DIREYS
32811 Ne 134th St (98019-7215)
PHONE..................................425 788-2026
Ken Irish, *Owner*
EMP: 3
SALES (est): 230K **Privately Held**
WEB: www.direys.com
SIC: 2431 Woodwork, interior & ornamental

(G-2984)
DUVALL GRAPHICS LLC
Also Called: Ef Print Copy Center
14524 Main St Ne Ste 111 (98019-8467)
PHONE..................................425 788-7578
William Falcon, *CEO*
EMP: 2 **EST:** 2007
SALES (est): 266.2K **Privately Held**
WEB: www.efprints.com
SIC: 2759 Advertising literature: printing

(G-2985)
ELEGANTLY YOURS
28000 Ne 142nd Pl (98019-8173)
PHONE..................................425 478-2873
Bethany Gibbs, *Principal*
EMP: 2 **EST:** 2011
SALES (est): 107.7K **Privately Held**
SIC: 3911 Jewelry apparel

(G-2986)
EVERGREEN CIRCUITS LLC
14023 284th Cir Ne (98019-8176)
P.O. Box 1304 (98019-1304)
PHONE..................................425 382-8412
Jay Beavers, *Mng Member*
EMP: 3
SALES (est): 132.5K **Privately Held**
SIC: 3842 Wheelchairs

(G-2987)
EVIL INDUSTRIES
31920 Ne Big Rock Rd (98019-7024)
PHONE..................................206 612-3293
Jason B Cullen, *Administration*
EMP: 2
SALES (est): 174.1K **Privately Held**
SIC: 3999 Barber & beauty shop equipment

(G-2988)
FERRIER CABINETS
20014 312th Ave Ne (98019-7904)
P.O. Box 1136 (98019-1136)
PHONE..................................425 788-0230
Gordon Ferrier, *Owner*
EMP: 2
SALES (est): 183.7K **Privately Held**
SIC: 2434 Wood kitchen cabinets

(G-2989)
GENERAL DYNAMICS CORPORATION
26802 Ne Virginia St (98019-8422)
PHONE..................................425 885-5010
EMP: 40
SALES (corp-wide): 36.1B **Publicly Held**
SIC: 3812 Search & navigation equipment
PA: General Dynamics Corporation
2941 Frview Pk Dr Ste 100
Falls Church VA 22042
703 876-3000

(G-2990)
GENGLER VETERINARY SVCS PLLC
Also Called: Duvall Veterinary Hospital
26415 Ne Valley St (98019-5023)
P.O. Box 56 (98019-0056)
PHONE..................................425 788-2620
Michelle Gengler, *Mng Member*
EMP: 15
SALES (est): 290.4K **Privately Held**
WEB: www.duvallvet.com
SIC: 0742 7372 Animal hospital services, pets & other animal specialties; application computer software

(G-2991)
ISLAND DOG SIGN COMPANY
14432 320th Ave Ne (98019-7410)
PHONE..................................206 381-0661
Kevin Jeffries, *President*
Richard Lyon, *Vice Pres*
EMP: 12
SALES (est): 1.5MM **Privately Held**
WEB: www.islanddogsigns.com
SIC: 3993 Signs & advertising specialties

(G-2992)
JAKS CUSTOM WOODWORK
17516 W Snoqualmie Riv (98019-9203)
PHONE..................................425 443-6210
Andrea Kosters, *Owner*
EMP: 2
SALES (est): 199K **Privately Held**
SIC: 2431 Millwork

(G-2993)
JERRYS IRON WORKS INC (PA)
16015 Main St Ne (98019-8582)
P.O. Box 334 (98019-0334)
PHONE..................................425 788-1467
Herman G Kaptein, *President*
EMP: 3 **EST:** 1966
SQ FT: 9,200
SALES: 2.2MM **Privately Held**
WEB: www.sanitech.net
SIC: 3589 3523 Garbage disposers & compactors, commercial; farm machinery & equipment; dairy equipment (farm)

(G-2994)
KENWORTHY MACHINE
30330 Ne 172nd St (98019-7806)
P.O. Box 1359 (98019-1359)
PHONE..................................425 788-2131
Mark Kenworthy, *Principal*
EMP: 4
SALES (est): 480.1K **Privately Held**
WEB: www.farm-ad.com
SIC: 3599 Machine shop, jobbing & repair

(G-2995)
MARILYNS RECYCLE INC
18525 W Snoqualmie Riv (98019-9204)
PHONE..................................425 788-1716
Marilyn D Young, *President*
Jerry Dejong, *President*
Marilyn De Jong, *Vice Pres*
EMP: 3
SALES (est): 549.9K **Privately Held**
SIC: 2611 Pulp manufactured from waste or recycled paper

(G-2996)
NORTHWEST OUTDOOR LIGHTING
26813 Ne Beadonhall St (98019-8423)
PHONE..................................425 633-6074
Mary Peterson, *Principal*
EMP: 2 **EST:** 2015
SALES (est): 134.5K **Privately Held**
SIC: 3648 Lighting equipment

(G-2997)
PENTZ DESIGN PATTERN FNDRY INC
14823 Main St Ne (98019-8439)
P.O. Box 69 (98019-0069)
PHONE..................................425 788-6490
Larry D Pentz, *President*
Stewart De Ome, *Vice Pres*
Ron Ahlegian, *VP Sales*
Rob Crawford, *Supervisor*
EMP: 41
SQ FT: 49,000
SALES (est): 5.7MM **Privately Held**
SIC: 3599 3369 3365 Machine shop, jobbing & repair; nonferrous foundries; aluminum & aluminum-based alloy castings

(G-2998)
PHONE FLARE INC
14023 284th Cir Ne (98019-8176)
PHONE..................................425 346-9230
Jay Beavers, *President*
Seth Talbott, *Treasurer*
EMP: 3
SALES (est): 141K **Privately Held**
SIC: 7372 7389 Business oriented computer software;

(G-2999)
R P SIGNS
14701 Main St Ne Ste C1 (98019-8443)
PHONE..................................425 788-6717
Ray Payne, *Owner*
Diane Payne, *Co-Owner*
EMP: 4 **EST:** 1998
SALES (est): 225K **Privately Held**
WEB: www.towsigns.com
SIC: 2759 Screen printing

(G-3000)
R P SIGNS SCREENPRINTING
32430 Ne 120th St (98019-7013)
PHONE..................................425 788-6717
EMP: 2
SALES (est): 75.8K **Privately Held**
SIC: 3993 Signs & advertising specialties

(G-3001)
SCRUPULOUS DESIGN
28326 Ne 146th St (98019-8136)
PHONE..................................425 788-1812
S W Law, *Principal*
EMP: 2 **EST:** 1996
SALES (est): 133.1K **Privately Held**
SIC: 3679 Electronic circuits

(G-3002)
SUNDOG LLC
26311 Ne Valley St 219 (98019-8435)
PHONE..................................206 313-8871
Dominick S Villella, *Owner*
▲ **EMP:** 3
SALES (est): 750K **Privately Held**
WEB: www.sundog.com
SIC: 2393 Textile bags

(G-3003)
WSB SHEETMETAL COMPANY
14701 Main St Ne Ste C3 (98019-8443)
PHONE..................................425 844-2061
Bill Bigleman, *President*
EMP: 4 **EST:** 1989
SALES (est): 490K **Privately Held**
SIC: 3585 Heating & air conditioning combination units

East Wenatchee
Douglas County

(G-3004)
4K LIFT SERVICES INC
459 Rock Island Rd (98802-5359)
P.O. Box 3239, Wenatchee (98807-3239)
PHONE..................................509 679-9997
Kregg Morrow, *President*
Kelly Morrow, *Vice Pres*
Korban Morrow, *Vice Pres*
EMP: 6
SALES (est): 900K **Privately Held**
SIC: 3537 5531 Lift trucks, industrial: fork, platform, straddle, etc.; truck equipment & parts

(G-3005)
A & E SYSTEMS
6350 Batterman Rd (98802-9327)
PHONE..................................509 886-1092
EMP: 3
SALES (est): 303.9K **Privately Held**
SIC: 7372 7371 Prepackaged Software Services Custom Computer Programing

(G-3006)
ACCOR TECHNOLOGY INC
3310 5th St Se (98802-9225)
PHONE..................................509 662-0608
Donna Terry, *Vice Pres*
EMP: 41
SALES (est): 9.4MM
SALES (corp-wide): 8.6MM **Privately Held**
WEB: www.accortechnology.com
SIC: 3494 3432 Valves & pipe fittings; plumbing fixture fittings & trim
PA: Accor Technology, Inc
608 State St S Ste 100
Kirkland WA 98033
425 453-5410

(G-3007)
APPLE OF MY PIE LLC
207 Goldcrest St (98802-9581)
PHONE..................................509 860-8881
EMP: 2
SALES (est): 85.9K **Privately Held**
SIC: 3571 Mfg Electronic Computers

(G-3008)
BARRETT SHEET METAL
435 Rock Island Rd Ste A (98802-5359)
P.O. Box 2297, Wenatchee (98807-2297)
PHONE..................................509 886-8708
Joseph Barrett, *Owner*
Kay Barrett, *Co-Owner*
Susan Barrett, *Co-Owner*
EMP: 2 **EST:** 2011
SALES (est): 93K **Privately Held**
SIC: 3441 Fabricated structural metal

(G-3009)
CASHMERE MANUFACTURING LLC
3759 Airport Way (98802-8721)
PHONE..................................509 888-2141
Thomas Kroon, *CEO*
Mike Krebs, *Prgrmr*
EMP: 20
SALES (est): 1.4MM **Privately Held**
SIC: 3599 3728 3369 Machine shop, jobbing & repair; aircraft parts & equipment; nonferrous foundries

(G-3010)
DOUGS DIESEL REPAIR
3703 N Clemons St (98802-9336)
P.O. Box 2778, Wenatchee (98807-2778)
PHONE..................................509 665-7480
Douglas Scaramozzino, *Principal*
EMP: 4
SALES (est): 556.9K **Privately Held**
SIC: 3713 Truck bodies & parts

(G-3011)
EMPIRE PRESS CO
Also Called: Water Empire Press
832 Valley Mall Pkwy D (98802-4496)
P.O. Box 1455, Wenatchee (98807-1455)
PHONE..................................509 886-8668
Donna Cassidy, *Branch Mgr*
EMP: 4
SALES (est): 163.3K
SALES (corp-wide): 513.4K **Privately Held**
SIC: 2711 Newspapers: publishing only, not printed on site
PA: Empire Press Co
550 Empire Blvd
Brooklyn NY 11225
718 756-9500

(G-3012)
ENTIAT VALLEY VINEYARDS LLC
406 23rd St Ne (98802-4050)
PHONE..................................509 884-1152
Garrett Grubbs, *Principal*
EMP: 2
SALES (est): 66K **Privately Held**
SIC: 2084 Wines

(G-3013)
FIBER TRENDS INC
301 2nd St Se (98802-5322)
PHONE..................................509 884-8631
Beverly Galeskas, *Owner*
Joe Galeskas, *Co-Owner*
◆ **EMP:** 2

▲ = Import ▼=Export
◆ =Import/Export

SALES (est): 135.4K **Privately Held**
WEB: www.fibertrends.com
SIC: 2295 Yarns, plastic coated: made from purchased yarns

(G-3014)
GLASS DOCTOR OF WENATCHEE
435b Rock Island Rd (98802-5359)
PHONE...................509 415-3400
Cassandra Franklin, *Owner*
EMP: 4
SALES (est): 118.4K **Privately Held**
SIC: 1793 3714 Glass & glazing work; windshield wiper systems, motor vehicle

(G-3015)
GOLD IMPRESSIONS
1417 Easthills Ter (98802-4624)
P.O. Box 4383, Wenatchee (98807-4383)
PHONE...................509 886-0866
Robert Wallace, *Owner*
EMP: 2
SALES (est): 58K **Privately Held**
WEB: www.goldimpressions.com
SIC: 3961 Costume jewelry

(G-3016)
GP GRADERS LLC
3721 Airport Way (98802-8721)
PHONE...................253 239-3727
Stuart Payne, *President*
▲ **EMP:** 18 **EST:** 2012
SALES (est): 8.2MM **Privately Held**
SIC: 3523 Grading, cleaning, sorting machines, fruit, grain, vegetable

(G-3017)
GREASE HEADS LUBE AND OIL LLC
1130 N Baker Ave (98802-4331)
PHONE...................509 930-3786
EMP: 2
SALES (est): 81.9K **Privately Held**
SIC: 1311 Crude petroleum & natural gas

(G-3018)
H2 PRE- CAST INC
3835 N Clemons St (98802-9337)
PHONE...................509 884-6644
Travis Garske, *President*
Clay Trewitt, *General Mgr*
Susan Haven, *Corp Secy*
EMP: 82
SQ FT: 1,700
SALES: 10MM **Privately Held**
WEB: www.h2precast.com
SIC: 3272 Concrete products, precast

(G-3019)
HEALING MOUNTAIN PUBG INC
430 Elva Way (98802-5418)
PHONE...................509 433-4719
Gary Piscopo, *President*
EMP: 4
SALES (est): 294.9K **Privately Held**
SIC: 2741 Miscellaneous publishing

(G-3020)
HORAN ESTATES WINERY
431 19th St Ne (98802-4213)
PHONE...................509 679-8705
EMP: 2
SALES (est): 83.7K **Privately Held**
SIC: 2084 Wines

(G-3021)
INPRINT PRINTING INC
962 Valley Mall Pkwy (98802-4402)
PHONE...................509 884-1454
Chris Mingo, *President*
Delis Mingo, *Admin Sec*
EMP: 8
SQ FT: 5,000
SALES (est): 1.3MM **Privately Held**
WEB: www.inprintprinting.com
SIC: 2752 Commercial printing, offset

(G-3022)
J S VAIL
435 Rock Island Rd A (98802-5359)
PHONE...................509 886-8708
Michael J Vail, *Principal*
EMP: 2

SALES (est): 275.7K **Privately Held**
SIC: 3444 Sheet metalwork

(G-3023)
M K HANSEN COMPANY
2216 Fancher Blvd (98802)
P.O. Box 2066, Wenatchee (98807-2066)
PHONE...................509 884-1396
Mike K Hansen, *President*
Margaret Hansen, *Treasurer*
EMP: 2 **EST:** 1975
SQ FT: 700
SALES: 210K **Privately Held**
WEB: www.mkhansen.com
SIC: 3822 3571 Auto controls regulating residntl & coml environmt & applncs; electronic computers

(G-3024)
MEDIA DIRECTED INC (PA)
Also Called: D M I
1150 N Grover Ave (98802-4546)
PHONE...................509 886-5759
Dale Lambert, *President*
Kathleen Lambert, *Vice Pres*
EMP: 4 **EST:** 1978
SALES: 370K **Privately Held**
SIC: 2741 Miscellaneous publishing

(G-3025)
METAL SMITH
450 Rock Island Rd (98802-5360)
PHONE...................509 884-4851
Daniel J Pattison, *President*
EMP: 12
SQ FT: 6,000
SALES (est): 786.1K **Privately Held**
SIC: 1711 3444 Refrigeration contractor; metal roofing & roof drainage equipment

(G-3026)
MITCHELL TRUCKING AND PAVING
Also Called: Mitchell Trucking & Paving
3223 Nw Alan Ave (98802-9548)
PHONE...................509 884-5928
Bonnie Mitchell, *President*
Jody Mitchell, *Vice Pres*
Ted Mitchell, *Vice Pres*
Kathy Mitchell, *Admin Sec*
EMP: 4
SALES (est): 2.3MM **Privately Held**
SIC: 2951 4212 1771 Asphalt & asphaltic paving mixtures (not from refineries); local trucking, without storage; concrete work

(G-3027)
NORTHWEST INTERNET
343 Grant Rd (98802-5333)
PHONE...................509 888-2020
Demeti Mandelis, *Owner*
EMP: 2
SALES (est): 96K **Privately Held**
SIC: 7372 Prepackaged software

(G-3028)
PACE INTERNATIONAL LLC
3765 N Clemons St Unit 6 (98802-9338)
PHONE...................800 936-6750
Peter Sanderson, *Principal*
EMP: 29 **Privately Held**
SIC: 2842 Specialty cleaning preparations
HQ: Pace International, Llc
5661 Branch Rd
Wapato WA 98951
800 936-6750

(G-3029)
PIPKIN-GOODFELLOW VENTURE LLC
4801 Contractors Dr (98802-8688)
P.O. Box 3181, Wenatchee (98807-3181)
PHONE...................509 884-2400
Arnie Pipkin,
Martin Barron,
EMP: 3 **EST:** 2012
SQ FT: 11,000
SALES (est): 208.7K **Privately Held**
SIC: 1442 Construction sand & gravel

(G-3030)
PURE EXTRACTS
5526 Industry Ln Ste 1 (98802-9601)
PHONE...................509 679-6556
EMP: 3 **EST:** 2017

SALES (est): 90K **Privately Held**
SIC: 3999 2836 ; extracts

(G-3031)
ROSEMOUNT SPECIALTY PDTS LLC (DH)
5545 Nelpar Dr (98802-8001)
PHONE...................509 881-2100
Jodie Hall, *Manager*
Daneille Mooney, *Manager*
EMP: 39
SALES (est): 11.3MM
SALES (corp-wide): 17.4B **Publicly Held**
SIC: 3823 Industrial instrmnts msrmnt display/control process variable
HQ: Rosemount Inc.
8200 Market Blvd
Chanhassen MN 55317
952 906-8888

(G-3032)
SALLY BEAUTY SUPPLY LLC
300 Simon St Se Ste 3 (98802-7720)
PHONE...................509 881-2120
Raquel Jones, *Manager*
EMP: 3 **Publicly Held**
SIC: 5087 3069 Beauty parlor equipment & supplies; capes, vulcanized rubber or rubberized fabric; brushes, rubber
HQ: Sally Beauty Supply Llc
3001 Colorado Blvd
Denton TX 76210
940 898-7500

(G-3033)
ULTIMATE RACK INC
331 Valley Mall Pkwy # 215 (98802-4831)
PHONE...................509 393-3526
Robert Oblon, *President*
EMP: 2 **EST:** 2010
SALES (est): 121K
SALES (corp-wide): 183.9K **Privately Held**
SIC: 3429 5021 Bicycle racks, automotive; ski racks, automotive; racks
PA: Travopoly Travel, Llc
3207 Skylane Dr Ste 110
Carrollton TX

(G-3034)
VAN DOREN SALES INC (PA)
10 Ne Cascade Ave (98802-8291)
P.O. Box 1746, Wenatchee (98807-1746)
PHONE...................509 886-1837
Brian Haun, *CEO*
Bret Pittsinger, *President*
Jeremy Loewen, *Sales Staff*
▲ **EMP:** 91
SQ FT: 75,000
SALES (est): 21.6MM **Privately Held**
WEB: www.vandorensales.com
SIC: 3523 5084 Farm machinery & equipment; industrial machinery & equipment

(G-3035)
WENATCHEE RED APPLE FLYERS
1123 2nd St Se (98802-5511)
PHONE...................509 881-7884
EMP: 2
SALES (est): 85.9K **Privately Held**
SIC: 3571 Electronic Computers, Nsk

Eastsound
San Juan County

(G-3036)
8STEM INC
118 Main St (98245-9635)
P.O. Box 370 (98245-0370)
PHONE...................360 317-7448
Bruce Pavitt,
EMP: 4
SALES (est): 108.2K **Privately Held**
SIC: 7372 7389 Application computer software;

(G-3037)
JAMES HELLAR CABINETRY
564 Eastman Rd (98245-9388)
PHONE...................360 376-5727
James Hellar, *Owner*
EMP: 2

SALES (est): 172.3K **Privately Held**
SIC: 2434 Wood kitchen cabinets

(G-3038)
KC MCCOY INC
Also Called: Bushwhackers Brushcutting
5290 Olga Rd (98245)
PHONE...................360 376-5619
Kevin Mc Coy, *President*
EMP: 2
SALES (est): 120K **Privately Held**
SIC: 3531 Road construction & maintenance machinery

(G-3039)
MARK E PADBURY
Also Called: Mark Padbury Construction
17 Jensen Rd (98245-9472)
PHONE...................360 376-6200
EMP: 2
SALES (est): 100K **Privately Held**
SIC: 2431 Manufactures Millwork

(G-3040)
MINDPLACE COMPANY
374 N Beach Rd Ste 2b (98245-8962)
P.O. Box 833 (98245-0833)
PHONE...................360 376-6494
Robert Austin, *President*
William Austin, *Shareholder*
Ftel George, *Shareholder*
Frank M Robinson, *Shareholder*
Diane Thome, *Shareholder*
EMP: 4
SALES (est): 800K **Privately Held**
SIC: 3829 3845 Thermometers & temperature sensors; electrocardiographs; electroencephalographs; electromyographs

(G-3041)
ORBIS COMPANY LLC
Also Called: Orbis World Globes
663 Gafford Ln (98245-9485)
P.O. Box 1148 (98245-1148)
PHONE...................360 376-4320
Eric James Morris, *President*
▲ **EMP:** 4
SALES (est): 438.1K **Privately Held**
SIC: 3999 Globes, geographical

(G-3042)
ORCAS ISLAND POTTERY
338 Old Pottery Rd (98245-9319)
PHONE...................360 376-2813
Syd Exton, *Owner*
EMP: 2
SALES (est): 160K **Privately Held**
WEB: www.orcasislandpottery.com
SIC: 3269 5719 Art & ornamental ware, pottery; pottery

(G-3043)
ORCAS MEMORIES LLC
2200 Buck Mountain Rd (98245-5654)
P.O. Box 165 (98245-0165)
PHONE...................650 325-9400
Rebecca McDonough, *Principal*
EMP: 3
SALES (est): 105.9K **Privately Held**
SIC: 2711 Newspapers

(G-3044)
PAPER JAM PUBLISHING CO LLP
10 Madrona St (98245)
PHONE...................360 376-3200
Robert J Kinney, *Principal*
EMP: 3
SALES (est): 127.8K **Privately Held**
SIC: 2731 Books: publishing only

(G-3045)
PAR 4 GOLF SERVICES
112 Discovery Way (98245-8505)
P.O. Box 1268 (98245-1268)
PHONE...................360 376-4462
Beatrice Vontobel, *Partner*
Cindy Elliott, *Partner*
EMP: 2
SALES (est): 129.2K **Privately Held**
SIC: 3949 7699 Shafts, golf club; golf club & equipment repair

Eastsound - San Juan County (G-3046) — GEOGRAPHIC SECTION

(G-3046)
SEA ISLAND CORP
340 Gravel Pit Rd (98245-9261)
PHONE..................360 376-4215
Rockwell Arnt, *President*
EMP: 12
SQ FT: 3,000
SALES (est): 1.3MM **Privately Held**
SIC: 1442 Construction sand & gravel

(G-3047)
SOUND PUBLISHING INC
Also Called: Island Sounder
217 Main St B (98245-5510)
PHONE..................360 376-4500
Elyse Van Den Bosch, *Branch Mgr*
EMP: 8 **Privately Held**
WEB: www.soundpublishing.com
SIC: 2711 2731 Newspapers: publishing only, not printed on site; book publishing
HQ: Sound Publishing, Inc.
11323 Commando Rd W Main
Everett WA 98204
360 394-5800

(G-3048)
TURTLEBACK PRESS
636 Wildrose Ln (98245-9221)
PHONE..................360 376-4625
Linda Henry, *Partner*
Pam Loew, *Partner*
EMP: 2
SALES (est): 105.4K **Privately Held**
WEB: www.turtlebackpress.com
SIC: 2731 Book publishing

Eatonville
Pierce County

(G-3049)
ADA SIGNAGE AND SPC INC
35511 Etnvlle Cutoff Rd E (98328)
PHONE..................253 651-1748
Mark Rosenkranz, *General Mgr*
EMP: 3
SALES (est): 218.5K **Privately Held**
SIC: 3993 7389 Signs & advertising specialties;

(G-3050)
BASIC HOMES LLC
Also Called: Landredi
109 Washinton Ave N (98328)
PHONE..................253 579-2724
William A Lewis,
William Lewis,
EMP: 3
SQ FT: 1,000
SALES (est): 173K **Privately Held**
SIC: 1611 1794 1799 2411 General contractor, highway & street construction; excavation & grading, building construction; fence construction; timber, cut at logging camp; mobile homes

(G-3051)
BOETTCHER & SONS INC
186 Dow Ridge Dr N (98328-8087)
P.O. Box 992 (98328-0992)
PHONE..................360 832-3943
Caleb Boettcher, *President*
Daniel Boeetcher, *Principal*
Benjamin Boettcher, *Principal*
EMP: 5
SALES (est): 480K **Privately Held**
SIC: 2411 1521 Logging; new construction, single-family houses

(G-3052)
CLIMACOVER INC
44128 Nsqually Ridge Dr E (98328-9218)
P.O. Box 4838, Spanaway (98387-4055)
PHONE..................360 458-1010
John Baum, *President*
James Akers, *Chairman*
Andrea Sodon, *Treasurer*
Erling Larsen, *Director*
Roger Whinnery, *Director*
▼ **EMP:** 6
SQ FT: 3,255
SALES (est): 280K **Privately Held**
SIC: 2394 Tarpaulins, fabric: made from purchased materials

(G-3053)
DON GLASER LOGGING
8707 366th St E (98328-9326)
PHONE..................206 462-9638
Gina Glaser, *Principal*
EMP: 2
SALES (est): 81.7K **Privately Held**
SIC: 2411 Logging

(G-3054)
DON PAINTER LOGGING INC
410 Madison Ave N (98328-9444)
P.O. Box 477 (98328-0477)
PHONE..................360 832-3683
Don Painter, *President*
EMP: 10
SALES (est): 894K **Privately Held**
SIC: 2411 Logging camps & contractors

(G-3055)
EATONVILLE DISPATCH NEWSPAPER
Also Called: South Pierce County Dispatch
133 Mashell Ave N (98328)
P.O. Box 248 (98328-0248)
PHONE..................360 832-4411
Michael Jefferies, *President*
EMP: 13 **EST:** 1983
SQ FT: 3,200
SALES (est): 477K **Privately Held**
WEB: www.dispatchnews.com
SIC: 2711 Newspapers: publishing only, not printed on site

(G-3056)
ERICKSON LOGGING INC
41306 90th Ave E (98328-9569)
P.O. Box 365, Gig Harbor (98335-0365)
PHONE..................360 832-8627
Kurt Erickson, *President*
EMP: 16 **EST:** 1996
SQ FT: 2,500
SALES (est): 3.6MM **Privately Held**
WEB: www.ericksonlogging.com
SIC: 2411 Logging camps & contractors

(G-3057)
F PS PALLET RECYCLING INC
7020 Ohop Valley Rd E (98328-9343)
PHONE..................253 312-7122
Freeman Pruitt, *President*
EMP: 7
SQ FT: 6,000
SALES (est): 595.8K **Privately Held**
WEB: www.fpspallets.com
SIC: 2448 Pallets, wood

(G-3058)
GREAT GATES NW INC
33911 Tanwax Ct E (98328-8692)
PHONE..................360 879-5554
EMP: 5
SALES (est): 358.5K **Privately Held**
SIC: 3315 1751 Fence gates posts & fittings: steel; window & door (prefabricated) installation

(G-3059)
HUBSTER LOGGING INC
4325 Chrstensen Muck Rd E (98328-9729)
PHONE..................253 200-7183
Jim Hubbard, *President*
EMP: 6 **EST:** 2011
SALES (est): 797.7K **Privately Held**
SIC: 2411 Logging camps & contractors

(G-3060)
JERRY NYBO CONSTRUCTION INC (PA)
7420 320th St E (98328-9793)
PHONE..................253 691-1797
Jerry Nybo, *President*
EMP: 5
SALES: 3MM **Privately Held**
SIC: 1521 3273 Single-family housing construction; ready-mixed concrete

(G-3061)
LOUDIN LOGGING LLC
8807 321st Street Ct E (98328-8912)
PHONE..................253 691-8679
Bradley S Loudin, *Principal*
EMP: 2
SALES (est): 138.8K **Privately Held**
SIC: 2411 Logging

(G-3062)
LYNCH CREEK QUARRY LLC
14115 419th St E (98328-9534)
PHONE..................360 832-4269
David Randles,
EMP: 4
SALES (est): 242.7K **Privately Held**
SIC: 5032 5261 2411 Stone, crushed or broken; lawn & garden supplies; logging
PA: Lynch Creek Quarry Llc
19209 Canyon Rd E
Puyallup WA 98375

(G-3063)
NORDKYN OUTFITTERS
5903 316th St E (98328-8612)
P.O. Box 1023, Graham (98338-1023)
PHONE..................253 847-4128
Jane Riffle, *Owner*
Rip Riffle, *Co-Owner*
M Nordkyn, *Administration*
▲ **EMP:** 3
SALES (est): 150K **Privately Held**
SIC: 3999 Pet supplies

(G-3064)
NORTHWEST DOCK SYSTEMS LLC
795 State Route 161 N (98328-7032)
PHONE..................360 832-2295
Ken Ames,
Mark Swartout,
EMP: 2
SALES (est): 800K **Privately Held**
SIC: 2499 3732 Floating docks, wood; boat building & repairing

(G-3065)
PACIFIC SPRING MFG CO
1607 434th St E (98328-9284)
PHONE..................360 832-3633
Brian Joseph Piper, *Principal*
EMP: 2
SALES (est): 139.9K **Privately Held**
SIC: 3999 Manufacturing industries

(G-3066)
PLAAS TIMBER LLC
41427 Orville Rd E (98328-8394)
P.O. Box 429 (98328-0429)
PHONE..................360 832-2440
Mike Plaas, *Partner*
Kattie Plaas, *Partner*
EMP: 15
SALES (est): 891K **Privately Held**
SIC: 2411 Logging

(G-3067)
PRECISION INDUSTRIES LLC
33915 Tanwax Ct E (98328-8692)
PHONE..................253 255-3814
Brian Leach, *Principal*
EMP: 2
SALES (est): 124.8K **Privately Held**
SIC: 3999 Manufacturing industries

(G-3068)
RAMSEY BROS LOGGING INC
5912 340th St E (98328-8617)
PHONE..................253 380-4971
Jeff Ramsey, *President*
EMP: 6 **EST:** 1969
SALES (est): 597.8K **Privately Held**
SIC: 2411 Logging camps & contractors

(G-3069)
T L FITZER LOGGING INC
11927 Clear Lake S Rd E (98328-9311)
P.O. Box 997 (98328-0997)
PHONE..................360 832-4949
Tracy Fitzer, *President*
EMP: 24
SQ FT: 900
SALES (est): 2.4MM **Privately Held**
SIC: 2411 Logging camps & contractors

(G-3070)
TOTAL SIGN SERVICE
44010 14th Ave E (98328-8280)
PHONE..................253 847-6868
Roger Drake, *Principal*
EMP: 3
SALES (est): 200.3K **Privately Held**
SIC: 3993 Signs & advertising specialties

Edgewood
Pierce County

(G-3071)
3 HATS
13120 55th St E (98372-9261)
PHONE..................253 606-3474
Barbara Eagle Patterson, *President*
EMP: 2
SALES (est): 110.6K **Privately Held**
SIC: 2353 Hats, caps & millinery

(G-3072)
BATP INC
2917 Meridian Ave E (98371-2110)
PHONE..................253 677-4706
Dorothy Bartelson, *Ch of Bd*
Bryan Bartelson, *President*
Scott Bartelson, *Vice Pres*
James Pizl, *CFO*
EMP: 3
SQ FT: 1,200
SALES: 1.6MM **Privately Held**
SIC: 6719 3715 Investment holding companies, except banks; truck trailers

(G-3073)
BIGONI STINER & ASSOC
2722 112th Ave E (98372-1856)
P.O. Box 1210, Milton (98354-1210)
PHONE..................253 826-5824
Dick Bigoni, *President*
Cal Steiner, *Corp Secy*
EMP: 2 **EST:** 1980
SALES (est): 200K **Privately Held**
SIC: 3999 Manufacturing industries

(G-3074)
CORWIN SCOTT THOMAS IMAG
422 106th Avenue Ct E (98372-1114)
PHONE..................253 350-6984
Thomas Corwin Walton, *Principal*
EMP: 2
SALES (est): 135.5K **Privately Held**
SIC: 3993 Signs & advertising specialties

(G-3075)
DIVERSIFIED DEFENSE
10710 48th St E Unit A (98372-5913)
PHONE..................253 327-0862
Aaron Kravik, *Principal*
EMP: 3
SALES (est): 196.6K **Privately Held**
SIC: 3812 Defense systems & equipment

(G-3076)
ENGINEERED PRODUCTS ENTPS
Also Called: E P E
12723 53rd Street Ct E (98372-9272)
PHONE..................253 826-6185
EMP: 10
SALES: 950K **Privately Held**
SIC: 8711 3429 Marine Engineers

(G-3077)
FAB SHOP LLC
Also Called: Fab Shop, The
10315 16th St E (98372-1337)
PHONE..................253 568-9124
Eric Bakke,
Ken Rush,
EMP: 23
SALES (est): 4.2MM **Privately Held**
WEB: www.thefabshop.com
SIC: 3599 5531 3713 Machine & other job shop work; machine shop, jobbing & repair; truck equipment & parts; truck bodies & parts

(G-3078)
FARWEST AIRCRAFT INC
1415 Meridian Ave E (98371-1057)
P.O. Box 1889, Milton (98354-1889)
PHONE..................253 568-1707
Jay D Marshall, *President*
Frank Gutfrucht, *President*
Tom Peterson, *Vice Pres*
▲ **EMP:** 32
SQ FT: 35,000

GEOGRAPHIC SECTION

Edmonds - Snohomish County (G-3112)

SALES (est): 8.1MM
SALES (corp-wide): 10MM **Privately Held**
WEB: www.farwestair.com
SIC: 3592 Valves, aircraft
PA: Jones Stevedoring Company
7245 W Marginal Way Sw
Seattle WA 98106
360 734-8960

(G-3079)
G B MACHINING INC
4415 102nd Ave E (98371-2717)
PHONE.................................253 848-8055
Gerhard Buchmann, *President*
EMP: 3
SALES (est): 211.6K **Privately Held**
SIC: 3599 Machine shop, jobbing & repair

(G-3080)
GOLDENROD INC
Also Called: Goldenrod Jewelry
2121 Meridian Ave E Ste 5 (98371-1024)
PHONE.................................253 840-8114
Diane L Hash, *President*
Diane Hash, *President*
Rodney Hash, *Vice Pres*
EMP: 2
SQ FT: 1,300
SALES: 300K **Privately Held**
WEB: www.goldenrodjewelry.com
SIC: 5944 3911 Jewelry, precious stones & precious metals; watches; jewelry apparel

(G-3081)
H & E BUILDING ENTERPRISES
Also Called: H & E Custom Cabinets
10318 32nd St E (98372-1750)
PHONE.................................253 848-3534
Ruben Estrada, *President*
EMP: 5
SALES: 500K **Privately Held**
SIC: 1751 2434 Cabinet building & installation; wood kitchen cabinets

(G-3082)
INNOVATIVE THERMAL SOLUTIONS
12201 23rd St E (98372-1652)
P.O. Box 544, Milton (98354-0544)
PHONE.................................253 830-4550
Brent Walker, *Principal*
EMP: 2
SALES (est): 224.2K **Privately Held**
SIC: 3585 Heating equipment, complete

(G-3083)
KANON ELECTRIC
1018 122nd Ave E (98372-1431)
PHONE.................................253 447-7831
EMP: 2
SALES (est): 97.2K **Privately Held**
SIC: 3699 Mfg Electrical Equipment/Supplies

(G-3084)
KRACKER TORTILLA DISTRIBUTION
916 118th Avenue Ct E (98372-1421)
PHONE.................................253 380-2690
Jeremy Knowles, *Principal*
EMP: 3
SALES (est): 161.7K **Privately Held**
SIC: 2099 Tortillas, fresh or refrigerated

(G-3085)
MITTENS BY ANN
4018 Caldwell Rd E (98372-9234)
PHONE.................................253 862-1050
Ann Miller, *Principal*
EMP: 2 EST: 2011
SALES (est): 107.4K **Privately Held**
SIC: 2381 Mittens, woven or knit: made from purchased materials

(G-3086)
MOOSE CANYON WINERY
9813 36th St E (98371-2651)
PHONE.................................253 225-1985
Dawne Swanson, *Principal*
EMP: 2 EST: 2016
SALES (est): 81.5K **Privately Held**
SIC: 2084 Wines

(G-3087)
NIGHTSIDE DISTILLERY LLC
2908 Meridian Ave E # 116 (98371-2190)
PHONE.................................253 906-4265
Raymond Bunk,
EMP: 6
SQ FT: 400
SALES (est): 223.9K **Privately Held**
SIC: 2085 Distilled & blended liquors

(G-3088)
NOVAK WINDOWS
11907 18th St E (98372-1677)
PHONE.................................253 332-4392
Bob Novak, *Principal*
EMP: 3
SALES (est): 227K **Privately Held**
SIC: 3442 Window & door frames

(G-3089)
PACIFIC SLOT CAR RACEWAYS LLC
2908 Meridian Ave E # 104 (98371-2196)
P.O. Box 421, Puyallup (98371-0044)
PHONE.................................253 446-5039
Rob McCusition, *Principal*
EMP: 5 EST: 2009
SALES (est): 425.3K **Privately Held**
SIC: 3644 Raceways

(G-3090)
R & R PRINTING INC
2908 Meridian Ave E (98371-2190)
PHONE.................................206 257-9438
Ronald Prasad, *President*
Rajendra Prasad, *Vice Pres*
EMP: 2
SALES: 240K **Privately Held**
SIC: 2752 Commercial printing, lithographic

(G-3091)
WB MOBILE MODULAR SERVICE
11005 20th St E (98372-1565)
PHONE.................................253 952-4630
Russell Williams, *Owner*
EMP: 2
SALES (est): 174.7K **Privately Held**
SIC: 3441 Fabricated structural metal

(G-3092)
WELDING BY CRAIG
4225 114th Ave E (98372-2316)
PHONE.................................253 307-3936
EMP: 2
SALES (est): 110K **Privately Held**
SIC: 7692 Welding repair

Edmonds
Snohomish County

(G-3093)
ALLNIGHT WHEELCHAIRS
7730 238th Pl Sw (98026-8858)
PHONE.................................425 774-6814
Thomas Cusworth, *Owner*
EMP: 3
SALES (est): 130K **Privately Held**
SIC: 3842 Wheelchairs

(G-3094)
AMBREW LLC
Also Called: American Brewing Company
180 W Dayton St (98020-7211)
PHONE.................................425 774-1717
Steve Navarro, *Mng Member*
EMP: 6
SQ FT: 5,000
SALES (est): 838.6K
SALES (corp-wide): 352.6K **Privately Held**
SIC: 2082 Malt beverages
PA: Pacific Brewing & Malting Co., Llc
914 A St 200
Tacoma WA 98402
253 442-0596

(G-3095)
APPLIED MFG & ENGRG TECH INC
Also Called: Ametech
6729 135th Pl Sw (98026-3333)
PHONE.................................253 852-5378
Paul Johnson, *President*
▲ EMP: 16 EST: 1980
SQ FT: 16,000
SALES (est): 3.2MM **Privately Held**
WEB: www.ametech.com
SIC: 3444 7692 3555 Sheet metal specialties, not stamped; welding repair; printing trades machinery

(G-3096)
BIG DOOR MUSIC PUBLISHING
6503 128th Pl Sw (98026-3165)
PHONE.................................206 890-1269
Kelly Springer, *Administration*
EMP: 2
SALES (est): 108.8K **Privately Held**
SIC: 2741 Miscellaneous publishing

(G-3097)
BNB INTERNATIONAL LLC
110 W Dayton St Ste 205 (98020-7210)
PHONE.................................425 712-1687
Tim Zhu, *Prdtn Mgr*
Barbara Shi,
Bean MA,
▲ EMP: 4
SALES (est): 380K **Privately Held**
SIC: 3714 Motor vehicle parts & accessories

(G-3098)
BROOKS PRODUCTS & SERVICES
6417 146th St Sw (98026-3520)
P.O. Box 2249, Lynnwood (98036-2249)
PHONE.................................425 742-4214
T J Brooks, *Owner*
Beverly Brooks, *Co-Owner*
EMP: 3
SALES (est): 200.2K **Privately Held**
WEB: www.brooksactivewear.com
SIC: 2396 Screen printing on fabric articles

(G-3099)
CAMOFLAGE
5812 159th St Sw (98026-4746)
PHONE.................................425 744-0764
Michael Mc Combe, *Owner*
EMP: 2
SALES (est): 119.7K **Privately Held**
SIC: 8748 3089 0781 Business consulting; planters, plastic; landscape services

(G-3100)
CHILD INC
7425 Olympic View Dr (98026-5554)
PHONE.................................425 775-9076
Dave Clobes, *President*
Julie Clobes, *President*
EMP: 2
SALES: 300K **Privately Held**
SIC: 1799 2426 5941 Playground construction & equipment installation; textile machinery accessories, hardwood; playground equipment

(G-3101)
CLINE MANUFACTURING JEWELERS
Also Called: Cline Custom Jewelers
105 5th Ave S (98020-3423)
PHONE.................................425 673-7979
Gerald Cline, *President*
Rebecca Cline, *Corp Secy*
Andrew Cline, *Vice Pres*
EMP: 8
SQ FT: 2,000
SALES (est): 1.5MM **Privately Held**
SIC: 3911 5944 Jewelry, precious metal; jewelry stores

(G-3102)
CR CALLEN LLC
17231 76th Ave W (98026-5006)
PHONE.................................206 363-7648
Brad Callen, *Mng Member*
EMP: 5
SQ FT: 3,000

SALES (est): 487K **Privately Held**
SIC: 2899 Chemical preparations

(G-3103)
CRAFT LABOR & SUPPORT SVCS LLC (PA)
7636 230th St Sw Apt B (98026-8480)
PHONE.................................206 304-4543
Peter L Madonna, *Mng Member*
Peter Madonna, *Manager*
EMP: 1
SALES (est): 10.3MM **Privately Held**
SIC: 3731 7389 Shipbuilding & repairing;

(G-3104)
CREATIVE CONCEPTS
6615 Marine View Dr (98026-3120)
PHONE.................................425 743-4671
Debbie Pedrola, *Co-Owner*
Bruce Pedrola, *Co-Owner*
EMP: 2
SALES: 100K **Privately Held**
SIC: 3589 Coffee brewing equipment

(G-3105)
CREATIVE ENTERPRISES INC
21014 70th Ave W (98026-7203)
PHONE.................................425 775-7010
Douglas Russell, *Principal*
EMP: 2 EST: 2012
SALES (est): 180.5K **Privately Held**
SIC: 3993 Signs & advertising specialties

(G-3106)
DENIM DREAMZ
19214 80th Ave W (98026-6210)
PHONE.................................425 712-1001
Christina Walker, *Principal*
EMP: 2
SALES (est): 120K **Privately Held**
SIC: 2211 Denims

(G-3107)
DRAKE INDUSTRIES LLC
17742 Talbot Rd (98026-5325)
PHONE.................................425 672-8266
EMP: 2 EST: 2010
SALES (est): 110K **Privately Held**
SIC: 3999 Mfg Misc Products

(G-3108)
DUREN CONTROLS
14328 Beverly Park Rd (98026-3921)
PHONE.................................206 745-4987
Tom Duren, *Owner*
EMP: 3
SALES (est): 224.5K **Privately Held**
SIC: 3625 Relays & industrial controls

(G-3109)
ENVIROSORB CO
8128 187th St Sw (98026-5843)
PHONE.................................425 778-7485
Richard B Eger, *Owner*
EMP: 2 EST: 1974
SALES: 100K **Privately Held**
WEB: www.envirosorb.co.za
SIC: 2869 Industrial organic chemicals

(G-3110)
ERIKSEN DIESEL REPAIR INC
7724 222nd St Sw (98026-7967)
PHONE.................................425 778-8237
Terry Eriksen, *President*
Peggy Eriksen, *Corp Secy*
▲ EMP: 2
SALES (est): 257.5K **Privately Held**
SIC: 3519 Diesel engine rebuilding

(G-3111)
FASCINATURALS LLC
Also Called: Washington State Gifts
23632 Highway 99 F107 (98026-9211)
PHONE.................................425 954-7151
EMP: 5
SALES (est): 360K **Privately Held**
SIC: 2844 8742 Mfg Toilet Preparations Mgmt Consulting Svcs

(G-3112)
FOLDZ WALLET LLC
111 Sunset Ave N Ste 104 (98020-3229)
PHONE.................................206 730-6381
Peter Roberts, *Principal*
EMP: 2

Edmonds - Snohomish County (G-3113)

SALES (est): 132.3K **Privately Held**
SIC: 3172 Wallets

(G-3113)
FOX PRINTING
5705 156th St Sw (98026-4617)
PHONE.....................206 595-7055
Kathleen Marden, *Owner*
EMP: 3
SALES (est): 132.8K **Privately Held**
SIC: 2752 Commercial printing, lithographic

(G-3114)
GENTLE DRAGON CARDS INC
18603 76th Ave W Ste 104 (98026-5808)
P.O. Box 31154, Seattle (98103-1154)
PHONE.....................206 546-3593
Mark Ukelson, *President*
Steve Wayne, *Treasurer*
John Yackshaw, *Admin Sec*
EMP: 2
SQ FT: 1,000
SALES (est): 218.6K **Privately Held**
SIC: 2771 Greeting cards

(G-3115)
HAMILTON JAN PRINTING SYSTEMS
120 W Dayton St Ste C8 (98020-4180)
PHONE.....................425 778-1975
Don Austin, *Owner*
EMP: 2
SALES (est): 191.9K **Privately Held**
SIC: 2752 Commercial printing, offset

(G-3116)
HAMILTON PRINITING
120 W Dayton St Ste C8 (98020-4180)
PHONE.....................425 778-1975
Don Austin, *Owner*
EMP: 2 EST: 2010
SALES (est): 130K **Privately Held**
SIC: 2759 Screen printing

(G-3117)
HAMILTON PRINTING SYSTEMS
22314 97th Ave W (98020-4535)
PHONE.....................425 778-1936
John Hamilton, *Principal*
EMP: 2
SALES (est): 132.6K **Privately Held**
SIC: 2752 Commercial printing, lithographic

(G-3118)
HELLA SHAGGY SOFTWARE LLC
10505 Nottingham Rd (98020-5185)
PHONE.....................206 533-1468
Robert Trahms, *Principal*
EMP: 2
SALES (est): 56.5K **Privately Held**
SIC: 7372 Prepackaged software

(G-3119)
HUNDMAN PUBLISHING INC
5115 Monticello Dr (98026-3449)
PHONE.....................425 742-1214
Robert Hundman, *President*
Ann Hundman, *Vice Pres*
EMP: 8
SQ FT: 1,800
SALES (est): 640K **Privately Held**
SIC: 2721 2731 Magazines: publishing only, not printed on site; book publishing

(G-3120)
INNOVAURA CORPORATION
7418 Soundview Dr (98026-5568)
PHONE.....................425 272-2702
Jeffrey Roe, *CEO*
Charles Lynde, *Director*
EMP: 2 EST: 2009
SALES (est): 233.4K **Privately Held**
SIC: 3825 3845 Test equipment for electronic & electric measurement; electromedical equipment

(G-3121)
JAMES BAY DISTILLERS LTD
10016 Edmonds Way C313 (98020-5107)
PHONE.....................703 930-8453
Ernest Troth, *Principal*
EMP: 2
SALES (est): 66K **Privately Held**
SIC: 2085 Distilled & blended liquors

(G-3122)
JAMES I MANNING
9003 220th St Sw (98026-8141)
PHONE.....................425 774-4275
James Manning, *Owner*
EMP: 2
SALES (est): 100K **Privately Held**
SIC: 3993 Signs & advertising specialties

(G-3123)
JETOPTERA INC
144 Railroad Ave Ste 100 (98020-4121)
PHONE.....................516 456-7609
Denis Dancaneit, *CEO*
Simina Farcasiu, *President*
Andrei Evulet, *Chief Engr*
EMP: 3 EST: 2015
SALES (est): 156.8K **Privately Held**
SIC: 3721 Research & development on aircraft by the manufacturer

(G-3124)
JIM MANNING
Also Called: Jim Manning & Associates
9003 220th St Sw (98026-8141)
PHONE.....................425 774-1964
James I Manning, *Owner*
EMP: 3 EST: 1977
SALES (est): 210K **Privately Held**
SIC: 3993 Neon signs; electric signs

(G-3125)
JOHN MARSHALL METALSMITH INC
23312 Robin Hood Dr (98020-5115)
PHONE.....................206 546-5643
John Marshall, *President*
Jane Marshall, *Vice Pres*
EMP: 2
SALES (est): 120K **Privately Held**
SIC: 3914 Silversmithing

(G-3126)
JOONGANG USA
Also Called: Korea Central Daily News
22727 Highway 99 Ste 204 (98026-8381)
PHONE.....................206 365-4000
Tae Won Kang, *President*
Olivia Kim, *Data Proc Exec*
▲ EMP: 400
SQ FT: 10,000
SALES (est): 15MM **Privately Held**
SIC: 2711 Newspapers, publishing & printing

(G-3127)
JOYFUL NOISE PUBLICATIONS
22506 92nd Ave W (98020-4506)
PHONE.....................425 774-7078
Allen Lund, *Owner*
Ellen Lund, *Co-Owner*
EMP: 2
SALES (est): 120K **Privately Held**
WEB: www.joyful-noise.com
SIC: 2741 Miscellaneous publishing

(G-3128)
K AND K INDUSTRIES LLC
172 Sunset Ave (98020-4134)
PHONE.....................425 951-0502
EMP: 2
SALES (est): 69.6K **Privately Held**
SIC: 3999 Manufacturing industries

(G-3129)
KOREAN SUNDAY NEWS OF SEATTLE
22727 Highway 99 (98026-8381)
PHONE.....................425 778-6747
Daniel Min, *Principal*
EMP: 3
SALES (est): 130.2K **Privately Held**
SIC: 2711 Newspapers, publishing & printing

(G-3130)
LIVING STONE INDUSTRIES INC
22812 90th Ave W (98026-8434)
PHONE.....................425 679-6278
Xiang Yuan Liu, *Principal*
EMP: 2 EST: 2008

SALES (est): 223.6K **Privately Held**
SIC: 3999 Manufacturing industries

(G-3131)
MAGNAPRO BUSINESS SYSTEMS INC
8515 224th St Sw (98026-8253)
PHONE.....................206 280-6222
Peter Kirkham, *President*
Laural Kirkham, *Corp Secy*
EMP: 2
SALES: 20K **Privately Held**
SIC: 5734 7371 5045 7372 Computer software & accessories; computer software development; custom computer programming services; computer software; computers; prepackaged software;

(G-3132)
MAKOTA CO
303 5th Ave S Ste 209 (98020-3626)
PHONE.....................206 226-1843
Dustin Doss, *President*
EMP: 7
SQ FT: 1,200
SALES: 160K **Privately Held**
SIC: 3949 Protective sporting equipment

(G-3133)
METAL FRICTIONS COMPANY INC
650 Birch St (98020-4633)
PHONE.....................425 776-0336
Dick Larson, *Owner*
EMP: 5
SQ FT: 3,100
SALES (est): 559.8K **Privately Held**
SIC: 3542 3751 3714 Brakes, metal forming; motorcycles & related parts; motor vehicle brake systems & parts

(G-3134)
METRIX SOFTWARE
123 4th Ave N (98020-3199)
PHONE.....................425 361-2415
EMP: 2
SALES (est): 73.2K **Privately Held**
SIC: 2759 2752 Publication printing; commercial printing, lithographic

(G-3135)
MODUS HEALTH LLC
123 2nd Ave S Ste 220 (98020-8450)
PHONE.....................703 835-0055
Douglas McCormack, *President*
EMP: 6
SQ FT: 750
SALES (est): 898.3K **Privately Held**
SIC: 3821 Clinical laboratory instruments, except medical & dental

(G-3136)
NESTOR ENTERPRISES LLC
Also Called: East and Nest
22620 95th Pl W (98020-4524)
PHONE.....................206 794-4989
Bradley Nestor,
Brittney Nestor,
EMP: 4
SALES (est): 237.8K **Privately Held**
SIC: 2211 7389 Pillowcases; table cover fabrics, cotton;

(G-3137)
NIELSEN BROS & SONS INC
Also Called: Nielsen Bros Rugs & Carpets
8130 240th St Sw (98026-5030)
PHONE.....................425 776-9191
Brett Anderson, *Manager*
EMP: 4
SQ FT: 4,300
SALES (corp-wide): 8.4MM **Privately Held**
SIC: 2273 Floor coverings, textile fiber; dyeing & finishing of tufted rugs & carpets
PA: Nielsen Bros & Sons Inc
8130 240th St Sw Apt B2
Edmonds WA 98026
206 783-5454

(G-3138)
NORTHWEST PLASTIC TECH LLC (PA)
10308 242nd Pl Sw (98020-5779)
PHONE.....................206 499-6292

Binh Le Herdrick, *Mng Member*
Larry Herdrick,
▲ EMP: 20
SALES: 10MM **Privately Held**
SIC: 3089 Cups, plastic, except foam

(G-3139)
NOVO CONTOUR INC
7015 147th St Sw (98026-3531)
PHONE.....................425 773-2673
EMP: 2
SALES (est): 166.8K **Privately Held**
SIC: 3841 Mfg Surgical/Medical Instruments

(G-3140)
OFFSHORE PRODUCTS INC
7905 192nd Pl Sw (98026-6123)
PHONE.....................206 567-5404
EMP: 2
SALES (est): 85.6K **Privately Held**
SIC: 3498 Fabricated pipe & fittings

(G-3141)
ORTHOCARE INNOVATIONS LLC (PA)
123 2nd Ave S Ste 220 (98020-8450)
PHONE.....................425 771-0797
Jonathan Maier, *Sr Software Eng*
Jung Kim, *Software Dev*
David Boone,
David Adams,
Douglas McCormack,
EMP: 15
SQ FT: 2,000
SALES (est): 3.5MM **Privately Held**
WEB: www.orthocareinnovations.com
SIC: 3842 8733 Surgical appliances & supplies; medical research

(G-3142)
P F M INDUSTRIES INC
Also Called: Pacific Fast Mail
111 Sunset Ave N (98020-3229)
P.O. Box 57 (98020-0057)
PHONE.....................425 776-3112
Donald H Drew, *President*
Verna Rauscher, *Exec Sec*
EMP: 6
SQ FT: 6,500
SALES: 15K **Privately Held**
SIC: 5092 2731 5085 Toys & hobby goods & supplies; books: publishing only; industrial supplies

(G-3143)
PEQUOD INC
7215 156th St Sw (98026-4528)
PHONE.....................425 742-7456
Rick Mezich, *Mng Member*
EMP: 2
SALES (est): 163.3K **Privately Held**
SIC: 3731 Fishing vessels, large: building & repairing

(G-3144)
PORTRAIT DISPLAYS INC
Also Called: Spectracal
123 2nd Ave S Ste 200 (98020-8449)
PHONE.....................206 420-7514
La Heberlein, *Manager*
EMP: 14
SALES (est): 908.2K **Privately Held**
SIC: 7379 7372 7371 Computer related maintenance services; prepackaged software; computer software development
PA: Portrait Displays, Inc.
6663 Owens Dr
Pleasanton CA 94588

(G-3145)
REVELATIONS YOGURT LLC
527 Main St (98020-3149)
PHONE.....................425 744-6012
Reilley Duvall, *Manager*
Debbie Duvall,
EMP: 12
SALES: 411.1K **Privately Held**
SIC: 2024 Yogurt desserts, frozen

GEOGRAPHIC SECTION

(G-3146)
REYNOLDS AND REYNOLDS COMPANY
Also Called: Dealer Net
17121 76th Ave W (98026-5005)
PHONE.....................425 985-0194
Peter M Wilson, *Manager*
EMP: 20
SALES (corp-wide): 1.5B **Privately Held**
WEB: www.reyrey.com
SIC: 2761 7372 5045 6159 Manifold business forms; application computer software; computers; machinery & equipment finance leasing; management consulting services
HQ: The Reynolds And Reynolds Company
1 Reynolds Way
Kettering OH 45430
937 485-2000

(G-3147)
RICHINS PRINTING INC
Also Called: American Printing
7530 Olympic View Dr # 101 (98026-5522)
PHONE.....................425 776-1800
Martin Richins, *President*
Julie Richins, *Vice Pres*
EMP: 3
SQ FT: 1,800
SALES: 375K **Privately Held**
SIC: 2752 Commercial printing, offset

(G-3148)
RIDGEWOOD INDUSTRIES INC
Also Called: Spectrum Graphics
23110 99th Ave W (98020-5083)
PHONE.....................425 774-0170
James Dasher II, *President*
Lynn Dasher, *Treasurer*
EMP: 13
SQ FT: 2,000
SALES (est): 1.8MM **Privately Held**
SIC: 2752 Commercial printing, lithographic

(G-3149)
ROBINS JEWELERS LTD
18604 80th Ave W (98026-5818)
PHONE.....................206 622-4337
Kenneth F Davidson, *President*
EMP: 3 EST: 1972
SQ FT: 700
SALES (est): 293.6K **Privately Held**
SIC: 3911 5944 Jewel settings & mountings, precious metal; jewelry, precious stones & precious metals

(G-3150)
RUSSELL SIGN COMPANY
21104 70th Ave W (98026-7203)
PHONE.....................425 775-7010
Doug Russell, *Owner*
EMP: 2
SALES (est): 76.9K **Privately Held**
SIC: 3993 Signs & advertising specialties

(G-3151)
SASSY PILLOWS
9007 Olympic View Dr (98026-5322)
PHONE.....................425 778-7783
Sheri Symonds, *Principal*
EMP: 2 EST: 2010
SALES (est): 113.5K **Privately Held**
SIC: 2299 Pillow fillings: curled hair, cotton waste, moss, hemp tow

(G-3152)
SBK PHARMA LLC
7315 212th St Sw Ste 100 (98026-7610)
PHONE.....................425 778-7778
Harikrishna Sajja, *Principal*
EMP: 5
SALES (est): 616.8K **Privately Held**
SIC: 2834 Pharmaceutical preparations

(G-3153)
SCRATCH DISTILLERY LLC
200 James St Apt 303 (98020-3573)
PHONE.....................425 442-7306
EMP: 7
SALES (est): 738.5K **Privately Held**
SIC: 2085 Distilled & blended liquors

(G-3154)
SEATTLE APPLIED SCIENCE INC
7015 147th St Sw (98026-3531)
PHONE.....................425 773-2673
Michael P Lau, *CEO*
EMP: 2
SALES (est): 170K **Privately Held**
SIC: 3841 Surgical & medical instruments

(G-3155)
SHIELDS AEROSPACE SERVICES LLC
614 6th Ave N Apt 18 (98020-3047)
P.O. Box 1744, Helendale CA (92342-1744)
PHONE.....................425 240-6079
James Shields, *Principal*
EMP: 2
SALES (est): 125.7K **Privately Held**
SIC: 3721 Aircraft

(G-3156)
SILVERFEATHER CREATIONS
18801 Sound View Pl (98020-2358)
PHONE.....................425 771-9389
Mark Silver, *President*
EMP: 2
SALES (est): 89.8K **Privately Held**
SIC: 2499 Novelties, wood fiber

(G-3157)
SLEEPING INDUSTRIES LLC
9523 232nd St Sw (98020-5028)
PHONE.....................360 201-4305
Nicole Ivancovich, *Principal*
EMP: 2
SALES (est): 104.7K **Privately Held**
SIC: 3999 Manufacturing industries

(G-3158)
SNO-KING SIGNS
Also Called: Sno King Signs
625 Aloha Way (98020-3018)
PHONE.....................425 775-0594
Randolph W Hutchins, *Principal*
EMP: 3
SALES (est): 267.4K **Privately Held**
SIC: 2759 3993 5046 Commercial printing; electric signs; neon signs; letters for signs, metal; neon signs

(G-3159)
TC SPAN AMERICA LLC
21020 70th Ave W (98026-7202)
PHONE.....................425 774-3881
Sara Kedrowski, *Human Res Dir*
Pam Reuhl, *Sales Staff*
Claire Conway, *Marketing Staff*
Terrence Conway, *Mng Member*
Ross Cheever, *Graphic Designe*
EMP: 15
SALES (est): 242K **Privately Held**
WEB: www.tcspanamerica.com
SIC: 2759 Screen printing

(G-3160)
VESTDAVIT INC
170 W Dayton St Ste 101 (98020-4162)
PHONE.....................425 355-4652
Magnus Oding, *Vice Pres*
EMP: 3 EST: 2017
SQ FT: 1,580
SALES (est): 152.8K **Privately Held**
SIC: 3536 Davits

(G-3161)
WATERFRONT SOLUTIONS INC
Also Called: Wfs Networks
820 12th Ave N (98020-2935)
P.O. Box 1736 (98020-1736)
PHONE.....................360 348-1874
Gail Court, *President*
Tom Tertocha, *Vice Pres*
EMP: 5
SALES (est): 580K **Privately Held**
WEB: www.wfsnetworks.com
SIC: 3669 Intercommunication systems, electric

(G-3162)
WELCO SALES LLC
18401 76th Ave W (98026-5826)
PHONE.....................425 771-9043
William Lund, *Administration*

EMP: 2
SALES (est): 73.2K **Privately Held**
SIC: 2759 2599 Publication printing; beds, not household use

(G-3163)
WREATHE HAVOC
17629 76th Ave W (98026-5401)
PHONE.....................206 979-6838
Helju Coder, *Principal*
EMP: 2
SALES (est): 94.1K **Privately Held**
SIC: 3999 Wreaths, artificial

(G-3164)
WYNDSOR CABINET GROUP LLC
200 2nd Ave N Apt 202 (98020-3158)
PHONE.....................425 775-9828
EMP: 2
SALES (est): 125.5K **Privately Held**
SIC: 2434 Wood kitchen cabinets

(G-3165)
YOU ARE BETTER PUBLISHING
716 Maple St (98020-3436)
PHONE.....................425 776-8640
Rob Loomis, *Principal*
EMP: 2 EST: 2011
SALES (est): 95K **Privately Held**
SIC: 2741 Miscellaneous publishing

(G-3166)
YOUTH WITH A MISSION
Also Called: Ywam Publishing
7825 230th St Sw (98026-8713)
P.O. Box 55787, Seattle (98155-0787)
PHONE.....................425 771-1153
Tom Bragg, *Manager*
EMP: 15
SALES (corp-wide): 160.7K **Privately Held**
WEB: www.ywam.com
SIC: 2731 Book publishing
PA: Youth With A Mission
7085 Battle Creek Rd Se
Salem OR
503 364-3837

Electric City
Grant County

(G-3167)
LUANN AYLING
Also Called: Bird's Auto Glass & Body Shop
37 W Coulee Blvd (99123-9707)
P.O. Box 426 (99123-0426)
PHONE.....................509 633-2839
Luann Ayling, *Owner*
EMP: 3
SALES: 500K **Privately Held**
SIC: 7532 3714 Top & body repair & paint shops; windshield frames, motor vehicle

(G-3168)
TAYLORS MARINE CENTER
Also Called: Taylor's Custom Exhaust
236 Coulee Blvd (99123)
P.O. Box 242 (99123-0242)
PHONE.....................509 633-2945
Owen Taylor, *Owner*
Claren Taylor, *Co-Owner*
EMP: 4
SQ FT: 3,600
SALES (est): 360.9K **Privately Held**
SIC: 3714 7533 5551 Mufflers (exhaust), motor vehicle; muffler shop, sale or repair & installation; motor boat dealers; marine supplies

Elk
Spokane County

(G-3169)
COLBURN ENTERPRISE
14310 E Blanchard Rd (99009-9688)
PHONE.....................509 292-2310
Larry Colburn, *Owner*
Sharon Colburn, *Co-Owner*
EMP: 2

SALES: 33K **Privately Held**
SIC: 2399 Horse harnesses & riding crops, etc.: non-leather

(G-3170)
JROTC DOG TAGS INC
Also Called: Jrotc.com
11906 E Dolly Ln (99009-5128)
PHONE.....................509 292-0410
Ernie Kiel, *President*
◆ EMP: 4 EST: 1999
SALES (est): 385K **Privately Held**
WEB: www.jrotcpride.com
SIC: 3999 3993 Identification tags, except paper; signs & advertising specialties

(G-3171)
K & S OIL FIELD SERVICES INC
4504 E Elk To Highway Rd (99009-8752)
PHONE.....................509 998-5738
EMP: 2
SALES (est): 81.9K **Privately Held**
SIC: 1311 Crude petroleum & natural gas

(G-3172)
MACARTHUR LOGGING
39510 N Madison Rd (99009-9666)
PHONE.....................509 675-8045
Jesse Macarthur, *Principal*
EMP: 2
SALES (est): 81.7K **Privately Held**
SIC: 2411 Logging

(G-3173)
MCNAMEE & SONS LOGGING
10310 E Bridges Rd (99009-9664)
PHONE.....................509 292-8656
EMP: 2
SALES (est): 154.9K **Privately Held**
SIC: 2411 Logging

(G-3174)
MICHAEL D WORLEY
Also Called: Worley Logging
5410 E Eloika Ln (99009-9779)
PHONE.....................509 290-0927
Michael Worley, *Principal*
EMP: 3
SALES (est): 221.2K **Privately Held**
SIC: 2411 Logging

(G-3175)
PRECAST BY DESIGN INC
133 Allen Rd (99009-9519)
PHONE.....................509 292-2988
Jeff Sprague, *Principal*
EMP: 5
SALES (est): 479K **Privately Held**
WEB: www.precastbd.com
SIC: 3272 Concrete products, precast

(G-3176)
SENSIBLE HORSEMANSHIP LLC
38303 N Chapman Rd (99009-8625)
PHONE.....................509 292-2475
Ann Kirk, *Mng Member*
EMP: 2
SALES (est): 115.4K **Privately Held**
SIC: 2752 Commercial printing, lithographic

(G-3177)
SPOKANE ROCK PRODUCTS INC
39102 N Newport Hwy (99009)
PHONE.....................509 292-2200
Neil Deatley, *Owner*
EMP: 10 **Privately Held**
WEB: www.spokanerock.com
SIC: 3273 Ready-mixed concrete
PA: Spokane Rock Products, Inc.
4418 E 8th Ave
Spokane Valley WA 99212

(G-3178)
WINES COMPANY
36103 N Conklin Rd (99009-9663)
PHONE.....................509 292-8820
David Wines, *Partner*
EMP: 2
SALES (est): 123K **Privately Held**
SIC: 2411 Logging camps & contractors

Elk - Spokane County (G-3179)

(G-3179)
WYCHWOOD INC
161 Bunge Rd (99009-9569)
PHONE.................................209 667-8188
Clair Hall, *CEO*
Clair Henley, *President*
Reginald Henley, *Vice Pres*
▲ EMP: 3
SALES (est): 184.1K **Privately Held**
WEB: www.wychwood.com
SIC: 3999 Pet supplies

Ellensburg
Kittitas County

(G-3180)
ADAMS APPLE CIDER LLC
221 Canyon Vista Way (98926-9153)
PHONE.................................509 933-1025
Joshua Adams, *Principal*
EMP: 2
SALES (est): 94.5K **Privately Held**
SIC: 3571 Cider, nonalcoholic

(G-3181)
ALTOS EZ MAT INC
703 N Wenas St (98926-2861)
PHONE.................................509 962-9212
Samuel Albright, *President*
▲ EMP: 6 EST: 1974
SQ FT: 5,000
SALES (est): 776.8K **Privately Held**
WEB: www.altosezmat.com
SIC: 3423 Hand & edge tools

(G-3182)
AMERICAN MACHINE WORKS
4621 Rader Rd 1 (98926-6942)
PHONE.................................509 968-4415
Charles Borin, *President*
Eleanor Borin, *Admin Sec*
EMP: 9 EST: 1974
SALES (est): 530K **Privately Held**
SIC: 3553 Woodworking machinery

(G-3183)
AMP ENGINEERING SERVICES LLC
702 E 7th Ave (98926-3215)
P.O. Box 2676, Issaquah (98027-0122)
PHONE.................................480 512-1186
Hector Pomales, *Principal*
EMP: 2
SALES (est): 104.2K **Privately Held**
SIC: 3822 7371 Temperature controls, automatic; building services monitoring controls, automatic; custom computer programming services

(G-3184)
BAHMILLER WOODWORKS
905 W Cascade Ct Unit 56 (98926-6562)
PHONE.................................509 929-6300
Jim Bahmiller, *Principal*
EMP: 2
SALES (est): 131.6K **Privately Held**
SIC: 2431 Millwork

(G-3185)
BUILDING SPECIALTY SYSTEMS (PA)
106 W Joanna Pl (98926-3084)
P.O. Box 1610, North Bend (98045-1610)
PHONE.................................425 483-6875
Todd Parker, *President*
EMP: 5
SALES: 800K **Privately Held**
WEB: www.bssionline.com
SIC: 5211 5032 2431 3442 Doors, wood or metal, except storm; building stone; garage doors, overhead: wood; fire doors, metal; rolling doors for industrial buildings or warehouses, metal

(G-3186)
CARIBOU CREEK LOGGING INC
1921 Riverbottom Rd (98926-8306)
PHONE.................................509 962-6700
Jane Czapiewski, *President*
Terry Clark, *Vice Pres*
EMP: 5
SALES (est): 524K **Privately Held**
SIC: 2411 Logging camps & contractors

(G-3187)
CASSANDRA WATTERSON
Also Called: ABC Forms
1411 Alford Rd (98926-7309)
PHONE.................................509 306-0205
Cassandra White, *Principal*
EMP: 3 EST: 2015
SALES (est): 111.6K **Privately Held**
SIC: 2752 Commercial printing, lithographic

(G-3188)
CEDAR MOUNTAIN WOODWRIGHTS
309 S Railroad Ave (98926-9699)
PHONE.................................509 933-2602
Michael Bello, *President*
EMP: 3
SALES (est): 437.4K **Privately Held**
SIC: 5211 2521 Cabinets, kitchen; cabinets, office: wood

(G-3189)
CENTRAL PARTY & COSTUME
203 W 7th Ave (98926-2816)
P.O. Box 241 (98926-1912)
PHONE.................................509 962-3934
Eva J Frink, *Principal*
EMP: 5 EST: 2010
SALES (est): 583.8K **Privately Held**
SIC: 2335 Wedding gowns & dresses

(G-3190)
COPY SHOP
724 E University Way (98926-2947)
PHONE.................................509 962-2679
David Oehlerich, *Owner*
David L Oehlerich, *Owner*
EMP: 4
SQ FT: 4,000
SALES (est): 985.5K **Privately Held**
SIC: 2752 7334 Commercial printing, offset; photocopying & duplicating services

(G-3191)
COX CANYON VINEYARDS
221 Canyon Vista Way (98926-9153)
PHONE.................................206 940-5086
EMP: 2
SALES (est): 79.4K **Privately Held**
SIC: 2084 Wines

(G-3192)
DAILY ELLENSBURG RECORD INC
Also Called: Daily Record, The
401 N Main St (98926-3107)
PHONE.................................509 925-1414
Dave Lord, *President*
EMP: 40 EST: 1909
SQ FT: 14,400
SALES (est): 2.1MM
SALES (corp-wide): 78.7MM **Privately Held**
WEB: www.kvnews.com
SIC: 2711 Newspapers: publishing only, not printed on site
PA: Pioneer Newspaper Service Llc
221 1st Ave W Ste 405
Seattle WA
206 284-4424

(G-3193)
DICK AND JANES SPOT
Also Called: Dick and Janes Spot Fine Arts
101 N Pearl St (98926-3324)
PHONE.................................509 925-3224
Jane Orleman, *Co-Owner*
Richard Elliott, *Co-Owner*
EMP: 3
SALES: 270K **Privately Held**
SIC: 8999 3993 Artist's studio; signs & advertising specialties

(G-3194)
ELLENSBURG CANYON WINERY LLC
221 Canyon Vista Way (98926-9153)
PHONE.................................509 933-3523
Gary Cox, *Owner*
EMP: 4
SALES (est): 274.6K **Privately Held**
SIC: 2084 Wines

(G-3195)
ELLENSBURG EYE & CNTACT LENS C
2201 W Dolarway Rd Ste 2 (98926-8228)
PHONE.................................509 925-1000
William Meyer, *Owner*
EMP: 7
SALES (est): 634.5K **Privately Held**
SIC: 3851 8011 Protective eyeware; offices & clinics of medical doctors

(G-3196)
ELLENSBURG FENCE CO
2603 W Willis Rd (98926-9648)
P.O. Box 898 (98926-1923)
PHONE.................................509 929-4090
Chris Gaidos, *Principal*
EMP: 3
SALES (est): 270.8K **Privately Held**
SIC: 1799 2411 Fence construction; rails, fence: round or split

(G-3197)
ELLENSBURG PALLET
208 S Willow St (98926-3562)
PHONE.................................509 962-1373
Valente Arellano, *Principal*
EMP: 3 EST: 2012
SALES (est): 233.2K **Privately Held**
SIC: 2448 Pallets, wood & wood with metal

(G-3198)
ERICKSON CUSTOM MEATS ✪
1840 Clarke Rd (98926-8555)
PHONE.................................509 962-6099
Mark Erickson, *Principal*
EMP: 2 EST: 2018
SALES (est): 62.3K **Privately Held**
SIC: 2011 Meat packing plants

(G-3199)
EVO INDUSTRIES LLC
2172 Fairview Rd (98926-7191)
PHONE.................................717 665-0406
River Moore, *Principal*
EMP: 2 EST: 2012
SALES (est): 89.4K **Privately Held**
SIC: 3999 Manufacturing industries

(G-3200)
EXECUTIVE MEDIA CORP
701 N Anderson St (98926-3150)
PHONE.................................509 933-2993
Gerard Vanderschauw, *President*
EMP: 5
SALES (est): 241.2K **Privately Held**
WEB: www.executivemediacorp.com
SIC: 2711 Newspapers

(G-3201)
GARIKO LLC
Also Called: Winegar's
1708 W University Way (98926-2377)
PHONE.................................509 933-1821
Gary Winegar,
Kori Winegar,
Richel Winegar,
EMP: 2
SQ FT: 2,500
SALES (est): 75.5K **Privately Held**
SIC: 5812 5149 2023 2024 Ice cream, soft drink & soda fountain stands; coffee shop; coffee & tea; ice cream mix, unfrozen: liquid or dry; ice cream & frozen desserts

(G-3202)
GIBSON & SON ROAD BUILDING INC
Also Called: Gibson & Son Excavation
1221 S Thorp Hwy (98926-8010)
PHONE.................................509 925-2017
Kristen Gibson, *President*
Louie Gibson, *Principal*
EMP: 10
SALES (est): 1.5MM **Privately Held**
WEB: www.gibsonandson.com
SIC: 2411 1611 Logging camps & contractors; general contractor, highway & street construction

(G-3203)
GIGGLYDOO LLC
Also Called: Meda Nova
907 N Hibbs Rd (98926-8374)
PHONE.................................425 344-5594
Ernie Kilburn,
EMP: 4
SALES (est): 164.1K **Privately Held**
SIC: 3089 Plastic processing; injection molding of plastics; thermoformed finished plastic products; novelties, plastic

(G-3204)
GORMAN INDUSTRIES
2214 W Dry Creek Rd (98926-9446)
PHONE.................................509 899-3933
Jeff Gorman, *Principal*
EMP: 2
SALES (est): 147.8K **Privately Held**
SIC: 3999 Manufacturing industries

(G-3205)
GRAVEL DOCTOR OF WASHINGTON ✪
421 Biltmore Dr (98926-5251)
PHONE.................................509 899-1608
EMP: 2 EST: 2018
SALES (est): 66K **Privately Held**
SIC: 1442 Construction sand & gravel

(G-3206)
GREEN SYNERGY
1508 N B St Apt 1304 (98926-5610)
PHONE.................................206 779-3324
Abdolhossein S Haghighi, *Owner*
EMP: 2
SALES (est): 88K **Privately Held**
SIC: 3799 Transportation equipment

(G-3207)
HAYTOOLS INC
1003 S Ruby St (98926-3755)
PHONE.................................509 933-1102
Duane Huppert, *Principal*
EMP: 3
SALES (est): 195.7K **Privately Held**
SIC: 3999 Atomizers, toiletry

(G-3208)
HOFSTRAND LOGGING INC
11333 Vantage Hwy (98926-7030)
PHONE.................................509 968-3197
Monte R Hofstrand, *President*
Susan Hofstrand, *Corp Secy*
EMP: 25
SALES: 1MM **Privately Held**
SIC: 2411 Logging camps & contractors

(G-3209)
JTS KETTLECORN
520 Blazing Sky Ln (98926-9176)
PHONE.................................509 962-2524
Teri Ellis, *Owner*
Jim Ellis, *Co-Owner*
EMP: 2
SALES (est): 96K **Privately Held**
SIC: 3589 Popcorn machines, commercial

(G-3210)
KELLER SUPPLY CO
2060 Vantage Hwy Ste 26 (98926-9531)
PHONE.................................509 925-2400
Vern Ball, *Manager*
EMP: 12
SALES (corp-wide): 327MM **Privately Held**
SIC: 5074 3432 Plumbing fittings & supplies; plumbing fixture fittings & trim
PA: Keller Supply Co
3209 17th Ave W
Seattle WA 98119
206 285-3300

(G-3211)
KNUTSON CRANE
6402 Manastash Rd (98926-7815)
PHONE.................................509 925-5438
Mike Knutson, *Principal*
EMP: 4
SALES (est): 384K **Privately Held**
SIC: 3536 Hoists, cranes & monorails

GEOGRAPHIC SECTION

Elma - Grays Harbor County (G-3243)

(G-3212)
LAWRENCE FRUIT INC
311 N Pearl St (98926-3363)
PHONE.................................509 925-1095
Joshua Lawrence, *Branch Mgr*
EMP: 3
SALES (est): 156K Privately Held
SIC: 2084 Wines
PA: Lawrence Fruit Inc
    13000 Road D Sw
    Royal City WA 99357

(G-3213)
LONGHORN INDUSTRIES
705 N Cle Elum St (98926-2838)
P.O. Box 1038 (98926-1926)
PHONE.................................509 899-5475
Teresa Long, *Principal*
EMP: 2
SALES (est): 98.9K Privately Held
SIC: 3999 Manufacturing industries

(G-3214)
MAJESTIC MONUMENT & STONE
214 Hanson Rd (98926-8904)
PHONE.................................509 699-8937
Ken Grannan, *Principal*
EMP: 3
SALES (est): 119.9K Privately Held
SIC: 3272 Monuments & grave markers, except terrazo

(G-3215)
MIKES RENTAL MACHINERY INC
Also Called: Anderson Machinery
501 S Main St (98926-3636)
P.O. Box 838 (98926-1922)
PHONE.................................509 925-6126
Michael Forman, *President*
Paulette Forman, *Admin Sec*
EMP: 38 EST: 1970
SQ FT: 8,000
SALES: 4.6MM Privately Held
SIC: 7359 7353 5082 5083 Equipment rental & leasing; heavy construction equipment rental; general construction machinery & equipment; agricultural machinery & equipment; haying machines: mowers, rakes, stackers, etc.

(G-3216)
PACIFIC PILOT SERVICES LLC
43 Red Mountain Dr (98926-9049)
PHONE.................................509 899-0858
Thomas Bull II, *Principal*
EMP: 3 EST: 2012
SALES (est): 148.3K Privately Held
SIC: 2711 Newspapers, publishing & printing

(G-3217)
PATRICK CORP
1043 W University Way (98926-2370)
PHONE.................................509 925-1300
Patrick Long, *Principal*
EMP: 2
SALES (est): 143.4K Privately Held
SIC: 3711 Fire department vehicles (motor vehicles), assembly of

(G-3218)
PAUTZKE BAIT CO INC
800 N Prospect St (98926-8370)
P.O. Box 36 (98926-1909)
PHONE.................................509 925-6154
Casey Kelley, *President*
Paula Williams, *Vice Pres*
Chris Shaffer, *Opers Staff*
Kelly Gerrits, *Admin Sec*
EMP: 5 EST: 1934
SQ FT: 22,000
SALES (est): 698.7K Privately Held
WEB: www.pautzke.com
SIC: 2091 2048 Fish eggs: packaged for use as bait; prepared feeds

(G-3219)
PERFECT BLEND LLC
8270 Tjossem Rd (98926-9621)
PHONE.................................509 968-3316
Patrick Burchard, *Branch Mgr*
EMP: 12
SALES (corp-wide): 11.5MM Privately Held
SIC: 5261 2873 Fertilizer; fertilizers: natural (organic), except compost
PA: Perfect Blend, Llc
    10900 Ne 8th St Ste 615
    Bellevue WA 98004
    509 488-5570

(G-3220)
PHOENIX TRUSS CORPORATION
2015 Hwy Old 10 (98926)
PHONE.................................509 925-3135
Ken Beedle, *President*
EMP: 23
SALES (est): 20.9K Privately Held
SIC: 2439 Trusses, except roof: laminated lumber

(G-3221)
PROTAC INC
110 W 6th Ave (98926-3106)
PHONE.................................509 962-5001
Brady Erickson, *President*
Leah Erickson, *Admin Sec*
EMP: 3
SALES (est): 286K Privately Held
SIC: 3826 Dust sampling & analysis equipment

(G-3222)
RAYFIELD ONEIL TIMBER CUTTERS
1307 N Vista Rd (98926-9585)
P.O. Box 1382 (98926-1904)
PHONE.................................509 925-2061
Dennis Rayfield, *President*
Doug O'Neil, *Partner*
EMP: 2
SALES (est): 164.8K Privately Held
SIC: 2411 Timber, cut at logging camp

(G-3223)
RONALD SAND & GRAVEL INC
1221 S Thorp Hwy (98926-8010)
P.O. Box 1088 (98926-1900)
PHONE.................................509 728-8605
EMP: 3
SALES (est): 105.8K Privately Held
SIC: 1442 Construction sand & gravel

(G-3224)
S&S TRANSPORTATION SERVICE
Also Called: S & S Transportation Services
1000 Emerson Rd (98926-8438)
PHONE.................................509 968-9825
James Sperline, *Owner*
EMP: 4
SALES (est): 337.5K Privately Held
SIC: 2911 Diesel fuels

(G-3225)
SHIRTWORKS
100 W 8th Ave (98926)
PHONE.................................509 925-3469
Kile Williams, *Co-Owner*
Kathy Williams, *Co-Owner*
EMP: 7
SQ FT: 2,000
SALES (est): 747.6K Privately Held
WEB: www.larsonfruit.com
SIC: 2759 Screen printing

(G-3226)
SLYFIELD ENTERPRISES
Also Called: Rocky Mountain Log Holmes
1331 Grindrod Rd (98926-5020)
PHONE.................................509 968-3456
Richard Slyfield, *Owner*
EMP: 2
SALES (est): 100.1K Privately Held
SIC: 1799 2452 Special trade contractors; log cabins, prefabricated, wood

(G-3227)
SPRINGBOARD WINERY LLC
5090 Naneum Rd (98926-6960)
PHONE.................................509 929-4247
Trista Daugherty, *Owner*
EMP: 5
SALES (est): 103.1K Privately Held
SIC: 2084 Wine cellars, bonded: engaged in blending wines

(G-3228)
STORLIE & GRAHAM CUTTING INC
2700 Willowdale Rd (98926-9383)
PHONE.................................509 962-6494
EMP: 3 EST: 2010
SALES (est): 120K Privately Held
SIC: 2411 Logging

(G-3229)
T & R LOG CO
306 S Lookout Mountain Dr (98926-9032)
PHONE.................................509 962-6590
EMP: 4
SALES (est): 260K Privately Held
SIC: 2411 Logging

(G-3230)
TECHNIPFMC US HOLDINGS INC
1621 Vantage Hwy (98926-9001)
PHONE.................................509 925-2500
Brad Beckstrom, *Manager*
EMP: 4
SALES (corp-wide): 12.6B Privately Held
WEB: www.fmctechnologies.com
SIC: 3533 Oil & gas field machinery
HQ: Fmc Technologies, Inc.
    11740 Katy Fwy Energy Tow
    Houston TX 77079
    281 591-4000

(G-3231)
THRALL & DODGE WINERY
111 Dodge Rd (98926-8452)
PHONE.................................509 925-4110
Troy Goodreau, *Principal*
EMP: 4
SALES (est): 241.8K Privately Held
SIC: 2084 Wines

(G-3232)
THRIFTY PAYLESS INC T/A
700 S Main St (98926-3641)
PHONE.................................509 925-4232
EMP: 2
SALES (est): 99.5K Privately Held
SIC: 2836 Vaccines & other immunizing products

(G-3233)
TOUCH OF WEST
2381 Cooke Canyon Rd (98926-5019)
PHONE.................................509 962-6410
Matt Webb, *Principal*
EMP: 4 EST: 2010
SALES (est): 442.9K Privately Held
SIC: 3645 Garden, patio, walkway & yard lighting fixtures: electric

(G-3234)
TRINITY FARMS INC
Also Called: Agricultural
2451 Number 81 Rd (98926-8195)
PHONE.................................509 968-4107
Michael Forman, *Owner*
Paulette Forman, *Co-Owner*
EMP: 5
SALES (est): 476.4K Privately Held
SIC: 0212 2875 0781 Beef cattle except feedlots; compost; landscape services

(G-3235)
TWIN CITY FOODS INC
501 W 4th Ave (98926-3082)
P.O. Box 478 (98926-1915)
PHONE.................................509 962-9806
Orin Page, *Plant Supt*
Tom Foster, *Manager*
EMP: 250
SALES (corp-wide): 213.6MM Privately Held
WEB: www.twincityfoods.com
SIC: 2037 2099 Vegetables, quick frozen & cold pack, excl. potato products; food preparations
PA: Twin City Foods, Inc.
    10120 269th Pl Nw
    Stanwood WA 98292
    206 515-2400

(G-3236)
V-CARE HEALTH SYSTEMS INC
2601 N Alder St (98926-5460)
PHONE.................................509 670-9068
Sandy Wheeler, *President*
EMP: 4 EST: 1995
SALES (est): 407.6K Privately Held
SIC: 3841 Medical instruments & equipment, blood & bone work

(G-3237)
WASHINGTON HAYKINGDOM INC
7931 Reecer Creek Rd (98926-6831)
PHONE.................................509 925-7000
Yvonne Lin, *Principal*
EMP: 4 EST: 2010
SALES (est): 384.9K Privately Held
SIC: 2048 Prepared feeds

(G-3238)
WESTERN METAL PRODUCTS LLC
2613 Hwy 97 (98926-8385)
PHONE.................................509 962-4895
Jason Bjorkman,
David Bjorkman,
EMP: 2
SALES (est): 337.2K Privately Held
SIC: 3441 Fabricated structural metal

(G-3239)
WHIPSAW BREWING LLC
704 N Wenas St (98926-2862)
P.O. Box 303 (98926-1913)
PHONE.................................360 463-0436
Debbie Tierney, *Principal*
EMP: 15
SALES (est): 2MM Privately Held
SIC: 2082 Malt beverages

Elma
Grays Harbor County

(G-3240)
ASCENSUS SPECIALTIES LLC
4800 State Rte 12 (98541)
PHONE.................................360 482-8819
Jim Beerbower, *Plant Mgr*
EMP: 68
SALES (corp-wide): 1.8B Privately Held
SIC: 2819 Industrial inorganic chemicals
HQ: Ascensus Specialties Llc
    2821 Northup Way Ste 275
    Bellevue WA 98004
    425 448-1679

(G-3241)
BAYVIEW REDI MIX INC
91 Schouweiler Rd (98541-9352)
P.O. Box 165, Aberdeen (98520-0044)
PHONE.................................360 482-3444
Greg Macomber, *Manager*
EMP: 9
SALES (est): 770.2K
SALES (corp-wide): 4.9MM Privately Held
WEB: www.bayviewredimix.com
SIC: 3273 Ready-mixed concrete
PA: Bayview Redi Mix, Inc.
    100 Hagara St
    Aberdeen WA 98520
    360 533-7372

(G-3242)
BILLY BOB CUSTOMS
68 Hurd Rd (98541-9349)
PHONE.................................360 637-9147
Chris Mull, *Principal*
▲ EMP: 5
SALES (est): 395.5K Privately Held
SIC: 3465 Body parts, automobile: stamped metal

(G-3243)
BROWN-MNNPLIS TNK-NRTHWEST LLC
100 Tower Blvd Ste 99 (98541-9169)
PHONE.................................360 482-1720
Charles Travelstead,
Michael L Morris,
EMP: 30
SQ FT: 40,000

Elma - Grays Harbor County (G-3244)

SALES (est): 4.2MM **Privately Held**
WEB: www.reliablesteelinc.com
SIC: 3443 3441 Tanks, standard or custom fabricated: metal plate; fabricated structural metal

(G-3244)
DAWLING SPAY RETRACTOR LLC
44 Butler Mill Rd (98541-9203)
PHONE................360 482-4970
EMP: 2
SALES (est): 86.6K **Privately Held**
SIC: 3841 Retractors

(G-3245)
EAGLES EDUCTL CONSULTING LLC
69 Raspberry Rd (98541-9113)
PHONE................360 482-6093
Steve Bridge, *Principal*
EMP: 2
SALES (est): 54K **Privately Held**
SIC: 3131 Quarters

(G-3246)
FUR TREE FORESTRY
1701 W Ford Loop Rd (98541-9722)
PHONE................360 426-6252
Dave Persell, *Owner*
EMP: 2
SALES (est): 154.7K **Privately Held**
SIC: 2411 Logging

(G-3247)
GIRARD WOOD PRODUCTS INC
10 Bear Rd (98541-8919)
PHONE................360 482-5151
Anthony Hubbs, *Sales Mgr*
Stan Henry, *Manager*
EMP: 60
SALES (est): 6.1MM
SALES (corp-wide): 16.7MM **Privately Held**
WEB: www.girardwoodproducts.com
SIC: 2448 Pallets, wood
PA: Girard Wood Products, Inc.
  802 E Main
  Puyallup WA 98372
  253 845-0505

(G-3248)
HARBOR PACIFIC BOTTLING INC (PA)
50 Schouweiler Tract Rd E (98541-9385)
PHONE................360 482-4820
Willis G Martin, *President*
Jackie Martin, *Business Mgr*
Tim Martin, *Vice Pres*
Dawn Dougherty, *Finance*
Justin Ehly, *Sales Staff*
EMP: 41 EST: 1957
SQ FT: 50,000
SALES (est): 6MM **Privately Held**
WEB: www.harborpacificbottling.com
SIC: 2086 Soft drinks: packaged in cans, bottles, etc.

(G-3249)
MARTIN COMPANY
4733 State Rte 12 (98541)
PHONE................360 482-2157
Kenneth Martin, *Partner*
Dennis Martin, *Partner*
EMP: 2
SALES (est): 174.6K **Privately Held**
SIC: 2499 Handles, poles, dowels & stakes: wood; poles, wood

(G-3250)
MURPHY COMPANY
Also Called: Murphy Plywood
505 Elma Mccleary Rd (98541-9439)
PHONE................360 482-2521
John R Murphy, *Branch Mgr*
EMP: 132
SALES (corp-wide): 113.3MM **Privately Held**
SIC: 2439 2436 Timbers, structural: laminated lumber; softwood veneer & plywood
PA: Murphy Company
  2350 Prairie Rd
  Eugene OR 97402
  541 461-4545

(G-3251)
NDC TIMBER INC
357 Cloquallum Rd (98541-9440)
PHONE................360 482-4645
Dell Carter, *President*
EMP: 23 EST: 1985
SQ FT: 36,000
SALES (est): 3.5MM **Privately Held**
WEB: www.ndctimber.com
SIC: 2411 Logging camps & contractors

(G-3252)
NESHKAW SAND AND GRAVEL LLC
290 W Lillie Rd (98541-9755)
PHONE................360 482-0274
Arlan F Cook, *Manager*
EMP: 3
SALES (est): 135.3K **Privately Held**
SIC: 1442 Construction sand & gravel

(G-3253)
NORTHWEST ROCK INC
55 Schouweiler Rd (98541)
PHONE................360 482-3550
Jason Messmer, *Manager*
EMP: 8
SALES (corp-wide): 8.7MM **Privately Held**
SIC: 1442 Construction sand & gravel
PA: Northwest Rock, Inc.
  642 Newskah Rd
  Aberdeen WA 98520
  360 533-3050

(G-3254)
RCD TIMBER INC
16 Hokanson Rd (98541-9151)
P.O. Box 520 (98541-0520)
PHONE................360 591-9078
EMP: 3
SALES (est): 154.5K **Privately Held**
SIC: 2448 Wood pallets & skids

(G-3255)
REBELL INDUSTRIES
310 W Haven Dr (98541-9515)
PHONE................360 495-4846
Randy Bell, *Principal*
EMP: 2
SALES (est): 118.2K **Privately Held**
SIC: 3999 Manufacturing industries

(G-3256)
RONALD JOHNSON
Also Called: Rj Equipment Service
861 S Bank Rd (98541-9143)
PHONE................360 482-4982
Ronald Johnson, *Owner*
Rena Johnson, *Owner*
EMP: 2
SALES (est): 261.3K **Privately Held**
SIC: 1711 7692 Mechanical contractor; welding repair

(G-3257)
TOBIN & RIEDESEL LOGGING LLC
161 Hokanson Rd (98541-9106)
P.O. Box 367, Aberdeen (98520-0091)
PHONE................360 482-8127
EMP: 43 EST: 2012
SQ FT: 600
SALES (est): 5.5MM **Privately Held**
SIC: 2411 Logging

(G-3258)
VAN ORMAN GUITARS LLC
179 S Union Rd (98541-9432)
PHONE................253 269-8660
Donny V Orman, *Owner*
▼ EMP: 2
SALES (est): 60K **Privately Held**
SIC: 3931 Guitars & parts, electric & non-electric

(G-3259)
WEYERHAEUSER COMPANY
505 Elma Mccleary Rd (98541-9439)
PHONE................360 482-2521
Allan Watters, *Manager*
EMP: 74
SALES (corp-wide): 7.4B **Publicly Held**
SIC: 2439 2436 Timbers, structural: laminated lumber; softwood veneer & plywood

PA: Weyerhaeuser Company
  220 Occidental Ave S
  Seattle WA 98104
  206 539-3000

(G-3260)
ZEPP RESOURCES
Also Called: Albert Zepp Logging
225 Dunlap Rd (98541-9241)
PHONE................360 470-4622
Albert Zepp, *Owner*
EMP: 12
SALES (est): 910.3K **Privately Held**
SIC: 2411 Logging camps & contractors

Eltopia
Franklin County

(G-3261)
AIR LIQUIDE
301 Summit Loop (99330-8715)
PHONE................509 793-9590
Dave Oleary, *Principal*
EMP: 3 EST: 2010
SALES (est): 244.9K **Privately Held**
SIC: 2813 Industrial gases

(G-3262)
ASNW INC
Also Called: Agri-Service Northwest
12731 Glade North Rd (99330-9746)
P.O. Box 299 (99330-0299)
PHONE................509 297-4272
Monte Buttars, *President*
Suzanne Buttars, *Treasurer*
EMP: 15
SALES (est): 4.7MM **Privately Held**
SIC: 3523 Farm machinery & equipment

Endicott
Whitman County

(G-3263)
C & V MACHINERY
1562 Swent Rd (99125-9771)
PHONE................509 657-3392
Helen Jane Hughes, *Owner*
Clarence Hughes, *Owner*
EMP: 2
SALES: 130K **Privately Held**
SIC: 3713 7532 3714 3523 Truck beds; body shop, trucks; trailer hitches, motor vehicle; farm machinery & equipment

(G-3264)
ENDICOTT TRUCK & TRACTOR
Po Box 46a (99125)
P.O. Box 46a
PHONE................509 657-3436
Roy Wolfe, *Owner*
EMP: 5
SALES: 15K **Privately Held**
SIC: 7538 2411 0291 5399 Truck engine repair, except industrial; logging; general farms, primarily animals; country general stores

(G-3265)
ENDICOTT WASTE WATER TREATMENT
102 Margin St (99125-8714)
PHONE................509 657-3407
Mike Isaacs, *Principal*
EMP: 2
SALES (est): 109.8K **Privately Held**
SIC: 3589 Water treatment equipment, industrial

(G-3266)
S & S WELDING & REPAIR
407 D St (99125-5121)
P.O. Box 178 (99125-0178)
PHONE................509 657-3340
Vern Strader, *Owner*
Barbara Strader, *Co-Owner*
EMP: 2
SALES: 50K **Privately Held**
SIC: 7692 7389 Welding repair;

Entiat
Chelan County

(G-3267)
MARVIN BATCHELLER
Also Called: MD Manufacturing
16981 Casey Ln (98822-7509)
PHONE................509 784-7018
Marvin Batcheller, *Owner*
Darcey Batcheller, *Co-Owner*
EMP: 2
SALES (est): 109.9K **Privately Held**
SIC: 2841 Soap & other detergents

(G-3268)
MULVANEY TRUCKING AND EXCAV
5980 Entiat River Rd (98822-9729)
PHONE................509 784-4502
EMP: 5
SALES (est): 267.6K **Privately Held**
SIC: 1795 2411 Wrecking And Demolition Work, Nsk

(G-3269)
NO GRASS WINERY
6701 Entiat River Rd (98822-9735)
PHONE................509 784-5101
Alan Moen, *Owner*
EMP: 2 EST: 2017
SALES (est): 68.6K **Privately Held**
SIC: 2084 Wines

(G-3270)
SAFE BATHTUB INC
3047 Hedding St (98822-9713)
PHONE................509 670-2711
Roger Gardner, *President*
EMP: 3
SALES: 500K **Privately Held**
SIC: 3088 7389 Tubs (bath, shower & laundry), plastic;

(G-3271)
SANFORD ART PRINTS
13464 Dunn St (98822-9701)
PHONE................509 784-1220
Dale Sanford, *Principal*
EMP: 2 EST: 2001
SALES (est): 139.9K **Privately Held**
SIC: 2752 Commercial printing, lithographic

(G-3272)
US CASTINGS LLC
14351 Shamel St (98822)
P.O. Box 678 (98822-0678)
PHONE................509 784-1001
John Koegler,
EMP: 75
SQ FT: 100,000
SALES (est): 18.5MM
SALES (corp-wide): 62.8MM **Privately Held**
WEB: www.us-castings.com
SIC: 3365 Aluminum & aluminum-based alloy castings
PA: Advanced Metals Group, L.L.C.
  18 Mystic Ln
  Malvern PA 19355
  610 408-8006

Enumclaw
King County

(G-3273)
410 QUARRY DIBELLA ENTPS INC
718 Griffin Ave (98022-3418)
PHONE................360 825-7505
Augustine B Dibella II, *President*
Kristin Dibella, *Vice Pres*
EMP: 7
SALES (est): 883.3K **Privately Held**
SIC: 1411 Dimension stone

(G-3274)
ACRYLIC ARTS & FABRICATION
1462 Blake St (98022-3428)
PHONE................360 802-0808

GEOGRAPHIC SECTION

Enumclaw - King County (G-3308)

EMP: 4 EST: 2012
SALES (est): 361K **Privately Held**
SIC: 3089 Mfg Plastic Products

(G-3275)
AFTER MARKET PRODUCTS INC
1751 Garrett St (98022-4440)
P.O. Box 578 (98022-0578)
PHONE.................................360 825-6500
Eric Anderson, *President*
▼ EMP: 15 EST: 2004
SQ FT: 18,000
SALES (est): 3.7MM **Privately Held**
SIC: 3728 Aircraft body assemblies & parts

(G-3276)
ALPACA MENTORS
30128 Se 402nd St (98022-7731)
PHONE.................................253 880-6469
EMP: 2
SALES (est): 79.2K **Privately Held**
SIC: 2231 Alpacas, mohair: woven

(G-3277)
B & B PARROTTS WELDING INC
2401 Cole St (98022-3648)
P.O. Box 222 (98022-0222)
PHONE.................................360 825-0565
William Parrott, *President*
EMP: 8
SQ FT: 12,623
SALES (est): 487.9K **Privately Held**
SIC: 1799 3441 Welding on site; fabricated structural metal

(G-3278)
B & G INDUSTRIES INC
501 Griffin Ave (98022-3422)
P.O. Box 495 (98022-0495)
PHONE.................................360 802-0363
Bill Hund, *President*
Gary Gustafson, *Vice Pres*
EMP: 16
SQ FT: 10,000
SALES (est): 1.5MM **Privately Held**
SIC: 3599 Machine shop, jobbing & repair

(G-3279)
BEST WAY CONCRETE
24959 Se 362nd Ln (98022-5808)
PHONE.................................360 825-5494
EMP: 2
SALES (est): 124.4K **Privately Held**
SIC: 7353 5211 3273 1771 Heavy Cnstn Equip Rent Ret Lumber/Building Mtrl Mfg Ready-Mixed Concrete Concrete Contractor

(G-3280)
CARTER LIFT BAG INC
Also Called: Carter Bag Co
29500 Se Green Riv (98022)
PHONE.................................360 886-2302
Jim Carter, *President*
Dave Blackburn, *Vice Pres*
Linda Carter, *Treasurer*
Dianna Blackburn, *Admin Sec*
▼ EMP: 4 EST: 1973
SALES (est): 412.4K **Privately Held**
WEB: www.carterbag.com
SIC: 3949 Skin diving equipment, scuba type

(G-3281)
CHATEAU PLATEAU WINERY INC
28925 Se 416th St (98022-9752)
PHONE.................................360 825-2466
David Asplund, *President*
EMP: 7
SALES (est): 459.8K **Privately Held**
SIC: 2084 Wines

(G-3282)
CLARK MACHINERY INC
36923 249th Ave Se (98022-8804)
PHONE.................................360 825-1840
Greg Johnson, *Principal*
EMP: 4
SALES (est): 406.7K **Privately Held**
SIC: 3569 General industrial machinery

(G-3283)
COURIER-HERALD
Also Called: Enumclaw Herald
1186 Myrtle Ave (98022-3502)
P.O. Box 157 (98022-0157)
PHONE.................................360 825-2555
John Natt, *Owner*
EMP: 12
SALES (est): 650.9K **Privately Held**
WEB: www.courierherald.com
SIC: 2711 Commercial printing & newspaper publishing combined; job printing & newspaper publishing combined

(G-3284)
CREATIVE WOOD SCULPTURES
28801 Se 480th St (98022-9357)
PHONE.................................360 825-6069
Joaquin Quezada, *Owner*
Donna Quezada, *Co-Owner*
EMP: 2
SALES (est): 50K **Privately Held**
SIC: 2499 Carved & turned wood

(G-3285)
DISCOVERY TOOLS
20921 Se 403rd St (98022-9164)
PHONE.................................253 288-1720
David Putman, *Owner*
EMP: 3
SALES (est): 90K **Privately Held**
SIC: 7379 7372 Computer related consulting services; educational computer software

(G-3286)
DIVERSIFIED PLASTICS WEST INC
Also Called: Dp West
2551 Cole St Ste E (98022-3645)
P.O. Box 1274 (98022-1274)
PHONE.................................360 825-7660
Barry L Reid, *President*
Brenda K Reid, *Treasurer*
EMP: 12
SALES (est): 750K **Privately Held**
WEB: www.dpwestinc.com
SIC: 3089 Injection molding of plastics

(G-3287)
DP WEST
2551 Cole St (98022-3647)
PHONE.................................360 825-7660
EMP: 5
SALES (est): 143.2K **Privately Held**
SIC: 3089 Mfg Plastic Products

(G-3288)
E B ASSOCIATES INC
1446 Lafromboise St (98022-2811)
PHONE.................................253 709-1433
Earl Barker, *President*
Marilyn Barker, *Vice Pres*
EMP: 2
SALES (est): 184.9K **Privately Held**
WEB: www.ebassociates.com
SIC: 7372 8748 Prepackaged software; business consulting

(G-3289)
ELDER LOGGING INC
1614 Cole St (98022-3508)
PHONE.................................360 825-7158
Jim Elder, *Principal*
EMP: 3
SALES (est): 410.6K **Privately Held**
SIC: 2411 Logging camps & contractors

(G-3290)
EROSION CTRL INNOVATIONS LLC
31002 Se Enumclaw (98022)
PHONE.................................206 962-9582
Brian Michael Malgarini, *Mng Member*
EMP: 5
SQ FT: 2,000
SALES (est): 280.9K **Privately Held**
SIC: 2436 2421 0782 Softwood veneer & plywood; sawmills & planing mills, general; lawn & garden services

(G-3291)
EXCEL PACKAGING SYSTEMS INC
3214 Wynalda Dr (98022-6413)
PHONE.................................360 825-7209
Vernon L Lee, *Principal*
EMP: 2 EST: 2012
SALES (est): 146K **Privately Held**
SIC: 2631 Container, packaging & boxboard

(G-3292)
GREEN SECTION 30 LLC
36000 Enumclaw Franklin R (98022)
PHONE.................................253 433-4130
David Morris,
Robert Morris,
EMP: 4
SALES (est): 622.9K **Privately Held**
SIC: 1311 Oil sand mining

(G-3293)
HILL AEROSYSTEMS INC
911 Battersby Ave (98022-9248)
PHONE.................................360 802-8300
Steve Hill, *President*
Lorimay Hill, *Vice Pres*
Tim Drake, *QC Mgr*
Suzie Van, *Human Res Mgr*
Suzie Van Eecke, *Human Res Mgr*
EMP: 90
SALES (est): 22.1MM **Privately Held**
WEB: www.hillstamping.com
SIC: 3469 Stamping metal for the trade

(G-3294)
IRON GATE SHOPPE
1108 Loraine St (98022-2134)
PHONE.................................360 791-3292
Don Ward, *Owner*
EMP: 9
SQ FT: 3,600
SALES (est): 700K **Privately Held**
WEB: www.irongateshoppe.com
SIC: 3446 3496 Fences, gates, posts & flagpoles; fences or posts, ornamental iron or steel; miscellaneous fabricated wire products

(G-3295)
J H HOLM
46909 286th Ave Se (98022-9320)
P.O. Box 12 (98022-0012)
PHONE.................................360 825-4276
John Holm, *Owner*
EMP: 2
SALES (est): 150K **Privately Held**
SIC: 2411 Logging camps & contractors

(G-3296)
J S OWILL INC
553 Roosevelt Ave Ste 203 (98022-2990)
PHONE.................................360 226-3637
EMP: 3 EST: 2017
SALES (est): 129K **Privately Held**
SIC: 3433 Mfg Heating Equipment-Non-electric

(G-3297)
JENSEN BARTON W INC
Also Called: Jensen Sand & Gravel
548 Dickson Ave (98022-2952)
PHONE.................................360 825-3750
Bart Jensen, *President*
Karen Jensen, *Vice Pres*
EMP: 15
SQ FT: 600
SALES (est): 1.3MM **Privately Held**
WEB: www.karenjensen.com
SIC: 4212 1611 1442 Local trucking, without storage; general contractor, highway & street construction; gravel mining

(G-3298)
KAM MANUFACTURING
2551 Cole St (98022-3647)
PHONE.................................360 625-8321
EMP: 2 EST: 2017
SALES (est): 87.7K **Privately Held**
SIC: 3999 Manufacturing industries

(G-3299)
KOVASH LOGGING LTD
43804 284th Ave Se (98022-9280)
PHONE.................................360 825-4263
John Kovash, *President*
EMP: 25 EST: 1979
SALES (est): 2.3MM **Privately Held**
SIC: 2411 Logging camps & contractors

(G-3300)
LIQUID INDUSTRY LLC
19311 Se 416th St (98022-9135)
P.O. Box 337 (98022-0337)
PHONE.................................206 718-3360
Nicole Bramson,
EMP: 3
SALES (est): 388.1K **Privately Held**
SIC: 2741 Miscellaneous publishing

(G-3301)
LOHR INDUSTRIES
27644 Se 401st St (98022-9722)
PHONE.................................360 802-4351
Terry Lohr, *Principal*
EMP: 2 EST: 2011
SALES (est): 147.9K **Privately Held**
SIC: 3999 Manufacturing industries

(G-3302)
LYLE W PULLING
1805 Lafromboise St (98022-2728)
PHONE.................................360 825-6129
EMP: 2
SALES (est): 110K **Privately Held**
SIC: 1389 Oil/Gas Field Services

(G-3303)
M & L MACHINE INC (PA)
355 Rainier Ave (98022-3409)
PHONE.................................360 825-4700
Mark G Mathieson, *President*
Sharon Meehan, *Office Mgr*
EMP: 4
SQ FT: 5,000
SALES (est): 700K **Privately Held**
WEB: www.mlmachine.com
SIC: 3599 Machine shop, jobbing & repair

(G-3304)
MAVIN MFG INC
58722 Lumpy Ln E (98022-8023)
PHONE.................................360 663-0354
Josh Mavin, *President*
Tom Mavin, *Admin Sec*
EMP: 2
SALES (est): 400K **Privately Held**
SIC: 3334 Primary aluminum

(G-3305)
MODULAR SOFTWARE SYSTEMS INC
33628 Se 348th St (98022-7622)
PHONE.................................360 886-8882
Gary Robert Palmer, *Principal*
EMP: 2 EST: 2012
SALES (est): 135.1K **Privately Held**
SIC: 7372 Prepackaged software

(G-3306)
MT PEAK ALPACAS LLC
47921 284th Ave Se (98022-7354)
PHONE.................................253 297-4083
EMP: 2
SALES (est): 73.4K **Privately Held**
SIC: 2231 Alpacas, mohair: woven

(G-3307)
NATURAL STONE RESTORERS
29227 Se 374th St (98022-6702)
P.O. Box 1315 (98022-1315)
PHONE.................................360 825-3199
EMP: 4
SALES (est): 404.3K **Privately Held**
SIC: 3531 Finishers & spreaders (construction equipment)

(G-3308)
NATURES INVENTORY LLC
2551 Cole St Ste S (98022-3646)
PHONE.................................425 775-2000
Louann Brandjes,
▲ EMP: 14
SQ FT: 5,000
SALES (est): 2.3MM **Privately Held**
WEB: www.naturesinventory.com
SIC: 2899 Oils & essential oils

(PA)=Parent Co (HQ)=Headquarters (DH)=Div Headquarters
✿ = New Business established in last 2 years

Enumclaw - King County (G-3309)

(G-3309)
NETHER INDUSTRIES INC
1633 Commerce St (98022-8247)
PHONE....................360 825-7940
Neal Sanders, *President*
Theresa Sanders, *Vice Pres*
◆ **EMP:** 22
SQ FT: 3,000
SALES (est): 6.1MM **Privately Held**
WEB: www.netherind.com
SIC: 3556 Food products machinery

(G-3310)
NIPR LLC
47614 260th Ave Se (98022-9391)
PHONE....................253 261-6840
Danielle Dukart, *Mng Member*
EMP: 7
SALES (est): 800.5K **Privately Held**
SIC: 3499 Fabricated metal products

(G-3311)
PARKER-HANNIFIN CORPORATION
Also Called: Cylinder Division
225 Battersby Ave (98022-8204)
PHONE....................360 802-1039
EMP: 300
SALES (corp-wide): 12B **Publicly Held**
SIC: 3593 Fluid power actuators, hydraulic or pneumatic
PA: Parker-Hannifin Corporation
6035 Parkland Blvd
Cleveland OH 44124
216 896-3000

(G-3312)
PURSUIT DISTILLING CO
2321 Cole St Ste 102 (98022-3651)
PHONE....................206 406-2263
EMP: 2
SALES (est): 62.3K **Privately Held**
SIC: 2085 Distilled & blended liquors

(G-3313)
Q OTM
1713 Garrett St Ste 2 (98022-3466)
PHONE....................360 802-3700
Willis Parker, *President*
EMP: 10
SALES (est): 865.7K **Privately Held**
WEB: www.qotm.com
SIC: 3541 Machine tools, metal cutting: exotic (explosive, etc.)

(G-3314)
QUALITY ON TIME MACHINING INC
1713 Garrett St Ste 2 (98022-3466)
PHONE....................360 802-3700
Willis A Parker, *President*
Micael A Parker, *Vice Pres*
EMP: 7
SALES (est): 1MM **Privately Held**
SIC: 3469 3728 3599 Machine parts, stamped or pressed metal; aircraft parts & equipment; machine shop, jobbing & repair

(G-3315)
R N C LATH & PLASTER
47902 288th Ave Se (98022-9388)
PHONE....................360 802-0938
Robert Corbett, *Principal*
EMP: 4 **EST:** 2008
SALES (est): 460.9K **Privately Held**
SIC: 3541 Lathes

(G-3316)
RAINIER GRAVEL
23028 Se 400th St (98022-8931)
P.O. Box 920 (98022-0920)
PHONE....................206 510-3451
Steve Pausheck, *Principal*
EMP: 3
SALES (est): 185.5K **Privately Held**
SIC: 1442 Construction sand mining

(G-3317)
REDEMPTION PRESS
1730 Railroad St (98022-3542)
P.O. Box 427 (98022-0427)
PHONE....................360 226-3488
Athena Dane Holtz, *Owner*
EMP: 2

SALES (est): 147.1K **Privately Held**
SIC: 2741 Miscellaneous publishing

(G-3318)
RON & LEOS WELDING SVCS INC
2221 Garrett St (98022-3452)
PHONE....................360 825-1221
Ron L Hardersen, *President*
Sherrie Hardersen, *Treasurer*
EMP: 8
SALES (est): 1MM **Privately Held**
WEB: www.weldingservice.com
SIC: 7692 Welding repair

(G-3319)
RUSH SAILS INC
Also Called: Neil Pryde Sails
16608 Crystal Dr E (98022-8062)
PHONE....................425 827-9648
Mary Rush, *President*
Scott Rush, *Corp Secy*
EMP: 4
SQ FT: 6,760
SALES: 300K **Privately Held**
WEB: www.dynamicsails.com
SIC: 2394 5091 Sails: made from purchased materials; sporting & recreation goods

(G-3320)
SKIERS INC
30015 Crystal Mountain Bl (98022-7929)
PHONE....................360 663-7777
EMP: 2
SALES (est): 75K **Privately Held**
SIC: 2064 Candy And Other Confectionery Products

(G-3321)
SOUND PUBLISHING INC
Also Called: Bonneylk/Sumner Courier-Herald
1627 Cole St (98022-3509)
PHONE....................360 825-2555
Bill Marcum, *Branch Mgr*
EMP: 7 **Privately Held**
WEB: www.soundpublishing.com
SIC: 2711 Newspapers: publishing only, not printed on site
HQ: Sound Publishing, Inc.
11323 Commando Rd W Main
Everett WA 98204
360 394-5800

(G-3322)
STAGEPLAN INC
1101 Battersby Ave (98022-3534)
PHONE....................360 825-2428
Ron D Alexander, *Ch of Bd*
Ron Alexander, *Ch of Bd*
Brian Pruitt, *Prdtn Mgr*
Kathy Carmichael, *Administration*
EMP: 22
SQ FT: 40,000
SALES: 3MM **Privately Held**
WEB: www.stageplan.com
SIC: 2541 Office fixtures, wood; display fixtures, wood; store fixtures, wood

(G-3323)
THRIFTY PAYLESS INC T/A
232 Roosevelt Ave (98022-8242)
PHONE....................360 825-2558
EMP: 2 **EST:** 2010
SALES (est): 96.3K **Privately Held**
SIC: 2836 Mfg Biological Products

(G-3324)
TIM CORLISS & SON INC
Also Called: Corliss Redi-Mix
29410 Hwy 410 (98022)
P.O. Box 487 (98022-0487)
PHONE....................360 825-2578
Toll Free:....................888   -
Scott Corliss, *President*
EMP: 7
SALES (corp-wide): 1.1MM **Privately Held**
SIC: 3273 5032 1442 Ready-mixed concrete; sand, construction; construction sand & gravel
PA: Tim Corliss & Son Inc
1050 Butte Ave Se
Pacific WA
253 833-3131

(G-3325)
TIN CAN DIVA
42905 260th Ave Se (98022-8336)
PHONE....................253 315-5587
Beverly Bass-Dunning, *Principal*
EMP: 2
SALES (est): 73.4K **Privately Held**
SIC: 3411 Tin cans

(G-3326)
WAPITI WOOLIES INC
58414 State Route 410 E (98022-8041)
PHONE....................360 663-2268
Robert W Grubb, *President*
EMP: 5
SQ FT: 3,000
SALES (est): 555K **Privately Held**
WEB: www.wapitiwoolies.com
SIC: 5699 2253 5812 Sports apparel; hats & headwear, knit; sweaters & sweater coats, knit; coffee shop

(G-3327)
WHITE RIVER DISTILLERS LLC
25714 Se 400th St (98022-6857)
PHONE....................253 219-5100
EMP: 3 **EST:** 2016
SALES (est): 134.2K **Privately Held**
SIC: 2085 Distilled & blended liquors

(G-3328)
WHITE RIVER FABRICATION LLC
2321 Cole St Ste 101 (98022-3651)
PHONE....................253 261-8718
Kevin Boyles,
Jonathan Thomas,
EMP: 3 **EST:** 2014
SALES (est): 265.9K **Privately Held**
SIC: 3429 7389 Clamps, couplings, nozzles & other metal hose fittings; metal cutting services

(G-3329)
WHITMAN CABINETS AND WDWKG
1732 Harding St (98022-2721)
PHONE....................360 825-6466
G Whitman, *Principal*
EMP: 2
SALES (est): 182.1K **Privately Held**
SIC: 2431 Millwork

Ephrata
Grant County

(G-3330)
AGREX INC
3031 Road E Nw (98823-9735)
PHONE....................509 787-4595
Joe Milkowski, *Vice Pres*
EMP: 25 **Privately Held**
WEB: www.agrex.com
SIC: 2048 Cereal-, grain-, & seed-based feeds; alfalfa, cubed
HQ: Agrex Inc.
8205 W 108th Ter Ste 200
Overland Park KS 66210
913 851-6300

(G-3331)
ARCHER-DANIELS-MIDLAND COMPANY
Also Called: ADM
16051 Rail Road St Nw (98823)
PHONE....................509 754-5266
EMP: 15
SALES (corp-wide): 64.3B **Publicly Held**
SIC: 2041 3999 Flour & other grain mill products; barber & beauty shop equipment
PA: Archer-Daniels-Midland Company
77 W Wacker Dr Ste 4600
Chicago IL 60601
312 634-8100

(G-3332)
CPM DEVELOPMENT CORPORATION
Also Called: Central Washington Concrete
2651 Hwy 282 W (98823)
P.O. Box 248 (98823-0248)
PHONE....................509 754-5287

Troy Holt, *General Mgr*
EMP: 8
SALES (corp-wide): 30.6B **Privately Held**
SIC: 1611 3273 Surfacing & paving; ready-mixed concrete
HQ: Cpm Development Corporation
5111 E Broadway Ave
Spokane Valley WA 99212
509 534-6221

(G-3333)
EPHRATA RACEWAY PARK LLC
14156 Rd B3nw Nw (98823)
P.O. Box 145 (98823-0145)
PHONE....................509 398-7110
Mike Witte, *Partner*
Rita Witte, *Manager*
EMP: 25
SALES (est): 2.5MM **Privately Held**
SIC: 3644 7948 Raceways; racing, including track operation

(G-3334)
EPRHATA OIL CHANGE EXPRESS
1254 Basin St Sw (98823-2129)
P.O. Box 128 (98823-0128)
PHONE....................509 398-8740
Derick Kapalo, *General Mgr*
EMP: 4
SALES (est): 160.3K **Privately Held**
SIC: 1311 Crude petroleum & natural gas

(G-3335)
GOTAGSCOM LLC
55 Alder St Nw Ste B1 (98823-1696)
PHONE....................509 754-2760
Shannon Stevens, *Partner*
Todd Stevens,
▲ **EMP:** 9
SALES (est): 800K **Privately Held**
SIC: 3993 Signs & advertising specialties

(G-3336)
GRAVEL FLAT CROP DUSTING LLC
155 D St Ne (98823-1765)
P.O. Box 1229 (98823-1229)
PHONE....................509 398-8617
EMP: 3
SALES (est): 140K **Privately Held**
SIC: 1442 Construction Sand/Gravel

(G-3337)
I-90 EXPRESS LLC
256 Basin St Nw Ste B (98823-2417)
PHONE....................509 855-6280
EMP: 3
SALES (est): 261.9K **Privately Held**
SIC: 4731 5963 3632 Freight transportation arrangement; beverage services, direct sales; household refrigerators & freezers

(G-3338)
INK DOCTOR PRINTING
303 Patrick Rd (98823-1540)
PHONE....................509 237-1644
EMP: 2 **EST:** 2017
SALES (est): 83.9K **Privately Held**
SIC: 2752 Commercial printing, lithographic

(G-3339)
JOURNAL-NEWS PUBLISHING CO (PA)
Also Called: Grant County Journal
29 Alder St Sw (98823-1873)
P.O. Box 998 (98823-0998)
PHONE....................509 754-4636
Jeffrey G Fletcher, *President*
William Ifft, *Vice Pres*
EMP: 12 **EST:** 1968
SQ FT: 10,000
SALES (est): 3.3MM **Privately Held**
WEB: www.cheneyfreepress.com
SIC: 2711 2759 2752 Commercial printing & newspaper publishing combined; commercial printing; commercial printing, lithographic

(G-3340)
KATANA INDUSTRIES INC
1980 Fairchild Ave (98823)
PHONE....................509 754-5600

GEOGRAPHIC SECTION
Everett - Snohomish County (G-3369)

Gene Tanaka, *President*
EMP: 100
SALES (est): 13.6MM **Privately Held**
SIC: 3449 Bars, concrete reinforcing; fabricated steel

(G-3341)
LENROC CO
16051 Railroad Ave (98823)
P.O. Box 786 (98823-0786)
PHONE..................................509 754-5266
Kurt Stephan, *President*
Linda Stephan, *Corp Secy*
Tim Hepner, *Vice Pres*
▲ **EMP:** 10
SQ FT: 20,000
SALES (est): 1.6MM **Privately Held**
SIC: 2873 2819 2048 Fertilizers: natural (organic), except compost; industrial inorganic chemicals; prepared feeds

(G-3342)
MATERIAL INC (PA)
Also Called: Ephrata Auto Parts
1050 Basin St Sw (98823-2078)
P.O. Box 756 (98823-0756)
PHONE..................................509 754-4695
Paul Swanson, *President*
Shirley Wixon, *Vice Pres*
EMP: 10 **EST:** 1946
SQ FT: 11,000
SALES (est): 7.7MM **Privately Held**
SIC: 5531 5013 3599 Automotive parts; automotive supplies & parts; machine shop, jobbing & repair

(G-3343)
NORCO INC
276 Enterprise St Se (98823-1970)
PHONE..................................509 754-3518
Ronald Oakes, *Manager*
EMP: 6
SALES (corp-wide): 413MM **Privately Held**
WEB: www.norco-inc.com
SIC: 7389 2813 Filling pressure containers; acetylene
PA: Norco, Inc.
 1125 W Amity Rd
 Boise ID 83705
 208 336-1643

(G-3344)
P AND S PRINT COMPANY LLC
56 C St Nw (98823-1636)
PHONE..................................509 398-6504
Stephen Reagan, *Principal*
EMP: 2
SALES (est): 83.9K **Privately Held**
SIC: 2752 Commercial printing, lithographic

(G-3345)
PURPLE COYOTE INC
16 Basin St Sw (98823-1865)
P.O. Box 335 (98823-0335)
PHONE..................................509 754-2488
Carl L Highland, *CEO*
EMP: 3
SQ FT: 2,000
SALES (est): 369.4K **Privately Held**
SIC: 2759 2752 2741 2731 Screen printing; laser printing; business form & card printing, lithographic; posters: publishing & printing; business service newsletters: publishing & printing; pamphlets: publishing & printing

(G-3346)
SANDRA STROUP
Also Called: Chain Stitchery
12199 Dodson Rd Nw (98823-9577)
PHONE..................................509 754-0822
Sandra Stroup, *Owner*
EMP: 2
SALES (est): 96.1K **Privately Held**
SIC: 2395 Embroidery & art needlework

(G-3347)
WHITMUS ENTERPRISES INC
16051 Railroad St Nw (98823)
PHONE..................................509 398-0144
Matthew Whitmus, *President*
EMP: 8
SALES (est): 235K **Privately Held**
SIC: 3999 Manufacturing industries

Ethel
Lewis County

(G-3348)
B&M LOGGING INC
1940 Us Highway 12 (98542-9724)
PHONE..................................360 985-0150
Jeff Ripley, *Manager*
EMP: 2
SALES (est): 119.9K **Privately Held**
SIC: 2411 Logging camps & contractors

(G-3349)
BUCKS LOGGING INC
2160 Us Highway 12 (98542-9726)
P.O. Box 518, Onalaska (98570-0518)
PHONE..................................360 985-0758
Brad Lyons, *President*
Bart Lyons, *Vice Pres*
Brent Lyons, *Treasurer*
EMP: 6
SALES (est): 892.1K **Privately Held**
SIC: 2411 Logging camps & contractors

(G-3350)
DAN MCMULLEN WELL DRILLING
119 Oyler Way (98542-9700)
PHONE..................................707 998-9252
Dan McMullen, *Owner*
EMP: 2
SALES (est): 174.4K **Privately Held**
SIC: 1381 1521 1542 Drilling water intake wells; general remodeling, single-family houses; new construction, single-family houses; commercial & office building, new construction; commercial & office buildings, renovation & repair

(G-3351)
SHIPP CONSTRUCTION INC
262 Larmon Rd (98542-9709)
PHONE..................................360 262-0197
Kenneth Shipp, *President*
EMP: 30
SQ FT: 1,728
SALES (est): 3MM **Privately Held**
SIC: 2411 1611 Logging; highway & street construction

(G-3352)
WA CUTTING AND LOGGING
1648 Us Highway 12 (98542-9717)
PHONE..................................360 520-0464
Bill Foister, *Owner*
EMP: 3
SALES (est): 313.1K **Privately Held**
SIC: 2411 Logging camps & contractors

Everett
Snohomish County

(G-3353)
A & W BOTTLING COMPANY INC
7620 Hardeson Rd (98203-6286)
PHONE..................................425 355-0100
R B Christiansen, *President*
EMP: 30 **EST:** 1980
SALES (est): 5.1MM **Privately Held**
SIC: 2086 5149 Bottled & canned soft drinks; groceries & related products

(G-3354)
A H LUNDBERG INC
Also Called: Lundberg, A H Inc Engineers
2803 1/2 Hewitt Ave (98201-3819)
P.O. Box 1386 (98206-1386)
PHONE..................................425 258-4617
Thomas Eckstrom, *President*
EMP: 3
SQ FT: 3,000
SALES (est): 485.4K **Privately Held**
WEB: www.ahlundberginc.com
SIC: 5084 8711 3554 3541 Pulp (wood) manufacturing machinery; consulting engineer; designing: ship, boat, machine & product; paper industries machinery; machine tools, metal cutting type

(G-3355)
AAA KARTAK CO
13214 4th Ave W (98204-6336)
PHONE..................................425 844-8555
Cameron Kartak, *Principal*
EMP: 3 **EST:** 2017
SALES (est): 103.6K **Privately Held**
SIC: 3231 Doors, glass: made from purchased glass

(G-3356)
AALBU BROTHERS OF EVERETT INC
1001 Harborview Ln (98203-1732)
PHONE..................................425 252-9751
Cal Ferguson, *President*
Larry Torve, *Vice Pres*
EMP: 6
SALES (est): 500K **Privately Held**
SIC: 3441 7692 7538 3713 Fabricated structural metal; welding repair; general truck repair; truck bodies (motor vehicles)

(G-3357)
ACHILLES USA INC (HQ)
Also Called: Achilles Inflatable Boats
1407 80th St Sw (98203-6295)
PHONE..................................425 353-7000
Takuo Suzuki, *President*
Makoto Mino, *Vice Pres*
David Kater, *Business Mgr*
Harold Von Spreckelsen, *Business Mgr*
Chad Turner, *Vice Pres*
◆ **EMP:** 171 **EST:** 1973
SALES (est): 36.2MM **Privately Held**
WEB: www.achillesusa.com
SIC: 3081 Polyvinyl film & sheet

(G-3358)
ACROWOOD CORPORATION
4425 S 3rd Ave (98203-2515)
P.O. Box 1028 (98206-1028)
PHONE..................................425 258-3555
Farhang Javid, *President*
Kendall Kreft, *Vice Pres*
Jun Tian, *Vice Pres*
David Barnhart, *Foreman/Supr*
Jay Denoma, *Purch Mgr*
▲ **EMP:** 60
SQ FT: 200,000
SALES (est): 23.1MM **Privately Held**
WEB: www.acrowood.com
SIC: 3531 Chippers: brush, limb & log

(G-3359)
AD SIGN DESIGN
2032 Lombard Ave B (98201-2330)
PHONE..................................425 259-3000
Kristina Damery, *Owner*
EMP: 2
SALES (est): 127K **Privately Held**
SIC: 3993 Signs & advertising specialties

(G-3360)
ADAPTIVE CARGO SOLUTIONS LLC
Also Called: ACS
11504 Airport Rd (98204-3743)
PHONE..................................240 475-6521
Donald Barnard,
Kenneth Miller,
Shirlene Ostrov,
EMP: 10
SALES (est): 559.9K **Privately Held**
SIC: 2655 3089 4731 3221 Fiber cans, drums & similar products; plastic containers, except foam; freight transportation arrangement; glass containers; commercial containers; transportation consultant

(G-3361)
ADVANCED TRAFFIC PRODUCTS INC
1122 Industry St Ste A (98203-7154)
PHONE..................................425 347-6208
Edie Smith, *President*
Edie L Smith, *President*
Michael C Smith, *Vice Pres*
EMP: 12
SQ FT: 6,000
SALES (est): 4.5MM **Privately Held**
WEB: www.advancedtraffic.com
SIC: 5082 3669 Construction & mining machinery; transportation signaling devices

(G-3362)
ADVANTAC TECHNOLOGIES LLC
11504 Airport Rd G (98204-3743)
PHONE..................................360 217-8500
Chris Venti, *Mng Member*
▲ **EMP:** 20
SQ FT: 25,000
SALES (est): 3.2MM **Privately Held**
WEB: www.ultimatesurvival.com
SIC: 3999 Education aids, devices & supplies

(G-3363)
AEROACOUSTICS INC
Also Called: Aeroacoustics Aircraft Systems
9802 29th Ave W Ste B104 (98204-1349)
PHONE..................................425 438-0215
Jim Larson, *President*
Duane Easterly, *Managing Dir*
Gary Gorder, *Vice Pres*
EMP: 6 **EST:** 1989
SALES (est): 300K **Privately Held**
WEB: www.aeroacoustics.com
SIC: 3728 4581 Aircraft body assemblies & parts; airports, flying fields & services

(G-3364)
AIR TECHNICS
12022 39th Dr Se (98208-5666)
PHONE..................................425 316-0587
Rich Fillerup, *Principal*
EMP: 2
SALES (est): 125.3K **Privately Held**
SIC: 3721 Aircraft

(G-3365)
AIRMAGNET INC
6920 Seaway Blvd (98203-5829)
PHONE..................................800 283-5853
EMP: 3
SALES (est): 249.2K **Privately Held**
SIC: 3823 Industrial instrmnts msrmnt display/control process variable

(G-3366)
ALEXANDER PRINTING CO INC
2807 Rockefeller Ave (98201-3524)
PHONE..................................425 252-4212
Brett Wynne, *President*
Julie Wynne, *Vice Pres*
EMP: 5 **EST:** 1947
SQ FT: 1,800
SALES (est): 824.5K **Privately Held**
SIC: 2621 2759 Printing paper; commercial printing

(G-3367)
ALL OCEAN SERVICES LLC (PA)
1205 Craftsman Way # 100 (98201-1594)
PHONE..................................206 632-7692
Alfred Favre, *Mng Member*
EMP: 3
SALES (est): 696.7K **Privately Held**
WEB: www.alloceanservices.com
SIC: 8744 8711 3731 3732 Facilities support services; engineering services; shipbuilding & repairing; patrol boats, building & repairing; boat building & repairing

(G-3368)
ALLSPEC FASTENERS INC
1912 W Mukilteo Blvd (98203-1522)
PHONE..................................512 263-2593
Christopher Crickmer, *Principal*
EMP: 2
SALES (est): 72.9K **Privately Held**
SIC: 3965 Fasteners

(G-3369)
AMERON INTERNATIONAL CORP
Ameron Pole Products & Systems
1130 W Marine View Dr (98201-1500)
PHONE..................................425 258-2616
Will Richardson, *Manager*
EMP: 50
SQ FT: 30,000
SALES (corp-wide): 8.4B **Publicly Held**
WEB: www.ameron.com
SIC: 3272 Prestressed concrete products

Everett - Snohomish County (G-3370) **GEOGRAPHIC SECTION**

HQ: Ameron International Corporation
7909 Parkwood Circle Dr
Houston TX 77036
713 375-3700

(G-3370)
APPLIED POWER & CONTROL INC
12432 Highway 99 Ste 82 (98204-5505)
P.O. Box 13382, Mill Creek (98082-1382)
PHONE.................................425 710-9911
Dennis Johnson, *President*
David Bechtel, *Vice Pres*
EMP: 5
SQ FT: 4,000
SALES (est): 560K **Privately Held**
WEB: www.appliedcontrols.com
SIC: 3613 Control panels, electric

(G-3371)
APPLIED TECHNICAL SVCS CORP (PA)
Also Called: A T S
6300 Merrill Creek Pkwy (98203-1577)
PHONE.................................425 249-5555
George Hamilton, *CEO*
Arnulfo Manriquez, *General Mgr*
Trevor Tonning, *Project Mgr*
Jami Lentz, *Purchasing*
Fatima Abdelkafi, *Engineer*
▲ **EMP:** 2
SQ FT: 38,000
SALES (est): 1.6MM **Privately Held**
WEB: www.atscorp.net
SIC: 3672 Printed circuit boards

(G-3372)
ARIEL SCREENPRINTING & DESIGN
2128 105th Pl Se (98208-4244)
PHONE.................................425 337-1918
Daniel R Birks, *Owner*
Kathy Birks, *Owner*
EMP: 2
SALES (est): 110K **Privately Held**
SIC: 2396 Screen printing on fabric articles

(G-3373)
ARMADILLO PRESS INC
9609 Belmont Dr (98208-2713)
PHONE.................................425 355-5588
Nancy Brown, *President*
Doyle Brown, *Vice Pres*
EMP: 2
SALES (est): 180K **Privately Held**
SIC: 2789 Bookbinding & related work

(G-3374)
AT YOUR SERVICE
Also Called: Color ME Frugal
10508 Rosewood Ave (98204-3680)
PHONE.................................425 348-9129
Kelli Rippee, *Owner*
George Rippee, *Co-Owner*
EMP: 2
SQ FT: 1,056
SALES (est): 83.6K **Privately Held**
SIC: 2782 Scrapbooks, albums & diaries

(G-3375)
AUROMA TECHNOLOGIES CO LLC
2211 W Casino Rd Ste A (98204-1456)
PHONE.................................425 582-8674
Yongfang Zhang, *President*
Lianfang Zhang, *Vice Pres*
Christiane Laakmann, *Admin Sec*
▲ **EMP:** 15 **EST:** 1994
SQ FT: 8,100
SALES (est): 4.5MM **Privately Held**
WEB: www.accesslaserco.com
SIC: 3699 Laser systems & equipment

(G-3376)
AUTOMOTIVE MACHINE SPECIALTIES
12432 Highway 99 Ste 77 (98204-5505)
PHONE.................................425 355-0802
James Hadaler, *President*
Lisa Hadaler, *Vice Pres*
EMP: 2
SALES (est): 174K **Privately Held**
SIC: 7539 6411 3599 Machine shop, automotive; insurance agents, brokers & service; machine shop, jobbing & repair

(G-3377)
AVN FLOOR & MILL WORK LLC
10124 9th Ave W Apt B106 (98204-3711)
PHONE.................................425 345-6071
Andrey Nazarchuk, *Principal*
EMP: 2
SALES (est): 112.9K **Privately Held**
SIC: 2431 Millwork

(G-3378)
AVTECHTYEE INC
Also Called: Tyee Aircraft
6500 Merrill Creek Pkwy (98203-5860)
PHONE.................................425 290-3100
Jorge Valladares, *President*
Kelli Kruse, *General Mgr*
Rachel Kosmin, *Mfg Mgr*
Corinne Sternberg, *Mfg Mgr*
Don Glass, *Research*
◆ **EMP:** 150
SQ FT: 45,000
SALES (est): 105MM
SALES (corp-wide): 3.8B **Publicly Held**
WEB: www.avtcorp.com
SIC: 3728 3648 3812 Aircraft parts & equipment; lighting equipment; search & navigation equipment
HQ: Transdigm, Inc.
4223 Monticello Blvd
Cleveland OH 44121

(G-3379)
B & C MANUFACTURING INC
Also Called: Advanced Designs
3419 Hayes St (98201-1928)
PHONE.................................425 787-8868
Bill Hodo, *President*
Cheryl Hodo, *Vice Pres*
EMP: 7
SQ FT: 3,200
SALES (est): 989K **Privately Held**
SIC: 3599 Machine shop, jobbing & repair

(G-3380)
B/E AEROSPACE INC
Also Called: Flight Structures
11404 Commando Rd W (98204-3535)
PHONE.................................360 657-5197
Mike Hugull, *Vice Pres*
April Aldrich, *Buyer*
Don Cook, *Engineer*
Art Escobar, *Engineer*
Robert Hyink, *Controller*
EMP: 300
SALES (corp-wide): 66.5B **Publicly Held**
WEB: www.beaerospace.com
SIC: 3728 8711 3812 Aircraft parts & equipment; consulting engineer; search & navigation equipment
HQ: B/E Aerospace, Inc.
1400 Corporate Center Way
Wellington FL 33414
561 791-5000

(G-3381)
B/E AEROSPACE INC
11404 Commando Rd W (98204-3535)
PHONE.................................425 923-2700
Amin J Khoury, *Ch of Bd*
EMP: 300
SALES (corp-wide): 66.5B **Publicly Held**
SIC: 2531 3728 3647 Seats, aircraft; aircraft parts & equipment; aircraft lighting fixtures
HQ: B/E Aerospace, Inc.
1400 Corporate Center Way
Wellington FL 33414
561 791-5000

(G-3382)
BAL & BAL 200803466 INC
Also Called: Signs Now Washington
11630 Arprt Rd Ste B-200 (98204)
PHONE.................................425 481-4900
David Bal, *Ch of Bd*
Rani Bal, *President*
EMP: 6
SQ FT: 5,000
SALES: 500K **Privately Held**
SIC: 3993 Signs & advertising specialties

(G-3383)
BALLARD TECHNOLOGY INC
Also Called: Astronics Ballard Technology
11400 Airport Rd Ste 201 (98204-8711)
PHONE.................................425 339-0281
Peter Gundermann, *Ch of Bd*
Kevin Chrisian, *Assistant VP*
Jason Harper, *Opers Staff*
Don Sprinkle, *Purch Mgr*
Greg Powers, *Engineer*
◆ **EMP:** 58
SQ FT: 22,000
SALES: 16MM
SALES (corp-wide): 803.2MM **Publicly Held**
WEB: www.ballardtech.com
SIC: 3728 3575 3812 Aircraft parts & equipment; computer terminals, monitors & components; search & navigation equipment
PA: Astronics Corporation
130 Commerce Way
East Aurora NY 14052
716 805-1599

(G-3384)
BB CITC LLC
Also Called: Birdbuffer
1420 80th St Sw Ste D (98203-6248)
PHONE.................................425 776-4950
Paul De La Port, *President*
Jason Wilbur, *Vice Pres*
EMP: 15
SQ FT: 8,757
SALES (est): 713.5K **Privately Held**
SIC: 3569 5999 Separators for steam, gas, vapor or air (machinery); theatrical equipment & supplies

(G-3385)
BERRY NEON CO INC
Also Called: Berry Signs Systems
7400 Hardeson Rd (98203-5840)
PHONE.................................425 776-8835
Ron Jacobs, *President*
Erik Stephanides, *Sales Staff*
Larissa Maninger, *Admin Asst*
EMP: 25
SQ FT: 3,500
SALES (est): 4.4MM **Privately Held**
WEB: www.berryneonsigns.com
SIC: 3993 1731 7629 Electric signs; neon signs; electrical work; electrical repair shops

(G-3386)
BERRY NUTTY
910 Se Everett Mall Way (98208-3709)
PHONE.................................425 265-1680
Berry Nutty, *Principal*
EMP: 4
SALES (est): 215.8K **Privately Held**
SIC: 2026 Yogurt

(G-3387)
BIG CREEK FISHERIES LLC
3900 Railway Ave (98201-3840)
PHONE.................................425 742-8609
John R Boggs, *Mng Member*
▼ **EMP:** 115
SQ FT: 3,000
SALES: 4MM **Privately Held**
SIC: 2092 Fresh or frozen packaged fish

(G-3388)
BIMBO BAKERY USA
909 Se Everett Mall Way E550 (98208-3749)
PHONE.................................425 347-3900
Mark Hoag, *Principal*
EMP: 6 **EST:** 2010
SALES (est): 494.2K **Privately Held**
SIC: 2051 Bread, cake & related products

(G-3389)
BLR AEROSPACE LLC
11002 29th Ave W (98204-1314)
PHONE.................................425 353-6591
Kevin Gwin, *CFO*
Guilherme De Moraes, *Sales Mgr*
Emily Brown, *Mktg Coord*
Robert J Desroche, *Mng Member*
Cameron Piercy, *Manager*
◆ **EMP:** 20
SALES (est): 4.9MM **Privately Held**
SIC: 3728 Aircraft parts & equipment

(G-3390)
BLUE PRINT
305 Bedrock Dr (98203-4246)
PHONE.................................425 870-5599

Jorge Rosales, *Principal*
EMP: 2
SALES (est): 83.9K **Privately Held**
SIC: 2752 Commercial printing, lithographic

(G-3391)
BLUE RIBBON PRINTING
12712 Admiralty Way (98204-5562)
PHONE.................................425 478-7628
EMP: 2
SALES (est): 83.9K **Privately Held**
SIC: 2752 Commercial printing, lithographic

(G-3392)
BLUE STREAK FINISHERS LLC
1520 80th St Sw Ste A (98203-7200)
PHONE.................................425 347-1944
Jack Giddens, *President*
Tim Giddens, *Corp Secy*
EMP: 80
SALES (est): 10.6MM
SALES (corp-wide): 103MM **Privately Held**
WEB: www.bluestreak-finishers.com
SIC: 3471 3479 Finishing, metals or formed products; painting of metal products
PA: Valence Surface Technologies Llc
1790 Hughes Landing Blvd
The Woodlands TX 77380
855 370-5920

(G-3393)
BMC WEST LLC
Also Called: BMC West Truss Plant
3200 35th Ave Ne (98201-8645)
PHONE.................................425 303-0661
Todd Grogen, *Systems Mgr*
EMP: 80 **Publicly Held**
SIC: 5211 2439 Lumber products; trusses, wooden roof
HQ: Bmc West, Llc
980 Hammond Dr Ste 500
Atlanta GA 30328
208 331-4300

(G-3394)
BOEING COMMERCIAL AIRPLANE
3003 W Casino Rd (98204-1910)
PHONE.................................425 237-2019
▲ **EMP:** 23
SALES: 8.6MM **Privately Held**
SIC: 3721 3728 Aircraft; military aircraft equipment & armament

(G-3395)
BOEING COMPANY
6200 23rd Dr W (98203-1576)
PHONE.................................425 407-1400
EMP: 4
SALES (corp-wide): 101.1B **Publicly Held**
SIC: 3721 Airplanes, fixed or rotary wing
PA: The Boeing Company
100 N Riverside Plz
Chicago IL 60606
312 544-2000

(G-3396)
BOEING COMPANY
3003 W Casino Rd (98204-1910)
PHONE.................................425 342-2121
Di Ann Sanchez, *Vice Pres*
Peter Alcorn, *Project Mgr*
Adam Grim, *Project Mgr*
Wayne Kremling, *Project Mgr*
Ioana Ursescu, *Project Mgr*
EMP: 5
SALES (corp-wide): 101.1B **Publicly Held**
SIC: 3721 Airplanes, fixed or rotary wing; motorized aircraft
PA: The Boeing Company
100 N Riverside Plz
Chicago IL 60606
312 544-2000

(G-3397)
BOEING COMPANY
2600 94th St Sw (98204-2153)
PHONE.................................312 544-2000
Maria Nelson, *Managing Dir*
Ruth Garcia, *Export Mgr*

▲ = Import ▼ = Export
◆ = Import/Export

GEOGRAPHIC SECTION
Everett - Snohomish County (G-3426)

Minsu Kim, *Engineer*
Janusz Szymanski, *Engineer*
Martin Cioffoletti, *Project Engr*
EMP: 996
SALES (corp-wide): 101.1B **Publicly Held**
SIC: 3721 3663 Airplanes, fixed or rotary wing; helicopters; research & development on aircraft by the manufacturer; airborne radio communications equipment
PA: The Boeing Company
100 N Riverside Plz
Chicago IL 60606
312 544-2000

(G-3398)
BOLT WOODWORKS CORP
3010 Everett Ave Unit A (98201-3881)
PHONE..................................206 734-5845
Jared Levi Levi Bolt, *Principal*
EMP: 2
SALES (est): 59.5K **Privately Held**
SIC: 2431 Millwork

(G-3399)
BOULDER GOLD LLC
2824 110th St Se (98208-7831)
PHONE..................................425 308-4316
Bryan Stephens,
EMP: 6
SALES (est): 249.5K **Privately Held**
SIC: 1041 Gold ores mining

(G-3400)
BRANDON COMPANY INC
12708 Alexander Rd (98204-5427)
PHONE..................................425 290-5327
Jeff Brandon, *President*
Mary Brandon, *Admin Sec*
EMP: 3
SQ FT: 1,000
SALES: 40K **Privately Held**
SIC: 3559 Electronic component making machinery

(G-3401)
BRIDGEWAYS
5801 23rd Dr W Ste 104 (98203-1587)
PHONE..................................425 513-2989
Donna Konicki, *Exec Dir*
Nancy Elliott, *Director*
Virginia Sprague, *Director*
EMP: 66
SQ FT: 8,256
SALES: 4.3MM **Privately Held**
WEB: www.bridgeways.org
SIC: 3599 8331 3812 3699 Machine shop, jobbing & repair; vocational rehabilitation agency; search & navigation equipment; electrical equipment & supplies; vocational counseling; mental health clinic, outpatient

(G-3402)
BUCHER AEROSPACE CORPORATION
1310 Industry St Ste 100 (98203-7124)
PHONE..................................425 355-2202
Francisco Aguilera, *CEO*
Hans Rudolf Burlet, *President*
Michael Schertler, *Engineer*
Thomas Hofer, *CFO*
EMP: 38
SQ FT: 45,000
SALES: 10MM **Privately Held**
WEB: www.bucheraero.com
SIC: 8711 3728 Acoustical engineering; aircraft parts & equipment

(G-3403)
BUILDERS EXCHANGE WASH INC
2607 Wetmore Ave (98201-2926)
PHONE..................................425 743-3244
Cheri French, *President*
Stuart French, *Vice Pres*
EMP: 11
SQ FT: 5,000
SALES (est): 1.3MM **Privately Held**
WEB: www.bxwa.com
SIC: 2721 Trade journals: publishing only, not printed on site

(G-3404)
BUSE TIMBER & SALES INC
3812 28th Pl Ne (98201-8602)
PHONE..................................425 258-2577
Tom Parks, *Principal*
Diana Martin, *Controller*
◆ **EMP:** 68
SQ FT: 6,000
SALES: 25.8MM **Privately Held**
WEB: www.busetimber.com
SIC: 2421 Lumber: rough, sawed or planed

(G-3405)
BUTLER TOOL & MANUFACTURING
Also Called: Butler Tools
12322 Highway 99 Ste 92 (98204-8548)
PHONE..................................425 348-7672
David Butler, *President*
Carolyn L Butler, *Corp Secy*
Carol Butler, *Vice Pres*
EMP: 8
SQ FT: 4,000
SALES: 750K **Privately Held**
SIC: 3599 Machine shop, jobbing & repair

(G-3406)
CABINET GUYS
10802 40th Ave Se (98208-5400)
PHONE..................................425 344-5882
John Thurston, *Principal*
EMP: 2
SALES (est): 203.4K **Privately Held**
SIC: 2434 Wood kitchen cabinets

(G-3407)
CADENCE AEROSPACE LLC
2300 Merrill Creek Pkwy (98203-5855)
PHONE..................................425 353-0405
EMP: 2
SALES (est): 86K **Privately Held**
SIC: 3721 Aircraft

(G-3408)
CADENCE AEROSPACE LLC
2600 94th St Sw Ste 150 (98204-2151)
PHONE..................................425 353-0405
Larry Resnick, *CEO*
Mike Coburn, *COO*
John Seguin, *Vice Pres*
Scott Willis, *Vice Pres*
Don Devore, *CFO*
EMP: 19
SALES (est): 5.7MM **Privately Held**
SIC: 3728 Aircraft parts & equipment

(G-3409)
CAMERON INTERNATIONAL CORP
834 80th St Sw Ste 300 (98203-7008)
PHONE..................................425 438-8726
EMP: 49
SALES (corp-wide): 9.8B **Publicly Held**
SIC: 3533 Mfg Oil/Gas Field Machinery
PA: Cameron International Corporation
1333 West Loop S Ste 1700
Houston TX 77041
713 513-3300

(G-3410)
CASCADE COFFEE INC (DH)
1525 75th St Sw Ste 100 (98203-7007)
PHONE..................................425 347-3995
Philip Johnson, *Chairman*
Greg Thayer, *Vice Pres*
Patrick Lyon, *QA Dir*
Fred Haines, *Engineer*
Jerry Klobertanz, *Engineer*
EMP: 15
SQ FT: 110,000
SALES (est): 18.5MM
SALES (corp-wide): 2.2B **Privately Held**
WEB: www.cascadecoffeeinc.com
SIC: 2095 5149 5499 7389 Coffee roasting (except by wholesale grocers); coffee, green or roasted; coffee; coffee service
HQ: Ds Services Of America, Inc.
2300 Windy Ridge Pkwy Se 500n
Atlanta GA 30339
770 933-1400

(G-3411)
CBI SERVICES LLC
5500 S 1st Ave (98203-4116)
PHONE..................................425 258-2350

Bruce Fabert, *Sales Mgr*
Raymond Maw, *Branch Mgr*
EMP: 50
SALES (corp-wide): 6.7B **Publicly Held**
SIC: 3443 1791 Fabricated plate work (boiler shop); structural steel erection
HQ: Cbi Services, Llc
14107 S Route 59
Plainfield IL 60544
815 439-6668

(G-3412)
CEDAR GROVE COMPOSTING INC
3620 36th Pl Ne (98201-8641)
PHONE..................................425 212-2515
Steve Banachero, *Branch Mgr*
EMP: 153 **Privately Held**
SIC: 2875 Compost
PA: Cedar Grove Composting, Inc.
7343 E Marginal Way S
Seattle WA 98108

(G-3413)
CEMEX CNSTR MTLS FLA LLC
Also Called: Northwest - Everett Landsale
6300 Glenwood Ave (98203-4247)
PHONE..................................425 513-6651
EMP: 3 **Privately Held**
SIC: 3273 Ready-mixed concrete
HQ: Cemex Construction Materials Florida, Llc
1501 Belvedere Rd
West Palm Beach FL 33406

(G-3414)
CEMEX CNSTR MTLS PCF LLC
Also Called: N.everett Asphalt Materials
222 W Marine View Dr (98201-1029)
PHONE..................................425 252-8600
EMP: 3 **Privately Held**
SIC: 3273 Ready-mixed concrete
HQ: Cemex Construction Materials Pacific, Llc
1501 Belvedere Rd
West Palm Beach FL 33406
561 833-5555

(G-3415)
CEPHER PUBLISHING GROUP LLC
1523 132nd St Se C-350 (98208-7200)
PHONE..................................406 889-7583
David Castro, *COO*
EMP: 6
SALES (est): 230.9K **Privately Held**
SIC: 2731 Books: publishing & printing

(G-3416)
CHILD EVNGELISM FELLOWSHIP INC
1832 Walnut St (98201-1904)
PHONE..................................425 252-6314
Jan Akam, *Director*
EMP: 41
SALES (corp-wide): 24.4MM **Privately Held**
SIC: 2752 Commercial printing, lithographic
PA: Child Evangelism Fellowship Incorporated
17482 Highway M
Warrenton MO 63383
636 456-4321

(G-3417)
CHURCHILL BROTHERS
1130 W Mar View Dr Ste C (98201)
PHONE..................................360 293-2700
Don Heirman, *Owner*
EMP: 5 **EST:** 1975
SQ FT: 3,000
SALES (est): 376.3K **Privately Held**
SIC: 2394 5091 Convertible tops, canvas or boat: from purchased materials; boat accessories & parts

(G-3418)
CINCINNATI INCORPORATED
2210 Hewitt Ave Ste 201 (98201-3767)
PHONE..................................425 263-9216
EMP: 44

SALES (corp-wide): 83.2MM **Privately Held**
SIC: 3542 Machine tools, metal forming type
PA: Cincinnati Incorporated
7420 Kilby Rd
Harrison OH 45030
513 367-7100

(G-3419)
CLEAR WATER COMPLIANCE LLC
Also Called: Clear Water Services
2525 W Casino Rd Ste 7a (98204-2112)
PHONE..................................425 412-5700
Chris Augustine, *President*
Saundra Nulkey, *Principal*
Cory Shelest,
EMP: 23
SALES (est): 9.3MM **Privately Held**
WEB: www.ch2ocsi.com
SIC: 3589 1799 8999 Sewage & water treatment equipment; dewatering; weather related services

(G-3420)
CLONERS MARKET INC
9817 28th Dr Se (98208-2951)
PHONE..................................425 218-0440
Matthew Ramsey, *President*
EMP: 4
SALES: 400K **Privately Held**
SIC: 2833 Drugs & herbs: grading, grinding & milling

(G-3421)
COASTAL MANUFACTURING INC
6700 Hardeson Rd Ste 103 (98203-7104)
PHONE..................................425 407-0624
Philip R Lepley, *President*
Dave Julius, *Opers Mgr*
EMP: 47
SQ FT: 30,000
SALES (est): 14.2MM **Privately Held**
WEB: www.coastal-mfg.com
SIC: 3444 3599 3469 3479 Sheet metal specialties, not stamped; machine shop, jobbing & repair; metal stampings; painting, coating & hot dipping

(G-3422)
COGENT HOLDINGS-1 LLC (PA)
Also Called: Berry Sign Systems
7400 Hardeson Rd (98203-5840)
PHONE..................................425 776-8835
Don Gerould, *President*
EMP: 7
SALES (est): 2.4MM **Privately Held**
SIC: 3993 5099 Signs & advertising specialties; signs, except electric

(G-3423)
COLOUR COACH
2026 Rucker Ave Apt B (98201-2257)
PHONE..................................206 478-6159
EMP: 2
SALES (est): 99.9K **Privately Held**
SIC: 3171 Handbags, women's

(G-3424)
COMMERCIAL DISPLAYERS
2916 100th St Sw Ste E (98204-1316)
PHONE..................................206 622-8039
Bernie Comer, *President*
EMP: 8
SALES (est): 837.2K **Privately Held**
SIC: 3993 Signs & advertising specialties

(G-3425)
CONTROL DYNAMICS INC
21 E Marine View Dr Ste G (98201-1276)
PHONE..................................800 738-5004
Eric M Moran, *President*
Gina Bryant, *Office Mgr*
EMP: 27
SQ FT: 15,000
SALES: 5MM **Privately Held**
SIC: 1731 3842 General electrical contractor; personal safety equipment

(G-3426)
COOK WELDING SERVICES
2626 119th St Sw Ste A1 (98204-6111)
PHONE..................................425 513-1263

Everett - Snohomish County (G-3427)   GEOGRAPHIC SECTION

EMP: 4
SALES: 500K **Privately Held**
SIC: 7692 Welding Repair

(G-3427)
CORNERSTONE PRSTHTICS ORTHTICS (PA)
1300 44th St Se (98203-2200)
PHONE..................................425 339-2559
Dave Hughes, *President*
David Hughes, *Vice Pres*
EMP: 15
SQ FT: 3,956
SALES (est): 2.8MM **Privately Held**
SIC: 3842 5999 Limbs, artificial; braces, elastic; braces, orthopedic; medical apparatus & supplies

(G-3428)
COUNTRYMAN SIGNS SCREEN PRTRS
Also Called: Countryman Signs/Screen Prtrs
5615 Broadway (98203-3925)
PHONE..................................425 355-1037
Gary Countryman, *Owner*
Jan Countryman, *Partner*
EMP: 3
SALES (est): 170K **Privately Held**
SIC: 7336 2396 2399 3993 Silk screen design; graphic arts & related design; screen printing on fabric articles; banners, made from fabric; signs & advertising specialties; commercial printing; decals: printing

(G-3429)
COVENANT ART GLASS INC
3232 Broadway (98201-4423)
PHONE..................................425 252-4232
Stanley Price, *President*
Colleen Price, *Vice Pres*
EMP: 6 **EST:** 1979
SALES (est): 340K **Privately Held**
WEB: www.covenantartglass.com
SIC: 3231 8299 Stained glass: made from purchased glass; arts & crafts schools; glass, leaded or stained

(G-3430)
CROSSROADS GROUP INC
Also Called: Crossroads Export
12618 Alexander Rd (98204-5429)
PHONE..................................206 855-3146
Jean-Marie Kabamba, *President*
Marshall Macnabb, *Analyst*
EMP: 1
SALES: 3MM **Privately Held**
SIC: 1481 Mine & quarry services, non-metallic minerals

(G-3431)
CRUCIBLE BREWING COMPANY
909 Se Everett Mall Way (98208-3746)
PHONE..................................425 374-7293
Shawn Dowling, *Principal*
EMP: 8
SALES (est): 281K **Privately Held**
SIC: 2082 Beer (alcoholic beverage)

(G-3432)
CRYSTALITE INC (PA)
3307 Cedar St (98201-4517)
PHONE..................................425 259-6000
Stephen Richter, *President*
Randy Wicklund, *Corp Secy*
Dennis Conway, *Vice Pres*
Cathy Hieb, *Controller*
Michael Gosner, *Sales Staff*
EMP: 49
SQ FT: 50,000
SALES: 10.3MM **Privately Held**
WEB: www.crystaliteinc.com
SIC: 3444 Skylights, sheet metal

(G-3433)
CRYSTALITE INC
3307 Cedar St (98201-4517)
PHONE..................................425 259-6000
Andy Nelson, *Branch Mgr*
EMP: 30
SALES (corp-wide): 10.3MM **Privately Held**
WEB: www.crystaliteinc.com
SIC: 3444 Skylights, sheet metal
PA: Crystalite, Inc.
3307 Cedar St
Everett WA 98201
425 259-6000

(G-3434)
CUTTING EDGE MANUFACTURING
3101 111th St Sw Ste L (98204-3590)
PHONE..................................425 348-0626
Chris Reed, *President*
EMP: 9
SALES (est): 1.6MM **Privately Held**
WEB: www.cuttingedge-mfg.com
SIC: 3449 Miscellaneous metalwork

(G-3435)
D & P PRODUCTS INC
1310 Industry St Ste 200 (98203-7124)
PHONE..................................425 551-1380
Michael Carr, *CEO*
Fred Johnson, *President*
EMP: 4
SQ FT: 2,000
SALES (est): 625K **Privately Held**
SIC: 3949 Exercise equipment; treadmills

(G-3436)
D&TOPM INC
11422 20 St Se (98205)
PHONE..................................425 334-7667
Delynn Kimberly, *Owner*
EMP: 2
SALES (est): 82.9K **Privately Held**
SIC: 3795 Tanks & tank components

(G-3437)
DAILY HERALD COMPANY (HQ)
1800 41st St Ste 300 (98203-2355)
P.O. Box 930 (98206-0930)
PHONE..................................425 339-3000
Gloria Fletcher, *President*
Larry Hanson, *President*
Daniel J Lynch, *Treasurer*
Veronica Dillon, *Admin Sec*
EMP: 97 **EST:** 1901
SQ FT: 10,000
SALES (est): 21.9MM
SALES (corp-wide): 2.7B **Publicly Held**
WEB: www.heraldnet.com
SIC: 2711 Commercial printing & newspaper publishing combined; newspapers, publishing & printing
PA: Graham Holdings Company
1300 17th St N Ste 1700
Arlington VA 22209
703 345-6300

(G-3438)
DAINES CORPORATION
Also Called: Baker Industries Northwest
12428 Highway 99 Ste 56 (98204-5502)
PHONE..................................425 212-3169
Ben Daines, *President*
Nick Daines, *Vice Pres*
EMP: 6
SQ FT: 6,000
SALES (est): 925.3K **Privately Held**
WEB: www.bakerindnw.com
SIC: 3449 Bars, concrete reinforcing: fabricated steel

(G-3439)
DATA QUEST LLC
1010 Se Everett Mall Way # 203 (98208-2855)
PHONE..................................360 568-8708
Shannon L Johnson, *Principal*
EMP: 2
SALES (est): 91.7K **Privately Held**
SIC: 2899

(G-3440)
DAVE YOCOMS WOOD CREATIONS
4121 119th St Se (98208-5344)
PHONE..................................425 220-5628
David Yocom, *Principal*
EMP: 2
SALES (est): 90.4K **Privately Held**
SIC: 2431 Millwork

(G-3441)
DCI METAL FINISHING LLC
6700 Hardeson Rd Ste 101 (98203-7104)
PHONE..................................425 347-7776
Mike Osburn, *President*
EMP: 14
SALES (est): 1.8MM **Privately Held**
SIC: 3471 Cleaning, polishing & finishing

(G-3442)
DESIGN CONSTRUCTION HERITG INC
1302 125th Pl Sw (98204-5650)
PHONE..................................206 634-1989
Don Harman, *President*
EMP: 2
SALES (est): 170K **Privately Held**
SIC: 3441 1542 Fabricated structural metal; nonresidential construction

(G-3443)
DIVE XTRAS
11520 Airport Rd (98204-3743)
PHONE..................................425 296-6570
Benjamin McGeever, *President*
EMP: 8
SALES (est): 2MM **Privately Held**
WEB: www.dive-xtras.com
SIC: 3949 Sporting & athletic goods

(G-3444)
DIVERSIFIED NORTHWEST INC (PA)
2941 Chestnut St (98201-3807)
PHONE..................................425 710-0753
James O'Dell, *President*
EMP: 13
SQ FT: 2,400
SALES (est): 2.5MM **Privately Held**
WEB: www.diversifiednw.com
SIC: 1623 3661 Underground utilities contractor; communication line & transmission tower construction; telephone & communication line construction; fiber optics communications equipment

(G-3445)
DOG ON IT PARKS INC
4818 Evergreen Way Ste B (98203-2879)
PHONE..................................425 512-8489
Cathy Max, *President*
Gary Max, *Vice Pres*
Shawn Avoy, *Prdtn Mgr*
EMP: 5 **EST:** 2010
SALES: 1.5MM **Privately Held**
SIC: 3559 Parking facility equipment & supplies

(G-3446)
DRAGONFIRE CANDLES LLC
911 93rd St Se (98208-3719)
PHONE..................................206 851-4235
Jamie Brunner, *Principal*
EMP: 2
SALES (est): 48K **Privately Held**
SIC: 3999 Candles

(G-3447)
DUNGENESS ENVMTL SOLUTIONS INC
909 Se Everett Mall Way (98208-3746)
PHONE..................................888 481-0326
Joel Van Ornum, *President*
EMP: 9
SALES (est): 203.2K **Privately Held**
SIC: 3823 Water quality monitoring & control systems

(G-3448)
DWAYNES SOFTWARE
15225 49th Ave Se (98208-8816)
PHONE..................................425 379-7741
Dwayne Dunlap, *Principal*
EMP: 2
SALES (est): 122.8K **Privately Held**
SIC: 7372 Prepackaged software

(G-3449)
DYNAMIC UTILITY SERVICES
13726 1st Pl W (98208-6919)
PHONE..................................425 742-1670
Danny Koingibbel, *Owner*
EMP: 2
SALES (est): 118.7K **Privately Held**
SIC: 3713 Utility truck bodies

(G-3450)
E TEEZ
1520 112th St Sw (98204-3757)
PHONE..................................425 645-9514
Eric Carey, *Manager*
EMP: 2
SALES (est): 111.6K **Privately Held**
SIC: 2759 Screen printing

(G-3451)
ECB CORP
Also Called: Omni Duct Systems
1515 75th St Sw (98203-7004)
PHONE..................................425 514-8334
Adam Barstad, *Principal*
EMP: 25
SALES (est): 3.3MM
SALES (corp-wide): 48.8MM **Privately Held**
SIC: 3444 Ducts, sheet metal
PA: Ecb Corp.
6400 Artesia Blvd
Buena Park CA 90620
714 385-8900

(G-3452)
EDJ PRECISION MACHINE INC
13317 Ash Way B-1 (98204-5014)
PHONE..................................425 745-3937
Edward A Mack, *President*
Maria Mack, *Treasurer*
EMP: 6
SQ FT: 3,909
SALES (est): 814.6K **Privately Held**
WEB: www.edjprecision.com
SIC: 3542 Machine tools, metal forming type

(G-3453)
ELDORADO STONE LLC
1200 Industry St Ste 100 (98203-7125)
PHONE..................................425 349-4107
EMP: 30 **Privately Held**
SIC: 3272 Concrete products, precast
HQ: Eldorado Stone Llc
1370 Grand Ave Bldg B
San Marcos CA 92078
800 925-1491

(G-3454)
ELECTRIC MIRROR LLC
6101 Assod Blvd Ste 101 (98203)
PHONE..................................425 776-4946
James V Mischel Jr, *CEO*
Donald Jacques, *COO*
Jon Johnston, *Vice Pres*
Joseph Clagett, *Buyer*
Stephen Lamachia, *Natl Sales Mgr*
◆ **EMP:** 400
SQ FT: 102,000
SALES (est): 72.6MM **Privately Held**
WEB: www.electricmirror.com
SIC: 3648 Lighting equipment

(G-3455)
ELECTRICAL PACKAGING CO INC
Also Called: Elpac
11627 Airport Rd Ste L (98204-8714)
PHONE..................................425 745-5466
Russell Roberts, *President*
Thomas G Carlisle, *Vice Pres*
Scott A Roberts, *Treasurer*
Tom Carlisle, *Manager*
Margaret L Roberts, *Admin Sec*
EMP: 11 **EST:** 1981
SQ FT: 5,500
SALES (est): 2.4MM **Privately Held**
SIC: 3613 Control panels, electric

(G-3456)
ELECTRONETICS LLC
1320 75th St Sw (98203-6254)
PHONE..................................425 355-1855
Mike Quinn, *Principal*
EMP: 56
SQ FT: 12,000
SALES: 8MM
SALES (corp-wide): 50.3MM **Privately Held**
WEB: www.americandataguard.com
SIC: 3612 Electronic meter transformers
PA: Northwest Center
7272 W Marginal Way S
Seattle WA 98108
206 285-9140

GEOGRAPHIC SECTION
Everett - Snohomish County (G-3483)

(G-3457)
ELECTRONIC COATING TECH INC
2615 W Casino Rd Ste 5g (98204-2108)
PHONE.................................425 265-2212
Tom Charlton, *President*
EMP: 4
SALES (corp-wide): 1.4MM **Privately Held**
SIC: 3479 Coating of metals & formed products; coating of metals with silicon
PA: Electronic Coating Technologies, Inc.
 1 Mustang Dr Ste 4
 Cohoes NY 12047
 518 688-2048

(G-3458)
ELPIS WORKS INC
3011 Grand Ave (98201-3910)
PHONE.................................206 317-4647
Blake Paine, *President*
EMP: 2
SALES (est): 233.8K **Privately Held**
SIC: 2521 Wood office furniture

(G-3459)
EMC NURSING SERVICES
5532 148th St Se (98208-9375)
PHONE.................................425 346-5982
Erin Chaney, *Principal*
EMP: 3
SALES (est): 188.2K **Privately Held**
SIC: 3572 Computer storage devices

(G-3460)
EMERALD CITY LABEL INC
834 80th St Sw Ste 100 (98203-7008)
PHONE.................................425 347-3479
Ted Shanley, *President*
EMP: 10
SQ FT: 5,570
SALES (est): 1.7MM **Privately Held**
WEB: www.emeraldcitylabel.com
SIC: 2671 2759 Packaging paper & plastics film, coated & laminated; labels & seals: printing

(G-3461)
ENCORE CABINETS INC
2115 39th St (98201-5022)
PHONE.................................425 259-0100
Kelly Baerwaldt, *Vice Pres*
EMP: 10
SALES (est): 1.1MM **Privately Held**
WEB: www.encorecabinets.com
SIC: 2434 Wood kitchen cabinets

(G-3462)
ESTERLINE TECHNOLOGIES CORP
Also Called: Esterline Ctrl Systems-Korry
11910 Beverly Park Rd (98204-3529)
PHONE.................................425 297-9624
Frank Houston, *President*
EMP: 32
SALES (corp-wide): 3.8B **Publicly Held**
SIC: 3728 Aircraft parts & equipment
HQ: Esterline Technologies Corp
 500 108th Ave Ne Ste 1500
 Bellevue WA 98004
 425 453-9400

(G-3463)
EVERETT BARK SUPPLY INC
11715 Highway 99 (98204-4809)
PHONE.................................425 353-9324
Rex Miller, *President*
EMP: 4
SALES (est): 371.9K **Privately Held**
SIC: 2499 5083 Mulch, wood & bark; landscaping equipment

(G-3464)
EVERETT TENT & AWNING INC
1625 E Mar View Dr Ste 1 (98201)
PHONE.................................425 252-8213
Tim Thomas, *President*
Shelly Thomas, *Treasurer*
EMP: 2
SALES: 235K **Privately Held**
SIC: 7699 2394 Tent repair shop; awning repair shop; awnings, fabric: made from purchased materials; tents: made from purchased materials

(G-3465)
EVERGREEN GRANITE & CAB SUP
8701 Evergreen Way Ste B (98208-2650)
PHONE.................................425 423-9681
James Louie, *Partner*
▲ **EMP:** 2
SALES (est): 261.4K **Privately Held**
SIC: 2434 Wood kitchen cabinets

(G-3466)
EVERGREEN PRINTING & GRAPHICS
Also Called: Evergreen Copy Service
10530 19th Ave Se Ste 103 (98208-4282)
PHONE.................................425 338-2900
Mel Simpson, *Ch of Bd*
Kim Simpson, *President*
EMP: 9 **EST:** 1980
SQ FT: 3,500
SALES (est): 94.5K **Privately Held**
WEB: www.epandg.com
SIC: 2752 Commercial printing, offset

(G-3467)
EVOLVING NUTRITION
Also Called: T.A.J.J.
9800 Harbour Pl Ste 208 (98203)
PHONE.................................425 355-5682
Tj Abbinanti, *Mng Member*
EMP: 10
SALES (est): 405.6K **Privately Held**
SIC: 8099 2023 5451 Nutrition services; dietary supplements, dairy & non-dairy based; dairy products stores

(G-3468)
FABTECH SYSTEMS LLC
3304 Hill Ave (98201-4522)
P.O. Box 2248 (98213-0248)
PHONE.................................425 349-9557
Greg Matson, *President*
EMP: 3
SALES (est): 704.5K **Privately Held**
WEB: www.fabtechsystems.com
SIC: 3842 Limbs, artificial; prosthetic appliances

(G-3469)
FAM WATERJET INC
12310 Highway 99 Ste 114 (98204-8033)
PHONE.................................425 353-6111
Amir Mehmedagic, *President*
EMP: 5 **EST:** 2014
SALES (est): 576.2K **Privately Held**
SIC: 3545 Machine tool accessories

(G-3470)
FARLEY DESIGHN AND INC
327 42nd St Sw (98203-2055)
PHONE.................................425 259-5946
Nancy Farley, *Owner*
EMP: 2 **EST:** 1998
SALES (est): 110K **Privately Held**
SIC: 2822 Synthetic rubber

(G-3471)
FIBRES INTERNATIONAL INC
Also Called: Fibres Internation Recycling
2600 94th St Sw Ste 100 (98204-2154)
PHONE.................................425 455-9811
Tony Rounds, *General Mgr*
EMP: 75 **Privately Held**
WEB: www.fibres.net
SIC: 4953 4212 3341 3231 Refuse collection & disposal services; local trucking, without storage; secondary nonferrous metals; products of purchased glass; pulp mills
PA: Fibres International, Inc.
 2600 94th St Sw Ste 100
 Everett WA 98204

(G-3472)
FIBRES INTERNATIONAL INC
2600 94th St Sw 100 (98204-2151)
PHONE.................................425 455-9811
Rich Yost, *Manager*
EMP: 20
SQ FT: 6,250 **Privately Held**
WEB: www.fibres.net
SIC: 4953 3231 Recycling, waste materials; products of purchased glass

PA: Fibres International, Inc.
 2600 94th St Sw Ste 100
 Everett WA 98204

(G-3473)
FIRST BOAT COMPANY
615 80th St Sw (98203-6273)
PHONE.................................425 931-9433
William B Tytus, *Principal*
EMP: 2 **EST:** 2007
SALES (est): 146.3K **Privately Held**
SIC: 3732 Boat building & repairing

(G-3474)
FLAKE PRINTING
4729 View Dr (98203-2429)
PHONE.................................425 210-6371
Lisa Flake, *Principal*
EMP: 2
SALES (est): 169.3K **Privately Held**
SIC: 2752 Commercial printing, lithographic

(G-3475)
FLIGHT STRUCTURES INC
11404 Commando Rd W Ste C (98204-3535)
PHONE.................................360 651-8537
Werner Lieberherr, *CEO*
EMP: 200 **EST:** 1975
SALES: 19.5MM
SALES (corp-wide): 66.5B **Publicly Held**
WEB: www.beaerospace.com
SIC: 3728 8711 Aircraft parts & equipment; consulting engineer
HQ: B/E Aerospace, Inc.
 1400 Corporate Center Way
 Wellington FL 33414
 561 791-5000

(G-3476)
FLUKE CORPORATION
9025 Evergreen Way (98204-7117)
PHONE.................................425 446-5600
Bill Parzybok, *Branch Mgr*
EMP: 14
SALES (corp-wide): 6.4B **Publicly Held**
SIC: 3823 Industrial process measurement equipment
HQ: Fluke Corporation
 6920 Seaway Blvd
 Everett WA 98203
 425 347-6100

(G-3477)
FLUKE CORPORATION
Also Called: Fluke Service Center
1420 75th St Sw (98203-6256)
PHONE.................................888 993-5853
Paul Caldarazzo, *Vice Pres*
Fred Michel, *Vice Pres*
Steve Hoch, *Opers Staff*
Pamela Bond, *Buyer*
Daniel Mak, *Engineer*
EMP: 33
SALES (corp-wide): 6.4B **Publicly Held**
SIC: 3823 Industrial process measurement equipment
HQ: Fluke Corporation
 6920 Seaway Blvd
 Everett WA 98203
 425 347-6100

(G-3478)
FLUKE ELECTRONICS CORPORATION (DH)
6920 Seaway Blvd (98203-5829)
P.O. Box 9090 (98206-9090)
PHONE.................................425 347-6100
Wes Pringle, *President*
Paul Heydron, *Vice Pres*
Ernie Lauber, *Vice Pres*
Salvatore Parlatore, *Vice Pres*
Laurence Smith, *Vice Pres*
▲ **EMP:** 1200 **EST:** 2001
SQ FT: 757,800
SALES (est): 457.5MM
SALES (corp-wide): 6.4B **Publicly Held**
SIC: 3825 3823 Test equipment for electronic & electric measurement; frequency synthesizers; volt meters; multimeters; industrial process measurement equipment; data loggers, industrial process type; thermometers, filled system: industrial process type

(G-3479)
FLUKE ELECTRONICS CORPORATION
Also Called: Fluke Networks
6920 Seaway Blvd (98203-5829)
PHONE.................................425 446-5610
Jeff Clark, *Project Mgr*
Randall Chenier, *Buyer*
Darla Grambo, *Buyer*
William Britz, *Engineer*
Brad Kremer, *Engineer*
EMP: 413
SALES (corp-wide): 6.4B **Publicly Held**
SIC: 3825 3823 Test equipment for electronic & electric measurement; frequency synthesizers; volt meters; multimeters; industrial process measurement equipment; data loggers, industrial process type; thermometers, filled system: industrial process type
HQ: Fluke Electronics Corporation
 6920 Seaway Blvd
 Everett WA 98203
 425 347-6100

(G-3480)
FLUKE ELECTRONICS CORPORATION
Also Called: Fluke Networks
9028 Evergreen Way (98204-7100)
PHONE.................................425 446-5858
Carolyn Schults, *Branch Mgr*
EMP: 413
SQ FT: 196,531
SALES (corp-wide): 6.4B **Publicly Held**
SIC: 3825 Test equipment for electronic & electric measurement
HQ: Fluke Electronics Corporation
 6920 Seaway Blvd
 Everett WA 98203
 425 347-6100

(G-3481)
FLUKE ELECTRONICS CORPORATION
Also Called: Fluke Networks
1420 75th St Sw (98203-6256)
P.O. Box 9090 (98206-9090)
PHONE.................................888 993-5853
Carol Kowalski, *Human Res Mgr*
Luis Silva, *Marketing Staff*
EMP: 30
SALES (corp-wide): 6.4B **Publicly Held**
SIC: 3825 3823 Test equipment for electronic & electric measurement; frequency synthesizers; volt meters; multimeters; industrial process measurement equipment; data loggers, industrial process type; thermometers, filled system: industrial process type
HQ: Fluke Electronics Corporation
 6920 Seaway Blvd
 Everett WA 98203
 425 347-6100

(G-3482)
FORGED FROM CARDBOARD
13810 Cascadian Way (98208-7346)
PHONE.................................425 399-0715
Jonathan Gooler, *Principal*
EMP: 2
SALES (est): 90.7K **Privately Held**
SIC: 2631 Cardboard

(G-3483)
FORTIVE CORPORATION (PA)
6920 Seaway Blvd (98203-5829)
PHONE.................................425 446-5000
Alan G Spoon, *Ch of Bd*
James A Lico, *President*
Peter C Underwood, *Senior VP*
Stacey A Walker, *Senior VP*
Lisa Curran, *Vice Pres*
EMP: 168
SALES: 6.4B **Publicly Held**
SIC: 3823 Industrial instrmnts msrmnt display/control process variable

Everett - Snohomish County (G-3484)

(G-3484)
FOSTER PRESS
430 91st Ave Ne Ste 3 (98205)
PHONE..................................425 334-9317
Vern Foster, *Owner*
EMP: 3
SALES (est): 256K **Privately Held**
WEB: www.fosterpress.com
SIC: 2791 2759 Typesetting; commercial printing

(G-3485)
FRASCOLD USA CORPORATION
5901 23rd Dr W Ste 101 (98203-1588)
PHONE..................................855 547-5600
Kristian Ellefsen, *CEO*
▲ **EMP:** 6
SQ FT: 6,528
SALES: 1.8MM **Privately Held**
SIC: 3585 Compressors for refrigeration & air conditioning equipment

(G-3486)
FTV BUSINESS SERVICES LLC
6920 Seaway Blvd (98203-5829)
PHONE..................................425 347-6100
James A Lico,
EMP: 10
SALES (est): 2.4MM
SALES (corp-wide): 6.4B **Publicly Held**
SIC: 3845 Electromedical apparatus
PA: Fortive Corporation
6920 Seaway Blvd
Everett WA 98203
425 446-5000

(G-3487)
FULL CIRCLE NATURAL PRODUCTS
5429 Lowell Larimer Rd (98208-9716)
PHONE..................................425 337-8844
Ken Goerhs, *President*
EMP: 3
SALES (est): 279.2K **Privately Held**
SIC: 2421 Sawdust & shavings

(G-3488)
FUNKO INC (PA)
2802 Wetmore Ave Ste 100 (98201-3562)
PHONE..................................425 783-3616
Brian Mariotti, *CEO*
Ken Brotman, *Ch of Bd*
Andrew Perlmutter, *President*
Tracy Daw, *Senior VP*
Russell Nickel, *CFO*
EMP: 15
SQ FT: 99,000
SALES: 686MM **Publicly Held**
SIC: 3944 Games, toys & children's vehicles

(G-3489)
FURION CELLARS LLC
2832 102nd Pl Se (98208-4478)
PHONE..................................425 314-8922
Micole Miller, *Mng Member*
EMP: 4 **EST:** 2005
SALES (est): 241.8K **Privately Held**
SIC: 2084 Wines

(G-3490)
GAMBIA PRESS UNION GPU-USA
2017 124th Pl Se (98208-6626)
PHONE..................................425 357-6483
Demba S Baldeh, *Principal*
EMP: 2
SALES (est): 99.8K **Privately Held**
SIC: 2741 Miscellaneous publishing

(G-3491)
GARDEN FRESH GOURMET FOODS INC
Also Called: Stockpot Soups
1200 Merrill Creek Pkwy (98203-7152)
PHONE..................................425 407-6400
Stan Polomski, *CEO*
Holly Flatt, *Opers Mgr*
Aryn Shillair, *Buyer*
Richard J Landers, *Director*
William O'Shea, *Director*
EMP: 200

SALES (est): 32.3MM
SALES (corp-wide): 8.6B **Publicly Held**
WEB: www.campbellsoups.com
SIC: 2035 5411 Seasonings & sauces, except tomato & dry; grocery stores
PA: Campbell Soup Company
1 Campbell Pl
Camden NJ 08103
856 342-4800

(G-3492)
GEARTROLOGY CORPORATION
3101 111th St Sw Ste A (98204-3590)
PHONE..................................425 347-1300
Gerry Rouillard, *President*
EMP: 4
SALES (est): 625.9K **Privately Held**
SIC: 3823 Industrial process control instruments

(G-3493)
GENERATIONS WINERY LLC
2001 120th Pl Se 3-303 (98208-6259)
PHONE..................................206 351-0933
Michael Tarabochia, *Principal*
EMP: 4
SALES (est): 156.4K **Privately Held**
SIC: 2084 Wines

(G-3494)
GENESIS WELLNESS
10604 26th Dr Se (98208-4419)
PHONE..................................425 337-3944
Phil S Bartlow, *Owner*
EMP: 2
SALES: 30K **Privately Held**
SIC: 1389 Oil & gas field services

(G-3495)
GENOA HEALTHCARE MASS LLC
Also Called: Genoa 5
3322 Broadway Ste 230 (98201-4425)
PHONE..................................425 789-3050
Bradley Luton, *Manager*
EMP: 7
SALES (corp-wide): 226.2B **Publicly Held**
WEB: www.genoahealthcare.com
SIC: 5912 2741 Drug stores; business service newsletters: publishing & printing
HQ: Genoa Healthcare of Massachusetts, Llc
707 S Grady Way Ste 700
Renton WA 98057
800 519-1139

(G-3496)
GET LIT LIGHTING LLC
9931 40th Pl Se (98205)
PHONE..................................425 772-1646
David Grant, *Principal*
EMP: 4
SALES (est): 237.4K **Privately Held**
SIC: 3645 Garden, patio, walkway & yard lighting fixtures: electric

(G-3497)
GIDDENS AEROSPACE INC
2600 94th St Sw 150 (98204-2151)
PHONE..................................425 353-0405
Robin Becker, *Manager*
EMP: 2
SALES (est): 269.3K **Privately Held**
SIC: 3728 Aircraft parts & equipment

(G-3498)
GIDDENS HOLDINGS INC (HQ)
2600 94th St Sw Ste 150 (98204-2153)
PHONE..................................425 353-0405
EMP: 7 **EST:** 2008
SALES (est): 48.2MM
SALES (corp-wide): 195.8MM **Privately Held**
SIC: 3728 Aircraft parts & equipment
PA: Cadence Aerospace, Llc
3150 E Miraloma Ave
Anaheim CA 92806
949 877-3630

(G-3499)
GIDDENS INDUSTRIES INC
2300 Merrill Creek Pkwy (98203-5855)
PHONE..................................425 353-0405
EMP: 4

SALES (corp-wide): 195.8MM **Privately Held**
SIC: 3728 Aircraft parts & equipment
HQ: Giddens Industries, Inc.
2600 94th St Sw Ste 150
Everett WA 98204
425 353-0405

(G-3500)
GIDDENS INDUSTRIES INC (DH)
2600 94th St Sw Ste 150 (98204-2151)
PHONE..................................425 353-0405
Curt Schroeder, *President*
Kevin D Brown, *Principal*
Ron Case, *Principal*
Donald Devore, *Principal*
Michael F Finley, *Principal*
EMP: 150
SQ FT: 155,000
SALES (est): 48.2MM
SALES (corp-wide): 195.8MM **Privately Held**
WEB: www.giddens.com
SIC: 3728 Aircraft parts & equipment
HQ: Giddens Holdings, Inc.
2600 94th St Sw Ste 150
Everett WA 98204
425 353-0405

(G-3501)
GLOBAL PRODUCT MFG CORP
Also Called: Labels International
12322 Highway 99 Ste 98 (98204-8548)
PHONE..................................425 512-9129
Cecilia Sivertson, *President*
Anthony Nguyen, *Vice Pres*
EMP: 12
SQ FT: 4,000
SALES (est): 1.2MM **Privately Held**
WEB: www.evergreenlabel.com
SIC: 2759 5199 Labels & seals: printing; general merchandise, non-durable

(G-3502)
GOODRICH AEROSTRUCTURES INTEGR
2615 94th St Sw (98204-2151)
PHONE..................................425 318-9276
EMP: 2
SALES (est): 86K **Privately Held**
SIC: 3728 Aircraft parts & equipment

(G-3503)
GOODRICH CORPORATION
Also Called: Goodrich Landing Gear
2701 94th St Sw (98204-2128)
PHONE..................................425 261-8700
Dave Brown, *Manager*
EMP: 40
SALES (corp-wide): 66.5B **Publicly Held**
WEB: www.bfgoodrich.com
SIC: 3728 Alighting (landing gear) assemblies, aircraft
HQ: Goodrich Corporation
2730 W Tyvola Rd
Charlotte NC 28217
704 423-7000

(G-3504)
GRAMPAS GARLIC SALT LLC
820 Cady Rd Apt J102 (98203-5023)
PHONE..................................425 513-0446
Daniel Klebold,
Ellen Mark,
EMP: 2
SALES (est): 98.2K **Privately Held**
SIC: 2099 Seasonings & spices

(G-3505)
GRASSROOTS OUTDOOR LLC
500 Se Everett Mall Way (98208-8110)
PHONE..................................425 210-5745
Francine Watts, *Manager*
Molly Sonne,
EMP: 6 **EST:** 2009
SALES (est): 894.2K **Privately Held**
SIC: 3949 Sporting & athletic goods

(G-3506)
GREAT LITTLE BOX CO INC
1500 Industry St Ste 100 (98203-7119)
PHONE..................................425 349-4522
Toll Free:..................................877 -
Brad Tindall, *President*
Bob Meggy, *President*
EMP: 9

SALES (est): 777.4K
SALES (corp-wide): 95.5MM **Privately Held**
WEB: www.greatlittlebox.com
SIC: 2653 5085 Boxes, corrugated: made from purchased materials; industrial supplies
PA: Great Little Box Company Ltd, The
11300 Twigg Pl
Richmond BC V6V 3
604 301-3700

(G-3507)
GROVE AND KANE INC
520 128th St Sw Ste A6 (98204-9350)
PHONE..................................425 407-3454
Karen Elaine Olsoy, *Principal*
EMP: 5 **EST:** 2014
SALES (est): 449.1K **Privately Held**
SIC: 2834 Dermatologicals

(G-3508)
HART SCIENTIFIC
6920 Seaway Blvd (98203-5829)
PHONE..................................425 446-5400
EMP: 2
SALES (est): 234.4K **Privately Held**
SIC: 3829 Measuring & controlling devices

(G-3509)
HENRYS DONUTS
2515 Broadway (98201-3020)
PHONE..................................425 258-6887
Tekly Pol, *Principal*
EMP: 12
SALES (est): 211.3K **Privately Held**
SIC: 5812 5499 2051 Eating places; beverage stores; doughnuts, except frozen

(G-3510)
HERALD CLASSIFIED WANT ADS
1213 California St (98201-3445)
PHONE..................................425 339-3100
Josh O'Connor, *Principal*
EMP: 2
SALES (est): 62.9K **Privately Held**
SIC: 2711 Newspapers

(G-3511)
HERITAGE ELECTRICAL GROUP INC
Also Called: Heritage Marine Electrical
2516 W Marine View Dr (98201-2730)
PHONE..................................425 774-7595
Paul Harris, *Principal*
Tom Mohoric, *Principal*
EMP: 3
SQ FT: 2,500
SALES (est): 121.3K **Privately Held**
SIC: 3613 Panel & distribution boards & other related apparatus

(G-3512)
HORIZON OF CHANGE
6328 W Beech St (98203-4233)
PHONE..................................425 355-1712
Tina Taylor, *Principal*
EMP: 2 **EST:** 2013
SALES (est): 67.9K **Privately Held**
SIC: 2711 Newspapers

(G-3513)
IN CANVAS
12428 Highway 99 Ste 46 (98204-5502)
PHONE..................................425 355-4102
Christiane Ekness, *Principal*
EMP: 2
SALES (est): 110K **Privately Held**
SIC: 2394 Canvas & related products

(G-3514)
INCONTROL SYSTEMS CORP
216 Heather Rd (98203-1911)
P.O. Box 963, Woodinville (98072-0963)
PHONE..................................425 424-9707
Maurice K Brown, *President*
EMP: 4
SQ FT: 1,500
SALES (est): 273.6K **Privately Held**
WEB: www.incontrolpos.com
SIC: 7371 3575 Computer software development; computer terminals, monitors & components

GEOGRAPHIC SECTION

Everett - Snohomish County (G-3544)

(G-3515)
INDUSTRIAL WELDING SERVICE
3425 103rd Pl Se (98208-4527)
PHONE..........................425 334-2686
Mark Metz, *Owner*
EMP: 2
SALES: 175K **Privately Held**
SIC: 3441 Building components, structural steel

(G-3516)
INNOVATIVE TECHNOLOGIES INC
21 E Marine View Dr Ste C (98201-1207)
PHONE..........................425 258-4773
Jim Phillips, *President*
John Howard, *Vice Pres*
Nick Wilson, *Engineer*
EMP: 8
SQ FT: 7,000
SALES (est): 900K **Privately Held**
SIC: 3087 2822 Custom compound purchased resins; synthetic rubber

(G-3517)
INTEGRATED PRINT SOLUTIONS INC
Also Called: Everett Print
2215 37th St (98201-4554)
PHONE..........................888 716-5666
Kelly Davidson, *President*
EMP: 2 EST: 2010
SALES (est): 267.6K **Privately Held**
SIC: 2752 Commercial printing, lithographic

(G-3518)
INTEGRATED TECHNOLOGIES INC
Also Called: Intec
1910 Merrill Creek Pkwy (98203-5859)
PHONE..........................425 349-2084
Ronald Saks, *President*
Robert C La Mantea, *CFO*
Rodney Wishart, *Shareholder*
Lawrence Dickinson, *Admin Sec*
EMP: 60
SQ FT: 28,000
SALES (est): 7.6MM
SALES (corp-wide): 355.8K **Privately Held**
SIC: 8734 3663 Product testing laboratories; satellites, communications
HQ: Lmi Aerospace, Inc.
    411 Fountain Lakes Blvd
    Saint Charles MO 63301
    636 946-6525

(G-3519)
INVITATIONINABOTTLECOM
12330 43rd Dr Se (98208-9122)
PHONE..........................800 489-8048
EMP: 2 EST: 2017
SALES (est): 101.8K **Privately Held**
SIC: 2759 Commercial printing

(G-3520)
J M C CABINETS & INTERIORS
3224 Mcdougall Ave (98201-4434)
P.O. Box 628 (98206-0628)
PHONE..........................425 258-1204
Neil Maddy, *President*
Walter B Myers, *Vice Pres*
Dawn Topp, *Office Mgr*
EMP: 32
SQ FT: 19,000
SALES (est): 6.8MM **Privately Held**
WEB: www.jmccabs.com
SIC: 5031 2434 Doors & windows; wood kitchen cabinets

(G-3521)
JACKYES ENTERPRISES INC
2604 119th St Sw (98204-4757)
PHONE..........................425 355-5997
Fax: 425 513-8673
EMP: 5
SQ FT: 6,000
SALES (est): 586.8K **Privately Held**
SIC: 3953 7389 5199 2395 Mfg Marking Devices Business Services Whol Nondurable Goods Pleating/Stitching Svcs

(G-3522)
JAMCO AMERICA INC (HQ)
1018 80th St Sw (98203-6278)
PHONE..........................425 347-4735
Norikazu Natsume, *President*
Don Grissitt, *Vice Pres*
Masamichi Kato, *Vice Pres*
David Nelson, *Vice Pres*
Mike Rayner, *Plant Mgr*
▲ EMP: 225
SQ FT: 48,000
SALES (est): 87MM **Privately Held**
WEB: www.jamcoamerica.com
SIC: 3728 Aircraft parts & equipment

(G-3523)
JAMCO AMERICA INC
720 80th St Sw Bldg A (98203-6217)
PHONE..........................425 347-4735
Aelisha, *Branch Mgr*
EMP: 5 **Privately Held**
SIC: 3728 Aircraft parts & equipment
HQ: Jamco America, Inc.
    1018 80th St Sw
    Everett WA 98203
    425 347-4735

(G-3524)
JOE CONSTANCE
Also Called: Constance Machine
1410 80th St Sw Ste F (98203-6200)
PHONE..........................425 347-8920
Joe Constance, *Owner*
EMP: 10
SQ FT: 4,300
SALES (est): 879.3K **Privately Held**
SIC: 3599 3465 7692 Machine shop, jobbing & repair; body parts, automobile: stamped metal; welding repair

(G-3525)
JOLLY FAMILY CORP (PA)
Also Called: Fastsigns
2802 Colby Ave (98201-3513)
PHONE..........................425 438-9350
EMP: 4
SALES (est): 753.7K **Privately Held**
SIC: 3993 Signs & advertising specialties

(G-3526)
JUDD & BLACK ELECTRIC INC
Also Called: Judd Black Applnce-Service Ctr
2808 Maple St (98201-3831)
PHONE..........................425 258-4557
Cheryl Olson, *Manager*
EMP: 15
SALES (corp-wide): 9.3MM **Privately Held**
SIC: 3639 3632 Major kitchen appliances, except refrigerators & stoves; household refrigerators & freezers
PA: Judd & Black Electric, Inc.
    3001 Hewitt Ave
    Everett WA
    425 258-2591

(G-3527)
K & D SERVICES INC (HQ)
2702 Oakes Ave (98201-3628)
P.O. Box 12040 (98206-2040)
PHONE..........................425 252-0906
Brooks Walton, *President*
Morrie Trautman, *Corp Secy*
Rob Pratt, *Manager*
EMP: 6
SQ FT: 1,200
SALES (est): 1.5MM **Privately Held**
SIC: 7363 3669 Manpower pools; transportation signaling devices

(G-3528)
K & H PRNTRS-LITHOGRAPHERS INC
Also Called: K & H Intgrted Print Solutions
7720 Hardeson Rd Ste A (98203-7000)
P.O. Box 388 (98206-0388)
PHONE..........................425 446-3300
Darren Loken, *President*
Jay Ackley, *President*
Steven J Hopp, *Senior VP*
Richard Haines, *Vice Pres*
Sandi Johns, *Project Mgr*
▲ EMP: 55 EST: 1908
SQ FT: 28,000
SALES (est): 15.5MM **Privately Held**
WEB: www.khprint.com
SIC: 2752 Commercial printing, offset

(G-3529)
KASILOF FISH COMPANY
Also Called: Ilovesalmon.com
1930 Merrill Creek Pkwy B (98203-5897)
PHONE..........................360 658-7552
Drew M Ellison, *President*
Patti Moore, *Vice Pres*
▲ EMP: 25
SQ FT: 22,000
SALES (est): 2.3MM
SALES (corp-wide): 2.3B **Privately Held**
WEB: www.ilovesalmon.com
SIC: 2091 Salmon, smoked
PA: Trident Seafoods Corporation
    5303 Shilshole Ave Nw
    Seattle WA 98107
    206 783-3818

(G-3530)
KERMITS WOOD PRODUCTS
13724 51st Dr Se (98208-9537)
PHONE..........................425 316-6823
Kermit Guest, *Owner*
EMP: 2
SALES (est): 142.4K **Privately Held**
SIC: 2541 Cabinets, except refrigerated: show, display, etc.: wood

(G-3531)
KMD INVESTED LLC
Also Called: Five Star Rv
13200 Highway 99 (98204-5424)
PHONE..........................425 741-9600
Kathy Alexander, *Principal*
Kristina Dunkin,
EMP: 2
SALES (est): 225.1K **Privately Held**
SIC: 3799 Recreational vehicles

(G-3532)
KORRY ELECTRONICS CO (DH)
11910 Beverly Park Rd (98203-3529)
PHONE..........................425 297-9700
Jason Childs, *President*
Fern Hansen, *General Mgr*
Phouang S Vixaysakd, *Exec VP*
Rob Gibbs, *Vice Pres*
Frank E Houston, *Vice Pres*
EMP: 650
SQ FT: 200,000
SALES (est): 103.8MM
SALES (corp-wide): 3.8B **Publicly Held**
SIC: 3613 Panel & distribution boards & other related apparatus
HQ: Esterline Technologies Corp
    500 108th Ave Ne Ste 1500
    Bellevue WA 98004
    425 453-9400

(G-3533)
L G ARTWORKS INC
12124 1st Ave Se (98208-5717)
PHONE..........................425 355-9143
Linda Gentry, *President*
Richard Gentry, *Vice Pres*
EMP: 7
SQ FT: 2,000
SALES (est): 516K **Privately Held**
SIC: 2791 7389 7374 Typesetting; design services; computer graphics service

(G-3534)
LARRY LISK
4220 Terrace Dr (98203-2206)
PHONE..........................425 252-5475
Larry Lisk, *Principal*
EMP: 2
SALES (est): 74.4K **Privately Held**
SIC: 2899 Chemical preparations

(G-3535)
LC LOGIC DEFENSE AND SPACE LLC
1818 101st Pl Sw (98204-3687)
PHONE..........................425 270-5169
Gerald Sterkel, *Principal*
EMP: 3
SALES (est): 177.3K **Privately Held**
SIC: 3812 Defense systems & equipment

(G-3536)
LEO WELDING FABRICATION
9502 36th Ave Se (98208-3006)
PHONE..........................425 379-5836
Leonardo Estrada, *Principal*
EMP: 2
SALES (est): 157.6K **Privately Held**
SIC: 7692 Welding repair

(G-3537)
LIVE SOUND & RECORDING CO LLC
9815 31st Ave Se (98208-4308)
P.O. Box 4067 (98204-0007)
PHONE..........................425 308-2868
Leroy Saunders,
EMP: 2
SALES (est): 100K **Privately Held**
SIC: 3651 Audio electronic systems

(G-3538)
LMI AEROSPACE INC
1910 Merrill Crekk Pkwy (98203)
PHONE..........................425 293-0340
EMP: 6 EST: 2016
SALES (est): 365.6K **Privately Held**
SIC: 3728 Aircraft parts & equipment

(G-3539)
LONE RANGER LLC
Also Called: Maverick International
11512 Airport Rd Ste 1 (98204-3753)
PHONE..........................425 355-7474
Randy Braa, *President*
Jerry Coffell, *Manager*
▲ EMP: 33
SQ FT: 18,000
SALES (est): 5.8MM **Privately Held**
WEB: www.mav.com
SIC: 3577 3578 3579 Encoders, computer peripheral equipment; coin counters; check writing, endorsing or signing machines

(G-3540)
LOVE NOODLE INC
7815 Evergreen Way Ste 2 (98203-6429)
PHONE..........................425 513-8888
EMP: 8
SALES (est): 409.9K **Privately Held**
SIC: 2098 Noodles (e.g. egg, plain & water), dry

(G-3541)
LS BREWING INC
Also Called: Lazy Boy Brewing Co
715 100th St Se Ste A1 (98203-3762)
PHONE..........................425 423-7700
Michael Scanlon, *President*
Shawn Lorang, *Vice Pres*
EMP: 2
SALES: 100K **Privately Held**
SIC: 2082 Beer (alcoholic beverage)

(G-3542)
M & I SYSTEMS INC
2936 Colby Ave (98201-4011)
PHONE..........................206 547-7899
CL Biles-Kennedy, *President*
EMP: 3
SALES (est): 424.9K **Privately Held**
WEB: www.misystems.com
SIC: 3613 5551 Panelboards & distribution boards, electric; marine supplies & equipment

(G-3543)
M E B MANUFACTURING
3410 Everett Ave (98201-3893)
PHONE..........................425 259-6074
Steve Thompson, *President*
EMP: 6
SQ FT: 5,000
SALES: 650K **Privately Held**
WEB: www.mebmfg.com
SIC: 3599 Machine shop, jobbing & repair

(G-3544)
MAIL N BEYOND
5714 134th Pl Se Ste A18 (98208-9421)
PHONE..........................425 379-6111
EMP: 9
SALES (est): 994.8K **Privately Held**
SIC: 2542 Mfg Partitions/Fixtures-Nonwood

Everett - Snohomish County (G-3545)

(G-3545)
MAPLE SYSTEMS INC
808 134th St Sw Ste 120 (98204-2300)
PHONE..............................425 745-3229
Larry St Peter, *President*
Jennifer Schuy, *Vice Pres*
Samuel Schuy, *Vice Pres*
Andre Zins, *Senior Buyer*
Daunne Ofarrell, *VP Finance*
EMP: 22
SQ FT: 11,500
SALES (est): 4.6MM **Privately Held**
WEB: www.maplesystem.com
SIC: 3625 Control equipment, electric

(G-3546)
METALISTICS INC
2626 119th St Sw Ste B4 (98204-6111)
PHONE..............................425 348-9377
Chris Gallagher, *Owner*
EMP: 7
SALES (est): 993.4K **Privately Held**
SIC: 3499 Fabricated metal products

(G-3547)
METICULOUS COATING APPLICATORS
4834 W Glenhaven Dr (98203-1733)
PHONE..............................206 251-3684
Douglas Aickle, *Principal*
EMP: 2
SALES (est): 172K **Privately Held**
SIC: 3479 Metal coating & allied service

(G-3548)
MOBILE ONE LUBE EX EVERETT
2411 Broadway (98201-3018)
PHONE..............................425 374-8862
Vince Nelson, *Principal*
EMP: 3
SALES (est): 285.1K **Privately Held**
SIC: 2992 Lubricating oils

(G-3549)
MODERN METALS LLC
13317 Ash Way Ste A1 (98204-5014)
PHONE..............................425 405-6994
Vadim Novozhilov, *Managing Dir*
Vitaliy Gutsalo, *Principal*
Sergey Gutsalo,
▲ **EMP:** 48
SALES: 6MM **Privately Held**
SIC: 3446 Architectural metalwork

(G-3550)
MODERN SIDING LLC
12322 Highway 99 Ste 214 (98204-8546)
PHONE..............................813 484-9498
Christopher Omdal,
Caroline Omdal,
EMP: 2
SALES (est): 185.6K **Privately Held**
SIC: 3562 1522 Roller bearings & parts; residential construction

(G-3551)
MORGAN AERO PRODUCTS INC
1450 80th St Sw (98203-6221)
PHONE..............................425 438-9600
Virgil Morgan Sr, *President*
Roger Bell, *Vice Pres*
EMP: 9
SQ FT: 20,000
SALES (est): 1.4MM **Privately Held**
WEB: www.morganaero.com
SIC: 3728 Aircraft parts & equipment

(G-3552)
NEXUS MARINE CORPORATION
3816 Railway Ave (98201-3838)
PHONE..............................425 252-8330
Nancy Sosnove, *President*
David Roberts, *Vice Pres*
EMP: 2
SQ FT: 6,000
SALES: 100K **Privately Held**
WEB: www.nexusmarine.com
SIC: 3732 5551 Motorboats, inboard or outboard: building & repairing; sailboats, building & repairing; boat dealers

(G-3553)
NORQUEST SEAFOODS INC
Also Called: Port Chatham Smoked Seafood's
1930 Merrill Creek Pkwy B (98203-5897)
PHONE..............................425 349-2563
Ken Ng, *Manager*
EMP: 90
SALES (corp-wide): 2.3B **Privately Held**
WEB: www.norquest.com
SIC: 2092 Fresh or frozen packaged fish
HQ: Norquest Seafoods, Inc.
5303 Shilshole Ave Nw
Seattle WA 98107

(G-3554)
NORTHSOUND SHOPPING
1213 California St (98201-3445)
PHONE..............................425 258-3455
EMP: 2
SALES (est): 67.3K **Privately Held**
SIC: 2711 Newspapers

(G-3555)
NORTHWEST AEROSPACE TECH INC (PA)
415 Riverside Rd (98201-1278)
PHONE..............................425 257-2044
Paul Sobotta, *President*
Jeff McShane, *Vice Pres*
Randy Overholser, *Engineer*
Judy Smith, *Accountant*
Julie Small, *Program Mgr*
EMP: 60
SQ FT: 20,000
SALES (est): 26.5MM **Privately Held**
WEB: www.natdesign.com
SIC: 8711 3728 Aviation &/or aeronautical engineering; aircraft parts & equipment

(G-3556)
NORTHWEST AEROSPACE TECH INC
2922 Chestnut St (98201-3808)
PHONE..............................425 212-5001
Paul Sobotta, *Branch Mgr*
EMP: 4
SALES (corp-wide): 26.5MM **Privately Held**
SIC: 3728 8711 Aircraft parts & equipment; aviation &/or aeronautical engineering
PA: Northwest Aerospace Technologies, Inc.
415 Riverside Rd
Everett WA 98201
425 257-2044

(G-3557)
NORTHWEST CENTER
Also Called: Electronetics
1320 75th St Sw (98203-6254)
PHONE..............................425 355-1855
Mike Carr, *Manager*
EMP: 30
SALES (corp-wide): 50.3MM **Privately Held**
WEB: www.americandataguard.com
SIC: 8331 8322 3599 Vocational training agency; sheltered workshop; child related social services; machine & other job shop work
PA: Northwest Center
7272 W Marginal Way S
Seattle WA 98108
206 285-9140

(G-3558)
NORTHWEST STAIR AND RAIL INC
12322 Highway 99 Ste 100 (98204-8548)
PHONE..............................425 348-7880
Gary Ellesson, *President*
Darla Ames, *Corp Secy*
Ted Ames, *Vice Pres*
EMP: 6 **EST:** 2005
SALES (est): 281.1K **Privately Held**
SIC: 3441 Fabricated structural metal

(G-3559)
OMEGA PRINTING
2110 Broadway Ste A (98201-2379)
PHONE..............................425 339-8538
Roger Wise, *Owner*
EMP: 3
SALES (est): 177.3K **Privately Held**
SIC: 2759 Commercial printing

(G-3560)
ONAMAC INDUSTRIES INC
Also Called: Onamac Machine Works
6300 Merrill Creek Pkwy B200 (98203-1577)
PHONE..............................425 743-6676
Richard Kenyon, *President*
Brice Massey, *Vice Pres*
Steve Ulvestad, *Mfg Staff*
Dan Bellman, *Engineer*
Jake Hardwick, *Engineer*
▲ **EMP:** 135
SALES (est): 27.4MM
SALES (corp-wide): 136.6MM **Privately Held**
WEB: www.onamac.com
SIC: 3599 Machine shop, jobbing & repair
PA: Selmet, Inc.
33992 Seven Mile Ln Se
Albany OR 97322
541 926-7731

(G-3561)
P APPLE LLC
7007 Beverly Blvd (98203-5225)
PHONE..............................206 290-9898
EMP: 2
SALES (est): 94.5K **Privately Held**
SIC: 3571 Mfg Electronic Computers

(G-3562)
P G I PUBLICATIONS INC
13410 Highway 99 Ste 205 (98204-5454)
PHONE..............................425 743-0110
EMP: 2
SALES (est): 135.6K **Privately Held**
SIC: 2759 Commercial Printing

(G-3563)
PAC SHIP
2000 W Marine View Dr (98207-0001)
PHONE..............................425 622-9030
EMP: 3
SALES (est): 160.6K **Privately Held**
SIC: 3731 Shipbuilding & repairing

(G-3564)
PACIFIC ORTHODONTIC LABORATORY
10830 19th Ave Se Ste D (98208-5181)
P.O. Box 2188, Lynnwood (98036-2188)
PHONE..............................425 224-4193
Doug Zahn, *President*
EMP: 7
SQ FT: 3,000
SALES (est): 967.9K **Privately Held**
SIC: 3843 8072 Orthodontic appliances; orthodontic appliance production

(G-3565)
PACIFIC PERFORMANCE COATINGS
2815 W Marine View Dr (98201-3423)
PHONE..............................425 339-5528
Chris Petersen, *Owner*
EMP: 2
SALES (est): 160.7K **Privately Held**
SIC: 3479 Coating of metals & formed products

(G-3566)
PACIFIC RADAR INC
12310 Highway 99 Ste 132 (98204-7556)
PHONE..............................425 775-0400
Dan R Asplund, *President*
Charles A Johnson, *Admin Sec*
EMP: 2 **EST:** 1997
SQ FT: 600
SALES: 550K **Privately Held**
SIC: 3812 4812 5551 Electronic detection systems (aeronautical); paging services; sailboats & equipment

(G-3567)
PACIFIC SHIP REPR FBRCTION INC
13228 4th Ave W Ste A (98204-6336)
PHONE..............................425 409-5060
David Moore, *CEO*
EMP: 21
SALES (corp-wide): 45.1MM **Privately Held**
SIC: 7699 3731 Professional instrument repair services; shipbuilding & repairing
PA: Pacific Ship Repair & Fabrication, Inc.
1625 Rigel St
San Diego CA 92113
619 232-3200

(G-3568)
PACIFIC TOPSOILS INC (PA)
805 80th St Sw (98203-6216)
PHONE..............................425 337-2700
Sandra L Forman, *President*
Sandra Forman, *CFO*
Jim McSpadden, *Controller*
Kathy Perdue, *Human Res Mgr*
Nonda Stoen, *Human Res Mgr*
EMP: 23 **EST:** 1978
SQ FT: 1,000
SALES: 31.9MM **Privately Held**
SIC: 2421 5032 5261 3524 Sawdust & shavings; sand, construction; sod; lawn & garden equipment; fertilizers, mixing only

(G-3569)
PARAGON MANUFACTURING CORP
2615 W Casino Rd Ste 4c (98204-1490)
PHONE..............................425 438-0800
Patrick Floyd, *President*
Mark Samuelson, *Vice Pres*
Alen Berstein, *Shareholder*
Mark Casebolt, *Shareholder*
EMP: 48
SQ FT: 7,200
SALES (est): 8MM **Privately Held**
SIC: 3679 Harness assemblies for electronic use: wire or cable; electronic circuits

(G-3570)
PASSAGE INC
Also Called: Contractor Equipment Rental
1720 75th St Sw (98203-6262)
PHONE..............................425 743-5600
Jason Decker, *Principal*
Donna Dake, *Director*
EMP: 2
SALES (est): 170K **Privately Held**
SIC: 3732 Yachts, building & repairing

(G-3571)
PERFORMANCE MARINE INC
930 W Marine View Dr (98201-1300)
PHONE..............................425 258-9292
Bill Hook, *President*
Rick Hook, *Corp Secy*
EMP: 12
SQ FT: 6,000
SALES: 2.8MM **Privately Held**
WEB: www.performarine.com
SIC: 5551 7699 3732 Motor boat dealers; outboard motors; marine engine repair; boat building & repairing

(G-3572)
PHILLIPS INDUSTRIAL SUPPLY INC
Also Called: Labels Plus
2407 106th St Sw (98204-3628)
PHONE..............................206 523-0477
Kathleen Carrera, *President*
EMP: 16
SQ FT: 12,000
SALES (est): 3.7MM **Privately Held**
WEB: www.labelsplus.com
SIC: 2672 5084 Labels (unprinted), gummed: made from purchased materials; packaging machinery & equipment

(G-3573)
PILKINGTON NORTH AMERICA INC
Also Called: Lof Service Center
10315 Airport Rd 101 (98204-3539)
PHONE..............................425 438-8442
Rustin Roper, *Manager*
EMP: 11 **Privately Held**
WEB: www.low-eglass.com
SIC: 3211 Flat glass
HQ: Pilkington North America, Inc.
811 Madison Ave Fl 3
Toledo OH 43604
419 247-3731

▲ = Import ▼=Export
◆ =Import/Export

Everett - Snohomish County (G-3603)

(G-3574)
PIXELAN WORKS
3427 104th Pl Se (98208-4540)
PHONE.................................425 379-0339
N Linnabary, *Partner*
EMP: 2
SALES (est): 150.5K **Privately Held**
SIC: 3993 Signs & advertising specialties

(G-3575)
PLC-MULTIPOINT INC
Also Called: P L C
3101 111th St Sw Ste F (98204-3590)
PHONE.................................425 353-7552
Norm Dittmann, *President*
Ingrid Dittmann, *Vice Pres*
Mary Beth Peavey, *Treasurer*
Mary Beth Schoeler, *Admin Sec*
Susan White, *Administration*
EMP: 9
SQ FT: 6,000
SALES (est): 880K **Privately Held**
WEB: www.plcmultipoint.com
SIC: 3672 3648 Printed circuit boards; lighting equipment

(G-3576)
PLS PACIFIC LASER SYSTEMS LLC
6920 Seaway Blvd (98203-5829)
PHONE.................................415 453-5780
D Michael Tramontin, *Mng Member*
Cynthia M Hersey, *Mng Member*
▲ **EMP:** 92
SQ FT: 27,000
SALES (est): 17.3MM **Privately Held**
WEB: www.plslaser.com
SIC: 3821 5211 3699 Laser beam alignment devices; lumber & other building materials; laser systems & equipment

(G-3577)
POCOCK RACING SHELLS INC
615 80th St Sw (98203-6273)
PHONE.................................425 438-9048
William B Tytus, *President*
Julie Hobson, *Project Mgr*
John Tytus, *Sales Staff*
Guedo Fanony, *Mktg Dir*
Dave Haworth, *Relations*
▲ **EMP:** 18 **EST:** 1911
SQ FT: 30,000
SALES (est): 1.3MM **Privately Held**
WEB: www.pocock.com
SIC: 3732 Rowboats, building & repairing

(G-3578)
POETRY NORTHWEST
2000 Tower St (98201-1352)
PHONE.................................425 388-9395
David Biespiel, *President*
Kevin Craft, *Exec Dir*
EMP: 3
SALES: 10K **Privately Held**
SIC: 2721 Magazines: publishing & printing

(G-3579)
POST TENSION CABLES INC (PA)
Also Called: P T C
10127 9th Ave W (98204-3777)
PHONE.................................425 745-1304
Carl Bumpass, *CEO*
Dawn Nearing, *President*
Jason Ng, *Project Mgr*
Judy Bumpass, *Treasurer*
EMP: 9
SQ FT: 4,000
SALES (est): 2MM **Privately Held**
SIC: 3315 Wire, steel: insulated or armored

(G-3580)
POWER EQUIPMENT SUPPLY LLC
1307 38th St Unit 6 (98201-4873)
PHONE.................................206 817-5627
Bishara Farhoud,
Stacy Calvert,
EMP: 2 **EST:** 2014
SALES (est): 157.8K **Privately Held**
SIC: 5015 3429 3599 2394 Automotive supplies, used; aircraft & marine hardware, inc. pulleys & similar items; propellers, ship & boat: machined; canvas boat seats; hand tools

(G-3581)
PR LIFTING LLC
3010 Everett Ave Unit A (98201-3881)
PHONE.................................425 214-4124
▲ **EMP:** 2 **EST:** 2014
SALES (est): 212.9K **Privately Held**
SIC: 3949 Sporting & athletic goods

(G-3582)
PRAXAIR INC
1111 Hewitt Ave (98201-3916)
PHONE.................................425 259-0188
Roy Pintacura, *Manager*
EMP: 3 **Privately Held**
SIC: 2813 Industrial gases
HQ: Praxair, Inc.
10 Riverview Dr
Danbury CT 06810
203 837-2000

(G-3583)
PRECISION DATA TECHNOLOGY INC
3409 Mcdougall Ave # 107 (98201-5040)
PHONE.................................425 259-9237
Larry Eccleston, *President*
Linda Anthony, *Opers Mgr*
EMP: 8
SALES (est): 1.1MM **Privately Held**
WEB: www.pdt-inc.com
SIC: 3829 3625 Measuring & controlling devices; electric controls & control accessories, industrial

(G-3584)
PRECISION ENGINES LLC
1523 132nd St Se Ste C (98208-7200)
PHONE.................................425 347-2800
Dave Cort, *Mng Member*
Scott Farabaugh,
▲ **EMP:** 75
SALES (est): 9.2MM **Privately Held**
WEB: www.precisionengines.com
SIC: 3724 Air scoops, aircraft

(G-3585)
PRINT HOUSE INC
3101 111th St Sw Ste A (98204-3590)
PHONE.................................425 742-1434
Eleanor L Costanza, *President*
EMP: 2
SQ FT: 3,000
SALES (est): 244K **Privately Held**
WEB: www.eprinthouse.com
SIC: 2752 Commercial printing, offset

(G-3586)
PROBARE INDUSTRIES LLC
927 132nd St Sw Apt C4 (98204-9353)
PHONE.................................206 334-9840
Lee Bragg, *Principal*
EMP: 2
SALES (est): 97.1K **Privately Held**
SIC: 3999 Manufacturing industries

(G-3587)
PROPELLER ARPRTS PINE FELD LLC
9724 32nd Dr W 2 (98204-1903)
PHONE.................................425 216-3010
EMP: 2
SALES (est): 63.4K **Privately Held**
SIC: 3366 Propellers

(G-3588)
PROPULSION CONTROLS ENGRG
920 W Marine View Dr (98201-1300)
PHONE.................................425 257-9065
Larry Horning, *General Mgr*
Mike Hass, *Prdtn Mgr*
EMP: 40
SALES (est): 2.4MM
SALES (corp-wide): 23.4MM **Privately Held**
WEB: www.pcehawaii.com
SIC: 7699 3731 Marine engine repair; shipbuilding & repairing
PA: Propulsion Controls Engineering
1620 Rigel St
San Diego CA 92113
619 235-0961

(G-3589)
QUALITEL CORPORATION
Also Called: Quality Electronic Assembly
11831 Beverly Park Rd A (98204-3526)
PHONE.................................425 423-8388
Tuanhai Hoang, *President*
Donna Sparks, *Corp Secy*
Hoa Van Hoang, *Vice Pres*
Sokhan Pan, *Engineer*
Michael McGrath, *Manager*
▲ **EMP:** 200
SALES (est): 83.5MM **Privately Held**
WEB: www.qualitelcorp.com
SIC: 3679 Electronic switches; electronic circuits

(G-3590)
QUALITY COUNTER
1625 E Marine View Dr (98201-1975)
PHONE.................................425 303-9180
Ali Merdassi, *President*
EMP: 8
SALES (est): 843K **Privately Held**
WEB: www.qualitycounter.com
SIC: 2541 Counter & sink tops

(G-3591)
QUANTUM WINDOWS AND DOORS INC
2720 34th St (98201-4500)
PHONE.................................425 259-6650
Jeff Klein, *CEO*
Hugh Matheson, *President*
Holly Guthrie, *Corp Secy*
Jeff Quillen, *Vice Pres*
Ryan Neal, *Admin Sec*
EMP: 75
SQ FT: 48,000
SALES (est): 14.7MM **Privately Held**
WEB: www.quantumwindows.com
SIC: 2431 Window frames, wood

(G-3592)
R C SYSTEMS INC
1609 England Ave (98203-1617)
PHONE.................................425 355-3800
Randy Carlstrom, *President*
Pamela Carlstrom, *Admin Sec*
▼ **EMP:** 2
SALES: 900K **Privately Held**
WEB: www.rcsys.com
SIC: 3577 3823 Computer peripheral equipment; computer interface equipment for industrial process control

(G-3593)
RACAL ACOUSTICS INC
11910 Beverly Park Rd (98204-3529)
PHONE.................................425 297-9700
Kevin Moschetti, *President*
Robert George, *Vice Pres*
Frank Houston, *Vice Pres*
EMP: 7
SQ FT: 800
SALES: 50K **Privately Held**
WEB: www.racalacoustics.com
SIC: 3661 Fiber optics communications equipment
PA: Racal Acoustics Limited
Unit 3 Waverley Industrial Estate
Harrow MIDDX HA1 4

(G-3594)
RAILMAKERS NORTHWEST
2944 Cedar St (98201-3722)
PHONE.................................425 259-9236
Judy Darst, *Owner*
EMP: 10 **EST:** 1974
SQ FT: 6,000
SALES (est): 1MM **Privately Held**
WEB: www.railmakersnw.com
SIC: 3732 5091 3446 Boat building & repairing; boat accessories & parts; architectural metalwork

(G-3595)
RAINIER BUILDING SUPPLY LLC
12414 Highway 99 (98204-5544)
PHONE.................................206 939-2591
Aleksandr Kovalchuk, *Mng Member*
Oleh Onyshchuk, *Mng Member*
EMP: 4
SALES (est): 614.8K **Privately Held**
SIC: 3441 Fabricated structural metal

(G-3596)
REBREATHERS USA LLC
12811 8th Ave W Ste D105 (98204-6370)
PHONE.................................425 789-1255
Barry K Shuster, *Principal*
EMP: 2
SALES (est): 180.8K **Privately Held**
SIC: 3714 Motor vehicle parts & accessories

(G-3597)
RED WING BRANDS AMERICA INC
221 Se Everett Mall Way (98208-3239)
PHONE.................................651 388-6233
EMP: 2
SALES (corp-wide): 576.4MM **Privately Held**
SIC: 3149 Children's footwear, except athletic
HQ: Red Wing Brands Of America, Inc.
314 Main St
Red Wing MN 55066
844 314-6246

(G-3598)
RESTORFX
1329 56th St Sw (98203-5919)
PHONE.................................425 286-5189
Surge Harton, *Principal*
EMP: 2
SALES (est): 125K **Privately Held**
SIC: 2842 Automobile polish

(G-3599)
REVIVE CABINET CLOSET PRO LLC
2615 W Casino Rd Ste 6b (98204-2113)
PHONE.................................425 382-0739
Mehran Tivay,
EMP: 2
SALES (est): 80.2K **Privately Held**
SIC: 2434 Wood kitchen cabinets

(G-3600)
ROCKWELL COLLINS INC
11404 Commando Rd W (98204-3535)
PHONE.................................425 923-2700
EMP: 4
SALES (corp-wide): 66.5B **Publicly Held**
SIC: 3812 Search & navigation equipment
HQ: Rockwell Collins, Inc.
400 Collins Rd Ne
Cedar Rapids IA 52498

(G-3601)
ROYAL DENTAL MANUFACTURING INC (PA)
12414 Highway 99 Ste 29 (98204-5599)
PHONE.................................425 743-0988
Harold Y Tai, *President*
Raymond H Tai, *Principal*
Gary Marrs, *Purchasing*
Laridan L Griffin, *Treasurer*
Howard Sorenson, *VP Sales*
▲ **EMP:** 70 **EST:** 1939
SQ FT: 31,000
SALES (est): 11.7MM **Privately Held**
SIC: 3843 Dental chairs

(G-3602)
ROYELL MANUFACTURING INC
3817 Smith Ave (98201-4547)
PHONE.................................425 259-9258
Jamie Yelle, *President*
Steve Schwecke, *COO*
Kim Hallett, *Purch Mgr*
Ali Akbarpour, *Data Proc Exec*
▲ **EMP:** 90
SQ FT: 35,000
SALES: 59.4MM **Privately Held**
WEB: www.royell.com
SIC: 3728 Aircraft parts & equipment

(G-3603)
SAFRAN ELEC & PWR USA LLC
Also Called: Labinal, Inc.
2300 Merrill Creek Pkwy # 100
(98203-5950)
PHONE.................................425 407-6700

Everett - Snohomish County (G-3604) — GEOGRAPHIC SECTION

Jorge Ortega, *General Mgr*
Ricardo Varela, *General Mgr*
Lonnie Thomas, *QC Mgr*
Leslee Baggette, *Manager*
EMP: 75 **EST:** 1997
SALES (est): 7.2MM
SALES (corp-wide): 833.4MM **Privately Held**
SIC: 3357 3315 Aircraft wire & cable, nonferrous; wire & fabricated wire products
HQ: Safran Electrical & Power
  Parc D Activite Andromede
  Blagnac 31700
  562 870-500

(G-3604)
SAFRAN VENTILATION SYSTEM USA
7501 Hardeson Rd (98203-6285)
PHONE 425 438-1378
Bruno Bergoend, *CEO*
Tracy Zmolik, *QC Mgr*
Nathalie Boschetti, *CFO*
Sarah Thesenvitz, *Finance Mgr*
Kevin Blydenburgh, *Marketing Staff*
EMP: 43
SQ FT: 20,000
SALES (est): 15.3MM
SALES (corp-wide): 833.4MM **Privately Held**
SIC: 3728 Aircraft parts & equipment
PA: Safran
  2 Bd Du General Martial Valin
  Paris 15e Arrondissement 75015
  140 608-080

(G-3605)
SCREEN PRINTING NORTHWEST INC
2526 Colby Ave (98201-2916)
PHONE 425 303-3381
Don Levin, *Principal*
EMP: 6
SALES: 800K **Privately Held**
SIC: 2759 Screen printing

(G-3606)
SCUTTLEBUTT BREWING CO LLC (PA)
3310 Cedar St (98201-4518)
PHONE 425 252-2829
Philip Bannan, *President*
EMP: 12
SALES (est): 1.3MM **Privately Held**
SIC: 2082 5149 5812 2086 Beer (alcoholic beverage); groceries & related products; eating places; bottled & canned soft drinks

(G-3607)
SEA-DOG CORPORATION (PA)
Also Called: Sea-Dog Line
3402 Smith Ave Ste C (98201-4592)
P.O. Box 479 (98206-0479)
PHONE 425 259-0194
Bradley M Nysether, *President*
Mark A Nysether, *Vice Pres*
◆ **EMP:** 55
SQ FT: 50,000
SALES (est): 16.8MM **Privately Held**
WEB: www.sea-dog.com
SIC: 5088 3429 Marine supplies; marine hardware

(G-3608)
SEASALT SUPERSTORE LLC (PA)
Also Called: Caravel Gourmet
11604 Airport Rd Ste D300 (98204-3752)
PHONE 425 249-2331
Merry Johnson, *Accountant*
Scott Mackie, *Mng Member*
Jenny Mackie, *Manager*
▲ **EMP:** 25
SQ FT: 10,000
SALES (est): 2.9MM **Privately Held**
SIC: 2099 5961 5499 Seasonings & spices; catalog & mail-order houses; spices & herbs

(G-3609)
SEATTLE ENGRAVING LLC
Also Called: Seattle Engraving Company
5626 Evergreen Way Ste 1 (98203-3628)
PHONE 425 212-9797
Lynn Sperry,
Donna Knowles-Sperry,
EMP: 4
SQ FT: 1,200
SALES (est): 453.6K **Privately Held**
WEB: www.seattleengraving.com
SIC: 3993 7389 Signs & advertising specialties; engraving service

(G-3610)
SHADD GLOBAL INDUSTRIES L
3616 Colby Ave Ste 774 (98201-4773)
PHONE 425 374-3946
EMP: 2
SALES (est): 77K **Privately Held**
SIC: 3999 Manufacturing industries

(G-3611)
SIMPLY JOYFUL LLC
215 100th St Sw (98204-2722)
PHONE 425 686-5311
Joy Graves, *Principal*
EMP: 2
SALES (est): 105.4K **Privately Held**
SIC: 2844 Toilet preparations

(G-3612)
SITELINES PK & PLAYGROUND PDTS
4818 Evergreen Way Ste B (98203-2879)
PHONE 425 355-5655
Gary W Max, *President*
EMP: 4
SALES (est): 283.3K **Privately Held**
SIC: 3949 Playground equipment

(G-3613)
SKEIN INTEGRATED SYSTEMS LLC
6300 Merrill Creek Pkwy (98203-1577)
PHONE 586 795-2000
Brian Bowers, *Manager*
EMP: 80
SALES (corp-wide): 37.7B **Privately Held**
SIC: 3724 Aircraft engines & engine parts
HQ: Skein Integrated Systems Llc
  22500 Key Dr
  Clinton Township MI 48036
  586 795-2000

(G-3614)
SNOHOMISH COUNTY BUS JURNL
1213 California St (98201-3445)
P.O. Box 930 (98206-0930)
PHONE 425 339-3000
Steve Hawef, *President*
EMP: 5
SALES: 500K **Privately Held**
WEB: www.snohomishcountybusinessjournal.com
SIC: 2711 Newspapers, publishing & printing

(G-3615)
SOFTEC SYSTEMS INC
917 134th St Sw Ste A6 (98204-9377)
PHONE 425 741-2055
Tomas Gonzalez, *President*
EMP: 6
SALES (est): 880K **Privately Held**
SIC: 3578 3577 Point-of-sale devices; computer peripheral equipment

(G-3616)
SOTERION CO
Also Called: Minuteman Press
3201 Rucker Ave Ste 2 (98201-4282)
PHONE 425 259-8181
Peter Faber, *President*
EMP: 4
SQ FT: 1,400
SALES (est): 458K **Privately Held**
WEB: www.soterion.com
SIC: 2752 Commercial printing, lithographic

(G-3617)
SOUND PUBLISHING INC (DH)
Also Called: Everett/Kitsap Press
11323 Commando Rd W Main (98204-3532)
PHONE 360 394-5800
Gloria G Fletcher, *President*
Lori Maxim, *Vice Pres*
Josh O'Connor, *Vice Pres*
Josh Oconnor, *Vice Pres*
EMP: 67
SQ FT: 25,000
SALES (est): 91.8MM **Privately Held**
WEB: www.soundpublishing.com
SIC: 2711 Newspapers: publishing only, not printed on site; newspapers, publishing & printing

(G-3618)
SOUND PUBLISHING INC
Also Called: Everett Press
11323 Commando Rd W Main (98204-3532)
PHONE 425 355-0717
Larry Babcock, *Branch Mgr*
EMP: 87 **Privately Held**
WEB: www.soundpublishing.com
SIC: 2759 2711 Commercial printing; newspapers, publishing & printing
HQ: Sound Publishing, Inc.
  11323 Commando Rd W Main
  Everett WA 98204
  360 394-5800

(G-3619)
SPRAYING SYSTEMS CO
1720 100th Pl Se Ste 102 (98208-3865)
PHONE 425 357-6327
Joe Albert, *Manager*
EMP: 4
SALES (corp-wide): 280.9MM **Privately Held**
WEB: www.spray.com
SIC: 3499 Nozzles, spray: aerosol, paint or insecticide
PA: Spraying Systems Co.
  200 W North Ave
  Glendale Heights IL 60139
  630 665-5000

(G-3620)
STAR MANUFACTURING INTL INC
Also Called: Lang Mfg Division
6500 Merrill Creek Pkwy (98203-5860)
PHONE 800 882-6368
Tracy Cumming, *General Mgr*
EMP: 102
SALES (corp-wide): 2.7B **Publicly Held**
SIC: 3556 3589 Food products machinery; cooking equipment, commercial
HQ: Star Manufacturing International Inc.
  250 Hobson St
  Smithville TN 37166
  800 264-7827

(G-3621)
STARK RAVING FOODS LLC
802 134th St Sw (98204-7314)
PHONE 425 361-7640
EMP: 2 **EST:** 2012
SALES (est): 311.5K **Privately Held**
SIC: 2656 Frozen food & ice cream containers

(G-3622)
STEVENS HOLDING COMPANY INC
6920 Seaway Blvd (98203-5829)
PHONE 425 446-4928
EMP: 2
SALES (est): 107.4K **Privately Held**
SIC: 3569 General industrial machinery

(G-3623)
SUPERMEDIA LLC
906 Se Everett Mall Way # 210 (98208-3744)
PHONE 425 423-7904
Mike Anderson, *Exec Dir*
EMP: 254
SALES (corp-wide): 1.8B **Privately Held**
SIC: 2741 Miscellaneous publishing
HQ: Supermedia Llc
  2200 W Airfield Dr
  Dfw Airport TX 75261
  972 453-7000

(G-3624)
SYNSOR LLC
1920 Merrill Creek Pkwy (98203-5859)
PHONE 425 551-1300
Richard Jackson, *CEO*
Guy Eden, *Vice Pres*
Kevin Watson, *Vice Pres*
Doug Owen, *Production*
Angelina Rouse, *CFO*
▲ **EMP:** 145
SQ FT: 130,000
SALES: 45MM
SALES (corp-wide): 265.2MM **Privately Held**
WEB: www.synsor.com
SIC: 2541 3585 Display fixtures, wood; cabinets, show & display, refrigerated
HQ: Premier Fixtures, Llc
  400 Oser Ave Ste 350
  Hauppauge NY 11788
  631 236-4100

(G-3625)
T D LASER ENGRAVING
10306 19th Pl W (98203-3659)
PHONE 425 347-6837
Debbie Staley, *Owner*
EMP: 2
SALES (est): 134.1K **Privately Held**
SIC: 3699 Laser systems & equipment

(G-3626)
TALCO SERVICES LLC
34th Ave Ne Bldg B (98201)
PHONE 425 259-0213
Gregory E Nordholm, *Mng Member*
Kirk Geary,
▲ **EMP:** 13
SQ FT: 14,000
SALES: 1.5MM **Privately Held**
SIC: 3441 Fabricated structural metal

(G-3627)
TAURUS AEROSPACE GROUP INC (PA)
3121 109th St Sw (98204-1318)
PHONE 425 423-6200
Larry Resnick, *CEO*
Terence R Montgomery, *CFO*
EMP: 7
SALES (est): 38.8MM **Privately Held**
SIC: 3599 Machine shop, jobbing & repair

(G-3628)
TERRY ALBRACHT
Also Called: Commercial Service & Repair
1035 N Park Dr (98203-1828)
PHONE 425 252-2997
Terry Albracht, *Owner*
EMP: 4
SQ FT: 1,000
SALES: 150K **Privately Held**
SIC: 3731 Military ships, building & repairing

(G-3629)
TERRYS MACHINE & MFG INC
1102 Shuksan Way Ste 200 (98203-7155)
PHONE 425 315-8866
Roger Sanford, *President*
Josh Brown, *General Mgr*
Darrell Emnott, *Engineer*
Mimi Moilanen, *Controller*
Jamie Morgan, *Accountant*
EMP: 14
SQ FT: 12,500
SALES (est): 3.5MM **Privately Held**
WEB: www.terrysmachine.com
SIC: 3599 Machine shop, jobbing & repair

(G-3630)
TERRYS PRECISION PRODUCTS LLC
1102 Shuksan Way (98203-7155)
PHONE 425 349-2700
Dirkson Charles, *Principal*
Mimi Moilanen, *Controller*
EMP: 3
SALES (est): 285.3K **Privately Held**
SIC: 3728 Aircraft parts & equipment

(G-3631)
TEX WARE
13827 51st Dr Se (98208-9543)
PHONE 425 337-3696
Ray Ruppert, *Principal*
EMP: 3 **EST:** 2010
SALES (est): 143.9K **Privately Held**
SIC: 2711 Newspapers, publishing & printing

▲ = Import ▼ = Export
◆ = Import/Export

GEOGRAPHIC SECTION

Everett - Snohomish County (G-3661)

(G-3632)
THICK FILM TECHNOLOGIES INC
3101 111th St Sw Ste R (98204-3590)
PHONE.....................425 347-0919
Kirk Goldenberger, *President*
EMP: 4
SQ FT: 3,300
SALES: 250K **Privately Held**
WEB: www.thickfilmtech.com
SIC: 3679 Electronic circuits

(G-3633)
TOOLLESS PLASTIC SOLUTIONS INC
1410 80th St Sw Ste C (98203-6200)
PHONE.....................425 493-1223
Bruno Haize, *President*
Kathy Abelson, *Opers Mgr*
Lena Chalfant-Godwin, *Opers Staff*
Scott Baggett, *Design Engr*
Kathy Harja, *CFO*
EMP: 22
SQ FT: 13,000
SALES (est): 2.6MM **Privately Held**
WEB: www.toolless.com
SIC: 3089 Plastic hardware & building products; injection molding of plastics

(G-3634)
TOTAL CNTRL LLC
5705 Evergreen Way # 204 (98203-6030)
PHONE.....................425 446-0342
Coleman Anderson,
EMP: 12 EST: 2017
SALES (est): 256K **Privately Held**
SIC: 7372 Prepackaged software

(G-3635)
TRAMCO INC
3100 112th St Sw (98204-3524)
PHONE.....................425 347-3030
EMP: 6
SALES (corp-wide): 706.3MM **Privately Held**
SIC: 3535 5063 3556 6512 Conveyors & conveying equipment; power transmission equipment, electric; food products machinery; commercial & industrial building operation
HQ: Tramco, Inc.
1020 E 19th St N
Wichita KS 67214
316 264-4604

(G-3636)
TRIAD PRODUCTS CORPORATION
12414 Highway 99 Ste 40 (98204-8008)
PHONE.....................425 514-8363
Gary I Jensen, *President*
Frank Garbarino, *Corp Secy*
EMP: 7 EST: 1965
SQ FT: 6,000
SALES: 810K **Privately Held**
SIC: 3498 3714 3429 3544 Tube fabricating (contract bending & shaping); motor vehicle parts & accessories; manufactured hardware (general); jigs & fixtures; surgical & medical instruments

(G-3637)
TRIDENT SEAFOODS CORPORATION
Also Called: Port Chatham Smoked Seafood
1930 Merrill Creek Pkwy B (98203-5897)
PHONE.....................425 407-4000
Debby Cox, *Business Anlyst*
Kevin Galley, *Manager*
EMP: 181
SALES (corp-wide): 2.3B **Privately Held**
SIC: 2092 Fresh or frozen packaged fish
PA: Trident Seafoods Corporation
5303 Shilshole Ave Nw
Seattle WA 98107
206 783-3818

(G-3638)
TURTLEWORKS
6721 60th St Se (98205)
PHONE.....................425 335-0394
Jan Armstrong, *Owner*
EMP: 2
SALES (est): 65K **Privately Held**
SIC: 3961 Costume jewelry, ex. precious metal & semiprecious stones

(G-3639)
TYEE AIRCRAFT INC
Also Called: Division of Avtechtyee, Inc.
6500 Merrill Creek Pkwy (98203-5860)
PHONE.....................425 290-3100
Kenneth Kates, *Controller*
Dana Sanders, *Consultant*
EMP: 2
SALES (est): 86K **Privately Held**
SIC: 3728 Aircraft parts & equipment

(G-3640)
UMBRA CUSCINETTI INCORPORATED
6707 Hardeson Rd (98203-7101)
PHONE.....................425 405-3500
Antonio Baldaccini, *Ch of Bd*
Robert Collett, *President*
Mariano Spigarelli, *President*
Leonardo Baldaccini, *Corp Secy*
Adam Nelson, *Vice Pres*
EMP: 90
SQ FT: 67,000
SALES (est): 59.1MM **Privately Held**
SIC: 3728 Aircraft assemblies, subassemblies & parts
HQ: Umbragroup Spa
Via Valter Baldaccini 1
Foligno PG 06034
074 234-81

(G-3641)
UNFORS RAYSAFE INC (DH)
6920 Seaway Blvd (98203-5829)
PHONE.....................508 435-5600
Kevin McMahon, *President*
Susanna Laursen, *Treasurer*
Carsten Browall, *Director*
▲ EMP: 45 EST: 1997
SQ FT: 12,200
SALES (est): 13.4MM
SALES (corp-wide): 19.8B **Publicly Held**
WEB: www.raysafe.com
SIC: 3841 Surgical & medical instruments
HQ: Unfors Raysafe Ab
Uggledalsvagen 29
Billdal 427 4
317 199-700

(G-3642)
UNIQUE ALLSCAPES
5129 Evergreen Way (98203-2869)
PHONE.....................425 309-6325
EMP: 2
SALES (est): 90.7K **Privately Held**
SIC: 2951 Asphalt paving mixtures & blocks

(G-3643)
UNIQUE BEVERAGE COMPANY LLC
Also Called: Cascade Ice Sparkling Water
7620 Hardeson Rd (98203-6286)
P.O. Box 2246 (98213-0246)
PHONE.....................425 267-0959
Mike Broadwell, *CEO*
Mark Christensen, *Executive*
EMP: 9
SQ FT: 40,000
SALES (est): 1.4MM **Privately Held**
SIC: 2086 Carbonated soft drinks, bottled & canned

(G-3644)
V F SERVICES INC JANSPORT
1202 Shuksan Way (98203-7105)
PHONE.....................425 407-4040
Rene Crow, *Principal*
EMP: 3
SALES (est): 165.5K **Privately Held**
SIC: 2325 Men's & boys' trousers & slacks

(G-3645)
VALVE ADJUSTERS CO INTL
10711 Washington Way (98204-3705)
PHONE.....................425 322-4241
Martin Evert, *Principal*
EMP: 2 EST: 2012
SALES (est): 130K **Privately Held**
SIC: 3592 Valves

(G-3646)
VANSH FOODS LLC
13414 11th Pl W (98204-6379)
PHONE.....................425 743-1043
Nipun Prashar, *Principal*
EMP: 2
SALES (est): 97.3K **Privately Held**
SIC: 2099 Food preparations

(G-3647)
VAPORTECH SOLUTIONS LLC
10011 3rd Ave Se Ste J (98208-3933)
PHONE.....................888 746-8955
Devin Longmore,
EMP: 10
SALES: 2MM **Privately Held**
SIC: 5169 2899 Chemicals & allied products; chemical preparations

(G-3648)
VAUPELL RAPID SOLUTIONS
Also Called: Vaupell NW Molding & Tooling
11323 Commando Rd W (98204-3532)
PHONE.....................206 784-9050
EMP: 7 **Privately Held**
SIC: 3728 Airframe assemblies, except for guided missiles
HQ: Vaupell Rapid Solutions
20 Executive Dr
Hudson NH 03051

(G-3649)
VECTORED SOLUTIONS INC
9800 29th Ave W Unit E101 (98204-1313)
PHONE.....................425 355-8038
Douglas Devries, *President*
Pameld Devries, *Vice Pres*
▲ EMP: 2
SALES (est): 341.4K **Privately Held**
SIC: 3721 Aircraft

(G-3650)
VERTICAL GARDENS NORTHWEST LLC
2808 16th St (98201-2114)
PHONE.....................425 891-7183
Matthew Keenan, *Principal*
▲ EMP: 2
SALES (est): 173K **Privately Held**
SIC: 2591 Blinds vertical

(G-3651)
WASHINGTON SCHL INFO PROC COOP
2121 W Casino Rd (98204-1472)
PHONE.....................425 349-6600
Marty Daybell, *CEO*
Ken Gersten, *Engineer*
Barbara Ollivier, *Database Admin*
George Horner, *Asst Director*
EMP: 105
SQ FT: 33,000
SALES (est): 22.4MM **Privately Held**
WEB: www.wsipc.com
SIC: 7372 7378 7371 Educational computer software; computer maintenance & repair; custom computer programming services

(G-3652)
WATERSTATION TECHNOLOGY LLC (PA)
2732 Grand Ave Ste 122 (98201-3416)
PHONE.....................877 475-7717
Dominic Simonelli, *Opers Staff*
Bryce Froberg, *Director*
Ryan Wear,
EMP: 2
SALES (est): 1MM **Privately Held**
SIC: 3589 Water purification equipment, household type

(G-3653)
WAYA GROUP INC
Also Called: Arrowcat Marine
1205 Craftsman Way # 111 (98201-1588)
PHONE.....................877 277-6999
Kim Stebbens, *President*
Robby Harty, *Vice Pres*
▲ EMP: 4 EST: 2011
SALES (est): 450.5K **Privately Held**
SIC: 3732 5091 5551 Motorboats, inboard or outboard: building & repairing; motorboats; inboard boats; inboard outdrive boats; outboard boats

(G-3654)
WELLS WW MILLWORK LLC
Also Called: W W Wells
3202 Mcdougall Ave (98201-4434)
PHONE.....................425 405-3252
Steve Oswald, *Mng Member*
EMP: 13
SQ FT: 20,000
SALES (est): 2.1MM **Privately Held**
SIC: 2434 2431 2521 Wood kitchen cabinets; millwork; wood office furniture

(G-3655)
WEST COAST MANUFACTURING INC
1515 75th St Sw Ste 600 (98203-7003)
PHONE.....................208 667-5121
Dan Barstad, *President*
Jake Neill, *Principal*
EMP: 5
SALES (est): 333.4K **Privately Held**
SIC: 3444 Sheet metalwork

(G-3656)
WESTERN SYSTEMS INC
1122 Industry St Ste B (98203-7154)
PHONE.....................425 438-1133
Michael C Smith, *President*
Robert W Nims, *President*
EMP: 25
SQ FT: 10,000
SALES (est): 9.3MM **Privately Held**
WEB: www.westerntrafficsystems.com
SIC: 3669 Traffic signals, electric

(G-3657)
WESTWOOD PRECISION INC
7509 Hardeson Rd (98203-6285)
PHONE.....................425 742-7011
Gordon Nisbet, *President*
James Clark, *Vice Pres*
Diane Rowberry, *Production*
Jim Hanson, *QC Mgr*
Carol McArthur, *Human Resources*
▲ EMP: 53
SQ FT: 15,000
SALES (est): 9.7MM **Privately Held**
WEB: www.westwoodprecision.com
SIC: 3599 Machine shop, jobbing & repair

(G-3658)
WH INTERNATIONAL CASTING LLC
6605 Hardeson Rd Ste 101 (98203-7118)
PHONE.....................425 498-7531
Kevin Ocallaghan, *Manager*
EMP: 2
SALES (corp-wide): 54.6MM **Privately Held**
SIC: 3321 Gray & ductile iron foundries
HQ: Wh International Casting, Llc
14821 Artesia Blvd
La Mirada CA 90638
562 521-0727

(G-3659)
WILLYS CANVAS WORKS
12315 4th Pl W (98204-8622)
PHONE.....................425 923-7810
EMP: 2
SALES (est): 126.6K **Privately Held**
SIC: 2394 Canvas & related products

(G-3660)
WINTRAN TRADING
3601 97th Pl Se (98208-3117)
PHONE.....................425 501-7818
Phuoc Nguyen, *President*
Win Nguyen, *Vice Pres*
Dat Nguyen, *CFO*
EMP: 5
SALES: 25K **Privately Held**
SIC: 2511 5211 Wood lawn & garden furniture; lumber & other building materials

(G-3661)
WIPRO GIVON USA INC
2300 Merrill Creek Pkwy # 300 (98203-5855)
PHONE.....................425 355-3330
Moran Yaari, *General Mgr*
Ronen Givon, *Chairman*
Gonen Letzter, *Corp Secy*
EMP: 44
SQ FT: 27,000

Everett - Snohomish County (G-3662) — GEOGRAPHIC SECTION

SALES (est): 9.8MM
SALES (corp-wide): 34.2MM **Privately Held**
WEB: www.jlmfg.com
SIC: 3728 Aircraft assemblies, subassemblies & parts
PA: Wipro Givon Limited
29 Levy Yosef
Kiryat Bialik 27511
488 131-00

(G-3662)
YK PRODUCTS LLC
12428 Highway 99 Ste 53 (98204-5502)
PHONE 425 244-5000
John Ackerman,
EMP: 5
SALES (est): 720K **Privately Held**
WEB: www.uscoldpatch.com
SIC: 2951 Asphalt & asphaltic paving mixtures (not from refineries)

(G-3663)
ZOAL & ASSOCIATES LLC
Also Called: Zoal Precission Machining
4609 Marble Ln (98203-2816)
PHONE 425 355-9590
EMP: 5
SALES (est): 186K **Privately Held**
SIC: 3599 Mfg Industrial Machinery

(G-3664)
ZODIAC AEROSPACE
6300 Merrill Creek Pkwy B100 (98203-1578)
PHONE 425 791-3302
EMP: 3
SALES (est): 286.9K **Privately Held**
SIC: 3728 Aircraft parts & equipment

(G-3665)
ZODIAC AEROSPACE
2204 Hewitt Ave (98201-3705)
PHONE 425 257-2044
Todd Driskell, *Manager*
EMP: 2
SALES (est): 86K **Privately Held**
SIC: 3728 Aircraft parts & equipment

Everson
Whatcom County

(G-3666)
ALRT CORPORATION
4040 Mt Baker Hwy (98247-9426)
PHONE 360 592-5300
William Westergreen, *President*
Gerald Hammer, *President*
Jill Yonkman, *VP Opers*
Rod Lofdahl, *Executive*
EMP: 65
SQ FT: 2,078
SALES (est): 8.4MM **Privately Held**
WEB: www.alrtcorp.com
SIC: 2411 1611 Logging camps & contractors; general contractor, highway & street construction

(G-3667)
AZ PRECISION MFG LLC
6872 Mission Rd (98247-9750)
PHONE 360 441-9008
Brian Cabbage,
Lori Cabbage,
EMP: 2
SQ FT: 5,000
SALES (est): 500K **Privately Held**
SIC: 3599 Machine shop, jobbing & repair

(G-3668)
BODES PRECAST INC
1861 E Pole Rd (98247-9614)
PHONE 360 354-3912
Ray Herringa, *President*
Rick Herringa, *Corp Secy*
EMP: 12
SALES (est): 1.8MM **Privately Held**
WEB: www.bodesprecast.com
SIC: 3272 5039 Concrete products, precast; septic tanks

(G-3669)
C & C WELDING INC
8716 Trapline Rd (98247-9349)
PHONE 360 966-4772
Alvin Weerdhuizen, *President*
EMP: 4
SALES (est): 250K **Privately Held**
SIC: 7692 Welding repair

(G-3670)
CH LEATHER & SUPPLY
7602 Nooksack Rd (98247-9514)
PHONE 360 966-0183
Carl Hippe, *Owner*
Marie Hippe, *Co-Owner*
Bruce Hippe, *Manager*
EMP: 2
SALES (est): 95.8K **Privately Held**
SIC: 3199 Equestrian related leather articles

(G-3671)
CHS-SUB WHATCOM INC
Also Called: Wfc Nooksack Convenience Store
102 Nooksack Ave (98276-8219)
P.O. Box 611, Lynden (98264-0611)
PHONE 360 966-4782
Phillip Hutton, *Opers Mgr*
Paulina Stauffer, *Branch Mgr*
EMP: 20
SALES (corp-wide): 31.9B **Publicly Held**
WEB: www.wfcoop.com
SIC: 2875 5191 Fertilizers, mixing only; farm supplies
HQ: Chs-Sub Whatcom, Inc.
402 Main St
Lynden WA 98264
360 354-2108

(G-3672)
COPPERTOP ENTERPRISES INC (PA)
Also Called: Christensen Net Works
401 Lincoln St Ste 102 (98247-9130)
PHONE 360 966-9622
Jeannie Davidson, *President*
Brian Davidson, *Principal*
Britt Holmes, *Vice Pres*
◆ EMP: 30
SQ FT: 6,000
SALES (est): 4.9MM **Privately Held**
WEB: www.cnwsports.com
SIC: 2258 3949 2298 Net & netting products; sporting & athletic goods; cordage & twine

(G-3673)
DIAMOND NETS INC
1064 E Pole Rd (98247-9640)
PHONE 360 354-1319
Les Powers, *President*
John Neal, *Vice Pres*
▲ EMP: 40
SQ FT: 23,000
SALES: 5MM **Privately Held**
WEB: www.diamondnets.com
SIC: 3949 2399 Sporting & athletic goods; fishing nets

(G-3674)
EPL FEED LLC
5996 Lawrence Rd (98247-9586)
P.O. Box 99, Sumas (98295-0099)
PHONE 360 988-5811
Steve Skogrand, *Branch Mgr*
EMP: 9
SALES (corp-wide): 4.6MM **Privately Held**
SIC: 2048 Prepared feeds
PA: Epl Feed, Llc
411 W Front St
Sumas WA 98295
360 988-5811

(G-3675)
EVERSON CORDAGE WORKS LLC
7180 Everson Goshen Rd (98247-9741)
PHONE 360 966-4613
Larry Powers, *Partner*
▲ EMP: 44
SQ FT: 85,000

SALES (est): 6.3MM **Privately Held**
WEB: www.catlinefishing.com
SIC: 2298 Fishing lines, nets, seines; made in cordage or twine mills

(G-3676)
GRANITE CONSTRUCTION COMPANY
7017 Everson Goshen Rd (98247-9740)
PHONE 360 676-2450
Jeff Nelson, *Manager*
EMP: 3
SALES (corp-wide): 3.3B **Publicly Held**
SIC: 1611 1771 2951 Highway & street construction; blacktop (asphalt) work; asphalt paving mixtures & blocks
HQ: Granite Construction Company
585 W Beach St
Watsonville CA 95076
831 724-1011

(G-3677)
GREAT WESTERN LUMBER COMPANY
7636 Goodwin Rd (98247-9469)
P.O. Box 159 (98247-0159)
PHONE 360 966-3061
Justin Hamilton, *Human Res Mgr*
Gerry Millman, *Manager*
Bobby Kelley, *Maintence Staff*
EMP: 65
SALES (est): 10MM
SALES (corp-wide): 11MM **Privately Held**
WEB: www.greatwesternlumber.net
SIC: 2421 2426 Lumber: rough, sawed or planed; hardwood dimension & flooring mills
PA: Great Western Lumber Company
9264 Manchester Rd
Saint Louis MO 63144
314 968-1700

(G-3678)
GROW NORTHWEST
7399 Goodwin Rd (98247-9466)
PHONE 360 398-1155
EMP: 2
SALES (est): 90.8K **Privately Held**
SIC: 5148 2721 Fresh fruits & vegetables; comic books: publishing only, not printed on site

(G-3679)
IRISH ACRES FOUNDATION QUARTER
2422 E Badger Rd (98247-9329)
PHONE 360 966-4677
Debra McGuire, *Principal*
EMP: 3
SALES (est): 225.5K **Privately Held**
SIC: 3131 Quarters

(G-3680)
KCPK TRUCKING INC
4076 Mt Baker Hwy (98247-9426)
PHONE 360 592-2260
Chuck Cooper, *Principal*
EMP: 2
SALES (est): 147.4K **Privately Held**
SIC: 2411 Logging

(G-3681)
LAND OLAKES INC
5996 Lawrence Rd (98247-9586)
PHONE 360 592-5115
James Colombo, *Manager*
EMP: 8
SALES (corp-wide): 10.4B **Privately Held**
WEB: www.landolakes.com
SIC: 0723 2048 5191 Feed milling custom services; prepared feeds; animal feeds
PA: Land O'lakes, Inc.
4001 Lexington Ave N
Arden Hills MN 55126
651 375-2222

(G-3682)
MILES SAND & GRAVEL COMPANY
Also Called: Concrete Nor'west
6513 Siper Rd (98247-9438)
PHONE 360 734-1956
Brad Davis, *Branch Mgr*
EMP: 25

SALES (corp-wide): 88MM **Privately Held**
SIC: 3273 5032 Ready-mixed concrete; sand, construction; gravel
PA: Miles Sand & Gravel Company
400 Valley Ave Ne
Puyallup WA 98372
253 833-3705

(G-3683)
MT BAKER STUMP GRINDING & GRAV
501 Shuksan Way (98247-9101)
PHONE 360 684-1695
Heidi Gudde, *Principal*
EMP: 2
SALES (est): 66K **Privately Held**
SIC: 1442 Construction sand & gravel

(G-3684)
NICHOL PRFMCE & CTRL AUTOMATIO
5649 Smith Creek Rd (98247-9485)
PHONE 360 961-2833
Robert Nichol, *Principal*
EMP: 4
SALES (est): 397.3K **Privately Held**
SIC: 3356 Nickel

(G-3685)
NYLATECH INCORPORATED (PA)
223 W Main St (98247-8256)
P.O. Box 455 (98247-0455)
PHONE 360 966-2838
Graeme Fraser, *President*
Dale Delmage, *Vice Pres*
Nate Merkt, *Sales Mgr*
Bill Fulton, *Admin Sec*
Isaac White, *Admin Sec*
▲ EMP: 13
SQ FT: 20,000
SALES (est): 2.5MM **Privately Held**
WEB: www.nylatech.com
SIC: 2821 Nylon resins

(G-3686)
PALLETS UNLIMITED
2007 Hampton Rd (98247-9364)
PHONE 360 354-1395
EMP: 4
SALES (est): 400.6K **Privately Held**
SIC: 2448 Pallets, wood & wood with metal

(G-3687)
REEVES CRICKET RANCH INC
3207 Hughes Rd (98247-9516)
P.O. Box 845 (98247-0845)
PHONE 360 966-3300
Clyde Reeves, *President*
EMP: 10
SALES (est): 856.9K **Privately Held**
WEB: www.reevescricketranch.com
SIC: 3949 0291 Sporting & athletic goods; general farms, primarily animals

(G-3688)
SAMSON ESTATES WINERY
1861 Van Dyk Rd (98247-9655)
PHONE 360 966-4526
Rob Dhaliwal, *Principal*
EMP: 7
SALES (est): 845.7K **Privately Held**
SIC: 2084 5921 Wines; wine

(G-3689)
SOUTH EVERSON LUMBER CO INC
Also Called: Selco
1615 Mission Rd (98247-8780)
P.O. Box 309 (98247-0309)
PHONE 360 966-2188
Hardarshan Johal, *President*
Kelly O'Toole, *Manager*
▼ EMP: 110
SQ FT: 140,000
SALES (est): 17.6MM
SALES (corp-wide): 97.4MM **Privately Held**
WEB: www.terminalforest.com
SIC: 2421 Custom sawmill
PA: Terminal Forest Products Ltd
12180 Mitchell Rd
Richmond BC V6V 1
604 717-1200

▲ = Import ▼ = Export
◆ = Import/Export

GEOGRAPHIC SECTION

Federal Way - King County (G-3721)

(G-3690)
SUE A PRIEBE
6759 Lunde Rd (98247-9635)
PHONE....................360 398-7647
Sue Priebe, *Principal*
EMP: 3
SALES (est): 122.3K **Privately Held**
SIC: 7692 Welding repair

(G-3691)
TELADAQ LLC
2040 Lindsay Rd (98247-8218)
PHONE....................661 373-1168
Anush A Abtahi,
EMP: 2
SALES (est): 136.3K **Privately Held**
SIC: 3511 Turbines & turbine generator sets

(G-3692)
TIPPECANOE BOATS LTD
4305 Nordum Rd (98247-9213)
PHONE....................360 966-7245
William T Lesh Jr, *President*
Cynthia Rogers, *Vice Pres*
EMP: 6
SQ FT: 3,200
SALES: 100K **Privately Held**
WEB: www.tboats.com
SIC: 3944 5092 Games, toys & children's vehicles; toys

(G-3693)
TWISTED METAL LLC
1212 Nooksack Ave (98276-8216)
PHONE....................360 966-5309
Humberto Elizondo, *Mng Member*
EMP: 3
SALES (est): 618.3K **Privately Held**
SIC: 3441 3446 3399 5039 Fabricated structural metal for bridges; railings, bannisters, guards, etc.; made from metal pipe; metal fasteners; metal guardrails

(G-3694)
ZENDER LOGGING CO INC
2181 Central Rd (98247-9755)
PHONE....................360 966-5693
Ken Zender, *President*
EMP: 25 **EST:** 1955
SALES (est): 2.1MM **Privately Held**
SIC: 2411 Logging

Fairchild Afb
Spokane County

(G-3695)
ENVISION INC
Also Called: Envision Express
610 N Depot Ave (99011-9685)
PHONE....................509 247-5732
Ken Dohmen, *Manager*
EMP: 6
SALES (corp-wide): 174.9MM **Privately Held**
WEB: www.envisionus.com
SIC: 2673 2676 Plastic bags: made from purchased materials; towels, paper: made from purchased paper
PA: Envision, Inc.
2301 S Water St
Wichita KS 67213
316 267-2244

Fairfield
Spokane County

(G-3696)
DW CORNWALL FARMS INC
21706 S Sands Rd (99012-9712)
PHONE....................509 291-5011
David W Cornwall, *President*
James Cornwall, *Corp Secy*
EMP: 5
SALES (est): 470K **Privately Held**
SIC: 2411 Logging

(G-3697)
PACIFIC NW FRMRS COOP INC
102 S Railroad Ave (99012-5000)
PHONE....................509 283-2124
Julee Huff, *Branch Mgr*
EMP: 10
SALES (corp-wide): 151.7MM **Privately Held**
SIC: 2099 5153 Food preparations; grains
PA: Pacific Northwest Farmers Cooperative Inc.
117 W Chestnut
Genesee ID 83832
208 285-1141

Fall City
King County

(G-3698)
ADVANCED FUEL SYSTEMS
29100 Se 43rd Pl (98024-7006)
PHONE....................425 526-7566
Edward Dunn, *Partner*
Stephen Walsh, *Partner*
EMP: 4
SQ FT: 2,200
SALES (est): 452.1K **Privately Held**
WEB: www.afsfuel.com
SIC: 5013 3443 5088 5172 Motor vehicle supplies & new parts; farm storage tanks, metal plate; tanks & tank components; aircraft fueling services

(G-3699)
ALMET METAL REFINISHING
32814 Se 76th St (98024-6709)
PHONE....................206 234-8555
Leonard Clemeson, *Owner*
EMP: 3
SALES (est): 188.5K **Privately Held**
SIC: 3471 Finishing, metals or formed products

(G-3700)
BEAM MACHINE
3023 362nd Ave Se (98024-9407)
PHONE....................425 222-5587
Theodore Mather, *Owner*
EMP: 2
SALES (est): 107.6K **Privately Held**
SIC: 2421 Sawmills & planing mills, general

(G-3701)
FALL CITY WELDING INC
33623 Se 43rd St (98024)
P.O. Box 535 (98024-0535)
PHONE....................425 222-5105
Michael Tawney, *President*
Renae Tawney, *Vice Pres*
EMP: 3
SQ FT: 2,400
SALES (est): 294.2K **Privately Held**
SIC: 7692 Welding repair

(G-3702)
HUNT HOSTED SOLUTIONS
Also Called: Hunt Interactive
5600 329th Ave Se (98024-6653)
PHONE....................425 222-0098
John Hunt, *Principal*
EMP: 3
SALES (est): 209.8K **Privately Held**
SIC: 7371 7375 2741 4813 Custom computer programming services; on-line data base information retrieval; ;

(G-3703)
MERCER MARINE INC
3911 Lake Wash Blvd Se (98024)
PHONE....................425 641-2090
Doug Burbridge, *President*
Margie Burbridge, *Vice Pres*
EMP: 17
SQ FT: 8,000
SALES (est): 527.3K **Privately Held**
SIC: 7699 5551 3732 Boat repair; outboard motors; marine supplies; boat building & repairing

(G-3704)
OCEAN INSTRUMENTS WASH LLC
Also Called: Ocean Instruments, Inc.
32617 Se 44th St (98024-8724)
PHONE....................425 281-1471
Shawn Hinz, *President*
EMP: 7
SQ FT: 6,000
SALES (est): 400K
SALES (corp-wide): 1.3MM **Privately Held**
WEB: www.oceaninstruments.com
SIC: 3812 Sonar systems & equipment
PA: Gravity Consulting, Llc
32617 Se 44th St
Fall City WA 98024
425 281-1471

(G-3705)
PACIFIC ENVIRONMENTAL INC
29100 Se 43rd Pl (98024-7006)
PHONE....................760 877-9796
EMP: 4
SQ FT: 2,200
SALES: 1MM **Privately Held**
SIC: 3822 Mfg Environmental Controls

(G-3706)
PRECISION ALIAS
30211 Se 40th St (98024-6513)
PHONE....................425 222-0744
EMP: 2
SALES (est): 108.9K **Privately Held**
SIC: 3599 Mfg Industrial Machinery

(G-3707)
RAINIER WOOD RECYCLERS INC (PA)
33216 Se Rdmnd Fall Cty (98024-5806)
PHONE....................425 222-0008
Tony Bennett, *President*
Robert Sargent, *General Mgr*
Ed Strauser, *CFO*
EMP: 24
SQ FT: 840
SALES (est): 3.1MM **Privately Held**
SIC: 2499 Sawdust, reground

(G-3708)
SIMPLICITY ABC LLC
7302 Lake Alice Rd Se (98024-6703)
PHONE....................425 250-1186
Suraphong Liengboonlertchai,
EMP: 2
SALES (est): 49.5K **Privately Held**
SIC: 7389 2511 Design services; children's wood furniture

(G-3709)
VERTX INDUSTRIES LLC
32319 Se 42nd Ln (98024-7804)
P.O. Box 1100, North Bend (98045-1100)
PHONE....................206 619-1479
EMP: 3 **EST:** 2010
SALES (est): 160K **Privately Held**
SIC: 3999 Mfg Misc Products

(G-3710)
WILLIAM GRSSIE WINE ESTTES LLC
35922 Se 46th St (98024-9700)
PHONE....................913 461-4601
William Grassie, *Principal*
EMP: 5
SALES (est): 413.6K **Privately Held**
SIC: 2084 Wines

Federal Way
King County

(G-3711)
A J R ENTERPRISES INC
Also Called: Delightful Treat Distributors
29819 5th Ave Sw (98023-3516)
PHONE....................253 946-1708
Allan K Stork, *President*
Janice Stork, *Vice Pres*
EMP: 2
SALES (est): 172.3K **Privately Held**
SIC: 2024 Ice cream & frozen desserts

(G-3712)
AD ONE CORP
30833 Pacific Hwy S (98003-4901)
PHONE....................253 942-3688
Byung K Chae, *Principal*
EMP: 2
SALES (est): 197.3K **Privately Held**
SIC: 3993 Advertising artwork

(G-3713)
AGM FABRIC PRODUCTS INC
27721 Pcf Hwy S Ste 101 (98003)
PHONE....................253 946-3200
John Halberg, *President*
Jan Vanamburg, *Principal*
EMP: 9
SQ FT: 1,200
SALES: 750K **Privately Held**
SIC: 2394 Canvas & related products

(G-3714)
ALLCO MANUFACTURING INC
31811 Pacific Hwy S (98003-5646)
PHONE....................702 616-2081
EMP: 2
SALES (est): 154.4K **Privately Held**
SIC: 3999 Atomizers, toiletry

(G-3715)
ALLRED HEATING COOLING ELC LLC
1020 Sw 334th St 205 (98023)
PHONE....................206 359-2164
Matthew Allred, *Mng Member*
Melanie Gilchrist, *Mng Member*
EMP: 10 **EST:** 2011
SALES: 1MM **Privately Held**
SIC: 3564 Filters, air; furnaces, air conditioning equipment, etc.

(G-3716)
ARROWS SIGN SERVICING LLC
34809 14th Pl Sw (98023-7021)
PHONE....................206 412-4922
Sophal Sim, *Principal*
EMP: 3
SALES (est): 318.2K **Privately Held**
SIC: 3993 Signs & advertising specialties

(G-3717)
ASBESTOS NORTHWEST
30620 Pacific Hwy S # 103 (98003-4888)
PHONE....................253 941-4343
Sarah Lafley, *Principal*
Cathy Butler, *Analyst*
EMP: 5
SALES (est): 328.1K **Privately Held**
SIC: 3292 Asbestos products

(G-3718)
BROWSEREPORT
28908 6th Ave S (98003-3605)
PHONE....................206 948-2640
Don Hyun, *Co-Owner*
Zach Bates, *Co-Owner*
EMP: 2 **EST:** 2012
SALES (est): 163.6K **Privately Held**
SIC: 7372 7389 Educational computer software;

(G-3719)
C T SALES INC
37405 Pacific Hwy S (98003-7454)
PHONE....................253 874-8737
David Anderson, *President*
EMP: 3
SALES (est): 287.5K **Privately Held**
SIC: 3272 Concrete products

(G-3720)
CALEDONIA BAY CABINETS INC
34251 18th Pl S (98003-6823)
PHONE....................253 905-7368
EMP: 2 **EST:** 2009
SALES (est): 161.1K **Privately Held**
SIC: 2434 Mfg Wood Kitchen Cabinets

(G-3721)
CARPET PLUS LLC
34515 16th Ave S (98003-6802)
PHONE....................253 874-0525
O Alex Kobets, *Mng Member*
Oleksander Alex Kobets, *Mng Member*
Alina Kobets,
Oleksandr Alex Kobets,

Federal Way - King County (G-3722)

EMP: 3
SALES: 1.7MM **Privately Held**
SIC: **5713** 2426 2273 Carpets; hardwood dimension & flooring mills; carpets, textile fiber

(G-3722)
CASCADE PRINTING DIRECT
1505 S 356th St Ste 110 (98003-3513)
PHONE..........................253 661-6213
Chuong Pham, *President*
Val Pham, *Vice Pres*
EMP: 4
SALES (est): 260K **Privately Held**
SIC: **2759** Commercial printing

(G-3723)
CHURCH & DWIGHT CO INC
350 S 333rd St Ste 102 (98003-6339)
PHONE..........................253 838-3385
Jeff Stephens, *Manager*
EMP: 2
SALES (corp-wide): 4.1B **Publicly Held**
WEB: www.churchdwight.com
SIC: **2812** Sodium bicarbonate
PA: Church & Dwight Co., Inc.
500 Charles Ewing Blvd
Ewing NJ 08628
609 806-1200

(G-3724)
COMPLETE MLLWK SOLUTIONS INC
33615 1st Way S Ste A (98003-4558)
PHONE..........................253 875-6769
Chong So, *President*
EMP: 2
SALES (est): 220K **Privately Held**
SIC: **2431** Millwork

(G-3725)
CORE TRAINING INDUSTRIES INC
103 S 297th Pl (98003-3629)
PHONE..........................206 250-2050
G W Corby, *Principal*
EMP: 2
SALES (est): 151.2K **Privately Held**
SIC: **3999** Manufacturing industries

(G-3726)
CQ2 ENTERPRISES
29618 Marine View Dr Sw (98023-3400)
PHONE..........................253 941-4488
Christine M Quist, *Principal*
EMP: 2 EST: 2010
SALES (est): 165.5K **Privately Held**
SIC: **3229** Pressed & blown glass

(G-3727)
CRYSTALLI INC (PA)
405 Sw 347th St (98003-8351)
PHONE..........................253 905-6784
Alexander Dehaan, *CEO*
Christine Carlson, *President*
EMP: 4 EST: 2015
SALES: 1.2MM **Privately Held**
SIC: **2339** Women's & misses' athletic clothing & sportswear

(G-3728)
CSL PLASMA INC
2200 S 314th St (98003-5087)
PHONE..........................253 275-2243
EMP: 7 **Privately Held**
SIC: **2836** Plasmas
HQ: Csl Plasma Inc.
900 Broken Sound Pkwy Nw # 4
Boca Raton FL 33487
561 981-3700

(G-3729)
DIRECT HIT GOLF FLAGS LLC
308 Sw 294th Pl (98023-3550)
PHONE..........................253 946-6263
Carole Bartlett, *President*
EMP: 2
SALES (est): 202.7K **Privately Held**
SIC: **2399** 3949 Flags, fabric; golf equipment

(G-3730)
DOMTAR PAPER COMPANY LLC
33663 Weyerhaeuser Way S (98001-9620)
PHONE..........................253 924-2345
EMP: 375
SALES (corp-wide): 301.1MM **Privately Held**
SIC: **2621** Paper mills
HQ: Domtar Paper Company, Llc
234 Kingsley Park Dr
Fort Mill SC 29715

(G-3731)
DOW JONES & COMPANY INC
600 S 334th St (98003-6344)
PHONE..........................253 661-8850
Frank Bruno, *Principal*
Mary Grooman, *Manager*
Mike Diblasio, *Technical Staff*
Marvin Clinesmith,
EMP: 32
SALES (corp-wide): 9B **Publicly Held**
SIC: **2711** Newspapers, publishing & printing
HQ: Dow Jones & Company, Inc.
1211 Avenue Of The Americ
New York NY 10036
609 627-2999

(G-3732)
DOYON TECHNICAL SERVICES LLC
33810 Weyerhaeuser Way S (98001-9624)
PHONE..........................253 344-5300
Kevin Slattery, *President*
Aaron Schutt, *Senior VP*
Shawn Barrows, *Vice Pres*
Kathleen Villars, *CFO*
Daniel S Osborn, *Treasurer*
EMP: 3
SQ FT: 32,286
SALES (est): 259.2K **Privately Held**
WEB: www.doyon-dgs.com
SIC: **3724** Aircraft engines & engine parts

(G-3733)
DR VENTURES INC
Also Called: UPS
1911 Sw Campus Dr (98023-6473)
PHONE..........................253 874-6583
Doug Reetz, *President*
Nannette Reetz, *Admin Sec*
EMP: 5
SALES (est): 425.6K **Privately Held**
SIC: **7389** 2752 Mailbox rental & related service; commercial printing, lithographic

(G-3734)
EC/NDT LLC
1020 S 344th St Ste 214 (98003-8713)
P.O. Box 24418 (98093-1418)
PHONE..........................253 815-0797
Richard Petter, *CEO*
EMP: 7 EST: 1998
SQ FT: 1,800
SALES (est): 1.3MM **Privately Held**
SIC: **3829** Measuring & controlling devices

(G-3735)
EVERGREEN EYE CENTER INC PS
716 S 348th St (98003-7000)
PHONE..........................206 212-2163
Robert A Tester MD, *Principal*
EMP: 11
SALES (est): 239.2K **Privately Held**
SIC: **2741** Miscellaneous publishing

(G-3736)
FAST SIGNS
Also Called: Fastsigns
34930 Enchanted Pkwy S # 170 (98003-8364)
PHONE..........................253 942-9444
Claudia Mizukami, *Principal*
EMP: 2
SALES (est): 164.6K **Privately Held**
SIC: **3993** Signs & advertising specialties

(G-3737)
FASTSIGNS INTERNATIONAL INC
34930 Encntd Pkwy S # 170 (98003-8364)
PHONE..........................253 835-9450
Claudia Mizukami, *Owner*
EMP: 3
SALES (corp-wide): 27.1MM **Privately Held**
SIC: **3993** 7319 5999 Signs & advertising specialties; display advertising service; banners
PA: Fastsigns International, Inc.
2542 Highlander Way
Carrollton TX 75006
888 285-5935

(G-3738)
FEDERAL WAY MEMORIAL FIELD
1300 S 308th St (98003-4708)
PHONE..........................253 945-5575
Greg Flynn, *Principal*
EMP: 2
SALES (est): 150.1K **Privately Held**
SIC: **2531** Stadium seating

(G-3739)
FEDERAL WAY SIGN
34205 18th Pl S (98003-6823)
PHONE..........................253 529-2011
Milan Michalek, *Principal*
EMP: 2
SALES (est): 283.7K **Privately Held**
SIC: **3993** Electric signs

(G-3740)
GELATELLO INC
1902 S Commons Ste A (98003-6018)
PHONE..........................425 214-1267
Faisal Qureshi, *Manager*
EMP: 9
SQ FT: 600
SALES (est): 418K **Privately Held**
SIC: **2052** Cones, ice cream

(G-3741)
GLOBAL DIRECT COMPONENTS LLC
1820 S 341st Pl (98003-6859)
PHONE..........................253 661-1100
Hun Honchoe,
EMP: 13
SALES (est): 1.8MM **Privately Held**
SIC: **5013** 3312 Automotive brakes; wheels

(G-3742)
GRAND D SIGNS
1082 S 316th St (98003-5331)
PHONE..........................253 929-9963
EMP: 2
SALES (est): 122.8K **Privately Held**
SIC: **3993** Signs & advertising specialties

(G-3743)
HOLMES FAMILY WINERY LLC
1625 S 374th Ct (98003-7593)
PHONE..........................253 906-6317
EMP: 2
SALES (est): 120.9K **Privately Held**
SIC: **2084** Wines

(G-3744)
I LOVE RAMEN JAPENESE NOODLE
31254 Pacific Hwy S (98003-5402)
PHONE..........................253 839-1115
EMP: 4 EST: 2010
SALES (est): 294.4K **Privately Held**
SIC: **2098** Noodles (e.g. egg, plain & water), dry

(G-3745)
INK WELL PRINTERS INC
2423 S 304th St (98003-4809)
PHONE..........................206 623-1701
Karen Caisse, *President*
Peter Caisse, *Vice Pres*
EMP: 3
SQ FT: 4,500
SALES: 200K **Privately Held**
SIC: **2752** Commercial printing, lithographic

(G-3746)
INTELLIGENT INDUSTRIES LLC
1900 Sw Campus Dr (98023-6533)
PHONE..........................206 372-7273
Nicholas Sutton, *Principal*
EMP: 2
SALES (est): 97.3K **Privately Held**
SIC: **3999** Manufacturing industries

(G-3747)
JUNTLABS LLC
416 Sw 353rd St (98023-8127)
PHONE..........................253 987-1750
Ryan Junt, *CEO*
John Hogan, *Principal*
Brian Junt, *Principal*
Heidi Junt, *Principal*
EMP: 5
SALES: 50K **Privately Held**
SIC: **3572** 7371 7389 Magnetic storage devices, computer; computer software development & applications;

(G-3748)
JW WOODWORKS
32408 2nd Ave Sw (98023-5605)
PHONE..........................206 719-4229
Jason Webber, *Principal*
EMP: 2 EST: 2012
SALES (est): 160K **Privately Held**
SIC: **2431** Millwork

(G-3749)
KYLE O MEARA
3857 Sw 339th St (98023-2973)
PHONE..........................206 874-2626
EMP: 2 EST: 2010
SALES (est): 150K **Privately Held**
SIC: **2431** Mfg Millwork

(G-3750)
LA WAFFLETZ LLC
2429 S 273rd Pl Apt 234 (98023-8249)
PHONE..........................206 432-7548
Rogerio Martinho,
EMP: 4 EST: 2014
SQ FT: 530
SALES (est): 139.8K **Privately Held**
SIC: **2051** Pies, bakery: except frozen

(G-3751)
LANDY CORPORATION
835 Sw 347th Pl (98003-8454)
PHONE..........................253 835-1427
Haiying Guo, *President*
EMP: 3 EST: 2009
SALES (est): 207.5K **Privately Held**
SIC: **3999** 5149 Pet supplies; pet foods

(G-3752)
LIFE CHRONICLES
30918 20th Ave S Apt B (98023-4362)
PHONE..........................253 508-8876
EMP: 2
SALES (est): 86.8K **Privately Held**
SIC: **2741** Miscellaneous publishing

(G-3753)
LLOYD ENTERPRISES INC (PA)
Also Called: Federal Way Sand & Gravel
34667 Pacific Hwy S (98003-6894)
P.O. Box 3889 (98063-3889)
PHONE..........................253 874-6692
Danny L Lloyd, *President*
Robert R Lloyd, *Chairman*
Randy Lloyd, *Vice Pres*
Jon Peterson, *Treasurer*
Luann Davis, *Admin Sec*
EMP: 90
SQ FT: 5,000
SALES: 19.1MM **Privately Held**
WEB: www.lloydenterprisesinc.com
SIC: **6552** 1623 1442 4212 Land subdividers & developers, commercial; underground utilities contractor; construction sand & gravel; local trucking, without storage

(G-3754)
LUPITAS
2124 Sw 336th St (98023-2883)
PHONE..........................253 838-6132
Victor Hernandez, *Principal*
EMP: 2
SALES (est): 77.2K **Privately Held**
SIC: **2051** 5411 Bread, cake & related products; grocery stores

GEOGRAPHIC SECTION

Federal Way - King County (G-3787)

(G-3755)
MARBLE PLSG STONE RSTRTION LLC
32749 6th Ave Sw (98023-5624)
PHONE.....................425 564-8284
Chhay Haong, *Principal*
EMP: 5 EST: 2010
SALES (est): 438K **Privately Held**
SIC: 3471 Polishing, metals or formed products

(G-3756)
MASONS CHEESECAKE CO LLC
32801 26th Ave Sw (98023-2895)
PHONE.....................206 602-4563
Michael Mason II, *Mng Member*
EMP: 2
SQ FT: 10,000
SALES (est): 86.4K **Privately Held**
SIC: 2051 Bakery: wholesale or wholesale/retail combined

(G-3757)
MCOBJECT LLC (PA)
33309 1st Way S Ste A208 (98003-6260)
PHONE.....................425 888-8505
Steven Graves, *Mng Member*
Alexander Krivolapov, *Exec Dir*
Andrei Gorine,
EMP: 14
SQ FT: 700
SALES (est): 2.2MM **Privately Held**
WEB: www.mcobject.com
SIC: 7372 Prepackaged software

(G-3758)
MICHAEL SHAW
29811 5th Ave Sw (98023-3516)
PHONE.....................206 669-7597
Michael Shaw, *Principal*
EMP: 2 EST: 2010
SALES (est): 355.3K **Privately Held**
SIC: 3829 Seismoscopes

(G-3759)
MINDCAST SOFTWARE
33530 1st Way S Ste 102 (98003-7332)
PHONE.....................425 341-0350
EMP: 2
SALES (est): 63.8K **Privately Held**
SIC: 7372 Prepackaged software

(G-3760)
MOUNTAIN TREE FARM COMPANY
2515 S 336th St (98001-9769)
P.O. Box 9777 (98063-9777)
PHONE.....................253 924-2345
EMP: 20
SALES (est): 907.6K
SALES (corp-wide): 6.3B **Publicly Held**
SIC: 2411 Logging Company
PA: Weyerhaeuser Company
    220 Occidental Ave S
    Seattle WA 98104
    206 539-3000

(G-3761)
NEW WORLD MARKET LP
2200 S 320th St Ste 1b (98003-5644)
PHONE.....................206 653-7754
EMP: 3 EST: 2014
SALES (est): 174K **Privately Held**
SIC: 2084 2082 Brandy spirits; beer (alcoholic beverage)

(G-3762)
NEXUS AEROSPACE
4034 S 329th St (98001-5164)
PHONE.....................253 797-0700
John Guest, *Administration*
EMP: 2
SALES (est): 112.5K **Privately Held**
SIC: 3721 Aircraft

(G-3763)
NIPPON DYNAWAVE PACKAGING CO
32001 32nd Ave S Ste 310 (98001-9791)
PHONE.....................360 414-3379
EMP: 3 **Privately Held**
SIC: 2675 2631 5113 Cutouts, paper or paperboard: made from purchased materials; packaging board; cups, disposable plastic & paper; paper & products, wrapping or coarse
HQ: Nippon Dynawave Packaging Company, Llc
    3401 Industrial Way
    Longview WA 98632
    360 425-2150

(G-3764)
NORTHWEST EQUIPMENT SALES INC
2011 S 341st Pl (98003-6861)
PHONE.....................253 835-1802
Russell Hibbard, *CEO*
Madison Hibbard, *Executive Asst*
EMP: 6
SALES (est): 780K **Privately Held**
SIC: 3531 Construction machinery

(G-3765)
NORTHWEST TRUCK & AUTO AC
Also Called: Northwest Air Conditioning
30014 5th Ave Sw (98023-3518)
PHONE.....................206 242-6034
Robert J Fulford, *Owner*
EMP: 10
SALES (est): 1MM **Privately Held**
SIC: 3563 7539 7538 Air & gas compressors including vacuum pumps; automotive air conditioning repair; general automotive repair shops

(G-3766)
NOUMENA LLC ✪
1010 S 312th St (98003-4766)
PHONE.....................206 451-3895
Tyrone A Butler,
EMP: 4 EST: 2018
SALES (est): 120.7K **Privately Held**
SIC: 3949 Team sports equipment

(G-3767)
OLYMPIC AEROSPACE INC
34210 9th Ave S Ste 116 (98003-6790)
PHONE.....................253 835-4984
Robert Harpster, *President*
EMP: 6
SALES (est): 1MM **Privately Held**
SIC: 3728 Aircraft parts & equipment

(G-3768)
OLYMPIC AREOSPACE INC
34729 5th Ave Sw (98023-8357)
P.O. Box 25127 (98093-2127)
PHONE.....................253 835-4984
R C Harpster, *President*
EMP: 3 EST: 2011
SALES (est): 333.2K **Privately Held**
SIC: 3728 Aircraft parts & equipment

(G-3769)
PATES RESTAURANT LLC
222 Sw 293rd St (98023-3535)
PHONE.....................253 334-7520
Clayton Pate, *Owner*
EMP: 11
SALES (est): 477K **Privately Held**
SIC: 3421 Table & food cutlery, including butchers'

(G-3770)
PERLAGE SYSTEMS INC
1020 S 344th St (98003-6726)
PHONE.....................253 632-0891
Donna Candiliere, *Manager*
EMP: 2 **Privately Held**
SIC: 3556 Beverage machinery
PA: Perlage Systems, Inc.
    1507 Western Ave Apt 606
    Seattle WA 98101

(G-3771)
PRECISION MACHINE WORKS
401 Sw 322nd St (98023-5632)
PHONE.....................253 661-8180
Mike Hoefel, *Principal*
EMP: 2
SALES (est): 185.4K **Privately Held**
SIC: 3599 Machine shop, jobbing & repair

(G-3772)
PREFERRED ORTHOTIC & PROSTHETC
Also Called: Karl Entenmann Cpo
34709 9th Ave S Ste A100 (98003-6723)
PHONE.....................253 838-6726
Carl Entenmann, *Vice Pres*
EMP: 6 **Privately Held**
SIC: 5999 3842 Orthopedic & prosthesis applications; surgical appliances & supplies
PA: Preferred Orthotic & Prosthetic Services Inc
    1901 S Cedar St Ste 202
    Tacoma WA 98405

(G-3773)
PREMIER SALES NORTHWEST INC
1505 S 356th St Ste 104 (98003-3513)
PHONE.....................206 763-9857
Vaughn Hodgins, *President*
EMP: 4
SALES (est): 452K **Privately Held**
SIC: 3446 Stairs, staircases, stair treads: prefabricated metal

(G-3774)
PYRAMIS AEROSPACE LLC
402 S 333rd St Ste 128 (98003-6073)
PHONE.....................206 407-3406
David Mojica, *Sales Staff*
Maria Rodriguez, *Mng Member*
Ana M Hernandez,
Maria A Hernandez,
EMP: 5
SALES (est): 543.6K **Privately Held**
SIC: 3721 5599 Aircraft; aircraft dealers

(G-3775)
RAMS CUSTOM CABINETS & WDWKG
33107 40th Ave S (98001-5175)
PHONE.....................253 952-2551
EMP: 4 EST: 2009
SALES (est): 270K **Privately Held**
SIC: 2431 Mfg Millwork

(G-3776)
REED PERFORMANCE HEADERS
33534 18th Ave S (98003-6822)
PHONE.....................253 838-7693
EMP: 2 EST: 2011
SALES (est): 110K **Privately Held**
SIC: 3542 Mfg Machine Tools-Forming

(G-3777)
RM METAL WORKS
Also Called: Ron Pircey Race Cars
37205 Pacific Hwy S (98003-7429)
PHONE.....................253 815-0652
Ron Pircey, *Principal*
EMP: 2
SALES (est): 216.9K **Privately Held**
SIC: 3711 Automobile assembly, including specialty automobiles

(G-3778)
RND SIGN AND DESIGN LLC
34737 27th Ave Sw (98023-3077)
P.O. Box 25672 (98093-2672)
PHONE.....................206 255-1963
David W Timme,
EMP: 3
SALES (est): 220.5K **Privately Held**
SIC: 3993 Signs & advertising specialties

(G-3779)
RUTH PUBLISHING LLC
32461 Military Rd S (98001-9634)
PHONE.....................253 351-2375
William Gizrilov, *General Mgr*
Alex Nikolsky,
Olena Nikolsky,
▲ EMP: 2
SALES (est): 168.4K **Privately Held**
SIC: 2731 Books: publishing only

(G-3780)
SAGEMAX BIOCERAMICS INC
34210 9th Ave S Ste 118 (98003-6790)
PHONE.....................253 214-0389
Shen Dang, *President*
◆ EMP: 34
SALES (est): 1MM
SALES (corp-wide): 818.2MM **Privately Held**
SIC: 8072 3843 Dental laboratories; dental equipment & supplies
PA: Ivoclar Vivadent Aktiengesellschaft
    Bendererstrasse 2
    Schaan 9494
    235 353-5

(G-3781)
SCHACHERE INDUSTRIES LLC
33427 Pacific Hwy S E1 (98003-6897)
PHONE.....................253 235-5205
EMP: 2
SALES (est): 120.8K **Privately Held**
SIC: 3999 Manufacturing industries

(G-3782)
SHARP SYNAPTICS LLC
700 Sw 368th St (98023-7264)
PHONE.....................253 927-2616
EMP: 5
SALES (est): 141.8K **Privately Held**
SIC: 7372 Prepackaged Software Services

(G-3783)
SHIRTZ TO GO INC
28717 Pacific Hwy S Ste 1 (98003-2974)
PHONE.....................206 242-4055
Bishop Deveraux, *Manager*
EMP: 4
SALES (corp-wide): 885K **Privately Held**
WEB: www.shirtztogo.com
SIC: 5611 2759 5699 Men's & boys' clothing stores; screen printing; T-shirts, custom printed
PA: Shirtz To Go Inc
    77 Wells Ave S
    Renton WA 98057
    206 949-5989

(G-3784)
SIGN GUYS INC
1714 S 341st Pl (98003-8997)
PHONE.....................253 942-3688
Byung Cha, *President*
EMP: 2
SQ FT: 1,000
SALES (est): 145.4K **Privately Held**
SIC: 3993 Signs & advertising specialties

(G-3785)
SLAM SIGNS
700 Sw 368th St (98023-7264)
PHONE.....................253 927-2616
EMP: 2
SALES (est): 129.3K **Privately Held**
SIC: 3993 Mfg Signs/Advertising Specialties

(G-3786)
SOUND PUBLISHING INC
Also Called: Little Nickel Classifieds
1010 S 336th St Ste 330 (98003-7354)
PHONE.....................253 437-6000
Lynette Portello, *Branch Mgr*
EMP: 8 **Privately Held**
WEB: www.soundpublishing.com
SIC: 2711 2721 2741 Newspapers: publishing only, not printed on site; periodicals: publishing only; shopping news: publishing only, not printed on site
HQ: Sound Publishing, Inc.
    11323 Commando Rd W Main
    Everett WA 98204
    360 394-5800

(G-3787)
SOUND PUBLISHING INC
Also Called: Federal Way Mirror
1010 S 336th St Ste 330 (98003-7354)
PHONE.....................253 925-5565
Kay Miller, *Advt Staff*
Rudi Alcott, *Branch Mgr*
EMP: 9 **Privately Held**
WEB: www.soundpublishing.com
SIC: 2711 Newspapers: publishing only, not printed on site
HQ: Sound Publishing, Inc.
    11323 Commando Rd W Main
    Everett WA 98204
    360 394-5800

Federal Way - King County (G-3788)

(G-3788)
SOUND PUBLISHING INC
Also Called: Kent Reporter
1010 S 336th St Ste 330 (98003-7354)
PHONE.................................253 872-6600
Mark Klaas, *Editor*
Polly Shepherd, *Branch Mgr*
EMP: 29 **Privately Held**
WEB: www.soundpublishing.com
SIC: 2711 Newspapers: publishing only, not printed on site
HQ: Sound Publishing, Inc.
11323 Commando Rd W Main
Everett WA 98204
360 394-5800

(G-3789)
SOUTH SOUND AQUAPONICS LLC
1847 S 310th St Unit B (98003-4956)
PHONE.................................206 510-0408
Brian D Norton, *Administration*
EMP: 2
SALES (est): 89.9K **Privately Held**
SIC: 0259 2095 5193 Duck farm; roasted coffee; nursery stock

(G-3790)
SPIRIT OF WINDS INCENSE ST
455 S 305th St (98003-4020)
PHONE.................................253 293-2743
Regis Belcher, *Principal*
EMP: 2 EST: 2014
SALES (est): 164.1K **Privately Held**
SIC: 2899 Incense

(G-3791)
SUN PRINTING
33304 Pcf Hwy S Ste 304 (98003)
PHONE.................................253 517-5017
Eric Hwang, *Owner*
Les Thompson, *Manager*
EMP: 2
SQ FT: 1,000
SALES (est): 203.1K **Privately Held**
SIC: 2752 2759 Commercial printing, lithographic; commercial printing

(G-3792)
SUNNE GROUP LTD INC
Also Called: Euro Amport
1302 S 293rd Pl (98003-3756)
PHONE.................................253 839-5240
Vito Rizzo, *President*
Anita Goransson, *Vice Pres*
▲ EMP: 2
SALES (est): 110.7K **Privately Held**
SIC: 2052 Cookies

(G-3793)
TAMU FOODS
1112 S 344th St (98003-6797)
PHONE.................................253 835-1855
Lydia Kariuki, *Owner*
EMP: 2
SALES: 50K **Privately Held**
SIC: 2099 Food preparations

(G-3794)
TESORO COMPANIES INC
3450 S 344th Way Ste 100 (98001-5931)
PHONE.................................253 896-8700
Joseph Sparino, *President*
EMP: 60 **Publicly Held**
SIC: 1311 2911 Crude petroleum & natural gas; petroleum refining
HQ: Tesoro Companies, Inc.
19100 Ridgewood Pkwy
San Antonio TX 78259
210 626-7390

(G-3795)
TEXAS INSTRUMENTS INC
3455 S 344th Way (98001-9560)
PHONE.................................253 927-0754
EMP: 2
SALES (est): 90K **Privately Held**
SIC: 3674 Microprocessors

(G-3796)
TOBACCO STATION-WA
34815 Pacific Hwy S # 201 (98003-8371)
PHONE.................................253 517-5618
Donald Frederick Urban, *Principal*
EMP: 2
SALES (est): 160.6K **Privately Held**
SIC: 2131 Smoking tobacco

(G-3797)
TRANSGOODS AMERICA INC
33400 9th Ave S Ste 114 (98003-2607)
PHONE.................................253 661-0440
Li Liu, *President*
Chun Lei Dong, *Vice Pres*
▲ EMP: 2
SALES (est): 234K
SALES (corp-wide): 5.7B **Privately Held**
SIC: 3743 5088 Railroad equipment; railroad equipment & supplies
PA: China Railway Materials Group Co., Ltd.
Guohai Plaza B,No.17,Fuxing Road,Haidian Dist.
Beijing 10003
105 189-5249

(G-3798)
TRINITY GLASS INTL INC (PA)
33615 1st Way S Ste A (98003-4558)
PHONE.................................800 803-8182
Jong Ham, *President*
Ki Ham, *Vice Pres*
Alex Lee, *CFO*
John Yi, *Technology*
Chong So, *Admin Sec*
◆ EMP: 85
SALES (est): 56.3MM **Privately Held**
WEB: www.trinityglassinternational.com
SIC: 2431 Doors, wood

(G-3799)
VALMET INC
34320 Pacific Hwy S (98003-6816)
PHONE.................................253 927-2200
Don Shull, *Manager*
EMP: 42
SALES (corp-wide): 3.8B **Privately Held**
WEB: www.metso.com
SIC: 3069 7629 Roll coverings, rubber; electrical repair shops
HQ: Valmet, Inc.
2425 Commerce Ave Ste 100
Duluth GA 30096
770 263-7863

(G-3800)
VETERANS EXPRESS
1300 Sw Campus Dr 14-7 (98023-5363)
PHONE.................................253 517-3798
EMP: 2
SALES (est): 102.2K **Privately Held**
SIC: 2741 8641 Misc Publishing Civic/Social Association

(G-3801)
VILMAS FAMILY CORPORATION
Also Called: Vilma Signs
30432 Military Rd S (98003-4849)
PHONE.................................253 941-9008
Vilma Stewart, *President*
Mariea Cohen, *Vice Pres*
Janet Stewart, *Treasurer*
EMP: 5
SQ FT: 3,000
SALES (est): 573.9K **Privately Held**
WEB: www.vilmasigns.com
SIC: 2396 3993 Screen printing on fabric articles; signs & advertising specialties

(G-3802)
WESTERN WASH SAFETY CONSLT
34213 31st Ave Sw (98023-7633)
P.O. Box 24743 (98093-1743)
PHONE.................................253 815-7920
Bruce D Johnson, *President*
Jacqueline Johnson, *Vice Pres*
EMP: 2
SALES (est): 250K **Privately Held**
SIC: 3842 Personal safety equipment

(G-3803)
WESTFALL GOODEN SFO CO
500 S 336th St (98003-6389)
PHONE.................................253 344-1025
Carolyn G Dunstone, *Principal*
EMP: 3 EST: 2012
SALES (est): 247K **Privately Held**
SIC: 2911 Petroleum refining

(G-3804)
XYZ MANUFACTURING
1611 Sw 325th Pl (98023-5419)
P.O. Box 26836 (98093-3836)
PHONE.................................206 402-1936
EMP: 2
SALES (est): 108.7K **Privately Held**
SIC: 3999 Manufacturing industries

(G-3805)
YOUNGS NEON SIGN CO
30318 13th Ave S (98003-4145)
PHONE.................................253 946-1286
Chang Lee, *Owner*
EMP: 2
SALES (est): 142.7K **Privately Held**
SIC: 5099 3993 Signs, except electric; neon signs

(G-3806)
YOUNGWOL NOODLE
31260 Pacific Hwy S (98003-5448)
PHONE.................................253 941-2002
Hay Young Kim, *Owner*
EMP: 4
SALES (est): 219.9K **Privately Held**
SIC: 2098 Noodles (e.g. egg, plain & water), dry

Ferndale
Whatcom County

(G-3807)
3DX INDUSTRIES INC
6920 Salashan Pkwy D101 (98248-8395)
PHONE.................................360 244-4339
Roger Jenssen, *President*
Jennie Canfield, *QC Mgr*
EMP: 3 EST: 1986
SALES (est): 480.1K **Privately Held**
WEB: www.key-mfg.com
SIC: 3541 Machine tools, metal cutting type

(G-3808)
3DX INDUSTRIES INC
6920 Salashan Pkwy D101 (98248-8395)
PHONE.................................360 244-4339
Roger Janssen, *President*
Earl W Abbott, *Executive*
EMP: 2
SQ FT: 8,588
SALES (est): 386.5K **Privately Held**
SIC: 1041 1044 Gold ores; silver ores

(G-3809)
ADVANCED ALL WHEEL DRIVE
2869 W 63rd Ln (98248-9697)
PHONE.................................360 746-8746
Tim Walker, *Principal*
EMP: 2
SALES (est): 174.2K **Privately Held**
SIC: 3312 Blast furnaces & steel mills

(G-3810)
ADVANCED ROUTER TECHNOLOGY
Also Called: ACS
1355 Pacific Pl Ste 117 (98248-7827)
PHONE.................................360 318-7534
Ron Rankin, *President*
EMP: 2 EST: 2010
SALES (est): 150.9K **Privately Held**
SIC: 3544 Dies & die holders for metal cutting, forming, die casting

(G-3811)
ALL AMERICAN METAL PRODUCTS
4999 Labounty Dr (98248-8915)
PHONE.................................360 380-6202
Sam Menzies, *President*
▲ EMP: 6
SQ FT: 1,479
SALES (est): 802.3K **Privately Held**
SIC: 3444 5033 Roof deck, sheet metal; downspouts, sheet metal; metal ventilating equipment; fiberglass building materials

(G-3812)
AMERICAN MANUFACTURING CORP
Also Called: American Group-Samson Division
2090 Thornton St (98248-9314)
PHONE.................................360 384-4669
Stephen Swiackey, *President*
EMP: 120
SALES (corp-wide): 153MM **Privately Held**
WEB: www.theamcgroup.com
SIC: 2298 Cordage: abaca, sisal, henequen, hemp, jute or other fiber; rope, except asbestos & wire
PA: American Manufacturing Corporation
555 Croton Rd Ste 200
King Of Prussia PA 19406
610 962-3770

(G-3813)
AMERICAN NETTINGS & FABRIC INC
2684 Delta Ring Rd (98248-8818)
P.O. Box 227, Custer (98240-0227)
PHONE.................................360 366-2630
Ross Bernard, *President*
Dorian Bernard, *Principal*
Dorothy Bernard, *Corp Secy*
◆ EMP: 10
SALES (est): 2MM **Privately Held**
SIC: 3089 Netting, plastic

(G-3814)
ANT FX INTERNATIONAL LLC
2625 Delta Ring Rd Ste 3 (98248-8818)
PHONE.................................253 302-7414
Nicholas Vaandering, *CEO*
Anthony Dowsett, *Principal*
Nadia Kotyakov, *Principal*
Justin Perry, *Principal*
Benjamin Tolman, *Principal*
EMP: 2 EST: 2017
SALES (est): 74.4K **Privately Held**
SIC: 2842 Automobile polish

(G-3815)
APPEL FARMS LLC
6605a Northwest Dr (98248-9456)
PHONE.................................360 384-4996
John Appel,
EMP: 11
SQ FT: 932
SALES (est): 1.3MM **Privately Held**
WEB: www.appelfarms.com
SIC: 2022 Cheese, natural & processed

(G-3816)
AQUATIC LIFE SCIENCES INC (PA)
1441 W Smith Rd (98248-8933)
PHONE.................................800 283-5292
Steve Becker, *CEO*
Jim Brackett, *President*
Jim Code, *Shareholder*
Robert Code, *Shareholder*
▲ EMP: 12
SALES (est): 2.8MM **Privately Held**
SIC: 2834 Veterinary pharmaceutical preparations

(G-3817)
BARLEANS FISHERY INC
3660 Slater Rd (98248-9518)
PHONE.................................360 384-0325
Cindy Smith, *President*
Ronan Smith, *Vice Pres*
EMP: 5 EST: 1972
SALES (est): 1.6MM **Privately Held**
WEB: www.barleansfishery.com
SIC: 5146 0912 2091 Fish & seafoods; salmon, catching of; fish, smoked

(G-3818)
BARLEANS ORGANIC OILS LLC
3660 Slater Rd (98248-9518)
PHONE.................................360 384-0485
Audrey Myers, *Purch Agent*
Bruce Barlean, *Mng Member*
David Barlean, *Mng Member*
Barbara Barlean,
▲ EMP: 175

GEOGRAPHIC SECTION

Ferndale - Whatcom County (G-3847)

SALES (est): 28.1MM Privately Held
WEB: www.barleans.com
SIC: 5499 2079 Health & dietetic food stores; vegetable refined oils (except corn oil)

(G-3819)
BUTLER DESIGN INC
7072 Kickerville Rd (98248-8795)
P.O. Box 6 (98248-0006)
PHONE..................................360 380-1651
John Butler, *President*
Ted Swanson, *Admin Sec*
EMP: 5
SQ FT: 10,000
SALES (est): 652.8K Privately Held
SIC: 2621 8999 Wallpaper (hanging paper); artist's studio

(G-3820)
C QUARTZ INC
Also Called: C-Quarts
5863 Portal Way Unit 104 (98248-9338)
P.O. Box 2508 (98248-2508)
PHONE..................................360 393-1254
Ronald Azevedo, *President*
Theresa Azevedo, *Vice Pres*
EMP: 2
SALES (est): 193.9K Privately Held
SIC: 3679 Quartz crystals, for electronic application

(G-3821)
C S ADVENTURECORP LLC
Also Called: Jbm Press
6470 Portal Manor Dr (98248-8378)
PHONE..................................425 679-1172
Clarissa Lacefield, *CEO*
Phil Lacefield Jr, *Chief Engr*
EMP: 2
SQ FT: 3,000
SALES: 50K Privately Held
SIC: 2759 Screen printing

(G-3822)
CANDELA TECHNOLOGIES INC
2417 Main St Ste 201 (98248-8834)
P.O. Box 3285 (98248-3260)
PHONE..................................360 380-1618
Ben Greear, *President*
Hun-Kyi Wynn, *Vice Pres*
Jed Reynolds, *Technology*
▼ EMP: 4
SQ FT: 2,500
SALES: 1.1MM Privately Held
WEB: www.candelatech.com
SIC: 7371 7372 Computer software development; business oriented computer software

(G-3823)
CARGILL INCORPORATED
5744 3rd Ave (98248-8392)
P.O. Box 39 (98248-0039)
PHONE..................................360 656-5784
Andrew Loder, *General Mgr*
EMP: 50
SALES (corp-wide): 114.7B Privately Held
WEB: www.cargill.com
SIC: 5191 2048 Feed; prepared feeds
PA: Cargill, Incorporated
    15407 Mcginty Rd W
    Wayzata MN 55391
    952 742-7575

(G-3824)
CARLS MOWER AND SAW
Also Called: Carl' S Mower and Saw
6209 Portal Way (98248-9362)
PHONE..................................360 384-0799
Carl Levien, *Owner*
Josh Levien, *General Mgr*
Clayton Levien, *Parts Mgr*
EMP: 6
SQ FT: 3,000
SALES: 225K Privately Held
WEB: www.carlsmowerandsaw.com
SIC: 5261 7699 3546 Lawnmowers & tractors; garden supplies & tools; power tool repair; saws & sawing equipment

(G-3825)
CASCADE DAFO INC
1360 Sunset Ave (98248-8913)
PHONE..................................360 543-9306

Cheryl Persse, *President*
Donald Buethorn, *Corp Secy*
Candace Buethorn, *Vice Pres*
William Weymer, *Plant Mgr*
Diane Hodgkins, *Research*
EMP: 300
SQ FT: 32,000
SALES (est): 47.9MM Privately Held
WEB: www.cascadedafo.com
SIC: 3842 Limbs, artificial; orthopedic appliances

(G-3826)
CASCADE JOINERY INC
1349 Pacific Pl Ste 103 (98248-8985)
P.O. Box 5807, Bellingham (98227-5807)
PHONE..................................360 527-0119
Craig Aument, *President*
John Miller, *Treasurer*
Susan Brown, *Bookkeeper*
Phil Kneisley, *Human Res Dir*
EMP: 10
SQ FT: 6,000
SALES: 1.5MM Privately Held
WEB: www.cascadejoinery.com
SIC: 1521 8711 2452 New construction, single-family houses; engineering services; prefabricated wood buildings

(G-3827)
CASCADE NETS INC
2138 Buchanan Loop (98248-9801)
PHONE..................................866 738-8071
Eric Jonsson, *President*
Tony Jonsson, *Vice Pres*
Debbie Willkie, *Admin Sec*
EMP: 6
SQ FT: 5,000
SALES: 1MM Privately Held
WEB: www.cascadenets.com
SIC: 2258 Net & netting products

(G-3828)
CASCADE PRSTHTICS ORTHTICS INC (PA)
1360 Sunset Ave (98248-8913)
PHONE..................................360 384-1858
Sheryl Persse, *CEO*
Candace Buethorn, *Vice Pres*
Don Buethorn, *Treasurer*
Heather Barthlow, *Office Mgr*
Sophia Evans, *Info Tech Mgr*
EMP: 15
SQ FT: 10,000
SALES (est): 1.8MM Privately Held
SIC: 3842 Prosthetic appliances

(G-3829)
CEDARVILLE SHAKE & SHINGLE MIL
3353 Breslin Ln (98248-8607)
PHONE..................................360 715-1856
James Underwood, *Principal*
EMP: 2
SALES (est): 86.7K Privately Held
SIC: 2429 Shingle mill

(G-3830)
CHEMCO ACQUISITION CORPORATION
4191 Grandview Rd (98248-8540)
P.O. Box 875 (98248-0875)
PHONE..................................360 366-3500
Fred Amundson, *CEO*
John Gibb, *President*
▲ EMP: 45
SALES: 3MM Privately Held
SIC: 2861 Gum & wood chemicals

(G-3831)
CJ MANUFACTURING I INC
7050 Portal Way Ste 140 (98248-9830)
PHONE..................................360 543-5297
David Edward Palka, *Administration*
EMP: 3
SALES (est): 196.2K Privately Held
SIC: 3999 Manufacturing industries

(G-3832)
CLEAR-FX LLC
Also Called: Clear Fx International
2625 Delta Ring Rd Ste 3 (98248-8818)
PHONE..................................800 408-3701
Nicholas Vaandering, *CEO*
Nadia Kotyakov, *Principal*

Justin Perry, *Principal*
Benjamin Tolman, *Principal*
EMP: 10
SALES (est): 1.1MM Privately Held
SIC: 2842 Automobile polish

(G-3833)
COOKES CANVAS & SEWING
5040 Pacific Hwy (98248-8922)
PHONE..................................360 384-1636
Fax: 360 384-2480
EMP: 2 EST: 2010
SALES (est): 72K Privately Held
SIC: 2211 Cotton Broadwoven Fabric Mill

(G-3834)
COTTAGE SIGN CO
6193 Hamilton Ave (98248-5407)
PHONE..................................360 312-1565
Jessica Richins, *Principal*
EMP: 2
SALES (est): 136.6K Privately Held
SIC: 3993 Signs & advertising specialties

(G-3835)
CUTSFORTH INC (PA)
5160 Industrial Pl # 101 (98248-7819)
PHONE..................................800 290-6458
Robert Cutsforth, *CEO*
Dustin L Cutsforth, *Vice Pres*
EMP: 38
SQ FT: 9,000
SALES: 12MM Privately Held
WEB: www.cutsforth.com
SIC: 3621 Commutators, electric motor

(G-3836)
DISTILLERS WAY LLC
5235 Industrial Pl (98248-7813)
PHONE..................................360 927-8781
EMP: 3
SALES (est): 74.1K Privately Held
SIC: 2085 Distilled & blended liquors

(G-3837)
EDT CORP
5345 Labounty Dr (98248-9438)
PHONE..................................360 574-7294
Carl G Klinge, *President*
Sue Meyer, *Corp Secy*
EMP: 10
SQ FT: 12,000
SALES (est): 2.9MM
SALES (corp-wide): 3.5B Publicly Held
WEB: www.edtcorp.com
SIC: 3089 Bearings, plastic
PA: The Timken Company
    4500 Mount Pleasant St Nw
    North Canton OH 44720
    234 262-3000

(G-3838)
EMB CREATE INC
4958 Pacific Hwy (98248-8921)
PHONE..................................360 384-8072
Laurie Irwin, *Principal*
Kim Cruz, *Mng Member*
EMP: 2
SALES (est): 140.5K Privately Held
WEB: www.embcreate.com
SIC: 2395 Embroidery products, except schiffli machine; embroidery & art needlework

(G-3839)
EVOLUTION TECHNOLOGIES USA
2657 Delta Ring Rd (98248-8818)
PHONE..................................360 392-8600
Stephen Liu, *President*
▲ EMP: 6
SALES: 500K Privately Held
SIC: 3842 2599 Wheelchairs; hospital beds

(G-3840)
FAST HORTICULTURAL SERVICES
Also Called: Red Barn Lavender
3106 Thornton Rd (98248-9296)
PHONE..................................360 393-7057
Marvin Fast, *Owner*
Lynn Fast, *Co-Owner*
EMP: 2

SALES (est): 133.2K Privately Held
WEB: www.redbarnlavender.com
SIC: 2844 Face creams or lotions

(G-3841)
FASTCAP LLC
5016 Pacific Hwy (98248-8922)
PHONE..................................888 443-3748
Paul A Akers, *Mng Member*
Leanne Akers,
◆ EMP: 20
SQ FT: 6,000
SALES (est): 5.3MM Privately Held
WEB: www.fastcap.com
SIC: 3089 2449 3643 Plastic containers, except foam; wood containers; current-carrying wiring devices

(G-3842)
FERNDALE CREAMERY CO LLC
2780 Aldergrove Rd (98248-8604)
PHONE..................................360 255-7062
William Wavnh, *Principal*
EMP: 5
SALES (est): 417.4K Privately Held
SIC: 2021 Creamery butter

(G-3843)
FERNDALE READY-MIX
5271 Creighton Rd (98248-9497)
PHONE..................................360 384-8087
Brad Dehaan, *Vice Pres*
EMP: 15
SALES (est): 2.2MM
SALES (corp-wide): 3.9MM Privately Held
WEB: www.ferndalereadymix.net
SIC: 3273 Ready-mixed concrete
PA: Ferndale Ready-Mix
    144 River Rd
    Lynden WA 98264
    360 354-1400

(G-3844)
FERNDALE RECORD INC
Also Called: West Side Record Journal
2004 Main St (98248-9468)
P.O. Box 153, Lynden (98264-0153)
PHONE..................................360 384-1411
Michael Lewis, *President*
Jan Brown, *Adv Mgr*
EMP: 3
SQ FT: 3,000
SALES (est): 214.7K Privately Held
SIC: 2711 2741 Newspapers: publishing only, not printed on site; shopping news: publishing only, not printed on site

(G-3845)
FERROTEK CORPORATION
7135 Delta Line Rd (98248-7704)
PHONE..................................360 366-7444
Klaus Klix, *President*
George Edwards, *Corp Secy*
Brian Philliber, *Vice Pres*
EMP: 15
SQ FT: 6,000
SALES (est): 3MM Privately Held
WEB: www.ferrotek.com
SIC: 3441 3711 1799 Fabricated structural metal; motor vehicles & car bodies; welding on site

(G-3846)
G R PLUME CO
1373 W Smith Rd (98248-8930)
P.O. Box 937 (98248-0937)
PHONE..................................360 384-2800
Gordon Plume, *President*
Robin Plume, *Admin Sec*
EMP: 10
SQ FT: 10,000
SALES: 2.5MM Privately Held
WEB: www.grplume.com
SIC: 1521 2439 2431 General remodeling, single-family houses; new construction, single-family houses; structural wood members; millwork

(G-3847)
GARRISON FUEL TECH
5897 Aspen Ave (98248-9252)
PHONE..................................360 739-2634
Anthony Garrison, *Principal*
EMP: 3 EST: 2014

Ferndale - Whatcom County (G-3848)

SALES (est): 188.2K **Privately Held**
SIC: 2869 Fuels

(G-3848)
GDS DIRECT COUNTERTOPS LTD
5506 Nielsen Ave Ste D (98248-8960)
PHONE 360 312-9688
Garret Murker, *President*
Dan Morecombe, *Treasurer*
▲ **EMP:** 2
SALES (est): 130K **Privately Held**
SIC: 2541 Counter & sink tops

(G-3849)
GREENBERRY INDUSTRIAL LLC
6980 Salashan Pkwy (98248-8314)
PHONE 360 366-3767
Troy Goodreau, *Branch Mgr*
EMP: 5
SQ FT: 49,430 **Privately Held**
SIC: 1711 1541 3443 3441 Mechanical contractor; industrial buildings & warehouses; fabricated plate work (boiler shop); fabricated structural metal
HQ: Greenberry Industrial Llc
600 Se Maritime Ave # 190
Vancouver WA 98661
360 567-0006

(G-3850)
HEALTHY PET LP
Also Called: Healthy Pet BB&T Johson Square
6960 Salashan Pkwy (98248-8314)
PHONE 360 734-7415
Ted Mischaikov, *CEO*
Bill Gunter, *Opers Staff*
Tom Redd, *Production*
Bill Van Antwerp, *Production*
Todd Catey, *Purchasing*
▲ **EMP:** 130
SALES (est): 36.3MM
SALES (corp-wide): 355.8K **Privately Held**
WEB: www.socksandpads.com
SIC: 3999 2899 Pet supplies; oil absorption equipment
HQ: J. Rettenmaier & Sohne Gmbh + Co. Kg
Holzmuhle 1
Rosenberg 73494
796 715-20

(G-3851)
HERTCO KITCHENS LLC
1810 Scout Pl (98248-8937)
PHONE 360 380-1100
Doug Blaschuk,
Xuong Dich,
Sven Lincke,
EMP: 70
SQ FT: 30,000
SALES (est): 6.8MM **Privately Held**
WEB: www.hertco.com
SIC: 2434 Wood kitchen cabinets

(G-3852)
HOME FIRE PREST LOGS LTD
6925 Salashan Pkwy (98248-8314)
PHONE 360 366-2200
Glenn Hermanson, *President*
Virginia Hermanson, *Director*
EMP: 13
SALES (est): 950K **Privately Held**
SIC: 3433 Logs, gas fireplace

(G-3853)
HOUSTORY PUBLISHING LLC
6161 Glacier Pl (98248-8321)
P.O. Box 1465 (98248-1465)
PHONE 877 962-6500
Michael Hiestand,
EMP: 3
SALES (est): 217K **Privately Held**
SIC: 2731 Books: publishing only

(G-3854)
HOWARD FABRICATION
6968 Dahlberg Rd (98248-9711)
PHONE 360 380-1721
Travis Howard, *Owner*
EMP: 3
SALES (est): 239.1K **Privately Held**
SIC: 3732 Non-motorized boat, building & repairing

(G-3855)
INDUSTRIAL DESIGN & EQP INC
Also Called: Indeco
1518 Slater Rd (98248-9121)
PHONE 360 671-9200
Craig Wasilewski, *President*
EMP: 7
SALES (est): 1.2MM **Privately Held**
WEB: www.indeco-usa.com
SIC: 3914 Stainless steel ware

(G-3856)
INFINITY BUILDING MTLS LLC
4084 Saltspring Dr (98248-9538)
PHONE 804 921-0810
William Church, *CEO*
Armistead Church, *Ch of Bd*
Scott Renneckar, *Ch of Bd*
EMP: 4
SALES (est): 196K **Privately Held**
SIC: 2436 2435 Softwood veneer & plywood; panels, hardwood plywood

(G-3857)
INNOVATIVE FREEZE DRIED FD LLC
6025 Portal Way (98248-9360)
PHONE 855 836-3233
Terry Sebastian, *Chairman*
EMP: 22
SALES: 5MM **Privately Held**
SIC: 2099 Food preparations

(G-3858)
INSTRUMENT & VALVE SERVICES CO
6920 Salashan Pkwy E208 (98248-8320)
PHONE 360 366-3645
Jim Boyles, *Principal*
EMP: 50
SALES (corp-wide): 17.4B **Publicly Held**
SIC: 3494 Valves & pipe fittings
HQ: Instrument and Valve Services Company
205 S Center St
Marshalltown IA 50158

(G-3859)
INTALCO ALUMINUM LLC
Also Called: Alcoa Intalco Works
4050 Mountain View Rd (98248-9683)
PHONE 360 384-7061
A Sue Zemba, *Vice Pres*
Patricia Martin, *Senior Buyer*
Peter Hong, *Treasurer*
Nicklaus A Oliver, *Admin Sec*
Roman Garcia, *Maintence Staff*
◆ **EMP:** 750
SQ FT: 181,250
SALES (est): 228.8MM
SALES (corp-wide): 13.4B **Publicly Held**
SIC: 3334 Ingots (primary), aluminum
PA: Alcoa Corporation
201 Isabella St Ste 500
Pittsburgh PA 15212
412 315-2900

(G-3860)
INTERNATIONAL ATHLETIC
Also Called: I A Rugby.com
2044 Main St (98248-9468)
P.O. Box 126 (98248-0126)
PHONE 360 384-6868
Jeffrey P Lombard, *Owner*
▲ **EMP:** 5
SQ FT: 5,000
SALES (est): 537.4K **Privately Held**
WEB: www.iarugby.com
SIC: 5941 5961 2396 2393 Soccer supplies; mail order house; screen printing on fabric articles; canvas bags

(G-3861)
J & S MANUFACTURING INC
Also Called: Baker Commodities
1508 Slater Rd (98248)
PHONE 360 384-5553
Dick Hawthorne, *President*
EMP: 2
SALES (est): 141.1K **Privately Held**
SIC: 2077 Animal & marine fats & oils

(G-3862)
J A LEASING INC
6067 Portal Way (98248-8345)
P.O. Box 397 (98248-0397)
PHONE 360 380-5290
Chuck Elashkar, *President*
EMP: 3
SALES (est): 293K **Privately Held**
SIC: 3537 Trucks, tractors, loaders, carriers & similar equipment

(G-3863)
J L POWDER CTG
6585 Vista Dr (98248-8715)
PHONE 360 380-3898
Jeff Lorenz, *Principal*
EMP: 3
SALES (est): 192.2K **Privately Held**
SIC: 3399 Powder, metal

(G-3864)
KITTY CRIBS LLC
1245 W Axton Rd (98248-9100)
PHONE 360 312-8102
William T Ransom, *Principal*
William Ransom, *Mng Member*
EMP: 2
SALES (est): 150.1K **Privately Held**
SIC: 2519 Household furniture

(G-3865)
LORENZ WELDING
2248 Aldergrove Rd (98248-9322)
PHONE 360 384-5258
EMP: 2
SALES (est): 114.3K **Privately Held**
SIC: 7692 1799 Welding Repair Shop & Portable Welding On Site

(G-3866)
LOU HINKLEY
Also Called: Daedalus Cabinets
7060 Portal Way Ste 120 (98248-9833)
PHONE 360 312-3604
Lou Hinkley, *Owner*
EMP: 2
SQ FT: 4,000
SALES (est): 140K **Privately Held**
SIC: 2517 Stereo cabinets, wood

(G-3867)
MANUFLAXSTERIT LLC
3660 Slater Rd (98248-9518)
PHONE 360 384-0485
Bruce Barlean,
▲ **EMP:** 70 **EST:** 2001
SALES (est): 10.2MM **Privately Held**
SIC: 2869 Fatty acid esters, aminos, etc.

(G-3868)
MEKLTEK ENGINEERING & MFG
Also Called: Micro Electronics
6229 Aldrich Rd (98248-9483)
PHONE 360 384-1607
Peter P Ruese, *Owner*
EMP: 2
SALES (est): 174.4K **Privately Held**
SIC: 3625 5065 Electric controls & control accessories, industrial; electronic parts & equipment

(G-3869)
MERCURIUS BIOFUELS LLC
3190 Bay Rd (98248-9691)
PHONE 360 941-7207
Michael Vevera, *General Mgr*
Karl Seck, *Mng Member*
EMP: 4
SALES (est): 402.2K **Privately Held**
SIC: 2899 Chemical preparations

(G-3870)
METRIE INC
5575 Nordic Pl (98248-9138)
PHONE 360 863-1730
EMP: 35
SALES (corp-wide): 202.9K **Privately Held**
SIC: 2431 Mfg Millwork
HQ: Metrie Inc.
2200 140th Ave E Ste 600
Sumner WA 98390
253 470-5050

(G-3871)
MIKE BRECKON
2722 Douglas Rd (98248-8907)
P.O. Box 2351 (98248-2351)
PHONE 360 380-0622
Mike Breckon, *Mng Member*
Lori Breckon,
EMP: 3
SQ FT: 1,782
SALES (est): 201.8K **Privately Held**
SIC: 2092 Fish, frozen: prepared

(G-3872)
MIRROR FINISH INCORPORATED
2508 Brown Rd (98248-9633)
PHONE 360 384-1710
Joshua Leibrant, *President*
Cheryl Mitchell, *Treasurer*
James O'Laire, *Shareholder*
EMP: 6
SQ FT: 160
SALES (est): 26K **Privately Held**
SIC: 2431 Door trim, wood

(G-3873)
MOBERG & COMPANY
6726 Northwest Dr (98248-9457)
PHONE 360 380-5257
Fred Moberg, *Owner*
EMP: 5
SQ FT: 1,027
SALES (est): 300K **Privately Held**
SIC: 2448 Cargo containers, wood & wood with metal

(G-3874)
MODERN ART WOODWORK LLC
6036 N Star Rd (98248-8702)
PHONE 360 303-6054
Rhonda Delaney, *Principal*
EMP: 4
SALES (est): 387.3K **Privately Held**
SIC: 2431 Millwork

(G-3875)
MOTHERWELL PRODUCTS USA INC
7074 Portal Way Ste 140 (98248-9840)
PHONE 360 366-2600
Kelly Motherwell, *President*
▲ **EMP:** 3
SQ FT: 4,000
SALES (est): 443.8K **Privately Held**
SIC: 3751 Motorcycles & related parts

(G-3876)
NEXTLEVEL TRAINING LLC
Also Called: Sirt
5160 Industrial Pl # 101 (98248-7819)
PHONE 360 933-4640
Michael Hughes, *Mng Member*
Steve Booth,
EMP: 7
SALES (est): 950K **Privately Held**
SIC: 3699 Electrical equipment & supplies

(G-3877)
NORTHWEST LIME CO LLC
6175 Aldrich Rd (98248-9427)
PHONE 360 815-0304
Bradley Youngquist, *Mng Member*
EMP: 2
SQ FT: 1,920
SALES: 375K **Privately Held**
SIC: 1411 Limestone & marble dimension stone

(G-3878)
NORTHWEST PAPER CONVERTERS INC
5441 Labounty Dr (98248-8936)
P.O. Box 223 (98248-0223)
PHONE 800 681-9748
Rick Anderson, *Principal*
▲ **EMP:** 10
SALES (est): 1.5MM **Privately Held**
SIC: 3554 7694 Paper mill machinery: plating, slitting, waxing, etc.; rewinding services

GEOGRAPHIC SECTION

Ferndale - Whatcom County (G-3909)

(G-3879)
NUOVO PARTS INC
Also Called: Wiseworth Canada
1465 Slater Rd (98248-8919)
PHONE 360 738-1888
Stan Thompson, *President*
EMP: 6
SALES (est): 5.4MM **Privately Held**
SIC: 3533 Oil & gas drilling rigs & equipment

(G-3880)
NUTRADRIED FOOD COMPANY LLC
Also Called: Moon Cheese
6920 Salashan Pkwy D111 (98248-8320)
PHONE 360 366-4567
Michael Pytlinski, *CEO*
Joseph Spinazola, *Senior VP*
Hung Huynh, *Controller*
EMP: 70
SALES (est): 6.3MM
SALES (corp-wide): 12.7MM **Privately Held**
SIC: 2022 Pastes, cheese
PA: Enwave Corporation
1668 Derwent Way Unit 1
Delta BC V3M 6
604 806-6110

(G-3881)
OPEN WATER SPLICING
5867 Portal Way Unit 103 (98248-9338)
PHONE 360 510-8059
Ray Froneberter,
EMP: 2
SQ FT: 2,000
SALES (est): 135K **Privately Held**
SIC: 2298 Slings, rope

(G-3882)
PACIFIC POWDER COATING INC
7072 Portal Way Ste 110 (98248-9839)
PHONE 360 383-9100
Tony Devries, *CEO*
Marcy Freese, *Admin Sec*
EMP: 2
SALES (est): 167.9K **Privately Held**
SIC: 3479 Coating of metals & formed products

(G-3883)
PATRIOT WOOD LLC
4122 Stuart Cir (98248-9001)
PHONE 360 393-7082
Arthur Pinney, *Principal*
EMP: 2
SALES (est): 187K **Privately Held**
SIC: 3993 Signs & advertising specialties

(G-3884)
PATS BLUE RIBBONS & TROPHIES
6738 Family Hill Ln (98248-8537)
PHONE 360 676-8292
Lloyd Anderson, *President*
Linda Hall, *Principal*
EMP: 10
SALES (est): 850K **Privately Held**
WEB: www.patsblueribbons.com
SIC: 5999 3479 Trophies & plaques; engraving jewelry silverware, or metal

(G-3885)
PERRY ENTERPRISES
Also Called: Perry Pallets
7200 Delta Line Rd Ste B (98248-9706)
PHONE 360 366-5239
Max L Perry, *Owner*
EMP: 28 **EST:** 1992
SQ FT: 5,000
SALES (est): 3.5MM **Privately Held**
SIC: 2448 Pallets, wood

(G-3886)
PHILLIPS 66 COMPANY
Tosco Northwest Company
3901 Unick Rd (98248-9003)
P.O. Box 8 (98248-0008)
PHONE 360 384-1011
Ronald Crutcher, *Engineer*
Curtis Whittle, *Engineer*
Dean Ratzlaff, *Project Engr*
Gary Goodman, *Manager*
EMP: 68
SALES (corp-wide): 114.2B **Publicly Held**
WEB: www.phillips66.com
SIC: 2911 Petroleum refining
HQ: Phillips 66 Company
2331 Citywest Blvd
Houston TX 77042
281 293-6600

(G-3887)
PIP BUILDING LLC
3777 Brown Rd (98248-9299)
PHONE 360 961-1702
Kyle Haggith, *Principal*
EMP: 2
SALES (est): 146.9K **Privately Held**
SIC: 2752 Commercial printing, offset

(G-3888)
PNW SELECT MARKETING GROUP LLC
1855 Main St (98248-9062)
PHONE 360 746-8270
Kim Schnackenberg,
Chuck Smith,
EMP: 3
SALES (est): 253.9K **Privately Held**
SIC: 2298 Cordage & twine

(G-3889)
POOR ITALIANS VINEYARD
7110 Valley View Rd (98248-8744)
PHONE 360 366-5970
Camille Royle, *Principal*
EMP: 2
SALES (est): 119.7K **Privately Held**
SIC: 2084 Wines, brandy & brandy spirits

(G-3890)
PRAXAIR INC
4466 Aldergrove Rd (98248-9619)
PHONE 360 371-2900
Cleve Guessford, *Manager*
EMP: 12 **Privately Held**
SIC: 2813 Industrial gases
HQ: Praxair, Inc.
10 Riverview Dr
Danbury CT 06810
203 837-2000

(G-3891)
PRIME WEST BEEF CO INC
7060 Portal Way Ste 140 (98248-9833)
PHONE 360 306-1831
John Sheehan, *Principal*
EMP: 3
SALES (est): 142.6K **Privately Held**
SIC: 2011 Boxed beef from meat slaughtered on site

(G-3892)
RELIABLE CONTROLS CORP USA
1465 Slater Rd (98248-8919)
PHONE 250 475-2036
Patrick Cronin, *Vice Pres*
EMP: 2
SALES: 950K **Privately Held**
SIC: 3822 Auto controls regulating residntl & coml environmt & applncs

(G-3893)
RESTORFX INTERNATIONAL INC
2625 Delta Ring Rd Ste 3 (98248-8818)
PHONE 800 404-4107
Nicholas Vaandering, *CEO*
Anthony Dowsett, *Principal*
Alexander Kotyakov, *Principal*
Vitaly Kotyakov, *Principal*
EMP: 2
SALES (est): 130.6K **Privately Held**
SIC: 2842 Automobile polish

(G-3894)
SAFE HOME SECURITY PRODUCTS
1736 Matz Rd (98248-9385)
PHONE 360 384-1239
Ed Wittmier, *Principal*
EMP: 2
SALES (est): 196.8K **Privately Held**
SIC: 3699 Security devices

(G-3895)
SALISH SCREENPRINTING
4283 Lummi Shore Dr (98248-9154)
PHONE 360 758-2287
Keith Tom, *Principal*
EMP: 2
SALES (est): 144.2K **Privately Held**
SIC: 2759 Screen printing

(G-3896)
SAMSON ROPE TECHNOLOGIES INC (DH)
2090 Thornton St (98248-9314)
PHONE 360 384-4669
Andrea Sturm, *CEO*
Jeremy Jordan, *President*
Mark Swiackey, *COO*
Rafael Chou, *Vice Pres*
Vincent Mascherino, *Vice Pres*
◆ **EMP:** 120 **EST:** 1997
SQ FT: 80,000
SALES: 95MM
SALES (corp-wide): 153MM **Privately Held**
WEB: www.samsonrope.com
SIC: 2298 Cordage & twine

(G-3897)
SARVEL BIOFUELS LUMMI CORP
4534 Haxton Way (98248-9126)
PHONE 360 362-0016
Thomas Crom, *CEO*
Vincent Misanes Sr, *President*
Douglas Robertson, *Director*
EMP: 5 **EST:** 2016
SALES (est): 299.3K **Privately Held**
SIC: 2875 Fertilizers, mixing only

(G-3898)
SAUDER MOULDINGS INC FERNDALE
5575 Nordic Pl (98248-9138)
PHONE 360 384-4774
E Lawrence Sauder, *President*
Pamela Campbell, *Admin Sec*
▼ **EMP:** 120
SALES (est): 10MM **Privately Held**
SIC: 2431 Moldings, wood: unfinished & prefinished

(G-3899)
SAWARNE LUMBER CO LTD
5530 Nordic Pl (98248-9138)
PHONE 360 380-1290
Kerry Sangara, *Manager*
EMP: 20
SALES (corp-wide): 17.3MM **Privately Held**
SIC: 2421 Sawmills & planing mills, general
PA: Sawarne Lumber Co. Ltd
1770 Burrard St Suite 280
Vancouver BC V6J 3
604 324-4666

(G-3900)
SCHWALDBE NORTH AMERICA
5501 Hovander Rd (98248-7835)
PHONE 360 384-6468
Klaus Moser, *Administration*
▲ **EMP:** 3
SALES (est): 239.8K **Privately Held**
SIC: 5995 3949 Optical goods stores; fencing equipment (sporting goods)

(G-3901)
SCITUS TECH SOLUTIONS LLC
7032 Portal Way R6 (98248-9822)
PHONE 360 202-9642
Erica Johnson,
EMP: 8
SALES (est): 534.7K **Privately Held**
SIC: 5999 3577 7699 Mobile telephones & equipment; bar code (magnetic ink) printers; repair services

(G-3902)
SCOTTS SHEET METAL
6169 Portal Way (98248-9303)
PHONE 360 384-3827
Scott Jensen, *Partner*
Scott Campbell, *Partner*
EMP: 5
SQ FT: 500
SALES: 49K **Privately Held**
SIC: 3441 1711 7692 Fabricated structural metal; heating & air conditioning contractors; welding repair

(G-3903)
SENSORLINK CORPORATION
1360 Stonegate Way (98248-7824)
PHONE 360 380-0592
Karen Roth, *CEO*
Gary Hielkema, *President*
Robin Mazur, *Human Res Mgr*
Michelle Hielkema, *Human Resources*
Teneya Tinsley, *Mktg Dir*
▼ **EMP:** 25
SQ FT: 30,000
SALES: 5.4MM **Privately Held**
WEB: www.sensorlink.com
SIC: 3825 Electrical energy measuring equipment

(G-3904)
SHERRI AND BRENT WRIGHT
Also Called: Digital Threads
7535 Hickory Ridge Ln (98248-8532)
P.O. Box 28188, Bellingham (98248-0188)
PHONE 360 366-3100
Sherri Wright, *Owner*
Brent Wright, *Co-Owner*
▲ **EMP:** 4
SALES (est): 435.7K **Privately Held**
SIC: 2284 2395 Embroidery thread; embroidery & art needlework

(G-3905)
SMC GEAR
6930 Salashan Pkwy (98248-8314)
PHONE 360 366-5534
EMP: 2 **EST:** 2016
SALES (est): 143.1K **Privately Held**
SIC: 3949 Sporting & athletic goods

(G-3906)
STAR NORTH WOODWORKS INC
Also Called: Northstar Woodworks
6186 Portal Way (98248-9363)
P.O. Box 1767 (98248-1767)
PHONE 360 384-0307
Frank Chambers, *President*
Mike Anderson, *Vice Pres*
Lorelei Chambers, *Treasurer*
EMP: 30
SQ FT: 20,000
SALES: 1.3MM **Privately Held**
WEB: www.northstarww.com
SIC: 2431 Doors, wood

(G-3907)
STARKENBURG SHAVINGS
1546 Slater Rd (98248-9121)
PHONE 360 734-8818
Sherman Starkenburg, *Owner*
EMP: 5
SALES (corp-wide): 1.3MM **Privately Held**
SIC: 5099 2421 Shavings, wood; sawdust & shavings
PA: Starkenburg Shavings
4013 Saltspring Dr
Ferndale WA 98248
360 384-6891

(G-3908)
SUMMIT RESCUE INC
Also Called: Seattle Manufacturing
6930 Salashan Pkwy (98248-8314)
PHONE 360 366-0221
Kathy Hughes, *President*
Chris Starr, *Engineer*
Don Enos, *Sales Executive*
EMP: 25 **EST:** 1967
SQ FT: 19,000
SALES (est): 3MM **Privately Held**
WEB: www.smcgear.net
SIC: 3949 Camping equipment & supplies

(G-3909)
SUNDANCE BEEF INTL INC
Also Called: Sundance Beef Co
7060 Portal Way Ste 140 (98248-9833)
PHONE 360 224-2333
John Sheehan, *President*
EMP: 4
SQ FT: 4,000

Ferndale - Whatcom County (G-3910)

SALES (est): 458.1K **Privately Held**
WEB: www.sundancebeef.com
SIC: 2011 5421 Boxed beef from meat slaughtered on site; meat markets, including freezer provisioners

(G-3910)
SUNSET FORGE LLC
3502 Bay Rd (98248-9605)
PHONE..................360 201-0160
Robert Thomas, *Principal*
EMP: 2 EST: 2010
SALES (est): 170.8K **Privately Held**
SIC: 3399 Primary metal products

(G-3911)
TECH-ROLL INC
5514 Nielsen Ave (98248-9467)
P.O. Box 959, Blaine (98231-0959)
PHONE..................360 371-4321
Ulf Hansson, *CEO*
Jeanette Hansson, *Vice Pres*
EMP: 2
SQ FT: 3,000
SALES: 845.3K **Privately Held**
SIC: 3568 Pulleys, power transmission

(G-3912)
TELEGRAPH FABRICATION
7343 Meadowmist Ln (98248-9794)
PHONE..................360 739-8170
Mark Razore, *Owner*
EMP: 2
SALES (est): 110K **Privately Held**
SIC: 3441 Fabricated structural metal

(G-3913)
TIDAL VISION PRODUCTS LLC
5506 Nielsen Ave Ste A (98248-8960)
PHONE..................907 988-8888
Craig Kasberg, *CEO*
EMP: 10
SALES (est): 450.4K **Privately Held**
SIC: 2869 2879 2899 2824 Industrial organic chemicals; agricultural chemicals; water treating compounds; organic fibers, noncellulosic; specialty leathers

(G-3914)
TNT SIGNS & DESIGN INC
6018 Portal Way (98248-9360)
PHONE..................360 384-3190
Ted Denessen, *Principal*
EMP: 2
SALES (est): 186.3K **Privately Held**
SIC: 3993 Signs, not made in custom sign painting shops

(G-3915)
TOTAL BUILDING PRODUCTS LLC (PA)
1810 Scout Pl (98248-8937)
PHONE..................360 380-1100
Sven Lincke, *Principal*
Ron Kocol, *Maintence Staff*
EMP: 10
SALES (est): 1.8MM **Privately Held**
WEB: www.totalbuildingproducts.com
SIC: 2434 Wood kitchen cabinets

(G-3916)
TREE ISLAND INDUSTRIES LTD
Also Called: Tree Island Fastener
6980 Salashan Loop (98248)
PHONE..................360 366-0988
Bill McAvoy, *Division Mgr*
EMP: 34
SALES (corp-wide): 178.3MM **Privately Held**
SIC: 3315 3452 Nails, spikes, brads & similar items; bolts, nuts, rivets & washers
HQ: Tree Island Industries Ltd
3933 Boundary Rd
Richmond BC V6V 1
604 524-2744

(G-3917)
TRIVAN TRUCK BODY LLC
1385 W Smith Rd (98248-8930)
PHONE..................360 380-0773
Marty Vandriel, *General Mgr*
Kris Veldman, *Plant Mgr*
Richard Hoving, *Project Mgr*
Bob Johnson, *Purchasing*
Ian Van Seters, *Sales Mgr*
EMP: 95

SQ FT: 43,000
SALES: 33.2MM **Privately Held**
WEB: www.trivan.net
SIC: 3713 Truck bodies (motor vehicles)

(G-3918)
TRIVAN TRUCK BODY TEXAS LLC
1385 W Smith Rd (98248-8930)
PHONE..................254 799-2360
Adrian Harthoorn, *Mng Member*
EMP: 53 EST: 2007
SQ FT: 35,000
SALES (est): 6.1MM **Privately Held**
SIC: 3713 Truck bodies (motor vehicles)

(G-3919)
TRUE MACHINE
Also Called: Jeffrey Lee Redington
5410 Barrett Rd Ste B107 (98248-8830)
PHONE..................425 610-9669
Jeff Redington, *Owner*
EMP: 4
SALES (est): 19.4K **Privately Held**
SIC: 3569 1731 Filters; computerized controls installation

(G-3920)
TUFF TRAILER INC
6742 Portal Way (98248-9326)
PHONE..................360 398-0300
Don Piccolo, *President*
Dan Piccolo, *Manager*
▲ EMP: 7
SQ FT: 10,000
SALES (est): 1.3MM **Privately Held**
WEB: www.webuildtrailers.com
SIC: 5599 3792 Utility trailers; automobile house trailer chassis

(G-3921)
ULTRASONICS INTERNATIONAL CORP
7044 Portal Way (98248-9828)
PHONE..................360 676-0056
David Mazur, *President*
Jerry Hample, *General Mgr*
◆ EMP: 7
SALES (est): 86.9K **Privately Held**
SIC: 3582 Commercial laundry equipment

(G-3922)
WALTON BEVERAGE CO
1350 Pacific Pl (98248-8985)
PHONE..................360 380-1660
John Walton, *President*
David McLeod, *Corp Secy*
Ford Carothers, *Vice Pres*
EMP: 130 EST: 1941
SQ FT: 40,000
SALES (est): 21.9MM **Privately Held**
SIC: 2086 5149 Soft drinks: packaged in cans, bottles, etc.; groceries & related products

(G-3923)
WESTERN CHEMICAL INCORPORATED
Also Called: Syndel USA
1441 W Smith Rd (98248-8933)
PHONE..................360 384-5898
Chris McReynolds, *CEO*
Ryan Becker, *Corp Secy*
◆ EMP: 10
SALES (est): 2.8MM **Privately Held**
SIC: 2834 Veterinary pharmaceutical preparations
PA: Aquatic Life Sciences, Inc.
1441 W Smith Rd
Ferndale WA 98248

(G-3924)
WESTERN YACHT SYSTEMS INC
1720 Kaas Rd (98248-9331)
PHONE..................360 384-3648
Dave Rasmussen, *President*
Peggy Naylor, *Manager*
EMP: 4
SALES (est): 270K **Privately Held**
SIC: 3732 7699 5088 Yachts, building & repairing; boat repair; marine crafts & supplies

(G-3925)
WILLIAMSON ILLUSTRATION
5989 Longdin Rd (98248-9417)
PHONE..................360 734-5497
James Williamson, *Owner*
Norma Appleton, *Owner*
EMP: 2
SALES (est): 107.9K **Privately Held**
WEB: www.williamson-labs.com
SIC: 2395 2499 Art goods for embroidering, stamped: purchased materials; picture & mirror frames, wood

(G-3926)
XAFAX CORPORATION
2045 Aldergrove Rd (98248-9306)
PHONE..................360 389-5630
Danny McDonald, *Project Mgr*
EMP: 7
SALES (est): 643.8K **Privately Held**
SIC: 3411 Beer cans, metal

Fife
Pierce County

(G-3927)
ABG
3719 70th Ave E Unit E (98424-3771)
PHONE..................253 896-1372
Brent Carl, *Owner*
EMP: 5 EST: 1995
SALES (est): 313K **Privately Held**
WEB: www.abg.com
SIC: 3449 3441 Bars, concrete reinforcing: fabricated steel; fabricated structural metal

(G-3928)
ALABAMA METAL INDUSTRIES CORP
3011 70th Ave E (98424-3609)
PHONE..................253 926-1600
Mark Comfort, *Branch Mgr*
EMP: 135
SQ FT: 320,000
SALES (corp-wide): 1B **Publicly Held**
WEB: www.amico-online.com
SIC: 3446 Open flooring & grating for construction
HQ: Alabama Metal Industries Corporation
3245 Fayette Ave
Birmingham AL 35208
205 787-2611

(G-3929)
ALTRIA
4512 70th Ave E (98424-3710)
PHONE..................253 922-4267
EMP: 2
SALES (est): 68K **Privately Held**
SIC: 5194 2111 Smoking tobacco; cigarettes

(G-3930)
AMERICAN NEWS COMPANY LLC
3995 70th Ave E Ste B (98424-3616)
PHONE..................866 466-7231
EMP: 2
SALES (est): 73.1K **Privately Held**
SIC: 2721 Magazines: publishing & printing

(G-3931)
AMERICAN VINYL INDUSTRIES INC
Also Called: Factory Direct Windows
6310 18th St E (98424-1502)
P.O. Box 682, Fox Island (98333-0682)
PHONE..................253 473-4731
John Verderico, *President*
Bob Ericcsen, *Shareholder*
EMP: 8
SQ FT: 1,100
SALES (est): 1.2MM **Privately Held**
SIC: 3089 1761 Windows, plastic; siding contractor

(G-3932)
AMES INTERNATIONAL INC
Also Called: Emily's Chocolate
4401 Industry Dr E Ste A (98424-1832)
PHONE..................253 946-4779

Amy Paulose, *President*
Susan Paulose, *Vice Pres*
◆ EMP: 75
SQ FT: 90,000
SALES (est): 16.9MM **Privately Held**
WEB: www.emilyschocolate.com
SIC: 2064 2066 2068 2034 Candy & other confectionery products; chocolate & cocoa products; salted & roasted nuts & seeds; dehydrated fruits, vegetables, soups
PA: Ames Foods Processors India Private Limited
X/558, Common Facility Centre
Ernakulam KER 68672

(G-3933)
ART MORRISON ENTERPRISES INC
5301 8th St E (98424-2712)
PHONE..................253 344-0161
Arthur M Morrison, *President*
Kevin Kosir, *Vice Pres*
Dion Olson, *Engineer*
Ronda Nelson, *Manager*
Steve Wang, *Info Tech Mgr*
EMP: 33
SQ FT: 9,000
SALES (est): 6.6MM **Privately Held**
WEB: www.artmorrison.com
SIC: 3714 5531 3711 Motor vehicle parts & accessories; automotive & home supply stores; motor vehicles & car bodies

(G-3934)
ART N STITCHES INC
5013 Pacific Hwy E Ste 13 (98424-3421)
PHONE..................253 248-1900
Marjorie Hoffine, *President*
Brenda Hackett, *Vice Pres*
Shana Burdick, *Admin Sec*
EMP: 3
SALES (est): 324.5K **Privately Held**
SIC: 7389 2395 Embroidering of advertising on shirts, etc.; embroidery products, except schiffli machine

(G-3935)
ASSOCIATED MATERIALS LLC
Also Called: Alside Supply
2801 78th Ave E (98424-4501)
PHONE..................425 481-7101
EMP: 7 **Privately Held**
SIC: 2541 5033 Mfg Wood Partitions/Fixtures Whol Roofing/Siding/Insulation
HQ: Associated Materials, Llc
3773 State Rd
Cuyahoga Falls OH 44223
330 929-1811

(G-3936)
B-A-PRO LLC
Also Called: Ba Pro Sports Product
2001 48th Avenue Ct E B (98424-3437)
PHONE..................253 861-3634
Kathy Parr, *Office Mgr*
Michael A Parr,
EMP: 3
SALES (est): 251.1K **Privately Held**
SIC: 3949 Sporting & athletic goods

(G-3937)
BARGREEN-ELLINGSON INC
2511 70th Ave E (98424-3691)
PHONE..................253 722-2573
Paul G Ellingson, *President*
Terry Arellano, *General Mgr*
Matt Wicks, *General Mgr*
Geoff Grothe, *Project Mgr*
Javier Galindo, *Warehouse Mgr*
EMP: 23
SALES (corp-wide): 129.8MM **Privately Held**
SIC: 5046 2541 Restaurant equipment & supplies; store & office display cases & fixtures
PA: Bargreen-Ellingson, Inc.
6626 Tacoma Mall Blvd B
Tacoma WA 98409
253 475-9201

(G-3938)
BENS PRECISION INSTRS INC
Also Called: B P I Medical
5417 12th St E Ste 100 (98424-1335)
PHONE..................253 883-5040

GEOGRAPHIC SECTION

Fife - Pierce County (G-3965)

Robert J Overmars, *President*
Ben Overmars, *Vice Pres*
Janneke Overmars, *Vice Pres*
EMP: 53
SQ FT: 15,000
SALES (est): 8.4MM **Privately Held**
WEB: www.bpimedical.com
SIC: **7699** 3841 Surgical instrument repair; surgical & medical instruments

(G-3939)
BJ II INC
Dt Express
1305 Alexander Ave E (98424-1108)
PHONE.................................253 926-8538
Benita Lam, *Manager*
EMP: 3
SALES (corp-wide): 2.2MM **Privately Held**
WEB: www.bjii.com
SIC: **2111** Cigarettes
PA: Bj Ii Inc
    4315 Pacific Hwy E
    Fife WA 98424
    253 922-6830

(G-3940)
BROWN & HALEY
3501 Industry Dr E Ste D (98424-1834)
PHONE.................................253 620-3000
Brad Degerman, *Principal*
EMP: 200
SALES (corp-wide): 6MM **Privately Held**
SIC: **2064** Candy & other confectionery products
PA: Brown & Haley
    110 E 26th St
    Tacoma WA 98421
    253 620-3067

(G-3941)
CENTERLINE FABRICATORS LLC
5912 15th St E (98424-1341)
P.O. Box 1938, Milton (98354-1938)
PHONE.................................253 922-3226
Bonnie J Watson, *Principal*
Joseph A Jordan,
William R Watson,
EMP: 3
SALES (est): 154.7K **Privately Held**
SIC: **3441** 3443 3498 Fabricated structural metal; reactor containment vessels, metal plate; pile shells, metal plate; pipe, large diameter; metal plate; fabricated pipe & fittings

(G-3942)
CFM CONSOLIDATED INC
Also Called: Flex-A-Lite Consolidated
7213 45th Street Ct E (98424-3714)
PHONE.................................253 922-2700
Lisa Chissus, *CEO*
EMP: 16
SALES (est): 3MM **Privately Held**
SIC: **3089** Injection molded finished plastic products

(G-3943)
CFM CONSOLIDATED INC
Also Called: Cascade Plastics
7009 45th Street Ct E (98424-3700)
PHONE.................................253 922-2700
Lisa Chissus, *CEO*
Michelle R Radin, *Admin Sec*
▲ EMP: 50
SQ FT: 43,000
SALES (est): 12.9MM
SALES (corp-wide): 5.3B **Publicly Held**
WEB: www.cascadeplastics.com
SIC: **3089** Injection molded finished plastic products
PA: Rpm International Inc.
    2628 Pearl Rd
    Medina OH 44256
    330 273-5090

(G-3944)
CM2931 LLC
4179 70th Ave E Ste B (98424-3706)
PHONE.................................253 447-7537
EMP: 37
SALES (corp-wide): 47MM **Privately Held**
SIC: **3273** Ready-mixed concrete

PA: Cm2931, Llc
    2875 Temple Ave
    Signal Hill CA 90755
    562 490-3800

(G-3945)
CONSOLIDATED PRESS LLC
2521 Pacific Hwy E Ste A (98424-1049)
PHONE.................................253 922-3195
Brian Lester, *Opers Mgr*
Jim Davis, *Branch Mgr*
EMP: 75
SALES (est): 6MM
SALES (corp-wide): 13.8MM **Privately Held**
WEB: www.conspress.com
SIC: **2752** Publication printing, lithographic
PA: Consolidated Press Llc
    600 S Spokane St
    Seattle WA 98134
    206 447-9659

(G-3946)
CRYSTAL DISTRIBUTION INC
Also Called: CDI
7218 45th Street Ct E # 104 (98424-3809)
PHONE.................................253 736-0016
David Welch, *Manager*
EMP: 10 **Privately Held**
SIC: **3444** Sheet metalwork
PA: Crystal Distribution Inc.
    17560 Tyler St Nw
    Elk River MN 55330

(G-3947)
CUSTOM CONTROLS CORPORATION
Also Called: Custom Electric & Controls
4630 16th St E Ste B24 (98424-2666)
PHONE.................................253 922-5874
Tom Gibelyou, *President*
Tom E Gibelyou, *President*
Sherrie Gibelyou, *Vice Pres*
Mel Locks, *CFO*
EMP: 10
SQ FT: 7,000
SALES (est): 2MM **Privately Held**
WEB: www.customcontrolsusa.com
SIC: **1731** 3625 General electrical contractor; relays & industrial controls

(G-3948)
DASHBOARD SKIMBOARDS LLC
2519 Pacific Hwy E Ste B (98424-1047)
PHONE.................................253 235-1811
Bryce Herminsen, *Branch Mgr*
▲ EMP: 2
SALES (est): 199.9K **Privately Held**
SIC: **3949** Skateboards

(G-3949)
DB SKIMBOARDS
Also Called: Origin Distribution
2519 Pacific Hwy E Ste B (98424-1047)
PHONE.................................253 235-1811
Blake Zimmerman, *Principal*
Nathan Pauli, *VP Sales*
▲ EMP: 10
SALES (est): 922.4K **Privately Held**
SIC: **3949** Sporting & athletic goods

(G-3950)
EMBLEMS & MORE X3
1401 52nd Ave E (98424-1221)
PHONE.................................253 248-2400
Linda Jackson, *Partner*
▲ EMP: 2
SQ FT: 1,200
SALES (est): 129.8K **Privately Held**
SIC: **2395** Emblems, embroidered

(G-3951)
ENERGY CONVERSIONS INC
6411 Pacific Hwy E (98424-1537)
PHONE.................................253 922-6670
Scott Jensen, *President*
Don Jensen Sr, *Principal*
Don Jensen Jr, *Principal*
Paul Jensen, *Vice Pres*
David Cook, *Senior Engr*
▼ EMP: 7
SQ FT: 18,000
SALES (est): 913.6K **Privately Held**
WEB: www.energyconversions.com
SIC: **3519** Diesel engine rebuilding

(G-3952)
FIFES VEHICLE VESSEL
4905 Pacific Hwy E Ste 2a (98424-2649)
PHONE.................................253 926-8227
Mike Flynn, *Owner*
Jean Flynn, *Co-Owner*
EMP: 4
SALES: 350K **Privately Held**
SIC: **3469** Automobile license tags, stamped metal

(G-3953)
FLUID CONTROLS AND COMPONENTS (PA)
5909 12th St E (98424-1364)
P.O. Box 1938, Milton (98354-1938)
PHONE.................................253 922-3226
Bonnie J Watson, *President*
William R Watson, *Vice Pres*
▲ EMP: 15
SQ FT: 600
SALES (est): 9.5MM **Privately Held**
WEB: www.fluidcontrols.net
SIC: **5074** 3498 Pipes & fittings, plastic; fabricated pipe & fittings

(G-3954)
GENSCO INC (PA)
4402 20th St E (98424-1803)
P.O. Box 2905, Tacoma (98401-2905)
PHONE.................................253 620-8203
Charles E Walters Jr, *President*
Charles E Walters Sr, *Chairman*
Ken R Bell, *Treasurer*
Eric Van Orden, *Sales Staff*
◆ EMP: 225
SQ FT: 225,000
SALES (est): 349.9MM **Privately Held**
WEB: www.gensco.com
SIC: **5074** 3444 Heating equipment (hydronic); sheet metalwork; ducts, sheet metal

(G-3955)
GIBRALTAR INDUSTRIES INC
Also Called: Norwesco
3011 70th Ave E (98424-3609)
PHONE.................................253 926-1600
Brian J Lipke, *Ch of Bd*
Stacey Kinzebach, *Executive*
EMP: 130
SALES (corp-wide): 1B **Publicly Held**
SIC: **3444** Sheet metalwork
PA: Gibraltar Industries, Inc.
    3556 Lake Shore Rd # 100
    Buffalo NY 14219
    716 826-6500

(G-3956)
GLOBALTECH PLASTICS LLC
5555 8th St E (98424-1316)
PHONE.................................253 327-1333
Tom Fleck, *President*
Dave Wheeler, *COO*
◆ EMP: 65
SQ FT: 42,000
SALES (est): 12.8MM **Privately Held**
WEB: www.globaltechplastics.com
SIC: **3089** Molding primary plastic; injection molding of plastics

(G-3957)
GRUMA CORPORATION
Also Called: Diane Foods
6611 Valley Ave E (98424-2250)
PHONE.................................253 896-4483
Martine Murillo, *Branch Mgr*
EMP: 200
SQ FT: 101,432 **Privately Held**
WEB: www.missionfoods.com
SIC: **2096** 0723 2099 Tortilla chips; flour milling custom services; food preparations
HQ: Gruma Corporation
    5601 Executive Dr Ste 800
    Irving TX 75038
    972 232-5000

(G-3958)
HONEY HOUSE NATURALS INC
7704 48th St E (98424-3732)
PHONE.................................253 926-8193
Ruth Ingles, *Principal*
Keri Willis, *Sales Mgr*
▲ EMP: 15
SQ FT: 3,000

SALES: 1.7MM **Privately Held**
SIC: **2844** Cosmetic preparations

(G-3959)
HOSHIZAKI WESTERN DIST CTR INC
7214 26th St E Ste 103 (98424-3778)
PHONE.................................253 922-8589
Dan Cazalet, *President*
EMP: 6 **Privately Held**
SIC: **3585** Refrigeration & heating equipment
HQ: Hoshizaki Western Distribution Center, Inc.
    790 Challenger St
    Brea CA 92821
    714 671-1423

(G-3960)
IKONIKA CORP
5013 Pcf Hwy E Unit 14 (98424)
PHONE.................................253 344-1523
Marek Rywacki, *President*
Kathy O'Brien-Rywacki, *Vice Pres*
EMP: 9
SALES (est): 1.7MM **Privately Held**
WEB: www.ikonika.com
SIC: **3613** 1731 Switchgear & switchboard apparatus; computerized controls installation

(G-3961)
JUMBO DTI CORPORATION
Also Called: Scoring Sports
2909 Pcf Hwy E Ste 101 (98424)
P.O. Box 1396, Tacoma (98401-1396)
PHONE.................................253 272-9764
Wolfgang Sauer, *President*
Mark Marinkovich, *VP Finance*
William Stoll, *VP Sales*
▲ EMP: 12
SQ FT: 56,000
SALES (est): 1MM **Privately Held**
WEB: www.dtisoccer.com
SIC: **5941** 3949 2339 Soccer supplies; sporting & athletic goods; women's & misses' outerwear

(G-3962)
KEPLER ABSORBENTS LLC (PA)
6808 26th St E (98424-3651)
PHONE.................................844 453-7537
John Toler,
EMP: 3
SALES (est): 1.3MM **Privately Held**
SIC: **5169** 2842 Chemicals & allied products; specialty cleaning, polishes & sanitation goods

(G-3963)
KUSHER LLC
Also Called: Kusher Bakery
7214 26th St E Ste 102 (98424-3778)
PHONE.................................800 445-0655
Anatoliy Zaika,
▲ EMP: 8
SALES (est): 849.4K **Privately Held**
SIC: **2052** Bakery products, dry

(G-3964)
L & L NURSERY SUPPLY INC
Also Called: L L Nursery Supply
2507 Frank Albert Rd E # 130 (98424-2700)
PHONE.................................909 591-0461
Annette Dhaenens, *Sales Mgr*
Dan Froli, *Manager*
EMP: 45
SALES (corp-wide): 184.4MM **Privately Held**
WEB: www.llnurserysupply.com
SIC: **5191** 5193 5169 5083 Chemicals, agricultural; flowers & florists' supplies; chemicals & allied products; farm & garden machinery; fertilizers, mixing only
PA: L & L Nursery Supply, Inc.
    2552 Shenandoah Way
    San Bernardino CA 92407
    909 591-0461

(G-3965)
LENNOX INDUSTRIES COMMERI
2105 70th Ave E Ste 300 (98424-1501)
PHONE.................................206 607-1585
EMP: 2

Fife - Pierce County (G-3966)

SALES (est): 79.9K **Privately Held**
SIC: 3585 Refrigeration & heating equipment

(G-3966)
LENNOX STORES (PARTSPLUS)
2105 70th Ave E Ste 100 (98424-1501)
PHONE..................................206 607-1818
EMP: 2
SALES (est): 79.9K **Privately Held**
SIC: 3585 Refrigeration & heating equipment

(G-3967)
M7M INVESTMENTS
Also Called: Milgard Mfg
1010 54th Ave E (98424-2731)
P.O. Box 11368, Tacoma (98411-0368)
PHONE..................................253 922-2030
James A Milgard, *Partner*
Gary E Milgard, *Partner*
EMP: 2
SQ FT: 78,000
SALES (est): 300K **Privately Held**
SIC: 6512 3231 Commercial & industrial building operation; products of purchased glass

(G-3968)
MAJORWIRE SCREEN MEDIA
7110 26th St E (98424-3772)
PHONE..................................253 327-1550
Jean Leblond, *President*
▲ EMP: 60
SALES (est): 13.3MM **Privately Held**
SIC: 3496 Miscellaneous fabricated wire products

(G-3969)
MATHESON TRI-GAS INC
510 53rd Ave E (98424-2740)
PHONE..................................253 284-9295
Barry Groves, *Branch Mgr*
EMP: 4 **Privately Held**
SIC: 2813 Nitrogen
HQ: Matheson Tri-Gas, Inc.
150 Allen Rd Ste 302
Basking Ridge NJ 07920
908 991-9200

(G-3970)
MCNICHOLS COMPANY
3400 Industry Dr E Ste B (98424-1853)
PHONE..................................253 922-4296
Ryan Sackmann, *Sales Staff*
Ray Sudduth, *Branch Mgr*
EMP: 13
SALES (corp-wide): 177.1MM **Privately Held**
SIC: 5051 3446 Steel; open flooring & grating for construction
PA: Mcnichols Company
2502 N Rocky Point Dr # 750
Tampa FL 33607
877 884-4653

(G-3971)
MILGARD MANUFACTURING INC (HQ)
Also Called: Milgard Windows
1010 54th Ave E (98424-2793)
PHONE..................................253 922-6030
Vishal Singh, *President*
Kenneth Cole, *Vice Pres*
Lawrence Leaman, *Vice Pres*
Stephen Moore, *Vice Pres*
John Sznewajs, *Vice Pres*
▲ EMP: 107
SQ FT: 140,000
SALES (est): 500.8MM
SALES (corp-wide): 8.3B **Publicly Held**
WEB: www.milgard.com
SIC: 3089 3442 Windows, plastic; sash, door or window: metal
PA: Masco Corporation
17450 College Pkwy
Livonia MI 48152
313 274-7400

(G-3972)
MILGARD MANUFACTURING INC
Also Called: Milgard Pultrusion
2935 70th Ave E (98424-3607)
P.O. Box 11368, Tacoma (98411-0368)
PHONE..................................253 922-4341
Lynn Steele, *Branch Mgr*
EMP: 575
SALES (corp-wide): 8.3B **Publicly Held**
WEB: www.milgard.com
SIC: 3089 2431 3442 Window frames & sash, plastic; windows & window parts & trim, wood; metal doors, sash & trim
HQ: Milgard Manufacturing Incorporated
1010 54th Ave E
Fife WA 98424
253 922-6030

(G-3973)
NEWGEM FOODS LLC
3600 Industry Dr E Ste A (98424-1835)
PHONE..................................209 948-1508
Thomas De Bord,
▲ EMP: 12 EST: 2004
SALES (est): 1.9MM **Privately Held**
SIC: 2099 Food preparations

(G-3974)
NOLL/NORWESCO LLC
3011 70th Ave E (98424-3609)
PHONE..................................253 926-1600
Gary Henry, *Mng Member*
EMP: 130 EST: 2007
SALES (est): 16MM
SALES (corp-wide): 1B **Publicly Held**
SIC: 3444 Sheet metalwork
PA: Gibraltar Industries, Inc.
3556 Lake Shore Rd # 100
Buffalo NY 14219
716 826-6500

(G-3975)
OCTAPHARMA PLASMA
5306 Pacific Hwy E Ste D (98424-3436)
PHONE..................................253 922-7753
EMP: 2
SALES (est): 74.4K **Privately Held**
SIC: 2836 Plasmas

(G-3976)
ORIENT FOOD PRODUCTION
Also Called: Orient Seafood Production
1494 46th Ave E (98424-1281)
PHONE..................................253 926-1389
Hoon Namkoong, *Owner*
EMP: 5
SALES (est): 422.8K **Privately Held**
SIC: 2092 Fresh or frozen packaged fish

(G-3977)
OVERHEAD DOOR CORPORATION
Also Called: Genie Pro Sales Center
2505 F Albert Rd E B127 (98424)
PHONE..................................253 520-8008
Jeff Sturlaugson, *General Mgr*
EMP: 6 **Privately Held**
WEB: www.overheaddoor.com
SIC: 3442 2431 Garage doors, overhead: metal; doors, wood
HQ: Overhead Door Corporation
2501 S State Hwy 121 Ste
Lewisville TX 75067
469 549-7100

(G-3978)
PARR CABINET OUTLET
Also Called: Parr Lumber
3500 20th St E Ste A (98424-1700)
PHONE..................................253 926-0505
Paul Feinauer, *Manager*
EMP: 9 **Privately Held**
SIC: 2434 Wood kitchen cabinets
PA: Parr Cabinet Outlet
6750 S 180th St 120
Tukwila WA 98188

(G-3979)
PERIODICO LARAZA
4505 Pacific Hwy E Ste 2 (98424-2638)
PHONE..................................253 961-5008
EMP: 3
SALES (est): 108.2K **Privately Held**
SIC: 2711 Newspapers

(G-3980)
PEXCO LLC
3110 70th Ave E (98424-3608)
PHONE..................................253 284-8000
Scott Vervalin, *Warehouse Mgr*
Peter Speer, *Manager*
EMP: 153
SALES (corp-wide): 7.7B **Privately Held**
SIC: 2821 Plastics materials & resins
HQ: Pexco Llc
2500 Northwinds Pkwy # 472
Alpharetta GA 30009
770 777-8540

(G-3981)
PM TESTING LABORATORY INC
3921 Pacific Hwy E (98424-1131)
PHONE..................................253 922-1321
Patrick M Murphie, *President*
David Gleason, *Controller*
Lauri Mc Bee, *Office Mgr*
EMP: 90
SQ FT: 11,000
SALES: 9MM **Privately Held**
SIC: 8734 3471 Metallurgical testing laboratory; finishing, metals or formed products

(G-3982)
POREX TECHNOLOGIES CORPORATION
Also Called: Filtrona Extrusion Tacoma
3110 70th Ave E (98424-3608)
PHONE..................................253 284-8000
Steven Spear, *Branch Mgr*
EMP: 249
SALES (corp-wide): 112.5MM **Privately Held**
SIC: 3082 3089 Unsupported plastics profile shapes; battery cases, plastic or plastic combination
PA: Porex Technologies Corporation
1625 Ashton Park Dr Ste A
South Chesterfield VA 23834
804 524-4983

(G-3983)
PORTAC INC
3600 Port Of Tacoma Rd # 302 (98424-1039)
P.O. Box 3471, Redmond (98073-3471)
PHONE..................................253 922-9900
Gary Takahashi, *President*
Y Fujita, *Vice Pres*
R W Ashby, *CFO*
▼ EMP: 14
SQ FT: 167,497
SALES (est): 2.1MM **Privately Held**
SIC: 2421 Lumber: rough, sawed or planed
HQ: Mitsui & Co. (U.S.A.), Inc.
200 Park Ave Fl 36
New York NY 10166
212 878-4000

(G-3984)
PSI ELECTRONICS LLC
Also Called: Puget Sound Instrument
5007 Pacific Hwy E Ste 5 (98424-2645)
PHONE..................................253 922-7890
Peter Ollodart, *Mng Member*
▼ EMP: 11
SALES: 3MM **Privately Held**
SIC: 5731 3663 3812 7629 Radios, two-way, citizens' band, weather, short-wave, etc.; marine radios & radar equipment; microwave communication equipment; infrared object detection equipment; telecommunication equipment repair (except telephones)

(G-3985)
PUGET SOUND QULTY COATINGS LLC
6307 7th Street Ct E (98424-1477)
PHONE..................................253 861-8871
James McMillan, *President*
James R McMillan,
EMP: 3
SALES: 50K **Privately Held**
SIC: 3479 Painting, coating & hot dipping

(G-3986)
RECALL
3995 70th Ave E Ste A (98424-3616)
PHONE..................................253 272-2813
EMP: 2
SALES (est): 160.4K **Privately Held**
SIC: 3999 Pet supplies

(G-3987)
RTC AEROSPACE - FIFE DIV INC
7215 45th Street Ct E (98424-3714)
PHONE..................................253 922-3806
Jason Darley, *President*
Luke Sorenson, *Chairman*
William Hart, *Vice Pres*
Salina Chowen, *Director*
▲ EMP: 79
SQ FT: 55,719
SALES: 18MM
SALES (corp-wide): 28.7MM **Privately Held**
WEB: www.jwdmachine.com
SIC: 3812 Acceleration indicators & systems components, aerospace
PA: Rtc Aerospace Llc
7215 45th Street Ct E
Fife WA 98424
918 407-0291

(G-3988)
RTC AEROSPACE LLC (PA)
7215 45th Street Ct E (98424-3714)
PHONE..................................918 407-0291
Jason Darley, *CEO*
EMP: 17
SQ FT: 63,000
SALES (corp-wide): 28.7MM **Privately Held**
SIC: 3728 Aircraft parts & equipment

(G-3989)
S & S SELDEN LLC
1802 62nd Ave E (98424-2508)
PHONE..................................253 922-5700
Syd Selden, *Principal*
EMP: 2
SALES (est): 447.7K **Privately Held**
SIC: 2426 Furniture stock & parts, hardwood

(G-3990)
SA CONSUMER PRODUCTS INC
4602 20th St E (98424-1926)
PHONE..................................888 792-4264
Thomas Fimmen, *Manager*
EMP: 2
SALES (corp-wide): 1.1MM **Privately Held**
SIC: 3499 Locks, safe & vault: metal
PA: Sa Consumer Products, Inc
3305 W 132nd St
Leawood KS 66209
888 792-4264

(G-3991)
SACO SALES LLC
Also Called: AlphaGraphics
4803 Pacific Hwy E Ste 2b (98424-3440)
PHONE..................................253 922-6349
Scott Dumas,
EMP: 8
SQ FT: 3,000
SALES: 700K **Privately Held**
SIC: 2759 2721 2731 Commercial printing; periodicals: publishing & printing; books: publishing & printing

(G-3992)
SIEMENS AG
5013 Pacific Hwy E (98424-2658)
PHONE..................................253 922-4297
EMP: 2
SALES (est): 88.3K **Privately Held**
SIC: 3661 Telephones & telephone apparatus

(G-3993)
SIGN-TECH ELC LTD LBLTY CO
Also Called: S T E Electrical Contractors
5113 Pacific Hwy E Ste 7 (98424-3428)
PHONE..................................253 922-2146
John Mendenhall,
Linda Mendenhall,
EMP: 21
SQ FT: 5,200
SALES: 1.3MM **Privately Held**
WEB: www.signtechelectric.com
SIC: 1731 3993 General electrical contractor; electric signs

(G-3994)
STICKERS NORTHWEST INC
5113 Pacific Hwy E Ste 7 (98424-3428)
PHONE..................................253 344-1236
EMP: 2
SALES (est): 105.6K **Privately Held**
SIC: 2759 Screen printing

GEOGRAPHIC SECTION

Fox Island - Pierce County (G-4022)

(G-3995)
TECH MARINE ENTERPRISES INC
5111 4th St E (98424-2703)
PHONE..................206 878-7878
Steve Parker, *President*
Stive Wasson, *Vice Pres*
Laurie Lukas, *Admin Sec*
EMP: 14 **EST:** 1972
SQ FT: 7,200
SALES (est): 1.4MM **Privately Held**
WEB: www.tech-marine.us
SIC: 3599 Machine shop, jobbing & repair

(G-3996)
TOTEM ELECTRIC
4310 70th Ave E (98424-9800)
PHONE..................253 327-1500
EMP: 2
SALES (est): 384K **Privately Held**
SIC: 3699 1731 Electrical equipment & supplies; electrical work

(G-3997)
WESTERN EQUIPMENT REPR & WLDG
115 54th Ave E (98424-2715)
PHONE..................253 922-8351
Gary Smith, *President*
Patricia Smith, *Corp Secy*
EMP: 3
SQ FT: 6,000
SALES (est): 220K **Privately Held**
SIC: 7692 7538 Welding repair; diesel engine repair; automotive

(G-3998)
WESTERN GRAPHICS INC
5009 Pacific Hwy E Ste 12 (98424-2643)
PHONE..................206 241-2526
Sam Santos, *President*
Nona Santos, *Corp Secy*
Joanne Santos, *Vice Pres*
EMP: 3 **EST:** 1957
SQ FT: 5,500
SALES (est): 300K **Privately Held**
WEB: www.westerngraphics.net
SIC: 3993 2396 2759 3544 Signs & advertising specialties; automotive & apparel trimmings; screen printing; decals; printing; special dies, tools, jigs & fixtures; art design services

(G-3999)
WIND TALKER INNOVATIONS INC
Also Called: Wti
5007 Pacific Hwy E Ste 4 (98424-3435)
PHONE..................253 883-3615
Ryan Luther, *President*
Matthew Perdew, *President*
EMP: 8
SALES (est): 431.7K **Privately Held**
SIC: 4899 3663 Data communication services; communication signal enhancement network system; radio receiver networks; airborne radio communications equipment

Fircrest
Pierce County

(G-4000)
BUDGET SIGNS INC
Also Called: Budgetbanners.com
1021 Fairway Dr (98466-5929)
PHONE..................253 473-1760
Terry Manley, *President*
EMP: 4
SQ FT: 2,000
SALES (est): 336.6K **Privately Held**
WEB: www.budgetbanners.com
SIC: 7389 3993 Sign painting & lettering shop; signs & advertising specialties

(G-4001)
COFFEE ON CANVAS
1003 Laurel Ct (98466-6522)
PHONE..................419 605-2529
Jonathan Norquist, *Principal*
EMP: 2
SALES (est): 73.4K **Privately Held**
SIC: 2211 Canvas

(G-4002)
MARTIN WILLIAM OWENS
Also Called: Owens Press
1320 Alameda Ave Ste B (98466-6500)
PHONE..................253 564-5950
Martin W Owens, *Owner*
EMP: 6
SALES (est): 438.4K **Privately Held**
SIC: 2752 Commercial printing, offset

(G-4003)
MILMOR LUMBER MANUFACTURING
Also Called: Miller Lumber Manufacturing
4520 Orchard St W (98466-6622)
PHONE..................253 474-1001
Kenneth Miller, *President*
Ronald Miller, *Vice Pres*
Steven Miller, *Vice Pres*
Barbara Miller, *Treasurer*
EMP: 4
SALES (est): 100K **Privately Held**
SIC: 2421 Sawmills & planing mills, general

(G-4004)
REESMAN CO
Also Called: Shaklee Athrzed Dstrs - Resman
606 Regents Blvd (98466-7043)
PHONE..................253 564-7997
Mike Reesman, *Owner*
Roberta Reesman, *Owner*
EMP: 2
SALES (est): 160K **Privately Held**
SIC: 5149 2023 Specialty food items; dietary supplements, dairy & non-dairy based

Ford
Stevens County

(G-4005)
FRANK SWIGER TRUCKING INC
5243 Ford Wellpinit Rd (99013)
PHONE..................509 258-7226
Frank Swiger, *President*
Stephanie Swiger, *Admin Sec*
EMP: 8
SALES (est): 1MM **Privately Held**
SIC: 4213 2411 Trucking, except local; timber, cut at logging camp

(G-4006)
TWO WINEY BITCHES WINERY
38278 Angels Landing Rd N (99013-9524)
PHONE..................509 796-3600
EMP: 2
SALES (est): 81.4K **Privately Held**
SIC: 2084 Wines

(G-4007)
WILLOW WIND ORGANIC FARMS INC
38278 Angels Landing Rd N (99013-9524)
PHONE..................509 796-4006
Roy Steve Walser, *President*
Margaret Walser, *Vice Pres*
▲ **EMP:** 8
SQ FT: 56,300
SALES: 10MM **Privately Held**
WEB: www.willowwindfarms.com
SIC: 2037 Vegetables, quick frozen & cold pack, excl. potato products; potato products, quick frozen & cold pack

Forks
Clallam County

(G-4008)
ANDEAVOR
Also Called: Tesoro
171 N Forks Ave (98331-9721)
PHONE..................360 374-2038
Debbie Arnold, *Manager*
EMP: 9 **Publicly Held**
WEB: www.tesoropetroleum.com
SIC: 1311 Crude petroleum production; natural gas production
HQ: Andeavor Llc
 19100 Ridgewood Pkwy
 San Antonio TX 78259
 210 626-6000

(G-4009)
D & H ENTERPRISES
442 Ski Dr (98331-9725)
P.O. Box 631 (98331-0631)
PHONE..................360 374-9500
Darrel S Gaydeski, *Owner*
Heidi Gaydeski, *Co-Owner*
EMP: 9
SALES: 900K **Privately Held**
SIC: 3713 1629 Utility truck bodies; timber removal

(G-4010)
JIM DAVIS
370 Evergreen Loop (98331-9680)
PHONE..................360 374-5659
Jim Davis, *President*
EMP: 2
SALES (est): 141.7K **Privately Held**
SIC: 2411 Logging

(G-4011)
KEN OLSON CUTTING
1441 Merchants Rd (98331-9253)
PHONE..................360 374-5052
Ken Olson, *Owner*
EMP: 3
SALES (est): 208.6K **Privately Held**
SIC: 2411 Logging

(G-4012)
MCCLANAHAN LUMBER INC
188421 Hwy 101 S (98331)
P.O. Box 1483 (98331-1483)
PHONE..................360 374-5887
Larry Mc Clanahan Sr, *President*
Judi McClanahan, *Vice Pres*
EMP: 3
SQ FT: 2,100
SALES (est): 386.7K **Privately Held**
WEB: www.mcclanahanlumber.com
SIC: 2421 5211 Lumber: rough, sawed or planed; planing mill products & lumber

(G-4013)
OLYMPIC GRAPHIC ARTS INC
Also Called: UPS Customer Center
640 S Forks Ave (98331-9014)
P.O. Box 1698 (98331-1698)
PHONE..................360 374-6020
Luetta Joyce Pajac, *President*
Paul Pagac, *Exec VP*
EMP: 6 **EST:** 1973
SQ FT: 2,500
SALES: 250K **Privately Held**
WEB: www.olympicprinting.com
SIC: 2752 5943 7336 2791 Commercial printing, offset; office forms & supplies; commercial art & graphic design; typesetting

(G-4014)
OLYMPIC VIEW PUBLISHING LLC
Also Called: Forks Forum-Peninsula Herald
490 S Forks Ave (98331-9155)
P.O. Box 300 (98331-0300)
PHONE..................360 374-3311
Sue Ellen Reedson, *Manager*
EMP: 4
SALES (corp-wide): 1.7MM **Privately Held**
WEB: www.sequimgazette.com
SIC: 2711 Newspapers: publishing only, not printed on site
PA: Olympic View Publishing Llc
 147 W Washington St
 Sequim WA 98382
 360 683-3311

(G-4015)
PLEINES LOGGING INC
1755 Bogachiel Way (98331-9692)
PHONE..................360 374-6373
Fred T Pleines, *President*
Lorraine Pleines, *Principal*
EMP: 3
SQ FT: 4,000
SALES (est): 51.8K **Privately Held**
SIC: 2411 Logging camps & contractors

(G-4016)
PUGET SOUND SURFACERS INC
1680 S Forks Ave (98331)
P.O. Box 1687 (98331-1687)
PHONE..................360 374-9590
Michael Shaw, *President*
Susan Shaw, *Corp Secy*
EMP: 8
SALES: 900K **Privately Held**
SIC: 3295 Minerals, ground or treated

(G-4017)
RAYONIER FOREST RESOURCES LP
Also Called: Rayonier NW Forest Resources
116 Quillayute Rd (98331-9408)
PHONE..................360 374-6565
Bill Peach, *Manager*
EMP: 12
SALES (corp-wide): 816.1MM **Publicly Held**
SIC: 0811 2411 Tree farm; logging camps & contractors
HQ: Forest Rayonier Resources Lp
 1 Rayonier Way
 Yulee FL 32097
 904 357-9100

Fox Island
Pierce County

(G-4018)
AUTOMATION MODULES INC
870 10th Ln (98333-9646)
PHONE..................253 549-4868
Kent Lachner, *President*
EMP: 2
SALES (est): 280K **Privately Held**
WEB: www.automationmodules.com
SIC: 3625 Industrial controls: push button, selector switches, pilot

(G-4019)
BROOKS TACTICAL SYSTEMS
Also Called: Brooks Industries
865 9th Ave (98333-9676)
PHONE..................253 549-2703
Brooks Speier, *Owner*
EMP: 10
SALES (est): 780K **Privately Held**
WEB: www.brookstactical.com
SIC: 2381 3842 3812 3728 Gloves, work: woven or knit, made from purchased materials; surgical appliances & supplies; search & navigation equipment; aircraft parts & equipment; motor vehicle parts & accessories

(G-4020)
FOX ISLAND EXCAVATION LLC
1101 Island Blvd (98333-9624)
P.O. Box 124 (98333-0124)
PHONE..................253 677-7291
Robert Desjardins, *Principal*
Ryan Desjardins, *Principal*
EMP: 2
SALES (est): 65.5K **Privately Held**
SIC: 1389 Excavating slush pits & cellars

(G-4021)
FOX ISLAND WOODWORKS
1323 Mowitsh Dr (98333-9636)
PHONE..................253 549-7019
Mark Wuesthoff, *Principal*
EMP: 2
SALES (est): 159.9K **Privately Held**
SIC: 2431 Millwork

(G-4022)
GLOBAL FIA INC (PA)
684 6th Ave (98333-9693)
P.O. Box 480 (98333-0480)
PHONE..................253 549-2223
Don Olson, *CEO*
Graham Marshall, *President*
Sharon Marshall, *Treasurer*
EMP: 4
SQ FT: 1,200
SALES: 700K **Privately Held**
WEB: www.globalfia.com
SIC: 3823 Industrial instrmnts msrmnt display/control process variable

Fox Island - Pierce County (G-4023) — GEOGRAPHIC SECTION

(G-4023)
PLANET HEADSET INC
811 Enati Way (98333-9721)
PHONE.....................253 238-0643
Patrick Murphy, *CEO*
Aude Lugern, *Vice Pres*
EMP: 2
SALES (est): 258.7K **Privately Held**
WEB: www.planetheadset.com
SIC: 3661 Headsets, telephone

(G-4024)
PRINS WILLIAMS ANALYTICS LLC
363 North Shore Blvd (98333-9713)
P.O. Box 653 (98333-0653)
PHONE.....................253 549-0740
David Williams, *Principal*
EMP: 2
SALES (est): 153K **Privately Held**
SIC: 2752 Commercial printing, lithographic

(G-4025)
SOPHIES TOUCH
1361 11th Ct (98333-9629)
PHONE.....................253 677-1061
Trena Page, *Principal*
EMP: 3
SALES (est): 169.6K **Privately Held**
SIC: 3999 Pet supplies

(G-4026)
TREIT EQUIPMENT CO INC
240 Shorewood Ct (98333-9725)
PHONE.....................253 549-2399
Mike Treit, *President*
EMP: 3
SALES (est): 257.5K **Privately Held**
SIC: 3589 Water filters & softeners, household type

Freeland
Island County

(G-4027)
BRIAN E STYKE
1861 Lancaster Rd (98249-9582)
PHONE.....................360 331-0527
Brian Styke, *President*
EMP: 2
SALES (est): 80.6K **Privately Held**
SIC: 2759 Commercial printing

(G-4028)
FREELAND CAFE
Main St (98249)
P.O. Box 154 (98249-0154)
PHONE.....................360 331-9945
Robert Bryant, *Partner*
▲ EMP: 12 EST: 1970
SALES (est): 402.2K **Privately Held**
SIC: 5812 5813 2253 Cafe; cocktail lounge; lounge, bed & leisurewear

(G-4029)
H&H PUBLICATIONS LLP
4160 Beach Dr (98249-9434)
PHONE.....................360 730-1206
John Horn, *Partner*
Philip Hansten, *Partner*
EMP: 2
SALES (est): 100K **Privately Held**
SIC: 2731 Books: publishing only

(G-4030)
ICE FLOE LLC
Also Called: Nichols Brothers Boat Builders
5400 Cameron Rd (98249-9782)
P.O. Box 580 (98249-0580)
PHONE.....................360 331-5500
Joe Russick, *Mng Member*
John Collins,
Mitchel D Usibelli,
Scott Vollmer,
▲ EMP: 161
SALES (est): 73.7MM **Privately Held**
SIC: 3732 Boat building & repairing

(G-4031)
ISLAND SASH & DOOR INC
18181 D State Rte 525 (98249)
PHONE.....................360 331-7752
David Serres, *President*
Anita Serres, *Admin Sec*
EMP: 12
SQ FT: 2,500
SALES: 3.4MM **Privately Held**
SIC: 2431 1751 Window sashes, wood; window & door (prefabricated) installation

(G-4032)
MA & KT INC
Also Called: Eco-Vac
5586 Double Bluff Rd (98249)
PHONE.....................360 321-4019
Mark Arnold, *President*
EMP: 2
SALES (est): 135.6K **Privately Held**
SIC: 3589 Service industry machinery

(G-4033)
MUTINY BAY BLUES LLC
5578 Mutiny Bay Rd (98249)
PHONE.....................360 678-4315
Britt Fletcher,
EMP: 5
SQ FT: 5,000
SALES (est): 579.5K **Privately Held**
SIC: 5149 2034 0722 Groceries & related products; dried & dehydrated fruits; berry crops, machine harvesting services

(G-4034)
MUTINY BAY SOFTWARE LLC
5645 Carie Ln (98249-8723)
PHONE.....................360 331-5170
Keith Davis, *Principal*
EMP: 2
SALES (est): 115.3K **Privately Held**
SIC: 7372 Prepackaged software

(G-4035)
NICHOLS DIVERSIFIED INDS LLC
1957 Lancaster Rd (98249-9524)
PHONE.....................360 331-7230
Justin M Nichols,
Alanna L Nichols,
EMP: 10
SQ FT: 4,925
SALES (est): 985.8K **Privately Held**
WEB: www.ndiboats.com
SIC: 3732 Boat building & repairing

(G-4036)
NORTH CROSS ALUMINUM LLC
4964 Mutiny Bay Rd (98249-9665)
PHONE.....................360 821-1481
Tim Leonard, *Bd of Directors*
EMP: 4
SALES (est): 273.4K **Privately Held**
SIC: 2741 Catalogs: publishing & printing

(G-4037)
THIRSTY CRAB BREWERY LLC
4670 Rhodie Ln (98249-9686)
PHONE.....................360 331-3667
Robert Stallone, *Principal*
EMP: 3
SALES (est): 96.5K **Privately Held**
SIC: 2082 Malt beverages

(G-4038)
TOVA COMPANY
1832 Scott Rd Ste C5 (98249-9475)
PHONE.....................800 729-2886
Chris Holder, *CEO*
Tammy Dupuy, *COO*
Lawrence Greenberg, *Research*
Andrew Greenberg,
Carol Kinschi,
EMP: 12
SALES: 1.3MM **Privately Held**
WEB: www.tova.net
SIC: 5045 7372 7371 Computer software; prepackaged software; computer software development & applications

(G-4039)
WHIDBEY ISLAND ICE CREAM LLC
1715 Main St (98249)
PHONE.....................425 359-6372
Ronald J Hecker, *Mng Member*
Florence L Hecker,
EMP: 5
SQ FT: 1,500
SALES (est): 399.3K **Privately Held**
SIC: 5143 2024 Ice cream & ices; ice cream & frozen desserts

(G-4040)
WHIDBEY ISLAND NTURAL PDTS INC
Also Called: Whidbey Island Soap Company
2133 Lancaster Rd (98249-9690)
PHONE.....................360 929-2461
Kimberly Tiller, *President*
EMP: 2
SQ FT: 300
SALES (est): 138.5K **Privately Held**
SIC: 2841 2844 Textile soap; toilet preparations; shampoos, rinses, conditioners: hair; perfumes & colognes; face creams or lotions

Friday Harbor
San Juan County

(G-4041)
BLUE MOON MARINE LLC
Also Called: Blue Moon Marine Botanicals
1945 White Point Rd (98250-8100)
PHONE.....................360 378-2498
Mark R Donohue,
Mark Donohue,
EMP: 5
SALES: 20K **Privately Held**
SIC: 2833 Medicinals & botanicals

(G-4042)
DIESEL AMERICA WEST INC
92 Little Rd (98250-7107)
P.O. Box 968 (98250-0968)
PHONE.....................360 378-4182
Nancy Raichlen, *President*
Chris Raichlen, *Vice Pres*
Steve Raichlen, *Vice Pres*
▼ EMP: 6
SQ FT: 1,180
SALES (est): 801.1K **Privately Held**
WEB: www.dawest.com
SIC: 3599 Machine & other job shop work

(G-4043)
DOUBLE VISION PARTNERS INC
Also Called: At Home Publication
276 Salmonberry Ln (98250-9660)
P.O. Box 1571 (98250-1571)
PHONE.....................360 378-4331
Claudia Lavaca, *President*
Claudia La Vaca, *President*
EMP: 3 EST: 1999
SALES (est): 50K **Privately Held**
WEB: www.athome1.com
SIC: 2731 Books: publishing & printing

(G-4044)
FALCON RCNNISSANCE SYSTEMS INC
72 Airport Circle Dr (98250-7153)
P.O. Box 2597 (98250-2597)
PHONE.....................360 378-3900
Richard S Rich, *President*
Philip J Anderson, *Vice Pres*
EMP: 2
SQ FT: 1,600
SALES (est): 124.6K **Privately Held**
WEB: www.falconrecon.com
SIC: 8731 3724 Electronic research; research & development on aircraft engines & parts

(G-4045)
FRIDAY HARBOR EXPORTS INC
343 Vista Way (98250-8471)
PHONE.....................360 378-6086
EMP: 3
SALES (est): 157.9K **Privately Held**
SIC: 2099 Food preparations

(G-4046)
FRIDAY HARBOR HOUSE OF JERKY
260 Spring St Ste 7 (98250-7254)
PHONE.....................360 207-9652
James Lineback, *Owner*
Cynthia Malin, *Co-Owner*
EMP: 4
SALES (est): 244.4K **Privately Held**
SIC: 5421 2013 5149 Meat markets, including freezer provisioners; snack sticks, including jerky: from purchased meat; specialty food items

(G-4047)
GEM WELDING & FABRICATION
64 Miner Ln (98250-8589)
PHONE.....................360 378-5818
Dennis Steckler, *President*
Janette Steckler, *Corp Secy*
EMP: 7
SALES (est): 410K **Privately Held**
SIC: 7692 3599 Welding repair; machine & other job shop work

(G-4048)
GLASSHAPE NORTH AMERICA LP
175 2nd St N (98250-7949)
PHONE.....................206 538-5416
EMP: 8 EST: 2014
SALES (est): 292.6K **Privately Held**
SIC: 3211 Plate & sheet glass

(G-4049)
GREEN ISLAND GROWERS LLC
142 Pemberton Pl (98250-7099)
PHONE.....................360 298-0438
Levi Clark, *Mng Member*
EMP: 2
SALES (est): 88.8K **Privately Held**
SIC: 0139 3999 ;

(G-4050)
HARDENED ARMS LLC
515 Tucker Ave (98250-8040)
PHONE.....................425 530-0837
Patrick Merlino, *Mng Member*
EMP: 25
SALES (est): 329.1K **Privately Held**
SIC: 5941 3484 Firearms; small arms

(G-4051)
LUXEL CORPORATION
60 Saltspring Dr (98250-9062)
P.O. Box 1879 (98250-1879)
PHONE.....................360 378-0064
Travis Ayers, *President*
Dianne Hall, *Business Mgr*
David Grove, *Engineer*
Ryan Smith, *Engineer*
Heidi Lopez, *Lab Dir*
EMP: 18 EST: 1973
SQ FT: 10,000
SALES (est): 4.3MM **Privately Held**
WEB: www.luxel.com
SIC: 3827 Optical instruments & lenses

(G-4052)
NANOPORT TECHNOLOGIES LLC
300 Cessna Ave (98250-9147)
PHONE.....................206 403-1714
Andrew Muray, *Principal*
EMP: 4 EST: 2007
SALES (est): 266.6K **Privately Held**
SIC: 3825 Test equipment for electronic & electric measurement

(G-4053)
PRINT EASY
158 Channel Heights Way (98250-8938)
PHONE.....................800 562-0888
Mary Campanella, *President*
EMP: 2
SALES (est): 225.6K **Privately Held**
SIC: 2752 Commercial printing, lithographic

(G-4054)
PRINTONYX INC
470 Reed St (98250-5017)
P.O. Box 654 (98250-0654)
PHONE.....................360 378-2069
Kristine Brown, *President*
David Brown, *Vice Pres*
EMP: 5
SQ FT: 2,200
SALES (est): 432.5K **Privately Held**
WEB: www.printonyx.com
SIC: 7334 2752 Blueprinting service; commercial printing, lithographic

GEOGRAPHIC SECTION

Gig Harbor - Pierce County (G-4084)

(G-4055)
RICHARD LAWSON CONSTRUCTION
1165 W Valley Rd (98250-7073)
PHONE.................360 378-4313
Richard L Lawson, *President*
Jim Sampson, *Project Mgr*
EMP: 23
SQ FT: 3,000
SALES (est): 3.5MM **Privately Held**
SIC: **1794** 5032 2952 3273 Excavation work; stone, crushed or broken; asphalt felts & coatings; ready-mixed concrete

(G-4056)
SAN JUAN ISLANDER
1010 Guard St (98250-9240)
P.O. Box 1118 (98250-1118)
PHONE.................360 378-2798
Sharon Kivisto, *Owner*
Matt Pranger, *Co-Owner*
EMP: 2
SALES (est): 130.4K **Privately Held**
WEB: www.sanjuanislander.com
SIC: **2711** Newspapers: publishing only, not printed on site

(G-4057)
SAN JUAN ISLANDS SCULPTURE PK
9083 Roche Harbor Rd (98250-5520)
PHONE.................360 370-0035
Rikki K Swin, *President*
Kathleen Wilson, *Exec Dir*
EMP: 7 EST: 2012
SALES (est): 332.9K **Privately Held**
SIC: **3299** Architectural sculptures: gypsum, clay, papier mache, etc.

(G-4058)
SAN JUAN NATURALS
745 Larson St Ste A (98250-8027)
P.O. Box 642 (98250-0642)
PHONE.................360 378-2648
EMP: 2
SALES (est): 69K **Privately Held**
SIC: **2731** Book Publishing

(G-4059)
SOUND PUBLISHING INC
Also Called: Journal of The San Juans
640 Mullis St (98250-7940)
P.O. Box 519 (98250-0519)
PHONE.................360 378-5696
Heather Spaulding, *Office Mgr*
Colleen Armstrong, *Branch Mgr*
EMP: 5 **Privately Held**
WEB: www.soundpublishing.com
SIC: **2711** Newspapers, publishing & printing; newspapers: publishing only, not printed on site
HQ: Sound Publishing, Inc.
11323 Commando Rd W Main
Everett WA 98204
360 394-5800

(G-4060)
STRATEGIC NEWS SERVICE LLC
Also Called: Technology Alliance Partners
38 Yew Ln (98250-8509)
P.O. Box 1969 (98250-1969)
PHONE.................360 378-1023
Mark Anderson, *CEO*
Sharon Morris, *Director*
Russ Daggatt, *Bd of Directors*
EMP: 10
SALES (est): 865.7K **Privately Held**
WEB: www.tapsns.com
SIC: **2741** Miscellaneous publishing

(G-4061)
SUMNER STAINED GLASS COMPANY
91 Cougar Ln (98250-8436)
PHONE.................360 378-2761
Gary Sumner, *Owner*
EMP: 4
SALES (est): 198.8K **Privately Held**
SIC: **5231** 3211 Glass; flat glass

(G-4062)
TROPIC BIRD LLC
618 Harrison St Apt T (98250-7992)
P.O. Box 1896 (98250-1896)
PHONE.................360 378-5234
EMP: 2 EST: 2011
SALES (est): 83K **Privately Held**
SIC: **2741** Misc Publishing

(G-4063)
VALLEY STEEL & STONE
2435 San Juan Valley Rd (98250-9414)
P.O. Box 2261 (98250-2261)
PHONE.................360 378-5758
John Brash, *Principal*
EMP: 2
SALES (est): 198.2K **Privately Held**
SIC: **1542** 3499 Nonresidential construction; fabricated metal products

(G-4064)
WHATZIT MACHINING INC
474a Dexter Ln (98250-5003)
PHONE.................360 378-6874
Shelley Shelton-Wilson, *President*
Woody Wilson, *Manager*
EMP: 2
SALES (est): 130K **Privately Held**
WEB: www.whatzit-inc.com
SIC: **3599** Machine shop, jobbing & repair

Fruitland
Stevens County

(G-4065)
DON LARSON LOGGING INC
5900b Larson Ln (99129-9723)
PHONE.................509 722-6612
Donald R Larson, *President*
Linda Larson, *Corp Secy*
EMP: 5
SALES: 800K **Privately Held**
SIC: **2421** 2411 Lath, made in sawmills in lathmills; logging

Garfield
Whitman County

(G-4066)
CASCADE ARCFT CONVERSIONS LLC
903 Grinnell Rd (99130-8714)
PHONE.................509 635-1212
Aaron Abbott, *Exec VP*
EMP: 6
SALES (est): 235.4K
SALES (corp-wide): 10.9MM **Privately Held**
SIC: **3724** Aircraft engines & engine parts
PA: Abbott Industries, Inc.
12801 Highway 75
Okmulgee OK 74447
918 756-8320

(G-4067)
CASCADE FLYING SERVICE LLC
903 Grinnell Rd (99130-8714)
PHONE.................509 635-1212
Aaron Abbott, *Exec VP*
EMP: 6
SQ FT: 12,000
SALES (est): 302.5K
SALES (corp-wide): 10.9MM **Privately Held**
SIC: **4581** 0721 5191 3724 Aircraft cleaning & janitorial service; crop dusting services; farm supplies; aircraft engines & engine parts
PA: Abbott Industries, Inc.
12801 Highway 75
Okmulgee OK 74447
918 756-8320

(G-4068)
ED KA MANUFACTURING INC
213 E Main St (99130-8742)
P.O. Box 37 (99130-0037)
PHONE.................509 635-1521
T J Mitzimberg, *President*
EMP: 6
SQ FT: 5,200
SALES (est): 1.2MM **Privately Held**
SIC: **3531** 3523 3599 3715 Backhoes, tractors, cranes, plows & similar equipment; planting, haying, harvesting & processing machinery; machine shop, jobbing & repair; custom machinery; truck trailers

(G-4069)
TOWN OF GARFIELD
405 W California St (99130)
PHONE.................509 635-1604
EMP: 2
SALES (est): 222.5K **Privately Held**
SIC: **3523** Loaders, farm type: manure, general utility

Gig Harbor
Pierce County

(G-4070)
5TH WAVE MOBILE TECH INC
4212 Burnham Dr (98332-1008)
P.O. Box 3427, Redmond (98073-3427)
PHONE.................425 898-8161
Jerry Fowlkes, *President*
Teresa Fowlkes, *Principal*
Steve Hardy, *Vice Pres*
EMP: 5
SQ FT: 3,000
SALES (est): 354.2K **Privately Held**
SIC: **7299** 7373 3577 Personal document & information services; systems integration services; bar code (magnetic ink) printers

(G-4071)
AMERICAN NEON INC
10610 Crescent Vly Dr Nw (98332-9335)
PHONE.................253 627-7446
Elisa Jacoby, *President*
EMP: 10 EST: 1977
SQ FT: 4,000
SALES: 877.9K **Privately Held**
WEB: www.americanneon.com
SIC: **3993** Neon signs; electric signs

(G-4072)
ANN SILVERS
1013 140th Street Ct Nw (98332-9619)
PHONE.................253 853-7049
Ann Marie Silvers, *Principal*
EMP: 2
SALES (est): 129.1K **Privately Held**
SIC: **2741** Miscellaneous publishing

(G-4073)
APPGEN BUSINESS SOFTWARE
3312 Rsdale St Nw Ste 203 (98335)
PHONE.................253 857-9400
EMP: 2
SALES (est): 93.1K **Privately Held**
SIC: **7372** Prepackaged software

(G-4074)
AUSTIN JORDAN INC
2809 White Cloud Ave Nw (98335-7619)
PHONE.................253 265-1903
Brian Blevins, *President*
EMP: 2
SALES (est): 160K **Privately Held**
WEB: www.austinjordan.com
SIC: **3531** Construction machinery

(G-4075)
BAILEY AND BAILEY INC
Also Called: New Memorial Direct
5246 Olympic Dr Nw 101 (98335-1763)
PHONE.................253 649-0568
Brad Bailey, *President*
Michelle Bailey, *Vice Pres*
EMP: 12
SALES (est): 585.3K **Privately Held**
SIC: **3281** 5094 5944 Marble, building: cut & shaped; jewelry & precious stones; jewelry, precious stones & precious metals

(G-4076)
BARNARD PRESS
14702 33rd Ave Nw (98332-9226)
PHONE.................253 851-2208
David Doty, *Owner*
EMP: 3
SALES (est): 147.4K **Privately Held**
SIC: **2741** Miscellaneous publishing

(G-4077)
BEAR CREEK COATINGS LLC
4212 32nd Avenue Ct Nw (98335-8579)
PHONE.................253 722-4220
Thomas Davis, *Principal*
EMP: 2
SALES (est): 97.4K **Privately Held**
SIC: **3479** Metal coating & allied service

(G-4078)
BEAR INC
Also Called: Wild Birds Unlimited
3120 Harborview Dr (98335-2124)
PHONE.................253 851-2575
James Ullrich, *President*
Suzanne Ullrich, *Vice Pres*
EMP: 5
SQ FT: 1,200
SALES (est): 577.8K **Privately Held**
SIC: **2048** Prepared feeds

(G-4079)
BELLA BELLA CUPCAKES LLC
5515 38th Ave (98335-8236)
PHONE.................253 509-3158
Donna Wharton, *Branch Mgr*
EMP: 10
SALES (corp-wide): 988.3K **Privately Held**
SIC: **2053** Cakes, bakery: frozen
PA: Bella Bella Cupcakes, Llc
10726 Silverdale Way Nw # 107
Silverdale WA 98383
360 908-8096

(G-4080)
BERING STREET STUDIO LLC
5227 Bering St Nw (98332-9794)
P.O. Box 2121 (98335-4121)
PHONE.................253 677-4870
Stephanie Lile, *Administration*
EMP: 2
SALES (est): 101.4K **Privately Held**
SIC: **3999** Preparation of slides & exhibits

(G-4081)
BIG SMOOTH INDUSTRIES LLC
8611 89th Ave Nw (98332-6321)
PHONE.................206 356-5888
EMP: 2
SALES (est): 74.6K **Privately Held**
SIC: **3999** Manufacturing industries

(G-4082)
BLUE MARINE LLC
11010 Harbor Hill Dr B507 (98332-8953)
PHONE.................253 225-8228
Jacob Fichter, *Principal*
EMP: 2
SALES (est): 131.5K **Privately Held**
SIC: **1629** 2491 Dams, waterways, docks & other marine construction; piles, foundation & marine construction: treated wood

(G-4083)
BLUER SKIES PUBLISHING LLC
11400 Olympus Way C104 (98332-8758)
P.O. Box 495, Tacoma (98401-0495)
PHONE.................813 675-7588
Candice Harris, *Principal*
EMP: 2
SALES (est): 47.9K **Privately Held**
SIC: **2741** Miscellaneous publishing

(G-4084)
CARDSWAPPER LLC
925 34th Ave Nw (98335-7855)
P.O. Box 1134, Mercer Island (98040-1134)
PHONE.................253 549-8600
Bryan Gula,
Steven Gula,
EMP: 5
SALES (est): 141.8K **Privately Held**
SIC: **7372** Application computer software

Gig Harbor - Pierce County (G-4085)

(G-4085)
CELLULAR TO GO INC
Also Called: Kettle Corn Machine
9724 90th Ave Nw (98332-6837)
PHONE...................253 255-1955
Greg Sweet, *President*
Darci Sweet, *Vice Pres*
EMP: 4
SALES (est): 46.8K **Privately Held**
SIC: 3589 Popcorn machines, commercial

(G-4086)
CHIPS & DEL CARVINGS IN WOOD
10014 135th St Nw (98329-7042)
PHONE...................253 858-4751
Delbert Hansen, *Owner*
EMP: 2
SALES (est): 96K **Privately Held**
SIC: 2499 Carved & turned wood

(G-4087)
CHOICE CARDIOVASCULAR PLLC
4423 Point Fosdick Dr Nw # 300 (98335-1794)
PHONE...................253 229-7003
Robert Emerick, *Mng Member*
EMP: 6
SALES (est): 733.1K **Privately Held**
SIC: 2834 Drugs acting on the cardiovascular system, except diagnostic

(G-4088)
CIGARETTO
5500 Olympic Dr Ste A107 (98335-1489)
PHONE...................253 851-2175
Ae Kim, *Principal*
EMP: 2
SALES (est): 152.1K **Privately Held**
SIC: 2111 5194 Cigarettes; smoking tobacco

(G-4089)
CIGARLAND GIG HARBOR
4949 Borgen Blvd (98332-7895)
PHONE...................253 851-5515
Anna Lee, *Principal*
EMP: 2
SALES (est): 180K **Privately Held**
SIC: 2111 2121 3999 5194 Cigarettes; cigars; cigarette & cigar products & accessories; tobacco & tobacco products

(G-4090)
CLEARWATER CABINET CO
6869 Kimball Dr (98335-1256)
PHONE...................253 853-3644
EMP: 2 EST: 2005
SALES (est): 150K **Privately Held**
SIC: 2434 Mfg Wood Kitchen Cabinets

(G-4091)
CNC SOFTWARE INC
Also Called: Education Office
5717 Wollochet Dr Nw 2a (98335-7369)
PHONE...................253 858-6677
Dan Newby, *Manager*
EMP: 4
SALES (corp-wide): 14.5MM **Privately Held**
WEB: www.mastercam.com
SIC: 7372 5045 Prepackaged software; computers, peripherals & software
PA: Cnc Software, Inc.
671 Old Post Rd
Tolland CT
800 228-2877

(G-4092)
COMMENCEMENT BAY COFFEE CO
8626 Dogwood Ln Nw (98332-6768)
PHONE...................253 851-8259
Keith Trichard, *President*
EMP: 7
SALES (est): 444.3K **Privately Held**
SIC: 2095 Coffee roasting (except by wholesale grocers)

(G-4093)
CUSTOM PRINTS NW LLC
13627 131st Street Ct Nw (98329-5352)
PHONE...................253 225-7725
Jessica-Rachel Rogg, *Principal*
EMP: 2
SALES (est): 83.9K **Privately Held**
SIC: 2752 Commercial printing, lithographic

(G-4094)
DELPHIS CREATIVE BUS SOLUTIONS
3421 42nd Ave Nw (98335-8005)
PHONE...................360 689-4063
Shannon Faulkner, *Principal*
EMP: 2
SALES (est): 162.2K **Privately Held**
SIC: 3714 Motor vehicle parts & accessories

(G-4095)
DOUGLAS L PERRY
Also Called: Pg Woodworks
9614 Starlet Ln Nw (98335-5809)
PHONE...................253 303-0537
Douglas L Perry, *Owner*
EMP: 2
SALES (est): 94.5K **Privately Held**
WEB: www.douglaslperry.com
SIC: 2511 2521 2531 2519 Wood household furniture; wood office furniture; church furniture; fiberglass & plastic furniture; reupholstery & furniture repair; office furniture repair & maintenance

(G-4096)
DYNA FLOW
3110 Judson St (98335-1254)
PHONE...................253 381-9736
EMP: 4
SALES (est): 232K **Privately Held**
SIC: 2869 Hydraulic fluids, synthetic base

(G-4097)
ECO TEC INC
18617 108th St Ct Kpn (98329)
P.O. Box 690, Vaughn (98394-0690)
PHONE...................253 884-6804
Herb Pearse, *President*
EMP: 2
SALES: 125K **Privately Held**
WEB: www.eco-tec-inc.com
SIC: 8748 0711 2899 Environmental consultant; soil chemical treatment services; chemical preparations

(G-4098)
ENDRESEN PRESSURE WASHING
9111 66th Ave Nw Trlr 124 (98332-8427)
PHONE...................253 858-7743
Scott Endresen, *Owner*
EMP: 5
SALES (est): 60K **Privately Held**
SIC: 3589 7349 Service industry machinery; building maintenance services

(G-4099)
FINGER PRINTS OF HIS GRACE
13621 11th Ave Nw (98332-7603)
PHONE...................253 514-6150
EMP: 2
SALES (est): 130K **Privately Held**
SIC: 2752 Commercial printing, lithographic

(G-4100)
FITZ CUSTOM MARINE
163 Maple Ln Nw (98335-5996)
PHONE...................253 732-5669
Dan Fitzgerald, *Owner*
EMP: 2
SALES (est): 190.1K **Privately Held**
SIC: 3732 Boat building & repairing

(G-4101)
FOR ART SAKE INC
3155 Harborview Dr (98335-2124)
PHONE...................253 858-8087
EMP: 2
SALES (est): 55.8K **Privately Held**
SIC: 5199 2741 Whol Nondurable Goods Misc Publishing

(G-4102)
FOR THE LOVE OF SPICE
3104 Harborview Dr (98335-2124)
PHONE...................253 858-0272
Windy Payne, *Owner*
EMP: 2
SALES (est): 97K **Privately Held**
SIC: 2099 Seasonings & spices

(G-4103)
FRANK J MADERA
Also Called: Madera Woodworking
2606 120th Street Ct Nw (98332-9420)
P.O. Box 202 (98335-0202)
PHONE...................253 858-7934
Frank J Madera, *Owner*
EMP: 6
SALES (est): 368.5K **Privately Held**
WEB: www.maderawoodworking.com
SIC: 2431 Woodwork, interior & ornamental

(G-4104)
GAMBLE LOGGING
11203 70th Ave Nw (98332-8570)
PHONE...................253 857-3294
John Gamble, *Owner*
EMP: 2
SALES (est): 190K **Privately Held**
SIC: 2411 Logging camps & contractors

(G-4105)
GARY R HOWE
Also Called: Gary Howe Construction
6512 117th Street Ct Nw (98332-8529)
PHONE...................253 857-5835
Gary R Howe, *Owner*
EMP: 5
SQ FT: 1,200
SALES (est): 427.6K **Privately Held**
WEB: www.garyhowe.com
SIC: 2434 1521 Wood kitchen cabinets; new construction, single-family houses; general remodeling, single-family houses

(G-4106)
GDP GROUP LTD SPC
6610 78th Avenue Ct Nw (98335-6287)
PHONE...................253 459-3447
Jerry Schwartz, *CEO*
John J Anderson II, *Ch of Bd*
EMP: 2
SALES (est): 121.8K **Privately Held**
SIC: 3523 7389 Hog feeding, handling & watering equipment;

(G-4107)
GIG HARBOR BOAT WORKS INC
9905 Peacock Hill Ave (98332-1076)
P.O. Box 765 (98335-0765)
PHONE...................253 851-2126
Steve Sorensen, *President*
EMP: 5
SALES (est): 688.2K **Privately Held**
WEB: www.ghboats.com
SIC: 3732 5551 Boat building & repairing; boat dealers

(G-4108)
GIMPY NINJA LLC
7107 40th St Nw (98335-6503)
PHONE...................253 282-9943
Corey Moore, *CEO*
Bernadine Moore, *COO*
EMP: 2 EST: 2015
SALES (est): 105K **Privately Held**
SIC: 2899 2992 3448 3537 Oil treating compounds; oil absorption equipment; lubricating oils & greases; prefabricated metal buildings; containers (metal), air cargo

(G-4109)
HALEY & BROS
Also Called: Cutters Point Coffee
4909 33rd Avenue Ct Nw (98335-8611)
PHONE...................253 851-4977
Brooke Payne, *CEO*
Cody Payne, *Business Mgr*
EMP: 9
SALES (est): 223.7K **Privately Held**
SIC: 5149 2095 Coffee, green or roasted; roasted coffee

(G-4110)
HANGER PRSTHETCS & ORTHO INC
Also Called: Hanger Clinic
3555 Erickson St (98335-1268)
PHONE...................253 372-7478
Sam Liang, *Branch Mgr*
EMP: 8
SALES (corp-wide): 1B **Publicly Held**
SIC: 3842 Limbs, artificial
HQ: Hanger Prosthetics & Orthotics, Inc.
10910 Domain Dr Ste 300
Austin TX 78758
512 777-3800

(G-4111)
HARBOR GRAPHICS INC
3123 56th St Nw Ste 3 (98335-1363)
PHONE...................253 858-7909
Bryan Barber, *President*
EMP: 4
SQ FT: 24,000
SALES (est): 500.4K **Privately Held**
WEB: www.harborgraphics.net
SIC: 2752 Commercial printing, lithographic

(G-4112)
HARBOR STEEL FABRICATION
5926 Sehmel Dr Nw (98332-8307)
PHONE...................253 858-8804
EMP: 2
SALES (est): 48K **Privately Held**
SIC: 3999 Manufacturing industries

(G-4113)
HARMON BREWING COMPANY L L C
Also Called: Hub Gig Harbor
1208 26th Ave Nw (98335-7808)
PHONE...................253 853-1585
EMP: 10
SALES (est): 250.8K
SALES (corp-wide): 2.3MM **Privately Held**
SIC: 5812 2082 Eating places; malt beverages
PA: Harmon Brewing Company L L C
1938 Pacific Ave
Tacoma WA 98402
253 383-2739

(G-4114)
HART SYSTEMS INC
4911 71st Street Ct Nw (98335-8314)
PHONE...................253 858-8481
Ronald D Hart, *President*
EMP: 2 EST: 1982
SQ FT: 920
SALES: 350K **Privately Held**
SIC: 3823 Pressure measurement instruments, industrial

(G-4115)
HASSLER & ASSOCIATES INC
Also Called: Northwest Marine Supplies
12408 Tanager Dr Nw (98332-7865)
PHONE...................253 851-3248
Carl Hassler, *President*
EMP: 5
SALES: 2MM **Privately Held**
SIC: 2842 Sanitation preparations

(G-4116)
HAWK INTERNATIONAL INC
10421 Burnham Dr Nw Ste 3 (98332-7876)
PHONE...................253 851-3444
James Gates, *President*
Judith Gates, *Admin Sec*
EMP: 5
SQ FT: 10,000
SALES (est): 343.2K **Privately Held**
SIC: 3999 Fire extinguishers, portable

(G-4117)
HELITRAK INC
1620 26th Ave Nw Ste A (98335-8829)
PHONE...................253 857-0890
Peter Hambling, *President*
John Mercer, *Principal*
Tammie Carlyle-Chin, *Vice Pres*
Thomas Hall, *Vice Pres*
June Mercer, *Admin Sec*
EMP: 9
SALES (est): 666.4K **Privately Held**
SIC: 7359 3721 Aircraft & industrial truck rental services; aircraft rental; helicopters

(G-4118)
HERITAGE DISTILLING CO INC
3207 57th Street Ct Nw (98335-7586)
PHONE...................253 509-0008
Justin Stiefel, *CEO*

▲ EMP: 1
SALES (est): 1.7MM Privately Held
SIC: 2085 Distillers' dried grains & solubles & alcohol

(G-4119)
HORSESHOE LAKE AUTO WRECK
9401 State Route 302 Nw (98329-7107)
P.O. Box 57, Olalla (98359-0057)
PHONE.................................253 857-3866
Leonard Larson, Owner
EMP: 2 EST: 2008
SALES (est): 321.8K Privately Held
SIC: 3531 Automobile wrecker hoists

(G-4120)
HORSESHOE LAKE ESTATES ASSN
9216 147th Street Ct Nw (98329-8749)
PHONE.................................253 851-3514
Shawn McNellis, Principal
EMP: 2 EST: 2012
SALES (est): 138.8K Privately Held
SIC: 3462 Horseshoes

(G-4121)
INSPIRED MONUMENTAL
1620 60th Avenue Ct Nw (98335-7523)
PHONE.................................253 468-4835
Troi Cockayne, Principal
EMP: 3 EST: 2011
SALES (est): 182.8K Privately Held
SIC: 3272 Monuments & grave markers, except terrazo

(G-4122)
INTERNATIONAL CHEM SYSTEMS INC
Also Called: Environmental Chem Solutions
3006 Judson St Ste 201 (98335-1226)
P.O. Box 2029 (98335-4029)
PHONE.................................253 263-8038
Robert Philpott, CEO
Edward Grubbs, President
James Figueira, Vice Pres
▼ EMP: 15
SQ FT: 3,000
SALES (est): 2.4MM Privately Held
WEB: www.ecschem.com
SIC: 2869 Industrial organic chemicals

(G-4123)
JI WOODWORK
3227 76th Ave Nw (98335-6450)
PHONE.................................360 790-4083
EMP: 2
SALES (est): 181.5K Privately Held
SIC: 2431 Millwork

(G-4124)
JL CABINET REFACING LLC
3227 76th Ave Nw (98335-6450)
PHONE.................................253 514-5975
John Lucas, Principal
EMP: 2
SALES (est): 167.1K Privately Held
SIC: 2434 Wood kitchen cabinets

(G-4125)
JON LONNING DRYWALL
14620 94th Ave Nw (98329-8828)
PHONE.................................253 851-4866
Jon Lonning, Owner
EMP: 2
SALES (est): 138K Privately Held
SIC: 1742 2411 Drywall; logging

(G-4126)
KIRSTEN GALLERY INC
6921 120th St Nw (98332-8563)
PHONE.................................206 522-2011
Richard J Kirsten, President
Nicolas Kirsten, Vice Pres
Kay Kirsten, Treasurer
Richard Kirsten, Administration
EMP: 5 EST: 1974
SALES (est): 500K Privately Held
WEB: www.kirstengallery.com
SIC: 5999 5199 2741 Art dealers; art goods; miscellaneous publishing

(G-4127)
KIT A JEWELER DESIGNED FOR YOU
3104 Harborview Dr (98335-2124)
P.O. Box 2433 (98335-4433)
PHONE.................................253 851-5546
Kit Kuhn, President
Kathy Kuhn, Vice Pres
EMP: 3
SQ FT: 750
SALES (est): 780K Privately Held
WEB: www.kitkuhn.com
SIC: 3911 Jewelry apparel

(G-4128)
KRANTZ NEWS SERVICE INC
Also Called: Kns Information Services
15407 41st Ave Nw (98332-8040)
PHONE.................................253 857-6590
Beckie Krantz, CEO
Dennis Krantz, Principal
EMP: 2 EST: 1989
SALES (est): 219.2K Privately Held
WEB: www.legicrawler.com
SIC: 8743 5045 7372 Public relations services; computer software; application computer software

(G-4129)
LCH ENTERPRISES
5315 Point Fosdick Dr Nw B (98335-1777)
PHONE.................................253 313-5665
Leigh Hurlburt, Principal
EMP: 4
SALES (est): 424.3K Privately Held
SIC: 5122 2844 Toilet soap; face creams or lotions

(G-4130)
LENNOX ERGONOMICS & CO
4203 74th Avenue Ct Nw (98335-6553)
PHONE.................................253 268-0830
Lennox Peters, Partner
Helen Peters, Partner
EMP: 2
SALES (est): 130.1K Privately Held
SIC: 3993 Signs & advertising specialties

(G-4131)
LETS RIDE LLC
5114 Point Fosdick Dr Nw (98335-1733)
PHONE.................................253 225-3630
▲ EMP: 3
SALES (est): 210K Privately Held
SIC: 3751 Mfg Motorcycles/Bicycles

(G-4132)
LIFESMART PUBLICATION
12913 50th Avenue Ct Nw (98332-7830)
PHONE.................................253 851-3169
Dennis Trittin, Principal
EMP: 2 EST: 2011
SALES (est): 105.1K Privately Held
SIC: 2741 Miscellaneous publishing

(G-4133)
LKA GOLD INCORPORATED (PA)
3724 47th Street Ct Nw (98335-8538)
PHONE.................................253 514-6661
Kye A Abraham, Ch of Bd
Nanette Abraham, Treasurer
EMP: 2
SQ FT: 750
SALES (est): 413K Publicly Held
SIC: 1041 1044 1031 1481 Gold ores mining; silver ores; lead & zinc ores; mine exploration, nonmetallic minerals

(G-4134)
MARDIE REES ARTIST LLC
13515 82nd Ave Nw (98329-8642)
PHONE.................................253 279-3244
Mardie Broderick, General Mgr
Jeremy Broderick, Principal
EMP: 3
SALES (est): 245.3K Privately Held
SIC: 3269 Pottery products

(G-4135)
MURDOCKS
5501 90th Ave Nw (98335-6254)
PHONE.................................253 858-9697
Murdock Martenson, Owner
EMP: 2

SALES (est): 130K Privately Held
SIC: 2434 Wood kitchen cabinets

(G-4136)
NORTHWEST METROLOGY LLC
5715 Wollochet Dr Nw (98335-7370)
PHONE.................................253 853-3183
Larry H Morris, CEO
Joy Morris, Manager
EMP: 15 EST: 1998
SALES (est): 3.3MM Privately Held
WEB: www.northwestmetrology.com
SIC: 3829 Measuring & controlling devices

(G-4137)
NWT3K OUTERWEAR
14919 118th Ave Nw (98329-5695)
PHONE.................................253 318-2371
Nick Marvik, Bd of Directors
▲ EMP: 2
SALES (est): 125.6K Privately Held
SIC: 3949 Snow skiing equipment & supplies, except skis

(G-4138)
OCEAN CARGO CONTAINER INC
3111 Harborview Dr (98335-2105)
PHONE.................................253 381-9098
Al Hayes, CEO
EMP: 3
SALES (est): 330K Privately Held
SIC: 5113 3412 3715 Boxes & containers; milk (fluid) shipping containers, metal; demountable cargo containers

(G-4139)
OLYMPIC HOME MODIFICATION LLC
4700 Point Fosdick Dr Nw (98335-1706)
PHONE.................................253 858-9941
Jeffrey Bond,
EMP: 5
SALES (est): 778.2K Privately Held
SIC: 3534 5999 1521 3999 Stair elevators, motor powered; wheelchair lifts; single-family home remodeling, additions & repairs; patio & deck construction & repair; wheelchair lifts

(G-4140)
ORIGINAL HEARTS
1114 138th St Nw (98332-9697)
PHONE.................................253 857-0700
Peter V Fernandez, Owner
EMP: 2
SALES (est): 70.4K Privately Held
SIC: 2771 Greeting cards

(G-4141)
PACIFIC STAGE LIGHTING
15504 131st Avenue Ct Nw (98329-4142)
PHONE.................................253 248-6344
Mike Reece, Principal
EMP: 2
SALES (est): 157.5K Privately Held
SIC: 3648 Stage lighting equipment

(G-4142)
PALMER HAYES OFFSHORE
7419 Rosedale St Nw (98335-6734)
PHONE.................................253 310-7162
Matt Palmer, Principal
EMP: 2 EST: 2010
SALES (est): 155K Privately Held
SIC: 3731 Offshore supply boats, building & repairing

(G-4143)
PENINSULA IRON
11020 State Route 302 Nw (98329-7022)
PHONE.................................253 857-8844
Keith Hillstrom, CEO
Kathy Hillstrom, President
EMP: 2
SQ FT: 8,500
SALES (est): 300K Privately Held
SIC: 3448 Prefabricated metal buildings

(G-4144)
PETTIBON BIO-MECHANICS INST (PA)
3208 50th Street Ct Nw 102b (98335-8590)
PHONE.................................360 748-4207
EMP: 3

SQ FT: 900
SALES (est): 3MM Privately Held
SIC: 3842 9999 Mfg Surgical Appliances/Supplies Nonclassified Establishment

(G-4145)
PIN FOUNDATIONS INC
Also Called: Diamond Pier
5114 Point Fosdick Dr Nw E60 (98335-1733)
PHONE.................................253 858-3844
Rick Gagliano, President
Olive Jeanne Ratcliffe Gaglian, Admin Sec
EMP: 6 EST: 1992
SALES (est): 213.1K Privately Held
WEB: www.pinfoundation.com
SIC: 3272 Concrete stuctural support & building material

(G-4146)
PIPEMASTERS INC
15807 130th Ave Nw (98329-4138)
PHONE.................................253 377-0717
Ron Cobb, President
EMP: 2
SALES (est): 212.4K Privately Held
SIC: 3432 Plumbing fixture fittings & trim

(G-4147)
POPE RESOURCES
4423 Point Fosdick Dr Nw (98335-1797)
PHONE.................................253 851-7009
John Chadwell, Principal
EMP: 2
SALES (est): 118.6K Privately Held
SIC: 2411 Timber, cut at logging camp

(G-4148)
PREMIER INDUSTRIES
11126 Vipond Dr Nw (98329-6905)
PHONE.................................253 514-0977
Sally McCannon, Principal
EMP: 3
SALES (est): 173.2K Privately Held
SIC: 3999 Manufacturing industries

(G-4149)
PRINTING HOPE
4918 38th Ave Nw (98335-8215)
PHONE.................................253 358-3348
Katie Wright, Principal
EMP: 2
SALES (est): 124.3K Privately Held
SIC: 2752 Commercial printing, lithographic

(G-4150)
RAINPLEX INC
1512 37th St Nw (98335-1555)
P.O. Box 527 (98335-0527)
PHONE.................................253 576-0157
Robert Backstein, President
Joshua Backstein, Vice Pres
EMP: 3 EST: 2016
SALES (est): 93.1K Privately Held
SIC: 7372 Prepackaged software

(G-4151)
RAYA PUBLISHING LLC
7718 Swanson Dr Nw (98335-6439)
PHONE.................................808 635-5908
Edith Stadig, Principal
EMP: 2 EST: 2012
SALES (est): 114K Privately Held
SIC: 2741 Miscellaneous publishing

(G-4152)
REAL CARRIAGE DOOR COMPANY
9803 44th Ave Nw (98332-7899)
PHONE.................................253 853-3815
Don Rees, President
▼ EMP: 4
SALES (est): 705.4K Privately Held
WEB: www.realcarriagedoors.com
SIC: 3231 Doors, glass: made from purchased glass

(G-4153)
RECLUSE LLC
10516 36th Street Ct Nw (98335-5815)
P.O. Box 463 (98335-0463)
PHONE.................................253 312-2169
Dan R Antilla, Principal

Gig Harbor - Pierce County (G-4154)

EMP: 2
SALES (est): 133.5K **Privately Held**
SIC: 3949 Sporting & athletic goods

(G-4154)
RED PERISCOPE TECHNOLOGIE
3467 Edwards Dr (98335-1151)
PHONE.................253 851-3968
EMP: 3
SALES (est): 183.1K **Privately Held**
SIC: 3827 Periscopes

(G-4155)
RILEY HOPKINS SCREEN PRINTING
196 Fir Dr Nw (98335-5933)
P.O. Box 1727 (98335-3727)
PHONE.................253 851-9078
P Hopkins, *Bd of Directors*
EMP: 2
SALES (est): 137.7K **Privately Held**
SIC: 2752 Commercial printing, lithographic

(G-4156)
ROGUE EMPIRE INC
Also Called: Fresh Northwest Design
915 26th Ave Nw (98335-8814)
PHONE.................253 857-5300
Scott Sehoenem, *President*
David Olive, *Managing Prtnr*
Joe Valosay, *Opers Mgr*
EMP: 10
SQ FT: 3,000
SALES (est): 1.1MM **Privately Held**
WEB: www.freshnorthwestdesign.com
SIC: 3231 Products of purchased glass

(G-4157)
ROYS SALSA LLC
6805 Rosedale St Nw (98335-6622)
PHONE.................253 514-3767
EMP: 2
SALES (est): 62.3K **Privately Held**
SIC: 2099 Dips, except cheese & sour cream based

(G-4158)
RUNWAY LIQUIDATION LLC
Also Called: Bcbg
5900 Greenbelt Rd (98335)
PHONE.................304 325-3603
EMP: 2
SALES (corp-wide): 645.5MM **Privately Held**
SIC: 2335 Women's, juniors' & misses' dresses
HQ: Runway Liquidation, Llc
2761 Fruitland Ave
Vernon CA 90058
323 589-2224

(G-4159)
SCOTT WOOD ASSOCIATES LLC
38 Raft Island Dr Nw (98335-5918)
PHONE.................253 509-3742
Scott Wood,
Holly Blash-Wood,
EMP: 2
SALES (est): 160K **Privately Held**
SIC: 2759 Thermography

(G-4160)
SENSORMATIC ELECTRONICS LLC
5775 Soundview Dr E101 (98335-2211)
PHONE.................253 851-6500
Bill McCubbins, *President*
Jim I Wilkerson, *Engineer*
John Morrison,
EMP: 56 **Privately Held**
WEB: www.sensormatic.com
SIC: 3812 Detection apparatus: electronic/magnetic field, light/heat
HQ: Sensormatic Electronics, Llc
6600 Congress Ave
Boca Raton FL 33487
561 912-6000

(G-4161)
SOUERS MANUFACTURING INC
Also Called: Souers Custom Plastics
915 26th Ave Nw Ste C8 (98335-8814)
PHONE.................253 735-2488
Justin Bice, *President*
Cary Bice, *Vice Pres*
Brent Johnson, *Opers Mgr*
EMP: 8
SALES (est): 1.4MM **Privately Held**
WEB: www.souersplastics.com
SIC: 2542 Partitions & fixtures, except wood

(G-4162)
SOUNDVIEW GRAPHICS LLC
3303 Jahn Ave Nw Ste 115 (98335-8050)
PHONE.................253 851-2007
William Massey, *Partner*
Deborah Massey, *Partner*
EMP: 2
SALES (est): 220K **Privately Held**
SIC: 2759 Screen printing

(G-4163)
SPARKLEHORSE LLC
6820 Kimball Dr Ste C (98335-5124)
P.O. Box 65532, University Place (98464-1532)
PHONE.................253 948-7772
Aaron Johnson,
EMP: 5
SALES (est): 296.8K **Privately Held**
SIC: 2082 Near beer

(G-4164)
SPECVIEW CORP (PA)
3100b Harborview Dr (98335-2124)
PHONE.................253 853-3199
Stephen Cooper, *President*
Steve Cooper, *Principal*
Nancy Cooper, *Corp Secy*
EMP: 2
SALES: 750K **Privately Held**
SIC: 7372 Application computer software

(G-4165)
TEAM SPORT SOFTWARE LLC
4415 Holly Ln Nw (98335-1433)
PHONE.................703 971-2005
David Hyde, *Principal*
EMP: 2
SALES (est): 129.4K **Privately Held**
SIC: 7372 Prepackaged software

(G-4166)
TECHNIPFMC US HOLDINGS INC
13409 53rd Ave Nw (98332-7870)
PHONE.................253 853-5060
EMP: 13
SALES (corp-wide): 12.6B **Privately Held**
WEB: www.fmctechnologies.com
SIC: 3556 Food products machinery
HQ: Fmc Technologies, Inc.
11740 Katy Fwy Energy Tow
Houston TX 77079
281 591-4000

(G-4167)
TOUCH & GO TEES
4917 63rd Ave Nw (98335-7383)
PHONE.................253 651-7505
EMP: 2
SALES (est): 73.2K **Privately Held**
SIC: 2759 Screen printing

(G-4168)
TRADITIONAL CONCEPTS
10626 Wright Bliss Rd Nw (98329-5773)
PHONE.................253 884-2818
Kim Mc Kibben, *Partner*
David Mc Kibben, *Partner*
Duane Mc Kibben, *Partner*
Kelly Mc Kibben, *Partner*
Mark Mc Kibben, *Partner*
EMP: 5
SALES (est): 675K **Privately Held**
SIC: 2431 2591 Windows & window parts & trim, wood; drapery hardware & blinds & shades

(G-4169)
TRI-POINT INDUSTRIES INC
10107 74th Ave Nw (98332-6801)
PHONE.................253 514-8890
Ty Lyles, *President*
EMP: 2
SALES (est): 115.8K **Privately Held**
SIC: 3999 Manufacturing industries

(G-4170)
TROCAR INVESTMENTS
9303 N Harborview Dr (98332-2158)
PHONE.................253 851-9206
Randy Eaton, *Administration*
EMP: 2
SALES (est): 86.6K **Privately Held**
SIC: 3841 Trocars

(G-4171)
VIBRATRIM LLC
5114 Point Fosdick Dr Nw (98335-1733)
PHONE.................253 238-0675
Donald Wickstrom,
▲ EMP: 2
SALES (est): 219.9K **Privately Held**
SIC: 3999 Vibrators, electric: designed for barber & beauty shops

(G-4172)
VISTAPRINT
11287 Borgen Loop (98332-5712)
PHONE.................617 838-2434
Corey McGrath, *Principal*
EMP: 2
SALES (est): 100.1K **Privately Held**
SIC: 2752 Commercial printing, lithographic

(G-4173)
WACHTLER INC
6659 Kimball Dr Ste D404 (98335-5141)
PHONE.................253 225-1904
William Wachtler, *President*
EMP: 3
SALES (est): 221.8K **Privately Held**
SIC: 2435 Panels, hardwood plywood

(G-4174)
WATERS EDGE GALLERY & FRAMERY
7808 Pioneer Way (98335-1133)
PHONE.................253 858-7449
Bill Fogarty, *Owner*
Aidan Fogarty, *Co-Owner*
EMP: 2
SQ FT: 900
SALES (est): 121.8K **Privately Held**
WEB: www.watersedgegallery.com
SIC: 5999 3999 Art dealers; picture frames, ready made; framed artwork

(G-4175)
WILKINS PRECISION INC
927 34th Ave Nw (98335-7855)
PHONE.................253 851-9736
Scott Wilkins, *President*
Kc Wilkins, *Vice Pres*
EMP: 2
SALES: 400K **Privately Held**
SIC: 3545 Precision measuring tools

(G-4176)
WOJTANOWICZ WOOD WORKS
5902 Reid Dr Nw (98335-1344)
PHONE.................253 225-2252
Joel Wojtanowicz, *Principal*
EMP: 2
SALES (est): 108.8K **Privately Held**
SIC: 2431 Millwork

(G-4177)
YO GS GH
4784 Borgen Blvd Ste E (98332-6764)
PHONE.................253 858-9647
Rudy Kaldor, *Principal*
EMP: 6
SALES (est): 350.8K **Privately Held**
SIC: 2024 Ice cream, bulk

Glenwood
Klickitat County

(G-4178)
C & H LOGGING INC
105 Trout Lake Hwy (98619-9037)
PHONE.................509 364-3420
Steven Hoodenpyl, *President*
James Fritchey, *Vice Pres*
EMP: 34
SALES (est): 3.4MM **Privately Held**
SIC: 2411 Logging camps & contractors

(G-4179)
ELK CREEK CONTRACTORS INC
25 Dean Ln (98619-9900)
P.O. Box 17 (98619-0017)
PHONE.................509 364-3692
Mary Dean, *President*
EMP: 10
SALES (est): 1.1MM **Privately Held**
SIC: 2411 Logging camps & contractors

(G-4180)
F AND F EXCAVATING AND LOGGING
1816 Bz Glenwood Hwy (98619-9051)
PHONE.................509 637-2551
EMP: 2
SALES (est): 84.3K **Privately Held**
SIC: 2411 Logging

(G-4181)
FELLER LOGGING INC
1788 Bz Glenwood Hwy (98619-9050)
PHONE.................509 364-3435
Allen Feller, *President*
Francis Feller, *Corp Secy*
EMP: 4 EST: 1970
SALES (est): 445.8K **Privately Held**
SIC: 2411 4789 Logging camps & contractors; log loading & unloading

(G-4182)
GLENWOOD TIMBER INC
9 Pine Vista Rd (98619-9033)
PHONE.................509 364-4158
Brad Gimlin, *President*
Brent Gimlin, *Vice Pres*
EMP: 2 EST: 1990
SALES (est): 198.5K **Privately Held**
SIC: 2411 Timber, cut at logging camp

(G-4183)
HANSEN & SPIES LOGGING INC
Also Called: Mt. Adams Forest Pdts & Svcs
18 Pine Vista Rd (98619-9033)
PHONE.................509 364-3385
Darrel E Spies, *President*
EMP: 12
SALES (est): 1.4MM **Privately Held**
SIC: 2411 Logging camps & contractors

(G-4184)
HELLROARING COMPANY
17 Ladiges Rd (98619-9023)
PHONE.................509 364-3522
Diane Carlson, *Owner*
EMP: 3
SALES (est): 20K **Privately Held**
SIC: 2395 2399 Embroidery & art needlework; hand woven & crocheted products

Gold Bar
Snohomish County

(G-4185)
ASSOCIATED SAND GRAVEL
44000 State Route 2 (98251)
PHONE.................425 348-6309
Graham Hardwick, *Principal*
EMP: 5 EST: 2008
SALES (est): 337.9K **Privately Held**
SIC: 1442 Construction sand & gravel

(G-4186)
AYURVEG INC
14811 Moonlight Dr (98251-9582)
P.O. Box 19767, Seattle (98109-6767)
PHONE.................360 863-2457
Rakesh Raniga, *President*
EMP: 3
SQ FT: 2,500
SALES: 600K **Privately Held**
SIC: 2099 5499 Food preparations; gourmet food stores

(G-4187)
FOSS STUMP GRINDING
16023 419th Ave Se (98251-9375)
PHONE.................360 799-2100
Clayton Foss, *Principal*
EMP: 2
SALES (est): 130K **Privately Held**
SIC: 3599 Grinding castings for the trade

GEOGRAPHIC SECTION

(G-4188)
G WOLF ENTERPRISES INC
Also Called: Wolf Pack
14811 Moonlight Dr (98251-9582)
PHONE..................................360 793-2988
George Wolf, *President*
EMP: 7
SALES (est): 540K **Privately Held**
SIC: 2033 Vegetables: packaged in cans, jars, etc.

(G-4189)
HANSON PRECISION INC
41729 164th St Se (98251-9531)
PHONE..................................360 793-0626
Jill Hanson, *Principal*
Jerry Hanson, *Officer*
EMP: 2
SQ FT: 2,000
SALES (est): 360K **Privately Held**
SIC: 3599 Machine shop, jobbing & repair

(G-4190)
PUGET SOUND CANVAS UPHOLS
17030 418th Ave Se (98251-4101)
PHONE..................................206 782-5974
Robin Burns, *Principal*
EMP: 2
SALES (est): 95K **Privately Held**
SIC: 2211 Canvas

(G-4191)
SNIPAHS LLC
16808 405th Dr Se (98251-9580)
PHONE..................................910 922-4693
Patrick Lewis, *Principal*
Alisson Lewis, *Principal*
EMP: 2
SALES (est): 75.4K **Privately Held**
SIC: 2033 7389 Vegetables & vegetable products in cans, jars, etc.;

Goldendale
Klickitat County

(G-4192)
ALEXANDER S SERVICE REPAIR
3123 S Columbos (98620)
P.O. Box 1408 (98620-1408)
PHONE..................................509 773-7010
John Alexander, *President*
EMP: 3
SALES (est): 275K **Privately Held**
SIC: 7699 3732 Lawn mower repair shop; motorized boat, building & repairing

(G-4193)
BISHOP-RED ROCK INC
221 W Main St (98620-9587)
P.O. Box 34 (98620-0034)
PHONE..................................509 773-5335
Edgar Holbrook, *President*
EMP: 7
SQ FT: 2,000
SALES (est): 750K **Privately Held**
SIC: 1442 Gravel & pebble mining

(G-4194)
CHRISTINE WOODCOCK
Also Called: Golden Graphics Sign Co
377 Ekone Rd (98620-2822)
PHONE..................................509 773-4747
Christine Woodcock, *Owner*
EMP: 2
SALES: 75K **Privately Held**
SIC: 3993 Signs & advertising specialties

(G-4195)
DWINELL LLC
Also Called: Dwinell Country Ales
206 W Broadway St (98620-9130)
P.O. Box 855 (98620-0855)
PHONE..................................312 343-8607
Jocelyn Leigh, *Manager*
Justin Leigh, *Manager*
EMP: 3
SALES (est): 91.3K **Privately Held**
SIC: 2082 Beer (alcoholic beverage)

(G-4196)
EMERALD TWIST INCORPORATED
459 Brentwood Rd (98620-2813)
PHONE..................................541 659-2189
Ryan Hamreus, *President*
Jerry Lapora, *Director*
EMP: 6
SALES (est): 338.7K **Privately Held**
SIC: 0139 3999 ;

(G-4197)
FARRER LOGGING CO
3275 Highway 142 (98620-3300)
PHONE..................................509 773-5069
James Farrer, *Owner*
EMP: 2
SALES (est): 201.5K **Privately Held**
SIC: 2411 Logging camps & contractors

(G-4198)
GOLDENDALE GRAPPLERS
111 Rimrock Rd (98620-3416)
PHONE..................................509 314-9975
Rachele Williams, *Principal*
EMP: 3
SALES (est): 148.8K **Privately Held**
SIC: 2711 Newspapers: publishing only, not printed on site

(G-4199)
GOLDENDALE SENTINEL INC
Also Called: Tirtan Publications
117 W Main St (98620-9526)
PHONE..................................509 773-3777
Leslie Marzeles, *President*
Andrew McNab, *President*
EMP: 5
SQ FT: 4,000
SALES (est): 219K **Privately Held**
WEB: www.goldendalesentinel.com
SIC: 2711 Newspapers: publishing only, not printed on site; commercial printing & newspaper publishing combined

(G-4200)
HOOD RIVER SAND GRAVEL
1030 W Broadway St (98620-3802)
PHONE..................................509 773-0314
EMP: 2
SALES (est): 66K **Privately Held**
SIC: 1442 Construction sand & gravel

(G-4201)
HOT RODS
105 W Main St (98620-9526)
PHONE..................................509 773-7005
Rod Hot, *Principal*
EMP: 4
SALES (est): 380.1K **Privately Held**
SIC: 2599 Bar, restaurant & cafeteria furniture

(G-4202)
LOG PROCESSORS INC
2020 Glenwood Hwy (98620-2200)
PHONE..................................509 773-3043
Kenneth Quantrell, *President*
Donald Quantrell, *President*
Cindy Quantrell, *Corp Secy*
EMP: 10
SALES (est): 1.2MM **Privately Held**
SIC: 2411 Logging camps & contractors

(G-4203)
MOUNTAINVIEW SCREEN PRINT
3255 Highway 142 (98620-3300)
PHONE..................................509 773-6290
EMP: 2
SALES (est): 100K **Privately Held**
SIC: 2752 Lithographic Commercial Printing

(G-4204)
MULRONY LOGGING LLC
192 Horseshoe Bend Rd (98620-3603)
PHONE..................................509 261-1549
Jasen Mulrony, *Administration*
EMP: 6 **EST:** 2016
SALES (est): 131.6K **Privately Held**
SIC: 2411 Logging camps & contractors

(G-4205)
PAULEY RODINE INC (PA)
Also Called: American Machines
405 S Columbus Ave (98620-9624)
P.O. Box 1379 (98620-1379)
PHONE..................................509 773-3200
Pauline H Nathan, *President*
Rodney Nathan, *Vice Pres*
EMP: 3
SQ FT: 2,500
SALES (est): 1.6MM **Privately Held**
WEB: www.american-machines.com
SIC: 5049 3441 Metal locating equipment & accessories; fabricated structural metal

(G-4206)
PIONEER ROCK & MONUMENT LLC
201 Crafton Rd (98620)
P.O. Box 348 (98620-0348)
PHONE..................................509 773-4702
Robert Rising,
Benjamin Rising,
Kristine Rising,
EMP: 3
SQ FT: 500
SALES (est): 137.5K **Privately Held**
SIC: 5999 3272 Monuments, finished to custom order; grave markers, concrete

(G-4207)
RAPID READYMIX CO (PA)
740 W Railroad Ave (98620)
P.O. Box 668, Bingen (98605-0668)
PHONE..................................509 773-5919
Patricia Riley, *President*
Matt Riley, *Vice Pres*
Matthew M Riley, *Vice Pres*
Patricia K Riley, *Admin Sec*
EMP: 7
SQ FT: 40,000
SALES (est): 783.3K **Privately Held**
SIC: 3273 Ready-mixed concrete

(G-4208)
RR PRODUCTS
29 Wildcat Rd (98620-2328)
PHONE..................................509 773-5227
Richard Post, *Owner*
EMP: 2
SALES: 50K **Privately Held**
SIC: 2861 Wood extract products

(G-4209)
THE MCCREDY COMPANY
126 W Main St (98620-9588)
PHONE..................................509 773-5340
Dan McCredy, *Owner*
EMP: 6
SALES: 220K **Privately Held**
SIC: 5231 5941 5092 5719 Paint; paint & painting supplies; sporting goods & bicycle shops; toys & games; housewares; costume jewelry

(G-4210)
TRADITIONAL HEIRLOOMS
117 N Columbus Ave (98620-9541)
PHONE..................................509 722-2620
Arthur Torsen, *Principal*
EMP: 2 **EST:** 2010
SALES (est): 104.3K **Privately Held**
SIC: 2511 Wood household furniture

(G-4211)
V&C LLC
Also Called: Maryhill Winery
9774 Highway 14 (98620-4648)
PHONE..................................509 773-1976
Doug Mile, *Accounts Mgr*
Cherie A Brooks,
Craig Leuthold,
Vickie Leuthold,
EMP: 15
SALES (est): 3.1MM **Privately Held**
WEB: www.maryhillwinery.com
SIC: 2084 Wines

(G-4212)
WAVING TREE VINEYARD & WINERY
2 Maryhill Hwy (98620-4604)
PHONE..................................509 773-6552
Atkins Parrente, *Principal*
EMP: 4

SALES (est): 344.8K **Privately Held**
SIC: 5921 2084 Wine; wines

(G-4213)
WEST COAST AUTOMATION CORP
Also Called: TLC Modular Homes
1600 S Roosevelt St (98620-9219)
PHONE..................................509 773-5055
Wes Wagner, *President*
Dave Wagner, *Vice Pres*
Rita Wagner, *Treasurer*
EMP: 24
SQ FT: 16,000
SALES: 2.5MM **Privately Held**
WEB: www.tlcmodularhomes.com
SIC: 3544 2452 Special dies & tools; modular homes, prefabricated, wood

(G-4214)
WILD FLAVORS INC
A.M. Todd
1501 S Columbus Ave (98620)
P.O. Box 310 (98620-0310)
PHONE..................................509 773-4008
David West, *Manager*
EMP: 6
SALES (corp-wide): 64.3B **Publicly Held**
SIC: 2087 Flavoring extracts & syrups
HQ: Wild Flavors, Inc.
   1261 Pacific Ave
   Erlanger KY 41018

Graham
Pierce County

(G-4215)
ALLWAYS LOGGING LLC
15801 264th St E (98338-8730)
P.O. Box 192, Packwood (98361-0192)
PHONE..................................360 893-2724
Fay Flanery,
Larry Flanery,
EMP: 4
SALES (est): 310.7K **Privately Held**
SIC: 2411 Logging

(G-4216)
APPLE EARTHWORKS LLC
11708 200th St E (98338-8805)
PHONE..................................253 847-3755
EMP: 2
SALES (est): 85.9K **Privately Held**
SIC: 3571 Mfg Electronic Computers

(G-4217)
BUILDERS FIRSTSOURCE INC
20810 Meridian Ave E (98338-8492)
PHONE..................................253 847-2900
Barney Palmer, *Branch Mgr*
EMP: 20
SALES (corp-wide): 7.7B **Publicly Held**
WEB: www.hopelumber.com
SIC: 2421 5031 3272 Building & structural materials, wood; lumber, plywood & millwork; concrete stuctural support & building material
PA: Builders Firstsource, Inc.
   2001 Bryan St Ste 1600
   Dallas TX 75201
   214 880-3500

(G-4218)
C & C MOBILE WELDING LLC
31206 129th Ave E (98338-7577)
PHONE..................................360 879-5623
Chris Campbell, *Principal*
EMP: 2 **EST:** 2010
SALES (est): 348.5K **Privately Held**
SIC: 7692 Welding repair

(G-4219)
C & M WOODWORKS
25606 69th Ave E (98338-8315)
PHONE..................................253 503-9440
Christine Humiston, *Principal*
EMP: 2
SALES (est): 85.2K **Privately Held**
SIC: 2431 Millwork

Graham - Pierce County (G-4220)

(G-4220)
CASCADE MOBILE MIX (PA)
Also Called: Cascade Mobile Mix Concrete
6723 304th St E (98338-9744)
PHONE.............................253 833-1956
Debbie Cooper, *Owner*
Jim Cooper, *Co-Owner*
EMP: 3
SALES (est): 345.6K **Privately Held**
SIC: 3273 Ready-mixed concrete

(G-4221)
CONSTRUCTION PARTS LLC
25302 Meridian Ave E (98338-7877)
PHONE.............................253 255-1775
Andrew Briggs, *Sales Mgr*
Ronald Briggs,
Marci Briggs,
EMP: 3
SALES: 240K **Privately Held**
SIC: 3531 Construction machinery

(G-4222)
CRUISER CREATIONS
23607 80th Avenue Ct E (98338-9818)
PHONE.............................360 832-7078
Jill Pollock,
EMP: 2 **EST:** 2013
SALES (est): 147.5K **Privately Held**
SIC: 2397 Schiffli machine embroideries

(G-4223)
D S HARDWOOD CORPORATION
4706 247th Street Ct E (98338-8337)
PHONE.............................509 369-3442
EMP: 3
SALES: 200K **Privately Held**
SIC: 2426 Retails Hardwood

(G-4224)
EATON CORP
5211 292nd St E (98338-9669)
PHONE.............................253 375-6013
EMP: 3
SALES (est): 129.6K **Privately Held**
SIC: 3625 Motor controls & accessories

(G-4225)
ERICKSON LOGGING
21806 103rd Avenue Ct E # 104 (98338-8115)
PHONE.............................253 846-2646
EMP: 3 **EST:** 1996
SALES (est): 180K **Privately Held**
SIC: 2411 Logging Contractor

(G-4226)
HOT OFF PRESS
13510 Kapowsin Hwy E (98338-7564)
P.O. Box 85, Kapowsin (98344-0085)
PHONE.............................253 255-2829
EMP: 4
SALES (est): 50K **Privately Held**
SIC: 2741 Miscellaneous publishing

(G-4227)
JACKSON OIL ANTHONY SCHNELL
19914 90th Avenue Ct E (98338-8253)
PHONE.............................253 847-2566
Anthony Schnell, *Owner*
EMP: 2
SALES (est): 96.4K **Privately Held**
SIC: 1311 Crude petroleum & natural gas

(G-4228)
JC FABWORKS LLC
23214 145th Avenue Ct E (98338-7618)
PHONE.............................253 389-5842
John Cole, *Mng Member*
Samantha Cole, *Mng Member*
EMP: 2
SALES: 250K **Privately Held**
SIC: 7692 7389 Welding repair;

(G-4229)
KAPOWSIN MEATS INC
29401 118th Ave E (98338-9008)
P.O. Box 542 (98338-0542)
PHONE.............................253 847-1777
EMP: 15
SALES: 2.1MM **Privately Held**
SIC: 2011 Meat Packing Plant

(G-4230)
LIBERTY CASEWORK LLC
22510 152nd Ave E (98338-8606)
P.O. Box 1341 (98338-1341)
PHONE.............................253 651-7891
Kimberly Smith, *President*
Leonard Smith, *Manager*
EMP: 2
SALES: 750K **Privately Held**
SIC: 2521 1731 Wood office filing cabinets & bookcases; electric power systems contractors

(G-4231)
MASTER VAC LLC
28002 138th Ave E (98338-6940)
P.O. Box 440, Kapowsin (98344-0440)
PHONE.............................253 875-0074
Becky Langley,
Garrett Langley,
Ricky Langley,
EMP: 5
SALES: 570K **Privately Held**
SIC: 7389 1081 1389 ; metal mining exploration & development services; construction, repair & dismantling services

(G-4232)
MCFADDEN & MCFADDEN LOGGING
29910 Webster Rd E (98338-9104)
PHONE.............................253 847-7695
Charles McFadden, *Partner*
EMP: 7
SALES (est): 620K **Privately Held**
SIC: 2411 Logging camps & contractors

(G-4233)
NITA N ACE LLC
22509 152nd Ave E (98338-8606)
P.O. Box 1981, Orting (98360-1981)
PHONE.............................253 209-4413
Allan Evans,
EMP: 2
SALES (est): 93K **Privately Held**
SIC: 3944 Games, toys & children's vehicles

(G-4234)
NORTHWEST MULTIPLE LISTING SVC
19510 104th Ave E (98338-6439)
PHONE.............................253 566-2331
Monica Beck, *Branch Mgr*
EMP: 2
SALES (corp-wide): 9.3MM **Privately Held**
WEB: www.nwmls.com
SIC: 2741 6531 Directories: publishing only, not printed on site; real estate agents & managers
PA: Northwest Multiple Listing Service Inc
  11430 Ne 120th St
  Kirkland WA 98034
  425 820-9200

(G-4235)
PRATER ENTERPRISES INC
26619 122nd Ave E (98338-8775)
PHONE.............................360 893-3620
EMP: 2
SALES (est): 106K **Privately Held**
SIC: 3556 Food products machinery

(G-4236)
Q A R RENDERING SERVICES INC
Also Called: Qar Redering Service In
23123 Meridian Ave E (98338-9157)
PHONE.............................253 847-7220
Justin Mothershead, *President*
Charlotte Mothershead, *Vice Pres*
Marcie Mothershead, *Admin Sec*
EMP: 2
SALES: 400K **Privately Held**
SIC: 4953 2077 Dead animal disposal; rendering

(G-4237)
ROSS METIER LLC
6011 256th St E (98338-9582)
PHONE.............................253 208-8777
Steve Ross,
EMP: 2 **EST:** 2014
SALES: 60K **Privately Held**
SIC: 3993 2813 Neon signs; neon

(G-4238)
SOVEREIGN MANUFACTURING
10506 193rd Street Ct E (98338-6451)
PHONE.............................253 318-7180
James Milford, *President*
EMP: 2
SALES (est): 156.5K **Privately Held**
SIC: 3999 Manufacturing industries

(G-4239)
SPECHT COATINGS
27917 129th Ave E (98338-8741)
PHONE.............................253 732-5662
Kellen Specht, *Administration*
EMP: 2 **EST:** 2017
SALES (est): 121.6K **Privately Held**
SIC: 3479 Metal coating & allied service

(G-4240)
ULTIMATE SHEEPSKIN
16014 245th St E (98338-5668)
PHONE.............................253 677-4384
EMP: 2 **EST:** 2016
SALES (est): 110.7K **Privately Held**
SIC: 2399 Fabricated textile products

(G-4241)
UNITED FARMS
23212 86th Ave E (98338-9109)
P.O. Box 40 (98338-0040)
PHONE.............................253 847-4230
Dale N Pedersen, *Owner*
EMP: 12 **EST:** 1957
SALES: 200K **Privately Held**
SIC: 3999 Pet supplies

Grand Coulee
Grant County

(G-4242)
ALL AMERICAN SPACER CO LLC
Also Called: Aasc
515 Division St (99133-8826)
P.O. Box 626 (99133-0626)
PHONE.............................509 633-3440
Mervin Monteith,
Mary Jo Monteith,
EMP: 5
SQ FT: 5,000
SALES (est): 370.4K **Privately Held**
SIC: 3599 Custom machinery

(G-4243)
MATERIAL INC
Also Called: Tri-City Auto Parts
141 Spokane Way (99133-9779)
P.O. Box 229 (99133-0229)
PHONE.............................509 633-1740
Jerry Maigha, *Manager*
EMP: 5
SALES (corp-wide): 7.7MM **Privately Held**
SIC: 5531 3599 Automotive parts; machine shop, jobbing & repair
PA: Material Inc
  1050 Basin St Sw
  Ephrata WA 98823
  509 754-4695

(G-4244)
STAR PUBLISHING INC
Also Called: Star Newspaper, The
3 Midway Ave (99133)
P.O. Box 150 (99133-0150)
PHONE.............................509 633-1350
Scott Hunter, *President*
Sheri Edwards, *Principal*
EMP: 7 **EST:** 1946
SALES (est): 509.8K **Privately Held**
WEB: www.grandcoulee.com
SIC: 2711 Newspapers: publishing only, not printed on site

Grandview
Yakima County

(G-4245)
BAKER COMMODITIES INC
150 Bridgeview Rd Fl 1 (98930-9677)
P.O. Box 359, Sunnyside (98944-0359)
PHONE.............................509 837-8686
Fred Roberts, *Manager*
EMP: 16
SALES (corp-wide): 161.3MM **Privately Held**
WEB: www.bakercommodities.com
SIC: 2077 2048 Tallow rendering, inedible; poultry feeds
PA: Baker Commodities, Inc.
  4020 Bandini Blvd
  Vernon CA 90058
  323 268-2801

(G-4246)
COVENTRY VALE WINERY INC
160602 Evans Rd (98930-9375)
P.O. Box 249 (98930-0249)
PHONE.............................509 882-4100
Clifford D Wyckoff, *Principal*
Liz McBride, *Human Resources*
David Wyckoff, *Office Mgr*
Edward P Siefert, *Office Mgr*
▲ **EMP:** 30
SQ FT: 2,300
SALES (est): 5MM **Privately Held**
SIC: 2084 2033 Wines; canned fruits & specialties

(G-4247)
DURADO ENTERPRISE
201 Walnut Ln (98930-9225)
PHONE.............................509 882-3247
Susan Durado, *Owner*
Frank Durado, *Co-Owner*
EMP: 2
SALES: 60K **Privately Held**
SIC: 2395 Embroidery & art needlework

(G-4248)
J M SMUCKER COMPANY
100 Forsell Rd (98930-8834)
P.O. Box 608 (98930-0608)
PHONE.............................509 882-1530
Stephen Masternak, *Production*
Randy Hecker, *Opers-Prdtn-Mfg*
EMP: 30
SALES (corp-wide): 7.8B **Publicly Held**
WEB: www.smuckers.com
SIC: 2033 2087 Canned fruits & specialties; flavoring extracts & syrups
PA: The J M Smucker Company
  1 Strawberry Ln
  Orrville OH 44667
  330 682-3000

(G-4249)
K & D MACHINE LLC
4651 N County Line Rd (98930-9086)
PHONE.............................509 882-2239
Dennis Weets, *Mng Member*
Aaron Weets, *Mng Member*
Janice Weets, *Mng Member*
EMP: 13
SALES: 2MM **Privately Held**
SIC: 3523 3599 Farm machinery & equipment; machine shop, jobbing & repair

(G-4250)
KOLLMAR INCORPORATED
410 O I E (98930-9336)
PHONE.............................509 882-3148
Sharon Kollmar, *President*
Alan Labelson, *Mktg Dir*
EMP: 25 **EST:** 1952
SQ FT: 3,000
SALES: 9.6MM **Privately Held**
SIC: 3444 Sheet metalwork

(G-4251)
LOWER VALLEY MACHINE SHOP
104 W 5th St (98930-1617)
P.O. Box 516 (98930-0516)
PHONE.............................509 882-3881
William Clarke, *Owner*
EMP: 10

GEOGRAPHIC SECTION

Granite Falls - Snohomish County (G-4277)

SQ FT: 90,000
SALES: 1MM **Privately Held**
SIC: 7699 3523 7692 7629 Farm machinery repair; industrial machinery & equipment repair; farm machinery & equipment; welding repair; electrical repair shops

(G-4252)
MARCHANT LADDERS INC
1311 W Wine Country Rd (98930-1043)
P.O. Box 661 (98930-0661)
PHONE...................................509 882-1912
Larry Marchant, *President*
Marion Marchant, *Corp Secy*
EMP: 5
SALES: 400K **Privately Held**
SIC: 3499 Metal ladders

(G-4253)
MICHELLE STE WINE ESTATES LTD
Also Called: Grandview Winery
205 W 5th St (98930-1618)
PHONE...................................509 882-3928
Gordon Hill, *Manager*
EMP: 10
SALES (corp-wide): 25.3B **Publicly Held**
WEB: www.columbia-crest.com
SIC: 2084 Wines
HQ: Michelle Ste Wine Estates Ltd
  14111 Ne 145th St
  Woodinville WA 98072
  425 488-1133

(G-4254)
PRECISION BUILDERS
901 W Robinson Rd (98930-9158)
PHONE...................................509 882-2232
Greg Richard, *Owner*
Clarie Richard, *Owner*
EMP: 2
SALES (est): 106.7K **Privately Held**
SIC: 3429 Builders' hardware

(G-4255)
SHONAN USA INC
702 Wallace Way (98930-8844)
P.O. Box 128 (98930-0128)
PHONE...................................509 453-0757
Akira Nozaka, *President*
EMP: 50
SQ FT: 27,000
SALES (est): 7.1MM **Privately Held**
WEB: www.shonanusa.com
SIC: 2086 Fruit drinks (less than 100% juice): packaged in cans, etc.

(G-4256)
VALLEY PUBLISHING COMPANY INC
Also Called: Grandview Printing
308 Division St (98930-1359)
PHONE...................................509 882-3712
John L Fournier Jr, *Owner*
EMP: 5
SALES (corp-wide): 1.1MM **Privately Held**
WEB: www.thegrandviewherald.com
SIC: 2711 Newspapers: publishing only, not printed on site
PA: Valley Publishing Company Inc
  613 7th St
  Prosser WA 99350
  509 786-1711

(G-4257)
WELCH FOODS INC A COOPERATIVE
Also Called: Grandview Plant
504 Birch Ave (98930-1601)
P.O. Box 38 (98930-0038)
PHONE...................................509 882-1711
Terry Chambers, *Manager*
Art Ortega, *Supervisor*
EMP: 50
SALES (corp-wide): 608.4MM **Privately Held**
WEB: www.welchs.com
SIC: 2033 Fruits: packaged in cans, jars, etc.; fruit juices: packaged in cans, jars, etc.
HQ: Welch Foods Inc., A Cooperative
  300 Baker Ave Ste 101
  Concord MA 01742
  978 371-1000

(G-4258)
WELCH FOODS INC A COOPERATIVE
401 Grandridge Rd (98930-1565)
PHONE...................................509 882-3112
Keith Naughton, *Branch Mgr*
EMP: 6
SALES (corp-wide): 608.4MM **Privately Held**
SIC: 2037 2033 Fruit juices; jams, jellies & preserves: packaged in cans, jars, etc.
HQ: Welch Foods Inc., A Cooperative
  300 Baker Ave Ste 101
  Concord MA 01742
  978 371-1000

(G-4259)
WYCKOFF FARMS INCORPORATED (PA)
Also Called: Milne Microdried
160602 Evans Rd (98930-9375)
P.O. Box 249 (98930-0249)
PHONE...................................509 882-3934
David W Wyckoff, *CEO*
Jay Holthus, *General Mgr*
David Wyckoff, *Trustee*
Court Wyckoff, *Vice Pres*
Kirby Redman, *Department Mgr*
▲ **EMP:** 49
SQ FT: 2,300
SALES (est): 88.8MM **Privately Held**
WEB: www.wyckoff-farms.com
SIC: 0191 2034 2037 2084 General farms, primarily crop; dehydrated fruits, vegetables, soups; frozen fruits & vegetables; wines

Granger
Yakima County

(G-4260)
CARGILL INCORPORATED
700 Ruehl Way (98932-9336)
PHONE...................................509 854-1035
James Ramey, *Branch Mgr*
EMP: 9
SALES (corp-wide): 114.7B **Privately Held**
WEB: www.cargill.com
SIC: 2048 Prepared feeds
PA: Cargill, Incorporated
  15407 Mcginty Rd W
  Wayzata MN 55391
  952 742-7575

(G-4261)
EATON HILL WINERY
530 Gurley Rd (98932-9432)
PHONE...................................509 854-2220
Edwin Stear, *Owner*
Joann Stear, *Co-Owner*
EMP: 4
SALES: 60K **Privately Held**
SIC: 2084 5921 Wines; wine & beer

(G-4262)
O L LUTHER CO
2901 Beam Rd (98932-9504)
PHONE...................................509 837-2527
O L Luther, *President*
Lorretta Luther, *Corp Secy*
Arnold Luther, *Vice Pres*
EMP: 5
SALES (est): 495.6K **Privately Held**
SIC: 1442 1794 Gravel mining; excavation & grading, building construction

(G-4263)
QUALITY LIQUID FEEDS INC
100 Bailey Ave (98932)
P.O. Box 1346 (98932-1346)
PHONE...................................509 854-2311
Eddie Post, *General Mgr*
EMP: 4
SALES (corp-wide): 148.2MM **Privately Held**
WEB: www.qlf.com
SIC: 2048 Prepared feeds

PA: Quality Liquid Feeds, Inc.
  3586 State Road 23
  Dodgeville WI 53533
  608 935-2345

(G-4264)
YAKIMA BAIT CO
Also Called: Worden's Lures
1000 Bailey Ave (98932-9488)
P.O. Box 310 (98932-0310)
PHONE...................................509 854-1311
Mark Masterson, *President*
Jeff Wiley, *Safety Mgr*
Rob Phillips, *Sales Mgr*
Sandra Johnson, *Admin Sec*
EMP: 175 **EST:** 1934
SQ FT: 50,000
SALES (est): 20.2MM **Privately Held**
WEB: www.yakimabait.com
SIC: 3949 5941 Fishing tackle, general; lures, fishing: artificial; sporting goods & bicycle shops

Granite Falls
Snohomish County

(G-4265)
BIC INC
10401 Mountain Loop Hwy (98252-9597)
P.O. Box 110 (98252-0110)
PHONE...................................360 691-1452
Steve Dickenson, *President*
Sig Mc Guire, *President*
EMP: 9
SQ FT: 10,000
SALES (est): 840K **Privately Held**
SIC: 3679 3714 Harness assemblies for electronic use: wire or cable; instrument board assemblies, motor vehicle

(G-4266)
CHECKMATE INDUSTRIES INC
8810 147th Ave Ne (98252-9249)
PHONE...................................360 691-1753
Dennis Schule, *President*
EMP: 3 **EST:** 2009
SALES (est): 383.1K **Privately Held**
SIC: 3625 Crane & hoist controls, including metal mill

(G-4267)
COBALT ENTERPRISES LLC (PA)
10913 Mountain Loop Hwy (98252-8500)
PHONE...................................360 691-2298
Fred Schule,
Paul Clark,
▲ **EMP:** 73
SQ FT: 20,000
SALES (est): 20MM **Privately Held**
WEB: www.cobaltent.com
SIC: 3728 Aircraft body assemblies & parts

(G-4268)
COBALT INVESTMENTS LLC
Also Called: Cobalt Finishing
10917 Mountain Loop Hwy (98252-8500)
P.O. Box 478 (98252-0478)
PHONE...................................360 691-2298
Fred Schule, *President*
Paul Clark, *Vice Pres*
EMP: 5
SQ FT: 7,000
SALES (est): 280.6K **Privately Held**
SIC: 3479 Metal coating & allied service

(G-4269)
COMPETITIVE DEVELOPMENT & MFG
19403 63rd Ave Ne (98252)
PHONE...................................360 691-7816
Harry A Wood, *President*
EMP: 10
SALES: 1.2MM **Privately Held**
SIC: 3444 Sheet metal specialties, not stamped

(G-4270)
COMPETITIVE DEVELOPMENT & MFG
Also Called: CDM
10905 Mountain Loop Hwy (98252-8500)
PHONE...................................360 691-7816

Harry Wood, *Owner*
EMP: 3
SALES: 700K **Privately Held**
SIC: 3444 Sheet metalwork

(G-4271)
EAGLE ROCK MANUFACTURING INC
12815 Mountain Loop Hwy (98252-9131)
PHONE...................................360 989-0863
EMP: 2
SALES (est): 91.9K **Privately Held**
SIC: 3999 Manufacturing industries

(G-4272)
FSX EQUIPMENT INC (PA)
10404 Mountain Loop Hwy (98252-9597)
P.O. Box 1617 (98252-1617)
PHONE...................................360 691-2999
Diane Waldo, *President*
Cole Waldo, *Vice Pres*
Matt Riley, *Design Engr*
Jeff Onstad, *Info Tech Mgr*
Jalene Lyman, *Admin Asst*
EMP: 17
SQ FT: 9,200
SALES (est): 4.4MM **Privately Held**
SIC: 3564 3589 Purification & dust collection equipment; air cleaning systems; dust or fume collecting equipment, industrial; high pressure cleaning equipment

(G-4273)
FSX EQUIPMENT INC
10909a Mountain Loop Hwy (98252-8500)
PHONE...................................360 691-2999
Diane Waldo, *Branch Mgr*
EMP: 3
SALES (corp-wide): 4.4MM **Privately Held**
SIC: 3564 Purification & dust collection equipment; air cleaning systems; dust or fume collecting equipment, industrial
PA: Fsx Equipment Inc.
  10404 Mountain Loop Hwy
  Granite Falls WA 98252
  360 691-2999

(G-4274)
FSX INCORPORATED
Also Called: Fume and Smoke Extraction
10404 Mountain Loop Hwy (98252-9597)
P.O. Box 1617 (98252-1617)
PHONE...................................360 691-2999
Diane L Waldo, *President*
Cole L Waldo, *Vice Pres*
Rob Salsgiver, *Technical Mgr*
Jeremy Anderson, *Natl Sales Mgr*
EMP: 6 **EST:** 1999
SQ FT: 7,000
SALES (est): 1.2MM **Privately Held**
WEB: www.fsxinc.com
SIC: 3569 Filters

(G-4275)
GARVIE INDUSTRIES LLC
13105 E Loop View Dr (98252-9587)
P.O. Box 1122 (98252-1122)
PHONE...................................360 691-1233
Daniel Garvie, *Principal*
EMP: 3
SALES (est): 121.1K **Privately Held**
SIC: 3999 Manufacturing industries

(G-4276)
GREEN MTN MINE OPER CO LLC
26709 Mountain Loop Hwy (98252-8928)
PHONE...................................206 451-7105
Melissa Kilcup, *Manager*
Spencer Kunath, *Manager*
Gene Juarez,
EMP: 4 **EST:** 2011
SALES (est): 213K **Privately Held**
SIC: 1221 Surface mining, bituminous

(G-4277)
HOOK LINE AND ESPRESSO
208 W Stanley St (98252)
PHONE...................................360 691-7095
Charles Wagner, *Owner*
EMP: 4
SALES (est): 187.8K **Privately Held**
SIC: 2095 Roasted coffee

(PA)=Parent Co (HQ)=Headquarters (DH)=Div Headquarters
✿ = New Business established in last 2 years

Granite Falls - Snohomish County (G-4278)

(G-4278)
JD FABRICATION
11307 Mountain Loop Hwy (98252-8503)
PHONE..................360 691-4550
EMP: 2
SALES (est): 100.2K **Privately Held**
SIC: 3999 Manufacturing industries

(G-4279)
LOOKER INDUSTRIES INC
7111 210th Dr Ne (98252-9388)
P.O. Box 1248 (98252-1248)
PHONE..................360 691-1596
Kara Looker, *Principal*
EMP: 3
SALES (est): 181.4K **Privately Held**
SIC: 3999 Barber & beauty shop equipment

(G-4280)
MDR PUBLISHING
501 Eagle View Dr (98252-8005)
PHONE..................360 691-5908
Mary Raichle, *Principal*
EMP: 2 EST: 2016
SALES (est): 59.2K **Privately Held**
SIC: 2741 Miscellaneous publishing

(G-4281)
MILLER SHINGLE COMPANY LLC
20820 Gun Club Rd (98252-9496)
P.O. Box 29 (98252-0029)
PHONE..................360 691-7727
Barry Miller,
Bruce Miller II,
EMP: 4
SQ FT: 10,000
SALES (est): 161.3K **Privately Held**
SIC: 2411 7389 2429 2421 Logging camps & contractors; log & lumber broker; shingle & shingle mills; sawmills & planing mills, general

(G-4282)
NORTHMAN LOGGING
3608 233rd Ave Ne (98252-9337)
PHONE..................425 870-4727
Matthew Fink, *Owner*
EMP: 2
SALES: 41.4K **Privately Held**
SIC: 2411 Logging camps & contractors

(G-4283)
PRO WHEEL RACING COMPONENTS
3729 Menzel Lake Rd (98252-9317)
PHONE..................360 691-6459
Gary Carter, *Owner*
▲ EMP: 10
SALES (est): 1.2MM **Privately Held**
SIC: 3751 Motorcycles & related parts

(G-4284)
QUESTECH UNLIMITED
509 E Stanley St (98252-8445)
PHONE..................360 691-2620
Jason Smith, *President*
Kimberly Smith, *Vice Pres*
▲ EMP: 26
SQ FT: 8,200
SALES (est): 3.9MM **Privately Held**
WEB: www.questech.us
SIC: 3599 Machine shop, jobbing & repair

(G-4285)
RICK CARLSON
Also Called: Lorric Logging
23212 Scotty Rd (98252-8701)
PHONE..................360 691-4421
EMP: 2
SALES (est): 110K **Privately Held**
SIC: 2411 Logging

(G-4286)
TARPLEY WOODWORKING
6615 Robe Menzel Rd (98252-9749)
PHONE..................360 631-1405
EMP: 2 EST: 2007
SALES (est): 123.8K **Privately Held**
SIC: 2431 Millwork

(G-4287)
VEATCH CUSTOM CABINETRY LLC
22620 29th Pl Ne (98252-9460)
PHONE..................425 418-3693
Michael Veatch, *Principal*
EMP: 2
SALES (est): 181.2K **Privately Held**
SIC: 2434 Wood kitchen cabinets

Grapeview
Mason County

(G-4288)
GREEN DIAMOND RESOURCE COMPANY
Also Called: Mason Lake Recreation Area
1050 E Mason Lake Dr W (98546-9757)
PHONE..................360 426-0737
EMP: 2
SALES (est): 239.6K **Privately Held**
SIC: 5031 2421 2411 Lumber: rough, dressed & finished; lumber: rough, sawed or planed; timber, cut at logging camp

(G-4289)
MILLERS QUALITY CABINETS
110 E Pirates Dr (98546-9632)
PHONE..................360 275-4349
Michael R Miller, *Owner*
Cindly L Miller, *Co-Owner*
EMP: 2
SALES (est): 119.7K **Privately Held**
SIC: 2434 Wood kitchen cabinets

(G-4290)
SIFFERMAN & SIFFERMAN
Also Called: Mason Marine Repair
2931 E Mason Lake Dr W (98546-9546)
PHONE..................360 426-0714
Edward J Sifferman, *Partner*
Stephen K Sifferman, *Partner*
EMP: 2
SALES (est): 160K **Privately Held**
SIC: 3732 Boat building & repairing

(G-4291)
UNITED STATES ELECTRIC CORP
1101 E Lake Trask Rd (98546-9751)
PHONE..................360 427-4218
EMP: 2
SALES (est): 102.5K **Privately Held**
SIC: 3699 1731 Mfg Electrical Equipment/Supplies Electrical Contractor

Grayland
Grays Harbor County

(G-4292)
BAINTER BAINTER & BAINTER LLC
Also Called: D B C Paving
3079 State Route 105 (98547)
PHONE..................360 267-5521
Carol Bainter, *Owner*
David Bainter, *Partner*
Kc Bainter,
▲ EMP: 3
SALES (est): 200K **Privately Held**
SIC: 1771 2951 Blacktop (asphalt) work; asphalt & asphaltic paving mixtures (not from refineries)

(G-4293)
F/V NATIVE STAR
1174 Wood Ln (98547-9510)
P.O. Box 894, Westport (98595-0894)
PHONE..................360 267-6348
Robert Brokhoff, *Owner*
EMP: 3 EST: 2000
SALES (est): 150K **Privately Held**
SIC: 3732 Fishing boats: lobster, crab, oyster, etc.: small

(G-4294)
FURFORD PICKER CO
2395 State Route 105 (98547-9720)
P.O. Box 391 (98547-0391)
PHONE..................360 267-3303
David Furford, *President*
EMP: 3
SALES (est): 360K **Privately Held**
SIC: 5083 3523 Farm & garden machinery; harvesters, fruit, vegetable, tobacco, etc.

Greenacres
Spokane County

(G-4295)
AUTOCRAFT INCORPORATED
525 S Cavalier Ct (99016-9605)
PHONE..................509 926-7002
David Jeffreys, *President*
Wanda Jeffries, *Admin Sec*
EMP: 2
SALES: 18K **Privately Held**
SIC: 2395 Quilting & quilting supplies; quilted fabrics or cloth; quilting, for the trade

(G-4296)
CURTISS R GRENZ
Also Called: Concrete Works
2620 S Corbin Cir (99016-7719)
PHONE..................509 893-0317
Curtis Grenz, *Co-Owner*
Laura Grenz, *Co-Owner*
EMP: 25 EST: 1995
SALES (est): 2.3MM **Privately Held**
WEB: www.concreteworksstatuary.com
SIC: 3272 Concrete products

(G-4297)
ELECTRIJET RESEARCH FOUNDATION
2812 S Steen Ln (99016-7780)
PHONE..................509 990-9474
Devin Glenn, *CEO*
Russell Fotheringham, *Director*
Paul McCarty, *Director*
EMP: 8 EST: 2015
SALES: 3.9K **Privately Held**
SIC: 8731 3812 9661 3764 Energy research; electronic research; acceleration indicators & systems components, aerospace; space research & development, government; guided missile & space vehicle propulsion unit parts

(G-4298)
FOLSOM INDUSTRIES INC
Also Called: Folsom Manufacturing
4015 S Conklin Rd (99016-8846)
PHONE..................509 921-6602
Mark Folsom, *President*
EMP: 10
SALES (est): 200K **Privately Held**
SIC: 3441 Fabricated structural metal

(G-4299)
HUNT FAMILY LTD PARTNERSHIP
6425 S Chapman Rd (99016-7810)
PHONE..................509 892-5287
EMP: 2 EST: 2017
SALES (est): 66K **Privately Held**
SIC: 1081 Exploration, metal mining

(G-4300)
PACIFIC NORTHWEST JEWELERS
Also Called: Pnj
3925 S Conklin Rd (99016-9712)
PHONE..................509 927-8923
Jim Mc Andrew, *Owner*
EMP: 5
SALES (est): 260K **Privately Held**
SIC: 3911 7631 5099 5199 Jewel settings & mountings, precious metal; jewelry repair services; firearms & ammunition, except sporting; dressed furs; women's accessory & specialty stores

(G-4301)
PACIFIC STEEL STRUCTURES LLC
19814 E Pheasant Dr (99016-9763)
PHONE..................509 921-5835
Jarrod Goodwin,
EMP: 3
SALES (est): 250K **Privately Held**
SIC: 3312 Blast furnaces & steel mills

(G-4302)
SCHELL PUMP SERVICE
4312 S Chapman Rd (99016-8732)
PHONE..................509 922-4756
Roger Schell, *Owner*
EMP: 3
SALES (est): 272.3K **Privately Held**
SIC: 3533 Water well drilling equipment

(G-4303)
VICTORIAN HEARTS
20419 E 1st Ave (99016-8616)
PHONE..................509 926-1425
Beverly Schultz, *Owner*
EMP: 2
SALES (est): 115.4K **Privately Held**
SIC: 2335 Dresses, paper: cut & sewn

Greenbank
Island County

(G-4304)
ALTAN INC
4605 Honeymoon Bay Rd (98253-6310)
PHONE..................360 331-1595
Glen Eisenbrey, *President*
Shannon Ophelan, *Manager*
EMP: 4
SALES (est): 332K **Privately Held**
WEB: www.altan.com
SIC: 2834 Proprietary drug products

(G-4305)
HERRINGTON MARINE TECH INC
959 Vashon St (98253-6420)
PHONE..................360 222-3106
Allen Herrington, *CEO*
Shelly Wallenberg, *CFO*
EMP: 4
SQ FT: 2,000
SALES (est): 376.1K **Privately Held**
SIC: 3699 Electrical equipment & supplies

(G-4306)
HOLMES HARBOR CELLARS LLC
4591 Honeymoon Bay Rd (98253-6309)
PHONE..................360 331-3544
Theresa Martinez,
EMP: 2
SALES (est): 120K **Privately Held**
SIC: 2084 Wines

(G-4307)
HOUSE REPORTER LLC
2674 Harbor Estates Rd (98253-6002)
PHONE..................360 678-4931
Joseph Pruitt, *Principal*
EMP: 4
SALES (est): 239K **Privately Held**
SIC: 2711 Newspapers, publishing & printing

(G-4308)
KLAS TECHNOLOGIES LLC
Also Called: Railtek Supply
959 Vashon St (98253-6420)
P.O. Box 625, Duvall (98019-0625)
PHONE..................360 678-8705
Kenneth Wallenberg Jr,
Shelly Wallenberg,
▲ EMP: 8 EST: 2008
SALES (est): 1.1MM **Privately Held**
WEB: www.railteksupply.com
SIC: 3647 Locomotive & railroad car lights

(G-4309)
PUZZLE PIECE ARTS
3076 Celestial Way (98253-9775)
PHONE..................360 678-3687
EMP: 2

SALES (est): 129.6K **Privately Held**
SIC: 3944 Mfg Games/Toys

(G-4310)
WHIDBEY ISLAND VINTNERS
4591 Honeymoon Bay Rd (98253-6309)
PHONE..................360 331-3544
Virginia Bloom, *Principal*
EMP: 2
SALES (est): 81.9K **Privately Held**
SIC: 2084 Wines

(G-4311)
WILDEBERRY LLC
Also Called: Whidbeyfresh
23923 Sr 525 (98253)
PHONE..................360 222-3626
Missy Villapudua,
John Villapudua,
EMP: 2
SALES (est): 122.1K **Privately Held**
SIC: 2035 7389 Pickles, sauces & salad dressings;

Hamilton
Skagit County

(G-4312)
DILLS CREEK INC
821 First St (98255)
P.O. Box 498 (98255-0498)
PHONE..................360 826-3841
Gordon Ray-Dills, *President*
Gordon Ray Dills, *President*
Barbara Dills, *Corp Secy*
EMP: 6
SALES: 433.2K **Privately Held**
SIC: 2411 Logging camps & contractors

(G-4313)
JANICKI INDUSTRIES INC
34240 State Route 20 (98255-7000)
PHONE..................360 856-5143
Andrew Lathrop, *Project Mgr*
Larry Elliott, *Branch Mgr*
EMP: 284 **Privately Held**
SIC: 3599 3545 Machine shop, jobbing & repair; machine tool attachments & accessories
PA: Janicki Industries, Inc.
719 Metcalf St
Sedro Woolley WA 98284

Hansville
Kitsap County

(G-4314)
BROOKE ENGRG PHOTOGRAPHIC EQP
Also Called: Brooke International
37567 Vista Key Dr Ne (98340-7771)
P.O. Box 300 (98340-0300)
PHONE..................360 638-2591
Jack Brooke, *Owner*
Cindy Brooke, *General Mgr*
▲ **EMP:** 15
SALES: 200K **Privately Held**
WEB: www.brookecutters.com
SIC: 3861 Printing equipment, photographic

(G-4315)
CASCADE PUBLICATIONS
40503 Skunk Bay Rd Ne (98340-7724)
PHONE..................360 638-0404
Barbara Wilson, *Owner*
▲ **EMP:** 2
SALES (est): 100.7K **Privately Held**
SIC: 2731 Book clubs: publishing & printing

(G-4316)
NEW TOUCH WOODWORKING
6331 Ne Ponderosa Blvd (98340-7733)
P.O. Box 331, Poulsbo (98370-0331)
PHONE..................360 930-1118
EMP: 2
SALES (est): 153.5K **Privately Held**
SIC: 2431 Millwork

(G-4317)
PINK SLUG PRESS
5454 Birch Ct Ne (98340-9716)
PHONE..................206 430-2637
Heidi Morgan, *Principal*
EMP: 2
SALES (est): 85.6K **Privately Held**
SIC: 2741 Miscellaneous publishing

(G-4318)
PRITCHARD WOODWORKS LLC
37120 Madrona Blvd Ne (98340-8709)
PHONE..................206 755-4503
Nolle Pritchard, *Administration*
EMP: 2
SALES (est): 138.8K **Privately Held**
SIC: 2431 Millwork

(G-4319)
SEVEN TWENTY EIGHT CL LLC
37000 Cypress Dr Ne (98340-9711)
PHONE..................206 484-7634
Renee Marie Hart,
EMP: 2
SALES (est): 67K **Privately Held**
SIC: 2389 Apparel & accessories

Harrah
Yakima County

(G-4320)
HARRAH FARM SHOP
Also Called: HFS Conveyors
3959 Harrah Rd (98933-9800)
P.O. Box 182 (98933-0182)
PHONE..................509 848-2941
Gene Hedden, *Owner*
EMP: 4
SALES (est): 479K **Privately Held**
SIC: 3535 Conveyors & conveying equipment

(G-4321)
STACH STEEL SUPPLY
3070 Harrah Rd (98933-9766)
PHONE..................509 848-2772
Kevin Stach, *Partner*
Adam Stach, *Partner*
EMP: 2
SALES (est): 421.6K **Privately Held**
SIC: 5051 7692 Steel; welding repair

Hatton
Adams County

(G-4322)
MONSANTO COMPANY
776 S Booker Rd (99344-9459)
PHONE..................509 488-0821
Tyler Postin, *General Mgr*
Tony Herrmann, *Branch Mgr*
EMP: 8
SALES (corp-wide): 45.3B **Privately Held**
WEB: www.monsanto.com
SIC: 2879 Agricultural chemicals
HQ: Monsanto Company
800 N Lindbergh Blvd
Saint Louis MO 63167
314 694-1000

Hobart
King County

(G-4323)
HB AEROSPACE LLC
28819 Se 208th St (98025)
P.O. Box 7 (98025-0007)
PHONE..................425 432-3440
Rosemary Brester,
EMP: 2
SALES (est): 198.5K **Privately Held**
WEB: www.hobartmachined.com
SIC: 3365 Aerospace castings, aluminum

(G-4324)
HOBART MACHINED PRODUCTS INC (PA)
28819 Se 208th St (98025)
P.O. Box 7 (98025-0007)
PHONE..................425 432-3440
Rosemary Brester, *President*
Larry Brewster, *Vice Pres*
EMP: 7
SQ FT: 4,000
SALES (est): 1MM **Privately Held**
SIC: 3599 Machine shop, jobbing & repair

Hoodsport
Mason County

(G-4325)
HOODSPORT WINERY INC
23501 N Us Highway 101 (98548-9605)
PHONE..................360 877-9894
Edwin Patterson, *Ch of Bd*
Peggy Patterson, *President*
EMP: 4
SQ FT: 4,000
SALES: 600K **Privately Held**
WEB: www.hoodsport.com
SIC: 2084 5921 Wines; wine

(G-4326)
STOTTLE WINERY TASTING ROOM
24180 N Us Highway 101 B (98548-9482)
PHONE..................360 877-2247
EMP: 2
SALES (est): 76.8K **Privately Held**
SIC: 2084 Wines

Hoquiam
Grays Harbor County

(G-4327)
ACE LOGGING INC
219 Ocean Beach Rd (98550-9528)
P.O. Box 784 (98550-0784)
PHONE..................360 537-6843
Josh Stoken, *President*
Justin Larsson, *Vice Pres*
EMP: 10
SALES: 500K **Privately Held**
SIC: 2411 Logging camps & contractors

(G-4328)
APRILS INDOOR GARDEN SUPPLIES
737 State Route 109 (98550-9740)
PHONE..................360 537-6850
Donald C Etue, *Owner*
April Etue, *Co-Owner*
EMP: 2
SALES (est): 75K **Privately Held**
SIC: 2499 Carved & turned wood

(G-4329)
BEST SHINGLE SALES INC
1100 5th St (98550)
PHONE..................360 532-5423
Terry A Kost,
Melissa Kost,
EMP: 5
SQ FT: 8,000
SALES (est): 1.5MM **Privately Held**
SIC: 2429 Shakes (hand split shingles); shingle mill; shingles, wood: sawed or hand split

(G-4330)
CARLYLE PRINTING
511 M St (98550-3421)
PHONE..................360 537-0266
EMP: 2
SALES (est): 141.4K **Privately Held**
SIC: 2752 Lithographic Commercial Printing

(G-4331)
DAHLSTROM LUMBER CO INC
1131 Airport Way (98550-2652)
P.O. Box 386 (98550-0386)
PHONE..................360 533-0448
Monte B Dahlstrom, *President*
Kirk A Dahlstrom, *Corp Secy*
Robert Bell, *Vice Pres*
▼ **EMP:** 20
SQ FT: 5,000
SALES (est): 2.7MM **Privately Held**
SIC: 2421 2499 5031 2426 Lumber: rough, sawed or planed; surveyors' stakes, wood; lumber, plywood & millwork; hardwood dimension & flooring mills

(G-4332)
DEEP CREEK LOGGING INC
1847 E Hoquiam Rd (98550-9105)
PHONE..................360 533-2390
Pete M Rabey, *President*
Cindy Rabey, *Corp Secy*
EMP: 8
SALES (est): 708.2K **Privately Held**
SIC: 2411 Logging camps & contractors

(G-4333)
DEREK MEFFORD
Also Called: Mefford and Sons Logging
2221 E Hoquiam Rd (98550-9112)
PHONE..................360 580-9166
Derek Mefford, *Principal*
EMP: 3
SALES (est): 173K **Privately Held**
SIC: 2411 Logging

(G-4334)
DOUBLE D LOGGING CO INC
612 L St (98550-3540)
PHONE..................360 533-7168
David Dupont, *President*
Sandi Dupont, *Admin Sec*
EMP: 7
SALES (est): 597.1K **Privately Held**
SIC: 2411 Logging camps & contractors

(G-4335)
DROLZ LOG AND ROCK INC
Also Called: Drolz Logging & Rock
95 Bowes Rd (98550-9417)
PHONE..................360 987-2343
Robert Drolz, *President*
Pauline Drolz, *Vice Pres*
EMP: 2
SALES: 100K **Privately Held**
SIC: 2411 4212 Logging camps & contractors; local trucking, without storage

(G-4336)
ENTERPRISES INTERNATIONAL INC (PA)
Blaine & Firman Sts (98550)
PHONE..................360 533-6222
Isabelle S Lamb, *Ch of Bd*
David Lamb, *President*
▲ **EMP:** 4
SQ FT: 300,000
SALES (est): 34.4MM **Privately Held**
SIC: 3569 5084 3555 3554 Baling machines, for scrap metal, paper or similar material; industrial machinery & equipment; printing trades machinery; paper industries machinery

(G-4337)
FUHRERS MACHINE LLC
309 10th St (98550-3802)
PHONE..................360 533-5517
Gary Fuhrer, *Mng Member*
EMP: 4
SALES: 200K **Privately Held**
SIC: 7692 3599 Welding repair; machine shop, jobbing & repair

(G-4338)
GRAYS HARBOR ELECTRONICS
2614 Simpson Ave (98550-2929)
P.O. Box 633, Grayland (98547-0633)
PHONE..................360 532-3474
Joe W Arndt, *President*
Regena Arndt, *President*
EMP: 7 **EST:** 1972
SQ FT: 5,200
SALES (est): 650K **Privately Held**
WEB: www.harborelectronics.net
SIC: 3571 7378 5731 Electronic computers; computer maintenance & repair; television sets; video recorders, players, disc players & accessories

Hoquiam - Grays Harbor County (G-4339)

(G-4339)
HARBOR GRAPHICS INC
Also Called: Washingtonian Print
608 8th St (98550-3523)
P.O. Box 699 (98550-0699)
PHONE..................360 532-1234
Jeanne Johnson, *President*
John McCoy, *Officer*
EMP: 4
SQ FT: 5,000
SALES (est): 360K **Privately Held**
WEB: www.harborgraphicscorp.com
SIC: 2752 2759 Commercial printing, offset; letterpress printing

(G-4340)
HARBOR MACHINE & FABRICATING
710 30th St (98550-4238)
P.O. Box 682, Aberdeen (98520-0146)
PHONE..................360 533-1188
Mikko Koski, *President*
Pentti Koski, *Admin Sec*
EMP: 10
SQ FT: 11,000
SALES (est): 750K **Privately Held**
WEB: www.harbormachine.com
SIC: 3599 7692 Machine shop, jobbing & repair; welding repair

(G-4341)
HEART HANDS PREGANACY CARE CTR
2638 Simpson Ave (98550-2929)
P.O. Box 32, Aberdeen (98520-0039)
PHONE..................360 532-1104
Judy Higginbotham, *Director*
EMP: 2
SALES (est): 140.7K **Privately Held**
SIC: 2835 Pregnancy test kits

(G-4342)
HOQUIAM BREWING CO
526 8th St (98550-3521)
PHONE..................360 637-8252
EMP: 2
SALES (est): 62.3K **Privately Held**
SIC: 2082 Malt beverages

(G-4343)
HOQUIAM PLYWOOD PRODUCTS INC
1000 Woodlawn Ave (98550-1140)
PHONE..................360 533-3060
Roger Burch, *President*
Austin Vanderhoot, *Vice Pres*
EMP: 113
SQ FT: 90,000
SALES (est): 14.8MM
SALES (corp-wide): 179.8MM **Privately Held**
SIC: 2436 Plywood, softwood
PA: Pacific States Industries, Incorporated
10 Madrone Ave
Morgan Hill CA 95037
408 779-7354

(G-4344)
IMAGE SIGNS AND DESIGN LLC
718 28th St Ste A (98550-4140)
PHONE..................360 533-0133
Jeff Edwards,
Chuck Edwards,
EMP: 3
SALES: 400K **Privately Held**
SIC: 3993 Signs & advertising specialties

(G-4345)
ISLAS CEDAR LLC
56 Blacktail Ln (98550-9710)
PHONE..................360 590-2176
Norberto Islas, *Principal*
EMP: 3
SALES (est): 230.8K **Privately Held**
SIC: 2411 Logging

(G-4346)
LEGACY AUTOMATION INC
Also Called: Lai
206 Firman Ave Ste P (98550-2000)
P.O. Box 636 (98550-0636)
PHONE..................360 538-2550
Isabelle S Lamb, *Ch of Bd*
David E Lamb, *President*
Larry Lock, *Corp Secy*
Jack B Sparks, *Treasurer*
▲ EMP: 11
SALES (est): 2.9MM **Privately Held**
WEB: www.legacyautomation.com
SIC: 3554 Pulp mill machinery

(G-4347)
LITTLE RIVER INC
92 Us Highway 101 (98550-9539)
P.O. Box 296 (98550-0296)
PHONE..................360 532-7490
Tom Mayr, *Principal*
EMP: 9
SALES (est): 1MM **Privately Held**
SIC: 2421 Sawmills & planing mills, general

(G-4348)
MAINTENANCE WELDING SERVICE
17 Fairfield Acres Rd (98550-9544)
PHONE..................360 533-4318
Jim Yowell, *President*
James Yowell Jr, *Vice Pres*
EMP: 4
SQ FT: 4,000
SALES (est): 480K **Privately Held**
SIC: 7692 3443 1799 7699 Welding repair; tanks, standard or custom fabricated: metal plate; welding on site; industrial machinery & equipment repair

(G-4349)
MOE HOWARD ENTERPRISES INC
Also Called: Little Hoquiam Shipyard
825 Queen Ave (98550-1060)
PHONE..................360 538-1622
Howard Moe, *President*
Margaret Moe, *Corp Secy*
Dawn Keogh, *Executive*
EMP: 29
SQ FT: 56,000
SALES (est): 4.7MM **Privately Held**
WEB: www.littlehoquiamshipyard.com
SIC: 3732 Boats, fiberglass: building & repairing

(G-4350)
OCEAN PROTEIN LLC
518 22nd St (98550-4040)
P.O. Box 696 (98550-0696)
PHONE..................360 538-7400
Aaron Dierks, *General Mgr*
Francis Miller,
Dennis Rydmam,
Sherry Vinson,
EMP: 35
SQ FT: 300
SALES (est): 5.4MM **Privately Held**
WEB: www.oceanprotein.com
SIC: 2077 Fish meal, except as animal feed

(G-4351)
OSZMAN SERVICE INC
2202 Bay Ave (98550-4000)
PHONE..................360 532-4552
Brian Oszman, *President*
Heleena Anderson, *Executive*
EMP: 6
SALES (est): 860.5K **Privately Held**
SIC: 3441 7692 Building components, structural steel; welding repair

(G-4352)
OVALSTRAPPING INCORPORATED (HQ)
Also Called: Oval International Division
206 Firman Ave (98550-2000)
P.O. Box 738 (98550-0738)
PHONE..................360 532-9101
David E Lamb, *President*
Jack Kidd, *Corp Secy*
Isabelle S Lamb, *Vice Pres*
Andrew Madderson, *Admin Sec*
▲ EMP: 39
SQ FT: 35,200
SALES: 5.3MM
SALES (corp-wide): 34.4MM **Privately Held**
WEB: www.ovalstrapping.com
SIC: 3069 3555 Medical & laboratory rubber sundries & related products; printing trades machinery

PA: Enterprises International Inc
Blaine & Firman Sts
Hoquiam WA 98550
360 533-6222

(G-4353)
PANELTECH INTERNATIONAL LLC
2999 John Stevens Way (98550-4242)
PHONE..................360 538-1480
Dave Wentworth, *Production*
Gregg Rupert, *Sales Staff*
Gale Dahlstrom,
Kirk Dahlstrom,
Monte Dahlstrom,
EMP: 23
SALES (est): 6.8MM **Privately Held**
SIC: 2672 2434 Coated & laminated paper; wood kitchen cabinets

(G-4354)
PANELTECH INTL HOLDINGS INC (HQ)
2999 John Stevens Way (98550-4242)
PHONE..................360 538-1480
Leroy D Nott, *President*
Ronald Iff, *Vice Pres*
Scott Olmstead, *CFO*
R Wade Mosby, *Director*
▲ EMP: 10
SALES (est): 3.6MM **Privately Held**
SIC: 2679 2611 2295 2655 Paper products, converted; pulp manufactured from waste or recycled paper; resin or plastic coated fabrics; containers, laminated phenolic & vulcanized fiber; rental of railroad cars

(G-4355)
PANELTECH PRODUCTS INC
2999 John Stevens Way (98550-4242)
PHONE..................360 538-1480
Leroy D Nott, *CEO*
Scott Olmstead, *CFO*
EMP: 39
SALES (est): 1.4MM **Privately Held**
SIC: 0831 2672 5961 Forest products; coated & laminated paper; fishing, hunting & camping equipment & supplies: mail order
HQ: Paneltech International Holdings, Inc.
2999 John Stevens Way
Hoquiam WA 98550

(G-4356)
RTS & BBC INC
911 3rd St (98550-3101)
PHONE..................360 239-1953
EMP: 2
SALES (est): 92.9K **Privately Held**
SIC: 2411 Logging

(G-4357)
SCHERMER CONSTRUCTION INC
299 Us Highway 101 (98550-9540)
P.O. Box 1783, Aberdeen (98520-0291)
PHONE..................360 533-5866
Doug Schermer, *President*
Sharon Schermer, *Vice Pres*
EMP: 21 EST: 1989
SALES (est): 3MM **Privately Held**
SIC: 1611 3531 Concrete construction: roads, highways, sidewalks, etc.; crushers, grinders & similar equipment

(G-4358)
SHIPYARD LLC
1303 C St (98550-2639)
P.O. Box 441 (98550-0441)
PHONE..................360 532-1990
Don Root, *President*
Kevin Duffy, *Accounts Exec*
Kelsey Dus, *Marketing Staff*
Ross Capers, *Director*
Mike Long, *Officer*
EMP: 3
SALES (est): 394.3K **Privately Held**
SIC: 3731 Shipbuilding & repairing

(G-4359)
SHIRT IMAGE EMBROIDERY
2200 Simpson Ave (98550-2749)
PHONE..................360 870-2837
Debi Luther, *Owner*
EMP: 2
SALES (est): 120.6K **Privately Held**
SIC: 2759 Screen printing

(G-4360)
SPRADLIN ROCK PRODUCTS INC
167 Us Highway 101 (98550-9539)
PHONE..................360 532-2994
T J Spradlin, *President*
EMP: 2
SALES (est): 216.1K **Privately Held**
SIC: 2411 Logging camps & contractors

(G-4361)
STOTT LOGGING INC
1102 Simpson Ave (98550-3823)
P.O. Box 714 (98550-0714)
PHONE..................360 533-2971
Dean M Stott, *President*
Robert E Byron, *Vice Pres*
Douglas M Schermer, *Treasurer*
Patrick H Byron, *Admin Sec*
EMP: 14
SALES (est): 2.1MM **Privately Held**
SIC: 2411 Logging camps & contractors

(G-4362)
WESTERN LAND TIMBER
66 Badger Rd (98550-9416)
PHONE..................360 987-2170
Thomas McBride, *Owner*
EMP: 30
SALES (est): 1.2MM **Privately Held**
SIC: 2411 Logging camps & contractors

(G-4363)
WOOD CRAFTS BY PEAR COMPANY
617 Kuhn Ave (98550-1011)
PHONE..................360 532-6246
Arthur Bell, *Owner*
EMP: 2
SALES (est): 74K **Privately Held**
SIC: 2499 Carved & turned wood

Humptulips
Grays Harbor County

(G-4364)
PACIFIC REIGN ENTERPRISES
5403 Us Highway 101 (98552-9720)
PHONE..................360 580-4447
Gerald Stajcar, *President*
Charles Stajcar, *President*
April Nicholson, *Corp Secy*
EMP: 3
SALES (est): 80K **Privately Held**
SIC: 2429 2411 Shakes (hand split shingles); shingle mill; logging camps & contractors

Hunters
Stevens County

(G-4365)
HUNTER CREEK PROPERTY LTD
6447 Springdale Hunter Rd (99137-9704)
PHONE..................509 675-4949
Dave Price, *Partner*
EMP: 3
SALES (est): 120.1K **Privately Held**
SIC: 2411 Timber, cut at logging camp

Hunts Point
King County

(G-4366)
CALENDARS NORTHWEST LLC (PA)
Also Called: Fuego
8314 Hunts Point Pl (98004-1004)
PHONE..................425 454-1145
Mark Colver, *Mng Member*
Kelly Smith,
EMP: 12

GEOGRAPHIC SECTION

Issaquah - King County (G-4395)

SALES (est): 1.6MM **Privately Held**
SIC: 3069 Sponge rubber & sponge rubber products

Husum
Klickitat County

(G-4367)
WIND RIVER CELLAR
196 Spring Creek Rd (98623)
PHONE..................................509 493-2324
Kris Goodwille, *Owner*
Joel Goodwillie, *Partner*
Joel Goodwille, *Co-Owner*
EMP: 2
SALES: 350K **Privately Held**
WEB: www.windrivercellars.com
SIC: 2084 Wines

Ilwaco
Pacific County

(G-4368)
CAPE DISSAPOINTMENT STATE PARK
Loop Robert Gray Dr (98624)
PHONE..................................360 642-3078
Evan Robert, *Manager*
Evan Roberts, *Manager*
EMP: 12
SALES (est): 1MM **Privately Held**
WEB: www.fortcanby.org
SIC: 2531 7011 7033 Picnic tables or benches, park; hotels & motels; trailer parks & campsites

(G-4369)
DOCKSIDE CANNERY
Port Of Ilwaco (98624)
P.O. Box 920 (98624-0920)
PHONE..................................360 642-8870
Sean Mortez, *President*
EMP: 3
SQ FT: 5,000
SALES (est): 203.9K **Privately Held**
SIC: 2091 5421 Canned & cured fish & seafoods; seafood markets

(G-4370)
FV FAST BREAK
314 Eliza Ave (98624)
PHONE..................................360 642-3753
Dan Oja, *President*
EMP: 3
SALES (est): 146.5K **Privately Held**
SIC: 3732 Fishing boats: lobster, crab, oyster, etc.: small

Inchelium
Ferry County

(G-4371)
CARL EMIL SEASTROM
Also Called: C & K General Contractors
190 Kewa Meteor Rd (99138)
P.O. Box 308 (99138-0308)
PHONE..................................509 722-5414
Carl E Seastrom, *Owner*
EMP: 12
SALES: 300K **Privately Held**
SIC: 2411 Logging

Index
Snohomish County

(G-4372)
WARREN HARTZ
Also Called: Silk From The Hartz
51211 Avenue A (98256-9700)
P.O. Box 165 (98256-0165)
PHONE..................................360 793-0691
Warren Hartz, *Owner*
Edie Hartz, *Co-Owner*
EMP: 2

SALES (est): 29.2K **Privately Held**
SIC: 2221 Silks, satins, taffetas & crepes

Indianola
Kitsap County

(G-4373)
SPARROW WOODWORKS LLC
9829 Ne Coyote Ln (98342-9792)
P.O. Box 261 (98342-0261)
PHONE..................................206 708-5615
Jewell John, *Principal*
John Jewell,
Mike Stuntz,
EMP: 2
SALES (est): 140K **Privately Held**
SIC: 2431 Millwork

(G-4374)
WASHINGTON PRECAST PRODUCTS
20519 Chief Sealth Dr Ne (98342-9745)
P.O. Box 266 (98342-0266)
PHONE..................................360 598-1631
William House, *President*
EMP: 3
SALES (est): 511.8K **Privately Held**
SIC: 3272 Concrete products, precast

Ione
Pend Oreille County

(G-4375)
KENNETH MAUPIN LOGGING CNSTR
Roy Maupin Rd 1 (99139)
P.O. Box 203 (99139-0203)
PHONE..................................509 442-3484
Kenneth Maupin, *Owner*
Kathy Maupin, *Co-Owner*
EMP: 4
SALES: 600K **Privately Held**
SIC: 1611 2411 Highway & street construction; logging

(G-4376)
VAN DYKE LOGGING INCORPORATED
Also Called: Boundary Creek Majestic
221 Mckay St (99139-5101)
P.O. Box 99, Metaline Falls (99153-0099)
PHONE..................................509 442-3852
Jim Van Dyke, *Owner*
Valerie Van Dyke, *Co-Owner*
EMP: 9
SQ FT: 1,800
SALES: 800K **Privately Held**
SIC: 2411 Logging camps & contractors

(G-4377)
WILLARD NEWMAN
Also Called: Willard Newman Logging
25282 Le Clerc Rd N (99139-9623)
PHONE..................................509 442-3265
Willard Newman, *Owner*
Patty Newman, *Owner*
EMP: 4
SALES (est): 119.5K **Privately Held**
SIC: 2411 Logging camps & contractors

Issaquah
King County

(G-4378)
ADALBERT & NAGY SAUSAGE CO LLC
13110 244th Ave Se (98027-7339)
PHONE..................................206 356-3305
EMP: 3
SALES (est): 99K **Privately Held**
SIC: 2011 Meat Packing Plant

(G-4379)
ALL SPORTS SCHOOL
4568 194th Ave Se (98027-9307)
PHONE..................................425 747-1511
EMP: 2

SALES (est): 87.2K **Privately Held**
SIC: 3715 Truck trailers

(G-4380)
APPLIED PRECISION LLC
1040 12th Ave Nw (98027-8929)
PHONE..................................425 557-1000
Ronald Suebert, *CEO*
Daniel Berry, *Exec VP*
Donald Snow, *Vice Pres*
Stephen D Reichenbach, *CFO*
Ian Kirk, *Regl Sales Mgr*
EMP: 150
SQ FT: 54,000
SALES (est): 20.8MM
SALES (corp-wide): 121.6B **Publicly Held**
WEB: www.appliedprecision.com
SIC: 3825 3674 Test equipment for electronic & electric measurement; light sensitive devices
HQ: Ge Healthcare Limited
Amersham Place
Amersham BUCKS HP7 9
149 454-0000

(G-4381)
APPLIED PRECISION HOLDINGS LLC
1040 12th Ave Nw (98027-8929)
PHONE..................................425 557-1000
Daniel Berry, *Exec VP*
Joseph Ahladis, *Senior VP*
Joseph J Victor Jr, *Senior VP*
Donald Snow, *Vice Pres*
Stephen D Reichenbach, *CFO*
EMP: 179
SQ FT: 53,000
SALES (est): 15.1MM **Privately Held**
SIC: 3825 3674 Semiconductor test equipment; light sensitive devices

(G-4382)
ARIGATO LLC
975 Ne Discovery Dr # 407 (98029-6229)
PHONE..................................713 492-3858
Chelsey Roney,
EMP: 2
SALES (est): 56.5K **Privately Held**
SIC: 7372 Application computer software

(G-4383)
ASSURED INDEPENDENCE LLC
2932 Ne Logan St (98029-7357)
PHONE..................................425 516-7400
Joseph Brooke,
EMP: 7
SALES (est): 313.1K **Privately Held**
SIC: 3069 Medical & laboratory rubber sundries & related products

(G-4384)
ATOMROCK LLC
1045 Ridgewood Cir Sw (98027-4638)
PHONE..................................425 281-2371
Kevin Tseng, *CEO*
EMP: 8
SALES: 20K **Privately Held**
SIC: 3571 Electronic computers

(G-4385)
BIOTANGENT DIAGNOSTICS LLC
580 Wilderness Peak Dr Nw (98027-5621)
PHONE..................................503 713-3339
EMP: 4
SALES (est): 256.7K **Privately Held**
SIC: 2835 3826 Mfg Diagnostic Substances Mfg Analytical Instruments

(G-4386)
BLUEFIRE LLC
16231 266th Ave Se (98027-6935)
PHONE..................................206 251-0698
Mary Fredrickson, *CEO*
Mark Fredrickson, *Chief Engr*
EMP: 3 EST: 2014
SALES (est): 157.9K **Privately Held**
SIC: 3571 Computers, digital, analog or hybrid

(G-4387)
BOEHMS CANDIES INC
Also Called: Edelweiss Chalet
255 Ne Gilman Blvd (98027-2903)
PHONE..................................425 392-6652
Helen Shafer, *President*
Bernard Garbusjuk, *Vice Pres*
Joanne Garbusjuk, *Admin Sec*
▲ EMP: 50
SQ FT: 16,000
SALES (est): 3.8MM **Privately Held**
WEB: www.boehmscandies.com
SIC: 5441 2064 Candy; chocolate candy, except solid chocolate

(G-4388)
BRAS THERMOGRAPHY
317 Nw Gilman Blvd (98027-2496)
PHONE..................................425 677-8430
Linda Bamber, *Principal*
EMP: 2
SALES (est): 162.5K **Privately Held**
SIC: 2759 Thermography

(G-4389)
BTPSURGICAL LLC
24218 Se 42nd Pl (98029-7516)
PHONE..................................425 657-0805
Leslie Olson, *Mng Member*
EMP: 2
SALES: 79K **Privately Held**
SIC: 3841 5999 Surgical & medical instruments; medical apparatus & supplies

(G-4390)
CASCADE INTGRTIVE MEDICINE LLC
450 Nw Gilman Blvd # 201 (98027-2722)
PHONE..................................425 391-5270
Rian N Shah, *President*
EMP: 3
SALES (est): 275.6K **Privately Held**
SIC: 8082 5499 2023 8049 Home health care services; vitamin food stores; dietary supplements, dairy & non-dairy based; nutritionist

(G-4391)
CHANNEL KOREA
22525 Se 64th Pl Ste 200 (98027-5307)
PHONE..................................425 557-5970
Eun An, *Principal*
EMP: 2
SALES (est): 139.7K **Privately Held**
SIC: 3663 Space satellite communications equipment

(G-4392)
CHARLES CERAR
630 Sw Ellerwood St (98027-4509)
PHONE..................................425 392-1821
Charles Donald Cerar, *Owner*
EMP: 2
SALES (est): 111.4K **Privately Held**
SIC: 2721 Periodicals: publishing only

(G-4393)
CHIC INK
4709 240th Ave Se (98029-7560)
PHONE..................................425 392-3943
EMP: 2
SALES (est): 150K **Privately Held**
SIC: 2759 Invitations: printing

(G-4394)
CINTERION WIRELESS MODU
22010 Se 51st St (98029-7298)
PHONE..................................630 517-0198
Joe Peterson, *Principal*
EMP: 2
SALES (est): 86.6K **Privately Held**
SIC: 3841 Surgical & medical instruments

(G-4395)
CM INNOVATIONS INC
Also Called: Crux Medical Innovations
1062 Ne High St Ste 8 (98029-7478)
PHONE..................................425 641-0460
EMP: 2
SALES (est): 214.7K **Privately Held**
SIC: 3841 Mfg Surgical/Medical Instruments

Issaquah - King County (G-4396)

(G-4396)
COMBAT FLIP FLOPS LLC
280 Ne Birch St (98027-3310)
PHONE....................206 913-9971
Andrew Sewrey, *Mng Member*
EMP: 3
SALES (est): 121.7K Privately Held
SIC: 3021 Sandals, rubber

(G-4397)
COMBAT FLIP FLOPS LLC
1422 Nw Gilman Blvd Ste 2 (98027)
PHONE....................206 913-9971
Matthew Griffin,
Donald Lee,
Andy Sewrey,
▲ EMP: 3 EST: 2012
SALES (est): 418.6K Privately Held
SIC: 3021 Sandals, rubber

(G-4398)
COMPETENTUM-USA LTD
1495 Nw Gilman Blvd # 14 (98027-5328)
PHONE....................425 996-4201
Natalia Soboleva, *CEO*
Keth Crotty, *Director*
Denis Kovalchu, *Director*
EMP: 15
SALES (est): 1.1MM
SALES (corp-wide): 1.8B Publicly Held
SIC: 7372 Educational computer software
PA: Epam Systems, Inc.
41 University Dr Ste 202
Newtown PA 18940
267 759-9000

(G-4399)
COMPUTER ASSISTED MESSAGE INC
400 Jasmine Pl Nw (98027-2639)
PHONE....................425 392-2496
Paul M Culwell, *President*
EMP: 16
SALES (est): 1.2MM Privately Held
WEB: www.computerassisted.com
SIC: 7389 7372 Mailing & messenger services; prepackaged software

(G-4400)
CREATIVE WINDOW CONCEPTS
2920 200th Ave Se (98075-7469)
PHONE....................425 351-2246
Moniqui Pauoin, *Owner*
EMP: 2
SALES (est): 211.7K Privately Held
WEB: www.cwcwindows.com
SIC: 2591 Drapery hardware & blinds & shades

(G-4401)
DAILY PLANT-IT
10603 Issaquah Hbart Rd Se (98027-5404)
PHONE....................425 677-4948
EMP: 4
SALES (est): 229.7K Privately Held
SIC: 2711 Newspapers, publishing & printing

(G-4402)
DARIGOLD INC
Also Called: Darigold Farms
611 Front St N (98027-2913)
P.O. Box 1308 (98027-0051)
PHONE....................425 392-6463
Kim Niino, *Manager*
EMP: 100
SALES (corp-wide): 1.4B Privately Held
WEB: www.darigold.com
SIC: 2021 2026 Creamery butter; cottage cheese; yogurt; cream, sour
HQ: Darigold, Inc.
5601 6th Ave S Ste 300
Seattle WA 98108
206 284-7220

(G-4403)
DATA SHAPING SOLUTIONS LLC
2428 35th Ave Ne (98029-3611)
PHONE....................425 837-4767
Vincent Granville,
Paris Granville,
EMP: 2
SALES (est): 143.2K Privately Held
WEB: www.datashaping.com
SIC: 2721 Statistical reports (periodicals): publishing & printing

(G-4404)
DEER PATH INDUSTRIAL TECH
14236 246th Pl Se (98027-8366)
P.O. Box 1463 (98027-0059)
PHONE....................425 391-9223
Gerri Steele, *President*
James D Grubel, *Vice Pres*
EMP: 2
SALES: 500K Privately Held
SIC: 5084 3569 Recycling machinery & equipment; filters & strainers, pipeline

(G-4405)
DELTA V CELLARS LLC
1050 1st Pl Se (98027-4641)
PHONE....................425 677-8487
Christopher Voorhees, *Principal*
EMP: 2
SALES (est): 62.3K Privately Held
SIC: 2084 Wines, brandy & brandy spirits

(G-4406)
DISMAN BAKNER NORTHWEST INC
2243 275th Ct Se (98075-7942)
PHONE....................425 837-3913
EMP: 2
SALES: 200K Privately Held
SIC: 3699 Mfg Electrical Equipment/Supplies

(G-4407)
DYNO RESOURCE CORP
26429 Se 152nd St (98027-8273)
PHONE....................425 391-6084
Steven Walker, *President*
EMP: 3
SALES (est): 310K Privately Held
WEB: www.dynoresource.com
SIC: 3829 Dynamometer instruments

(G-4408)
EARTH SOAP COMPANY
24759 Se 56th St (98029-7623)
PHONE....................425 677-8540
Christina Britts, *Principal*
EMP: 2 EST: 2010
SALES (est): 160.1K Privately Held
SIC: 2841 Soap & other detergents

(G-4409)
EDMUND LUCY
1205 Oakcreek Pl Nw (98027-8664)
PHONE....................425 703-4155
EMP: 2
SALES (est): 62.9K Privately Held
SIC: 2711 Newspapers

(G-4410)
EYEON LLC
20603 Se 136th St (98027-8437)
PHONE....................425 652-9556
William Mickel, *President*
EMP: 2
SALES: 40K Privately Held
WEB: www.eyepole.com
SIC: 3827 Optical test & inspection equipment

(G-4411)
FAIRWOOD COMMERCE CENTER LLP
20728 Se 119th St (98027-8547)
PHONE....................206 903-9200
Brad Solly, *Principal*
EMP: 2
SALES (est): 102.5K Privately Held
SIC: 2499 Wood products

(G-4412)
FANTASY GLASS WORKS INC
7932 Rnton Issaquah Rd Se (98027-5443)
P.O. Box 2391 (98027-0108)
PHONE....................425 557-6642
John Stefani, *CEO*
Gail Vandemoere, *President*
EMP: 3
SALES (est): 223.5K Privately Held
SIC: 3229 5231 Glassware, art or decorative; glass

(G-4413)
FIELDS FABRICATION CORPORATION
Also Called: Tuff Boat
11138 Upper Preston Rd Se (98027-8713)
PHONE....................425 222-5905
Edward Fields, *President*
EMP: 3
SQ FT: 2,500
SALES: 500K Privately Held
WEB: www.tuffboat.com
SIC: 3732 Boat building & repairing

(G-4414)
FINANCIAL MANAGEMENT SYSTEMS
1420 Nw Gilman Blvd # 2729 (98027-5394)
PHONE....................425 881-8687
Samuel J Bisignano, *President*
EMP: 2
SALES (est): 160K Privately Held
WEB: www.micromuni.com
SIC: 7372 7374 Operating systems computer software; data processing & preparation

(G-4415)
FIRESTEED CORPORATION (PA)
Also Called: Firesteed Cellars
375 1st Pl Nw (98027-3220)
PHONE....................503 623-8683
Howard Rossbach, *President*
E G Morgan, *Vice Pres*
Patricia Dash, *Comptroller*
Curtis Hine, *Human Resources*
Deborah Chapman, *Manager*
▲ EMP: 5
SQ FT: 1,500
SALES (est): 464.2K Privately Held
WEB: www.firesteed.com
SIC: 2084 5149 Wines; mineral or spring water bottling

(G-4416)
GALLATIN INTERNATIONAL LLC
22525 Se 64th Pl Ste 244 (98027-5383)
PHONE....................425 557-4356
Todd L Shaw,
▲ EMP: 2
SQ FT: 2,000
SALES: 10MM Privately Held
SIC: 2092 Seafoods, frozen: prepared

(G-4417)
GARCIA INK CORP
Also Called: Minuteman Press
180 Ne Juniper St (98027-2505)
PHONE....................425 391-4950
Damon Garcia, *President*
EMP: 9
SALES (est): 460.6K Privately Held
SIC: 2752 Commercial printing, offset

(G-4418)
GENE L HENRY INC
1175 Nw Gilman Blvd B16 (98027-5399)
PHONE....................425 392-1485
Gene Henry, *Principal*
EMP: 5 EST: 2010
SALES (est): 427.4K Privately Held
SIC: 3578 Coin counters

(G-4419)
GENERAL ELECTRIC COMPANY
1605 Nw Sammamish Rd # 110 (98027-5378)
PHONE....................425 557-3022
Scott Chapman, *Manager*
EMP: 177
SALES (corp-wide): 121.6B Publicly Held
SIC: 3844 X-ray apparatus & tubes
PA: General Electric Company
41 Farnsworth St
Boston MA 02210
617 443-3000

(G-4420)
GIRT JOHN
Also Called: John Girt & Associates
4629 191st Ave Se (98027-9316)
PHONE....................206 399-4977
John Girt, *Owner*
EMP: 2

SALES (est): 160K Privately Held
SIC: 7372 Prepackaged software

(G-4421)
GLOBAL SOFTWARE SYSTEMS INC
23349 Se 51st Pl (98029-6808)
PHONE....................425 427-8215
EMP: 2 EST: 2000
SALES: 150K Privately Held
SIC: 7371 7372 Custom Computer Programing Prepackaged Software Services

(G-4422)
GLOBALMAX ASSOCIATES INC
1672202 25th Pl Ne (98027)
PHONE....................425 392-4848
Denny Liao, *President*
▲ EMP: 15
SQ FT: 1,000
SALES: 1.5MM Privately Held
SIC: 3089 2392 Novelties, plastic; household furnishings

(G-4423)
GOLDEN CREEK LLC
17321 270th Ave Se (98027-6907)
PHONE....................425 830-4343
Rex Foxford, *Principal*
EMP: 2
SALES (est): 132.3K Privately Held
SIC: 3949 Fishing equipment

(G-4424)
GRETTE CUSTOM WOODWORKING
27022 Se 162nd Pl (98027-6903)
PHONE....................425 392-8584
Dan Grette, *Owner*
Virginia Grette, *Co-Owner*
EMP: 2
SALES: 80K Privately Held
SIC: 2499 Laundry products, wood

(G-4425)
HANSON LEHIGH INC
6600 230th Ave Se (98027-2524)
PHONE....................425 867-1234
Barry Meade, *Branch Mgr*
EMP: 5
SALES (corp-wide): 20.6B Privately Held
SIC: 3273 Ready-mixed concrete
HQ: Hanson Lehigh Inc
300 E John Carpenter Fwy
Irving TX 75062

(G-4426)
HOWLING WOLF DRUMS
24834 Se Mirrormont Way (98027-7314)
PHONE....................425 391-2540
EMP: 2
SALES (est): 120K Privately Held
SIC: 3931 Mfg Musical Instruments

(G-4427)
HYDROPEPTIDE LLC
295 Ne Gilman Blvd # 201 (98027-2906)
PHONE....................425 458-1072
Steve Peck, *President*
Michael Huber, *Opers Mgr*
Stacey Cepeda, *Office Mgr*
▲ EMP: 11
SQ FT: 4,000
SALES (est): 2.6MM Privately Held
SIC: 2844 Towelettes, premoistened

(G-4428)
IN THE ZONE PROMOTIONS
25722 Se Tiger Mtn Rd (98027-8357)
PHONE....................425 246-6313
Jason Jackowich, *Owner*
EMP: 3
SALES: 450K Privately Held
SIC: 3993 Signs & advertising specialties

(G-4429)
INNOCOR INC
1180 Nw Maple St (98027-8106)
PHONE....................844 824-9348
EMP: 4
SALES (corp-wide): 209.9MM Privately Held
SIC: 3086 Plastics foam products

GEOGRAPHIC SECTION

Issaquah - King County (G-4461)

HQ: Innocor, Inc.
200 Schulz Dr Ste 2
Red Bank NJ 07701

(G-4430)
ISSAQUAH LANSCAPING INC
45 1st Pl Nw (98027)
P.O. Box 1442 (98027-0059)
PHONE..................................425 392-6123
David Rogers, *President*
EMP: 4
SALES: 700K **Privately Held**
WEB: www.issaquahlandscaping.com
SIC: 0782 3229 Landscape contractors; bulbs for electric lights

(G-4431)
ISSAQUAH SIGNS INC
60 Nw Gilman Blvd Ste C (98027-2480)
PHONE..................................425 391-3010
Steven Lambert, *President*
EMP: 6
SALES (est): 345K **Privately Held**
SIC: 3993 Signs & advertising specialties

(G-4432)
IXIA SPORTS INC
1420 Nw Gilman Blvd (98027-5394)
PHONE..................................425 417-6454
Charles Kim, *Principal*
EMP: 4
SALES (est): 348.5K **Privately Held**
SIC: 3949 Sporting & athletic goods

(G-4433)
J & K WOODWORKS
391 Sw Forest Dr (98027-4623)
PHONE..................................425 392-3758
James Crabtree, *Principal*
EMP: 2
SALES (est): 157.8K **Privately Held**
SIC: 2431 Millwork

(G-4434)
JULIES DESIGNS
30500 Se 79th St (98027-8700)
PHONE..................................206 727-3341
Julie Adam, *Owner*
EMP: 3
SALES (est): 95.2K **Privately Held**
SIC: 2395 Art goods for embroidering, stamped: purchased materials

(G-4435)
JX CRYSTALS INC
1105 12th Ave Nw Ste A2 (98027-8968)
PHONE..................................425 392-5237
Lewis M Fraas, *President*
Lewis Fraas, *President*
Jany Xiang-Fraas, *Vice Pres*
▲ **EMP:** 5
SQ FT: 14,000
SALES (est): 781.6K **Privately Held**
WEB: www.jxcrystals.com
SIC: 3674 5074 Wafers (semiconductor devices); solar cells; infrared sensors, solid state; heating equipment & panels, solar

(G-4436)
L M CUPCAKES LLC
250 1st Ave Ne (98027-3322)
PHONE..................................425 427-9558
Lisa W Johnson, *Principal*
EMP: 6
SALES (est): 522.6K **Privately Held**
SIC: 2051 Bread, cake & related products

(G-4437)
LAKESIDE INDUSTRIES INC (PA)
6505 226th Pl Se Ste 200 (98027-8905)
P.O. Box 7016 (98027-7016)
PHONE..................................425 313-2600
Timothy Lee Jr, *CEO*
Michael J Lee, *President*
Robert Dennis, *Division Mgr*
Tony Hammett, *Division Mgr*
Pat Van Eaton, *Superintendent*
▲ **EMP:** 80
SQ FT: 24,000
SALES (est): 326.4MM **Privately Held**
WEB: www.lakesideind.com
SIC: 1611 2951 5032 Highway & street paving contractor; asphalt & asphaltic paving mixtures (not from refineries); gravel

(G-4438)
LG INDUSTRIES LLC
60 Nw Gilman Blvd Ste D (98027-2480)
PHONE..................................425 557-7993
Hamid Shaysete, *Principal*
EMP: 2
SALES (est): 118.1K **Privately Held**
SIC: 3999 Manufacturing industries

(G-4439)
LINC TECHNOLOGY CORPORATION
Also Called: Data-Linc Group
1125 12th Ave Nw Ste B2 (98027-8966)
PHONE..................................425 882-2206
Michel Maes, *President*
James Steffey, *Vice Pres*
EMP: 30
SQ FT: 13,000
SALES (est): 4.3MM **Privately Held**
SIC: 3669 3661 Intercommunication systems, electric; telephone & telegraph apparatus

(G-4440)
LINKS BUSINESS GROUP LLC
700 Nw Gilman Blvd (98027-5395)
PHONE..................................425 961-0565
EMP: 2 **EST:** 2010
SALES (est): 110K **Privately Held**
SIC: 7372 Prepackaged Software Services

(G-4441)
LUCKYHORSE INDUSTRIES
18848 Se 42nd St (98027-9366)
P.O. Box 16666, Seattle (98116-0666)
PHONE..................................206 227-3383
EMP: 2
SALES (est): 185.1K **Privately Held**
SIC: 3999 Manufacturing industries

(G-4442)
LUFKIN INDUSTRIES LLC
1595 Nw Gilman Blvd Ste 7 (98027-5329)
PHONE..................................425 295-7676
EMP: 425
SALES (corp-wide): 121.6B **Publicly Held**
SIC: 3561 Pumps & pumping equipment
HQ: Lufkin Industries, Llc
601 S Raguet St
Lufkin TX 75904
936 634-2211

(G-4443)
MANGOAPPS INC
1495 11th Ave Nw (98027-5319)
PHONE..................................425 274-9950
Anup Kejriwal, *CEO*
Ashish Agarwal, *Vice Pres*
Ajit Hirekar, *Accounts Mgr*
Vishwa Malhotra, *CTO*
EMP: 51
SALES (est): 2.7MM **Privately Held**
SIC: 7372 Application computer software

(G-4444)
MARK HUMMEL
Also Called: Mk Machining
19434 Se 118th St (98027-8594)
PHONE..................................425 271-7156
Mark Hummel, *Owner*
Karen Hummel, *Co-Owner*
EMP: 2
SALES (est): 144.2K **Privately Held**
SIC: 3599 Machine shop, jobbing & repair

(G-4445)
MARKETING MASTERS INC
1871 Nw Gilman Blvd (98027-8116)
P.O. Box 675 (98027-0025)
PHONE..................................425 454-5610
Richard F Gauron, *President*
Jacques Gauron, *Vice Pres*
Andre Gauron, *Treasurer*
Kathy St Marie, *Manager*
EMP: 16
SQ FT: 15,000
SALES (est): 5.1MM **Privately Held**
SIC: 3728 5088 Aircraft parts & equipment; aircraft equipment & supplies

(G-4446)
MCCAIN INC
8172 304th Ave Se (98027-8889)
PHONE..................................760 734-5086
EMP: 3
SALES (corp-wide): 177.9K **Privately Held**
SIC: 3669 Traffic signals, electric
HQ: Mccain, Inc.
2365 Oak Ridge Way
Vista CA 92081
760 727-8100

(G-4447)
MECHATRONICS INC (PA)
8152 304th Ave Se (98027-8889)
P.O. Box 5012, Preston (98050-5012)
PHONE..................................425 222-5900
Kent G Ross, *President*
Julie Cushman, *Senior VP*
William P Messenger, *Director*
Edward P Knopf, *Admin Sec*
▲ **EMP:** 130
SQ FT: 40,000
SALES (est): 102.7MM **Privately Held**
WEB: www.mechatronicsinc.com
SIC: 5085 5063 3564 Bearings; electronic wire & cable; blowers & fans

(G-4448)
MENASHA PACKAGING COMPANY LLC
22530 Se 64th Pl Ste 210 (98027-5353)
PHONE..................................425 677-7788
EMP: 151
SALES (corp-wide): 1.7B **Privately Held**
SIC: 2653 Corrugated & solid fiber boxes
HQ: Menasha Packaging Company, Llc
1645 Bergstrom Rd
Neenah WI 54956
920 751-1000

(G-4449)
MICROSOFT CORPORATION
21930 Se 51st Pl (98029-8238)
PHONE..................................425 882-8080
EMP: 35
SALES (corp-wide): 110.3B **Publicly Held**
SIC: 7372 Prepackaged software
PA: Microsoft Corporation
1 Microsoft Way
Redmond WA 98052
425 882-8080

(G-4450)
MIX CREATIONS
20524 Se 26th St (98075-9628)
PHONE..................................425 392-1123
EMP: 2 **EST:** 2001
SALES (est): 140K **Privately Held**
SIC: 2253 Knit Outerwear Mill

(G-4451)
MOUNT FURY CO INC
1592 Nw Maple St (98027-8973)
P.O. Box 2763 (98027-0127)
PHONE..................................425 391-0747
Daniel F Pope, *President*
Frances Pope, *Admin Sec*
EMP: 2
SQ FT: 900
SALES: 250K **Privately Held**
WEB: www.mtfuryco.com
SIC: 3823 Industrial process control instruments

(G-4452)
NBTY INC
22526 Se 64th Pl (98027-5368)
PHONE..................................425 369-1771
EMP: 2 **EST:** 2013
SALES (est): 106.5K **Privately Held**
SIC: 2833 Medicinals & botanicals

(G-4453)
NEON ELECTRIC SIGN CO
23834 Se 111th St (98027-8320)
PHONE..................................206 405-4001
Roger Ligrano, *Partner*
EMP: 5
SALES (est): 414.7K **Privately Held**
SIC: 3993 Electric signs

(G-4454)
NORTH PACIFIC INDUSTRIAL
457 1st Ave Nw (98027-2804)
PHONE..................................425 251-0335
Steve Wemk, *Owner*
Lue Pestl, *General Mgr*
EMP: 2
SALES: 68K **Privately Held**
SIC: 3589 Sandblasting equipment

(G-4455)
NOVO FOGO
13217 255th Ave Se (98027-8371)
P.O. Box 903 (98027-0033)
PHONE..................................425 256-2527
Dragos Axinte, *Owner*
EMP: 2
SALES (est): 62.3K **Privately Held**
SIC: 2085 Distilled & blended liquors

(G-4456)
OMNIM2M LLC
4826 194th Ave Se (98027-9326)
PHONE..................................425 278-4090
Gary Schmidt, *Managing Dir*
Ajay Sikka, *Mng Member*
EMP: 10
SQ FT: 3,000
SALES: 3MM
SALES (corp-wide): 181.3K **Privately Held**
SIC: 7372 Business oriented computer software
PA: Traqiq, Inc.
201 Santa Monica Blvd # 300
Santa Monica CA 90401
310 752-7773

(G-4457)
PACIFIC ORTHOTIC LLC
1527 Sycamore Dr Se (98027-4806)
PHONE..................................425 417-3742
Eric Stephenson, *Principal*
EMP: 2 **EST:** 2016
SALES (est): 105.5K **Privately Held**
SIC: 3842 Orthopedic appliances

(G-4458)
PEACEFUL SOLE
320 Newport Way Nw (98027-3119)
PHONE..................................425 652-7043
EMP: 2
SALES (est): 130K **Privately Held**
SIC: 3843 Mfg Dental Equipment/Supplies

(G-4459)
PERRY STAINED GLASS STUDIO
470 Front St N Ste 3 (98027-2914)
PHONE..................................425 392-1600
James Perry, *Owner*
Elizabeth Perry, *Co-Owner*
EMP: 3
SALES (est): 200K **Privately Held**
SIC: 3231 Stained glass: made from purchased glass

(G-4460)
PRESTON WOODCRAFT LLC
23514 Se 137th St (98027-8324)
PHONE..................................425 749-8074
Abel Richardson, *Principal*
EMP: 2 **EST:** 2012
SALES (est): 133.8K **Privately Held**
SIC: 2511 Wood household furniture

(G-4461)
PROCTER & GAMBLE COMPANY
1180 Nw Maple St (98027-8106)
PHONE..................................425 313-3511
Mary Stuckenschneider, *Manager*
Rajeev Agarwal, *Manager*
EMP: 150
SALES (corp-wide): 66.8B **Publicly Held**
WEB: www.pg.com
SIC: 2844 2676 3421 2842 Deodorants, personal; towels, napkins & tissue paper products; razor blades & razors; specialty cleaning preparations; soap: granulated, liquid, cake, flaked or chip
PA: The Procter & Gamble Company
1 Procter And Gamble Plz
Cincinnati OH 45202
513 983-1100

Issaquah - King County

(G-4462)
PROGRESSIVE PRINTING SOLUTIONS
700 Nw Gilman Blvd Ste E (98027-5395)
P.O. Box 2337, Redmond (98073-2337)
PHONE...................................425 867-1296
Kent Osborne, *Principal*
Nancy Osborne, *Principal*
EMP: 2
SALES (est): 180K **Privately Held**
SIC: 2759 Commercial printing

(G-4463)
PURPLETRAIL
1495 11th Ave Nw (98027-5319)
PHONE...................................425 292-1811
EMP: 2
SALES (est): 28.1K **Privately Held**
SIC: 5947 2759 Greeting cards; promotional printing

(G-4464)
READY WELD
13620 233rd Way Se (98027-6406)
P.O. Box 2061 (98027-0092)
PHONE...................................425 391-4211
Michael D Sailing, *Owner*
EMP: 10
SALES (est): 195.8K **Privately Held**
SIC: 7692 Welding repair

(G-4465)
REDMOND WLDERS FABRICATORS INC
30244 Se High Point Way (98027-8820)
P.O. Box 999, Preston (98050-0999)
PHONE...................................425 222-6330
Chris Brilz, *President*
Jim Brilz, *Principal*
EMP: 20
SQ FT: 11,000
SALES (est): 4.9MM **Privately Held**
WEB: www.redmondwelders.com
SIC: 3441 Fabricated structural metal

(G-4466)
REFRESH PRTG & PROMOTIONS LLC
40 5th Ave Ne (98027-3432)
PHONE...................................425 391-3223
Allen Flintoft,
EMP: 4
SALES (est): 366.1K **Privately Held**
SIC: 2752 Commercial printing, lithographic

(G-4467)
RIMINI SOFTWARE LLC
16650 246th Pl Se (98027-8403)
PHONE...................................425 785-8819
Tim Van Houten, *President*
EMP: 2
SALES (est): 127.8K **Privately Held**
SIC: 7372 Prepackaged software

(G-4468)
RIPLEY SOFTWARE
996 Ne High St (98029-7479)
PHONE...................................501 773-5519
EMP: 2 EST: 2016
SALES (est): 65.5K **Privately Held**
SIC: 7372 Prepackaged software

(G-4469)
RLEYH SOFTWARE LLC
21293 Se 42nd Pl (98029-9511)
PHONE...................................425 837-4643
Francois Cantonnet,
Vinit Jain,
EMP: 2
SALES (est): 75.2K **Privately Held**
SIC: 7374 7371 7372 Data processing & preparation; custom computer programming services; computer software writing services; home entertainment computer software

(G-4470)
RONDYS INC (PA)
Also Called: Idaho Lime
5647 229th Ave Se (98029-8908)
PHONE...................................425 392-6324
Vern W Hall, *President*
Wilburn Hall, *Vice Pres*
Bonnie Elerding, *Admin Sec*
EMP: 5
SALES (est): 549.9K **Privately Held**
SIC: 0912 0913 1422 1041 Finfish; crabs, catching of; crushed & broken limestone; gold ores

(G-4471)
SAN MAR CORPORATION
Sanmar
30500 Se 79th St (98027-8700)
PHONE...................................206 727-3200
EMP: 135
SALES (corp-wide): 1.6B **Privately Held**
SIC: 2326 5137 Men's & boys' work clothing; sweaters, women's & children's
PA: San Mar Corporation
22833 Se Black Nugget Rd # 130
Issaquah WA 98029
206 727-3200

(G-4472)
SECURITAY INC
1095 Sunrise Pl Sw (98027-4639)
PHONE...................................425 392-0203
David Mowers, *President*
Jeffrey Spelman, *Principal*
EMP: 3
SALES (est): 236.3K **Privately Held**
SIC: 5045 7372 Computer software; application computer software

(G-4473)
SHADEWAVE
14532 255th Ave Se (98027-7325)
PHONE...................................425 557-7788
Dennis Braunston, *Owner*
EMP: 4
SALES (est): 184.9K **Privately Held**
SIC: 3843 Dental equipment & supplies

(G-4474)
SIEMENS INDUSTRY INC
22010 Se 51st St (98029-7298)
PHONE...................................208 883-8330
Juan Cantu, *Area Mgr*
Gary Potraz, *Manager*
EMP: 6
SALES (corp-wide): 95B **Privately Held**
WEB: www.sibt.com
SIC: 3585 3825 Refrigeration & heating equipment; instruments to measure electricity
HQ: Siemens Industry, Inc.
1000 Deerfield Pkwy
Buffalo Grove IL 60089
847 215-1000

(G-4475)
SIEMENS MED SOLUTIONS USA INC
Ultrasound Division - Issaquah
22010 Se 51st St (98029-7298)
P.O. Box 7002 (98027-7002)
PHONE...................................425 392-9180
Ganesh Sivananthan, *Engineer*
Martin Klein, *CFO*
Russell Braymen, *Manager*
Michael Gilmore, *Manager*
Ken Swanson, *Technology*
EMP: 152
SALES (corp-wide): 95B **Privately Held**
WEB: www.siemensmedical.com
SIC: 3841 7371 3845 Diagnostic apparatus, medical; custom computer programming services; electromedical equipment
HQ: Siemens Medical Solutions Usa, Inc.
40 Liberty Blvd
Malvern PA 19355
888 826-9702

(G-4476)
SIEMENS PRODUCT LIFE MGMT SFTW
Also Called: Siemens PLM Software
22010 Se 51st St (98029-7298)
PHONE...................................425 507-1900
Tony Affuso, *Principal*
EMP: 34
SALES (corp-wide): 95B **Privately Held**
WEB: www.ugs.com
SIC: 7372 Business oriented computer software
HQ: Siemens Product Lifecycle Management Software Inc.
5800 Granite Pkwy Ste 600
Plano TX 75024
972 987-3000

(G-4477)
SOCK OUTLET
1420 Nw Gilman Blvd (98027-5394)
PHONE...................................435 787-8888
EMP: 33
SALES (corp-wide): 2.5MM **Privately Held**
SIC: 2252 Socks
PA: The Sock Outlet
2929 N Main St
Logan UT 84341
435 787-8889

(G-4478)
SODA POP MINIATURES LLC
1895 10th Ave Ne (98029-5417)
PHONE...................................425 260-4638
Christopher Birkenhagen, *Principal*
EMP: 3
SALES (est): 181.6K **Privately Held**
SIC: 3999 Miniatures

(G-4479)
SOFTWARE IN 34TH ST
22014 Se 34th St (98075-9241)
PHONE...................................425 557-7953
John Grigg, *Principal*
EMP: 2 EST: 2001
SALES (est): 121.1K **Privately Held**
SIC: 7372 Prepackaged software

(G-4480)
SOLCON INC
Also Called: Quick Medical Gs
30200 Se 79th St Unit 120 (98027-8792)
PHONE...................................425 222-5963
Scott Hanna, *President*
Warren Strasen, *Vice Pres*
Eileen Brisbine, *CFO*
Michael Lautenslager, *Controller*
Bonnie Lambert, *Sales Staff*
▲ EMP: 41
SQ FT: 9,000
SALES (est): 7.6MM **Privately Held**
WEB: www.quickmedical.com
SIC: 5999 5047 3596 Medical apparatus & supplies; medical & hospital equipment; scales & balances, except laboratory

(G-4481)
SOURCE DYNAMICS INC
Also Called: Source Insight
22525 Se 64th Pl Ste 260 (98027-5387)
PHONE...................................425 557-3630
Ray Gram, *President*
EMP: 3
SALES (est): 267.9K **Privately Held**
WEB: www.sourcedyn.com
SIC: 7372 7371 Prepackaged software; custom computer programming services

(G-4482)
STEPPIR ANTENNA SYSTEMS INC
14135 233rd Pl Se (98027-6441)
PHONE...................................425 391-1999
▲ EMP: 3
SALES (est): 290K **Privately Held**
SIC: 3812 Mfg Search/Navigation Equipment

(G-4483)
STREAMLINE INTERNATIONAL
200 W Sunset Way (98027-0081)
P.O. Box 1766 (98027-0072)
PHONE...................................425 392-2350
EMP: 2
SALES (est): 118.9K **Privately Held**
SIC: 2759 Commercial Printing

(G-4484)
T-ZERO RACING INC
7700 300th Ave Se Unit A2 (98027-8791)
PHONE...................................425 222-5800
Charles A Lyford IV, *President*
Laurie Lyford, *Admin Sec*
EMP: 4
SALES (est): 463.6K **Privately Held**
WEB: www.t-zeroracing.com
SIC: 3465 Tops, automobile: stamped metal

(G-4485)
US SIGN GIRL
772 Big Tree Dr Nw (98027-5616)
PHONE...................................801 644-1108
EMP: 2 EST: 2011
SALES (est): 110K **Privately Held**
SIC: 3993 Mfg Signs/Advertising Specialties

(G-4486)
VECTRA FITNESS INC
18840 Se 42nd St (98027-9366)
PHONE...................................425 291-9550
W D Maclean, *President*
W D Mac Lean, *President*
Doug Maclean, *Principal*
Robert A Rasmussen, *Corp Secy*
A Buell Ish, *Vice Pres*
◆ EMP: 120
SALES (est): 13.8MM **Privately Held**
WEB: www.vectrafitness.com
SIC: 3949 5941 Exercise equipment; exercise equipment

(G-4487)
VERSALY GAMES INC
1065 1st Pl Se (98027-4641)
PHONE...................................425 577-0208
Matthew Feldman, *Principal*
EMP: 2
SALES (est): 120K **Privately Held**
SIC: 7372 Prepackaged software

(G-4488)
WARNERS CABINETS
33516 Se 114th St (98027-8743)
PHONE...................................425 222-7386
Todd Warner, *Owner*
EMP: 4
SALES (est): 350K **Privately Held**
SIC: 5712 2434 Furniture stores; wood kitchen cabinets

(G-4489)
WHALEN FURNITURE MANUFACTURING
1605 Nw Sammamish Rd # 111 (98027-5378)
PHONE...................................425 427-0115
Luis Villasenor, *President*
EMP: 2 EST: 2011
SALES (est): 158.6K **Privately Held**
SIC: 5021 3999 Furniture; manufacturing industries

(G-4490)
XEXTEX CORPORATION USA
Also Called: X'Tex
70 E Sunset Way Ste 188 (98027-3813)
PHONE...................................425 392-3848
Jerry M Brownstein, *President*
Brent Hepner, *Vice Pres*
Herb Pearse, *Director*
Tom Coyner, *Admin Sec*
EMP: 4
SALES: 1MM **Privately Held**
WEB: www.xextex.com
SIC: 1382 3999 Oil & gas exploration services; barber & beauty shop equipment

Kalama
Cowlitz County

(G-4491)
AIR LIQUIDE AMERICA LP
185 Eastwind Rd (98625)
PHONE...................................360 673-1400
Scott Moon, *Branch Mgr*
EMP: 2
SALES (corp-wide): 125.9MM **Privately Held**
SIC: 2813 Hydrogen; nitrogen; oxygen, compressed or liquefied
HQ: Air Liquide America L.P.
9811 Katy Fwy Ste 100
Houston TX 77024
713 624-8000

GEOGRAPHIC SECTION

Kelso - Cowlitz County (G-4519)

(G-4492)
ARCH WOOD PROTECTION INC
532 Hendrickson Dr (98625-9650)
P.O. Box 340 (98625-0300)
PHONE..................360 673-5099
Pam Griffin, *Manager*
EMP: 6
SALES (corp-wide): 5.5B **Privately Held**
SIC: 2899 2861 Chemical preparations; gum & wood chemicals
HQ: Arch Wood Protection, Inc.
5660 New Northside Dr
Atlanta GA 30328
678 627-2000

(G-4493)
BENNU GLASS LLC
2310 N Hendrickson Dr (98625-9546)
PHONE..................360 524-4970
Gerald Lemieux,
Trish Garringer,
EMP: 13
SQ FT: 166,000
SALES (est): 3.4MM **Privately Held**
SIC: 3221 Bottles for packing, bottling & canning: glass

(G-4494)
CE METAL FABRICATION
2632 N Hendrickson Dr (98625-9513)
PHONE..................360 673-9663
Joe Christiansen,
EMP: 10
SALES (est): 242.2K **Privately Held**
SIC: 1081 Metal mining exploration & development services

(G-4495)
CHEVRON KALAMA
344 Ne Frontage Rd (98625)
P.O. Box 187 (98625-0200)
PHONE..................360 673-2972
Jim Hendrickson, *Owner*
EMP: 15
SALES (est): 1MM **Privately Held**
SIC: 5541 5411 7999 3578 Filling stations, gasoline; convenience stores; lottery tickets, sale of; automatic teller machines (ATM)

(G-4496)
COLUMBIA METAL FAB CNSTR INC
1265 Nw 3rd St (98625-9703)
PHONE..................360 989-0201
Jeremie Singer, *Principal*
EMP: 2
SALES (est): 86.6K **Privately Held**
SIC: 3441 Fabricated structural metal

(G-4497)
EAST WEST GENERAL INC
Also Called: Absolute Concrete Colors
1265 Hendrickson Dr (98625-8401)
PHONE..................360 673-6404
Clark Goodrich, *President*
Byron Goodrich, *Corp Secy*
EMP: 8
SQ FT: 8,000
SALES (est): 1.2MM **Privately Held**
SIC: 3272 5032 Concrete products, precast; concrete building products

(G-4498)
ECOTECH RECYCLING LLC
2601 N Hendrickson Dr A (98625-9571)
PHONE..................360 673-3860
Renie Duvall, *CEO*
▲ EMP: 23 EST: 2008
SQ FT: 40,000
SALES: 1.2MM **Privately Held**
SIC: 5094 5065 8748 4953 Precious metals; electronic parts; environmental consultant; refuse systems; refuse collection & disposal services; recycling, waste materials; ; secondary nonferrous metals

(G-4499)
EMERALD KALAMA CHEMICAL LLC
Also Called: Emerald Performance Materials
1296 3rd St Nw (98625-9563)
PHONE..................360 673-2550
Edward T Gotch, *CEO*
EMP: 150
SALES (corp-wide): 557.5MM **Privately Held**
SIC: 2865 Cyclic crudes & intermediates
HQ: Emerald Kalama Chemical, Llc
1499 Se Tech Center Pl # 300
Vancouver WA 98683
360 673-2550

(G-4500)
ENB LOGGING & CONSTRUCTION
Also Called: E N B Logging
1743 Cloverdale Rd (98625-9724)
P.O. Box 808 (98625-0800)
PHONE..................360 673-2696
Edward N Bryant Jr, *President*
EMP: 11
SALES (est): 1.1MM **Privately Held**
SIC: 2411 Logging

(G-4501)
IMSA STEEL CORP
Also Called: Steelscape
222 W Kalama River Rd (98625-9420)
PHONE..................360 673-8200
Cesar Jarero, *President*
EMP: 316
SALES (est): 22.3MM **Privately Held**
SIC: 3479 3441 Coating of metals & formed products; fabricated structural metal
PA: Bluescope Steel Limited
88 Ricketts Rd
Mount Waverley VIC 3000

(G-4502)
KALAMA PRECISION MACHINE
1629 S Cloverdale Rd (98625-9603)
P.O. Box 580 (98625-0600)
PHONE..................360 673-1255
Julie Lockwood, *Owner*
Samuel Lockwood, *Co-Owner*
EMP: 3
SQ FT: 1,152
SALES (est): 262.5K **Privately Held**
WEB: www.kalamaprecision.com
SIC: 3599 Machine shop, jobbing & repair

(G-4503)
KALAMA RIVER ROAD QUARRY
460 Kalama River Rd (98625-9448)
PHONE..................360 673-0795
EMP: 2
SALES (est): 88.1K **Privately Held**
SIC: 1429 Crushed & broken stone

(G-4504)
LONZA INC
532 Hendrickson Dr (98625-9650)
P.O. Box 340 (98625-0300)
PHONE..................360 673-5099
Pam Griffin, *Manager*
EMP: 2
SALES (est): 74.4K **Privately Held**
SIC: 2899 Chemical preparations

(G-4505)
NORTHWEST INNOVATION WORKS KA
380 W Marine Dr (98625-9500)
PHONE..................360 673-7800
EMP: 16
SALES (est): 850.7K **Privately Held**
SIC: 2869 Methyl alcohol, synthetic methanol

(G-4506)
PAN-PACIFIC ENERGY CORP
Also Called: Northwest Innovation Works
380 W Marine Dr (98625-9500)
PHONE..................360 673-7800
Simon Zhang, *CEO*
Edward Sappin, *CFO*
▼ EMP: 15
SQ FT: 7,000
SALES (est): 1.6MM
SALES (corp-wide): 2.2MM **Privately Held**
SIC: 2869 Methyl alcohol, synthetic methanol; high purity grade chemicals, organic
PA: Shanghai Bi Ke Clean Energy Technology Co., Ltd.
Room 2301-2303,Free International Square,No.76,Pujian Road,Pudon Shanghai 20012
216 106-0100

(G-4507)
RSG FOREST PRODUCTS INC (PA)
Also Called: Gram Lumber Company
985 Nw 2nd St (98625-9647)
PHONE..................360 673-2825
Robert C Sanders, *President*
Samuel E Sanders, *Corp Secy*
Bob Redd, *Sales Mgr*
Kirk Harrison, *Manager*
John Schmit, *Manager*
▲ EMP: 225
SQ FT: 4,000
SALES (est): 145.8MM **Privately Held**
WEB: www.rsgfp.com
SIC: 2421 2499 Lumber: rough, sawed or planed; fencing, wood

(G-4508)
SOMARAKIS INC (PA)
552 Hendrickson Dr (98625-9650)
P.O. Box 430 (98625-0500)
PHONE..................360 574-6722
John Somarakis, *President*
Matt Hildebrand, *General Mgr*
▲ EMP: 10
SQ FT: 20,000
SALES (est): 26.2MM **Privately Held**
SIC: 5084 8711 3563 3561 Pulp (wood) manufacturing machinery; paper manufacturing machinery; engineering services; air & gas compressors; pumps & pumping equipment

(G-4509)
STEELSCAPE LLC (PA)
222 W Kalama River Rd (98625-9420)
PHONE..................360 673-8200
Sarah Deukmejian, *President*
Dj Schmidt, *Vice Pres*
Mike Wire, *Vice Pres*
Richard Desc Teaux, *Plant Mgr*
Brendan Brophy, *Manager*
▲ EMP: 175 EST: 1991
SQ FT: 800,000
SALES (est): 192.8MM **Privately Held**
WEB: www.steelscape.com
SIC: 3479 Aluminum coating of metal products

(G-4510)
STEELSCAPE LLC
220 W Kalama River Rd (98625-9420)
P.O. Box 1098 (98625-1000)
PHONE..................360 673-8200
Richard Wechsler, *Manager*
EMP: 200
SALES (corp-wide): 192.8MM **Privately Held**
SIC: 3479 3312 Aluminum coating of metal products; blast furnaces & steel mills
PA: Steelscape, Llc
222 W Kalama River Rd
Kalama WA 98625
360 673-8200

(G-4511)
STEELSCAPE WASHINGTON LLC
222 W Kalama River Rd (98625-9420)
PHONE..................360 673-8200
Sarah Deukmejian, *President*
EMP: 250
SALES (est): 5.4MM
SALES (corp-wide): 192.8MM **Privately Held**
SIC: 3479 Aluminum coating of metal products
PA: Steelscape, Llc
222 W Kalama River Rd
Kalama WA 98625
360 673-8200

Keller
Ferry County

(G-4512)
FRED NANAMKIN
Also Called: Lone Rock Contracting
11960 S Highway 21 (99140-9512)
P.O. Box 204 (99140-0204)
PHONE..................509 634-8110
Fred Nanamkin Jr, *Owner*
EMP: 2
SALES (est): 176.5K **Privately Held**
SIC: 2411 1794 1521 Logging camps & contractors; excavation work; general remodeling, single-family houses

(G-4513)
JESSE W PALMER
Also Called: JWP Construction
115 Frosty Meadows Rd (99140)
PHONE..................509 634-1494
Jesse Palmer, *Owner*
EMP: 10
SALES (est): 286.2K **Privately Held**
SIC: 1799 8711 2951 Construction site cleanup; fire protection engineering; road materials, bituminous (not from refineries)

(G-4514)
SAN POIL LOGGING
12153 S Highway 21 (99140-9514)
PHONE..................509 634-8112
Joe Vanslyker, *Owner*
EMP: 2 EST: 2001
SALES: 500K **Privately Held**
SIC: 2411 Logging camps & contractors

Kelso
Cowlitz County

(G-4515)
5-STAR ENTERPRISES INC
513 Colorado St (98626-5525)
P.O. Box 765 (98626-0066)
PHONE..................360 577-0829
Emmett R Johnson, *CEO*
Vicki M Johnson, *President*
EMP: 4
SQ FT: 1,200
SALES: 250K **Privately Held**
SIC: 3444 Gutters, sheet metal

(G-4516)
APPLIED APPLICATIONS INTL LLC
500 Colorado St (98626-5593)
PHONE..................360 425-7900
Alan Pilger, *Mng Member*
▲ EMP: 14
SALES (est): 1.3MM **Privately Held**
SIC: 2653 Sheets, corrugated: made from purchased materials

(G-4517)
AZ IMPRINT
305 W Main St Ste B (98626-1354)
PHONE..................360 578-2476
Tony Werner, *Principal*
EMP: 2
SALES (est): 117.6K **Privately Held**
SIC: 3577 Printers & plotters

(G-4518)
BITE BUDDY LLC
1813 S 13th Ave (98626-2850)
PHONE..................360 749-4781
Mike Little, *President*
EMP: 2 EST: 2014
SALES (est): 140.9K **Privately Held**
SIC: 3089 Novelties, plastic

(G-4519)
C & C LOGGING LLC
2207 Talley Way (98626-5510)
PHONE..................360 636-0300
Frank R Chandler,
Onuma Soepamin, *Administration*
Lee Anne Beech,
EMP: 80

Kelso - Cowlitz County (G-4520) — GEOGRAPHIC SECTION

SALES: 20MM **Privately Held**
SIC: 2411 Logging camps & contractors

(G-4520)
CONNER INDUSTRIES
1390 Mount Pleasant Rd (98626-9212)
PHONE..................360 261-0265
Elmer Conner, *Principal*
EMP: 2
SALES (est): 106.3K **Privately Held**
SIC: 3999 Manufacturing industries

(G-4521)
COWLITZ CONT & DIECUTTING INC
2228 Talley Way (98626-5540)
P.O. Box 727 (98626-0062)
PHONE..................360 577-8748
Gwen Clark, *President*
Ralph Clark, *CFO*
EMP: 15
SQ FT: 31,000
SALES: 1.2MM **Privately Held**
WEB: www.cowlitzcontainer.com
SIC: 2675 Die-cut paper & board

(G-4522)
COWLITZ FENCE CO
2401 Talley Way Ste B (98626-5550)
P.O. Box 367, Longview (98632-7232)
PHONE..................360 577-6110
James Steward, *President*
Angela Steward, *Vice Pres*
EMP: 5
SALES: 800K **Privately Held**
SIC: 5211 3312 1799 Fencing; fence posts, iron & steel; fence construction

(G-4523)
DE ROSIER TRUCKING INC
3627 Pleasant Hill Rd (98626-9778)
PHONE..................360 577-1636
Scott De Rosier, *President*
Lane De Rosier, *Corp Secy*
Neil De Rosier, *Vice Pres*
EMP: 22
SALES: 1.9MM **Privately Held**
SIC: 1429 4212 4213 Igneous rock, crushed & broken-quarrying; dump truck haulage; trucking, except local

(G-4524)
ELLIOT ATTACHMENTS INC
244 Milwaukee Pl Unit 2 (98626-1453)
PHONE..................360 636-2203
Dennis Page, *President*
Bonnie Page, *Admin Sec*
▲ EMP: 4 EST: 1999
SALES: 1.5MM **Privately Held**
SIC: 3531 Construction machinery attachments

(G-4525)
F H SULLIVAN CO INC
Also Called: Fh Sullivan Company
2219 Talley Way (98626-5510)
PHONE..................360 442-4222
EMP: 20
SQ FT: 17,000
SALES: 2MM **Privately Held**
SIC: 1751 2599 5712 2434 Carpentry Contractor Mfg Furniture/Fixtures Ret Furniture Mfg Wood Kitchen Cabinet

(G-4526)
FOSTER POULTRY FARMS
1700 S 13th Ave (98626-2849)
PHONE..................360 425-8957
Dave McNiel, *Safety Mgr*
Joe Wright, *Maint Spvr*
Sandra Pineda, *Production*
April Spaulding, *Purch Mgr*
Ricardo Guzman, *Engineer*
EMP: 800
SALES (corp-wide): 3B **Privately Held**
WEB: www.fosterfarms.com
SIC: 2015 Chicken slaughtering & processing; turkey processing & slaughtering
PA: Foster Poultry Farms
 1000 Davis St
 Livingston CA 95334
 209 394-6914

(G-4527)
HADALLER LOGGING INC
1290 Walnut St (98626-2717)
PHONE..................360 425-0602
Jason Hadaller, *Principal*
EMP: 15
SALES (est): 2.6MM **Privately Held**
SIC: 2411 Logging camps & contractors

(G-4528)
HEATON PRINTING
3829 Pleasant Hill Rd (98626-9781)
PHONE..................360 353-3720
EMP: 2
SALES (est): 97.8K **Privately Held**
SIC: 2752 Commercial printing, lithographic

(G-4529)
INFINITY DIGITAL LLC
233 Lasalle Dr (98626-8850)
PHONE..................715 298-3530
Jeff Anderson, *Mng Member*
EMP: 4
SALES (est): 365.4K **Privately Held**
SIC: 7372 Prepackaged software

(G-4530)
J L & O ENTERPRISES INC
2632 Mt Brynion Rd (98626-9556)
PHONE..................360 636-5427
James L Oldis, *President*
EMP: 2
SALES: 200K **Privately Held**
SIC: 2411 Logging

(G-4531)
JAMES SMITH TRUCKING
1404 Rose Valley Rd (98626-9663)
PHONE..................360 423-1027
James M Smith, *Owner*
EMP: 6
SALES (est): 359.8K **Privately Held**
SIC: 1611 4212 2411 General contractor, highway & street construction; local trucking, without storage; logging

(G-4532)
JULIE CAKE FISHERIES INC
124 Trapper Ln (98626-9652)
PHONE..................360 636-3621
Earl Mitchell, *President*
Barbara Mitchell, *Corp Secy*
EMP: 2
SALES (est): 86.6K **Privately Held**
SIC: 2092 Fresh or frozen packaged fish

(G-4533)
KAPER II INC
Also Called: Woody's Accessories
2212 Parrott Way (98626-5523)
PHONE..................360 423-4404
Richard Renshaw, *President*
Ronald Renshaw, *CFO*
Matt Rasmussen, *Manager*
Laura Seelye, *Manager*
▲ EMP: 30
SQ FT: 23,000
SALES: 5.4MM **Privately Held**
WEB: www.kaper2.com
SIC: 3714 Motor vehicle wheels & parts

(G-4534)
KING GRAPHICS
1906 Westside Hwy (98626-1933)
PHONE..................360 423-9781
Don King, *Owner*
EMP: 2
SALES (est): 101.4K **Privately Held**
SIC: 7389 3993 Lettering & sign painting services; signs & advertising specialties

(G-4535)
LIBERTY LOGGING INC
142 Westminster Dr (98626-1897)
PHONE..................360 423-5454
Fax: 360 423-5983
EMP: 2 EST: 2008
SALES (est): 120K **Privately Held**
SIC: 2411 Logging

(G-4536)
MALONE INDUSTRIES LLC
838 Carroll Rd (98626-9461)
PHONE..................360 636-1383
EMP: 2 EST: 2003
SALES (est): 75K **Privately Held**
SIC: 3999 Mfg Misc Products

(G-4537)
MATTS CUSTOM MEATS
705 N Maple Hill Rd (98626-9479)
PHONE..................360 414-1073
Matthew M Franett, *Principal*
EMP: 3
SALES (est): 270.1K **Privately Held**
SIC: 2011 Meat packing plants

(G-4538)
MINUTEMAN PRESS
402 W Main St (98626-1118)
PHONE..................360 577-3257
Carla Vorse, *President*
EMP: 4
SALES: 150K **Privately Held**
SIC: 2752 Commercial printing, lithographic

(G-4539)
NOR-TECH FABRICATING LLC
2510 Talley Way (98626-5517)
PHONE..................360 232-0144
Stephanie Beck, *Principal*
Jerry Storedahl,
Kimball Storedahl,
EMP: 25
SALES (est): 6.1MM **Privately Held**
SIC: 3441 Fabricated structural metal

(G-4540)
NYGARDS CUSTOM CABINETRY
1602 Pacific Ave N Ste B (98626-3947)
PHONE..................360 425-1777
Boyd A Nygard, *Owner*
EMP: 2
SQ FT: 2,400
SALES: 200K **Privately Held**
SIC: 2599 Cabinets, factory

(G-4541)
PAPE MACHINERY INC
Also Called: John Deere Authorized Dealer
2504 Talley Way (98626-5517)
PHONE..................360 575-9959
Jordan Pape, *CEO*
Scot Boatright, *Branch Mgr*
EMP: 15
SALES (corp-wide): 606.3MM **Privately Held**
WEB: www.papemh.com
SIC: 7699 3599 5082 Aircraft & heavy equipment repair services; carnival machines & equipment, amusement park; construction & mining machinery
HQ: Pape' Machinery, Inc.
 355 Goodpasture Island Rd # 300
 Eugene OR 97401
 541 683-5073

(G-4542)
PLEASANT HILL SAWMILL
5412 Pleasant Hill Rd (98626-9332)
PHONE..................360 274-7888
Louis Brockmoller, *Principal*
EMP: 3
SALES (est): 162.4K **Privately Held**
SIC: 2421 Sawmills & planing mills, general

(G-4543)
QUALITY BREWING INCORPORATED
Also Called: Brew Express
159 Hale Barber Rd (98626-8816)
P.O. Box 1726, Longview (98632-8058)
PHONE..................866 268-5953
Phillip Gardner, *Vice Pres*
Marcella Spencer, *Admin Sec*
▲ EMP: 3 EST: 2009
SALES (est): 443.1K **Privately Held**
SIC: 3589 Coffee brewing equipment

(G-4544)
QUALITY CABINETS PLUS INC
2411 Talley Way (98626-5514)
PHONE..................360 423-1242
Kevin Schrepel, *President*
Gerald W Norton, *Vice Pres*
Laura Norton, *Treasurer*
Lane Schrepel, *Admin Sec*
EMP: 5
SQ FT: 2,200
SALES (est): 680.1K **Privately Held**
SIC: 2511 2521 Wood household furniture; cabinets, office: wood

(G-4545)
R E B MAGNETICS
3321 Mount Pleasant Rd (98626-9274)
PHONE..................360 636-4693
Kristy Woodhams, *Owner*
Russell Byers, *Co-Owner*
EMP: 2
SALES: 65K **Privately Held**
WEB: www.rebmag.com
SIC: 3993 3944 7336 Signs & advertising specialties; board games, puzzles & models, except electronic; silk screen design

(G-4546)
S & R SHEET METAL INC
1300 Walnut St (98626-2719)
PHONE..................360 425-7020
Mark Laufer, *President*
EMP: 60
SQ FT: 15,000
SALES (est): 7.7MM **Privately Held**
WEB: www.srsheetmetal.com
SIC: 1761 3444 Sheet metalwork; sheet metalwork

(G-4547)
SIGN PRINT 360 LLC
305 W Main St Ste B (98626-1354)
PHONE..................360 578-2476
Shannon Werner, *Principal*
EMP: 2
SALES (est): 133.1K **Privately Held**
SIC: 2752 Commercial printing, lithographic

(G-4548)
SIGNSMART USA (PA)
Also Called: Sign Smart
305 W Main St Ste B (98626-1354)
PHONE..................360 578-2476
Tony Warner, *Owner*
Tony Werner, *Principal*
EMP: 3
SQ FT: 2,500
SALES (est): 221.2K **Privately Held**
WEB: www.signsmart-usa.com
SIC: 3993 5999 Signs & advertising specialties; banners, flags, decals & posters

(G-4549)
SPECIALTY CONCRETE
312 Hazel St (98626-1410)
PHONE..................360 577-4555
Jeff Deal, *Owner*
April Deal, *Co-Owner*
EMP: 4
SALES (est): 750K **Privately Held**
SIC: 3273 Ready-mixed concrete

(G-4550)
SPEEDY LITHO INC
403 Catlin St (98626-1101)
PHONE..................360 425-3610
James R Wilson, *President*
Kathy Wilson, *Admin Sec*
EMP: 6
SQ FT: 5,000
SALES (est): 805.8K **Privately Held**
SIC: 2752 Commercial printing, offset

(G-4551)
STEEL PAINTERS INC
Also Called: Steel Painter Division
700 Colorado St Ste A (98626-5541)
PHONE..................360 425-7720
Chris Mayeda, *President*
EMP: 20
SQ FT: 17,000
SALES (est): 2.4MM **Privately Held**
SIC: 3479 3312 Painting of metal products; structural & rail mill products

(G-4552)
STOWE WOODWARD LLC
Also Called: Stove-Woodward Co
2209 Talley Way (98626-5510)
PHONE..................360 636-0330
Robert L Deckon, *Manager*
EMP: 35
SALES (corp-wide): 6.9B **Privately Held**
SIC: 3069 Roll coverings, rubber

GEOGRAPHIC SECTION

HQ: Stowe Woodward Llc
8537 Six Forks Rd Ste 300
Raleigh NC 27615

(G-4553)
SUPERIOR WLDG FABRICATION LLC
516 Oak St (98626-2610)
PHONE..................360 430-6766
EMP: 3
SALES (est): 203.4K Privately Held
SIC: 7692 Welding repair

(G-4554)
TED GRUBER SOFTWARE INC
212 Beasley Rd (98626-8802)
PHONE..................702 735-1980
Ted Gruber, *President*
EMP: 2
SALES (est): 144.1K Privately Held
WEB: www.fastgraph.com
SIC: 7372 Prepackaged software

(G-4555)
THREE RIVERS INDUSTRIAL MCH
Also Called: Delta Industries
700 Colorado St Ste A (98626-5541)
PHONE..................360 578-1114
Christopher Mayeda, *President*
EMP: 7
SALES (est): 644.2K Privately Held
SIC: 3599 7629 Machine shop, jobbing & repair; electrical repair shops

(G-4556)
TRAMWELD LLC
1605 Burcham St (98626-4803)
PHONE..................360 425-1240
Lya Crammell, *Mng Member*
Joey Crammell, *Mng Member*
EMP: 2
SALES (est): 174.7K Privately Held
SIC: 7692 Welding repair

(G-4557)
TRAVELING DESIGNS
2412 Kingfisher Ln (98626-5413)
PHONE..................360 695-5887
Steven Hill, *Owner*
Mae Beth Hill, *Owner*
EMP: 2
SALES (est): 116K Privately Held
WEB: www.travelingdesigns.com
SIC: 2269 Printing of narrow fabrics

(G-4558)
US ATTACHMENTS INC
211 Hazel St (98626-1435)
P.O. Box 1921, Lake Oswego OR (97035-0616)
PHONE..................360 501-4484
James Monroe, *President*
Mona Varnet, *Office Mgr*
▲ EMP: 18
SQ FT: 7,500
SALES: 3MM Privately Held
SIC: 3537 Forklift trucks

(G-4559)
WESTERN FABRICATION CENTER LLC
700 Colorado St Ste A (98626-5541)
PHONE..................360 575-1500
James McCracken, *Project Mgr*
Bob Dugger, *Foreman/Supr*
Tina Thompson, *Office Mgr*
Chris Mayada,
EMP: 15
SALES (est): 3.8MM Privately Held
WEB: www.westernfab.com
SIC: 3449 Bars, concrete reinforcing: fabricated steel

(G-4560)
WESTOM TOOLS
520 Haussler Rd (98626-3014)
PHONE..................360 355-6741
Brian Westom, *Principal*
EMP: 2
SALES (est): 140.6K Privately Held
SIC: 3599 Industrial machinery

(G-4561)
XERIUM TECHNOLOGIES INC
2209 Talley Way (98626-5510)
PHONE..................360 636-0330
EMP: 4
SALES (corp-wide): 6.9B Privately Held
SIC: 2221 Broadwoven fabric mills, man-made
HQ: Andritz Fabrics And Rolls Inc.
14101 Capital Blvd
Youngsville NC 27596
919 526-1400

(G-4562)
YACHT SPECIALTIES
111 Speer Dr (98626-9620)
PHONE..................360 423-9995
Lonnie D Rogers, *Principal*
EMP: 2
SALES (est): 157.1K Privately Held
SIC: 3732 Yachts, building & repairing

Kenmore
King County

(G-4563)
A & P FASTENERS INC (PA)
6824 Ne 154th Ct (98028-4657)
PHONE..................425 486-9562
William D Anderson, *President*
Camella Anderson, *Vice Pres*
Dana Borgmann, *Treasurer*
EMP: 3
SALES (est): 955.8K Privately Held
WEB: www.aandpfasteners.com
SIC: 5085 3965 Fasteners, industrial: nuts, bolts, screws, etc.; fasteners

(G-4564)
ALMX-SECURITY INC
6527 Ne 192nd Pl (98028-3457)
PHONE..................425 485-3801
Alan Maclachlan, *President*
EMP: 3
SALES: 1MM Privately Held
SIC: 5084 3669 Safety equipment; signaling apparatus, electric

(G-4565)
ARTACA CO
8619 Ne 169th St (98028-3936)
PHONE..................425 398-0122
Kamiar Bahri, *Principal*
EMP: 2
SALES (est): 86.6K Privately Held
SIC: 3441 Fabricated structural metal

(G-4566)
ARTISAN INSTRUMENTS INC
Also Called: A O K Manufacturing
6450 Ne 183rd St (98028-7910)
PHONE..................425 486-6555
H W Carlson, *President*
Mark Anderson, *Vice Pres*
EMP: 17
SQ FT: 4,500
SALES (est): 2MM Privately Held
SIC: 3931 Organs, all types: pipe, reed, hand, electronic, etc.; guitars & parts, electric & nonelectric

(G-4567)
BUCKLEY INDUSTRIES
7238 Ne 147th Pl (98028-4936)
PHONE..................425 286-6443
EMP: 2 EST: 2010
SALES (est): 87K Privately Held
SIC: 3999 Mfg Misc Products

(G-4568)
CALPORTLAND COMPANY
6423 Ne 175th St (98028-4808)
P.O. Box 82224 (98028-0224)
PHONE..................425 486-3281
EMP: 68 Privately Held
SIC: 3241 Portland cement
HQ: Calportland Company
2025 E Financial Way
Glendora CA 91741
626 852-6200

(G-4569)
CLEAN AS A WHISTLE
16638 Juanita Dr Ne 101g (98028-6330)
PHONE..................425 354-9719
Jeremias Bandeira, *Principal*
EMP: 2
SALES (est): 136.7K Privately Held
SIC: 3999 Whistles

(G-4570)
CUSTOM MADE DRAPERIES ETC
7524 Ne 175th St Ste 4 (98028-2503)
PHONE..................425 485-2724
Steve Carlson, *Owner*
EMP: 4
SQ FT: 1,250
SALES (est): 190K Privately Held
SIC: 2391 5714 Draperies, plastic & textile: from purchased materials; draperies

(G-4571)
EPICENTER PRESS INC
6524 Ne 181st St Ste 2 (98028-4851)
P.O. Box 82368 (98028-0368)
PHONE..................425 485-6822
B G Olson, *Ch of Bd*
Kent Sturgis, *President*
▲ EMP: 5
SQ FT: 800
SALES (est): 725.7K Privately Held
WEB: www.epicenterpress.com
SIC: 2731 Books: publishing only

(G-4572)
EVAN MARTIN LURE INC
16308 Inglewood Rd Ne (98028-3908)
PHONE..................425 478-7163
Evan Seitz, *Principal*
EMP: 2
SALES (est): 128.6K Privately Held
SIC: 3949 Sporting & athletic goods

(G-4573)
EVER-MARK LLC
7330 Ne Bothel Way 202 (98028)
PHONE..................425 486-7200
Sandra Quiring, *Owner*
EMP: 5
SALES: 1.2MM Privately Held
WEB: www.evermarkllc.com
SIC: 2759 Promotional printing

(G-4574)
EXOTEC
15974 82nd Pl Ne (98028-4411)
PHONE..................425 488-0691
Arnold Wilson, *Principal*
EMP: 4
SALES (est): 304.5K Privately Held
SIC: 3089 Injection molding of plastics

(G-4575)
GILDEANE GROUP
Also Called: Cultural Diversity At Work Onl
6015 Ne 205th St (98028-1951)
PHONE..................206 362-0336
Carlos B Gil, *President*
Barbara Deane, *Vice Pres*
EMP: 5
SALES (est): 458.5K Privately Held
WEB: www.gildeane.com
SIC: 2721 5961 8742 7361 Trade journals: publishing & printing; books, mail order (except book clubs); training & development consultant; human resource consulting services; employment agencies

(G-4576)
GLAXOSMITHKLINE LLC
18707 63rd Ave Ne (98028-3319)
PHONE..................206 856-5663
Gsk Glaxosmithkline, *Branch Mgr*
EMP: 26
SALES (corp-wide): 39.5B Privately Held
SIC: 2834 Pharmaceutical preparations
HQ: Glaxosmithkline Llc
5 Crescent Dr
Philadelphia PA 19112
215 751-4000

(G-4577)
GOOSEWORKS MEDIA LLC
8016 Ne 152nd Ct (98028-5606)
PHONE..................425 487-8766
Eric Brod, *President*
EMP: 2
SALES (est): 120K Privately Held
SIC: 7372 Application computer software

(G-4578)
GRENLAR HOLDINGS INC
Also Called: Grenlar Construction
16636 Simonds Rd Ne (98028-4413)
PHONE..................425 419-4430
Noemi Aguilar-Grenzebach, *CEO*
Kalen Grenzebach, *COO*
EMP: 2
SALES (est): 307.5K Privately Held
SIC: 1542 3448 1522 1541 Commercial & office buildings, renovation & repair; school building construction; specialized public building contractors; commercial & office building contractors; prefabricated metal buildings; apartment building construction; industrial buildings, new construction

(G-4579)
HENDERSON CABINET REFINISHING
7825 Ne 192nd St (98028-2630)
PHONE..................206 963-0874
John Henderson, *President*
Carol Madoerin, *Vice Pres*
EMP: 2
SALES: 100K Privately Held
SIC: 2434 Wood kitchen cabinets

(G-4580)
HERFF JONES LLC
Also Called: Grad Products
6134 Ne Bothell Way (98028-8939)
P.O. Box 82462 (98028-0462)
PHONE..................425 488-7213
Fax: 425 488-4557
EMP: 2
SALES (corp-wide): 1.1B Privately Held
SIC: 2752 Lithographic Commercial Printing
HQ: Herff Jones, Llc
4501 W 62nd St
Indianapolis IN 46268
800 419-5462

(G-4581)
HILL WOODWORKING
6869 Ne 153rd Pl (98028-4925)
PHONE..................425 488-7943
Douglas Hill, *Owner*
EMP: 2
SALES: 150K Privately Held
SIC: 3553 1521 Woodworking machinery; single-family housing construction

(G-4582)
HOMCHICK MICHAEL STONE WORK
Also Called: Michael Homchick Stoneworks
6834 Ne 175th St (98028-3502)
PHONE..................425 481-2783
Micheal E Homchick, *President*
▲ EMP: 37
SALES (est): 5MM Privately Held
WEB: www.homchickstoneworks.com
SIC: 3281 Granite, cut & shaped

(G-4583)
J & R MERCANTILE
Also Called: J&R Mercantile
18815 56th Ave Ne (98028-8738)
PHONE..................425 486-6402
Robin Nelson, *Partner*
Allen Nelson, *Partner*
EMP: 2
SALES (est): 240K Privately Held
WEB: www.datacurrent.com
SIC: 3452 2395 Pins; embroidery & art needlework

(G-4584)
J L INNOVATIONS INC
17511 68th Ave Ne Ste 2 (98028-2504)
PHONE..................425 823-8540
EMP: 4 EST: 1991

Kenmore - King County (G-4585)

SALES (est): 510K **Privately Held**
SIC: **5191** 3999 Whol Farm Supplies Mfg Misc Products

(G-4585)
JET CITY PRINTING INC
6134 Ne Bothell Way (98028-8948)
PHONE 425 485-8611
Gerald Dugan, *President*
EMP: 6
SQ FT: 11,000
SALES (est): 976K **Privately Held**
SIC: **2752** 7334 Commercial printing, offset; photocopying & duplicating services

(G-4586)
KANAWAY SEAFOODS INC (DH)
Also Called: Alaska General Seafoods
6425 Ne 175th St (98028-4808)
PHONE 425 485-7755
Gordon Lindquist, *President*
Dick Loid, *Plant Mgr*
Sandy Souter, *Manager*
▼ EMP: 78
SALES (est): 97.9MM
SALES (corp-wide): 19B **Privately Held**
WEB: www.akgen.com
SIC: **2092** Fresh or frozen packaged fish
HQ: Pattison, Jim Industries Ltd
1067 Cordova St W Suite 1800
Vancouver BC V6C 1
604 688-6764

(G-4587)
KENMORE AIR HARBOR INC (PA)
Also Called: Kenmore Air Seaplanes
6321 Ne 175th St (98028-4898)
P.O. Box 82064 (98028-0064)
PHONE 425 486-3224
Gregg Munro, *President*
Todd Banks, *President*
Marjorie Greene, *Vice Pres*
Leslie Banks, *Admin Sec*
EMP: 95 EST: 1946
SALES (est): 15.1MM **Privately Held**
WEB: www.kenmoreair.com
SIC: **4581** 4512 5599 8299 Airport; air transportation, scheduled; aircraft dealers; flying instruction; aircraft

(G-4588)
KENMORE VIOLINS
7330 Ne Bothell Way # 201 (98028-6525)
PHONE 425 481-5638
Dave Scott, *Principal*
EMP: 2
SALES (est): 141.7K **Privately Held**
WEB: www.kenmoreviolins.com
SIC: **3931** Violins & parts

(G-4589)
KNIGHTS EDGE SOFTWARE
15356 Juanita Dr Ne (98028-4601)
PHONE 425 488-3552
Ken Hines, *Principal*
EMP: 2
SALES (est): 150.7K **Privately Held**
SIC: **7372** Prepackaged software

(G-4590)
LOW ORBIT PUBLICATIONS
5605 Ne 184th St (98028-8752)
PHONE 425 398-0598
EMP: 2
SALES (est): 120K **Privately Held**
SIC: **2741** Misc Publishing

(G-4591)
MCBEE METAL FABRICATORS INC
20117 73rd Ave Ne (98028-2008)
PHONE 425 486-1410
Bill McBee, *President*
Todd McBee, *Vice Pres*
EMP: 2
SALES (est): 230K **Privately Held**
SIC: **3315** Welded steel wire fabric

(G-4592)
MICHIELS INTERNATIONAL INC (PA)
Also Called: Seahurst Lumber Company
5701 Ne Bothell Way Ste 2 (98028-9400)
P.O. Box 82554 (98028-0554)
PHONE 206 365-4060
Frank Michiels, *President*
Tiger Joe Michiels, *Principal*
Robert Michiels, *Chairman*
Jim Beyer, *Vice Pres*
▲ EMP: 4
SQ FT: 1,600
SALES (est): 597.9K **Privately Held**
WEB: www.tigerjoe.com
SIC: **5031** 2421 Lumber: rough, dressed & finished; building materials, exterior; building materials, interior; sawmills & planing mills, general

(G-4593)
MINDWARE INC
15435 86th Ave Ne (98028-4769)
PHONE 425 415-3921
Bill Higgins, *Managing Dir*
EMP: 2
SALES (est): 122.6K **Privately Held**
SIC: **2741** Miscellaneous publishing

(G-4594)
NORTHWEST WOODWORKING LLC
8003 Ne 151st Ct (98028-5602)
PHONE 425 488-9597
Gary Shupe, *Principal*
EMP: 4
SALES (est): 165.4K **Privately Held**
SIC: **2431** Millwork

(G-4595)
OFNER AND COMPANY
8037 Ne 169th St (98028-3950)
PHONE 425 485-0437
Thomas Ofner, *Owner*
EMP: 2
SQ FT: 2,200
SALES: 200K **Privately Held**
SIC: **3911** 5944 Jewelry, precious metal; jewelry, precious stones & precious metals

(G-4596)
OPEN MOBILE SOLUTIONS INC
6442 Ne 192nd Pl (98028-3322)
PHONE 206 290-2314
Jai Jaisimha, *Principal*
EMP: 2 EST: 2012
SALES (est): 212.5K **Privately Held**
SIC: **7372** Application computer software

(G-4597)
PASSION WORKS LLC
Also Called: Eric The Closet Guy
6830 Ne Bothell Way (98028-3546)
PHONE 425 260-7777
Eric Rootvik, *Principal*
EMP: 2
SQ FT: 2,000
SALES (est): 122.3K **Privately Held**
SIC: **2541** Cabinets, lockers & shelving

(G-4598)
PIERRES DOCK INC
Also Called: Pierres Polaris
7504 Ne 175th St Ste 8 (98028-2507)
PHONE 425 488-8600
Everett Pierre, *President*
John Peterson, *Vice Pres*
Jason Martin, *Manager*
EMP: 6
SALES (est): 764.8K **Privately Held**
WEB: www.pierrespolaris.com
SIC: **7699** 3732 Marine engine repair; boat building & repairing

(G-4599)
PORTLOCK SOFTWARE
20002 73rd Ave Ne (98028-2007)
PHONE 425 247-0545
Chase Hanley, *Principal*
EMP: 2 EST: 2010
SALES (est): 193.4K **Privately Held**
SIC: **7372** Prepackaged software

(G-4600)
PROTECT-A-COVER INC
8112 Ne 145th Pl (98028-4755)
PHONE 425 408-1072
Marc F Hall, *President*
EMP: 2
SALES (est): 190K **Privately Held**
SIC: **2452** Farm buildings, prefabricated or portable: wood

(G-4601)
RAPHOE PRESS
6116 Ne 190th St (98028-3213)
PHONE 425 486-5036
Patrick Bennett, *Principal*
EMP: 5 EST: 2001
SALES (est): 118.5K **Privately Held**
SIC: **2741** Miscellaneous publishing

(G-4602)
SAN JUAN PUBLISHING
18414 57th Ave Ne (98028-8708)
PHONE 425 485-2813
Michael McCloskey, *Owner*
EMP: 2
SALES (est): 59.2K **Privately Held**
SIC: **2741** Miscellaneous publishing

(G-4603)
SAVAGE GUN COATING
15405 63rd Ave Ne (98028-4317)
PHONE 206 485-4125
Weston Henderson, *Principal*
EMP: 2
SALES (est): 79.9K **Privately Held**
SIC: **3479** Metal coating & allied service

(G-4604)
SES USA INC (PA)
Also Called: Safety Emergency Systems
6527 Ne 192nd Pl (98028-3457)
PHONE 425 485-3801
EMP: 2
SQ FT: 4,000
SALES: 2MM **Privately Held**
SIC: **3669** 5084 Mfg & Whol Signaling Sysytems

(G-4605)
SHINE MARBLE CO INC
20414 80th Ave Ne (98028-2109)
PHONE 425 444-5832
Demitrie Dintilie, *CEO*
EMP: 10
SALES (est): 837.1K **Privately Held**
SIC: **3281** Marble, building: cut & shaped

(G-4606)
SOCKS IN A BOX LLC
7938 Ne 181st Pl (98028-4501)
PHONE 425 533-8316
Curtis McGann, *Principal*
EMP: 3
SALES (est): 224.6K **Privately Held**
SIC: **2252** Socks

(G-4607)
SOUTHSHORE PRSTHTICS ORTHOTICS
Also Called: South Shore Rehabilitation
6509 Ne 181st St (98028-4801)
PHONE 206 440-1811
Steve Colwell, *Owner*
EMP: 3
SALES (est): 220.4K **Privately Held**
SIC: **3842** Prosthetic appliances

(G-4608)
T & D MACHINE INC
8030 Ne Bothell Way Ste A (98028-1899)
PHONE 425 486-8338
Gary Taylor, *President*
Robert Inks, *Vice Pres*
EMP: 2
SQ FT: 5,700
SALES (est): 190K **Privately Held**
SIC: **3599** Machine shop, jobbing & repair

(G-4609)
T-PRINTS LLC
6830 Ne 153rd Pl (98028-4925)
PHONE 425 780-9380
Tran Pohl, *Principal*
EMP: 4

SALES (est): 225.2K **Privately Held**
SIC: **2752** Commercial printing, lithographic

Kennewick
Benton County

(G-4610)
ABOVE AND BEYOND CNSTR LLC
411 N Underwood St (99336-3025)
PHONE 509 521-8081
Timothy Miller, *Co-Owner*
EMP: 2
SALES (est): 113.5K **Privately Held**
SIC: **2431** 1522 2541 1799 Woodwork, interior & ornamental; remodeling, multi-family dwellings; cabinets, lockers & shelving; kitchen & bathroom remodeling

(G-4611)
ADAMS PLACE COUNTRY GOURMET
193910 E Game Farm Rd (99337-6823)
PHONE 509 582-8564
Leslie Adams, *President*
Gerry Adams, *Admin Sec*
EMP: 9
SALES: 350K **Privately Held**
WEB: www.adamsplacecountrygourmet.com
SIC: **2066** Chocolate candy, solid

(G-4612)
AG ENGINEERING & DEVELOPMENT
1515 E 7th Ave (99337-9605)
PHONE 509 582-8900
Thayne B Wiser, *President*
Steve A Blodgett, *Corp Secy*
Clod D Rawlins, *Vice Pres*
EMP: 15
SQ FT: 27,500
SALES (est): 2.8MM **Privately Held**
WEB: www.dammerdiker.com
SIC: **3523** Farm machinery & equipment

(G-4613)
AGRIUM US INC
227515 E Bowles Rd (99337-8673)
PHONE 509 586-5500
Robert Campbell, *Vice Pres*
Don Larue, *Manager*
Steve Laird, *Info Tech Mgr*
EMP: 120
SALES (corp-wide): 8.8B **Privately Held**
SIC: **2873** 5191 2879 2869 Nitrogenous fertilizers; fertilizer & fertilizer materials; agricultural chemicals; industrial organic chemicals; industrial inorganic chemicals
HQ: Agrium U.S. Inc.
5296 Harvest Lake Dr
Loveland CO 80538

(G-4614)
AGRIUM US INC
227108 E Perkins Rd (99337)
PHONE 509 586-5355
Don Larue, *Branch Mgr*
EMP: 120
SALES (corp-wide): 8.8B **Privately Held**
SIC: **2873** 5191 Nitrogenous fertilizers; farm supplies
HQ: Agrium U.S. Inc.
5296 Harvest Lake Dr
Loveland CO 80538

(G-4615)
AMERA SALES INC
Also Called: Amera Cosmetics
6403 W Rio Grande Ave (99336-7680)
PHONE 509 735-1531
Fax: 509 783-0910
EMP: 7
SQ FT: 10,000
SALES (est): 530K **Privately Held**
SIC: **2844** Mfg Nail & Skin Care Products

(G-4616)
AMERISTAR 124
2610 W Kennewick Ave (99336-3123)
PHONE 509 783-7518
EMP: 3

GEOGRAPHIC SECTION

Kennewick - Benton County (G-4645)

SALES (est): 144.2K **Privately Held**
SIC: 3471 Plating & polishing

(G-4617)
ANDEAVOR
Also Called: Tesoro
22 S Gum St (99336-4054)
PHONE..................................509 586-2117
Paula Brooks, *Manager*
EMP: 7 **Publicly Held**
WEB: www.tesoropetroleum.com
SIC: 1311 Crude petroleum production; natural gas production
HQ: Andeavor Llc
  19100 Ridgewood Pkwy
  San Antonio TX 78259
  210 626-6000

(G-4618)
APOLLO SHEET METAL INC (PA)
1201 W Columbia Dr (99336-3459)
P.O. Box 7287 (99336-0617)
PHONE..................................509 586-1104
Angie Haisch, *CEO*
Bruce Ratchford, *President*
Dave Dallas, *Division Mgr*
Ken Hagen, *General Mgr*
Cory Bond, *Superintendent*
EMP: 1000
SQ FT: 50,000
SALES (est): 158.5MM **Privately Held**
WEB: www.apollosm.com
SIC: 1711 3444 Mechanical contractor; sheet metalwork

(G-4619)
ARMSTRONG & ASSOCIATES LLC
Also Called: Aa-Its
2528 W 6th Pl (99336-4729)
PHONE..................................253 548-6148
Gary D Armstrong, *President*
EMP: 2
SALES (est): 102.2K **Privately Held**
SIC: 8748 3571 7373 Systems analysis & engineering consulting services; electronic computers; value-added resellers, computer systems

(G-4620)
ARTICLAND ICE (PA)
Also Called: Inland Ice
125 N Washington St (99336-3736)
PHONE..................................509 582-5808
Roger Pearson, *President*
EMP: 5
SQ FT: 2,000
SALES (est): 1.6MM **Privately Held**
SIC: 2097 5999 5989 5169 Manufactured ice; ice; coal; chemicals & allied products

(G-4621)
ATOMIC SCREEN PRINTING & EMB
Also Called: Atomic Vinyl Signs & Banners
329 W Columbia Dr (99336-3655)
PHONE..................................509 585-2866
Laura Walden, *President*
Brent Walden, *Principal*
Chris Walden, *Principal*
Greg Walden, *Principal*
Karolyn Walden, *Principal*
EMP: 20
SALES (est): 2.6MM **Privately Held**
WEB: www.atomicink.net
SIC: 2759 Screen printing

(G-4622)
B & B EXPRESS PRINTING (PA)
7519 W Kennewick Ave A (99336-7745)
PHONE..................................509 783-7383
Bruce Rawlins, *President*
Bill Henry, *Vice Pres*
Terri Rawlins, *Marketing Mgr*
EMP: 9
SQ FT: 5,000
SALES (est): 971.5K **Privately Held**
WEB: www.bbprinting.com
SIC: 2752 7334 2759 Commercial printing, offset; photocopying & duplicating services; commercial printing

(G-4623)
BADGER MOUNTAIN INC
Also Called: Badger Mtn Vnyrd Powers Winery
1106 N Jurupa St (99336-7337)
PHONE..................................509 627-4986
Greg Powers, *President*
Tim De Cook, *Admin Sec*
EMP: 11
SALES (est): 5.2MM **Privately Held**
WEB: www.badgermtnvineyard.com
SIC: 5182 2084 0172 Wine; wines; grapes

(G-4624)
BADGER MOUNTAIN VINEYARDS LLC
110 Jurupa St (99338)
PHONE..................................509 627-4986
Kelly Gallacher, *Marketing Staff*
Bill Powers,
EMP: 7
SALES (est): 607.9K **Privately Held**
SIC: 2084 Wines

(G-4625)
BARTHOLOMEW WINERY INC
10319 W 17th Pl (99338-4525)
PHONE..................................206 755-5296
Bart Fawbush, *President*
Chona Fawbush, *Vice Pres*
EMP: 2
SALES: 150K **Privately Held**
SIC: 5182 5921 2084 Wine; wine; wines

(G-4626)
BARTHOLOMEW WINERY INC
421 E Columbia Dr Bldg B (99336-3712)
PHONE..................................206 755-5296
Bart Fawbush, *President*
Chona Fawbush, *Vice Pres*
EMP: 13
SALES (est): 68.6K **Privately Held**
SIC: 2084 Wines

(G-4627)
BASIC MACHINING & ELECTRONICS
404 E 3rd Ave (99336-4028)
PHONE..................................509 308-6341
Bernie Vinther, *Partner*
Brenda Vinther, *Partner*
EMP: 2
SALES: 6K **Privately Held**
SIC: 3599 Industrial machinery

(G-4628)
BAUMS CANDY
Also Called: Baum's House of Chocolate
513 N Edison St Ste D (99336-2217)
PHONE..................................509 967-9340
Katherine Baumgarten, *Owner*
EMP: 3
SALES (est): 199.1K **Privately Held**
SIC: 2064 5441 Candy & other confectionery products; candy

(G-4629)
BENTONFRANKLIN COUNTIES IAN BF
7207 W Deschutes Ave (99336-7777)
PHONE..................................509 783-5284
Joyce Ninnemann, *Principal*
EMP: 2
SALES (est): 209K **Privately Held**
SIC: 3011 Tires & inner tubes

(G-4630)
BETTENDORFS PRINTING & DESIGN
14 S Benton St (99336-3801)
PHONE..................................509 586-7473
Judy Bettendorf, *Owner*
EMP: 4
SQ FT: 4,600
SALES (est): 538.4K **Privately Held**
SIC: 2752 Commercial printing, offset

(G-4631)
BIOGUARD RESEARCH & DEV
10815 Cottonwood Dr (99336-7472)
PHONE..................................509 628-0170
Peter V Voris, *Principal*
Dominic Cataldo, *Principal*
EMP: 4 EST: 1997
SQ FT: 2,000
SALES (est): 380K **Privately Held**
WEB: www.bioguardtech.com
SIC: 2821 Vinyl resins

(G-4632)
BLACKHAWK SYNERGIES INC
816 S Yolo St (99336-9607)
PHONE..................................509 627-9726
EMP: 2 EST: 2014
SALES (est): 160K **Privately Held**
SIC: 1382 Oil/Gas Exploration Services

(G-4633)
BROCKMAN MACHINE WORKS LLC
6820 W Deschutes Ave (99336-7763)
PHONE..................................509 735-1354
Randy Brockman,
EMP: 10 EST: 2003
SQ FT: 6,000
SALES (est): 746.7K **Privately Held**
SIC: 3599 Machine & other job shop work

(G-4634)
BROTHERHOOD BREWING CO LLC
107 W 48th Ave (99337-4444)
PHONE..................................509 585-6765
Zach Hayward, *Principal*
EMP: 2
SALES (est): 62.3K **Privately Held**
SIC: 2082 Malt beverages

(G-4635)
BRUKER AXS HANDHELD INC
Also Called: Bruker Elemental
415 N Quay St (99336-7783)
PHONE..................................509 783-9850
John Landefeld, *President*
EMP: 45
SQ FT: 20,000
SALES (est): 10MM
SALES (corp-wide): 1.9B **Publicly Held**
WEB: www.keymastertech.com
SIC: 3826 Analytical instruments
HQ: Bruker Axs Inc.
  5465 E Cheryl Pkwy
  Fitchburg WI 53711
  800 234-9729

(G-4636)
BUDGET PRINTING CENTER
7010 W Okanogan Pl (99336-5076)
PHONE..................................509 736-7511
Patricia Ashby, *Partner*
David Ashby, *Partner*
EMP: 7
SQ FT: 6,000
SALES (est): 650K **Privately Held**
SIC: 2752 5999 2759 3953 Commercial printing, offset; rubber stamps; commercial printing; marking devices; bookbinding & related work

(G-4637)
BUILDERS FIRSTSOURCE INC
3919 W Clearwater Ave (99336-2633)
PHONE..................................509 783-8148
Jean Raybun, *General Mgr*
EMP: 70
SALES (corp-wide): 7.7B **Publicly Held**
WEB: www.lumbermens.net
SIC: 5072 2439 5211 Builders' hardware; structural wood members; electrical construction materials
PA: Builders Firstsource, Inc.
  2001 Bryan St Ste 1600
  Dallas TX 75201
  214 880-3500

(G-4638)
CADWELL LABORATORIES INC
909 N Kellogg St (99336-7688)
PHONE..................................509 735-6481
Carlton M Cadwell, *President*
Kendell Millbauer, *General Mgr*
Theresa Sickler, *General Mgr*
Patrick Jensen, *COO*
John C Cadwell, *Vice Pres*
EMP: 74
SQ FT: 28,000
SALES (est): 14.6MM
SALES (corp-wide): 26.9MM **Privately Held**
WEB: www.cadwell.com
SIC: 3845 3841 Electromedical equipment; surgical & medical instruments
PA: Cadwell Industries, Inc.
  909 N Kellogg St
  Kennewick WA 99336
  509 735-6481

(G-4639)
CAKES BE WE
2625 W Bruneau Pl (99336-3168)
PHONE..................................509 460-1399
Fonny Michaud,
EMP: 4 EST: 2010
SALES: 76K **Privately Held**
SIC: 5461 7372 Cakes; application computer software

(G-4640)
CANNON LAUREE
1204 S Clodfelter Rd (99338-9121)
PHONE..................................509 627-0505
Robert Cannon, *President*
Lauree Cannon, *Vice Pres*
Charlie Cannon, *Manager*
EMP: 9
SALES (est): 750K **Privately Held**
SIC: 3545 Tools & accessories for machine tools

(G-4641)
CANNON MACHINE PRODUCTS INC
1204 S Clodfelter Rd (99338-9121)
PHONE..................................509 627-0505
Robert Cannon, *President*
Lauree Cannon, *Vice Pres*
EMP: 8
SQ FT: 4,600
SALES: 894.6K **Privately Held**
WEB: www.cannonmch.com
SIC: 3599 Machine shop, jobbing & repair

(G-4642)
CARBITEX INC
1426 E 3rd Ave Bldg B (99337-9601)
PHONE..................................509 591-9775
Ron Boninger, *CEO*
Junus A Khan, *Principal*
Stefan Rosvall, *Principal*
Aaron Grundmeier, *CFO*
EMP: 2 EST: 2012
SALES (est): 122.8K **Privately Held**
SIC: 2824 Fluorocarbon fibers

(G-4643)
CARTRIDGE WORLD
1360 N Louisiana St Ste B (99336-7171)
PHONE..................................509 469-9711
EMP: 2
SALES (est): 119.8K **Privately Held**
SIC: 5112 5734 2899 Whol Stationery/Office Supplies Ret Computers/Software Mfg Chemical Preparations

(G-4644)
CI SUPPORT LLC
Also Called: Ci Shred
900 S Dayton St (99336-5667)
P.O. Box 7346 (99336-0617)
PHONE..................................509 586-6090
Michael Dunlop, *CFO*
EMP: 4
SALES (est): 362.5K **Privately Held**
SIC: 3589 Shredders, industrial & commercial

(G-4645)
COLUMBIA BASIN ICE LLC
6300 W Deschutes Ave A106 (99336-7732)
PHONE..................................509 736-9583
David McDaniels,
Thomas Obrien,
Andrew Sorn,
EMP: 45
SQ FT: 15,000
SALES: 1.7MM **Privately Held**
SIC: 2097 Manufactured ice

Kennewick - Benton County (G-4646)

(G-4646)
COLUMBIA BASIN PROSTHETIC
Also Called: Prosthetic & Orthotic Services
2624a W Deschutes Ave A (99336-3003)
P.O. Box 662, Walla Walla (99362-0016)
PHONE.................................509 737-8322
Steven Kimball, *President*
Jodi Kimball, *Vice Pres*
EMP: 7
SALES (est): 915.4K **Privately Held**
SIC: 3842 Limbs, artificial

(G-4647)
COLUMBIA CULTURED MARBLE INC
1601 S Washington St (99337-4850)
PHONE.................................509 582-5660
Barry Barnhart, *President*
Nathan Barnhart, *Vice Pres*
Karen Barnhart, *CFO*
EMP: 9 EST: 1970
SALES (est): 1.1MM **Privately Held**
WEB: www.columbiamarble.com
SIC: 3281 1743 3088 2821 Bathroom fixtures, cut stone; terrazzo, tile, marble, mosaic work; plastics plumbing fixtures; plastics materials & resins; wood kitchen cabinets

(G-4648)
COLUMBIA CULTURED MBL II LLC
1601 1/2 S Washington St (99337-4850)
PHONE.................................509 582-5660
Karen Barnhart,
EMP: 7
SALES (est): 336.5K **Privately Held**
SIC: 3281 Cut stone & stone products

(G-4649)
COLUMBIA RIVER MFG SVCS LLC
1030 N Center Pkwy (99336-7160)
PHONE.................................801 652-3008
Kyle Kafentzis,
EMP: 4
SALES (est): 125.1K **Privately Held**
SIC: 3999 Manufacturing industries

(G-4650)
CORY A STEMP
Also Called: Print Wearhouse, The
222 W Kennewick Ave (99336-3828)
PHONE.................................509 491-3847
Cory Stemp, *Owner*
EMP: 3
SALES (est): 246.8K **Privately Held**
SIC: 2759 7389 Screen printing; textile & apparel services

(G-4651)
CUSTOM WELDING & ORNA IR LLC
118 N Gum St (99336-3703)
P.O. Box 6702 (99336-0639)
PHONE.................................509 947-8863
Julian Veagas,
Joseph Pock,
EMP: 2
SALES: 195K **Privately Held**
SIC: 7692 Welding repair

(G-4652)
D W PAPE INC
Also Called: Ditch Witch of Washington
722 N Hartford St (99336-3513)
PHONE.................................509 586-0522
Jordan Pape, *CEO*
Chris Wetle, *President*
Bert Merit, *Manager*
EMP: 4
SALES (corp-wide): 606.3MM **Privately Held**
SIC: 5082 3531 General construction machinery & equipment; backhoes, tractors, cranes, plows & similar equipment
HQ: D W Pape Inc
355 Goodpasture Island Rd
Eugene OR 97401
541 683-5073

(G-4653)
DELTA C DYNAMICS LLC
2839 W Kennewick Ave (99336-2927)
PHONE.................................888 704-3626
Ping P Bullock,
Sean P Bullock,
EMP: 2
SALES (est): 138.8K **Privately Held**
SIC: 2759 Engraving

(G-4654)
DIVERSIFIED MARKETING INTL LLC
Also Called: Bi-Directional Microwave
1807 S Garfield St (99337-4846)
PHONE.................................509 585-9377
Aaron Davis,
EMP: 1
SQ FT: 5,800
SALES: 1MM **Privately Held**
SIC: 5065 3663 Communication equipment; modems, computer; microwave communication equipment

(G-4655)
DODGER AND POWERS WINES
1106 N Jurupa St (99338-7337)
PHONE.................................509 627-4986
EMP: 2
SALES (est): 124.3K **Privately Held**
SIC: 2084 Mfg Wines/Brandy/Spirits

(G-4656)
DORIS J JOHNSON
739 S Tacoma Pl (99336-5277)
PHONE.................................509 586-3646
Doris J Johnson, *Owner*
EMP: 3
SALES (est): 158.3K **Privately Held**
SIC: 1442 Gravel mining

(G-4657)
ELECTRONIC SYSTEMS TECH INC
Also Called: Esteem Wireless Modems
415 N Quay St Ste B1 (99336-7783)
PHONE.................................509 735-9092
Michael Eller, *President*
EMP: 10
SQ FT: 8,600
SALES: 1.4MM **Privately Held**
WEB: www.esteem.com
SIC: 3661 3571 Modems; electronic computers

(G-4658)
EMBROIDERY BY DESIGN
3705 S Dennis St (99337-3129)
PHONE.................................509 582-2858
Bryan Jones, *Principal*
EMP: 2
SALES (est): 83.7K **Privately Held**
SIC: 2395 Embroidery & art needlework

(G-4659)
EMERALD AUTOMATION LLC
9228 W Clearwater Dr (99336-8622)
PHONE.................................509 783-1369
Dave Hussey, *CEO*
Rob McIntyre, *Engineer*
Kevin Bubar,
▲ EMP: 23
SQ FT: 4,000
SALES: 2.5MM **Privately Held**
WEB: www.emeraldautomation.com
SIC: 3565 Packing & wrapping machinery

(G-4660)
ENCASED SPECIALTY MFG LLC
Also Called: Encased Presentation
4605 S Toro Ct (99338-8819)
PHONE.................................509 396-0755
Derrick K Perrins,
EMP: 3
SALES (est): 330K **Privately Held**
SIC: 2441 Boxes, wood

(G-4661)
ENERGY NORTHWEST
92308 S Nine Canyon Rd (99337-7201)
PHONE.................................509 585-3677
◆ EMP: 3 EST: 2010
SALES (est): 317.9K **Privately Held**
SIC: 3511 Turbines & turbine generator sets & parts

(G-4662)
ESPRIT GRPHIC CMMNICATIONS INC
110 N Cascade St (99336-3850)
P.O. Box 5493 (99336-0493)
PHONE.................................509 586-7858
Nicholas Novakovich, *President*
Shannon Novakovich, *Vice Pres*
John Keller, *Manager*
EMP: 13
SQ FT: 7,500
SALES (est): 2.3MM **Privately Held**
WEB: www.espritinc.net
SIC: 2752 Commercial printing, offset

(G-4663)
ESTERBROOK INC
3311 W Clearwater Ave B110 (99336-2710)
PHONE.................................509 783-6826
Larry Dickman, *President*
Elaine Dickman, *General Mgr*
Vicky Schmitt, *Manager*
EMP: 4
SALES (est): 3MM **Privately Held**
SIC: 3634 Electric housewares & fans

(G-4664)
ESTM INC
Also Called: Reliance Pharmacy
133 N Ely St Ste C1 (99336-2941)
PHONE.................................509 545-0596
Tamer Elsammak, *President*
Eslam Mohamed, *Principal*
EMP: 3
SALES (est): 164K **Privately Held**
SIC: 2834 Pharmaceutical preparations

(G-4665)
FARMHAND WINERY
8101 W 10th Ave (99336-9567)
PHONE.................................509 308-7203
EMP: 2
SALES (est): 74.4K **Privately Held**
SIC: 2084 Wines

(G-4666)
GABRIELLES GLASSWORKS
4102 S Green St (99337-2671)
PHONE.................................509 585-9394
EMP: 2
SALES (est): 110K **Privately Held**
SIC: 3211 Mfg Flat Glass

(G-4667)
GINNY HARDINGS EQUINE CLASSICS
228710 E Lechelt Rd (99337-7532)
PHONE.................................509 582-7924
Ginny Hardings, *Owner*
EMP: 2 EST: 1994
SALES (est): 153.4K **Privately Held**
SIC: 3952 Paints, except gold & bronze: artists'

(G-4668)
GOLD PLATING SPECIALIST
Also Called: Rick's Mr Chips
600 W Entiat Ave (99336-3536)
PHONE.................................509 582-3430
EMP: 3
SALES (est): 147K **Privately Held**
SIC: 3471 Plating/Polishing Service

(G-4669)
HERITAGE PROFESSIONAL LDSCPG
Also Called: Heritage Home Accents & Floral
1350 N Louisiana St (99336-7177)
P.O. Box 7225 (99336-0616)
PHONE.................................509 737-8580
Randall Mendenhall, *Branch Mgr*
EMP: 9 **Privately Held**
WEB: www.heritagelandscaping.com
SIC: 2392 5992 Household furnishings; florists
PA: Heritage Professional Landscaping, Inc
2816 W 27th Ave
Kennewick WA 99337

(G-4670)
HIGH DESERT MAINTENANCE INC
525 E Bruneau Ave (99336-3725)
PHONE.................................509 531-8341
Paul Dobrovolsky, *President*
EMP: 5
SALES (est): 593.5K **Privately Held**
SIC: 7692 Welding repair

(G-4671)
HOLDIMAN SOFTWARE
105 N Mayfield St (99336-3332)
PHONE.................................509 582-5085
Devin Holdiman, *Principal*
EMP: 2 EST: 2014
SALES (est): 131.7K **Privately Held**
SIC: 7372 Prepackaged software

(G-4672)
HRH DOOR CORP
Also Called: Wayne - Dalton of Yakima
440 N Quay St (99336-7734)
PHONE.................................509 575-0832
Joe Wild, *Office Mgr*
EMP: 13
SALES (corp-wide): 600.8MM **Privately Held**
WEB: www.waynedalton.com
SIC: 5211 3699 Garage doors, sale & installation; door opening & closing devices, electrical
PA: Hrh Door Corp.
1 Door Dr
Mount Hope OH 44660
850 208-3400

(G-4673)
ICE HARBOR BREWING COMPANY
350 Clover Island Dr (99336-3678)
PHONE.................................509 586-3181
Teff Canaday, *Manager*
EMP: 21 **Privately Held**
SIC: 2082 5812 Beer (alcoholic beverage); eating places
PA: Ice Harbor Brewing Company
206 N Benton St Ste C
Kennewick WA 99336

(G-4674)
ICE HARBOR BREWING COMPANY (PA)
206 N Benton St Ste C (99336-3608)
PHONE.................................509 545-0927
William R Jaquish, *President*
Michael J Hall, *Vice Pres*
EMP: 24
SQ FT: 7,000
SALES (est): 3.5MM **Privately Held**
WEB: www.iceharbor.com
SIC: 2082 5149 Beer (alcoholic beverage); wine makers' equipment & supplies

(G-4675)
IMAGES
2527 W Kennewick Ave # 106 (99336-3102)
PHONE.................................509 736-9508
Thomas Koepnick, *Owner*
EMP: 3
SALES: 225K **Privately Held**
WEB: www.imagespromo.com
SIC: 8743 2752 Promotion service; promotional printing, lithographic; advertising posters, lithographed

(G-4676)
INNOVATEK INC
3806 W 40th Pl (99337-2603)
P.O. Box 6816 (99336-0601)
PHONE.................................509 375-1093
Patricia Irving, *CEO*
Kathryn Rightor, *CFO*
EMP: 9 EST: 1997
SALES: 1.2MM **Privately Held**
WEB: www.tekkie.com
SIC: 8731 3621 Energy research; environmental research; power generators

(G-4677)
IRON HORSE VAC LLC
1915 S Oak St (99337-6105)
PHONE.................................509 586-2446
Daniel Stewart,

GEOGRAPHIC SECTION
Kennewick - Benton County (G-4708)

Tammy Stewart,
EMP: 3
SALES (est): 484K **Privately Held**
SIC: 3531 7699 Buckets, excavating: clamshell, concrete, dragline, etc.; septic tank cleaning service

(G-4678)
IRONDOG INDUSTRIES LLC
819 W 25th Ave (99337-4248)
PHONE.................................509 586-0479
EMP: 2 **EST:** 2010
SALES (est): 128.3K **Privately Held**
SIC: 3999 Manufacturing industries

(G-4679)
IW INTERNATIONAL INC
Also Called: Intermountain West Intl
9304 W Clearwater Dr A (99336-8612)
PHONE.................................509 735-8411
T Dean Moody, *President*
Chris Moody, *Vice Pres*
Darran Moody, *Vice Pres*
EMP: 46
SQ FT: 5,000
SALES (est): 11.6MM **Privately Held**
SIC: 3211 1742 Insulating glass, sealed units; window glass, clear & colored; insulation, buildings

(G-4680)
JENNETH TECHNOLOGIES INC
Also Called: Northwest Fiberglass
4408 W 7th Ave (99336-4147)
PHONE.................................509 547-8977
EMP: 2 **EST:** 1991
SQ FT: 3,600
SALES: 100K **Privately Held**
SIC: 3732 Fiberglass Repair

(G-4681)
KARL-SONS LLC
28409 Country Meadows Ln (99338-7517)
PHONE.................................509 627-0152
EMP: 2
SALES (est): 129.6K **Privately Held**
SIC: 3841 Surgical & medical instruments

(G-4682)
KENNEWICK PRESS LLC
Also Called: Minuteman Press
7201 W Clearwater Ave (99336-1694)
PHONE.................................509 491-3801
Michael Duffy,
Tristan Weetch, *Graphic Designe*
Phyllis Shovelski,
EMP: 5
SQ FT: 1,510
SALES (est): 613K **Privately Held**
SIC: 2752 Commercial printing, lithographic

(G-4683)
KITCHEN CABINET AND GRANITE
7903 W Grandridge Blvd (99336-7827)
PHONE.................................509 783-9500
Qi Chen, *Principal*
EMP: 2
SALES (est): 201.9K **Privately Held**
SIC: 2434 Wood kitchen cabinets

(G-4684)
KRISTEN ROSE WINERY
109 E 27th Ave (99337-5537)
PHONE.................................509 586-4830
Kirsten Rose, *Principal*
EMP: 2 **EST:** 2007
SALES (est): 113.9K **Privately Held**
SIC: 2084 Wines, brandy & brandy spirits

(G-4685)
LAMB WESTON INC
8701 W Gage Blvd (99336-1034)
P.O. Box 1900, Pasco (99302-1900)
PHONE.................................509 735-4651
Jim Kaip, *COO*
Kim Cupelli, *Vice Pres*
Sharon Miller, *Vice Pres*
Eryk Spytek, *Vice Pres*
Shelby Reed, *Export Mgr*
EMP: 310
SALES (corp-wide): 3.4B **Publicly Held**
SIC: 2037 Potato products, quick frozen & cold pack

HQ: Lamb Weston Inc
599 S Rivershore Ln
Eagle ID 83616

(G-4686)
LAMB WESTON SALES INC
8701 W Gage Blvd (99336-1034)
P.O. Box 1900, Pasco (99302-1900)
PHONE.................................509 735-4651
EMP: 250
SALES (corp-wide): 3.4B **Publicly Held**
SIC: 2037 Potato products, quick frozen & cold pack; fruits, quick frozen & cold pack (frozen)
HQ: Lamb Weston Sales Inc
599 S Rivershore Ln
Eagle ID 83616
208 938-1047

(G-4687)
LARRY S AYRE
37304 S Lemon Dr (99337-9181)
PHONE.................................509 582-8925
EMP: 3
SALES (est): 120K **Privately Held**
SIC: 2099 Mfg Food Preparations

(G-4688)
LEE ENTERPRISES INCORPORATED
Also Called: Tri-Cities Wheel Deals
3321 W Kennewick Ave # 190 (99336-2957)
PHONE.................................509 783-5555
Mike Wise, *Manager*
EMP: 8
SALES (corp-wide): 596.5MM **Publicly Held**
WEB: www.lee.net
SIC: 2711 2741 Newspapers: publishing only, not printed on site; miscellaneous publishing
PA: Lee Enterprises, Incorporated
201 N Harrison St Ste 600
Davenport IA 52801
563 383-2100

(G-4689)
LEGACY MILL AND CABINET LLC
6855 W Clearwater Blvd (99336-5011)
PHONE.................................509 440-4884
EMP: 4
SALES (est): 303K
SALES (corp-wide): 1.8MM **Privately Held**
SIC: 2434 Wood kitchen cabinets
PA: Legacy Mill And Cabinet Llc
900 N 400 W Ste 3
North Salt Lake UT 84054
801 292-0795

(G-4690)
MADRETIERRA CANDLE COMPANY LLC
2922 Brian Ln (99338-9307)
PHONE.................................786 374-5913
Silvia Isaac, *Principal*
EMP: 2
SALES (est): 62.5K **Privately Held**
SIC: 3999 Candles

(G-4691)
MANUFACTURING SERVICES INC
1023 N Kellogg St (99336-7661)
PHONE.................................509 735-8444
Michael S Brown, *President*
EMP: 38 **EST:** 1979
SQ FT: 15,000
SALES: 7.8MM **Privately Held**
SIC: 3679 Rheostats, for electronic end products

(G-4692)
MARTIN BUSINESS SYSTEMS
1010 E 23rd Ave Bldg B (99337-5521)
P.O. Box 6567 (99336-0628)
PHONE.................................509 582-3159
Joanne Martin, *Owner*
Neil Martin, *Owner*
EMP: 2
SALES: 200K **Privately Held**
SIC: 5943 2759 5947 Office forms & supplies; commercial printing; souvenirs

(G-4693)
MCCLATCHY NEWSPAPERS INC
Also Called: Tri-City Herald
333 W Canal Dr (99336-3811)
PHONE.................................509 582-1500
Cheryl Ebright Dell, *Publisher*
Jack Briggs, *Branch Mgr*
EMP: 132
SALES (corp-wide): 807.2MM **Publicly Held**
WEB: www.sacbee.com
SIC: 2711 2759 Newspapers, publishing & printing; commercial printing
HQ: Mcclatchy Newspapers, Inc.
2100 Q St
Sacramento CA 95816
916 321-1855

(G-4694)
MID-COLUMBIA NEWSPAPER PUBHS ✪
9228 W Clearwater Dr (99336-8622)
PHONE.................................509 845-5253
Dennis Cresswell, *President*
EMP: 2 **EST:** 2018
SALES (est): 62.9K **Privately Held**
SIC: 2711 Newspapers

(G-4695)
MJV MFG
1920 S Taft St (99338-1483)
PHONE.................................509 735-1662
Mark J Verwest, *Principal*
EMP: 2
SALES (est): 111.4K **Privately Held**
SIC: 3999 Manufacturing industries

(G-4696)
MOMS CARMEL APPLES & MORE LLC
5610 W Clearwater Ave (99336-1903)
PHONE.................................509 515-8153
EMP: 2
SALES (est): 168.9K **Privately Held**
SIC: 3571 Candy & other confectionery products

(G-4697)
MURDOCK ROACH INC
4708 W 4th Ct (99336-4180)
PHONE.................................509 302-1054
Susan Roach, *CEO*
Mitchell Roach, *President*
EMP: 2
SALES (est): 180K **Privately Held**
SIC: 3272 Grave markers, concrete

(G-4698)
MUSTANG SIGNS LLC
Also Called: Mustang Sign Group
10379 W Clearwater Ave (99336-8641)
PHONE.................................509 735-4607
Hal Smith, *Owner*
Violeta Smith, *Co-Owner*
Lauran Wang, *Co-Owner*
Mac Gayler, *Consultant*
EMP: 10
SQ FT: 6,000
SALES (est): 482.2K **Privately Held**
WEB: www.mustangsigns.com
SIC: 7336 3993 7312 7389 Graphic arts & related design; signs & advertising specialties; outdoor advertising services;

(G-4699)
NATURAL ESSENCES
210506 E 193 Pr Se (99337-7055)
PHONE.................................509 820-3242
Selena Albertsen-Benavidez, *Principal*
EMP: 2 **EST:** 2015
SALES (est): 127.7K **Privately Held**
SIC: 2844 Toilet preparations

(G-4700)
NEIL F LAMPSON INC (PA)
607 E Columbia Dr (99336-3778)
P.O. Box 6510 (99336-0502)
PHONE.................................509 586-0411
William N Lampson, *Ch of Bd*
Jenny Lampson, *Vice Pres*
Mary Lampson, *Treasurer*
◆ **EMP:** 150
SQ FT: 22,000

SALES (est): 31.4MM **Privately Held**
SIC: 3531 1799 4213 3537 Backhoes, tractors, cranes, plows & similar equipment; rigging & scaffolding; heavy machinery transport; industrial trucks & tractors; cranes & aerial lift equipment, rental or leasing

(G-4701)
NEW FOUNDATION PRESS
114 Vista Way (99336-3119)
PHONE.................................509 783-5237
EMP: 2 **EST:** 2011
SALES (est): 78K **Privately Held**
SIC: 2741 Misc Publishing

(G-4702)
NICKEL ONE AD NEWSPAPER (PA)
Also Called: Nickel The
501 S Volland St (99336-4108)
P.O. Box 488, Longview (98632-7317)
PHONE.................................360 423-3141
Dave Bragg, *Owner*
EMP: 5
SALES (est): 572.5K **Privately Held**
WEB: www.thenickel.net
SIC: 2711 2721 2741 Newspapers, publishing & printing; periodicals; miscellaneous publishing

(G-4703)
NO GRAF NETWORK INC
8524 W Gage Blvd (99336-8241)
PHONE.................................509 531-1334
Randy Campbell, *Principal*
EMP: 2
SALES (est): 194.4K **Privately Held**
SIC: 3479 Coating, rust preventive

(G-4704)
OLYMPUS SCIENTIFIC SOLUTIONS (DH)
421 N Quay St (99336-7735)
PHONE.................................509 735-7550
Fabrice Cancre, *CEO*
Mark A Miller, *Vice Pres*
Andrew Thomas, *Engineer*
Randall Kenien, *Sales Staff*
Michael Pinchback, *Sales Staff*
EMP: 42
SQ FT: 26,000
SALES (est): 7.5MM **Privately Held**
SIC: 3829 Physical property testing equipment; stress, strain & flaw detecting/measuring equipment; ultrasonic testing equipment

(G-4705)
PAUL PARISH LIMITED
4806 S Reed St (99337-2731)
PHONE.................................509 735-9820
Paul Parish, *President*
Linda Parish, *Vice Pres*
EMP: 2
SQ FT: 7,200
SALES: 1MM **Privately Held**
SIC: 8748 3999 7389 3711 Business consulting; wheelchair lifts; balloons, novelty & toy; motor vehicles & car bodies

(G-4706)
PENS BY BILL
34115 Cantera St (99338-9207)
PHONE.................................509 628-3288
William Sheehan, *Principal*
EMP: 2
SALES (est): 131.7K **Privately Held**
SIC: 3993 Signs & advertising specialties

(G-4707)
PREMIER WOODWORKS LLC
100 W Canal Dr (99336-3818)
PHONE.................................509 591-0839
Juan Palomino, *Mng Member*
EMP: 9
SQ FT: 5,000
SALES (est): 1.4MM **Privately Held**
SIC: 2431 Wood kitchen cabinets

(G-4708)
PRINT PLUS INC
Also Called: Pss Rubber Stamp
2514 W Kennewick Ave (99336-3125)
PHONE.................................509 735-6303

Kennewick - Benton County (G-4709) — GEOGRAPHIC SECTION

Kenny Koehoer, *Manager*
EMP: 2   **Privately Held**
SIC: 2752 3953 Commercial printing, offset; embossing seals & hand stamps
PA: Print Plus Inc
  2514 W Kennewick Ave
  Kennewick WA 99336

(G-4709)
PRINT PLUS INC (PA)
Also Called: P S S Rubber Stamps
2514 W Kennewick Ave (99336-3125)
PHONE 509 735-6303
Colleen Johnson, *CEO*
Eric Johnson, *Vice Pres*
EMP: 6
SQ FT: 4,380
SALES (est): 831K **Privately Held**
SIC: 2752 Commercial printing, offset

(G-4710)
PROFESSIONAL NETWORK SOLUTIONS
905 S Sharron St (99336-5209)
PHONE 509 308-0318
Garrett Hope, *Owner*
EMP: 2
SALES (est): 118.1K **Privately Held**
SIC: 3825 Network analyzers

(G-4711)
PUGET SOUND PIPE AND SUPPLY CO
5950 W Brinkley Rd (99338-2001)
PHONE 509 783-0474
Mark Chindavat, *Branch Mgr*
EMP: 14
SALES (corp-wide): 95.3MM **Privately Held**
SIC: 3317 Steel pipe & tubes
PA: Puget Sound Pipe And Supply Company
  7816 S 202nd St
  Kent WA 98032
  206 682-9350

(G-4712)
QUALITY SIGN SERVICE INC
Also Called: Qss
9312 W 10th Ave (99336-8521)
PHONE 509 586-0585
Daniel Glenn Washam, *President*
Glenn Ross Washam, *Treasurer*
EMP: 12
SALES (est): 1.4MM **Privately Held**
SIC: 3993 Electric signs

(G-4713)
RALLITO DE LUNA TORTILLA
213803 E 200 Pr Se (99337-7067)
PHONE 509 586-8691
EMP: 2 **EST:** 2011
SALES (est): 55K **Privately Held**
SIC: 2099 Mfg Food Preparations

(G-4714)
RAM PIPING INDUSTRIES INC
Also Called: Ram Mechanical
109416 E Windward Ln (99338-9223)
PHONE 509 586-0801
Roy Cole, *President*
Barbara Cole, *Manager*
EMP: 10
SQ FT: 5,000
SALES (est): 1.5MM **Privately Held**
WEB: www.ramindustries.com
SIC: 3443 1711 Pipe, large diameter: metal plate; mechanical contractor

(G-4715)
REDD INDUSTRIES LLC
802 N Keller St (99336-2406)
PHONE 509 572-5752
EMP: 3
SALES (est): 124.2K **Privately Held**
SIC: 3999 Mfg Misc Products

(G-4716)
REESE CONCRETE PRODUCTS MFG
Also Called: Reese Construction Pdts Mfg
1606 S Ely St (99337-2833)
PHONE 509 586-3704
Dan Westermeyer, *Vice Pres*
Steve Landon, *Vice Pres*
EMP: 13
SQ FT: 80,000
SALES (est): 2MM **Privately Held**
SIC: 3272 5999 Pipe, concrete or lined with concrete; concrete products, pre-cast

(G-4717)
REFRESCO BEVERAGES US INC
10 E Bruneau Ave (99336-3772)
PHONE 509 582-5200
Ramon Ruesga, *Branch Mgr*
EMP: 45
SALES (corp-wide): 242.1K **Privately Held**
WEB: www.jliebfoods.com
SIC: 2086 Carbonated beverages, nonalcoholic: bottled & canned
HQ: Refresco Beverages Us Inc.
  8112 Woodland Center Blvd
  Tampa FL 33614
  813 313-1800

(G-4718)
RESEARCH REACTR SFTY/ANYLST SV
6808 W 15th Ave (99338-1206)
PHONE 509 783-6860
Robert C Nelson, *Owner*
EMP: 2
SALES (est): 209.9K **Privately Held**
WEB: www.rrsas.com
SIC: 3612 8732 Current limiting reactors, electrical; research services, except laboratory

(G-4719)
RIVERSANDS DISTILLERY
19 W Canal Dr (99336-3821)
P.O. Box 4748, West Richland (99353-4012)
PHONE 509 492-1015
EMP: 3
SALES (est): 165.3K **Privately Held**
SIC: 2085 Distilled & blended liquors

(G-4720)
RSS KENNEWICK
8390 W Gage Blvd (99336-8105)
PHONE 206 441-9907
EMP: 2
SALES (est): 83.9K **Privately Held**
SIC: 2752 Commercial printing, lithographic

(G-4721)
RUNWAY LIQUIDATION LLC
Also Called: Bcbg
3177 Long Beach Rd (99336)
PHONE 304 645-2799
EMP: 2
SALES (corp-wide): 645.5MM **Privately Held**
SIC: 2335 Women's, juniors' & misses' dresses
HQ: Runway Liquidation, Llc
  2761 Fruitland Ave
  Vernon CA 90058
  323 589-2224

(G-4722)
RUNWAY LIQUIDATION LLC
Also Called: Bcbg
6003 Big Tree Rd (99338)
PHONE 304 825-6364
EMP: 2
SALES (corp-wide): 645.5MM **Privately Held**
SIC: 2335 Women's, juniors' & misses' dresses
HQ: Runway Liquidation, Llc
  2761 Fruitland Ave
  Vernon CA 90058
  323 589-2224

(G-4723)
RUNWAY LIQUIDATION LLC
Also Called: Bcbg
2020 116th Ave Ne (99336)
PHONE 304 636-2020
EMP: 2
SALES (corp-wide): 645.5MM **Privately Held**
SIC: 2335 Women's, juniors' & misses' dresses
HQ: Runway Liquidation, Llc
  2761 Fruitland Ave
  Vernon CA 90058
  323 589-2224

(G-4724)
SAFE DEFENSE LLC
8406 W Deschutes Ave (99336-1630)
PHONE 509 430-5731
Howard Hunt, *Bd of Directors*
EMP: 2
SALES (est): 137.2K **Privately Held**
SIC: 3812 Defense systems & equipment

(G-4725)
SALLY BEAUTY SUPPLY LLC
3180 W Clearwatr Ave C (99336-2767)
PHONE 509 783-7292
Caryn Steward, *Principal*
EMP: 4 **Publicly Held**
SIC: 5087 3069 Beauty parlor equipment & supplies; capes, vulcanized rubber or rubberized fabric; brushes, rubber
HQ: Sally Beauty Supply Llc
  3001 Colorado Blvd
  Denton TX 76210
  940 898-7500

(G-4726)
SANDVIK SPECIAL METALS LLC
235407 E Sr 397 (99337-7709)
P.O. Box 6027 (99336-0027)
PHONE 509 734-4000
Orjan Blom, *President*
Erika Hedberg, *Project Engr*
David Mortensen, *Finance*
Gary Grade, *Mng Member*
Ken Idler, *Mng Member*
▲ **EMP:** 130
SQ FT: 150,000
SALES (est): 27.9MM
SALES (corp-wide): 11.1B **Privately Held**
SIC: 3356 2819 Titanium; nuclear fuel & cores, inorganic
HQ: Sandvik, Inc.
  17-02 Nevins Rd
  Fair Lawn NJ 07410
  201 794-5000

(G-4727)
SIGN CRAFTERS INC
Also Called: Signs Now
627 N Kellogg St Ste A (99336-4922)
PHONE 509 783-8718
Robert Ogata, *President*
Laura Ogata, *Vice Pres*
EMP: 5
SQ FT: 8,000
SALES (est): 500K **Privately Held**
SIC: 3993 5999 1799 Signs & advertising specialties; banners; sign installation & maintenance

(G-4728)
SIRJMR INC
Also Called: Treasure Valley Coffee Company
1351 E 3rd Ave Ste C (99337-6308)
P.O. Box 6145 (99336-0145)
PHONE 509 582-2683
Susan Roskelley, *President*
John Roskelley, *Vice Pres*
EMP: 28
SALES (est): 1.1MM **Privately Held**
SIC: 2095 7389 5149 Roasted coffee; coffee service; coffee & tea

(G-4729)
SPECTROGLYPH LLC
101904 Wiser Pkwy Ste 104 (99338-1257)
PHONE 415 793-1242
Mikhail Delov,
EMP: 3
SALES (est): 52.6K **Privately Held**
SIC: 3826 Analytical instruments

(G-4730)
STATEWIDE PUBG - WASH INC
5009 W Clearwatr Ave K (99336-4986)
PHONE 509 734-1186
Phillip Johnson, *President*
Phillip Thompson, *President*
Shane Thomas, *Production*
June Kernaghan, *Sales Mgr*
Lydia Fairchild, *Accounts Mgr*
EMP: 10
SALES (est): 1MM **Privately Held**
SIC: 2741 Telephone & other directory publishing

(G-4731)
SUN RIVER VINTNERS LLC
1030 N Center Pkwy (99336-7160)
PHONE 509 627-3100
Marc Le Grand, *Principal*
EMP: 4
SALES (est): 158.4K **Privately Held**
SIC: 2084 Wines

(G-4732)
TERRA VINUM LLC
2514 S Irving St (99338-1926)
PHONE 509 628-7799
Tonnie S Stinson, *President*
EMP: 7 **EST:** 2009
SALES (est): 542.3K **Privately Held**
SIC: 2084 Wines

(G-4733)
TESSENDERLO KERLEY INC
Also Called: Tki
233807 E Straightbank Rd (99337-7708)
PHONE 509 586-9148
Jeff Strickland, *Opers-Prdtn-Mfg*
EMP: 23
SALES (corp-wide): 428.8MM **Privately Held**
WEB: www.mprserve.com
SIC: 2874 2819 5191 Phosphatic fertilizers; industrial inorganic chemicals; fertilizer & fertilizer materials
HQ: Tessenderlo Kerley, Inc.
  2255 N 44th St Ste 300
  Phoenix AZ 85008
  602 889-8300

(G-4734)
TEVADA PUBLISHING INC
Also Called: Giant Nickel Want ADS
4812 W Clearwater Ave (99336-2119)
PHONE 509 783-5455
Elon Bragg, *President*
EMP: 18
SQ FT: 1,500
SALES (est): 2.5MM **Privately Held**
WEB: www.giantnickel.com
SIC: 2621 2741 Newsprint paper; miscellaneous publishing

(G-4735)
THRIFTY PAYLESS INC T/A
101 N Ely St (99336-2941)
PHONE 509 783-1438
EMP: 2 **EST:** 2010
SALES (est): 94.5K **Privately Held**
SIC: 2836 Vaccines & other immunizing products

(G-4736)
TOP QUALITY WOODWORKS LLC
3131 W Hood Ave Apt A105 (99336-2742)
PHONE 509 551-3658
Ismael Olivera, *Principal*
EMP: 2 **EST:** 2016
SALES (est): 59.5K **Privately Held**
SIC: 2431 Millwork

(G-4737)
TOPTEC SOFTWARE LLC
Also Called: Mdtoolbox
8524 W Gage Blvd A137 (99336-8241)
PHONE 206 331-4420
Michael Conner,
EMP: 2
SALES (corp-wide): 450K **Privately Held**
SIC: 7372 Prepackaged software
PA: Toptec Software, Llc
  1766 Fowler St Ste D
  Richland WA 99352
  206 331-4420

(G-4738)
TRI-CITY GLASS INC
304 E Columbia Dr (99336-3798)
PHONE 509 586-0454
Larry Wise, *President*
Gloria Wise, *Admin Sec*
EMP: 6
SQ FT: 5,000

▲ = Import ▼ = Export
◆ = Import/Export

SALES (est): 1.1MM **Privately Held**
SIC: 5231 3429 1751 5031 Glass; door opening & closing devices, except electrical; window & door installation & erection; doors & windows; mirrors; fiberglass doors

(G-4739)
TRI-CITY MODEL RAILROADERS
101 N Quebec St (99336-5093)
PHONE..................................509 987-7000
Richard J Anema, *Principal*
EMP: 2
SALES (est): 71K **Privately Held**
SIC: 2711 Newspapers, publishing & printing

(G-4740)
TRIAD COMSURAL PRINTING CORP
Also Called: Tri-City Herald
333 W Canal Dr (99336-3811)
PHONE..................................509 582-1466
Jerry Hug, *Manager*
EMP: 10
SALES (est): 1.3MM **Privately Held**
WEB: www.annedoyle.com
SIC: 2759 2752 Newspapers: printing; commercial printing, lithographic

(G-4741)
TRICOMP PUBLISHING
Also Called: Tri City Journal of Business
8919 W Grandridge Blvd (99336-7218)
PHONE..................................509 737-8778
Melanie Schmitt, *Vice Pres*
EMP: 4
SALES (est): 313.4K **Privately Held**
WEB: www.tcajob.com
SIC: 2711 Commercial printing & newspaper publishing combined; newspapers, publishing & printing

(G-4742)
TRU DOOR INC
5601 W Clearwater Ave # 101 (99336-4953)
PHONE..................................509 545-8773
Mark Mitchell, *President*
Barbara Zigler, *Vice Pres*
EMP: 17 **EST:** 1979
SQ FT: 25,000
SALES (est): 2.7MM **Privately Held**
SIC: 5031 5211 3442 2431 Doors; doors, storm: wood or metal; doors, wood or metal, except storm; metal doors, sash & trim; millwork

(G-4743)
VULCAN GLOBAL LLC
Also Called: Vulcan Global Solutions
2014 W 6th Ave (99336-5146)
PHONE..................................509 528-2000
Thomas Hogan,
EMP: 2
SALES (est): 92.7K **Privately Held**
SIC: 2813 3569 5169 1542 Industrial gases; gas producers, generators & other gas related equipment; compressed gas; commercial & office building contractors

(G-4744)
WELCH FOODS INC A COOPERATIVE
Also Called: Welch's
10 E Bruneau Ave (99336-3772)
PHONE..................................509 582-1010
Richard Western, *Branch Mgr*
EMP: 166
SALES (corp-wide): 608.4MM **Privately Held**
WEB: www.welchs.com
SIC: 2033 2035 Fruit juices: packaged in cans, jars, etc.; jams, including imitation: packaged in cans, jars, etc.; jellies, edible, including imitation: in cans, jars, etc.; fruit juices: concentrated, hot pack; pickles, sauces & salad dressings
HQ: Welch Foods Inc., A Cooperative
300 Baker Ave Ste 101
Concord MA 01742
978 371-1000

(G-4745)
WHITELATCH-HOCH LLC
Also Called: Le Chateau Winery
313 W Kennewick Ave (99336-3827)
PHONE..................................509 956-9311
Richmond J Hoch,
EMP: 5
SALES (est): 551.7K **Privately Held**
SIC: 5182 2084 Wine; wines

(G-4746)
WHITES CUSTOM WOODWORKING LLC
510 E 31st Ct (99337-5634)
PHONE..................................509 582-9474
Jody White, *Bd of Directors*
EMP: 2 **EST:** 2012
SALES (est): 164.3K **Privately Held**
SIC: 2431 Millwork

Kent
King County

(G-4747)
25 BITS INC
13628 Se 208th St (98042)
PHONE..................................206 861-3836
Steven Mahoney, *President*
Alice Mahoney, *Admin Sec*
EMP: 2
SQ FT: 500
SALES: 60K **Privately Held**
SIC: 2023 Dietary supplements, dairy & non-dairy based

(G-4748)
3D MAIL RESULTS
6205 S 231st St (98032-1802)
PHONE..................................253 859-7310
Travis Lee, *Principal*
EMP: 2
SALES (est): 125.3K **Privately Held**
SIC: 2752 Commercial printing, lithographic

(G-4749)
7 OCEAN EXPRESS INC
25617 129th Ave Se (98030-7979)
PHONE..................................206 250-9239
Harinderbir Singh, *Principal*
EMP: 4
SALES (est): 250K **Privately Held**
SIC: 2741 Miscellaneous publishing

(G-4750)
A & M PRCSION MSURING SVCS INC (PA)
8320 S 208th St Ste H104 (98032-1335)
PHONE..................................425 432-7554
Anthony Elis, *President*
Steve Albrecht, *Director*
Donald L Nelson Jr, *Director*
EMP: 15
SALES (est): 3.3MM **Privately Held**
SIC: 3549 3728 7549 7389 Metalworking machinery; aircraft assemblies, sub-assemblies & parts; inspection & diagnostic service, automotive; inspection & testing services

(G-4751)
A 1 DOORS INC
8711 S 222nd St (98031-1927)
PHONE..................................604 591-1044
Kirpal Basra, *Principal*
EMP: 8
SALES (est): 1.2MM **Privately Held**
SIC: 2431 Door frames, wood

(G-4752)
A 1 PALLETS INC
7752 S 259th St (98032-7316)
PHONE..................................253 395-3119
Daniel Nehls, *President*
EMP: 20
SALES (est): 3.7MM **Privately Held**
SIC: 2448 Pallets, wood

(G-4753)
AAYERS
20119 59th Pl S Ste 102 (98032-2141)
PHONE..................................253 872-5108

EMP: 2
SALES (est): 155.2K **Privately Held**
SIC: 2499 Decorative wood & woodwork

(G-4754)
ABB INC
18425 72nd Ave S (98032-1010)
PHONE..................................253 280-9900
EMP: 5
SALES (corp-wide): 36.4B **Privately Held**
SIC: 3612 Transformers, except electric
HQ: Abb Inc.
305 Gregson Dr
Cary NC 27511

(G-4755)
ACACIA CONTROLS INC
1819 Central Ave S Ste 37 (98032-7506)
PHONE..................................253 277-1206
Kristi Waite, *Governor*
EMP: 6
SALES (est): 270.6K **Privately Held**
SIC: 3672 3679 3643 Printed circuit boards; electronic circuits; current-carrying wiring devices

(G-4756)
ACCESS PRINTING INC
Also Called: Coolest Graphics
19219 W Valley Hwy M106 (98032-2111)
PHONE..................................425 656-0563
Delaney Bascom, *President*
Jennifer Bascom, *Admin Sec*
EMP: 3 **EST:** 1997
SQ FT: 1,000
SALES (est): 32K **Privately Held**
WEB: www.accessprintedmedia.com
SIC: 2752 Commercial printing, offset; photo-offset printing; photolithographic printing

(G-4757)
ACCURUS AEROSPACE KENT LLC
5416 S 226th St (98032-1890)
PHONE..................................253 872-8541
Joel Nielsen, *President*
Joan Sundqvist, *Vice Pres*
EMP: 70
SQ FT: 50,000
SALES (est): 11.2MM
SALES (corp-wide): 152.7MM **Privately Held**
SIC: 3728 Aircraft parts & equipment
PA: Accurus Aerospace Corporation
12716 E Pine St
Tulsa OK 74116
918 438-3121

(G-4758)
ACI COMMUNICATIONS INC
23307 66th Ave S (98032-1827)
PHONE..................................253 854-9802
John Tai, *President*
Shannon Shaw, *Accountant*
Say Sot, *Director*
Phim Kaiponen, *Administration*
◆ **EMP:** 20
SQ FT: 15,956
SALES (est): 4.3MM **Privately Held**
WEB: www.acicomms.com
SIC: 3663 Amplifiers, RF power & IF

(G-4759)
ADEMCO INC
Also Called: ADI Global Distribution
7617 S 180th St (98032-1048)
PHONE..................................253 872-7128
William Staggs, *Manager*
EMP: 9
SALES (corp-wide): 4.8B **Publicly Held**
WEB: www.adilink.com
SIC: 5063 3669 3822 Electrical apparatus & equipment; emergency alarms; auto controls regulating residntl & coml environmt & applncs
HQ: Ademco Inc.
1985 Douglas Dr N
Golden Valley MN 55422
800 468-1502

(G-4760)
ADVANCE PATTERN & TOOLING INC
30218 188th Ave Se (98042-9246)
PHONE..................................253 638-0300

Greg Dielmen, *President*
Gregory Dielman, *President*
Olga Thomas, *Vice Pres*
EMP: 3
SQ FT: 3,200
SALES (est): 350K **Privately Held**
SIC: 3569 Filters

(G-4761)
AE DOWNS ENTERPRISES INC
22227 76th Ave S (98032-1924)
P.O. Box 2139, Renton (98056-0139)
PHONE..................................206 295-9831
Alfred Downs, *President*
Barbara Downs, *Treasurer*
EMP: 28
SQ FT: 26,000
SALES (est): 3MM **Privately Held**
WEB: www.aedowns.com
SIC: 2517 1751 2434 Wood television & radio cabinets; cabinet & finish carpentry; vanities, bathroom: wood

(G-4762)
AEROFAB NDT LLC
8629 S 212th St (98031-1910)
PHONE..................................253 395-8706
Fran Stearns, *Mng Member*
Charles Lafoure,
Doug Melvin,
Quang Nguyen,
Paul Schroeder,
EMP: 5
SALES: 608.7K **Privately Held**
SIC: 3369 Aerospace castings, nonferrous: except aluminum

(G-4763)
AEROSPACE INTERNATIONAL LLC
Also Called: Aerospace Solutions Intl
12329 Se 238th Pl (98031-3734)
P.O. Box 5464 (98064-5464)
PHONE..................................206 334-7426
Ajith Titus,
Saramma Titus,
EMP: 2
SALES (est): 243.3K **Privately Held**
SIC: 3728 7389 Aircraft parts & equipment;

(G-4764)
AEROSPACE MLTXIS MACHINING INC
Also Called: Aerospace Manufacturing
7020 Oberto Dr (98032-7014)
PHONE..................................253 856-1068
John Glowezyk, *Owner*
EMP: 15
SQ FT: 30,000
SALES (est): 2.1MM **Privately Held**
SIC: 3569 Sifting & screening machines

(G-4765)
AFL IG LLC (DH)
Also Called: AFL Hyperscale
8039 S 192nd St Ste 100 (98032-5027)
PHONE..................................425 291-4200
Paul Robinson, *President*
Pth Ventures LLC,
EMP: 28
SALES (est): 27MM **Privately Held**
SIC: 3679 Harness assemblies for electronic use: wire or cable
HQ: America Fujikura Ltd
170 Ridgeview Cir
Duncan SC 29334
800 235-3423

(G-4766)
AIRGAS USA LLC
8008 S 222nd St (98032-1943)
PHONE..................................253 872-7000
Joe Reynolds, *Manager*
EMP: 30
SQ FT: 21,798
SALES (corp-wide): 125.9MM **Privately Held**
WEB: www.airliquide.com
SIC: 5169 2813 2097 Compressed gas; industrial gases; manufactured ice
HQ: Airgas Usa, Llc
259 N Radnor Chester Rd # 100
Radnor PA 19087
610 687-5253

Kent - King County

(G-4767)
ALADDIN MANUFACTURING CORP
23210 71st Pl S Ste 101 (98032-3914)
PHONE...................................253 395-3277
Mark Schroeder, *Manager*
EMP: 30
SALES (corp-wide): 9.9B **Publicly Held**
SIC: **2273** 5023 Carpets, textile fiber; home furnishings
HQ: Aladdin Manufacturing Corporation
160 S Industrial Blvd
Calhoun GA 30701
706 629-7721

(G-4768)
ALASKAN COPPER COMPANIES INC (HQ)
Also Called: Alaskan Copper & Brass Co
27402 72nd Ave S (98032-7366)
P.O. Box 3546, Seattle (98124-3546)
PHONE...................................206 623-5800
William M Rosen, *Ch of Bd*
Kermit Rosen Jr, *President*
Rob Rosen, *General Mgr*
Donald Rosen, *Vice Pres*
Douglas C Rosen, *Vice Pres*
▲ EMP: 350 EST: 1913
SQ FT: 300,000
SALES (est): 131.5MM **Privately Held**
WEB: www.alascop.com
SIC: **3498** 3443 Fabricated pipe & fittings; fabricated plate work (boiler shop); heat exchangers, condensers & components; industrial vessels, tanks & containers

(G-4769)
ALASKAN COPPER COMPANIES INC
Also Called: Alaskon Copper & Brass Company
27402 72nd Ave S (98032-7366)
PHONE...................................206 623-5800
EMP: 26 **Privately Held**
SIC: **3498** 3443 Fabricated pipe & fittings; fabricated plate work (boiler shop)
HQ: Alaskan Copper Companies, Inc.
27402 72nd Ave S
Kent WA 98032
206 623-5800

(G-4770)
ALCO INVESTMENT COMPANY (PA)
Also Called: Alaskan Copper Works
27402 72nd Ave S (98032-7366)
P.O. Box 3546, Seattle (98124-3546)
PHONE...................................206 623-5800
William Rosen, *Ch of Bd*
Kermit Rosen Jr, *President*
Donald Rosen, *Vice Pres*
Douglas Rosen, *Vice Pres*
Alan J Rosen, *Treasurer*
▲ EMP: 200
SQ FT: 300,000
SALES: 154MM **Privately Held**
SIC: **3498** 3443 Fabricated pipe & fittings; fabricated plate work (boiler shop)

(G-4771)
ALL NATURAL BOTANICALS INC (PA)
835 Central Ave N (98032-2015)
PHONE...................................253 939-2600
Andrew Rizzo, *President*
▲ EMP: 6
SALES (est): 1.3MM **Privately Held**
WEB: www.allnatbo.com
SIC: **2844** Face creams or lotions

(G-4772)
ALLEGIS CORPORATION
19821 87th Ave S (98031-1262)
PHONE...................................425 242-6680
John Johnson, *Principal*
Ray Foslid, *Manager*
EMP: 4
SALES (corp-wide): 36.1MM **Privately Held**
SIC: **3599** Amusement park equipment
PA: Allegis Corporation
8001 Central Ave Ne
Minneapolis MN 55432
763 780-4333

(G-4773)
ALMET INCORPORATED
959 5th Ave S (98032-5825)
P.O. Box 399 (98035-0399)
PHONE...................................253 852-1690
Robert K Lillie, *President*
Virginia Lillie, *Admin Sec*
EMP: 19
SQ FT: 17,500
SALES (est): 3.1MM **Privately Held**
SIC: **3398** Metal heat treating

(G-4774)
ALWAYS PURE WATER TREATMENT SY
14405 Se 266th St (98042-8112)
PHONE...................................253 631-0294
Steve Gestahl, *Owner*
EMP: 3
SALES (est): 163.2K **Privately Held**
SIC: **3589** Water treatment equipment, industrial

(G-4775)
AMARAL MUSIC
10619 Se 261st Pl E201 (98030-6750)
PHONE...................................206 853-9847
Cesar Amaral, *President*
EMP: 2
SALES (est): 93K **Privately Held**
SIC: **2741** Miscellaneous publishing

(G-4776)
AMERICAN AIR FILTER CO INC
22338 68th Ave S (98032-1948)
PHONE...................................253 395-8860
Brett Arlt, *Branch Mgr*
EMP: 3 **Privately Held**
SIC: **3564** Filters, air: furnaces, air conditioning equipment, etc.
HQ: American Air Filter Company, Inc.
9920 Corporate Campus Dr
Louisville KY 40223
502 637-0011

(G-4777)
AMERICAN MFG & ENGIN
1513 Central Ave S Ste B (98032-7435)
PHONE...................................253 520-5865
Dean Spears, *Owner*
EMP: 12
SQ FT: 5,000
SALES (est): 700K **Privately Held**
WEB: www.amecnc.com
SIC: **3999** Tape measures

(G-4778)
AMERICAN PRIDE CORPORATION
21838 84th Ave S (98032-1959)
P.O. Box 1226 (98035-1226)
PHONE...................................253 850-1212
Sikander Sekhon, *President*
EMP: 12
SALES (est): 2.1MM **Privately Held**
SIC: **3713** Dump truck bodies

(G-4779)
AMERICAN PRINTING AND PUBG
5844 S 194th St (98032-2126)
PHONE...................................253 395-3349
Alan Dewitt, *President*
Paula Stringer, *Sales Staff*
Judi Dewitt, *Admin Sec*
EMP: 6
SQ FT: 3,000
SALES (est): 905K **Privately Held**
WEB: www.ampub.net
SIC: **2731** 2893 2759 2752 Books: publishing only; printing ink; commercial printing; commercial printing, lithographic; book printing

(G-4780)
AMICA INC
19625 62nd Ave S Ste C110 (98032-1109)
PHONE...................................253 872-9600
Sadia Kerim, *Principal*
▲ EMP: 6
SALES (est): 679.8K **Privately Held**
SIC: **2752** Commercial printing, offset

(G-4781)
AMMERAAL BELTECH INC
Also Called: Ammeraal Belting
6841 S 220th St Ste D (98032-1921)
PHONE...................................510 352-3770
EMP: 10 **Privately Held**
SIC: **3496** Mfg Misc Fabricated Wire Products
HQ: Ammeraal Beltech, Inc.
7501 Saint Louis Ave
Skokie IL 60076
847 673-6720

(G-4782)
ANDERSON & VREELAND INC
20206 87th Ave S (98031-1280)
PHONE...................................419 636-5002
Michael Gayda, *Manager*
EMP: 4
SALES (corp-wide): 73.7MM **Privately Held**
WEB: www.andersonvreeland.com
SIC: **5084** 3555 Printing trades machinery, equipment & supplies; printing plates
PA: Anderson & Vreeland, Inc.
8 Evans St
Fairfield NJ 07004
973 227-2270

(G-4783)
ANDERSON ELECTRIC CONTROLS
Also Called: Anderson Controls
8639 S 212th St (98031-1910)
PHONE...................................206 575-4444
Gary Anderson, *President*
Dean Shull, *Vice Pres*
EMP: 20
SQ FT: 12,000
SALES (est): 6.3MM **Privately Held**
WEB: www.aecontrols.com
SIC: **3625** 3613 Relays & industrial controls; switchgear & switchboard apparatus

(G-4784)
ANGEL SCREEN PRINTING
8459 S 208th St (98031-1208)
PHONE...................................253 872-3040
EMP: 2
SALES (est): 162.5K **Privately Held**
SIC: **2759** Commercial Printing

(G-4785)
ANNE & MOLLYS INC
Also Called: Mostly Muffins
22330 68th Ave S (98032-1948)
PHONE...................................253 872-8390
Molly Bolanos, *President*
Ann Marie Flaherty, *Vice Pres*
EMP: 98
SQ FT: 18,000
SALES (est): 11.9MM **Privately Held**
WEB: www.mostlymuffins.com
SIC: **2051** Bread, cake & related products

(G-4786)
APPLICATOR TECHNOLOGY INC
24854 116th Ave Se (98030-6546)
P.O. Box 5297 (98064-5297)
PHONE...................................253 859-9501
Ernest W Cushing, *President*
Carol Cushing, *Vice Pres*
Kim Cushing, *Treasurer*
EMP: 2 EST: 1974
SALES (est): 250K **Privately Held**
WEB: www.rapidrinser.com
SIC: **3639** 5087 Floor waxers & polishers, electric: household; cleaning & maintenance equipment & supplies

(G-4787)
ARBON EQUIPMENT CORPORATION
Also Called: Arbon Eqpment Crprtn/Rite-Hite
22718 58th Pl S (98032-4666)
PHONE...................................253 395-7099
Russ Berkman, *Manager*
Brian Hevly, *Manager*
EMP: 15
SALES (corp-wide): 779.4MM **Privately Held**
WEB: www.arbonequipment.com
SIC: **3537** 3449 5084 5085 Loading docks: portable, adjustable & hydraulic; miscellaneous metalwork; materials handling machinery; industrial supplies
HQ: Arbon Equipment Corporation
8900 N Arbon Dr
Milwaukee WI 53223
414 355-2600

(G-4788)
ARBON EQUIPMENT CORPORATION
22613 68th Ave S (98032-1981)
PHONE...................................253 796-0004
Ken Wildman, *Manager*
EMP: 20
SALES (corp-wide): 779.4MM **Privately Held**
WEB: www.arbonequipment.com
SIC: **3537** 3449 Loading docks: portable, adjustable & hydraulic; miscellaneous metalwork
HQ: Arbon Equipment Corporation
8900 N Arbon Dr
Milwaukee WI 53223
414 355-2600

(G-4789)
ARCTIC CIRCLE ENTERPRISES LLC
Also Called: Polar Graphics
19801 87th Ave S Bldg D (98031-1262)
PHONE...................................253 872-8525
Shuji Murasaki, *Vice Pres*
EMP: 100
SALES (corp-wide): 28.7MM **Privately Held**
WEB: www.aceak.com
SIC: **2331** 2321 2353 2396 T-shirts & tops, women's: made from purchased materials; men's & boys' furnishings; hats, caps & millinery; automotive & apparel trimmings; pleating & stitching; screen printing
HQ: Arctic Circle Enterprises Llc
3812 Spenard Rd
Anchorage AK 99517
907 272-4366

(G-4790)
ARGUS DEFENSE LLC
23402 59th Pl S (98032-6404)
PHONE...................................206 707-6373
Kenneth C P Mesler, *Administration*
EMP: 4
SALES (est): 277.7K **Privately Held**
SIC: **3812** Defense systems & equipment

(G-4791)
ARMSTRONG NW
18414 80th Ct S (98032-2516)
PHONE...................................425 251-0353
Chris Chandler, *Principal*
Heath Deweber, *Manager*
EMP: 3 EST: 2009
SALES (est): 235.5K **Privately Held**
SIC: **3272** Floor slabs & tiles, precast concrete

(G-4792)
ARROWDISC LLC
23008 68th Ave S (98032-8417)
P.O. Box 98852, Seattle (98198-0852)
PHONE...................................253 518-3900
Carl Haglund,
▲ EMP: 70
SQ FT: 65,000
SALES: 9.4MM **Privately Held**
WEB: www.arrowdisc.com
SIC: **3652** Compact laser discs, prerecorded

(G-4793)
ASSA ABLOY AB
Also Called: Assa Abloy Northwest Svc Ctr
20112 72nd Ave S (98032-2338)
PHONE...................................253 872-8174
EMP: 7
SALES (corp-wide): 9.3B **Privately Held**
SIC: **7692** Welding repair

GEOGRAPHIC SECTION Kent - King County (G-4823)

PA: Assa Abloy Ab
Klarabergsviadukten 90
Stockholm 111 6
850 648-500

(G-4794)
ASSOCIATED AIRCRAFT & MAR SVCS
17627 Se 292nd Pl (98042-5709)
P.O. Box 8052 (98042-0048)
PHONE.....................253 631-3082
Charles Gundlach, Owner
Janet Gundlach, Co-Owner
EMP: 2
SALES: 120K **Privately Held**
SIC: 3724 Aircraft engines & engine parts

(G-4795)
ASTRONICS CSTM CTRL CNCPTS INC
Also Called: Astronics CCC
6020 S 190th St (98032-2130)
PHONE.....................206 575-0933
Bill Weaver, CEO
EMP: 100
SQ FT: 85,000
SALES (est): 20.3MM
SALES (corp-wide): 803.2MM **Publicly Held**
WEB: www.custom-control.com
SIC: 3577 8711 3663 3728 Computer peripheral equipment; engineering services; radio & TV communications equipment; aircraft parts & equipment; computer software development & applications
PA: Astronics Corporation
130 Commerce Way
East Aurora NY 14052
716 805-1599

(G-4796)
ATKORE INTERNATIONAL GROUP INC
7819 S 206th St (98032-1354)
PHONE.....................253 478-3199
EMP: 5 **Publicly Held**
SIC: 3441 Fabricated structural metal
PA: Atkore International Group Inc.
16100 Lathrop Ave
Harvey IL 60426

(G-4797)
ATLAS COPCO COMPRESSORS LLC
22649 83rd Ave S (98032-1990)
PHONE.....................425 251-1040
Mike Conwell, Branch Mgr
EMP: 19
SALES (corp-wide): 10.5B **Privately Held**
SIC: 3563 Air & gas compressors
HQ: Atlas Copco Compressors Llc
300 Technology
Rock Hill SC 29730
866 472-1015

(G-4798)
AURORA HARDWOOD SEATTLE LLC
18630 72nd Ave S (98032-1039)
PHONE.....................253 236-8985
Jingke Lin,
Gang Wang,
EMP: 6
SALES (est): 623K **Privately Held**
SIC: 2426 Flooring, hardwood

(G-4799)
AUTO SPRING SERVICE INC
Also Called: Emerald Brake and Muffler
26460 Pacific Hwy S (98032-6930)
PHONE.....................253 839-3780
Jerry Prokop, President
Joanne Prokop, Vice Pres
EMP: 2
SQ FT: 2,000
SALES (est): 160K **Privately Held**
SIC: 7692 7539 Welding repair; machine shop, automotive

(G-4800)
AUTOMATIC PRODUCTS CO INC
5858 S 194th St (98032-2126)
PHONE.....................253 872-0203
Joel M Gregory, President
Angela Gregory, Admin Sec
▲ **EMP:** 70
SQ FT: 44,000
SALES (est): 15.6MM **Privately Held**
WEB: www.automatic-products.com
SIC: 3451 Screw machine products

(G-4801)
AUTOMATIC PRODUCTS MFG CO LLC
25329 74th Ave S (98032-6037)
PHONE.....................253 395-7173
Joel Gregory, Mng Member
EMP: 8
SQ FT: 20,000
SALES (est): 1.5MM **Privately Held**
WEB: www.cycleslider.com
SIC: 5084 3599 3441 Machinists' precision measuring tools; machine shop, jobbing & repair; fabricated structural metal

(G-4802)
AVERY DENNISON CORPORATION
Avery Dennison Materials Group
21604 86th Ave S (98031-1909)
PHONE.....................253 872-6993
Janet Sweeney, Manager
EMP: 10
SALES (corp-wide): 7.1B **Publicly Held**
WEB: www.avery.com
SIC: 2672 Coated & laminated paper
PA: Avery Dennison Corporation
207 N Goode Ave
Glendale CA 91203
626 304-2000

(G-4803)
AVIA MARINE COMPANY
1309 Central Ave S Ste E (98032-7407)
P.O. Box 925 (98035-0925)
PHONE.....................253 373-1644
John Gehlman, President
Lonny Power, Vice Pres
Vickie Power, Admin Sec
▼ **EMP:** 3 **EST:** 1956
SQ FT: 4,000
SALES (est): 460.9K **Privately Held**
SIC: 3429 Aircraft hardware; marine hardware

(G-4804)
AWARD DENTAL II LLC (PA)
22430 134th Pl Se (98042-3296)
PHONE.....................253 520-0100
Yongjae Kim, Principal
EMP: 4
SALES (est): 626.5K **Privately Held**
SIC: 3843 Enamels, dentists'

(G-4805)
B & B ELECTRIC MOTORS INC
22114 68th Ave S (98032-1912)
PHONE.....................206 763-3538
Bill Masri, President
Barbara A Masri, Corp Secy
EMP: 4
SQ FT: 5,100
SALES: 1.1MM **Privately Held**
WEB: www.bbelectricmotors.com
SIC: 7694 Electric motor repair

(G-4806)
BALL
1220 2nd Ave N (98032-2946)
PHONE.....................253 854-9950
Bob Leifester, Principal
Regan Rosettie, Human Res Mgr
EMP: 5
SALES (est): 350.5K **Privately Held**
SIC: 3411 Metal cans

(G-4807)
BANCHEROS GLASS AND ETCHING
22653 83rd Ave S (98032-1990)
PHONE.....................253 854-4877
Ric Banchero, President
Delight Banchero, Treasurer
▲ **EMP:** 2
SQ FT: 3,600
SALES (est): 315.1K **Privately Held**
WEB: www.bancheros.com
SIC: 1793 3231 Glass & glazing work; ornamental glass: cut, engraved or otherwise decorated

(G-4808)
BARCO INC
Also Called: Barco Wiper Supply Co
7979 S 180th St (98032-1051)
PHONE.....................425 251-3530
Fred Barber, President
EMP: 10
SALES (est): 850K **Privately Held**
SIC: 2211 2259 Towels, dishcloths & washcloths: cotton; towels, washcloths & dishcloths: knit

(G-4809)
BARRERAS PRECISION FABG LLC
8483 S 228th St (98031-2430)
PHONE.....................253 850-6227
EMP: 3 **EST:** 2007
SALES: 500K **Privately Held**
SIC: 3441 Structural Metal Fabrication

(G-4810)
BATECH LLC
Also Called: Machine & Fabrication Inds
7032 S 196th St Ste A-110 (98032-2185)
PHONE.....................253 395-3630
Stijn Vandegaer, General Mgr
Tyler Husby, Prdtn Mgr
Karen Epley, Accounts Mgr
EMP: 35
SQ FT: 12,000
SALES: 7MM **Privately Held**
SIC: 3599 Machine shop, jobbing & repair

(G-4811)
BEES IN BURBS
18911 Se 236th Pl (98042-4849)
PHONE.....................425 432-0546
Norman Holcomb, Principal
EMP: 2 **EST:** 2011
SALES (est): 184.9K **Privately Held**
SIC: 2499 Beekeeping supplies, wood

(G-4812)
BELL MACHINE INC
14510 171st Ave Se (98032)
PHONE.....................425 254-1173
Fred Bell, President
▲ **EMP:** 7 **EST:** 1968
SQ FT: 6,000
SALES (est): 1MM **Privately Held**
SIC: 3599 Machine shop, jobbing & repair

(G-4813)
BENSON SMOKE
21006 108th Ave Se (98031-2199)
PHONE.....................253 859-6120
Eden ME, Manager
EMP: 2 **EST:** 2010
SALES (est): 198.6K **Privately Held**
SIC: 2131 Smoking tobacco

(G-4814)
BLACK BOX CORPORATION
6918 S 220th St (98032-1906)
PHONE.....................800 733-0274
Pat Kaufman, Manager
EMP: 5 **Privately Held**
SIC: 3577 Computer peripheral equipment
HQ: Black Box Corporation
1000 Park Dr
Lawrence PA 15055
724 746-5500

(G-4815)
BLUE ORIGIN LLC (PA)
21218 76th Ave S (98032-2442)
PHONE.....................253 872-0411
Erika Wagner, Business Mgr
Todd Hartmann, Project Mgr
David Robb, Site Mgr
Robert Peterson, Production
Jim Reed, Production
▲ **EMP:** 100
SQ FT: 53,000
SALES (est): 42.8MM **Privately Held**
WEB: www.blueorigin.com
SIC: 3761 Space vehicles, complete

(G-4816)
BODY BUILDERS GYM EQUIPMENT
12003 Se 248th St (98030-5009)
PHONE.....................253 631-8274
Christain Mosieur, President

EMP: 2
SALES: 60K **Privately Held**
SIC: 3949 5941 7699 Gymnasium equipment; gymnasium equipment; recreational sporting equipment repair services

(G-4817)
BOEING COMMERCIAL AIRPLANE
8118 S 208th St (98032-1328)
PHONE.....................206 662-9615
Gary Bond, Engineer
EMP: 2
SALES (est): 153.5K **Privately Held**
SIC: 3721 Airplanes, fixed or rotary wing

(G-4818)
BOEING COMPANY
18-01 Bldg 2nd (98032)
PHONE.....................312 544-2000
Joel Funfar, Vice Pres
Michael Giuntoli, Project Mgr
Gene Huh, Project Mgr
Christian Davies, Facilities Mgr
Joann Wells, QC Mgr
EMP: 25
SALES (corp-wide): 101.1B **Publicly Held**
SIC: 3721 Aircraft
PA: The Boeing Company
100 N Riverside Plz
Chicago IL 60606
312 544-2000

(G-4819)
BOEING COMPANY
20403 68th Ave S (98032-2316)
P.O. Box 3707, Seattle (98124-2207)
PHONE.....................253 872-5545
Jim Hornsby, Principal
Richard Badgley, Research
Fernando Griego, Engineer
Rajan Joshi, Engineer
Brett Lewis, Engineer
EMP: 996
SALES (corp-wide): 101.1B **Publicly Held**
SIC: 3721 Aircraft
PA: The Boeing Company
100 N Riverside Plz
Chicago IL 60606
312 544-2000

(G-4820)
BOX MAKER INC
6230 S 190th St (98032-3102)
PHONE.....................425 291-1291
Dwight Sawtell, Branch Mgr
EMP: 8
SALES (corp-wide): 172.1MM **Privately Held**
SIC: 2653 Boxes, corrugated: made from purchased materials
PA: The Box Maker Inc
6412 S 190th St
Kent WA 98032
425 251-0655

(G-4821)
BRADLEY SAXTON
6718 S 216th St (98032-1388)
PHONE.....................800 643-3512
Bradley Saxton, Principal
EMP: 6
SALES (est): 24K **Privately Held**
SIC: 2531 School furniture

(G-4822)
BREEDT PROD TOOLING DESIGN LLC
811 1st Ave S (98032-6139)
PHONE.....................253 859-1100
Ruan Breedt, COO
Andries Breedt,
EMP: 15
SALES (est): 3.4MM **Privately Held**
SIC: 3544 Special dies, tools, jigs & fixtures

(G-4823)
BRIDPORT-AIR CARRIER INC (DH)
Also Called: Amsafe Bridport
1819 Central Ave S # 109 (98032-7501)
PHONE.....................253 872-7205

Kent - King County (G-4824)

Keith McConnell, *President*
▲ **EMP:** 21
SQ FT: 18,000
SALES (est): 5.5MM
SALES (corp-wide): 225.3B **Publicly Held**
WEB: www.bridportinflatables.com
SIC: 2394 2296 2399 2298 Canvas & related products; tire cord & fabrics; seat belts, automobile & aircraft; cordage & twine; strapping webs

(G-4824)
BROUSSARDS CREOLE FOODS INC
23915 135th Pl Se (98042-3279)
P.O. Box 6312 (98064-6312)
PHONE 253 638-2098
Stephanie Durham, *President*
Ike Durham, *Vice Pres*
EMP: 3
SALES (est): 460.6K **Privately Held**
WEB: www.broussardscreolefoods.com
SIC: 5149 2099 Spices & seasonings; seasonings & spices

(G-4825)
BTS EXCHANGE LLC
Also Called: Independent Dealer Accessories
1213 4th Ave N (98032-2939)
PHONE 253 859-5450
Kevin Madin, *General Mgr*
Tamara Shoemaker,
EMP: 6
SQ FT: 15,000
SALES (est): 865.5K **Privately Held**
WEB: www.idatruck.com
SIC: 5531 5084 3713 Truck equipment & parts; lift trucks & parts; utility truck bodies

(G-4826)
BUFFALO INDUSTRIES LLC (PA)
7979 S 180th St (98032-1051)
PHONE 206 682-9900
Rodger Koefod, *Opers Mgr*
Mark Benezra,
William Lavaris,
▼ **EMP:** 27
SALES (est): 9.6MM **Privately Held**
WEB: www.buffaloexportllc.com
SIC: 5093 5198 2299 Scrap & waste materials; paints; fibers, textile: recovery from textile mill waste & rags

(G-4827)
BUYKEN METAL PRODUCTS INC
1216 4th Ave N (98032-2940)
PHONE 253 852-0634
Mark De Laurenti, *President*
Julie E D De Laurenti, *Corp Secy*
EMP: 48
SALES (est): 8.7MM **Privately Held**
WEB: www.buyken.com
SIC: 3469 3312 3441 3444 Metal stampings; tool & die steel & alloys; special dies, tools, jigs & fixtures; sheet metalwork; architectural metalwork; fabricated structural metal

(G-4828)
C & S WELDING INC
Also Called: AAA Welding Co
22610 85th Pl S (98031-2469)
PHONE 253 520-2095
Rally Snider, *President*
Luann Sneider, *Vice Pres*
Jeff Hall, *Treasurer*
EMP: 7
SQ FT: 5,000
SALES: 800K **Privately Held**
SIC: 3441 7692 Building components, structural steel; welding repair

(G-4829)
C J & M TRANSPORT INC
27430 72nd Ave S (98032-7366)
PHONE 206 510-8296
Dave Sherwood, *General Mgr*
David Smetzler, *Manager*
EMP: 11
SALES (est): 780K **Privately Held**
SIC: 3441 Railroad car racks, for transporting vehicles: steel

(G-4830)
C M F INDUSTRIES INC
20614 84th Ave S (98032-1224)
PHONE 425 282-5065
Bruce Maupin, *President*
▲ **EMP:** 4
SALES (est): 551.2K **Privately Held**
WEB: www.cmfind.com
SIC: 3999 Manufacturing industries

(G-4831)
C&J INDUSTRIES INC
Also Called: Buyken Metal Products
1216 4th Ave N (98032-2940)
PHONE 253 852-0634
Craig Hanela, *President*
EMP: 30
SALES (est): 1MM **Privately Held**
SIC: 2295 Metallizing of fabrics

(G-4832)
CACHANILLA DESIGN
21110 84th Ave S Ste 202 (98032-1200)
PHONE 425 207-6396
Perdomo Arnoldo, *Principal*
EMP: 2
SALES (est): 129.9K **Privately Held**
SIC: 5699 2395 T-shirts, custom printed; embroidery products, except schiffli machine

(G-4833)
CADENA PRINTING
27120 121st Pl Se (98030-8808)
PHONE 253 951-7545
EMP: 2
SALES (est): 83.9K **Privately Held**
SIC: 2752 Commercial printing, lithographic

(G-4834)
CAESARSTONE USA INC
Also Called: Caesar Stone
7832 S 198th St (98032-1127)
PHONE 425 251-8668
Mark Wallace, *Principal*
EMP: 12
SALES (corp-wide): 24.5MM **Privately Held**
WEB: www.caesarstoneus.com
SIC: 1499 Quartz crystal (pure) mining
PA: Caesarstone Usa, Inc.
9275 Corbin Ave Ste 100
Northridge CA 91324
818 779-0999

(G-4835)
CAMS-USA INC
30245 148th Ave Se (98042-9368)
P.O. Box 7869, Covington (98042-0047)
PHONE 253 639-3890
Yelena Pavlenko, *President*
▼ **EMP:** 10
SQ FT: 10,000
SALES (est): 963.1K **Privately Held**
SIC: 5999 3086 3271 3281 Foam & foam products; plastics foam products; ashlar, cast stone; interior & ornamental woodwork & trim

(G-4836)
CARLISLE INC
Also Called: Carlisle Interconnect Tech
7911 S 188th St Ste 100 (98032-1099)
PHONE 425 251-0700
John Berlin, *President*
Joseph Lipscomb, *Principal*
Brent Whisenant, *Principal*
Bill Eliot, *Engineer*
Jonathan OH, *Engineer*
EMP: 750
SQ FT: 61,000
SALES (est): 188.2MM
SALES (corp-wide): 4.4B **Publicly Held**
WEB: www.carlisle.com
SIC: 3643 5065 5063 Current-carrying wiring devices; electronic parts & equipment; wire & cable
HQ: Carlyle Holdings, Inc.
7911 S 188th St Ste 100
Kent WA 98032

(G-4837)
CARLISLE INTERCONNECT TECH INC
24023 104th Ave Se (98030-4975)
PHONE 425 656-5235
EMP: 3
SALES (corp-wide): 4.4B **Publicly Held**
SIC: 3679 3357 Harness assemblies for electronic use: wire or cable; nonferrous wiredrawing & insulating
HQ: Carlisle Interconnect Technologies, Inc.
100 Tensolite Dr
Saint Augustine FL 32092

(G-4838)
CARLISLE INTERCONNECT TECH INC
7911 S 188th St Ste 100 (98032-1099)
PHONE 425 291-3991
Erwin Widjaja, *Production*
Brett Clutter, *Engineer*
Daniel Lagueux, *Engineer*
Thuan Nguyen, *Engineer*
John Berlin, *Branch Mgr*
EMP: 360
SALES (corp-wide): 4.4B **Publicly Held**
SIC: 3679 3357 Harness assemblies for electronic use: wire or cable; nonferrous wiredrawing & insulating
HQ: Carlisle Interconnect Technologies, Inc.
100 Tensolite Dr
Saint Augustine FL 32092

(G-4839)
CARLYLE HOLDINGS INC (HQ)
7911 S 188th St Ste 100 (98032-1099)
PHONE 425 251-0700
David Roberts, *Ch of Bd*
John Berlin, *President*
Carol A O'Mack, *President*
Diane M Johansson, *Corp Secy*
Kevin Zdimal, *Treasurer*
EMP: 173
SQ FT: 62,000
SALES (est): 188.2MM
SALES (corp-wide): 4.4B **Publicly Held**
SIC: 3643 5065 5063 Current-carrying wiring devices; electronic parts & equipment; wire & cable
PA: Carlisle Companies Incorporated
16430 N Scottsdale Rd # 400
Scottsdale AZ 85254
480 781-5000

(G-4840)
CASCADE CABINETRY LLC
19411 66th Ave S (98032-1173)
PHONE 253 395-6670
Phil Birk, *Mng Member*
EMP: 4
SALES (est): 504.4K **Privately Held**
SIC: 2434 Wood kitchen cabinets

(G-4841)
CASCADE GASKET & MFG CO INC
8825 S 228th St (98031-2499)
PHONE 253 854-1800
Lee Ellen Terry, *President*
Michael Moran, *General Mgr*
Carol Terry, *Vice Pres*
EMP: 164
SQ FT: 20,000
SALES (est): 41MM **Privately Held**
WEB: www.cascadegasket.com
SIC: 3069 3053 Molded rubber products; gaskets, all materials

(G-4842)
CASCADE METALLURGICAL INC
21213 76th Ave S (98032-2443)
P.O. Box 848 (98035-0848)
PHONE 253 838-0477
William Blackburn, *President*
David Blackburn, *President*
Daniel Ederer, *Vice Pres*
EMP: 25
SQ FT: 11,000
SALES (est): 5.8MM **Privately Held**
WEB: www.cascademet.com
SIC: 3398 Metal heat treating

(G-4843)
CECO DOOR PRODUCTS
7230 S 227th Pl (98032-1907)
PHONE 253 872-8174
Glen Spiker, *Principal*
EMP: 3 **EST:** 2005
SALES (est): 337.8K **Privately Held**
SIC: 3442 Screen & storm doors & windows

(G-4844)
CEDAR MOUNTAIN SPA COVERS (PA)
Also Called: Cedar Mountain Spa Cover Mfg
22717 72nd Ave S Ste 105 (98032-2403)
PHONE 253 872-8993
Doug Potter, *Owner*
EMP: 16
SQ FT: 1,200
SALES (est): 1.5MM **Privately Held**
SIC: 2394 Liners & covers, fabric: made from purchased materials

(G-4845)
CEDARTONE SPECIALTIES INC
26843 51st Pl S (98032-6211)
PHONE 253 852-6628
Edward R Probyn, *Ch of Bd*
Gary Couling, *President*
Karen Gillmore-Beal, *Corp Secy*
Jack Menzies, *Vice Pres*
EMP: 200
SALES: 9.7MM
SALES (corp-wide): 76.2MM **Privately Held**
SIC: 2499 5031 Fencing, wood; lumber, plywood & millwork
PA: E.R. Probyn Ltd
601 Sixth St Unit 350
New Westminster BC V3L 3
604 526-8545

(G-4846)
CENTRAL ADMXTURE PHRM SVCS INC
Also Called: C A P S
7044 S 220th St (98032-1910)
PHONE 253 395-8700
Michael Wright, *Branch Mgr*
EMP: 20
SALES (corp-wide): 2.6MM **Privately Held**
WEB: www.capspharmacy.com
SIC: 2834 5122 Pharmaceutical preparations; pharmaceuticals
HQ: Central Admixture Pharmacy Services, Inc.
2525 Mcgaw Ave
Irvine CA 92614

(G-4847)
CENTRIX INC
1022 W Valley Hwy (98032-3913)
PHONE 253 872-4773
Travis McClure, *CEO*
EMP: 54
SQ FT: 57,000
SALES: 10MM **Privately Held**
SIC: 3965 Fasteners

(G-4848)
CENVEO INC
6520 S 190th St Ste 100 (98032-2156)
PHONE 503 224-7777
Nancy Vaughn, *Controller*
Jerry Young, *Accounts Exec*
Dan Morris, *CTO*
James Miller, *Technology*
Jeffrey Boyer, *Programmer Anys*
EMP: 4
SALES (est): 404.6K **Privately Held**
SIC: 2329 Men's & boys' clothing

(G-4849)
CENVEO WORLDWIDE LIMITED
6520 S 190th St Ste 100 (98032-2156)
PHONE 206 576-4300
Steve Markf, *Branch Mgr*
EMP: 500
SALES (corp-wide): 1.9B **Privately Held**
WEB: www.mail-well.com
SIC: 5112 2677 Envelopes; envelopes

GEOGRAPHIC SECTION **Kent – King County (G-4877)**

HQ: Cenveo Worldwide Limited
200 First Stamford Pl # 2
Stamford CT 06902
203 595-3000

(G-4850)
CERTAINTEED GYPSUM INC
Also Called: Bpb Gypsum
8655 S 187th St (98031-1217)
PHONE..................................425 291-9099
Dan Cusick, *Branch Mgr*
EMP: 94
SALES (corp-wide): 215.9MM **Privately Held**
WEB: www.bpb-na.com
SIC: 3275 Gypsum products
HQ: Certainteed Gypsum, Inc.
20 Moores Rd
Malvern PA 19355

(G-4851)
CHINOOK ELEVATOR SOLUTIONS
824 3rd Ave N (98032-3017)
PHONE..................................425 213-0784
Sean Benning, *Principal*
EMP: 3 **EST:** 2014
SALES (est): 317.7K **Privately Held**
SIC: 1796 3534 Elevator installation & conversion; elevators & equipment

(G-4852)
CHRISTIE LITES SEATTLE LLC
7815 S 208th St Ste 101 (98032-1303)
PHONE..................................206 223-7200
Huntly Christie, *President*
EMP: 10
SALES (est): 369.4K
SALES (corp-wide): 20.2MM **Privately Held**
SIC: 3648 Lighting equipment
PA: Christie Lites Enterprises Usa, Llc
6990 Lake Ellenor Dr
Orlando FL 32809
407 856-0016

(G-4853)
CLEAN-SHOT ARCHERY INC
6849 S 220th St (98032-1921)
P.O. Box 88901, Seattle (98138-2901)
PHONE..................................425 242-5970
Larry Bay, *Principal*
Marc Durand, *Vice Pres*
▲ **EMP:** 4
SALES (est): 422.1K **Privately Held**
SIC: 3949 Archery equipment, general

(G-4854)
CNC DIVERSIFIED MANUFACTURING
311 Railroad Ave S (98032-5936)
PHONE..................................253 852-6869
John Glowczyk, *President*
EMP: 2
SALES (est): 107.4K **Privately Held**
SIC: 3569 General industrial machinery

(G-4855)
COATES HEATER COMPANY INC
840 5th Ave S (98032-5866)
P.O. Box 1750 (98035-1750)
PHONE..................................253 872-7256
Gary A Heinen, *President*
EMP: 9
SALES (est): 1.4MM **Privately Held**
WEB: www.coatesheaters.com
SIC: 3569 Heaters, swimming pool: electric

(G-4856)
COATES INNOVATIONS LLC
Also Called: Support The Foot
14607 Se 267th St (98042-8109)
P.O. Box 7982 (98042-0048)
PHONE..................................907 617-5801
Lori Coates,
Christopher Coates,
EMP: 3
SALES (est): 283.4K **Privately Held**
SIC: 3842 7389 Surgical appliances & supplies;

(G-4857)
COLORGRAPHICS
6520 S 190th St Ste 100 (98032-2156)
PHONE..................................206 576-4300
EMP: 2 **EST:** 2012
SALES (est): 160K **Privately Held**
SIC: 2752 Lithographic Commercial Printing

(G-4858)
COMPASS AEROSPACE NORTHWEST, I
821 3rd Ave S (98032-6129)
PHONE..................................253 852-9700
▲ **EMP:** 55
SALES (est): 12.3MM **Privately Held**
WEB: www.lamsco.com
SIC: 3728 Aircraft parts & equipment

(G-4859)
COMPUTER SYSTEMS SALES & SVCS
Also Called: Csssi
12946 Se Kent Kangley Rd # 300 (98030-7940)
P.O. Box 95, Romance AR (72136-0095)
PHONE..................................206 979-1731
Marty Curtis, *President*
▲ **EMP:** 2
SALES (est): 311.3K **Privately Held**
SIC: 3564 Air purification equipment

(G-4860)
COMPUTER TECHNOLOGY LINK CORP
Also Called: Ctl
22409 72nd Ave S (98032-1905)
PHONE..................................253 872-3608
Fax: 253 872-4177
EMP: 2
SALES (corp-wide): 13.1MM **Privately Held**
SIC: 3577 5045 Mfg & Whol Computer Peripheral Equipment
PA: Computer Technology Link Corp.
9700 Sw Harvest Ct # 100
Beaverton OR 97005
503 646-3733

(G-4861)
CONAGRA BRANDS INC
Also Called: Bakery Chef Seattle
6320 S 190th St (98032-1178)
PHONE..................................425 251-0761
EMP: 230
SALES (corp-wide): 7.9B **Publicly Held**
SIC: 2053 Frozen bakery products, except bread
PA: Conagra Brands, Inc.
222 Merchandise Mart Plz
Chicago IL 60654
312 549-5000

(G-4862)
CONCUT INC (HQ)
Also Called: Concut Diamond Products
6815 S 220th St (98032-1921)
PHONE..................................253 872-3507
Jim Mayer, *President*
James D Mayer, *Vice Pres*
Diana Reamy, *Admin Sec*
▲ **EMP:** 38
SQ FT: 9,000
SALES (est): 6MM
SALES (corp-wide): 13.9MM **Privately Held**
WEB: www.concutusa.com
SIC: 3545 3531 3425 Diamond cutting tools for turning, boring, burnishing, etc.; construction machinery; saw blades & handsaws
PA: Dixie Diamond Manufacturing, Inc.
205 Buxton Ct Nw
Lilburn GA 30047
770 921-2464

(G-4863)
CONESTOGA WOOD SPC CORP
Sunriver Industries
6122 S 228th St (98032-1849)
PHONE..................................253 437-1320
Robert Bertch, *President*
EMP: 2
SALES (corp-wide): 213MM **Privately Held**
SIC: 2491 2541 2431 1751 Wood products, creosoted; wood partitions & fixtures; millwork; cabinet & finish carpentry; manufactured hardware (general)

PA: Conestoga Wood Specialties Corporation
245 Reading Rd
East Earl PA 17519
717 445-6701

(G-4864)
CONTINENTAL MILLS INC
7851 S 192nd St (98032-1198)
P.O. Box 88176, Seattle (98138-2176)
PHONE..................................206 816-7799
Chris Rodebaugh, *Branch Mgr*
Judy Else, *Manager*
EMP: 150
SALES (corp-wide): 237.6MM **Privately Held**
WEB: www.crustease.com
SIC: 2045 Flours & flour mixes, from purchased flour
PA: Continental Mills, Inc.
18100 Andover Park W
Tukwila WA 98188
206 816-7000

(G-4865)
CONTRACT SEW & REPAIR INC
Also Called: Adult Care Products
23001 54th Ave S (98032-6443)
PHONE..................................253 395-7910
Sheila Brush, *President*
EMP: 16
SALES (est): 750K **Privately Held**
WEB: www.csr123.com
SIC: 7389 5136 5137 2395 Sewing contractor; men's & boys' clothing; women's & children's clothing; embroidery & art needlework

(G-4866)
COWLITZ RIVER SOFTWARE INC
1851 Central Pl S Ste 118 (98030-7507)
PHONE..................................253 856-3111
Lucy Mann, *President*
EMP: 6
SALES (est): 530K **Privately Held**
WEB: www.cowlitz.com
SIC: 7372 Prepackaged software

(G-4867)
CP FILMS CUSTOM PRINTED FILMS
26910 140th Ave Se (98042-8053)
PHONE..................................253 261-9404
EMP: 2
SALES (est): 217.2K **Privately Held**
SIC: 2671 Mfg Packaging Paper/Film

(G-4868)
CUSTOM HYDRAULIC & MACHINE INC
Also Called: Custom Machine
22911 86th Ave S (98031-2493)
P.O. Box 630, Somerset PA (15501-0630)
PHONE..................................253 854-4666
Robert Kirst, *President*
EMP: 13
SQ FT: 17,000
SALES (est): 3.3MM **Privately Held**
WEB: www.customhydraulic.com
SIC: 3599 3593 3492 3052 Machine shop, jobbing & repair; fluid power cylinders & actuators; fluid power valves & hose fittings; rubber & plastics hose & beltings

(G-4869)
DABS M&A LLC
Also Called: Dabs Manufacturing & Assembly
8622 S 228th St (98031-2449)
PHONE..................................253 872-2200
Georganna Clifford, *Trustee*
Ella Darlene Russell, *Trustee*
Melanie Russell, *Trustee*
Andrew Russell, *Manager*
EMP: 21
SALES (est): 941.1K **Privately Held**
SIC: 3728 Aircraft body & wing assemblies & parts

(G-4870)
DABS MANUFACTURING & ASSEMBLY
8622 S 228th St (98031-2449)
PHONE..................................253 872-2200

Craig Pruss, *President*
EMP: 17
SQ FT: 8,000
SALES (est): 887.5K **Privately Held**
SIC: 3599 3812 Amusement park equipment; search & navigation equipment; acceleration indicators & systems components, aerospace

(G-4871)
DAVIS WIRE CORPORATION
19411 80th Ave S (98032-1134)
PHONE..................................253 872-8910
Dan Berkstresser, *Branch Mgr*
EMP: 10 **Privately Held**
WEB: www.daviswire.com
SIC: 3315 3496 Wire, ferrous/iron; miscellaneous fabricated wire products
HQ: Davis Wire Corporation
5555 Irwindale Ave
Irwindale CA 91706
626 969-7651

(G-4872)
DEAN POWELL & MAGDA VELARDE
25848 33rd Ave S (98032-5643)
PHONE..................................253 535-4195
Dean Powell, *Owner*
EMP: 2
SALES (est): 115.1K **Privately Held**
SIC: 2434 Wood kitchen cabinets

(G-4873)
DIGITAL CONTROL INCORPORATED (PA)
19625 62nd Ave S Ste B103 (98032-1107)
PHONE..................................425 251-0701
John Mercer, *Ch of Bd*
Peter Hambling, *President*
Tammie Carlyle-Chinn, *Treasurer*
Thomas J Hall, *Admin Sec*
▲ **EMP:** 65
SQ FT: 12,000
SALES (est): 11.4MM **Privately Held**
WEB: www.digital-control.com
SIC: 3545 3812 Boring machine attachments (machine tool accessories); search & navigation equipment

(G-4874)
DITCO INC
106 E Titus St (98032-5912)
PHONE..................................253 854-1002
James M Bitondo, *General Mgr*
Tom Greive, *Engineer*
EMP: 15
SQ FT: 3,000
SALES (est): 2.1MM **Privately Held**
WEB: www.ditco.net
SIC: 3699 3594 Electrical equipment & supplies; fluid power pumps & motors

(G-4875)
DIVERSIFIED SYSTEMS GROUP INC
26601 79th Ave S (98032-7319)
PHONE..................................425 947-1500
Bob Sambrook, *Owner*
EMP: 4 **EST:** 2016
SALES (est): 260.7K **Privately Held**
SIC: 3572 3695 Disk drives, computer; computer software tape & disks: blank, rigid & floppy

(G-4876)
DOMENICS PRINTING INC
Also Called: Digital Print Services
1819 Central Ave S Ste 80 (98032-7508)
PHONE..................................425 251-4925
Domenic Tassielli, *President*
Kathy Tassielli, *Vice Pres*
▲ **EMP:** 8
SQ FT: 7,300
SALES (est): 987.9K **Privately Held**
SIC: 2752 Commercial printing, offset

(G-4877)
DONGALEN ENTERPRISES INC
Also Called: Interstate Plastics
22435 68th Ave S (98032-2444)
PHONE..................................253 395-4885
David Mosbach, *Manager*
EMP: 7

Kent - King County (G-4878)

SALES (corp-wide): 142.2MM **Privately Held**
SIC: 5162 3089 Plastics products; plastic processing
PA: Dongalen Enterprises, Inc.
330 Commerce Cir
Sacramento CA 95815
916 422-3110

(G-4878)
DRIVERS LICENSE EXAMINING
25410 74th Ave S (98032-6011)
PHONE 253 872-2782
Deborah Morrison, *Principal*
EMP: 2
SALES (est): 106.5K **Privately Held**
SIC: 3469 Automobile license tags, stamped metal

(G-4879)
DUO WEAR INC
7857 S 180th St (98032-1050)
PHONE 425 251-0760
Tashi Sherpa, *President*
Tseten Sherpa, *Admin Sec*
▲ EMP: 6
SALES (est): 1.1MM **Privately Held**
WEB: www.duowear.com
SIC: 2329 2339 Men's & boys' sportswear & athletic clothing; women's & misses' outerwear

(G-4880)
DUT PROTECTIVE COATINGS I
1215 2nd Ave N (98032-2945)
PHONE 253 520-3374
Don Devaney, *President*
EMP: 2
SALES (est): 124.4K **Privately Held**
SIC: 3479 Painting, coating & hot dipping

(G-4881)
EAGLE BEV & ACCESSORY PDTS LLC
Also Called: Calson Industries
19220 64th Ave S (98032-1152)
PHONE 253 867-6134
Jamaal Dequier, *Warehouse Mgr*
Aisha Kabani, *Mng Member*
Almas Kabani,
Sadru Kabani,
▲ EMP: 80
SALES (est): 25.3MM **Privately Held**
WEB: www.calsonindustries.com
SIC: 2087 2656 Syrups, drink; straws, drinking: made from purchased material

(G-4882)
EAST HILL OPTOMETRY
Also Called: Lum, Arthur B Od
11120 Se Kent Kangley Rd (98030-7708)
PHONE 253 859-0942
Arthur Lum, *Owner*
EMP: 3
SQ FT: 2,316
SALES (est): 260.4K **Privately Held**
SIC: 8042 3851 5995 Specialized optometrists; ophthalmic goods; opticians

(G-4883)
EASY FOLD FIXTURES
19219 W Valley Hwy M110 (98032-2133)
PHONE 425 209-0167
Chris Dukelow, *President*
Toby Turlay, *Director*
EMP: 10
SALES (est): 1MM **Privately Held**
SIC: 2653 Corrugated boxes, partitions, display items, sheets & pad

(G-4884)
EDGEBANDING SERVICES INC
6876 S 220th St (98032-1963)
PHONE 866 395-7002
Jay Byson, *Branch Mgr*
EMP: 10
SALES (corp-wide): 44.8MM **Privately Held**
SIC: 2541 Counter & sink tops
PA: Edgebanding Services, Inc.
828 W Cienega Ave
San Dimas CA 91773
909 599-2336

(G-4885)
EE PRINTING LLC
8258 S 192nd St (98032-1195)
PHONE 425 656-1250
Wesley Nguyen, *Sales Mgr*
Thao Nguyen,
EMP: 2
SALES: 350K **Privately Held**
SIC: 7331 2752 Direct mail advertising services; commercial printing, offset

(G-4886)
EFCO CORP
1004 3rd Ave S (98032-6101)
PHONE 253 852-3800
Paul Jennings, *Manager*
EMP: 12
SALES (corp-wide): 256.4MM **Privately Held**
SIC: 5051 7353 3443 3444 Steel; heavy construction equipment rental; fabricated plate work (boiler shop); concrete forms, sheet metal
HQ: Efco Corp
1800 Ne Broadway Ave
Des Moines IA 50313
515 266-1141

(G-4887)
ELECTRICAL SERVICES & SEC INC
2408 S 272nd St (98032-6944)
PHONE 206 276-6629
Thomas Burrell, *President*
Anna Burrell, *Vice Pres*
EMP: 2
SALES: 250K **Privately Held**
SIC: 7539 7382 3669 Electrical services; security systems services; emergency alarms

(G-4888)
ELECTROFINISHING INC
22630 88th Ave S Ste A (98031-2432)
PHONE 253 850-0540
Ned Raymond, *President*
EMP: 8
SALES (est): 1MM **Privately Held**
SIC: 3471 Electroplating of metals or formed products

(G-4889)
ELITE GROUP MANAGEMENT CORP
Also Called: Elite Group Ballistics
14200 Se 272nd St F203 (98042-8050)
PHONE 253 631-1175
Roy Chenaur, *President*
Ian Coleman, *Vice Pres*
EMP: 2 EST: 2012
SALES (est): 160K **Privately Held**
SIC: 3842 Bulletproof vests

(G-4890)
ELKAY PLASTICS CO INC
6425 S 224th St (98032-2456)
PHONE 425 251-1488
Anne Bayne, *Sales Staff*
Jake Kalagian, *Branch Mgr*
Mike Balacuit, *Manager*
Araceli Gonzalez, *Manager*
EMP: 15
SALES (corp-wide): 98.2MM **Privately Held**
WEB: www.elkayplastics.com
SIC: 2673 Plastic bags: made from purchased materials
PA: Elkay Plastics Co., Inc.
6000 Sheila St
Commerce CA 90040
323 722-7073

(G-4891)
EMBROIDERY PLUS LLC
15022 Se 282nd Pl (98042-4587)
PHONE 253 630-2616
Merlin Blehm, *Mng Member*
Ashley Blehm,
Bonnie Blehm,
EMP: 8
SQ FT: 800
SALES (est): 443.8K **Privately Held**
SIC: 5136 5137 2395 Men's & boys' outerwear; women's & children's sportswear & swimsuits; embroidery & art needlework

(G-4892)
EMERALD CITY GRAPHICS INC
23328 66th Ave S (98032-1827)
PHONE 253 520-2600
Mark Steiner, *Principal*
Joe Davis, *Chairman*
Jeff Pierce, *Vice Pres*
Neil Stonestreet, *Prdtn Mgr*
Ron Anderson, *Purch Agent*
▲ EMP: 97 EST: 1981
SQ FT: 42,000
SALES (est): 23.4MM
SALES (corp-wide): 6.8B **Publicly Held**
WEB: www.emeraldcg.com
SIC: 2752 Commercial printing, offset
HQ: Consolidated Graphics, Inc.
5858 Westheimer Rd # 200
Houston TX 77057
713 787-0977

(G-4893)
ENLIGHTING STRUCK DESIGN LLC
146 Washington Ave N (98032-4400)
P.O. Box 6240 (98064-6240)
PHONE 206 229-9438
Eli Struck, *Mng Member*
EMP: 3
SALES: 450K **Privately Held**
SIC: 2759 7389 3479 Promotional printing; apparel designers, commercial; etching & engraving

(G-4894)
ENVISION MANUFACTURING & SERVI
25326 39th Pl S (98032-5605)
PHONE 253 941-1739
Michael Johnson, *Principal*
EMP: 4
SALES (est): 320K **Privately Held**
SIC: 3082 Unsupported plastics profile shapes

(G-4895)
ENVISION MANUFACTURING CO
1104 4th Ave N (98032-2942)
PHONE 206 963-7352
EMP: 2
SALES (est): 90.5K **Privately Held**
SIC: 3999 Manufacturing industries

(G-4896)
ERIKS ◆
7748 S 200th St (98032-1104)
PHONE 253 395-4770
EMP: 3 EST: 2018
SALES (est): 118.7K **Privately Held**
SIC: 3594 Pumps, hydraulic, aircraft

(G-4897)
ESTERLINE TECHNOLOGIES CORP
8127 S 216th St (98032-1996)
PHONE 253 796-4527
EMP: 3
SALES (corp-wide): 3.8B **Publicly Held**
SIC: 3728 Aircraft assemblies, subassemblies & parts; panel assembly (hydromatic propeller test stands), aircraft
HQ: Esterline Technologies Corp
500 108th Ave Ne Ste 1500
Bellevue WA 98004
425 453-9400

(G-4898)
ETZ INDUSTRIES LLC
24103 138th Ave Se (98042-5187)
PHONE 253 630-2915
Erich Zerr, *Principal*
EMP: 2
SALES (est): 90.3K **Privately Held**
SIC: 3999 Manufacturing industries

(G-4899)
EVERGREEN ENGRAVERS
1819 Central Ave S Ste 24 (98032-7515)
PHONE 253 852-6766
Jeff Hilton, *President*
Ling Hilton, *Admin Sec*
EMP: 4
SQ FT: 8,000
SALES: 700K **Privately Held**
SIC: 3555 Engraving machinery & equipment, except plates

(G-4900)
EXOTIC METALS FORMING CO LLC (PA)
Also Called: Emfco
5411 S 226th St (98032-4842)
PHONE 253 220-5900
Mark Simon, *General Mgr*
Katherine Binder, *Principal*
Bill Binder, *Vice Pres*
Doug Gines, *Vice Pres*
Christian Dewey, *Buyer*
▲ EMP: 277
SQ FT: 275,000
SALES (est): 76.3MM **Privately Held**
WEB: www.exoticmetals.com
SIC: 3728 3724 Aircraft assemblies, subassemblies & parts; aircraft engines & engine parts

(G-4901)
EXOTIC METALS FORMING CO LLC
6020 S 226th St (98032-4814)
PHONE 253 395-3710
EMP: 6
SALES (corp-wide): 76.3MM **Privately Held**
SIC: 3728 Aircraft parts & equipment
PA: Exotic Metals Forming Company Llc
5411 S 226th St
Kent WA 98032
253 220-5900

(G-4902)
EZ LINE CABINETS
26433 104th Ave Se D302 (98030-7664)
PHONE 206 775-2226
Halil Zenuni, *Principal*
EMP: 2
SALES (est): 89.6K **Privately Held**
SIC: 2434 Wood kitchen cabinets

(G-4903)
FAMILY ENDURANCE CORPORATION
Also Called: Gavco
8805 S 190th St (98031-1270)
PHONE 253 872-3900
Colin Lester Martin, *President*
Freida L Voss, *Treasurer*
EMP: 15
SQ FT: 15,000
SALES (est): 2.4MM **Privately Held**
SIC: 2521 Wood office furniture

(G-4904)
FASTSIGNS
7825 S 180th St (98032-1050)
PHONE 206 575-2110
Sam Spiller, *Principal*
EMP: 5
SALES (est): 634.2K **Privately Held**
SIC: 3993 Signs & advertising specialties

(G-4905)
FASTSIGNS OF AUBURN
9912 S 244th St (98030-5037)
PHONE 360 480-1097
EMP: 2
SALES (est): 72.6K **Privately Held**
SIC: 3993 Signs & advertising specialties

(G-4906)
FEDEX OFFICE & PRINT SVCS INC
5901 S 226th St (98032-4861)
PHONE 253 872-5539
EMP: 10
SALES (corp-wide): 69.6B **Publicly Held**
SIC: 7389 5099 2752 Packaging & labeling services; signs, except electric; commercial printing, lithographic
HQ: Fedex Office And Print Services, Inc.
7900 Legacy Dr
Plano TX 75024
800 463-3339

(G-4907)
FIRESIDE HEARTH & HOME INC (PA)
21402 84th Ave S (98032-1961)
PHONE 425 251-9447
Williark Nirk, *President*
Keri Rodriguez, *Vice Pres*

GEOGRAPHIC SECTION

Kent - King County (G-4936)

EMP: 18
SQ FT: 31,000
SALES (est): 2.1MM **Privately Held**
WEB: www.firesidehearthandhome.com
SIC: 3272 5999 Fireplace & chimney material: concrete; air purification equipment

(G-4908)
FIRST IMPRESSIONS CO INC
25818 117th Pl Se (98030-7831)
PHONE..................................206 372-0361
Bruce L Johnson, *Principal*
EMP: 2 EST: 2012
SALES (est): 200.8K **Privately Held**
SIC: 3541 Lathes

(G-4909)
FLOW INTERNATIONAL CORPORATION (DH)
23500 64th Ave S (98032-2618)
PHONE..................................253 850-3500
David Savage, *CEO*
D Ick Leblanc, *President*
Dick Leblanc, *President*
Richard Leblanc, *President*
Jerry L Calhoun, *Chairman*
◆ EMP: 350 EST: 1970
SALES (est): 264.9MM
SALES (corp-wide): 162.7MM **Privately Held**
WEB: www.fresherunderpressure.com
SIC: 3561 Pumps & pumping equipment; pumps, domestic: water or sump
HQ: Shape Technologies Group, Inc.
23500 64th Ave S
Kent WA 98032
253 246-3200

(G-4910)
FLOW INTERNATIONAL CORPORATION
22165 68th Ave S (98032-1937)
PHONE..................................812 590-4922
EMP: 3
SALES (corp-wide): 162.7MM **Privately Held**
SIC: 3561 Pumps, domestic: water or sump
HQ: Flow International Corporation
23500 64th Ave S
Kent WA 98032
253 850-3500

(G-4911)
FLOW INTERNATIONAL CORPORATION
Also Called: Flow Robotic Systems
23430 64th Ave S (98032-2305)
P.O. Box 3737, Allentown PA (18106-0737)
PHONE..................................253 850-3501
Mike Arena, *General Mgr*
EMP: 300
SALES (corp-wide): 162.7MM **Privately Held**
WEB: www.fresherunderpressure.com
SIC: 3569 Robots, assembly line: industrial & commercial
HQ: Flow International Corporation
23500 64th Ave S
Kent WA 98032
253 850-3500

(G-4912)
FLOWERS BKG CO THOMASVILLE INC
7817 S 210th St (98032-2302)
PHONE..................................253 433-4455
EMP: 2
SALES (corp-wide): 3.9B **Publicly Held**
SIC: 2051 Bakery: wholesale or wholesale/retail combined
HQ: Flowers Baking Co. Of Thomasville, Inc.
1919 Flowers Cir
Thomasville GA 31757
229 226-9110

(G-4913)
FLUID MOTION LLC
Also Called: Ranger Tugs
25802 Pacific Hwy S (98032-5514)
PHONE..................................253 839-5213
Dolan David, *Purchasing*
Joe Blodgett, *Engineer*
Jerry Foote, *CFO*
John Livingston, *Mng Member*
▲ EMP: 24 EST: 1958
SQ FT: 15,000
SALES (est): 6.9MM **Privately Held**
WEB: www.solaraboats.com
SIC: 3732 Boats, fiberglass: building & repairing

(G-4914)
FLUX DRIVE INC
23412 68th Ave S (98032-1811)
PHONE..................................253 826-9002
Philip Corbin III, *President*
▲ EMP: 10
SALES (est): 1.6MM **Privately Held**
SIC: 3542 Magnetic forming machines

(G-4915)
FOLDCRAFT CO
Jh Carr
8311 S 200th St (98032-1113)
PHONE..................................253 437-1355
Michael Rychert, *Branch Mgr*
EMP: 35
SALES (corp-wide): 7.2MM **Privately Held**
SIC: 2599 Bar, restaurant & cafeteria furniture
PA: Foldcraft Co.
14400 Southcross Dr W
Burnsville MN 55306
507 789-5111

(G-4916)
FOREMOST PRINTING
21411 100th Ave Se (98031-2065)
PHONE..................................206 861-6576
EMP: 2
SALES (est): 101.5K **Privately Held**
SIC: 2752 Commercial printing, lithographic

(G-4917)
FORREST PAINT CO
1741 Central Ave S (98032-7415)
PHONE..................................253 854-6372
Steve Grimsby, *General Mgr*
Debbie Brooks, *Branch Mgr*
EMP: 10
SALES (est): 1MM
SALES (corp-wide): 57.5MM **Privately Held**
WEB: www.forrestpaint.com
SIC: 2851 Paints & allied products
PA: Forrest Paint Co.
1011 Mckinley St
Eugene OR 97402
541 868-1222

(G-4918)
FORTIS MANUFACTURING INC
6823 S 220th St (98032-1921)
PHONE..................................253 277-3211
Jin A A Hwang, *President*
John Hwang, *Chairman*
EMP: 2
SALES (est): 175.2K **Privately Held**
SIC: 3949 Shooting equipment & supplies, general

(G-4919)
FXI INC
Also Called: Foamex
19635 78th Ave S (98032-1118)
PHONE..................................253 872-0170
Mahmood Davani, *Manager*
EMP: 100 **Privately Held**
SIC: 3086 Insulation or cushioning material, foamed plastic
HQ: Fxi, Inc.
1400 N Providence Rd # 2000
Media PA 19063

(G-4920)
G&S TRADING INTERNATIONAL
11201 Se 272nd Pl (98030-9043)
PHONE..................................253 859-1097
▲ EMP: 2 EST: 2002
SALES (est): 110K **Privately Held**
SIC: 2273 Mfg Carpets/Rugs

(G-4921)
GAFFER GLASS USA LIMITED
19622 70th Ave S Ste 4 (98032-1162)
PHONE..................................253 395-3361
John Leggott, *Principal*
Lacey Dollahite, *Sales Staff*
▲ EMP: 3
SALES (est): 326K **Privately Held**
SIC: 5039 3211 Glass construction materials; flat glass

(G-4922)
GENERAL ELECTRIC COMPANY
6925 S 194th St (98032-3105)
PHONE..................................253 395-1798
Brick Kincade, *Manager*
EMP: 10
SALES (corp-wide): 121.6B **Publicly Held**
SIC: 3613 Switchgear & switchboard apparatus
PA: General Electric Company
41 Farnsworth St
Boston MA 02210
617 443-3000

(G-4923)
GLOBAL MARINE SPECIALTIES INC
12932 Se Kent Kangley Rd (98030-7940)
PHONE..................................206 414-0819
Arthur S Rose, *President*
EMP: 2
SALES (est): 145.4K **Privately Held**
SIC: 3732 Boat building & repairing

(G-4924)
GLOBAL SPORTSWEAR CORPORATION
19122 84th Ave S Ste A (98032-1207)
PHONE..................................253 813-9788
Wai Tai Cho, *Principal*
▲ EMP: 4
SALES (est): 287.5K **Privately Held**
SIC: 2329 Men's & boys' sportswear & athletic clothing

(G-4925)
GRAPHIC IMPRESSIONS INC
7908 S 228th St (98032-3911)
PHONE..................................253 872-0555
Craig Robinson, *President*
Lisa Closterman, *Controller*
EMP: 42
SQ FT: 24,000
SALES: 4MM **Privately Held**
WEB: www.graphicimpressionsinc.com
SIC: 3544 2675 2759 2796 Paper cutting dies; die-cut paper & board; embossing on paper; platemaking services; metal stampings

(G-4926)
GRATING PACIFIC LLC
19411 66th Ave S (98032-1173)
PHONE..................................253 872-7733
Ron Robertson,
EMP: 6
SALES (corp-wide): 21.1MM **Privately Held**
WEB: www.gratingpacific.com
SIC: 3446 5085 Gratings, open steel flooring; industrial supplies
HQ: Grating Pacific, Llc
2775 N Front St
Woodburn OR 97071
503 980-2060

(G-4927)
GRAVES SPRAY SUPPLY INC
1862 Ives Ave (98032-7502)
PHONE..................................253 854-2660
Jim Jumior, *President*
EMP: 9
SQ FT: 68,236
SALES (est): 1.4MM **Privately Held**
WEB: www.venusmagnum.com
SIC: 3089 Plastics products

(G-4928)
GREEN RIVER COLLEGE
417 Ramsay Way Ste 112 (98032-4502)
PHONE..................................253 856-9595
Mary Ragland, *Director*
EMP: 25
SALES (corp-wide): 4.8MM **Privately Held**
WEB: www.greenriver.ctc.edu
SIC: 8222 8742 3661 Community college; management consulting services; fiber optics communications equipment

PA: Green River College
12401 Se 320th St
Auburn WA 98092
253 833-9111

(G-4929)
GRIND ALL INC
22638 85th Pl S (98031-2469)
PHONE..................................253 854-6117
Charles P Williams, *President*
Janyce Williams, *Manager*
EMP: 7
SQ FT: 6,400
SALES (est): 125K **Privately Held**
SIC: 3599 Machine shop, jobbing & repair

(G-4930)
GROUND SOURCE ENERGY NW
10600 Se 212th St (98031-2047)
PHONE..................................253 852-5926
Mark Humphrey, *Principal*
EMP: 2
SALES (est): 145.6K **Privately Held**
SIC: 1382 Oil & gas exploration services

(G-4931)
GUIDES CHICE AP SPCIALISTS LLC
18930 Se 236th Pl (98042-4849)
P.O. Box 920, Maple Valley (98038-0920)
PHONE..................................206 931-3838
Mike Alquist,
Carolyn Alquist,
▲ EMP: 4 EST: 2007
SALES (est): 420.5K **Privately Held**
SIC: 2329 Men's & boys' sportswear & athletic clothing

(G-4932)
HAPPY DONUT
10214 Se 240th St Ste A (98031-5123)
PHONE..................................253 852-3286
Koung Thon, *Owner*
EMP: 3
SALES (est): 138.8K **Privately Held**
SIC: 5461 2051 Doughnuts; doughnuts, except frozen

(G-4933)
HARBISONWALKER INTL INC
20408 87th Ave S I (98031-1201)
PHONE..................................253 872-2552
Paul Morel, *Branch Mgr*
EMP: 22
SALES (corp-wide): 703.8MM **Privately Held**
WEB: www.hwr.com
SIC: 3255 Clay refractories
HQ: Harbisonwalker International, Inc.
1305 Cherrington Pkwy # 100
Moon Township PA 15108

(G-4934)
HARRIS MACHINE LLC
1819 Central Ave S Ste 12 (98032-7514)
PHONE..................................253 347-6230
Jason Harris,
EMP: 6
SALES (est): 346.4K **Privately Held**
SIC: 3545 Machine tool accessories

(G-4935)
HARVEYS SKIN DIVING SUPPLIES
Also Called: Skindiver Suits
2505 S 252nd St (98032-5405)
PHONE..................................206 824-1114
Larry L Grohs, *President*
Harvey L Grohs, *Chairman*
Wilma J Grohs, *Corp Secy*
▲ EMP: 50
SQ FT: 22,000
SALES (est): 6.4MM **Privately Held**
WEB: www.harveys-divesuits.com
SIC: 3069 2329 2339 Wet suits, rubber; ski & snow clothing: men's & boys'; ski jackets & pants: women's, misses' & juniors'

(G-4936)
HC LASERLIGN INC
10842 Se 208th St Ste 531 (98031-2091)
PHONE..................................253 852-2001
Glenn Larsen, *President*
Tom Ohtami, *Admin Sec*

Kent - King County (G-4937)

EMP: 2 EST: 1999
SALES (est): 254K Privately Held
SIC: 3826 Laser scientific & engineering instruments

(G-4937)
HEARTWARMER DESIGNS
12018 Se 219th Ct (98031-3902)
PHONE..........................253 630-7408
Terri Brown, Owner
EMP: 5
SALES: 12K Privately Held
SIC: 3999 Sewing kits, novelty

(G-4938)
HEATHER & COMPANY FOR IBS LLC
Also Called: Heather's Tummy Care
19203 78th Ave S (98032)
PHONE..........................206 264-8069
Heather Van Vorous,
William Van Vorous,
▲ EMP: 10
SQ FT: 25,000
SALES (est): 2.1MM Privately Held
SIC: 2833 Cinchona & derivatives

(G-4939)
HEIRET PUBLICATIONS
20845 102nd Ave Se (98031-2059)
PHONE..........................253 852-1254
EMP: 2
SALES (est): 110K Privately Held
SIC: 2741 Misc Publishing

(G-4940)
HEXAGON METROLOGY INC
19625 62nd Ave S (98032-1103)
PHONE..........................253 872-2443
Todd Meek, Principal
EMP: 7
SALES (corp-wide): 4.3B Privately Held
SIC: 3823 3545 Industrial instrmnts msrmnt display/control process variable; precision measuring tools
HQ: Hexagon Metrology, Inc.
250 Circuit Dr
North Kingstown RI 02852
401 886-2000

(G-4941)
HEXCEL CORPORATION
19819 84th Ave S (98032-1233)
P.O. Box 97004 (98064-9704)
PHONE..........................253 872-7500
Russ Thurman, General Mgr
Brian Fingarson, Opers Mgr
Christopher Hlebichuk, Opers Staff
Guy Edson, Purch Agent
Juergen Gietz, Engineer
EMP: 120
SALES (corp-wide): 2.1B Publicly Held
WEB: www.hexcel.com
SIC: 3728 Aircraft parts & equipment
PA: Hexcel Corporation
281 Tresser Blvd Ste 1503
Stamford CT 06901
203 969-0666

(G-4942)
HILLSHIRE BRANDS COMPANY
20230 70th Ave S (98032-2354)
PHONE..........................253 437-3700
Victoria Odden, Branch Mgr
EMP: 100
SALES (corp-wide): 40B Publicly Held
SIC: 2013 Sausages & other prepared meats
HQ: The Hillshire Brands Company
400 S Jefferson St Fl 1
Chicago IL 60607
312 614-6000

(G-4943)
HILLSHIRE BRANDS COMPANY
Also Called: A La Francaise Bakery
20360 70th Ave S (98032)
PHONE..........................253 395-3444
Peter Lee, Manager
EMP: 11
SALES (corp-wide): 40B Publicly Held
SIC: 2013 Sausages & other prepared meats

HQ: The Hillshire Brands Company
400 S Jefferson St Fl 1
Chicago IL 60607
312 614-6000

(G-4944)
HOGAN CONSTRUCTION INC
28621 183rd Ct Se (98042-5324)
PHONE..........................206 290-5553
Joseph Hogan, President
EMP: 2 EST: 2011
SALES: 100K Privately Held
SIC: 2431 Woodwork, interior & ornamental

(G-4945)
HY-SECURITY GATE INC
Also Called: Hysecurity
6705 S 209th St Ste 101 (98032-2327)
PHONE..........................253 867-3700
Brian Denault, President
▲ EMP: 45
SALES (est): 13.4MM Privately Held
WEB: www.hy-security.com
SIC: 3699 Door opening & closing devices, electrical

(G-4946)
HYDRO SYSTEMS USA INC
Also Called: Hydro Precision Aero
7028 S 204th St (98032-1321)
PHONE..........................253 876-2100
Jonathan Edwards, President
Matthias Bay, Buyer
Sonya Ernst, Buyer
Damon Frashure, Project Engr
Suzanne Haywood, CFO
◆ EMP: 158
SQ FT: 60,000
SALES: 41MM
SALES (corp-wide): 96.1K Privately Held
WEB: www.hydrousaco.com
SIC: 3728 Aircraft parts & equipment
PA: Hydro Holding Kg
Ahfeldstr. 10
Biberach
783 578-70

(G-4947)
HYTEK FINISHES CO
Also Called: Esterline
8127 S 216th St (98032-1996)
PHONE..........................253 872-7160
Curtis C Reusser, CEO
Alain Durand, President
Mary Rosen, President
Robert D George, Vice Pres
Tom Heine, Vice Pres
EMP: 200
SQ FT: 93,000
SALES (est): 37.9MM
SALES (corp-wide): 3.8B Publicly Held
WEB: www.hytekfinishes.com
SIC: 3471 Finishing, metals or formed products
HQ: Esterline Technologies Corp
500 108th Ave Ne Ste 1500
Bellevue WA 98004
425 453-9400

(G-4948)
IB WOOD INC
22414 72nd Ave S (98032-1904)
PHONE..........................253 395-8886
Doug Wood, President
Jim McCall, Project Mgr
EMP: 5
SQ FT: 8,000
SALES (est): 639.2K Privately Held
WEB: www.ibwood.com
SIC: 2541 5021 5712 Cabinets, lockers & shelving; store & office display cases & fixtures; household furniture; customized furniture & cabinets

(G-4949)
INDEPENDENT AERO SPACE SVCS
25051 128th Pl Se (98030-6520)
PHONE..........................702 237-9953
EMP: 2
SALES: 500K Privately Held
SIC: 3721 Mfg Aircraft

(G-4950)
INDUSTRIAL REPAIR SERVICE INC
7016 S 196th St (98032-2185)
PHONE..........................253 395-8852
Larry Sadler, President
EMP: 8
SQ FT: 5,000
SALES (est): 1.2MM Privately Held
SIC: 3599 Machine shop, jobbing & repair

(G-4951)
INDUSTRIAL SCREENPRINT INC
Also Called: Miller Studio
1505 Central Ave S (98032-7419)
PHONE..........................253 735-5111
Vincent S Miller, President
▲ EMP: 4
SALES: 600K Privately Held
SIC: 2759 7336 Screen printing; graphic arts & related design

(G-4952)
INGERSOLL-RAND COMPANY
20121 72nd Ave S (98032-2351)
PHONE..........................253 931-8600
John Scofield, Manager
EMP: 20 Privately Held
WEB: www.ingersoll-rand.com
SIC: 3563 Air & gas compressors
HQ: Ingersoll-Rand Company
800 Beaty St Ste B
Davidson NC 28036
704 655-4000

(G-4953)
INGERSOLL-RAND COMPANY
20017 72nd Ave S (98032-2300)
PHONE..........................253 398-3900
Dan Munko, Principal
Jose Maria Lopez Izquierdo, Human Resources
EMP: 120 Privately Held
WEB: www.ingersoll-rand.com
SIC: 3561 Pumps & pumping equipment
HQ: Ingersoll-Rand Company
800 Beaty St Ste B
Davidson NC 28036
704 655-4000

(G-4954)
INSTRUMENT SALES AND SVC INC
7051 S 234th St (98032-2965)
PHONE..........................253 796-5400
Patrick Mayo, Manager
EMP: 50
SQ FT: 4,500
SALES (corp-wide): 30.8MM Privately Held
WEB: www.ouriss.net
SIC: 5013 3714 7539 5731 Truck parts & accessories; motor vehicle parts & accessories; automotive sound system service & installation; sound equipment, automotive
HQ: Instrument Sales And Service, Inc.
17880 Ne Airport Way
Portland OR 97230

(G-4955)
INSTRUMENTATION NORTHWEST INC
Also Called: Inw
19026 72nd Ave S (98032-1005)
PHONE..........................425 822-4434
Gregg Gustafson, Ch of Bd
EMP: 24
SQ FT: 5,900
SALES (est): 58.5K Privately Held
WEB: www.inwusa.com
SIC: 3823 Industrial instrmnts msrmnt display/control process variable

(G-4956)
INTERLOCK INDUSTRIES INC
20213 84th Ave S (98032-1204)
PHONE..........................253 872-5750
Thomas Croffett, Manager
EMP: 2
SALES (corp-wide): 390.6MM Privately Held
WEB: www.metalsales.us.com
SIC: 3444 Roof deck, sheet metal

PA: Interlock Industries, Inc.
545 S 3rd St Ste 310
Louisville KY 40202
502 569-2007

(G-4957)
INTERNATIONAL PAPER COMPANY
1225 6th Ave N (98032-2933)
PHONE..........................253 372-1360
Sean Hatcher, CEO
EMP: 73
SALES (corp-wide): 23.3B Publicly Held
WEB: www.internationalpaper.com
SIC: 2621 Paper mills
PA: International Paper Company
6400 Poplar Ave
Memphis TN 38197
901 419-9000

(G-4958)
INTERPLASTIC CORPORATION
Also Called: Corezyn
22237 76th Ave S (98032-1924)
PHONE..........................253 872-8067
Paul Selle, Branch Mgr
EMP: 30
SALES (corp-wide): 271.4MM Privately Held
WEB: www.interplastic.com
SIC: 2821 Plastics materials & resins
PA: Interplastic Corporation
1225 Willow Lake Blvd
Saint Paul MN 55110
651 481-6860

(G-4959)
INTERSTATE INDUSTRIES INC
1217 4th Ave N Ste 103 (98032-2939)
PHONE..........................206 387-2364
Lorne Smith, President
EMP: 2
SALES (est): 289.6K Privately Held
SIC: 3999 Atomizers, toiletry

(G-4960)
INTERSTATE INDUSTRIES INC
8320 S 259th St (98030-7428)
PHONE..........................425 226-2135
Lorne Smith, President
EMP: 3
SALES (est): 160.4K Privately Held
SIC: 3999 Manufacturing industries

(G-4961)
ISC INC
Also Called: Isernio Sausage Company
8222 S 228th St (98032-2928)
PHONE..........................253 395-5465
Stephen Bates, President
Frank Isernio, President
George Paleologou, Chairman
Richard Hempler, Director
William Kalutycz, Admin Sec
EMP: 28
SQ FT: 15,000
SALES: 20MM Privately Held
WEB: www.isernio.com
SIC: 2013 5812 Sausages from purchased meat; eating places

(G-4962)
ISSAK SHAMSO
Also Called: Puget Sound Dumpster Services
25122 117th Ct Se (98030-6582)
PHONE..........................253 457-2964
Awale Farah, Owner
Shamso Issak, Branch Mgr
EMP: 2
SALES (est): 116.6K Privately Held
SIC: 3443 Dumpsters, garbage

(G-4963)
J & R COMMERCIAL INC
Also Called: Cams-USA
30245 148th Ave Se (98042-9368)
P.O. Box 7869, Covington (98042-0047)
PHONE..........................253 639-3890
Yelena Pavlenko, President
EMP: 6
SQ FT: 4,750
SALES (est): 511.5K Privately Held
WEB: www.jrcommercial.com
SIC: 3999 3086 3272 Stage hardware & equipment, except lighting; plastics foam products; ashlar, cast stone

▲ = Import ▼ = Export
◆ = Import/Export

GEOGRAPHIC SECTION
Kent - King County (G-4992)

(G-4964)
JANUARY COMPANY
5851 S 194th St (98032-2125)
PHONE.....................253 872-9919
Jim Ding, *CEO*
Gerald Sung, *Partner*
Randolf Sung, *Partner*
EMP: 40 **EST:** 1976
SQ FT: 35,000
SALES (est): 8.5MM **Privately Held**
SIC: 2013 2099 2038 Sausages from purchased meat; food preparations; frozen specialties
PA: Tall Tree Foods Holdings, Inc.
400 Hamilton Ave Ste 230
Palo Alto CA 94301

(G-4965)
JASPREET SINGH
11827 Se 266th Pl (98030-8602)
PHONE.....................253 239-3250
Jaspreet Singh, *Administration*
EMP: 2
SALES (est): 85.9K **Privately Held**
SIC: 3577 Computer peripheral equipment

(G-4966)
JC GLOBAL SUPPLY LLC
25223 132nd Pl Se (98042-6615)
PHONE.....................253 275-6093
Janice M Chau,
EMP: 3
SQ FT: 2,000
SALES (est): 210.4K **Privately Held**
SIC: 5112 4783 5943 3086 Stationery & office supplies; containerization of goods for shipping; office forms & supplies; packaging & shipping materials, foamed plastic; fiber shipping & mailing containers; computer software & accessories

(G-4967)
JC MANUFACTURING
23454 30th Ave S (98032-2825)
PHONE.....................206 870-3827
Jeff Cissel, *Principal*
EMP: 4
SALES (est): 227.3K **Privately Held**
SIC: 3599 Machine shop, jobbing & repair

(G-4968)
JLT PARTNERS INC (PA)
25811 74th Ave S (98032-6021)
PHONE.....................800 325-7513
Terry Morse, *President*
Larry Morse, *Vice Pres*
Jeff Morse, *Shareholder*
◆ **EMP:** 1
SALES (est): 1.3MM **Privately Held**
WEB: www.morseindustries.com
SIC: 3441 Fabricated structural metal

(G-4969)
JMTEK LLC
Also Called: Usbdrive
25426 74th Ave S (98032-6011)
PHONE.....................425 251-9400
Sorithya Eap, *Sales Associate*
Kyu Lee,
▲ **EMP:** 25
SALES (est): 4.8MM **Privately Held**
WEB: www.jmtek.com
SIC: 3572 Computer storage devices

(G-4970)
JOHNS MANVILLE CORPORATION
Also Called: N R G Barriers
21234 76th Ave S (98032-2442)
PHONE.....................800 654-3103
Michael Slee, *Manager*
EMP: 75
SALES (corp-wide): 225.3B **Publicly Held**
SIC: 3086 3296 2952 Insulation or cushioning material, foamed plastic; mineral wool; asphalt felts & coatings
HQ: Johns Manville Corporation
717 17th St Ste 800
Denver CO 80202
303 978-2000

(G-4971)
JOVIPAK CORPORATION
19625 62nd Ave S Ste C101 (98032-1112)
PHONE.....................206 575-1656
Jo-Ann Rovig, *President*
EMP: 14
SQ FT: 50,000
SALES (est): 1.6MM **Privately Held**
WEB: www.jovipak.com
SIC: 2211 Surgical fabrics, cotton

(G-4972)
K ROUNDS LLC
115 E Willis St (98032-5930)
PHONE.....................206 452-0466
David Lam, *Mng Member*
▲ **EMP:** 7 **EST:** 2012
SALES (est): 375K **Privately Held**
SIC: 2821 5091 Plastics materials & resins; sporting & recreation goods

(G-4973)
KDL ENTERPRISES INC
Also Called: Western Skylights
7818 S 194th St (98032-1163)
PHONE.....................253 395-3113
Don Hess, *CEO*
Jeff Bartlett, *General Mgr*
Dennis Hartup, *Vice Pres*
EMP: 25
SQ FT: 25,000
SALES (est): 4.2MM **Privately Held**
WEB: www.kdlenterprises.com
SIC: 3211 3444 Skylight glass; sheet metalwork

(G-4974)
KELLOGG COMPANY
21229 72nd Ave S (98032-1916)
PHONE.....................253 872-3826
Idona Kellogg, *Branch Mgr*
EMP: 29
SALES (corp-wide): 13.5B **Publicly Held**
WEB: www.kelloggs.com
SIC: 2043 Cereal breakfast foods
PA: Kellogg Company
1 Kellogg Sq
Battle Creek MI 49017
269 961-2000

(G-4975)
KENT CHAMBER OF COMMERCE INC
524 W Meeker St Ste 1 (98032-5766)
P.O. Box 128 (98035-0128)
PHONE.....................253 854-1770
Marcelle Pechler, *Director*
EMP: 9
SQ FT: 1,825
SALES: 359.4K **Privately Held**
SIC: 8611 2721 Chamber of Commerce; periodicals

(G-4976)
KILOMTERS TO MILES SPEEDO EXCH
21218 76th Ave S (98032-2442)
PHONE.....................253 872-3839
EMP: 2
SALES (est): 85.6K **Privately Held**
SIC: 3491 Industrial Valves, Nsk

(G-4977)
KINGS COMMAND FOODS LLC (DH)
7622 S 188th St (98032-1021)
PHONE.....................425 251-6788
Ryan Small, *VP Opers*
Mark Wallace, *Purch Mgr*
Tom Wigington, *Purchasing*
Angelina Boland, *QC Mgr*
Jerry Clark, *QC Mgr*
EMP: 120
SQ FT: 24,000
SALES (est): 72MM
SALES (corp-wide): 3B **Privately Held**
SIC: 2013 Sausages & other prepared meats
HQ: American Foods Group, Llc
500 S Washington St
Green Bay WI 54301
320 759-5900

(G-4978)
KIRK DIAL OF SEATTLE
112 Central Ave N (98032-4521)
PHONE.....................253 852-5125
Seung IL Lee, *Owner*
EMP: 6
SALES (est): 280K **Privately Held**
SIC: 7631 3873 Watch repair; watches, clocks, watchcases & parts

(G-4979)
KLUNE INDUSTRIES INC
21719 84th Ave S (98032-1969)
PHONE.....................253 872-7488
EMP: 183
SALES (corp-wide): 225.3B **Publicly Held**
SIC: 3728 Aircraft parts & equipment
HQ: Klune Industries, Inc.
7323 Coldwater Canyon Ave
North Hollywood CA 91605
818 503-8100

(G-4980)
KMT US HOLDING COMPANY INC (DH)
23500 64th Ave S (98032-2618)
PHONE.....................620 856-2151
Duane Johnson, *CEO*
Brett Lawrie, *Vice Pres*
▲ **EMP:** 1
SALES (est): 11.3MM
SALES (corp-wide): 162.7MM **Privately Held**
SIC: 3569 Baling machines, for scrap metal, paper or similar material
HQ: Shape Technologies Group, Inc.
23500 64th Ave S
Kent WA 98032
253 246-3200

(G-4981)
KNOLL TREE CARE & LOGGING
27029 167th Pl Se (98042)
PHONE.....................253 630-1520
EMP: 3 **EST:** 2000
SALES (est): 190K **Privately Held**
SIC: 2411 Logging

(G-4982)
KONECRANES INC
Also Called: Crane Pro Services
8735 S 212th St (98031-1921)
PHONE.....................253 872-9696
Mary Jo Landdeck, *Manager*
EMP: 10
SALES (corp-wide): 3.6B **Privately Held**
WEB: www.kciusa.com
SIC: 3536 Hoists, cranes & monorails
HQ: Konecranes, Inc.
4401 Gateway Blvd
Springfield OH 45502

(G-4983)
KRAFT FOODS
19032 62nd Ave S (98032-1128)
PHONE.....................253 395-4237
EMP: 2
SALES (est): 62.3K **Privately Held**
SIC: 2022 Processed cheese

(G-4984)
KRAFT HEINZ FOODS COMPANY
26401 79th Ave S (98032-7321)
PHONE.....................800 255-5750
Bruce Rowe, *Exec VP*
EMP: 200
SQ FT: 54,660
SALES (corp-wide): 26.2B **Publicly Held**
SIC: 2032 Canned specialties
HQ: Kraft Heinz Foods Company
1 Ppg Pl Fl 34
Pittsburgh PA 15222
412 456-5700

(G-4985)
KYLIE BS PASTRY CASE LLC
11124 Se 272nd Pl (98030-9037)
PHONE.....................206 935-6335
Kylie Bacungan, *Principal*
EMP: 4
SALES (est): 97.9K **Privately Held**
SIC: 2051 Bakery: wholesale or wholesale/retail combined

(G-4986)
L & P SCREEN PRINTING
3420 S 271st St (98032-7092)
PHONE.....................253 859-8787
Mike Haugsven, *Principal*
EMP: 2
SALES (est): 94.1K **Privately Held**
SIC: 2759 Screen printing

(G-4987)
LABEL MASTERS INC
22261 68th Ave S (98032-1914)
PHONE.....................425 869-2422
Kent F Osborne, *President*
David Iler, *Opers Mgr*
Walter Bantle, *Manager*
EMP: 6
SALES: 350K **Privately Held**
SIC: 2759 Labels & seals: printing

(G-4988)
LANKTREE LAND SURVEYING INC
Also Called: Lanktree Equipment and Supply
25510 74th Ave S (98032-6014)
PHONE.....................253 653-6423
Trevor Lanktree, *President*
Revor Lanktree, *President*
EMP: 14
SQ FT: 6,400
SALES (est): 643.5K **Privately Held**
SIC: 8713 2499 Surveying services; surveyors' stakes, wood

(G-4989)
LARSON-JUHL US LLC
18401 72nd Ave S (98032-1010)
PHONE.....................206 433-6002
Doyug Farnham, *Branch Mgr*
EMP: 43
SQ FT: 15,000
SALES (corp-wide): 225.3B **Publicly Held**
SIC: 2499 Picture frame molding, finished
HQ: Larson-Juhl Us Llc
3900 Steve Reynolds Blvd
Norcross GA 30093
770 279-5200

(G-4990)
LATIUM USA TRADING INC
Also Called: Metal Building Products
7041 S 234th St (98032-2965)
PHONE.....................253 850-4530
Matt Strickland, *General Mgr*
EMP: 6
SALES (corp-wide): 46.7MM **Privately Held**
SIC: 3448 Prefabricated metal buildings
PA: Latium Usa Trading Llc
5005 Veterans Mem Hwy
Holbrook NY 11741
631 563-4000

(G-4991)
LAUREL GRAPHICS FABRICATION CO
22417 76th Ave S (98032-2450)
PHONE.....................253 872-7617
Keith Finnelly, *President*
Ralph Ortiz, *Vice Pres*
EMP: 20
SQ FT: 18,000
SALES (est): 3.7MM **Privately Held**
WEB: www.laurelgraphics.com
SIC: 2759 Screen printing

(G-4992)
LEGEND DATA SYSTEMS INC
Also Called: Legend ID
18024 72nd Ave S (98032-1065)
P.O. Box 88787, Seattle (98138-2787)
PHONE.....................425 251-1670
Matt McDaniel, *President*
Brenda Wise, *Vice Pres*
EMP: 14
SQ FT: 4,000
SALES (est): 2.5MM **Privately Held**
WEB: www.legenddatasystems.com
SIC: 5999 2759 Business machines & equipment; commercial printing

Kent - King County (G-4993)

(G-4993)
LEWIS AND CLARK PUBLISHING
13203 Se 233rd St (98042-3239)
PHONE..................253 631-8712
Marie Campbell, *Owner*
Spence Campbell, *Co-Owner*
EMP: 2
SALES (est): 122.2K Privately Held
SIC: 2741 Miscellaneous publishing

(G-4994)
LEWIS-GOETZ AND COMPANY INC
Also Called: Valley Rubber & Gasket
7748 S 200th St (98032-1104)
PHONE..................206 623-5650
Matt Morris, *Branch Mgr*
EMP: 10 Privately Held
SIC: 5085 3053 3052 Hose, belting & packing; gaskets & seals; gaskets, packing & sealing devices; rubber & plastics hose & beltings
HQ: Eriks North America, Inc.
650 Washington Rd Ste 500
Pittsburgh PA 15228
800 937-9070

(G-4995)
LIFTEX
19632 70th Ave S Ste 1 (98032-2176)
PHONE..................253 395-4458
Sherry Evans, *Principal*
EMP: 3
SALES (est): 311.4K Privately Held
SIC: 3625 Crane & hoist controls, including metal mill

(G-4996)
LILIBETE LLC
23044 148th Ave Se Ste 10 (98042-3842)
PHONE..................206 407-6890
Lilibete Upjohn,
EMP: 2 EST: 2017
SALES (est): 91.5K Privately Held
SIC: 3613 5084 8733 8742 Control panels, electric; safety equipment; safety research, noncommercial; management consulting services; programmers, process type

(G-4997)
LITHO-CRAFT INC
Also Called: Ultrakote
7820 S 228th St (98032-2962)
PHONE..................253 872-9161
Todd Christian, *Manager*
EMP: 3
SALES (corp-wide): 8MM Privately Held
WEB: www.lcprint.com
SIC: 2752 2672 Commercial printing, offset; coated & laminated paper
PA: Litho-Craft, Inc.
21021 66th Ave W
Lynnwood WA
206 789-7151

(G-4998)
LJS PLANTS & CRAFTS
21622 105th Pl Se (98031-2582)
PHONE..................253 854-9407
Linda Johnson, *Owner*
EMP: 2
SALES (est): 126.9K Privately Held
SIC: 3944 5193 Craft & hobby kits & sets; flowers & florists' supplies

(G-4999)
M-K-D DISTRIBUTORS INC
Also Called: Dreyers Grand Ice Cream NW
18404 72nd Ave S (98032-1010)
PHONE..................425 251-0809
David Mutzel, *President*
Kenneth Mutzel, *Corp Secy*
EMP: 200
SALES (est): 23.1MM Privately Held
SIC: 5143 2024 Ice cream & ices; ice cream & frozen desserts

(G-5000)
MAGNUM VENUS PRODUCTS INC
Also Called: Magnum Venus Products
1862 Ives Ave (98032-7599)
PHONE..................253 854-2660
Bob Clay, *Manager*
EMP: 80
SALES (corp-wide): 34MM Privately Held
WEB: www.gsscs.org
SIC: 3563 Air & gas compressors
PA: Magnum Venus Products, Inc.
2030 Falling Waters Rd # 350
Knoxville TN 37922
865 686-5670

(G-5001)
MAIL WELL ENVELOPE
6520 S 190th St Ste 100 (98032-2156)
PHONE..................206 576-4300
Bjelland Clara, *Principal*
EMP: 2
SALES (est): 154.6K Privately Held
SIC: 2752 Commercial printing, lithographic

(G-5002)
MAN DIESEL NORTH AMERICA INC
Also Called: Man Diesel Interval
6608 S 211th St Ste 101 (98032-2329)
PHONE..................253 479-6800
EMP: 5
SALES (est): 687.1K Privately Held
SIC: 3531 3519 Marine related equipment; marine engines

(G-5003)
MANINIS LLC
22408 72nd Ave S (98032-1904)
PHONE..................206 686-4600
Jerome Goldberg,
Robby Bach,
EMP: 18
SALES: 2MM Privately Held
SIC: 2098 Macaroni & spaghetti

(G-5004)
MAPLEHURST BAKERIES LLC
Plush Pippin
21331 88th Pl S (98031-1922)
PHONE..................253 872-7300
Kris Vagata, *Branch Mgr*
EMP: 70
SALES (corp-wide): 36.8B Privately Held
SIC: 2051 Cakes, pies & pastries
HQ: Maplehurst Bakeries, Llc
50 Maplehurst Dr
Brownsburg IN 46112
317 858-9000

(G-5005)
MEMBANE SOLUTIONS CORP
20021 80th Ave S (98032-1209)
PHONE..................253 487-5134
EMP: 2 EST: 2017
SALES (est): 248.5K Privately Held
SIC: 3569 General industrial machinery

(G-5006)
MERCHANT INVESTMENTS INC
Also Called: Global Venture
7412 S 262nd St (98032-7300)
PHONE..................425 235-8675
Hakim Merchant, *President*
Brandi Bird, *Accountant*
Kent Jackson, *Executive*
Nargis Merchant, *Admin Sec*
▲ **EMP:** 46
SQ FT: 40,000
SALES (est): 15.8MM Privately Held
SIC: 2679 2759 Labels, paper: made from purchased material; labels & seals: printing

(G-5007)
METAL SALES MANUFACTURING CORP
20213 84th Ave S (98032-1204)
P.O. Box 1008 (98035-1008)
PHONE..................253 872-5750
Russ Dayton, *General Mgr*
EMP: 18
SALES (corp-wide): 390.6MM Privately Held
SIC: 5051 3444 2952 Metals service centers & offices; sheet metalwork; asphalt felts & coatings
HQ: Metal Sales Manufacturing Corporation
545 S 3rd St Ste 200
Louisville KY 40202
502 855-4300

(G-5008)
METALS USA BUILDING PDTS LP
7041 S 234th St D (98032-2965)
PHONE..................425 251-0589
Fax: 425 251-6856
EMP: 10
SALES (corp-wide): 9.7B Publicly Held
SIC: 3444 Mfg Aluminum Awnings & Handrails
HQ: Metals Usa Building Products Lp
955 Columbia St
Brea CA 92821
713 946-9000

(G-5009)
MEYER ENGINEERED MATERIALS LLC
Also Called: Grind-All
22638 85th Pl S (98031-2469)
PHONE..................253 854-6117
Darcy Meyer,
EMP: 7
SALES: 500K Privately Held
SIC: 3399 Primary metal products

(G-5010)
MICHELIN MOUNTING CENTER
20840 84th Ave S (98032-1222)
PHONE..................253 872-0868
Randy Marks, *Manager*
EMP: 7
SALES (est): 520K Privately Held
SIC: 3011 Airplane tires, pneumatic

(G-5011)
MIKRON INDUSTRIES INC
1034 6th Ave N (98032-2991)
PHONE..................253 854-8020
Wade Hall, *Production*
Andrea West, *Production*
Jeff Franson, *Engineer*
Amy Noble, *Human Res Mgr*
Cheryl Roettger, *Human Res Mgr*
EMP: 111 Publicly Held
SIC: 3272 Concrete products
HQ: Mikron Industries, Inc.
2505 Meridian Pkwy # 250
Durham NC 27713
713 961-4600

(G-5012)
MODULAR ARTS INC
8207 S 192nd St (98032-1129)
PHONE..................206 788-4210
EMP: 5
SALES (est): 399.9K Privately Held
SIC: 3089 Mfg Plastic Products

(G-5013)
MOHAWK ESV INC
23210 71st Pl S (98032-3914)
PHONE..................253 395-3277
Jeffrey Lorberbaum, *Principal*
EMP: 9
SALES (est): 898.8K Privately Held
SIC: 2273 Carpets & rugs

(G-5014)
MOHAWK INDUSTRIES INC
23210 71st Pl S Ste 101 (98032-3914)
PHONE..................253 395-3277
Frank McMurtry, *Principal*
EMP: 4
SALES (corp-wide): 9.9B Publicly Held
SIC: 2273 Finishers of tufted carpets & rugs
PA: Mohawk Industries, Inc.
160 S Industrial Blvd
Calhoun GA 30701
706 629-7721

(G-5015)
MONDELEZ GLOBAL LLC
Also Called: Nabisco
19032 62nd Ave S (98032-1128)
PHONE..................253 395-4237
EMP: 9 Publicly Held
SIC: 2053 Frozen bakery products, except bread
HQ: Mondelez Global Llc
3 N Pkwy Ste 300
Deerfield IL 60015
847 943-4000

(G-5016)
MOOSOO CORPORATION
Also Called: Indian Popcorn
7818 S 212th St Ste A110 (98032-1302)
PHONE..................866 966-6766
Moosoo Ahn, *President*
Mihee Ahn, *Vice Pres*
Kyung Lee, *Manager*
EMP: 9 EST: 2014
SQ FT: 18,000
SALES: 2MM Privately Held
SIC: 2064 5145 Popcorn balls or other treated popcorn products; popcorn & supplies

(G-5017)
MYOTRONICS-NOROMED INC
Also Called: Myo-Tronics
5870 S 194th St (98032-2126)
PHONE..................206 243-4214
Fray Adib, *President*
Robert Jankelson, *Principal*
Roland Jankelson, *Principal*
Larry Morris, *CFO*
▲ **EMP:** 18
SALES (est): 1.9MM Privately Held
WEB: www.myotronics.com
SIC: 3843 3845 3841 Dental tools; electromedical equipment; surgical & medical instruments

(G-5018)
NELSON TRUCK EQUIPMENT CO INC (PA)
20063 84th Ave S (98032-1229)
PHONE..................253 395-3825
Roy W Nelson, *President*
Claudia Dingerson, *Vice Pres*
Neil Crater, *Admin Sec*
▲ **EMP:** 45
SQ FT: 50,000
SALES: 15MM Privately Held
SIC: 5013 3713 5531 Truck parts & accessories; truck & bus bodies; truck equipment & parts

(G-5019)
NESTLE DREYERS ICE CREAM CO
Also Called: Dreyer's Grand Ice Cream
18404 72nd Ave S (98032-1010)
PHONE..................425 251-0809
Louren Richey, *Manager*
EMP: 70
SALES (corp-wide): 92B Privately Held
WEB: www.dreyersinc.com
SIC: 5143 2024 Ice cream & ices; ice cream & frozen desserts
HQ: Nestle Dreyer's Ice Cream Company
5929 College Ave
Oakland CA 94618
510 594-9466

(G-5020)
NEUMEIER ENGINEERING INC
22610 88th Ave S (98031-2434)
PHONE..................253 854-3635
Heinz Neumeier, *President*
Helene Neumeier, *Corp Secy*
Mark Neumeier, *Vice Pres*
Martin Neumeier, *Vice Pres*
EMP: 28
SQ FT: 12,000
SALES (est): 5.6MM Privately Held
SIC: 3599 8711 3812 3769 Machine shop, jobbing & repair; engineering services; search & navigation equipment; guided missile & space vehicle parts & auxiliary equipment

(G-5021)
NEW WEST GYPSUM INC
Also Called: New West Gypsum USA
8657 S 190th St (98031-1270)
PHONE..................253 380-1079
Richard McCamley, *Vice Pres*
Curby Hyland, *Branch Mgr*
EMP: 12
SALES (corp-wide): 3.8MM Privately Held
SIC: 3275 4953 Gypsum products; refuse systems

GEOGRAPHIC SECTION   Kent - King County (G-5049)

PA: Cloverdale Disposal Ltd
5620 198 St
Langley BC V3A 7
604 534-9983

(G-5022)
NEWTOWN INC
23001 54th Ave S (98032-6443)
PHONE.................................253 395-9028
William Wong, *President*
Nona M Wong, *Admin Sec*
▲ **EMP:** 12
SALES (est): 1.2MM **Privately Held**
WEB: www.newtown.net
SIC: 2389 5137 Apparel for handicapped; women's & children's sportswear & swimsuits

(G-5023)
NICHOLSON MANUFACTURING CO
8300 S 206th St (98032-1214)
PHONE.................................206 291-8849
EMP: 4
SALES (corp-wide): 41.4MM **Privately Held**
SIC: 3553 Woodworking machinery
HQ: Nicholson Manufacturing Co Inc
200 S Orcas St
Seattle WA 98108
206 682-2752

(G-5024)
NITE-HAWK SWEEPERS LLC
19713 58th Pl S (98032-3106)
PHONE.................................253 872-2077
Brad Morris,
Tracy Day,
EMP: 18
SQ FT: 10,000
SALES (est): 3.8MM
SALES (corp-wide): 1B **Publicly Held**
WEB: www.nitehawksweepers.com
SIC: 3559 3711 Parking facility equipment & supplies; motor vehicles & car bodies
PA: Alamo Group Inc.
1627 E Walnut St
Seguin TX 78155
830 379-1480

(G-5025)
NORHTWEST STONE PROS
3922 S 241st St (98032-2845)
PHONE.................................206 824-2458
EMP: 3 **EST:** 2005
SALES (est): 150K **Privately Held**
SIC: 3281 Mfg Cut Stone/Products

(G-5026)
NORSTAR SPECIALTY FOODS INC
Also Called: Real Foods
8030 S 228th St (98032-2987)
PHONE.................................206 764-4499
Gerald Isaac, *President*
Janice T B Isaac, *President*
EMP: 30
SQ FT: 6,000
SALES (est): 9MM **Privately Held**
SIC: 2053 5149 Frozen bakery products, except bread; groceries & related products

(G-5027)
NORTH AMERICAN COMPOSITES CO
22239 76th Ave S (98032-1924)
PHONE.................................253 351-9994
Jarred Clark, *Branch Mgr*
EMP: 7
SALES (corp-wide): 271.4MM **Privately Held**
SIC: 2821 Plastics materials & resins
HQ: North American Composites Company
300 Apollo Dr
Circle Pines MN 55014
651 766-6892

(G-5028)
NORTHWEST AUTOMATICS INC
25219 74th Ave S (98032-6007)
PHONE.................................253 852-9006
John M Ketola, *President*
Marien Ketola, *Vice Pres*
Gary Olsen, *Opers Mgr*
Diane R Morgan, *Treasurer*
Cristina Ketola, *Admin Sec*
EMP: 8
SQ FT: 3,000
SALES (est): 1.5MM **Privately Held**
SIC: 3599 Machine shop, jobbing & repair

(G-5029)
NORTHWEST CARBIDE TOOL & SVC
1120 4th Ave N (98032-2942)
PHONE.................................253 872-7848
Mark Monte, *President*
EMP: 2
SALES (est): 214.1K **Privately Held**
SIC: 3999 3545 Custom pulverizing & grinding of plastic materials; machine tool accessories

(G-5030)
NORTHWEST CREATIONS
13106 Se 234th St (98031-3626)
PHONE.................................253 709-4504
Doug Cowan, *Principal*
EMP: 2
SALES (est): 147.3K **Privately Held**
SIC: 3499 Novelties & giftware, including trophies

(G-5031)
NORTHWEST FINE ART PRINTING
26601 79th Ave S (98032-7319)
PHONE.................................425 947-1501
EMP: 2
SALES (est): 83.9K **Privately Held**
SIC: 2752 Commercial printing, lithographic

(G-5032)
NORTHWEST LASER SYSTEMS INC
19219 68th Ave S Ste M105 (98032-2111)
PHONE.................................877 623-1342
Timothy Jasper, *President*
EMP: 2
SALES (est): 206.3K **Privately Held**
SIC: 3699 Laser welding, drilling & cutting equipment

(G-5033)
NORTHWEST LININGS & GEO
20824 77th Ave S (98032-1361)
PHONE.................................253 872-0244
Scott W Newton, *President*
Rodney Allen, *Vice Pres*
Kirk Lilleskare, *Vice Pres*
Kevin Allen, *Project Mgr*
Brett Holmstrom, *Project Mgr*
◆ **EMP:** 25
SQ FT: 24,000
SALES (est): 20.8MM **Privately Held**
WEB: www.northwestlinings.com
SIC: 5131 3443 Textiles, woven; water tanks, metal plate

(G-5034)
NORTHWEST PIONEER INC (PA)
Also Called: Pioneer Packaging
6006 S 228th St (98032-1806)
PHONE.................................253 872-9693
Robert M Steele, *President*
▲ **EMP:** 53
SQ FT: 47,000
SALES: 35MM **Privately Held**
WEB: www.pioneerpackaging.com
SIC: 5113 7319 2679 Corrugated & solid fiber boxes; distribution of advertising material or sample services; paper products, converted

(G-5035)
NORTHWEST POWDER SOULTIONS
7818 S 194th St (98032-1163)
PHONE.................................253 395-6282
Jeff Bartlett, *Owner*
EMP: 2
SALES (est): 210.6K **Privately Held**
SIC: 3399 Powder, metal

(G-5036)
NORTHWEST TERRITORIAL MINT LLC
Also Called: Medallic Art Company
841 Central Ave N Ste 200 (98032-2058)
P.O. Box 2148, Auburn (98071-2148)
PHONE.................................253 833-7780
Paul Wagner, *COO*
Matthew Lee, *Human Resources*
Don Routh, *Sales Mgr*
Diane Hopkins, *Supervisor*
Steve Mayer, *Supervisor*
EMP: 10 **Privately Held**
WEB: www.nwtmint.com
SIC: 3999 Barber & beauty shop equipment
PA: Northwest Territorial Mint Llc
80 Airpark Vista Blvd
Dayton NV 89403

(G-5037)
NORWOOD-WANG INC
Also Called: Puget Sound Cutting
1522 Central Ave S (98032-7420)
PHONE.................................206 304-8769
Stephanie Wang, *Principal*
EMP: 2
SALES (est): 230K **Privately Held**
SIC: 3541 Machine tools, metal cutting type

(G-5038)
NW CLOSETS
22024 68th Ave S (98032-1939)
PHONE.................................253 246-7596
Garrett Wodruff, *Principal*
EMP: 10
SALES (est): 856.4K **Privately Held**
SIC: 2515 Foundations & platforms

(G-5039)
NW FILTERS
5525 S 231st Pl (98032-6408)
PHONE.................................253 859-4099
EMP: 2 **EST:** 2011
SALES (est): 110K **Privately Held**
SIC: 3569 Mfg General Industrial Machinery

(G-5040)
NW LIGHTING SOLUTIONS LLC
1819 Central Ave S # 126 (98032-7501)
PHONE.................................253 246-2959
William Cowart, *Mng Member*
EMP: 2 **EST:** 2014
SALES (est): 117.6K **Privately Held**
SIC: 3648 5063 Arc lighting fixtures; lighting fixtures

(G-5041)
OBERTO SNACKS INC (HQ)
Also Called: OH Boy Oberto
7060 Oberto Dr (98032-7014)
PHONE.................................253 437-6100
Tom Hernquist, *CEO*
Heather Waller, *Business Mgr*
Mark Falconi, *Vice Pres*
Steve Haft, *Vice Pres*
Mike Tull, *Vice Pres*
▲ **EMP:** 250 **EST:** 1918
SQ FT: 40,000
SALES: 149.4MM
SALES (corp-wide): 2.2B **Privately Held**
WEB: www.smokecraft.com
SIC: 2013 Sausages from purchased meat; snack sticks, including jerky: from purchased meat
PA: Premium Brands Holdings Corporation
10991 Shellbridge Way Unit 100
Richmond BC V6X 3
604 656-3100

(G-5042)
OLDCASTLE MATERIALS INC
20609 77th Ave S (98032-1311)
PHONE.................................253 872-9466
Don Litzenberger, *Manager*
EMP: 50
SALES (corp-wide): 30.6B **Privately Held**
WEB: www.centralpremix.com
SIC: 3273 5211 Ready-mixed concrete; masonry materials & supplies
HQ: Oldcastle Materials, Inc.
900 Ashwood Pkwy Ste 700
Atlanta GA 30338

(G-5043)
OLIVER MACHINERY COMPANY
6902 S 194th St (98032-3108)
PHONE.................................253 867-0334
Marc Cox, *Principal*
▲ **EMP:** 4
SALES (est): 853.6K **Privately Held**
WEB: www.olivermachinery.net
SIC: 3559 5084 Degreasing machines, automotive & industrial; woodworking machinery

(G-5044)
OLYMPIC MOUNTAIN PRODUCTS INC
8655 S 208th St (98031-1214)
PHONE.................................253 850-2343
Jeff Stice, *CEO*
Jeffrey Stice Sr, *Vice Pres*
Sheri Goranson, *Project Mgr*
Kristi Cramer, *Marketing Staff*
◆ **EMP:** 27
SQ FT: 38,130
SALES (est): 12.2MM **Privately Held**
WEB: www.omplabs.com
SIC: 2841 5199 2844 Soap: granulated, liquid, cake, flaked or chip; candles; toilet preparations

(G-5045)
OMAX CORPORATION
21409 72nd Ave S (98032-1944)
PHONE.................................253 872-2300
John Bosco Cheung, *President*
Stephen Bruner, *Vice Pres*
John Henry Olsen, *Vice Pres*
Steve O'Brien, *VP Mfg*
Greg Berft, *Warehouse Mgr*
◆ **EMP:** 250
SQ FT: 53,000
SALES (est): 116.3MM
SALES (corp-wide): 465.6MM **Privately Held**
WEB: www.omax.com
SIC: 3545 3561 Cutting tools for machine tools; pumps & pumping equipment
PA: Hypertherm, Inc.
21 Great Hollow Rd
Hanover NH 03755
603 643-3441

(G-5046)
ORILLIA SMOKE
18111 E Valley Hwy D102 (98032-1071)
PHONE.................................425 656-1219
Chris Nam, *Principal*
EMP: 3
SALES (est): 181.5K **Privately Held**
SIC: 3999 Cigarette & cigar products & accessories

(G-5047)
ORNAMENTAL IRON SPECIALISTS
27221 135th Ave Se (98042-9072)
PHONE.................................253 630-0328
Daryl Runnestrand, *President*
EMP: 2
SALES (est): 150K **Privately Held**
SIC: 3446 Grillwork, ornamental metal; stairs, staircases, stair treads: prefabricated metal; railings, bannisters, guards, etc.: made from metal pipe

(G-5048)
ORORA PACKAGING SOLUTIONS
Also Called: Landsburg In Orora North Amer
20208 72nd Ave S (98032-2322)
PHONE.................................253 796-6200
Joseph Saylor, *Manager*
EMP: 15 **Privately Held**
SIC: 5113 2653 Paper & products, wrapping or coarse; boxes, corrugated: made from purchased materials
HQ: Orora Packaging Solutions
6600 Valley View St
Buena Park CA 90620
714 562-6000

(G-5049)
OROWEAT
7054 S 220th St (98032-1910)
PHONE.................................253 872-8237
Eric Rice, *Principal*

Kent - King County (G-5050)

EMP: 2
SALES (est): 90.3K **Privately Held**
SIC: 2051 Cakes, bakery: except frozen

(G-5050)
PACIFIC ENVIROMENTS CORP
25331 33rd Pl S (98032-5631)
PHONE...........................408 836-7581
Felipe Fernandez, *CEO*
Mario Bonilla, *President*
EMP: 20
SALES: 251K **Privately Held**
SIC: 2542 Fixtures, office: except wood

(G-5051)
PACIFIC FUEL AND CONVENIENCE
Also Called: Circle K
13122 Se 240th St (98031-5001)
PHONE...........................253 631-8512
Glenda Rose, *Principal*
EMP: 3 EST: 2011
SALES (est): 195.8K **Privately Held**
SIC: 2869 5411 Fuels; convenience stores

(G-5052)
PACIFIC KNIGHT EMBLEM & INSIG
11358 Se 211th Ln Apt 39 (98031-1139)
P.O. Box 6111 (98064-6111)
PHONE...........................206 354-2060
Brett Bingham,
EMP: 6
SALES: 23K **Privately Held**
SIC: 5699 2399 5999 3999 Uniforms & work clothing; emblems, badges & insignia; police supply stores; identification badges & insignia; badges, metal: policemen, firemen, etc.;

(G-5053)
PACIFIC MAT & COML FLRG LLC
18414 80th Ct S (98032-2516)
P.O. Box 1382 (98035-1382)
PHONE...........................800 345-6287
Will McHarness, *Accounts Mgr*
Mark Mitchell, *Accounts Mgr*
Josh Park, *Accounts Mgr*
John Ferguson, *Mng Member*
▲ EMP: 40
SQ FT: 30,000
SALES (est): 41.4MM **Privately Held**
SIC: 5023 2451 Carpets; floor cushion & padding; mobile homes

(G-5054)
PACIFIC METAL FABRICATION INC
833 1st Ave S (98032-6139)
P.O. Box 5184 (98064-5184)
PHONE...........................253 833-3362
Marvin L Davis, *President*
Margaret Davis, *Vice Pres*
Cara Howes, *Vice Pres*
Dan Gant, *Project Mgr*
Janine Zeitler, *Office Mgr*
▲ EMP: 7 EST: 1975
SQ FT: 4,000
SALES (est): 1.7MM **Privately Held**
WEB: www.pacmetalfab.com
SIC: 3444 Sheet metalwork

(G-5055)
PACIFIC METALLURGICAL INC
925 5th Ave S (98032-5825)
P.O. Box 399 (98035-0399)
PHONE...........................206 292-9205
Catherine Fallen, *President*
Robert Lillie, *Finance*
Burt Tooke, *Maintence Staff*
Regina Brown, *Receptionist*
EMP: 34
SQ FT: 18,000
SALES (est): 8MM **Privately Held**
WEB: www.pacmet.com
SIC: 3398 Metal heat treating

(G-5056)
PACIFIC METER & EQUIPMENT INC
8001 S 222nd St (98032-1942)
PHONE...........................253 872-3374
Russell Smith, *President*
Destiney Carr, *Office Mgr*
EMP: 6
SALES (est): 1.6MM **Privately Held**
WEB: www.pacificmeter.com
SIC: 5084 3714 5999 Meters, consumption registering; propane conversion equipment, motor vehicle; alcoholic beverage making equipment & supplies

(G-5057)
PACIFIC PAPER TUBE INC
7850 S 196th St (98032-1143)
PHONE...........................253 872-7981
Tim McKee, *Manager*
EMP: 15
SALES (corp-wide): 23.4MM **Privately Held**
WEB: www.pacificpapertube.com
SIC: 2655 Fiber cans, drums & similar products
PA: Pacific Paper Tube, Inc.
4343 E Fremont St
Stockton CA 95215
510 562-8823

(G-5058)
PACMET
1205 5th Ave S (98032-6023)
PHONE...........................253 854-4241
Doug Allan, *Principal*
Maria Olea, *Assistant*
EMP: 2
SALES (est): 117K **Privately Held**
SIC: 3471 Finishing, metals or formed products

(G-5059)
PANEL ARTZ
20462 84th Ave S (98032-1201)
PHONE...........................253 277-1040
Karl A Weiss, *Principal*
EMP: 2
SALES (est): 65.4K **Privately Held**
SIC: 2491 Flooring, treated wood block

(G-5060)
PASSPORT FOOD GROUP LLC
Also Called: House of Bee
6931 S 234th St (98032-2920)
PHONE...........................253 520-9299
Mark L'Esperance, *Branch Mgr*
EMP: 25
SALES (corp-wide): 41.7MM **Privately Held**
SIC: 2099 Packaged combination products: pasta, rice & potato
PA: Passport Food Group, Llc
2539 E Philadelphia St
Ontario CA 91761
909 627-7312

(G-5061)
PATIO PLANTINGS
12810 Se 245th St (98030-5054)
PHONE...........................253 631-6131
Lori Morley, *Principal*
EMP: 2
SALES (est): 178.3K **Privately Held**
SIC: 3645 Garden, patio, walkway & yard lighting fixtures: electric

(G-5062)
PAULA S CHOICE
23215 66th Ave S (98032-1880)
PHONE...........................425 988-2931
Shana Seorozhee, *Principal*
EMP: 4
SALES (est): 240.6K **Privately Held**
SIC: 2844 Face creams or lotions; cosmetic preparations

(G-5063)
PBS SUPPLY CO INC
Also Called: Krw Specialties
7013 S 216th St (98032-1932)
PHONE...........................253 395-5550
David R Strecker, *Admin Sec*
EMP: 18
SALES: 5MM **Privately Held**
WEB: www.pbssupply.com
SIC: 3952 2493 2541 Boards, drawing, artists'; bulletin boards, cork; store & office display cases & fixtures

(G-5064)
PERFORMNCE FIRE PROTECTION INC
15322 Se 240th St (98042-4108)
PHONE...........................253 778-8039
Mitch Stemm, *President*
Jamey Gabbard, *Shareholder*
EMP: 4
SALES (est): 618.4K **Privately Held**
SIC: 3669 Fire detection systems, electric

(G-5065)
PETNET SOLUTIONS INC
Also Called: P E T Net Solution
7048 S 188th St Bldg 1 (98032-1055)
PHONE...........................425 656-1640
Joshua Nutting, *Manager*
EMP: 4
SALES (corp-wide): 95B **Privately Held**
SIC: 2835 Radioactive diagnostic substances
HQ: Petnet Solutions, Inc.
810 Innovation Dr
Knoxville TN 37932
865 218-2000

(G-5066)
PITNEY BOWES INC
19005 64th Ave S Ste 175 (98032-5404)
P.O. Box 1479, Portland OR (97207-1479)
PHONE...........................253 395-8717
Doug Macdonald, *Principal*
EMP: 65
SALES (corp-wide): 3.5B **Publicly Held**
SIC: 3579 7359 Postage meters; business machine & electronic equipment rental services
PA: Pitney Bowes Inc.
3001 Summer St Ste 3
Stamford CT 06905
203 356-5000

(G-5067)
PLASTICS DYNAMICS INC
Also Called: Gourmet Display
6004 S 190th St Ste 102 (98032-2170)
PHONE...........................206 762-2164
Rick Edris, *President*
Tony Schueler, *Corp Secy*
Rita Edris, *Treasurer*
Mark Vollmar, *Senior Mgr*
▲ EMP: 30
SQ FT: 30,000
SALES (est): 4.2MM **Privately Held**
WEB: www.gourmetdisplay.com
SIC: 3089 Plastic kitchenware, tableware & houseware; plastic containers, except foam

(G-5068)
PMC INC
Also Called: Venus Gusmer
1862 Ives Ave (98032-7502)
PHONE...........................206 854-2660
Ron Rivers, *Branch Mgr*
EMP: 80
SQ FT: 8,000
SALES (corp-wide): 2.5B **Privately Held**
SIC: 3296 Fiberglass insulation
HQ: Pmc, Inc.
12243 Branford St
Sun Valley CA 91352
818 896-1101

(G-5069)
POLAR FUSION LLC
Also Called: Tiger Tail USA
10605 Se 240th St (98031-4903)
PHONE...........................206 395-7811
Katheryn Hobnick, *Opers Mgr*
EMP: 8
SALES (corp-wide): 50K **Privately Held**
SIC: 3634 Massage machines, electric, except for beauty/barber shops
PA: Polar Fusion Llc
2737 72nd Ave S Ste 106
Kent WA 98030
206 779-5238

(G-5070)
POLAR FUSION LLC (PA)
2737 72nd Ave S Ste 106 (98030)
PHONE...........................206 779-5238
Spring Faussett, *President*
Adam Faussett, *Vice Pres*
EMP: 8
SQ FT: 5,000
SALES (est): 50K **Privately Held**
WEB: www.polarfusion.com
SIC: 3999 Barber & beauty shop equipment

(G-5071)
POLYDROP LLC
22431 76th Ave S (98032-2450)
PHONE...........................206 601-2191
Volha Hrechka,
Heather Milligan,
Danilo Pozzo,
EMP: 8 EST: 2013
SQ FT: 6,000
SALES (est): 173.7K **Privately Held**
SIC: 3087 Custom compound purchased resins

(G-5072)
POLYFORM US LTD
7030 S 224th St (98032-1986)
PHONE...........................253 872-0300
Jan Beyer-Olsen, *President*
Knut Beyer Olsen, *Principal*
Phyllis Johnson, *Treasurer*
Tom Case, *Sales Mgr*
Lisa Baespflug, *Sales Executive*
◆ EMP: 57
SQ FT: 50,230
SALES (est): 14.3MM **Privately Held**
WEB: www.polyformus.com
SIC: 3089 Buoys & floats, plastic

(G-5073)
POPPLETON ELECTRIC & MCHY CO
24831 110th Pl Se (98030-2816)
PHONE...........................206 762-9160
Robert Mc Laughlin, *President*
Sean Sullivan, *Corp Secy*
Jack Richmond, *Vice Pres*
EMP: 10
SQ FT: 10,000
SALES: 1.7MM **Privately Held**
WEB: www.poppletonelectric.com
SIC: 1731 7694 General electrical contractor; electric motor repair

(G-5074)
POWERGUARD CORPORATION
6506 S 209th St Ste 200 (98032-2313)
PHONE...........................206 764-8882
EMP: 2
SQ FT: 3,700
SALES: 250.4K **Privately Held**
SIC: 3679 Mfg Back Up Power Supplies

(G-5075)
PRECISION COUNTER TECH INC
6409 S 194th St (98032-2165)
P.O. Box 387, Wilsonville OR (97070-0387)
PHONE...........................425 486-8629
Michael W Ahlstrom, *President*
EMP: 9 EST: 2009
SALES: 222.2K
SALES (corp-wide): 34.2MM **Privately Held**
SIC: 3131 Counters
PA: Precision Countertops Inc.
26200 Sw 95th Ave Ste 303
Wilsonville OR 97070
503 660-3023

(G-5076)
PRECISION COUNTERTOPS INC
20866 89th Ave S Bldg Q (98031-1235)
PHONE...........................253 867-5317
Ken Bartolotta, *Branch Mgr*
EMP: 25
SALES (corp-wide): 34.2MM **Privately Held**
WEB: www.precisioncountertops.com
SIC: 5031 2541 Plywood; particleboard; table or counter tops, plastic laminated
PA: Precision Countertops Inc.
26200 Sw 95th Ave Ste 303
Wilsonville OR 97070
503 660-3023

(G-5077)
PRECISION DRIVESHAFT INC
20835 102nd Pl Se (98031-2072)
PHONE...........................253 236-5640
Toll Free:...........................888
Jean B Soularie, *President*

GEOGRAPHIC SECTION
Kent - King County (G-5104)

EMP: 2
SALES (est): 210K **Privately Held**
SIC: 3714 7539 Drive shafts, motor vehicle; powertrain components repair services

(G-5078)
PRECISION SPRING STAMPING CORP
Also Called: Pressco Products
22617 85th Pl S (98031-2469)
P.O. Box 2090, Sumner (98390-0460)
PHONE 253 852-6911
Sean McHugh, *President*
Christine McHugh, *Corp Secy*
Todd Petchnick, *Vice Pres*
Christine Petchnick, *Admin Sec*
EMP: 35 EST: 1965
SQ FT: 13,000
SALES (est): 7.4MM **Privately Held**
SIC: 3545 3469 5084 Milling machine attachments (machine tool accessories); metal stampings; machine tools & accessories

(G-5079)
PREFERRED BUSINESS SOLUTIONS
7691 S 180th St (98032-1048)
PHONE 425 251-1202
Ron Cox, *President*
EMP: 2
SALES (est): 84.4K **Privately Held**
SIC: 5044 3579 Copying equipment; paper handling machines

(G-5080)
PRENTIS LITERARY LLC
25322 36th Pl S (98032-5683)
PHONE 425 260-7753
Leslie Varney, *Principal*
EMP: 2
SALES (est): 62.9K **Privately Held**
SIC: 2711 Newspapers

(G-5081)
PRIME WEST OF WASHINGTON INC
1819 Central Ave S Ste 80 (98032-7508)
PHONE 360 424-5783
John Ruhlman, *President*
Steve Harmon, *Principal*
Steve Rust, *Exec VP*
Nancy Ruhlman, *Admin Sec*
EMP: 22
SALES (est): 2.4MM **Privately Held**
WEB: www.primewest.com
SIC: 7319 8611 7336 7311 Display advertising service; business associations; commercial art & graphic design; advertising agencies; typesetting

(G-5082)
PRINTING CONTROL SERVICES INC
Also Called: Printing Control Graphics
23328 66th Ave S (98032-1827)
PHONE 206 575-4114
Carl Vonder-Haar, *President*
Nancy Charpentier, *Controller*
Harlan Morgan, *Sales Staff*
EMP: 70 EST: 1974
SALES (est): 10.4MM
SALES (corp-wide): 6.8B **Publicly Held**
WEB: www.ocpc.com
SIC: 2752 Commercial printing, offset
HQ: Consolidated Graphics, Inc.
5858 Westheimer Rd # 200
Houston TX 77057
713 787-0977

(G-5083)
PRO FINISH INC
Also Called: Pro Finish Autobody & Auto Sls
1506 Central Ave S (98032-7420)
PHONE 253 850-9422
Jesse T Thatcher, *President*
Erin N Thatcher, *Admin Sec*
EMP: 3
SQ FT: 7,000
SALES (est): 662.4K **Privately Held**
WEB: www.profinishinc.com
SIC: 7532 5521 3471 Body shop, automotive; automobiles, used cars only; finishing, metals or formed products

(G-5084)
PROFESSIONAL PLASTICS INC
6412 S 196th St (98032-1169)
PHONE 714 446-6500
Keith Sremaniak, *CFO*
Samantha Jepsen, *VP Sales*
EMP: 2 EST: 2015
SALES (est): 81.8K **Privately Held**
SIC: 2821 Plastics materials & resins

(G-5085)
PROGRESSIVE INTERNATIONAL CORP (HQ)
20435 72nd Ave S Ste 400 (98032-2358)
PHONE 253 850-6111
Bill Reibl, *CEO*
Kurt Bergquist, *President*
Mike Hagen, *Business Mgr*
Jim Campbell, *Vice Pres*
Marie Chin, *Vice Pres*
◆ EMP: 75 EST: 1998
SQ FT: 235,000
SALES (est): 17MM
SALES (corp-wide): 11.1MM **Privately Held**
SIC: 3365 5023 Cooking/kitchen utensils, cast aluminum; kitchenware

(G-5086)
PROVAIL
21019 66th Ave S (98032-2311)
PHONE 206 363-7303
Dave Ohrick, *Manager*
EMP: 29
SALES (corp-wide): 11.3MM **Privately Held**
WEB: www.provail.org
SIC: 3549 Metalworking machinery
PA: Provail
12550 Aurora Ave N
Seattle WA 98133
206 363-7303

(G-5087)
PUGET BINDERY INC
7820 S 228th St (98032-2962)
PHONE 206 621-8898
Richard T Bayless, *President*
Robert E Bayless, *Vice Pres*
EMP: 25
SQ FT: 16,000
SALES (est): 4.2MM **Privately Held**
WEB: www.pugetbindery.com
SIC: 2789 Binding only: books, pamphlets, magazines, etc.

(G-5088)
PUGET SOUND STEEL CO INC
906 3rd Ave S (98032-6194)
PHONE 253 854-3600
Constance Macalino, *President*
Dave Haglund, *General Mgr*
Harold Paulson, *Principal*
Shirley Robertson, *Principal*
Lisa New, *Accounting Mgr*
▲ EMP: 22
SQ FT: 18,000
SALES (est): 7.2MM **Privately Held**
SIC: 3312 3441 3316 Rods, iron & steel: made in steel mills; fabricated structural metal; cold finishing of steel shapes

(G-5089)
PUNJAB SIGNS & PRINTING
22307 122nd Ave Se (98031-2388)
PHONE 425 501-3336
EMP: 2
SALES (est): 130K **Privately Held**
SIC: 2752 Lithographic Commercial Printing

(G-5090)
PURE SAFETY GROUP INC
6305 S 231st St (98032-1872)
PHONE 253 854-5877
EMP: 2
SALES (corp-wide): 3.2MM **Privately Held**
SIC: 5099 3429 Safety equipment & supplies; wood & wood by-products; harness hardware
PA: Pure Safety Group, Inc.
9201 Winkler Dr
Houston TX 77017
713 928-3936

(G-5091)
QUALLS STUD WELDING PDTS INC (PA)
7820 S 210th St Ste C103 (98032-2418)
P.O. Box 68887, Seattle (98168-0887)
PHONE 425 656-9787
Joseph B Quall, *CEO*
Jay E Koski, *President*
D Jean Quall, *Corp Secy*
Andrew Quall, *Vice Pres*
Lisa L Quall, *Treasurer*
EMP: 3
SALES (est): 13.7MM **Privately Held**
WEB: www.studweldprod.com
SIC: 5084 7692 Welding machinery & equipment; welding repair

(G-5092)
QUEEN CITY SHTMTL & ROOFG INC
22030 84th Ave S (98032-2468)
PHONE 206 623-6020
Diane Puetz, *President*
Chad Puetz, *Vice Pres*
Mark Puetz, *Vice Pres*
Rick Puetz, *Vice Pres*
Oscar W Puetz, *Shareholder*
EMP: 25 EST: 1945
SQ FT: 5,000
SALES (est): 4.2MM **Privately Held**
SIC: 1761 3444 1799 Roofing contractor; sheet metalwork; sheet metalwork; waterproofing

(G-5093)
QUEST INTEGRITY USA LLC (HQ)
Also Called: Quest Integrity Group
19823 58th Pl S Ste 100 (98032-2183)
PHONE 253 893-7070
Jeffrey Ott, *CEO*
Milton Altenberg, *Ch of Bd*
Robert De Lorenzo, *Vice Pres*
Ted L Anderson, *CTO*
Robert A Difulgentiz,
EMP: 59
SALES (est): 5.9MM
SALES (corp-wide): 1.2B **Publicly Held**
SIC: 7389 7372 Inspection & testing services; prepackaged software
PA: Team, Inc.
13131 Dar Ashford Ste 600
Sugar Land TX 77478
281 331-6154

(G-5094)
QUEST PRODUCTS LLC
Also Called: Oracoat
19017 62nd Ave S (98032-1185)
PHONE 425 451-9876
Jeff Haley, *Manager*
EMP: 12
SALES (corp-wide): 30.4MM **Privately Held**
SIC: 2844 Oral preparations
HQ: Quest Products, Llc
8201 104th St Ste 200
Pleasant Prairie WI 53158
800 650-0113

(G-5095)
QUICK SIGNS AND DESIGNS
12368 Se 221st St (98031-2395)
PHONE 253 929-4488
Devin Ramsey, *Principal*
EMP: 2
SALES (est): 139.4K **Privately Held**
SIC: 3993 Signs & advertising specialties

(G-5096)
RAG MAN LLC
3821 S 250th Pl (98032-4182)
PHONE 206 653-7125
Byron Beck, *Owner*
EMP: 4
SALES: 2MM **Privately Held**
WEB: www.ragmanrags.com
SIC: 2211 5699 5932 Towels, dishcloths & washcloths: cotton; uniforms & work clothing; used merchandise stores

(G-5097)
RAM BIGHORN BREWERY KENT
512 Ramsay Way (98032-4509)
PHONE 253 520-3881
Deshawn Richardson, *Principal*
EMP: 4
SALES (est): 294.3K **Privately Held**
SIC: 2082 Beer (alcoholic beverage)

(G-5098)
RAMCO CONSTRUCTION TOOLS INC (PA)
21213 76th Ave S (98032-2443)
P.O. Box 1007 (98035-1007)
PHONE 253 796-3051
William D Blackburn, *Ch of Bd*
David Blackburn, *President*
Millie Pullen, *Finance Mgr*
Jeremy Burks, *Info Tech Dir*
▲ EMP: 12
SQ FT: 30,000
SALES (est): 5MM **Privately Held**
WEB: www.ramcotools.com
SIC: 3532 Drills, bits & similar equipment

(G-5099)
RAMCO CONSTRUCTION TOOLS INC
1217 4th Ave N (98032-2939)
PHONE 253 796-3051
David Blackburn, *Manager*
EMP: 15
SALES (corp-wide): 5MM **Privately Held**
SIC: 3532 Drills, bits & similar equipment
PA: Ramco Construction Tools, Inc.
21213 76th Ave S
Kent WA 98032
253 796-3051

(G-5100)
RAY SUMMERLIN
Also Called: Schaeffer Specialized Lubr
29805 148th Ave Se (98042-9371)
PHONE 253 638-0733
Ray Summerlin, *Owner*
EMP: 2
SALES: 300K **Privately Held**
SIC: 2992 Lubricating oils & greases

(G-5101)
REDONDO RV STORAGE & SERVICE
Also Called: Redondo R V Storage
27641 Pacific Hwy S (98032)
PHONE 253 941-3662
Won WI, *Owner*
Ron Miguel, *Manager*
EMP: 2
SALES (est): 178.5K **Privately Held**
SIC: 3716 4225 Motor homes; general warehousing

(G-5102)
RICE LAKE WEIGHING SYSTEMS INC
Measurement Systems Intl
19201 62nd Ave S (98032-1133)
PHONE 206 433-0199
Philip Gray, *Branch Mgr*
EMP: 33
SALES (corp-wide): 138.5MM **Privately Held**
SIC: 3596 Weighing machines & apparatus
PA: Rice Lake Weighing Systems, Inc.
230 W Coleman St
Rice Lake WI 54868
715 234-9171

(G-5103)
RK TITANIUM LLC
27031 114th Ave Se (98030-7859)
PHONE 253 886-1377
EMP: 2
SALES (est): 90.8K **Privately Held**
SIC: 3356 Titanium

(G-5104)
ROBBINS COMPANY
Also Called: Robbins PBM
5866 S 194th St (98032-2126)
PHONE 253 872-0500
Joe Roby, *Vice Pres*
EMP: 35
SQ FT: 24,229
SALES (corp-wide): 14.9MM **Privately Held**
WEB: www.robbinstbm.com
SIC: 3531 Tunnelling machinery

Kent - King County (G-5105)

HQ: The Robbins Company
29100 Hall St Ste 100
Solon OH 44139
440 248-3303

(G-5105)
ROLLN DOUGH LTD (PA)
Also Called: Great American Bagel, The
20620 84th Ave S (98032-1224)
PHONE.................................206 763-4300
Young Chung, *Owner*
EMP: 30
SALES (est): 4.7MM **Privately Held**
SIC: 2051 5411 Bakery: wholesale or wholesale/retail combined; delicatessens

(G-5106)
ROSELLINI DISTRIBUTION INC
Also Called: Pac Dry Ice
8637 S 212th St (98031-1910)
P.O. Box 25577, Federal Way (98093-2577)
PHONE.................................253 867-5648
Adam Rosellini, *President*
▲ **EMP:** 8
SALES (est): 1.1MM **Privately Held**
WEB: www.rosellinidistribution.com
SIC: 2813 Dry ice, carbon dioxide (solid)

(G-5107)
ROTARY OFFSET PRESS INC
Also Called: Seattle Times Publications
6600 S 231st St (98032-1847)
PHONE.................................253 813-9900
Michael Shepard, *President*
C S Kelly, *President*
Frank Blethen, *Chairman*
K L Hatch, *Vice Pres*
Ken Hatch, *Vice Pres*
EMP: 140
SALES (est): 19.2MM
SALES (corp-wide): 226.3MM **Privately Held**
WEB: www.rotaryoffsetpress.com
SIC: 2752 7331 Commercial printing, offset; mailing service
HQ: Seattle Times Company
1000 Denny Way Ste 501
Seattle WA 98109
206 464-2111

(G-5108)
ROTTLER MANUFACTURING COMPANY
8029 S 200th St (98032-1114)
PHONE.................................253 872-7050
Andrew Rottler, *President*
John C Rottler, *Corp Secy*
Erica Rainwater, *Purch Mgr*
Kevin Ameline, *Engineer*
Ed Kiebler, *Sales Mgr*
◆ **EMP:** 50 **EST:** 1922
SQ FT: 40,000
SALES (est): 16.8MM **Privately Held**
SIC: 3541 3549 Drilling & boring machines; honing & lapping machines; metalworking machinery

(G-5109)
S & BS BOUTIQUE
22721 126th Pl Se (98031-3666)
PHONE.................................253 631-2718
EMP: 2 **EST:** 2003
SALES (est): 140K **Privately Held**
SIC: 3559 Mfg Misc Industry Machinery

(G-5110)
S & S WELDING INC
22131 68th Ave S (98032-1937)
P.O. Box 1505 (98035-1505)
PHONE.................................206 793-9943
Thomas Stucke, *President*
Bonnie Stucke, *Vice Pres*
Jamey McKinley, *Manager*
Rob Vanderford, *Manager*
Christie Richards, *Assistant*
EMP: 36
SQ FT: 21,600
SALES (est): 10.3MM **Privately Held**
WEB: www.ssweld.com
SIC: 3446 3441 Architectural metalwork; fabricated structural metal

(G-5111)
SABRE INDUSTRIES
26609 79th Ave S (98032-7319)
PHONE.................................253 246-7132
EMP: 3 **EST:** 2013
SALES (est): 195.2K **Privately Held**
SIC: 3999 Manufacturing industries

(G-5112)
SACO SALES
29304 204th Pl Se (98042-6889)
PHONE.................................253 277-1568
Scott Dumas, *Owner*
EMP: 2 **EST:** 2012
SALES (est): 115.7K **Privately Held**
SIC: 3451 Screw machine products

(G-5113)
SAFE SYSTEMS INC
Also Called: Steel Abrasive Finishing Eqp
18420 68th Ave S Ste 202 (98032-1093)
PHONE.................................425 251-8662
Glenn Seaverns, *President*
Todd Robinson, *Accounts Mgr*
EMP: 12
SQ FT: 15,000
SALES (est): 3MM **Privately Held**
WEB: www.safesys.com
SIC: 3589 Sandblasting equipment

(G-5114)
SAMUEL EDWARDS
Also Called: Op-Air Engineering
22415 41st Ave S (98032-1898)
PHONE.................................253 988-0219
Samuel Edwards, *Owner*
EMP: 2
SALES (est): 179.3K **Privately Held**
SIC: 3728 Aircraft parts & equipment

(G-5115)
SAN GENNARO FOODS INC
Also Called: Polenta
19255 80th Ave S (98032-1135)
PHONE.................................253 872-1900
Jerry Mascio, *President*
Julio Jimenez, *Opers Mgr*
EMP: 14
SQ FT: 20,000
SALES (est): 2.6MM **Privately Held**
WEB: www.polenta.net
SIC: 2041 Corn meal

(G-5116)
SANSUEB SOFTWARE LLC
17019 Se 240th St (98042-5569)
P.O. Box 369, Clarkston (99403-0369)
PHONE.................................253 630-5208
Brad Belmondo,
Bob Barr,
EMP: 2 **EST:** 1999
SALES (est): 135K **Privately Held**
WEB: www.sansueb.com
SIC: 7372 Prepackaged software

(G-5117)
SAWBOX LLC
8623 S 212th St (98031-1910)
PHONE.................................253 277-0506
DEA McClure, *Mng Member*
Grant McClure,
EMP: 2
SQ FT: 6,000
SALES (est): 90.4K **Privately Held**
SIC: 2521 Cabinets, office: wood

(G-5118)
SEA LECT PRODUCTS
821 3rd Ave S (98032-6193)
PHONE.................................253 520-2598
Kelly Koontz, *Owner*
▲ **EMP:** 2
SALES (est): 198.4K **Privately Held**
SIC: 3444 Sheet metalwork

(G-5119)
SEA WEST PRODUCTS INC
8801 S 228th St (98031-2437)
PHONE.................................253 854-2942
Cecil Green, *President*
Joan Green, *Principal*
Bruce Green, *Vice Pres*
Sean Green, *Shareholder*
EMP: 12 **EST:** 1976
SQ FT: 10,000
SALES (est): 1.4MM **Privately Held**
WEB: www.seawestproducts.com
SIC: 3728 Aircraft parts & equipment

(G-5120)
SEASONINGSNET LLC
8001 S 194th St (98032-1126)
P.O. Box 746 (98035-0746)
PHONE.................................253 237-0550
Rita Sutter, *Opers Mgr*
Tyler Jones, *Executive*
Nancy R Jones,
EMP: 17
SQ FT: 30,000
SALES (est): 3.4MM **Privately Held**
SIC: 2099 Seasonings & spices

(G-5121)
SEATAC AUTOMOTIVE
24805 Pacific Hwy S (98032-5441)
PHONE.................................253 839-0309
Stan Lee, *Principal*
David Ott, *Manager*
EMP: 2 **EST:** 2007
SALES (est): 131.6K **Privately Held**
SIC: 7694 7538 7319 Rebuilding motors, except automotive; engine repair; coupon distribution

(G-5122)
SEATTLE KOMBUCHA COMPANY LLC
1819 Central Ave S C49 (98032-7501)
PHONE.................................425 985-2364
Wayne Greenfield, *Mng Member*
EMP: 3
SALES (est): 131.7K **Privately Held**
SIC: 2085 Cocktails, alcoholic

(G-5123)
SEATTLE PACIFIC INDUSTRIES
Also Called: Unionbay Sportswear Juniors
21216 72nd Ave S (98032-1916)
P.O. Box 58710, Seattle (98138-1710)
PHONE.................................253 872-8822
Connie Maynard, *Manager*
EMP: 100
SALES (est): 7.2MM
SALES (corp-wide): 101.6MM **Privately Held**
WEB: www.unionbay.com
SIC: 5136 5137 2339 Sportswear, men's & boys'; sportswear, women's & children's; women's & misses' outerwear
PA: Seattle Pacific Industries, Inc.
1633 Westlake Ave N Ste 3
Seattle WA 98109
253 872-8822

(G-5124)
SEATTLE PRECISION FORM INC
8210 S 222nd St (98032-1943)
P.O. Box 1909, Issaquah (98027-0079)
PHONE.................................253 872-8356
Douglas Ayres, *President*
Dale Hacker, *Vice Pres*
Virginia Ayres, *Treasurer*
Sandra Hacker, *Admin Sec*
EMP: 4
SQ FT: 2,000
SALES (est): 520K **Privately Held**
WEB: www.seattlemovers.org
SIC: 3599 Electrical discharge machining (EDM)

(G-5125)
SEATTLE PRINT HOUSE LLC
26213 116th Ave Se C201 (98030-8643)
PHONE.................................503 841-7755
Ozgur Kaya, *Principal*
EMP: 2 **EST:** 2016
SALES (est): 117.6K **Privately Held**
SIC: 2752 Commercial printing, lithographic

(G-5126)
SEED FACTORY NORTHWEST INC
8439 S 208th St Bldg M (98031-1208)
PHONE.................................253 395-8813
Wally Strickland, *Manager*
EMP: 7
SALES (corp-wide): 2.9MM **Privately Held**
WEB: www.seedfactory.com
SIC: 2048 Bird food, prepared

PA: Seed Factory Northwest, Inc.
4319 Jessup Rd
Ceres CA 95307
209 634-8522

(G-5127)
SEQUOYAH ELECTRIC
1319 Central Ave S (98032-7412)
PHONE.................................253 520-2064
EMP: 2 **EST:** 2007
SALES (est): 140K **Privately Held**
SIC: 3699 Mfg Electrical Equipment/Supplies

(G-5128)
SHARK STAINLESS SYSTEMS INC
19717 62nd Ave S Ste E102 (98032-1153)
P.O. Box 906, Bellevue (98009-0906)
PHONE.................................866 960-9779
Brian Witz, *President*
Robert Hobart, *Vice Pres*
▲ **EMP:** 3
SQ FT: 7,000
SALES: 800K **Privately Held**
WEB: www.sharkstainless.com
SIC: 2434 Wood kitchen cabinets

(G-5129)
SHERPA ADVENTURE GEAR LLC
7857 S 180th St (98032-1050)
PHONE.................................425 251-0760
Tashi Sherpa, *President*
Tom Hammond, *Marketing Staff*
Stephanie Van Evera, *Manager*
▲ **EMP:** 11
SALES (est): 16.2K **Privately Held**
WEB: www.sherpaadventuregear.com
SIC: 2329 2339 Men's & boys' sportswear & athletic clothing; women's & misses' athletic clothing & sportswear

(G-5130)
SIDETRACK DISTILLERY
27010 78th Ave S (98032-7354)
PHONE.................................206 963-5079
EMP: 3 **EST:** 2013
SALES (est): 123.1K **Privately Held**
SIC: 2085 Distilled & blended liquors

(G-5131)
SIGN BY TOMMORROW KENT
22005 68th Ave S (98032-1917)
PHONE.................................253 872-7844
Craig Pasquinelli, *Principal*
EMP: 3
SALES (est): 302.8K **Privately Held**
SIC: 3993 Signs & advertising specialties

(G-5132)
SIGN PRINTS INC
Also Called: Sign Prin6s
27106 46th Ave S (98032-7147)
PHONE.................................253 854-7841
Brian Hayashi, *Owner*
EMP: 2
SALES (est): 215.9K **Privately Held**
WEB: www.signprints.com
SIC: 3993 Signs & advertising specialties

(G-5133)
SKOOKEM AEROSPACE MFG
21019 66th Ave S (98032-2311)
PHONE.................................206 365-8027
EMP: 2
SALES (est): 77.4K **Privately Held**
SIC: 3812 Electronic field detection apparatus (aeronautical)

(G-5134)
SKYIDRONES LLC
18929 Se 292nd Pl (98042-9262)
PHONE.................................253 347-7261
Thomas Allen, *Principal*
EMP: 2
SALES (est): 102.7K **Privately Held**
SIC: 3721 Motorized aircraft

(G-5135)
SMITH BROTHERS FARMS INC (PA)
Also Called: Smith Brother Feed Lot
32030 4th Ave Sw (98032)
PHONE.................................253 852-1000

▲ = Import ▼ = Export
◆ = Import/Export

Scott Highland, *President*
Alson Kemp, *Chairman*
Todd Behan, *Vice Pres*
Greg Kessiner, *Treasurer*
Terra Behan, *Director*
EMP: 35 **EST:** 1920
SQ FT: 4,000
SALES (est): 25.7MM **Privately Held**
WEB: www.smithbrothersfarms.com
SIC: 2026 0211 Fluid milk; beef cattle feedlots

(G-5136)
SMITH FABRICATION INC
1609 Central Ave S Ste 13 (98032-7447)
PHONE 253 854-4367
Stephen M Smith, *President*
EMP: 4
SQ FT: 6,000
SALES (est): 640.7K **Privately Held**
WEB: www.smithfabinc.com
SIC: 3444 Sheet metal specialties, not stamped

(G-5137)
SMOKE PLUS
23635 104th Ave Se (98031-3315)
PHONE 206 579-3661
John H Kim, *Owner*
Duk Hwenz, *Owner*
EMP: 2
SALES (est): 145.7K **Privately Held**
SIC: 2111 Cigarettes

(G-5138)
SOLUTIONS WITH INNOVATION
6757 S 216th St (98032-1389)
PHONE 253 872-0783
Frank Sorba, *Principal*
EMP: 3
SALES (est): 68.6K **Privately Held**
SIC: 2037 Frozen fruits & vegetables

(G-5139)
SOOS CREEK WINE CELLARS LLC
24012 172nd Ave Se (98042-5280)
PHONE 253 631-8775
David Larsen,
Cecile Larsen,
EMP: 2
SALES: 300K **Privately Held**
WEB: www.sooscreekwine.com
SIC: 2084 Wines

(G-5140)
SOUND MACHINE PRODUCTS INC
22645 76th Ave S (98032-1922)
P.O. Box 1327 (98035-1327)
PHONE 253 872-5876
Mark Parhaniemi, *President*
Tom Evans, *Prdtn Mgr*
EMP: 12 **EST:** 1985
SQ FT: 10,000
SALES (est): 2.2MM **Privately Held**
WEB: www.soundmachineproducts.com
SIC: 3599 Machine shop, jobbing & repair

(G-5141)
SOUND MANUFACTURING INC
5820 S 228th St (98032-1810)
P.O. Box 5097 (98064-5097)
PHONE 253 872-8007
Chris Jensen, *President*
Val Williams, *Managing Dir*
EMP: 43
SQ FT: 24,000
SALES (est): 5.1MM **Privately Held**
SIC: 3089 3599 3083 Molding primary plastic; machine shop, jobbing & repair; laminated plastics plate & sheet

(G-5142)
SOUND SPRING INC
830 3rd Ave S (98032-6128)
PHONE 253 859-9499
Alfred Kerns, *President*
Pat Kerns, *Vice Pres*
EMP: 10
SQ FT: 6,500
SALES (est): 1.1MM **Privately Held**
WEB: www.soundspringinc.com
SIC: 3495 3469 3496 3493 Wire springs; ornamental metal stampings; miscellaneous fabricated wire products; steel springs, except wire

(G-5143)
SPACEWALL WEST INC
Also Called: Spacewall Northwest
25315 74th Ave S (98032-6013)
PHONE 253 852-0203
Gary Mills, *President*
EMP: 9
SQ FT: 21,702
SALES (corp-wide): 4.1MM **Privately Held**
WEB: www.spacewallwest.com
SIC: 2541 2542 5046 Display fixtures, wood; fixtures: display, office or store: except wood; store fixtures
PA: Spacewall West, Inc.
4509 Stonegate Indus Blvd
Stone Mountain GA 30083
770 442-8157

(G-5144)
SPEARMAN CORP KENT DIVISION
7020 Oberto Dr (98032-7014)
PHONE 253 236-5980
Alexander Spearman, *President*
EMP: 15
SALES (est): 527.7K **Privately Held**
SIC: 3728 Refueling equipment for use in flight, airplane

(G-5145)
SPEARMAN CORPORATION (PA)
7020 Oberto Dr (98032-7014)
P.O. Box 1657, Tacoma (98401-1657)
PHONE 360 651-9281
Alex Spearman, *Ch of Bd*
Dave Hill, *Engineer*
EMP: 22
SALES (est): 4.7MM **Privately Held**
SIC: 3728 Aircraft parts & equipment

(G-5146)
SPECIALIZED MACHINE WORKS
20021 80th Ave S (98032-1209)
PHONE 206 715-5901
Sherri Hanson, *Office Mgr*
EMP: 2
SALES (est): 177.8K **Privately Held**
SIC: 3599 Machine shop, jobbing & repair

(G-5147)
SPECIALIZED PHARMACEUTICALS
325 W Gowe St (98032-5892)
PHONE 253 859-3702
EMP: 3 **EST:** 2011
SALES (est): 231.8K **Privately Held**
SIC: 2834 Pharmaceutical preparations

(G-5148)
SPECIALTY SHEET METAL INC
11409 Se 218th Pl (98031-1305)
PHONE 253 872-5718
Fax: 253 872-5519
EMP: 10
SQ FT: 7,000
SALES (est): 1.3MM **Privately Held**
SIC: 3444 Mfg Sheet Metalwork

(G-5149)
SPECIALTY WIPERS INC (PA)
7979 S 180th St (98032-1051)
PHONE 425 251-3530
Fred Barber, *President*
▲ **EMP:** 4
SQ FT: 50,000
SALES (est): 1.5MM **Privately Held**
WEB: www.specialtywipers.com
SIC: 2273 Carpets & rugs

(G-5150)
SPILLER CORPORATION
7825 S 180th St (98032-1050)
PHONE 206 575-2110
Sam Spiller, *Owner*
EMP: 2
SALES (est): 198.9K **Privately Held**
SIC: 3993 Signs & advertising specialties

(G-5151)
SPLENDID INTL USA CORP
8647 S 212th St (98031-1910)
PHONE 253 813-5692
Victor Lin, *President*
EMP: 4
SQ FT: 6,000
SALES (est): 6.8MM **Privately Held**
SIC: 3272 Building stone, artificial: concrete

(G-5152)
STARGATE INC
19625 62nd Ave S Ste B103 (98032-1107)
PHONE 425 251-0701
Peter Hambling, *President*
Lorrie Hambling, *Director*
June Mercer, *Admin Sec*
◆ **EMP:** 6
SALES (est): 1.7MM
SALES (corp-wide): 11.4MM **Privately Held**
WEB: www.digital-control.com
SIC: 3679 3812 Electronic circuits; search & navigation equipment
PA: Digital Control Incorporated
19625 62nd Ave S Ste B103
Kent WA 98032
425 251-0701

(G-5153)
STECK TECHNICAL PUBLICATIONS
12613 Se 228th Ct (98031-3751)
PHONE 253 630-7279
Diane Steck, *Principal*
EMP: 2
SALES (est): 117.3K **Privately Held**
SIC: 2741 Miscellaneous publishing

(G-5154)
STEEL RULE CONCEPTS LLC
19221 62nd Ave S (98032-1133)
P.O. Box 88199, Seattle (98138-2199)
PHONE 905 475-0324
Rick Bernard,
EMP: 9
SQ FT: 4,100
SALES (est): 1.3MM **Privately Held**
WEB: www.steelruleconcepts.com
SIC: 3544 Dies & die holders for metal cutting, forming, die casting

(G-5155)
STELIA AEROSPACE NORTH AMERICA
8407 S 259th St Ste 303 (98030-7536)
PHONE 253 852-4055
Kevin Steck, *Vice Pres*
EMP: 4
SALES (est): 426.1K **Privately Held**
WEB: www.compositesatlantic.com
SIC: 3549 Wiredrawing & fabricating machinery & equipment, ex. die

(G-5156)
STERLITECH CORPORATION
22027 70th Ave S (98032-1911)
PHONE 253 437-0844
Mark Spatz, *President*
Charles Shaw, *Engineer*
Kristina Shahbazian, *Sales Mgr*
Ron Carr, *Sales Staff*
Kensen Hirohata, *Sales Staff*
◆ **EMP:** 20
SQ FT: 10,000
SALES (est): 4.4MM **Privately Held**
WEB: www.sterlitech.com
SIC: 3069 Medical & laboratory rubber sundries & related products

(G-5157)
STOCKTON CUL DE SAC
10955 Se 224th Pl (98031-2633)
PHONE 253 854-9358
James R R Teeters, *Principal*
EMP: 2
SALES (est): 70.6K **Privately Held**
SIC: 3915 Jewelers' materials & lapidary work

(G-5158)
STONEWAY ELECTRIC SUPPLY CO
7011 S 234th St (98032-2965)
PHONE 253 859-0224
Eric McGinnis, *Manager*
EMP: 14
SALES (corp-wide): 1.2B **Privately Held**
WEB: www.stoneway.com
SIC: 5063 3625 Electrical supplies; motor control accessories, including overload relays
HQ: Stoneway Electric Supply Co.
402 N Perry St
Spokane WA 99202
509 535-2933

(G-5159)
STOROPACK INC
20414 87th Ave S (98031-1201)
PHONE 253 872-6844
Jim Nevis, *Manager*
EMP: 10
SALES (corp-wide): 535.4MM **Privately Held**
WEB: www.storopack.com
SIC: 3086 Packaging & shipping materials, foamed plastic
HQ: Storopack, Inc.
4758 Devitt Dr
West Chester OH 45246
513 874-0314

(G-5160)
STRICTLY IC
24920 43rd Ave S (98032-4160)
PHONE 253 941-6611
Robert Washburn, *Principal*
EMP: 2
SALES (est): 109.6K **Privately Held**
SIC: 2741 Miscellaneous publishing

(G-5161)
SUN RISE DENTAL
10216 Se 256th St Ste 108 (98030-6437)
PHONE 253 856-3384
Nasser Barghi DDS, *Principal*
EMP: 2
SALES (est): 248.9K **Privately Held**
SIC: 3843 Enamels, dentists'

(G-5162)
SUNOCO INC
8039 S 192nd St (98032-5027)
PHONE 253 872-8500
EMP: 4
SALES (corp-wide): 54B **Publicly Held**
SIC: 2893 2911 2869 2865 Printing ink; petroleum refining; industrial organic chemicals; phenol, alkylated & cumene; petroleum terminals
HQ: Sunoco, Inc.
3801 West Chester Pike
Newtown Square PA 19073
215 977-3000

(G-5163)
SUNSTREAM CORPORATION (PA)
22149 68th Ave S (98032-1937)
PHONE 253 395-0500
Kenneth Hey, *President*
Julie Gazda, *Vice Pres*
Deborah Hey, *Vice Pres*
Loern Halverson, *Engineer*
Chris Ketzel, *CFO*
◆ **EMP:** 24
SQ FT: 3,200
SALES (est): 5.9MM **Privately Held**
WEB: www.sunstreamcorp.com
SIC: 3536 Boat lifts

(G-5164)
SWIFTCARB
1720 Central Ave S (98032-7416)
PHONE 800 227-9876
Brian Swiftcarb, *Technical Staff*
EMP: 2 **EST:** 2016
SALES (est): 85.2K **Privately Held**
SIC: 3545 Cutting tools for machine tools

(G-5165)
SYNCHRONOUS AEROSPACE
821 3rd Ave S (98032-6129)
PHONE 253 852-9700

Kent - King County (G-5166)

EMP: 2
SALES (est): 119.3K Privately Held
SIC: 3728 Aircraft parts & equipment

(G-5166)
T & A SUPPLY COMPANY INC (PA)
6807 S 216th St (98032-2440)
P.O. Box 927 (98035-0927)
PHONE..................................206 282-3770
Owen E Strecker Jr, *President*
Greg Szalay, *Principal*
Nikki Cross, *Safety Mgr*
Ralph Richner, *Facilities Mgr*
Tom McMakin, *Opers Staff*
◆ EMP: 84
SALES (est): 108MM Privately Held
SIC: 1771 5023 1752 2431 Flooring contractor; floor coverings; carpets; floor cushion & padding; resilient floor coverings: tile or sheet; wood floor installation & refinishing; doors & door parts & trim, wood

(G-5167)
T & A SUPPLY COMPANY INC
Also Called: Pacific Mat Co
6821 S 216th St Bldg A (98032-2440)
P.O. Box 927 (98035-0927)
PHONE..................................253 872-3682
Mike Wegener, *Principal*
Kathleen Miller, *CIO*
EMP: 9
SALES (corp-wide): 108MM Privately Held
SIC: 5023 1771 1752 2431 Floor coverings; flooring contractor; wood floor installation & refinishing; millwork; boards: planning, display, notice
PA: T & A Supply Company, Inc.
6807 S 216th St
Kent WA 98032
206 282-3770

(G-5168)
T & S DENTAL GROUP CORP
Also Called: Choice Dental Laboratory
1303 Central Ave S # 202 (98032-7403)
PHONE..................................714 720-5511
Seong Keor Kim, *President*
Seong Kim, *President*
Kevin Kim, *Marketing Staff*
Chun Chol Kim, *Admin Sec*
EMP: 4 EST: 2015
SALES (est): 81.8K Privately Held
SIC: 8021 3843 Offices & clinics of dentists; teeth, artificial (not made in dental laboratories)

(G-5169)
T J POTTERY
26620 Pacific Hwy S (98032-6926)
PHONE..................................253 946-1974
Jose Rivera, *Owner*
EMP: 2
SALES: 60K Privately Held
SIC: 3269 5199 Figures: pottery, china, earthenware & stoneware; statuary

(G-5170)
TACOMA SCREW PRODUCTS INC
22123 84th Ave S (98032-2462)
PHONE..................................253 395-9770
Brian Miller, *Manager*
Bryan Miller, *Manager*
EMP: 6
SALES (corp-wide): 42.4MM Privately Held
WEB: www.tacomascrew.com
SIC: 3451 5085 5072 Screw machine products; fasteners, industrial: nuts, bolts, screws, etc.; bolts, nuts & screws
PA: Tacoma Screw Products, Inc.
2001 Center St
Tacoma WA 98409
253 572-3444

(G-5171)
TAURUS POWER AND CONTROLS INC
8714 S 222nd St (98031-1915)
PHONE..................................425 656-4170
David Coons, *Manager*
EMP: 3
SALES (corp-wide): 7.1MM Privately Held
WEB: www.tauruspower.com
SIC: 3625 Electric controls & control accessories, industrial
PA: Taurus Power And Controls Inc.
9999 Sw Avery St
Tualatin OR 97062
503 692-9004

(G-5172)
TAYLOR FARMS NORTHWEST LLC
Also Called: Real Foods
8030 S 228th St Bldg A (98032-2987)
PHONE..................................206 764-4499
Bruce Taylor, *CEO*
Garth Borman, *COO*
Thomas Bryan, *CFO*
EMP: 10
SQ FT: 122,856
SALES (est): 2.8MM Privately Held
SIC: 2099 Ready-to-eat meals, salads & sandwiches
PA: Taylor Fresh Foods, Inc
150 Main St Ste 400
Salinas CA 93901

(G-5173)
TECHNA NDT LLC
6707 S 216th St (98032-1389)
PHONE..................................253 872-2415
Kelly T Phelps,
Kelly Phelps,
◆ EMP: 17
SQ FT: 12,000
SALES (est): 3.2MM Privately Held
WEB: www.technandt.com
SIC: 3829 Measuring & controlling devices

(G-5174)
TECHNICAL MOLDED PLASTICS INC
Also Called: T M P
18506a 80th Pl S Ste A (98032-1069)
PHONE..................................425 251-9710
Charles Green, *President*
▲ EMP: 35
SQ FT: 30,000
SALES (est): 6.2MM Privately Held
WEB: www.tmp1.com
SIC: 3089 Injection molded finished plastic products

(G-5175)
TECT AEROSPACE LLC
19420 84th Ave S (98032-1240)
PHONE..................................253 872-7045
Jim Ripka, *Principal*
Glenn Warren, *Plant Mgr*
Tim Madison, *Buyer*
Mike Needam, *Info Tech Mgr*
EMP: 100
SALES (corp-wide): 45MM Privately Held
SIC: 3728 Aircraft body & wing assemblies & parts
HQ: Tect Aerospace, Llc
300 W Douglas Ave Ste 100
Wichita KS 67202
316 425-3638

(G-5176)
TELEPRESS INC (PA)
19241 62nd Ave S (98032-1133)
P.O. Box 1085 (98035-1085)
PHONE..................................425 392-1660
Daren Loken, *President*
Michael Allen, *CFO*
Shellie Holst, *Accounts Mgr*
Valicia Valiani, *Accounts Mgr*
Shannon Lykken, *Sales Staff*
EMP: 40
SQ FT: 12,000
SALES (est): 9.1MM Privately Held
WEB: www.telepress.com
SIC: 2752 Commercial printing, lithographic

(G-5177)
TEREX UTILITIES INC
Also Called: Terex Utilities West
7829 S 206th St (98032-1354)
PHONE..................................206 764-5025
Kevin Crowder, *Production*
Brian Clark, *Engineer*
Wayne Miller, *Manager*
Beau Anderson, *Manager*
EMP: 41
SALES (corp-wide): 5.1B Publicly Held
WEB: www.terexutilities.com
SIC: 3699 Electrical equipment & supplies
HQ: Terex Utilities, Inc.
12805 Sw 77th Pl
Tigard OR 97223
503 620-0611

(G-5178)
THERMAL NORTHWEST INC
6020 S 226th St (98032-4814)
PHONE..................................253 520-8899
Terry M Osthus, *President*
EMP: 10
SALES (est): 1.4MM Privately Held
SIC: 3292 Blankets, insulating for aircraft asbestos

(G-5179)
THREE SIGMA MANUFACTURING INC
22604 58th Pl S (98032-4603)
P.O. Box 97059, Redmond (98073-9759)
PHONE..................................253 395-1125
Kenneth Frankel, *President*
EMP: 21
SQ FT: 18,040
SALES (est): 3.1MM Privately Held
WEB: www.threesigma.net
SIC: 3599 Machine shop, jobbing & repair

(G-5180)
TIEGRRR STRAPS INC
27005 Cardiff Ave (98032-7600)
P.O. Box 1719 (98035-1719)
PHONE..................................253 520-0303
Michael Brenneman, *President*
Lisa Brenneman, *Vice Pres*
▲ EMP: 7
SQ FT: 1,000
SALES (est): 370K Privately Held
SIC: 2221 5131 Polyester broadwoven fabrics; piece goods & other fabrics

(G-5181)
TONYS CUSTOM CABINETS
24504 148th Ln Se (98042-4139)
PHONE..................................425 444-1086
Judith Parkins, *Principal*
EMP: 2 EST: 2006
SALES (est): 207.9K Privately Held
SIC: 2434 Wood kitchen cabinets

(G-5182)
TORK LIFT INTERNATIONAL INC (PA)
Also Called: Torklift International
322 Railroad Ave N (98032-4531)
PHONE..................................253 479-0115
Jack Kay, *President*
Chad Winslow, *Research*
Candice Boutilier, *Mktg Dir*
Joel Crawford, *Mktg Dir*
Jay Taylor, *Manager*
▲ EMP: 10 EST: 2005
SALES (est): 2.6MM Privately Held
SIC: 3714 Motor vehicle parts & accessories

(G-5183)
TORKLIFT CENTRAL WLDG KENT INC
322 Railroad Ave N (98032-4531)
PHONE..................................253 854-1832
Matt Lynch, *Vice Pres*
EMP: 4
SALES (est): 180.2K
SALES (corp-wide): 11.9MM Privately Held
SIC: 7692 Welding repair
PA: Torklift Central Welding Of Kent, Inc.
315 Central Ave N
Kent WA 98032
253 854-1832

(G-5184)
TOTAL RECLAIM INCORPORATED (PA)
7021 S 220th St (98032-1900)
PHONE..................................206 343-7443
Jeff Zirkle, *President*
Craig Lorch, *Treasurer*
▼ EMP: 129
SALES (est): 13.2MM Privately Held
WEB: www.totalreclaim.com
SIC: 3559 5084 Recycling machinery; recycling machinery & equipment

(G-5185)
TOUCHFIRE INC
20206 87th Ave S (98031-1280)
PHONE..................................425 466-4177
Steven Isaac, *CEO*
Bradley Melmon, *Director*
▲ EMP: 3
SALES: 1MM Privately Held
SIC: 3575 Keyboards, computer, office machine

(G-5186)
TOUCHMARK PRINTING
7859 S 180th St (98032-1050)
PHONE..................................206 420-4607
Kelly Cannon, *Principal*
EMP: 2
SALES (est): 161.1K Privately Held
SIC: 2759 Commercial printing

(G-5187)
TRAIGHT INDUSTRIES
14181 Se 255th St (98042-6621)
PHONE..................................253 630-1489
Scott Waight, *Principal*
▲ EMP: 2
SALES (est): 137.9K Privately Held
SIC: 3999 Manufacturing industries

(G-5188)
TRANSCO NORTHWEST INC (PA)
22211 76th Ave S (98032-1924)
P.O. Box 88002, Seattle (98138-2002)
PHONE..................................425 251-5422
Richard Brown Jr, *President*
Richard Brown Sr, *Vice Pres*
Joe Gill, *Vice Pres*
Dave McClain, *Project Dir*
Collin Cakarnis, *CFO*
▲ EMP: 20
SQ FT: 22,000
SALES (est): 18MM Privately Held
WEB: www.transconorthwest.com
SIC: 5085 5084 3535 Industrial supplies; conveyor systems; conveyors & conveying equipment

(G-5189)
TRANSCOLD DISTRIBUTION USA INC
6858 S 190th St (98032-1033)
PHONE..................................604 519-0600
John Joseph Coughlan, *President*
Linida Tjondrosejio, *CFO*
EMP: 3
SALES (est): 684.6K Privately Held
SIC: 2024 Ice cream & frozen desserts

(G-5190)
TRI-TEC MANUFACTURING LLC
6915 S 234th St (98032-2920)
PHONE..................................425 251-8777
Mark Haller, *President*
EMP: 33
SALES (corp-wide): 8.5MM Privately Held
WEB: www.tritecmfg.com
SIC: 3491 Valves, automatic control
PA: Tri-Tec Manufacturing, Llc
6915 S 234th St
Kent WA 98032
425 251-8777

(G-5191)
TRUE CUSTOM CABINETRY
22225 76th Ave S (98032-1924)
PHONE..................................206 909-4454
Ben Feely, *Principal*
EMP: 5
SALES (est): 358.1K Privately Held
SIC: 2434 Wood kitchen cabinets

(G-5192)
TUDOR GAMES INC
6852 S 224th St (98032-1901)
PHONE..................................800 914-8836
Doug Strohm, *CEO*
Wyatt Strohm, *Warehouse Mgr*

GEOGRAPHIC SECTION

Kent - King County (G-5221)

EMP: 8 EST: 2012
SALES: 1.5MM Privately Held
SIC: 3944 Games, toys & children's vehicles

(G-5193)
U S SCALE INCORPORATED
Also Called: Meridian Scale Service
8702 S 222nd St (98031-1915)
PHONE 253 872-4803
Toll Free: ....888 -
Todd Thompson, *President*
Jim Hague, *Vice Pres*
EMP: 8
SALES: 1.2MM Privately Held
WEB: www.usscale.com
SIC: 5046 3596 Scales, except laboratory; counting scales; weighing machines & apparatus

(G-5194)
UNIFIED SCREENING & CRUSHING
22020 72nd Ave S (98032-1964)
PHONE 253 872-6595
Austin Gwyther, *General Mgr*
EMP: 5
SALES (corp-wide): 15.6MM Privately Held
SIC: 3523 Feed grinders, crushers & mixers
PA: Unified Screening & Crushing - Mn, Inc.
3350 Highway 149
Eagan MN 55121
651 454-8835

(G-5195)
UNIFIED SCRNING CRSHING-WA LLC
22020 72nd Ave S (98032-1964)
PHONE 800 562-1971
Thomas Charles Lentsch,
EMP: 5
SALES (est): 187.8K Privately Held
SIC: 3559 Screening equipment, electric

(G-5196)
UNISOURCE MANUFACTURING INC
1037 4th Ave N (98032-2943)
PHONE 253 854-0541
EMP: 2 EST: 2012
SALES (est): 157.3K Privately Held
SIC: 8742 5084 3999 3569 Industrial & labor consulting services; hydraulic systems equipment & supplies; manufacturing industries; general industrial machinery

(G-5197)
UNITED SORBENTS SEATTLE LLC (HQ)
Also Called: United Sorbents Midwest
18821 90th Ave S (98031-2400)
PHONE 425 656-4440
Donald Rogahn, *Partner*
Yeanna Woo, *Partner*
◆ EMP: 50
SQ FT: 55,000
SALES (est): 22.4MM Privately Held
WEB: www.unitedsorbents.com
SIC: 2842 Sweeping compounds, oil or water absorbent, clay or sawdust

(G-5198)
UNIVERSAL SIGN AND GRAPHICS
Also Called: Chaos Graphics
14408 Se 256th Pl (98042-3630)
PHONE 253 630-0400
Brad Taylor, *Owner*
Kim Taylor, *Vice Pres*
EMP: 3
SALES (est): 22K Privately Held
SIC: 3993 Signs & advertising specialties

(G-5199)
VALLEY MACHINE SHOP INC
Also Called: VMS
1166 6th Ave N (98032-2936)
PHONE 425 226-5040
Victor Dalosto, *President*
Valarie Dalosto, *Corp Secy*
EMP: 40 EST: 1974
SQ FT: 10,000
SALES (est): 7.3MM Privately Held
SIC: 3599 3812 3728 Machine shop, jobbing & repair; search & navigation equipment; aircraft parts & equipment

(G-5200)
VERLINDAS
22510 43rd Ave S (98032-8470)
PHONE 253 437-5217
Linda Leonard, *Owner*
EMP: 3
SALES (est): 100K Privately Held
SIC: 3942 Stuffed toys, including animals

(G-5201)
VINTAGE QUILTING
20004 106th Ave Se (98031-5501)
PHONE 253 852-6596
Sylvia Jacobus, *Principal*
EMP: 2
SALES (est): 205.1K Privately Held
SIC: 3552 Cloth spreading machines

(G-5202)
VISHAY PRECISION GROUP INC
5920 S 194th St (98032-1196)
PHONE 253 872-1910
EMP: 4
SALES (corp-wide): 299.7MM Publicly Held
SIC: 3676 Electronic resistors
PA: Vishay Precision Group, Inc.
3 Great Valley Pkwy # 150
Malvern PA 19355
484 321-5300

(G-5203)
VITAL SIGNS NOTARY
14641 Se 276th Pl (98042-9130)
PHONE 206 387-6622
Gregory Bell, *Owner*
EMP: 2
SALES (est): 112.8K Privately Held
SIC: 3993 Signs & advertising specialties

(G-5204)
W R MEADOWS INC
826 3rd Ave S (98032-6128)
PHONE 707 745-6666
EMP: 2
SALES (est): 125.8K Privately Held
SIC: 3272 Concrete products

(G-5205)
WALMAN OPTICAL COMPANY
20417 80th Ave S (98032-1257)
P.O. Box 88804, Seattle (98138-2804)
PHONE 253 872-7137
Roger Bruce, *Branch Mgr*
EMP: 36
SALES (corp-wide): 404.2MM Privately Held
SIC: 5995 3229 5049 3851 Optical goods stores; pressed & blown glass; optical goods; ophthalmic goods
PA: The Walman Optical Company
801 12th Ave N Ste 1
Minneapolis MN 55411
612 520-6000

(G-5206)
WASHIGTON FIELD SERVICES INC
11325 Se 264th Pl (98030-7124)
PHONE 253 813-6681
Steve Hayes, *President*
Carol Hayes, *Vice Pres*
EMP: 6
SALES (est): 500K Privately Held
SIC: 1389 Gas field services

(G-5207)
WASHINGTON IGNITION INTERLOCK
Also Called: Affordable Ignition Interlock
23452 30th Ave S Ste 102 (98032-2820)
PHONE 206 824-6849
Mary Pellegrini, *Partner*
EMP: 2
SALES (est): 154.3K Privately Held
SIC: 3694 Ignition apparatus & distributors

(G-5208)
WASHINGTON POTTERY CO
18815 72nd Ave S (98032-1040)
PHONE 425 656-7277
Donald Wilson, *President*
Kathy Wilson, *Corp Secy*
Dan Surber, *Sales Mgr*
Brian Ehle, *Sales Associate*
▲ EMP: 9
SQ FT: 20,000
SALES (est): 888.2K Privately Held
WEB: www.washingtonpottery.com
SIC: 5193 3269 Planters & flower pots; flower pots, red earthenware

(G-5209)
WASHINGTON POWERSCREEN INC
7915 S 261st St (98032-7313)
PHONE 253 236-4153
Patrick F Lowe, *President*
▲ EMP: 8
SQ FT: 6,000
SALES (est): 2.4MM
SALES (corp-wide): 555.1K Privately Held
WEB: www.powerscreen-wa.com
SIC: 3531 Crushers, grinders & similar equipment
HQ: Terex Gb Limited
200 Coalisland Road
Dungannon BT71
288 771-8500

(G-5210)
WEST COAST FIBER INC
832 3rd Ave S (98032-6128)
P.O. Box 249, Sumner (98390-0050)
PHONE 253 850-5606
Byron Larson, *President*
Patricia Larson, *Vice Pres*
EMP: 10
SQ FT: 14,000
SALES: 1.5MM Privately Held
SIC: 2392 Pillows, bed: made from purchased materials

(G-5211)
WEST COAST LAMINATING LLC
8939 S 190th St Ste 104 (98031-1212)
PHONE 253 395-5225
Brian Reitz, *Manager*
EMP: 12
SALES (corp-wide): 94.5MM Privately Held
WEB: www.westcoastlaminating.com
SIC: 2452 2434 2541 Panels & sections, prefabricated, wood; wood kitchen cabinets; table or counter tops, plastic laminated
HQ: West Coast Laminating, Llc
5602 Bickett St
Vernon CA 90058
323 585-9201

(G-5212)
WEST COAST PAPER COMPANY (PA)
Also Called: Wcp Solutions
6703 S 234th St Ste 120 (98032-2903)
PHONE 253 850-1900
Teresa Russell, *President*
Keith Spurdon, *General Mgr*
Chris Hansch, *COO*
Stephanie Quinn, *Vice Pres*
Jon Thompson, *Vice Pres*
▲ EMP: 20 EST: 1930
SQ FT: 6,800
SALES (est): 242.4MM Privately Held
WEB: www.wcpsolutinos.com
SIC: 5085 5169 5084 2677 Industrial supplies; chemicals & allied products; packaging machinery & equipment; envelopes

(G-5213)
WESTERN CLEAR VIEW RAILING
7818 S 194th St (98032-1163)
PHONE 253 395-3113
Krista Bartlet, *Owner*
EMP: 30 EST: 2001
SALES (est): 2.9MM Privately Held
SIC: 3446 Stairs, staircases, stair treads: prefabricated metal

(G-5214)
WESTMARK INDUSTRIES INC
Also Called: Diagraph of The Northwest
19115 68th Ave S Ste H101 (98032-2110)
PHONE 425 251-8444
Mike Offer, *President*
Chris Ferris, *Purch Agent*
John Deveiteo, *Marketing Staff*
Brad Ulrich, *Technical Staff*
Kim Hubbard, *Representative*
EMP: 3
SALES (corp-wide): 14.3MM Privately Held
WEB: www.westmarkind.com
SIC: 2672 Labels (unprinted), gummed: made from purchased materials; tape, pressure sensitive: made from purchased materials
PA: Westmark Industries, Inc.
6701 Mcewan Rd
Lake Oswego OR 97035
503 620-0945

(G-5215)
WHISD CRAFT
10825 Se 233rd Pl (98031-3443)
PHONE 253 850-7126
Diane Whitlock, *Owner*
Stephen Whitlock, *Manager*
EMP: 3
SALES (est): 150.3K Privately Held
SIC: 2499 Decorative wood & woodwork

(G-5216)
WHITEFAB
22803 86th Ave S (98031-2466)
PHONE 253 277-4047
Dave White, *Principal*
David White, *Principal*
EMP: 5
SALES (est): 747.6K Privately Held
SIC: 3469 Metal stampings

(G-5217)
WIREKAT ENTERPRISES
18531 Se 224th St (98042-7231)
PHONE 425 413-6946
Kevin Thomas, *Principal*
EMP: 2
SALES (est): 200.6K Privately Held
SIC: 3674 Light emitting diodes

(G-5218)
WORD UP PUBLISHING
1600 Central Ave S (98032-7459)
PHONE 253 859-7002
Michael Miller, *President*
EMP: 2 EST: 2011
SALES (est): 91.1K Privately Held
SIC: 2741 Miscellaneous publishing

(G-5219)
WRIGHT BUSINESS FORMS INC
7015 S 212th St (98032-1369)
PHONE 253 872-0200
Robert Williams, *Manager*
EMP: 50
SALES (corp-wide): 400.7MM Publicly Held
WEB: www.wrightbg.com
SIC: 2761 5943 Manifold business forms; office forms & supplies
HQ: Wright Business Graphics Llc
18440 Ne San Rafael St
Portland OR 97230
800 547-8397

(G-5220)
ZEBRA PRINTING
18439 E Valley Hwy # 103 (98032-1205)
PHONE 425 656-3700
Fax: 425 656-3703
EMP: 2 EST: 2011
SALES (est): 160K Privately Held
SIC: 2752 Lithographic Commercial Printing

(G-5221)
ZERO ONE VINTNERS
7050 S 216th St (98032-1932)
PHONE 206 601-2407
EMP: 2
SALES (est): 64.8K Privately Held
SIC: 2084 Wines, brandy & brandy spirits

Kettle Falls
Ferry County

(G-5222)
COLUMBIA NAVIGATION INC
365 2nd Ave (99160-9421)
P.O. Box 636 (99141-0636)
PHONE 509 684-4335
Eric Weatherman, *President*
EMP: 6
SQ FT: 1,500
SALES: 850K **Privately Held**
SIC: **1629** 4449 2493 2411 Marine construction; log rafting & towing; reconstituted wood products; logging

Kettle Falls
Stevens County

(G-5223)
3 LAKES FLY FISHING
910 E Riverview Ln (99141-8687)
P.O. Box 462 (99141-0462)
PHONE 509 675-4200
Mike Matney, *Owner*
EMP: 2
SALES (est): 83K **Privately Held**
SIC: **2399** Fishing nets

(G-5224)
BEARDSLEE LOGGING
3200 Hill Loop Rd (99141-8733)
PHONE 509 675-2400
Barry Beardslee, *Owner*
EMP: 2
SALES (est): 223.1K **Privately Held**
WEB: www.lightening.com
SIC: **2411** Logging camps & contractors

(G-5225)
BOBOLINK SOFTWARE
1723 Mountain Garden Way (99141-8840)
PHONE 509 684-2800
EMP: 2 EST: 2010
SALES (est): 124.4K **Privately Held**
SIC: **7372** Prepackaged Software Services

(G-5226)
BOISE CASCADE COMPANY
1274 S Boise Rd (99141-9792)
PHONE 509 738-3200
Richard D Just, *Manager*
EMP: 65
SALES (corp-wide): 5B **Publicly Held**
SIC: **2436** 2435 Plywood, softwood; hardwood veneer & plywood
PA: Boise Cascade Company
1111 W Jefferson St # 300
Boise ID 83702
208 384-6161

(G-5227)
BRIAN MARTELL
Also Called: Martell & Martell
2 Baxter Ln (99141-9403)
PHONE 509 738-3041
Brian Martell, *Owner*
David Martell, *Co-Owner*
EMP: 2
SALES (est): 96K **Privately Held**
WEB: www.martellmartell.com
SIC: **2411** Logging

(G-5228)
CHINA BEND VINEYARDS
Also Called: Victories Organic Gardens
3751 Vineyard Way (99141-8852)
PHONE 509 732-6123
William Bart Alexander, *Owner*
Victory I Alexander, *Owner*
EMP: 6
SQ FT: 2,400
SALES: 150K **Privately Held**
WEB: www.chinabend.com
SIC: **0172** 2084 Grapes; wines

(G-5229)
COLUMBIA CEDAR INC (PA)
24419 Highway 395 N (99141-9559)
PHONE 509 738-4711
Ralph Schmidt, *President*
Merry Schmidt, *Corp Secy*
Angela Monette, *Controller*
EMP: 82
SALES (est): 15.7MM **Privately Held**
WEB: www.columbiacedar.com
SIC: **2421** Lumber: rough, sawed or planed

(G-5230)
DALE BRADEEN LOGGING
3934 Highway 20 E (99141)
PHONE 509 738-6132
Dale Bradeen, *Owner*
EMP: 5
SALES (est): 250K **Privately Held**
SIC: **2411** Logging camps & contractors

(G-5231)
DJ CREATIONS
815 W Old Kettle Rd (99141-9676)
P.O. Box 958 (99141-0958)
PHONE 509 738-6200
Denna Balcom, *Partner*
Jody Balcom, *Partner*
EMP: 2
SALES (est): 98.6K **Privately Held**
SIC: **2621** Stationery, envelope & tablet papers

(G-5232)
HAULIN SOMETHIN INC
2084 Northprt Flat Crk Rd (99141-8759)
PHONE 509 738-4144
EMP: 2
SALES (est): 92.2K **Privately Held**
SIC: **2411** Logging

(G-5233)
KAISERS WELDING & MFG
410 Larch St (99141-5062)
P.O. Box 994 (99141-0994)
PHONE 509 738-6855
Karl Kaiser, *Owner*
Howard Kaiser, *Owner*
EMP: 2
SALES (est): 89.9K **Privately Held**
SIC: **7692** 3429 Welding repair; manufactured hardware (general)

(G-5234)
KETTLE RIVER BOAT WORKS LLC
1190 W Old Kettle Rd (99141-8690)
Rural Route 2 Box 5, Boyds (99107)
PHONE 509 738-2872
EMP: 2 EST: 2009
SALES (est): 83K **Privately Held**
SIC: **3732** Boatbuilding/Repairing

(G-5235)
LEAKE LOGGING INC
Also Called: Real Steel Recycling
883b Vanasse Rd (99141-9711)
PHONE 509 738-3033
Rick Leake, *President*
Sue Leake, *Corp Secy*
EMP: 3
SALES (est): 150K **Privately Held**
SIC: **2411** 7389 Logging camps & contractors;

(G-5236)
MAGIC EARTH
80 Martin Creek Dr (99141-9531)
PHONE 509 738-2801
Lonnie Leonard, *Principal*
EMP: 2
SALES (est): 62.6K **Privately Held**
SIC: **3295** Minerals, ground or treated

(G-5237)
NEW TEC LLC
Also Called: Newtec
970 Highway 395 N (99141-9660)
P.O. Box 1029 (99141-1029)
PHONE 509 738-6621
Dan Leighton,
Sandy Leighton,
EMP: 15
SQ FT: 10,000
SALES (est): 3.2MM **Privately Held**
SIC: **7699** 3532 3553 Industrial machinery & equipment repair; mining machinery; woodworking machinery

(G-5238)
NORTHERN ALES INC
325 W 3rd Ave (99141)
P.O. Box 993 (99141-0993)
PHONE 509 738-6913
Andrea Hedrick, *CEO*
Nanci Griffith, *Principal*
Stephen Hedrick, *Treasurer*
EMP: 8
SALES (est): 721.2K **Privately Held**
SIC: **2082** Beer (alcoholic beverage)

(G-5239)
NORTHWEST WOOD PRODUCTS INC
850 W Old Kettle Rd (99141-9676)
P.O. Box 330 (99141-0330)
PHONE 509 738-6190
Art House, *President*
Shirley House, *Treasurer*
EMP: 6
SQ FT: 15,000
SALES (est): 565.2K **Privately Held**
SIC: **2499** Engraved wood products

(G-5240)
RAW ADVANTAGE INC
1156 Highway 25 S (99141)
PHONE 509 738-3344
ARA Bush, *Principal*
EMP: 2
SALES (est): 177.7K **Privately Held**
SIC: **2048** 5199 Prepared feeds; pet supplies

(G-5241)
SUMMIT LAKE LABS LLC
8 Enzyme Ln (99141-9472)
PHONE 509 738-4313
Dave Gaynor,
Phillip Gaynor,
EMP: 15 EST: 2010
SALES (est): 2.4MM **Privately Held**
SIC: **2023** Dietary supplements, dairy & non-dairy based

(G-5242)
TARBERT LOGGING INC
1505 W Old Kettle Rd (99141)
PHONE 509 738-6567
Larry Tarbert, *President*
EMP: 16
SALES (est): 1.6MM **Privately Held**
SIC: **2411** Logging camps & contractors

(G-5243)
WHITE STONE CALCIUM CORP (PA)
Also Called: White Stone Co
Rittinger Rd (99141)
PHONE 509 738-6571
Don Grubb, *President*
Jim Bennett, *Vice Pres*
Dave Wilcox, *Treasurer*
EMP: 6
SALES (est): 1.3MM **Privately Held**
SIC: **1429** Dolomitic marble, crushed & broken-quarrying

Keyport
Kitsap County

(G-5244)
RAYTHEON COMPANY
610 Dowell St Bldg 894 (98345-7601)
PHONE 360 394-3434
Glenda Ledford, *Manager*
James Lanzafame, *Technology*
Dana Schroedel, *Technology*
Liza Desir, *Sr Software Eng*
Garrett Flynn, *Sr Software Eng*
EMP: 200
SALES (corp-wide): 27B **Publicly Held**
SIC: **3812** Sonar systems & equipment
PA: Raytheon Company
870 Winter St
Waltham MA 02451
781 522-3000

(G-5245)
RAYTHEON COMPANY
610 Dowell St Bldg 894 (98345-7601)
P.O. Box 500 (98345-0500)
PHONE 360 697-6600
Jon Rudlang, *Finance*
EMP: 450
SALES (corp-wide): 27B **Publicly Held**
SIC: **3812** Sonar systems & equipment
PA: Raytheon Company
870 Winter St
Waltham MA 02451
781 522-3000

(G-5246)
RAYTHEON COMPANY
610 Dowell St (98345-7601)
P.O. Box 500 (98345-0500)
PHONE 360 394-7559
William Watts, *Vice Pres*
Mariana Vawter, *Branch Mgr*
EMP: 172
SALES (corp-wide): 27B **Publicly Held**
SIC: **3812** Defense systems & equipment
PA: Raytheon Company
870 Winter St
Waltham MA 02451
781 522-3000

(G-5247)
UNITED STATES DEPT OF NAVY
Naval Undersea Warfare Ctr Div
610 Dowell St (98345-7601)
PHONE 360 396-2340
Elizabeth Kerstetter, *Engineer*
Mary Townsend-Manning, *Manager*
EMP: 175 **Publicly Held**
SIC: **9711** 3357 Navy; aircraft wire & cable, nonferrous
HQ: United States Department Of The Navy
1200 Navy Pentagon
Washington DC 20350

Kingston
Kitsap County

(G-5248)
BLUE HOME THERMAL IMAGING LLC
33640 Widmark Rd Ne (98346-7648)
P.O. Box 1963 (98346-1963)
PHONE 360 638-0838
Jon Wood, *Principal*
EMP: 2
SALES (est): 212.9K **Privately Held**
SIC: **2591** Venetian blinds

(G-5249)
BRIARWOOD FURNITURE LTD INC
28680 State Hwy 104 Ne (98346-8400)
PHONE 425 868-7707
Terry Johnson, *President*
EMP: 2
SALES: 200K **Privately Held**
WEB: www.briarwoodfurniture.com
SIC: **2511** 5712 Wood household furniture; furniture stores

(G-5250)
CASEY BURNS FLUTES
9962 Ne Shrty Campbell Rd (98346-9614)
P.O. Box 882 (98346-0882)
PHONE 360 297-4020
EMP: 2
SALES (est): 144.4K **Privately Held**
SIC: **3931** Mfg Musical Instruments

(G-5251)
FLYING WRENCH SVC
Also Called: Flying Wrench Services
31516 Commercial Ave Ne (98346-7667)
P.O. Box 1361 (98346-1361)
PHONE 360 638-0044
Joe Kiernan, *President*
EMP: 11
SALES (est): 2.1MM **Privately Held**
SIC: **7699** 7692 Aircraft & heavy equipment repair services; welding repair

GEOGRAPHIC SECTION

Kirkland - King County (G-5283)

(G-5252)
FORSYTH ENTERPRISES
25770 Miller Bay Rd Ne (98346-9359)
PHONE..................360 297-2684
Michael Forsyth, *Owner*
Monica Forsyth, *Co-Owner*
EMP: 2 **EST:** 1983
SALES: 68K **Privately Held**
SIC: 1629 2411 Timber removal; logging

(G-5253)
GAMBLE BAY TIMBER
26131 Bond Rd Ne (98346-9415)
P.O. Box 278, Port Gamble (98364-0278)
PHONE..................360 297-0555
Jeremy J Anunson, *Owner*
EMP: 9
SQ FT: 950
SALES: 125K **Privately Held**
SIC: 2411 Logging camps & contractors

(G-5254)
GLOBAL ENTERPRISE INTL
Also Called: Synenergy Triad North America
26257 Montera Loop Ne (98346-9442)
PHONE..................303 928-3208
EMP: 10
SALES (est): 657K **Privately Held**
SIC: 2869 Operative Builders

(G-5255)
KATHLEEN M SOLE
Also Called: Real World Publications
12835 Ne Marine View Dr (98346-9162)
P.O. Box 7302 (98346-0030)
PHONE..................360 297-4650
Kathleen M Sole, *Owner*
EMP: 2
SALES (est): 450K **Privately Held**
WEB: www.whatstherule.com
SIC: 2731 Book publishing

(G-5256)
KINGSTON MAIL CENTER INC
Also Called: Kingston Mail & Print
8202 Ne Stat Hwy 104 10 (98346)
PHONE..................360 297-2173
Amy Spray, *President*
EMP: 2
SALES (est): 392.2K **Privately Held**
SIC: 4731 3444 Shipping documents preparation; mail (post office) collection or storage boxes, sheet metal

(G-5257)
KITSAP BUSINESS SERVICES INC
Also Called: Kingston Mail and Print
8202 Ne State Hwy (98346)
PHONE..................360 297-2173
Amy Spray, *Officer*
EMP: 5
SALES (est): 503.6K **Privately Held**
SIC: 7334 3993 4731 Photocopying & duplicating services; signs, not made in custom sign painting shops; agents, except

(G-5258)
NORTHSTAR INVESTMENT CO
Also Called: Pierside Promotions
25923 Washington Blvd Ne (98346-7632)
P.O. Box 569 (98346-0569)
PHONE..................360 297-2260
David Kutz, *Owner*
◆ **EMP:** 2
SQ FT: 1,000
SALES (est): 179.1K **Privately Held**
SIC: 5199 7389 2731 Advertising specialties; embroidering of advertising on shirts, etc.; book publishing

(G-5259)
OLYMPIC PRINTER RESOURCES INC
Also Called: Olympic Technology Resources
26127 Calvary Ln Ne # 200 (98346-8485)
PHONE..................360 297-8384
Harry Petersen, *President*
Erik Petersen, *Vice Pres*
▲ **EMP:** 10
SQ FT: 4,800
SALES (est): 1.5MM **Privately Held**
WEB: www.olyprinter.com
SIC: 3955 Print cartridges for laser & other computer printers

(G-5260)
PACIFIC NETTING PRODUCTS INC
25993 United Rd Ne (98346-8480)
PHONE..................360 697-5540
Glenn Kramer, *President*
David Erickson, *Vice Pres*
▲ **EMP:** 12 **EST:** 1997
SQ FT: 15,000
SALES (est): 2.8MM **Privately Held**
WEB: www.pacificnettingproducts.com
SIC: 2258 Lace & warp knit fabric mills

(G-5261)
PENINSULA TRUSS CO
26343 Bond Rd Ne Unit A-1 (98346-8495)
PHONE..................360 297-6026
David Jory, *General Mgr*
Debbie Loudin, *Principal*
EMP: 4
SALES (est): 471.8K **Privately Held**
SIC: 2439 Trusses, wooden roof

(G-5262)
SCOTT MCCLURE
Also Called: Scott's Tool & Die
27837 Lindvog Rd (98346)
P.O. Box 1665 (98346-1665)
PHONE..................360 297-7007
Scott McClure, *Owner*
EMP: 4
SQ FT: 3,000
SALES (est): 201K **Privately Held**
WEB: www.scottstool.com
SIC: 3312 Tool & die steel

(G-5263)
SCOTTS HOME & ROOFING SERVICE
9750 Ne Kingston Farm Rd (98346-8620)
PHONE..................360 297-7524
Kelly Scott, *Owner*
EMP: 5 **EST:** 2001
SALES: 700K **Privately Held**
SIC: 1761 2411 Roofing contractor; logging

(G-5264)
STEELE AND ASSOCIATES INC
Also Called: Steelevest Co
26112 Iowa Ave Ne (98346-7634)
P.O. Box 7304 (98346-0050)
PHONE..................360 297-4555
Sandra Steele, *President*
Lynn Steele, *Vice Pres*
Lisa France, *Treasurer*
▼ **EMP:** 4
SQ FT: 1,000
SALES (est): 594.1K **Privately Held**
WEB: www.steelevest.com
SIC: 2311 5699 Vests: made from purchased materials; customized clothing & apparel

(G-5265)
SYNERGY WELDING INC
20818 Stephen Ct Ne (98346-9131)
PHONE..................360 881-0204
David J Lyon, *President*
EMP: 3
SALES (est): 279.6K **Privately Held**
SIC: 1799 7692 Welding on site; welding repair

(G-5266)
TWO SYLVIAS PRESS
11264 Hwy 305 Ste 204 (98346)
PHONE..................360 447-8735
Kelli Agodon, *Partner*
Annette Spaulding-Convy, *Partner*
EMP: 2
SALES: 24.7K **Privately Held**
SIC: 2731 Books: publishing only

Kirkland
King County

(G-5267)
ABSOLUTE GM LLC
11809 Ne 116th St (98034-7105)
PHONE..................425 814-1011
Vlad Khan, *President*

Anna Sayapina, *Bookkeeper*
EMP: 32 **EST:** 2009
SQ FT: 22,000
SALES: 2.2MM **Privately Held**
SIC: 1799 3281 Counter top installation; granite, cut & shaped

(G-5268)
ACCOR TECHNOLOGY INC (PA)
608 State St S Ste 100 (98033-6602)
PHONE..................425 453-5410
Jerry O'Neil, *President*
EMP: 50
SALES (est): 8.6MM **Privately Held**
WEB: www.accortechnology.com
SIC: 3494 Sprinkler systems, field

(G-5269)
ADVANCED CASTER CORPORATI
8606 Ne 138th St (98034-1714)
PHONE..................425 821-6574
Arthur Vacca, *President*
Tami Vacca, *Sales Staff*
Guy Wilson, *Admin Sec*
Art Vacca, *Master*
EMP: 7
SALES (est): 1.1MM **Privately Held**
SIC: 3562 Casters

(G-5270)
ADVANCED COATING SOLUTIONS LLC
218 Maint St 429 (98033)
PHONE..................425 785-0902
Richard Stratton, *Managing Dir*
EMP: 3
SALES: 550K **Privately Held**
WEB: www.latitude47.com
SIC: 3479 Painting, coating & hot dipping

(G-5271)
ADVANCED PRTCTIVE COATINGS LLC
10220 Ne Points Dr # 315 (98033-7864)
PHONE..................425 818-2820
Seth Thomas, *Principal*
EMP: 2
SALES (est): 120.1K **Privately Held**
SIC: 3479 Metal coating & allied service

(G-5272)
AEES INC
4040 Lk Wa Blvd Ne # 150 (98033-7874)
PHONE..................425 803-2170
EMP: 3
SALES (corp-wide): 1B **Privately Held**
SIC: 3679 Electronic loads & power supplies
HQ: Aees Inc.
36555 Corp Dr Ste 300
Farmington Hills MI 48331

(G-5273)
AERIES ENTERPRISES LLC
1100 Carillon Pt (98033-7412)
PHONE..................425 739-9997
William Monkman, *CEO*
Lou Mills, *Treasurer*
EMP: 9
SALES (est): 942.4K **Privately Held**
SIC: 3812 Aircraft/aerospace flight instruments & guidance systems

(G-5274)
AG TREE SERVICE LLC
218 Main St (98033-6108)
PHONE..................425 830-8820
Adam Guy,
EMP: 3
SALES: 150K **Privately Held**
SIC: 2411 Logging

(G-5275)
ALLSTAR SPECIALTY DESIGNS
9308 Ne 126th Pl (98034-2774)
PHONE..................425 820-0285
Sherman Leach, *Owner*
Mikkei Leach, *Co-Owner*
EMP: 2
SALES (est): 100K **Privately Held**
SIC: 2395 Embroidery & art needlework

(G-5276)
ALMAX MANUFACTURING CO
Also Called: Almax USA
903 5th Ave Ste 101 (98033-6348)
PHONE..................425 889-8708
Alan Burk, *President*
Robert Deppiesse, *Vice Pres*
▲ **EMP:** 2
SQ FT: 1,000
SALES (est): 340.9K **Privately Held**
SIC: 3672 Printed circuit boards

(G-5277)
AMERICAN DIGITAL
8525 120th Ave Ne Ste 301 (98033-5866)
PHONE..................800 765-2580
R Cats, *Principal*
EMP: 3 **EST:** 2016
SALES (est): 172.6K **Privately Held**
SIC: 3669 Communications equipment

(G-5278)
AMHI INC
11812 Ne 116th St (98034-7100)
PHONE..................425 883-4040
Margaret Ames, *Manager*
EMP: 2
SALES (est): 88.3K **Privately Held**
SIC: 3634 Electric housewares & fans

(G-5279)
APPATTACH INC
9704 132nd Ave Ne (98033-5222)
PHONE..................425 202-5676
James Depoy, *CEO*
Jim Stackman, *Vice Pres*
Cameron Altenhof-Long, *CTO*
EMP: 2
SALES (est): 68.4K **Privately Held**
SIC: 7372 Application computer software

(G-5280)
ARNESON FUELS LLC
12117 105th Ave Ne (98034-3815)
PHONE..................425 823-1096
Everett Arneson, *President*
EMP: 3
SALES (est): 246.5K **Privately Held**
SIC: 2869 Fuels

(G-5281)
ASSETIC INC
3240 Carillon Pt (98033-7308)
PHONE..................425 658-6603
Brad Campbell, *General Mgr*
Suzanne Sanders, *Principal*
Lawrence George, *Manager*
EMP: 2
SALES (est): 98.6K **Privately Held**
SIC: 7372 Prepackaged software

(G-5282)
ASTRONICS ADVANCES ELECTRONIC
13625 Ne 126th Pl (98034-8757)
PHONE..................425 895-4622
Mark A Peabody, *Vice Pres*
EMP: 2
SALES (est): 270.1K **Privately Held**
SIC: 3825 Instruments to measure electricity

(G-5283)
ASTRONICS ADVNCD ELECTRNC SYS
Also Called: Astronics-Aes
12950 Willows Rd Ne (98034-8769)
PHONE..................425 881-1700
Peter Gundermann, *President*
Mark A Peabody, *President*
James S Kramer, *Exec VP*
Diana Suzuki, *Vice Pres*
Dave Burney, *CFO*
▲ **EMP:** 520
SQ FT: 49,000
SALES: 180.8MM
SALES (corp-wide): 803.2MM **Publicly Held**
SIC: 3728 Aircraft parts & equipment
PA: Astronics Corporation
130 Commerce Way
East Aurora NY 14052
716 805-1599

Kirkland - King County (G-5284)

(G-5284)
ASTRONICS CORPORATION
12950 Willows Rd Ne (98034-8769)
PHONE...................................425 881-1700
Mark Peabody, *Manager*
EMP: 350
SALES (corp-wide): 803.2MM **Publicly Held**
SIC: 3825 Instruments to measure electricity
PA: Astronics Corporation
130 Commerce Way
East Aurora NY 14052
716 805-1599

(G-5285)
AUSCLEAN TECHNOLOGY INC
8554 122nd Ave Ne 244 (98033-5831)
PHONE...................................360 563-9244
Ross Wigney, *President*
Wendy Wigney, *Vice Pres*
Keith Wigney, *Project Mgr*
EMP: 8
SALES (est): 1.4MM **Privately Held**
SIC: 3589 Vacuum cleaners & sweepers, electric: industrial

(G-5286)
AVIO CORPORATION
Also Called: Avio Support
8525 120th Ave Ne Ste 300 (98033-5866)
PHONE...................................425 739-6800
Gordon Kirkland, *President*
Kenneth Kirkland, *Corp Secy*
Anne Pernaa, *Accounts Mgr*
EMP: 5
SQ FT: 18,000
SALES (est): 866.9K **Privately Held**
SIC: 5088 3648 Aircraft & parts; lighting equipment

(G-5287)
AVOCENT REDMOND CORP
Also Called: Vertiv
11335 Ne 122nd Way # 140 (98034-6933)
PHONE...................................425 861-5858
Samuel Saracino, *Senior VP*
Douglass Pritchett, *CFO*
C Dave Perry, *VP Sales*
▲ **EMP:** 84
SQ FT: 36,000
SALES (est): 12.3MM
SALES (corp-wide): 322.9MM **Privately Held**
WEB: www.avocent.com
SIC: 3829 3577 Measuring & controlling devices; computer peripheral equipment
HQ: Avocent Corporation
4991 Corporate Dr Nw
Huntsville AL 35805
256 430-4000

(G-5288)
BARKING DOG INC
Also Called: Fastsigns
12644 Ne 85th St (98033-8045)
PHONE...................................425 822-6542
Greg Shugarts, *President*
EMP: 9
SALES: 1.4MM **Privately Held**
SIC: 3993 2759 Signs & advertising specialties; commercial printing

(G-5289)
BBTLINE LLC
10907 Ne 133rd St (98034-5310)
PHONE...................................425 273-3712
Mark Derbyshire, *Principal*
EMP: 2
SALES (est): 121.7K **Privately Held**
SIC: 3663 Radio & TV communications equipment

(G-5290)
BELLEVUE DOOR & MILLWORK CO
12805 141st Ave Ne (98034-8734)
P.O. Box 455 (98083-0455)
PHONE...................................425 885-3009
Gerald La Jeunesse, *President*
Michael T Craig, *Corp Secy*
William J Craig, *Vice Pres*
EMP: 3
SQ FT: 2,400
SALES: 250K **Privately Held**
SIC: 2431 Doors, wood

(G-5291)
BITTITAN INC
218 Main St Ste 719 (98033-6108)
PHONE...................................206 428-6030
Geeman Yip, *CEO*
Gabriela Bialoszewski, *Office Mgr*
EMP: 15 **Privately Held**
SIC: 7372 Business oriented computer software
PA: Bittitan, Inc.
1120 112th Ave Ne Ste 300
Bellevue WA 98004

(G-5292)
BLADEGALLERY INC
Also Called: Epicurean Edge
107 Central Way (98033-6107)
PHONE...................................425 889-5980
Daniel O'Malley, *President*
▲ **EMP:** 5
SALES (est): 578.7K **Privately Held**
SIC: 3421 Cutlery

(G-5293)
BLUEFIN MARINE LLC
7429 Ne 129th St (98034-5729)
PHONE...................................206 276-4087
Dave Bechtel,
EMP: 3
SQ FT: 1,600
SALES: 660K **Privately Held**
SIC: 3643 3613 Rail bonds, electric: for propulsion & signal circuits; time switches, electrical switchgear apparatus

(G-5294)
BOCADA LLC
5555 Lakeview Dr Ste 201 (98033-7444)
PHONE...................................425 818-4400
Mark Silverman, *Ch of Bd*
Nancy Hurley, *President*
Henry Albrecht, *Vice Pres*
Michael Bauer, *Vice Pres*
Elizabeth Morgan, *Vice Pres*
EMP: 50
SALES (est): 6.5MM **Privately Held**
WEB: www.bocada.com
SIC: 7372 Business oriented computer software

(G-5295)
BOEING COMPANY
12605 94th Ave Ne (98034-2761)
PHONE...................................425 417-5612
Roeseler Billy, *Principal*
EMP: 895
SALES (corp-wide): 101.1B **Publicly Held**
SIC: 3721 Airplanes, fixed or rotary wing
PA: The Boeing Company
100 N Riverside Plz
Chicago IL 60606
312 544-2000

(G-5296)
BOUCHARD LAKE WINERY LLC
12205 Ne 64th St (98033-8554)
PHONE...................................425 803-5076
Gerald Warnken, *Principal*
EMP: 2
SALES (est): 131.8K **Privately Held**
SIC: 2084 Wines

(G-5297)
CARBON NORTHWEST
7422 Ne 120th Pl (98034-2409)
PHONE...................................425 820-0873
Sara St John, *Owner*
EMP: 3
SALES (est): 160.5K **Privately Held**
SIC: 2819 Industrial inorganic chemicals

(G-5298)
CASCIOPPO BROS MEATS INC
Also Called: Cascioppo Bros Italian Mt Mkt
13613 Ne 126th Pl Ste 310 (98034-8722)
PHONE...................................206 784-6121
Tony Casioppi, *President*
EMP: 10 **EST:** 1974
SQ FT: 1,500
SALES: 1MM **Privately Held**
SIC: 2013 5421 Sausages & other prepared meats; meat markets, including freezer provisioners

(G-5299)
CASE ENTERPRISES
12201 Ne 70th St (98034-8541)
PHONE...................................425 827-2056
Betty M Case, *Owner*
Alvin Case, *Co-Owner*
EMP: 2
SALES (est): 117.2K **Privately Held**
SIC: 2741 Miscellaneous publishing

(G-5300)
CEDERGREEN CELLARS INC
11315 Ne 65th St (98033-7114)
PHONE...................................425 827-7244
Kevin Cedergreen, *President*
EMP: 2
SALES (est): 62.3K **Privately Held**
SIC: 2084 Wines, brandy & brandy spirits

(G-5301)
CELL SYSTEMS CORPORATION
12815 Ne 124th St Ste A (98034-8313)
PHONE...................................425 823-1010
Carl Soderland, *CEO*
Jim Luff, *Persnl Mgr*
EMP: 6
SQ FT: 4,000
SALES (est): 803.4K **Privately Held**
SIC: 8731 2835 Biotechnical research, commercial; in vitro & in vivo diagnostic substances

(G-5302)
CENTER TRADE CORPORATION
5400 Carillon Pt Fl 4 (98033-7357)
PHONE...................................206 992-2374
Ali Nassersaeid, *President*
EMP: 5
SALES (est): 416.2K **Privately Held**
SIC: 3728 4581 Aircraft parts & equipment; airports, flying fields & services

(G-5303)
CHARLES LOOMIS INC
11828 Ne 112th St (98033-4511)
PHONE...................................425 823-4560
Charles Loomis, *President*
Laura Loomis, *Exec VP*
EMP: 18 **EST:** 1968
SQ FT: 30,000
SALES: 4.5MM **Privately Held**
WEB: www.charlesloomis.com
SIC: 3646 Commercial indusl & institutional electric lighting fixtures

(G-5304)
CHOIX PUBLISHING
12635 93rd Pl Ne (98034-5911)
PHONE...................................425 821-2752
EMP: 2 **EST:** 2011
SALES (est): 85K **Privately Held**
SIC: 2741 Misc Publishing

(G-5305)
CINEMATIX LLC
11332 Ne 122nd Way # 100 (98034-6949)
PHONE...................................425 533-1024
Murugesan Ganesan, *Principal*
EMP: 2
SALES (est): 75.2K **Privately Held**
SIC: 7372 7812 Home entertainment computer software; motion picture & video production

(G-5306)
CIRRATO TECHNOLOGIES INC
5400 Carillon Pt Fl 4 (98033-7357)
PHONE...................................425 999-4500
Gorm Halberg-Lange, *CEO*
Tony Svensson, *President*
Randal Pinney, *Vice Pres*
Mats Wennberg, *Vice Pres*
EMP: 6
SALES (est): 409.6K **Privately Held**
SIC: 7372 Application computer software
PA: Round The Corner Intressenter Ab
Hogbovagen 19
Ekero
709 200-999

(G-5307)
CLARIFICATION TECHOLOGY INC
Also Called: Filter Corp, The
9805 Ne 116th St Ste A200 (98034-4245)
PHONE...................................425 820-4850
Robin Bernard, *Vice Pres*
▲ **EMP:** 5
SALES (est): 742.8K **Privately Held**
SIC: 3599 Oil filters, internal combustion engine, except automotive

(G-5308)
CLOSEST TO THE PIN INC
11605 Ne 116th St (98033-7103)
PHONE...................................425 820-2297
Andy Roberts, *Principal*
EMP: 3 **EST:** 2012
SALES (est): 181.9K **Privately Held**
SIC: 3452 Pins

(G-5309)
CNC TOOLING SOLUTIONS INC
13820 116th Pl Ne (98034-2152)
PHONE...................................425 250-6295
Lucian Cocos, *President*
EMP: 5
SALES (est): 390K **Privately Held**
SIC: 3545 5084 Machine tool accessories; machine tools & metalworking machinery

(G-5310)
COBALT UTILITY PRODUCTS
8711 Ne 119th St (98034-6022)
PHONE...................................425 823-0715
Mark Mason, *Principal*
EMP: 3
SALES (est): 172.2K **Privately Held**
SIC: 3824 Fluid meters & counting devices

(G-5311)
CONTROL TECHNOLOGY INC
12817 Ne 126th Pl (98034-7721)
PHONE...................................425 823-3878
WEI-Hung KAO, *President*
Vern Braly, *Vice Pres*
Russell KAO, *Software Engr*
EMP: 7
SQ FT: 2,500
SALES (est): 2.1MM **Privately Held**
WEB: www.control-tech.com
SIC: 3823 Industrial instrmnts msrmnt display/control process variable

(G-5312)
CONTROLS GROUP THE INC
Also Called: Logix
10518 Ne 68th St Ste 103 (98033-7003)
PHONE...................................425 828-4149
Jim Conant, *President*
▲ **EMP:** 5
SALES (est): 580K **Privately Held**
WEB: www.logix-controls.com
SIC: 3625 3822 Control equipment, electric; auto controls regulating residntl & coml environmt & applncs

(G-5313)
COOLPC INCORPORATED
Also Called: Cooler Guys
11630 Slater Ave Ne Ste 6 (98034-4100)
PHONE...................................425 821-6400
Andrew Anderson, *President*
Mark Webster, *General Mgr*
▲ **EMP:** 6
SQ FT: 2,000
SALES (est): 548.5K **Privately Held**
SIC: 3724 Cooling systems, aircraft engine

(G-5314)
COSMIC CREAMERY LLC
8218 126th Ave Ne Apt E34 (98033-8093)
PHONE...................................425 633-7742
Kelly Berger, *Principal*
EMP: 3
SALES (est): 124K **Privately Held**
SIC: 2021 Creamery butter

(G-5315)
COSTOM WOODWORK
1312 3rd St (98033-5535)
PHONE...................................425 828-2579
Constantine Mavromatis, *Owner*
EMP: 3

GEOGRAPHIC SECTION
Kirkland - King County (G-5349)

SALES (est): 316.4K **Privately Held**
SIC: 2431 Millwork

(G-5316)
CRAFTY WOODWORKING
9234 128th Ave Ne (98033-5930)
PHONE..................................425 822-9618
EMP: 2 EST: 2008
SALES (est): 110K **Privately Held**
SIC: 2431 Mfg Millwork

(G-5317)
CREATIVE LABEL INCORPORATED
18005 Ne 68th St (98034)
PHONE..................................425 821-8810
Robert Kiger, *President*
EMP: 6
SQ FT: 7,000
SALES (est): 89.8K **Privately Held**
SIC: 2759 Labels & seals: printing

(G-5318)
CRH MEDICAL CORPORATION
Also Called: Crh O'Regan System
4040 Lake Washington Blvd (98033-7874)
PHONE..................................425 284-7890
Edward Wright, *CEO*
Anthony F Holler, *Ch of Bd*
Iian Cleator, *Principal*
David A Johnson, *Principal*
Bergein F Overholt, *Principal*
EMP: 15 EST: 2008
SALES (est): 96.3K **Privately Held**
SIC: 3841 Surgical & medical instruments

(G-5319)
CUSTOM FIRESCREEN INC
12700 Ne 124th St Ste 15 (98034-8304)
PHONE..................................425 821-4800
Rick Dailey, *President*
Jan Dailey, *Vice Pres*
EMP: 2
SQ FT: 9,600
SALES (est): 180K **Privately Held**
SIC: 3599 Machine shop, jobbing & repair

(G-5320)
DEFENSIVE DRIVING SCHOOL INC (PA)
10505 Ne 38th Pl Bldg 9 (98033-7926)
PHONE..................................425 643-0116
JC Fawcett, *President*
EMP: 6
SALES (est): 786.3K **Privately Held**
WEB: www.driving-school.com
SIC: 8299 3469 Automobile driving instruction; automobile license tags, stamped metal

(G-5321)
DISTILLER LLC
10510 Northup Way Ste 300 (98033-7928)
PHONE..................................206 659-4759
EMP: 2
SALES (est): 111.1K **Privately Held**
SIC: 2085 Mfg Distilled/Blended Liquor

(G-5322)
DON MACINTOSH
Also Called: Mac Plaque Awards
14422 87th Ave Ne (98034-5022)
PHONE..................................425 821-1499
Don Macintosh, *Owner*
EMP: 2
SQ FT: 1,000
SALES: 40K **Privately Held**
SIC: 3999 Plaques, picture, laminated

(G-5323)
DUMAS HOLDINGS LLC
Also Called: Simply Brilliant Press
5400 Carillon Pt (98033-7357)
PHONE..................................425 576-4227
Scott Heilmann, *Partner*
Scott Ellis, *Partner*
EMP: 5
SALES (est): 519.9K **Privately Held**
SIC: 7389 2752 2741 7374 Printers' services: folding, collating; commercial printing, offset; poster & decal printing, lithographic; business service newsletters: publishing & printing; computer graphics service

(G-5324)
DUNGENESS DEVELOPMENT ASSOC (PA)
Also Called: East Point Seafood
11805 N Creek Pkwy S (98034)
PHONE..................................425 481-0600
Joel V Ornum, *President*
Joel Van Ornum, *President*
◆ EMP: 45
SQ FT: 25,000
SALES (est): 5.3MM **Privately Held**
WEB: www.dungenessassoc.com
SIC: 2091 Seafood products: packaged in cans, jars, etc.

(G-5325)
DUPONT CO
11203 100th Ave Ne (98033-4417)
PHONE..................................425 260-0257
EMP: 2
SALES (est): 115.6K **Privately Held**
SIC: 2879 Agricultural chemicals

(G-5326)
DYNAMIC DESIGNS JEWELRY INC
11711 Ne 67th Pl (98033-8432)
P.O. Box 2342 (98083-2342)
PHONE..................................425 827-7722
Jeanette Betton, *President*
EMP: 2
SALES: 250K **Privately Held**
SIC: 5944 3911 Jewelry, precious stones & precious metals; jewelry, precious metal

(G-5327)
DYSON INC
12815 Ne 124th St Ste N (98034-8313)
PHONE..................................425 968-2456
EMP: 2 EST: 2015
SALES (est): 176.5K **Privately Held**
SIC: 3635 Household vacuum cleaners

(G-5328)
ECHODYNE CORP
12112 115th Ave Ne Ste A (98034-6958)
PHONE..................................206 713-1216
Eben Frankenberg, *Principal*
William Graves, *Vice Pres*
Skyler Martens, *Design Engr*
Andrea Radosevich, *General Counsel*
EMP: 75 EST: 2014
SALES (est): 7MM **Privately Held**
SIC: 3812 Search & navigation equipment

(G-5329)
ECO CARTRIDGE STORE
11316 Ne 124th St (98034-4303)
PHONE..................................425 820-3570
Vic Swan, *Principal*
EMP: 2
SALES (est): 218.7K **Privately Held**
WEB: www.ecocartridgestore.com
SIC: 3482 Cartridges, 30 mm. & below

(G-5330)
EL DORADO TORTILLAS LLC
11842 Ne 112th St (98034-4511)
PHONE..................................719 459-2576
Jose Roxas, *Mng Member*
EMP: 4
SALES (est): 149.4K **Privately Held**
SIC: 2099 Tortillas, fresh or refrigerated

(G-5331)
EMERALD CITY LIGHTING
12613 Ne 112th Pl (98034-4110)
PHONE..................................206 234-8554
Mark Schuster, *Principal*
EMP: 4
SALES (est): 155.9K **Privately Held**
SIC: 3648 Lighting equipment

(G-5332)
EMERALD CITY WATER LLC
10925 81st Pl Ne (98034-3567)
PHONE..................................425 821-0800
Brian Talfreyman,
EMP: 4
SALES: 800K **Privately Held**
WEB: www.emeraldcitymultisport.com
SIC: 3589 Water filters & softeners, household type

(G-5333)
EQUIPMENT INC
218 Main St Ste 730 (98033-6108)
PHONE..................................206 826-9577
EMP: 2
SALES (est): 91.6K **Privately Held**
SIC: 2741 Internet Publishing And Broadcasting

(G-5334)
EVERGREEN HOUSE INC
13645 Ne 126th Pl (98034-8705)
PHONE..................................425 821-1005
Thomas Neilson, *President*
John Alexander, *General Mgr*
William Ahlgrim, *Vice Pres*
EMP: 15
SQ FT: 5,000
SALES (est): 3.7MM **Privately Held**
SIC: 3444 3231 3448 Skylights, sheet metal; products of purchased glass; greenhouses: prefabricated metal

(G-5335)
EVERGREEN ORTHPD RES LAB LLC
Also Called: Operativ
11317 Ne 120th St (98034-6907)
PHONE..................................425 284-7262
Dr Craig McAllister, *Mng Member*
Jennifer Henderson,
Mark Kuiper,
Casey Sullivan,
Wayne Summers,
EMP: 7
SALES (est): 402.6K **Privately Held**
SIC: 3841 Surgical & medical instruments

(G-5336)
FARNWORTH GROUP
Also Called: Culinary Arts
8707 123rd Ln Ne (98033-5873)
PHONE..................................425 894-8643
EMP: 2
SALES (est): 100K **Privately Held**
SIC: 2041 Gluten-Free Product R&D

(G-5337)
FASHION EMBROIDERY INC
13625 Ne 126th Pl Ste 430 (98034-8738)
PHONE..................................425 820-7125
Angela Van Derpool, *President*
Angela Vanderpool, *President*
EMP: 5
SALES (est): 250K **Privately Held**
SIC: 2395 7389 Emblems, embroidered; embroidering of advertising on shirts, etc.

(G-5338)
FETHA STYX LLC
Also Called: Fetha Styx Custom Fishing Rods
6825 122nd Ave Ne (98033-8527)
PHONE..................................425 242-0014
EMP: 2 EST: 2002
SALES (est): 750K **Privately Held**
SIC: 3949 Mfg Sporting/Athletic Goods

(G-5339)
FLOAT TECHNOLOGIES LLC
790 6th St S Ste 100 (98033-6762)
PHONE..................................916 947-6646
EMP: 2
SALES (est): 80K **Privately Held**
SIC: 7372 Prepackaged Software Services

(G-5340)
FLYING DOG ENTERTAINMENT LLC
Also Called: Skip's Dip
13911 121st Ave Ne (98034-2138)
PHONE..................................206 372-5553
George Saling, *CEO*
EMP: 4
SALES (est): 253.4K **Privately Held**
SIC: 2035 Pickles, sauces & salad dressings

(G-5341)
FOLLOWONE INC
Also Called: Followone.com
8512 122nd Ave Ne Ste 300 (98033-5831)
PHONE..................................206 518-8844
Cristian Popescu, *CEO*
EMP: 15 EST: 2014

SALES: 100K **Privately Held**
SIC: 7372 Business oriented computer software

(G-5342)
FORTUN FOODS INC
Also Called: Fortuns Finshg Sauces & Soups
6513 132nd Ave Ne Ste 394 (98033-8628)
PHONE..................................425 827-1977
Kevin G Fortun, *CEO*
David L Kirkham, *CFO*
Richard Sariraksa, *CFO*
EMP: 14
SALES (est): 2.1MM **Privately Held**
WEB: www.fortunfoods.com
SIC: 5149 2099 2034 Sauces; soups, except frozen; sauces: dry mixes; soup powders

(G-5343)
FREAKN GENIUS INC
14152 77th Ave Ne (98034-0703)
PHONE..................................425 301-4258
EMP: 5
SALES (est): 296.7K **Privately Held**
SIC: 7372 7389 Application computer software;

(G-5344)
FREEMO INC
5019 112th Ave Ne Apt B (98033-7750)
PHONE..................................425 280-9661
Leigh Hunt, *CEO*
EMP: 4 EST: 2014
SQ FT: 2,500
SALES (est): 119K **Privately Held**
SIC: 7372 Publishers' computer software

(G-5345)
FSS HOLDINGS LLC
Also Called: Ironfire Design & Fabrication
13600 Ne 126th Pl Ste D (98034-8720)
PHONE..................................425 820-5455
Frank Sciabica, *Mng Member*
EMP: 8
SALES (est): 87.4K **Privately Held**
WEB: www.ironfiredesign.com
SIC: 3462 Iron & steel forgings

(G-5346)
GARDEN BUCKET LLC
512 6th St S Ste 201 (98033-6764)
PHONE..................................425 828-6500
Simon Ross, *Principal*
EMP: 4
SQ FT: 100
SALES (est): 222.3K **Privately Held**
SIC: 3089 Planters, plastic

(G-5347)
GEMINI MANAGEMENT LTD
8525 120th Ave Ne (98033-5866)
PHONE..................................425 739-6800
Ken Kirkland, *President*
EMP: 7
SQ FT: 2,500
SALES (est): 1.5MM
SALES (corp-wide): 15.7MM **Privately Held**
SIC: 3728 Aircraft parts & equipment
PA: Aviosupport, Inc.
   8525 120th Ave Ne Ste 300
   Kirkland WA 98033
   425 739-6800

(G-5348)
GHOST RIDGE SOFTWARE INC
5510 Lakeview Dr Apt D (98033-7364)
PHONE..................................425 646-4822
EMP: 2 EST: 1999
SALES (est): 170K **Privately Held**
SIC: 7372 Prepackaged Software Services

(G-5349)
GLOBAL FIRE RESPONSE & SAFETY
1100 Carillon Pt (98033-7412)
PHONE..................................701 774-2022
EMP: 5
SALES (est): 313.4K **Privately Held**
SIC: 1389 Oil/Gas Field Services

Kirkland - King County (G-5350) — GEOGRAPHIC SECTION

(G-5350)
GLOBAL MARINE LOGISTICS LLC
12638 Ne 70th St (98033-8537)
PHONE 206 854-0201
Richard Stabbert, *President*
EMP: 50
SALES (est): 3MM **Privately Held**
WEB: www.globalmarinelogistics.com
SIC: 3531 Construction machinery

(G-5351)
GOODRICH CORPORATION
Also Called: UTC Aerospace Systems
4020 Lake Wash Blvd Ne (98033-7862)
PHONE 425 822-9851
Gary Van Derkooy, *Manager*
EMP: 15
SALES (corp-wide): 66.5B **Publicly Held**
WEB: www.hamilton-standard.com
SIC: 3728 Aircraft parts & equipment
HQ: Goodrich Corporation
    2730 W Tyvola Rd
    Charlotte NC 28217
    704 423-7000

(G-5352)
GRAPECITY INC
401 Parkplace Ctr Ste 411 (98033-6200)
PHONE 425 828-4440
EMP: 2 **Privately Held**
SIC: 2741 Miscellaneous publishing
HQ: Grapecity, Inc.
    201 S Highland Ave Fl 3
    Pittsburgh PA 15206

(G-5353)
GREATER INTELLIGENCE INC (PA)
6710 108th Ave Ne Ste 354 (98033-7050)
PHONE 703 989-2281
Coleman White, *Principal*
Tracy Mandell, *Vice Pres*
Corey Mandell, *CTO*
EMP: 8 EST: 2015
SALES (est): 2.1MM **Privately Held**
SIC: 7372 Application computer software

(G-5354)
GREEN KARMA INC
8124 Ne 122nd Pl (98034-5836)
PHONE 206 786-1988
Cheryl Chandler, *Principal*
EMP: 2
SALES (est): 119.1K **Privately Held**
SIC: 2759 Screen printing

(G-5355)
GRIPTONITE INC
12421 Willows Rd Ne # 200 (98034-8751)
PHONE 425 825-6800
Daniel Elenbas, *Principal*
EMP: 200
SALES (est): 5.6MM
SALES (corp-wide): 366.5MM **Publicly Held**
SIC: 7371 3944 Computer software writing services; electronic games & toys
PA: Glu Mobile Inc.
    875 Howard St Ste 100
    San Francisco CA 94103
    415 800-6100

(G-5356)
GROWLIFE INC (PA)
5400 Carillon Pt (98033-7357)
PHONE 866 781-5559
Marco Hegyi, *Ch of Bd*
Joseph Barnes, *Senior VP*
Mark E Scott, *CFO*
Foday Deen, *Controller*
EMP: 13
SALES (est): 4.5MM **Publicly Held**
SIC: 0181 3674 Flowers: grown under cover (e.g. greenhouse production); light emitting diodes

(G-5357)
HAPPY TAB LLC
319 7th Ln S (98033-6914)
PHONE 773 231-8223
EMP: 2 EST: 2015
SALES (est): 92.1K **Privately Held**
SIC: 7372 Prepackaged Software Services

(G-5358)
HIRSCHLER MFG INC
915 6th St S (98033-6797)
PHONE 425 827-9384
Gerald Hirschler, *President*
Craig Myre, *Vice Pres*
Grant Schneider, *Vice Pres*
EMP: 20
SQ FT: 20,000
SALES: 8.8MM **Privately Held**
WEB: www.hirschler.com
SIC: 3728 Aircraft assemblies, subassemblies & parts

(G-5359)
HOLM BREWING ENTERPISES LLC
11701 Ne 73rd St (98033-8106)
PHONE 425 827-9307
Scott Holm, *Principal*
EMP: 4
SALES (est): 204K **Privately Held**
SIC: 2082 Malt beverages

(G-5360)
HOUGHTON PLAZA
935 6th St S (98033-6712)
PHONE 425 298-4857
EMP: 3
SALES (est): 212.1K **Privately Held**
SIC: 2026 Yogurt

(G-5361)
HOYLU INC (PA)
720 4th Ave Ste 220 (98033-8154)
PHONE 425 269-3299
Karl Wiersholm, *President*
EMP: 4
SALES (est): 1.2MM **Privately Held**
SIC: 7372 Prepackaged software

(G-5362)
HOYLU INC
7624 116th Ave Ne (98033-8101)
PHONE 425 829-2316
EMP: 2
SALES (est): 83.2K **Privately Held**
SIC: 7372 Prepackaged software

(G-5363)
HUMBAY HEALTH LLC
5729 Lakeview Dr (98033-7443)
PHONE 425 922-0200
Bob Nelson, *Mng Member*
EMP: 2
SALES (est): 180K **Privately Held**
SIC: 3728 Oxygen systems, aircraft

(G-5364)
HYPERFISH INC
3410 Carillon Pt (98033-7317)
PHONE 425 332-6567
Brian Cook, *CEO*
Chris Johnson, *CTO*
EMP: 13
SALES (est): 165.2K
SALES (corp-wide): 3.8MM **Privately Held**
SIC: 7372 Business oriented computer software
PA: Livetiles Corp.
    137 W 25th St Fl 6
    New York NY 10001
    917 472-7887

(G-5365)
I1 SENSORTECH INC
Also Called: I1 Biometrics
12020 113th Ave Ne (98034-6938)
PHONE 425 372-7811
Gary Rubens, *President*
Ray Rhodes, *Vice Pres*
EMP: 13 EST: 2014
SALES (est): 1.8MM **Privately Held**
SIC: 3842 Personal safety equipment

(G-5366)
ICARUS AERO COMPONENTS LLC
11818 97th Ln Ne (98034-8967)
PHONE 386 299-0529
Lisa Renter, *Principal*
EMP: 2
SALES (est): 170K **Privately Held**
SIC: 3728 7389 Aircraft assemblies, sub-assemblies & parts;

(G-5367)
IMPERIAL PUBLISHING
8112 Ne 131st St (98034-2523)
PHONE 800 210-5033
Stewart Klein, *Principal*
EMP: 2
SALES (est): 111.1K **Privately Held**
SIC: 2741 Miscellaneous publishing

(G-5368)
INSIGHTS WORKS INC
14408 118th Ave Ne (98034-1160)
PHONE 425 577-2206
Bruce Gabrielle, *Principal*
EMP: 4
SALES (est): 238.3K **Privately Held**
SIC: 7372 Prepackaged software

(G-5369)
INTELLIGENTEFFECTS LLC
4315 Lake Washington Blvd (98033-7888)
PHONE 323 206-0499
Binyam Kebede,
EMP: 2 EST: 2017
SALES (est): 56.5K **Privately Held**
SIC: 7372 Prepackaged software

(G-5370)
INTUITIVE MFG SYSTEMS INC (HQ)
12131 113th Ave Ne # 200 (98034-6944)
PHONE 425 821-0740
Sara Gillam, *CEO*
Chuck Gillam, *President*
Barbara J Carey, *Chairman*
J Patrick Carey, *Chairman*
Amy Wilcox, *Exec VP*
EMP: 85
SQ FT: 12,000
SALES (est): 7.7MM
SALES (corp-wide): 594.8MM **Privately Held**
WEB: www.intuitivemfg.com
SIC: 7371 7372 Computer software development; prepackaged software
PA: Aptean, Inc.
    4325 Alexander Dr Ste 100
    Alpharetta GA 30022
    770 351-9600

(G-5371)
ITS A WRAP WASHINGTON INC
Also Called: Interior Art & Frame
11004 Ne 68th St Apt 913 (98033-7164)
PHONE 425 827-2000
Ken Worsham, *President*
EMP: 4
SALES: 100K **Privately Held**
SIC: 7699 5999 2752 Picture framing, custom; flags; photo-offset printing

(G-5372)
JEMCO CMPNENTS FABRICATION INC
603 5th Pl S (98033-6673)
PHONE 425 827-7611
Stan Moore, *President*
Jane Moore, *Vice Pres*
EMP: 90
SQ FT: 100,000
SALES: 25MM **Privately Held**
WEB: www.jemcoinc.com
SIC: 3599 3444 Custom machinery; machine shop, jobbing & repair; sheet metalwork

(G-5373)
JH MARINE LLC
109 2nd St S Apt 435 (98033-9002)
PHONE 425 241-6801
Jon Edwards,
Holly Palmer,
EMP: 2 EST: 2013
SALES (est): 163.2K **Privately Held**
SIC: 8711 2392 5551 Designing: ship, boat, machine & product; boat cushions; boat dealers

(G-5374)
JMJ CUSTOM FINISHES
8432 Ne 131st Pl (98034-2679)
PHONE 425 820-4376
Matt Stclair, *Owner*
EMP: 2
SALES (est): 224.1K **Privately Held**
SIC: 3423 Edge tools for woodworking: augers, bits, gimlets, etc.

(G-5375)
KESTRA MEDICAL TECH INC
3933 Lake Washington Blvd (98033-7806)
PHONE 425 279-8002
Brian Webster, *President*
Traci Umberger, *Officer*
EMP: 9
SALES (est): 1.3MM **Privately Held**
SIC: 3841 Surgical & medical instruments

(G-5376)
KFJ INDUSTRIES LLC
9133 126th Ave Ne (98033-5902)
PHONE 425 922-2889
Bon Nguyen, *Principal*
EMP: 2
SALES (est): 170.5K **Privately Held**
SIC: 3999 Manufacturing industries

(G-5377)
KONA GOLD CORP
18388 Redmond Fall Cy Rd (98033)
P.O. Box 2946, Redmond (98073-2946)
PHONE 425 836-0389
EMP: 2
SALES (est): 61K **Privately Held**
SIC: 2844 5122 Mfg Toilet Preparations Whol Drugs/Sundries

(G-5378)
LA MESA FICTION
6619 132nd Ave Ne (98033-8627)
PHONE 206 459-2664
Cristina Dugoni, *Principal*
EMP: 2
SALES (est): 73K **Privately Held**
SIC: 2731 Book publishing

(G-5379)
LANCS INDUSTRIES HOLDINGS LLC
Also Called: Bop Filters
12704 Ne 124th St Ste 36 (98034-8397)
PHONE 425 823-6634
Lewis Byrd,
EMP: 56
SALES (est): 5MM **Privately Held**
SIC: 3999 Manufacturing industries

(G-5380)
LANCS INDUSTRIES INC (PA)
12704 Ne 124th St Ste 36 (98034-8397)
PHONE 425 823-6634
Lewis Byrd, *President*
Priscilla R Wiest, *Corp Secy*
Ron Therrien, *Vice Pres*
Diego Rangel, *Opers Mgr*
Erwin Sastra, *Controller*
▲ EMP: 34
SQ FT: 10,000
SALES (est): 6.9MM **Privately Held**
WEB: www.lancsindustries.com
SIC: 3842 Clothing, fire resistant & protective

(G-5381)
LANDIS GYR
11425 Ne 120th St (98034-6922)
PHONE 425 458-9363
Rachel Breeden, *Principal*
EMP: 4 EST: 2010
SALES (est): 381.5K **Privately Held**
SIC: 3825 Instruments to measure electricity

(G-5382)
LANDSOL LLC
11447 120th Ave Ne # 300 (98034-4539)
PHONE 425 242-5198
Wagner Stoppa, *Mng Member*
Mauricio Stoppa, *Mng Member*
EMP: 12
SQ FT: 1,350

SALES (est): 1.7MM **Privately Held**
SIC: 3271 0782 0781 Blocks, concrete: landscape or retaining wall; landscape contractors; landscape services; landscape planning services

(G-5383)
LATITUDE BLUE PRESS LLC
109 2nd St S Apt 433 (98033-9002)
PHONE.................................360 421-1934
Shawn Breeding,
▲ **EMP:** 2
SALES (est): 119.6K **Privately Held**
SIC: 2731 Books: publishing only

(G-5384)
LEATHER GUARD DIV INT RENOVATN
Also Called: Interiors Renovation
11246 Ne 87th St (98033-5746)
PHONE.................................425 827-4895
Kurt Perry, *President*
EMP: 2
SALES (est): 110K **Privately Held**
SIC: 7699 3554 Leather goods, cleaning & repair; coating & finishing machinery, paper

(G-5385)
LEATHERBACK PUBLISHING INC
681 7th Ave (98033-5627)
PHONE.................................425 822-1202
Grant Cundy, *President*
Audrey Gretch, *Controller*
Dan Heringer, *Accounts Mgr*
Bill McNally, *Accounts Mgr*
Liz Pearl, *Representative*
EMP: 27
SQ FT: 12,000
SALES (est): 5MM **Privately Held**
WEB: www.leatherback.net
SIC: 2752 Commercial printing, offset

(G-5386)
LEHENENGO AEROSPACE INC
1312 4th St (98033-5502)
PHONE.................................425 256-1376
Richard Williamson, *Principal*
EMP: 2
SALES (est): 113.7K **Privately Held**
SIC: 3721 Aircraft

(G-5387)
LEON GREEN CO FINE WOODWORKING
11130 117th Pl Ne (98033-5008)
PHONE.................................425 822-8210
Leon Green, *President*
EMP: 2
SALES (est): 230.4K **Privately Held**
WEB: www.leoncompany.com
SIC: 2434 Wood kitchen cabinets

(G-5388)
LFR AEROSPACE
9735 Ne 138th Pl (98033-1808)
PHONE.................................516 330-0633
EMP: 2
SALES (est): 100.2K **Privately Held**
SIC: 3721 Aircraft

(G-5389)
M I S CONSTRUCTION SOFTWARE
11319 Ne 120th St (98034-6907)
PHONE.................................425 882-3027
Thomas Moore, *President*
Stanley Goldsmith, *Vice Pres*
Libby Ballard, *Office Mgr*
EMP: 7
SQ FT: 2,100
SALES (est): 799K **Privately Held**
WEB: www.mischievouscomputer.com
SIC: 7372 7371 7373 Prepackaged software; custom computer programming services; computer integrated systems design

(G-5390)
M S I ENGINEERING CORPORATION
Also Called: MSI
603 5th Pl S (98033-6673)
PHONE.................................425 827-6797

Dan Miller, *President*
Stan Moore, *President*
EMP: 10
SALES (est): 619.9K **Privately Held**
SIC: 3479 Etching & engraving

(G-5391)
M&S CUSTOM REMODELING
12821 Ne 108th Pl (98033-4759)
P.O. Box 1743, Ocean Shores (98569-1743)
PHONE.................................425 739-0262
EMP: 5
SALES: 400K **Privately Held**
SIC: 1389 Exterior And Interior Remodeling

(G-5392)
MADSAM PRINTING LLC
12700 Ne 124th St (98034-8316)
PHONE.................................425 445-1949
Ron Smith, *Principal*
EMP: 2 **EST:** 2017
SALES (est): 92.3K **Privately Held**
SIC: 2752 Commercial printing, lithographic

(G-5393)
MAELSTROM INTERACTIVE
10501 Ne 114th Ln (98033-4426)
PHONE.................................206 841-6071
Katherine Vanderheiden, *CEO*
Scott Vanderheiden, *COO*
EMP: 2 **EST:** 2014
SALES (est): 105.8K **Privately Held**
SIC: 7372 7389 Educational computer software;

(G-5394)
MAGNET MAGAZINE
11319 Ne 103rd St (98033-5178)
PHONE.................................206 977-7696
EMP: 3
SALES (est): 200K **Privately Held**
SIC: 2721 Periodicals-Publishing/Printing

(G-5395)
MAMMA-KIN LLC
9009 Ne 117th Pl (98034-6120)
PHONE.................................425 922-9505
Vivian Muehlen, *President*
▲ **EMP:** 3
SALES (est): 296.3K **Privately Held**
SIC: 3944 Carriages, baby

(G-5396)
MARINE RESTORATION & CNSTR LLC
6116 114th Ave Ne (98033-7235)
P.O. Box 208, Fall City (98024-0208)
PHONE.................................425 576-8661
Mark Henderson, *Owner*
EMP: 8
SALES (est): 766.8K **Privately Held**
SIC: 3536 Boat lifts

(G-5397)
MARK RYAN WINERY LLC (PA)
11025 117th Pl Ne (98033-5025)
PHONE.................................425 481-7070
Mark Ryan McNeilly,
EMP: 13
SALES (est): 1.6MM **Privately Held**
SIC: 2084 Wines

(G-5398)
MARSHALL DT COMPANY
13600 Ne 126th Pl Ste B (98034-8720)
PHONE.................................425 869-2525
Todd Marshall, *President*
Tia Marshall, *Vice Pres*
EMP: 10
SQ FT: 6,000
SALES (est): 1MM **Privately Held**
WEB: www.dtprint.com
SIC: 2752 Commercial printing, lithographic

(G-5399)
MECADAQ AEROSPACE LLC
Also Called: Meca Aerospace
915 6th St S (98033-6712)
PHONE.................................714 442-9703
Julien Dubecq, *President*
▲ **EMP:** 10

SALES: 1MM
SALES (corp-wide): 1.4MM **Privately Held**
SIC: 3545 Precision tools, machinists'
HQ: Mecadaq Tarnos
Pole Technologique Jean Be
Tarnos 40220

(G-5400)
MEDIDA HEALTH LLC
6126 130th Ave Ne (98033-8603)
PHONE.................................425 985-5214
Kenneth Krossa, *Principal*
Nelson Del Rio, *Principal*
EMP: 5
SALES (est): 190K **Privately Held**
SIC: 7372 Business oriented computer software

(G-5401)
MICROQUILL SOFTWARE PUBLISHING
10512 Ne 68th St Ste 101 (98033-7062)
PHONE.................................425 827-7200
Thomas Marvin, *President*
Mark Suver, *Vice Pres*
EMP: 5
SALES (est): 338.7K **Privately Held**
WEB: www.microquill.com
SIC: 7372 7371 Application computer software; custom computer programming services

(G-5402)
MICROSOFT CORPORATION
434 Kirkland Way (98033)
PHONE.................................206 724-8130
Roan Kang, *Marketing Mgr*
Kelsey Garner, *Director*
EMP: 35
SALES (corp-wide): 110.3B **Publicly Held**
SIC: 7372 Prepackaged software
PA: Microsoft Corporation
1 Microsoft Way
Redmond WA 98052
425 882-8080

(G-5403)
MIKE HOUSTON
950 18th Ave W (98033-4884)
PHONE.................................425 889-0682
EMP: 2 **EST:** 1997
SALES (est): 150K **Privately Held**
SIC: 7372 Prepackaged Software Services

(G-5404)
MITSUBISHI ELECTRIC & ELEC USA
127 10th St S (98033-6795)
PHONE.................................425 202-7671
▲ **EMP:** 4
SALES (est): 332.6K **Privately Held**
SIC: 5065 3699 Sound equipment, electronic; electrical equipment & supplies

(G-5405)
MONOLITHIC POWER SYSTEMS INC (PA)
4040 Lake Wash Blvd Ne (98033-7874)
PHONE.................................425 296-9956
Michael R Hsing, *Ch of Bd*
Maurice Sciammas, *Senior VP*
Saria Tseng, *Vice Pres*
Ivor Hendry, *Design Engr Mgr*
Eddie Chu, *Engineer*
▲ **EMP:** 140
SQ FT: 106,000
SALES: 582.3MM **Publicly Held**
WEB: www.monolithicpower.com
SIC: 3674 8711 Semiconductors & related devices; engineering services

(G-5406)
N-VEE EMBROIDERY
14428 75th Ave Ne (98034-4930)
PHONE.................................425 246-3125
Naomi Newell, *Principal*
EMP: 2 **EST:** 2016
SALES (est): 53.2K **Privately Held**
SIC: 2395 Embroidery & art needlework

(G-5407)
NABTESCO AEROSPACE INC
12413 Willows Rd Ne (98034-8766)
PHONE.................................425 602-8400
Isao Ohashi, *President*
Desree Griffin, *Human Resources*
Karen Brothers, *Manager*
Bill Walkling, *Manager*
Scott Winter, *Manager*
▲ **EMP:** 48 **EST:** 1976
SQ FT: 30,000
SALES: 90MM **Privately Held**
WEB: www.nabtescoaero.com
SIC: 3728 3812 3593 Aircraft assemblies, subassemblies & parts; search & navigation equipment; fluid power cylinders & actuators
PA: Nabtesco Corporation
2-7-9, Hirakawacho
Chiyoda-Ku TKY 102-0

(G-5408)
NBK ASSOCIATES INC
Also Called: Dadoes
6472 Ne 135th Pl (98034-1626)
PHONE.................................216 408-8685
Nathan Kundtz, *CEO*
Kyu Hwang, *COO*
EMP: 2
SALES (est): 45.6K **Privately Held**
SIC: 8731 8711 8243 7371 Commercial physical research; engineering services; data processing schools; custom computer programming services; prepackaged software

(G-5409)
NEIL LEVINSON ENTERPRISES
Also Called: N L Enterprises
11631 Ne 95th St (98033-5101)
PHONE.................................425 828-3833
Neil Levinson, *Owner*
EMP: 2
SALES (est): 232.1K **Privately Held**
SIC: 2434 5031 Wood kitchen cabinets; hardboard

(G-5410)
NETACQUIRE CORPORATION
12000 115th Ave Ne (98034-6900)
PHONE.................................425 821-3100
Preston Hauck, *President*
John Bono, *Vice Pres*
Mark Roseberry, *Vice Pres*
EMP: 26
SQ FT: 14,707
SALES (est): 6.3MM **Privately Held**
WEB: www.netacquire.com
SIC: 3577 Decoders, computer peripheral equipment

(G-5411)
NO QUARTER LLC
11250 Kirkland Way # 103 (98033-3422)
PHONE.................................206 412-4311
EMP: 2
SALES (est): 54K **Privately Held**
SIC: 3131 Quarters

(G-5412)
NORTHWEST CELLARS LLC (PA)
11909 124th Ave Ne (98034-8112)
PHONE.................................866 421-9463
Robert Delf,
EMP: 15
SALES (est): 1.9MM **Privately Held**
SIC: 2084 Wine cellars, bonded: engaged in blending wines; wines

(G-5413)
NORTHWEST EYE DESIGN LLC
Also Called: Erickson Labs Northwest
12911 120th Ave Ne C10 (98034-3086)
PHONE.................................425 823-1861
Toll Free:.................................888 -
Christie Erickson, *Mng Member*
EMP: 8
SALES (est): 542.2K **Privately Held**
WEB: www.ericksonlabs.com
SIC: 3851 Ophthalmic goods

Kirkland - King County

(G-5414)
NOVEL INC
4020 Lake Washington Blvd (98033-7862)
PHONE..................................425 956-3096
Brayden Olson, *CEO*
McLean Capital Corporation, *Shareholder*
Nairbo Investments, *Shareholder*
EMP: 20
SQ FT: 6,222
SALES (est): 2MM **Privately Held**
SIC: 3944 5945 Video game machines, except coin-operated; toys & games

(G-5415)
O-NETICS LTD
14144 76th Pl Ne (98034-5069)
PHONE..................................425 823-2279
Susan Purvine, *President*
Harold Purvine, *Vice Pres*
EMP: 5
SALES: 250K **Privately Held**
SIC: 3612 Power & distribution transformers

(G-5416)
OIL SPILLS SERVICES INC
12422 68th Ave Ne (98034-5706)
P.O. Box 548 (98083-0548)
PHONE..................................425 823-6500
EMP: 2
SALES (est): 270K **Privately Held**
SIC: 3533 5169 4959 Mfg Oil Spill Equipment Manufacturers Representative Oil Spill Products

(G-5417)
OMEGA ARCHITECTURAL PDTS INC (PA)
Also Called: Omega Aerospace Products
517 6th St S (98033-6717)
PHONE..................................425 821-7222
Mike Cotter, *President*
EMP: 2
SQ FT: 10,000
SALES (est): 705.1K **Privately Held**
SIC: 3599 Crankshafts & camshafts, machining

(G-5418)
OMEGA LABS INC
10916 101st Pl Ne (98033-4418)
PHONE..................................425 296-0886
Mary Oemig, *Principal*
Eric Oemig,
EMP: 2 **EST:** 2012
SALES (est): 159.7K **Privately Held**
SIC: 7372 7374 Educational computer software; data processing service

(G-5419)
OMNI TECHNOLOGY
7427 Ne 144th Pl (98034-4920)
PHONE..................................425 823-9295
Edward Ott, *Owner*
EMP: 3
SALES (est): 200K **Privately Held**
SIC: 3613 8711 Power connectors, electric; engineering services

(G-5420)
ON SITE SAFETY INC
1100 Carillon Pt (98033-7412)
PHONE..................................970 876-1908
Royce Bradford, *Office Mgr*
EMP: 7
SALES (est): 638.6K **Privately Held**
SIC: 5999 5099 1389 Safety supplies & equipment; safety equipment & supplies; oil field services

(G-5421)
ON-SITE SAFETY INC
1100 Carillon Pt (98033-7412)
PHONE..................................701 774-2022
EMP: 6
SALES (est): 462K **Privately Held**
SIC: 1389 5999 Oil/Gas Field Services Ret Misc Merchandise

(G-5422)
ORION MFG LLC
210 10th St Apt 6 (98033-6361)
PHONE..................................206 979-5511
Weihoa Long,
EMP: 2 **EST:** 2012
SALES (est): 117.4K **Privately Held**
SIC: 3999 Manufacturing industries

(G-5423)
P&M PRODUCTS INC
Also Called: EZ Grill
6619 132nd Ave Ne Ste 206 (98033-8627)
PHONE..................................425 939-8349
▲ **EMP:** 6
SALES (est): 1.1MM **Privately Held**
SIC: 5023 3631 Whol Homefurnishings Mfg Household Cooking Equipment/Barbeque Grills Easy Light Charcoal & Grilling Accessories

(G-5424)
PACCAR INC
10630 Ne 38th Pl (98033-7909)
P.O. Box 1000 (98083-1000)
PHONE..................................425 828-5000
Bob Christiansen, *Manager*
EMP: 250
SQ FT: 250,000
SALES (corp-wide): 23.5B **Publicly Held**
SIC: 3711 3714 Truck & tractor truck assembly; motor vehicle parts & accessories
PA: Paccar Inc
777 106th Ave Ne
Bellevue WA 98004
425 468-7400

(G-5425)
PACRIM TECHNOLOGIES LLC
11321 Ne 120th St Bldg W (98034-6907)
PHONE..................................425 284-7300
Jill McCallum, *President*
EMP: 2
SALES (est): 90.7K **Privately Held**
SIC: 2911 Fuel additives

(G-5426)
PAGE AEROSPACE INC
4020 Lake Wash Blvd Ne (98033-7862)
PHONE..................................425 650-1459
EMP: 2
SALES (est): 173.9K **Privately Held**
SIC: 3721 Aircraft

(G-5427)
PALO ALTO HEALTH SCIENCES INC
12020 113th Ave Ne (98034-6938)
PHONE..................................925 594-8404
Simon Thomas, *COO*
EMP: 18
SQ FT: 3,500
SALES (est): 2.3MM **Privately Held**
SIC: 3845 Electromedical equipment

(G-5428)
PARADISE STUDIOS
11410 Ne 124th St (98034-4305)
PHONE..................................360 789-5744
Bethel Raya, *Principal*
EMP: 3
SALES (est): 175.4K **Privately Held**
SIC: 2515 Studio couches

(G-5429)
PARAGON ENERGY SOLUTIONS
5511 105th Ave Ne (98033-7405)
PHONE..................................425 445-6471
Gary L Henderson, *Principal*
EMP: 3
SALES: 100K **Privately Held**
SIC: 3433 Heating equipment, except electric

(G-5430)
PATERIC SOFTWARE
13029 Ne 126th Pl (98034-7723)
PHONE..................................425 814-4949
Eric Minsky, *Partner*
EMP: 9
SALES (est): 638K **Privately Held**
SIC: 7372 Prepackaged software

(G-5431)
PCS MILL WORK INC (PA)
116 Slater St Ste 9 (98033-6788)
PHONE..................................425 820-5688
Loren Perrigo, *President*
EMP: 33
SQ FT: 15,000
SALES (est): 2.6MM **Privately Held**
WEB: www.pcsmillwork.com
SIC: 2431 3429 Mantels, wood; staircases & stairs, wood; manufactured hardware (general)

(G-5432)
PEEL DAVID AND ASSOCIATES
Also Called: Washington Healthcare News
631 8th Ave (98033-5661)
PHONE..................................425 577-8980
David Peel, *Principal*
EMP: 3 **EST:** 2010
SALES (est): 400K **Privately Held**
SIC: 2721 Periodicals

(G-5433)
PGRI INCORPORATED
218 Main St Ste 203 (98033-6108)
PHONE..................................425 449-3000
Paul Jason, *CEO*
EMP: 2
SALES (est): 149.3K **Privately Held**
SIC: 2721 Magazines: publishing only, not printed on site

(G-5434)
PINNION INC
821 Kirkland Ave Ste 100 (98033-6311)
PHONE..................................206 577-3070
Steve Gahler, *CEO*
Michael Yerkovich, *President*
EMP: 12
SQ FT: 2,000
SALES (est): 809.9K **Privately Held**
SIC: 7372 8713 Publishers' computer software; surveying services

(G-5435)
PLANNED SOLUTIONS LLC
807 Lake St S (98033-6439)
PHONE..................................425 827-4277
Peter Robertson, *Principal*
EMP: 2
SALES (est): 110K **Privately Held**
SIC: 2499 Decorative wood & woodwork

(G-5436)
PLUNK LLC
4313 106th Pl Ne (98033-7919)
PHONE..................................425 770-1287
Ross Holeman, *President*
EMP: 4 **EST:** 2017
SQ FT: 2,000
SALES (est): 156.7K **Privately Held**
SIC: 2879 Insecticides & pesticides

(G-5437)
PLUSSOFT INC
11637 Ne 148th Ct (98034-4640)
PHONE..................................425 821-8776
Peter Girotat, *President*
EMP: 4
SALES (est): 257.7K **Privately Held**
SIC: 3695 Computer software tape & disks: blank, rigid & floppy

(G-5438)
POLYTHERMICS LLC
11628 73rd Pl Ne (98034-2432)
PHONE..................................425 823-5568
John Neukirchen,
EMP: 2
SALES (est): 220K **Privately Held**
SIC: 2821 Plastics materials & resins

(G-5439)
POSABIT INC
1128 8th St (98033-5666)
PHONE..................................903 641-7604
Ryan Hamlin, *Principal*
Laurie Rosini, *Ch Credit Ofcr*
Kelsey Teel, *Manager*
EMP: 10
SQ FT: 2,500
SALES (est): 393K **Privately Held**
SIC: 7372 Prepackaged software

(G-5440)
PRAXAIR INC
11216 120th Ave Ne (98033-4535)
PHONE..................................425 821-2423
Nathan Davis, *Manager*
EMP: 2 **Privately Held**
SIC: 2813 Industrial gases
HQ: Praxair, Inc.
10 Riverview Dr
Danbury CT 06810
203 837-2000

(G-5441)
PREVENCIO INC
11335 Ne 122nd Way # 105 (98034-6933)
PHONE..................................425 576-1200
Rhonda Rhyne, *CEO*
Gary Franks, *COO*
EMP: 7
SQ FT: 1,000
SALES (est): 655K **Privately Held**
SIC: 2835 In vitro diagnostics

(G-5442)
PRINTERS SHOPPER LLC
12832 Ne 70th Pl (98033-8535)
P.O. Box 2941 (98083-2941)
PHONE..................................425 822-7766
Kurt T Coralline,
Ian Coralline,
EMP: 2
SQ FT: 1,000
SALES: 350K **Privately Held**
WEB: www.theprintersshopper.com
SIC: 5199 3861 Art goods & supplies; graphic arts plates, sensitized

(G-5443)
PRODECO LLC
12832 Ne 70th Pl (98033-8535)
P.O. Box 82778, Kenmore (98028-0778)
PHONE..................................425 827-2573
Kurt Coralin,
EMP: 3
SALES (est): 320.2K **Privately Held**
SIC: 3555 Printing trades machinery

(G-5444)
PROMEDEV LLC
Also Called: Relief Factor
11335 Ne 122nd Way # 140 (98034-6919)
PHONE..................................800 500-8384
Jerry Mixon, *Mng Member*
Mike Cleek, *Program Mgr*
EMP: 6
SALES (est): 1.7MM **Privately Held**
SIC: 2834 Medicines, capsuled or ampuled

(G-5445)
PROSTHTIC SPECIALISTS WASH LLC
1111417 124th Ave Ne 10 (98033)
PHONE..................................425 576-5050
Sanjay Perti, *Owner*
EMP: 3
SALES (est): 219.3K **Privately Held**
SIC: 3842 Limbs, artificial

(G-5446)
PUGET SOUND WOOD WINDOWS LLC
603 Market St (98033-5422)
PHONE..................................425 828-9736
Matt Sheffer,
EMP: 4
SQ FT: 800
SALES (est): 578.5K **Privately Held**
WEB: www.pugetsoundexteriorsinc.com
SIC: 2431 5211 Windows & window parts & trim, wood; windows, storm: wood or metal

(G-5447)
PUGET SOUND WORKSHOP LLC
14207 100th Ave Ne (98034-5126)
P.O. Box 1694, Bothell (98041-1694)
PHONE..................................425 821-7345
EMP: 8
SALES (est): 140.1K **Privately Held**
SIC: 2399 Mfg Fabricated Textile Products

(G-5448)
PULSAIR SYSTEMS INC
13643 Ne 126th Pl (98034-8705)
P.O. Box 562, Bellevue (98009-0562)
PHONE..................................425 455-1263
Richard E Parks, *President*
John Parks, *Prdtn Mgr*
John Voorhies, *Sales Staff*
EMP: 5
SQ FT: 4,500

GEOGRAPHIC SECTION

Kirkland - King County (G-5479)

SALES (est): 981.1K **Privately Held**
WEB: www.pulsair.com
SIC: 3569 8711 5172 Liquid automation machinery & equipment; consulting engineer; lubricating oils & greases

(G-5449)
R D WING CO INC
517 6th St S (98033-6717)
PHONE.....................425 821-7222
Rick Wing, *President*
EMP: 15
SQ FT: 16,000
SALES (est): 102.4MM **Privately Held**
SIC: 3599 Machine shop, jobbing & repair

(G-5450)
RACEWAY ELECTRIC
8136 Ne 115th Ct (98034-3504)
PHONE.....................206 459-5894
EMP: 2
SALES (est): 88.3K **Privately Held**
SIC: 3644 Raceways

(G-5451)
REDMOND COMMUNICATIONS INC
Also Called: Directions On Microsoft
1410 Market St Ste 200 (98033-5409)
PHONE.....................425 739-4669
Jeff Parker, *President*
Mona Wolf, *Opers Mgr*
EMP: 12
SQ FT: 2,050
SALES (est): 1.2MM **Privately Held**
WEB: www.directionsonmicrosoft.com
SIC: 2741 2721 Newsletter publishing; periodicals

(G-5452)
RHINO STEEL CORPORATION
4030 Lake Washington Blvd (98033-7870)
PHONE.....................425 443-2322
EMP: 2 EST: 2017
SALES (est): 85.2K **Privately Held**
SIC: 3542 Headers

(G-5453)
RUCKUS WIRELESS INC
Also Called: Arris
8815 122nd Ave Ne (98033-5828)
PHONE.....................425 896-6000
EMP: 20
SALES (corp-wide): 6.6B **Privately Held**
SIC: 3661 3663 3357 Mfg Telephone/Graph Eqip Mfg Radio/Tv Comm Equip
HQ: Ruckus Wireless, Inc.
350 W Java Dr
Sunnyvale CA 94089
650 265-4200

(G-5454)
RUNWAY LIQUIDATION LLC
Also Called: Bcbg
2202 W Artesia Blvd (98230)
PHONE.....................304 598-4888
EMP: 2
SALES (corp-wide): 645.5MM **Privately Held**
SIC: 2335 Women's, juniors' & misses' dresses
HQ: Runway Liquidation, Llc
2761 Fruitland Ave
Vernon CA 90058
323 589-2224

(G-5455)
S2 PROTO TYPES INC
12446 Ne 75th St (98033-8206)
PHONE.....................425 822-0858
Ted Svendsen, *President*
Peter Sorrenson, *Vice Pres*
EMP: 2
SALES (est): 200K **Privately Held**
SIC: 2531 School furniture

(G-5456)
SEATTLE SYNCHRO
11410 Ne 124th St (98034-4305)
PHONE.....................206 856-5239
Eva Gonzalez, *President*
EMP: 3
SALES (est): 225.6K **Privately Held**
SIC: 3621 Synchros

(G-5457)
SECORD PRINTING INC
11332 120th Ave Ne # 119 (98033-4537)
PHONE.....................425 883-2182
Jay Secord, *President*
Dean Secord, *Vice Pres*
EMP: 5
SQ FT: 10,000
SALES (est): 749.8K **Privately Held**
WEB: www.secordprinting.com
SIC: 2752 Commercial printing, offset

(G-5458)
SELECT SELLING INC (HQ)
Also Called: TAS Group
550 Kirkland Way Ste 101 (98033-6240)
PHONE.....................425 895-8959
Donal Daly, *CEO*
Patricia Elliot, *President*
Tim Foster, *Senior Partner*
Scott Jackson, *Senior Partner*
Krissy Koza, *Senior Partner*
EMP: 31
SALES (est): 10.5MM **Privately Held**
WEB: www.thetasgroup.com
SIC: 7372 Business oriented computer software

(G-5459)
SERVABLY INC
Also Called: Syncromsp
11410 Ne 124th St Ste 270 (98034-4305)
PHONE.....................425 216-3333
Robert Reichner II, *CEO*
Ian Alexander, *COO*
Troy Anderson, *Vice Pres*
EMP: 4
SALES (est): 216.3K **Privately Held**
SIC: 7372 Business oriented computer software

(G-5460)
SIGN MAKERS INC
Also Called: Tactile Signs
99 10th St S (98033-6731)
PHONE.....................425 828-0688
Kevin Chisman, *President*
EMP: 6
SALES (est): 829.2K **Privately Held**
SIC: 3993 Signs & advertising specialties

(G-5461)
SILICON DESIGNS INC
Also Called: Sdi
13905 Ne 128th St (98034-8768)
PHONE.....................425 391-8329
John Cole, *President*
Russ Ballantyne, *Facilities Mgr*
Dawn Schmidt, *Mfg Staff*
Alyson Graff, *Purch Agent*
Marie Grinolds, *Human Res Mgr*
EMP: 43
SQ FT: 60,000
SALES (est): 6.5MM **Privately Held**
WEB: www.silicondesigns.com
SIC: 8711 3825 3823 Electrical or electronic engineering; test equipment for electronic & electric measurement; industrial instrmnts msrmnt display/control process variable

(G-5462)
SILVAN CRAFT INC
Also Called: Walker Custom Cabinets
11844 Ne 112th St (98033-4511)
PHONE.....................425 827-7050
Dobum Kim, *President*
EMP: 6
SQ FT: 8,000
SALES: 600K **Privately Held**
SIC: 2434 Wood kitchen cabinets

(G-5463)
SIMUTECH INTERNATIONAL INC
10205 136th Ave Ne (98033-5213)
PHONE.....................360 490-4029
Gary Carlberg, *CEO*
Brian C Horsfield, *Corp Secy*
Edward L Soule, *Vice Pres*
EMP: 4
SALES (est): 476.6K **Privately Held**
WEB: www.clc6000.com
SIC: 3554 5084 Coating & finishing machinery, paper; industrial machinery & equipment

(G-5464)
SITKA 2 PUBLISHING LLC
13326 119th Ave Ne Ste A (98034-2159)
P.O. Box 2604 (98083-2604)
PHONE.....................425 522-4231
Charles W Hitz, *Administration*
EMP: 2
SALES (est): 99.9K **Privately Held**
SIC: 2741 Miscellaneous publishing

(G-5465)
SOFTRESOURCES LLC
11411 Ne 124th St Ste 270 (98034-4341)
PHONE.....................425 216-4030
Elaine Watson, *Mng Member*
Pamela Ettien, *Manager*
Ron Loos, *Director*
Spencer Arnesen,
Christine Panian,
EMP: 7
SQ FT: 6,000
SALES (est): 770.7K **Privately Held**
WEB: www.softresources.com
SIC: 7372 Business oriented computer software

(G-5466)
SOMERSET SOFTWARE
520 6th Ave Apt 4003 (98033-5683)
PHONE.....................425 822-1951
EMP: 2
SALES (est): 140K **Privately Held**
SIC: 7372 Prepackaged Software Services

(G-5467)
SOUND PUBLISHING INC
Also Called: Bothell Rprter Knmore Reporter
11630 Slater Ave Ne Ste 9 (98034-4100)
PHONE.....................425 483-3732
Julie Thompsen, *Branch Mgr*
EMP: 7 **Privately Held**
WEB: www.soundpublishing.com
SIC: 2711 Newspapers: publishing only, not printed on site
HQ: Sound Publishing, Inc.
11323 Commando Rd W Main
Everett WA 98204
360 394-5800

(G-5468)
SOUNDNINE INC
10825 Ne 112th St (98033-4507)
PHONE.....................206 245-4463
Darius Miller, *President*
◆ EMP: 4 EST: 2011
SALES (est): 458.4K **Privately Held**
SIC: 3823 Transmitters of process variables, stand. signal conversion

(G-5469)
SPRY FOX LLC
8730 Ne 124th St (98034-2644)
PHONE.....................425 835-3320
David Edery, *CEO*
Daniel Cook,
EMP: 2
SALES (est): 175.4K **Privately Held**
SIC: 7372 Home entertainment computer software

(G-5470)
SPRY HIVE INDUSTRIES
1113 6th St (98033-5640)
PHONE.....................425 503-9790
Paul Scarpa, *Principal*
EMP: 2
SALES (est): 144K **Privately Held**
SIC: 3999 Manufacturing industries

(G-5471)
STRATAGEN SYSTEMS INC
4040 Lake Washington Blvd (98033-7874)
PHONE.....................425 821-8454
Mike Nienhuis, *President*
Vari Ghai, *Admin Sec*
EMP: 40 EST: 1998
SALES (est): 4.9MM **Privately Held**
WEB: www.stratagen.com
SIC: 7372 Business oriented computer software

(G-5472)
SUBARU OF AMERICA INC
Also Called: Fuji Heavy Industries
4040 Lake Washington Blvd (98033-7874)
PHONE.....................425 822-0762
Kahiko Hayakawa, *Manager*
EMP: 5 **Privately Held**
SIC: 3728 Aircraft parts & equipment
HQ: Subaru Of America, Inc.
1 Subaru Dr
Camden NJ 08103
856 488-8500

(G-5473)
SYSTEMS ENGINEERING INC
4327 105th Ave Ne (98033-7913)
PHONE.....................206 633-4972
Sylvia M Scott, *President*
James Nash, *Vice Pres*
EMP: 7
SQ FT: 20,000
SALES (est): 1MM **Privately Held**
WEB: www.systemscontrols.com
SIC: 7699 3625 5088 Marine engine repair; marine & navy auxiliary controls; marine propulsion machinery & equipment

(G-5474)
T14 INC
Also Called: T14 Creations
10211 112th Ave Ne (98033-5142)
PHONE.....................425 829-8213
EMP: 3
SALES (est): 197.3K **Privately Held**
SIC: 3944 Mfg Games/Toys

(G-5475)
TABLEAU SOFTWARE INC
720 4th Ave Ste 120 (98033-8136)
PHONE.....................206 634-5610
Michael Clark, *Sales Staff*
David Jones, *Sales Staff*
April Kauffman, *Sales Staff*
Chris Appel, *Technician*
EMP: 11
SALES (corp-wide): 1.1B **Publicly Held**
SIC: 7372 Prepackaged software
PA: Tableau Software, Inc.
1621 N 34th St
Seattle WA 98103
206 633-3400

(G-5476)
TABLESAFE INC
12220 113th Ave Ne # 220 (98034-6915)
PHONE.....................206 516-6100
Gordon Gardiner, *CEO*
Steve McKean, *COO*
Gary McGrath, *Exec VP*
Livia Stoica, *Project Mgr*
Debra Evans, *Manager*
EMP: 52
SALES (est): 6.4MM **Privately Held**
SIC: 3571 Computers, digital, analog or hybrid

(G-5477)
TELOS SALES CORPORATION
11733 Holmes Point Dr Ne (98034-3444)
PHONE.....................425 890-2755
Eric Ullery, *Principal*
EMP: 2
SALES (est): 214.6K **Privately Held**
SIC: 7372 Prepackaged software

(G-5478)
TELSPACE LLC
Also Called: Telmage Consulting
5400 Carillon Pt (98033-7357)
PHONE.....................425 953-2801
Jeremy Geis,
Cody Hershey,
Paris Holt,
Ryan Reed,
Jeremy Sands,
EMP: 24
SQ FT: 10,370
SALES (est): 1.3MM **Privately Held**
WEB: www.telspace.com
SIC: 8748 7372 Telecommunications consultant; prepackaged software

(G-5479)
TESLAVISION
401 Parkplace Ctr Ste 319 (98033-6200)
PHONE.....................425 822-6535
EMP: 3 EST: 2009
SALES (est): 250K **Privately Held**
SIC: 3993 Mfg Signs/Advertising Specialties

Kirkland - King County (G-5480)

(G-5480)
TETRACHROME SOFTWARE
14058 120th Ave Ne (98034-1426)
PHONE.....................425 825-1708
Ryan Seghers, *Principal*
EMP: 2
SALES (est): 85.1K **Privately Held**
SIC: 7372 Prepackaged software

(G-5481)
THESOFTWAREWORXCOM
12205 Ne 138th Pl (98034-2227)
PHONE.....................425 825-3814
EMP: 2
SALES (est): 107.4K **Privately Held**
SIC: 3561 Mfg Pumps/Pumping Equipment

(G-5482)
THYSSENKRUPP ELEVATOR CORP
12530 135th Ave Ne (98034-8709)
P.O. Box 2699 (98083-2699)
PHONE.....................425 828-3110
Steve Vining, *Manager*
EMP: 22
SALES (corp-wide): 39.8B **Privately Held**
WEB: www.tyssenkrupp.com
SIC: 3999 3534 Wheelchair lifts; elevators & moving stairways
HQ: Thyssenkrupp Elevator Corporation
11605 Haynes Bridge Rd # 650
Alpharetta GA 30009
678 319-3240

(G-5483)
TIMS MANUFACTURING CORP
11902 124th Ave Ne (98034-8111)
PHONE.....................425 392-2616
Timothy Tim David Thorning, *Principal*
EMP: 2
SALES (est): 130.3K **Privately Held**
SIC: 3999 Manufacturing industries

(G-5484)
TISSUE REGENERATION SYSTEMS
5400 Carillon Pt (98033-7357)
PHONE.....................425 576-4032
William J Fitzsimmons, *Principal*
EMP: 2
SALES (est): 221K **Privately Held**
SIC: 3841 Surgical & medical instruments

(G-5485)
TRACKTION SOFTWARE CORPORATION
10820 Ne 108th St (98033-5033)
PHONE.....................425 273-3376
James Woodburn, *CEO*
EMP: 3
SALES (est): 168.1K **Privately Held**
SIC: 7372 7389 Prepackaged software;

(G-5486)
TUBE CRAZY
218 Main St (98033-6108)
PHONE.....................206 931-7764
EMP: 2
SALES (est): 110K **Privately Held**
SIC: 1389 Oil/Gas Field Services

(G-5487)
TYSON NUTRACEUTICALS INC
Also Called: Daoust & Daoust
6531 132nd Ave Ne (98033-8628)
PHONE.....................425 869-1192
Gene Daoust, *Manager*
EMP: 2
SALES (corp-wide): 4.8MM **Privately Held**
WEB: www.tysonnutraceuticals.com
SIC: 2834 Pharmaceutical preparations
PA: Tyson Nutraceuticals, Inc.
3535 Lomita Blvd Ste A
Torrance CA
310 325-5600

(G-5488)
UNICON INC
11834 Ne 90th St (98033-5814)
P.O. Box 2919, Redmond (98073-2919)
PHONE.....................425 454-2466
O Hauge, *President*
EMP: 5
SALES (est): 790.5K **Privately Held**
WEB: www.unicon.net
SIC: 3829 Measuring & controlling devices

(G-5489)
VIDOR
13002 Ne 101st Pl (98033-5274)
PHONE.....................425 827-9967
EMP: 2
SALES (est): 100K **Privately Held**
SIC: 2731 Books-Publishing/Printing

(G-5490)
VIOGUARD LLC
12220 113th Ave Ne # 100 (98034-6952)
PHONE.....................425 406-8009
Larry Ranta, *President*
John Sharpes, *VP Mfg*
Ken Sullivan, *VP Sales*
Craig Ranta, *CTO*
EMP: 12
SALES (est): 1.7MM **Privately Held**
SIC: 3841 Surgical & medical instruments

(G-5491)
WAKEFIELD ART
11203 100th Ave Ne (98033-4417)
PHONE.....................425 260-0257
Janet Wakefield, *Owner*
Rod Wakefield, *Manager*
EMP: 2
SALES (est): 130.4K **Privately Held**
SIC: 2851 Lead-in-oil paints

(G-5492)
WASHINGTON VG INC
13600 Ne 126th Pl Ste A (98034-8720)
PHONE.....................425 823-4518
Guy McFarland, *Ch of Bd*
Bonnie Brice, *President*
Vivian McFarland, *Corp Secy*
Tom Beatty, *Engineer*
▲ EMP: 12
SQ FT: 7,000
SALES (est): 2.5MM **Privately Held**
WEB: www.veegee.com
SIC: 5049 3944 Laboratory equipment, except medical or dental; science kits: microscopes, chemistry sets, etc.

(G-5493)
WAVE HOLDCO CORPORATION
401 Kirkland Parkpl (98033)
PHONE.....................425 576-8200
Daniel Huffman, *Technology*
EMP: 2
SALES (est): 95.3K **Privately Held**
SIC: 3663 Radio & TV communications equipment

(G-5494)
WESTERN PNEUMATIC TUBE CO LLC (HQ)
835 6th St S (98033-6759)
PHONE.....................425 822-8271
Surin Mahaltra,
Chuck Haggard,
Jeff Knowles,
Dany Wanner,
◆ EMP: 45
SQ FT: 80,000
SALES (est): 27MM
SALES (corp-wide): 4.2B **Publicly Held**
WEB: www.wptube.com
SIC: 3317 Tubes, wrought: welded or lock joint
PA: Leggett & Platt, Incorporated
1 Leggett Rd
Carthage MO 64836
417 358-8131

(G-5495)
WNTR SKI ACADEMY LLC
Also Called: Cordova
614 10th Ave W (98033-4838)
PHONE.....................425 829-1384
Jane Seim,
Cody Seim,
◆ EMP: 7
SALES (est): 303.8K **Privately Held**
SIC: 5699 2211 Designers, apparel; apparel & outerwear fabrics, cotton

(G-5496)
WOLFF DEFENSE
4040 Lake Wash Blvd Ne (98033-7874)
PHONE.....................425 284-2000
EMP: 2
SALES (est): 105.6K **Privately Held**
SIC: 3812 Defense systems & equipment

(G-5497)
WOOD CARE SYSTEMS
719 Kirkland Ave (98033-6319)
PHONE.....................425 827-6000
Jim Remfroe, *Principal*
▲ EMP: 6
SALES (est): 456.1K **Privately Held**
WEB: www.ewoodcare.com
SIC: 2491 Wood preserving

(G-5498)
WORLDWIDE DGITAL SOLUTIONS INC
Also Called: Send4print.com
11251 120th Ave Ne # 142 (98033-4538)
PHONE.....................425 605-0923
Zaid Chishti, *President*
Sofia Chishti, *Chairman*
▲ EMP: 5 EST: 2011
SQ FT: 1,000
SALES (est): 60K **Privately Held**
SIC: 2752 Commercial printing, lithographic

(G-5499)
ZEMAX LLC (PA)
10230 Ne Pints Dr Ste 540 (98033)
PHONE.....................425 305-2800
Mark Nicholson, *CEO*
Alison Yates, *Engineer*
Jeff Decillia, *CFO*
Dan Hamann, *Risk Mgmt Dir*
EMP: 51
SQ FT: 1,000
SALES (est): 9.5MM **Privately Held**
SIC: 7372 Prepackaged software

(G-5500)
ZERO ONE VINTNERS
131 Lake St S (98033-6517)
PHONE.....................425 242-0735
EMP: 2
SALES (est): 68.6K **Privately Held**
SIC: 2084 Wines, brandy & brandy spirits

(G-5501)
ZHONGTAO
11228 Ne 143rd Ct (98034-1019)
PHONE.....................425 344-9373
EMP: 3 EST: 2010
SALES (est): 196.8K **Privately Held**
SIC: 3465 Mfg Automotive Stampings

La Center
Clark County

(G-5502)
BME LOGGING LLC
32214 Ne 82nd Ave (98629-2837)
PHONE.....................360 931-6797
Brandon M Endres,
EMP: 3 EST: 2012
SALES (est): 235.7K **Privately Held**
SIC: 2411 Logging

(G-5503)
CUSICHACA ALPACAS
33404 Ne 24th Ave (98629-2657)
PHONE.....................360 936-3259
Andy Rukliss, *Principal*
EMP: 2
SALES (est): 160.5K **Privately Held**
SIC: 2231 Alpacas, mohair: woven

(G-5504)
FARM BUILT FAB LLC
216 Ne 349th St (98629-3230)
PHONE.....................360 213-8458
EMP: 3
SALES: 200K **Privately Held**
SIC: 3441 1541 7389 Fabricated structural metal; factory construction; prefabricated building erection, industrial;

(G-5505)
HI-LINELEATHER
12013 Ne 368th St (98629-4304)
PHONE.....................360 263-7898
Kenneth Lone, *Owner*
EMP: 2
SALES (est): 85.8K **Privately Held**
SIC: 3199 Leather goods

(G-5506)
HIGHLAND MACHINE WORKS
5405 Ne 399th St (98629-4723)
PHONE.....................360 263-1216
Phillip Kinsella, *Owner*
Lyndalin Kinsella, *Co-Owner*
EMP: 2
SALES (est): 75K **Privately Held**
SIC: 3599 Machine shop, jobbing & repair

(G-5507)
J & L MACHINING AND MORE LLC
1352 E 14th Cir (98629-5584)
PHONE.....................503 317-8284
Jonathan Manire, *Co-Owner*
EMP: 2
SALES (est): 102.6K **Privately Held**
SIC: 3599 Crankshafts & camshafts, machining

(G-5508)
J TS TRACTOR WORK
35808 Ne 84th Ave (98629-4261)
PHONE.....................360 263-3016
John Taylor, *Owner*
EMP: 2
SALES (est): 215.4K **Privately Held**
SIC: 3531 1799 Tractors, construction; posthole digging

(G-5509)
MCLAREN DESTINY
Also Called: Destiny Dawn Spirituality
116 W 10th St (98629-9520)
PHONE.....................971 217-5877
Destiny McLaren, *Owner*
Bryce McLaren, *Manager*
EMP: 2
SALES (est): 67.3K **Privately Held**
SIC: 3999 5722 Candles; household appliance stores

(G-5510)
ON THE LEVEL CUSTOM CABINETS
9217 Ne 316th St (98629-2803)
PHONE.....................360 666-9058
Kevin J Roggenkamp, *Principal*
EMP: 4
SALES (est): 210K **Privately Held**
SIC: 2434 Wood kitchen cabinets

(G-5511)
PACIFIC ALLY LLC
Also Called: Docudriven
419 E Cedar Ave Ste A201 (98629-5482)
PHONE.....................360 760-4266
Dion Labadie, *Sales Associate*
Bruce Randall,
EMP: 4
SALES (est): 463.5K **Privately Held**
SIC: 8742 7374 7373 7372 Management consulting services; data processing service; optical scanning data service; value-added resellers, computer systems; business oriented computer software; document & office records storage

(G-5512)
PENTECH INDUSTRIES LLC
36806 Ne Holling Ave (98629-4280)
P.O. Box 455 (98629-0455)
PHONE.....................360 989-7903
Tom Pender, *Principal*
EMP: 2 EST: 2012
SALES (est): 104.3K **Privately Held**
SIC: 3999 Manufacturing industries

(G-5513)
RAMCO MECHANICAL CUTTING LTD
Also Called: Fairview Equipment
5616 Ne 399th St (98629-4724)
P.O. Box 890 (98629-0890)
PHONE.....................360 263-1967

GEOGRAPHIC SECTION

Mark Chord, *President*
Wendy Chord, *Admin Sec*
EMP: 24
SALES (est): 2.7MM **Privately Held**
SIC: 2411 Logging camps & contractors

(G-5514)
RHYTHMICAL STEEL
3908 Ne 397th Cir (98629-4622)
PHONE..................................360 263-3141
Dennis Martin, *Owner*
Sharon Martin, *Co-Owner*
EMP: 2
SALES: 23K **Privately Held**
WEB: www.rhythmicalsteel.com
SIC: 3931 Drums, parts & accessories (musical instruments)

(G-5515)
SALMON CREEK INDUSTRIES INC
34506 Nw 11th Ave (98629-3134)
PHONE..................................360 921-5143
Fred Hollis, *President*
Bette Lou Hollis, *Admin Sec*
EMP: 2
SALES (est): 195.9K **Privately Held**
SIC: 3548 Welding & cutting apparatus & accessories

(G-5516)
TDB HOLDINGS LLC
3214 Ne 394th St (98629-4863)
PHONE..................................360 600-5506
Timothy Homola, *Principal*
EMP: 2
SALES (est): 81.7K **Privately Held**
SIC: 2411 Logging

(G-5517)
TIMEZONE RACEWAY PARK
6900 Ne 374th St (98629-4130)
PHONE..................................360 450-3730
Rick Stcyr, *Branch Mgr*
EMP: 5
SALES (corp-wide): 584.4K **Privately Held**
SIC: 3644 Raceways
PA: Timezone Raceway Park
29718 Ne 132nd Ave
Battle Ground WA 98604
360 687-5100

(G-5518)
VAN BRYNNS WHEELCHAIR
8319 Ne 316th St (98629-2800)
PHONE..................................360 687-8546
Ann Franck, *Executive Asst*
EMP: 3 **EST:** 2012
SALES (est): 153.3K **Privately Held**
SIC: 3842 Wheelchairs

(G-5519)
WHITE & ZUMSTEIN INC
35006 Nw Seibler Dr (98629-3008)
P.O. Box 1439, Woodland (98674-1301)
PHONE..................................360 263-6114
Gene White, *President*
David White, *Corp Secy*
Cindy White, *Vice Pres*
EMP: 18
SALES (est): 1.8MM **Privately Held**
SIC: 2411 Logging

La Conner
Skagit County

(G-5520)
ALPAC COMPONENTS CO
110 Caledonia (98257)
P.O. Box 40404, Bellevue (98015-4404)
PHONE..................................360 466-2024
Fax: 360 466-4150
EMP: 23 **EST:** 1996
SALES (est): 1.6MM **Privately Held**
SIC: 2435 Mfg Hardwood Veneer/Plywood

(G-5521)
COLD SEA REFRIGERATION INC
758 Tillamuk Dr (98257-9611)
P.O. Box 1388, Burlington (98233-0617)
PHONE..................................360 466-5850
Bruce Wyman, *President*
Donald Holman, *Vice Pres*
EMP: 6
SQ FT: 2,800
SALES: 550K **Privately Held**
SIC: 5078 3585 Commercial refrigeration equipment; refrigeration equipment, complete

(G-5522)
COMPTEX INC
125 Sherman St (98257-4760)
P.O. Box 1228 (98257-1228)
PHONE..................................360 466-5453
Eric Schaub, *President*
Don Shortt, *Vice Pres*
▲ **EMP:** 10
SQ FT: 30,000
SALES (est): 1.6MM **Privately Held**
SIC: 2221 3229 Fiberglass fabrics; glass fibers, textile

(G-5523)
CUSTOM FAB
65 Kalama Pl (98257-9637)
PHONE..................................360 466-1199
Charles Ray, *Owner*
Amanda Ray, *Co-Owner*
EMP: 2
SALES (est): 129.5K **Privately Held**
SIC: 3499 Novelties & specialties, metal

(G-5524)
MARITIME FABRICATIONS INC (PA)
Also Called: La Conner Maritime Service
920 Pearl Jensen Way (98257-4720)
PHONE..................................360 466-3629
Ed Oczkewicz, *President*
Isaac Oczkewicz, *General Mgr*
Nancy Oczkewicz, *Vice Pres*
EMP: 36
SALES (est): 2.5MM **Privately Held**
WEB: www.laconnermaritime.com
SIC: 7699 3949 3599 Boat repair; fishing equipment; machine shop, jobbing & repair

(G-5525)
MAVRIK MARINE INC
780 Pearl Jensen Way (98257-4754)
PHONE..................................360 296-4051
Zachery Battle, *President*
Russ Wilson, *Vice Pres*
EMP: 80
SQ FT: 45,000
SALES (est): 20.5MM **Privately Held**
SIC: 3731 Shipbuilding & repairing

(G-5526)
SWINOMISH FISH CO INC
11455 Moorage Way (98257)
PHONE..................................360 466-0176
▼ **EMP:** 9
SALES (est): 1.4MM **Privately Held**
SIC: 2092 5142 Mfg/Whol Frozen And Can Sea Food

(G-5527)
TRITON AEROSPACE LLC
813 S 2nd St (98257)
PHONE..................................360 466-4160
Ron Halterman, *Mng Member*
Thomas Hsueh, *Mng Member*
EMP: 11
SALES (est): 1.6MM **Privately Held**
SIC: 3728 Aircraft parts & equipment

Lacey
Thurston County

(G-5528)
ABC PRINTING INC
7009 Martin Way E (98516-5537)
P.O. Box 3309 (98509-3309)
PHONE..................................360 456-4545
Robert Kagy, *President*
Michael Shupe, *Sales Mgr*
EMP: 24
SQ FT: 15,000
SALES: 3MM **Privately Held**
WEB: www.abcprinting.net
SIC: 2752 Commercial printing, offset

(G-5529)
ABOUT PRINTING AND APPAREL
5709 Lacey Blvd Se (98503-2495)
PHONE..................................360 584-9159
Adan Tepale-Vazquez, *Principal*
EMP: 3
SALES (est): 82.7K **Privately Held**
SIC: 5699 2759 Miscellaneous apparel & accessories; commercial printing

(G-5530)
ACCESS US OIL & GAS INC
665 Woodland Sq Loop Se (98503-1009)
PHONE..................................206 792-7575
Michael Mattox, *Principal*
EMP: 2
SALES (est): 156K **Privately Held**
SIC: 1382 Oil & gas exploration services

(G-5531)
ALL PRO SCREEN PRTG & EMB LLC
8300 28th Ct Ne (98516-7143)
PHONE..................................360 438-0304
Thomas Whitney, *Principal*
EMP: 6 **EST:** 2007
SALES (est): 511.2K **Privately Held**
SIC: 2759 Screen printing

(G-5532)
AMISH LOG HOMES
6360 Carpenter Rd Se (98503-2457)
PHONE..................................360 491-4132
EMP: 2
SALES (est): 170K **Privately Held**
SIC: 2452 Prefabricated Wood Buildings

(G-5533)
ARTISTIC TALENTS STYLING SALON
5233 Lacey Blvd Se (98503-2443)
PHONE..................................360 456-0100
Gloria Zvirzdy, *Owner*
EMP: 6
SALES (est): 118.1K **Privately Held**
SIC: 7231 3634 Hairdressers; massage machines, electric, except for beauty/barber shops

(G-5534)
ASKA COMPANY
4706 Pacific Ave Se (98503-1216)
PHONE..................................360 753-4233
Ken Naganuma, *President*
Brett Ferguson, *Vice Pres*
▲ **EMP:** 3
SQ FT: 10,000
SALES: 650K **Privately Held**
SIC: 3089 Molding primary plastic
PA: Aska Company Co.,Ltd.
4004, Kotaka
Kato HYO 679-0

(G-5535)
BAIR CONSTRUCTION INC
Also Called: A-1 Concrete Supplies
8464 30th Ave Ne (98516-7124)
PHONE..................................360 491-2285
Toll Free:..................................888 -
David Bair, *President*
Terese Bair, *Vice Pres*
EMP: 4
SQ FT: 7,000
SALES (est): 872.6K **Privately Held**
SIC: 5032 5211 7359 3444 Concrete & cinder building products; masonry materials & supplies; equipment rental & leasing; concrete forms, sheet metal

(G-5536)
CALLISONS INC (PA)
Also Called: I. P. Callison & Sons Division
2400 Callison Rd Ne (98516-3154)
PHONE..................................360 412-3340
Jim Burgett, *Principal*
Greg Biza, *Principal*
Karsten Kohrs, *Principal*
Robert Mazur, *Principal*
Robert Motta, *Principal*
◆ **EMP:** 40
SQ FT: 100,000
SALES (est): 24.6MM **Privately Held**
WEB: www.ipcallison.com
SIC: 2899 5193 Oils & essential oils; peppermint oil; spearmint oil; florists' supplies

(G-5537)
CAPITAL HEATING & COOLING INC
1218 Carpenter Rd Se (98503-2411)
P.O. Box 3387 (98509-3387)
PHONE..................................360 491-7450
William Schmidtke, *President*
Dean Schmidtke, *Vice Pres*
Chuck Schmidtke, *Treasurer*
Erin Schmidtke, *Admin Sec*
EMP: 35 **EST:** 1937
SQ FT: 10,000
SALES (est): 8.4MM **Privately Held**
WEB: www.capitalsheetmetal.com
SIC: 1761 1711 3444 Sheet metalwork; ventilation & duct work contractor; warm air heating & air conditioning contractor; sheet metalwork

(G-5538)
CAPITOL OPTICAL CORP
Also Called: Vsp
8719 Commerce Place Dr Ne D (98516-1362)
PHONE..................................360 352-7502
Steve Mullen, *President*
EMP: 24
SQ FT: 1,000
SALES (est): 2.9MM **Privately Held**
SIC: 3851 5995 Lens grinding, except prescription: ophthalmic; optical goods stores

(G-5539)
CARE ENGRAVING COMPANY
2131 Agate Ct Se (98503-8611)
PHONE..................................360 456-0831
Roger L Kehr, *Owner*
EMP: 2
SALES (est): 50K **Privately Held**
SIC: 2759 Engraving

(G-5540)
CARTRIDGE CARE INC
1314 Lebanon St Se (98503-2456)
PHONE..................................360 459-8845
Chris Erickson, *President*
Sasha Erickson, *Vice Pres*
EMP: 3
SQ FT: 1,200
SALES: 150K **Privately Held**
SIC: 5112 3699 Laserjet supplies; laser systems & equipment

(G-5541)
CISCO SYSTEMS INC
4160 6th Ave Se Ste 203 (98503-1039)
PHONE..................................360 352-3657
EMP: 2
SALES (corp-wide): 47.1B **Publicly Held**
SIC: 3577 Mfg Internetworking Systems
PA: Cisco Systems, Inc.
170 W Tasman Dr
San Jose CA 95134
408 526-4000

(G-5542)
CLEAR VIEW AUTO & WINDOW GLASS
4207 Pacific Ave Se (98503-1114)
PHONE..................................360 539-5909
John Pazar, *Owner*
EMP: 3
SALES (est): 204.8K **Privately Held**
SIC: 3211 7536 Window glass, clear & colored; automotive glass replacement shops

(G-5543)
CURTS PRINTING
1613 Diamond Loop Se (98503-2968)
PHONE..................................360 456-3041
Curt Highsmith, *Owner*
EMP: 3
SALES (est): 190K **Privately Held**
SIC: 2752 Commercial printing, lithographic

Lacey - Thurston County (G-5544) GEOGRAPHIC SECTION

(G-5544)
CUZD INDUSTRIES
5707 Lacey Blvd Se (98503-7228)
PHONE.................................360 742-3126
Mark Lunde, CEO
EMP: 2
SALES (est): 116.4K Privately Held
SIC: 3999 Manufacturing industries

(G-5545)
D & J MARKETING INC
4108 Kyro Rd Se (98503-4612)
PHONE.................................360 413-9173
Doug Karman, President
Judy Karman, Vice Pres
EMP: 2
SALES (est): 20K Privately Held
WEB: www.djmarketingonline.com
SIC: 2759 Promotional printing

(G-5546)
EJIMCOM
833 Westminster Ct Ne (98516-6318)
PHONE.................................360 459-4785
James Fehlig, Principal
EMP: 2 EST: 2016
SALES (est): 90K Privately Held
SIC: 3674 Semiconductors & related devices

(G-5547)
ELDORADO AG
Also Called: A G EL DORADO
5707 Lacey Blvd Se # 100 (98503-7228)
PHONE.................................360 491-0394
Humberto Aguilar, Owner
EMP: 2
SALES (est): 110K Privately Held
SIC: 5944 3911 Jewelry, precious stones & precious metals; jewelry, precious metal

(G-5548)
ELECTRINO GROUP INC
4401 37th Ave Se Unit 14 (98503-3575)
PHONE.................................360 491-9373
Gordon Ziegler, CEO
EMP: 4
SALES (est): 232.8K Privately Held
SIC: 3462 Nuclear power plant forgings, ferrous

(G-5549)
ELEGANZA DESIGNS INC
7127 Bailey St Se (98513-5013)
PHONE.................................360 499-2710
James M Duffy III, President
James Duffy, President
EMP: 2
SALES (est): 87K Privately Held
SIC: 2499 2493 7389 Engraved wood products; reconstituted wood products; interior design services

(G-5550)
FORKLIFT TRAINING CENTER INC -
8830 Tallon Ln Ne (98516-6656)
PHONE.................................360 515-0696
EMP: 2 EST: 2016
SALES (est): 132.7K Privately Held
SIC: 3537 Forklift trucks

(G-5551)
G B E PUBLISHERS INC
2030 Cardinal Ln Se (98503-2509)
PHONE.................................360 438-5779
EMP: 2
SALES (est): 59.2K Privately Held
SIC: 2741 Miscellaneous publishing

(G-5552)
G L KLUH & SONS JEWELERS INC (PA)
Also Called: Kluh Jewelers
810 Sleater Kinney Rd Se A (98503-1127)
PHONE.................................360 491-3530
Matt Kluh, President
Gregory L Kluh, President
Dennis Craig, Manager
EMP: 10
SALES (est): 785.7K Privately Held
SIC: 5944 7631 3911 Jewelry, precious stones & precious metals; watch, clock & jewelry repair; jewelry apparel

(G-5553)
GLACIER WATER SERVICES INC
6290 Gravel Ln Ne (98516-1322)
PHONE.................................360 413-7272
Rual Tjoa, Manager
EMP: 2
SALES (corp-wide): 286MM Publicly Held
WEB: www.glacierwater.com
SIC: 3581 5499 8741 Automatic vending machines; water: distilled mineral or spring; management services
HQ: Glacier Water Services, Inc.
1385 Park Center Dr
Vista CA 92081
760 560-1111

(G-5554)
HAWKBIRD AUTO AN BOAT LISTING
Also Called: Hawks Prrie Auto Boat Lcensing
1401 Marvin Rd Ne Ste 105 (98516-5711)
PHONE.................................360 491-3015
Ronalee K Mattern, Owner
EMP: 3
SALES (est): 199.6K Privately Held
SIC: 3469 Automobile license tags, stamped metal

(G-5555)
HITECH PUBLICATIONS GROUP
5005 22nd Ave Se (98503-7050)
PHONE.................................520 378-1155
Carl Lawrence, Principal
EMP: 2
SALES (est): 83.9K Privately Held
SIC: 2752 Commercial printing, lithographic

(G-5556)
HUMMINGBIRD PRECISION MCH CO
Also Called: Hummingbird Scientific
2610 Willamette Dr Ne A (98516-1329)
PHONE.................................360 252-2737
Norman Salmon, President
EMP: 13
SQ FT: 4,500
SALES (est): 1.2MM Privately Held
SIC: 3599 3826 Machine shop, jobbing & repair; microscopes, electron & proton

(G-5557)
HUMMINGBIRD SCIENTIFIC LLC
2610 Willamette Dr Ne A (98516-1329)
PHONE.................................360 252-2737
Norman Salmon, President
Ramee Salmon, Treasurer
Eric Stach, CTO
Daan Hein Alsem, Director
EMP: 13
SQ FT: 3,000
SALES (est): 2.2MM Privately Held
WEB: www.hummingbirdscientific.com
SIC: 3826 Microscopes, electron & proton

(G-5558)
I-5 DESIGN BUILD INC
Also Called: I-5 Design and Manufacture
8751 Commerce Place Dr Ne (98516-1326)
PHONE.................................360 459-3200
Duncan Williams, President
Dave Waters, Vice Pres
John Oconnor, Admin Sec
EMP: 100
SQ FT: 12,000
SALES: 29MM Privately Held
WEB: www.i5design.com
SIC: 7389 1542 7336 3646 Interior design services; custom builders, non-residential; graphic arts & related design; ornamental lighting fixtures, commercial; electric signs

(G-5559)
IGT GLOBAL SOLUTIONS CORP
7860 29th Ave Ne Ste B (98516-7122)
PHONE.................................360 412-2140
Shannon Moberly, Branch Mgr
EMP: 25 Privately Held
WEB: www.gtech.com
SIC: 3575 Computer terminals
HQ: Igt Global Solutions Corporation
10 Memorial Blvd
Providence RI 02903
401 392-1000

(G-5560)
INTEGRAL FABRICATIONS LLC
Also Called: Puget Sound Welding
1420 Marvin Rd Ne (98503-3878)
PHONE.................................360 831-9353
James Brooks,
EMP: 5
SALES: 500K Privately Held
SIC: 7692 Welding repair

(G-5561)
JVS PUBLICATIONS LLC
5320 Marvin Rd Ne (98516-2149)
PHONE.................................360 412-0516
EMP: 2
SALES (est): 59.2K Privately Held
SIC: 2741 Miscellaneous publishing

(G-5562)
KADDY
9327 Classic Dr Ne (98516-3191)
PHONE.................................360 438-3636
Delbert J Parkinson, Owner
EMP: 2
SALES: 20K Privately Held
SIC: 2631 Cardboard

(G-5563)
KF INDUSTRIES LLC
1123 Sleater Kinney Rd Se (98503-2300)
PHONE.................................360 628-8473
EMP: 2
SALES (est): 102.1K Privately Held
SIC: 3999 Manufacturing industries

(G-5564)
LAWMAN INDUSTRIES LLC
Also Called: Stair Company The
2629 Reinhardt Ln Ne O (98516-3157)
PHONE.................................360 915-7807
EMP: 3
SALES (est): 184.5K Privately Held
SIC: 3999 Manufacturing industries

(G-5565)
LIPSTICK MISSION
9510 Bentley Ct Ne (98516-3196)
PHONE.................................360 455-3212
Courtney Buechler, Principal
EMP: 2
SALES (est): 74.4K Privately Held
SIC: 2844 Lipsticks

(G-5566)
MEDLINE INDUSTRIES INC
3770 Hogum Bay Rd Ne (98516-3137)
PHONE.................................360 491-0241
EMP: 2
SALES (corp-wide): 6B Privately Held
SIC: 3842 Surgical appliances & supplies
PA: Medline Industries, Inc.
3 Lakes Dr
Northfield IL 60093
847 949-5500

(G-5567)
NORTH PCF IGN INTERLOCK SVC
2633 Willamette Dr Ne G (98516-1323)
PHONE.................................360 480-4919
EMP: 2
SALES (est): 129K Privately Held
SIC: 3694 Engine electrical equipment

(G-5568)
NORTHWEST WLDG FABRICATION INC
3900 12th Ave Se Ste A (98503-2255)
PHONE.................................360 338-0923
Kathy Bodnar, CEO
Chuck Bryant, Vice Pres
Jessica Bryant, Admin Sec
EMP: 5
SALES (est): 224.1K Privately Held
SIC: 7692 Welding repair

(G-5569)
NOTEADSCOM INC
3900 12th Ave Se (98503-2255)
PHONE.................................360 705-4548
EMP: 3
SALES (est): 347.1K Privately Held
SIC: 7319 2752 Distribution of advertising material or sample services; commercial printing, lithographic

(G-5570)
NUTSHELL
4748 Lakeshore Ln Se (98513-4589)
PHONE.................................360 438-1054
Bonnie Vandver, Principal
EMP: 2
SALES (est): 129.2K Privately Held
SIC: 3915 Jewelers' materials & lapidary work

(G-5571)
O-TOWN BREWING LLC
4414 Montclair Dr Se (98503-3541)
PHONE.................................360 701-4706
Bryan Trunnell, Principal
EMP: 2
SALES (est): 62.3K Privately Held
SIC: 2082 Malt beverages

(G-5572)
OFFICEMAX NORTH AMERICA INC
1200 Marvin Rd Ne (98516-3800)
PHONE.................................360 455-4068
Brian Slavach, Branch Mgr
EMP: 28
SALES (corp-wide): 11B Publicly Held
WEB: www.copymax.net
SIC: 5943 2711 Stationery stores; job printing & newspaper publishing combined
HQ: Officemax North America, Inc.
263 Shuman Blvd
Naperville IL 60563

(G-5573)
PACIFIC NORTHWEST DRONE SVCS
5445 Balustrade Blvd Se (98513-5032)
PHONE.................................509 679-0863
Michael Atkinson, Principal
EMP: 2
SALES (est): 100.2K Privately Held
SIC: 3721 Motorized aircraft

(G-5574)
PACIFIC NORTHWEST TECHNOLOGY
8294 28th Ct Ne Ste 500 (98516-7141)
PHONE.................................360 493-8344
Phong Nguyen, Owner
Phong Ngyun, Owner
EMP: 5
SQ FT: 1,800
SALES: 420K Privately Held
WEB: www.pntinc.com
SIC: 3596 Truck (motor vehicle) scales

(G-5575)
PATRIOT TOWING RECOVERY
5868 Pacific Ave Se Ste B (98503-1309)
PHONE.................................360 890-9288
William Hynes,
EMP: 4
SALES (est): 306.7K Privately Held
SIC: 3993 7549 Signs & advertising specialties; towing services; towing service, automotive; road service, automotive

(G-5576)
PFIZER INC
9018 Campus Glen Dr Ne (98516-3898)
PHONE.................................360 701-0799
Brady Adams, Principal
EMP: 225
SALES (corp-wide): 53.6B Publicly Held
SIC: 2834 Pharmaceutical preparations
PA: Pfizer Inc.
235 E 42nd St
New York NY 10017
212 733-2323

(G-5577)
PNW AEROSPACE LLC
5709 Lacey Blvd Se # 202 (98503-2495)
PHONE.................................360 292-0909
Shem Muirhead,
Michael Lovely,
EMP: 3

GEOGRAPHIC SECTION

SALES (est): 341.8K **Privately Held**
SIC: **3728** Aircraft body assemblies & parts

(G-5578)
PRINTING WASHINGTON STATE DEPT
Also Called: Copy Center 6
300 Desmond Dr Se (98503-1274)
PHONE...................................360 407-6013
David Darrah, *Principal*
EMP: 2 **Privately Held**
SIC: **2759** 9199 Commercial printing; general government administration;
HQ: Washington State Department Of Printing
7580 New Market St Sw
Tumwater WA 98501
360 753-6820

(G-5579)
PURE HEALTH PRODUCTS LLC
8450 30th Ave Ne (98516-7176)
PHONE...................................360 688-7034
Pasqual Ferro, *President*
David Posel, *COO*
Stan Teeple, *CFO*
EMP: 5
SQ FT: 5,000
SALES (est): 244.5K **Privately Held**
SIC: **2023** Dietary supplements, dairy & non-dairy based
PA: Canbiola, Inc.
960 S Broadway Ste 120
Hicksville NY 11801

(G-5580)
QUANTUM SOLUTIONS INC
9119 Classic Dr Ne (98516-9247)
PHONE...................................360 491-0757
EMP: 2
SALES (est): 85.9K **Privately Held**
SIC: **3572** Computer storage devices

(G-5581)
R T LONDON COMPANY
Also Called: Rt London-Norse
8605 Commerce Place Dr Ne (98516-3813)
PHONE...................................360 943-5090
Bale Akley, *Manager*
EMP: 30
SALES (est): 4.9MM
SALES (corp-wide): 29.5MM **Privately Held**
WEB: www.rtlondon.com
SIC: **2521** Wood office furniture
PA: R. T. London Company
1642 Broadway Ave Nw # 1
Grand Rapids MI 49504
616 364-4800

(G-5582)
RUNWAY LIQUIDATION LLC
Also Called: Bcbg
44555 Woodward Ave (98503)
PHONE...................................304 748-2055
EMP: 2
SALES (corp-wide): 645.5MM **Privately Held**
SIC: **2335** Women's, juniors' & misses' dresses
HQ: Runway Liquidation, Llc
2761 Fruitland Ave
Vernon CA 90058
323 589-2224

(G-5583)
RY INVESTMENTS INC
5238 56th Ave Se (98503-9006)
PHONE...................................360 701-1261
Mike Whitlatch, *President*
EMP: 2 EST: 2012
SALES (est): 114K **Privately Held**
SIC: **7379** 7371 7372 ; custom computer programming services; custom computer programming services; application computer software

(G-5584)
SALISH SEA ORGANIC LIQUEURS
2641 Willamette Dr Ne (98516-1360)
PHONE...................................360 890-4927
F Sandy Desner, *Administration*
EMP: 4

SALES (est): 332.9K **Privately Held**
SIC: **2086** Bottled & canned soft drinks

(G-5585)
SEALY MATTRESS MFG CO INC
2626 Willamette Dr Ne (98516-3810)
PHONE...................................360 413-6902
EMP: 200
SQ FT: 140,000
SALES (corp-wide): 2.7B **Publicly Held**
SIC: **2515** Mfg Mattresses And Boxsprings
HQ: Sealy Mattress Manufacturing Company, Inc.
1 Office Parkway Rd
Trinity NC 27370
336 861-3500

(G-5586)
SEVIER LOGGING LLC
4570 Avery Ln Se (98503-5608)
PHONE...................................360 791-5527
EMP: 5
SALES (est): 418.4K **Privately Held**
SIC: **2411** Logging

(G-5587)
SIGN A RAMA
Also Called: Sign-A-Rama
2633 Willamette Dr Ne H (98516-1323)
PHONE...................................360 915-9207
Jeff Klingberg, *Owner*
EMP: 4
SALES (est): 318.5K **Privately Held**
SIC: **3993** Signs & advertising specialties

(G-5588)
SIGNATURE VASE
921 Ulery St Se (98503-1348)
PHONE...................................253 951-3357
Phuong Le, *Owner*
EMP: 2 EST: 2013
SALES (est): 104.7K **Privately Held**
SIC: **3229** 7389 Vases, glass;

(G-5589)
SOULIER SOUTHBAY LLC
Also Called: South Bay Press
4003 8th Ave Se (98503-1102)
PHONE...................................360 459-3015
Doug Soulier, *Owner*
Wade Boulton, *Manager*
EMP: 7
SQ FT: 2,400
SALES (est): 400K **Privately Held**
WEB: www.southbaypress.com
SIC: **2791** 2752 Typesetting, computer controlled; commercial printing, lithographic

(G-5590)
SOUND PUBLISHING INC
Also Called: Little Nickel Classifieds
7128 Holmes Island Rd Se (98503-3436)
PHONE...................................360 786-6973
Gina Alford, *Branch Mgr*
EMP: 3 **Privately Held**
WEB: www.soundpublishing.com
SIC: **2711** 2721 2741 Newspapers: publishing only, not printed on site; periodicals: publishing only; shopping news: publishing only, not printed on site
HQ: Sound Publishing, Inc.
11323 Commando Rd W Main
Everett WA 98204
360 394-5800

(G-5591)
SOUNDWORKS U S A INC
Also Called: Jerden Records
8300 28th Ct Ne Ste 400 (98516-7126)
P.O. Box 4608, Rollingbay (98061-0608)
PHONE...................................425 882-3344
Gerald B Dennon, *President*
Robert Wikstrom, *COO*
EMP: 4 EST: 1992
SALES: 250K **Privately Held**
WEB: www.soundworks.net
SIC: **3652** 5099 Pre-recorded records & tapes; tapes & cassettes, prerecorded

(G-5592)
SOUTH SOUND CONTRACTORS LLC
4010 8th Ave Se (98503-1129)
P.O. Box 8450 (98509-8450)
PHONE...................................360 688-5101

Jeffrey Blume, *President*
EMP: 12 EST: 2017
SALES (est): 249.6K **Privately Held**
SIC: **1389** Construction, repair & dismantling services

(G-5593)
SPECIALTY EMBROIDERY
1925 Sorrel Ln Se (98503-5316)
PHONE...................................509 924-1579
Carolyn Standen, *Principal*
EMP: 2
SALES (est): 73.2K **Privately Held**
SIC: **2759** Commercial printing

(G-5594)
THOMAS TREE SVC & LOGGING
4401 37th Ave Se Unit 53 (98503-3561)
PHONE...................................360 561-9589
Kevin Thomas, *Principal*
EMP: 3 EST: 2010
SALES (est): 243K **Privately Held**
SIC: **2411** Logging

(G-5595)
TNT SIGNS INC
Also Called: Fastsigns
4609 Lacey Blvd Se (98503-5720)
PHONE...................................360 438-3800
Grace Kendall, *President*
EMP: 4
SALES (est): 487.3K **Privately Held**
SIC: **3993** Signs & advertising specialties

(G-5596)
TOUCH SKY KITES
7635 11th Ave Se (98503-1822)
P.O. Box 3760 (98509-3760)
PHONE...................................360 459-2063
Gerry Pennell, *Owner*
EMP: 2
SALES (est): 124K **Privately Held**
SIC: **3944** Kites

(G-5597)
TRU-TRUSS INC
2750 Hogum Bay Rd Ne (98503-3123)
PHONE...................................360 491-8024
Jack L Harmon, *President*
Jeanie Harmon, *Corp Secy*
Chad Walker, *Opers Staff*
EMP: 20
SQ FT: 6,000
SALES (est): 2.7MM **Privately Held**
WEB: www.tru-truss.com
SIC: **2439** Trusses, wooden roof

(G-5598)
VENUS LABORATORIES INC
Earth Friendly Products
8735 Commerce Place Dr Ne (98516-1364)
PHONE...................................360 455-8933
Matthew Arkin, *Branch Mgr*
EMP: 30
SALES (corp-wide): 76.7MM **Privately Held**
SIC: **2841** Soap & other detergents
PA: Venus Laboratories, Inc.
111 S Rohlwing Rd
Addison IL 60101
630 595-1900

(G-5599)
WASHINGTON ASSN BLDG OFFICIALS
Also Called: Wabo
4405 7th Ave Se Ste 205 (98503-1055)
P.O. Box 7310, Olympia (98507-7310)
PHONE...................................360 628-8321
Julie Rogers, *Director*
EMP: 10
SALES (est): 803.6K **Privately Held**
WEB: www.wabo.org
SIC: **7389** 2721 Building inspection service; periodicals

(G-5600)
WASHINGTON ASSN OF SHERIFFS
3060 Willamette Dr Ne # 200 (98516-6267)
PHONE...................................360 438-6618
Larry Erickson, *Exec Dir*
Steve Strachan, *Exec Dir*
Steven Briggs, *Coordinator*

EMP: 27
SQ FT: 20,000
SALES: 14.4MM **Privately Held**
SIC: **2499** Policemen's clubs, wood

(G-5601)
WATFORD TANIKKA
Also Called: Deep Roots Foods
8535 Commerce Place Dr Ne (98516-1367)
PHONE...................................360 499-6327
Tanikka Watford, *Owner*
EMP: 2
SALES: 60K **Privately Held**
WEB: www.easternorganics.com
SIC: **5149** 2043 2096 0723 Natural & organic foods; cereal breakfast foods; potato chips & similar snacks; fruit (fresh) packing services; vegetable packing services; bread, cake & related products

(G-5602)
XEROX
8535 Commerce Place Dr Ne A (98516-1367)
PHONE...................................360 923-8640
EMP: 2
SALES (est): 104K **Privately Held**
SIC: **3577** Computer peripheral equipment

(G-5603)
ZORN MANUFACTURING CO
6714 Shincke Rd Ne (98506-9687)
PHONE...................................360 456-4747
EMP: 2
SALES (est): 74.6K **Privately Held**
SIC: **3999** Manufacturing industries

Lacrosse
Whitman County

(G-5604)
UNCAGED CREATIONS LLC
1954 Penawawa Rd (99143-9773)
PHONE...................................509 397-3873
Anita Lopes, *Principal*
EMP: 2
SALES (est): 124K **Privately Held**
SIC: **2771** Greeting cards

Lake Forest Park
King County

(G-5605)
BALANCE CONSTRUCTION INC
Also Called: Ramparts
17016 32nd Ave Ne (98155-5322)
PHONE...................................206 364-5555
Joseph K Louis, *President*
EMP: 2
SQ FT: 300
SALES (est): 197.9K **Privately Held**
WEB: www.ramparts.com
SIC: **3999** Wheelchair lifts

(G-5606)
BENJAMIN D SCHREINER
Also Called: Estate Iron Work
18245 47th Pl Ne (98155-4309)
PHONE...................................206 417-4663
Benjamin D Schreiner, *Owner*
Pamela L Schreiner, *Co-Owner*
EMP: 7
SALES: 532.1K **Privately Held**
SIC: **3446** 7389 Architectural metalwork;

(G-5607)
BETH DONALLEY
Also Called: Cbf
18541 35th Ave Ne (98155-2703)
PHONE...................................206 366-8445
Beth Donalley, *Owner*
EMP: 7
SALES (est): 170.8K **Privately Held**
SIC: **5131** 2395 Labels; embroidery & art needlework

(G-5608)
BOB BRACHT LLC
16522 37th Ave Ne (98155-5439)
PHONE...................................206 678-5168

Lake Forest Park - King County (G-5609)

Robert Bracht,
EMP: 2
SALES (est): 124K **Privately Held**
SIC: 2759 7371 Commercial printing; computer software development

(G-5609)
CLOWERS CORPORATION
Also Called: Sandland Construction
16160 41st Ave Ne (98155-6726)
PHONE.................................206 420-1202
Jason Clowers, *President*
EMP: 5
SQ FT: 9,000
SALES: 500K **Privately Held**
SIC: 1541 1241 0783 Renovation, remodeling & repairs: industrial buildings; warehouse construction; coal mining services; tree trimming services for public utility lines

(G-5610)
CUSTOM MASONRY & STOVE INC
17824 28th Ave Ne (98155-4006)
PHONE.................................206 524-4714
Derek Lober, *President*
Robi Lober, *Corp Secy*
EMP: 5
SALES (est): 450K **Privately Held**
WEB: www.custommasonryandstoves.com
SIC: 1741 3433 Masonry & other stonework; heating equipment, except electric

(G-5611)
DECATUR INDUSTRIES INC
19536 44th Ave Ne (98155-2807)
PHONE.................................206 368-3178
Michel Goffin, *Principal*
EMP: 2 **EST:** 2012
SALES (est): 118.6K **Privately Held**
SIC: 3999 Manufacturing industries

(G-5612)
DIGNON CO INC (PA)
Also Called: Hoonah Cold Storage
17851 29th Ave Ne (98155-4011)
PHONE.................................206 448-6677
William A Dignon, *President*
▲ **EMP:** 3
SQ FT: 655
SALES (est): 3.2MM **Privately Held**
SIC: 2092 4222 Fresh or frozen packaged fish; warehousing, cold storage or refrigerated

(G-5613)
GEM EAST CORPORATION
Also Called: Northwest Jewelers
5418 Ne 200th Pl (98155-1814)
PHONE.................................206 441-1700
Patrick Druxman, *Ch of Bd*
Hal S Staehle, *President*
Tim Druxman, *Vice Pres*
Thomas C Barrigan, *Treasurer*
EMP: 34 **EST:** 1928
SALES (est): 3.6MM **Privately Held**
WEB: www.gemeast.com
SIC: 3911 Jewelry, precious metal

(G-5614)
HILDEBRAND CONSULTING
20215 41st Pl Ne (98155-1646)
PHONE.................................206 465-1729
David Hilderbrand, *Owner*
Bryan Hildebrand, *Owner*
Theresa Hildebrand, *Owner*
EMP: 3
SALES: 100K **Privately Held**
SIC: 7373 7372 Computer integrated systems design; prepackaged software

(G-5615)
INSTANT GRATIFICATION LLP
20266 37th Ave Ne (98155-1657)
PHONE.................................206 361-2966
David Lyman, *Principal*
EMP: 4
SALES (est): 319.7K **Privately Held**
SIC: 2752 Commercial printing, lithographic

(G-5616)
JET CITY ELECTRONICS INC
17709 Beach Dr Ne (98155-4516)
PHONE.................................206 529-0351
John Fallisgaard, *President*
EMP: 5
SQ FT: 1,000
SALES (est): 487.7K
SALES (corp-wide): 7.4MM **Privately Held**
WEB: www.jetcityelectronics.com
SIC: 3674 Semiconductors & related devices
PA: Fox Enterprises, Inc.
5570 Enterprise Pkwy
Fort Myers FL 33905
239 693-0099

(G-5617)
JOSEPH ARTESE DESIGN
16003 34th Ave Ne (98155-6507)
PHONE.................................206 365-4326
EMP: 3 **EST:** 1970
SALES: 200K **Privately Held**
SIC: 3732 Boatbuilding/Repairing

(G-5618)
KELSEYS COLLECTION INC
3010 Ne 193rd St (98155-2544)
PHONE.................................206 355-4333
Charles Bright, *President*
EMP: 2
SALES: 100K **Privately Held**
SIC: 2426 5712 Carvings, furniture: wood; customized furniture & cabinets

(G-5619)
L & B SERVICE LLC
Also Called: Wickman Electric
4209 Ne 169th Ct (98155-5647)
P.O. Box 30831, Seattle (98113-0831)
PHONE.................................206 650-4607
Lindsey Wickman,
EMP: 2
SALES (est): 179.9K **Privately Held**
SIC: 3931 Reeds, organ

(G-5620)
MAHLER & ASSOC INC
3322 Ne 200th Ct (98155-1541)
PHONE.................................206 365-3800
Keith Mahler, *President*
EMP: 2
SALES (est): 230K **Privately Held**
SIC: 3663 Marine radio communications equipment

(G-5621)
MATRIX VISIONS LLC
20302 44th Ave Ne (98155-1624)
PHONE.................................206 368-3824
Salim Rabaa,
EMP: 2
SALES (est): 95.8K **Privately Held**
SIC: 3674 Integrated circuits, semiconductor networks, etc.

(G-5622)
NORTH PARK HEATING COMPANY INC
19204 Ballinger Way Ne (98155-2499)
PHONE.................................206 365-1414
David Hughes, *President*
Teresa Hughes, *Admin Sec*
EMP: 16
SQ FT: 10,000
SALES (est): 1.8MM **Privately Held**
SIC: 1711 1761 3444 Warm air heating & air conditioning contractor; sheet metalwork; forming machine work, sheet metal

(G-5623)
OUT ON A LIMB TREE CO
17576 Ballinger Way Ne (98155-5516)
PHONE.................................206 938-3779
Kathy E Holzer, *Administration*
EMP: 3
SALES (est): 430.8K **Privately Held**
SIC: 3842 Limbs, artificial

(G-5624)
SANDY JO FRANKS
18212 Ballinger Way Ne (98155-4237)
PHONE.................................206 367-2669
Sandy Franks, *Principal*
EMP: 2
SALES (est): 159.2K **Privately Held**
SIC: 3721 Aircraft

(G-5625)
TITAN INDUSTRIES USA LLC
18473 Ballinger Way Ne (98155-4238)
PHONE.................................206 466-1300
Andrew Shumate, *Principal*
EMP: 2
SALES (est): 112.8K **Privately Held**
SIC: 3999 Manufacturing industries

(G-5626)
V S P JEWELRY DESIGN GALLERY
17171 Bothell Way Ne A137 (98155-4228)
PHONE.................................206 367-7310
Wai Keung Lee, *Owner*
Yee Lee, *Co-Owner*
EMP: 2
SALES: 110K **Privately Held**
SIC: 3911 5944 Jewelry, precious metal; jewelry, precious stones & precious metals

(G-5627)
WAX ORCHARDS INC
3041 Ne 166th St (98155-5337)
PHONE.................................800 634-6132
Anna E Sestrap, *President*
Anna Swain, *Treasurer*
EMP: 3
SQ FT: 13,000
SALES: 400K **Privately Held**
WEB: www.waxorchards.com
SIC: 1541 2066 Food products manufacturing or packing plant construction; chocolate coatings & syrup

(G-5628)
WOLFETONE PICKUPS CO
18944 40th Pl Ne (98155-2810)
PHONE.................................206 417-3548
Robert Sturm, *Principal*
EMP: 2
SALES (est): 72.9K **Privately Held**
SIC: 3931 Musical instruments

Lake Stevens
Snohomish County

(G-5629)
ABC WATER SPECIALTY INC
2918 Cavalero Rd (98258-4518)
PHONE.................................425 355-9826
Christine Purdy, *President*
William Purdy, *Vice Pres*
EMP: 2
SALES (est): 216.3K **Privately Held**
SIC: 3531 Backhoes

(G-5630)
ACF IDEA WORKS INC
3830 97th Dr Se (98258-5708)
PHONE.................................425 335-0958
Pary Hanke, *Principal*
EMP: 2 **EST:** 2011
SALES (est): 127K **Privately Held**
SIC: 3545 Scales, measuring (machinists' precision tools)

(G-5631)
ANDERSON FINE WOODS
2811 121st Ave Se (98258-5188)
PHONE.................................425 422-2753
Randy Anderson, *President*
Lea Hughes Anderson, *Vice Pres*
EMP: 7
SALES: 150K **Privately Held**
SIC: 2431 1751 Interior & ornamental woodwork & trim; carpentry work

(G-5632)
APEX FINISHING LLC
9015 Vernon Rd Ste 3 (98258-2432)
PHONE.................................425 334-6281
Lorenzo Ariz, *Principal*
EMP: 5 **EST:** 2009
SALES (est): 427.5K **Privately Held**
SIC: 3471 Cleaning, polishing & finishing

(G-5633)
BARMON DOOR & PLYWOOD INC
Also Called: Barmon Door & Millwork
2508 Hartford Dr (98258)
PHONE.................................425 334-1222
EMP: 20
SQ FT: 32,000
SALES (est): 2MM **Privately Held**
SIC: 2431 3442 Mfg Millwork Mfg Metal Doors/Sash/Trim

(G-5634)
BIG ROCK INDUSTRIES
10610 115th Ave Ne (98258-8931)
PHONE.................................360 659-3308
Ed Wood, *Principal*
EMP: 3
SALES (est): 130.5K **Privately Held**
SIC: 3999 Manufacturing industries

(G-5635)
BRAVEN METALS LLC
2315 N Machias Rd (98258-9344)
PHONE.................................206 963-2234
EMP: 3
SALES (est): 481.5K **Privately Held**
SIC: 2611 Mechanical pulp, including groundwood & thermomechanical

(G-5636)
C DAVIS SOFTWARE CON
9004 1st Pl Se (98258-3372)
PHONE.................................847 436-6225
Craig Davis, *Owner*
EMP: 2 **EST:** 2015
SALES (est): 75.2K **Privately Held**
SIC: 7372 Prepackaged software

(G-5637)
CCS BAKING CO
8416 25th St Ne (98258-6496)
PHONE.................................206 200-5195
EMP: 4
SALES (est): 154.4K **Privately Held**
SIC: 2051 Bread, cake & related products

(G-5638)
CLAYPORT POTTERY
11710 60th St Ne (98258-8715)
PHONE.................................425 335-0678
Ralph Whitman, *Owner*
EMP: 2
SALES (est): 95.5K **Privately Held**
SIC: 3269 5023 Pottery household articles, except kitchen articles; pottery

(G-5639)
CLEANPWR
930 Sunnyside Blvd (98258-3124)
PHONE.................................425 334-6100
Joseph B Heineck, *Principal*
EMP: 3
SALES (est): 243.6K **Privately Held**
SIC: 3433 Solar heaters & collectors

(G-5640)
COORDINATING SERVICES INC
Also Called: Reel News, The
621 State Route 9 Ne (98258-8525)
PHONE.................................425 334-8966
Jim Goerg, *President*
EMP: 2
SALES (est): 117.6K **Privately Held**
SIC: 2711 Newspapers: publishing only, not printed on site

(G-5641)
CORTEX MANUFACTURING INC
421 S Davies Rd (98258-8536)
PHONE.................................425 334-2277
Andrew Jones, *CEO*
Brenda Vroman, *Admin Sec*
EMP: 2
SALES (est): 245.7K **Privately Held**
SIC: 3841 Surgical & medical instruments

(G-5642)
D & D LOGGING
4528 116th Ave Ne (98258-9087)
PHONE.................................425 308-2063
Bruce Carmichael, *Principal*
EMP: 3
SALES (est): 154.7K **Privately Held**
SIC: 2411 Logging camps & contractors

GEOGRAPHIC SECTION

(G-5643)
DE JONG SAWDUST & SHAVINGS
3413 Old Hartford Rd (98258-9280)
PHONE..................425 252-1566
Cory De Jong, *Owner*
EMP: 15 **EST:** 1949
SQ FT: 1,568
SALES (est): 1.3MM **Privately Held**
SIC: 2499 5199 2875 5261 Wood products; nondurable goods; fertilizers, mixing only; top soil; garden supplies; sawdust & shavings

(G-5644)
DOZING & DITCHING
4528 116th Ave Ne (98258-9087)
PHONE..................425 308-2063
Bruce Carmichael, *Principal*
EMP: 2
SALES (est): 81.7K **Privately Held**
SIC: 2411 Logging

(G-5645)
GROUNDHOG MINES LLC
1825 S Lake Stevens Rd (98258-1960)
PHONE..................425 609-6901
Gregory Ellis, *
EMP: 4
SALES (est): 144.2K **Privately Held**
SIC: 1241 Coal mining services

(G-5646)
HYDROGEN 2O2 LLC
16410 84th St Ne (98258-9060)
PHONE..................704 906-3770
Steve Adkins, *Principal*
EMP: 2
SALES (est): 135.2K **Privately Held**
SIC: 2813 Hydrogen

(G-5647)
IMPACT PROPERTY MGNT
9506 4th St Ne Ste 101 (98258-7988)
P.O. Box 1158 (98258-1158)
PHONE..................425 334-6341
Marcus A Tageant, *President*
EMP: 2
SALES (est): 212K **Privately Held**
SIC: 6531 1389 Real estate managers; oil field services

(G-5648)
INK IT YOUR WAY
10827 27th St Se (98258-5179)
PHONE..................425 789-1669
Pamela Lemieux, *Owner*
EMP: 2 **EST:** 2010
SALES (est): 134.8K **Privately Held**
SIC: 2759 Screen printing

(G-5649)
INTERGRATED AEROSPACE LLC
3316 Old Hartford Rd (98258-8184)
PHONE..................360 691-2298
EMP: 2
SALES (est): 86K **Privately Held**
SIC: 3728 Aircraft body assemblies & parts

(G-5650)
ISAKSEN SCALE MODELS
Also Called: Scale Model Boats
7419 25th St Ne (98258-3143)
PHONE..................425 334-2807
Gary Isaksen, *Owner*
EMP: 2
SALES (est): 105.8K **Privately Held**
SIC: 3999 Boat models, except toy

(G-5651)
JACOBS LADDER PAINTING INC
11304 Vernon Rd (98258-9405)
PHONE..................425 754-3202
Jacob Evans, *President*
Angela Evans, *Admin Sec*
EMP: 2
SALES (est): 143.6K **Privately Held**
SIC: 3479 Painting, coating & hot dipping

(G-5652)
JOBSITE STUD WELDING INC
3302 Old Hartford Rd (98258-8699)
PHONE..................425 656-9783
Jay E Koski, *President*
Andrew Quall, *Vice Pres*
Lisa Quall, *Treasurer*
Jamie Koski, *Admin Sec*
EMP: 7
SALES (est): 959.8K **Privately Held**
SIC: 7692 Welding repair

(G-5653)
KEVIN W LANTZ
Also Called: Lantz Cellars
3001 S Lake Stevens Rd (98258-5618)
PHONE..................425 770-2599
Kevin W Lantz, *Principal*
EMP: 2
SALES (est): 121.3K **Privately Held**
SIC: 2084 Wines

(G-5654)
LEXINGTON PUBLISHING COMPANY
1614 113th Dr Se (98258-2012)
PHONE..................800 774-1170
Jessica Loberg-Marty, *Owner*
EMP: 2 **EST:** 2011
SALES (est): 92.1K **Privately Held**
SIC: 2741 Miscellaneous publishing

(G-5655)
LEYDA COMPUTERS
11103 22nd Pl Ne (98258-8401)
PHONE..................425 335-1273
Matthew Leyda, *President*
EMP: 3
SALES (est): 260K **Privately Held**
WEB: www.leyda.com
SIC: 3575 7379 Computer terminals; computer related consulting services

(G-5656)
LIFESIGNS PLUS
10024 38th Pl Se (98258-5739)
PHONE..................425 330-3710
EMP: 2 **EST:** 2011
SALES (est): 133.9K **Privately Held**
SIC: 3993 Signs & advertising specialties

(G-5657)
LIFT SOLUTIONS INC
1806 S Lake Stevens Rd (98258-7959)
PHONE..................360 862-8328
John Castano, *President*
Jed Shapiro, *Vice Pres*
Parker Castano, *Project Mgr*
EMP: 7
SQ FT: 1,400
SALES (est): 1.5MM **Privately Held**
SIC: 3728 8742 Elevators, aircraft; marketing consulting services

(G-5658)
LITTLE MEXICO ORNAMENTAL IRON
3509 139th Ave Ne (98258-9772)
PHONE..................425 334-1082
Lonnie Serrano, *President*
EMP: 3
SQ FT: 3,800
SALES (est): 300K **Privately Held**
SIC: 1799 3446 Ornamental metal work; stairs, staircases, stair treads: prefabricated metal

(G-5659)
LONG SEPTIC SERVICES
2910 Old Hartford Rd (98258-8990)
P.O. Box 259 (98258-0259)
PHONE..................253 852-0550
Dave Eldredge, *Partner*
EMP: 50
SQ FT: 1,000
SALES (est): 2.9MM **Privately Held**
SIC: 3272 1711 Septic tanks, concrete; septic system construction

(G-5660)
LOWRIDGE ON SITE TECH LLC
1925 N Machias Rd (98258-9259)
P.O. Box 1179 (98258-1179)
PHONE..................877 476-8823
Patsy Camanez, *Office Mgr*
Richard D Eldredge, *
David M Lowe, *
EMP: 5
SALES: 2MM **Privately Held**
SIC: 3089 Septic tanks, plastic

(G-5661)
MILES SAND & GRAVEL COMPANY
Also Called: Concrete Nor'west
15415 84th St Ne (98258-8822)
PHONE..................360 435-5511
Jerry Simons, *Manager*
EMP: 19
SALES (est): 1.6MM
SALES (corp-wide): 88MM **Privately Held**
SIC: 3273 Ready-mixed concrete
PA: Miles Sand & Gravel Company
400 Valley Ave Ne
Puyallup WA 98372
253 833-3705

(G-5662)
MILL CREEK SPINE INJURY INC PS
1112 76th Ave Ne (98258-3201)
PHONE..................425 344-6835
Ryan L Doerge, *Owner*
EMP: 2
SALES (est): 114.7K **Privately Held**
SIC: 3821 Clinical laboratory instruments, except medical & dental

(G-5663)
MOMMA DOT PUBLISHING LLC
11632 18th St Se (98258-2044)
PHONE..................425 322-3486
Dotty Nuetzmann, *Principal*
EMP: 2
SALES (est): 59.2K **Privately Held**
SIC: 2741 Miscellaneous publishing

(G-5664)
NIKA MINES LLC
1825 S Lake Stevens Rd (98258-1960)
PHONE..................425 609-6901
Gregory Ellis, *
EMP: 3
SALES (est): 120.4K **Privately Held**
SIC: 1241 Coal mining services

(G-5665)
OSTER LOGGING INC
1205 N Machias Rd (98258-9720)
PHONE..................425 397-0585
D Oster, *Principal*
EMP: 3
SALES (est): 260K **Privately Held**
SIC: 2411 Logging camps & contractors

(G-5666)
PACIFIC ART PRESS INC
10730 Vernon Rd (98258-8500)
PHONE..................425 778-8095
Margo Leiter, *President*
Al Leiter, *Vice Pres*
Joyce Putnam, *Office Admin*
EMP: 8
SQ FT: 7,380
SALES (est): 1.3MM **Privately Held**
WEB: www.pacificartpress.com
SIC: 2752 Commercial printing, offset

(G-5667)
PACIFIC LOGGING LLC
8425 123rd Ave Ne (98258-8817)
PHONE..................425 508-9150
EMP: 4
SALES (est): 305K **Privately Held**
SIC: 2411 Logging camps & contractors

(G-5668)
PADDED SPACES LLC
2104 82nd Dr Ne (98258-6465)
PHONE..................872 222-7767
Benjamin Palmer, *
Cathy Palmer, *
▲ **EMP:** 7
SALES (est): 723.9K **Privately Held**
SIC: 3161 Camera carrying bags

(G-5669)
PIN CITY WRESTLING CLUB
13101 20th St Ne (98258-9785)
PHONE..................425 327-8518
Burke Barnes, *Principal*
EMP: 4
SALES (est): 274.5K **Privately Held**
SIC: 3452 Pins

(G-5670)
RADIORACKS AVIATION SYSTEMS
Also Called: Radiorax
11616 125th Ave Ne (98258-8307)
PHONE..................360 651-1200
Mark Landes, *Principal*
EMP: 3
SALES (est): 150K **Privately Held**
WEB: www.radiorax.com
SIC: 3728 Aircraft parts & equipment

(G-5671)
REMEMBER FILTERCOM
8418 13th Pl Se (98258-3694)
PHONE..................425 359-7905
Beau French, *Owner*
EMP: 2
SALES (est): 190K **Privately Held**
SIC: 3569 Filters

(G-5672)
TOBACCO CITY
731 State Route 9 Ne # 103 (98258-1914)
PHONE..................425 377-1658
Uyoo Chung, *President*
EMP: 2
SALES (est): 180.7K **Privately Held**
SIC: 2111 Cigarettes

(G-5673)
VETERAN AWARDS INC
3416 97th Dr Se (98258-5728)
P.O. Box 413, Snohomish (98291-0413)
PHONE..................360 925-6019
Geoffrey Surprenant, *President*
EMP: 4 **EST:** 2013
SALES: 150K **Privately Held**
SIC: 3231 3229 Ornamental glass: cut, engraved or otherwise decorated; Christmas tree ornaments: made from purchased glass; decorated glassware: chipped, engraved, etched, etc.; art glass: made from purchased glass; optical glass

(G-5674)
WILSONS CUSTOM CABINETS INC
13008 27th Pl Ne (98258-6484)
P.O. Box 461 (98258-0461)
PHONE..................425 334-3522
Jim Wilson, *President*
Stephanie Wilson, *Corp Secy*
EMP: 5
SQ FT: 6,500
SALES: 1MM **Privately Held**
SIC: 2434 Wood kitchen cabinets

(G-5675)
WOODWORK UNLIMITED INC
2608 Hartford Dr (98258-9220)
PHONE..................425 334-5702
John V Holdaway, *President*
Michal Holdaway, *Admin Sec*
EMP: 3
SALES: 250K **Privately Held**
SIC: 2434 Wood kitchen cabinets

Lake Tapps
Pierce County

(G-5676)
ALPINE INDUSTRIES LLC
18215 9th St E Ste 110 (98391-6409)
PHONE..................253 261-1500
EMP: 2
SALES (est): 66.1K **Privately Held**
SIC: 3999 Manufacturing industries

(G-5677)
CHERRYS JUBILEE
3618 Deer Island Dr E (98391-9496)
PHONE..................253 862-6751
Jewel Lind, *Owner*
EMP: 2
SALES (est): 92.7K **Privately Held**
SIC: 2099 Food preparations

(G-5678)
EXPRESSIVE PROMOTIONS
17505 51st Street Ct E (98391-6737)
PHONE..................253 863-4211

Lake Tapps - Pierce County (G-5679)

Greg Hiron, *Owner*
Bambi Hiron, *Co-Owner*
EMP: 2
SALES: 40K **Privately Held**
SIC: 2759 Promotional printing

(G-5679)
JJ ENTERPRISES
21320 Snag Island Dr E (98391-8706)
PHONE..................................253 862-8854
John Whitehead, *Partner*
EMP: 2
SALES (est): 115.1K **Privately Held**
SIC: 3599 Machine shop, jobbing & repair

(G-5680)
KELLEY BLOCKS LLC
17810 17th St E (98391-9447)
P.O. Box 1908, Milton (98354-1908)
PHONE..................................253 922-9848
Mike Kelley,
EMP: 4
SALES (est): 418.3K **Privately Held**
SIC: 3271 Blocks, concrete or cinder: standard

(G-5681)
LARRY WAITS NEMESIS
Also Called: Nemesis Metal Fabrication Repr
405 202nd Ave E (98391-6282)
PHONE..................................253 863-4444
Larry Waits Nemesis, *Owner*
EMP: 3
SALES (est): 255K **Privately Held**
SIC: 3441 Fabricated structural metal

(G-5682)
M2 ANESTHESIA PLLC ❂
20704 Snag Island Dr E (98391-8712)
PHONE..................................206 605-5933
Marlon Michel MD, *President*
EMP: 4 **EST:** 2019
SALES (est): 139.2K **Privately Held**
SIC: 3841 Anesthesia apparatus

(G-5683)
PAPEC
18310 17th St E (98391-9452)
PHONE..................................253 862-6148
Fax: 253 862-6463
EMP: 3
SALES (est): 160K **Privately Held**
SIC: 3812 Mfg Search/Navigation Equipment

(G-5684)
PETROLEUM SVC & SOLUTIONS LLC
416 196th Ave E (98391-9381)
P.O. Box 115, Auburn (98071-0115)
PHONE..................................253 987-5143
Kory Holm, *Mng Member*
EMP: 2
SALES: 100K **Privately Held**
SIC: 3586 Measuring & dispensing pumps

(G-5685)
PHUNNYBAGGSCOM
Also Called: Afterglowpowercompany.com
2702 181st Ave E (98391-9423)
PHONE..................................253 709-9481
Kenneth Rounds, *Owner*
EMP: 3
SALES (est): 161.3K **Privately Held**
SIC: 3999 Manufacturing industries

(G-5686)
STEVE HAZELWOOD & SON TRUCKING
4703 Ridgewest Dr E (98391-9181)
PHONE..................................253 863-5721
Steven Hazelwood, *President*
EMP: 2
SALES (est): 204.3K **Privately Held**
SIC: 2411 Logging

(G-5687)
WEST COAST FIRE & RESCUE INC
18322 9th St E (98391-6413)
PHONE..................................253 826-9852
Tracy Hoffman, *President*
EMP: 5
SALES: 500K **Privately Held**
SIC: 3999 Manufacturing industries

Lakebay
Pierce County

(G-5688)
BLEND WINE SHOP
8914 Key Peninsula Hwy Nw (98349-9326)
PHONE..................................253 884-9688
Jeff Minch, *Principal*
EMP: 4 **EST:** 2016
SALES (est): 45.5K **Privately Held**
SIC: 8748 5181 2085 Business consulting; beer & ale; distilled & blended liquors

(G-5689)
GLORIOUS COMFORT
14820 38th Street Kp S (98349-9354)
PHONE..................................253 884-1465
EMP: 2
SALES (est): 85K **Privately Held**
SIC: 2392 Mfg Household Furnishings

(G-5690)
PARADISE TECHNOLGY INC
5715 151st Avenue Ct Nw (98349-9500)
PHONE..................................253 370-3682
James Brauneis, *President*
Laurie Brauneis, *Admin Sec*
EMP: 2
SALES: 18.8K **Privately Held**
SIC: 3679 Electronic circuits

(G-5691)
TRADER BAY LTD
17020 Rouse Rd Sw (98351-9730)
P.O. Box 429 (98349-0429)
PHONE..................................253 884-5249
Lindsey Babich, *Owner*
EMP: 100
SQ FT: 2,000
SALES: 1MM **Privately Held**
SIC: 3556 2092 Meat, poultry & seafood processing machinery; fresh or frozen packaged fish

Lakewood
Pierce County

(G-5692)
10-20 SERVICES INC
10111 South Tacoma Way D5 (98499-4666)
PHONE..................................253 503-6000
Lannes Clay Williamson II, *President*
Rodney Reum, *Corp Secy*
EMP: 2
SALES (est): 179.9K **Privately Held**
SIC: 2253 2499 5136 Jackets, knit; shoe & boot products, wood; uniforms, men's & boys'

(G-5693)
253 CUSTOM TEES
9614 40th Ave Sw (98499-4302)
PHONE..................................253 244-7117
EMP: 2
SALES (est): 82.7K **Privately Held**
SIC: 2759 Screen printing

(G-5694)
3V PRECISION MACHINING INC
10025 Lakewood Dr Sw H4 (98499-3878)
PHONE..................................253 584-3888
Peter Boucher, *President*
EMP: 9
SQ FT: 4,000
SALES (est): 1.1MM **Privately Held**
SIC: 3599 Machine shop, jobbing & repair

(G-5695)
ACE STAMP & ENGRAVING
10510 Bridgeport Way Sw # 6 (98499-4830)
PHONE..................................253 582-3322
Thomas Joseph, *Owner*
EMP: 2
SALES (est): 72.6K **Privately Held**
SIC: 3953 Marking devices

(G-5696)
ALASKA WATHERVANE SEAFOODS LLC
3871 Steilacoom Blvd Sw C (98499-4559)
PHONE..................................253 582-2580
James Stone, *Mng Member*
Glenn Mikkelsen,
EMP: 9 **EST:** 2016
SQ FT: 2,500
SALES (est): 651.1K **Privately Held**
SIC: 2092 Seafoods, fresh: prepared

(G-5697)
ALL THINGS NEW LLC
8404 83rd Ave Sw Ste H (98498-6079)
PHONE..................................253 255-4954
Anthony Oury, *Principal*
EMP: 2
SALES (est): 164.1K **Privately Held**
SIC: 2426 Flooring, hardwood

(G-5698)
ANGELS PALLETS
2520 112th St S (98499-8891)
PHONE..................................253 426-1770
EMP: 3
SALES (est): 157.3K **Privately Held**
SIC: 2448 Pallets, wood & wood with metal

(G-5699)
ARCOMM INC
Also Called: NW Design Center
4421 98th Street Ct Sw (98499-5967)
P.O. Box 39700 (98496-3700)
PHONE..................................253 581-9800
Alan Reames, *President*
EMP: 8
SQ FT: 13,000
SALES: 5MM **Privately Held**
SIC: 5023 5713 1799 5211 Kitchen tools & utensils; floor coverings; floor covering stores; counter top installation; bathroom fixtures, equipment & supplies; wood kitchen cabinets

(G-5700)
ATKINS MACHINES LLC
Also Called: Pulley Boys
10526 Steele St S Ste B (98499-8743)
PHONE..................................253 588-2350
David Atkins,
EMP: 4
SALES (est): 425.7K **Privately Held**
SIC: 3569 5088 General industrial machinery; pulleys

(G-5701)
AZ ARTS INC
9802 40th Ave Sw (98499-4306)
PHONE..................................253 584-8155
Maruice Thevenroux, *President*
Shannon Olmsted, *Vice Pres*
EMP: 10
SALES (est): 494.1K **Privately Held**
WEB: www.azarts.com
SIC: 2395 Embroidery & art needlework

(G-5702)
BEDKERS PRTBLE WLDG FBRICATION
3802 87th St Sw (98499-4514)
PHONE..................................253 581-7077
Phillip Bedker, *President*
Aaron Bedker, *Vice Pres*
Liz Bedker, *Admin Sec*
EMP: 4
SALES (est): 546.7K **Privately Held**
SIC: 3441 Fabricated structural metal

(G-5703)
BITE ME INC
3827 100th St Sw Ste E (98499-4420)
PHONE..................................253 244-7194
Casey Cantwell, *Principal*
EMP: 20
SALES (est): 2.5MM **Privately Held**
SIC: 2052 Bakery products, dry

(G-5704)
BMC WEST LLC
Also Called: B M C Building Materials Ctr
9721 40th Ave Sw (98499-4303)
PHONE..................................360 943-8050
Tim Gallagher, *Manager*
EMP: 50 **Publicly Held**
SIC: 5211 5031 2439 Door & window products; lumber, plywood & millwork; structural wood members
HQ: Bmc West, Llc
980 Hammond Dr Ste 500
Atlanta GA 30328
208 331-4300

(G-5705)
BORAL ROOFING LLC
10920 Steele St S (98499-8877)
PHONE..................................253 581-3666
Dave Mills, *Manager*
EMP: 30
SQ FT: 31,264 **Privately Held**
WEB: www.monierlifetile.com
SIC: 3272 Roofing tile & slabs, concrete
HQ: Boral Roofing Llc
7575 Irvine Center Dr # 100
Irvine CA 92618
949 756-1605

(G-5706)
CBS CABINET CENTER
4425 100th St Sw Ste B (98499-5980)
PHONE..................................253 582-8088
Mike Ritchie, *Principal*
EMP: 2
SALES (est): 142.3K **Privately Held**
SIC: 2434 Wood kitchen cabinets

(G-5707)
CONOCOPHILLIPS COMPANY
Also Called: Brown Bear Car Wash
10913 Bridgeport Way Sw (98499-3511)
PHONE..................................253 584-0583
Paula Wind, *Manager*
EMP: 10
SALES (corp-wide): 38.7B **Publicly Held**
WEB: www.phillips66.com
SIC: 5541 2911 5411 Filling stations, gasoline; petroleum refining; convenience stores, chain
HQ: Conocophillips Company
925 N Eldridge Pkwy
Houston TX 77079
281 293-1000

(G-5708)
CONSOLIDATED FOOD MANAGEMENT
Also Called: CFM
4500 Steilacoom Blvd Sw (98499-4004)
PHONE..................................253 589-5654
Ted Hamby, *General Mgr*
Mike Anderson, *Director*
EMP: 3
SALES (est): 197.5K **Privately Held**
WEB: www.cf-m.com
SIC: 2099 Food preparations

(G-5709)
CUSTOM BILT HOLDINGS LLC
2418 104th Street Ct S G (98499-8718)
P.O. Box 1777, Kent (98035-1777)
PHONE..................................253 872-7330
Dennis Kurtz, *Manager*
EMP: 26
SALES (corp-wide): 40MM **Privately Held**
SIC: 5084 7629 3444 1761 Industrial machinery & equipment; electrical repair shops; sheet metalwork; gutter & downspout contractor; asphalt felts & coatings
PA: Custom Bilt Holdings, Llc
3001 Skyway Cir N Ste 160
Irving TX 75038
214 699-4876

(G-5710)
CUSTOM CHOICE DOOR LLC
8607 Durango St Sw Ste B (98499-4433)
P.O. Box 98716 (98496-8716)
PHONE..................................253 472-0963
Ted Matthews, *Principal*
EMP: 1
SALES (est): 2.8MM
SALES (corp-wide): 12.1MM **Privately Held**
SIC: 2431 Door frames, wood
PA: Homewood Holdings, Llc
6 Lytle Place Dr
Abilene TX 79602
325 676-3240

GEOGRAPHIC SECTION

Lakewood - Pierce County (G-5742)

(G-5711)
DEJAY PRODUCTS LLC
8016 Durango St Sw Ste B6 (98499-4591)
PHONE..................206 784-8200
Micheal Goldstein, *Mng Member*
Jackie Goldstein,
EMP: 2
SQ FT: 3,636
SALES: 300K **Privately Held**
WEB: www.dejaygold.com
SIC: 3999 Framed artwork; engraving service; trophies & plaques

(G-5712)
DODGE SYSTEMS LLC
2710 104th Street Ct S A (98499-6770)
PHONE..................253 405-3967
Monty Dodge, *President*
Roger Christofferson, *Vice Pres*
Lisa Dodge, *Treasurer*
James Adams, *Director*
Travis Dodge, *Director*
EMP: 6
SALES (est): 369.5K **Privately Held**
SIC: 3429 Builders' hardware

(G-5713)
DOREMUS & FAHEY PUBLISHING
12414 Glenwood Ave Sw (98499-1104)
PHONE..................253 507-8848
David Doremus, *Principal*
EMP: 4
SALES (est): 204.4K **Privately Held**
SIC: 2741 Miscellaneous publishing

(G-5714)
DOUG SKRIVAN
10914 93rd Ave Sw (98498-3723)
PHONE..................253 584-7323
Doug Skrivan, *Owner*
EMP: 2
SALES (est): 90.7K **Privately Held**
SIC: 2911 Petroleum refining

(G-5715)
DUTENA BLANKETS
9122 South Tacoma Way # 102 (98499-4406)
PHONE..................253 581-0312
Dutena Lee, *Owner*
▲ **EMP:** 2
SALES (est): 113.2K **Privately Held**
SIC: 2392 Household furnishings

(G-5716)
E POWER SYSTEMS & BATTERY INC
Also Called: Wli Recycling
10321 Lakeview Ave Sw (98499-4224)
PHONE..................253 267-1965
SE Choi, *Ch of Bd*
Louis Lamonte, *President*
EMP: 4
SQ FT: 4,200
SALES (est): 660.8K **Privately Held**
SIC: 5015 5093 3691 Batteries, used: automotive; ferrous metal scrap & waste; lead acid batteries (storage batteries)

(G-5717)
E2 SYSTEMS LLC
3006 96th St S (98499-9395)
PHONE..................253 284-3707
Mike Doyle, *Mng Member*
EMP: 5
SALES (est): 363.2K **Privately Held**
SIC: 3699 Security devices

(G-5718)
EAST PENN MANUFACTURING CO
10803 South Tacoma Way (98499-4605)
PHONE..................253 983-9622
Steve Johnson, *Branch Mgr*
EMP: 3
SALES (corp-wide): 2.5B **Privately Held**
SIC: 3691 Storage batteries
PA: East Penn Manufacturing Co.
  102 Deka Rd
  Lyon Station PA 19536
  610 682-6361

(G-5719)
ENERGY BATTERY SYSTEMS INC
10321 Lakeview Ave Sw (98499-4224)
PHONE..................253 267-1965
Louis Lamonte, *President*
SE Choi, *Chairman*
EMP: 3
SALES (est): 263.4K **Privately Held**
SIC: 3691 Lead acid batteries (storage batteries)

(G-5720)
EXTRUSION TECHNOLOGY GROUP INC
2411 104th Street Ct S (98499-8740)
PHONE..................253 583-8283
Maurice Force, *President*
Noel Force, *Vice Pres*
EMP: 7 **EST:** 2000
SQ FT: 5,000
SALES (est): 1.6MM **Privately Held**
SIC: 3082 Unsupported plastics profile shapes

(G-5721)
FAST LANE AUTO SPORTS
8328 South Tacoma Way (98499-4537)
PHONE..................253 584-3676
Eric Kin, *Owner*
Raymond Hong, *Owner*
EMP: 3
SALES (est): 130K **Privately Held**
SIC: 2395 Pleating & stitching

(G-5722)
FELLER CUSTOM COATINGS
6352 School St Sw (98499-1319)
PHONE..................360 551-2045
Donald Feller, *Principal*
EMP: 2 **EST:** 2017
SALES (est): 110.5K **Privately Held**
SIC: 3479 Metal coating & allied service

(G-5723)
FRESH IMPRESSIONS BY HONEY D
7520 John Dower Rd W (98499-8163)
PHONE..................253 503-7887
EMP: 3 **EST:** 2011
SALES (est): 150K **Privately Held**
SIC: 3291 Mfg Abrasive Products

(G-5724)
G A NEWS
11120 Gravelly Lake Dr Sw # 7 (98499-1337)
PHONE..................253 471-9888
EMP: 2
SALES (est): 73.1K **Privately Held**
SIC: 2721 Periodicals

(G-5725)
GETTING PERSONAL IMPRINTING
4021 100th St Sw Ste B (98499-4319)
PHONE..................253 302-5566
Dj Brown, *Owner*
Judi Brown, *Principal*
EMP: 2
SALES (est): 130K **Privately Held**
SIC: 2759 Imprinting

(G-5726)
GLACIER PACKAGING INC
9403 43rd Avenue Ct Sw (98499-5968)
P.O. Box 2334, Tacoma (98401-2334)
PHONE..................253 272-4682
Richard S Le Duc, *President*
Pete Wingard, *Manager*
EMP: 12
SQ FT: 62,000
SALES (est): 4.2MM **Privately Held**
WEB: www.glacierpkg.com
SIC: 2671 Packaging paper & plastics film, coated & laminated

(G-5727)
GREER STEEL INC
3117 107th St S (98499-8717)
PHONE..................253 581-4100
Mark E Greer, *President*
David Greer, *Vice Pres*
Stephen Helms, *Vice Pres*
Linda D Helms, *Director*
EMP: 27
SQ FT: 25,000
SALES (est): 14.3MM
SALES (corp-wide): 25.6MM **Privately Held**
SIC: 5051 3443 Steel; tanks, standard or custom fabricated; metal plate
PA: Greer Tank, Inc.
  3140 Lakeview Dr
  Fairbanks AK 99701
  907 452-1711

(G-5728)
INFINITY SIGN & MARKETING INC
10025 South Tacoma Way H4 (98499-4635)
PHONE..................253 539-6771
Anthony Belandi, *President*
Mark Queen, *Vice Pres*
Danielle D Smith, *Office Mgr*
Jami Wilson, *Shareholder*
EMP: 5 **EST:** 2007
SQ FT: 2,400
SALES (est): 503.4K **Privately Held**
SIC: 3993 Signs & advertising specialties

(G-5729)
JADRON TOOLS
8211 118th Street Ct Sw (98498-5531)
PHONE..................253 862-3908
Benjamin Jadron, *Principal*
EMP: 3
SALES (est): 108.4K **Privately Held**
SIC: 3599 Industrial machinery

(G-5730)
JMD PROPERTY PRESERVATION
9710 Forest Ave Sw (98498-2734)
PHONE..................267 713-2277
EMP: 2
SALES (est): 74K **Privately Held**
SIC: 0782 3423 Lawn/Garden Services Mfg Hand/Edge Tools

(G-5731)
JOY GLBAL LNGVIEW OPRTIONS LLC
3107 106th St S Ste 105 (98499-6704)
PHONE..................253 588-1726
EMP: 3 **Privately Held**
SIC: 3532 Trucks (dollies), mining
HQ: Joy Global Longview Operations Llc
  2400 S Macarthur Dr
  Longview TX 75602
  903 237-7000

(G-5732)
LAK WOODWORKS
9827 Wildwood Ave Sw (98498-2732)
PHONE..................253 495-0611
EMP: 2
SALES (est): 117.6K **Privately Held**
SIC: 2431 Millwork

(G-5733)
LAKEWOOD COUNTER TOPS INC
10513 Lakeview Ave Sw (98499-4228)
P.O. Box 98074 (98496-8074)
PHONE..................253 588-8550
Richard Whinnery, *President*
Roger Whinnery, *Vice Pres*
Cathy Tunnell, *Shareholder*
EMP: 14 **EST:** 1954
SQ FT: 10,000
SALES (est): 2.2MM **Privately Held**
WEB: www.lakewoodcountertops.com
SIC: 2541 1799 Counter & sink tops; counter top installation

(G-5734)
LAKEWOOD HOLDINGS INC
Also Called: Comfort Design Windows & Doors
11101 South Tacoma Way B (98499-4616)
PHONE..................253 284-4897
Clayton Christenson, *President*
EMP: 9
SALES (est): 209.8K **Privately Held**
SIC: 3442 Window & door frames

(G-5735)
LAKEWOOD PRINTING INC
9625 Gravelly Lake Dr Sw (98499-2698)
PHONE..................253 582-6670
Jim Barber Jr, *President*
Brian Huey, *Vice Pres*
EMP: 11
SQ FT: 2,250
SALES (est): 1.2MM **Privately Held**
WEB: www.lakewoodprinting.com
SIC: 2752 Commercial printing, offset

(G-5736)
LARSEN SIGN COMPANY
Also Called: Foam Graphics
9411 Lakeview Ave Sw (98499-4300)
PHONE..................253 581-4313
Paul Larsen, *Owner*
EMP: 3
SQ FT: 1,500
SALES (est): 150K **Privately Held**
SIC: 3993 7389 2395 Signs & advertising specialties; sign painting & lettering shop; pleating & stitching

(G-5737)
MITCHELL LEWIS & STAVER
2624 112th St S Ste D3 (98499-8868)
PHONE..................253 589-2141
David Brown, *Owner*
EMP: 3
SALES (est): 236K **Privately Held**
SIC: 5084 3561 Pumps & pumping equipment; pumps & pumping equipment

(G-5738)
MOLD DMAGE RMVAL PROS LAKEWOOD
14902 Union Ave Sw Ste C (98498-7701)
PHONE..................253 343-0497
EMP: 2 **EST:** 2010
SALES (est): 120K **Privately Held**
SIC: 3544 Mfg Dies/Tools/Jigs/Fixtures

(G-5739)
MORNING SUN INC
10828 Gravelly Lake Dr Sw # 212 (98499-1346)
PHONE..................253 922-6589
Morning Sun, *Principal*
EMP: 4
SALES (est): 260.7K **Privately Held**
SIC: 1221 Bituminous coal & lignite-surface mining

(G-5740)
NATIONAL SPECIALTIES LLC
12829 Pacific Hwy Sw (98499-1030)
PHONE..................253 581-4908
Jordan Austin, *Mng Member*
▲ **EMP:** 7
SALES (est): 1MM **Privately Held**
SIC: 3552 Embroidery machines

(G-5741)
NEWLY WEDS FOODS INC
4421 98th Street Ct Sw C (98499-5967)
P.O. Box 99460, Tacoma (98496-0460)
PHONE..................253 584-9270
John Bailey, *Manager*
Lamar Duncan, *Manager*
EMP: 80
SALES (corp-wide): 116.5MM **Privately Held**
WEB: www.newlywedsfoods.com
SIC: 2099 2045 2041 2034 Food preparations; prepared flour mixes & doughs; flour & other grain mill products; dehydrated fruits, vegetables, soups
PA: Newly Weds Foods, Inc.
  4140 W Fullerton Ave
  Chicago IL 60639
  773 489-7000

(G-5742)
NORTHWEST FLYER INC
5611 76th St W (98499-8650)
P.O. Box 39099 (98496-3099)
PHONE..................253 471-9888
Dave Parkhurst, *Principal*
EMP: 3
SALES (est): 119.1K **Privately Held**
SIC: 2711 Newspapers

Lakewood - Pierce County (G-5743)

(G-5743)
NW PROPELLER OPERATIONS INC
10902 25th Ave S (98499-8879)
PHONE 253 858-5061
Dieter Przygoda, *President*
John Schuett, *Vice Pres*
▲ EMP: 4
SALES: 2.3MM **Privately Held**
SIC: 3366 5088 Propellers, ship; propellers, ship: cast bronze; transportation equipment & supplies

(G-5744)
PACIFIC MACHINE INC
8601 38th Ave Sw (98499-4561)
PHONE 253 383-3838
Jim Tschimperle, *President*
EMP: 9
SQ FT: 10,500
SALES (est): 1.5MM **Privately Held**
WEB: www.pacmacinc.com
SIC: 3599 Machine shop, jobbing & repair

(G-5745)
PAKTEK INC
Also Called: Toolpak
7307 82nd Street Ct Sw (98499-6389)
PHONE 253 584-4914
J Alan Billingsley, *CEO*
Mark Blanchard, *President*
▲ EMP: 23
SQ FT: 2,300
SALES (est): 2.4MM **Privately Held**
WEB: www.toolpak.com
SIC: 2393 Textile bags

(G-5746)
PALACE
8718 South Tacoma Way A1 (98499-4597)
PHONE 253 581-0880
EMP: 6 EST: 2010
SALES (est): 488.1K **Privately Held**
SIC: 3421 Table & food cutlery, including butchers'

(G-5747)
PREFLEX DIGITAL PREPRESS SVCS
4620 95th St Sw Ste B (98499-5964)
P.O. Box 99008 (98496-0008)
PHONE 253 583-9100
Mike McAuley, *CEO*
Mike Ellis, *President*
EMP: 12
SQ FT: 25,000
SALES (est): 3.1MM **Privately Held**
SIC: 3555 2796 Printing plates; platemaking services

(G-5748)
PREMIUM SIGN INC
8203 South Tacoma Way (98499-4535)
PHONE 253 267-0547
Sin O Kang, *Principal*
EMP: 2 EST: 2009
SALES (est): 162.5K **Privately Held**
SIC: 3993 Signs & advertising specialties

(G-5749)
PRINTERS BLOC
9814 Wildwood Ave Sw (98498-2733)
PHONE 253 576-6043
Cristina Blocher, *Principal*
EMP: 4
SALES (est): 243.1K **Privately Held**
SIC: 2752 Commercial printing, offset

(G-5750)
QUIET GIANT BREWING CO LLC
10505 Rainier Ave Sw (98499-4761)
P.O. Box 39216 (98496-3216)
PHONE 253 584-8373
Russell Dunham, *Principal*
EMP: 2
SALES (est): 62.3K **Privately Held**
SIC: 2082 Malt beverages

(G-5751)
RENEWABLE ENERGY TECH INC
Also Called: Regenx Systems
10321 Lakeview Ave Sw (98499-4224)
PHONE 253 267-1965
Louis Lamonte, *President*
Andrei Novakovskiy, *Principal*
Howard Sant, *Principal*
EMP: 2
SQ FT: 6,000
SALES (est): 117.6K **Privately Held**
SIC: 3621 Storage battery chargers, motor & engine generator type

(G-5752)
ROBS SPRNKLR SVC INSTALLATION
8103 Steilacoom Blvd Sw (98498-6154)
PHONE 253 581-6491
Robert Mooreson, *Owner*
EMP: 3 EST: 1996
SALES: 200K **Privately Held**
SIC: 3432 Lawn hose nozzles & sprinklers

(G-5753)
SALSA WITH A KICK
11609 Cloverdale Ct Sw (98499-1264)
PHONE 253 820-7622
EMP: 2
SALES (est): 67.3K **Privately Held**
SIC: 2099 Dips, except cheese & sour cream based

(G-5754)
SHADOW MASTER
Also Called: Speedzone By Shadow Master
11018 Bridgeport Way Sw (98499-3514)
PHONE 253 984-0559
Chin Kanze, *Owner*
EMP: 2
SALES (est): 140.5K **Privately Held**
SIC: 1799 5999 3651 Glass tinting, architectural or automotive; alarm signal systems; audio electronic systems

(G-5755)
SHELTERLOGIC CORP
9317 47th Ave Sw Bldg 9 (98499-5949)
PHONE 253 985-0026
EMP: 6
SALES (corp-wide): 150MM **Privately Held**
SIC: 3448 Prefabricated metal buildings
HQ: Shelterlogic Corp.
150 Callender Rd
Watertown CT 06795
860 945-6442

(G-5756)
SMART CABLE COMPANY
7403 Lakewood Dr W Ste 14 (98499-7951)
PHONE 253 474-9967
Don Carr, *President*
EMP: 7
SQ FT: 1,200
SALES (est): 961.6K **Privately Held**
WEB: www.smart-cable.com
SIC: 3496 3577 Cable, uninsulated wire: made from purchased wire; computer peripheral equipment

(G-5757)
SOCK PEDDLERS
6122 Motor Ave Sw (98499-1529)
PHONE 253 267-0148
EMP: 2
SALES (est): 73.4K **Privately Held**
SIC: 2252 Socks

(G-5758)
SOUTH TACOMA GLASS SPECIALISTS
Also Called: Sunwrist To Go
8915 Lakeview Ave Sw (98499-4342)
PHONE 253 582-2401
Guy Hemley, *Owner*
EMP: 22
SALES (est): 3MM **Privately Held**
WEB: www.southtacomaglassspecialists.com
SIC: 3714 3211 Wipers, windshield, motor vehicle; window glass, clear & colored

(G-5759)
SPECIALTY PRODUCTS INC (HQ)
Also Called: SPI
2410 104th Street Ct S D (98499-8701)
PHONE 253 588-7101
Dan Helton, *President*
Charles Weatherford, *Vice Pres*
Curt Josaitis, *Admin Sec*
◆ EMP: 24
SQ FT: 15,000
SALES (est): 5.1MM **Privately Held**
WEB: www.specialty-products.com
SIC: 2851 Polyurethane coatings

(G-5760)
TACOMA GLASS MANUFACTURING INC
4424 98th Street Ct Sw B (98499-5982)
PHONE 253 581-7679
Michael Campbell, *President*
Steven Wood, *Vice Pres*
Jeff Tregoning, *CFO*
Jeffrey Tregoning, *Admin Sec*
EMP: 29
SALES (est): 5.4MM **Privately Held**
SIC: 3211 Flat glass

(G-5761)
TACOMA TOFU INC
51 Westlake Ave Sw (98498-5827)
PHONE 253 627-5085
James Van Wie, *President*
Sandy Johnson, *Corp Secy*
Ron Johnson, *Vice Pres*
▲ EMP: 8
SQ FT: 1,800
SALES (est): 616.4K **Privately Held**
SIC: 2099 Tofu, except frozen desserts

(G-5762)
TACTICAL TAILOR INC
2916 107th St S (98499-1636)
PHONE 253 984-7854
Justin Coffey, *President*
Anita Coffey, *Admin Sec*
◆ EMP: 71
SQ FT: 55,000
SALES: 11MM **Privately Held**
WEB: www.tacticaltailor.com
SIC: 2221 Nylon broadwoven fabrics

(G-5763)
TUFF TS CONNECTION SCREEN PRTG (PA)
8012 South Tacoma Way (98499-4500)
PHONE 253 588-8897
Louis Hunter, *Owner*
EMP: 2
SALES (est): 251.3K **Privately Held**
SIC: 5699 5136 5137 2396 T-shirts, custom printed; shirts, men's & boys'; sportswear, women's & children's; screen printing on fabric articles

(G-5764)
ULTRA CARBON
10203 Lakeview Ave Sw (98499-4222)
PHONE 253 922-4266
Gregory Shampine, *Principal*
EMP: 4
SALES (est): 527.8K **Privately Held**
SIC: 3714 Motor vehicle parts & accessories

(G-5765)
WASHINGTON TENT & AWNING INC
3419 Chapel St S (98499-8884)
P.O. Box 98809 (98496-8809)
PHONE 253 581-7177
Bernard Ruff, *President*
Jamie Williams, *Vice Pres*
Dan Williams, *Treasurer*
EMP: 6
SQ FT: 7,000
SALES (est): 549K **Privately Held**
WEB: www.washingtontentandawning.com
SIC: 2394 7389 Awnings, fabric: made from purchased materials; sewing contractor; awnings; awnings

(G-5766)
WEST FORK TIMBER CO LLC
3819 100th St Sw Ste 5b (98499-4478)
PHONE 253 383-5871
EMP: 14
SQ FT: 800
SALES (est): 850K **Privately Held**
SIC: 2411 Logging

(G-5767)
WESTWYND PUBLISHING LLC
9709 73rd St Sw (98498-3303)
PHONE 253 588-3066
Neil Delisanti, *Principal*
EMP: 2
SALES (est): 84K **Privately Held**
SIC: 2741 Miscellaneous publishing

(G-5768)
WISDOM ELITE LLC
10614 Westwood Dr Sw (98499-4826)
P.O. Box 25552, Federal Way (98093-2552)
PHONE 806 201-3953
Anthony Aparicio,
Margarita Aparicio,
EMP: 2
SALES (est): 164.4K **Privately Held**
SIC: 2844 5149 Face creams or lotions; flavourings & fragrances

(G-5769)
WLI RECYCLING INC
10321 Lakeview Ave Sw (98499-4224)
PHONE 253 267-1965
Louis Lamonte, *President*
Amy Choi, *Bd of Directors*
EMP: 2
SQ FT: 4,000
SALES (est): 363.3K **Privately Held**
SIC: 5013 3691 Automotive batteries; lead acid batteries (storage batteries)

(G-5770)
X PRESS INK CO
4001 100th St Sw (98499-4309)
PHONE 253 588-1818
EMP: 2 EST: 2011
SALES (est): 83K **Privately Held**
SIC: 2741 Misc Publishing

Langley
Island County

(G-5771)
BUY MONTHLY DEALS
4357 Peaceful Pl (98260-9648)
PHONE 360 321-6748
Christopher Wilson, *Principal*
EMP: 3 EST: 2015
SALES (est): 78.6K **Privately Held**
SIC: 2711 Newspapers

(G-5772)
CADEE DISTILLERY LLC
12 De Bruyn Ave (98260-9316)
P.O. Box 857, Clinton (98236-0857)
PHONE 360 969-5565
EMP: 4
SALES (est): 199.2K **Privately Held**
SIC: 2085 Distilled & blended liquors

(G-5773)
CENTER FOR TOUCH DRAWING
628 1st St (98260-9602)
P.O. Box 1595 (98260-1595)
PHONE 360 221-5745
Deborah Coff-Chapin, *Owner*
EMP: 2
SALES: 110K **Privately Held**
WEB: www.touchdrawing.com
SIC: 2731 Books: publishing only

(G-5774)
CHASE SCIENTIFIC CO
5619 Winona Ln (98260-8624)
P.O. Box 1487 (98260-1487)
PHONE 360 221-8455
Frank Chase, *Owner*
EMP: 2
SALES (est): 227.4K **Privately Held**
WEB: www.chase2000.com
SIC: 3825 7379 Digital test equipment, electronic & electrical circuits; computer related consulting services

(G-5775)
COSMIC RESOURCES
3939 Saratoga Rd (98260-9621)
P.O. Box 913 (98260-0913)
PHONE 360 730-8574
Barbara Matteson, *Partner*

GEOGRAPHIC SECTION

Robert Matteson, *Partner*
EMP: 2
SALES: 70K **Privately Held**
WEB: www.cosmicresources.net
SIC: 5094 3915 Jewelers' findings; jewelers' materials & lapidary work

(G-5776)
DAVID GRAY FURNITUREMAKER INC
5227 Crawford Rd (98260-8525)
PHONE...................360 321-4514
David Gray, *President*
Bayle Gray, *Admin Sec*
EMP: 4
SALES: 270K **Privately Held**
WEB: www.dgfurnituremakers.com
SIC: 2511 Wood household furniture

(G-5777)
FLANAGAN WOODWORKS INC
5180 Nighthawk Rd (98260-9572)
PHONE...................360 221-3352
Michael Flanagan, *Principal*
EMP: 2
SALES (est): 179.2K **Privately Held**
SIC: 2431 Millwork

(G-5778)
GIRAFFE PROJECT
197 2nd St Ste A (98260)
P.O. Box 759 (98260-0759)
PHONE...................360 221-7989
Ann Medlock, *COO*
Mary E Keblusek, *Deputy Dir*
EMP: 8
SALES: 101.7K **Privately Held**
WEB: www.giraffe.org
SIC: 2711 Newspapers: publishing only, not printed on site

(G-5779)
GREY GULL CERAMICS
5177 Blacktail Ln (98260-8225)
P.O. Box 363, Freeland (98249-0363)
PHONE...................360 321-1582
Linda Lutch, *Partner*
EMP: 2
SALES (est): 162.3K **Privately Held**
SIC: 3952 Colors, artists': water & oxide ceramic glass

(G-5780)
HOFFMANN PETRA
Also Called: Heron Creek Press
5088 Lakeside Dr (98260-8260)
PHONE...................360 321-4733
Petra Hoffmann, *Owner*
EMP: 2
SALES (est): 117.8K **Privately Held**
SIC: 8748 2731 Publishing consultant; book publishing

(G-5781)
HONOLDS ORNAMENTAL IRONWORK
2635 Dreamland Ln (98260-8150)
PHONE...................206 779-0668
Jim Honold, *Principal*
EMP: 2
SALES (est): 88.9K **Privately Held**
SIC: 3446 Architectural metalwork

(G-5782)
MANY RIVERS COMPANY
221 2nd St Bldg 13 (98260-8664)
P.O. Box 868 (98260-0868)
PHONE...................360 221-1324
David Whyte, *Owner*
EMP: 5 **EST:** 1993
SQ FT: 1,000
SALES: 900K **Privately Held**
SIC: 2731 Book publishing

(G-5783)
MILLMAN INDUSTRIES LLC
2104 Millman Rd (98260-9751)
PHONE...................425 471-0854
Marc Kukuk, *Principal*
EMP: 2
SALES (est): 140.4K **Privately Held**
SIC: 3999 Manufacturing industries

(G-5784)
SCHWAGER DESIGN & CONSTRUCTION
3800 E Harbor Rd (98260-9663)
PHONE...................360 221-8165
Bruce H Schwager, *Co-Owner*
Christine Schwager, *Co-Owner*
EMP: 2
SALES: 50K **Privately Held**
SIC: 2434 Wood kitchen cabinets

(G-5785)
SIMPLELINE INC
Also Called: Headsets Connect
2576 Myra Pl (98260-9227)
P.O. Box 103, Freeland (98249-0103)
PHONE...................888 743-7903
Mario Falso, *Vice Pres*
EMP: 2
SALES (est): 221.4K **Privately Held**
WEB: www.gotbelts.com
SIC: 5044 3661 Office equipment; telephones & telephone apparatus; headsets, telephone

(G-5786)
SPOILED DOG WINERY
5881 Maxwelton Rd (98260-9518)
PHONE...................360 321-6226
EMP: 3
SALES (est): 83.5K **Privately Held**
SIC: 2084 Wines

(G-5787)
WHIDBEY ISLAND VINYARD WINERY
5237 Langley Rd (98260-9557)
PHONE...................360 221-2040
Gregory Osenbach, *Owner*
Elizabeth Osenbach, *Co-Owner*
EMP: 3
SQ FT: 1,400
SALES: 150K **Privately Held**
WEB: www.whidbeyislandwinery.com
SIC: 2084 5812 Wines; eating places

(G-5788)
WILLIAMSON BROCK WLDG MCH SP
Also Called: Welding &MAchine Shop
5017 Bayview Rd (98260-9775)
PHONE...................360 321-3227
Brock Williamson, *Owner*
Elizabeth Williamson, *Principal*
EMP: 2
SALES (est): 147.2K **Privately Held**
SIC: 7692 Welding repair

(G-5789)
WOMSLEY LOGGING COMPANY
Also Called: Womsley Enterprises
4869 Lakeside Dr (98260-8258)
PHONE...................360 321-5321
David Womsley, *Owner*
S Womsley, *Principal*
EMP: 6 **EST:** 1978
SALES (est): 541.6K **Privately Held**
SIC: 2411 Logging camps & contractors

Latah
Spokane County

(G-5790)
COUNTRY FLICKER CANDLE CO
20411 E Wheeler Rd (99018-9541)
PHONE...................509 286-3031
Ashley Pottratz, *Principal*
EMP: 2
SALES (est): 63.7K **Privately Held**
SIC: 3999 Candles

(G-5791)
HOFFMAN MANUFACTURING
602 W Spring Valley Rd (99018-6000)
PHONE...................509 286-3200
Justin Hoffman, *Owner*
Taylor Mishalanie, *Engineer*
EMP: 3
SALES (est): 450K **Privately Held**
SIC: 3441 Fabricated structural metal

(G-5792)
JAKES SMALL MCH FBRICATION SP
150 E Coplen St (99018-6501)
PHONE...................509 286-3690
Jake Buckner, *Principal*
EMP: 2
SALES (est): 81.4K **Privately Held**
SIC: 3599 Machine shop, jobbing & repair

Leavenworth
Chelan County

(G-5793)
37 CELLARS
1261 Dempsey Rd (98826-5804)
P.O. Box 520 (98826-0520)
PHONE...................509 679-0668
Charles R Egner, *Manager*
EMP: 4 **EST:** 2010
SALES (est): 254.7K **Privately Held**
SIC: 2084 Wines

(G-5794)
ALPINE CABINET
507 Cedar St (98826-1113)
PHONE...................509 679-6380
Nancy Bywater-Johnson, *President*
EMP: 2 **EST:** 2010
SALES (est): 192.1K **Privately Held**
SIC: 2434 Wood kitchen cabinets

(G-5795)
ANN H MCCORMICK PHD
10454 Fox Rd (98826-9515)
PHONE...................650 451-8020
Ann H McCormick, *CEO*
EMP: 2
SALES (est): 56.5K **Privately Held**
SIC: 7372 Educational computer software

(G-5796)
BERGDORF CELLARS
939 Front St (98826-1427)
PHONE...................509 548-7638
Gary Robertson, *Principal*
EMP: 4
SALES (est): 210.8K **Privately Held**
SIC: 2084 Wines

(G-5797)
BURGESS LOGGING INC
18600 River Rd (98826-9294)
PHONE...................509 763-3119
William T Burgess, *President*
William E Burgess, *President*
Bill Burgess, *Vice Pres*
Jean Burgess, *Admin Sec*
EMP: 15
SALES (est): 1.5MM **Privately Held**
SIC: 2411 2421 Logging camps & contractors; sawmills & planing mills, general

(G-5798)
DVINERY
617 Front St (98826-1363)
PHONE...................509 548-7059
Nat Sharpe, *Manager*
EMP: 2
SALES (est): 132.1K **Privately Held**
SIC: 2084 Wines

(G-5799)
EAGLE CREEK WINERY
10037 Eagle Creek Rd (98826-9113)
PHONE...................509 548-7059
Edw Rutledge, *Principal*
Edward Rutledge, *Executive Asst*
EMP: 2
SALES (est): 150K **Privately Held**
SIC: 2084 Wines

(G-5800)
EIGER SKYLINE INC
5332 Old Bluett Rd (98826)
P.O. Box 184 (98826-0184)
PHONE...................509 548-6808
Hans Trummer, *President*
Sandra Trummer, *Corp Secy*
EMP: 5
SALES (est): 469.8K **Privately Held**
SIC: 2411 Logging camps & contractors

(G-5801)
EUROPEAN WROUGHT IRON
9351 E Leavenworth Rd (98826-9357)
PHONE...................509 548-4879
Jan Uchytil, *Owner*
EMP: 2
SALES (est): 187.2K **Privately Held**
SIC: 3446 1799 Stairs, staircases, stair treads: prefabricated metal; ornamental metal work

(G-5802)
EVOLUTION REVOLUTION LLC
22584 Meadow Creek Rd (98826)
PHONE...................623 703-5042
Derrick Passertti, *Manager*
EMP: 2
SALES (est): 130K **Privately Held**
SIC: 2326 Men's & boys' work clothing

(G-5803)
GINGERBREAD FACTORY
828 Commercial St (98826-1317)
P.O. Box 366 (98826-0366)
PHONE...................509 548-6592
Carol Stolmeier-Seaman, *Owner*
Carol Ann Stolmeier-Seaman, *Owner*
EMP: 7
SQ FT: 900
SALES (est): 243.1K **Privately Held**
WEB: www.gingerbreadfactory.com
SIC: 5461 2045 5947 Bakeries; gingerbread mix, prepared: from purchased flour; gift shop

(G-5804)
GRONLUND LOGGING INC
236 Mine St (98826-1017)
PHONE...................509 548-5039
Ernie Gronlund, *President*
EMP: 3
SALES (est): 220K **Privately Held**
SIC: 2411 Logging camps & contractors

(G-5805)
H & D LOGGING COMPANY INC
11797 Chumstick Hwy (98826-9212)
PHONE...................509 548-7358
Steve Lemons, *President*
Paula Lemons, *Admin Sec*
EMP: 17
SALES: 3MM **Privately Held**
SIC: 2411 4789 Timber, cut at logging camp; skidding logs; log loading & unloading

(G-5806)
HIGH CASCADE INCORPORATED
12285 Allen Rd (98826-9547)
PHONE...................509 763-2195
Benjamin Barke, *President*
Robin Barke, *Corp Secy*
EMP: 2
SALES (est): 153.8K **Privately Held**
SIC: 1081 5999 Metal mining services; monuments & tombstones

(G-5807)
ICICLE RIDGE WINERY
821 Front St (98826-1382)
PHONE...................509 548-7019
Louie Wagoner, *Principal*
EMP: 2
SALES (est): 113K
SALES (corp-wide): 160K **Privately Held**
SIC: 2084 Wines
PA: Icicle Ridge Winery
8977 North Rd
Peshastin WA 98847
509 548-7019

(G-5808)
KESTREL VINTNERS
843 Front St Ste B1 (98826-1381)
PHONE...................509 548-7348
Randy Nichols, *Branch Mgr*
EMP: 4
SALES (est): 244.2K
SALES (corp-wide): 1.4MM **Privately Held**
SIC: 2084 Wines

Leavenworth - Chelan County (G-5809)

PA: Kestrel Vintners
2890 Lee Rd
Prosser WA 99350
509 786-2675

(G-5809)
LASTING MEMORIES
110 Park Ave (98826-1019)
PHONE................................509 548-6393
Paula Muyer, *Partner*
Larry Muyer, *Partner*
EMP: 2
SALES (est): 129K **Privately Held**
SIC: 3469 Porcelain enameled products & utensils

(G-5810)
NAPEEQUA VINTNERS
18820 Beaver Valley Rd (98826-9162)
P.O. Box 343, Manson (98831-0343)
PHONE................................509 763-1600
David Morris, *Principal*
Dave Morris, *Executive Asst*
EMP: 4 **EST:** 2010
SALES (est): 257.8K **Privately Held**
SIC: 2084 Wines

(G-5811)
NCW MEDIA INC (PA)
Also Called: Cashmere Valley Record
215 14th St (98826-1411)
P.O. Box 39 (98826-0039)
PHONE................................509 548-5286
William E Forhan, *President*
Carol Forhan, *Vice Pres*
Jeff Walter, *Admin Sec*
EMP: 5 **EST:** 1906
SQ FT: 1,800
SALES: 2MM **Privately Held**
WEB: www.leavenworthecho.com
SIC: 2711 Newspapers: publishing only, not printed on site

(G-5812)
PAULTY MFG LLC
960 Us Highway 2 # 1037 (98826-1652)
P.O. Box 265, Peshastin (98847-0265)
PHONE................................509 470-1791
Ty Bourgeois, *Principal*
EMP: 2
SALES (est): 141.9K **Privately Held**
SIC: 3999 Manufacturing industries

(G-5813)
PLAIN CELLARS LLC
18749 Alpine Acres Rd (98826-9500)
PHONE................................509 548-5412
Bob Sage, *Mng Member*
EMP: 10
SALES: 400K **Privately Held**
SIC: 2084 5921 5182 Wines; wine; wine

(G-5814)
QUILTERS HEAVEN LLC
917 Commercial St (98826-1413)
PHONE................................800 253-8990
Deann Howie, *Administration*
EMP: 2
SALES (est): 171.9K **Privately Held**
SIC: 3731 Lighthouse tenders, building & repairing

(G-5815)
SCHEIBLER BROS INC
15600 Chumstick Hwy (98826-9101)
P.O. Box 242 (98826-0242)
PHONE................................509 548-7115
Mary Scheibler, *CEO*
Moritz O Scheibler Jr, *President*
▼ **EMP:** 8
SQ FT: 4,500
SALES (est): 1.4MM **Privately Held**
SIC: 3555 Printing presses

(G-5816)
SKYKOMISH KNIFE WORKS
19475 Us Highway 2 (98826-9227)
PHONE................................509 763-3117
Elliott Wakefield, *Owner*
EMP: 3 **EST:** 2012
SALES (est): 120K **Privately Held**
SIC: 3421 Knife blades & blanks

(G-5817)
TWO RIVERS SAND AND GRAVEL
22750 Lake Wenatchee Hwy (98826-9552)
PHONE................................509 763-3280
Bruce Dickenson, *President*
Barbara Dickenson, *Corp Secy*
Kirk Dickenson, *Vice Pres*
EMP: 9
SQ FT: 1,200
SALES (est): 935K **Privately Held**
SIC: 5032 3273 Sand, construction; ready-mixed concrete

(G-5818)
US MAT SYSTEMS LLC
17400 Winton Rd (98826-9254)
PHONE................................509 763-4000
Mike Wold, *President*
EMP: 18
SALES (est): 5.4MM **Privately Held**
SIC: 3533 Oil & gas drilling rigs & equipment

Lewis McChord
Pierce County

(G-5819)
ANDREW MCDONALD
2668 Columbia Ave Apt B (98433-1083)
PHONE................................253 964-5020
Andrew McDonald, *Principal*
EMP: 2
SALES (est): 87.2K **Privately Held**
SIC: 3711 Motor vehicles & car bodies

Lewis Mcchord
Pierce County

(G-5820)
HONEYWELL INTERNATIONAL INC
Rainier Dr (98433)
PHONE................................253 966-0203
EMP: 2
SALES (corp-wide): 41.8B **Publicly Held**
SIC: 3724 Aircraft engines & engine parts
PA: Honeywell International Inc.
115 Tabor Rd
Morris Plains NJ 07950
973 455-2000

Lewis McChord
Pierce County

(G-5821)
PACIFIC NORTHWEST WOVENS LLC
2659 S 5th St (98433-1009)
PHONE................................714 392-0634
Heather Smith, *Mng Member*
Brittany Land-Cross, *Mng Member*
Wynter Weaver, *Mng Member*
EMP: 3 **EST:** 2016
SALES (est): 113.3K **Privately Held**
SIC: 2361 Girls' & children's dresses, blouses & shirts

Liberty Lake
Spokane County

(G-5822)
ACCRA-FAB INC (PA)
Also Called: Accra Fab
23201 E Appleway Ave (99019-6029)
P.O. Box 641 (99019-0641)
PHONE................................509 922-3300
Gregory Konkol, *President*
Don Bolling, *QC Mgr*
John Coker, *Engineer*
EMP: 84
SQ FT: 155,000
SALES (est): 30.1MM **Privately Held**
WEB: www.accrafab.com
SIC: 3444 Sheet metalwork

(G-5823)
ACCRA-FAB INC
23201 E Knox Ave (99019)
PHONE................................509 922-3300
Don J Hemmer, *Branch Mgr*
EMP: 146
SALES (corp-wide): 30.1MM **Privately Held**
SIC: 3444 Sheet metalwork
PA: Accra-Fab, Inc.
23201 E Appleway Ave
Liberty Lake WA 99019
509 922-3300

(G-5824)
AGILENT TECHNOLOGIES INC
24001 E Mission Ave (99019-3001)
P.O. Box 2500, Spokane (99220)
PHONE................................509 921-3525
Jim Rundle, *President*
EMP: 60
SQ FT: 74,500
SALES (corp-wide): 4.9B **Publicly Held**
WEB: www.agilent.com
SIC: 3825 Instruments to measure electricity
PA: Agilent Technologies, Inc.
5301 Stevens Creek Blvd
Santa Clara CA 95051
408 345-8886

(G-5825)
ALTEK INC
22819 E Appleway Ave (99019-9514)
PHONE................................509 921-0597
Michael Marzetta, *President*
Jeff Logan, *General Mgr*
Alan Marzetta, *Chairman*
Robert H Lamp, *Admin Sec*
▲ **EMP:** 115
SQ FT: 140,000
SALES (est): 46.7MM **Privately Held**
WEB: www.altek.net
SIC: 3599 3089 3544 Machine shop, jobbing & repair; injection molding of plastics; dies, plastics forming; industrial molds

(G-5826)
APRICOTS & LOLLIPOPS
24013 E Maxwell Ave (99019-8624)
PHONE................................509 216-0325
EMP: 2
SALES (est): 70.4K **Privately Held**
SIC: 2064 Lollipops & other hard candy

(G-5827)
AVELLA LLC
24817 E Liberty Creek Rd (99019-9718)
PHONE................................509 217-0347
▲ **EMP:** 2
SALES (est): 180.6K **Privately Held**
SIC: 2434 Wood kitchen cabinets

(G-5828)
CLOUDSTREAM MEDIA INC (PA)
Also Called: Solaracast
24402 E 3rd Ave (99019-9657)
PHONE................................858 245-0034
Jeff O'Shea, *CEO*
Michael Sakakeeny, *Managing Dir*
EMP: 2
SALES: 2.3MM **Privately Held**
SIC: 3651 Audio electronic systems

(G-5829)
CROWN MEDIA & PRINTING INC
24222 E Pinehurst Ln (99019-9676)
P.O. Box 606 (99019-0606)
PHONE................................509 315-8114
H Richard Shutts, *President*
EMP: 4
SALES (est): 333.8K **Privately Held**
SIC: 2752 Commercial printing, offset

(G-5830)
DIFFERENT DRUMMERS
320 N Mitchell Dr (99019-9413)
PHONE................................509 216-2098
Donald Caron, *Principal*
EMP: 2
SALES (est): 101.9K **Privately Held**
SIC: 2741 Miscellaneous publishing

(G-5831)
ELECTRIJET FLIGHT SYSTEMS INC
23403 E Mission Ave Ste 2 (99019-7553)
PHONE................................509 990-9474
Devin Samuelson, *President*
Nathan Brown, *CFO*
EMP: 8
SQ FT: 1,000
SALES (est): 364.7K **Privately Held**
SIC: 8711 3519 3829 3621 Aviation &/or aeronautical engineering; jet propulsion engines; pressure & vacuum indicators, aircraft engine; thrust power indicators, aircraft engine; storage battery chargers, motor & engine generator type

(G-5832)
FRENCKEN AMERICA INC
22924 E Appleway Ave (99019-9514)
P.O. Box 828 (99019-0828)
PHONE................................509 924-9777
Darren Helm, *Managing Dir*
Scott Bruno, *Prdtn Mgr*
Teresa Mann, *Buyer*
Joshua Soule, *Buyer*
Ian Hees, *Engineer*
EMP: 50
SQ FT: 17,000
SALES (est): 13.3MM
SALES (corp-wide): 379.8MM **Privately Held**
WEB: www.usmotion.com
SIC: 3569 8711 Assembly machines, non-metalworking; electrical or electronic engineering
HQ: Frencken Europe B.V.
Hurksestraat 16
Eindhoven 5652
402 507-507

(G-5833)
GRAND TEMPLE
618 S Liberty Cir (99019-9726)
PHONE................................509 715-7876
Kriangkrai Chingchairit,
EMP: 3
SALES (est): 91.3K **Privately Held**
SIC: 2099 5499 5149 Food preparations; miscellaneous food stores; specialty food items

(G-5834)
HUNDRED HORSE PANELS LLC
Also Called: Qualiteq
23305 E Knox Ave Bldg B (99019-9461)
PHONE................................509 227-5686
Doug Lauer, *Mng Member*
EMP: 8
SALES: 2MM **Privately Held**
SIC: 3613 Control panels, electric

(G-5835)
HUNT MINING CORP
23800 E Appleway Ave (99019-9807)
PHONE................................509 290-5659
Tim Hunt, *CEO*
Kenneth B Atwood, *CFO*
Bob Little, *CFO*
EMP: 3
SALES (est): 158.8K **Privately Held**
SIC: 1081 Exploration, metal mining

(G-5836)
HUNTMOUNTAIN RESOURCES LTD
Also Called: (A DEVELOPMENT STAGE ENTERPRISE)
1611 N Molter Rd Ste 201 (99019-9484)
PHONE................................509 290-5659
Tim Hunt, *Ch of Bd*
Matthew J Hughes, *COO*
Bryn Harman, *CFO*
EMP: 10
SALES (est): 699K **Privately Held**
WEB: www.huntmountain.com
SIC: 1499 Precious stones mining

(G-5837)
INTELLITOUCH COMMUNICATONS
24310 E 3rd Ave (99019-9656)
PHONE................................858 457-3300
Michael Sakakeeny, *President*
EMP: 6

GEOGRAPHIC SECTION

Liberty Lake - Spokane County (G-5866)

SALES (est): 481.3K **Privately Held**
SIC: **3931** Musical instruments, electric & electronic

(G-5838)
ITRON INC (PA)
2111 N Molter Rd (99019-9469)
PHONE.....................................509 924-9900
Philip C Mezey, *President*
Eryn McCulloch, *President*
Ralph Harms, *Business Mgr*
Thomas L Deitrich, *COO*
Michel C Cadieux, *Senior VP*
◆ **EMP:** 500 **EST:** 1977
SALES: 2.3B **Publicly Held**
WEB: www.siliconenergy.com
SIC: **3829** 7371 Measuring & controlling devices; computer software development & applications

(G-5839)
ITRON BRAZIL II LLC
2111 N Molter Rd (99019-9469)
PHONE.....................................509 924-9900
EMP: 3 **EST:** 2013
SALES (est): 141.2K
SALES (corp-wide): 2.3B **Publicly Held**
SIC: **3829** Measuring & controlling devices
PA: Itron, Inc.
2111 N Molter Rd
Liberty Lake WA 99019
509 924-9900

(G-5840)
ITRON INTERNATIONAL INC
2111 N Molter Rd (99019-9469)
PHONE.....................................866 374-8766
Philip Mezey, *President*
EMP: 3 **EST:** 2012
SALES (est): 201.4K
SALES (corp-wide): 2.3B **Publicly Held**
SIC: **3829** Measuring & controlling devices
PA: Itron, Inc.
2111 N Molter Rd
Liberty Lake WA 99019
509 924-9900

(G-5841)
ITRON US GAS LLC
2111 N Molter Rd (99019-9469)
PHONE.....................................509 924-9900
EMP: 2
SALES (est): 160K **Privately Held**
SIC: **3825** Instruments to measure electricity

(G-5842)
LAKE CITY NATUROPATHIC CARE IN
21950 E Country Vista Dr # 600 (99019-6005)
PHONE.....................................509 590-1343
Julia Stevens, *Principal*
EMP: 4
SALES (est): 391K **Privately Held**
SIC: **2899** Salt

(G-5843)
LHC2 INC
Also Called: Eigen Wireless
23326 E 2nd Ave (99019-9421)
PHONE.....................................509 723-4517
Robert J Conley, *President*
Dan Lohman, *General Mgr*
Royden M Honda, *Treasurer*
Royden Honda, *Treasurer*
Jon Thorpe, *Asst Treas*
EMP: 8
SALES (est): 716.2K **Privately Held**
WEB: www.lhc2.com
SIC: **8711** 3663 3679 Consulting engineer; radio broadcasting & communications equipment; antennas, receiving

(G-5844)
LIBERTY LAKE POWERSPORTS LLC
Also Called: Allsport Polaris
19505 E Broadway Ave (99016-8842)
PHONE.....................................509 926-5044
Diane Blacklidge, *Controller*
Eric K Holt,
Lorali K Holt,
EMP: 3

SALES (est): 327.3K **Privately Held**
SIC: **3751** 5571 Motorcycles & related parts; motorcycle accessories; motorcycle dealers

(G-5845)
MARIO & SON INC
2750 Eagle Ln (99019-5047)
PHONE.....................................509 536-6079
Mario J Marcella, *CEO*
Jeffery Marcella, *President*
Michael C Marcella, *Vice Pres*
▲ **EMP:** 20
SQ FT: 45,000
SALES (est): 2.6MM **Privately Held**
WEB: www.marioandson.com
SIC: **3281** 5032 Cut stone & stone products; brick, stone & related material

(G-5846)
MINDS-I INC
22819 E Appleway Ave (99019-9514)
PHONE.....................................509 252-5725
Michael Marzetta, *President*
Christy Marzetta, *Vice Pres*
▲ **EMP:** 2
SQ FT: 140,000
SALES (est): 242.6K **Privately Held**
SIC: **3089** Injection molding of plastics

(G-5847)
MK20 INC
Also Called: Professional Crane Inspections
25025 E Appleway Ave (99019)
P.O. Box 160 (99019-0160)
PHONE.....................................509 226-5302
Robert Odea, *President*
EMP: 6
SALES (est): 850K **Privately Held**
SIC: **3536** Hoists, cranes & monorails

(G-5848)
NORDSON SELECT INC
22425 E Appleway Ave Fl 1 (99019-8508)
PHONE.....................................509 924-4898
Michael F Hilton, *President*
EMP: 33
SALES (est): 3.4MM
SALES (corp-wide): 2.2B **Publicly Held**
SIC: **3563** Spraying outfits: metals, paints & chemicals (compressor); robots for industrial spraying, painting, etc.
PA: Nordson Corporation
28601 Clemens Rd
Westlake OH 44145
440 892-1580

(G-5849)
OFFSET SOLAR LLC
2111 N Molter Rd (99019-9469)
PHONE.....................................866 376-9559
Samuel Hampsch, *Mng Member*
Konrad Billetz, *Mng Member*
EMP: 40
SALES (est): 5.2MM **Privately Held**
SIC: **5211** 3433 Solar heating equipment; solar heaters & collectors

(G-5850)
PACIFIC GRINDING
2100 N Winrock St (99019-5093)
PHONE.....................................208 412-5945
EMP: 2
SALES (est): 106K **Privately Held**
SIC: **3999** Custom pulverizing & grinding of plastic materials

(G-5851)
PAWPULAR COMPANIONS BOUTI
21950 E Country Vista Dr # 100 (99019-6006)
PHONE.....................................509 850-6070
Carl Crowell, *Principal*
EMP: 3
SALES (est): 225.3K **Privately Held**
SIC: **3999** Pet supplies

(G-5852)
PC OPEN INCORPORATED
Also Called: Openeye
23221 E Knox Ave (99019-5069)
PHONE.....................................509 777-6736
Richard Ryan Sheppard, *President*
Doug Cherney, *Business Mgr*
Jack Lynch, *COO*

Megan Taylor, *Purch Agent*
Scott Kingsford, *Technical Mgr*
▲ **EMP:** 120
SQ FT: 27,000
SALES (est): 39.6MM **Privately Held**
WEB: www.pcopen.com
SIC: **3699** Security control equipment & systems

(G-5853)
PERIDOT PUBLISHING LLC
2310 N Molter Rd Ste 309 (99019-8630)
PHONE.....................................509 242-7752
Josh Johnson, *Owner*
EMP: 2
SALES (est): 100K **Privately Held**
SIC: **2741** Miscellaneous publishing

(G-5854)
PREMIER MANUFACTURING INC
1711 N Madson St (99019-8544)
P.O. Box 566 (99019-0566)
PHONE.....................................509 927-9860
Keri Ann Collins, *President*
Kevin L Collins, *Vice Pres*
Bonnie Lormis, *Treasurer*
Charles Leonard Lormis, *Admin Sec*
EMP: 85
SQ FT: 53,000
SALES (est): 26.3MM **Privately Held**
SIC: **3444** Sheet metalwork

(G-5855)
PROTO TECHNOLOGIES INC
22808 E Appleway Ave A (99019-9514)
PHONE.....................................509 891-4747
Rory Nay, *President*
Albert Williams, *Opers Mgr*
Stephen Ball, *Sales Staff*
Greg Nay, *Executive*
EMP: 52
SQ FT: 26,000
SALES (est): 4.5MM **Privately Held**
WEB: www.prototech.com
SIC: **3089** 3069 3497 3599 Molding primary plastic; thermoformed finished plastic products; castings, rubber; magnesium & magnesium-base alloy foil; hose, flexible metallic

(G-5856)
QUANTUM NORTHWEST INC
Also Called: Quantum Development Group
22910 E Appleway Ave # 4 (99019-8605)
PHONE.....................................509 624-9290
Enoch W Small PHD, *President*
EMP: 8
SQ FT: 2,000
SALES (est): 1.5MM **Privately Held**
WEB: www.qnw.com
SIC: **3827** Optical instruments & lenses

(G-5857)
SANDY BEACH MOBILE VILLA LLC
326 S Sandy Beach Ln (99019-9600)
PHONE.....................................509 255-6222
Howard Dolphin, *Partner*
Mary Dolphin,
EMP: 2
SALES: 100K **Privately Held**
SIC: **2451** Mobile homes

(G-5858)
SAUTHER & ASSOC INC
Also Called: Banner Advertising
2208 N Swing Ln (99019)
PHONE.....................................509 922-7828
Bill Sauther, *President*
Jane Sauther, *Treasurer*
EMP: 29
SQ FT: 10,000
SALES (est): 1.3MM **Privately Held**
WEB: www.banner123.com
SIC: **7313** 2759 Printed media advertising representatives; advertising literature: printing

(G-5859)
SCANIVALVE CORP
1722 N Madson St (99019-8544)
PHONE.....................................509 891-9970
Addison Pemberton, *President*
Evangeline Pemberton, *Corp Secy*
Jim C Pemberton, *Vice Pres*

EMP: 38
SQ FT: 30,000
SALES (est): 9.7MM **Privately Held**
WEB: www.scanivalve.com
SIC: **3823** Pressure measurement instruments, industrial; temperature measurement instruments, industrial

(G-5860)
SCREEN TEK INC
22902 E Appleway Ave (99019-9514)
PHONE.....................................509 928-8322
Jerry Frislie, *President*
Barbara Frislie, *Vice Pres*
EMP: 30
SQ FT: 13,000
SALES (est): 1.5MM **Privately Held**
SIC: **2759** 3993 2752 2396 Screen printing; signs & advertising specialties; commercial printing, lithographic; automotive & apparel trimmings

(G-5861)
T T I ACQUISITION CORP
Also Called: Translation Technologies
1421 N Meadowwood Ln # 40 (99019-7616)
PHONE.....................................509 358-2036
Robert Sorenson, *CEO*
Sankar Jayaram, *Vice Pres*
Dan Evans, *Human Res Dir*
Tim Boden, *Marketing Staff*
Micheal Mc Donald, *CTO*
EMP: 10
SALES (est): 1.2MM **Privately Held**
SIC: **5734** 5045 7372 Computer & software stores; computer software; prepackaged software

(G-5862)
TEKOA SOFTWARE INC
16201 E Ind Ave Ste 2750 (99019)
PHONE.....................................509 340-3580
Allan Snodgrass, *President*
EMP: 4
SQ FT: 1,150
SALES: 500K **Privately Held**
SIC: **7372** Prepackaged software

(G-5863)
TELECT INC (PA)
22245 E Appleway Blvd Ste (99019)
P.O. Box 665 (99019-0665)
PHONE.....................................509 926-6000
Wayne Williams, *President*
Bill Williams, *Chairman*
Walt Takisaki, *Vice Pres*
Thomas C Simpson, *Director*
Judith Williams, *Admin Sec*
▲ **EMP:** 245
SQ FT: 52,000
SALES (est): 150MM **Privately Held**
WEB: www.fiberlan.com
SIC: **3661** Telephones & telephone apparatus; switching equipment, telephone

(G-5864)
TIBCO SOFTWARE INC
2310 N Molter Rd Ste 300 (99019-8621)
PHONE.....................................650 846-1000
Marc Sattler, *Principal*
Samantha Guan, *Analyst*
EMP: 15
SALES (corp-wide): 885.6MM **Privately Held**
WEB: www.tibco.com
SIC: **7372** Prepackaged software
HQ: Tibco Software Inc.
3307 Hillview Ave
Palo Alto CA 94304

(G-5865)
TSUNAMI PRODUCTS INC
1711 N Madson St (99019-8544)
PHONE.....................................509 868-5731
Kevin Collins, *President*
EMP: 2 **EST:** 2017
SALES (est): 88.3K **Privately Held**
SIC: **3621** Motors & generators

(G-5866)
VALLEY ORTHOPEDICS INC
509 N Homestead Dr (99019-7580)
PHONE.....................................509 922-5040
EMP: 3
SQ FT: 2,000

Liberty Lake - Spokane County (G-5867)

SALES: 260K **Privately Held**
SIC: **8069** 3842 Orthopedic Clinic & Mfg Orthopedic Braces

(G-5867)
WESTERBERG & ASSOCIATES INC
1421 N Meadowwood Ln # 20 (99019-5037)
P.O. Box 567 (99019-0567)
PHONE.................................509 951-4399
Yolanda Westerberg, *CEO*
Nickolas Westerberg, *President*
EMP: 4
SALES: 220K **Privately Held**
SIC: **8331** 2411 2731 Job training & vocational rehabilitation services; poles, posts & pilings: untreated wood; book publishing

(G-5868)
WHEELCHAIR ADL SOLUTIONS
23614 E Sprague Ave (99019-9621)
PHONE.................................509 228-8293
Matt Allen, *Principal*
EMP: 3
SALES (est): 130K **Privately Held**
SIC: **3842** Wheelchairs

(G-5869)
XOCECO USA
225 N Holiday Hills Dr (99019-5049)
PHONE.................................509 808-2480
EMP: 2
SALES (est): 72.5K **Privately Held**
SIC: **5064** 3663 Television sets; marine radio communications equipment

---

Lilliwaup
Mason County

(G-5870)
BLOOMFIELD LIGHT INDUSTRIES
40 N Lon Webb Rd (98555-9712)
PHONE.................................360 877-5718
EMP: 2 **EST:** 2010
SALES (est): 83.4K **Privately Held**
SIC: **3999** Mfg Misc Products

(G-5871)
HAL BURTON PUBLISHING & DIST
61 N Picnic Dr (98555-9793)
PHONE.................................360 877-0613
Harold Burton, *Principal*
EMP: 2
SALES (est): 102.5K **Privately Held**
SIC: **2741** Miscellaneous publishing

(G-5872)
NORA HAUGAN
Also Called: Nora Enterprises
950 N Colony Surf Dr (98555-9784)
PHONE.................................360 877-0602
Nora Haugan, *Owner*
EMP: 2
SALES: 30K **Privately Held**
SIC: **8721** 3961 Accounting services, except auditing; jewelry apparel, non-precious metals

---

Long Beach
Pacific County

(G-5873)
EAST OREGONIAN PUBLISHING CO
205 Bolstad Ave Ste (98631)
P.O. Box 427 (98631-0427)
PHONE.................................360 642-8181
Matt Winters, *Manager*
EMP: 7
SALES (corp-wide): 15.4MM **Privately Held**
WEB: www.eastoregonrealestate.com
SIC: **2711** Newspapers, publishing & printing

PA: East Oregonian Publishing Co Inc
1400 Broadway St Ne
Salem OR
541 276-2211

(G-5874)
ENERGY CONSULTING SERVICES LLC
1504 196th St (98631-7032)
PHONE.................................701 580-9732
Lea Cote, *Administration*
EMP: 2
SALES (est): 167.4K **Privately Held**
SIC: **1311** 7389 Crude petroleum & natural gas production;

(G-5875)
PACIFIC COAST TOOLS LLC
1306 197th St (98631-7019)
PHONE.................................360 244-5087
Raymond L Kramer, *Administration*
EMP: 4
SALES (est): 165.6K **Privately Held**
SIC: **3799** Transportation equipment

(G-5876)
PENINSULA SHEET METAL INC
312 6th St Ne (98631-3926)
P.O. Box 501 (98631-0501)
PHONE.................................360 642-2102
Dale Jacobson, *President*
Jean Jacobson, *Corp Secy*
EMP: 2
SALES (est): 253.2K **Privately Held**
SIC: **3444** Sheet metalwork

(G-5877)
PIERSON & SON CONSTRUCTION
18000 Sandridge Rd (98631-6903)
PHONE.................................360 642-2796
Woody J Pierson, *President*
Carol Pierson, *Vice Pres*
EMP: 3
SALES: 500K **Privately Held**
SIC: **1794** 2411 Excavation work; logging camps & contractors

(G-5878)
STARVATION ALLEY SOCIA
Also Called: Starvation Alley Farms
15202 Birch St (98631-6203)
PHONE.................................503 440-0970
Jared Oakes,
EMP: 2
SALES (est): 132.3K **Privately Held**
SIC: **2033** Fruit juices: packaged in cans, jars, etc.

Longbranch
Pierce County

(G-5879)
NCE INC
Also Called: Harvest Timber Company
5005 Mahncke Rd Sw (98351-9557)
P.O. Box 59, Lakebay (98349-0059)
PHONE.................................253 884-6255
Glen Ehrhardt, *President*
EMP: 3
SALES (est): 330K **Privately Held**
WEB: www.harvest-timber.com
SIC: **3996** Hard surface floor coverings

(G-5880)
SUMMITCLIMB INC
5212 Whiskey Beach Ln Sw (98351-9569)
P.O. Box 123, Lakebay (98349-0123)
PHONE.................................360 570-0715
Murari K Sharma, *Principal*
EMP: 3
SALES (est): 218.2K **Privately Held**
SIC: **2515** Foundations & platforms

Longview
Cowlitz County

(G-5881)
ABC PRINTERS INC
1291 Industrial Way (98631-1022)
PHONE.................................360 423-6991
Cecil Sonny Martin, *Partner*
Kay Benson, *Partner*
Larry Benson, *Partner*
Cecil Martin, *Partner*
Pam Martin, *Partner*
EMP: 4
SQ FT: 4,000
SALES (est): 480.6K **Privately Held**
SIC: **2752** Commercial printing, offset

(G-5882)
ADVANTAGE SCREEN PRINTING
1706 12th Ave (98632-3939)
PHONE.................................360 425-7343
Rick Huckaby, *Owner*
EMP: 2
SALES (est): 195.6K **Privately Held**
SIC: **2752** Commercial printing, offset

(G-5883)
AESSEAL INC
960 Industrial Way Ste 8 (98632-1041)
PHONE.................................360 414-0118
Tom Grove, *Branch Mgr*
EMP: 4
SALES (est): 297.9K
SALES (corp-wide): 232.8MM **Privately Held**
SIC: **2754** Seals: gravure printing
HQ: Aesseal Inc.
355 Dunavant Dr
Rockford TN 37853

(G-5884)
AIR PRO HEATING & COOLING LLC
Also Called: Honeywell Authorized Dealer
967 3rd Ave Ste A (98632-3373)
PHONE.................................360 423-9165
Ernest Halleck, *Principal*
Ernie Halleck,
EMP: 16
SALES (est): 1.2MM **Privately Held**
SIC: **1711** 1761 3444 7699 Heating systems repair & maintenance; heating & air conditioning contractors; warm air heating & air conditioning contractor; architectural sheet metal work; flues & pipes, stove or furnace: sheet metal; gas appliance repair service

(G-5885)
ALDER GROVE DISTRIBUTORS
1559 32nd Ave (98632-3300)
PHONE.................................360 423-3138
Donna Madsen, *Owner*
Kenneth Hadson, *Co-Owner*
EMP: 2
SALES: 10K **Privately Held**
SIC: **2771** Greeting cards

(G-5886)
AWARDS N MORE USA INC
825 Hillcrest Dr (98632-5640)
PHONE.................................360 577-3646
Christine Jones, *President*
EMP: 2
SALES: 150K **Privately Held**
WEB: www.awardsnmoreusainc.com
SIC: **3479** Engraving jewelry silverware, or metal

(G-5887)
AXIALL CORPORATION
3541 Industrial Way (98632-9286)
PHONE.................................360 577-3232
EMP: 65 **Publicly Held**
SIC: **2821** Plastics materials & resins
HQ: Axiall Corporation
1000 Abernathy Rd # 1200
Atlanta GA 30328
304 455-2200

(G-5888)
BIG C INDUSTRIES LLC
3339 Washington Way (98632-1942)
PHONE.................................844 406-2442
Tom Ball, *Vice Pres*
Ronda Cross,
EMP: 9 **EST:** 2015
SQ FT: 7,200
SALES (est): 505.7K **Privately Held**
SIC: **3441** 3449 3446 Building components, structural steel; expansion joints (structural shapes), iron or steel; bars, concrete reinforcing: fabricated steel; curtain walls for buildings, steel; fences or posts, ornamental iron or steel

(G-5889)
BONNIE PRESS
115 Crown Point Rd (98632-5918)
PHONE.................................360 807-4442
Bonnie Press, *Principal*
EMP: 4
SALES (est): 7.9K **Privately Held**
SIC: **2741** Miscellaneous publishing

(G-5890)
BRECHT-PACIFIC PUBLISHING INC
884 11th Ave (98632-2402)
PHONE.................................360 425-4671
EMP: 40
SALES: 1.3MM **Privately Held**
SIC: **7311** 7336 2741 Advertising Agency Commercial Art/Graphic Design Misc Publishing

(G-5891)
BUD CLARY PROPERTIES LLC
1030 Commerce Ave (98632-2514)
PHONE.................................800 899-1926
James E Clary, *Principal*
EMP: 2
SALES (est): 197.3K **Privately Held**
SIC: **1382** Oil & gas exploration services

(G-5892)
C H W ENTERPRISES INC
1341 Industrial Way (98632-1017)
P.O. Box 722 (98632-7464)
PHONE.................................360 425-8700
Spencer C Wiggins, *President*
EMP: 15
SALES (corp-wide): 2.9MM **Privately Held**
SIC: **7699** 3621 Industrial machinery & equipment repair; motors & generators
PA: C. H. W. Enterprises, Inc
1331 Baltimore St
Longview WA 98632
360 425-8700

(G-5893)
CALPORTLAND COMPANY
1100 3rd Ave (98632-3205)
PHONE.................................360 423-8112
James Repman, *President*
EMP: 4 **Privately Held**
SIC: **3273** Ready-mixed concrete
HQ: Calportland Company
2025 E Financial Way
Glendora CA 91741
626 852-6200

(G-5894)
CARAUSTAR INDUSTRIES INC
620 11th Ave (98632-1619)
P.O. Box 3016 (98632)
PHONE.................................360 423-3420
Carl Depalna, *Vice Pres*
Chuck Miller, *Engineer*
Judith Paine, *Human Res Mgr*
EMP: 30
SALES (corp-wide): 3.8B **Publicly Held**
WEB: www.newarkpaperboardproducts.com
SIC: **2679** 2672 2631 Paper products, converted; coated & laminated paper; coated paperboard
HQ: Caraustar Industries, Inc.
5000 Austell Powder Sprin
Austell GA 30106
770 948-3101

GEOGRAPHIC SECTION

(G-5895)
CASCADE ALES COMPANY
3621 Oak St (98632-4728)
PHONE.................................360 520-6040
George Seiler, *Owner*
EMP: 9
SALES (est): 400K **Privately Held**
SIC: 2082 5813 Beer (alcoholic beverage); tavern (drinking places)

(G-5896)
CASCADE HYDRAULICS AND MACHINE
420 Industrial Way (98632-1006)
P.O. Box 2787 (98632-8768)
PHONE.................................360 423-1082
David Fleming, *President*
Harold Fleming, *Shareholder*
EMP: 25
SQ FT: 12,000
SALES (est): 2.7MM **Privately Held**
SIC: 3599 Machine shop, jobbing & repair

(G-5897)
CASUAL FRIDAYS
3232 Nebraska St (98632-4229)
PHONE.................................360 425-8841
Dan Shuflin, *Partner*
Barbara Shuflin, *Partner*
EMP: 3 **EST:** 1995
SALES: 80K **Privately Held**
SIC: 5699 2395 Customized clothing & apparel; emblems, embroidered

(G-5898)
CASUAL FRIDAYS CUSTOM E M B
3232 Nebraska St (98632-4229)
PHONE.................................360 425-8841
Barbara Shuflin, *Owner*
Dan Shuflin, *Co-Owner*
EMP: 2
SQ FT: 1,000
SALES (est): 89.5K **Privately Held**
SIC: 2395 Embroidery & art needlework

(G-5899)
CHRISTIAN HAMILTON
Also Called: H Enterprises
3376 Olive Way (98632-4244)
PHONE.................................360 442-4900
Christian Hamilton, *Owner*
EMP: 2
SALES (est): 49.3K **Privately Held**
SIC: 5961 8748 1731 7699 Computer equipment & electronics, mail order; catalog sales; systems engineering consultant, ex. computer or professional; computer installation; scale repair service; electrical equipment repair services; electronic computers

(G-5900)
COLUMBIA RIVER READER
1333 14th Ave (98632-3701)
PHONE.................................360 636-6097
Sue Piper, *Publisher*
Susan Piper, *Principal*
EMP: 4 **EST:** 2012
SALES (est): 231.4K **Privately Held**
SIC: 2711 Newspapers

(G-5901)
COLUMBIA TARP LINER & SUP CO
3048 Lindsey Dr (98632-5405)
P.O. Box 1674 (98632-8018)
PHONE.................................360 577-1834
EMP: 2
SALES: 50K **Privately Held**
SIC: 2394 Mfg Canvas/Related Products

(G-5902)
COPRINTCO BUSINESS FORMS INC
1146 15th Ave Ste 100 (98632-3175)
P.O. Box 6 (98632-7006)
PHONE.................................360 425-1810
Amy Sides, *CFO*
EMP: 25
SQ FT: 25,000
SALES (est): 4MM **Privately Held**
WEB: www.coprintco.net
SIC: 2752 2759 Business forms, lithographed; envelopes; printing

(G-5903)
COWLITZ RIVER RIGGING INC
1540 Industrial Way (98632-1018)
PHONE.................................360 425-6720
Dennis Wallace, *President*
Chris Wallace, *Vice Pres*
Scott Wallace, *Vice Pres*
Wayne Wallace, *Vice Pres*
EMP: 14
SQ FT: 20,000
SALES (est): 2.6MM **Privately Held**
WEB: www.loggingsupply.com
SIC: 5251 3496 Tools; miscellaneous fabricated wire products

(G-5904)
CREW CUSTOM HOLSTERS
2824 Fir St (98632-2025)
PHONE.................................360 270-3588
EMP: 2
SALES (est): 126.4K **Privately Held**
SIC: 3199 Holsters, leather

(G-5905)
CRW TIMBER
540 22nd Ave (98632-1308)
PHONE.................................360 425-4858
EMP: 3 **EST:** 2005
SALES (est): 170K **Privately Held**
SIC: 2411 Logging

(G-5906)
DOCUMENT MGT ARCHIVES LLC
1021 Columbia Blvd (98632-1024)
P.O. Box 488 (98632-7317)
PHONE.................................360 501-5047
Patricia Rodman,
EMP: 4 **EST:** 1998
SALES (est): 480.9K **Privately Held**
SIC: 3589 Shredders, industrial & commercial

(G-5907)
DONALD R JACOBSON
Also Called: Jacobson Logging
2525 Germany Creek Rd (98632-4380)
PHONE.................................360 425-4346
Donald R Jacobson, *Owner*
EMP: 2
SALES (est): 88.3K **Privately Held**
SIC: 0851 2411 Reforestation services; logging camps & contractors

(G-5908)
E L F SOFTWARE DISTRIBUTORS
156 Monticello Dr (98632-9543)
PHONE.................................360 577-6163
Betty Erickson, *President*
John Freerks, *Corp Secy*
EMP: 5
SQ FT: 2,200
SALES (est): 269.1K **Privately Held**
SIC: 7372 7371 Prepackaged software; computer software development

(G-5909)
EPSON TOYOCOM SEATTLE INC
1850 Prudential Blvd (98632-9828)
PHONE.................................360 200-5537
Shin Hashimoto, *President*
◆ **EMP:** 11 **EST:** 2000
SALES (est): 1.8MM **Privately Held**
SIC: 3679 Electronic crystals
PA: Seiko Epson Corporation
  3-3-5, Owa
  Suwa NAG 392-0

(G-5910)
FABRICAST VALVE LLC
1061 Industrial Way (98632-1030)
PHONE.................................360 425-0306
Jon Hansen, *Manager*
Steve Norby,
Sid Somers,
▲ **EMP:** 17
SALES (est): 4.1MM **Privately Held**
SIC: 3491 Industrial valves

(G-5911)
FLOURISH SKIN & LASER LLC (PA)
625 9th Ave Ste 230 (98632-2465)
PHONE.................................360 636-1411
Mary Boaglio, *Mng Member*
Amy Hannahs,
EMP: 12
SALES (est): 2.2MM **Privately Held**
SIC: 3845 Laser systems & equipment, medical

(G-5912)
GORLEYS PRECISION MACHINE
2302 Lee Ave (98632-5031)
PHONE.................................360 423-4567
EMP: 10
SQ FT: 5,000
SALES (est): 1MM **Privately Held**
SIC: 3599 7692 Mfg Industrial Machinery Welding Repair

(G-5913)
GUARDIAN INTERLOCK SYSTEMS
560 Industrial Way (98632-1008)
PHONE.................................360 423-4766
EMP: 2
SALES (est): 153.2K **Privately Held**
SIC: 3829 Mfg Measuring/Controlling Devices

(G-5914)
HANGER INC
Also Called: Hanger Clinic
1516 Hudson St Ste 105 (98632-3046)
PHONE.................................360 423-6049
Sam Liang, *President*
Tim Vanas, *Manager*
Tim Zanas, *Manager*
Ally Nillis, *Director*
EMP: 5
SALES (corp-wide): 1B **Publicly Held**
SIC: 3842 Surgical appliances & supplies
PA: Hanger, Inc.
  10910 Domain Dr Ste 300
  Austin TX 78758
  512 777-3800

(G-5915)
HANGER PRSTHETCS & ORTHO INC
1516 Hudson St Ste 105 (98632-3046)
PHONE.................................360 423-6049
Tim Zanas, *Branch Mgr*
Sheryl Price, *Director*
EMP: 5
SALES (corp-wide): 1B **Publicly Held**
SIC: 3842 Orthopedic appliances; limbs, artificial
HQ: Hanger Prosthetics & Orthotics, Inc.
  10910 Domain Dr Ste 300
  Austin TX 78758
  512 777-3800

(G-5916)
HASA INC
3539 Industrial Way (98632-9286)
P.O. Box 1173 (98632-7693)
PHONE.................................360 578-9300
Arlen Proctor, *Branch Mgr*
EMP: 25
SALES (corp-wide): 72.3MM **Privately Held**
WEB: www.hasapool.com
SIC: 2812 Chlorine, compressed or liquefied
PA: Hasa, Inc.
  23119 Drayton St
  Santa Clarita CA 91350
  661 259-5848

(G-5917)
IMPERIUM RENEWABLES INC (HQ)
821 3rd Ave (98632-2105)
PHONE.................................360 532-2387
John Plaza, *President*
Mark Warner, *President*
▲ **EMP:** 5
SQ FT: 27,300
SALES (est): 10.8MM
SALES (corp-wide): 2.3B **Publicly Held**
WEB: www.imperiumrenewables.com
SIC: 2869 Fuels
PA: Renewable Energy Group, Inc.
  416 S Bell Ave
  Ames IA 50010
  515 239-8000

(G-5918)
INNOCOR FOAM TECHNOLOGIES LLC
1205 Prudential Blvd (98632-9822)
PHONE.................................360 575-8844
EMP: 10
SALES (corp-wide): 209.9MM **Privately Held**
SIC: 3069 Bathmats, rubber
HQ: Innocor Foam Technologies, Llc
  200 Schulz Dr Ste 2
  Red Bank NJ 07701

(G-5919)
INTERFOR US INC
540 3rd Ave (98632-1652)
P.O. Box 1398 (98632-7824)
PHONE.................................360 575-3600
Doug Caffall, *Branch Mgr*
EMP: 100
SALES (corp-wide): 1.6B **Privately Held**
WEB: www.simpsondoor.com
SIC: 2411 2421 Wooden logs; piling, wood; untreated; lumber: rough, sawed or planed
HQ: Interfor U.S. Inc.
  700 Westpark Dr Ste 100
  Peachtree City GA 30269
  360 788-2299

(G-5920)
JANS CERAMICS
Also Called: Fern's Feature Pens Doll Molds
1223 Commerce Ave (98632-3026)
PHONE.................................360 425-3540
Janet Norton, *Owner*
EMP: 2
SQ FT: 2,700
SALES (est): 128.4K **Privately Held**
SIC: 3269 5719 5947 Art & ornamental ware, pottery; pottery; gift shop

(G-5921)
K L COOK INC
Also Called: Signmaster
1317 15th Ave (98632-3705)
PHONE.................................360 423-0195
Charles Rak, *President*
EMP: 4
SQ FT: 1,000
SALES: 145K **Privately Held**
SIC: 3993 Signs, not made in custom sign painting shops

(G-5922)
KENS ENGRAVING EMPORIUM INC
1165 Commerce Ave (98632-3024)
PHONE.................................360 578-0844
EMP: 3 **EST:** 2006
SQ FT: 2,000
SALES: 80K **Privately Held**
SIC: 2759 Commercial Printing

(G-5923)
KITCHENS ETC
904 12th Ave (98632-2508)
PHONE.................................360 430-4272
Kerri Scroggins, *Principal*
EMP: 4
SALES (est): 341.4K **Privately Held**
SIC: 2434 Wood kitchen cabinets

(G-5924)
KOEHLER ENTERPRISE INC
Also Called: Eagle Cliffs Distilery
160 Whitewater Rd (98632-8197)
PHONE.................................360 261-0390
John Koehler, *CEO*
Laura Koehler, *Vice Pres*
EMP: 3 **EST:** 2010
SALES (est): 210.8K **Privately Held**
SIC: 3944 Craft & hobby kits & sets

(G-5925)
LAKESIDE INDUSTRIES INC
500 Tennant Way (98632-2449)
P.O. Box 576 (98632-7372)
PHONE.................................360 423-6882
Ron Green, *Branch Mgr*

Longview - Cowlitz County (G-5926)

EMP: 50
SALES (corp-wide): 326.4MM **Privately Held**
WEB: www.lakesideind.com
SIC: 1611 2951 5032 Highway & street paving contractor; asphalt & asphaltic paving mixtures (not from refineries); gravel
PA: Lakeside Industries, Inc.
6505 226th Pl Se Ste 200
Issaquah WA 98027
425 313-2600

(G-5926)
LEE PUBLICATIONS INC
Also Called: Daily News
770 11th Ave (98632-2412)
PHONE 360 577-2500
EMP: 12
SALES (corp-wide): 656.7MM **Publicly Held**
SIC: 2711 Newspapers-Publishing/Printing
HQ: Lee Publications, Inc.
201 N Harrison St Ste 600
Davenport IA 52801
563 383-2100

(G-5927)
LITTLE INDIAN EMBROIDERY
527 Coal Creek Rd (98632-9154)
PHONE 360 414-4165
Teri Skinner, *Owner*
EMP: 4
SALES (est): 197.2K **Privately Held**
SIC: 2395 Embroidery products, except schiffli machine; embroidery & art needlework

(G-5928)
LIVING WATERS LOGGING LLC
921 Hudson St (98632-3141)
PHONE 360 749-6333
EMP: 2
SALES (est): 81.7K **Privately Held**
SIC: 2411 Logging

(G-5929)
LONGVIEW AUTO WRECKING
Also Called: Alphase Used Autos
2001 38th Ave (98632-9441)
PHONE 360 423-9327
Charles Wallace, *Owner*
EMP: 3
SALES (est): 277.9K **Privately Held**
SIC: 3536 5521 5093 Hoists, cranes & monorails; used car dealers; scrap & waste materials

(G-5930)
LONGVIEW FIBRE PPR & PACKG INC (DH)
Also Called: Kapstone
300 Fibre Way (98632-1199)
P.O. Box 639 (98632-7411)
PHONE 360 425-1550
Roger W Stone, *CEO*
Matthew Kaplan, *President*
Randy Nebel, *Principal*
Lou Loosbrock, *Vice Pres*
Andrea K Tarbox, *CFO*
◆ **EMP:** 809
SQ FT: 100,000
SALES (est): 407.8MM
SALES (corp-wide): 16.2B **Publicly Held**
WEB: www.longviewfibre.com
SIC: 2653 Corrugated & solid fiber boxes
HQ: Kapstone Paper And Packaging Corporation
1000 Abernathy Rd
Atlanta GA 30328
770 448-2193

(G-5931)
MARK 3 LOGGING
2151 Delaware St (98632-2233)
PHONE 360 577-8833
Bart Kilgore, *President*
Julie Kilgore, *Principal*
EMP: 2
SALES (est): 202K **Privately Held**
SIC: 2411 Logging camps & contractors

(G-5932)
MOORE-CLARK USA INC (DH)
Also Called: Bio-Oregon
1140 Industrial Way (98632-1021)
PHONE 360 425-6715
Ron Gowan, *CEO*
◆ **EMP:** 38
SALES (est): 4.5MM **Privately Held**
SIC: 3999 Pet supplies
HQ: Nutreco N.V.
Stationsstraat 77
Amersfoort
334 226-100

(G-5933)
NELSON-BALL PAPER PRODUCTS
Also Called: Newark Paperboard Products
620 11th Ave (98632-1619)
PHONE 360 423-3420
Fred P Thompson Jr, *CEO*
Andy M Stewart III, *President*
Juan Del Valle, *Vice Pres*
Eugene C Thomas, *Vice Pres*
▼ **EMP:** 167
SQ FT: 66,000
SALES (est): 18.7MM **Privately Held**
SIC: 2655 2679 Tubes, fiber or paper: made from purchased material; cores, fiber: made from purchased material; paper products, converted

(G-5934)
NETZERO ENERGY LLC
Also Called: Dynamic Energy Solutions
1339 Commerce Ave Ste 314 (98632-3729)
PHONE 360 636-5337
Barry Redman, *CEO*
Greg Wright, *President*
EMP: 3
SQ FT: 1,500
SALES (est): 350K **Privately Held**
SIC: 1731 3646 3648 3641 Lighting contractor; commercial indusl & institutional electric lighting fixtures; floodlights; street lighting fixtures; electric light bulbs, complete; tubes, electric light

(G-5935)
NIPPON DYNAWAVE PACKG CO LLC (HQ)
Also Called: Nippon Dynawave Packaging Co.
3401 Industrial Way (98632-9285)
PHONE 360 425-2150
John Carpenter, *President*
EMP: 540
SALES (est): 22.1MM **Privately Held**
SIC: 2657 2631 5113 2621 Paperboard backs for blister or skin packages; packaging board; cups, disposable plastic & paper; paper & products, wrapping or coarse; wrapping & packaging papers; pulp mills

(G-5936)
NIPPON PAPER INDS USA CO LTD (DH)
Also Called: Parent Is Nppon Ppr Inds Japan
3401 Industrial Way (98632-9285)
P.O. Box 271, Port Angeles (98362-0044)
PHONE 360 457-4474
Yoshifumi Nagaura, *President*
Steve Johnson, *Vice Pres*
Minori Yabu, *Treasurer*
Cathy Price, *Admin Sec*
◆ **EMP:** 8
SQ FT: 3,000
SALES (est): 62.9MM **Privately Held**
SIC: 2621 2421 Paper mills; wood chips, produced at mill
HQ: Daishowa North America Corporation
510 Burrard St
Vancouver BC
604 684-4326

(G-5937)
NORTH PACIFIC PAPER CO LLC
Also Called: Norpac
3001 Industrial Way (98632-1057)
P.O. Box 2069 (98632-8191)
PHONE 360 636-6400
Craig Anneberg, *CEO*
Nick Karavolos, *Vice Pres*
Judy Werner, *Buyer*
Karl CPM, *Manager*
Scott Dalquist, *Manager*
◆ **EMP:** 410 **EST:** 1976
SQ FT: 100,000
SALES (est): 221.8MM **Privately Held**
SIC: 5084 3554 2621 Paper manufacturing machinery; paper mill machinery: plating, slitting, waxing, etc.; newsprint paper
HQ: Np Paper Company, Llc
3001 Industrial Way
Longview WA 98632
360 636-6400

(G-5938)
NP PAPER COMPANY LLC (HQ)
3001 Industrial Way (98632-1057)
P.O. Box 2069 (98632-8191)
PHONE 360 636-6400
Tony W Lee, *Principal*
EMP: 3
SALES (est): 386.3MM **Privately Held**
SIC: 2621 Newsprint paper

(G-5939)
NW COFFEE ROSTERS LLC
Also Called: Zojo Coffee
1335 14th Ave (98632-3701)
PHONE 360 442-4111
EMP: 12
SALES (est): 53.2K **Privately Held**
SIC: 5499 2095 Ret Misc Foods Mfg Roasted Coffee

(G-5940)
PACIFIC DOOR & WINDOW INC
1041 Columbia Blvd (98632-1054)
PHONE 360 577-9121
Boyd R Burns, *President*
EMP: 11 **EST:** 1979
SQ FT: 11,000
SALES (est): 1.4MM **Privately Held**
SIC: 2431 2434 5211 Doors, wood; wood kitchen cabinets; windows, storm: wood or metal

(G-5941)
PACIFIC FIBRE PRODUCTS INC (PA)
20 Fibre Way (98632-1038)
P.O. Box 278 (98632-7173)
PHONE 360 577-7112
Larry Lemmons, *President*
EMP: 100
SQ FT: 1,500
SALES (est): 26.4MM **Privately Held**
SIC: 2421 Chipper mill

(G-5942)
PET MEDIA PLUS LLC
1502 9th Ave (98632-4113)
PHONE 360 425-0188
George Ford, *Principal*
EMP: 3
SALES (est): 207.5K **Privately Held**
SIC: 5199 5149 3999 Pet supplies; pet foods; pet supplies

(G-5943)
PETERSON MANUFACTURING CO
1005 California Way (98632-1614)
PHONE 360 425-4170
Donald Peterson, *President*
JD Peterson, *Vice Pres*
Thomas N Peterson, *Vice Pres*
Robert W Peterson, *Treasurer*
EMP: 13 **EST:** 1923
SQ FT: 7,500
SALES (est): 1.3MM **Privately Held**
SIC: 2421 3953 2434 Planing mill, independent: except millwork; furniture dimension stock, softwood; marking devices; wood kitchen cabinets

(G-5944)
POTTER-WEBSTER CO
1110 Columbia Blvd Ste A (98632-1052)
PHONE 360 577-9632
Scott Meyer, *Manager*
EMP: 6
SALES (corp-wide): 16.6MM **Privately Held**
WEB: www.potterwebster.com
SIC: 3537 3714 3566 Industrial trucks & tractors; motor vehicle parts & accessories; speed changers, drives & gears
PA: Potter-Webster Co.
41 Ne Walker St
Portland OR 97211
503 283-3392

(G-5945)
PROGRAPHYX
735 Commerce Ave (98632-2415)
PHONE 360 636-1595
Calvin Dowd, *Owner*
EMP: 2
SALES (est): 143.8K **Privately Held**
SIC: 2395 Embroidery products, except schiffli machine

(G-5946)
R & R RODS
4543 Columbia Heights Rd (98632-9563)
PHONE 360 423-7935
Randy Thompson, *Owner*
Robert Sherade, *Partner*
EMP: 2
SALES (est): 124K **Privately Held**
SIC: 3949 Rods & rod parts, fishing

(G-5947)
REPROGRAPHICS INC
1444 12th Ave (98632-3822)
P.O. Box 125 (98632-7077)
PHONE 360 423-1237
Tom Gunn, *President*
Pat Gunn, *Vice Pres*
Beth Gunn, *Admin Sec*
EMP: 6
SQ FT: 4,500
SALES (est): 500K **Privately Held**
WEB: www.reproprinting.com
SIC: 2752 Commercial printing, offset

(G-5948)
RODDA PAINT CO
Also Called: Rodda Paint Longview Lv55
541 California Way (98632-1609)
PHONE 360 423-4990
Callie Gieseke, *Principal*
EMP: 6
SALES (corp-wide): 237.5MM **Privately Held**
WEB: www.roddapaint.com
SIC: 2851 5198 5023 5231 Paints & paint additives; paints; paint brushes, rollers, sprayers; wallcoverings; window furnishings; window covering parts & accessories; paint; paint brushes, rollers, sprayers & other supplies; wallcoverings; window furnishings
HQ: Rodda Paint Co.
6107 N Marine Dr Ste 3
Portland OR 97203
503 521-4300

(G-5949)
ROEMER ELECTRIC STEEL FOUNDRY
523 7th Ave (98632-1653)
PHONE 360 423-1330
Lowell Roemer, *President*
George S Roemer Jr, *Vice Pres*
EMP: 36 **EST:** 1929
SQ FT: 21,000
SALES (est): 6.1MM **Privately Held**
SIC: 3325 3543 3369 Alloy steel castings, except investment; foundry patternmaking; nonferrous foundries

(G-5950)
SAINT SQUARE PUBLISHING
Also Called: St2 Publishing
191 Inglewood Dr (98632-5778)
PHONE 360 636-2645
Timothy Trinkle, *Partner*
Steve Selby, *Partner*
Thomas Sitts, *Partner*
EMP: 3
SALES: 40K **Privately Held**
WEB: www.st2pub.com
SIC: 2731 Book publishing

GEOGRAPHIC SECTION

Lopez Island - San Juan County (G-5981)

(G-5951)
SCREEN PRINT NORTHWEST INC
Also Called: Spnw
1141 Commerce Ave (98632-3024)
PHONE...................360 577-1534
Jillene Holter, *President*
Jim Holter, *Vice Pres*
EMP: 4
SQ FT: 7,200
SALES: 450K **Privately Held**
SIC: 2396 5099 3993 Screen printing on fabric articles; novelties, durable; signs & advertising specialties

(G-5952)
SERVICE SURPLUS & CRAFTS
112 Clark Creek Ln (98632-9623)
PHONE...................360 636-0250
Darrel Eisele, *Partner*
Cynthia Eisele, *Partner*
EMP: 2
SALES (est): 130K **Privately Held**
SIC: 2741 Miscellaneous publishing

(G-5953)
SILICON & SOLAR MFG LLC
1401 Industrial Way # 100 (98632-1037)
PHONE...................360 703-0701
Renie Duvall,
EMP: 19
SALES (est): 1.6MM **Privately Held**
SIC: 3496 Miscellaneous fabricated wire products

(G-5954)
SLAPSHOT USA LTD LIABILITY CO
2637 Maplewood Dr (98632-4604)
PHONE...................360 560-0245
Randy Teig, *Owner*
EMP: 3
SALES (est): 120.6K **Privately Held**
SIC: 3483 7389 Ammunition, except for small arms;

(G-5955)
SOLVAY CHEMICALS INC
3500 Industrial Way (98632-9482)
P.O. Box 2099 (98632-8213)
PHONE...................360 425-1114
W R Reade, *Branch Mgr*
Richard Reymont, *Supervisor*
EMP: 45
SALES (corp-wide): 12.8MM **Privately Held**
SIC: 2819 2812 Peroxides, hydrogen peroxide; sodium bicarbonate
HQ: Solvay Chemicals, Inc.
3737 Buffalo Speedway
Houston TX 77098
713 525-6800

(G-5956)
SPECIALTY MOTORS MFG LLC
641 California Way (98632-1611)
P.O. Box 157 (98632-7098)
PHONE...................360 423-9880
Louis A Hunziker, *Partner*
Sharon Gottfryd, *Partner*
EMP: 4
SALES (est): 631K **Privately Held**
WEB: www.specialtymotorsmfg.com
SIC: 3443 3569 3536 3546 Tanks, standard or custom fabricated: metal plate; jacks, hydraulic; boat lifts; chain saws, portable

(G-5957)
STUART ORTHOTICS LLC
1555 3rd Ave Ste B (98632-3268)
PHONE...................360 577-3505
Victoria Miller, *Partner*
David Stuart, *Partner*
EMP: 2
SALES (est): 206.9K **Privately Held**
SIC: 3842 5661 Foot appliances, orthopedic; custom & orthopedic shoes

(G-5958)
SURE TRAX LLC
5005 Mt Solo Rd (98632-9211)
PHONE...................360 430-8343
Jerry McRary, *President*
EMP: 3
SALES: 250K **Privately Held**
SIC: 3842 Traction apparatus

(G-5959)
TENACIOUS HGS JAMS
447 23rd Ave (98632-1313)
PHONE...................360 747-4080
Aimee Rios, *Principal*
EMP: 3
SALES (est): 143K **Privately Held**
SIC: 2033 Jams, jellies & preserves: packaged in cans, jars, etc.

(G-5960)
TOP NOTCH MANUFACTURING CO
Also Called: Action West
1556 3rd Ave (98632-3229)
PHONE...................360 577-9150
Mark J Kuning, *President*
Patty J Kuning, *Vice Pres*
EMP: 2
SALES (est): 200.1K **Privately Held**
SIC: 3669 3993 3444 Transportation signaling devices; signs & advertising specialties; sheet metalwork

(G-5961)
TRIUMPH AEROSTRUCTURES LLC
4029 Industrial Way (98632-9461)
PHONE...................310 355-3826
EMP: 2 **Publicly Held**
SIC: 3721 Aircraft
HQ: Triumph Aerostructures, Llc
300 Austin Blvd
Red Oak TX 75154

(G-5962)
V O PRINTERS INC
1213 14th Ave (98632-3018)
PHONE...................360 577-0038
Thuy Vo, *President*
Anh Nguyen, *Vice Pres*
EMP: 8
SQ FT: 5,000
SALES: 644.6K **Privately Held**
SIC: 2752 2791 Commercial printing, offset; typesetting

(G-5963)
WAHOO FABRICATION
1171 3rd Ave (98632-3204)
PHONE...................360 353-3478
EMP: 2
SALES (est): 127.2K **Privately Held**
SIC: 3599 Mfg Industrial Machinery

(G-5964)
WAITE SPECIALITY MCH WORK INC
1356 Tennant Way (98632-2424)
PHONE...................360 577-0777
Steve Waite, *President*
Bob Thompson, *COO*
Rob Conner, *Project Mgr*
Jake Kelsey, *Project Mgr*
Harry Herod, *Sales Associate*
EMP: 75
SQ FT: 25,000
SALES (est): 1.7MM **Privately Held**
WEB: www.waitespecialty.com
SIC: 5051 3599 Iron & steel (ferrous) products; machine & other job shop work

(G-5965)
WESTROCK COMPANY
300 Fibre Way (98632-1199)
PHONE...................360 575-5256
EMP: 2
SALES (est): 236.2K **Privately Held**
SIC: 2621 Specialty or chemically treated papers

(G-5966)
WEYERHAEUSER COMPANY
Also Called: Weyhaeuser Co
3401 Industrial Way (98632-9285)
PHONE...................360 425-2150
Don Shilly, *Principal*
EMP: 400
SALES (corp-wide): 7.4B **Publicly Held**
SIC: 0811 2411 Timber tracts; logging
PA: Weyerhaeuser Company
220 Occidental Ave S
Seattle WA 98104
206 539-3000

(G-5967)
WEYERHAEUSER COMPANY
120 Industrial Way (98632-1004)
PHONE...................360 577-6678
Kim Newbury, *Branch Mgr*
EMP: 220
SALES (corp-wide): 7.4B **Publicly Held**
SIC: 2421 2426 Sawmills & planing mills, general; hardwood dimension & flooring mills
PA: Weyerhaeuser Company
220 Occidental Ave S
Seattle WA 98104
206 539-3000

(G-5968)
WHITTEN GROUP INTERNATIONAL
2622 Lilac St (98632-3525)
PHONE...................360 560-3319
Ronald W Whitten, *President*
Ron Whitten, *President*
EMP: 12
SQ FT: 3,000
SALES: 100.2MM **Privately Held**
SIC: 5172 3559 Service station supplies, petroleum; petroleum refinery equipment

(G-5969)
WIEST LOGGING
1616 Abernathy Creek Rd (98632-9765)
PHONE...................360 423-3560
Andy Wiest, *Owner*
Jan Wiest, *Partner*
EMP: 2
SALES (est): 135.9K **Privately Held**
SIC: 2411 Logging camps & contractors

(G-5970)
YUM YUM DONUT SHOPS INC
Also Called: Winchell's Donut House
1560 15th Ave (98632-3918)
PHONE...................360 423-0150
Dee Jessup, *Manager*
EMP: 9 **Privately Held**
SIC: 5461 2045 2051 Doughnuts; doughnut mixes, prepared: from purchased flour; bread, cake & related products
PA: Yum Yum Donut Shops, Inc.
18830 San Jose Ave
City Of Industry CA 91748

Loomis
Okanogan County

(G-5971)
BULLFROG LAND CO INC
1930 Loomis Oroville Rd (98827-9717)
PHONE...................509 223-3055
Jerry Cooksey, *President*
Robert W Cook, *Vice Pres*
EMP: 2
SALES (est): 190K **Privately Held**
SIC: 6552 2411 Subdividers & developers; logging

(G-5972)
RONALD G WAHL
Also Called: North Central Cabinets
300 Chopaka Rd (98827-9714)
PHONE...................509 223-3957
Ronald G Wahl, *Owner*
Loren G Wahl, *Manager*
EMP: 2
SALES: 100K **Privately Held**
SIC: 2434 Wood kitchen cabinets

(G-5973)
WILL LOGGING & CONSTRUCTION
2049 Sinlahekin Rd (98827-9702)
P.O. Box 178 (98827-0178)
PHONE...................509 223-3560
Gary A Will, *Owner*
EMP: 12
SALES (est): 1MM **Privately Held**
SIC: 2411 1542 Logging camps & contractors; nonresidential construction

Loon Lake
Stevens County

(G-5974)
BIG LLOYDE
4044 Pine Meadows Dr (99148-8709)
PHONE...................509 233-2293
EMP: 2
SALES (est): 136.3K **Privately Held**
SIC: 3931 Mfg Musical Instruments

(G-5975)
KRITTER KOOKIES LTD
4106 Gardenspot Rd (99148-9751)
P.O. Box 189 (99148-0189)
PHONE...................509 233-8414
Cassy Morrow, *President*
John Morrow, *Vice Pres*
EMP: 2
SALES (est): 103.3K **Privately Held**
WEB: www.kritterkookies.com
SIC: 2048 Dry pet food (except dog & cat)

(G-5976)
OTTER CREEK INDUSTRIES L L C
4578 E Deer Lake Rd A (99148-9629)
PHONE...................509 954-3998
Joseph M Lenz, *Principal*
EMP: 3
SALES (est): 176.5K **Privately Held**
SIC: 3999 Manufacturing industries

(G-5977)
REACH FOR SKY SATELLITE SERVIC
17 N Main Ave (99148)
PHONE...................509 276-9340
Michael Tyner,
Marie Tyner,
EMP: 2 EST: 2007
SALES (est): 166.7K **Privately Held**
SIC: 5731 3663 Antennas, satellite dish; satellites, communications

Lopez Island
San Juan County

(G-5978)
ARBORDOUN
744 Richardson Rd (98261-8026)
PHONE...................360 468-2508
Susan Bill, *Owner*
EMP: 5
SALES (est): 140K **Privately Held**
WEB: www.arbordoun.com
SIC: 2844 Cosmetic preparations

(G-5979)
BARN OWL BAKERY INC
108 Grayling Ln (98261-8601)
PHONE...................360 468-3492
Sage Dilts, *Principal*
EMP: 4
SALES (est): 67.7K **Privately Held**
SIC: 5461 2051 Bakeries; bread, cake & related products

(G-5980)
CUSTOM WOOD FINISHES
4559 Center Rd (98261-8013)
PHONE...................360 468-4383
EMP: 2
SALES (est): 110K **Privately Held**
SIC: 2431 Mfg Millwork

(G-5981)
EDGEWALKER WOODWORKS LTD
653 Shark Reef Rd (98261-8202)
PHONE...................360 468-2839
Paul Nave, *Owner*
Mary Ann Redds, *Owner*
EMP: 2
SALES (est): 89.5K **Privately Held**
SIC: 2392 Household furnishings

Lopez Island - San Juan County (G-5982)

(G-5982)
EIDOS STAINED GLASS
242 Raven Hill Rd (98261-8523)
PHONE 360 468-3577
Steven Wrubleski, *Owner*
EMP: 2
SALES (est): 74K **Privately Held**
WEB: www.eidostainedglass.com
SIC: 3231 Stained glass: made from purchased glass

(G-5983)
HAPPY THOUGHTS
12 Dolphin Ln (98261-8346)
PHONE 360 468-2880
Karly Leyde, *Principal*
EMP: 2
SALES (est): 120.4K **Privately Held**
SIC: 2335 Bridal & formal gowns

(G-5984)
KESTREL TOOL
180 Snowberry Ln (98261-8122)
PHONE 360 468-2103
Gregg Blomberg, *Owner*
EMP: 4
SALES (est): 318.2K **Privately Held**
WEB: www.kestreltool.com
SIC: 3423 5072 5251 5085 Edge tools for woodworking: augers, bits, gimlets, etc.; hand tools; tools, hand; tools

(G-5985)
LOPEZ REDI MIX INC
2969 Fisherman Bay Rd (98261-8513)
PHONE 360 468-2485
Rose Farris, *President*
EMP: 5 **EST:** 1976
SALES (est): 350K **Privately Held**
SIC: 3273 3272 5211 Ready-mixed concrete; septic tanks, concrete; tanks, concrete; solid concreting units, concrete; precast terrazo or concrete products; sand & gravel

(G-5986)
RON HALL
Also Called: Paper Scissors On The Rock
214 Lopez Rd (98261-8851)
P.O. Box 448 (98261-0448)
PHONE 360 468-2294
Ron Hall, *Owner*
EMP: 6
SQ FT: 2,400
SALES (est): 300K **Privately Held**
SIC: 7336 7313 2678 Graphic arts & related design; radio, television, publisher representatives; stationery products

(G-5987)
TIGER PRESS
659 Port Stanley Rd (98261-8505)
P.O. Box 12254, Mill Creek (98082-0254)
PHONE 360 468-3737
Jerry Whitbeck, *Owner*
EMP: 4
SALES (est): 211.1K **Privately Held**
SIC: 2759 2752 Commercial printing; commercial printing, lithographic

(G-5988)
WAUGH ENTERPRISES LLC
1008 Dill Rd Ste C (98261-8893)
P.O. Box 691 (98261-0691)
PHONE 360 468-4372
David Randall Waugh,
Annie Waugh,
EMP: 4
SALES: 74K **Privately Held**
SIC: 2099 Sauces: gravy, dressing & dip mixes

(G-5989)
WINDOWSCAPE DESIGNS
948 Cross Rd (98261-8374)
PHONE 360 468-3510
George Willis, *Owner*
Anne Willis, *Co-Owner*
EMP: 2
SALES (est): 29.2K **Privately Held**
SIC: 3231 Stained glass: made from purchased glass

Lowden
Walla Walla County

(G-5990)
LOWDEN SCHOOLHOUSE CORPORATION
Also Called: L Ecole N 41 Street
41 Lowden School Rd (99360)
P.O. Box 111 (99360-0111)
PHONE 509 525-0940
Martin Clubb, *President*
Megan Clubb, *Corp Secy*
Deborah D Frol, *Vice Pres*
▲ **EMP:** 15
SQ FT: 23,500
SALES (est): 2.1MM **Privately Held**
WEB: www.lecole.com
SIC: 2084 Wines

(G-5991)
RED GOAT FABRICATION INC
12339 W Highway 12 (99360-9748)
PHONE 509 240-2896
Gary McColley, *Principal*
EMP: 2
SALES (est): 120.1K **Privately Held**
SIC: 7692 Welding repair

(G-5992)
WOODWARD CANYON WINERY INC
11920 W Highway 12 (99360-9710)
PHONE 509 525-4129
Richard Small, *President*
Darcey Lynn Fugman-Small, *Vice Pres*
Jaymee Leamer, *Controller*
EMP: 10
SALES (est): 1MM **Privately Held**
WEB: www.woodwardcanyon.com
SIC: 2084 Wines

Lummi Island
Whatcom County

(G-5993)
SCHNEIDER DRAINFIELD DES
2455 Tuttle Ln (98262-8646)
PHONE 360 758-7353
Stephan Schneider, *Principal*
EMP: 3
SALES (est): 244K **Privately Held**
SIC: 3272 Concrete products

Lyle
Klickitat County

(G-5994)
AMERY ROCK & CONSTRUCTION INC
Also Called: Amery Rock and Construction
51 Hartland Rd (98635-9413)
PHONE 509 365-4122
Tom W Amery, *Owner*
James Amery, *Vice Pres*
EMP: 3
SALES (est): 180K **Privately Held**
SIC: 1429 Grits mining (crushed stone)

(G-5995)
COLUMBIA GORGE WINERY INC
6 Lyle Snowden Rd (98635-9535)
PHONE 509 365-2900
Richard Dobson, *Principal*
EMP: 7
SALES (est): 582.4K **Privately Held**
SIC: 2084 Wines

(G-5996)
KLICKITAT CANYON WINERY
6 Lyle Snowden Rd (98635-9535)
PHONE 509 365-2900
Robin Dobson, *Principal*
EMP: 2
SALES (est): 106.7K **Privately Held**
SIC: 2084 Wines

Lyman
Skagit County

(G-5997)
STAR INDUSTRIES CORP INC
8129 Pipeline Rd (98263)
PHONE 360 826-3895
Matt Gunther, *Principal*
EMP: 2 **EST:** 2013
SALES (est): 106.1K **Privately Held**
SIC: 3999 Barber & beauty shop equipment

Lynden
Whatcom County

(G-5998)
A 2 Z MFG LLC
7157 Guide Meridian Rd A (98264-9213)
PHONE 360 398-2126
Tom Swartwood, *Principal*
EMP: 8
SALES (est): 959.3K **Privately Held**
SIC: 3999 Candles

(G-5999)
AARON LIBOLT
110 Park View Dr (98264-9561)
PHONE 360 441-0662
Aaron Libolt, *Owner*
EMP: 2 **EST:** 2017
SALES (est): 73.4K **Privately Held**
SIC: 3452 Bolts, nuts, rivets & washers

(G-6000)
ALS CUSTOM WOODWORKING
548 E Wiser Lake Rd (98264-9455)
PHONE 360 354-2407
Alan Macphee, *Principal*
EMP: 2
SALES (est): 157.4K **Privately Held**
SIC: 2431 Millwork

(G-6001)
AQ USA INC
210 Duffner Dr Ste A (98264-9483)
PHONE 800 663-8303
Michael Ross, *Director*
Marc Ross, *Director*
EMP: 4
SQ FT: 4,500
SALES (est): 250K **Privately Held**
SIC: 2834 Pharmaceutical preparations

(G-6002)
ARTISTIC IRON FURNITURE MFRS
Also Called: Andean Imports
6965 Guide Meridian Rd (98264-9000)
P.O. Box 262 (98264-0262)
PHONE 360 398-9351
Ismael Gomberoff, *President*
EMP: 10
SALES (est): 1.2MM **Privately Held**
SIC: 2514 6794 0174 0161 Metal household furniture; franchises, selling or licensing; citrus fruits; vegetables & melons; architectural metalwork

(G-6003)
BRANDS RECO
211 Grover St (98264-1415)
PHONE 360 428-8985
EMP: 2
SALES (est): 92.3K **Privately Held**
SIC: 2752 Commercial printing, lithographic

(G-6004)
C N C REPAIR & SALES INC
1770 Front St Ste 142 (98264-2103)
PHONE 408 331-1970
James Leuba, *President*
EMP: 9
SALES (est): 799.3K **Privately Held**
SIC: 3541 Machine tool replacement & repair parts, metal cutting types

(G-6005)
CASCADE CONCRETE
8987 Jasmine Ln (98264-9174)
P.O. Box 1006 (98264-6106)
PHONE 360 354-8901
Daren Deboer, *Owner*
EMP: 2 **EST:** 1989
SALES (est): 160K **Privately Held**
SIC: 3272 Concrete products, precast

(G-6006)
CEDARBROOK
Also Called: Barging In Europe
145 E Cedar Dr (98264-9516)
PHONE 360 354-5770
Roger Van Dyken, *Owner*
Marlene Van Dyken, *Co-Owner*
Roger Dyken, *Author*
EMP: 2
SALES (est): 10K **Privately Held**
WEB: www.barginginineurope.com
SIC: 2731 Book publishing

(G-6007)
CHS-SUB WHATCOM INC (HQ)
Also Called: Whatcom Farmers Coop
402 Main St (98264-1324)
P.O. Box 611 (98264-0611)
PHONE 360 354-2108
Don Eucker, *CEO*
Dave Henderson, *Division Mgr*
Kim Bouma, *Principal*
Phil Hutton, *Principal*
Darrin Wisbey, *Principal*
EMP: 40
SQ FT: 25,000
SALES (est): 81.6MM **Privately Held**
SALES (corp-wide): 32.6B **Publicly Held**
WEB: www.wfcoop.com
SIC: 2875 5191 5999 Fertilizers, mixing only; farm supplies; feed & farm supply
PA: Chs Inc.
5500 Cenex Dr
Inver Grove Heights MN 55077
651 355-6000

(G-6008)
CHS-SUB WHATCOM INC
Also Called: Wfc Lynden Convenience Store
300 Main St (98264-1361)
P.O. Box 611 (98264-0611)
PHONE 360 354-1198
Torri Silva, *Branch Mgr*
EMP: 8
SALES (corp-wide): 31.9B **Publicly Held**
WEB: www.wfcoop.com
SIC: 2875 5191 Fertilizers, mixing only; farm supplies
HQ: Chs-Sub Whatcom, Inc.
402 Main St
Lynden WA 98264
360 354-2108

(G-6009)
CLARKS BERRY FARM INC (PA)
632 Birch Bay Lynden Rd (98264-9486)
PHONE 360 354-1294
John Clark, *President*
Brent Clark, *Vice Pres*
Barbara Clark, *Admin Sec*
◆ **EMP:** 20
SQ FT: 4,000
SALES (est): 3.3MM **Privately Held**
SIC: 2037 0171 Fruits, quick frozen & cold pack (frozen); raspberry farm

(G-6010)
CREON LLC
7358 Lankhaar Rd (98264-9462)
PHONE 360 318-1559
Dave Korthuis,
EMP: 7
SALES (est): 1.1MM **Privately Held**
SIC: 3499 Fabricated metal products

(G-6011)
CUSTOM WOODWORKING
6867 Vail Dr (98264-9637)
P.O. Box 2200, Ferndale (98248-2200)
PHONE 360 739-3961
Jeff Schulteis, *Principal*
EMP: 2
SALES (est): 163.4K **Privately Held**
SIC: 2431 Millwork

GEOGRAPHIC SECTION

Lynden - Whatcom County (G-6043)

(G-6012)
DAI ENVIRONMENTAL SERVICES
752 Loomis Trail Rd (98264-9110)
PHONE...................360 354-1134
Frank Devries, *President*
Marilyn Devries, *Owner*
Ivan Devries, *Vice Pres*
Jeff Penpas, *Vice Pres*
Angela Bosman, *Admin Sec*
EMP: 25
SALES (est): 3.7MM **Privately Held**
SIC: 1389 0171 Oil field services; raspberry farm

(G-6013)
DARI-TECH INC
8540 Benson Rd (98264-9711)
PHONE...................360 354-6900
David De Waard, *President*
Ryan De Waard, *Vice Pres*
◆ **EMP:** 49
SQ FT: 28,200
SALES (est): 13.7MM **Privately Held**
WEB: www.daritech.com
SIC: 5999 3523 Farm equipment & supplies; farm machinery & equipment

(G-6014)
ELENBAAS COMPANY INC (PA)
421 Birch Bay Lynden Rd (98264-9410)
PHONE...................360 354-3577
Dennis W Elenbaas, *President*
Glen Elenbaas, *Vice Pres*
Rex Warolin, *CFO*
Richard J Elenbaas, *Admin Sec*
EMP: 35
SALES (est): 20.1MM **Privately Held**
WEB: www.elenbaasco.com
SIC: 2048 5999 Feed concentrates; feed & farm supply

(G-6015)
EXCEL INDUSTRIES INCORPORATED
1400 Yarrow Ct (98264-3904)
PHONE...................360 790-3577
Donald R Kurz, *Principal*
EMP: 2
SALES (est): 97.6K **Privately Held**
SIC: 3999 Manufacturing industries

(G-6016)
FAIRLANE HELICOPTERS INC
284 Pollman Cir (98264-9016)
P.O. Box 632 (98264-0632)
PHONE...................360 398-1015
Keith Smith, *Principal*
EMP: 2
SALES (est): 114.9K **Privately Held**
SIC: 3721 Helicopters

(G-6017)
FERNDALE READY-MIX (PA)
144 River Rd (98264-9419)
PHONE...................360 354-1400
Larry Vanwerven, *President*
Brad De Haan, *Vice Pres*
Brad Dehaan, *Vice Pres*
EMP: 15
SQ FT: 6,000
SALES (est): 3.9MM **Privately Held**
WEB: www.ferndalereadymix.net
SIC: 3273 5032 Ready-mixed concrete; sand, construction; gravel

(G-6018)
FISHTRAP CREEK LIGHTING LLC
307 19th St (98264-1702)
PHONE...................360 354-7900
Randy Smit,
EMP: 4
SALES (est): 235.1K **Privately Held**
SIC: 3648 Lighting equipment

(G-6019)
FLORA INC
805 E Badger Rd (98264-9502)
P.O. Box 73 (98264-0073)
PHONE...................360 354-2110
Thomas Greither, *President*
Summer Sit, *QC Mgr*
Tom Ball, *Sales Staff*
Jose Furtado, *Sales Staff*
Sid Gluckman, *Marketing Staff*
◆ **EMP:** 100
SALES (est): 20.5MM
SALES (corp-wide): 62.2MM **Privately Held**
WEB: www.florahealth.com
SIC: 2099 Food preparations
PA: Flora Manufacturing And Distributing Ltd
7400 Fraser Park Dr
Burnaby BC V5J 5
604 436-6000

(G-6020)
HEIRLOOM CUSTOM CABINETS INC
406 E Wiser Lake Rd (98264-9454)
PHONE...................360 354-7851
Robert Matter, *President*
EMP: 4
SALES (est): 356.4K **Privately Held**
SIC: 2434 2511 1751 Wood kitchen cabinets; wood household furniture; cabinet & finish carpentry

(G-6021)
HIGH DEFINITION AUDIO VIDEO
7029 Guide Meridian Rd (98264-9669)
PHONE...................360 398-8265
David Carpenter, *Owner*
EMP: 2
SALES (est): 134K **Privately Held**
SIC: 3651 Household audio & video equipment

(G-6022)
HOLZ ENTERPRISES INC
Also Called: Holz Racing Products
6226 Chasteen Rd (98264-9609)
PHONE...................360 398-7006
Mark Holz, *President*
EMP: 6
SQ FT: 3,200
SALES (est): 690K **Privately Held**
WEB: www.holzracingproducts.com
SIC: 3799 Snowmobiles

(G-6023)
INVESTURE - WA INC
Also Called: Rader Farms
1270 E Badger Rd (98264-9503)
PHONE...................360 354-6574
Terry McDaniel, *CEO*
Steven Sklar, *Senior VP*
Steve Weinberger, *CFO*
EMP: 80 **EST:** 1961
SQ FT: 80,000
SALES (est): 24.8MM
SALES (corp-wide): 723.8MM **Privately Held**
WEB: www.raderfarms.com
SIC: 2037 0171 Frozen fruits & vegetables; raspberry farm
HQ: Inventure Foods, Inc.
900 High St
Hanover PA 17331

(G-6024)
J CALMAN INDUSTRIES
176 W King Tut Rd (98264-9623)
PHONE...................360 398-1932
James Lee Calman, *Owner*
EMP: 5
SALES (est): 750K **Privately Held**
SIC: 5084 3731 Industrial machinery & equipment; offshore supply boats, building & repairing

(G-6025)
J K PROPERTIES INC
Also Called: Lamby Nursery Collection
1309 Woodfield Dr (98264-9358)
PHONE...................360 354-6719
John Geleynse, *General Mgr*
▲ **EMP:** 2
SALES (est): 275.3K **Privately Held**
SIC: 2676 Infant & baby paper products

(G-6026)
JD BARGEN INDUSTRIES LLC
Also Called: Lynden Door
2077 Main St (98264-9186)
P.O. Box 528 (98264-0528)
PHONE...................360 354-5676
Ted Bargen, *Principal*
EMP: 3 **EST:** 1978
SALES (est): 259.7K **Privately Held**
SIC: 3999 Manufacturing industries

(G-6027)
K & S WOODWORKS LLC
9641 Benson Rd (98264-9712)
PHONE...................360 354-1043
Kolin Veldman, *Principal*
EMP: 4
SALES (est): 477.8K **Privately Held**
SIC: 2431 Millwork

(G-6028)
K&B CUSTOM RODS & TACKLE
821 Garden Dr (98264-1028)
PHONE...................360 354-1945
William Vancleve, *Owner*
Cynthia Vancleve, *Co-Owner*
EMP: 2 **EST:** 1984
SALES (est): 80.8K **Privately Held**
SIC: 5941 3949 Bait & tackle; rods & rod parts, fishing

(G-6029)
KORVAN INDUSTRIES INC
270 Birch Bay Lynden Rd (98264-9408)
PHONE...................360 354-1500
Herb Korthuis, *President*
Scott Korthuis, *Vice Pres*
Jon Olson, *Treasurer*
Dorothy Otter, *Admin Sec*
▲ **EMP:** 75
SQ FT: 30,000
SALES (est): 9.1MM **Privately Held**
WEB: www.korvan.com
SIC: 3523 3599 Harvesters, fruit, vegetable, tobacco, etc.; custom machinery

(G-6030)
LAKESIDE GARDENS
130 Misty Waters Ln (98264-9262)
PHONE...................360 483-8889
EMP: 2
SALES (est): 73.2K **Privately Held**
SIC: 2759 Commercial Printing, Nec

(G-6031)
LEWIS PUBLISHING COMPANY INC
Also Called: Lynden Tribune Print and Pubg
113 6th St (98264-1901)
P.O. Box 153 (98264-0153)
PHONE...................360 354-4444
Michael Lewis, *President*
Aaron Schiffman, *General Mgr*
Mary Jo Lewis, *Corp Secy*
Steve Engholm, *Prdtn Mgr*
Kester Mitze, *Adv Mgr*
EMP: 30 **EST:** 1914
SQ FT: 10,000
SALES (est): 4.5MM **Privately Held**
SIC: 2752 2711 Offset & photolithographic printing; newspapers, publishing & printing

(G-6032)
LYNDEN DOOR INC (PA)
2077 Main St (98264-9186)
P.O. Box 528 (98264-0528)
PHONE...................360 354-5676
Theodore Bargen, *President*
Steve Berkompas, *Business Mgr*
Kevin Ardt, *Vice Pres*
Dave Hiebert, *Vice Pres*
Jennifer Winder, *Production*
▲ **EMP:** 50 **EST:** 1978
SQ FT: 10,000
SALES (est): 13MM **Privately Held**
WEB: www.lyndendoor.com
SIC: 2431 Doors, wood

(G-6033)
LYNDEN LIQUOR AGENCY 570
610 Front St (98264-1925)
PHONE...................360 354-4744
Pat Kohl, *Owner*
EMP: 2
SALES (est): 230K **Privately Held**
SIC: 5921 2085 Hard liquor; vodka (alcoholic beverage)

(G-6034)
LYNDEN MEAT COMPANY LLC
1936 Front St (98264-1708)
PHONE...................360 354-5227
Richard Allan,
Brett Biesheuvel,
Richard A Biesheuvel Jr,
EMP: 10
SQ FT: 6,400
SALES (est): 298K **Privately Held**
SIC: 0751 5199 2097 Slaughtering: custom livestock services; ice, manufactured or natural; manufactured ice

(G-6035)
LYNDEN PRECAST LLC
8987 Jasmine Ln (98264-9174)
PHONE...................360 354-8901
EMP: 3
SALES (est): 305.7K **Privately Held**
SIC: 3272 Precast terrazo or concrete products

(G-6036)
MAINLAND MACHINERY LLC
9458 Depot Rd (98264-9579)
PHONE...................360 354-2348
Gary Friesen, *President*
Etta Friesen, *Manager*
EMP: 2
SALES (est): 214.8K **Privately Held**
SIC: 3599 5084 Machine shop, jobbing & repair; industrial machinery & equipment

(G-6037)
MATERIAL GIRLS QUILTING
1124 Birch Bay Lynden Rd (98264-9220)
PHONE...................360 354-2930
Sharon Coots, *Owner*
EMP: 2
SALES (est): 65.4K **Privately Held**
SIC: 2395 Quilting, for the trade

(G-6038)
MT BAKER MANUFACTURING
1689 Aaron Dr (98264-3919)
PHONE...................360 778-1238
EMP: 2
SALES (est): 135.3K **Privately Held**
SIC: 3999 Mfg Misc Products

(G-6039)
NEVADA LITHIUM CORP
9443 Axlund Rd (98264-9705)
PHONE...................360 318-8352
John Hiner, *President*
EMP: 2
SALES (est): 187.8K **Privately Held**
SIC: 3648 Miners' lamps

(G-6040)
NORTHWEST WATER TREATMENT LLC
8600 Bender Rd (98264-1004)
PHONE...................360 354-2044
Lance Nieuwsma, *Partner*
Dan Nieuwsma,
Marlae Nieuwsma,
EMP: 2
SALES (est): 230K **Privately Held**
SIC: 3589 Water filters & softeners, household type

(G-6041)
OCEANWEST RVM LLC
1205 E Badger Rd (98264-9376)
PHONE...................503 569-6969
Dave Kuypers, *Principal*
EMP: 2
SALES (est): 80.8K **Privately Held**
SIC: 3429 5531 Marine hardware; automotive parts

(G-6042)
ORIGINALS BY CHAD JWLY DESIGN
521 Front St Ste 101 (98264-1922)
PHONE...................360 318-0210
Chad Shoemaker, *Owner*
EMP: 2
SALES (est): 122.3K **Privately Held**
SIC: 3911 7631 Jewelry, precious metal; jewelry repair services

(G-6043)
OXBO INTERNATIONAL CORPORATION
270 Birch Bay Lynden Rd (98264-9408)
PHONE...................360 354-1500
John Olfon, *Manager*

Lynden - Whatcom County (G-6044)

EMP: 100
SALES (corp-wide): 51.4MM **Privately Held**
WEB: www.oxbocorp.com
SIC: 3523 Planting, haying, harvesting & processing machinery
HQ: Oxbo International Corporation
 7275 Batavia Byron Rd
 Byron NY 14422
 585 548-2665

(G-6044)
PACIFIC NORTHWEST PACKERS INC
9900 Hammer Rd (98264-9532)
P.O. Box 98 (98264-0098)
PHONE.................................360 354-0776
Jagtar Alamwala, *President*
Satwinder K Alamwala, *Admin Sec*
EMP: 20
SALES (est): 1MM **Privately Held**
SIC: 0723 2037 Fruit (fresh) packing services; frozen fruits & vegetables

(G-6045)
PARTS WAREHOUSE INC
309 Judson Street Aly (98264-1931)
PHONE.................................360 354-4722
Alan Kennedy, *President*
Cindy Heins, *Vice Pres*
▲ **EMP:** 8
SQ FT: 4,000
SALES (est): 1.3MM **Privately Held**
SIC: 3843 5047 Dental equipment & supplies; dental equipment & supplies

(G-6046)
PERDUE FOODS LLC
Also Called: Harchery Division
6323 Guide Meridian Rd (98264-9615)
PHONE.................................360 398-2911
Robin Visser, *Manager*
EMP: 18
SALES (corp-wide): 6B **Privately Held**
SIC: 2015 0254 0252 0251 Poultry slaughtering & processing; poultry hatcheries; chicken eggs; broiler, fryer & roaster chickens
HQ: Perdue Foods Llc
 31149 Old Ocean City Rd
 Salisbury MD 21804

(G-6047)
PRINT STOP INC
514 Front St (98264-1974)
PHONE.................................360 354-5100
Craig Hersman, *President*
EMP: 9 **EST:** 1974
SALES (est): 1.4MM **Privately Held**
SIC: 2752 Commercial printing, offset; offset & photolithographic printing

(G-6048)
RECO CORPORATE SPORTSWEAR INC
210 Nooksack Ave Ste 102 (98264-1544)
P.O. Box 754 (98264-0754)
PHONE.................................360 354-2134
Mark Rutledge, *President*
Brandon Rutledge, *Vice Pres*
EMP: 4
SALES: 250K **Privately Held**
SIC: 2395 2759 Embroidery products, except schiffli machine; screen printing

(G-6049)
RIVERSIDE CABINET CO INC
1145 Polinder Rd (98264-9439)
PHONE.................................360 354-3070
Dan Mathis, *President*
EMP: 4
SALES (est): 450.1K **Privately Held**
SIC: 2434 Wood kitchen cabinets

(G-6050)
ROSS GROUP OF COMPANIES INC
210 Duffner Dr (98264-9483)
PHONE.................................800 663-8303
Michael Ross, *Director*
EMP: 2
SALES (est): 74.4K **Privately Held**
SIC: 2834 Pharmaceutical preparations

(G-6051)
S & H AUTO PARTS INC (PA)
Also Called: Carquest Auto Parts
8123 Guide Meridian Rd (98264-9230)
P.O. Box 633 (98264-0633)
PHONE.................................360 354-4468
Ron Zylstra, *President*
Ed Weidenaar, *Manager*
EMP: 5
SQ FT: 3,300
SALES (est): 1.2MM **Privately Held**
SIC: 5531 5013 3599 Automotive parts; automotive supplies & parts; machine shop, jobbing & repair

(G-6052)
SANDCASTLE SANDBLASTING
Also Called: Illustrated Illusions
861 19th St (98264-9769)
PHONE.................................360 354-5087
Starla Voth, *Partner*
Nolan Roth, *Partner*
EMP: 2
SALES (est): 114.9K **Privately Held**
SIC: 3231 3281 Decorated glassware: chipped, engraved, etched, etc.; monument or burial stone, cut & shaped

(G-6053)
SOURCE ENGINEERING LLC (HQ)
8858 Guide Meridian Rd (98264-9133)
P.O. Box 553 (98264-0553)
PHONE.................................360 383-5129
Theodore Bargen, *Mng Member*
EMP: 35
SQ FT: 2,500
SALES (est): 800K
SALES (corp-wide): 13MM **Privately Held**
SIC: 3312 3535 8711 Stainless steel; conveyors & conveying equipment; mechanical engineering
PA: Lynden Door, Inc.
 2077 Main St
 Lynden WA 98264
 360 354-5676

(G-6054)
SPOONK SPACE INC
164 Bay Lyn Dr Ste F (98264-9238)
PHONE.................................360 392-8067
Natasha Frykman, *President*
Hans Frykman, *Admin Sec*
▲ **EMP:** 6
SALES (est): 905.6K **Privately Held**
SIC: 2273 Mats & matting

(G-6055)
STITCH N WOOD
501 Wood Creek Dr (98264-1109)
PHONE.................................360 354-1211
Rick Faupel, *Owner*
EMP: 3
SALES (est): 132.4K **Privately Held**
SIC: 2499 Decorative wood & woodwork

(G-6056)
TONY PECARIC
Also Called: Karlene
236 Pyramid Ln (98264-9649)
PHONE.................................360 398-9885
Tony Pecaric, *Owner*
Maureen Pecaric, *Co-Owner*
EMP: 2
SALES: 50K **Privately Held**
SIC: 3732 Fishing boats: lobster, crab, oyster, etc.: small

(G-6057)
TRI COUNTY DEAD STOCK
714 E Front St (98264-1614)
PHONE.................................360 354-3173
Linsey Hoekstra, *Principal*
EMP: 3
SALES (est): 224K **Privately Held**
SIC: 2077 Rendering

(G-6058)
VANDERPOL BUILDING COMPONENTS
841 E Badger Rd (98264-9502)
PHONE.................................360 354-5883
Jeffrey C Vanderpol, *President*
EMP: 10
SQ FT: 27,300
SALES (est): 3.4MM **Privately Held**
WEB: www.vanderpol.com
SIC: 3448 1521 2439 Trusses & framing: prefabricated metal; single-family housing construction; structural wood members

(G-6059)
VANS CABINETS LLC
Also Called: Van's Cabinet Shop
426 E Wiser Lake Rd (98264-9454)
PHONE.................................360 354-5845
Bob Van Hofwegen, *Owner*
EMP: 3
SALES (est): 461.5K **Privately Held**
SIC: 2434 Wood kitchen cabinets

(G-6060)
VICTORY MILLWORK LLC
2077 Main St (98264-9186)
P.O. Box 528 (98264-0528)
PHONE.................................360 592-6090
Ted Bargen, *Mng Member*
EMP: 50
SALES (est): 1.7MM **Privately Held**
SIC: 2431 Millwork

(G-6061)
Z RECYCLERS INC
6129 Guide Meridian Rd (98264-9614)
P.O. Box 648 (98264-0648)
PHONE.................................360 398-2161
Tim Zawicki, *President*
Dan Thompson, *Treasurer*
Chris Thompson, *Admin Sec*
EMP: 10
SQ FT: 1,000
SALES (est): 3.6MM **Privately Held**
SIC: 5093 3341 Nonferrous metals scrap; secondary nonferrous metals

Lynnwood
Snohomish County

(G-6062)
2H PROTECTIVE COATINGS INC
16824 44th Ave W (98037-3111)
PHONE.................................425 346-3306
Kookchun Han, *Principal*
EMP: 2 **EST:** 2012
SALES (est): 106.7K **Privately Held**
SIC: 3479 Metal coating & allied service

(G-6063)
99 SMOKERS PARADISE
20829 Highway 99 (98036-7376)
PHONE.................................425 775-8081
EMP: 2
SALES (est): 138.7K **Privately Held**
SIC: 3999 Mfg Misc Products

(G-6064)
A & R ENTERPRISE
Also Called: A & R Entps A Div A & R PR
4210 198th St Sw Ste 100 (98036-6756)
PHONE.................................425 453-0010
Alan Cohen, *President*
Ricka Cohen, *Vice Pres*
Michelle Allyn, *Manager*
Ricki Cohen, *Prgrmr*
EMP: 3
SALES (est): 335.1K **Privately Held**
SIC: 2759 2752 Commercial printing; commercial printing, lithographic

(G-6065)
A D G DATA SYSTEMS INC
21021 66th Ave W (98036-7303)
PHONE.................................425 771-7603
Gabor Miklos, *President*
EMP: 2
SALES (est): 871.6K **Privately Held**
SIC: 2752 Commercial printing, lithographic

(G-6066)
A D G PRINTING
19031 36th Ave W Ste D (98036-5763)
PHONE.................................425 771-7603
Adam Springer, *Owner*
EMP: 2
SALES (est): 173.5K **Privately Held**
SIC: 2752 Commercial printing, offset

(G-6067)
ABSOLUTE GRAPHIX INC
19231 36th Ave W Ste F (98036-5763)
PHONE.................................425 771-6087
EMP: 3 **EST:** 1990
SALES (est): 250K **Privately Held**
SIC: 2759 7336 Screen Printing & Commercial Art

(G-6068)
ALASKA UNITED PARTNERSHIP
3721 148th St Sw (98087-5515)
PHONE.................................425 741-3350
Harry Lamb, *Partner*
EMP: 2
SQ FT: 2,191
SALES (est): 144.3K **Privately Held**
SIC: 3661 Fiber optics communications equipment

(G-6069)
ALDERWOOD PARK
18031 36th Ave W (98037-3848)
PHONE.................................425 774-5266
Teresa Carver, *Principal*
EMP: 4
SALES (est): 285.9K **Privately Held**
SIC: 2392 Household furnishings

(G-6070)
ALDERWOOD SIGNS
2231 196th St Sw (98036-7068)
PHONE.................................425 744-6555
Steve L Fritsch, *Owner*
Maggie Fritsch, *Co-Owner*
EMP: 4
SQ FT: 2,800
SALES: 450K **Privately Held**
WEB: www.alderwoodsigns.com
SIC: 3993 Signs & advertising specialties

(G-6071)
ALL SEASONS STUMP GRINDING
20609 53rd Ave W (98036-7617)
PHONE.................................425 775-7977
John Merkel, *Owner*
EMP: 2
SALES (est): 242.9K **Privately Held**
SIC: 3599 Grinding castings for the trade

(G-6072)
ALLVIEW SERVICES INC
2215 S Castle Way (98036-8338)
PHONE.................................425 483-6103
Walter Schaplow, *President*
EMP: 3
SALES: 150K **Privately Held**
SIC: 3571 Electronic computers

(G-6073)
ALPHAPRINT INC
Also Called: AlphaGraphics
19011 36th Ave W Ste E (98036-5752)
PHONE.................................425 771-1140
Lisa Burnett, *General Mgr*
Mark Bonne, *Info Tech Dir*
EMP: 3
SALES (corp-wide): 14.8MM **Privately Held**
SIC: 2752 7331 Commercial printing, offset; direct mail advertising services
PA: Alphaprint, Inc.
 3131 Elliott Ave Ste 100
 Seattle WA 98121
 206 448-9100

(G-6074)
AMERICAN POWDER WORKS ◆
13127 Beverly Park Rd (98087-5129)
PHONE.................................360 220-3104
EMP: 3 **EST:** 2018
SALES (est): 157.2K **Privately Held**
SIC: 3471 Plating & polishing

(G-6075)
AMERICAN RAILWORKS
13127 Beverly Park Rd (98087-5129)
PHONE.................................425 582-8990
Seth Macgillivray, *Administration*
EMP: 9
SALES (est): 1.4MM **Privately Held**
SIC: 3446 Architectural metalwork

GEOGRAPHIC SECTION
Lynnwood - Snohomish County (G-6106)

(G-6076)
ARROW INTERNATIONAL INC
Trade Products
2807 Lincoln Way (98087-5620)
P.O. Box 898 (98046-0898)
PHONE..................................425 745-3700
Clem Chantiam, *CEO*
EMP: 400
SALES (corp-wide): 235.9MM **Privately Held**
WEB: www.arrowgames.com
SIC: 2759 Promotional printing; tickets: printing
PA: Arrow International, Inc.
   9900 Clinton Rd
   Cleveland OH 44144
   216 961-3500

(G-6077)
ARROW INTERNATIONAL INC
Also Called: Specialty Manufacturer
2807 Lincoln Way (98087-5620)
PHONE..................................425 407-1475
Lane Gormley, *VP Opers*
Rob Tekel, *Marketing Staff*
EMP: 70
SALES (corp-wide): 235.9MM **Privately Held**
WEB: www.arrowgames.com
SIC: 2752 2675 Commercial printing, lithographic; die-cut paper & board
PA: Arrow International, Inc.
   9900 Clinton Rd
   Cleveland OH 44144
   216 961-3500

(G-6078)
ATLANTIS PUBLICATIONS INC
18120 71st Ave W (98037-4145)
PHONE..................................206 497-0894
EMP: 2 **EST**: 2011
SALES (est): 101.5K **Privately Held**
SIC: 2741 Miscellaneous publishing

(G-6079)
B3 BREAKFAST & BURGER BAR
4027 196th St Sw (98036-6714)
PHONE..................................425 672-3666
EMP: 7
SALES (est): 340.6K **Privately Held**
SIC: 2064 Breakfast bars

(G-6080)
BAILEY TOOL INC
Also Called: Bailey Tool & Die
3605 132nd St Sw Ste 2 (98087-5137)
PHONE..................................425 745-8427
Al Bailey, *President*
EMP: 5
SALES (est): 469.7K **Privately Held**
SIC: 3599 Machine shop, jobbing & repair

(G-6081)
BANG & JACK MONTGOMERY
1826 192nd Pl Sw (98036-4840)
PHONE..................................360 403-9444
Linda Montgomery, *President*
EMP: 2
SALES (est): 96.2K **Privately Held**
SIC: 3571 Electronic computers

(G-6082)
BAYER HEALTHCARE LLC
2625 162nd St Sw (98087-3263)
PHONE..................................425 245-1392
Donna B Hoskins, *Branch Mgr*
EMP: 134
SALES (corp-wide): 45.3B **Privately Held**
SIC: 2834 Pharmaceutical preparations
HQ: Bayer Healthcare Llc
   100 Bayer Blvd
   Whippany NJ 07981
   862 404-3000

(G-6083)
BENCHMARK INJECTION MOLDING
3605 132nd St Sw Ste 1 (98087-5137)
PHONE..................................425 263-9171
Art Olsen, *Owner*
EMP: 2
SALES (est): 169.9K **Privately Held**
WEB: www.benchmarkmolding.com
SIC: 3089 Injection molding of plastics

(G-6084)
BLUE SEAL INC
15006 35th Ave W Ste A (98087-5016)
PHONE..................................360 568-2098
Brad Bradshaw, *President*
EMP: 3
SALES (est): 663.3K **Privately Held**
SIC: 2891 Adhesives & sealants

(G-6085)
BOYD COFFEE COMPANY
21009 63rd Ave W (98036-8557)
PHONE..................................425 744-1394
Randy Studds, *Manager*
EMP: 4
SALES (corp-wide): 606.5MM **Publicly Held**
WEB: www.boydscoffeestore.com
SIC: 2095 5141 Roasted coffee; groceries, general line
HQ: Boyd Coffee Company
   19730 Ne Sandy Blvd
   Portland OR 97230
   503 666-4545

(G-6086)
CAMWEST INC
2228 133rd St Sw (98087-6069)
PHONE..................................425 776-7900
Terry J Campbell, *President*
EMP: 3
SALES (est): 170.3K **Privately Held**
SIC: 1311 Crude petroleum & natural gas

(G-6087)
CARSOS PASTA COMPANY INC
5530 208th St Sw (98036-7633)
P.O. Box 77003, Seattle (98177-0003)
PHONE..................................206 283-8227
Dave Parson, *President*
Kim Scarth, *General Mgr*
Carson Kaiser-Brown, *Administration*
▲ **EMP**: 20
SALES (est): 3.5MM **Privately Held**
SIC: 2098 5149 Noodles (e.g. egg, plain & water), dry; pasta & rice

(G-6088)
CASCADE MOUNTAIN BLENDS NW LLC
4320 196th St Sw Ste B (98036-6754)
PHONE..................................425 275-3344
William Anderson,
EMP: 4
SALES (est): 433.4K **Privately Held**
SIC: 2099 Seasonings: dry mixes

(G-6089)
CCS COMPUTER SYSTEMS INC
2100 196th St Sw Ste 112 (98036-7000)
PHONE..................................425 672-4806
Dan Mc Cormick, *President*
Marilyn Mc Cormick, *Vice Pres*
EMP: 10
SQ FT: 4,500
SALES (est): 1.8MM **Privately Held**
WEB: www.ccscentral.com
SIC: 5045 1731 7378 7372 Computers, peripherals & software; computer installation; computer peripheral equipment repair & maintenance; prepackaged software; custom computer programming services

(G-6090)
CELESTIAL MONITORING CORP
2100 196th St Sw Ste 109 (98036-7000)
PHONE..................................800 477-2506
Pierre Gouvin, *Branch Mgr*
EMP: 3
SALES (est): 2.8B **Privately Held**
SIC: 3823 Pressure measurement instruments, industrial
HQ: Celestial Monitoring Corp.
   24 Celestial Dr Ste B
   Narragansett RI 02882
   401 782-1045

(G-6091)
CEMEX CNSTR MTLS PCF LLC
Also Called: Northwest - Lynnwood Office
20700 44th Ave W Ste 240 (98036-7735)
P.O. Box 2037, Everett (98213-0037)
PHONE..................................425 355-2111
Bryan Fowler, *General Mgr*
EMP: 40 **Privately Held**
SIC: 3271 Blocks, concrete or cinder: standard; blocks, concrete: acoustical
HQ: Cemex Construction Materials Pacific, Llc
   1501 Belvedere Rd
   West Palm Beach FL 33406
   561 833-5555

(G-6092)
CHEERS TO LIFE
20722 33rd Ave W (98036-7890)
PHONE..................................425 697-2966
Paul Lablanc, *Principal*
EMP: 3
SALES (est): 225.6K **Privately Held**
SIC: 2254 Shirts & t-shirts (underwear), knit

(G-6093)
CHERBO PUBLISHING GROUP INC
20006 Cedar Valley Rd # 101 (98036-6334)
PHONE..................................818 783-0040
EMP: 14
SQ FT: 3,500
SALES (est): 1.4MM **Privately Held**
SIC: 2731 Books-Publishing/Printing

(G-6094)
COENZYME-A TECHNOLOGIES INC
Also Called: Coa
12512 Beverly Park Rd B1 (98087-1516)
PHONE..................................425 438-8586
Nick Skourans, *President*
EMP: 12 **EST**: 2001
SALES (est): 1.4MM **Privately Held**
SIC: 2048 8011 Mineral feed supplements; offices & clinics of medical doctors

(G-6095)
COIN MARKET LLC
1120 164th St Sw Ste J (98087-8190)
PHONE..................................425 745-1659
George Marley,
EMP: 4
SALES (est): 275.3K **Privately Held**
SIC: 5999 7389 3911 Coins; appraisers, except real estate; mountings, gold or silver: pens, leather goods, etc.

(G-6096)
COLORIFIC PORCELAIN
6329 176th St Sw (98037-2959)
PHONE..................................425 743-1591
Jeanette Gullikson, *Owner*
Ralph Gullikson, *Co-Owner*
EMP: 4
SALES (est): 170K **Privately Held**
SIC: 5945 3264 Ceramics supplies; porcelain electrical supplies

(G-6097)
CONNECTZONECOM LLC
5030 208th St Sw Ste B (98036-7642)
PHONE..................................425 212-4400
Daniel Oberholtzer, *Mng Member*
◆ **EMP**: 35 **EST**: 2006
SQ FT: 6,000
SALES (est): 4MM **Privately Held**
SIC: 3229 5063 5051 Pressed & blown glass; electronic wire & cable; cable, wire

(G-6098)
CONNELLY SKIS INC (HQ)
Also Called: Proline
20621 52nd Ave W (98036-7611)
P.O. Box 716 (98046-0716)
PHONE..................................425 775-5416
Robert Archer, *Principal*
Jeffrey Banister, *Principal*
Denis Hoyt, *Vice Pres*
◆ **EMP**: 50
SQ FT: 42,000
SALES (est): 7.3MM
SALES (corp-wide): 143.8MM **Privately Held**
WEB: www.connellyskis.com
SIC: 3949 Water skiing equipment & supplies, except skis
PA: Kent Sporting Goods Company, Inc.
   433 Park Ave
   New London OH 44851
   419 929-7021

(G-6099)
COUNTING STICK SOFTWARE LLC
15015 29th Ave W (98087-2455)
P.O. Box 14189, Mill Creek (98082-2189)
PHONE..................................425 750-1028
Jeremy Baer,
EMP: 2 **EST**: 2013
SALES (est): 230K **Privately Held**
SIC: 7372 7389 Publishers' computer software;

(G-6100)
CRANE AEROSPACE INC
16706 13th Ave W (98037-8503)
P.O. Box 97027 (98046-9727)
PHONE..................................425 743-1313
Jim Herning, *Branch Mgr*
EMP: 36
SALES (corp-wide): 3.3B **Publicly Held**
SIC: 3728 Aircraft parts & equipment
HQ: Crane Aerospace, Inc.
   100 Stamford Pl
   Stamford CT 06902

(G-6101)
CROSSROADS SIGN & GRAPHIC
16406 7th Pl W (98037-8100)
PHONE..................................425 481-9411
Jeff Thomas, *Owner*
EMP: 4
SALES (est): 295.8K **Privately Held**
SIC: 3993 Signs, not made in custom sign painting shops

(G-6102)
CUSTOM SENSOR DESIGN INC
2006 196th St Sw Ste 102 (98036-7042)
PHONE..................................425 778-4980
Charles F Haasl, *President*
Kenneth L Lysen, *Vice Pres*
EMP: 7
SQ FT: 7,000
SALES: 500K **Privately Held**
SIC: 3829 Measuring & controlling devices

(G-6103)
CYPRESS MICROSYSTEMS INC
Also Called: Cypress Semi Conductor
2700 162nd St Sw Bldg D (98087-3200)
PHONE..................................425 787-4400
Mark Hastings, *Engineer*
Rajiv Singh, *Engineer*
Talia Helle, *Corp Comm Staff*
Dee Bender, *Office Mgr*
Gagan Luthra, *Manager*
EMP: 19
SALES (est): 3.3MM **Privately Held**
SIC: 3674 Semiconductors & related devices

(G-6104)
CYPRESS SEMICONDUCTOR CORP
Also Called: Washington Design Center
2700 162nd St Sw Bldg D (98087-3200)
PHONE..................................425 787-4400
Pushek Madaan, *Marketing Mgr*
Regina Gonzales, *Branch Mgr*
EMP: 13
SALES (corp-wide): 2.4B **Publicly Held**
WEB: www.cypress.com
SIC: 3674 Semiconductors & related devices
PA: Cypress Semiconductor Corporation
   198 Champion Ct
   San Jose CA 95134
   408 943-2600

(G-6105)
D & D MILLWORK INC
Also Called: Arvid's Woods
19420 21st Ave W (98036-4858)
PHONE..................................800 627-8437
Darin White, *President*
David E Wilson Jr, *Principal*
EMP: 18
SALES: 2.9MM **Privately Held**
SIC: 2431 Millwork

(G-6106)
DEEP SEA FISHERIES
15030 Highway 99 (98087-2318)
PHONE..................................206 743-3381
Fax: 425 742-8699

EMP: 4
SALES (est): 224.4K **Privately Held**
SIC: 2092 Mfg Fresh/Frozen Packaged Fish

(G-6107)
DESIGN CRAFT UPHOLSTERY INC
19704 Cypress Way (98036-7036)
PHONE.....................425 775-7620
Allan Kaas, *President*
Michelle Kaas, *Vice Pres*
EMP: 4
SQ FT: 1,900
SALES (est): 393.5K **Privately Held**
SIC: 2512 7641 Upholstered household furniture; upholstery work

(G-6108)
DIRECT MAILING SOLUTIONS
21021 66th Ave W (98036-7303)
PHONE.....................425 739-4568
Brian Webber, *President*
EMP: 2
SALES (est): 160K **Privately Held**
SIC: 7331 2759 Mailing service; commercial printing

(G-6109)
DISCOVERY PRODUCTS CORPORATION
13619 Mukilteo Speedway (98087-1626)
PHONE.....................877 530-2999
Dennis A Clark, *CEO*
Robb Kruger, *COO*
▼ EMP: 9
SQ FT: 6,000
SALES (est): 1.7MM **Privately Held**
WEB: www.discoveryproducts.com
SIC: 2842 Specialty cleaning preparations

(G-6110)
DIY TABLE LEGS LLC
20927 13th Pl W (98036-8712)
PHONE.....................206 659-8669
Antonio STA Teresa, *Principal*
EMP: 4 EST: 2017
SALES (est): 126.4K **Privately Held**
SIC: 2511 Wood household furniture

(G-6111)
EDMONDS ATHLETIC SUPPLY CO
20815 67th Ave W Ste 102 (98036-7359)
PHONE.....................425 778-7322
George Meyring, *Manager*
EMP: 5
SALES (corp-wide): 1.4MM **Privately Held**
SIC: 5941 2759 Team sports equipment; screen printing
PA: Edmonds Athletic Supply Co
514 Main St
Edmonds WA

(G-6112)
EDMONDS PRINTING CO INC
6715 210th St Sw Ste C (98036-7330)
PHONE.....................425 775-7907
Gordon Gegax, *President*
Jeanie Gegax, *Treasurer*
EMP: 6
SALES (est): 560K **Privately Held**
SIC: 2752 Commercial printing, offset

(G-6113)
EIGHT STAR GROUP OF AMERICA
17725 11th Pl W (98037-3323)
PHONE.....................206 243-8888
David Hwang, *President*
▲ EMP: 3
SALES (est): 302.9K **Privately Held**
SIC: 3711 Chassis, motor vehicle

(G-6114)
ELDEC CORPORATION (DH)
Also Called: Crane Aerospace & Electronics
16700 13th Ave W (98037-8503)
P.O. Box 97027 (98046-9727)
PHONE.....................425 743-1313
Brendan Curran, *President*
Max Mitchell, *Chairman*
Michael Brady, *Vice Pres*
Chris Cook, *Vice Pres*
Rick Jones, *Vice Pres*
◆ EMP: 586
SQ FT: 196,000
SALES (est): 167MM
SALES (corp-wide): 3.3B **Publicly Held**
WEB: www.eldec.com
SIC: 3812 3728 3824 3769 Aircraft/aerospace flight instruments & guidance systems; aircraft control instruments; aircraft control systems, electronic; aircraft parts & equipment; fluid meters & counting devices; guided missile & space vehicle parts & auxiliary equipment; semiconductors & related devices; switchgear & switchboard apparatus

(G-6115)
EUSTIS CO INC
Also Called: Pyrocom Co
12407b Mukilteo Speedway (98087-1531)
P.O. Box 1095, Mukilteo (98275-1095)
PHONE.....................425 423-9996
William W Paulson, *President*
Jim Hall, *Treasurer*
Jesse Falcon, *Sales Mgr*
EMP: 36 EST: 1962
SQ FT: 10,000
SALES (est): 7.7MM **Privately Held**
WEB: www.eustispyrocom.com
SIC: 3829 5084 5049 Thermocouples; controlling instruments & accessories; measuring & testing equipment, electrical; scientific recording equipment

(G-6116)
EVEN FLOW HEATING A/C & RFRGN
17317 38th Ave W (98037-7545)
P.O. Box 2184 (98036-2184)
PHONE.....................425 381-0400
Alan Tuerschner, *President*
EMP: 2
SALES (est): 240K **Privately Held**
SIC: 3585 Parts for heating, cooling & refrigerating equipment

(G-6117)
EVER GREEN DONUTS
20101 44th Ave W Ste F (98036-6745)
PHONE.....................425 673-5331
Ngoc Le Thanh, *Owner*
EMP: 2
SALES (est): 71.6K **Privately Held**
SIC: 5461 2051 Doughnuts; doughnuts, except frozen

(G-6118)
EVERYTHING QUARTERLY LLC
2901 211th St Sw (98036-8945)
PHONE.....................425 478-2173
Miriam Davis, *Principal*
EMP: 3
SALES (est): 212.5K **Privately Held**
SIC: 2721 Periodicals

(G-6119)
FENCE QUARTER LLC
16824 44th Ave W Ste 130 (98037-3111)
PHONE.....................800 205-0128
EMP: 2
SALES (est): 77.4K **Privately Held**
SIC: 3131 Quarters

(G-6120)
FORMAL WEAR INC
Also Called: Tuxedo Park
19231 36th Ave W Ste P (98036-5763)
PHONE.....................425 776-1088
Don Berger, *President*
Jason Berger, *Vice Pres*
▲ EMP: 8
SQ FT: 4,000
SALES: 800K **Privately Held**
WEB: www.tuxpark.com
SIC: 2311 2323 Tuxedos: made from purchased materials; men's & boys' neckwear

(G-6121)
FORWORD INPUT INC
20615 36th Pl W (98036-9365)
PHONE.....................206 227-0191
Clifford Kushler, *CEO*
EMP: 12
SALES (est): 489.5K **Privately Held**
SIC: 7372 Prepackaged software

(G-6122)
FRANK J MARTIN COMPANY
18424 Highway 99 (98037-4455)
P.O. Box 1277 (98046-1250)
PHONE.....................206 523-7665
Gerald Martin, *President*
Patricia Martin, *Corp Secy*
Michael McLeod, *Vice Pres*
Justin Wiltse, *Warehouse Mgr*
Arlen Horst, *CFO*
▲ EMP: 35
SQ FT: 22,000
SALES (est): 28.4MM **Privately Held**
WEB: www.fjmartin.com
SIC: 5072 3699 1629 Hardware; security devices; drainage system construction

(G-6123)
GAIS BAKERY
430 164th St Sw (98087-8114)
PHONE.....................425 743-2460
Kathy Leach, *Manager*
EMP: 2
SALES (est): 62.3K **Privately Held**
SIC: 2051 Bread, cake & related products

(G-6124)
GALAXY HOBBY INC
19332 60th Ave W (98036-5112)
PHONE.....................425 670-0454
Bob Jacobson, *President*
Laurie Jacobson, *Vice Pres*
EMP: 9
SALES (est): 771.5K **Privately Held**
WEB: www.galaxyhobby.com
SIC: 3999 5945 Models, general, except toy; models, toy & hobby

(G-6125)
GAMBLIN ENTERPRISES INC
Also Called: All American Metal Finishing
5609 176th St Sw (98037-2816)
PHONE.....................206 795-3817
Dave Amlin, *President*
EMP: 5
SALES: 670K **Privately Held**
WEB: www.allamericanmetalfinishing.com
SIC: 3471 Plating of metals or formed products

(G-6126)
GARAGE
3000 184th St Sw Ste 230 (98037-4719)
PHONE.....................425 640-6021
EMP: 2 **Privately Held**
SIC: 5651 5632 5621 2299 Family clothing stores; women's dancewear, hosiery & lingerie; women's clothing stores; jute & flax textile products

(G-6127)
GENERAL AEROSPACE INC
7127 196th St Sw Ste 201 (98036-5078)
PHONE.....................425 422-5462
EMP: 2
SALES (est): 152.6K **Privately Held**
SIC: 3721 Aircraft

(G-6128)
GENERAL STEAMSHIP INTL LTD
19020 33rd Ave W Ste 365 (98036-4754)
PHONE.....................425 329-1040
Kelly Atkinson, *Manager*
EMP: 5
SALES (corp-wide): 35.1MM **Privately Held**
SIC: 3731 4731 Cargo vessels, building & repairing; agents, shipping
PA: General Steamship International, Ltd.
575 Rdwd Hwy Frntg Rd 200
Mill Valley CA 94941
562 988-9000

(G-6129)
GENZYME CORPORATION
2625 162nd St Sw (98087-3263)
PHONE.....................425 245-1221
John Daigneault, *Engineer*
Tim Andrews, *Branch Mgr*
Steven McAdams, *Security Mgr*
EMP: 93 **Privately Held**
SIC: 2835 Enzyme & isoenzyme diagnostic agents
HQ: Genzyme Corporation
50 Binney St
Cambridge MA 02142
617 252-7500

(G-6130)
GILLESPIE POLYGRAPH
16825 48th Ave W Ste 218 (98037-6404)
PHONE.....................425 775-9015
Terry J Ball, *Owner*
Terry Ball, *Owner*
EMP: 2
SALES (est): 210.9K **Privately Held**
SIC: 3829 7381 Polygraph devices; lie detection service

(G-6131)
GLENNS WELDING AND MFG INC
Also Called: Glenn's Welding & R V Supply
15330 Meadow Rd (98087-6415)
PHONE.....................425 743-2226
Dale Ingraham, *President*
Mark Ingraham, *Vice Pres*
EMP: 20 EST: 1949
SQ FT: 6,000
SALES: 2.5MM **Privately Held**
WEB: www.gweld.com
SIC: 3446 3441 7692 3469 Railings, bannisters, guards, etc.: made from metal pipe; fabricated structural metal; welding repair; metal stampings; sheet metalwork

(G-6132)
HARRIS-FORD INC (PA)
Also Called: Harris Isuzu
20006 64th Ave W (98036-5906)
P.O. Box 867 (98046-0867)
PHONE.....................425 678-0391
Beckey Stupey, *President*
James P Pierre, *President*
Luk Blackwell, *General Mgr*
Rebecca Bright, *Vice Pres*
Michael Shane Pierre, *Vice Pres*
EMP: 138
SQ FT: 10,000
SALES (est): 46.1MM **Privately Held**
WEB: www.harrisford.com
SIC: 5511 5012 7532 7515 Automobiles, new & used; pickups, new & used; automobiles & other motor vehicles; top & body repair & paint shops; passenger car leasing; used car dealers; motor vehicle parts & accessories

(G-6133)
HBSW INC
Also Called: Thryll
200 147th Pl Se (98087-6265)
PHONE.....................217 377-9043
Michael Hendrickson, *CEO*
Monal Shah, *Vice Pres*
Eric Bueser, *CFO*
Jeffrey Waller, *Admin Sec*
EMP: 4
SALES (est): 210K **Privately Held**
SIC: 7372 7389 Application computer software;

(G-6134)
HELIPOWER HELICOPTER INC
3822 134th Pl Sw (98087-1640)
PHONE.....................425 232-0972
Young J Woo, *Vice Pres*
EMP: 2
SALES (est): 150.5K **Privately Held**
SIC: 3721 Aircraft

(G-6135)
HONEYWELL INTERNATIONAL INC
16201 25th Ave W (98087-2520)
PHONE.....................425 921-4598
EMP: 22
SALES (corp-wide): 41.8B **Publicly Held**
SIC: 3724 Aircraft engines & engine parts
PA: Honeywell International Inc.
115 Tabor Rd
Morris Plains NJ 07950
973 455-2000

(G-6136)
HYDRAMASTER
6323 204th St Sw (98036-6012)
PHONE.....................425 775-7276
Steven Brandt, *Branch Mgr*

EMP: 2
SALES (corp-wide): 18.9MM Privately Held
SIC: 3635 Household vacuum cleaners
HQ: Hydramaster Llc
  11015 47th Ave W
  Mukilteo WA 98275
  425 775-7272

(G-6137)
INDUSTRIAL COATINGS
2831 156th St Sw (98087-6355)
PHONE.....................425 742-3415
EMP: 2
SALES (est): 69.9K Privately Held
SIC: 3479 Galvanizing of iron, steel or end-formed products

(G-6138)
INJECTIDRY SYSTEMS INC
3223 164th St Sw Ste N (98087-3214)
P.O. Box 9, Kirkland (98083-0009)
PHONE.....................425 822-3851
Ernie Storrer, President
Eric Storrer, General Mgr
Jane Storrer, Vice Pres
▲ EMP: 9
SALES (est): 1.8MM Privately Held
WEB: www.injectidry.com
SIC: 3564 Ventilating fans: industrial or commercial

(G-6139)
INTERMEC INC (HQ)
16201 25th Ave W (98087-2520)
PHONE.....................425 348-2600
Allen J Lauer, Ch of Bd
Steven B Sample, Principal
Oren G Shaffer, Principal
Larry D Yost, Principal
Yukio Morikubo, Senior VP
▲ EMP: 15
SALES (est): 703MM
SALES (corp-wide): 41.8B Publicly Held
WEB: www.unova.com
SIC: 3577 Bar code (magnetic ink) printers
PA: Honeywell International Inc.
  115 Tabor Rd
  Morris Plains NJ 07950
  973 455-2000

(G-6140)
INTERMEC TECHNOLOGIES CORP (HQ)
16201 25th Ave W (98087-2520)
PHONE.....................425 348-2600
John Waldron, President
Gene Shultice, Principal
Michael Colwell, Vice Pres
John J Tus, Treasurer
Robert A Krulisky, Asst Treas
▲ EMP: 800 EST: 1966
SQ FT: 312,000
SALES (est): 479.3MM
SALES (corp-wide): 41.8B Publicly Held
WEB: www.intermec.net
SIC: 3577 2759 Computer peripheral equipment; printers, computer; optical scanning devices; readers, sorters or in-scribers, magnetic ink; labels & seals: printing
PA: Honeywell International Inc.
  115 Tabor Rd
  Morris Plains NJ 07950
  973 455-2000

(G-6141)
INTERNTIONAL SEAFOODS ALSK INC
Also Called: Kodiak Seafood
3500 188th St Sw Ste 502 (98037-4746)
PHONE.....................206 284-4830
Kay McCready, Manager
EMP: 5
SALES (corp-wide): 598.4MM Privately Held
SIC: 2092 Seafoods, fresh: prepared; seafoods, frozen: prepared
HQ: International Seafoods Of Alaska, Inc.
  517 Shelikof St
  Kodiak AK 99615
  907 486-4768

(G-6142)
J & M DIESEL INC
3418 121st St Sw (98087-1502)
PHONE.....................425 353-3050
Mike Noel, President
Greg Noel, Vice Pres
Gregory Noel, Treasurer
EMP: 10
SQ FT: 1,920
SALES: 1.2MM Privately Held
WEB: www.jmdiesel.com
SIC: 3519 Diesel engine rebuilding

(G-6143)
JAMES LUND
Also Called: Northwest Enterprises
1804 142nd St Sw (98087-6013)
PHONE.....................425 742-9135
James Lund, Owner
EMP: 3
SALES (est): 170K Privately Held
WEB: www.nwent.com
SIC: 2759 Commercial printing

(G-6144)
JENSEN RACE CARS
15032 Highway 99 (98087-2318)
PHONE.....................425 745-8000
Jessie Jensen, Principal
EMP: 2 EST: 2009
SALES (est): 169K Privately Held
SIC: 3711 Automobile assembly, including specialty automobiles

(G-6145)
K & T MACHINE INCORPORATED
12315 Mukilteo Speedway H (98087-1553)
PHONE.....................425 347-2157
Ken Rowe, President
▲ EMP: 4
SALES (est): 390K Privately Held
SIC: 3599 Machine shop, jobbing & repair

(G-6146)
K H B INC
Also Called: Shoreline Graphics
5010 194th St Sw (98036-5449)
PHONE.....................425 771-0881
EMP: 6
SALES (est): 500K Privately Held
SIC: 2752 Lithographic Printing

(G-6147)
KELLIS CREATIONS
3404 132nd St Sw (98087-5133)
PHONE.....................206 371-7130
Kelli Morse, Principal
EMP: 5
SALES (est): 330.3K Privately Held
SIC: 2053 Cakes, bakery: frozen

(G-6148)
KENCO MANUFACTURING INC (PA)
Also Called: Kenco Cabinet and Fixture Mfg
13614 Manor Way (98087-1905)
PHONE.....................425 743-1080
Ken Paterson, President
EMP: 4 EST: 1976
SALES (est): 431.4K Privately Held
WEB: www.kenco-ws.com
SIC: 2434 Wood kitchen cabinets

(G-6149)
KHAN MACHINE TOOL COMPANY LTD
19510 21st Ave W Ste B (98036-4867)
PHONE.....................206 784-9694
Mohammed A Khan, President
Zia Khan, Vice Pres
EMP: 8
SQ FT: 6,500
SALES (est): 1.2MM Privately Held
WEB: www.khanmachine.com
SIC: 3599 Machine shop, jobbing & repair

(G-6150)
KICK ASS PUZZLES
3807 Serene Way (98087-5205)
PHONE.....................425 275-2381
Lynne Springer, Principal
EMP: 2
SALES (est): 60K Privately Held
SIC: 3944 Puzzles

(G-6151)
KIRA AVIATION SERVICES LLC
Also Called: Kira Operations Support
4208 198th St Sw Ste 104c (98036-6736)
PHONE.....................425 361-1060
Richard Rinehart, CEO
EMP: 2
SALES (est): 144.5K Privately Held
SIC: 3728 Aircraft parts & equipment

(G-6152)
KJAR INDUSTRIAL
6320 208th St Sw (98036-7550)
PHONE.....................206 992-7151
EMP: 2
SALES (est): 81.4K Privately Held
SIC: 3599 Mfg Industrial Machinery

(G-6153)
KONGSBERG UNDERWATER TECH INC
Also Called: Simrad Fisheries
19210 33rd Ave W Ste B (98036-4749)
PHONE.....................425 712-1107
Tom Healy, President
Craig Rominger, Controller
Karen Rappleye, Accounting Mgr
Mike Hillers, Sales Staff
Rob Kluver, CTO
▲ EMP: 40
SALES (est): 22MM
SALES (corp-wide): 1.7B Privately Held
SIC: 3812 Sonar systems & equipment
HQ: Kongsberg Digital As
  Drengsrudbekken 12
  Asker 1383
  529 858-02

(G-6154)
KVAMME LTD
15806 Highway 99 Ste 1 (98087-1400)
PHONE.....................425 787-1669
EMP: 2
SALES (est): 64.5K Privately Held
SIC: 2394 Canvas & related products

(G-6155)
L & E TUBING LLC
Also Called: Lafarge & Egge
5820 188th St Sw Ste D (98037-4349)
PHONE.....................425 778-4123
Louis Hoffmann,
John Graham,
EMP: 30
SALES (est): 7.5MM Privately Held
SIC: 3444 Sheet metalwork

(G-6156)
LANDD VENTURES INC
Also Called: Fastsigns
2921 Alderwood Mall Blvd # 104 (98036-4737)
PHONE.....................425 775-9709
Lisa Wilson, President
EMP: 5
SALES (est): 511.2K Privately Held
SIC: 3993 Signs & advertising specialties

(G-6157)
LEIDOS INC
12424 Beverly Park Rd A2 (98087-1517)
PHONE.....................425 267-5600
Mark Burrows, Manager
EMP: 20
SALES (corp-wide): 10.1B Publicly Held
WEB: www.saic.com
SIC: 8731 7371 7373 8742 Commercial physical research; energy research; environmental research; medical research, commercial; computer software development; systems engineering, computer related; training & development consultant; recording & playback apparatus, including phonograph; integrated circuits, semiconductor networks, etc.
HQ: Leidos, Inc.
  11951 Freedom Dr Ste 500
  Reston VA 20190
  571 526-6000

(G-6158)
LITERARY FATALE
4627 192nd St Sw (98036-5508)
PHONE.....................425 239-2126
Heather Reasby, Principal

EMP: 2
SALES (est): 72.2K Privately Held
SIC: 2741 Miscellaneous publishing

(G-6159)
LOEWEN GROUP LLC
Also Called: Fastsigns
2921 Alderwood Mall Blvd # 104 (98036-4737)
PHONE.....................425 775-9709
Linda Niemi, Principal
EMP: 4
SALES (est): 400K Privately Held
SIC: 3993 Signs & advertising specialties

(G-6160)
LUPINE VINEYARDS LLC
18020 67th Ave W (98037-4214)
PHONE.....................206 915-5862
Robert Anderson, Mng Member
EMP: 2
SALES (est): 122.3K Privately Held
SIC: 0172 2084 Grapes; wines

(G-6161)
MAD CONCRETE CUTTING & CORING
4320196st Sw B Pmb 1424 (98036)
PHONE.....................206 367-0263
Daniel Thompson, President
EMP: 3
SALES (est): 290K Privately Held
SIC: 2899 Concrete curing & hardening compounds

(G-6162)
METAL MASTERS NORTHWEST INC
20926 63rd Ave W Ste A (98036-7402)
PHONE.....................425 775-4481
Craig Jeppesen, President
Tim Eaves, Vice Pres
Timothy Eaves, Vice Pres
EMP: 9
SQ FT: 12,050
SALES: 2MM Privately Held
WEB: www.metalmastersnw.com
SIC: 3312 Stainless steel

(G-6163)
METTLER TOLEDO NW
6911 216th St Sw Ste B (98036-7337)
PHONE.....................425 774-3510
Gary Minor, Principal
EMP: 2
SALES (est): 160.3K Privately Held
SIC: 7372 Prepackaged software

(G-6164)
MIRA TECHNOLOGY
20833 67th Ave W Ste 101 (98036-7365)
PHONE.....................425 678-0183
Amir Varamini, President
Chris Soukup, Manager
EMP: 5
SALES (est): 447.3K Privately Held
SIC: 3355 1731 Aluminum wire & cable; fiber optic cable installation

(G-6165)
MMUSA INC
Also Called: Coenzyme A Technologies
12512 Beverly Park Rd 15-16 (98087-1516)
PHONE.....................360 306-5383
Amir Zeibak, CEO
EMP: 2
SALES (est): 326.4K Privately Held
SIC: 5091 2048 Fitness equipment & supplies; feed supplements; mineral feed supplements

(G-6166)
MONDELLO PUBLISHING
3929 205th Pl Sw (98036-8803)
PHONE.....................425 775-9695
Bruce Vaneedenter, Owner
EMP: 2
SALES (est): 110.2K Privately Held
SIC: 2741 Miscellaneous publishing

(G-6167)
MOSAICSNMORE
614 Logan Rd (98036-7242)
PHONE.....................425 273-3216

Lynnwood - Snohomish County (G-6168)   GEOGRAPHIC SECTION

Roberta James, *Owner*
EMP: 2
SALES (est): 127.4K Privately Held
SIC: 3253 Ceramic wall & floor tile

(G-6168)
NEON SYSTEMS INC
1729 143rd Pl Sw (98087-6016)
PHONE..................425 501-6447
John Weiss, *President*
Drew Susan, *Director*
EMP: 3
SALES (est): 200.1K Privately Held
SIC: 3993 Neon signs

(G-6169)
NEUTEK INC
5214 201st Pl Sw (98036-6329)
PHONE..................206 660-0056
Mike Pantelich, *CEO*
Mike Monaghan, *Vice Pres*
EMP: 4
SALES: 100K Privately Held
SIC: 3496 Miscellaneous fabricated wire products

(G-6170)
NORTHWEST FLEXO SPC LLC
Also Called: Advanced Labels NW
2100 196th St Sw Ste 131 (98036-7082)
PHONE..................425 776-4315
Kevin Kj, *Opers Dir*
Caitlin Archipley, *Accounts Mgr*
Richard Key, *Mktg Dir*
Jeff McCorkle, *Mktg Dir*
EMP: 2
SALES (est): 90.7K Privately Held
SIC: 2679 7389 Converted paper products; packaging & labeling services

(G-6171)
NOVATECH INSTRUMENTS INC
4210 198th St Sw Ste 204 (98036-6737)
PHONE..................206 284-0704
EMP: 2
SALES (est): 138.9K Privately Held
SIC: 3825 Instruments to measure electricity

(G-6172)
OLSONS BAKING COMPANY LLC
Also Called: Signature Bakery
6414 204th St Sw Ste 100 (98036-5966)
P.O. Box 3488 (98046-3488)
PHONE..................425 774-9164
Charles M Olson, *President*
Maurice S Olson Jr,
Maurice Olson,
EMP: 150
SQ FT: 55,000
SALES (est): 30.1MM Privately Held
SIC: 2051 2053 Bakery: wholesale or wholesale/retail combined; bakery products, partially cooked (except frozen); biscuits, baked: baking powder & raised; cakes, bakery: except frozen; frozen bakery products, except bread

(G-6173)
OLYMPUS LOCK INC
18424 Highway 99 (98037-4455)
P.O. Box 1277 (98046-1250)
PHONE..................206 362-3290
Gerald E Martin, *President*
Patricia A Martin, *Corp Secy*
Frank J Martin, *Director*
▲ **EMP:** 22
SQ FT: 14,000
SALES (est): 3.5MM Privately Held
WEB: www.olympus-lock.com
SIC: 3429 Keys, locks & related hardware

(G-6174)
OMEN BOARD INDUSTRIES LLC
5001 208th St Sw Ste 102 (98036-7637)
PHONE..................425 967-3434
▲ **EMP:** 3 **EST:** 2014
SALES (est): 244.9K Privately Held
SIC: 3999 Manufacturing industries

(G-6175)
OPTIMUM PRECISION INC
6324 202nd St Sw (98036-6065)
PHONE..................425 778-1455
Jeffrey Barker, *President*

Kathleen Barker, *Corp Secy*
EMP: 5
SALES (est): 768.4K Privately Held
SIC: 3444 Sheet metal specialties, not stamped

(G-6176)
PACIFIC COAST MARINE LLC
16531 13th Ave W Ste A106 (98037-8500)
PHONE..................425 743-9550
Scott Howell, *President*
Darren Loken, *General Mgr*
Paul Hill,
EMP: 69
SALES (est): 7.1MM Privately Held
SIC: 3442 Window & door frames

(G-6177)
PACIFIC COAST MARINE INDS INC
Also Called: P M C
16531 13th Ave W Ste A106 (98037-8500)
PHONE..................425 743-9550
Paul Price, *President*
Scott W Nicholson, *President*
Paul Price, *President*
R Scott Howell, *Vice Pres*
Stephen D Smith, *Treasurer*
▲ **EMP:** 80
SQ FT: 60,000
SALES (est): 11.5MM
SALES (corp-wide): 41.4MM Privately Held
WEB: www.pcmii.com
SIC: 3444 3442 3429 Sheet metalwork; metal doors, sash & trim; manufactured hardware (general)
PA: Northern Industrial, Inc.
200 S Orcas St
Seattle WA 98108
206 682-2752

(G-6178)
PEE WEE PROS LTD LIABILITY CO
12925 Beverly Park Rd (98087-5127)
PHONE..................206 276-6707
Kyle Lien,
EMP: 2 **EST:** 2013
SALES (est): 120K Privately Held
SIC: 3949 Football equipment & supplies, general

(G-6179)
PEREGRINE MANUFACTURING INC
19504 24th Ave W Ste 105 (98036-4868)
PHONE..................425 673-5600
Kirk Wallace, *President*
Barbara Wallace, *Admin Sec*
EMP: 7 **EST:** 1998
SQ FT: 2,500
SALES (est): 1.6MM Privately Held
SIC: 3566 3545 3462 Drives, high speed industrial, except hydrostatic; gears, power transmission, except automotive; machine tool accessories; iron & steel forgings

(G-6180)
PETOSA ACCORDIONS INC
19503 56th Ave W Ste B (98036-5225)
PHONE..................206 632-2700
Joe Petosa Sr, *President*
Joe Petosa Jr, *Corp Secy*
Kristy Petosa, *Vice Pres*
▲ **EMP:** 7
SQ FT: 5,000
SALES (est): 1MM Privately Held
WEB: www.petosa.com
SIC: 3931 5736 Accordions & parts; musical instrument stores

(G-6181)
PLASTIC SALES & SERVICE INC
5522 208th St Sw (98036-7633)
PHONE..................206 524-8312
Ruben Rael, *President*
John Canfield, *General Mgr*
Patricia Rael, *Vice Pres*
Bo Alvizo, *Admin Asst*
EMP: 19
SQ FT: 14,000

SALES (est): 2MM Privately Held
WEB: www.plasticsales.com
SIC: 7692 7299 7389 2759 Welding repair; stitching services; laminating service; screen printing; acrylic fibers; automotive & apparel trimmings

(G-6182)
POLISH NAIL SPA
20101 44th Ave W Ste A (98036-6745)
PHONE..................425 771-1458
Cathrine Vo, *Principal*
EMP: 2
SALES (est): 147.3K Privately Held
SIC: 2844 Manicure preparations

(G-6183)
POSERA USA INC (PA)
6016 204th St Sw Ste A (98036-4016)
PHONE..................206 364-8686
Michel Cote, *President*
James Gillis, *President*
Bill Neptune, *Vice Pres*
William Neptune, *Vice Pres*
Frances Nickell, *Opers Mgr*
EMP: 120
SQ FT: 5,500
SALES (est): 19MM Privately Held
WEB: www.posera.com
SIC: 5044 3578 Cash registers; cash registers

(G-6184)
PRECISION MACHINE & TOOL INC
2813 148th St Sw (98087-5804)
PHONE..................425 745-6229
Richard Junco, *President*
EMP: 7
SQ FT: 8,000
SALES (est): 1MM Privately Held
SIC: 3599 7692 1799 Machine shop, jobbing & repair; welding repair; welding on site

(G-6185)
R ELLERSICK BREWING CO
5030 208th St Sw (98036-7642)
PHONE..................425 374-7248
Rick Ellersick, *Principal*
EMP: 9
SALES (est): 798.8K Privately Held
SIC: 2082 Beer (alcoholic beverage)

(G-6186)
R S MANUFACTURING INC
5728 204th St Sw Ste 100 (98036-7554)
PHONE..................425 774-1211
Rob Stevenson, *President*
EMP: 20
SQ FT: 8,000
SALES (est): 3.5MM Privately Held
SIC: 2521 2541 2434 Cabinets, office: wood; wood partitions & fixtures; wood kitchen cabinets

(G-6187)
REBEC LLC
Also Called: Prestine Environmental
3511 132nd St Sw Ste 1 (98087-5141)
P.O. Box 658, Edmonds (98020-0658)
PHONE..................425 745-4177
Timothy W Reber, *Mng Member*
EMP: 7
SALES (est): 1.2MM Privately Held
WEB: www.rebec.com
SIC: 3532 4953 Amalgamators (metallurgical or mining machinery); recycling, waste materials

(G-6188)
REFOCUS LASER ENGRAVING-DESIGN
21420 Locust Way (98036-8632)
PHONE..................541 998-2047
EMP: 2
SALES (est): 73.1K Privately Held
SIC: 2796 Platemaking Services

(G-6189)
ROBERT GEE VIOLINS
19330 7th Ave W (98036-4915)
PHONE..................425 776-4002
Robert Gee, *Owner*
EMP: 2

SALES (est): 103.2K Privately Held
SIC: 3931 Violins & parts

(G-6190)
RUTILLO CHAVES
4202 198th St Sw Ste 3 (98036-6730)
PHONE..................425 775-0651
Rutillo Chaves, *Principal*
Rutillo O Chaves, *Fmly & Gen Dent*
EMP: 2
SALES (est): 187.8K Privately Held
SIC: 3843 Enamels, dentists'

(G-6191)
S & W MANAGEMENT CO INC
Also Called: Auntie Anne's
3000 184th St Sw Ste 856 (98037-4723)
PHONE..................425 771-6850
Scott Barbour, *Manager*
EMP: 20
SALES (corp-wide): 8MM Privately Held
SIC: 5461 5963 2096 2051 Pretzels; direct selling establishments; potato chips & similar snacks; bread, cake & related products
PA: S & W Management Co Inc
20300 19th Ave Ne
Shoreline WA

(G-6192)
SCRATCH DISTILLERY LLC
20818 44th Ave W Ste 201 (98036-7709)
PHONE..................425 673-5541
William Wood, *Principal*
EMP: 3 **EST:** 2014
SALES (est): 136.4K Privately Held
SIC: 2085 Distilled & blended liquors

(G-6193)
SEABOARD CABINET COMPANY INC
5728 204th St Sw Ste 400 (98036-7554)
PHONE..................425 776-2000
James Sciscoe, *President*
EMP: 12
SQ FT: 15,000
SALES (est): 1.1MM Privately Held
WEB: www.seaboardcabinet.com
SIC: 2434 2521 2517 Wood kitchen cabinets; wood office furniture; wood television & radio cabinets

(G-6194)
SHELDON CUSTOM CABINETS LTD
20626 50th Ave W (98036-7639)
PHONE..................425 778-0043
Randall Sheldon, *President*
Lavonne Sheldon, *Treasurer*
EMP: 8
SQ FT: 6,300
SALES: 430K Privately Held
SIC: 2434 Wood kitchen cabinets

(G-6195)
SHIRTS ILLUSTRATED
12315 Mukilteo Speedway J (98087-1553)
PHONE..................425 742-3844
Matthew Fowler, *Mng Member*
EMP: 2
SQ FT: 1,500
SALES: 200K Privately Held
SIC: 7389 2759 Embroidering of advertising on shirts, etc.; screen printing

(G-6196)
SILVER HORDE FISHING SUPPLIES (PA)
20910 63rd Ave W (98036-7402)
P.O. Box 150 (98046-0150)
PHONE..................425 778-2640
Barrett F Morrison, *President*
Marilyn Morrison, *Treasurer*
▲ **EMP:** 6 **EST:** 1947
SQ FT: 3,000
SALES (est): 749.1K Privately Held
WEB: www.silverhorde.com
SIC: 3949 Fishing tackle, general

(G-6197)
SINBON TECHNOLOGIES WEST
6925 216th St Sw Ste D (98036-7358)
PHONE..................425 712-8500
Thomas Mullins, *Owner*
▲ **EMP:** 2

GEOGRAPHIC SECTION

SALES (est): 200K Privately Held
SIC: 3629 Electronic generation equipment

(G-6198)
SITEC COATINGS
4700 176th St Sw (98037-3419)
PHONE.....................360 840-9979
David Pauser, *Administration*
EMP: 2 EST: 2014
SALES (est): 98.7K Privately Held
SIC: 3479 Metal coating & allied service

(G-6199)
SMART START
18908 Highway 99 (98036-5218)
PHONE.....................425 967-5699
EMP: 2
SALES (est): 106.9K Privately Held
SIC: 3694 Ignition apparatus & distributors

(G-6200)
SMOKE PLUS CIGAR
3333 184th St Sw (98037-4724)
PHONE.....................425 673-1390
Dori Taft, *Principal*
EMP: 2 EST: 2010
SALES (est): 125.6K Privately Held
SIC: 5993 2013 Tobacco stores & stands; sausages & other prepared meats

(G-6201)
SNO KING RECYCLING INC
16123 Highway 99 (98087-1430)
P.O. Box 2711, Kirkland (98083-2711)
PHONE.....................425 582-2919
Michael Kane, *President*
EMP: 5
SQ FT: 5,000
SALES (est): 560K Privately Held
SIC: 5093 4953 2679 Bottles, waste; ferrous metal scrap & waste; waste paper; recycling, waste materials; corrugated paper: made from purchased material

(G-6202)
SNO KING STAMP
19832 Highway 99 (98036-6042)
P.O. Box 626 (98046-0626)
PHONE.....................425 771-9373
Kelly Sheehan, *President*
EMP: 2
SQ FT: 4,000
SALES (est): 206.5K Privately Held
WEB: www.sno-kingstamp.com
SIC: 3953 5999 7389 Embossing seals & hand stamps; rubber stamps; engraving service

(G-6203)
SOG SPECIALTY KNIVES & TLS LLC (HQ)
6521 212th St Sw (98037-7411)
PHONE.....................425 771-6230
Gerald T Heinlen, *CEO*
Robi Gupta, *Vice Pres*
Greg Matty, *Controller*
Harrison Frye, *Sales Staff*
John N Belniak,
◆ EMP: 65
SALES (est): 28.7MM
SALES (corp-wide): 59.6MM Publicly Held
WEB: www.sogknives.com
SIC: 3421 Knives: butchers', hunting, pocket, etc.
PA: Gladstone Investment Corp
1521 Westbranch Dr # 100
Mc Lean VA 22102
703 287-5800

(G-6204)
SPEEDY SIGNS
19106 Highway 99 Ste A (98036-5238)
PHONE.....................425 771-1700
James Park, *Principal*
EMP: 2 EST: 2011
SALES (est): 187.5K Privately Held
SIC: 3993 Electric signs

(G-6205)
SQUIRES MACHINE INC
19510 21st Ave W Ste B (98036-4867)
PHONE.....................425 672-7101
Rod Hemuth, *President*
EMP: 7
SQ FT: 4,000

SALES (est): 757.6K Privately Held
SIC: 3599 Machine shop, jobbing & repair

(G-6206)
SUPERIOR STONE MANUFACTURING
15105 Highway 99 Ste B (98087-2344)
PHONE.....................425 312-2968
EMP: 2
SALES (est): 66.7K Privately Held
SIC: 3999 Manufacturing industries

(G-6207)
TAMER LABORATORIES INC
16825 48th Ave W Ste 310 (98037-6407)
PHONE.....................206 364-6761
Steven Llyod, *CEO*
Macit Gurol, *Ch of Bd*
Robert Burns, *President*
Jim Zue, *COO*
EMP: 15
SQ FT: 6,600
SALES (est): 2.1MM Privately Held
SIC: 2869 Perfumes, flavorings & food additives

(G-6208)
TECHNICAL SYSTEMS INC (PA)
2303 196th St Sw Ste B (98036-7071)
PHONE.....................425 678-4142
Gary Conley, *President*
Brad Peistrup, *President*
Bob J Kotjan, *Vice Pres*
Matthew Scott, *Vice Pres*
EMP: 45
SQ FT: 22,000
SALES (est): 24.2MM Privately Held
WEB: www.tsicontrols.com
SIC: 3823 Panelboard indicators, recorders & controllers: receiver

(G-6209)
TED GAY
Also Called: Line X Custom Bed Liners
17709 Highway 99 (98037-3612)
PHONE.....................425 742-9566
Teg Gay, *Owner*
EMP: 2
SALES (est): 110K Privately Held
SIC: 3714 Pickup truck bed liners

(G-6210)
TINCAN STUDIO LLC
13308 Wigen Rd (98087-1636)
PHONE.....................559 906-3521
Ernest Leitch,
EMP: 2
SALES: 1K Privately Held
SIC: 7371 3944 Computer software development; games, toys & children's vehicles

(G-6211)
TOMATESA ENTERPRISES LLC
Also Called: Ultrafino Panama Hat
6333 212th St Sw (98036-7499)
P.O. Box 612, Mountlake Terrace (98043-0612)
PHONE.....................425 778-6708
Lorena Ashton,
Ivonne Jurado,
Yuri Parreno,
EMP: 4
SALES (est): 440K Privately Held
SIC: 8748 2353 Business consulting; panama hats

(G-6212)
TRANSACT COMMUNICATIONS INC (PA)
5105 200th St Sw Ste 200 (98036-6397)
PHONE.....................425 977-2100
Richard H Passovoy, *President*
William Donnelly, *Exec Dir*
EMP: 13 EST: 1994
SQ FT: 4,000
SALES (est): 2.4MM Privately Held
WEB: www.transact.com
SIC: 7371 2741 Computer software development;

(G-6213)
TUBS TO GO INC
Also Called: Portable Baptistry
12314 Beverly Park Rd # 119 (98087-1513)
PHONE.....................425 348-7888
Ronald Tosh, *President*
Constance Tosh, *Vice Pres*
EMP: 7
SALES (est): 770K Privately Held
WEB: www.portablebaptistry.com
SIC: 3432 8661 Plastic plumbing fixture fittings, assembly; non-church religious organizations

(G-6214)
TURNER EXHIBITS INC
5631 208th St Sw Ste B (98036-7513)
PHONE.....................425 776-4930
Stephen Groves, *President*
Gregory Cain, *Vice Pres*
EMP: 24
SQ FT: 18,000
SALES (est): 3MM Privately Held
WEB: www.turnerexhibits.com
SIC: 7389 2541 1751 Exhibit construction by industrial contractors; wood partitions & fixtures; store fixture installation

(G-6215)
VARSITY COMMUNICATIONS INC
4114 198th St Sw Ste 5 (98036-6742)
PHONE.....................425 412-7070
Ralph Boyle, *CEO*
Dick Stephens, *President*
Kirk Tourtillote, *Vice Pres*
Bobbi Kramer, *CFO*
Sandra J Boyle, *Admin Sec*
EMP: 18
SQ FT: 5,000
SALES (est): 1.9MM Privately Held
WEB: www.varsitycommunications.com
SIC: 2721 7389 Magazines: publishing only, not printed on site; advertising, promotional & trade show services

(G-6216)
VERITAS CUSTOM WOODWORKS
17725 17th Ave W (98037-4012)
PHONE.....................425 346-5576
Byron Heward, *Principal*
EMP: 2 EST: 2013
SALES (est): 119.7K Privately Held
SIC: 2431 Millwork

(G-6217)
VIETNAM FILTER PROJECT
14831 19th Ave W (98087-6027)
PHONE.....................425 772-5401
EMP: 2
SALES (est): 216.5K Privately Held
SIC: 3569 Mfg General Industrial Machinery

(G-6218)
VINDICO PRINTING AND DESIGN
2100 196th St Sw Ste 117 (98036-7081)
PHONE.....................425 329-4739
EMP: 2
SALES (est): 92.3K Privately Held
SIC: 2759 Screen printing

(G-6219)
VINYL LAB NW LLC
16401 43rd Pl W (98087-6803)
PHONE.....................425 870-8702
Brett Lane, *Principal*
EMP: 2 EST: 2012
SALES (est): 140.1K Privately Held
SIC: 3993 Signs & advertising specialties

(G-6220)
VULCAN SOFTWARE LLC
14416 18th Ave W (98087-6047)
PHONE.....................206 407-3057
Phil Kramer,
EMP: 2
SALES: 150K Privately Held
SIC: 7372 Application computer software

(G-6221)
WARM PRODUCTS INC (PA)
Also Called: Warm Company, The
5529 186th Pl Sw (98037-4325)
PHONE.....................425 248-2424
James F Chumbley, *President*
Erica Johnson, *Vice Pres*
Ron Stafford, *Vice Pres*
Dawn Tereira, *Vice Pres*
Irina Thompson, *Vice Pres*
◆ EMP: 39
SQ FT: 38,000
SALES (est): 8.3MM Privately Held
WEB: www.warmcompany.com
SIC: 2297 Nonwoven fabrics

(G-6222)
WESMAR COMPANY INC
5720 204th St Sw (98036-7554)
PHONE.....................206 783-5344
Daryl Funston, *President*
Cathie Farrell, *Area Mgr*
Robert Gore, *Area Mgr*
Kevin Graham, *Area Mgr*
Jesus Heredia, *Area Mgr*
▲ EMP: 66
SALES: 14.7MM Privately Held
WEB: www.wesmarcompany.com
SIC: 2842 Specialty cleaning, polishes & sanitation goods

(G-6223)
WESTERN TYPOGRAPHERS INC
6327 204th St Sw 201 (98036-6012)
PHONE.....................425 967-4700
Warren B Funnel, *President*
Warren B Funnell, *President*
Lorence I Funnell, *Treasurer*
EMP: 6
SQ FT: 2,400
SALES (est): 58K Privately Held
SIC: 2759 Commercial printing

(G-6224)
WHAB TECHNOLOGIES LLC
13716 Manor Way (98087-1903)
PHONE.....................800 506-2770
Aaron Butt, *Mng Member*
Wade Hults, *Mng Member*
EMP: 2 EST: 2013
SALES (est): 25K Privately Held
SIC: 7372 7374 Application computer software; computer graphics service

(G-6225)
WHITE SIGNS
15107 Highway 99 (98087-2319)
PHONE.....................425 745-0760
Nobuygn Myung, *Principal*
▲ EMP: 2
SALES (est): 228.5K Privately Held
SIC: 3993 Electric signs

(G-6226)
WOODCRAFT INC
5015 208th St Sw Ste 3 (98037-7649)
PHONE.....................800 225-1153
Steve Zajaczkowski, *President*
Mary Jajaczkowski, *Vice Pres*
EMP: 5
SALES: 699.5K Privately Held
SIC: 2511 Wood household furniture

(G-6227)
XOCECO USA
4100 194th St Sw (98036-4613)
PHONE.....................425 670-3968
John Merrell, *Vice Pres*
EMP: 2
SALES (est): 119.4K Privately Held
SIC: 3663 Radio & TV communications equipment

Mabton
Yakima County

(G-6228)
GREEN VALLEY MANAGEMENT LLC
101 Green Valley Rd Ste A (98935-9471)
PHONE.....................509 830-5240
EMP: 2

Mabton - Yakima County (G-6229)

SALES (est): 48.8K **Privately Held**
SIC: **0139** 3999 8741 ; ; management services

(G-6229)
L STOP-N-GO
330 South St (98935-0207)
PHONE..................................509 896-6089
EMP: 2
SALES (est): 90.7K **Privately Held**
SIC: **2911** Petroleum refining

Malaga
Chelan County

(G-6230)
ALCOA WENATCHEE LLC
6200 Malaga Alcoa Hwy (98828-9784)
PHONE..................................509 663-9246
Brian Stokes, *Sr Corp Ofcr*
Phil Rassmussen, *Manager*
EMP: 393
SALES (corp-wide): 13.4B **Publicly Held**
SIC: **3353** Aluminum sheet, plate & foil
HQ: Alcoa Wenatchee Llc
   201 Isabella St Ste 500
   Pittsburgh PA 15212
   412 553-4545

(G-6231)
AMG ALUMINUM NORTH AMERICA LLC
4400 Kawecki Rd (98828-9718)
PHONE..................................509 663-2165
Katia Marcoux, *Safety Mgr*
Chuck Plugstun, *Manager*
Bernie Cain, *Director*
Tom Pickett, *Maintence Staff*
EMP: 55
SALES (corp-wide): 1B **Privately Held**
WEB: www.kballoys.com
SIC: **3355** 3677 3334 Aluminum rod & bar; aluminum ingot; electronic coils, transformers & other inductors; primary aluminum
HQ: Amg Aluminum North America, Llc
   435 Devon Park Dr Ste 200
   Wayne PA 19087
   610 293-2501

(G-6232)
MICAHS CUSTOM WORKS LLC
56 Hurds River Ranch Ln (98828-7800)
P.O. Box 104 (98828-0104)
PHONE..................................509 665-9631
Micah England, *Mng Member*
EMP: 3
SQ FT: 60,000
SALES (est): 750K **Privately Held**
SIC: **3715** Trailer bodies

(G-6233)
UFP WASHINGTON LLC
Also Called: Nepa Pallet and Container
4234 Malaga Alcoa Hwy (98828-9727)
PHONE..................................509 663-1988
Tim Gosser, *Branch Mgr*
EMP: 11
SALES (corp-wide): 4.4B **Publicly Held**
SIC: **2448** 2441 Pallets, wood; nailed wood boxes & shook
HQ: Ufp Washington, Llc
   12027 3 Lakes Rd
   Snohomish WA 98290
   360 568-3185

Malo
Ferry County

(G-6234)
KNUTZ LOGGING & FARMING
1940 N Saint Peters Crk (99150)
P.O. Box 13 (99150-0013)
PHONE..................................509 779-4713
William Knutz, *Owner*
EMP: 5
SALES (est): 298.9K **Privately Held**
SIC: **2411** Logging camps & contractors

(G-6235)
ROBERT LLOYD ZERCK
17424 N Highway 21 (99150-9700)
PHONE..................................509 779-4820
Robert Zerck, *Principal*
EMP: 6
SALES (est): 406.3K **Privately Held**
SIC: **2411** Logging

(G-6236)
ZERCKS LOGGING LLC
17424 N Highway 21 (99150-9700)
PHONE..................................509 779-4820
EMP: 3
SALES (est): 176.1K **Privately Held**
SIC: **2411** Logging

Malott
Okanogan County

(G-6237)
FAR WEST MACHINE INC
21 Three Devils Rd (98829)
P.O. Box H (98829-0160)
PHONE..................................509 422-0312
Mike Poole, *President*
Vicky Poole, *Corp Secy*
EMP: 2
SALES (est): 341K **Privately Held**
SIC: **3599** Machine shop, jobbing & repair

Manson
Chelan County

(G-6238)
AMOS ROME VINEYARDS
700 Wapato Lake Rd (98831-9552)
PHONE..................................206 890-4482
EMP: 2
SALES (est): 80.3K **Privately Held**
SIC: **2084** Wines

(G-6239)
ATAM COMPANY LLC
Also Called: Atam Winery
148 High Blossom Ln (98831-4501)
PHONE..................................509 687-4421
Denis Atam, *Principal*
EMP: 3
SALES (est): 256.4K **Privately Held**
SIC: **2084** Wines

(G-6240)
BENSON VINEYARDS
754 Winesap Ave (98831-9581)
PHONE..................................509 687-0313
Scott Benson, *Owner*
EMP: 6
SALES (est): 356.8K **Privately Held**
WEB: www.bensonvineyards.com
SIC: **2084** Wines

(G-6241)
CHARLES LYBECKER
2478 Totem Pole Rd (98831-9513)
PHONE..................................509 687-0555
Charles Lybecker, *Principal*
EMP: 2
SALES (est): 108.4K **Privately Held**
SIC: **2084** Wines

(G-6242)
CHELAN VINTNERS
121 Furey Ave (98831-9731)
PHONE..................................509 630-8504
Heather Beattiger, *Principal*
EMP: 2
SALES (est): 64.9K **Privately Held**
SIC: **2084** Wines, brandy & brandy spirits

(G-6243)
CROWDER FAMILY WINERY
546 Klate Rd (98831-9747)
PHONE..................................509 834-3270
Jefferey Crowder, *Principal*
EMP: 2
SALES (est): 87.7K **Privately Held**
SIC: **2084** Wines

(G-6244)
HARD ROW TO HOE VINEYARDS
300 Ivan Morse Rd (98831-9468)
P.O. Box 159, Chelan (98816-0159)
PHONE..................................509 687-3000
Don Phelps, *Principal*
EMP: 3
SALES (est): 290.1K **Privately Held**
SIC: **2084** Wines

(G-6245)
STEVEN JON KLUDT
200 Quetilquasoon Rd (98831-9667)
PHONE..................................509 687-4000
Ben Williams, *Principal*
EMP: 15
SALES (est): 945.4K **Privately Held**
SIC: **2084** Wines, brandy & brandy spirits

(G-6246)
TILDIO WINERY LLC
70 E Wapto Rd (98831)
P.O. Box 303 (98831-0303)
PHONE..................................509 687-8463
Milum Perry, *Principal*
EMP: 2
SALES (est): 173.3K **Privately Held**
SIC: **2084** Wines

(G-6247)
TIPSY CANYON WINERY
270 Upper Joe Creek Rd (98831-9515)
PHONE..................................425 306-4844
EMP: 2
SALES (est): 126.3K **Privately Held**
SIC: **2084** Wines

Maple Falls
Whatcom County

(G-6248)
BEE HIVE CANDLES INC
8582 Tilbury Rd (98266-8275)
PHONE..................................360 599-9725
Darian Wesolowski, *Principal*
EMP: 3
SALES (est): 254.9K **Privately Held**
WEB: www.beehivecandles.com
SIC: **3999** Candles

(G-6249)
CLAUSON QUARRY LLC
Also Called: Clauson Lime
8899 Silver Lake Rd (98266-7912)
PHONE..................................360 599-2731
Charlie Clauson, *Principal*
EMP: 9
SQ FT: 100
SALES (est): 429.9K **Privately Held**
SIC: **1422** Crushed & broken limestone

(G-6250)
SAFETY REFLECTION
6250 Juniper Ln (98266-8224)
P.O. Box 2326 (98266-2326)
PHONE..................................360 599-1874
EMP: 3
SALES (est): 220.3K **Privately Held**
SIC: **3842** Clothing, fire resistant & protective

(G-6251)
SPEC TECH INDUSTRIES INC
622 Sprague Valley Dr (98266-7827)
PHONE..................................360 303-9077
Mark Garst, *President*
Patty Solomon, *Principal*
EMP: 4
SALES (est): 400.6K **Privately Held**
SIC: **3489** Guns or gun parts, over 30 mm.

Maple Valley
King County

(G-6252)
A-K PRINTING
27207 Witte Rd Se (98038-3224)
P.O. Box 619 (98038-0619)
PHONE..................................253 391-1784
EMP: 2

SALES (est): 92.3K **Privately Held**
SIC: **2752** Commercial printing, lithographic

(G-6253)
AFFORDBLE TRCTR BCKHOE SVC LLC
28819 Se 216th Way (98038-7730)
PHONE..................................360 306-1533
Scott Kling, *Principal*
EMP: 2 EST: 2016
SALES (est): 91K **Privately Held**
SIC: **3531** Backhoes

(G-6254)
AIRCRAFT PROPULSION SYSTEMS
25316 232nd Ave Se (98038-6899)
P.O. Box 629, Ravensdale (98051-0629)
PHONE..................................425 413-4127
Betty Nelson, *President*
EMP: 2
SALES: 140K **Privately Held**
SIC: **3728** 5088 Aircraft propellers & associated equipment; transportation equipment & supplies

(G-6255)
ALB FRAMING GALLERY & GIFT
20515 292nd Ave Se (98038-7809)
PHONE..................................425 432-5505
EMP: 2 EST: 1988
SALES (est): 80K **Privately Held**
SIC: **3952** 5999 Mfg Lead Pencils/Art Goods Ret Misc Merchandise

(G-6256)
ALPACA THIS LLC
23116 244th Ave Se (98038-6776)
PHONE..................................425 432-7227
Kelley Jarvis, *Principal*
EMP: 2
SALES (est): 110.4K **Privately Held**
SIC: **2231** Alpacas, mohair: woven

(G-6257)
AMERICAN FOREST LANDS
24012 Se 276th St (98038-8116)
PHONE..................................425 432-5004
C Dickinson, *Principal*
EMP: 2
SALES: 190K **Privately Held**
SIC: **2411** 4212 Logging camps & contractors; lumber (log) trucking, local

(G-6258)
AMERICAN FOREST LANDS WASH ✪
21410 Se 248th St (98038-8514)
PHONE..................................425 358-5235
EMP: 2 EST: 2018
SALES (est): 81.7K **Privately Held**
SIC: **2411** Logging

(G-6259)
AUTOMATED TECH SOLUTIONS LLC
22240 257th Ave Se (98038-7621)
PHONE..................................425 999-1297
Victor Bagnall, *Principal*
Patrick McGinnis, *Principal*
Jacob Wrolson, *Principal*
EMP: 3 EST: 2015
SALES (est): 180K **Privately Held**
SIC: **3674** 3822 Infrared sensors, solid state; ultra-violet sensors, solid state; thermostats & other environmental sensors; temperature sensors for motor windings

(G-6260)
BILLABONG PUBLISHING & ME
24405 222nd Ave Se (98038-6023)
PHONE..................................206 391-8300
Carol Carine, *Owner*
EMP: 4
SALES (est): 240.1K **Privately Held**
SIC: **2741** Miscellaneous publishing

(G-6261)
BOEING COMPANY
25215 Se 184th St (98038-7304)
PHONE..................................425 413-3400
Randy Hanford, *Manager*
EMP: 500

GEOGRAPHIC SECTION

Maple Valley - King County (G-6295)

SALES (corp-wide): 101.1B **Publicly Held**
SIC: **3721** 3663 3764 3812 Airplanes, fixed or rotary wing; radio & TV communications equipment; guided missile & space vehicle propulsion unit parts; search & navigation equipment
PA: The Boeing Company
100 N Riverside Plz
Chicago IL 60606
312 544-2000

(G-6262)
BRASS KEY INC
24418 Se 177th St (98038-7341)
P.O. Box 967 (98038-0967)
PHONE..........................866 325-6840
Mary Gustaff, *President*
Judy Mullins, *Managing Dir*
▲ EMP: 26
SQ FT: 10,000
SALES (est): 3.7MM **Privately Held**
WEB: www.brass-key.com
SIC: **3944** 5945 3942 Games, toys & children's vehicles; hobby, toy & game shops; dolls & stuffed toys

(G-6263)
CHEVRON CORPORATION
27201 216th Ave Se (98038-3245)
PHONE..........................425 413-8881
EMP: 2
SALES (corp-wide): 166.3B **Publicly Held**
SIC: **2911** Petroleum refining
PA: Chevron Corporation
6001 Bollinger Canyon Rd
San Ramon CA 94583
925 842-1000

(G-6264)
CHOOCH ENTERPRISES INC
20002 Se 236th St (98038-8613)
P.O. Box 1200 (98038-1200)
PHONE..........................425 273-4794
Michael O'Connell, *President*
▲ EMP: 2
SALES (est): 154.7K **Privately Held**
SIC: **1081** Preparing shafts or tunnels, metal mining

(G-6265)
COOPER POWER SYSTEMS INC
26733 227th Ave Se (98038-5821)
PHONE..........................206 499-9473
Jeff Lindgren, *Manager*
EMP: 2
SALES (est): 171.8K **Privately Held**
SIC: **3699** Electrical equipment & supplies

(G-6266)
CUSTOM FABRICATION TECH LLC
24712 234th Way Se (98038-8362)
PHONE..........................206 949-0212
Brandon Collins, *Principal*
EMP: 2
SALES (est): 180.7K **Privately Held**
SIC: **3499** Novelties & giftware, including trophies

(G-6267)
DYNAMIC SOFTWARE INNOVATIONS
22949 Se 280th Pl (98038-8128)
PHONE..........................425 432-5313
EMP: 2 EST: 2010
SALES (est): 110K **Privately Held**
SIC: **7372** Prepackaged Software Services

(G-6268)
ENGINE & AIRCRAFT STRATEGIES
22129 234th Ave Se (98038-8445)
PHONE..........................425 432-2800
Dave Tegeler, *President*
EMP: 2
SALES (est): 83.9K **Privately Held**
SIC: **3812** Search & navigation equipment

(G-6269)
FIBREARTS INC
Also Called: Ozbolt Storer, Marylou
19709 Maxwell Rd Se (98038-8929)
PHONE..........................425 432-1454
Marylou Ozbolt-Storer, *President*
EMP: 7
SQ FT: 2,000
SALES (est): 800.2K **Privately Held**
SIC: **2337** 2385 Women's & misses' suits & coats; raincoats, except vulcanized rubber: purchased materials

(G-6270)
FORTYNINE INDUSTRIES
24712 197th Ave Se (98038-8623)
PHONE..........................253 632-3081
Justin Anderson, *Principal*
EMP: 2
SALES (est): 139.7K **Privately Held**
SIC: **3999** Manufacturing industries

(G-6271)
GROUND PRINT LLC
21310 Se 271st Pl (98038-6129)
PHONE..........................206 852-2622
Kyle Miller, *Principal*
EMP: 2
SALES (est): 92.3K **Privately Held**
SIC: **2752** Commercial printing, lithographic

(G-6272)
HACIENDA CUSTOM WOODWORK LLC
23213 239th Pl Se (98038-5526)
PHONE..........................206 922-9330
Elda L Villalobos, *Administration*
EMP: 2
SALES (est): 65.4K **Privately Held**
SIC: **2431** Millwork

(G-6273)
HONEYWELL INTERNATIONAL INC
27438 236th Pl Se (98038-8130)
PHONE..........................425 413-2453
EMP: 2
SALES (est): 86K
SALES (corp-wide): 40.5B **Publicly Held**
SIC: **3724** Aircraft Engines And Engine Parts
PA: Honeywell International Inc.
115 Tabor Rd
Morris Plains NJ 07950
973 455-2000

(G-6274)
HURKIN LLC
Also Called: Hurkin Software
25500 212th Pl Se (98038-7546)
P.O. Box 992 (98038-0992)
PHONE..........................425 437-0100
Keno Granger,
EMP: 3
SALES: 50K **Privately Held**
SIC: **7372** 7389 Prepackaged software;

(G-6275)
IAN ENTERPRISES LLC
25918 234th Ave Se (98038-4710)
PHONE..........................425 413-0371
John C Turner, *President*
Kathy Turner,
EMP: 2
SALES: 850K **Privately Held**
SIC: **2833** Animal based products

(G-6276)
INFORMATION MANAGEMENT TECH
2082 Se 213th St (98038)
PHONE..........................425 322-5078
Diane Pak, *President*
EMP: 5
SALES (est): 348K **Privately Held**
SIC: **2759** Imprinting

(G-6277)
IRON HORSE HAY & FEED
19435 244th Ave Se (98038-8815)
PHONE..........................425 432-0636
Joleen Williams, *Owner*
EMP: 3
SALES (est): 213.3K **Privately Held**
SIC: **2048** 5191 Prepared feeds; animal feeds

(G-6278)
JAVA JAVA COFFEE COMPANY INC (PA)
23130 224th Pl Se Ste 101 (98038-8261)
PHONE..........................425 432-5261
Brenda Habenicht, *President*
Brett Habenicht, *Vice Pres*
EMP: 6
SALES (est): 200K **Privately Held**
SIC: **5812** 5149 2095 Coffee shop; coffee & tea; coffee roasting (except by wholesale grocers)

(G-6279)
KASON PET SUPPLY
27203 216th Ave Se Ste 8 (98038-3273)
PHONE..........................360 886-2306
Rashon Cureton, *Principal*
EMP: 4
SALES (est): 198.9K **Privately Held**
SIC: **3999** Pet supplies

(G-6280)
LIFE SIZE 3 D ANIMAL TARG
24803 Se 208th St (98038-8809)
PHONE..........................206 432-9147
EMP: 2 EST: 2011
SALES (est): 120K **Privately Held**
SIC: **2899** Mfg Chemical Preparations

(G-6281)
MAAS PUBLICATIONS LLC
23419 Se 250th Pl (98038-7941)
PHONE..........................425 445-7845
Maas Travis, *Bd of Directors*
EMP: 2
SALES (est): 127.5K **Privately Held**
SIC: **2741** Miscellaneous publishing

(G-6282)
MAPLE VALLEY SIGNS INC
Also Called: Covington Signs
23220 Maple Valley Hwy (98038)
P.O. Box 3 (98038-0003)
PHONE..........................425 413-1430
Amy M Kuipers, *President*
EMP: 2
SQ FT: 2,500
SALES: 250K **Privately Held**
SIC: **3993** Signs & advertising specialties

(G-6283)
NORTHWEST PIPE ORGAN
22808 253rd Ave Se (98038-5176)
P.O. Box 1193 (98038-1193)
PHONE..........................425 432-5039
EMP: 2
SALES: 65K **Privately Held**
SIC: **3931** 5736 Manufactures And Retails Pipe Organs

(G-6284)
P & RS MOBILE SERVICES INC
Also Called: P & R'S Mobile Charpening
22616 Se 283rd St (98038-8271)
PHONE..........................425 652-1394
Todd Stuth, *President*
Patricia Stuth, *Admin Sec*
EMP: 5
SALES: 460K **Privately Held**
SIC: **3822** Electric air cleaner controls, automatic

(G-6285)
P G K INC
23030 244th Ave Se (98038-6776)
P.O. Box 263, Hobart (98025-0263)
PHONE..........................425 432-0945
Michael Woodruff, *President*
Lisa Woodruff, *Vice Pres*
EMP: 5
SALES (est): 634.1K **Privately Held**
WEB: www.pgkco.com
SIC: **3822** 3625 Liquid level controls, residential or commercial heating; relays & industrial controls

(G-6286)
PACIFIC FLUID SOLUTIONS INC
25005 234th Pl Se (98038-7940)
P.O. Box 1037 (98038-1037)
PHONE..........................425 432-6535
Scott Severse, *Principal*
EMP: 6
SALES (est): 857.9K **Privately Held**
SIC: **3589** Water treatment equipment, industrial

(G-6287)
PACIFIC OUTDOOR PRODUCTS INC
22415 Se 231st St (98038-5000)
P.O. Box 50 (98038-0050)
PHONE..........................425 432-6000
Sam Emmons, *President*
Shelley Emmons, *Vice Pres*
EMP: 12
SQ FT: 30,000
SALES (est): 1.1MM **Privately Held**
WEB: www.pacificoutdoor.com
SIC: **3949** Playground equipment

(G-6288)
PAPER MUSES
26216 Se 230th St (98038-6741)
PHONE..........................425 241-3710
Susan Kelder, *Principal*
EMP: 2 EST: 2010
SALES (est): 135.1K **Privately Held**
SIC: **2759** Commercial printing

(G-6289)
PIECEMEAL PUBLISHING LLC
26547 222nd Ave Se (98038-7406)
PHONE..........................425 432-3043
Erik Korhel, *Principal*
EMP: 2 EST: 2012
SALES (est): 218.7K **Privately Held**
SIC: **2741** Miscellaneous publishing

(G-6290)
PINK POWER PRINTING
23149 Se 184th St (98038-7202)
PHONE..........................425 295-4324
Heidi Pink, *Principal*
EMP: 2
SALES (est): 137.8K **Privately Held**
SIC: **2752** Commercial printing, lithographic

(G-6291)
QUALITY STAIRS AND WOODWORKING
22833 Se 287th Pl (98038-3147)
PHONE..........................425 358-4196
Joseph Johnson, *Principal*
EMP: 2
SALES (est): 103K **Privately Held**
SIC: **2431** Millwork

(G-6292)
ROOM MAKER
22218 Se Bain Rd (98038-6522)
PHONE..........................425 432-3324
Jim Thompson, *Owner*
EMP: 3
SQ FT: 1,000
SALES (est): 176K **Privately Held**
SIC: **2541** 2434 1799 Cabinets, except refrigerated: show, display, etc.: wood; wood kitchen cabinets; counter top installation

(G-6293)
SOLAR GUARD COATINGS INC
22126 238th Pl Se (98038-8451)
PHONE..........................425 413-0545
EMP: 2
SALES (est): 106.8K **Privately Held**
SIC: **3479** Coating/Engraving Service

(G-6294)
TIN CAN ROCKET LLC
24275 229th Ave Se (98038-5162)
PHONE..........................206 427-9260
Carole Harris, *Principal*
EMP: 3
SALES (est): 205.1K **Privately Held**
SIC: **3411** Tin cans

(G-6295)
TWO HARPS
25360 237th Pl Se (98038-8331)
PHONE..........................425 432-4128
Nancey Harp, *Owner*
Irvin Harp, *Owner*
EMP: 2
SALES (est): 97K **Privately Held**
SIC: **2395** Emblems, embroidered

Maple Valley - King County (G-6296)

(G-6296)
UNITED MANUFACTURING PRODUCTS
20317 244th Ave Se (98038-8817)
PHONE....................425 433-1141
R Dewey Lambert, *President*
Diane Lambert, *Corp Secy*
EMP: 6
SQ FT: 10,000
SALES (est): 801K **Privately Held**
SIC: 3599 Machine shop, jobbing & repair

(G-6297)
VISION WOODWORKS
21639 290th Ave Se (98038-7739)
PHONE....................425 432-6772
Adrian Burwell, *Owner*
Reuben Burwell, *Project Engr*
EMP: 4
SALES (est): 330K **Privately Held**
WEB: www.visionwoodworks.com
SIC: 2434 Wood kitchen cabinets

(G-6298)
VITAMIN SHOPPE INDUSTRIES INC
Also Called: Super Supplement
26710 Maple Vlly Blck Dia (98038-8392)
PHONE....................855 235-9431
EMP: 3 **Publicly Held**
SIC: 2834 Hormone preparations
HQ: Vitamin Shoppe Industries Inc
  300 Harmon Meadow Blvd
  Secaucus NJ 07094
  201 868-5959

(G-6299)
WEST COAST ATHLETIC LLC
Also Called: West Coast Goalkeeping
23220 Maple Valley B (98038)
PHONE....................425 413-9200
Shawn Norris, *Mng Member*
EMP: 7
SALES: 1.4MM **Privately Held**
SIC: 3949 Sporting & athletic goods

(G-6300)
WILD HORSE GRAPHICS
21036 Se 232nd St (98038-8727)
PHONE....................425 413-5080
Terry L Schliebe, *President*
EMP: 3
SALES (est): 211.8K **Privately Held**
SIC: 7336 7319 2759 Graphic arts & related design; advertising; screen printing

(G-6301)
WILD WOOD SPLITTING
25124 215th Pl Se (98038-8539)
PHONE....................206 909-8342
Michael Hill, *Principal*
EMP: 2
SALES (est): 178.8K **Privately Held**
SIC: 2431 Millwork

(G-6302)
WILLINGHAM INC
20008 244th Ave Se (98038-8816)
PHONE....................425 432-9867
Jason Willingham, *President*
Leah Monroe, *Bookkeeper*
EMP: 15
SALES (est): 85.5K **Privately Held**
SIC: 2399 5013 7532 Seat covers, automobile; seat covers; upholstery & trim shop, automotive

(G-6303)
WRAPPER PRESS
23010 Se 222nd St (98038-8403)
PHONE....................425 443-4389
EMP: 3
SALES (est): 133K **Privately Held**
SIC: 2741 Miscellaneous publishing

Marblemount
Skagit County

(G-6304)
CINDY LOUS ARTISAN JAMS
61363 State Route 20 (98267-9749)
PHONE....................360 873-4178
EMP: 2
SALES (est): 67.3K **Privately Held**
SIC: 2033 Jams, jellies & preserves: packaged in cans, jars, etc.

(G-6305)
MICHELLAINE LEE LARRY BERGSMA
Also Called: Discount Fence
7349 Ranger Station Rd (98267-9758)
PHONE....................360 873-4005
Michellaine Lee, *Partner*
Larry Bergsma, *Partner*
EMP: 2
SALES (est): 206.7K **Privately Held**
SIC: 2411 3315 2499 3089 Rails, fence: round or split; chain link fencing; snow fence, wood; fences, gates & accessories: plastic; fences, gates, posts & flagpoles

(G-6306)
SARA JUNE HASKIN
60623 Beverly Pl (98267)
PHONE....................360 873-4257
Sara Haskin, *Owner*
EMP: 3
SALES (est): 117.4K **Privately Held**
SIC: 3841 7389 Surgical stapling devices;

(G-6307)
SKAGIT PUBLISHING
5763 Honeysuckle Ln (98267-9736)
PHONE....................360 424-3251
Vallerie Feltus, *Principal*
EMP: 19
SALES (est): 1.7MM **Privately Held**
SIC: 2741 Miscellaneous publishing

Marlin
Grant County

(G-6308)
MARLIN TRAILERS
22955 Road 22 Ne (98832-9720)
PHONE....................509 345-2316
Steve Cannon, *Owner*
Alberta Cannon, *Partner*
EMP: 3
SALES (est): 80.5K **Privately Held**
SIC: 3715 Trailers or vans for transporting horses

Marysville
Snohomish County

(G-6309)
A & S MANUFACTURING ENTPS
5902 46th St Ne (98270-9534)
PHONE....................425 334-6606
Stephanie Junot, *Principal*
EMP: 2
SALES (est): 123.4K **Privately Held**
SIC: 3999 Manufacturing industries

(G-6310)
ACRO MACHINING INC
15303 39th Ave Ne (98271-8902)
P.O. Box 3187, Arlington (98223-3187)
PHONE....................360 659-6401
Daniel Edmonds, *President*
Jeremy Hagen, *Vice Pres*
Noreen Edmonds, *Admin Sec*
EMP: 70
SQ FT: 24,000
SALES (est): 17.1MM **Privately Held**
WEB: www.acromachining.net
SIC: 3599 Machine shop, jobbing & repair

(G-6311)
AEROCELL CORPORATION
12806 State Ave (98271-7849)
P.O. Box 443 (98270-0443)
PHONE....................360 653-2211
James Downey, *CEO*
Joe Moran, *President*
Ron Fredson, *CFO*
Clark Valentine, *Treasurer*
Lechia Dean, *Human Res Mgr*
▲ **EMP:** 160
SQ FT: 107,000
SALES (est): 28.8MM **Privately Held**
SIC: 3728 3812 Aircraft parts & equipment; search & navigation equipment

(G-6312)
ARROW MACHINING COMPANY INC
7224 44th Ave Ne (98270-3717)
P.O. Box 768 (98270-0768)
PHONE....................360 659-0342
Joseph Shipp, *President*
Clint Osborn, *Vice Pres*
EMP: 27
SQ FT: 9,500
SALES (est): 4.1MM **Privately Held**
WEB: www.arrowmachining.com
SIC: 3599 Machine shop, jobbing & repair

(G-6313)
ARTISAN FINISHING SYSTEMS INC
14219 Smokey Point Blvd # 6 (98271-8906)
PHONE....................360 658-0686
Wallace Thomas, *President*
EMP: 9
SALES (est): 1MM **Privately Held**
WEB: www.artisanfinishingsystems.com
SIC: 3479 3471 Coating of metals & formed products; finishing, metals or formed products

(G-6314)
AURORA QUALITY BUILDINGS INC
14418 Smokey Point Blvd (98271-7864)
PHONE....................360 658-9967
Ward Holme, *President*
Holly Holmes, *Sales Staff*
EMP: 7
SQ FT: 1,000
SALES: 900K **Privately Held**
WEB: www.auroraqualitybuildings.com
SIC: 2434 Wood kitchen cabinets

(G-6315)
BARNES WOOD INC
1065 Beach Ave (98270-4224)
PHONE....................360 658-0145
Gary Barnes, *President*
Nancy Barnes, *Corp Secy*
EMP: 6
SQ FT: 6,712
SALES (est): 540K **Privately Held**
WEB: www.barneswood.com
SIC: 2511 Wood household furniture

(G-6316)
BENDING SOLUTIONS INCORPORATED
Also Called: BSI
3815 124th St Ne (98271-8775)
P.O. Box 1126 (98271-1126)
PHONE....................360 651-2443
D Steve Larson, *President*
EMP: 25
SQ FT: 22,000
SALES (est): 6.3MM **Privately Held**
WEB: www.bendingsolutions.com
SIC: 3444 Sheet metalwork

(G-6317)
BLANCHARD ABRASIVES
13120 State Ave (98271-7822)
P.O. Box 468 (98270-0468)
PHONE....................360 653-5273
Liam Brosnan, *President*
James Kean, *President*
Donald Tischer, *VP Finance*
EMP: 15
SALES (est): 762.8K
SALES (corp-wide): 797.8MM **Privately Held**
WEB: www.radiac.com
SIC: 3291 Wheels, grinding: artificial
HQ: Radiac Abrasives, Inc.
  1015 S College St
  Salem IL 62881
  618 548-4200

(G-6318)
C&D ZODIAC INC
12810 State Ave (98271-7849)
P.O. Box 443 (98270-0443)
PHONE....................360 653-2211
Stephen Zimmerman, *President*
Lecia Dean, *Human Res Mgr*
Bradley Young, *Manager*
John Maglione, *Admin Sec*
Norman Hussey, *Analyst*
▲ **EMP:** 57 **EST:** 2005
SALES (est): 13.3MM **Privately Held**
SIC: 3728 Aircraft parts & equipment

(G-6319)
CABINET FX
6516 66th St Ne (98270-5307)
PHONE....................425 879-6690
Pete Munoz, *Principal*
EMP: 2
SALES (est): 229.3K **Privately Held**
SIC: 2434 Wood kitchen cabinets

(G-6320)
CAN AM COATINGS
1110 5th St (98270-4500)
PHONE....................360 386-9692
Marcelle Robbins, *Principal*
Todd Robbins, *Opers Mgr*
EMP: 2
SALES (est): 107.3K **Privately Held**
SIC: 3479 Metal coating & allied service

(G-6321)
CAN AM FABRICATION INC
4803 56th Pl Ne (98270-5702)
P.O. Box 412 (98270-0412)
PHONE....................360 653-2245
Monte Nybo, *President*
Roger Schemenauer, *Vice Pres*
EMP: 6 **EST:** 1979
SQ FT: 14,000
SALES: 1MM **Privately Held**
SIC: 3441 Fabricated structural metal

(G-6322)
CASCADE AVIATION SERVICES INC
15318 39th Ave Ne (98271-8902)
PHONE....................425 493-1707
Paul Vallins, *President*
Brad Bustad, *Vice Pres*
Bradley Bustad, *Admin Sec*
EMP: 35
SALES (est): 6.1MM **Privately Held**
WEB: www.cascade-aviation.com
SIC: 3728 Aircraft parts & equipment

(G-6323)
CHAMELEON PRINTS
5008 60th Ave Ne (98270-7535)
PHONE....................425 493-3071
Kristopher Ames, *Principal*
EMP: 2
SALES (est): 238.2K **Privately Held**
SIC: 2752 Commercial printing, lithographic

(G-6324)
CHARA CREATIONS
5810 74th St Ne A (98270-3926)
PHONE....................360 658-0574
Sandra Grembos, *Owner*
Robert W Grembos, *Co-Owner*
EMP: 2
SALES (est): 98K **Privately Held**
SIC: 2221 Textile mills, broadwoven: silk & manmade, also glass

(G-6325)
CHETS CABINETS
7728 47th Ave Ne (98270-3744)
PHONE....................360 659-7500
Mark Jensen, *Owner*
EMP: 4
SQ FT: 9,000
SALES (est): 401.3K **Privately Held**
SIC: 2434 Wood kitchen cabinets

(G-6326)
CLARK OFFICE PRODUCTS INC
Also Called: Cloes Blue Book
12407 48th Dr Ne (98271-8657)
PHONE....................360 657-2018
Frank W Fadden, *President*

GEOGRAPHIC SECTION

Marysville - Snohomish County (G-6359)

EMP: 5
SQ FT: 10,000
SALES (est): 650K Privately Held
SIC: 5112 2752 Office supplies; business form & card printing, lithographic

(G-6327)
COMPUTER CLINIC NORTHWEST INC
1239 State Ave (98270-3601)
P.O. Box 932 (98270-0932)
PHONE..................360 658-1234
Sam Mohammed, *President*
EMP: 3
SALES: 360K Privately Held
WEB: www.computerclinicusa.com
SIC: 5734 7372 Computer peripheral equipment; application computer software

(G-6328)
COVLET MACHINE & DESIGN INC
13115 41st Ave Ne (98271-7808)
PHONE..................360 658-1977
Robert L Black Jr, *President*
EMP: 12
SQ FT: 9,000
SALES: 1.2MM Privately Held
SIC: 3542 Machine tools, metal forming type

(G-6329)
DANS MACHINE WORKS
13305 41st Ave Ne (98271-7848)
PHONE..................360 403-0887
Daniel G Sprouse, *Owner*
EMP: 3 EST: 1990
SALES (est): 121K Privately Held
SIC: 3599 Machine shop, jobbing & repair

(G-6330)
DISPLAY MANUFACTURING LLC
Also Called: Display Mfg
3803 136th St Ne (98271-7816)
PHONE..................360 653-0990
David Sharp,
Tina Sharp,
EMP: 6
SQ FT: 7,000
SALES (est): 940.8K Privately Held
WEB: www.displaymfg.com
SIC: 2541 5046 Store & office display cases & fixtures; store fixtures

(G-6331)
DOUBLE D MFG LLC
3710b 136th St Ne (98271-7820)
PHONE..................206 954-8099
Kellian England, *Partner*
▲ EMP: 6
SQ FT: 400
SALES (est): 717.9K Privately Held
SIC: 3724 3728 Engine mount parts, aircraft; flaps, aircraft wing

(G-6332)
EJ USA INC
13127 State Ave (98271-7851)
PHONE..................360 651-6144
Roger Plautz, *Marketing Staff*
EMP: 5 Privately Held
WEB: www.ejiw.com
SIC: 3321 Gray & ductile iron foundries
HQ: Ej Usa, Inc.
    301 Spring St
    East Jordan MI 49727
    800 874-4100

(G-6333)
EPICORE
11127 47th Ave Ne (98271-8338)
PHONE..................360 659-1986
Steve Griffin, *President*
EMP: 2
SALES (est): 56.5K Privately Held
SIC: 7372 Prepackaged software

(G-6334)
FIVES N AMERCN COMBUSTN INC
6912 77th Ave Ne (98270-6523)
PHONE..................360 659-7432
Cynthia Jamesstrakele, *Branch Mgr*
EMP: 43
SALES (corp-wide): 871.2K Privately Held
SIC: 3433 Heating equipment, except electric
HQ: Fives North American Combustion, Inc.
    4455 E 71st St
    Cleveland OH 44105
    216 271-6000

(G-6335)
FOUR BARR INDUSTRIES
4124 134th St Ne (98270-7838)
PHONE..................360 659-8182
Marilynn Barr, *Owner*
Robert Barr, *Co-Owner*
EMP: 7
SALES: 1.4MM Privately Held
SIC: 3672 Printed circuit boards

(G-6336)
FRASERS BRONZE FOUNDRY INC
5625 48th Dr Ne Apt D (98270-5711)
PHONE..................877 264-1064
Kevin Fraser, *President*
Brian Fisher, *Vice Pres*
Anne Fraser, *Admin Sec*
▼ EMP: 7
SQ FT: 4,200
SALES (est): 1.1MM Privately Held
WEB: www.fraserbronze.com
SIC: 3366 3365 Bronze foundry; brass foundry; aluminum foundries

(G-6337)
FUND RR LLC
6502 55th Dr Ne (98270-6102)
PHONE..................425 530-7120
Robert Roberts, *Mng Member*
Russell Bare,
EMP: 2
SALES: 100K Privately Held
SIC: 7372 Prepackaged software

(G-6338)
GALE INDUSTRIES
13520 45th Ave Ne (98271-7823)
PHONE..................360 659-7674
Larry Aris, *Principal*
EMP: 2
SALES (est): 95K Privately Held
SIC: 3999 Manufacturing industries

(G-6339)
GARMIRE IRON WORKS INC
5620 48th Dr Ne (98270-5720)
PHONE..................360 651-1001
James Rebar, *President*
EMP: 6
SQ FT: 4,800
SALES (est): 940.3K Privately Held
SIC: 3317 Steel pipe & tubes

(G-6340)
GRANDMA EDNAS
9214 State Ave (98270-2265)
P.O. Box 1584 (98270-1584)
PHONE..................425 200-5435
Debbie Martson, *Principal*
EMP: 3 EST: 2016
SALES (est): 201.1K Privately Held
SIC: 2099 Food preparations

(G-6341)
GRIZZLY FIRESTARTERS NORTH
10310 State Ave (98271-7212)
PHONE..................360 659-3948
Ken Staab, *Branch Mgr*
EMP: 2 Privately Held
SIC: 2499 5099 5989 Logs of sawdust & wood particles, pressed; wood & wood by-products; wood (fuel)
PA: Grizzly Firestarters North
    35177 Deer Creek Rd
    Mount Vernon WA 98274

(G-6342)
GROVE CHURCH
4705 Grove St (98270-4422)
P.O. Box 651, Snohomish (98291-0651)
PHONE..................360 386-5760
Nik Baumgart, *President*
EMP: 5
SQ FT: 42,969

SALES (est): 645.3K Privately Held
WEB: www.marysvillefirst.org
SIC: 8661 7372 Assembly of God Church; application computer software

(G-6343)
HD STRUCTURES LLC
6922 69th Pl Ne (98270-7791)
PHONE..................425 327-3931
Daniel Hoffman, *Owner*
EMP: 2
SALES (est): 158.8K Privately Held
SIC: 2499 Laundry products, wood

(G-6344)
HENRYS DONUTS
1289 State Ave Ste A (98270-3696)
PHONE..................360 653-4044
Phay Vanh, *Owner*
EMP: 2
SALES (est): 57.7K Privately Held
SIC: 5461 2051 Doughnuts; doughnuts, except frozen

(G-6345)
HOLLIBAUGH MANUFACTURING
12524 54th Ave Ne (98271-9004)
PHONE..................360 653-8612
Charles Hollibaugh, *Owner*
EMP: 4
SQ FT: 10,000
SALES: 250K Privately Held
SIC: 3999 5999 Hot tubs; spas & hot tubs

(G-6346)
J SALGADO LLC
9701 35th Ave Ne (98270-7203)
PHONE..................425 367-3188
EMP: 4
SALES (est): 374.2K Privately Held
SIC: 2752 Commercial printing, lithographic

(G-6347)
KIEU DANH
Also Called: DK Precision Machine
3707 124th St Ne Ste 6 (98271-8770)
PHONE..................360 548-9649
Danh Kieu, *Owner*
EMP: 2 EST: 2017
SQ FT: 1,246
SALES (est): 145.7K Privately Held
SIC: 2431 Millwork

(G-6348)
KINEMATICS MARINE EQP INC
5625 48th Dr Ne Ste B (98270-5711)
PHONE..................360 659-5415
Ed Luttrell, *President*
James Davis, *Manager*
EMP: 4
SQ FT: 2,500
SALES: 1MM Privately Held
WEB: www.kinematicsmarine.com
SIC: 5084 3531 3599 Hydraulic systems equipment & supplies; marine related equipment; capstans, ship; ship winches; custom machinery; machine shop, jobbing & repair

(G-6349)
LA MICHOACANA
1511 3rd St (98270-5001)
PHONE..................360 658-1635
Rodney Cuthbert, *Principal*
EMP: 3
SALES (est): 118.4K Privately Held
SIC: 5411 2096 Grocery stores; tortilla chips

(G-6350)
LACOTO INDUSTRIES INC
7610 80th Ave Ne (98270-8007)
PHONE..................360 658-9668
George Lindgren, *President*
EMP: 2
SALES (est): 16.1K Privately Held
SIC: 3429 Keys, locks & related hardware

(G-6351)
LAKOTA INDUSTRIES INC
4001 132nd Pl Ne (98271-7884)
PHONE..................360 659-5333
Dan Fleshman, *Principal*
EMP: 6

SALES (est): 660K Privately Held
SIC: 3599 Machine shop, jobbing & repair

(G-6352)
LAMAR TECHNOLOGIES LLC
14900 40th Ave Ne (98271-8914)
PHONE..................360 651-8869
Scott Grafenauer,
▲ EMP: 10 EST: 1998
SQ FT: 9,600
SALES (est): 2.2MM Privately Held
WEB: www.lamartech.com
SIC: 3728 Aircraft parts & equipment

(G-6353)
LASTING IMPRESSIONS INC
1423 6th St (98270-4516)
PHONE..................360 659-1255
Steve D Chilson, *President*
Karmin Kippen, *Treasurer*
Nancy Chilson, *Admin Sec*
EMP: 7
SQ FT: 8,000
SALES (est): 981.1K Privately Held
WEB: www.lastingimp.com
SIC: 2759 5199 Screen printing; advertising specialties

(G-6354)
MADRONA LOG HM REPR & CARE LLC
5609 71st Ave Ne (98270-8824)
PHONE..................360 202-2842
Travis Bird,
EMP: 2
SALES (est): 178.7K Privately Held
SIC: 1521 1389 1541 Single-family home remodeling, additions & repairs; general remodeling, single-family houses; construction, repair & dismantling services; renovation, remodeling & repairs: industrial buildings

(G-6355)
MAILBOX JUNCTION
Also Called: Mail Box Junction
1242 State Ave Ste I (98270-3695)
PHONE..................360 658-2445
Randy Wirther, *Owner*
Pat Enlow, *Owner*
EMP: 3
SALES (est): 271.7K Privately Held
SIC: 2542 Mail racks & lock boxes, postal service: except wood

(G-6356)
MARYSVILLE AWARDS INC
1826 4th St Ste 101 (98270-5039)
PHONE..................360 653-4811
Connie Kukull, *CEO*
Steven Kukull, *Co-Owner*
EMP: 3
SALES (est): 266.5K Privately Held
WEB: www.marysvilleawards.com
SIC: 5999 8322 3479 Trophies & plaques; youth center; engraving jewelry silverware, or metal

(G-6357)
MARYSVILLE PRINTING INC
1509 6th St (98270-4709)
PHONE..................360 658-9195
Huong Nation, *President*
EMP: 5
SALES (est): 466.6K Privately Held
WEB: www.marysvilleprinting.net
SIC: 2759 2396 Commercial printing; automotive & apparel trimmings

(G-6358)
MCVAYS MOBILE WELDING LLC
4100 134th St Ne (98271-7838)
PHONE..................360 657-0360
Bernard F McVays,
EMP: 5
SALES (est): 507.3K Privately Held
WEB: www.mcvaysmobilewelding.com
SIC: 7692 3441 3449 Welding repair; fabricated structural metal; bars, concrete reinforcing: fabricated steel

(G-6359)
METAL WERKS INC
5625 47th Ave Ne Ste D (98270-5167)
PHONE..................360 651-0300
Michael Hobeck, *President*

Marysville - Snohomish County (G-6360)

Audrey Hobeck, *Corp Secy*
EMP: 18
SQ FT: 10,000
SALES: 2.5MM **Privately Held**
WEB: www.metalwerksinc.com
SIC: 2542 3499 Racks, merchandise display, for storage: except wood; ladder assemblies, combination workstand: metal

(G-6360)
MIND MODULATIONS
Also Called: Mindmods
8507 78th Ave Ne (98270-8061)
PHONE 626 863-7379
Gary Bense, *Owner*
EMP: 2
SALES (est): 130K **Privately Held**
SIC: 4813 3845 ; audiological equipment, electromedical; electrotherapeutic apparatus

(G-6361)
MORGAN BRANCH CNC INC
3923 88th St Ne Ste Q (98270-7258)
PHONE 360 435-7170
Guy Kinkead, *President*
Lorraine Kinkead, *Corp Secy*
EMP: 3
SQ FT: 3,000
SALES: 400K **Privately Held**
SIC: 3599 Machine shop, jobbing & repair

(G-6362)
MUTUAL MATERIALS COMPANY
1410 Grove St (98270-3637)
PHONE 425 353-9686
Gary Hollahan, *President*
EMP: 7
SALES (corp-wide): 44.8MM **Privately Held**
SIC: 5211 3272 1741 Masonry materials & supplies; concrete products, precast; retaining wall construction
PA: Mutual Materials Company
605 119th Ave Ne
Bellevue WA 98005
425 452-2300

(G-6363)
NORTHEND TRUCK EQUIPMENT LLC
14919 40th Ave Ne (98271-8949)
PHONE 360 653-6066
Greg Stewart, *President*
EMP: 40
SALES (est): 1.6MM
SALES (corp-wide): 12.4MM **Privately Held**
WEB: www.northendtruck.com
SIC: 3713 Truck bodies (motor vehicles)
PA: Osw Equipment & Repair, Llc
20812 Broadway Ave
Snohomish WA 98296
425 483-9863

(G-6364)
NORTHWEST COMPOSITES INC (PA)
12810 State Ave (98271-7849)
PHONE 360 653-2211
James Downey, *Ch of Bd*
Joseph Moran, *President*
▲ **EMP:** 42
SQ FT: 100,000
SALES (est): 33.5MM **Privately Held**
SIC: 3089 Plastic processing

(G-6365)
PACIFIC LOGGING INC
3603 136th St Ne (98271-7845)
P.O. Box 1439 (98270-1439)
PHONE 425 334-3600
Robert Hild, *President*
Maurice Geibel, *Vice Pres*
EMP: 45
SALES (est): 4MM **Privately Held**
SIC: 2411 Logging camps & contractors

(G-6366)
PACIFIC PREPAC INC
Also Called: Hendrickson Farms
3925 134th St Ne (98271-7813)
PHONE 360 653-1661
Michael Bennett, *President*
Dan Hendrickson, *President*
Lynn Hendrickson, *Admin Sec*
EMP: 35
SQ FT: 10,400
SALES (est): 3.9MM **Privately Held**
SIC: 2033 Vegetables & vegetable products in cans, jars, etc.

(G-6367)
PACIFIC SKIFFS NW INC
Also Called: Pacific Boats
5611 48th Dr Ne Ste 5 (98270-5786)
P.O. Box 1249 (98270-1249)
PHONE 360 658-7111
Daniel King, *President*
Julie Parks, *President*
EMP: 8
SQ FT: 12,500
SALES: 1.2MM **Privately Held**
WEB: www.pacificboats.com
SIC: 3732 Boat building & repairing

(G-6368)
PETERSON TOOLS
4414 128th Pl Ne (98271-8730)
PHONE 425 870-0137
Natalie G Peterson, *President*
EMP: 2
SALES (est): 98.6K **Privately Held**
SIC: 3599 Industrial machinery

(G-6369)
PLATINUM RAIL PUBLICATIONS LLC
5811 75th Ave Ne (98270-9062)
PHONE 360 658-2485
Pamela Clapp, *President*
EMP: 2 **EST:** 2010
SALES (est): 106.9K **Privately Held**
SIC: 2741 Miscellaneous publishing

(G-6370)
POLARIS MANUFACTURING INC
Also Called: Polaris Machining
103 Cedar Ave (98270-4930)
PHONE 360 653-7676
Michael Bontatibus, *CEO*
EMP: 42
SQ FT: 15,000
SALES (est): 7.9MM **Privately Held**
WEB: www.polarismachining.com
SIC: 3444 3545 Sheet metalwork; precision tools, machinists'

(G-6371)
PRECISION AIRMOTIVE LLC
14800 40th Ave Ne (98271-8952)
PHONE 360 659-7348
Mike Allen, *CEO*
Cindi McCarter, *Manager*
EMP: 50 **EST:** 1974
SQ FT: 38,000
SALES (est): 8.2MM **Privately Held**
WEB: www.precisionairmotive.com
SIC: 3724 7699 Aircraft engines & engine parts; engine repair & replacement, non-automotive

(G-6372)
PUGET SOUND BREATHALYZERS
3402 65th Dr Ne (98270-9024)
PHONE 425 359-9515
Bryan Lutz, *Principal*
EMP: 2
SALES (est): 152.4K **Privately Held**
SIC: 3829 Breathalyzers

(G-6373)
QUIL CEDA TANNING CO INC
3922 88th St Ne (98270-7230)
P.O. Box 466 (98270-0466)
PHONE 360 659-1333
Charles Warden, *President*
Mike Warden, *Treasurer*
EMP: 6 **EST:** 1933
SQ FT: 4,800
SALES (est): 766.6K **Privately Held**
SIC: 3111 Tanneries, leather

(G-6374)
RADIAC ABRASIVES INC
Pacific Grinding Co
13120 Smokey Point Blvd (98271-7822)
PHONE 360 659-6276
James Burkepile, *Manager*
EMP: 70
SQ FT: 91,540
SALES (corp-wide): 797.8MM **Privately Held**
WEB: www.radiac.com
SIC: 3291 Wheels, abrasive
HQ: Radiac Abrasives, Inc.
1015 S College St
Salem IL 62881
618 548-4200

(G-6375)
RADIAC ABRASIVES INC
Pacific Grinding Wheel Co
13120 State Ave (98271-7822)
PHONE 360 659-6201
Charles Tunt, *CEO*
EMP: 90
SALES (corp-wide): 797.8MM **Privately Held**
SIC: 3291 Abrasive products
HQ: Radiac Abrasives, Inc.
1015 S College St
Salem IL 62881
618 548-4200

(G-6376)
RADIAC ABRASIVES INC
Pacific Grinding Wheel Co Div
13120 State Ave (98271-7822)
PHONE 360 659-6201
James Burkepile, *Manager*
EMP: 80
SALES (corp-wide): 797.8MM **Privately Held**
WEB: www.radiac.com
SIC: 3545 3291 Machine tool accessories; wheels, abrasive
HQ: Radiac Abrasives, Inc.
1015 S College St
Salem IL 62881
618 548-4200

(G-6377)
REALITY PLASTICS INC
4700 56th Pl Ne Ste D (98270-5721)
PHONE 360 653-3949
Steven J Stasney, *President*
EMP: 7
SQ FT: 4,000
SALES (est): 805.2K **Privately Held**
WEB: www.realitysandwich.com
SIC: 3089 Injection molding of plastics

(G-6378)
ROC RACING INC
14702 Smokey Point Blvd A (98271-8918)
PHONE 360 658-4353
Randy Cole, *Principal*
EMP: 4 **EST:** 2010
SALES (est): 433.6K **Privately Held**
SIC: 3429 Bicycle racks, automotive

(G-6379)
ROCK PLACE
1622 3rd St (98270-5004)
PHONE 425 220-1110
EMP: 2 **EST:** 2016
SALES (est): 74.3K **Privately Held**
SIC: 5032 3281 Building blocks; cut stone & stone products

(G-6380)
RUBBER GRANULATORS INC
3811 152nd St Ne (98271-8909)
P.O. Box 692, Snohomish (98291-0692)
PHONE 360 658-7754
Milton Chryst, *President*
Steven Chryst, *Vice Pres*
Susan Chryst, *Treasurer*
Diane Chryst, *Admin Sec*
EMP: 5 **EST:** 1978
SQ FT: 5,000
SALES (est): 858.6K **Privately Held**
WEB: www.rubbergranulators.com
SIC: 3069 Reclaimed rubber (reworked by manufacturing processes)

(G-6381)
SAFRAN CABIN INC
Also Called: Engineered Materials
12806 State Ave (98271-7849)
PHONE 360 653-2600
Mike Pound, *General Mgr*
EMP: 223
SALES (corp-wide): 833.4MM **Privately Held**
SIC: 3728 3443 Aircraft parts & equipment; fabricated plate work (boiler shop)
HQ: Safran Cabin Inc.
5701 Bolsa Ave
Huntington Beach CA 92647
714 934-0000

(G-6382)
SAFRAN CABIN INC
12810 State Ave (98271-7849)
PHONE 360 653-2211
Cindy Rainer, *Branch Mgr*
EMP: 99
SALES (corp-wide): 833.4MM **Privately Held**
SIC: 3728 Aircraft parts & equipment
HQ: Safran Cabin Inc.
5701 Bolsa Ave
Huntington Beach CA 92647
714 934-0000

(G-6383)
SEACLEAR INDUSTRIES MFG INC
3923 88th St Ne Ste H (98270-7258)
PHONE 360 659-2700
Scott Sperbeck, *President*
EMP: 12
SALES (est): 870K **Privately Held**
SIC: 3442 Louver windows, metal

(G-6384)
SEATTLE TIMES - MARYSVILLE
14506 Smokey Point Blvd (98271-7887)
PHONE 360 925-6324
EMP: 3
SALES (est): 113.7K **Privately Held**
SIC: 2711 Newspapers, publishing & printing

(G-6385)
SLUMBER EASE MATTRESS CO INC
Also Called: Slumber Ease Mattress Factory
1327 8th St (98270-4205)
PHONE 360 657-1654
Nick Rothrock, *President*
Rex Pardo, *Vice Pres*
EMP: 6
SQ FT: 13,200
SALES: 600K **Privately Held**
SIC: 2515 5021 5712 Mattresses & foundations; bedsprings; mattresses; bedding & bedsprings; mattresses

(G-6386)
SMOKEY POINT CUSTOM CABINETS
Also Called: Cascade Cabinets
14620 Smokey Point Blvd (98271-7866)
PHONE 360 659-6233
Rick Kazen, *President*
Anne Kazen, *Treasurer*
EMP: 15
SQ FT: 7,000
SALES (est): 1.7MM **Privately Held**
SIC: 2434 5712 Wood kitchen cabinets; cabinet work, custom

(G-6387)
SMOKEY POINT LOG HOMES INC
15026 Smokey Point Blvd (98271-7874)
PHONE 360 659-7122
EMP: 4
SQ FT: 360
SALES: 100K **Privately Held**
SIC: 2452 Mfg Prefabricated Wood Buildings

(G-6388)
SOUND METAL WORKS LTD
14721 16th Ave Nw (98271-8122)
PHONE 360 659-0999
James Peterson, *Principal*
EMP: 12 **EST:** 2010
SALES (est): 1.3MM **Privately Held**
SIC: 3444 1761 Sheet metalwork; sheet metalwork

GEOGRAPHIC SECTION

McCleary - Grays Harbor County (G-6418)

(G-6389)
SOUND PUBLISHING INC
Also Called: Marysville Globe
1085 Cedar Ave (98270-4232)
PHONE.....................360 659-1300
Stuart Chernis, *Branch Mgr*
EMP: 14 **Privately Held**
WEB: www.soundpublishing.com
SIC: 2711 Newspapers: publishing only, not printed on site
HQ: Sound Publishing, Inc.
11323 Commando Rd W Main
Everett WA 98204
360 394-5800

(G-6390)
SPEEDWAY MARINE INC
15008 Smokey Point Blvd F (98271-8912)
PHONE.....................360 658-1288
Tony Brown, *President*
Janae Brown, *Vice Pres*
EMP: 2
SQ FT: 1,200
SALES (est): 100K **Privately Held**
SIC: 5551 3732 Marine supplies; motorboats, inboard or outboard: building & repairing

(G-6391)
SUN NEWS INC
Also Called: Marysville Globe
6720a 60th Pl Ne (98270-8929)
P.O. Box 145 (98270-0145)
PHONE.....................360 659-1300
Robert Marshall, *President*
Kristopher Passey, *Corp Secy*
EMP: 50 **EST:** 1891
SQ FT: 4,000
SALES (est): 2.4MM **Privately Held**
WEB: www.marysvilleglobe.com
SIC: 2711 2752 Job printing & newspaper publishing combined; commercial printing, lithographic

(G-6392)
SUNCOAST POST-TENSION LTD
13520 45th Ave Ne (98271-7823)
PHONE.....................360 651-2769
EMP: 2
SALES (corp-wide): 2.8B **Privately Held**
SIC: 3315 Cable, steel: insulated or armored
HQ: Suncoast Post-Tension, Ltd.
509 N Sam Houston Pkwy E # 300
Houston TX 77060
281 445-8886

(G-6393)
SUPERIOR SOLE WLDG FABRICATION
7402 44th Ave Ne (98270-3780)
P.O. Box 1589 (98270-1589)
PHONE.....................360 653-2565
J Andrew Sole, *President*
Rita Sole, *Corp Secy*
EMP: 8
SQ FT: 7,700
SALES (est): 1.1MM **Privately Held**
SIC: 7692 3446 Welding repair; stairs, staircases, stair treads: prefabricated metal

(G-6394)
TECHPOINT MANUFACTURING INC
7823 51st Pl Ne (98270-8968)
PHONE.....................425 387-0305
John Landau, *Principal*
EMP: 2 **EST:** 2016
SALES (est): 94.5K **Privately Held**
SIC: 3999 Manufacturing industries

(G-6395)
THOMAS MACHINE & FOUNDRY INC
13100 41st Ave Ne (98271-7808)
PHONE.....................360 651-9100
Charles Thomas Jr, *President*
Richard W Thomas, *Vice Pres*
William B Thomas Jr, *Vice Pres*
Terence Dahl, *Shareholder*
Daniel J Thomas, *Admin Sec*
EMP: 60 **EST:** 1948
SQ FT: 23,000
SALES: 4MM **Privately Held**
WEB: www.tmaf.com
SIC: 3365 3599 3369 Aluminum & aluminum-based alloy castings; machine shop, jobbing & repair; nonferrous foundries

(G-6396)
TOP LEFT INDUSTRIES
8712 57th Dr Ne (98270-3211)
PHONE.....................360 914-1400
Andy McHale, *Principal*
EMP: 2
SALES (est): 90K **Privately Held**
SIC: 3999 Manufacturing industries

(G-6397)
TRUHUMIC ENVMTL SOLUTIONS LLC
9617 48th Dr Ne Ste B (98270-2309)
P.O. Box 1862 (98270-1862)
PHONE.....................425 232-6903
Dan Anderson, *Mng Member*
EMP: 2 **EST:** 2012
SALES (est): 148.6K **Privately Held**
SIC: 2879 5191 2899 7389 Trace elements (agricultural chemicals); fertilizers & agricultural chemicals; water treating compounds;

(G-6398)
TURNING POINT MACHINING INC
710 Ash Ave (98270-4539)
PHONE.....................425 252-7300
Bob Evans, *President*
Glenna Evans, *Vice Pres*
EMP: 5
SQ FT: 3,000
SALES: 650K **Privately Held**
SIC: 3599 Machine shop, jobbing & repair

(G-6399)
VANDERMEER FOREST PRODUCTS INC
1364 State Ave Bldg B (98270-3605)
PHONE.....................360 657-2518
Andy Wilson, *Branch Mgr*
EMP: 3
SALES (corp-wide): 13.5MM **Privately Held**
SIC: 0831 2421 Forest products; lumber: rough, sawed or planed
PA: Vandermeer Forest Products, Inc.
5110 196th St Sw Ste 200
Lynnwood WA 98036
425 774-3544

(G-6400)
WARREN WELDING
8824 60th St Ne (98270-7084)
PHONE.....................425 761-1777
Trent Warren, *Administration*
EMP: 2
SALES (est): 190.8K **Privately Held**
SIC: 7692 Welding repair

(G-6401)
WHITEWALL BREWING LLC
14524 Smokey Point Blvd # 1 (98271-8921)
PHONE.....................360 454-0464
Aaron Wight, *Mng Member*
EMP: 3
SALES (est): 187.3K **Privately Held**
SIC: 2084 Wines

(G-6402)
WHITLEY EVERGREEN INC
14219 Smokey Point Blvd (98271-8906)
PHONE.....................360 653-5790
Al Long, *General Mgr*
Brian Walker, *General Mgr*
John Kremm, *Managing Dir*
Hank Kennedy, *Prdtn Mgr*
Fred Nelson, *Purch Dir*
EMP: 25 **Privately Held**
WEB: www.schooldesign.com
SIC: 2452 Prefabricated wood buildings
HQ: Whitley Evergreen Inc
201 W First St
South Whitley IN 46787
260 723-5131

(G-6403)
ZODIAC AROSPC ENGINEERED MTLS
12806 State Ave (98271-7849)
PHONE.....................360 653-2600
EMP: 5
SALES (est): 742.8K **Privately Held**
SIC: 3728 Aircraft parts & equipment

Mattawa
Grant County

(G-6404)
COPTRACKER INC
26619 Road U Sw (99349-8292)
PHONE.....................214 542-2351
Jeffrey V Cox, *Principal*
EMP: 2 **EST:** 2016
SALES (est): 85.8K **Privately Held**
SIC: 7372 Prepackaged software

(G-6405)
CPM DEVELOPMENT CORPORATION
Also Called: Central Pre-Mix Concrete
31002 Hwy 243 S (99349)
PHONE.....................509 932-4525
Troy Holt, *General Mgr*
EMP: 6
SALES (corp-wide): 30.6B **Privately Held**
WEB: www.centralpremix.com
SIC: 3273 Ready-mixed concrete
HQ: Cpm Development Corporation
5111 E Broadway Ave
Spokane Valley WA 99212
509 534-6221

(G-6406)
GINKGO FOREST WINERY LLC
Also Called: Ginkco Distillery
22561 Rd T27 Sw (99349)
PHONE.....................509 932-0082
Lois Thiede, *Vice Pres*
Michael Thiede, *Mng Member*
EMP: 6
SALES: 250K **Privately Held**
SIC: 5921 2084 Wine; wines

(G-6407)
GO PLANIT LLC
415 Airport Way Sw (99349-1950)
PHONE.....................206 227-0660
Karen Chiaramonte, *Owner*
Cecilio Rodriguez, *Owner*
EMP: 2
SALES (est): 74.2K **Privately Held**
SIC: 3451 3484 3494 3599 Screw machine products; small arms; valves & pipe fittings; machine & other job shop work; bolts, nuts, rivets & washers;

(G-6408)
HIGH LIFTT LLC
415 Airport Way Sw (99349-1950)
PHONE.....................425 216-3050
Karen Chiaramonte,
EMP: 3
SALES (est): 109.4K **Privately Held**
SIC: 3599 7389 Machine & other job shop work;

(G-6409)
J&S CRUSHING
Also Called: River's Edge Winery
22132 Road T 7 Sw 7 T (99349)
PHONE.....................509 787-3537
EMP: 2
SALES (est): 117.1K **Privately Held**
SIC: 2084 Wines

(G-6410)
MATTAWA WOOD PRODUCTS CORP
Also Called: Wood Box Factory
23961 Road T.2 Sw (99349-8201)
P.O. Box 1836 (99349-0900)
PHONE.....................509 932-6420
Terry Lee Roller, *President*
EMP: 4
SQ FT: 6,000
SALES (est): 310K **Privately Held**
WEB: www.woodboxfactory.com
SIC: 2441 Boxes, wood

(G-6411)
NORTHWEST COMPOST LLC
26395 Road U Sw (99349-8206)
PHONE.....................509 932-0215
EMP: 2
SALES (est): 81.8K **Privately Held**
SIC: 2875 Compost

(G-6412)
ROSEBUD RANCHES
21954 Road I Sw (99349-8219)
PHONE.....................509 932-4617
Roy Dobson, *Owner*
Sharon K Dobson, *Manager*
EMP: 30
SALES (est): 1.4MM **Privately Held**
SIC: 0172 2084 Grapes; wines

(G-6413)
WAHLUKE WINE COMPANY INC
23934 Road T.1 Sw (99349)
PHONE.....................509 932-0030
Don T Milbrandt Jr, *President*
Jerry Charles Milbrandt, *Vice Pres*
▲ **EMP:** 22
SALES (est): 3.7MM **Privately Held**
SIC: 2084 Wines

Mazama
Okanogan County

(G-6414)
LOST RIVER WINERY LLC (PA)
699 Lost River Rd (98833-9709)
PHONE.....................509 996-2888
John Morgan, *Mng Member*
Liam Doyle,
Barbara Houfe,
EMP: 3
SALES: 450K **Privately Held**
WEB: www.lostriverwinery.com
SIC: 2084 Wines

McCleary
Grays Harbor County

(G-6415)
DUGGER AND ASSOCIATES INC
Also Called: Urns Throgh Time
336 E Beck St (98557-9511)
PHONE.....................425 785-6940
Donald Gugger, *President*
Pam Sinclair-Nixon, *Vice Pres*
EMP: 2
SALES: 50K **Privately Held**
SIC: 3299 7379 Vases & urns, gypsum & papier mache; computer related consulting services

(G-6416)
GREYBEARD PUBLISHING
1125 W Simpson Ave (98557-9670)
PHONE.....................360 495-4107
David Beshears, *Principal*
EMP: 2
SALES (est): 138.4K **Privately Held**
SIC: 2741 Miscellaneous publishing

(G-6417)
JOE GORDON LOGGING INC
194 State Route 108 (98557-9503)
P.O. Box 1055 (98557-1055)
PHONE.....................360 470-1631
Joe Gordon, *President*
EMP: 5
SALES (est): 412.5K **Privately Held**
SIC: 2411 Logging camps & contractors

(G-6418)
M & M LOGGING
828 Mox Chehalis Rd (98557-9408)
PHONE.....................360 280-5973
Michael Mc Closkey, *CEO*
EMP: 3
SALES (est): 184.4K **Privately Held**
SIC: 2411 Logging

(PA)=Parent Co (HQ)=Headquarters (DH)=Div Headquarters
✿ = New Business established in last 2 years

2019 Washington Manufacturers Register

McCleary - Grays Harbor County (G-6419)

(G-6419)
SANDYS NIFTY TEES
9 Mcconkey Ave (98557-9686)
PHONE 360 861-8669
Sandra Elliott, *Principal*
EMP: 2 **EST:** 2017
SALES (est): 99.2K **Privately Held**
SIC: 2759 Screen printing

(G-6420)
SIMPSON DOOR COMPANY
400 W Simpson Ave (98557-9600)
PHONE 360 495-3291
James A Fielder, *Branch Mgr*
EMP: 480
SALES (est): 48.3MM **Privately Held**
WEB: www.simpsondoor.com
SIC: 2431 Millwork
PA: Simpson Door Company
400 W Simpson Ave
Mccleary WA

(G-6421)
WITTCO SEPARATION SYSTEMS INC
260 Mccleary Rd (98557-9303)
P.O. Box 626 (98557-0626)
PHONE 360 495-3100
EMP: 2
SQ FT: 24,000
SALES: 200K **Privately Held**
SIC: 3532 Mfg Separating Machinery

Mead
Spokane County

(G-6422)
AIRCRAFT CARGO PODS
18105 N Sands Rd (99021-8724)
PHONE 509 238-1165
Roy Keck, *Owner*
EMP: 5
SALES (est): 272K **Privately Held**
SIC: 3731 Cargo vessels, building & repairing

(G-6423)
ALL AMERICAN CORPORATION
Also Called: All American Homes
14525 N Newport Hwy (99021-9636)
P.O. Box 502, Richland (99352-0502)
PHONE 509 315-9951
James D Weber, *President*
EMP: 18
SQ FT: 2,000
SALES (est): 1.7MM **Privately Held**
SIC: 6552 3462 Subdividers & developers; anchors, forged

(G-6424)
AMERICAN CONTAINER HOMES INC
14525 N Newport Hwy (99021-9636)
P.O. Box 502, Richland (99352-0502)
PHONE 509 531-3286
James Weber, *President*
EMP: 5
SALES (est): 498.1K **Privately Held**
SIC: 3448 Prefabricated metal buildings

(G-6425)
BITPEG SOFTWARE INC
14818 N Peone Pines Dr (99021-9409)
PHONE 509 290-5216
Charles Heintzelman, *Principal*
EMP: 2
SALES (est): 98.8K **Privately Held**
SIC: 7372 Prepackaged software

(G-6426)
C & E SPRINKLER
4911 E Greenleaf Ave (99021-9421)
P.O. Box 9492, Spokane (99209-9492)
PHONE 509 466-2020
Craig Eastburg, *Owner*
EMP: 3
SALES (est): 223.4K **Privately Held**
WEB: www.cesprinklerremodel.com
SIC: 3494 Sprinkler systems, field

(G-6427)
CHARLES WASHINGTON
15010 N Neptune Ln (99021-9392)
PHONE 509 466-9098
Charles Washington, *Principal*
EMP: 3 **EST:** 2010
SALES (est): 218.6K **Privately Held**
SIC: 2411 Logging

(G-6428)
GLOBAL HARVEST FOODS LTD
Also Called: Global Harvest of Colorado
3116 E Graves Rd Ste 300 (99021)
PHONE 509 466-0539
EMP: 9
SALES (corp-wide): 6.2MM **Privately Held**
SIC: 2048 Bird food, prepared
HQ: Global Harvest Foods, Ltd.
16000 Christensen Rd # 300
Tukwila WA 98188

(G-6429)
HIEROPHANT MEADERY LLC
16602 N Day Mt Spokane Rd (99021-8764)
PHONE 509 294-0134
EMP: 5
SALES (est): 292.3K **Privately Held**
SIC: 2084 Wines

(G-6430)
HIGHWAY GRIND INC
14009 N Newport Hwy (99021-9224)
PHONE 509 466-5061
EMP: 2
SALES (est): 228K **Privately Held**
SIC: 3599 Mfg Industrial Machinery

(G-6431)
MANGO INK
4601 E Pineglen Rd (99021-9048)
PHONE 509 990-9085
Ryan Miller, *Owner*
Heidi Miller, *Co-Owner*
EMP: 2
SALES (est): 132.8K **Privately Held**
SIC: 2759 Invitations: printing

(G-6432)
METAL ROOFING & SIDING SUP INC
13906 N Newport Hwy (99021-9631)
PHONE 509 466-6854
Daniel McDonald, *President*
Carol McDonald, *Vice Pres*
EMP: 10
SQ FT: 14,000
SALES (est): 2.2MM **Privately Held**
SIC: 3547 Rolling mill machinery

(G-6433)
MIRAMAC METALS INC
13906 N Newport Hwy (99021-9631)
PHONE 509 483-5331
Carol A McDonald, *President*
Carol McDonald, *President*
Jennifer Lynn Suela-Mcdonald, *Admin Sec*
EMP: 19
SALES (est): 4.6MM **Privately Held**
SIC: 3531 Roofing equipment

(G-6434)
N2 STORAGE SYSTEMS INC
4227 E Chris Ct (99021-9355)
P.O. Box 460 (99021-0460)
PHONE 509 981-8097
Tammera L McClure, *President*
Charles J Clark, *President*
EMP: 4
SALES: 50K **Privately Held**
SIC: 3469 Boxes, stamped metal

(G-6435)
OK SOCK LLC
4815 E Patricia Rd (99021-9498)
PHONE 509 209-6598
Kyle Peterson, *Partner*
EMP: 3
SALES (est): 172.2K **Privately Held**
SIC: 2252 Socks

(G-6436)
SIMCHUK KARENE
Also Called: Hidden Acres
16802 N Applewood Ln (99021-9100)
PHONE 509 238-2830
Karene Simchuk, *Owner*
EMP: 4
SALES (est): 234.8K **Privately Held**
SIC: 2033 5441 0171 0175 Jams, including imitation: packaged in cans, jars, etc.; jellies, edible, including imitation: in cans, jars, etc.; fruits & fruit products in cans, jars, etc.; confectionery produced for direct sale on the premises; raspberry farm; apple orchard; flavoring extracts & syrups

(G-6437)
SPOKANE CUSTOM CABINETS INC
4515 E Bixel Ct (99021-9411)
PHONE 509 487-8416
Rob Saccomanno, *President*
Pamela Saccomanno, *Treasurer*
EMP: 2
SALES (est): 240.5K **Privately Held**
SIC: 2434 Wood kitchen cabinets

(G-6438)
SUPER SURIS ALPACAS
16219 N Day Mt Spokane Rd (99021-9704)
PHONE 509 475-5110
EMP: 2 **EST:** 2012
SALES (est): 127.8K **Privately Held**
SIC: 2231 Alpacas, mohair: woven

Medical Lake
Spokane County

(G-6439)
AMERICAN POSTAGE SCALE CORP (PA)
Also Called: APS
16120 W Silver Lake Rd (99022-8500)
P.O. Box 3915, Spokane (99220-3915)
PHONE 509 299-6144
Ronald Cook, *Principal*
Olga Cook, *Vice Pres*
EMP: 5
SALES (est): 653.1K **Privately Held**
SIC: 3579 5961 Postage meters; stamps, mail order

(G-6440)
DIRECT FIRE SUPPRESSION SYSTEM
620 N Grant Ave (99022-9108)
P.O. Box 665 (99022-0665)
PHONE 509 215-0852
Melissa Neece,
Shelby Neece,
EMP: 2
SALES (est): 82.3K **Privately Held**
SIC: 7382 5099 3999 Fire alarm maintenance & monitoring; fire extinguishers; fire extinguishers, portable

(G-6441)
HANDYWORKS INC
Also Called: Common Ground Pottery
405 E Fellows St (99022-5025)
PHONE 509 299-4918
Arthur Kulibert, *President*
Donna Kulibert, *Vice Pres*
EMP: 2
SALES (est): 118.4K **Privately Held**
SIC: 3269 Art & ornamental ware, pottery

(G-6442)
MIKE NILLES
7302 S Ladd Rd (99022-9406)
PHONE 509 299-3653
Mike Nilles, *Owner*
EMP: 2
SALES (est): 163.4K **Privately Held**
SIC: 0111 0119 2411 Wheat; cash grains; logging

(G-6443)
PACIFIC DEALER SERVICES
6315 S Brooks Rd (99022-8947)
PHONE 509 299-7269
Mark Wegner, *Owner*
EMP: 2
SQ FT: 828,511
SALES: 350K **Privately Held**
SIC: 2759 Business forms: printing

(G-6444)
R & R WOODWORKING INC
23719 W Manila Rd (99022-9622)
PHONE 509 279-9345
Ronald Burris, *Principal*
EMP: 2
SALES (est): 209K **Privately Held**
SIC: 2431 Millwork

(G-6445)
VINTAGE IDAHO PRINTS
19711 W Mcfarlane Rd (99022-5013)
PHONE 509 217-8453
Chris Bovey, *Principal*
EMP: 2
SALES (est): 83.9K **Privately Held**
SIC: 2752 Commercial printing, lithographic

Medina
King County

(G-6446)
BIKELID LLC
3430 Evergreen Point Rd (98039-1021)
P.O. Box 408 (98039-0408)
PHONE 206 963-7585
Steve Voorhees, *Ch of Bd*
Coert Voorhees, *Managing Prtnr*
Robert Duberow, *COO*
Bernard Anthen, *CFO*
Kimberly Pettit,
EMP: 8
SQ FT: 3,000
SALES: 250K **Privately Held**
SIC: 3949 Protective sporting equipment

(G-6447)
BYTE BROTHERS
1004 84th Ave Ne (98039-4805)
PHONE 425 917-8380
Darrell A Igelmund, *President*
▲ **EMP:** 20
SQ FT: 10,000
SALES (est): 3.8MM **Privately Held**
WEB: www.bytebros.com
SIC: 3577 Computer peripheral equipment

(G-6448)
CLAUDON INC
935 88th Ave Ne (98039-4832)
PHONE 425 454-2912
Kathy Claudon, *President*
Brian Claudon, *Corp Secy*
EMP: 2
SALES: 700K **Privately Held**
WEB: www.claudon.com
SIC: 3556 Meat, poultry & seafood processing machinery

(G-6449)
JAY PATHY
2455 80th Ave Ne (98039-1501)
P.O. Box 3 (98039-0003)
PHONE 425 890-9526
Jay Pathy, *Principal*
EMP: 2
SALES (est): 88.3K **Privately Held**
SIC: 3669 Communications equipment

(G-6450)
LACHINI WINERY (PA)
7720 Ne 24th St (98039-2351)
PHONE 503 864-4553
Ronald Lachini Jr, *Owner*
▼ **EMP:** 2
SALES (est): 210.7K **Privately Held**
WEB: www.lachinivineyards.com
SIC: 2084 Wines

(G-6451)
LUNDQUIST JOEGIL
Also Called: Literacy Unlmited Publications
8621 Ne 6th St (98039-5302)
PHONE 425 454-5830
Joegil Lundquist, *Owner*
Jeanne Lundquist, *Co-Owner*

EMP: 4
SALES: 90K Privately Held
WEB: www.literacyunlimited.com
SIC: 2731 Books: publishing only

(G-6452)
MARY MEDINA LLC
Also Called: Techtether
7835 Ne 14th St (98039-3108)
PHONE...................................206 719-1730
Mary Bennett,
Carol Johnsen,
Mary Maron,
▲ EMP: 3
SALES: 1MM Privately Held
WEB: www.marymedina.com
SIC: 3663 Mobile communication equipment

(G-6453)
NEPOWARE CORPORATION
Also Called: Neposmart
2647 79th Ave Ne (98039-1516)
PHONE....................................425 802-8821
Richard Ang, CEO
Catherine Ang, Director
EMP: 5
SALES (est): 343.6K Privately Held
SIC: 5731 7389 3651 Radio, television & electronic stores; ; household audio & video equipment

Mercer Island
King County

(G-6454)
AORTICA CORPORATION
6200 Se 27th St (98040-2404)
PHONE....................................425 209-0272
Richard Van Bibber, Vice Pres
EMP: 3
SQ FT: 3,000
SALES (est): 538.7K Privately Held
SIC: 3841 Surgical & medical instruments

(G-6455)
AWARE SOFTWARE INC
4534 Ferncroft Rd (98040-3820)
PHONE....................................206 232-5709
David J Ross, Principal
EMP: 2
SALES (est): 95.1K Privately Held
SIC: 7372 Prepackaged software

(G-6456)
BRAZIER LUMBER COMPANY INC
8444 N Mercer Way (98040-3134)
PHONE....................................206 441-8184
Stephen Brazier, President
EMP: 2
SQ FT: 1,600
SALES: 5.5MM Privately Held
SIC: 5031 2421 Lumber: rough, dressed & finished; lumber: rough, sawed or planed

(G-6457)
BUMPERCHUTE CO
8815 Se 74th Pl (98040-5765)
PHONE....................................206 232-8189
Renee Christenson, President
Bill Christenson, Vice Pres
EMP: 2
SALES (est): 195K Privately Held
WEB: www.bumperchute.com
SIC: 2394 Canvas awnings & canopies

(G-6458)
COHERENT KNOWLEDGE SYSTEMS LLC
5 Wembley Ln (98040-4330)
PHONE....................................206 519-6410
Benjamin Grosof, Principal
Janine Bloomfield, Opers Staff
EMP: 6
SALES (est): 366.5K Privately Held
SIC: 7372 7371 Business oriented computer software; educational computer software; computer software systems analysis & design, custom; computer software development

(G-6459)
CONTINUUM CREATIVE LLC ✪
2760 76th Ave Se Apt 406 (98040-2768)
PHONE....................................404 985-6648
EMP: 2 EST: 2018
SALES (est): 56.5K Privately Held
SIC: 7372 Application computer software

(G-6460)
DUMB LUCK LLC
8333 Se 68th St (98040-5210)
PHONE....................................206 406-1011
William Elliott McNary,
Nolan McHugh,
EMP: 2
SALES (est): 108.4K Privately Held
SIC: 7372 Application computer software

(G-6461)
EMERALD CITY PROMOTIONS LLC
2741 72nd Ave Se (98040-2619)
PHONE....................................206 271-2880
Arthur D Smith, Mng Member
EMP: 9
SALES (est): 1.1MM Privately Held
WEB: www.emeraldcitypromo.com
SIC: 2064 Chocolate candy, except solid chocolate; nuts, candy covered

(G-6462)
FABRICATIONS INC
3010 77th Ave Se Ste 107 (98040-2829)
P.O. Box 691 (98040-0691)
PHONE....................................888 808-9878
Larry Clark, President
EMP: 3
SALES (est): 167.8K Privately Held
SIC: 2326 2211 2392 Aprons, work, except rubberized & plastic: men's; bed sheeting, cotton; tablecloths & table settings

(G-6463)
FLYING SOFA LLC
6040 86th Ave Se (98040-4944)
PHONE....................................206 275-3935
Glenn Dierkes,
EMP: 2 EST: 2011
SALES (est): 132K Privately Held
SIC: 7372 7389 Application computer software;

(G-6464)
GRACE HARVEST & ASSOC LLC
8245 Se 36th St (98040-3030)
PHONE....................................206 973-2363
Grace Vhou,
Natasha Gao,
◆ EMP: 10
SALES (est): 970K Privately Held
SIC: 5122 2844 5999 7389 Cosmetics, perfumes & hair products; cosmetic preparations; hair care products;

(G-6465)
GREENLITE HEAVY INDUSTRIES LLC
6801 96th Ave Se (98040-5407)
PHONE....................................206 226-3523
Michael McGuffin, Principal
EMP: 2
SALES (est): 142.8K Privately Held
SIC: 3999 Manufacturing industries

(G-6466)
HONEYWELL INTERNATIONAL INC
9555 Se 36th St (98040-3703)
PHONE....................................360 253-8100
EMP: 2
SALES (corp-wide): 41.8B Publicly Held
SIC: 3724 Aircraft engines & engine parts
PA: Honeywell International Inc.
    115 Tabor Rd
    Morris Plains NJ 07950
    973 455-2000

(G-6467)
INDUSTRIAL CRATING & PACKING
Also Called: Industrial Containers Div
4821 84th Ave Se (98040-4615)
PHONE....................................425 226-9200
Tom Kalil, President
Carmen Arzo, Owner
P Arzo, Principal
▲ EMP: 14 EST: 1950
SQ FT: 50,000
SALES (est): 2.3MM Privately Held
WEB: www.indcrate.com
SIC: 2441 5085 4783 2653 Boxes, wood; packing, industrial; packing & crating; corrugated & solid fiber boxes

(G-6468)
INNOVATIVE SOLUTIONS INTL
8441 Se 68th St Ste 312 (98040-5235)
PHONE....................................206 365-7200
Frank Sorba, President
Andrew Sorba, Vice Pres
Bonnie Sorba, Admin Sec
EMP: 18
SALES (est): 3.7MM Privately Held
SIC: 2099 Food preparations

(G-6469)
JPHOTONICS INC
5041 W Mercer Way (98040-4629)
PHONE....................................206 397-3702
Qinggen Chen, CEO
EMP: 5
SALES (est): 483.4K Privately Held
SIC: 3661 Fiber optics communications equipment

(G-6470)
LED SOFTWARE
Also Called: Computer Enhancement
7515 86th Ave Se (98040-5740)
PHONE....................................206 232-2812
EMP: 2 EST: 1991
SALES (est): 150K Privately Held
SIC: 7372 Prepackaged Software Services

(G-6471)
LIFECODEX PUBLISHING
7221 87th Ave Se (98040-5742)
P.O. Box 58 (98040-0058)
PHONE....................................206 453-0235
Daniel Lapin, Mng Member
Susan Lapin,
EMP: 4
SALES (est): 224.7K Privately Held
SIC: 2741 Miscellaneous publishing

(G-6472)
MAMMOTH MEDIA INC
Also Called: Food For Tots Publishing
7650 Se 27th Ave Unit 307 (98040-3061)
PHONE....................................206 275-3183
Janice Woolley, President
EMP: 3
SALES: 70K Privately Held
SIC: 2741 Miscellaneous publishing

(G-6473)
MEMBERS CLUB AT ALDARRA
3853 Island Crest Way (98040-3548)
PHONE....................................206 232-8580
Patrick Schulties, Branch Mgr
EMP: 5
SALES (corp-wide): 4.1MM Privately Held
SIC: 2731 7997 Book publishing; golf club, membership
PA: Members Club At Aldarra
    29125 Se Duthie Hill Rd
    Sammamish WA 98075
    425 222-7828

(G-6474)
MICHAEL W SHERER
4741 Fernridge Ln (98040-4700)
PHONE....................................206 230-8541
Michael Sherer, Principal
EMP: 2
SALES (est): 88.9K Privately Held
SIC: 3089 Plastics products

(G-6475)
O S WINERY LLC
6743 80th Ave Se (98040-5221)
PHONE....................................206 243-3427
Robert Sullivan, Mng Member
Rob Sullivan, Administration
William Owen,
▲ EMP: 2

SALES (est): 209.2K Privately Held
WEB: www.oswinery.com
SIC: 2084 Wines

(G-6476)
OBERON PHARMA
8339 Se 57th St (98040-4906)
PHONE....................................206 713-5467
Jeffrey Oster, Principal
EMP: 2
SALES (est): 110K Privately Held
SIC: 2834 Pharmaceutical preparations

(G-6477)
OH CHOLOCOLATE LLC
2703 76th Ave Se (98040-2735)
PHONE....................................206 232-4974
Nola Wyse, Mng Member
Margo Masaoka,
EMP: 21
SQ FT: 600
SALES (est): 1.8MM Privately Held
WEB: www.ohchocolate.com
SIC: 2064 5441 Candy & other confectionery products; candy, nut & confectionery stores

(G-6478)
OUTSMART OFFICE SOLUTIONS INC
7683 Se 27th St Ste 185 (98040-2804)
P.O. Box 170157, San Francisco CA (94117-0157)
PHONE....................................888 688-8154
George Pieper, CEO
Dawn Ackerman, President
EMP: 5
SQ FT: 1,000
SALES: 400K Privately Held
SIC: 1799 2893 Office furniture installation; printing ink

(G-6479)
PHARMA TERRA INC
3440 W Mercer Way (98040-3313)
P.O. Box 486 (98040-0486)
PHONE....................................800 215-3957
Robert Adamowski, CEO
Omar Lalani, President
EMP: 2
SALES (est): 190K Privately Held
SIC: 2023 Dietary supplements, dairy & non-dairy based

(G-6480)
POLARIS MANUFACTURING INC
3816 Greenbrier Ln (98040-3728)
PHONE....................................206 230-9235
Michael Bontatibus, Principal
EMP: 2
SALES (est): 128.5K Privately Held
SIC: 3999 Manufacturing industries

(G-6481)
PUGET SOUND FOODS INC
8245 Se 59th St (98040-4908)
PHONE....................................206 232-2757
John Lettengarver, CEO
EMP: 15
SALES (est): 1MM Privately Held
SIC: 2099 Spices, including grinding

(G-6482)
SCHAFER WINERY LLC (PA)
Also Called: Amaurice Cellars
4402 E Mercer Way (98040-3828)
PHONE....................................425 985-7000
Tom Schafer, General Mgr
A Thomas Schafer,
EMP: 10
SALES (est): 2MM Privately Held
SIC: 2084 Wine cellars, bonded: engaged in blending wines

(G-6483)
SEATTLE DRONE SALES LLC
8203 Avalon Dr (98040-5612)
PHONE....................................206 858-2764
EMP: 2 EST: 2015
SALES (est): 92.9K Privately Held
SIC: 3721 Motorized aircraft

Mercer Island - King County (G-6484)

(G-6484)
SHOWALTER SYSTEMS INC
3047 78th Ave Se Ste 203 (98040-2847)
P.O. Box 654 (98040-0654)
PHONE..................................206 236-6276
Steve Showalter, *Principal*
EMP: 3
SALES (est): 330K **Privately Held**
SIC: 7373 3823 Systems integration services; industrial process measurement equipment

(G-6485)
SPAZ INDUSTRIES LLC
2445 74th Ave Se (98040-2632)
PHONE..................................206 890-7079
EMP: 2 **EST:** 2017
SALES (est): 89.1K **Privately Held**
SIC: 3999 Manufacturing industries

(G-6486)
STORYBOX STUDIOS LLC
5608 89th Ave Se (98040-5031)
PHONE..................................206 310-2626
EMP: 3
SALES: 750K **Privately Held**
SIC: 3944 Production Studio Games/Toys

(G-6487)
TUCKER GARNER CA
7256 Holly Hill Dr (98040-5344)
PHONE..................................206 236-0856
Tucker Garner, *Principal*
EMP: 3
SALES (est): 195.5K **Privately Held**
SIC: 1382 Oil & gas exploration services

(G-6488)
TYPESETTER CORPORATION
Also Called: Image East
9675 Se 36th St Ste 110 (98040-3723)
PHONE..................................425 455-3055
Frances Simperman, *President*
Chris Beasley, *President*
Frances Rogers, *President*
Mike Young, *General Mgr*
EMP: 13
SQ FT: 10,000
SALES (est): 1.4MM **Privately Held**
WEB: www.printex-press.com
SIC: 2759 2791 Commercial printing; typesetting

(G-6489)
WHITE MATTER LLC
4431 Ferncroft Rd (98040-3817)
PHONE..................................510 409-0144
Timothy Blanche,
EMP: 6 **EST:** 2014
SALES (est): 856.2K **Privately Held**
SIC: 3672 Printed circuit boards

Mesa
Franklin County

(G-6490)
AGRI-TRAC INC
201 1st Ave (99343)
PHONE..................................509 265-4327
Spencer Kim Haws, *President*
Thomas Clyde, *Vice Pres*
Ben Casper, *Treasurer*
Robert Clyde, *Admin Sec*
EMP: 8
SQ FT: 16,500
SALES (est): 1.2MM **Privately Held**
SIC: 3523 Fertilizing, spraying, dusting & irrigation machinery

(G-6491)
D B EXPRESS LLC
220 Park Ave (99343)
P.O. Box 223 (99343-0223)
PHONE..................................509 265-4511
EMP: 2 **EST:** 2006
SALES (est): 120K **Privately Held**
SIC: 2741 Misc Publishing

(G-6492)
EASTERDAY DIESEL MANUFACTURING
51 Bellflower Rd (99343-8503)
PHONE..................................509 269-4577
Bill Easterday, *Owner*
EMP: 2 **EST:** 1997
SQ FT: 3,600
SALES (est): 198.7K **Privately Held**
SIC: 3535 7538 Conveyors & conveying equipment; engine repair, except diesel: automotive

(G-6493)
GIESBRECHT & SONS LLC
1061 Hollingsworth Rd (99343-9552)
PHONE..................................509 269-4087
EMP: 6 **EST:** 2014
SALES (est): 284.4K **Privately Held**
SIC: 3999 Manufacturing industries

(G-6494)
LEE H KOEHN
2671 Colonial Rd (99343-9714)
PHONE..................................509 265-4367
Lee E Koehn, *Owner*
EMP: 2
SALES (est): 210K **Privately Held**
SIC: 3523 0211 Driers (farm): grain, hay & seed; beef cattle feedlots

(G-6495)
SAGE HILL NORTHWEST INC (PA)
5230 Hollingsworth Rd (99343-9537)
PHONE..................................509 269-4966
Michael Davidson, *President*
Troy Withers, *Marketing Staff*
Earline Mathis, *Manager*
Chino Melo, *Information Mgr*
◆ **EMP:** 10
SQ FT: 44,000
SALES (est): 1.7MM **Privately Held**
SIC: 2048 6519 Hay, cubed; farm land leasing

(G-6496)
SHEFFIELD CIDER INC
4665 Sheffield Rd (99343-9715)
PHONE..................................509 269-4610
Nolan Empey, *Principal*
▲ **EMP:** 2 **EST:** 2009
SALES (est): 169.8K **Privately Held**
SIC: 2099 7389 Cider, nonalcoholic;

Metaline Falls
Pend Oreille County

(G-6497)
CITY OF SATTLE-CITY LIGHT DEPT
Also Called: Boundary Power House
10382 Boundary Rd (99153-9736)
P.O. Box 219 (99153-0219)
PHONE..................................509 446-3083
Lonnie Johnson, *Manager*
EMP: 40 **Privately Held**
WEB: www.energysmartservices.com
SIC: 3621 4911 Motors & generators; electric services
HQ: The City Of Seattle-City Light Department
  700 5th Ave Ste 3200
  Seattle WA 98104
  206 684-3200

(G-6498)
SWEET CREEK CREATIONS
219 E 5th Ave (99153-9717)
P.O. Box 307 (99153-0307)
PHONE..................................509 446-2429
Patricia Zimmerman, *Partner*
Shirley Botzheim, *Partner*
EMP: 2
SQ FT: 1,440
SALES: 160K **Privately Held**
SIC: 2385 2331 3999 5949 Raincoats, except vulcanized rubber: purchased materials; blouses, women's & juniors': made from purchased material; flowers, artificial & preserved; fabric stores piece goods; notions, including trim; gift, novelty & souvenir shop

(G-6499)
TECK AMERICAN INCORPORATED
Also Called: Pend Oreille Mine
1382 Pend Oreille Mine Rd (99153-9708)
P.O. Box 7 (99153-0007)
PHONE..................................509 446-5308
David Riggle, *Branch Mgr*
EMP: 80
SALES (corp-wide): 9.5B **Privately Held**
SIC: 1081 Metal mining services
HQ: Teck American Incorporated
  501 N Riverpoint Blvd # 300
  Spokane WA 99202
  509 747-6111

(G-6500)
WASHINGTON TECK INCORPORATED
1382 Pend Oreille Mine Rd (99153-9708)
P.O. Box 7 (99153-0007)
PHONE..................................509 446-4516
Dale Andres, *President*
Leslie Panther, *Vice Pres*
Phillip Pesek, *Vice Pres*
EMP: 275
SALES (est): 79.9K
SALES (corp-wide): 9.5B **Privately Held**
SIC: 1081 Exploration, metal mining
HQ: Teck American Incorporated
  501 N Riverpoint Blvd # 300
  Spokane WA 99202
  509 747-6111

Mica
Spokane County

(G-6501)
MUTUAL MATERIALS COMPANY
10627 S Highway 27 (99023-6059)
PHONE..................................509 924-2120
Joe Taff, *Manager*
EMP: 50
SALES (corp-wide): 44.8MM **Privately Held**
SIC: 3251 3255 Structural brick & blocks; clay refractories
PA: Mutual Materials Company
  605 119th Ave Ne
  Bellevue WA 98005
  425 452-2300

Mill Creek
Snohomish County

(G-6502)
CADMAN (SEATTLE) INC
Also Called: Lehigh Hanson
18427 Bothell Everett Hwy (98012)
PHONE..................................425 316-9100
Bill Sayer, *President*
EMP: 185
SALES (corp-wide): 20.6B **Privately Held**
SIC: 3273 Ready-mixed concrete
HQ: Cadman, Inc.
  7554 185th Ave Ne Ste 100
  Redmond WA 98052

(G-6503)
CAMINOVA INC
15325 34th Dr Se (98012-5037)
PHONE..................................206 919-2110
Hyung Lim, *Principal*
EMP: 2
SALES: 950K **Privately Held**
SIC: 7372 Prepackaged software

(G-6504)
CONSTRUCTIVISION INC
17010 9th Ave Se (98012-6311)
PHONE..................................425 741-4413
Leon Johnson, *President*
EMP: 2
SALES (est): 104.8K **Privately Held**
WEB: www.constructivision.com
SIC: 7372 7371 Prepackaged software; custom computer programming services

(G-6505)
CRYSTAL POINT INC
15833 Mill Creek Blvd (98082-0019)
P.O. Box 12247 (98082-0247)
PHONE..................................425 487-3656
Chris Stephens, *President*
Fred Stephens, *Exec VP*
EMP: 17
SQ FT: 8,200
SALES (est): 2MM **Privately Held**
WEB: www.crystalpoint.com
SIC: 7372 Business oriented computer software

(G-6506)
DEFSEC SOLUTIONS LLC
914 164th St Se Ste B12 (98012-6339)
PHONE..................................855 933-3732
Greg Wisdom, *COO*
Anna Truss,
EMP: 2
SALES (est): 200K **Privately Held**
SIC: 5734 8243 7372 Computer software & accessories; software training, computer; prepackaged software

(G-6507)
DINNERS READY
2932 143rd St Se (98012-5011)
PHONE..................................425 337-7955
Pim Peterson, *Principal*
EMP: 5
SALES (est): 26.2K **Privately Held**
SIC: 3273 Ready-mixed concrete

(G-6508)
DOSE OIL LLC
2302 140th Pl Se (98012-1304)
PHONE..................................954 494-7976
Thomas E Gregory Jr, *Administration*
EMP: 2
SALES (est): 105.5K **Privately Held**
SIC: 1311 Crude petroleum & natural gas

(G-6509)
EVOLUTION COVERS
4109 161st St Se (98012-3105)
PHONE..................................425 478-2043
EMP: 2 **EST:** 2009
SALES (est): 112.4K **Privately Held**
SIC: 2394 Canvas & related products

(G-6510)
FANIPIN KOREA CORP
2320 162nd St Se (98012-7835)
PHONE..................................425 218-6555
Jinsik Cho, *Principal*
EMP: 2
SALES (est): 62.9K **Privately Held**
SIC: 2711 Newspapers

(G-6511)
FLORIAN DESIGN
16212 Bothell Everett Hwy (98012-1603)
PHONE..................................425 742-7212
Florian Wells, *Partner*
Kevin Sweeney, *Partner*
EMP: 4
SALES (est): 300K **Privately Held**
WEB: www.floriangreenhouse.com
SIC: 7389 2385 Apparel designers, commercial; waterproof outerwear

(G-6512)
GLOBAL VISION
4307 147th Pl Se (98012-4714)
PHONE..................................425 985-9325
Anzhela Pizhuk, *Owner*
EMP: 2
SALES (est): 75K **Privately Held**
SIC: 7372 Prepackaged software

(G-6513)
HUNTRON INC
Also Called: Huntron Instruments
15720 Main St Ste 100 (98012-1555)
PHONE..................................425 743-3171
William Curry, *President*
James Crosson, *Vice Pres*
Thomas Stewart, *Vice Pres*
Don Parry, *Controller*
Allen Howard, *Shareholder*
EMP: 11
SQ FT: 15,000

SALES (est): 4.2MM **Privately Held**
WEB: www.huntron.com
SIC: 3825 5065 Test equipment for electronic & electric measurement; electronic parts

(G-6514)
JP PUBLICATIONS
16212 Bothell Everett Hwy (98012-1603)
PHONE.....................................425 835-0021
EMP: 2 **EST:** 2010
SALES (est): 95K **Privately Held**
SIC: 2741 Misc Publishing

(G-6515)
KRELL SOFTWARE INC
1805 Village Green Dr # 24 (98012-1374)
PHONE.....................................425 298-9519
Stephen S Troxell, *President*
EMP: 2
SALES (est): 121.1K **Privately Held**
WEB: www.krell-software.com
SIC: 7372 Business oriented computer software

(G-6516)
LRT INC (PA)
Also Called: Aircraft Maintenance & Support
15712 Mill Creek Blvd # 1 (98012-1573)
P.O. Box 12366 (98082-0366)
PHONE.....................................425 742-0333
Jackie Toombs, *President*
Larry Toombs, *Exec VP*
EMP: 3
SQ FT: 25,000
SALES: 3.1MM **Privately Held**
WEB: www.lrt-inc.com
SIC: 3728 5091 Aircraft parts & equipment; boat accessories & parts

(G-6517)
MERCER PRODUCTS & MFG CO (HQ)
15712 Mill Creek Blvd (98012-1573)
P.O. Box 12366 (98082-0366)
PHONE.....................................425 742-0333
Jackie Toombs, *President*
Larry Toombs, *Exec VP*
EMP: 3
SALES (est): 407.6K **Privately Held**
SIC: 3728 Aircraft parts & equipment

(G-6518)
NW HARDWOODS LLC
13423 39th Dr Se (98012-8946)
PHONE.....................................206 784-9369
EMP: 3
SALES (est): 173.5K **Privately Held**
SIC: 2435 Mfg Hardwood Veneer/Plywood

(G-6519)
OSBOURNE SQUARE DENTAL
13209 44th Ave Se 201 (98012-8985)
PHONE.....................................425 225-5757
Gurieerpal Bajwa, *Owner*
Gurinderpal Bajwa, *Principal*
EMP: 4
SALES (est): 374.3K **Privately Held**
SIC: 3843 Enamels, dentists'

(G-6520)
PKFASHIONS INC
13300 Bothell Everett Hwy # 628 (98012-5312)
PHONE.....................................425 359-6510
Paige K Fortner, *CEO*
▲ **EMP:** 2
SALES: 150K **Privately Held**
SIC: 2339 Women's & misses' accessories

(G-6521)
PROFESSIONAL HARDWOOD FLOORS
4205 141st St Se (98012-8942)
PHONE.....................................425 741-1017
Ivan Pilat, *Owner*
EMP: 7
SALES (est): 647.8K **Privately Held**
WEB: www.prohardwoods.com
SIC: 2426 2439 Flooring, hardwood; structural wood members

(G-6522)
RC & CO
15603 Main St Ste 101 (98012-9003)
PHONE.....................................425 774-7511
Raymond C Elliott, *President*
Sherrie Elliott, *Treasurer*
EMP: 4
SALES (est): 345.8K **Privately Held**
WEB: www.chrislee21.com
SIC: 7631 3911 Jewelry repair services; jewelry, precious metal

(G-6523)
ROOFERPRO SOFTWARE LLC
914 164th St Se Unit 110 (98012-6385)
PHONE.....................................425 503-4298
David Urban, *Mng Member*
EMP: 2
SALES (est): 124K **Privately Held**
SIC: 7372 Business oriented computer software

(G-6524)
RUNNING 26 INC
15603 Main St (98012-9003)
PHONE.....................................425 948-6495
Shelby Schenck, *Owner*
EMP: 3
SALES (est): 224.1K **Privately Held**
SIC: 3949 Sporting & athletic goods

(G-6525)
SEALTH AERO MARINE CO
16001 Mill Creek Blvd (98012-1542)
PHONE.....................................425 481-0727
John Andrew, *President*
Diane Matuska, *Corp Secy*
John Van Broekhoven, *Vice Pres*
Kim Sullivan, *Relations*
EMP: 30
SQ FT: 20,000
SALES (est): 7.4MM **Privately Held**
WEB: www.sealth.com
SIC: 3429 3812 Marine hardware; aircraft hardware; search & navigation equipment

(G-6526)
SEATTLE CURTAIN MFG CO
104 12th Ave (98012)
PHONE.....................................206 324-0692
Morris Capeluto, *President*
Jewel Capeluto, *Corp Secy*
Ralph A Capeluto, *Vice Pres*
EMP: 35 **EST:** 1930
SQ FT: 20,000
SALES (est): 3MM **Privately Held**
WEB: www.seattlecurtain.com
SIC: 2391 5023 2591 2392 Draperies, plastic & textile: from purchased materials; window furnishings; venetian blinds; drapery hardware & blinds & shades; household furnishings

(G-6527)
SEATTLE POMADE CO
13401 Dumas Rd Apt G304 (98012-5514)
PHONE.....................................206 348-3972
Andrew Parry, *Principal*
EMP: 4 **EST:** 2015
SALES (est): 304.6K **Privately Held**
SIC: 2844 Toilet preparations

(G-6528)
SEATTLE VIET TIMES INC
102 167th St Sw (98012-4920)
P.O. Box 14111 (98082-2111)
PHONE.....................................425 678-8872
Ha Ngo, *President*
EMP: 5
SALES (est): 321.8K **Privately Held**
SIC: 2721 7389 Periodicals: publishing only;

(G-6529)
SNO RIVER MANUFACTURING
3105 Silver Crest Dr (98012-5632)
PHONE.....................................425 338-5200
EMP: 2
SALES (est): 97K **Privately Held**
SIC: 3999 Mfg Misc Products

(G-6530)
SPORTSOFT INC
914 164th St Se (98012-6385)
PHONE.....................................425 822-4613
Leslie Totten, *President*
EMP: 5
SALES (est): 566.5K **Privately Held**
SIC: 3577 Bar code (magnetic ink) printers

Milton
Pierce County

(G-6531)
4 OVER LLC
Also Called: 4over
300 Meridian E (98354-9338)
PHONE.....................................818 246-1170
EMP: 5
SALES (corp-wide): 190.6MM **Privately Held**
SIC: 2759 7336 Commercial printing; commercial art & graphic design
HQ: 4 Over, Llc
5900 San Fernando Rd D
Glendale CA 91202
818 246-1170

(G-6532)
ANDERSEN MODELS INTERNATIONAL
Also Called: AMI
1302 28th Avenue Ct (98354-7007)
PHONE.....................................253 952-2135
Donna Anderson, *Owner*
EMP: 2 **EST:** 1983
SALES (est): 125.4K **Privately Held**
SIC: 3842 Models, anatomical

(G-6533)
CALHOUN TANKS AND SERVICES
301 Porter Way (98354-9690)
PHONE.....................................253 517-7356
EMP: 3
SALES (est): 160.4K **Privately Held**
SIC: 3443 Fabricated plate work (boiler shop)

(G-6534)
EMERALD CITY EMBROIDERY
509 22nd Avenue Ct (98354-9417)
PHONE.....................................253 922-8838
James Gunn, *Owner*
EMP: 2
SALES (est): 98.4K **Privately Held**
WEB: www.emcityem.com
SIC: 2395 Embroidery products, except schiffli machine

(G-6535)
INTERIOR FORM TOPS INC
1420 Meridian E Ste 5 (98354-9387)
PHONE.....................................253 927-8171
Gary Skinner, *President*
Rory Skinner, *Vice Pres*
Terry Carlton, *Treasurer*
Steve Vanstone, *Technology*
EMP: 30
SQ FT: 10,000
SALES (est): 4MM **Privately Held**
WEB: www.interiorformtops.com
SIC: 2541 3083 Table or counter tops, plastic laminated; laminated plastics plate & sheet

(G-6536)
MORLEY MACHINE TOOL ALGNMT INC
800 Fife Way (98354-8838)
PHONE.....................................253 926-1515
Tony Morley, *President*
Stephen Smith, *COO*
Jan Morley, *CFO*
EMP: 20
SQ FT: 9,000
SALES (est): 3.8MM **Privately Held**
WEB: www.morleymta.com
SIC: 7699 5049 3559 Mechanical instrument repair; precision tools; sewing machines & hat & zipper making machinery

(G-6537)
NTH DEGREE INC
1009 Xavier St (98354-8935)
PHONE.....................................253 926-6705
Mike Pittman, *Branch Mgr*
EMP: 2
SALES (corp-wide): 58.8MM **Privately Held**
WEB: www.nthdegree.com
SIC: 3999 Barber & beauty shop equipment
PA: Nth Degree, Inc.
3237 Satellite Blvd # 600
Duluth GA 30096
404 296-5282

Mineral
Lewis County

(G-6538)
REMBOS HIPRO
121 Maple Ln (98355)
P.O. Box 170 (98355-0170)
PHONE.....................................360 492-3100
EMP: 4
SALES (est): 296.6K **Privately Held**
SIC: 3053 Gaskets, packing & sealing devices

Moclips
Grays Harbor County

(G-6539)
GRIFFITHS INC
Also Called: Shake & Shingle 208
208 Otis Ave (98562)
PHONE.....................................360 276-4122
Craig Griffiths, *President*
EMP: 6
SQ FT: 19,000
SALES (est): 441.8K **Privately Held**
SIC: 2429 2411 Shakes (hand split shingles); shingle mill; logging camps & contractors

Monroe
Snohomish County

(G-6540)
A & I MANUFACTURING INC
17476 147th St Se Ste E (98272-1075)
P.O. Box 1269 (98272-4269)
PHONE.....................................360 805-0858
Mike Degraff, *President*
Tama Degraff, *Treasurer*
Tamar Degraff, *Treasurer*
▲ **EMP:** 27
SQ FT: 12,000
SALES (est): 4.1MM **Privately Held**
SIC: 2591 Mini blinds

(G-6541)
A AND R CABINETS & WDWKG L L C
22223 Yeager Rd (98272-8648)
PHONE.....................................360 863-8417
EMP: 2
SALES (est): 155.9K **Privately Held**
SIC: 2431 Mfg Millwork

(G-6542)
ADI SOLAR CORPORATION
14815 Chain Lake Rd Ste H (98272-8775)
PHONE.....................................206 484-2879
Wayne Bliesner, *President*
Gerald Fargo, *Vice Pres*
EMP: 2
SQ FT: 3,600
SALES: 500K **Privately Held**
SIC: 3724 Research & development on aircraft engines & parts

(G-6543)
AFCO PERFORMANCE GROUP LLC
Also Called: Longacre Racing Products
101 E Main St Ste 206 (98272-1519)
PHONE.....................................360 453-2030
Jeff Scales, *Branch Mgr*
EMP: 5
SALES (corp-wide): 1.8MM **Privately Held**
SIC: 3714 5531 Motor vehicle parts & accessories; automotive parts

Monroe - Snohomish County (G-6544)

PA: Afco Performance Group, Llc
977 Hyrock Blvd
Boonville IN 47601
812 897-0900

(G-6544)
AFFORDABLE ELECTRONICS INC
Also Called: A E I
16001 234th St Se (98272-9359)
PHONE....................425 484-0964
Michael Myhre, *President*
Kim Myhre, *Vice Pres*
EMP: 3
SALES (est): 245.7K **Privately Held**
WEB: www.aeisecure.com
SIC: 3699 Security control equipment & systems

(G-6545)
ALL POINTS EAST
21420 189th Ave Se (98272-9439)
PHONE....................360 863-8971
EMP: 2 **EST:** 2004
SALES (est): 100K **Privately Held**
SIC: 2511 Mfg Wood Household Furniture

(G-6546)
ALR SPECIALTY COATINGS LLC
27008 137th St Se (98272-7842)
PHONE....................206 713-2070
EMP: 2
SALES (est): 100K **Privately Held**
SIC: 3479 Coating/Engraving Service

(G-6547)
AMERICAN DREAM HOMES & CR
Also Called: American Dream Product
17404 147th St Se Ste C (98272-2714)
PHONE....................360 863-9340
Paul Tortorice, *Owner*
Halina Tortorice, *Partner*
EMP: 8
SQ FT: 4,000
SALES: 500K **Privately Held**
WEB: www.adp-usa.com
SIC: 2499 Novelties, wood fiber

(G-6548)
AMERICAN ROOF INC
Also Called: Super Anchor Safety
17731 147th St Se (98272-1030)
PHONE....................360 668-3206
Steven Nichols, *President*
Paul Lagerstedt, *VP Sales*
▲ **EMP:** 16
SQ FT: 5,200
SALES (est): 3.7MM **Privately Held**
WEB: www.superanchor.com
SIC: 3569 Firefighting apparatus & related equipment

(G-6549)
AMIGO ARTS LLC
17461 147th St Se (98272-2728)
PHONE....................425 443-5744
Pablo Guerrero, *Principal*
EMP: 2
SALES (est): 183.6K **Privately Held**
SIC: 3993 Signs & advertising specialties

(G-6550)
ANNIVERSARY YEAR PRESS
15820 291st Ave Se (98272-8909)
PHONE....................360 348-7945
Curtis Wright, *Principal*
EMP: 2
SALES (est): 97K **Privately Held**
SIC: 2741 Miscellaneous publishing

(G-6551)
BEDFORD INDUSTRIES INC
Also Called: Oberg International
16726 146th St Se Ste 135 (98272-2937)
PHONE....................360 805-9099
David Ledoux, *President*
EMP: 5
SQ FT: 25,100
SALES (est): 974.6K **Privately Held**
WEB: www.bedfordindustries.com
SIC: 3532 Crushers, stationary

(G-6552)
BELTECNO INC
16726 Tye St Se (98272-1059)
PHONE....................360 512-4000
Hiroshi Suzuki, *Ch of Bd*
Bill Weaver, *President*
Norm Zahler, *Vice Pres*
Takashi Suzuki, *Treasurer*
John Dacy, *Admin Sec*
EMP: 8
SQ FT: 190,000
SALES (est): 595.2K **Privately Held**
SIC: 2434 2511 Wood kitchen cabinets; wood household furniture
HQ: Beltecno Co.,Ltd.
3-5-27, Nishiki, Naka-Ku
Nagoya AIC 460-0

(G-6553)
BIG ROCK INDUSTRIES LLC
17391 Tye St Se (98272-1047)
PHONE....................425 314-8710
EMP: 3
SALES (est): 166.2K **Privately Held**
SIC: 3999 Manufacturing industries

(G-6554)
BINGHAM MANUFACTURING INC
Also Called: Bingham Industries
17401 147th St Se Ste C (98272-2747)
PHONE....................360 863-1170
Gary Bingham, *President*
Jeremy Bingham, *President*
▼ **EMP:** 9
SQ FT: 10,000
SALES (est): 1.4MM **Privately Held**
WEB: www.binghammfg.com
SIC: 3589 Water treatment equipment, industrial

(G-6555)
BLUE WATER PUBLISHERS LLC
22727 161st Ave Se (98272-7302)
PHONE....................360 805-6474
Kathleen Aitkins, *Principal*
Eric Johnson, *Sales Staff*
James Aitkins,
EMP: 2
SALES: 300K **Privately Held**
WEB: www.bluewaterpublishers.com
SIC: 2721 Magazines: publishing & printing

(G-6556)
BLUEBERRY MERINGUE SOFTWARE
16824 Stackpole Rd (98272-9407)
PHONE....................425 830-5414
Scott Kupec, *Principal*
EMP: 2 **EST:** 2014
SALES (est): 119.1K **Privately Held**
SIC: 7372 Prepackaged software

(G-6557)
BMT - USA LLC
Also Called: Bmt USA
14532 169th Dr Se Ste 142 (98272-2936)
PHONE....................360 863-2252
Kevin Hallgrimson, *General Mgr*
Alan Perry, *Regl Sales Mgr*
Scott Noteboom,
Rick Ellison, *Admin Sec*
▲ **EMP:** 20
SALES (est): 5.4MM **Privately Held**
WEB: www.bmtus.com
SIC: 3821 Sterilizers

(G-6558)
BRICKING SOLUTIONS
1144 Village Way (98272-2026)
PHONE....................360 794-1277
Bill Barraugh, *President*
Mike Pirollo, *Controller*
◆ **EMP:** 3
SALES (est): 390.1K
SALES (corp-wide): 6.1B **Privately Held**
SIC: 3255 Brick, clay refractory
HQ: Washington Brokk Inc
1144 Village Way
Monroe WA 98272

(G-6559)
BROWNFIELD MANUFACTURING INC
16705 Tye St Se (98272-1059)
P.O. Box 556, Snohomish (98291-0556)
PHONE....................360 568-0572
Debbi Brownfield, *President*
EMP: 40
SQ FT: 15,000
SALES (est): 5.9MM **Privately Held**
WEB: www.brownfieldent.com
SIC: 3444 Sheet metalwork

(G-6560)
BULLDOG PRINTING LLC
10528 Friar Creek Rd (98272-7209)
PHONE....................360 217-7317
Georganne Sward, *Principal*
EMP: 2 **EST:** 2017 **Privately Held**
SIC: 2752 Commercial printing, lithographic

(G-6561)
BYWATER WELDING
12115 Wagner Rd (98272-8744)
PHONE....................360 794-4618
Michael Bywater, *Owner*
EMP: 2
SALES: 150K **Privately Held**
SIC: 7692 Welding repair

(G-6562)
CALIFORNIA INDUSTRIAL FACILITI
Also Called: Camss Shelters
13960 179th Ave Se (98272-1107)
P.O. Box 2459, Kirkland (98083-2459)
PHONE....................360 863-9333
Douglas Hotes, *President*
John Hotes, *Admin Sec*
▲ **EMP:** 19
SQ FT: 30,000
SALES (est): 4MM **Privately Held**
WEB: www.camssshelters.com
SIC: 2295 Coated fabrics, not rubberized

(G-6563)
CUTTING EDGE ENGRAVING INC
12621 251st Ave Se (98272-8612)
PHONE....................360 863-2184
Mary Colleen Ketz, *Administration*
EMP: 2
SALES (est): 135.4K **Privately Held**
SIC: 3479 Etching & engraving

(G-6564)
DEK ENTERPRISES INC
Also Called: Signco
17288 Beaton Rd Se (98272-2758)
P.O. Box 430 (98272-0430)
PHONE....................360 794-8614
Dick Steimert, *President*
Eric Steimert, *Vice Pres*
EMP: 7
SQ FT: 10,000
SALES (est): 586.7K **Privately Held**
WEB: www.deksignco.com
SIC: 3993 Signs & advertising specialties

(G-6565)
DELUXE
14640 172nd Dr Se (98272-1076)
PHONE....................360 794-3157
EMP: 3 **EST:** 2017
SALES (est): 41.9K **Privately Held**
SIC: 8742 2782 Marketing consulting services; checkbooks

(G-6566)
DMS MOTORSPORTS
17461 147th Ave Se (98272-2728)
PHONE....................360 863-3807
David D Bennitt, *Principal*
EMP: 2
SALES (est): 148.3K **Privately Held**
SIC: 3713 Car carrier bodies

(G-6567)
EARTHBOUND CORPORATION
17361 Tye St Se (98272-1047)
PHONE....................360 863-0722
Thomas Espinosa, *President*
Edward Chin, *Vice Pres*
Gary Hampton, *Manager*
EMP: 15
SQ FT: 12,000
SALES: 10MM **Privately Held**
SIC: 8711 3399 Structural engineering; metal fasteners

(G-6568)
EMBROIDERY FOR SOUL
18600 State Route 2 Ste A (98272-1430)
PHONE....................425 319-1269
Elizheva Lazella, *Partner*
Jeffery Dwor, *Partner*
EMP: 2
SQ FT: 1,400
SALES (est): 84.5K **Privately Held**
SIC: 2396 2389 Apparel & other linings, except millinery; costumes; hospital gowns; burial garments; academic vestments (caps & gowns)

(G-6569)
EMERSON ELECTRIC CO
115 W Main St (98272-1809)
PHONE....................360 805-0590
EMP: 4
SALES (corp-wide): 17.4B **Publicly Held**
SIC: 3823 Industrial instrmnts msrmnt display/control process variable
PA: Emerson Electric Co.
8000 West Florissant Ave
Saint Louis MO 63136
314 553-2000

(G-6570)
EVS MANUFACTURING INC
14253 169th Dr Se Ste 799 (98272-2923)
PHONE....................360 863-6413
Denise Root, *President*
Tammy Covello, *Purchasing*
EMP: 6 **EST:** 2013
SALES: 840K **Privately Held**
SIC: 3714 3679 3613 Motor vehicle electrical equipment; automotive wiring harness sets; video triggers, except remote control TV devices; control panels, electric

(G-6571)
EXPRESSIONS SIGNS INC
Also Called: Northwest Wholesale Signs
17201 Beaton Rd Se (98272-1071)
PHONE....................425 844-6415
Bryant Stoddard, *President*
EMP: 2
SALES (est): 296.8K **Privately Held**
SIC: 3993 Signs & advertising specialties

(G-6572)
FACTORS GROUP MFG INC
14224 167th Ave Se (98272-2810)
PHONE....................360 243-3500
EMP: 3
SALES (est): 75.4K **Privately Held**
SIC: 2099 Ready-to-eat meals, salads and sandwiches

(G-6573)
FITHIAN WLDG & FABRICATION LLC
21407 179th Pl Se (98272-9227)
PHONE....................206 658-3732
EMP: 3
SALES (est): 92.6K **Privately Held**
SIC: 7692 3446 Welding repair; stairs, fire escapes, balconies, railings & ladders

(G-6574)
FREELOCALPOKER CO
319 S Blakeley St (98272-2260)
PHONE....................360 794-5173
Michael Guild Sr, *Owner*
EMP: 3
SALES (est): 147.9K **Privately Held**
SIC: 3944 Poker chips

(G-6575)
HEAVENLY SOAP
115 3/4 W Main St (98272-1831)
PHONE....................206 349-7982
Patti Gibbons, *Owner*
EMP: 2
SALES (est): 176.3K **Privately Held**
SIC: 2841 Soap & other detergents

GEOGRAPHIC SECTION

Monroe - Snohomish County (G-6607)

(G-6576)
HEAVY DUTY TRANSAXLE INC
16891 146th St Se (98272-2916)
PHONE.................................360 794-2021
Steve Manion, *Principal*
EMP: 2
SALES (est): 438K **Privately Held**
SIC: 3537 Forklift trucks

(G-6577)
HIDE-A-HOSE INC
14490 167th Ave Se C (98272-2915)
PHONE.................................425 750-7636
Gary Driztuen, *CEO*
Rod Drizstuen, *President*
Roger Harmon, *Vice Pres*
▲ **EMP:** 7
SALES: 600K **Privately Held**
WEB: www.hideahose.biz
SIC: 3052 Vacuum cleaner hose, rubber

(G-6578)
HOLMES AND ASSOCIATES
19916 Old Owen Rd 177 (98272-9778)
PHONE.................................360 793-9723
Ken Holmes, *Owner*
EMP: 2
SALES (est): 136.5K **Privately Held**
SIC: 3679 8711 7389 Electronic circuits; engineering services; design services

(G-6579)
HOOFSBEAT BLANKETS
220 N Woods St (98272-1595)
PHONE.................................206 390-0016
Sarah Gunberson, *Owner*
EMP: 6
SALES (est): 200K **Privately Held**
SIC: 3582 Commercial laundry equipment

(G-6580)
INNOVATIVE SALON PRODUCTS INC
Also Called: Loma Hair Care
154 Village Ct Ste 172 (98272-2107)
PHONE.................................360 805-0794
David Hanen, *President*
Imelda Berg, *Corp Secy*
Dave Opitz, *Vice Pres*
▲ **EMP:** 9
SALES (est): 2MM **Privately Held**
SIC: 2844 Hair preparations, including shampoos

(G-6581)
IRON HOP BREWING CO LLC
19639 141st Pl Se (98272-8885)
PHONE.................................360 421-8138
Erin Hively, *Principal*
EMP: 3
SALES (est): 74.3K **Privately Held**
SIC: 2082 Beer (alcoholic beverage)

(G-6582)
JP INNOVATIONS LLC
101 E Main St Ste 207 (98272-1519)
P.O. Box 879 (98272-0879)
PHONE.................................360 805-3124
Gus Tombros, *Engineer*
Jeff Pierce,
EMP: 5
SQ FT: 3,000
SALES (est): 893.1K **Privately Held**
WEB: www.jpinnovations.com
SIC: 3699 Laser systems & equipment

(G-6583)
JSMD KEY PRODUCTS LLC
Also Called: Shur - Ooc
14517 Fryelands Blvd Se (98272-2942)
PHONE.................................360 805-4140
James Larson,
David Larson,
Sheir Larson,
EMP: 7 **EST:** 1998
SQ FT: 4,500
SALES (est): 900.3K **Privately Held**
SIC: 2261 Screen printing of cotton broad-woven fabrics

(G-6584)
KC FINE CABINETRY
11718 Wagner Rd (98272-9733)
PHONE.................................425 359-8491
Clint Noyes, *Owner*
Kimberly Noyes, *Co-Owner*
EMP: 2
SALES (est): 155.1K **Privately Held**
SIC: 2434 Wood kitchen cabinets

(G-6585)
KEN ROBINSON PUBLICATIONS INC
Also Called: Monroe Monitor
125 E Main St Ste 202 (98272-1543)
P.O. Box 80156, Seattle (98108-0156)
PHONE.................................360 794-7116
Kenneth Robinson, *President*
Polly Keary, *Editor*
Debra Robinson, *Corp Secy*
EMP: 4 **EST:** 1967
SQ FT: 3,000
SALES (est): 246.2K
SALES (corp-wide): 3.2MM **Privately Held**
SIC: 2711 Commercial printing & newspaper publishing combined
PA: Pacific Publishing Co
 636 S Alaska St
 Seattle WA
 206 461-1300

(G-6586)
KERN CONSTRUCTION INC
21616 230th St Se (98272-8004)
P.O. Box 65 (98272-0065)
PHONE.................................360 805-5598
Daniel R Kern, *President*
Jeanine Kern, *Vice Pres*
EMP: 4
SALES (est): 295.9K **Privately Held**
WEB: www.ebs-northwest.com
SIC: 1799 2499 Kitchen cabinet installation; decorative wood & woodwork

(G-6587)
KHANN INDUSTRIES CORP
Also Called: Spirit Trailer
1138 Village Way (98272-2026)
PHONE.................................360 794-1033
Norman Keith Batie, *President*
Elizabeth Zimmerman, *Vice Pres*
EMP: 7
SQ FT: 7,000
SALES: 800K **Privately Held**
SIC: 2392 Household furnishings

(G-6588)
KOOL CHANGE PRINTING INC
220 N Woods St (98272-1595)
PHONE.................................360 794-9019
Lora Perrine, *President*
Ken Perrine, *Vice Pres*
EMP: 4
SQ FT: 2,500
SALES: 500K **Privately Held**
WEB: www.koolchangeprinting.com
SIC: 2752 2759 Commercial printing, offset; commercial printing

(G-6589)
KOPPENBERG ENTERPRISES INC
14751 N Kelsey St Ste 105 (98272-1458)
PHONE.................................360 793-1600
Kim Koppenberg, *President*
Julie Koppenberg, *Admin Sec*
EMP: 16
SQ FT: 6,500
SALES (est): 2.1MM **Privately Held**
WEB: www.koppenbergenterprises.com
SIC: 3281 Monument or burial stone, cut & shaped

(G-6590)
LAKESIDE INDUSTRIES INC
14282 Galaxy Way (98272)
PHONE.................................360 794-7779
Gail Land, *Branch Mgr*
EMP: 50
SALES (corp-wide): 326.4MM **Privately Held**
WEB: www.lakesideind.com
SIC: 1611 2951 5032 Highway & street paving contractor; asphalt & asphaltic paving mixtures (not from refineries); gravel
PA: Lakeside Industries, Inc.
 6505 226th Pl Se Ste 200
 Issaquah WA 98027
 425 313-2600

(G-6591)
LES WARE BACKHOE
11923 Bollenbaugh Hill Rd (98272-7678)
PHONE.................................425 508-2252
EMP: 2
SALES (est): 197.5K **Privately Held**
SIC: 3531 Backhoes

(G-6592)
LEVEL 5 INC
12430 Wagner Rd (98272-7744)
PHONE.................................425 260-3440
Dennis Boyle, *Principal*
EMP: 2
SALES (est): 119.4K **Privately Held**
SIC: 2273 Carpets & rugs

(G-6593)
LIGHTSHINE SOFTWARE LLC
22305 230th St Se (98272-8012)
PHONE.................................425 231-9320
Miles Ulrich, *Principal*
EMP: 2
SALES (est): 168.3K **Privately Held**
SIC: 7372 Prepackaged software

(G-6594)
M24 INDUSTRIES LLC
21030 151st Ave Se (98272-9182)
P.O. Box 1197 (98272-4197)
PHONE.................................360 348-3578
Matthew Olsen, *Principal*
EMP: 2 **EST:** 2014
SALES (est): 107.8K **Privately Held**
SIC: 3999 Manufacturing industries

(G-6595)
MADERA COMPONENTS LLC
17146 Beaton Rd Se Ste 4 (98272-2749)
PHONE.................................800 404-8746
Russel Hermes,
Robert Vazquez,
▲ **EMP:** 2
SALES (est): 312.6K **Privately Held**
SIC: 2439 Trusses, wooden roof

(G-6596)
MERRILL CORPORATION
14640 172nd Dr Se (98272-1082)
PHONE.................................360 794-3157
Greg Schnatterly, *Principal*
EMP: 130
SALES (corp-wide): 566.6MM **Privately Held**
WEB: www.merrillcorp.com
SIC: 2759 3993 2761 2752 Commercial printing; signs & advertising specialties; manifold business forms; commercial printing, lithographic; packaging paper & plastics film, coated & laminated; automotive & apparel trimmings
PA: Merrill Corporation
 1 Merrill Cir
 Saint Paul MN 55108
 651 646-4501

(G-6597)
MINNYSONODA CORPORATION
Also Called: Morris Magnets
14428 167th Ave Se (98272-2915)
PHONE.................................360 863-8141
William E Peterson, *President*
Jeffery Cannon, *Vice Pres*
Chiho Min, *Treasurer*
Callie Kite, *Accounts Mgr*
Rhonda Riester, *Accounts Exec*
EMP: 16
SQ FT: 5,000
SALES: 1.5MM **Privately Held**
WEB: www.morrismagnets.com
SIC: 3961 Keychains, except precious metal

(G-6598)
MONROE DOOR & MILLWORK INC
17350 Tye St Se (98272-1067)
PHONE.................................360 863-9882
Peter Bingham, *President*
EMP: 10
SQ FT: 8,000
SALES (est): 2.6MM **Privately Held**
SIC: 5031 2431 Doors; millwork

(G-6599)
MOONLITE MACHINING INC
508 Powell St (98272-2230)
PHONE.................................360 863-8535
Jason Trim, *Principal*
EMP: 2
SALES (est): 153.6K **Privately Held**
SIC: 3599 Machine shop, jobbing & repair

(G-6600)
MOONLITE MACHINING INC
17700 147th St Se Ste H (98272-2732)
PHONE.................................360 794-6622
David Bulliman, *Principal*
EMP: 7
SALES (est): 863.7K **Privately Held**
SIC: 3599 Machine shop, jobbing & repair

(G-6601)
NEW STAR TECHNOLOGY INC
Also Called: Titan Manufacturing, Inc
17461 147th St Se Ste 6a (98272-1070)
PHONE.................................425 350-7611
Mike Brindamour, *President*
Jamie Brindamour, *Vice Pres*
EMP: 4
SQ FT: 16,000
SALES (est): 320K **Privately Held**
SIC: 3469 Machine parts, stamped or pressed metal

(G-6602)
NORTHWEST INC
Also Called: Urethane Technologies
17461 147th St Se Ste 15 (98272-2735)
P.O. Box 1212 (98272-4212)
PHONE.................................360 794-7473
Kevin Hoff, *Principal*
David Macke, *Principal*
EMP: 2
SALES (est): 419.7K **Privately Held**
SIC: 3089 Molding primary plastic

(G-6603)
PACER DESIGN BY SHARP PDTS INC
17072 Tye St Se Ste 195 (98272-2764)
PHONE.................................360 217-8120
Paul Sharp, *President*
Kathleen Sharp, *Treasurer*
EMP: 16
SQ FT: 12,000
SALES: 2MM **Privately Held**
SIC: 3444 Sheet metalwork

(G-6604)
PEARCE DESIGN
14512 167th Ave Se (98272-2820)
PHONE.................................425 481-5214
Joseph Pearce, *Owner*
EMP: 6
SALES (est): 212.9K **Privately Held**
SIC: 3599 Machine shop, jobbing & repair

(G-6605)
PERFORMANCE CNSTR EQP INC
7522 Woods Creek Rd (98272-8636)
PHONE.................................360 794-6220
Debbie Rowe, *Principal*
▲ **EMP:** 5
SALES (est): 350.1K **Privately Held**
SIC: 3531 Construction machinery

(G-6606)
PHOENIX POWER CONTROL INC
16778 146th St Se Ste 190 (98272-2940)
PHONE.................................360 794-8550
Herb Vernon, *President*
Herbert E Vernon, *President*
John K Claybrook, *Vice Pres*
EMP: 16
SQ FT: 3,600
SALES (est): 2.3MM **Privately Held**
WEB: www.phoenixcontrol.com
SIC: 3613 8711 Switchgear & switchboard apparatus; engineering services

(G-6607)
POWER BREAKER LLC SEATTLE
15153 175th Ave Se (98272-2718)
PHONE.................................425 286-4276

Monroe - Snohomish County (G-6608)   GEOGRAPHIC SECTION

EMP: 2
SALES (est): 115K **Privately Held**
SIC: 3699 Electrical equipment & supplies

(G-6608)
PPR INDUSTRIES CORPORATION
Also Called: Precision
17045 Tye St Se (98272-2756)
P.O. Box 1150 (98272-4150)
PHONE 360 863-9500
Helmut Wegener, *President*
Wes Erickson, *Manager*
▲ **EMP:** 44
SQ FT: 87,000
SALES (est): 7MM **Privately Held**
WEB: www.prp.com
SIC: 3714 Windshield frames, motor vehicle

(G-6609)
PUZZLE PIECES BOOKKEEPING
20379 Corbridge Rd Se (98272-8668)
PHONE 360 217-7140
Angie Baumgartner, *Principal*
EMP: 2
SALES (est): 125.4K **Privately Held**
SIC: 3944 Puzzles

(G-6610)
QUALITY FUEL TRLR & TANK INC
Also Called: Advanced Fuel Systems
22117 161st Ave Se (98272-9171)
PHONE 425 526-7566
Edward Dunn, *President*
Stephen Walsh, *Vice Pres*
EMP: 4
SQ FT: 2,200
SALES: 1MM **Privately Held**
WEB: www.qualityfueltrailers.com
SIC: 3715 3443 5089 7519 Truck trailers; industrial vessels, tanks & containers; fuel tanks (oil, gas, etc.); metal plate; tanks & tank components; recreational vehicle rental; recreational vehicles, motor homes & trailers; petroleum storage tanks, pumping & draining

(G-6611)
R L INDUSTRIES (PA)
Also Called: Millwork Concepts
14582 172nd Dr Se (98272-2742)
PHONE 360 794-1621
Roy Cline, *CEO*
Ronald Hunt, *President*
James Burch, *General Mgr*
EMP: 15
SQ FT: 33,000
SALES: 2.6MM **Privately Held**
WEB: www.millworkconcepts.com
SIC: 2431 5211 Moldings & baseboards, ornamental & trim; moldings, wood: unfinished & prefinished; millwork & lumber

(G-6612)
RAINBOW METALS INC
Also Called: University Brass
17301 Beaton Rd Se (98272-1032)
PHONE 360 794-3691
Jerry D Peterson, *President*
Chris Seresey, *Vice Pres*
EMP: 3
SQ FT: 3,600
SALES: 242K **Privately Held**
SIC: 3366 Castings (except die): bronze

(G-6613)
RANGER TUGS
18310 Cascade View Dr Se (98272-1142)
PHONE 360 794-7430
EMP: 2
SALES (est): 205.8K **Privately Held**
SIC: 3732 Boats, fiberglass: building & repairing

(G-6614)
REFLECT-A-LIFE INC
20415 Rimrock Rd (98272-9413)
P.O. Box 2162, Tacoma (98401-2162)
PHONE 253 693-8662
David A Zornes, *President*
Anna L Zornes, *Principal*
EMP: 4
SALES (est): 626.3K **Privately Held**
WEB: www.reflect-a-life.com
SIC: 3089 Plastic hardware & building products

(G-6615)
ROBERTS PRECISION MACHINE INC
1166 Village Way Ste B (98272-2026)
PHONE 360 805-1000
Roberts Vandyke Brown Jr, *President*
Diana R Brown, *Vice Pres*
EMP: 10
SQ FT: 9,600
SALES: 1.2MM **Privately Held**
WEB: www.robertsprecision.com
SIC: 3812 3451 3728 3599 Acceleration indicators & systems components, aerospace; screw machine products; aircraft parts & equipment; machine & other job shop work

(G-6616)
SCHOEBEN & SCHOEBEN INC
Also Called: Metal Tech
14792 172nd Dr Se (98272-1028)
PHONE 360 794-1945
Arthur Schoeben, *President*
Alan Schoeben, *Vice Pres*
Pamela Schoeben, *Treasurer*
EMP: 25
SQ FT: 24,000
SALES: 1.7MM **Privately Held**
WEB: www.metal-tech.net
SIC: 3471 Finishing, metals or formed products

(G-6617)
SENIOR OPERATIONS LLC
Also Called: Damar Aero Systems
14767 172nd Dr Se (98272-1033)
P.O. Box 9 (98272-0009)
PHONE 360 794-4448
Charles Elder, *CEO*
Michelle Kloss, *Production*
Robyn Taylor, *Buyer*
Brice Nassey, *CFO*
Mindy Marsh, *Administration*
▲ **EMP:** 160 **EST:** 1973
SQ FT: 60,000
SALES (est): 45.1MM
SALES (corp-wide): 1.3B **Privately Held**
WEB: www.damarmachine.com
SIC: 3369 3365 Aerospace castings, non-ferrous: except aluminum; aerospace castings, aluminum
PA: Senior Plc
 59-61 High Street
 Rickmansworth HERTS WD3 1

(G-6618)
SHUR-LOC FABRIC SYSTEM
14517 Fryelands Blvd Se (98272-2942)
PHONE 360 805-4140
EMP: 2
SALES (est): 136.3K **Privately Held**
SIC: 2759 Screen printing

(G-6619)
SIMPOS
21414 Ricci Rd (98272-9119)
PHONE 360 794-4658
Bob Smitz, *Principal*
EMP: 2
SALES (est): 144.7K **Privately Held**
SIC: 7372 Prepackaged software

(G-6620)
SKY VALLEY FOODS INC
17288 Beaton Rd Se Ste C (98272-2759)
PHONE 360 805-1430
Richard Schindler, *President*
Danielle Martin, *Office Mgr*
EMP: 4
SALES (est): 344.7K **Privately Held**
SIC: 2099 Food preparations

(G-6621)
SNO-MON STAMPING INC
20927 Calhoun Rd (98272-8750)
PHONE 360 794-6304
Brian J Thorpe, *President*
Brian Thorpe, *President*
Darlene Thorpe, *Admin Sec*
EMP: 3
SALES: 500K **Privately Held**
SIC: 3599 Machine & other job shop work

(G-6622)
SNOQUALMIE VALLEY LOGGING INC
25308 Ben Howard Rd (98272-8913)
PHONE 360 794-8205
EMP: 2
SALES (est): 162.9K **Privately Held**
SIC: 2411 Logging

(G-6623)
SPECTYR INDUSTRIES CORP
14327 169th Dr Se Ste 154 (98272-2963)
PHONE 360 863-7720
EMP: 2
SALES (est): 126K **Privately Held**
SIC: 3999 Manufacturing industries

(G-6624)
SPENCER LLC
17381 Tye St Se Ste 4 (98272-2751)
PHONE 360 805-2500
William Spencer, *Plant Mgr*
Carl Spencer,
EMP: 9
SALES (est): 877.6K **Privately Held**
SIC: 2434 Wood kitchen cabinets

(G-6625)
SPENCER CABINETRY
17381 Tye St Se Ste 4 (98272-2751)
PHONE 360 794-8344
Dorotea Spencer, *Mng Member*
Carl Spencer, *Mng Member*
EMP: 2
SALES (est): 750K **Privately Held**
SIC: 2434 Wood kitchen cabinets

(G-6626)
SRP TRANSPORT INC
21005 Brown Rd (98272-8734)
PHONE 425 770-3031
Steven Peters, *President*
EMP: 4
SALES: 300K **Privately Held**
SIC: 3799 7549 Carriages, horse drawn; towing service, automotive

(G-6627)
STARSHINE PRODUCTS
17251 Tye St Se Ste A-7 (98272-1023)
PHONE 425 238-9820
Gc Ackley, *Principal*
EMP: 2
SALES (est): 114.5K **Privately Held**
SIC: 2759 Screen printing

(G-6628)
SUNBACKER FIBERGLASS INC
Also Called: Sunbacker Fbrgls Repr Fbrction
17453 147th St Se Ste 1 (98272-1092)
PHONE 360 794-5547
Alfred G Lewis III, *President*
Ruby Lewis, *Vice Pres*
EMP: 5
SQ FT: 13,000
SALES: 800K **Privately Held**
SIC: 3089 3732 7319 2221 Plastic processing; boat building & repairing; display advertising service; fiberglass fabrics

(G-6629)
T EIGHT FINCING LLC
Also Called: Tee-Eight Log
13224 191st Ave Se (98272-7728)
PHONE 360 794-7369
Thomas Trombley,
Tim Trombley,
EMP: 2 **EST:** 1975
SALES (est): 89K **Privately Held**
SIC: 2499 5211 Fencing, wood; fencing

(G-6630)
THRIFTY PAYLESS INC T/A
18906 State Route 2 (98272-1415)
PHONE 360 794-0943
EMP: 2 **EST:** 2010
SALES (est): 98.4K **Privately Held**
SIC: 2836 Mfg Biological Products

(G-6631)
TITAN MFG
17461 147th St Se (98272-2728)
PHONE 360 863-1808
EMP: 2
SALES (est): 82.8K **Privately Held**
SIC: 3999 Manufacturing industries

(G-6632)
TJI II LLC
Also Called: Damar Machine
14767 172nd Dr Se (98272-1033)
PHONE 360 794-4448
Charles Elder, *Mng Member*
EMP: 160
SQ FT: 57,168
SALES (est): 465.8K **Privately Held**
WEB: www.tji-holdings.com
SIC: 3812 Search & navigation equipment

(G-6633)
TOOLCRAFT INC
17700 147th St Se Ste E (98272-2732)
PHONE 360 794-5512
Karl Niemela, *President*
Steve Wittenberg, *Opers Mgr*
EMP: 15
SQ FT: 2,400
SALES: 950K **Privately Held**
SIC: 3728 3812 3714 3599 Aircraft parts & equipment; search & navigation equipment; motor vehicle parts & accessories; machine shop, jobbing & repair

(G-6634)
TRONDAK INC
Also Called: Aqua Seal
17631 147th St Se Ste 7 (98272-1049)
PHONE 360 794-8250
Dan Metcalf, *President*
EMP: 6 **EST:** 1970
SQ FT: 4,000
SALES (est): 1MM **Privately Held**
WEB: www.u-40.com
SIC: 2899 5941 Waterproofing compounds; sporting goods & bicycle shops

(G-6635)
VOISS WOOD PRODUCTS INC
14582 172nd Dr Se Ste 5 (98272-2742)
PHONE 360 794-1062
Stephen Voiss, *CEO*
Maria Voiss, *Vice Pres*
EMP: 7
SALES (est): 1.2MM **Privately Held**
SIC: 2431 Millwork

(G-6636)
WET NOSES NATURAL DOG TREAT CO
Also Called: Doggy Delirious
14439 167th Ave Se (98272-2915)
PHONE 360 794-7950
Jasmine Lybrand, *President*
Lance Lybrand, *Principal*
Gail Howerton, *Human Res Mgr*
Laura Smith, *Human Res Mgr*
Sara Paynter-Mercer, *Manager*
EMP: 33
SALES (est): 7.9MM **Privately Held**
SIC: 2047 2048 Dog food; prepared feeds

(G-6637)
WIARD H GROENEVELD
29126 Fern Bluff Rd (98272-8907)
PHONE 360 793-1638
Wiard H Groeneveld, *Owner*
EMP: 2
SALES (est): 109.7K **Privately Held**
SIC: 0241 2411 Dairy farms; logging

(G-6638)
WINTER MATTIAS
Also Called: Jester Built
500c E Main St (98272-1515)
PHONE 206 579-5275
Mattias Winter, *Owner*
EMP: 2
SALES (est): 135.3K **Privately Held**
SIC: 3499 Fabricated metal products

(G-6639)
WOLFKILL FEED & FERT CORP (PA)
217 E Stretch St (98272-1520)
P.O. Box 578 (98272-0578)
PHONE.................................360 794-7065
Merritt Wolfkill, *President*
▲ **EMP: 12 EST:** 1938
SQ FT: 65,000
SALES: 5.1MM **Privately Held**
SIC: 2875 2048 Fertilizers, mixing only; livestock feeds

(G-6640)
WYNAKOS MACHINE INC
17461 147th St Se Ste 7 (98272-1070)
PHONE.................................360 794-9057
Mike Waynakos, *President*
Mike Wynakos, *President*
Cindy Wynakos, *Vice Pres*
EMP: 6
SQ FT: 1,800
SALES: 350K **Privately Held**
SIC: 3599 3484 Machine shop, jobbing & repair; small arms; machine guns or machine gun parts, 30 mm. & below; guns (firearms) or gun parts, 30 mm. & below; pistols or pistol parts, 30 mm. & below

Montesano
Grays Harbor County

(G-6641)
A & RS LOGGING INC
195 Brady Loop Rd E (98563-9519)
PHONE.................................360 249-4017
Richard Raubuch, *President*
Stanley Raubuch, *Principal*
EMP: 12
SALES (est): 1MM **Privately Held**
SIC: 2411 Logging camps & contractors

(G-6642)
BLACKBEAR PONTOONS FABRICATION
Also Called: Blackbear Outdoors
117 Camp Creek Rd (98563-9301)
PHONE.................................206 372-9998
Scott J Melton, *President*
Tammy Melton, *Senior VP*
EMP: 2
SALES (est): 146K **Privately Held**
SIC: 3069 Pontoons, rubber

(G-6643)
D & M MACHINE DIVISION INC
12 Monte Brady Rd (98563-9521)
PHONE.................................360 249-3366
David Milbourn, *President*
Paul Milbourn, *Opers Staff*
Melody Milbourn, *Admin Sec*
EMP: 10
SALES (est): 2MM **Privately Held**
WEB: www.slashbuster.com
SIC: 3531 3524 Excavators: cable, clamshell, crane, derrick, dragline, etc.; lawn & garden equipment

(G-6644)
EAST COUNTY MACHINE LLC
426 S Fleet St (98563-4407)
PHONE.................................360 249-4114
Don Melton,
EMP: 5
SALES (est): 508.7K **Privately Held**
SIC: 3545 Shaping tools (machine tool accessories)

(G-6645)
MACMILLAN & COMPANY
511 N Main St (98563-2403)
PHONE.................................360 249-1148
Robert Macmillan, *President*
Carol Macmillan, *Vice Pres*
EMP: 18
SALES (est): 1.5MM **Privately Held**
SIC: 2411 2426 Logging camps & contractors; hardwood dimension & flooring mills

(G-6646)
MACMILLAN AND COMPANY
33 Sylvia Ridge Ln (98563-9372)
PHONE.................................360 470-1535
Robert Macmillan, *President*
Carol Macmillan, *Vice Pres*
EMP: 20
SALES (est): 1.9MM **Privately Held**
SIC: 2411 Timber, cut at logging camp

(G-6647)
MARNIS PETAL PUSHERS
114 S Main St (98563-3709)
PHONE.................................360 249-8382
Donald Joseph Sandifur, *Principal*
EMP: 2
SALES (est): 188.9K **Privately Held**
SIC: 3545 Pushers

(G-6648)
MNR LOGGING LLC
330 W Pioneer Ave (98563-4412)
P.O. Box 310 (98563-0310)
PHONE.................................360 249-2213
EMP: 2
SALES (est): 81.7K **Privately Held**
SIC: 2411 Logging

(G-6649)
NETHERFIELD PUBLISHING LLC
409 N River St (98563-2405)
PHONE.................................360 903-8512
Keani Kaye Gifford, *Owner*
EMP: 2 **EST:** 2015
SALES (est): 45.4K **Privately Held**
SIC: 2741 Miscellaneous publishing

(G-6650)
NORTHWEST HYDROPRINT
305 W Arland Ave (98563-4344)
P.O. Box 272 (98563-0272)
PHONE.................................360 249-2220
Tammy Melton, *Owner*
EMP: 5
SALES (est): 598.1K **Privately Held**
SIC: 3577 Printers & plotters

(G-6651)
NORTHWEST ROCK INC
155 Wynooche Rd W (98563)
PHONE.................................360 249-2245
Jason Messmer, *Manager*
EMP: 8
SALES (corp-wide): 8.7MM **Privately Held**
SIC: 1442 1611 Construction sand mining; general contractor, highway & street construction
PA: Northwest Rock, Inc.
642 Newskah Rd
Aberdeen WA 98520
360 533-3050

(G-6652)
PACIFIC COAST CASCARA BARK CO
Also Called: Esses Cascara Bark
520 W Pioneer Ave (98563-4319)
PHONE.................................360 249-3503
Russell D Esses, *Partner*
Dorothy Esses, *Partner*
Sherman Esses, *Partner*
▼ **EMP:** 6
SALES (est): 620K **Privately Held**
SIC: 2833 Medicinals & botanicals

(G-6653)
PHOENIX SIGN COMPANY
112 Clemons Rd (98563-9634)
PHONE.................................360 532-1111
Faron Lash, *Owner*
EMP: 5
SALES (est): 376.9K **Privately Held**
SIC: 3993 Electric signs

(G-6654)
ROBERT WICKES OD
Also Called: Montesano Vision Center
118 S Main St (98563-3709)
PHONE.................................360 249-3485
Robert Wickes, *Owner*
EMP: 3
SALES (est): 242.9K **Privately Held**
SIC: 5995 3841 Opticians; optometers

(G-6655)
RUFF CUTS CUSTOM SAWING LLC
157 Clemons Rd (98563-9668)
PHONE.................................360 249-3926
Karla J Smith, *Principal*
EMP: 2
SALES (est): 141.1K **Privately Held**
SIC: 2421 Sawmills & planing mills, general

(G-6656)
S J OLSEN PUBLISHING INC
Also Called: Montesano Vidette
109 W Marcy Ave (98563-3615)
PHONE.................................360 249-3311
S J Olsen, *President*
Jeanne Olsen, *Vice Pres*
EMP: 11
SALES (est): 439.9K **Privately Held**
SIC: 2711 8111 Newspapers: publishing only, not printed on site; legal services

(G-6657)
SATELLITE SIGN DESIGN
951 N Stephenson Dr (98563-1314)
PHONE.................................360 986-0067
EMP: 2
SALES (est): 145.6K **Privately Held**
SIC: 3993 Signs & advertising specialties

(G-6658)
SAWTOOTH LOGGING
81 Winkleman Rd N (98563-9726)
PHONE.................................360 249-6255
Richard Sholes, *Owner*
EMP: 2
SALES (est): 116.5K **Privately Held**
SIC: 2411 Logging camps & contractors

(G-6659)
STEWART & STEWART LAW OFF PS
Also Called: Stewart, James M
101 S 1st St (98563-3601)
PHONE.................................360 249-4342
William J Stewart, *President*
James M Stewart, *Corp Secy*
EMP: 3 **EST:** 1970
SQ FT: 3,968
SALES (est): 250K **Privately Held**
SIC: 8111 2411 General practice attorney, lawyer; logging

(G-6660)
TAYLOR DENTAL STUDIO
433 E Spruce Ave (98563-3104)
PHONE.................................360 249-4329
Kathryn Taylor, *Owner*
EMP: 2
SALES (est): 150K **Privately Held**
SIC: 3843 Denture materials

(G-6661)
TOBIN AND RIEDESEL LOGGING LLC
100 Brumfield Ave (98563-4343)
PHONE.................................360 249-8184
EMP: 2
SALES (est): 81.7K **Privately Held**
SIC: 2411 Wooden logs

(G-6662)
TRACYS PRINT SHOP
210 E Pioneer Ave (98563-4507)
PHONE.................................360 249-5575
Cully Ecklund, *Owner*
EMP: 2
SALES (est): 184.7K **Privately Held**
WEB: www.tracegoldsmith.com
SIC: 2752 Commercial printing, offset

(G-6663)
UNIVERSAL REFINER CORPORATION
458 Wynooche Valley Rd (98563-9738)
P.O. Box 151 (98563-0151)
PHONE.................................360 249-4415
John Hughes, *President*
Karen Gates, *Corp Secy*
Karen Hughes, *Corp Secy*
EMP: 2
SALES: 300K **Privately Held**
WEB: www.universalrefiner.com
SIC: 3559 3541 Cryogenic machinery, industrial; machine tools, metal cutting type

(G-6664)
VAUGHAN CO INC (PA)
364 Monte Elma Rd (98563-9798)
PHONE.................................360 249-4042
Larry Vaughan, *Ch of Bd*
Glenn Dorsch, *President*
Dale Vaughan, *President*
Dierick Bryan, *Regional Mgr*
Patricia A Cornwell, *Corp Secy*
▲ **EMP:** 104
SQ FT: 60,000
SALES: 31.8MM **Privately Held**
WEB: www.rotamix.com
SIC: 3561 Industrial pumps & parts

(G-6665)
VENNCO RUBBER INC
285 Geissler Rd (98563-9640)
PHONE.................................360 249-6924
Robin L Venn, *President*
EMP: 6
SALES: 276K **Privately Held**
SIC: 2822 Synthetic rubber

(G-6666)
WYNOOCHEE RIVER WINERY ✿
79 Wheeler Rd (98563-9735)
PHONE.................................360 580-4452
Denise Schupbach, *Principal*
EMP: 2 **EST:** 2018
SALES (est): 117.2K **Privately Held**
SIC: 2084 Wines

Morton
Lewis County

(G-6667)
ALTA FOREST PRODUCTS LLC
318 State Route 7 (98356-9607)
PHONE.................................360 219-0008
Howard Hoffman, *Manager*
EMP: 300 **Privately Held**
SIC: 2421 Sawmills & planing mills, general
HQ: Alta Forest Products Llc
810 Nw Alta Way
Chehalis WA 98532
360 219-0008

(G-6668)
EAST COUNTY JOURNAL
278 Main St (98356-9200)
P.O. Box 1099 (98356-0018)
PHONE.................................360 496-5993
Frank Devaul, *President*
EMP: 5
SQ FT: 1,700
SALES (est): 247.7K **Privately Held**
SIC: 2711 2752 Newspapers: publishing only, not printed on site; commercial printing, offset

(G-6669)
FLUID POWER SERVICE INC
102 Crumb Rd 33 (98356-9510)
P.O. Box 1249 (98356-1249)
PHONE.................................360 496-6888
Art Minnear, *President*
Gaylene Minnear, *Treasurer*
EMP: 2
SQ FT: 500
SALES: 300K **Privately Held**
SIC: 7699 3531 Hydraulic equipment repair; construction machinery; forestry related equipment

(G-6670)
NUMERIC CONTROL LLC
204 2nd St (98356-9804)
P.O. Box 916 (98356-0916)
PHONE.................................360 269-1497
Randall B Smith, *Mng Member*
EMP: 2 **EST:** 2007
SALES: 250K **Privately Held**
SIC: 3569 3821 Centrifuges, industrial; centrifuges, laboratory

Morton - Lewis County (G-6671)

(G-6671)
NW FIBRE LLC
324 Davis Lake Rd (98356-9414)
P.O. Box 758, Ridgefield (98642-0758)
PHONE..................................360 887-8418
EMP: 10 EST: 2011
SALES (est): 1.1MM Privately Held
SIC: 2421 Sawmill/Planing Mill

(G-6672)
RICHARDSON COATINGS LLC
5930 State Route 508 (98356-9707)
PHONE..................................253 861-7611
Jim Richardson, Principal
EMP: 2
SALES (est): 131.2K Privately Held
SIC: 3479 Metal coating & allied service

(G-6673)
S&S REPAIR
382 Butts Rd (98356-9766)
PHONE..................................360 496-5533
Tony Snedigar, Owner
EMP: 2
SALES (est): 114.5K Privately Held
SIC: 3541 Machine tools, metal cutting type

(G-6674)
WILSON OPERATIONS
324 Davis Lake Rd (98356-9414)
PHONE..................................360 496-6565
Vic Brown, Principal
EMP: 2 EST: 2007
SALES (est): 120K Privately Held
SIC: 2411 Logging

Moses Lake
Grant County

(G-6675)
2 M COMPANY INC
1026 W 3rd Ave (98837-2601)
PHONE..................................509 765-0867
Bill Mills, Branch Mgr
EMP: 6
SALES (corp-wide): 1.3B Publicly Held
SIC: 3561 Pumps & pumping equipment
HQ: 2 M Company, Inc.
   5249 Holiday Ave
   Billings MT 59101
   406 245-1490

(G-6676)
A & H PRINTERS INC
1030 W Marina Dr (98837-2699)
PHONE..................................509 765-0283
Stephanie Biallas, President
Roger Biallas, Corp Secy
EMP: 5
SQ FT: 1,800
SALES (est): 706.2K Privately Held
SIC: 2752 7334 Commercial printing, offset; photocopying & duplicating services

(G-6677)
A A A REDI MIX II INC
Also Called: AAA Readymix
7001 Stratford Rd Ne (98837)
P.O. Box 1044 (98837-0155)
PHONE..................................509 765-1923
Pamp Maiers, President
Barbara Maiers, Vice Pres
EMP: 10
SQ FT: 5,000
SALES (est): 1.4MM Privately Held
SIC: 3273 Ready-mixed concrete

(G-6678)
ADL CATTLE GROWERS LLC
6751 Road 16 Ne (98837-8945)
PHONE..................................509 765-0584
Denise C Lembcke, Principal
EMP: 2
SQ FT: 2,226
SALES (est): 188.8K Privately Held
SIC: 3523 Cattle feeding, handling & watering equipment

(G-6679)
ASIMI
3322 Road N Ne (98837-9505)
PHONE..................................509 766-9641

Reidar Langmo, Principal
EMP: 3
SALES (est): 309.4K Privately Held
SIC: 3674 Silicon wafers, chemically doped

(G-6680)
ASTAREAL INC
Also Called: Astareal Technologies, Inc.
7761 Randolph Rd Ne (98837-7922)
P.O. Box 1119 (98837-0168)
PHONE..................................509 855-4370
Takashi Douguchi, President
Akitoshi Kitamura, Vice Pres
Shinya Uchiyama, Admin Sec
▲ EMP: 34
SALES (est): 6.9MM Privately Held
SIC: 2023 Dietary supplements, dairy & non-dairy based
PA: Fuji Chemical Industries Co., Ltd.
   55, Yokohoonji, Kamiichimachi
   Nakaniikawa-Gun TYM 930-0

(G-6681)
ATF MFG LLC
5024 Mcconihe Rd Ne (98837-9338)
PHONE..................................509 762-2421
Brandy Grigg,
EMP: 2 EST: 2017
SALES (est): 106.7K
SALES (corp-wide): 3.7MM Privately Held
SIC: 3999 Atomizers, toiletry
PA: Grigg Apiaries, Inc.
   5024 Mcconihe Rd Ne
   Moses Lake WA 98837
   509 762-2421

(G-6682)
AUTOMATED AG SYSTEMS LLC
145 N Hamilton Rd (98837-5602)
PHONE..................................813 786-7282
Stephen R Mason, Mng Member
EMP: 2 EST: 2007
SALES (est): 287.4K Privately Held
SIC: 3541 Home workshop machine tools, metalworking

(G-6683)
BADNASTY PAINTBALL
11064 Road K Ne (98837-8963)
PHONE..................................509 998-0984
Jake Crotsley, Manager
EMP: 2
SALES (est): 107.4K Privately Held
SIC: 3949 Camping equipment & supplies

(G-6684)
BASIC AMERICAN INC
Also Called: Basic American Foods
538 Potato Frontage Rd Se (98837-8500)
PHONE..................................509 765-8601
EMP: 125
SALES (corp-wide): 443.9MM Privately Held
WEB: www.baf.com
SIC: 2034 2099 Potato products, dried & dehydrated; food preparations
PA: Basic American, Inc.
   2999 Oak Rd Ste 800
   Walnut Creek CA 94597
   925 472-4438

(G-6685)
BASIC AMERICAN INC
Also Called: Basic American Food
538 Potato Frontage Rd Se (98837-8500)
PHONE..................................509 765-7807
Paul Landon, Branch Mgr
EMP: 180
SALES (corp-wide): 443.9MM Privately Held
WEB: www.baf.com
SIC: 0723 2034 Potato curing services; dehydrated fruits, vegetables, soups
PA: Basic American, Inc.
   2999 Oak Rd Ste 800
   Walnut Creek CA 94597
   925 472-4438

(G-6686)
BASIN PALLETT INC
657 Road N Ne (98837-9592)
P.O. Box 1939 (98837-0339)
PHONE..................................509 765-8083
Roy Dirks, President

Wendy Dirks, Admin Sec
EMP: 11
SQ FT: 2,656
SALES (est): 2MM Privately Held
SIC: 2448 Pallets, wood

(G-6687)
BLUEWATER INDUSTRIES INC
3283 Bell Rd Ne (98837-9550)
PHONE..................................509 765-4623
Doug Stanford, President
Sandy Stanford, Admin Sec
EMP: 10
SALES (est): 836.4K Privately Held
SIC: 3599 Machine & other job shop work

(G-6688)
BRM MARKETING LLC
1045 E June Dr (98837-8853)
PHONE..................................509 350-5844
Barbara Morgan, Principal
EMP: 3 EST: 2012
SALES (est): 120K Privately Held
SIC: 2875 Compost

(G-6689)
BUSBY INTERNATIONAL INC
12600 Road 3 Ne (98837-4902)
P.O. Box 1457 (98837-0225)
PHONE..................................509 765-1313
Mike Mansfield, President
Mary Gregory, Corp Secy
EMP: 20
SQ FT: 32,500
SALES (est): 2.2MM Privately Held
WEB: www.e-busby.com
SIC: 3715 Trailer bodies

(G-6690)
CENTER FOR DENTAL IMPLANTS
1308 S Pioneer Way (98837-2410)
PHONE..................................509 765-5141
Thomas J Laney, Principal
EMP: 2
SALES (est): 125.5K Privately Held
SIC: 3843 Enamels, dentists'

(G-6691)
CENTRAL WASHINGTON SIGN CO
10158 Kinder Rd Ne (98837-3479)
P.O. Box D (98837-0013)
PHONE..................................509 765-1818
Duane Jenks, Owner
EMP: 4
SALES (est): 155.2K Privately Held
SIC: 3993 Signs & advertising specialties

(G-6692)
CHEMI-CON MATERIALS CORP
9053 Graham St Ne (98837-9334)
PHONE..................................509 762-8788
Hisataka Muramatsu, President
Shunichi Saeki, President
Celaine Luckey, Treasurer
Celaine L Ringstad, Treasurer
Mitchell Delabarre, Admin Sec
◆ EMP: 62
SALES (est): 18.1MM Privately Held
SIC: 3353 Foil, aluminum
PA: Nippon Chemi-Con Corporation
   5-6-4, Osaki
   Shinagawa-Ku TKY 141-0

(G-6693)
CHICAGO TITLE INSURANCE CO
1025 S Pioneer Way Ste C (98837-2265)
PHONE..................................509 765-8820
William Bell, Branch Mgr
EMP: 2
SALES (corp-wide): 7.5B Publicly Held
SIC: 2329 5137 Men's & boys' sportswear & athletic clothing; women's & children's clothing
HQ: Chicago Title Insurance Company
   601 Riverside Ave
   Jacksonville FL 32204

(G-6694)
COLBASIA CABINETS INC
1228 E Wheeler Rd B (98837-1860)
PHONE..................................509 765-0718
Dale G Good, President
Cindy M Good, Vice Pres

EMP: 4 EST: 1979
SALES (est): 362.6K Privately Held
SIC: 2434 Vanities, bathroom: wood

(G-6695)
COLUMBIA BASIN MACHINE CO INC
612 W 3rd Ave (98837-2098)
PHONE..................................509 765-6212
Delone Krueger, President
Eileen Krueger, Vice Pres
EMP: 9
SQ FT: 13,000
SALES: 765K Privately Held
SIC: 3599 Machine shop, jobbing & repair

(G-6696)
COLUMBIA BASIN PUBLISHING CO
Also Called: Basin Business Journal
813 W 3rd Ave (98837-2008)
P.O. Box 910 (98837-0136)
PHONE..................................509 765-4561
Duane Hagadone, President
Lynne Lynch, Editor
Mike Riggs, Council Mbr
EMP: 55 EST: 1941
SQ FT: 4,200
SALES (est): 3.2MM
SALES (corp-wide): 308.5MM Privately Held
WEB: www.columbiabasinherald.com
SIC: 2711 Commercial printing & newspaper publishing combined; newspapers, publishing & printing
PA: Hagadone Investment Co Inc
   111 S 1st St
   Coeur D Alene ID 83814
   208 667-3431

(G-6697)
COLUMBIA BASIN SIGN AND LTG
320 S Alder St (98837-1787)
P.O. Box 790 (98837-0118)
PHONE..................................509 764-8121
Michael Garland, Principal
EMP: 2
SALES (est): 216.8K Privately Held
SIC: 3993 Signs & advertising specialties

(G-6698)
COURTRIGHT ENTERPRISES INC
3385 Road M.2 Ne Ste 6 (98837-8628)
P.O. Box 1266 (98837-0190)
PHONE..................................509 764-9600
John Courtright, CEO
Susan Courtright, CFO
▼ EMP: 25
SQ FT: 978,000
SALES: 4.4MM Privately Held
WEB: www.courtrightent.com
SIC: 3532 Auger mining equipment

(G-6699)
CPM DEVELOPMENT CORPORATION
Also Called: Central Washington Concrete
5278 Hwy 17 N (98837)
P.O. Box 248, Ephrata (98823-0248)
PHONE..................................509 762-5366
Troy Holt, General Mgr
EMP: 7
SALES (corp-wide): 30.6B Privately Held
SIC: 1771 3273 Concrete work; ready-mixed concrete
HQ: Cpm Development Corporation
   5111 E Broadway Ave
   Spokane Valley WA 99212
   509 534-6221

(G-6700)
CRESAP ORTHOTICS & PROSTHETICS
835 E Colonial Ave Ste 10 (98837-4617)
PHONE..................................509 764-8500
Sean Cresap, President
EMP: 4 Privately Held
SIC: 3842 Orthopedic appliances
PA: Cresap Orthotics & Prosthetics Inc
   630 N Chelan Ave Ste A5
   Wenatchee WA 98801

GEOGRAPHIC SECTION

Moses Lake - Grant County (G-6729)

(G-6701)
D & L FOUNDRY INC
12970 Road 3 Ne (98837-4902)
P.O. Box 1319 (98837-0194)
PHONE.....................509 765-7952
Jason McGowan, *President*
John Leftwich, *President*
Scott McLaughlin, *Vice Pres*
Linda Cooper, *Shareholder*
Kelly Leftwich, *Shareholder*
▲ **EMP:** 120
SQ FT: 40,000
SALES (est): 27.6MM **Privately Held**
SIC: 3321 Gray iron castings

(G-6702)
D & N FARMS PARTNERSHIP
137 Fairmont Ln (98837-2558)
PHONE.....................509 771-1714
Nichole Greninger, *Partner*
Daryl Greninger, *Executor*
EMP: 2
SALES (est): 62.3K **Privately Held**
SIC: 2051 Bread, all types (white, wheat, rye, etc): fresh or frozen

(G-6703)
D AND D ELECTRIC MOTOR SVC INC
Also Called: D&D RC Hobbies
4320 Airway Dr Ne (98837-1002)
P.O. Box 1314 (98837-0199)
PHONE.....................509 762-6136
John Day, *President*
Rose Day, *Vice Pres*
EMP: 5 **EST:** 1998
SALES: 450K **Privately Held**
SIC: 7694 5063 Electric motor repair; motors, electric

(G-6704)
DESERT GRAPHICS INC
1626 W Broadway Ave Ste A (98837-3948)
PHONE.....................509 765-8082
Agnes R Holloway, *Ch of Bd*
Bonnie Frost, *President*
EMP: 4
SQ FT: 4,800
SALES: 400K **Privately Held**
WEB: www.desertgraphicsinc.net
SIC: 2759 Screen printing

(G-6705)
DFI MP EROH LLC
Also Called: Dynamic Food Ingredients
13583 Wheeler Rd Ne Ste D (98837-8656)
PHONE.....................206 499-2687
Benjamin Sykora, *CFO*
Paul Magnotto,
Jonathan Stapley,
EMP: 3
SALES (est): 141.3K **Privately Held**
SIC: 2869 Sweeteners, synthetic

(G-6706)
DNA GROWERS LLC
16833 Road 8 Ne (98837-9559)
P.O. Box 2181 (98837-0581)
PHONE.....................509 793-6606
Doug Spurbeck, *Mng Member*
Andrew Simmonds,
EMP: 2
SALES (est): 73.4K **Privately Held**
SIC: 3423 7389 Garden & farm tools, including shovels;

(G-6707)
EASTSIDE WELDING & FABRICATION
10828 Road 5.2 Ne (98837-9021)
PHONE.....................509 765-6434
Pamela Stowers, *President*
EMP: 2
SALES: 140K **Privately Held**
SIC: 3441 Fabricated structural metal

(G-6708)
FIVE FOOD INC
Also Called: Kuki Collection
2801 W Broadway Ave (98837-2905)
PHONE.....................509 855-6914
Surinder Singh, *President*
Harjit Singh, *Vice Pres*
Sunney Singh, *Admin Sec*
▲ **EMP:** 4

SALES (est): 231.2K **Privately Held**
SIC: 2676 3086 3714 Towels, napkins & tissue paper products; plastics foam products; air conditioner parts, motor vehicle

(G-6709)
FLODIN INC
13624 N Frontage Rd E (98837-9320)
PHONE.....................509 766-2996
John Flodin, *President*
EMP: 30
SQ FT: 24,000
SALES (est): 4.1MM **Privately Held**
SIC: 3556 Smokers, food processing equipment

(G-6710)
GENERAL DYNAMICS ORDNA
9256 Randolph Rd Ne (98837-9397)
PHONE.....................509 762-5381
Chris Montoya, *Manager*
Wade Schmidt, *Manager*
EMP: 70
SQ FT: 5,000
SALES (corp-wide): 36.1B **Publicly Held**
SIC: 3764 3769 3537 Guided missile & space vehicle propulsion unit parts; guided missile & space vehicle parts & auxiliary equipment; industrial trucks & tractors
HQ: General Dynamics Ordnance And Tactical Systems, Inc.
11399 16th Ct N Ste 200
Saint Petersburg FL 33716
727 578-8100

(G-6711)
GENIE INDUSTRIES INC
8987 Graham St Ne (98837-9334)
PHONE.....................425 881-1800
Sabino Serrato, *Production*
Brian Healy, *Manager*
Jeff Benz, *Manager*
EMP: 31
SALES (corp-wide): 5.1B **Publicly Held**
SIC: 3536 Hand hoists; hoists
HQ: Genie Industries, Inc.
18340 Ne 76th St
Redmond WA 98052
425 881-1800

(G-6712)
GENIE MANUFACTURING INC
8987 Graham St Ne D5820 (98837-9334)
PHONE.....................509 762-3200
George Santiago, *General Mgr*
Tom Scevers, *Manager*
Tommy Seavers, *Manager*
Benito Candanoza, *Director*
Steve Chandler, *Manager*
EMP: 210
SALES (corp-wide): 5.1B **Publicly Held**
WEB: www.geniekorea.com
SIC: 3531 Aerial work platforms: hydraulic/elec. truck/carrier mounted
HQ: Genie Manufacturing, Inc.
18340 Ne 76th St
Redmond WA 98052
425 881-1800

(G-6713)
HARRYS RADIATOR SHOP INC
Also Called: Lake Plating
607 E Broadway Ave (98837-1725)
PHONE.....................509 765-8581
Harry H Stern, *President*
Joanne Stern, *Admin Sec*
EMP: 5
SQ FT: 1,500
SALES (est): 430.3K **Privately Held**
SIC: 7539 3471 Radiator repair shop, automotive; chromium plating of metals or formed products

(G-6714)
HELENA CHEMICAL COMPANY
9519 Vernal Ave Se (98837-9052)
PHONE.....................509 539-5761
Jerry Ellis, *Branch Mgr*
EMP: 8 **Privately Held**
WEB: www.helenachemical.com
SIC: 2879 Agricultural chemicals
HQ: Helena Agri-Enterprises, Llc
255 Schilling Blvd # 300
Collierville TN 38017
901 761-0050

(G-6715)
INLAND TARP & COVER INC
4172 N Frontage Rd E (98837-4901)
PHONE.....................509 766-7024
Glen Knopp, *President*
John Beeman, *Division Mgr*
Matt Purcell, *Sales Mgr*
Ben Stonecypher Jr, *Sales Staff*
Torger Myran, *Manager*
▲ **EMP:** 7
SALES (est): 1.4MM **Privately Held**
SIC: 2394 Canvas & related products
PA: Inland Tarp & Liner, Llc
4172 N Frontage Rd E
Moses Lake WA 98837

(G-6716)
INTERNATIONAL PAPER COMPANY
13594 Wheeler Rd Ne (98837-9150)
P.O. Box 1369 (98837-0208)
PHONE.....................509 765-0262
Tom Rossi, *Branch Mgr*
EMP: 102
SALES (corp-wide): 23.3B **Publicly Held**
WEB: www.internationalpaper.com
SIC: 2653 Boxes, corrugated: made from purchased materials
PA: International Paper Company
6400 Poplar Ave
Memphis TN 38197
901 419-9000

(G-6717)
JERRY FRY
830 E Broadway Ave (98837-5932)
PHONE.....................509 765-4367
Jerry Fry, *Principal*
EMP: 2
SALES (est): 171.3K **Privately Held**
SIC: 3568 Power transmission equipment

(G-6718)
JOYSON SAFETY SYSTEMS
Also Called: Inflation Systems
9138 Randolph Rd Ne (98837-9397)
PHONE.....................509 762-5549
Don Tersky, *Branch Mgr*
EMP: 140
SALES (corp-wide): 8B **Privately Held**
SIC: 3491 3714 3842 Compressed gas cylinder valves; motor vehicle parts & accessories; surgical appliances & supplies
HQ: Joyson Safety Systems Acquisition Llc
2500 Innovation Dr
Auburn Hills MI 48326
248 373-8040

(G-6719)
JR SIMPLOT COMPANY
14124 Wheeler Rd Ne (98837-9119)
PHONE.....................509 765-3443
Steve Hennig, *Principal*
EMP: 50
SALES (corp-wide): 4.9B **Privately Held**
WEB: www.simplot.com
SIC: 2099 2037 Food preparations; frozen fruits & vegetables
PA: J.R. Simplot Company
1099 W Front St
Boise ID 83702
208 780-3287

(G-6720)
JUSTUS BAG COMPANY INC
1312 W Broadway Ave (98837-2610)
PHONE.....................509 765-6981
Darin R Justus, *Branch Mgr*
EMP: 2
SALES (corp-wide): 5.9MM **Privately Held**
SIC: 2211 Bags & bagging, cotton
PA: Justus Bag Company, Inc.
11205 E Trent Ave
Spokane Valley WA 99206
509 924-8353

(G-6721)
KIOWNA PUBLISHING INC
390 Dream St Se (98837-8262)
P.O. Box 1095 (98837-0164)
PHONE.....................509 947-0675
William Byers, *President*
Thomi Ditch, *Principal*
▲ **EMP:** 4

SALES (est): 75K **Privately Held**
WEB: www.kionapublishing.com
SIC: 2721 2731 Magazines: publishing only, not printed on site; book publishing

(G-6722)
M 1 TANKS INC
13058 N Frontage Rd Ne (98837-7902)
PHONE.....................509 766-2914
Denise Morgan, *President*
Jim Morgan, *Vice Pres*
EMP: 4
SALES: 600K **Privately Held**
SIC: 3272 Septic tanks, concrete

(G-6723)
MAKK MOTORING LLC
10766 Road 9 Ne (98837-9007)
PHONE.....................509 855-2638
Nicole Mackey, *Principal*
EMP: 2
SALES (est): 140.7K **Privately Held**
SIC: 3714 Exhaust systems & parts, motor vehicle

(G-6724)
MCDOWALL BROS INSULATION
Also Called: McDowall & Son Construction
4896 Mcconihe Rd Ne (98837-9338)
PHONE.....................509 762-9530
Calvin D McDowall, *Owner*
EMP: 3
SALES (est): 229K **Privately Held**
SIC: 0139 3999 1542 1541 ; ; commercial & office building contractors; industrial buildings, new construction

(G-6725)
METRON POWDERCOATING INC
2000 Wheeler Rd Ne (98837-5110)
PHONE.....................509 766-1278
Ronald Karlsten, *Principal*
EMP: 2
SALES (est): 126.9K **Privately Held**
SIC: 3479 Coating of metals & formed products

(G-6726)
MONSANTO
912 S Dahlia Dr (98837-2216)
PHONE.....................509 760-0707
EMP: 2
SALES (est): 74.4K **Privately Held**
SIC: 2879 Agricultural chemicals

(G-6727)
MOSES LAKE INDUSTRIES INC (HQ)
8248 Randolph Rd Ne (98837-9328)
PHONE.....................509 762-5336
Tsurahide Cho, *Ch of Bd*
Hiroyuki ERA, *President*
Michael Harvey, *President*
Toshitsura Cho, *Chairman*
Laura Sofield, *QC Dir*
◆ **EMP:** 75
SQ FT: 20,250
SALES (est): 19.3MM **Privately Held**
WEB: www.mlindustries.com
SIC: 2869 Industrial organic chemicals

(G-6728)
MOSES LAKE SHEET METAL INC
1130 E Wheeler Rd (98837-1866)
P.O. Box 550 (98837-0083)
PHONE.....................509 765-1614
Bob Massart, *President*
EMP: 26
SQ FT: 29,000
SALES (est): 3MM **Privately Held**
SIC: 3444 Sheet metalwork

(G-6729)
MOUNTAINVIEW POLARIS INC
507 E 3rd Ave (98837-1711)
PHONE.....................509 765-9340
Wes Melcher, *President*
EMP: 2
SALES (est): 205.4K **Privately Held**
SIC: 3799 Snowmobiles

Moses Lake - Grant County (G-6730)

(G-6730)
NATIONAL FROZEN FOODS CORP
14406 Road 3 Se (98837-9090)
P.O. Box A (98837-0010)
PHONE..................509 766-0793
Gary Ash, *Branch Mgr*
EMP: 40
SALES (corp-wide): 228.8MM **Privately Held**
SIC: **2099** 2037 Vegetables, peeled for the trade; frozen fruits & vegetables
PA: National Frozen Foods Corporation
1600 Frview Ave E Ste 200
Seattle WA 98102
206 322-8900

(G-6731)
NORCO INC
2757 Road N Ne (98837-9581)
PHONE..................509 764-5032
Sean Welch, *Branch Mgr*
EMP: 3
SALES (corp-wide): 413MM **Privately Held**
SIC: **5084** 5169 7352 2813 Welding machinery & equipment; safety equipment; industrial gases; medical equipment rental; industrial gases
PA: Norco, Inc.
1125 W Amity Rd
Boise ID 83705
208 336-1643

(G-6732)
NORTH RIDGE MACHINE LLC
9531 Beacon Rd Ne (98837-4332)
PHONE..................509 765-8928
Jerry Hendrickson, *Mng Member*
Gayle Hendrickson, *Mng Member*
EMP: 6
SQ FT: 6,000
SALES: 250K **Privately Held**
SIC: **7699** 3599 Pumps & pumping equipment repair; machine shop, jobbing & repair

(G-6733)
NOURYON PULP & PRFMCE CHEM LLC
2701 Road N Ne (98837-9581)
PHONE..................509 765-6400
Pat Baly, *Branch Mgr*
EMP: 171
SALES (corp-wide): 110.5MM **Privately Held**
SIC: **2819** Industrial inorganic chemicals
PA: Nouryon Pulp And Performance Chemicals Llc
1850 Parkway Pl Se # 1200
Marietta GA 30067
770 578-0858

(G-6734)
PACIFIC COCA COLA BOTTLING
Also Called: Coca-Cola
5803 Patton Blvd Ne (98837-3229)
PHONE..................509 762-6987
Brent Larkin, *Principal*
EMP: 3
SALES (est): 148.5K **Privately Held**
SIC: **2086** Bottled & canned soft drinks

(G-6735)
PACIFIC NORTHWEST MECH LLC
1740 W Pheasant St (98837-2780)
P.O. Box 357 (98837-0056)
PHONE..................509 765-9606
Seth Gerber, *Project Mgr*
Lee Gerber,
Sue C Gerber,
EMP: 15
SQ FT: 7,200
SALES (est): 3.3MM **Privately Held**
WEB: www.pnwm.com
SIC: **3441** Fabricated structural metal

(G-6736)
PALMER INDUSTRIES LLC
11835 Chris Dr Ne (98837-9099)
PHONE..................509 989-1069
Sarah Palmer, *Principal*
EMP: 2

SALES (est): 119.8K **Privately Held**
SIC: **3999** Manufacturing industries

(G-6737)
PARKER-HANNIFIN CORPORATION
5803 Patton Blvd Ne Ste E (98837-3229)
P.O. Box 487 (98837-0074)
PHONE..................509 764-5430
EMP: 2
SALES (corp-wide): 12B **Publicly Held**
SIC: **3594** Fluid power pumps & motors
PA: Parker-Hannifin Corporation
6035 Parkland Blvd
Cleveland OH 44124
216 896-3000

(G-6738)
PARKER-HANNIFIN CORPORATION
5803 Patton Blvd Ne (98837-3229)
PHONE..................509 764-5430
EMP: 2
SALES (corp-wide): 14.3B **Publicly Held**
SIC: **3594** Fluid power pumps & motors
PA: Parker-Hannifin Corporation
6035 Parkland Blvd
Cleveland OH 44124
216 896-3000

(G-6739)
PROWELD FABRICATION LLC
7609 Mcbeth Ln Ne (98837-1877)
P.O. Box 645, Issaquah (98027-0024)
PHONE..................425 835-6477
Valentin Lovin, *Principal*
EMP: 2
SALES (est): 122.5K **Privately Held**
SIC: **3446** Architectural metalwork

(G-6740)
R AND DEE COATINGS LLC
900 N Grape Dr (98837-1477)
PHONE..................509 771-1111
EMP: 4
SALES (est): 281.9K **Privately Held**
SIC: **3479** Metal coating & allied service

(G-6741)
REC SILICON INC
3322 Road N Ne (98837-9505)
PHONE..................509 765-2106
Tore Torvund, *CEO*
Jan Johannessen, *President*
Ole Enger, *Chairman*
Kurt Levens, *Vice Pres*
Ron Reis, *Vice Pres*
▲ EMP: 60
SALES (est): 21.1MM **Privately Held**
SIC: **3674** 3295 2813 Metal oxide silicon (MOS) devices; minerals, ground or treated; industrial gases
PA: Rec Silicon Asa
Fornebuveien 84
Lysaker 1366

(G-6742)
REC SILICON INC
1800 Road N Ne (98837-9816)
PHONE..................509 793-9015
EMP: 7 **Privately Held**
SIC: **3674** Semiconductors & related devices
HQ: Rec Silicon Inc
1616 S Pioneer Way
Moses Lake WA 98837
509 793-9000

(G-6743)
REC SILICON INC (HQ)
1616 S Pioneer Way (98837-2487)
PHONE..................509 793-9000
James Bowen, *Governor*
James May II, *Governor*
Francine Sullivan, *Governor*
Tore Torvund, *Governor*
Jens Ulltveit-Moe, *Governor*
◆ EMP: 12
SALES (est): 291.6MM **Privately Held**
WEB: www.sgsilicon.com
SIC: **3339** Silicon & chromium

(G-6744)
REC SOLAR GRADE SILICON LLC
3322 Road N Ne (98837-9505)
PHONE..................509 765-2106
Chuck Sutton, *Vice Pres*
Jeff Johnson, *Vice Pres*
Deeanna Worley, *Vice Pres*
▲ EMP: 175
SALES (est): 62.8MM **Privately Held**
WEB: www.sgsilicon.com
SIC: **3339** Silicon & chromium
HQ: Rec Silicon Inc
1616 S Pioneer Way
Moses Lake WA 98837
509 793-9000

(G-6745)
REYES COCA-COLA BOTTLING LLC
6819 22nd Ave Ne (98837-3286)
PHONE..................509 762-5480
Brent Larkin, *Manager*
EMP: 13
SALES (corp-wide): 713.8MM **Privately Held**
SIC: **2086** Bottled & canned soft drinks
PA: Reyes Coca-Cola Bottling, L.L.C.
3 Park Plz Ste 600
Irvine CA 92614
213 744-8616

(G-6746)
ROYAL REGISTER
813 W 3rd Ave (98837-2008)
P.O. Box 910 (98837-0136)
PHONE..................509 770-8221
EMP: 2
SALES (est): 62.9K **Privately Held**
SIC: **2711** Newspapers

(G-6747)
SGL ATOMOTIVE CARBN FIBERS LLC
8781 Randolph Rd Ne (98837-7920)
PHONE..................509 762-4600
Steve Swanson, *General Mgr*
Skyler Hoffer, *Production*
Thaydra Claunch, *Purchasing*
John Anderson, *Engineer*
Dennis Henline, *Project Engr*
◆ EMP: 52
SQ FT: 154,000
SALES (est): 11MM **Privately Held**
SIC: **3624** Fibers, carbon & graphite

(G-6748)
SGL COMPOSITES LLC
8781 Randolph Rd Ne (98837-7920)
PHONE..................704 593-5177
Andreas Wuellner, *CEO*
Steven Swanson, *Vice Pres*
Benoit Labelle, *CFO*
Marcel Remp, *Info Tech Mgr*
▲ EMP: 5
SQ FT: 25,000
SALES (est): 1.7MM
SALES (corp-wide): 1.2B **Privately Held**
SIC: **3624** Carbon & graphite products
HQ: Sgl Carbon, Llc
10715 David Taylor Dr # 460
Charlotte NC 28262
704 593-5100

(G-6749)
SHIRTBUILDERS INC
206 S Fir St (98837-1978)
PHONE..................509 765-3885
John Jeninga, *President*
Karen Jeninga, *Vice Pres*
EMP: 3
SALES (est): 290K **Privately Held**
WEB: www.shirtbuilders.com
SIC: **2396** Screen printing on fabric articles

(G-6750)
SIGNS NOW OF MOSES LAKE INC
1626 W Broadway Ave Ste C (98837-3948)
PHONE..................509 765-8955
Patrick Simmons, *President*
EMP: 6
SALES (est): 400K **Privately Held**
SIC: **3993** 5199 Signs & advertising specialties; advertising specialties

(G-6751)
SPECIALIZED SAFETY PDTS LLC
Also Called: SSP Eyewear
6082 22nd Ave Ne Spc 1 (98837-3220)
P.O. Box 1958 (98837-0358)
PHONE..................509 707-0068
Jennifer Bechtel, *Marketing Staff*
Michael Bechtel,
EMP: 3
SQ FT: 5,500
SALES (est): 297.2K **Privately Held**
SIC: **3851** Ophthalmic goods

(G-6752)
TARGET MEDIA PARTNERS
Also Called: Nickel Saver
1428 S Pioneer Way (98837-2484)
PHONE..................509 765-5681
Sue Tebow, *Manager*
EMP: 9
SALES (corp-wide): 27.7MM **Privately Held**
WEB: www.targetmediapartners.com
SIC: **5192** 2741 Newspapers; miscellaneous publishing
HQ: Target Media Partners
5200 Lankershim Blvd # 350
North Hollywood CA 91601
323 930-3123

(G-6753)
TEN PIN BREWING COMPANY
1165 N Stratford Rd (98837-1514)
PHONE..................509 750-0396
BJ Garbe, *CEO*
EMP: 4
SALES (est): 106.4K **Privately Held**
SIC: **3585** Beer dispensing equipment

(G-6754)
TOTALWAVE FITNESS LLC
1300 W Marina Dr Apt 27 (98837-3923)
PHONE..................509 361-9089
Robert Jackson, *Principal*
EMP: 2
SALES (est): 129K **Privately Held**
SIC: **5091** 3949 Fitness equipment & supplies; exercise equipment

(G-6755)
UAV SYSTEMS DEVELOPMENT CORP
Also Called: Unmanned Aerial Systems Dev
509 N Bluff West Dr (98837-4923)
PHONE..................803 767-1351
Ruben Delvalle, *CEO*
R J Santiago, *Development*
EMP: 418
SALES (est): 365.4K **Privately Held**
SIC: **3728** 7389 3721 Target drones; mapmaking or drafting, including aerial; airplanes, fixed or rotary wing

(G-6756)
VERNS MOSES LAKE MEATS INC
3954 Mae Valley Rd Ne (98837-9596)
PHONE..................509 765-5671
Larry Ellestad, *President*
Tom Ellestad, *Corp Secy*
EMP: 15
SQ FT: 1,500
SALES (est): 2.7MM **Privately Held**
SIC: **5147** 5421 0751 2011 Meats, cured or smoked; meat markets, including freezer provisioners; slaughtering: custom livestock services; meat packing plants

(G-6757)
WEST WORLDWIDE SERVICES INC
151 S Hamilton Rd (98837-9534)
PHONE..................509 764-2177
Travis Laidl, *Branch Mgr*
EMP: 2
SQ FT: 30,000
SALES (corp-wide): 1.1MM **Privately Held**
SIC: **3011** Truck or bus inner tubes
PA: West Worldwide Services, Inc.
26378 289th Pl
Adel IA 50003
515 202-8424

▲ = Import ▼ = Export
◆ = Import/Export

GEOGRAPHIC SECTION

(G-6758)
WH INTERNATIONAL CASTING LLC
5075 Randolph Rd Ne (98837-3203)
PHONE.................................562 521-0727
Donald Hu, *President*
EMP: 2
SALES (corp-wide): 54.6MM **Privately Held**
SIC: 3321 Gray & ductile iron foundries
HQ: Wh International Casting, Llc
   14821 Artesia Blvd
   La Mirada CA 90638
   562 521-0727

Mossyrock
Lewis County

(G-6759)
BRINDLE TECHNICAL LOGGING INC
451 Winston Creek Rd (98564-9687)
PHONE.................................360 985-7459
Jerry Lee Brindle Jr, *President*
EMP: 3
SALES (est): 98.8K **Privately Held**
SIC: 2411 Logging

(G-6760)
BRINTECH INC
451 Winston Creek Rd (98564-9687)
PHONE.................................360 985-7459
Jerry Lee Brindle Jr, *President*
EMP: 6
SALES (est): 662.6K **Privately Held**
SIC: 2411 Logging

(G-6761)
EVERGREEN COOLING TECH INC (PA)
148-33 Bear Ridge Rd (98564)
P.O. Box 108 (98564-0108)
PHONE.................................360 983-3691
Jeffery Padrta, *President*
Marry Padrta, *Vice Pres*
▲ EMP: 8
SQ FT: 5,000
SALES: 5MM **Privately Held**
SIC: 3443 Cooling towers, metal plate

(G-6762)
KIONA CREEK TIMBER INC
105 Caytee Cv (98564-9721)
PHONE.................................360 983-3786
Samuel R Kilmer, *President*
Sam Kilmer, *Owner*
EMP: 6
SALES (est): 420K **Privately Held**
SIC: 2411 Timber, cut at logging camp

(G-6763)
NEILSON ORGANIC COMPOST
195 Wilson Rd (98564-9611)
PHONE.................................360 983-8125
Mike Neilson, *Owner*
EMP: 3
SALES (est): 267.9K **Privately Held**
SIC: 2875 Compost

(G-6764)
PRECISION CUSTOMER WOODWORKING
180 Mossyrock Rd W (98564-9655)
PHONE.................................360 983-3297
Randy Sasser, *Principal*
EMP: 2 EST: 2011
SALES (est): 191.1K **Privately Held**
SIC: 2431 Millwork

(G-6765)
R HARPER INC
323 Hadaller Rd (98564-9614)
PHONE.................................360 985-0306
Rick Harper, *President*
EMP: 9
SALES: 650K **Privately Held**
SIC: 2411 Logging

(G-6766)
SALMON CREEK MEATS
139 Koons Rd (98564-9716)
PHONE.................................360 985-7822
Joe Markholt, *Partner*
EMP: 2 EST: 1998
SALES (est): 144.2K **Privately Held**
SIC: 2015 Chicken, processed: cooked

(G-6767)
WINSTON QUARRY INC
269 Winston Creek Rd (98564-9665)
P.O. Box 518, Onalaska (98570-0518)
PHONE.................................360 985-0487
Bart Lyons, *President*
EMP: 6
SALES (est): 642K **Privately Held**
SIC: 1442 Construction sand & gravel

Mount Vernon
Skagit County

(G-6768)
A U CORNERSTONE INC
401 S 1st St Ste 201 (98273-3806)
P.O. Box 1127 (98273-1127)
PHONE.................................360 336-5234
Lynn Strauss, *CEO*
Sean McCarty, *President*
Bonnie Mc Carty, *Office Mgr*
Barbara Strauss, *Admin Sec*
EMP: 6
SQ FT: 1,200
SALES: 500K **Privately Held**
WEB: www.aucornerstone.com
SIC: 5094 3911 7631 Jewelry; jewelry, precious metal; jewelry repair services

(G-6769)
ACTION PAGES CONSOLIDATED INC
2021 E College Way # 101 (98273-2373)
PHONE.................................360 848-0870
David Lindsey, *President*
Lori Halverson, *Sales Staff*
EMP: 20
SALES (est): 2.4MM **Privately Held**
SIC: 2741 Directories, telephone: publishing & printing

(G-6770)
ALL IN CNSTR & LDSCPG LLC
430 N 30th St (98273-3674)
PHONE.................................360 840-7990
Jack Clevenger, *Principal*
EMP: 2 EST: 2016
SALES (est): 34.6K **Privately Held**
SIC: 0781 1799 3446 2411 Landscape services; fence construction; fences, gates, posts & flagpoles; rails, fence: round or split

(G-6771)
ASAP SIGN & DESIGN
Also Called: ASAP Sign & Banner
1202 S 2nd St Ste B (98273-4858)
PHONE.................................360 757-1570
Timothy Lindeman, *Partner*
Brian Cypher, *Partner*
Jacquelyn Lindeman, *Partner*
EMP: 4
SALES: 360K **Privately Held**
SIC: 3993 5999 2759 Signs & advertising specialties; banners, flags, decals & posters; screen printing

(G-6772)
AUTO BODY SPECIALTIES
2407 Old Highway 99 S Rd # 996 (98273-9094)
PHONE.................................360 424-1313
Don White, *Principal*
EMP: 2
SALES (est): 94.2K **Privately Held**
SIC: 7532 3713 Body shop, automotive; truck bodies & parts

(G-6773)
BAD APPLE
2320 N Laventure Rd (98273-5813)
PHONE.................................360 899-5183
EMP: 2 EST: 2013
SALES (est): 206.4K **Privately Held**
SIC: 3571 Mfg Electronic Computers

(G-6774)
BARKER DRILLING
20793 English Rd (98274-7567)
PHONE.................................425 252-4686
Brent Barker, *Owner*
Linda Barker, *Co-Owner*
EMP: 2
SALES (est): 226.3K **Privately Held**
SIC: 1381 1781 Service well drilling; water well drilling

(G-6775)
BAYVIEW COMPOSITES LLC
13593 Bayview Edison Rd (98273-8231)
PHONE.................................360 466-4160
Dacia Hsueh, *COO*
Thomas Hsueh,
EMP: 78
SALES: 1,000K **Privately Held**
SIC: 2951 Composition blocks for paving

(G-6776)
BAZOOKA GOLD MINING CO LLC
17720 Moore Rd (98273-6586)
PHONE.................................360 202-5953
Rod Bonnifield,
Donn Lee,
EMP: 2
SALES (est): 105.1K **Privately Held**
SIC: 1041 Gold ores mining

(G-6777)
BBC BIOCHEMICAL CORPORATION
409 Eleanor Ln (98273-4518)
P.O. Box 1320 (98273-1320)
PHONE.................................360 542-8400
Adrian Biesecker, *President*
Laura Biesecker, *CFO*
Ashley Stuart, *Info Tech Mgr*
▲ EMP: 108
SQ FT: 57,000
SALES (est): 23.7MM **Privately Held**
WEB: www.bbcus.com
SIC: 3821 5169 2869 2819 Laboratory equipment: fume hoods, distillation racks, etc.; industrial chemicals; laboratory chemicals, organic; chemicals, reagent grade: refined from technical grade

(G-6778)
BEAVER LAKE QUARRY INC
14322 Beaver Lake Rd (98273-8065)
PHONE.................................360 856-5870
Charles Tewalt, *President*
EMP: 4
SALES (est): 216.9K **Privately Held**
SIC: 1429 Volcanic rock, crushed & broken-quarrying

(G-6779)
BEE KEEPER GORDONS GOLD
17084 Dunbar Rd (98273-8763)
PHONE.................................360 202-9523
Gordon Moran, *Owner*
EMP: 3
SALES (est): 97.3K **Privately Held**
SIC: 3999 Beekeepers' supplies

(G-6780)
BERTELSEN WINERY & TASTING RM
20598 Starbird Rd (98274-7534)
PHONE.................................360 445-2300
EMP: 3
SALES (est): 118.9K **Privately Held**
SIC: 2084 Wines

(G-6781)
BLADE CHEVERLOT RV
111 Stewart Rd (98273-9628)
PHONE.................................360 982-2370
EMP: 2 EST: 2011
SALES (est): 129.2K **Privately Held**
SIC: 3799 All terrain vehicles (ATV)

(G-6782)
CALIBER PRECISION INC
1824 Railroad Ave (98273-4953)
P.O. Box 2769 (98273-7769)
PHONE.................................360 333-7602
Benjamin Orton, *President*
Paul Budd, *Corp Secy*
EMP: 6
SALES (est): 3MM **Privately Held**
SIC: 3599 Machine shop, jobbing & repair

(G-6783)
CASCADE PRSTHTICS ORTHTICS INC
Also Called: Cascade Prosthetic & Orthotics
17670 Dunbar Rd (98273-8752)
PHONE.................................360 428-4003
Debbie Donaldson, *Manager*
EMP: 2
SALES (corp-wide): 1.8MM **Privately Held**
SIC: 3842 5999 Prosthetic appliances; orthopedic & prosthesis applications
PA: Cascade Prosthetics And Orthotics, Inc.
   1360 Sunset Ave
   Ferndale WA 98248
   360 384-1858

(G-6784)
CHILD EVNGELISM FELLOWSHIP INC
1404 Riverside Dr Ste B (98273-2487)
P.O. Box 3137, Ferndale (98248-3137)
PHONE.................................360 424-1014
Ross Elden, *Branch Mgr*
EMP: 41
SALES (corp-wide): 24.4MM **Privately Held**
SIC: 2752 Commercial printing, lithographic
PA: Child Evangelism Fellowship Incorporated
   17482 Highway M
   Warrenton MO 63383
   636 456-4321

(G-6785)
CNS INDUSTRIES INC
4301 Apache Dr (98273-9171)
PHONE.................................360 424-1624
Seungchul Suh, *President*
EMP: 2
SALES (est): 110.4K **Privately Held**
SIC: 3999 Manufacturing industries

(G-6786)
CREATIVE CONCRETE PRODUCTS LLC
Also Called: Nu Driveways
115 Lind St (98273-4979)
PHONE.................................360 419-9909
David Imus, *Mng Member*
Richard Imus, *Mng Member*
EMP: 5
SALES: 600K **Privately Held**
WEB: www.creativeconcreteproducts.com
SIC: 3272 Precast terrazo or concrete products

(G-6787)
DAVES TV & APPLIANCE INC
Also Called: Anaco TV & Appliances
230 Belmont Ter (98274-4520)
PHONE.................................360 293-5129
David Evans, *President*
EMP: 5
SQ FT: 2,500
SALES: 350K **Privately Held**
SIC: 3639 Major kitchen appliances, except refrigerators & stoves

(G-6788)
DELAVAL INC
3709 Old Highway 99 S Rd (98273-9019)
PHONE.................................360 428-1744
Arlene Nevin, *Safety Dir*
Bill Jilisen, *Branch Mgr*
Doug Lambert, *Manager*
EMP: 15
SALES (corp-wide): 7.5B **Privately Held**
SIC: 3523 Farm machinery & equipment
HQ: Delaval Inc.
   11100 N Congress Ave
   Kansas City MO 64153
   816 891-7700

(G-6789)
DIAMOND BLUE MANUFACTURING CO
3709 Old Highway 99 S Rd (98273-9019)
PHONE.................................360 428-1744
Ken Johnson, *General Mgr*

Mount Vernon - Skagit County (G-6790)

Bill Jilesen, *General Mgr*
EMP: 40
SQ FT: 48,000
SALES (est): 7.1MM **Privately Held**
SIC: 3523 Dairy equipment (farm)

(G-6790)
DIVERSIFIED MFG TECHOLOGIES
1817 Railroad Ave Bldg A (98273-4959)
PHONE 360 424-9300
Seth Tromburg, *Principal*
EMP: 2
SQ FT: 8,800
SALES (est): 218.7K **Privately Held**
SIC: 3999 Barber & beauty shop equipment

(G-6791)
DOTSON DOORS LLC
3012 Withers Pl (98274-6186)
PHONE 253 326-6047
EMP: 2
SALES (est): 88.9K **Privately Held**
SIC: 3442 Metal doors, sash & trim

(G-6792)
EDCO INC
14508 Ovenell Rd (98273-8266)
PHONE 360 424-6600
Leslie Smith, *President*
◆ **EMP:** 47
SQ FT: 30,000
SALES: 8MM **Privately Held**
WEB: www.edcoonline.com
SIC: 3441 3535 3599 3443 Fabricated structural metal; conveyors & conveying equipment; machine & other job shop work; fabricated plate work (boiler shop)

(G-6793)
ERVIN H TENNYSON
Also Called: Cascading Waterscapes
100 E Washington St (98273-3903)
PHONE 360 445-2434
Ervin H Tennyson, *President*
EMP: 4
SALES (est): 252.7K **Privately Held**
WEB: www.cascadingwaterscapes.com
SIC: 3569 5261 5083 Filters; nurseries & garden centers; landscaping equipment

(G-6794)
EXCEL DAIRY SERVICE INC (PA)
2725 Old Highway 99 S Rd (98273-9040)
PHONE 360 848-9494
Clyde Fox, *President*
EMP: 31
SQ FT: 6,000
SALES: 9.2MM **Privately Held**
SIC: 3523 Dairy equipment (farm)

(G-6795)
FARMSTRONG LLC
Also Called: Farmstrong Brewing Co.
110 Stewart Rd (98273-9628)
PHONE 360 873-8852
Kelsey Lott, *Manager*
Todd Owsley,
EMP: 2
SALES (est): 62.3K **Privately Held**
SIC: 2082 5181 5813 Beer (alcoholic beverage); beer & other fermented malt liquors; beer garden (drinking places)

(G-6796)
FARRENEWELDING
22128 State Route 9 # 89 (98274-9364)
PHONE 360 941-5571
Jesse Farrens, *Principal*
EMP: 2
SALES (est): 40.2K **Privately Held**
SIC: 7692 Welding repair

(G-6797)
FLY BY NIGHT EXPRESS FREI
1910 Forest Dr (98273-5647)
PHONE 360 420-0844
Ryan Mackey, *Principal*
EMP: 4
SALES (est): 268.9K **Privately Held**
SIC: 2741 Miscellaneous publishing

(G-6798)
FRANKS CUSTOM WHEELS
1221 Riverside Dr (98273-2489)
PHONE 360 333-6887
EMP: 4 **EST:** 2010
SALES (est): 408.5K **Privately Held**
SIC: 3312 Blast Furnace-Steel Works

(G-6799)
GLACIER PEAK WINERY
13821 Best Rd (98273-4766)
PHONE 360 419-9107
EMP: 2
SALES (est): 85.9K **Privately Held**
SIC: 2084 Wines

(G-6800)
GOODWINDS LLC
1829 Railroad Ave (98273-4959)
PHONE 206 362-6151
Leland Holeman,
EMP: 3 **EST:** 2008
SALES (est): 611K **Privately Held**
SIC: 3089 Molding primary plastic

(G-6801)
GRANITE BOATWORKS INC
11071 Josh Green Ln # 105 (98273-4729)
PHONE 360 466-1280
Scott Roberts, *Principal*
EMP: 2
SALES (est): 254K **Privately Held**
SIC: 3732 Boat building & repairing

(G-6802)
GRIZZLY FIRESTARTERS NORTH (PA)
35177 Deer Creek Rd (98274-8261)
PHONE 360 652-2100
Ken Staab, *Owner*
Angela Staab, *Co-Owner*
EMP: 3
SALES (est): 80K **Privately Held**
SIC: 2499 5099 5989 Logs of sawdust & wood particles, pressed; wood & wood by-products; wood (fuel)

(G-6803)
HALLMARK REFINING CORPORATION
Also Called: H R C Refining
1016 Dale Ln (98274-9553)
P.O. Box 1446 (98273-1446)
PHONE 360 428-5880
Anthony N Senff, *President*
Mark Osborn, *Export Mgr*
Keith Erwin, *Purch Agent*
Ron Jakosh, *Controller*
Adam Ball, *IT/INT Sup*
▼ **EMP:** 57
SQ FT: 65,000
SALES (est): 12.3MM **Privately Held**
WEB: www.hallmarkrefining.com
SIC: 5084 3339 4212 3561 Pollution control equipment, air (environmental); pollution control equipment, water (environmental); gold refining (primary); silver refining (primary); local trucking, without storage; pumps & pumping equipment; fabricated plate work (boiler shop); secondary nonferrous metals

(G-6804)
INDUSTRIAL ELECTRIC CO INC
Also Called: Mount Vernon Electric Mtr Svcs
1120 W Division St (98273-3230)
PHONE 360 424-3239
Fax: 360 424-3230
EMP: 2
SQ FT: 3,000
SALES (corp-wide): 191.8K **Privately Held**
SIC: 7694 1731 7699 5999 Armature Rewinding Electrical Contractor Repair Services Ret Misc Merchandise
PA: Industrial Electrical Company, Inc.
2701 Hewitt Ave
Everett WA
425 293-0659

(G-6805)
JOAN F SCHLEH
Also Called: Skagit Valley Cheese
17198 Dunbar Rd (98273-8762)
PHONE 360 424-4112
Joan Schleh, *Owner*
Joan Shleh, *Owner*
Steve Shleh, *Manager*
EMP: 2
SALES (est): 70.5K **Privately Held**
SIC: 2022 0291 7389 Cheese, natural & processed; livestock farm, general;

(G-6806)
LA EXCAV & SELECT LOG INC
Also Called: La Excavation
13361 Teak Ln (98273-8571)
P.O. Box 302, Clearlake (98235-0302)
PHONE 360 856-4111
Lincoln Aldridge, *President*
Heidi Aldridge, *Vice Pres*
EMP: 5
SALES: 200K **Privately Held**
SIC: 1794 2411 7389 Excavation work; logging;

(G-6807)
LITHTEX NORTHWEST LLC
2226 Market St (98273-5451)
PHONE 360 424-5945
EMP: 4
SALES (est): 327.9K
SALES (corp-wide): 3.1MM **Privately Held**
SIC: 2752 Commercial printing, offset
PA: Lithtex Northwest L.L.C.
2000 Kentucky St
Bellingham WA 98229
360 676-1977

(G-6808)
M A C I INC
Also Called: Industrial Maintenance & Cnstr
2525 Old Highway 99 S Rd (98273-9093)
PHONE 360 424-7013
Arthur Mantei, *President*
EMP: 39
SQ FT: 2,600
SALES: 3.5MM **Privately Held**
WEB: www.imacinc.com
SIC: 7623 1771 1623 1531 Refrigeration service & repair; concrete work; water, sewer & utility lines; operative builders; gas field services; building site preparation

(G-6809)
MACGREGOR PUBLISHING CO
1100 Roosevelt Ave Ste B (98273-2427)
PHONE 800 581-5040
Linda Mac Gregor, *Partner*
Mac Mac Gregor, *Partner*
Mac Macgregor, *Principal*
EMP: 45
SQ FT: 7,500
SALES (est): 2.5MM **Privately Held**
WEB: www.plaidnet.com
SIC: 2741 2731 Directories: publishing only, not printed on site; pamphlets: publishing only, not printed on site

(G-6810)
MARTIN MARIETTA MATERIALS INC
Also Called: Pacific Quarry
20411 E Hickox Rd (98274-7731)
PHONE 360 424-3441
Bob Wiggens, *Manager*
EMP: 15
SQ FT: 1,304 **Publicly Held**
WEB: www.martinmarietta.com
SIC: 1422 Crushed & broken limestone
PA: Martin Marietta Materials Inc
2710 Wycliff Rd
Raleigh NC 27607

(G-6811)
MARTIN MARIETTA MATERIALS INC
Also Called: Beaver Lake Quarry
14322 Beaver Lake Rd (98273-8065)
PHONE 360 856-5870
Leland Reese, *Branch Mgr*
EMP: 4 **Publicly Held**
WEB: www.martinmarietta.com
SIC: 1422 Crushed & broken limestone
PA: Martin Marietta Materials Inc
2710 Wycliff Rd
Raleigh NC 27607

(G-6812)
MEDICAL PDTS FOR COMFORT INC
Also Called: Med Products Comfort
2301 Martin Rd (98273-5841)
PHONE 360 770-2005
EMP: 3
SALES (est): 220K **Privately Held**
SIC: 3842 Mfg Surgical Appliances/Supplies

(G-6813)
MEYER SIGN & ADVERTISING CO
2608 Old Highway 99 S Rd (98273-9092)
PHONE 360 424-1325
Martin P Boer, *Owner*
Gregg Collins, *Project Mgr*
EMP: 10 **EST:** 1956
SALES (est): 1.2MM **Privately Held**
WEB: www.meyersign.com
SIC: 7319 7389 3993 Display advertising service; sign painting & lettering shop; signs & advertising specialties

(G-6814)
MOUNTAIN TOP INC
Also Called: Copy & Print Store
1726 Riverside Dr (98273-5415)
PHONE 360 416-3333
Zahir Faruqi, *President*
EMP: 5 **EST:** 1990
SALES (est): 671.7K **Privately Held**
SIC: 2759 7334 Decals: printing; photocopying & duplicating services

(G-6815)
MR TS TROPHIES
17691 State Route 536 (98273-3272)
P.O. Box 1148 (98273-1148)
PHONE 360 424-9339
Dawn Latimer, *Manager*
EMP: 6
SALES (corp-wide): 1.2MM **Privately Held**
WEB: www.mrtstrophies.com
SIC: 5699 5999 3479 2395 Sports apparel; trophies & plaques; engraving jewelry silverware, or metal; embroidery products, except schifli machine
PA: Mr T's Trophies
7900 Ne Bothell Way
Bothell WA 98028
425 485-2858

(G-6816)
NATIONAL WIRECRAFT COMPANY INC
Also Called: Vergon Medical Products
1012 W Division St (98273-3228)
PHONE 360 424-1129
▲ **EMP:** 15 **EST:** 1964
SQ FT: 30,000
SALES: 2MM **Privately Held**
SIC: 3496 3449 Mfg Miscellaneous Fabricated Wire Products Mfg Miscellaneous Metalwork

(G-6817)
NATIONAL WIRECRAFT COMPANY INC
Also Called: Wirefab Company
1012 W Division St (98273-3228)
PHONE 360 424-1129
Terry Sanderson, *President*
▲ **EMP:** 15
SQ FT: 30,000
SALES (est): 2.2MM **Privately Held**
SIC: 3496 Miscellaneous fabricated wire products

(G-6818)
NORTHWIND INDUSTRIES
4417 Landmark Dr (98274-8733)
PHONE 360 424-6689
Marvin Wilbur, *Principal*
EMP: 2 **EST:** 2008
SALES (est): 101.8K **Privately Held**
SIC: 3999 Manufacturing industries

(G-6819)
OSBORNE WOODWORKS
13848 Avon Allen Rd (98273-6909)
PHONE 360 428-0245
Jeff Osborne, *Principal*

▲ = Import ▼ = Export
◆ = Import/Export

GEOGRAPHIC SECTION — Mount Vernon - Skagit County (G-6850)

EMP: 2
SALES (est): 231K **Privately Held**
SIC: 2431 Millwork

(G-6820)
PACCAR INC
12479 Farm To Market Rd (98273-9690)
PHONE..................................360 757-5357
Margaret Sullivan, *Manager*
EMP: 150
SALES (corp-wide): 23.5B **Publicly Held**
WEB: www.paccar.com
SIC: 3711 Truck & tractor truck assembly
PA: Paccar Inc
   777 106th Ave Ne
   Bellevue WA 98004
   425 468-7400

(G-6821)
PAM S BUBBLE MOBILE
17027 Lake View Blvd (98274-8176)
PHONE..................................360 630-5511
Pam Julian, *Principal*
EMP: 2
SALES (est): 102.7K **Privately Held**
SIC: 3999 Pet supplies

(G-6822)
PASEK CELLARS WINERY INC
2629 Old Hwy 99 S Ste B (98273-9092)
PHONE..................................888 350-9463
Gene D Pasek, *President*
Kathy L Pasek, *Vice Pres*
David James, *Admin Sec*
EMP: 2
SALES (est): 220.3K **Privately Held**
WEB: www.pasekcellars.com
SIC: 2084 Wines

(G-6823)
PERDUE FOODS LLC
Also Called: Draper Valley Farms
1000 Jason Ln (98273-2490)
PHONE..................................360 424-7947
EMP: 475
SALES (corp-wide): 6B **Privately Held**
SIC: 0254 2015 Chicken hatchery; chicken, processed
HQ: Perdue Foods Llc
   31149 Old Ocean City Rd
   Salisbury MD 21804

(G-6824)
PETRZELKA BROS INC
Also Called: Pbi
2320 Cedar Ct (98273-3617)
P.O. Box 1334 (98273-1334)
PHONE..................................360 424-8095
John Petrzelka, *President*
Joel Petrzelka, *Corp Secy*
Paul Petrzelka, *Vice Pres*
EMP: 7
SQ FT: 5,000
SALES: 620K **Privately Held**
SIC: 3732 3949 5551 5941 Fishing boats: lobster, crab, oyster, etc.: small; fishing equipment; motor boat dealers; fishing equipment

(G-6825)
PRESTIGE FINE JEWELRY
3601 Mohawk Dr (98273-3766)
PHONE..................................206 623-0085
Deborah Blaurock, *President*
EMP: 7
SQ FT: 1,500
SALES: 700K **Privately Held**
SIC: 3911 5944 Jewelry, precious metal; jewelry, precious stones & precious metals

(G-6826)
PRINTWISE INC
Also Called: Print Streams
2226 Market St Unit Main (98273-5451)
PHONE..................................360 424-5945
Bob Singer, *President*
Debbra Singer, *Vice Pres*
EMP: 12
SQ FT: 45,000
SALES: 1.3MM **Privately Held**
WEB: www.printwiseinc.com
SIC: 2752 Commercial printing, lithographic

(G-6827)
PROFORMA CRTIVE PRTG SOLUTIONS
2119 N Trumpeter Dr (98273-8967)
PHONE..................................360 848-7714
Bob Lama, *Owner*
Maureen Lama, *Co-Owner*
EMP: 2 EST: 2000
SALES: 800K **Privately Held**
SIC: 5734 2759 Computer software & accessories; promotional printing

(G-6828)
RIVER CITY SCREENPRINTING
222 Anderson Rd Ste D (98273-9033)
PHONE..................................360 428-8985
Kyle Davis, *Owner*
Barbara Davis, *COO*
EMP: 5
SALES (est): 484.4K **Privately Held**
WEB: www.rivercityscreenprint.com
SIC: 2759 Screen printing

(G-6829)
ROOFING SERVICES INC
Also Called: R S I
1005 W Hazel St (98273-6504)
P.O. Box 699 (98273-0699)
PHONE..................................425 347-1146
Larry Trim, *President*
Brent Yeadon, *Vice Pres*
Gayle Yeadon, *Treasurer*
EMP: 12
SQ FT: 12,000
SALES: 1.7MM **Privately Held**
WEB: www.rsimetal.com
SIC: 3444 Sheet metalwork

(G-6830)
ROZEMA BOAT WORKS INC
11130 Bayview Edison Rd (98273-8216)
PHONE..................................360 757-6004
Dirk Rozema, *President*
Jason Rozema, *Corp Secy*
▲ EMP: 10
SQ FT: 10,000
SALES (est): 2.4MM **Privately Held**
SIC: 3731 3444 Shipbuilding & repairing; sheet metalwork

(G-6831)
ROZEMA ENTERPRISES INC
Also Called: Rozema Boat Works
11130 Bayview Edison Rd (98273-8216)
PHONE..................................360 757-6004
Barbara Rozema, *President*
Clarence Rozema, *Corp Secy*
EMP: 9
SQ FT: 7,000
SALES (est): 770K **Privately Held**
WEB: www.rozemaboatworks.com
SIC: 7359 5551 3732 3731 Equipment rental & leasing; boat dealers; boat building & repairing; shipbuilding & repairing

(G-6832)
SALISH POST ENTERPRISES LLC
Also Called: Skagit Vly Malting & Brewing
10788 Seaview Ln (98273-7200)
PHONE..................................360 391-5492
Wayne Carpenter,
EMP: 4
SALES (est): 198K **Privately Held**
SIC: 2083 Malt

(G-6833)
SARCO PRECISION
2816 Old Highway 99 S Rd # 4 (98273-9054)
PHONE..................................360 424-0605
Stephen Jungquist, *Owner*
EMP: 11
SQ FT: 7,000
SALES (est): 1MM **Privately Held**
SIC: 3599 Machine shop, jobbing & repair

(G-6834)
SCHENK PACKING CO INC
1321 S 6th St (98273-4919)
PHONE..................................360 336-2128
Doug Richter, *Branch Mgr*
EMP: 20

SALES (corp-wide): 18.7MM **Privately Held**
SIC: 5142 4222 2011 Packaged frozen goods; refrigerated warehousing & storage; beef products from beef slaughtered on site
PA: Schenk Packing Co., Inc.
   8204 288th St Nw
   Stanwood WA 98292
   360 629-3939

(G-6835)
SHUTTLESYSTEM LLC
3302 Cedardale Rd E500 (98274-9548)
PHONE..................................425 551-1335
Paul M Allen,
John D Horning,
Edward J Kramer,
▲ EMP: 10
SALES (est): 1MM **Privately Held**
SIC: 2511 Wood household furniture

(G-6836)
SIGN DEPARTMENT INC
919 E College Way Ste A (98273-5627)
PHONE..................................360 708-3823
Jenna R Urban, *Principal*
EMP: 2 EST: 2012
SALES (est): 142.1K **Privately Held**
SIC: 3993 Signs & advertising specialties

(G-6837)
SKAGIT CELLARS LLC
3200 Shelly Hill Rd (98274-6134)
PHONE..................................360 708-2801
EMP: 4
SALES (est): 250.6K **Privately Held**
SIC: 2084 Wines

(G-6838)
SKAGIT CITY SIGNS INC
Also Called: Sign Pro of Skagit Valley
224 Stewart Rd Ste 201 (98273-9687)
PHONE..................................360 848-8888
Danielle Lawson, *President*
Chad Lawson, *Vice Pres*
EMP: 4 EST: 2009
SALES: 400K **Privately Held**
SIC: 3993 Signs & advertising specialties

(G-6839)
SKAGIT POWDER COATING
14805 Jackpot Ln (98273-3274)
PHONE..................................360 428-0413
Andy Blankinship, *President*
Jennifer Blankinship, *Admin Mgr*
EMP: 9
SALES (est): 1.2MM **Privately Held**
SIC: 3479 Coating of metals & formed products

(G-6840)
SKAGIT READY MIX
Also Called: Smokey Point Conrete
14658 Ovenell Rd (98273-8232)
PHONE..................................360 856-0422
EMP: 7
SALES (est): 32.3K **Privately Held**
SIC: 3273 Ready-mixed concrete

(G-6841)
SKAGIT SEED SERVICES INC
17297 Hulbert Rd (98273-7189)
P.O. Box 276, La Conner (98257-0276)
PHONE..................................360 466-3191
Thomas B Hulbert, *CEO*
Jack D Hulbert, *CEO*
Kathleen Hulbert, *Treasurer*
Rene Hulbert, *Admin Sec*
EMP: 6
SALES (est): 601.7K **Privately Held**
SIC: 3999 5191 Seeds, coated or treated, from purchased seeds; farm supplies

(G-6842)
SKAGITS BEST SALSA
21146 Falcon Ct (98274-7041)
PHONE..................................360 610-9022
Jill Rohrs, *Principal*
EMP: 3
SALES (est): 212.8K **Privately Held**
SIC: 2099 Dips, except cheese & sour cream based

(G-6843)
SMILEYS INC
18022 State Route 536 (98273-3248)
P.O. Box 737 (98273-0737)
PHONE..................................360 424-7338
G Dale Smiley, *President*
Donna Smiley, *Vice Pres*
EMP: 10
SQ FT: 16,000
SALES: 2MM **Privately Held**
WEB: www.smileysstudio.com
SIC: 7699 3441 2353 Farm machinery repair; fabricated structural metal; hats, caps & millinery

(G-6844)
TEAM INC
3302 Cedardale Rd Ste D5 (98274-9502)
P.O. Box 2449 (98273-7449)
PHONE..................................360 848-0353
Tom Tweed, *Manager*
EMP: 22
SALES (corp-wide): 1.2B **Publicly Held**
SIC: 3398 3567 Metal heat treating; heating units & devices, industrial: electric; fuel-fired furnaces & ovens
HQ: Team, Inc.
   5095 Paris St
   Denver CO 80239

(G-6845)
TECH MACHINING USA LLC
1117 Dale Ln Ste D (98274-9604)
PHONE..................................425 754-8221
Chris Branch, *Mng Member*
Natasha Branch,
EMP: 2
SALES (est): 94.5K **Privately Held**
SIC: 3544 Special dies, tools, jigs & fixtures

(G-6846)
THE EUCLID CHEMICAL COMPANY
13527 Farm & Market Rd (98273)
PHONE..................................360 848-1202
Jim Holden, *Branch Mgr*
EMP: 2
SALES (corp-wide): 5.3B **Publicly Held**
SIC: 2899 Chemical preparations
HQ: The Euclid Chemical Company
   19218 Redwood Rd
   Cleveland OH 44110
   800 321-7628

(G-6847)
TRAILREADY PRODUCTS LLC
1005 W Hazel St (98273-6504)
P.O. Box 699 (98273-0699)
PHONE..................................425 353-6776
Larry Trim,
▼ EMP: 10
SALES (est): 1.2MM **Privately Held**
SIC: 2396 Automotive & apparel trimmings

(G-6848)
TRITON HOLDINGS INC
13593 Bayview Edison Rd (98273-8231)
PHONE..................................360 466-4160
Thomas Hsuet, *President*
Paolo Jurkobichas, *Vice Pres*
Theodore Ginsburg, *CFO*
EMP: 15
SALES (est): 3.1MM **Privately Held**
WEB: www.bayviewedisonindustries.com
SIC: 3441 Fabricated structural metal

(G-6849)
TRUMPETER PUBLIC HOUSE
416 Myrtle St (98273-3850)
PHONE..................................360 588-4515
Paul Springer, *Principal*
EMP: 4 EST: 2007
SALES (est): 332.4K **Privately Held**
SIC: 2741 Miscellaneous publishing

(G-6850)
VALLEY AUTOMOTIVE MACHINE
331 E Blackburn Rd (98273-9027)
PHONE..................................360 336-9722
Tim Petersen, *Owner*
Timothy Petersen, *Owner*
EMP: 5
SQ FT: 3,000

Mount Vernon - Skagit County (G-6851)

SALES: 600K **Privately Held**
SIC: 7539 5013 5084 3599 Machine shop, automotive; automotive supplies & parts; engines & parts, diesel; machine shop, jobbing & repair

(G-6851)
VALLEY CABINETS & MORE INC
18362 Burkland Rd (98274-9056)
PHONE..................................360 428-0916
Philip Ernest Hagman, *President*
Debora E Hagman, *Corp Secy*
EMP: 7
SQ FT: 2,800
SALES: 1.2MM **Privately Held**
SIC: 2434 2517 2521 2541 Wood kitchen cabinets; home entertainment unit cabinets, wood; wood office filing cabinets & bookcases; cabinets, office: wood; counter & sink tops; table or counter tops, plastic laminated

(G-6852)
VEHICLE LICENSING
700 S 2nd St Ste 201 (98273-3879)
PHONE..................................360 336-9348
Michael Woodmansee, *President*
EMP: 2
SALES (est): 103.4K **Privately Held**
SIC: 3469 Automobile license tags, stamped metal

(G-6853)
VICTORY ENTERPRISES LLC
1510 Windsor Dr (98273-5659)
PHONE..................................360 420-1161
Steve Grubbs, *CEO*
EMP: 2
SALES (est): 126.7K **Privately Held**
SIC: 7372 Application computer software

(G-6854)
WASHINGTON ALDER LLC
13421 Farm To Market Rd (98273-8273)
PHONE..................................360 542-1900
Richard Tinney,
Jim Allen,
Paula K Norman,
David Syre,
Kay Syre,
▲ EMP: 98
SALES (est): 13.2MM **Privately Held**
WEB: www.wa-alder-llc.com
SIC: 2421 Lumber: rough, sawed or planed

(G-6855)
WHOLE ENERGY FUELS CORPORATION
20 Alder Ln (98273-2424)
PHONE..................................888 600-8611
Hugh Stephenson, *Manager*
EMP: 2
SALES (corp-wide): 4.2MM **Privately Held**
SIC: 2869 Glycerin
PA: Whole Energy Fuels Corporation
2950 Newmarket St Ste 101
Bellingham WA 98226
888 600-8611

(G-6856)
WOLLIN WOODWORKING INC
725 N 1st St (98273-2814)
PHONE..................................360 929-5895
Tyler Wollin, *Principal*
EMP: 3 EST: 2012
SALES (est): 171K **Privately Held**
SIC: 2431 Millwork

Mountlake Terrace
Snohomish County

(G-6857)
ANGSTROM INNOVATIONS INC
4103 223rd St Sw (98043-3647)
PHONE..................................425 750-6329
Dave Ashcroft, *COO*
EMP: 2
SALES (est): 158.2K **Privately Held**
SIC: 2899 7389 Insulating compounds;

(G-6858)
ARCTIC PRINTING & GRAPHICS INC
22314 70th Ave W Ste 6 (98043-2190)
PHONE..................................425 967-0700
Michael Stelma, *President*
EMP: 10
SALES (est): 1.7MM **Privately Held**
WEB: www.arcticprinting.com
SIC: 2752 Commercial printing, offset

(G-6859)
AUDIOCONTROL INC (PA)
22410 70th Ave W Ste 1 (98043-2182)
PHONE..................................425 775-8461
Alexander Camara, *CEO*
Joan McEwen, *Purchasing*
▲ EMP: 32
SALES (est): 6.4MM **Privately Held**
SIC: 3651 Audio electronic systems

(G-6860)
FANTAZIMO FOOD
7102 229th Pl Sw (98043-2308)
PHONE..................................206 484-8232
Peter Gradwohl, *Principal*
EMP: 3
SALES: 120K **Privately Held**
WEB: www.tallecom.com
SIC: 2099 Food preparations

(G-6861)
GOOD WEAR LEATHER COAT COMPANY
5703 215th Pl Sw (98043-3151)
PHONE..................................206 724-6325
EMP: 3
SALES (est): 239.3K **Privately Held**
SIC: 3199 Leather goods

(G-6862)
HAIN REFRIGERATED FOODS INC
Also Called: Greek Gods
21707 66th Ave W (98043-2103)
P.O. Box 1994, Woodinville (98072-1994)
PHONE..................................425 485-2476
Basel Nassar, *CEO*
Irwin D Simon, *President*
Stephanos Margaritis, *Principal*
EMP: 18
SQ FT: 3,750
SALES: 107MM **Publicly Held**
SIC: 2024 5143 Ice cream & ice milk; yogurt
PA: The Hain Celestial Group Inc
1111 Marcus Ave Ste 100
New Hyde Park NY 11042

(G-6863)
HAPPILY EVER AFTER
23508 65th Pl W (98043-2914)
PHONE..................................206 226-8814
Heather A Caspar, *Owner*
EMP: 2
SALES (est): 87.9K **Privately Held**
SIC: 2335 Bridal & formal gowns

(G-6864)
MAXART INC
Also Called: Printing Plus
22410 70th Ave W Ste 12 (98043-2182)
PHONE..................................425 778-1108
P Michael Torres, *President*
Phillip Michael Torres, *President*
EMP: 5
SQ FT: 5,000
SALES: 600K **Privately Held**
WEB: www.prtgplus.com
SIC: 2752 Commercial printing, offset

(G-6865)
PACIFIC PIPE & PUMP LLC
24121 56th Ave W (98043-5503)
PHONE..................................425 640-0376
Nils Petter Dragoy, *Mng Member*
Anne Lise Brooks,
Nils Petter,
▲ EMP: 13
SQ FT: 6,000
SALES: 3.5MM **Privately Held**
WEB: www.pacificpipeonline.com
SIC: 5251 3731 Pumps & pumping equipment; shipbuilding & repairing

(G-6866)
PAUL MIDDLEWOOD
21315 52nd Ave W Apt G144 (98043-3087)
PHONE..................................425 778-4771
Paul Middlewood, *Manager*
EMP: 2 EST: 2017
SALES (est): 62.9K **Privately Held**
SIC: 2711 Newspapers

(G-6867)
RYCO EQUIPMENT INC
6810 220th St Sw (98043-2122)
PHONE..................................425 744-0444
Robert M Ryan, *President*
Dennis J Delahunt, *Vice Pres*
EMP: 20
SQ FT: 15,000
SALES (est): 5.4MM **Privately Held**
SIC: 3556 Smokers, food processing equipment

(G-6868)
SEA COM CORPORATION
7030 220th St Sw (98043-2164)
PHONE..................................425 771-2182
Ralph Muckelrath, *President*
◆ EMP: 13
SALES: 950K **Privately Held**
SIC: 3663 Radio & TV communications equipment

(G-6869)
STELLAR MANAGEMENT INC
22608 44th Ave W (98043-4533)
PHONE..................................206 724-3973
Payal Palta, *President*
EMP: 5
SALES: 250K **Privately Held**
SIC: 6411 7372 Insurance agents, brokers & service; application computer software

(G-6870)
SUNN PHARMACEUTICALS LLC
23303 56th Ave W (98043-4717)
PHONE..................................425 835-0418
EMP: 4 EST: 2011
SALES (est): 150K **Privately Held**
SIC: 2834 Mfg Pharmaceutical Preparations

(G-6871)
SYMETRIX INC
Also Called: Lucid Technologies
6408 216th St Sw Ste A (98043-2093)
PHONE..................................425 640-3331
Dane Butcher, *President*
Kurt Laetz, *CFO*
Julie Ogden, *Admin Sec*
▲ EMP: 38 EST: 1977
SQ FT: 10,000
SALES (est): 8MM **Privately Held**
WEB: www.symetrixaudio.com
SIC: 3679 3663 Recording & playback apparatus, including phonograph; radio & TV communications equipment

(G-6872)
TECHNICAL MARINE AND INDUS LLC
24121 56th Ave W (98043-5503)
PHONE..................................206 717-4466
Troy Bills, *Mng Member*
EMP: 2
SALES: 500K **Privately Held**
SIC: 3731 Shipbuilding & repairing

(G-6873)
VERTICAL VISUAL SOLUTIONS
7036 220th St Sw (98043-2125)
PHONE..................................425 361-1562
Brian Wimer, *Owner*
EMP: 3
SALES (est): 270.9K **Privately Held**
SIC: 5311 2499 7374 Department stores; signboards, wood; computer graphics service

Moxee
Yakima County

(G-6874)
ALEXANDRIA MOULDING INC (HQ)
101 Grant Way (98936-9787)
P.O. Box 169 (98936-0169)
PHONE..................................509 248-2120
Andre Cholette, *President*
Jeff Munly, *General Mgr*
Kera Albertson, *Area Mgr*
John Mac Donald, *Vice Pres*
Martin Hurlbut, *Finance Mgr*
◆ EMP: 246
SQ FT: 205,000
SALES (est): 61.4MM
SALES (corp-wide): 334MM **Privately Held**
WEB: www.alexandriamoulding.com
SIC: 2431 Millwork
PA: Moulure Alexandria Moulding Inc
20352 Power Dam Rd
Alexandria ON K0C 1
613 525-2784

(G-6875)
BLUELINE EQUIPMENT CO LLC
105 N Spokane St (98936-9641)
P.O. Box 1108 (98936-1108)
PHONE..................................509 248-8411
Gregg Marrs, *Principal*
EMP: 34
SALES (corp-wide): 18.9MM **Privately Held**
SIC: 3523 Farm machinery & equipment
HQ: Blueline Equipment Co., Llc
1605 E Mead Ave
Yakima WA 98903
509 248-8411

(G-6876)
C AND R COATINGS LLC
5260 State Route 24 (98936-9762)
PHONE..................................509 949-8515
EMP: 2
SALES (est): 69.9K **Privately Held**
SIC: 3479 Metal coating & allied service

(G-6877)
FAR WEST FABRICATORS INC
7537 Postma Rd (98936-9706)
PHONE..................................509 453-1663
Tye Walker, *Purch Mgr*
EMP: 2
SALES (est): 86.6K **Privately Held**
SIC: 3441 Fabricated structural metal

(G-6878)
FARWEST OPERATING LLC
7537 Postma Rd (98936-9706)
PHONE..................................509 453-1663
Norm Thomas, *CEO*
EMP: 80
SALES (est): 3.6MM **Privately Held**
SIC: 3444 3599 7692 3479 Sheet metalwork; machine & other job shop work; welding repair; coating of metals & formed products; metal cutting services

(G-6879)
JR SIMPLOT COMPANY
Also Called: Simplot Grower Solutions
7528 Postma Rd (98936-9706)
P.O. Box 9 (98936-0009)
PHONE..................................509 248-5756
Dennis Bohanan, *Sls & Mktg Exec*
John Cullen, *Manager*
Dennis Bohannan, *Manager*
Don Page, *Manager*
EMP: 10
SALES (corp-wide): 4.9B **Privately Held**
WEB: www.simplot.com
SIC: 5191 2879 2875 Chemicals, agricultural; agricultural chemicals; fertilizers, mixing only
PA: J.R. Simplot Company
1099 W Front St
Boise ID 83702
208 780-3287

GEOGRAPHIC SECTION

Mukilteo - Snohomish County (G-6905)

(G-6880)
KRONOS MICRONUTRIENTS LP
213 W Moxee Ave (98936-9635)
P.O. Box 1167 (98936-1167)
PHONE..................................509 248-4911
Mark Whitfield, *Partner*
John Bowen, *Partner*
Robert Bowen, *Partner*
▲ **EMP:** 3
SALES (est): 715.2K
SALES (corp-wide): 7.2MM **Privately Held**
SIC: 2875 Fertilizers, mixing only
PA: Cameron Chemicals, Inc.
4530 Prof Cir Ste 201
Virginia Beach VA 23455
757 487-0656

(G-6881)
MARK SHOLTYS
Also Called: Daily Crave Espresso
4809 Beauchene Rd (98936-9734)
PHONE..................................509 930-1725
Mark Sholtys, *Owner*
EMP: 2
SQ FT: 2,260
SALES (est): 85.8K **Privately Held**
SIC: 2095 Roasted coffee

(G-6882)
MOXEE INNOVATIONS CORPORATION
Also Called: Mic
207b W Charron Rd (98936-9647)
P.O. Box 38 (98936-0038)
PHONE..................................509 575-6322
Howard Walker, *President*
EMP: 6
SQ FT: 70,000
SALES (est): 1MM **Privately Held**
SIC: 3568 Power transmission equipment

(G-6883)
NATIONAL FOOD CORPORATION
Also Called: Northwest Egg Sales
1752 Deering Off Rd (98936)
PHONE..................................509 457-4031
Linda Rixe, *Owner*
EMP: 11
SALES (corp-wide): 333.2MM **Privately Held**
WEB: www.natlfood.com
SIC: 0252 2015 Chicken eggs; egg processing
PA: National Food Corporation
728 134th St Sw Ste 103
Everett WA 98204
425 349-4257

(G-6884)
PERRAULT MANUFACTURING INC
5700 Beauchene Rd (98936-9459)
PHONE..................................509 248-9905
Ken Perrault, *President*
Chuck Perrault, *Vice Pres*
EMP: 2
SALES: 200K **Privately Held**
SIC: 3523 Harvesters, fruit, vegetable, tobacco, etc.; sprayers & spraying machines, agricultural

(G-6885)
SHARPS WELDING & MUFFLER CTR
Also Called: Sharp's Fabricating & Muffler
212 E Moxee Ave (98936)
PHONE..................................509 452-2101
William T Sharp, *Owner*
Patricia Sharp, *Co-Owner*
EMP: 4
SALES (est): 226.8K **Privately Held**
SIC: 7533 7692 3444 Muffler shop, sale or repair & installation; welding repair; sheet metalwork

(G-6886)
SICKSPEED INC
508 Baker St (98936-9018)
PHONE..................................509 833-3768
Jason Jordan, *President*
▲ **EMP:** 7
SALES (est): 717.8K **Privately Held**
SIC: 3711 Automobile bodies, passenger car, not including engine, etc.

(G-6887)
SNAPIDLE
207b W Charron Rd (98936-9647)
P.O. Box 38 (98936-0038)
PHONE..................................509 575-6322
Randy Walker, *CEO*
Howard Walker, *CEO*
EMP: 5
SALES (est): 500K **Privately Held**
WEB: www.snapidle.com
SIC: 3568 Power transmission equipment

(G-6888)
ULTRA YIELD MICRONUTRIENTS INC
213 W Moxee Ave (98936-9635)
PHONE..................................509 248-4911
Robert Bowen, *Ch of Bd*
Mark Whitfield, *President*
John Bowen, *Vice Pres*
EMP: 3
SQ FT: 8,000
SALES (est): 646.2K
SALES (corp-wide): 7.2MM **Privately Held**
SIC: 2873 Nitrogenous fertilizers
PA: Cameron Chemicals, Inc.
4530 Prof Cir Ste 201
Virginia Beach VA 23455
757 487-0656

Mukilteo
Snohomish County

(G-6889)
ACCURATE SHEET METAL INC
Also Called: A S M
4301 Russell Rd (98275-5485)
P.O. Box 126 (98275-0126)
PHONE..................................425 745-6786
Carol Peterson, *President*
Sloane Scott, *Buyer*
Paula Blood, *Controller*
EMP: 27
SQ FT: 25,000
SALES (est): 6.6MM **Privately Held**
SIC: 3444 3312 Sheet metalwork; structural shapes & pilings, steel

(G-6890)
AERO MAC INC
4602 Chennault Beach Rd D1 (98275-5016)
PHONE..................................425 348-4140
Kimberly Ducker, *President*
Dick Carlburg, *Vice Pres*
Rollyn Ducker, *Treasurer*
Jayne Carlburg, *Admin Sec*
EMP: 6
SALES (est): 500K **Privately Held**
WEB: www.aeromac.com
SIC: 2399 Banners, pennants & flags

(G-6891)
AIRWORTHNESS DRCTIVE SOLUTIONS
9461 53rd Ave W (98275-3344)
P.O. Box 855 (98275-0855)
PHONE..................................425 876-9742
Gordon Tylosky, *President*
EMP: 3
SALES (est): 400K **Privately Held**
SIC: 3728 Aircraft assemblies, subassemblies & parts

(G-6892)
ALLIED GRINDERS INC (PA)
Also Called: Allied Ice
11431 Cyrus Way (98275-5402)
PHONE..................................425 493-1313
John M Grosso, *President*
Sherry Parks-Grosso, *Corp Secy*
EMP: 12
SQ FT: 6,000
SALES (est): 3.4MM **Privately Held**
SIC: 5983 2097 5999 Fuel oil dealers; manufactured ice; ice

(G-6893)
APPLIED FINISHING INC
4216 Russell Rd (98275-5418)
PHONE..................................425 513-2505
Randall Bickle, *President*
Michael Alligood, *Vice Pres*
Joseph Brown, *Shareholder*
EMP: 22
SQ FT: 15,000
SALES (est): 2.8MM **Privately Held**
WEB: www.appliedfinishing.com
SIC: 3479 3089 3471 Coating of metals & formed products; plastic processing; finishing, metals or formed products

(G-6894)
ASKO INDUSTRIAL REPAIR
12128 Cyrus Way Ste B (98275-5700)
PHONE..................................206 284-2659
David G Kelley, *President*
Dean Mc Carty, *General Mgr*
EMP: 10
SQ FT: 8,000
SALES (est): 1MM
SALES (corp-wide): 15.2MM **Privately Held**
SIC: 7699 3728 Hydraulic equipment repair; aircraft parts & equipment
PA: Asko Processing, Inc.
434 N 35th St
Seattle WA 98103
206 634-2080

(G-6895)
ASKO PROCESSING INC
Asko Industrial Repair
12128 Cyrus Way Ste B (98275-5700)
PHONE..................................206 284-2659
Dave Kelly, *President*
EMP: 15
SALES (corp-wide): 15.2MM **Privately Held**
WEB: www.askogroup.com
SIC: 7699 3599 Hydraulic equipment repair; machine shop, jobbing & repair
PA: Asko Processing, Inc.
434 N 35th St
Seattle WA 98103
206 634-2080

(G-6896)
ASKO PROCESSING INC
Asko Selective Plating
12128 Cyrus Way Ste B (98275-5700)
PHONE..................................206 298-9730
Fred Tobin, *Manager*
EMP: 3
SALES (corp-wide): 15.2MM **Privately Held**
WEB: www.askogroup.com
SIC: 3471 Electroplating of metals or formed products
PA: Asko Processing, Inc.
434 N 35th St
Seattle WA 98103
206 634-2080

(G-6897)
BEACON PUBLISHING INC
806 5th St (98275-1628)
PHONE..................................425 347-1711
Paul Archipley, *President*
Linda Chittum, *Vice Pres*
EMP: 15
SALES (est): 980.2K **Privately Held**
SIC: 2711 Newspapers: publishing only, not printed on site

(G-6898)
BM PRGRM & MACHINING SVC INC
Also Called: RB Enterprises
11620 49th Pl W (98275-4255)
P.O. Box 2512, Lynnwood (98036-2512)
PHONE..................................425 743-5373
Binh Mach, *President*
EMP: 10
SQ FT: 8,000
SALES: 940K **Privately Held**
SIC: 3599 Machine shop, jobbing & repair

(G-6899)
BOEING COMPANY
8630 53rd Pl W (98275-3139)
PHONE..................................425 493-8267
Wilmarie Villanueva, *Branch Mgr*
EMP: 895
SALES (corp-wide): 101.1B **Publicly Held**
SIC: 3721 Airplanes, fixed or rotary wing
PA: The Boeing Company
100 N Riverside Plz
Chicago IL 60606
312 544-2000

(G-6900)
BOEING COMPANY
8415 Paine Field Blvd (98275-3239)
PHONE..................................425 266-0616
Charles Carter, *Program Mgr*
Kitt Burton, *Admin Asst*
Dawn Wachter, *Administration*
EMP: 5
SALES (corp-wide): 101.1B **Publicly Held**
SIC: 3721 Aircraft
PA: The Boeing Company
100 N Riverside Plz
Chicago IL 60606
312 544-2000

(G-6901)
C JOHNSON LUMBER COMPANY INC
610 Possession View Ln (98275-2246)
P.O. Box 363 (98275-0363)
PHONE..................................425 353-4222
Cliff Johnson, *President*
EMP: 2
SALES: 4.5MM **Privately Held**
SIC: 2421 Flooring (dressed lumber), softwood

(G-6902)
C4 ENTERPRISES INC
Also Called: Ram Technologies
4605 116th St Sw (98275-5301)
P.O. Box 27 (98275-0027)
PHONE..................................425 347-9200
Greg Wright, *President*
Susie Wright, *CFO*
◆ **EMP:** 35
SQ FT: 46,000
SALES (est): 8.9MM **Privately Held**
WEB: www.ramtechnologies.com
SIC: 3086 Packaging & shipping materials, foamed plastic

(G-6903)
CLEANMASTER
Also Called: Division of Hydramaster
11015 47th Ave W (98275-5019)
PHONE..................................425 775-7272
Steve Brandt, *President*
Bruce Beckmann, *CFO*
EMP: 120
SQ FT: 45,000
SALES (est): 6MM
SALES (corp-wide): 18.9MM **Privately Held**
WEB: www.hydramaster.com
SIC: 3635 Household vacuum cleaners
HQ: Hydramaster Llc
11015 47th Ave W
Mukilteo WA 98275
425 775-7272

(G-6904)
COMPONENT PRODUCTS CORPORATION
11623 Cyrus Way (98275-5405)
PHONE..................................425 355-6800
John R Stone, *President*
Janet Stone, *CFO*
EMP: 13
SQ FT: 5,500
SALES (est): 3MM **Privately Held**
WEB: www.cpc-web.com
SIC: 3728 Aircraft parts & equipment

(G-6905)
COR-TREAD LLC
4493 Russell Rd Ste H (98275-5479)
PHONE..................................425 268-6377
David Smith,
EMP: 2
SALES (est): 62.5K **Privately Held**
SIC: 3999 Manufacturing industries

Mukilteo - Snohomish County (G-6906)

(G-6906)
COX ORTHOTICS INC
4400 Chennault Beach Rd (98275-5047)
PHONE.................................425 493-8015
David Cox, *President*
Kenneth L Cox, *Vice Pres*
EMP: 8
SQ FT: 5,000
SALES: 829K **Privately Held**
WEB: www.coxorthotics.com
SIC: 3842 Foot appliances, orthopedic

(G-6907)
COYOTE CLEANING SYSTEMS INC
4208 Russell Rd Ste J (98275-5425)
PHONE.................................425 776-8002
James M O'Connor, *President*
Mary F O'Connor, *Vice Pres*
EMP: 6
SQ FT: 5,000
SALES (est): 880K **Privately Held**
WEB: www.coyotescrubber.com
SIC: 5087 3541 7349 5999 Janitors' supplies; buffing & polishing machines; building component cleaning service; floor waxing; cleaning equipment & supplies

(G-6908)
CR ENTERPRISES NW LLC
4617 Chennault Beach Rd (98275-5015)
P.O. Box 94 (98275-0094)
PHONE.................................425 290-3800
George Giordano, *Principal*
EMP: 5 EST: 2014
SQ FT: 10,000
SALES (est): 698.7K **Privately Held**
SIC: 3441 Fabricated structural metal

(G-6909)
CURRY CUSTOM CABINETS CORP
4408 Chennault Beach Rd B (98275-5046)
PHONE.................................425 315-9355
EMP: 9 EST: 1999
SQ FT: 6,000
SALES: 800K **Privately Held**
SIC: 2434 2431 1751 Mfg Wood Kitchen Cabinets Mfg Millwork Carpentry Contractor

(G-6910)
CURVETEC MFG
4433 Russell Rd Ste 112 (98275-5445)
PHONE.................................425 760-2844
EMP: 2
SALES (est): 129.8K **Privately Held**
SIC: 3999 Manufacturing industries

(G-6911)
DIAMOND KNOT BREWERY INC
621 Front St (98275-1557)
PHONE.................................425 355-4488
Andy Eason, *President*
Brian Sollenberger, *President*
Robert D Maphet, *Vice Pres*
Andrew Eason, *Branch Mgr*
▲ **EMP:** 7
SALES (est): 734.1K **Privately Held**
WEB: www.diamondknot.com
SIC: 2082 5149 7389 Beer (alcoholic beverage); groceries & related products;

(G-6912)
DIAMOND KNOT BREWING CO INC (PA)
Also Called: Diamond Knot Craft Brewing
4602 Chennault Beach Rd B2
(98275-5016)
PHONE.................................425 355-4488
Robert Maphet, *President*
Andrew Eason, *Corp Secy*
Patrick Ringe, *Vice Pres*
EMP: 95 EST: 1994
SALES: 5.3MM **Privately Held**
WEB: www.diamondknot.com
SIC: 5813 5812 2087 Bars & lounges; grills (eating places); beverage bases

(G-6913)
DIAMOND KNOT BREWING CO INC
Also Called: Diamond Knot Craft Brewing
4602 Chennault Beach Rd B2 (98275-5016)
PHONE.................................425 315-0703
Partrick Ringe, *Branch Mgr*
EMP: 10
SALES (corp-wide): 5.3MM **Privately Held**
SIC: 2082 Ale (alcoholic beverage)
PA: Diamond Knot Brewing Co., Inc.
4602 Chennault Beach Rd B2
Mukilteo WA 98275
425 355-4488

(G-6914)
DIAMOND KNOT BREWING CO INC
621 Front St (98275-1557)
PHONE.................................425 355-4488
Andrew Eason, *Branch Mgr*
EMP: 27
SALES (corp-wide): 5.3MM **Privately Held**
SIC: 2082 5812 Ale (alcoholic beverage); American restaurant
PA: Diamond Knot Brewing Co., Inc.
4602 Chennault Beach Rd B2
Mukilteo WA 98275
425 355-4488

(G-6915)
DLM INC
Also Called: Magicare Services
9800 Harbour Pl Ste 114 (98275-4749)
PHONE.................................425 348-3204
Mark Midkiff, *Ch of Bd*
Diane Midkiff, *Treasurer*
EMP: 15
SQ FT: 8,000
SALES (est): 2.4MM **Privately Held**
WEB: www.fabricpanels.com
SIC: 1742 3471 Acoustical & ceiling work; solar reflecting insulation film; electroplating of metals or formed products

(G-6916)
DURHAM GEO-ENTERPRISES INC
Also Called: Slope Indicator
12123 Harbour Reach Dr (98275-5306)
PHONE.................................770 465-7557
Robert Pitman, *Principal*
EMP: 45 **Privately Held**
WEB: www.durhamgeo.com
SIC: 3829 Instrumentation for reactor controls, auxiliary
PA: Durham Geo-Enterprises, Inc.
2175 W Park Ct
Stone Mountain GA 30087

(G-6917)
DYNAMIC SAFETY LLC
9700 Harbour Pl Ste 218 (98275-4746)
PHONE.................................425 290-9399
Jason Dai, *President*
EMP: 6
SALES (est): 548K **Privately Held**
SIC: 3728 Aircraft parts & equipment

(G-6918)
DYNESCO CORPORATION INC (PA)
Also Called: Dynesco Lighting Services
12242 Championship Cir (98275-5035)
PHONE.................................360 256-0116
Gary Weyman, *President*
EMP: 3
SQ FT: 1,000
SALES: 210K **Privately Held**
SIC: 3646 Commercial indusl & institutional electric lighting fixtures

(G-6919)
EDS AUTOMOTIVE AND MACHINE SP
Also Called: Ed's Automotive & Machine Shop
8622 44th Ave W (98275-3226)
PHONE.................................425 355-7268
Edward Trihey, *Owner*
EMP: 2

SALES (est): 180K **Privately Held**
SIC: 3519 7538 Internal combustion engines; general automotive repair shops

(G-6920)
ELECTROIMPACT INC
4413 Chennault Beach Rd (98275-5048)
PHONE.................................425 348-8090
Peter Zieve, *President*
EMP: 100
SALES (corp-wide): 200MM **Privately Held**
WEB: www.electroimpact.com
SIC: 3542 3769 3546 3429 Machine tools, metal forming type; guided missile & space vehicle parts & auxiliary equipment; power-driven handtools; manufactured hardware (general)
PA: Electroimpact Inc.
4413 Chennault Beach Rd
Mukilteo WA 98275
425 348-8090

(G-6921)
ELECTROIMPACT INC
4630 Chennault Beach Rd F (98275-5014)
PHONE.................................425 348-8090
Keith Zealey, *Manager*
EMP: 10
SALES (corp-wide): 200MM **Privately Held**
SIC: 3542 Machine tools, metal forming type
PA: Electroimpact Inc.
4413 Chennault Beach Rd
Mukilteo WA 98275
425 348-8090

(G-6922)
ELECTROIMPACT INC (PA)
4413 Chennault Beach Rd (98275-5048)
PHONE.................................425 348-8090
Peter Zieve, *President*
Michael Zieve, *Vice Pres*
Alex Jones, *Engineer*
Christopher Sutton, *Project Engr*
Justin Fletcher, *Electrical Engi*
◆ **EMP:** 500
SQ FT: 100,000
SALES: 200MM **Privately Held**
WEB: www.electroimpact.com
SIC: 3542 Riveting machines

(G-6923)
EMERALD CITY CABINET CO LLC
11417 Cyrus Way (98275-5481)
PHONE.................................425 429-7887
Darrin Krouse, *Mng Member*
EMP: 2
SALES (est): 17.6K **Privately Held**
SIC: 2434 Wood kitchen cabinets

(G-6924)
EMERALD HILLS COFFEE INC
11502 Cyrus Way (98275-5404)
PHONE.................................800 562-6015
EMP: 3
SALES (est): 123.9K **Privately Held**
SIC: 2095 5812 Coffee extracts; coffee shop

(G-6925)
EVERGREEN FORMS SERVICES
Also Called: Evergreen Print Solutions
9800 Harbour Pl Ste 202 (98275-4749)
PHONE.................................425 740-2927
William McDonnell, *President*
Sue McDonnell, *Corp Secy*
EMP: 5
SQ FT: 2,500
SALES (est): 536.3K **Privately Held**
WEB: www.evergreenps.com
SIC: 2761 Unit sets (manifold business forms)

(G-6926)
EVERGREEN PACIFIC PUBLISHING
4204 Russell Rd Ste M (98275-5424)
PHONE.................................425 493-1451
Paul Hamstra, *Principal*
▲ **EMP:** 2
SALES (est): 145.5K **Privately Held**
SIC: 2741 Miscellaneous publishing

(G-6927)
GBJC INC
Also Called: Mukilteo Coffee Company
10809 47th Ave W A (98275-5001)
P.O. Box 862, Langley (98260-0862)
PHONE.................................360 321-5262
Gary Smith, *President*
Beth Smith, *Corp Secy*
Jerry Kaloper, *Vice Pres*
▲ **EMP:** 5
SQ FT: 5,000
SALES (est): 610K **Privately Held**
SIC: 2095 5149 5499 Roasted coffee; coffee & tea; beverage stores

(G-6928)
GLOBODYNE INDUSTRIES INC
4679 Arbors Cir (98275-6086)
PHONE.................................425 321-9471
EMP: 2
SALES (est): 118.5K **Privately Held**
SIC: 3999 Manufacturing industries

(G-6929)
GOMPF BRACKETS INC (PA)
12426 Mukilteo Speedway (98275-5731)
PHONE.................................425 348-5002
Lee Gompf, *President*
Shirley Gompf, *Vice Pres*
▲ **EMP:** 15
SQ FT: 23,000
SALES (est): 1.9MM **Privately Held**
WEB: www.bracket.com
SIC: 3441 3469 3444 2396 Fabricated structural metal; metal stampings; sheet metalwork; automotive & apparel trimmings

(G-6930)
HARBOUR POINTE GOLF LLC
Also Called: Harbour Pointe Golf Assn
11817 Harbour Pointe Blvd (98275-5200)
PHONE.................................425 355-6060
Mark Rhodes, *Mng Member*
EMP: 6 EST: 2007
SALES (est): 23.9K **Privately Held**
SIC: 3949 Shafts, golf club

(G-6931)
HD PACIFIC INC (PA)
Also Called: Hanson Ding Pacific
4606 107th St Sw (98275-4706)
PHONE.................................425 481-3031
Eugene Ding, *President*
Yujian Zeng, *Accountant*
▲ **EMP:** 18
SQ FT: 20,000
SALES: 5MM **Privately Held**
WEB: www.hdpacific.com
SIC: 3674 Semiconductors & related devices

(G-6932)
HF ACQUISITION CO LLC
Also Called: Healthfirst
11629 49th Pl W (98275-4255)
PHONE.................................800 331-1984
Christian Nye, *Controller*
Don Cohen, *Officer*
James Breslawski,
EMP: 30
SALES (est): 5.9MM
SALES (corp-wide): 13.2B **Publicly Held**
SIC: 3842 3843 Surgical appliances & supplies; dental equipment & supplies
PA: Henry Schein, Inc.
135 Duryea Rd
Melville NY 11747
631 843-5500

(G-6933)
HIGHER POWER SUPPLIES INC
Also Called: Industrial Fans Direct
9700 Harbour Pl Ste 128 (98275-4746)
PHONE.................................425 438-0990
Bryan Holmes, *President*
Douglas Date, *General Mgr*
Niklas Halladay, *Sales Mgr*
Julie Post, *Info Tech Mgr*
▼ **EMP:** 6
SQ FT: 2,600
SALES: 4.6MM **Privately Held**
WEB: www.higherpowersupplies.com
SIC: 5999 3564 Cleaning equipment & supplies; blowers & fans; ventilating fans; industrial or commercial

GEOGRAPHIC SECTION

Mukilteo - Snohomish County (G-6961)

(G-6934)
HIMALAYAN CORPORATION
Also Called: Himalayan Dog Chew
4480 Chennault Beach Rd (98275-5020)
PHONE.................................425 322-4295
Sujan Shrestha, *CEO*
Suman Shrestha, *President*
Jill Flores, *Opers Mgr*
Laureen Maninger, *Accounting Mgr*
Nishes Shrestha, *Admin Sec*
▲ **EMP:** 56 **EST:** 2008
SQ FT: 37,000
SALES: 9.6MM **Privately Held**
SIC: 2047 Dog food

(G-6935)
HONEYCUTT MACHINE INC
12402 Evergreen Dr (98275-5708)
PHONE.................................425 493-0525
Mike Luitgaarden, *President*
EMP: 35
SQ FT: 15,000
SALES (est): 5.4MM **Privately Held**
WEB: www.honeycuttmachine.com
SIC: 3599 Machine shop, jobbing & repair

(G-6936)
HONEYCUTT MANUFACTURING LLC
12402 Evergreen Dr (98275-5708)
PHONE.................................425 493-0525
Ronald Honeycutt, *President*
Sheri Honeycutt, *Corp Secy*
Tim Honeycutt, *Sales Staff*
EMP: 33
SQ FT: 15,000
SALES: 6MM **Privately Held**
SIC: 3599 Machine shop, jobbing & repair

(G-6937)
HOWATT COMPANY INC
12212 Cyrus Way (98275-5702)
P.O. Box 14877, Mill Creek (98082-2877)
PHONE.................................425 743-4682
EMP: 18
SQ FT: 16,000
SALES: 2.3MM **Privately Held**
SIC: 3069 2273 2449 Mfg Fabricated Rubber Products Mfg Carpets/Rugs Mfg Wood Containers

(G-6938)
HYDRAMASTER LLC (HQ)
Also Called: Hydramaster North America Inc
11015 47th Ave W (98275-5019)
PHONE.................................425 775-7272
Josh Howard, *President*
Doyle Bloss, *Vice Pres*
Robert Dobbs, *Vice Pres*
Chris Ryan, *Project Mgr*
Mikkel Joensen, *Finance Dir*
◆ **EMP:** 65
SQ FT: 66,000
SALES (est): 18.9MM **Privately Held**
WEB: www.hydramaster.com
SIC: 3582 3635 Rug cleaning, drying or napping machines: commercial; carpet shampooer

(G-6939)
ICG CORP
4403 Russell Rd Ste 116 (98275-5423)
PHONE.................................425 315-0200
Fred Martens, *Principal*
EMP: 2 **EST:** 2002
SALES (est): 131.4K **Privately Held**
SIC: 3965 Fasteners

(G-6940)
ID INTEGRATION INC (PA)
Also Called: ID Integration
13024 Beverly Park Rd # 104 (98275-5857)
PHONE.................................425 438-2533
Gary Moe, *President*
EMP: 12
SQ FT: 3,300
SALES (est): 1.6MM **Privately Held**
WEB: www.id-integration.com
SIC: 3825 7373 2759 8711 Test equipment for electronic & electric measurement; computer integrated systems design; commercial printing; engineering services

(G-6941)
IDL PRECISION MACHINING LLC
11600 49th Pl W Ste A (98275-4256)
PHONE.................................425 315-8080
Robert Peha, *President*
Dean Handaly, *Principal*
EMP: 47
SQ FT: 5,000
SALES (est): 9.2MM **Privately Held**
SIC: 3599 Machine shop, jobbing & repair

(G-6942)
IMMUNOBIOSCIENCE CORP
12121 Harbour Rch Dr 11 (98275)
PHONE.................................425 367-4601
Bader Siddiki, *President*
Nikki Siddiki, *Vice Pres*
EMP: 3
SQ FT: 2,200
SALES: 200K **Privately Held**
SIC: 2836 Biological products, except diagnostic

(G-6943)
INSTA-LEARN BY STEP INC
11324 Mukilteo Spdwy # 4 (98275-5439)
P.O. Box 3177, Edmonds (98020-0045)
PHONE.................................425 355-9830
Millie Morgan, *President*
Ronald Morgan, *Vice Pres*
EMP: 3
SALES (est): 281.5K **Privately Held**
WEB: www.insta-learn.com
SIC: 3999 Education aids, devices & supplies

(G-6944)
INTERIOR CONSTRUCTION SPC
Also Called: I C S
11527 Cyrus Way Ste 1 (98275-5446)
PHONE.................................425 745-8343
Ernest Gonzalez Jr, *President*
EMP: 10
SQ FT: 8,000
SALES (est): 1.1MM **Privately Held**
SIC: 2431 5031 Millwork; doors

(G-6945)
IVARS INC
Also Called: Ivar's Commissary
11777 Cyrus Way (98275-5406)
PHONE.................................425 493-1402
Kevin Stalcup, *Plant Mgr*
Frank Madigan, *CFO*
Tom Ward, *Accounts Exec*
Peg Hamill, *Sales Staff*
Walt Pillman, *Director*
EMP: 20
SQ FT: 25,000
SALES (corp-wide): 42.8MM **Privately Held**
WEB: www.ivars.com
SIC: 2038 Soups, frozen
PA: Ivar's, Inc.
1001 Alaskan Way Ste 109
Seattle WA
206 587-6500

(G-6946)
JUMBO FOODS INC
Also Called: Emerald Hills Coffee
11502 Cyrus Way (98275-5404)
P.O. Box 1100 (98275-1100)
PHONE.................................425 355-1103
William Mynar, *CEO*
Stephen Giles, *President*
Susan Oliver, *Corp Secy*
EMP: 200
SQ FT: 22,000
SALES (est): 31.3MM **Privately Held**
SIC: 2099 5145 5149 Sandwiches, assembled & packaged: for wholesale market; snack foods; coffee, green or roasted

(G-6947)
KAASCO INC
Also Called: Kaas Tailored
13000 Beverly Park Rd A (98275-5852)
PHONE.................................425 412-2460
Jeff Kaas, *President*
Darrin Wright, *Prdtn Mgr*
Tom Thompson, *Purchasing*
Ken Govertsen, *Manager*
Jason Smith, *Manager*
▲ **EMP:** 150
SQ FT: 48,000

SALES: 14.2MM **Privately Held**
WEB: www.kaastailored.com
SIC: 2512 Living room furniture: upholstered on wood frames

(G-6948)
KING MACHINE LLC
11710 Cyrus Way (98275-5452)
PHONE.................................425 743-5464
EMP: 10
SALES: 539.9K **Privately Held**
SIC: 3599 3569 Machine shop, jobbing & repair; lubrication machinery, automatic

(G-6949)
LINEAR CONTROLS INC
Also Called: L C I
9461 53rd Ave W (98275-3344)
P.O. Box 855 (98275-0855)
PHONE.................................425 876-9742
Gordon Tylosky, *President*
EMP: 4
SALES: 75K **Privately Held**
WEB: www.linearcontrolsinc.com
SIC: 3728 Aircraft assemblies, subassemblies & parts

(G-6950)
LOCKNANE INC
11417 Cyrus Way Ste 3 (98275-5481)
PHONE.................................425 493-8300
Duane Locknane, *CEO*
Brent Locknane, *President*
Duane R Locknane, *Chairman*
Susan Locknane, *Corp Secy*
Tara Locknname, *Admin Sec*
▲ **EMP:** 30
SALES (est): 4.3MM **Privately Held**
WEB: www.locknane.com
SIC: 2385 2329 2339 2326 Aprons, waterproof: made from purchased materials; jackets (suede, leatherette, etc.), sport: men's & boys'; jackets, untailored: women's, misses' & juniors'; men's & boys' work clothing; men's & boys' suits & coats

(G-6951)
LORTONE INC
12130 Cyrus Way (98275-5700)
PHONE.................................425 493-1600
Doug Guthrie, *President*
Kathleen O Guthrie, *Vice Pres*
EMP: 12
SQ FT: 15,000
SALES (est): 3.1MM **Privately Held**
WEB: www.lortone.com
SIC: 3541 5085 Grinding, polishing, buffing, lapping & honing machines; lapidary equipment

(G-6952)
MANTA NETWORK TECHNOLOGIES LLC
12172 Wilmington Way (98275-6019)
PHONE.................................202 713-0508
Ricky Rivera, *Mng Member*
EMP: 2
SALES (est): 118K **Privately Held**
SIC: 3357 7376 7379 8742 Fiber optic cable (insulated); computer facilities management; computer related consulting services; management consulting services; business consulting;

(G-6953)
MANUFACTURING & DESIGN INC
4420 Russell Rd Ste A (98275-5460)
PHONE.................................425 356-2648
Greg Hansen, *President*
EMP: 5
SQ FT: 4,500
SALES: 661K **Privately Held**
SIC: 3599 Machine shop, jobbing & repair

(G-6954)
MUKILTEO BEACON
806 5th St (98275-1628)
PHONE.................................425 347-5634
Paul Archipley, *Owner*
EMP: 9 **EST:** 1990
SQ FT: 3,030

SALES (est): 360.8K **Privately Held**
WEB: www.mukilteobeacon.com
SIC: 2711 Newspapers, publishing & printing

(G-6955)
NEW TECH INDUSTRIES INC
7911 44th Ave W (98275-2799)
PHONE.................................425 374-3814
Joanne Bigelow, *President*
EMP: 30
SQ FT: 24,000
SALES (est): 5.3MM **Privately Held**
WEB: www.newtechind.com
SIC: 3599 3544 Machine & other job shop work; special dies, tools, jigs & fixtures

(G-6956)
NORTHWAY PRODUCTS INC
Also Called: Northway Prdcts/Mthers Contrls
11027 47th Ave W (98275-5019)
PHONE.................................425 493-1127
Philip Kulishov, *CEO*
EMP: 25
SQ FT: 17,000
SALES: 3.2MM
SALES (corp-wide): 1.4MM **Privately Held**
SIC: 3599 Machine shop, jobbing & repair
HQ: American Metal Manufacturing Company
11027 47th Ave W
Mukilteo WA 98275
425 493-1127

(G-6957)
NORTHWESTERN FUEL LDSCPG SUPS
Also Called: Super Cedar Firestarters
4493 Russell Rd Ste A (98275-5479)
PHONE.................................425 743-1550
Lara May Lambert, *Owner*
Thomas Reynolds, *Manager*
EMP: 2
SQ FT: 10,000
SALES: 700K **Privately Held**
WEB: www.nwfuel.com
SIC: 2869 Fuels

(G-6958)
NOVANTA INC
Also Called: Synrad
4600 Campus Pl (98275-5305)
PHONE.................................425 349-1359
Melissa Corpuz, *Buyer*
EMP: 125 **Publicly Held**
SIC: 3699 Laser systems & equipment
PA: Novanta Inc.
125 Middlesex Tpke
Bedford MA 01730

(G-6959)
OLIVE SEATTLE OIL CO
10317 Marine View Dr (98275-4507)
P.O. Box 1854, Woodinville (98072-1854)
PHONE.................................425 740-6055
Raman Patel, *President*
▲ **EMP:** 3
SALES (est): 221.3K **Privately Held**
SIC: 2079 Olive oil

(G-6960)
OMNITEC DESIGN INC
4640 Campus Pl Ste 100 (98275-5311)
PHONE.................................425 290-3922
Pavel Mazac, *President*
Kathleen Mazac Stack, *Vice Pres*
EMP: 10
SQ FT: 8,000
SALES (est): 1.8MM **Privately Held**
WEB: www.omnitecdesign.com
SIC: 3564 Air cleaning systems

(G-6961)
ORCA BEVERAGE INC
11903 Cyrus Way Ste 5 (98275-5456)
PHONE.................................425 349-5655
Mike Bourgeois, *Owner*
Charles Funk, *CFO*
Mabel Snow, *Assistant*
◆ **EMP:** 13
SQ FT: 3,000

Mukilteo - Snohomish County (G-6962)

SALES (est): 2.3MM **Privately Held**
WEB: www.orcabeverage.com
SIC: 2086 Soft drinks: packaged in cans, bottles, etc.; carbonated soft drinks, bottled & canned

(G-6962)
ORION INDUSTRIES
13008 Beverly Park Rd (98275-5846)
PHONE..................................425 355-1253
EMP: 129
SALES (corp-wide): 28.7MM **Privately Held**
SIC: 3444 8331 Sheet metalwork; vocational training agency
PA: Orion Industries
   1590 A St Ne
   Auburn WA 98002
   253 661-7805

(G-6963)
PAC WEST SALES INC
11112 47th Ave W (98275-5023)
PHONE..................................425 493-9680
Gary Babb, *President*
Kelly Fahey, *Vice Pres*
EMP: 10
SALES (est): 1.7MM **Privately Held**
SIC: 3432 5074 Plumbing fixture fittings & trim; plumbing fittings & supplies

(G-6964)
PANTHERCORN STUDIOS
Also Called: Panthercorn Publishing
12199 Village Center Pl # 103 (98275-5313)
PHONE..................................425 501-9717
EMP: 2
SALES (est): 87.9K **Privately Held**
SIC: 7372 3944 Prepackaged Software Services Mfg Games/Toys

(G-6965)
PIC SENTRY RAIL INC
Also Called: Glasrail
4215a Russell Rd Ste A (98275-5417)
PHONE..................................425 349-3606
Jack S Junnell, *President*
Jack Junell, *President*
Dan Junell, *Manager*
EMP: 4
SALES (est): 630.3K **Privately Held**
WEB: www.glasrail.com
SIC: 3089 Awnings, fiberglass & plastic combination

(G-6966)
PLEXUS MANUFACTURING INC
4416 Russell Rd (98275-5422)
PHONE..................................425 355-2997
John Thompson, *President*
Lola Thompson, *Corp Secy*
Daniel W Thompson, *Vice Pres*
EMP: 7
SQ FT: 11,520
SALES (est): 790K **Privately Held**
SIC: 3089 Injection molding of plastics

(G-6967)
POWDER COATING INC
Also Called: Craig Craft Powder Coating
11324 Mukilteo Speedway # 7 (98275-5440)
PHONE..................................425 743-4393
Debbie McGeehan, *President*
EMP: 8
SQ FT: 8,500
SALES (est): 1MM **Privately Held**
WEB: www.powdercoatinginc.com
SIC: 3479 3471 Coating, rust preventive; sand blasting of metal parts

(G-6968)
PRODUCTION PLATING INC
4412 Russell Rd (98275-5498)
PHONE..................................425 347-4635
Patrick Keating, *President*
Pat Keating, *Vice Pres*
Marc Wislen, *Vice Pres*
Ronia Billerbeck, *Controller*
Shobby Reynoldson, *Accountant*
◆ EMP: 61
SQ FT: 50,000
SALES (est): 8.6MM **Privately Held**
WEB: www.productionplating.com
SIC: 3471 3479 Electroplating of metals or formed products; coating of metals & formed products

(G-6969)
QUALITY CONCRETE PRODUCTS INC
4200 78th St Sw (98275-2826)
P.O. Box 1609 (98275-7809)
PHONE..................................425 355-5510
Michael O Haug, *President*
Carol Haug, *Admin Sec*
EMP: 20
SALES (est): 3MM
SALES (corp-wide): 30.6B **Privately Held**
SIC: 3272 Concrete products, precast; manhole covers or frames, concrete; covers, catch basin: concrete
HQ: Oldcastle Infrastructure, Inc.
   1002 15th St Sw Ste 110
   Auburn WA 98001
   253 833-2777

(G-6970)
QUEEN CITY PLATING COMPANY INC
11914 Cyrus Way (98275-5408)
PHONE..................................425 315-1992
Richard Frisch, *President*
Gayle Brown, *Vice Pres*
EMP: 6
SQ FT: 5,000
SALES: 723K **Privately Held**
WEB: www.queencityplating.com
SIC: 3471 Electroplating of metals or formed products

(G-6971)
RED ELECTRIC
4433 Russell Rd (98275-5483)
PHONE..................................425 670-7035
EMP: 2
SALES (est): 97.2K **Privately Held**
SIC: 3699 1731 Mfg Electrical Equipment/Supplies Electrical Contractor

(G-6972)
RICH NATURE NUTRACEUTICAL LABS
Also Called: Rich Nature Lab
9700 Harbour Pl Ste 128 (98275-4746)
PHONE..................................425 493-1885
Jinnan Zhang, *President*
Xiaoping Zhang, *Vice Pres*
▲ EMP: 16
SQ FT: 20,000
SALES (est): 2.7MM **Privately Held**
SIC: 2824 Organic fibers, noncellulosic

(G-6973)
RICH NATURE ORGANIC
9700 Harbour Pl Ste 128 (98275-4746)
P.O. Box 1701 (98275-7901)
PHONE..................................425 315-7000
EMP: 2
SALES (est): 108.3K **Privately Held**
SIC: 2099 Food preparations

(G-6974)
S & I PROPELLERS INC
3610 South Rd Ste 100 (98275-5734)
PHONE..................................425 745-1700
Dianne Ives, *President*
EMP: 2 EST: 2009
SALES (est): 208.9K **Privately Held**
SIC: 3366 Propellers

(G-6975)
S3J ELCTRNICS ACQUISITION CORP
Also Called: Momentum Lighting
10323 53rd Ave W (98275-4305)
PHONE..................................716 206-1309
Kristi Doody, *Officer*
William Schmitz, *Officer*
EMP: 6
SALES (est): 950.4K **Privately Held**
SIC: 3646 Commercial indusl & institutional electric lighting fixtures

(G-6976)
SEATTLE AREA TEES
9700 Harbour Pl Ste 130 (98275-4746)
PHONE..................................425 314-3814
Teri Janes, *Principal*
EMP: 2
SALES (est): 98.8K **Privately Held**
SIC: 2759 Screen printing

(G-6977)
SITTAUER INDUSTRIES INC
Also Called: Quality Otbard Boring Sleeving
3610 South Rd Ste 101 (98275-5734)
PHONE..................................425 741-1125
Donn Sittauer, *President*
John Sittauer, *Vice Pres*
EMP: 2 EST: 1991
SALES (est): 125K **Privately Held**
SIC: 3599 Machine shop, jobbing & repair

(G-6978)
SPINNERRACK LLC
10706 57th Pl W (98275-4620)
PHONE..................................425 268-1084
James Demonakos,
EMP: 2
SALES (est): 64.7K **Privately Held**
SIC: 3999 Manufacturing industries

(G-6979)
STANLEY ACCESS TECH LLC
4433 Russell Rd Ste 105 (98275-5483)
PHONE..................................425 493-0482
Dick Dow, *Branch Mgr*
EMP: 7
SALES (corp-wide): 13.9B **Publicly Held**
SIC: 3699 Door opening & closing devices, electrical
HQ: Stanley Access Technologies Llc
   65 Scott Swamp Rd
   Farmington CT 06032

(G-6980)
STR8 SHEET FABRICATIONS LLC
4493 Russell Rd Ste D (98275-5479)
PHONE..................................425 789-1755
Will Webber Jr, *Manager*
EMP: 5 EST: 2014
SALES (est): 537.2K **Privately Held**
SIC: 3444 Sheet metalwork

(G-6981)
SYSTEMS INTERFACE INC
10802 47th Ave W (98275-5000)
PHONE..................................425 481-1225
Scott Demers, *President*
Thoresen Bussinger, *Chairman*
Kathleen Bussinger, *Corp Secy*
Robert H Schnommer, *Vice Pres*
Tj McDermott, *Project Mgr*
EMP: 45
SQ FT: 15,000
SALES (est): 21.6MM **Privately Held**
WEB: www.systems-interface.com
SIC: 3823 Industrial process control instruments

(G-6982)
TML INNOVATIVE PRODUCTS LLC
12333 Evergreen Dr (98275-5707)
PHONE..................................425 290-3994
Thanh Hoang,
EMP: 15
SALES (est): 2.3MM **Privately Held**
SIC: 3634 Coffee makers, electric: household

(G-6983)
TRAVIS INDUSTRIES INC (PA)
Also Called: Lopi
12521 Harbour Reach Dr (98275-5317)
PHONE..................................425 609-2500
Kurt W F Rumens, *President*
Travis W Garske, *Vice Pres*
Sandness Ken, *Vice Pres*
Ken Sandness, *Vice Pres*
Alan Atemboski, *Research*
▲ EMP: 260
SQ FT: 475,000
SALES (est): 42.7MM **Privately Held**
WEB: www.lopistoves.com
SIC: 3433 Stoves, wood & coal burning; logs, gas fireplace

(G-6984)
TRI COASTAL INDUSTRIES
4204 Russell Rd (98275-5424)
PHONE..................................425 353-4384
Bill Britt, *Principal*
EMP: 2
SALES (est): 147K **Privately Held**
SIC: 3999 Manufacturing industries

(G-6985)
UNIENERGY TECHNOLOGIES LLC
Also Called: U E T
4333 Harbour Pt Blvd Sw (98275-5461)
PHONE..................................425 290-8898
Gary Yang, *CEO*
Scott Koznek, *Controller*
Liyu LI, *CTO*
EMP: 55
SQ FT: 20,000
SALES (est): 12.1MM **Privately Held**
SIC: 3691 Storage batteries

(G-6986)
US MARINE CHEMISTS & ENGRG
4986 Dover Ct (98275-6020)
P.O. Box 63 (98275-0063)
PHONE..................................206 200-6912
Philip Dovinh, *Principal*
EMP: 2
SALES (est): 231.1K **Privately Held**
SIC: 3519 Marine engines

(G-6987)
VAN ESSEN INSTRUMENTS DIVISION
12123 Harbour Reach Dr (98275-5306)
PHONE..................................520 203-3445
EMP: 2 EST: 2016
SALES (est): 129.1K **Privately Held**
SIC: 3829 Measuring & controlling devices

(G-6988)
VARTAN PRODUCT SUPPORT LLC
Mukilteo Speedway Ste 204 (98275)
PHONE..................................425 374-8914
Christian Vartan,
EMP: 44
SALES (est): 5.7MM **Privately Held**
SIC: 3449 Landing mats, aircraft: metal

(G-6989)
VIMLY BENEFIT SOLUTIONS INC
12121 Harbour Reach Dr (98275-5314)
P.O. Box 6 (98275-0006)
PHONE..................................425 771-7359
Shannon Jurdana, *CEO*
Tiffanie Quincy, *Accounts Mgr*
Lisa Hamilton, *Sales Staff*
Alex Munoz, *Sales Staff*
Tiffany Hudspeth, *Director*
EMP: 85
SALES (est): 4.4MM **Privately Held**
WEB: www.bsitpa.com
SIC: 8748 8742 6411 7372 Employee programs administration; management consulting services; insurance agents, brokers & service; business oriented computer software

(G-6990)
WAFT CORP
Also Called: Scaler Sales Comp
9806 Marine View Dr (98275-4110)
PHONE..................................425 743-4601
Wallace Trana, *President*
EMP: 10
SALES (est): 861.2K **Privately Held**
SIC: 3822 8741 5065 Electric heat proportioning controls, modulating controls; management services; electronic parts & equipment

(G-6991)
WESTERN SPECIALTIES CO
7924 40th Ave W (98275-2817)
PHONE..................................425 353-9282
Brenda Anderson, *Owner*
Graydon Anderson, *Co-Owner*
EMP: 3
SQ FT: 3,000

GEOGRAPHIC SECTION

SALES (est): 220K **Privately Held**
WEB: www.raincity.com
SIC: 2396 Screen printing on fabric articles

(G-6992)
WIZARD INTERNATIONAL INC
Also Called: Wizard Shipping & Receiving
4600 116th St Sw (98275-5301)
PHONE..............................425 551-4300
Lloyd Everard, *President*
Albert Dahl, *General Mgr*
Wilbur Wridge, *Vice Pres*
Tony Tanis, *Purchasing*
Michael Talcott, *Engineer*
◆ EMP: 65
SQ FT: 10,000
SALES (est): 13.3MM **Privately Held**
WEB: www.wizardint.com
SIC: 3579 7359 Paper handling machines; business machine & electronic equipment rental services

Naches
Yakima County

(G-6993)
ALLAN BROS INC
Also Called: Allan Brothers
31 Allan Rd (98937-9781)
PHONE..............................509 653-2625
George Allan, *Corp Secy*
Dave Allan, *Vice Pres*
Tom Allan, *Manager*
EMP: 100 EST: 1880
SQ FT: 1,500
SALES (est): 50.3MM **Privately Held**
SIC: 0723 4222 2087 2033 Fruit (fresh) packing services; warehousing, cold storage or refrigerated; fruits, crushed: for fountain use; fruits: packaged in cans, jars, etc.

(G-6994)
BYRON AUTOMATION LLC
70 Locust Ln (98937-8801)
P.O. Box 700 (98937-0700)
PHONE..............................509 653-2100
Scott Main, *CEO*
▲ EMP: 15
SQ FT: 35,000
SALES (est): 3.6MM **Privately Held**
WEB: www.byronnelsoncompany.com
SIC: 8711 3535 Mechanical engineering; robotic conveyors

(G-6995)
CITY OF NACHES
10237 Us Highway 12 (98937-9254)
PHONE..............................509 653-1400
Randy Shepard, *President*
EMP: 2 EST: 2010
SALES (est): 110K **Privately Held**
SIC: 2741 Directories, telephone: publishing & printing

(G-6996)
FOUNTAINE ESTATES WINERY
151 Rowe Hill Dr (98937-9631)
PHONE..............................509 972-8123
Amy Robert, *Owner*
EMP: 4
SALES (est): 258K **Privately Held**
SIC: 2084 Wines

(G-6997)
H B Q INC
Also Called: Horseshoe Bend Quarry
3001 State Rte 410 (98937)
P.O. Box 1000 (98937-1000)
PHONE..............................509 653-1939
Ken R Williamson, *President*
Renee Williamson, *Corp Secy*
David Williamson, *Vice Pres*
EMP: 3
SALES (est): 404.3K **Privately Held**
SIC: 1429 Boulder, crushed & broken-quarrying

(G-6998)
JOHN KNUTSON LAPIDARY
13731 Old Naches Hwy (98937-9740)
PHONE..............................509 653-2111
John Knutson, *Principal*

EMP: 2
SALES (est): 110.7K **Privately Held**
SIC: 3915 Jewelers' materials & lapidary work

(G-6999)
KRAGWORKS LLC
26 Orchard St (98937-9776)
PHONE..............................208 871-6413
Justin Pease,
Matt Yeager,
EMP: 2
SALES (est): 56.5K **Privately Held**
SIC: 7372 Application computer software

(G-7000)
NOLAN & SONS NORTHWEST INC
281 Deer View Ln (98937-9437)
P.O. Box 187 (98937-0187)
PHONE..............................509 658-2604
Gail A Nolan, *President*
George D Nolan, *Vice Pres*
EMP: 3
SQ FT: 18,000
SALES (est): 426.6K **Privately Held**
SIC: 3523 5084 Grading, cleaning, sorting machines, fruit, grain, vegetable; food industry machinery

(G-7001)
PCS INDUSTRIES LLC
6401 State Route 410 (98937-9118)
P.O. Box 777 (98937-0777)
PHONE..............................509 406-5852
Jason Herndon, *Principal*
EMP: 2
SALES (est): 91.1K **Privately Held**
SIC: 3999 Manufacturing industries

(G-7002)
QUICK MARKET INC
9951 Us Highway 12 (98937-9720)
PHONE..............................509 653-2268
Makhan Lehel, *Principal*
EMP: 3
SALES (est): 202.6K **Privately Held**
SIC: 5411 2011 Convenience stores; meat packing plants

(G-7003)
SIMMONS DENSIFIED FUELS INC
8871 State Route 410 (98937)
PHONE..............................509 453-6008
Ronald Simmons, *President*
Gerald Simmons, *Vice Pres*
EMP: 4 EST: 1939
SQ FT: 4,616
SALES (est): 337.1K **Privately Held**
SIC: 2421 Wood chips, produced at mill

(G-7004)
SPINNER WOOD PRODUCTS LLC
Also Called: J & J Wood Products
10533 Old Naches Hwy (98937-9774)
P.O. Box 1361, Yakima (98907-1361)
PHONE..............................509 653-2222
Ed Jewett,
EMP: 6 EST: 2012
SALES (est): 677K
SALES (corp-wide): 24.1MM **Privately Held**
SIC: 2448 2449 Pallets, wood; wood containers
PA: H. R. Spinner Corporation
115 S 1st Ave
Yakima WA 98902
509 453-9111

(G-7005)
SPIRIT IN WOOD LLC
11180 State Route 410 (98937-9412)
PHONE..............................509 961-3061
Brin Austin, *Principal*
EMP: 2
SALES (est): 159.7K **Privately Held**
SIC: 2431 Millwork

(G-7006)
TEAM CHINOOK SALES
380 Old River Rd (98937-9557)
PHONE..............................509 949-0929
Ty Brown, *Principal*

EMP: 2
SALES (est): 127.2K **Privately Held**
SIC: 3799 Snowmobiles

(G-7007)
TRICKINNEX TREE TRIMMING & FAL
10383 Old Naches Hwy (98937-9758)
PHONE..............................509 653-1937
Josh Mullinax, *Mng Member*
Patrick Trickey, *Mng Member*
EMP: 2
SALES (est): 300K **Privately Held**
SIC: 0783 2411 Planting, pruning & trimming services; logging

(G-7008)
X BOLT SIGNS LLC
111 Blue Spruce Ln (98937-9616)
P.O. Box 10, Selah (98942-0010)
PHONE..............................509 945-6780
Robert Hill, *Administration*
EMP: 3
SALES (est): 226K **Privately Held**
SIC: 3993 Signs & advertising specialties

(G-7009)
YAKIMA PRESS COMPANY LLC
361 Charlie Ln (98937-7700)
PHONE..............................509 480-0642
EMP: 2 EST: 2011
SALES (est): 105.7K **Privately Held**
SIC: 2741 Misc Publishing

Nahcotta
Pacific County

(G-7010)
HECKES CLAMS INC
Also Called: Heckes Oyster Co
28107 Sandridge Rd (98637)
P.O. Box 1657, Ocean Park (98640-1657)
PHONE..............................360 665-4371
John Heckes, *President*
EMP: 4
SALES (est): 328K **Privately Held**
SIC: 2092 Shellfish, fresh: shucked & packed in nonsealed containers

Napavine
Lewis County

(G-7011)
MCCAIN TIMBER & BRIDGE INC
205 Ruger Ln (98532-4500)
PHONE..............................360 520-6595
Daniel McCain, *President*
EMP: 3
SALES (est): 282.2K **Privately Held**
SIC: 1521 1623 1795 2491 Single-family housing construction; underground utilities contractor; wrecking & demolition work; bridges, treated wood; concrete construction: roads, highways, sidewalks, etc.; bridge construction

Naselle
Pacific County

(G-7012)
C & J LOGGING CO INC
800 State Route 4 (98638-8539)
P.O. Box 798, Ilwaco (98624-0798)
PHONE..............................360 484-7256
Charles Torppa, *President*
Judy Torppa, *Vice Pres*
EMP: 25
SALES (est): 1.5MM **Privately Held**
SIC: 2411 Wooden logs

(G-7013)
JOHN M SMITH
Also Called: Naselle Machine
17 Torppa Rd (98638-8544)
PHONE..............................360 484-7738
John M Smith, *Owner*
Marjorie Smith, *Co-Owner*
EMP: 2

SALES (est): 89K **Privately Held**
SIC: 3599 3911 Machine & other job shop work; jewelry, precious metal

(G-7014)
JOHNSON FORESTRY CONTRACTING
1192 State Route 4 (98638-8511)
PHONE..............................360 484-3311
Harvey M Johnson Jr, *President*
Harvey Johnson, *Vice Pres*
Jeannine Johnson, *Admin Sec*
EMP: 5
SALES (est): 500K **Privately Held**
SIC: 4212 2411 Lumber & timber trucking; logging camps & contractors

(G-7015)
KILPONEN BROS LOGGING INC
9 Cougar Park Ln (98638-8510)
PHONE..............................360 484-7758
Cliff Kilponen, *President*
Jerry Kilponen, *Partner*
EMP: 5
SALES (est): 240K **Privately Held**
SIC: 2411 Wooden logs

(G-7016)
LAND CO LLC
172 Knappton Rd (98638-8614)
P.O. Box 176 (98638-0176)
PHONE..............................360 484-7712
Lorne Wirkkala, *Mng Member*
EMP: 2
SALES (est): 180K **Privately Held**
SIC: 2411 6552 Logging; land subdividers & developers, commercial

(G-7017)
NASELLE ROCK & ASPHALT COMPANY (PA)
50 Crusher Ln (98638-8540)
P.O. Box 5 (98638-0005)
PHONE..............................360 484-3443
Brian Wirkkala, *CEO*
Arnie Wirkkala, *President*
EMP: 18 EST: 1945
SALES: 3MM **Privately Held**
SIC: 2951 1411 Asphalt & asphaltic paving mixtures (not from refineries); basalt, dimension-quarrying

(G-7018)
PACIFIC FORCE MGT & HARVEST
213 Knappton Rd Ste A (98638-8613)
P.O. Box 126 (98638-0126)
PHONE..............................360 484-3854
Howard Wirkkala Jr, *President*
EMP: 3
SALES (est): 50K **Privately Held**
SIC: 2411 Logging camps & contractors

(G-7019)
RAINY DAY ARTISTRY
Also Called: Rainy Day T-Shirt Gallery
178 Government Rd (98638-8605)
PHONE..............................360 484-3681
Jill Merrill, *President*
EMP: 2
SQ FT: 2,000
SALES (est): 225.8K **Privately Held**
WEB: www.rainydayartistry.com
SIC: 2396 5699 Screen printing on fabric articles; T-shirts, custom printed

(G-7020)
STAMBAUGHS HUNGRY HARBOR ENTPS
Also Called: Deflector Marine Rudder
47 Hungry Harbor Ln (98638-8622)
PHONE..............................360 777-8289
Lowell Stambaugh, *Owner*
EMP: 3
SALES: 200K **Privately Held**
SIC: 3732 Boats, fiberglass: building & repairing

(G-7021)
WESTERLUND LOG HANDLERS LLC
496 Parpala Rd (98638-8629)
PHONE..............................503 325-9877
David Westerlund, *Mng Member*
▼ EMP: 40

Nespelem - Okanogan County (G-7022) GEOGRAPHIC SECTION

SALES (est): 5.3MM **Privately Held**
SIC: 2411 Logging

Nespelem
Okanogan County

(G-7022)
MCCLURE RANCH
21 N Star Rd (99155)
P.O. Box 683 (99155-0683)
PHONE..................................509 634-4685
Gary McClure, *Partner*
EMP: 2
SALES (est): 75K **Privately Held**
SIC: 0291 2411 General farms, primarily animals; logging

Newcastle
King County

(G-7023)
AGDECOR
6947 Coal Creek Pkwy Se (98059-3136)
PHONE..................................425 255-2271
EMP: 4
SALES (est): 172.4K **Privately Held**
SIC: 3431 Bathroom fixtures, including sinks

(G-7024)
ARTEMISIA BIOMEDICAL INC
7908 127th Ave Se (98056-9140)
PHONE..................................425 444-5619
Michael V Kuran, *CEO*
EMP: 2
SALES (est): 183.4K **Privately Held**
SIC: 2834 Pharmaceutical preparations

(G-7025)
AVADO INC
6947 Coal Creek Pkwy Se # 242 (98059-3136)
PHONE..................................415 662-8236
Dave Chase, *Principal*
Bassam Saliba, *Principal*
EMP: 2 EST: 2010
SALES (est): 116.4K
SALES (corp-wide): 705MM **Privately Held**
SIC: 7372 Business oriented computer software
HQ: Webmd, Llc
395 Hudson St Fl 3
New York NY 10014

(G-7026)
BELLA CUPCAKE COUTURE LLC
6909 125th Ave Se (98056-1211)
PHONE..................................425 260-3224
Carrie Middlemiss, *CEO*
Ben Middlemiss, *Vice Pres*
EMP: 4 EST: 2008
SALES (est): 489.4K **Privately Held**
SIC: 2621 7359 7389 Greaseproof wrapping paper; party supplies rental services;

(G-7027)
DEES COMMUNICATIONS CORP
14221 Se 78th Way (98059-3242)
PHONE..................................425 276-5269
Louis Champan, *President*
Kay Champan, *Vice Pres*
EMP: 2
SQ FT: 2,400
SALES (est): 220K **Privately Held**
WEB: www.dees.com
SIC: 3695 3661 Computer software tape & disks: blank, rigid & floppy; telephones & telephone apparatus

(G-7028)
DOUG & JUNE HOLT
12769 Se 73rd Pl (98056-1315)
PHONE..................................425 228-6067
June Holt, *Principal*
EMP: 3
SALES (est): 273.6K **Privately Held**
SIC: 3429 Manufactured hardware (general)

(G-7029)
ETHEN FOODS INC
8612 137th Ave Se (98059-3493)
PHONE..................................206 778-0931
Yuh-Sen Chiou, *CEO*
Li-Ll Liang, *Vice Pres*
EMP: 8
SALES (est): 698.3K **Privately Held**
SIC: 2099 Tea blending; syrups

(G-7030)
GLARUS GROUP INC
6947 Coal Creek Pkwy Se (98059-3136)
PHONE..................................425 572-5907
John D Hammerly, *CEO*
Robert W Moisan, *President*
Gary Rosenwald, *Vice Pres*
EMP: 9
SQ FT: 4,100
SALES (est): 2.7MM **Privately Held**
SIC: 7372 4911 8748 7379 Utility computer software; ; systems analysis & engineering consulting services; energy conservation consultant; computer related consulting services; management consulting services

(G-7031)
INSTANT ACCESS VIDEOCOM
12814 Se 80th Way (98056-1746)
PHONE..................................425 273-3496
Michael McMillian, *Principal*
EMP: 2
SALES (est): 149.1K **Privately Held**
SIC: 2752 Commercial printing, lithographic

(G-7032)
INTRADATA INC
6947 Coal Creek Pkwy Se # 17 (98059-3136)
PHONE..................................425 836-8654
EMP: 9
SALES (est): 150K **Privately Held**
SIC: 7372 Prepackaged Software Services

(G-7033)
LEGAL + PLUS SOFTWARE GROUP
Also Called: Legal Plus
6947 Coal Creek Pkwy Se (98059-3136)
PHONE..................................206 286-3600
Fax: 206 283-8445
EMP: 2
SALES (est): 138.9K **Privately Held**
SIC: 7372 Prepackaged Software Services

(G-7034)
LEGAL+PLUS SOFTWARE GROUP INC
6947 Coal Creek Pkwy Se # 35 (98059-3136)
PHONE..................................206 286-3600
Timothy Sooter, *CEO*
Stephen Sooter, *President*
EMP: 5 EST: 1988
SALES (est): 814.1K **Privately Held**
WEB: www.legalplus.com
SIC: 7372 Business oriented computer software

(G-7035)
MAGNUM OPUS SOFTWARE & CO
8021 128th Ave Se (98056-1797)
PHONE..................................425 227-7712
Peter W George, *Principal*
EMP: 2
SALES (est): 109K **Privately Held**
SIC: 7372 Prepackaged software

(G-7036)
MYSTIC WOODWORKING
11428 Se 82nd St (98056-1646)
PHONE..................................425 736-1416
EMP: 2
SALES (est): 85.2K **Privately Held**
SIC: 2431 Millwork

(G-7037)
NORTHWEST BREWERY WORKS INC
7757 142nd Way Se (98059-3258)
PHONE..................................425 255-0698
Cliff Hall, *Principal*
EMP: 2
SALES (est): 134.4K **Privately Held**
SIC: 2099 Food preparations

(G-7038)
PLANO BROS PAVING INC (PA)
9219 Coal Creek Pkwy Se (98059-3328)
PHONE..................................425 226-8210
H Drew Plano, *President*
John C Plano, *Vice Pres*
EMP: 5
SALES: 750K **Privately Held**
SIC: 1794 3531 Excavation work; pavers

(G-7039)
SHERPA FOODS SPC
6947 Coal Creek Pkwy Se (98059-3136)
PHONE..................................425 243-9278
Renzin Yuthok, *CEO*
Josh Schroeter, *President*
Edmond Sanctis,
EMP: 10 EST: 2015
SALES (est): 160K **Privately Held**
SIC: 2043 Cereal breakfast foods

(G-7040)
SHOCKWAVE MEDICAL INC
15309 Se 82nd St (98059-9223)
PHONE..................................425 736-3946
John Adams, *Principal*
Brett McCabe, *Engineer*
Kevin Brounstein, *Mktg Dir*
EMP: 4
SALES (est): 255.6K **Privately Held**
SIC: 3841 Diagnostic apparatus, medical

(G-7041)
TEAMWEST LTD
7701 142nd Way Se (98059-3258)
PHONE..................................425 227-8525
John Brant, *President*
EMP: 3
SALES (est): 230K **Privately Held**
SIC: 3949 Sporting & athletic goods

(G-7042)
WITHIN POWER PUBLISHING
9231 118th Pl Se (98056-2010)
PHONE..................................425 241-4214
Carmela Ramaglia, *Principal*
EMP: 4 EST: 2010
SALES (est): 254.2K **Privately Held**
SIC: 2741 Miscellaneous publishing

Newman Lake
Spokane County

(G-7043)
DANIEL ONEILL
Also Called: At-Spex Lmo Test Solutions
14318 N Meadow Ln (99025-8407)
PHONE..................................509 939-7916
Danny Oneill, *Owner*
EMP: 8
SALES (est): 406.6K **Privately Held**
SIC: 3825 7389 Digital test equipment, electronic & electrical circuits;

(G-7044)
DAVIS TOOL INC
6309 N Harvard Rd (99025-8633)
PHONE..................................509 891-5568
Neil Davis, *President*
Penny Davis, *Admin Sec*
EMP: 2
SALES (est): 313.4K **Privately Held**
SIC: 3089 Injection molding of plastics

(G-7045)
GORDON GRUEL
Also Called: G M K
25720 E Princeton Ave (99025-9302)
PHONE..................................509 226-1309
Gordon Gruel, *Owner*
EMP: 3
SALES: 70K **Privately Held**
SIC: 2759 Commercial printing

(G-7046)
HENTEC INDUSTRIES INC
Also Called: RPS Automation
25517 E Kildea Rd (99025-5115)
P.O. Box 251, Otis Orchards (99027-0251)
PHONE..................................509 891-1680
Reid Henry, *President*
Jessica Henry, *Corp Secy*
▼ EMP: 25
SQ FT: 10,000
SALES: 2.5MM **Privately Held**
SIC: 3548 Soldering equipment, except hand soldering irons

(G-7047)
IRON RANGERS LLC
8401 N Haye Ln (99025-8480)
PHONE..................................509 891-9355
Daniel Osborne,
EMP: 2
SALES: 150K **Privately Held**
SIC: 3499 Fabricated metal products

(G-7048)
JAMISON SIGNS INC
25211 E Trent Ave (99025-6300)
PHONE..................................509 226-2000
Ken Jamison, *President*
Alicia Chantry, *Graphic Designe*
EMP: 6
SQ FT: 8,000
SALES (est): 676.8K **Privately Held**
SIC: 3993 Signs, not made in custom sign painting shops

(G-7049)
NORTHERN MOUNTAIN METALS LLC
Also Called: Cnc Plasma Cutting
25323 E Eddy Ln (99025-9446)
PHONE..................................509 226-1957
Lenny Chase, *Mng Member*
EMP: 2
SALES (est): 162.4K **Privately Held**
SIC: 3444 Sheet metalwork

(G-7050)
NOVA GRAPHICS
5715 N Malta St (99025-9675)
PHONE..................................509 251-2575
Nicola Novakovich, *Owner*
EMP: 2
SALES (est): 69.6K **Privately Held**
SIC: 2721 Periodicals

(G-7051)
PIPE VLVES FTTNGS WRLDWIDE INC
21319 E Harvard Vistas Ln (99025-5101)
PHONE..................................509 991-7191
Jeffrey Wood, *President*
Anna M Wood, *Vice Pres*
EMP: 8
SALES (est): 1.8MM **Privately Held**
SIC: 2679 Pipes & fittings, fiber: made from purchased material

(G-7052)
TIMBERLINE TRUSS AND SUP INC
25414 E Rowan Ave (99025-9631)
P.O. Box 148 (99025-0148)
PHONE..................................509 226-0100
Rory McDonlad, *President*
EMP: 10
SALES (est): 1.2MM **Privately Held**
SIC: 2439 Trusses, wooden roof

Newport
Pend Oreille County

(G-7053)
ALL SEASON OVERHEAD DOOR
9261 Coyote Trl (99156-9308)
PHONE..................................509 218-8303
EMP: 2
SALES (est): 88.9K **Privately Held**
SIC: 3442 Metal doors, sash & trim

▲ = Import ▼ = Export
◆ = Import/Export

GEOGRAPHIC SECTION

(G-7054)
BRUSHWOOD INDUSTRIES LTD
102 Levitch Rd (99156-8799)
PHONE.................................509 447-2266
Steve Yergens, *President*
EMP: 2
SALES (est): 79.8K Privately Held
SIC: 3999 Manufacturing industries

(G-7055)
CHARLO TIMBERLANDS INC
Pend Oreille River Homes (99156)
P.O. Box 783 (99156-0783)
PHONE.................................509 447-3671
Bradford Jason Waterman, *President*
Lois C Waterman, *Corp Secy*
Holly Morgan, *Vice Pres*
EMP: 4
SALES (est): 175.9K Privately Held
SIC: 0811 2411 Timber tracts, hardwood; timber tracts, softwood; logging

(G-7056)
COBBLESTONE INDUSTRIES LLC
1066 Coyote Trl (99156-8845)
PHONE.................................509 447-4518
Linda Rose, *Principal*
EMP: 2
SALES (est): 105.5K Privately Held
SIC: 3999 Manufacturing industries

(G-7057)
DYNAMIC SPECIALTIES
442 City View Ln (99156-8800)
PHONE.................................509 447-2755
IMO Jones, *Owner*
EMP: 2
SALES (est): 161.5K Privately Held
SIC: 7389 3993 Textile & apparel services; brokers, contract services; letters for signs, metal

(G-7058)
GREG ROBERTSON LOGGING INC
322 S Washington Ave (99156-9671)
P.O. Box 629 (99156-0629)
PHONE.................................208 660-3616
Lois Ernst, *Principal*
EMP: 3
SALES (est): 216.9K Privately Held
SIC: 2411 Logging camps & contractors

(G-7059)
J L SHRMAN EXCVTG ROCK CRSHING
1512 Ashenfelter Bay Rd (99156-8604)
PHONE.................................509 447-4214
Pam Sherman, *President*
Jeff Sherman, *Vice Pres*
EMP: 12
SALES (est): 850K Privately Held
SIC: 1429 5032 Igneous rock, crushed & broken-quarrying; gravel; sand, construction

(G-7060)
MASON MEAT PACKING CO
1871 Green Rd (99156-8580)
PHONE.................................509 447-3788
Neil Mason, *Owner*
EMP: 4
SQ FT: 900
SALES (est): 170K Privately Held
SIC: 0751 2011 5421 5159 Slaughtering: custom livestock services; meat packing plants; meat markets, including freezer provisioners; hides

(G-7061)
MONK LOGGING INC
547 Quail Loop (99156-8703)
PHONE.................................509 447-4526
EMP: 5
SALES (est): 430K Privately Held
SIC: 2411 Logging

(G-7062)
NEWPORT EQUIPMENT ENTPS INC
328772 Highway 2 (99156-9260)
PHONE.................................509 447-4688
Steven Smith, *President*
Deborah Smith, *Vice Pres*
EMP: 28
SQ FT: 4,500
SALES: 5MM Privately Held
SIC: 2411 Logging

(G-7063)
OUT OF WOODS PRINTING LLC
300 W 2nd St (99156-9075)
PHONE.................................509 447-2590
EMP: 2
SALES (est): 92.3K Privately Held
SIC: 2752 Commercial printing, lithographic

(G-7064)
PETROGLYPH PRINTING & SIGNS
300 W 2nd St (99156-9075)
PHONE.................................509 447-2590
Lisa Ratliff, *Owner*
EMP: 3
SALES (est): 238.4K Privately Held
SIC: 3993 Signs & advertising specialties

(G-7065)
SAFRAN CABIN INC
501 N Newport Ave (99156-9253)
PHONE.................................509 447-4122
Kevin Kempe, *Branch Mgr*
Travis Hanson, *Manager*
Jennifer Prueher, *Manager*
Natalie Roberg, *Director*
EMP: 223
SALES (corp-wide): 833.4MM Privately Held
SIC: 3728 Aircraft assemblies, subassemblies & parts
HQ: Safran Cabin Inc.
    5701 Bolsa Ave
    Huntington Beach CA 92647
    714 934-0000

(G-7066)
SNOW VALLEY FURNITURE
631 Diamond Creek Rd (99156-8514)
PHONE.................................509 292-8880
Jennie Cuthire, *Owner*
EMP: 10
SALES (est): 645K Privately Held
SIC: 2511 Wood household furniture

Nine Mile Falls
Spokane County

(G-7067)
ADVANCED PLASTIC & METAL WLDNG
12012 N Landt Farms Ln (99026-8726)
PHONE.................................509 466-1986
George Tippner, *Owner*
EMP: 2
SALES (est): 88.9K Privately Held
SIC: 3089 Plastics products

(G-7068)
BOATWORKS LONG LAKE
323 E Shore Rd (99026-9351)
PHONE.................................509 979-0936
Eric Farmer, *Owner*
EMP: 3
SALES (est): 128.1K Privately Held
SIC: 3732 Boat building & repairing

(G-7069)
COME ON GET HOPPY
6431 Lakeview Dr (99026-9539)
PHONE.................................509 276-6288
Paul Stettler, *Principal*
EMP: 3
SALES (est): 110.3K Privately Held
SIC: 2082 Malt beverages

(G-7070)
CONCRETE & AGGREGATE SUPPLY CO
Also Called: Conagsco
6533 Long Lake Dr (99026-9543)
P.O. Box 225, Harrington (99134-0225)
PHONE.................................253 853-2887
EMP: 2
SALES: 250K Privately Held
SIC: 3273 Mfg Ready-Mixed Concrete

(G-7071)
D&S INNOVATIVE ENTERPRISES
15819 N Inch Rd (99026-9676)
PHONE.................................509 467-2032
Susan Burgi, *Principal*
Dennis Burgi, *Principal*
EMP: 2
SALES (est): 68.7K Privately Held
SIC: 3999 Pet supplies

(G-7072)
DK MACHINING LLC
11325 W Meadowview Ln (99026-9419)
PHONE.................................509 991-6110
Kris Matthews, *General Mgr*
Kristopher Matthews, *Mng Member*
David Wilkes, *Mng Member*
EMP: 2
SALES: 150K Privately Held
SIC: 7699 3444 Industrial machinery & equipment repair; precision instrument repair; sheet metalwork

(G-7073)
ETSOUTDOORS
21223 W Four Mound Rd (99026-9710)
PHONE.................................509 481-3938
Edward Smith, *Principal*
EMP: 2
SALES (est): 161.1K Privately Held
SIC: 3949 Golf equipment

(G-7074)
FAM USA INC
18324 N West Shore Rd (99026-8635)
P.O. Box 185 (99026-0185)
PHONE.................................509 468-2677
Thomas Col, *President*
EMP: 5
SALES (est): 380K Privately Held
SIC: 1081 Metal mining services

(G-7075)
FOREVER GREEN SPRINKLERS
20727 N Calhoun Ln (99026-8657)
P.O. Box 429 (99026-0429)
PHONE.................................509 796-2676
Joseph Sander, *Co-Owner*
Lisa Sander, *Co-Owner*
EMP: 7
SALES (est): 804.1K Privately Held
SIC: 3432 Lawn hose nozzles & sprinklers

(G-7076)
HK WINDOW FASHIONS
8814 N Abrey L White Pkwy (99026-9286)
PHONE.................................509 466-4202
Wayne Kenny, *Partner*
EMP: 2
SALES (est): 144.7K Privately Held
SIC: 2591 Window blinds

(G-7077)
J AND S IRONWORKS LLC
6398 Highway 291 (99026)
PHONE.................................509 276-5887
John Labere, *Mng Member*
Shirley Labere,
EMP: 3
SALES (est): 281.6K Privately Held
SIC: 3446 Architectural metalwork

(G-7078)
MACHSTEM INC
Also Called: Machstem International
12611 W Greenfield Rd (99026-9357)
PHONE.................................801 259-3305
Leah Fayal, *CEO*
Andrew Fayal, *Principal*
Tayva Hart, *Admin Sec*
EMP: 5
SALES (est): 155.3K Privately Held
SIC: 8748 7389 3325 3423 Educational consultant; personal service agents, brokers & bureaus; steel foundries; alloy steel castings, except investment; mechanics' hand tools; civil service training school; specialty education

(G-7079)
MICO WELDING & MACHINING INC
16332 N Saddlewood Rd (99026-9463)
PHONE.................................509 467-5082
Mike Judd, *President*
EMP: 3
SALES: 90K Privately Held
WEB: www.mico-machine.com
SIC: 3451 3452 3089 Screw machine products; bolts, nuts, rivets & washers; washers, plastic

(G-7080)
NINE MILE POWER STATION
9602 W Old Charles Rd (99026-9625)
P.O. Box 3727, Spokane (99220-3727)
PHONE.................................509 466-5322
EMP: 3 EST: 2007
SALES (est): 274.6K Privately Held
SIC: 3621 Generators & sets, electric

(G-7081)
PACIFIC NORTHWEST IRON LLC
6196 Moriah Dr (99026-8310)
PHONE.................................509 499-0668
Kristene McCarthy, *Mng Member*
Kevin McCarthy,
EMP: 5
SALES: 140K Privately Held
SIC: 1791 3441 7389 Iron work, structural; fabricated structural metal;

(G-7082)
PRO TINT LLC
13409 W Shore Rd (99026-9366)
PHONE.................................509 468-8468
Edward Hatch, *Principal*
EMP: 2
SALES (est): 114.4K Privately Held
SIC: 3211 Window glass, clear & colored

(G-7083)
RON C ENGLAND
Also Called: Airquip
6633 Long Lake Dr (99026-9542)
PHONE.................................509 276-9150
Ron C England, *Owner*
Dora England, *Principal*
EMP: 2
SALES (est): 130K Privately Held
WEB: www.airquipco.com
SIC: 8748 3563 5084 Business consulting; air & gas compressors; vacuum (air extraction) systems, industrial; processing & packaging equipment

(G-7084)
UNIVERSAL ENGINE HEATER CO
6333b Rocky Pines Way (99026-5018)
P.O. Box 250 (99026-0250)
PHONE.................................509 276-5923
Cory Miedema, *CEO*
Aj Kline, *President*
EMP: 3 EST: 1945
SQ FT: 5,000
SALES: 250K Privately Held
SIC: 3714 3724 Motor vehicle engines & parts; engine heaters, aircraft

(G-7085)
WESTEK MARKETING LLC
7415 W Ridgecrest Ave (99026-8620)
PHONE.................................425 888-1988
Mark Enfield, *CEO*
Jesse Enfield, *President*
EMP: 5
SALES: 2MM Privately Held
WEB: www.westekmarketing.com
SIC: 3651 7359 Audio electronic systems; video cassette recorder & accessory rental

Nooksack
Whatcom County

(G-7086)
CHS-SUB WHATCOM INC
Also Called: Wfc Nooksack Country Store
106 Nooksack Ave (98276)
PHONE.................................360 966-4193

Cindy Tjoelker, *Manager*
EMP: 5
SALES (corp-wide): 32.6B **Publicly Held**
WEB: www.wfcoop.com
SIC: 2875 5191 Fertilizers, mixing only; farm supplies
HQ: Chs-Sub Whatcom, Inc.
   402 Main St
   Lynden WA 98264
   360 354-2108

(G-7087)
SWIFT INDUSTRIES
101 W Madison St (98276-7048)
P.O. Box 4546 (98276-0546)
PHONE.................................360 966-9697
Ron Hydorn, *Principal*
EMP: 8 **EST:** 2008
SALES (est): 643.8K **Privately Held**
SIC: 3999 Manufacturing industries

Nordland
Jefferson County

(G-7088)
BAYVIEW PUMPS
121 Robbins Rd (98358-9646)
P.O. Box 370, Port Hadlock (98339-0370)
PHONE.................................360 301-3600
Steven Grace, *President*
EMP: 4
SALES (est): 520.4K **Privately Held**
SIC: 3533 Water well drilling equipment

Normandy Park
King County

(G-7089)
ADD CORPORATION
Also Called: Unify
618 Sw 185th St (98166-3913)
PHONE.................................206 452-7498
Sandeep Walia, *CEO*
EMP: 65
SALES (est): 2.2MM **Privately Held**
SIC: 7372 7373 Business oriented computer software; computer systems analysis & design

(G-7090)
AMAZON TOOL SHED
19701 1st Pl Sw (98166-4007)
PHONE.................................206 429-2185
EMP: 2 **Privately Held**
SIC: 3599 Mfg Industrial Machinery

(G-7091)
DYNOLAB
643 Sw Normandy Rd (98166-3909)
PHONE.................................206 243-8877
Hal Middleton, *Owner*
EMP: 3
SALES: 50K **Privately Held**
SIC: 3829 8711 Dynamometer instruments; electrical or electronic engineering

(G-7092)
FPS WEST INC
17020 Sylvester Rd Sw (98166-3434)
PHONE.................................206 242-4888
Andrew Batcho, *Principal*
EMP: 3
SALES (est): 216K **Privately Held**
SIC: 3999 Manufacturing industries

(G-7093)
FRACTAL FILTERS LLC
1126 Sw 168th St (98166-3439)
PHONE.................................206 854-0968
Nicholas Wong, *Principal*
EMP: 2
SALES (est): 150.3K **Privately Held**
SIC: 3827 Prisms, optical

(G-7094)
FREEDOM SNACKS LLC
19803 1st Ave S Ste 103 (98148-2410)
PHONE.................................253 886-1838
Veronica Cockerham,
EMP: 6 **EST:** 2011

SALES (est): 179.2K **Privately Held**
SIC: 5963 2099 Snacks, direct sales; food preparations

(G-7095)
J & G INDUSTRIES INC
18124 Riviera Pl Sw (98166-3856)
PHONE.................................206 246-3782
Jooinder P Singh, *President*
EMP: 2
SALES (est): 119.8K **Privately Held**
SIC: 3999 Barber & beauty shop equipment

(G-7096)
PHILLIPS PUBLISHING GROUP
19679 Marine View Dr Sw (98166-4117)
PHONE.................................206 429-2429
EMP: 2
SALES (est): 73.1K **Privately Held**
SIC: 2721 Comic books: publishing only, not printed on site

(G-7097)
ROJOS FAMOUS INC
19901 1st Ave S (98148-2411)
PHONE.................................206 592-6581
Robert Selfridge, *CEO*
EMP: 6
SALES (est): 374.7K **Privately Held**
SIC: 2099 Food preparations

(G-7098)
SAMOA MARITIME COMPANY
18627 1st Ave S (98148-2001)
PHONE.................................206 246-1182
▼ **EMP:** 2
SALES (est): 2.6MM **Privately Held**
SIC: 1611 3273 5032 Highway/Street Construction Mfg Ready-Mixed Concrete Whol Brick/Stone Material

(G-7099)
SVENDSEN BROTHERS FISH INC
18629 2nd Ave Sw (98166-4009)
PHONE.................................206 767-4258
EMP: 12
SALES (est): 1.3MM **Privately Held**
SIC: 2091 Mfg Canned/Cured Fish/Seafood

(G-7100)
ZZAPHORIA SPIRITS
20614 4th Ave Sw (98166-4228)
PHONE.................................206 450-1353
Zane Gilbert, *Manager*
EMP: 2
SALES (est): 116.8K **Privately Held**
SIC: 2084 Wines, brandy & brandy spirits

North Bend
King County

(G-7101)
BALLBOY LLC
42202 Se 108th St (98045-8933)
PHONE.................................425 281-9152
Kris Reid,
EMP: 3 **EST:** 2011
SALES (est): 169.5K **Privately Held**
SIC: 3999 Pet supplies

(G-7102)
BLUE PRINTS PLUS
301 W North Bend Way (98045-8163)
PHONE.................................425 888-8815
EMP: 2
SALES (est): 91.5K **Privately Held**
SIC: 2752 Commercial printing, lithographic

(G-7103)
CABINET AESTHETICS
13827 436th Ave Se (98045-9364)
PHONE.................................808 268-1822
EMP: 2
SALES (est): 94.2K **Privately Held**
SIC: 2434 Wood kitchen cabinets

(G-7104)
CARLS POWDER COATING
46722 Se 161st St (98045-8798)
PHONE.................................425 864-7950
Ellen Landdeck, *Principal*
EMP: 2
SALES (est): 69.9K **Privately Held**
SIC: 3479 Metal coating & allied service

(G-7105)
CASCADE TOY LTD (PA)
10405 428th Ave Se (98045-9498)
PHONE.................................425 888-4600
Dave Perry, *President*
Joanne Perry, *Corp Secy*
▲ **EMP:** 15
SALES (est): 1.2MM **Privately Held**
WEB: www.cascadetoy.com
SIC: 3942 Stuffed toys, including animals

(G-7106)
CASCADE TREE SERVICE LLC
915 Snoqualm Pl (98045-9143)
P.O. Box 2453 (98045-2453)
PHONE.................................425 241-9326
Katie Swanson,
EMP: 2
SALES (est): 279.9K **Privately Held**
SIC: 2411 0783 Timber, cut at logging camp; ornamental shrub & tree services; pruning services, ornamental bush; tree trimming services for public utility lines; removal services, bush & tree

(G-7107)
CHIP AWAY BATHTUB REPAIR
46533 Se 156th Pl (98045-8707)
P.O. Box 1504 (98045-1504)
PHONE.................................425 246-1306
Sherrill Williamson, *Principal*
EMP: 2
SALES (est): 234.1K **Privately Held**
WEB: www.chipbrown.net
SIC: 3272 Bathtubs, concrete

(G-7108)
CHOUETTE VINEYARDS LLC
42311 Se 141st St (98045-8974)
PHONE.................................206 229-5167
Grant McDonald, *Principal*
EMP: 2
SALES (est): 86.8K **Privately Held**
SIC: 2084 Wines, brandy & brandy spirits

(G-7109)
COMMSCOPE TECHNOLOGIES LLC
1546 Boalch Ave Nw Ste 60 (98045-8127)
PHONE.................................425 888-2370
EMP: 12 **Publicly Held**
WEB: www.andrew.com
SIC: 3663 Radio & TV communications equipment
HQ: Commscope Technologies Llc
   4 Westbrook Corporate Ctr
   Westchester IL 60154
   708 236-6600

(G-7110)
D SQUARE ENERGY LLC
201 W North Bend Way (98045-8196)
PHONE.................................425 888-2882
Donald Nevens Dunavant, *CEO*
Jenette Dunavant, *President*
EMP: 12
SALES (est): 3.5MM **Privately Held**
WEB: www.dsquaregenerators.com
SIC: 3621 Motors & generators

(G-7111)
GATE TECHNOLOGIES LLC
825 Ne 6th St (98045-8929)
PHONE.................................206 229-9947
Mark Gates, *Principal*
EMP: 5
SALES (est): 339.4K **Privately Held**
SIC: 7372 Operating systems computer software

(G-7112)
GENIE INDUSTRIES INC
47020 Se 144th St (98045-9095)
PHONE.................................425 888-4600
Jaap Eric, *Branch Mgr*
EMP: 20

SALES (corp-wide): 5.1B **Publicly Held**
SIC: 3536 Hand hoists; hoists
HQ: Genie Industries, Inc.
   18340 Ne 76th St
   Redmond WA 98052
   425 881-1800

(G-7113)
IPR-NOW INC
45839 Se 137th St (98045-8863)
PHONE.................................425 888-6190
Richard Schramm, *President*
EMP: 9
SALES: 950K **Privately Held**
WEB: www.ipr-now.com
SIC: 7372 Prepackaged software

(G-7114)
K&J MFG INC
1001 Riverside Dr Se (98045-7904)
PHONE.................................425 503-2174
Gregory Birchall, *Owner*
Josephine A Birchall, *Principal*
EMP: 2
SALES: 300K **Privately Held**
SIC: 3999 Manufacturing industries

(G-7115)
MATSON LLC
45620 Se N Bend Way (98045)
P.O. Box 1820 (98045-1820)
PHONE.................................425 888-6212
Jim Hills, *Mng Member*
David Grassman,
Kenneth Matson,
▲ **EMP:** 20
SQ FT: 30,000
SALES (est): 3.9MM
SALES (corp-wide): 2.2B **Publicly Held**
WEB: www.corrys.com
SIC: 2879 Pesticides, agricultural or household
PA: Central Garden & Pet Company
   1340 Treat Blvd Ste 600
   Walnut Creek CA 94597
   925 948-4000

(G-7116)
MIKE BRANDEBERRY
Also Called: Brandeberry Logging
980 Mountain View Blvd Se (98045-9120)
P.O. Box 6270, Kamuela HI (96743-6270)
PHONE.................................206 524-9656
Mike Brandeberry, *Owner*
EMP: 10
SALES (est): 703.5K **Privately Held**
SIC: 2411 5099 Logging camps & contractors; logs, hewn ties, posts & poles

(G-7117)
NISSEN WOODWORKS
46325 Se 140th St (98045-8620)
PHONE.................................425 216-3575
Peter Nissen, *Principal*
EMP: 2
SALES (est): 175K **Privately Held**
SIC: 2431 Millwork

(G-7118)
NOBU INTEGRATIVE MEDICINE LLC
301 W North Bend Way # 104 (98045-8163)
PHONE.................................425 363-2970
Michelle Walter,
EMP: 2 **EST:** 2014
SALES (est): 217.2K **Privately Held**
SIC: 2834 8049 Hormone preparations; dermatologicals; naturopath

(G-7119)
NORTH BEND AUTOMOTIVES
43306 Se North Bend Way (98045-8636)
PHONE.................................425 888-4522
Dennie Dennis, *Owner*
EMP: 5 **EST:** 2000
SALES (est): 473.9K **Privately Held**
SIC: 3599 7538 Machine shop, jobbing & repair; general automotive repair shops

(G-7120)
POETRY POSTERS
224 Ne 6th St (98045-8924)
PHONE.................................425 831-5809
EMP: 2 **EST:** 2000

SALES (est): 110K **Privately Held**
SIC: 2741 Misc Publishing

(G-7121)
POOPLESS IN SEATTLE
817 Pickett Ave Ne (98045-7910)
PHONE..................................425 444-6930
Amada Gerber, *Principal*
EMP: 2
SALES (est): 147.9K **Privately Held**
SIC: 3999 Pet supplies

(G-7122)
SERIOUS CYBERNETICS LLC
42010 Se 149th Pl (98045-9040)
PHONE..................................646 247-3642
EMP: 2 EST: 2012
SALES (est): 180K **Privately Held**
SIC: 7372 Prepackaged Software Services

(G-7123)
SILICON DIGITAL INDUSTRIES INC
1127 Se 10th St (98045-9183)
PHONE..................................360 332-1349
Christopher Bigelow, *Principal*
Christopher N Bigelow, *Principal*
EMP: 2 EST: 2012
SALES (est): 148K **Privately Held**
SIC: 3999 Manufacturing industries

(G-7124)
SNO-VALLEY DREAM FACTORY LLC
101 W North Bend Way # 207 (98045-8150)
PHONE..................................408 888-8183
Luke Marusiak, *Mng Member*
EMP: 3
SALES (est): 94K **Privately Held**
SIC: 5411 3631 Grocery stores, chain; barbecues, grills & braziers (outdoor cooking)

(G-7125)
SOLOMON LOGGING LLC ○
14412 447th Ave Se (98045-9773)
PHONE..................................425 292-0745
EMP: 2 EST: 2019
SALES (est): 81.7K **Privately Held**
SIC: 2411 Logging

(G-7126)
SWIRL
426 Main Ave S (98045-8215)
PHONE..................................425 292-0909
Michael Kuntz, *Owner*
Loren Kuntz, *Co-Owner*
EMP: 3
SALES (est): 247.8K **Privately Held**
SIC: 2024 Yogurt desserts, frozen

(G-7127)
TANADA CORPORATION
Also Called: Farma Tech International
1546 Boalch Ave Nw Ste 30 (98045-8127)
PHONE..................................425 396-1050
Peter Cook, *President*
John Cook, *Chairman*
▲ EMP: 4
SALES: 1.5MM **Privately Held**
WEB: www.farmatech.com
SIC: 2879 Pesticides, agricultural or household

(G-7128)
THIRTNSPADES METAL FABRICATION
43723 Se 149th St (98045-9322)
PHONE..................................425 831-6126
EMP: 2
SALES (est): 120K **Privately Held**
SIC: 3499 Mfg Misc Fabricated Metal Products

(G-7129)
TONKIN REPLICAS INC
45127 Se 140th St (98045-9743)
P.O. Box 302 (98045-0302)
PHONE..................................206 542-6919
Jack Tonkin, *CEO*
Eric Anderson, *President*
▲ EMP: 20

SALES (est): 4MM **Privately Held**
WEB: www.tonkinreplicas.com
SIC: 3542 Die casting machines

(G-7130)
UMLAUT SOFTWARE INC
870 Snoqualm Pl (98045-9142)
PHONE..................................919 321-8324
Erik Dickelman, *President*
EMP: 3 EST: 2008
SALES (est): 176K **Privately Held**
SIC: 7372 Application computer software

(G-7131)
WELDING SHOP INC
939 Nw 14th St (98045-9404)
PHONE..................................425 888-0911
Bill Kramer, *President*
EMP: 3
SQ FT: 5,000
SALES (est): 200K **Privately Held**
SIC: 7692 Welding repair

(G-7132)
ZOOKA
44027 Se Tanner Rd Ste A (98045-8440)
PHONE..................................425 363-3922
EMP: 4
SALES (est): 249.3K **Privately Held**
SIC: 3949 Sporting & athletic goods

North Bonneville
Skamania County

(G-7133)
SILVER STAR INDUSTIES INC (PA)
Also Called: Silver Star Industries
409 Evergreen Dr (98639-4619)
P.O. Box 8 (98639-0008)
PHONE..................................509 427-8800
Matthew Califf, *President*
Elaine J Califf, *Vice Pres*
Treva Spears, *Purch Mgr*
Casey Campbell, *CFO*
Richard Mahar, *CFO*
EMP: 100
SQ FT: 70,000
SALES: 15MM **Privately Held**
WEB: www.silverstarcabinets.com
SIC: 2541 Store fixtures, wood

(G-7134)
SILVER STAR INDUSTIES INC
Also Called: Silver Star Cabinets
505 Evergreen Dr (98639-4620)
P.O. Box B (98639)
PHONE..................................509 427-8800
Micah Tilman, *Branch Mgr*
EMP: 40
SALES (corp-wide): 15MM **Privately Held**
WEB: www.silverstarcabinets.com
SIC: 2541 Cabinets, except refrigerated: show, display, etc.: wood
PA: Silver Star Industies Inc.
409 Evergreen Dr
North Bonneville WA 98639
509 427-8800

(G-7135)
SLINGSHOT SPORTS LLC
390 Evergreen Dr Ste Ef (98639-4618)
P.O. Box 1395, Stevenson (98648-1395)
PHONE..................................509 427-4950
Jim Kimball, *CFO*
Jeff Logosz,
Tony Logosz,
Breff McLauglin,
John Ratchye,
◆ EMP: 16
SQ FT: 5,000
SALES (est): 2.4MM **Privately Held**
WEB: www.slingshotkiteboarding.com
SIC: 3949 3944 Sporting & athletic goods; games, toys & children's vehicles

(G-7136)
VOLCANIC MANUFACTURING LLC
Also Called: Volcanic Bikes
28 Cbd Mall St (98639-4614)
P.O. Box 334 (98639-0334)
PHONE..................................509 427-8623
Eric Kackley,
▲ EMP: 6
SALES (est): 667.9K **Privately Held**
SIC: 5941 3751 Sporting goods & bicycle shops; bicycle & bicycle parts; frames, motorcycle & bicycle

Northport
Stevens County

(G-7137)
HEARFORM SOFTWARE LLC
3339 Highway 25 N Lot 44 (99157-9735)
P.O. Box 1268 (99157-1268)
PHONE..................................888 453-8806
Michael Huskey, *Principal*
EMP: 2
SALES (est): 151.3K **Privately Held**
SIC: 7372 Application computer software

(G-7138)
HEMPHILL BROTHERS INC
Also Called: Northport Limestone
4183 Wright Rd (99157-9729)
P.O. Box 27 (99157-0027)
PHONE..................................509 732-4481
Pete Sherve, *Branch Mgr*
EMP: 5
SALES (est): 615K
SALES (corp-wide): 6.6MM **Privately Held**
SIC: 3531 1422 Crushers, grinders & similar equipment; crushed & broken limestone
PA: Hemphill Brothers Inc
375 Ericksen Ave Ne
Bainbridge Island WA 98110
206 842-0748

Oak Harbor
Island County

(G-7139)
BASTION BREWING COMPANY LLC
2990 Advance Dr (98277-9196)
PHONE..................................360 420-8223
Joseph Behan, *Principal*
EMP: 3
SALES (est): 74.8K **Privately Held**
SIC: 2082 Malt beverages

(G-7140)
BAY PRINTING INC
1131 Se Ely St Ste 101 (98277-4070)
PHONE..................................360 679-3816
Jack Stiltz, *President*
EMP: 2
SQ FT: 3,176
SALES (est): 422.6K **Privately Held**
SIC: 2752 Commercial printing, lithographic

(G-7141)
BAYVIEW ENGINEERING INDS LLC
618 Oak St Ste C (98277-3542)
PHONE..................................360 421-2126
Ronald C Voegeli,
EMP: 2
SALES (est): 317.6K **Privately Held**
SIC: 3728 Rudders, aircraft

(G-7142)
BLOOD EAGLE WEAPONRY LLC
2800 Ne Goldie St (98277-2727)
PHONE..................................360 929-9567
Aaron Michael Fletcher,
EMP: 2

SALES (est): 73.4K **Privately Held**
SIC: 3484 5099 Guns (firearms) or gun parts, 30 mm. & below; firearms & ammunition, except sporting

(G-7143)
BTE PRINTING INC
Also Called: Whidbey Printers
1330 Sw Barlow St Ste 1 (98277-3101)
PHONE..................................360 675-8837
Becky King, *President*
Eric King, *Vice Pres*
EMP: 3
SALES (est): 275K **Privately Held**
SIC: 2752 2759 Commercial printing, offset; commercial printing

(G-7144)
CUSTOM CABINET DESIGN
632 Erin Park Rd (98277-2705)
PHONE..................................360 679-8729
Toll Free:..................................877 -
Paul Wilson, *Partner*
Doug Bowden, *Partner*
EMP: 2
SALES (est): 211.7K **Privately Held**
SIC: 2434 Wood kitchen cabinets

(G-7145)
CUTTING EDGE WOODWORKS LLC
1141 Balda Rd (98277-7620)
PHONE..................................360 929-5386
Terry L Krueger, *Administration*
EMP: 2
SALES (est): 187.5K **Privately Held**
SIC: 2431 Millwork

(G-7146)
DARBONNIER TACTICAL SUPPLY LLC (PA)
Also Called: Dts
951 Ne 21st Ct (98277-2715)
PHONE..................................360 672-0216
Shawn Kurtz, *COO*
Brittni Darbonnier, *Info Tech Mgr*
EMP: 2
SALES (est): 473.1K **Privately Held**
SIC: 5941 7218 5699 2385 Sporting goods & bicycle shops; flame & heat resistant clothing supply; uniforms & work clothing; customized clothing & apparel; raincoats, except vulcanized rubber: purchased materials; gloves: leather: work; welders' gloves; cases, carrying; traveling bags

(G-7147)
DAYTON TRAISTER CO INC
Also Called: Mark II Safety
4778 Monkey Hill Rd (98277-9769)
PHONE..................................360 675-3421
Gregory Roberts, *President*
Claudette A Greene, *Treasurer*
EMP: 2
SALES (est): 240.7K **Privately Held**
WEB: www.daytraco.com
SIC: 3484 5941 Guns (firearms) or gun parts, 30 mm. & below; sporting goods & bicycle shops

(G-7148)
DENNIS NELSON
Also Called: America Fiber Optic Technology
695 Maplewood Loop (98277-7714)
PHONE..................................360 320-4237
Dennis Nelson, *Owner*
EMP: 1
SALES: 25MM **Privately Held**
SIC: 3674 3229 Light emitting diodes; fiber optics strands

(G-7149)
ELEMENT
656 Se Bayshore Dr (98277-5739)
PHONE..................................360 682-5649
Mike Kummerfeldt, *Principal*
EMP: 33 EST: 2007
SALES (est): 1.6MM **Privately Held**
SIC: 2819 Industrial inorganic chemicals

(G-7150)
FARSTAD INDUSTRIES LLC
796 Gun Club Rd (98277-3632)
PHONE..................................360 316-9485

Oak Harbor - Island County (G-7151)

EMP: 2
SALES (est): 99.1K **Privately Held**
SIC: 3999 Manufacturing industries

(G-7151)
FC PLATING INC
321 E Henni Rd (98277-9416)
PHONE....................................360 679-4665
Forest Dolph, *President*
EMP: 2
SQ FT: 4,000
SALES (est): 150K **Privately Held**
SIC: 3471 Plating of metals or formed products

(G-7152)
FIREPAK OIL AND GAS INDS LLC
164 Nw Jib St (98277-2299)
PHONE....................................360 679-1747
EMP: 2
SALES (corp-wide): 470.2K **Privately Held**
WEB: www.pyrogen.com
SIC: 1389 Cementing oil & gas well casings
PA: Firepak Oil And Gas Industries, L.L.C.
11717 Bedford St
Houston TX 77031
713 952-1996

(G-7153)
IDEX HEALTH & SCIENCE LLC
Also Called: Upchurch Scientific
619 Oak St (98277-3553)
P.O. Box 1529 (98277-1529)
PHONE....................................360 679-2528
Jason Polly, *Engineer*
Andrea Rivers, *Sales Staff*
EMP: 122
SALES (corp-wide): 2.4B **Publicly Held**
SIC: 3494 3823 3826 Valves & pipe fittings; industrial instrmnts msrmnt display/control process variable; analytical instruments
HQ: Idex Health & Science Llc
600 Park Ct
Rohnert Park CA 94928
707 588-2000

(G-7154)
INJECT TOOL & DIE INC
657 Oak St (98277-3552)
PHONE....................................360 679-6160
Rex D Block, *President*
Robert Scott, *Principal*
Dianna K Block, *Corp Secy*
EMP: 4
SQ FT: 3,200
SALES: 650K **Privately Held**
WEB: www.injecttool.com
SIC: 3544 Forms (molds), for foundry & plastics working machinery; special dies & tools

(G-7155)
KING AEROSPACE INC
3690 N Ranger St (98278-4926)
PHONE....................................360 257-6610
EMP: 3
SALES (est): 250.1K **Privately Held**
SIC: 3812 Aircraft/aerospace flight instruments & guidance systems

(G-7156)
KRIEG CONCRETE PRODUCTS INC
35717 State Route 20 (98277-9584)
P.O. Box 2218 (98277-6218)
PHONE....................................360 675-2727
Karl Krieg, *President*
Darlyne Krieg, *Corp Secy*
Chuck Krieg, *Vice Pres*
EMP: 15 EST: 1922
SQ FT: 215,000
SALES (est): 1.9MM **Privately Held**
SIC: 3273 3272 1442 Ready-mixed concrete; precast terrazo or concrete products; gravel mining

(G-7157)
M & M CRAFTWORKS
687 Maplewood Loop (98277-7714)
PHONE....................................360 675-9138
Judith Myers, *Owner*
Gorge Myers, *Owner*

EMP: 2
SALES (est): 100K **Privately Held**
SIC: 3732 Tenders (small motor craft), building & repairing

(G-7158)
MELT CANDLE COMPANY LLC
1022 Diane Ave (98277-8225)
PHONE....................................360 200-0993
EMP: 2
SALES (est): 124.4K **Privately Held**
SIC: 3999 Candles

(G-7159)
MILES SAND & GRAVEL COMPANY
Also Called: Concrete Norwest
3199 N Oak Harbor Rd (98277)
PHONE....................................360 675-2626
Joe Short, *Manager*
EMP: 12
SALES (est): 890.1K
SALES (corp-wide): 88MM **Privately Held**
SIC: 3273 Ready-mixed concrete
PA: Miles Sand & Gravel Company
400 Valley Ave Ne
Puyallup WA 98372
253 833-3705

(G-7160)
NORTHWEST WELDING ACADEMY LLC
1233 Nw Elwha St 2 (98277-3802)
PHONE....................................325 574-3212
Martin Mares, *Principal*
EMP: 5
SALES (est): 90.6K **Privately Held**
SIC: 7692 Welding repair

(G-7161)
POWDER RIVER DRAFTING
1788 Conifer Ln (98277-8421)
PHONE....................................360 679-9859
Sarah Wakefield, *Owner*
Donald Harper, *Agent*
EMP: 2
SALES: 90K **Privately Held**
WEB: www.3ddrafting.com
SIC: 2077 Tallow rendering, inedible

(G-7162)
PRUDENT PRODUCTS INC
883 Nw 2nd Ave (98277-4435)
PHONE....................................360 445-2556
Jim Maher, *CEO*
EMP: 2 EST: 2017
SALES: 250K **Privately Held**
SIC: 3999 Manufacturing industries

(G-7163)
RELENTLESS PUBLISHING LLC
361 Se Neil St (98277-5026)
PHONE....................................360 929-7530
Gregory S Hancock, *Principal*
EMP: 2
SALES (est): 92K **Privately Held**
SIC: 2741 Music book & sheet music publishing

(G-7164)
SAYITRIGHT LLC
Also Called: Sayitright Media
3122 Angela Ln (98277-9002)
PHONE....................................401 682-7630
Joseph Andrade,
EMP: 2 EST: 2013
SALES (est): 89.9K **Privately Held**
SIC: 7372 Application computer software

(G-7165)
TECHNICAL SERVICES INC
Also Called: T S I
1150 Ne 21st Ct (98277-2717)
P.O. Box 1527 (98277-1527)
PHONE....................................360 675-1322
Dee Boothe, *President*
Calvin Boothe, *President*
Nicole Boothe, *Vice Pres*
Chris Edenburn, *Opers Mgr*
Mardy Ashbrook, *Prdtn Mgr*
▲ EMP: 102
SALES (est): 29.4MM **Privately Held**
WEB: www.technicalservices.net
SIC: 3679 Electronic circuits

(G-7166)
VON GREY CUSTOM CABINETS INC
920 Silver Lake Rd (98277-9045)
PHONE....................................360 679-8641
Larry Von Grey, *President*
Peter Von Grey, *Vice Pres*
▲ EMP: 2
SALES: 200K **Privately Held**
SIC: 2434 5211 Wood kitchen cabinets; cabinets, kitchen

(G-7167)
WASHINGTON IRON WORKS INC
3144 Ne Halyard Ln (98277-4814)
PHONE....................................360 679-4868
Michael Nagel, *President*
Nagel Tammie, *Treasurer*
EMP: 12
SALES (est): 970K **Privately Held**
SIC: 7692 Welding repair

(G-7168)
WEST QUARTER HORSES LLC
1593 Baker Ranch Ln (98277-3338)
PHONE....................................360 969-0791
Barbara West, *Principal*
EMP: 3
SALES (est): 65.4K **Privately Held**
SIC: 3131 Quarters

(G-7169)
WEST ROAD CANDLES
1504 Sw 2nd Ct (98277-2280)
PHONE....................................360 682-5822
Cary Anderson, *Principal*
EMP: 2
SALES (est): 113.5K **Privately Held**
SIC: 3999 Candles

(G-7170)
WHIDBEY AUTO PARTS INC
Also Called: NAPA Auto Parts
1370 Sw Barlow St (98277-3158)
PHONE....................................360 675-5946
Doyle Osborne, *Owner*
EMP: 7
SALES (est): 770.5K **Privately Held**
SIC: 5531 3599 Automobile & truck equipment & parts; machine shop, jobbing & repair

(G-7171)
WHIDBEY CRUZERS
953 Se 4th Ave (98277-5219)
P.O. Box 1875 (98277-1875)
PHONE....................................253 299-6442
Lynn Holmes, *President*
EMP: 2
SALES (est): 139.4K **Privately Held**
SIC: 3714 Transmission housings or parts, motor vehicle

(G-7172)
WHIDBEY MARKETPLACE & NEWS LLC
390 Ne Midway Blvd B203 (98277-2642)
PHONE....................................360 682-2341
Eric Marshall, *Principal*
EMP: 2
SALES (est): 120.3K **Privately Held**
SIC: 2741 Miscellaneous publishing

(G-7173)
WHIDBEY SIGN CO
751 Ne Midway Blvd (98277-2665)
PHONE....................................360 720-2015
Jeff Humphrey, *Owner*
EMP: 3
SALES (est): 120.4K **Privately Held**
SIC: 3993 Signs & advertising specialties

Oakville
Grays Harbor County

(G-7174)
FRED B MOE LOGGING CO
110 Elma Gate Rd E (98568-9614)
PHONE....................................360 273-6049
Fred B Moe, *Principal*
EMP: 3

SALES (est): 125.8K **Privately Held**
SIC: 2411 Logging

(G-7175)
GRAPHITE GUITAR SYSTEMS
13043 195th Ave Sw (98568-9633)
PHONE....................................360 273-7744
Gerald Dorsch, *Owner*
EMP: 3
SALES: 150K **Privately Held**
SIC: 3931 Musical instruments

(G-7176)
UNITED GAMES
40 Cedar Creek Rd (98568-9643)
PHONE....................................360 470-6480
Beth Eaton, *Principal*
EMP: 2
SALES (est): 88.3K **Privately Held**
SIC: 3625 Motor controls & accessories

(G-7177)
WILLIS ENTERPRISES INC (PA)
208 Park St (98568-9630)
P.O. Box 457 (98568-0457)
PHONE....................................360 273-9266
Paul Willis, *President*
Pat Tagman, *Principal*
Rich Lane, *Buyer*
Robert Nelson, *Project Engr*
▼ EMP: 6
SQ FT: 1,500
SALES (est): 25MM **Privately Held**
SIC: 2421 Chipper mill

Ocean Park
Pacific County

(G-7178)
AIRCRAFT SHEEPSKIN COMPANY
35404 I Pl (98640-5830)
PHONE....................................800 874-5747
Kathleen Williams, *Owner*
▼ EMP: 7 EST: 1987
SQ FT: 2,600
SALES: 100K **Privately Held**
SIC: 3111 Shearling (prepared sheepskin)

(G-7179)
DIANA THOMPSON
Also Called: Harmony Soapworks
34704 T Ln (98640)
P.O. Box 233, Oysterville (98641-0233)
PHONE....................................360 665-0102
Diana Thompson, *Owner*
EMP: 2
SALES (est): 167.5K **Privately Held**
WEB: www.harmonysoapworks.com
SIC: 2841 Soap & other detergents

(G-7180)
DONNIES PENINSULA SIGN
35504 J Pl (98640-5834)
P.O. Box 741 (98640-0741)
PHONE....................................360 642-4512
Don Sartwell, *Owner*
EMP: 2
SALES (est): 84.3K **Privately Held**
SIC: 2499 Signboards, wood

(G-7181)
DYERS CONSTRUCTION & EXCAV
Also Called: Dyer's Firefighter Cnstr
23621 Birch Ln (98640-3872)
PHONE....................................903 486-1881
Dewayne L Dyer, *Owner*
EMP: 2
SALES (est): 159.3K **Privately Held**
SIC: 1611 1389 1522 1794 General contractor, highway & street construction; construction, repair & dismantling services; residential construction; excavation work; construction machinery

(G-7182)
PHONE VAULT
22516 Pacific Way (98640-3427)
PHONE....................................360 867-8535
Robert Stritof, *Owner*
EMP: 2

GEOGRAPHIC SECTION

SALES (est): 134.2K **Privately Held**
WEB: www.phonevault.com
SIC: 3272 Burial vaults, concrete or precast terrazzo

(G-7183)
WIEGARDT BROS INC
Also Called: Jolly Roger Seafoods
3215 273rd St (98640-4467)
P.O. Box 309 (98640-0309)
PHONE.................................360 665-4111
Fritz Wiegardt, *President*
EMP: 40
SQ FT: 4,500
SALES (est): 4.7MM **Privately Held**
SIC: 2091 2092 Oysters: packaged in cans, jars, etc.; fresh or frozen packaged fish

Ocean Shores
Grays Harbor County

(G-7184)
BEACH BEE INC
Also Called: North Bch Prtg & Scrapbooking
698 Ocean Shores Blvd Nw (98569-9317)
P.O. Box 1428 (98569-1428)
PHONE.................................360 289-2244
Artemisa Garcia, *President*
EMP: 2
SALES (est): 170K **Privately Held**
SIC: 5943 2752 Office forms & supplies; commercial printing, lithographic

(G-7185)
DANCING CLOUDS LLC
540 Meadow Ave Ne (98569-9691)
P.O. Box 129, Gold Hill OR (97525-0129)
PHONE.................................360 289-0790
Margaret Stermer-Cox,
Margaret G Stermer-Cox,
Robert Stermer-Cox,
EMP: 2
SALES (est): 151.2K **Privately Held**
WEB: www.e-worldproductions.com
SIC: 3993 Advertising artwork

(G-7186)
MUCH MORE EMBROIDERY
643 E Chance A La Mer Ne (98569-9669)
PHONE.................................360 289-0955
Marge Avery, *Owner*
EMP: 12
SALES (est): 347.5K **Privately Held**
SIC: 2395 Embroidery & art needlework

(G-7187)
N J L INC
779 Cardinal Ave Ne (98569-9711)
P.O. Box 1805 (98569-1805)
PHONE.................................360 590-8100
Juan Contreras, *President*
EMP: 2
SALES (est): 182K **Privately Held**
SIC: 2429 Special product sawmills

(G-7188)
NORTH BEACH MEDIA INC
Also Called: North Coast News, The
668 Ocean Shores Blvd Nw (98569-9346)
P.O. Box 1869 (98569-1869)
PHONE.................................360 289-2441
John Huge, *President*
Angelo Bruscas, *Editor*
EMP: 5
SALES (est): 226.1K **Privately Held**
SIC: 2711 Newspapers, publishing & printing

(G-7189)
PAGE LAST PUBLISHING
100 Ocean Shores Blvd Nw (98569-9721)
PHONE.................................360 289-4165
Michele Minich, *Principal*
EMP: 2 EST: 2017
SALES (est): 59.2K **Privately Held**
SIC: 2741 Miscellaneous publishing

Odessa
Lincoln County

(G-7190)
I 90 ENTERPRISES INC
8 S 5th St (99159-5000)
PHONE.................................509 988-0380
Wade S Walter, *Principal*
EMP: 3
SALES (est): 321K **Privately Held**
SIC: 3563 Air & gas compressors

(G-7191)
ODESSA RECORD
1 W 1st Ave (99159)
PHONE.................................509 982-2632
Donald E Walter, *Owner*
EMP: 3
SQ FT: 2,500
SALES (est): 172.2K **Privately Held**
SIC: 2711 Job printing & newspaper publishing combined

(G-7192)
SPECTRUM MANUFACTURING
2194 N Schoonover Rd (99159-9729)
PHONE.................................509 982-2257
Peter Hofer, *President*
EMP: 8
SALES (est): 657.8K **Privately Held**
SIC: 3999 Manufacturing industries

(G-7193)
VOISE SUSAGE BY SCHUMACHER INC
7 S lst St (99159)
PHONE.................................509 982-2956
Jason Dean Schumacher, *President*
Chandra Schumacher, *Vice Pres*
EMP: 2
SALES (est): 142.7K **Privately Held**
SIC: 2013 Sausages from purchased meat

Okanogan
Okanogan County

(G-7194)
ALL WEATHER MOBILE WELDING
1871b Old Highway 97 (98840-8222)
P.O. Box 748 (98840-0748)
PHONE.................................509 422-3789
Aaron Morgan, *Partner*
Jennifer Drader, *Partner*
EMP: 2
SALES (est): 103.4K **Privately Held**
SIC: 7692 Welding repair

(G-7195)
CUSTOM BUILDING SERVICES INC
22525 Highway 20 (98840-8242)
PHONE.................................509 422-5746
David Richard Petitt, *President*
Teri Petitt, *Treasurer*
EMP: 2
SALES (est): 400K **Privately Held**
SIC: 1542 1521 8712 2452 Commercial & office building, new construction; commercial & office buildings, renovation & repair; new construction, single-family houses; general remodeling, single-family houses; house designer; log cabins, prefabricated, wood; kitchen & bathroom remodeling; roofing contractor

(G-7196)
DIEBELS WELDING & MACHINE
Also Called: Patriot Steel & Supply
269 Conconully Rd (98840-9771)
PHONE.................................509 422-0457
Darrel Diebel, *President*
EMP: 6
SQ FT: 2,400
SALES (est): 688.1K **Privately Held**
SIC: 3599 5531 Machine shop, jobbing & repair; automotive parts

(G-7197)
INDUSTRIAL IRON WORKS
1871 Old Highway 97 (98840-8222)
PHONE.................................509 322-0072
Aaron Morgan, *Principal*
EMP: 3
SALES (est): 180.6K **Privately Held**
SIC: 7692 Welding repair

(G-7198)
JONES LOGGING AND CNSTR LLC
17 Jones Rd (98840-8245)
PHONE.................................509 422-3147
Bill E Jones, *Partner*
Dorian Jones, *Partner*
Dory Jones, *Partner*
Sterling Jones, *Partner*
EMP: 15 EST: 1970
SALES (est): 1.7MM **Privately Held**
SIC: 2411 1611 1794 Logging; surfacing & paving; excavation work

(G-7199)
LUCKY DOG WOODWORKING
421 Cameron Lake Loop Rd (98840-9513)
P.O. Box 593, Entiat (98822-0593)
PHONE.................................507 218-6767
Tyler Kulsrud, *Principal*
EMP: 2 EST: 2013
SALES (est): 128K **Privately Held**
SIC: 2431 Millwork

(G-7200)
MITZNER LOGGING
Also Called: Mitzner Logging and Cattle
22585 Highway 20 (98840-8242)
P.O. Box 432, Malott (98829-0432)
PHONE.................................509 422-6834
Steven E Mitzner, *Owner*
Laurel J Mitzner, *Co-Owner*
EMP: 6
SALES (est): 400K **Privately Held**
SIC: 2411 0212 Logging camps & contractors; beef cattle except feedlots

(G-7201)
MONUMENTAL TASK
1033 7th Ave S (98840-9746)
PHONE.................................509 449-8286
Douglas Woodrow, *Owner*
EMP: 3
SALES (est): 192.5K **Privately Held**
SIC: 3272 Monuments & grave markers, except terrazo

(G-7202)
OKANOGAN ARMS CO LLC
105 W Oak St Okanogan Wa (98840)
PHONE.................................509 422-4123
Kole Pitts, *Owner*
EMP: 2 EST: 2017
SALES (est): 80.8K **Privately Held**
SIC: 3484 Machine guns or machine gun parts, 30 mm. & below

(G-7203)
OKANOGAN VALLEY CONCRETE INC
2145 Elmway (98840-9621)
P.O. Box 1296 (98840-1296)
PHONE.................................509 422-3211
David Freels, *President*
Terry Paslay, *Vice Pres*
Jinx Freels, *Treasurer*
EMP: 6
SQ FT: 1,200
SALES (est): 737K **Privately Held**
SIC: 3273 5032 5211 1711 Ready-mixed concrete; stone, crushed or broken; gravel; masonry materials & supplies; septic system construction

(G-7204)
WASHINGTON TRACTOR INC
1 Patrol St (98840)
PHONE.................................509 422-3030
James Hale, *Principal*
EMP: 17
SALES (corp-wide): 129.6MM **Privately Held**
SIC: 3523 5083 5261 7699 Farm machinery & equipment; farm & garden machinery; lawnmowers & tractors; farm machinery repair; heavy construction equipment rental
PA: Washington Tractor, Incorporated
2700 136th Avenue Ct E
Sumner WA 98390
253 863-4436

Olalla
Kitsap County

(G-7205)
CHOICE CONSTRUCTION INC
8139 Se Millihanna Rd (98359-9613)
P.O. Box 63, Port Orchard (98366-0063)
PHONE.................................360 340-2206
Joseph P Krecker, *President*
EMP: 10
SALES (est): 950K **Privately Held**
SIC: 2452 Prefabricated wood buildings

(G-7206)
INTEK MANUFACTURING INC
3257 Se Gliding Hawk Way (98359-5500)
PHONE.................................253 857-5073
Mark Kendal, *President*
Mark Kendall, *President*
EMP: 3
SQ FT: 2,400
SALES (est): 180K **Privately Held**
SIC: 3599 Machine & other job shop work

(G-7207)
JB TIMBERLINE LOGGING
11501 Se Black Rd (98359-9769)
P.O. Box 546 (98359-0546)
PHONE.................................360 871-0956
John Anderson, *Principal*
EMP: 2
SALES (est): 168.9K **Privately Held**
SIC: 2411 Logging

(G-7208)
MAGICAL STRINGS
9052 Se Willock Rd (98359-9660)
P.O. Box 1240 (98359-1240)
PHONE.................................253 857-3716
Philip Boulding, *Owner*
Pamela Boulding, *Co-Owner*
EMP: 2
SALES (est): 76.1K **Privately Held**
WEB: www.magicalstrings.com
SIC: 8299 3931 7929 Music school; musical instruments; popular music groups or artists

(G-7209)
RONALD FINNEY
Also Called: North Woods Productions
3252 Se Nelson Rd (98359-8525)
PHONE.................................253 857-7635
Ron Finney, *Owner*
EMP: 2
SALES (est): 140.1K **Privately Held**
WEB: www.northwoods-graphics.com
SIC: 2759 Commercial printing

(G-7210)
SMITH LOGGING & MONKEY BUS
13698 Fagerud Rd Se (98359-9523)
PHONE.................................253 857-5900
Dennis Smith, *Owner*
EMP: 2 EST: 2017
SALES (est): 81.7K **Privately Held**
SIC: 2411 Logging

(G-7211)
TEACHING 2020 LLC
10631 Orchard Ave Se (98359-9797)
PHONE.................................253 232-6822
EMP: 2
SALES (est): 67.8K **Privately Held**
SIC: 7372 Prepackaged Software Services

(G-7212)
WHITE CLOUD ALPACAS
8535 Se Willock Rd (98359-9693)
PHONE.................................253 853-6984

Harlie Hanke, *Owner*
EMP: 2
SALES (est): 141.6K **Privately Held**
SIC: 2211 7389 Alpacas, cotton;

Olga
San Juan County

(G-7213)
BAY CITY MOLD INSPECTION SVCS
32 Codfish Ln (98279-9578)
PHONE.............................415 925-0801
Robert Minton, *President*
EMP: 2
SALES (est): 180.7K **Privately Held**
SIC: 3544 Industrial molds

(G-7214)
ELIZA K TROWBRIDGE
Also Called: Island Thyme Herbs and Flowers
53 4th St (98279)
P.O. Box 99 (98279-0099)
PHONE.............................360 376-5152
Eliza K Trowbridge, *Owner*
Chris Morris, *Co-Owner*
EMP: 5
SALES (est): 66K **Privately Held**
SIC: 2841 5122 Soap & other detergents; toilet soap

(G-7215)
LOPEZ ISLAND CHAMBER COMMERCE
532 Point Lawrence Rd (98279-9509)
P.O. Box 102, Lopez Island (98261-0102)
PHONE.............................360 468-4664
Jennifer Welch, *Owner*
EMP: 2
SALES: 98.4K **Privately Held**
SIC: 2099 Food preparations

(G-7216)
MT PICKETT WOODWORKING
517 Picketts Ln (98279-9594)
PHONE.............................360 376-2449
Gary Sisson, *Owner*
EMP: 3
SALES (est): 245.1K **Privately Held**
SIC: 3553 Cabinet makers' machinery

(G-7217)
ORCAS ISLAND TONEWOODS
679 Roehls Hill Rd (98279-9310)
PHONE.............................360 376-2747
Casey Wood, *Principal*
EMP: 2
SALES (est): 149.6K **Privately Held**
SIC: 2431 Millwork

(G-7218)
PICKETT SPRING
Hc 172 (98279)
PHONE.............................360 376-6982
Thomas Leonard, *Owner*
EMP: 2
SALES (est): 200.2K **Privately Held**
SIC: 3449 Miscellaneous metalwork

(G-7219)
SMALLDOG NET SOLUTIONS INC
808 Pioneer Hill Rd (98279-9555)
PHONE.............................360 376-6056
Christopher Sutton, *Principal*
EMP: 2 EST: 2011
SALES (est): 144.2K **Privately Held**
SIC: 7372 Application computer software

(G-7220)
WHALESTOOTH PUBLISHING
131 Bond Mill Rd (98279-9401)
PHONE.............................360 376-2784
Thomas Tillman, *Owner*
Tom Tillman, *Director*
EMP: 3
SALES (est): 182.4K **Privately Held**
WEB: www.divinghistory.com
SIC: 8748 2741 Publishing consultant; miscellaneous publishing

Olympia
Thurston County

(G-7221)
ADVANCED DRAINAGE SYSTEMS INC
Also Called: Hancor
6001 Belmore St Sw (98512-7921)
P.O. Box 352 (98507-0352)
PHONE.............................360 943-3313
Graham Wilkin, *Branch Mgr*
EMP: 20
SALES (est): 3.2MM **Privately Held**
SIC: 3084 Plastics pipe

(G-7222)
ALLEN BROS DIVING LOGGING
8049 Stmboat Island Rd Nw (98502-8611)
PHONE.............................360 866-3643
William L Allen, *Principal*
EMP: 3
SALES (est): 184.3K **Privately Held**
SIC: 2411 Logging

(G-7223)
ALLIED DAILY NEWSPAPERS WASH
1110 Capitol Way S # 300 (98501-2251)
P.O. Box 29 (98507-0029)
PHONE.............................360 943-9960
Rowland Thompson, *Director*
EMP: 2 EST: 2001
SALES (est): 333.1K **Privately Held**
SIC: 2711 Newspapers, publishing & printing

(G-7224)
AMERICAN BNCHMARK MCH WRKS LLC
Also Called: Abmw
926 Unit A 79th St Se 79 A (98501)
PHONE.............................360 584-9303
Steve Jacobson, *CEO*
EMP: 5
SQ FT: 7,000
SALES: 325K **Privately Held**
SIC: 3841 7389 Medical instruments & equipment, blood & bone work; design services; engraving service

(G-7225)
ANDERSON & MIDDLETON COMPANY (PA)
111 Market St Ne Ste 360 (98501-1070)
PHONE.............................360 533-2410
James C Middleton, *CEO*
Rick Middleton, *President*
Kevin James, *General Mgr*
Richard W Middleton, *Vice Pres*
Doug Hockett Jr, *Facilities Mgr*
EMP: 16
SQ FT: 1,500
SALES (est): 13.8MM **Privately Held**
WEB: www.delanofarms.com
SIC: 2411 Timber, cut at logging camp

(G-7226)
ANDERSON WOODWORKS
2646 Delphi Rd Sw (98512-9306)
PHONE.............................360 923-2203
Brian Anderson, *Principal*
EMP: 2 EST: 2012
SALES (est): 213.8K **Privately Held**
SIC: 2431 Millwork

(G-7227)
ANGELA J BOWEN & ASSOC LLC
2010 Caton Way Sw Ste 203 (98502-8201)
P.O. Box 11459 (98508-1459)
PHONE.............................360 252-2440
Angela Bowen, *CEO*
EMP: 8
SALES (est): 629.3K **Privately Held**
SIC: 3949 Shafts, golf club

(G-7228)
APEX MARKETING STRATEGY
1612 Easthill Pl Nw (98502-8523)
PHONE.............................360 402-6487
Sam Barer, *Owner*
EMP: 8
SALES (est): 328.4K **Privately Held**
WEB: www.apexstrategy.com
SIC: 2759 Publication printing

(G-7229)
ARM INC
2002 Caton Way Sw (98502-1119)
PHONE.............................408 576-1500
EMP: 127 **Privately Held**
SIC: 3674 Integrated circuits, semiconductor networks, etc.
HQ: Arm, Inc.
150 Rose Orchard Way
San Jose CA 95134

(G-7230)
ARO-TEK LTD (PA)
4024 113th Ave Sw (98512-9161)
PHONE.............................360 754-2770
Morris K Dagley, *Principal*
EMP: 5
SALES (est): 598.7K **Privately Held**
SIC: 7699 5091 3949 Gunsmith shop; sporting & recreation goods; sporting & athletic goods

(G-7231)
ARTILLERY GRAPHIC DESIGN & SCR
12305 Littlerock Rd Sw (98512-9238)
PHONE.............................360 709-3351
EMP: 2
SALES (est): 104.1K **Privately Held**
SIC: 2752 Commercial printing, lithographic

(G-7232)
ASH HOLLOW WINERY LLC
Also Called: Ash Hollow Vineyard
519 Mission Dr Ne (98506-3237)
PHONE.............................509 529-7565
Thomas A Glase, *General Mgr*
Steve Thompson, *Manager*
EMP: 2
SALES (est): 169.3K **Privately Held**
WEB: www.ashhollow.com
SIC: 2084 Wines

(G-7233)
AWAKENED HEART
1213 19th Ave Se (98501-3005)
PHONE.............................360 556-6168
EMP: 2 EST: 2010
SALES (est): 87K **Privately Held**
SIC: 2833 Mfg Medicinal/Botanical Products

(G-7234)
BARDON INC
512 Seahawk St Se (98503-1454)
PHONE.............................360 455-1790
Donna Bartley, *President*
Blaine Bartley, *Vice Pres*
EMP: 2
SALES: 20K **Privately Held**
SIC: 3914 Trophies, plated (all metals)

(G-7235)
BAYVIEW PRO AUDIO INC
Also Called: Cascade Microphones
630 Oleary St Nw (98502-8875)
PHONE.............................360 867-1798
Mike Chiriac, *President*
Kathleen Shimshock, *Corp Secy*
◆ EMP: 4
SQ FT: 2,000
SALES (est): 538.4K **Privately Held**
WEB: www.bayviewproaudio.com
SIC: 3651 Household audio & video equipment

(G-7236)
BLACK LK BB CAMP CNFERENCE CTR
6521 Fairview Rd Sw (98512-7052)
PHONE.............................360 539-5337
Steve Ewert, *Director*
EMP: 14
SALES: 1.4MM **Privately Held**
WEB: www.blacklakebiblecamp.com
SIC: 8661 2411 Covenant & Evangelical Church; religious instruction; logging

(G-7237)
BLACKBOARD CYPHR EDUC CONSLTNG
1316 Central St Se (98501-2522)
PHONE.............................360 870-8429
Steven Welliever, *Principal*
EMP: 2
SALES (est): 73K **Privately Held**
SIC: 7372 Educational computer software

(G-7238)
BLUE MARTINI SOFTWARE
7205 105th Ave Sw (98512-8561)
PHONE.............................360 754-2207
Rob Neibauer, *Principal*
EMP: 2
SALES (est): 134.1K **Privately Held**
SIC: 7372 Prepackaged software

(G-7239)
BOLANDER SIGN CO
Also Called: Blonder Signs
1311 4th Ave E (98506-4245)
PHONE.............................360 943-2447
Mellissa Jenkins, *Owner*
EMP: 2
SQ FT: 3,000
SALES (est): 110K **Privately Held**
WEB: www.bolandersign.com
SIC: 3993 Signs & advertising specialties

(G-7240)
BOTANICAL BLU L L C
3749 36th Loop Nw (98502-3504)
PHONE.............................360 866-8251
Barbara L Blue, *Principal*
EMP: 2
SALES (est): 126.4K **Privately Held**
SIC: 2833 Medicinal chemicals

(G-7241)
BRIAN D AMES
7424 Puget Beach Rd Ne (98516-9169)
PHONE.............................360 561-5119
Brian D Ames, *Principal*
EMP: 3
SALES (est): 180.7K **Privately Held**
SIC: 2411 Logging

(G-7242)
BRIGHTWIRE NETWORKS LLC
2102 Carriage St Sw Ste J (98502-1049)
PHONE.............................360 528-6017
Todd Whitley,
Gordon Carlisle,
EMP: 7
SQ FT: 18,000
SALES: 1MM **Privately Held**
WEB: www.brightwirenetworks.com
SIC: 3825 Network analyzers

(G-7243)
BROWN & BALSLEY SIGN CO
Also Called: American Banner & Sign Co
1927 State Ave Ne (98506-4651)
PHONE.............................360 705-3099
Tim Brown, *Partner*
EMP: 2
SALES (est): 147K **Privately Held**
SIC: 3993 Signs, not made in custom sign painting shops

(G-7244)
BUDD BAY EMBROIDERY INC
6906 Martin Way E (98516-5567)
PHONE.............................360 709-0483
John Grantham, *President*
EMP: 10 EST: 1996
SQ FT: 2,500
SALES (est): 1.4MM **Privately Held**
WEB: www.buddbay.com
SIC: 7389 2396 Advertising, promotional & trade show services; embroidering of advertising on shirts, etc.; automotive & apparel trimmings

(G-7245)
BUDD BAY HOMES
7029 Boston Harbor Rd Ne (98506-9202)
PHONE.............................360 357-6064
Steve Fudurich, *Owner*
EMP: 2
SALES (est): 160K **Privately Held**
SIC: 2431 Doors & door parts & trim, wood

GEOGRAPHIC SECTION

Olympia - Thurston County (G-7279)

(G-7246)
BUDWIZ INC
921 Lkrdge Way Sw Ste 301 (98502)
PHONE 360 508-2771
Daniel McMahon, *CEO*
EMP: 2
SALES (est): 69.9K Privately Held
SIC: 7372 7389 Application computer software;

(G-7247)
CASCADIA HOMEBREW
211 4th Ave E (98501-1104)
PHONE 360 943-2337
EMP: 5
SALES (est): 289.8K Privately Held
SIC: 2082 Beer (alcoholic beverage)

(G-7248)
CHEHALIS BREWING GROUP LLC
222 Capitol Way N Ste 111 (98501-8211)
PHONE 360 628-8259
EMP: 4 **EST:** 2014
SALES (est): 254K Privately Held
SIC: 2085 Distilled & blended liquors

(G-7249)
CHIMERAS LLC
8120 Delphi Rd Sw (98512-2160)
PHONE 360 754-9217
Shelley Stomieroski,
EMP: 4
SALES: 230K Privately Held
SIC: 2844 Cosmetic preparations

(G-7250)
COBBS LLC
313 5th Ave Se Ste C (98501-1191)
PHONE 360 302-2692
Stephen Cobb, *Owner*
EMP: 2
SALES (est): 162.2K Privately Held
SIC: 5149 2064 Pet foods; natural & organic foods; specialty food items; chocolate candy, except solid chocolate

(G-7251)
COINFORCECOM LLC
9111 Yelm Hwy Se (98513-6319)
PHONE 253 682-2825
Jordan Haines,
Donna Haines,
EMP: 6
SQ FT: 1,300
SALES: 2MM Privately Held
WEB: www.coinforce.com
SIC: 3999 Coins & tokens, non-currency

(G-7252)
COLOR ME HOUSE INC
Also Called: CMH
1801 East Bay Dr Ne Apt J (98506-3266)
PHONE 360 742-8646
April McCray, *President*
EMP: 2
SALES (est): 126.4K Privately Held
WEB: WWW.COLORMEHOUSE.COM
SIC: 3952 7389 Crayons: chalk, gypsum, charcoal, fusains, pastel, wax, etc.;

(G-7253)
COLUMBIA GRANITE LLC
5209 Boulevard Ext Rd Se (98501-4967)
PHONE 360 943-4072
Jim Gilmore,
Joe Ashlock,
EMP: 8
SALES: 2.4MM Privately Held
SIC: 1411 Granite, dimension-quarrying

(G-7254)
COMMUNITY VALUES MAGAZINE
3619 Owl Ln Ne (98516-2740)
PHONE 360 459-8292
Lee Townsend, *Publisher*
Babbet Townsend, *Principal*
EMP: 2
SALES (est): 190.8K Privately Held
SIC: 2721 Magazines: publishing only, not printed on site

(G-7255)
CONTECH ENGNERED SOLUTIONS LLC
606 Columbia St Nw # 210 (98501-1085)
PHONE 360 357-9735
Doug Maxwell, *Manager*
EMP: 13 Privately Held
SIC: 3443 Fabricated plate work (boiler shop)
HQ: Contech Engineered Solutions Llc
9025 Centre Pointe Dr # 400
West Chester OH 45069
513 645-7000

(G-7256)
CORNERSTONE REAL PROPERTY
4731 Center Ln Ne (98516-9216)
PHONE 360 455-0862
Robert Hodgman, *Owner*
EMP: 4
SALES (est): 247.9K Privately Held
SIC: 2431 Millwork

(G-7257)
COSTUME ATLIER MSQUE PETTYCOTE
620 Legion Way Se (98501-1425)
PHONE 360 819-4296
Mishka Navarre, *Mng Member*
Ricky German,
EMP: 2
SALES (est): 131.7K Privately Held
SIC: 2389 7299 Theatrical costumes; clothing rental services

(G-7258)
CRAWFORD ENTERPRISES
2204 Westwind Dr Nw (98502-9725)
PHONE 360 866-4972
Bonnie L Crawford, *Owner*
EMP: 2
SALES (est): 130K Privately Held
SIC: 2411 Logging

(G-7259)
CREATIVE COLLECTIONS CO INC
Also Called: J & L Company
1633 Kaiser Rd Nw (98502-8513)
PHONE 360 866-8840
Lina Wiatt, *President*
▲ **EMP:** 26
SQ FT: 10,000
SALES: 3MM Privately Held
SIC: 5131 2844 3069 5199 Hair accessories; shampoos, rinses, conditioners: hair; rubber hair accessories; curlers, hair, rubber; hairbrushes; costume jewelry

(G-7260)
CREMA DEVELOPMENT LLC
3834 Starling Dr Nw (98502-3223)
PHONE 360 918-6978
Carter Barnes,
Deanna Barnes,
EMP: 2
SALES (est): 62.1K Privately Held
SIC: 7372 7371 Application computer software; custom computer programming services

(G-7261)
CROWN CORK & SEAL USA INC
1202 Fones Rd Se (98501-2716)
PHONE 360 491-4900
Troy Lovett, *Opers Mgr*
Dave Rivard, *Technical Staff*
EMP: 220
SALES (corp-wide): 11.1B Publicly Held
WEB: www.crowncork.com
SIC: 3411 Metal cans
HQ: Crown Cork & Seal Usa, Inc.
770 Township Line Rd # 100
Yardley PA 19067
215 698-5100

(G-7262)
CUSTOM SHEET METAL INC
3231 46th Ave Ne (98506-9602)
PHONE 360 754-5220
Brian Pruett, *President*
EMP: 3
SALES (est): 415.4K Privately Held
SIC: 3444 Sheet metalwork

(G-7263)
D G PARROTT & SON
Also Called: Parrott D G Son McHnsts Mnfact
209 Thurston Ave Ne (98501-1171)
PHONE 360 352-8242
Steve Parrott, *Owner*
EMP: 7
SALES (est): 538.8K Privately Held
SIC: 3599 Machine shop, jobbing & repair

(G-7264)
DAUGHTERS OF MARY
1921 Parkwood Dr Se (98501-3059)
PHONE 360 943-2186
Jill Hulbert, *President*
Helga Natterer, *Vice Pres*
Alice Janny, *Treasurer*
EMP: 4
SALES (est): 340K Privately Held
WEB: www.daughtersofmary.com
SIC: 3911 3961 5999 Bracelets, precious metal; costume jewelry; religious goods

(G-7265)
DAVID LITTLEJOHN LOGGING
11946 Case Rd Sw (98512-9127)
PHONE 360 352-5858
David Littlejohn, *Partner*
EMP: 5
SALES (est): 540K Privately Held
SIC: 2411 Logging camps & contractors

(G-7266)
DECK BUILDERS
5641 Maytown Rd Sw (98512-9242)
PHONE 360 709-9225
Kim Katwijk, *President*
Linda Katwijk, *Vice Pres*
EMP: 2
SALES: 350K Privately Held
WEB: www.deck-builders.com
SIC: 2789 Deckling books, cards or paper

(G-7267)
DELTA GRIND LLC
9105 Martin Way E (98516-5994)
PHONE 360 459-8205
EMP: 2 **EST:** 2016
SALES (est): 81.4K Privately Held
SIC: 3599 Grinding castings for the trade

(G-7268)
DERMA MEDICAL SPA
3025 Limited Ln Nw (98502-2613)
PHONE 360 350-5321
Amanda Berg, *Director*
EMP: 3
SALES (est): 85.3K Privately Held
SIC: 7991 8011 3845 Spas; medical centers; laser systems & equipment, medical

(G-7269)
DESCO PLASTICS LLC
7235 40th Ct Ne (98516-2745)
PHONE 360 413-7787
Dave Higgs,
EMP: 2
SQ FT: 2,400
SALES (est): 190.1K Privately Held
WEB: www.descoplastics.com
SIC: 3089 Plastics products

(G-7270)
DIAMOND TECH INNOVATIONS INC
Also Called: Dti Exact
1043 Kaiser Rd Sw (98512-5585)
PHONE 360 866-1337
Theodore Jernigan, *President*
Mike Greely, *Vice Pres*
Tyrel Rothell, *Engineer*
Tanya Jernigan, *CFO*
Jessica Jernigan, *Mktg Dir*
▲ **EMP:** 45
SALES: 7.4MM
SALES (corp-wide): 22.4MM Privately Held
SIC: 3429 3915 Clamps, couplings, nozzles & other metal hose fittings; diamond cutting & polishing
PA: Bourn & Koch, Inc.
2500 Kishwaukee St
Rockford IL 61104
815 965-4013

(G-7271)
DINGEYS LLC
700 Capitol Way S (98501)
PHONE 360 789-0853
Teresa Ricklick, *Owner*
EMP: 5
SALES (est): 441.2K Privately Held
SIC: 2599 Food wagons, restaurant

(G-7272)
DONT STOP PRINTING
1803 Cameo Ct Nw (98502-4054)
PHONE 360 292-8610
Mark Malsbary, *Founder*
EMP: 2
SALES (est): 146.3K Privately Held
SIC: 2752 Commercial printing, offset

(G-7273)
DOT4KIDS
1925 54th Ln Se (98501-4774)
PHONE 503 884-8838
Meena Sambandam, *CEO*
EMP: 2
SALES (est): 34.7K Privately Held
SIC: 8699 8641 7372 Charitable organization; youth organizations; application computer software

(G-7274)
ELEMENT ELECTRIC LLC
629 Hawks Glen Dr Se (98513-1770)
PHONE 360 304-9918
Burke Mee, *Principal*
EMP: 2
SALES (est): 74.4K Privately Held
SIC: 2819 Elements

(G-7275)
ELEMENTS OF IRON & WOOD LLC
4525 72nd Ave Ne (98516-9511)
PHONE 360 789-0840
EMP: 2
SALES (est): 74.4K Privately Held
SIC: 2819 Elements

(G-7276)
EMPIRE PACKING
Also Called: Northwest Processing
7430 32nd Ave Ne (98516-3188)
PHONE 360 459-3745
Debra Robinson, *President*
Michelle Kelling, *Manager*
EMP: 80
SALES (est): 5.9MM Privately Held
SIC: 2011 Meat packing plants

(G-7277)
ENERTEC BAS
Also Called: Building Automation Systems
628 Plymouth St Sw (98502-5311)
PHONE 360 786-1257
Cynthia Johnstone, *President*
Robin Johnstone, *Vice Pres*
Carol Morehead, *Vice Pres*
John Morehead, *Vice Pres*
EMP: 4
SALES (est): 772.3K Privately Held
WEB: www.enertec-bas.com
SIC: 3822 1731 1711 Building services monitoring controls, automatic; electrical work; heating & air conditioning contractors; warm air heating & air conditioning contractor

(G-7278)
ERGO DESIGN INC (PA)
3441 93rd Ave Sw (98512-1103)
PHONE 360 427-5779
Bruce W Kemppainen, *President*
EMP: 4
SALES (est): 370K Privately Held
SIC: 3572 Computer storage devices

(G-7279)
ERNEST R HOWALD INC
1645 Marvin Rd Se (98503-1968)
PHONE 360 491-1758
Norbert Howald, *President*
Brigiette Howald, *Corp Secy*
Alf Howald, *Vice Pres*
Ernest R Howald, *Vice Pres*
EMP: 4
SQ FT: 3,600

Olympia - Thurston County (G-7280)

SALES (est): 377.2K **Privately Held**
SIC: **1751** 2434 Cabinet building & installation; wood kitchen cabinets

(G-7280)
EXIT PUZZLES
109 State Ave Ne (98501-1130)
PHONE.....................360 930-9686
EMP: 2
SALES (est): 64.6K **Privately Held**
SIC: **3944** Puzzles

(G-7281)
EXTREME CAPACITOR INC
Also Called: X-Cap
1835 Cedarbury Ln Sw (98512-5515)
PHONE.....................360 878-9749
▼ EMP: 7
SALES (est): 561.4K **Privately Held**
SIC: **3675** Mfg Electronic Capacitors

(G-7282)
FASTENER TRAINING
10111 Tilley Rd S (98512-9143)
PHONE.....................562 400-3009
Dallas Puckett, *Principal*
EMP: 2
SALES (est): 84.7K **Privately Held**
SIC: **3965** Fasteners

(G-7283)
FINAS SALSA
3509 Autumnwood Ct Se (98501-6604)
PHONE.....................360 951-5218
Josefina Pilon, *Principal*
EMP: 3
SALES (est): 121.5K **Privately Held**
SIC: **2099** Dips, except cheese & sour cream based

(G-7284)
FINELY FINISHED LLC
3534 49th Ave Sw (98512-6602)
PHONE.....................360 709-0602
Anamarie C Seidel, *Mng Member*
Cory Seidel,
EMP: 2
SALES (est): 180K **Privately Held**
SIC: **2782** Scrapbooks

(G-7285)
FIRST STRIKE LLC
924 Capitol Way S Ste 105 (98501-1210)
P.O. Box 11219 (98508-1219)
PHONE.....................360 285-4000
◆ EMP: 3 EST: 2010
SQ FT: 1,000
SALES (est): 120K **Privately Held**
SIC: **3999** Government Contractor And/Or Vendor

(G-7286)
FISH BREWING CO (HQ)
Also Called: Fish Tale Ales
515 Jefferson St Se (98501-1467)
PHONE.....................360 943-3650
Lyle Morse, *Ch of Bd*
Scott Hansen, *President*
EMP: 19
SQ FT: 15,000
SALES (est): 3MM
SALES (corp-wide): 3.3MM **Privately Held**
SIC: **2082** 5947 5813 5812 Beer (alcoholic beverage); ale (alcoholic beverage); gift, novelty & souvenir shop; drinking places; eating places
PA: Washington Wine & Beverage Co Inc
14701 148th Ave Ne
Woodinville WA 98072
425 485-2437

(G-7287)
FISHTAIL PUB
515 Jefferson St Se (98501-1467)
PHONE.....................360 943-3650
Lyle Morse, *Principal*
EMP: 50
SALES (est): 554.9K **Privately Held**
SIC: **5813** 2082 Bar (drinking places); beer (alcoholic beverage)

(G-7288)
FLYINGVIOLIN INC
8648 Fenwick Loop Se (98513-3414)
PHONE.....................209 595-9709
Josephine Petetra Olson, *CEO*
EMP: 2
SALES (est): 117.5K **Privately Held**
SIC: **3931** Violins & parts

(G-7289)
FOOTEPRINTS INCORPORATED
Also Called: Minuteman Press
1025 Black Lake Blvd Sw (98502-1120)
PHONE.....................360 754-8779
Clothele Foote, *President*
James Foote, *Corp Secy*
EMP: 2
SQ FT: 3,200
SALES: 800K **Privately Held**
SIC: **2752** Commercial printing, lithographic

(G-7290)
FOOTEPRINTS INC
Also Called: Minuteman Press
4404 Martin Way E Ste 2 (98516-5365)
PHONE.....................360 491-8195
Clothele Foote, *President*
James Foote, *Admin Sec*
EMP: 2
SQ FT: 1,500
SALES (est): 265.6K **Privately Held**
SIC: **2752** Commercial printing, lithographic

(G-7291)
FORTERRA INC
1414 Cherry St Se (98501-2341)
P.O. Box 7508 (98507-7508)
PHONE.....................360 943-1600
EMP: 3 EST: 2016
SALES (est): 331.6K **Privately Held**
SIC: **3272** Concrete products

(G-7292)
GABRIELLE ENGLAND INC
1520 Woodard Ct Nw (98502-3112)
PHONE.....................360 956-1017
Gabrielle England, *President*
Mohamed Elsokkary, *Vice Pres*
Glen Sawray, *Treasurer*
EMP: 3
SALES (est): 267.5K **Privately Held**
WEB: www.gabrielleengland.com
SIC: **3281** Cut stone & stone products

(G-7293)
GALIVAN LOGGING INC
2138 Overhulse Rd Nw (98502-4048)
PHONE.....................360 866-1431
Patricia Galivan, *Owner*
EMP: 3
SALES (est): 200K **Privately Held**
SIC: **2411** Logging camps & contractors

(G-7294)
GARYS GARDEN GATE
1900 93rd Ave Sw (98512-9155)
PHONE.....................360 357-5607
Gary Waldherr, *Owner*
EMP: 8
SALES (est): 892.2K **Privately Held**
WEB: www.garysgardengate.com
SIC: **3446** Ornamental metalwork

(G-7295)
GEORGIA-PACIFIC LLC
1203 Fones Rd Se (98501-2715)
PHONE.....................360 491-1310
Scott White, *General Mgr*
Emily Ouhl, *Safety Mgr*
Jim Gillihan, *QC Mgr*
Eric King, *Controller*
Lain Long, *Marketing Staff*
EMP: 140
SQ FT: 245,046
SALES (corp-wide): 42.6B **Privately Held**
WEB: www.gp.com
SIC: **2653** Boxes, corrugated: made from purchased materials
HQ: Georgia-Pacific Llc
133 Peachtree St Nw
Atlanta GA 30303
404 652-4000

(G-7296)
GLACIER AVIATION INC (PA)
Also Called: Glacier Jet Center
7645 Old Hwy 99 Ne (98501)
PHONE.....................360 705-3214
Michael Thielen, *President*
EMP: 18
SALES (est): 1.3MM **Privately Held**
SIC: **8331** 3721 Job training & vocational rehabilitation services; helicopters

(G-7297)
GLENN WALDREN
Also Called: Micro Data Bus Forms & Prtg
2612 Yelm Hwy Se Ste D (98501-4826)
PHONE.....................360 570-8400
Glenn Waldren, *Owner*
EMP: 2 EST: 1978
SALES (est): 110K **Privately Held**
SIC: **2621** 5734 Business form paper; computer & software stores

(G-7298)
GRANDVIEW SCREEN USA INC
2121 Crestline Blvd Nw (98502-4320)
P.O. Box 2466 (98507-2466)
PHONE.....................360 481-3490
EMP: 2
SALES (est): 92.3K **Privately Held**
SIC: **2752** Commercial printing, lithographic

(G-7299)
GRAPHIC COMMUNICATIONS (PA)
Also Called: Greg's Graphic & Printing Co
109 Columbia St Nw (98501-1053)
PHONE.....................360 786-5110
Doug Souliere, *President*
Greggory R Souliere, *Vice Pres*
Carolyn Crabill,
EMP: 10
SQ FT: 1,800
SALES (est): 1.1MM **Privately Held**
WEB: www.gcprint.com
SIC: **2759** Commercial printing

(G-7300)
GROOVE INCORPORATED
6715 Martin Way E (98516-6507)
PHONE.....................360 786-9605
Andrea Patton, *President*
EMP: 2
SALES (est): 127.2K **Privately Held**
SIC: **2499** Picture frame molding, finished

(G-7301)
GUYS PLASMA NW LLC
9611 Summerfield Loop Se (98513-6682)
PHONE.....................360 878-9826
Paul Julbes, *Principal*
EMP: 2
SALES (est): 115.6K **Privately Held**
SIC: **2836** Plasmas

(G-7302)
HANCOR INC
6001 Belmore St Sw (98512-7921)
PHONE.....................360 943-3313
Marv Gregs, *Manager*
EMP: 50
SALES (corp-wide): 1.3B **Publicly Held**
SIC: **3082** 3084 Tubes, unsupported plastic; plastics pipe
HQ: Hancor, Inc.
4640 Trueman Blvd
Hilliard OH 43026
614 658-0050

(G-7303)
HANSEN MARINE REPAIR & RIGGING
4433 61st Ave Ne (98516-9501)
PHONE.....................360 705-1252
EMP: 2
SALES (est): 87K **Privately Held**
SIC: **3731** Shipbuilding/Repairing

(G-7304)
HARTLEY JEWELERS
Also Called: Hartley Co
6640 Klein St Nw (98502-3360)
PHONE.....................360 754-6161
Rick Hartley, *Partner*
Linda Hartley, *Partner*
EMP: 8
SALES (est): 864.2K **Privately Held**
WEB: www.hartleyjewelers.com
SIC: **5944** 3911 7631 Jewelry, precious stones & precious metals; jewelry, precious metal; jewelry repair services

(G-7305)
HARVEST HELPER
2747 Pacific Ave Se (98501-2097)
PHONE.....................360 515-5491
EMP: 2
SALES (est): 111.7K **Privately Held**
SIC: **3999** Manufacturing industries

(G-7306)
HICKS LOGGING CHRISTMAS T
3721 Fuller Ln Se (98501-5059)
PHONE.....................253 208-8914
EMP: 3
SALES (est): 134.5K **Privately Held**
SIC: **2411** Logging

(G-7307)
HOLBROOK INC (PA)
Also Called: Holbrook Logging Sort Yard
1576 Marine Dr Ne (98501-6905)
PHONE.....................360 754-9390
Richard Holbrook, *President*
Jerry Holbrook, *Vice Pres*
Ylan Trivison, *Director*
Terry Moore, *Admin Sec*
EMP: 37
SQ FT: 1,300
SALES: 8MM **Privately Held**
WEB: www.holbrook.com
SIC: **2411** 2421 Logging camps & contractors; lumber stacking or sticking

(G-7308)
HOLROYD COMPANY INC
828 Old Pacific Hwy Se (98513-9513)
P.O. Box 39009, Lakewood (98496-3009)
PHONE.....................253 474-0725
Chris Vaughn, *Manager*
EMP: 50
SALES (corp-wide): 16.7MM **Privately Held**
WEB: www.holroyd.com
SIC: **3273** Ready-mixed concrete
PA: Holroyd Company, Inc.
7216 Lakewood Dr W
Tacoma WA 98499
253 474-0725

(G-7309)
HOLY LAMB ORGANICS INC
4431 Boston Harbor Rd Ne (98506-2442)
P.O. Box 309, Oakville (98568-0309)
PHONE.....................360 402-5781
Willow Luisa Whitton, *President*
EMP: 4
SALES (est): 402.7K **Privately Held**
SIC: **2392** Household furnishings

(G-7310)
J R SETINA MANUFACTURING CO
2926 Yelm Hwy Se (98501-4832)
PHONE.....................360 491-6197
Terry Setina, *President*
Ryan Bredeson, *Administration*
▼ EMP: 80
SQ FT: 85,000
SALES (est): 25.9MM **Privately Held**
WEB: www.setina.com
SIC: **3089** 3465 3444 Aquarium accessories, plastic; automotive parts, plastic; awnings, fiberglass & plastic combination; body parts, automobile: stamped metal; fenders, automobile: stamped or pressed metal; metal housings, enclosures, casings & other containers

(G-7311)
JEWELRY BOUTIQUE LLC (PA)
Also Called: Helen Ficalora
6753 Bellevista Pl Nw (98502-3398)
PHONE.....................360 866-2278
Helen Ficaroa,
Robert Ficaroa,
▲ EMP: 4
SALES (est): 1.9MM **Privately Held**
SIC: **3911** 5094 5961 Jewelry, precious metal; jewelry; jewelry, mail order; computers & peripheral equipment, mail order

GEOGRAPHIC SECTION

Olympia - Thurston County (G-7345)

(G-7312)
JOHN MEEK LOGGING
3748 80th Ave Se (98501-9511)
PHONE..................................360 491-6976
John E Meek, *Owner*
EMP: 4
SALES: 1MM **Privately Held**
SIC: 2411 Logging camps & contractors

(G-7313)
JOHNSONS MACHINE AND PRFMCE SP
1510 93rd Ave Sw (98512-9102)
PHONE..................................360 352-4465
Randy Rosar, *Owner*
EMP: 3
SALES (est): 221.5K **Privately Held**
SIC: 3599 7539 Machine shop, jobbing & repair; machine shop, automotive

(G-7314)
JOOM 3D
7636 Rixie St Se (98501-5668)
PHONE..................................413 566-6330
Renee Gillard, *CEO*
Paul Tinari, *Principal*
EMP: 2
SALES (est): 94.7K **Privately Held**
SIC: 2452 3448 3559 Prefabricated buildings, wood; prefabricated metal buildings; cement making machinery

(G-7315)
KEITH COOPER LOGGING INC
3846 Mari Ln Se (98513-9315)
PHONE..................................360 459-3553
Keith Cooper, *Principal*
EMP: 2 EST: 2016
SALES (est): 89.8K **Privately Held**
SIC: 2411 Logging

(G-7316)
KENNEDY CREEK POTTERY
12320 Summit Lake Rd Nw (98502-9401)
PHONE..................................360 866-3937
David Siemens, *Owner*
EMP: 2 EST: 2000
SALES (est): 65.5K **Privately Held**
SIC: 3269 5719 Pottery products; pottery

(G-7317)
LAKE SUNSET LLC
1816 Lenox Ct Nw (98502-3113)
PHONE..................................718 683-2269
EMP: 2
SALES (est): 90.4K **Privately Held**
SIC: 2541 Wood partitions & fixtures

(G-7318)
LAKESIDE INDUSTRIES INC
11125 Durgin Rd Se (98513-9525)
PHONE..................................360 491-5460
Dean Smith, *Branch Mgr*
EMP: 50
SALES (corp-wide): 326.4MM **Privately Held**
WEB: www.lakesideind.com
SIC: 1611 2951 5032 Highway & street paving contractor; asphalt & asphaltic paving mixtures (not from refineries); gravel
PA: Lakeside Industries, Inc.
6505 226th Pl Se Ste 200
Issaquah WA 98027
425 313-2600

(G-7319)
LATTINS COUNTRY CIDER
9402 Rich Rd Se (98501-9822)
PHONE..................................360 491-7328
Carolyn G Lattin, *President*
Sherrie Cohlemann, *Mng Member*
Debbie Lattin, *Mng Member*
EMP: 25 EST: 1972
SQ FT: 3,760
SALES (est): 750K **Privately Held**
SIC: 2099 2051 Cider, nonalcoholic; bakery: wholesale or wholesale/retail combined

(G-7320)
LAVAL
4802 31st Ave Se (98503-3636)
PHONE..................................360 491-8118
Laval Houskeeper, *Principal*
EMP: 4
SALES (est): 110K **Privately Held**
SIC: 2051 Bakery: wholesale or wholesale/retail combined

(G-7321)
LEGACY PLASTICS L L C
7235 40th Ct Ne (98516-2745)
PHONE..................................360 413-7787
D R Higgs, *Bd of Directors*
EMP: 3
SALES (est): 197.7K **Privately Held**
SIC: 3089 Injection molding of plastics

(G-7322)
LENNOX INC
2302 Harrison Ave Nw (98502-4543)
PHONE..................................360 970-8954
Palmer Higa, *Principal*
EMP: 2
SALES (est): 106.4K **Privately Held**
SIC: 3585 Refrigeration & heating equipment

(G-7323)
LIFE RECOVERY SOLUTIONS INC
711 Capitol Way S Ste 204 (98501-1267)
PHONE..................................208 771-2161
Gail Stevenson, *CEO*
Edward Stevenson, *President*
EMP: 2
SALES (est): 147.1K **Privately Held**
SIC: 7372 Application computer software

(G-7324)
LOADING DOCKS SUPPLY LLC
Also Called: Delaware Supply
5405 Keating Rd Nw (98502-9536)
PHONE..................................360 866-7063
Janet Buechel,
▼ EMP: 6
SALES (est): 655K **Privately Held**
SIC: 3537 Loading docks: portable, adjustable & hydraulic

(G-7325)
LONG LIFE CANDLES
Also Called: Long Life Bees Wax Candles
810 Oleary St Nw (98502-9588)
PHONE..................................360 866-1127
Talbot Uehlinger, *Partner*
Deena Manif, *Partner*
EMP: 2
SALES (est): 106K **Privately Held**
SIC: 3999 Candles

(G-7326)
LUES DEBEAKING
4114 Fir Tree Rd Se (98501-9617)
PHONE..................................360 438-9207
Luella Huber, *Owner*
EMP: 2
SALES (est): 50K **Privately Held**
SIC: 2015 Chicken slaughtering & processing

(G-7327)
M AND J DISTRIBUTION
5847 Braywood Ln Se (98513-9039)
PHONE..................................360 455-4675
Michael Schaler, *Owner*
Jillian Schaler, *Co-Owner*
EMP: 2
SALES (est): 101.5K **Privately Held**
SIC: 2051 Bread, all types (white, wheat, rye, etc): fresh or frozen

(G-7328)
M B G MANAGEMENT SERVICES
3521 Hollywood Dr Ne (98516-1415)
PHONE..................................360 493-0522
Ron Kuest, *President*
Patricia Kuest, *Corp Secy*
EMP: 3
SALES (est): 303.3K **Privately Held**
WEB: www.spirituallead.com
SIC: 8742 2731 Business consultant; pamphlets: publishing only, not printed on site

(G-7329)
MADSEN FAMILY CELLARS
1916 Allegro Dr Se (98501-3747)
PHONE..................................360 357-3015
Dana Madsen, *Principal*
EMP: 2 EST: 2010
SALES (est): 204.8K **Privately Held**
SIC: 2084 Wines

(G-7330)
MADSEN FAMILY CELLARS ✿
2633 Reinhardt Ln Ne D (98516-3158)
PHONE..................................360 339-8371
EMP: 2 EST: 2019
SALES (est): 62.3K **Privately Held**
SIC: 2084 Wines, brandy & brandy spirits

(G-7331)
MAL INC
Also Called: Aaron's Septic Svc
7225 Pacific Ave Se (98503-6750)
PHONE..................................360 491-2900
Teresa Grimsley, *President*
EMP: 70
SALES (est): 13.9MM **Privately Held**
SIC: 3569 3561 7699 Filters; pumps & pumping equipment; pumps & pumping equipment repair

(G-7332)
MAUGHAN PROSTHETIC ORTHOTIC S
208 Lilly Rd Ne Ste A (98506-6100)
P.O. Box 1546, Graham (98338-1546)
PHONE..................................360 338-0284
Justin Maughan, *President*
Brett Barnts, *Vice Pres*
EMP: 4 EST: 2012
SQ FT: 2,362
SALES (est): 343.5K **Privately Held**
SIC: 3842 5999 Limbs, artificial; orthopedic & prosthesis applications

(G-7333)
MCCLATCHY NEWSPAPERS INC
Also Called: Olympian
522 Franklin St Se (98501-1336)
PHONE..................................360 754-5400
Bob Retter, *Branch Mgr*
EMP: 117
SALES (corp-wide): 807.2MM **Publicly Held**
WEB: www.sacbee.com
SIC: 2711 2752 Newspapers: publishing only, not printed on site; commercial printing, lithographic
HQ: Mcclatchy Newspapers, Inc.
2100 Q St
Sacramento CA 95816
916 321-1855

(G-7334)
MCLEOD PILOT CAR & HOT SHT SVC
6430 Guerin St Sw (98512-2247)
PHONE..................................360 701-5827
Larry McLeod, *Principal*
EMP: 2
SALES (est): 107.6K **Privately Held**
SIC: 1389 Hot shot service

(G-7335)
MECHANICAL SPECIALTIES LLC
1000 85th Ave Se (98501-5707)
PHONE..................................360 273-7604
Rob Schales, *General Mgr*
Brian A Reynolds, *Mng Member*
EMP: 3
SQ FT: 2,800
SALES: 500K **Privately Held**
WEB: www.nwhelicopters.com
SIC: 3728 3599 Aircraft assemblies, subassemblies & parts; machine shop, jobbing & repair

(G-7336)
MECHANICAL SPECILITIES
975 85th Ave Se (98501-5762)
PHONE..................................360 273-7604
Rob Schales, *Mng Member*
EMP: 3
SALES (est): 165.6K **Privately Held**
SIC: 3721 Helicopters

(G-7337)
MED-CORE SERVICES INC
6706 Martin Way E Ste 1 (98516-5540)
PHONE..................................360 455-5425
Rene Clontz, *President*
John Marshall, *Officer*
EMP: 5
SALES (est): 610.9K **Privately Held**
SIC: 2813 8099 Oxygen, compressed or liquefied; medical services organization

(G-7338)
MEDIA HOLDINGS LLC
Also Called: Media Direct
3130 Madrona Beach Rd Nw (98502-8869)
PHONE..................................503 313-0676
Ron Ellwanger, *Mng Member*
Linda Ellwanger,
EMP: 6
SALES (est): 692K **Privately Held**
WEB: www.mediadirect.com
SIC: 3652 Compact laser discs, prerecorded

(G-7339)
MICHAEL ASHFORD DESIGN
Also Called: Evergreen Studios
6543 Alpine Dr Sw (98512-2007)
PHONE..................................360 352-0694
Michael Ashford, *Owner*
Cathy Ashford, *Co-Owner*
EMP: 3
SALES (est): 160.2K **Privately Held**
WEB: www.evergreenstudios.com
SIC: 3645 Residential lighting fixtures

(G-7340)
MINUTEMAN FUND OF WASHINGTON
3521 17th Way Se (98501-2935)
PHONE..................................253 584-5411
EMP: 3
SALES (est): 26.2K **Privately Held**
SIC: 2752 Commercial printing, offset

(G-7341)
MISS MFFTTS MYSTCAL CPCKES LLC
625 Black Lake Blvd Sw (98502-5066)
PHONE..................................360 890-4403
Rachel Young, *Mng Member*
EMP: 2
SALES (est): 325.1K **Privately Held**
SIC: 2051 Bread, cake & related products

(G-7342)
MONTES LOGGING & FIREWOOD
7607 Kmrlyn Prairie Ln Se (98513-5656)
PHONE..................................360 943-3181
EMP: 3 EST: 1971
SALES (est): 220K **Privately Held**
SIC: 2411 Logging

(G-7343)
MORICE ENGINEERING
8120 Delphi Rd Sw (98512-2160)
PHONE..................................360 754-9217
Justin Morice, *Owner*
Sherly Morice, *Co-Owner*
◆ EMP: 2
SQ FT: 3,000
SALES (est): 230.1K **Privately Held**
SIC: 3556 Milk machinery, dry milk processing machinery

(G-7344)
MOUNT EVERGREEN INDUSTRIES
4200 Boston Harbor Rd Ne (98506-2439)
PHONE..................................360 584-9620
Paul Glasgow, *Vice Pres*
EMP: 2
SALES (est): 107.7K **Privately Held**
SIC: 3999 Manufacturing industries

(G-7345)
MQS GROUP LLC
301 18th Ave Se (98501-2301)
PHONE..................................360 956-9114
John Saunders, *Principal*
EMP: 3 EST: 2011
SALES (est): 251.4K **Privately Held**
SIC: 3695 Computer software tape & disks: blank, rigid & floppy

Olympia - Thurston County (G-7346)

(G-7346)
MURPHY & DAD INC
Also Called: Total Battery & Automotive Sup
3480 Martin Way E (98506-5034)
PHONE..................360 438-2747
Brent Murphy, *President*
Fawn Murphy, *Vice Pres*
EMP: 2
SALES (est): 275.1K **Privately Held**
SIC: 3694 Battery charging generators, automobile & aircraft

(G-7347)
MVR TIMBER CUTTING INC
12028 Dream St Sw (98512-1074)
PHONE..................360 459-7409
Montie Rask, *President*
Gina Rask, *Admin Sec*
EMP: 14
SALES (est): 2.9MM **Privately Held**
SIC: 2411 Timber, cut at logging camp

(G-7348)
NATIONAL HSPTLITY RSOURCES LLC
1242 Milbanke Dr Se (98513-7722)
PHONE..................360 413-1654
Joseph Navarra,
EMP: 3
SALES (est): 227.8K **Privately Held**
SIC: 2844 Toilet preparations

(G-7349)
OAK BROS CURVED GLASS
Also Called: Oak Brothers
7510 Fair Oaks Rd Se (98513-5125)
PHONE..................253 752-4055
EMP: 2 **EST:** 1976
SQ FT: 1,200
SALES (est): 119.9K **Privately Held**
SIC: 3229 Mfg Pressed/Blown Glass

(G-7350)
OILTRAP ENVIRONMENTAL PDTS INC
8904 Kimmie St Sw (98512-7641)
PHONE..................360 943-6495
Dale Nelson, *President*
Mike Davis, *President*
Marit Nelson, *Corp Secy*
EMP: 12
SQ FT: 10,000
SALES (est): 2.8MM **Privately Held**
WEB: www.oiltrap.com
SIC: 3589 8711 Water treatment equipment, industrial; engineering services

(G-7351)
OLD PLANK WOODWORKS
3141 60th Loop Se (98501-5376)
PHONE..................360 455-7366
Eileen Stanley, *Principal*
EMP: 2
SALES (est): 164K **Privately Held**
SIC: 2431 Millwork

(G-7352)
OLY KRAUT LLC
2300 Friendly Grove Rd Ne (98506-3508)
P.O. Box 1234 (98507-1234)
PHONE..................360 561-4532
Summer Bock, *Principal*
EMP: 4
SALES (est): 354.7K **Privately Held**
SIC: 2033 Canned fruits & specialties

(G-7353)
OLYMPIA POWDER COAT
1015 85th Ave Se (98501-5706)
PHONE..................360 570-9100
Don Rollman, *Partner*
Roger Rollman, *Partner*
EMP: 3
SQ FT: 10,500
SALES (est): 290K **Privately Held**
WEB: www.olympiapowdercoating.com
SIC: 3479 Coating of metals & formed products

(G-7354)
OLYMPIA SHEET METAL INC
Also Called: Honeywell Authorized Dealer
7635 Betti Ln Ne (98516-4511)
PHONE..................360 491-1123
Helga Rebitzer, *President*
EMP: 25
SQ FT: 7,000
SALES (est): 5.3MM **Privately Held**
SIC: 3444 Sheet metalwork

(G-7355)
OLYMPIAN NEWSPAPER
Also Called: Gannett Co
11 Duffel St Ne (98506)
PHONE..................360 754-5402
Bob Ritter, *Principal*
EMP: 3
SALES (est): 165K **Privately Held**
SIC: 2711 Newspapers: publishing only, not printed on site

(G-7356)
OLYMPIC ARMS INC
624 Old Pacific Hwy Se (98513-9505)
PHONE..................360 456-3471
Robert C Schuetz, *President*
Brian Schuetz, *Vice Pres*
Doris Ann Schuetz, *Treasurer*
Diane Haupert, *Admin Sec*
EMP: 60
SQ FT: 22,000
SALES (est): 8.4MM **Privately Held**
WEB: www.olyarms.com
SIC: 3484 Guns (firearms) or gun parts, 30 mm. & below; rifles or rifle parts, 30 mm. & below

(G-7357)
OLYMPIC CREST COFFEE ROASTERS
Also Called: Street Corner Caffe
5800 Pacific Ave Se (98503-1336)
PHONE..................360 459-5756
Charles R Kennedy, *Owner*
EMP: 4
SALES (est): 264.5K **Privately Held**
SIC: 2095 5812 Coffee roasting (except by wholesale grocers); coffee shop

(G-7358)
OLYMPIC IRON WORKS
3105 Marvin Rd Ne (98516-1403)
PHONE..................360 491-2500
Michael O' Rear,
Nancy Carter,
Roger Ledesma,
Gary Tokos,
EMP: 12
SQ FT: 12,000
SALES (est): 2.7MM **Privately Held**
SIC: 3441 Fabricated structural metal

(G-7359)
OLYMPIC MILLWORK
1521 Thomas St Nw (98502-3111)
PHONE..................360 480-6650
Robert Bly, *Principal*
EMP: 2
SALES (est): 152.9K **Privately Held**
SIC: 2431 Millwork

(G-7360)
OLYSUNRISE COMPOST CONCIERGE
206 Lilly Rd Ne Apt L10 (98506-5021)
PHONE..................360 551-0674
Heather Wood, *Principal*
EMP: 2
SALES (est): 74.4K **Privately Held**
SIC: 2875 Compost

(G-7361)
OMICRON INVESTMENT CORPORATION (PA)
6736 78th Ave Ne (98516-9571)
PHONE..................360 413-7569
Hernan G Etcheto, *President*
Hernan Etcheto, *President*
EMP: 9
SQ FT: 27,000
SALES (est): 1.1MM **Privately Held**
SIC: 2022 Natural cheese

(G-7362)
ONE ATTA TIME DOLL CO
6519 Lazy St Sw (98512-7122)
PHONE..................360 956-1091
Lois McCall, *Partner*
Jerry McCall, *Partner*
EMP: 2

SALES (est): 110K **Privately Held**
SIC: 5945 3942 Dolls & accessories; dolls & stuffed toys

(G-7363)
OTHER WORLDS
3921 Shincke Rd Ne (98506-9669)
PHONE..................360 459-2323
Keith Neissel, *Owner*
EMP: 3
SALES (est): 120K **Privately Held**
WEB: www.chimezone.com
SIC: 3931 8999 Percussion instruments & parts; stained glass art

(G-7364)
P I P PRINTING INC
Also Called: PIP Printing
3530 Martin Way E (98506-5424)
P.O. Box 64782, Tacoma (98464-0782)
PHONE..................360 456-4742
Richard Bringhurst, *President*
Walter E Duke, *President*
EMP: 10
SQ FT: 1,500
SALES (est): 500K **Privately Held**
SIC: 7334 2752 2759 Photocopying & duplicating services; commercial printing, lithographic; commercial printing

(G-7365)
PACIFIC STONE & TILE LLC
2770 Mottman Rd Sw Ste A (98512-5648)
PHONE..................360 352-3960
Musong Kim,
Lloyd B Heyland,
Katty Hinton,
EMP: 17 **EST:** 1999
SALES (est): 2.4MM **Privately Held**
SIC: 3281 1743 Marble, building: cut & shaped; marble installation, interior

(G-7366)
PATTERNS IN NATURE LLC
1826 Arbutus St Ne (98506-3204)
PHONE..................360 918-2629
Eugene Walker, *Principal*
EMP: 2
SALES (est): 117.3K **Privately Held**
SIC: 3543 Industrial patterns

(G-7367)
PAUL E SEVIER
Also Called: Eaton Creek Tree Farm
9721 Yelm Hwy Se (98513-9029)
PHONE..................360 491-1334
Paul E Sevier, *Owner*
EMP: 6
SALES (est): 511.6K **Privately Held**
SIC: 2411 4212 Logging; lumber (log) trucking, local

(G-7368)
PERKINS TIMBER LLC
Also Called: Perkins Lonnie Tmbr & Lnd Clng
4125 Dent Rd Sw (98512-6628)
PHONE..................360 754-2892
Lonnie Perkins, *Mng Member*
EMP: 2
SALES: 250K **Privately Held**
SIC: 2411 Logging camps & contractors

(G-7369)
PHILOS PRESS
8038a N Bcntnnial Loop Se (98503-1708)
PHONE..................360 456-5106
Laura Beausoleil, *Owner*
EMP: 2
SALES (est): 110K **Privately Held**
SIC: 2741 Miscellaneous publishing

(G-7370)
PICKLES PRINTING
5046 Viewridge Dr Se (98501-5138)
PHONE..................360 456-3230
Steve Dilley, *Principal*
EMP: 2
SALES (est): 172.7K **Privately Held**
SIC: 2752 Commercial printing, offset

(G-7371)
PLANTSPLUS
2244 65th Ln Nw (98502-3468)
PHONE..................360 628-8368
Eric J Olmstead, *Administration*
EMP: 2

SALES (est): 228.3K **Privately Held**
SIC: 3556 Homogenizing machinery: dairy, fruit, vegetable

(G-7372)
PRINT ROGUE LLC
1280 Partridge Dr Nw (98502-8907)
PHONE..................360 791-0914
Nick Milligan, *Principal*
EMP: 2
SALES (est): 92.1K **Privately Held**
SIC: 2752 Commercial printing, lithographic

(G-7373)
PRINTING UNLIMITED
2232 63rd Ct Sw (98512-7204)
PHONE..................360 357-8936
Scott Pidone, *Owner*
EMP: 2
SALES (est): 98.3K **Privately Held**
SIC: 2752 Commercial printing, lithographic

(G-7374)
PROFESSIONAL BUSINESS SVC INC
Also Called: Olympia Copy and Printing
704 Franklin St Se (98501-1345)
PHONE..................360 352-3000
Gary Fair, *President*
James Haran, *Exec VP*
Suzanne Fair, *Marketing Staff*
EMP: 10 **EST:** 1971
SQ FT: 8,000
SALES (est): 1.6MM **Privately Held**
WEB: www.olycopy.com
SIC: 2752 5112 5021 5045 Commercial printing, offset; office supplies; office furniture; computers, peripherals & software

(G-7375)
R L SMITH LOGGING INC
14612 State Route 8 W (98502-9447)
PHONE..................360 943-6540
Roger Smith, *President*
Carmen Smith, *Treasurer*
EMP: 16
SQ FT: 10,000
SALES (est): 2.3MM **Privately Held**
SIC: 2411 Logging camps & contractors

(G-7376)
R VISION ANTQ & RESTORATION
1911 Farwell Ave Nw (98502-4205)
PHONE..................360 280-0328
EMP: 2 **EST:** 2011
SALES (est): 127.3K **Privately Held**
SIC: 2431 Millwork

(G-7377)
RANDOM WALK GROUP LLC
501 Columbia St Nw Ste H (98501-1062)
PHONE..................206 724-3621
Keith Rossma, *Partner*
EMP: 2
SALES (est): 170K **Privately Held**
SIC: 6282 3812 8731 7371 Investment research; aircraft/aerospace flight instruments & guidance systems; commercial physical research; commercial research laboratory; computer software development & applications

(G-7378)
RAVEN RADIO THEATER
Also Called: Calling Crane Publishing
7605 Boston Harbor Rd Ne (98506-9749)
PHONE..................360 943-3206
Joe McHugh, *Owner*
EMP: 2 **EST:** 1986
SALES (est): 106.5K **Privately Held**
WEB: www.callingcrane.com
SIC: 2741 Miscellaneous publishing

(G-7379)
RAY R L VIOLIN SHOP LLC
925 State Ave Ne (98506-3956)
PHONE..................360 570-1085
Robert Ray,
Jon Hanson,
Tess Ray,
▲ **EMP:** 5
SQ FT: 800

GEOGRAPHIC SECTION

Olympia - Thurston County (G-7414)

SALES (est): 533.9K **Privately Held**
SIC: 5099 5736 3931 Musical instruments; musical instrument stores; string instruments & parts

(G-7380)
RCM ENTERPRISE LLC
Also Called: Naked Prosthetics
614 4th Ave E (98501-1113)
PHONE.................................888 977-6693
Robert B Thompson,
EMP: 2 EST: 2010
SALES (est): 227K **Privately Held**
SIC: 3842 Prosthetic appliances

(G-7381)
RED CREEK EMBROIDERY LLC
Also Called: Red Creek Apparel and Prom
1025 Black Lake Blvd Sw 1f (98502-1120)
PHONE.................................360 956-1792
Rebecca Robison, *Co-Owner*
Dennis Robison,
EMP: 2
SQ FT: 3,500
SALES: 200K **Privately Held**
WEB: www.redcreekapparel.com
SIC: 2395 Art goods for embroidering, stamped: purchased materials

(G-7382)
REDWOOD SUBS LLC (PA)
4316 Leavelle St Nw (98502-3639)
PHONE.................................217 493-9499
Adam Teske, *Principal*
EMP: 4
SALES (est): 654K **Privately Held**
SIC: 2499 Wood products

(G-7383)
RETURN MY LIFE LLC
4400 Fire Willow Way Nw (98502-8181)
PHONE.................................360 584-9799
Arthur Hunter, *Principal*
EMP: 3
SALES (est): 144.8K **Privately Held**
SIC: 2711 Newspapers

(G-7384)
REVELATION BUSINESS SERVI
9902 Hampshire Ct Se (98513-4241)
PHONE.................................360 456-1376
EMP: 2
SALES (est): 83.9K **Privately Held**
SIC: 2752 Commercial printing, lithographic

(G-7385)
RGD ENTERPRISES INC
Also Called: Laser One
8937 27th Ave Se (98513-4250)
PHONE.................................360 923-9582
Jerry Davenport, *President*
Ron Davenport, *Vice Pres*
EMP: 5
SALES (est): 351.7K **Privately Held**
SIC: 3861 3955 Toners, prepared photographic (not made in chemical plants); print cartridges for laser & other computer printers

(G-7386)
RICHMOND SYSTEMS INC
Also Called: Specialty Steel Fabricators
3721 Griffin Ln Se (98501-2192)
PHONE.................................360 455-8284
George Richmond, *Ch of Bd*
EMP: 24
SQ FT: 6,000
SALES (est): 3.6MM **Privately Held**
WEB: www.richmondsystems.com
SIC: 3599 8711 Machine & other job shop work; industrial engineers; construction & civil engineering

(G-7387)
ROBERT ROGERS
Also Called: Rogers Bob Blldzg & Log Trckg
3631 113th Ave Sw (98512-9160)
PHONE.................................360 352-9408
Robert Rogers, *Owner*
EMP: 5
SALES (est): 272K **Privately Held**
SIC: 1629 1794 2411 Earthmoving contractor; excavation work; logging

(G-7388)
ROGERS & ASSOCIATES
7905 Martin Way E (98516-5719)
P.O. Box 5370, Lacey (98509-5370)
PHONE.................................360 455-1534
Steve Rogers, *Owner*
EMP: 2
SALES: 900K **Privately Held**
SIC: 2434 Wood kitchen cabinets

(G-7389)
RUGID COMPUTER
6305 Elizan Dr Nw (98502-9694)
PHONE.................................360 866-0909
Don Bedlington, *Principal*
EMP: 3 EST: 2016
SALES (est): 104K **Privately Held**
SIC: 3571 Electronic computers

(G-7390)
RW MORSE CO
1515 Lakemoor Loop Sw (98512-5534)
P.O. Box 12302 (98508-2302)
PHONE.................................360 943-8600
Rw Morse, *Owner*
▲ EMP: 2
SALES (est): 85.7K **Privately Held**
SIC: 2731 Book publishing

(G-7391)
SALTED VINEGAR STUDIOS
9616 Regency Loop Se (98513-6851)
PHONE.................................931 302-0404
Pamela McFarland, *Principal*
EMP: 2
SALES (est): 65.4K **Privately Held**
SIC: 2099 Vinegar

(G-7392)
SCHMID FAMILY ENGRAVING LLC
3420 Yorkshire Dr Se (98513-4264)
PHONE.................................360 491-0997
EMP: 2 EST: 2010
SALES (est): 176K **Privately Held**
SIC: 3479 Coating/Engraving Service

(G-7393)
SIGN JUNKIES
13906 Vue St Sw (98512-5929)
PHONE.................................360 273-7553
Greg Leach, *Principal*
EMP: 2
SALES (est): 91.9K **Privately Held**
SIC: 3993 Signs & advertising specialties

(G-7394)
SIGNDEZIGN LLC
2407 Harrison Ave Nw A (98502-4591)
P.O. Box 1666 (98507-1666)
PHONE.................................360 709-0505
Bridget Shreve,
EMP: 3
SQ FT: 2,400
SALES (est): 251.6K **Privately Held**
SIC: 3993 Signs & advertising specialties

(G-7395)
SIMPLY WONDER LLC
4719 69th Ave Nw (98502-9603)
P.O. Box 12591 (98508-2591)
PHONE.................................360 866-2482
Patricia Kay, *Partner*
EMP: 3
SALES (est): 175.5K **Privately Held**
SIC: 2731 Book publishing

(G-7396)
SKILLMAN BROTHERS INC
Also Called: Skillman Bob Hauling & Logging
5541 Stmboat Island Rd Nw (98502-9681)
PHONE.................................360 866-7083
Robert Skillman Jr, *President*
EMP: 8
SALES (est): 606.4K **Privately Held**
SIC: 2411 Logging camps & contractors

(G-7397)
SKINMEDICA INC
3645 Sunset Beach Dr Nw (98502-3537)
PHONE.................................760 448-3600
Adele Reese, *Principal*
EMP: 2
SALES (est): 74.4K **Privately Held**
SIC: 2834 Pharmaceutical preparations

(G-7398)
SO YOU WANT TO WRITE
5508 Peninsula Dr Se (98513-9230)
PHONE.................................760 771-8940
Ann McIndoo, *Principal*
EMP: 2
SALES (est): 113.3K **Privately Held**
SIC: 2741 Miscellaneous publishing

(G-7399)
SPIN TEES
2008 Harrison Ave Nw # 101 (98502-4572)
PHONE.................................360 515-0543
Alex Jones, *Owner*
EMP: 2
SALES (est): 196.8K **Privately Held**
SIC: 2759 Screen printing

(G-7400)
SPINAL SPECIALTIES
2024 Caton Way Sw Ste A (98512-1119)
PHONE.................................253 861-7329
Patrick O'Neil, *Owner*
EMP: 2 EST: 2012
SALES (est): 142.2K **Privately Held**
SIC: 3842 5999 Implants, surgical; orthopedic & prosthesis applications

(G-7401)
SUNRISEBUSWERK
4315 Cooper Point Rd Nw (98502-3613)
PHONE.................................360 866-7240
Clara Williams, *Principal*
EMP: 2 EST: 2003
SALES (est): 133.5K **Privately Held**
SIC: 2499 Decorative wood & woodwork

(G-7402)
SUPER-KELLER INDUSTRIES LLC
1918 Smmit Lk Shore Rd Nw (98502)
PHONE.................................360 459-1059
Christina Keller, *Principal*
EMP: 2 EST: 2017
SALES (est): 71.4K **Privately Held**
SIC: 3999 Manufacturing industries

(G-7403)
SUPERFANCY INDUSTRIES
1808 5th Ave Se (98501-1804)
PHONE.................................360 556-9762
Erika Lari, *Administration*
EMP: 2
SALES (est): 112.1K **Privately Held**
SIC: 3999 Manufacturing industries

(G-7404)
SYMBOL SERVERS
416 Washington St Se (98501-6971)
PHONE.................................360 819-5132
Marlene Bremner, *Partner*
William Curtis, *Partner*
EMP: 2 EST: 2016
SALES (est): 72.5K **Privately Held**
SIC: 3953 5699 Screens, textile printing; stencils, painting & marking; T-shirts, custom printed

(G-7405)
THRIFTY PAYLESS INC T/A
305 Cooper Point Rd Nw (98502-4436)
PHONE.................................360 754-8014
EMP: 3
SALES (est): 140K **Privately Held**
SIC: 2836 Vaccines & other immunizing products

(G-7406)
THURSTON CO TRANSFER STATION
Also Called: Aways Connection
2420 Hogum Bay Rd Ne (98516-3875)
PHONE.................................360 459-1901
John Cox, *Manager*
EMP: 22
SALES (est): 1MM **Privately Held**
SIC: 4212 3443 Garbage collection & transport, no disposal; dumpsters, garbage

(G-7407)
TILLAMOOK COUNTRY SMOKER LLC
7040 Pacific Ave Se (98503-1474)
P.O. Box 3120, Bay City OR (97107-3120)
PHONE.................................360 456-2640
Joan Jackson, *Sales Staff*
Kari Tally, *Manager*
EMP: 5
SQ FT: 1,200
SALES (corp-wide): 75.9MM **Privately Held**
WEB: www.tcsjerky.com
SIC: 2013 Snack sticks, including jerky: from purchased meat
PA: Tillamook Country Smoker, Llc
8250 Warren St
Bay City OR 97107
800 325-2220

(G-7408)
TIN CUP LLC
117 Lilly Rd Ne (98506-5028)
PHONE.................................360 866-1580
Kimberly J Kelly, *Principal*
EMP: 3
SALES (est): 208.9K **Privately Held**
SIC: 3356 Tin

(G-7409)
TOKE POINT FISHERIES INC
10415 Stardust Ln Se (98501-9760)
PHONE.................................360 753-6917
EMP: 4
SALES (est): 199.8K **Privately Held**
SIC: 2092 Mfg Fresh/Frozen Packaged Fish

(G-7410)
TOPIA PRESS LTD
1508 Bowman Ave Nw (98502-4605)
PHONE.................................360 754-4449
Douglas McGregor, *Principal*
EMP: 2
SALES (est): 130.3K **Privately Held**
SIC: 2741 Miscellaneous publishing

(G-7411)
TOUCHE BEAUTY BAR LLC
1912 State Ave Ne (98506-4652)
PHONE.................................360 972-2345
Jenell Arnold, *Owner*
EMP: 9
SALES (est): 876.6K **Privately Held**
SIC: 3199 7231 Spats; beauty shops; unisex hair salons

(G-7412)
TOWN SMOKE PLUS
3700 Martin Way E Ste 109 (98506-5052)
PHONE.................................360 456-8234
Scott Hwang, *Owner*
EMP: 3
SALES (est): 219.2K **Privately Held**
SIC: 3443 Smokestacks, boiler plate

(G-7413)
TRANSPORTATION WASH STATE DEPT
Also Called: Engineering Publications
310 Maple Park Dr (98504-0001)
P.O. Box 47408 (98504-7408)
PHONE.................................360 705-7428
Lynn Hicks, *Manager*
Steven Vandor, *Director*
EMP: 4 **Privately Held**
WEB: www.wsdot.wa.gov
SIC: 2741 9451 Miscellaneous publishing; administration of veterans' affairs;
HQ: Washington State Department Of Transportation
310 Maple Park Ave Se
Olympia WA 98501

(G-7414)
TRIPLE R ENTERPRISES INC
1025 Kiwi Ct Nw (98502-4477)
PHONE.................................360 491-1600
Doug Jones, *President*
Robert Wright, *Vice Pres*
EMP: 3
SALES: 1MM **Privately Held**
WEB: www.justonce.com
SIC: 2851 Vinyl coatings, strippable

Olympia - Thurston County (G-7415)

(G-7415)
TUIGIS TEK LLC
3419 Gibraltar Ct Se (98501-6615)
PHONE 360 943-9133
Hop Tu, *CEO*
EMP: 5 **EST:** 2001
SALES: 150K **Privately Held**
SIC: 3571 7373 Computers, digital, analog or hybrid; computer-aided engineering (CAE) systems service

(G-7416)
TYLER TECHNOLOGIES INC
2114 Caton Way Sw (98502-1177)
PHONE 360 352-0922
John Schlotfeldt, *Principal*
Rowan Polly, *Technical Staff*
EMP: 25
SALES (corp-wide): 935.2MM **Publicly Held**
SIC: 7372 Prepackaged software
PA: Tyler Technologies, Inc.
5101 Tennyson Pkwy
Plano TX 75024
972 713-3700

(G-7417)
UP4U INC
3034 Cloverfield Dr Se (98501-3631)
PHONE 206 660-8498
Yolanka Wulff, *President*
Bruno Mombrinie, *Admin Sec*
EMP: 2 **EST:** 2015
SALES (est): 103K **Privately Held**
SIC: 3721 Aircraft

(G-7418)
USA MILK PROCESSING LLC
120 State Ave Ne Ste 1014 (98501-1131)
PHONE 202 657-5399
Paul L Strickland, *Principal*
Paul Strickland, *Bd of Directors*
EMP: 5 **EST:** 2015
SALES (est): 201.7K **Privately Held**
SIC: 2023 Dry, condensed, evaporated dairy products

(G-7419)
VALMET INC
9730 Lathrop Indus Dr (98512-1063)
PHONE 360 753-8831
EMP: 3
SALES (corp-wide): 3.8B **Privately Held**
SIC: 3554 Paper industries machinery
HQ: Valmet, Inc.
2425 Commerce Ave Ste 100
Duluth GA 30096
770 263-7863

(G-7420)
WASHINGTON CNCIL PLICE SHERIFF
200 Union Ave Se (98501-1322)
PHONE 360 352-8224
Bill Hanson, *Exec Dir*
EMP: 3
SQ FT: 4,200
SALES: 535.9K **Privately Held**
SIC: 8621 2721 Professional membership organizations; magazines: publishing only, not printed on site

(G-7421)
WASHINGTON MEDIA SERVICES INC
407 West Bay Dr Nw (98502-4831)
P.O. Box 7184 (98507-7184)
PHONE 360 754-4543
Joyce M Williams, *President*
Joyce M Willms, *President*
EMP: 5
SQ FT: 1,400
SALES (est): 562.7K **Privately Held**
WEB: www.charliesphoto.com
SIC: 2721 2791 4813 7221 Periodicals: publishing & printing; typesetting; ; photographic studios, portrait; information retrieval services; advertising agencies

(G-7422)
WASHINGTON NEWSPAPER PUBLISHER
1204 4th Ave E Ste 4 (98506-4276)
P.O. Box 389, Port Townsend (98368-0389)
PHONE 360 515-0974
Keven Graves, *Vice Pres*
EMP: 3
SALES (est): 94.1K **Privately Held**
SIC: 2711 Newspapers: publishing only, not printed on site

(G-7423)
WEDDINGS SOCHIC
441 Cougar St Se (98503-6709)
PHONE 360 438-6540
EMP: 2
SALES (est): 120K **Privately Held**
SIC: 2335 Mfg Women's/Misses' Dresses

(G-7424)
WESTERLY WOOD WORKING
6920 Zangle Rd Ne (98506-9796)
PHONE 360 480-4840
Jeff Kloppel, *Principal*
EMP: 2
SALES (est): 71.9K **Privately Held**
SIC: 2499 Decorative wood & woodwork

(G-7425)
WEYERHAEUSER COMPANY
Also Called: Containers Division
7727 Union Mill Rd Se (98503)
P.O. Box 101 (98507-0101)
PHONE 360 491-1200
Bill Schille, *Manager*
EMP: 135
SQ FT: 158,213
SALES (corp-wide): 7.4B **Publicly Held**
SIC: 2653 Boxes, corrugated: made from purchased materials
PA: Weyerhaeuser Company
220 Occidental Ave S
Seattle WA 98104
206 539-3000

(G-7426)
WILLIAM H OLSON INC (PA)
Also Called: Grays Harbor Cabinet
2203 Pacific Ave Se (98501-2028)
PHONE 360 249-3691
William H Olson, *President*
EMP: 5
SQ FT: 10,000
SALES (est): 985.2K **Privately Held**
WEB: www.harborcabinets.com
SIC: 5712 2434 Cabinets, except custom made: kitchen; wood kitchen cabinets

(G-7427)
WILLIAM H OLSON INC
Also Called: Harbor Cabinet
2203 Pacific Ave Se (98501-2028)
PHONE 360 754-2858
Ralfh Box, *Manager*
EMP: 3
SALES (corp-wide): 985.2K **Privately Held**
WEB: www.harborcabinets.com
SIC: 5712 2434 Cabinets, except custom made: kitchen; wood kitchen cabinets
PA: William H. Olson, Inc.
2203 Pacific Ave Se
Olympia WA 98501
360 249-3691

(G-7428)
WINDTONES LLC
2203 Wilkins Pl Se (98501-3133)
PHONE 360 349-9083
Steve G Robertson, *Administration*
Steve Roberts,
EMP: 2
SALES (est): 139.6K **Privately Held**
SIC: 3931 Chimes & parts (musical instruments)

(G-7429)
WINDY ACRES
9546 Glory Dr Se (98513-4803)
PHONE 360 491-2177
Gary Bigler, *Owner*
EMP: 2
SALES (est): 66.5K **Privately Held**
SIC: 0219 3552 General livestock; spinning machines, textile

(G-7430)
WOOD CREATIONS
4303 68th Ave Ne (98516-9510)
PHONE 360 491-1616
Robert Sauls, *Principal*
EMP: 2
SALES (est): 116K **Privately Held**
SIC: 2431 Millwork

(G-7431)
WORLD KNIVES LTD
2103 Harrison Ave Nw 2-646 (98502-2636)
P.O. Box 2092 (98507-2092)
PHONE 866 862-5233
Chris Hyde, *Principal*
EMP: 2
SALES (est): 210K **Privately Held**
SIC: 3949 Hunting equipment

(G-7432)
ZIGLERS WELDING SHOP INC
Also Called: Zeigler's Welding & Hitch Shop
322 Capitol Way N (98501-1023)
PHONE 360 357-6077
Jeff Hilts, *President*
EMP: 9
SALES (est): 860K **Privately Held**
SIC: 7692 Welding repair

OMAK
Okanogan County

(G-7433)
ARTHUR D FULFORD JR
Also Called: Fulford Logging
Nichols Rd (98841)
PHONE 509 826-2225
Arthur D Fulford Jr, *Owner*
EMP: 3
SALES (est): 243K **Privately Held**
SIC: 2411 Logging camps & contractors

(G-7434)
BACKWOODS
Also Called: Joe Thomas Supply
32 Omak River Rd (98841-9641)
PHONE 509 826-0758
Guthrie Joseph Thomas, *Owner*
EMP: 3
SALES (est): 317.4K **Privately Held**
WEB: www.watertroughs.com
SIC: 3523 Water troughs

(G-7435)
BILLS MARINE SERVICE
33 Hopfer Rd (98841-9367)
PHONE 509 826-5564
EMP: 2
SALES: 95K **Privately Held**
SIC: 7694 5551 7699 5088 Armature Rewinding Ret Boats Repair Services Whol Trans Equip

(G-7436)
CHRONICLE
Also Called: Okanogan Chronicle
618 Okoma Dr (98841)
PHONE 509 826-1110
Judy Z Smith, *Principal*
EMP: 30 **EST:** 1910
SQ FT: 3,000
SALES (est): 1.6MM **Privately Held**
WEB: www.omakchronicle.com
SIC: 2711 Newspapers: publishing only, not printed on site

(G-7437)
COMMUNITY NETWORKERS LLC
Also Called: Havillah Road Printing
208 S Main St (98841-9755)
PHONE 509 826-5154
Kim Vassar,
Corina Radford,
EMP: 5
SQ FT: 5,700
SALES (est): 318.2K **Privately Held**
SIC: 7336 5947 2759 Commercial art & graphic design; gift shop; commercial printing

(G-7438)
CONCRETE CREATIONS
64 Danker Cutoff (98841)
P.O. Box 106 (98841-0106)
PHONE 509 826-5409
Brian Maclean, *Owner*
Kelly Maclean, *Co-Owner*
EMP: 2
SALES (est): 100K **Privately Held**
SIC: 3272 5211 5083 Concrete products; masonry materials & supplies; landscaping equipment

(G-7439)
NORTH CASCADES BROADCASTING
Also Called: K O M W AM
320 Emery Dr (98841-9237)
P.O. Box 151 (98841-0151)
PHONE 509 826-0100
John Andrist, *President*
Becki Andrist, *Vice Pres*
EMP: 9 **EST:** 1982
SQ FT: 4,000
SALES (est): 640K **Privately Held**
WEB: www.komw.net
SIC: 4832 2711 Radio broadcasting stations; newspapers

(G-7440)
OMAK MACHINE SHOP INC
505 Okoma Dr (98841-9251)
P.O. Box 1625 (98841-1625)
PHONE 509 826-1030
Albert Apple, *President*
June Apple, *Treasurer*
EMP: 5
SQ FT: 4,000
SALES (est): 450K **Privately Held**
SIC: 5083 3599 Irrigation equipment; machine shop, jobbing & repair

(G-7441)
OMAK WOOD PRODUCTS LLC
1100 E 8th Ave (98841-9481)
PHONE 360 432-5048
Rob Habura, *CEO*
EMP: 32
SALES (est): 5.8MM **Privately Held**
SIC: 2499 Applicators, wood

(G-7442)
R AND D HOME AND GARDEN INC
317 S Main St (98841-9718)
PHONE 509 826-1730
Nicholas E Rodger, *President*
EMP: 2
SALES (est): 104.6K **Privately Held**
SIC: 3423 Garden & farm tools, including shovels

(G-7443)
ROCKWALL CELLARS
110 Nichols Rd (98841-9771)
PHONE 509 826-0201
Dumbo, *Principal*
EMP: 4
SALES (est): 384.2K **Privately Held**
SIC: 2084 Wines

(G-7444)
STAMPEDE FOREST PRODUCTS INC
1100 E 8th Ave D (98841-9481)
PHONE 509 557-3014
Terry Johnson, *President*
John Taylor, *Vice Pres*
Ted Skinner, *Director*
EMP: 14 **EST:** 2013
SQ FT: 800
SALES (est): 1.6MM **Privately Held**
SIC: 2491 Structural lumber & timber, treated wood

(G-7445)
TJ LOGGING LLC
29572 Us Highway 97 (98841-9413)
PHONE 509 826-5203
Tom Jones,

GEOGRAPHIC SECTION

Orting - Pierce County (G-7475)

EMP: 3
SALES (est): 311.6K Privately Held
SIC: 2411 Logging

Onalaska
Lewis County

(G-7446)
BIRCHFIELD WINERY INC
Also Called: Virgil L L C Fax Company
921 Middle Fork Rd (98570-9710)
PHONE...................................360 280-8998
Virgil Fox, *President*
EMP: 2
SALES (est): 84.8K Privately Held
SIC: 2084 Wines

(G-7447)
BUTTEVILLE LUMBER CO
1680 Hwy 508 (98570)
P.O. Box 687 (98570-0687)
PHONE...................................360 978-6098
Daniel Clare, *President*
Don Rouse, *Vice Pres*
Casey Rouse, *Admin Sec*
▲ EMP: 30 EST: 1982
SQ FT: 320
SALES (est): 4.3MM Privately Held
SIC: 2421 Sawmills & planing mills, general

(G-7448)
J & O TIMBER FALLING INC
116 Cattle Dr (98570-9663)
P.O. Box 176 (98570-0176)
PHONE...................................360 978-4590
John Weiler, *President*
Owen Fickett, *Vice Pres*
EMP: 2
SALES (est): 196.4K Privately Held
SIC: 2411 Timber, cut at logging camp

(G-7449)
J&L ENTERPRISES INC
635 Middle Fork Rd (98570-9545)
PHONE...................................360 262-3735
Jim Sabin, *President*
EMP: 2
SALES (est): 131.7K Privately Held
SIC: 3531 Dozers, tractor mounted: material moving

(G-7450)
J&M RIFLE WORKS
Also Called: Johnson Cams
704 Burnt Ridge Rd (98570-9456)
PHONE...................................360 985-0445
Keith Johnson, *Owner*
EMP: 2
SALES: 100K Privately Held
WEB: www.johnsoncams.com
SIC: 3542 Machine tools, metal forming type

(G-7451)
M H R A CORP
Also Called: All Metal Wldg & Fabrication
156 Moonridge Ln (98570-9473)
PHONE...................................360 978-6878
Bob Aiken, *CEO*
Michelle Healy, *President*
EMP: 5
SQ FT: 1,700
SALES (est): 605.9K Privately Held
SIC: 3441 Fabricated structural metal

(G-7452)
PARIYATTI
Also Called: PARIYATTI BOOKSTORE
867 Larmon Rd (98570-9534)
PHONE...................................360 978-4998
Brihas Sarathy, *Exec Dir*
EMP: 6
SALES: 424.8K Privately Held
SIC: 8641 2759 Civic social & fraternal associations; publication printing

(G-7453)
PRIES LOGGING
561 Burnt Ridge Rd (98570)
PHONE...................................360 985-0044
Eric Pries, *Principal*
EMP: 6

SALES (est): 584.5K Privately Held
SIC: 2411 Logging camps & contractors

(G-7454)
WRIGHT ENTERPRISES
103 Shanklin Rd (98570-9414)
P.O. Box 65 (98570-0065)
PHONE...................................360 985-7060
Marla Hirtzel, *President*
EMP: 2
SALES (est): 120K Privately Held
SIC: 2759 Screen printing

Orcas
San Juan County

(G-7455)
ACCESS EQUIPMENT LLC
Also Called: Hoistpartsnow
283 Killebrew Lake Rd (98280)
P.O. Box 82 (98280-0082)
PHONE...................................360 376-2679
Geoff Nelson, *General Mgr*
Matthew Engel,
EMP: 2
SALES (est): 319.1K Privately Held
SIC: 3536 Mine hoists

(G-7456)
TURN PT LGHTHUSE PRSRVTION SOC
5 Liberty Ln (98280)
PHONE...................................360 376-5246
Margaret Jonas, *President*
EMP: 2 EST: 2009
SALES (est): 147.7K Privately Held
SIC: 3731 Lighthouse tenders, building & repairing

Orondo
Douglas County

(G-7457)
GREAT GRAPHICS & SIGNS INC
33 Kyms Way (98843-9821)
P.O. Box 224 (98843-0224)
PHONE...................................206 948-9480
Kym Sweepe, *President*
EMP: 15
SALES: 500K Privately Held
WEB: www.greatgraphicsandsigns.com
SIC: 3993 7389 Signs & advertising specialties;

(G-7458)
NOVIELLO VINEYARDS LLC
272 Vineyard Dr (98843-9508)
PHONE...................................509 784-0544
Ana Stern, *Principal*
EMP: 4
SALES (est): 104.8K Privately Held
SIC: 2084 Wines

(G-7459)
PINE CANYON GROWERS LLC
8 Orondo Loop Rd (98843-9676)
P.O. Box 135 (98843-0135)
PHONE...................................509 888-7017
Starla Graham,
Andy Feil,
Ryan Hickery,
Josh Lawrence,
EMP: 87
SALES (est): 9.3MM Privately Held
SIC: 2631 Container, packaging & boxboard

(G-7460)
ROCKY POND WINERY
116 Orchard Pl (98843-9808)
PHONE...................................206 458-9119
David Dufenhorst, *President*
EMP: 2 EST: 2016
SALES (est): 81.3K Privately Held
SIC: 2084 Wines

Oroville
Okanogan County

(G-7461)
ALPINE BREWING CO
821 14th Ave (98844-9387)
P.O. Box 2320 (98844-2320)
PHONE...................................509 476-9662
Bart T Araubeck, *Partner*
EMP: 3
SALES (est): 271.3K Privately Held
SIC: 2082 Malt beverages

(G-7462)
CARBON CYCLE CRUSH LLC
224 Appleway Ave (98844)
P.O. Box 2147 (98844-2147)
PHONE...................................509 476-3667
EMP: 2
SALES (est): 260K Privately Held
SIC: 1382 Oil/Gas Exploration Services

(G-7463)
COPPER MOUNTAIN VINEYARDS
33349c Us Highway 97 (98844)
P.O. Box 604 (98844-0604)
PHONE...................................509 476-2762
David Taber, *Owner*
EMP: 2
SALES: 40K Privately Held
SIC: 2084 Wines

(G-7464)
DOUBLE A LOGGING INC
10 Verbeck Rd (98844)
PHONE...................................509 476-2907
Tom Acord, *President*
Diane Acord, *Vice Pres*
EMP: 15
SALES: 360K Privately Held
SIC: 2411 Logging

(G-7465)
ESTHER BRCQUES WNERY VNYRD LLC
38 Swanson Mill Rd (98844-9789)
PHONE...................................509 476-2861
Steven Colvin, *Principal*
EMP: 5
SALES (est): 319.8K Privately Held
SIC: 8733 8731 5921 2084 Noncommercial research organizations; commercial research laboratory; wine; wines

(G-7466)
FUNCTION WORKS
1872 Chesaw Rd (98844-9694)
PHONE...................................206 219-5636
Jennifer Saltzman, *Owner*
EMP: 2
SALES (est): 146.2K Privately Held
SIC: 3999 Manufacturing industries

(G-7467)
INTERNATIONAL BAR CODING
441 11th Ave (98844-9817)
PHONE...................................800 661-5570
EMP: 10
SALES (est): 580K Privately Held
SIC: 8748 3577 Business Consulting Services Mfg Computer Peripheral Equipment

(G-7468)
K & S GARDEN
2101 Highland Dr (98844-9700)
PHONE...................................509 476-3287
Stacy Moser, *Owner*
EMP: 2
SALES (est): 103.5K Privately Held
SIC: 3423 Garden & farm tools, including shovels

(G-7469)
MORNINGSTAR BUSINESS GROUP INC
3 814 Central Ave (98844)
PHONE...................................509 476-2944
Marilyn Mellis, *President*
EMP: 4

SALES (est): 21.7K Privately Held
WEB: www.air-adventure.com
SIC: 2389 Apparel & accessories

(G-7470)
OROVILLE GAZETTE INC
Also Called: Okanogan Vly Gazette Tribune
1420 Main St (98844-9385)
P.O. Box 250 (98844-0250)
PHONE...................................509 476-3602
Bill Forhan, *President*
EMP: 4 EST: 1960
SALES (est): 190K Privately Held
SIC: 2711 5943 Commercial printing & newspaper publishing combined; office forms & supplies

(G-7471)
OROVILLE REMAN & RELOAD INC
301 9th St (98844-9237)
P.O. Box 1610 (98844-1610)
PHONE...................................509 476-2935
Ron Gorman, *President*
John M Gorman, *Vice Pres*
EMP: 35 EST: 1964
SQ FT: 7,200
SALES (est): 3.8MM
SALES (corp-wide): 83.5MM Privately Held
WEB: www.orovillewashington.com
SIC: 4789 2441 3577 2421 Freight car loading & unloading; box shook, wood; computer peripheral equipment; sawmills & planing mills, general; commercial printing
PA: Gorman Bros. Lumber Ltd
3900 Dunfield Rd
West Kelowna BC V4T 1
250 768-5131

(G-7472)
ROBERT E MILLER
Also Called: Miller & Sons Logging
211 Chesaw Rd (98844)
PHONE...................................509 485-3032
Robert E Miller, *Partner*
Jeff Miller, *Partner*
EMP: 2
SALES (est): 92.4K Privately Held
SIC: 0212 2411 Beef cattle except feedlots; logging

Orting
Pierce County

(G-7473)
AUTOMATIC DOOR SOLUTIONS LLC
19602 153rd Ave E (98360-9496)
PHONE...................................253 802-0888
Andrew Buman,
Emily Buman,
EMP: 3
SALES (est): 57.6K Privately Held
SIC: 7699 3429 1751 3699 Door & window repair; door opening & closing devices, except electrical; window & door installation & erection; door opening & closing devices, electrical; doors, sliding

(G-7474)
BLAZEN METAL WORKS
22511 162nd St E (98360)
PHONE...................................360 897-2053
Susan Anderson, *Owner*
EMP: 2
SALES: 12K Privately Held
SIC: 3446 Architectural metalwork

(G-7475)
CANDY FIX
14414 133rd Street Ct E (98360-9512)
PHONE...................................253 770-8242
Tammy Klein, *Principal*
EMP: 7
SALES (est): 676.1K Privately Held
SIC: 2064 Candy & other confectionery products

Orting - Pierce County (G-7476)

(G-7476)
CONTEMPORARY WOODWORKS LLC
15619 223rd Ave E (98360-9148)
PHONE.................................360 897-2162
John Heffernan, *Principal*
EMP: 2
SALES (est): 224.1K Privately Held
SIC: 2431 Millwork

(G-7477)
COUNTY OF PIERCE
Also Called: Pierce County River Imprv
20520 162nd Ave (98360)
PHONE.................................360 893-2844
Timothy Ramsaur, *Branch Mgr*
EMP: 16 Privately Held
WEB: www.tpchd.org
SIC: 9511 1429 Water control & quality agency, government; riprap quarrying
PA: County Of Pierce
950 Fawcett Ave Ste 100
Tacoma WA 98402
253 798-7285

(G-7478)
D & R QUALITY COATINGS INC
401 Brown Way Se (98360-9465)
PHONE.................................253 209-5441
Daniel Smith, *Principal*
EMP: 2 EST: 2014
SALES (est): 128.9K Privately Held
SIC: 3479 Metal coating & allied service

(G-7479)
FAMILY ROOTS PUBLISHING CO LLC
Also Called: Salt Lake Christmas Tool
220 Bridge St Sw Ste 2 (98360)
P.O. Box 1682 (98360-1682)
PHONE.................................801 949-7259
Leland Meitzler,
EMP: 7
SALES (est): 616K Privately Held
SIC: 2741 Miscellaneous publishing

(G-7480)
HOBART CORPORATION
19220 State Route 162 E (98360-9236)
PHONE.................................360 893-5554
Steve Staton, *Principal*
EMP: 200
SALES (corp-wide): 14.7B Publicly Held
WEB: www.hobartcorp.com
SIC: 3556 5046 Bakery machinery; bakery equipment & supplies
HQ: Hobart Llc
701 S Ridge Ave
Troy OH 45374
937 332-3000

(G-7481)
INTEGRITY DENTAL LLC
15605 196th St E (98360)
PHONE.................................253 691-7292
Shiela Whaley, *Mng Member*
EMP: 2
SALES (est): 115.3K Privately Held
SIC: 3843 7699 Dental equipment; compressor repair

(G-7482)
ITW FOOD EQUIPMENT GROUP LLC
Baxter Manufacturing
19220 State Rd 162 E (98360)
PHONE.................................360 893-5554
Bob Schumann, *Branch Mgr*
EMP: 31
SALES (corp-wide): 14.7B Publicly Held
SIC: 3556 Bakery machinery; ovens, bakery
HQ: Itw Food Equipment Group Llc
701 S Ridge Ave
Troy OH 45374

(G-7483)
JABEZ MARPAC CONSTRUCTION JV1
13322 142nd Ave E (98360-9560)
PHONE.................................253 735-2000
Jesse Cherian, *Managing Prtnr*
EMP: 30
SALES: 950K Privately Held
SIC: 3441 Fabricated structural metal

(G-7484)
LIFE SPRING PRESS
207 Michell Ln Ne (98360-7448)
PHONE.................................360 872-8452
EMP: 2 EST: 2010
SALES (est): 110K Privately Held
SIC: 2741 Misc Publishing

(G-7485)
MJM MANUFACTURING
19105 205th St E (98360-9354)
PHONE.................................305 620-2020
Mathew Murphy, *Owner*
Jamie Murphy, *Co-Owner*
EMP: 2
SALES (est): 72.7K Privately Held
SIC: 3999 Manufacturing industries

(G-7486)
QUICK CUT INC
416 Kensington Ave Nw (98360-9428)
PHONE.................................360 893-0689
Rod Karppinen, *President*
Tim Lindula, *Vice Pres*
EMP: 5
SALES (est): 125K Privately Held
WEB: www.quickcutsanders.com
SIC: 3589 Floor sanding machines, commercial

(G-7487)
THOMAS L NORMAN CNSTR & LOG
22805 133rd Street Ct E (98360-9614)
PHONE.................................253 312-7858
Thomas Norman, *Principal*
EMP: 3
SALES (est): 221.5K Privately Held
SIC: 2411 Logging

(G-7488)
WASHINGTON ROCK QUARRIES INC
29104 Camp 1 Rd E (98360-9712)
P.O. Box 1806 (98360-1806)
PHONE.................................360 893-7701
Harry Hart, *Branch Mgr*
EMP: 10
SALES (est): 1MM
SALES (corp-wide): 22.2MM Privately Held
SIC: 5032 1442 Stone, crushed or broken; construction sand & gravel
PA: Washington Rock Quarries Inc.
21711 103rd Avenue Ct E C302
Graham WA 98338
253 262-1661

(G-7489)
WRITING HANDS
1206 Williams St Nw (98360-8457)
PHONE.................................360 893-1606
Joe Langowski, *Owner*
EMP: 2
SALES (est): 88.1K Privately Held
SIC: 2759 Advertising literature: printing

Othello
Adams County

(G-7490)
AG SPRAY EQUIPMENT INC
81 E Pine St (99344-1041)
PHONE.................................509 488-6631
EMP: 20
SALES (corp-wide): 138.4MM Privately Held
SIC: 3523 Mfg Farm Machinery/Equipment
HQ: Ag. Spray Equipment, Inc.
3303 Pembroke Rd
Hopkinsville KY 42240
270 886-0296

(G-7491)
CENEX SUPPLY & MARKETING INC
528 S Booker Rd (99344-9420)
PHONE.................................509 488-5261
Lorry Anderson, *General Mgr*
EMP: 2 EST: 2009
SALES (est): 119.5K Privately Held
SIC: 5099 2873 5172 Durable goods; fertilizers: natural (organic), except compost; diesel fuel

(G-7492)
CHS INC
Also Called: C H S
1296 S Broadway Ave (99344-1833)
P.O. Box 469 (99344-0469)
PHONE.................................509 488-9681
Royal Muller, *Manager*
EMP: 10
SALES (corp-wide): 31.9B Publicly Held
WEB: www.cenexharveststates.com
SIC: 2075 5191 5153 Soybean oil, cake or meal; seeds: field, garden & flower; grains
PA: Chs Inc.
5500 Cenex Dr
Inver Grove Heights MN 55077
651 355-6000

(G-7493)
CPM DEVELOPMENT CORPORATION
Also Called: Central Washington Concrete
804 E Broadway Ave (99344)
PHONE.................................509 488-2614
Troy Holt, *General Mgr*
EMP: 3
SALES (corp-wide): 30.6B Privately Held
SIC: 1771 3273 Concrete work; ready-mixed concrete
HQ: Cpm Development Corporation
5111 E Broadway Ave
Spokane Valley WA 99212
509 534-6221

(G-7494)
ELEMENT
1199 W Cunningham Rd (99344-9004)
PHONE.................................425 941-5373
EMP: 2
SALES (est): 46.7K Privately Held
SIC: 0139 3999 2819 ; ; elements

(G-7495)
FABTECH MANUFACTURING LLC
1787 S Broadway Ave (99344-9503)
P.O. Box 326 (99344-0326)
PHONE.................................509 488-1950
Warren Small,
EMP: 2
SALES: 250K Privately Held
SIC: 3441 Fabricated structural metal

(G-7496)
FRENCH MAN HILLS QUARRY
9498 Road H Se (99344-9620)
PHONE.................................509 346-2111
Alfredo Cruz, *Principal*
EMP: 2
SALES (est): 120.5K Privately Held
SIC: 1481 Mine & quarry services, nonmetallic minerals

(G-7497)
JOELS MACHINE SHOP
1980 S Broadway Ave (99344-9506)
PHONE.................................509 488-3234
Joel Rios, *Owner*
EMP: 2
SALES (est): 137.3K Privately Held
SIC: 3599 Machine shop, jobbing & repair

(G-7498)
JR SIMPLOT COMPANY
Also Called: Simplot Grower Solutions
531 S Booker Rd (99344-9419)
P.O. Box 509 (99344-0509)
PHONE.................................509 488-2132
Ronda Wilkins, *Manager*
EMP: 40
SALES (corp-wide): 4.9B Privately Held
WEB: www.simplot.com
SIC: 2874 2875 Phosphatic fertilizers; fertilizers, mixing only
PA: J.R. Simplot Company
1099 W Front St
Boise ID 83702
208 780-3287

(G-7499)
JR SIMPLOT COMPANY
Also Called: Food Group
1200 N Broadway Ave (99344-9067)
PHONE.................................509 765-5663
EMP: 40
SQ FT: 3,300
SALES (corp-wide): 4.9B Privately Held
WEB: www.simplot.com
SIC: 2037 2099 Frozen fruits & vegetables; food preparations
PA: J.R. Simplot Company
1099 W Front St
Boise ID 83702
208 780-3287

(G-7500)
KILLIAN KORN INC
1615 E Catalpa St (99344-1547)
P.O. Box 344 (99344-0344)
PHONE.................................800 528-7861
Dennis Killian, *President*
Gordon Killian, *Vice Pres*
EMP: 5
SALES (est): 352.6K Privately Held
WEB: www.killiankorn.com
SIC: 2064 5441 Popcorn balls or other treated popcorn products; popcorn, including caramel corn

(G-7501)
LAND OLAKES INC
449 W Mcmanomon Rd (99344)
P.O. Box 250 (99344-0250)
PHONE.................................509 488-5208
Bruce Becker, *Branch Mgr*
EMP: 12
SALES (corp-wide): 10.4B Privately Held
WEB: www.landolakes.com
SIC: 2048 Prepared feeds
PA: Land O'lakes, Inc.
4001 Lexington Ave N
Arden Hills MN 55126
651 375-2222

(G-7502)
MCCAIN FOODS USA INC
100 Lee St (99344)
PHONE.................................509 488-9611
Dave Rawlings, *Technical Mgr*
Dan Paradis, *Manager*
Anthony Devereux, *Manager*
Leroy Enger, *Manager*
Angie Pineda, *Manager*
EMP: 600
SQ FT: 50,000
SALES (corp-wide): 19.5B Privately Held
WEB: www.mccainusa.com
SIC: 2037 2099 2038 2034 Potato products, quick frozen & cold pack; food preparations; frozen specialties; dehydrated fruits, vegetables, soups
HQ: Mccain Foods Usa, Inc.
1 Tower Ln Ste Uppr
Oakbrook Terrace IL 60181
630 955-0400

(G-7503)
PERFECT BLEND LLC
771 Kulm Rd (99344-9139)
PHONE.................................509 488-5570
Patrick Burchard, *Manager*
EMP: 25
SQ FT: 43,560
SALES (corp-wide): 11.5MM Privately Held
SIC: 2873 5191 Fertilizers: natural (organic), except compost; fertilizer & fertilizer materials
PA: Perfect Blend, Llc
10900 Ne 8th St Ste 615
Bellevue WA 98004
509 488-5570

(G-7504)
RALLITO DE LUNA
2105 W Bench Rd (99344-8914)
PHONE.................................509 488-4272
EMP: 2
SALES (corp-wide): 288.1K Privately Held
SIC: 2099 Mfg Food Preparations
PA: Rallito De Luna
6411 Burden Blvd
Pasco WA 99301
509 547-7737

GEOGRAPHIC SECTION

(G-7505)
SIGNS OF GRACE
430 S 16th Ave (99344-1542)
PHONE..................................509 488-5081
EMP: 2
SALES (est): 140.4K **Privately Held**
SIC: 3993 Signs & advertising specialties

(G-7506)
SVZ USA WASHINGTON INC
Also Called: Svz Industrial Fruit
1700 N Broadway Ave (99344-8918)
P.O. Box 715 (99344-0715)
PHONE..................................509 488-6563
Jenny Billups, *President*
Anouk Ter Laak, *Chairman*
Ger Bemer, *Chairman*
Guido Kamps, *Business Mgr*
Erin McCulloch, *Business Mgr*
◆ EMP: 50
SALES (est): 12.5MM
SALES (corp-wide): 2.3B **Privately Held**
WEB: www.svz-usa.com
SIC: 2033 Fruit purees: packaged in cans, jars, etc.
HQ: S.V.Z. Industrial Products B.V.
Reduitlaan 41
Breda 4814
765 049-494

(G-7507)
T L C CUSTOM MEATS INC
93 N Desdemona Dr (99344-1100)
PHONE..................................509 488-9953
Kenneth Dockins, *President*
Rita Dockins, *Vice Pres*
EMP: 6
SQ FT: 2,400
SALES: 215K **Privately Held**
SIC: 2011 Meat packing plants

(G-7508)
UDABOMB BATH BOMBS
215 N 14th Ave (99344-1217)
PHONE..................................509 331-4100
Heather Quigley, *Principal*
EMP: 2
SALES (est): 88.8K **Privately Held**
SIC: 2844 Bath salts

(G-7509)
WEST COLUMBIA CARRIERS LLC
435 N Desdemona Ave (99344-1115)
PHONE..................................509 488-5000
Enedelia Cantu, *Manager*
EMP: 2 EST: 2009
SALES (est): 165K **Privately Held**
SIC: 3537 Trucks, tractors, loaders, carriers & similar equipment

(G-7510)
WILLAMETTE VALLEY LUMBER LLC (PA)
1885 W Herman Rd (99344-9016)
PHONE..................................509 331-0442
Justin Yancey, *Principal*
EMP: 12 EST: 2014
SALES (est): 6MM **Privately Held**
SIC: 2421 Lumber stacking or sticking; lumber: rough, sawed or planed

(G-7511)
YANCEY PALLET INC
1885 W Herman Rd (99344-9016)
PHONE..................................509 331-0442
Ron Yancey, *President*
Justin Yancey, *Vice Pres*
Lyann Yancey, *Admin Sec*
EMP: 80
SQ FT: 40,000
SALES (est): 2.5MM **Privately Held**
WEB: www.yanceypallet.com
SIC: 2448 Pallets, wood

Otis Orchards
Spokane County

(G-7512)
BOART LONGYEAR
21312 E Gilbert Ave (99027-9240)
PHONE..................................509 926-9575
Frank Waddingta, *Sales Mgr*
EMP: 2
SALES (est): 83.2K **Privately Held**
SIC: 3544 1081 Special dies, tools, jigs & fixtures; metal mining services

(G-7513)
CASE42
22606 E Heroy Ave (99027-9317)
PHONE..................................509 270-3500
Dave McClave, *Branch Mgr*
EMP: 4
SALES (est): 390.9K
SALES (corp-wide): 139.5K **Privately Held**
SIC: 3523 Farm machinery & equipment
PA: Case42
10014 E Montgomery Dr # 1
Spokane Valley WA 99206
509 270-3500

(G-7514)
INSPECTION PLUS
21312 E Gilbert Ave (99027-9240)
PHONE..................................509 534-9290
Rob Wysong, *Owner*
Stacy Wysong, *Co-Owner*
EMP: 4
SQ FT: 2,800
SALES (est): 344.2K **Privately Held**
SIC: 3599 Machine shop, jobbing & repair

(G-7515)
NO NAME BOOT COMPANY
4213 N Starr Rd (99027-8730)
PHONE..................................509 226-1980
Leonard Smith, *Owner*
Melody Smith, *Co-Owner*
EMP: 2
SALES (est): 90K **Privately Held**
SIC: 3149 Children's footwear, except athletic

(G-7516)
PROFESSIONAL CRANE INSPECTIONS
24810 E Wellesley Ave (99027-9770)
PHONE..................................509 226-5302
Paul D Mc Queen, *CEO*
Bob O'Dea, *President*
EMP: 2
SALES (est): 178K **Privately Held**
SIC: 1799 3531 Athletic & recreation facilities construction; crane carriers

(G-7517)
ROSS CREEK LOGGING INC
18908 E Lincoln Rd (99027-8237)
PHONE..................................509 926-0415
Greg Malloy, *President*
Tracie Malloy, *Vice Pres*
EMP: 2
SALES (est): 205.1K **Privately Held**
SIC: 2411 Logging camps & contractors

(G-7518)
START 2 FINISH COATINGS INC
24424 E Wellesley Ave (99027-9766)
PHONE..................................509 481-8898
EMP: 2
SALES (est): 120.6K **Privately Held**
SIC: 3479 Metal coating & allied service

(G-7519)
TOUGH OUTDOOR PRODUCTS LLC
24801 E Wellesley Ave (99027-9769)
PHONE..................................509 621-0034
EMP: 10
SALES (est): 740K **Privately Held**
SIC: 3499 Mfg Misc Fabricated Metal Products

(G-7520)
TROPICAL SAUNA
5205 N Harvard Rd (99027-9282)
P.O. Box 815 (99027-0815)
PHONE..................................509 927-7898
J J Makool, *President*
EMP: 2
SALES (est): 158.2K **Privately Held**
WEB: www.tropicalsauna.com
SIC: 2452 Sauna rooms, prefabricated, wood

(G-7521)
USJADE LLC
3606 N Garry Rd (99027-9300)
PHONE..................................509 535-3411
EMP: 2 EST: 2009
SALES (est): 89K **Privately Held**
SIC: 3915 Mfg Jewelers' Materials

Pacific
King County

(G-7522)
AMERICAN STRUCTURES DESIGN INC
218 Stewart Rd Se (98047-2132)
PHONE..................................253 833-4343
Mark E Weissenbuehler, *President*
EMP: 8
SALES (est): 1.7MM **Privately Held**
SIC: 3441 Fabricated structural metal

(G-7523)
AMREP INC
427 5th Ave Nw (98047-1006)
PHONE..................................253 939-6265
Gabriel Ghibaudo, *Branch Mgr*
EMP: 2
SALES (corp-wide): 43.3MM **Privately Held**
SIC: 3713 Truck & bus bodies
PA: Amrep, Inc.
1555 S Cucamonga Ave
Ontario CA 91761
909 923-0430

(G-7524)
CEDAR RECYCLING INC
Also Called: Rusty Rack Guys, The
411 West Valley Hwy S (98047-1302)
PHONE..................................253 863-5353
Jerald D Eck, *President*
EMP: 12
SQ FT: 2,000
SALES (est): 3.5MM **Privately Held**
WEB: www.pacificrimhandling.com
SIC: 3559 Recycling machinery

(G-7525)
DUDLEY FAMILY GROUP INC
Also Called: Solid Surface Solutions
1350 Thornton Ave Sw B (98047-2112)
PHONE..................................253 863-9282
Alan Dudley, *President*
EMP: 2
SQ FT: 10,000
SALES (est): 62.6K **Privately Held**
SIC: 3281 Granite, cut & shaped

(G-7526)
ENVIRONMENTAL TECH GROUP
201 Frontage Rd N (98047-1003)
PHONE..................................253 804-2507
Victor Deluechi, *President*
EMP: 12
SALES (est): 975.8K **Privately Held**
SIC: 3556 Fish & shellfish processing machinery

(G-7527)
ENVIRONMENTAL TECHNOLOGIES INC
201 Frontage Rd N Ste C (98047-1003)
PHONE..................................253 804-2507
Victor Deluechi, *President*
EMP: 11
SQ FT: 16,000
SALES (est): 1.9MM **Privately Held**
SIC: 3594 Fluid power pumps

(G-7528)
GURGLEPOT INC
120 County Line Rd 101 (98047)
PHONE..................................253 670-6240
Matthew B Ellison, *President*
▲ EMP: 3 EST: 2010
SALES (est): 305.9K **Privately Held**
SIC: 3269 Cookware: stoneware, coarse earthenware & pottery

(G-7529)
HYDRA-COM INC
136 Stewart Rd Se Bldg 2 (98047-2143)
PHONE..................................253 862-9140
Darryl E Cushing, *President*
EMP: 8 EST: 1979
SALES: 260K **Privately Held**
SIC: 3519 5084 Marine engines; industrial machinery & equipment

(G-7530)
IDEA COMPANY
Also Called: Mugs and More
743 Valentine Ave Se (98047-2124)
PHONE..................................253 891-8140
Doug Anderson, *Owner*
EMP: 5
SQ FT: 4,000
SALES: 250K **Privately Held**
SIC: 3911 3229 Jewelry, precious metal; glassware, art or decorative

(G-7531)
MARRIED TO METAL
1563 Thornton Ave Sw D (98047-2149)
PHONE..................................206 244-2238
Kelly Twedt, *Owner*
EMP: 4
SALES (est): 327K **Privately Held**
SIC: 3499 5023 Metal household articles; decorative home furnishings & supplies

(G-7532)
MODERN BUILDING SYSTEMS INC
1550 Thornton Ave Sw (98047-2114)
PHONE..................................800 682-1422
Ken Mero, *Branch Mgr*
EMP: 10
SALES (corp-wide): 18.8MM **Privately Held**
SIC: 2452 Prefabricated buildings, wood
PA: Modern Building Systems, Inc.
9493 Porter Rd Se Ste D
Aumsville OR 97325
503 749-4949

(G-7533)
MORPAC INDUSTRIES INC (PA)
117 Frontage Rd N Ste A (98047-1052)
PHONE..................................253 735-8922
Heidi E Morgan, *Ch of Bd*
Erika Morgan, *Vice Pres*
Peter Morgan, *Shareholder*
Peter L Morgan, *Shareholder*
Christine Dixon, *Admin Sec*
▲ EMP: 40
SQ FT: 18,000
SALES: 9.5MM **Privately Held**
WEB: www.morpac.com
SIC: 3613 3699 3531 Switchgear & switchboard apparatus; electrical equipment & supplies; construction machinery; winches

(G-7534)
NORFIL LLC
1335 Valentine Ave Se (98047-2105)
PHONE..................................253 863-5888
Doren Spinner,
EMP: 35 EST: 2012
SQ FT: 25,000
SALES (est): 1.9MM **Privately Held**
SIC: 3724 Aircraft engines & engine parts

(G-7535)
NORMS TRUCK & EQUIPMENT INC
361 Roy Rd Sw (98047-2133)
PHONE..................................253 833-8339
Norman Bilbrey, *President*
Keith Bilbrey, *Vice Pres*
Kevin Bilbrey, *Vice Pres*
EMP: 12
SQ FT: 6,000
SALES (est): 1.2MM **Privately Held**
SIC: 7539 7532 3713 Frame & front end repair services; truck painting & lettering; truck bodies & parts

(G-7536)
NW UTILITY SERVICES LLC
228 Frontage Rd S Ste A (98047-1018)
P.O. Box 1008, Sumner (98390-0190)
PHONE..................................253 891-7802

Pacific - King County (G-7537)

William L Garoutte,
Mary Garoutte,
EMP: 35
SQ FT: 5,000
SALES: 8.7MM **Privately Held**
SIC: 1623 1731 3699 Underground utilities contractor; electrical work; general electrical contractor; sound signaling devices, electrical

(G-7537)
PANELSUPPLIERS
116 2nd Ave Se (98047-1132)
PHONE.................................253 217-1668
Thomas McSheery, *Principal*
Denise Sirven, *Principal*
EMP: 5
SALES: 300K **Privately Held**
SIC: 3272 Concrete products

(G-7538)
PARKERS TRUCK & EQUIPMENT REPR
Also Called: Parker Truck
116 Frontage Rd N (98047-1024)
PHONE.................................253 833-3696
Tim Parker, *President*
Martha V Parker, *Corp Secy*
EMP: 4
SQ FT: 4,200
SALES (est): 330K **Privately Held**
SIC: 7538 3441 5084 General truck repair; fabricated structural metal; engines & parts, diesel

(G-7539)
PRECISION IRON WORKS INC
102 Frontage Rd S (98047-1041)
PHONE.................................253 887-5555
Steve Leighton, *President*
Waylon Owens, *Vice Pres*
EMP: 41
SQ FT: 6,500
SALES (est): 9.6MM **Privately Held**
SIC: 3441 Fabricated structural metal

(G-7540)
SONIQ AEROSPACE LP
175 Roy Rd Sw Bldg A (98047-2150)
PHONE.................................253 750-4592
Dustin Ronk, *Partner*
EMP: 5
SALES (est): 696.6K **Privately Held**
SIC: 3812 Aircraft/aerospace flight instruments & guidance systems

(G-7541)
WOOD SHED INC
373 Pacific Ave N (98047-1260)
P.O. Box 815, Milton (98354-0815)
PHONE.................................253 405-8890
Austin Shepherd, *President*
EMP: 5
SALES (est): 400K **Privately Held**
SIC: 2411 Logging

Packwood
Lewis County

(G-7542)
COUNTY OF LEWIS
Also Called: Lewis County Fire Dst No 10
12953 Us Highway 12 (98361-9792)
P.O. Box 270 (98361-0270)
PHONE.................................360 494-4123
Lonnie Goble, *Chief*
EMP: 2 **Privately Held**
SIC: 3711 Fire department vehicles (motor vehicles), assembly of
PA: County Of Lewis
   351 Nw North St
   Chehalis WA 98532
   360 740-1192

(G-7543)
HIGHWAY SHOPPERS
12975 Us Highway 12 (98361-9792)
PHONE.................................360 494-7641
Dave Bunting, *Owner*
EMP: 6
SQ FT: 700

SALES (est): 342.3K **Privately Held**
WEB: www.highwayshopper.com
SIC: 2741 5947 Shopping news: publishing only, not printed on site; gift shop

Palouse
Whitman County

(G-7544)
CRAIG FLEENER
2722 Lawson Rd (99161-9767)
PHONE.................................509 872-3016
Craig Fleener, *Owner*
EMP: 3
SALES (est): 220.8K **Privately Held**
SIC: 3523 7389 Driers (farm): grain, hay & seed;

(G-7545)
MISS MAGS LLC
100 W Church St (99161)
PHONE.................................208 301-0549
EMP: 2
SALES (est): 111.2K **Privately Held**
SIC: 2047 Mfg Dog Food

(G-7546)
NOAHS ARK FOODS LLC
330 E Harrison St (99161-5112)
PHONE.................................509 595-8642
Mindy Hicks, *Mng Member*
Michael Hicks,
EMP: 2 **EST:** 2011
SQ FT: 600
SALES: 1.2K **Privately Held**
SIC: 2096 7389 Potato chips & similar snacks;

(G-7547)
QUALITY DRAPERY SERVICE
120 S Bridge St (99161)
P.O. Box 8 (99161-0008)
PHONE.................................509 878-1371
John Gearheart, *Owner*
Lynne Gearhart, *Co-Owner*
EMP: 2
SALES: 37K **Privately Held**
SIC: 2591 Shade, curtain & drapery hardware

Parker
Yakima County

(G-7548)
COLUMBIA READY MIX INC
371 Parker Ridge Rd (98939)
PHONE.................................509 453-2063
Leonard Sali, *President*
Steve Sali, *Vice Pres*
EMP: 80
SQ FT: 7,500
SALES: 3MM **Privately Held**
SIC: 3273 Ready-mixed concrete

(G-7549)
PACE INTERNATIONAL LLC
Also Called: Evergreen Products Division
N Track Rd (98939)
PHONE.................................509 877-2830
Gerald Byers, *Manager*
EMP: 10 **Privately Held**
WEB: www.paceint.com
SIC: 2879 Agricultural chemicals
HQ: Pace International, Llc
   5661 Branch Rd
   Wapato WA 98951
   800 936-6750

(G-7550)
WAUPACA NORTHWOODS LLC
Also Called: Waupaca Materials
81 N Track Rd (98939)
PHONE.................................509 877-2830
Jerald Buyers, *Manager*
EMP: 65
SALES (corp-wide): 30.6B **Privately Held**
SIC: 2879 2842 2873 Agricultural chemicals; specialty cleaning, polishes & sanitation goods; nitrogenous fertilizers

HQ: Waupaca Northwoods, Llc
   N2564 County Road Qq
   Waupaca WI 54981
   800 365-4032

Pasco
Franklin County

(G-7551)
AMERICA WEST ENVMTL SUPS
3300 E A St (99301-6409)
P.O. Box 730 (99301-1211)
PHONE.................................509 547-2240
EMP: 7
SQ FT: 1,500
SALES (est): 606.2K **Privately Held**
SIC: 0711 0782 3826 Mfg Dust Control Deicers And Environmental Products

(G-7552)
AMERON INTERNATIONAL CORP
1828 W Lewis St (99301-4958)
PHONE.................................509 547-3689
Larry Halloway, *Branch Mgr*
EMP: 120
SALES (corp-wide): 8.4B **Publicly Held**
WEB: www.ameron.com
SIC: 3479 3353 Coating, rust preventive; aluminum sheet, plate & foil
HQ: Ameron International Corporation
   7909 Parkwood Circle Dr
   Houston TX 77036
   713 375-3700

(G-7553)
BERRY HAVEN LLC
Also Called: Gwenies Ckies Hmemade Goodness
3834 Dogwood Rd (99301-8609)
PHONE.................................509 521-4902
Megan Williams,
EMP: 2 **EST:** 2013
SALES (est): 197.7K **Privately Held**
SIC: 5149 2051 0171 Crackers, cookies & bakery products; pickles, preserves, jellies & jams; bakery: wholesale or wholesale/retail combined; raspberry farm

(G-7554)
BOGERT AVIATION INC
3606 N Swallow Ave # 100 (99301-3788)
PHONE.................................509 736-1513
Richard Bogert, *Principal*
Catherine Bogert, *CFO*
EMP: 5
SQ FT: 1,000
SALES (est): 300K **Privately Held**
WEB: www.bogert-av.com
SIC: 3728 4581 3545 Aircraft assemblies, subassemblies & parts; aircraft servicing & repairing; machine tool attachments & accessories

(G-7555)
BOGERT INTERNATIONAL INC
3606 N Swallow Ave # 300 (99301-3788)
PHONE.................................509 736-1512
Richard W Bogert, *President*
Catherine Bogert, *Corp Secy*
Suzan Bogert, *Vice Pres*
Warren Hughs, *Supervisor*
EMP: 8
SQ FT: 2,500
SALES: 900K **Privately Held**
SIC: 3714 Hydraulic fluid power pumps for auto steering mechanism

(G-7556)
BOGERT MANUFACTURING INC
Also Called: Safe Jack
3606 N Swallow Ave # 200 (99301-3788)
PHONE.................................509 735-2106
Richard W Bogert, *President*
Catherine Bogert, *Treasurer*
EMP: 19
SALES (est): 90K **Privately Held**
WEB: www.bmihydraulics.com
SIC: 3594 Fluid power pumps & motors

(G-7557)
CABIN FEVER MEDIA
1736 N 21st Ave (99301-3307)
PHONE.................................509 544-2155
Dee Combs, *Owner*
EMP: 3
SALES (est): 111.9K **Privately Held**
WEB: www.cfever.com
SIC: 2711 Newspapers, publishing & printing

(G-7558)
CENTRAL HOSE AND FITTINGS INC
2214 N 4th Ave (99301-3731)
PHONE.................................509 547-6460
Loren Peterson, *President*
Don Adams, *Vice Pres*
Drenan Adams, *Treasurer*
George Laiblin, *Admin Sec*
EMP: 10
SALES (est): 1.7MM **Privately Held**
SIC: 5251 5085 5084 3492 Hardware; hose, belting & packing; industrial fittings; hydraulic systems equipment & supplies; hose & tube fittings & assemblies, hydraulic/pneumatic

(G-7559)
CENTRAL MACHINERY SALES INC
1802 E James St (99301-4273)
P.O. Box 2838 (99302-2838)
PHONE.................................509 547-9003
Steven Stredwick, *Manager*
EMP: 16 **Privately Held**
WEB: www.centralmachinery.com
SIC: 3523 3531 5082 Farm machinery & equipment; construction machinery; contractors' materials
PA: Central Machinery Sales, Inc.
   1201 Yonezawa Blvd
   Moses Lake WA 98837

(G-7560)
CLAAR CELLARS LLC
1081 Glenwood Rd (99301-8665)
PHONE.................................509 266-4449
Robert Whitelatch, *Partner*
Crista Whitelatch, *Partner*
▲ **EMP:** 8
SQ FT: 10,000
SALES (est): 1MM **Privately Held**
WEB: www.claarcellars.com
SIC: 2084 Wine cellars, bonded: engaged in blending wines; wines

(G-7561)
COCA-COLA BOTTLING CO
1225 Road 34 (99301)
P.O. Box 2405 (99302-2405)
PHONE.................................509 547-6712
Mat Sanders, *Branch Mgr*
EMP: 70
SALES (corp-wide): 55.1MM **Privately Held**
SIC: 2086 Bottled & canned soft drinks
HQ: Coca-Cola Bottling Co.-Yakima &Tri-Cities, Inc.
   607 E R St
   Yakima WA 98901
   509 248-1855

(G-7562)
COLUMBIA CHAIN BELT INC
Also Called: Sullivan Manufacturing Co
308 E B Cir (99301-6402)
PHONE.................................509 546-2000
Paul Sullivan, *Ch of Bd*
Suzanne Sullivan, *President*
Greg Sullivan, *Vice Pres*
EMP: 4
SALES (est): 576.9K **Privately Held**
SIC: 3535 Belt conveyor systems, general industrial use

(G-7563)
COLUMBIA PALLET LLC
1651 Se Road 33 (99301-3894)
PHONE.................................509 430-9647
Lynn Zamudio,
Rafael Ezquivel Zanudio,
EMP: 5
SALES (est): 219.1K **Privately Held**
SIC: 2448 Pallets, wood

GEOGRAPHIC SECTION

Pasco - Franklin County (G-7594)

(G-7564)
COLUMBIA RIGGING CORPORATION
2407 E A St (99301-4010)
P.O. Box 2717 (99302-2717)
PHONE 509 545-4657
James Kyle Lewis, *President*
EMP: 4
SQ FT: 4,000
SALES (est): 700.6K **Privately Held**
SIC: **3496** 3536 Miscellaneous fabricated wire products; chain, welded; slings, lifting; made from purchased wire; hoisting slings

(G-7565)
CONAGRA FODS CLMBIA BASE BLNDS
Also Called: Conagra Foods-Lamb Weston
3330 Travel Plaza Way (99301-9791)
PHONE 509 544-2111
Todd Obermeyer, *Principal*
EMP: 88
SALES (est): 6.2MM
SALES (corp-wide): 7.9B **Publicly Held**
WEB: www.conagra.com
SIC: **2011** Lamb products from lamb slaughtered on site
PA: Conagra Brands, Inc.
222 Merchandise Mart Plz
Chicago IL 60654
312 549-5000

(G-7566)
CONAGRA FOODS SPECIALTY POTATO
960 N Glade Rd (99301-9390)
PHONE 509 547-8851
Doug Bruce, *Principal*
EMP: 2
SALES (est): 248K **Privately Held**
SIC: **2499** Food handling & processing products, wood

(G-7567)
CONNELL SAND & GRAVEL INC
6220 N Burlington St (99301-9498)
PHONE 509 545-4066
Tony Hille, *Owner*
EMP: 10
SALES (corp-wide): 5.5MM **Privately Held**
SIC: **3273** Ready-mixed concrete
PA: Connell Sand & Gravel, Inc.
200 W Date St
Connell WA 99326
509 234-3221

(G-7568)
CONSOLIDATED PUMP & SUPPLY
2305 N Capitol Ave (99301-9539)
PHONE 509 543-7241
Doug Campbell, *Manager*
EMP: 4
SALES (est): 485K **Privately Held**
SIC: **3561** 5084 Pumps & pumping equipment; pumps & pumping equipment

(G-7569)
CRAFT WALL OF OREGON INC
2090 Crane Ave (99301)
PHONE 509 547-2436
EMP: 9
SALES (corp-wide): 1.2MM **Privately Held**
SIC: **2439** Mfg Structural Wood Members
PA: Craft Wall Of Oregon Inc
3727 14th St
Lewiston ID 83501
208 743-5776

(G-7570)
CRF FROZEN FOODS LLC
1825 N Commercial Ave (99301-9533)
P.O. Box 2508 (99302-2508)
PHONE 509 542-0318
◆ EMP: 42
SALES (est): 18.1MM **Privately Held**
WEB: www.bybeefoods.com
SIC: **2037** Vegetables, quick frozen & cold pack, excl. potato products

(G-7571)
CRF METAL WORKS LLC
3120 Travel Plaza Way (99301-9800)
PHONE 509 430-7609
Jay Brantingham, *Mng Member*
EMP: 15
SALES (est): 4.6MM **Privately Held**
SIC: **3441** Fabricated structural metal

(G-7572)
CUBBYS ELC MTR & PUMP REPR
1716 W A St (99301-5151)
PHONE 509 544-9317
Toll Free: ....888 -
Henry Koontz, *President*
Viola Koontz, *Vice Pres*
EMP: 2
SALES (est): 110K **Privately Held**
SIC: **7694** Electric motor repair

(G-7573)
CUMMINS INC
Also Called: Cummins Northwest
1708 E James St (99301-5937)
PHONE 541 276-2561
Eric Smith, *Branch Mgr*
EMP: 6
SALES (corp-wide): 23.7B **Publicly Held**
SIC: **5084** 3519 Engines & parts, diesel; internal combustion engines
PA: Cummins Inc.
500 Jackson St
Columbus IN 47201
812 377-5000

(G-7574)
CURNUTT INC
8607 Packard Dr (99301-6647)
PHONE 208 520-2598
Florence Curnutt, *President*
Don Curnutt, *Vice Pres*
EMP: 6
SALES (est): 819.7K **Privately Held**
SIC: **2851** 1742 7389 Polyurethane coatings; insulation, buildings;

(G-7575)
CUSTOM COAT
927 S Lindsay St (99301-5804)
P.O. Box 227, Lewiston ID (83501-0227)
PHONE 509 542-9431
Johnny Conn, *Principal*
EMP: 2
SALES (est): 198.4K **Privately Held**
SIC: **3399** Silver powder

(G-7576)
DIESEL PRFMCE UNLIMITED LLC
6804 Franklin Rd (99301-1947)
PHONE 509 546-9997
Chad Riley,
Scott Howell,
EMP: 2
SQ FT: 1,244
SALES: 300K **Privately Held**
WEB: www.urx.com
SIC: **2911** Diesel fuels

(G-7577)
DINA HELMTS
Also Called: Hurrican Hut A Trpcl Sno Dlr
7904 Wrigley Dr (99301-7923)
PHONE 509 521-9866
EMP: 4 EST: 2014
SALES (est): 130K **Privately Held**
SIC: **2024** Mfg Ice Cream/Frozen Desert

(G-7578)
DM COATING LLC
804 W Marie St (99301-4138)
PHONE 509 420-0961
Dennis G Cassens, *Administration*
EMP: 2
SALES (est): 109.4K **Privately Held**
SIC: **3479** Metal coating & allied service

(G-7579)
EMPIRE RUBBER & SUPPLY CO
1428 W A St (99301-5127)
PHONE 509 547-0026
Bob Dunn, *Manager*
EMP: 13

SALES (corp-wide): 12.7MM **Privately Held**
WEB: www.empire-rubber.com
SIC: **5085** 3535 3429 5084 Rubber goods, mechanical; conveyors & conveying equipment; manufactured hardware (general); conveyor systems
PA: Empire Rubber & Supply Co.
80 Se Taylor St
Portland OR 97214
503 235-8461

(G-7580)
EUCON CORPORATION
3300 E A St (99301-6409)
PHONE 509 547-4402
Ron Hjaltalin, *Branch Mgr*
EMP: 61
SALES (corp-wide): 83.3MM **Privately Held**
WEB: www.euconcorp.com
SIC: **1442** Construction sand & gravel
PA: Eucon Corporation
4201 Snake River Ave
Lewiston ID 83501
509 533-1615

(G-7581)
FAYE GEAR RHONDA
Also Called: Eckler Mountain Sawmill
3711 Antigua Dr (99301-8252)
PHONE 509 380-0950
Rhonda Faye Gear, *Owner*
Robert Gear, *Manager*
EMP: 2
SALES (est): 73.2K **Privately Held**
SIC: **2421** Sawmills & planing mills, general

(G-7582)
FOSTER FAMILY FARM
11006 W Court St (99301-6514)
PHONE 509 543-9330
Chris Foster, *Principal*
Teresa Robertson,
EMP: 60
SALES: 2MM **Privately Held**
SIC: **0161** 2035 Asparagus farm; vegetables, pickled

(G-7583)
FRANCISCO GOMEZ VINEYARD SVCS
712 W Park St (99301-5219)
PHONE 559 567-7013
EMP: 2
SALES (est): 70.4K **Privately Held**
SIC: **2084** Wines

(G-7584)
GEMMELLS WLDG FABRICATION LLC
505 S 26th Ave (99301-4748)
PHONE 509 547-5200
Jaime Contreras, *Mng Member*
Dax Gemmell,
EMP: 7
SALES (est): 278.9K **Privately Held**
SIC: **3443** 3542 Fabricated plate work (boiler shop); machine tools, metal forming type

(G-7585)
GEN-X ENERGY GROUP INC
2705 Saint Andrews Loop B (99301-3378)
PHONE 509 547-2447
Scott Johnson, *President*
Joe Stanton, *Principal*
Ray Beneavides, *Corp Secy*
Ramon Benavides, *Vice Pres*
Brian Moreno, *Vice Pres*
EMP: 7
SQ FT: 3,500
SALES (est): 1.6MM **Privately Held**
WEB: www.genxenergies.com
SIC: **2869** Industrial organic chemicals

(G-7586)
GIBBS TRAILER MFG & REPR
320 S Main Ave (99301-4398)
PHONE 509 547-8241
Daniel Marquez, *Manager*
Brian Marquez, *Manager*
EMP: 2
SQ FT: 10,000

SALES (est): 120K **Privately Held**
SIC: **3715** 7539 Truck trailers; trailer repair

(G-7587)
GOOD NEWS CHURCH
Also Called: Hungrygen Church
3203 W Sylvester St (99301-4658)
PHONE 509 544-0938
Vasily Parkhogyuk, *Principal*
▲ EMP: 8
SALES (est): 174.9K **Privately Held**
SIC: **2711** 8661 Newspapers, publishing & printing; churches, temples & shrines

(G-7588)
GORDON BROTHERS CELLARS INC
671 Levey Rd (99301-9711)
PHONE 509 547-6331
Jeffrey Gordon, *President*
Vicki Gordon, *Vice Pres*
▲ EMP: 20
SALES (est): 3.4MM **Privately Held**
SIC: **2084** Wines

(G-7589)
HEALTHIER LIVING PRODUCTS
9315 Chapel Hill Blvd F6101 (99301-8266)
PHONE 509 582-6346
Dale Ballard, *Principal*
EMP: 2
SALES (est): 138.5K **Privately Held**
SIC: **3589** Water treatment equipment, industrial

(G-7590)
HORIZON FLIGHT
20 Piekarski Rd (99301-9708)
PHONE 509 521-4244
Keith Middleton, *Principal*
EMP: 3
SALES (est): 196.8K **Privately Held**
SIC: **3728** Airframe assemblies, except for guided missiles

(G-7591)
HYDRO CONSULTING LLC
615 S Oregon Ave (99301-4320)
P.O. Box 4844 (99302-4844)
PHONE 509 302-1034
Thomas Matheson,
James Powers,
EMP: 2
SQ FT: 8,000
SALES (est): 240K **Privately Held**
SIC: **5162** 1771 3556 Resins; grouting work; cutting, chopping, grinding, mixing & similar machinery

(G-7592)
INTEGRITY FIRST COATINGS LLC
6405 Chapel Hill Blvd D202 (99301-3274)
PHONE 509 619-9983
Jasmine Dominguez, *Principal*
EMP: 2 EST: 2012
SALES (est): 108.1K **Privately Held**
SIC: **3479** Metal coating & allied service

(G-7593)
INTERSTATE CONCRETE AND ASP CO
Also Called: American Rock Products
11919 Harris Rd (99301-8950)
PHONE 509 547-2380
Wade Blagg, *General Mgr*
EMP: 50
SALES (corp-wide): 30.6B **Privately Held**
SIC: **3273** Ready-mixed concrete
HQ: Interstate Concrete And Asphalt Company
8849 W Wyoming Ave
Rathdrum ID 83858
208 765-1144

(G-7594)
J T COATINGS INC
4510 Saint Paul Ct (99301-6144)
PHONE 509 944-1669
Tyler Spencer, *Principal*
EMP: 4
SALES (est): 384.7K **Privately Held**
SIC: **3479** Metal coating & allied service

(PA)=Parent Co (HQ)=Headquarters (DH)=Div Headquarters
✪ = New Business established in last 2 years

2019 Washington Manufacturers Register

Pasco - Franklin County (G-7595)   GEOGRAPHIC SECTION

(G-7595)
JESUS ROMERO
Also Called: La Jalpita
202 W Lewis St (99301-5646)
PHONE..................................509 545-9551
Jesus Romero, *Owner*
EMP: 7
SALES (est): 489.1K **Privately Held**
WEB: www.lajalpita.com
SIC: 2024 5451 Ice cream & frozen desserts; ice cream (packaged)

(G-7596)
KNIGHTS WELDING
1718 W A St (99301-5151)
PHONE..................................509 412-1103
Pat Knight, *Owner*
Randy Knight, *Co-Owner*
EMP: 6 EST: 2013
SALES: 250K **Privately Held**
SIC: 7692 5039 3449 Welding repair; architectural metalwork; miscellaneous metalwork

(G-7597)
KRAFT
4171 Alder Rd (99301-8872)
PHONE..................................509 375-2992
EMP: 2
SALES (est): 62.3K **Privately Held**
SIC: 2022 Processed cheese

(G-7598)
LAMB WESTON INC
960 N Glade Rd (99301-9390)
P.O. Box 2324 (99302-2324)
PHONE..................................509 547-8851
Donny Krautscheid, *Manager*
Douglas Kaanapu, *Director*
EMP: 646
SALES (corp-wide): 3.4B **Publicly Held**
SIC: 2038 2037 5148 2034 Frozen specialties; frozen fruits & vegetables; potatoes, fresh; dehydrated fruits, vegetables, soups
HQ: Lamb Weston Inc
  599 S Rivershore Ln
  Eagle ID 83616

(G-7599)
LARSEN MACHINE
914 S Maitland Ave (99301-5807)
P.O. Box 3457 99302 (99301)
PHONE..................................509 545-0346
Larry Larsen, *Owner*
Jan Larsen, *Corp Secy*
EMP: 2
SQ FT: 6,000
SALES: 100K **Privately Held**
SIC: 3599 Machine shop, jobbing & repair

(G-7600)
LEGGARI PRODUCTS LLC
3105 E Ainsworth Ave Warehouse (99301)
PHONE..................................509 727-2979
Tim Krumland, *Principal*
EMP: 4
SALES (est): 349.2K **Privately Held**
SIC: 2821 Epoxy resins

(G-7601)
LONNIES SIGN SERVICE
1900 W A St (99301-5149)
PHONE..................................509 543-7446
Lonnie Uribe, *Principal*
EMP: 3
SALES (est): 244.5K **Privately Held**
SIC: 3993 Signs & advertising specialties

(G-7602)
MEGAN NIEFORTH
Also Called: Lucky Ice Cream Company
5011 Sinai Dr (99301-8120)
PHONE..................................509 380-6543
Megan Nieforth, *Owner*
EMP: 4
SALES (est): 120K **Privately Held**
SIC: 2024 Ice cream & frozen desserts

(G-7603)
MONARCH MACHINE AND TL CO INC
Also Called: Monarch Metals
410 S Oregon Ave (99301-4317)
PHONE..................................509 547-7753
Douglas J Winters, *President*
Dennis H Shepard, *Vice Pres*
Dorothy J Clark, *Admin Sec*
EMP: 25
SQ FT: 27,000
SALES (est): 6MM **Privately Held**
SIC: 3441 3599 5085 5082 Fabricated structural metal; machine shop, jobbing & repair; industrial supplies; general construction machinery & equipment

(G-7604)
NORTHWEST AG PDTS LLC
Also Called: N A P Chemical
821 S Chestnut Ave (99301-5605)
PHONE..................................509 547-8234
David Bergevin, *President*
EMP: 22
SQ FT: 23,000
SALES (est): 5MM
SALES (corp-wide): 138.9MM **Privately Held**
WEB: www.nap-chem.com
SIC: 2879 2874 2875 Soil conditioners; trace elements (agricultural chemicals); phosphatic fertilizers; fertilizers, mixing only
PA: Verdesian Life Sciences, Llc
  1001 Winstead Dr Ste 480
  Cary NC 27513
  919 825-1901

(G-7605)
NORTHWEST GRINDING CO LLC
1125 E Spokane St (99301-4271)
P.O. Box 3022 (99302-3022)
PHONE..................................509 727-5774
EMP: 3 EST: 2016
SALES (est): 158.4K **Privately Held**
SIC: 3999 Custom pulverizing & grinding of plastic materials

(G-7606)
NUTRIEN AG SOLUTIONS INC
3486 N Glade Rd (99301-9389)
PHONE..................................509 547-9771
Jim Osmond, *Manager*
EMP: 8
SALES (corp-wide): 8.8B **Privately Held**
WEB: www.cropproductionservices.com
SIC: 5261 5083 2879 2875 Fertilizer; farm & garden machinery; agricultural chemicals; fertilizers, mixing only
HQ: Nutrien Ag Solutions, Inc.
  3005 Rocky Mountain Ave
  Loveland CO 80538
  970 685-3300

(G-7607)
OCHOA BROTHERS INC
812 S Myrtle Ave (99301-5611)
PHONE..................................509 544-6553
Juan P Ochoa, *Principal*
EMP: 4 EST: 2012
SALES (est): 425.7K **Privately Held**
SIC: 3559 Semiconductor manufacturing machinery

(G-7608)
OREGON POTATO COMPANY
Also Called: Freeze Pack
400 Commercial Ave (99301)
P.O. Box 2087 (99302-2087)
PHONE..................................509 547-8772
Tim Tippett, *Branch Mgr*
EMP: 50 **Privately Held**
SIC: 2034 Potato products, dried & dehydrated
PA: Oregon Potato Company
  6610 W Court St Ste B
  Pasco WA 99301

(G-7609)
OREGON POTATO COMPANY (PA)
Also Called: Washington Potato Company
6610 W Court St Ste B (99301-2010)
P.O. Box 3110 (99302-3110)
PHONE..................................509 545-4545
Frank S Tiegs, *President*
Tim M Tippett, *Vice Pres*
▼ EMP: 3
SQ FT: 55,000
SALES (est): 185.3MM **Privately Held**
SIC: 2034 Potato products, dried & dehydrated

(G-7610)
OXBO INTERNATIONAL CORPORATION
Also Called: Byron Enterprises
815 N Oregon Ave (99301-4242)
PHONE..................................509 544-0362
Don Carter, *Sales Staff*
Brad Bonny, *Manager*
EMP: 9
SALES (corp-wide): 51.4MM **Privately Held**
WEB: www.oxbocorp.com
SIC: 3523 5083 Farm machinery & equipment; farm & garden machinery
HQ: Oxbo International Corporation
  7275 Batavia Byron Rd
  Byron NY 14422
  585 548-2665

(G-7611)
PACIFIC HIDE & FUR DEPOT
Also Called: Pacific Steel
925 N Oregon Ave (99301-4243)
P.O. Box 3035 (99302-3035)
PHONE..................................509 545-0688
Charle Isaac, *Manager*
EMP: 30
SALES (corp-wide): 391.3MM **Privately Held**
WEB: www.pacific-steel.com
SIC: 5051 3541 3433 3421 Tubing, metal; machine tools, metal cutting type; heating equipment, except electric; cutlery
PA: Pacific Hide & Fur Depot
  5 River Dr S
  Great Falls MT 59405
  406 771-7222

(G-7612)
PALLET SERVICES INC ◆
1430 N Glade Rd (99301-5079)
PHONE..................................509 543-3541
EMP: 4 EST: 2018
SALES (est): 300.7K **Privately Held**
SIC: 2448 Wood pallets & skids

(G-7613)
PASCO MACHINE COMPANY
518 W Columbia St (99301-5579)
PHONE..................................509 547-2448
Jason Story, *President*
EMP: 17
SQ FT: 16,000
SALES (est): 3.6MM **Privately Held**
WEB: www.pascomachineco.com
SIC: 3599 Machine shop, jobbing & repair

(G-7614)
PASCO PROCESSING LLC
5815 N Industrial Way (99301-9388)
PHONE..................................509 544-6700
Douglas Byers,
Paul Saras,
Frank Tiegs,
Tim Tippett,
EMP: 72
SALES (est): 25.5MM **Privately Held**
SIC: 0723 3599 Potato curing services; machine & other job shop work

(G-7615)
PEPSI COLA BOTTLING CO PASCO (HQ)
Also Called: Pepsi-Cola
2525 W Hopkins St (99301-4730)
P.O. Box 111, Yakima (98907-0111)
PHONE..................................509 545-8585
Rodger D Noel, *President*
Larry Estes, *Admin Sec*
EMP: 39
SQ FT: 7,500
SALES (est): 4.9MM
SALES (corp-wide): 97MM **Privately Held**
SIC: 2086 Bottled & canned soft drinks
PA: The Noel Corporation
  1001 S 1st St
  Yakima WA 98901
  509 248-4545

(G-7616)
PEPSI COLA BOTTLING CO PASCO
Also Called: Pepsi-Cola
2525 W Hopkins St (99301-4730)
P.O. Box 2531 (99302-2531)
PHONE..................................509 248-1313
Bill Tilton, *Manager*
EMP: 25
SALES (corp-wide): 97MM **Privately Held**
SIC: 5149 3585 Soft drinks; soda fountain & beverage dispensing equipment & parts
HQ: Pepsi Cola Bottling Company Of Pasco
  2525 W Hopkins St
  Pasco WA 99301
  509 545-8585

(G-7617)
PLASMA BIOLIFE SERVICES L P
7430 Wrigley Dr (99301-5286)
PHONE..................................509 545-3008
EMP: 6
SALES (corp-wide): 15.1B **Privately Held**
SIC: 2836 Plasmas
HQ: Biolife Plasma Services L.P.
  1200 Lakeside Dr
  Bannockburn IL

(G-7618)
PRAIRIE ELECTRIC INC
6931 Road 76 (99301-9599)
PHONE..................................509 545-1752
Randy Brown, *President*
EMP: 69
SALES (corp-wide): 46.2MM **Privately Held**
SIC: 3699 1731 Electrical equipment & supplies; electrical work
PA: Prairie Electric, Inc.
  6000 Ne 88th St
  Vancouver WA 98665
  360 573-2750

(G-7619)
PROGRESSIVE MACHINE INC
318 E B Cir (99301-6402)
PHONE..................................509 547-4062
Joseph A Alvarez, *President*
EMP: 17
SQ FT: 12,400
SALES (est): 3.2MM **Privately Held**
WEB: www.progressivemachine.com
SIC: 3599 Machine shop, jobbing & repair

(G-7620)
R N S FARMS INC
281 Cottonwood Dr (99301-8762)
PHONE..................................509 545-6775
Rodger Wolf, *President*
Norma Wolf, *Corp Secy*
Steve Wolf, *Vice Pres*
EMP: 2
SALES (est): 276.2K **Privately Held**
SIC: 3523 Planting, haying, harvesting & processing machinery

(G-7621)
RADA INC
Also Called: Rada & Sons
2707 E Lewis St (99301-4333)
PHONE..................................509 547-7232
Doug Rada, *President*
Debbie Rada, *Corp Secy*
EMP: 5
SQ FT: 4,992
SALES: 500K **Privately Held**
SIC: 1711 3272 Septic system construction; septic tanks, concrete

(G-7622)
RESERS FINE FOODS INC
Also Called: Pasco Potato Processing
5310 N Industrial Way (99301-9547)
PHONE..................................509 543-4911
Alvin Reser, *President*
EMP: 100
SALES (corp-wide): 1.7B **Privately Held**
SIC: 2099 Food preparations
PA: Reser's Fine Foods, Inc.
  15570 Sw Jenkins Rd
  Beaverton OR 97006
  503 643-6431

GEOGRAPHIC SECTION

Pasco - Franklin County (G-7650)

(G-7623)
RICHARDS PACKAGING INC
2105 E Ainsworth St (99301-5848)
PHONE.....................509 545-8690
Terry Edward, *Owner*
EMP: 3
SALES (corp-wide): 241.1MM **Privately Held**
SIC: 5999 5023 3229 2086 Alarm & safety equipment stores; glassware; pressed & blown glass; bottled & canned soft drinks
HQ: Richards Packaging, Inc.
2321 Ne Argyle St Ste D
Portland OR 97211
503 290-0000

(G-7624)
ROYAL PRESTIGE
104 S Oregon Ave Ste D (99301-4312)
PHONE.....................509 544-0330
Gabriel Plancarte, *Owner*
EMP: 5
SALES (est): 434.7K **Privately Held**
SIC: 3321 Cooking utensils, cast iron

(G-7625)
SBD INC
Also Called: Safeguard
2521 W Sylvester St (99301-4536)
P.O. Box 2186 (99302-2186)
PHONE.....................509 545-8845
Jan Francis, *President*
David Cruzen, *Treasurer*
EMP: 5
SALES (est): 531.8K **Privately Held**
SIC: 2754 2759 Commercial printing, gravure; promotional printing; envelopes: printing; tags: printing; screen printing

(G-7626)
SEMMATERIALS LP
3152 Selph Landing Rd (99301-8840)
PHONE.....................509 545-9864
Stan R Brogdon, *Manager*
EMP: 7
SALES (corp-wide): 2.5B **Publicly Held**
WEB: www.semgroup.com
SIC: 2951 Asphalt paving mixtures & blocks
HQ: Semmaterials, L.P.
6520 S Yale Ave Ste 700
Tulsa OK 74136
918 524-8100

(G-7627)
SEVEN UP BTLG CO TRI CITIES
2106 W Frontage Rd (99301-4703)
PHONE.....................509 547-1660
Greg Scherck, *Manager*
EMP: 17
SALES (est): 835.9K **Privately Held**
SIC: 2086 Bottled & canned soft drinks

(G-7628)
SEVEN UP DR PEPER BOTTLING CO
Also Called: Swires 7up
2106 W Frontage Rd (99301-4703)
PHONE.....................509 547-1660
Greg Scherck, *Manager*
EMP: 16 EST: 2001
SALES (est): 1.5MM **Privately Held**
SIC: 2086 Soft drinks: packaged in cans, bottles, etc.

(G-7629)
SHOWCASE SPECIALTIES INC
Also Called: Pasco Silk Screeners
702 W Lewis St (99301-5540)
PHONE.....................509 547-3344
Teresa Day, *President*
EMP: 5
SQ FT: 2,500
SALES (est): 530.1K **Privately Held**
SIC: 5699 5521 5511 2759 T-shirts, custom printed; automobiles, used cars only; pickups, new & used; screen printing; transit advertising services; embroidery products, except schiffli machine

(G-7630)
SMILEY INDUSTRIAL LLC
1315 N Oregon Ave (99301-5962)
PHONE.....................509 302-8792
Scott Smiley,
EMP: 2
SALES (est): 109K **Privately Held**
SIC: 3399 Primary metal products

(G-7631)
SMK TRI-CITIES INC
1125 E Hillsboro St (99301-9500)
P.O. Box 2548 (99302-2548)
PHONE.....................509 547-0412
Patrick Flumerfelt, *President*
EMP: 50
SALES (est): 9.6MM **Privately Held**
SIC: 3444 Sheet metalwork

(G-7632)
STAR RENTALS INC
1912 W A St (99301-5196)
P.O. Box 2611 (99302-2611)
PHONE.....................509 545-8521
Marty Schur, *Sales Staff*
Ted Merrill, *Branch Mgr*
Kent Scheminske, *Branch Mgr*
Mike Trejbal, *Branch Mgr*
Rob Rathbone, *Manager*
EMP: 15
SALES (corp-wide): 45.7MM **Privately Held**
WEB: www.starrentals.com
SIC: 7359 7353 5082 3444 Tool rental; heavy construction equipment rental; contractors' materials; concrete forms, sheet metal
HQ: Star Rentals, Inc.
1919 4th Ave S
Seattle WA 98134
206 622-7880

(G-7633)
STAR WEST SATELLITE
1320 W A St (99301-5126)
PHONE.....................509 545-4996
Roman Uzarraga, *Principal*
EMP: 2
SALES (est): 152.5K **Privately Held**
SIC: 3663 Space satellite communications equipment

(G-7634)
STEAM ENGINE METAL ART
5412 Koufax Ln (99301-7856)
P.O. Box 309, Mountain View HI (96771-0309)
PHONE.....................509 302-9941
Thomas Gilmore, *Principal*
EMP: 2
SALES (est): 143.6K **Privately Held**
SIC: 3511 Steam engines

(G-7635)
SULLIVAN MANUFACTURING INC
Also Called: Aero Outdoors
316 E B Cir (99301-6402)
PHONE.....................509 545-8000
Paul Sullivan, *CEO*
Suzanne Sullivan, *President*
▲ **EMP:** 7
SALES (est): 652.3K **Privately Held**
WEB: www.aerooutdoors.com
SIC: 3949 Decoys, duck & other game birds

(G-7636)
SYNGENTA SEEDS INC
5516 N Industrial Way (99301-9522)
PHONE.....................509 543-8000
Kevin Lane, *General Mgr*
EMP: 150
SALES (corp-wide): 64.2B **Privately Held**
SIC: 2074 2075 2076 5191 Cottonseed oil mills; soybean oil mills; vegetable oil mills; seeds: field, garden & flower; agricultural chemicals
HQ: Syngenta Seeds, Llc
11055 Wayzata Blvd
Hopkins MN 55305
612 656-8500

(G-7637)
TELCO WIRING & REPAIR INC
613 N Road 27 (99301-4520)
P.O. Box 2503 (99302-2503)
PHONE.....................509 547-4300
Vernon Powers, *President*
Dusty Powers, *Vice Pres*
Herbert Powers, *Treasurer*
Martha Powers, *Admin Sec*
Brad Brest, *Technician*
EMP: 8
SQ FT: 2,000
SALES (est): 875.8K **Privately Held**
SIC: 1731 7629 5065 3661 Telephone & telephone equipment installation; telephone set repair; telecommunication equipment repair (except telephones); telephone equipment; fiber optics communications equipment

(G-7638)
TIMKEN MOTOR & CRANE SVCS LLC
Also Called: H&N Electric
4224 E B St (99301-6418)
PHONE.....................509 547-1691
Tamme Ward, *Manager*
EMP: 45
SALES (corp-wide): 3.5B **Publicly Held**
SIC: 5063 1731 7694 3613 Motors, electric; general electrical contractor; electric motor repair; switchgear & switchboard apparatus; cranes, industrial plant
HQ: Timken Motor & Crane Services, Llc
4850 Moline St
Denver CO 80239
303 623-8658

(G-7639)
TISPORT LLC
Also Called: Tilite
2701 W Court St (99301-3911)
P.O. Box 3970 (99302-3970)
PHONE.....................509 416-4245
David Lippes, *CEO*
Richard Forman, *President*
Josh Anderson, *Vice Pres*
John Roach, *Vice Pres*
Ken Winward, *Vice Pres*
▲ **EMP:** 150 EST: 1997
SQ FT: 60,000
SALES (est): 30.7MM **Privately Held**
SIC: 3842 Wheelchairs; atomizers, medical

(G-7640)
TITANIUM SPORTS TECH LLC
2701 W Court St (99301-3911)
P.O. Box 3970 (99302-3970)
PHONE.....................509 586-6117
Peter Rockefeller, *Warehouse Mgr*
David Scott Lippes,
EMP: 80
SALES (est): 10.1MM **Privately Held**
SIC: 3449 Miscellaneous metalwork

(G-7641)
TOMAR INDUSTRIES
560 Ione Rd (99301-8726)
PHONE.....................509 266-8384
EMP: 2
SALES (est): 71.4K **Privately Held**
SIC: 3999 Manufacturing industries

(G-7642)
TORTILLERIA VALPARAISO
1108 W Sylvester St (99301-4809)
PHONE.....................509 542-1340
Raul Tabuyo, *Owner*
EMP: 3
SALES (est): 190.1K **Privately Held**
SIC: 2099 Tortillas, fresh or refrigerated

(G-7643)
TRI CITY PALLETS
335 E B Cir (99301-6402)
P.O. Box 5633 (99302-5600)
PHONE.....................509 543-7500
Evaristo J Sanchez, *Principal*
EMP: 8
SALES (est): 1MM **Privately Held**
SIC: 2448 Pallets, wood & wood with metal

(G-7644)
TRUSS CO
355 N Commercial Ave (99301-9563)
PHONE.....................509 547-2436
EMP: 8 EST: 2016
SALES (est): 1MM **Privately Held**
SIC: 2439 Trusses, wooden roof

(G-7645)
TWIN CITY FOODS INC
5405 N Industrial Way (99301-9547)
PHONE.....................509 546-0850
Steve Sundberg, *Branch Mgr*
EMP: 272
SALES (corp-wide): 213.6MM **Privately Held**
WEB: www.twincityfoods.com
SIC: 2037 Frozen fruits & vegetables
PA: Twin City Foods, Inc.
10120 269th Pl Nw
Stanwood WA 98292
206 515-2400

(G-7646)
UNITED WESTERN TECH CORP (PA)
Also Called: Uniwest
122 S 4th Ave (99301-5507)
PHONE.....................509 544-0720
Mark Gehlen, *President*
Kurt Oldson, *Vice Pres*
George Nuxoll, *Engineer*
Darlene Cross, *Bookkeeper*
Mike Lewis, *Manager*
EMP: 47
SQ FT: 10,000
SALES (est): 4.8MM **Privately Held**
SIC: 3829 Measuring & controlling devices

(G-7647)
VALMONT NORTHWEST INC (HQ)
4225 N Capitol Ave (99301-2536)
PHONE.....................509 547-1623
Leonard Adams, *President*
Glen Adams, *President*
Dan Winder, *Human Res Mgr*
EMP: 10 EST: 1965
SQ FT: 1,000
SALES (est): 5.4MM
SALES (corp-wide): 2.7B **Publicly Held**
SIC: 3523 5085 Farm machinery & equipment; industrial supplies
PA: Valmont Industries, Inc.
1 Valmont Plz Ste 500
Omaha NE 68154
402 963-1000

(G-7648)
VERDESIAN LIFE SCIENCE US LLC
821 S Chestnut Ave (99301-5605)
PHONE.....................919 825-1901
EMP: 19
SALES (corp-wide): 138.9MM **Privately Held**
SIC: 1479 Fertilizer mineral mining
HQ: Verdesian Life Science U.S., Llc
1001 Winstead Dr Ste 480
Cary NC 27513
919 825-1901

(G-7649)
VIVID LEARNING SYSTEMS INC
5728 Bedford St (99301-8214)
PHONE.....................509 545-1800
Matthew Hammer, *CEO*
EMP: 70
SQ FT: 11,000
SALES: 7.5MM **Privately Held**
WEB: www.learnatvivid.com
SIC: 8331 7372 Job training services; prepackaged software
PA: American Safety And Health Institute, Inc.
1450 Westec Dr
Eugene OR 97402

(G-7650)
VIVOS INC
Also Called: Rdgl
11316 W Court St (99301-6517)
PHONE.....................509 736-4000
James C Katzaroff, *Ch of Bd*
L Bruce Jolliff, *CFO*
Michael Pollack, *CFO*
EMP: 6
SALES (est): 7.1K **Privately Held**
SIC: 2819 Isotopes, radioactive

Pasco - Franklin County (G-7651)

GEOGRAPHIC SECTION

(G-7651)
WESTERN HYDRO LLC
1116 N Oregon Ave (99301-5964)
PHONE..................................509 546-9999
Paul Haderer, *CEO*
EMP: 2
SALES (corp-wide): 1.3B **Publicly Held**
SIC: 3561 Pumps & pumping equipment
HQ: Western Hydro Llc
2034 Research Dr
Livermore CA 94550
559 275-3305

(G-7652)
WESTERN MATERIALS INC
317 S 5th Ave (99301-5596)
PHONE..................................509 547-3301
Dennis Villman, *Manager*
EMP: 55
SALES (corp-wide): 39.4MM **Privately Held**
SIC: 5033 5032 5031 5211 Roofing & siding materials; drywall materials; brick, except refractory; lumber, plywood & millwork; roofing material; lumber products; brick; concrete products, precast
PA: Western Materials, Inc.
1202 S 1st St
Yakima WA 98901
509 575-3000

(G-7653)
WESTERN STATES ASPHALT LLC
3152 Selph Landing Rd (99301-8840)
PHONE..................................509 545-9864
Stan Brogdon, *Branch Mgr*
EMP: 4
SALES (corp-wide): 8.5MM **Privately Held**
SIC: 3531 Asphalt plant, including gravel-mix type
HQ: Western States Asphalt, Llc
4327 N Thor St
Spokane WA 99217
509 487-4560

(G-7654)
WILKERSON WELD & FBRCN INC
1100 E Columbia St B-7 (99301-4355)
P.O. Box 5421, Kennewick (99336-0421)
PHONE..................................509 545-3181
Todd Wilkerson, *President*
EMP: 7
SALES (est): 968.2K **Privately Held**
SIC: 3548 Resistance welders, electric

(G-7655)
WLDG WILKERSON & FABRICATION
1100 E Columbia St D7 (99301-4355)
PHONE..................................509 438-9667
Todd A Wilkerson, *Principal*
EMP: 2
SALES (est): 170K **Privately Held**
SIC: 3444 Sheet metalwork

(G-7656)
WRIGHT SURGICAL ARTS LLC
5908 Bedford St (99301-6605)
PHONE..................................509 792-1404
Dr Joson Wright, *Principal*
EMP: 3 EST: 2015
SALES (est): 146.5K **Privately Held**
SIC: 3841 3842 7231 Saws, surgical; autoclaves, hospital & surgical; facial salons

Pateros
Okanogan County

(G-7657)
AIR METAL FABRICATORS INC
28 Buckhorn Mountain Rd (98846)
PHONE..................................509 923-2274
Kenneth E Orford, *President*
Vicki S Orford, *Vice Pres*
EMP: 5
SALES: 500K **Privately Held**
SIC: 3728 4581 Aircraft parts & equipment; aircraft servicing & repairing

Paterson
Benton County

(G-7658)
LAMB WESTON INC
Also Called: Watts Brothers Frozen Foods
187107 S Watts Rd (99345)
PHONE..................................509 875-2423
Randy Bayuk, *Manager*
EMP: 246
SALES (corp-wide): 3.4B **Publicly Held**
WEB: www.conagra.com
SIC: 2099 Food preparations
HQ: Lamb Weston Inc
599 S Rivershore Ln
Eagle ID 83616

(G-7659)
MICHELLE STE WINE ESTATES LTD
Also Called: Columbia Crest Winery
178810 Hwy 221 (99345)
P.O. Box 231 (99345-0231)
PHONE..................................509 875-4227
Joe Fraser, *Vice Pres*
Evette Mendalez, *Human Res Mgr*
Dennis Burnett, *Lab Dir*
EMP: 10
SALES (corp-wide): 25.3B **Publicly Held**
WEB: www.columbia-crest.com
SIC: 2084 Wines
HQ: Michelle Ste Wine Estates Ltd
14111 Ne 145th St
Woodinville WA 98072
425 488-1133

(G-7660)
MICHELLE STE WINE ESTATES LTD
Hwy 221 Columbia Crest Dr (99345)
P.O. Box 231 (99345-0231)
PHONE..................................509 875-2061
EMP: 10
SALES (corp-wide): 25.3B **Publicly Held**
SIC: 2084 Wines
HQ: Michelle Ste Wine Estates Ltd
14111 Ne 145th St
Woodinville WA 98072
425 488-1133

Pe Ell
Lewis County

(G-7661)
WEYERHAEUSER COMPANY
1098 Muller Rd (98572-9728)
PHONE..................................360 291-3229
Dennis McClure, *Manager*
EMP: 200
SALES (corp-wide): 7.4B **Publicly Held**
SIC: 0811 2411 Tree farm; logging
PA: Weyerhaeuser Company
220 Occidental Ave S
Seattle WA 98104
206 539-3000

Peshastin
Chelan County

(G-7662)
HUNEY JUN LLC
10090 Main St 3 (98847-9770)
PHONE..................................805 903-2011
Molly Hemler,
EMP: 4
SALES (est): 137.6K **Privately Held**
SIC: 3999 Manufacturing industries

(G-7663)
ICICLE RIDGE WINERY (PA)
8977 North Rd (98847-9521)
PHONE..................................509 548-7019
Lou Wagoner, *Owner*
EMP: 2
SALES: 160K **Privately Held**
WEB: www.icicleridgewinery.com
SIC: 2084 Wines

(G-7664)
THIN AIR LOGGING LLC
3000 Ingalls Creek Rd (98847-9433)
PHONE..................................509 670-8139
Shaun Brender,
EMP: 2
SALES (est): 171.7K **Privately Held**
SIC: 2411 Logging

(G-7665)
WATERRA USA INC
5108 Mountain Hm Rnch Rd (98847)
P.O. Box 576 (98847-0576)
PHONE..................................360 738-3366
John McAdam, *President*
Cameron Smith, *Vice Pres*
EMP: 2
SQ FT: 3,000
SALES: 500K **Privately Held**
WEB: www.waterra.com
SIC: 3561 Pumps & pumping equipment

(G-7666)
WEDGE MOUNTAIN WINERY
9534 Saunders Rd (98847-9727)
PHONE..................................509 548-7068
Charles Mc Kee, *Principal*
EMP: 4
SALES (est): 304.3K **Privately Held**
WEB: www.wedgemountainwinery.com
SIC: 2084 Wines

Point Roberts
Whatcom County

(G-7667)
BUBBLES BAKERY
1981 Wellington Rd (98281-9539)
PHONE..................................360 945-1816
Pamela Sheppard, *Owner*
EMP: 2
SALES (est): 59K **Privately Held**
WEB: www.pointbob.net
SIC: 2841 Soap & other detergents

(G-7668)
INTERWORLD ELEC CMPT INDS INC
1480 Gulf Rd Ste 837 (98281-9020)
P.O. Box 1280 (98281-1280)
PHONE..................................425 223-4311
Gerald Cassel, *President*
EMP: 5
SQ FT: 600
SALES: 1MM **Privately Held**
SIC: 5065 3699 Electronic parts; particle accelerators, high voltage

(G-7669)
MARKE WOODWORKING
1528 Panorama Dr (98281-9002)
P.O. Box 99 (98281-0099)
PHONE..................................360 945-4023
EMP: 2 EST: 2008
SALES (est): 130K **Privately Held**
SIC: 2431 Mfg Millwork

(G-7670)
THOMAS MAYER
Also Called: Graphcomm Services
1886 Washington Dr (98281-9613)
PHONE..................................360 945-0354
Thomas Mayer, *Owner*
EMP: 2
SALES (est): 25K **Privately Held**
SIC: 2759 Commercial printing

Pomeroy
Garfield County

(G-7671)
DAVE LEDGERWOOD
Also Called: K and D Asso
61 Hutchens Hill Rd (99347-9655)
P.O. Box 963 (99347-0963)
PHONE..................................509 843-3677
Dave Ledgerwood, *Owner*
EMP: 2
SALES (est): 124.3K **Privately Held**
SIC: 2841 Textile soap

(G-7672)
EAST WASHINGTONIAN
933 Highway 12 W (99347)
PHONE..................................509 843-1313
Mike Tom, *Owner*
Tery Tom, *Co-Owner*
EMP: 3
SQ FT: 1,000
SALES (est): 76K **Privately Held**
SIC: 2711 2759 Newspapers, publishing & printing; commercial printing

(G-7673)
HEALTH RESEARCH
62 7th St (99347-1700)
PHONE..................................509 843-2385
Ben Roberts, *Owner*
Nikki Jones, *Co-Owner*
EMP: 10
SQ FT: 3,000
SALES: 500K **Privately Held**
WEB: www.healthresearchbooks.com
SIC: 2731 Books: publishing only

(G-7674)
HELENA AGRI-ENTERPRISES LLC
Also Called: Central Ferry
82 Central Ferry Rd (99347-8653)
P.O. Box 603, Pullman (99163-0603)
PHONE..................................509 549-3566
Chris Railey, *General Mgr*
EMP: 11 **Privately Held**
SIC: 2875 Fertilizers, mixing only
HQ: Helena Agri-Enterprises, Llc
255 Schilling Blvd # 300
Collierville TN 38017
901 761-0050

(G-7675)
MCGREGOR COMPANY
601 Central Ferry Rd (99347-8623)
PHONE..................................509 549-3635
Jeff Becker, *Branch Mgr*
EMP: 2
SALES (corp-wide): 220.7MM **Privately Held**
SIC: 2873 Nitrogenous fertilizers
PA: The Mcgregor Company
401 Colfax Airport Rd
Colfax WA 99111
509 397-4355

(G-7676)
PRINTING PERFECTION
836 W Main St (99347)
PHONE..................................509 843-7455
Candice Quarles, *Principal*
EMP: 2
SALES (est): 189.7K **Privately Held**
SIC: 2752 Commercial printing, lithographic

(G-7677)
SCOGGIN & SCOGGIN
969 Mountain Rd (99347-9792)
PHONE..................................509 843-1251
EMP: 2
SALES: 50K **Privately Held**
SIC: 3537 Mfg Industrial Trucks/Tractors

Port Angeles
Clallam County

(G-7678)
ADVERTISING SIGNS & MORE
Also Called: A S M Signs
1327 E 1st St Ste A (98362-4650)
PHONE..................................360 452-7785
Michael Millar, *Owner*
EMP: 3
SQ FT: 3,000
SALES (est): 256.6K **Privately Held**
WEB: www.asmsigns.com
SIC: 3993 Signs & advertising specialties

(G-7679)
AIRBORNE ECS LLC
Also Called: Aecs
2007 S O St (98363-1328)
PHONE..................................319 538-1051
William Lee, *President*
◆ EMP: 10

▲ = Import ▼ = Export
◆ = Import/Export

SQ FT: 5,000
SALES: 11MM Privately Held
SIC: 3594 3728 3548 3621 Fluid power pumps & motors; aircraft parts & equipment; arc welders, transformer-rectifier; motors & generators; clock springs, precision; search & navigation equipment

(G-7680)
AK LOGGING LUMBER & MILLWORK
4223 S Fey Rd (98363-9467)
P.O. Box 2072 (98362-0377)
PHONE..................................360 461-3764
Gregory Lippincott, *President*
EMP: 2
SALES (est): 198.2K Privately Held
SIC: 2411 Logging camps & contractors

(G-7681)
ALAN LOGHRY EXCAVATION INC
1553 Township Line Rd (98362-7441)
PHONE..................................360 461-0660
Alan Loghry, *President*
Paula Loghry, *Corp Secy*
▼ EMP: 3
SALES: 800K Privately Held
SIC: 1794 2411 Excavation work; logging

(G-7682)
ALL IN WOOD
845 Shore Rd (98362-7101)
PHONE..................................360 457-8337
Stephen Portner, *Principal*
EMP: 2
SALES (est): 245.4K Privately Held
SIC: 2542 Cabinets: show, display or storage: except wood

(G-7683)
ALLEN LOGGING CO
2818 S Cherry St (98362-6969)
P.O. Box 1660 (98362-0033)
PHONE..................................360 374-6000
Lloyd J Allen, *President*
Bertha Allen, *Vice Pres*
EMP: 50
SQ FT: 43,000
SALES: 10MM Privately Held
SIC: 2421 Wood chips, produced at mill; building & structural materials, wood

(G-7684)
ANGELES COMPOSITE TECH INC
Also Called: Acti
2138 W 18th St (98363-5123)
PHONE..................................360 452-6776
Thomas Panamaroff, *CEO*
Michael Rauch, *President*
Ron Unger, *Chairman*
Alan Wang, *Materials Mgr*
Glenn Murrain, *QC Mgr*
EMP: 99
SQ FT: 75,000
SALES: 18.8MM
SALES (corp-wide): 113.5MM Privately Held
WEB: www.angelescomposite.com
SIC: 3083 Thermoplastic laminates: rods, tubes, plates & sheet
HQ: Shimtech Industries U.S., Inc.
29101 The Old Rd
Valencia CA 91355
661 295-8620

(G-7685)
ANGELES MACHINE WORKS INC
404 E 2nd St (98362-3119)
P.O. Box 765 (98362-0133)
PHONE..................................360 457-0011
Randall Frick, *President*
Steven Frick, *Vice Pres*
EMP: 5
SQ FT: 5,000
SALES (est): 400K Privately Held
SIC: 3599 Machine shop, jobbing & repair

(G-7686)
ARMSTRONG MARINE USA INC
151 Octane Ln (98362-8171)
PHONE..................................360 457-5752
Byron Bolton, *CEO*
Brad Armstrong, *COO*
EMP: 51 EST: 2017
SQ FT: 40,000
SALES: 12MM Privately Held
SIC: 3732 Boat building & repairing

(G-7687)
ARROW MARINE SERVICES INC
830 Boathaven Dr (98362-2101)
PHONE..................................360 457-1544
Jeramey Johnson, *Manager*
EMP: 6 EST: 2015
SALES (est): 386.1K Privately Held
SIC: 3443 Industrial vessels, tanks & containers

(G-7688)
BAKER ENTERPRISES
172 Snow Ln (98362-7204)
PHONE..................................360 452-1349
Anita Baker, *Owner*
Charles Baker, *Co-Owner*
EMP: 2
SALES (est): 94K Privately Held
SIC: 3264 Magnets, permanent: ceramic or ferrite

(G-7689)
BALAMETRICS INC
815 S Oak St (98362-7739)
P.O. Box 2716 (98362-0331)
PHONE..................................360 452-2842
Frank Belgau, *President*
Beverly Belgau, *Corp Secy*
EMP: 3
SALES (est): 200K Privately Held
WEB: www.balametrics.com
SIC: 3999 Education aids, devices & supplies

(G-7690)
BETTER BOATS INC
Also Called: Lee Shore Boats
2271 W Edgewood Dr (98363-9573)
P.O. Box 154 (98362-0021)
PHONE..................................360 797-1244
James Erick Schneider, *President*
Linda Schneider, *Principal*
Dena Schneider, *Vice Pres*
James C Schneider, *Vice Pres*
EMP: 18
SALES: 430K Privately Held
SIC: 3732 Sailboats, building & repairing

(G-7691)
CANVAS SHOPPE
255650 Highway 101 (98362-9297)
PHONE..................................360 457-2773
Rajesh Singh, *Principal*
EMP: 2
SALES (est): 124.2K Privately Held
SIC: 2394 Canvas & related products

(G-7692)
CAUDILL BROS DISTILLERY
125 Motor Ave (98362-2500)
PHONE..................................360 460-6172
EMP: 2
SALES (est): 62.3K Privately Held
SIC: 2085 Distilled & blended liquors

(G-7693)
CAUDILL DISTILLERY
1329 W 10th St (98363-5501)
PHONE..................................360 457-0947
Michael Caudill, *Principal*
EMP: 4 EST: 2017
SALES (est): 233.3K Privately Held
SIC: 2085 Distilled & blended liquors

(G-7694)
COMPOSITE RECYCLING TECH CTR
2220 W 18th St (98363-1521)
PHONE..................................360 819-1204
Robert Larsen, *CEO*
EMP: 8
SALES (est): 69.5K Privately Held
SIC: 3559 Recycling machinery

(G-7695)
COPY CAT GRAPHICS
3234 E Highway 101 (98362-9073)
P.O. Box 2348 (98362-0303)
PHONE..................................360 452-3635
Ted Groves,
EMP: 4
SALES (est): 404.2K Privately Held
WEB: www.copycatgraphics.com
SIC: 7336 3993 Graphic arts & related design; signs & advertising specialties

(G-7696)
CUSTOM FIBERGLASS MFR
4107 Newell Rd (98363)
PHONE..................................360 457-5092
Jody Coman, *Owner*
Judy Coman, *Owner*
EMP: 2
SALES (est): 148.7K Privately Held
SIC: 3732 Boats, fiberglass: building & repairing; fishing boats: lobster, crab, oyster, etc.: small

(G-7697)
DJS PENS
3013 Obrien Rd (98362-7431)
PHONE..................................360 565-0145
Dennis Johnson, *Owner*
Nancy Johnson, *Co-Owner*
EMP: 2
SALES: 30K Privately Held
SIC: 3951 Ball point pens & parts

(G-7698)
DREAMERS WOODS (PA)
102 Holly Hill Rd (98363-8857)
PHONE..................................360 477-5888
Eric A Berson, *Principal*
EMP: 4
SALES (est): 607.3K Privately Held
SIC: 2431 Millwork

(G-7699)
DUDLEYS FINE ENGRAVING
918 E 8th St (98362-6421)
PHONE..................................360 417-9415
EMP: 2 EST: 2001
SALES (est): 77K Privately Held
SIC: 2499 Mfg Wood Products

(G-7700)
DUNGENESS BREWING CO
4017 S Mount Angeles Rd (98362-8966)
PHONE..................................360 775-1877
Michael Sager, *Principal*
EMP: 2
SALES (est): 62.3K Privately Held
SIC: 2082 Malt beverages

(G-7701)
ECHO SPRINGS PUBLISHING
1503 E 3rd St (98362-4801)
PHONE..................................360 417-1346
Gordon Anderson, *Principal*
EMP: 2
SALES (est): 62.9K Privately Held
SIC: 2711 Newspapers

(G-7702)
EDWARDS LOGGING CO
2019 E Maddock Rd (98362-9348)
PHONE..................................360 457-7330
David B Edwards, *Owner*
EMP: 13
SALES (est): 947.8K Privately Held
SIC: 2411 4212 Logging camps & contractors; local trucking, without storage

(G-7703)
ERICKSON BUSHELING INC
964 Freshwater Bay Rd (98363-8877)
PHONE..................................360 928-3232
David E Erickson, *President*
June Erickson, *Corp Secy*
Margaret Erickson, *Vice Pres*
EMP: 3
SALES (est): 300K Privately Held
SIC: 2411 Logging camps & contractors

(G-7704)
EVERGREEN FIBRE INC
Also Called: Herman Brothers Log & Cnstr
404 Eclipse West Dr (98363)
PHONE..................................360 452-2670
Bill Herman, *Corp Secy*
EMP: 20
SALES (corp-wide): 10.7MM Privately Held
SIC: 2411 Logging

HQ: Evergreen Fibre, Inc
2095 Blue Mountain Rd
Port Angeles WA 98362
360 452-3341

(G-7705)
EVERGREEN FIBRE INC (HQ)
2095 Blue Mountain Rd (98362-9203)
PHONE..................................360 452-3341
Steven A Hermann, *President*
William T Hermann, *Corp Secy*
Fred Hermann, *Vice Pres*
EMP: 12
SQ FT: 1,500
SALES (est): 3.6MM
SALES (corp-wide): 10.7MM Privately Held
SIC: 2411 Wood chips, produced in the field
PA: Hermann Brothers Logging & Construction, Incorporated
2095 Blue Mountain Rd
Port Angeles WA 98362
360 452-3341

(G-7706)
FKC CO LTD
2708 W 18th St (98363-1349)
PHONE..................................360 452-9472
Roger Olson, *President*
Keith Lawler, *Counsel*
James Capell, *Vice Pres*
Keith Wallar, *Vice Pres*
Andre Harper, *Project Mgr*
◆ EMP: 14
SQ FT: 8,500
SALES (est): 3.2MM Privately Held
WEB: www.fkcscrewpress.com
SIC: 3451 2759 Screw machine products; screen printing

(G-7707)
FLETCHER BOATS INC
292 Wellman Rd (98363-9412)
PHONE..................................360 452-8430
EMP: 2
SALES (est): 208.6K Privately Held
SIC: 3732 5551 Boatbuilding/Repairing Ret Boats

(G-7708)
HARBOR ACTION INC
Also Called: Pf Industries
166 Alice Rd (98363-9405)
PHONE..................................360 417-1316
Byron Woolsey, *CEO*
Lillian Woolsey, *President*
EMP: 15
SQ FT: 4,000
SALES (est): 1.9MM Privately Held
WEB: www.blisp.com
SIC: 1542 2441 3544 3537 Nonresidential construction; boxes, wood; special dies, tools, jigs & fixtures; industrial trucks & tractors

(G-7709)
HERMANN BROS LOG & CNSTR INC (PA)
2095 Blue Mountain Rd (98362-9203)
PHONE..................................360 452-3341
Fred A Hermann, *President*
William T Hermann, *Corp Secy*
Michael W Hermann, *Vice Pres*
Steven A Hermann, *Vice Pres*
EMP: 55 EST: 1968
SQ FT: 10,000
SALES (est): 10.7MM Privately Held
SIC: 4212 2421 Animal & farm product transportation services; wood chips, produced at mill

(G-7710)
HIGH TIDE SEAFOODS INC
808 Marine Dr (98363-2104)
P.O. Box 2141 (98362-0407)
PHONE..................................360 452-8488
Ernest J Vail, *President*
EMP: 30 EST: 1976
SQ FT: 10,000
SALES (est): 3.8MM Privately Held
SIC: 2092 Fish, frozen: prepared

Port Angeles - Clallam County (G-7711)

(G-7711)
HOOD RIVER CANDLE WORKS
413 Hillstrom Rd (98363-8668)
PHONE.................503 213-4487
Guy M Stokley, *Principal*
EMP: 2
SALES (est): 110.8K Privately Held
SIC: 3999 Candles

(G-7712)
HURWORTH LOGGING
713 Gasman Rd (98362-9526)
PHONE.................360 457-4776
Sam Hurworth, *Owner*
EMP: 2
SALES (est): 120K Privately Held
SIC: 2411 Logging camps & contractors

(G-7713)
INSPIRED
124 W 1st St Ste B (98362-2603)
PHONE.................360 504-2590
Merala Heins, *Owner*
EMP: 2
SALES (est): 76K Privately Held
SIC: 5947 2389 Gift shop; men's miscellaneous accessories

(G-7714)
INTERFOR US INC
243701 W Highway 101 (98363-9810)
PHONE.................360 457-6266
Rick Fortunaso, *General Mgr*
Joe Rodgers, *Vice Pres*
Steve Grawl, *Branch Mgr*
EMP: 210
SALES (corp-wide): 1.6B Privately Held
WEB: www.interfor.com
SIC: 2421 Sawmills & planing mills, general
HQ: Interfor U.S. Inc.
    700 Westpark Dr Ste 100
    Peachtree City GA 30269
    360 788-2299

(G-7715)
INTERFOR US INC
243701 W Highway 101 (98363-9810)
PHONE.................360 327-3377
EMP: 33
SALES (corp-wide): 1.5B Privately Held
SIC: 0811 2421 5031 Timber Tract Operationsawmill And Planning Mill Wholesale Lumber And Plywood An Millwork
HQ: Interfor U.S. Inc.
    2219 Rimland Dr Ste 201
    Bellingham WA 30269
    360 788-2299

(G-7716)
JACKSON SIGNS & GRAPHICS
Also Called: Jackson's Signs & Art Studio
472 Mount Pleasant Rd (98362-9332)
PHONE.................360 457-3703
Jack Smart, *Owner*
EMP: 2
SALES (est): 122.5K Privately Held
SIC: 3993 7336 Signs, not made in custom sign painting shops; chart & graph design

(G-7717)
JESSE BAY CABINETRY
175 S Bayview Ave Unit 21 (98362-8345)
PHONE.................360 417-8122
Jesse Bay, *Principal*
EMP: 4
SALES (est): 371.8K Privately Held
SIC: 2434 Wood kitchen cabinets

(G-7718)
JIG & LURE
826 Marine Dr (98363-2104)
PHONE.................360 457-2745
EMP: 3
SALES (est): 137.7K Privately Held
SIC: 3949 Sporting & athletic goods

(G-7719)
JOHNNIE MONTICE
Also Called: Captain T'S
114 E Front St (98362-2907)
P.O. Box 993 (98362-0806)
PHONE.................360 452-6549
Johnnie Montice, *Owner*
▲ EMP: 5
SQ FT: 7,500
SALES: 300K Privately Held
WEB: www.captaints.com
SIC: 2759 2395 5651 Screen printing; embroidery & art needlework; family clothing stores

(G-7720)
JUDD TIMBER CUTTING LLC
1283 Crescent Beach Rd (98363-7135)
PHONE.................360 928-9011
Larry Judd,
Marva Jean Judd,
EMP: 2
SALES (est): 81.7K Privately Held
SIC: 2411 Logging

(G-7721)
JUSTICE SYSTEMS PRESS
32 Chessie Ln (98362-9147)
P.O. Box 2852 (98362-0334)
PHONE.................360 417-8845
Barbara Birkland, *President*
Steven Kernes, *Co-Owner*
Steve Kernes, *Vice Pres*
EMP: 2
SALES (est): 129.6K Privately Held
SIC: 2731 Books: publishing only

(G-7722)
K & M WDWRKERS PORT ANGLES INC
Also Called: K & M Woodworkers Port Angeles
1619 S Butler St (98363-1339)
PHONE.................360 457-9773
Ken Strain, *President*
EMP: 2
SALES: 72K Privately Held
SIC: 2434 Wood kitchen cabinets

(G-7723)
LEFT COAST COMPOSITES
60 Montrose Pl (98362-9198)
PHONE.................305 923-4590
Joseph Kitchell, *Principal*
EMP: 2
SALES (est): 151.9K Privately Held
SIC: 3732 Boat building & repairing

(G-7724)
MCKINLEY PAPER COMPANY
1815 Marine Dr (98362-1836)
PHONE.................360 457-4474
Mary French, *Controller*
EMP: 24 Privately Held
SIC: 2621 Paper mills
HQ: Mckinley Paper Company
    7850 Jefferson St Ne # 150
    Albuquerque NM 87109

(G-7725)
MERRILL & RING INC
813 E 8th St (98362-6418)
P.O. Box 1058 (98362-0181)
PHONE.................360 452-2367
Fax: 360 452-2015
EMP: 23
SALES (corp-wide): 11.3MM Privately Held
SIC: 2421 6552 Sawmill/Planing Mill Subdivider/Developer
PA: Merrill & Ring Inc.
    813 E 8th St
    Port Angeles WA 98362
    425 778-7900

(G-7726)
MODERN YACHT JOINERY
1023 King St (98363-8546)
P.O. Box 1291 (98362-0240)
PHONE.................360 928-0214
John Bert, *Principal*
EMP: 4 EST: 2008
SALES (est): 361.6K Privately Held
SIC: 2431 Millwork

(G-7727)
NIPPON PAPER INDS USA CO LTD
1902 Marine Dr (98363-1803)
PHONE.................360 457-4474
EMP: 10 Privately Held
SIC: 2611 Pulp mills
HQ: Nippon Paper Industries Usa Co., Ltd.
    3401 Industrial Way
    Longview WA 98632
    360 457-4474

(G-7728)
OLYMPIC CELLARS LLC
Also Called: Lighting Ridge Investments
255410 Highway 101 (98362-9200)
PHONE.................360 452-0160
Kathy Charlton, *Partner*
EMP: 5
SALES (est): 457K Privately Held
WEB: www.olympiccellars.com
SIC: 2084 Wines

(G-7729)
OLYMPIC DISTILLERS LLC
356 Freshwater Bay Rd (98363-8871)
PHONE.................360 920-9645
Svend Larsson, *Principal*
EMP: 2
SALES (est): 106K Privately Held
SIC: 3556 Distillery machinery

(G-7730)
OLYSIGNS
12 Findley Rd (98362-8174)
PHONE.................360 417-5254
Wade Leinaar, *Partner*
Tom Leinaar, *Principal*
EMP: 2
SALES (est): 180.6K Privately Held
SIC: 3993 Signs, not made in custom sign painting shops

(G-7731)
ONE TIME WELDING
2917 W Edgewood Dr (98363-9587)
PHONE.................360 452-8532
EMP: 2 EST: 1995
SALES (est): 110K Privately Held
SIC: 7692 Welding Repair

(G-7732)
ORACLE FISHERIES LLC
1485 Deer Park Rd (98362-8263)
PHONE.................360 477-9829
EMP: 2
SALES (est): 62.1K Privately Held
SIC: 7372 Prepackaged software

(G-7733)
OUT ON A LIMB ENTERPRISES
430 W 5th St (98362-2223)
PHONE.................360 457-8479
Christinia Lawrence, *Owner*
EMP: 2
SALES (est): 125.4K Privately Held
SIC: 3842 Limbs, artificial

(G-7734)
OZETTE INDUSTRIES LLC
133 Doyle Rd (98363-9416)
P.O. Box 1873 (98362-0281)
PHONE.................360 460-4272
Vernon Pritchard, *Principal*
EMP: 3 EST: 2015
SALES (est): 239.4K Privately Held
SIC: 3999 Manufacturing industries

(G-7735)
PEN PRINT INC
230 E 1st St Ste A (98362-2938)
PHONE.................360 457-3404
Cindy Souders, *President*
EMP: 5
SQ FT: 2,500
SALES: 200K Privately Held
WEB: www.penprintinc.com
SIC: 2759 2752 Commercial printing; commercial printing, lithographic

(G-7736)
PENINSULA LUBRICANTS
1230 W 17th St (98363-7010)
PHONE.................360 452-8376
Richard Dearinger, *Principal*
EMP: 3
SALES (est): 213.8K Privately Held
SIC: 2992 Oils & greases, blending & compounding

(G-7737)
PORT ANGELES HARDWOOD LLC
333 Eclipse Ind Pkwy (98363)
PHONE.................360 452-6041
Ron Wilson, *Manager*
◆ EMP: 2
SALES (est): 466.6K Privately Held
SIC: 2421 Sawmills & planing mills, general

(G-7738)
PRISMOID OPTICAL LABORATORY
Also Called: Bec's Specs
216 E 5th St Ste A (98362-3008)
P.O. Box 774 (98362-0134)
PHONE.................360 417-1244
Rebecca E Doherty, *President*
EMP: 2
SALES (est): 189.2K Privately Held
SIC: 3851 5995 5048 Lenses, ophthalmic; optical goods stores; ophthalmic goods

(G-7739)
RISE N GRIND
3231 E Highway 101 (98362-9073)
PHONE.................360 452-9335
Donna Roark, *CEO*
EMP: 2
SALES (est): 122.6K Privately Held
SIC: 3599 Grinding castings for the trade

(G-7740)
RODOCKER WOODWORKS LLC
1011 W 11th St (98363-7208)
PHONE.................360 775-1620
EMP: 2 EST: 2014
SALES (est): 59.5K Privately Held
SIC: 2431 Millwork

(G-7741)
RYGAARD LOGGING INC (PA)
401 Monroe Rd (98362-9328)
PHONE.................360 457-4941
Gabriel Rygaard, *President*
Craig Rygaard, *Vice Pres*
Jason Rygaard, *Shareholder*
Katherine Rygaard, *Admin Sec*
EMP: 12
SQ FT: 10,000
SALES (est): 1.3MM Privately Held
SIC: 2411 Logging camps & contractors

(G-7742)
S&L PORTABLE SAWMILL LLC
3578 Monroe Rd (98362-8969)
P.O. Box 1205 (98362-0200)
PHONE.................360 417-3085
EMP: 9
SALES (est): 640.4K Privately Held
SIC: 2421 Sawmill/Planing Mill

(G-7743)
SANCTUARY CORPORATION
Also Called: Phoenix Dragon Limited
182 N Ridge View Dr (98362-8455)
PHONE.................360 477-4384
Keith Comeau, *President*
EMP: 2
SALES (est): 97.6K Privately Held
SIC: 3479 2796 Etching & engraving; steel line engraving for the printing trade

(G-7744)
SMOOTHIE ESSENTIALS
213 W 13th St (98362-7719)
PHONE.................360 452-8060
Sheila Gregg, *Principal*
EMP: 4
SALES (est): 277K Privately Held
SIC: 2037 Frozen fruits & vegetables

(G-7745)
SPECIALTY WOODWORKS
124 N Gales St (98362-8732)
PHONE.................360 670-6280
EMP: 2 EST: 2014
SALES (est): 84K Privately Held
SIC: 2431 Millwork

GEOGRAPHIC SECTION

Port Ludlow - Jefferson County (G-7777)

(G-7746)
SPILLMASTERS X LLC
322 Christmas Tree Ln (98363-9599)
PHONE..................360 461-7910
Bret Hendren,
EMP: 2
SALES (est): 61.6K **Privately Held**
SIC: 2823 Cellulosic manmade fibers

(G-7747)
STROMSKI REPAIR AND WELDING
541 Erving Jacobs Rd (98362-9240)
PHONE..................360 452-1661
Francis Stromski, *Owner*
Evelyne Stromski, *Co-Owner*
EMP: 2
SALES (est): 69.5K **Privately Held**
SIC: 7692 Welding repair

(G-7748)
TC LUMBER
3943 Eden Valley Rd (98363-8832)
PHONE..................360 452-2612
Merton Corey, *Partner*
George Thompson, *Partner*
EMP: 2
SALES (est): 163.9K **Privately Held**
SIC: 2411 Logging camps & contractors

(G-7749)
THINKING CAP SOLUTIONS IN
3122 Old Olympic Hwy (98362-8199)
PHONE..................360 452-6159
Elizabeth Batz, *Manager*
EMP: 2
SALES (est): 90.9K **Privately Held**
WEB: www.ice-alert.com
SIC: 2731 Book publishing

(G-7750)
THRIFTY PAYLESS INC T/A
1940 E 1st St Ste 110 (98362-4990)
PHONE..................360 457-3456
EMP: 2 **EST:** 2010
SALES (est): 98.4K **Privately Held**
SIC: 2836 Vaccines & other immunizing products

(G-7751)
VERTICAL LIFT SOLUTIONS
763 Oxenford Rd (98363-8866)
P.O. Box 2760 (98362-0332)
PHONE..................360 928-1126
EMP: 2 **EST:** 2011
SALES (est): 93K **Privately Held**
SIC: 2591 Mfg Drapery Hardware/Blinds

(G-7752)
VIGOR INDUSTRIAL LLC
Also Called: Vigor Alaska
202 N Cedar St Ste 1 (98362-2205)
P.O. Box 1425 (98362-0262)
PHONE..................360 457-8470
Roy McKay, *General Mgr*
EMP: 25
SALES (corp-wide): 599.5MM **Privately Held**
SIC: 3731 Shipbuilding & repairing
PA: Vigor Industrial Llc
   5555 N Channel Ave # 71
   Portland OR 97217
   503 247-1777

(G-7753)
WASHINGTON MARINE REPAIR LLC
202 N Cedar St Ste 1 (98363-2205)
P.O. Box 1425 (98362-0262)
PHONE..................360 457-8470
Frank J Foti, *CEO*
David R Whitcomb, *COO*
Lon V Leneve, *CFO*
Julie Skirvin, *Admin Sec*
▲ **EMP:** 30
SQ FT: 6,000
SALES (est): 3.1MM
SALES (corp-wide): 599.5MM **Privately Held**
WEB: www.vigorindustrial.com
SIC: 3731 Shipbuilding & repairing
PA: Vigor Industrial Llc
   5555 N Channel Ave # 71
   Portland OR 97217
   503 247-1777

(G-7754)
WESTPORT LLC
3500 E Highway 101 (98362-9148)
PHONE..................360 452-5095
Pam Foust, *Executive Asst*
EMP: 226
SALES (corp-wide): 40.5MM **Privately Held**
SIC: 3732 Yachts, building & repairing
PA: Westport, L.L.C.
   637 Marine Dr
   Port Angeles WA 98363
   360 452-5095

(G-7755)
WESTPORT LLC
2140 W 18th St 1050 (98363-5123)
PHONE..................360 452-5095
Jennifer Swogger, *Human Res Mgr*
EMP: 12
SALES (corp-wide): 40.5MM **Privately Held**
SIC: 3732 Yachts, building & repairing
PA: Westport, L.L.C.
   637 Marine Dr
   Port Angeles WA 98363
   360 452-5095

Port Gamble
Kitsap County

(G-7756)
ACORN TREE AND STUMP SERVICES
17-A Hwy 104 (98364)
PHONE..................360 509-0145
Carl John Koepp, *Owner*
EMP: 5
SALES: 80K **Privately Held**
SIC: 2411 Logging

(G-7757)
OLYMPIC OUTDOOR CENTER
Also Called: Olympic Kayak Co
32379 Rainier Ave Ne (98364-1204)
P.O. Box 236 (98364-0236)
PHONE..................360 297-4659
John Kuntz, *Owner*
EMP: 40
SQ FT: 3,000
SALES (est): 4.8MM **Privately Held**
WEB: www.olympicoutdoorcenter.com
SIC: 5551 7999 7359 3732 Kayaks; canoes; rafting tours; instruction schools, camps & services; equipment rental & leasing; boat building & repairing

Port Hadlock
Jefferson County

(G-7758)
GRAYMARK INDUSTRIES INC
3655 Oak Bay Rd (98339-9730)
PHONE..................360 437-5121
Dee Meek, *Principal*
EMP: 2
SALES (est): 67K **Privately Held**
SIC: 3999 Manufacturing industries

(G-7759)
HEAVENLY MOUNTAIN STUDIOS
26 Leighbrook Ln (98365-8745)
PHONE..................360 437-2298
Virginia Ford, *Owner*
EMP: 3
SALES (est): 133.1K **Privately Held**
SIC: 2515 Studio couches

(G-7760)
MERLINS WORKSHOP LLC
251 Brighton St (98339-8508)
PHONE..................206 817-9677
Michael K Hoskins,
EMP: 3
SALES: 100K **Privately Held**
SIC: 3599 Industrial machinery

(G-7761)
NAVAL MAGAZINE CODE 4214
100 Indn Island Annex Rd (98339-9723)
PHONE..................360 396-2187
EMP: 3
SALES (est): 154.4K **Privately Held**
SIC: 2721 Periodicals

(G-7762)
SIGN STATION
11602 Rhody Dr (98339-9772)
PHONE..................360 379-2954
Gary Shannon, *Principal*
EMP: 2
SALES (est): 186.6K **Privately Held**
SIC: 3713 Truck bodies & parts

Port Ludlow
Jefferson County

(G-7763)
A THOUSAND HILLS INC
103 S Bayview Dr (98365-9471)
PHONE..................360 437-9805
John Parent, *Owner*
EMP: 3
SALES: 270K **Privately Held**
WEB: www.athousandhills.com
SIC: 3822 Hydronic controls

(G-7764)
CALPORTLAND COMPANY
360 Quarry Rd (98365-9459)
PHONE..................206 764-3000
EMP: 2 **Privately Held**
SIC: 3241 Cement, hydraulic
HQ: Calportland Company
   2025 E Financial Way
   Glendora CA 91741
   626 852-6200

(G-7765)
E MCS2
53 Keller Ln (98365-9607)
PHONE..................971 295-4641
Mishele Smith, *Principal*
EMP: 2
SALES (est): 85.9K **Privately Held**
SIC: 3572 Computer storage devices

(G-7766)
GIRAFFE FAMILY PRESS
45 Jackson Ln (98365-9668)
PHONE..................360 437-8018
EMP: 2 **EST:** 2002
SALES (est): 81K **Privately Held**
SIC: 2741 Misc Publishing

(G-7767)
HIGHER MIND INCENSE
3871 Larson Lake Rd (98365-9754)
PHONE..................541 702-1560
Evan Purcell, *Principal*
EMP: 2
SALES (est): 96.1K **Privately Held**
SIC: 2899 Incense

(G-7768)
JOHNSON MARINE
291 Mats View Rd (98365-9403)
P.O. Box 65406 (98365-0406)
PHONE..................360 437-0467
Errol Johnson, *Owner*
EMP: 2 **EST:** 2017
SALES (est): 104K **Privately Held**
SIC: 3519 Internal combustion engines

(G-7769)
KRISTINES
7251 Oak Bay Rd (98365-9441)
PHONE..................360 437-0136
Kristine L Jasiecki, *Owner*
Ronald V Jasiecki, *Owner*
EMP: 3
SALES (est): 343.2K **Privately Held**
SIC: 5021 2511 2434 2521 Furniture; wood household furniture; wood kitchen cabinets; cabinets, office: wood

(G-7770)
LUDLOW MORTGAGE INC
7446 Oak Bay Rd (98365-9445)
P.O. Box 65486 (98365-0486)
PHONE..................360 437-1344
Sterling C Couch III, *President*
EMP: 3
SQ FT: 3,000
SALES: 150K **Privately Held**
WEB: www.irshelp.com
SIC: 3663 Radio & TV communications equipment

(G-7771)
OAK BAY TECHNOLOGIES INC
521 Verner Ave (98365-9422)
P.O. Box 65494 (98365-0494)
PHONE..................360 437-0718
Mark K Mc Kibbin, *President*
EMP: 5
SQ FT: 1,000
SALES (est): 449.9K **Privately Held**
WEB: www.oakbay.com
SIC: 3663 7371 Radio broadcasting & communications equipment; custom computer programming services

(G-7772)
PORT ORCHARD SAND & GRAVEL
9868 State Route 104 (98365-9592)
PHONE..................360 681-2526
Dean Moergeli, *Owner*
EMP: 40 **EST:** 1999
SALES (est): 1MM **Privately Held**
SIC: 1442 Construction sand & gravel

(G-7773)
SEATTLE KITCHEN CABINET INC
7446 Oak Bay Rd (98365-9445)
P.O. Box 65486 (98365-0486)
PHONE..................360 437-1344
Gary Burt, *Principal*
EMP: 2
SALES (est): 89.6K **Privately Held**
SIC: 2434 Wood kitchen cabinets

(G-7774)
SHINE MICRO INC
9405 Oak Bay Rd Unit A (98365-8269)
P.O. Box 340, Port Gamble (98364-0340)
PHONE..................360 437-2503
Mark M Johnson, *President*
Judith Johnson, *CFO*
Steve Marquis, *Technician*
EMP: 14
SALES: 1MM **Privately Held**
WEB: www.shinemicro.com
SIC: 8748 3629 Business consulting; electronic generation equipment

(G-7775)
SHINE QUARRY INC
9861 State Route 104 (98365-9592)
PHONE..................360 437-2415
Danae Larrance, *President*
EMP: 12
SQ FT: 800
SALES (est): 823.8K **Privately Held**
SIC: 1429 Igneous rock, crushed & broken-quarrying

(G-7776)
SIGN ME UP INC
605 Shine Rd (98365-9279)
PHONE..................360 271-8070
Barbara Smith, *Principal*
EMP: 2 **EST:** 2012
SALES (est): 128.7K **Privately Held**
SIC: 3993 Signs & advertising specialties

(G-7777)
SILVERGEN INC
170 Embody Rd (98365-8772)
PHONE..................360 732-5091
Trem William, *President*
K M Williams, *President*
Tren Williams, *President*
Kathleen McDermott, *Corp Secy*
EMP: 2
SALES (est): 245.8K **Privately Held**
WEB: www.silvergen.com
SIC: 3621 Power generators

Port Ludlow - Jefferson County (G-7778)

(G-7778)
STERLING ENVMTL RESOURCES
7446 Oak Bay Rd (98365-9445)
PHONE..................360 437-1344
Sterling C Couch III, *President*
EMP: 60
SALES (est): 3.8MM **Privately Held**
SIC: 3731 Shipbuilding & repairing

(G-7779)
STEWART LOGGING
300 N Bay Way (98365-9451)
P.O. Box 38, Port Hadlock (98339-0038)
PHONE..................360 437-2905
Charles Stewart, *Owner*
EMP: 2
SALES (est): 53.2K **Privately Held**
SIC: 2411 0781 Logging camps & contractors; landscape services

---

Port Orchard
Kitsap County

(G-7780)
A GOOD YARN SHOP
1140 Bethel Ave Ste 101 (98366-3299)
PHONE..................360 876-0157
Debbie Macomber, *President*
EMP: 12
SALES (est): 1.5MM **Privately Held**
SIC: 2284 Sewing thread

(G-7781)
AAA SUPERLUBES INC
1860 California Ave Se (98366-8709)
PHONE..................425 353-4901
Dannie O Thumma, *Principal*
EMP: 3
SALES (est): 263.2K **Privately Held**
SIC: 2911 Oils, lubricating

(G-7782)
AAHED LOGISTICS LLC
2570 Alaska Ave E (98366-8213)
PHONE..................757 395-7063
Kristin Mickelson, *Principal*
EMP: 3
SALES (est): 219.6K **Privately Held**
SIC: 3568 3052 3566 Power transmission equipment; v-belts, rubber; gears, power transmission, except automotive

(G-7783)
ADHESIVE & PACKAGING SYSTEMS
12938 Woodside Ln Sw (98367-7179)
PHONE..................360 876-9278
Tim Bamburg, *President*
EMP: 3
SALES (est): 150.9K **Privately Held**
SIC: 2631 Container, packaging & boxboard

(G-7784)
AIR MOD INC
11840 Ridge Rim Trl Se (98367-8717)
PHONE..................360 895-0910
EMP: 2
SALES (est): 152K **Privately Held**
SIC: 3612 Mfg Transformers

(G-7785)
ALASKA MARINE REFRIGERATION
Also Called: AMR Enviromental Services
4390 Cottonwood Dr Se (98367-9028)
P.O. Box 533, Manchester (98353-0533)
PHONE..................360 871-4414
Karen Mc Gee, *President*
Melinda Kelly, *Executive*
EMP: 12
SALES (est): 1.6MM **Privately Held**
SIC: 7623 1711 3585 Refrigeration repair service; refrigeration contractor; refrigeration equipment, complete

(G-7786)
AMERICAN IMAGE DISPLAYS
5571 Watauga Beach Dr E (98366-8063)
PHONE..................425 556-9511
Joe Dugan, *Production*
Michele Gibbs-Luna, *Accounts Exec*
Charles Dugan,
Terri Adugan,
Terri Dugan,
EMP: 10
SALES (est): 1.6MM **Privately Held**
WEB: www.american-image.com
SIC: 3993 5199 7389 7319 Displays & cutouts, window & lobby; advertising specialties; advertising, promotional & trade show services; display advertising service

(G-7787)
AMERICAN LASER WORKS
1860 California Ave Se (98366-8709)
PHONE..................360 871-3738
Nelson Wagner, *Owner*
EMP: 3
SALES (est): 50K **Privately Held**
WEB: www.americanlaserworks.com
SIC: 3993 Signs & advertising specialties

(G-7788)
APPAGARE SOFTWARE INC
8970 Wyvern Dr Se (98367-9054)
P.O. Box 762, Burley (98322-0762)
PHONE..................253 857-4675
Eric Guenther, *Principal*
EMP: 5
SALES (est): 375.8K **Privately Held**
SIC: 7372 Prepackaged software

(G-7789)
ARROWOOD MINI STORAGE
6530 Se Mile Hill Dr (98366-8724)
PHONE..................360 769-7400
Allan Campbell, *Partner*
Kathy Campbell, *Partner*
EMP: 3
SQ FT: 27,820
SALES (est): 265.6K **Privately Held**
SIC: 2511 Storage chests, household: wood

(G-7790)
B C TRAFFIC
2501 Se Mile Hill Dr (98366-3500)
PHONE..................360 895-1000
Thio A Budiman, *Principal*
EMP: 7
SALES (est): 862.4K **Privately Held**
SIC: 3669 Transportation signaling devices

(G-7791)
B K WELDING AND FABRICATION
Also Called: Bk Welding
6412 Se Sedgwick Rd (98366-9797)
PHONE..................360 871-0490
Barbra Kovacs, *Partner*
Belag Kovacs, *Partner*
EMP: 2
SQ FT: 2,400
SALES: 100K **Privately Held**
SIC: 3446 7692 1799 Railings, bannisters, guards, etc.: made from metal pipe; fences or posts, ornamental iron or steel; welding repair; welding on site

(G-7792)
BADGE BOYS AWARDS & ENGRAVING
3220 Se Puffin Ln (98367-9581)
PHONE..................360 876-8414
EMP: 3
SALES (est): 178.5K **Privately Held**
SIC: 5999 5199 5099 2759 Ret Misc Merchandise Whol Nondurable Goods Whol Durable Goods Commercial Printing

(G-7793)
BEST GUESS SOFTWARE
4306 Pioneer Pl Se (98366-1537)
PHONE..................360 876-3272
EMP: 2
SALES: 100K **Privately Held**
SIC: 7372 Prepackaged Software Services

(G-7794)
BETTY OGUIN
Also Called: J B Creations
1880 Sidney Ave (98366-2448)
PHONE..................360 876-0803
Betty O'Guin, *Owner*
EMP: 2
SALES: 20K **Privately Held**
SIC: 2399 Book covers, fabric

(G-7795)
BLACKWATERS METAL
8471 Glenwood Rd Sw (98367-7501)
PHONE..................425 213-0154
Bob Delaney, *Principal*
EMP: 2
SALES (est): 140.9K **Privately Held**
SIC: 3231 Ornamental glass: cut, engraved or otherwise decorated

(G-7796)
BREMERTON TRAP & SKEET CLUB
4956 State Highway 3 Sw (98367)
PHONE..................360 674-2438
Tom Hamilton, *President*
EMP: 2
SQ FT: 4,658
SALES: 56.8K **Privately Held**
WEB: www.bremertontrapandskeet.com
SIC: 7999 2411 Recreation services; logging

(G-7797)
CHARLES HANSON
Also Called: Colonial Heirlooms Manchester
8043 E Seaview Dr (98366-8514)
PHONE..................360 871-2173
Charles Henson, *Owner*
EMP: 2
SALES (est): 100K **Privately Held**
SIC: 2511 2657 Wood household furniture; folding paperboard boxes

(G-7798)
COMPOST MANUFACTURING ALLIANCE
1771 Vista Rama Dr E (98366-8352)
PHONE..................206 755-8309
Susan Thoman, *Principal*
EMP: 2
SALES (est): 74.4K **Privately Held**
SIC: 2875 Compost

(G-7799)
CONFIG-SYSTEMS
9481 Se Miller Creek Rd (98367-5905)
PHONE..................360 871-8091
J Grubbs, *COO*
EMP: 2 **Privately Held**
SIC: 3599 Industrial machinery

(G-7800)
CRAZY J
4452 Sw Hunter Ln (98377-7789)
P.O. Box 21, Burley (98322-0021)
PHONE..................360 876-6618
Jonathan Jolly, *Owner*
Patt K Jolly, *Co-Owner*
EMP: 2
SALES (est): 77.9K **Privately Held**
SIC: 3999 Stringing beads

(G-7801)
CREATIVE IMAGERY
7347 E Collins Rd (98366-8304)
PHONE..................360 871-6529
Heiko Vogler, *Owner*
EMP: 2
SALES (est): 168K **Privately Held**
SIC: 3993 Signs & advertising specialties

(G-7802)
DESIGNS UNLIMITED
5384 E Collins Rd (98366-8329)
PHONE..................360 792-1372
Diana Linne, *Owner*
Charles I Linne, *Co-Owner*
EMP: 5
SQ FT: 3,000
SALES (est): 563K **Privately Held**
WEB: www.designsunlimitedco.com
SIC: 2284 2759 7336 Embroidery thread; screen printing; graphic arts & related design

(G-7803)
DIFFERENTIAL ENERGY GLOBAL LTD
1540 Leader Intl Dr (98367)
PHONE..................360 895-1184
Richard A Flaherty, *President*
Catherine Flaherty, *Vice Pres*
▲ EMP: 9
SQ FT: 2,600
SALES (est): 1.3MM **Privately Held**
SIC: 3641 Electric lamps & parts for specialized applications

(G-7804)
DON BOEHME & SONS LOGGING
7084 Se King Rd (98367-8630)
PHONE..................360 871-1571
Don Boehme, *President*
JB Bohme, *Vice Pres*
Joan Boehme, *Admin Sec*
EMP: 3
SALES (est): 250K **Privately Held**
SIC: 2411 Logging camps & contractors

(G-7805)
EAGLE HARBOR PRINT CO LLC
9676 Glenwood Rd Sw (98367-9403)
PHONE..................970 441-0000
A Gregory Dreiling, *Bd of Directors*
EMP: 2
SALES (est): 119.4K **Privately Held**
SIC: 2752 Commercial printing, lithographic

(G-7806)
EAGLES NEST
14423 Glenwood Rd Sw (98367-7771)
PHONE..................360 876-9522
John Laundry, *Owner*
EMP: 2
SALES (est): 121.3K **Privately Held**
SIC: 2426 Carvings, furniture: wood

(G-7807)
ELEANOR WILEY
9992 Fairview Lake Rd Sw (98367-9213)
PHONE..................360 698-5077
EMP: 2
SALES (est): 98.5K **Privately Held**
SIC: 3479 Coating/Engraving Service

(G-7808)
ERS GROUP INC
10201 Horizon Ln Se Ste A (98367-8189)
PHONE..................360 895-1318
Eileen Rogers, *President*
EMP: 5
SALES: 140K **Privately Held**
SIC: 2329 2339 5699 Men's & boys' sportswear & athletic clothing; women's & misses' outerwear; sports apparel

(G-7809)
FINE ARTS LITHO
1014 Bay St Ste 6 (98366-5243)
PHONE..................360 876-5649
Jeff White, *Owner*
Kristy White, *Co-Owner*
EMP: 3
SQ FT: 1,000
SALES: 350K **Privately Held**
WEB: www.fineartslitho.com
SIC: 2759 2752 Screen printing; commercial printing, lithographic

(G-7810)
FRAN HUNTER
15384 Glenwood Rd Sw (98367-7775)
PHONE..................253 876-0434
Fran Hunter, *Principal*
EMP: 2
SALES (est): 90.8K **Privately Held**
SIC: 3341 Secondary nonferrous metals

(G-7811)
GREENLAND INDUSTRIES LLC
2327 Se Sedgwick Rd (98366-9555)
P.O. Box 215, Southworth (98386-0215)
PHONE..................503 841-1835
Lidys Ellingson, *President*
EMP: 5
SALES (est): 260.4K **Privately Held**
SIC: 1542 3271 7389 Commercial & office building, new construction; blocks, concrete; landscape or retaining wall;

(G-7812)
GTR TECHNOLOGIES INC
1420 Lumsden Rd (98367-9189)
PHONE..................360 876-2974

GEOGRAPHIC SECTION

Port Orchard - Kitsap County (G-7843)

Tony Branham, *President*
▲ **EMP:** 10
SALES (est): 2.2MM **Privately Held**
SIC: 3571 Computers, digital, analog or hybrid

(G-7813)
HELIUM DEVELOPMENT LLC
3043 Se Travera Dr (98366-1519)
PHONE 360 550-3322
EMP: 3
SALES (est): 135.6K **Privately Held**
SIC: 2813 Helium

(G-7814)
IDEAL COMMERCIAL UNIFORMS
1008 Bethel Ave Ste C (98366-4236)
PHONE 360 876-1767
Gloria Rosario, *Owner*
EMP: 2
SALES (est): 104.1K **Privately Held**
SIC: 5699 2759 5621 2395 Uniforms; letterpress & screen printing; ready-to-wear apparel, women's; art goods for embroidering, stamped: purchased materials; art design services; advertising, promotional & trade show services

(G-7815)
ILLUSION WEAR CAPES
Also Called: Haunted Quigit Sound
6101 Sunnyslope Rd Sw (98367-7436)
PHONE 360 674-2357
Sandra Kimball, *Owner*
EMP: 4
SALES (est): 218.3K **Privately Held**
SIC: 2337 Women's & misses' capes & jackets

(G-7816)
IMC-INNVTIVE MKTG CNNCTION LLC
Also Called: Www.bestbuyhorsetack.com
3377 Bethel Rd Se Ste 107 (98366-5608)
PHONE 360 895-0178
Kathy Yaskin,
Michael Yaskin,
EMP: 2
SALES (est): 125.8K **Privately Held**
SIC: 2399 5961 Horse & pet accessories, textile; horse harnesses & riding crops, etc.: non-leather;

(G-7817)
INK FOR YOU TATTOO
3590 Westminster Dr Se (98366-5815)
PHONE 360 649-6972
Samantha Eaton, *Principal*
EMP: 2
SALES (est): 88.3K **Privately Held**
SIC: 3625 Motor controls & accessories

(G-7818)
J&M HEAVY CNSTR & LOG CO LLC
14385 Wild Tree Ave Se (98367-4553)
P.O. Box 84, Burley (98322-0084)
PHONE 360 747-2735
Martin Flateland, *Principal*
EMP: 3 **EST:** 2009
SALES (est): 242.9K **Privately Held**
SIC: 2411 Logging

(G-7819)
JERRY HART & SON LOGGING
4028 Stohlton Rd Se (98366-8962)
PHONE 360 871-7037
Jerry Hart, *President*
EMP: 2
SALES (est): 191.6K **Privately Held**
SIC: 2411 Logging camps & contractors

(G-7820)
JIM LEMONS DOORS & CABINETS
205 Bethel Ave (98366-5215)
PHONE 360 871-4001
James H Lemon, *Owner*
EMP: 3
SQ FT: 3,500
SALES (est): 180K **Privately Held**
SIC: 2431 7699 Garage doors, overhead: wood; door frames, wood; garage door repair

(G-7821)
JOHNSON FABRICATION
3041 Anderson Hill Rd Sw (98367-7504)
PHONE 360 874-2679
EMP: 2 **EST:** 2009
SALES (est): 159.8K **Privately Held**
SIC: 3441 Fabricated structural metal

(G-7822)
KADCO TACKLE MANUFACTURING
10634 Woodchuck Ln Se (98367-8252)
P.O. Box 2271 (98366-0749)
PHONE 253 857-5033
Ken Randall, *Owner*
EMP: 2 **EST:** 1987
SALES (est): 100K **Privately Held**
SIC: 3949 Fishing equipment

(G-7823)
KITC RADIO INC
Also Called: Maga Talk 1400
1700 Se Mile Hill Dr # 243 (98366-3554)
PHONE 360 876-1400
Alan Gottlieb, *President*
Paul Lyle, *General Mgr*
Mike Siegel, *Correspondent*
EMP: 4
SALES (est): 206.8K **Privately Held**
SIC: 7999 3663 Riding & rodeo services; radio & TV communications equipment

(G-7824)
KITSAP SCREEN PRINTING LLC
Also Called: Kitsap Screen Prtg Embroderry
3995 Bethel Rd Se Ste 4 (98366-1976)
PHONE 360 876-5101
Dwayne Jones, *Managing Prtnr*
Carl Graf, *Partner*
EMP: 4
SQ FT: 2,200
SALES (est): 330K **Privately Held**
SIC: 2396 Screen printing on fabric articles

(G-7825)
LEADER MANUFACTURING INC
1540 Leader Intl Dr (98367)
PHONE 360 895-1184
Richard A Flaherty, *President*
Leader Manufacturing, *President*
Anne Brown, *Vice Pres*
Catherine Townsend Flaherty, *Vice Pres*
▼ **EMP:** 40
SQ FT: 93,000
SALES (est): 4MM **Privately Held**
WEB: www.theleader.com
SIC: 2511 3446 3648 3674 Wood household furniture; architectural metalwork; lighting equipment; semiconductors & related devices; commercial indusl & institutional electric lighting fixtures; signs & advertising specialties
PA: Leader International Corporation
1525 Vivian Ct
Port Orchard WA

(G-7826)
LT RACING
6487 Knight Dr Se (98367-8015)
PHONE 360 871-2259
Les Tinius, *Owner*
EMP: 2
SALES (est): 100K **Privately Held**
SIC: 3751 Motorcycle accessories

(G-7827)
MARIE-LUCE ENTERPRISES
840 Prospect St (98366-5337)
PHONE 360 876-7925
Marge Gissberg, *Owner*
EMP: 2
SALES (est): 98.9K **Privately Held**
SIC: 2844 Concentrates, perfume

(G-7828)
MAY MOBILE MARINE TECH
Also Called: Riley, Monty Allen
13440 Reindeer Ln Sw (98367-9214)
PHONE 360 552-2561
Monty Riley, *Owner*
EMP: 2
SALES (est): 66.5K **Privately Held**
SIC: 3519 Internal combustion engines

(G-7829)
MISCHEL BROS LOGGING INC
1933 Sw Berry Lake Rd (98367-9314)
PHONE 360 649-7101
Jerome Mischel, *President*
Kenneth Mischel, *Vice Pres*
Judy Mischel, *Treasurer*
Clarisse Mischel, *Admin Sec*
EMP: 4
SALES: 100K **Privately Held**
SIC: 2411 Logging camps & contractors

(G-7830)
MITCHELL DOOR AND TRIM INC
Also Called: Mitchell Door & Trim
3812 Bancroft Rd E (98366-8349)
PHONE 360 874-8901
Rita Mitchell, *President*
Larry Mitchell, *Vice Pres*
EMP: 15 **EST:** 1990
SALES: 1MM **Privately Held**
SIC: 2431 1751 Doors & door parts & trim, wood; window & door (prefabricated) installation

(G-7831)
MYSEPS
7312 Mccrmick Wods Dr Sw (98367-7476)
PHONE 858 231-2774
Scott Detavernier, *Principal*
EMP: 2
SALES (est): 73.2K **Privately Held**
SIC: 2759 Commercial printing

(G-7832)
MYYEARLOOK
6749 Se Skycrest Ln (98366-8787)
PHONE 303 523-2468
Julie Doran, *CEO*
EMP: 3
SALES (est): 151.5K **Privately Held**
SIC: 2741

(G-7833)
NORRIS TECHNIQUES
Also Called: Nortec
1528 Puget Dr E (98366-8545)
PHONE 360 871-1458
Kathy Norris Woodside, *Owner*
Gerald Woodside, *Co-Owner*
EMP: 2
SALES (est): 112K **Privately Held**
SIC: 3911 Jewelry, precious metal

(G-7834)
NORTH WEST COATING & SVCS LLC
2745 Mckinley Pl Se (98366-2325)
PHONE 360 649-1548
EMP: 2
SALES (est): 105.4K **Privately Held**
SIC: 3479 Metal coating & allied service

(G-7835)
NORTHWEST WATER SYSTEMS INC
7245 Bethel Burley Rd Se (98367-9599)
P.O. Box 123 (98366-0123)
PHONE 360 876-0958
Ron Wiley, *President*
EMP: 2
SALES (est): 435.3K **Privately Held**
WEB: www.nwwatersystems.com
SIC: 3823 Water quality monitoring & control systems

(G-7836)
OLSONS GASKETS
3059 Opdal Rd E (98366-8108)
PHONE 360 871-1207
Francis Olson, *Partner*
Linda Olson, *Partner*
EMP: 2
SALES: 40K **Privately Held**
WEB: www.olsonsgaskets.com
SIC: 5531 3714 5015 Automotive parts; motor vehicle engines & parts; motor vehicle parts, used

(G-7837)
OMOHUNDRO CO KITSAP COMPOSITES
1525 Vivian Ct (98367-6400)
PHONE 360 519-3047
Cynthia Sparks, *CEO*

Mark Sparks, *President*
EMP: 75 **EST:** 2014
SQ FT: 40,000
SALES (est): 11.9MM **Privately Held**
WEB: www.omoco.com
SIC: 3812 3663 3679 3728 Radar systems & equipment; antennas, transmitting & communications; microwave communication equipment; satellites, communications; antennas, receiving; fins, aircraft; blades, aircraft propeller: metal or wood; panel assembly (hydromatic propeller test stands), aircraft; guided missile & space vehicle parts & auxiliary equipment; guided missile & space vehicle parts & aux eqpt, rsch & dev; nose cones, guided missiles; air scoops, aircraft

(G-7838)
ORPILLA SANTIAGO
Also Called: T & J Basic Design
3161 Se Villa Carmel Dr (98366-1111)
PHONE 360 876-1976
Saniago Orpilla, *Owner*
EMP: 2 **EST:** 2000
SALES (est): 117K **Privately Held**
SIC: 2284 2499 Embroidery thread; decorative wood & woodwork

(G-7839)
OUTSIDE IN WOODWORKS LLC
1470 Se Vallair Ct (98366-5607)
PHONE 208 403-9067
Joey Olsen, *Principal*
EMP: 2
SALES (est): 85.2K **Privately Held**
SIC: 2431 Millwork

(G-7840)
PACIFIC COAST EVERGREEN INC (PA)
5158 Bethel Rd Se (98367-7826)
P.O. Box 727 (98366-0727)
PHONE 360 876-2061
Richard Berg, *President*
Karen Berg, *Corp Secy*
Leslie Hoyt, *Vice Pres*
Becky Hoyt, *Manager*
◆ **EMP:** 22
SQ FT: 25,000
SALES (est): 2.7MM **Privately Held**
WEB: www.pacificcoastevergreens.com
SIC: 5193 2499 Florists' supplies; decorative wood & woodwork

(G-7841)
PACIFIC WESTERN TIMBERS INC
5555 Cruiser Loop Sw (98367)
PHONE 360 674-2700
John Wagner, *President*
Peter Wagner, *Vice Pres*
▲ **EMP:** 12
SALES (est): 2MM **Privately Held**
SIC: 2491 Structural lumber & timber, treated wood

(G-7842)
PRINTING SERVICES INC
3480 Bethel Rd Se Ste A (98366-5665)
PHONE 253 858-5350
Brad Potter, *President*
Merry Potter, *Vice Pres*
Anna Payne, *Graphic Designe*
EMP: 5
SQ FT: 1,800
SALES (est): 530K **Privately Held**
WEB: www.myprintsource.net
SIC: 2752 2759 Commercial printing, offset; photo-offset printing; post cards, picture: printing; visiting cards (including business): printing; advertising literature: printing; decals: printing

(G-7843)
PROGOURMET FOODS LLC
3643 Beach Dr E (98366-8118)
PHONE 360 769-7420
Brian Warkentin,
Karlo Flores,
▲ **EMP:** 3
SALES (est): 324.6K **Privately Held**
SIC: 2066 Chocolate & cocoa products

Port Orchard - Kitsap County (G-7844)

(G-7844)
R K I
9240 Emerald Dr Se (98367-8539)
PHONE..................360 876-0937
Ronald James, *Principal*
Karen James, *Co-Owner*
EMP: 2
SALES (est): 175.8K **Privately Held**
SIC: 3552 7371 Embroidery machines; custom computer programming services

(G-7845)
RDC ENTERPRISES LLC
3325 Merganser Ln Se (98367-9594)
PHONE..................360 265-0723
James Thompson,
EMP: 2
SALES (est): 180.5K **Privately Held**
SIC: 7692 Welding repair

(G-7846)
RESOURCE ACCOUNTING SVCS INC
8737 Glenwood Rd Sw (98367-7090)
PHONE..................860 608-0457
EMP: 2
SALES (est): 77.4K **Privately Held**
SIC: 3161 Luggage

(G-7847)
SHORELINE CUSTOM CANVAS & AUTO
5056 Sw Lake Helena Rd (98367-9281)
PHONE..................360 874-2702
EMP: 2
SALES (est): 179.4K **Privately Held**
SIC: 2211 Canvas

(G-7848)
SINCLAIR COMPANIES
Also Called: Sinclair Apartments The
414 Sw Hayworth Dr (98367-5001)
PHONE..................360 874-6772
EMP: 102
SALES (corp-wide): 3.9B **Privately Held**
SIC: 2911 Petroleum refining
PA: The Sinclair Companies
550 E South Temple
Salt Lake City UT 84102
801 524-2700

(G-7849)
SOIL SCIENCE PRODUCTS LLC
2713 Anderson Hill Rd Sw (98367-7503)
PHONE..................360 876-3734
Linda Penovich, *Principal*
EMP: 5
SALES: 50K **Privately Held**
SIC: 2874 Phosphatic fertilizers

(G-7850)
SOUND PUBLISHING INC
Also Called: Port Orchard Independent
2497 Bethel Rd Se Ste 102 (98366-4889)
PHONE..................360 876-4414
Shawn McDonalds, *Branch Mgr*
EMP: 9
SQ FT: 3,000 **Privately Held**
WEB: www.soundpublishing.com
SIC: 2711 Newspapers: publishing only, not printed on site
HQ: Sound Publishing, Inc.
11323 Commando Rd W Main
Everett WA 98204
360 394-5800

(G-7851)
SOUTH SOUND SCREEN PRINTING
3370 Arvick Rd Se (98366-8834)
PHONE..................360 871-4206
Kenneth R Edwards, *Owner*
EMP: 2
SALES: 14K **Privately Held**
SIC: 2389 Apparel & accessories

(G-7852)
SPRING CREEK ENTERPRISES
7997 Van Decar Rd Se (98367-9562)
PHONE..................360 876-8884
Carol Anne Northfield, *Owner*
EMP: 2
SALES (est): 70.7K **Privately Held**
WEB: www.springcreek-engraving.com
SIC: 2759 3993 Engraving; signs & advertising specialties

(G-7853)
TIN FOIL HAT PRODUCTIONS
3420 Se Navigation Ln (98366-6347)
PHONE..................619 208-5469
Mark Allen, *Principal*
EMP: 2
SALES (est): 89.8K **Privately Held**
SIC: 3497 Tin foil

(G-7854)
UNIQUE TS PRINTING
1750 Jackson Ave Se # 16 (98366-3459)
PHONE..................253 686-3669
Edson London, *Principal*
EMP: 2
SALES (est): 92.3K **Privately Held**
SIC: 2752 Commercial printing, lithographic

(G-7855)
VERTICAL WELDER
4851 Geiger Rd Se (98367-9350)
PHONE..................360 265-5457
Douglas Thompson, *Principal*
EMP: 2 **EST:** 2010
SALES (est): 165.6K **Privately Held**
SIC: 2591 Blinds vertical

(G-7856)
WATERMARK ART & FRAMING
3857 E Nautical Cove Way (98366-4841)
PHONE..................360 871-2906
Marti Green, *Owner*
EMP: 2
SALES (est): 80.4K **Privately Held**
SIC: 3999 Framed artwork

(G-7857)
WESTERN TIMBER INC
6845 Se King Rd (98367-8631)
P.O. Box 654 (98366-0654)
PHONE..................360 769-0639
David G Berry, *President*
EMP: 4
SALES (est): 430K **Privately Held**
SIC: 2411 Logging camps & contractors

Port Townsend
Jefferson County

(G-7858)
A H TOM PUBLISHING
538 Calhoun St (98368-8109)
PHONE..................360 385-2059
Thomas Camfield, *Owner*
EMP: 2
SALES (est): 77.7K **Privately Held**
SIC: 2731 Book publishing

(G-7859)
ABSOLUTE CONCRETEWORKS LLC
490 Sunset Blvd (98368-8911)
PHONE..................360 297-5055
Steven J Silberman,
Kristina Silberman,
EMP: 5
SALES (est): 420K **Privately Held**
SIC: 3272 3229 Concrete products, precast; glass fiber products

(G-7860)
ADMIRALTY PRECISION LLC
321 Otto St (98368-9391)
PHONE..................360 344-2212
Elliott Yakush,
EMP: 3 **EST:** 2014
SALES (est): 249.7K **Privately Held**
SIC: 3599 Machine shop, jobbing & repair

(G-7861)
AMPERSAN PRESS INC
750 Lake St (98368-2216)
PHONE..................360 379-5187
E R Haller, *Owner*
EMP: 4 **EST:** 1973

SALES (est): 228.3K **Privately Held**
WEB: www.ampersandpress.com
SIC: 2731 Book publishing

(G-7862)
ANAPHORA PRESS
3110 San Juan Ave (98368-5012)
PHONE..................360 379-4004
EMP: 2
SALES (est): 99K **Privately Held**
SIC: 2741 Misc Publishing

(G-7863)
ANDERSEN MACHINE SHOP INC
2702 Washington St (98368-4615)
P.O. Box 1569, Port Hadlock (98339-1569)
PHONE..................360 379-1031
Ulfar Andersen, *President*
Halla Andersen, *Vice Pres*
EMP: 2 **EST:** 1991
SALES: 120K **Privately Held**
SIC: 3599 Machine shop, jobbing & repair

(G-7864)
ARMSTRONG CONSOLIDATED LLC
Also Called: Aci Boats
2900 Washington St (98368-1801)
PHONE..................360 477-7558
Abraham Armstrong, *President*
EMP: 4
SQ FT: 4,000
SALES: 1.8MM **Privately Held**
SIC: 3732 Boat building & repairing

(G-7865)
ATLAS BIMETAL LABS INC
Also Called: Atlas Technologies,
305 Glen Cove Rd (98368-9795)
PHONE..................360 385-3123
Richard Bothell, *President*
Justin Bothell, *Vice Pres*
Austin Henry, *Sales Engr*
Allegra Bothell, *Comms Dir*
EMP: 20
SQ FT: 2,200
SALES (est): 4.8MM **Privately Held**
SIC: 3821 Laboratory apparatus & furniture

(G-7866)
BAD HABIT LTD
1005 Lawrence St (98368-6523)
P.O. Box 797 (98368-0797)
PHONE..................360 385-3101
Peter Boeschenstein, *President*
EMP: 5
SALES (est): 513.1K **Privately Held**
WEB: www.baddhabit.com
SIC: 2396 Screen printing on fabric articles

(G-7867)
BARBARA BOGART
716 Taylor St (98368-5530)
PHONE..................360 385-0815
Barbara Bogart, *Exec Officer*
EMP: 2
SALES (est): 72.9K **Privately Held**
SIC: 2512 Upholstered household furniture

(G-7868)
BEAR WILDFIRE
Also Called: Alpen Fire Cider
220 Pocket Ln (98368-8833)
PHONE..................360 379-8915
Steve Bishop, *Managing Prtnr*
Nancy Bishop, *Partner*
Philippe Bishop, *Partner*
EMP: 7
SALES: 80K **Privately Held**
SIC: 2084 Wines

(G-7869)
BLUE STREAK WOODWORKS
1039 Jackson St (98368-4509)
PHONE..................360 379-0414
Seth Rolland, *Owner*
EMP: 2
SALES (est): 171.4K **Privately Held**
WEB: www.sethrolland.com
SIC: 2431 Millwork

(G-7870)
BOWET & POET INC
Also Called: Christine Hemp
5445 Kuhn St (98368-1614)
PHONE..................360 385-9005
Christine Hemp, *Principal*
Ole Kanestrom, *Principal*
EMP: 2 **EST:** 2003
SALES: 100K **Privately Held**
SIC: 3931 8699 Violins & parts; personal interest organization

(G-7871)
CANNON ENGINEERING SOLUTIONS
1463 W Uncas Rd (98368-8709)
PHONE..................360 840-6731
EMP: 3 **EST:** 2016
SALES (est): 114.3K **Privately Held**
SIC: 3423 7692 7699 7389 Garden & farm tools, including shovels; welding repair; agricultural equipment repair services; boat repair; marine engine repair;

(G-7872)
COPPER CANYON PRESS
Fort Worden State Park (98368)
P.O. Box 271 (98368-0271)
PHONE..................360 385-4925
Randy Sturgis, *Finance Mgr*
Kris Becker, *Exec Dir*
EMP: 9
SQ FT: 1,440
SALES: 1.4MM **Privately Held**
WEB: www.coppercanyonpress.org
SIC: 2741 Miscellaneous publishing

(G-7873)
CORVIDAE PRESS
403 U St (98368-3506)
PHONE..................360 379-1934
Debra Brochin, *Principal*
EMP: 2 **EST:** 2012
SALES (est): 96K **Privately Held**
SIC: 2741 Miscellaneous publishing

(G-7874)
CRAFTSMEN UNITED INC
3109 Jefferson St (98368-4613)
P.O. Box 1542 (98368-0051)
PHONE..................360 379-2500
Daniel D Wiggins, *President*
Jim Warner, *Vice Pres*
EMP: 10
SALES: 3.5MM **Privately Held**
SIC: 1629 3441 Marine construction; fabricated structural metal

(G-7875)
CROWN PAPER GROUP INC (PA)
100 Mill Rd (98368-2246)
PHONE..................360 385-3170
Steven Klinger, *CEO*
Matthew Denton, *CFO*
EMP: 12
SALES (est): 341MM **Privately Held**
SIC: 2621 Paper mills

(G-7876)
DAILY CONNER
250 Madison St (98368-5738)
P.O. Box 861 (98368-0861)
PHONE..................360 643-0056
Conner Daily, *Principal*
EMP: 3
SALES (est): 126.7K **Privately Held**
SIC: 2711 Newspapers, publishing & printing

(G-7877)
DAVES MOBILE WELDING LLC
Also Called: DMW & Marine Repair
304 10th St Bldg 4 (98368-1820)
P.O. Box 1911 (98368-0063)
PHONE..................360 302-0069
David Fletcher,
Carney Mick-Hager,
EMP: 5
SALES: 140K **Privately Held**
SIC: 7692 3731 Welding repair; shipbuilding & repairing

Port Townsend - Jefferson County (G-7912)

(G-7878)
DELOZIER RECOVERY SERVICES
211 Taylor St Ste 37 (98368-5758)
PHONE 360 385-1258
Lisa Delozier, *Owner*
EMP: 2
SALES (est): 144.8K **Privately Held**
SIC: 2819 Chemicals, reagent grade: refined from technical grade

(G-7879)
DENTZEL CAROUSEL CO
843 53rd St (98368-1503)
PHONE 360 385-1068
EMP: 2
SALES (est): 100K **Privately Held**
SIC: 3599 Mfg Industrial Machinery

(G-7880)
DL LOGOS ✪
275 Otto St Ste A (98368-9780)
PHONE 360 385-3101
EMP: 2 EST: 2019
SALES (est): 83.9K **Privately Held**
SIC: 2752 Commercial printing, lithographic

(G-7881)
DREAM IT INC (PA)
Also Called: Itali Lambertini
818 Corona St (98368-4920)
PHONE 360 379-1070
Tim Lambert, *Owner*
Sheryly Morgenstern, *Vice Pres*
EMP: 2
SALES (est): 288.8K **Privately Held**
SIC: 3911 Jewelry apparel

(G-7882)
EV DRIVES
1240 W Sims Way (98368-3058)
PHONE 360 302-5226
▲ EMP: 10
SALES (est): 970.9K **Privately Held**
SIC: 3621 Motors, electric

(G-7883)
FERAL HOUSE INC
1240 W Sims Way Ste 124 (98368-3058)
PHONE 323 666-3311
Adam Parfrey, *Principal*
◆ EMP: 6 EST: 2009
SALES (est): 735.7K **Privately Held**
SIC: 2721 Periodicals

(G-7884)
FERAL HOUSE INC
1240 W Sims Way Ste 124 (98368-3058)
PHONE 323 666-3311
Adam Parfray, *President*
▲ EMP: 4
SALES (est): 252.5K **Privately Held**
WEB: www.feralhouse.com
SIC: 2731 Book publishing

(G-7885)
FOXBAT HEAVY INDUSTRIES INC
886 55th St (98368-1201)
PHONE 425 890-0410
Darren McClelland, *President*
EMP: 2 EST: 2012
SALES (est): 112.6K **Privately Held**
SIC: 3999 Barber & beauty shop equipment

(G-7886)
GENERATIONS DENTAL
642 Harrison St (98368-6518)
PHONE 360 379-1591
Greg Barry, *Principal*
EMP: 2
SALES (est): 176K **Privately Held**
SIC: 3843 Enamels, dentists'

(G-7887)
HANAZONO ASIAN NOODLE
225 Taylor St Fl 1 (98368-5716)
PHONE 360 385-7622
Kaori Hull, *Owner*
EMP: 6
SALES (est): 220K **Privately Held**
SIC: 2098 Noodles (e.g. egg, plain & water), dry

(G-7888)
HANSENCRAFTS LLC
710 E Pk Ave Port Twnsnd (98368)
PHONE 360 747-7746
Kevin Hansen, *Principal*
EMP: 2
SALES (est): 378.1K **Privately Held**
SIC: 3552 Fiber & yarn preparation machinery & equipment

(G-7889)
HAVEN BOATWORKS LLC
305 8th St (98368-1840)
P.O. Box 1430 (98368-0033)
PHONE 360 385-5727
Stephen Gale, *Owner*
EMP: 3
SALES (corp-wide): 1.3MM **Privately Held**
SIC: 3732 Boat building & repairing
PA: Haven Boatworks, L.L.C.
305 8th St
Port Townsend WA 98368
360 385-5727

(G-7890)
HAVEN BOATWORKS LLC (PA)
Also Called: John Deere Authorized Dealer
305 8th St (98368-1840)
P.O. Box 1430 (98368-0033)
PHONE 360 385-5727
Tom Foley, *Principal*
EMP: 11
SALES (est): 1.3MM **Privately Held**
SIC: 3732 5082 Boat building & repairing; construction & mining machinery

(G-7891)
INSIDE REAL ESTATE
151 Windship Dr (98368-2513)
PHONE 360 379-0139
Anne Burkhart, *Principal*
EMP: 2
SALES (est): 62.9K **Privately Held**
SIC: 2711 Newspapers

(G-7892)
ISLAND BLUEBACK INC
220 Lincoln St (98368-4515)
PHONE 360 385-0871
James Prance, *President*
EMP: 2
SALES (est): 79.2K **Privately Held**
SIC: 0921 3949 7389 Fishing preserves; sporting & athletic goods; personal service agents, brokers & bureaus

(G-7893)
JERRY P OSBORNE
Also Called: Osborne Enterprises
918 Holcomb St (98368-2923)
P.O. Box 255 (98368-0255)
PHONE 360 385-1200
Jerry Osborne, *Owner*
Barbara Hahn, *Office Mgr*
EMP: 3
SALES (est): 235.6K **Privately Held**
WEB: www.jerryosborne.com
SIC: 2731 Book publishing

(G-7894)
KATHERINE OTTAWAY DR
2120 Lawrence St (98368-7925)
PHONE 360 385-3826
Katherine T Ottaway, *Principal*
EMP: 3
SALES (est): 135.8K **Privately Held**
SIC: 2711 Newspapers

(G-7895)
LEE SHORE BOATS INC
950 30th St (98368-4901)
PHONE 360 385-1491
Jay Brevik, *President*
EMP: 3
SALES (est): 350K **Privately Held**
WEB: www.leeshoreboats.com
SIC: 3732 Boat building & repairing

(G-7896)
MAIZEFIELD COMPANY
Also Called: Maizefield Mantels
203 Frederick St (98368-9742)
P.O. Box 336 (98368-0336)
PHONE 360 385-6789
Robert S Eggert, *Owner*
EMP: 7
SALES (est): 280K **Privately Held**
WEB: www.maizefield.com
SIC: 1521 2431 General remodeling, single-family houses; mantels, wood

(G-7897)
MARKETECH INTERNATIONAL INC
11 Westridge Ct (98368-9504)
PHONE 360 379-6707
Beth A Juran, *President*
EMP: 4
SALES (est): 352.9K **Privately Held**
SIC: 3674 Semiconductors & related devices

(G-7898)
MITCHELL OSBORNE
Also Called: Mitchell Osborne Photography
321 Cherry St (98368-6336)
PHONE 360 379-2427
Mitchell Osborne, *Owner*
EMP: 4
SQ FT: 2,000
SALES (est): 170K **Privately Held**
SIC: 7335 2741 Commercial photography; miscellaneous publishing

(G-7899)
NEW FOUND METALS INCORPORATED
240 Airport Rd (98368-9726)
PHONE 360 385-3315
Richard O Walcome, *President*
▲ EMP: 3 EST: 1975
SQ FT: 1,500
SALES (est): 210K **Privately Held**
WEB: www.newfoundmetals.com
SIC: 3429 5088 Marine hardware; marine crafts & supplies

(G-7900)
NORTH WINDS WELDING & MET
13576 Airport Cutoff Rd (98368-9320)
PHONE 360 379-0487
Randy Krofick, *Principal*
EMP: 5
SALES (est): 254.5K **Privately Held**
SIC: 7692 Welding repair

(G-7901)
NORTHWEST PUBLICATIONS INC
Also Called: Inside Golf Newspaper
460 Dennis Blvd (98368-9412)
P.O. Box 1890 (98368-0060)
PHONE 360 379-4080
Bob Marlatt, *President*
Kathy Marlatt, *Manager*
EMP: 2
SALES (est): 250K **Privately Held**
SIC: 2711 Commercial printing & newspaper publishing combined

(G-7902)
NORTHWEST SAILS & CANVAS INC
1238 Blaine St (98368-6506)
PHONE 360 301-3204
Sean Rankins, *Director*
EMP: 2
SALES (est): 136.1K **Privately Held**
SIC: 2211 Canvas

(G-7903)
OLD SALT MERCHANTS LLC
30 E Rhododendron Dr (98368-9483)
P.O. Box 97375, Lakewood (98497-0375)
PHONE 888 995-7258
Anika Colvin, *Principal*
EMP: 2
SALES (est): 90K **Privately Held**
SIC: 2899 Salt

(G-7904)
OLYMPIC PENINSULA IMPLANTS
1119 Lawrence St (98368-6525)
PHONE 360 385-5121
Julie Waholbrook, *Principal*
EMP: 2
SALES (est): 154.4K **Privately Held**
SIC: 3843 Enamels, dentists'

(G-7905)
OM LLC REINSTATED 2005
60 Huckleberry Pl (98368-9418)
PHONE 360 821-1802
Sandra Hicks, *Administration*
EMP: 2
SALES (est): 150.9K **Privately Held**
SIC: 2299 Textile goods

(G-7906)
PACIFIC NORTHWEST TIMBERS LLC
130 Seton Rd (98368-9305)
P.O. Box 1931 (98368-0065)
PHONE 360 379-2792
Marc Mandel, *Mng Member*
EMP: 3
SALES (est): 317.5K **Privately Held**
SIC: 2421 Sawmills & planing mills, general

(G-7907)
POINT WILSON CO INC
131 Cape George Dr (98368-9468)
P.O. Box 464 (98368-0464)
PHONE 360 385-7625
Niel Dacquisto, *President*
Sandra Lau, *Vice Pres*
▲ EMP: 2
SALES (est): 92K **Privately Held**
WEB: www.pointwilson.com
SIC: 3949 5091 Fishing tackle, general; flies, fishing: artificial; fishing tackle

(G-7908)
PORT TOWNSEND BREWING CO
330 10th St Ste C (98368-1815)
PHONE 360 385-9967
Guy R Sands, *President*
Kim Sands, *Treasurer*
EMP: 2
SQ FT: 1,200
SALES (est): 208.2K **Privately Held**
WEB: www.porttownsendbrewing.com
SIC: 2082 5149 Beer (alcoholic beverage); groceries & related products

(G-7909)
PORT TOWNSEND COMMUNITY
1101 Cherry St (98368-4057)
P.O. Box 1814 (98368-0219)
PHONE 360 385-0120
Richard L Shaneyfelt, *Principal*
EMP: 2
SALES (est): 79.7K **Privately Held**
SIC: 2211 Canvas

(G-7910)
PORT TOWNSEND FOUNDRY LLC
251 Otto St (98368-9780)
PHONE 360 385-6425
Peter R Langley, *Mng Member*
Cathy Langley,
EMP: 12
SQ FT: 1,152
SALES (est): 1.6MM **Privately Held**
WEB: www.porttownsendfoundry.com
SIC: 3369 Nonferrous foundries

(G-7911)
PORT TOWNSEND HOLDINGS CO INC (HQ)
100 Mill Rd (98368-2246)
PHONE 360 385-3170
Steven Klinger, *Chairman*
Matthew Denton, *CFO*
Brad Madison, *Treasurer*
EMP: 300
SQ FT: 1,500
SALES (est): 329.5MM **Privately Held**
SIC: 2611 2653 Pulp mills; corrugated & solid fiber boxes

(G-7912)
PORT TOWNSEND PAPER CORP (DH)
100 Mill Rd (98368-2246)
PHONE 360 385-3170
Steven Klinger, *CEO*
Matthew Denton, *CFO*
Brad Madison, *Treasurer*
◆ EMP: 282

Port Townsend - Jefferson County (G-7913)

SALES: 326.5MM **Privately Held**
WEB: www.ptpc.com
SIC: 2631 Paperboard mills
HQ: Port Townsend Holdings Company, Inc.
100 Mill Rd
Port Townsend WA 98368
360 385-3170

(G-7913)
PORT TOWNSEND PUBLISHING CO
Also Called: Leader, The
226 Adams St (98368-5706)
P.O. Box 552 (98368-0552)
PHONE..................................360 385-2900
Scott Wilson, *President*
EMP: 26
SQ FT: 5,950
SALES (est): 1.5MM **Privately Held**
WEB: www.ptleader.com
SIC: 2711 Newspapers, publishing & printing; newspapers: publishing only, not printed on site

(G-7914)
PORT TOWNSEND SAILS INC
Also Called: Hasse & Company
315 Jackson St (98368-5607)
PHONE..................................360 385-1640
Carol Hasse, *President*
EMP: 14
SQ FT: 3,000
SALES: 375K **Privately Held**
WEB: www.porttownsendsails.com
SIC: 5551 2394 3732 Sails & equipment; sails: made from purchased materials; boat building & repairing

(G-7915)
PORT TOWNSEND SCHOOL OF WOODWO
Also Called: Ptsw
200 Battery Way (98368-3621)
PHONE..................................303 910-0016
Kacie Guthrie, *Principal*
Tim Lawson, *Exec Dir*
EMP: 2 EST: 2014
SALES: 397.9K **Privately Held**
SIC: 2431 Millwork

(G-7916)
PORT TOWNSEND SHIPWRIGHTS COOP
919 Haines Pl (98368-1823)
P.O. Box 1163 (98368-0963)
PHONE..................................360 385-6138
Jeff Galey, *President*
Todd Lee, *Vice Pres*
David Griswold, *Treasurer*
Ric Brenden, *Admin Sec*
EMP: 40
SQ FT: 1,400
SALES: 653.1K **Privately Held**
SIC: 3732 Boat building & repairing

(G-7917)
PORT TOWNSEND VINEYARDS WINERY
1812 Fir St (98368-3831)
PHONE..................................360 385-0694
EMP: 2
SALES (est): 90K **Privately Held**
SIC: 2084 Wines

(G-7918)
PORT TOWNSEND WINERY LLC
2640 W Sims Way (98368-2252)
PHONE..................................360 344-8155
Jens Coppenrath, *Principal*
EMP: 2
SALES (est): 62.3K **Privately Held**
SIC: 2084 Wines, brandy & brandy spirits; wines

(G-7919)
PROCESS MEDIA INC
1240 W Sims Way (98368-3058)
PHONE..................................323 666-3377
Adam Parfrey, *President*
EMP: 2
SALES (est): 85K **Privately Held**
SIC: 2731 Book publishing

(G-7920)
PT SHIRT
940 Water St (98368-5747)
PHONE..................................360 385-1911
Susan Euro, *Principal*
EMP: 3
SALES (est): 274.1K **Privately Held**
SIC: 2254 Shirts & t-shirts (underwear), knit

(G-7921)
PYGMY BOATS INC
Also Called: Pygmy Kayak
355 Hudson St (98368-5614)
P.O. Box 1529 (98368-0048)
PHONE..................................360 385-6143
John Lockwood, *President*
Candace Monroe, *Director*
EMP: 5
SQ FT: 1,800
SALES (est): 340K **Privately Held**
WEB: www.pygmyboats.com
SIC: 3732 5551 Kayaks, building & repairing; boat dealers

(G-7922)
RAIN SHADOW WOODWORKS INC
130 Seton Rd (98368-9305)
P.O. Box 336 (98368-0336)
PHONE..................................360 385-6789
Sebastian Eggert, *Owner*
EMP: 4 EST: 2011
SALES (est): 287.2K **Privately Held**
SIC: 2431 Millwork

(G-7923)
REYNOLD GREY & ASSOCIATES
321 Otto St (98368-9391)
PHONE..................................360 385-1167
Grey Pohl, *Owner*
EMP: 2
SQ FT: 2,600
SALES (est): 130K **Privately Held**
SIC: 3599 Machine shop, jobbing & repair

(G-7924)
REYNOLD GREY MCHINING SVCS INC
Also Called: RG Machining
321 Otto St (98368-9391)
PHONE..................................360 385-1167
Gregory J Mika, *President*
Marcy Y Mika, *Vice Pres*
Donna Kramer, *Admin Sec*
EMP: 7
SALES (est): 604.1K **Privately Held**
SIC: 3548 Welding apparatus

(G-7925)
SHELTER PEAK PUBLISHING LLC
1654 Cherry St (98368-3704)
P.O. Box 1718 (98368-0160)
PHONE..................................360 460-0751
EMP: 2
SALES (est): 62.9K **Privately Held**
SIC: 2711 Newspapers

(G-7926)
SKIDMORE & SKIDMORE INC
1929 Hill St (98368-7715)
PHONE..................................360 379-6385
Vincent Skidmore, *Principal*
EMP: 4
SALES (est): 428K **Privately Held**
SIC: 3553 Cabinet makers' machinery

(G-7927)
SOS PRINTING
710 Q St (98368-3829)
PHONE..................................360 385-4194
Dan Huntingford, *Owner*
EMP: 5 EST: 1978
SALES: 521K **Privately Held**
SIC: 2752 7334 5943 Commercial printing, offset; photocopying & duplicating services; office forms & supplies

(G-7928)
SOUND SAILS
290 10th St (98368-1816)
P.O. Box 312 (98368-0312)
PHONE..................................360 385-3881
Ellen Falconer, *President*
EMP: 2
SQ FT: 950
SALES: 150K **Privately Held**
SIC: 2394 Sails: made from purchased materials

(G-7929)
SPECIALTY WOODWORKING
235 Hancock St (98368-3014)
PHONE..................................360 379-1222
EMP: 2
SALES (est): 142.4K **Privately Held**
SIC: 2431 Millwork

(G-7930)
SPINDRIFT ROWING LLC
762 W Park Ave (98368-2276)
PHONE..................................360 344-2233
Sonya Baumstein, *Partner*
Andrew Cull, *Partner*
EMP: 2
SQ FT: 2,000
SALES (est): 217.6K **Privately Held**
SIC: 3732 5551 Non-motorized boat, building & repairing; boat dealers

(G-7931)
STAR COPY & REPROGRAPHICS CTR
625 Tyler St (98368-6536)
PHONE..................................360 385-1022
Mike Kenna, *Owner*
EMP: 30
SALES (est): 2.3MM **Privately Held**
WEB: www.printery.com
SIC: 2759 Commercial printing

(G-7932)
TOSS BRION YACHT RIGGING INC
Also Called: Brion Toss Rigging
313 Jackson St (98368-5607)
PHONE..................................360 385-1080
Brion Toss, *President*
Christian Gruye, *Co-Owner*
EMP: 4
SALES (est): 630K **Privately Held**
WEB: www.briontoss.com
SIC: 3731 3732 1799 Marine rigging; boat building & repairing; rigging & scaffolding

(G-7933)
TOWNSEND BAY MARINE LLC
919 Haines Pl (98368-1823)
P.O. Box 2067 (98368-0249)
PHONE..................................360 385-3981
Paul Zeusche,
Bill Nance,
David W Pratt,
▲ EMP: 16 EST: 1999
SQ FT: 35,000
SALES: 6MM **Privately Held**
WEB: www.townsendbay.com
SIC: 3732 7699 Boat building & repairing; boat repair

(G-7934)
TOWNSEND BAY SOAP CO LLC
1634 Jackson St (98368-3914)
PHONE..................................360 379-4140
Robert F Middelburg, *Principal*
EMP: 2
SALES (est): 128.4K **Privately Held**
SIC: 2841 Soap: granulated, liquid, cake, flaked or chip

(G-7935)
TOWNSEND LTR FOR DCTORS PTENTS
911 Tyler St (98368-6541)
PHONE..................................360 385-6021
Jonathan Collin, *President*
Barbara Smith, *General Mgr*
EMP: 12
SALES (est): 1.2MM **Privately Held**
WEB: www.tldp.com
SIC: 2721 Magazines: publishing & printing

(G-7936)
TRADITIONAL BOAT WORKS INC
538 Fillmore St (98368-6609)
PHONE..................................360 379-6502
Douglas Jones, *President*
EMP: 2 EST: 2013

SALES (est): 94.6K **Privately Held**
SIC: 3732 Boat building & repairing

(G-7937)
USL TECHNOLOGIES LLC
260 Kala Heights Dr (98368-9506)
P.O. Box 289 (98368-0289)
PHONE..................................360 379-0684
John P Downing Jr, *President*
EMP: 6
SALES (est): 410K **Privately Held**
SIC: 3827 Light sources, standard

(G-7938)
WATERMARK BINDERIES
1510 Hastings Ave (98368-5912)
P.O. Box 175, Nordland (98358-0175)
PHONE..................................360 379-0186
Virginia Marston, *Owner*
Ned Herbert, *Co-Owner*
EMP: 2
SALES (est): 88K **Privately Held**
SIC: 2789 Binding only: books, pamphlets, magazines, etc.

(G-7939)
ZEPHYRWERKS ◆
521 Snagstead Way (98368-9668)
PHONE..................................360 385-2720
EMP: 2 EST: 2019
SALES (est): 73.4K **Privately Held**
SIC: 3429 Manufactured hardware (general)

(G-7940)
ZIRKUS INC
910 Calhoun St (98368-8016)
P.O. Box 309 (98368-0309)
PHONE..................................360 385-5478
Glenn Lyons, *President*
Christine Busch-Lyons, *Treasurer*
EMP: 2
SALES: 120K **Privately Held**
SIC: 5944 3911 Jewelry stores; pins (jewelry), precious metal

Poulsbo
Kitsap County

(G-7941)
A MILLICAN CRANE SERVICE INC
180 Nw Beaver Rdg (98370-9112)
P.O. Box 300, Port Gamble (98364-0300)
PHONE..................................360 779-6723
Andrew Millican, *President*
Jackie Millican, *Treasurer*
EMP: 7 EST: 1996
SQ FT: 28,932
SALES (est): 1.2MM **Privately Held**
SIC: 4119 4213 3531 Local rental transportation; heavy hauling; crane carriers

(G-7942)
ACCUMAR CORPORATION
1180 Nw Finn Hill Rd (98370-9712)
PHONE..................................360 779-7795
Scott Sprague, *President*
William Carter, *Vice Pres*
Nathan Smith, *Admin Sec*
EMP: 7
SALES (est): 1.2MM **Privately Held**
SIC: 3536 Boat lifts

(G-7943)
ANCHOR CNC LLC
7660 Ne Harbor View Dr (98370-7782)
PHONE..................................360 516-3501
Phillip Vandenbrink, *Principal*
EMP: 2
SALES (est): 123.3K **Privately Held**
SIC: 3599 Industrial machinery

(G-7944)
ANDERSONS REBUILDING
17296 Lemolo Shore Dr Ne (98370-8707)
PHONE..................................360 779-5287
Don Anderson, *Owner*
EMP: 2
SALES: 89K **Privately Held**
SIC: 7532 3632 Body shop, automotive; refrigerators, mechanical & absorption: household

(G-7945)
ARTISTS EDGE INC
18723 State Hwy 305 Ne (98370-8769)
P.O. Box 206, Silverdale (98383-0206)
PHONE...............................360 779-2337
William Greenlaw, *President*
EMP: 6
SALES (corp-wide): 654K **Privately Held**
WEB: www.artistsedge.com
SIC: 2499 5947 Picture & mirror frames, wood; artcraft & carvings
PA: Artists' Edge Inc
  9960 Silverdale Way Nw # 5
  Silverdale WA 98383
  360 698-3113

(G-7946)
BARKER CREEK PUBLISHING INC
5686 Ne Minder Rd Ste 205 (98370-5809)
P.O. Box 2610 (98370-2610)
PHONE...............................360 881-0292
Carolyn Hurst, *President*
Steve Perry, *Vice Pres*
▲ **EMP:** 11
SQ FT: 7,500
SALES (est): 971.2K **Privately Held**
WEB: www.barkercreek.com
SIC: 2731 5961 Books: publishing only; catalog & mail-order houses

(G-7947)
BATTERY INFORMATICS INC
19491 Willet Ln Ne (98370-8051)
P.O. Box 501 (98370-0501)
PHONE...............................443 534-7671
Bjorn Frogner, *President*
Andrei Afanasiev, *Vice Pres*
Matthew Murbach, *Admin Sec*
EMP: 4
SALES (est): 130.9K **Privately Held**
SIC: 7372 Utility computer software

(G-7948)
BLUE FROG SOLAR LLC
1015 Ne Hostmark St # 104 (98370-6204)
PHONE...............................206 855-5149
Kelly Samson,
EMP: 2 **EST:** 2011
SALES (est): 254.2K **Privately Held**
SIC: 5211 3629 Solar heating equipment; inverters, nonrotating: electrical

(G-7949)
BLUE SKY PRINTING LLC
19036 Front St Ne (98370-7354)
P.O. Box 242 (98370-0242)
PHONE...............................360 779-2681
Deane Smith, *Mng Member*
Erin Payson, *Graphic Designe*
Melissa Smith,
EMP: 7
SQ FT: 3,800
SALES (est): 1MM **Privately Held**
WEB: www.blueskyprinting.com
SIC: 2752 Commercial printing, offset

(G-7950)
BOATWORKS GALLERY LLC
1563 Archway Ct (98370-9497)
P.O. Box 1568 (98370-0179)
PHONE...............................360 626-1284
Julann E Campbell, *Principal*
EMP: 2 **EST:** 2014
SALES (est): 155.2K **Privately Held**
SIC: 3732 Boat building & repairing

(G-7951)
BRIGHTWORK SPECIALTY PRINTING
2046 Nw Tregaten Ln (98370-7101)
PHONE...............................360 930-0218
Cheryl Esposito, *Owner*
EMP: 2
SALES (est): 25K **Privately Held**
SIC: 2759 Commercial printing

(G-7952)
BROWBANDSBYDESIGNCOM
2823 Ne Cedar Creek Way (98370-4500)
PHONE...............................360 779-9339
Jim Owens, *Principal*
EMP: 2

SALES (est): 113.4K **Privately Held**
SIC: 2399 Pet collars, leashes, etc.: non-leather

(G-7953)
BRUCE & WALTER WEBSTER
Also Called: Miller Bay Excavating
6009 Ne Gunderson Rd (98370-8838)
P.O. Box 1406 (98370-0140)
PHONE...............................360 697-3975
Bruce Wendell Webster, *President*
EMP: 2
SALES (est): 197.6K **Privately Held**
SIC: 2411 1794 Logging camps & contractors; excavation work

(G-7954)
CEDAR FARMS LLC
17582 Noll Rd Ne (98370-7631)
PHONE...............................360 779-3575
Jack Donaldson, *Partner*
EMP: 7 **EST:** 1978
SALES (est): 714.7K **Privately Held**
SIC: 2421 5211 5031 Kiln drying of lumber; lumber products; lumber: rough, dressed & finished

(G-7955)
COREY SIGN & DISPLAY INC
5654 Ne Minder Rd Ste 101 (98370-5826)
PHONE...............................360 297-5490
Scott Corey, *President*
EMP: 4
SALES: 150K **Privately Held**
SIC: 2759 Screen printing

(G-7956)
CRIMSON COVE LLC
22273 Stottlemeyer Rd Ne (98370-8957)
PHONE...............................360 598-2683
Mark Desalvo, *Principal*
EMP: 6
SALES (est): 511.1K **Privately Held**
SIC: 2013 Sausages & other prepared meats

(G-7957)
DAILY TOILS & TROUBLES
18657 State Hwy 305 Ne (98370-8418)
PHONE...............................360 337-9028
EMP: 3
SALES (est): 132.5K **Privately Held**
SIC: 2711 Newspapers-Publishing/Printing

(G-7958)
DLI ENGINEERING CORPORATION
Also Called: Azima Dli
1050 Ne Hostmark St # 101 (98370-7538)
PHONE...............................206 842-7656
Joe Vandyke, *President*
William Watts, *Corp Secy*
EMP: 14
SQ FT: 11,000
SALES (est): 2.5MM
SALES (corp-wide): 3.6MM **Privately Held**
WEB: www.dliengineering.com
SIC: 8711 3829 Marine engineering; vibration meters, analyzers & calibrators
PA: Azima, Inc.
  300 Tradecenter Ste 4610
  Woburn MA 01801
  206 842-7656

(G-7959)
DOGFISH BAY STUDIOS LLC ✪
18062 Viking Way Nw (98370-8306)
PHONE...............................772 335-8711
EMP: 2 **EST:** 2019
SALES (est): 67K **Privately Held**
SIC: 2339 Women's & misses' outerwear

(G-7960)
EACCELERATION CORP (PA)
Also Called: Stop-Sign/Eanthology
1050 Ne Hostmark St # 210 (98370-7538)
PHONE...............................360 697-9260
Diana T Ballard, *Ch of Bd*
Clinton Ballard, *President*
Melonie Miccio, *Vice Pres*
Mark Peterson, *Marketing Staff*
Joshua Lizon, *Software Dev*
EMP: 23
SQ FT: 48,593

SALES (est): 10.5MM **Privately Held**
WEB: www.eacceleration.com
SIC: 7372 Business oriented computer software

(G-7961)
EDGETOWN PUBG & PRODUCTIONS
19657 Front St Ne Apt 1 (98370-6245)
PHONE...............................360 626-1242
EMP: 2
SALES (est): 80K **Privately Held**
SIC: 2741 Misc Publishing

(G-7962)
EVANS BOARD SHOP
2037 Ne Templar Ln (98370-7941)
PHONE...............................360 297-4445
Evans Matan, *Owner*
EMP: 2
SALES (est): 100K **Privately Held**
SIC: 3949 Water sports equipment

(G-7963)
FERN HOLLOW LLC
20726 State Highway 305 N (98370-8085)
PHONE...............................360 504-2323
Ray Allwine, *Owner*
EMP: 2
SALES (est): 134.7K **Privately Held**
SIC: 2335 Wedding gowns & dresses

(G-7964)
GROUNDS FOR CHANGE INC
15773 Gorge Ln Ne Ste 204 (98370)
PHONE...............................360 779-0401
Kelsey Marshall, *President*
Jenny Dewitt, *Office Mgr*
EMP: 8
SQ FT: 3,000
SALES (est): 707.2K **Privately Held**
WEB: www.groundsforchange.com
SIC: 5499 2095 Coffee; coffee, ground: mixed with grain or chicory

(G-7965)
HARDROCK INCORPORATED
17672 Widme Rd (98370)
PHONE...............................360 779-3700
Bill Arness, *President*
Larry Todd, *Vice Pres*
EMP: 30
SALES (est): 4.1MM **Privately Held**
SIC: 3273 Ready-mixed concrete

(G-7966)
INTERLOCKING SOFTWARE CORP
19472 Powder Hill Pl Ne (98370-7473)
PHONE...............................360 394-5900
James Nall, *President*
EMP: 3
SALES (est): 148.8K **Privately Held**
WEB: www.interlockingsoftware.com
SIC: 7372 Prepackaged software

(G-7967)
J & J ENGINEERING INC
22797 Holgar Ct Ne (98370-9108)
P.O. Box 1551 (98370-0178)
PHONE...............................360 779-3853
Jan C Hoover, *President*
EMP: 10
SQ FT: 3,000
SALES (est): 1.5MM **Privately Held**
WEB: www.jjengineering.com
SIC: 3845 Patient monitoring apparatus

(G-7968)
JANTZ ENGINEERING
20555 Pugh Rd Ne (98370-9021)
PHONE...............................360 598-2773
Carl Jantz, *Owner*
EMP: 2
SQ FT: 9,000
SALES (est): 100K **Privately Held**
WEB: www.jantz4x4.com
SIC: 3714 3694 Axles, motor vehicle; engine electrical equipment

(G-7969)
K STAUFFER MANUFACTURING LLC
18082 Miss Ellis Loop Ne (98370-7315)
P.O. Box 2344, Martindale PA (17549-0344)
PHONE...............................360 626-1462
Gregory Johnston, *Principal*
EMP: 2
SALES (est): 113.6K **Privately Held**
SIC: 3999 Manufacturing industries

(G-7970)
KINGSTON COMMUNITY NEWS
19351 8th Ave Ne Ste 205 (98370-8710)
P.O. Box 278 (98370-0278)
PHONE...............................360 779-4464
Lorrie Maxim, *Vice Pres*
EMP: 30
SALES (est): 678.7K **Privately Held**
SIC: 2711 Commercial printing & newspaper publishing combined; newspapers, publishing & printing

(G-7971)
KITSAP POWDER COATING LLC
5734 Ne Minder Rd Bldg B (98370-8896)
PHONE...............................360 297-0015
Dale Gerber,
EMP: 8
SQ FT: 9,500
SALES (est): 924.4K **Privately Held**
WEB: www.kitsappowdercoating.com
SIC: 3479 Coating of metals & formed products

(G-7972)
KORBEN MATHIS WOODWORKING INC
3081 Ne Lincoln Rd (98370-8944)
PHONE...............................360 598-6797
Christopher C Vernon-Cole, *President*
EMP: 2
SALES (est): 111.7K **Privately Held**
SIC: 2431 Millwork

(G-7973)
LASER REFLECTIONS
18800 Front St Ne (98370-7351)
PHONE...............................206 818-2940
Bernadette Olson, *Principal*
EMP: 2
SALES (est): 121.6K **Privately Held**
SIC: 2515 Studio couches

(G-7974)
LAVRY ENGINEERING
15775 George Ln Ne (98370-7888)
PHONE...............................360 598-9757
Dan Lavry, *Principal*
EMP: 6
SALES (est): 464.8K **Privately Held**
SIC: 7812 3651 5064 Motion picture & video production; household audio & video equipment; electrical entertainment equipment

(G-7975)
LEIDOS INC
26279 Twelv Trees Ln Nw (98370)
PHONE...............................360 394-8870
EMP: 4
SALES (corp-wide): 5B **Publicly Held**
SIC: 8731 7371 7373 8742 Coml Physical Research Computer Programming Svc
HQ: Leidos, Inc.
  11951 Freedom Dr Ste 500
  Reston VA 20190
  571 526-6000

(G-7976)
LOCKHEED MARTIN CORPORATION
40 Trailers (98370)
PHONE...............................360 779-4682
EMP: 2
SALES (est): 86K **Publicly Held**
SIC: 3721 Aircraft
PA: Lockheed Martin Corporation
  6801 Rockledge Dr
  Bethesda MD 20817

Poulsbo - Kitsap County (G-7977) GEOGRAPHIC SECTION

(G-7977)
LOCKHEED MARTIN CORPORATION
40 Trailers (98370)
PHONE..................................360 779-4682
EMP: 2 **Publicly Held**
SIC: 3721 Aircraft
PA: Lockheed Martin Corporation
6801 Rockledge Dr
Bethesda MD 20817

(G-7978)
LR WOODWORKING
5686 Ne Minder Rd Ste 101 (98370-5809)
PHONE..................................281 813-1169
Luke Rasmus, *Principal*
EMP: 6
SALES (est): 279.3K **Privately Held**
SIC: 2431 Millwork

(G-7979)
MACKICHAN SOFTWARE INC (PA)
19689 7th Ave Ne 183238 (98370-8091)
PHONE..................................360 394-6033
Barry Mackichan, *CEO*
Lynda Mackichan, *Admin Sec*
EMP: 17 EST: 1998
SQ FT: 3,000
SALES (est): 1.8MM **Privately Held**
WEB: www.mackichan.com
SIC: 3695 7372 Computer software tape & disks: blank, rigid & floppy; prepackaged software

(G-7980)
MAD CUSTOM COATING
22239 Big Valley Rd Ne (98370-9116)
PHONE..................................360 621-6525
EMP: 2
SALES (est): 96.3K **Privately Held**
SIC: 3479 Metal coating & allied service

(G-7981)
MAINE COTTAGE INC
15771 Gorge Ln Ne Ste 202 (98370)
PHONE..................................866 366-3505
Laurence M Strassner, *President*
Lauren M Russell, *Co-President*
EMP: 8
SALES (est): 770.8K **Privately Held**
SIC: 2511 Wood household furniture

(G-7982)
MARKAY CABINETS INC
24950 Stottlemeyer Rd Ne (98370-8893)
P.O. Box 968 (98370-0020)
PHONE..................................360 779-3443
William Davison, *President*
Judith Davison, *Corp Secy*
EMP: 18
SALES (est): 2.3MM **Privately Held**
SIC: 2599 2521 2517 2434 Cabinets, factory; wood office furniture; wood television & radio cabinets; wood kitchen cabinets

(G-7983)
MICROBIAL MAGIC LLC
Also Called: Soilsoup
19689 7th Ave Ne (98370-8091)
PHONE..................................360 297-2224
Kent Rosenberg, *CEO*
EMP: 2
SALES (est): 240.2K **Privately Held**
SIC: 3523 2875 Farm machinery & equipment; compost

(G-7984)
MILEAGE MAXER LLC
23787 Montecarlo Pl Nw (98370-9458)
PHONE..................................360 550-5809
EMP: 3
SALES (est): 147.1K **Privately Held**
SIC: 2869 Fuels

(G-7985)
MORA LLC
Also Called: Mora Iced Creamery
22195 Viking Ave Nw C (98370-4903)
PHONE..................................206 855-1112
Jerry Perez, *President*
▲ EMP: 25

SALES (est): 2.8MM **Privately Held**
SIC: 2024 7389 Ice cream & frozen desserts;

(G-7986)
MORGAN STEEL & METAL WORKS
170 Nw Beaver Rdg (98370-9112)
PHONE..................................360 301-6611
Henry Morgan, *Principal*
EMP: 7 EST: 2012
SQ FT: 4,000
SALES (est): 1MM **Privately Held**
SIC: 3449 3441 1791 Miscellaneous metalwork; fabricated structural metal; structural steel erection

(G-7987)
NORTHWEST CABINET & REFACING
22407 Foss Rd Ne (98370-6560)
PHONE..................................970 497-8230
EMP: 2
SALES (est): 134.9K **Privately Held**
SIC: 2434 Wood kitchen cabinets

(G-7988)
NORTHWEST CABINETRY & DESIGN
1975 Ne Laurie Vei Loop (98370-8580)
PHONE..................................360 434-0740
Terry Waddell, *Owner*
EMP: 3
SALES (est): 300K **Privately Held**
SIC: 2434 Wood kitchen cabinets

(G-7989)
OLYMPIC MUSICAL INSTRUMEN
23022 Miller Bay Rd Ne (98370-7745)
PHONE..................................360 779-4620
Carolyn Hackmann, *Principal*
Cali Hackmann, *CFO*
EMP: 2
SALES (est): 80K **Privately Held**
SIC: 3931 Musical instruments

(G-7990)
PACIFIC NETTING PRODUCTS INC
3203 Ne Totten Rd Ste D (98370-8600)
PHONE..................................360 697-5540
Glenn Kramer, *Principal*
EMP: 3 EST: 2011
SALES (est): 194.4K **Privately Held**
SIC: 2258 Net & netting products

(G-7991)
PALADIN DATA SYSTEMS CORP
19362 Powder Hill Pl Ne (98370-6244)
PHONE..................................360 779-2400
James A Nall, *President*
Dan Burton, *COO*
Robert Johnston, *Exec VP*
Gary Anderson, *CFO*
Ellen Briggs, *Controller*
EMP: 56
SQ FT: 20,000
SALES (est): 7.4MM **Privately Held**
SIC: 7372 Prepackaged software

(G-7992)
PROLINE PRINTER SERVICES
2049 Ptarmigan Ln Nw (98370-8299)
PHONE..................................360 697-2336
EMP: 2 EST: 2003
SALES (est): 94K **Privately Held**
SIC: 2759 Commercial Printing

(G-7993)
PROTOTEK CORP
19044b Jensen Way Ne (98370)
P.O. Box 1700 (98370-0225)
PHONE..................................360 779-1310
Lawrence Smith, *President*
Kent Tarpley, *Sales Mgr*
EMP: 12
SQ FT: 2,000
SALES (est): 1.9MM **Privately Held**
WEB: www.prototek.net
SIC: 3669 3812 Metal detectors; search & navigation equipment

(G-7994)
PUGET SOUND PRECISION INC
6113 Ne Minder Rd (98370-8852)
P.O. Box 950, Kingston (98346-0950)
PHONE..................................360 297-3939
Kevin Lahn, *Owner*
EMP: 14
SQ FT: 6,000
SALES (est): 950K **Privately Held**
WEB: www.pugetsoundprecision.com
SIC: 3599 Machine shop, jobbing & repair

(G-7995)
R MATHEWS OPTICAL WORKS INC
26280 Twelve Trees Ln Nw A (98370-7199)
PHONE..................................360 697-6160
Robert Mathews, *President*
Marilyn Mathews, *Corp Secy*
EMP: 5
SALES (est): 971.9K **Privately Held**
WEB: www.mathewsoptical.com
SIC: 3827 Optical instruments & lenses

(G-7996)
RONALD F PHILLIPS
22244 Port Gamble Rd Ne (98370-8817)
PHONE..................................360 779-5614
EMP: 3 EST: 2010
SALES (est): 180K **Privately Held**
SIC: 2875 Mfg Fertilizers-Mix Only

(G-7997)
SEATECH PUBLICATIONS INC
2622 Ne Lillehammer Ln (98370-9085)
PHONE..................................360 394-1911
Molly Mansker, *Principal*
EMP: 6
SALES (est): 461.3K **Privately Held**
WEB: www.seatechpubs.com
SIC: 2741 Miscellaneous publishing

(G-7998)
SEATTLE SYSTEMS
26296 Twelve Trees Ln Nw (98370-9435)
PHONE..................................360 598-8916
EMP: 2
SALES (est): 166.7K **Privately Held**
SIC: 3842 Surgical appliances & supplies

(G-7999)
SHUNYATA RESEARCH CORPORATION
26273 Twelve Trees Ln Nw D (98370-7172)
PHONE..................................360 598-9935
Caelin Gabriel, *President*
Teya Gabriel, *Vice Pres*
▲ EMP: 17
SQ FT: 5,400
SALES (est): 3.4MM **Privately Held**
WEB: www.shunyata.com
SIC: 3651 Household audio & video equipment

(G-8000)
SKYHAWK PRESS LLC
Also Called: Anfield Shop
1230 Nw Finn Hill Rd D (98370-9712)
PHONE..................................360 598-2211
EMP: 5
SALES (est): 142.6K **Privately Held**
SIC: 2759 5331 Commercial Printing Variety Store

(G-8001)
SLAYS POULSBO BAKERY INC
Also Called: Poulsbo Bake Shop
18924 Front St Ne (98370-7353)
P.O. Box 279 (98370-0279)
PHONE..................................360 779-2798
Marion Sluys, *Owner*
EMP: 35
SQ FT: 4,592
SALES (est): 2.4MM **Privately Held**
SIC: 2052 2051 5461 Cookies & crackers; bread, cake & related products; bread

(G-8002)
SMYTH PAUL ENTERPRISES INC
Also Called: Smyth Lumber Mills
22922 Indianola Rd Ne (98370-7780)
PHONE..................................360 598-3262

Paul Smyth, *President*
Rhonda Smyth, *Corp Secy*
Denver Smyth, *Vice Pres*
EMP: 6
SALES (est): 783.7K **Privately Held**
SIC: 2421 Lumber: rough, sawed or planed

(G-8003)
SOUND PUBLISHING INC
Also Called: North Kitsap Herald
19351 8th Ave Ne Ste 205 (98370-8710)
P.O. Box 278 (98370-0278)
PHONE..................................360 779-4464
Robert Smith, *Editor*
Donna Etchey, *Branch Mgr*
Robert Zollna, *Manager*
EMP: 15 **Privately Held**
WEB: www.soundpublishing.com
SIC: 2711 2731 Newspapers: publishing only, not printed on site; book publishing
HQ: Sound Publishing, Inc.
11323 Commando Rd W Main
Everett WA 98204
360 394-5800

(G-8004)
SOUND PUBLISHING HOLDING INC (DH)
19351 8th Ave Ne Ste 106 (98370-8710)
PHONE..................................360 394-5800
David Black, *CEO*
EMP: 30
SALES (est): 200.2MM **Privately Held**
SIC: 2711 Newspapers, publishing & printing
HQ: Black Press Group Ltd
3175 Beach Dr
Victoria BC V8R 6
250 480-3220

(G-8005)
STORMY SEAS INC
26287 Twelve Trees Ln Nw (98370-9435)
P.O. Box 1570 (98370-0179)
PHONE..................................360 779-4439
Michael A Jackson, *President*
EMP: 14
SQ FT: 4,000
SALES (est): 1.1MM **Privately Held**
WEB: www.stormyseas.com
SIC: 2385 Waterproof outerwear

(G-8006)
TELOS3 LLC
22277 Stottlemeyer Rd Ne (98370-8957)
PHONE..................................360 900-9274
Edward Joshua Lafferty, *Administration*
EMP: 5
SALES (est): 479.2K **Privately Held**
SIC: 7372 Prepackaged software

(G-8007)
THERMION INC
5815 Ne Minder Rd (98370-8814)
PHONE..................................360 297-5150
Rich Goessman, *Branch Mgr*
EMP: 4
SALES (corp-wide): 2.9MM **Privately Held**
SIC: 3563 Spraying outfits: metals, paints & chemicals (compressor)
PA: Thermion Inc.
5815 Ne Minder Rd
Poulsbo WA 98370
360 692-6469

(G-8008)
THERMION INC
5813 Ne Minder Rd (98370-8814)
PHONE..................................360 692-6469
Becky Goessman, *Manager*
EMP: 2
SALES (corp-wide): 2.9MM **Privately Held**
SIC: 3563 Spraying outfits: metals, paints & chemicals (compressor)
PA: Thermion Inc.
5815 Ne Minder Rd
Poulsbo WA 98370
360 692-6469

(G-8009)
THERMION INC
5811 Ne Minder Rd (98370-8814)
PHONE..................................360 362-1273
EMP: 3

▲ = Import ▼ = Export
◆ = Import/Export

GEOGRAPHIC SECTION

SALES (est): 322.6K **Privately Held**
SIC: 3563 Air & gas compressors

(G-8010)
THERMION INC (PA)
5815 Ne Minder Rd (98370-8814)
P.O. Box 780, Silverdale (98383-0780)
PHONE.................................360 692-6469
Frank Rogers, *CEO*
Allen Rogers, *President*
Rich Goesman, *Vice Pres*
Rich Goessman, *Vice Pres*
◆ EMP: 4
SQ FT: 1,500
SALES (est): 2.9MM **Privately Held**
SIC: 3563 Spraying outfits: metals, paints & chemicals (compressor)

(G-8011)
TMF INC
26273 Twelve Trees Ln Nw B (98370-7172)
PHONE.................................360 598-1750
Chris Wood, *President*
David L Poggi, *Co-Owner*
Eric P Potts, *Vice Pres*
EMP: 12
SALES: 2MM **Privately Held**
WEB: www.tmf-inc.com
SIC: 3545 Precision tools, machinists'

(G-8012)
TRULIFE INC
26284 Twelve Trees Ln Nw (98370-9435)
PHONE.................................360 697-5656
Anna Reyes-Potts, *Branch Mgr*
EMP: 250 **Privately Held**
SIC: 3842 7371 Prosthetic appliances; custom computer programming services
HQ: Trulife Inc.
 2010 E High St
 Jackson MI 49203
 517 787-1600

(G-8013)
TV JONES INC
Also Called: TV Jones Guitars and Pickups
18916 3rd Ave Ne (98370-7495)
P.O. Box 2802 (98370-2802)
PHONE.................................360 930-0418
Thomas V Jones, *President*
Elizabeth Jones, *Vice Pres*
▲ EMP: 2
SALES (est): 225.9K **Privately Held**
SIC: 3931 7389 Guitars & parts, electric & nonelectric;

(G-8014)
UTILITY SUPPLY GROUP
24355 Nordvie Pl Nw (98370-7184)
PHONE.................................360 626-1086
EMP: 2 EST: 2012
SALES (est): 118K **Privately Held**
SIC: 5063 3699 Electrical apparatus & equipment; electrical equipment & supplies

(G-8015)
VALCO INSTRUMENTS COMPANY LP
26295 Twelve Trees Ln Nw (98370-9435)
PHONE.................................360 697-9199
Kathy Miller, *Production*
Mike Minner, *Branch Mgr*
Kristie Parker, *Administration*
EMP: 5
SALES (corp-wide): 68.9MM **Privately Held**
SIC: 3823 On-stream gas/liquid analysis instruments, industrial
PA: Valco Instruments Company, Inc
 7811 Westview Dr
 Houston TX 77055
 713 688-9345

(G-8016)
VALTECH
610 Nw Gurley Ct (98370-9749)
PHONE.................................360 779-6748
Ben Valenta, *Principal*
EMP: 3
SALES (est): 234.8K **Privately Held**
SIC: 3572 Computer storage devices

(G-8017)
VICI METRONICS INC
26295 Twelve Trees Ln Nw (98370-9435)
PHONE.................................360 697-9199
Stanley Stearns, *President*
Naveen Chaudhary, *General Mgr*
Santos Puente, *General Mgr*
EMP: 22
SQ FT: 10,000
SALES (est): 4.4MM
SALES (corp-wide): 68.9MM **Privately Held**
WEB: www.vici.com
SIC: 3823 On-stream gas/liquid analysis instruments, industrial; industrial flow & liquid measuring instruments
PA: Valco Instruments Company, Inc
 7811 Westview Dr
 Houston TX 77055
 713 688-9345

(G-8018)
VIVA PUBLISHING
1995 Miss Ellis Loop Ne (98370-7594)
P.O. Box 1874 (98370-0268)
PHONE.................................360 394-3756
John Vitale, *Principal*
EMP: 2 EST: 2008
SALES (est): 139.2K **Privately Held**
SIC: 2741 Miscellaneous publishing

(G-8019)
WATSON FURNITURE GROUP INC (PA)
Also Called: Watson Desking
26246 Twelve Trees Ln Nw (98370-9435)
PHONE.................................360 394-1300
Clif McKenzie, *President*
Clif Mc Kenzie, *President*
Daniel Warn, *Vice Pres*
Kelly Mc Donald, *Controller*
▲ EMP: 150
SQ FT: 68,500
SALES (est): 27.4MM **Privately Held**
WEB: www.watsondesking.com
SIC: 2521 2531 Panel systems & partitions (free-standing), office; wood; public building & related furniture

(G-8020)
WATSON FURNITURE GROUP INC
Also Called: Watson Dispatch
26246 Twelve Trees Ln Nw (98370-9435)
PHONE.................................360 394-1300
James Falk, *Principal*
EMP: 9
SALES (corp-wide): 27.4MM **Privately Held**
WEB: www.watsondesking.com
SIC: 2531 Public building & related furniture
PA: Watson Furniture Group, Inc.
 26246 Twelve Trees Ln Nw
 Poulsbo WA 98370
 360 394-1300

(G-8021)
WIZZ SIGNS
20373 Viking Ave Nw D (98370-7193)
PHONE.................................360 779-3103
Diana Wolf, *Owner*
EMP: 4
SALES (est): 240K **Privately Held**
SIC: 3993 Signs & advertising specialties

(G-8022)
WOODWORK TATTOO AND GALLERY
19494 7th Ave Ne Ste 144 (98370-8097)
PHONE.................................360 626-1965
Kyle Wood, *Principal*
EMP: 2 EST: 2014
SALES (est): 103.2K **Privately Held**
SIC: 2431 Millwork

Prescott
Walla Walla County

(G-8023)
CATAPULT SOLUTIONS
1070 Sharp Rd (99348-9683)
PHONE.................................509 849-2660
Larry Pitcher, *Principal*
EMP: 2
SALES (est): 134.2K **Privately Held**
SIC: 3599 Catapults

Preston
King County

(G-8024)
BECK PACK SYSTEMS INC
7700 300th Ave (98050)
P.O. Box 709 (98050-0709)
PHONE.................................425 222-9515
Michele Pfeffer, *President*
▲ EMP: 20
SALES (est): 3.9MM
SALES (corp-wide): 392.1K **Privately Held**
SIC: 2011 Bacon, slab & sliced from meat slaughtered on site
HQ: Beck Pack Systems A/S
 Sandemandsvej 6
 ROnne 3700
 569 525-22

(G-8025)
FINEST ACCESSORIES INC
30545 Se 84th St Rm 5 (98050)
PHONE.................................425 831-7001
Dillon McCarten, *Manager*
EMP: 7
SALES (corp-wide): 4.6MM **Privately Held**
SIC: 3089 Novelties, plastic
PA: The Finest Accessories Inc
 349 E 3rd St
 North Bend WA
 425 831-7001

(G-8026)
POWDER VISION INC
8110 304th Ave Se (98050)
P.O. Box 947 (98050-0947)
PHONE.................................425 222-6363
John R Still, *President*
J R Still, *President*
EMP: 6
SQ FT: 7,300
SALES (est): 500K **Privately Held**
WEB: www.powdervision.com
SIC: 3471 3479 Sand blasting of metal parts; coating of metals & formed products

(G-8027)
TALKING RAIN BEVERAGE COMPANY
30520 Se 84th St (98050)
P.O. Box 549 (98050-0549)
PHONE.................................425 222-4900
Chris Hall, *CEO*
Marcus Smith, *President*
Kevin M Klock, *Principal*
Donald Kline, *Chairman*
Christopher Hall, *Vice Pres*
▼ EMP: 65
SQ FT: 60,000
SALES (est): 43.8MM **Privately Held**
WEB: www.talkingrain.com
SIC: 2086 Mineral water, carbonated: packaged in cans, bottles, etc.; carbonated beverages, nonalcoholic: bottled & canned

Prosser
Benton County

(G-8028)
AIRPORT RANCH ESTATES LLC (PA)
Also Called: Airfield Estates Winery
560 Merlot Dr (99350-6721)
PHONE.................................509 786-7401
Michael Miller,
Lori Miller,
Marcus Miller,
EMP: 14
SALES (est): 2MM **Privately Held**
SIC: 2084 Wines

(G-8029)
ALEXANDRIA NICOLE CELLARS LLC
158422 W Sonova Rd (99350-9363)
PHONE.................................509 786-3497
Jose Yanez, *Foreman/Supr*
Karen Day, *Accountant*
Ali Boyle, *Mktg Dir*
Jared Boyle, *Mng Member*
EMP: 10
SALES (est): 1.6MM **Privately Held**
SIC: 5921 2084 Wine; wines

(G-8030)
B & B EQUIPMENT CO INC
County Rte 12 (99350)
PHONE.................................509 786-3838
Patricia Beierle, *President*
EMP: 15
SQ FT: 3,000
SALES (est): 2.2MM **Privately Held**
WEB: www.bbeqp.com
SIC: 3599 3556 Machine shop, jobbing & repair; food products machinery

(G-8031)
BUNNELL FAMILY CELLAR
548 Cabernet Ct (99350-6733)
P.O. Box 806 (99350-0806)
PHONE.................................509 786-2197
Susan Bunnell, *Principal*
EMP: 4 EST: 2010
SALES (est): 178.7K **Privately Held**
SIC: 2084 Wines, brandy & brandy spirits

(G-8032)
CHERRY CHUKAR COMPANY (PA)
Also Called: Chukar Cherry
320 Wine Country Rd (99350-9797)
P.O. Box 510 (99350-0510)
PHONE.................................509 786-2055
Pamela Auld, *President*
Tommy Montgomery, *VP Sales*
Teresa Garcia, *Marketing Mgr*
Jill Dixson, *Manager*
Kathleen Young, *Manager*
▲ EMP: 36
SQ FT: 14,000
SALES (est): 7.1MM **Privately Held**
WEB: www.chukar.com
SIC: 2034 5961 5499 5149 Fruits, dried or dehydrated, except freeze-dried; fruit, mail order; dried fruit; dried or canned foods

(G-8033)
CHINOOK WINES
220 Wittkopf Loop (99350-5016)
P.O. Box 387 (99350-0387)
PHONE.................................509 786-2725
Clay Mackey, *Partner*
Kay Simon, *Partner*
EMP: 4
SALES: 320K **Privately Held**
WEB: www.chinookwines.com
SIC: 2084 5921 Wines; wine

(G-8034)
CLOUDS VINEYARD LLC
160589 W Sonova Rd (99350-9330)
P.O. Box 567 (99350-0567)
PHONE.................................509 830-2785
Jose Yanez, *Principal*
EMP: 2 EST: 2013

Prosser - Benton County (G-8035) — GEOGRAPHIC SECTION

SALES (est): 110.2K Privately Held
SIC: 2084 Wines, brandy & brandy spirits

(G-8035)
COLUMBIA VALLEY COMPOST LLC
251 S Wamba Rd (99350-9516)
P.O. Box 1703 (99350-0835)
PHONE..................................509 551-7202
Dan Nickolaus, COO
Paul Ash,
Daniel Nickolaus,
EMP: 2
SALES (est): 252.5K Privately Held
SIC: 2875 Compost

(G-8036)
COYOTE CANYON WINERY LLC
Also Called: H/H Estates Reserve
80 Mckinley Springs Rd (99350-9307)
PHONE..................................509 786-7686
Mathew A Gray,
Mike Andrews,
EMP: 2
SALES (est): 215.9K Privately Held
SIC: 2084 5961 5182 Wines; fruit, mail order; wine

(G-8037)
CRYOVAC INC
170202 W Apricot Rd (99350-8234)
PHONE..................................509 539-2923
EMP: 140
SALES (corp-wide): 4.7B Publicly Held
SIC: 3086 Packaging & shipping materials, foamed plastic
HQ: Cryovac, Inc.
    2415 Cascade Pointe Blvd
    Charlotte NC 28208
    980 430-7000

(G-8038)
DE KLEINE MACHINE COMPANY LLC
209 Sw San Juan Ct (99350-9420)
P.O. Box 907 (99350-0907)
PHONE..................................509 832-1108
EMP: 3
SALES: 250K Privately Held
SIC: 8731 3523 7373 Agricultural research; harvesters, fruit, vegetable, tobacco, etc.; computer-aided design (CAD) systems service; computer-aided engineering (CAE) systems service

(G-8039)
DEAD CANYON VINEYARD LLC
31902 N Crosby Rd (99350-8763)
PHONE..................................509 786-2665
EMP: 2
SALES (est): 76.8K Privately Held
SIC: 2084 Wines

(G-8040)
DEAD OAK DISTILLING LLC
172006 Dogwood Pr Nw (99350-8316)
P.O. Box 732, Grandview (98930-0732)
PHONE..................................509 882-2794
Brian Morton, Principal
EMP: 3
SALES (est): 73.3K Privately Held
SIC: 2085 Distilled & blended liquors

(G-8041)
DESERT WIND VINEYARD
2258 Wine Country Rd (99350-6732)
PHONE..................................509 786-7277
Greg Fries, Owner
Lisa Jenkins, Vice Pres
Carolyn Knee, Manager
EMP: 25
SALES (est): 1.7MM Privately Held
SIC: 2084 Wines

(G-8042)
HOGUE CELLARS LTD
3090 Wittkopf Loop (99350-6566)
PHONE..................................509 786-4557
Michael Hogue, Ch of Bd
Gary Hogue, President
Ron Harley, Treasurer
Waid Wolfe, Admin Sec
▲ EMP: 60
SQ FT: 8,000
SALES (est): 7.3MM
SALES (corp-wide): 8.1B Publicly Held
WEB: www.hoguecellars.com
SIC: 2084 5947 Wines; gift shop
PA: Constellation Brands, Inc.
    207 High Point Dr # 100
    Victor NY 14564
    585 678-7100

(G-8043)
INTERSTATE CONCRETE AND ASP CO
Also Called: American Rock Products
2505 Dump Rd (99350)
PHONE..................................509 547-2380
EMP: 2
SALES (corp-wide): 30.6B Privately Held
SIC: 3273 Ready-mixed concrete
HQ: Interstate Concrete And Asphalt Company
    8849 W Wyoming Ave
    Rathdrum ID 83858
    208 765-1144

(G-8044)
JAG ENTERPRIZES INC
Also Called: Identities Green Printing
154008 W Johnson Rd (99350-9351)
PHONE..................................509 832-2836
Richard Gordon, President
EMP: 3
SQ FT: 1,800
SALES: 85K Privately Held
SIC: 7389 2261 Advertising, promotional & trade show services; printing of cotton broadwoven fabrics

(G-8045)
JV DESIGNS INC
1520 Meade Ave (99350-1450)
P.O. Box 1409 (99350-0800)
PHONE..................................509 786-2588
Jim Vance, CEO
Dorothy L Vance, President
EMP: 3
SALES: 300K Privately Held
SIC: 7389 3556 Drafting service, except temporary help; food products machinery

(G-8046)
KESTREL VINTNERS (PA)
2890 Lee Rd (99350-5520)
PHONE..................................509 786-2675
Cindy Walker, Owner
Martino Trost, General Mgr
▲ EMP: 15
SALES (est): 1.4MM Privately Held
WEB: www.kestrelwines.com
SIC: 2084 Wines

(G-8047)
KRIMSTEN PUBLISHING LLC (PA)
Also Called: Www.multiplication.com
65 W Old Inland Empire (99350-9708)
P.O. Box 48 (99350-0048)
PHONE..................................509 786-7978
Alan Walker, Webmaster
Kimberly Saxton, Director
EMP: 3
SQ FT: 2,000
SALES: 740K Privately Held
SIC: 2731 7371 Books: publishing only; custom computer programming services

(G-8048)
LAMB WESTON HOLDINGS INC
506 6th St (99350-1170)
PHONE..................................509 786-2700
EMP: 140
SALES (corp-wide): 3.4B Publicly Held
SIC: 2037 Potato products, quick frozen & cold pack; fruits, quick frozen & cold pack (frozen)
PA: Lamb Weston Holdings Inc
    599 S Rivershore Ln
    Eagle ID 83616
    208 938-1047

(G-8049)
LAMB WESTON HOLDINGS INC
1125 Sheridan Ave (99350-1133)
PHONE..................................509 882-1417
Michael White, Branch Mgr
EMP: 24
SALES (corp-wide): 3.4B Publicly Held
SIC: 2099 Food preparations
PA: Lamb Weston Holdings Inc
    599 S Rivershore Ln
    Eagle ID 83616
    208 938-1047

(G-8050)
MARTINEZ AND MARTINEZ WINERY
357 Port Ave Ste C (99350-5017)
PHONE..................................509 786-2424
Andrew Martinez, Owner
Monica Martinez, Co-Owner
EMP: 2 EST: 2009
SALES (est): 159.7K Privately Held
SIC: 2084 Wines

(G-8051)
MARTINEZ VINEYARD LLC
1919 Miller Ave (99350-1532)
PHONE..................................509 786-2424
Monica Tudor, Principal
EMP: 4 EST: 2011
SALES (est): 320.5K Privately Held
SIC: 2084 Wines, brandy & brandy spirits

(G-8052)
MCKINLEY SPRINGS LLC
1201 Alderdale Rd (99350-9301)
PHONE..................................509 894-4528
Doug Rowell,
Dana Andrews,
Rob Andrews,
Scott Andrews,
Sandy Rowell,
EMP: 8
SALES (est): 816.6K Privately Held
WEB: www.mckinleysprings.com
SIC: 2084 Wines

(G-8053)
MERCER RANCHES INC (PA)
Also Called: Mercer Ranch Imperial
46 Sonova Rd (99350-9312)
PHONE..................................509 894-4773
Milton Mercer Jr, President
Russ Rasmussen, Corp Secy
Richard T Beightel, Vice Pres
EMP: 100
SQ FT: 50,000
SALES (est): 13.1MM Privately Held
SIC: 0191 2099 General farms, primarily crop; vegetables, peeled for the trade

(G-8054)
MERCER WINE ESTATES LLC (PA)
3100 Lee Rd (99350-6572)
PHONE..................................509 786-2097
Ronald N Harle,
▲ EMP: 12
SALES (est): 1.8MM Privately Held
SIC: 2084 Wines

(G-8055)
MERCER WINE ESTATES LLC
Also Called: Mercer Estate Winery
32302 N Mcdonald Rd (99350-6605)
PHONE..................................509 832-2810
David Forsyth, Branch Mgr
EMP: 11 Privately Held
SIC: 2084 Wines
PA: Mercer Wine Estates, Llc
    3100 Lee Rd
    Prosser WA 99350

(G-8056)
MID-VALLEY MILLING INC
N Hinzerling Rd (99350)
PHONE..................................509 786-1300
Dennis Cavin, President
Mike Spegeman, Vice Pres
EMP: 5
SQ FT: 600
SALES: 750K Privately Held
SIC: 2048 Prepared feeds

(G-8057)
MILBRANDT VINEYARDS INC
508 Cabernet Ct (99350-6733)
PHONE..................................509 788-0030
Butch Milbrandt, Owner
Scott Worrall, Export Mgr
Robin Chiprez, Controller
Heather Price, Sales Dir
Stacy Bellew, Pub Rel Staff
EMP: 10
SALES (est): 1.4MM Privately Held
SIC: 2084 Wines
PA: Milbrandt Vineyards, Inc.
    23934 Road T.1 Sw
    Mattawa WA 99349

(G-8058)
MILNE ASEPTICS LLC
804 Bennett Ave (99350-1267)
P.O. Box 111 (99350-0111)
PHONE..................................509 786-2240
David Wyckoff,
Andi Klein,
Court Wyckoff,
Roman Wyckoff,
▲ EMP: 15
SQ FT: 10,000
SALES (est): 2.8MM Privately Held
SIC: 2087 Beverage bases, concentrates, syrups, powders & mixes

(G-8059)
MILNE FRUIT PRODUCTS INC
804 Bennett Ave (99350-1267)
P.O. Box 111 (99350-0111)
PHONE..................................509 786-0019
Michael Sorenson, President
Diane Moon, General Mgr
John J Schroedder, Vice Pres
Allen Roberts, Opers Staff
Jodi Burger, Purchasing
◆ EMP: 80
SQ FT: 105,000
SALES (est): 28.3MM
SALES (corp-wide): 88.8MM Privately Held
WEB: www.milnefruit.com
SIC: 2037 Fruit juice concentrates, frozen; vegetables, quick frozen & cold pack, excl. potato products
PA: Wyckoff Farms, Incorporated
    160602 Evans Rd
    Grandview WA 98930
    509 882-3934

(G-8060)
OLD TIMERS PORK RINDS ○
129907 W Hanks Rd (99350-7704)
PHONE..................................509 438-8999
Brent Baker, Principal
EMP: 2 EST: 2018
SALES (est): 62.3K Privately Held
SIC: 2096 Pork rinds

(G-8061)
OLSEN ESTATES LLC
46002 N District Line Rd (99350-5620)
PHONE..................................509 973-2203
▲ EMP: 25
SALES: 170K Privately Held
SIC: 2084 Mfg Wines/Brandy/Spirits

(G-8062)
PONTIN DEL ROZA WINERY
Also Called: Pontin Farms
35502 N Hinzerling Rd (99350-8762)
PHONE..................................509 786-4449
Nesto Pontin, Owner
Delores Pontin, Co-Owner
Scott Pontin, Manager
EMP: 3
SALES: 300K Privately Held
SIC: 2084 Wines

(G-8063)
PROSSER GRANDVIEW-PUBLISHERS
Also Called: Prosser Record Bulletin
613 7th St (99350-1459)
PHONE..................................509 786-1711
Sourier John, President
Dianne Buxton, Manager
EMP: 17 EST: 1928
SQ FT: 3,600
SALES (est): 800K Privately Held
WEB: www.recordbulletin.com
SIC: 2711 Newspapers

(G-8064)
RIVERAERIE CELLARS
548 Cabernet Ct (99350-6733)
PHONE..................................509 786-2197
Susan Bunnell, Principal

▲ = Import ▼ = Export
◆ = Import/Export

GEOGRAPHIC SECTION

Pullman - Whitman County (G-8094)

EMP: 7 EST: 2010
SALES (est): 683.7K Privately Held
SIC: 2084 Wines

(G-8065)
ROS WINE COMPANY LLC (PA)
Also Called: Smasne Cellars
28126 N Hansen Rd (99350-7773)
PHONE..................................509 301-0627
Robert Smasne,
Alan Busacca,
EMP: 8
SQ FT: 600
SALES (est): 888.5K Privately Held
SIC: 2084 Wines

(G-8066)
SNOQUALMIE VINEYARDS
660 Frontier Rd (99350-5507)
PHONE..................................509 786-2104
Joy Andersen, Principal
EMP: 30
SALES (est): 1.7MM Privately Held
WEB: www.snoqualmievineyards.com
SIC: 2084 Wines

(G-8067)
TASTE OF HEAVEN BAKING LLC
1604 Meade Ave (99350-1448)
PHONE..................................509 786-3657
Chris Flodin, Mng Member
Glenna Dragoo,
EMP: 2
SALES: 46K Privately Held
SIC: 2051 Bakery: wholesale or wholesale/retail combined

(G-8068)
TINSLEY WELDING INCORPORATED
133401 W Johnson Rd (99350-7504)
PHONE..................................509 786-4000
Wallace Tinsley, President
Michael Tinsley, Vice Pres
EMP: 3
SQ FT: 4,200
SALES: 500K Privately Held
SIC: 7692 Welding repair

(G-8069)
TREE TOP INC
Also Called: Juice Operations
2780 Lee Rd (99350-5541)
PHONE..................................509 786-2926
David Watkins, Vice Pres
Bryan Aaberg, Engineer
Rosemarie Michaels, Human Res Dir
Ray Hager, Executive
EMP: 200
SALES (corp-wide): 399.9MM Privately Held
SIC: 2037 2033 Fruit juice concentrates, frozen; apple sauce: packaged in cans, jars, etc.
PA: Tree Top, Inc.
220 E 2nd Ave
Selah WA 98942
509 697-7251

(G-8070)
TRI-STATE MACHINERY INC
1531 Stacy Ave (99350-1183)
P.O. Box 103 (99350-0103)
PHONE..................................509 786-0400
James Deaton, President
Irma Deaton, President
EMP: 6
SALES: 300K Privately Held
SIC: 3556 Food products machinery

(G-8071)
TWIN CITY FOODS INC
506 6th St (99350-1170)
PHONE..................................509 786-2700
Gary Krebs, Branch Mgr
EMP: 450
SALES (corp-wide): 213.6MM Privately Held
WEB: www.twincityfoods.com
SIC: 2037 4222 2099 Fruits, quick frozen & cold pack (frozen); vegetables, quick frozen & cold pack, excl. potato products; storage, frozen or refrigerated goods; food preparations

PA: Twin City Foods, Inc.
10120 269th Pl Nw
Stanwood WA 98292
206 515-2400

(G-8072)
VALLEY CABINET SHOP INC
22502 S Ward Gap Rd (99350-6582)
PHONE..................................509 786-2717
John F Brown, CEO
Marvin Studdard, President
Pauline Mills, Vice Pres
Susan Brown, Treasurer
Debra Studdard, Admin Sec
EMP: 10 EST: 1950
SQ FT: 9,000
SALES (est): 1.3MM Privately Held
SIC: 2434 5712 Wood kitchen cabinets; cabinets, except custom made: kitchen

(G-8073)
VALLEY PUBLISHING COMPANY INC (PA)
Also Called: Nickel Ads-Fournier Newspaper
613 7th St (99350-1459)
P.O. Box 750 (99350-0750)
PHONE..................................509 786-1711
John L Fournier Jr, President
John L Fournier III, Corp Secy
Dianne Buxton, Manager
EMP: 13
SALES (est): 1.1MM Privately Held
WEB: www.thegrandviewherald.com
SIC: 2711 2752 5943 Commercial printing & newspaper publishing combined; commercial printing, offset; office forms & supplies

(G-8074)
WALLFAM INC
Also Called: Hinzerling Winery
1520 Sheridan Ave (99350-1140)
PHONE..................................509 786-2163
Michael A Wallace, President
EMP: 4
SQ FT: 4,000
SALES (est): 400.5K Privately Held
WEB: www.hinzerling.com
SIC: 2084 8742 Wines; industry specialist consultants

(G-8075)
WARRINERS ORIGINALS INC
15702 N Rothrock Rd (99350-7609)
PHONE..................................509 973-2705
Lester Warriners, President
EMP: 2
SALES (est): 147.5K Privately Held
SIC: 3942 Dolls, except stuffed toy animals

(G-8076)
WHITSTRAN BREWING COMPANY INC
1427 Wine Country Rd (99350-1148)
PHONE..................................509 786-4922
Lawrence Barbus, CEO
EMP: 4
SALES (est): 320.2K Privately Held
SIC: 2082 Beer (alcoholic beverage)

(G-8077)
WILLOW CREST WINERY (PA)
Also Called: Willow Crest Winery Estates
590 Willow Dr (99350)
PHONE..................................509 786-7999
David Minick, President
Mandy Minick, Vice Pres
EMP: 2
SALES (est): 210.7K Privately Held
WEB: www.willowcrestwinery.com
SIC: 2084 Wines

(G-8078)
WITS CELLARS
2880 Lee Rd (99350-5508)
PHONE..................................509 786-1311
EMP: 2
SALES (est): 62.3K Privately Held
SIC: 2084 Mfg Wines/Brandy/Spirits

(G-8079)
WM BOLTHOUSE FARMS INC
10 Sonova Rd (99350-9312)
PHONE..................................509 894-4460
EMP: 7

SALES (corp-wide): 8.6B Publicly Held
SIC: 0191 2035 General farms, primarily crop; dressings, salad: raw & cooked (except dry mixes)
HQ: Wm. Bolthouse Farms, Inc.
7200 E Brundage Ln
Bakersfield CA 93307
661 366-7209

Pullman
Whitman County

(G-8080)
ABR INC
425 Nw Albion Dr (99163-7000)
PHONE..................................509 334-2968
Scott Adams, CEO
EMP: 5
SALES (est): 537.8K Privately Held
SIC: 2835 In vitro & in vivo diagnostic substances

(G-8081)
ABT 360 LLC
1615 Ne Eastgate Blvd G1w (99163-5303)
PHONE..................................509 592-8144
Kathy Shearer, Mng Member
Alyssa Hood,
EMP: 2 EST: 2017
SQ FT: 2,000
SALES: 100K Privately Held
SIC: 2834 Pharmaceutical preparations

(G-8082)
ADAPTELLIGENCE LLC
525 Nw Aspen Ct (99163-5387)
PHONE..................................509 432-1812
Lawrence Holder,
Diane Cook,
EMP: 2 EST: 2015
SALES (est): 75.2K Privately Held
SIC: 7372 7389 Application computer software;

(G-8083)
ALL FABRICATION AND SUPPLY LLC
1904 Airport Rd (99163-8969)
PHONE..................................509 334-1905
Bill Christian,
Kathryn L Christian,
William Boyd Christian,
EMP: 3
SALES (est): 410.4K Privately Held
SIC: 3441 Fabricated structural metal

(G-8084)
AYNANO TECHNOLOGY LLC
1805 Nw Ventura Dr (99163-3559)
PHONE..................................208 596-9865
Suat Ay,
Safak Ay,
Sakire Arslan Ay,
EMP: 3
SALES (est): 60.7K Privately Held
SIC: 8731 3822 7371 7373 Energy research; electronic research; thermostats & other environmental sensors; computer software systems analysis & design, custom; computer integrated systems design

(G-8085)
BILLS WELDING & MACHINE SHOP
700 S Grand Ave (99163-2193)
PHONE..................................509 334-2222
Chuck Gearhiser, President
Gail Gearhiser, Corp Secy
Allen Hood, Vice Pres
EMP: 8
SQ FT: 6,000
SALES (est): 922K Privately Held
SIC: 3599 3523 5051 Machine shop, jobbing & repair; farm machinery & equipment; steel

(G-8086)
BUNCHGRASS FOLKTOYS INC
835 Se Spring St (99163-2243)
PHONE..................................509 334-5143
EMP: 2
SALES (est): 99K Privately Held
SIC: 3944 Mfg Games/Toys

(G-8087)
DIGILENT INC (HQ)
1300 Ne Henley Ct Ste 3 (99163-5662)
P.O. Box 428 (99163-0428)
PHONE..................................509 338-3784
Clint Cole, President
Gene Apperson, Vice Pres
Jim Odell, Opers Staff
Sam Kristoff, Engineer
Larissa Swanland, Marketing Staff
▲ EMP: 13 EST: 2000
SQ FT: 1,000
SALES (est): 2.4MM
SALES (corp-wide): 1.3B Publicly Held
WEB: www.digilentinc.com
SIC: 3999 Education aids, devices & supplies
PA: National Instruments Corporation
11500 N Mopac Expy
Austin TX 78759
512 683-0100

(G-8088)
DOW AGROSCIENCE
2001 Country Club Rd (99163-8868)
PHONE..................................509 332-3650
▲ EMP: 4
SALES (est): 399.4K Privately Held
SIC: 2879 Agricultural chemicals

(G-8089)
DRM HOLDINGS INC
Also Called: Merry Cellars
1300 Ne Henley Ct (99163-5662)
P.O. Box 1833, Billings MT (59103-1833)
PHONE..................................509 338-4699
Patrick Merry, President
EMP: 6
SALES (est): 562.8K Privately Held
SIC: 5921 2084 Wine; wine cellars, bonded: engaged in blending wines

(G-8090)
FUNDAMENTALS PUBLISHING
1335 Sw Lost Trail Dr (99163-5661)
PHONE..................................509 334-8787
EMP: 2
SALES (est): 103.4K Privately Held
SIC: 2741 Miscellaneous publishing

(G-8091)
HOLDER SOFTWARE
525 Nw Aspen Ct (99163-5387)
P.O. Box 966 (99163-0966)
PHONE..................................509 338-0692
Lawrence Holder, Principal
EMP: 2
SALES (est): 121.8K Privately Held
SIC: 7372 Prepackaged software

(G-8092)
INSTY-PRINTS
1652 S Grand Ave (99163-4906)
PHONE..................................509 334-4275
Chris Farnham, Manager
EMP: 2
SALES (est): 90.5K Privately Held
SIC: 2752 Commercial printing, lithographic

(G-8093)
INTELIPEDICS LLC
725 Nw Charlotte St (99163-3012)
PHONE..................................509 432-4036
Gary Fielding, Principal
EMP: 3
SALES (est): 167.4K Privately Held
SIC: 3842 Surgical appliances & supplies

(G-8094)
J & H PRINTING INC
223 E Main St (99163-2618)
PHONE..................................509 332-0782
Jon Zia, President
Frances L Devlin, President
Fred Devlin, Manager
EMP: 3
SQ FT: 2,000
SALES: 275K Privately Held
SIC: 2621 5099 5999 Printing paper; brass goods; alcoholic beverage making equipment & supplies

---

(PA)=Parent Co (HQ)=Headquarters (DH)=Div Headquarters
✪ = New Business established in last 2 years

2019 Washington Manufacturers Register

Pullman - Whitman County (G-8095)

(G-8095)
JESTERNICK SYSTEMS LLC
1520 Sw Casey Ct (99163-5368)
PHONE..................................509 338-4837
Jeremy Nickles, *Principal*
EMP: 2 **EST:** 2008
SALES (est): 164.4K Privately Held
SIC: 3949 Playground equipment

(G-8096)
KLAR SCIENTIFIC LLC
790 Se Sherwood Ct (99163-2400)
PHONE..................................509 330-2103
Matthew McCluskey,
EMP: 5
SALES (est): 278K Privately Held
SIC: 3826 Laser scientific & engineering instruments

(G-8097)
LL3 LLC
801 Rose Creek Rd (99163-8767)
PHONE..................................509 332-2109
Ron Lidey, *President*
EMP: 5
SALES (est): 400K Privately Held
SIC: 1081 Metal mining exploration & development services

(G-8098)
METRIGUARD TECHNOLOGIES INC
2465 Ne Hopkins Ct (99163-5616)
P.O. Box 399 (99163-0399)
PHONE..................................509 332-7526
Jani Roivainen, *President*
Daniel A Uskoski, *Vice Pres*
Don Sverdrup, *Purch Agent*
Todd Kurle, *Buyer*
Steve Redinger, *Buyer*
▲ **EMP:** 28
SQ FT: 11,000
SALES (est): 6.6MM
SALES (corp-wide): 174.8MM Privately Held
WEB: www.metriguard.com
SIC: 3825 Instruments to measure electricity
PA: Raute Oyj
  Rautetie 2
  Nastola 15550
  382 911-

(G-8099)
MODULIEN INC
255 Se Dexter St (99163-2308)
PHONE..................................208 874-2219
Cindy Choy, *CEO*
Brian Kraft, *COO*
EMP: 3
SALES (est): 158.3K Privately Held
SIC: 2833 Medicinal chemicals

(G-8100)
PHOTON BIOSCIENCES LLC
445 S Grand Ave (99163-2751)
P.O. Box 1203 (99163-1260)
PHONE..................................509 595-0159
James Brozik,
Chulhee Kang,
EMP: 2
SALES (est): 86.7K Privately Held
SIC: 2835 Hemotology diagnostic agents; in vitro diagnostics; in vivo diagnostics; cytology & histology diagnostic agents

(G-8101)
POE ASPHALT PAVING INC
5991 Sr 270 (99163)
P.O. Box 784 (99163-0784)
PHONE..................................509 334-6400
Brad Griffith, *Branch Mgr*
EMP: 25
SALES (corp-wide): 34.2MM Privately Held
WEB: www.poeasphalt.com
SIC: 1611 2951 Highway & street paving contractor; asphalt paving mixtures & blocks
PA: Poe Asphalt Paving, Inc.
  302 15th St
  Clarkston WA 99403
  509 758-5561

(G-8102)
PROTIUM INNOVATIONS LLC
425 Se Dexter St (99163-2312)
PHONE..................................206 854-8792
Patrick Adam,
Ian Richardson,
Elijah Shoemake,
EMP: 3
SALES (est): 149K Privately Held
SIC: 8711 3728 8731 Mechanical engineering; fuel tanks, aircraft; commercial physical research

(G-8103)
RECKLESS CHARM
1200 Ne Cove Way (99163-4607)
PHONE..................................253 355-1420
Kelli Brown, *Principal*
EMP: 2
SALES (est): 121.2K Privately Held
SIC: 3199 Leather goods

(G-8104)
RED ROCK CREEK INC
845 Se Greenhill Rd (99163-2416)
PHONE..................................509 765-1664
Trudy Demeerleer, *CEO*
EMP: 12
SQ FT: 30,000
SALES: 1.4MM Privately Held
SIC: 2519 Furniture, household: glass, fiberglass & plastic

(G-8105)
RENAISSANCE FINE WOODWORKING
525 Se Highland Way (99163-2505)
PHONE..................................509 334-7008
Thomas Rodgers, *Principal*
EMP: 2
SALES (est): 298K Privately Held
SIC: 2431 Interior & ornamental woodwork & trim

(G-8106)
SCHWEITZER ENGRG LABS INC
2440 Ne Hopkins Ct (99163-5616)
PHONE..................................509 332-1890
Thomas P Roth, *President*
Jean Hill, *Business Mgr*
Theresa Soto, *Business Mgr*
Kamal Garg, *Project Mgr*
Sherry Jackson, *Opers Staff*
EMP: 22
SALES (corp-wide): 1.1B Privately Held
SIC: 3825 Instruments to measure electricity
PA: Schweitzer Engineering Laboratories Inc.
  2440 Ne Hopkins Ct
  Pullman WA 99163
  509 332-1890

(G-8107)
SEL DEVELOPMENT LLC
2440 Ne Hopkins Ct (99163-5616)
PHONE..................................509 332-1890
Edmund O Schweitzer III, *President*
EMP: 12
SALES (est): 1.1MM
SALES (corp-wide): 1.1B Privately Held
SIC: 3612 Current limiting reactors, electrical
PA: Schweitzer Engineering Laboratories Inc.
  2440 Ne Hopkins Ct
  Pullman WA 99163
  509 332-1890

(G-8108)
SIEMENS INDUSTRY INC
6 Odonnell Rd B (99163-7013)
PHONE..................................208 883-8330
Gary Potrarz, *Manager*
EMP: 87
SALES (corp-wide): 95B Privately Held
SIC: 3822 Air conditioning & refrigeration controls
HQ: Siemens Industry, Inc.
  1000 Deerfield Pkwy
  Buffalo Grove IL 60089
  847 215-1000

(G-8109)
SIMPLE INTELLIGENCE LLC
925 Ne Lake St Apt B (99163-4474)
PHONE..................................425 418-9803
Lorin Vandegrift, *CEO*
Alan Vandegrift, *President*
Mitchell Scott, *CFO*
EMP: 6
SALES (est): 410.8K Privately Held
SIC: 3721 Aircraft

(G-8110)
SWING FLY PRESS LLC
430 Se Dilke St (99163-2529)
P.O. Box 1426 (99163-1381)
PHONE..................................616 540-3836
Zack Williams, *Principal*
EMP: 5
SALES (est): 83.8K Privately Held
SIC: 2711 Newspapers

(G-8111)
WASHINGTON STATE UNIVERSITY
Also Called: Bulletin Office
2 Cooper Bldg (99164-0001)
P.O. Box 645912 (99164-5912)
PHONE..................................509 335-2947
Dawn Dewitt, *Dean*
Daniel Teraguchi, *Dean*
Randi Wasik, *Dean*
Jennifer Cook, *Opers Mgr*
Nigel Pickering, *Research*
EMP: 10
SALES (corp-wide): 750MM Privately Held
WEB: www.wsu.edu
SIC: 2759 8221 Publication printing; university
PA: Washington State University Inc
  240 French Adm Bldg
  Pullman WA 99164
  509 335-2022

(G-8112)
WASHINGTON STATE UNIVERSITY
Also Called: University Publications/Prntng
Cooper Publications Bldg (99164-0001)
PHONE..................................509 335-3518
Ed Sala, *Branch Mgr*
EMP: 60
SALES (corp-wide): 750MM Privately Held
WEB: www.wsu.edu
SIC: 2752 2731 2721 8221 Commercial printing, lithographic; book publishing; periodicals; university
PA: Washington State University Inc
  240 French Adm Bldg
  Pullman WA 99164
  509 335-2022

(G-8113)
WASHINGTON STATE UNIVERSITY
Also Called: Ferdinand's
Food Quality Bldg Rm 101 (99164-0001)
P.O. Box 646392 (99164-6392)
PHONE..................................509 335-4014
Russ Salvadalena, *Manager*
EMP: 70
SALES (corp-wide): 750MM Privately Held
WEB: www.wsu.edu
SIC: 2023 2024 2022 Dry, condensed, evaporated dairy products; ice cream & frozen desserts; cheese, natural & processed
PA: Washington State University Inc
  240 French Adm Bldg
  Pullman WA 99164
  509 335-2022

(G-8114)
WASHINGTON STATE UNIVERSITY
Also Called: Students Publication
113 Murrow Comm Ctr (99164-0001)
P.O. Box 642510 (99164-2510)
PHONE..................................509 335-4573
Al Donnelly, *General Mgr*
EMP: 106
SALES (corp-wide): 750MM Privately Held
WEB: www.wsu.edu
SIC: 2711 8221 Newspapers; university
PA: Washington State University Inc
  240 French Adm Bldg
  Pullman WA 99164
  509 335-2022

(G-8115)
WAWAWAI CANYON WINERY
5602 State Route 270 (99163-8708)
P.O. Box 124, Uniontown (99179-0124)
PHONE..................................509 338-4916
Ben Moffett, *Principal*
EMP: 2
SALES (est): 131.9K Privately Held
SIC: 2084 Wines

(G-8116)
WSU BULLETIN OFFICE
2580 Nw Grimes Way (99164-0001)
P.O. Box 645912 (99164-5912)
PHONE..................................509 335-2857
Marta Coursey, *Director*
EMP: 12
SALES (est): 426.4K Privately Held
SIC: 2711 Newspapers, publishing & printing

Puyallup
Pierce County

(G-8117)
AEROFORGE INC (PA)
609 N Levee Rd (98371-3223)
PHONE..................................253 286-2525
Evan Brown, *President*
Teresa Gartner, *Sales Mgr*
Kevin Antholt, *Sales Staff*
Adrian Hill, *Sales Staff*
Michelle Wilson, *Sales Staff*
EMP: 32
SQ FT: 56,000
SALES (est): 53.8MM Privately Held
WEB: www.airspares.com
SIC: 5088 3429 Aircraft & parts; aircraft hardware

(G-8118)
AEROFORGE MANUFACTURING INC
Also Called: Aerostar Engineering, Inc.
609 N Levee Rd (98371-3223)
PHONE..................................253 286-2525
Evan Brown, *President*
EMP: 48
SQ FT: 15,000
SALES: 41.4K
SALES (corp-wide): 53.8MM Privately Held
WEB: www.airspares.com
SIC: 3728 3812 Aircraft parts & equipment; search & navigation equipment
PA: Aeroforge, Inc.
  609 N Levee Rd
  Puyallup WA 98371
  253 286-2525

(G-8119)
AIR PRODUCTS AND CHEMICALS INC
1500 39th Ave Se (98374-2268)
PHONE..................................253 845-4000
Randy Clancy, *Branch Mgr*
EMP: 6
SALES (corp-wide): 8.9B Publicly Held
WEB: www.airproducts.com
SIC: 5169 5084 2869 Industrial gases; welding machinery & equipment; amines, acids, salts, esters
PA: Air Products And Chemicals, Inc.
  7201 Hamilton Blvd
  Allentown PA 18195
  610 481-4911

(G-8120)
ALL ELECTRIC MOTOR SERVICE
5507 Milwaukee Ave E (98372-2761)
PHONE..................................253 845-1938
Michael Thayer, *President*
EMP: 3
SQ FT: 4,000

GEOGRAPHIC SECTION

Puyallup - Pierce County (G-8153)

SALES: 269.5K **Privately Held**
SIC: 5999 7694 Engine & motor equipment & supplies; electric motor repair

(G-8121)
ALL SYSTEMS INTEGRATED INC
Also Called: A S I
315 7th St Ne (98372-5022)
PHONE.................253 770-5570
Michael Lindbo, *President*
Dave Zeth, *Technician*
EMP: 10
SALES (est): 907.5K **Privately Held**
WEB: www.asinw.com
SIC: 3629 Electronic generation equipment

(G-8122)
AMERICAN PETRO ENVMTL SVCS LLC
402 Valley Ave Nw Ste 108 (98371-3310)
PHONE.................253 538-5252
Shannon Mazza, *Exec VP*
Michael P Mazza,
EMP: 2
SALES (est): 1.2MM **Privately Held**
WEB: www.apes-inc.com
SIC: 8748 1382 Environmental consultant; oil & gas exploration services

(G-8123)
AQUA REC INC
14019 Meridian E (98375-5618)
PHONE.................253 770-9447
Stella Bennett, *Manager*
EMP: 4
SALES (corp-wide): 7.4MM **Privately Held**
WEB: www.aquarec.com
SIC: 3949 3429 7389 Swimming pools, except plastic; fireplace equipment, hardware: andirons, grates, screens; swimming pool & hot tub service & maintenance
PA: Aqua Rec, Inc.
   1407 Puyallup Ave
   Tacoma WA 98421
   253 682-1792

(G-8124)
AQUA-LIFT INC
7502 116th St E (98373-4709)
P.O. Box 937 (98371-0249)
PHONE.................253 845-4010
Lonnie Davis, *President*
Myrna Lee Davis, *Vice Pres*
EMP: 2
SALES: 1MM **Privately Held**
SIC: 3536 2899 Boat lifts; plastic wood

(G-8125)
B G BENDER INC
Also Called: Valley Machine & Manufacturing
1109 Valley Ave Nw (98371-2598)
PHONE.................253 848-3742
Bruce Bender, *President*
EMP: 2
SALES: 100K **Privately Held**
SIC: 3599 7692 Machine shop, jobbing & repair; welding repair

(G-8126)
BACK TO BASICS LEAN MFG
9101 166th St E (98375-6228)
PHONE.................253 353-4281
Tony Rodriguez, *Principal*
EMP: 2 EST: 2017
SALES (est): 65.5K **Privately Held**
SIC: 3999 Manufacturing industries

(G-8127)
BAD BREATH GARLIC CO
Also Called: Gnarly Garlic Dip
17404 Meridian E (98375-6234)
PHONE.................253 223-1835
Ryan Heather, *Owner*
EMP: 3 EST: 2017
SALES (est): 57.5K **Privately Held**
SIC: 2099 Dips, except cheese & sour cream based

(G-8128)
BAKER MANUFACTURING INC
11121 Valley Ave E (98372-5971)
PHONE.................253 840-8610
David Baker, *President*
EMP: 15
SQ FT: 4,500
SALES (est): 2.9MM **Privately Held**
WEB: www.bakermfginc.com
SIC: 3599 Machine shop, jobbing & repair; machine & other job shop work

(G-8129)
BELLANDI SIGNS INC
11515 120th Ave E (98374-2217)
PHONE.................253 841-1144
Marty Bellandi, *President*
EMP: 2 EST: 1975
SALES (est): 359.1K **Privately Held**
SIC: 7389 3993 Sign painting & lettering shop; signs & advertising specialties

(G-8130)
BIGFOOT PIPE & PILING LLC
15422 Canyon Rd E (98375-7476)
PHONE.................425 882-1000
Don Karchmer,
EMP: 2
SALES (est): 90.8K **Privately Held**
SIC: 3317 5051 Steel pipe & tubes; piling, iron & steel

(G-8131)
BIGWOODS SCREEN PRINTING
16203 70th Ave E (98375-7279)
PHONE.................253 208-3990
Gerald Grandbois, *Principal*
EMP: 2 EST: 2013
SALES (est): 183.1K **Privately Held**
SIC: 2752 Commercial printing, lithographic

(G-8132)
BOEING AROSPC OPERATIONS INC
12901 133rd Ave E (98374-4858)
PHONE.................253 773-9906
EMP: 4
SALES (corp-wide): 101.1B **Publicly Held**
SIC: 3721 Aircraft
HQ: Boeing Aerospace Operations, Inc.
   6001 S A Depo Blvd Ste E
   Oklahoma City OK 73150
   405 622-6000

(G-8133)
BRITE LIGHT WELDING INC
Also Called: Brite Light Wldg Frabrication
5526 184th St E Ste G (98375-2416)
P.O. Box 1122, Graham (98338-1122)
PHONE.................253 875-6291
Ralph Thompson, *President*
EMP: 30
SALES (est): 666.9K **Privately Held**
SIC: 7692 Welding repair

(G-8134)
CD FABRICATION
11914 119th Ave E (98374-4005)
PHONE.................253 273-2005
Geoff Wright, *Principal*
EMP: 2
SALES (est): 149.5K **Privately Held**
SIC: 3599 Machine shop, jobbing & repair

(G-8135)
CONATION TECHNOLOGIES LLC
101 S Meridian Ste B (98371-5900)
PHONE.................253 864-8234
Colleen Ward, *Managing Prtnr*
Jean Richaud,
▲ EMP: 4
SALES (est): 648.5K **Privately Held**
SIC: 3674 Integrated circuits, semiconductor networks, etc.; photovoltaic devices, solid state

(G-8136)
CONCRETE PRODUCTS INC
5415 189th St E (98375-2364)
PHONE.................253 864-2774
Patrick Sibborn, *Sales Mgr*
EMP: 2
SALES (est): 91.3K **Privately Held**
SIC: 3272 Concrete products

(G-8137)
COPPER RIVER SMOKING CO
240 15th St Se (98372-3411)
PHONE.................253 446-0634
Andi Whary, *President*
Barney Alanis, *Manager*
▲ EMP: 5 EST: 1997
SALES (est): 100.9K
SALES (corp-wide): 1.1MM **Privately Held**
SIC: 2092 Fresh or frozen packaged fish
PA: Trapper's Creek, Inc.
   5650 B St
   Anchorage AK 99518
   907 561-8088

(G-8138)
CRAFTWORK COATINGS
11803 130th Avenue Ct E (98374-5038)
PHONE.................253 508-9358
John Swauger, *Principal*
EMP: 2 EST: 2016
SALES (est): 75.5K **Privately Held**
SIC: 3479 Metal coating & allied service

(G-8139)
CURLY CLUTCH LLC
7110 121st Street Ct E (98373-8826)
P.O. Box 732045 (98373-0047)
PHONE.................253 732-3647
Carson Duda, *Mng Member*
EMP: 9
SQ FT: 6,300
SALES (est): 300K **Privately Held**
SIC: 3634 Curling irons, electric

(G-8140)
DAVIDSON PROSTHETICS LLC
11919 Canyon Rd E (98373-4456)
PHONE.................253 770-6578
Greg Davidson,
EMP: 3
SALES (est): 295.6K **Privately Held**
SIC: 3842 Clothing, fire resistant & protective; limbs, artificial

(G-8141)
DEBBIE ZACHARY
Also Called: Sand Blasted Art
1210 22nd St Se (98372-4146)
PHONE.................253 848-5011
Debbie Zachary, *Owner*
EMP: 2
SALES (est): 40K **Privately Held**
WEB: www.sandblastedart.com
SIC: 3231 Decorated glassware: chipped, engraved, etched, etc.

(G-8142)
DEBORAH DESIGNS
1910 28th Avenue Ct Sw (98373-1362)
PHONE.................253 848-3274
EMP: 2
SALES (est): 113.5K **Privately Held**
SIC: 3911 Mfg Precious Metal Jewelry

(G-8143)
DF INDUSTRIES INC
16802 116th Avenue Ct E (98374-9119)
PHONE.................253 445-7940
Dale Fusch, *President*
EMP: 2 EST: 2012
SALES (est): 85.1K **Privately Held**
SIC: 3999 Manufacturing industries

(G-8144)
DIAMOND POLISHING SYSTEMS
8801 Canyon Rd E (98371-6311)
PHONE.................253 770-0508
Dale Hoyt, *Owner*
EMP: 5
SALES (est): 640.7K **Privately Held**
SIC: 3471 Polishing, metals or formed products

(G-8145)
DORMAKABA USA INC
6319 112th St E Ste 102 (98373-4300)
PHONE.................253 864-4484
Neil Davaz, *Branch Mgr*
EMP: 15
SALES (corp-wide): 2.8B **Privately Held**
SIC: 3429 Builders' hardware
HQ: Dormakaba Usa Inc.
   100 Dorma Dr
   Reamstown PA 17567
   717 336-3881

(G-8146)
DRUID MOUNTAIN DRONES
2121 5th Ave Nw (98371-5124)
PHONE.................206 321-4771
Jennifer Moen, *Principal*
EMP: 2
SALES (est): 102.7K **Privately Held**
SIC: 3721 Motorized aircraft

(G-8147)
E & S CUSTOM CABINETS INC
1204 39th Ave Sw (98373-3843)
PHONE.................253 405-2732
G Edward Knoben, *President*
Ed Knoben, *Executive*
EMP: 32
SQ FT: 12,800
SALES (est): 3.8MM **Privately Held**
SIC: 2434 Wood kitchen cabinets

(G-8148)
EDGEWOOD MONUMENTS
111 W Meeker (98371-5375)
PHONE.................253 561-2498
EMP: 2
SALES (est): 126.5K **Privately Held**
SIC: 3272 Monuments & grave markers, except terrazo

(G-8149)
EDS GARAGE & WELDING
10813 Valley Ave E (98372-2548)
PHONE.................253 845-8741
Fax: 253 845-0754
EMP: 3 EST: 1967
SQ FT: 2,000
SALES (est): 170K **Privately Held**
SIC: 7538 7692 General Auto Repair Welding Repair

(G-8150)
EVERYTHING PRINTS
15301 76th Avenue Ct E (98375-6984)
PHONE.................360 447-8217
Clark Bartron, *Principal*
EMP: 2
SALES (est): 132.5K **Privately Held**
SIC: 2752 Commercial printing, lithographic

(G-8151)
F RUCKMAN ENTERPRISES
Also Called: Ruckman's
14002 Canyon Rd E (98373-5202)
PHONE.................253 531-9132
Frank Ruckman, *Partner*
Mary Lou Ruckman, *Partner*
EMP: 30
SQ FT: 7,200
SALES (est): 2.2MM **Privately Held**
SIC: 2434 2431 Wood kitchen cabinets; millwork

(G-8152)
FEDEX OFFICE & PRINT SVCS INC
101 37th Ave Se Ste B (98374-1205)
PHONE.................253 841-3557
EMP: 23
SALES (corp-wide): 69.6B **Publicly Held**
WEB: www.kinkos.com
SIC: 7334 2752 Photocopying & duplicating services; commercial printing, lithographic
HQ: Fedex Office And Print Services, Inc.
   7900 Legacy Dr
   Plano TX 75024
   800 463-3339

(G-8153)
FIREHOUSE CUSTOM CABINETS
12603 146th St E (98374-3567)
PHONE.................253 864-4894
Brad Wesenberg, *Principal*
EMP: 2 EST: 2007
SALES (est): 168.8K **Privately Held**
SIC: 2434 Wood kitchen cabinets

Puyallup - Pierce County (G-8154)

(G-8154)
FRANKS CUSTOM COATINGS LLC
9105 118th St E (98373-3819)
PHONE 253 973-4361
Frank Besaw, *Principal*
EMP: 2
SALES (est): 99K **Privately Held**
SIC: 3479 Metal coating & allied service

(G-8155)
GAZEBO & PORCHWORKS
Also Called: Gazebo & Porch Works
728 9th Ave Sw (98371-6744)
PHONE 253 380-0918
Frederick G McDonald, *Owner*
Rey McDonald, *Co-Owner*
EMP: 2
SALES (est): 126.2K **Privately Held**
SIC: 2431 Ornamental woodwork: cornices, mantels, etc.; woodwork, interior & ornamental

(G-8156)
GIRARD MANAGEMENT GROUP LLC
802 E Main (98372-3364)
PHONE 253 845-0505
Scott Vipond, *Mng Member*
EMP: 100
SALES (est): 6.6MM **Privately Held**
SIC: 2448 Pallets, wood

(G-8157)
GIRARD WOOD PRODUCTS INC (PA)
802 E Main (98372-3364)
P.O. Box 830 (98371-0075)
PHONE 253 845-0505
Scott M Vipond, *President*
Steven J Vipond, *Vice Pres*
Gaby Perez, *Human Res Dir*
Greg R Vipond, *Admin Sec*
EMP: 50 **EST:** 1961
SQ FT: 50,000
SALES (est): 16.7MM **Privately Held**
WEB: www.girardwoodproducts.com
SIC: 2448 4953 Pallets, wood; skids, wood; refuse systems

(G-8158)
GLAZY DAZE CERAMICS
6814 96th St E (98371-6102)
PHONE 253 770-2979
Pamela Block, *Principal*
EMP: 2 **EST:** 2010
SALES (est): 108.8K **Privately Held**
SIC: 3269 Pottery products

(G-8159)
GLEN HIDDEN MHC LLC
15616 76th Ave E (98375-7602)
PHONE 253 537-9383
EMP: 2
SALES (est): 120K **Privately Held**
SIC: 2451 Mobile homes

(G-8160)
GRIEF INC
Also Called: Grief Store, The
4227 S Meridian Ste C-363 (98373-3603)
PHONE 253 929-0649
Robert Sims, *CEO*
Robert A Sims, *CEO*
Darcie D Sims, *President*
Greg M Franklin, *CFO*
Alicia S Franklin, *Admin Sec*
▲ EMP: 3
SQ FT: 2,000
SALES (est): 200K **Privately Held**
WEB: www.griefinc.com
SIC: 8742 5049 5192 2741 Personnel management consultant; training & development consultant; school supplies; books, periodicals & newspapers; miscellaneous publishing

(G-8161)
HERBRAND COMPANY
Also Called: Herbrand-Mcgowan Timber
315 39th Ave Sw Ste 6 (98373-3690)
PHONE 253 848-7700
Keith N Herbrand, *President*
Dan Miller, *Principal*
Becky Narayan, *Office Mgr*
EMP: 10
SALES (est): 1.6MM **Privately Held**
SIC: 2411 Logging

(G-8162)
HOSE PRO
12424 80th Ave E (98373-4839)
PHONE 253 448-1304
Ray Rios, *Principal*
Keri Street, *Principal*
EMP: 2
SALES (est): 225.2K **Privately Held**
SIC: 3492 Hose & tube fittings & assemblies, hydraulic/pneumatic; hose & tube couplings, hydraulic/pneumatic

(G-8163)
HS PRINT WORKS DIFFICULT
9918 162nd Street Ct E # 13 (98375-6283)
PHONE 253 251-0045
William Halgen, *Owner*
Mark Saathoff, *Owner*
EMP: 3
SQ FT: 2,400
SALES: 250K **Privately Held**
SIC: 2759 Screen printing

(G-8164)
IDEAL INDUSTRIES INTL INC
17914 93rd Ave E (98375-9698)
PHONE 360 761-9958
EMP: 2
SALES (est): 103.2K **Privately Held**
SIC: 3999 Manufacturing industries

(G-8165)
IDX CORPORATION
Also Called: Idx Seattle
1601 Industrial Park Way # 101 (98371-3242)
PHONE 253 445-9000
EMP: 195
SALES (corp-wide): 394.6MM **Privately Held**
SIC: 2542 Office & store showcases & display fixtures
PA: Idx Corporation
1 Rider Trail Plaza Dr
Earth City MO 63045
314 739-4120

(G-8166)
INDEPENDENT CHUTE COMPANY
Also Called: Independent Company
6113 176th St E Bldg B (98375-2370)
PHONE 206 321-8911
William Miller, *Principal*
EMP: 3
SALES (est): 160.4K **Privately Held**
SIC: 3444 Coal chutes, prefabricated sheet metal; mail chutes, sheet metal; hoppers, sheet metal; laundry hampers, sheet metal

(G-8167)
INDEPENDENT TECH SERVICE LLC
9918 162nd Street Ct E # 1 (98375-6283)
PHONE 253 891-1976
Chad Eberhart, *Mng Member*
EMP: 4
SALES: 365K **Privately Held**
WEB: www.itsfabrication.com
SIC: 3842 Limbs, artificial

(G-8168)
INK SMITHS SCREEN PRINTING LLC
312 N Meridian (98371-8634)
PHONE 253 446-7126
Lance D Hart,
EMP: 2
SALES (est): 83.9K **Privately Held**
SIC: 2752 Commercial printing, lithographic

(G-8169)
INTEGRITY PRINTING LLC
2102 E Main Ste 111 (98372-3205)
PHONE 253 841-3161
Henry Hayes, *Principal*
EMP: 4
SALES (est): 460K **Privately Held**
SIC: 2759 Commercial printing

(G-8170)
JUST SALSA
6328 121st Street Ct E (98373-4404)
PHONE 253 455-4618
Alev Meyer, *Principal*
EMP: 3 **EST:** 2016
SALES (est): 121.5K **Privately Held**
SIC: 2099 Dips, except cheese & sour cream based

(G-8171)
KAES ENTERPRISES LLC
16707 129th Avenue Ct E (98374-8840)
PHONE 800 252-5237
Christopher Kaes,
EMP: 28
SQ FT: 250
SALES (est): 2.7MM **Privately Held**
WEB: www.kaesenterprises.com
SIC: 1731 4911 3281 1542 Electric power systems contractors; generation, electric power; granite, cut & shaped; custom builders, non-residential

(G-8172)
KIBBEY BATTERY SERVICE INC
2906 E Main (98372-3168)
PHONE 253 845-9155
Jack Campbell, *President*
EMP: 2
SQ FT: 800
SALES: 300K **Privately Held**
SIC: 3691 5531 3692 Storage batteries; automotive tires; primary batteries, dry & wet

(G-8173)
KTS MEDIA INC
Also Called: Sign Connections
15309 88th Avenue Ct E (98375-2113)
PHONE 253 845-0771
Katherine Simons, *President*
EMP: 2
SALES (est): 172.4K **Privately Held**
SIC: 3993 Signs & advertising specialties

(G-8174)
L & L PRINTING INC
1430 E Main Ste E (98372-3139)
PHONE 253 848-5546
Brian Snell, *President*
Larry Snell, *President*
Cindy Snell, *Admin Sec*
EMP: 6 **EST:** 1979
SALES (est): 646.3K **Privately Held**
WEB: www.llprinting.com
SIC: 2759 2752 Letterpress printing; commercial printing, lithographic

(G-8175)
L J SMITH INC
1212 Valley Ave Nw 300 (98371-2500)
PHONE 253 435-9120
Bob Pury, *Branch Mgr*
EMP: 13
SALES (corp-wide): 300.2MM **Privately Held**
WEB: www.ljsmith.com
SIC: 2431 Staircases, stairs & railings
HQ: L. J. Smith, Inc.
35280 Scio Bowerston Rd
Bowerston OH 44695
740 269-2221

(G-8176)
LASERFAB INC (PA)
5406 184th St E Ste D (98375-2489)
PHONE 509 762-0400
Kevin T Frazer, *President*
Mark Allen, *President*
Kevin Frazer, *President*
Rollie Mercer, *President*
Alan White, *Principal*
EMP: 15
SQ FT: 33,000
SALES: 12.4MM **Privately Held**
WEB: www.laserfabusa.com
SIC: 3699 Laser welding, drilling & cutting equipment

(G-8177)
LEDFORD INDUSTRIES LLC
16126 Meridian Ave (98375)
PHONE 253 446-6508
Michael Ledford, *Mng Member*
EMP: 3

SALES: 229.5K **Privately Held**
SIC: 3999 Barber & beauty shop equipment

(G-8178)
LOCKE PRECISION LLC
14119 Pioneer Way E Ste B (98372-3607)
PHONE 253 904-8615
David M Locke, *Mng Member*
EMP: 15
SQ FT: 10,000
SALES (est): 825K **Privately Held**
SIC: 3599 Machine shop, jobbing & repair

(G-8179)
LOOKER & ASSOCIATES INC
5625 189th St E (98375-7203)
P.O. Box 44944, Tacoma (98448-0944)
PHONE 253 210-5200
Duncan Sturrock, *President*
Douglas R Looker, *Admin Sec*
EMP: 50 **EST:** 1974
SQ FT: 2,000
SALES (est): 4.4MM **Privately Held**
SIC: 1771 2951 Blacktop (asphalt) work; asphalt & asphaltic paving mixtures (not from refineries)

(G-8180)
LSI LOGISTIC SVC SOLUTIONS LLC
Also Called: L S I
4326 86th Ave E (98371-2563)
PHONE 253 872-8970
Nic Klamke, *President*
EMP: 10
SQ FT: 2,000
SALES: 2MM **Privately Held**
SIC: 4225 2621 3579 Miniwarehouse, warehousing; wrapping & packaging papers; mail tying (bundling) machines

(G-8181)
LYNCH CREEK QUARRY LLC (PA)
19209 Canyon Rd E (98375-2310)
PHONE 360 832-4269
David Randles,
EMP: 4
SQ FT: 2,000
SALES (est): 1.6MM **Privately Held**
SIC: 1442 Construction sand & gravel

(G-8182)
MASTER MILLWORK INC
11603 Canyon Rd E (98373-4361)
PHONE 253 770-2023
Gary Monette, *President*
EMP: 45
SQ FT: 15,000
SALES (est): 4.4MM **Privately Held**
WEB: www.master-millwork.com
SIC: 2431 2434 Millwork; wood kitchen cabinets

(G-8183)
MASTER PRECASTER INC
212 10th St Se (98372-3403)
PHONE 253 770-9119
Fred Beyers, *President*
Linda Beyers, *Vice Pres*
EMP: 6
SQ FT: 10,000
SALES (est): 726.3K **Privately Held**
SIC: 3272 Concrete products, precast

(G-8184)
MAURICES INCORPORATED
3500 S Meridian (98373-3779)
PHONE 253 845-5577
EMP: 4 **Privately Held**
SIC: 5621 5137 2389 Women's clothing stores; women's & children's clothing; apparel for handicapped
HQ: Maurices Incorporated
425 W Superior St
Duluth MN 55802
218 727-8431

(G-8185)
MAVEN WATERSPORTS DESIGNS LLC
18203 73rd Ave E (98375-1858)
PHONE 360 481-2521
EMP: 2 **EST:** 2016

GEOGRAPHIC SECTION
Puyallup - Pierce County (G-8216)

SALES (est): 86K Privately Held
SIC: 3732 Boat building & repairing

(G-8186)
MC PUBLISHING LLC
16818 86th Ave E (98375-9606)
PHONE.................................253 678-3105
EMP: 2
SALES (est): 103.1K Privately Held
SIC: 2741 Miscellaneous publishing

(G-8187)
MCCAULEY INTERNATIONAL INC
12408 138th Street Ct E (98374-3252)
P.O. Box 73365 (98373-0365)
PHONE.................................253 229-8900
Euguni Samochimen, *President*
EMP: 4
SALES (est): 260K Privately Held
SIC: 3651 Audio electronic systems

(G-8188)
MCCAULEY SOUND INC
16607 Meridian E (98375-6203)
P.O. Box 731024 (98373-0030)
PHONE.................................253 848-0363
Thomas McCauley, *President*
Evgueni Samochine, *Vice Pres*
Bill Lisa, *Prdtn Mgr*
Svetlana Samochina, *Bookkeeper*
▲ EMP: 25 EST: 1979
SQ FT: 6,000
SALES (est): 3.7MM Privately Held
WEB: www.mccauleysound.com
SIC: 3651 Speaker systems

(G-8189)
METAL TECH METALWORKS INC
9918 162nd Street Ct E (98375-6283)
PHONE.................................253 435-5885
Matthew Steinman, *President*
EMP: 3
SALES (est): 180K Privately Held
SIC: 7692 Welding repair

(G-8190)
MGS SOFTWARE LLC
14415 115th Avenue Ct E (98374-3467)
PHONE.................................253 841-1573
Bruce Barker, *Principal*
EMP: 2
SALES (est): 128.3K Privately Held
SIC: 7372 Prepackaged software

(G-8191)
MICHAEL DRESDNER
3303 28th St Se (98374-4115)
PHONE.................................253 770-1664
Michael Dresdner, *Principal*
EMP: 2
SALES (est): 98.1K Privately Held
SIC: 2499 Decorative wood & woodwork

(G-8192)
MILES RESOURCES LLC
400 Valley Ave Ne (98372-2516)
PHONE.................................253 383-3585
Cedric Brooks, *President*
Mike Bradley, *General Mgr*
Pat McBride, *Project Mgr*
Jeff Williams, *Project Mgr*
Brad Deakins, *CFO*
EMP: 200
SALES (est): 28.7MM Privately Held
SIC: 1771 1611 2951 Blacktop (asphalt) work; highway & street construction; asphalt & asphaltic paving mixtures (not from refineries)

(G-8193)
MILES SAND & GRAVEL COMPANY (PA)
Also Called: Concrete Nor'west Division
400 Valley Ave Ne (98372-2516)
PHONE.................................253 833-3705
Walter Miles, *President*
Tom Butler, *General Mgr*
Lisa Kittilsby, *Vice Pres*
Frank Miles, *Vice Pres*
Tim Kittilsby, *CFO*
EMP: 300
SQ FT: 3,000

SALES (est): 88MM Privately Held
SIC: 3273 5032 Ready-mixed concrete; sand, construction; gravel

(G-8194)
MILLER ELECTRIC MFG CO
7102 98th Street Ct E (98373-1234)
PHONE.................................253 212-5346
Nicholas Miller, *Branch Mgr*
EMP: 207
SALES (corp-wide): 14.7B Publicly Held
SIC: 3548 Welding apparatus
HQ: Miller Electric Mfg. Llc
1635 W Spencer St
Appleton WI 54914
920 734-9821

(G-8195)
MINUTEMAN PRESS INTL INC
2102 E Main Ste 111 (98372-5697)
PHONE.................................253 841-3161
William Colborn, *CEO*
EMP: 6
SALES (corp-wide): 23.4MM Privately Held
SIC: 2752 Commercial printing, offset
PA: Minuteman Press International, Inc.
61 Executive Blvd
Farmingdale NY 11735
631 249-1370

(G-8196)
MULTI APP COATINGS LLC
9801 126th St E (98373-3447)
PHONE.................................253 841-1256
Scott Bee, *Principal*
EMP: 2 EST: 2011
SALES (est): 101K Privately Held
SIC: 3479 Metal coating & allied service

(G-8197)
NATURAL WONDER PUBLISHING ✪
10710 Rampart Dr E (98374-2066)
PHONE.................................253 905-1583
EMP: 2 EST: 2018
SALES (est): 59.2K Privately Held
SIC: 2741 Miscellaneous publishing

(G-8198)
NELSON S CABINET INSTALLA
2210 27th Ave Se (98374-1441)
PHONE.................................253 770-3975
EMP: 2 EST: 2011
SALES (est): 110K Privately Held
SIC: 2434 Mfg Wood Kitchen Cabinets

(G-8199)
NEWS TRIBUNE THE 1950 S
822 E Main (98372-3364)
PHONE.................................253 841-2481
EMP: 3 EST: 2010
SALES (est): 127.8K Privately Held
SIC: 2711 Newspapers-Publishing/Printing

(G-8200)
NORMA INDUSTRIES
133 23rd St Se (98372-4117)
P.O. Box 905, Sumner (98390-0160)
PHONE.................................253 208-1728
Andy Fitterer, *Owner*
EMP: 5
SALES (est): 280K Privately Held
SIC: 3084 3523 5084 5046 Plastics pipe; farm machinery & equipment; industrial machinery & equipment; commercial equipment

(G-8201)
NORTHWEST CAB & COUNTERTOP LLC
14611 Meridian E Ste A (98375-6697)
PHONE.................................253 446-7193
Anthony Lenberg, *Principal*
EMP: 2
SALES (est): 183.1K Privately Held
SIC: 2434 Wood kitchen cabinets

(G-8202)
NORTHWEST CASCADE INC (PA)
Also Called: Honeybuckets
10412 John Bananola Way E (98374-9333)
P.O. Box 73399 (98373-0399)
PHONE.................................253 848-2371

Carl Liliequest, *President*
Tom Rogers, *Opers Staff*
Michael Sanford, *Engineer*
Melinda Wells, *Credit Mgr*
Denise Rice, *Sales Staff*
EMP: 180
SQ FT: 2,400
SALES (est): 127.9MM Privately Held
WEB: www.nwcascade.com
SIC: 1623 7359 7699 3272 Underground utilities contractor; portable toilet rental; septic tank cleaning service; septic tanks, concrete; septic system construction

(G-8203)
NORTHWEST CSTM CRATING BOX INC
10227 139th Street Ct E C2 (98374-6702)
PHONE.................................253 232-3244
Jennifer Summers, *President*
EMP: 2
SALES (est): 100K Privately Held
SIC: 2441 Nailed wood boxes & shook

(G-8204)
NORTHWEST ENVMTL & EQP INC
Also Called: NW Contractor Services
2319 E Pioneer Ste B (98372-3531)
PHONE.................................253 435-5115
Steve Barker, *President*
Karen Barker, *Corp Secy*
EMP: 5
SQ FT: 3,000
SALES (est): 1MM Privately Held
WEB: www.nwenviro.com
SIC: 3589 3823 5084 Commercial cleaning equipment; water quality monitoring & control systems; industrial machinery & equipment

(G-8205)
NORTHWEST ENVMTL SOLUTIONS INC
Also Called: N E S
15021 136th Ave E (98374-9460)
P.O. Box 1583, Sumner (98390-0330)
PHONE.................................253 241-6213
Kevin Wilkerson, *CEO*
EMP: 5
SALES (est): 650K Privately Held
SIC: 1389 Oil & gas field services

(G-8206)
NORTHWEST LCKNUT SPECIALTY INC
2323 7th St Se Apt R102 (98374-1131)
PHONE.................................253 604-4860
Jennifer M Derr, *President*
EMP: 2
SALES (est): 190K Privately Held
SIC: 3965 Fasteners

(G-8207)
NORTHWEST PRECAST LLC
212 10th St Se (98372-3403)
PHONE.................................253 770-9119
Timothy McGourty, *Owner*
Pam Kramlich, *Human Resources*
Mark Cooper, *Marketing Staff*
EMP: 30
SALES (est): 4.1MM
SALES (corp-wide): 2.5MM Privately Held
SIC: 3272 Concrete products, precast
PA: Northwest Precast, Llc.
2313 W Overland Rd
Boise ID 83705
208 331-8200

(G-8208)
NORTHWEST SERVICES
2019 86th Avenue Ct E (98371-1553)
PHONE.................................253 922-6475
Jackie Hoyt, *Owner*
EMP: 3
SALES (est): 302.9K Privately Held
SIC: 3715 Truck trailers

(G-8209)
OLD WOODWORKING INC
2203 Inter Ave Ste D (98372-3439)
PHONE.................................253 770-3650
EMP: 4 EST: 2005

SALES (est): 340K Privately Held
SIC: 2431 Mfg Millwork

(G-8210)
ONLY SOLUTIONS CABINET INSTALL
12517 164th St E (98374-9522)
PHONE.................................253 848-8358
Troy Murray, *Principal*
EMP: 3 EST: 2010
SALES (est): 150K Privately Held
SIC: 2491 Structural lumber & timber, treated wood

(G-8211)
OVERLOAD ELECTRIC WINDING SVCS
6119 56th Avenue Ct E (98371-4996)
PHONE.................................253 848-8900
Marilyn J Holway, *President*
Richard Holway, *Corp Secy*
EMP: 2
SALES (est): 100K Privately Held
SIC: 7694 Rewinding stators; electric motor repair

(G-8212)
P & J MACHINING INC
2601 Inter Ave (98372-3430)
P.O. Box 310 (98371-0032)
PHONE.................................253 841-0500
Paul D Hogoboom, *President*
EMP: 94 EST: 1979
SALES (est): 17.9MM Privately Held
WEB: www.pnjmachining.com
SIC: 3599 Machine shop, jobbing & repair

(G-8213)
P&A METAL FAB INC
1629 28th St Se (98372-5188)
PHONE.................................253 435-8947
Phil Aronson, *Branch Mgr*
EMP: 2
SALES (est): 133.4K Privately Held
SIC: 3444 Sheet metalwork
PA: Kyoshin Giken Y.K.
140-3, Hirai
Yamaguchi YMG 753-0

(G-8214)
P&J MACHINING INC
2607 Inter Ave (98372-3430)
PHONE.................................253 841-0500
Teri Hammons, *Principal*
Lori Hogoboom, *Principal*
Michael Hogoboom, *Principal*
Paul Hogoboom, *Principal*
EMP: 3 EST: 2015
SALES (est): 367.7K Privately Held
SIC: 3599 Machine shop, jobbing & repair

(G-8215)
PAC RITE INC
418 Valley Ave Nw Ste 105 (98371-3312)
P.O. Box 796, Auburn (98071-0796)
PHONE.................................253 833-7071
Al Dietz, *President*
Tracy Dietz, *Vice Pres*
EMP: 6
SALES (est): 960.1K Privately Held
SIC: 3086 2655 5113 Packaging & shipping materials, foamed plastic; fiber cans, drums & similar products; paper tubes & cores

(G-8216)
PACIFIC COAST SHOWCASE INC
Also Called: Idx
1601 Industrial Park Way # 101 (98371-3242)
PHONE.................................253 445-9000
William Naidenovich, *President*
Robert Cox, *Vice Pres*
Steve Page, *Controller*
▲ EMP: 160
SQ FT: 220,000
SALES (est): 22.8MM
SALES (corp-wide): 394.6MM Privately Held
WEB: www.idxseattle.com
SIC: 2541 2431 Store fixtures, wood; interior & ornamental woodwork & trim

Puyallup - Pierce County (G-8217) — GEOGRAPHIC SECTION

PA: Idx Corporation
1 Rider Trail Plaza Dr
Earth City MO 63045
314 739-4120

(G-8217)
PACIFIC CREST BUILDING PDTS
4227 S Meridian Ste C114 (98373-3603)
PHONE..................253 447-7686
John Horton, *President*
Shufen Zhou, *Director*
▲ EMP: 10 EST: 2016
SALES (est): 4.4MM **Privately Held**
SIC: 2431 Doors, wood

(G-8218)
PACIFIC NW PROBE & DRLG INC
7613 188th Street Ct E (98375-2368)
PHONE..................253 651-2477
Robert Warner, *Principal*
EMP: 4
SALES (est): 359.1K **Privately Held**
SIC: 1381 Service well drilling

(G-8219)
PARAMETRIX INC (PA)
1019 39th Ave Se Ste 100 (98374-2115)
PHONE..................206 394-3700
Jeff Peacock, *President*
Diane Lenius, *Vice Pres*
Robin McManus, *Vice Pres*
Darlene Brown, *CFO*
Holli Moeini, *Treasurer*
EMP: 70 EST: 1974
SQ FT: 29,000
SALES (est): 100.7MM **Privately Held**
WEB: www.parametrix.com
SIC: 8748 8711 8742 1389 Environmental consultant; sanitary engineers; business consultant; construction, repair & dismantling services; cargo loading & unloading services

(G-8220)
PDQ SIGNS
13702 Dana Ln E (98373-5327)
PHONE..................253 531-8010
Tom Brinkly, *Partner*
EMP: 2 EST: 1997
SALES (est): 130K **Privately Held**
SIC: 3993 Signs & advertising specialties

(G-8221)
PERFECTION POWDER COATING & FA
5402 184th St E Ste D (98375-2488)
PHONE..................253 875-0010
Michael H Crandall, *President*
EMP: 6
SALES (est): 734.4K **Privately Held**
SIC: 3479 Coating of metals & formed products

(G-8222)
PERKINS PERFORMANCE
11203 Benston Dr E # 110 (98372-2881)
PHONE..................253 389-9669
Jason Perkins, *Principal*
EMP: 4
SALES (est): 329.5K **Privately Held**
SIC: 3842 Welders' hoods

(G-8223)
PINNACLE STEEL FABRICATORS
14021 Pioneer Way E (98372-3667)
PHONE..................253 770-1690
Dain L Powell, *President*
Donna A Powell, *Corp Secy*
EMP: 13
SQ FT: 7,000
SALES (est): 1.3MM **Privately Held**
SIC: 3441 Fabricated structural metal

(G-8224)
PREMIER STAINLESS INSTALLERS
8719 178th Street Ct E (98375-6242)
PHONE..................253 370-0521
Mike Murphy, *Owner*
EMP: 2
SALES (est): 192.5K **Privately Held**
SIC: 3469 Kitchen fixtures & equipment: metal, except cast aluminum

(G-8225)
PRINT SOLUTIONS
10213 139th Street Ct E B2 (98374-3894)
PHONE..................253 435-1928
Bob Thomas, *Owner*
EMP: 2
SALES (est): 540K **Privately Held**
SIC: 2759 Screen printing

(G-8226)
PRO SALES INCORPORATED (PA)
917 Valley Ave Nw Ste C (98371-2528)
PHONE..................253 852-6046
Gregory S Wood, *President*
Alan Sanders, *Vice Pres*
Luther Saige, *Enginr/R&D Asst*
Maria Wood, *Treasurer*
Christine Sandmire, *Accounting Mgr*
▲ EMP: 30
SQ FT: 10,170
SALES (est): 14.6MM **Privately Held**
WEB: www.prosalesinc.com
SIC: 3556 Food products machinery

(G-8227)
PUGET SOUND SAFETY
10720 Woodland Ave E (98373-4183)
PHONE..................253 770-8888
Bret Tkacs, *Principal*
EMP: 7
SALES (est): 847.6K **Privately Held**
SIC: 3751 Motorcycles & related parts

(G-8228)
PUYALLUP CASKET COMPANY INC
11725 Valley Ave E (98372-5976)
PHONE..................253 845-1883
Louis G Geisert, *President*
▲ EMP: 8
SALES (est): 720K **Privately Held**
SIC: 3995 Burial caskets

(G-8229)
PUYALLUP SEPTIC PUMPING
1214 6th Ave Sw (98371-5726)
PHONE..................253 785-6553
EMP: 2
SALES (est): 107.4K **Privately Held**
SIC: 3561 1711 Pumps & pumping equipment; septic system construction

(G-8230)
QSP PACKERS LLC
2316 Inter Ave Ste D (98372-3419)
P.O. Box 1544, Sumner (98390-0320)
PHONE..................253 770-0315
Ron Ronald,
Mark Hartley,
Ron Roland,
EMP: 2
SQ FT: 2,000
SALES (est): 1MM **Privately Held**
WEB: www.qsppackers.com
SIC: 3559 3532 3533 Semiconductor manufacturing machinery; mining machinery; water well drilling equipment

(G-8231)
QUALITY USED TIRES AND WHEELS
7602 River Rd E (98371-3845)
PHONE..................253 446-6002
Silvestre Llamas, *Owner*
EMP: 2
SALES (est): 147.8K **Privately Held**
SIC: 3312 Wheels

(G-8232)
QUILTING FAIRY LLC
13507 Meridian E Ste O (98373-9132)
PHONE..................253 845-0462
Suzette Gallagher, *Administration*
EMP: 5
SALES (est): 75K **Privately Held**
SIC: 2211 Table cover fabrics, cotton

(G-8233)
R&J INDUSTRIES LLC
Also Called: Cap Supplies
402 Valley Ave Nw Ste 105 (98371-3310)
PHONE..................253 466-3627
Roger Atkinson, *Mng Member*
EMP: 7 EST: 2008
SALES (est): 1MM **Privately Held**
SIC: 3429 5031 5712 Cabinet hardware; kitchen cabinets; cabinet work, custom

(G-8234)
RANDLES SAND & GRAVEL INC (PA)
5802 192nd St E (98375-5500)
PHONE..................253 531-6800
David Randles, *President*
Helen Randles, *Treasurer*
EMP: 75 EST: 1960
SQ FT: 2,000
SALES (est): 23.7MM **Privately Held**
SIC: 1442 Construction sand & gravel

(G-8235)
RANDOMALITIES
15302 76th Avenue Ct E (98375-6983)
PHONE..................253 954-5704
Andrew Druschba, *Principal*
EMP: 4 EST: 2015
SALES (est): 83.8K **Privately Held**
SIC: 2711 Newspapers

(G-8236)
REM & AES LLC
15821 136th Avenue Ct E (98374-9687)
PHONE..................580 284-3410
Christopher Kelley, *Principal*
Kenneth Flores, *COO*
EMP: 2
SALES (est): 88.6K **Privately Held**
SIC: 4581 7349 3582 7389 Aircraft cleaning & janitorial service; hospital housekeeping; building cleaning service; ironers, commercial laundry & drycleaning;

(G-8237)
RICHARDSON BOTTLING COMPANY (PA)
Also Called: Mountain Mist
5410 189th St E (98375-2316)
P.O. Box 44427, Tacoma (98448-0427)
PHONE..................253 535-6447
Neil H Richardson, *President*
Paul K Fischer, *General Mgr*
Paul Fischer, *General Mgr*
Ricky Richardson, *Principal*
Paula M Richardson, *Vice Pres*
EMP: 30
SQ FT: 5,000
SALES (est): 25.3MM **Privately Held**
SIC: 2086 Water, pasteurized: packaged in cans, bottles, etc.

(G-8238)
ROD THUNFIELD & CUSTOM
16616 71st Ave E (98375-7258)
PHONE..................253 536-0373
John Versamack, *Partner*
EMP: 2
SALES (est): 173.8K **Privately Held**
SIC: 3089 Automotive parts, plastic

(G-8239)
ROYAL CABINETS
10324 Canyon Rd E (98373-1013)
PHONE..................253 267-5071
Dan McGinn, *President*
EMP: 2
SALES (est): 155.4K **Privately Held**
SIC: 2434 Wood kitchen cabinets

(G-8240)
ROYAL CABINETS INC
5410 96th St E (98371-6106)
PHONE..................253 536-6879
Dan McGinn, *President*
Julie McGinn, *Corp Secy*
EMP: 9
SALES (est): 1.1MM **Privately Held**
SIC: 2434 Wood kitchen cabinets

(G-8241)
RT INDUSTRIES
12524 127th St E (98374-3666)
PHONE..................253 219-8246
EMP: 2
SALES (est): 110.1K **Privately Held**
SIC: 3999 Manufacturing industries

(G-8242)
RW PRECAST INC
12216 138th Ave E (98374-4537)
P.O. Box 731209 (98373-0050)
PHONE..................253 770-0100
Ross Connors, *President*
EMP: 18
SALES (est): 1.4MM **Privately Held**
SIC: 3272 Precast terrazo or concrete products

(G-8243)
S&S INDUSTRIES LLC
17127 115th Ave E (98374-9574)
PHONE..................360 500-9942
Sandi Grimnes, *Principal*
EMP: 2 EST: 2014
SALES (est): 95.1K **Privately Held**
SIC: 3999 Manufacturing industries

(G-8244)
SAINT-GOBAIN PRFMCE PLAS CORP
507 N Levee Rd (98371-3224)
PHONE..................253 466-5400
John Downs, *Plant Mgr*
EMP: 115
SALES (corp-wide): 215.9MM **Privately Held**
WEB: www.plastics.saint-gobain.com
SIC: 3089 Thermoformed finished plastic products; plastic processing
HQ: Saint-Gobain Performance Plastics Corporation
31500 Solon Rd
Solon OH 44139
440 836-6900

(G-8245)
SALSA 7
506 N Meridian (98371-8639)
PHONE..................253 445-6525
EMP: 2
SALES (est): 70.4K **Privately Held**
SIC: 2099 Dips, except cheese & sour cream based

(G-8246)
SCOTT RL AND ASSOCIATES
11126 117th Street Ct E (98374-2142)
PHONE..................253 604-4006
Rl Scott, *Principal*
EMP: 3
SALES (est): 164K **Privately Held**
SIC: 3053 Packing materials

(G-8247)
SEAMAX ENTERPRISES INC
4227 S Meridian (98373-3603)
PHONE..................206 323-8886
Gary Chen, *President*
▲ EMP: 12
SQ FT: 90,000
SALES: 3MM **Privately Held**
SIC: 2452 Sauna rooms, prefabricated, wood

(G-8248)
SEATAC PACKAGING MFG CORP
901 N Levee Rd (98371-3220)
PHONE..................253 682-6588
Scott Huang, *President*
Stephanie Huang, *Treasurer*
David Huang, *Admin Sec*
▲ EMP: 75
SQ FT: 86,000
SALES (est): 19.3MM **Privately Held**
WEB: www.seatacpackaging.com
SIC: 2674 Paper bags: made from purchased materials

(G-8249)
SEATTLE ECO COATINGS
9722 Canyon Rd E (98373-1060)
PHONE..................253 539-1113
Scott Steckler, *President*
EMP: 2
SALES (est): 165.9K **Privately Held**
SIC: 2952 Coating compounds, tar

(G-8250)
SEATTLE SEAMS
13617 165th St E (98374-9134)
PHONE..................206 251-8231

GEOGRAPHIC SECTION

Quilcene - Jefferson County (G-8282)

Randy Hazelton, *Principal*
EMP: 2
SALES (est): 64.5K **Privately Held**
SIC: 2393 Textile bags

(G-8251)
SEATTLE TURBINE INC
Also Called: Seattle Turbine Parts
16706 103rd Avenue Ct E (98374-3766)
PHONE.................................253 770-7567
Ray Frye, *President*
▲ EMP: 3 EST: 1999
SQ FT: 3,000
SALES (est): 320K **Privately Held**
SIC: 3728 Aircraft parts & equipment

(G-8252)
SEW ATHLETIC JACKETS AND MORE
12110 Meridian E (98373-3407)
PHONE.................................253 446-7115
Bruce Lewis, *Owner*
EMP: 2
SALES (est): 64.2K **Privately Held**
SIC: 5699 2395 Customized clothing & apparel; embroidery & art needlework

(G-8253)
SHAW ROAD DEVELOPMENT LLC (PA)
1001 Shaw Rd (98372-7437)
PHONE.................................253 845-9544
Daniel R Absher,
Thomas L Absher,
Clark E Helle,
Gregory Helle,
Bradley Sayre,
EMP: 1
SQ FT: 12,000
SALES (est): 1MM **Privately Held**
SIC: 2452 Panels & sections, prefabricated, wood

(G-8254)
SHOPE ENTERPRISES INC
1618 E Main (98372-3142)
PHONE.................................253 848-1551
Gary L Hall, *President*
Gary Pattee, *Vice Pres*
Stacey Tejel, *Admin Sec*
EMP: 45
SQ FT: 12,000
SALES (est): 8.3MM **Privately Held**
WEB: www.shopeconcrete.com
SIC: 3272 Concrete products, precast

(G-8255)
SOUTH HILL CABINETS
8418 75th Ave E (98371-6516)
PHONE.................................253 848-2026
Michael Rupp, *Principal*
EMP: 2
SALES (est): 178.2K **Privately Held**
SIC: 2434 Wood kitchen cabinets

(G-8256)
SULLY N A SAINT-GOBAIN
507 N Levee Rd (98371-3224)
PHONE.................................253 466-5417
Robert Hoffman, *Principal*
EMP: 6 EST: 2015
SALES (est): 576.2K **Privately Held**
SIC: 3089 Thermoformed finished plastic products

(G-8257)
SUMNER LAWN N SAW LLC
9318 State Route 162 E (98372-4117)
PHONE.................................253 435-9284
Rick Longnicker, *Mng Member*
EMP: 10
SALES (est): 603.2K **Privately Held**
WEB: www.sumnerlawn.com
SIC: 5261 5251 7699 3546 Lawnmowers & tractors; chainsaws; lawn mower repair shop; engine parts & replacement, non-automotive; saws & sawing equipment;

(G-8258)
SWEENY INDUSTRIES
13915 120th St E (98374-2421)
PHONE.................................510 701-0384
Niall Sweeny, *Owner*
EMP: 2 EST: 2010

SALES: 76K **Privately Held**
SIC: 3999 Barber & beauty shop equipment

(G-8259)
SWEENY INDUSTRIES ✪
17202 110th Ave E (98374-9509)
PHONE.................................253 446-7298
Niall Sweeny, *Principal*
EMP: 2 EST: 2018
SALES (est): 126.9K **Privately Held**
SIC: 3999 Manufacturing industries

(G-8260)
T&C CONCEPTS LLC
5609 114th Avenue Ct E (98372-2720)
PHONE.................................253 298-2104
James Bill, *Principal*
EMP: 2
SALES (est): 94.5K **Privately Held**
SIC: 3444 Awnings & canopies

(G-8261)
TAGORBI PUBLISHING LLC
13802 93rd Ave E (98373-6200)
PHONE.................................253 466-3214
Rayna Stiner, *Principal*
EMP: 2
SALES (est): 63.9K **Privately Held**
SIC: 2741 Miscellaneous publishing

(G-8262)
TAYLOR-MADE PRINTING INC
217 W Stewart (98371-4393)
PHONE.................................253 881-1624
Aaron Taylor, *President*
EMP: 5
SALES (est): 749.8K **Privately Held**
SIC: 2752 Commercial printing, offset

(G-8263)
THUNDER SPECIALTY PRINTING
8308 Woodland Ave E (98371-5535)
PHONE.................................253 921-7647
EMP: 2
SALES (est): 156K **Privately Held**
SIC: 2752 Commercial printing, lithographic

(G-8264)
TI NORTHWEST CORP
121 23rd St Se (98372-4117)
PHONE.................................253 445-4104
Susan Matthews, *President*
EMP: 18
SQ FT: 5,000
SALES (est): 2.4MM **Privately Held**
SIC: 3444 3441 1711 Sheet metalwork; fabricated structural metal; plumbing, heating, air-conditioning contractors

(G-8265)
UCOINITCOM LLC
18517 111th Ave E (98374-8864)
PHONE.................................253 271-0656
James Peters,
EMP: 2
SALES (est): 108K **Privately Held**
SIC: 3999 Manufacturing industries

(G-8266)
UNICON INTERNATIONAL INC
Also Called: UNICON INTERNATIONAL INCORPORATED
7502 135th Street Ct E (98373-5363)
PHONE.................................253 539-7533
John Piwtorak, *Principal*
EMP: 51
SALES (corp-wide): 17.8MM **Privately Held**
WEB: www.unicon-intl.com
SIC: 2448 Cargo containers, wood & wood with metal
PA: Unicon International, Inc.
   241 Outerbelt St
   Columbus OH 43213
   614 861-7070

(G-8267)
UP TO GRADE CONCRETE PRODUCTS
811 7th St Nw (98371-4141)
PHONE.................................253 845-3677
Jan Kuhchick, *Owner*
EMP: 13

SALES (est): 1MM **Privately Held**
SIC: 3272 Concrete products

(G-8268)
URETHANE CAST PARTS INC
5612 163rd St E (98375-9003)
PHONE.................................253 539-4282
Joe Schramm, *President*
EMP: 4
SQ FT: 10,000
SALES (est): 449.7K **Privately Held**
SIC: 3089 Molding primary plastic

(G-8269)
US SIGN ONE LLC
7808 River Rd E (98371-3841)
PHONE.................................253 236-8074
Tuan Le, *Administration*
EMP: 2
SALES (est): 67.4K **Privately Held**
SIC: 3993 Signs & advertising specialties

(G-8270)
VALLEY PRINTING INC
4601 6th Street Pl Se A (98374-5789)
PHONE.................................253 845-0960
William Olson, *Principal*
EMP: 2
SALES (est): 126.6K **Privately Held**
SIC: 2752 Commercial printing, offset

(G-8271)
VAN HORN MFD HOMES
15216 91st Avenue Ct E (98375-6891)
PHONE.................................253 370-7263
Mary V Horn, *Principal*
EMP: 2
SALES (est): 86.7K **Privately Held**
SIC: 2451 Mobile homes

(G-8272)
VANCOUVER DOOR COMPANY INC
203 5th St Nw (98371-4334)
P.O. Box 1418 (98371-0198)
PHONE.................................253 845-9581
Louise Hill, *President*
Lanny Glace, *Senior VP*
Gary Johnson, *Purchasing*
EMP: 30
SQ FT: 50,000
SALES (est): 5.8MM **Privately Held**
WEB: www.vancouverdoorco.com
SIC: 2431 Doors, wood

(G-8273)
VM SOLUTIONS INC
Also Called: Vm Products
11208 62nd Ave E (98373-4348)
P.O. Box 44926, Tacoma (98448-0926)
PHONE.................................253 841-2939
Dave Brown, *President*
Percival Tapia, *Opers Mgr*
Tom Reep, *Sales Staff*
EMP: 11
SQ FT: 10,500
SALES: 450K
SALES (corp-wide): 4.8MM **Privately Held**
WEB: www.vmproducts.net
SIC: 3825 Current measuring equipment
PA: United Western Technologies Corp.
   122 S 4th Ave
   Pasco WA 99301
   509 544-0720

(G-8274)
VRIEZE & OLSON CUSTOM WDWKG
2313 E Pioneer (98372-3527)
PHONE.................................253 445-9733
Larry Vrieze, *President*
Ron Olson, *Vice Pres*
Kevin Reagan, *Sales Staff*
EMP: 14 EST: 1997
SALES (est): 1MM **Privately Held**
SIC: 2541 2431 Cabinets, except refrigerated: show, display, etc.: wood; millwork

(G-8275)
W & S ENTERPRISES
12602 106th Avenue Ct E (98374-2711)
PHONE.................................253 848-9189
Warren Bayard, *Owner*
Sheila Bayarrad, *Partner*

EMP: 2
SALES (est): 140.2K **Privately Held**
SIC: 2434 Wood kitchen cabinets

(G-8276)
WAL MED INC
11302 164th St E (98374-9760)
PHONE.................................253 845-6633
Nancy O'Farrell, *President*
Jane Smitherman, *Corp Secy*
EMP: 8
SQ FT: 8,000
SALES (est): 933.9K **Privately Held**
SIC: 2992 5122 Lubricating oils & greases; drugs, proprietaries & sundries

(G-8277)
WATTS SPECIALTIES LLC
2323 E Pioneer Ste A (98372-3502)
PHONE.................................253 848-9288
James Collins, *President*
Teresa Collins, *Vice Pres*
▲ EMP: 10
SALES (est): 2.8MM **Privately Held**
SIC: 3548 Welding & cutting apparatus & accessories

(G-8278)
WEGNERS WIRE INC
7308 139th Street Ct E (98373-8218)
PHONE.................................253 535-0945
Art Wegner, *President*
Kathlyn Betzig, *Chairman*
EMP: 3
SALES (est): 100K **Privately Held**
SIC: 3679 Harness assemblies for electronic use: wire or cable

(G-8279)
WESTERN ENERGY GROUP INC
9817 132nd Street Ct E D (98373-9118)
PHONE.................................253 306-4748
Aaron Segovia, *CEO*
EMP: 2
SALES (est): 125.1K **Privately Held**
SIC: 1389 Oil & gas field services

Quil Ceda Village
Snohomish County

(G-8280)
BLAZE METRICS LLC
8825 34th Ave Ne L-190 (98271-8085)
PHONE.................................206 972-3890
Richard Becker,
EMP: 7
SALES: 1.8MM **Privately Held**
SIC: 3845 Electromedical equipment

(G-8281)
ROY PABLO
Also Called: Cosalish Design & Lighting
8825 34th Ave Ne (98271-8085)
PHONE.................................425 750-9941
Roy Pablo, *Owner*
EMP: 3 EST: 2017
SALES (est): 197.4K **Privately Held**
SIC: 3993 3646 7389 1542 Electric signs; neon signs; commercial indusl & institutional electric lighting fixtures; ; commercial & office building contractors

Quilcene
Jefferson County

(G-8282)
DOE RUN STUDIOS
Also Called: Custom and Production Woodwork
13th Doe Run Rd (98376)
PHONE.................................360 765-0935
Kathleen Kler, *Owner*
David Haakenson, *Co-Owner*
EMP: 2
SALES: 35K **Privately Held**
SIC: 2499 3479 Decorative wood & woodwork; engraving jewelry silverware, or metal

Quilcene - Jefferson County (G-8283)

(G-8283)
DUNCAN J WOODWORKING
50 Cemetary Rd (98376-8555)
PHONE.................................360 765-0745
James Duncan, *Owner*
EMP: 2
SALES (est): 194K **Privately Held**
SIC: 2431 Millwork

(G-8284)
HANDLY & PHILLIPS LOGGING INC
Also Called: P & G Timber
Camelot Rd (98376)
P.O. Box 373 (98376-0373)
PHONE.................................360 765-3578
Pat Handly, *Principal*
EMP: 3
SALES (est): 190K **Privately Held**
SIC: 2411 Logging camps & contractors

(G-8285)
KEN DRESSLER
Also Called: Quilcene Marine
1731 Linger Longer Rd (98376-9523)
P.O. Box 98 (98376-0098)
PHONE.................................360 765-3131
Ken Dressler, *Owner*
EMP: 3 EST: 1996
SALES (est): 135K **Privately Held**
SIC: 3731 Lighters, marine: building & repairing

(G-8286)
KITH D LAZELLES NTURE PHTGRPHY
1634 Toandos Rd (98376)
P.O. Box 192 (98376-0192)
PHONE.................................360 765-3697
Keith D Lazelle, *Owner*
EMP: 2
SALES (est): 80K **Privately Held**
WEB: www.keithlazelle.com
SIC: 2741 7221 Art copy & poster publishing; photographer, still or video

(G-8287)
PENNY CREEK QUARRY
450 Penny Creek Rd (98376-8533)
PHONE.................................360 765-3413
R Gary Philips, *Owner*
Mary Philips, *Co-Owner*
Kris Maki, *Manager*
EMP: 7 EST: 1990
SALES (est): 790.6K **Privately Held**
SIC: 1422 Cement rock, crushed & broken-quarrying

Quincy
Grant County

(G-8288)
ANCIENT LAKE WINE COMPANY LLC
795 Beverly Burke Rd N (98848-9090)
PHONE.................................509 787-2022
Jerry Milbrandt, *Mng Member*
Janie Milbrandt,
EMP: 12 EST: 2014
SALES (est): 950K **Privately Held**
SIC: 5182 2084 Wine; wines

(G-8289)
BASIN NATION AG LLC
8858 Road U Nw (98848-9630)
PHONE.................................509 289-9030
Scott Hodges, *Principal*
EMP: 2 EST: 2009
SALES (est): 100K **Privately Held**
SIC: 3589 Water treatment equipment, industrial

(G-8290)
BLUELINE EQUIPMENT CO LLC
Also Called: Kubota Authorized Dealer
603 Frontage Rd (98848)
PHONE.................................509 785-2595
Gregg Marrs, *Branch Mgr*
EMP: 2
SALES (corp-wide): 11.5MM **Privately Held**
SIC: 3523 Farm machinery & equipment
HQ: Blueline Equipment Co., Llc
1605 E Mead Ave
Yakima WA 98903
509 248-8411

(G-8291)
CASCADE RIDGE INDUSTRIES
3559 Road K Nw (98848-9748)
PHONE.................................509 237-1534
Patrick C Miller, *Principal*
EMP: 3
SALES (est): 163.2K **Privately Held**
SIC: 3999 Manufacturing industries

(G-8292)
CAVE B ESTATE WINERY
344 Silica Rd Nw (98848-9468)
PHONE.................................509 785-3500
Miranda Porterfield, *Principal*
EMP: 2
SALES (est): 155.9K **Privately Held**
SIC: 2084 Wines

(G-8293)
CENTRAL MARKET INCORPORATED
726 Central Ave S (98848-1358)
PHONE.................................509 787-5100
Allan Dearie, *CEO*
EMP: 7
SALES (est): 477.8K **Privately Held**
SIC: 2099 Food preparations

(G-8294)
CENTURION ENTERPRISES
Also Called: Code 3
107 D St Sw (98848-1210)
P.O. Box 725 (98848-0725)
PHONE.................................509 787-2345
George A Nutter, *President*
Pam Nutter, *Owner*
EMP: 2 EST: 1980
SALES (est): 120K **Privately Held**
SIC: 2396 5949 Screen printing on fabric articles; sewing, needlework & piece goods

(G-8295)
CROCKERS FISH OIL INC
214 6th Ave Ne (98848-9666)
PHONE.................................509 787-4983
Richard Freese, *President*
EMP: 2
SALES (est): 200K **Privately Held**
SIC: 2077 5191 5261 Fish oil; chemicals, agricultural; fertilizer & fertilizer materials; fertilizer

(G-8296)
DODSON RD ORCHARD LLC
Also Called: Jones Produce Dehy
903 A St Se (98848-1586)
P.O. Box 487 (98848-0487)
PHONE.................................509 787-3537
Mike Jones, *Principal*
EMP: 60
SALES (est): 5.9MM **Privately Held**
SIC: 2034 2099 Dehydrated fruits, vegetables, soups; food preparations

(G-8297)
ERICKSON TANK & PUMP LLC
Also Called: Erickson, Erick R
800 Road P.5 Sw (98848-8835)
PHONE.................................509 785-2955
Erick R Erickson, *Partner*
Erick L Erickson, *Partner*
EMP: 12
SALES (est): 2.5MM **Privately Held**
WEB: www.ericksontank.com
SIC: 3561 3443 Pumps, domestic: water or sump; fabricated plate work (boiler shop)

(G-8298)
ERRANT CELLARS
303 N St Sw (98848-1659)
PHONE.................................509 289-9660
EMP: 4 EST: 2012
SALES (est): 210.2K **Privately Held**
SIC: 2084 Wines

(G-8299)
GRIGG FARMS LLC (PA)
12139 Road 6 Nw (98848-9732)
PHONE.................................509 787-3225
Lorin A Grigg, *Mng Member*
EMP: 20
SALES (est): 2.7MM **Privately Held**
SIC: 0723 0161 3999 Vegetable packing services; onion farm; advertising curtains

(G-8300)
IMERYS MINERALS CALIFORNIA INC
16419 Road 10.5 Nw (98848-9667)
P.O. Box 636 (98848-0636)
PHONE.................................509 787-4575
Ron Matthews, *Facilities Mgr*
John Moritz, *Branch Mgr*
EMP: 69
SALES (corp-wide): 3MM **Privately Held**
SIC: 1459 3295 Clays (common) quarrying; minerals, ground or treated
HQ: Imerys Minerals California, Inc.
2500 San Miguelito Rd
Lompoc CA 93436

(G-8301)
LAMB WESTON INC
1005 E St Sw (98848-1931)
P.O. Box 368 (98848-0368)
PHONE.................................509 787-3567
Pam Nutter, *Branch Mgr*
EMP: 509
SALES (corp-wide): 3.4B **Publicly Held**
SIC: 2099 Food preparations
HQ: Lamb Weston Inc
599 S Rivershore Ln
Eagle ID 83616

(G-8302)
LLC PUTNAM BROTHERS
16995 Frenchman Hills Rd (98848-9561)
PHONE.................................509 679-4981
Sean E Putnam, *Principal*
EMP: 2
SALES (est): 150.9K **Privately Held**
SIC: 3993 Signs & advertising specialties

(G-8303)
MATERIAL INC
Also Called: Quincy Auto Parts
305 F St Se (98848-1445)
P.O. Box 66 (98848-0066)
PHONE.................................509 787-4585
Armando Martinez, *Manager*
EMP: 4
SALES (corp-wide): 7.7MM **Privately Held**
SIC: 5531 5013 3599 Automotive parts; motor vehicle supplies & new parts; machine shop, jobbing & repair
PA: Material Inc
1050 Basin St Sw
Ephrata WA 98823
509 754-4695

(G-8304)
MICROSOFT CORPORATION
501 Port Industrial Way (98848-1074)
PHONE.................................509 787-6900
Nicol Chadek, *Sales Staff*
Darayl Amundson, *Branch Mgr*
Brendan Acheson, *Manager*
Brandon Diersch, *Manager*
Scott McBride, *Manager*
EMP: 100
SALES (corp-wide): 110.3B **Publicly Held**
WEB: www.microsoft.com
SIC: 7372 Application computer software
PA: Microsoft Corporation
1 Microsoft Way
Redmond WA 98052
425 882-8080

(G-8305)
MONUMENT APPLES LLC
13762 Road 11 Nw (98848-9672)
PHONE.................................509 787-5700
EMP: 2
SALES (est): 85.9K **Privately Held**
SIC: 3571 Personal computers (microcomputers)

(G-8306)
PIONEER METAL WORKS INC
512 F St Se (98848-1498)
PHONE.................................509 787-4425
Ralph Andrews, *President*
Sharon Andrews, *Corp Secy*
EMP: 9 EST: 1978
SQ FT: 9,000
SALES (est): 1MM **Privately Held**
WEB: www.pioneermetalworks.com
SIC: 7538 7692 General automotive repair shops; welding repair

(G-8307)
QUINCY FOODS LLC
222 Columbia Way (98848-9072)
P.O. Box 127 (98848-0127)
PHONE.................................509 787-4521
George Smith,
▲ EMP: 5
SALES (est): 1.2MM
SALES (corp-wide): 972.1MM **Privately Held**
SIC: 2037 Frozen fruits & vegetables
PA: Norpac Foods, Inc.
3225 25th St Se
Salem OR 97302
503 480-2100

(G-8308)
QUINCY FRESH FRUIT LLC
1015 Industrial Pkwy (98848)
PHONE.................................509 787-7100
EMP: 15 EST: 2012
SALES (est): 3.5MM **Privately Held**
SIC: 2033 Fruits: packaged in cans, jars, etc.

(G-8309)
SAINT LAURENT WINERY
9224 Road S Nw (98848-8964)
PHONE.................................509 787-3700
EMP: 2 EST: 2007
SALES (est): 100K **Privately Held**
SIC: 2084 Mfg Wines/Brandy/Spirits

(G-8310)
WASHINGTON FRUIT & PRODUCE CO
19253 Road 5 Sw (98848-9809)
PHONE.................................509 932-7981
Nick Plath, *President*
EMP: 50
SALES (est): 2.1MM **Privately Held**
SIC: 2037 Frozen fruits & vegetables

(G-8311)
WASHINGTON JONES TASTING ROOM
2101 F St Sw (98848-1926)
PHONE.................................509 787-8108
EMP: 2
SALES (est): 89.9K **Privately Held**
SIC: 2084 Wines

Rainier
Thurston County

(G-8312)
COLBURN TIMBER INC
115 Rainier Estates Ct Se (98576-9518)
P.O. Box 435, South Bend (98586-0435)
PHONE.................................360 875-6565
Kevin Colburn, *President*
EMP: 3
SALES (est): 149.9K **Privately Held**
SIC: 2411 Logging

(G-8313)
DC ENGINEERING CONSULTING INC
15946 Woodbrook Ln Se (98576-9670)
P.O. Box 2768, Yelm (98597-2768)
PHONE.................................360 932-2367
Douglas Cabrera, *President*
EMP: 2 EST: 2017
SALES (est): 54.1K **Privately Held**
SIC: 7389 8711 3625 ; engineering services; electrical or electronic engineering; energy conservation engineering; relays & industrial controls

GEOGRAPHIC SECTION

Raymond - Pacific County (G-8347)

(G-8314)
DMFRANK PUBLICATION
404 California Ave N (98576-9567)
PHONE..................................360 446-6113
Diane Frank, *Principal*
EMP: 4 EST: 2008
SALES (est): 258.2K Privately Held
SIC: 2741 Miscellaneous publishing

(G-8315)
FROM FIELD
16909 Rivendale Ln Se (98576-9623)
PHONE..................................360 446-7689
EMP: 2
SALES (est): 162.3K Privately Held
SIC: 2741 Miscellaneous publishing

(G-8316)
LB STEELE CABINET CO
12935 Reo Rd Se (98576-9712)
PHONE..................................360 446-4114
L B Steele, *Principal*
EMP: 2
SALES (est): 293.7K Privately Held
SIC: 2434 Wood kitchen cabinets

(G-8317)
LIVING FREE
Also Called: Living Free Press
13144 Horizon Pionr Rd Se (98576-5003)
PHONE..................................360 446-3032
Betty A Johnson, *Owner*
EMP: 2
SALES (est): 100.2K Privately Held
SIC: 2731 Books: publishing only

(G-8318)
MOUNTAIN SIDE SAND & GRAV LLC
307 Binghampton St Se (98576-9577)
P.O. Box 610 (98576-0610)
PHONE..................................360 701-1241
Howard Wheeler, *Principal*
EMP: 2
SALES (est): 66K Privately Held
SIC: 1442 Construction sand & gravel

(G-8319)
NORMANDIE WOODWORKS
10915 128th Ave Se (98576-9711)
PHONE..................................360 446-0352
Hervieux Bruno, *President*
EMP: 2
SALES (est): 170.8K Privately Held
SIC: 2431 Woodwork, interior & ornamental

(G-8320)
PROJECT MACHINE INC
13424 State Route 507 (98576-9730)
P.O. Box 1086 (98576-1086)
PHONE..................................360 446-2858
Earl Fain, *President*
EMP: 2
SALES (est): 111.6K Privately Held
SIC: 3599 Machine shop, jobbing & repair

(G-8321)
REDWOOD INSTRUMENT CO
Also Called: Rico Instruments
17248 Rivendale Ln Se # 5 (98576-9600)
PHONE..................................360 446-2860
Peter Newgard, *President*
Eunice Newgard, *Vice Pres*
EMP: 5
SQ FT: 864
SALES: 50K Privately Held
WEB: www.ricoleaktest.com
SIC: 3841 3812 Surgical & medical instruments; aircraft flight instruments

(G-8322)
RV ALPACAS
10801 133rd Ave Se (98576-9761)
PHONE..................................253 431-6747
EMP: 2
SALES (est): 92.7K Privately Held
SIC: 2231 Alpacas, mohair: woven

(G-8323)
WEYERHAEUSER COMPANY
Also Called: Oregon Division-Raw Materials
16506 Vail Loop Se (98576-9647)
P.O. Box 889 (98576-0889)
PHONE..................................360 446-2420
Pat Brennan, *Branch Mgr*
EMP: 150
SALES (corp-wide): 7.4B Publicly Held
SIC: 2411 0851 Logging camps & contractors; forestry services
PA: Weyerhaeuser Company
220 Occidental Ave S
Seattle WA 98104
206 539-3000

Randle
Lewis County

(G-8324)
CEDAR GROVE WOOD SPECIALTY
109 Cedar Grove Rd (98377-9000)
PHONE..................................360 494-5295
Rhonda Oborne, *Principal*
EMP: 2
SALES (est): 145.1K Privately Held
SIC: 2449 Wood containers

(G-8325)
HAMPTON DIST COMPANIES LLC
Also Called: Hampton Lumber Cowlitz
10166 Us Highway 12 (98377)
P.O. Box 189 (98377-0189)
PHONE..................................360 496-5115
Ken Rankin, *Manager*
EMP: 100
SALES (corp-wide): 39.8MM Privately Held
SIC: 2421 Planing mills
PA: Hampton Distribution Companies, Llc
9600 Sw Barnes Rd Ste 200
Portland OR 97225
503 297-7691

(G-8326)
KAREN NICHOLS
Also Called: Dusty Shelf
995 Peters Rd (98377-9617)
PHONE..................................360 497-2778
Karen Nichols, *Owner*
EMP: 2
SALES (est): 86.8K Privately Held
SIC: 3229 Tableware, glass or glass ceramic

(G-8327)
RANDLE STEEL & MACHINE INC
117 Kehoe Rd (98377-9202)
PHONE..................................360 497-7477
Edith Bemis, *President*
Daniel Bemis, *Admin Sec*
EMP: 6
SQ FT: 6,000
SALES (est): 330K Privately Held
SIC: 3599 Machine shop, jobbing & repair

Ravensdale
King County

(G-8328)
AENEAS VALLEY CNSTR & LOG
27027 316th Ave Se (98051-9503)
PHONE..................................206 391-8408
Ronny Markus, *Principal*
EMP: 3
SALES (est): 240.2K Privately Held
SIC: 2411 Logging

(G-8329)
AEROFAB INC
27924 Se 268th St (98051-8814)
PHONE..................................253 863-8402
Jamie Tindall, *President*
EMP: 2 EST: 2010
SALES (est): 196.2K Privately Held
SIC: 3531 Construction machinery

(G-8330)
BAYER HEALTHCARE LLC
29335 333rd Ave Se (98051-9068)
PHONE..................................360 886-8182
EMP: 3
SALES (corp-wide): 45.3B Privately Held
SIC: 2834 Pharmaceutical preparations
HQ: Bayer Healthcare Llc
100 Bayer Blvd
Whippany NJ 07981
862 404-3000

(G-8331)
BAYNE JUNCTION WOODWORKS
32750 343rd Ave Se (98051-8940)
P.O. Box 106 (98051-0106)
PHONE..................................360 886-8908
EMP: 3 EST: 2014
SALES (est): 210.7K Privately Held
SIC: 2431 Millwork

(G-8332)
BREMMEYER LOGGING (PA)
27034 Se Kent Kangley Rd (98051-9584)
P.O. Box 245 (98051-0245)
PHONE..................................425 432-9310
Bill Bremmeyer, *Owner*
EMP: 20
SQ FT: 3,000
SALES (est): 1.2MM Privately Held
SIC: 2411 Logging camps & contractors

(G-8333)
BULLOCK MACHINING CO
26212 244th Ave Se (98051-9767)
PHONE..................................425 432-8261
Robert Bullock, *Partner*
Dorene Bullock, *Partner*
EMP: 3
SALES (est): 230K Privately Held
SIC: 3599 Machine & other job shop work

(G-8334)
EDINGER MFG INC
24705 Se Summit Landsbrg (98051)
PHONE..................................425 413-4008
Loretta Edinger, *Principal*
EMP: 2
SALES (est): 120K Privately Held
SIC: 3999 Manufacturing industries

(G-8335)
ELKWOOD CUSTOM CABINETRY LLC
32022 Se Rtreat Knsket Rd (98051-9054)
PHONE..................................360 886-1989
Kenneth Winkler, *Principal*
EMP: 2 EST: 2008
SALES (est): 174.5K Privately Held
SIC: 2434 Wood kitchen cabinets

(G-8336)
GO2ORIGINS LLC
29232 305th Ct Se (98051-9087)
P.O. Box 488 (98051-0488)
PHONE..................................425 413-4134
Stacy Jayne King-Murrey,
EMP: 2
SALES (est): 225.8K Privately Held
SIC: 3089 1531 7389 Casting of plastic; ; design, commercial & industrial

(G-8337)
GREEN RIVER WELDING
33830 Se Grn Rvr Hdwrks R (98051-8913)
PHONE..................................253 632-7551
Eric Phillip Konop, *President*
EMP: 3
SALES (est): 115.7K Privately Held
SIC: 7692 Welding repair

(G-8338)
OLYMPIC EMBROIDERY
28815 Se 258th St (98051-8607)
P.O. Box 1359 (98051-1218)
PHONE..................................425 413-2848
Brian Duncan, *Principal*
EMP: 20 EST: 1998
SALES (est): 1MM Privately Held
WEB: www.olympicembroidery.com
SIC: 2395 Embroidery products, except schiffli machine; embroidery & art needlework

(G-8339)
PROJUL INC (PA)
27924 Se 268th St (98051-8814)
PHONE..................................844 776-5853
Kurt Clayson, *President*
EMP: 2

SALES: 500K Privately Held
SIC: 7372 Business oriented computer software

(G-8340)
RESERVE INDUSTRIES CORPORATION
Also Called: Reserve Silica
28131 Rvnsdale Blck Diamn (98051-8212)
P.O. Box 99 (98051-0099)
PHONE..................................425 432-1241
Pete Cawlfield, *Branch Mgr*
EMP: 5
SQ FT: 2,811
SALES (corp-wide): 2MM Privately Held
WEB: www.reservesilica.com
SIC: 1446 Silica sand mining
PA: Reserve Industries Corporation
20 First Plaza Ctr Nw # 308
Albuquerque NM 87102
505 247-2384

Raymond
Pacific County

(G-8341)
AUNT DONNAS
1725 Ocean Ave (98577-2813)
PHONE..................................206 519-0143
EMP: 2
SALES (est): 105.7K Privately Held
SIC: 0139 3999 ;

(G-8342)
BAYVIEW REDI MIX INC
2835 Ocean Ave (98577-4909)
P.O. Box 165, Aberdeen (98520-0044)
PHONE..................................360 875-9993
Darin Prince, *Branch Mgr*
EMP: 3
SALES (corp-wide): 4.9MM Privately Held
SIC: 3273 Ready-mixed concrete
PA: Bayview Redi Mix, Inc.
100 Hagara St
Aberdeen WA 98520
360 533-7372

(G-8343)
BEANS & ROCKS LLC (PA)
Also Called: Hawk's Superior Rock
60 Hines Valley Rd (98577)
PHONE..................................360 942-5414
Rosalyn Erickson,
EMP: 10
SALES (est): 460.9K Privately Held
SIC: 1442 5032 Gravel mining; gravel

(G-8344)
C D BOAT WORKS
1001 Harrison Ave (98577-4404)
PHONE..................................360 942-3669
EMP: 2 EST: 2011
SALES (est): 75K Privately Held
SIC: 3732 Boatbuilding/Repairing

(G-8345)
CHRIS BARBER APPLE
2101 Henkle St (98577-4016)
PHONE..................................360 875-8112
EMP: 2
SALES (est): 85.9K Privately Held
SIC: 3571 Mfg Electronic Computers

(G-8346)
COLBURN TIMBER INC
1262 Sr6 (98577)
PHONE..................................360 208-4501
Kevin T Colburn, *Principal*
EMP: 10
SALES (est): 1.1MM Privately Held
SIC: 2411 Logging

(G-8347)
EVERGREEN PRODUCTION LLC
2870 Ocean Ave Bldg 1 (98577-4906)
P.O. Box 254, South Bend (98586-0254)
PHONE..................................206 818-5054
David Jett, *CEO*
Neil Halpern, *Principal*
Cory Mason, *Principal*
Drew Satterlee, *Principal*
EMP: 6 EST: 2013

Raymond - Pacific County (G-8348)

SQ FT: 11,250
SALES (est): 154.8K Privately Held
SIC: 0139 2079 ; edible oil products, except corn oil

(G-8348)
FAR WEST INC
401 Monohon Landing Rd (98577-9209)
PHONE..................360 942-3270
Scott Stephens, *President*
Arvor Hadlock, *Vice Pres*
Norma Stephens, *Treasurer*
EMP: 3
SALES: 268K Privately Held
SIC: 2411 Logging

(G-8349)
FLANNERY PUBLICATIONS LLC
168 Stauffer Rd (98577-9310)
PHONE..................360 942-0060
Flannery Properties, *Principal*
EMP: 2
SALES (est): 135.9K Privately Held
SIC: 2741 Miscellaneous publishing

(G-8350)
GREEN LABS LLC
45 Raymond South Bend Rd (98577-9624)
PHONE..................360 875-5556
Cristina Toader, *Mng Member*
Fabian Toader, *Mng Member*
EMP: 2
SALES (est): 155.2K Privately Held
SIC: 0139 3999 ;

(G-8351)
GRIGSBY SOFTWARE DEVELOPM
656 Barnhart St Ste C (98577-3504)
PHONE..................360 942-5240
EMP: 2 EST: 2011
SALES (est): 80K Privately Held
SIC: 7372 Prepackaged Software Services

(G-8352)
HALFMOON PUBLISHING LLC
105 Half Moon Creek Rd (98577-9389)
PHONE..................360 934-5387
Heidi Friese, *Principal*
EMP: 2
SALES (est): 89.6K Privately Held
SIC: 2741 Miscellaneous publishing

(G-8353)
HIGH COUNTRY WOODWORKS
122 S Fork Rd (98577-9395)
PHONE..................360 942-2996
Tony Betker, *Owner*
EMP: 2
SALES (est): 169.5K Privately Held
SIC: 2431 Millwork

(G-8354)
HIWAY 6 SHAKE & SHINGLE
2868 State Route 6 (98577-9348)
PHONE..................360 934-5442
Larry Collins, *Partner*
EMP: 2
SALES (est): 113.6K Privately Held
SIC: 2429 Shakes (hand split shingles)

(G-8355)
JASPER PUBLISHING LLC
168 Stauffer Rd (98577-9310)
PHONE..................360 875-8383
EMP: 2
SALES (est): 66K Privately Held
SIC: 2711 Newspapers

(G-8356)
NU WAY FLUME & EQUIPMENT CO (PA)
161 Elkhorn Rd (98577-9255)
PHONE..................360 942-3581
Charles H Overbay, *President*
Steve Jurca, *Vice Pres*
EMP: 2
SALES (est): 236.2K Privately Held
SIC: 3443 Flumes, metal plate

(G-8357)
PATRIOTIC PACKING
1649 Larson Rd (98577-9693)
P.O. Box 109 (98577-0109)
PHONE..................360 942-3054

Jim Lev, *Owner*
EMP: 2
SALES (est): 95K Privately Held
SIC: 2011 Meat packing plants

(G-8358)
SIGHTMAN
538 Ostman Rd (98577-9634)
PHONE..................360 934-5886
EMP: 3
SALES (est): 140K Privately Held
SIC: 3826 Mfg Analytical Instruments

(G-8359)
SWAKANE WINERY
63 Old Bullard Rd (98577-9383)
PHONE..................509 881-9688
EMP: 7
SALES (est): 401.4K Privately Held
SIC: 2084 Wines

(G-8360)
WEYERHAEUSER COMPANY
51 Ellis St (98577-1740)
PHONE..................360 942-6302
Louis Nadolny, *Manager*
EMP: 175
SALES (corp-wide): 7.4B Publicly Held
SIC: 2421 Lumber: rough, sawed or planed
PA: Weyerhaeuser Company
    220 Occidental Ave S
    Seattle WA 98104
    206 539-3000

(G-8361)
WILLAPA LOGGING COMPANY INC
2770 Ocean Ave (98577-4916)
P.O. Box 232 (98577-0232)
PHONE..................360 875-5670
Richard Oatfield, *President*
EMP: 50
SQ FT: 900
SALES (est): 6.5MM Privately Held
SIC: 2411 5031 1611 Logging camps & contractors; lumber: rough, dressed & finished; highway & street construction

(G-8362)
WILLAPA MARINE PRODUCTS INC
2 Green Creek Rd (98577-9362)
P.O. Box 157, Menlo (98561-0157)
PHONE..................360 942-2151
Steve Evertson, *President*
Lora Sanchez, *Vice Pres*
▲ EMP: 6
SALES (est): 66.5K Privately Held
SIC: 3531 Marine related equipment

(G-8363)
WILLAPA PRINTING
422 Franklin St (98577-1833)
PHONE..................360 942-5580
Michelle Layman, *Owner*
EMP: 2 EST: 2011
SALES (est): 210.9K Privately Held
SIC: 2752 Commercial printing, offset

Redmond
King County

(G-8364)
8TH SHORE INC (PA)
4016 148th Ave Ne (98052-5165)
PHONE..................425 681-1157
Chun Lu, *CEO*
EMP: 7 EST: 2014
SALES: 10K Privately Held
SIC: 7372 Prepackaged software

(G-8365)
A TEREX GENIE COMPANY
18465 Ne 68th St Bldg 17 (98052-3325)
PHONE..................800 536-1800
Echo Summers, *Principal*
Diemtrang Pham, *Sales Staff*
EMP: 9
SALES (est): 1.7MM Privately Held
SIC: 3536 Hand hoists; hoists

(G-8366)
AAPKISPACE LLC
11425 179th Ct Ne (98052-7427)
PHONE..................425 614-6465
Rekha Arikere, *Principal*
EMP: 2 EST: 2016
SALES (est): 76.3K Privately Held
SIC: 2741 Miscellaneous publishing

(G-8367)
ACE IRON WORKS
1323 Rdmond Fall Cy Rd Ne (98053-9236)
PHONE..................206 903-6161
Jim Athan, *Owner*
EMP: 5
SQ FT: 1,050,000
SALES (est): 336.1K Privately Held
SIC: 7692 Welding repair

(G-8368)
ACG SOFTWARE
13632 Ne 94th St (98052-6430)
PHONE..................425 828-1456
Mark Moore, *Principal*
EMP: 2
SALES (est): 114.4K Privately Held
SIC: 7372 Prepackaged software

(G-8369)
ACRYLIC CONCEPTS INC
17932 Ne 65th St (98052-4963)
PHONE..................425 881-3603
Scott Crane, *President*
EMP: 2
SQ FT: 5,000
SALES: 325K Privately Held
SIC: 3083 Plastic finished products, laminated

(G-8370)
ADVANCED DIGITAL INFO CORP (HQ)
Also Called: Adic
11431 Willows Rd Ne (98052-3069)
PHONE..................425 881-8004
Peter H Van Oppen, *Ch of Bd*
Jonathan Otis, *Vice Pres*
Charles Stonecipher, *Vice Pres*
Jon Gacek, *CFO*
William Britts, *Products*
EMP: 300
SALES (est): 83.5MM
SALES (corp-wide): 339.3MM Privately Held
SIC: 3572 Computer storage devices
PA: Quantum Corporation
    224 Airport Pkwy Ste 550
    San Jose CA 95110
    408 944-4000

(G-8371)
ADVANTAGE PRECISION GRAPHICS
9474 Redmond Woodinville (98052-3671)
PHONE..................425 285-9787
Brian Goodman, *President*
EMP: 12
SALES: 500K Privately Held
SIC: 2396 Automotive & apparel trimmings

(G-8372)
AERO SAFETY GRAPHICS INC
6104 208th Ave Ne (98053-7810)
PHONE..................425 957-0712
Peter C Bonneau, *President*
Dorothy Bonneau, *Admin Sec*
EMP: 5
SQ FT: 3,000
SALES (est): 548K Privately Held
WEB: www.aerosafetygraphics.com
SIC: 2759 Commercial printing

(G-8373)
AEROJET ROCKETDYNE INC
11411 139th Pl Ne (98052-2025)
PHONE..................425 885-5000
Roger Myers, *General Mgr*
James Ellinthorpe, *Business Mgr*
Bill Cahill, *Project Mgr*
David Collins, *Mfg Staff*
David Carter, *Engrg Dir*
EMP: 41
SALES (corp-wide): 1.9B Publicly Held
SIC: 3728 Aircraft parts & equipment

HQ: Aerojet Rocketdyne, Inc.
    2001 Aerojet Rd
    Rancho Cordova CA 95742
    916 355-4000

(G-8374)
AGILE ADVANTAGE INC
8201 164th Ave Ne (98052-7604)
PHONE..................425 629-6361
Brent Barton, *President*
Chris Sterling, *Vice Pres*
EMP: 41
SALES (est): 137.9K
SALES (corp-wide): 20.8B Publicly Held
SIC: 7372 Prepackaged software
HQ: Rally Software Development Corp.
    3333 Walnut St
    Boulder CO 80301
    303 565-2800

(G-8375)
AGM INDUSTRIES INC
2690 152nd Ave Ne # 632 (98052-5782)
PHONE..................716 256-9470
Ravi Gajula, *CEO*
EMP: 5 EST: 2017
SALES (est): 431.3K Privately Held
SIC: 3999 Manufacturing industries

(G-8376)
ALCATEL-LUCENT USA INC
10675 Willows Rd Ne # 250 (98052-2530)
PHONE..................425 497-2400
EMP: 50
SALES (corp-wide): 884MM Privately Held
SIC: 7372 Computer Services
HQ: Alcatel-Lucent Usa Inc.
    600 Mountain Ave Ste 700
    New Providence NJ 07974

(G-8377)
ALCIDE CORPORATION
8561 154th Ave Ne (98052-3557)
PHONE..................425 882-2555
Joseph Sasenick, *Ch of Bd*
Jan Poczobutt, *Vice Pres*
Dr G Kere Kemp, *Officer*
EMP: 50
SQ FT: 6,751
SALES: 21.9MM
SALES (corp-wide): 14.6B Publicly Held
SIC: 2834 2842 5122 Veterinary pharmaceutical preparations; druggists' preparations (pharmaceuticals); disinfectants, household or industrial plant; drugs, proprietaries & sundries
PA: Ecolab Inc.
    1 Ecolab Pl
    Saint Paul MN 55102
    800 232-6522

(G-8378)
ALKI SPORTS LLC (PA)
16101 Ne 87th St (98052-3505)
P.O. Box 989 (98073-0989)
PHONE..................206 898-1305
Chad Baerwaldt,
EMP: 12
SQ FT: 60,000
SALES (est): 1.5MM Privately Held
SIC: 5941 5699 5661 3949 Team sports equipment; sports apparel; footwear, athletic; sporting & athletic goods; automotive & apparel trimmings

(G-8379)
ALL-PRO SERVICES RAN LLC
16541 Redmond Way 1004c (98052-4492)
PHONE..................425 746-4829
Nancy Slayton,
EMP: 9
SQ FT: 500
SALES (est): 652K Privately Held
SIC: 3564 Air cleaning systems

(G-8380)
ALLIED STEEL FABRICATORS INC
4604 148th Ave Ne (98052-5123)
PHONE..................425 861-9558
Nancy Exe, *President*
EMP: 27
SQ FT: 10,000

GEOGRAPHIC SECTION

Redmond - King County (G-8410)

SALES (est): 7.2MM **Privately Held**
SIC: 3441 3446 Fabricated structural metal; architectural metalwork

(G-8381)
ALTIX NORTH AMERICA INC
8201 164th Ave Ne Ste 200 (98052-7615)
PHONE..................................425 285-4477
Sylvain Dromaint, *President*
EMP: 4
SALES (est): 205.9K
SALES (corp-wide): 16.7MM **Privately Held**
SIC: 3569 Lubrication equipment, industrial
PA: Altix
Altix Automa Tech Voie De L Oree
Val De Reuil 27100
232 633-636

(G-8382)
APPAREL DUDE PRINTING
13770 Ne 75th Pl (98052-4030)
PHONE..................................425 283-3051
Samon Nowparvar, *Principal*
EMP: 2 EST: 2016
SALES (est): 92.3K **Privately Held**
SIC: 2752 Commercial printing, lithographic

(G-8383)
AQUATRONIX LLC
Also Called: Aquasense
16625 Redmond Way M367 (98052-4444)
PHONE..................................425 881-8600
Grant McKay, *Mng Member*
EMP: 3 EST: 1998
SALES (est): 397.9K **Privately Held**
SIC: 3494 Sprinkler systems, field

(G-8384)
ARCHIVE SOLUTION PROVIDERS
22822 Ne 58th Pl (98053-8341)
PHONE..................................425 440-0328
EMP: 2
SALES (est): 104.1K **Privately Held**
SIC: 7372 Prepackaged software

(G-8385)
ARGENT CHEMICAL LABS INC (PA)
8702 152nd Ave Ne (98052-3506)
P.O. Box 2053 (98073-2053)
PHONE..................................425 885-3777
Elliott Lieberman, *President*
Beatriz F Shanahan, *Vice Pres*
▲ EMP: 9
SQ FT: 16,000
SALES (est): 904.4K **Privately Held**
WEB: www.argent-labs.com
SIC: 2899 Chemical preparations

(G-8386)
ARS NOVA SOFTWARE
16770 Ne 79th St Ste 201 (98052-4413)
P.O. Box 3370 (98073-3370)
PHONE..................................425 869-0625
Dennis J Evans, *Owner*
EMP: 5
SALES: 700K **Privately Held**
SIC: 7371 7372 Computer software development; prepackaged software

(G-8387)
ARTIKS INC
16120 Ne 57th St (98052-4839)
PHONE..................................206 849-4335
John Schraub, *Principal*
EMP: 2
SALES (est): 90.4K **Privately Held**
SIC: 2522 Office furniture, except wood

(G-8388)
AURORAVIEW LLC (PA)
8201 164th Ave Ne Ste 200 (98052-7615)
PHONE..................................206 724-5953
Guy Shalom, *Principal*
Jasmin Kutes, *Vice Pres*
EMP: 11
SALES (est): 2.1MM **Privately Held**
SIC: 3812 Magnetic field detection apparatus

(G-8389)
AUTOMATED MECHANICAL CONTROLS
9630 153rd Ave Ne (98052-2546)
PHONE..................................425 881-8226
Rod Kirkwood, *President*
EMP: 2
SALES (est): 161.1K **Privately Held**
WEB: www.amcntc.com
SIC: 3829 Measuring & controlling devices

(G-8390)
AUTOMATED METAL TECH INC
15340 Ne 92nd St Ste C (98052-3521)
PHONE..................................425 895-9733
Mike Hulett, *President*
▲ EMP: 16 EST: 1998
SQ FT: 8,500
SALES (est): 2.6MM **Privately Held**
SIC: 3444 Sheet metalwork

(G-8391)
AVAC INC
18350 Redmond Way L (98052-5012)
PHONE..................................425 869-2822
Jeff Serex, *Principal*
EMP: 2
SALES (est): 170.2K **Privately Held**
SIC: 3829 Measuring & controlling devices

(G-8392)
AVERE SYSTEMS INC
1 Microsoft Way (98052-8300)
PHONE..................................425 706-7507
Ronald Bianchini Jr, *CEO*
David Stephenson, *President*
John Dean, *CFO*
Al Dawson, *Manager*
Justin McCann, *Technical Staff*
EMP: 100
SALES (est): 14.1MM
SALES (corp-wide): 110.3B **Publicly Held**
SIC: 3572 Computer storage devices
PA: Microsoft Corporation
1 Microsoft Way
Redmond WA 98052
425 882-8080

(G-8393)
AVIATION SPARES & SVCS INTL CO (PA)
Also Called: Global Inflight Products
8920 152nd Ave Ne (98052-3508)
PHONE..................................425 869-7799
Zine A Badissy, *President*
Najiba Badissy, *Vice Pres*
▲ EMP: 15
SQ FT: 15,582
SALES (est): 8.1MM **Privately Held**
WEB: www.assic.com
SIC: 5088 3728 Aircraft equipment & supplies; aircraft parts & equipment

(G-8394)
AVID PRODUCTS LLC
18344 Redmond Way (98052-5012)
PHONE..................................888 271-3616
Brian Park, *Principal*
EMP: 4 EST: 2012
SALES (est): 332.6K **Privately Held**
SIC: 3089 Injection molding of plastics

(G-8395)
AVITECH INTERNATIONAL CORP
15377 Ne 90th St (98052-3562)
PHONE..................................425 885-3863
Jyh-Cherng Gong, *President*
Miinhwa Gong, *President*
Jenny Lu, *Treasurer*
▲ EMP: 19
SALES: 3.8MM **Privately Held**
WEB: www.avitechvideo.com
SIC: 5099 3999 Video & audio equipment; barber & beauty shop equipment

(G-8396)
BAE SYSTEMS CONTROLS INC
Also Called: Platform Solutions Sector
8510 154th Ave Ne (98052-3500)
PHONE..................................607 770-2000
Paul Chisholm, *Manager*
Mark Drechsler, *Director*
EMP: 30

SALES (corp-wide): 21.6B **Privately Held**
WEB: www.drs-ss.com
SIC: 3812 Aircraft/aerospace flight instruments & guidance systems
HQ: Bae Systems Controls Inc.
1098 Clark St
Endicott NY 13760
607 770-2000

(G-8397)
BASIS SOFTWARE INC
Also Called: Surphaser
18103 Ne 68th St Ste C100 (98052-8593)
PHONE..................................425 861-9390
Peter M Petrov, *President*
EMP: 4
SQ FT: 2,300
SALES: 2MM **Privately Held**
WEB: www.surphaser.com
SIC: 3829 3821 Measuring & controlling devices; laser beam alignment devices

(G-8398)
BE MEYERS & CO INC (PA)
9461 Willows Rd Ne # 100 (98052-3577)
PHONE..................................425 881-6648
Brad E Meyers, *CEO*
Nancy E Meyers, *Corp Secy*
Michael Alvis, *Vice Pres*
Rick Athwal, *Production*
Ken Chaney, *Senior Buyer*
EMP: 200
SQ FT: 165,000
SALES (est): 43.6MM **Privately Held**
WEB: www.bemeyers.com
SIC: 3827 Optical instruments & lenses

(G-8399)
BECO INC
15715 Ne 56th Way (98052-4848)
PHONE..................................425 885-2603
Roger Baker, *President*
Anne L Baker, *Vice Pres*
EMP: 2
SALES (est): 160K **Privately Held**
SIC: 3829 Measuring & controlling devices

(G-8400)
BELGATE PRINTING & COPY INC
3817 W Lk Smmmish Pkwy Ne (98052-5802)
PHONE..................................425 451-9048
Norm Leque, *President*
Gail Leque, *Corp Secy*
EMP: 11
SALES: 1.1MM **Privately Held**
WEB: www.belgateprinting.com
SIC: 2759 2752 Commercial printing; commercial printing, lithographic

(G-8401)
BELLEVUE INSTANT SIGN
21903 Ne 18th St (98074-4105)
PHONE..................................425 451-8218
Joseph Pelonio, *Owner*
Kathleen Pelino, *Co-Owner*
EMP: 2
SQ FT: 1,000
SALES: 200K **Privately Held**
SIC: 3993 Signs, not made in custom sign painting shops

(G-8402)
BETZ CELLARS LLC
Also Called: Betz Family Winery
13244 Woodinville Redmond (98052-2020)
PHONE..................................425 861-9823
Stephen Griessel, *Mng Member*
Bridgit Griessel,
▲ EMP: 6
SALES (est): 740.9K **Privately Held**
SIC: 2084 Wines

(G-8403)
BIO-RAD LABORATORIES INC
6565 185th Ave Ne (98052-5039)
PHONE..................................425 881-8300
Donald Diamond, *Vice Pres*
Christopher Harner, *Safety Dir*
Linda Lathrop, *QA Dir*
Ernst Jorgensen, *Engineer*
Barbara Fithian, *Human Res Dir*
EMP: 200

SALES (corp-wide): 2.2B **Publicly Held**
WEB: www.bio-rad.com
SIC: 2835 3826 In vitro diagnostics; blood testing apparatus
PA: Bio-Rad Laboratories, Inc.
1000 Alfred Nobel Dr
Hercules CA 94547
510 724-7000

(G-8404)
BIRDWELL MACHINE LLC
17445 Ne 70th St Ste 160 (98052-4914)
PHONE..................................425 881-1916
Mike Birdwell, *Mng Member*
EMP: 7
SALES: 120K **Privately Held**
WEB: www.birdwellmachine.com
SIC: 3599 Machine shop, jobbing & repair

(G-8405)
BIZLOGR INC
8201 164th Ave Ne Ste 200 (98052-7615)
PHONE..................................800 366-4484
Stefan Negritoiu, *CEO*
Charles Kindel, *President*
EMP: 2
SALES (est): 120.7K **Privately Held**
SIC: 7372 Business oriented computer software

(G-8406)
BLUE COTTAGE JAMS
21701 Ne 73rd Pl (98053-7703)
PHONE..................................425 836-9580
Brian J Martin, *Principal*
EMP: 2
SALES (est): 129.3K **Privately Held**
WEB: www.martincasa.com
SIC: 2033 Jams, including imitation: packaged in cans, jars, etc.

(G-8407)
BOSTON SCEINTIFICS
6645 185th Ave Ne (98052-5038)
PHONE..................................608 323-3377
Ken Cowan, *Principal*
EMP: 2
SALES (est): 86.6K **Privately Held**
SIC: 3841 Surgical & medical instruments

(G-8408)
BRAVURA SOFTWARE LLC
6763 191st Pl Ne (98052-0542)
P.O. Box 3041 (98073-3041)
PHONE..................................425 881-7305
Matthew Block, *Principal*
EMP: 2
SALES (est): 164.3K **Privately Held**
SIC: 7372 Application computer software

(G-8409)
BRIGHTVOLT INC (PA)
8201 164th Ave Ne Ste 325 (98052-7604)
PHONE..................................863 603-7640
John Todd Peters, *CEO*
Michael W Mahan, *Exec VP*
John Davis, *Senior VP*
James P McDougall, *Vice Pres*
James Pope, *Vice Pres*
▲ EMP: 51
SALES (est): 3.6MM **Privately Held**
WEB: www.solicore.com
SIC: 3691 Nickel cadmium storage batteries

(G-8410)
BROCKETT OCEAN SERVICES INC
17455 Ne 67th Ct Ste 120 (98052-7910)
P.O. Box 2978 (98073-2978)
PHONE..................................425 869-1834
Tedd Brockett, *President*
Ted Brockett, *President*
Brockett Donald, *Vice Pres*
Pam Roell, *Purchasing*
Todd S John, *Engineer*
EMP: 10
SQ FT: 10,000
SALES (est): 800K
SALES (corp-wide): 2MM **Privately Held**
WEB: www.soundocean.com
SIC: 8711 3812 Consulting engineer; nautical instruments

Redmond - King County (G-8411)

PA: Okeanus Science & Technology Llc
2261 Denley Rd
Houma LA 70363
985 346-4666

(G-8411)
BRYAN ZIPPRO
Also Called: Zippro Press
9943 181st Ave Ne (98052-6903)
PHONE..............................425 881-9780
Bryan Zippro, *Owner*
Mike Zippro, *Partner*
EMP: 3
SQ FT: 1,000
SALES: 250K **Privately Held**
WEB: www.zippro.net
SIC: 2752 Commercial printing, lithographic

(G-8412)
BUNNY BEAR PRESS
11667 168th Ct Ne (98052-2342)
P.O. Box 71, Kirkland (98083-0071)
PHONE..............................425 894-0944
Abina Segal, *Owner*
EMP: 2
SALES (est): 107.8K **Privately Held**
SIC: 2741 Miscellaneous publishing

(G-8413)
CADMAN INC (DH)
Also Called: Cadman Administration
7554 185th Ave Ne Ste 100 (98052-8566)
P.O. Box 97038 (98073-9738)
PHONE..............................425 867-1234
James Derkatch, *President*
Rob Johnson, *Vice Pres*
Bill Sayer, *Vice Pres*
Linda George, *Treasurer*
Kari Keaton, *Train & Dev Mgr*
▲ **EMP:** 350
SQ FT: 4,060
SALES (est): 115.7MM
SALES (corp-wide): 20.6B **Privately Held**
SIC: 3273 Ready-mixed concrete

(G-8414)
CADMAN (ROCK) INC (DH)
18816 Ne 80th St (98052-3372)
PHONE..............................425 867-1234
Alan R Watt, *President*
Richard T Harper, *Treasurer*
N Bruce Kulla, *Admin Sec*
EMP: 60
SALES (est): 10.8MM
SALES (corp-wide): 20.6B **Privately Held**
WEB: www.cadman.com
SIC: 1411 1442 Dimension stone; sand mining; gravel mining

(G-8415)
CADMAN HOLDING COMPANY INC
7735 178th Pl Ne (98052-4921)
PHONE..............................425 868-1234
Richard Kline, *President*
Laurence Colegate Jr, *Vice Pres*
Alan R Watt, *Vice Pres*
N Bruce Kulla, *Admin Sec*
EMP: 4 **EST:** 1934
SALES (est): 373.2K
SALES (corp-wide): 20.6B **Privately Held**
SIC: 3273 5211 1411 1442 Ready-mixed concrete; sand & gravel; granite, dimension-quarrying; gravel mining; sand, construction
HQ: Hanson Lehigh Inc
300 E John Carpenter Fwy
Irving TX 75062

(G-8416)
CASABA SECURITY LLC
16625 Redmond Way Ste M (98052-4499)
PHONE..............................888 869-6708
Samuel Bucholtz, *Mng Member*
Jason Glassberg,
Brian Lewis,
Chris Weber,
EMP: 2
SALES (est): 57.2K **Privately Held**
SIC: 7372 Application computer software

(G-8417)
CASCADE SOFTWARE CORP
11874 175th Pl Ne (98052-2821)
PHONE..............................425 558-9017
Arumugam Rammanohar, *Principal*
EMP: 2 **EST:** 2012
SALES (est): 142.7K **Privately Held**
SIC: 7372 Prepackaged software

(G-8418)
CHINOOK ACOUSTICS INC
14842 Ne 95th St (98052-2541)
PHONE..............................425 307-1976
Kristie Forrest, *President*
EMP: 7
SALES (est): 957.1K **Privately Held**
SIC: 2391 Draperies, plastic & textile: from purchased materials

(G-8419)
CHONDREX INC
2607 151st Pl Ne (98052-5522)
PHONE..............................425 702-6365
Takaki Waritani, *President*
Hiroyuki Iwai, *Chairman*
Lorraine Masse, *Corp Secy*
EMP: 5
SQ FT: 3,626
SALES (est): 1.1MM **Privately Held**
WEB: www.chondrex.com
SIC: 2836 Biological products, except diagnostic

(G-8420)
CINQ CELLARS LLC
21407 Ne Union Hill Rd (98053-7714)
PHONE..............................206 954-4626
V Marc Droppert, *Mng Member*
EMP: 5 **EST:** 2012
SALES (est): 110K **Privately Held**
SIC: 5921 2084 Wine; wines

(G-8421)
CITRIX SYSTEMS INC
15809 Bear Creek Pkwy (98052-1542)
PHONE..............................425 895-4700
Frank SRP, *Engineer*
Sujo Varghese, *Engineer*
Nicole Czarnecki, *Sales Staff*
John Harris, *Sales Staff*
Bill Bistany, *Manager*
EMP: 8
SALES (corp-wide): 2.9B **Publicly Held**
WEB: www.citrix.com
SIC: 7372 Prepackaged software
PA: Citrix Systems, Inc.
851 W Cypress Creek Rd
Fort Lauderdale FL 33309
954 267-3000

(G-8422)
CONCORDIA COFFEE COMPANY INC
Also Called: Concordia Coffee Systems
6812 185th Ave Ne (98052-6712)
PHONE..............................425 453-2800
David Isett, *President*
Wayne Stearns, *Vice Pres*
Angie Prichard, *Materials Mgr*
David Davis, *Parts Mgr*
Gery Jaggars, *Engineer*
◆ **EMP:** 31
SQ FT: 25,000
SALES (est): 7.2MM
SALES (corp-wide): 2.7B **Publicly Held**
WEB: www.concordiacoffee.com
SIC: 2086 Bottled & canned soft drinks
PA: The Middleby Corporation
1400 Toastmaster Dr
Elgin IL 60120
847 741-3300

(G-8423)
CONNX SOLUTIONS INC
2039 152nd Ave Ne (98052-5521)
PHONE..............................425 519-6600
Fax: 425 519-6601
EMP: 23
SALES (est): 3.2MM **Privately Held**
SIC: 7372 Prepackaged Software Services

(G-8424)
CONSTELLATION HOMEBUILDER SYST
8343 154th Ave Ne Ste 200 (98052-6182)
PHONE..............................888 723-2222
Dexter Salna, *President*
Chris Graham, *Vice Pres*
Bonnie Wilhelm, *CFO*
EMP: 5

SALES (est): 954.7K
SALES (corp-wide): 3B **Privately Held**
SIC: 8741 7372 Business management; business oriented computer software
HQ: Constellation Homebuilder Systems Corp
75 Frontenac Dr
Markham ON L3R 6
888 723-2222

(G-8425)
CONTEXT REALITY INC
Also Called: Context Vr
8040 161st Ave Ne 225 (98052-3807)
PHONE..............................425 241-5860
Dmitri Bouianov, *CEO*
EMP: 2
SALES (est): 56.5K **Privately Held**
SIC: 7372 Business oriented computer software

(G-8426)
CORNERSTONE ATTACHE GROUP INC
Also Called: Vacupractor
15127 Ne 24th St Ste 185 (98052-5544)
PHONE..............................425 577-2713
Henry Paul Hagen, *Owner*
Paul Hagen, *Principal*
EMP: 2
SALES: 100K **Privately Held**
SIC: 3842 Surgical appliances & supplies

(G-8427)
CORY SIVERSON
Also Called: Siverson Design
18398 Redmond Way (98052-5012)
PHONE..............................425 869-8303
Cory Siverson, *Owner*
EMP: 2
SQ FT: 1,000
SALES: 250K **Privately Held**
WEB: www.siversondesign.com
SIC: 3678 Electronic connectors

(G-8428)
COUGAR HILLS LLC
14366 Woodnvll Redmond Ne (98052-2006)
PHONE..............................425 398-9999
Luv Peyton, *Branch Mgr*
EMP: 2
SALES (corp-wide): 2.1MM **Privately Held**
SIC: 2084 Wines
PA: Cougar Hills, Llc
50 Frenchtown Rd
Walla Walla WA 99362
509 529-5980

(G-8429)
CRANE ELECTRONICS INC (DH)
Also Called: Fka Interpoint
10301 Willows Rd Ne (98052-2529)
PHONE..............................425 882-3100
Brendan Curran, *Vice Pres*
Donna Bliss, *General Mgr*
Augustus Dupont, *Vice Pres*
Justine Bormann, *Engineer*
Frank Grabner, *Engineer*
▲ **EMP:** 260
SQ FT: 55,000
SALES (est): 88.7MM
SALES (corp-wide): 3.3B **Publicly Held**
WEB: www.stellarinteractivesolutions.com
SIC: 3679 Electronic loads & power supplies; oscillators

(G-8430)
CRANE ELECTRONICS INC
10301 Willows Rd Ne (98052-2529)
PHONE..............................425 882-3100
Rt Crane Jr, *Branch Mgr*
EMP: 2
SALES (corp-wide): 3.3B **Publicly Held**
SIC: 3679 Electronic loads & power supplies
HQ: Crane Electronics, Inc.
10301 Willows Rd Ne
Redmond WA 98052
425 882-3100

(G-8431)
CUTTINGBOARD LLC
2739 152nd Ave Ne (98052-5554)
PHONE..............................253 234-7569

Grant Yuan, *CEO*
▲ **EMP:** 2
SALES (est): 64K **Privately Held**
SIC: 3263 Commercial tableware or kitchen articles, fine earthenware

(G-8432)
DARKLIGHT INC (PA)
8201 164th Ave Ne (98052-7604)
PHONE..............................509 940-1818
Daniel Wachtler, *CEO*
Tom Bruderman, *Principal*
G Louis Graziadio III, *Principal*
Ryan Hohimer, *Principal*
Howard Ko, *Principal*
EMP: 6
SQ FT: 4,000
SALES (est): 866.5K **Privately Held**
SIC: 7372 Application computer software

(G-8433)
DATA I/O CORPORATION (PA)
6645 185th Ave Ne Ste 100 (98052-6431)
PHONE..............................425 881-6444
Alan B Howe, *Ch of Bd*
Anthony Ambrose, *President*
Joel S Hatlen, *COO*
Dwayne Jones, *Opers Mgr*
David Christie, *Engineer*
▲ **EMP:** 103 **EST:** 1972
SQ FT: 20,460
SALES: 29.2MM **Publicly Held**
WEB: www.dataio.com
SIC: 3679 3674 3823 Electronic circuits; semiconductors & related devices; programmers, process type

(G-8434)
DAUNTLESS INC ◆
8355 165th Ave Ne (98052-3914)
PHONE..............................206 494-3338
Clark Musser, *CEO*
Brady Miller, *COO*
EMP: 26 **EST:** 2018
SALES (est): 2.5MM **Privately Held**
SIC: 7372 Business oriented computer software

(G-8435)
DAVID LYNN SMOOTHIES LLC
16717 Redmond Way (98052-4450)
PHONE..............................907 242-4564
David Werdal, *Principal*
EMP: 3
SALES (est): 188.2K **Privately Held**
SIC: 2037 Frozen fruits & vegetables

(G-8436)
DAYS GONE BY CABINETRY
6305 252nd Pl Ne (98053-2633)
PHONE..............................425 868-5132
Brent Frizzell, *Principal*
EMP: 2
SALES (est): 205.1K **Privately Held**
SIC: 2434 Wood kitchen cabinets

(G-8437)
DELILLE CELLARS INC
14208 Wdnvlle Rdmnd Rd Ne (98052)
P.O. Box 2233, Woodinville (98072-2233)
PHONE..............................425 489-0544
Jay Soloff, *CEO*
Greg Lill, *Owner*
Chris Upchurch, *Chairman*
EMP: 8
SQ FT: 5,000
SALES (est): 1.2MM **Privately Held**
WEB: www.delillecellars.com
SIC: 2084 Wines

(G-8438)
DESEMA COMPANY
7241 185th Ave Ne # 2222 (98073-3801)
PHONE..............................425 202-7572
Timothy Mitchell, *Owner*
EMP: 2
SALES (est): 160K **Privately Held**
SIC: 5045 7371 7372 7373 Computers, peripherals & software; custom computer programming services; computer software development; prepackaged software; computer integrated systems design; computer facilities management

GEOGRAPHIC SECTION

Redmond - King County (G-8466)

(G-8439)
DESIGN HARDWOOD PRODUCTS INC (PA)
Also Called: Woodwise
15060 Ne 95th St (98052-2507)
PHONE.....................425 869-0859
John Goss, *President*
Gary Martin, *Vice Pres*
EMP: 13
SQ FT: 20,000
SALES (est): 1.7MM **Privately Held**
SIC: 3471 2851 Cleaning, polishing & finishing; paints & allied products

(G-8440)
DESIGN HARDWOOD PRODUCTS INC
15050 Ne 95th St (98052-2507)
PHONE.....................425 869-0859
John Gross, *President*
EMP: 7 **Privately Held**
SIC: 2842 Specialty cleaning, polishes & sanitation goods
PA: Design Hardwood Products Inc
  15060 Ne 95th St
  Redmond WA 98052

(G-8441)
DIGITAL ANGLERS LLC
16708 Ne 103rd Pl (98052-3141)
P.O. Box 3584 (98073-3584)
PHONE.....................206 819-7010
Aaron Borg, *Principal*
EMP: 2 **EST:** 2012
SALES (est): 120K **Privately Held**
SIC: 3949 Fishing equipment

(G-8442)
DIVERSIFIED SYSTEMS GROUP INC
8700 148th Ave Ne (98052-3482)
P.O. Box 1114, Issaquah (98027-0042)
PHONE.....................425 947-1500
Robert Sambrook, *President*
Janice Sambrook, *Vice Pres*
Larry Piccinino, *Prdtn Mgr*
Jan Hemmen, *Credit Mgr*
Ashley Sambrook, *Sales Staff*
▲ **EMP:** 25
SALES (est): 3.5MM **Privately Held**
WEB: www.dsgi.com
SIC: 7379 7372 2759 Disk & diskette conversion service; prepackaged software; screen printing

(G-8443)
DOSE SAFETY INC
17904 Ne 26th St (98052-5847)
PHONE.....................206 276-3385
Richard Kircher, *CEO*
Robert Kircher, *Partner*
Donald Matheson, *Partner*
EMP: 5
SALES (est): 490K **Privately Held**
WEB: www.kontact.com
SIC: 7372 Operating systems computer software

(G-8444)
DUTCH HARBOR SEAFOODS LTD
Also Called: F V Alyeska
15400 Ne 90th St Ste 200 (98052-3533)
P.O. Box 97019 (98073-9719)
PHONE.....................425 881-8181
Terry Shaff, *President*
EMP: 40
SALES (est): 3.2MM **Privately Held**
SIC: 2092 Seafoods, fresh: prepared

(G-8445)
EASTSIDE MASONRY PRODUCTS INC
19015 Ne 80th St (98052)
PHONE.....................425 868-0303
Herb Nyquist, *President*
Iain Rooney, *Vice Pres*
Garth Thomas, *Vice Pres*
Tom Thomas, *Shareholder*
EMP: 50
SQ FT: 1,000
SALES (est): 6.8MM **Privately Held**
WEB: www.eastsidemasonry.com
SIC: 3271 5032 Blocks, concrete or cinder: standard; brick, stone & related material

(G-8446)
ECHONOUS INC
8310 154th Ave Ne Ste 200 (98052-6180)
PHONE.....................425 482-6213
Kevin Goodwin, *CEO*
Michael Blaivas, *Chief Mktg Ofcr*
Yoon Shin, *Admin Sec*
EMP: 30
SQ FT: 30,500
SALES (est): 4.3MM **Privately Held**
SIC: 3841 Surgical & medical instruments

(G-8447)
ELDEC CORPORATION
Also Called: Crane Aerospace & Electronics
10301 Willows Rd Ne (98052-2529)
PHONE.....................425 882-3100
Lou Bieck, *Branch Mgr*
EMP: 5
SALES (corp-wide): 3.3B **Publicly Held**
SIC: 3812 Aircraft control instruments
HQ: Eldec Corporation
  16700 13th Ave W
  Lynnwood WA 98037
  425 743-1313

(G-8448)
ELEVATION EXHIBITS LLC
8117 166th Ave Ne (98052-3945)
PHONE.....................774 696-2549
Jim Burke, *Branch Mgr*
EMP: 20 **Privately Held**
SIC: 3993 Displays, paint process
PA: Elevation Exhibits, Llc
  905 Hartford Tpke
  Shrewsbury MA 01545

(G-8449)
ENNCO DISPLAY SYSTEMS INC
6975 176th Ave Ne Ste 350 (98052-7905)
PHONE.....................425 883-1650
Jan S Ennis, *President*
Bryce Sills, *Opers Staff*
EMP: 10
SQ FT: 10,500
SALES (est): 1.8MM **Privately Held**
WEB: www.ennco.com
SIC: 2542 2541 Showcases (not refrigerated): except wood; showcases, except refrigerated: wood

(G-8450)
ENTRAQ MEDICAL
11898 178th Pl Ne (98052-2989)
PHONE.....................425 495-5143
Kshama Kumar, *Owner*
EMP: 3
SALES (est): 102.1K **Privately Held**
SIC: 3069 7389 Medical & laboratory rubber sundries & related products;

(G-8451)
ENVELOPES UNLIMITED INC
7114 180th Ave Ne B107 (98052-4970)
P.O. Box 7118, Bellevue (98008-1118)
PHONE.....................425 451-9622
Cindy Oakes, *President*
Glenn Oakes, *Exec VP*
EMP: 8 **EST:** 1980
SQ FT: 8,400
SALES: 1.4MM **Privately Held**
WEB: www.envelopesunlimited.com
SIC: 2759 Envelopes: printing

(G-8452)
EPOCH DESIGN LLC (PA)
Also Called: Futon Factory
17617 Ne 65th St Unit 2 (98052-4979)
PHONE.....................425 284-0880
Christopher Erickson, *Manager*
David Bolles,
John Deraspe,
Monica Deraspe,
Susan Deraspe,
▲ **EMP:** 16
SQ FT: 45,000
SALES (est): 3.4MM **Privately Held**
WEB: www.epochbydesign.com
SIC: 2512 2541 Upholstered household furniture; cabinets, lockers & shelving

(G-8453)
ESCAPE FUEL GAME ONE LLC
9660 173rd Pl Ne (98052-6961)
PHONE.....................425 883-8054
Charles Zapata, *Principal*
EMP: 3
SALES (est): 150.1K **Privately Held**
SIC: 2869 Fuels

(G-8454)
EUROPEAN CREATIONS INC
24243 Ne Vine Maple Way (98053-5675)
PHONE.....................425 898-0685
Mark Poleschuk, *President*
Ilya Poleschuk, *Admin Sec*
EMP: 6 **EST:** 1978
SALES (est): 620K **Privately Held**
WEB: www.europeancreations.com
SIC: 5944 3911 5094 Jewelry, precious stones & precious metals; jewelry, precious metal; jewelry & precious stones

(G-8455)
EXCELERATE SYSTEMS LLC
2205 152nd Ave Ne (98052-5519)
PHONE.....................425 605-8515
David Bennett, *CEO*
Victor Pichardo, *Vice Pres*
EMP: 11
SALES (est): 1MM **Privately Held**
SIC: 7372 Prepackaged software

(G-8456)
F5 LLC
1 Microsoft Way (98052-8300)
PHONE.....................425 882-8080
EMP: 5
SALES (est): 121K **Privately Held**
SIC: 7372 Prepackaged software

(G-8457)
FANTASY INDEX MAGAZINES LLC
Also Called: Fantasy Football Index
12524 177th Ave Ne (98052-2109)
P.O. Box 15277, Seattle (98115-0277)
PHONE.....................206 527-4444
Bruce Taylor,
Ian Allan,
EMP: 5
SALES (est): 708.2K **Privately Held**
SIC: 2721 7389 Magazines: publishing & printing;

(G-8458)
FARM AQUISITION RES & MGT LLC
13651 Woodinville Rdmnd (98052-2017)
PHONE.....................425 869-0624
Roger Calhoon, *Principal*
EMP: 2
SQ FT: 1,120
SALES (est): 97K **Privately Held**
WEB: www.farmllc.com
SIC: 0762 2721 Farm management services; periodicals

(G-8459)
FARMER BROS CO
Also Called: Farmer Brother's Coffee
8660 Willows Rd Ne (98052-3498)
PHONE.....................425 881-7030
George Zaikowski, *Branch Mgr*
EMP: 20
SQ FT: 16,560
SALES (corp-wide): 606.5MM **Publicly Held**
WEB: www.farmerbros.com
SIC: 2095 5812 3634 2099 Coffee roasting (except by wholesale grocers); coffee shop; electric housewares & fans; food preparations; groceries, general line; commercial equipment
PA: Farmer Bros. Co.
  1912 Farmer Brothers Dr
  Northlake TX 76262
  888 998-2468

(G-8460)
FERGUSON MERCHANDISING LLC (PA)
Also Called: Ben Franklin Crafts Frames Sp
15756 Redmond Way (98052-3830)
PHONE.....................425 883-2050
Shirley Ferguson, *CEO*
David Ferguson,
Neil Ferguson,
Robert C Ferguson,
▲ **EMP:** 55
SQ FT: 17,000
SALES (est): 4.7MM **Privately Held**
WEB: www.craftsandframes.com
SIC: 5945 5999 7699 2499 Arts & crafts supplies; hobbies; picture frames, ready made; picture framing, custom; picture & mirror frames, wood

(G-8461)
FINISHING UNLIMITED INC
9165 151st Ave Ne (98052-3512)
PHONE.....................425 881-7300
Russell L Mahan, *President*
Russell Mahan, *General Mgr*
EMP: 4
SQ FT: 10,000
SALES (est): 627.9K **Privately Held**
SIC: 3471 Chromium plating of metals or formed products; plating of metals or formed products

(G-8462)
FLUENTPRO SOFTWARE CORPORATION
8201 164th Ave Ne Ste 200 (98052-7615)
P.O. Box 1971, North Bend (98045-1971)
PHONE.....................855 358-3688
Anton Kravtsov, *CEO*
Oleg Snurnikov, *COO*
Manny Levy, *Project Mgr*
EMP: 1
SALES (est): 3.7MM **Privately Held**
SIC: 7371 7372 7379 Computer software systems analysis & design, custom; computer software development & applications; prepackaged software; application computer software; business oriented computer software;

(G-8463)
FORGERON CELLARS
14344 Woodinville Redmond (98052-2006)
PHONE.....................425 908-7683
EMP: 2
SALES (est): 88K **Privately Held**
SIC: 2084 Wines

(G-8464)
FORREST SOUND PRODUCTS LLC
15115 Ne 90th St 4a (98052-3560)
PHONE.....................425 881-1111
Charles Roetcisoender, *Project Mgr*
Ben Forrest, *Mng Member*
Benjamin F Forrest, *Mng Member*
Mary Ippolito, *Info Tech Mgr*
Doug Bixel,
▲ **EMP:** 8
SALES (est): 1.8MM **Privately Held**
WEB: www.forrestsound.com
SIC: 1742 3446 Acoustical & ceiling work; partitions & supports/studs, including acoustical systems

(G-8465)
FRAMATOME INC
10865 Willows Rd Ne (98052-2502)
PHONE.....................425 250-2775
EMP: 11
SALES (corp-wide): 4.2MM **Privately Held**
SIC: 8742 5812 3612 Management consulting services; eating places; transformers, except electric
HQ: Framatome Inc.
  3315 Old Forest Rd
  Lynchburg VA 24501

(G-8466)
FREDERICKS APPLIANCE CENTERS
7509 159th Pl Ne (98052-4380)
PHONE.....................425 885-0000
Eric Blakemore, *President*
Margaret Blakemore, *Vice Pres*
EMP: 20
SALES (est): 3.4MM **Privately Held**
SIC: 3639 Floor waxers & polishers, electric: household; major kitchen appliances, except refrigerators & stoves

Redmond - King County (G-8467)

(G-8467)
FUKUDA DENSHI USA INC
17725 Ne 65th St Ste C (98052-4911)
PHONE......................425 881-7737
Keisuke Nagata, *President*
Daijiro Shirai, *Principal*
Yuri Konishi, *Financial Exec*
John Burrell, *Sales Mgr*
Andrew Danner, *Sales Staff*
EMP: 50
SQ FT: 22,000
SALES (est): 10MM **Privately Held**
WEB: www.fukuda.com
SIC: 3841 5047 Surgical & medical instruments; medical & hospital equipment
PA: Fukuda Denshi Co.,Ltd.
3-39-4, Hongo
Bunkyo-Ku TKY 113-0

(G-8468)
GAEMS INC
2517 152nd Ave Ne Bldg 16 (98052-5574)
PHONE......................855 754-2367
Dean Mercier, *CEO*
Karyn Jovanovich, *Principal*
Todd Jovanovich, *Principal*
◆ **EMP:** 10
SQ FT: 5,000
SALES (est): 1.3MM **Privately Held**
SIC: 3944 Electronic game machines, except coin-operated; electronic games & toys

(G-8469)
GARLIC CRUSH
16095 Cleveland St (98052-1548)
PHONE......................425 968-2539
EMP: 2
SALES (est): 53.5K **Privately Held**
SIC: 5431 2084 Fruit & vegetable markets; wines

(G-8470)
GE STEAM POWER INC
10865 Willows Rd Ne (98052-2502)
PHONE......................860 688-1911
Tim Curran, *President*
John Benne, *Plant Mgr*
Derya Yalim, *Engineer*
David Andersen, *Manager*
Reginald Mendis, *Manager*
EMP: 4
SALES (corp-wide): 121.6B **Publicly Held**
SIC: 3463 Pump, compressor, turbine & engine forgings, except auto
HQ: Ge Steam Power, Inc.
175 Addison Rd
Windsor CT 06095
866 257-8664

(G-8471)
GENIE HOLDINGS INC (HQ)
Also Called: Genie, A Terex Company
18340 Ne 76th St (98052-5020)
P.O. Box 97030 (98073-9730)
PHONE......................425 881-1800
Ronald M Defeo, *President*
Tim Ford, *President*
Kevin Bradley, *Vice Pres*
Eric I Cohen, *Vice Pres*
Robert Wylie, *Vice Pres*
◆ **EMP:** 1
SALES (est): 641MM
SALES (corp-wide): 5.1B **Publicly Held**
WEB: www.genieindustries.com
SIC: 3536 Hand hoists; hoists
PA: Terex Corporation
200 Nyala Farms Rd Ste 2
Westport CT 06880
203 222-7170

(G-8472)
GENIE INDUSTRIES INC (DH)
18340 Ne 76th St (98052-5020)
P.O. Box 97030 (98073-9730)
PHONE......................425 881-1800
Matthew S Fearon, *President*
Tim Ford, *Principal*
Gene Dougherty, *Vice Pres*
Eric I Cohen, *Vice Pres*
Robert Wylie, *Vice Pres*
◆ **EMP:** 1750 **EST:** 1966
SQ FT: 200,000
SALES (est): 481.2MM
SALES (corp-wide): 5.1B **Publicly Held**
SIC: 3536 Hand hoists; hoists
HQ: Genie Holdings, Inc.
18340 Ne 76th St
Redmond WA 98052
425 881-1800

(G-8473)
GENIE INDUSTRIES INC
18700 Ne 65th St (98052-4943)
PHONE......................425 881-1800
Gregory Monce, *Research*
Robert Hasegawa, *Manager*
EMP: 21
SALES (corp-wide): 5.1B **Publicly Held**
SIC: 3536 Hand hoists
HQ: Genie Industries, Inc.
18340 Ne 76th St
Redmond WA 98052
425 881-1800

(G-8474)
GENIE INDUSTRIES INC
Also Called: Phoenix Equipment Co
6464 185th Ave Ne Ste 200 (98052-5048)
PHONE......................254 714-0088
John Carhart, *Branch Mgr*
EMP: 140
SALES (corp-wide): 5.1B **Publicly Held**
SIC: 3536 Hoists, cranes & monorails
HQ: Genie Industries, Inc.
18340 Ne 76th St
Redmond WA 98052
425 881-1800

(G-8475)
GENIE MANUFACTURING INC (DH)
18340 Ne 76th St (98052-5020)
P.O. Box 97030 (98073-9730)
PHONE......................425 881-1800
Robert Wilkerson, *President*
Tim Ford, *President*
Yuiet Ireland, *Accountant*
▲ **EMP:** 1500
SALES (est): 89.8MM
SALES (corp-wide): 5.1B **Publicly Held**
WEB: www.geniekorea.com
SIC: 3531 Aerial work platforms: hydraulic/elec. truck/carrier mounted
HQ: Genie Holdings, Inc.
18340 Ne 76th St
Redmond WA 98052
425 881-1800

(G-8476)
GEORGE ANDERSON COMPANY
4821 272nd Ave Ne (98053-8703)
P.O. Box 176, Carnation (98014-0176)
PHONE......................425 333-0707
George Anderson, *Owner*
Mary Anderson, *Co-Owner*
EMP: 5
SALES: 960K **Privately Held**
SIC: 2411 Logging camps & contractors

(G-8477)
GIBRALTAR MAINT & CNSTR INC
Also Called: Avara Construction
15341 Ne 90th St S (98052-3562)
PHONE......................206 365-4440
Benjamin Petter, *President*
Sam McCgills, *Senior VP*
Jason Jensen, *Vice Pres*
EMP: 4
SALES (est): 643.5K **Privately Held**
SIC: 1389 1531 1541 Construction, repair & dismantling services; ; industrial buildings & warehouses

(G-8478)
GLORI PUBLISHING LLC
18612 Ne 25th St (98052-5950)
PHONE......................425 202-7714
EMP: 2
SALES (est): 56.5K **Privately Held**
SIC: 2741 Misc Publishing

(G-8479)
GNW CORPORATION
15333 Ne 92nd St (98052-3517)
PHONE......................425 869-6218
EMP: 4 **EST:** 2009
SALES (est): 350K **Privately Held**
SIC: 2431 Mfg Millwork

(G-8480)
GOLFCO INTERNATIONAL INC
18009 Ne 76th St (98052-5023)
PHONE......................425 861-7755
John Davis, *President*
Martin Doyle, *Vice Pres*
▲ **EMP:** 7 **EST:** 1993
SALES (est): 841.6K **Privately Held**
WEB: www.golfcointl.com
SIC: 3949 Golf equipment

(G-8481)
GORDON BECKER CONSTRUCTION
Also Called: Beckers Custom Cabinets
8535 152nd Ave Ne (98052-3510)
PHONE......................425 883-8545
Gordon Becker, *President*
EMP: 3
SQ FT: 5,000
SALES: 260K **Privately Held**
WEB: www.gordonbecker.com
SIC: 2434 Wood kitchen cabinets

(G-8482)
GORDON EXPORTS LLC
15912 Ne 41st St (98052-5266)
PHONE......................503 313-6544
Andrew Gordon, *Principal*
EMP: 1
SALES: 5MM **Privately Held**
SIC: 3432 Plumbing fixture fittings & trim

(G-8483)
GREAT NORTHWEST INDUSTRIES
Also Called: Great NW Storm Screen Door Co
5421 157th Dr Ne (98052-5212)
PHONE......................425 861-9768
Rick Edwards, *President*
EMP: 10
SQ FT: 6,000
SALES: 750K **Privately Held**
SIC: 2431 2434 Millwork; wood kitchen cabinets

(G-8484)
GREEN OFFICE SUPPLIES
704 228th Ave Ne (98074-7222)
PHONE......................408 871-8887
EMP: 2
SALES (est): 150K **Privately Held**
SIC: 3555 Mfg Printing Trades Machinery

(G-8485)
GREENWOOD CLEAN ENERGY INC (PA)
7114 180th Ave Ne B101 (98052-4970)
P.O. Box 2524 (98073-2524)
PHONE......................888 788-3090
German Burtscher, *CEO*
Michael Kuehner, *Principal*
EMP: 5
SALES (est): 757.3K **Privately Held**
SIC: 3433 Heating equipment, except electric

(G-8486)
H C U INC
15362 Ne 96th Pl (98052)
PHONE......................425 885-0564
Klaus Holler, *President*
▲ **EMP:** 1
SQ FT: 2,880
SALES (est): 1.5MM **Privately Held**
SIC: 3469 Machine parts, stamped or pressed metal

(G-8487)
HANCOCKS BAKERY
16150 Ne 85th St Ste 105 (98052-3540)
PHONE......................425 885-3780
John Hancock, *Owner*
Vicky Hancock, *Co-Owner*
EMP: 2
SALES (est): 67K **Privately Held**
SIC: 2051 Bakery: wholesale or wholesale/retail combined

(G-8488)
HARBINGER KNOWLEDGE PDTS INC
16770 Ne 79th St Ste 100 (98052-4413)
PHONE......................425 861-8400
Vikas Joshi, *CEO*
Seema Chaudhary, *President*
Umesh Kanade, *General Mgr*
Mahesh Keni, *Vice Pres*
Prashant Khambekar, *Vice Pres*
EMP: 4
SALES (est): 472.6K **Privately Held**
SIC: 7372 Business oriented computer software

(G-8489)
HAZELWOOD FARM LLC
Also Called: Vn Graphics
14831 Ne 87th St (98052-3485)
PHONE......................425 454-5165
Samuel Courtney, *General Mgr*
Thomas L Courtney, *Mng Member*
Jordan Bush, *Administration*
EMP: 16
SQ FT: 8,500
SALES (est): 2.4MM **Privately Held**
WEB: www.vngraphics.com
SIC: 3555 2796 2791 Printing plates; platemaking services; typesetting

(G-8490)
HELION ENERGY INC
8210 154th Ave Ne Ste 100 (98052-6178)
PHONE......................425 332-7463
David Kirtley, *CEO*
Chris Pihl, *COO*
Brian Campbell, *Engineer*
Mark Van Order, *CFO*
Scott Kimball, *Manager*
▲ **EMP:** 22
SALES (est): 1MM **Privately Held**
SIC: 3699 High-energy particle physics equipment

(G-8491)
HERZOG ENVELOPE INC
17644 Ne 65th St (98052-4904)
P.O. Box 583, Woodinville (98072-0583)
PHONE......................206 618-6765
Jack Herzog, *President*
EMP: 6
SQ FT: 3,000
SALES (est): 390K **Privately Held**
SIC: 2759 2752 Envelopes: printing; commercial printing, lithographic

(G-8492)
HESTIA CELLARS
28335 Ne Quail Creek Dr (98053-3102)
PHONE......................425 333-4270
Shannon Jones, *Manager*
EMP: 7 **EST:** 2010
SALES (est): 440.2K **Privately Held**
SIC: 2084 Wines

(G-8493)
HILLEBERG INC
Also Called: Hilleberg The Tentmaker
14790 Ne 95th St (98052-2519)
PHONE......................425 883-0101
Petra Hilleberg, *President*
▲ **EMP:** 9 **EST:** 2000
SALES (est): 1.2MM **Privately Held**
WEB: www.hilleberg.com
SIC: 5999 2394 Tents; tents: made from purchased materials

(G-8494)
HILTON ACQUISITION COMPANY LLC
14520 Ne 91st St (98052-6553)
PHONE......................425 883-7000
Matt Dezurik, *Principal*
EMP: 13 **EST:** 2014
SALES (est): 2.6MM **Privately Held**
SIC: 3491 Industrial valves

(G-8495)
HOME DESIGN EXPO
18425 Ne 95th St Unit 195 (98052-2941)
PHONE......................425 864-6313
Jerry Reep, *Administration*
EMP: 2
SALES (est): 91.3K **Privately Held**
SIC: 3993 Signs & advertising specialties

GEOGRAPHIC SECTION
Redmond - King County (G-8526)

(G-8496)
HONEYWELL INTERNATIONAL INC
15001 Ne 36th St (98052-5317)
PHONE.....................425 885-3711
David F Green, *Manager*
EMP: 463
SALES (corp-wide): 41.8B **Publicly Held**
WEB: www.honeywell.com
SIC: 3724 Aircraft engines & engine parts
PA: Honeywell International Inc.
115 Tabor Rd
Morris Plains NJ 07950
973 455-2000

(G-8497)
HONEYWELL INTERNATIONAL INC
15001 Ne 36th St (98052-5317)
PHONE.....................425 885-8944
Larry Fitzgerald, *Branch Mgr*
EMP: 3
SALES (corp-wide): 41.8B **Publicly Held**
WEB: www.honeywell.com
SIC: 3724 Aircraft engines & engine parts
PA: Honeywell International Inc.
115 Tabor Rd
Morris Plains NJ 07950
973 455-2000

(G-8498)
HONEYWELL INTERNATIONAL INC
15001 Ne 36th St (98052-5317)
PHONE.....................425 885-3711
Lynn Blair, *Branch Mgr*
EMP: 60
SALES (corp-wide): 41.8B **Publicly Held**
WEB: www.honeywell.com
SIC: 3724 Aircraft engines & engine parts
PA: Honeywell International Inc.
115 Tabor Rd
Morris Plains NJ 07950
973 455-2000

(G-8499)
HONEYWELL INTERNATIONAL INC
6670 185th Ave Ne (98052-5038)
PHONE.....................425 885-3711
Stuart Donaldson, *Branch Mgr*
EMP: 657
SALES (corp-wide): 41.8B **Publicly Held**
WEB: www.honeywell.com
SIC: 3724 Aircraft engines & engine parts
PA: Honeywell International Inc.
115 Tabor Rd
Morris Plains NJ 07950
973 455-2000

(G-8500)
HONEYWELL INTERNATIONAL INC
15001 Ne 36th St (98052-5317)
P.O. Box 97001 (98073-9701)
PHONE.....................425 885-3711
Dawn Lovely, *Manager*
EMP: 754
SALES (corp-wide): 41.8B **Publicly Held**
WEB: www.honeywell.com
SIC: 2821 3724 Plastics materials & resins; aircraft engines & engine parts
PA: Honeywell International Inc.
115 Tabor Rd
Morris Plains NJ 07950
973 455-2000

(G-8501)
HORIZON PROFESSIONAL CMPT SVCS
Also Called: Healthwind Horizon
8410 154th Ave Ne (98052-3800)
PHONE.....................425 883-6588
Craig Shaver, *President*
Larry Chapman, *Shareholder*
EMP: 10
SQ FT: 3,740
SALES (est): 989.3K **Privately Held**
WEB: www.horizonsoft.com
SIC: 7372 7376 Business oriented computer software; computer facilities management

(G-8502)
HOUGH SOFTWARE CONSULTING
8820 166th Ave Ne (98052-3712)
PHONE.....................425 881-2339
EMP: 2
SALES (est): 150K **Privately Held**
SIC: 7372 Prepackaged Software Services

(G-8503)
HYDROFLOW USA LLC
15301 Ne 90th St (98052-3562)
P.O. Box 543, Woodinville (98072-0543)
PHONE.....................425 497-3900
Tal Journo,
EMP: 10
SALES (est): 1.2MM **Privately Held**
SIC: 3589 Water treatment equipment, industrial

(G-8504)
HYTECH POWER INC
15340 Ne 92nd St Ste D (98052-3521)
PHONE.....................425 890-1180
Phillip Jennings, *CEO*
Daniel Breilh, *Manager*
EMP: 12
SALES (est): 657.5K **Privately Held**
SIC: 3714 Motor vehicle engines & parts

(G-8505)
IDD AEROSPACE CORP
Also Called: Zodiac Lighting Solutions
18225 Ne 76th St (98052-5021)
PHONE.....................425 885-0617
Donald Hayes, *Maint Spvr*
Yannick Giraud, *CFO*
Lori Brewer, *Human Res Mgr*
Steve Matriotti, *Manager*
Les Thorpe, *Manager*
EMP: 160
SQ FT: 32,000
SALES (est): 44.3MM
SALES (corp-wide): 833.4MM **Privately Held**
WEB: www.idd.zodiac.com
SIC: 3728 3647 3812 Panel assembly (hydromatic propeller test stands), aircraft; aircraft lighting fixtures; search & navigation equipment
HQ: Zodiac Us Corporation
1747 State Route 34
Wall Township NJ 07727
732 681-3527

(G-8506)
IMAGICORPS INC
10500 231st Way Ne (98053-5896)
PHONE.....................425 869-0599
Thomas W Hutchinson, *President*
EMP: 37
SQ FT: 23,500
SALES (est): 16MM **Privately Held**
WEB: www.imagicorps.com
SIC: 5046 8742 2542 2541 Display equipment, except refrigerated; marketing consulting services; fixtures: display, office or store: except wood; display fixtures, wood; signs & advertising specialties

(G-8507)
INNER FENCE HOLDINGS INC
16701 Ne 80th St Ste 204 (98052-3937)
PHONE.....................888 922-8277
Derek Del Conte, *Principal*
EMP: 5
SQ FT: 1,200
SALES (est): 340.8K **Privately Held**
SIC: 7372 Application computer software

(G-8508)
INNOVATIVE ADVANTAGE INC
15353 Ne 90th St (98052-3562)
PHONE.....................206 910-7528
Richard Morris, *President*
Dave Garing, *President*
Greg Smith, *Vice Pres*
Sally Morris, *Admin Sec*
EMP: 7
SALES (est): 1.3MM **Privately Held**
SIC: 3651 Home entertainment equipment, electronic

(G-8509)
INSOMANIA SOFTWARE
11758 175th Pl Ne (98052-2811)
PHONE.....................425 837-1525
Abdulwajid Mohamed, *Principal*
EMP: 2
SALES (est): 117.5K **Privately Held**
SIC: 7372 Prepackaged software

(G-8510)
INTEGRATED COMPUTER SYSTEMS
Also Called: I C S Support
8541 154th Ave Ne (98052-3557)
PHONE.....................425 820-6120
Jeff Mack, *President*
EMP: 12
SQ FT: 5,000
SALES (est): 1.7MM **Privately Held**
WEB: www.ics-support.com
SIC: 7372 Business oriented computer software

(G-8511)
INTEGRITY PRESS INC
1211 210th Ave Ne (98074-6614)
PHONE.....................425 868-3120
EMP: 5
SQ FT: 2,100
SALES (est): 600K **Privately Held**
SIC: 2754 Gravure Commercial Printing

(G-8512)
INTENTIONET INC
16625 Redmond Way M241 (98052-4444)
PHONE.....................206 579-6567
ARI Fogel, *CEO*
Ratul Mahajan, *President*
Jitendra Padhye, *Treasurer*
EMP: 2 **EST:** 2015
SALES (est): 65.5K **Privately Held**
SIC: 7372 7379 Utility computer software;

(G-8513)
INTERIOR WDWKG SPECIALISTS INC
15337 Ne 92nd St (98052-3517)
PHONE.....................425 881-1328
Doug W Hepner, *President*
Dan Cummings, *Vice Pres*
Tracy L Hepner, *Treasurer*
EMP: 45
SQ FT: 32,000
SALES: 8.9MM **Privately Held**
WEB: www.interiorwoodworking.com
SIC: 2431 Millwork

(G-8514)
INVENTPRISE LLC
18133 Ne 68th St Ste D150 (98052-8511)
PHONE.....................206 858-8472
Pradip Jhate, *COO*
Subhash Kapre,
EMP: 12
SALES: 3.9MM **Privately Held**
SIC: 2836 Vaccines

(G-8515)
ITO ENTERPRISES INC ✪
17717 Ne 108th Way (98052-2889)
PHONE.....................425 556-0819
EMP: 2 **EST:** 2019
SALES (est): 73.2K **Privately Held**
SIC: 2759 Commercial printing

(G-8516)
ITRAQ INC
8201 164th Ave Ne Ste 200 (98052-7615)
PHONE.....................844 694-8727
Roman Isakov, *CEO*
EMP: 4
SALES (est): 12MM **Privately Held**
SIC: 7371 3699 Computer software development & applications; electrical equipment & supplies

(G-8517)
JAACO CORPORATION
18080 Ne 68th St Ste C130 (98052-8513)
PHONE.....................425 952-4205
Chen Wui-Ying, *President*
Chia Shyang-Wen, *Admin Sec*
▲ **EMP:** 2

SALES (est): 304.8K **Privately Held**
SIC: 3315 Nails, spikes, brads & similar items

(G-8518)
JACK JUST ENTERPRISES LLC
Also Called: UPS Store 5427
23515 Ne Novelt (98053)
PHONE.....................425 836-7755
Jack Graham,
EMP: 4
SQ FT: 1,000
SALES (est): 420K **Privately Held**
SIC: 4215 2542 Package delivery, vehicular; postal lock boxes, mail racks & related products

(G-8519)
JESTER CELLARS
7581 Old Redmond Rd Apt 1 (98052-4288)
PHONE.....................425 785-9217
Chris Loeliger, *Principal*
EMP: 2
SALES (est): 144.5K **Privately Held**
SIC: 2084 Wines

(G-8520)
JOHNNYSTAND
26462 Ne 53rd St (98053-2712)
PHONE.....................206 412-2982
Jonathan A Bork, *Principal*
EMP: 2
SALES (est): 187.6K **Privately Held**
WEB: www.johnnystand.com
SIC: 2521 Wood office furniture

(G-8521)
JOMAR HOLDINGS INC
Also Called: Eagle Ins
16541 Redmond Way (98052-4492)
PHONE.....................425 881-7125
Russell Colley, *President*
Russ Cooley, *Principal*
EMP: 2
SALES (est): 230K **Privately Held**
WEB: www.eagleims.com
SIC: 2752 Publication printing, lithographic

(G-8522)
JPH INDUSTRIES LLC
14820 Redmond Way (98052-6843)
PHONE.....................425 269-8966
EMP: 2
SALES (est): 76.7K **Privately Held**
SIC: 3999 Manufacturing industries

(G-8523)
JTC AEROSPACE LLC
10018 184th Ave Ne (98052-6905)
PHONE.....................425 869-6812
EMP: 2
SALES (est): 77.4K **Privately Held**
SIC: 3812 Search & navigation equipment

(G-8524)
JUD CALVARY INC
Also Called: Mama Jo's Gourmet Sauce
10309 155th Pl Ne (98052-2515)
PHONE.....................708 323-8758
Josephine Siaw, *President*
Jesus Birikorang, *Principal*
Jesus Judahbram, *Principal*
EMP: 2
SALES (est): 197.7K **Privately Held**
SIC: 2035 2068 Pickles, sauces & salad dressings; salted & roasted nuts & seeds; seeds: dried, dehydrated, salted or roasted; nuts: dried, dehydrated, salted or roasted

(G-8525)
KONTAK LLC
21311 Ne 101st Ct (98053-7644)
PHONE.....................425 442-5929
Bart Norton, *CEO*
David O'Connor, *Chief Engr*
EMP: 2
SALES (est): 76.9K **Privately Held**
SIC: 3629 Electrochemical generators (fuel cells)

(G-8526)
KYMETA CORPORATION (PA)
12277 134th Ct Ne Ste 100 (98052-2431)
PHONE.....................425 896-3700
Nathan Kundtz, *CEO*

Redmond - King County (G-8527) GEOGRAPHIC SECTION

S Douglas Hutcheson, *Ch of Bd*
Walter Z Berger, *President*
John Schilling, *Exec VP*
Rash Jhanjee, *Vice Pres*
EMP: 100 **EST:** 2017
SQ FT: 50,000
SALES (est): 36MM **Privately Held**
SIC: 3663 Satellites, communications; television antennas (transmitting) & ground equipment

(G-8527)
KYMETA CORPORATION
12277 134th Ct Ne Ste 100 (98052-2431)
PHONE..................425 896-3700
Nathan Kundtz PHD, *Branch Mgr*
EMP: 70
SALES (corp-wide): 36MM **Privately Held**
SIC: 3663 Satellites, communications; television antennas (transmitting) & ground equipment
PA: Kymeta Corporation
12277 134th Ct Ne Ste 100
Redmond WA 98052
425 896-3700

(G-8528)
LADY 12 LLC
27928 Ne 5th St (98053-9203)
PHONE..................425 218-3080
Brandelyn Tafoya,
Tiffany Brown,
Nicole Evans,
EMP: 2
SALES (est): 175.7K **Privately Held**
SIC: 5699 5621 2211 5961 Sports apparel; ready-to-wear apparel, women's; apparel & outerwear fabrics, cotton; women's apparel, mail order; clothing & apparel carrying cases

(G-8529)
LASER GUIDANCE INC
14746 Ne 95th St (98052-2519)
P.O. Box 2139 (98073-2139)
PHONE..................206 679-3909
David Mark Shemwell, *President*
Dave Shemwell, *President*
Alan A Vetter, *Vice Pres*
EMP: 5
SQ FT: 2,100
SALES: 350K **Privately Held**
WEB: www.laserguidance.com
SIC: 3648 Outdoor lighting equipment

(G-8530)
LASER TECHNIQUES COMPANY LLC
Also Called: Ltc
11431 Willows Rd Ne # 100 (98052-3069)
PHONE..................425 885-0607
James Doyle,
EMP: 15
SQ FT: 15,000
SALES (est): 3.2MM **Privately Held**
WEB: www.laser-ndt.com
SIC: 3699 8711 Laser systems & equipment; consulting engineer

(G-8531)
LEADING EDGE LABELING INC
14612 Ne 91st St (98052-3436)
P.O. Box 802, Bothell (98041-0802)
PHONE..................425 821-4137
Kevin Halls, *President*
Jill S Halls, *Admin Sec*
EMP: 33
SQ FT: 3,500
SALES (est): 5.4MM **Privately Held**
WEB: www.labels4u.com
SIC: 2672 5085 5084 2671 Labels (unprinted), gummed: made from purchased materials; industrial supplies; industrial machinery & equipment; packaging paper & plastics film, coated & laminated

(G-8532)
LEANCODE INC
Also Called: Plugable Technologies
8511 154th Ave Ne (98052-3557)
PHONE..................425 533-5219
Michael Roberts, *Mng Member*
Bernie Thompson,
▲ **EMP:** 15
SALES (est): 3.9MM **Privately Held**
SIC: 3577 3572 Input/output equipment, computer; computer auxiliary storage units

(G-8533)
LEVETEC SURFACE PREP MCHY LLC
Also Called: Avenger USA
20245 Ne Redmond Fall Cty (98053-4815)
PHONE..................425 629-8200
Wayne Wheller,
▲ **EMP:** 4
SALES: 1MM **Privately Held**
WEB: www.levetec.com
SIC: 3541 Buffing & polishing machines

(G-8534)
LIONFORT SOFTWARE INC
18570 Ne 58th Ct K1081 (98052-6757)
PHONE..................425 698-7403
Harish Rane, *Owner*
EMP: 2
SALES (est): 56.5K **Privately Held**
SIC: 7372 Prepackaged software

(G-8535)
LITTLE BEAN COFFEE LLC
Also Called: Rivertrail Roasters
11924 158th Ave Ne (98052-2633)
PHONE..................425 829-8289
Ryan McLaughlin,
EMP: 3
SALES (est): 147.1K **Privately Held**
SIC: 2095 5812 5963 Roasted coffee; American restaurant; food service, coffee-cart

(G-8536)
LODER INSTRUMENT COMPANY INC
15143 Ne 90th St (98052-3560)
PHONE..................425 869-3861
John Loder, *President*
William Loder, *President*
Richard Loder, *Treasurer*
Juanita Loder, *Admin Sec*
EMP: 8
SALES (est): 533.5K **Privately Held**
SIC: 3599 3821 Machine shop, jobbing & repair; laboratory apparatus & furniture

(G-8537)
LOG CABIN CRAFTS
9114 171st Ave Ne (98052-3726)
PHONE..................425 885-9049
Lauri Heath, *Owner*
EMP: 2
SALES (est): 61.9K **Privately Held**
SIC: 3944 Craft & hobby kits & sets

(G-8538)
LOUDSCOOP INC
4018 173rd Ct Ne (98052-5706)
PHONE..................425 391-7159
Nishant Dani, *President*
EMP: 2 **EST:** 2010
SALES (est): 123.2K **Privately Held**
SIC: 7372 Prepackaged software

(G-8539)
LUCKY SCOOTER PARTS LLC
6855 176th Ave Ne B-235 (98052-5243)
PHONE..................425 558-0715
Brian Jeide,
▲ **EMP:** 7
SALES (est): 850.1K **Privately Held**
SIC: 3751 Motor scooters & parts

(G-8540)
LUMPINEE INC
8900 161st Ave Ne (98052-7551)
PHONE..................425 497-8383
EMP: 10
SALES (corp-wide): 1.7MM **Privately Held**
SIC: 3469 Kitchen fixtures & equipment: metal, except cast aluminum
PA: Lumpinee Inc.
23 Mercer St
Seattle WA 98109
206 281-8883

(G-8541)
LUNDBERG LLC
8271 154th Ave Ne 250 (98052-3878)
PHONE..................425 283-5070
Douglas Giarde, *President*
Peter Englund, *Engineer*
▼ **EMP:** 48
SQ FT: 15,000
SALES: 50MM
SALES (corp-wide): 1.5B **Privately Held**
SIC: 8711 3559 Energy conservation engineering; chemical machinery & equipment
HQ: Dustex Llc
60 Chastain Center Blvd N
Kennesaw GA 30144
770 429-5575

(G-8542)
M&L INDUSTRIES INC
4401 268th Ave Ne (98053-8715)
PHONE..................425 894-7147
Leanne Donaldson, *Principal*
EMP: 2
SALES (est): 155.4K **Privately Held**
SIC: 3999 Manufacturing industries

(G-8543)
MAC & JACKS BREWERY INC
17825 Ne 65th St (98052-4993)
PHONE..................425 558-9697
Malcolm Rankin, *President*
Jack Schropp, *Vice Pres*
Ken Nabors, *Manager*
Steve Nolan, *Executive*
▲ **EMP:** 17
SQ FT: 9,000
SALES (est): 3.4MM **Privately Held**
WEB: www.macandjacks.com
SIC: 2082 Ale (alcoholic beverage); beer (alcoholic beverage)

(G-8544)
MACKIE DESIGNS INC
25121 Ne 67th Pl (98053-2640)
PHONE..................425 868-0555
Greg Mackie, *Principal*
EMP: 2
SALES (est): 138.5K **Privately Held**
SIC: 5065 5064 3679 3651 Electronic parts & equipment; electrical entertainment equipment; electronic components; household audio & video equipment

(G-8545)
MAGNIX USA INC
6724 185th Ave Ne (98052-6733)
PHONE..................206 304-8129
Roei Ganzarski, *CEO*
Scott Sandler, *CFO*
EMP: 7
SALES (est): 375.6K **Privately Held**
SIC: 3643 Rail bonds, electric: for propulsion & signal circuits

(G-8546)
MAIL BOX & SHIPPING CENTER
Also Called: Mail Box & Shipping Center The
8040 161st Ave Ne (98052-3807)
PHONE..................425 869-1448
Vincent Cronin, *Mng Member*
EMP: 2
SALES (est): 188K **Privately Held**
SIC: 2542 Mail racks & lock boxes, postal service: except wood

(G-8547)
MANGO AND LIME DESIGN LLC
9117 151st Ave Ne (98052-3512)
P.O. Box 3188 (98073-3188)
PHONE..................425 985-8994
MEI Ferguson, *Principal*
▲ **EMP:** 2
SALES (est): 155.3K **Privately Held**
SIC: 7389 3274 Design services; lime

(G-8548)
MARCIA HARDY
3458 W Ames Lake Dr Ne (98053-9107)
PHONE..................425 880-4460
Marcia Hardy, *Principal*
EMP: 2
SALES (est): 56.5K **Privately Held**
SIC: 7372 Prepackaged software

(G-8549)
MARINE HARDWARE INC (PA)
14560 Ne 91st St (98052-6553)
P.O. Box 3099 (98073-3099)
PHONE..................425 883-0651
John F Pugh, *President*
Don Starbuck, *Opers Staff*
Melanie Filip, *Purch Mgr*
Nick J Librande, *Controller*
Melinda Booth, *Sales Staff*
◆ **EMP:** 30
SQ FT: 20,000
SALES (est): 3.8MM **Privately Held**
WEB: www.marinehardware.com
SIC: 3429 3433 Marine hardware; heating equipment, except electric; stoves, wood & coal burning

(G-8550)
MARK LASTING TECHNOLOGY
5310 240th Ave Ne (98053-2542)
PHONE..................425 836-4317
John W Hayenga, *Partner*
EMP: 2
SALES (est): 183.2K **Privately Held**
SIC: 3993 Signs & advertising specialties

(G-8551)
MARKARTS INC
Also Called: Mark Thmpson Mscal Vntrloqists
13821 181st Ln Ne (98052-1152)
P.O. Box 2321 (98073-2321)
PHONE..................425 895-0651
Mary Thompson, *President*
EMP: 2
SALES (est): 153.7K **Privately Held**
WEB: www.markarts.net
SIC: 2741 8661 Miscellaneous publishing; religious organizations

(G-8552)
MARVELL SEMICONDUCTOR INC
10545 Willows Rd Ne (98052-2505)
PHONE..................408 222-2500
EMP: 4 **Privately Held**
SIC: 3674 Semiconductors & related devices
HQ: Marvell Semiconductor, Inc.
5488 Marvell Ln
Santa Clara CA 95054

(G-8553)
MAVERICK SPORTS MEDICINE INC
Also Called: Pro-TEC Athletics
18080 Ne 68th St Ste A150 (98052-0573)
PHONE..................425 497-0887
Jeff Rodgers, *President*
Kathryn Fletcher, *Vice Pres*
Keith Strasburg, *Vice Pres*
▲ **EMP:** 24
SQ FT: 10,500
SALES (est): 2.4MM **Privately Held**
WEB: www.pro-tecathletics.com
SIC: 3949 Exercise equipment; winter sports equipment; protective sporting equipment

(G-8554)
MEDTRONIC INC
11811 Willows Rd Ne (98052-2003)
P.O. Box 97006 (98073-9706)
PHONE..................425 867-4000
Lin Provost, *Technical Mgr*
Steve Silkes, *Branch Mgr*
Matthew Quinn, *Director*
EMP: 16 **Privately Held**
SIC: 3845 Electromedical equipment
HQ: Medtronic, Inc.
710 Medtronic Pkwy
Minneapolis MN 55432
763 514-4000

(G-8555)
MELLANOX TECHNOLOGIES INC
8648 154th Ave Ne (98052-3556)
PHONE..................512 239-8282
EMP: 5
SALES (corp-wide): 293.8MM **Privately Held**
SIC: 3674 Semiconductors & related devices

GEOGRAPHIC SECTION

Redmond - King County (G-8583)

HQ: Mellanox Technologies, Inc.
350 Oakmead Pkwy
Sunnyvale CA 94085
408 970-3400

(G-8556)
MICHAEL CHAPMAN
8500 148th Ave Ne (98052-6556)
PHONE.....................425 881-0907
Michael Chapman, *Principal*
EMP: 2
SALES (est): 85.6K Privately Held
SIC: 3491 Industrial valves

(G-8557)
MICRO STANDARD
18133 Ne 68th St (98052-6718)
PHONE.....................425 882-1722
Jordan Malkin, *Vice Pres*
EMP: 2
SALES (est): 221.9K Privately Held
SIC: 3571 Electronic computers

(G-8558)
MICROSOFT CORPORATION
4200 150th Ave Ne (98052-5302)
PHONE.....................425 705-6218
James Frazier, *Branch Mgr*
EMP: 100
SALES (corp-wide): 110.3B Publicly Held
WEB: www.microsoft.com
SIC: 7372 Application computer software
PA: Microsoft Corporation
1 Microsoft Way
Redmond WA 98052
425 882-8080

(G-8559)
MICROSOFT CORPORATION
15563 Ne 31st St (98052-5385)
PHONE.....................425 706-0040
Steven Ballmer, *Branch Mgr*
Kunal Goel, *Software Dev*
EMP: 35
SALES (corp-wide): 110.3B Publicly Held
SIC: 7372 Prepackaged software
PA: Microsoft Corporation
1 Microsoft Way
Redmond WA 98052
425 882-8080

(G-8560)
MICROSOFT CORPORATION
15010 Ne 36th Way (98052-5317)
PHONE.....................425 706-6640
EMP: 35
SALES (corp-wide): 110.3B Publicly Held
SIC: 7372 Prepackaged software
PA: Microsoft Corporation
1 Microsoft Way
Redmond WA 98052
425 882-8080

(G-8561)
MICROSOFT CORPORATION
15120 Ne 40th St (98052-5308)
PHONE.....................425 861-0581
EMP: 35
SALES (corp-wide): 110.3B Publicly Held
SIC: 7372 Prepackaged software
PA: Microsoft Corporation
1 Microsoft Way
Redmond WA 98052
425 882-8080

(G-8562)
MICROSOFT CORPORATION
16070 Ne 36th Way Bldg 33 (98052-6301)
PHONE.....................425 706-0033
EMP: 35
SALES (corp-wide): 110.3B Publicly Held
SIC: 7372 Prepackaged software
PA: Microsoft Corporation
1 Microsoft Way
Redmond WA 98052
425 882-8080

(G-8563)
MICROSOFT CORPORATION
3009 157th Pl Ne (98052-8301)
PHONE.....................425 882-8080
EMP: 35
SALES (corp-wide): 110.3B Publicly Held
SIC: 7372 Prepackaged software
PA: Microsoft Corporation
1 Microsoft Way
Redmond WA 98052
425 882-8080

(G-8564)
MICROSOFT CORPORATION
3925 159th Ave Ne (98052-6309)
PHONE.....................360 863-0642
Glyn Desmond, *President*
EMP: 35
SALES (corp-wide): 110.3B Publicly Held
SIC: 7372 Prepackaged software
PA: Microsoft Corporation
1 Microsoft Way
Redmond WA 98052
425 882-8080

(G-8565)
MICROSOFT CORPORATION
5000 148th Ave Ne Ste 100 (98052-5100)
PHONE.....................425 867-6537
EMP: 35
SALES (corp-wide): 110.3B Publicly Held
SIC: 7372 Prepackaged software
PA: Microsoft Corporation
1 Microsoft Way
Redmond WA 98052
425 882-8080

(G-8566)
MICROSOFT CORPORATION
3635 156th Ave Ne Bldg 11 (98052)
PHONE.....................425 882-8080
EMP: 599
SALES (corp-wide): 110.3B Publicly Held
SIC: 7372 Application computer software
PA: Microsoft Corporation
1 Microsoft Way
Redmond WA 98052
425 882-8080

(G-8567)
MICROSOFT CORPORATION
15050 Ne 36th St Bldg 110 (98052-5387)
PHONE.....................425 882-8080
EMP: 599
SALES (corp-wide): 110.3B Publicly Held
SIC: 7372 Application computer software
PA: Microsoft Corporation
1 Microsoft Way
Redmond WA 98052
425 882-8080

(G-8568)
MICROSOFT CORPORATION
15220 Ne 40th St (98052-5323)
PHONE.....................425 882-8080
EMP: 599
SALES (corp-wide): 110.3B Publicly Held
SIC: 7372 Application computer software
PA: Microsoft Corporation
1 Microsoft Way
Redmond WA 98052
425 882-8080

(G-8569)
MICROSOFT CORPORATION
3801 Ne 39th St Bldg 17 (98052)
PHONE.....................425 882-8080
EMP: 599
SALES (corp-wide): 110.3B Publicly Held
SIC: 7372 Application computer software
PA: Microsoft Corporation
1 Microsoft Way
Redmond WA 98052
425 882-8080

(G-8570)
MICROSOFT CORPORATION
4350 150th Ave Ne (98052)
PHONE.....................425 828-8080
EMP: 599
SALES (corp-wide): 110.3B Publicly Held
SIC: 7372 Application computer software
PA: Microsoft Corporation
1 Microsoft Way
Redmond WA 98052
425 882-8080

(G-8571)
MICROSOFT CORPORATION
3600 159th Ave Ne Bldg 16 (98052)
PHONE.....................425 882-8080
EMP: 599
SALES (corp-wide): 110.3B Publicly Held
SIC: 7372 Application computer software
PA: Microsoft Corporation
1 Microsoft Way
Redmond WA 98052
425 882-8080

(G-8572)
MICROSOFT CORPORATION
4650 154th Pl Ne Bldg 85 (98052)
PHONE.....................425 882-8080
EMP: 599
SALES (corp-wide): 110.3B Publicly Held
SIC: 7372 Application computer software
PA: Microsoft Corporation
1 Microsoft Way
Redmond WA 98052
425 882-8080

(G-8573)
MICROSOFT CORPORATION
3860 Ne 39th St Bldg 18 (98052)
PHONE.....................425 882-8080
EMP: 599
SALES (corp-wide): 110.3B Publicly Held
SIC: 7372 Application computer software
PA: Microsoft Corporation
1 Microsoft Way
Redmond WA 98052
425 882-8080

(G-8574)
MICROSOFT CORPORATION
3925 Ne 39th St Bldg 21 (98052)
PHONE.....................425 882-8080
EMP: 599
SALES (corp-wide): 110.3B Publicly Held
SIC: 7372 Application computer software
PA: Microsoft Corporation
1 Microsoft Way
Redmond WA 98052
425 882-8080

(G-8575)
MICROSOFT CORPORATION
3600 156th Ave Ne Bldg 24 (98052)
PHONE.....................425 882-8080
EMP: 599
SALES (corp-wide): 110.3B Publicly Held
SIC: 7372 Application computer software
PA: Microsoft Corporation
1 Microsoft Way
Redmond WA 98052
425 882-8080

(G-8576)
MICROSOFT CORPORATION
4900 154th Pl Ne Bldg 86 (98052)
PHONE.....................425 882-8080
EMP: 599
SALES (corp-wide): 110.3B Publicly Held
SIC: 7372 Application computer software
PA: Microsoft Corporation
1 Microsoft Way
Redmond WA 98052
425 882-8080

(G-8577)
MICROSOFT CORPORATION
4001 156th Ave Ne Bldg 50 (98052)
PHONE.....................425 882-8080
Mitch Gray, *Marketing Mgr*
EMP: 599
SALES (corp-wide): 110.3B Publicly Held
SIC: 7372 Application computer software
PA: Microsoft Corporation
1 Microsoft Way
Redmond WA 98052
425 882-8080

(G-8578)
MICROSOFT CORPORATION
4500 154th Pl Ne Bldg 84 (98052)
PHONE.....................425 882-8080
EMP: 599
SALES (corp-wide): 110.3B Publicly Held
SIC: 7372 Application computer software
PA: Microsoft Corporation
1 Microsoft Way
Redmond WA 98052
425 882-8080

(G-8579)
MICROSOFT CORPORATION
15595 Ne 36th St Bldg 44 (98052-5312)
PHONE.....................425 882-8080
Vladimir Bakhmetyev, *Technology*
EMP: 3
SALES (corp-wide): 110.3B Publicly Held
SIC: 7372 Application computer software
PA: Microsoft Corporation
1 Microsoft Way
Redmond WA 98052
425 882-8080

(G-8580)
MICROSOFT CORPORATION (PA)
1 Microsoft Way (98052-8300)
PHONE.....................425 882-8080
Satya Nadella, *CEO*
John W Thompson, *Ch of Bd*
Jean-Philippe Courtois, *Exec VP*
Kathleen T Hogan, *Exec VP*
Margaret L Johnson, *Exec VP*
EMP: 3783
SQ FT: 5,000,000
SALES: 110.3B Publicly Held
WEB: www.microsoft.com
SIC: 7372 7371 3577 7375 Prepackaged software; operating systems computer software; business oriented computer software; application computer software; computer software development; computer peripheral equipment; information retrieval services

(G-8581)
MICROSOFT CORPORATION
22836 Ne 84th Pl (98053-1967)
PHONE.....................206 816-0190
Yuvraj Budhraja, *Branch Mgr*
EMP: 2
SALES (corp-wide): 110.3B Publicly Held
SIC: 7372 Prepackaged software
PA: Microsoft Corporation
1 Microsoft Way
Redmond WA 98052
425 882-8080

(G-8582)
MICROSOFT CORPORATION
17760 Ne 67th Ct (98052-4966)
P.O. Box 3011, Bothell (98041-3011)
PHONE.....................425 556-9348
Annie Spencer, *Corp Comm Staff*
Rajat Minocha, *Manager*
Sangeeta Mudnal, *Manager*
Jim Naroski, *Manager*
Amit Sharma, *Manager*
EMP: 35
SALES (corp-wide): 110.3B Publicly Held
WEB: www.microsoft.com
SIC: 7372 Prepackaged software
PA: Microsoft Corporation
1 Microsoft Way
Redmond WA 98052
425 882-8080

(G-8583)
MICROSOFT PAYMENTS INC
1 Microsoft Way (98052-8300)
PHONE.....................425 722-0528
Keith R Dolliver, *CEO*
Benjamin Orndorff, *Director*
George Zinn, *Director*
EMP: 10
SALES (est): 1.1MM
SALES (corp-wide): 110.3B Publicly Held
SIC: 7372 Business oriented computer software

Redmond - King County (G-8584)

PA: Microsoft Corporation
1 Microsoft Way
Redmond WA 98052
425 882-8080

(G-8584)
MICROSOFT TECH LICENSING LLC
1 Microsoft Way (98052-8300)
PHONE....................425 882-8080
Geoffrey Hoggard, *Principal*
EMP: 2 **EST:** 2014
SALES (est): 56.5K **Privately Held**
SIC: 7372 Operating systems computer software

(G-8585)
MICROSTAR LABORATORIES INC (PA)
Also Called: Microstar Instruments
16310 Ne 85th St Ste 201 (98052-3525)
PHONE....................425 453-2345
Ian Lewis, *President*
Neil Fenichel, *Chairman*
Loretta Lopez, *Vice Pres*
Mike McFeters, *Vice Pres*
EMP: 34
SQ FT: 14,400
SALES (est): 5.1MM **Privately Held**
WEB: www.mstarlabs.com
SIC: 3577 7371 Computer peripheral equipment; custom computer programming services

(G-8586)
MICROSURGICAL TECHNOLOGY INC
Also Called: MST
8415 154th Ave Ne (98052-3863)
P.O. Box 2679 (98073-2679)
PHONE....................425 861-4002
Jeff Castillo, *President*
Robert May, *Vice Pres*
Charles Stellmon, *Engineer*
Kenneth J Wiljanen, *Engineer*
Gwyn Boone, *Human Res Dir*
EMP: 73
SQ FT: 10,000
SALES (est): 15.3MM
SALES (corp-wide): 1.5B **Privately Held**
WEB: www.microsurgical.com
SIC: 3841 Surgical instruments & apparatus
PA: Halma Public Limited Company
Misbourne Court
Amersham BUCKS HP7 0
149 472-1111

(G-8587)
MICROVISION INC
6244 185th Ave Ne Ste 100 (98052-6413)
PHONE....................425 936-6847
Perry M Mulligan, *CEO*
Brian V Turner, *Ch of Bd*
Sumit Sharma, *COO*
David J Westgor, *Vice Pres*
Dean Brown, *Engineer*
EMP: 107
SQ FT: 31,142
SALES: 17.6MM **Privately Held**
WEB: www.mvis.com
SIC: 3679 3577 Electronic loads & power supplies; optical scanning devices

(G-8588)
MIDDY MARINE PRODUCTS INC
Also Called: Middy Plastic Products
9320 151st Ave Ne (98052-3515)
PHONE....................425 883-4600
Lawrence Roalsvig, *President*
M V Judd, *Corp Secy*
EMP: 2
SQ FT: 23,000
SALES: 490K **Privately Held**
SIC: 3082 3083 Unsupported plastics profile shapes; window sheeting, plastic

(G-8589)
MILESTONE PRODUCTS CO
15127 Ne 24th St Ste 332 (98052-5544)
PHONE....................425 882-1987
Jason Williams, *President*
Jo Anna J Birmingham, *Manager*
Lydja Williams, *Admin Sec*
▲ **EMP:** 11
SQ FT: 5,000
SALES (est): 1.4MM **Privately Held**
WEB: www.milestonesproducts.com
SIC: 3944 5092 5032 3952 Craft & hobby kits & sets; toys & hobby goods & supplies; brick, stone & related material; lead pencils & art goods; concrete products; products of purchased glass

(G-8590)
MINDRAY MEDICAL USA CORP
Also Called: Mindray North America
8620 154th Ave Ne 130 (98052-3556)
PHONE....................425 881-0361
Peter Hsu, *President*
Cathy Gao, *Human Res Dir*
Bill Dwyer, *Sales Dir*
Bryan Gilder, *Sales Staff*
Chris Jennings, *Sales Staff*
▲ **EMP:** 21
SALES (est): 2.8MM
SALES (corp-wide): 1.9B **Privately Held**
SIC: 3845 Electromedical equipment
PA: Shenzhen Mindray Bio-Medical Electronics Co., Ltd.
Mindray Building, Keji South No.12 Road, High-Tech Inductrial Zo
Shenzhen 51805
755 818-8881

(G-8591)
MISAPPLIED SCIENCES INC
16128 Ne 87th St (98052-3505)
PHONE....................425 999-9582
Paul Dietz, *CEO*
Albert Ng, *President*
David Thompson, *COO*
EMP: 3
SALES (est): 225.3K **Privately Held**
SIC: 3993 Electric signs

(G-8592)
N R G ENTERPRISES INC
10826 183rd Ave Ne (98052-2871)
PHONE....................425 556-3993
Albert Spokoiny, *President*
Matthew Townsend, *Vice Pres*
EMP: 97
SALES (est): 6.4MM
SALES (corp-wide): 1.4MM **Privately Held**
SIC: 3589 5075 Water filters & softeners, household type; air filters
PA: Hanvest Holding Gmbh
Heinrich-Hertz-Str. 4
Taunusstein 65232
612 874-60

(G-8593)
NEWLINE SOFTWARE INC
8201 164th Ave Ne Ste 320 (98052-7604)
PHONE....................425 442-1126
Kory Gill, *Principal*
EMP: 2
SALES (est): 136.3K **Privately Held**
SIC: 7372 Prepackaged software

(G-8594)
NICK JACKSON CO INC
17725 Ne 65th St Ste A110 (98052-7911)
PHONE....................425 481-1381
Nick Jackson, *President*
Kim Jackson, *Vice Pres*
EMP: 10
SQ FT: 2,500
SALES (est): 1MM **Privately Held**
WEB: www.nickjacksonco.com
SIC: 3536 Davits

(G-8595)
NIDEKKEN LTD
18348 Redmond Way (98052-5012)
PHONE....................425 885-1587
Gintas Taras, *President*
Mitch Taras, *Corp Secy*
EMP: 12
SQ FT: 3,800
SALES (est): 1.1MM **Privately Held**
WEB: www.nidekken.com
SIC: 2321 2325 Men's & boys' dress shirts; men's & boys' trousers & slacks

(G-8596)
NINTENDO SOFTWARE TECHNOLOGY
5001 150th Ave Ne (98052-5121)
P.O. Box 957 (98073-0957)
PHONE....................425 497-7500
Shigeki Yamashiro, *President*
EMP: 40
SQ FT: 1,400
SALES (est): 2.9MM **Privately Held**
WEB: www.nintendo.com
SIC: 7371 7372 Computer software development & applications; prepackaged software
PA: Nintendo Co., Ltd.
11-1, Hokotatecho, Kamitoba, Minami-Ku
Kyoto KYO 601-8

(G-8597)
NOONUM LLC
6449 191st Pl Ne (98052-0546)
PHONE....................425 894-1202
Shankar Vaidyanathan, *Administration*
EMP: 6 **EST:** 2015
SALES (est): 170.6K **Privately Held**
SIC: 7372 Application computer software

(G-8598)
NORTHWEST EXECUTIVE CORP (PA)
Also Called: Eagle Print
8108 138th Ave Ne (98052-1924)
PHONE....................425 883-9010
Ward Truess, *President*
EMP: 4
SQ FT: 1,150
SALES (est): 423.1K **Privately Held**
SIC: 7334 2752 6552 Photocopying & duplicating services; cards, lithographed; land subdividers & developers, commercial

(G-8599)
NORTHWEST GRANITE AND MBL LLC
9289 151st Ave Ne (98052-3511)
PHONE....................206 228-6881
Sergey Bekchiu, *Principal*
EMP: 10
SALES (est): 1.8MM **Privately Held**
SIC: 3281 1743 Table tops, marble; curbing, granite or stone; terrazzo, tile, marble, mosaic work

(G-8600)
NOVATECH INSTRUMENTS INC
12207 184th Ave Ne (98052-2213)
PHONE....................206 301-8986
Steve Swift, *President*
EMP: 3
SALES (est): 357.8K **Privately Held**
WEB: www.novatech-instr.com
SIC: 3825 Digital test equipment, electronic & electrical circuits

(G-8601)
NOW IMPRESSIONS INC
7126 180th Ave Ne C104 (98052-4971)
PHONE....................425 881-5911
Kent Osborne, *President*
Kent F Osborne, *President*
Nancy Osborne, *Vice Pres*
EMP: 6
SALES (est): 818.9K **Privately Held**
WEB: www.nowimpressions.com
SIC: 2761 2752 5112 5111 Continuous forms, office & business; commercial printing, lithographic; manifold business forms; printing paper

(G-8602)
NW FINE ART PRINTING
8700 148th Ave Ne (98052-3482)
P.O. Box 1114, Issaquah (98027-0042)
PHONE....................425 947-1539
EMP: 2
SALES (est): 134.8K **Privately Held**
SIC: 2752 Commercial printing, offset

(G-8603)
ONERADIO CORPORATION
15330 Ne 66th Ct (98052-4711)
PHONE....................206 393-2900
Mohan Vaghul, *CEO*
John Sahr, *Treasurer*
Tony Goodson, *Admin Sec*
EMP: 3 **EST:** 2016
SALES (est): 146.7K **Privately Held**
SIC: 3663 Radio broadcasting & communications equipment; receivers, radio communications

(G-8604)
ORYAN MARINE LLC
Also Called: O Ryan Water Sports Ski School
9045 Willows Rd Ne (98052-6589)
PHONE....................425 485-2871
Oscar Smith, *Principal*
Danielle Smith, *Marketing Mgr*
EMP: 12
SALES (est): 911.5K **Privately Held**
SIC: 3949 Water skis

(G-8605)
OXISCIENCE LLC
17455 Ne 67th Ct Ste 100 (98052-7910)
PHONE....................425 777-5488
Simon Johnston, *CEO*
EMP: 5
SQ FT: 1,500
SALES (est): 370K **Privately Held**
SIC: 2842 Sanitation preparations, disinfectants & deodorants

(G-8606)
PACIFIC BIOSCIENCE LABS INC
Also Called: Clarisonic
17425 Ne Union Hill Rd # 150 (98052-6190)
PHONE....................888 525-2747
Frederic Roze, *President*
Alice Brown, *Editor*
Paul Connors, *Vice Pres*
Christopher J Corbett, *Vice Pres*
Lisa M Gigliotti, *Vice Pres*
▲ **EMP:** 149
SQ FT: 20,000
SALES (est): 32.8MM
SALES (corp-wide): 4.4B **Privately Held**
WEB: www.clarisonic.com
SIC: 3841 Surgical & medical instruments
HQ: L'oreal Usa, Inc.
10 Hudson Yards
New York NY 10001
212 818-1500

(G-8607)
PACIFIC NW AROSPC ALIANCE
16911 Ne 95th St (98052-3748)
PHONE....................425 885-0290
Kevin Steck, *Principal*
EMP: 2
SALES: 46.5K **Privately Held**
SIC: 3812 Aircraft/aerospace flight instruments & guidance systems

(G-8608)
PACIFIC TCHNICAL SOLUTIONS INC
16541 Redmond Way 364 (98052-4492)
PHONE....................425 489-5700
Mark Zamalloa, *President*
EMP: 13
SALES (corp-wide): 4.5MM **Privately Held**
SIC: 3663 5065 Mobile communication equipment; communication equipment
PA: Pacific Technical Solutions, Inc.
1901 10th St Ste 500
Plano TX 75074
888 820-3508

(G-8609)
PACIFIC TOOL INC
Also Called: Pti
15235 Ne 92nd St (98052-3518)
PHONE....................425 882-1970
Bobby Holt, *CEO*
Frank L Garbarino, *President*
Scott Garbarino, *CFO*
EMP: 55 **EST:** 1966
SQ FT: 5,000
SALES (est): 12.4MM **Privately Held**
WEB: www.pacifictool.com
SIC: 3544 3599 Special dies & tools; machine shop, jobbing & repair

GEOGRAPHIC SECTION

Redmond - King County (G-8638)

(G-8610)
PAGEMARK TECHNOLOGY INC
17317 Ne 129th St (98052-1299)
PHONE.................................425 444-3735
Randair Porter, *CEO*
Zach Hector, *VP Bus Dvlpt*
EMP: 12
SALES (est): 783.2K **Privately Held**
SIC: 7372 Prepackaged software

(G-8611)
PAIZO INC
7120 185th Ave Ne Ste 120 (98052-0577)
PHONE.................................425 289-0060
Lisa Stevens, *CEO*
Gabriel Waluconis, *Project Mgr*
Jeff Alvarez, *CFO*
Jenny Bendel, *Director*
Pierce Watters, *Director*
▲ **EMP:** 37
SALES (est): 5.6MM **Privately Held**
WEB: www.paizo.com
SIC: 2731 5961 Books: publishing only; toys & games (including dolls & models), mail order

(G-8612)
PAIZO PUBLISHING LLC
7120 185th Ave Ne Ste 120 (98052-0577)
PHONE.................................425 289-0060
Lisa Stevens,
EMP: 2 **EST:** 2016
SALES (est): 80.4K **Privately Held**
SIC: 2721 Periodicals

(G-8613)
PANASONIC CORP NORTH AMERICA
Also Called: Panasonic Ind Dev Sales Co Div
15317 Ne 90th St (98052-3562)
PHONE.................................425 883-9290
Anthony Komeya, *Branch Mgr*
EMP: 4 **Privately Held**
SIC: 7694 Electric motor repair
HQ: Panasonic Corporation Of North America
2 Riverfront Plz Ste 200
Newark NJ 07102
201 348-7000

(G-8614)
PARAMOUNT CHEMICAL SPC INC
14762 Ne 95th St (98052-2519)
P.O. Box 124 (98073-0124)
PHONE.................................425 882-2673
John Latta, *President*
Erin L Latta, *Corp Secy*
EMP: 47
SQ FT: 2,500
SALES: 7MM **Privately Held**
WEB: www.kidsnpetsbrand.com
SIC: 2842 Cleaning or polishing preparations

(G-8615)
PARENTASOFT LLC
8201 164th Ave Ne Ste 200 (98052-7615)
PHONE.................................425 877-8574
Matthew Braun, *CEO*
Maria Braun, *CFO*
EMP: 2
SALES (est): 134.3K **Privately Held**
SIC: 7372 7389 Application computer software; home entertainment computer software; utility computer software; educational computer software;

(G-8616)
PARKER-HANNIFIN CORPORATION
Also Called: Cost Center
14690 Ne 9th St Ste 104 (98052)
PHONE.................................425 284-2925
Laura Lane McCants, *Manager*
EMP: 7
SALES (corp-wide): 12B **Publicly Held**
WEB: www.parker.com
SIC: 3594 Fluid power pumps & motors
PA: Parker-Hannifin Corporation
6035 Parkland Blvd
Cleveland OH 44124
216 896-3000

(G-8617)
PC CONSULTING & DEVELOPMENT
25819 Ne 25th St (98053-9076)
PHONE.................................425 836-0645
Rod Roadifer, *President*
EMP: 2
SALES (est): 117.2K **Privately Held**
WEB: www.pdlog.com
SIC: 7372 Prepackaged software

(G-8618)
PERFINT HEALTHCARE CORP USA
8201 164th Ave Ne Ste 200 (98052-7615)
PHONE.................................425 629-9207
EMP: 4
SALES: 450K **Privately Held**
SIC: 3841 Mfg Surgical/Medical Instruments

(G-8619)
PERMA-CHINK SYSTEMS INC (PA)
17635 Ne 67th Ct (98052-4944)
PHONE.................................425 885-6050
Richard Dunstan, *President*
◆ **EMP:** 15
SQ FT: 6,000
SALES (est): 9.2MM **Privately Held**
WEB: www.stuc-o-flex.com
SIC: 3299 2851 Stucco; wood stains

(G-8620)
PERSONAL MEDICAL CORP
8672 154th Ave Ne (98052-3556)
PHONE.................................425 497-1044
Kevin Connolly, *President*
EMP: 4
SALES: 1MM **Privately Held**
SIC: 3841 Surgical & medical instruments

(G-8621)
PHYSIO-CONTROL INTL INC
11811 Willows Rd Ne (98052-2015)
PHONE.................................425 867-4000
Mitch Parrish, *CEO*
Brian D Webster, *President*
Mathieu Badard, *General Mgr*
Dale Pearson, *General Mgr*
Erik Von Schenck, *General Mgr*
EMP: 1800
SALES (est): 370.2K
SALES (corp-wide): 13.6B **Publicly Held**
SIC: 3845 Defibrillator; pacemaker, cardiac
PA: Stryker Corporation
2825 Airview Blvd
Portage MI 49002
269 385-2600

(G-8622)
PIN HSIAO & ASSOCIATES LLC (PA)
Also Called: Antonina's Bakery
2535 152nd Ave Ne (98052-5537)
P.O. Box 40177, Bellevue (98015-4177)
PHONE.................................425 637-3357
Pin Hsiao, *CEO*
Tonya Gordeeva, *Controller*
Kay Conley, *Sales Dir*
EMP: 5
SALES (est): 12MM **Privately Held**
WEB: www.antoninasbakery.com
SIC: 2051 Bakery: wholesale or wholesale/retail combined

(G-8623)
PINPOINT LLC
16541 Redmond Way Ste 170 (98052-4492)
PHONE.................................425 442-4764
Randall Hooker, *Director*
Donald Gunn, *Director*
▲ **EMP:** 2
SALES (est): 190K **Privately Held**
SIC: 3579 Mailing machines

(G-8624)
PLASTICREATIONS INC
16541 Redmond Way (98052-4492)
PHONE.................................425 558-1075
Tom Johnson, *President*
EMP: 6
SALES (est): 545.3K **Privately Held**
WEB: www.plasticreations.com
SIC: 2821 Plastics materials & resins

(G-8625)
PLATALYTICS INC
6128 145th Ct Ne (98052-4681)
PHONE.................................916 835-9584
Asad Faizi, *CEO*
Asim Ranjha, *Principal*
EMP: 35 **EST:** 2013
SQ FT: 15,000
SALES (est): 845K **Privately Held**
SIC: 7372 Application computer software

(G-8626)
PLAYNETWORK INC (DH)
8727 148th Ave Ne (98052-3483)
PHONE.................................425 497-8100
Craig Hubbell, *CEO*
John Crooke, *Development*
Walt Tatum, *Sales Staff*
Nicole Rikkinen, *Marketing Staff*
Shari Green, *Manager*
▼ **EMP:** 175
SQ FT: 12,657
SALES (est): 65MM
SALES (corp-wide): 96.9MM **Privately Held**
WEB: www.playnetwork.com
SIC: 3651 Audio electronic systems
HQ: The Octave Music Group Inc
850 3rd Ave Ste 15th
New York NY 10022
212 991-6540

(G-8627)
POLARIS GLOVE & SAFETY IN
309 Nw 88st (98073)
P.O. Box 401 (98073-0401)
PHONE.................................206 789-5887
Pede Fanci, *Owner*
EMP: 3
SALES (est): 217.7K **Privately Held**
SIC: 3613 Panel & distribution boards & other related apparatus

(G-8628)
PPCS INC
Also Called: Minuteman
16292 Redmond Way (98052-3825)
PHONE.................................425 883-7464
JD Klein, *Principal*
EMP: 2
SALES (est): 189.8K **Privately Held**
SIC: 2752 Commercial printing, offset

(G-8629)
PPG INDUSTRIES INC
9135 Willows Rd Ne (98052-3407)
PHONE.................................425 885-3848
Shawn Carpentier, *Branch Mgr*
EMP: 4
SALES (corp-wide): 15.3B **Publicly Held**
SIC: 2851 Paints & allied products
PA: Ppg Industries, Inc.
1 Ppg Pl
Pittsburgh PA 15272
412 434-3131

(G-8630)
PRACTEC LLC
17625 Ne 65th St Ste 125 (98052-7914)
PHONE.................................425 881-8202
Robert Smrecansky, *Materials Mgr*
Kyle Haffner,
EMP: 16 **EST:** 1995
SALES: 300K **Privately Held**
WEB: www.practecllc.com
SIC: 3825 7629 Test equipment for electronic & electric measurement; electrical equipment repair services

(G-8631)
PRINT CONCIERGE
7241 185th Ave Ne (98073-3801)
PHONE.................................206 801-9996
EMP: 2
SALES (est): 83.9K **Privately Held**
SIC: 2752 Commercial printing, lithographic

(G-8632)
PROBI USA INC (HQ)
Also Called: Nutraceutix
9609 153rd Ave Ne (98052-2522)
PHONE.................................425 883-9518
Peter Nahlstedt, *CEO*
Tim Gamble, *President*
Randy Schoenfeldt, *President*
Richard Marriott, *CFO*
EMP: 9 **EST:** 1997
SQ FT: 41,624
SALES (est): 9MM
SALES (corp-wide): 3.6B **Privately Held**
SIC: 2023 Dietary supplements, dairy & non-dairy based
PA: Symrise Ag
Muhlenfeldstr. 1
Holzminden 37603
553 190-0

(G-8633)
PROCTOR INTERNATIONAL LLC (PA)
Also Called: Proctor & Associates
15305 Ne 95th St (98052-2517)
PHONE.................................425 881-7000
D Fred Proctor, *President*
EMP: 4
SQ FT: 20,000
SALES (est): 4.4MM **Privately Held**
WEB: www.proctorinc.com
SIC: 3661 7372 3429 Telephones & telephone apparatus; prepackaged software; manufactured hardware (general)

(G-8634)
PROLOGIX LLC
Also Called: Prologix Instruments
16541 Redmond Way 421c (98052-4492)
PHONE.................................425 829-8199
Abdul Nizar, *Mng Member*
EMP: 5
SALES (est): 245.8K **Privately Held**
SIC: 3577 Computer peripheral equipment

(G-8635)
PROMETHEUS ENERGY COMPANY
8511 154th Ave Ne Bldg L (98052-3557)
PHONE.................................425 558-9100
Jim Aivalis, *CEO*
Bradley R Bodwell, *Senior VP*
Doug Buchanan, *Purch Mgr*
Augie Catalano, *CFO*
Len York, *CFO*
EMP: 14
SALES (est): 3.2MM **Privately Held**
SIC: 1321 Natural gas liquids production

(G-8636)
PROMETHEUS ENERGY GROUP INC
8511 154th Ave Ne Bldg 1 (98052-3557)
PHONE.................................425 558-9100
Matt Barclay, *Manager*
EMP: 7
SALES (corp-wide): 35.2MM **Privately Held**
SIC: 1321 Natural gas liquids production
HQ: Prometheus Energy Group, Inc.
10305 Richmond Ave # 825
Houston TX 77042

(G-8637)
PROTO-DESIGN INC
Also Called: Pdi Tooling 2000
17824 Ne 65th St (98052-4902)
PHONE.................................425 558-0600
Wolf Blechschmidt, *President*
EMP: 11 **EST:** 1974
SQ FT: 8,500
SALES (est): 2.4MM **Privately Held**
WEB: www.proto-design.com
SIC: 3545 3544 Machine tool accessories; special dies, tools, jigs & fixtures

(G-8638)
PS2 GROUP LLC
18689 Ne 55th St (98052-6100)
PHONE.................................206 714-3025
Susan Kitzmiller, *Owner*
Susan A Kitzmiller, *Owner*
EMP: 4
SALES: 5MM **Privately Held**
SIC: 2732 Book printing

Redmond - King County (G-8639)

(G-8639)
QUICK PRESSURE LLC (PA)
15600 Redmond Way Ste 101 (98052-3862)
PHONE..................................206 219-5567
Ron Cook, *Mng Member*
LI Qi Yu,
EMP: 5
SQ FT: 200
SALES: 84K **Privately Held**
SIC: 3823 Pressure measurement instruments, industrial

(G-8640)
QUIET WING AEROSPACE LLC
12324 134th Ct Ne (98052-2433)
PHONE..................................425 451-8565
Philip Kirk, *Principal*
Om Prakash, *Principal*
Peter Swift, *Principal*
EMP: 7
SALES (est): 1MM **Privately Held**
SIC: 3728 Aircraft parts & equipment

(G-8641)
QWARDO INC
9440 171st Ave Ne (98052-3723)
PHONE..................................425 753-8865
Srinivas Penumaka, *CEO*
EMP: 3 **Privately Held**
SIC: 7372 Utility computer software; application computer software

(G-8642)
R3BAR LLC
26005 Ne 34th St (98053-3005)
P.O. Box 9867, Seattle (98109-0867)
PHONE..................................647 296-6265
Sylvester Walters,
Douglas Christie,
Michael Knight,
Timothy Manson,
EMP: 4
SALES: 100K **Privately Held**
SIC: 3949 7389 Gymnasium equipment;

(G-8643)
RADIANT VISION SYSTEMS LLC
18640 Ne 67th Ct (98052-6728)
PHONE..................................425 844-0152
Douglas Kreysar, *COO*
Hal Yamazaki, *Vice Pres*
EMP: 135
SQ FT: 11,000
SALES (est): 27.5MM **Privately Held**
WEB: www.radiantimaging.com
SIC: 3827 Optical instruments & lenses

(G-8644)
RAINIER WELDING INCORPORATED
19020 Ne 84th St (98053-9406)
PHONE..................................425 868-1300
Richard Forster, *President*
EMP: 25
SQ FT: 30,000
SALES (est): 7.3MM **Privately Held**
SIC: 3443 Fabricated plate work (boiler shop)

(G-8645)
RALSTON CUNNINGHAM ASSOCIATES
4050 148th Ave Ne (98052-5165)
PHONE..................................425 455-0316
William C Willard Jr, *President*
Charles Bond, *Vice Pres*
EMP: 3
SQ FT: 2,700
SALES: 1MM **Privately Held**
SIC: 2241 5131 3965 Webbing, braids & belting; belt & buckle assembly kits; buckles & buckle parts

(G-8646)
REDMOND TOWN CENTER
7525 166th Ave Ne (98052-7828)
PHONE..................................425 702-9168
EMP: 14
SALES (est): 2.9MM **Privately Held**
SIC: 3949 Mfg Sporting/Athletic Goods

(G-8647)
RELIANCE INC
6416 208th Ave Ne (98053-7807)
PHONE..................................615 218-3929
Rustamkhan Pathan, *CEO*
EMP: 10 **EST:** 2016
SALES (est): 289.6K **Privately Held**
SIC: 7371 7372 8742 8732 Computer software development & applications; computer software development; computer software systems analysis & design, custom; computer software writing services; application computer software; business oriented computer software; business planning & organizing services; new business start-up consultant; business consultant; business analysis; business management

(G-8648)
REMOTE CONTROL TECHNOLOGY INC
14736 Ne 95th St (98052-2519)
PHONE..................................425 216-7555
R Stockton Rush, *CEO*
David Buicko, *Corp Secy*
EMP: 8
SQ FT: 3,500
SALES: 1MM **Privately Held**
WEB: www.remotecontroltech.com
SIC: 3823 Computer interface equipment for industrial process control

(G-8649)
RESEARCH NETS INCORPORATED
8545 152nd Ave Ne (98052-3510)
P.O. Box 249, Bothell (98041-0249)
PHONE..................................425 821-7345
Fax: 425 775-5122
EMP: 8
SQ FT: 4,000
SALES: 750K **Privately Held**
SIC: 2399 Mfg Fishing Nets

(G-8650)
REXEL CAPITOL LIGHT
17618 Ne 130th Ct (98052-1120)
PHONE..................................425 861-0200
EMP: 2
SALES (est): 119.5K **Privately Held**
SIC: 5063 3646 3645 Lighting fixtures, commercial & industrial; commercial indusl & institutional electric lighting fixtures; residential lighting fixtures

(G-8651)
RIKKI USA INC
14590 Ne 95th St (98052-2550)
PHONE..................................425 881-6881
Hirofumi Fukawa, *President*
Masahiro Terada, *Vice Pres*
Yakasuki Terada, *Vice Pres*
Takashi Shimada, *CFO*
EMP: 17
SQ FT: 10,000
SALES (est): 2MM **Privately Held**
SIC: 2035 Dressings, salad: raw & cooked (except dry mixes)
HQ: Yamasa Corporation U.S.A
3500 Fairview Indus Dr Se
Salem OR 97302

(G-8652)
RIOS BRICK PAVERS
5833 236th Ave Ne (98053-2507)
PHONE..................................206 271-3447
Juan Rios, *Principal*
EMP: 4
SALES (est): 544.6K **Privately Held**
SIC: 3531 Pavers

(G-8653)
ROASTMASTERS LLC
Also Called: Caffe Lusso
17725 Ne 65th St 150 (98052-4931)
PHONE..................................425 284-2327
Philip Meech, *Mng Member*
Joyce Meech,
Wayne Meech,
EMP: 3
SALES (est): 417.8K **Privately Held**
SIC: 3556 Roasting machinery: coffee, peanut, etc.

(G-8654)
ROD CARR SAILMAKER
3011 177th Ave Ne (98052-5825)
PHONE..................................425 881-2846
Rod Carr, *Owner*
EMP: 2
SALES (est): 119.3K **Privately Held**
WEB: www.carrsails.com
SIC: 2394 5551 Sails: made from purchased materials; boat dealers

(G-8655)
ROTOVAC CORPORATION
14615 Ne 91st St Ste C (98052-3553)
PHONE..................................425 883-6746
Clifford Monson, *President*
Nick Long, *Corp Secy*
Charles Monson, *Vice Pres*
Chuck Monson, *Vice Pres*
Jeff Bryson, *Sales Mgr*
◆ **EMP:** 24
SQ FT: 11,000
SALES (est): 5.9MM **Privately Held**
WEB: www.cleaning-carpet.com
SIC: 3635 Carpet shampooer

(G-8656)
SALIRE CORPORATION
Also Called: Salire Partners
16541 Redmond Way Ste 180 (98052-4492)
PHONE..................................425 284-0679
Tony Kevin, *CEO*
EMP: 20 **EST:** 2001
SALES: 2.7MM **Privately Held**
WEB: www.salire.com
SIC: 7372 Business oriented computer software

(G-8657)
SAMUEL & COMPANY INC
Also Called: Market Spice
14690 Ne 95th St Ste 102 (98052-1014)
PHONE..................................425 883-1220
Nancy Dewitt, *General Mgr*
EMP: 5
SALES (corp-wide): 4.3MM **Privately Held**
SIC: 2099 Tea blending
PA: Samuel & Company, Inc.
5141 N 40th St Ste 500
Phoenix AZ 85018
602 840-2990

(G-8658)
SEATTLE SOUND & VIBRATION
14810 Ne 95th St (98052-2541)
PHONE..................................425 497-0660
David Forrest, *Owner*
EMP: 2 **EST:** 2015
SALES (est): 160.7K **Privately Held**
SIC: 3625 Relays & industrial controls

(G-8659)
SEATTLE SPORT SCIENCES INC (PA)
15320 Ne 92nd St (98052-3517)
PHONE..................................425 939-0015
Jeff Alger, *President*
R Scott Chaykin, *CFO*
EMP: 10
SQ FT: 19,000
SALES (est): 1.8MM **Privately Held**
SIC: 3949 Soccer equipment & supplies

(G-8660)
SENSITECH INC (DH)
Also Called: Ryan Instruments
8801 148th Ave Ne (98052-3492)
PHONE..................................425 883-7926
Fax: 425 883-3766
EMP: 42
SALES (est): 14MM
SALES (corp-wide): 57.2B **Publicly Held**
SIC: 7389 3823 3089 Business Services Mfg Process Control Instruments Mfg Plastic Products
HQ: Sensitech Inc.
800 Cummings Ctr Ste 258x
Beverly MA 01915
978 927-7033

(G-8661)
SENSITECH INC
Also Called: Ryan Instruments
8801 148th Ave Ne (98052-3492)
PHONE..................................425 883-7926
Mike Hurton, *President*
Jeff Drovdahl, *QC Mgr*
EMP: 160
SALES (corp-wide): 66.5B **Publicly Held**
SIC: 7389 3823 3089 Inspection & testing services; temperature measurement instruments, industrial; injection molding of plastics
HQ: Sensitech Inc.
800 Cummings Ctr Ste 258x
Beverly MA 01915

(G-8662)
SENSORIA HEALTH INC
15600 Redmond Way Ste 205 (98052-3862)
PHONE..................................425 533-2928
Maurizio Macagno, *Principal*
Davide Vigano, *Principal*
EMP: 8
SALES (est): 395.5K **Privately Held**
SIC: 3841 Surgical & medical instruments

(G-8663)
SERVICE CORP INTERNATIONAL
Also Called: SCI
7200 180th Ave Ne (98052-4923)
PHONE..................................425 885-2414
J C Barr, *Manager*
EMP: 3
SALES (corp-wide): 3.1B **Publicly Held**
SIC: 3281 5999 Burial vaults, stone; monuments, finished to custom order
PA: Service Corporation International
1929 Allen Pkwy
Houston TX 77019
713 522-5141

(G-8664)
SIGN ASSOCIATES INC
6825 176th Ave Ne Ste 125 (98052-7903)
PHONE..................................425 885-6100
Glenn Heyes, *President*
Rod Heyes, *Vice Pres*
Tim Heyes, *Vice Pres*
EMP: 5
SQ FT: 7,300
SALES (est): 601.7K **Privately Held**
WEB: www.signassociatesinc.com
SIC: 3993 Signs, not made in custom sign painting shops

(G-8665)
SIGN PROS INC
17425 Ne 70th St (98052-6187)
P.O. Box 2518 (98073-2518)
PHONE..................................425 885-3204
Ken Foltz, *President*
Richard Thakorlal, *Accounting Mgr*
EMP: 13
SALES (est): 2.2MM **Privately Held**
WEB: www.signpros.net
SIC: 3993 Signs, not made in custom sign painting shops

(G-8666)
SIGNAL INTERFACE GROUP
16310 Ne 85th St (98052-3525)
PHONE..................................425 467-7146
EMP: 5 **EST:** 2009
SALES (est): 644K **Privately Held**
SIC: 3577 Computer peripheral equipment

(G-8667)
SIGNORAMA
8563 154th Ave Ne (98052-3557)
PHONE..................................425 861-9341
EMP: 2 **EST:** 2017
SALES (est): 86.8K **Privately Held**
SIC: 3993 Mfg Signs/Advertising Specialties

(G-8668)
SIGNOSTICS INC
8310 154th Ave Ne Ste 200 (98052-6180)
PHONE..................................425 402-0971
Kevin Goodwin, *CEO*
EMP: 17

SALES (est): 4.4MM **Privately Held**
SIC: 3841 Surgical & medical instruments

(G-8669)
SIMPLE AGILE CORPORATION
4045 168th Ave Ne (98052-5477)
PHONE..................................425 985-1096
Ashok Singh, *CEO*
EMP: 2
SALES (est): 114.9K **Privately Held**
SIC: 7372 7389 Application computer software;

(G-8670)
SIRASCOM INC
11121 Willows Rd Ne # 200 (98052-1016)
PHONE..................................425 497-3300
Peter Junger, *Principal*
EMP: 2
SALES (est): 135.8K **Privately Held**
SIC: 7372 Prepackaged software

(G-8671)
SKY RIVER BREWING INC
14270 Woodinville Redmond (98052-2008)
PHONE..................................360 793-6761
Denise Ingalls, *President*
Dereck Ingalls, *Treasurer*
EMP: 3
SQ FT: 2,000
SALES (est): 308.5K **Privately Held**
WEB: www.skyriverbrewing.com
SIC: 2084 Wines

(G-8672)
SKY RIVER MEADERY
14270 Woodinvll Redmd Rd (98052-2008)
PHONE..................................425 242-3815
Glenda Downs, *Marketing Staff*
EMP: 11
SALES (est): 1.4MM **Privately Held**
SIC: 2084 Wines

(G-8673)
SOFTWARE AG USA INC
Also Called: Connx Solutions
2039 152nd Ave Ne (98052-5521)
PHONE..................................425 519-6600
Ann Lee, *Engineer*
Nick Pizzitola, *Marketing Staff*
EMP: 23
SALES (corp-wide): 991MM **Privately Held**
SIC: 7372 Business oriented computer software
HQ: Software Ag Usa, Inc.
11700 Plaza America Dr # 700
Reston VA 20190
703 860-5050

(G-8674)
SPACE EXPLORATION TECH CORP
Also Called: Spacex
18390 Ne 6th St (98052)
PHONE..................................425 867-9910
Jack Connor, *Senior Mgr*
EMP: 875
SALES (corp-wide): 1B **Privately Held**
SIC: 3761 Rockets, space & military, complete
PA: Space Exploration Technologies Corp.
1 Rocket Rd
Hawthorne CA 90250
310 363-6000

(G-8675)
SPACE EXPLORATION TECH CORP
Also Called: Spacex Redmond Rr02
23020 Ne Alder Crest Dr (98053-5874)
PHONE..................................425 602-2255
EMP: 250
SALES (corp-wide): 1B **Privately Held**
SIC: 3761 Rockets, space & military, complete
PA: Space Exploration Technologies Corp.
1 Rocket Rd
Hawthorne CA 90250
310 363-6000

(G-8676)
SPARKON INC
16430 Ne 50th St (98052-5292)
PHONE..................................425 273-3904

Bryan Starbuck, *CEO*
EMP: 2 EST: 2013
SALES (est): 93.1K **Privately Held**
SIC: 7372 Prepackaged software

(G-8677)
SPARTAN INDUSTRIES L L C
13244 Ne 108th St (98052-2449)
PHONE..................................425 822-2071
Arlene Howe,
Doug Howe,
EMP: 2
SQ FT: 2,000
SALES (est): 61K **Privately Held**
WEB: www.spartan-industries.com
SIC: 3728 Aircraft assemblies, subassemblies & parts

(G-8678)
SPECTRALUX CORPORATION
Also Called: Spectralux Avionics
12335 134th Ct Ne (98052-2433)
PHONE..................................425 285-3000
Elwood Hertzog, *CEO*
Frank Hummel, *Engineer*
John Bustad, *Manager*
Brian Brooks, *Director*
Tom Henderson, *Director*
EMP: 85 EST: 1973
SQ FT: 33,000
SALES (est): 17.3MM **Privately Held**
SIC: 3812 Aircraft/aerospace flight instruments & guidance systems

(G-8679)
SRS MEDICAL CORP (HQ)
8672p 154th Ave Ne (98052-3556)
PHONE..................................425 882-1101
David Mohoney, *Vice Pres*
Lee Brody, *Vice Pres*
EMP: 10
SALES (est): 754.9K **Privately Held**
WEB: www.srsmedical.com
SIC: 3841 Medical instruments & equipment, blood & bone work

(G-8680)
STAFFORD PRESS INC (PA)
Also Called: Western Tag and Label
14612 Ne 91st St (98052-3436)
PHONE..................................425 861-5856
David Long, *President*
Kim Long, *Vice Pres*
EMP: 13
SQ FT: 7,000
SALES (est): 1.8MM **Privately Held**
WEB: www.staffordpress.com
SIC: 2759 2752 2671 Labels & seals: printing; commercial printing, lithographic; packaging paper & plastics film, coated & laminated

(G-8681)
STAT CORPORATION
Also Called: Precision Press
14770 Ne 95th St (98052-2519)
PHONE..................................425 883-4181
John Bowers, *President*
James Bowers, *President*
John Bower Sr, *Vice Pres*
Andrea Parr, *CTO*
Andrea Bowers, *Admin Sec*
EMP: 16
SQ FT: 3,500
SALES (est): 2.1MM **Privately Held**
WEB: www.precisionpress.com
SIC: 7336 2752 7334 2759 Graphic arts & related design; commercial printing, offset; photocopying & duplicating services; commercial printing

(G-8682)
STEPHEN L NELSON INC
8434 154th Ave Ne Fl 2 (98052-3800)
PHONE..................................425 885-9499
Stephen L Nelson, *President*
Matt Donohoe, *Accountant*
EMP: 5
SQ FT: 1,600
SALES (est): 320K **Privately Held**
SIC: 2759 Commercial printing

(G-8683)
STONEWOOD INC
9009 Avondale Rd Ne I118 (98052-3383)
PHONE..................................425 417-5533

Daniel R West, *Principal*
EMP: 4
SALES (est): 306.4K **Privately Held**
SIC: 2434 Wood kitchen cabinets

(G-8684)
STRATEGIC ROBOTIC SYSTEMS INC
18394 Redmond Way (98052-5012)
PHONE..................................425 285-9229
Jesse Rodocker, *President*
Tracey Rodocker, *Admin Sec*
EMP: 6
SALES (est): 166.4K **Privately Held**
SIC: 3812 Search & detection systems & instruments

(G-8685)
STRAWBERRY KIDS LLC
16647 Ne 48th St (98052-5482)
PHONE..................................425 605-8883
Manjiri Kharkar,
Sujeet Kharkar,
▲ EMP: 2 EST: 2012
SALES (est): 145.9K **Privately Held**
SIC: 2396 7389 Linings, apparel: made from purchased materials;

(G-8686)
SUGIMOTO SEICHA USA INC
Also Called: Sugimoto America
4070 148th Ave Ne Bldg M (98052-5165)
PHONE..................................425 558-5552
Kyohei Sugimoto, *President*
▲ EMP: 3
SQ FT: 1,000
SALES: 500K **Privately Held**
WEB: www.sugimotousa.com
SIC: 2099 Tea blending
PA: Sugimoto Seicha.,Co.Ltd.
242-1, Yokooka
Shimada SZO 428-0

(G-8687)
T3 TECHNIQUE LLC
22330 Ne 54th St (98053-8239)
PHONE..................................425 785-0361
Christopher Scott Schimke, *Principal*
EMP: 4
SALES (est): 347K **Privately Held**
SIC: 3714 Motor vehicle parts & accessories

(G-8688)
TENSORMAKE CORPORATION
Also Called: Oneclick.ai
2128 204th Pl Ne (98074-4390)
PHONE..................................206 659-6139
Yuan Shen, *CEO*
Ning Jiang, *CFO*
EMP: 2
SALES (est): 56.5K **Privately Held**
SIC: 7372 Business oriented computer software

(G-8689)
TERATO PRODUCTS LLC
2605 151st Pl Ne (98052-5522)
PHONE..................................425 702-6365
Neil Larson,
Kuniakia Terato,
EMP: 2
SALES (est): 190K **Privately Held**
SIC: 2023 5122 5499 Dietary supplements, dairy & non-dairy based; vitamins & minerals; vitamin food stores

(G-8690)
TEREX CORPORATION
17275 Ne 67th Ct (98052-4952)
PHONE..................................800 536-1800
EMP: 10
SALES (corp-wide): 5.1B **Publicly Held**
SIC: 3537 3531 Industrial trucks & tractors; lift trucks, industrial: fork, platform, straddle, etc.; stackers, power (industrial truck stackers); straddle carriers, mobile; cranes
PA: Terex Corporation
200 Nyala Farms Rd Ste 2
Westport CT 06880
203 222-7170

(G-8691)
THUNDERBIRD PACIFIC CORP
Also Called: Thunderbird Mining Systems
2635 151st Pl Ne (98052-5562)
PHONE..................................425 869-2727
John F Vynne, *President*
Barbara Vynne, *Corp Secy*
Barbara Ruiz, *Office Mgr*
EMP: 8
SQ FT: 2,500
SALES (est): 1.3MM **Privately Held**
WEB: www.tbirdpac.com
SIC: 3532 Mining machinery

(G-8692)
TIME 4 FUN LLC
21410 Ne 84th St (98053-2262)
PHONE..................................425 836-5037
Scott Swanson, *Principal*
EMP: 2
SALES (est): 210.6K **Privately Held**
SIC: 3732 Yachts, building & repairing

(G-8693)
TNTGAMBLE INC (PA)
Also Called: Nutraceutix
9609 153rd Ave Ne (98052-2522)
PHONE..................................425 883-9518
Steve Moger, *President*
Tim J Gamble, *President*
Tony Blanch, *Director*
Randy Schoenfeldt, *Director*
EMP: 23
SQ FT: 20,000
SALES (est): 15.7MM **Privately Held**
WEB: www.nutraceutix.com
SIC: 2023 Dietary supplements, dairy & non-dairy based

(G-8694)
TRIM SEAL USA INC (PA)
17371 Ne 67th Ct Ste A2 (98052-4920)
PHONE..................................425 867-1522
Dan Semien, *President*
George Hudson, *Controller*
EMP: 3
SALES (est): 14.1MM **Privately Held**
SIC: 2782 Looseleaf binders & devices

(G-8695)
TRIUMPH GROUP INC
22922 Ne Alder Crest Dr (98053-5894)
PHONE..................................425 636-9000
Brian Robertson, *Marketing Staff*
EMP: 10 **Publicly Held**
SIC: 3728 Aircraft parts & equipment
PA: Triumph Group, Inc.
899 Cassatt Rd Ste 210
Berwyn PA 19312

(G-8696)
TRUTHTELLER WINERY
7581 Old Redmond Rd Apt 1 (98052-4288)
PHONE..................................425 985-3568
Dawn Loeliger, *Principal*
EMP: 2 EST: 2017
SALES (est): 91.2K **Privately Held**
SIC: 2084 Wines

(G-8697)
UNDERHORSE ENTERTAINMENT INC
6007 150th Ct Ne (98052-4757)
PHONE..................................760 216-0164
EMP: 2 EST: 2010
SALES (est): 140K **Privately Held**
SIC: 7372 Prepackaged Software

(G-8698)
UNITED VOLLEYBALL SUPPLY LLC
14615 Ne 91st St Ste B (98052-3553)
PHONE..................................425 576-8835
Mason Brown, *Partner*
Jesse Brown, *Principal*
EMP: 13
SALES (est): 1.7MM **Privately Held**
SIC: 3949 Sporting & athletic goods

(G-8699)
UNIVERSAL AVONICS SYSTEMS CORP
Also Called: Research and Development Div
11351 Willows Rd Ne (98052-2552)
PHONE..................................425 821-2800

Redmond - King County (G-8700)

Ted Naimer, *Owner*
Jane Morrow, *Senior Buyer*
Nicholas Foster, *Engineer*
Wes Halstead, *Engineer*
Rene Spani, *Engineer*
EMP: 130
SALES (corp-wide): 961MM **Privately Held**
WEB: www.uasc-id.com
SIC: 3829 8731 3812 Measuring & controlling devices; commercial physical research; search & navigation equipment
HQ: Universal Avionics Systems Corporation
3260 E Universal Way
Tucson AZ 85756
520 295-2300

(G-8700)
UPPER CUT WOODWORKS LLC
23515 Ne Novelty Hill Rd (98053-1996)
PHONE......................425 785-4817
Daniel Peterson, *President*
EMP: 2 **EST:** 2010
SALES (est): 145.9K **Privately Held**
SIC: 2431 Millwork

(G-8701)
US BUILDERS TEAM LLC
7438 159th Pl Ne (98052-4332)
PHONE......................425 466-2611
Mike Nykreim,
EMP: 4
SQ FT: 2,450
SALES (est): 178.7K **Privately Held**
SIC: 2451 1531 Mobile buildings: for commercial use; operative builders

(G-8702)
VALCON GAMES LLC
16701 Ne 80th St Ste 204 (98052-3937)
PHONE......................425 223-4672
Colon Gordon,
Glenn Halseth,
▲ **EMP:** 7
SALES (est): 12MM **Privately Held**
SIC: 2741 Miscellaneous publishing

(G-8703)
VEHICLE MONITOR CORPORATION
6825 176th Ave Ne Ste 100 (98052-4983)
PHONE......................425 881-5560
Donald Lawe, *President*
Jeff Ottesen, *Engineer*
Don Lawe, *CIO*
Peter Von Der Porten, *Admin Sec*
EMP: 14
SQ FT: 5,000
SALES (est): 3.3MM **Privately Held**
WEB: www.vehiclemonitorcorp.com
SIC: 3714 Motor vehicle electrical equipment

(G-8704)
VERGENT SOFTWARE
27915 Ne 26th St (98053-3116)
PHONE......................425 880-4158
Chris Kinsman, *Principal*
EMP: 2 **EST:** 2007
SALES (est): 151.5K **Privately Held**
SIC: 7372 Prepackaged software

(G-8705)
VIPER R/C SOLUTIONS INC
Also Called: Viper RC Solutions
2731 152nd Ave Ne (98052-5554)
PHONE......................425 968-5389
WEI Lih Chung, *President*
Chih-Yuan Shen, *Vice Pres*
Hsiao-Hsien Wang, *Admin Sec*
EMP: 5 **EST:** 2010
SALES (est): 536.2K **Privately Held**
SIC: 3621 Motors, electric

(G-8706)
VOICELEVER INC
7349 148th Ave Ne (98052-4148)
PHONE......................425 864-7676
Stephen Rondel, *CEO*
EMP: 53
SALES (est): 5.8MM **Privately Held**
SIC: 3571 Electronic computers

(G-8707)
VOLOMETRIX INC
1 Microsoft Way (98052-8300)
PHONE......................425 706-7507
Benjamin O Orndorff, *President*
EMP: 4
SALES (est): 707K
SALES (corp-wide): 110.3B **Publicly Held**
SIC: 8742 7372 Management consulting services; business oriented computer software
PA: Microsoft Corporation
1 Microsoft Way
Redmond WA 98052
425 882-8080

(G-8708)
WALLBEDS NORTHWEST INC (PA)
Also Called: Universal Wallbeds
17646 Ne 65th St (98052-4904)
PHONE......................425 284-6692
Jack Schuster, *President*
▲ **EMP:** 20
SALES (est): 2.1MM **Privately Held**
WEB: www.wallbedsnorthwest.com
SIC: 2519 2511 Household furniture, except wood or metal: upholstered; wood household furniture

(G-8709)
WASHINGTON GRAPHICS LLC
Also Called: Washington Screnprint Graphics
15340 Ne 92nd St Ste B (98052-3521)
PHONE......................425 376-0877
Robert Morgan,
EMP: 15
SQ FT: 20,000
SALES: 2.2MM **Privately Held**
WEB: www.washingtonscreenprint.com
SIC: 5199 5999 2759 Posters & decals; posters; banners, flags, decals & posters; banners; screen printing

(G-8710)
WASHINGTON PUBLISHING HSE LLC
Also Called: Adsiduous
16035 Ne 117th Way (98052-5472)
PHONE......................425 406-9891
Sreenivasan Trikkur, *CEO*
Mahidhar Reddy, *CFO*
EMP: 10
SALES: 5.4MM **Privately Held**
SIC: 2741 Miscellaneous publishing

(G-8711)
WESTERN INDUSTRIAL TOOLING INC
Also Called: Western Industrial Products
14511 Ne 87th St (98052-3431)
PHONE......................425 883-6644
Tom Miller, *President*
EMP: 23
SQ FT: 25,000
SALES (est): 4.9MM **Privately Held**
WEB: www.westernindustrial.com
SIC: 3599 Machine shop, jobbing & repair

(G-8712)
WESTROCK RKT COMPANY
8720 148th Ave Ne (98052-3482)
PHONE......................425 885-5851
Lisa McCord, *Manager*
EMP: 20
SALES (corp-wide): 16.2B **Publicly Held**
WEB: www.rocktenn.com
SIC: 2653 Partitions, solid fiber: made from purchased materials
HQ: Westrock Rkt, Llc
1000 Abernathy Rd Ste 125
Atlanta GA 30328
770 448-2193

(G-8713)
WHYTE & SONS INCORPORATED
11609 172nd Ave Ne (98052-2244)
PHONE......................425 885-3571
Gilbert Whyte, *Owner*
Gordon Whyte, *Vice Pres*
Bonnie Whyte, *Treasurer*
Myrna Whyte, *Treasurer*
EMP: 2
SALES (est): 210K **Privately Held**
SIC: 1794 3273 Excavation work; ready-mixed concrete

(G-8714)
WILDCARD PROPERTIES LLC
Also Called: Studio Wildcard
8383 158th Ave Ne Ste 200 (98052-3838)
PHONE......................425 296-0896
Douglas Kennedy, *CEO*
Jesse Rapczak, *President*
EMP: 35 **EST:** 2016
SALES (est): 1.2MM **Privately Held**
SIC: 7372 Home entertainment computer software

(G-8715)
WILDTANGENT INC
18578 Ne 67th Ct Bldg 5 (98052-6711)
PHONE......................425 497-4500
Matt Shea, *CEO*
Robert M Peronto, *President*
Dave Madden, *Exec VP*
Aj Redmer, *Vice Pres*
Alan Dishlip, *CFO*
EMP: 75
SQ FT: 38,000
SALES (est): 14.4MM **Privately Held**
WEB: www.hollywood3d.com
SIC: 7372 7371 Prepackaged software; custom computer programming services

(G-8716)
WOITCHEK PRINTING LLC
Also Called: Hot Off The Press
7126 180th Ave Ne C104 (98052-4971)
PHONE......................425 869-8212
Fred Woitchek, *President*
Andrew Koeppen, *Sales Staff*
Helen Woitchek,
EMP: 4
SALES (est): 525.7K **Privately Held**
SIC: 2752 Commercial printing, offset

(G-8717)
WOOD DESIGN
Also Called: Richard Demeules
11421 206th Ave Ne (98053-5131)
PHONE......................425 883-8842
Richard Demeules, *Owner*
EMP: 3
SALES (est): 298.9K **Privately Held**
SIC: 2441 Boxes, wood

(G-8718)
XENSOURCE INC
8461 154th Ave Ne (98052-3863)
PHONE......................425 881-9479
Ali Rouhfar, *Principal*
EMP: 2
SALES (est): 90K **Privately Held**
SIC: 7372 Prepackaged software

(G-8719)
XEROX CORP XEROX CORPORAT
18005 Ne 68th St Ste A120 (98052-8508)
PHONE......................425 947-7046
EMP: 6
SALES (est): 37.7K **Privately Held**
SIC: 3861 Photographic equipment & supplies

(G-8720)
XKL LLC
12020 113th Ave Ne 100 (98052)
PHONE......................425 869-9050
Leonard Bosack,
EMP: 40
SQ FT: 11,000
SALES (est): 10.6MM **Privately Held**
WEB: www.xkl.com
SIC: 3661 3674 Telephone & telegraph apparatus; semiconductors & related devices

(G-8721)
ZETA SOFTWARE INC
15606 Ne 40th St Apt I136 (98052-7011)
PHONE......................503 371-4340
Gopi B Muthineni, *Principal*
EMP: 2
SALES (est): 138.6K **Privately Held**
SIC: 7372 Prepackaged software

(G-8722)
ZIPWIRE INCORPORATED
8201 164th Ave Ne Ste 200 (98052-7615)
PHONE......................425 591-4924
Jason Kap, *Principal*
EMP: 3
SALES (est): 170.2K **Privately Held**
SIC: 7372 Application computer software

(G-8723)
ZOOKA SPORTS CORPORATION
8447 154th Ave Ne (98052-3863)
PHONE......................425 861-0111
Doug Murdock, *President*
Richard Wearn, *Vice Pres*
EMP: 4
SQ FT: 6,000
SALES (est): 290K **Privately Held**
WEB: www.zooka.com
SIC: 3949 Team sports equipment

Renton
King County

(G-8724)
A-1 PRO SIGN
5024 Ne 23rd St (98059-4129)
PHONE......................425 765-8836
EMP: 2 **EST:** 2009
SALES (est): 146.9K **Privately Held**
SIC: 3993 Signs & advertising specialties

(G-8725)
AAA VICTORY VENDING INC
12824 Se 170th St (98058-6140)
P.O. Box 171 (98057-0171)
PHONE......................425 235-0378
Stanley Abbott, *President*
EMP: 2
SALES (est): 190K **Privately Held**
SIC: 3021 Rubber & plastics footwear

(G-8726)
ACCURATE MODELS
19214 140th Ave Se (98058-7734)
PHONE......................253 630-3126
Tony Huber, *Principal*
EMP: 2
SALES (est): 157.9K **Privately Held**
SIC: 3944 Games, toys & children's vehicles

(G-8727)
ACORN CUSTOM CABINETRY INC
7211 132nd Pl Se (98056)
P.O. Box 190, Hobart (98025-0190)
PHONE......................425 235-8366
Kathy Anderson, *President*
EMP: 50
SQ FT: 17,500
SALES (est): 5.4MM **Privately Held**
SIC: 2434 5712 2521 2517 Wood kitchen cabinets; cabinet work, custom; wood office furniture; wood television & radio cabinets

(G-8728)
ADVADRI LLC
14127 W Lk Kathleen Dr Se (98059-7705)
PHONE......................425 228-7558
EMP: 2 **EST:** 2010
SALES (est): 130K **Privately Held**
SIC: 2385 Mfg Waterproof Outerwear

(G-8729)
AERO-SPACE PORT INTL GROUP INC
1600 Lind Ave Sw Ste 220 (98057-3305)
PHONE......................425 264-1000
Andy Chen, *President*
EMP: 3
SALES (est): 281.3K **Privately Held**
SIC: 3812 Acceleration indicators & systems components, aerospace

(G-8730)
AFFORDABLE BLACKFLOW TESTERS
18308 Se 145th St (98059-8006)
PHONE......................425 269-9064
Inga Flaherty, *Bd of Directors*

GEOGRAPHIC SECTION
Renton - King County (G-8758)

EMP: 2 EST: 2007
SALES (est): 140K Privately Held
SIC: 1389 Testing, measuring, surveying & analysis services

(G-8731)
AGILENT TECHNOLOGIES INC
14410 Se Petrovitsky Rd (98058-8900)
PHONE..............................425 255-6320
Catherine Balthazaar, Branch Mgr
EMP: 3
SALES (corp-wide): 4.9B Publicly Held
SIC: 3825 Instruments to measure electricity
PA: Agilent Technologies, Inc.
5301 Stevens Creek Blvd
Santa Clara CA 95051
408 345-8886

(G-8732)
AIM AEROSPACE INC
705 Sw 7th St (98057-2915)
P.O. Box 9011 (98057-3004)
PHONE..............................425 235-2750
Daniele Cagnatel, President
Jeff C Smith, Chairman
Robert A Green, Treasurer
Hans O Ulland, Admin Sec
▲ EMP: 150
SQ FT: 122,000
SALES (est): 23.7MM Privately Held
WEB: www.aim-aerospace.com
SIC: 3728 Aircraft assemblies, subassemblies & parts

(G-8733)
AIM GROUP USA INC (PA)
Also Called: Aim Aerospace
705 Sw 7th St (98057-2915)
P.O. Box 9011 (98057-3004)
PHONE..............................425 235-2750
Mark Potensky, President
Jeff Smith, Chairman
Ken Gamble, Vice Pres
Michael Pratt, VP Opers
Carl Dahl, Prdtn Mgr
EMP: 150
SQ FT: 129,500
SALES (est): 168.2MM Privately Held
SIC: 3728 Aircraft body & wing assemblies & parts

(G-8734)
AIRWAVZ INC
Also Called: Airwavz.tv
9628 123rd Ave Se (98058-2413)
PHONE..............................206 696-6649
Bonnie Beeman, CEO
EMP: 2
SALES (est): 170.6K Privately Held
SIC: 3663 5734 Radio broadcasting & communications equipment; computer & software stores

(G-8735)
ALEDDRA INC
Also Called: Aleddra Led Lighting
2210 Lind Ave Sw Ste 109 (98057-3326)
PHONE..............................425 430-4555
Benson Shen, Ch of Bd
Elena Wang, President
Patrick Yu, President
Matthew Maa, VP Sales
▲ EMP: 9
SALES (est): 1MM Privately Held
SIC: 3646 Commercial indusl & institutional electric lighting fixtures

(G-8736)
ALEDDRA INC
Also Called: Aleddra Led Lighting
2210 Lind Ave Sw Ste 109 (98057-3326)
PHONE..............................425 430-4555
Patrick Yu, President
Benson Shen, Principal
Elena Wang, Treasurer
EMP: 9
SALES (est): 382.3K Privately Held
SIC: 3646 Commercial indusl & institutional electric lighting fixtures

(G-8737)
ALEXANDER INDUSTRIES LLC
4033 Ne Sunset Blvd Ste 5 (98056-3368)
PHONE..............................253 686-6066
Miles Alexander, Principal

EMP: 2
SALES (est): 131.6K Privately Held
SIC: 3999 Manufacturing industries

(G-8738)
ALLIANCE PACKAGING LLC
Also Called: Graphic Sheet Packaging
1000 Sw 43rd St (98057-4832)
PHONE..............................425 291-3500
Scott Younger, General Mgr
EMP: 200 Privately Held
WEB: www.alliancepackaging.net
SIC: 2653 3086 Boxes, corrugated: made from purchased materials; packaging & shipping materials, foamed plastic
HQ: Alliance Packaging, Llc
1000 Sw 43rd St
Renton WA 98057
425 291-3500

(G-8739)
ALLPAK CONTAINER LLC (HQ)
1100 Sw 27th St (98057-2624)
PHONE..............................425 227-0400
Drew Sanders, Information Mgr
Hans Koch,
▲ EMP: 97
SQ FT: 125,000
SALES (est): 21.7MM
SALES (corp-wide): 27.3MM Privately Held
WEB: www.allpak.com
SIC: 2653 3993 5113 2671 Boxes, corrugated: made from purchased materials; signs & advertising specialties; corrugated & solid fiber boxes; packaging paper & plastics film, coated & laminated
PA: Golden West Packaging Group Llc
8333 24th Ave
Sacramento CA 95826
404 345-8365

(G-8740)
ALLPAK CONTAINER LLC
800 Sw 27th St (98057-4965)
PHONE..............................509 535-4112
Terry Piger, Manager
EMP: 25
SALES (corp-wide): 27.3MM Privately Held
WEB: www.allpak.com
SIC: 2653 Boxes, corrugated: made from purchased materials
HQ: Allpak Container, Llc
1100 Sw 27th St
Renton WA 98057
425 227-0400

(G-8741)
ALPHAPHARMA INC
865 Rainier Ave N (98057-5379)
PHONE..............................206 413-5122
Suliman Al-Fayoumi, Administration
EMP: 3
SALES (est): 189K Privately Held
SIC: 2834 Pharmaceutical preparations

(G-8742)
AMERICAN DRPERY BLIND CRPT INC
1040 Thomas Ave Sw (98057-2922)
PHONE..............................425 793-4477
Brett Swinson, Branch Mgr
EMP: 35
SALES (corp-wide): 27MM Privately Held
SIC: 2391 2591 Draperies, plastic & textile: from purchased materials; drapery hardware & blinds & shades
PA: American Drapery Blind & Carpet, Inc.
700 S 3rd St
Renton WA 98057
360 676-1121

(G-8743)
AMERICAN DRPERY BLIND CRPT INC (PA)
700 S 3rd St (98057-2542)
P.O. Box 896 (98057-0896)
PHONE..............................360 676-1121
Donald Richmond, President
Denny Sean Thostrud, President
Joseph McBride, Vice Pres
Joe McBride, VP Opers
Shannon Colleen O'Day, Admin Sec
EMP: 115

SQ FT: 35,000
SALES (est): 27MM Privately Held
SIC: 2591 5713 2391 5023 Mini blinds; carpets; draperies, plastic & textile: from purchased materials; home furnishings

(G-8744)
ANDYMAN ONLINE
4009 Ne 6th Ct (98056-3972)
PHONE..............................425 761-5921
Andy Assareh, Administration
EMP: 2
SALES (est): 87.2K Privately Held
SIC: 3711 Motor vehicles & car bodies

(G-8745)
APEX TOOL GROUP LLC
1020 Thomas Ave Sw (98057-2922)
PHONE..............................425 226-4491
EMP: 128
SALES (corp-wide): 14B Privately Held
SIC: 3546 Power-driven handtools
HQ: Apex Tool Group, Llc
910 Ridgebrook Rd Ste 200
Sparks Glencoe MD 21152

(G-8746)
APPERSON INC
851 Sw 34th St (98057-4815)
PHONE..............................206 336-1015
Bill Apperson, Branch Mgr
EMP: 30
SALES (corp-wide): 22MM Privately Held
WEB: www.appersonprint.com
SIC: 2761 Continuous forms, office & business
PA: Apperson, Inc.
17315 Studebaker Rd # 209
Cerritos CA 90703
562 356-3333

(G-8747)
APPERSON PRINT MANAGEMENT
851 Sw 34th St Bldg B (98057-4815)
PHONE..............................425 251-1850
Bill Apperson, Owner
EMP: 2
SALES (est): 216.7K Privately Held
SIC: 2759 Commercial printing

(G-8748)
ASCENDANCE POLE & AERIAL ARTS
724 S 3rd St Ste A (98057-2542)
PHONE..............................425 256-2246
Cynthia Tee, President
Margarette Nation, Vice Pres
Candice Vaivadas, Admin Sec
EMP: 4
SALES (est): 33.1K Privately Held
SIC: 7911 5699 7372 Dance studio & school; sports apparel; application computer software

(G-8749)
AVI MARIE HAIR COLLECTION LLC
2223 Benson Rd S Apt D102 (98055-8837)
PHONE..............................425 409-9924
Aviel Marie, Principal
EMP: 2
SALES (est): 80.9K Privately Held
SIC: 8742 7299 3999 Sales (including sales management) consultant; hair weaving or replacement; hair & hair-based products

(G-8750)
BADEN SPORTS INC
3401 Lind Ave Sw (98057-4924)
PHONE..............................253 925-0500
Michael Schindler, CEO
Richard Scott, Manager
EMP: 11
SALES (corp-wide): 15MM Privately Held
SIC: 3949 Balls: baseball, football, basketball, etc.
PA: Baden Sports, Inc.
34114 21st Ave S
Renton WA 98057
253 925-0500

(G-8751)
BASKIN ROBBINS 1361
Also Called: Baskin-Robbins
520 Rainier Ave S (98057-2411)
PHONE..............................425 226-3113
Dennis Lock, Principal
EMP: 9
SALES (est): 180.7K Privately Held
SIC: 5812 2024 Ice cream stands or dairy bars; ice cream & frozen desserts

(G-8752)
BAYVIEW PUBLISHING LLC
16409 Se 166th Ter (98058-4219)
PHONE..............................425 282-4640
EMP: 2 Privately Held
SIC: 2741 Misc Publishing
PA: Bayview Publishing, Llc
14201 Se Petrovitsky Rd
Renton WA
206 406-4810

(G-8753)
BC PAVERS INC
1916 Jones Ave Ne (98056-2660)
P.O. Box 3401 (98056-0015)
PHONE..............................425 413-2110
Brian Crooks, President
Jennifer Crooks, Admin Sec
EMP: 4
SALES (est): 68.4K Privately Held
SIC: 3531 Pavers

(G-8754)
BEACON MACHINE INC
420 Olympia Ave Ne (98056-3900)
PHONE..............................425 226-8460
Karen Arango, President
EMP: 3 EST: 1957
SQ FT: 1,800
SALES (est): 250K Privately Held
SIC: 3599 Machine shop, jobbing & repair

(G-8755)
BHARAT RATAN LLC
19030 116th Ave Se (98058-7159)
PHONE..............................206 458-3322
Ashok Monga, Mng Member
EMP: 3
SALES (est): 91.3K Privately Held
SIC: 2023 Dietary supplements, dairy & non-dairy based

(G-8756)
BOEING COMPANY
700 S Renton Village Pl (98057-3235)
PHONE..............................206 662-6863
Wayne Hixson, Branch Mgr
EMP: 996
SALES (corp-wide): 101.1B Publicly Held
SIC: 3721 Airplanes, fixed or rotary wing
PA: The Boeing Company
100 N Riverside Plz
Chicago IL 60606
312 544-2000

(G-8757)
BOEING COMPANY
1901 Oakesdale Ave Sw (98057-2623)
P.O. Box 3707, Seattle (98124-2207)
PHONE..............................206 766-2770
Kurt Ferstl, Counsel
Peter Lohr, Opers Dir
Jeff Hunt, Opers Mgr
Greg Batcher, Opers Staff
Roxane Asay, Buyer
EMP: 700
SALES (corp-wide): 101.1B Publicly Held
SIC: 3721 Airplanes, fixed or rotary wing
PA: The Boeing Company
100 N Riverside Plz
Chicago IL 60606
312 544-2000

(G-8758)
BOEING COMPANY
555 Monster Rd Sw (98057-2937)
PHONE..............................206 544-2374
Glenn Webb, Branch Mgr
EMP: 2
SALES (corp-wide): 101.1B Publicly Held
SIC: 3721 Aircraft

Renton - King County (G-8759)

PA: The Boeing Company
100 N Riverside Plz
Chicago IL 60606
312 544-2000

(G-8759)
BOEING COMPANY
800 N 6th St (98057-5411)
PHONE 425 306-8112
Michael Waltz, *Manager*
Steven Gillette, *Administration*
EMP: 5
SQ FT: 3,311,489
SALES (corp-wide): 101.1B **Publicly Held**
SIC: 3721 Airplanes, fixed or rotary wing
PA: The Boeing Company
100 N Riverside Plz
Chicago IL 60606
312 544-2000

(G-8760)
BOEING COMPANY
800 Logan Ave N (98055)
P.O. Box 3707, Seattle (98124-2207)
PHONE 206 689-4059
David Stutz, *Project Mgr*
Abigail C Lee, *Manager*
Dustin Doyle, *Analyst*
EMP: 196
SALES (corp-wide): 101.1B **Publicly Held**
SIC: 3812 Defense systems & equipment; missile guidance systems & equipment
PA: The Boeing Company
100 N Riverside Plz
Chicago IL 60606
312 544-2000

(G-8761)
BOEING COMPANY
801 Sw 41st St (98055)
PHONE 253 657-5616
Joellen Wrasper, *Manager*
EMP: 996
SALES (corp-wide): 101.1B **Publicly Held**
SIC: 3721 Airplanes, fixed or rotary wing
PA: The Boeing Company
100 N Riverside Plz
Chicago IL 60606
312 544-2000

(G-8762)
BOEING COMPANY
635 Park Ave N Bldg 101 (98057-5583)
PHONE 206 655-1131
Susan Vaughn, *Accountant*
Beauclair Carla, *Manager*
Thang Doan, *Software Dev*
EMP: 996
SALES (corp-wide): 101.1B **Publicly Held**
SIC: 3721 Airplanes, fixed or rotary wing
PA: The Boeing Company
100 N Riverside Plz
Chicago IL 60606
312 544-2000

(G-8763)
BOEING EMPLOYEES FLYING ASSN
840 W Perimeter Rd (98057-5346)
PHONE 425 271-2332
Donald Fogler, *Principal*
EMP: 3
SALES: 1.2MM **Privately Held**
SIC: 3721 Aircraft

(G-8764)
BP MARKETING
1200 N 27th Pl (98056-1473)
P.O. Box 516 (98057-0516)
PHONE 509 475-7125
Mark Johnson, *Owner*
EMP: 2
SALES (est): 121.3K **Privately Held**
SIC: 2013 Prepared beef products from purchased beef

(G-8765)
BUNKER HILL DIAGNOSTICS
718 S 38th Ct (98055)
PHONE 206 579-1440
Glenn Meyer, *Principal*
EMP: 5

SALES (est): 250K **Privately Held**
SIC: 3625 Relays & industrial controls

(G-8766)
CABI
17525 190th Ave Se (98058-0735)
PHONE 425 413-8772
Teresa Bates, *Principal*
EMP: 3
SALES (est): 276.8K **Privately Held**
SIC: 3679 Electronic loads & power supplies

(G-8767)
CAPE GREIG LLC
900 Powell Ave Sw (98057-2907)
PHONE 206 545-9501
EMP: 5
SALES (est): 303.3K **Privately Held**
SIC: 2091 Canned & cured fish & seafoods

(G-8768)
CASTLE BRIDGE WINERY
18706 137th Ct Se (98058-8058)
PHONE 425 251-0983
Bob Schlosser, *Principal*
EMP: 4
SALES (est): 493.6K **Privately Held**
SIC: 2084 Wines

(G-8769)
CEDAR RIVER CELLARS
2525 Ferndale Ave Ne (98056-8308)
PHONE 206 229-2104
Heather Nasarow, *Owner*
EMP: 4
SALES (est): 343.8K **Privately Held**
SIC: 2084 Wines

(G-8770)
CFC FISH COMPANY LLC
Also Called: Salmon Bay Processors
900 Powell Ave Sw (98057-2907)
PHONE 253 478-5160
Robert O'Bryant, *President*
Lyla Sackett, *Treasurer*
◆ EMP: 13
SALES (est): 33MM
SALES (corp-wide): 33.4MM **Privately Held**
WEB: www.cannonfish.com
SIC: 5146 2092 Fish, frozen, unpackaged; fresh or frozen packaged fish
PA: E & E Foods, Inc.
900 Powell Ave Sw
Renton WA 98057
206 768-8979

(G-8771)
CHERRY DE PON (PA)
365 S Grady Way (98057-3206)
PHONE 425 226-5246
Nghia Pham, *Principal*
EMP: 4
SALES (est): 747.6K **Privately Held**
SIC: 2024 Ice cream, bulk

(G-8772)
CHUNDER BAG
18116 W Lake Desire Dr Se (98058-9526)
PHONE 253 987-6224
Jen Samson, *Principal*
EMP: 2
SALES (est): 97.9K **Privately Held**
SIC: 2673 Plastic bags: made from purchased materials

(G-8773)
CNA MANUFACTURING SYSTEMS INC
230 S Tobin St (98057-5307)
PHONE 425 988-3905
Larry Cook, *Principal*
EMP: 9
SALES (est): 973K **Privately Held**
SIC: 3544 Special dies, tools, jigs & fixtures

(G-8774)
COCA-COLA REFRESHMENTS
300 Sw 27th St (98057-3380)
PHONE 425 226-6004
EMP: 2

SALES (est): 116.4K **Privately Held**
SIC: 5149 5078 2086 Beverages, except coffee & tea; refrigerated beverage dispensers; bottled & canned soft drinks

(G-8775)
CORKYCELLARS LLC
14518 Se 142nd St (98059-5518)
PHONE 425 226-5479
Michael R Jacobson,
Dainne Jacobson,
EMP: 2
SALES (est): 170K **Privately Held**
SIC: 2084 Wines

(G-8776)
CREATIVE MICROSYSTEMS INC
15224 Se Rnton Issquah Rd (98059-6205)
P.O. Box 2410 (98056-0410)
PHONE 425 235-4335
Larry Santi, *President*
Debbi Santi, *Treasurer*
EMP: 11
SQ FT: 6,000
SALES (est): 1.2MM **Privately Held**
WEB: www.loadman.com
SIC: 3596 3823 Truck (motor vehicle) scales; industrial process measurement equipment

(G-8777)
CUSTOM PRESSED TEES LLC
617 S 3rd St Ste B (98057-7514)
PHONE 425 264-5909
EMP: 2
SALES (est): 132.1K **Privately Held**
SIC: 2759 Screen printing

(G-8778)
D CROCKETT SURFBOARDS
16916 155th Pl Se (98058-8668)
PHONE 425 430-9947
EMP: 2 EST: 2012
SALES (est): 120K **Privately Held**
SIC: 3949 Mfg Sporting/Athletic Goods

(G-8779)
DAG INDUSTRIES INC
5210 Ne 23rd Ct (98059-4156)
PHONE 425 228-4962
Rob Green, *Vice Pres*
EMP: 7
SALES (est): 703.8K **Privately Held**
SIC: 3446 Fences or posts, ornamental iron or steel

(G-8780)
DAUNTLESS SOFTWARE INC
4702 Ne 1st Pl (98059-4970)
PHONE 206 489-4942
Elizabeth Murakami, *Principal*
EMP: 2
SALES (est): 136.4K **Privately Held**
SIC: 7372 Prepackaged software

(G-8781)
DAVID T MITCHELL
Also Called: Mitchell Technologies
14229 143rd Ave Se (98059-5548)
PHONE 425 227-7111
David T Mitchell, *Owner*
EMP: 4
SALES (est): 352.6K **Privately Held**
SIC: 3679 7389 Electronic circuits;

(G-8782)
DEFENSE SALES INTL LLC
1934 Shattuck Ave S (98055-4248)
PHONE 206 999-8684
Thomas Ogden,
EMP: 1
SQ FT: 800
SALES: 2.8MM **Privately Held**
SIC: 3728 5941 3484 3711 Aircraft parts & equipment; ammunition; guns (firearms) or gun parts, 30 mm. & below; universal carriers, military, assembly of

(G-8783)
DESIMONE OIL AND VINEGAR MKT
20134 Se 192nd St (98058-0280)
PHONE 253 709-5576
John Hittman, *Principal*
EMP: 2

SALES (est): 62.3K **Privately Held**
SIC: 2099 Vinegar

(G-8784)
DISTANT LANDS TRADING CO
801 Houser Way N (98057-5506)
PHONE 800 758-4437
Alton McEwen, *CEO*
Russell Kramer, *President*
Henry Stein, *President*
Michael Obrien, *CFO*
EMP: 5
SALES (est): 767.5K **Privately Held**
SIC: 2095 Roasted coffee
HQ: Ito En (North America) Inc.
20 Jay St Ste 530
Brooklyn NY 11201
718 250-4000

(G-8785)
DISTRIBUTION INTERNATIONAL INC
700 Powell Ave Sw (98057-2911)
PHONE 425 228-4111
Brian Bauer, *Branch Mgr*
EMP: 320
SALES (corp-wide): 445.2MM **Privately Held**
SIC: 5033 3086 1742 Insulation materials; insulation or cushioning material, foamed plastic; acoustical & insulation work
PA: Distribution International, Inc.
9000 Railwood Dr
Houston TX 77078
713 428-3740

(G-8786)
DOJO LLC
15627 Se 178th St (98058-9003)
PHONE 203 903-0079
EMP: 2
SALES (est): 112.5K **Privately Held**
SIC: 7372 Prepackaged software

(G-8787)
DOW PUBLISHING LLC
1210 N 42nd Pl (98056-2170)
PHONE 425 572-6540
William Dow, *Administration*
EMP: 2
SALES (est): 137.4K **Privately Held**
SIC: 2741 Miscellaneous publishing

(G-8788)
DREAMWORKS PRINTING INC
1250 Sw 43rd St (98057-4833)
PHONE 425 970-4625
Jonathan Foote, *Manager*
EMP: 3
SQ FT: 1,300
SALES: 400K **Privately Held**
SIC: 2759 Commercial printing

(G-8789)
E & E FOODS INC (PA)
Also Called: Pacific Star Seafoods
900 Powell Ave Sw (98057-2907)
PHONE 206 768-8979
Randy Patrick, *President*
Tadayuki Goto, *Vice Pres*
Yuk Lan LI, *CFO*
Jeremiah Judd, *Accounts Mgr*
Jon Roche, *Supervisor*
EMP: 30 EST: 2016
SQ FT: 76,900
SALES (est): 33.4MM **Privately Held**
SIC: 2092 5146 Seafoods, fresh: prepared; fish & seafoods

(G-8790)
EASYXAFS LLC
879 Rainier Ave N A103 (98057-5378)
PHONE 208 697-4076
Devon Mortensen, *Mng Member*
William Holden,
Gerald Seidler,
EMP: 7 EST: 2015
SALES (est): 131.4K **Privately Held**
SIC: 3826 Analytical instruments

GEOGRAPHIC SECTION

(G-8791)
EATON ELECTRIC HOLDINGS LLC
1020 Thomas Ave Sw (98057-2922)
PHONE..................................425 271-9237
Richard Schumacher, *Principal*
EMP: 100 **Privately Held**
WEB: www.cooperus.com
SIC: 3546 Power-driven handtools
HQ: Eaton Electric Holdings Llc
  1000 Eaton Blvd
  Cleveland OH 44122
  440 523-5000

(G-8792)
ELECTRO EROSION SPECIALTIES
242 Sw 43rd St (98057-4936)
PHONE..................................425 251-9440
Roy Weder, *President*
EMP: 3
SALES (est): 400K **Privately Held**
SIC: 3599 3559 Machine shop, jobbing & repair; electronic component making machinery

(G-8793)
ELLISON FLUID SYSTEMS INC
350 Airport Way (98057-5332)
PHONE..................................425 271-3220
Ben Ellison, *President*
Nancy Ellison, *Corp Secy*
Marty Ellison, *Vice Pres*
EMP: 2
SALES (est): 270K **Privately Held**
WEB: www.ellison-tbi.com
SIC: 3728 5013 Aircraft parts & equipment; motor vehicle supplies & new parts

(G-8794)
EMS & SALES LLC
12221 164th Ave Se (98059-6414)
PHONE..................................253 208-9062
Zbigniew Bauer, *Managing Dir*
Margaret Blank Bauer,
EMP: 5
SALES (est): 211.8K **Privately Held**
SIC: 3451 Screw machine products

(G-8795)
ENGINEERING SOLUTIONS INC
1201 Monster Rd Sw # 240 (98057-2954)
PHONE..................................206 241-9395
Robert Merrill, *President*
EMP: 10
SALES: 1.7MM **Privately Held**
WEB: www.engsolinc.com
SIC: 3571 3577 5734 8711 Electronic computers; computer peripheral equipment; computer peripheral equipment; electrical or electronic engineering

(G-8796)
EXPRESS IMAGING SYSTEMS LLC
Also Called: Evluma
3600 Lind Ave Sw Ste 140 (98057-4934)
PHONE..................................206 720-1798
Steve Mills, *Sales Dir*
Keith Miller,
▲ EMP: 15
SQ FT: 6,000
SALES: 5.4MM **Privately Held**
SIC: 3861 7371 Photographic equipment & supplies; computer software development

(G-8797)
EXTREME HARDWOOD FLOORS
12611 177th Pl Se (98059-6600)
PHONE..................................425 985-6735
Lorraine Ester, *Principal*
EMP: 2 EST: 2007
SALES (est): 181K **Privately Held**
SIC: 2426 1771 Flooring, hardwood; flooring contractor

(G-8798)
EZ LIP LLC
2218 Se 2nd Pl (98056-8867)
PHONE..................................425 753-6814
Stefan Stoynov,
EMP: 3 EST: 2011
SALES (est): 302.4K **Privately Held**
SIC: 3069 Rubber automotive products

(G-8799)
FINISHING TOUCHES
17832 W Lake Desire Dr Se (98058-9562)
PHONE..................................425 277-6079
Jeffrey Whitmore, *Owner*
EMP: 3
SALES (est): 290K **Privately Held**
SIC: 2431 Staircases & stairs, wood

(G-8800)
FIRST METALS INC
Also Called: First Metal and Supply
430 Olympia Ave Ne (98056-3900)
PHONE..................................303 915-2426
Pedro Aguilar, *CEO*
EMP: 7
SQ FT: 2,850
SALES: 2.5MM **Privately Held**
SIC: 3444 Sheet metalwork

(G-8801)
FLORIDA TILE INC
Also Called: Florida Tile 73
1012 Sw 41st St (98057-4808)
PHONE..................................206 767-9819
Jack Branson, *Regional Mgr*
EMP: 9
SALES (corp-wide): 6.6K **Privately Held**
WEB: www.floridatile.com
SIC: 3253 Wall tile, ceramic
HQ: Florida Tile, Inc.
  998 Governors Ln Ste 300
  Lexington KY 40513
  859 219-5200

(G-8802)
FORGER3D LLC
821 Dayton Ave Ne (98056-3640)
PHONE..................................425 440-0662
Sergey Singov, *Principal*
EMP: 2 EST: 2016
SALES (est): 122.8K **Privately Held**
SIC: 2752 Advertising posters, lithographed

(G-8803)
FOUR GENERALS BREWING
229 Wells Ave S (98057-2131)
PHONE..................................425 282-4360
EMP: 3 EST: 2016
SALES (est): 120K **Privately Held**
SIC: 2082 Malt beverages

(G-8804)
FREEMAN COMPANIES
1030 Sw 34th St Ste D (98057-4810)
PHONE..................................425 656-1255
EMP: 2
SALES (est): 213.7K **Privately Held**
SIC: 3599 Mfg Industrial Machinery

(G-8805)
GARY L JORDANGER
2301 Ne 28th St (98056-2221)
PHONE..................................425 271-2617
Jordanger Gary, *Principal*
EMP: 2
SALES (est): 97.6K **Privately Held**
SIC: 3231 Products of purchased glass

(G-8806)
GENUINE PARTS COMPANY
Also Called: Olympic Brake Supply
907 Thomas Ave Sw (98057-2931)
PHONE..................................206 575-8100
Lj Kaufman, *General Mgr*
Michelle Mellott, *Controller*
EMP: 30
SALES (corp-wide): 18.7B **Publicly Held**
SIC: 5013 3714 Automotive supplies & parts; motor vehicle brake systems & parts
PA: Genuine Parts Company
  2999 Wildwood Pkwy
  Atlanta GA 30339
  770 953-1700

(G-8807)
GLOBAL INDUSTRIES INC
820 Sw 34th St Ste A (98057-4806)
P.O. Box 111256, Tacoma (98411-1256)
PHONE..................................425 291-9282
Russ Curry, *Manager*
EMP: 4

SALES (corp-wide): 134.6MM **Privately Held**
WEB: www.evolvefurnituregroup.com
SIC: 2522 5021 Office furniture, except wood; furniture
PA: Global Industries, Inc.
  17 W Stow Rd
  Marlton NJ 08053
  856 596-3390

(G-8808)
GLOBAL PRESS
927 Harrington Ave Ne (98056-3013)
PHONE..................................425 254-9323
EMP: 4
SALES (est): 240K **Privately Held**
SIC: 2741 Misc Publishing

(G-8809)
GMAN INDUSTRIES LTD
18530 Se 145th St (98059-8001)
PHONE..................................425 228-2518
Gary A Ford, *Principal*
EMP: 2
SALES (est): 165.4K **Privately Held**
SIC: 3999 Manufacturing industries

(G-8810)
GRAPEVINE HATS LLC
10815 Se 184th Ln (98055-7104)
P.O. Box 6106, Bellevue (98008-0106)
PHONE..................................206 940-3896
Cindy Parsons, *Principal*
EMP: 2 EST: 2009
SALES (est): 106.7K **Privately Held**
SIC: 2353 Hats, caps & millinery

(G-8811)
GRAPHIC COMMUNICATIONS INC
Also Called: Sir Speedy
4208 Lind Ave Sw (98057-4943)
PHONE..................................425 251-8680
Edward S Denn, *President*
EMP: 8
SQ FT: 7,292
SALES (est): 650K **Privately Held**
SIC: 2752 7374 7334 Commercial printing, offset; computer graphics service; photocopying & duplicating services

(G-8812)
GRAPHIC PACKAGING INTL INC
Also Called: Altivity Packaging
601 Monster Rd Sw (98057-2966)
PHONE..................................425 235-3300
Rick Nordi, *General Mgr*
EMP: 133 **Publicly Held**
SIC: 2631 2657 Folding boxboard; folding paperboard boxes
HQ: Graphic Packaging International, Llc
  1500 Riveredge Pkwy # 100
  Atlanta GA 30328

(G-8813)
GRAYBAR ELECTRIC COMPANY INC
300 Sw 27th St Ste B (98057-3380)
PHONE..................................425 203-1500
EMP: 34
SALES (corp-wide): 7.2B **Privately Held**
SIC: 5063 3699 Electrical supplies; electrical equipment & supplies
PA: Graybar Electric Company, Inc.
  34 N Meramec Ave
  Saint Louis MO 63105
  314 573-9200

(G-8814)
GRAYS HARBOR PAPER LLC
451 Sw 10th St Ste 107 (98057-2981)
PHONE..................................877 548-3424
EMP: 18
SALES (est): 4.1MM **Privately Held**
SIC: 2621 Fine paper

(G-8815)
GTC INNOVATIONS LLC
14201 Se Petrovitsky Rd A3 (98058-8986)
PHONE..................................866 241-3149
Greg Thayer, *Principal*
EMP: 3
SALES (est): 199.2K **Privately Held**
SIC: 3559 Automotive related machinery

(G-8816)
HACIENDA CUSTOM WOODWORK LLC
17226 120th Ter Se (98058-6239)
PHONE..................................206 922-9330
Elda Villalobos, *Mng Member*
EMP: 4
SALES (est): 441.6K **Privately Held**
SIC: 2431 Millwork

(G-8817)
HARPER ENGINEERING COMPANY
700 Sw 7th St (98057-2919)
PHONE..................................425 255-0414
Robert Hazel, *President*
EMP: 75
SQ FT: 20,000
SALES (est): 19.2MM **Privately Held**
WEB: www.harperengineering.com
SIC: 3728 Aircraft parts & equipment

(G-8818)
HOMESTEAD MACHINE
15025 Se 116th St (98059-6026)
PHONE..................................425 228-1851
David Wilken, *Owner*
EMP: 2
SALES (est): 142.7K **Privately Held**
SIC: 3599 Machine shop, jobbing & repair

(G-8819)
HONEYWELL INTERNATIONAL INC
4150 Lind Ave Sw (98057-4973)
PHONE..................................760 339-5592
Nancy Luna, *President*
EMP: 699
SALES (corp-wide): 41.8B **Publicly Held**
SIC: 3724 Aircraft engines & engine parts
PA: Honeywell International Inc.
  115 Tabor Rd
  Morris Plains NJ 07950
  973 455-2000

(G-8820)
HONEYWELL INTERNATIONAL INC
4150 Lind Ave Sw (98057-4973)
PHONE..................................425 251-9511
Kim Cox, *Manager*
EMP: 150
SQ FT: 9,806
SALES (corp-wide): 41.8B **Publicly Held**
WEB: www.honeywell.com
SIC: 7699 7629 3812 Aircraft flight instrument repair; electrical repair shops; search & navigation equipment
PA: Honeywell International Inc.
  115 Tabor Rd
  Morris Plains NJ 07950
  973 455-2000

(G-8821)
HONEYWELL INTERNATIONAL INC
4150 Lind Ave Sw (98057-4973)
PHONE..................................425 251-9511
David Deer, *Principal*
EMP: 145
SALES (corp-wide): 41.8B **Publicly Held**
WEB: www.honeywell.com
SIC: 3571 4581 Electronic computers; airports, flying fields & services
PA: Honeywell International Inc.
  115 Tabor Rd
  Morris Plains NJ 07950
  973 455-2000

(G-8822)
HUNTER FISH ENTERPRISES
19808 144th Pl Se (98058-9434)
PHONE..................................253 852-8357
Jack Moore, *Owner*
Eileen Moore, *Co-Owner*
EMP: 4
SALES (est): 247.5K **Privately Held**
SIC: 3699 5941 Fly traps, electrical; sporting goods & bicycle shops

(G-8823)
INDIGO VINYLWORKS LLC
12828 Se 161st St (98058-5323)
PHONE..................................425 463-7460

James Romano, *Principal*
EMP: 2
SALES (est): 140.1K **Privately Held**
SIC: 3993 Signs & advertising specialties

(G-8824)
INDUSTRIAL SYSTEMS LABORATORY
58 Logan Ave S (98057-2039)
PHONE..................................425 226-7585
James Dawson, *Owner*
EMP: 2
SQ FT: 1,200
SALES (est): 277.7K **Privately Held**
WEB: www.islab.com
SIC: 7372 Application computer software

(G-8825)
INFINITE CASTE
3800 Ne Sunset Blvd (98056-3305)
PHONE..................................206 335-4058
EMP: 2
SALES (est): 68K **Privately Held**
SIC: 3961 Mfg Costume Jewelry

(G-8826)
INKWELL LLC (PA)
Also Called: Inkwell Property Management
709 S 32nd St (98055-5097)
PHONE..................................425 277-3655
Ricardo Lockhart, *Principal*
Natalie Lockhart, *Mng Member*
EMP: 7
SALES (est): 1MM **Privately Held**
SIC: 2752 Commercial printing, lithographic

(G-8827)
INSIGNIA SIGN INC
325 Burnett Ave N (98057-5616)
P.O. Box 2849 (98056-0849)
PHONE..................................425 917-2109
Cindy Thomson, *President*
Bryan Thomson, *Vice Pres*
EMP: 12
SALES (est): 1.4MM **Privately Held**
SIC: 3993 Signs & advertising specialties

(G-8828)
INTEGRITY INDUSTRIES INC
2210 Lind Ave Sw Ste 109 (98057-3326)
P.O. Box 739 (98057-0739)
PHONE..................................425 264-9401
Spencer Woods, *CEO*
Michael Callaghan, *President*
EMP: 2
SALES: 950K **Privately Held**
SIC: 2899 Chemical preparations

(G-8829)
J & R MTLCRAFT FABRICATORS INC
1220 N 5th St (98057-5550)
PHONE..................................425 254-0392
Joe Mosselli, *President*
Ron Porter, *Vice Pres*
EMP: 8
SALES (est): 1.5MM **Privately Held**
SIC: 3444 Sheet metal specialties, not stamped

(G-8830)
J FILLIPS LLC
3405 Se 7th St (98058-2890)
P.O. Box 1111 (98057-1111)
PHONE..................................425 277-1011
Judith Fillips, *Owner*
EMP: 3 EST: 2002
SALES (est): 307.5K **Privately Held**
SIC: 3534 3669 Elevators & equipment; intercommunication systems, electric

(G-8831)
J R STONE SERVICES
12244 155th Ave Se (98059-6311)
PHONE..................................425 227-8513
Romiudo Lins, *Owner*
EMP: 3
SALES (est): 285K **Privately Held**
SIC: 3281 Granite, cut & shaped

(G-8832)
JAVA TRADING CO LLC
Also Called: Distant Lands Coffee
801 Houser Way N (98057-5506)
PHONE..................................425 917-2920
Yosuke Honjo, *CEO*
Kazuhiro Hoshi, *President*
Yoshiyuki Takahashi, *Senior VP*
Koichiro Murase, *Vice Pres*
Kirk Hill, *Plant Mgr*
▲ EMP: 200
SQ FT: 115,000
SALES (est): 122.8MM **Privately Held**
WEB: www.javatradingco.com
SIC: 5149 2095 Coffee, green or roasted; roasted coffee

(G-8833)
JOT PRODUCTS CO
130 Main Ave S Apt 404 (98057-2156)
PHONE..................................206 331-6677
William Douglas Conklin, *Owner*
EMP: 2
SALES: 50K **Privately Held**
SIC: 2099 Sauces: dry mixes

(G-8834)
K SPORTS MANUFACTURING INC
5501 Ne 1st Pl (98059-4974)
PHONE..................................206 251-5211
Khai Nguyen, *Principal*
EMP: 2 EST: 2015
SALES (est): 109.1K **Privately Held**
SIC: 3999 Manufacturing industries

(G-8835)
K&W ENTERPRISES INC
2433 Jones Ave Ne (98056-2274)
PHONE..................................425 255-4316
Paul R Watt, *President*
Elizabeth Kalasountas, *Treasurer*
Nancy L Watt, *Admin Sec*
EMP: 4
SQ FT: 1,600
SALES: 125K **Privately Held**
WEB: www.nylongear.com
SIC: 2399 Belting & belt products

(G-8836)
KB HANKS ENTERPRISES
524 Olympia Ave Se (98058-2876)
PHONE..................................425 221-1040
Kevins Hanks, *Owner*
EMP: 4
SALES: 50K **Privately Held**
SIC: 2759 Engraving

(G-8837)
KINGTIME LLC
4112 Ne 24th St (98059-3637)
PHONE..................................206 375-7422
Yutian Guo, *Principal*
EMP: 2
SALES (est): 172.9K **Privately Held**
SIC: 3571 Electronic computers

(G-8838)
KP LLC
555 Monster Rd Sw (98057-2937)
PHONE..................................425 204-6355
Susan Dahl, *Accounts Exec*
Susan Bowles, *Marketing Mgr*
Sean Henderson, *Manager*
Michaell Hoerler, *Manager*
Jim Hunter, *Manager*
EMP: 200
SQ FT: 30,000
SALES (est): 31.6MM
SALES (corp-wide): 120MM **Privately Held**
WEB: www.kpcorporation.com
SIC: 2752 7331 2759 Lithographing on metal; direct mail advertising services; commercial printing
PA: Kp Llc
    13951 Washington Ave
    San Leandro CA 94578
    510 346-0729

(G-8839)
L & R INDUSTRIES LLC
11876 Se 160th St (98058-5318)
P.O. Box 58832 (98058-1832)
PHONE..................................425 226-2780

Lynn Faul,
Sandra Faul,
EMP: 2
SALES (est): 200K **Privately Held**
SIC: 3728 Aircraft parts & equipment

(G-8840)
LANDING GEAR WORK LLC
295 E Perimeter Rd (98057-5329)
PHONE..................................509 884-9546
Thomas Anderson, *CEO*
EMP: 2
SALES (est): 267.9K **Privately Held**
SIC: 3728 Alighting (landing gear) assemblies, aircraft

(G-8841)
LAYFIELD PLASTICS INCORPORATED
4001 Oakesdale Ave Sw (98057-4818)
PHONE..................................425 254-1075
Thomas Rose, *CEO*
Brian Fraser, *Vice Pres*
Gary Pinkerton, *Vice Pres*
▲ EMP: 5
SQ FT: 14,925
SALES (est): 5.7MM
SALES (corp-wide): 3.7MM **Privately Held**
SIC: 3081 1541 5162 Unsupported plastics film & sheet; industrial buildings & warehouses; plastics film
HQ: Layfield Group Limited
    11131 Hammersmith Gate
    Richmond BC V7A 5
    604 275-5588

(G-8842)
LDL- SOFTWARE INC
5129 Ne 4th Ct (98059-4566)
PHONE..................................425 652-1473
Larry Leach, *Principal*
EMP: 2
SALES (est): 116.1K **Privately Held**
SIC: 7372 Prepackaged software

(G-8843)
LIFT AV LLC
1533 Ilwaco Ave Ne (98059-4234)
PHONE..................................425 242-7339
EMP: 2 EST: 2010
SALES (est): 17K **Privately Held**
SIC: 3629 Mfg Electrical Industrial Apparatus

(G-8844)
LIGHTEL TECHNOLOGIES INC
2210 Lind Ave Sw Ste 100 (98057-3326)
PHONE..................................425 277-8000
Benson Shen, *CEO*
Pai-Sheng Shen, *President*
Patrick Yu, *General Mgr*
Mark Curran, *Vice Pres*
Sharon Huang, *Vice Pres*
▲ EMP: 40
SQ FT: 12,000
SALES (est): 7.1MM **Privately Held**
WEB: www.lighteltech.com
SIC: 3674 3646 Semiconductors & related devices; commercial indusl & institutional electric lighting fixtures

(G-8845)
LIONHEART INDUSTRIES LLC
14138 204th Ave Se (98059-8924)
PHONE..................................888 552-4743
William Maclean,
EMP: 3
SALES (est): 256.5K **Privately Held**
SIC: 5099 3484 Firearms & ammunition, except sporting; machine guns; small arms; machine guns & grenade launchers; pistols or pistol parts, 30 mm. & below

(G-8846)
LUMICOR INC
Also Called: Schober
1400 Monster Rd Sw Ste A (98057-2902)
PHONE..................................425 255-4000
Dan Lessard, *President*
Angela Foster, *Project Mgr*
Kaya Saldajeno, *Project Mgr*
Andrew Adams, *Production*
Amanda Lloyd, *Production*
▲ EMP: 80

SQ FT: 42,377
SALES (est): 20.4MM **Privately Held**
WEB: www.lumicor.com
SIC: 3728 3089 Aircraft parts & equipment; laminating of plastic

(G-8847)
MANUFACTURERS MINERAL COMPANY
1215 Monster Rd Sw (98057-2962)
PHONE..................................425 228-2120
James D Adderson, *President*
Vickie Adderson, *Corp Secy*
Michael Adderson, *Vice Pres*
EMP: 11
SQ FT: 1,000
SALES (est): 1.6MM **Privately Held**
SIC: 3295 1429 3281 1442 Minerals, ground or treated; marble, crushed & broken-quarrying; cut stone & stone products; construction sand & gravel

(G-8848)
MARTIAN PUBLISHING LLC
5320 Ne 17th Pl (98059-4377)
PHONE..................................425 572-0743
Duanna Sloss, *Principal*
EMP: 2 EST: 2013
SALES (est): 128.1K **Privately Held**
SIC: 2741 Miscellaneous publishing

(G-8849)
MASTER STUCCO HC
15228 Se 176th Pl (98058-9053)
PHONE..................................425 793-0576
Horacio Castellanos, *Principal*
EMP: 3
SALES (est): 150K **Privately Held**
SIC: 3299 Stucco

(G-8850)
MASTROGIANNIS DISTILLERY LLC
123 Vashon Ct Ne (98059-5238)
PHONE..................................206 383-2463
Ilias Mastrogiannis, *Principal*
EMP: 4
SALES (est): 236.2K **Privately Held**
SIC: 2085 Distilled & blended liquors

(G-8851)
MEDIA INCORPORATED
Also Called: Media Inc Sign Manufacturing
16508 164th Pl Se (98058-4216)
PHONE..................................425 251-5145
Lee Maxwell, *President*
Nacy Maxwell, *Vice Pres*
EMP: 4
SQ FT: 1,400
SALES (est): 400K **Privately Held**
WEB: www.media-ada.com
SIC: 3993 Signs & advertising specialties

(G-8852)
MEP LABS LLC
1513 Dayton Ct Ne (98056-2766)
PHONE..................................206 229-2525
Michael Purfield, *Co-Owner*
Enos Kline, *Co-Owner*
Paula Ladd, *Co-Owner*
EMP: 3 EST: 2017
SALES (est): 142.1K **Privately Held**
SIC: 2835 In vitro diagnostics

(G-8853)
METEORCOMM LLC
1201 Sw 7th St (98057-5213)
PHONE..................................253 872-2521
Robert Turnbull, *CEO*
Mike Byrne, *Mfg Mgr*
Jacob Chapman, *Engineer*
Mark Davies, *Engineer*
Daniel Feren, *Engineer*
EMP: 150
SQ FT: 25,400
SALES (est): 23.4MM **Privately Held**
WEB: www.meteorcomm.com
SIC: 3663 Radio broadcasting & communications equipment; space satellite communications equipment

(G-8854)
MICROSCAN MFG LLC
700 Sw 39th St (98057-2316)
PHONE..................................425 226-5700

EMP: 3
SALES (est): 160K **Privately Held**
SIC: 3999 Mfg Misc Products

(G-8855)
MILLION TREE PRJ FOR SOMALIA
2223 Smithers Ave S (98055-4208)
PHONE..................................206 731-9164
EMP: 2 EST: 2015
SALES (est): 124.8K **Privately Held**
SIC: 3822 8699 Mfg Environmental Controls Membership Organization

(G-8856)
MINUTEMAN PRESS RENTON
1120 Sw 16th St Ste 1a (98057-2639)
PHONE..................................425 251-0781
EMP: 2
SALES (est): 83.9K **Privately Held**
SIC: 2752 Commercial printing, lithographic

(G-8857)
NEW AGE PROCESSORS LLC
200 Sw 34th St (98057-4940)
PHONE..................................425 656-0174
Mark Isebrands,
Gerry Krieger,
Randy Lucas,
John Pagel,
EMP: 6
SALES (est): 11.2K **Privately Held**
SIC: 3674 Microprocessors

(G-8858)
NEWTON SECURITY INC
443 Sw 41st St (98057-4926)
PHONE..................................425 251-9494
John Bramblete, *President*
Tony Edington, *Principal*
Carl Witty, *Vice Pres*
EMP: 30
SALES (est): 3.3MM **Privately Held**
WEB: www.newtonsecurityinc.com
SIC: 3699 Security control equipment & systems; security devices

(G-8859)
NORTH PCF INDUS COATINGS LLC
2900 Lind Ave Sw Ste B (98057-3386)
P.O. Box 112629, Anchorage AK (99511-2629)
PHONE..................................907 865-8400
Jeffrey Mark Wilson, *President*
Lue Pestl, *General Mgr*
Mark McRobie, *Superintendent*
EMP: 2
SALES (est): 83.1K **Privately Held**
SIC: 1799 3479 Sandblasting of building exteriors; aluminum coating of metal products

(G-8860)
NORTHWEST SYNERGISTIC SOFTWARE
14024 W Lk Kathleen Dr Se (98059-7715)
PHONE..................................425 271-1491
Robert Clardy, *Principal*
EMP: 2 EST: 2010
SALES (est): 90.2K **Privately Held**
SIC: 7372 Prepackaged software

(G-8861)
NYEBERG MACHINE
17022 Se 136th St (98059-7009)
PHONE..................................425 235-9675
Mark Nyberg, *Principal*
EMP: 3
SALES (est): 110K **Privately Held**
SIC: 3599 Machine shop, jobbing & repair

(G-8862)
OBERTO
101 Sw 41st St Ste D (98057-4974)
PHONE..................................425 251-4563
Sehun Park, *Principal*
EMP: 3
SALES (est): 484.8K **Privately Held**
SIC: 2011 Meat packing plants

(G-8863)
OLD SOUL CANDLE COMPANY LLC
11903 Se 165th St (98058-5347)
PHONE..................................206 915-0224
Stefanie McIrvin, *Principal*
EMP: 2
SALES (est): 62.5K **Privately Held**
SIC: 3999 Candles

(G-8864)
ONG INNOVATIONS LLC
14201 Se Petrovitsky Rd (98058-8986)
PHONE..................................253 777-0186
Sean Ong, *Mng Member*
Neisha Ong,
EMP: 2
SALES (est): 50K **Privately Held**
SIC: 7372 7389 Application computer software;

(G-8865)
OPTICON INC
2220 Lind Ave Sw Ste 100 (98057-3327)
PHONE..................................425 651-2120
Nick Kamio, *President*
▲ EMP: 20
SQ FT: 20,000
SALES (est): 5.4MM **Privately Held**
WEB: www.opticonusa.com
SIC: 3577 5045 7378 8711 Optical scanning devices; computers; computer & data processing equipment repair/maintenance; engineering services
PA: Optoelectronics Co.,Ltd.
    4-12-17, Tsukagoshi
    Warabi STM 335-0

(G-8866)
ORVELLA INDUSTRIES CORP
1055 Blaine Ave Ne Unit C (98056-8725)
PHONE..................................206 778-2743
Chad Orvella, *Principal*
EMP: 2 EST: 2012
SALES (est): 106.8K **Privately Held**
SIC: 3999 Manufacturing industries

(G-8867)
OSMONICS INC
16814 163rd Pl Se (98058-8650)
PHONE..................................425 204-5508
Jeff Fleming, *Principal*
EMP: 2 EST: 2001
SALES (est): 219.3K **Privately Held**
WEB: www.gesm.ge.com
SIC: 3569 General industrial machinery

(G-8868)
OUT OF BOX MANUFACTURING LLC
1600 Sw 43rd St Ste 200 (98057-4819)
PHONE..................................253 214-7448
Chad Budvarson, *CEO*
Molly Dahlman, *Materials Mgr*
Mike Lopez, *Sales Mgr*
Samantha Perrin, *Admin Asst*
Allison Budvarson,
EMP: 26 EST: 2008
SALES (est): 7.1MM **Privately Held**
SIC: 3672 Printed circuit boards

(G-8869)
OUTDOOR SPECIALTIES LLC
17886 W Spring Lake Dr Se (98058-0612)
PHONE..................................425 432-0507
Edward Heikell, *Principal*
EMP: 4
SALES (est): 340.1K **Privately Held**
SIC: 3861 Motion picture film

(G-8870)
PACCAR INC
750 Houser Way N (98057-5573)
P.O. Box 1000, Kirkland (98083-1000)
PHONE..................................425 254-4400
Ed Caudill, *Branch Mgr*
Krista Van Gaver, *Manager*
EMP: 180
SALES (corp-wide): 23.5B **Publicly Held**
WEB: www.paccar.com
SIC: 3711 Truck & tractor truck assembly
PA: Paccar Inc
    777 106th Ave Ne
    Bellevue WA 98004
    425 468-7400

(G-8871)
PACCAR INC
1601 N 8th St (98057-5507)
P.O. Box 9001 (98057-9001)
PHONE..................................425 227-5800
Tony McQuary, *Plant Mgr*
Dave Caplan, *Plant Mgr*
Donna Hodeo, *Controller*
Kendell Bonner, *VP Finance*
Amber Eslinger, *Human Res Mgr*
EMP: 319
SALES (corp-wide): 23.5B **Publicly Held**
WEB: www.paccar.com
SIC: 3711 3537 Truck & tractor truck assembly; industrial trucks & tractors
PA: Paccar Inc
    777 106th Ave Ne
    Bellevue WA 98004
    425 468-7400

(G-8872)
PACIFIC INTERCONNECTION LLC
1022 N 33rd Pl (98056-1932)
PHONE..................................425 277-9527
Jeanne Wong, *Sales Staff*
Vincent Kim,
EMP: 3
SALES (est): 269.2K **Privately Held**
SIC: 3229 Glass fiber products; fiber optics strands

(G-8873)
PACIFIC SALES & SERVICE
17701 108th Ave Se 1010 (98055-6448)
P.O. Box 336 (98057-0336)
PHONE..................................425 271-9000
EMP: 3
SQ FT: 1,600
SALES (est): 100K **Privately Held**
SIC: 3999 Mfg Misc Products

(G-8874)
PAN ABODE CEDAR HOMES INC
1100 Maple Ave Sw (98057-3172)
PHONE..................................425 255-8260
Kevin Sloan, *President*
Ronald D Davis, *Vice Pres*
Pat King, *Vice Pres*
EMP: 48
SQ FT: 4,000
SALES (est): 9MM **Privately Held**
WEB: www.panabodehomes.com
SIC: 5039 2452 8712 2431 Prefabricated buildings; prefabricated buildings, wood; house designer; millwork

(G-8875)
PAN ABODE HOMES INC
1100 Maple Ave Sw (98057-3172)
PHONE..................................425 255-8260
Kevin Sloan, *President*
Russ Barney, *Corp Secy*
Ron Davis, *Vice Pres*
▼ EMP: 50 EST: 1952
SQ FT: 4,000
SALES (est): 1MM **Privately Held**
SIC: 5211 5039 8712 2452 Modular homes; prefabricated buildings; house designer; prefabricated buildings, wood

(G-8876)
PATRICK E & PATRICIA M LYDON
Also Called: Compliance Industries
14521 164th Pl Se (98059-7903)
PHONE..................................425 226-3216
Patrick Lydon, *Principal*
EMP: 2
SALES (est): 113.2K **Privately Held**
SIC: 3993 Signs & advertising specialties

(G-8877)
PETER K GROSSMAN
240 Sw 43rd St (98057-4936)
PHONE..................................206 824-6626
Peter K Grossman, *Principal*
EMP: 2
SALES (est): 131.4K **Privately Held**
SIC: 3599 Industrial machinery

(G-8878)
PF FISHPOLE HOISTS INC
238 Sw 43rd St (98057-4936)
PHONE..................................206 767-3887
William D Bishop, *President*
EMP: 5
SQ FT: 4,000
SALES (est): 848K **Privately Held**
SIC: 3537 Aircraft loading hoists

(G-8879)
PINNACLE PRINTING FOUNDATION
13613 Se 188th St (98058-8043)
PHONE..................................425 271-7089
Robert Walkley, *President*
EMP: 3
SALES: 44.8K **Privately Held**
SIC: 2752 Commercial printing, lithographic

(G-8880)
PIXOTEC LLC
15917 Se Fairwood Blvd (98058-8631)
PHONE..................................425 255-0789
Skip Echert,
R David Lucas,
EMP: 2
SALES (est): 170K **Privately Held**
WEB: www.slicerdicer.com
SIC: 7372 Prepackaged software

(G-8881)
PK GRAPHICS INC
Also Called: Print Mart
1120 Sw 16th St Ste 1a (98057-2639)
PHONE..................................425 251-8083
Robert Vetch, *President*
EMP: 4
SQ FT: 3,800
SALES: 400K **Privately Held**
SIC: 2752 Commercial printing, offset

(G-8882)
PRECISION PAINT
14248 Se Fairwood Blvd (98058-8538)
PHONE..................................425 235-0340
George C Seeman, *Owner*
EMP: 4 EST: 1997
SQ FT: 5,999
SALES (est): 230K **Privately Held**
SIC: 2851 Paints & allied products

(G-8883)
PRECISION TOOLING AND DIE
800 Sw 27th St (98057-4965)
PHONE..................................253 872-8217
EMP: 8
SALES (est): 719.8K **Privately Held**
SIC: 3544 Mfg Dies/Tools/Jigs/Fixtures

(G-8884)
PRECISION WELDING
2213 Aberdeen Ave Ne (98056-2623)
PHONE..................................425 271-7490
Harry Hughes, *Owner*
EMP: 2
SALES: 30K **Privately Held**
SIC: 7692 Welding repair

(G-8885)
PREMIUM WORLD FOOD CORPORATION
1672 Lake Youngs Way Se (98058-3816)
PHONE..................................206 267-8914
EMP: 3
SALES (est): 205.4K **Privately Held**
SIC: 2099 Mfg Food Preparations

(G-8886)
PYRAMID GRINDING
5851 Ne 4th St (98059-4857)
P.O. Box 2377 (98056-0377)
PHONE..................................425 254-1820
Tyler Wallace, *Superintendent*
EMP: 3
SALES (est): 361.8K **Privately Held**
SIC: 3599 Grinding castings for the trade

(G-8887)
QUALITY POLISHING AND PLATING
21010 196th Ave Se (98058-0543)
PHONE..................................425 432-5500
Karen Depasquale, *Owner*
EMP: 3
SALES (est): 140.6K **Privately Held**
SIC: 3471 Plating of metals or formed products

Renton - King County (G-8888) — GEOGRAPHIC SECTION

(G-8888)
R & A MANUFACTURING INC
13603 196th Ave Se (98059-7837)
PHONE..............................425 228-2109
Archie A Hodge, *President*
EMP: 5
SALES (est): 407.2K **Privately Held**
SIC: 3465 7539 Automotive stampings; frame & front end repair services

(G-8889)
R & R GRAPHICS INC
203 Airport Way (98057-5335)
PHONE..............................206 406-3604
Ron Guthrie, *Partner*
EMP: 4
SQ FT: 1,920
SALES (est): 277.8K **Privately Held**
WEB: www.gorenton.com
SIC: 3993 Signs & advertising specialties

(G-8890)
RADIAN AEROSPACE INC
2210 Ilwaco Ave Ne (98059-4151)
PHONE..............................425 235-1936
Curtis Gifford, *Principal*
EMP: 2
SALES (est): 282.7K **Privately Held**
SIC: 3721 Research & development on aircraft by the manufacturer

(G-8891)
RAINIER CLINICAL RESEARCH CTR
723 Sw 10th St Ste 100 (98057-5211)
PHONE..............................425 251-1720
Joanne C Phillips, *President*
Michelle Powell, *Administration*
EMP: 23
SALES (est): 4.2MM **Privately Held**
WEB: www.rainier-research.com
SIC: 2834 Pharmaceutical preparations

(G-8892)
REFUGE MUSIC
16710 133rd Pl Se (98058-6964)
P.O. Box 111 (98057-0111)
PHONE..............................425 271-4278
Gavin Fish, *Owner*
Brenda Fysh, *Partner*
EMP: 2
SALES (est): 64.7K **Privately Held**
WEB: www.refugemusic.com
SIC: 2731 Book publishing

(G-8893)
RENTON PRINTERY INCORPORATED
315 S 3rd St (98057-2092)
P.O. Box 4034 (98057-4034)
PHONE..............................425 235-1776
Myrol P Sweeney, *CEO*
Jeanne L Sweeney, *Treasurer*
EMP: 6
SQ FT: 500
SALES (est): 770K **Privately Held**
SIC: 2752 Commercial printing, offset

(G-8894)
RETIP LLC
5216 Ne 7th Ct (98059-4476)
PHONE..............................206 612-5538
EMP: 3
SALES (est): 71.1K **Privately Held**
SIC: 7372 Prepackaged Software Services

(G-8895)
RJ SPORTS INC
Also Called: Play It Again Sports 10280
17622 108th Ave Se (98055-6451)
PHONE..............................425 227-8777
Ron Jones, *President*
EMP: 6
SQ FT: 3,200
SALES (est): 655.3K **Privately Held**
SIC: 5941 3949 Sporting goods & bicycle shops; sporting & athletic goods

(G-8896)
ROGER HABON
Also Called: The Habon Company
17801 Se 146th St (98058-8016)
PHONE..............................206 240-0122
Roger Habon, *Owner*
EMP: 2

SALES (est): 135.2K **Privately Held**
SIC: 3612 Transformers, except electric

(G-8897)
ROGERS CUSTOM WOODWORKING
19042 Se 161st St (98058-0943)
PHONE..............................425 757-1799
EMP: 2
SALES (est): 85.2K **Privately Held**
SIC: 2431 Millwork

(G-8898)
ROSEMOUNT INC
800 Sw 34th St Ste L (98057-4807)
PHONE..............................206 329-8600
Sarah Amaly, *Manager*
EMP: 25
SALES (corp-wide): 17.4B **Publicly Held**
WEB: www.paineelectronics.com
SIC: 3823 Pressure measurement instruments, industrial
HQ: Rosemount Inc.
   8200 Market Blvd
   Chanhassen MN 55317
   952 906-8888

(G-8899)
ROSEMOUNT SPECIALTY PDTS LLC
800 Sw 34th St Ste L (98057-4807)
PHONE..............................206 329-8600
EMP: 26
SALES (corp-wide): 17.4B **Publicly Held**
SIC: 3823 Industrial instrmnts msrmnt display/control process variable
HQ: Rosemount Specialty Products, Llc
   5545 Nelpar Dr
   East Wenatchee WA 98802
   509 881-2100

(G-8900)
S M MARKETING SPECIALTIES
853 Jericho Pl Ne (98059-4472)
PHONE..............................206 230-0710
Stanley S Morhaime, *Partner*
EMP: 2
SALES (est): 190K **Privately Held**
SIC: 3953 Cancelling stamps, hand: rubber or metal

(G-8901)
S SMITH
15205 140th Way Se J101 (98058-7846)
PHONE..............................425 529-9244
S Smith, *Principal*
EMP: 5
SALES (est): 251.6K **Privately Held**
SIC: 1389 Oil field services

(G-8902)
SAMSONITE LLC
1030 Sw 34th St Ste D (98057-4810)
PHONE..............................253 395-1017
James Wasson, *Branch Mgr*
EMP: 4050
SALES (corp-wide): 177.9K **Privately Held**
SIC: 3161 Luggage
HQ: Samsonite Llc
   575 West St Ste 110
   Mansfield MA 02048
   508 851-1400

(G-8903)
SAVE SMOKE
17170 116th Ave Se (98058-5948)
PHONE..............................425 793-5030
Sang H Lee, *Principal*
EMP: 4
SALES (est): 230K **Privately Held**
SIC: 3669 Smoke detectors

(G-8904)
SAVON CASKETS AND URNS
460 Shelton Pl Ne (98056-8553)
PHONE..............................206 390-3797
Nicholas McNeil, *Owner*
EMP: 2
SALES (est): 100K **Privately Held**
SIC: 5087 3281 Caskets; urns, cut stone

(G-8905)
SAVOY CANDLES LLC
339 Burnett Ave S Apt 312 (98057-7510)
PHONE..............................205 281-9031
Latonya Savoy, *Administration*
EMP: 2 EST: 2016
SALES (est): 48K **Privately Held**
SIC: 3999 Candles

(G-8906)
SCHWARTZ BROTHERS RESTAURANTS
Also Called: Schwartz Brothers Bakery
1010 Sw 34th St (98057-4813)
PHONE..............................206 623-3134
Rachid Ovardi, *Manager*
EMP: 200
SALES (corp-wide): 38.5MM **Privately Held**
WEB: www.spazzo.com
SIC: 2051 5149 2052 Bread, cake & related products; groceries & related products; cookies & crackers
PA: Schwartz Brother's Restaurants
   325 118th Ave Se Ste 106
   Bellevue WA 98005
   425 455-3948

(G-8907)
SCUTTERS
14331 148th Pl Se (98059-7357)
PHONE..............................425 350-7480
Wiley Scutt, *Principal*
EMP: 3
SALES (est): 155.2K **Privately Held**
SIC: 2061 Raw cane sugar

(G-8908)
SEATTLE EGG ROLL CORP
106 Lake Ave S Ste B (98057-2087)
PHONE..............................425 226-6256
Paul Huang, *President*
EMP: 6
SALES (est): 530K **Privately Held**
SIC: 2099 Food preparations

(G-8909)
SHAWNEE CONSTRUCTION LLC
Also Called: Howell Creations
2613 Meadow Ave N (98056-2526)
PHONE..............................425 430-4232
Denton C Howell,
EMP: 2
SQ FT: 17,000
SALES: 1.5MM **Privately Held**
SIC: 2441 Cases, wood

(G-8910)
SHINE ON SIGNS & GRAPHICS INC
259 Sw 41st St (98057-4930)
PHONE..............................253 243-7777
Nancy Wilson, *CEO*
Harry Wilson, *President*
EMP: 2
SALES (est): 171K **Privately Held**
SIC: 3993 Letters for signs, metal

(G-8911)
SHOEZANDMORECOM LLC
17735 105th Pl Se (98055-8439)
PHONE..............................216 544-1745
David Holt, *CEO*
EMP: 10
SALES (est): 274.7K **Privately Held**
SIC: 2711 7822 7389 4832 Newspapers: publishing only, not printed on site; video tapes, recorded: wholesale; personal service agents, brokers & bureaus; educational

(G-8912)
SIEMENS
830 Sw 34th St (98057-4820)
PHONE..............................425 251-0858
EMP: 2
SALES (est): 70.8K **Privately Held**
SIC: 5063 3699 Whol Electrical Equipment Mfg Electrical Equipment/Supplies

(G-8913)
SKY SIGNS INC
12428 169th Ave Se (98059-6501)
PHONE..............................425 417-9063

John Carson, *President*
Lori Carson, *Vice Pres*
EMP: 2
SALES (est): 190K **Privately Held**
SIC: 3993 7319 Signs & advertising specialties; aerial advertising services

(G-8914)
SMART TECH 3D PRINTING
4006 Lincoln Ave Ne (98056-4200)
PHONE..............................425 614-6451
Atif Sattar, *Principal*
EMP: 2
SALES (est): 86.6K **Privately Held**
SIC: 2752 Commercial printing, lithographic

(G-8915)
SODEXO
245 Sw 41st St (98057-4930)
PHONE..............................425 656-2860
Patrick E Connolly, *President*
EMP: 4 EST: 2014
SALES (est): 375.2K **Privately Held**
SIC: 3721 5963 Airplanes, fixed or rotary wing; food services, direct sales

(G-8916)
SOUND BUILDING SUPPLY INC
2701 E Valley Rd (98057-3306)
P.O. Box 329 (98057-0329)
PHONE..............................425 264-0264
Richard Thome, *CEO*
▲ EMP: 45
SQ FT: 45,000
SALES: 20MM
SALES (corp-wide): 2MM **Privately Held**
WEB: www.soundbuildingsupply.com
SIC: 3444 5031 5033 Sheet metalwork; lumber, plywood & millwork; roofing & siding materials
PA: Sbs Holding Co.
   2701 E Valley Rd
   Renton WA 98057
   425 264-0264

(G-8917)
SOUZ LLC
5000 Lake Washington Blvd B102 (98056-5037)
PHONE..............................206 428-8332
Sergy Kuyan, *Principal*
▲ EMP: 5
SALES (est): 317.5K **Privately Held**
SIC: 2711 Newspapers: publishing only, not printed on site

(G-8918)
SP HOLDINGS INC (PA)
Also Called: Econo Box
1000 Sw 43rd St (98057-4832)
PHONE..............................425 291-3500
Mark Held, *President*
Gordon Younger, *Chairman*
Tony Boisen, *Treasurer*
Scott Younger, *Admin Sec*
EMP: 250
SALES (est): 153.4MM **Privately Held**
SIC: 5113 2653 Corrugated & solid fiber boxes; boxes, corrugated: made from purchased materials

(G-8919)
STARMAN METAL FABRICATIONS LLC
17300 Se 132nd St (98059-7034)
PHONE..............................425 235-1431
Mark Starman, *Principal*
EMP: 7
SALES (est): 556.2K **Privately Held**
WEB: www.starmanmetalfab.com
SIC: 3441 5949 Fabricated structural metal; fabric stores piece goods

(G-8920)
STONES BY MARIE INC
1202 N 10th Pl Apt 1413 (98057-5645)
PHONE..............................206 643-1520
Aviel Marie, *Shareholder*
EMP: 6
SALES (est): 330K **Privately Held**
SIC: 3961 7389 Costume jewelry, ex. precious metal & semiprecious stones;

GEOGRAPHIC SECTION

Renton - King County (G-8954)

(G-8921)
STYLE PLUS LLC
15760 143rd Ave Se (98058-6307)
PHONE....................206 920-9223
Sanin Mirvic,
Ismir Mirvic,
▲ EMP: 35
SALES: 22MM Privately Held
SIC: 2511 2512 Wood household furniture; upholstered household furniture

(G-8922)
SUBMETER SOLUTIONS INC
45 Logan Ave S (98057-2039)
PHONE....................425 228-6831
Jeff Lowry, Principal
EMP: 2
SALES (est): 370.9K Privately Held
SIC: 3825 Meters, power factor & phase angle

(G-8923)
SUNSET COMPANY LLC
16444 Se 135th St (98059-6921)
PHONE....................425 351-0839
Doris Yepez, Principal
Luis L Yepez, Principal
EMP: 2
SALES: 65K Privately Held
SIC: 7692 1791 Welding repair; structural steel erection

(G-8924)
SUPERIOR SLABJACKING INC
1603 Glennwood Ave Se (98058-3839)
PHONE....................425 970-3986
Shannon Dodge, Principal
EMP: 2
SALES (est): 198.2K Privately Held
SIC: 3531 Mud jacks

(G-8925)
SUSTAINABLE FIBER TECH LLC
234 Sw 43rd St Ste Mb (98057-4969)
PHONE....................206 818-4130
Mark Lewis,
EMP: 4 EST: 2016
SALES (est): 222K Privately Held
SIC: 2611 Mechanical pulp, including groundwood & thermomechanical

(G-8926)
TENTH GENERATION SOFTWARE
305 Lynnwood Ave Se (98056-5825)
PHONE....................425 226-1939
Donald Lightfoot, Principal
EMP: 2
SALES (est): 110.1K Privately Held
SIC: 7372 Prepackaged software

(G-8927)
THERMAL SOLAR PANELS
1405 N 34th St (98056-1959)
PHONE....................425 445-0244
James Van Avery, Owner
EMP: 3
SALES (est): 160K Privately Held
SIC: 3443 Tanks, standard or custom fabricated: metal plate

(G-8928)
TIGHT GROUP TARGETS LLC
15829 Se 167th Pl (98058-8279)
PHONE....................206 227-0201
Derrick Washington,
EMP: 4
SALES (est): 120.7K Privately Held
SIC: 3949 5961 Target shooting equipment;

(G-8929)
TODO FLORES ENTERPRISES LLC
14019 Se 159th Pl (98058-7810)
PHONE....................206 450-5123
Charles Ahlfors, Principal
EMP: 2
SALES (est): 139.1K Privately Held
SIC: 3841 Surgical & medical instruments

(G-8930)
TRIMLITE LLC
901 Sw 39th St (98057-4831)
PHONE....................425 251-8685

Ross Murray,
▲ EMP: 20
SALES (est): 3.6MM Privately Held
SIC: 3229 Glassware, art or decorative

(G-8931)
TRIMLITE SEATTLE INC
901 Sw 39th St (98057-4831)
PHONE....................425 251-8685
Fax: 425 251-8999
▲ EMP: 50
SQ FT: 50,000
SALES (est): 4.5MM Privately Held
SIC: 3229 5031 Mfg Pressed/Blown Glass Whol Lumber/Plywd/Millwk

(G-8932)
TRIO NATIVE AMERICAN ENTPS LLC
239 Sw 41st St (98057-4930)
PHONE....................206 728-8181
Dennis Brooks, Info Tech Mgr
Jeff Quint,
EMP: 8
SALES (est): 807.2K Privately Held
SIC: 3577 Printers & plotters

(G-8933)
TROJAN LITHOGRAPH CORPORATION
800 Sw 27th St (98057-4965)
PHONE....................425 873-2200
Wayne Millage, President
James Davis, Vice Pres
Bruce Hutcheon, Vice Pres
Donald C Atkinson, Treasurer
Donna Merrell, Manager
▲ EMP: 150 EST: 1994
SQ FT: 108,000
SALES (est): 27.7MM
SALES (corp-wide): 997.8MM Privately Held
WEB: www.trojanlitho.com
SIC: 2671 2752 2657 Packaging paper & plastics film, coated & laminated; commercial printing, lithographic; folding paperboard boxes
PA: Arbor Private Investment Co, Llc
676 N Michigan Ave # 3410
Chicago IL 60611
312 981-3770

(G-8934)
TRUE CUSTOM CABINETRY INC
15255 206th Ave Se (98059-9053)
PHONE....................425 919-1966
EMP: 4
SALES (est): 235.3K Privately Held
SIC: 2434 Wood kitchen cabinets

(G-8935)
ULTIMATE MTAL FABRICATIONS LLC
330 Sw 43rd St Ste D (98057-4900)
PHONE....................206 356-9666
Daniel Skobelev,
▲ EMP: 17
SALES: 950K Privately Held
SIC: 3449 Miscellaneous metalwork

(G-8936)
ULTRA PAPER CO LLC
15729 142nd Pl Se (98058-6319)
PHONE....................425 443-5505
EMP: 2 EST: 2012
SALES (est): 220K Privately Held
SIC: 2679 Mfg Converted Paper Products

(G-8937)
UNIQUE WREATHS
375 Union Ave Se Unit 94 (98059-5170)
PHONE....................206 355-2103
Barbara Martinson, Principal
EMP: 2
SALES (est): 62.5K Privately Held
SIC: 3999 Wreaths, artificial

(G-8938)
USA OIL LLC
3002 Ne Sunset Blvd (98056-3102)
PHONE....................425 226-5555
EMP: 2 EST: 2016 Privately Held
SIC: 1311 Crude petroleum & natural gas

(G-8939)
UV SYSTEMS INC
16605 127th Ave Se (98058-5549)
PHONE....................425 228-9988
Don E Newsome, President
Alma Newsome, Admin Sec
EMP: 2
SALES (est): 280K Privately Held
WEB: www.uvsystems.com
SIC: 5063 7389 3641 Lighting fixtures; ; ultraviolet lamps

(G-8940)
VALLEY AERO MFG
314 Williams Ave S # 4141 (98057-9700)
PHONE....................206 841-9652
Andrew Bradford, Principal
EMP: 2 EST: 2016
SALES (est): 90K Privately Held
SIC: 3999 Manufacturing industries

(G-8941)
VALLEY BUGLER LLC
15554 207th Pl Se (98059-9029)
PHONE....................360 414-1246
Michelle Myre,
EMP: 5
SALES (est): 166.3K Privately Held
SIC: 2711 Newspapers: publishing only, not printed on site

(G-8942)
WARRINGTON PUBLICATIONS
11100 Se Petrovitsky Rd A104 (98055-5686)
PHONE....................425 793-9629
Robert Cabell, Principal
EMP: 2
SALES (est): 117.6K Privately Held
SIC: 2741 Miscellaneous publishing

(G-8943)
WAX BARN INC
13009 172nd Ave Se (98059-8647)
PHONE....................425 228-8537
Vicki Mayfield, President
EMP: 10 EST: 1995
SQ FT: 1,000
SALES: 370K Privately Held
WEB: www.waxbarn.com
SIC: 3999 Candles

(G-8944)
WEST COAST STAIR COMPANY
16908 Se May Valley Rd (98059-5927)
PHONE....................206 406-4927
Jason Chamion, Principal
EMP: 2
SALES (est): 216.2K Privately Held
SIC: 3822 Building services monitoring controls, automatic

(G-8945)
WHAER INC
16405 Se 145th St (98059-7944)
P.O. Box 53121, Bellevue (98015-3121)
PHONE....................919 946-5720
Samuel Berger, CEO
Shana Harden, Principal
Jared Johnson, Chief Mktg Ofcr
EMP: 3 EST: 2016
SALES (est): 78.2K Privately Held
SIC: 7372 7389 Prepackaged software;

(G-8946)
WHAT S NEXT
4403 Se 4th St (98059-5118)
PHONE....................425 235-1696
EMP: 2
SALES: 25K Privately Held
SIC: 3949 Mfg Sporting/Athletic Goods

(G-8947)
WHITE LIGHT PUBLICATIONS LLC
Also Called: Northwest Cars & Trucks Mag
1201 Monster Rd Sw # 430 (98057-2996)
PHONE....................206 575-4236
Daniel L Aubrey,
Dan Aubrey,
Donna Aubrey,
Greg Borland,
EMP: 43 EST: 1999
SQ FT: 2,976

SALES (est): 3.8MM Privately Held
SIC: 2721 Magazines: publishing only, not printed on site

(G-8948)
WILO INC
Also Called: Minuteman Press
16958 Woodside Dr Se (98058-4205)
PHONE....................425 793-4862
David L Randolph, President
EMP: 2
SALES (est): 203.1K Privately Held
SIC: 2752 Commercial printing, offset

(G-8949)
WIZARDS OF COAST LLC (HQ)
1600 Lind Ave Sw Ste 400 (98057-3374)
P.O. Box 707 (98057-0707)
PHONE....................425 226-6500
Christian Cocks, CEO
Kim Graham, Project Mgr
Liz Larson, Prdtn Mgr
Crystal Carrow, Opers Staff
Randall Crews, Buyer
▲ EMP: 300
SQ FT: 180,000
SALES (est): 313.8MM
SALES (corp-wide): 4.5B Publicly Held
SIC: 3944 7371 Board games, children's & adults'; computer software development & applications
PA: Hasbro, Inc.
1027 Newport Ave
Pawtucket RI 02861
401 431-8697

(G-8950)
WRIGHT DESIGNS
Also Called: Wright T Company, The
17701 108th Ave Se (98055-6448)
PHONE....................800 866-1245
EMP: 4
SALES (est): 236K Privately Held
SIC: 2211 Cotton Broadwoven Fabric Mill

(G-8951)
XTREME PET PRODUCTS LLC
200 S Tobin St Ste D (98057-5338)
PHONE....................206 772-2000
Larry Thompson, Principal
▲ EMP: 3
SALES (est): 229.6K Privately Held
SIC: 5999 3999 Pets; pet supplies

(G-8952)
YKK (USA) INC
1300 Sw 7th St Ste 109 (98057-5225)
PHONE....................425 277-2503
Lee Dygert, Manager
EMP: 5 Privately Held
SIC: 3965 5072 Zipper; hardware
HQ: Ykk (U.S.A.), Inc.
1300 Cobb Industrial Dr
Marietta GA 30066
770 427-5521

(G-8953)
YOUNGS MARKET OF WASHINGTON
3215 Lind Ave Sw (98057-3320)
P.O. Box 9300 (98057-9300)
PHONE....................206 808-6124
Mark Levine, President
▲ EMP: 20
SALES (est): 2.3MM Privately Held
SIC: 2082 Beer (alcoholic beverage)

(G-8954)
ZILA WORKS LLC
4308 Ne 19th St (98059-3840)
PHONE....................425 777-6813
Janis Puracal,
Evan Bouchier,
Kerrie Carbary,
Jared Devine,
Heather Pierce,
EMP: 6
SALES (est): 294.2K Privately Held
SIC: 2821 Thermoplastic materials

Republic - Ferry County (G-8955)

Republic
Ferry County

(G-8955)
ADAMERA MINERALS LLC
55 Gold Mountain Rd (99166-8744)
PHONE...................509 237-7731
Mark Kolebaba, *CEO*
Mark Brown, *Ch of Bd*
Katherine Meginley,
EMP: 10
SALES (est): 338K **Privately Held**
SIC: 1081 Metal mining services

(G-8956)
DIGITAL DOCUMENTS INC
771 S Keller St (99166-5016)
P.O. Box 1117 (99166-1117)
PHONE...................509 775-2425
Gregory Sheffield, *President*
EMP: 2
SALES: 100K **Privately Held**
SIC: 2759 Commercial printing

(G-8957)
GRUBSTAKE EMC
13 Pine Grove St (99166-9629)
PHONE...................509 775-2041
EMP: 2
SALES (est): 85.9K **Privately Held**
SIC: 3572 Computer storage devices

(G-8958)
HAMILTON EQUIPMENT
148 N Portland St (99166-8807)
PHONE...................509 775-3445
William Hamilton, *Owner*
EMP: 2
SALES (est): 135.9K **Privately Held**
SIC: 3484 Guns (firearms) or gun parts, 30 mm. & below

(G-8959)
KINROSS GOLD USA INC
Also Called: Kettle River Operations
363 Fish Hatchery Rd (99166-8711)
PHONE...................509 775-3157
Gina Jardine, *Vice Pres*
Roy Swander, *Project Mgr*
Falcon Price, *Opers Mgr*
Sharon Smith, *Purch Agent*
Jacquelyn J Nutt, *Branch Mgr*
EMP: 109
SQ FT: 100,000
SALES (corp-wide): 3.2B **Privately Held**
SIC: 1041 Gold ores mining
HQ: Kinross Gold Usa, Inc
5075 S Syracuse St
Denver CO 80237

Rice
Stevens County

(G-8960)
QUILLISASCUT CHEESE CO
2409 Pleasant Valley Rd (99167-9706)
PHONE...................509 738-2011
Lora Lea Misterly, *Owner*
Richard Misterly, *Co-Owner*
EMP: 2
SALES: 92K **Privately Held**
WEB: www.quillisascutcheese.com
SIC: 2022 5812 Natural cheese; eating places

(G-8961)
RICKEY CANYON VINEYARD
2025 Rickey Canyon Rd (99167-9753)
PHONE...................206 718-9318
Robert S Lewis, *Principal*
EMP: 2
SALES (est): 118.8K **Privately Held**
SIC: 2084 Wines, brandy & brandy spirits

Richland
Benton County

(G-8962)
A1 SERVICES
1617 Hunt Ave (99354-2643)
PHONE...................509 946-6269
Howard Brager, *Owner*
EMP: 2
SALES: 100K **Privately Held**
SIC: 3911 Jewelry apparel

(G-8963)
ABADAN REPO GRAPHICS
79 Aaron Dr Ste 100 (99352-4522)
PHONE...................509 946-7697
Frank Hall, *Manager*
EMP: 30
SALES (est): 2.9MM **Privately Held**
SIC: 3579 7334 2759 Office machines; photocopying & duplicating services; commercial printing

(G-8964)
ACCENT SIGNS & ENGRAVING INC
72 Wellsian Way (99352-4111)
PHONE...................509 946-8998
Martin Huard, *CEO*
EMP: 2
SALES (est): 142.4K **Privately Held**
SIC: 3993 Signs, not made in custom sign painting shops

(G-8965)
ACCENT SIGNS INC
700 S 46th Ave (99353-9103)
PHONE...................509 967-7446
Mark Huard, *President*
EMP: 3
SALES (est): 286.9K **Privately Held**
WEB: www.accentsignsnaples.com
SIC: 3993 Signs & advertising specialties

(G-8966)
AEM-NETWORK LLC
1840 Terminal Dr (99354-4923)
PHONE...................509 946-0813
EMP: 4 **EST:** 2004
SALES (est): 240K **Privately Held**
SIC: 3541 Disttribution

(G-8967)
ARMOR PERFORMANCE COATING LLC
1857 Bronco Ln (99354-4968)
PHONE...................509 551-1294
Valerie Griffin, *Principal*
Peter Griffin,
Charles Hyndman II,
EMP: 2
SALES (est): 130K **Privately Held**
SIC: 3479 Etching & engraving

(G-8968)
ASSURWARE INC
497 Winesap Ct (99352-5741)
PHONE...................509 531-8336
Thomas P McKenna Jr, *CEO*
EMP: 5
SALES: 1,000K **Privately Held**
SIC: 3571 Electronic computers

(G-8969)
AVANTECH INC
2155 Robertson Dr (99354-5306)
PHONE...................509 943-6706
EMP: 90
SALES (corp-wide): 11.7MM **Privately Held**
SIC: 3441 7363 Fabricated structural metal; help supply services
PA: Avantech, Inc.
2050 American Italian Way
Columbia SC 29209
803 407-7171

(G-8970)
B&B CUSTOM METALS LLC
2700 Salk Ave (99354-1787)
PHONE...................425 308-8478
EMP: 2
SALES (est): 177.2K **Privately Held**
SIC: 3441 Fabricated structural metal

(G-8971)
BARNARD-GRIFFIN INC
Also Called: Barnard Griffin Winery
878 Tulip Ln (99352-8588)
PHONE...................509 627-0266
Rob Griffin, *President*
Deborah Barnard, *Corp Secy*
▲ **EMP:** 10
SQ FT: 15,000
SALES (est): 1.3MM **Privately Held**
WEB: www.barnardgriffin.com
SIC: 2084 Wines

(G-8972)
BAS INC
Also Called: Minuteman Press
214 Torbett St Ste F (99354-2651)
PHONE...................509 943-2611
Bruce Seghers, *President*
EMP: 5
SQ FT: 4,000
SALES: 500K **Privately Held**
SIC: 2752 Commercial printing, lithographic

(G-8973)
BLACK DOG INDUSTRIES
2019 Butler Loop (99354-4970)
PHONE...................509 946-6400
Laurie Dobush, *Bd of Directors*
▲ **EMP:** 3
SALES (est): 219.2K **Privately Held**
SIC: 3999 Barber & beauty shop equipment

(G-8974)
BLACKBIRDS NEST
2035 Howell Ave (99354-2009)
PHONE...................509 946-1978
Jacob Dowell, *Owner*
Marion Dowell, *Co-Owner*
EMP: 2
SALES: 7K **Privately Held**
SIC: 2381 Fabric dress & work gloves

(G-8975)
BLUE STAR ENTERPRISES NW INC
2019 Butler Loop (99354-4970)
PHONE...................509 946-9388
Robert Dobush, *President*
Laurie Dobush, *Vice Pres*
EMP: 15
SQ FT: 5,000
SALES: 2.6MM **Privately Held**
SIC: 1781 3533 Water well drilling; water well drilling equipment

(G-8976)
BOOKWALTER WINERY LLC
Also Called: J Bookwalter Wines
894 Tulip Ln (99352-8588)
PHONE...................509 627-5000
Caleb Foster, *General Mgr*
Gary Chervenell, *Mng Member*
David Hernand,
▲ **EMP:** 18
SQ FT: 3,450
SALES (est): 3.3MM **Privately Held**
WEB: www.bookwalterwines.com
SIC: 2084 Wines

(G-8977)
BOULDER ESTATES WINERY
336 Broadmoor St (99352-9600)
PHONE...................509 628-1209
Lynn Ball, *Owner*
Jim Ball, *Principal*
EMP: 2
SALES (est): 86.7K **Privately Held**
WEB: www.boulderwineblog.com
SIC: 2084 Wines

(G-8978)
BROTHERS JEWELERS INC
430 Grge Wash Way Ste 102 (99352)
PHONE...................509 946-7989
Mark Smith, *President*
Scott Smith, *Vice Pres*
EMP: 3
SALES (est): 250K **Privately Held**
SIC: 7631 3911 Jewelry repair services; jewelry, precious metal

(G-8979)
BUCKMASTER CELLARS
1600 Brantingham Rd (99352-7626)
PHONE...................509 627-1321
Mark A Buckmaster, *Principal*
EMP: 2
SALES (est): 87K **Privately Held**
WEB: www.buckmastercellars.com
SIC: 2084 Wines

(G-8980)
CHEMCHEK INSTRUMENTS INC
1845 Terminal Dr Ste 101 (99354-4959)
PHONE...................509 943-5000
Barbara Miller-Collins, *President*
Roberta Sanders, *CFO*
EMP: 4
SALES (est): 370K **Privately Held**
WEB: www.chemchek.com
SIC: 3829 Kinematic test & measuring equipment

(G-8981)
CLARKS COUNTRY KITCHEN
84104 N Harrington Rd (99353-9245)
PHONE...................509 586-6909
Margaret Clark, *Co-Owner*
William Clark, *Co-Owner*
EMP: 3
SALES (est): 128.4K **Privately Held**
SIC: 2064 5441 Candy & other confectionery products; confectionery

(G-8982)
CLEAN-VANTAGE
3100 Willow Pointe Dr (99354-2614)
PHONE...................509 392-2793
Ken Petersen, *Principal*
EMP: 2
SALES: 100K **Privately Held**
SIC: 2869 Industrial organic chemicals

(G-8983)
COLUMBIA INDUS COATINGS LLC
1212 Columbia Park Trl (99352-4760)
P.O. Box 140 (99352-0140)
PHONE...................509 531-7310
Miguel Aguilar,
Jonathan Duarte,
Luke Duarte,
Member Durte,
EMP: 3 **EST:** 2017
SALES (est): 57.1K **Privately Held**
SIC: 2851 Paints & allied products

(G-8984)
COMMUNITY THRIFT SHOP LLC
395 Wright Ave (99352-3951)
PHONE...................509 438-1302
Dustin Stordahl,
Nathan Pack,
EMP: 2
SALES: 15K **Privately Held**
SIC: 5999 7372 Miscellaneous retail stores; application computer software

(G-8985)
COWIN IN-SITU SCIENCE LLC
2500 George Washington (99354-1656)
PHONE...................509 392-1329
EMP: 2
SALES: 150K **Privately Held**
SIC: 3999 Mfg Misc Products

(G-8986)
CUSTOM PUBLICATIONS WASH LLC
Also Called: Real Estate Book, The
1950 Keene Rd Bldg M (99352-7754)
P.O. Box 4808, Pasco (99302-4808)
PHONE...................509 628-3500
Devonna Rehwalt,
Karl Rehwalt,
EMP: 2
SALES (est): 144.4K **Privately Held**
SIC: 2741 Miscellaneous publishing

(G-8987)
DESERT LEATHERCRAFT LLC
2532 Banyon St (99352-4117)
PHONE...................509 392-2589
Kurt Johnson, *Principal*
EMP: 2

GEOGRAPHIC SECTION
Richland - Benton County (G-9017)

SALES (est): 126.5K **Privately Held**
SIC: 3199 Leather goods

(G-8988)
DIGITAL IMAGE
2950 George Washington Wa (99352-1630)
PHONE..................................509 375-6001
Bob Davis, *Partner*
Grant McCallum, *General Ptnr*
Gabrielle Casarella, *Manager*
EMP: 6
SALES (est): 420K **Privately Held**
WEB: www.thedigitalimage.com
SIC: 2759 Commercial printing

(G-8989)
DKR WOOD WORKING
1639 April Loop (99354-2476)
PHONE..................................509 943-2273
Dean Moore, *Principal*
EMP: 2
SALES (est): 132.1K **Privately Held**
SIC: 2431 Millwork

(G-8990)
DWHITTLE SHOP INC
4322 S 47th Ave (99353-8778)
PHONE..................................509 627-3050
Raymond M Umlauf, *President*
Debbie Umlauf, *Admin Sec*
EMP: 3
SALES: 220K **Privately Held**
SIC: 2434 1751 Wood kitchen cabinets; cabinet & finish carpentry

(G-8991)
EAGLE PRINTING INC
Also Called: Eagle Prtg & Graphic Design
214 Torbett St Ste F (99354-2651)
PHONE..................................509 943-2611
David Henry, *Owner*
EMP: 5
SALES: 500.5K **Privately Held**
WEB: www.eagleprinting.com
SIC: 2752 7336 Commercial printing, offset; graphic arts & related design

(G-8992)
EFC EQUIPMENT LLC
Also Called: EFC Equipment Feed and Pet
2155 Stevens Dr (99354-1847)
PHONE..................................509 713-7230
Harold B Bond,
Susan L Bond,
EMP: 4
SALES (est): 483.8K **Privately Held**
SIC: 3523 5261 5999 Tractors, farm; lawn & garden equipment; pet food

(G-8993)
ELITE ATHLETICS TRAINING LLC
1221 Columbia Park Trl (99352-4766)
PHONE..................................509 221-1898
EMP: 3
SALES (est): 54.4K **Privately Held**
SIC: 7991 7372 Athletic club & gymnasiums, membership; application computer software

(G-8994)
ETHOS BAKERY LLC
2150 Keene Rd (99352-7726)
PHONE..................................509 942-8799
Angela Kora,
Scot Minor,
EMP: 6 EST: 2011
SALES (est): 277.6K **Privately Held**
SIC: 5149 2021 5812 Bakery products; pizza supplies; creamery butter; caterers

(G-8995)
EUGENE P LAMM JR
Also Called: Pit Bull Fabrication
807 Snow Ave (99352-3755)
PHONE..................................509 460-1240
Eugene P Lamm Jr, *Owner*
EMP: 2
SALES (est): 107.8K **Privately Held**
SIC: 3441 Fabricated structural metal

(G-8996)
FIDELITAS
318 Wellhouse Loop (99352-4152)
PHONE..................................509 521-1553
Jess Zander, *General Mgr*
Charlie Hoppes, *Principal*
▲ EMP: 4
SALES (est): 180K **Privately Held**
SIC: 2084 Wines

(G-8997)
FINNEGAN FROST
2150 Keene Rd (99352-7726)
PHONE..................................509 572-2477
Jeong Al Lee, *Principal*
EMP: 3 EST: 2012
SALES (est): 158K **Privately Held**
SIC: 2026 Yogurt

(G-8998)
FIRE DEF TECH SAFETY PDTS INC
1588 Sagewood St (99352-7694)
PHONE..................................509 619-0261
Jacek Kobiesa, *President*
Richard Stephens, *Treasurer*
EMP: 4
SALES (est): 278.8K **Privately Held**
SIC: 3569 Firefighting apparatus & related equipment

(G-8999)
FROG HOLLOW PRESS L L C
1111 Jadwin Ave (99352-3434)
PHONE..................................509 943-3331
Patricia Chvatal, *Manager*
EMP: 2
SALES (est): 72.2K **Privately Held**
SIC: 2741 Miscellaneous publishing

(G-9000)
G & M MACHINE LLC
205 Wellsian Way (99352-4114)
PHONE..................................509 946-3201
Scott Gorham, *President*
Thomas Hay, *Engineer*
Jeremiah Rogers, *Engineer*
EMP: 2
SALES: 300K **Privately Held**
SIC: 3565 3599 Bag opening, filling & closing machines; machine shop, jobbing & repair

(G-9001)
GF BLENDS INC
2151 Henderson Loop (99354-5303)
PHONE..................................509 375-0909
Glen Call, *President*
Julie Call, *Vice Pres*
Mette Warnick, *Admin Sec*
EMP: 6
SQ FT: 2,800
SALES: 60K **Privately Held**
SIC: 2041 Flour & other grain mill products

(G-9002)
GLEN COVE PRESS LLC
456 Palm Dr (99352-7672)
P.O. Box 65 (99352-0065)
PHONE..................................509 318-5934
Kristen A Jenson, *Administration*
EMP: 2
SALES (est): 70K **Privately Held**
SIC: 2741 Miscellaneous publishing

(G-9003)
GRAPHIC ADVERTISING SVCS INC
3120 River Park Dr (99354-8500)
PHONE..................................425 688-9980
Jim Wagner, *President*
Elizabeth Wagner, *Corp Secy*
EMP: 12
SALES (est): 1.3MM **Privately Held**
WEB: www.graphicadserv.com
SIC: 2791 2796 7336 2752 Typesetting; platemaking services; graphic arts & related design; commercial printing, offset

(G-9004)
HANGER PRSTHETCS & ORTHO INC
949 Stevens Dr (99352-3508)
PHONE..................................509 946-2520
Andy Lambert, *Manager*
EMP: 7
SALES (corp-wide): 1B **Publicly Held**
SIC: 3842 Orthopedic appliances
HQ: Hanger Prosthetics & Orthotics, Inc.
10910 Domain Dr Ste 300
Austin TX 78758
512 777-3800

(G-9005)
HARRINGTON TROPHIES
717 Jadwin Ave (99352-4217)
PHONE..................................509 943-2593
Norma Harrington, *Co-Owner*
John Harrington, *Co-Owner*
EMP: 3
SALES (est): 190K **Privately Held**
WEB: www.harringtonstrophies.com
SIC: 5999 3479 Trophies & plaques; engraving jewelry silverware, or metal

(G-9006)
HILINE ENGRG & FABRICATION INC
2105 Aviator St (99354-4942)
PHONE..................................509 943-9043
Troy Stokes, *President*
Tami Stokes, *Corp Secy*
Sean S Stevens, *Purch Mgr*
Lance Whitney, *Purch Mgr*
Michael Gimera, *Treasurer*
EMP: 43
SQ FT: 16,000
SALES (est): 7.3MM **Privately Held**
WEB: www.hilineeng.com
SIC: 3699 8711 3441 3443 Electrical equipment & supplies; mechanical engineering; fabricated structural metal; water tanks, metal plate; pile shells, metal plate; machine shop, jobbing & repair

(G-9007)
HUMMING HEMP LLC
723 The Parkway (99352-4259)
PHONE..................................503 559-6476
Max Schneider, *Principal*
EMP: 6
SALES (est): 429K **Privately Held**
SIC: 2099 Food preparations

(G-9008)
INDULGE LLC
219 Ontario Ct (99352-7616)
PHONE..................................360 589-7226
Sue Spooner, *CEO*
EMP: 3 EST: 2016
SALES (est): 71.9K **Privately Held**
SIC: 2052 Bakery products, dry

(G-9009)
INGREDION INCORPORATED
216 University Dr (99354-4501)
PHONE..................................509 375-1261
Kraig Powers, *Branch Mgr*
EMP: 4
SALES (corp-wide): 5.8B **Publicly Held**
SIC: 2046 Wet corn milling
PA: Ingredion Incorporated
5 Westbrook Corporate Ctr # 500
Westchester IL 60154
708 551-2600

(G-9010)
INNOVA MFG LLC
Also Called: Innova Precision Machining Mfg
1840 Terminal Dr (99354-4923)
PHONE..................................509 946-7461
Novjot Sandhu,
Prabhjot Sandhu,
Sandeep Singh,
EMP: 3
SALES (est): 240K **Privately Held**
SIC: 3599 3545 Machine shop, jobbing & repair; precision tools, machinists'

(G-9011)
INTERNTONAL HEARTH MELTING LLC
Also Called: ATI Richland Operations
3101 Kingsgate Way (99354-2188)
PHONE..................................509 371-2500
Rj Harshman, *Principal*
▲ EMP: 70
SALES (est): 11.7MM **Publicly Held**
WEB: www.h2membrane.com
SIC: 3462 3356 Iron & steel forgings; non-ferrous rolling & drawing
HQ: Oregon Metallurgical, Llc
1000 Six Ppg Pl
Pittsburgh PA 15222
541 967-9000

(G-9012)
INTERSTATE CONCRETE AND ASP CO
Also Called: American Rock Products
2590 Hagen Rd (99354-4504)
PHONE..................................509 375-1021
EMP: 2
SALES (corp-wide): 30.6B **Privately Held**
SIC: 3273 Ready-mixed concrete
HQ: Interstate Concrete And Asphalt Company
8849 W Wyoming Ave
Rathdrum ID 83858
208 765-1144

(G-9013)
ISORAY INC (PA)
350 Hills St Ste 106 (99354-5511)
PHONE..................................509 375-1202
Lori A Woods, *CEO*
Michael W McCormick, *Ch of Bd*
William Cavanagh III, *COO*
Jonathan Hunt, *CFO*
Jennifer Streeter, *VP Human Res*
EMP: 38
SQ FT: 15,300
SALES: 5.9MM **Publicly Held**
WEB: www.isoray.com
SIC: 3841 Diagnostic apparatus, medical

(G-9014)
ISORAY MEDICAL INC
350 Hills St Ste 106 (99354-5511)
PHONE..................................509 375-1202
Dwight Babcock, *President*
Lori Holmes-Woods, *Vice Pres*
Griffin Hanberg, *Prdtn Mgr*
Jonathan R Hunt, *CFO*
Jesse Dunn, *Accountant*
EMP: 35
SQ FT: 15,000
SALES: 5MM **Privately Held**
WEB: www.isoraymedical.com
SIC: 3841 Diagnostic apparatus, medical

(G-9015)
JMH ENTERPRISES
Also Called: Jmh Promotions
127 Meadow Hills Dr (99352-8461)
PHONE..................................509 628-2191
Gerald Hathaway, *Owner*
Valerie Hathaway, *CFO*
EMP: 3
SALES: 1MM **Privately Held**
WEB: www.jmhpromo.com
SIC: 5199 8742 2759 2395 Advertising specialties; incentive or award program consultant; screen printing; embroidery products, except schiffli machine

(G-9016)
KAISER ALUMINUM FAB PDTS LLC
2425 Stevens Dr (99354-1877)
PHONE..................................509 375-0900
EMP: 51
SALES (corp-wide): 1.5B **Publicly Held**
SIC: 3334 Primary aluminum
HQ: Kaiser Aluminum Fabricated Products, Llc
27422 Portola Pkwy # 200
Foothill Ranch CA 92610

(G-9017)
KAISER ALUMINUM FAB PDTS LLC
2425 Stevens Dr (99354-1877)
PHONE..................................509 375-0900
Melinda Ellsworth, *Vice Pres*
Joseph Ames, *Manager*
Jason Rayder,
EMP: 14
SALES (est): 2.5MM **Privately Held**
SIC: 3354 Aluminum extruded products

Richland - Benton County (G-9018)

(G-9018)
KENNEWICK COMPUTER COMPANY
Also Called: Positive Software Compan
2290 Robertson Dr (99354-5320)
PHONE...................509 371-0600
EMP: 6 EST: 2015
SALES: 482K Privately Held
SIC: 7371 7372 Custom Computer Programing Prepackaged Software Services

(G-9019)
KRN SERVICES
1761 George Wash Way 28 (99354-2303)
PHONE...................509 366-3431
Curtis Nickolaus, Partner
Paul Kelly, Partner
Darrell Robison, Partner
EMP: 3
SALES (est): 253.8K Privately Held
SIC: 3679 7389 Electronic circuits; electronic switches;

(G-9020)
LAMB WESTON INC
2013 Saint St (99354-5302)
PHONE...................509 375-4181
Mark Dorsey, Manager
EMP: 8
SALES (corp-wide): 3.4B Publicly Held
SIC: 2037 Frozen fruits & vegetables
HQ: Lamb Weston Inc
599 S Rivershore Ln
Eagle ID 83616

(G-9021)
LAMB WESTON INC
2005 Saint St (99354-5302)
PHONE...................509 713-7200
EMP: 2
SALES (corp-wide): 3.4B Publicly Held
SIC: 2037 Frozen fruits & vegetables
HQ: Lamb Weston Inc
599 S Rivershore Ln
Eagle ID 83616

(G-9022)
LINDA J MOHR (PA)
Also Called: Mohr & Associates
1440 Agnes St (99352-3918)
PHONE...................509 946-0941
Linda Mohr, Owner
Charles Mohr, Co-Owner
Chris Mulkey, Prdtn Mgr
EMP: 7
SALES: 400K Privately Held
SIC: 8711 3829 Consulting engineer; nuclear radiation & testing apparatus

(G-9023)
LUMBERMENS TRUSS
Also Called: Builders Lumber-Truss Division
4213 S 47th Ave (99353-6715)
PHONE...................509 627-0495
Ronald Hoaglin, President
John Stringen, Regional Mgr
EMP: 28
SQ FT: 15,000
SALES (est): 2.5MM Privately Held
SIC: 2439 Trusses, wooden roof

(G-9024)
MARKET VINEYARDS (PA)
1950 Keene Rd Bldg S (99352-7754)
PHONE...................509 396-4798
Daniel Charles Schulte, Principal
EMP: 2
SALES (est): 188.7K Privately Held
SIC: 2084 Wines

(G-9025)
MATTRESS MANUFACTURING PRIZE
1910 Butler Loop (99354-4944)
PHONE...................509 946-1194
EMP: 3
SALES (est): 111.7K Privately Held
SIC: 5712 3999 Ret Furniture Mfg Misc Products

(G-9026)
MEDIAMAX
213 Ontario Ct (99352-7616)
PHONE...................509 627-2358
Steven Oats, Owner
EMP: 2 EST: 1992
SALES (est): 144.3K Privately Held
SIC: 2759 7331 Publication printing; direct mail advertising services

(G-9027)
MOHR TEST AND MEASUREMENT LLC (HQ)
2105 Henderson Loop (99354-5303)
PHONE...................509 946-0941
Marc Pirello, Electrical Engi
Noel Egert, Office Mgr
Charles L Mohr,
Linda J Mohr,
EMP: 21 EST: 2011
SQ FT: 4,500
SALES (est): 357.1K
SALES (corp-wide): 400K Privately Held
SIC: 3825 3556 8711 Engine electrical test equipment; food products machinery; engineering services
PA: Linda J Mohr
1440 Agnes St
Richland WA 99352
509 946-0941

(G-9028)
MOHR TEST AND MEASUREMENT LLC
1440 Agnes St (99352-3918)
PHONE...................888 852-0408
EMP: 3
SALES (corp-wide): 400K Privately Held
SIC: 3556 8711 Food products machinery; engineering services
HQ: Mohr Test And Measurement, Llc
2105 Henderson Loop
Richland WA 99354
509 946-0941

(G-9029)
MONSON RANCHES
Also Called: Munson Ranches
16304 Dallas Rd (99352-7750)
PHONE...................509 628-3880
Evelyn Gore, Branch Mgr
EMP: 41
SALES (corp-wide): 4MM Privately Held
WEB: www.gooseridge.com
SIC: 0172 2084 Grapes; wines
PA: Monson Ranches
63615 E Jacobs Rd Ne
Benton City WA 99320
509 627-1618

(G-9030)
MORAVEK BIOCHEMICALS INC
2770 Salk Ave (99354-1673)
PHONE...................509 375-5124
John Heaney, Manager
EMP: 5
SALES (corp-wide): 4.1MM Privately Held
SIC: 2819 Industrial inorganic chemicals
PA: Moravek Biochemicals, Inc.
577 Mercury Ln
Brea CA 92821
714 990-2018

(G-9031)
NHTHREE LLC
1161 Viewmoor Ct (99352-7642)
P.O. Box 202 (99352-0202)
PHONE...................509 396-2082
John Holbrook,
Jason Ganley,
Douglas McKinley,
EMP: 3
SALES (est): 271.5K Privately Held
SIC: 2873 Nitrogenous fertilizers

(G-9032)
OUR COUNTRY BEADS
302 N 62nd Ave (99353-9704)
PHONE...................509 967-3953
Robert Welch, Owner
Sandra Welch, Co-Owner
EMP: 2
SALES (est): 87.7K Privately Held
SIC: 3999 Stringing beads

(G-9033)
PACIFIC WIRELESS SYSTEMS LLC
135 Patton St (99354-1618)
P.O. Box 1250 (99352-1250)
PHONE...................509 375-3533
Doreen Thompson, Principal
Dean Thompson, Manager
EMP: 2
SALES (est): 318.6K Privately Held
SIC: 3825 Spectrum analyzers

(G-9034)
PENFORD PRODUCTS CO
Penwest Foods
216 1st St (99354-5500)
PHONE...................509 375-1261
Craig Powers, Managing Dir
Mick Persinger, Manager
EMP: 20
SALES (corp-wide): 5.8B Publicly Held
WEB: www.penx.com
SIC: 2046 5499 Potato starch; health & dietetic food stores
HQ: Penford Products Co.
1001 1st St Sw
Cedar Rapids IA 52404
319 398-3700

(G-9035)
PLASTIC INJECTION MOLDING INC
2695 Battelle Blvd (99354-2193)
PHONE...................509 375-4260
Kenneth Williams, President
Kenneth A Williams, President
Sharon Williams, Vice Pres
▲ EMP: 6
SQ FT: 5,000
SALES (est): 976.7K Privately Held
WEB: www.moldingjobs.com
SIC: 3089 Injection molding of plastics

(G-9036)
PRINGLES POWER-VAC INC
2395 Robertson Dr (99354-5307)
P.O. Box 561 (99352-0561)
PHONE...................509 375-0500
Dave Lasater, President
Julie Lasater, Corp Secy
EMP: 5
SALES (est): 646.6K Privately Held
SIC: 3999 7349 Pipe cleaners; building maintenance services

(G-9037)
RADIX WINERY
4340 Highview St (99352-4571)
PHONE...................419 283-7924
Marco De Santis, Principal
EMP: 2
SALES (est): 85.9K Privately Held
SIC: 2084 Wines

(G-9038)
RATTLESNAKE MTN BREWING CO
2696 N Columbia Ctr Blvd (99352-4853)
PHONE...................509 783-5747
Kyle Chism, General Mgr
Evan Hudspeth, General Mgr
EMP: 25
SQ FT: 7,200
SALES (est): 577.1K Privately Held
SIC: 5813 5812 2082 Bars & lounges; eating places; malt beverages

(G-9039)
RIVERSIDE CLUB
3000 N Riverside Dr (99353-5261)
PHONE...................509 967-5756
Robert Knox, Owner
EMP: 2 EST: 1987
SALES (est): 91.4K Privately Held
SIC: 3949 Strings, tennis racket

(G-9040)
SECURED INC
413 Adams St (99352-4428)
PHONE...................508 361-0928
LI Tan, President
EMP: 2
SALES (est): 56.5K Privately Held
SIC: 7372 Application computer software

(G-9041)
SIGN FRACTURE CARE INTL
451 Hills St Ste B (99354-5502)
PHONE...................509 371-1107
Lewis Zirkie Jr, President
Sandra Gladstone, Opers Mgr
Richard Grizzell, Opers Mgr
Dule Mehic, Design Engr
Jeanne Dillner, Treasurer
EMP: 42
SALES: 5.1MM Privately Held
SIC: 3841 Surgical & medical instruments

(G-9042)
SUN SOLUTIONS INC
1370 Jadwin Ave Ste 134 (99354-3428)
PHONE...................509 946-7107
Mark Dade, President
Yu-Hang Dade, Vice Pres
EMP: 3
SALES (est): 360.7K Privately Held
WEB: www.sun-solutionsinc.com
SIC: 3442 Screens, window, metal

(G-9043)
SUN SPIRITS DISTILLERY LLC
Also Called: Solar Spirits Distillery
2409 Robertson Dr (99354-5310)
PHONE...................509 371-1622
Kris Lapp,
James Batdorf,
Khurshed Sharifov,
Brett Spooner,
EMP: 6 EST: 2013
SQ FT: 2,100
SALES (est): 401.7K Privately Held
SIC: 2085 Distilled & blended liquors

(G-9044)
TK MACHINE
1893 Airport Way (99354-4910)
PHONE...................509 946-2363
Tim Jones, Principal
Shelly Prewett, Vice Pres
EMP: 7 EST: 2007
SALES (est): 1.1MM Privately Held
SIC: 3599 Machine shop, jobbing & repair

(G-9045)
TOPTEC SOFTWARE LLC (PA)
Also Called: Mdtoolbox
1766 Fowler St Ste D (99352-4843)
PHONE...................206 331-4420
Michael Conner,
Angela Conner,
EMP: 7 EST: 2010
SALES: 450K Privately Held
SIC: 7372 Business oriented computer software

(G-9046)
TOTAL HOME CONTROL
1231 Brentwood Ave (99352-8533)
PHONE...................509 628-1673
Jim Snyder, Owner
Deborah Snyder, Co-Owner
EMP: 2
SALES (est): 100.5K Privately Held
SIC: 4911 3491 Electric services; automatic regulating & control valves

(G-9047)
TRI-CITY CABINETS LLC
1940 Butler Loop (99354-4944)
PHONE...................509 946-5614
EMP: 4 EST: 2011
SQ FT: 5,000
SALES (est): 415.8K Privately Held
SIC: 2434 Mfg Wood Kitchen Cabinets

(G-9048)
TRI-CITY TEES & SCREEN PRTG ◆
1834 Marshall Ave (99354-2460)
PHONE...................509 420-6993
EMP: 2 EST: 2018
SALES (est): 83.9K Privately Held
SIC: 2752 Commercial printing, lithographic

GEOGRAPHIC SECTION

Ridgefield - Clark County (G-9080)

(G-9049)
UNITED STATES DOSIMETRY TECH
660 George Washington Way A (99352-4246)
PHONE...................509 946-8738
Rita Winegardner, *President*
Mike Winegardner, *Admin Sec*
EMP: 6
SQ FT: 2,000
SALES (est): 275K **Privately Held**
SIC: 3829 5199 5084 5047 Personnel dosimetry devices; badges; instruments & control equipment; hospital equipment & furniture; testing laboratories

(G-9050)
VISTA PRECISION SOLUTIONS INC
2350 Lindberg Loop (99354-4967)
PHONE...................908 829-3471
EMP: 2
SALES (corp-wide): 2.4MM **Privately Held**
SIC: 1389 Detection & analysis service, gas
PA: Vista Precision Solutions, Inc.
2350 Lindberg Loop
Richland WA 99354
509 943-2484

(G-9051)
WASHINGTON BIO-OILS INC
2720 Crimson Way (99354)
PHONE...................509 713-3299
Jeffry Canin, *CEO*
Hanwu Lei, *Treasurer*
EMP: 3
SALES (est): 160.5K **Privately Held**
SIC: 2869 Industrial organic chemicals

(G-9052)
WASHINGTON STATE UNIVERSITY
Also Called: Ktnw Channel 31
2710 Crimson Way Ste 101 (99354-1671)
PHONE...................509 372-7400
Tony Wright, *General Mgr*
EMP: 5
SALES (corp-wide): 750MM **Privately Held**
WEB: www.wsu.edu
SIC: 3663 8221 Studio equipment, radio & television broadcasting; university
PA: Washington State University Inc
240 French Adm Bldg
Pullman WA 99164
509 335-2022

(G-9053)
WAUTOMA WINES LLC
1022 Meadow Hills Dr (99352-8661)
PHONE...................509 378-1163
J Munnell, *Bd of Directors*
EMP: 4
SALES (est): 235.9K **Privately Held**
SIC: 2084 Wines

(G-9054)
WINERY COMPLIANCE NORTHWE
2257 Morris Ave (99352-5114)
PHONE...................509 528-0905
Maureen Swaney, *Principal*
EMP: 7
SALES (est): 458.8K **Privately Held**
WEB: www.winerycompliancenw.com
SIC: 2084 Wines

(G-9055)
WORLD TRENDS HOLDINGS LLC
4170 Norris St (99352-9638)
PHONE...................559 474-2361
Rafael Nerell,
Jamilette Nerrell,
EMP: 2 **EST:** 2017
SALES (est): 59.2K **Privately Held**
SIC: 2741 Miscellaneous publishing

(G-9056)
YAKIMA ORTHTICS PROSTHETICS PC
Also Called: Tri-Cities Orthotics Prosetics
317 Wellsian Way (99352-4116)
PHONE...................509 943-8561
Marjorie Lott, *Owner*
Michael G Brockway, *Principal*
EMP: 3
SALES (est): 128.5K
SALES (corp-wide): 1.3MM **Privately Held**
SIC: 5999 3842 Orthopedic & prosthesis applications; limbs, artificial
PA: Yakima Orthotics & Prosthetics Pc
313 S 9th Ave
Yakima WA 98902
509 248-8040

(G-9057)
ZERO GRAVITY BLDRS STUDIO LLC
1865 Bronco Ln (99354-4968)
PHONE...................509 942-8439
Amber Hanchete,
Daniel Hanchete,
Scott Hanchete,
EMP: 2 **EST:** 2007
SALES (est): 227.4K **Privately Held**
SIC: 3721 Aircraft

Ridgefield
Clark County

(G-9058)
ABC SHEET METAL INC
3714 Nw 166th St (98642-5964)
P.O. Box 6042, Vancouver (98668-6042)
PHONE...................360 574-4884
Brian Warder, *President*
Phyllis Warder, *CFO*
EMP: 2
SALES (est): 190K **Privately Held**
SIC: 3444 Sheet metalwork

(G-9059)
ADRENALINE PRODUCTS LLC
16003 Ne 25th Ave (98642-8217)
PHONE...................503 805-4525
William Naemura, *Principal*
EMP: 2
SALES (est): 152.1K **Privately Held**
SIC: 3721 Airplanes, fixed or rotary wing

(G-9060)
ALPACAS PARADISE PT
31800 Nw 9th Ave (98642-9702)
PHONE...................360 263-2092
EMP: 2
SALES (est): 73.4K **Privately Held**
SIC: 2231 Alpacas, mohair: woven

(G-9061)
ALPHA IRON LLC
5823 S 6th Way (98642-3204)
PHONE...................360 823-1777
James N Buchan,
Lisa Buchan,
Mike Stewart,
EMP: 20
SALES (est): 5.3MM **Privately Held**
SIC: 3441 Fabricated structural metal for bridges

(G-9062)
ATK MANUFACTURING INC
2837 S 10th Way (98642-8369)
PHONE...................951 660-1218
EMP: 2
SALES (est): 86K **Privately Held**
SIC: 3764 Propulsion units for guided missiles & space vehicles

(G-9063)
B & J METAL FAB
31211 Nw Paradise Park Rd (98642-7983)
PHONE...................360 887-8548
Willman Spitzer, *President*
EMP: 3
SALES (est): 424.5K **Privately Held**
SIC: 3444 Sheet metalwork

(G-9064)
B AND D WHIRLIES
Also Called: B & D Storage
3318 Ne 239th St (98642-8881)
PHONE...................360 887-8471
William Faley, *Owner*
EMP: 2
SALES (est): 90K **Privately Held**
SIC: 3599 4226 0212 Weather vanes; special warehousing & storage; beef cattle except feedlots

(G-9065)
BACKYARD BOUNTY CO-OP
809 Nw 164th St (98642-9478)
PHONE...................360 574-6937
Mary Siebert, *President*
EMP: 2
SALES (est): 89.9K **Privately Held**
SIC: 2033 Fruit juices: fresh

(G-9066)
BELSHIRE INDUSTRIES
27603 Ne 10th Ave (98642-8781)
PHONE...................360 910-9209
Steve Shirey, *Owner*
EMP: 4
SALES (est): 250K **Privately Held**
WEB: www.belshireconcrete.com
SIC: 3999 Manufacturing industries

(G-9067)
BETHANY VINEYARD & WINERY
4115 Ne 259th St (98642-9749)
PHONE...................360 887-3525
Walt Houser, *Owner*
EMP: 2
SALES (est): 125.3K **Privately Held**
WEB: www.bethanyvineyards.com
SIC: 2084 Wines

(G-9068)
BIG C INDUSTRIES LLC
30305 Nw 18th Pl (98642-5224)
PHONE...................360 773-5873
Ronda Bross, *CEO*
EMP: 6
SALES (est): 603.3K **Privately Held**
SIC: 3999 Manufacturing industries

(G-9069)
BRIDGE CITY ARBORS INC
18708 Nw 61st Ave (98642-9005)
PHONE...................360 600-3803
Dana Dokken, *President*
EMP: 2
SALES (est): 154.2K **Privately Held**
SIC: 3545 Machine tool accessories

(G-9070)
CCI CASEWORKS INC
7509 S 5th St Ste 109 (98642-7157)
PHONE...................360 953-9641
Tim Blaker, *President*
Constance Blaker, *Vice Pres*
Tara Blaker, *Admin Sec*
EMP: 8 **EST:** 2010
SALES (est): 834.7K **Privately Held**
SIC: 2522 Filing boxes, cabinets & cases: except wood

(G-9071)
CHERRY GROVE CABINETS
22107 Ne 41st Ct (98642-8907)
PHONE...................360 687-8820
Doug Smith, *Owner*
EMP: 2
SALES (est): 196.8K **Privately Held**
SIC: 2434 Wood kitchen cabinets

(G-9072)
CHURCH AND DWIGHT
10 S 56th Pl (98642-3428)
PHONE...................360 816-7400
▲ **EMP:** 12 **EST:** 2013
SALES (est): 2.5MM **Privately Held**
SIC: 2841 Detergents, synthetic organic or inorganic alkaline

(G-9073)
COLORED METAL ROOFING
30515 Nw Paradise Park Rd (98642-7982)
PHONE...................360 887-4524
Scott Rolls, *Owner*
Barbara Melroy, *Owner*
EMP: 2 **EST:** 2001
SALES (est): 104.1K **Privately Held**
WEB: www.onsitecolormetalroofing.com
SIC: 3444 Sheet metalwork

(G-9074)
COMMERCIAL CABINET WORKS
5901 S 11th St (98642-4801)
PHONE...................360 857-3130
P R Marsh, *President*
Chuck Day, *General Mgr*
EMP: 2
SALES (est): 303.9K **Privately Held**
SIC: 2541 Cabinets, except refrigerated: show, display, etc.: wood

(G-9075)
CONFLUENCE VINEYARDS
19111 Nw 67th Ave (98642-9630)
PHONE...................360 887-2343
Gregory Weber, *Principal*
EMP: 4
SALES (est): 308.5K **Privately Held**
SIC: 2084 Wines

(G-9076)
CORWIN BEVERAGE CO (PA)
Also Called: Pepsi Cola Btlg Co Vancouver
219 S Timm Rd (98642-3343)
PHONE...................360 696-0766
Nancy L Bjerkman, *President*
Kyle W Corwin, *Principal*
Zachary Nizam-Aldine, *Director*
EMP: 80 **EST:** 1940
SQ FT: 8,000
SALES (est): 15.5MM **Privately Held**
SIC: 2086 Carbonated soft drinks, bottled & canned

(G-9077)
CORWIN BEVERAGE CO
Also Called: Pepsico
219 S Timm Rd (98642-3343)
PHONE...................360 696-0766
Mike Randall, *Manager*
EMP: 30
SALES (est): 3MM
SALES (corp-wide): 15.5MM **Privately Held**
SIC: 2086 Carbonated soft drinks, bottled & canned
PA: Corwin Beverage Co.
219 S Timm Rd
Ridgefield WA 98642
360 696-0766

(G-9078)
DANIEL E FRANCE
Also Called: France Special Tools
30111 Ne Timmen Rd (98642-8768)
PHONE...................360 263-2888
Daniel E France, *Owner*
Gabriel Temme, *Manager*
EMP: 2 **EST:** 1973
SQ FT: 2,500
SALES (est): 90K **Privately Held**
WEB: www.francespecialtool.com
SIC: 3544 Special dies, tools, jigs & fixtures

(G-9079)
DONALD R HOLLISTER TRCKG INC
1912 Ne 279th St (98642-8778)
PHONE...................360 887-8418
EMP: 4
SALES (est): 613.3K **Privately Held**
SIC: 3537 Industrial Trucks And Tractors

(G-9080)
ELKHART PLASTICS
6111 S 6th Way (98642-3338)
PHONE...................360 887-2230
Joan Wyngarden, *Principal*
EMP: 100
SQ FT: 140,000
SALES (corp-wide): 149.3MM **Privately Held**
SIC: 3089 8711 Plastic containers, except foam; engineering services
PA: Elkhart Plastics, Inc.
3300 N Kenmore St
South Bend IN 46628
574 232-8066

Ridgefield - Clark County (G-9081)

(G-9081)
ERSHIGS INC
Also Called: Attbaar Division
5985 S 6th Way (98642-3337)
PHONE...................360 887-3580
Joe W Volz, General Mgr
EMP: 50 **Privately Held**
SIC: 3089 Plastic processing
HQ: Ershigs, Inc.
  742 Marine Dr
  Bellingham WA 98225
  360 733-2620

(G-9082)
FLOWSERVE CORPORATION
7075 S 5th St (98642-7120)
PHONE...................360 573-5211
Don Backous, Manager
EMP: 17
SALES (corp-wide): 3.8B **Publicly Held**
SIC: 3561 Industrial pumps & parts
PA: Flowserve Corporation
  5215 N Oconnor Blvd Connor
  Irving TX 75039
  972 443-6500

(G-9083)
FOREST VIEW INC
607 Ne 224th Cir (98642-8229)
PHONE...................360 909-9890
Pavel Litvinov, Principal
EMP: 2
SALES (est): 278.5K **Privately Held**
SIC: 2452 Log cabins, prefabricated, wood

(G-9084)
G G CONSULTANTS
5604 Nw 234th St (98642-9626)
PHONE...................541 223-9519
Glen Greenwood, Owner
EMP: 11
SALES (est): 725.5K **Privately Held**
SIC: 3829 Vibration meters, analyzers & calibrators

(G-9085)
GLENBAR ALPACAS INC
20801 Ne 50th Ave (98642-8691)
PHONE...................360 574-5428
Barbara Zimmerly, Principal
EMP: 2
SALES (est): 135.8K **Privately Held**
SIC: 2211 Alpacas, cotton

(G-9086)
GOUGER CELLARS
26506 Ne 10th Ave (98642-9743)
PHONE...................360 693-2700
Gary Gouger, Principal
EMP: 7 **EST:** 2010
SALES (est): 596.5K **Privately Held**
SIC: 2084 Wines

(G-9087)
GREENCE INC
2 S 56th Pl (98642-3425)
PHONE...................360 727-3528
Ron C Blank, President
EMP: 2
SALES (est): 132.4K **Privately Held**
SIC: 8711 3674 Building construction consultant; semiconductors & related devices

(G-9088)
HEARTS IN MOTION MINISTRIES
309 Ne 189th St (98642-8864)
PHONE...................360 798-0275
Beverly Nielson, Director
EMP: 5
SALES (est): 46.1K **Privately Held**
SIC: 8661 7372 Churches, temples & shrines; application computer software

(G-9089)
IMCO INC
15812 Ne 10th Ave (98642-5727)
PHONE...................360 694-7121
Doug Gillingham, President
Donald Grothe, Corp Secy
Jeff Gillingham, Opers Mgr
Marsha Grothe, Director
EMP: 12
SQ FT: 7,100
SALES (est): 2MM **Privately Held**
SIC: 3613 Control panels, electric

(G-9090)
INDUSTRIAL CONTROL DEV INC
Also Called: Icd High Performance Coating
7350 S Union Ridge Pkwy (98642-7884)
PHONE...................360 546-2286
Larry D Vockler, President
Kris Vockler, Vice Pres
Patricia Vockler, CFO
Jamie Morgan,
▲ **EMP:** 36
SQ FT: 36,000
SALES (est): 8.1MM **Privately Held**
WEB: www.icdcoatings.com
SIC: 2851 Paints & allied products

(G-9091)
KAKADU TRADERS AUSTRALIA INC
17217 Nw 61st Ave (98642-5984)
PHONE...................360 836-5820
Stuart Whillas, President
Elsa Lynch, Vice Pres
▲ **EMP:** 18
SQ FT: 8,000
SALES (est): 3.6MM **Privately Held**
WEB: www.kakaduaustralia.com
SIC: 5136 5137 2389 Men's & boys' outerwear; women's & children's outerwear; men's miscellaneous accessories

(G-9092)
KINETIC SOLUTIONS INTL
7509 S 5th St Ste 110 (98642-7157)
PHONE...................503 490-8642
Dustin Jamieson, Principal
EMP: 2
SALES (est): 107.4K **Privately Held**
SIC: 3569 General industrial machinery

(G-9093)
KOI POND CELLARS
24211 Ne 41st Ave (98642-8842)
P.O. Box 483 (98642-0483)
PHONE...................360 281-2716
Michelle Parker, Owner
EMP: 2
SALES: 100K **Privately Held**
SIC: 2084 Wines

(G-9094)
MICRO DIMENSION INC
5617 S 6th Way (98642-3333)
PHONE...................360 887-0620
Byron Bates, President
EMP: 6
SQ FT: 6,000
SALES: 1MM **Privately Held**
SIC: 3599 Machine shop, jobbing & repair

(G-9095)
N W SOUND & SECURITY TECH LLC
Also Called: NW Sound & Security Tech
16315 Ne Union Rd (98642-5613)
PHONE...................360 213-1619
Jeff Pedersen, Partner
Jeff Pederson, Manager
EMP: 10
SALES (est): 1.2MM **Privately Held**
WEB: www.nwsst.com
SIC: 3699 Security devices

(G-9096)
NORTHWEST NATURAL PRODUCTS INC
10 S 56th Pl (98642-3428)
PHONE...................360 737-6800
Kathryn Jones, President
Martin Rifkin, Vice Pres
Rick Falconer, CFO
◆ **EMP:** 140
SQ FT: 106,000
SALES (est): 51.8MM
SALES (corp-wide): 4.1B **Publicly Held**
WEB: www.nwnaturalproducts.com
SIC: 5122 2834 Vitamins & minerals; vitamin, nutrient & hematinic preparations for human use
HQ: Avid Health, Inc.
  6350 Ne Campus Dr
  Vancouver WA 98661
  360 737-6800

(G-9097)
NUTRITION NOW INC
10 S 56th Pl (98642-3428)
PHONE...................360 737-6800
Martin Rifkin, President
Kathryn Jones, Vice Pres
David M Kaye, Director
▲ **EMP:** 90
SQ FT: 15,000
SALES (est): 11.3MM
SALES (corp-wide): 4.1B **Publicly Held**
WEB: www.nutritionnow.com
SIC: 2834 Vitamin, nutrient & hematinic preparations for human use
HQ: Avid Health, Inc.
  6350 Ne Campus Dr
  Vancouver WA 98661
  360 737-6800

(G-9098)
PACIFIC CREST BUILDING SUPPLY
Also Called: Pacific Crest Custom Cabinetry
5901 S 11th St (98642-4801)
PHONE...................360 857-3120
Peter R Marsh, President
Kraig Tront, General Mgr
EMP: 40
SQ FT: 18,000
SALES (est): 8.5MM **Privately Held**
SIC: 2434 Wood kitchen cabinets

(G-9099)
PACIFIC POWER GROUP LLC
Also Called: Pacific Power Products
6100 S 6th Way (98642-3339)
P.O. Box 640 (98642-0640)
PHONE...................360 887-5980
EMP: 45
SALES (corp-wide): 18.1MM **Privately Held**
SIC: 3621 5063 Mfg Motors/Generators Whol Electrical Equipment
HQ: Pacific Power Group, Llc
  805 Broadway St Ste 700
  Vancouver WA 98660
  360 887-7400

(G-9100)
PACIFIC POWER GROUP LLC
Also Called: Pacific Power Products
6100 S 6th Way (98642-3339)
PHONE...................360 887-5980
Andy Machin, Manager
EMP: 81
SALES (corp-wide): 18.1MM **Privately Held**
SIC: 3519 5084 Diesel engine rebuilding; engines & parts, diesel
HQ: Pacific Power Group, Llc
  805 Broadway St Ste 700
  Vancouver WA 98660
  360 887-7400

(G-9101)
PAUL SCHURMAN MACHINE INC
23201 Ne 10th Ave (98642-8175)
P.O. Box 999 (98642-0999)
PHONE...................360 887-3193
Matthew Houghton, President
EMP: 17 **EST:** 1959
SQ FT: 25,000
SALES (est): 3.8MM **Privately Held**
WEB: www.schurmanmfg.com
SIC: 3599 Custom machinery; machine shop, jobbing & repair

(G-9102)
PIPER 2600 INVESTMENTS LLC ✪
2600 Nw 329th St (98642-9775)
PHONE...................971 409-7596
EMP: 2 **EST:** 2019
SALES (est): 62.3K **Privately Held**
SIC: 2051 Bread, cake & related products

(G-9103)
PORTLAND PLASTICS
6111 S 6th Way (98642-3338)
PHONE...................360 887-2230
Jack Welter, President
◆ **EMP:** 400
SALES (est): 64.7MM
SALES (corp-wide): 149.3MM **Privately Held**
WEB: www.bonarplastics.com
SIC: 2673 3089 2671 3537 Bags: plastic, laminated & coated; plastic containers, except foam; packaging paper & plastics film, coated & laminated; industrial trucks & tractors
PA: Elkhart Plastics, Inc.
  3300 N Kenmore St
  South Bend IN 46628
  574 232-8066

(G-9104)
POWERHUSE BRNDS CONSULTING LLC
Also Called: Giff Card Network
17007 Ne 30th Ave (98642-8028)
P.O. Box 2397, Vancouver (98668-2397)
PHONE...................503 317-4925
Matt Davies,
EMP: 4 **EST:** 2017
SALES: 500K **Privately Held**
SIC: 8742 2741 7389 Marketing consulting services; miscellaneous publishing;

(G-9105)
RAZ ARTHUR JOHN
20800 Nw Krieger Rd (98642-9643)
PHONE...................360 518-2665
Arthur Raz, Principal
EMP: 18
SALES (est): 3.9MM **Privately Held**
SIC: 1081 Metal mining services

(G-9106)
RED TAIL WOODWORKS
16305 Nw 41st Ave (98642-5923)
PHONE...................360 852-6883
B Crawford, Exec Dir
Bruce Crawford, Exec Dir
EMP: 2 **EST:** 2012
SALES: 5K **Privately Held**
SIC: 2431 Woodwork, interior & ornamental

(G-9107)
REFLECTION VINEYARDS LLC
2286 S 31st Ct (98642-9096)
PHONE...................360 904-4800
Allison Vanarnam, Principal
EMP: 3
SALES (est): 165.7K **Privately Held**
SIC: 2084 Wines

(G-9108)
RIETDYKS MILLING COMPANY
512 Nw Carty Rd (98642-9425)
PHONE...................360 887-8874
Don Hegge, President
Lucy Hegge, Admin Sec
EMP: 5
SQ FT: 2,000
SALES: 700K **Privately Held**
SIC: 5191 5999 2048 Feed; feed & farm supply; feed premixes

(G-9109)
S E INDUSTRIES LLC
2401 S 17th Way (98642-9284)
PHONE...................503 519-2160
Jaret Alan Sutherland, Principal
EMP: 2 **EST:** 2012
SALES (est): 120.4K **Privately Held**
SIC: 3999 Manufacturing industries

(G-9110)
SCHURMANS GAS & GLASS
Also Called: Gas N' Glass
18109 Nw Krieger Rd (98642-8003)
PHONE...................360 573-3669
Roger Schurman, Owner
EMP: 4
SALES (est): 220K **Privately Held**
WEB: www.gasnglass.com
SIC: 3993 Signs & advertising specialties

(G-9111)
SINOTECHUSA INC
7509 S 5th St Ste 102 (98642-7157)
PHONE...................360 566-2880
Timothy Armstrong, Principal
Jared Armstrong, Principal
▲ **EMP:** 6 **EST:** 2011

GEOGRAPHIC SECTION

Rochester - Thurston County (G-9143)

SALES (est): 759.9K **Privately Held**
SIC: **5033** 3089 Roofing, asphalt & sheet metal; injection molding of plastics; extruded finished plastic products

(G-9112)
SOBEL GUITARS
716 Nw 179th St (98642-5754)
PHONE..................................505 699-4032
Christopher Sobel, *Administration*
EMP: 2 EST: 2015
SALES (est): 49.6K **Privately Held**
SIC: **3931** Musical instruments

(G-9113)
STAVALAURA VINYARDS
29503 Nw 41st Ave (98642-9776)
PHONE..................................360 887-1476
Joseph Leadingham, *Mng Member*
Beverly Leadingham,
EMP: 2
SALES (est): 110.1K **Privately Held**
SIC: **2084** Wines

(G-9114)
STRONG SNAX INC
6405 Nw 170th Cir (98642-9201)
PHONE..................................360 953-3753
Cameron Jay Crawford, *President*
EMP: 5
SALES (est): 410.2K **Privately Held**
SIC: **2834** 5085 8099 Chlorination tablets & kits (water purification); staplers & tackers; nutrition services

(G-9115)
THIRTEEN SHEETS LLC
Also Called: Fleet Sheets
3012 Nw 199th St (98642-9560)
PHONE..................................888 676-5270
Larry Dunn,
EMP: 2
SALES: 140K **Privately Held**
SIC: **2299** 7389 Broadwoven fabrics: linen, jute, hemp & ramie;

(G-9116)
THREE BROTHERS VINEYARD A
802 Nw 297th Cir (98642-8727)
PHONE..................................503 702-5549
EMP: 2
SALES (est): 75.9K **Privately Held**
SIC: **2084** Wines

(G-9117)
TYLER TECHNOLOGIES INC
Also Called: Taylor Technologies
415 N Allen Creek Dr (98642-8279)
PHONE..................................360 852-6696
David Taylor, *Branch Mgr*
EMP: 23
SALES (corp-wide): 935.2MM **Publicly Held**
SIC: **7372** Prepackaged software
PA: Tyler Technologies, Inc.
5101 Tennyson Pkwy
Plano TX 75024
972 713-3700

(G-9118)
URBAN STONEWORKS LLC
252 N Green Gables Loop (98642-2803)
PHONE..................................808 333-6675
Scott Kruckenberg,
Todd Burkart,
EMP: 4
SALES (est): 111.3K **Privately Held**
SIC: **1411** Limestone & marble dimension stone

(G-9119)
VULCAN PERFORMANCE
2112 Ne 236th St (98642-8848)
PHONE..................................360 450-4237
EMP: 4 EST: 2013
SALES (est): 361.7K **Privately Held**
SIC: **3714** Motor vehicle parts & accessories

(G-9120)
WINDBREAK INC
2515 Ne 163rd St (98642-7975)
PHONE..................................817 306-9587
EMP: 2
SALES (est): 77.4K **Privately Held**
SIC: **3131** Footwear cut stock

Ritzville
Adams County

(G-9121)
FLYING ARTS RANCH INC
Also Called: Grafika Korps
106 N Washington St (99169-2326)
PHONE..................................509 659-1819
John Rankin, *President*
EMP: 3
SALES (est): 167.8K **Privately Held**
SIC: **5999** 3993 7336 5699 Art dealers; signs & advertising specialties; chart & graph design; miscellaneous apparel & accessories

(G-9122)
RUSER PUBLICATIONS INC
Also Called: Ritzville Adams County Journal
216 W Railroad Ave (99169-2309)
P.O. Box 288 (99169-0288)
PHONE..................................509 659-1020
Dee Ruser, *President*
Dwayne Ruser, *Owner*
Steven McFadden, *Principal*
EMP: 4
SQ FT: 2,500
SALES (est): 170K **Privately Held**
SIC: **2711** 2752 Job printing & newspaper publishing combined; commercial printing, lithographic

(G-9123)
TEXAS JOHNS
1455 W 1st Ave (99169)
PHONE..................................509 659-1402
Irene Doherty, *Partner*
John Doherty, *Partner*
EMP: 22
SQ FT: 2,520
SALES (est): 360.9K **Privately Held**
SIC: **5812** 2032 American restaurant; caterers; ethnic foods: canned, jarred, etc.

Riverside
Okanogan County

(G-9124)
CRESCENT MOON STUDIOS INC
Also Called: Mac Flynn
780 Tunk Creek Rd (98849-9605)
P.O. Box 117 (98849-0117)
PHONE..................................509 322-7730
Heidi Willard, *Principal*
EMP: 2
SALES: 100K **Privately Held**
SIC: **2731** 7371 Books: publishing only; computer software development & applications

(G-9125)
DENRICK TEES
514 Chewiliken Valley Rd (98849-9686)
PHONE..................................509 429-6675
Daniel J Wilson, *Owner*
EMP: 2
SALES (est): 99.8K **Privately Held**
SIC: **2759** Screen printing

(G-9126)
ROMINE FUEL INC
105 Frank Rd (98849)
P.O. Box 1451, Oroville (98844-1451)
PHONE..................................509 476-3610
Jason Romine, *Principal*
EMP: 4
SALES (est): 395.3K **Privately Held**
SIC: **2869** Fuels

(G-9127)
TECH HEAVY INDUSTRIES INC
Also Called: Tech Industrial Services
7 Stansbury Rd (98849-9667)
P.O. Box 1338, Tonasket (98855-1338)
PHONE..................................509 557-8492
Brandon Wood, *CEO*
Martha Mary Wood, *President*

EMP: 2
SQ FT: 2,400
SALES: 1.3MM **Privately Held**
SIC: **3443** 3484 Tanks, standard or custom fabricated: metal plate; small arms

(G-9128)
TY ENTERPRISES
26 Rosewood Ln (98849-9671)
PHONE..................................509 826-6597
EMP: 2
SALES (est): 80.4K **Privately Held**
SIC: **3251** Mfg Brick/Structural Tile

Rochester
Thurston County

(G-9129)
CASCADIA VENOM COLLECTION
13831 Littlerock Rd Sw (98579-9706)
P.O. Box 126, Littlerock (98556-0126)
PHONE..................................360 556-3177
Stephanie Techner, *Principal*
EMP: 2
SALES (est): 74.4K **Privately Held**
SIC: **2836** Venoms

(G-9130)
CHETTIES WOODWORKING LLC
5939 184th Ln Sw (98579-8773)
P.O. Box 692 (98579-0692)
PHONE..................................360 500-9099
Chesley White, *Principal*
EMP: 2 EST: 2013
SALES (est): 125K **Privately Held**
SIC: **2431** Millwork

(G-9131)
DNLVI BUSINESS SOLUTIONS
7838 195th Ave Sw (98579-8700)
P.O. Box 908 (98579-0908)
PHONE..................................360 827-5210
EMP: 3
SALES (est): 176.5K **Privately Held**
SIC: **2759** Commercial printing

(G-9132)
FLYING COW CREAMERY LLC
209 Hyppa Rd E (98579-8932)
PHONE..................................360 273-1045
Selma Bjarnabottir,
EMP: 2 EST: 2012
SQ FT: 2,000
SALES: 25K **Privately Held**
SIC: **2026** Yogurt

(G-9133)
GUADALUPE FOODS INC
12231 Independence Rd Sw (98579-9606)
PHONE..................................360 736-0298
Bill Lepman, *President*
EMP: 3
SALES (est): 134.2K **Privately Held**
SIC: **2099** Food preparations

(G-9134)
K & L LOGGING
12935 Taylor Rd Sw (98579-8400)
PHONE..................................360 273-9916
Kenneth L Taylor, *Owner*
EMP: 4
SALES (est): 213.7K **Privately Held**
SIC: **2411** Logging camps & contractors

(G-9135)
LANDRACE LABS
5845 192nd Ave Sw (98579-7968)
PHONE..................................360 273-9277
EMP: 3
SALES (est): 185.6K **Privately Held**
SIC: **3999** 8731 ; commercial research laboratory

(G-9136)
MCFARLAND CASCADE HOLDINGS INC
18146 Dallas St Sw (98579-9563)
PHONE..................................360 273-5541
EMP: 3

SALES (corp-wide): 1.6B **Privately Held**
SIC: **2491** 6552 6531 Poles & pole crossarms, treated wood; land subdividers & developers, commercial; real estate managers
HQ: Mcfarland Cascade Holdings, Inc.
1640 E Marc St
Tacoma WA 98421
253 572-3033

(G-9137)
MILMAN ENGINEERING INC
19207 Guava St Sw (98579-8712)
PHONE..................................360 273-5080
Michael G Kimbrel, *President*
EMP: 4
SQ FT: 10,800
SALES (est): 569.2K **Privately Held**
SIC: **3541** 3599 1521 1542 Tapping machines; machine & other job shop work; single-family housing construction; farm building construction

(G-9138)
NORTH FORK TIMBER COMPANY CORP
Also Called: Pls Pole Yard
18146 Dallas St Sw (98579-9563)
PHONE..................................360 273-5541
Bill Latunen, *Sales/Mktg Mgr*
EMP: 7
SQ FT: 1,840
SALES (corp-wide): 9.9MM **Privately Held**
SIC: **2411** 2421 Logging camps & contractors; sawmills & planing mills, general
PA: North Fork Timber Company Corporation
417 W Main St Ste C
Centralia WA 98531
360 748-8333

(G-9139)
PUGET SOUND LOGGING
16516 Littlerock Rd Sw (98579-9527)
P.O. Box 268 (98579-0268)
PHONE..................................253 310-5923
Heidi Whalen, *Principal*
EMP: 2 EST: 2017
SALES (est): 81.7K **Privately Held**
SIC: **2411** Logging

(G-9140)
SAM BICKLE LOGGING INC
Also Called: Bickle Land & Timber
201 Jylha Rd (98579-8917)
PHONE..................................360 273-5886
Sam Bickle, *President*
EMP: 7 EST: 1971
SALES (est): 556.3K **Privately Held**
SIC: **2411** Logging camps & contractors

(G-9141)
TOP NOTCH TRAILER MFG
Also Called: Top Notch Trailers
19541 Elderberry St Sw (98579-9249)
PHONE..................................360 273-0468
Gordon Cooper, *President*
Darren Lloyd, *Vice Pres*
Donald McCormick, *Vice Pres*
Nancy Ford, *Office Mgr*
Joanne Lambert, *Admin Sec*
EMP: 10
SALES: 1.6MM **Privately Held**
WEB: www.topnotchtrailers.com
SIC: **3799** 5599 5013 5084 Trailers & trailer equipment; utility trailers; trailer parts & accessories; trailers, industrial

(G-9142)
TRUEPOINT METALWORKS WLDG INC
9616 James Rd Sw (98579-9362)
PHONE..................................360 273-3412
Brad Tarbet, *President*
EMP: 3
SQ FT: 4,500
SALES (est): 459.4K **Privately Held**
WEB: www.truepointmetalworks.com
SIC: **3444** Sheet metalwork

(G-9143)
VERNS RENT IT
19302 Elderberry St Sw (98579-9249)
PHONE..................................360 458-3302
Debra Fisk, *President*

Rochester – Thurston County (G-9144)

EMP: 2
SALES (est): 13.2K **Privately Held**
SIC: 3448 Prefabricated metal buildings

(G-9144)
WELD-TECH FABRICATION INC
10320 James Rd Sw (98579-9354)
PHONE..............................425 591-5912
Nikolay Nenkov, *President*
EMP: 5
SALES (est): 342.2K **Privately Held**
SIC: 3441 7389 Fabricated structural metal;

(G-9145)
WHOLESALE FORMS INC
17449 Jordan St Sw (98579-8525)
PHONE..............................800 826-7095
Tannley Goldberg, *President*
Marshall Goldberg, *Vice Pres*
Richard Fiedler, *Manager*
EMP: 5
SQ FT: 1,000
SALES (est): 573.6K **Privately Held**
WEB: www.wholesaleforms.com
SIC: 2759 5111 2672 2679 Business forms: printing; printing & writing paper; labels (unprinted), gummed: made from purchased materials; labels, paper: made from purchased material

(G-9146)
WILLIAMS ELITE MACHINING & MFG
9200 Applegate Loop Sw (98579-8567)
PHONE..............................253 228-2288
Louis Williams, *Owner*
EMP: 6
SALES (est): 466.6K **Privately Held**
SIC: 3532 Mining machinery

(G-9147)
WILSON DAIRY
2560 Lincoln Creek Rd (98579-8909)
PHONE..............................360 736-6001
Laurence Wilson, *Owner*
EMP: 2
SALES (est): 200K **Privately Held**
SIC: 3523 Dairy equipment (farm)

Rock Island
Douglas County

(G-9148)
COLUMBIA COVE LLC
1805 Columbia Cove Ln S (98850-9570)
PHONE..............................360 739-7373
Gerard Pierre, *Principal*
Molly Hanson, *Administration*
EMP: 2 EST: 2016
SALES (est): 57.6K **Privately Held**
SIC: 0175 0721 3556 Cherry orchard; tree orchards, cultivation of; presses, food: cheese, beet, cider & sugarcane

(G-9149)
SPECIALTY CHEMICAL PDTS LLC
100 S 4th St (98850)
P.O. Box 68 (98850-0068)
PHONE..............................509 884-4900
James Trunzo,
Kim Babbitts,
EMP: 3
SALES (est): 358.8K **Privately Held**
SIC: 2911 Aromatic chemical products

(G-9150)
STANDARD PALLET CO
5604 Nature Shore Dr (98850-9585)
PHONE..............................509 670-0632
James E Brock, *President*
EMP: 8
SQ FT: 1,000
SALES (est): 475.8K **Privately Held**
SIC: 7699 2448 Pallet repair; pallets, wood & wood with metal

Rockford
Spokane County

(G-9151)
HYDROSTRAW LLC (PA)
22110 S Sr 27 (99030-9724)
PHONE..............................509 291-6000
Ron Edwards, *President*
Edward Lee, *Vice Pres*
▼ EMP: 20
SQ FT: 2,500
SALES (est): 3.9MM **Privately Held**
WEB: www.hydrostraw.com
SIC: 3999 Straw goods

Rockport
Skagit County

(G-9152)
HO STAFFORD LOGGING
52748 Main St (98283-9765)
PHONE..............................360 853-8816
Craig Sjostrom, *Principal*
EMP: 3
SALES (est): 292.5K **Privately Held**
SIC: 2411 Logging

Roosevelt
Klickitat County

(G-9153)
SIEMENS GMESA RNWBLE ENRGY INC
1131 Dot Rd (99356-9752)
PHONE..............................509 896-5246
EMP: 2
SALES (corp-wide): 95B **Privately Held**
SIC: 3511 Turbines & turbine generator sets
HQ: Siemens Gamesa Renewable Energy, Inc.
3500 Quadrangle Blvd
Orlando FL 32817
407 736-2000

Rosalia
Whitman County

(G-9154)
COOPERATIVE AG PRODUCERS INC (PA)
Also Called: Northwest Pea & Bean Company
120 W Fifth St (99170-7007)
P.O. Box 295 (99170-0295)
PHONE..............................509 523-3032
Jackie Tee, *President*
Chad Denny, *Vice Pres*
Ida Clausen, *Treasurer*
Robert Goldsworthy, *Admin Sec*
EMP: 20 EST: 1998
SALES (est): 44.7MM **Privately Held**
SIC: 5153 2048 Grains; livestock feeds

(G-9155)
KILE MACHINE & MANUFACTURING
401 Squires Rd (99170-8608)
PHONE..............................509 569-3814
Ronald Kile, *President*
Ron Kile, *Principal*
Sharon Kile, *Corp Secy*
▼ EMP: 4 EST: 1974
SALES (est): 487.8K **Privately Held**
SIC: 0111 0119 3523 7699 Wheat; barley farm; farm machinery & equipment; farm machinery repair

Roslyn
Kittitas County

(G-9156)
ROSLYN BREWING CO INC
208 W Pennsylvania Ave (98941-3401)
P.O. Box 24 (98941-0024)
PHONE..............................509 649-2232
Dino Enrico, *Owner*
EMP: 4
SALES (est): 362.7K **Privately Held**
WEB: www.roslynbrewery.com
SIC: 2082 Beer (alcoholic beverage)

Roy
Pierce County

(G-9157)
BOARD SYSTEMS
8611 312th St S (98580-8753)
PHONE..............................253 307-0166
Michael Baker, *Partner*
Robert Carlman, *Partner*
EMP: 2
SALES (est): 121.1K **Privately Held**
SIC: 3999 Manufacturing industries

(G-9158)
COASTAL CLAYWORKS
33121 82nd Ave S (98580-8437)
PHONE..............................315 405-5077
Katherine Kedenburg, *Principal*
EMP: 2
SALES (est): 100.5K **Privately Held**
SIC: 3269 Stoneware pottery products

(G-9159)
FAT DADDYS FABRICATION LLC
28014 14th Ave E (98580-9571)
PHONE..............................253 677-8005
EMP: 2
SALES (est): 157.8K **Privately Held**
SIC: 3441 3443 3312 1731 Fabricated structural metal; fabricated plate work (boiler shop); rails, steel or iron; fiber optic cable installation

(G-9160)
HARTS LAKE TRADING POST
Also Called: Harts Lake Furrier
35816 58th Ave S (98580-8213)
PHONE..............................360 458-3477
Angelo Platoni, *Owner*
Amanda Platoni, *Co-Owner*
EMP: 3
SQ FT: 2,800
SALES (est): 248.8K **Privately Held**
SIC: 2371 2386 Fur goods; leather & sheep-lined clothing

(G-9161)
INTERNATIONAL CARBIDE CORP
32022 8th Ave S (98580-9640)
PHONE..............................800 422-8665
Bruce A Mackey, *President*
Chris Mackey, *Vice Pres*
Stuart Mackey, *Vice Pres*
Steve Mackey, *Treasurer*
Julie Mackey, *Admin Sec*
EMP: 10 EST: 1950
SQ FT: 3,500
SALES: 570K **Privately Held**
WEB: www.icctool.com
SIC: 3545 2282 3423 Cutting tools for machine tools; knitting yarn: twisting, winding or spooling; hand & edge tools

(G-9162)
MCKENNA DOOR AND MILLWORK
35009 46th Ave S (98580-7623)
P.O. Box 689, McKenna (98558-0689)
PHONE..............................360 458-5467
Gordon Leblanc Sr, *President*
Gordon Le Blanc Sr, *President*
Jennifer Le Blanc, *Vice Pres*
EMP: 6

SALES (est): 947.7K **Privately Held**
SIC: 2431 Doors, wood; doors & door parts & trim, wood

(G-9163)
MOORE MANUFACTURING LLC
38513 Allen Rd S (98580-9129)
PHONE..............................360 400-3277
Thomas Moore, *Bd of Directors*
EMP: 2 EST: 2012
SALES (est): 105.7K **Privately Held**
SIC: 3999 Manufacturing industries

(G-9164)
PROFESSIONAL PRACTICE SYSTEMS
Also Called: Opto
29622 48th Ave S (98580-8734)
P.O. Box 45192, Tacoma (98448-5192)
PHONE..............................253 531-8944
Ronald Bussinger, *CEO*
Scott Bussinger, *President*
Trucilla Bussinger, *Corp Secy*
EMP: 12
SQ FT: 4,500
SALES (est): 980K **Privately Held**
WEB: www.opto.com
SIC: 7371 5045 7372 Computer software systems analysis & design, custom; computers, peripherals & software; prepackaged software

(G-9165)
TARRA LLC
34214 102nd Ave S (98580-9459)
PHONE..............................360 458-4842
Donna Rebelez, *Principal*
EMP: 2
SALES (est): 165.6K **Privately Held**
SIC: 3861 Motion picture film

(G-9166)
WILCOX FARMS INC
40400 Harts Lake Vly Rd (98580-9182)
PHONE..............................360 458-6903
J T Wilcox, *Principal*
EMP: 15
SALES (corp-wide): 156.1MM **Privately Held**
SIC: 2026 0252 Fluid milk; chicken eggs
PA: Wilcox Farms, Inc.
40400 Harts Lake Vly Rd
Roy WA 98580
360 458-7774

Royal City
Grant County

(G-9167)
CALLAHAN MANUFACTURING INC
219 Balsom St (99357)
P.O. Box 205 (99357-0205)
PHONE..............................509 346-2208
Nancy Callahan, *President*
Dean Callahan, *Vice Pres*
EMP: 20 EST: 1968
SQ FT: 5,000
SALES: 1MM **Privately Held**
WEB: www.callahanhoist.com
SIC: 3523 3536 Farm machinery & equipment; hoists

(G-9168)
CASCADE ORGANIC FLOUR LLC
Also Called: Cascade Organic Farms
310 Camelia St Ne (99357)
P.O. Box 187 (99357-0187)
PHONE..............................509 855-7450
Justin Brown,
EMP: 10
SALES (est): 815.4K **Privately Held**
SIC: 2041 5153 Flour & other grain mill products; grain & field beans

(G-9169)
H A MILTON CORP
Also Called: Quick Tape
2140 Road 12 Sw (99357-9730)
PHONE..............................509 346-1192
David Hamilton, *President*
EMP: 3

SQ FT: 1,000
SALES (est): 220K **Privately Held**
SIC: 2241 Fabric tapes

(G-9170)
JET FARMS INC
5314 Road 13.9 Sw (99357-9734)
PHONE..................................509 346-2588
Jeff Cochran, *President*
Terry Cochran, *Vice Pres*
EMP: 15
SQ FT: 9,500
SALES (est): 2.1MM **Privately Held**
WEB: www.jetfarms.com
SIC: 2087 0139 Flavoring extracts & syrups; mint farm

(G-9171)
LAWRENCE CELLARS LLC
Also Called: Grd Vintners
13000 Road D Sw (99357-9776)
PHONE..................................509 346-2585
Joshua Lawrence,
Lisa Lawrence,
EMP: 3
SALES (est): 11.5K **Privately Held**
SIC: 2084 Wines

(G-9172)
MICHAELS TOUCH
14041 Crook Loop Sw (99357-9139)
P.O. Box 123 (99357-0123)
PHONE..................................509 346-9478
Micheal Flerchinger, *Owner*
Sharon Flerchinger, *Corp Secy*
EMP: 2
SALES (est): 65.7K **Privately Held**
WEB: www.michaelstouch.com
SIC: 7692 Welding repair

(G-9173)
P & DS IMG-N-THAT SPCALTY PRTG
10805 Road 13.5 Sw (99357-9658)
PHONE..................................509 346-1170
EMP: 2 EST: 2008
SALES (est): 120K **Privately Held**
SIC: 2752 Lithographic Commercial Printing

(G-9174)
ROYAL RIDGE FRT COLD STOR LLC (PA)
13215 Road F Sw (99357-9613)
P.O. Box 428 (99357-0428)
PHONE..................................509 346-1520
Craig Riley, *Prdtn Mgr*
Jeff Posey, *QC Mgr*
Terry Ihnen, *CFO*
Bryce Dorsing, *Mng Member*
Jenny Pena, *Manager*
◆ EMP: 99
SQ FT: 60,000
SALES (est): 34.8MM **Privately Held**
WEB: www.royalridgefruits.com
SIC: 2034 2037 Dehydrated fruits, vegetables, soups; frozen fruits & vegetables

(G-9175)
SOARING SUNS PROPERTIES LLC
4591 Road 13.6 Sw (99357-9770)
PHONE..................................509 346-9515
Cindy Niessner,
EMP: 2
SALES (est): 98.3K **Privately Held**
SIC: 2084 Wine cellars, bonded: engaged in blending wines

(G-9176)
SUMMIT COMPONENTS LLC
15509 Road 11 Sw (99357-9511)
PHONE..................................509 750-6629
Brandon Jenks, *Principal*
EMP: 3 EST: 2010
SALES (est): 236.1K **Privately Held**
SIC: 2439 Structural wood members

(G-9177)
TWIN CITY FOODS INC
12884 Beverly Burke Rd Sw (99357-9419)
PHONE..................................509 346-1483
Gary Pedersen, *Branch Mgr*
EMP: 237

SALES (corp-wide): 213.6MM **Privately Held**
SIC: 2037 Frozen fruits & vegetables
PA: Twin City Foods, Inc.
10120 269th Pl Nw
Stanwood WA 98292
206 515-2400

Ruston
Pierce County

(G-9178)
SECONDHAND HOUND
5609 N 51st St (98407-3109)
PHONE..................................253 232-9432
Joel Green, *Owner*
EMP: 2
SALES (est): 108.8K **Privately Held**
SIC: 3999 Pet supplies

Salkum
Lewis County

(G-9179)
BALDWIN LOGGING INCORPORATED
124 Jordan Rd (98582-9602)
P.O. Box 292 (98582-0292)
PHONE..................................360 520-4484
EMP: 3
SALES (est): 163.2K **Privately Held**
SIC: 2411 Logging

(G-9180)
MARTRONICS CORPORATION
500 Wilcox Rd (98582)
P.O. Box 200 (98582-0200)
PHONE..................................360 985-2999
Dean A Marshall, *President*
Marie Marshall, *Vice Pres*
▲ EMP: 20
SQ FT: 7,500
SALES (est): 2.5MM **Privately Held**
WEB: www.martronicscorporation.com
SIC: 3953 Marking devices

(G-9181)
VIPER TACTICAL LLC
107 Jordan Rd (98582-9602)
PHONE..................................425 341-0529
Scott Malcom, *President*
EMP: 2
SQ FT: 1,680
SALES (est): 167K **Privately Held**
SIC: 3714 3799 Motor vehicle parts & accessories; trailers & trailer equipment

Sammamish
King County

(G-9182)
A AND V INC
20141 Ne 28th Pl (98074-4538)
PHONE..................................425 968-5881
Lanphuong T Vu, *President*
EMP: 2 EST: 2017
SALES (est): 117.2K **Privately Held**
SIC: 2842 Specialty cleaning preparations

(G-9183)
AARD TECHNOLOGY LLC
2816 234th Ave Se (98075-6043)
PHONE..................................425 785-0682
Allan Biegaj, *Principal*
EMP: 5
SALES (est): 423.8K **Privately Held**
SIC: 3674 Semiconductors & related devices

(G-9184)
ANALI INCORPORATED
20333 Ne 34th Ct (98074-4319)
PHONE..................................425 284-1829
Sally J Wallace, *President*
Lynn K Ducken Goldstein, *Vice Pres*
◆ EMP: 18
SQ FT: 7,000

SALES (est): 2.1MM **Privately Held**
WEB: www.anali.com
SIC: 2392 Tablecloths & table settings

(G-9185)
ARTFUL DRAGON PRESS LLC
22113 Ne 28th Place Samma (98074)
PHONE..................................800 630-1117
Terry Page, *Manager*
Terrence Page,
▲ EMP: 3
SALES (est): 253.6K **Privately Held**
SIC: 2721 Magazines: publishing & printing

(G-9186)
ASABOOKS INC
24233 Se 39th St (98029-7564)
PHONE..................................425 885-1889
Kim Chau Tsnag, *President*
▲ EMP: 2
SALES (est): 136.5K **Privately Held**
SIC: 2335 Wedding gowns & dresses

(G-9187)
BABY SIGNS BY LAURIE HALS
2801 247th Ave Se (98075-9407)
PHONE..................................425 557-6537
Wes Halstead, *Principal*
EMP: 2
SALES (est): 123.9K **Privately Held**
SIC: 3993 Signs & advertising specialties

(G-9188)
BEAVER LAKE WOODWORKS
1919 E Beaver Lake Dr Se (98075-7905)
PHONE..................................425 391-0661
Joseph McConnell, *Principal*
EMP: 4
SALES (est): 342K **Privately Held**
SIC: 2431 Millwork

(G-9189)
BELLA TUTTO INC
1100 206th Pl Ne (98074-6661)
PHONE..................................425 898-8680
Isabella Tobiason, *President*
EMP: 2
SALES (est): 220K **Privately Held**
SIC: 2253 Collar & cuff sets, knit

(G-9190)
BILLDON LLC
Also Called: Billy Footwear
22703 Se 18th St (98075-9503)
PHONE..................................425 736-4316
Darin Donalsdon,
William Price III,
EMP: 5 EST: 2014
SALES (est): 331.7K **Privately Held**
SIC: 3144 3143 2211 Women's footwear, except athletic; men's footwear, except athletic; apparel & outerwear fabrics, cotton

(G-9191)
BOMBORA GLOBAL LLC
4825 240th Ave Se (98029-7511)
PHONE..................................206 617-6996
John R Hoss, *Mng Member*
Kyle Clayhold,
Trisha Hoss,
EMP: 5
SALES (est): 260.5K **Privately Held**
SIC: 3599 Amusement park equipment

(G-9192)
BOUTIQUE ON WHEELS
2837 234th Ave Se (98075-6043)
PHONE..................................425 369-9324
James Shim, *Principal*
EMP: 2
SALES (est): 147.3K **Privately Held**
SIC: 3312 Blast furnaces & steel mills

(G-9193)
BRAD PENDLETON SOFTWARE LLC
23402 Ne 23rd St (98074-4438)
PHONE..................................425 898-0309
Bradley Pendleton, *Principal*
EMP: 2
SALES (est): 95.1K **Privately Held**
SIC: 7372 Prepackaged software

(G-9194)
CADENCE NEUROSCIENCE INC
2036 223rd Pl Ne (98074-4134)
PHONE..................................425 681-6863
Kent Leyde, *CEO*
Warren Sheffield, *Admin Sec*
EMP: 2
SALES (est): 113.5K **Privately Held**
SIC: 3845 Electroencephalographs

(G-9195)
CALKINS PUBLISHING COMPANY LLC
2125 Sahalee Dr E Smmmishe (98074-6319)
PHONE..................................425 836-3548
Richard Calkins, *Principal*
EMP: 2 EST: 2011
SALES (est): 102.4K **Privately Held**
SIC: 2741 Miscellaneous publishing

(G-9196)
CHARGE SOLUTIONS LLC
24630 Se 24th St (98075-9457)
PHONE..................................425 381-7922
Alejandro Campos,
EMP: 2
SALES (est): 88.3K **Privately Held**
SIC: 3629 7389 Battery chargers, rectifying or nonrotating;

(G-9197)
CHEKIN MD LLC
722 210th Pl Se (98074-7306)
PHONE..................................425 894-9896
Maliha Burney,
EMP: 2 EST: 2014
SALES (est): 116.6K **Privately Held**
SIC: 7372 7389 Application computer software;

(G-9198)
COLLEGE PORTFOLIOS
26301 Se 31st St (98075-9148)
PHONE..................................425 427-0126
Lisa Abraham, *Principal*
EMP: 2
SALES (est): 173.5K **Privately Held**
SIC: 3172 Personal leather goods

(G-9199)
CONNERLEE VINEYARDS INC ✪
22913 Se 25th Pl (98075-9486)
PHONE..................................509 932-4267
EMP: 2 EST: 2018
SALES (est): 109.3K **Privately Held**
SIC: 2084 Wines

(G-9200)
CRIMSON CANVAS ARTS
4207 254th Pl Se (98029-7778)
PHONE..................................610 235-7605
Priyanka Parmanand, *Principal*
EMP: 2
SALES (est): 54.9K **Privately Held**
SIC: 2211 Canvas

(G-9201)
DIGI RESOURCES LLC
4115 205th Ave Se (98075-9600)
PHONE..................................888 775-3444
Denise Lagasse, *Opers Staff*
Elwood W Hertzog III,
EMP: 11
SALES: 900K **Privately Held**
WEB: www.digitalgiftstore.com
SIC: 3823 Digital displays of process variables

(G-9202)
DOUBLE UP LLC
22626 Ne Inglewood Hill R (98074-5011)
PHONE..................................908 398-9088
Beverly Bates, *Principal*
EMP: 2 EST: 2016
SALES (est): 62.9K **Privately Held**
SIC: 2711 Newspapers

(G-9203)
ELECTROMAGNETIC SOFTWARE
3206 218th Ave Se (98075-9539)
PHONE..................................425 557-4716
Barry Hansen, *Owner*
EMP: 2

Sammamish - King County (G-9204)

SALES (est): 142K **Privately Held**
SIC: 7372 Prepackaged software

(G-9204)
EMERSON PROCESS MANAGEMENT
3911 240th Pl Se (98029-6301)
PHONE...................................425 391-8565
EMP: 3
SALES (corp-wide): 17.4B **Publicly Held**
SIC: 3823 Industrial instrmnts msrmnt display/control process variable
HQ: Emerson Process Management Power & Water Solutions, Inc.
200 Beta Dr
Pittsburgh PA 15238
412 963-4000

(G-9205)
ETS-LINDGREN INC
22117 Ne 10th Pl (98074-6863)
PHONE...................................425 868-2558
Janet Oneil, *Branch Mgr*
EMP: 3
SALES (corp-wide): 771.5MM **Publicly Held**
SIC: 3825 Instruments to measure electricity
HQ: Ets-Lindgren Inc.
1301 Arrow Point Dr
Cedar Park TX 78613
512 531-6400

(G-9206)
FIDDLE AND FERN
3010 278th Ct Se (98075-4211)
PHONE...................................206 898-4165
Annalisa Johnson, *Administration*
EMP: 2
SALES (est): 113.9K **Privately Held**
SIC: 2844 Toilet preparations

(G-9207)
FLUID PROCESS ENGINEERING LLC
22931 Ne 27th Pl (98074-8918)
P.O. Box 2949, Redmond (98073-2949)
PHONE...................................425 868-0899
Richard Styles, *Mng Member*
EMP: 3
SALES: 1MM **Privately Held**
SIC: 3599 Amusement park equipment

(G-9208)
GEORADAR IMAGING
21418 E Main St (98074-7002)
PHONE...................................425 392-7688
Wendy Schall, *Owner*
EMP: 5
SALES: 200K **Privately Held**
WEB: www.georadarimaging.com
SIC: 3826 Infrared analytical instruments

(G-9209)
GLYCOCEPT INC
300 211th Pl Se (98074-7046)
PHONE...................................425 647-7446
Ronald Dudek, *President*
Eric Sundberg, *Vice Pres*
Beatriz Trastoy, *Vice Pres*
EMP: 3
SALES (est): 168.5K **Privately Held**
SIC: 2836 Biological products, except diagnostic

(G-9210)
GRACE AVI & LOGISTICS SUPPORT
21402 Se 16th Pl (98075-7119)
PHONE...................................425 269-9424
Mark T Richardson, *Principal*
Brian Kayner, *Principal*
EMP: 3
SALES (est): 1,000K **Privately Held**
WEB: www.grace-aviation.com
SIC: 3721 Aircraft

(G-9211)
GREENDISK INC
4404 211th Ct Ne (98074-9359)
PHONE...................................425 392-8700
David Beschen, *Principal*
EMP: 2
SALES (est): 140K **Privately Held**
SIC: 2759 Commercial printing

(G-9212)
H20 FACTOR
1340 229th Pl Ne (98074-6507)
PHONE...................................425 868-4017
Joe Kearney, *CEO*
EMP: 5
SALES (est): 196.3K **Privately Held**
SIC: 3949 Water sports equipment

(G-9213)
HALF FAMILIES ENTERPRISES LLC
20910 Ne 17th St (98074-4202)
PHONE...................................425 629-3232
EMP: 2
SALES (est): 111.4K **Privately Held**
SIC: 3651 Speaker systems

(G-9214)
HAOLIFTS INDUSTRIES
221 259th Ave Ne (98074-3478)
PHONE...................................425 836-3968
EMP: 2 EST: 2011
SALES (est): 110K **Privately Held**
SIC: 3999 Mfg Misc Products

(G-9215)
HARBOR VASCULAR INC
22445 Se 31st Pl (98075-9266)
PHONE...................................425 420-6009
Damon Peirce, *CEO*
EMP: 3
SALES (est): 122.5K **Privately Held**
SIC: 7371 3841 7389 Computer software development & applications; medical instruments & equipment, blood & bone work;

(G-9216)
HELIUM
21728 Se 3rd Pl (98074-7052)
PHONE...................................206 650-4822
Andrew Pham, *Principal*
EMP: 3
SALES (est): 123.2K **Privately Held**
SIC: 2813 Helium

(G-9217)
HEXAGON BLUE
19301 Se 16th St (98075-9615)
P.O. Box 1790, Issaquah (98027-0073)
PHONE...................................425 890-5351
Mary Jesse, *Partner*
Jennifer Cherif, *Partner*
EMP: 2
SALES (est): 160K **Privately Held**
SIC: 2741 Miscellaneous publishing

(G-9218)
I2NNOVATIONS LLC
3020 Issaqh Pine Lk Rd Se (98075-7253)
PHONE...................................425 298-3143
Vish Thirumurthy,
EMP: 2
SALES (est): 170K **Privately Held**
SIC: 8742 3672 7371 Marketing consulting services; printed circuit boards; computer software development & applications

(G-9219)
ICON CELLARS LLC
21821 Ne 30th Pl (98074-6358)
PHONE...................................425 223-7300
James Gamer, *Principal*
EMP: 4
SALES (est): 238.3K **Privately Held**
SIC: 2084 Wines

(G-9220)
INNOV8 CABIN SOLUTIONS LLC
24212 Se 21st St (98075-8164)
PHONE...................................425 241-8378
Jason Danforth,
EMP: 4
SALES (est): 252.1K **Privately Held**
SIC: 3812 Air traffic control systems & equipment, electronic

(G-9221)
J AS WINERY
25435 Se 42nd St (98029-7781)
PHONE...................................206 409-4841
Richard V Mettler, *Administration*
EMP: 4

SALES (est): 83K **Privately Held**
SIC: 2084 Wines

(G-9222)
JAYAM SOFTWARE
21324 Se 3rd St (98074-7027)
PHONE...................................425 208-6467
Karthigeyan Seetharaman, *Administration*
EMP: 2
SALES (est): 93.3K **Privately Held**
SIC: 7372 Prepackaged software

(G-9223)
JIAN WU
23121 Ne 19th Dr (98074-6585)
PHONE...................................425 706-9852
EMP: 2 EST: 2005
SALES (est): 200K **Privately Held**
SIC: 3695 Mfg Magnetic/Optical Recording Media

(G-9224)
K&M BUSINESS SYSTEMS INC
1603 248th Ave Se (98075-9450)
PHONE...................................425 557-7789
Kathy Miller, *President*
EMP: 2
SALES: 200K **Privately Held**
SIC: 3581 Automatic vending machines

(G-9225)
KAENAA CORP
Also Called: Qi-Infinity
2337 237th Pl Ne (98074-2300)
PHONE...................................425 283-3072
Sumeet Swami, *President*
EMP: 9 EST: 2011
SALES (est): 922.7K **Privately Held**
SIC: 3621 3089 Generators for storage battery chargers; battery cases, plastic or plastic combination

(G-9226)
KNOX CELLARS
Also Called: Knox Cellars Nativ Pollinators
4601 244th Pl Se (98029-6539)
PHONE...................................425 392-7536
Lisa Knovich, *Partner*
EMP: 2
SALES (est): 87.2K **Privately Held**
SIC: 3999 Beekeepers' supplies

(G-9227)
KUO SOFTWARE LLC
27906 Se 24th Way (98075-4119)
PHONE...................................425 961-0197
Guy Kuo, *Principal*
EMP: 2
SALES (est): 132.9K **Privately Held**
SIC: 7372 Prepackaged software

(G-9228)
L3 SYSTEMS INC
21401 Se 37th St (98075-9281)
P.O. Box 2954, Redmond (98073-2954)
PHONE...................................425 836-5438
Larry M Bateman, *President*
Larry Bateman, *President*
EMP: 2
SALES: 260K **Privately Held**
WEB: www.l3sys.com
SIC: 3699 Electrical equipment & supplies

(G-9229)
MAGAZINE FOR GIGGING MUSICANS
23629 Ne 7th Ct (98074-3616)
PHONE...................................425 503-0421
Arny Bailey, *Principal*
EMP: 2
SALES (est): 73.1K **Privately Held**
SIC: 2721 Periodicals

(G-9230)
MARKETECH
Also Called: Write Spark
558 241st Ln Se (98074-3681)
PHONE...................................425 391-1886
Janice King, *Owner*
EMP: 3
SALES (est): 140K **Privately Held**
WEB: www.writespark.com
SIC: 2741 Miscellaneous publishing

(G-9231)
MATERSMOST SOFTWARE LLC
1312 270th Way Se (98075-5970)
PHONE...................................425 392-6165
Aiwen Guo, *Principal*
EMP: 3
SALES (est): 297.1K **Privately Held**
SIC: 7372 Prepackaged software

(G-9232)
MCNERNEY ENTERPRISES LLC
Also Called: Merrie & Macs
253 E Lk Smmmish Pkwy Se (98074-3812)
PHONE...................................206 850-5023
Charles McNerney,
EMP: 2
SALES (est): 62.3K **Privately Held**
SIC: 2033 Barbecue sauce: packaged in cans, jars, etc.

(G-9233)
MICROSOFT CORPORATION
23436 Ne 6th Pl (98074-3655)
PHONE...................................425 281-6768
David Lalor, *Branch Mgr*
EMP: 2
SALES (corp-wide): 110.3B **Publicly Held**
SIC: 7372 Prepackaged software
PA: Microsoft Corporation
1 Microsoft Way
Redmond WA 98052
425 882-8080

(G-9234)
MICROSOFT CORPORATION
20542 Ne 26th St (98074-4350)
PHONE...................................425 633-4929
John Westworth, *Branch Mgr*
EMP: 2
SALES (corp-wide): 110.3B **Publicly Held**
SIC: 7372 Prepackaged software
PA: Microsoft Corporation
1 Microsoft Way
Redmond WA 98052
425 882-8080

(G-9235)
MODELING DYNAMICS INC
2721 226th Ave Ne (98075-9531)
PHONE...................................425 392-2262
W R Wright, *CEO*
EMP: 2
SALES: 300K **Privately Held**
SIC: 7372 Prepackaged software

(G-9236)
NORCOM INC
24608 Ne 3rd Pl (98074-3472)
PHONE...................................425 868-9973
Thomas Bozarth, *President*
EMP: 2
SALES (est): 223.7K **Privately Held**
WEB: www.norcom-inc.com
SIC: 7372 Prepackaged software

(G-9237)
NORTH SKY GAMES INC
Also Called: Northern Sky Games
3741 246th Ave Se (98029-6561)
PHONE...................................425 283-9647
Nicolas Payette, *President*
EMP: 2
SALES (est): 62.1K **Privately Held**
SIC: 7372 Home entertainment computer software

(G-9238)
OE TWO INDUSTRIES LLC
3211 216th Ct Se (98075-9546)
PHONE...................................425 657-0958
John Welliver, *Principal*
EMP: 2
SALES (est): 86.1K **Privately Held**
SIC: 3999 Manufacturing industries

(G-9239)
OKA WOODWORKS INC
22840 Ne 26th St (98074-8936)
PHONE...................................425 221-2573
Jonathan T Oka, *President*
EMP: 8
SALES: 500K **Privately Held**
SIC: 2431 Millwork

GEOGRAPHIC SECTION

Seatac - King County (G-9273)

(G-9240)
PETROGAS LIFT TECH LLC
2317 Sahalee Dr E (98074-6317)
PHONE..................................425 891-7403
Valentin Ispas, *Administration*
EMP: 2
SALES (est): 82.4K Privately Held
SIC: 1389 Oil field services

(G-9241)
PICOTE SOLUTIONS INC
20810 Se 18th Pl (98075-9228)
PHONE..................................425 505-0646
Jutta Ehder-Lokkinen, *President*
Katka Wilkinson, *Vice Pres*
EMP: 10
SALES (est): 1.1MM Privately Held
SIC: 3423 Plumbers' hand tools

(G-9242)
PLATEAU JEWELERS INC
2830 228th Ave Se Ste B (98075-9300)
PHONE..................................425 313-0657
Kelly Jensen, *President*
Susan Jensen, *Vice Pres*
EMP: 8
SQ FT: 1,000
SALES (est): 1.2MM Privately Held
WEB: www.plateaujewelers.com
SIC: 5944 3961 Jewelry, precious stones & precious metals; costume jewelry, ex. precious metal & semiprecious stones

(G-9243)
REFRELENT SOFTWARE LAB
4230 194th Pl Ne (98074-4659)
PHONE..................................425 898-9657
Evgeny Veselov, *Principal*
EMP: 2
SALES (est): 76.2K Privately Held
SIC: 7372 Prepackaged software

(G-9244)
S & G ENGRAVING
22539 Ne 18th St (98074-6511)
PHONE..................................425 868-4169
Stanley M White, *Owner*
EMP: 2
SALES (est): 127.1K Privately Held
SIC: 2796 Engraving platemaking services

(G-9245)
SAMMAMISH
22739 Se 29th St (98075-9532)
PHONE..................................425 295-7300
EMP: 2
SALES (est): 85.9K Privately Held
SIC: 3571 Personal computers (microcomputers)

(G-9246)
SAVOTTA TECH LLC
1234 244th Pl Se (98075-6087)
PHONE..................................425 505-9951
Antti Akkanen, *CEO*
EMP: 3
SALES: 25K Privately Held
SIC: 7372 7389 Application computer software;

(G-9247)
SHILSHOLE BIOSCIENCE INC
27213 Se 27th St (98075-7944)
PHONE..................................206 459-8341
Craig Philips, *Principal*
EMP: 3 **EST:** 2017
SALES (est): 123.2K Privately Held
SIC: 2834 Chlorination tablets & kits (water purification)

(G-9248)
SIMPATICO CELLARS
1718 224th Ct Ne (98074-4157)
PHONE..................................408 667-9658
EMP: 2
SALES (est): 62.3K Privately Held
SIC: 2084 Wines, brandy & brandy spirits

(G-9249)
STONEY CREEK BREWING CO LLC
19186 Ne 43rd Ct (98074-4655)
PHONE..................................425 836-0958
Catherine M Car, *Administration*
Catherine Carothers, *Administration*
EMP: 5
SALES (est): 407.3K Privately Held
SIC: 2082 2084 Malt beverages; wines

(G-9250)
STRATTON WOODWORKS
420 222nd Ave Ne (98074-7118)
PHONE..................................425 968-2455
Steven Stratton, *Principal*
EMP: 4
SALES (est): 402.9K Privately Held
SIC: 2431 Millwork

(G-9251)
SWEATER STONE INC
21103 Se 24th St (98075-7444)
P.O. Box 467, Issaquah (98027-0018)
PHONE..................................425 392-2747
Fred Menath, *President*
EMP: 4
SQ FT: 3,000
SALES (est): 364.8K Privately Held
WEB: www.sweaterstone.com
SIC: 3999 Novelties, bric-a-brac & hobby kits

(G-9252)
THERAPEUTAE PUBLISHING LLC
414 235th Ave Ne (98074-7224)
PHONE..................................425 242-1580
EMP: 2 **EST:** 2012
SALES (est): 110K Privately Held
SIC: 2741 Misc Publishing

(G-9253)
THINKING MAN SOFTWARE CORP
26518 Se 19th Ct (98075-7973)
PHONE..................................425 313-0607
Kris Chambers, *Principal*
EMP: 4
SALES (est): 231.7K Privately Held
SIC: 7372 Prepackaged software

(G-9254)
TINMAN SOFTWARE
22019 Ne 15th St (98074-6820)
PHONE..................................425 417-2142
Vincent Erickson, *Owner*
EMP: 2 **EST:** 2012
SALES (est): 104.8K Privately Held
SIC: 7372 Prepackaged software

(G-9255)
TINMAN SYSTEMS INC
22618 Se 47th Pl (98075-6808)
PHONE..................................425 802-9035
Karl Hirsch, *President*
Al Hirsch, *Vice Pres*
EMP: 2
SALES (est): 140.3K Privately Held
SIC: 7372 Prepackaged software

(G-9256)
V 4 SOFTWARE LLC
4271 E Lake Sammamish (98075)
PHONE..................................813 870-6666
Scott Miller,
EMP: 2
SALES (est): 56.5K Privately Held
SIC: 7372 Prepackaged software

(G-9257)
VIAR VISUAL COMMUNICATIONS
20867 Se 20th St (98075-7406)
PHONE..................................425 391-8443
Jorge Avila, *Principal*
EMP: 2 **EST:** 2014
SQ FT: 1,600
SALES (est): 95.2K Privately Held
SIC: 4899 5046 2741 3993 Data communication services; signs, electrical; posters: publishing & printing; signs & advertising specialties; letters for signs, metal; signs, except electric

(G-9258)
WHITE CELLARS
1307 240th Way Se (98075-8155)
PHONE..................................425 246-1419
Gus White, *Principal*
EMP: 2 **EST:** 2010

SALES (est): 105.4K Privately Held
SIC: 2084 Wines

(G-9259)
WOODONE-US CORP
23209 Se 27th St (98075-9458)
PHONE..................................206 850-0230
Bruce Wilson Connally, *President*
EMP: 2
SALES (est): 240K Privately Held
SIC: 3537 Trucks: freight, baggage, etc.: industrial, except mining

(G-9260)
WWW QUALITYLACECOM
2031 248th Pl Se (98075-6052)
PHONE..................................425 996-0523
Sunil Goparaju, *Principal*
◆ **EMP:** 2
SALES (est): 138.5K Privately Held
SIC: 3425 Saws, hand: metalworking or woodworking

(G-9261)
XERITON CORPORATION
Also Called: Bluephone
336 228th Ave Ne Ste 301 (98074-7290)
PHONE..................................425 369-2279
David Plummer, *CEO*
EMP: 25
SQ FT: 3,500
SALES (est): 1.5MM Privately Held
WEB: www.sharewareonline.com
SIC: 7372 Prepackaged software

(G-9262)
ZSOLUTIONZ LLC
415 210th Pl Se (98074-7083)
PHONE..................................425 502-6970
Sunil Koduri, *CEO*
Shalani Koduri, *COO*
EMP: 3 **EST:** 2012
SQ FT: 150
SALES (est): 150K Privately Held
SIC: 7373 7379 7372 7371 Systems software development services; computer related consulting services; ; application computer software; computer software development & applications

Seabeck
Kitsap County

(G-9263)
CUSTOM MOLDING CO INC
14812 Nw Eagles View Dr (98380-8630)
PHONE..................................360 830-0108
Jerry Mercogliano, *President*
EMP: 10 **EST:** 1952
SQ FT: 12,000
SALES: 600K Privately Held
SIC: 2431 Moldings, wood: unfinished & prefinished

(G-9264)
GO VERTICAL CORPORATION
14881 Nw Goeske Ln (98380-9261)
PHONE..................................360 830-5447
EMP: 2
SALES (est): 132.8K Privately Held
SIC: 2591 Mfg Drapery Hardware/Blinds

(G-9265)
JAUCH QUARTZ AMERICA INC
14601 Nw Arabian Way (98380-8806)
PHONE..................................360 633-7200
Nandor Forgacs, *President*
Thomas Vaeth, *Treasurer*
Kayla Cheney, *Marketing Staff*
Christian Schwenk, *Admin Sec*
EMP: 2
SALES (est): 664.7K Privately Held
SIC: 5065 3679 Electronic parts; quartz crystals, for electronic application

(G-9266)
KITSAP VINYL DECK & RAIL LLC
15712 Nw Hite Center Rd (98380-9200)
P.O. Box 871 (98380-0871)
PHONE..................................360 830-5959
Bria Steele, *President*
EMP: 2

SALES (est): 184.8K Privately Held
SIC: 1521 3446 1799 Patio & deck construction & repair; stairs, staircases, stair treads: prefabricated metal; waterproofing

(G-9267)
LEEWARD INDUSTRIES INC
8475 Leeward Ave Nw (98380-8818)
PHONE..................................360 830-0765
Michael Hancock, *Principal*
EMP: 2
SALES (est): 101.1K Privately Held
SIC: 3999 Manufacturing industries

(G-9268)
MAGIC MOUNTAINS SERVICES INC
Also Called: Signs
10078 Brush Arbor Ln Nw (98380-9700)
PHONE..................................360 830-0634
Mary Richardson, *President*
EMP: 2
SALES: 80K Privately Held
SIC: 3993 Signs & advertising specialties

(G-9269)
NORTHWEST CUSTOM PODIUMS INC
667 Wyatt Ln W (98380-9404)
PHONE..................................360 830-5858
Chris Mutchler, *Principal*
EMP: 2
SALES (est): 154.6K Privately Held
SIC: 2431 Millwork

(G-9270)
R RAMJET INC
11400 Nw Quiet Wtrs Way N (98380-8722)
P.O. Box 559 (98380-0559)
PHONE..................................541 312-1648
EMP: 2
SALES (est): 77.4K Privately Held
SIC: 3812 Mfg Search/Navigation Equipment

Seatac
King County

(G-9271)
A ONE ORNAMENTAL IRON WORKS
19232 39th Ave S (98188-5316)
PHONE..................................206 622-4033
Gordon Jarnig, *President*
EMP: 5
SQ FT: 5,700
SALES (est): 725.8K Privately Held
SIC: 3446 Architectural metalwork

(G-9272)
AHTNA ENGINEERING SERVICES LLC
19540 Intl Blvd Ste 201 (98188-5474)
PHONE..................................425 864-1695
Bernie Wong,
Krystal Nelson,
EMP: 99
SALES: 950K
SALES (corp-wide): 23.3MM Privately Held
SIC: 8711 3825 Engineering services; instruments to measure electricity
PA: Ahtna Engineering Services Llc
110 W 38th Ave Ste 200a
Anchorage AK 99503
907 646-2969

(G-9273)
ATOMIC CRATE & CASE INC
18927 16th Ave S (98188-5104)
PHONE..................................425 264-0336
Kenneth Moninski, *President*
EMP: 7
SALES (est): 313.6K Privately Held
SIC: 2449 Rectangular boxes & crates, wood

Seatac - King County (G-9274)

(G-9274)
BFC ARCHITECTURAL METALS INC
19034 Des Moines Mem Dr S (98148-1930)
PHONE.................................206 763-0530
Michael Cochran, *President*
Pamela Evans-Cochran, *Vice Pres*
EMP: 12
SALES (est): 1.6MM **Privately Held**
WEB: www.bfcmetals.com
SIC: 2542 3446 Partitions & fixtures, except wood; ornamental metalwork

(G-9275)
BOEING COMMERCIAL AIRPLANES
2201 S 142nd St (98168-3713)
P.O. Box 3707, Seattle (98124-2207)
PHONE.................................206 662-9615
EMP: 7
SALES: 317.1K **Privately Held**
SIC: 3721 Aircraft

(G-9276)
BOEING COMPANY
2201 S 142nd St W10 (98168-3713)
PHONE.................................206 662-9615
Darce Lamb, *President*
Mary M Lemmerman, *Business Anlyst*
Carolyn Grecia, *Manager*
Van Zeitz, *Manager*
Ric C Ruhlman, *Agent*
EMP: 1005
SALES (corp-wide): 101.1B **Publicly Held**
SIC: 3721 3663 Airplanes, fixed or rotary wing; radio & TV communications equipment
PA: The Boeing Company
100 N Riverside Plz
Chicago IL 60606
312 544-2000

(G-9277)
BOEING COMPANY
2141 S 211th St (98198-5179)
PHONE.................................253 657-0675
EMP: 2
SALES (est): 117.4K **Privately Held**
SIC: 3721 Aircraft

(G-9278)
BOEING COMPANY
17930 International Blvd (98188-4231)
PHONE.................................312 544-2000
Tom Goldade, *Branch Mgr*
Petra Critchfield, *Manager*
Lorrie Sivich, *Manager*
Danny Miller, *Administration*
EMP: 996
SALES (corp-wide): 101.1B **Publicly Held**
SIC: 3721 Airplanes, fixed or rotary wing
PA: The Boeing Company
100 N Riverside Plz
Chicago IL 60606
312 544-2000

(G-9279)
BUCKEYE INTERNATIONAL INC
Also Called: Buckeye Cleaning Center
18902 13th Pl S (98148-2340)
PHONE.................................206 575-1185
Troy Reiter, *Branch Mgr*
EMP: 3
SALES (corp-wide): 121.5MM **Privately Held**
WEB: www.buckeyeinternational.com
SIC: 2842 2841 2899 2812 Specialty cleaning preparations; detergents, synthetic organic or inorganic alkaline; chemical preparations; alkalies & chlorine
PA: Buckeye International, Inc.
2700 Wagner Pl
Maryland Heights MO 63043
314 291-1900

(G-9280)
DAVINCIS WORKSHOP LLC
18040 Des Moines Mem Dr S (98148-1941)
PHONE.................................206 244-7000
Kurt Nordquist,
EMP: 5
SALES: 390K **Privately Held**
WEB: www.davincis.org
SIC: 3541 Electrolytic metal cutting machine tools

(G-9281)
DRAGONDYNE PUBLISHING
13625 26th Pl S (98168-3807)
PHONE.................................206 619-1577
Sheri Turnley, *Principal*
EMP: 4
SALES (est): 57.1K **Privately Held**
SIC: 2741 Miscellaneous publishing

(G-9282)
EX OFFICIO LLC
17801 International Blvd (98158-1202)
PHONE.................................206 242-9696
Jim Stoohey, *Manager*
EMP: 3
SALES (corp-wide): 8.6B **Publicly Held**
SIC: 2329 Riding clothes:, men's, youths' & boys'
HQ: Ex Officio Llc
4202 6th Ave S Unit Main
Seattle WA 98108
206 283-1471

(G-9283)
FAIRBANKS MORSE LLC
Also Called: Fairbanks Morse Engine
18926 13th Pl S (98148-2387)
PHONE.................................206 246-8133
Thomas Stull, *Manager*
EMP: 18
SALES (corp-wide): 1.5B **Publicly Held**
SIC: 3519 Diesel, semi-diesel or duel-fuel engines, including marine
HQ: Fairbanks Morse, Llc
701 White Ave
Beloit WI 53511
800 356-6955

(G-9284)
FILSON MANUFACTURING INC
18923 16th Ave S (98188-5104)
PHONE.................................206 805-3730
EMP: 2
SALES (est): 97.7K **Privately Held**
SIC: 2389 Apparel & accessories

(G-9285)
GIANT METALS INC
Also Called: Giant Resources Co.
19280 11th Pl S Apt 3 (98148-2273)
PHONE.................................206 592-0963
Lin Xie, *President*
EMP: 7
SQ FT: 4,000
SALES: 2MM **Privately Held**
WEB: www.giantmetals.com
SIC: 5015 1011 5093 5052 Automotive supplies, used; iron ores; metal scrap & waste materials; coal & coke

(G-9286)
HEARTHSIDE USA LLC
2231 S 208th St Ste D (98198-5174)
PHONE.................................206 745-0850
EMP: 7 **Privately Held**
SIC: 2099 Food preparations
HQ: Hearthside Usa, Llc
3333 Finley Rd Ste 800
Downers Grove IL 60515
978 716-2530

(G-9287)
KARDIEL INC
2021 S 208th St (98198-5175)
PHONE.................................916 999-1050
Jason Paul Kilmer, *CEO*
◆ **EMP:** 9
SALES (est): 1.8MM **Privately Held**
SIC: 2521 Wood office chairs, benches & stools

(G-9288)
LES BOULANGERS ASSOCIES INC
18842 13th Pl S (98148-2342)
PHONE.................................206 241-9343
Michel Robert, *President*
Fattima Xasan, *Prdtn Mgr*
Amedeo Cocco, *Purch Mgr*
Chantal Robert, *Marketing Staff*
Robert Nathe, *Manager*
EMP: 47
SQ FT: 30,000
SALES (est): 7.3MM **Privately Held**
WEB: www.lba-inc.com
SIC: 2053 2051 Frozen bakery products, except bread; bread, cake & related products

(G-9289)
MATSUSHITA AVIONICS CO
Also Called: Panasonic Avionics
18601 28th Ave S Ste 108 (98158-1302)
PHONE.................................206 246-6200
Fred Pankey, *Manager*
EMP: 2
SALES (est): 159.4K **Privately Held**
SIC: 3728 Aircraft power transmission equipment

(G-9290)
MODEL A WHEEL COLORS
1400 S 192nd St (98148-2314)
PHONE.................................206 264-4944
EMP: 2
SALES (est): 151.5K **Privately Held**
SIC: 3714 Motor vehicle parts & accessories

(G-9291)
MONROE MACHINED PRODUCTS INC
Also Called: Unite Stares Arospace
1422 S 192nd St (98148-2314)
PHONE.................................206 242-4898
Bhrett A Monroe, *President*
Boyd L Monroe, *Vice Pres*
EMP: 30
SQ FT: 40,000
SALES: 4MM **Privately Held**
WEB: www.monroemachinedproducts.com
SIC: 3599 3429 3721 Machine shop, jobbing & repair; manufactured hardware (general); aircraft

(G-9292)
MUSEUM RESOURCE LLC
19102 Des Moines Mem Dr S (98148-1932)
PHONE.................................206 547-4047
Doug Tillotson, *Mng Member*
Dale Naachand,
EMP: 7
SALES: 800K **Privately Held**
SIC: 2441 2542 Cases, wood; cabinets: show, display or storage: except wood

(G-9293)
NORTHWEST PAPER BOX MFRS INC
Also Called: Universal Paper Box
855 S 192nd St Ste 100 (98148-2294)
PHONE.................................206 782-7105
EMP: 26
SALES (corp-wide): 13.9MM **Privately Held**
SIC: 2652 3089 Setup paperboard boxes; boxes, plastic
PA: Northwest Paper Box Mfrs., Inc.
5617 N Basin Ave
Portland OR 97217
503 240-2800

(G-9294)
NOVA GRAPHICS
14427 26th Ave S (98168-4209)
PHONE.................................206 248-3489
Robert Laughlin, *President*
EMP: 5
SALES (est): 370K **Privately Held**
SIC: 2759 Commercial printing

(G-9295)
OLSEN CABINET & MILLWORK
12860 23rd Ave S (98168-3057)
PHONE.................................206 242-1188
Ace W Elmer, *Owner*
EMP: 3
SQ FT: 5,000
SALES (est): 238.2K **Privately Held**
SIC: 2431 Millwork

(G-9296)
OPPORTUNITY INTERACTIVE INC
19604 Intl Blvd Ste 101 (98188-5454)
PHONE.................................206 870-1880
Aaron Schuh, *President*
Greg Gargan, *Vice Pres*
EMP: 10
SALES (est): 1.2MM **Privately Held**
SIC: 7372 Business oriented computer software

(G-9297)
PACCAR INC
Also Called: Paccar Seatac
1500 S 184th St (98158-1304)
PHONE.................................206 214-0418
EMP: 2
SALES (corp-wide): 23.5B **Publicly Held**
SIC: 3711 Motor vehicles & car bodies
PA: Paccar Inc
777 106th Ave Ne
Bellevue WA 98004
425 468-7400

(G-9298)
PACIFIC NORTHWEST INDUSTRIES
21414 30th Ave S (98198-6030)
PHONE.................................206 841-3144
EMP: 2
SALES (est): 130.2K **Privately Held**
SIC: 3999 Manufacturing industries

(G-9299)
PICKENS FUEL CORP
19425 28th Ave S (98188-5124)
PHONE.................................206 824-8181
Chris Bailey, *Principal*
EMP: 3 EST: 2012
SALES (est): 163.7K **Privately Held**
SIC: 2869 Fuels

(G-9300)
PROSHOPPERS NW
17604 41st Ave S (98188-4150)
PHONE.................................206 852-1127
Dan Winters, *Owner*
EMP: 2 EST: 2013
SALES (est): 186.8K **Privately Held**
SIC: 3171 Handbags, women's

(G-9301)
QUALITY MACHINE & HYDRAULIC
19202 Des Moines Mem Dr S (98148-2240)
PHONE.................................206 244-5674
Milo Mateer Jr, *President*
EMP: 5
SQ FT: 11,000
SALES (est): 560.2K **Privately Held**
SIC: 3599 Machine shop, jobbing & repair

(G-9302)
QUALITY METAL SPINNING CO
4031 S 168th St (98188-3161)
PHONE.................................206 242-6751
Douglas Vincent, *Owner*
Susan Vincent, *Co-Owner*
EMP: 2 EST: 1952
SQ FT: 1,800
SALES (est): 159.6K **Privately Held**
SIC: 3469 Spinning metal for the trade

(G-9303)
SEATTLE CUSTOM PRINTING
18938 13th Pl S (98148-2340)
PHONE.................................206 268-0443
EMP: 2
SALES (est): 83.9K **Privately Held**
SIC: 2752 Commercial printing, lithographic

(G-9304)
SHOW QUALITY METAL FINISH
18924 13th Pl S (98148-2340)
PHONE.................................206 762-6717
EMP: 5
SALES (est): 448K **Privately Held**
SIC: 3471 Plating And Polishing

GEOGRAPHIC SECTION Seattle - King County (G-9338)

(G-9305)
SHOW QUALITY METAL FINISHING
18924 13th Pl S (98148-2340)
PHONE..................206 762-6717
Donald L Meth Jr, *President*
EMP: 4
SQ FT: 7,000
SALES (est): 446.9K **Privately Held**
SIC: 3471 Finishing, metals or formed products; plating of metals or formed products

(G-9306)
SMARTE CARTE INC
17801 International Blvd (98158-1202)
PHONE..................206 431-0844
Robert Prow, *Branch Mgr*
EMP: 4 **Privately Held**
SIC: 2531 School furniture
HQ: Smarte Carte, Inc.
 912 W 12th St
 Dallas TX 75208
 214 946-4000

(G-9307)
TRANSPORT LOGISTICS INC
19600 Intl Blvd Ste 102 (98188-5481)
PHONE..................206 824-0667
EMP: 2 EST: 2016
SALES (est): 91.5K **Privately Held**
SIC: 3577 Computer peripheral equipment

(G-9308)
UNITED STARS AEROSPACE INC
1422 S 192nd St (98148-2314)
PHONE..................253 859-4540
Richard E Harig, *President*
David Schmitt, *Corp Secy*
EMP: 30
SQ FT: 30,000
SALES (est): 2.6MM
SALES (corp-wide): 0 **Privately Held**
WEB: www.unitedstarsaerospace.com
SIC: 3599 Machine shop, jobbing & repair
PA: United Stars, Inc.
 1546 Henry Ave
 Beloit WI 53511
 608 368-4625

(G-9309)
VUE INTERNATIONALK LTD
3237 S 202nd St (98198-5749)
PHONE..................206 878-1061
GE Vue, *Owner*
Anne Vue, *Owner*
EMP: 2
SALES (est): 89.6K **Privately Held**
SIC: 2329 Riding clothes:, men's, youths' & boys'

(G-9310)
WOODWORKS CNSTR & CABINETS
17019 33rd Ave S (98188-4445)
PHONE..................253 846-1918
Dennis L Mc Connell, *Owner*
EMP: 3
SALES (est): 190K **Privately Held**
SIC: 2434 Wood kitchen cabinets

(G-9311)
WORLDWIDE BOTANICALS INC
Also Called: Katharsis
4463 S 175th St (98188-3643)
PHONE..................206 518-1878
Bryan Hieronymus, *CEO*
EMP: 5 EST: 2012
SALES (est): 371K **Privately Held**
SIC: 2833 Organic medicinal chemicals: bulk, uncompounded

(G-9312)
X L F AEROSPACE LLC
19550 Intl Blvd Ste 205 (98188-5436)
PHONE..................206 592-2249
EMP: 2
SALES (est): 100.2K **Privately Held**
SIC: 3721 Aircraft

(G-9313)
XANFAB INC
19108 Des Moines Mem Dr (98148-1932)
PHONE..................206 717-2185
Christopher Reddy,
EMP: 5 EST: 2016
SALES (est): 645.1K **Privately Held**
SIC: 3672 Printed circuit boards

Seattle
King County

(G-9314)
1 WORLD GLOBES & MAPS LLC
Also Called: 1-World Globes
1605 S Jackson St (98144-2110)
PHONE..................206 781-1400
Paul Norrell, *Marketing Staff*
Davia Bailey,
▲ EMP: 6
SQ FT: 5,000
SALES (est): 909.2K **Privately Held**
WEB: www.1worldglobes.com
SIC: 5999 2741 Maps & charts; posters: publishing & printing, atlas, map & guide publishing; maps: publishing & printing

(G-9315)
11 TIMES CREATIVE LLC
6609 Woodlawn Ave N (98103-5429)
PHONE..................206 523-2985
Carly Lennstrom, *Principal*
EMP: 2
SALES (est): 62.9K **Privately Held**
SIC: 2711 Newspapers

(G-9316)
12 SCENTS
6311 Fauntleroy Way Sw (98136-1817)
PHONE..................206 588-0314
Lara Gustavson, *Principal*
EMP: 3 EST: 2015
SALES (est): 205.4K **Privately Held**
SIC: 2844 Toilet preparations

(G-9317)
12TH AVENUE IRON INC
1423 S Dearborn St (98144-2801)
PHONE..................206 325-0792
Stephen Marks, *President*
Mark Christiansen, *Vice Pres*
EMP: 5
SALES: 800K **Privately Held**
SIC: 3462 Iron & steel forgings

(G-9318)
2 C MEDIA LLC
10047 38th Ave Ne (98125-7812)
PHONE..................206 522-7211
Ed Messerly,
EMP: 25
SALES (est): 2.3MM **Privately Held**
WEB: www.cellcjb.cjb.net
SIC: 7379 7372 7819 Computer related consulting services; prepackaged software; video tape or disk reproduction

(G-9319)
206 INDUSTRIES LLC
1248 Ne 88th St (98115-3127)
PHONE..................206 390-8449
Andrew Oakley, *Principal*
EMP: 3
SALES (est): 178.5K **Privately Held**
SIC: 3999 Manufacturing industries

(G-9320)
2X4 INDUSTRIES
208 Ne 44th St (98105-6113)
PHONE..................253 205-0359
Aaron Dukehart, *Principal*
EMP: 3
SALES (est): 211K **Privately Held**
SIC: 3999 Manufacturing industries

(G-9321)
3 HOWLS
426 S Massachusetts St (98134-1517)
PHONE..................206 747-8400
Will Maschmeier, *Owner*
EMP: 4
SALES (est): 276.5K **Privately Held**
SIC: 2085 Distilled & blended liquors

(G-9322)
4M SIGMA CORPORATION
1900 W Emerson Pl Ste 208 (98119-1649)
P.O. Box 99330 (98139-0330)
PHONE..................206 285-9181
John Pauli, *President*
▼ EMP: 4
SQ FT: 1,700
SALES (est): 400K **Privately Held**
SIC: 3577 8711 Computer peripheral equipment; consulting engineer

(G-9323)
4R AVIATION LLC
14 W Roy St (98119-3828)
PHONE..................206 336-9415
Paul Riddell, *Principal*
EMP: 2
SALES (est): 142.3K **Privately Held**
SIC: 3721 Research & development on aircraft by the manufacturer

(G-9324)
5 BY 5 SOFTWARE VENTURES LTD
8023 18th Ave Ne (98115-4427)
PHONE..................206 779-6234
Barry Varga, *Principal*
EMP: 2
SALES (est): 56.5K **Privately Held**
SIC: 7372 Prepackaged software

(G-9325)
613 INDUSTRIES INC
4726 11th Ave Ne Apt 403 (98105-4679)
PHONE..................612 823-3606
EMP: 2
SALES (est): 100.6K **Privately Held**
SIC: 3999 Manufacturing industries

(G-9326)
A & A PRINTING INC
222 S Orcas St (98108-2441)
PHONE..................206 285-1700
Atef Matni, *President*
Aida Matni, *Corp Secy*
EMP: 23
SQ FT: 6,500
SALES (est): 3.7MM **Privately Held**
SIC: 2752 Lithographing on metal; commercial printing, offset

(G-9327)
A WELL BALANCED HOME LLC
Also Called: Barf Boutique, The
24 Roy St 474 (98109-4018)
PHONE..................206 280-5532
Kelli Lee,
EMP: 2
SALES (est): 262.8K **Privately Held**
SIC: 2673 5047 5947 Bags: plastic, laminated & coated; medical equipment & supplies; gift, novelty & souvenir shop

(G-9328)
AAAB CONSULTING LLC
217 1st Ave S Unit 4003 (98194-9401)
PHONE..................206 612-7041
Lon Israely,
EMP: 2
SALES: 2MM **Privately Held**
SIC: 7382 7372 Security systems services; business oriented computer software

(G-9329)
AACO INCORPORATED
9626 Rainier Ave S (98118-5935)
PHONE..................206 722-1571
Davis Crone, *President*
Leslee Lemka, *General Mgr*
EMP: 8 EST: 1980
SALES (est): 920K **Privately Held**
SIC: 3812 Aircraft/aerospace flight instruments & guidance systems

(G-9330)
AAIRE PARTICLE CONTROL CO INC
420 S 96th St Ste 25 (98108-4925)
P.O. Box 58262 (98138-1262)
PHONE..................206 767-6692
John Burrage, *President*
EMP: 5
SQ FT: 1,400
SALES: 250K **Privately Held**
SIC: 3564 7699 Filters, air: furnaces, air conditioning equipment, etc.; filter cleaning

(G-9331)
AASTHA INC
Also Called: Seattle Printing
105 Yesler Way (98104-2525)
PHONE..................206 382-4118
EMP: 4
SQ FT: 2,500
SALES (est): 400K **Privately Held**
SIC: 2759 Commercial Printing

(G-9332)
ABB INSTALLATION PRODUCTS INC
1101 N Northlake Way # 101 (98103-8950)
PHONE..................206 548-1595
Mike Coccaro, *Branch Mgr*
EMP: 25
SALES (corp-wide): 36.4B **Privately Held**
WEB: www.tnb.com
SIC: 3643 Connectors & terminals for electrical devices
HQ: Abb Installation Products Inc.
 860 Ridge Lake Blvd
 Memphis TN 38120
 901 252-5000

(G-9333)
ABCD MARINE
346 Nw 89th St (98117-2103)
PHONE..................206 527-3428
EMP: 2
SALES: 120K **Privately Held**
SIC: 3731 Shipbuilding/Repairing

(G-9334)
ABRACADABRA PRINTING INC
6250 Stanley Ave S (98108-2812)
PHONE..................206 343-9087
Joe Roberson, *President*
Kevin Graves, *General Mgr*
Mel Roberson, *Vice Pres*
Nancy Roberson, *Treasurer*
EMP: 6
SQ FT: 1,900
SALES: 450K **Privately Held**
WEB: www.abracadabraprinting.com
SIC: 2752 3993 2759 Commercial printing, offset; advertising novelties; commercial printing

(G-9335)
ABSOLUTE SPORTSWEAR
1900 W Nickerson St # 213 (98119-1661)
PHONE..................206 890-1531
Steve King, *Principal*
EMP: 2 EST: 2001
SALES (est): 95.3K **Privately Held**
SIC: 2759 Commercial printing

(G-9336)
ACCLAIM SIGN & DISPLAY PARTNER
1149 Nw 52nd St (98107-5130)
PHONE..................206 706-3900
Rose Waterman, *Owner*
James Crichfield, *Graphic Designe*
EMP: 8 EST: 2011
SALES (est): 802.5K **Privately Held**
SIC: 3993 Electric signs

(G-9337)
ACCORDENT TECHNOLOGIES INC
6905 39th Ave Sw (98136-1906)
PHONE..................310 374-7491
EMP: 16
SALES (corp-wide): 856.9MM **Publicly Held**
SIC: 7372 Computer Software Development
HQ: Accordent Technologies, Inc.
 300 N Cntntl Blvd Ste 200
 El Segundo CA 90245
 310 374-7491

(G-9338)
ACCURATE SURFACE GRINDING
430 S 96th St Ste 1 (98108-4926)
PHONE..................206 762-5205

Seattle - King County (G-9339)

Peter Radunovich, *Owner*
Steve Rudunovich, *Co-Owner*
EMP: 2
SQ FT: 1,750
SALES (est): 218.5K **Privately Held**
SIC: 3531 Surfacers, concrete grinding

(G-9339)
ACCURATE TOOL & DIE INC
11291 35th Ave Sw (98146-1802)
PHONE...............................206 244-0745
Donald Larsen, *CEO*
John Larsen, *President*
EMP: 11
SQ FT: 1,000
SALES (est): 1.9MM **Privately Held**
SIC: 3599 Machine shop, jobbing & repair

(G-9340)
ACE GALVANIZING INC (PA)
429 S 96th St (98108-4995)
PHONE...............................206 762-0330
David Breiwick, *President*
Loren McConnell, *Principal*
Corine Breiwick, *Admin Sec*
EMP: 40
SQ FT: 37,000
SALES (est): 5.7MM **Privately Held**
SIC: 3479 Galvanizing of iron, steel or end-formed products; painting, coating & hot dipping

(G-9341)
ACEFACE PRINTING
4333 Leary Way Nw (98107-4538)
PHONE...............................206 427-2272
EMP: 2 **EST:** 2008
SALES (est): 110K **Privately Held**
SIC: 2752 Lithographic Commercial Printing

(G-9342)
ACHIEVE LIFE SCIENCES INC
520 Pike St Ste 2250 (98101-4013)
PHONE...............................425 686-1500
Richard Stewart, *CEO*
EMP: 2
SALES (corp-wide): 3.7MM **Privately Held**
SIC: 2834 Pharmaceutical preparations
PA: Achieve Life Sciences, Inc
400-1001 Broadway W
Vancouver BC V6H 4
604 736-3678

(G-9343)
ACS TECHNOLOGIES GROUP INC
1505 Westlake Ave N (98109-3050)
PHONE...............................843 413-8032
Tom Rogers, *Branch Mgr*
EMP: 65
SALES (corp-wide): 75.4MM **Privately Held**
SIC: 7372 Prepackaged software
PA: Acs Technologies Group, Inc.
180 Dunbarton Dr
Florence SC 29501
843 662-1681

(G-9344)
ACTION COMMUNICATIONS INC
5700 6th Ave S Ste 101 (98108-2510)
PHONE...............................206 625-1234
Tony Cheng, *Branch Mgr*
EMP: 2
SALES (corp-wide): 4.8MM **Privately Held**
SIC: 3663 4899 Airborne radio communications equipment; data communication services
PA: Action Communications, Inc.
11630 Airport Rd Ste 300
Everett WA 98204
425 348-9121

(G-9345)
ACTIVATED CONTENT
2125 Western Ave Ste 200 (98121-2181)
PHONE...............................206 448-3260
EMP: 5 **EST:** 2004
SALES (est): 560K **Privately Held**
SIC: 7372 Prepackaged Software Services

(G-9346)
ACTIVELY LEARN INC
220 2nd Ave S Fl 4 (98104-2222)
PHONE...............................857 540-6670
Jay Goyal, *CEO*
Sean Kerawala, *Project Mgr*
Michael Diroberts, *Manager*
Kelly Healey, *Manager*
EMP: 2 **EST:** 2012
SALES (est): 218.5K
SALES (corp-wide): 64.2MM **Privately Held**
SIC: 7372 Educational computer software
PA: Achieve3000, Inc.
1985 Cedarbridge Ave # 3
Lakewood NJ 08701
732 367-5505

(G-9347)
ACU-LINE CORPORATION
Also Called: Acu-Line Chemical Machining
434 N 35th St (98103-8607)
PHONE...............................206 634-1618
Kenneth Krueger, *President*
David Kelly, *Corp Secy*
▲ **EMP:** 4
SQ FT: 3,200
SALES: 400K **Privately Held**
WEB: www.aculineetch.com
SIC: 3479 Etching & engraving

(G-9348)
ADAM WELCH
1740 Melrose Ave Unit 606 (98122-2070)
PHONE...............................206 329-8697
EMP: 2
SALES (est): 83.9K **Privately Held**
SIC: 2752 Commercial Printing, Lithographic

(G-9349)
ADD THREE INC
500 E Pike St Ste 200a (98122-3886)
PHONE...............................206 568-3772
Paul Uhlir, *CEO*
Jason Llorin, *Vice Pres*
Brian Rauschenbach, *Chief Mktg Ofcr*
Victoria Yeung, *Account Dir*
EMP: 30
SQ FT: 6,000
SALES (est): 2.5MM **Privately Held**
SIC: 7372 Operating systems computer software

(G-9350)
ADE HOLDING INC (HQ)
4420 14th Ave Nw (98107-4616)
PHONE...............................206 789-3600
Peter B Hill, *President*
Terry Schusted, *QC Mgr*
Robert K Humphryes, *CFO*
◆ **EMP:** 91
SQ FT: 58,000
SALES (est): 20.3MM
SALES (corp-wide): 181.2MM **Privately Held**
SIC: 3519 5088 5551 Diesel, semi-diesel or duel-fuel engines, including marine; marine crafts & supplies; boat dealers
PA: Valley Power Systems, Inc.
425 S Hacienda Blvd
City Of Industry CA 91745
626 333-1243

(G-9351)
ADHESA-PLATE MANUFACTURING CO
4000 7th Ave S (98108-5208)
P.O. Box 84723 (98124-6023)
PHONE...............................206 682-0141
Craig Mitchell, *President*
Ed Reiter, *Prdtn Mgr*
Suzie Coar, *Executive*
EMP: 22 **EST:** 1954
SQ FT: 9,000
SALES (est): 3.1MM **Privately Held**
WEB: www.adhesaplate.com
SIC: 3993 2759 2752 2672 Name plates: except engraved, etched, etc..: metal; commercial printing; commercial printing, lithographic; coated & laminated paper

(G-9352)
ADHESIVE PRODUCTS INC
945 S Doris St (98108-2729)
PHONE...............................206 762-7459

Rico Peretti, *Executive*
EMP: 10
SALES (corp-wide): 5.7MM **Privately Held**
WEB: www.crafterspick.com
SIC: 2891 2672 2671 Adhesives; coated & laminated paper; packaging paper & plastics film, coated & laminated
PA: The Adhesive Products Inc
520 Cleveland Ave
Albany CA 94710
510 526-7616

(G-9353)
ADOBE SYSTEMS INCORPORATED
801 N 34th St (98103-8882)
PHONE...............................206 675-7000
Vince Brown, *Branch Mgr*
EMP: 500
SALES (corp-wide): 9B **Publicly Held**
WEB: www.adobe.com
SIC: 7372 8711 Prepackaged software; engineering services
PA: Adobe Inc.
345 Park Ave
San Jose CA 95110
408 536-6000

(G-9354)
ADVANCE SIGN DESIGN INC
6501 6th Ave Nw (98117-5016)
PHONE...............................206 789-6051
Jeff Thompson, *President*
Brad Thompson, *Treasurer*
EMP: 5
SQ FT: 3,000
SALES (est): 552.2K **Privately Held**
SIC: 3993 Signs, not made in custom sign painting shops

(G-9355)
ADVANGELISTS LLC (HQ)
701 5th Ave Fl 75 (98104-7097)
PHONE...............................734 546-4989
Deepankr Katyal, *CEO*
EMP: 4
SALES (est): 931.2K
SALES (corp-wide): 1.4MM **Publicly Held**
SIC: 7336 7372 Creative services to advertisers, except writers; utility computer software
PA: Mobiquity Technologies, Inc.
35 Torrington Ln
Shoreham NY 11786
516 246-9422

(G-9356)
ADVERTISING SERVICES INTL LLC
Also Called: Ad Services
10000 Lake City Way Ne (98125-7734)
PHONE...............................206 623-6963
Ed Millman, *Mng Member*
EMP: 3
SQ FT: 1,900
SALES (est): 295.6K **Privately Held**
WEB: www.adservices.com
SIC: 7336 2791 Graphic arts & related design; typesetting

(G-9357)
AFAR INTERACTIVE INC
701 5th Ave Ste 3600 (98104-7010)
PHONE...............................425 442-5101
Zhihong Mao, *Director*
EMP: 5
SQ FT: 1,000
SALES (est): 184.5K **Privately Held**
SIC: 2741 7372 ; application computer software; educational computer software

(G-9358)
AG CREATIVE PUBLISHING
1727 14th Ave Apt 10 (98122-2653)
PHONE...............................206 375-0934
Anthony Greer, *Principal*
EMP: 2
SALES (est): 45.4K **Privately Held**
SIC: 2741 Miscellaneous publishing

(G-9359)
AGILE DATA TECHNOLOGY INC
2125 Western Ave Ste 488 (98121-3137)
PHONE...............................206 280-9512
Scott Isaacks, *President*

Scott Jenkins, *CFO*
EMP: 3
SQ FT: 1,100
SALES: 416.1K **Privately Held**
SIC: 3229 Fiber optics strands

(G-9360)
AIRCLEAN TECHNOLOGIES INC (PA)
Also Called: AIRCLEAN ENERGY
4725 W Marginal Way Sw (98106-1514)
P.O. Box 46017 (98146-0017)
PHONE...............................206 860-4930
William Hunter, *President*
Patrick Paul, *Chairman*
Kelly Hunter, *Manager*
EMP: 14
SQ FT: 6,000
SALES: 15.6MM **Privately Held**
WEB: www.aircleantech.com
SIC: 3511 Turbines & turbine generator sets

(G-9361)
AIRCON SOFT
Also Called: Julian RAD Software
1925 Ne 143rd St (98125-3236)
PHONE...............................206 851-8476
Said Sanayebaksherad, *Owner*
EMP: 3
SALES: 800K **Privately Held**
SIC: 7372 Prepackaged software

(G-9362)
AIRLOCK LLC
5007 43rd Ave S (98118-2305)
PHONE...............................206 992-3996
Guy Davis, *Principal*
EMP: 4
SALES (est): 360.8K **Privately Held**
SIC: 3443 Airlocks

(G-9363)
AJAXX DESIGN INC
Also Called: Ajaxx 63
8917 35th Ave Ne (98115-3612)
PHONE...............................206 522-4545
William Sherman, *President*
Andrew Fraser, *Vice Pres*
◆ **EMP:** 4
SQ FT: 1,500
SALES (est): 432.9K **Privately Held**
WEB: www.ajaxx63.com
SIC: 2253 5699 5136 T-shirts & tops, knit; shirts, custom made; T-shirts, custom printed; caps, men's & boys'; shirts, men's & boys'

(G-9364)
ALAN AND LINDA MURRAY LLC
6319 22nd Ave Ne (98115-6919)
PHONE...............................206 527-0841
Alan Murray, *Owner*
EMP: 4
SALES (est): 233.1K **Privately Held**
SIC: 2431 Window shutters, wood

(G-9365)
ALASKA DISTRIBUTORS CO
1728 4th Ave S (98134-1502)
PHONE...............................206 682-1517
EMP: 3
SALES (est): 200K **Privately Held**
SIC: 5182 2085 Whol Wine/Distilled Beverages Mfg Distilled/Blended Liquor

(G-9366)
ALASKA STAR INC
4019 21st Ave W Ste 200 (98199-1251)
PHONE...............................206 282-0988
Don Giles, *President*
Joy V Voorst, *Persnl Mgr*
EMP: 60 **EST:** 1977
SALES: 3.6MM
SALES (corp-wide): 268.6MM **Privately Held**
WEB: www.icicleseafoods.com
SIC: 2092 Seafoods, fresh: prepared
HQ: Icicle Seafoods, Inc.
4019 21st Ave W Ste 300
Seattle WA 98199
206 282-0988

GEOGRAPHIC SECTION

Seattle - King County (G-9396)

(G-9367)
ALASKAN COPPER COMPANIES INC
628 S Hanford St (98134-2123)
PHONE..................................206 623-5800
Monica Martinson, *Manager*
EMP: 2 **Privately Held**
SIC: 3498 3443 Fabricated pipe & fittings; fabricated plate work (boiler shop)
HQ: Alaskan Copper Companies, Inc.
   27402 72nd Ave S
   Kent WA 98032
   206 623-5800

(G-9368)
ALASKAN COPPER COMPANIES INC
Also Called: Alaskan Copper & Brass Company
3200 6th Ave S (98134-2106)
PHONE..................................206 623-5800
EMP: 2 **Privately Held**
SIC: 5051 3354 Metals Service Centers And Offices
HQ: Alaskan Copper Companies, Inc.
   27402 72nd Ave S
   Kent WA 98032
   206 623-5800

(G-9369)
ALBER SEAFOODS INC
900 1st Ave S Ste 202 (98134-1236)
PHONE..................................360 642-3773
Max Boland, *Branch Mgr*
EMP: 7 **Privately Held**
SIC: 2092 Seafoods, fresh: prepared; seafoods, frozen: prepared
HQ: Alber Seafoods, Inc.
   45 Pier Ste B4
   San Francisco CA 94111

(G-9370)
ALCHEMY GOODS LLC
1723 1st Ave S (98134-1403)
PHONE..................................206 484-9469
Eli Reich, *Owner*
EMP: 9
SQ FT: 2,000
SALES: 500K **Privately Held**
SIC: 3171 Handbags, women's

(G-9371)
ALETHEIA THERAPEUTICS LLC
901 Boren Ave Ste 701 (98104-3508)
PHONE..................................206 473-2435
Michael J Sibrava, *Manager*
EMP: 3
SALES (est): 155.7K **Privately Held**
SIC: 2834 Pharmaceutical preparations

(G-9372)
ALEUTIAN SPRAY REVERSE LLC
2157 N Northlake Way # 210 (98103-9184)
PHONE..................................206 784-5000
Chris Swasand, *President*
Craig Cross,
EMP: 6
SALES: 950K **Privately Held**
SIC: 2092 Fresh or frozen packaged fish

(G-9373)
ALEX DAISLEY
Also Called: Stock and Pantry
1122 E Pike St (98122-3916)
PHONE..................................206 623-5555
Alex Daisley, *Principal*
EMP: 2
SQ FT: 800
SALES (est): 118.6K **Privately Held**
SIC: 5192 5023 2392 5199 Books; decorative home furnishings & supplies; cushions & pillows; gifts & novelties; vases, pottery; pottery household articles, except kitchen articles; kitchen, bathroom & household ware: wood

(G-9374)
ALGAS-SDI INTERNATIONAL LLC
151 S Michigan St (98108-3225)
PHONE..................................206 789-5410
Randy Ervin, *President*
Douglas Perks,
◆ EMP: 100

SQ FT: 25,000
SALES (est): 24.5MM **Privately Held**
WEB: www.algas-sdi.com
SIC: 3569 Gas producers, generators & other gas related equipment

(G-9375)
ALGORITHMIA INC
1925 Post Aly Ste 3c (98101-1028)
PHONE..................................415 741-1491
Diego Oppenheimer, *CEO*
John Combs, *Vice Pres*
Kenneth F Daniel, *CTO*
Kyle Gonzales-Leitch, *Graphic Designe*
EMP: 9
SQ FT: 2,500
SALES (est): 399.1K **Privately Held**
SIC: 7372 Utility computer software

(G-9376)
ALICE E MARWICK
706 Belmont Ave E Apt 203 (98102-5978)
PHONE..................................206 329-9565
Bruce Marotta, *Founder*
EMP: 2 EST: 2017
SALES (est): 73.1K **Privately Held**
SIC: 2721 Periodicals

(G-9377)
ALKI FOUNDRY
3600 E Marginal Way S # 11 (98134-1140)
PHONE..................................206 794-4074
Hahn Rossman, *Principal*
EMP: 4
SALES (est): 449.6K **Privately Held**
SIC: 3441 Fabricated structural metal

(G-9378)
ALKI PRESS LLC
2420 54th Pl Sw Apt 31 (98116-1871)
PHONE..................................206 854-1148
EMP: 2
SALES (est): 97K **Privately Held**
SIC: 2741 Misc Publishing

(G-9379)
ALL FUR ONE
2400 Warren Ave N (98109-2024)
PHONE..................................206 281-8412
Dara Jenkins, *Principal*
EMP: 2 EST: 2011
SALES (est): 101.5K **Privately Held**
SIC: 3999 Furs

(G-9380)
ALL METAL ARTS SEATTLE
3047 18th Ave S (98144-5811)
PHONE..................................206 200-9496
EMP: 3
SALES (est): 215.7K **Privately Held**
SIC: 3842 Mfg Surgical Appliances/Supplies

(G-9381)
ALLIED BODY WORKS INC
Also Called: Walker Blocker
625 S 96th St (98108-4914)
PHONE..................................206 763-7811
Richard C Minice, *President*
Beverly Minice, *Corp Secy*
Pat Robinson, *Purch Agent*
Roger Neal, *Sales Staff*
▲ EMP: 12 EST: 1948
SQ FT: 25,000
SALES (est): 3.7MM **Privately Held**
WEB: www.alliedbody.com
SIC: 5012 3713 7532 Trailers for trucks, new & used; truck bodies; truck & bus bodies; body shop, trucks

(G-9382)
ALLIED TECHNICAL SERVICES CORP
10840 Myers Way S (98168-1368)
PHONE..................................206 763-3316
John Shockley, *President*
EMP: 10 EST: 1956
SQ FT: 7,400
SALES (est): 830K **Privately Held**
SIC: 7692 Welding repair

(G-9383)
ALLSPORTS CAGES & NETTING LLC
4514 Sw Trenton St (98136-2455)
P.O. Box 167, Southworth (98386-0167)
PHONE..................................206 933-8987
Ron Anderson,
EMP: 3
SALES: 500K **Privately Held**
SIC: 3949 Baseball equipment & supplies, general

(G-9384)
ALMEDA COTTAGE INC
2400 W Bertona St (98199-2207)
PHONE..................................206 285-1674
Romulo Almeda, *President*
Ester Almeda, *Vice Pres*
EMP: 46
SQ FT: 3,500
SALES: 500K **Privately Held**
SIC: 3589 5064 8748 Commercial cooking & foodwarming equipment; electrical appliances, television & radio; business consulting

(G-9385)
ALOE 2000
Also Called: Aloe Square
10224 Richwood Ave Nw (98177-5443)
PHONE..................................206 420-8785
Kala Agarwala, *President*
Om Agarwal, *Vice Pres*
EMP: 2
SALES (est): 280K **Privately Held**
WEB: www.aloe2000.com
SIC: 2023 Dietary supplements, dairy & non-dairy based

(G-9386)
ALPHA BIOPARTNERS LLC
2308 Eyres Pl W (98199-3812)
PHONE..................................405 603-1917
William Hagstrom, *Principal*
EMP: 2
SALES (est): 94.2K **Privately Held**
SIC: 2836 Biological products, except diagnostic

(G-9387)
ALPHAGRAPHICS
3131 Elliott Ave Ste 100 (98121-3043)
PHONE..................................206 343-5037
Chuck Stempler, *President*
Dave Parsons, *Project Mgr*
Mike Votava, *Marketing Mgr*
Kinsey Loudon, *Sr Project Mgr*
EMP: 5
SQ FT: 1,400
SALES (est): 393.5K **Privately Held**
SIC: 2752 Commercial printing, offset

(G-9388)
ALPINE IMMUNE SCIENCES INC (PA)
201 Elliott Ave W Ste 230 (98119-4230)
PHONE..................................206 788-4545
Mitchell H Gold, *Ch of Bd*
Stanford Peng, *President*
Paul Rickey, *CFO*
Wayne Gombotz, *CTO*
EMP: 38
SQ FT: 11,158
SALES: 705K **Publicly Held**
SIC: 2834 Pharmaceutical preparations

(G-9389)
ALRY PUBLICATIONS LLC
1321 Seneca St Apt 2107 (98101-3258)
PHONE..................................206 274-8204
EMP: 2
SALES (est): 59.2K **Privately Held**
SIC: 2741 Miscellaneous publishing

(G-9390)
ALUMINUM TECHNOLOGIES INC
Also Called: Altech
3017 12th Ave S (98144-5704)
PHONE..................................206 323-6900
Nick Papini, *President*
Marilyn E Papini, *Vice Pres*
EMP: 3
SALES: 860K **Privately Held**
SIC: 3297 5085 Nonclay refractories; refractory material

(G-9391)
AMDOCS QPASS INC
2211 Elliott Ave Ste 400 (98121-3625)
PHONE..................................206 447-6000
John J Horgan, *President*
EMP: 15
SALES (est): 3MM **Privately Held**
SIC: 7373 7371 7372 Computer integrated systems design; custom computer programming services; prepackaged software
HQ: Amdocs, Inc.
   1390 Timberlake Manor Pkwy
   Chesterfield MO 63017
   314 212-7000

(G-9392)
AMERICAN FLEX & EXHAUST PDTS
Also Called: American Flex & Exhaust Pdts
1121 Nw 45th St (98107-4627)
PHONE..................................206 789-1353
Greg Bowman, *President*
Peter Grines, *Vice Pres*
EMP: 7
SQ FT: 4,000
SALES (est): 686.4K **Privately Held**
SIC: 3732 3731 Boat building & repairing; shipbuilding & repairing

(G-9393)
AMERICAN LABELMARK COMPANY
Also Called: Labelmaster Software
400 E Pine St Ste 325 (98122-2315)
PHONE..................................206 256-0889
Dwight Curtis, *President*
EMP: 25
SALES (corp-wide): 71.6MM **Privately Held**
WEB: www.alc-net.com
SIC: 7372 Publishers' computer software
PA: American Labelmark Company Inc
   5724 N Pulaski Rd
   Chicago IL 60646
   773 478-0900

(G-9394)
AMERICAN PLASTIC MFG INC
526 S Monroe St (98108-4349)
PHONE..................................206 763-1055
Quang Vuong, *CEO*
Holmes Ken, *Mktg Dir*
Jewel Vuong, *Office Mgr*
▲ EMP: 15
SQ FT: 15,000
SALES (est): 3.4MM **Privately Held**
WEB: www.americanplasticmfg.com
SIC: 2673 Plastic bags: made from purchased materials

(G-9395)
AMERICAN SEAFOODS COMPANY LLC (DH)
2025 1st Ave Ste 900 (98121-2154)
PHONE..................................206 448-0300
Micheal Hyde, *President*
◆ EMP: 83
SQ FT: 15,341
SALES (est): 114.6MM **Privately Held**
WEB: www.americanseafoods.com
SIC: 0921 2092 0912 Fish hatcheries; fresh or frozen packaged fish; fish, frozen: prepared; fish fillets; pollack, catching of
HQ: American Seafoods Group Llc
   2025 1st Ave Ste 900
   Seattle WA 98121
   206 374-1515

(G-9396)
AMERICAN WINE TRADE INC (PA)
Also Called: Hedges Family Estate
900 Lenora St Apt 103 (98121-2755)
P.O. Box 999, Snoqualmie (98065-0999)
PHONE..................................206 357-0607
Tom Hedges, *President*
Anne-Marie Hedges, *Corp Secy*
Boo Walker, *Sales Staff*
▲ EMP: 27
SQ FT: 1,800
SALES (est): 4.4MM **Privately Held**
SIC: 2084 Wines

Seattle - King County (G-9397)   GEOGRAPHIC SECTION

(G-9397)
AMGEN INC
1201 Amgen Ct W (98119-3105)
PHONE..................206 265-7504
Steve Fritz, *General Mgr*
Gregg Dalton, *Counsel*
Jane-Law Huang, *Counsel*
Elsa Lemoine, *Counsel*
Greg-Law Mintz, *Counsel*
EMP: 800
SALES (corp-wide): 23.7B **Publicly Held**
SIC: 2834 Pharmaceutical preparations
PA: Amgen Inc.
  1 Amgen Center Dr
  Thousand Oaks CA 91320
  805 447-1000

(G-9398)
AMIGOS SKATEBOARDS LLC
33 S Hanford St (98134-1807)
PHONE..................901 289-9044
EMP: 2
SALES (est): 111.1K **Privately Held**
SIC: 3949 Skateboards

(G-9399)
AMNIS LLC
645 Elliott Ave W Ste 100 (98119-3960)
PHONE..................206 374-7000
David Basiji, *CEO*
David Perry, *President*
Igor Kozodoy, *Engineer*
EMP: 30
SQ FT: 25,000
SALES (est): 4.1MM **Publicly Held**
WEB: www.amnis.com
SIC: 3826 Analytical instruments
HQ: Iris Biotech Llc
  212 Technology Blvd
  Austin TX 78727
  512 219-8020

(G-9400)
AMPLE POWER COMPANY LLC
2442 Nw Market St 43 (98107-4137)
PHONE..................206 789-0827
Ruth Ishihaia, *Mng Member*
Ken Knight,
EMP: 8
SALES (est): 937K **Privately Held**
SIC: 3629 3822 Battery chargers, rectifying or nonrotating; temperature controls, automatic

(G-9401)
AMY STEVENS
6720 11th Ave Nw (98117-5213)
PHONE..................206 706-2528
Amy Stevens, *Administration*
EMP: 2
SALES (est): 85.9K **Privately Held**
SIC: 3571 Electronic computers

(G-9402)
ANANSE PRESS
1504 32nd Ave S (98144-3918)
PHONE..................206 325-8205
Donald Mumford, *Partner*
Esther Mumford, *Partner*
EMP: 2
SALES (est): 200K **Privately Held**
SIC: 2731 Book publishing

(G-9403)
ANGELWEAR
4411 11th Ave S (98108-1468)
PHONE..................206 230-9594
Angela Jones, *Principal*
EMP: 2
SALES (est): 145.2K **Privately Held**
SIC: 3911 Jewelry, precious metal

(G-9404)
ANNAPURNA GLASS & WOOD INC
4317 Bagley Ave N (98103-7626)
P.O. Box 31502 (98103-1502)
PHONE..................206 525-0777
Ed Brown, *President*
Judy Franco, *Admin Sec*
EMP: 2
SALES (est): 230K **Privately Held**
SIC: 1793 3231 Glass & glazing work; leaded glass; stained glass: made from purchased glass

(G-9405)
ANNOINTED OIL INC
12422 8th Ave S (98168-2207)
PHONE..................206 242-6925
Patricia Hughes, *Principal*
EMP: 2
SALES (est): 90.1K **Privately Held**
SIC: 1311 Crude petroleum & natural gas

(G-9406)
ANTICA FARMACISTA LLC
119 Pine St Ste 301 (98101-1592)
PHONE..................206 329-3966
Liana Robertshaw, *Sales/Mktg Dir*
Susanne Pruitt, *CFO*
Shelley Callaghan,
▲ **EMP:** 7
SQ FT: 1,800
SALES (est): 1.4MM **Privately Held**
WEB: www.anticafarmacista.com
SIC: 2844 Cosmetic preparations

(G-9407)
ANVIL HOUSE LLC
6532 57th Ave S (98118-3400)
PHONE..................406 579-3042
Michael Combs,
EMP: 2
SALES (est): 203.4K **Privately Held**
SIC: 3548 Electrodes, electric welding

(G-9408)
APE ARTISAN LEATHER
3858 31st Ave W (98199-1714)
PHONE..................206 399-0967
Armand Poole, *Principal*
EMP: 2
SALES (est): 124.1K **Privately Held**
SIC: 3199 Leather goods

(G-9409)
APEX RAILING SOLUTIONS
1505 S 93rd St Ste Bh (98108-5114)
PHONE..................206 452-3281
William Larson, *Owner*
EMP: 8
SALES (est): 550K **Privately Held**
SIC: 3441 Fabricated structural metal

(G-9410)
APP GRINDER LLC
Also Called: Better Than Good Games
5225a 19th Ave Sw (98106-1354)
PHONE..................206 293-9632
Neil Johnston, *Principal*
EMP: 2
SALES (est): 114.2K **Privately Held**
SIC: 7372 Application computer software

(G-9411)
APPLE FOR HIRE
2905 S Dakota St (98108-1618)
PHONE..................206 722-3205
EMP: 2 EST: 2016
SALES (est): 94.5K **Privately Held**
SIC: 3571 Mfg Electronic Computers

(G-9412)
APPLEWHITE AERO LLC
309 S Clvrdle Ste D17 (98108)
P.O. Box 46955 (98146-0955)
PHONE..................206 762-5285
Paul Applewhite, *President*
EMP: 2
SALES (est): 439.1K **Privately Held**
SIC: 3812 Aircraft/aerospace flight instruments & guidance systems

(G-9413)
APTEVO BIOTHERAPEUTICS LLC
2401 4th Ave Ste 1050 (98121-3460)
PHONE..................206 838-0500
Marvin White, *President*
Jeff Lamothe, *CFO*
Amy Beatty-Yasutake, *Administration*
EMP: 3
SALES (est): 198.5K
SALES (corp-wide): 23MM **Publicly Held**
SIC: 2833 Drugs & herbs: grading, grinding & milling
PA: Aptevo Therapeutics Inc.
  2401 4th Ave Ste 1050
  Seattle WA 98121
  206 838-0500

(G-9414)
APTEVO THERAPEUTICS INC (PA)
2401 4th Ave Ste 1050 (98121-3460)
PHONE..................206 838-0500
Marvin L White, *President*
Jane Gross, *Senior VP*
Randy J Maddux, *Senior VP*
Toshiye Ishisaka, *Project Mgr*
Jonathan Clapper, *Research*
EMP: 59
SQ FT: 51,000
SALES: 23MM **Publicly Held**
SIC: 2834 Pharmaceutical preparations

(G-9415)
AQUATIC SPECIALTY SERVICES
1605 S 93rd St Ste Ef (98108-5112)
PHONE..................206 275-0694
Dan Richards, *President*
Teresa T Meinzinger-Richards, *Owner*
EMP: 5
SALES (est): 788.8K **Privately Held**
WEB: www.aquaticspecialtyservices.com
SIC: 7389 3589 Swimming pool & hot tub service & maintenance; swimming pool filter & water conditioning systems

(G-9416)
AQUEDUCT CRITICAL CARE INC
1301 5th Ave Ste 3405 (98101-2630)
PHONE..................425 984-6090
Thomas Clement, *President*
Michael Behlke, *CFO*
EMP: 13
SALES (est): 2.2MM **Privately Held**
SIC: 3841 Surgical & medical instruments

(G-9417)
AQUEDUCT NEUROSCIENCES INC
7513 55th Pl Ne (98115-6381)
PHONE..................206 661-1538
Thomas Clement, *CEO*
Samuel Browd, *Principal*
Richard Wohns, *Director*
EMP: 2
SALES (est): 200K **Privately Held**
SIC: 3845 Electromedical equipment

(G-9418)
ARABELLA SOFTWARE LLC
1624 42nd Ave E Apt A (98112-3823)
PHONE..................206 963-6460
James Stearns, *Principal*
EMP: 4
SALES (est): 151.3K **Privately Held**
SIC: 7372 7389 Prepackaged software;

(G-9419)
ARCHER USA INC
Also Called: Archer Mobile USA
2025 1st Ave Ste Garage (98121-2100)
PHONE..................206 567-5343
Matthew Harris, *President*
Steve Alskie, *President*
Jim O'Brien, *CFO*
EMP: 36
SALES (est): 3.9MM **Privately Held**
WEB: www.iloopmobile.com
SIC: 7372 Prepackaged software

(G-9420)
ARCHITECT DAVID VANDERVORT
2000 Frview Ave E Ste 103 (98102)
PHONE..................206 784-1614
David Vandervort, *Owner*
EMP: 7
SALES (est): 680K **Privately Held**
SIC: 8712 3446 Architectural services; acoustical suspension systems, metal

(G-9421)
ARCHIVALRY
1708 26th Ave E (98112-3014)
PHONE..................206 420-3899
Benjamin Vogt, *Principal*
EMP: 6
SALES (est): 243.5K **Privately Held**
SIC: 2253 T-shirts & tops, knit

(G-9422)
ARCTIC CIRCLE HOLDINGS LLC (HQ)
419 Occidental Ave S S (98104-3853)
PHONE..................206 625-9226
Paul Serventi, *Mng Member*
EMP: 2
SALES (est): 14.8MM
SALES (corp-wide): 28.7MM **Privately Held**
SIC: 2395 7336 5199 2396 Emblems, embroidered; embroidery products, except schiffli machine; art design services; advertising specialties; automotive & apparel trimmings
PA: Intracorp Capital, L.L.C.
  419 Occidental Ave S # 300
  Seattle WA 98104
  206 625-9226

(G-9423)
ARCTIC FJORD INC
2727 Alaskan Way Pier 69 (98121-1107)
PHONE..................206 547-6557
Douglas L Christensen, *President*
Walter Pereyra, *Chairman*
H Samuelson Jr, *Vice Pres*
Michael Haggarty, *Treasurer*
Stan Hovik, *Director*
▼ **EMP:** 130
SALES (est): 9MM **Privately Held**
SIC: 0912 2092 Finfish; fresh or frozen packaged fish

(G-9424)
ARCTIC STORM INC
2727 Alaskan Way Pier 69 (98121-1107)
PHONE..................206 547-6557
Doug Christensen, *President*
Walter T Pereyra, *Chairman*
Do-Young Yun, *Vice Pres*
Peter Albee, *Engineer*
Michael Haggarty, *CFO*
◆ **EMP:** 50
SQ FT: 3,000
SALES (est): 3.9MM **Privately Held**
SIC: 0912 2092 Pollack, catching of; fresh or frozen packaged fish

(G-9425)
ARDAGH GLASS INC
5801 E Marginal Way S (98134-2413)
PHONE..................765 741-7985
Doug Coburn, *Plt & Fclts Mgr*
EMP: 600
SQ FT: 414,070
SALES (corp-wide): 242.1K **Privately Held**
WEB: www.sgcontainers.com
SIC: 3221 Glass containers
HQ: Ardagh Glass Inc.
  10194 Crosspoint Blvd
  Indianapolis IN 46256

(G-9426)
ARDEZAN CHOCOLATE LLC
2313 4th Ave N (98109-2112)
P.O. Box 22389 (98122-0389)
PHONE..................206 244-4440
EMP: 3
SALES (est): 172K **Privately Held**
SIC: 2066 Mfg Chocolate/Cocoa Products

(G-9427)
ARGENT FABRICATION LLC
1125 Nw 46th St (98107-4633)
PHONE..................206 438-0068
Curtis Eckman,
EMP: 15
SALES (est): 628.8K **Privately Held**
SIC: 3446 Architectural metalwork

(G-9428)
ARGO BLOWER & MFG CO
5400 E Marginal Way S # 1 (98134-2442)
PHONE..................206 762-9336
Al Schuehle, *President*
Karen Frank, *Admin Sec*
EMP: 16 EST: 1931
SQ FT: 10,000

GEOGRAPHIC SECTION

Seattle - King County (G-9457)

SALES (est): 4.4MM **Privately Held**
WEB: www.argoblower.com
SIC: 3564 7699 3441 Blower filter units (furnace blowers); dust or fume collecting equipment, industrial; ventilating fans: industrial or commercial; industrial machinery & equipment repair; fabricated structural metal

(G-9429)
ARIO INC
5333 9th Ave Ne (98105-3616)
PHONE.................................206 852-4877
Brian Hoskins, *President*
Dale Dell'ario, *CTO*
EMP: 4
SALES (est): 200K **Privately Held**
SIC: 3695 7389 Computer software tape & disks: blank, rigid & floppy;

(G-9430)
ARITEX USA INC
2101 4th Ave Ste 1370 (98121-2340)
PHONE.................................425 922-3819
David Erickson, *President*
EMP: 6 EST: 2015
SALES (est): 630.3K **Privately Held**
SIC: 3559 Automotive related machinery
HQ: Aritex Cading Sa
    Calle Del Progres 319
    Badalona 08918
    933 984-111

(G-9431)
ARNQUIST MUSICAL DESIGNS
5700 Ann Arbor Ave Ne (98105-2118)
PHONE.................................206 420-1639
Mark Arnquist, *President*
Prudence Arnquist, *Vice Pres*
Jurgen Thiede, *CFO*
EMP: 2
SALES: 500K **Privately Held**
SIC: 3931 Guitars & parts, electric & non-electric

(G-9432)
ARRAYS SOFTWARE LLC
1517 12th Ave Ste 304 (98122-3956)
PHONE.................................206 414-8250
EMP: 2
SALES (est): 130.2K **Privately Held**
SIC: 7372 Prepackaged software

(G-9433)
ARS NOVA PRESS INC DBA ARS NOV
515 N 62nd St (98103-5617)
PHONE.................................206 783-9671
Glenn D Greenwood, *President*
EMP: 2 EST: 2012
SALES: 2.6K **Privately Held**
SIC: 2741 Miscellaneous publishing

(G-9434)
ARSOBSCURA BK BNDING RSTRATION
214 1st Ave S Ste B11 (98104-3437)
P.O. Box 4424 (98194-0424)
PHONE.................................206 340-8810
Joel Radcliffe, *Owner*
EMP: 2
SALES: 60K **Privately Held**
SIC: 2789 Binding only: books, pamphlets, magazines, etc.

(G-9435)
ART BRASS AEROSPACE FINSHG INC
313 S Findlay St (98108-2429)
PHONE.................................206 209-3010
Danny Millette, *General Mgr*
Danny Milette, *Vice Pres*
Judy Hale, *QC Mgr*
EMP: 6
SALES (est): 118.3K **Privately Held**
SIC: 3429 3471 Aircraft hardware; cleaning, polishing & finishing

(G-9436)
ART BRASS PLATING INC
313 S Findlay St (98108-2429)
PHONE.................................206 767-4443
Mike Merryfield, *President*
Rob Codling, *General Mgr*
Dean Allstrom, *Shareholder*
EMP: 58
SQ FT: 15,000
SALES (est): 7.4MM **Privately Held**
WEB: www.artbrassplating.com
SIC: 3471 Plating of metals or formed products; cleaning, polishing & finishing

(G-9437)
ART OF SHAVING - FL LLC
600 E Pine St (98122-2324)
PHONE.................................206 737-8370
EMP: 4
SALES (corp-wide): 66.8B **Publicly Held**
SIC: 5999 2844 3421 5122 Hair care products; toilet preparations; razor blades & razors; razor blades
HQ: The Art Of Shaving - Fl Llc
    6100 Blue Lagoon Dr # 150
    Miami FL 33126

(G-9438)
ART ON FILE INC
1837 E Shelby St (98112-2021)
PHONE.................................206 329-9607
Rob Wilkinson, *President*
Colleen Chartier, *Vice Pres*
EMP: 2
SALES (est): 180K **Privately Held**
WEB: www.artonfile.com
SIC: 5961 2741 Mail order house; arts & crafts equipment & supplies, mail order; miscellaneous publishing

(G-9439)
ARTCO SIGN CO INC
108 S Brandon St (98108-2230)
P.O. Box 1660, Milton (98354-1660)
PHONE.................................206 622-5262
Damon C Moore, *President*
EMP: 6
SQ FT: 2,500
SALES (est): 650.8K **Privately Held**
WEB: www.artcosigns.com
SIC: 3993 Signs & advertising specialties

(G-9440)
ARTISAN BAKING COMPANY
109 Ne 65th St (98115-6403)
PHONE.................................206 240-4713
Leon Jackson, *Principal*
EMP: 5
SALES (est): 266.3K **Privately Held**
SIC: 2051 Bread, cake & related products

(G-9441)
ASAHIPEN AMERICA INC
Also Called: Aspen Paint
1128 Sw Spokane St (98134-1128)
PHONE.................................206 371-7931
Tatsuo Nishi, *President*
Hieeya Tanaka, *Director*
EMP: 14
SQ FT: 35,000
SALES (est): 2.4MM **Privately Held**
WEB: www.aspenpaints.com
SIC: 2851 Paints & allied products
PA: Asahipen Corporation
    4-1-12, Tsurumi, Tsurumi-Ku
    Osaka OSK 538-0

(G-9442)
ASCAP
3206 S Irving St (98144-3939)
PHONE.................................206 324-0561
Evelyn Anderson, *Manager*
EMP: 7
SALES (est): 360K **Privately Held**
SIC: 2741 Music, sheet: publishing & printing

(G-9443)
ASH GROVE CEMENT COMPANY
3801 E Marginal Way S (98134-1147)
PHONE.................................206 623-5596
Craig Puljan, *Opers-Prdtn-Mfg*
Tryg Grey, *Engineer*
Lonnie Jacobs, *Engineer*
Nick Hildebrandt, *Plant Engr*
EMP: 81
SQ FT: 2,000
SALES (corp-wide): 30.6B **Privately Held**
WEB: www.ashgrove.com
SIC: 3241 Masonry cement
HQ: Ash Grove Cement Company
    11011 Cody St Ste 300
    Overland Park KS 66210
    913 451-8900

(G-9444)
ASKO PROCESSING INC (PA)
434 N 35th St (98103-8689)
PHONE.................................206 634-2080
David G Kelly, *President*
D Michael Kelly, *Vice Pres*
Kent Kessler, *Prdtn Mgr*
John Franks, *Manager*
Gauin Moore, *Supervisor*
▲ EMP: 12 EST: 1967
SQ FT: 12,000
SALES (est): 15.2MM **Privately Held**
WEB: www.askogroup.com
SIC: 3471 3479 Electroplating of metals or formed products; anodizing (plating) of metals or formed products; coating of metals & formed products

(G-9445)
ASTAMED
2200 Alaskan Way Ste 200 (98121-3602)
PHONE.................................206 812-0270
EMP: 2 EST: 2015
SALES (est): 107.5K **Privately Held**
SIC: 2023 Mfg Dry/Evaporated Dairy Products

(G-9446)
ASTRAKE INC
2137 N 61st St (98103-5718)
P.O. Box 31442 (98103-1442)
PHONE.................................503 470-4470
Ed Garrahy, *President*
EMP: 2 EST: 2014
SALES (est): 130.2K **Privately Held**
SIC: 7373 3625 3823 Computer integrated systems design; marine & navy auxiliary controls; fluidic devices, circuits & systems for process control

(G-9447)
ASTRAL HOLDINGS INC (HQ)
5506 6th Ave S (98108-2552)
PHONE.................................206 762-4800
Andrew T Harris, *President*
EMP: 3
SALES (est): 36.1MM
SALES (corp-wide): 23.6MM **Privately Held**
SIC: 5094 3911 Watches & parts; jewelry, precious metal
PA: Shrenuj And Company Limited
    Hw 7011-13
    Mumbai MH 40005
    222 363-8002

(G-9448)
AT ONCE SALES SOFTWARE INC
3131 Wstn Ave Ste A486b (98121)
PHONE.................................509 845-2453
EMP: 2
SALES (est): 86.2K **Privately Held**
SIC: 7372 Prepackaged Software Services

(G-9449)
ATACS PRODUCTS INC
850 S Cambridge St (98108-4920)
P.O. Box 88237 (98138-2237)
PHONE.................................206 433-9000
Richard L Imus, *President*
Lou Bergan, *Chairman*
EMP: 11
SQ FT: 225,000
SALES (est): 1.5MM **Privately Held**
WEB: www.atacs.com
SIC: 3728 5169 3537 2891 Aircraft parts & equipment; adhesives, chemical; sealants; industrial trucks & tractors; adhesives & sealants

(G-9450)
ATECH SERVICES LLC
Also Called: Pacific NW Met Fabricators
4215 23rd Ave W (98199-1210)
PHONE.................................206 453-3182
Nathan Palmer, *CFO*
Richard Clymer, *Mng Member*
Bristol Bay Economic Developme,
Alaskan Leader Group LLC,
EMP: 206
SQ FT: 14,000
SALES: 2MM **Privately Held**
SIC: 3441 Fabricated structural metal

(G-9451)
ATHIRA PHARMA INC
4000 Mason Rd Ste 300 (98195-0001)
P.O. Box 352141 (98195-2141)
PHONE.................................206 221-8112
Leen Kawas, *CEO*
Kevin Church, *Research*
Glenna Mileson, *CFO*
Hans J Moebius, *Chief Mktg Ofcr*
EMP: 11
SALES (est): 240.1K **Privately Held**
SIC: 2834 8731 Pharmaceutical preparations; biological research

(G-9452)
ATHLETIC AWARDS COMPANY INC
Also Called: Athleticsawards.com
817 Republican St (98109-4715)
PHONE.................................206 624-3995
Monty D Holmes, *President*
Ben Holmes, *Principal*
Shirley J Holmes, *Corp Secy*
Dave Mercer, *Marketing Staff*
▲ EMP: 9
SQ FT: 7,000
SALES: 1.6MM **Privately Held**
WEB: www.athleticawards.com
SIC: 5999 5199 7389 3499 Trophies & plaques; advertising specialties; lettering & sign painting services; novelties & giftware, including trophies; trophies

(G-9453)
ATHLETIC CASES
999 3rd Ave Ste 2525 (98104-4032)
PHONE.................................206 569-8677
Michael Donia, *Principal*
EMP: 2
SALES (est): 85.9K **Privately Held**
SIC: 3523 Farm machinery & equipment

(G-9454)
ATLAS CERAMIC
8448 17th Ave Sw (98106-2306)
PHONE.................................206 280-0041
Danielle Gordon, *Principal*
EMP: 2
SALES (est): 115.4K **Privately Held**
SIC: 3269 Pottery products

(G-9455)
ATLAS CONSTRUCTION SPC CO INC
4044 22nd Ave W (98199-1205)
PHONE.................................206 283-2000
David R Connors, *Principal*
Dan Guyen, *Principal*
Jennifer Wistrom, *Export Mgr*
Vince Kisena, *Sales Staff*
Jami Mitchell, *Sales Staff*
EMP: 22 EST: 1957
SQ FT: 20,000
SALES (est): 11MM **Privately Held**
WEB: www.atlasconstructionspecialties.com
SIC: 5032 3599 3272 Concrete building products; ties, form: metal; concrete products

(G-9456)
ATOMIC FABRICATIONS LLC
1605 S 93rd St (98108-5112)
PHONE.................................206 767-8036
Patrick Speleers, *Mng Member*
EMP: 8
SALES (est): 850K **Privately Held**
SIC: 3443 3448 Atomic waste casks; prefabricated metal buildings

(G-9457)
ATOSSA GENETICS INC (PA)
107 Spring St (98104-1005)
PHONE.................................206 325-6086
Steven C Quay, *Ch of Bd*
Kyle Guse, *CFO*
Julie Chan, *Accountant*
Andrew Miller, *Technology*
Ben R Chen, *Bd of Directors*
EMP: 4
SQ FT: 192

Seattle - King County (G-9458)   GEOGRAPHIC SECTION

SALES (est): 6.6K **Publicly Held**
WEB: atossagenetics.com
SIC: 2834 3841 Pharmaceutical preparations; catheters

(G-9458)
ATTACHMATE CORPORATION (HQ)
Also Called: Attachmate Wrq
705 5th Ave S Ste 1000 (98104-4450)
PHONE 206 217-7100
Jeff Hawn, *CEO*
Vern Gustafson, *President*
Kathleen Owens, *President*
Telved Devlet, *Vice Pres*
Sergio Toshio Mituiwa, *Vice Pres*
EMP: 273
SQ FT: 137,000
SALES (est): 245MM **Privately Held**
SIC: 7373 7371 7372 Systems integration services; systems software development services; computer software development; prepackaged software

(G-9459)
ATTACHMATE INTL SLS CORP (DH)
705 5th Ave S Ste 1000 (98104-4450)
PHONE 206 217-7500
EMP: 3
SALES (est): 1MM **Privately Held**
SIC: 7373 7371 7372 Systems integration services; systems software development services; computer software development; prepackaged software
HQ: Attachmate Corporation
 705 5th Ave S Ste 1000
 Seattle WA 98104
 206 217-7100

(G-9460)
ATWOOD ADHESIVES INC
945 S Doris St (98108-2729)
PHONE 206 762-7455
Paul C Shattuck, *President*
Donald Higgins, *Marketing Staff*
Laurel Mangan, *Manager*
▲ **EMP:** 8 **EST:** 1946
SQ FT: 11,000
SALES (est): 1.4MM
SALES (corp-wide): 5.7MM **Privately Held**
WEB: www.crafterspick.com
SIC: 2891 Adhesives
PA: The Adhesive Products Inc
 520 Cleveland Ave
 Albany CA 94710
 510 526-7616

(G-9461)
AU GAVROCHE INC
2001 W Grfield St Ste C92 (98119)
PHONE 206 284-8770
Gerard Casavamt, *President*
Brenda Mutin, *Vice Pres*
EMP: 5
SALES: 500K **Privately Held**
WEB: www.gavroche-thailande.com
SIC: 2051 5149 Bakery: wholesale or wholesale/retail combined; groceries & related products

(G-9462)
AUCTION EDGE INC
1424 4th Ave Ste 920 (98101-2224)
PHONE 206 858-4808
David Weld, *CEO*
Aaron McConkey, *Project Mgr*
John Green, *Program Mgr*
Scott Ford, *Manager*
Mark Richardson, *CTO*
EMP: 35
SALES (est): 5.9MM **Privately Held**
SIC: 7372 7389 Prepackaged software; auction, appraisal & exchange services

(G-9463)
AURA ACCESSORIES INC (PA)
714 E Pike St Unit 509s (98122-4885)
PHONE 208 850-1603
Paul Kalousek, *CEO*
EMP: 2
SALES (est): 236.2K **Privately Held**
SIC: 3999 Cigarette & cigar products & accessories

(G-9464)
AUSTIN CHASE COFFEE INC (HQ)
4001 21st Ave W (98199-1201)
PHONE 206 281-8040
Phillip Sancken, *President*
Tucker McHugh, *Vice Pres*
▲ **EMP:** 5
SQ FT: 1,000
SALES (est): 1.6MM **Privately Held**
WEB: www.austinchasecoffee.com
SIC: 2095 5812 Roasted coffee; coffee shop

(G-9465)
AUSTIN-MAC INC
2739 6th Ave S (98134-2193)
P.O. Box 3746 (98124-3746)
PHONE 206 624-7066
David Martin, *President*
Elizabeth Martin, *Treasurer*
EMP: 19
SQ FT: 21,000
SALES (est): 5.4MM **Privately Held**
WEB: www.austinmacinc.com
SIC: 3535 Conveyors & conveying equipment

(G-9466)
AUTHOR-IT SOFTWARE CORPORATION
1109 1st Ave Ste 500 (98101-2988)
P.O. Box 21169 (98111-3169)
PHONE 888 999-1021
George Northup, *CEO*
Steve Davis, *President*
George Redenbaugh, *CFO*
Rob Vance, *CTO*
EMP: 14
SALES (est): 952.7K **Privately Held**
SIC: 7379 7372 7371 Computer related consulting services; prepackaged software; computer software development; software programming applications

(G-9467)
AUTOMATIC FUNDS TRANSFER SVCS
151 S Lander St Ste C (98134-1889)
P.O. Box 34108 (98124-1108)
PHONE 206 254-0975
Eric Johnson, *President*
Nick Briney, *Vice Pres*
Rick Soth, *Vice Pres*
Shirley Zaic, *Admin Sec*
EMP: 30
SQ FT: 8,000
SALES (est): 2.4MM **Privately Held**
WEB: www.afts.com
SIC: 7374 2782 Computer processing services; blankbooks & looseleaf binders

(G-9468)
AVALARA INC (PA)
255 S King St Ste 1800 (98104-2832)
PHONE 206 826-4900
Scott M McFarlane, *Ch of Bd*
EMP: 70
SALES: 272.1MM **Publicly Held**
WEB: www.avalara.com
SIC: 7372 Prepackaged software

(G-9469)
AVALYN PHARMA INC (PA)
701 Pike St Ste 1500 (98101-3926)
PHONE 206 707-0340
Bruce Montgomery, *CEO*
Nancy McKinley, *Vice Pres*
Mark Surber, *Security Dir*
EMP: 13 **EST:** 2011
SALES (est): 1.9MM **Privately Held**
SIC: 2834 Drugs acting on the respiratory system

(G-9470)
AVANTBIO CORPORATION
1011 Ne 103rd St (98125-7521)
PHONE 360 521-8904
Paul Cook, *Principal*
EMP: 3
SALES (est): 206.4K **Privately Held**
SIC: 2834 Pharmaceutical preparations

(G-9471)
AVIATION PARTNERS INC (PA)
7299 Perimeter Rd S Ste A (98108-3806)
P.O. Box 81107 (98108-1107)
PHONE 206 762-1171
Joseph S B Clark, *Ch of Bd*
Jeff Hannie, *Principal*
Gary Dunn, *Vice Pres*
Hank Thompson, *VP Opers*
Chip Kiehn, *Sales Dir*
▲ **EMP:** 15
SQ FT: 5,000
SALES (est): 4MM **Privately Held**
SIC: 3728 Wing assemblies & parts, aircraft

(G-9472)
AVISTAR AEROSPACE LLC
603 Stewart St Ste 1020 (98101-1226)
PHONE 206 838-6869
David Rubens, *President*
Anu Goel, *Principal*
EMP: 5
SQ FT: 2,000
SALES (est): 443.1K **Privately Held**
SIC: 3728 Aircraft parts & equipment

(G-9473)
B & G MACHINE INC (PA)
6400 Corson Ave S (98108-3444)
P.O. Box 80483 (98108-0483)
PHONE 206 767-6071
John C Bianchi, *President*
Karen Bianchi, *Vice Pres*
▲ **EMP:** 40 **EST:** 1953
SQ FT: 26,000
SALES (est): 10.2MM **Privately Held**
WEB: www.bandgmachine.com
SIC: 3599 5084 Machine shop, jobbing & repair; engines & transportation equipment

(G-9474)
B C T INC
3433 4th Ave S (98134-1904)
PHONE 206 343-9355
Bill Knapp, *President*
Barbara Knapp, *Vice Pres*
Katie K Hill, *Treasurer*
Kirk W Knapp, *Admin Sec*
EMP: 30
SALES (est): 1.3MM **Privately Held**
SIC: 2752 5112 Commercial printing, offset; stationery & office supplies

(G-9475)
B-SIDE SOFTWARE LLC
620 N 34th St Apt 410 (98103-8680)
PHONE 206 708-6973
Brandon Paddock, *Principal*
EMP: 2
SALES (est): 102.2K **Privately Held**
SIC: 7372 Business oriented computer software

(G-9476)
BAD BAGS INC
Also Called: Best American Duffel
5527 56th Ave S (98118-2514)
PHONE 206 722-0916
Malcolm Vetterlein, *President*
▲ **EMP:** 2
SQ FT: 250
SALES (est): 210K **Privately Held**
WEB: www.badbags.com
SIC: 2393 5963 Duffle bags, canvas: made from purchased materials; direct sales, telemarketing

(G-9477)
BAKED LLC
2604 California Ave Sw (98116-2459)
PHONE 206 307-4847
Natalie Vorpahl, *Principal*
EMP: 8
SALES (est): 546.5K **Privately Held**
SIC: 2051 Bread, cake & related products

(G-9478)
BAKER COMMODITIES INC
Also Called: Baker Cmmdties Inc/Seattle Div
5795 S 130th Pl (98178-4602)
P.O. Box 58368 (98138-1368)
PHONE 206 243-4781
Dick Hinthorne, *Manager*
EMP: 70
SQ FT: 17,352
SALES (corp-wide): 161.3MM **Privately Held**
WEB: www.bakercommodities.com
SIC: 2077 2048 Animal & marine fats & oils; prepared feeds
PA: Baker Commodities, Inc.
 4020 Bandini Blvd
 Vernon CA 90058
 323 268-2801

(G-9479)
BALLARD ELECTRIC
1080 W Ewing St (98119-1422)
PHONE 800 873-3526
Bonghot Damron, *Owner*
EMP: 4
SALES (est): 315.9K **Privately Held**
SIC: 7694 5999 Electric motor repair; engine & motor equipment & supplies

(G-9480)
BALLARD EXTRACTS
7741 9th Ave Nw (98117-4106)
PHONE 206 499-4476
EMP: 3
SALES (est): 161.7K **Privately Held**
SIC: 2836 Mfg Biological Products

(G-9481)
BALLARD ORNAMENTAL IRONWORKS
1510 Nw Ballard Way (98107-4711)
PHONE 206 782-3343
Douglas Farage, *President*
David Farage, *Vice Pres*
EMP: 7
SQ FT: 4,700
SALES (est): 902.5K **Privately Held**
WEB: www.ballardiron.com
SIC: 3446 Fences or posts, ornamental iron or steel

(G-9482)
BALLARD OUTDOOR
5484 Shilshole Ave Nw (98107-4022)
PHONE 206 552-0760
Waldo Vega, *Principal*
EMP: 13
SALES (est): 1.6MM **Privately Held**
SIC: 2759 Commercial printing

(G-9483)
BALLARD PRINTING
1112 Nw Ballard Way (98107-4638)
PHONE 206 782-7892
Jacob Bhak, *Partner*
Paul Bhak, *Partner*
EMP: 4
SALES (est): 473.1K **Privately Held**
SIC: 2752 Commercial printing, offset

(G-9484)
BALLARD SHEET METAL WORKS INC
4763 Ballard Ave Nw (98107-4810)
PHONE 206 784-0545
David Simpson, *President*
Douglas Simpson, *Principal*
Walt Hageman, *Corp Secy*
Mary Simpson, *Vice Pres*
EMP: 20
SQ FT: 10,000
SALES (est): 4.8MM **Privately Held**
WEB: www.ballardsheetmetal.com
SIC: 3444 Sheet metal specialties, not stamped

(G-9485)
BALLARD SOCK CRITTERS
6537 19th Ave Nw (98117-5701)
PHONE 206 218-9215
Traci Timmons, *Principal*
EMP: 3
SALES (est): 198.3K **Privately Held**
SIC: 2252 Socks

(G-9486)
BALLEYWOOD CREAMERY
717 Nw 70th St Apt 102 (98117-5060)
PHONE 206 920-5173
EMP: 3
SALES (est): 175.5K **Privately Held**
SIC: 2021 Creamery butter

GEOGRAPHIC SECTION

Seattle - King County (G-9518)

(G-9487)
BALROS INDUSTRIES
1015 Queen Anne Ave N # 102
(98109-3665)
PHONE..................................206 963-6114
Adam Goldstein, *Principal*
EMP: 2
SALES (est): 64.5K **Privately Held**
SIC: 3999 Manufacturing industries

(G-9488)
BAMBOO HARDWOODS INC
6405 Roosevelt Way Ne (98115-6617)
PHONE..................................800 607-2414
Mikey McAllister, *Manager*
EMP: 2 **Privately Held**
WEB: www.bamboohardwoods.com
SIC: 2426 2439 Dimension, hardwood;
  structural wood members
PA: Bamboo Hardwoods, Inc.
  4100 4th Ave S
  Seattle WA 98134

(G-9489)
BAMBOO HARDWOODS INC (PA)
4100 4th Ave S (98134-2310)
PHONE..................................206 264-2414
Doug Lewis, *President*
David Keegan, *COO*
Andrew Diehl, *Purchasing*
Hugh Gallagher, *CFO*
▲ **EMP:** 20
SQ FT: 45,000
SALES (est): 2.6MM **Privately Held**
WEB: www.bamboohardwoods.com
SIC: 2426 1629 Dimension, hardwood;
  waste water & sewage treatment plant
  construction

(G-9490)
BANANA BLOSSOM PRESS
1805 N 107th St Unit 101 (98133-1918)
PHONE..................................206 719-3887
Maria Gonzales-Millsap, *Principal*
EMP: 2 **EST:** 2009
SALES (est): 91K **Privately Held**
SIC: 2741 Miscellaneous publishing

(G-9491)
BARBANC
1506 11th Ave (98122-3904)
PHONE..................................206 552-0852
Justin Krause, *President*
EMP: 2
SALES (est): 125.1K **Privately Held**
SIC: 2499 Decorative wood & woodwork

(G-9492)
BARDAHL MANUFACTURING CORP (PA)
1400 Nw 52nd St (98107-5131)
P.O. Box 70607 (98127-0607)
PHONE..................................206 783-4851
Hugh Mc Niel, *President*
Evelyn Bardahl McNeil, *Vice Pres*
Eric Bardahl Nicolaysen, *Admin Sec*
◆ **EMP:** 37
SQ FT: 40,000
SALES (est): 6.8MM **Privately Held**
WEB: www.bardahleurope.com
SIC: 2992 Lubricating oils & greases

(G-9493)
BARN2DOOR INC
3648 Burke Ave N (98103-8337)
PHONE..................................206 459-4338
Janelle Maiocco, *CEO*
Crystal Hoyer, *COO*
EMP: 5
SALES (est): 172.6K **Privately Held**
SIC: 7373 7372 Computer-aided system
  services; application computer software

(G-9494)
BARRETT ENCLOSURES INC
12045 Bartlett Ave Ne (98125-5836)
PHONE..................................206 285-8100
John Barrett, *President*
Shane Leazer, *Vice Pres*
EMP: 3
SQ FT: 12,000
SALES: 660K **Privately Held**
WEB: www.barrettenclosures.com
SIC: 2394 Canopies, fabric: made from
  purchased materials; canvas boat seats

(G-9495)
BARSHAY SOFTWARE INC
1916 Pike Pl Ste 12-41 (98101-1056)
PHONE..................................206 370-2393
Oleg Barshay, *Principal*
EMP: 2 **EST:** 2009
SALES (est): 153.4K **Privately Held**
SIC: 7372 Prepackaged software

(G-9496)
BARTHOLOMEW WINERY
3100 Arprt Way S Unit 10 (98134)
PHONE..................................206 395-8460
EMP: 2
SALES (est): 93.1K **Privately Held**
SIC: 2084 Wines

(G-9497)
BASEBALL CLUB OF SEATTLE LLLP
Also Called: Seattle Mariners Baseball Club
1800 4th Ave (98101-1119)
PHONE..................................206 346-4327
Yuko Iwahashi, *Branch Mgr*
EMP: 1721
SALES (corp-wide): 124.9MM **Privately Held**
SIC: 3949 Baseball equipment & supplies,
  general
PA: The Baseball Club Of Seattle Lllp
  1250 1st Ave S
  Seattle WA 98134
  206 346-4000

(G-9498)
BASIC TOPICALS LLC
1631 15th Ave W (98119-2994)
PHONE..................................206 397-3309
EMP: 3
SALES (est): 163.3K **Privately Held**
SIC: 2844 Toilet preparations

(G-9499)
BASTET SCREEN PRINTING
1223 Sw Myrtle St (98106-1940)
PHONE..................................360 880-2717
Jesi Rae Hill, *Owner*
EMP: 2
SALES (est): 83.9K **Privately Held**
SIC: 2752 Commercial printing, lithographic

(G-9500)
BATCH 206 DISTILLERY LLC
1417 Elliott Ave W (98119-3104)
PHONE..................................206 216-2803
Jeff Steichen, *Partner*
EMP: 8
SALES (est): 701K **Privately Held**
SIC: 2085 Distilled & blended liquors

(G-9501)
BAVARIAN MEAT PRODUCTS INC (PA)
2934 Western Ave (98121-1021)
PHONE..................................206 448-3540
Manny Dupper, *President*
Robert Hofstater, *Manager*
Jamie Simmons, *Manager*
▲ **EMP:** 18
SQ FT: 7,200
SALES: 1.7MM **Privately Held**
SIC: 2013 5421 5147 Sausages from purchased meat; meat markets, including freezer provisioniers; meats & meat products

(G-9502)
BAYER HLTHCARE PHRMCTICALS LLC
Also Called: Berlex Biosciences Division
1191 2nd Ave Ste 1200 (98101-2952)
PHONE..................................862 404-3000
Mark Reuben, *Ch of Bd*
Robert C Chabora, *Vice Pres*
Jorge R Engel, *Vice Pres*
Wolfgang Kunze, *Vice Pres*
John Nicholson, *Treasurer*
EMP: 400
SALES (est): 6.2MM
SALES (corp-wide): 45.3B **Privately Held**
WEB: www.berleximaging.com
SIC: 2834 Chlorination tablets & kits (water purification)
HQ: Bayer Healthcare Pharmaceuticals Inc.
  100 Bayer Blvd
  Whippany NJ 07981
  862 404-3000

(G-9503)
BCTLD LLC
Also Called: Captive Spirits
1518 Nw 52nd St Unit Main (98107-3872)
PHONE..................................206 650-6408
Ben Capdevielle,
Todd Leabman,
Benjamin Meager,
Holly Robinson,
EMP: 7
SQ FT: 1,500
SALES: 200K **Privately Held**
SIC: 2084 Wines, brandy & brandy spirits

(G-9504)
BCWEST LLC
Also Called: B C W
2755 Airport Way S (98134-2112)
P.O. Box 3938 (98124-3938)
PHONE..................................206 323-8100
EMP: 22
SQ FT: 320,000
SALES (est): 3.6MM **Privately Held**
WEB: www.bcw-inc.com
SIC: 2754 Labels: gravure printing

(G-9505)
BEAN COLLECTION COFFEE INC
14307 Greenwood Ave N (98133-6880)
PHONE..................................206 382-1966
Ed Shi, *President*
EMP: 4
SALES (est): 341.8K **Privately Held**
SIC: 2095 5149 5812 Coffee roasting (except by wholesale grocers); coffee, green or roasted; eating places

(G-9506)
BEAR & WOLF LLC
Also Called: Bear & Wolf Salmon Co
4209 21st Ave W Ste 400 (98199-1254)
PHONE..................................206 281-7777
Sean O'Leary,
Peter Kuttel,
◆ **EMP:** 15
SALES (est): 2.1MM **Privately Held**
WEB: www.bearwolf.com
SIC: 2092 Fresh or frozen packaged fish

(G-9507)
BEATS4LEGENDS
4125 38th Ave S (98118-1317)
PHONE..................................253 218-5075
EMP: 2
SALES (est): 140K **Privately Held**
SIC: 3861 Mfg Photographic Equipment/Supplies

(G-9508)
BEDROCK INDUSTRIES INC
4021 13th Ave W (98119-1350)
PHONE..................................206 283-7625
Maria Ruano, *President*
EMP: 10
SALES (est): 1MM **Privately Held**
WEB: www.bedrockindustries.com
SIC: 2221 3231 3281 Glass & fiberglass broadwoven fabrics; products of purchased glass; cut stone & stone products

(G-9509)
BELLTOWN PRTG & GRAPHICS INC
Also Called: Minuteman Press
2505 3rd Ave Ste 150 (98121-1497)
PHONE..................................206 448-8919
Yong Hwan Seo, *Principal*
Young Hwan Kim, *Principal*
EMP: 4
SALES (est): 622.9K **Privately Held**
SIC: 2752 Commercial printing, lithographic

(G-9510)
BELS INTERNATIONAL CORPORATION
Also Called: Espi's Sausage & Tocino Co
29 S Hanford St (98134-1807)
PHONE..................................206 722-3365
Felisarin Layug, *President*
Eugene Layug, *Vice Pres*
EMP: 12
SQ FT: 4,000
SALES: 500K **Privately Held**
WEB: www.espisfoods.com
SIC: 2013 Sausages & other prepared meats

(G-9511)
BEMIS COMPANY INC
256 Ne 50th St (98105-4836)
PHONE..................................206 632-2246
Michelle Klink, *Principal*
EMP: 2
SALES (est): 77.4K **Privately Held**
SIC: 3081 Unsupported plastics film & sheet

(G-9512)
BENJAMIN ANDERSON
4416 47th Ave Sw (98116-4006)
PHONE..................................206 228-8174
Benjamin Anderson, *Executive*
EMP: 2
SALES (est): 85.9K **Privately Held**
SIC: 3572 Computer storage devices

(G-9513)
BENJAMIN MOORE INC
1213 S King St (98144-2024)
PHONE..................................206 329-8607
Benjamin Moore, *President*
EMP: 8
SALES (est): 764.9K **Privately Held**
WEB: www.benjaminmooreglass.com
SIC: 3229 7336 Pressed & blown glass; commercial art & graphic design

(G-9514)
BENTLEY MILLS INC
2424 S Graham St (98108-2968)
PHONE..................................206 622-8228
Kenneth Chu, *Branch Mgr*
EMP: 3
SALES (corp-wide): 222.2MM **Privately Held**
SIC: 2273 Carpets & rugs
PA: Bentley Mills, Inc.
  14641 Don Julian Rd
  City Of Industry CA 91746
  626 333-4585

(G-9515)
BERGMAN LLC
733 17th Ave E (98112-3921)
PHONE..................................206 910-0138
Ann Bergman, *Manager*
▲ **EMP:** 2
SALES (est): 126.2K **Privately Held**
SIC: 2731 Book publishing

(G-9516)
BERNSTEIN WOODWORKS
2916 19th Ave S (98144-5828)
PHONE..................................206 605-1796
Daniel Bernstein, *Principal*
EMP: 2 **EST:** 2008
SALES (est): 150K **Privately Held**
SIC: 2431 Millwork

(G-9517)
BEST PRACTICES WIKI
2231 Nw 64th St (98107-2442)
PHONE..................................206 708-1572
Terry Gardiner, *Principal*
EMP: 2
SALES (est): 90.5K **Privately Held**
SIC: 2752 Commercial printing, lithographic

(G-9518)
BETSY BELLS NATYURAL SOLUTIONS
Also Called: Betsy Bell Skaklee
4455 51st Ave Sw (98116-4028)
PHONE..................................206 933-1889
Elisabeth Bell, *Owner*
Charles Finney, *Co-Owner*

Seattle - King County (G-9519)

EMP: 2
SALES: 38K **Privately Held**
SIC: 2834 5122 5499 Vitamin preparations; vitamins & minerals; health & dietetic food stores

(G-9519)
BGE LTD
Also Called: Beppa
7700 6th Ave Nw (98117-4038)
PHONE..................206 789-2128
Rebecca Edwards, *Branch Mgr*
EMP: 12
SALES (corp-wide): 1.8MM **Privately Held**
SIC: 2339 3965 Athletic clothing: women's, misses' & juniors'; fasteners, buttons, needles & pins
PA: Bge, Ltd.
1908 E Republican St
Seattle WA

(G-9520)
BIBBI CO LLC
922 Nw 50th St (98107-3655)
PHONE..................206 453-4152
Birgir Johannesson, *Principal*
EMP: 2
SALES (est): 137.9K **Privately Held**
SIC: 3545 Scales, measuring (machinists' precision tools)

(G-9521)
BICYCLE QUARTERLY
2116 Western Ave (98121-2110)
PHONE..................206 789-0424
Jan Heine, *Principal*
EMP: 4 EST: 2011
SALES (est): 160.3K **Privately Held**
SIC: 2741 Miscellaneous publishing

(G-9522)
BIG DERBY DISTILLING CO
Also Called: Copperworks Distilling Co
1250 Alaskan Way (98101-3439)
PHONE..................206 504-7604
Jason Parker, *President*
Jeff Kanof, *Vice Pres*
EMP: 7
SALES (est): 522.4K **Privately Held**
SIC: 2084 2085 Wines, brandy & brandy spirits; distilled & blended liquors

(G-9523)
BIG DIPPER WAX WORKS
700 S Orchard St (98108-3427)
PHONE..................206 767-7322
Brent Roose, *Owner*
Chelsea Johnson, *Accounts Exec*
▲ EMP: 2
SALES (est): 210K **Privately Held**
WEB: www.bigdipperwaxworks.com
SIC: 3999 Candles; chairs, hydraulic, barber & beauty shop

(G-9524)
BIG FISH PREMIUM LLC
906 Alaskan Way Ste 700 (98104-1010)
PHONE..................206 269-3573
Omar Amin, *Mng Member*
Carey Dijulio,
EMP: 10 EST: 2017
SALES: 4MM **Privately Held**
SIC: 7372 Prepackaged software
HQ: Big Fish Games, Inc.
333 Elliott Ave W Ste 200
Seattle WA 98104
206 213-5753

(G-9525)
BIG SKY PUBLISHING CO (HQ)
Also Called: Bozeman Daily Chronicle
221 1st Ave W Ste 405 (98119-4238)
PHONE..................406 587-4491
Stephany Pressly, *President*
▲ EMP: 11
SALES (est): 12.7MM
SALES (corp-wide): 78.7MM **Privately Held**
SIC: 2711 Newspapers, publishing & printing
PA: Pioneer Newspaper Service Llc
221 1st Ave W Ste 405
Seattle WA
206 284-4424

(G-9526)
BIG TIME BREWERY COMPANY INC
Also Called: Big Time Brewery & Alehouse
4133 University Way Ne (98105-6213)
PHONE..................206 545-4509
Reid Martin, *President*
Armaned Jones, *General Mgr*
EMP: 20
SQ FT: 4,000
SALES (est): 2.4MM **Privately Held**
WEB: www.bigtimebrewery.com
SIC: 2082 5812 5813 Beer (alcoholic beverage); American restaurant; drinking places

(G-9527)
BILINGUAL BOOKS INC
1719 W Nickerson St (98119-1633)
PHONE..................206 284-4211
Kristine Kershul, *CEO*
Rich Bushnell, *Editor*
Anna Baller, *Corp Secy*
EMP: 9
SQ FT: 3,000
SALES: 2MM **Privately Held**
WEB: www.bbks.com
SIC: 2731 Books: publishing only

(G-9528)
BILL DIBENEDETTO
620 W Olympic Pl Apt 308 (98119-3666)
P.O. Box 16351 (98116-0351)
PHONE..................206 963-0499
Bill Dibenedetto, *Principal*
EMP: 2
SALES (est): 56.5K **Privately Held**
SIC: 7372 Prepackaged software

(G-9529)
BINING HEALTH INC
701 5th Ave Ste 5500 (98104-7096)
PHONE..................604 540-8288
Gursahib Bining, *President*
EMP: 2
SALES (est): 86.6K **Privately Held**
SIC: 3841 Surgical & medical instruments

(G-9530)
BIOSONICS INC
2356 W Commodore Way # 100 (98199-1258)
PHONE..................206 782-2211
Timothy Acker, *President*
Debbie McKinnon, *Purchasing*
EMP: 11 EST: 1978
SQ FT: 8,500
SALES: 3MM **Privately Held**
WEB: www.biosonicsinc.com
SIC: 3812 8748 Search & navigation equipment; fishery consultant

(G-9531)
BIOSONICS TELEMETRY LP
2356 W Commodore Way # 100 (98199-1258)
PHONE..................206 783-9356
Tim Acker, *Partner*
Beverly Acker, *Partner*
EMP: 2
SALES (est): 166.9K **Privately Held**
SIC: 3812 Search & navigation equipment

(G-9532)
BIRKLOR LLC
Also Called: Fastsigns
12700 Aurora Ave N Ste A (98133-7520)
PHONE..................206 368-7331
Steven Birklid,
EMP: 2
SQ FT: 2,100
SALES (est): 72.6K **Privately Held**
SIC: 3993 Signs & advertising specialties

(G-9533)
BISCOTTEA BAKING COMPANY LLC
4209 21st Ave W Ste 400 (98199-1254)
PHONE..................206 695-2614
Daniel Leston, *CFO*
Laurance Milner,
▲ EMP: 6 EST: 2011
SQ FT: 2,000
SALES (est): 2MM **Privately Held**
SIC: 2052 5499 Cookies & crackers; coffee; tea
PA: Bear Trading Enterprises Llc
4209 21st Ave W Ste 400
Seattle WA 98199

(G-9534)
BIT PUSHER LLC
400 N 34th St (98103-8600)
PHONE..................206 457-5242
EMP: 2 EST: 2011
SALES (est): 134.2K **Privately Held**
SIC: 3545 Pushers

(G-9535)
BIZZYBEE LLC
4337 15th Ave Ne Apt 712 (98105-5828)
PHONE..................206 707-9417
Boris Kogon, *Mng Member*
EMP: 7
SALES (est): 36.7K **Privately Held**
SIC: 7221 3531 Photographic studios, portrait; construction machinery

(G-9536)
BLACK & DECKER CORPORATION
2100 Airport Way S (98134-1604)
PHONE..................206 624-4228
John Satter, *Manager*
EMP: 10
SALES (corp-wide): 13.9B **Publicly Held**
WEB: www.blackanddecker.com
SIC: 3546 Power-driven handtools
HQ: The Black & Decker Corporation
701 E Joppa Rd
Towson MD 21286
410 716-3900

(G-9537)
BLACK MAGIC BEVERAGES LLC
13749 Midvale Ave N (98133-7009)
PHONE..................206 632-7257
Kia Karimi, *Mng Member*
EMP: 5
SALES (est): 282.4K **Privately Held**
SIC: 2085 Cocktails, alcoholic

(G-9538)
BLACK SHEEP CREAMERY
100 4th Ave N (98109-4905)
P.O. Box 293, Adna (98522-0293)
PHONE..................360 520-3397
Brad Gregory, *Owner*
Meg Gregory, *Owner*
EMP: 2
SALES: 120K **Privately Held**
SIC: 2022 Cheese, natural & processed

(G-9539)
BLASER CASTING CORPORATION
5700 3rd Ave S (98108-2417)
PHONE..................206 767-7800
Andrew Foley, *President*
EMP: 30
SALES (est): 1.8MM **Privately Held**
SIC: 3089 Injection molding of plastics

(G-9540)
BLASER DIE CASTING CO (PA)
Also Called: Continental Brass
5700 3rd Ave S (98108-2417)
P.O. Box 80286 (98108-0286)
PHONE..................206 767-7800
Sean E S Foley, *President*
P T Foley, *President*
Andrew B Foley, *Vice Pres*
Kevin Callan, *Admin Sec*
Kevin W Foley, *Admin Sec*
▲ EMP: 60
SQ FT: 30,000
SALES (est): 39.8MM **Privately Held**
WEB: www.blaser-die.com
SIC: 3429 5072 Furniture hardware; hardware

(G-9541)
BLETHEN CORPORATION (PA)
1120 John St (98109-5321)
PHONE..................206 464-2471
Frank A Blethen, *President*
Tim Williams, *Marketing Mgr*
EMP: 225
SALES (est): 226.3MM **Privately Held**
SIC: 2711 Newspapers, publishing & printing

(G-9542)
BLINK DEVICE COMPANY LLC
1530 Westlake Ave N (98109-3095)
PHONE..................206 708-6043
EMP: 10
SALES (est): 1.1MM **Privately Held**
SIC: 3674 Solid state electronic devices

(G-9543)
BLOCKPARTYGG LLC
3801 Stone Way N Apt 207 (98103-8070)
PHONE..................206 409-6562
Ron Forbes,
EMP: 2
SALES (est): 56.5K **Privately Held**
SIC: 7372 Home entertainment computer software

(G-9544)
BLOKABLE INC (PA)
Also Called: Blokable
1136 Poplar Pl S (98144-2834)
PHONE..................800 928-6778
EMP: 7 EST: 2015
SQ FT: 6,000
SALES (est): 5MM **Privately Held**
SIC: 2452 Mfg Prefabricated Wood Buildings

(G-9545)
BLOWING SANDS
5805 14th Ave Nw (98107-2936)
PHONE..................206 783-5314
David Smith, *Owner*
EMP: 2
SALES (est): 168.6K **Privately Held**
SIC: 3229 Pressed & blown glass

(G-9546)
BLUCAPP INC
Also Called: Rivet Hammer
6315 Ne Radford Dr # 3412 (98115-8715)
PHONE..................206 629-8887
Robert L Thordarson, *CEO*
EMP: 14
SALES (est): 1MM **Privately Held**
SIC: 7372 7371 Business oriented computer software; computer software development & applications

(G-9547)
BLUE DOG BAKERY GROUP INC
3302 Fuhrman Ave E # 202 (98102-7115)
PHONE..................206 323-6958
Kyle Polanski, *CEO*
Eric Koppelman, *Vice Pres*
Bart Anderson, *CFO*
Mika Shimazu, *Marketing Staff*
Heidi Lopez, *Manager*
EMP: 15
SQ FT: 1,200
SALES: 30MM **Privately Held**
WEB: www.bluedogbakery.com
SIC: 2047 Dog food

(G-9548)
BLUE HERON GROUP INC
Also Called: Washington Machine Works
5211 1st Ave S (98108-2205)
PHONE..................206 767-2688
Richard Stewart, *President*
Carmela Grandinetti, *Treasurer*
EMP: 14
SALES (est): 110.8K **Privately Held**
SIC: 3599 Machine shop, jobbing & repair

(G-9549)
BLUE INK
13030 Linden Ave N (98133-7587)
PHONE..................206 588-0739
Todd Korb, *Principal*
EMP: 3
SALES (est): 229.5K **Privately Held**
SIC: 2759 Commercial printing

GEOGRAPHIC SECTION

Seattle - King County (G-9579)

(G-9550)
BLUE LANTERN PUBLISHING INC (PA)
3645 Interlake Ave N (98103-8104)
PHONE 206 632-7075
Harold D Darling, *President*
Jason Meyer, *Purch Mgr*
Sandra Darling, *Shareholder*
◆ **EMP:** 6
SQ FT: 4,400
SALES (est): 840.4K **Privately Held**
WEB: www.gooddogcarl.com
SIC: 2731 Books: publishing only

(G-9551)
BLUE LANTERN PUBLISHING INC
Also Called: Laughing Elephant
3645 Interlake Ave N (98103-8104)
PHONE 206 447-9229
Benjamin Darling, *Marketing Staff*
EMP: 5
SQ FT: 6,480 **Privately Held**
WEB: www.gooddogcarl.com
SIC: 2731 2771 2741 Book publishing; greeting cards; miscellaneous publishing
PA: Blue Lantern Publishing, Inc.
3645 Interlake Ave N
Seattle WA 98103

(G-9552)
BLUE NORTH FOREST PRODUCTS LLC
2930 Westlake Ave N # 300 (98109-1968)
PHONE 208 935-2547
Michael F Burns,
Herb Hazen,
Bill Mulligan,
EMP: 10
SALES (est): 2.1MM **Privately Held**
SIC: 2421 Sawmills & planing mills, general

(G-9553)
BLUE NORTH TRADING COMPANY LLC
2940 Westlake Ave N # 302 (98109-1969)
PHONE 206 352-9252
Lance Magnuson, *Director*
Michael F Burns,
◆ **EMP:** 2
SALES (est): 356.2K **Privately Held**
SIC: 2261 Sponging cotton broadwoven cloth for the trade

(G-9554)
BLUE WATER PROJECTS INC
Also Called: Waypoint Sign Company
1505 S 93rd St Ste Ba (98108-5153)
PHONE 206 452-1332
Kevin Jeffries, *CEO*
Bob Ellis, *Project Mgr*
Steve McCallum, *Manager*
Flo Richardson, *Business Dir*
EMP: 17
SALES (est): 1.2MM **Privately Held**
SIC: 3993 Signs & advertising specialties

(G-9555)
BLUECOSMO INC
Also Called: Bluecsmo Stllite Cmmunications
4746 44th Ave Sw Ste 201 (98116-4476)
PHONE 877 258-3496
Jonathan M Saad, *President*
◆ **EMP:** 5
SQ FT: 1,100
SALES (est): 544.3K **Privately Held**
WEB: www.bluecosmo.com
SIC: 4812 4813 3663 7359 Cellular telephone services; voice telephone communications; mobile communication equipment; mobile communication equipment rental; antennas, receiving, satellite dishes; antennas, satellite dish

(G-9556)
BLUELINE EQUIPMENT CO LLC
105 S Spokane St (98134)
PHONE 509 248-8411
EMP: 2
SALES (corp-wide): 11.5MM **Privately Held**
SIC: 3523 Farm machinery & equipment

HQ: Blueline Equipment Co., Llc
1605 E Mead Ave
Yakima WA 98903
509 248-8411

(G-9557)
BLUESEVENTY LLC
118 Nw Canal St Ste A (98107-4933)
PHONE 206 547-5273
John Duguette, *Mng Member*
John Duguette, *Mng Member*
Tim Moxey, *Mng Member*
▲ **EMP:** 9
SQ FT: 500
SALES (est): 699.4K **Privately Held**
SIC: 2253 Bathing suits & swimwear, knit

(G-9558)
BLUEWAVE TECHNOLOGIES LLC
1546 Nw 56th St Ste 564 (98107-5209)
PHONE 800 636-1428
Don Carr, *Principal*
EMP: 2
SALES (est): 62.1K **Privately Held**
SIC: 7372 7382 Application computer software; security systems services

(G-9559)
BOAT-TECH
600 W Nickerson St (98119-1531)
PHONE 206 281-9828
Matt McGuane, *Owner*
Matt Mc Guane, *Owner*
EMP: 2
SALES (est): 186.3K **Privately Held**
WEB: www.boat-tech.com
SIC: 3732 Boat building & repairing

(G-9560)
BODYPOINT INC
558 1st Ave S Ste 300 (98104-3806)
PHONE 206 405-4555
David A Hintzman, *President*
Matthew Kosh, *Vice Pres*
▲ **EMP:** 35
SQ FT: 20,000
SALES (est): 6.2MM **Privately Held**
WEB: www.bodypoint.com
SIC: 3841 5047 Surgical & medical instruments; medical & hospital equipment

(G-9561)
BODYSENSE INC (PA)
4000 Sw 104th St (98146-1153)
PHONE 206 988-1719
Connie Colbert, *President*
Lucinda Morton, *Vice Pres*
Margery Jette, *Admin Sec*
EMP: 3
SQ FT: 4,000
SALES (est): 450.1K **Privately Held**
WEB: www.bodysenseinc.com
SIC: 3949 Masks: hockey, baseball, football, etc.

(G-9562)
BOEING CLASSIC
800 Occidental Ave S (98134-1200)
P.O. Box 3707 (98124-2207)
PHONE 206 381-7804
Michelle De, *Manager*
EMP: 3 **EST:** 2012
SALES (est): 263K **Privately Held**
SIC: 3721 Airplanes, fixed or rotary wing

(G-9563)
BOEING COMPANY
7701 14th Ave S (98108-3517)
P.O. Box 3707 (98124-2207)
PHONE 206 655-1131
Kevin McAllister, *President*
Scott A Campbell, *Vice Pres*
Matt Cooper, *Vice Pres*
Michael P Delaney, *Vice Pres*
Mark D Jenks, *Vice Pres*
EMP: 54000
SALES (corp-wide): 101.1B **Publicly Held**
SIC: 3721 3663 3761 Airplanes, fixed or rotary wing; helicopters; research & development on aircraft by the manufacturer; airborne radio communications equipment; guided missiles, complete

PA: The Boeing Company
100 N Riverside Plz
Chicago IL 60606
312 544-2000

(G-9564)
BOOM NOODLE CORP UV
2675 Ne Village Ln (98105-5029)
PHONE 206 525-2675
EMP: 13
SALES (est): 860K **Privately Held**
SIC: 2098 Mfg Macaroni/Spaghetti

(G-9565)
BOOMERANG BOXER LLC
468a Ne Thornton Pl (98125-8022)
PHONE 206 227-6569
EMP: 2
SALES (est): 56.9K **Privately Held**
SIC: 3949 Mfg Sporting/Athletic Goods

(G-9566)
BOTANICAL COLORS LLC
4020 Leary Way Nw Ste 300 (98107-5019)
PHONE 206 518-7073
EMP: 2
SALES (est): 83.9K **Privately Held**
SIC: 2865 Mfg Cyclic Crudes/Intermediates/Dyes

(G-9567)
BOTANICAL COLORS LLC
10550 Phinney Ave N (98133-8729)
PHONE 206 518-7073
Katherine Hattori,
EMP: 2 **EST:** 2010
SALES (est): 220.1K **Privately Held**
SIC: 2865 Dyes, synthetic organic

(G-9568)
BOUNDLESS ENTERPRISES INC
Also Called: 48 Degrees North
6327 Seaview Ave Nw (98107-2664)
PHONE 206 789-7350
Gary Wright, *Principal*
Richard D Hazeltton, *Principal*
Karen Higginson, *Assoc Editor*
EMP: 4
SQ FT: 1,500
SALES (est): 429.3K **Privately Held**
WEB: www.48north.com
SIC: 2721 Magazines: publishing only, not printed on site

(G-9569)
BOUNDLESS IMMIGRATION INC
240 2nd Ave S Ste 300 (98104-2250)
PHONE 855 268-6353
Doug Rand, *President*
EMP: 12
SALES (est): 1.4MM **Privately Held**
SIC: 2731 Book publishing

(G-9570)
BOURGEOIS BITS LLC
3417 Evanston Ave N # 313 (98103-8626)
PHONE 434 535-2487
David Peck,
Nicholas Robinson,
Peter Sagerson,
EMP: 3 **EST:** 2010
SALES (est): 172.7K **Privately Held**
SIC: 7372 Utility computer software

(G-9571)
BOUTIQUE IMPORTS LLC
8530 20th Ave Nw (98117-3524)
PHONE 206 650-5555
Dwight D Proteau,
Jacqueline L Proteau,
Antonino Sasa,
EMP: 2
SALES (est): 75.4K **Privately Held**
SIC: 2084 Wines

(G-9572)
BOWHEAD MANUFACTURING CO LLC
1011 Sw Kickwat Ste 104 (98134)
PHONE 206 957-5321
Jeff Guentzel, *Principal*
EMP: 5
SALES (corp-wide): 788.5MM **Privately Held**
SIC: 3069 Rubberized fabrics

HQ: Bowhead Manufacturing Company Llc
1000 Shiloh Rd Ste 500
Plano TX 75074
256 382-3260

(G-9573)
BOWMAN-MORTON MFG & MCH INC
7500 W Marginal Way S (98108-4142)
PHONE 206 524-8890
Scott Morton, *President*
EMP: 10
SQ FT: 5,000
SALES (est): 1.5MM **Privately Held**
SIC: 3441 3599 Fabricated structural metal; machine shop, jobbing & repair

(G-9574)
BP ARCO SEATTLE TERMINAL
Also Called: BP Logistics
1652 Sw Lander St (98134-1029)
PHONE 206 623-4637
Sammy Makalena, *Site Mgr*
EMP: 7
SALES (est): 367.2K **Privately Held**
SIC: 2911 Petroleum refining

(G-9575)
BRAD O CONNOR WOODWORKING
4022 52nd Ave Sw (98116-3621)
PHONE 206 302-8424
Bradley James Oconnor, *Principal*
EMP: 4
SALES (est): 362.2K **Privately Held**
SIC: 2431 Millwork

(G-9576)
BRADY WORLDWIDE INC
100 S Massachusetts St (98134-1401)
PHONE 800 854-6832
Katherine Hudson, *Branch Mgr*
EMP: 45
SALES (corp-wide): 1.1B **Publicly Held**
WEB: www.varitronicsystems.com
SIC: 3999 Identification badges & insignia
HQ: Brady Worldwide, Inc.
6555 W Good Hope Rd
Milwaukee WI 53223

(G-9577)
BRADY WORLDWIDE INC
1560 1st Ave S (98134-1402)
PHONE 206 323-8100
Dana Milkie, *Branch Mgr*
EMP: 45
SALES (corp-wide): 1.1B **Publicly Held**
WEB: www.varitronicsystems.com
SIC: 3999 Identification badges & insignia
HQ: Brady Worldwide, Inc.
6555 W Good Hope Rd
Milwaukee WI 53223

(G-9578)
BRANOM OPERATING COMPANY LLC
Also Called: Branom Instrument Co.
5500 4th Ave S (98108-2419)
PHONE 206 762-6050
Michael Lauer, *Mng Member*
Marty Weaver, *Manager*
EMP: 30
SALES: 10.5MM **Privately Held**
SIC: 3822 3823 Building services monitoring controls, automatic; water quality monitoring & control systems

(G-9579)
BRAVO PUBLICATIONS INC
Also Called: Banquet and Event
4817 California Ave Sw (98116-4414)
P.O. Box 2478, Friday Harbor (98250-2478)
PHONE 206 937-3264
Marion Clifton, *Owner*
Teresa Russell, *Sales Mgr*
EMP: 4 **Privately Held**
WEB: www.bravoportland.com
SIC: 2741 Directories: publishing only, not printed on site
PA: Bravo Publications Inc
311 B Ave Ste B
Lake Oswego OR 97034

Seattle - King County (G-9580)

(G-9580)
BRE & CAR INDUSTRIES LLC
924 S 117th Ct (98168-2186)
PHONE..................206 268-0204
Carlene Briones, *Principal*
EMP: 2
SALES (est): 83.2K **Privately Held**
SIC: 3999 Manufacturing industries

(G-9581)
BREAK FROM REALITY GAMES LLC
3273 Sw Avalon Way Unit A (98126-2647)
PHONE..................513 884-4940
Eric Salyers, *Mng Member*
Alex Barbieri
▲ EMP: 3 EST: 2013
SALES: 110K **Privately Held**
SIC: 3944 Board games, children's & adults'

(G-9582)
BREEZY UPHOLSTERY & CANVAS
23 Dravus St (98109-1604)
PHONE..................206 545-8538
Shawn Breese, *Owner*
EMP: 4
SALES (est): 330.7K **Privately Held**
SIC: 2273 2221 Carpets & rugs; upholstery fabrics, manmade fiber & silk

(G-9583)
BRIAN GANNON
7757 16th Ave Nw (98117-5420)
PHONE..................206 782-2276
Brian Gannon, *Principal*
EMP: 2
SALES (est): 62.3K **Privately Held**
SIC: 2068 Salted & roasted nuts & seeds

(G-9584)
BRIAN MURPHY
2023 E Roy St (98112-4038)
PHONE..................206 323-8001
Brian Murphy, *Administration*
EMP: 2
SALES (est): 62.9K **Privately Held**
SIC: 2711 Newspapers

(G-9585)
BRIDGESTONE HOSEPOWER LLC
Also Called: Fittings
5979 4th Ave S (98108-3209)
PHONE..................206 767-4670
John P Clarkson, *President*
EMP: 20 **Privately Held**
SIC: 5085 3494 3492 3429 Industrial fittings; hose, belting & packing; valves & pipe fittings; fluid power valves & hose fittings; manufactured hardware (general); laminated plastics plate & sheet
HQ: Bridgestone Hosepower, Llc
50 Industrial Loop N
Orange Park FL 32073
904 264-1267

(G-9586)
BRINDLE PRESS LLC
117 E Louisa St (98102-3203)
PHONE..................360 434-3302
EMP: 2 EST: 2017
SALES (est): 63.4K **Privately Held**
SIC: 2741 Miscellaneous publishing

(G-9587)
BRITISH FOOTPATHS
9521 45th Ave Ne (98115-2603)
PHONE..................206 525-2466
Fred Austin, *Principal*
EMP: 2
SALES (est): 138.7K **Privately Held**
SIC: 2711 Newspapers, publishing & printing

(G-9588)
BROOKS RAND INC
Also Called: Brooks Rand Instruments
4415 6th Ave Nw (98107-4416)
PHONE..................206 632-6206
Collin Davies, *CEO*
EMP: 8
SALES (est): 1.6MM **Privately Held**
SIC: 3826 Analytical instruments

(G-9589)
BROOMFLDS WLDG MET FABRICATION
Also Called: Broomfelds Mar Exhaust Seattle
5104 Ballard Ave Nw (98107-4856)
PHONE..................206 784-9267
Edmond L Broomfield Jr, *President*
Lisa Lagumina, *Admin Sec*
EMP: 5
SQ FT: 1,600
SALES: 800K **Privately Held**
WEB: www.broomfields.com
SIC: 3441 7699 7692 3429 Fabricated structural metal; welding equipment repair; welding repair; manufactured hardware (general)

(G-9590)
BROWN SUGAR BAKING COMPANY LLC
308 22nd Ave S Ste 101 (98144-2260)
P.O. Box 28536 (98118-8536)
PHONE..................202 558-8422
Dennis Comer, *Managing Dir*
Lillian Hill, *Principal*
Eddie Hill Jr, *Materials Mgr*
Joanne Hill, *Treasurer*
EMP: 4
SQ FT: 605
SALES (est): 244.9K **Privately Held**
SIC: 2053 5149 2051 2052 Frozen bakery products, except bread; crackers, cookies & bakery products; pies, bakery: except frozen; rolls, bread type: fresh or frozen; cookies

(G-9591)
BSPACE CORPORATION (PA)
500 Yale Ave N 105 (98109-5680)
PHONE..................208 559-7806
David Burcham, *President*
Christa Budinoff, *Vice Pres*
EMP: 4
SALES (est): 886.9K **Privately Held**
SIC: 3761 3724 3764 Guided missiles & space vehicles; aircraft engines & engine parts; guided missile & space vehicle propulsion unit parts

(G-9592)
BUCKY INC
6700 Riverside Dr (98188-4748)
PHONE..................206 545-8790
▲ EMP: 25
SQ FT: 17,000
SALES (est): 2.4MM **Privately Held**
SIC: 2392 Mfg Household Furnishings

(G-9593)
BUDO INDUSTRIES LLC
2727 34th Ave S (98144-5560)
PHONE..................206 349-8085
EMP: 2 EST: 2011
SALES (est): 100K **Privately Held**
SIC: 3999 Mfg Misc Products

(G-9594)
BUDO LLC
6212 Woodlawn Ave N (98103-5717)
PHONE..................206 854-1161
Josh Karp, *Principal*
EMP: 3
SALES (est): 133.7K **Privately Held**
SIC: 2711 Newspapers

(G-9595)
BUFFALO INDUSTRIES INC
99 S Spokane St (98134-2218)
PHONE..................206 682-9900
Larry Benezra, *President*
Wil Lavaris, *Accounting Mgr*
Matt Benesch, *VP Sales*
Glenn Welsh, *Manager*
EMP: 5
SALES (est): 59.9K **Privately Held**
SIC: 2392 2326 3842 Polishing cloths, plain; overalls & coveralls; applicators, cotton tipped

(G-9596)
BUILDER BOX LLC
Also Called: Hardsuit Labs
4025 Delridge Way Sw # 210 (98106-1249)
PHONE..................206 778-4753
Andrew Kipling,
Russell Nelson,
EMP: 30 EST: 2014
SQ FT: 7,000
SALES (est): 1.9MM **Privately Held**
SIC: 7371 7372 Computer software development & applications; home entertainment computer software

(G-9597)
BUILDING ENVLOPE INNVTIONS LLC
Also Called: B E I
1115 N 97th St (98103-3311)
PHONE..................206 985-3788
Stacey Grund,
EMP: 4
SALES (est): 545.3K **Privately Held**
SIC: 2891 Adhesives & sealants

(G-9598)
BULLENE SIGN
2801 1st Ave Apt 1005 (98121-1139)
PHONE..................425 260-3311
EMP: 2
SALES (est): 120K **Privately Held**
SIC: 3993 Mfg Signs/Advertising Specialties

(G-9599)
BURG CRIMINAL & DUI DEFENSE
720 3rd Ave Ste 2015 (98104-1814)
PHONE..................206 467-3190
EMP: 3
SALES (est): 184.6K **Privately Held**
SIC: 3812 Defense systems & equipment

(G-9600)
BURIED HATCHET TOOL CO LLC
1310 N Menford Pl (98103-7520)
PHONE..................253 677-9730
Robin Fay, *Principal*
EMP: 2
SALES (est): 98.6K **Privately Held**
SIC: 3599 Industrial machinery

(G-9601)
BUSH WOODCRAFT
Also Called: Bush Woodcraft Shoji Doors
841 Rainier Ave S (98144-2837)
PHONE..................206 323-2020
Mike Fujii, *Owner*
EMP: 2
SALES (est): 194.3K **Privately Held**
WEB: www.shojiscreens.com
SIC: 2431 Millwork

(G-9602)
BUTTER LONDON LLC
2401 Utah Ave S Ste 320 (98134-1431)
PHONE..................206 624-1085
Leslie Freytag, *President*
Rene Contreras, *Manager*
EMP: 5
SALES (corp-wide): 15.6MM **Privately Held**
WEB: www.butterlondon.com
SIC: 5999 2844 Toilet preparations; toilet preparations
PA: Butter London Llc
2101 4th Ave Ste 1650
Seattle WA 98121
206 525-0847

(G-9603)
CABINETS & COUNTERTOPS LLC
3030 64th Ave Sw (98116-2783)
PHONE..................206 933-9385
Terry M Steele,
EMP: 4
SALES (est): 5MM **Privately Held**
SIC: 2434 Wood kitchen cabinets

(G-9604)
CADWALLADER AND STERN LLC
1122 E Pike St (98122-3916)
PHONE..................206 931-8018
Alan Cadwallader, *Principal*
EMP: 2
SALES (est): 57.4K **Privately Held**
SIC: 2731 Books: publishing & printing

(G-9605)
CAFFE APPASSIONATO INC (PA)
Also Called: Austin Chase Coffee
4001 21st Ave W (98199-1201)
PHONE..................206 281-8040
Philip Sancken, *President*
Tucker McHugh, *Exec VP*
Thomas McHugh, *Vice Pres*
Rasmussen Kurt, *Engineer*
▲ EMP: 30
SQ FT: 6,000
SALES (est): 4.8MM **Privately Held**
SIC: 2095 5812 Roasted coffee; coffee shop

(G-9606)
CALIB DESIGNS LLC
4225 Francis Ave N Apt A (98103-7130)
P.O. Box 1519, Port Townsend (98368-0047)
PHONE..................206 548-9217
James Johnson, *Partner*
Glenn Jansen,
EMP: 2
SALES (est): 131.7K **Privately Held**
SIC: 3999 Barber & beauty shop equipment

(G-9607)
CALLISON ARCHITECTURE LLC
1420 5th Ave Ste 2400 (98101-1345)
PHONE..................206 623-4646
John Jastrem, *CEO*
EMP: 2
SALES (est): 126.3K
SALES (corp-wide): 6.6MM **Privately Held**
SIC: 3446 Architectural metalwork
PA: Arcadis N.V.
Gustav Mahlerplein 97 103
Amsterdam
202 011-011

(G-9608)
CALLISONS INC
Also Called: Sherwood Forest Farms
520 Pike St Ste 2500 (98101-4083)
PHONE..................206 545-3900
Walter Clayton, *President*
EMP: 10
SALES (corp-wide): 24.6MM **Privately Held**
WEB: www.ipcallison.com
SIC: 2899 Oils & essential oils; peppermint oil; spearmint oil
PA: Callisons, Inc.
2400 Callison Rd Ne
Lacey WA 98516
360 412-3340

(G-9609)
CALPORTLAND
5975 E Marginal Way S (98134-2414)
P.O. Box 1730 (98111-1730)
PHONE..................206 764-3000
Allen Hamblen, *President*
EMP: 2 **Privately Held**
SIC: 3273 Ready-mixed concrete
HQ: Calportland
20601 Ne Marine Dr
Fairview OR 97024

(G-9610)
CALPORTLAND COMPANY
5900 W Marginal Way Sw (98106-1500)
PHONE..................206 764-3075
Allen Hamblen, *Branch Mgr*
EMP: 68 **Privately Held**
SIC: 3273 Ready-mixed concrete
HQ: Calportland Company
2025 E Financial Way
Glendora CA 91741
626 852-6200

(G-9611)
CALYPSO MEDICAL TECH INC
2101 4th Ave Ste 500 (98121-2348)
PHONE..................206 254-0600
Edward Vertatschitsch, *President*
Mark Querry, *Vice Pres*
Susana Dilonex, *Project Mgr*
Matthew Moree, *Auditor*
Shelby Catteau, *Accounts Mgr*
▼ EMP: 175
SQ FT: 40,000

GEOGRAPHIC SECTION
Seattle - King County (G-9641)

SALES (est): 20.7MM
SALES (corp-wide): 2.9B **Publicly Held**
WEB: www.calypsomedical.com
SIC: **3845** Medical cleaning equipment, ultrasonic
PA: Varian Medical Systems, Inc.
3100 Hansen Way
Palo Alto CA 94304
650 493-4000

(G-9612)
CAMBRIA CORPORATION
1328 N 128th St (98133-7639)
PHONE 206 782-8380
Douglas M Johnson, *President*
Eric Cheney, *Corp Secy*
Brigitte Fortin, *Vice Pres*
▲ EMP: 7
SQ FT: 8,000
SALES (est): 1.4MM **Privately Held**
WEB: www.cambriacorp.net
SIC: **3823** Industrial process control instruments

(G-9613)
CAMILLE
2333 W Plymouth St Apt 1 (98199-4135)
PHONE 206 284-0407
Princess Camille, *Principal*
EMP: 2 **EST:** 2010
SALES (est): 103.3K **Privately Held**
SIC: **2844** Toilet preparations

(G-9614)
CAMPBELL MARITIME INC
1515 Fairview Ave E (98102-3718)
PHONE 206 794-0232
Brian Campbell, *Owner*
EMP: 2
SALES (est): 218.2K **Privately Held**
WEB: www.campbellmaritime.com
SIC: **3731** Barges, building & repairing

(G-9615)
CAMPUSCE CORPORATION
1201 3rd Ave Ste 1580 (98101-3093)
PHONE 206 686-8003
Loren Pace, *CEO*
Rebekah Koutny, *Editor*
Edward Vincent, *Editor*
Mark Morgan, *Assistant VP*
Daniel Herda, *Vice Pres*
EMP: 7
SALES (est): 636.2K **Privately Held**
WEB: www.campusce.com
SIC: **7372** Application computer software

(G-9616)
CANELLE CITRON
10438 40th Ave Sw (98146-1172)
P.O. Box 2403 (98111-2403)
PHONE 206 241-4657
Lori Brankey, *Principal*
EMP: 2
SALES (est): 90K **Privately Held**
SIC: **3674** Semiconductors & related devices

(G-9617)
CANNABIS LEAF INCORPORATED
4500 9th Ave Ne (98105-4737)
PHONE 206 430-6250
Laurie Stephenson, *CEO*
EMP: 2
SALES (est): 75K **Privately Held**
SIC: **1081** Metal mining services

(G-9618)
CANNON BALL INDUSTRIES
3411 Nw 59th St (98107-3352)
PHONE 206 781-1833
Jensen Graham, *Principal*
EMP: 2
SALES (est): 102.9K **Privately Held**
SIC: **3999** Manufacturing industries

(G-9619)
CANOE RIDGE VINEYARD
Also Called: Precept Wine
1910 Frview Ave E Ste 400 (98102)
PHONE 206 267-5252
Andrew Browne, *CEO*
Mark Harmann, *Senior VP*
Phil Kazanjian, *Senior VP*
David J Minick, *Vice Pres*

EMP: 4
SALES (est): 83K **Privately Held**
SIC: **2084** **5182** Wines; wine

(G-9620)
CANVAS
600 Elliott Ave W (98119-4075)
PHONE 206 829-9858
EMP: 4
SALES (est): 388K **Privately Held**
SIC: **2211** Canvas

(G-9621)
CANVAS SUPPLY CO INC
4711 Ballard Ave Nw (98107-4810)
PHONE 206 784-0711
Robert A McLauchlan, *President*
Brian A McLauchlan, *Vice Pres*
▲ EMP: 25 **EST:** 1959
SQ FT: 10,000
SALES (est): 2.1MM **Privately Held**
SIC: **2394** **2515** **5999** **5039** Canvas & related products; mattresses & bedsprings; awnings; awnings

(G-9622)
CANVAS TRADITIONS
5267 Shilshole Ave Nw # 106 (98107-4840)
PHONE 206 313-0223
Lee Barton, *Bd of Directors*
EMP: 4 **EST:** 2008
SALES (est): 271K **Privately Held**
SIC: **2211** Canvas

(G-9623)
CAPE POINT PRESS LLC
7406 Latona Ave Ne Unit B (98115-4000)
PHONE 206 324-2126
Kathleen Farquharson, *Principal*
EMP: 2
SALES (est): 123.3K **Privately Held**
SIC: **2741** Miscellaneous publishing

(G-9624)
CAPITAL INDUSTRIES INC
5801 3rd Ave S (98108-3205)
P.O. Box 80983 (98108-0983)
PHONE 206 762-8585
Ronald Taylor, *President*
Tim Lambert, *President*
Ronald S Taylor, *President*
David Taylor Jr, *Vice Pres*
William Garrity, *Treasurer*
◆ EMP: 100
SQ FT: 100,000
SALES (est): 35.5MM **Privately Held**
WEB: www.capitalind.com
SIC: **3469** **3713** **3465** Garbage cans, stamped & pressed metal; truck bodies & parts; fenders, automobile: stamped or pressed metal

(G-9625)
CAPITAL TOOL CO
91 S Royal Brougham Way (98134-1219)
PHONE 206 240-7470
Eric Peterson, *Principal*
EMP: 2
SALES (est): 83.2K **Privately Held**
SIC: **3544** Special dies, tools, jigs & fixtures

(G-9626)
CAPSTAN FUND
800 5th Ave Ste 4100 (98104-3100)
PHONE 206 626-0800
Douglas D Adkins, *Partner*
George C Textor Jr, *Partner*
EMP: 4
SQ FT: 2,000
SALES (est): 605.5K **Privately Held**
SIC: **6282** **3589** Investment advisory service; cooking equipment, commercial

(G-9627)
CARBON AEROSPACE
1318 Nw Woodbine Way (98177-5244)
PHONE 206 697-3832
EMP: 2 **EST:** 2014
SALES (est): 104.8K **Privately Held**
SIC: **3721** Aircraft

(G-9628)
CARDEAS PHARMA CORPORATION
2025 1st Ave Ste 1200 (98121-3119)
P.O. Box 534, Medina (98039-0534)
PHONE 206 973-1026
A Bruce Montgomery, *CEO*
EMP: 12
SALES (est): 1.7MM **Privately Held**
SIC: **2834** Pharmaceutical preparations

(G-9629)
CARDINAL HEALTH INC
421 S Michigan St (98108-3313)
PHONE 206 763-8500
Mary Johnson, *Manager*
EMP: 25
SALES (corp-wide): 136.8B **Publicly Held**
SIC: **3829** **8099** Medical diagnostic systems, nuclear; health screening service
PA: Cardinal Health, Inc.
7000 Cardinal Pl
Dublin OH 43017
614 757-5000

(G-9630)
CARDINAL HEALTH 414 LLC
5030 1st Ave S Ste 110 (98134-2438)
PHONE 206 763-4411
EMP: 9
SALES (corp-wide): 136.8B **Publicly Held**
SIC: **2835** **2834** Radioactive diagnostic substances; pharmaceutical preparations
HQ: Cardinal Health 414, Llc
7000 Cardinal Pl
Dublin OH 43017
614 757-5000

(G-9631)
CARE ZONE INC
1463 E Republican St (98112-4517)
PHONE 888 407-7785
Jonathan Schwartz, *Principal*
Katea Ravega, *Counsel*
Trent Gruenwald, *Marketing Staff*
EMP: 6
SALES (est): 461.7K **Privately Held**
SIC: **7372** Prepackaged software

(G-9632)
CARE ZONE INC
Also Called: Carezone
1520 Bellevue Ave Ste 202 (98122-7602)
PHONE 206 707-9127
Jonathan Schwartz, *CEO*
Walter Smith, *Vice Pres*
Jennifer Hsieh, *Finance*
Lito Nicolai, *Software Dev*
EMP: 50 **EST:** 2010
SQ FT: 4,000
SALES (est): 2.5MM **Privately Held**
SIC: **7372** Application computer software

(G-9633)
CARL ZAPFFE INC (PA)
12004 Aurora Ave N (98133-8250)
PHONE 206 364-1919
William Thompson, *Owner*
Audrey C Thompson, *Corp Secy*
Thad Thompson, *Treasurer*
EMP: 6
SQ FT: 3,500
SALES (est): 564.8K **Privately Held**
WEB: www.silverpros.com
SIC: **7699** **3914** **3471** Replating shop, except silverware; plated ware (all metals); plating & polishing

(G-9634)
CARNITECH US INC
1112 Nw Leary Way (98107-5133)
PHONE 206 781-1827
Henrik Rasmussen, *President*
▲ EMP: 4
SALES (est): 690K **Privately Held**
SIC: **3556** Food products machinery

(G-9635)
CAROL BRADEN INC
2224 E Miller St (98112-2214)
PHONE 206 715-9397
Carol Braden, *President*
EMP: 2

SALES (est): 675K **Privately Held**
SIC: **2836** Culture media

(G-9636)
CARRY GEAR SOLUTIONS LLC
2125 Western Ave Ste 300 (98121-3137)
PHONE 206 957-6800
Renee Pitra, *Mng Member*
Dave Henderson,
▲ EMP: 33
SQ FT: 3,000
SALES (est): 3.3MM **Privately Held**
WEB: www.carrygearsolutions.com
SIC: **2393** Textile bags

(G-9637)
CARSOE US INC
1112 Nw Leary Way (98107-5133)
PHONE 206 408-5869
Mikkel K Jacobsen, *President*
EMP: 8 **EST:** 2016
SALES (est): 187.8K
SALES (corp-wide): 410.9K **Privately Held**
SIC: **3535** Conveyors & conveying equipment
HQ: Carsoe A/S
Mineralvej 6-8
Aalborg
982 426-24

(G-9638)
CARSON/CORBETT LLC
2010 Airport Way S (98134-1603)
PHONE 206 624-8266
Ron Hudson, *Branch Mgr*
EMP: 5
SALES (est): 409.8K **Privately Held**
SIC: **3299** Architectural sculptures: gypsum, clay, papier mache, etc.
PA: Carson/Corbett, L.L.C.
1531 Ne 89th St
Seattle WA 98115

(G-9639)
CARSON/CORBETT LLC (PA)
1531 Ne 89th St (98115-3140)
PHONE 206 524-9782
Andrew Carson, *Mng Member*
Shelly Corbett,
EMP: 4
SALES (est): 736.3K **Privately Held**
WEB: www.fotowork.com
SIC: **3299** **5719** Architectural sculptures: gypsum, clay, papier mache, etc.; pictures, wall

(G-9640)
CASCADE DESIGNS INC (PA)
4000 1st Ave S (98134-2301)
PHONE 206 505-9500
John D Burroughs, *Ch of Bd*
Patrick Diller, *Business Mgr*
Donald Sublett, *Mfg Staff*
Paul Smith, *Engineer*
Jonathan Shapas, *Sales Staff*
▲ EMP: 300
SQ FT: 200,000
SALES (est): 110.8MM **Privately Held**
WEB: www.cascadedesigns.com
SIC: **2515** **3089** **3949** **8733** Mattresses & bedsprings; air mattresses, plastic; camping equipment & supplies; research institute

(G-9641)
CASCADE DESIGNS INC
Also Called: Msr Global Health
3800 1st Ave S (98134-2235)
PHONE 206 505-9500
Tim Davis, *Director*
EMP: 5
SALES (corp-wide): 110.8MM **Privately Held**
SIC: **2834** **3589** **3949** Chlorination tablets & kits (water purification); water treatment equipment, industrial; camping equipment & supplies
PA: Cascade Designs, Inc.
4000 1st Ave S
Seattle WA 98134
206 505-9500

Seattle - King County (G-9642)   GEOGRAPHIC SECTION

(G-9642)
CASCADE DESIGNS INC
Varilite
4000 1st Ave S (98134-2301)
PHONE..................................206 505-9500
Susan Cwiertnia, *Branch Mgr*
EMP: 20
SALES (corp-wide): 110.8MM **Privately Held**
SIC: 2399 3842 Sleeping bags; wheelchairs
PA: Cascade Designs, Inc.
4000 1st Ave S
Seattle WA 98134
206 505-9500

(G-9643)
CASCADE PUBLISHING INC
Also Called: Compass Productions
1546 Nw 56th St Ste 495 (98107-5209)
P.O. Box 99189, Lakewood (98496-0189)
PHONE..................................206 430-6021
Mark S Piteo-Tarpy, *President*
Claes Furusjo, *Shareholder*
Daniel Mullen, *Shareholder*
EMP: 5 **EST:** 2013
SALES (est): 600K **Privately Held**
SIC: 5192 2731 Books; book publishing

(G-9644)
CASE MIX ANALYSIS INC
200 W Thomas St Ste 150 (98119-4215)
PHONE..................................206 285-2576
Fax: 206 285-4317
EMP: 4
SALES (corp-wide): 1.2MM **Privately Held**
SIC: 3273 8748 Mfg Ready-Mixed Concrete Business Consulting Services
PA: Case Mix Analysis Inc
18 Keith Hill Rd
Grafton MA 01519
508 839-0305

(G-9645)
CASEY COMMUNICATIONS INC
Also Called: Casey Publications
800 5th Ave Ste 4100 (98104-3100)
PHONE..................................206 448-5902
Paul Casey, *President*
EMP: 1 **EST:** 1988
SQ FT: 300
SALES: 1.5MM **Privately Held**
WEB: www.caseycommunications.net
SIC: 8748 2711 4833 Business consulting; newspapers, publishing & printing; television broadcasting stations

(G-9646)
CATHERINE TOMLINSON
Also Called: Restoration
7729 31st Ave Nw (98117-4643)
PHONE..................................206 789-4405
Catherine Tomlinson, *Owner*
EMP: 3
SALES (est): 110K **Privately Held**
SIC: 3269 Art & ornamental ware, pottery

(G-9647)
CATHOLIC NORTHWEST PROGRESS
710 9th Ave (98104-2017)
PHONE..................................206 382-4850
Greg Magnoni, *Principal*
EMP: 13
SALES (est): 720K **Privately Held**
SIC: 2711 Newspapers

(G-9648)
CATHOLIC PRINTERY INC
6327 W Marginal Way Sw (98106-1525)
P.O. Box 81026 (98108-1026)
PHONE..................................206 767-0660
Kieth R Sterling, *President*
Tom Perri, *Exec VP*
EMP: 30 **EST:** 1975
SQ FT: 13,000
SALES: 1.6MM **Privately Held**
WEB: www.catholicprintery.com
SIC: 2759 2791 2789 2752 Circulars: printing; envelopes: printing; typesetting; bookbinding & related work; commercial printing, lithographic

(G-9649)
CC FILSON CO (HQ)
1741 1st Ave S (98134-1403)
P.O. Box 34020 (98124-1020)
PHONE..................................206 624-4437
Alan Kirk, *CEO*
▲ **EMP:** 159 **EST:** 1897
SQ FT: 36,000
SALES (est): 49.6MM
SALES (corp-wide): 28.2MM **Privately Held**
SIC: 2326 2329 2353 3161 Men's & boys' work clothing; hunting coats & vests, men's; hats, caps & millinery; luggage; catalog & mail-order houses; men's & boys' clothing stores
PA: Filson Holdings, Inc.
1555 4th Ave S
Seattle WA 98134
206 622-3147

(G-9650)
CELGENE CORPORATION
1616 Eastlake Ave E S (98102-3788)
PHONE..................................415 839-7058
EMP: 68
SALES (corp-wide): 15.2B **Publicly Held**
SIC: 2834 Pharmaceutical preparations
PA: Celgene Corporation
86 Morris Ave
Summit NJ 07901
908 673-9000

(G-9651)
CELLARTRACKER LLC
1535 9th Ave W (98119-3226)
PHONE..................................206 601-7226
Eric Levine,
EMP: 2
SALES (est): 101K **Privately Held**
SIC: 2741

(G-9652)
CENTER FOR PROSTHETIC (PA)
Also Called: C P O
411 12th Ave Ste 200 (98122-5599)
PHONE..................................206 328-4276
Jose E Ignacio, *President*
Douglas L Pinkley, *Treasurer*
EMP: 15
SQ FT: 7,500
SALES (est): 2.1MM **Privately Held**
WEB: www.cpo.biz
SIC: 3842 Limbs, artificial; prosthetic appliances

(G-9653)
CENTER FOR RELIGIOUS HUMANISM
Also Called: JOURNAL OF THE ARTS & RELIGION
3307 3rd Ave W (98119-1940)
PHONE..................................206 281-2988
Gregory Wolfe, *President*
Mary Kenagy, *Manager*
EMP: 10
SQ FT: 640
SALES: 606K **Privately Held**
WEB: www.imagejournal.org
SIC: 2741 Miscellaneous publishing

(G-9654)
CENTRAL FABRICATORS INC
4758 Ballard Ave Nw (98107-4817)
PHONE..................................206 633-4762
Edmond Gregerson, *President*
▲ **EMP:** 10 **EST:** 1953
SQ FT: 14,000
SALES: 900K **Privately Held**
WEB: www.centralfabinc.com
SIC: 5051 3444 Sheets, metal; sheet metalwork

(G-9655)
CENTURY 21 PROMOTIONS INC (PA)
Also Called: Fahrenheit Headwear
2601 W Commodore Way (98199-1263)
PHONE..................................206 282-8827
Jeffrey Hoch, *President*
Irv Hoch, *Vice Pres*
Janet Hansen, *CFO*
Noelle Craddock, *Sales Staff*
Michael Fahlstrom, *Manager*
◆ **EMP:** 26
SQ FT: 38,000
SALES (est): 2.6MM **Privately Held**
WEB: www.century21promotions.com
SIC: 2353 Hats & caps

(G-9656)
CERADYNE INC
6701 6th Ave S (98108-3438)
PHONE..................................206 763-2170
EMP: 2
SALES (corp-wide): 32.7B **Publicly Held**
SIC: 3299 3671 Ceramic fiber; cathode ray tubes, including rebuilt
HQ: Ceradyne, Inc.
1922 Barranca Pkwy
Irvine CA 92606
949 862-9600

(G-9657)
CERTAINTEED GYPSUM INC
Also Called: Bpb Gypsum
5931 E Marginal Way S (98134-2414)
PHONE..................................206 763-1441
Ellis C Goebel, *Branch Mgr*
EMP: 130
SALES (corp-wide): 215.9MM **Privately Held**
WEB: www.bpb-na.com
SIC: 3275 Wallboard, gypsum
HQ: Certainteed Gypsum, Inc.
20 Moores Rd
Malvern PA 19355

(G-9658)
CERTAINTEED GYPSUM MFG INC
Also Called: Bpb Gypsum Inc
5931 E Marginal Way S (98134-2414)
PHONE..................................949 282-5300
David Englehardt, *CEO*
EMP: 600
SALES (est): 4.7MM
SALES (corp-wide): 1B **Privately Held**
SIC: 3275 Wallboard, gypsum
HQ: Pertemps Recruitment Partnership Limited
Meriden Hall
Coventry W MIDLANDS CV7 7
118 950-0580

(G-9659)
CERTIFIED BRANCHING HABIT
Also Called: Certified Jeans
8821 Renton Ave S (98118-4918)
PHONE..................................206 286-9685
David Davison, *Principal*
EMP: 4
SQ FT: 1,600
SALES (est): 230K **Privately Held**
SIC: 2329 2339 5136 5137 Men's & boys' sportswear & athletic clothing; women's & misses' outerwear; men's & boys' clothing; women's & children's clothing

(G-9660)
CERTIFLY LLC
24 Roy St Ste 169 (98109-4018)
PHONE..................................888 415-9119
Jerome Reyes, *Mng Member*
EMP: 5
SALES: 155K **Privately Held**
SIC: 7371 7372 Computer software development & applications; application computer software

(G-9661)
CES ENTERPRISES
1428 10th Ave (98122-3805)
PHONE..................................206 443-1742
EMP: 2
SALES (est): 170.7K **Privately Held**
SIC: 3625 Motor controls & accessories

(G-9662)
CETRESTEC INC
Also Called: Cetacean Research Technology
7021 6th Ave Nw (98117-4938)
PHONE..................................206 650-8676
Joseph R Olson, *President*
EMP: 2
SQ FT: 750
SALES (est): 476.7K **Privately Held**
WEB: www.cetaceanresearch.com
SIC: 5734 3699 7379 Software, computer games; underwater sound equipment; computer related consulting services

(G-9663)
CETS LLC
1441 N Northlake Way # 214 (98103-8988)
PHONE..................................206 992-6993
Thomas Jordan, *Mng Member*
EMP: 3 **EST:** 2016
SALES (est): 161.4K **Privately Held**
SIC: 3613 Control panels, electric

(G-9664)
CHADAO TEA CO INC
3700 Corliss Ave N (98103-9117)
PHONE..................................206 335-6585
Ghim Sim Chua, *President*
EMP: 8
SQ FT: 6,100
SALES: 250K **Privately Held**
SIC: 2095 Roasted coffee

(G-9665)
CHAMBONG INDUSTRIES LLC
358 29th Ave (98122-6216)
PHONE..................................608 335-1882
Randy Leslein, *Principal*
EMP: 2
SALES (est): 101K **Privately Held**
SIC: 3999 Manufacturing industries

(G-9666)
CHARCOIR CORPORATION
3537 Sw Rose St (98126-3439)
PHONE..................................213 379-4040
Michael Leone, *President*
EMP: 5
SALES (est): 777.6K **Privately Held**
SIC: 2819 Charcoal (carbon), activated

(G-9667)
CHARLES FRIEDMAN
2841 Nw 70th St (98117-6240)
PHONE..................................206 781-0608
Charles Friedman, *Principal*
EMP: 3
SALES (est): 192.7K **Privately Held**
SIC: 3999 Framed artwork

(G-9668)
CHARLES PARRIOTT
3918 S Ferdinand St (98118-1740)
PHONE..................................206 725-1765
Charles Parriott, *Owner*
Constance Parriott, *Principal*
▲ **EMP:** 2
SALES (est): 108.2K **Privately Held**
SIC: 3231 Stained glass: made from purchased glass

(G-9669)
CHARLIES COAT LLC
735 35th Ave (98122-5203)
PHONE..................................206 323-2191
Tracy Bradley, *Principal*
EMP: 2 **EST:** 2011
SALES (est): 110.6K **Privately Held**
SIC: 2335 Women's, juniors' & misses' dresses

(G-9670)
CHAUNCEY AND SHIRAH BELL INC
Also Called: Nine Seeds
6212 39th Ave Ne (98115-7416)
PHONE..................................206 437-7556
Chauncey F Bell, *CEO*
EMP: 2 **EST:** 2001
SALES: 250K **Privately Held**
SIC: 8742 3582 Business consultant; dryers, laundry: commercial, including coin-operated; extractors, commercial laundry

(G-9671)
CHEMITHON CORPORATION (HQ)
5430 W Marginal Way Sw (98106-1598)
PHONE..................................206 937-9954
Burton Brooks, *President*
Gerald G Toussaint, *President*
Colin Gregg, *Regional Mgr*
Keith Thompson, *District Mgr*

GEOGRAPHIC SECTION

Seattle - King County (G-9704)

Augie Catalano, *Vice Pres*
▼ EMP: 50
SQ FT: 41,845
SALES (est): 15.7MM **Privately Held**
SIC: 3559 Refinery, chemical processing & similar machinery

(G-9672)
CHEMITHON ENTERPRISES INC (PA)
5430 W Marginal Way Sw (98106-1598)
PHONE.................................206 937-9954
Burton Brooks, *President*
Peter Riley, *COO*
Augie Catalano, *CFO*
Agostino Catalano, *Treasurer*
Norman Foster, *VP Mktg*
EMP: 103
SQ FT: 41,845
SALES (est): 20MM **Privately Held**
SIC: 3559 5084 5085 1541 Refinery, chemical processing & similar machinery; industrial machinery & equipment; industrial supplies; industrial buildings & warehouses

(G-9673)
CHEYENNE SCALE CO INC
1613 Sw 114th St (98146-3563)
P.O. Box 47041 (98146-7041)
PHONE.................................206 933-7904
Cheyenne Humphries, *President*
EMP: 3
SALES (est): 230K **Privately Held**
SIC: 3545 Scales, measuring (machinists' precision tools)

(G-9674)
CHI-SQUARE LABS LLC
2107 W Barrett St (98199-2928)
PHONE.................................206 282-8246
Michael Cook, *Principal*
EMP: 4
SALES (est): 131.3K **Privately Held**
SIC: 7372 Prepackaged software

(G-9675)
CHIHULY INC (PA)
1111 Nw 50th St (98107-5120)
PHONE.................................206 781-8707
Dale Chihuly, *President*
Tom Lind, *Project Mgr*
Christopher Roberts, *Accountant*
Janet Lennon, *Human Resources*
Britt Cornett, *Manager*
▲ EMP: 150
SQ FT: 30,000
SALES (est): 19.5MM **Privately Held**
WEB: www.chihuly.com
SIC: 3229 Glassware, art or decorative

(G-9676)
CHIMCARE WEST SEATTLE
4742 42nd Ave Sw (98116-4553)
PHONE.................................206 673-2203
EMP: 2
SALES (est): 74.4K **Privately Held**
SIC: 2842 Specialty cleaning, polishes & sanitation goods

(G-9677)
CHIMINERA LLC
5023 16th Ave Ne (98105-4228)
PHONE.................................401 326-2820
Joel Smith, *Chief Engr*
EMP: 2 EST: 2016
SALES (est): 60.6K **Privately Held**
SIC: 7372 7389 Utility computer software;

(G-9678)
CHIN MUSIC PRESS INC
2621 24th Ave W (98199-3407)
PHONE.................................206 457-8752
Bruce Rutledge, *President*
EMP: 2
SALES (est): 166.1K **Privately Held**
WEB: www.chinmusicpress.com
SIC: 2741 Miscellaneous publishing

(G-9679)
CHOKE SHIRT COMPANY
920 S Holgate St Ste 109 (98134-1623)
PHONE.................................206 624-4444
Angela Prosper, *Production*
Jeff Gonzales, *Manager*
▼ EMP: 7

SALES (est): 491.4K **Privately Held**
SIC: 2759 Screen printing

(G-9680)
CHOUKETTE
5028 Wilson Ave S (98118-2085)
PHONE.................................206 466-6906
Ludovic Guillaume, *Principal*
EMP: 4
SALES (est): 156.5K **Privately Held**
SIC: 2051 Doughnuts, except frozen

(G-9681)
CHROMAWORKS CORPORATION
Also Called: Color One
4240 Gilman Pl W Ste A (98199-1248)
PHONE.................................206 622-7107
Laura Livingston, *Owner*
EMP: 2
SALES (est): 80K **Privately Held**
SIC: 2741 Art copy: publishing & printing

(G-9682)
CHROME INDUSTRIES
1117 1st Ave (98101-2909)
PHONE.................................206 682-1343
EMP: 2 EST: 2017
SALES (est): 124.2K **Privately Held**
SIC: 3999 Manufacturing industries

(G-9683)
CHRYSANTHEMUM
4820 Rainier Ave S (98118-1718)
PHONE.................................206 722-1031
EMP: 4
SALES (est): 314.6K **Privately Held**
SIC: 2361 Girls' & children's blouses & shirts

(G-9684)
CINEVEND INC
3518 Fremont Ave N # 580 (98103-8814)
PHONE.................................206 388-3784
Gregory Kriegler, *President*
▲ EMP: 2
SQ FT: 300
SALES (est): 184.9K **Privately Held**
SIC: 3581 7359 Automatic vending machines; vending machine rental

(G-9685)
CIRCLE SYSTEMS INC
1001 4th Ave Ste 3200 (98154-1003)
PHONE.................................206 682-3783
Steve Dubnoff, *President*
Marian Lowe, *Vice Pres*
EMP: 2
SALES (est): 300K **Privately Held**
SIC: 7371 7372 Computer software development; prepackaged software

(G-9686)
CISCO SYSTEMS INC
2901 3rd Ave Ste 600 (98121-1000)
PHONE.................................206 256-3229
Matthew Moran, *Branch Mgr*
Brian Gore, *Technical Staff*
Skip Macaskill, *Executive*
EMP: 691
SALES (corp-wide): 49.3B **Publicly Held**
WEB: www.cisco.com
SIC: 3577 Computer peripheral equipment
PA: Cisco Systems, Inc.
170 W Tasman Dr
San Jose CA 95134
408 526-4000

(G-9687)
CITY LITES NEON INC
Also Called: City Lights Sign Company
902 Nw 49th St (98107-3653)
PHONE.................................206 789-4747
Martha Davis, *President*
EMP: 6
SQ FT: 3,000
SALES (est): 618.9K **Privately Held**
SIC: 3993 Neon signs

(G-9688)
CLARIO MEDICAL
2033 6th Ave Ste 333 (98121-2592)
PHONE.................................206 315-5410
EMP: 3

SALES (corp-wide): 1.2MM **Privately Held**
SIC: 7372 Prepackaged Software Services
PA: Clario Medical Imaging, Inc.
2033 6th Ave Ste 333
Seattle WA 98121
206 315-5410

(G-9689)
CLARK SECURITY PRODUCTS INC
2760 4th Ave S (98134-1913)
PHONE.................................206 467-3000
Nick Bruno, *Principal*
EMP: 2 EST: 2009
SALES (est): 89.9K **Privately Held**
SIC: 5099 3429 Locks & lock sets; locks or lock sets

(G-9690)
CLASSIC IMPRESSIONS
5800 Corson Ave S (98108-2606)
PHONE.................................206 766-9121
Ted Rayl, *President*
EMP: 30
SQ FT: 10,000
SALES (est): 1.5MM **Privately Held**
WEB: www.classicimpressions.com
SIC: 2759 2396 2395 Screen printing; automotive & apparel trimmings; pleating & stitching

(G-9691)
CLEAN REPUBLIC SODO LLC
920 S Holgate St Ste 106 (98134-1623)
PHONE.................................206 682-7499
Michael Shope, *CEO*
Ryan Ellison, *Partner*
Jussi Lyons, *Partner*
Yong Hou, *Founder*
▲ EMP: 4
SALES (est): 242K **Privately Held**
SIC: 3751 Motorcycles, bicycles & parts

(G-9692)
CLEANING CONSULTANTS SERVICES
Also Called: CCS Lock & Key
3693 E Marginal Way S (98134-1150)
P.O. Box 98757 (98198-0757)
PHONE.................................206 682-9748
William Griffin, *President*
EMP: 4
SQ FT: 4,000
SALES (est): 300K **Privately Held**
WEB: www.cleaningbusiness.com
SIC: 8742 2731 2721 7382 General management consultant; books: publishing & printing; magazines: publishing & printing; security systems services; educational aids & electronic training materials

(G-9693)
CLEAR COATED
1006 15th Ave E Apt 2 (98112-3943)
PHONE.................................425 495-2369
Miriam Rigby, *Principal*
EMP: 2
SALES (est): 140.1K **Privately Held**
SIC: 3949 Sporting & athletic goods

(G-9694)
CLEAR CUT PLASTICS INC
507 N 36th St (98103-8613)
PHONE.................................206 545-9131
Charles Robinson, *President*
Anne Robinson, *Vice Pres*
Linda Deutsch, *Manager*
▲ EMP: 5
SQ FT: 5,800
SALES (est): 550K **Privately Held**
WEB: www.clearcutplastics.com
SIC: 3089 Plastic containers, except foam; plastic hardware & building products

(G-9695)
CLEAR YOUR CLUTTER LLC
618 Nw 87th St (98117-3131)
PHONE.................................206 784-1515
R Julia F Rudden, *Principal*
EMP: 2 EST: 2010
SALES (est): 132.4K **Privately Held**
SIC: 3949 Sporting & athletic goods

(G-9696)
CLIENT SERVICE CENTER
6333 1st Ave S (98108-3228)
PHONE.................................206 237-0821
EMP: 2
SALES (est): 104.1K **Privately Held**
SIC: 3721 Airplanes, fixed or rotary wing

(G-9697)
CLIPPER SEAFOODS LTD
641 W Ewing St (98119-1528)
PHONE.................................206 284-1162
Dave Little, *President*
Paul Gilliland, *Vice Pres*
Brian Motoyama, *Purch Mgr*
Larry Pihl, *CFO*
Charles Bates, *Treasurer*
◆ EMP: 200
SQ FT: 2,000
SALES (est): 49.5MM **Privately Held**
SIC: 2092 8731 Fresh or frozen packaged fish; environmental research

(G-9698)
CLOTHWORKS TEXTILES INC
6301 W Marginal Way Sw (98106-1525)
PHONE.................................206 762-7886
Ted Hoffman, *President*
▲ EMP: 22
SALES (est): 6MM **Privately Held**
SIC: 2211 Broadwoven fabric mills, cotton

(G-9699)
CLOUD CITY SKATEBOARDS
3270 California Ave Sw (98116-3305)
PHONE.................................206 403-1882
EMP: 2 EST: 2012
SALES (est): 91K **Privately Held**
SIC: 3949 Mfg Sporting/Athletic Goods

(G-9700)
CLOUDCOREO INC
2727 Fairview Ave E # 15 (98102-3151)
PHONE.................................206 851-0130
EMP: 2
SALES (est): 156.2K **Privately Held**
SIC: 7372 Application computer software

(G-9701)
CLOUDLIFT CELLARS
312 S Lucile St (98108-2434)
PHONE.................................206 622-2004
Tom Stangeland, *Principal*
EMP: 3
SALES (est): 84.3K **Privately Held**
SIC: 2084 Wines

(G-9702)
CNT TECHNOLOGIES INC
4216 Ne 70th St (98115-6043)
PHONE.................................206 522-2256
Thomas Puzzo, *CEO*
Randolph Tremper, *President*
EMP: 4
SALES (est): 293.1K **Privately Held**
SIC: 2284 Thread from natural fibers

(G-9703)
COACH CHEETAH INC
1711 12th Ave Ste 1090 (98122-3289)
PHONE.................................206 914-8313
Travis Picou,
Evan Johnson,
EMP: 2 EST: 2014
SALES (est): 85.8K **Privately Held**
SIC: 7373 7371 7372 7389 Systems software development services; computer software development & applications; prepackaged software; business oriented computer software; utility computer software;

(G-9704)
COAL HEADWEAR LLC
4917 14th Ave Nw (98107-5142)
PHONE.................................206 632-1601
Jake Hanson, *Principal*
▲ EMP: 10
SQ FT: 1,000
SALES (est): 1MM **Privately Held**
SIC: 2353 2339 2389 Hats, caps & millinery; women's & misses' accessories; men's miscellaneous accessories

Seattle - King County (G-9705)

(G-9705)
COASTAL CRUISE GUIDES
Also Called: Coastal Cruise Tour Guides
3828 26th Ave W (98199-1550)
PHONE 206 448-4488
George King, *Owner*
EMP: 2
SALES (est): 147.2K **Privately Held**
SIC: 2741 Telephone & other directory publishing

(G-9706)
COASTAL STAR INC
4019 21st Ave W Ste 200 (98199-1251)
PHONE 206 282-0988
Don Giles, *President*
EMP: 60
SQ FT: 8,000
SALES (est): 2.4MM
SALES (corp-wide): 268.6MM **Privately Held**
WEB: www.icicleseafoods.com
SIC: 2092 Fresh or frozen packaged fish
HQ: Icicle Seafoods, Inc.
4019 21st Ave W Ste 300
Seattle WA 98199
206 282-0988

(G-9707)
COASTLINE FABRICATORS INC (PA)
8151 Occidental Ave S (98108-4210)
PHONE 206 763-5035
Allan Smyth, *President*
Joe Devlin, *Vice Pres*
EMP: 7
SQ FT: 17,000
SALES (est): 733K **Privately Held**
WEB: www.coastlinefabricators.com
SIC: 3443 Industrial vessels, tanks & containers; heat exchangers, condensers & components

(G-9708)
COBALT GROUP INC (HQ)
Also Called: National Interad
605 5th Ave S Ste 800 (98104-3888)
PHONE 206 269-6363
John Holt, *CEO*
Scott Mathews, *COO*
Mark Dunn, *Vice Pres*
Phil Turner, *Vice Pres*
Lauren Haven, *Opers Staff*
EMP: 480
SQ FT: 23,500
SALES (est): 69.8MM
SALES (corp-wide): 13.3B **Publicly Held**
WEB: www.partsvoice.com
SIC: 7372 Business oriented computer software
PA: Automatic Data Processing, Inc.
1 Adp Blvd Ste 1 # 1
Roseland NJ 07068
973 974-5000

(G-9709)
COCOA FUTURE SPC
3422 19th Ave S (98144-6706)
PHONE 206 877-3347
Kimberly Wilson, *Principal*
EMP: 3
SALES (est): 175.4K **Privately Held**
SIC: 2066 Chocolate

(G-9710)
CODE PUBLISHING COMPANY INC
9410 Roosevelt Way Ne (98115-2844)
PHONE 206 527-6831
Margaret Bustion, *President*
William Ferensen, *President*
Rosamund Hodge, *Web Dvlpr*
EMP: 18
SQ FT: 4,000
SALES (est): 1.6MM **Privately Held**
WEB: www.codepublishing.com
SIC: 2731 Pamphlets: publishing & printing

(G-9711)
COFFEE CATCHER LLC
Also Called: Kaffeologie
9516 Palatine Ave N (98103-3020)
PHONE 202 704-2868
John Custer,
Nathaniel Jones,
EMP: 6
SQ FT: 900
SALES: 239.3K **Privately Held**
SIC: 3589 Coffee brewing equipment

(G-9712)
COGNEX
2001 6th Ave (98121-2855)
PHONE 206 448-2343
EMP: 3
SALES (est): 176.4K **Privately Held**
SIC: 3823 Industrial instrmnts msrmnt display/control process variable

(G-9713)
COINSTAX LLC
1700 Westlake Ave N # 200 (98109-3012)
PHONE 206 629-8831
Colin Mackie,
EMP: 2
SALES (est): 124.3K **Privately Held**
SIC: 7372 Prepackaged software

(G-9714)
COLLINS MACHINE INC
1429 S Cloverdale St (98108-4826)
PHONE 206 767-4149
Mike Collins, *President*
EMP: 4
SQ FT: 2,000
SALES: 300K **Privately Held**
SIC: 3599 Machine shop, jobbing & repair

(G-9715)
COLOR ART PRINTING INC
Also Called: Color Art Press
9451 Delridge Way Sw (98106-2734)
PHONE 206 762-0784
William Renn, *President*
EMP: 4 **EST:** 1970
SQ FT: 3,200
SALES (est): 423K **Privately Held**
SIC: 2752 Commercial printing, offset

(G-9716)
COMMERCIAL CHEMTECH INC
309 S Cloverdale St D5 (98108-4568)
PHONE 206 932-0841
Ed H Campbell, *President*
Katie Miller, *Director*
EMP: 6
SALES (est): 750K **Privately Held**
WEB: www.commercialchemtech.com
SIC: 2819 Industrial inorganic chemicals

(G-9717)
COMMERCIAL PLASTICS CORP
3414 4th Ave S (98134-1905)
PHONE 206 682-4832
Bruce Bruner, *President*
Mary Lou Bruner, *Vice Pres*
▲ **EMP:** 17
SQ FT: 30,000
SALES (est): 2.4MM **Privately Held**
WEB: www.commercialplasticscorp.com
SIC: 3089 3993 3851 3732 Injection molding of plastics; signs & advertising specialties; ophthalmic goods; boat building & repairing

(G-9718)
COMMITTEE FOR CHILDREN
2815 2nd Ave Ste 400 (98121-3207)
PHONE 206 343-1223
Richard Israel, *COO*
Joan Duffell, *Exec Dir*
EMP: 65
SQ FT: 25,693
SALES (est): 19.7MM **Privately Held**
SIC: 2731 7812 Textbooks: publishing & printing; educational motion picture production; training motion picture production; video tape production

(G-9719)
COMMON INDUSTRIES LLC
6548 Palatine Ave N (98103-5230)
PHONE 206 963-6649
John Gerich, *Principal*
EMP: 3
SALES (est): 153.5K **Privately Held**
SIC: 3999 Candles

(G-9720)
COMMON TONE ARTS
3827 Meridian Ave N (98103-8344)
PHONE 206 251-8260
Brian Chin, *Director*
Kimberly Chin,
EMP: 3
SALES (est): 253.8K **Privately Held**
SIC: 3599 Machine shop, jobbing & repair

(G-9721)
COMPACTORS NW
7345 9th Ave Nw (98117-4102)
PHONE 206 747-7316
Trevor Backlin, *Principal*
EMP: 2 **EST:** 2016
SALES (est): 82.5K **Privately Held**
SIC: 3589 Service industry machinery

(G-9722)
COMPANION BAKING LLC
4411 42nd Ave Sw (98116-4222)
PHONE 206 856-4080
Joanne Jacobs, *Principal*
EMP: 4
SALES (est): 143.1K **Privately Held**
SIC: 2051 Bread, cake & related products

(G-9723)
COMPANY K LLC
620 Nw 44th St (98107-4431)
PHONE 206 632-0509
Jack Kearney, *Mng Member*
Scott Roberts, *Data Proc Exec*
EMP: 5
SQ FT: 1,800
SALES: 850K **Privately Held**
WEB: www.companyk.com
SIC: 5021 2511 Furniture; unassembled or unfinished furniture, household: wood

(G-9724)
COMPENDIUM INCORPORATED (PA)
2100 N Pacific St (98103-9126)
PHONE 206 812-1640
Kobi Yamada, *President*
Dan Zadra, *Founder*
Jim Darragh, *Treasurer*
Tote Yamada, *VP Sales*
Tammy Monday, *Marketing Staff*
▲ **EMP:** 42
SQ FT: 6,720
SALES (est): 9MM **Privately Held**
WEB: www.compendiuminc.com
SIC: 2771 Greeting cards

(G-9725)
COMSCORE INC
316 Occidental Ave S # 200 (98104-2864)
PHONE 206 447-1860
Will Hodgman, *Principal*
EMP: 50
SALES (corp-wide): 419.4MM **Publicly Held**
SIC: 7372 Business oriented computer software
PA: Comscore, Inc.
11950 Democracy Dr # 600
Reston VA 20190
703 438-2000

(G-9726)
CONDOR TECHNICAL SERVICES
Also Called: Condor Electronics
10007 Aurora Ave N (98133-9328)
PHONE 206 633-5190
Peter Toms, *Owner*
Nick Nation, *Service Mgr*
EMP: 7
SQ FT: 2,400
SALES (est): 455.3K **Privately Held**
WEB: www.condor-electronics.com
SIC: 7629 3651 Electronic equipment repair; household audio equipment

(G-9727)
CONGLOBAL INDUSTRIES LLC
Also Called: ITEL Terminals of Seattle
1818 S 93rd St (98108-5121)
PHONE 206 624-8180
Mark Gonzalez, *Manager*
EMP: 35
SALES (corp-wide): 183.7MM **Privately Held**
WEB: www.cgini.com
SIC: 4231 5099 3731 Trucking terminal facilities; containers: glass, metal or plastic; shipbuilding & repairing
HQ: Conglobal Industries, Llc
8200 185th St Ste A
Tinley Park IL 60487

(G-9728)
CONGLOBAL INDUSTRIES LLC
1 S Idaho St (98134-1118)
PHONE 206 624-8180
Todd Sundeften, *Manager*
EMP: 58
SALES (corp-wide): 183.7MM **Privately Held**
WEB: www.cgini.com
SIC: 7699 3537 Nautical repair services; industrial trucks & tractors
HQ: Conglobal Industries, Llc
8200 185th St Ste A
Tinley Park IL 60487

(G-9729)
CONGRUENT SOFTWARE
1001 W Howe St (98119-2971)
PHONE 206 301-0553
Mani Krishnamurthy, *Principal*
EMP: 2
SALES (est): 109.4K **Privately Held**
SIC: 7372 Business oriented computer software

(G-9730)
CONSOLIDATED PRESS LLC (PA)
600 S Spokane St (98134-2229)
PHONE 206 447-9659
Gary R Stone, *CEO*
Greg Andersen, *Business Mgr*
Rob Pollard, *Business Mgr*
Bonnie Hansen, *Project Mgr*
Dedee Manning, *Prdtn Mgr*
EMP: 50 **EST:** 1930
SQ FT: 37,000
SALES (est): 13.8MM **Privately Held**
WEB: www.conspress.com
SIC: 2752 2789 Publication printing, lithographic; catalogs, lithographed; newspapers, lithographed only; commercial printing, offset; bookbinding & related work

(G-9731)
CONSTANCY PRESS LLC
4532 48th Ave Ne (98105-3824)
PHONE 206 522-7513
John Sidles, *Principal*
▲ **EMP:** 4
SALES (est): 236.7K **Privately Held**
SIC: 2741 Miscellaneous publishing

(G-9732)
CONTINENTAL HOLDINGS III
480 S Kenyon St (98108-4324)
PHONE 425 502-7055
EMP: 2
SALES (est): 70.5K **Privately Held**
SIC: 3999 6719 ; holding companies

(G-9733)
CONTINUOUS CASTING CO
2724 6th Pl S (98134-2129)
PHONE 206 623-7688
Helen C Kloess, *President*
EMP: 11
SQ FT: 6,000
SALES (est): 1.4MM **Privately Held**
SIC: 3543 3544 Foundry cores; special dies, tools, jigs & fixtures

(G-9734)
CONTOUR INC
3131 Western Ave Ste 410 (98121-1036)
PHONE 206 792-5226
Paul Warburg, *President*
Marc Barros, *Principal*
Jason Green, *Principal*
Steven Moore, *Chairman*
Jeremy Andrus, *Director*
◆ **EMP:** 17 **EST:** 2007
SALES (est): 2.5MM **Privately Held**
SIC: 3861 Cameras & related equipment

GEOGRAPHIC SECTION
Seattle - King County (G-9766)

(G-9735)
CONVERGENT TECHNOLOGY
2646 Magnolia Blvd W (98199-3004)
PHONE..................................206 352-5357
Technology Convergent, *Administration*
EMP: 2
SALES (est): 86.6K **Privately Held**
SIC: 3841 Surgical & medical instruments

(G-9736)
COOKE AQUACULTURE PACIFIC LLC (DH)
Also Called: Icicle Seafoods
4019 21st Ave W Ste 300 (98199-1251)
PHONE..................................206 282-0988
EMP: 17
SALES (est): 2MM
SALES (corp-wide): 268.6MM **Privately Held**
SIC: 2092 Shellfish, frozen: prepared
HQ: Icicle Seafoods, Inc.
4019 21st Ave W Ste 300
Seattle WA 98199
206 282-0988

(G-9737)
COOKE SEAFOOD USA INC
4207 9th Ave Nw (98107-4542)
PHONE..................................206 282-0988
EMP: 5
SALES (corp-wide): 268.6MM **Privately Held**
SIC: 2092 Fresh or frozen packaged fish
HQ: Cooke Seafood Usa, Inc.
2000 Nrthgate Cmmrce Pkwy
Suffolk VA 23435
757 673-4500

(G-9738)
COOPER T KIRSCH GLASS LLC
3821 Beach Dr Sw Apt 202 (98116-3567)
PHONE..................................206 718-8183
Cooper Kirsch,
EMP: 2
SALES (est): 62.5K **Privately Held**
SIC: 3999 Manufacturing industries

(G-9739)
COPY BREAK
7725 24th Ave Nw (98117-4412)
PHONE..................................206 782-7506
Paul G Janders, *Owner*
Earl Nelson, *Partner*
EMP: 5
SALES (est): 595.8K **Privately Held**
WEB: www.copywritingbasics101.com
SIC: 2752 2759 7334 Commercial printing, offset; commercial printing; photocopying & duplicating services

(G-9740)
COPY CO
616 6th Ave S (98104-2815)
PHONE..................................206 622-4050
Rick Andersen, *Principal*
Cathy Powell, *Vice Pres*
EMP: 2
SALES (est): 198.2K **Privately Held**
SIC: 2752 Commercial printing, offset

(G-9741)
CORONA DECOR COMPANY
6133 6th Ave S (98108-3309)
P.O. Box 81184 (98108-1184)
PHONE..................................206 763-1600
R H Brecht Sandlian, *President*
Frank Ramirez, *Director*
EMP: 10
SQ FT: 25,000
SALES (est): 1.2MM **Privately Held**
WEB: www.coronadecor.com
SIC: 2392 Cushions & pillows

(G-9742)
CORONADO BIOSCIENCES
1700 7th Ave (98101-1397)
PHONE..................................206 826-7168
Rj Tesi, *CEO*
EMP: 3
SALES (est): 182.1K **Privately Held**
SIC: 2834 Pharmaceutical preparations

(G-9743)
CORPORATE VAT MANAGEMENT INC
122 S Jackson St Ste 330 (98104-2895)
PHONE..................................206 292-0300
Jim Kelly, *CEO*
John H Powell, *President*
EMP: 8
SQ FT: 4,000
SALES (est): 748K **Privately Held**
WEB: www.autovat.com
SIC: 7372 Prepackaged software

(G-9744)
CORUS ESTATES & VINEYARDS LLC (HQ)
1910 Frview Ave E Ste 500 (98102)
PHONE..................................206 728-9063
Stan Baty, *CEO*
Ken McCabe, *President*
Brandon Baty,
Daniel Baty,
Stanley Baty,
EMP: 2
SQ FT: 1,000
SALES (est): 768.6K
SALES (corp-wide): 72.6MM **Privately Held**
WEB: www.corusbrands.com
SIC: 2084 5182 Wines; wine & distilled beverages
PA: Precept Brands Llc
1910 Frview Ave E Ste 400
Seattle WA 98102
206 267-5252

(G-9745)
CORVUS AND COLUMBA LLC
177 Western Ave W (98119-4211)
PHONE..................................206 673-7860
Michael Aylesworth, *Managing Prtnr*
William Gibbs, *Principal*
EMP: 2
SALES (est): 228.2K **Privately Held**
SIC: 3599 Custom machinery

(G-9746)
COUNTERBALANCE POETRY
2040 13th Ave W Apt 26 (98119-2754)
PHONE..................................206 282-2677
Jeffrey A Cantrell, *President*
EMP: 2
SALES (est): 7K **Privately Held**
WEB: www.counterbalancearts.org
SIC: 2741 Miscellaneous publishing

(G-9747)
COUNTRY CLOTHIERS
3817 Aurora Ave N (98103-8702)
PHONE..................................206 632-3319
Chris Vander Yacht, *Owner*
EMP: 2
SALES: 10K **Privately Held**
SIC: 2361 2369 2341 5641 Girls' & children's dresses, blouses & shirts; girls' & children's outerwear; women's & children's underwear; children's & infants' wear stores

(G-9748)
COUNTY OF KING
Also Called: Printing Dept
821 2nd Ave Ste 1100 (98104-1572)
PHONE..................................206 263-3113
Tutti Compton, *Branch Mgr*
EMP: 20 **Privately Held**
SIC: 2752 9199 Commercial printing, lithographic; general government administration;
PA: County Of King
401 5th Ave Ste 3
Seattle WA 98104
206 296-4040

(G-9749)
COURAGEOUS HEART HEALING LLC
7901 Delridge Way Sw 22d (98106-3423)
PHONE..................................541 517-6222
Jennifer Harkness, *Principal*
EMP: 3 **EST:** 2012
SALES (est): 253.7K **Privately Held**
SIC: 3845 Surgical support systems: heart-lung machine, exc. iron lung

(G-9750)
COVERITY
701 5th Ave (98104-7097)
PHONE..................................206 467-5967
EMP: 2
SALES (est): 108.9K **Privately Held**
SIC: 7372 Prepackaged software

(G-9751)
CRAY INC (PA)
901 5th Ave Ste 1000 (98164-2058)
PHONE..................................206 701-2000
Stephen C Kiely, *Ch of Bd*
Gary Geissler, *President*
Peter J Ungaro, *President*
John Dinning, *Senior VP*
Charles A Morreale, *Senior VP*
▲ **EMP:** 600
SQ FT: 51,643
SALES: 455.9MM **Publicly Held**
SIC: 3571 7379 Electronic computers; computer related maintenance services

(G-9752)
CREEPCOCOM
4504 Woodlawn Ave N Apt 1 (98103-6778)
PHONE..................................206 547-7020
Brent Watanabe, *CEO*
EMP: 2
SALES (est): 90K **Privately Held**
SIC: 3679 Electronic components

(G-9753)
CRIMPD LLC
9321 57th Ave S (98118-5524)
PHONE..................................847 436-0433
Peter Klimek, *Mng Member*
EMP: 2
SALES: 50K **Privately Held**
SIC: 7372 7371 Application computer software; computer software development & applications

(G-9754)
CROIX INDUSTRIES LTD
4306 3rd Ave Nw (98107-4401)
PHONE..................................206 528-5555
Michael Croix, *Principal*
EMP: 2 **EST:** 2008
SALES (est): 167K **Privately Held**
SIC: 3999 Barber & beauty shop equipment

(G-9755)
CROSS AND CROWN CHURCH
4554 12th Ave Ne (98105-4524)
P.O. Box 70343 (98127-0343)
PHONE..................................206 498-3551
EMP: 7
SALES: 1.5MM **Privately Held**
SIC: 8661 7372 Religious organizations; application computer software

(G-9756)
CROWD COW INC
801 3rd Ave Ste 325 (98104-1658)
PHONE..................................717 333-0740
Michelle Newbery, *CFO*
Joseph Heitzeberg, *Director*
Ethan Lowry, *Director*
EMP: 6
SALES (est): 339.8K **Privately Held**
SIC: 2011 Beef products from beef slaughtered on site

(G-9757)
CROWN BLACK CAR
715 4th Ave N Apt 36 (98109-4248)
PHONE..................................206 722-7696
EMP: 2
SALES (est): 140K **Privately Held**
SIC: 3713 Mfg Truck/Bus Bodies

(G-9758)
CRUCIBLE NW WOODWORKS LLC
3933 S Edmunds St (98118-1715)
PHONE..................................206 661-3545
Dave Hamilton, *Principal*
EMP: 2 **EST:** 2012
SALES (est): 188.1K **Privately Held**
SIC: 2431 Millwork

(G-9759)
CRUCIBLE WINES LLC
4434 Sw 101st St (98146-1058)
PHONE..................................206 605-2953
EMP: 2
SALES (est): 180K **Privately Held**
SIC: 2084 Mfg Wines/Brandy/Spirits

(G-9760)
CRYSTAL BARONE
Also Called: Barone Engraving
1907 4th Ave (98101-1106)
PHONE..................................206 621-7810
Michele Barone, *Owner*
Wendy Barone, *Co-Owner*
▲ **EMP:** 3
SQ FT: 1,000
SALES: 200K **Privately Held**
WEB: www.baronecrystal.net
SIC: 3231 Cut & engraved glassware: made from purchased glass

(G-9761)
CSR MARINE INC
4701 Shilshole Ave Nw (98107-4802)
PHONE..................................206 632-2001
Tim Ryan, *President*
Scott Anderson, *Vice Pres*
EMP: 35
SQ FT: 3,000
SALES: 5MM **Privately Held**
WEB: www.csrmarine.com
SIC: 7532 3732 Top & body repair & paint shops; boat building & repairing

(G-9762)
CTI BIOPHARMA CORP (PA)
3101 Western Ave Ste 800 (98121-4096)
PHONE..................................206 282-7100
Richard Love, *Ch of Bd*
Laurent Fischer, *Ch of Bd*
Bruce J Seeley, *COO*
Louis A Bianco, *Exec VP*
Matthew Plunkett, *Exec VP*
EMP: 90
SQ FT: 66,000
SALES: 26.2MM **Publicly Held**
SIC: 2834 8733 Pharmaceutical preparations; biotechnical research, noncommercial

(G-9763)
CUCINA FRESCA INC
8300 Military Rd S # 120 (98108-3950)
PHONE..................................206 903-0825
Jamie Beattie, *President*
Pat Clingman, *Vice Pres*
EMP: 17
SQ FT: 3,500
SALES (est): 1.5MM **Privately Held**
WEB: www.cucinafresca.com
SIC: 2099 2098 Pasta, uncooked: packaged with other ingredients; macaroni & spaghetti

(G-9764)
CUDDLETUNES COM
2508 Lorentz Pl N (98109-2034)
PHONE..................................206 284-4991
Michael Robinson, *Principal*
EMP: 2
SALES (est): 116.1K **Privately Held**
SIC: 2741 Miscellaneous publishing

(G-9765)
CURRENT DRIVES LLC
2622 Nw Market St Ste B (98107-4106)
PHONE..................................206 697-6073
EMP: 4
SALES (est): 307.8K **Privately Held**
SIC: 3714 Motor vehicle parts & accessories

(G-9766)
CUSTOM COMPUTER CREAT CCC LLC
5260 University Way Ne # 501 (98105-3681)
PHONE..................................800 295-3381
Daniel Wheeler,
EMP: 4

Seattle - King County (G-9767)

SALES (est): 214.1K **Privately Held**
SIC: 5734 5045 7372 8748 Computer & software stores; computers, peripherals & software; application computer software; systems analysis & engineering consulting services; computer related consulting services; computer software development & applications

(G-9767)
CUSTOM MECH SOLUTIONS INC
Also Called: CMS
2810 Eastlake Ave E (98102-3008)
PHONE 206 973-3900
Greg Adams, *President*
Craig Center, *Vice Pres*
Crystal Faulkner, *Project Mgr*
Jennifer Kondziola, *Project Mgr*
Aaron Arnold, *Engineer*
EMP: 16
SALES (est): 8.7MM **Privately Held**
SIC: 3585 Refrigeration & heating equipment

(G-9768)
CUSTOM METAL SPINNING LLC
9330 15th Ave S Ste Dc (98108-5106)
PHONE 206 762-2707
Ken Burke, *Mng Member*
EMP: 3
SQ FT: 2,100
SALES: 4MM **Privately Held**
SIC: 3469 Spinning metal for the trade

(G-9769)
CUSTOM MFG AMBASSADOR LLC
1422 E Union St Apt 304 (98122-4181)
PHONE 206 963-9853
EMP: 2
SALES (est): 90.1K **Privately Held**
SIC: 3999 Manufacturing industries

(G-9770)
CUSTOM OCULAR PROSTHETICS
10212 5th Ave Ne Ste 210 (98125-7471)
PHONE 206 522-4222
Gregory T Sankey, *Owner*
Brian Koceski, *Office Mgr*
EMP: 3
SQ FT: 1,000
SALES: 350K **Privately Held**
SIC: 3842 8011 5999 Prosthetic appliances; offices & clinics of medical doctors; orthopedic & prosthesis applications

(G-9771)
CUSTOM SEAFOOD SERVICES INC
Also Called: C & C Meats
1818 Westlake Ave N # 302 (98109-2707)
PHONE 360 267-2666
Chris Heckman, *President*
EMP: 25
SALES (est): 4.7MM **Privately Held**
WEB: www.customseafoodservices.com
SIC: 2092 Fresh or frozen packaged fish

(G-9772)
CUSTOM SMOOTHIE
808 2nd Ave (98104-1548)
PHONE 206 462-6264
EMP: 3
SALES (est): 147K **Privately Held**
SIC: 2086 Bottled And Canned Soft Drinks, Nsk

(G-9773)
CUTTING TOOL CONTROL INC
1411 Nw 51st St (98107-5128)
PHONE 206 789-7277
Bruce Lowry, *President*
EMP: 10 **EST:** 1979
SQ FT: 2,000
SALES (est): 1.1MM **Privately Held**
WEB: www.cuttingtoolcontrol.com
SIC: 3545 Cutting tools for machine tools

(G-9774)
CWC INDUSTRIES LLC A WASHINGTO
7918 Aurora Ave N (98103-4756)
PHONE 206 528-8090
EMP: 2 **EST:** 2016

SALES (est): 89.2K **Privately Held**
SIC: 3999 Manufacturing industries

(G-9775)
CYRUS BIOTECHNOLOGY INC
500 Union St Ste 320 (98101-4035)
PHONE 503 489-8460
Lucas Nivon, *President*
Yifan Song,
EMP: 4 **EST:** 2014
SALES (est): 360.6K **Privately Held**
SIC: 7371 7372 Software programming applications; application computer software

(G-9776)
D & L SCREEN PRINTING
9047 12th Ave Nw (98117-3326)
PHONE 206 781-1977
Steve Horvath, *Owner*
EMP: 5
SQ FT: 4,000
SALES: 300K **Privately Held**
SIC: 2759 Commercial printing

(G-9777)
D A GRAPHICS INC
Also Called: Seal Shield
1902 Occidental Ave S (98134-1413)
PHONE 206 760-5886
Dave Vaillancourt, *President*
Beth Beeman, *Accountant*
▲ **EMP:** 6
SQ FT: 11,500
SALES (est): 450K **Privately Held**
WEB: www.dagraphics.com
SIC: 3993 2396 5699 5719 Signs & advertising specialties; screen printing on fabric articles; customized clothing & apparel; glassware; commercial printing

(G-9778)
D A M SALSA LLC
7533 21st Ave Ne (98115-4501)
PHONE 206 527-0300
Rita Martinez, *Administration*
EMP: 3
SALES (est): 131.5K **Privately Held**
SIC: 2099 Dips, except cheese & sour cream based

(G-9779)
D D M CORPORATION
2657 20th Ave W (98199-2907)
PHONE 206 282-3422
Shirley A Mehrer, *President*
Donald D Mehrer, *Vice Pres*
Morris B Mehrer, *Treasurer*
Ronald R Coble, *Admin Sec*
EMP: 2
SQ FT: 6,000
SALES (est): 256.8K **Privately Held**
SIC: 3553 Sanding machines, except portable floor sanders: woodworking

(G-9780)
D DS HARDWOOD FLOORS
7009 Covello Dr S (98108-3628)
PHONE 206 726-8808
Ngon Nguyen, *Principal*
EMP: 2
SALES (est): 145.1K **Privately Held**
SIC: 5211 2426 1771 1752 Lumber products; flooring, hardwood; flooring contractor; floor laying & floor work

(G-9781)
D FLOURED LLC
Also Called: Nuflours
518 15th Ave E (98112-4513)
PHONE 206 395-4623
Phebe Rossi,
Amanda Bedell,
EMP: 14
SALES (est): 145.9K **Privately Held**
SIC: 5461 2051 Bakeries; cakes, bakery: except frozen

(G-9782)
D S THERMAL
632 Nw 77th St (98117-4046)
PHONE 206 789-2271
Devon Skelton, *Principal*
EMP: 2 **EST:** 2008

SALES (est): 191.9K **Privately Held**
SIC: 3578 Accounting machines & cash registers

(G-9783)
DA VINCIS GARAGE LLC
1301 Spring St Apt 10b (98104-1351)
PHONE 206 579-1333
Matthew Carlson,
EMP: 2 **EST:** 2012
SALES (est): 101.2K **Privately Held**
SIC: 7372 7389 Application computer software;

(G-9784)
DAHLIA PRESS
7910 16th Ave Sw (98106-1841)
PHONE 206 229-0817
Stephanie Clarke, *Principal*
EMP: 3
SALES (est): 193.7K **Privately Held**
SIC: 2741 Miscellaneous publishing

(G-9785)
DAILY DESSERT LLC
4550 38th Ave Sw Apt 612 (98126-2778)
PHONE 757 746-7744
EMP: 3
SALES (est): 143.3K **Privately Held**
SIC: 2711 Newspapers-Publishing/Printing

(G-9786)
DAIRY EXPORT CO INC (DH)
635 Elliott Ave W (98119-3911)
P.O. Box 34377 (98124-1377)
PHONE 206 284-7220
Steven Rowe, *Vice Pres*
Stephen R Boyd, *Vice Pres*
EMP: 3
SQ FT: 160,300
SALES: 1.4B
SALES (corp-wide): 1.4B **Privately Held**
SIC: 5191 5083 2033 Animal feeds; farm implements; fruit juices: packaged in cans, jars, etc.
HQ: Darigold, Inc.
   5601 6th Ave S Ste 300
   Seattle WA 98108
   206 284-7220

(G-9787)
DALE M SHAFMAN LLC
Also Called: Northwest Wood Design
1762 Airport Way S Ste B (98134-1618)
PHONE 206 499-4408
Dale Shafman,
EMP: 3
SQ FT: 30,000
SALES (est): 177.5K **Privately Held**
SIC: 2511 Wood household furniture

(G-9788)
DALYS INC (PA)
Also Called: Daly's Wood Finishing Products
3525 Stone Way N (98103-8923)
PHONE 425 454-3093
Herbert C Paulson, *President*
Robin T Daly, *Admin Sec*
Robin Daly, *Admin Sec*
EMP: 45 **EST:** 1948
SQ FT: 24,500
SALES (est): 5.9MM
SALES (corp-wide): 8.7MM **Privately Held**
WEB: www.dalys.com
SIC: 5231 2851 Paint; wallpaper; paints & allied products; paints & paint additives; varnishes; stains: varnish, oil or wax

(G-9789)
DAMN GOOD PEPPER
567 John St (98109-5042)
PHONE 206 675-0540
EMP: 2
SALES (est): 87.3K **Privately Held**
SIC: 2099 Food preparations

(G-9790)
DANALCO INC
Also Called: Hanz Extremity Wear
11721 Fremont Ave N (98133-8234)
PHONE 626 303-4019
EMP: 22
SQ FT: 12,500

SALES (est): 3MM **Privately Held**
SIC: 2252 2381 2221 Mfg Hosiery Mfg Fabric Gloves Manmade Broadwoven Fabric Mill

(G-9791)
DANDELION & TEA LLC
1500 Sw Myrtle St (98106-1952)
PHONE 206 353-2048
Heather Shaver, *Principal*
EMP: 2
SALES (est): 105.2K **Privately Held**
SIC: 2841 Soap & other detergents

(G-9792)
DARBY WINERY
9615 57th Ave S (98118-5801)
PHONE 206 954-4700
Darby English, *Owner*
EMP: 2
SALES (est): 147.3K **Privately Held**
SIC: 2084 Wines

(G-9793)
DARIGOLD INC
Darigold Ingredients
1130 Rainier Ave S (98144-2842)
P.O. Box 80627 (98108-0627)
PHONE 206 722-2655
Todd Aarons, *Manager*
Jacqueline Langford, *Manager*
Brad Zorb, *Manager*
Kenneth Bailey, *Director*
EMP: 300
SQ FT: 169,487
SALES (corp-wide): 1.4B **Privately Held**
WEB: www.darigold.com
SIC: 2026 Fluid milk
HQ: Darigold, Inc.
   5601 6th Ave S Ste 300
   Seattle WA 98108
   206 284-7220

(G-9794)
DARK COAST PRESS CO
1433 Nw 64th St Apt 306 (98107-2268)
PHONE 206 902-0906
Aaron Talwar, *Principal*
EMP: 2 **EST:** 2010
SALES (est): 116.7K **Privately Held**
SIC: 2741 Miscellaneous publishing

(G-9795)
DARK STAR CANDLE COMPANY
10035 9th Ave Sw (98146-3817)
PHONE 206 280-5902
Daniela Ramallo, *Principal*
EMP: 2
SALES (est): 62K **Privately Held**
SIC: 3999 Candles

(G-9796)
DARUMA GRAPHICS
Also Called: PIP Printing
11325 Pinehurst Way Ne (98125-6331)
PHONE 206 365-5644
Victor Koga, *President*
Kathy Koga, *Vice Pres*
EMP: 7
SQ FT: 2,000
SALES: 600K **Privately Held**
SIC: 2752 Commercial printing, offset

(G-9797)
DATREX INC
309 S Cloverdale St (98108-4568)
PHONE 206 762-9070
Kathy Basehart, *Branch Mgr*
EMP: 3
SALES (est): 327.1K
SALES (corp-wide): 7.5MM **Privately Held**
WEB: www.datrex.com
SIC: 3429 5088 Marine hardware; marine supplies
PA: Datrex, Inc.
   13878 Highway 165
   Kinder LA 70648
   337 738-4511

(G-9798)
DAVE PECK SOFTWARE DEVELOPMENT
2901 Ne Blakeley St Apt 5 (98105-3164)
PHONE 206 931-7572
David Peck, *Principal*

▲ = Import ▼=Export
◆ =Import/Export

GEOGRAPHIC SECTION

EMP: 2 EST: 2010
SALES (est): 94.7K **Privately Held**
SIC: 7372 Prepackaged software

(G-9799)
DAVID LORING
10434 Forest Ave S (98178-2606)
PHONE.....................206 772-5004
David Loring, *Owner*
EMP: 2 EST: 2016
SALES (est): 62.3K **Privately Held**
SIC: 2084 Wines, brandy & brandy spirits

(G-9800)
DAVID GULASSA & CO INC
Also Called: Gullassa
6 Dravus St (98109-1603)
P.O. Box 70387 (98127-0387)
PHONE.....................206 283-1810
Barrett Sheppard, *President*
EMP: 26
SQ FT: 6,500
SALES (est): 2.6MM **Privately Held**
WEB: www.gulassaco.com
SIC: 2514 2511 3444 Household furniture: upholstered on metal frames; wood household furniture; sheet metalwork

(G-9801)
DAVID T VANZANDT CO
1119 Nw 60th St (98107-2919)
PHONE.....................206 789-7294
David T Vanzandt, *Owner*
EMP: 2
SALES (est): 136.7K **Privately Held**
WEB: www.vanzandtviolins.com
SIC: 3931 Violins & parts

(G-9802)
DAVIS SIGN COMPANY INC
4025 7th Ave S (98108-5240)
PHONE.....................206 287-9800
Scott Davis, *President*
Mary Jewett, *Info Tech Mgr*
EMP: 5
SALES (est): 597.2K **Privately Held**
WEB: www.davissign.com
SIC: 3993 Signs, not made in custom sign painting shops

(G-9803)
DAWN FOOD PRODUCTS INC
1001 John St Ste 101 (98109-5320)
PHONE.....................206 623-7740
Mark Esperance, *Opers-Prdtn-Mfg*
EMP: 40
SALES (corp-wide): 1.6B **Privately Held**
WEB: www.dawnfoods.com
SIC: 2099 2087 2045 Dessert mixes & fillings; flavoring extracts & syrups; prepared flour mixes & doughs
HQ: Dawn Food Products, Inc.
3333 Sargent Rd
Jackson MI 49201

(G-9804)
DAWN FOOD PRODUCTS INC
6901 Fox Ave S (98108-3420)
PHONE.....................206 763-1711
Jane Lohry, *Opers-Prdtn-Mfg*
Arnie Eilertsen, *Maintence Staff*
Tau Fola, *Maintence Staff*
EMP: 88
SALES (corp-wide): 1.6B **Privately Held**
WEB: www.dawnfoods.com
SIC: 2045 Prepared flour mixes & doughs
HQ: Dawn Food Products, Inc.
3333 Sargent Rd
Jackson MI 49201

(G-9805)
DBA EUROIMPORT COMPANY INC
Also Called: Pedag USA
309 S Cloverdale St E10 (98108-4568)
P.O. Box 80624 (98108-0624)
PHONE.....................206 763-7303
David Shinder, *President*
Rose Dembo, *Vice Pres*
▲ EMP: 6
SQ FT: 2,500
SALES (est): 933.9K **Privately Held**
WEB: www.dbaeuroimport.com
SIC: 3131 Boot & shoe accessories

(G-9806)
DBCS INNOVATIONS
6558 43rd Ave Ne (98115-7538)
PHONE.....................206 919-2249
EMP: 2 EST: 2015
SALES (est): 90K **Privately Held**
SIC: 3944 Games, toys & children's vehicles

(G-9807)
DCW NEWS AGENCY INC
501 S Jackson St Ste 303 (98104-2897)
P.O. Box 25572 (98165-1072)
PHONE.....................206 682-2888
Da-Chung Weng, *President*
EMP: 2
SALES (est): 170K **Privately Held**
SIC: 2621 Catalog, magazine & newsprint papers

(G-9808)
DEAF SPOTLIGHT
404 E Harrison St Apt 204 (98102-5248)
PHONE.....................206 466-4693
Patty Liang, *Principal*
EMP: 2
SALES (est): 222K **Privately Held**
SIC: 3648 Spotlights

(G-9809)
DECA STORIES LLC
3247 S Edmunds St (98118-1725)
PHONE.....................302 219-0373
McKenzie W Funk,
EMP: 8 EST: 2013
SALES (est): 199.6K **Privately Held**
SIC: 2731 Book clubs: publishing & printing

(G-9810)
DECENT EXPOSURES INC
12554 Lake City Way Ne (98125-4425)
PHONE.....................206 364-4540
Pat Marcus, *President*
EMP: 10
SQ FT: 2,300
SALES (est): 920K **Privately Held**
WEB: www.decentexposures.com
SIC: 2254 5961 2341 2322 Underwear, knit; women's apparel, mail order; women's & children's underwear; men's & boys' underwear & nightwear

(G-9811)
DECKER FOUNDRY
2654 Sw 112th St (98146-1939)
PHONE.....................206 225-9000
Laura Decker, *Principal*
EMP: 5 EST: 2010
SALES (est): 404.6K **Privately Held**
SIC: 3325 Steel foundries

(G-9812)
DECORATIVE METAL ARTS
45 S Spokane St (98134-2218)
PHONE.....................206 782-4009
Michael Rydinski,
EMP: 8
SALES (est): 895.4K **Privately Held**
SIC: 3444 1799 Sheet metalwork; ornamental metal work

(G-9813)
DEEP CELL INDUSTRIES
111 S Jackson St (98104-3111)
PHONE.....................206 909-3858
EMP: 3
SALES (est): 197.1K **Privately Held**
SIC: 3999 Manufacturing industries

(G-9814)
DEEP OCEAN EXPEDITIONS LLC
4601 Shilshole Ave Nw (98107-4718)
PHONE.....................801 390-7025
Robert D McCallum, *General Mgr*
Jason Fitschen, *Principal*
Joe Smith, *Principal*
EMP: 2
SALES (est): 210K **Privately Held**
SIC: 3731 Barges, building & repairing

(G-9815)
DEFENSESTORM INC
710 2nd Ave Ste 310 (98104-1763)
PHONE.....................858 228-1903
Edgardo Nazario, *Principal*
Alex Hernandez, *Vice Pres*
Terrie O'Hanlon, *Chief Mktg Ofcr*
EMP: 4
SALES (est): 396.1K **Privately Held**
SIC: 3812 Defense systems & equipment

(G-9816)
DEL RIO FOOD PROCESSING CORP
Also Called: Del-Rio Grocery Store
9808 16th Ave Sw (98106-2829)
PHONE.....................206 767-9102
Rogelio Riojas, *President*
EMP: 17
SQ FT: 3,600
SALES (est): 2.8MM **Privately Held**
SIC: 5141 2099 5142 Food brokers; food preparations; packaged frozen goods

(G-9817)
DELESTINE DESIGNS
4024 Ne 57th St (98105-2244)
PHONE.....................206 524-6980
EMP: 2
SALES (est): 150K **Privately Held**
SIC: 3089 Mfg Plastic Products

(G-9818)
DELTA MARINE INDUSTRIES INC
1608 S 96th St (98108-5198)
PHONE.....................206 763-0760
Ivor Jones, *Principal*
Jack Jones, *VP Opers*
Chris Jones, *Project Mgr*
Perry Berggren, *Purch Agent*
Frank Lee, *Engineer*
▲ EMP: 300 EST: 1967
SALES (est): 122.2MM **Privately Held**
WEB: www.deltamarine.com
SIC: 3732 Yachts, building & repairing; boats, fiberglass: building & repairing

(G-9819)
DEMOCRACY LIVE INC (PA)
2900 Ne Blakeley St Ste B (98105-3100)
PHONE.....................855 655-8683
Bryan Finney, *President*
Joseph Brotherton, *Chairman*
EMP: 10
SALES (est): 982.6K **Privately Held**
SIC: 3579 5734 5087 Voting machines; software, business & non-game; voting machines

(G-9820)
DENDREON CORPORATION
1208 Eastlake Ave E (98102-3703)
PHONE.....................877 256-4545
James Caggiano, *CEO*
John Hudson, *Manager*
EMP: 400
SALES (corp-wide): 215.7MM **Privately Held**
SIC: 2834 Pharmaceutical preparations
HQ: Dendreon Corporation
1208 Eastlake Ave E
Seattle WA 98102

(G-9821)
DENDREON CORPORATION (HQ)
1208 Eastlake Ave E (98102-3703)
PHONE.....................206 256-4545
Craig Jalbert, *President*
Kurt Elster, *President*
▼ EMP: 205
SQ FT: 112,915
SALES (est): 155.4MM
SALES (corp-wide): 215.7MM **Privately Held**
WEB: www.dendreon.com
SIC: 2834 Pharmaceutical preparations
PA: Sanpower Group Co., Ltd.
No.68, Ruanjian Avenue, Yuhuatai District
Nanjing 21001
258 327-4887

(G-9822)
DENNY MOUNTAIN MEDIA LLC
1300 N Northlake Way # 200 (98103-8987)
P.O. Box 2330, North Bend (98045-2330)
PHONE.....................425 831-7130
Jill Sherensky, *CEO*
EMP: 82
SALES (est): 5.5MM **Privately Held**
WEB: www.dennymountain.com
SIC: 2741 7374 8742 ; computer graphics service; marketing consulting services

(G-9823)
DENNY PARK GLASS STUDIO LLC
818 John St (98109-5129)
PHONE.....................206 388-5725
Phillip A O'Reilly, *President*
EMP: 12
SALES (est): 780K **Privately Held**
SIC: 3231 Products of purchased glass

(G-9824)
DEP HOMES CORPORATION
800 23rd Ave S (98144-3022)
PHONE.....................206 322-1241
Cao Huynh, *President*
EMP: 2 EST: 2013
SALES (est): 1MM **Privately Held**
SIC: 3443 5074 1752 Housing cabinets for radium, metal plate; water heaters & purification equipment; access flooring system installation

(G-9825)
DESCARTES SYSTEMS (USA) LLC
Also Called: Shiprush
2014 E Madison St Ste 400 (98122-2965)
PHONE.....................206 812-7874
EMP: 12
SALES (corp-wide): 237.4MM **Privately Held**
SIC: 7372 7371 Business oriented computer software; custom computer programming services
HQ: Descartes Systems (Usa) Llc
2030 Powers Ferry Rd Se
Atlanta GA 30339

(G-9826)
DEVLIN DESIGNING BOATBUILDERS
3010 37th Ave Sw (98126-2213)
PHONE.....................360 866-0164
Sam S Devlin, *President*
EMP: 7
SQ FT: 4,800
SALES (est): 1MM **Privately Held**
SIC: 8711 3732 Designing: ship, boat, machine & product; boat building & repairing

(G-9827)
DIAMOND MACHINE WORKS INC
2122 W Elmore St (98199-1242)
PHONE.....................206 633-3960
Glenn Swan, *President*
Theresa Swan, *Corp Secy*
Bjorn Swan, *Vice Pres*
Dave Pruett, *Manager*
Michael Staggs, *Technology*
EMP: 20
SQ FT: 18,000
SALES: 4MM **Privately Held**
SIC: 3728 3821 Aircraft parts & equipment; sample preparation apparatus

(G-9828)
DIGITAL IMPRESSIONS INC
Also Called: Digicopy N Print
9 Denny Way (98109-4908)
PHONE.....................206 443-1234
Kamran Salahuddin, *President*
EMP: 5
SQ FT: 3,000
SALES (est): 677.9K **Privately Held**
SIC: 7334 7336 2752 7374 Photocopying & duplicating services; graphic arts & related design; commercial printing, offset; computer time-sharing

(G-9829)
DIGITAL PRODUCT STUDIO LLC
8332 Mary Ave Nw (98117-4240)
PHONE.....................206 484-8439
Aaron Andersen,
Craig Swanson,
George Varanakis,
EMP: 6 EST: 2016

Seattle - King County (G-9830)

SALES (est): 50.7K **Privately Held**
SIC: 7371 2741 Custom computer programming services;

(G-9830)
DIMENSIONAL IMAGING INC
1475 Elliott Ave W (98119-3104)
PHONE..................................206 285-0450
Cathy Shilts, *President*
Joel Hagopian, *Vice Pres*
EMP: 3
SQ FT: 3,500
SALES: 250K **Privately Held**
WEB: www.dimaging.net
SIC: 3479 Etching & engraving

(G-9831)
DIMENSIONAL PRODUCTS INC (PA)
1467 Elliott Ave W (98119-3104)
PHONE..................................206 352-9065
Jim Allen, *CEO*
Brian Philips, *CFO*
EMP: 12
SQ FT: 10,000
SALES (est): 1.6MM **Privately Held**
WEB: www.dimprod.com
SIC: 7374 3953 5084 Computer graphics service; screens, textile printing; printing trades machinery, equipment & supplies

(G-9832)
DINESYNC INC
999 3rd Ave Ste 700 (98104-4039)
PHONE..................................206 620-2550
Boyd Ferris, *President*
Tim Browne, *CFO*
EMP: 4
SALES: 10K **Privately Held**
SIC: 7371 7372 Computer software development & applications; business oriented computer software

(G-9833)
DIRECT CONNECT GROUP (DCG) LLC (PA)
Also Called: DCG ONE
4401 E Marginal Way S (98134-1116)
P.O. Box 3905 (98124-3905)
PHONE..................................206 784-6892
Terry Storms, *CEO*
Lyle Peniston, *Facilities Dir*
Sue Berg, *Project Mgr*
David Carns, *Opers Staff*
Sharon Estes, *Production*
▲ EMP: 270
SALES: 63.6MM **Privately Held**
SIC: 2752 7331 8742 2677 Commercial printing, lithographic; direct mail advertising services; marketing consulting services; envelopes; catalog showrooms

(G-9834)
DIRECT PROCESS METAL FABG
154 N 35th St Apt 103 (98103-8627)
PHONE..................................206 276-6014
Denny Jensen, *Owner*
EMP: 2
SALES (est): 91.6K **Privately Held**
SIC: 3441 Fabricated structural metal

(G-9835)
DIRTY COUCH LLC (PA)
Nw 46th St (98107)
PHONE..................................203 303-8661
Jonathan M Cargille, *Principal*
Robert L Nelson, *Principal*
Francis E Swiderski, *Principal*
EMP: 4
SALES (est): 325.6K **Privately Held**
SIC: 2082 Beer (alcoholic beverage)

(G-9836)
DISTILLERY A CREATIVE LLC
317 Nw 50th St (98107-3522)
PHONE..................................206 696-0597
Alicia M Thornber, *Administration*
EMP: 2
SALES (est): 66K **Privately Held**
SIC: 2085 Distilled & blended liquors

(G-9837)
DISTILLERY LOFT EVENTS
1735 Westlake Ave N (98109-3055)
PHONE..................................206 262-1022
EMP: 2
SALES (est): 62.3K **Privately Held**
SIC: 2085 Distilled & blended liquors

(G-9838)
DISTILLERY PROVISIONS LLC
3257 25th Ave W (98199-2815)
PHONE..................................206 861-5350
EMP: 3
SALES (est): 165.4K **Privately Held**
SIC: 2085 Distilled & blended liquors

(G-9839)
DJANGOBOOKSCOM
4002 Ne 45th St (98105)
PHONE..................................206 528-9873
Michael Horowitz, *Principal*
EMP: 2 EST: 2010
SALES (est): 135.4K **Privately Held**
SIC: 2731 Book publishing

(G-9840)
DOCUMENTARY MEDIA LLC
3250 41st Ave Sw (98116-3445)
PHONE..................................206 935-9292
Peter Beck,
Barry Provorse,
▲ EMP: 2
SALES (est): 167.9K **Privately Held**
SIC: 2731 Books: publishing only

(G-9841)
DOG HOUSE LEATHERS
715 E Pike St (98122-3719)
PHONE..................................206 257-0231
Jess Heness, *Owner*
EMP: 3
SALES (est): 340K **Privately Held**
SIC: 3199 Leather goods

(G-9842)
DOGFISH SOFTWARE CORPORATION
216 1st Ave S Ste 200 (98104-3454)
PHONE..................................206 395-9050
Daniel Zimmerman, *President*
Barbara Bree, *Exec VP*
EMP: 5
SALES (est): 500.4K **Privately Held**
SIC: 7372 Application computer software

(G-9843)
DOGSDREAM CORPORATION
8408 Aurora Ave N (98103-4358)
PHONE..................................425 737-2810
EMP: 2 EST: 2011
SALES (est): 111.3K **Privately Held**
SIC: 3999 Pet supplies

(G-9844)
DOLANS DOG DOODADS LLC
10808 Myers Way S (98168-1368)
PHONE..................................206 257-4518
Paul Dolan, *Mng Member*
Mary Dolan, *Director*
EMP: 7 EST: 2010
SALES: 650K **Privately Held**
SIC: 3199 3842 Dog furnishings: collars, leashes, muzzles, etc.: leather; limbs, artificial

(G-9845)
DOMANICO CELLARS LLC
1403 Dexter Ave N (98109-3534)
PHONE..................................206 465-9406
Jason Domanico, *Mng Member*
Jesse Andrews, *Correspondent*
EMP: 5
SALES (est): 266.7K **Privately Held**
SIC: 2084 Wines

(G-9846)
DOMESTIQUE
6560 5th Pl S (98108-3434)
PHONE..................................206 545-3769
William Travers, *President*
EMP: 4
SALES: 125K **Privately Held**
SIC: 2339 5949 Aprons, except rubber or plastic: women's, misses', juniors'; sewing, needlework & piece goods

(G-9847)
DONNELLEY FINANCIAL LLC
999 3rd Ave Ste 1500 (98104-1148)
PHONE..................................206 853-5460
Brian Quinn, *Managing Dir*
Monica Brown, *Manager*
EMP: 16
SALES (corp-wide): 963MM **Publicly Held**
SIC: 2752 Commercial printing, offset
HQ: Donnelley Financial, Llc
35 W Wacker Dr
Chicago IL 60601
844 866-4337

(G-9848)
DOSE SAFETY CO
2925 28th Ave W (98199-2705)
PHONE..................................206 282-7086
Robert Kircher, *Principal*
EMP: 2
SALES (est): 109.7K **Privately Held**
SIC: 7372 Prepackaged software

(G-9849)
DOUG D FROLAND
Also Called: Froland Marine Fab
10600 8th Ave S (98168-1577)
PHONE..................................206 932-8433
Doug D Froland, *Principal*
Douglas Froland, *Principal*
EMP: 7
SALES (est): 510K **Privately Held**
SIC: 3441 Fabricated structural metal

(G-9850)
DOUGLASS CERTIFIED PROSTHETICS
10740 Meridian Ave N G2 (98133-9010)
PHONE..................................206 363-7790
J Kirk Douglass, *President*
EMP: 5
SQ FT: 2,200
SALES (est): 657.3K **Privately Held**
WEB: www.douglasscpo.com
SIC: 3842 Prosthetic appliances; braces, orthopedic

(G-9851)
DR DANS ALTERNATIVE FUEL WERKS
Also Called: Dr Dan Bio Diesel
912 Nw 50th St (98107-3634)
PHONE..................................206 783-5728
Dan L Freeman, *President*
EMP: 6
SALES (est): 490K **Privately Held**
WEB: www.fuelwerks.com
SIC: 7539 2911 Automotive repair shops; diesel fuels

(G-9852)
DR SOFTWARE LLC
5123 47th Ave Ne (98105-2924)
PHONE..................................206 526-1371
Gregory R Miller, *Administration*
EMP: 2
SALES (est): 112.3K **Privately Held**
SIC: 7372 Prepackaged software

(G-9853)
DRACHEN DESIGN INC
Also Called: Drachen Foundation
3131 Western Ave Ste 321 (98121-3035)
PHONE..................................206 282-4349
Ali Fujino, *Director*
EMP: 3
SALES (corp-wide): 314.2K **Privately Held**
WEB: www.drachen.org
SIC: 3944 Kites
PA: Drachen Design Inc
128 S Tejon St Ste 406
Colorado Springs CO 80903
719 632-7447

(G-9854)
DRAMA NINE LLP
531 Malden Ave E (98112-4573)
PHONE..................................206 949-2953
EMP: 2 EST: 2009
SALES (est): 84K **Privately Held**
SIC: 3999 Mfg Misc Products

(G-9855)
DRESSER-RAND COMPANY
Dresser-Rand Services Division
225 S Lucile St (98108-2433)
PHONE..................................206 762-7660
Rick Peeler, *Branch Mgr*
EMP: 15
SQ FT: 20,092
SALES (corp-wide): 95B **Privately Held**
WEB: www.dresser-rand.com
SIC: 3511 Turbines & turbine generator sets
HQ: Dresser-Rand Company
500 Paul Clark Dr
Olean NY 14760
716 375-3000

(G-9856)
DUANE RUUD
Also Called: Commercial Fabric Mfg
2223 Occidental Ave S (98134-5103)
PHONE..................................206 682-1082
Duane Ruud, *Owner*
EMP: 10
SQ FT: 6,000
SALES: 580K **Privately Held**
WEB: www.commercialfabric.com
SIC: 7389 2394 Sewing contractor; canvas & related products

(G-9857)
DUCK SOFTWARE LLC
5626 42nd Ave Sw (98136-1511)
PHONE..................................206 935-9722
Dale Stammen, *Principal*
EMP: 2 EST: 2011
SALES (est): 108.4K **Privately Held**
SIC: 7372 Prepackaged software

(G-9858)
DUNCAN MACDONALD VIOLINS LLC
2 W Smith St (98119-2317)
PHONE..................................206 352-7219
Lisa M Yanak, *Principal*
EMP: 3
SALES (est): 225.4K **Privately Held**
SIC: 3931 Violins & parts

(G-9859)
DUNCAN STONE LLC
7331 21st Ave Nw (98117-5624)
PHONE..................................360 820-0823
Andrew Barr,
EMP: 2
SALES (est): 62.5K **Privately Held**
SIC: 3999 Manufacturing industries

(G-9860)
DUNGENESS DEVELOPMENT ASSOC
Also Called: East Point Seafood
2288 W Commodore Way # 205 (98199-1491)
PHONE..................................360 875-5507
Joel Van Ornem, *Owner*
EMP: 15
SALES (est): 2MM
SALES (corp-wide): 5.3MM **Privately Held**
WEB: www.dungenessassoc.com
SIC: 2091 2092 Canned & cured fish & seafoods; fresh or frozen packaged fish
PA: Dungeness Development Associates Inc
11805 N Creek Pkwy S
Kirkland WA 98034
425 481-0600

(G-9861)
DUSTY STRINGS CO (PA)
3450 16th Ave W Ste 200 (98119-1667)
PHONE..................................206 634-1656
Ray L Mooers, *President*
Susan F Mooers, *Corp Secy*
▲ EMP: 30
SQ FT: 170,500
SALES (est): 5.2MM **Privately Held**
WEB: www.dustystrings.com
SIC: 5736 5099 3931 String instruments; musical instruments parts & accessories; string instruments & parts

GEOGRAPHIC SECTION

Seattle - King County (G-9893)

(G-9862)
DUTHIE ENTERPRISES INC
Also Called: Standard Steel Fabricating Co
8155 1st Ave S (98108-4202)
P.O. Box 80907 (98108-0907)
PHONE..................................206 767-3314
W James Duthie, *President*
Kevin M Duthie, *Corp Secy*
W Greg Duthie, *Vice Pres*
EMP: 24
SQ FT: 16,000
SALES (est): 5.1MM **Privately Held**
SIC: 3441 Fabricated structural metal

(G-9863)
DUWAMISH MARINE SERVICES LLC
5600 W Marginal Way Sw (98106-1520)
P.O. Box 13368, Des Moines (98198-1006)
PHONE..................................206 870-3027
Kyle McCleary,
EMP: 8
SALES: 950K **Privately Held**
SIC: 3731 Shipbuilding & repairing

(G-9864)
DYNAMIC AUTOMOTIVE DISTRS
Also Called: Honest Jack
7269 Rainier Ave S (98118-3863)
PHONE..................................206 725-4474
Fred Silverman, *CEO*
Jack C Eastey Jr, *President*
Angela Eastey, *Corp Secy*
Ricardo Eastey, *Vice Pres*
EMP: 4
SQ FT: 4,500
SALES (est): 569.5K **Privately Held**
SIC: 5531 5411 5013 3599 Automotive parts; grocery stores, independent; automotive supplies & parts; machine shop, jobbing & repair

(G-9865)
DYNAVEST INC
2201 3rd Ave Apt 2604 (98121-2007)
PHONE..................................206 728-0777
EMP: 45 **EST**: 1995
SALES (est): 4.4MM **Privately Held**
SIC: 3823 Mfg Measurement Equipment

(G-9866)
E R BALABAN CUSTOM FABRICATION
411 W Republican St (98119-4030)
PHONE..................................206 883-5030
Eric Balaban, *Principal*
EMP: 2
SALES (est): 170.3K **Privately Held**
SIC: 3499 Novelties & giftware, including trophies

(G-9867)
E-GREEN BUILDING SYSTEMS
8421 32nd Ave Sw (98126-3703)
PHONE..................................206 219-9236
Benjamin T Cook, *Principal*
EMP: 9 **EST**: 2007
SALES (est): 826.6K **Privately Held**
SIC: 2421 Building & structural materials, wood

(G-9868)
EAGLE HARBOR TECHNOLOGIES INC
169 Western Ave W Ste 263 (98119-4211)
PHONE..................................206 402-5241
Timothy M Ziemba, *CEO*
John Carscadden, *Vice Pres*
Kyle McEleney, *Research*
James Prager, *Research*
Trevor Ziemba, *Admin Sec*
EMP: 11
SQ FT: 3,000
SALES (est): 1.4MM **Privately Held**
SIC: 8733 3679 Physical research, non-commercial; electronic circuits

(G-9869)
EAGLES NEST HOLDING INC
Also Called: Fastsigns
12700 Aurora Ave N (98133-7520)
PHONE..................................206 368-7331
Wayne Flesjer, *President*
EMP: 3

SALES (est): 220K **Privately Held**
SIC: 3993 Signs & advertising specialties

(G-9870)
EARSHOT LLC
1517 12th Ave Ste 101 (98122-3956)
PHONE..................................917 822-6074
Amy Spinelli, *Mng Member*
EMP: 4
SALES (est): 158.4K **Privately Held**
SIC: 7372 Educational computer software

(G-9871)
EASTERN MERCHANDISE CO INC
2701 2nd Ave (98121-1270)
PHONE..................................206 448-4466
Allen Klein, *President*
▲ **EMP**: 8
SQ FT: 8,000
SALES (est): 1.2MM **Privately Held**
SIC: 3911 5094 Jewelry, precious metal; precious stones & metals

(G-9872)
EASTERN NEWS INC
6221 39th Ave S (98118-3123)
PHONE..................................206 760-9168
Phuong Dong, *Principal*
EMP: 5 **EST**: 2011
SALES (est): 271.6K **Privately Held**
SIC: 2711 Newspapers, publishing & printing

(G-9873)
EASTSIDE PARENT
1530 Westlake Ave N # 600 (98109-3095)
PHONE..................................206 441-0191
Linda Watson, *Principal*
EMP: 2
SALES (est): 114.2K **Privately Held**
SIC: 2721 Magazines: publishing only, not printed on site

(G-9874)
ECLIPSE INC
1005 E Roy St Apt 12 (98102-4694)
PHONE..................................754 581-1513
EMP: 2
SALES (est): 73.4K **Privately Held**
SIC: 3433 Heating equipment, except electric

(G-9875)
ECLIPSE TECHNOLOGY LLC
219 1st Ave S Ste 400 (98104-2551)
PHONE..................................406 270-6366
Travis Pine, *Mng Member*
Blake Spout,
EMP: 2
SALES: 1MM **Privately Held**
SIC: 7371 7372 Computer software development & applications; application computer software

(G-9876)
ECM MARITIME SERVICES LLC
603 Stewart St Ste 803 (98101-1264)
PHONE..................................206 780-9980
Paul O'Brien, *Branch Mgr*
EMP: 2 **Privately Held**
SIC: 3731 6411 Shipbuilding & repairing; inspection & investigation services, insurance
PA: Ecm Maritime Services Llc
   1 Selleck St Ste 5
   Norwalk CT 06855

(G-9877)
ECO CHEMICAL INC (PA)
6600 Ursula Pl S (98108-2850)
P.O. Box 80823 (98108-0823)
PHONE..................................206 448-7930
Mark Cheirrtt, *President*
Mark Cheirrett, *President*
▼ **EMP**: 10
SQ FT: 500
SALES (est): 1.6MM **Privately Held**
WEB: www.ecochemical.com
SIC: 2851 Paints: oil or alkyd vehicle or water thinned

(G-9878)
ECO INC
Also Called: Ballard Smoke Shop
5439 Ballard Ave Nw (98107-4052)
PHONE..................................206 784-6611
Tom Economou, *President*
Pete Economou, *Treasurer*
EMP: 13 **EST**: 1971
SALES (est): 1.5MM **Privately Held**
SIC: 2813 5812 5813 Industrial gases; eating places; drinking places

(G-9879)
ECOBALANZA LLC
4919 17th Ave Nw (98107-4726)
P.O. Box 17183 (98127-0883)
PHONE..................................888 220-6020
Aimee Robinson, *Mng Member*
▲ **EMP**: 4 **EST**: 2002
SQ FT: 1,200
SALES (est): 150K **Privately Held**
SIC: 2512 Upholstered household furniture

(G-9880)
ECONET INC (PA)
3005 1st Ave (98121-1010)
PHONE..................................360 486-8300
B William Lee, *President*
Randy Banzino, *President*
Maria Lopez, *Manager*
▲ **EMP**: 36
SALES (est): 53.4MM **Privately Held**
SIC: 2844 2833 Cosmetic preparations; medicinals & botanicals

(G-9881)
ECORSYS INC
5000 22nd Ave Ne (98105-5720)
PHONE..................................347 282-6888
Kanglei Yu, *Principal*
EMP: 2
SALES (est): 90K **Privately Held**
SIC: 3674 Microcircuits, integrated (semiconductor)

(G-9882)
EDEN LABS LLC
309 S Cloverdale St D10 (98108-4568)
PHONE..................................888 626-3271
A C Braddock, *CEO*
Nick Marvin, *Production*
Ruth Winbauer, *Marketing Staff*
Joel Gordon, *Manager*
Melissa Braddock, *Officer*
EMP: 10 **EST**: 2002
SQ FT: 5,000
SALES (est): 1.9MM **Privately Held**
SIC: 8731 3821 Commercial research laboratory; distilling apparatus, laboratory type

(G-9883)
EDERER LLC (DH)
3701 S Norfolk St Ste A (98118-5650)
PHONE..................................800 464-1320
Jerry Olsen, *CEO*
Mark Wrightsman, *President*
▲ **EMP**: 10
SQ FT: 60,000
SALES (est): 6.4MM
SALES (corp-wide): 244.7MM **Privately Held**
WEB: www.ederer.par.com
SIC: 3536 Cranes, industrial plant; cranes, overhead traveling
HQ: Par Systems, Llc
   707 County Road E W
   Shoreview MN 55126
   651 528-5258

(G-9884)
EDITORIAL CONSULTANTS INC ✪
911 E Allison St (98102-3805)
PHONE..................................206 329-6499
EMP: 2 **EST**: 2019
SALES (est): 73.2K **Privately Held**
SIC: 2759 Commercial printing

(G-9885)
EDWIN LAIRD
Also Called: Air Cargo Management Group
2033 6th Ave Ste 830 (98121-2589)
PHONE..................................206 587-6537
Edwin C Laird, *Owner*

Charles Kauffman, *Assoc Editor*
EMP: 8 **EST**: 1977
SQ FT: 2,000
SALES (est): 827.3K **Privately Held**
WEB: www.cargofacts.com
SIC: 8748 2721 2741 Business consulting; periodicals; miscellaneous publishing

(G-9886)
EFESTE
1730 1st Ave S (98134-1404)
PHONE..................................206 535-6997
EMP: 2
SALES (est): 62.3K **Privately Held**
SIC: 2084 Brandy & brandy spirits

(G-9887)
EFFECTIVE DESIGN STUDIO LLC
1932 1st Ave Ste 605 (98101-1051)
PHONE..................................206 328-8989
Fax: 206 328-2285
EMP: 7
SQ FT: 3,000
SALES (est): 650K **Privately Held**
SIC: 3993 Mfg Signs/Advertising Specialties

(G-9888)
EFFORTLESS ATMS LLC
219 E Garfield St Apt 212 (98102-3762)
PHONE..................................206 456-4130
Andrew Rennhack,
Roland Chaiton,
EMP: 2
SALES (est): 110K **Privately Held**
SIC: 2032 Canned specialties

(G-9889)
EH ENTERPRISES MANAGEMENT INC (PA)
Also Called: Evergreen Herbal
3922 6th Ave S (98108-5201)
PHONE..................................206 596-8600
Marco Hoffman, *President*
EMP: 17
SQ FT: 10,000
SALES: 1.5MM **Privately Held**
SIC: 2048 Feed concentrates

(G-9890)
EIGHT BELLS WINERY
6213 Roosevelt Way Ne B (98115-6614)
PHONE..................................206 294-4131
EMP: 2
SALES (est): 79.4K **Privately Held**
SIC: 2084 Wines

(G-9891)
EIKI DIGITAL SYSTEMS INC
5701 6th Ave S (98108-2568)
P.O. Box 98161 (98198-0161)
PHONE..................................206 957-2626
Takao Niimura, *President*
EMP: 2
SALES (est): 115.1K **Privately Held**
SIC: 2759 Commercial printing

(G-9892)
ELARM INC
3114 15th Ave S (98144-5730)
PHONE..................................206 395-9604
Daniel Pickford, *CEO*
EMP: 6
SALES (est): 263.8K **Privately Held**
SIC: 7375 3571 Information retrieval services; minicomputers

(G-9893)
ELECTRONIC CHARTS CO INC
4241 21st Ave W Ste 107 (98199-1250)
PHONE..................................206 282-4990
Byron Verbon, *President*
Jim Brantingham, *Principal*
James Brantingham, *Vice Pres*
Robert Bark, *Sales/Mktg Dir*
EMP: 3
SALES (est): 348.1K **Privately Held**
WEB: www.electroniccharts.com
SIC: 3812 7336 Navigational systems & instruments; commercial art & graphic design

Seattle - King County (G-9894)

(G-9894)
ELECTRONIC PRGRM & DESIGN
Also Called: E P A D
7114 17th Ave Sw (98106-1807)
P.O. Box 81163 (98108-1163)
PHONE..................................206 767-7262
Matthew H Shaw, *President*
EMP: 5
SALES (est): 562.7K **Privately Held**
WEB: www.tantime.com
SIC: 8742 3679 8748 Industry specialist consultants; electronic circuits; business consulting

(G-9895)
ELEMENT 6
2562 Thorndyke Ave W # 301 (98199-3540)
PHONE..................................206 282-0877
Rusty Williams, *Principal*
EMP: 3
SALES (est): 181.1K **Privately Held**
SIC: 2819 Industrial inorganic chemicals

(G-9896)
ELEMENT 8
2717 Western Ave Apt 6010 (98121-1163)
PHONE..................................208 870-8471
EMP: 2 EST: 2016
SALES (est): 74.4K **Privately Held**
SIC: 2819 Mfg Industrial Inorganic Chemicals

(G-9897)
ELEMENT GROUP INC
6506 Sycamore Ave Nw (98117-4846)
PHONE..................................206 784-3355
William Bauer, *Vice Pres*
EMP: 3
SALES (est): 150.4K **Privately Held**
SIC: 2819 Industrial inorganic chemicals

(G-9898)
ELKINS DISTRIBUTION INC
Also Called: Old World Cone
12602 1st Ave S (98168-2617)
PHONE..................................206 241-0333
Andi Elkins, *President*
▼ EMP: 3
SALES (est): 357K **Privately Held**
WEB: www.oldworldcone.com
SIC: 2052 Cones, ice cream

(G-9899)
ELLIOTT BAY BICYCLES INC
2116 Western Ave (98121-2110)
PHONE..................................206 441-9998
Bill Davidson, *President*
Robert Freeman, *Vice Pres*
EMP: 10 EST: 1974
SQ FT: 7,000
SALES (est): 900K **Privately Held**
WEB: www.elliottbaybicycles.com
SIC: 5941 3751 Bicycle & bicycle parts, bicycles & related parts

(G-9900)
ELLIOTT BAY BREWING COMPANY
Also Called: Elliott Bay Brewery & Pub
4720 California Ave Sw (98116-4413)
PHONE..................................206 246-4211
Todd Carden, *President*
Bret Norton, *Vice Pres*
EMP: 31
SALES (est): 3.9MM **Privately Held**
WEB: www.elliottbaybrewing.com
SIC: 2082 5813 5812 Beer (alcoholic beverage); drinking places; eating places

(G-9901)
ELLIOTT BAY HOLDING CO LLC
Also Called: Elliott Bay Industries
7500 W Marginal Way S (98108-4142)
PHONE..................................206 762-6560
Illona Miller, *Owner*
EMP: 5
SALES: 1MM **Privately Held**
SIC: 3599 Custom machinery

(G-9902)
ELLIOTT BAY RECORDING COMPANY
932 12th Ave (98122-4412)
PHONE..................................206 709-9626
EMP: 2
SALES: 50K **Privately Held**
SIC: 3679 Mfg Electronic Components

(G-9903)
ELMOR INC
2300 W Elmore St (98199-1245)
PHONE..................................206 213-0111
Joe Williams, *CEO*
EMP: 2 EST: 1987
SALES (est): 117.6K **Privately Held**
SIC: 3699 Electrical equipment & supplies

(G-9904)
ELN COMMUNICATIONS INC
814 6th Ave S (98134-1304)
PHONE..................................206 256-0420
Jf Roberts III, *President*
Daniel Dingess, *Vice Pres*
EMP: 2
SALES (est): 170K **Privately Held**
SIC: 3663 Digital encoders

(G-9905)
ELSOM CELLARS LLC
3023 Fauntleroy Ave Sw (98126-2318)
PHONE..................................425 298-3082
Jody Elsom,
EMP: 7 EST: 2008
SALES (est): 552.7K **Privately Held**
SIC: 2084 Wines

(G-9906)
ELSOM CLLARS WINERY 3PP PNW HQ
2960 4th Ave S (98134-1203)
PHONE..................................775 848-1771
EMP: 2
SALES (est): 90.4K **Privately Held**
SIC: 2084 Wines

(G-9907)
ELYSIAN BREWING COMPANY INC
5510 Airport Way S (98108-2255)
PHONE..................................206 767-0210
Andrew Goeler, *President*
EMP: 11
SALES (corp-wide): 1.5B **Privately Held**
SIC: 2082 Malt beverages
HQ: Elysian Brewing Company, Inc.
6010 Airport Way S
Seattle WA 98108

(G-9908)
ELYSIAN BREWING COMPANY INC (DH)
6010 Airport Way S (98108-2716)
PHONE..................................206 860-3977
Andrew Goeler, *President*
Garry Tappana, *Vice Pres*
David West, *Treasurer*
Jonathan Knowles, *Executive*
Thomas Larson, *Admin Sec*
▲ EMP: 30
SALES (est): 8.1MM
SALES (corp-wide): 1.5B **Privately Held**
WEB: www.elysianbrewing.com
SIC: 2082 5812 Ale (alcoholic beverage); beer (alcoholic beverage); eating places
HQ: Anheuser-Busch Companies, Llc
1 Busch Pl
Saint Louis MO 63118
314 632-6777

(G-9909)
EMC CORPORATION
505 1st Ave S Ste 600 (98104-3284)
PHONE..................................206 623-1227
Phillip Pao, *Manager*
Travis Lane, *Software Engr*
Skyler Sell, *Software Dev*
EMP: 70
SALES (corp-wide): 90.6B **Publicly Held**
SIC: 3572 Computer storage devices
HQ: Emc Corporation
176 South St
Hopkinton MA 01748
508 435-1000

(G-9910)
EMC ELECTRO MECHANICAL COMPANY
5002 2nd Ave S (98134-2432)
PHONE..................................206 767-9307
Adam Chukri, *Owner*
EMP: 3
SALES (est): 360.7K **Privately Held**
SIC: 3537 Forklift trucks

(G-9911)
EMERALD CITY SOFTWARE LLC
1234 Nw 118th St (98177-4629)
PHONE..................................206 321-5252
Ken Hill, *Principal*
EMP: 2 EST: 2010
SALES (est): 154.4K **Privately Held**
SIC: 7372 Prepackaged software

(G-9912)
EMERALD GALVANIZING INC
621 Nw 41st St (98107-5032)
PHONE..................................206 782-8300
Randall D Breiwick, *President*
EMP: 9
SALES (est): 1.2MM **Privately Held**
SIC: 3479 Galvanizing of iron, steel or end-formed products

(G-9913)
EMERALD SERVICES INC (DH)
Also Called: Emerald Recycling
6851 E Marginal Way S (98108-3408)
PHONE..................................206 430-7795
Alan S McKim, *CEO*
Mark G Bouldin, *President*
Frank Flanegan, *General Mgr*
Jim Munnell, *General Mgr*
Eric W Gerstenberg, *COO*
▲ EMP: 200
SALES (est): 149.3MM
SALES (corp-wide): 3.3B **Publicly Held**
WEB: www.emeraldnw.com
SIC: 4953 7699 2911 8748 Refuse collection & disposal services; waste cleaning services; petroleum refining; environmental consultant; portable toilet rental
HQ: Safety-Kleen Systems, Inc.
2600 N Central Expy # 400
Richardson TX 75080
972 265-2000

(G-9914)
EMERALD TOOL INC
8009 7th Ave S (98108-4365)
PHONE..................................206 767-5670
Gary Walker, *President*
Leonard Walker, *Vice Pres*
Susan Walker, *Admin Sec*
EMP: 7
SQ FT: 14,000
SALES (est): 2MM **Privately Held**
WEB: www.emeraldtool.com
SIC: 7699 5085 5072 3423 Knife, saw & tool sharpening & repair; tools; saw blades; edge tools for woodworking: augers, bits, gimlets, etc.; power-driven handtools; machine tool accessories

(G-9915)
EMERGENT DETECTION INC
3656 Whitman Ave N (98103-8720)
PHONE..................................206 391-4876
Eric Fogel, *CEO*
EMP: 3
SALES (est): 194.2K **Privately Held**
SIC: 3845 Electromedical equipment

(G-9916)
EMERGING MKTS CMMNICATIONS LLC
Also Called: Mtn Satellite Communications
101 Stewart St Ste 800 (98101-2059)
PHONE..................................206 454-8300
Fax: 206 838-7708
EMP: 5
SALES (corp-wide): 114.1MM **Privately Held**
SIC: 3663 Mfg Radio/Tv Communication Equipment
PA: Emerging Markets Communications, Llc
3044 N Commerce Pkwy
Miramar FL 33025
954 538-4000

(G-9917)
EMERY BURTON LLC
1534 1st Ave S (98134-1466)
PHONE..................................206 323-7351
Van Bjorkland, *Mng Member*
Roger Affe,
EMP: 4
SALES (est): 289.5K **Privately Held**
SIC: 2771 Greeting cards

(G-9918)
EMULATE THERAPEUTICS INC
24 Roy St Ste 437 (98109-4018)
PHONE..................................206 708-2288
Charles Cobbs, *Ch of Bd*
Chris E Rivera, *President*
Lisa C Butters, *COO*
Kenneth M Ferguson, *Security Dir*
Donna Morgan Murray, *Risk Mgmt Dir*
EMP: 9
SQ FT: 1,200
SALES (est): 2MM **Privately Held**
SIC: 3845 Electrotherapeutic apparatus

(G-9919)
ENCOMPASS PRINT SOLUTIONS LLC
309 S Cloverdale St C38 (98108-4579)
PHONE..................................425 922-6170
Jennifer Morrison, *Mng Member*
EMP: 2
SALES (est): 319.3K **Privately Held**
SIC: 2752 Commercial printing, offset

(G-9920)
ENCORE PUBLISHING INC
Also Called: Encore Media Group
87 Wall St (98121-1330)
PHONE..................................206 443-0445
Paul Heppner, *President*
EMP: 7
SQ FT: 1,100
SALES (est): 850K **Privately Held**
SIC: 2741 Miscellaneous publishing

(G-9921)
ENDEX NEWSPAPER LLC
1535 11th Ave Fl 3 (98122-3933)
PHONE..................................206 322-4194
Tim Keck, *Principal*
EMP: 4
SALES (est): 267.1K **Privately Held**
SIC: 2711 5994 Newspapers, publishing & printing; newsstand

(G-9922)
ENER-G FOODS INC (PA)
5960 1st Ave S (98108-3248)
PHONE..................................206 767-3928
Sam Wylde III, *President*
Marie Palermo Wylde, *Vice Pres*
Heather Caille, *Director*
Cely Cleto, *Admin Sec*
▲ EMP: 47 EST: 1948
SQ FT: 30,000
SALES (est): 10.9MM **Privately Held**
WEB: www.ener-g.com
SIC: 2051 2052 2041 5961 Bread, cake & related products; cookies & crackers; flour; food, mail order

(G-9923)
ENERG2 INC
100 Ne Northlake Way (98105-6869)
PHONE..................................206 465-7243
Eric Luebbe, *CEO*
Jack Santo, *CFO*
Leanne McInerny, *Office Mgr*
Aaron Feaver, *CTO*
EMP: 19
SALES (est): 5.8MM **Privately Held**
SIC: 2819 Industrial inorganic chemicals

(G-9924)
ENERG2 TECHNOLOGIES INC
100 Ne Northlake Way (98105-6869)
PHONE..................................206 547-0445
Eric Luebbe, *CEO*
Henry Costantino, *Vice Pres*
Tom Kieffer, *Vice Pres*
Phil Souza, *Vice Pres*
Chris Hohman, *Engineer*
EMP: 32
SALES (est): 4.1MM **Privately Held**
SIC: 2819 Industrial inorganic chemicals

(G-9925)
ENERGSOFT INC
701 17th Ave Apt 201 (98122-4667)
PHONE..................................425 246-1675

GEOGRAPHIC SECTION

Seattle - King County (G-9957)

Viacheslav Agafonov, *President*
EMP: 6
SALES (est): 132.9K **Privately Held**
SIC: 7372 Prepackaged software

(G-9926)
ENERGYSAVVY INC
506 2nd Ave Ste 1900 (98104-2300)
PHONE......................206 462-2206
Aaron Goldfeder, *President*
Scott Case, *COO*
Michael Rigney, *Senior VP*
David Wolpa, *Vice Pres*
Kim Guilbault, *Opers Mgr*
EMP: 34
SALES (est): 3.7MM **Privately Held**
SIC: 7371 7372 Computer software development & applications; prepackaged software

(G-9927)
ENPRECIS INC (PA)
111 S Jackson St Ste 400 (98104-3112)
PHONE......................206 274-0122
Ed Shapero, *CEO*
Vincent Dupray, *General Mgr*
Jacques Dacosta, *Vice Pres*
Paul Miller, *Project Mgr*
Brad Anderson, *Sales Staff*
EMP: 24 **EST:** 2006
SALES (est): 7.1MM **Privately Held**
SIC: 7372 Business oriented computer software

(G-9928)
ENRAVEL INC
3014 Nw 75th St (98117-4652)
PHONE......................206 414-8884
Brian Schowengerdt, *CEO*
EMP: 5
SALES (est): 422.7K **Privately Held**
SIC: 3577 Computer peripheral equipment

(G-9929)
ENT SOLUTIONS INC
118 Sw 116th St Unit D13 (98146-2369)
PHONE......................206 769-1735
Bryn Patton, *President*
EMP: 2
SALES (est): 186.2K **Privately Held**
SIC: 3841 Surgical & medical instruments

(G-9930)
ENTIRELY INC
505 Broadway E Unit 123 (98102-5023)
PHONE......................206 979-9092
Adam Benzion, *CEO*
Wally Ho,
EMP: 2
SALES (est): 122.1K **Privately Held**
SIC: 7372 Business oriented computer software

(G-9931)
ENTROPY KILLER SOFTWARE
4222 Meridian Ave N (98103-7602)
PHONE......................206 526-2488
EMP: 2
SALES (est): 130K **Privately Held**
SIC: 7372 Prepackaged Software Services

(G-9932)
ENVELOPE CONVERTING SERVICE
Also Called: E C S
6603 Ursula Pl S (98108-2851)
PHONE......................206 767-3653
Tim McClenahan, *President*
Barb McClenahan, *Business Mgr*
EMP: 9
SALES (est): 2.1MM **Privately Held**
WEB: www.envelopeconverting.com
SIC: 2677 Envelopes

(G-9933)
ENVIRONMENTAL FINCL INFO SVCS
Also Called: Efis
2832 Magnolia Blvd W (98199-2411)
PHONE......................206 283-4210
Alexander Stewart, *President*
EMP: 4
SALES (est): 341.3K **Privately Held**
WEB: www.efisinfo.com
SIC: 2759 Publication printing

(G-9934)
EPICRU VINTNERS LLC
4501 2nd Ave Nw (98107-4320)
PHONE......................206 829-9714
Michael Arnette, *Principal*
EMP: 2
SALES (est): 101.2K **Privately Held**
SIC: 2084 Wines, brandy & brandy spirits

(G-9935)
EPPING-JORDAN FINE WDWKG LLC
4721 W Roberts Way (98199-1824)
PHONE......................206 588-2700
Mark Epping-Jordan, *Principal*
EMP: 4 **EST:** 2012
SALES (est): 329.6K **Privately Held**
SIC: 2431 Millwork

(G-9936)
ERIC GIBBS SOFTWARE
2918 Nw Esplanade (98117-2621)
PHONE......................206 784-0741
Eric P Gibbs, *Principal*
EMP: 2
SALES (est): 68.4K **Privately Held**
SIC: 7372 Prepackaged software

(G-9937)
ERICKA J THIELKE
Also Called: Fittersweet
6816 17th Ave Ne (98115-6845)
PHONE......................206 214-7530
Ericka Thielke, *Owner*
EMP: 3
SALES (est): 65.8K **Privately Held**
SIC: 2053 7389 Frozen bakery products, except bread;

(G-9938)
ERICS WOODWORK
141 Nw 80th St (98117-3038)
PHONE......................206 860-6174
Erik G Lord, *Principal*
EMP: 3
SALES (est): 216K **Privately Held**
SIC: 2499 Decorative wood & woodwork

(G-9939)
ESOTERIC SOFTWARE LLC
4011 23rd Ave Sw (98106-1261)
PHONE......................206 618-3331
Nathan Sweet,
EMP: 2
SALES (est): 48.4K **Privately Held**
SIC: 7372 Prepackaged software

(G-9940)
ESP PRINTING INC
Also Called: E S P Complete Printing Svc
4700 9th Ave Nw (98107-4528)
PHONE......................425 251-6240
David Cooke, *President*
EMP: 30
SALES (est): 4.3MM **Privately Held**
SIC: 2752 2791 2789 Commercial printing, lithographic; typesetting; bookbinding & related work

(G-9941)
ESQUEL APPAREL INC
1109 1st Ave Ste 204 (98101-2979)
PHONE......................206 223-7338
Betsy Hentz, *Manager*
EMP: 4 **Privately Held**
SIC: 2389 Men's miscellaneous accessories
HQ: Esquel Apparel, Inc
   14 E 33rd St Apt 3n
   New York NY 10016
   212 481-0886

(G-9942)
ESTERLINE TECHNOLOGIES CORP
901 Dexter Ave N (98109-3515)
PHONE......................206 281-1312
Mark Cochran, *Business Mgr*
Janice Chung, *Production*
Brian Baker, *Engineer*
Kevin Parson, *Engineer*
Nathan Wortinger, *Engineer*
EMP: 10

SALES (corp-wide): 3.8B **Publicly Held**
SIC: 3825 Test equipment for electronic & electric measurement
HQ: Esterline Technologies Corp
   500 108th Ave Ne Ste 1500
   Bellevue WA 98004
   425 453-9400

(G-9943)
EVANS - HAMILTON INC
4608 Union Bay Pl Ne (98105-4027)
PHONE......................206 526-5622
Kevin Redman, *Manager*
EMP: 7
SALES (corp-wide): 12.7MM **Privately Held**
SIC: 8748 3577 Business consulting; data conversion equipment, media-to-media: computer
PA: Evans - Hamilton, Inc.
   411 N Sam Houston Pkwy E
   Houston TX 77060
   281 448-6188

(G-9944)
EVAS CRACKERS LLC
1137 22nd Ave E (98112-3516)
PHONE......................206 353-5691
Eric Copenhaver, *Administration*
EMP: 3 **EST:** 2016
SALES (est): 157.9K **Privately Held**
SIC: 2052 Pretzels

(G-9945)
EVELO INC
Also Called: Evelo Electric Bicycle Company
1411 34th Ave (98122-3333)
PHONE......................877 991-7272
Yevgeniy Mordkovich, *President*
Boris Mordkovich, *Vice Pres*
EMP: 14
SALES (est): 156.5K **Privately Held**
SIC: 3699 Cleaning equipment, ultrasonic, except medical & dental

(G-9946)
EVERGREEN TIMBER CORP
8823 Renton Ave S Ste 2 (98118-4918)
PHONE......................206 579-2925
◆ **EMP:** 10
SQ FT: 1,000
SALES: 1.7MM **Privately Held**
SIC: 2411 5031 5099 Logging Whol Lumber/Plywood/Millwork Whol Durable Goods

(G-9947)
EVERGREENS SALAD
823 3rd Ave (98104-1650)
PHONE......................206 973-4400
EMP: 6 **EST:** 2015
SALES (est): 499.3K **Privately Held**
SIC: 2099 Salads, fresh or refrigerated

(G-9948)
EVERPATH INC
Also Called: Skilljar
720 Olive Way Ste 700 (98101-1853)
PHONE......................206 682-7259
Sandi Lin, *CEO*
Samuel Sunderaraj, *VP Sales*
Adrienne Domingus, *Software Engr*
Jay Martinage, *Executive*
EMP: 6
SALES (est): 708.5K **Privately Held**
SIC: 7372 Business oriented computer software

(G-9949)
EVOLUTION PRESS INC
2525 W Commodore Way (98199-1229)
PHONE......................206 783-5522
Scott Hill, *President*
EMP: 4
SALES (est): 475.3K **Privately Held**
WEB: www.evolutionpress.net
SIC: 2752 Commercial printing, lithographic

(G-9950)
EVRNU SPC
3200 1st Ave S Ste 200 (98134-1856)
PHONE......................206 466-5269
Stacy Flynn, *CEO*
Christopher Stanev, *Principal*
Karen Barrier, *Opers Staff*

EMP: 2
SQ FT: 1,700
SALES (est): 169.2K **Privately Held**
SIC: 2282 Manmade & synthetic fiber yarns: twisting, winding, etc.

(G-9951)
EX OFFICIO LLC (DH)
Also Called: Marmot
4202 6th Ave S Unit Main (98108-1739)
PHONE......................206 283-1471
Bill Conradt, *Vice Pres*
Steve Skidmore, *Finance Mgr*
Steve Bendzk, *Mng Member*
Kathleen O'Brien, *Manager*
Monte H Baier,
▲ **EMP:** 8
SALES (est): 8.6MM
SALES (corp-wide): 8.6B **Publicly Held**
SIC: 2339 2329 Women's & misses' outerwear; men's & boys' sportswear & athletic clothing

(G-9952)
EXCEPTIONALLY SMART
Also Called: Esin Games
500 Union St Ste 420 (98101-4041)
PHONE......................206 321-0721
EMP: 2
SALES (est): 130K **Privately Held**
SIC: 7372 Prepackaged Software Services

(G-9953)
EXO LABS INC
3131 Wstn Ave Ste M325 (98121)
PHONE......................206 659-1249
Michael Baum, *President*
Jeff Stewart, *Vice Pres*
Dainia Edwards, *Engineer*
George Cawman, *Marketing Staff*
EMP: 5
SQ FT: 1,600
SALES: 1MM **Privately Held**
SIC: 7372 Prepackaged software

(G-9954)
EXOMOTION LLC
Also Called: Thomashilfen
7936 Exodental Ave S (98108)
PHONE......................206 763-0754
Angela Darlene Hawthorne, *President*
Andrew Woehr, *COO*
▲ **EMP:** 4
SALES: 1.1MM
SALES (corp-wide): 355.8K **Privately Held**
SIC: 2531 2599 2515 3842 Seats, automobile; beds, not household use; mattresses, containing felt, foam rubber, urethane, etc.; wheelchairs
HQ: Thomas Hilfen Fur Korperbehinderte Gmbh & Co. Medico Kg
   Walkmuhlenstr. 1
   Bremervorde 27432
   476 188-60

(G-9955)
EXORVISION INC
3417 Evanston Ave N # 402 (98103-8626)
PHONE......................206 254-0220
Oddvar Huslid, *President*
Reying Huslid, *Vice Pres*
▲ **EMP:** 6
SALES (est): 1MM **Privately Held**
WEB: www.exorvision.com
SIC: 3577 Computer peripheral equipment

(G-9956)
EXPENSIVE CARDBOARD
2401 Sw Brandon St # 208 (98106-3522)
PHONE......................214 564-2670
Ron Keiser, *Principal*
EMP: 2
SALES (est): 99.8K **Privately Held**
SIC: 2631 Cardboard

(G-9957)
F&S INDUSTRIES LLC
1416 N 50th St (98103-6733)
PHONE......................206 501-5347
Alan Forst, *Principal*
EMP: 2 **EST:** 2015
SALES (est): 104.6K **Privately Held**
SIC: 3999 Manufacturing industries

Seattle - King County (G-9958)

(G-9958)
F/V NEAHKAHNIE LLC
2727 Alaskan Way Pier 69 (98121-1107)
PHONE...................206 547-6557
EMP: 2
SALES (est): 132.7K **Privately Held**
SIC: 3731 Fishing vessels, large: building & repairing

(G-9959)
F5 NETWORKS INC (PA)
401 Elliott Ave W Ste 500 (98119-4003)
PHONE...................206 272-5555
Alan J Higginson, *Ch of Bd*
Francois Locoh-Donou, *President*
Tom Fountain, *Exec VP*
Steve McMillan, *Exec VP*
Scot Rogers, *Exec VP*
EMP: 123
SQ FT: 320,000
SALES: 2.1B **Publicly Held**
WEB: www.f5.com
SIC: 7373 7372 Computer integrated systems design; prepackaged software

(G-9960)
FABRIFORM LLC
3300 Airport Way S (98134-2118)
PHONE...................206 587-5303
Jim Parkes, *President*
Robert J Parkes, *President*
Harvey Wright, *Chairman*
Joseph Bianchi, *Vice Pres*
Mike Clacy, *Vice Pres*
EMP: 25
SQ FT: 27,000
SALES (est): 8.4MM **Privately Held**
WEB: www.fabriform.com
SIC: 3089 Plastic hardware & building products; plastic processing

(G-9961)
FACTORY TRAWLER SUPPLY INC (PA)
4257 24th Ave W (98199-1214)
PHONE...................206 285-6732
Stan Simonson, *President*
Bill Orr, *Principal*
Bill Sage, *Vice Pres*
EMP: 2
SALES (est): 1.7MM **Privately Held**
SIC: 5084 2399 4222 7359 Fish processing machinery, equipment & supplies; fishing nets; warehousing, cold storage or refrigerated; equipment rental & leasing

(G-9962)
FACTS NEWSPAPER
1112 34th Ave (98122-5139)
PHONE...................206 324-0552
Marla Beaver, *Owner*
Lavanonne Beaver, *Co-Owner*
EMP: 2
SQ FT: 5,000
SALES (est): 122.3K **Privately Held**
SIC: 2711 Newspapers: publishing only, not printed on site

(G-9963)
FAIRY FLOSS
13728 Interlake Ave N (98133-7104)
PHONE...................206 364-3218
Darren Nelson, *Owner*
EMP: 2 EST: 2017
SALES (est): 78.7K **Privately Held**
SIC: 3843 Dental equipment & supplies

(G-9964)
FALCONSTOR SOFTWARE INC
601 Union St (98101-2341)
PHONE...................206 652-3312
Natalie Evans, *Branch Mgr*
EMP: 4
SALES (corp-wide): 17.8MM **Publicly Held**
SIC: 7372 Prepackaged software
PA: Falconstor Software, Inc.
2 Huntington Quadrangle
Melville NY 11747
631 777-5188

(G-9965)
FALL LINE WINERY LLC
2960 4th Ave S Ste 107 (98134-1203)
PHONE...................206 406-4249
EMP: 2
SALES (est): 100.9K **Privately Held**
SIC: 2084 Wines

(G-9966)
FAMILIAN NORTHWEST SEATTLE 07
7115 W Marginal Way Sw (98106-1911)
PHONE...................206 767-7700
Fax: 206 763-3090
EMP: 4 EST: 2008
SALES (est): 290K **Privately Held**
SIC: 3431 Mfg Metal Sanitary Ware

(G-9967)
FAMILY TREASURES
909 2nd Ave N Apt 301 (98109-3795)
PHONE...................206 282-1194
May Yeung, *Owner*
EMP: 3
SALES (est): 21K **Privately Held**
SIC: 3944 Craft & hobby kits & sets

(G-9968)
FANTAGRAPHICS BOOKS INC (PA)
Also Called: Eros Comix
7563 Lake City Way Ne (98115-4218)
P.O. Box 25070 (98165-1970)
PHONE...................206 524-1967
Gary Groth, *President*
Kim Thompson, *Vice Pres*
Greg Zura, *Sales Mgr*
Stephanie Olczyk, *Cust Mgr*
Dan Dean, *Technology*
▲ EMP: 25
SQ FT: 4,500
SALES (est): 2.7MM **Privately Held**
WEB: www.fantagraphics.com
SIC: 2721 5942 Trade journals: publishing only, not printed on site; comic books: publishing only, not printed on site; book stores

(G-9969)
FANTASY SPORTS VAULT
3210 California Ave Sw (98116-3305)
PHONE...................206 219-9833
EMP: 2 EST: 2011
SALES (est): 120K **Privately Held**
SIC: 3272 Mfg Concrete Products

(G-9970)
FAQA
1725 Ne 115th St (98125-6573)
PHONE...................206 362-5916
Edmund Freeman, *Principal*
EMP: 2
SALES (est): 172.2K **Privately Held**
SIC: 3441 Fabricated structural metal

(G-9971)
FARADAY PHARMACEUTICALS INC
1616 Eastlake Ave E # 560 (98102-3788)
PHONE...................206 946-1989
Stephen A Hill, *CEO*
Mark B Roth, *President*
Brian Blackman, *CFO*
Simon J Tulloch, *Chief Mktg Ofcr*
EMP: 4
SALES (est): 2.1MM **Privately Held**
SIC: 2834 Pharmaceutical preparations

(G-9972)
FARIS LLC
2233 15th Ave W (98119-2417)
PHONE...................206 992-6453
Faris Du Graf, *President*
EMP: 2 EST: 2015
SALES (est): 54.6K **Privately Held**
SIC: 3911 Jewelry apparel

(G-9973)
FASHION SALES INC
2617 2nd Ave Ste B (98121-1211)
PHONE...................206 441-3282
Douglas Lo, *President*
EMP: 3
SQ FT: 1,300
SALES (est): 347.5K **Privately Held**
SIC: 2329 2331 Knickers, dress (separate): men's & boys'; women's & misses' blouses & shirts

(G-9974)
FAST FLASHINGS LLC
13760 32nd Ave Ne (98125-8314)
PHONE...................425 827-8367
Ian McGlynn, *Branch Mgr*
EMP: 3
SALES (corp-wide): 2MM **Privately Held**
SIC: 3446 Architectural metalwork
PA: Fast Flashings, Llc
13760 32nd Ave Ne
Seattle WA 98125
206 364-3612

(G-9975)
FAST FLASHINGS LLC (PA)
13760 32nd Ave Ne (98125-8314)
PHONE...................206 364-3612
Ian McGlynn, *President*
EMP: 8
SQ FT: 5,500
SALES: 2MM **Privately Held**
WEB: www.fastflashings.com
SIC: 3446 Architectural metalwork

(G-9976)
FASTDATAIO INC
601 Union St (98101-2341)
PHONE...................888 707-3346
Alen Capalik, *CEO*
EMP: 10 EST: 2017
SALES (est): 221.8K **Privately Held**
SIC: 7372 Application computer software

(G-9977)
FASTSIGNS
1515 9th Ave Ste 4 (98101-1814)
PHONE...................206 682-2129
Lance Holmes, *President*
EMP: 4
SALES (est): 159.7K **Privately Held**
SIC: 3993 Signs & advertising specialties

(G-9978)
FASTSIGNS
4721 University Way Ne (98105-4412)
PHONE...................206 886-3860
EMP: 2
SALES (est): 150.5K **Privately Held**
SIC: 3993 Signs & advertising specialties

(G-9979)
FEATHER AND SKULL
317 Nw 41st St Apt 208 (98107-5065)
PHONE...................206 227-7951
Noel Bores, *Principal*
EMP: 2
SALES (est): 99.5K **Privately Held**
SIC: 3911 Jewelry, precious metal

(G-9980)
FEDERAL MARINE & DEF SVCS LLC (PA)
8000 5th Ave S (98108-4303)
P.O. Box 80966 (98108-0966)
PHONE...................206 322-5529
Rocky Becker, *Manager*
Jason Walker,
Deborah Sandeman,
EMP: 25
SQ FT: 2,500
SALES (est): 4.5MM **Privately Held**
SIC: 3731 Shipbuilding & repairing

(G-9981)
FEDEX OFFICE & PRINT SVCS INC
735 Pike St Ste 11 (98101-2310)
PHONE...................206 467-1767
Mark Werling, *Branch Mgr*
EMP: 25
SALES (corp-wide): 69.6B **Publicly Held**
WEB: www.kinkos.com
SIC: 7334 2789 2752 2759 Photocopying & duplicating services; bookbinding & related work; commercial printing, lithographic; commercial printing
HQ: Fedex Office And Print Services, Inc.
7900 Legacy Dr
Plano TX 75024
800 463-3339

(G-9982)
FEDEXOFFICE
1400 6th Ave (98101-2318)
PHONE...................206 467-5885

Brian Philips, *Principal*
EMP: 2
SALES (est): 119.3K **Privately Held**
SIC: 7389 7334 5099 2752 Packaging & labeling services; photocopying & duplicating services; signs, except electric; commercial printing, lithographic

(G-9983)
FEMININA GROUP INC
Also Called: Genneve
85 S Atlantic St Ste 203 (98134-1220)
PHONE...................310 237-5733
Jill Angelo, *CEO*
EMP: 2
SALES: 120K **Privately Held**
SIC: 2676 8099 Feminine hygiene paper products; health screening service

(G-9984)
FENIX INDUSTRIES INC
11552 6th Ave Nw (98177-4727)
PHONE...................206 695-2582
EMP: 2
SALES (est): 110K **Privately Held**
SIC: 3999 Mfg Misc Products

(G-9985)
FENOLOGICA BIOSCIENCES INC
720 Broadway (98122-4302)
PHONE...................206 726-1200
Sean Macleod, *CEO*
John Wecker, *Bd of Directors*
EMP: 4
SALES (est): 162.8K **Privately Held**
SIC: 3826 Analytical optical instruments

(G-9986)
FIALAB INSTRUMENTS INC
2151 N Northlake Way # 100 (98103-9178)
PHONE...................206 258-2290
Henning Hasle, *President*
Ilkka Lahdesmaki, *General Mgr*
EMP: 9
SQ FT: 3,000
SALES (est): 1.7MM **Privately Held**
WEB: www.fialab.com
SIC: 3826 Analytical instruments

(G-9987)
FIBERDYNE AEROSPACE
1222 S Angelo St Ste A (98108-2719)
PHONE...................206 326-8581
EMP: 3
SALES (est): 131.3K **Privately Held**
SIC: 3728 Aircraft parts & equipment

(G-9988)
FIDO N-SCRATCH
5012 41st Ave Sw (98136-1204)
PHONE...................206 588-2111
Melanie Carroll, *Owner*
EMP: 3
SALES (est): 162.8K **Privately Held**
SIC: 5199 3999 Pet supplies; pet supplies

(G-9989)
FIELD ROAST GRAIN MEAT CO SPC
3901 7th Ave S (98108-5206)
PHONE...................800 311-9797
Dan Curtin, *President*
Glynn Omoto, *Purch Mgr*
▲ EMP: 220
SALES (est): 45.9MM
SALES (corp-wide): 2.6B **Privately Held**
SIC: 2013 5149 2011 2041 Roast beef from purchased meat; coffee, green or roasted; meat packing plants; flour & other grain mill products
PA: Maple Leaf Foods Inc
6985 Financial Dr
Mississauga ON L5N 0
905 285-5000

(G-9990)
FIFTH STAR LABS LLC
626 Randolph Pl (98122-6454)
PHONE...................206 369-3956
EMP: 2 EST: 2013
SALES (est): 142.1K **Privately Held**
SIC: 7372 7389 Prepackaged Software Services Business Services At Non-Commercial Site

GEOGRAPHIC SECTION

Seattle - King County (G-10020)

(G-9991)
FIGUREHEAD BREWING COMPANY LLC
1710 Nw 61st St (98107-2358)
PHONE....................206 492-7981
Robert Monroe, *Principal*
EMP: 3
SALES (est): 68.6K Privately Held
SIC: 2082 Malt beverages

(G-9992)
FILMATERIA STUDIOS INC
Also Called: TV Books
3440 California Ave Sw (98116-3379)
PHONE....................206 938-6791
William T Jeakle, *President*
Thomas T Crouch, *President*
Brian Rees, *Editor*
EMP: 3
SQ FT: 1,500
SALES (est): 375.5K Privately Held
WEB: www.filmateria.com
SIC: 7812 2731 8748 7374 Video production; motion picture production; books: publishing only; business consulting; computer graphics service; television program, including commercial producers

(G-9993)
FILSON MANUFACTURING INC
1741 1st Ave S (98134-1403)
PHONE....................206 242-9579
EMP: 2
SALES (est): 129.9K Privately Held
SIC: 5611 3161 5961 2326 Men's & boys' clothing stores; luggage; catalog & mail-order houses; men's & boys' work clothing

(G-9994)
FIRE PROTECTION INC
12045 31st Ave Ne (98125-5501)
P.O. Box 12642, Mill Creek (98082-0642)
PHONE....................206 440-5763
Roy Cats, *Principal*
EMP: 3 **EST:** 2010
SALES (est): 208.2K Privately Held
SIC: 3669 Fire detection systems, electric

(G-9995)
FIRST CABIN YACHTS INC
3221 W Elmore St (98199-4404)
PHONE....................206 595-6657
Paul La Russa, *President*
EMP: 2 **EST:** 1995
SALES: 100K Privately Held
SIC: 3732 Yachts, building & repairing

(G-9996)
FIRST CHOICE MARKETING INC
10355 Sand Point Way Ne (98125-8155)
PHONE....................206 306-1100
Tony Tudisco, *President*
EMP: 5
SQ FT: 2,500
SALES (est): 630K Privately Held
WEB: www.firstchoicemarketing.com
SIC: 3676 Electronic resistors

(G-9997)
FISH TRANSPORT SYSTEMS LLC
2001 W Grfeld St Bldg 156 (98119)
PHONE....................206 801-3565
Vincent Bryan III, *CEO*
Tom Shearer, *President*
Vincent E Bryan Jr,
Todd Deligan,
EMP: 5 **EST:** 2010
SQ FT: 5,000
SALES: 1MM Privately Held
SIC: 3535 Conveyors & conveying equipment

(G-9998)
FISHER PUBLICATIONS INC
8803 42nd Ave Sw (98136-2520)
PHONE....................206 923-2000
Robert Fisher, *Principal*
EMP: 2
SALES (est): 104.5K Privately Held
SIC: 2741 Miscellaneous publishing

(G-9999)
FISHERMENS NEWS INC
Also Called: The Fishermen's News
2201 W Commodore Way (98199-1223)
PHONE....................206 282-7545
Peter Philipf, *CEO*
Chris Philipf, *Principal*
Laura Hicks, *Manager*
EMP: 7
SALES (est): 466.1K Privately Held
WEB: www.fishermensnews.com
SIC: 2711 Newspapers: publishing only, not printed on site

(G-10000)
FISHING VESSEL OWNERS MAR WAY (PA)
Also Called: Fvo In Seattle
1511 W Thurman St (98119-1623)
PHONE....................206 282-6421
Donald G Lindblad, *President*
Dan Larsen, *Corp Secy*
Larry Englom, *Vice Pres*
EMP: 18 **EST:** 1910
SQ FT: 20,000
SALES (est): 1.7MM Privately Held
WEB: www.fvo.com
SIC: 3731 3599 3732 Fishing vessels, large: building & repairing; machine shop, jobbing & repair; boat building & repairing

(G-10001)
FIVE STAR INDUSTRIES LLC
2440 W Commodore Way # 201 (98199-1484)
PHONE....................206 706-2754
John Lucchesini, *Mng Member*
EMP: 3
SALES (est): 464.3K Privately Held
SIC: 7389 3999 Metal cutting services; manufacturing industries

(G-10002)
FIX BROTHERS INC
1332 Sw 113th St (98146-3505)
PHONE....................206 246-5127
Larry Fix, *President*
EMP: 3
SALES (est): 310K Privately Held
SIC: 3463 Plumbing fixture forgings, non-ferrous

(G-10003)
FLAGSHIP CUSTOM PUBLISHING LLC
1416 Nw 46th St (98107-4622)
PHONE....................310 245-9550
Tim Greenwell, *Business Dir*
George Fuller,
EMP: 7
SALES (est): 277.6K Privately Held
SIC: 2741 Miscellaneous publishing

(G-10004)
FLAMESPRAY NORTHWEST INC
250 S Chicago St (98108-4366)
PHONE....................206 508-6779
Joseph G Orint, *President*
Chester Orint, *Assistant VP*
Sheryl Orint, *Treasurer*
Gary Pattie, *Manager*
EMP: 17
SQ FT: 6,000
SALES (est): 2.3MM Privately Held
SIC: 7699 3479 Industrial machinery & equipment repair; coating of metals & formed products

(G-10005)
FLEXE INC
83 S King St Ste 600 (98104-2851)
PHONE....................855 733-7788
Karl Siebrecht, *CEO*
Edmond Yue, *COO*
Adrian Grigg, *VP Bus Dvlpt*
Ryan Morel, *Marketing Staff*
Simmonds Dan, *Software Engr*
EMP: 5
SALES (est): 700.9K Privately Held
SIC: 4225 7372 General warehousing; business oriented computer software

(G-10006)
FLOURISH CHURCH RAINIER VALLEY
5231 39th Ave S Apt 212 (98118-6148)
PHONE....................206 769-7950
Jevon Washington, *President*
Jordan Taylor, *Treasurer*
Russell McCutcheon, *Admin Sec*
EMP: 3
SALES (est): 38.9K Privately Held
SIC: 8661 7372 Churches, temples & shrines; application computer software

(G-10007)
FLOWPLAY INC
1008 Western Ave Ste 300 (98104-1025)
PHONE....................206 903-0457
Derrick Morton, *CEO*
Craig Robinson, *Vice Pres*
Joe Sauer, *Vice Pres*
Douglas Pearson, *CTO*
EMP: 16
SQ FT: 6,000
SALES (est): 2.4MM Privately Held
WEB: www.flowplay.com
SIC: 3944 Electronic games & toys

(G-10008)
FLUTEWORKS
1029 Ne 69th St (98115-6623)
PHONE....................206 729-1903
Courtney Westcott, *Partner*
Peter Noy, *Partner*
EMP: 2
SALES (est): 130K Privately Held
SIC: 3931 7699 Flutes & parts; musical instrument repair services

(G-10009)
FLYING LAB SOFTWARE LLC
1905 Queen Anne Ave N # 300 (98109-2500)
PHONE....................206 272-9815
Paul Cannifs,
EMP: 10
SALES (est): 733.2K Privately Held
SIC: 7372 7371 Prepackaged software; custom computer programming services

(G-10010)
FOG TITE METER SEAL INC
Also Called: Fog Tite Meter Seal Co
4819 W Marginal Way Sw (98106-1516)
PHONE....................206 935-8000
Donald L Glidden, *President*
Greg Glidden, *Principal*
Roy Heric, *Vice Pres*
EMP: 35 **EST:** 1952
SQ FT: 11,500
SALES (est): 5.2MM Privately Held
SIC: 3272 Meter boxes, concrete; covers, catch basin: concrete

(G-10011)
FOLEY SIGN COMPANY INC
572 Mercer St (98109-4618)
PHONE....................206 324-3040
Mark Metcalf, *President*
EMP: 12
SQ FT: 25,000
SALES (est): 1.3MM Privately Held
SIC: 7389 2499 3993 Sign painting & lettering shop; signboards, wood; signs & advertising specialties

(G-10012)
FORFJORD SUPPLY CO
9015 Dibble Ave Nw (98117-3208)
PHONE....................206 784-8171
Debbie Furford, *Manager*
Julie Brenden, *Manager*
EMP: 3 **EST:** 1949
SALES (est): 300K Privately Held
SIC: 3462 5088 Anchors, forged; transportation equipment & supplies

(G-10013)
FORM LIGHTING AND CONTROLS LLC
1601 5th Ave (98101-3621)
PHONE....................206 854-8689
Antonio Giacobbe, *Mng Member*
EMP: 6

SALES (est): 386.9K Privately Held
SIC: 3646 Commercial indusl & institutional electric lighting fixtures

(G-10014)
FOSS MARINE HOLDINGS INC
450 Alaskan Way S Ste 706 (98104-2785)
PHONE....................206 381-5800
Paul E Stevens, *CEO*
Gary Faber, *Senior VP*
Scott Merritt, *Senior VP*
Arthur J Volkle Jr, *Vice Pres*
Kirstin L Sandaas, *CFO*
EMP: 6
SALES (est): 345.9K Privately Held
SIC: 4492 3443 4482 Towing & tugboat service; liners/lining; ferries operating across rivers or within harbors

(G-10015)
FOSS MARITIME COMPANY LLC (HQ)
450 Alaskan Way S Ste 706 (98104-2785)
PHONE....................206 281-3800
John Parrott, *President*
Paul E Stevens, *President*
Paul Stevens, *Chairman*
Scott Merritt, *COO*
Glenn K Y Hong, *Senior VP*
◆ **EMP:** 60 **EST:** 1889
SQ FT: 18,000
SALES (est): 224.5MM
SALES (corp-wide): 2B Privately Held
WEB: www.foss-maritime.com
SIC: 4412 4424 4492 4491 Deep sea foreign transportation of freight; deep sea domestic transportation of freight; coastwide transportation, freight; intercoastal transportation, freight; marine towing services; tugboat service; waterfront terminal operation; shipbuilding & repairing; environmental cleanup services
PA: Saltchuk Resources, Inc.
450 Alaskan Way S Ste 708
Seattle WA 98104
206 652-1111

(G-10016)
FOUAD FARHAT
720 Olive Way Ste 810 (98101-1836)
PHONE....................206 628-0404
Fred Farhat, *Principal*
EMP: 2
SALES (est): 113.8K Privately Held
SIC: 3843 Enamels, dentists'

(G-10017)
FOUR SEASONS GOURMET FOOD PROC
10325 Aurora Ave N (98133-9227)
PHONE....................847 636-9879
Pericles Tarsinos, *President*
EMP: 3
SALES (est): 213.2K Privately Held
SIC: 2099 Food preparations

(G-10018)
FOXFACERABBITFISH LLC
1403 S Hanford St (98144-6305)
PHONE....................206 856-7222
Guy Whitmore, *Owner*
EMP: 2
SALES (est): 97.9K Privately Held
SIC: 7819 7929 7372 Sound (effects & music production), motion picture; popular music groups or artists; home entertainment computer software

(G-10019)
FRAME IT LTD
539 Ne Northgate Way F (98125)
PHONE....................206 364-7477
Juanita Schmidt, *President*
Rhonda Brallier, *President*
EMP: 4
SALES (est): 243.3K Privately Held
SIC: 2499 5999 3999 Picture & mirror frames, wood; picture frames, ready made; barber & beauty shop equipment

(G-10020)
FRANK LAU JEWELRY INC
1010 E Miller St (98102-4045)
PHONE....................206 323-6343
Frank Lau, *President*
Joanna Lau, *Corp Secy*

Seattle - King County (G-10021)   GEOGRAPHIC SECTION

EMP: 3
SQ FT: 2,000
SALES: 1.2MM **Privately Held**
SIC: 3911 5094 Jewelry, precious metal; jewelry & precious stones

(G-10021)
FRANKENSTEIN INCORPORATED
2563 24th Ave W (98199-3404)
PHONE..................................206 915-1011
Jack Chaffin, *Principal*
EMP: 2
SIC: 2599 Cabinets, factory

(G-10022)
FRANS CHOCOLATES LTD (PA)
5900 Airport Way S (98108-2776)
PHONE..................................206 322-0233
Fran Bigelow, *President*
▲ EMP: 30
SQ FT: 6,500
SALES (est): 8.2MM **Privately Held**
SIC: 2066 5441 5961 Chocolate; candy; food, mail order

(G-10023)
FREDRICKSONS FURN & CABINETS
Also Called: Karl Ronald Fredrickson
8307 22nd Ave Nw (98117-3531)
PHONE..................................206 782-5310
Ron Fredrickson, *Owner*
Ingrid I Fredrickson, *Co-Owner*
EMP: 2
SALES: 125K **Privately Held**
SIC: 1751 2426 Cabinet building & installation; furniture dimension stock, hardwood

(G-10024)
FREMONT FINE ARTS FOUNDRY INC
Also Called: Fremont Foundry
154 N 35th St Apt 203 (98103-8628)
PHONE..................................206 588-6981
Peter Bevis, *President*
Dani Nelson, *Manager*
EMP: 5
SQ FT: 14,500
SALES (est): 259.8K **Privately Held**
SIC: 7999 3366 Art gallery, commercial; bronze foundry

(G-10025)
FREMONT PRINTING CO
3504 Fremont Ave N (98103-8414)
PHONE..................................206 632-3759
Lisa Gayton, *Principal*
EMP: 2
SALES (est): 114K **Privately Held**
SIC: 2752 Commercial printing, lithographic

(G-10026)
FRESH FLOURS
6015 Phinney Ave N (98103-5577)
PHONE..................................206 297-3300
Etsuko Minematsu, *Principal*
EMP: 8
SALES (est): 585.5K **Privately Held**
SIC: 2051 Bakery, for home service delivery

(G-10027)
FRESH FRUIT JUICE LLC
1043 S Jackson St (98104-3029)
PHONE..................................206 329-5979
EMP: 4
SALES (est): 212.7K **Privately Held**
SIC: 2037 Fruit juices

(G-10028)
FROGCHART PRESS
41 Dravus St Apt 205 (98109-1662)
PHONE..................................206 284-7156
EMP: 2 EST: 2008
SALES (est): 92K **Privately Held**
SIC: 2741 Misc Publishing

(G-10029)
FRONT PANEL EXPRESS LLC
5959 Corson Ave S Ste I (98108-2605)
PHONE..................................206 768-0602
Diane Haensel, *Managing Dir*
Christian Bloess,
Heinz Hanssen,
Joerg Schaeffer,
Kai Schaeffer,
▲ EMP: 10
SQ FT: 10,000
SALES (est): 1.6MM **Privately Held**
WEB: www.frontpanelexpress.com
SIC: 3448 Panels for prefabricated metal buildings

(G-10030)
FRONTSIDE GRIND LLC
12000 Des Moines Mem Dr S (98168-2228)
PHONE..................................206 246-5697
Manuel Ostermann, *Principal*
EMP: 2
SALES (est): 107.9K **Privately Held**
SIC: 3599 Grinding castings for the trade

(G-10031)
FROYO FRESH
701 5th Ave Ste 106 (98104-7016)
PHONE..................................206 447-4599
Hye Young Choung, *Principal*
EMP: 3
SALES (est): 138.5K **Privately Held**
SIC: 2026 Yogurt

(G-10032)
FRUHLA LLC
4033 Wallingford Ave N (98103-8218)
PHONE..................................206 633-4652
Christopher Steck, *Principal*
EMP: 4 EST: 2011
SALES (est): 240.8K **Privately Held**
SIC: 2741 Miscellaneous publishing

(G-10033)
FSI INC
4601 6th Ave S (98108-1716)
P.O. Box 1630, Port Angeles (98362-0807)
PHONE..................................360 452-9194
Kenneth Louie, *President*
Bob Moe, *Vice Pres*
EMP: 3
SALES (est): 95K **Privately Held**
SIC: 2899 Fire retardant chemicals

(G-10034)
FTI CONSULTING TECH SFTWR
Also Called: Attenex
1111 3rd Ave (98101-3292)
PHONE..................................206 373-6500
Kimra Hawley, *CEO*
Joseph White, *Exec VP*
Jr Jesson, *Senior VP*
Eric Friedman, *Vice Pres*
Mike Kinnaman, *Vice Pres*
EMP: 73
SQ FT: 17,000
SALES (est): 7.1MM
SALES (corp-wide): 2B **Publicly Held**
WEB: www.attenex.com
SIC: 7372 Prepackaged software
PA: Fti Consulting, Inc.
555 12th St Nw Ste 3
Washington DC 20004
202 312-9100

(G-10035)
FUEL COFFEE (PA)
1705 N 45th St (98103-6801)
PHONE..................................206 634-2700
Cassie Office, *Manager*
EMP: 4
SALES (est): 404.1K **Privately Held**
SIC: 2869 Fuels

(G-10036)
FUEL100 LLC
2624 E Aloha St (98112-4122)
PHONE..................................206 898-4904
Michelle Halsne, *Bd of Directors*
EMP: 4
SALES (est): 266.9K **Privately Held**
SIC: 2869 Fuels

(G-10037)
FULL SPECTRUM ANALYTICS INC
22525 Se 64th Pl (98115)
PHONE..................................206 729-0775
Louis Devita, *Branch Mgr*
EMP: 3 **Privately Held**
SIC: 3826 Analytical instruments
PA: Full Spectrum Group, Llc
1252 Quarry Ln
Pleasanton CA 94566

(G-10038)
FUNCTIONAL PATTERNS LLC
2820 Elliott Ave (98121-1168)
PHONE..................................619 565-3955
Naudimar Eloy Aguilar, *CEO*
EMP: 2
SALES (est): 95.2K **Privately Held**
SIC: 3543 Industrial patterns

(G-10039)
FUNKO GAMES LLC (HQ)
5030 Roosevelt Way Ne (98105-3611)
PHONE..................................206 547-7155
Kathy Faulk, *Principal*
Alan Pruzan,
Andrew Forrest,
Jay Wheatley,
EMP: 14
SALES (est): 1.2MM
SALES (corp-wide): 686MM **Publicly Held**
WEB: www.forrest-pruzan.com
SIC: 3944 Board games, puzzles & models, except electronic
PA: Funko, Inc.
2802 Wetmore Ave Ste 100
Everett WA 98201
425 783-3616

(G-10040)
FURNITURE BY FOSS
Also Called: Foss Furniture
811 Nw 47th St (98107-4534)
PHONE..................................206 783-3626
Harold Foss, *Partner*
Arthur Foss, *Partner*
Eric Foss, *Partner*
EMP: 3 EST: 1967
SQ FT: 10,000
SALES (est): 300K **Privately Held**
SIC: 2521 2511 Wood office furniture; wood household furniture

(G-10041)
FURTIM THERAPEUTICS LLC
4000 Mason Rd Ste 304 (98105)
PHONE..................................425 273-1035
Shaoyi Jiang, *President*
EMP: 2
SALES (est): 81.8K **Privately Held**
SIC: 2834 Pharmaceutical preparations

(G-10042)
FUSSY CLOUD PUPPET SLAM
925 14th Ave Apt 1 (98122-4511)
PHONE..................................206 235-9109
Nicholas Hubbard, *Principal*
EMP: 2
SALES (est): 83.1K **Privately Held**
SIC: 3999 Puppets & marionettes

(G-10043)
FUZE CREATE LLC
10423 3rd Ave S (98168-1377)
PHONE..................................425 212-8807
Charles Harvey Jr, *Mng Member*
EMP: 2
SALES: 3MM **Privately Held**
SIC: 3089 2499 3499 3999 Plastic containers, except foam; reed, rattan, wicker & willow ware, except furniture; furniture parts, metal; cigarette & cigar products & accessories; caps: cloth, straw & felt

(G-10044)
G AND T RENEWABLES
12619 2nd Ave S (98168-2676)
PHONE..................................206 412-2352
Gary Gerde, *Partner*
EMP: 4
SALES: 594K **Privately Held**
SIC: 2992 Lubricating oils & greases

(G-10045)
G C P LLC
Also Called: G C P Manufacturing
958 N 127th St (98133-8031)
PHONE..................................206 781-1162
Michael Hooper, *President*
EMP: 7
SQ FT: 3,700
SALES (est): 895.2K **Privately Held**
WEB: www.gcpinc.com
SIC: 2851 Marine paints

(G-10046)
GALLIVAN GALLIVAN & OMELIA (PA)
Also Called: GG&o
1511 3rd Ave Ste 910 (98101-1683)
PHONE..................................206 652-1441
Justin D Farmer, *President*
Robert Souders, *Project Mgr*
Bill Gallivan, *Marketing Staff*
Barry C O'Melia, *Director*
Jim Vandermeer, *Director*
EMP: 12
SALES: 590K **Privately Held**
WEB: www.gallivanlawfirm.com
SIC: 3812 Detection apparatus: electronic/magnetic field, light/heat

(G-10047)
GARDNER BOAT REPAIR INC
2442 Nw Market St Ste 404 (98107-4137)
PHONE..................................206 784-0854
William Gardner, *President*
EMP: 8
SQ FT: 2,000
SALES (est): 926.7K **Privately Held**
SIC: 3731 Fishing vessels, large: building & repairing

(G-10048)
GARPIKE INC
Also Called: Solipsis Publishing
1947 Broadway E (98102-4254)
PHONE..................................206 719-7820
Gerard Lasalle, *President*
EMP: 12
SALES: 1MM **Privately Held**
SIC: 2741 Miscellaneous publishing

(G-10049)
GARY MERLINO CNSTR CO INC (PA)
Also Called: Stoneway Construction Supply
9125 10th Ave S (98108-4600)
PHONE..................................206 763-9552
Gary M Merlino, *President*
Dan Raymond, *President*
Mike Abbott, *Superintendent*
Don Merlino, *Vice Pres*
Charlie Oliver, *Vice Pres*
EMP: 350
SQ FT: 15,000
SALES (est): 158.5MM **Privately Held**
WEB: www.stonewayconcrete.com
SIC: 1611 1623 3273 General contractor, highway & street construction; water main construction; sewer line construction; ready-mixed concrete

(G-10050)
GARY MERLINO CNSTR CO INC
Also Called: Stoneway Concrete
9216 8th Ave S (98108-4608)
PHONE..................................206 763-2134
Don Merlino, *President*
Dave Alston, *Vice Pres*
EMP: 15
SALES (corp-wide): 158.5MM **Privately Held**
WEB: www.stonewayconcrete.com
SIC: 3273 5032 3281 3272 Ready-mixed concrete; brick, stone & related material; cut stone & stone products; concrete products; construction sand & gravel
PA: Gary Merlino Construction Co., Inc.
9125 10th Ave S
Seattle WA 98108
206 763-9552

(G-10051)
GASLLC LTD LIABILITY COMPANY
Also Called: Golden Alaska Seafoods
2200 Alaskan Way Ste 420 (98121-1684)
PHONE..................................206 441-1990
Mark Franklin, *Mng Member*
Joseph Fleming,
◆ EMP: 115

GEOGRAPHIC SECTION

Seattle - King County (G-10081)

SALES (est): 26.3MM **Privately Held**
WEB: www.goldenalaska.com
SIC: **2092** Seafoods, fresh: prepared; seafoods, frozen: prepared

(G-10052)
GATHEREDTABLE INC
506 2nd Ave Ste 2300 (98104-2347)
P.O. Box 4503 (98194-0503)
PHONE..................................206 735-4886
Mary Egan, *CEO*
EMP: 16
SQ FT: 5,000
SALES (est): 1.3MM **Privately Held**
SIC: **7372** Application computer software

(G-10053)
GAVRIEL JECAN
1944 1st Ave S (98134-1406)
PHONE..................................206 332-0993
Gavriel Jecan, *Principal*
EMP: 2
SALES (est): 62.3K **Privately Held**
SIC: **2087** Flavoring extracts & syrups

(G-10054)
GB ACQUISITION INC
Also Called: Craftworks
600 Pine St Ste 401 (98101-3709)
PHONE..................................206 405-4205
Paula Webb, *Manager*
EMP: 9 **Privately Held**
SIC: **2082** 5812 Malt beverages; eating places
HQ: Gb Acquisition, Inc.
8001 Arista Pl Fl 5
Broomfield CO 80021

(G-10055)
GE HEALTHCARE INC
925 4th Ave Ste 400 (98104-1136)
PHONE..................................206 622-9558
Mike Ramer, *General Mgr*
Santhosh Raman, *Director*
EMP: 500
SALES (corp-wide): 121.6B **Publicly Held**
WEB: www.idx.com
SIC: **7371** 7372 Computer software systems analysis & design, custom; prepackaged software
HQ: Ge Healthcare Inc.
100 Results Way
Marlborough MA 01752
800 526-3593

(G-10056)
GE TOTTEN & ASSOCIATES LLC
514 N 86th St (98103-3723)
P.O. Box 25007 (98165-1907)
PHONE..................................206 788-0188
George E Totten, *President*
EMP: 3
SALES (est): 370.3K **Privately Held**
SIC: **3826** Thermal analysis instruments, laboratory type

(G-10057)
GEEKWIRE LLC (PA)
123 Nw 36th St Ste 203 (98107-4958)
PHONE..................................206 913-7926
Cara Kuhlman, *Advt Staff*
John Cook, *Mng Member*
Daniel Rossi, *Officer*
EMP: 15 EST: 2011
SQ FT: 5,500
SALES (est): 1.7MM **Privately Held**
SIC: **2741** Shopping news: publishing only, not printed on site

(G-10058)
GEMELLI PRESS LLC
9600 Stone Ave N (98103-2802)
PHONE..................................360 420-7721
Michelle Fabio, *Editor*
EMP: 2
SALES (est): 105.1K **Privately Held**
SIC: **2741** Miscellaneous publishing

(G-10059)
GEN-TECH LLC
250 Nw 39th St Ste 5 (98107-4962)
PHONE..................................206 634-3399
Erling Skaar,
EMP: 7

SALES (est): 784.1K **Privately Held**
SIC: **3621** Motors & generators

(G-10060)
GENESIS ADVANCED TECHNOLOGIES
654 S Lucile St (98108-2640)
PHONE..................................206 762-8383
Gary L Koh, *CEO*
Carolyn Koh, *COO*
▲ EMP: 11
SQ FT: 6,050
SALES (est): 1.8MM **Privately Held**
WEB: www.genesisloudspeakers.com
SIC: **3651** Loudspeakers, electrodynamic or magnetic
PA: Genesis Advanced Technologies Pte. Limited
71 Ubi Road 1
Singapore

(G-10061)
GENOA HEALTHCARE LLC
3639 Martin L King Jr Way (98144-6847)
PHONE..................................206 971-9707
EMP: 2
SALES (corp-wide): 226.2B **Publicly Held**
SIC: **2834** Pharmaceutical preparations
HQ: Genoa Healthcare Llc
707 S Grady Way Ste 700
Renton WA 98057

(G-10062)
GEO LASTOMIRSKY CERAMIC A
4203 4th Ave Nw (98107-5013)
PHONE..................................206 782-4695
Geo Francis Latomirsky, *Owner*
George Francis Lastomirsky, *Principal*
EMP: 2
SALES (est): 117.6K **Privately Held**
SIC: **3269** 3952 Pottery products; colors, artists': water & oxide ceramic glass

(G-10063)
GEOGENIUS LLC
1501 4th Ave Ste 301 (98101-1660)
PHONE..................................206 838-8125
F Berg,
EMP: 2 EST: 2010
SALES (est): 99K **Privately Held**
SIC: **3589** Service industry machinery

(G-10064)
GEORGE BROOM SONS INC
2440 W Commodore Way # 100 (98199-1482)
PHONE..................................206 282-0800
George Broom, *President*
Sharon Broom, *Admin Sec*
EMP: 5 EST: 1895
SQ FT: 3,200
SALES (est): 360K **Privately Held**
SIC: **2394** 3496 5131 Tarpaulins, fabric: made from purchased materials; woven wire products; fiberglass fabrics

(G-10065)
GEOSPACE PRODUCTS COMPANY INC
Also Called: Geospace International
3931 Leary Way Nw (98107-5043)
PHONE..................................206 547-2556
Dennis Binkley, *President*
Martje Binkley, *Vice Pres*
▲ EMP: 2
SALES (est): 735.6K **Privately Held**
WEB: www.geospaceplay.com
SIC: **3944** Games, toys & children's vehicles

(G-10066)
GERRY NEWCOMB
3511 Interlake Ave N (98103-8915)
PHONE..................................206 633-0154
Gerry Newcomb, *Owner*
EMP: 2
SALES (est): 78.2K **Privately Held**
WEB: www.gerrynewcomb.com
SIC: **3253** 5945 Ceramic wall & floor tile; hobby, toy & game shops

(G-10067)
GESTSURE TECHNOLOGIES LTD
2200 Alaskan Way (98121-1689)
PHONE..................................800 510-2485
Jamie Tremaine, *President*
Greg Brigley, *Vice Pres*
Sharon Fan, *Admin Sec*
EMP: 2 EST: 2012
SALES (est): 160K **Privately Held**
SIC: **3841** Surgical & medical instruments

(G-10068)
GHL ARCHITECTURAL MILLWORK LLC
1938 Occidental Ave S (98134-1413)
P.O. Box 16313 (98116-0313)
PHONE..................................206 467-5004
Tavis Gaudt, *Mng Member*
Leonard Lambert,
EMP: 5
SALES (est): 973.6K **Privately Held**
SIC: **2431** Millwork

(G-10069)
GHOST INSPECTOR INC
1601 5th Ave Ste 1100 (98101-3603)
PHONE..................................206 395-3635
EMP: 2
SALES (est): 33.8K **Privately Held**
SIC: **7372** Business oriented computer software

(G-10070)
GILEAD SCIENCES INC
2107 E Republican St (98112-4003)
PHONE..................................206 728-5090
A Bruce Montgomery, *Principal*
EMP: 100
SALES (corp-wide): 22.1B **Publicly Held**
WEB: www.gilead.com
SIC: **2834** 8731 Pharmaceutical preparations; biotechnical research, commercial
PA: Gilead Sciences, Inc.
333 Lakeside Dr
Foster City CA 94404
650 574-3000

(G-10071)
GILS ALUMINUM & SHELL CORE SP
533 S Holden St (98108-4361)
PHONE..................................206 762-1726
Gilbert Dyson, *Owner*
EMP: 6
SQ FT: 19,000
SALES (est): 646.2K **Privately Held**
SIC: **3363** 3543 Aluminum die-castings; foundry cores

(G-10072)
GINACOR INC
513 31st Ave (98122-6321)
P.O. Box 19437 (98109-1437)
PHONE..................................206 860-1595
Monica Jones, *President*
EMP: 15
SALES (est): 1.5MM **Privately Held**
SIC: **3841** 5047 5999 Surgical & medical instruments; medical & hospital equipment; medical apparatus & supplies

(G-10073)
GIRANDOLA
Also Called: Girandola Center
A-242 14419 Grnwood Ave N Greenwood (98133)
PHONE..................................206 289-0523
Tiffany McVetty, *CEO*
Mark McVeety,
Tiffany McVeety,
EMP: 2
SALES (est): 122.1K **Privately Held**
SIC: **8732** 2741 8742 8748 Market analysis, business & economic research; technical manuals: publishing only, not printed on site; management consulting services; economic consultant

(G-10074)
GIRLIE PRESS INC
1658 21st Ave (98122-2908)
PHONE..................................206 720-1237
Risa Blythe, *President*
EMP: 8

SALES (est): 1.5MM **Privately Held**
WEB: www.girliepress.com
SIC: **2759** 2752 Letterpress printing; commercial printing, lithographic

(G-10075)
GLACIER BAY FISHERIES LLC
1200 Westlake Ave N # 900 (98109-3543)
PHONE..................................206 298-1200
John Bundy,
▼ EMP: 15
SQ FT: 2,000
SALES (est): 492.3K **Privately Held**
SIC: **0912** 2091 Finfish; canned & cured fish & seafoods

(G-10076)
GLACIER NORTHWEST INC
Also Called: Kenmore Pre-Mix
6423 175th St Ne (98155)
PHONE..................................425 486-3281
Jim Retman, *Manager*
EMP: 38 **Privately Held**
WEB: www.glaciernw.com
SIC: **3272** 3273 1442 Concrete products; ready-mixed concrete; construction sand & gravel
HQ: Glacier Northwest, Inc.
5975 E Marginal Way S
Seattle WA 98134
206 764-3000

(G-10077)
GLACIER NORTHWEST INC
5900 W Marginal Way Sw (98106-1500)
P.O. Box 1730 (98111-1730)
PHONE..................................206 764-3075
Steve Penswick, *Manager*
EMP: 10 **Privately Held**
WEB: www.glaciernw.com
SIC: **3273** Ready-mixed concrete
HQ: Glacier Northwest, Inc.
5975 E Marginal Way S
Seattle WA 98134
206 764-3000

(G-10078)
GLANT TEXTILES CORPORATION (PA)
3031 S Walden St Ste 102 (98144-6952)
PHONE..................................206 725-4444
Gary Glant, *President*
Sylvia Augustavo, *Info Tech Mgr*
EMP: 24
SQ FT: 21,000
SALES (est): 2.6MM **Privately Held**
WEB: www.glant.com
SIC: **2211** Upholstery, tapestry & wall coverings: cotton

(G-10079)
GLASSHOUSE STUDIO
Also Called: Glass House Studio
311 Occidental Ave S (98104-2839)
PHONE..................................206 682-9939
Mark Monson, *President*
Craig Maxwell, *Corp Secy*
Chris Sternberg-Powidzki, *Vice Pres*
EMP: 8
SQ FT: 4,500
SALES (est): 520K **Privately Held**
WEB: www.glasshouse-studio.com
SIC: **3229** 5719 Glassware, art or decorative; lamp parts & shades, glass; vases, glass; glassware; lamps & lamp shades

(G-10080)
GLASSIQUE
10509 Aurora Ave N (98133-8811)
PHONE..................................206 963-4400
Richard Heath, *Owner*
EMP: 2 EST: 2009
SALES (est): 160.9K **Privately Held**
SIC: **2511** China closets

(G-10081)
GLASSY BABY LLC (PA)
3406 E Union St (98122-3374)
PHONE..................................206 568-7368
Lee Rhodes, *Principal*
JP Liddle, *Vice Pres*
Jody Riley, *Manager*
Dabney Rohrbach, *Manager*
EMP: 30
SALES (est): 5.6MM **Privately Held**
SIC: **3999** Candles

Seattle - King County (G-10082)

(G-10082)
GLI INTERACTIVE LLC (PA)
Also Called: Motion Workshop
304 Alaskan Way S Ste 302 (98104-2782)
PHONE..................................206 201-2708
Erik Bakke,
Luke Tokheim,
EMP: 2
SALES (est): 275.3K **Privately Held**
SIC: 3829 Physical property testing equipment

(G-10083)
GLOBAL EMERGENT TECH LLC
318 17th Ave S (98144-2153)
PHONE..................................425 999-9021
Rolland Gregg,
EMP: 2 **EST:** 2015
SALES (est): 180.8K **Privately Held**
SIC: 1542 1711 3621 4911 Greenhouse construction; solar energy contractor; storage battery chargers, motor & engine generator type; ; combination utilities

(G-10084)
GLOBAL INCORPORATED
7619 5th Ave S (98108-4117)
PHONE..................................206 763-4424
EMP: 15
SQ FT: 22,500
SALES (est): 1.6MM **Privately Held**
SIC: 3443 6282 3444 3441 Mfg Fabricated Plate Wrk Investment Advisory Svcs Mfg Sheet Metalwork Structural Metal Fabrctn

(G-10085)
GLOBALWXDATACOM
4119 Sw Kenyon St (98136-2332)
PHONE..................................425 644-4010
John Schmidt, *Principal*
EMP: 2
SALES (est): 56.5K **Privately Held**
SIC: 7372 Prepackaged software

(G-10086)
GLOBE
Also Called: Globe Books The
5220 University Way Ne B (98105-3542)
PHONE..................................206 527-2480
John Siscoe, *President*
Carolyn Siscoe, *Vice Pres*
Carolyn G Siscoe, *Vice Pres*
EMP: 2 **EST:** 1979
SQ FT: 400
SALES (est): 88.1K **Privately Held**
SIC: 5932 5942 5735 2789 Book stores, secondhand; records, secondhand; book stores; records; bookbinding & repairing: trade, edition, library, etc.

(G-10087)
GLOBO PRODUCTIONS VOICEOVER
575 Highland Dr (98109-3416)
PHONE..................................206 992-0483
Jaime Mendez, *Principal*
EMP: 2 **EST:** 2011
SALES (est): 136.9K **Privately Held**
SIC: 3651 Electronic kits for home assembly: radio, TV, phonograph

(G-10088)
GLOBYS INC (PA)
705 5th Ave S Ste 700 (98104-4439)
PHONE..................................206 352-3055
Derek Edwards, *CEO*
Mark Sten, *Senior VP*
Dwayne Edwards, *Treasurer*
Carrie Klauss, *Marketing Staff*
EMP: 90 **EST:** 2007
SALES (est): 13.6MM **Privately Held**
SIC: 7372 Prepackaged software

(G-10089)
GLYKON TECHNOLOGIES GROUP LLC
24 Roy St Ste 401 (98109-4018)
PHONE..................................510 289-4331
Dallas L Clouatre, *Mng Member*
Daniel L Clouatre,
Brad J Douglass,
▲ **EMP:** 2 **EST:** 2012
SALES (est): 168.1K **Privately Held**
SIC: 2833 Medicinals & botanicals

(G-10090)
GM NAMEPLATE INC
Supergraphics
2201 15th Ave W (98119-2417)
PHONE..................................206 284-2201
Jim Allen, *Branch Mgr*
EMP: 115
SALES (corp-wide): 315.4MM **Privately Held**
SIC: 3479 Name plates: engraved, etched, etc.
PA: Gm Nameplate, Inc.
2040 15th Ave W
Seattle WA 98119
206 284-2200

(G-10091)
GO DESIGNS
3417 21st Ave W (98199-2304)
PHONE..................................206 719-0936
Chris Dickensons, *Owner*
EMP: 3
SALES (est): 122.3K **Privately Held**
SIC: 2261 Screen printing of cotton broadwoven fabrics

(G-10092)
GODDARD WOODWORKING LLCPETR GO
3645 36th Ave S (98144-7106)
PHONE..................................206 920-8675
Peter Goddard, *Principal*
EMP: 4
SALES (est): 394.5K **Privately Held**
SIC: 2431 Millwork

(G-10093)
GOLD MINE OF JEWELRY INC
Also Called: Gold Mine Jewelry
1405 1st Ave (98101-2017)
PHONE..................................206 622-3333
John Winters, *President*
EMP: 2
SALES (est): 267.9K **Privately Held**
SIC: 5944 3911 Jewelry, precious stones & precious metals; jewelry, precious metal

(G-10094)
GOLDEN CHILD INC
2829 Sw 106th St (98146-1269)
PHONE..................................206 901-9502
Christopher Khun, *Principal*
EMP: 2
SALES (est): 69.2K **Privately Held**
SIC: 2711 Newspapers

(G-10095)
GOLDEN SHAMROCK INC
4005 20th Ave W Ste 218 (98199-1290)
PHONE..................................206 282-5825
Paul J Duffy, *President*
Dahl P Duffy, *Vice Pres*
EMP: 2
SQ FT: 800
SALES (est): 2.5MM **Privately Held**
WEB: www.goldenshamrock.com
SIC: 0913 2092 Crabs, catching of; crab meat, fresh: packaged in nonsealed containers; crabmeat, frozen

(G-10096)
GOLDFINCH PRESS
2308 N 62nd St (98103-5723)
PHONE..................................206 696-2933
Lisa Schaefbauer, *Administration*
EMP: 2
SALES (est): 113.8K **Privately Held**
SIC: 2741 Miscellaneous publishing

(G-10097)
GOLDFISH PRESS
Also Called: Chrysanthemum Literary Society
4545 42nd Ave Sw Apt 211 (98116-4243)
PHONE..................................206 380-4181
Koon Woon, *Principal*
Susan Steiner, *Principal*
EMP: 2
SALES (est): 72.1K **Privately Held**
SIC: 2741 Miscellaneous publishing

(G-10098)
GOMOTIVE INC
1501 4th Ave Ste 550 (98101-3234)
PHONE..................................206 462-6379
Michael Richards, *CEO*
David Watson, *Admin Sec*
EMP: 2 **EST:** 2012
SALES: 500K **Privately Held**
SIC: 7372 Application computer software

(G-10099)
GOOD PET FOOD INC
Also Called: Eureka Pet Food
214 1st Ave S Ste G7 (98104-2598)
PHONE..................................310 430-3833
Rhonda Hobgood, *President*
EMP: 2
SALES (est): 62.3K **Privately Held**
SIC: 2047 5149 Cat food; pet foods

(G-10100)
GOODALL PRODUCTIONS INC
5018 8th Ave Ne (98105-3603)
P.O. Box 18677 (98118-0677)
PHONE..................................206 722-0544
Roy Goodall, *President*
Marcia Goodall, *Vice Pres*
EMP: 4
SQ FT: 1,200
SALES: 160K **Privately Held**
WEB: www.goodallcards.com
SIC: 2771 7335 Greeting cards; commercial photography

(G-10101)
GOODMAR GROUP LLC
Also Called: Studio 3 Signs
1117b Nw 54th St (98107-3740)
PHONE..................................206 622-8204
Mike Goodwin, *Mng Member*
Michael Goodwin, *Info Tech Mgr*
EMP: 3
SALES (est): 341K **Privately Held**
WEB: www.s3signs.com
SIC: 3993 Signs, not made in custom sign painting shops

(G-10102)
GORILLA SCREEN PRINTING
2232c 1st Ave S (98134-1408)
PHONE..................................206 621-1728
Brandon Lennert, *Owner*
EMP: 5
SALES (est): 453.8K **Privately Held**
WEB: www.gorillaprintshop.com
SIC: 2759 Screen printing

(G-10103)
GOURMET MIXES INC
Also Called: Demitris Blody Mary Seasonings
8230 5th Ave S Ste A (98108-4557)
P.O. Box 84123 (98124-5423)
PHONE..................................206 764-6006
Demitri Pallis, *President*
Iska Pallios, *Assistant*
EMP: 7
SQ FT: 10,000
SALES (est): 543.6K **Privately Held**
SIC: 2087 Cocktail mixes, nonalcoholic

(G-10104)
GRAIN CRAFT INC
3235 16th Ave Sw (98134-1023)
PHONE..................................206 898-3079
Bryce Seidl, *Principal*
Dan Bahr, *Marketing Staff*
EMP: 100
SALES (corp-wide): 320.5MM **Privately Held**
SIC: 2041 5149 2048 2043 Flour; bakery products; prepared feeds; cereal breakfast foods
PA: Grain Craft, Inc.
201 W Main St Ste 203
Chattanooga TN 37408
423 265-2313

(G-10105)
GRAN QUARTZ TRADING INC
6001 6th Ave S (98108-3307)
PHONE..................................206 973-7640
EMP: 7
SALES (corp-wide): 21.5MM **Privately Held**
SIC: 5085 3559 Industrial supplies; stone working machinery
PA: Gran Quartz Trading, Inc.
4963 S Royal Atlanta Dr
Tucker GA 30084
770 621-9777

(G-10106)
GRAND CENTRAL BAKERY INC (PA)
Also Called: Grand Central Baking Company
21 S Nevada St (98134-1121)
PHONE..................................206 768-0320
Gwen Bassetti, *President*
Gillian Allen-White, *General Mgr*
Bob Kerr, *Business Mgr*
Laura Heinlein, *Prdtn Mgr*
Meghan Stuart, *Pub Rel Mgr*
EMP: 58
SQ FT: 13,000
SALES (est): 40.9MM **Privately Held**
SIC: 5149 5461 5812 2051 Bakery products; bakeries; cafeteria; delicatessen (eating places); bakery: wholesale or wholesale/retail combined

(G-10107)
GRAND IMAGE LTD (PA)
4730 Ohio Ave S (98134-2326)
PHONE..................................206 624-0444
Larry Winn, *President*
▲ **EMP:** 11
SQ FT: 2,000
SALES (est): 1.4MM **Privately Held**
WEB: www.grandimage.com
SIC: 2711 2741 Commercial printing & newspaper publishing combined; miscellaneous publishing

(G-10108)
GRATRACK
901 Occidental Ave S (98134-1218)
PHONE..................................571 357-4728
Craig Clark, *Principal*
EMP: 2
SALES (est): 108.9K **Privately Held**
SIC: 7372 Prepackaged software

(G-10109)
GRAVEL TONES PRODUCTIONS INC
1236 3rd Ave N (98109-3280)
PHONE..................................248 202-5757
Dante Bonaduce, *Principal*
EMP: 4 **EST:** 2012
SALES (est): 189K **Privately Held**
SIC: 1442 Construction sand & gravel

(G-10110)
GRAVELROAD LLC
1124 Nw 57th St (98107-3719)
PHONE..................................760 840-7174
Jon Newman, *Administration*
EMP: 6
SALES (est): 328.1K **Privately Held**
SIC: 1442 Construction sand & gravel

(G-10111)
GRAVITY SQUARE INC
5041 46th Ave Ne (98105-2918)
PHONE..................................206 524-0063
Ian Turek, *Principal*
EMP: 2
SALES (est): 97.6K **Privately Held**
SIC: 3678 Electronic connectors

(G-10112)
GRAYPANTS INC
3220 1st Ave S Ste 400 (98134-1852)
PHONE..................................206 420-3912
Jonathan Junker, *President*
Eleanor Smitherman, *Sales Mgr*
▲ **EMP:** 8
SQ FT: 3,000
SALES: 1MM **Privately Held**
SIC: 3646 3645 Ornamental lighting fixtures, commercial; garden, patio, walkway & yard lighting fixtures: electric

(G-10113)
GREAT KING OF AMERICAS LLC
2701 1st Ave Ste 310 (98121-1285)
PHONE..................................206 957-0987
Douglas Lan,
◆ **EMP:** 5
SALES (est): 664.4K **Privately Held**
WEB: www.greatkinggroup.com
SIC: 2329 Men's & boys' sportswear & athletic clothing

GEOGRAPHIC SECTION
Seattle - King County (G-10145)

(G-10114)
GREAT SUN CORP
5930 1st Ave S (98108-3248)
PHONE....................206 329-8027
Kevin Ta, *President*
▲ **EMP:** 11
SALES (est): 1.8MM **Privately Held**
WEB: www.greatsuncorp.com
SIC: 3312 Stainless steel

(G-10115)
GREEN BROTHERS OF SEATTLE LLC
603 Stewart St Ste 616 (98101-1235)
PHONE....................303 295-7669
James Hunter, *President*
EMP: 2
SALES (est): 90.7K **Privately Held**
SIC: 2611 Pulp manufactured from waste or recycled paper

(G-10116)
GREEN HILLS SOFTWARE LLC
800 5th Ave Ste 4100 (98104-3100)
PHONE....................206 447-1373
Sharon Gilpin, *Principal*
EMP: 4
SALES (corp-wide): 16.3MM **Privately Held**
SIC: 7372 Application computer software
HQ: Green Hills Software Llc
  30 W Sola St
  Santa Barbara CA 93101
  805 965-6044

(G-10117)
GREEN LAKE BREWING COMPANY LLC
Also Called: Fremont Brewing Co.
3409 Woodland Park Ave N (98103-8925)
PHONE....................206 300-9337
Matthew Lincecum, *Owner*
EMP: 53 **EST:** 2008
SALES (est): 11MM **Privately Held**
SIC: 2082 Malt beverages

(G-10118)
GREENFIRE CANDLES LLC
4302 Greenwood Ave N (98103-7022)
PHONE....................206 240-9225
Jennifer Loewen, *Principal*
EMP: 2 **EST:** 2013
SALES (est): 104.6K **Privately Held**
SIC: 3999 Candles

(G-10119)
GREENLAND INC
815 S Weller St Ste 103 (98104-3047)
PHONE....................206 623-2577
Chris Sodchuen, *President*
Qing Gia, *Vice Pres*
EMP: 14
SQ FT: 1,900
SALES (est): 1.9MM **Privately Held**
WEB: www.greenland.com
SIC: 2099 2086 Tea blending; bottled & canned soft drinks

(G-10120)
GREENLEAF FOODS SPC
4011 6th Ave S (98108-5202)
PHONE....................206 762-5961
Jennifer Hryciw, *Marketing Mgr*
EMP: 50
SALES (corp-wide): 2.6B **Privately Held**
SIC: 2013 Roast beef from purchased meat
HQ: Greenleaf Foods, Spc
  180 E Park Ave Ste 300
  Elmhurst IL 60126
  800 268-3708

(G-10121)
GREENLEAF FOODS SPC
3901 7th Ave S (98108-5206)
PHONE....................206 762-5961
EMP: 3
SALES (corp-wide): 2.6B **Privately Held**
SIC: 2013 Roast beef from purchased meat
HQ: Greenleaf Foods, Spc
  180 E Park Ave Ste 300
  Elmhurst IL 60126
  800 268-3708

(G-10122)
GREENWOOD CIDER CO LLC
10015 Lake Cy Way Ne 10 (98125)
PHONE....................360 961-2902
Ryan Short,
Marshall Petryni,
Andrew Short,
EMP: 2
SQ FT: 312
SALES (est): 62.3K **Privately Held**
SIC: 2084 Wines

(G-10123)
GREMLIN INC
Also Called: Soldano Custom Amplification
4233 21st Ave W Fl 2 (98199-1202)
PHONE....................206 781-4636
Michael J Soldano Jr, *President*
EMP: 4
SQ FT: 4,000
SALES (est): 578.7K **Privately Held**
WEB: www.soldano.com
SIC: 3651 5736 Amplifiers: radio, public address or musical instrument; musical instrument stores

(G-10124)
GREYWOOD MANOR LLC
11833 3rd Ave S (98168-2033)
PHONE....................206 949-1362
Eric Butler, *Principal*
EMP: 2 **EST:** 2015
SALES (est): 66.1K **Privately Held**
SIC: 2499 Wood products

(G-10125)
GRIST MAGAZINE INC
1201 Western Ave Ste 410 (98101-2987)
PHONE....................206 876-2020
Charles N Giller, *President*
Susan L Kaufman, *Treasurer*
Kendra Howe, *Director*
Patrick Schmitt, *Director*
Kristen Wolf, *Director*
EMP: 25
SALES: 3.5MM **Privately Held**
SIC: 2721 Magazines: publishing only, not printed on site

(G-10126)
GROUP 2 INC
4442 27th Ave W (98199-1220)
PHONE....................206 378-0900
Dan Wakefield, *Principal*
EMP: 2
SALES (est): 220K **Privately Held**
SIC: 3732 Boat building & repairing

(G-10127)
GROUPFABRIC INC
819 Virginia St Unit 3007 (98101-4431)
PHONE....................425 681-2927
EMP: 2
SALES (est): 101.5K **Privately Held**
SIC: 7372 Prepackaged software

(G-10128)
GROW PLASTICS LLC
7734 15th Ave Ne (98115-4336)
PHONE....................206 954-4564
Michael Waggoner, *CEO*
EMP: 2
SALES (est): 186.6K **Privately Held**
SIC: 3089 8733 8711 Thermoformed finished plastic products; biotechnical research, noncommercial; engineering services

(G-10129)
GSF PUBLICATIONS
3507 Nw 60th St (98107-2641)
PHONE....................206 789-7548
EMP: 2 **EST:** 2008
SALES (est): 120K **Privately Held**
SIC: 2741 Misc Publishing

(G-10130)
GT RECORDING
9921 Aurora Ave N (98103-3269)
PHONE....................206 783-6911
Gordon Murray, *Owner*
EMP: 4
SALES (est): 320.5K **Privately Held**
WEB: www.gtrecording.com
SIC: 2759 3652 Commercial printing; prerecorded records & tapes

(G-10131)
GUESS   INC
600 Pine St Ste 220 (98101-3704)
PHONE....................206 682-7005
EMP: 25
SALES (corp-wide): 2.4B **Publicly Held**
SIC: 2325 5136 5621 Mfg Men's/Boy's Trousers Whol Men's/Boy's Clothing Ret Women's Clothing
PA: Guess , Inc.
  1444 S Alameda St
  Los Angeles CA 90021
  213 765-3100

(G-10132)
GUIDO PERLA & ASSOCIATES INC
Also Called: GPA
701 5th Ave Ste 1200 (98104-7007)
PHONE....................206 463-2217
Alex M Loudon, *President*
George Karantsavelos, *General Mgr*
Guido F Perla, *Chairman*
Dan Koch, *Vice Pres*
David Pasciuti, *Vice Pres*
EMP: 31
SQ FT: 18,000
SALES (est): 4.9MM **Privately Held**
WEB: www.gpai.com
SIC: 8711 8712 3731 Consulting engineer; marine engineering; architectural services; shipbuilding & repairing

(G-10133)
GURIAN INSTRUMENTS INC
5350 30th Ave Nw Ste H (98107-5813)
PHONE....................206 467-7990
Michael Gurian, *President*
Barbara Weiss, *Vice Pres*
Ron Ferguson, *Treasurer*
▲ **EMP:** 9
SALES (est): 690K **Privately Held**
WEB: www.gurianinstruments.com
SIC: 3931 3544 String instruments & parts; special dies & tools

(G-10134)
H BROTHERS INC
1425 Broadway 480 (98122-3854)
PHONE....................206 999-9837
John Hostetler, *CEO*
Daniel Hostetler, *CFO*
EMP: 2 **EST:** 2006
SALES: 1.5MM **Privately Held**
SIC: 2741 7389 Miscellaneous publishing;

(G-10135)
HADO LABS LLC
5604 28th Ave Nw (98107-4111)
PHONE....................425 891-7124
Matthew Branthwaite,
Catherine Hubert,
EMP: 2
SALES (est): 110.6K **Privately Held**
SIC: 7372 Application computer software

(G-10136)
HAM INDUSTRIES
303 Nw 97th St (98117-2034)
PHONE....................360 201-8439
Samuel Abrams, *Principal*
EMP: 2
SALES (est): 87.2K **Privately Held**
SIC: 3999 Manufacturing industries

(G-10137)
HAMMER & TONGS LLC
1500 N 100th St (98133-9422)
PHONE....................206 526-0549
Christopher James, *Principal*
EMP: 2
SALES (est): 110K **Privately Held**
SIC: 1389 Construction, repair & dismantling services

(G-10138)
HANGING CANVAS
1027 California Ln Sw (98116-1612)
PHONE....................206 937-3525
Marilyn Ullin, *Principal*
EMP: 2
SALES (est): 234.1K **Privately Held**
SIC: 2211 Canvas

(G-10139)
HANSEN FABRICATION
4254 23rd Ave W (98199-1211)
PHONE....................206 283-9181
John Gunnarsson, *President*
EMP: 3
SQ FT: 5,000
SALES: 150K **Privately Held**
WEB: www.hansenfabrication.com
SIC: 3531 3732 Construction machinery; boat building & repairing

(G-10140)
HARBOR ISLAND MCH WORKS INC
3431 11th Ave Sw (98134-1007)
PHONE....................206 682-7637
Michael T Defaccio, *President*
Lauren T De Faccio, *Vice Pres*
Mark A Defaccio, *Treasurer*
Lisa Defaccio, *Admin Sec*
EMP: 20 **EST:** 1950
SQ FT: 26,238
SALES (est): 4.2MM **Privately Held**
WEB: www.harborislandmachine.com
SIC: 3599 Machine shop, jobbing & repair

(G-10141)
HARBOR ISLAND SUPPLY CORP
230 S Chicago St (98108-4366)
PHONE....................206 762-1900
Janice Thomas, *President*
Janice Alexander, *President*
Jeff McGee, *Vice Pres*
John McGee, *Treasurer*
Wayne Alexander, *Admin Sec*
▲ **EMP:** 12
SQ FT: 22,000
SALES (est): 2.3MM **Privately Held**
WEB: www.harboranodes.com
SIC: 3429 5088 5551 Marine hardware; marine supplies; marine supplies

(G-10142)
HARMONIOUS DEVELOPMENT LLC
4548 20th Ave Ne Apt 203 (98105-3362)
PHONE....................425 248-5794
Cameron Jacobson,
EMP: 2
SALES (est): 68.1K **Privately Held**
SIC: 7372 7389 Home entertainment computer software;

(G-10143)
HARRINGTON TOWER SERVICES
3515 S Ferdinand St (98118-1733)
P.O. Box 18201 (98118-0201)
PHONE....................206 760-9191
Joseph Harrington, *President*
EMP: 4
SALES: 200K **Privately Held**
WEB: www.harringtontower.com
SIC: 3441 Tower sections, radio & television transmission

(G-10144)
HARRISON GRAY PUBLISHING LLC
5801 Phinney Ave N # 403 (98103-5862)
P.O. Box 30752 (98113-0752)
PHONE....................206 783-5682
EMP: 2 **EST:** 2011
SALES (est): 87K **Privately Held**
SIC: 2741 Misc Publishing

(G-10145)
HART CROWSER INC (PA)
3131 Elliott Ave Ste 600 (98121-1047)
PHONE....................206 324-9530
Mike Bailey, *CEO*
Daivd G Winter, *Vice Pres*
Marissa Goodman, *Engineer*
Robert Jenson, *CFO*
Paula Houston, *Human Res Dir*
EMP: 70

Seattle - King County (G-10146) — GEOGRAPHIC SECTION

SALES (est): 23.6MM **Privately Held**
WEB: www.hartcrowser.com
SIC: 8748 1081 1241 1481 Environmental consultant; metal mining services; metal mining exploration & development services; mine development, metal; coal mining services; mine preparation services; anthracite mining services, contract basis; mine & quarry services, nonmetallic minerals

(G-10146)
HATCH & KIRK INC (PA)
927 Nw 50th St (98107-4888)
PHONE.................................206 783-2766
Bob Hoelscher, *Ch of Bd*
Michael Korotkin, *President*
Leslie Isernio, *Corp Secy*
Cathy Hatch Daniels, *Shareholder*
Marshall Hatch, *Shareholder*
◆ **EMP:** 15
SQ FT: 160,000
SALES (est): 11.5MM **Privately Held**
WEB: www.hatchkirk.com
SIC: 5084 3519 7699 Engines & parts, diesel; marine engines; engines, diesel & semi-diesel or dual-fuel; engine repair & replacement, non-automotive

(G-10147)
HATTERDASHERY
1862 E Shelby St (98112-2022)
PHONE.................................206 322-6149
Michael Loeffler, *Owner*
EMP: 3
SQ FT: 2,000
SALES: 50K **Privately Held**
WEB: www.hatterdashery.com
SIC: 5611 2353 Hats, men's & boys'; hats & caps

(G-10148)
HATTINGH HOLDINGS INC
Also Called: Northwest Prosthetic
600 Broadway Ste 190 (98122-5371)
PHONE.................................206 323-4040
John Hattingh, *President*
Michele Hattingh, *CFO*
EMP: 30
SQ FT: 6,500
SALES (est): 2.5MM
SALES (corp-wide): 1B **Publicly Held**
WEB: www.nwpoc.com
SIC: 3842 Prosthetic appliances
HQ: Hanger Prosthetics & Orthotics, Inc.
 10910 Domain Dr Ste 300
 Austin TX 78758
 512 777-3800

(G-10149)
HAUGE & HASSAIN INCORPORATED
1140 Nw 46th St (98107-4632)
PHONE.................................206 789-8842
Wayne Lennstrom, *President*
Lane Christopherson, *Sales Executive*
EMP: 34
SQ FT: 4,650
SALES: 3MM **Privately Held**
WEB: www.haugeinc.com
SIC: 1721 5231 2851 Residential painting; wallcovering contractors; paint, glass & wallpaper; paints & allied products

(G-10150)
HAUN MADE LLC
Also Called: Tacoma Woodworks
16 S Michigan St Ste A (98108-3256)
PHONE.................................253 242-6105
Colin Huan, *Mng Member*
EMP: 5 **EST:** 2016
SALES: 300K **Privately Held**
SIC: 2599 5031 5712 Cabinets, factory; kitchen cabinets; cabinet work, custom

(G-10151)
HAVRE DAILY NEWS (HQ)
221 1st Ave W Ste 405 (98119-4238)
PHONE.................................206 284-4424
David Lord, *President*
Mike Gugliotto, *Principal*
Jeffrey Hood, *Principal*
EMP: 3 **EST:** 1963
SQ FT: 2,000
SALES (est): 614.9K
SALES (corp-wide): 78.7MM **Privately Held**
WEB: www.havredailynews.com
SIC: 2711 Newspapers: publishing only, not printed on site
PA: Pioneer Newspaper Service Llc
 221 1st Ave W Ste 405
 Seattle WA
 206 284-4424

(G-10152)
HAWAIIAN EARTH PRODUCTS
7343 E Marginal Way S (98108-3513)
PHONE.................................808 682-5895
EMP: 5 **EST:** 2010
SALES (est): 520.6K **Privately Held**
SIC: 2875 Compost

(G-10153)
HAYWARD GORDON US INC (HQ)
1541 S 92nd Pl (98108-5116)
PHONE.................................206 767-5660
John Gordon, *President*
EMP: 4 **EST:** 2014
SALES (est): 21.5MM
SALES (corp-wide): 41.9MM **Privately Held**
SIC: 3463 Pump, compressor, turbine & engine forgings, except auto
PA: Hayward Gordon Ulc
 5 Brigden Gate
 Georgetown ON L7G 0
 905 693-8595

(G-10154)
HEADLIGHT SOFTWARE INC
2143 N 64th St (98103-5441)
PHONE.................................206 985-4431
EMP: 2
SALES (est): 111.4K **Privately Held**
SIC: 7372 Business oriented computer software

(G-10155)
HEALIONICS CORPORATION
2121 N 35th St (98103-9103)
PHONE.................................206 432-9060
Mike Connolly, *CEO*
EMP: 8
SQ FT: 7,000
SALES (est): 1.4MM **Privately Held**
SIC: 2836 Biological products, except diagnostic

(G-10156)
HEALTH GUARDIAN INC
3216 Magnolia Blvd W (98199-2415)
PHONE.................................206 999-8153
Mark Querry, *CEO*
EMP: 2 **EST:** 2011
SALES (est): 137.9K **Privately Held**
SIC: 7372 Business oriented computer software

(G-10157)
HEARST CORPORATION
Seattle Post Intelligencer
101 Elliott Ave W (98119-4236)
P.O. Box 1909 (98111-1909)
PHONE.................................206 448-8000
Roger Oglesby, *Editor*
Tim West, *Accounts Mgr*
John Killian, *Sales Staff*
Shannon Fears, *Producer*
EMP: 165
SALES (corp-wide): 6.3B **Privately Held**
WEB: www.hearstcorp.com
SIC: 2711 Newspapers, publishing & printing
PA: The Hearst Corporation
 300 W 57th St Fl 42
 New York NY 10019
 212 649-2000

(G-10158)
HEARST SEATTLE MEDIA LLC
Also Called: Seattlepi.com
2901 3rd Ave Ste 120 (98121-1042)
PHONE.................................206 448-8000
Karl Johnson, *Principal*
EMP: 6
SALES (est): 372K
SALES (corp-wide): 6.3B **Privately Held**
SIC: 2711 Newspapers, publishing & printing
PA: The Hearst Corporation
 300 W 57th St Fl 42
 New York NY 10019
 212 649-2000

(G-10159)
HEBERT SAM-E LLC
427 Bellevue Ave E # 301 (98102-4764)
PHONE.................................206 650-4489
Rolland Hebert, *Manager*
Sohail Malik, *Manager*
EMP: 3
SALES (est): 123.2K **Privately Held**
SIC: 2834 Pharmaceutical preparations

(G-10160)
HEIRLOOM QUALITY MODERN LLC
2409 E Pine St (98122-3041)
PHONE.................................206 291-7331
Matthew Cary, *Principal*
EMP: 9
SALES (est): 1MM **Privately Held**
SIC: 2421 Furniture dimension stock, softwood

(G-10161)
HEJ LLC
Also Called: Home Energy Japan
2414 Sw Andover St D201 (98106-1153)
PHONE.................................425 652-9183
Ted Thomas,
EMP: 4
SALES: 950K **Privately Held**
SIC: 3511 Turbines & turbine generator sets

(G-10162)
HELCORP INTERACTIVE LLC
606 W Galer St (98119-3253)
PHONE.................................917 446-8506
Brian Helfrich, *Principal*
EMP: 2 **EST:** 2014
SALES (est): 141.4K **Privately Held**
SIC: 7372 Prepackaged software

(G-10163)
HELM INDUSTRIES LLC
550 Ne Ravenna Blvd Apt 5 (98115-6436)
PHONE.................................206 419-3973
EMP: 2 **EST:** 2014
SALES (est): 84.7K **Privately Held**
SIC: 3999 Manufacturing industries

(G-10164)
HEMEL BOARD COMPANY
224 Pontius Ave N Apt 510 (98109-5575)
PHONE.................................206 261-2781
Stephen Dekoch, *Principal*
Shirish Mulherkar, *Vice Pres*
EMP: 6 **EST:** 2010
SQ FT: 1,890
SALES (est): 373.6K **Privately Held**
SIC: 3949 Sporting & athletic goods

(G-10165)
HEMLOCK PRINTERS USA INC
318 1st Ave S Ste 300 (98104-2597)
PHONE.................................206 241-8311
Frits Kouwenhoven, *Vice Pres*
EMP: 5
SQ FT: 1,500
SALES (corp-wide): 1.7MM **Privately Held**
WEB: www.hemlock.com
SIC: 2759 Commercial printing
PA: Hemlock Printers Ltd
 7050 Buller Ave
 Burnaby BC V5J 4
 604 438-2456

(G-10166)
HENRY PRODUCTS INCORPORATED
Also Called: Henrybuilt
4632 Ohio Ave S (98134-2361)
P.O. Box 80764 (98108-0764)
PHONE.................................206 624-5656
Scott Hudson, *CEO*
Chris Barriatua, *Vice Pres*
Sarah Viars, *Production*
Joseph Goodwin, *Engineer*
Kelly Jasper, *Business Anlyst*
EMP: 64
SALES (est): 9.1MM **Privately Held**
WEB: www.henrybuilt.com
SIC: 2511 Kitchen & dining room furniture

(G-10167)
HERBIVORE BOTANICALS LLC
1620 N 45th St Apt 205 (98103-6755)
PHONE.................................206 226-5008
Julia Wills, *Branch Mgr*
EMP: 2
SALES (corp-wide): 530K **Privately Held**
SIC: 2844 Toilet preparations
PA: Herbivore Botanicals, Llc
 80 Vine St Apt 201
 Seattle WA 98121
 206 441-7509

(G-10168)
HEXA MATERIALS LLC
707 N 64th St (98103-5633)
PHONE.................................541 337-3669
Richard Schure,
Dorian Goettler,
EMP: 2
SALES (est): 106.9K **Privately Held**
SIC: 3624 3675 Carbon & graphite products; electronic capacitors

(G-10169)
HEYLO
145 S Horton St Ste 100 (98134-1869)
PHONE.................................440 522-4674
EMP: 2
SALES (est): 117.1K **Privately Held**
SIC: 3999

(G-10170)
HIGH RISE SOFTWARE GROUP INC
3859 Beach Dr Sw (98116-3507)
PHONE.................................206 290-6087
James Fattore, *Principal*
EMP: 2 **EST:** 2011
SALES (est): 94.6K **Privately Held**
SIC: 7372 Prepackaged software

(G-10171)
HIGHER AGE PRESS
5222 University Way Ne 304a (98105-3553)
PHONE.................................425 891-9129
Jake Hansen, *Principal*
EMP: 2 **EST:** 2016
SALES (est): 59.2K **Privately Held**
SIC: 2741 Miscellaneous publishing

(G-10172)
HIGHLANDS WELDING REPAIR INC (PA)
2001 W Garfield St (98119-3115)
PHONE.................................206 283-0080
Esteban Ramirez, *President*
Ciracio Ramirez, *Vice Pres*
EMP: 2
SQ FT: 2,600
SALES: 400K **Privately Held**
SIC: 3441 3499 7692 3731 Fabricated structural metal; barricades, metal; welding repair; sailing vessels, commercial: building & repairing

(G-10173)
HILLIARDS BEER LLC
6711 1st Ave Nw (98117-4828)
PHONE.................................206 257-4486
Ryan Hilliard,
EMP: 13
SQ FT: 16,500
SALES (est): 1.2MM **Privately Held**
SIC: 2082 Beer (alcoholic beverage)

(G-10174)
HILLTOP MANAGEMENT INC
Also Called: Zebra Print and Copy
4151 Fauntleroy Way Sw (98126-2672)
PHONE.................................206 933-5900
Amar Yusaf, *Principal*
EMP: 4
SALES (est): 438K **Privately Held**
SIC: 2752 Color lithography; commercial printing, offset

GEOGRAPHIC SECTION — Seattle - King County (G-10207)

(G-10175)
HIRELYTICS LLC
1828 25th Ave Unit B (98122-3024)
PHONE.................................843 900-4473
Benjamin Stull,
Shawn Murphy,
Kamal Suffoletta,
EMP: 3 EST: 2014
SALES (est): 213.7K **Privately Held**
SIC: 7372 7389 Application computer software; business oriented computer software;

(G-10176)
HISPANIC YELLOW PAGES
324 Nw 47th St (98107-4445)
PHONE.................................206 297-8532
Ramon Rodriguez, *Principal*
EMP: 2
SALES (est): 62.9K **Privately Held**
SIC: 2711 Newspapers

(G-10177)
HJALMAR INDUSTRIES INC
1535 Nw Ballard Way (98107-4712)
PHONE.................................360 957-4302
EMP: 2
SALES (est): 86.9K **Privately Held**
SIC: 3999 Manufacturing industries

(G-10178)
HOLLY PRESS INC
115 Warren Ave N Apt 110 (98109-4996)
PHONE.................................206 623-2444
James R Burdett, *President*
Elliott W Burdett Jr, *Vice Pres*
Audrey Burdett, *Admin Sec*
EMP: 5
SQ FT: 4,000
SALES (est): 584.1K **Privately Held**
SIC: 2752 Commercial printing, offset

(G-10179)
HOLLYWOOD TRIANGLE PRODUCTIONS
1301 1st Ave Apt 709 (98101-2140)
PHONE.................................323 301-3003
Virgil Wade, *CEO*
Jessica Kennington, *CFO*
EMP: 2
SALES (est): 160K **Privately Held**
SIC: 7313 2741 Electronic media advertising representatives;

(G-10180)
HOMESTEAD BOOK CO
6101 22nd Ave Nw (98107-2413)
P.O. Box 17444 (98127-1144)
PHONE.................................206 782-4532
EMP: 5
SQ FT: 3,000
SALES (est): 610K **Privately Held**
WEB: www.homesteadbook.com
SIC: 5192 2731 Books; books: publishing only

(G-10181)
HOOK & LADDER PRINTING CO LLC
2229 Waverly Way E (98112-2333)
P.O. Box 22048 (98122-0048)
PHONE.................................206 568-0588
Janet Jones, *Mng Member*
EMP: 2
SALES (est): 100K **Privately Held**
WEB: www.hookandladderprinting.com
SIC: 2752 Commercial printing, offset

(G-10182)
HOSS A W & SONS FURN & MFG
9221 Roosevelt Way Ne (98115-2841)
PHONE.................................206 522-1229
Lawrence R Hoss, *President*
Larry Hoss, *Principal*
Allan W Hoss, *Vice Pres*
EMP: 12
SQ FT: 4,000
SALES: 1.5MM **Privately Held**
SIC: 7641 2391 5712 Reupholstery; furniture refinishing; draperies, plastic & textile: from purchased materials; furniture stores

(G-10183)
HOT GLASS COLOR & SUPPLY
2225 5th Ave (98121-1807)
PHONE.................................206 448-1199
Cliff Goodman, *Owner*
▼ EMP: 3
SQ FT: 6,480
SALES (est): 237K **Privately Held**
WEB: www.hotglasscolor.com
SIC: 3229 Glassware, art or decorative

(G-10184)
HOT OIL COMPANY LLC
1428 Queen Anne Ave N (98109-3189)
PHONE.................................509 338-5678
Max Larue, *CEO*
EMP: 3
SALES (est): 91.3K **Privately Held**
SIC: 2079 Edible oil products, except corn oil

(G-10185)
HOT SHOT SITE DOTS
3032 Sw Charlestown St (98126-2525)
PHONE.................................206 604-8980
EMP: 2 EST: 2010
SALES (est): 100K **Privately Held**
SIC: 1389 Oil/Gas Field Services

(G-10186)
HOUSE OF LASHES
10522 Lake City Way Ne C104 (98125-7750)
PHONE.................................206 522-5277
Suzie Raghouber, *Principal*
EMP: 2 EST: 2012
SALES (est): 171.3K **Privately Held**
SIC: 3851 Eyes, glass & plastic

(G-10187)
HOW PICKLE GOT OUT OF A JAM
821 20th Ave S (98144-2919)
PHONE.................................206 940-6532
EMP: 2
SALES (est): 105.8K **Privately Held**
SIC: 2035 Pickled fruits & vegetables

(G-10188)
HOWARD LAMP COMPANY
1912 N 45th St (98103-6805)
PHONE.................................425 776-7914
Ian Howard, *Owner*
▲ EMP: 2
SALES (est): 220K **Privately Held**
SIC: 3645 Residential lighting fixtures

(G-10189)
HOWELLCORP
1200 Westlake Ave N Ste 1 (98109-3543)
P.O. Box 84183 (98124-5483)
PHONE.................................206 954-8011
Nicholas Howell, *CEO*
EMP: 10 EST: 2011
SALES (est): 913.4K **Privately Held**
SIC: 3841 Surgical & medical instruments

(G-10190)
HP INC
2401 4th Ave Ste 500 (98121-1498)
PHONE.................................650 857-1501
Alan Levy, *President*
Dj Rackham, *Opers Staff*
EMP: 14
SALES (corp-wide): 58.4B **Publicly Held**
SIC: 3571 Personal computers (microcomputers)
PA: Hp Inc.
   1501 Page Mill Rd
   Palo Alto CA 94304
   650 857-1501

(G-10191)
HRH PRESS
6521 Greenwood Ave N (98103-5223)
PHONE.................................206 781-1279
Heidi Rose Hespelt, *Owner*
EMP: 2
SALES (est): 59.2K **Privately Held**
SIC: 2741 Miscellaneous publishing

(G-10192)
HTC AMERICA INNOVATION INC
308 Occidental Ave S # 300 (98104-2822)
PHONE.................................425 679-5318
Peter Chou, *CEO*
Craig Parietti, *Vice Pres*
EMP: 500
SALES (est): 70.1MM
SALES (corp-wide): 768.1MM **Privately Held**
SIC: 3661 Headsets, telephone; telephone sets, all types except cellular radio
PA: Htc Corporation
   23, Hsing Hua Rd.,
   Taoyuan City TAY 33068
   337 532-52

(G-10193)
HUMMINGBIRD PRESS
10113 Radford Ave Nw (98177-5437)
PHONE.................................617 921-6502
Catherine Keating, *Principal*
EMP: 2 EST: 2012
SALES (est): 123.5K **Privately Held**
SIC: 2741 Miscellaneous publishing

(G-10194)
HUSKEY PRINTING & ENVELOP
11405 10th Ave Sw (98146-2267)
PHONE.................................206 901-1792
Chris Huskey, *Owner*
EMP: 4
SALES (est): 174.6K **Privately Held**
SIC: 2752 Commercial printing, lithographic

(G-10195)
HUSSEY SOFTWARE LLC
7465 Corliss Ave N (98103-4932)
P.O. Box 31545 (98103-1545)
PHONE.................................206 409-0959
Thomas Hussey, *Administration*
EMP: 2 EST: 2009
SALES (est): 153.9K **Privately Held**
SIC: 7372 Application computer software

(G-10196)
HYDROACOUSTIC TECHNOLOGY INC
715 Ne Northlake Way (98105-6429)
PHONE.................................206 633-3383
John Ehernberg, *President*
Bruce Ransom, *Vice Pres*
Sam Johnston, *Vice Pres*
Tracey Steig, *Admin Sec*
EMP: 15
SQ FT: 8,000
SALES (est): 1.7MM **Privately Held**
WEB: www.htisonar.com
SIC: 8748 3812 Fishery consultant; sonar systems & equipment

(G-10197)
HYDROBEE SPC
5534 30th Ave Ne (98105-5502)
PHONE.................................206 491-0945
William Hamner, *President*
Dane Roth, *Vice Pres*
EMP: 2 EST: 2013
SQ FT: 500
SALES (est): 168.5K **Privately Held**
SIC: 3511 Turbines & turbine generator sets

(G-10198)
HYPERFIZZICS
3948 S Brandon St B (98118-6130)
PHONE.................................904 253-5137
Richard Smith, *Partner*
Shethy Stuckey, *General Ptnr*
EMP: 2
SALES (est): 101K **Privately Held**
SIC: 2086 Carbonated beverages, nonalcoholic: bottled & canned

(G-10199)
I CONCEPT SIGNS LLC
700 S Orchard St (98108-3427)
PHONE.................................206 658-1158
David C Fanta, *Administration*
EMP: 5
SALES (est): 83.9K **Privately Held**
SIC: 3993 Signs & advertising specialties

(G-10200)
ICICLE SEAFOODS INC (DH)
Also Called: Seward Fisheries
4019 21st Ave W Ste 300 (98199-1299)
P.O. Box 79003 (98119-7903)
PHONE.................................206 282-0988
Peter Buck, *Corp Secy*
John Woodruff, *COO*
Libby Moore, *Manager*
Glenn Cooke, *Director*
◆ EMP: 75
SQ FT: 8,000
SALES (est): 207.9MM
SALES (corp-wide): 268.6MM **Privately Held**
WEB: www.icicleseafoods.com
SIC: 2092 2091 Shellfish, frozen: prepared; fish, frozen: prepared; salmon: packaged in cans, jars, etc.
HQ: Cooke Seafood Usa, Inc.
   2000 Nrthgate Cmmrce Pkwy
   Suffolk VA 23435
   757 673-4500

(G-10201)
ICOPYRIGHT INC
4742 42nd Ave Sw 615 (98116-4553)
PHONE.................................206 484-8561
EMP: 2 EST: 2012
SALES (est): 173K **Privately Held**
SIC: 7372 Business oriented computer software

(G-10202)
ID LABEL INC
3250 Arprt Way S Ste 410 (98134)
PHONE.................................206 323-8100
Jeff Chandler, *Branch Mgr*
EMP: 16 **Privately Held**
SIC: 2759 Commercial printing
PA: Id Label, Inc.
   425 Park Ave
   Lake Villa IL 60046

(G-10203)
IDEATIONS DESIGN INC
4214 24th Ave W (98199-1216)
P.O. Box 99575 (98139-0575)
PHONE.................................206 281-0067
Dave Hancock, *President*
▲ EMP: 2
SALES (est): 275.4K **Privately Held**
WEB: www.divealert.com
SIC: 3949 Skin diving equipment, scuba type

(G-10204)
IFOODDECISIONSCIENCES INC
500 Yale Ave N Fl 1 (98109-5680)
PHONE.................................206 219-3703
Diane Wetherington, *CEO*
Timorthy Giacometti, *Vice Pres*
Helen Bekris, *Research*
EMP: 25
SALES (est): 607.2K **Privately Held**
SIC: 7372 Business oriented computer software

(G-10205)
ILLUME
4878 Beacon Ave S (98108-1567)
P.O. Box 94386 (98124-6686)
PHONE.................................206 566-5375
EMP: 4
SALES (est): 455.5K **Privately Held**
SIC: 3441 Fabricated structural metal

(G-10206)
IM PRINTING
1800 Federal Ave E (98102-4237)
PHONE.................................206 300-7511
EMP: 2
SALES (est): 83.9K **Privately Held**
SIC: 2752 Commercial printing, lithographic

(G-10207)
IMAGINE COLOR SERVICE LLC
4215 21st Ave W Ste 100 (98199-1253)
PHONE.................................206 281-5703
Andrew Larson, *Managing Prtnr*
Kristy Lindgren, *Project Mgr*
Steve Quade, *Project Mgr*
Jean Schier, *CFO*
Alison Walker, *Manager*
EMP: 30
SQ FT: 3,600
SALES: 4.9MM **Privately Held**
WEB: www.imaginecs.com
SIC: 2796 Color separations for printing

Seattle - King County (G-10208)   GEOGRAPHIC SECTION

(G-10208)
IMAGINE VISUAL SERVICE LLC
4215 21st Ave W Ste 100 (98199-1253)
PHONE...................................206 281-5703
Jean Schier,
Michael Anderson,
Ron Eggers,
Andy Larsen,
EMP: 8
SALES (est): 640K **Privately Held**
SIC: 2752 Commercial printing, lithographic

(G-10209)
IMMUNE DESIGN CORP (PA)
1616 Eastlake Ave E (98102-3788)
PHONE...................................206 682-0645
Ed Penhoet, *Ch of Bd*
Carlos Paya, *President*
Stephen Brady, *Exec VP*
Sergey Yurasov, *Chief Mktg Ofcr*
Jan Ter Meulen, *Security Dir*
EMP: 56 **EST:** 2008
SQ FT: 20,133
SALES: 2.2MM **Privately Held**
SIC: 2834 8731 Pharmaceutical preparations; commercial physical research; biotechnical research, commercial

(G-10210)
IMMUNEX CORPORATION
51 University St (98101-3614)
PHONE...................................206 551-5169
Roger Pearlmutter, *President*
Michael Mumford, *President*
Douglas E Williams, *President*
Peggy V Phillips, *COO*
Steve M Odre, *Vice Pres*
EMP: 700
SQ FT: 120,000
SALES (est): 86.6MM
SALES (corp-wide): 23.7B **Publicly Held**
WEB: www.immunex.com
SIC: 2836 2834 8731 Biological products, except diagnostic; pharmaceutical preparations; drugs affecting parasitic & infective diseases; biotechnical research, commercial
PA: Amgen Inc.
1 Amgen Center Dr
Thousand Oaks CA 91320
805 447-1000

(G-10211)
IMPEL NEUROPHARMA INC
Also Called: Impel Biopharmaceuticals
201 Elliott Ave W Ste 260 (98119-4265)
PHONE...................................206 568-1466
Jon Congleton, *President*
Lynn C Gold, *Senior VP*
John Hoekman, *Vice Pres*
Maria Jeleva, *Opers Staff*
John Leaman, *CFO*
EMP: 6
SALES (est): 2.2MM **Privately Held**
SIC: 2834 8733 Pharmaceutical preparations; medical research

(G-10212)
IMPINJ INC (PA)
400 Frview Ave N Ste 1200 (98109)
PHONE...................................206 517-5300
Chris Diorio, *CEO*
Vincent Bianco, *Counsel*
Jeff Dossett, *Exec VP*
Hussein Mecklai, *Exec VP*
Rob Collins, *Vice Pres*
EMP: 201
SQ FT: 70,000
SALES: 122.6MM **Publicly Held**
WEB: www.impinj.com
SIC: 3674 7372 Semiconductor circuit networks; prepackaged software

(G-10213)
IMPINJ INC
716 N 34th St (98103-8801)
PHONE...................................206 834-1098
EMP: 4
SALES (est): 391.6K **Privately Held**
SIC: 3674 Semiconductors And Related Devices, Nsk

(G-10214)
IMPINJ INC
400 Fairview Ave N # 1200 (98109-5371)
PHONE...................................206 315-4449
Clayton Cullum, *Manager*
EMP: 19
SALES (corp-wide): 122.6MM **Publicly Held**
SIC: 3674 Semiconductor circuit networks
PA: Impinj, Inc.
400 Frview Ave N Ste 1200
Seattle WA 98109
206 517-5300

(G-10215)
IMPLICIT BIOSCIENCE INC
1600 E Jefferson St # 505 (98122-5698)
PHONE...................................650 851-3133
Garry Redlich, *CEO*
Daniel Parry, *CFO*
EMP: 3
SALES (est): 393.9K **Privately Held**
SIC: 2834 Druggists' preparations (pharmaceuticals)

(G-10216)
IMPRESSION PRINTING CO INC
222 S Lucile St (98108-2432)
PHONE...................................206 762-6211
Michael B Klinke, *President*
Herbert Lockard, *President*
Bryce Lockhard, *Vice Pres*
EMP: 3 **EST:** 1960
SQ FT: 6,800
SALES (est): 583.4K **Privately Held**
WEB: www.impressionprintingonline.com
SIC: 2752 2759 Letters, circular or form: lithographed; letterpress printing

(G-10217)
IMPULSE AUDIO INC
9911 37th Ave Sw (98126-4015)
P.O. Box 46217 (98146-0217)
PHONE...................................206 650-0075
David May, *Principal*
EMP: 2
SALES (est): 264.9K **Privately Held**
SIC: 3651 Household audio & video equipment

(G-10218)
IN AN INSTANT
5438 35th Ave Sw (98126-2822)
PHONE...................................206 465-0644
Kelly Morris, *Principal*
EMP: 2
SALES (est): 128.2K **Privately Held**
SIC: 2752 Commercial printing, lithographic

(G-10219)
IN AN INSTANT ART LLC
1941 1st Ave S Ste 2g (98134-1418)
PHONE...................................206 294-3570
Kelly Roxx, *Principal*
EMP: 2
SALES (est): 191.2K **Privately Held**
SIC: 2752 Commercial printing, lithographic

(G-10220)
INCENTIVES BY DESIGN INC
1920 Occidental Ave S A (98134-1429)
PHONE...................................206 623-4310
Richard A Hirshberg, *President*
William Hirshberg, *Vice Pres*
Marci French, *Manager*
EMP: 9
SQ FT: 4,000
SALES (est): 1.5MM **Privately Held**
WEB: www.incentivesbydesign.com
SIC: 3993 Signs & advertising specialties

(G-10221)
INDENA USA INC
601 Union St Ste 330 (98101-2372)
PHONE...................................206 340-6140
Greg Ris, *CEO*
Philippe Bertrand, *Prdtn Dir*
Giovanni Appendino, *Research*
Giovanni Esposito, *Controller*
Cosimo Palumbo, *Sales Staff*
EMP: 6
SALES (est): 865.3K **Privately Held**
SIC: 2834 Extracts of botanicals: powdered, pilular, solid or fluid
HQ: Indena Spa
Viale Ortles 12
Milano MI 20139
025 749-61

(G-10222)
INDEPENDENT BREWERS UNTD CORP
91 S Royal Brougham Way (98134-1219)
PHONE...................................206 682-8322
Robert Haskell, *Branch Mgr*
EMP: 16 **Privately Held**
SIC: 2082 Malt beverages
HQ: Independent Brewers United Corporation
431 Pine St Ste G12
Burlington VT 05401
802 862-6114

(G-10223)
INDEPENDENT PACKERS CORP
Also Called: Itc
2001 W Grfeld St Ste C102 (98119)
PHONE...................................206 285-6000
Jeffery Buske, *President*
▲ **EMP:** 60
SALES (est): 12MM **Privately Held**
SIC: 2092 Seafoods, fresh: prepared; seafoods, frozen: prepared

(G-10224)
INDEPENDENT WOODWORKS
4546 45th Ave Sw (98116-4155)
PHONE...................................206 239-8577
Suzy Knutson, *Principal*
EMP: 4
SALES (est): 226.1K **Privately Held**
SIC: 2431 Millwork

(G-10225)
INDEX PUBLISHING (PA)
Also Called: Stranger, The
1535 11th Ave Ste 300 (98122-3933)
PHONE...................................206 323-7101
Tim Keck, *President*
Nokes Emily, *Editor*
Julia Raban, *Editor*
Chelcie Blackmun, *Production*
Erica Tarrant, *Production*
EMP: 75
SQ FT: 8,600
SALES (est): 4.7MM **Privately Held**
WEB: www.naughtynw.com
SIC: 2711 Newspapers: publishing only, not printed on site

(G-10226)
INDIE FLIX INC
4314 E Madison St (98112-2797)
PHONE...................................206 829-9112
Scilla Andreen, *President*
EMP: 15
SALES (est): 1.1MM **Privately Held**
SIC: 3861 Motion picture film

(G-10227)
INDIGO VINYLWORKS LLC
309 S Cloverdale St B4 (98108-4500)
PHONE...................................425 278-4411
EMP: 2
SALES (est): 116.9K **Privately Held**
SIC: 3993 Signs & advertising specialties

(G-10228)
INDULO INC
100 20th Ave E Apt 10 (98112-5349)
PHONE...................................206 383-0373
Attila Melegh, *CEO*
EMP: 2
SALES (est): 62.1K **Privately Held**
SIC: 7372 Application computer software

(G-10229)
INDUSTRIAL AUTOMATION INC
1421 S 93rd St (98108-5107)
PHONE...................................206 763-1025
Tom McKown, *President*
John Reynolds, *Safety Mgr*
EMP: 35
SQ FT: 15,000
SALES (est): 8.2MM **Privately Held**
WEB: www.iagse.com
SIC: 3423 Hand & edge tools

(G-10230)
INDUSTRIAL CERAMICS INC
815 1st Ave (98104-1404)
PHONE...................................905 878-2848
John Lawrence, *President*
Dominica Misale, *General Mgr*
Shawn Stewart, *Technical Staff*
EMP: 2
SALES (est): 170.9K
SALES (corp-wide): 4.1MM **Privately Held**
SIC: 3297 5085 Graphite refractories: carbon bond or ceramic bond; industrial supplies
PA: Industrial Ceramics Limited
851 Nipissing Rd
Milton ON
905 878-2848

(G-10231)
INDUSTRIAL CONTAINER SVCS LLC
Also Called: I C S
7152 1st Ave S (98108-4102)
PHONE...................................206 763-2345
Rick Cabuco, *Branch Mgr*
EMP: 43
SALES (corp-wide): 1.1B **Privately Held**
WEB: www.iconserv.com
SIC: 3443 3412 Fabricated plate work (boiler shop); metal barrels, drums & pails
HQ: Industrial Container Services Llc
2600 Mtland Ctr Pkwy 20 # 200
Maitland FL 32751
407 930-4182

(G-10232)
INDUSTRIAL GENEROSITY INC
159 S Jackson St Ste 200 (98104-4433)
PHONE...................................206 336-2268
Thomas Riley, *CEO*
EMP: 2
SALES (est): 138.9K **Privately Held**
SIC: 7372 5731 Application computer software; consumer electronic equipment

(G-10233)
INFOHARVEST INC
8238 15th Ave Ne (98115-4340)
P.O. Box 25155 (98165-2055)
PHONE...................................206 686-2729
Phillip Murphy, *President*
Tamara Oki, *General Mgr*
EMP: 3
SQ FT: 2,300
SALES (est): 400K **Privately Held**
WEB: www.infoharvest.com
SIC: 7372 7371 Prepackaged software; custom computer programming services

(G-10234)
INFORMATION BUILDERS INC
Also Called: Iway Software
1420 5th Ave Ste 3250 (98101-1380)
PHONE...................................206 624-9055
EMP: 15
SALES (corp-wide): 260.4MM **Privately Held**
WEB: www.informationbuilders.com
SIC: 7372 Prepackaged software
PA: Information Builders, Inc.
2 Penn Plz Fl 28
New York NY 10121
212 736-4433

(G-10235)
INKER PRINTS LLC
210 S Mead St (98108-2438)
PHONE...................................206 499-7379
EMP: 2
SALES (est): 92.3K **Privately Held**
SIC: 2752 Commercial printing, lithographic

(G-10236)
INKWELL SCREENPRINTING
1055 S Director St (98108-4702)
PHONE...................................206 551-1713
Tamara Snellenberg-Fraser, *Principal*
EMP: 2
SALES (est): 106.7K **Privately Held**
SIC: 2759 Screen printing

GEOGRAPHIC SECTION

Seattle - King County (G-10267)

(G-10237)
INLET PETROLEUM SOLVENTS
1191 2nd Ave Ste 1800 (98101-2996)
P.O. Box 79018 (98119-7918)
PHONE.................................907 274-3835
EMP: 5
SALES (est): 194.5K **Privately Held**
SIC: 2911 Solvents

(G-10238)
INLINE DESIGN LLC (PA)
1420 Terry Ave Unit 2304 (98101-1985)
PHONE.................................425 405-5505
Jad Honein, *Mng Member*
◆ **EMP:** 11
SALES: 3.1MM **Privately Held**
SIC: 3446 Railings, prefabricated metal

(G-10239)
INNOFRESH LLC
2707 33rd Ave S (98144-5551)
PHONE.................................206 438-3541
Matthew Moore,
EMP: 2
SALES (est): 200K **Privately Held**
SIC: 3569 Industrial shock absorbers

(G-10240)
INNOVATE FOR ALL SPC
4000 1st Ave S (98134-2301)
PHONE.................................425 681-2191
Patrick Diller, *President*
EMP: 2
SALES (est): 750K **Privately Held**
SIC: 3999 Manufacturing industries

(G-10241)
INSECT SHIELD LLC
3201 1st Ave S Ste 350 (98134-1846)
PHONE.................................206 624-9307
Rick Himmering, *Branch Mgr*
EMP: 6
SALES (corp-wide): 6MM **Privately Held**
WEB: www.buzzoates.com
SIC: 2329 Hunting coats & vests, men's
PA: Insect Shield, Llc
814 W Market St
Greensboro NC 27401
336 272-4157

(G-10242)
INSECT SKATEBOARDS INC
7536 Dibble Ave Nw (98117-5125)
PHONE.................................206 706-8882
Steve Hopper, *Principal*
EMP: 2
SALES (est): 145.3K **Privately Held**
WEB: www.insectskateboards.com
SIC: 3949 Skateboards

(G-10243)
INSIDE OUT MEDICINE INC
2026 N 77th St (98103-4906)
PHONE.................................206 920-8959
Maria Cho, *CEO*
Adam Goldin, *Director*
Hao-Tam Tran, *Director*
EMP: 3 **EST:** 2011
SALES (est): 162.8K **Privately Held**
SIC: 7372 Application computer software

(G-10244)
INSIGHTFUL CORPORATION (DH)
1700 Westlake Ave N # 500 (98109-3012)
PHONE.................................206 283-8802
Sachin Chawla, *Ch of Bd*
Jeffrey E Coombs, *President*
Murray E Laidley, *Vice Pres*
Ann Parker-Way, *Vice Pres*
Richard P Barber, *CFO*
EMP: 85
SQ FT: 27,370
SALES (est): 9.3MM
SALES (corp-wide): 885.6MM **Privately Held**
WEB: www.insightful.com
SIC: 7372 Application computer software

(G-10245)
INSTANT CHEER ILLSTRATIONS LLC
3844 Ne 85th St (98115-3719)
PHONE.................................206 999-5515
Karla Johnson, *Principal*
EMP: 2
SALES (est): 175.6K **Privately Held**
SIC: 2752 Commercial printing, lithographic

(G-10246)
INTEGRATED MARINE SYSTEMS INC
Also Called: Wescold Systems
4816 15th Ave Nw (98107-4717)
P.O. Box 2028, Port Townsend (98368-0099)
PHONE.................................360 385-0077
Arne Ness, *President*
Mark Burn, *Vice Pres*
Jerry Downing, *Treasurer*
Kurt Ness, *Admin Sec*
EMP: 25
SQ FT: 6,400
SALES (est): 4.2MM **Privately Held**
SIC: 3585 Refrigeration equipment, complete

(G-10247)
INTELLIGENT LIDS LLC
505 Bdwy Way S Unit 457 (98102)
PHONE.................................206 920-6484
Traci Tenneson,
Bill Tenneson,
EMP: 5
SALES (est): 388.2K **Privately Held**
SIC: 3089 Caps, plastic

(G-10248)
INTERIOR ENVIRONMENTS INC
3450 4th Ave S (98134-1905)
PHONE.................................206 432-8800
David J Brzusek, *President*
Brenda Douglas, *Director*
EMP: 25
SQ FT: 45,000
SALES (est): 3MM **Privately Held**
SIC: 2521 Wood office furniture

(G-10249)
INTERNATIONAL CNSTR EQP INC
Also Called: I C E
8101 Occidental Ave S (98108-4210)
PHONE.................................206 764-4787
Michael Clark, *Branch Mgr*
EMP: 4
SQ FT: 1,296
SALES (corp-wide): 31.4MM **Privately Held**
WEB: www.iceusa.com
SIC: 3531 7353 Construction machinery; earth moving equipment, rental or leasing
PA: International Construction Equipment, Inc.
301 Warehouse Dr
Matthews NC 28104
704 821-8200

(G-10250)
INTERNATIONAL EXAMINER
409 Maynard Ave S Ste 203 (98104-2959)
PHONE.................................206 624-3925
Nila Kim, *Principal*
EMP: 5
SALES (est): 287.7K **Privately Held**
WEB: www.iexaminer.org
SIC: 2711 Newspapers, publishing & printing

(G-10251)
INTERNATIONAL PAINT LLC
1621 S 92nd Pl (98108-5118)
PHONE.................................206 763-5884
Chris Heide, *Sales Staff*
Nick Salesky, *Marketing Staff*
Laurie Hill, *Branch Mgr*
EMP: 12
SALES (corp-wide): 11.3B **Privately Held**
WEB: www.epiglass.com
SIC: 2851 Paints & allied products
HQ: International Paint Llc
6001 Antoine Dr
Houston TX 77091
713 682-1711

(G-10252)
INTERWORKS US LLC
6075 California Ave Sw (98136-1612)
PHONE.................................206 934-1074
Digby Williams, *Principal*
EMP: 2 **EST:** 2016
SALES (est): 122.4K **Privately Held**
SIC: 7372 Prepackaged software

(G-10253)
INTRIGUE CHOCOLATES CO
76 S Washington St (98104-2568)
PHONE.................................206 829-8810
Aaron Barthel, *Principal*
EMP: 7 **EST:** 2009
SALES (est): 416.7K **Privately Held**
SIC: 5149 2066 Chocolate; chocolate

(G-10254)
INTRINSYC SOFTWARE (USA) INC
600 University St # 3600 (98101-1176)
PHONE.................................604 678-3734
Glenda M Dorchak, *Principal*
EMP: 3
SALES (est): 330.8K **Privately Held**
SIC: 3695 Computer software tape & disks: blank, rigid & floppy

(G-10255)
INVESTIGATEWEST
401 Mercer St (98109-4640)
PHONE.................................206 441-4288
EMP: 8
SALES (est): 479.8K **Privately Held**
SIC: 2711 Newspapers-Publishing/Printing

(G-10256)
INVIO INC
Also Called: Invio Clinical
325 Harvard Ave E Apt 200 (98102-5454)
P.O. Box 12065 (98102-0065)
PHONE.................................206 915-3563
J Dmitri Poppa, *CEO*
James Poppa, *CEO*
EMP: 4
SALES (est): 130.9K **Privately Held**
SIC: 7372 Business oriented computer software

(G-10257)
IOCOLOR LLP
929 N 130th St Ste 8 (98133-7500)
PHONE.................................206 223-1845
Gary Hawkey, *Partner*
Ed Marquand, *Partner*
John Bailey, *Manager*
▲ **EMP:** 8
SALES (est): 912K **Privately Held**
WEB: www.iocolor.com
SIC: 2721 Magazines: publishing & printing

(G-10258)
IOCURRENTS INC
159 Western Ave W (98119-4247)
PHONE.................................206 494-0099
Cosmo King, *President*
Bhaskar Bhattacharyya, *CTO*
EMP: 5
SQ FT: 100
SALES (est): 121.8K **Privately Held**
SIC: 7375 3812 Information retrieval services; search & navigation equipment

(G-10259)
IRISH FOUNDRY & MFG INC
45 S Spokane St (98134-2218)
PHONE.................................206 623-7147
Charles A Irish, *President*
Gail Irish, *Vice Pres*
EMP: 8
SALES (est): 1.1MM **Privately Held**
WEB: www.irishfoundry.com
SIC: 3365 3366 7389 Aluminum & aluminum-based alloy castings; castings (except die): bronze;

(G-10260)
ISILON SYSTEMS LLC
Also Called: EMC Isilon
505 1st Ave S (98104-3284)
PHONE.................................206 315-7500
Paul Dacier, *President*
Christopher Boyd, *Regional Mgr*
Linda Hang, *Opers Staff*
Prasad Mohapatra, *Production*
Robert Bogdan, *Engineer*
▲ **EMP:** 356 **EST:** 2001
SQ FT: 66,000
SALES (est): 57.7MM
SALES (corp-wide): 90.6B **Publicly Held**
WEB: www.isilon.com
SIC: 3674 3572 Semiconductors & related devices; computer auxiliary storage units
HQ: Emc Corporation
176 South St
Hopkinton MA 01748
508 435-1000

(G-10261)
ISS (WEST) INC
801 2nd Ave Ste 1108 (98104-1524)
PHONE.................................206 470-3754
Yoshio Nakamura, *President*
Judith Nakamura, *Admin Sec*
EMP: 4
SQ FT: 1,000
SALES (est): 748.2K **Privately Held**
WEB: www.isswestinc.com
SIC: 3315 Steel wire & related products

(G-10262)
ITC USA LLC
603 Stewart St Ste 200 (98101-1249)
PHONE.................................206 669-3442
Dustin Winegardner,
EMP: 13
SQ FT: 2,400
SALES (est): 5.5MM **Privately Held**
SIC: 7213 8741 2389 Linen supply, clothing; business management; apparel for handicapped
HQ: Itc Accessories B.V.
Burgemeester Stramanweg 101
Amsterdam 1101
852 738-456

(G-10263)
IUNU INC
558 1st Ave S Ste 100 (98104-3832)
PHONE.................................253 307-1858
Adam Greenberg, *CEO*
EMP: 7
SALES (est): 403.2K **Privately Held**
SIC: 0762 7372 3646 Farm management services; business oriented computer software; commercial indusl & institutional electric lighting fixtures

(G-10264)
J & D MACHINE & GEAR INC
624 S Findlay St (98108-2618)
P.O. Box 80262 (98108-0262)
PHONE.................................206 762-3274
Jeffrey Epler, *President*
Joyce Epler, *Corp Secy*
Janet E Epler, *Vice Pres*
EMP: 8 **EST:** 1976
SQ FT: 2,000
SALES (est): 870K **Privately Held**
SIC: 3599 Machine shop, jobbing & repair

(G-10265)
J A JACK & SONS INC (DH)
5427 Ohio Ave S (98134-2419)
P.O. Box 80786 (98108-0786)
PHONE.................................206 762-7622
Paul Harrington, *President*
John W Miller, *Vice Pres*
Keval Patel, *Admin Sec*
▲ **EMP:** 13
SQ FT: 5,000
SALES (est): 8.2MM
SALES (corp-wide): 1.4B **Publicly Held**
SIC: 1422 Limestones, ground
HQ: Harrison Gypsum, Llc
1550 Double C Dr
Norman OK 73069
405 366-9500

(G-10266)
J AND T PRTECTIVE COATINGS LLC
8823 41st Ave Sw (98136-2555)
PHONE.................................206 498-6147
EMP: 2 **EST:** 2017
SALES (est): 96.3K **Privately Held**
SIC: 3479 Metal coating & allied service

(G-10267)
J BOZEAT & ASSOCIATES LLC
7333 California Ave Sw (98136-2112)
PHONE.................................206 937-5719
John Bozeat,
EMP: 2

Seattle - King County (G-10268)

SALES: 250K **Privately Held**
SIC: 3625 Actuators, industrial

(G-10268)
J C ROSS CO INC
Also Called: M&M Grinding
10840 Myers Way S (98168-1368)
PHONE...................................206 241-0715
Marc Pearce, *President*
EMP: 5
SQ FT: 1,500
SALES (est): 608.4K **Privately Held**
SIC: 3544 Special dies & tools; punches, forming & stamping

(G-10269)
J D OTT CO INC
2244 6th Ave S (98134-2002)
PHONE...................................206 749-0777
Rex Ott, *President*
Joshua Ott, *General Mgr*
Joseph Conrad, *Production*
Brian Cleveland, *Purchasing*
Rick Sandberg, *Network Mgr*
EMP: 108 EST: 1943
SQ FT: 75,000
SALES (est): 23.6MM **Privately Held**
WEB: www.jdott.com
SIC: 3728 3441 Aircraft parts & equipment; fabricated structural metal

(G-10270)
J K FABRICATION INC
3101 W Commodore Way (98199-1159)
PHONE...................................206 297-7400
James Kreider, *President*
EMP: 5
SQ FT: 3,000
SALES (est): 630K **Privately Held**
SIC: 3496 Miscellaneous fabricated wire products

(G-10271)
J L R DESIGN GROUP INC
557 Roy St Ste 175a (98109-4257)
PHONE...................................206 625-0070
Les Jones, *President*
Garrett Lennon, *Consultant*
EMP: 3
SQ FT: 2,000
SALES (est): 264.1K **Privately Held**
SIC: 2499 Kitchen, bathroom & household ware: wood

(G-10272)
J M CELLARS COMPANY (PA)
3329 W Laurelhurst Dr Ne (98105-5344)
PHONE...................................206 321-0052
John Bigelow, *President*
Sarah Eskenazi, *Director*
▲ EMP: 2
SALES (est): 658.4K **Privately Held**
WEB: www.jmcellars.com
SIC: 2084 7389 Wines;

(G-10273)
J M HUBER CORPORATION
5427 Ohio Ave S (98134-2419)
P.O. Box 80786 (98108-0786)
PHONE...................................206 762-4263
Steve Eckhart, *Manager*
EMP: 2
SALES (corp-wide): 916.2MM **Privately Held**
WEB: www.huber.com
SIC: 1455 Kaolin mining
PA: J.M. Huber Corporation
499 Thornall St Ste 8
Edison NJ 08837
732 603-3630

(G-10274)
J WANAMAKER CABINETRY & WDWRK
430 S 96th St (98108-4926)
PHONE...................................206 762-3494
James Wanamaker, *Principal*
EMP: 2
SALES (est): 192.2K **Privately Held**
SIC: 2431 Millwork

(G-10275)
J&DS DOWN HOME ENTPS INC
309 S Cloverdale St A13 (98108-4568)
PHONE...................................206 388-3395
Dave Lefkow, *President*
EMP: 5
SALES (est): 523.4K **Privately Held**
SIC: 2099 Seasonings: dry mixes

(G-10276)
JABIL DEF & AROSPC SVCS LLC
135 S Brandon St (98108-2231)
PHONE...................................206 257-0243
EMP: 2
SALES (corp-wide): 22.1B **Publicly Held**
SIC: 3672 Printed circuit boards
HQ: Jabil Defense And Aerospace Services, Llc
10500 Dr M L K Jr St N Mlk
Saint Petersburg FL 33716
727 577-9749

(G-10277)
JABIL INC
135 S Brandon St (98108-2231)
PHONE...................................206 257-0243
EMP: 4
SALES (corp-wide): 22.1B **Publicly Held**
SIC: 3672 Printed circuit boards
PA: Jabil Inc.
10560 Dr Martin Luther
Saint Petersburg FL 33716
727 577-9749

(G-10278)
JACKSON YUKON
3429 Airport Way S (98134-2139)
PHONE...................................206 349-8566
Keith Jackson, *Principal*
EMP: 2 EST: 2008
SALES (est): 130.3K **Privately Held**
SIC: 2064 Candy & other confectionery products

(G-10279)
JADEFLOWER CERAMICS
5025 22nd Ave Ne (98105-5706)
PHONE...................................253 720-6036
Rebekka Ferbrache, *Principal*
EMP: 2 EST: 2011
SALES (est): 91.1K **Privately Held**
SIC: 3269 Pottery products

(G-10280)
JAM DEVELOPERS INC
Also Called: Cogenix
2101 4th Ave Ste 1530 (98121-2316)
PHONE...................................206 448-5225
Mike Treat, *CEO*
Jim Whitlock, *Consultant*
EMP: 20
SALES: 2MM **Privately Held**
WEB: www.cogenix.com
SIC: 7372 Educational computer software

(G-10281)
JAMAR INDUSTRIES LLC
6014 21st Ave S (98108-2940)
P.O. Box 80052 (98108-0052)
PHONE...................................206 725-3409
Ogden Samual, *Bd of Directors*
EMP: 2 EST: 2010
SALES (est): 102.6K **Privately Held**
SIC: 3999 Manufacturing industries

(G-10282)
JAMES KOEHNLINE
2405 Nw 67th St Unit 303 (98117-5857)
P.O. Box 30134 (98113-0134)
PHONE...................................206 783-6846
James Koehnline, *Principal*
EMP: 2
SALES (est): 74.4K **Privately Held**
SIC: 2821 Plastics materials & resins

(G-10283)
JAMES MOORE ◆
726 N 46th St .(98103-6505)
PHONE...................................206 799-0399
Michael Meagher, *Chairman*
EMP: 2 EST: 2018
SALES (est): 85.9K **Privately Held**
SIC: 3571 Electronic computers

(G-10284)
JAMIE KINNEY
3620 Burke Ave N Apt 1 (98103-8350)
PHONE...................................206 953-9302
Jamie Kinney, *Principal*
EMP: 2
SALES (est): 87.2K **Privately Held**
SIC: 3711 Motor vehicles & car bodies

(G-10285)
JAN SCIENTIFIC INC
Also Called: Jansi
4726 11th Ave Ne Ste 101 (98105-4678)
PHONE...................................206 632-1814
V Nagarajan, *CEO*
EMP: 2
SALES (est): 700K **Privately Held**
SIC: 8999 3827 Scientific consulting; optical instruments & lenses

(G-10286)
JAYWICK WOODWORKS LLC
5551 16th Ave S (98108-2826)
PHONE...................................206 793-7208
Jason Wickham, *Principal*
EMP: 2
SALES (est): 88.3K **Privately Held**
SIC: 2431 Millwork

(G-10287)
JAZZIE SOFTWARE
4815 Calif Ave Sw Apt 210 (98116-4468)
PHONE...................................206 905-7411
Tim Young, *Owner*
EMP: 2
SALES (est): 126K **Privately Held**
SIC: 7372 Prepackaged software

(G-10288)
JEEVA WIRELESS INC
4000 Mason Rd Ste 300 (98195-0001)
P.O. Box 352141 (98195-2141)
PHONE...................................206 214-6177
Joshua Smith, *Principal*
Shyamnath Gollakota, *Principal*
Vamsi Talla, *Principal*
Bryce Kellogg, *Info Tech Mgr*
EMP: 6 EST: 2015
SALES (est): 304.3K **Privately Held**
SIC: 3663 Telemetering equipment, electronic

(G-10289)
JEFF POTTER
6207 Linden Ave N Apt 1 (98103-5676)
PHONE...................................206 819-4224
Jeff Potter, *Principal*
EMP: 2
SALES (est): 62.3K **Privately Held**
SIC: 2015 Poultry slaughtering & processing

(G-10290)
JEFFREY JAMES LLC
Also Called: Jeffrey James Botanical
201 Mcgraw St (98109-2041)
PHONE...................................562 541-6976
Jeffrey James, *President*
EMP: 5
SQ FT: 1,200
SALES (est): 182.1K **Privately Held**
SIC: 2844 Cosmetic preparations

(G-10291)
JELLYFISH BREWING COMPANY
7566 Roosevelt Way Ne (98115-4221)
PHONE...................................206 517-4497
Thomas Stevens, *Principal*
EMP: 7
SALES (est): 110.5K **Privately Held**
SIC: 2082 Malt beverages

(G-10292)
JERI -OHS
10420 65th Ave S (98178-2505)
PHONE...................................206 722-5918
Geri M Flynn, *Owner*
George H Flynn, *Co-Owner*
EMP: 4 EST: 1992
SALES (est): 146.4K **Privately Held**
WEB: www.jeri-ohs.com
SIC: 3161 3356 Traveling bags; tin

(G-10293)
JET CITY IMAGING LLC
Also Called: US Printing
6501 E Marginal Way S B (98108-3221)
PHONE...................................206 447-0600
Bruce Wiggins,
EMP: 2
SQ FT: 4,200
SALES (est): 339.5K **Privately Held**
SIC: 2752 Commercial printing, offset

(G-10294)
JET CITY VTG TEES
5122 S Dawson St (98118-2122)
PHONE...................................310 500-0577
Brendon Mendoza, *Principal*
EMP: 2 EST: 2017
SALES (est): 83.6K **Privately Held**
SIC: 2759 Screen printing

(G-10295)
JET PARTS ENGINEERING LLC
4772 Ohio Ave S (98134-2326)
PHONE...................................206 281-0963
Anu Goel, *Principal*
Arpana Goel, *Principal*
EMP: 28
SQ FT: 5,500
SALES (est): 7MM **Privately Held**
WEB: www.jetpartsengineering.com
SIC: 3728 Aircraft parts & equipment

(G-10296)
JGC FOOD CO LLC (HQ)
1425 4th Ave Ste 420 (98101-2218)
PHONE...................................206 622-0420
Joshua Green III, *CEO*
EMP: 10
SALES (est): 102.1MM
SALES (corp-wide): 170.6MM **Privately Held**
SIC: 2099 2092 Food preparations; fresh or frozen fish or seafood chowders, soups & stews
PA: Joshua Green Corporation
1425 4th Ave Ste 420
Seattle WA
206 622-0420

(G-10297)
JJ 206 LLC (PA)
Also Called: Juju Joints
2228 1st Ave Ste B (98121-3621)
PHONE...................................206 453-0186
EMP: 8
SALES: 875K **Privately Held**
SIC: 3674 7371 Solid state electronic devices; computer software development

(G-10298)
JJ&D SIGNS INC
Also Called: Heath Northwest
727 S 96th St (98108-4922)
PHONE...................................206 623-3100
EMP: 7
SQ FT: 10,000
SALES (est): 590.4K **Privately Held**
SIC: 3993 Signs And Advertising Specialties

(G-10299)
JM SOFTWARE
3413 Nw 57th St (98107-3350)
PHONE...................................206 453-3544
Justin Myers, *Principal*
EMP: 2
SALES (est): 120.6K **Privately Held**
SIC: 7372 Prepackaged software

(G-10300)
JODAL MANUFACTURING
1410 Sw 102nd St (98146-3755)
P.O. Box 80424 (98108-0424)
PHONE...................................206 763-8848
Joe Ditschinger, *Owner*
EMP: 3
SQ FT: 2,000
SALES: 90K **Privately Held**
SIC: 3449 3599 Bars, concrete reinforcing: fabricated steel; machine shop, jobbing & repair

(G-10301)
JOHN DEELY
7047 19th Ave Ne (98115-5703)
PHONE...................................206 527-8218
John Deely, *Principal*
EMP: 2
SALES (est): 88.3K **Privately Held**
SIC: 3661 Telephone & telegraph apparatus

GEOGRAPHIC SECTION

(G-10302)
JOHNSON CONTROLS
9520 10th Ave S Ste 100 (98108-5068)
PHONE 206 291-1400
Darrel Sackwar, *Manager*
EMP: 111 **Privately Held**
WEB: www.simplexgrinnell.com
SIC: 3669 1731 1711 Emergency alarms; fire detection & burglar alarm systems specialization; fire sprinkler system installation
HQ: Johnson Controls Fire Protection Lp
6600 Congress Ave
Boca Raton FL 33487
561 988-7200

(G-10303)
JOHNSON WARD WINERY
1445 Elliott Ave W (98119-3104)
PHONE 206 284-2635
Charles Johnson, *Bd of Directors*
EMP: 5
SALES (est): 263.6K **Privately Held**
SIC: 5149 2084 Wine makers' equipment & supplies; wines

(G-10304)
JOINTMETRIX MEDICAL LLC
4111 E Madison St Ste 68 (98112-3241)
PHONE 425 246-7799
David Marver, *CEO*
EMP: 5 **EST:** 2011
SALES (est): 352.9K **Privately Held**
SIC: 3841 7389 Diagnostic apparatus, medical;

(G-10305)
JONATHAN QUINN BARNETT LTD
116 Vine St (98121-1439)
PHONE 206 322-2152
Jonathan Barnett, *President*
EMP: 6
SALES (est): 548.2K **Privately Held**
WEB: www.jqbltd.com
SIC: 3732 5091 Boat building & repairing; sporting & recreation goods

(G-10306)
JONBOY CARAMELS LLC
4900 9th Ave Nw Ste 100 (98107-3659)
PHONE 206 850-4225
Jason Alm, *Mng Member*
Jonathan Sue,
EMP: 5
SALES (est): 190K **Privately Held**
SIC: 2064 Candy & other confectionery products

(G-10307)
JONES SODA CO
66 S Hanford St Ste 150 (98134-1868)
PHONE 206 624-3357
Michael M Fleming, *Ch of Bd*
Jennifer L Cue, *President*
Eric Chastain, *COO*
Max Schroedl, *CFO*
EMP: 25
SQ FT: 6,500
SALES: 12.5MM **Privately Held**
WEB: www.jonessoda.com
SIC: 2086 Soft drinks: packaged in cans, bottles, etc.; carbonated soft drinks, bottled & canned

(G-10308)
JOURNAL OF JAPANESE STUDIES
Also Called: SOCIETY FOR JAPANESE STUDIES
University Of Washington (98195-0001)
P.O. Box 353650 (98195-3650)
PHONE 206 543-9302
Marie Anchorvoguy, *Principal*
John Treat, *Principal*
Martha Walsh, *Principal*
Kenneth Pyle, *Chairman*
EMP: 3
SALES: 95.9K **Privately Held**
SIC: 2721 Trade journals: publishing & printing

(G-10309)
JOYLUX INC
1430 34th Ave (98122-3334)
PHONE 206 219-6444
Colette D Courtion, *CEO*
Peter Weiss, *CFO*
Colette Courtion, *Officer*
EMP: 10
SALES: 1.5MM **Privately Held**
SIC: 3841 Surgical & medical instruments

(G-10310)
JPMORGAN CHASE BANK NAT ASSN
20 Mercer St (98109-4006)
PHONE 206 505-1501
EMP: 2
SALES (corp-wide): 131.4B **Publicly Held**
SIC: 3644 Insulators & insulation materials, electrical
HQ: Jpmorgan Chase Bank, National Association
1111 Polaris Pkwy
Columbus OH 43240
614 436-3055

(G-10311)
JRJ INC
Also Called: Northern Land Management
9517 35th Ave Ne 1a (98115-2570)
P.O. Box 48, Granite Falls (98252-0048)
PHONE 360 691-2528
Jeff Burnett, *CEO*
EMP: 18 **EST:** 1992
SALES (est): 1MM **Privately Held**
SIC: 2411 Logging

(G-10312)
JUBILEE WOODWORKS LLC
832 16th Ave (98122-4528)
PHONE 206 734-0344
Mark A Johnson, *President*
EMP: 2
SALES (est): 127.4K **Privately Held**
SIC: 2431 Millwork

(G-10313)
JUDITH AMES FURNITURE
2118 E Olive St (98122-2936)
PHONE 206 324-8538
Judith Ames, *Owner*
EMP: 2
SALES (est): 90.4K **Privately Held**
SIC: 2599 Furniture & fixtures

(G-10314)
JUICE & JAM INC
Also Called: Juice and Jam
520 Pike St Ste 1440 (98101-4001)
PHONE 206 734-5136
Nathan Brown, *President*
Kristen Brown, *Vice Pres*
EMP: 2
SALES (est): 67.6K **Privately Held**
SIC: 7929 7819 2741 Jazz music group or artists; sound (effects & music production), motion picture; music book & sheet music publishing

(G-10315)
JULIAS GLOWS
11602 59th Ave S (98178-2946)
PHONE 206 722-0411
Julia Coleman, *Principal*
EMP: 2
SALES (est): 117.8K **Privately Held**
SIC: 3999 Candles

(G-10316)
JUNK CAR REMOVAL 1
5903 11th Ave Nw (98107-2906)
PHONE 206 369-7832
Ken Stoddard, *Principal*
EMP: 2
SALES (est): 174.9K **Privately Held**
SIC: 3531 Automobile wrecker hoists

(G-10317)
JUNO THERAPEUTICS INC (HQ)
400 Dexter Ave N Ste 1200 (98109-5094)
PHONE 206 582-1600
Hans E Bishop, *President*
Craig Beasley, *Vice Pres*
Michael Covington, *Vice Pres*
James Howard, *Vice Pres*
Amy Mills, *Vice Pres*
EMP: 24
SQ FT: 298,700
SALES: 111.8MM
SALES (corp-wide): 15.2B **Publicly Held**
SIC: 2836 8731 Biological products, except diagnostic; biotechnical research, commercial
PA: Celgene Corporation
86 Morris Ave
Summit NJ 07901
908 673-9000

(G-10318)
JUST BIOTHERAPEUTICS INC
401 Terry Ave N (98109-5263)
PHONE 206 651-5094
James N Thomas, *CEO*
Yining Zhao, *Partner*
Victor P Fung, *COO*
Jason Eckert, *Engineer*
Suzanne Jones, *Controller*
EMP: 70
SALES (est): 2.8MM **Privately Held**
SIC: 2836 8731 Biological products, except diagnostic; biotechnical research, commercial

(G-10319)
JUSTIN-GRACE INC
7950 Seward Park Ave S (98118-4251)
PHONE 206 992-4292
Jerry Bannon, *Principal*
EMP: 2
SALES (est): 56.5K **Privately Held**
SIC: 7372 Prepackaged software

(G-10320)
K J M ELECTRIC CO INC
521 S Monroe St (98109-4350)
P.O. Box 2270, Issaquah (98027-0102)
PHONE 206 624-5294
Kamal Joe Masri, *President*
Magda England, *Vice Pres*
EMP: 9 **EST:** 1975
SQ FT: 7,000
SALES (est): 744.2K **Privately Held**
SIC: 7694 1731 Electric motor repair; electrical work

(G-10321)
K&G SCENTS
11433 70th Pl S (98178-3004)
PHONE 206 380-1831
Anthony Gowdy, *Principal*
EMP: 2 **EST:** 2013
SALES (est): 103.5K **Privately Held**
SIC: 2844 Toilet preparations

(G-10322)
K2 SPORTS LLC (PA)
Also Called: K2 Sports USA
413 Pine St Ste 300 (98101-3670)
PHONE 206 805-4800
Rudi Gothenquist, *Manager*
Joe Lawler,
◆ **EMP:** 180 **EST:** 1970
SQ FT: 160,000
SALES (est): 7.3MM **Privately Held**
WEB: www.k2ski.com
SIC: 3949 5091 Snow skis; winter sports equipment; sporting & recreation goods; skiing equipment

(G-10323)
K2 SPORTS LLC
4501 6th Ave S (98108-1704)
PHONE 206 805-4800
Anthony De Rocco, *President*
EMP: 5
SALES (corp-wide): 7.3MM **Privately Held**
SIC: 3949 Snow skis; winter sports equipment
PA: K2 Sports, Llc
413 Pine St Ste 300
Seattle WA 98101
206 805-4800

(G-10324)
KACI WOODWORKS LLC
4225 Francis Ave N Apt B (98103-7130)
PHONE 206 601-0395
Hakim Kaci, *Principal*
EMP: 3
SALES (est): 113.6K **Privately Held**
SIC: 2431 Millwork

(G-10325)
KAMI STEEL US INC
Also Called: Kami Tech
2001 W Grfeld St Ste C110 (98119)
PHONE 206 283-9655
Claus Eskildsen, *President*
Ann Christiensen, *Manager*
▲ **EMP:** 10
SALES: 1.7MM **Privately Held**
WEB: www.kamisteel.com
SIC: 3556 Fish & shellfish processing machinery

(G-10326)
KAMILCHE COMPANY (PA)
1301 5th Ave Ste 2700 (98101-2675)
PHONE 206 224-5800
Colin Moseley, *President*
Reed Jr Wm G, *Vice Pres*
Colley Nancy L, *Treasurer*
Bill Pedersen, *Finance Dir*
Kyle Alexander, *Accounts Mgr*
◆ **EMP:** 2
SQ FT: 33,000
SALES (est): 242.9MM **Privately Held**
SIC: 2621 2611 2421 2435 Paper mills; pulp mills; lumber: rough, sawed or planed; plywood, hardwood or hardwood faced; doors, wood

(G-10327)
KAPSTONE SEATTLE
5901 E Marginal Way S (98134-2414)
PHONE 206 762-7170
Lance Meyer, *Manager*
EMP: 7 **EST:** 2013
SALES (est): 1.1MM **Privately Held**
SIC: 2653 Corrugated & solid fiber boxes

(G-10328)
KARLAS HAND BINDERY INC
Also Called: Global Fulfillment
4 S Idaho St (98134-1119)
PHONE 206 405-3350
Julie Hiatt, *CEO*
Robyn Bayless, *Vice Pres*
Randy Gray, *Director*
▲ **EMP:** 20
SQ FT: 47,000
SALES (est): 1.6MM **Privately Held**
WEB: www.gloful.com
SIC: 2789 7389 7319 Binding & repair of books, magazines & pamphlets; subscription fulfillment services: magazine, newspaper, etc.; coupon distribution

(G-10329)
KASTORIA INC
4420 Burke Ave N (98103-7536)
PHONE 206 633-4170
Linda Marie, *President*
EMP: 4
SALES (est): 210K **Privately Held**
SIC: 2032 5142 Canned specialties; packaged frozen goods

(G-10330)
KATERRA INC
901 5th Ave Ste 3210 (98164-2064)
PHONE 650 422-3572
Brad Knight, *CEO*
EMP: 913
SALES (corp-wide): 125MM **Privately Held**
SIC: 1389 Construction, repair & dismantling services
PA: Katerra Inc.
2494 Sand Hill Rd Ste 100
Menlo Park CA 94025
650 422-3572

(G-10331)
KATZ MEDIA GROUP INC
Also Called: Katz Television Group
701 5th Ave Ste 4200 (98104-7047)
PHONE 206 777-1800
Paul Claeys, *VP Sales*
EMP: 9 **Publicly Held**
WEB: www.ctvsales.com
SIC: 3663 Radio receiver networks
HQ: Katz Media Group, Inc.
125 W 55th St Fl 11
New York NY 10019

Seattle - King County (G-10332)

(G-10332)
KAVU INC (PA)
Also Called: Kavu World
1515 Nw 51st St (98107-4735)
PHONE..................................206 456-9305
Barry Barr, *President*
Nicholas Young, *Production*
Desiree Hastie, *Design Engr*
Joe Pinsoneault, *Treasurer*
Hai Nguyen, *Marketing Staff*
▲ **EMP:** 16
SALES (est): 1.4MM **Privately Held**
WEB: www.kavu.com
SIC: 2353 Hats & caps

(G-10333)
KC WHEELWRIGHT
2258 15th Ave W (98119-2418)
PHONE..................................206 799-9822
EMP: 3
SALES (est): 268.3K **Privately Held**
SIC: 2836 Mfg Biological Products

(G-10334)
KEAN CENTER
811 1st Ave Ste 475 (98104-1454)
PHONE..................................206 465-4879
Mark Lawless, *Principal*
EMP: 3 **EST:** 2007
SALES (est): 244K **Privately Held**
SIC: 3841 Skin grafting equipment

(G-10335)
KEMEERA INCORPORATED
Also Called: Seattle Office and Prod Ctr
4302 Stone Way N (98103-7421)
PHONE..................................206 582-1062
EMP: 25
SALES (corp-wide): 26.9MM **Privately Held**
SIC: 5045 3577 Printers, computer; printers, computer
PA: Kemeera Incorporated
620 3rd St
Oakland CA 94607
510 281-9000

(G-10336)
KENCO CONSTRUCTION INC (PA)
Also Called: Kci
101 Nickerson St Ste 330 (98109-1620)
P.O. Box 70568 (98127-0568)
PHONE..................................206 783-3300
Ken Macdonald, *President*
Ian Elliott, *VP Opers*
Linda Schrubbe, *Controller*
EMP: 28
SQ FT: 2,400
SALES: 7.6MM **Privately Held**
WEB: www.kencoci.com
SIC: 2522 Panel systems & partitions, office: except wood

(G-10337)
KENNETH A EDLEMAN
Also Called: Teeter's Metal Fabricators
9422 Roosevelt Way Ne (98115-2844)
PHONE..................................206 524-2814
Kenneth A Edleman, *Owner*
Kenneth Edleman, *Owner*
EMP: 2
SQ FT: 2,700
SALES: 200K **Privately Held**
WEB: www.teetersmetalfab.com
SIC: 3444 3351 Sheet metal specialties, not stamped; copper rolling & drawing

(G-10338)
KENTUCKY CHROME INDUSTRIES
3245 31st Ave W (98199-2739)
PHONE..................................816 522-1783
Greg Franklin, *Principal*
EMP: 2 **EST:** 2014
SALES (est): 108.9K **Privately Held**
SIC: 3999 Manufacturing industries

(G-10339)
KEVIN PHILBIN YACHT DETAIL
2842 Nw 67th St (98117-6235)
PHONE..................................206 949-0162
Kevin Philbin, *Principal*
EMP: 2

SALES (est): 187.3K **Privately Held**
SIC: 3732 Boat building & repairing

(G-10340)
KEYPICT
6507 57th Ave Ne (98115-7830)
PHONE..................................206 522-5201
Steve Flenniken, *Principal*
EMP: 2
SALES (est): 136.3K **Privately Held**
SIC: 7372 Prepackaged software

(G-10341)
KHEPER GAMES INC
440 S Holgate St (98134-1505)
PHONE..................................206 782-2201
Brian Pellham, *President*
Tony Pellham, *VP Opers*
Cathy Ziegler, *Sales Staff*
Jacob Brady, *Graphic Designe*
▲ **EMP:** 13
SQ FT: 14,000
SALES (est): 2.2MM **Privately Held**
WEB: www.khepergames.com
SIC: 3944 Games, toys & children's vehicles

(G-10342)
KIADIS PHARMA US CORPORATION
1812 10th Ave E (98102-4215)
PHONE..................................585 397-1074
Arthur Lahr, *CEO*
Amy Sullivan, *Senior VP*
Scott A Holmes, *CFO*
Dirk De Naeyer, *Officer*
Robert Friesen, *Officer*
EMP: 6
SALES (est): 409.2K
SALES (corp-wide): 6.9MM **Privately Held**
SIC: 2834 Pharmaceutical preparations
PA: Kiadis Pharma N.V.
Paasheuvelweg 25 A
Amsterdam
202 405-250

(G-10343)
KILN CORE HOLDINGS LLC
601 Union St Ste 4950 (98101-3951)
PHONE..................................206 859-1114
EMP: 3 **EST:** 2014
SALES (est): 158.6K **Privately Held**
SIC: 3559 Kilns

(G-10344)
KINDEX PHARMACEUTICALS INC
800 5th Ave Ste 4100 (98104-3100)
PHONE..................................206 922-2912
Jeffrey Bland, *CEO*
Neile Grayson, *Vice Pres*
Lincoln Bouillon, *CFO*
EMP: 3
SALES (est): 344.8K **Privately Held**
SIC: 2834 Chlorination tablets & kits (water purification); druggists' preparations (pharmaceuticals)

(G-10345)
KING ELECTRICAL MFG CO
9131 10th Ave S (98108-4612)
PHONE..................................206 762-0400
Robert E Wilson, *President*
Brad Wilson, *Vice Pres*
Stan Batten, *Mfg Staff*
Robert Wilson II, *Treasurer*
Sara Killham, *Cust Svc Mgr*
▲ **EMP:** 100 **EST:** 1958
SQ FT: 150,000
SALES (est): 27.3MM **Privately Held**
WEB: www.king-electric.com
SIC: 3634 3585 3567 Heating units, electric (radiant heat): baseboard or wall; heating equipment, complete; heating & air conditioning combination units; industrial furnaces & ovens

(G-10346)
KISKA SEA NORTHERN LLC
2157 N Northlake Way # 210 (98103-9184)
PHONE..................................206 784-5000
Chris Swasand, *President*
Craig Cross, *Administration*
EMP: 6

SALES (est): 345.2K **Privately Held**
SIC: 2092 Fresh or frozen packaged fish

(G-10347)
KNITWEAR NETWORK INC
1507 30th Ave S Lowr (98144-3905)
PHONE..................................206 353-1337
Helen Sharp, *President*
EMP: 2 **EST:** 1992
SQ FT: 400
SALES: 500K **Privately Held**
SIC: 2253 Sweaters & sweater coats, knit

(G-10348)
KNOLL INC
1200 5th Ave Ste 2000 (98101-3100)
PHONE..................................206 624-0174
Karen Webb, *Principal*
Lisa Cooper, *Branch Mgr*
EMP: 10 **Publicly Held**
WEB: www.knoll.com
SIC: 2521 Wood office furniture
PA: Knoll, Inc.
1235 Water St
East Greenville PA 18041

(G-10349)
KNOW LABS INC (PA)
500 Union St Ste 810 (98101-2332)
PHONE..................................206 903-1351
Phillip A Bosua, *CEO*
Ronald P Erickson, *Ch of Bd*
Mark Tapsak, *Vice Pres*
EMP: 15
SQ FT: 943
SALES: 4.3MM **Publicly Held**
WEB: www.visualant.net
SIC: 3829 Measuring & controlling devices

(G-10350)
KOCH MACHINE INC
10623 16th Ave Sw (98146-2077)
PHONE..................................206 241-7178
Fax: 206 244-0344
EMP: 3
SQ FT: 2,600
SALES: 320K **Privately Held**
SIC: 3599 5088 Mfg Industrial Machinery Whol Transportation Equipment

(G-10351)
KOF ENTERPRISES LLC
Also Called: King's Oriental Foods
1328 S Weller St (98144-2051)
PHONE..................................206 328-2972
John Cao, *President*
▲ **EMP:** 10
SALES (est): 1.5MM **Privately Held**
SIC: 2035 2045 2099 Soy sauce; prepared flour mixes & doughs; packaged combination products: pasta, rice & potato

(G-10352)
KOKAKO SOFTWARE
1409 N 41st St (98103-8141)
PHONE..................................425 922-1115
EMP: 2 **EST:** 2010
SALES (est): 107.5K **Privately Held**
SIC: 7372 Prepackaged Software Services

(G-10353)
KOLLMAR SHEET METAL WORKS INC
941 S Nebraska St (98108-2747)
PHONE..................................206 283-2330
Jordan Lorz, *President*
EMP: 4 **EST:** 2011
SALES: 800K **Privately Held**
SIC: 3444 Sheet metal specialties, not stamped

(G-10354)
KONNEKTI INCORPORATED
2621 2nd Ave Unit 1001 (98121-1256)
PHONE..................................925 878-5083
Shawn Fallah, *President*
EMP: 5
SALES (est): 128.9K **Privately Held**
SIC: 7372 Application computer software

(G-10355)
KOPIUS ENERGY SOLUTIONS LLC
8837 39th Ave Sw (98136-2511)
PHONE..................................425 322-2853
John Plaza,
EMP: 3 **EST:** 2015
SALES (est): 146.6K **Privately Held**
SIC: 2869 Industrial organic chemicals

(G-10356)
KOREA TIMES LOS ANGELES INC
Also Called: Korean Times
12532 Aurora Ave N (98133-8036)
PHONE..................................206 622-2229
Yeo Cheun Yun, *Manager*
EMP: 20
SQ FT: 9,070
SALES (corp-wide): 83.9MM **Privately Held**
WEB: www.koreatimeshawaii.com
SIC: 5963 2711 Newspapers, home delivery, not by printers or publishers; newspapers
PA: The Korea Times Los Angeles Inc
3731 Wilshire Blvd
Los Angeles CA 90010
323 692-2000

(G-10357)
KOTELNIKOV ZINAIDA
1908 Pike Pl (98101-1013)
PHONE..................................206 728-6195
Zinaida Kotelnikov, *Principal*
EMP: 2
SALES (est): 73.1K **Privately Held**
SIC: 2051 Bakery: wholesale or wholesale/retail combined

(G-10358)
KRISPY KREME DOUGHNUTS
12505 Aurora Ave N (98133-8037)
PHONE..................................206 316-7090
Gerard Centioli, *Principal*
EMP: 6
SALES (est): 109.4K **Privately Held**
SIC: 5461 2051 Doughnuts; doughnuts, except frozen

(G-10359)
KRONOS INCORPORATED
Also Called: Kronos Northwest
701 5th Ave Ste 4200 (98104-7047)
PHONE..................................206 696-1505
Jeannie Ryan, *Branch Mgr*
EMP: 25
SALES (corp-wide): 1.1B **Privately Held**
WEB: www.kronos.com
SIC: 7372 Business oriented computer software
HQ: Kronos Incorporated
900 Chelmsford St # 312
Lowell MA 01851
978 250-9800

(G-10360)
KRYKI SPORTS
200 W Comstock St Apt 202 (98119-3595)
PHONE..................................206 660-7359
Mike Hone, *Owner*
EMP: 4 **EST:** 2010
SALES (est): 271.4K **Privately Held**
SIC: 3465 Body parts, automobile: stamped metal

(G-10361)
KUGHLER CO INC
4601 Shilshole Ave Nw Main (98107-4718)
PHONE..................................206 789-0667
Thomas Kughler, *Manager*
EMP: 4 **EST:** 1957
SALES (est): 556.8K **Privately Held**
WEB: www.kughler.com
SIC: 3537 Lift trucks, industrial: fork, platform, straddle, etc.

(G-10362)
KURT BLUME
Also Called: Art Publishing Direct
511 N 73rd St (98103-5132)
PHONE..................................206 371-9337
Kurt Blume, *Owner*
EMP: 2

GEOGRAPHIC SECTION
Seattle - King County (G-10396)

SALES (est): 72K **Privately Held**
SIC: 2731 Book publishing

(G-10363)
KUSHCO
Also Called: Custom Hats and Apparels
11431 Rainier Ave S (98178-3954)
PHONE..................................206 772-9333
Bryan Smith,
Javarie Mohr,
Robin Smith,
EMP: 3
SQ FT: 1,500
SALES: 60K **Privately Held**
SIC: 5699 2326 5137 Customized clothing & apparel; men's & boys' work clothing; women's & children's clothing

(G-10364)
KUSHCO CLOTHING LLC
Also Called: Custom Hats & Apparel
11431 Rainier Ave S (98178-3954)
PHONE..................................206 772-9333
Bryan Earl Smith,
Javarie Mohr,
Robyn Smith,
EMP: 3 EST: 2015
SQ FT: 1,400
SALES (est): 20K **Privately Held**
SIC: 2353 Hats & caps

(G-10365)
KUSINA FILLIPINA
Also Called: Kusina Filipina Rest & Bky
7612 S 135th St (98178-5154)
PHONE..................................206 322-9433
Amando Vicencio, *Owner*
EMP: 6
SQ FT: 2,000
SALES (est): 281K **Privately Held**
SIC: 5812 2052 7841 5947 Eating places; bakery products, dry; video tape rental; gift shop

(G-10366)
KUSTOM PRINTING INC
Also Called: Star Printing
3243 20th Ave W (98199-2301)
PHONE..................................206 282-8400
Fax: 206 283-1213
EMP: 12
SQ FT: 9,000
SALES (est): 1.5MM **Privately Held**
SIC: 2752 Lithographic Commercial Printing

(G-10367)
LA MARZOCCO INTERNATIONAL LLC
1553 Nw Ballard Way (98107-4712)
PHONE..................................206 706-9104
▲ EMP: 6
SALES (est): 840K **Privately Held**
SIC: 3589 Mfg Service Industry Machinery

(G-10368)
LA MEXICANA INC (PA)
Also Called: Lamexicana Tortilla Factory
10020 14th Ave Sw (98146-3703)
PHONE..................................206 763-1488
Keith Bloxham, *President*
Sandra Bloxham, *Treasurer*
EMP: 50
SQ FT: 14,000
SALES (est): 9.9MM **Privately Held**
WEB: www.habero.com
SIC: 2099 5499 Tortillas, fresh or refrigerated; sauces: gravy, dressing & dip mixes; gourmet food stores

(G-10369)
LABEL COMPANY INC
430 S 96th St Ste 8 (98108-4926)
P.O. Box 338, Lynnwood (98046-0338)
PHONE..................................206 568-6000
James Yoo, *President*
▲ EMP: 3
SQ FT: 10,000
SALES: 1MM **Privately Held**
SIC: 2679 Labels, paper: made from purchased material

(G-10370)
LACHSELIAN DISTILLERY
1712 1st Ave S (98134-1404)
PHONE..................................206 743-8070
Tracy Bell, *Principal*
EMP: 4
SALES (est): 224.9K **Privately Held**
SIC: 2899 Distilled water

(G-10371)
LAFARGE NORTH AMERICA INC
5400 W Marginal Way Sw (98106-1517)
PHONE..................................206 937-8025
Joe Pennings, *Manager*
Monty Wilson, *Supervisor*
EMP: 100
SALES (corp-wide): 27.6B **Privately Held**
WEB: www.lafargenorthamerica.com
SIC: 3241 Cement, hydraulic
HQ: Lafarge North America Inc.
8700 W Bryn Mawr Ave
Chicago IL 60631
773 372-1000

(G-10372)
LAGUNAMOON BEAUTY INTL LTD LLC
12345 Lake City Way Ne (98125-5401)
PHONE..................................480 925-7577
Jianzhong Yang, *Governor*
EMP: 10
SALES (est): 318K **Privately Held**
SIC: 6799 7372 Commodity contract trading companies; application computer software

(G-10373)
LAGUNITAS
1550 Nw 49th St (98107-4731)
PHONE..................................206 784-2230
EMP: 5 EST: 2017
SALES (est): 354K **Privately Held**
SIC: 2082 Malt beverages

(G-10374)
LAMMY INDUSTRIES INC
Also Called: Sony Sewing Co
25 S Hanford St (98134-1807)
PHONE..................................206 654-0010
Mike Nguyen, *President*
EMP: 35
SQ FT: 30,000
SALES (est): 1.9MM **Privately Held**
SIC: 7389 3161 2393 Sewing contractor; luggage; textile bags

(G-10375)
LANE CHESTNUT PRINTS
10001 49th Ave Ne (98125-8131)
PHONE..................................206 397-3108
EMP: 2
SALES (est): 160K **Privately Held**
SIC: 2752 Lithographic Commercial Printing

(G-10376)
LANE MT SILICA CO (HQ)
5427 Ohio Ave S (98134-2419)
PHONE..................................206 762-7622
Thomas Hemphill, *President*
Dale Snow, *Treasurer*
EMP: 3 EST: 1959
SQ FT: 5,000
SALES (est): 6.6MM **Privately Held**
SIC: 1446 Silica mining
PA: Hemphill Brothers Inc
375 Ericksen Ave Ne
Bainbridge Island WA 98110
206 842-0748

(G-10377)
LANTERN BREWING LLC
938 N 95th St (98103-3206)
PHONE..................................206 729-5350
Chris Engdahl,
EMP: 7
SALES (est): 503.4K **Privately Held**
SIC: 2082 Malt beverages

(G-10378)
LARSEN EQUIPMENT DESIGN INC
1117 Nw 52nd St (98107-5130)
PHONE..................................206 789-5121
Erik Larsen, *President*
Pamela Larsen, *CFO*
EMP: 9
SQ FT: 3,000
SALES (est): 600K **Privately Held**
WEB: www.larsenequipment.com
SIC: 3541 Lathes, metal cutting & polishing

(G-10379)
LATITUDE 47 DISTILLERS
2801 1st Ave Apt 1005 (98121-1139)
PHONE..................................206 794-0852
EMP: 2
SALES (est): 88.2K **Privately Held**
SIC: 2085 Distilled & blended liquors

(G-10380)
LAUD SOCIAL INC
1802 11th Ave (98122-2421)
PHONE..................................213 797-0744
Thomas Kirkby, *CEO*
EMP: 3 EST: 2015
SALES (est): 138.1K **Privately Held**
SIC: 7372 Application computer software

(G-10381)
LAURA TOWNSEND-FABER
5730 Ne 60th St (98115-7918)
PHONE..................................206 517-5739
Laura M Townsend-Faber, *Owner*
EMP: 2
SALES (est): 81.4K **Privately Held**
SIC: 2392 Comforters & quilts: made from purchased materials

(G-10382)
LAURELCREST II LLC (PA)
12033 12th Ave Nw (98177-4620)
PHONE..................................206 922-3634
Michael Bernstein, *CEO*
▲ EMP: 5
SALES (est): 507.4K **Privately Held**
SIC: 2299 Jute & flax textile products

(G-10383)
LAURELHURST CELLARS LLC
3935 9th Ave S (98108-5210)
PHONE..................................206 992-2875
Greg Smallwood, *Principal*
Dave Halbgewachs, *Principal*
EMP: 2
SALES (est): 129.3K **Privately Held**
SIC: 2084 5921 Wines; wine

(G-10384)
LAVENDER HEART LTD (PA)
3212 Cascadia Ave S (98144-7000)
PHONE..................................206 568-4441
Holly Henderson, *President*
Elizabeth Nakamisha, *Vice Pres*
EMP: 4
SALES (est): 626.5K **Privately Held**
SIC: 3999 5947 Artificial trees & flowers; gift shop

(G-10385)
LAWRENCE MILNER
Also Called: Biscottea
3020 W Garfield St (98199-4244)
PHONE..................................360 860-1924
Lawrence Milner, *Owner*
▲ EMP: 2
SALES (est): 133.6K **Privately Held**
SIC: 2051 Breads, rolls & buns

(G-10386)
LAWSUITE TECHNOLOGIES LLC
506 2nd Ave Ste 1400 (98104-2329)
PHONE..................................206 349-2227
Alexandra Kennedy,
EMP: 4
SQ FT: 200
SALES (est): 136.1K **Privately Held**
SIC: 7372 Application computer software

(G-10387)
LAWYER AVENUE
4701 Sw Admiral Way (98116-2340)
PHONE..................................425 243-7958
William Kane, *Director*
Richard Carlton, *Deputy Dir*
EMP: 4
SALES (est): 180.5K **Privately Held**
SIC: 2741 Miscellaneous publishing

(G-10388)
LAZERWOOD INDUSTRIES
1103 E Pike St (98122-3915)
PHONE..................................206 650-2367
Erick Waldman, *Principal*
EMP: 3
SALES (est): 128.7K **Privately Held**
SIC: 3999 Manufacturing industries

(G-10389)
LE BIJOU CORPORATION
1424 4th Ave Ste 712 (98101-2217)
PHONE..................................206 622-9453
Carlos Costabel, *President*
EMP: 2
SQ FT: 645
SALES (est): 209K **Privately Held**
SIC: 3915 5094 Jewelers' castings; jewelry

(G-10390)
LE LABO
921 E Pine St (98122-3843)
PHONE..................................206 420-2835
EMP: 2
SALES (est): 107.4K **Privately Held**
SIC: 2844 Perfumes & colognes

(G-10391)
LEAD CAT PRESS LLC
1200 Boylston Ave Apt 302 (98101-2813)
PHONE..................................206 349-3226
Susan Palmer, *Principal*
EMP: 2
SALES (est): 139.7K **Privately Held**
SIC: 2741 Miscellaneous publishing

(G-10392)
LEADSCORZ INC
10 Harrison St Ste 311 (98109-4509)
PHONE..................................206 899-4665
Patrick Murphy, *President*
EMP: 8
SALES: 1MM **Privately Held**
SIC: 7372 Application computer software

(G-10393)
LEAF CELLARS LLC
Also Called: Cadence
9320 15th Ave S Ste Cf (98108-5105)
PHONE..................................206 860-6888
Benjamin Smith,
Gaye McNutt,
EMP: 2
SQ FT: 5,000
SALES (est): 238.3K **Privately Held**
WEB: www.cadencewinery.com
SIC: 2084 Wine cellars, bonded: engaged in blending wines; wines

(G-10394)
LEAFTAIL LABS LLC
1417 Nw 54th St Ste 337 (98107-3574)
PHONE..................................206 399-4233
Jessica Coombs,
EMP: 2
SALES (est): 73K **Privately Held**
SIC: 7372 7389 Home entertainment computer software;

(G-10395)
LEAVELOGIC INC
2008a California Ave Sw (98116-1954)
PHONE..................................757 655-3283
EMP: 5 EST: 2016
SALES (est): 393.1K **Privately Held**
SIC: 7372 Prepackaged software

(G-10396)
LECLERCQ MARINE CONSTRUCTION
1080 W Ewing St (98119-1422)
PHONE..................................206 283-8555
Samuel D Leclercq, *President*
Steve Peckham, *Manager*
EMP: 20 EST: 1974
SQ FT: 10,000
SALES (est): 2.2MM **Privately Held**
WEB: www.leclercqmarine.com
SIC: 7699 3732 Boat repair; boat building & repairing

Seattle - King County (G-10397) — GEOGRAPHIC SECTION

(G-10397)
LECOQ MACHINE WORK INC
1605 S 93rd St Ste G2 (98108-5112)
PHONE 206 762-4606
Marc Lecoq, *President*
Jacques Lecoq, *President*
▲ **EMP:** 8
SALES (est): 1MM **Privately Held**
SIC: 3599 Machine shop, jobbing & repair

(G-10398)
LEEDS LOOK LISTEN INC
1300 N Northlake Way # 200 (98103-8987)
PHONE 208 252-6075
Gary Leeds, *CEO*
Jerome Mandelbaum, *CFO*
Joseph Leeds, *CTO*
EMP: 4
SALES (est): 169.6K **Privately Held**
SIC: 3651 Loudspeakers, electrodynamic or magnetic

(G-10399)
LEGACY CREATIONS
903 W Newell St (98119-2246)
PHONE 206 286-1827
Rand Babcock, *President*
EMP: 2
SALES (est): 240K **Privately Held**
SIC: 2631 3499 Container, packaging & boxboard; novelties & giftware, including trophies

(G-10400)
LEGACY VULCAN LLC
5915 Delridge Way Sw (98106-3510)
PHONE 206 284-7717
EMP: 26 **Publicly Held**
WEB: www.vulcanmaterials.com
SIC: 1422 Crushed & broken limestone
HQ: Legacy Vulcan, Llc
1200 Urban Center Dr
Vestavia AL 35242
205 298-3000

(G-10401)
LEMMINO INC
6520 29th Ave Sw (98126-2954)
PHONE 571 229-3854
Raphael Mun, *CEO*
EMP: 3
SALES (est): 126K **Privately Held**
SIC: 7372 7389 Business oriented computer software;

(G-10402)
LENCO MOBILE INC
2025 1st Ave Ste 320 (98121-2158)
PHONE 800 557-4148
Matthew Harris, *Ch of Bd*
Srinivas Kandikattu, *COO*
Christopher Stanton, *Admin Sec*
EMP: 62
SQ FT: 2,700
SALES (est): 15.2MM **Privately Held**
WEB: www.suttercapital.com
SIC: 7372 7371 Prepackaged software; custom computer programming services

(G-10403)
LEO ROUX LLC
9016 38th Ave Sw (98126-3839)
PHONE 512 565-3406
EMP: 2
SALES (est): 102.4K **Privately Held**
SIC: 2311 Men's & boys' suits & coats

(G-10404)
LEOPONA INC
Also Called: Audiosocket
3518 Fremont Ave N 400 (98103-8814)
PHONE 206 701-7931
Jenn Miller, *President*
EMP: 11
SALES (est): 750K **Privately Held**
SIC: 2741 6794 Music book & sheet music publishing; music licensing & royalties

(G-10405)
LEOS WELDING & GAB LLC
4451 26th Ave W (98199-1218)
PHONE 425 343-6920
Leonardo Estrada, *Principal*
EMP: 3
SALES (est): 169.8K **Privately Held**
SIC: 7692 Welding repair

(G-10406)
LETS PLAY STELLA LLC
14045 24th Ave Ne (98125-3401)
PHONE 206 365-6249
Jane Peck, *Manager*
EMP: 2
SALES: 120K **Privately Held**
SIC: 2741 Music books: publishing & printing

(G-10407)
LETTER & SPHERE LLC
2415 Ne 65th St (98115-7050)
PHONE 206 473-7534
Anna Bisignano, *Principal*
EMP: 2
SALES (est): 69.2K **Privately Held**
SIC: 2711 Newspapers

(G-10408)
LETTERPRESS DISTILLING LLC
85 S Atlantic St (98134-1220)
PHONE 206 227-4522
Skip Tognetti, *Owner*
EMP: 3
SALES (est): 302.1K **Privately Held**
SIC: 2759 Letterpress printing

(G-10409)
LEV DESIGN
1818 Westlake Ave N Ste 1 (98109-2777)
PHONE 425 417-2758
John Bergquist, *Owner*
EMP: 2
SALES: 100K **Privately Held**
SIC: 3441 Fabricated structural metal

(G-10410)
LEVEL SKY BOATWORKS
9718 21st Ave Nw (98117-2417)
PHONE 206 789-5655
Tom Forsythe, *Owner*
EMP: 4
SALES (est): 270K **Privately Held**
SIC: 3732 Boat building & repairing

(G-10411)
LEVIATHAN GAMES INC
524 Ne 96th Pl (98115-2134)
PHONE 206 432-9949
Wyeth Ridgway, *Principal*
EMP: 2 EST: 2011
SALES (est): 109.8K **Privately Held**
SIC: 7372 Home entertainment computer software

(G-10412)
LEVINGTON TRANE
3401 W Government Way (98199-1391)
PHONE 206 352-2453
EMP: 2
SALES (est): 79.9K **Privately Held**
SIC: 3585 Parts for heating, cooling & refrigerating equipment

(G-10413)
LIBROFM INC
4533 Ne 55th St C (98105-2937)
P.O. Box 70525 (98127-0525)
PHONE 206 730-2463
EMP: 3
SALES (est): 55.8K **Privately Held**
SIC: 7371 2731 Computer software development & applications; books: publishing only

(G-10414)
LID SIGNS LLC
8915 27th Ave Ne (98115-3437)
PHONE 206 290-7536
EMP: 2 EST: 2012
SALES (est): 99K **Privately Held**
SIC: 3993 Signs & advertising specialties

(G-10415)
LIFTER APPS LLC
6312 Calif Ave Sw Apt 409 (98136-1868)
PHONE 206 289-0407
EMP: 2 EST: 2016
SALES (est): 56.5K **Privately Held**
SIC: 7372 Prepackaged software

(G-10416)
LIGHTBANK STUDIO
2200 N Pacific St (98103-9127)
PHONE 206 409-0939
EMP: 2
SALES (est): 75.6K **Privately Held**
SIC: 3999 Stage hardware & equipment, except lighting

(G-10417)
LIGHTHOUSE FOR THE BLIND INC (PA)
Also Called: Skillcraft
2501 S Plum St (98144-4711)
P.O. Box 14959 (98114-0959)
PHONE 206 322-4200
Brad Wiens, *CEO*
Steve Harrison, *General Mgr*
Pat Ohara, *General Mgr*
Masaki Watson, *Principal*
Ron Wagner, *Vice Pres*
▲ **EMP:** 350
SQ FT: 152,000
SALES: 84.3MM **Privately Held**
SIC: 8331 3444 Vocational rehabilitation agency; job training services; sheet metalwork

(G-10418)
LIGHTHOUSE ROASTERS INC
400 N 43rd St (98103-7106)
PHONE 206 633-4775
Ed Leebrick, *President*
Mileaux Welty, *Corp Secy*
EMP: 11
SALES (est): 1.5MM **Privately Held**
SIC: 2095 5499 5149 5812 Coffee roasting (except by wholesale grocers); coffee; coffee, green or roasted; coffee shop

(G-10419)
LIGHTING GROUP NORTHWEST INC
5700 6th Ave S Ste 215 (98108-2511)
P.O. Box 80585 (98108-0585)
PHONE 206 298-9000
Rich Wilkens, *President*
EMP: 4
SALES (est): 480K **Privately Held**
SIC: 3646 Commercial indusl & institutional electric lighting fixtures

(G-10420)
LIGHTSMITH CONSULTING LLC
Also Called: Transparent Classroom
10100 4th Ave Nw (98177-4928)
PHONE 312 953-1193
Jeremy Lightsmith, *Mng Member*
EMP: 6 EST: 2010
SALES: 600K **Privately Held**
SIC: 7372 Educational computer software

(G-10421)
LIKEBRIGHT INC
122 Nw 36th St (98107-4921)
PHONE 206 669-2536
Nick Soman, *CEO*
EMP: 5
SALES (est): 339.8K **Privately Held**
SIC: 7372 Prepackaged software

(G-10422)
LILL CREATES
6234 33rd Ave Ne (98115-7307)
PHONE 206 355-4409
E Johnson, *Principal*
EMP: 2
SALES (est): 155.6K **Privately Held**
SIC: 7372 Home entertainment computer software

(G-10423)
LINDAL CEDAR HOMES INC (PA)
Also Called: Lindal Building Products
4300 S 104th Pl (98178-2081)
PHONE 206 725-0900
Michael Harris, *President*
Douglas F Lindal, *President*
Christina Lindal, *Exec VP*
Martin J Lindal, *Vice Pres*
Bret Knutson, *Opers Mgr*
▲ **EMP:** 60
SQ FT: 13,000
SALES (est): 37.1MM **Privately Held**
WEB: www.lindal.com
SIC: 1751 2452 Window & door (prefabricated) installation; prefabricated buildings, wood

(G-10424)
LINDMARK MACHINE WORKS INC
3626 E Marginal Way S (98134-1130)
PHONE 206 624-0777
Gary Lindmark, *President*
EMP: 14
SALES (corp-wide): 1.5MM **Privately Held**
SIC: 3599 Machine shop, jobbing & repair
PA: Lindmark Machine Works Inc
49 S Spokane St
Seattle WA
206 624-0777

(G-10425)
LINEDATA SERVICES
Also Called: Linedata Capital Stream
501 N 34th St Ste 301 (98103-8856)
PHONE 206 545-9522
EMP: 5
SALES (corp-wide): 7MM **Privately Held**
SIC: 7372 Prepackaged Software Services
PA: Linedata Services
19 Rue D Orleans
Neuilly Sur Seine 92200
147 776-825

(G-10426)
LITERARYROAD COM
6523 California Ave Sw (98136-1833)
PHONE 206 909-1672
EMP: 2
SALES (est): 115.9K **Privately Held**
SIC: 2732 Books: printing only

(G-10427)
LITFUSE PUBLICITY GROUP
1311 12th Ave S Apt C102 (98144-3471)
PHONE 206 947-3743
Lead Hen, *Owner*
EMP: 2 EST: 2012
SALES (est): 133.6K **Privately Held**
SIC: 2741 Miscellaneous publishing

(G-10428)
LITHO INC
348 Nw 54th St (98107-3556)
PHONE 206 632-0211
Ed Brooks, *Principal*
▲ **EMP:** 4 EST: 1995
SALES (est): 348.1K **Privately Held**
SIC: 2752 Commercial printing, lithographic

(G-10429)
LITTLE BAY INC
Also Called: Marley Natural
2701 Eastlake Ave E 3 (98102-3104)
PHONE 646 300-3694
Brandon Kennedy, *President*
Bob Marley, *Principal*
EMP: 3 EST: 2014
SALES (est): 145K **Privately Held**
SIC: 2844 Face creams or lotions

(G-10430)
LIVE MUSIC PROJECT
Also Called: Lmp
2019 Fairview Ave E (98102-3579)
PHONE 206 329-8125
Shaya Lyon, *Principal*
EMP: 4
SALES (est): 213.6K **Privately Held**
SIC: 2741 Miscellaneous publishing

(G-10431)
LIVINGSTON PRINTING INC
Also Called: Windward Press
504 N 85th St (98103-3721)
PHONE 206 382-1117
David K Livingston, *President*
Mary Kay Livingston, *Vice Pres*
EMP: 13
SQ FT: 12,000
SALES (est): 1.2MM **Privately Held**
SIC: 2752 Commercial printing, offset

GEOGRAPHIC SECTION

Seattle - King County (G-10462)

(G-10432)
LIZ TRAN
940 26th Ave (98122-4916)
PHONE..................................206 720-7165
Liz Tran, *Principal*
EMP: 2
SALES (est): 99.1K **Privately Held**
SIC: 3999 Framed artwork

(G-10433)
LJ BACKDOOR INC
Also Called: Construction Unlimited Inc of
10033 13th Ave Sw (98146-3726)
P.O. Box 66632 (98166-0632)
PHONE..................................206 767-2434
Lionel A Fuher, *President*
Michael Graves, *Vice Pres*
EMP: 40
SQ FT: 7,800
SALES (est): 5.8MM **Privately Held**
SIC: 2431 2434 Doors & door parts & trim, wood; wood kitchen cabinets

(G-10434)
LOGO HOUSE
2507 S Orcas St (98108-3065)
PHONE..................................206 890-3051
William John McIntyre, *Manager*
EMP: 2
SALES (est): 169.1K **Privately Held**
SIC: 2759 Screen printing

(G-10435)
LOMAX INDUSTRIES LLC
1700 Summit Ave Apt 201 (98122-2159)
PHONE..................................206 687-7499
Phillip Lomax, *Principal*
EMP: 2
SALES (est): 85.3K **Privately Held**
SIC: 3999 Manufacturing industries

(G-10436)
LONG SHADOWS VINTNERS LLC (PA)
3861 1st Ave S C (98134-2203)
PHONE..................................509 526-0905
Dane Narbaitz, *Principal*
Allen Shoup,
Anthony Von Mandle,
Charles Michael Williamson,
Matt Oakley, *Assistant*
EMP: 15
SQ FT: 1,000
SALES (est): 3.1MM **Privately Held**
SIC: 2084 Wines

(G-10437)
LONGVIEW FIBRE PPR & PACKG INC
Capstone Container
5901 E Marginal Way S (98134-2414)
PHONE..................................206 762-7170
Rick Morgan, *Branch Mgr*
EMP: 90
SQ FT: 120,000
SALES (corp-wide): 3.3B **Publicly Held**
WEB: www.longviewfibre.com
SIC: 2411 2631 2653 Wooden logs; container board; boxes, corrugated: made from purchased materials; boxes, solid fiber: made from purchased materials
HQ: Longview Fibre Paper And Packaging, Inc.
    300 Fibre Way
    Longview WA 98632
    360 425-1550

(G-10438)
LONJINA DESIGN AND PRINT
3817 Sw 105th St (98146-1159)
PHONE..................................206 852-6197
Charles Fielding, *Principal*
EMP: 2
SALES (est): 150.6K **Privately Held**
SIC: 2752 Commercial printing, lithographic

(G-10439)
LOOMIS PLASTICS CORPORATION
Also Called: The Loomis Company
3931 1st Ave S (98134-2236)
PHONE..................................206 292-0111
Charles J Loomis, *President*
Doug Bryan, *Director*
EMP: 35
SQ FT: 30,000
SALES (est): 3.8MM **Privately Held**
SIC: 3089 3993 Injection molding of plastics; plastic boats & other marine equipment; signs & advertising specialties

(G-10440)
LOOP CORP
Also Called: The Loop
568 1st Ave S (98104-4419)
P.O. Box 4680 (98194-0680)
PHONE..................................206 499-0679
Jonathon Loop, *President*
Angela Brown, *Sales Staff*
Patricia Phelps, *Officer*
Sheffield Phelps, *Officer*
Patricia Loop, *Admin Sec*
EMP: 9
SQ FT: 50,000
SALES (est): 580K **Privately Held**
SIC: 2521 2522 Wood office furniture; office furniture, except wood

(G-10441)
LOOP DEVICES INC
113 Cherry St Ste 70880 (98104-2205)
PHONE..................................206 965-9828
Michael Bettua, *CEO*
EMP: 4 **EST:** 2015
SALES (est): 185.3K **Privately Held**
SIC: 3663 Microwave communication equipment

(G-10442)
LORACHE CAD/IT SERVICES LLC
11707 87th Ave S Aofc (98178-4005)
PHONE..................................206 328-4227
Lisa Alexander, *General Mgr*
Barry Cobb, *Mng Member*
Carol Versey-Cobb,
EMP: 10
SQ FT: 1,500
SALES (est): 1.1MM **Privately Held**
SIC: 8741 7373 1389 Construction management; computer integrated systems design; construction, repair & dismantling services

(G-10443)
LORELEI II INC
2944 Nw Esplanade (98117-2621)
PHONE..................................206 783-6045
Eric W Olsen, *President*
EMP: 5
SALES (est): 520K **Privately Held**
SIC: 3732 Fishing boats: lobster, crab, oyster, etc.: small

(G-10444)
LOUISVILLE LADDER
920 S Doris St (98108-2728)
PHONE..................................206 762-4888
Rob Norwood, *Owner*
EMP: 2 **EST:** 2013
SALES (est): 175K **Privately Held**
SIC: 3446 Ladders, for permanent installation: metal

(G-10445)
LPR PARK LLC
1601 5th Ave Ste 1100 (98101-3603)
PHONE..................................888 884-9507
Darius Cincys, *President*
EMP: 5
SALES (est): 117.2K **Privately Held**
SIC: 7372 Application computer software

(G-10446)
LUCKY BREAK WISHBONE CORP
4400 Sw Roxbury Pl (98136-2738)
PHONE..................................206 933-8700
Ken Ahroni, *President*
EMP: 7
SQ FT: 10,000
SALES: 1MM **Privately Held**
WEB: www.luckybreakwishbone.com
SIC: 3089 Novelties, plastic

(G-10447)
LUCKY LEADERS
12039 Palatine Ave N (98133-8111)
PHONE..................................206 363-2208
Don Croghan, *Owner*
Lilly S Croghan, *Co-Owner*
EMP: 2
SALES (est): 99K **Privately Held**
SIC: 3949 5091 Fishing tackle, general; fishing equipment & supplies; fishing tackle

(G-10448)
LULABOP INC
7920 1/2 Seward Pk Ave S (98118-4251)
PHONE..................................206 225-0049
EMP: 3
SQ FT: 1,000
SALES (est): 153.9K **Privately Held**
SIC: 3496 Clips & fasteners, made from purchased wire

(G-10449)
LUMATAX INC
240 2nd Ave S Ste 300 (98104-2250)
PHONE..................................206 450-2004
Robert Schulte, *CEO*
EMP: 5
SALES (est): 141.8K **Privately Held**
SIC: 7372 Business oriented computer software

(G-10450)
LUMENEX LLC
Also Called: Altruen
317 32nd Ave (98122-6329)
PHONE..................................206 909-3474
Gino D'Cafango, *COO*
Andrew Mellon, *Manager*
▲ **EMP:** 2
SALES: 5K **Privately Held**
SIC: 3646 Commercial indusl & institutional electric lighting fixtures

(G-10451)
LUMENOMICS INC (PA)
500 Mercer St C2 (98109-4654)
PHONE..................................206 327-9037
Martha Hoffer, *President*
Carlee Swihart, *Vice Pres*
Heather Sharp, *VP Sales*
EMP: 49
SALES (est): 8MM **Privately Held**
SIC: 3444 3648 2591 Skylights, sheet metal; lighting equipment; shade, curtain & drapery hardware

(G-10452)
LUMISANDS INC
800 Ne 42nd St Apt 303 (98105-0001)
PHONE..................................206 403-7887
Changchang Tu, *CEO*
Chang-Chang Tu, *CEO*
Ji Hoo, *CFO*
EMP: 2
SALES (est): 129.3K **Privately Held**
SIC: 2899 Chemical preparations

(G-10453)
LUNDGREN ENTERPRISES
2442 Nw Market St (98107-4137)
PHONE..................................206 789-1122
Craig Lundgren, *Principal*
Brian Cornish, *Sales Staff*
EMP: 8
SALES (est): 1.1MM **Privately Held**
SIC: 3442 Screen & storm doors & windows

(G-10454)
LX PACKAGING & PRINTING SVC
9108 35th Ave Ne (98115-3617)
PHONE..................................206 714-5479
EMP: 2
SALES (est): 140K **Privately Held**
SIC: 2752 Lithographic Commercial Printing

(G-10455)
LYELL IMMUNOPHARMA INC
500 Fairview Ave N # 200 (98109-5541)
PHONE..................................206 909-3809
Hans Bishop, *Principal*
Richard Klausner, *Principal*
EMP: 2
SALES (est): 74.4K **Privately Held**
SIC: 2834 Pharmaceutical preparations

(G-10456)
M&L RESEARCH INC
Also Called: Jobfindersites
4701 Sw Admiral Way Ste 4 (98116-2340)
PHONE..................................877 321-8766
Leona Guthrie, *Principal*
EMP: 2
SALES (est): 128.8K **Privately Held**
SIC: 2741

(G-10457)
M-SPACE INC
2727 39th Ave Sw (98116-2504)
PHONE..................................253 779-0101
Joesph Miller, *President*
EMP: 4
SQ FT: 5,000
SALES (est): 310K **Privately Held**
SIC: 3229 Pressed & blown glass

(G-10458)
MACH 2 ARTS INC
914 Nw 50th St (98107-3634)
PHONE..................................206 953-0575
Haarald Peterson, *President*
EMP: 5 **EST:** 2015
SQ FT: 2,000
SALES (est): 162K **Privately Held**
SIC: 3299 3999 8412 Architectural sculptures: gypsum, clay, papier mache, etc.; preparation of slides & exhibits; museums & art galleries

(G-10459)
MACH TRANSONIC LLC
Also Called: Mxs
5520 31st Ave Ne (98105-2301)
PHONE..................................206 853-6909
Fred B Holt, *Mng Member*
EMP: 4
SALES (est): 219K **Privately Held**
SIC: 3823 Industrial process measurement equipment

(G-10460)
MACHINISTS INC (PA)
7600 5th Ave S (98108-4116)
P.O. Box 80505 (98108-0505)
PHONE..................................206 763-0990
Hugh La Bossier, *President*
Thomas Jackson, *Project Mgr*
Jarrod Braack, *Purchasing*
Rick Bradbury, *Director*
Johnn Galbraith, *Director*
EMP: 200
SQ FT: 20,000
SALES: 32.3MM **Privately Held**
WEB: www.machinistsinc.com
SIC: 3599 1799 Machine shop, jobbing & repair; sandblasting of building exteriors

(G-10461)
MACHINISTS INC
509 S Austin St (98108-4120)
P.O. Box 80505 (98108-0505)
PHONE..................................206 763-0840
Hugh La Bossier, *President*
Dave Miner, *Sales Mgr*
EMP: 40
SALES (est): 4.2MM
SALES (corp-wide): 32.3MM **Privately Held**
WEB: www.machinistsinc.com
SIC: 3599 3544 3441 Machine shop, jobbing & repair; special dies, tools, jigs & fixtures; fabricated structural metal
PA: Machinists, Inc.
    7600 5th Ave S
    Seattle WA 98108
    206 763-0990

(G-10462)
MACHINISTS INC
8201 7th Ave S (98108-4367)
PHONE..................................206 763-1036
Hugh La Bossier, *President*
EMP: 20
SALES (est): 1.5MM
SALES (corp-wide): 32.3MM **Privately Held**
WEB: www.machinistsinc.com
SIC: 3599 Machine shop, jobbing & repair

Seattle - King County (G-10463) GEOGRAPHIC SECTION

PA: Machinists, Inc.
7600 5th Ave S
Seattle WA 98108
206 763-0990

(G-10463)
MAD FIBER
1604 N 34th St (98103-9002)
P.O. Box 6563, Providence RI (02940-6563)
PHONE..................206 402-3925
Ric Hjertberg, *Principal*
▲ **EMP:** 8
SALES (est): 900.2K **Privately Held**
SIC: 3312 Wheels

(G-10464)
MADBOY INDUSTRIES
902 1st Ave S (98134-1204)
PHONE..................206 707-9394
EMP: 2
SALES (est): 171.1K **Privately Held**
SIC: 3999 Manufacturing industries

(G-10465)
MADRONA SPECIALTY FOODS LLC (PA)
Also Called: La Panzanella
18300 Cascade Ave S # 260 (98188-4746)
PHONE..................206 903-0500
Paul Pigott,
Maureen Pigott,
▲ **EMP:** 25
SQ FT: 25,000
SALES (est): 4MM **Privately Held**
SIC: 2052 5149 Cracker meal & crumbs; crackers

(G-10466)
MAGNETIC PENETRANT SVCS CO INC
Also Called: Mapsco
8135 1st Ave S (98108-4202)
PHONE..................206 762-5855
Frank Milette, *President*
Rick Reese, *Vice Pres*
Mary Walls, *Manager*
Matt Cade, *Administration*
▲ **EMP:** 72
SQ FT: 20,000
SALES (est): 7.6MM **Privately Held**
SIC: 3479 7389 8734 3471 Painting, coating & hot dipping; inspection & testing services; testing laboratories; plating & polishing

(G-10467)
MAGNOLIA DESKTOP COMPUTING LLC
2549 34th Ave W (98199-3223)
PHONE..................206 282-7161
Max Foster, *Partner*
Carmelita C Foster, *Partner*
EMP: 4
SQ FT: 1,100
SALES: 100K **Privately Held**
WEB: www.magdesk.com
SIC: 7379 7372 Computer related maintenance services; application computer software

(G-10468)
MAGNOLIA MEDICAL TECH INC
200 W Mercer St Ste 500 (98119-5908)
PHONE..................206 673-2500
Gregory Bullington, *President*
John Havard, *Vice Pres*
Brad Nelson, *Vice Pres*
Toni Eco-Wilbur, *Marketing Mgr*
Richard Patton MD, *Admin Sec*
EMP: 20
SQ FT: 500
SALES (est): 1.7MM **Privately Held**
SIC: 3841 Medical instruments & equipment, blood & bone work

(G-10469)
MAINSTEM INC
612 S Lucile St (98108-2623)
PHONE..................844 623-4084
Allen Nguyen, *CEO*
John-Michael Kasten, *COO*
Craig McCallum, *CFO*
Garrett Hampton, *CTO*
EMP: 17

SALES: 2MM **Privately Held**
SIC: 5961 7371 7372 ; computer software development & applications; business oriented computer software

(G-10470)
MALCOM DRILLING
100 S King St (98104-3844)
PHONE..................206 623-0776
Glen W Snyder, *Principal*
EMP: 2
SALES (est): 143.2K **Privately Held**
SIC: 1381 Service well drilling

(G-10471)
MANASTASH LOGGING INC
2314 Alki Ave Sw (98116-1820)
PHONE..................206 937-8311
Michael August, *President*
EMP: 6
SALES (est): 311.5K **Privately Held**
SIC: 2411 Logging

(G-10472)
MANTEC SERVICES INC (PA)
4400 24th Ave W (98199-1236)
PHONE..................206 285-5656
Lamar Havens, *President*
Bonnie Havens, *Vice Pres*
James Havens, *Vice Pres*
Krystyn Havens, *Vice Pres*
▲ **EMP:** 25
SQ FT: 15,000
SALES (est): 3.4MM **Privately Held**
WEB: www.mantecservicesinc.com
SIC: 3496 3679 3086 Cable, uninsulated wire; made from purchased wire; electronic circuits; plastics foam products

(G-10473)
MANUFACTURING TECHNOLOGY INC
Also Called: Mfg Tech
7709 5th Ave S (98108-4301)
PHONE..................206 763-3161
Martin Lyman, *President*
EMP: 8
SQ FT: 4,000
SALES (est): 1.3MM **Privately Held**
WEB: www.mfgtech.com
SIC: 3728 3545 Aircraft parts & equipment; machine tool accessories

(G-10474)
MARCO GLOBAL INC
4242 22nd Ave W (98199-1293)
PHONE..................206 298-4758
Hans Schmidt, *President*
Richard W Boehm, *Vice Pres*
Barbara Gabrielsen-Miles, *Admin Sec*
▲ **EMP:** 40
SALES: 10MM **Privately Held**
SIC: 3949 Fishing equipment

(G-10475)
MAREL SEATTLE INC
2001 W Garfield St C106 (98119-3115)
PHONE..................206 781-1827
Arni Oddur Thordarson, *CEO*
Henrik Rasmussen, *President*
Haukur Johannesson, *General Mgr*
Sigsteinn Grtarsson, *COO*
Erik Kaman, *CFO*
▲ **EMP:** 94
SQ FT: 25,000
SALES (est): 26.9MM
SALES (corp-wide): 1.3B **Privately Held**
WEB: www.carnitech.com
SIC: 3556 Dehydrating equipment, food processing
HQ: Marel Salmon A/S
Juelstrupparken 14
StOvring 9530
989 215-11

(G-10476)
MARGARET OLEARY INC
2609 Ne Village Ln (98105-5029)
PHONE..................206 729-5934
Margaret O Leary, *CEO*
EMP: 4 **Privately Held**
SIC: 2339 5621 Service apparel, washable: women's; ready-to-wear apparel, women's

PA: Margaret O'leary, Inc.
50 Dorman Ave
San Francisco CA 94124

(G-10477)
MARGATE SOFTWARE LLC
809 Olive Way Apt 1903 (98101-1998)
PHONE..................206 381-9120
Pedro Margate, *Principal*
EMP: 2 **EST:** 2012
SALES (est): 144.8K **Privately Held**
SIC: 7372 Prepackaged software

(G-10478)
MARINE CNSTR & DESIGN CO (PA)
4259 22nd Ave W (98199-1206)
PHONE..................206 285-3200
Peter G Schmidt, *President*
Dick Boehm, *General Mgr*
John Hedlan, *CFO*
◆ **EMP:** 30
SQ FT: 163,000
SALES (est): 2.8MM **Privately Held**
SIC: 3949 Fishing equipment

(G-10479)
MARINE DIESEL INC
9448 17th Ave Sw Unit B1 (98106-2709)
PHONE..................206 767-9594
Royal Ruetter, *President*
EMP: 2
SQ FT: 4,000
SALES (est): 210K **Privately Held**
SIC: 3469 Machine parts, stamped or pressed metal

(G-10480)
MARINE ENGINE REPAIR CO INC
Also Called: Mer Equipment
2400 W Commodore Way (98199-1228)
PHONE..................206 286-1817
Robert Allen, *President*
Chris Clonch, *Sales Staff*
Dustin Jones, *Manager*
Herb Knight, *Manager*
Jody Fox, *Admin Sec*
◆ **EMP:** 24 **EST:** 1964
SQ FT: 23,500
SALES: 5MM **Privately Held**
WEB: www.merequipment.com
SIC: 3621 5013 5088 Generator sets: gasoline, diesel or dual-fuel; generators & sets, electric; exhaust systems (mufflers, tail pipes, etc.); marine propulsion machinery & equipment

(G-10481)
MARINE FLUID SYSTEMS INC
801 Nw 42nd St Ste 202 (98107-4503)
PHONE..................206 706-0858
Dana Bostwick, *President*
◆ **EMP:** 10
SQ FT: 110,000
SALES (est): 1.6MM **Privately Held**
WEB: www.marinefluid.com
SIC: 3731 Shipbuilding & repairing

(G-10482)
MARINE LUMBER SERVICE INC
Also Called: George Schuster
525 S Chicago St (98108-4320)
P.O. Box 80964 (98108-0964)
PHONE..................206 767-4730
Patrick Oar, *CEO*
Todd Marker, *President*
John Bray, *Vice Pres*
Guy Merriman, *CFO*
Kurt Bray, *Shareholder*
▲ **EMP:** 15
SQ FT: 3,200
SALES (est): 7.4MM **Privately Held**
WEB: www.marinelumberservice.com
SIC: 5031 2493 Lumber: rough, dressed & finished; plywood; reconstituted wood products

(G-10483)
MARINE RECURITING
4735 E Marginal Way S # 1238 (98134-2388)
PHONE..................206 763-5050
Sum Kim, *CEO*
EMP: 2

SALES (est): 86K **Privately Held**
SIC: 3743 Railroad equipment

(G-10484)
MARINE SERVICENTER INC (PA)
2442 Westlake Ave N (98109-2209)
PHONE..................206 323-2405
James Rard, *President*
Gina Rard, *Vice Pres*
Patrick Harrigan, *Consultant*
▲ **EMP:** 8
SQ FT: 1,000
SALES (est): 2.7MM **Privately Held**
WEB: www.marinesc.com
SIC: 7699 5551 5091 3732 Boat repair; boat dealers; sporting & recreation goods; boat building & repairing

(G-10485)
MARITIME PACIFIC BREWING CO
1111 Nw Ballard Way (98107-4639)
P.O. Box 17812 (98127-1812)
PHONE..................206 782-6181
George Hancock, *President*
Colin Hunter, *Accounts Mgr*
EMP: 19
SALES (est): 2.3MM **Privately Held**
SIC: 2082 Beer (alcoholic beverage); ale (alcoholic beverage)

(G-10486)
MARK ANTHONY BRANDS INC
Also Called: Mike's Hard Lemonade
316 1st Ave S (98104-2506)
PHONE..................206 267-4444
Kevin Kotecki, *President*
Brian Amicon, *President*
Victor Giacomin, *Treasurer*
Paul Jansky, *Marketing Staff*
Anya Dange, *Manager*
▲ **EMP:** 90
SALES (est): 18.5MM
SALES (corp-wide): 73MM **Privately Held**
WEB: www.mikeshardlemonade.com
SIC: 2084 2085 5182 Wines, brandy & brandy spirits; distilled & blended liquors; wine & distilled beverages
PA: Pelecanus Holdings Ltd
887 Great Northern Way Suite 101
Vancouver BC V5T 4
604 263-9994

(G-10487)
MARK MUZI
6027 Ne 57th St (98105-2007)
PHONE..................206 523-6954
Mark Muzi, *Principal*
EMP: 2
SALES (est): 56.5K **Privately Held**
SIC: 7372 Prepackaged software

(G-10488)
MARKET OPTICAL (PA)
1906 Pike Pl Ste 8 (98101-1055)
PHONE..................206 448-7739
Ruvane Richman, *Owner*
EMP: 5 **EST:** 1982
SQ FT: 900
SALES (est): 491K **Privately Held**
SIC: 3851 5995 Lenses, ophthalmic; eyeglasses, prescription

(G-10489)
MARKEY MACHINERY CO INC (PA)
7266 8th Ave S (98108-3403)
PHONE..................206 622-4697
Blaine Dempke, *President*
Robert A Lecoque, *Vice Pres*
Ross Murray, *Project Mgr*
Jeffrey Epler, *Engineer*
EMP: 42
SQ FT: 2,618
SALES: 21.6MM **Privately Held**
WEB: www.markeymachinery.com
SIC: 3531 Marine related equipment; ship winches; capstans, ship

(G-10490)
MARKEY MACHINERY CO INC
Also Called: Markey Machinery Co-Plant No 2
7266 8th Ave S (98108-3403)
PHONE..................206 763-0383
Art Wheatley, *Manager*

GEOGRAPHIC SECTION
Seattle - King County (G-10521)

EMP: 17
SQ FT: 20,000
SALES (corp-wide): 21.6MM **Privately Held**
WEB: www.markeymachinery.com
SIC: 3531 3429 Marine related equipment; manufactured hardware (general)
PA: Markey Machinery Co. Inc.
7266 8th Ave S
Seattle WA 98108
206 622-4697

(G-10491)
MARNINSAYLOR LLC
2400 S Hill St Apt 1 (98144-4700)
PHONE 307 360-6165
EMP: 3
SALES (est): 219.2K **Privately Held**
SIC: 3944 Games, toys & children's vehicles

(G-10492)
MARQMETRIX INC
2157 N Northlake Way # 240 (98103-9186)
PHONE 206 971-3625
Larry Joireman, *Director*
EMP: 12
SALES (est): 2.9MM **Privately Held**
SIC: 3823 Industrial process measurement equipment

(G-10493)
MARTIN BLANK STUDIOS
4407 6th Ave Nw (98107-4416)
PHONE 206 621-9733
Martin Blank, *Owner*
EMP: 10
SALES (est): 590K **Privately Held**
WEB: www.martinblankstudios.com
SIC: 3229 Pressed & blown glass

(G-10494)
MARTIN SIGNS & FABRICATION
122 S Mead St (98108-2436)
PHONE 206 768-5183
Martin King, *President*
Kathy King, *Vice Pres*
EMP: 6
SQ FT: 3,824
SALES (est): 731K **Privately Held**
SIC: 3993 Electric signs

(G-10495)
MARYMOOR PRESS INC
7577 S Laurel St (98178-2609)
PHONE 425 867-9073
Cindy Courtmanch, *President*
EMP: 3
SALES (est): 417.9K **Privately Held**
WEB: www.marymoorpress.com
SIC: 2752 Commercial printing, offset

(G-10496)
MASONS SUPPLY COMPANY
5210 1st Ave S (98108-2204)
PHONE 206 883-5550
EMP: 2
SALES (est): 73.4K
SALES (corp-wide): 41.6MM **Privately Held**
SIC: 3432 Faucets & spigots, metal & plastic
PA: Masons Supply Company
2637 Se12th Ave
Portland OR 97202
503 234-4321

(G-10497)
MASTER SWITCH LLC
1929 42nd Ave E (98112-3201)
PHONE 206 769-9560
David Wilkinson, *Principal*
EMP: 3
SALES (est): 184.7K **Privately Held**
SIC: 3679 Electronic switches

(G-10498)
MASTERCRAFT METAL FINISHING
1175 Harrison St (98109-5318)
PHONE 206 622-6380
Jim Gaviglio, *President*
EMP: 5
SQ FT: 4,000
SALES: 600K **Privately Held**
SIC: 3471 Plating of metals or formed products; polishing, metals or formed products

(G-10499)
MASTERPRESS INC
10717 Midvale Ave N (98133-8911)
PHONE 206 524-1444
Ronald Shigeno, *President*
Gloria Shigeno, *Corp Secy*
EMP: 44
SQ FT: 29,000
SALES (est): 7.1MM **Privately Held**
WEB: www.masterpress.net
SIC: 3679 2759 Electronic switches; labels & seals: printing; decals: printing

(G-10500)
MAT SALLEH SATAY LLC
1711 N 45th St (98103-6801)
PHONE 206 547-0597
EMP: 3
SALES (est): 246.4K **Privately Held**
SIC: 2273 Mfg Carpets/Rugs

(G-10501)
MATHSOFT INC
1700 Westlake Ave N # 500 (98109-3012)
PHONE 206 283-8802
Ronald Stevens, *Director*
EMP: 2
SALES (est): 133.6K **Privately Held**
SIC: 7372 Prepackaged software

(G-10502)
MAULCOR INC
Also Called: Amaroq Technologies
2906 S Jackson St (98144-2523)
PHONE 773 696-2783
Stephan Sendelbach, *President*
EMP: 3
SALES (est): 153.4K **Privately Held**
SIC: 2311 2326 2381 3541 Men's & boys' uniforms; military uniforms, men's & youths': purchased materials; overalls & coveralls; gloves, work: woven or knit, made from purchased materials; saws & sawing machines

(G-10503)
MAVAM LLC
Also Called: Mavam Espresso
309 S Cloverdale St D7 (98108-4571)
PHONE 360 789-0639
Michael Myers,
Matthew Shaw,
Terrance D Ziniewicz,
EMP: 3 **EST:** 2015
SALES (est): 146.7K **Privately Held**
SIC: 3634 Coffee makers, electric: household

(G-10504)
MAX MONITOR & PUBLICATIONS LLC
3121 W Government Way (98199-1402)
PHONE 206 280-6489
Malcolm Witter,
EMP: 2 **EST:** 2012
SALES (est): 112.8K **Privately Held**
SIC: 2741 Miscellaneous publishing

(G-10505)
MCCOY INTERNATIONAL LTD
4241 21st Ave W Ste 300 (98199-1250)
PHONE 206 284-7734
Michael Patneaude, *President*
Don Carswell, *Vice Pres*
EMP: 4
SQ FT: 1,616
SALES: 10MM **Privately Held**
WEB: www.mccoyintl.com
SIC: 2329 Men's & boys' sportswear & athletic clothing; men's & boys' athletic uniforms

(G-10506)
MCCREA CELLARS INC
7533 34th Ave Sw (98126-3342)
PHONE 206 938-8643
Susan McCrea, *Principal*
EMP: 5
SALES (est): 346.1K **Privately Held**
SIC: 2084 Wine cellars, bonded: engaged in blending wines; wines

(G-10507)
MCG HEALTH LLC (DH)
901 5th Ave Ste 2000 (98164-2076)
PHONE 206 389-5300
Jon Shreve, *CEO*
Bob Katter, *Exec VP*
Nick Beard, *Senior VP*
Lynn Nemiccolo, *Vice Pres*
Jann Einfeld, *Project Mgr*
EMP: 30
SALES: 9.1MM
SALES (corp-wide): 6.3B **Privately Held**
SIC: 7389 7372 7379 Mailing & messenger services; prepackaged software; publishers' computer software;
HQ: Hearst Business Media Corp
2620 Barrett Rd
Gainesville GA 30507
770 532-4111

(G-10508)
MCKINNON INTERNATIONAL
1101 N Northlake Way # 7 (98103-8948)
PHONE 206 633-1616
Jonathan M Kinnon, *President*
Jonathan Mc Kinnon, *President*
▲ **EMP:** 2
SALES: 1MM **Privately Held**
WEB: www.mckinnoninternational.com
SIC: 3556 Food products machinery

(G-10509)
MCKINSTRY CO LLC (PA)
5005 3rd Ave S (98134-2423)
P.O. Box 24567 (98124-0567)
PHONE 206 762-3311
Dean Allen, *CEO*
Jen Nichols, *COO*
John V Lossow, *Safety Dir*
Ed Wells, *Project Mgr*
Chuck Davidson, *Facilities Mgr*
▲ **EMP:** 500
SQ FT: 20,000
SALES: 450MM **Privately Held**
WEB: www.mckinstry.com
SIC: 1711 1623 3446 3444 Plumbing contractors; ventilation & duct work contractor; heating & air conditioning contractors; pipeline construction; architectural metalwork; sheet metalwork

(G-10510)
MCMENAMINS INC
Also Called: Mc Menamins Pub
200 Roy St Ste 105 (98109-4110)
PHONE 206 285-4722
Mike McManenmins, *Owner*
EMP: 14
SALES (corp-wide): 230.4MM **Privately Held**
WEB: www.hoteloregon.com
SIC: 2082 5812 Malt beverages; eating places
PA: Mcmenamins, Inc.
430 N Killingsworth St
Portland OR 97217
503 223-0109

(G-10511)
MEADOWBROOK MANUFACTURING LLC
4025 Leary Way Nw (98107-5045)
PHONE 206 297-1029
EMP: 2 **EST:** 2009
SALES (est): 156.2K **Privately Held**
SIC: 3999 Manufacturing industries

(G-10512)
MEASUREMENT TECHNOLOGY NW INC (PA)
4220 24th Ave W (98199-1216)
PHONE 206 634-1308
F T O'Neill, *President*
F Timothy O'Neill, *President*
Katherine Burns, *Corp Secy*
Richard Burke, *Vice Pres*
Rick Burke, *Vice Pres*
EMP: 26
SQ FT: 7,000
SALES (est): 8.7MM **Privately Held**
WEB: www.mtnw-usa.com
SIC: 3829 Measuring & controlling devices

(G-10513)
MEAT & BREAD US INC
1201 10th Ave (98122-4209)
PHONE 604 819-1728
EMP: 4
SALES (est): 87.9K **Privately Held**
SIC: 2011 Meat packing plants

(G-10514)
MEDITERRANEAN EXPRESS
1417 Broadway (98122-3854)
P.O. Box 50604, Bellevue (98015-0604)
PHONE 206 860-3989
Khal Beleh, *Principal*
EMP: 4
SALES (est): 272.4K **Privately Held**
SIC: 2741 Miscellaneous publishing

(G-10515)
MEMORY BOX INC
Also Called: Poppystamps
10232 63rd Ave S (98178-2307)
PHONE 206 722-8438
Monica M Brethauer, *President*
David Brethauer, *Vice Pres*
▲ **EMP:** 4
SALES (est): 479.9K **Privately Held**
SIC: 2621 Stationery, envelope & tablet papers

(G-10516)
MEND
4117 34th Ave S (98118-1305)
PHONE 949 355-9925
Susie Herr, *Principal*
EMP: 2
SALES (est): 89K **Privately Held**
SIC: 3915 Jewelers' materials & lapidary work

(G-10517)
MERVIN MANUFACTURING INC
3400 Stone Way N Ste 200 (98103-8983)
PHONE 206 204-7800
Greg Hughes, *Vice Pres*
Jeremy Hatt, *CFO*
Doug Vensel, *Supervisor*
EMP: 2 **EST:** 2007
SALES (est): 196.4K **Privately Held**
SIC: 3949 Skateboards

(G-10518)
MESSENGER CORPORATION
Also Called: M3
37 S Hudson St (98134-2416)
PHONE 206 623-4525
William Davis, *President*
Barbara F Davis, *Vice Pres*
EMP: 30
SQ FT: 9,000
SALES (est): 3.8MM **Privately Held**
SIC: 7389 3993 Sign painting & lettering shop; signs, not made in custom sign painting shops

(G-10519)
METABOLIC GLOBAL
4214 Stone Way N (98103-7432)
PHONE 206 660-7243
Keven Mann, *Manager*
EMP: 2
SALES (est): 62.3K **Privately Held**
SIC: 2099 Food preparations

(G-10520)
METAL ONE AMERICA INC
1201 3rd Ave Ste 3700 (98101-3072)
PHONE 206 223-2273
Akio Uchida, *President*
Terry Neikirk, *Vice Pres*
Darek Kusnierewicz, *Sales Mgr*
▲ **EMP:** 2
SALES (est): 182.2K **Privately Held**
WEB: www.metaloneamerica.com
SIC: 3317 Steel pipe & tubes

(G-10521)
METAL SOLUTIONS LLC
5212 6th Ave S (98108-2222)
PHONE 206 767-5587
Steve Northey, *Mng Member*
EMP: 52
SALES (est): 300K **Privately Held**
SIC: 3441 Fabricated structural metal

Seattle - King County (G-10522)

(G-10522)
METAL WORKS NORTHWEST
3834 4th Ave S (98134-2210)
PHONE..................206 624-4766
Rod Leppa, *Principal*
EMP: 2
SALES (est): 122.1K **Privately Held**
SIC: 3441 Fabricated structural metal

(G-10523)
METRICSTORY INCORPORATED
12302 Sand Point Way Ne (98125-5841)
PHONE..................206 755-4511
Joshua Gebhardt, *Principal*
EMP: 4 EST: 2015
SALES (est): 189.3K **Privately Held**
SIC: 3826 Analytical instruments

(G-10524)
METRIX CREATE SPACE
623 Broadway E (98102-5025)
PHONE..................206 357-9406
EMP: 2
SALES (est): 134.7K **Privately Held**
SIC: 2759 Laser printing

(G-10525)
MEYER WELLS INC
421 3rd Ave W (98119-4001)
PHONE..................206 282-0076
John Wells, *President*
Seth Meyer, *Vice Pres*
Amanda Coccaro, *Marketing Mgr*
David Kienholz, *Manager*
Loie Docter, *Consultant*
EMP: 26
SALES (est): 2.7MM **Privately Held**
SIC: 2519 2421 2522 Furniture, household: glass, fiberglass & plastic; sawmills & planing mills, general; office furniture, except wood

(G-10526)
MEZICH ALLEGIANCE INC
1445 Nw 56th St (98107-3726)
PHONE..................206 782-1767
Rick Mezich, *President*
EMP: 5
SALES (est): 480K **Privately Held**
SIC: 3732 Fishing boats: lobster, crab, oyster, etc.: small

(G-10527)
MICHAEL D LYNNE
Also Called: Practical Trauma
624 S Lander St Ste 20d (98134-2009)
PHONE..................800 587-2313
Michael Lynne, *Owner*
EMP: 9
SQ FT: 1,500
SALES (est): 98K **Privately Held**
WEB: www.practicaltrauma.com
SIC: 3842 First aid, snake bite & burn kits

(G-10528)
MICRACULTURE LLC
4608 1st Ave Ne (98105-4804)
PHONE..................202 838-7645
Sarah Pellkofer, *Administration*
EMP: 3
SALES (est): 155.7K **Privately Held**
SIC: 2873 Fertilizers: natural (organic), except compost

(G-10529)
MICRAMETAL INC
810 Nw 45th St (98107-4515)
PHONE..................206 508-1405
EMP: 2
SALES: 190K **Privately Held**
SIC: 3674 Mfg Semiconductors/Related Devices

(G-10530)
MICRO CURRENT TECHNOLOGY INC
Also Called: Bio-Therapeutic
2244 1st Ave S (98134-1408)
PHONE..................206 938-5800
David Suzuki, *President*
Jim Suzuki, *Treasurer*
Alex Wu, *Sales Staff*
Tawney Briggs, *Executive Asst*
▲ EMP: 25

SALES (est): 5.1MM **Privately Held**
SIC: 2844 Face creams or lotions

(G-10531)
MICRO CURRENT TECHNOLOGY INC
Also Called: Bio-Therapeutic
4822 California Ave Sw (98116-4415)
PHONE..................206 938-5288
David Suzuki, *President*
▲ EMP: 30
SQ FT: 4,000
SALES (est): 3.5MM **Privately Held**
WEB: www.biotherapeutic.com
SIC: 3679 Electronic circuits

(G-10532)
MICRO FOCUS SOFTWARE INC
Also Called: Novell
705 5th Ave S Ste 1000 (98104-4450)
PHONE..................206 217-7100
Nahla Kintzer, *Branch Mgr*
EMP: 566
SALES (corp-wide): 1.2B **Privately Held**
SIC: 7372 Prepackaged software
PA: Micro Focus Software Inc.
1800 Novell Pl
Provo UT 84606
801 861-7000

(G-10533)
MICROBIOLOGIQUE INC (PA)
Also Called: Pl Biologique
8315 Lake City Way Ne (98115-4411)
PHONE..................206 714-5275
Dalia Alfi, *Exec VP*
▲ EMP: 12 EST: 2013
SALES (est): 1.4MM **Privately Held**
SIC: 3826 Analytical instruments

(G-10534)
MICROHAOPS INC
8041 Stroud Ave N (98103-4530)
PHONE..................206 595-6426
Mark Benjamin, *CEO*
Mark M Benjamin, *President*
Jeffry Canin, *Bd of Directors*
EMP: 3
SALES (est): 312.5K **Privately Held**
SIC: 3589 Sewage & water treatment equipment

(G-10535)
MICRON TECHNOLOGY INC
506 2nd Ave (98104-2343)
PHONE..................206 294-7015
EMP: 9
SALES (est): 1.1MM **Privately Held**
SIC: 3674 Semiconductors & related devices

(G-10536)
MICROSOFT CORPORATION
200 W Thomas St Ste 300 (98119-4218)
PHONE..................206 290-9669
Ana Ruiz, *Administration*
EMP: 2
SALES (est): 56.5K **Privately Held**
SIC: 7372 Prepackaged software

(G-10537)
MICROSOFT CORPORATION
562 1st Ave S Ste 400 (98104-3816)
PHONE..................425 533-6624
Katherine Chong, *Branch Mgr*
Melissa Powell, *Manager*
EMP: 2
SALES (corp-wide): 110.3B **Publicly Held**
SIC: 7372 Prepackaged software
PA: Microsoft Corporation
1 Microsoft Way
Redmond WA 98052
425 882-8080

(G-10538)
MICROSOFT CORPORATION
320 Westlake Ave N (98109-5232)
PHONE..................206 883-5474
Justin Hall, *Technology*
Cliff Reeves, *Director*
EMP: 35
SALES (corp-wide): 110.3B **Publicly Held**
SIC: 7372 Prepackaged software

PA: Microsoft Corporation
1 Microsoft Way
Redmond WA 98052
425 882-8080

(G-10539)
MID MOUNTAIN MATERIALS INC (PA)
5602 2nd Ave S (98108-2409)
P.O. Box 80266 (98108-0266)
PHONE..................206 762-7600
Donald Knapp, *Ch of Bd*
John R Knapp, *President*
Gretchen Reimbold, *Senior VP*
Fred Willcutt, *Opers Mgr*
▲ EMP: 41
SQ FT: 70,000
SALES (est): 11.1MM **Privately Held**
WEB: www.mid-mountain.com
SIC: 2299 2295 2298 3053 Coir yarns & roving; coated fabrics, not rubberized; cordage & twine; gaskets, packing & sealing devices; glass fibers, textile; narrow fabric mills

(G-10540)
MIGHTY AI LLC
1411 4th Ave Ste 1100 (98101-1431)
PHONE..................425 753-3167
Daryn Nakhuda, *CEO*
Isaac Kato, *President*
Teresa Kotwis, *CFO*
EMP: 40 EST: 2014
SALES (est): 719.9K
SALES (corp-wide): 11.2B **Publicly Held**
SIC: 7372 Prepackaged software
PA: Uber Technologies, Inc.
1455 Market St Fl 4
San Francisco CA 94103
415 612-8582

(G-10541)
MIHALISIN/WALLING STUDIO
4418 Sw College St (98116-2122)
PHONE..................206 923-1037
Julie Mihalisin, *Owner*
EMP: 2
SQ FT: 1,850
SALES: 80K **Privately Held**
WEB: www.mihalisinwalling.com
SIC: 3299 Architectural sculptures: gypsum, clay, papier mache, etc.

(G-10542)
MIKE MONTGOMERY
Also Called: Unite Seattle Publishing
1820 Minor Ave Apt 419 (98101-1454)
PHONE..................206 306-4599
Mike Montgomery, *Owner*
EMP: 2
SALES (est): 67.9K **Privately Held**
SIC: 2741 Miscellaneous publishing

(G-10543)
MILLER & MILLER BOATYARD CO
2700 W Commodore Way B (98199-1264)
PHONE..................206 285-5958
Paul Miller, *President*
Peggy Miller, *Admin Sec*
EMP: 9
SALES (est): 750K **Privately Held**
SIC: 7699 3732 Boat repair; boat building & repairing

(G-10544)
MILO & GABBY LLC
8721 Golden Gardens Dr Nw (98117-3942)
PHONE..................206 257-1957
Karen Keller, *Principal*
▲ EMP: 2 EST: 2010
SALES (est): 170K **Privately Held**
SIC: 2211 Pillowcases

(G-10545)
MINIMA SOFTWARE LLC
1629 Harvard Ave Apt 512 (98122-2265)
PHONE..................206 659-9646
EMP: 2
SALES (est): 110K **Privately Held**
SIC: 7372 Prepackaged software

(G-10546)
MINTAKA INSTRUMENTS LLC
3050 Nw 63rd St (98107-2521)
PHONE..................206 783-1414
David Burch, *Partner*
EMP: 3 EST: 2014
SQ FT: 1,500
SALES (est): 189.8K **Privately Held**
SIC: 3812 Nautical instruments

(G-10547)
MINUTEMAN PRESS
10300 Greenwood Ave N (98133-9144)
PHONE..................206 577-9199
EMP: 2
SALES (est): 83.9K **Privately Held**
SIC: 2752 Commercial printing, lithographic

(G-10548)
MISTY MOUNTAIN MANUFACTURING
Also Called: Jensen Lee
6264 Stanley Ave S (98108-2812)
PHONE..................206 763-4055
Regina Crumbaker, *President*
Gregory J Crumbaker, *Corp Secy*
Greg Crumbaker, *CPA*
EMP: 26 EST: 1975
SQ FT: 7,000
SALES (est): 2.9MM **Privately Held**
WEB: www.mistymtn.com
SIC: 2393 2399 2326 Canvas bags; aprons, breast (harness); banners, pennants & flags; men's & boys' work clothing

(G-10549)
MJ DIRECTIONS LLC
Also Called: Marijuana Venture Magazine
4000 Airport Way S (98108-5217)
PHONE..................425 656-3621
Greg James, *Mng Member*
EMP: 8 EST: 2014
SALES (est): 449.7K **Privately Held**
SIC: 2721 Magazines: publishing & printing

(G-10550)
MK OPTIMIZATION AND CTRL LLC
3645 Ashworth Ave N (98103-8116)
PHONE..................509 656-3321
Melvin Koch,
Nan Holmes,
EMP: 5
SALES (est): 332.2K **Privately Held**
SIC: 3823 Industrial process control instruments

(G-10551)
MK PERRIGO REALTOR
1112 19th Ave E (98112-3505)
PHONE..................425 478-6694
EMP: 3
SALES (est): 157K **Privately Held**
SIC: 2834 Pharmaceutical preparations

(G-10552)
MODEL ONE
1817 N 49th St (98103-6839)
PHONE..................206 383-0380
Gregory Menikoff, *Owner*
EMP: 2
SALES (est): 276.9K **Privately Held**
SIC: 3543 Industrial patterns

(G-10553)
MODELWERKS INC
655 S Andover St (98108-5234)
PHONE..................206 340-6007
Jon Stamm, *President*
Sandra Coulter, *Corp Secy*
EMP: 12
SQ FT: 8,000
SALES (est): 1.1MM **Privately Held**
WEB: www.modelwerks.com
SIC: 8711 3544 Engineering services; forms (molds), for foundry & plastics working machinery

(G-10554)
MODERN PATTERN WORKS INC
Also Called: Modern Coach
255 S Austin St (98108-4119)
PHONE..................206 762-2227
Gerald Kelson, *President*

GEOGRAPHIC SECTION

Seattle - King County (G-10587)

Ed Kelson, *Vice Pres*
EMP: 3
SQ FT: 10,000
SALES (est): 210K **Privately Held**
SIC: 3543 Industrial patterns

(G-10555)
MODUMETAL INC (PA)
1443 N Northlake Way (98103-8920)
PHONE.................................877 632-4242
Christina Lomasney, *President*
William Reynolds, *General Mgr*
Joel Baldwin, *Counsel*
Brian Durkin, *Facilities Mgr*
Daniel Casioppo, *Engineer*
EMP: 26
SQ FT: 1,000
SALES (est): 8.6MM **Privately Held**
WEB: www.modumetal.com
SIC: 8732 3339 Research services, except laboratory; tin-base alloys (primary)

(G-10556)
MOGUL EXPRESS
701 5th Ave Ste 5800 (98104-7014)
PHONE.................................206 386-8070
Donald Elmer, *Principal*
EMP: 4
SALES (est): 218.6K **Privately Held**
SIC: 2741 Miscellaneous publishing

(G-10557)
MOLLY MOONS HOMEMADE ICE CREAM (PA)
1622 N 45th St (98103-6702)
PHONE.................................206 547-5105
Molly Moons, *Principal*
EMP: 3
SALES (est): 517.8K **Privately Held**
SIC: 2024 Ice cream & frozen desserts

(G-10558)
MOLLYS SALADS LLC
4636 E Marginal Way S (98134-2382)
P.O. Box 80007 (98108-0007)
PHONE.................................206 512-3075
Stefan Kalb, *CEO*
Molly Ayre-Svingen,
Richard Buchanan,
Bertrand De Boutray,
EMP: 6
SQ FT: 2,000
SALES (est): 882.3K **Privately Held**
SIC: 3999 5149 5148 Advertising curtains; sandwiches; vegetables

(G-10559)
MONOLITHIC POWER SYSTEMS INC
101 Elliott Ave W Ste 500 (98119-4292)
PHONE.................................408 826-0600
EMP: 4
SALES (est): 296K **Privately Held**
SIC: 3674 Read-only memory (ROM)

(G-10560)
MONSTER CONCEPTS INC
1406 Nw 53rd St Ste 1a (98107-3731)
PHONE.................................206 706-6730
Mark Hulscher, *President*
EMP: 3
SALES (est): 225.2K **Privately Held**
SIC: 3599 8711 8748 Machine shop, jobbing & repair; machine tool design; systems analysis & engineering consulting services

(G-10561)
MONUMENT WHEELWORKS LLC
335 Nw 49th St (98107-3544)
PHONE.................................206 856-9509
Andrew Jorgensen, *Principal*
EMP: 3
SALES (est): 195.4K **Privately Held**
SIC: 3272 Monuments & grave markers, except terrazo

(G-10562)
MORGAN ELECTRIC & PLUMBING INC
3627 Stone Way N (98103-8093)
PHONE.................................206 547-1617
Russell S Morgan, *President*
Randy Morgan, *Manager*
EMP: 13

SALES (corp-wide): 4.1MM **Privately Held**
WEB: www.morgansonline.com
SIC: 5211 2434 5999 8111 Cabinets, kitchen; wood kitchen cabinets; plumbing & heating supplies; malpractice & negligence law; motels; hardware
PA: Morgan Electric & Plumbing, Inc.
    8055 15th Ave Nw
    Seattle WA 98117
    425 814-4551

(G-10563)
MORNING DEW CANDLES
10802 Lake Ridge Dr S (98178-2640)
PHONE.................................206 772-5611
Ellyn Johnson, *Principal*
EMP: 2
SALES (est): 191.5K **Privately Held**
WEB: www.morningdewcandles.com
SIC: 3999 Candles

(G-10564)
MOSS GREEN INC
3635 Thorndyke Ave W B (98119-1640)
PHONE.................................206 285-4020
Russ Harvey, *President*
Kris Edwards, *Corp Secy*
EMP: 12
SALES: 1MM **Privately Held**
SQ FT: 4,500
WEB: www.mossgreen.net
SIC: 2759 2396 Screen printing; automotive & apparel trimmings

(G-10565)
MOTEK INC
1849 N 53rd St (98103-6115)
PHONE.................................206 632-7795
Michael Krasik, *President*
EMP: 7 **EST:** 1981
SALES: 1.5MM **Privately Held**
WEB: www.motek.com
SIC: 3669 3577 Emergency alarms; computer peripheral equipment

(G-10566)
MPL INNOVATIONS INC (PA)
2505 2nd Ave (98121-1452)
PHONE.................................425 398-1310
Michael Mitrovich, *President*
Earl Carey, *Principal*
Martin McQuaid, *Admin Sec*
◆ **EMP:** 5
SQ FT: 3,000
SALES (est): 2.3MM **Privately Held**
WEB: www.mpltechnology.com
SIC: 2992 Lubricating oils & greases

(G-10567)
MSC PRINT HOUSE
3300 Wallingford Ave N (98103-9039)
PHONE.................................206 708-1423
EMP: 2
SALES (est): 182.6K **Privately Held**
SIC: 2752 Commercial printing, lithographic

(G-10568)
MULTI SCORE INC
Also Called: Multi Score Manufacturing
10327 44th Ave Ne (98125-8117)
PHONE.................................206 524-7591
Hugh Lade, *President*
Carol Lade, *Corp Secy*
EMP: 7 **EST:** 1956
SQ FT: 8,000
SALES (est): 620K **Privately Held**
SIC: 3553 Woodworking machinery

(G-10569)
MULTICO RATING SYSTEMS
610 12th Ave E (98102-5116)
PHONE.................................206 357-3928
Charlie Anderson, *Owner*
EMP: 14
SALES (est): 1.8MM **Privately Held**
SIC: 7371 7372 Computer software development; prepackaged software

(G-10570)
MULTIMODAL HEALTH INC
13 10 Mainor Ave 502 (98101)
PHONE.................................651 245-2326
Brian Mogen, *President*
EMP: 4

SALES (est): 119K **Privately Held**
SIC: 7372 Prepackaged software

(G-10571)
MURPHY JP CONSTRUCTION
8430 Fauntleroy Pl Sw (98136-2410)
PHONE.................................425 222-7299
J P Murphy, *Owner*
EMP: 4
SALES (est): 470K **Privately Held**
SIC: 1521 1389 Single-family housing construction; construction, repair & dismantling services

(G-10572)
MURPHY RUNA INC
5416 Shilshole Ave Nw (98107-4022)
PHONE.................................206 782-2664
Bryan Northrop, *President*
EMP: 3
SALES (est): 350K **Privately Held**
SIC: 2434 Wood kitchen cabinets

(G-10573)
MUSCLECLUB 4 MEN
1806 8th Ave Apt 214 (98101-1317)
PHONE.................................206 624-9785
William Fisher, *Principal*
EMP: 2
SALES (est): 90K **Privately Held**
SIC: 3674 Semiconductors & related devices

(G-10574)
MUSEUM QUALITY DISCOUNT FRMNG (PA)
Also Called: Beards Framing
1964 4th Ave S (98134-1504)
PHONE.................................206 624-1057
Adrian Hanauer, *Ch of Bd*
Steven Dodd, *President*
Thomas Riley, *CFO*
Terry Beard, *Shareholder*
Reed Koch, *Shareholder*
▲ **EMP:** 15
SQ FT: 4,000
SALES (est): 20.6MM **Privately Held**
WEB: www.mqf.com
SIC: 3952 5023 Frames for artists' canvases; frames & framing, picture & mirror

(G-10575)
MUSTAD LONGLINE INC
4240 Gilman Pl W Ste B (98199-1248)
PHONE.................................206 284-4376
Jan Foss, *President*
Bruce Sadow, *Accountant*
Steve Cromwell, *VP Sales*
Diane Stewart, *Office Mgr*
▲ **EMP:** 2 **EST:** 2000
SQ FT: 6,000
SALES (est): 295.6K **Privately Held**
WEB: www.mustadlongline.com
SIC: 3949 Rods & rod parts, fishing
HQ: Mustad Autoline As
    Raufossvegen 40
    Gjovik 2821

(G-10576)
MUSTARD AND CO LLC
4501 Shilshole Ave Nw # 205 (98107-4708)
PHONE.................................734 904-9877
Bryan Mitchiner, *Administration*
EMP: 6
SALES (est): 518.9K **Privately Held**
SIC: 2099 Food preparations

(G-10577)
MUTUAL INDUSTRIES INC
9832 17th Ave Sw Ste Es (98106-2713)
PHONE.................................206 767-6647
Eric Chau, *President*
Hien Chau, *Vice Pres*
▲ **EMP:** 5
SALES (est): 685.9K **Privately Held**
SIC: 3444 1761 Sheet metalwork; sheet metalwork

(G-10578)
MY CITY WISE LLC
Also Called: Wise Publishing Group
7724 35th Ave Ne # 15528 (98115-9955)
PHONE.................................206 409-0818
Max Wells,
EMP: 7

SALES (est): 400K **Privately Held**
SIC: 2721 Magazines: publishing only, not printed on site

(G-10579)
MY LOCAL CO
Also Called: My Local Honey
8328 Earl Ave Nw (98117-4530)
PHONE.................................360 989-6903
Michael Falter, *Principal*
Matthew Larson, *Principal*
EMP: 10 **EST:** 2015
SALES (est): 377.2K **Privately Held**
SIC: 2099 Honey, strained & bottled

(G-10580)
MYBOCK MANUFACTURING LLC
3515 Sw Ocean View Dr # 106 (98146-1800)
PHONE.................................716 913-4157
David Myka, *Bd of Directors*
EMP: 2
SALES (est): 105K **Privately Held**
SIC: 3999 Manufacturing industries

(G-10581)
MYINTERZONE
9735 8th Ave Nw (98117-2206)
PHONE.................................206 679-4566
Terry Allen, *Principal*
EMP: 2
SALES (est): 81.9K **Privately Held**
SIC: 1311 Crude petroleum & natural gas

(G-10582)
MYOVISION
13545 Erickson Pl Ne S (98125-3896)
PHONE.................................800 969-6961
Mark Marcarian, *Sales Staff*
EMP: 6
SALES (est): 682K **Privately Held**
SIC: 3845 CAT scanner (Computerized Axial Tomography) apparatus

(G-10583)
MYSTIC LTD
Also Called: Sheets Unlimited
301 Sw 27th St (98101)
P.O. Box 91302 (98111-9402)
PHONE.................................425 251-5959
Gordon Younger, *Principal*
▲ **EMP:** 93
SQ FT: 200,000
SALES (est): 53MM **Privately Held**
WEB: www.mysticsheets.com
SIC: 2653 Sheets, corrugated: made from purchased materials

(G-10584)
NANCY ZWIEBACK
643 Nw 114th Pl (98177-4735)
PHONE.................................206 306-0411
EMP: 3
SALES (est): 180.7K **Privately Held**
SIC: 2052 Mfg Cookies/Crackers

(G-10585)
NANOFIBER TECH INC
1420 5th Ave Ste 2200 (98101-1346)
PHONE.................................206 781-9288
Edith Hwang, *President*
Dean Chiang, *Vice Pres*
Janet Feng, *Treasurer*
EMP: 3 **EST:** 2002
SALES (est): 303.8K **Privately Held**
SIC: 2656 Paper cups, plates, dishes & utensils

(G-10586)
NANOOK LODGE
1900 W Nickerson St (98119-1661)
PHONE.................................206 200-8233
EMP: 2
SALES (est): 76K **Privately Held**
SIC: 2399 Mfg Fabricated Textile Products

(G-10587)
NATIONAL COLOR
769 Hayes St Ste 101 (98109-3064)
PHONE.................................206 281-9400
Bradley A Thomson, *President*
Bradley A Thomsonbrad Thomson, *President*
Chad Quail, *Graphic Designe*
EMP: 11

Seattle - King County (G-10588)   GEOGRAPHIC SECTION

SALES (est): 860K **Privately Held**
WEB: www.national-color.com
SIC: 2759 7336 Commercial printing; commercial art & graphic design

(G-10588)
NATIONAL FROZEN FOODS CORP (PA)
Also Called: Pac/Gro and Associates
1600 Frview Ave E Ste 200 (98102)
P.O. Box 9366 (98109-0366)
PHONE..........................206 322-8900
Richard Grader, *President*
Bill Obryan, *General Mgr*
Robert Ashmun, *Vice Pres*
John Bafus, *Vice Pres*
Jonathan Bafus, *Vice Pres*
◆ EMP: 1009 **EST:** 1912
SQ FT: 12,000
SALES (est): 228.8MM **Privately Held**
SIC: 2037 Frozen fruits & vegetables

(G-10589)
NATIONAL PRODUCTS INC (PA)
Also Called: N P I
8410 Dallas Ave S (98108-4423)
PHONE..........................206 763-8361
Jeffrey Carnevali, *President*
Aaron Hersey, *Vice Pres*
Karl Ozolin, *Vice Pres*
Chad Remmers, *Vice Pres*
Michael Turner, *CFO*
▲ EMP: 154
SQ FT: 12,000
SALES (est): 7.1MM **Privately Held**
SIC: 3429 Marine hardware

(G-10590)
NATIONAL SIGN CORPORATION (PA)
Also Called: Signpac Northwest Division
1255 Westlake Ave N (98109-3531)
PHONE..........................206 282-0700
Timothy Zamberlin, *President*
Steve Zamberlin, *Vice Pres*
George Zamberlin, *Admin Sec*
EMP: 49
SQ FT: 30,000
SALES (est): 6.3MM **Privately Held**
SIC: 3993 7359 7629 Electric signs; sign rental; electrical repair shops

(G-10591)
NATURAL MACHINES INC
925 4th Ave Ste 2900 (98104-1158)
PHONE..........................206 747-9483
Emilio Sepulveda, *CEO*
Lynette Kucsma, *Vice Pres*
EMP: 11
SALES (est): 462.7K **Privately Held**
SIC: 3639 Major kitchen appliances, except refrigerators & stoves

(G-10592)
NATURAL MATTERS INC
3451 24th Ave W Apt 522 (98199-2218)
PHONE..........................206 387-7054
Peter Boyle, *Principal*
EMP: 2
SALES (est): 86.6K **Privately Held**
SIC: 2099 Food preparations

(G-10593)
NATURAL PET PANTRY
309 S Cloverdale St (98108-4568)
PHONE..........................206 762-5575
Jacque Haggard, *Principal*
EMP: 5
SALES (est): 348.9K **Privately Held**
SIC: 5149 2047 Pet foods; dog & cat food

(G-10594)
NATUS MEDICAL INCORPORATED
Also Called: Olympic Medical
5900 1st Ave S (98108-3248)
PHONE..........................206 767-3500
Elsie Smith, *QC Mgr*
Patsy Rogerson, *Human Res Mgr*
Ted Weiler, *Manager*
Richard Wombold, *Info Tech Mgr*
Tony Heimerman, *Recruiter*
EMP: 16

SALES (corp-wide): 530.8MM **Publicly Held**
SIC: 3845 Electromedical equipment
PA: Natus Medical Incorporated
6701 Koll Center Pkwy # 120
Pleasanton CA 94566
925 223-6700

(G-10595)
NAUST MARINE USA INC
4816 15th Ave Nw (98107-4717)
PHONE..........................206 484-5710
Helgi Kristjansson, *President*
▲ EMP: 10
SALES (est): 1.1MM **Privately Held**
SIC: 3531 Marine related equipment
HQ: Naust Marine Ehf.
Midhellu 4
Hafnarfirdi 221
414 808-0

(G-10596)
NAVAN ENTERPRISES LLC
Also Called: Chip Pros
8224 16th Ave Ne (98115-4368)
PHONE..........................206 214-6227
Vanessa Phillips,
EMP: 2
SALES: 79K **Privately Held**
SIC: 3714 7699 Windshield frames, motor vehicle; repair services

(G-10597)
NAVIT LLC
500 Yale Ave N Ste 400 (98109-5680)
PHONE..........................425 647-3580
Shannon Krueger,
EMP: 4
SALES (est): 249.2K **Privately Held**
SIC: 7372 Application computer software

(G-10598)
NELSON TRUCK EQUIPMENT CO INC
14325 Aurora Ave N (98133-6916)
PHONE..........................206 622-3825
Sindy Potts, *Manager*
EMP: 10
SALES (est): 827.2K
SALES (corp-wide): 15MM **Privately Held**
SIC: 5531 5561 5084 3713 Truck equipment & parts; recreational vehicle dealers; winches; truck bodies & parts
PA: Nelson Truck Equipment Co., Inc.
20063 84th Ave S
Kent WA 98032
253 395-3825

(G-10599)
NEON LABS INC
5511 28th Ave Nw (98107-4159)
PHONE..........................415 854-8795
EMP: 3
SALES (est): 123.2K **Privately Held**
SIC: 2813 Neon

(G-10600)
NEON TACO
209 Broadway E (98102-5723)
PHONE..........................323 577-3045
EMP: 3
SALES (est): 123.2K **Privately Held**
SIC: 2813 Neon

(G-10601)
NEPTUNE GLOBAL LLC
Also Called: Neptune Industries
2124 3rd Ave Ste 201 (98121-2376)
PHONE..........................310 752-9992
Nichole Leigh, *Principal*
Nia Kajumulo, *Principal*
EMP: 2
SALES (est): 106.8K **Privately Held**
SIC: 3999 Barber & beauty shop equipment

(G-10602)
NETWORK COLLABORATIVE 4 LLC
3601 Fremont Ave N # 314 (98103-2709)
PHONE..........................206 898-5869
Jim Alekson, *Mng Member*
Willie Prince, *Mng Member*
EMP: 10

SALES (est): 229.5K **Privately Held**
SIC: 5199 2899 Nondurable goods; chemical preparations

(G-10603)
NEWSDATA LLC (HQ)
4241 21st Ave W Ste 306 (98199-1250)
PHONE..........................206 285-4848
Michael Shepherd, *CEO*
EMP: 16
SALES (est): 386.3K
SALES (corp-wide): 54.7MM **Privately Held**
SIC: 2741 Newsletter publishing
PA: Ruralite Services, Inc.
5605 Ne Elam Young Pkwy
Hillsboro OR 97124
503 357-2105

(G-10604)
NEWTONIA PUBLISHING LLC
2201 3rd Ave Apt 2201 # 2201 (98121-2037)
PHONE..........................206 790-6628
Lynne Walker, *Manager*
EMP: 2
SALES (est): 138K **Privately Held**
SIC: 2741 Miscellaneous publishing

(G-10605)
NEXTGEN APPS CO
111 W Prospect St (98119-3535)
PHONE..........................206 395-6770
William Van Valkenberg, *President*
Bruce J Holmes, *Vice Pres*
EMP: 2
SALES (est): 62.1K **Privately Held**
SIC: 7372 Prepackaged software

(G-10606)
NGUOI VIET NGAY NAY
7101 Mlk Jr Way S (98118-3594)
PHONE..........................206 725-8384
Long K Nguyen, *President*
EMP: 4
SALES (est): 234.3K **Privately Held**
SIC: 2711 Newspapers

(G-10607)
NICHOLSON MANUFACTURING CO (HQ)
200 S Orcas St (98108-2441)
PHONE..........................206 682-2752
Scott Howell, *CEO*
Scott W Nicholson, *President*
Peter Bowers, *Traffic Mgr*
Steve Gosse, *Buyer*
Paul Nishimura, *CFO*
EMP: 55
SQ FT: 50,000
SALES (est): 16.4MM
SALES (corp-wide): 41.4MM **Privately Held**
WEB: www.nmwa.com
SIC: 3553 5084 3544 3537 Woodworking machinery; industrial machinery & equipment; special dies, tools, jigs & fixtures; industrial trucks & tractors; farm machinery & equipment
PA: Northern Industrial, Inc.
200 S Orcas St
Seattle WA 98108
206 682-2752

(G-10608)
NIFTYBRICK SOFTWARE
1807 E Pike St Unit C (98122-2888)
PHONE..........................206 588-5696
Mark Aiken, *Principal*
EMP: 4 **EST:** 2010
SALES (est): 250.1K **Privately Held**
SIC: 7372 Prepackaged software

(G-10609)
NIKE INC
2649 Ne 46th St (98105-5041)
PHONE..........................206 527-3554
EMP: 4
SALES (corp-wide): 36.4B **Publicly Held**
SIC: 3021 Rubber & plastics footwear
PA: Nike, Inc.
1 Sw Bowerman Dr
Beaverton OR 97005
503 671-6453

(G-10610)
NIMBUS TECHNOLOGIES LLC
4348 9th Ave Ne Apt 101 (98105-1739)
PHONE..........................206 724-5507
EMP: 2
SALES (est): 140K **Privately Held**
SIC: 3827 Mfg Optical Instruments/Lenses

(G-10611)
NITWIT LICE REMOVAL
12551 1st Ave Nw (98177-4403)
PHONE..........................206 327-5782
EMP: 2
SALES (est): 110K **Privately Held**
SIC: 3999 Mfg Misc Products

(G-10612)
NK WOODWORKING LLC (PA)
1605 S 93rd St Ste Eg3 (98108-5112)
PHONE..........................206 257-4395
Phoebe Schraer, *Sales Staff*
Nathie Katzoff, *Mng Member*
EMP: 2
SALES (est): 464.4K **Privately Held**
SIC: 2431 Millwork

(G-10613)
NLPCORE LLC
921 N 82nd St (98103-4321)
PHONE..........................206 883-7616
Varun Mittal, *Owner*
Naveen Garg, *Principal*
EMP: 2
SALES (est): 122K **Privately Held**
SIC: 7372 7389 Application computer software; utility computer software;

(G-10614)
NOBELUS LLC
1414 S Director St (98108-4834)
PHONE..........................800 895-2747
EMP: 4
SALES (corp-wide): 23.1MM **Privately Held**
SIC: 5112 5084 3081 Blank books; cement making machinery; film base, cellulose acetate or nitrocellulose plastic
PA: Nobelus Llc
4841 Lumber Ln Ste 103
Knoxville TN 37921
800 895-2747

(G-10615)
NOBLE GAS NEON COMPANY
11435 Rainier Ave S (98178-3954)
PHONE..........................206 708-6290
Matt Dilling, *Owner*
EMP: 2 **EST:** 2012
SALES (est): 112.7K **Privately Held**
SIC: 2813 Neon

(G-10616)
NOBLE NEON
11435 Rainier Ave S (98178-3954)
PHONE..........................206 708-6290
Lia Hall, *Manager*
EMP: 2
SALES (est): 152.9K **Privately Held**
SIC: 3993 Neon signs

(G-10617)
NODA SOFTWARE
170 Melrose Ave E (98102-5552)
PHONE..........................206 726-1125
EMP: 2 **EST:** 2011
SALES (est): 110K **Privately Held**
SIC: 7372 Prepackaged Software Services

(G-10618)
NOEL INC
7359 23rd Ave Nw (98117-5661)
PHONE..........................206 784-1894
Noel Gilbrough, *Principal*
EMP: 2
SALES (est): 110.5K **Privately Held**
SIC: 2371 Fur goods

(G-10619)
NOON INTERNATIONAL LLC
5506 6th Ave S Ste 101 (98108-2552)
PHONE..........................206 283-8400
Elizabeth Johnson, *Vice Pres*
Veronica Brown, *Accountant*
EMP: 10

▲ = Import ▼=Export
◆ =Import/Export

SALES (est): 110.5K **Privately Held**
SIC: 2037 Frozen fruits & vegetables

(G-10620)
NORBERG PRESS INC
4700 42nd Ave Sw Ste 160 (98116-4561)
PHONE..................................206 938-3905
▲ EMP: 3
SALES (est): 340.3K **Privately Held**
SIC: 2752 Lithographic Commercial Printing

(G-10621)
NORMANDY PRESS LLC
1616 11th Ave W (98119-2904)
PHONE..................................206 285-2881
EMP: 2 EST: 2012
SALES (est): 120K **Privately Held**
SIC: 2741 Misc Publishing

(G-10622)
NORQUEST SEAFOODS INC (HQ)
Also Called: Silver Lining Seafoods
5303 Shilshole Ave Nw (98107-4021)
PHONE..................................206 281-7022
Gerard A Dowd, *President*
Terry Gardiner, *President*
Charles H Bundrant, *Chairman*
John N Garner, *Vice Pres*
Allen K Kimball, *Vice Pres*
▲ EMP: 40
SQ FT: 8,000
SALES (est): 7MM
SALES (corp-wide): 2.3B **Privately Held**
WEB: www.norquest.com
SIC: 2092 Fresh or frozen packaged fish
PA: Trident Seafoods Corporation
  5303 Shilshole Ave Nw
  Seattle WA 98107
  206 783-3818

(G-10623)
NORTH AMERICAN POST PUBLISHING
Also Called: Hokubei Hochi
519 6th Ave S Ste 200 (98104-2878)
P.O. Box 3173 (98114-3173)
PHONE..................................206 726-6460
Tomio Moriguchi, *President*
EMP: 4
SQ FT: 5,000
SALES (est): 400K **Privately Held**
WEB: www.napost.com
SIC: 2711 Commercial printing & newspaper publishing combined

(G-10624)
NORTH INDUSTRIES INC
Also Called: Torrid Manufacturing Company
10826 Glen Acres Dr S (98168-1557)
PHONE..................................206 940-0842
James North, *President*
Kelly T North, *Vice Pres*
EMP: 3 EST: 1985
SQ FT: 20,000
SALES (est): 493.3K **Privately Held**
WEB: www.marinewaterheaters.com
SIC: 3444 3443 3433 3732 Metal ventilating equipment; heat exchangers, condensers & components; heating equipment, except electric; boat building & repairing; manufactured hardware (general)

(G-10625)
NORTH PACIFIC CRANE CO LLC (PA)
10734 Lake City Way Ne (98125-6760)
PHONE..................................206 361-7064
Joseph James, *VP Sales*
Joseph R James, *Mng Member*
Keddy Kleinbergs, *Manager*
▼ EMP: 12
SQ FT: 2,000
SALES (est): 1.8MM **Privately Held**
WEB: www.northpacificcrane.com
SIC: 3536 Hoists, cranes & monorails

(G-10626)
NORTH PACIFIC SEAFOODS INC (HQ)
Also Called: Alaska Pacific Seafood
4 Nickerson St Ste 400 (98109-1699)
P.O. Box 31179 (98103-1179)
PHONE..................................206 726-9900
Masayuki Yano, *CEO*
John Garner, *President*
Tomonobu Miki, *President*
Jeff Backlund, *Vice Pres*
Leauri Moore, *Vice Pres*
◆ EMP: 39
SQ FT: 18,000
SALES (est): 331.3MM **Privately Held**
WEB: www.ssssitka.com
SIC: 2091 Canned & cured fish & seafoods

(G-10627)
NORTH STAR CASTEEL PDTS INC (PA)
820 S Bradford St (98108-5241)
PHONE..................................206 622-0068
Kurtis Gray, *President*
William C Gibb, *Principal*
Nancy J Gray, *Vice Pres*
Nancy Gray, *Vice Pres*
Kurt Gray, *CFO*
EMP: 40
SQ FT: 45,000
SALES (est): 8.3MM **Privately Held**
WEB: www.northstarcasteel.com
SIC: 3325 5072 Alloy steel castings, except investment; chains

(G-10628)
NORTH STAR CASTEEL PDTS INC
3401 Colorado Ave S (98134-1806)
PHONE..................................206 621-1039
Juan Solano, *Principal*
EMP: 9
SALES (est): 1.2MM
SALES (corp-wide): 8.3MM **Privately Held**
SIC: 3369 White metal castings (lead, tin, antimony), except die
PA: North Star Casteel Products, Inc.
  820 S Bradford St
  Seattle WA 98108
  206 622-0068

(G-10629)
NORTH WEST BARRICADES & SIGNS
Also Called: North West Flagging
11229 16th Ave Sw (98146-3580)
PHONE..................................206 243-8004
David Michaels, *Owner*
EMP: 21 EST: 2014
SALES (est): 528.8K **Privately Held**
SIC: 3993 Signs, not made in custom sign painting shops

(G-10630)
NORTHCOAST YACHTS INC
1141 Fairview Ave N (98109-4418)
PHONE..................................253 383-3803
Stephen Yadvish, *President*
EMP: 45
SQ FT: 50,000
SALES (est): 17.5MM **Privately Held**
SIC: 3732 Yachts, building & repairing

(G-10631)
NORTHERN INDUSTRIAL INC (PA)
Also Called: Nicholson Manufacturing
200 S Orcas St (98108-2441)
PHONE..................................206 682-2752
Scott Howell, *CEO*
Scott Nicholson, *President*
Paul Nishimura, *CFO*
Thomas W Nicholson, *Shareholder*
◆ EMP: 50
SQ FT: 50,000
SALES (est): 41.4MM **Privately Held**
WEB: www.nmwa.com
SIC: 2421 3553 Sawmills & planing mills, general; sawmill machines

(G-10632)
NORTHERN LIGHTS INC (DH)
4420 14th Ave Nw (98107-4616)
PHONE..................................206 789-3600
H Clark Lee, *CEO*
Peter B Hill Jr, *President*
Kit Purdy, *President*
Brian Vesely, *General Mgr*
Nathan Price, *Vice Pres*
◆ EMP: 75 EST: 1971
SQ FT: 58,000
SALES (est): 20.3MM
SALES (corp-wide): 181.2MM **Privately Held**
WEB: www.lugger.com
SIC: 3519 5088 5551 Diesel, semi-diesel or duel-fuel engines, including marine; marine crafts & supplies; marine propulsion machinery & equipment; boats, non-recreational; marine supplies; boat dealers; outboard motors; marine supplies & equipment
HQ: Ade Holding, Inc.
  4420 14th Ave Nw
  Seattle WA 98107
  206 789-3600

(G-10633)
NORTHERN WAVE LLC
Also Called: Northern Wave Seafood
1818 Westlake Ave N # 420 (98109-2707)
PHONE..................................206 217-4518
Andrey Svininnikov, *Principal*
▲ EMP: 10
SALES (est): 396.7K **Privately Held**
SIC: 2092 Fresh or frozen packaged fish

(G-10634)
NORTHLAKE SHIPYARD INC
1441 N Northlake Way # 100 (98103-8951)
PHONE..................................206 632-1441
E Peter Kelly, *President*
Peter Kelly, *President*
James Kelly, *Business Mgr*
Richard Kelly Jr, *Vice Pres*
Mick Maddock, *Opers Mgr*
EMP: 10
SALES (est): 500K **Privately Held**
WEB: www.northlakeshipyard.com
SIC: 3731 Shipbuilding & repairing

(G-10635)
NORTHLIGHT COMMUNICATIONS
11395 5th Ave Ne (98125-6170)
PHONE..................................425 493-1903
Bob Tarcea, *Owner*
Vincent Kiteley, *Co-Owner*
EMP: 11
SALES: 475K **Privately Held**
SIC: 2731 Book publishing

(G-10636)
NORTHLIGHT POWER LLC
83 S King St Ste 200 (98104-2875)
PHONE..................................206 780-3551
Dana Zentz, *Vice Pres*
EMP: 4 EST: 2011
SALES (est): 398.4K **Privately Held**
SIC: 3674 Solar cells

(G-10637)
NORTHWEST ARCHITECTURAL LEAGUE
Also Called: ARCADE
1201 Alaskan Way Ste 200 (98101-2913)
PHONE..................................206 971-5596
Kurt Wolken, *President*
Scott Allen, *Vice Pres*
Linda Pruitt, *Treasurer*
Den Rankin, *Admin Sec*
EMP: 8
SALES: 190.2K **Privately Held**
SIC: 2721 Periodicals: publishing & printing

(G-10638)
NORTHWEST BUILDING TECH INC
215 S Austin St (98108-4119)
PHONE..................................206 767-4012
Jeff Hayford, *President*
EMP: 50
SQ FT: 23,000
SALES (est): 6.6MM **Privately Held**
WEB: www.nwbti.com
SIC: 2541 2542 Display fixtures, wood; partitions & fixtures, except wood

(G-10639)
NORTHWEST CENTER (PA)
7272 W Marginal Way S (98108-4140)
P.O. Box 80827 (98108-0827)
PHONE..................................206 285-9140
Richard Valerio, *General Mgr*
Pat Butler, *Vice Pres*
Michael Leslie, *Opers Staff*
Sara Walsh, *Hum Res Coord*
Jennifer Nash, *Marketing Staff*
▲ EMP: 168
SQ FT: 16,000
SALES (est): 50.3MM **Privately Held**
WEB: www.americandataguard.com
SIC: 8331 8322 3599 7211 Vocational training agency; sheltered workshop; child related social services; social services for the handicapped; machine & other job shop work; power laundries, family & commercial; packaging & labeling services

(G-10640)
NORTHWEST CPITL APPRCATION INC (PA)
1200 Westlake Ave N # 310 (98109-3543)
PHONE..................................206 689-5615
Brad Creswell, *Co-President*
E Perot Bissell, *Co-President*
Lisa Mortell, *Controller*
EMP: 601
SQ FT: 3,800
SALES (est): 91.1MM **Privately Held**
SIC: 2611 Pulp produced from wood base

(G-10641)
NORTHWEST DAIRY ASSOCIATION (PA)
5601 6th Ave S Ste 300 (98108-2544)
P.O. Box 80627 (98108-0627)
PHONE..................................206 284-7220
Jim Werkhoven, *CEO*
Randy Lindley, *Corp Secy*
Steve Rowe, *Vice Pres*
◆ EMP: 150
SQ FT: 68,000
SALES (est): 1.4B **Privately Held**
WEB: www.nwdairy.com
SIC: 2023 2026 2022 5143 Dry, condensed, evaporated dairy products; cream, aerated; cheese, natural & processed; dairy products, except dried or canned

(G-10642)
NORTHWEST EURO LLC
2620 W Commodore Way B (98199-1490)
PHONE..................................206 981-8002
EMP: 2
SALES (est): 74.4K **Privately Held**
SIC: 2842 Automobile polish

(G-10643)
NORTHWEST FAMILY STRANDS
14337 Interlake Ave N (98133-7107)
PHONE..................................206 779-8997
Rebecca C Brittle, *Owner*
EMP: 13
SALES (est): 450K **Privately Held**
SIC: 3961 Costume jewelry

(G-10644)
NORTHWEST FLY FISHING LLC
600 1st Ave Ste 202a (98104-2238)
P.O. Box 1209, Winthrop (98862-1209)
PHONE..................................206 667-9359
Scott Lindner, *Mktg Dir*
Steve Cole, *Mng Member*
EMP: 7
SALES (est): 750.1K **Privately Held**
WEB: www.nwflyfishing.net
SIC: 2721 Magazines: publishing only, not printed on site

(G-10645)
NORTHWEST FROZEN LLC
Also Called: BANZAI
3623 6th Ave S Ste 200 (98134-2200)
PHONE..................................206 388-3551
Philip Sinz, *Mng Member*
James Foreman,

▲ EMP: 43
SQ FT: 33,338
SALES: 11.7MM **Privately Held**
SIC: 2038 Frozen specialties

(G-10646)
NORTHWEST LABEL/DESIGN INC
3225 20th Ave W (98199-2301)
PHONE.................................206 282-5568
Mike Perry, *President*
Evelyn Perry, *Vice Pres*
Angie Carroll, *Manager*
EMP: 24
SQ FT: 6,000
SALES (est): 4.1MM **Privately Held**
WEB: www.nwlabel.com
SIC: 2759 2672 Labels & seals: printing; coated & laminated paper

(G-10647)
NORTHWEST LABOR INDUSTRIES
6204 Latona Ave Ne (98115-6553)
PHONE.................................206 388-6135
EMP: 2
SALES (est): 116.9K **Privately Held**
SIC: 3999 Manufacturing industries

(G-10648)
NORTHWEST LAMINATING CO INC (PA)
1136 Nw 51st St (98107-5125)
PHONE.................................206 789-5536
Brad Huber, *President*
Dave Wailes, *General Mgr*
Kimberly Huber, *Corp Secy*
Herbert O Huber, *Vice Pres*
Joel Hazel, *Branch Mgr*
▲ EMP: 11 **EST:** 1954
SQ FT: 11,000
SALES (est): 3.5MM **Privately Held**
SIC: 5162 3083 Plastics sheets & rods; laminated plastic sheets

(G-10649)
NORTHWEST PEAKS BREWERY LLC
4912 17th Ave Nw Ste B (98107-4725)
PHONE.................................206 853-0525
Kevin Carl Klein,
EMP: 3 **EST:** 2010
SALES (est): 150K **Privately Held**
SIC: 2082 Beer (alcoholic beverage)

(G-10650)
NORTHWEST PRESS LLC
2621 E Madison St (98112-4711)
PHONE.................................646 926-6427
Charles Christensen,
EMP: 2
SALES (est): 131.5K **Privately Held**
SIC: 2731 Book publishing

(G-10651)
NORTHWEST RUNNER
Also Called: Rudow Specialty Publishing
6310 Ne 74th St Ste 217e (98115-8169)
PHONE.................................206 527-5301
Martin Rudow, *Owner*
Club Northwest, *Co-Owner*
EMP: 2
SALES: 600K **Privately Held**
WEB: www.nwrunner.com
SIC: 2721 8011 Magazines: publishing & printing; offices & clinics of medical doctors

(G-10652)
NORTHWEST TECHNOLOGIES
5415 Ne 55th St (98105-2867)
PHONE.................................206 528-5353
Michael G Fox, *Owner*
▲ EMP: 3
SALES (est): 600K **Privately Held**
SIC: 5734 7371 7372 7378 Computer peripheral equipment; computer software development; prepackaged software; computer maintenance & repair; computer peripheral equipment

(G-10653)
NORTHWESTERN INDUSTRIES INC (HQ)
2500 W Jameson St (98199-1294)
PHONE.................................206 285-3140
Yoshiyuki Fujii, *CEO*
Tim McQuade, *President*
Darrell Aldrich, *Vice Pres*
Rick Nelson, *Vice Pres*
John Butler, *Plant Mgr*
▲ EMP: 20
SQ FT: 64,240
SALES (est): 5MM **Privately Held**
WEB: www.nwiglass.com
SIC: 3211 3231 Window glass, clear & colored; tempered glass; insulating glass, sealed units; laminated glass; products of purchased glass

(G-10654)
NORTON SOUND FISH COMPANY LLC
1200 Westlake Ave N # 900 (98109-3529)
PHONE.................................206 298-1200
Erik Breivik,
John Bundy,
EMP: 40
SALES (est): 6MM **Privately Held**
SIC: 0912 2091 Finfish; canned & cured fish & seafoods

(G-10655)
NORWEST BUSINESS FORMS & SUPS
3836 Sw Orchard St (98126-3244)
PHONE.................................206 938-4387
Kevin Padon, *Owner*
EMP: 4
SQ FT: 1,000
SALES (est): 308.1K **Privately Held**
SIC: 5112 2752 Business forms; computer paper; envelopes; stationery; commercial printing, lithographic

(G-10656)
NOSTOPSIGN LLC
1200 E Pike St Unit 215 (98122-4344)
PHONE.................................213 422-1750
Kang IL Koh, *CEO*
EMP: 2 **EST:** 2016
SQ FT: 110
SALES (est): 52.7K **Privately Held**
SIC: 7372 Application computer software; home entertainment computer software

(G-10657)
NOTA BENE CELLARS LTD
9320 15th Ave S (98108-5105)
PHONE.................................206 762-5581
Timothy W Narby, *Principal*
EMP: 4
SALES (est): 186K **Privately Held**
SIC: 2084 Wines

(G-10658)
NOVA FISHERIES INC
Also Called: Nova Fisheries & Market Coop
2532 Yale Ave E (98102-3208)
PHONE.................................206 781-2000
Robert Simon, *President*
◆ EMP: 5
SQ FT: 4,000
SALES (est): 638.5K **Privately Held**
WEB: www.novafish.com
SIC: 2092 6799 Fish, frozen: prepared; seafoods, frozen: prepared; venture capital companies

(G-10659)
NOVARTIS VCCNES DAGNOSTICS INC
201 Elliott Ave W Ste 150 (98119-4230)
PHONE.................................862 778-2100
Francois Lebel, *Site Mgr*
EMP: 155
SALES (corp-wide): 39.5B **Privately Held**
WEB: www.chiron.com
SIC: 2834 Pharmaceutical preparations
HQ: Novartis Vaccines And Diagnostics, Inc.
   475 Green Oaks Pkwy
   Holly Springs NC 27540
   617 871-7000

(G-10660)
NOVELTY HILL WINERY LLC
1000 2nd Ave Ste 3700 (98104-1053)
PHONE.................................206 664-2522
Mike Januik, *Principal*
EMP: 2
SALES (est): 270K **Privately Held**
SIC: 2084 Wines

(G-10661)
NOVUSTONE LLC
3100 Airport Way S # 71 (98134-2138)
PHONE.................................206 457-4443
Matt Muhsam, *Opers Mgr*
Aaron Cohen,
EMP: 2
SALES: 277K **Privately Held**
SIC: 3272 Cast stone, concrete

(G-10662)
NPM LLC
1080 W Ewing Pl Ste D (98119-1498)
PHONE.................................206 782-8999
Bill Forsell, *Principal*
EMP: 5
SALES (est): 251.9K **Privately Held**
SIC: 7699 3731 Nautical repair services; shipbuilding & repairing

(G-10663)
NRC ENVIRONMENTAL SERVICES INC
9520 10th Ave S Ste 150 (98108-5067)
PHONE.................................206 607-3000
Jim Riedel, *Branch Mgr*
EMP: 70
SALES (corp-wide): 360.1MM **Publicly Held**
SIC: 1389 Lease tanks, oil field: erecting, cleaning & repairing
HQ: Nrc Environmental Services, Inc.
   1605 Ferry Pt
   Alameda CA 94501

(G-10664)
NUANCE COMMUNICATIONS INC
821 2nd Ave Ste 1200 (98104-1568)
PHONE.................................781 565-5000
Charles Berger, *President*
Ryan Granard, *Vice Pres*
Vince Iannotti, *Engineer*
Troy Mathern, *Manager*
Matthew Crabtree, *Software Engr*
EMP: 150 **Publicly Held**
SIC: 7372 Application computer software
PA: Nuance Communications, Inc.
   1 Wayside Rd
   Burlington MA 01803

(G-10665)
NUBBLE ROAD MUSIC & PUBG LLC
8712 18th Ave Nw (98117-3514)
PHONE.................................206 283-0696
Kristin Chambers, *Principal*
EMP: 4
SALES (est): 189.1K **Privately Held**
SIC: 2741 Miscellaneous publishing

(G-10666)
NUCOR CORPORATION
Nucor Steel Seattle Div
2424 Sw Andover St (98106-1100)
PHONE.................................206 933-2222
Douglas J Jellison, *General Mgr*
Denise Jenkins, *Buyer*
Jamie Spivey, *Human Res Dir*
Ed Shilley, *Supervisor*
EMP: 110
SALES (corp-wide): 25B **Publicly Held**
WEB: www.nucor.com
SIC: 3325 3449 3441 3312 Steel foundries; miscellaneous metalwork; fabricated structural metal; blast furnaces & steel mills
PA: Nucor Corporation
   1915 Rexford Rd Ste 400
   Charlotte NC 28211
   704 366-7000

(G-10667)
NUCOR STEEL SEATTLE INC (HQ)
Also Called: Nucor Steel Bar Mills Group
2424 Sw Andover St (98106-1100)
PHONE.................................206 933-2222
James Darsey, *President*
John Ferriola, *Chairman*
James Frias, *Vice Pres*
Dan Gallagher, *Manager*
A Rae Eagle, *Admin Sec*
▲ EMP: 140
SALES (est): 55.1MM
SALES (corp-wide): 25B **Publicly Held**
WEB: www.nucor-seattle.com
SIC: 3312 Blast furnaces & steel mills
PA: Nucor Corporation
   1915 Rexford Rd Ste 400
   Charlotte NC 28211
   704 366-7000

(G-10668)
NUGENT GIS & ENVIRONMENTAL SVC
1925 7th Ave W (98119-2815)
PHONE.................................206 324-0059
John Nugent, *CEO*
EMP: 2
SALES (est): 156.9K **Privately Held**
SIC: 3822 Auto controls regulating residntl & coml environmt & applncs

(G-10669)
NUID INC
5111 Latona Ave Ne (98105-3741)
PHONE.................................360 927-4682
Ethan Landau, *Principal*
EMP: 6
SALES (est): 251.5K **Privately Held**
SIC: 3699 Security devices

(G-10670)
NUTRIFASTER INC
209 S Bennett St (98108-2226)
PHONE.................................206 767-5054
Bert Robins, *President*
Michael Robins, *Vice Pres*
Adam Kauffman, *Sales Mgr*
▲ EMP: 8
SQ FT: 5,000
SALES (est): 1.6MM **Privately Held**
WEB: www.nutrifaster.com
SIC: 3634 3556 Juice extractors, electric; food products machinery

(G-10671)
NUUN & COMPANY INC
800 Maynard Ave S Ste 102 (98134-1334)
P.O. Box 3312 (98114-3312)
PHONE.................................206 219-9237
Kevin Rutherford, *President*
Molly McGuire, *Cust Mgr*
Amanda Tuttle, *Sales Staff*
Nate Underwood, *Sales Staff*
Peter Beels, *Marketing Staff*
EMP: 60
SALES (est): 9.9MM **Privately Held**
SIC: 2834 Tablets, pharmaceutical

(G-10672)
NW ASIAN WEEKLY
412 Maynard Ave S (98104-2917)
PHONE.................................206 223-5559
Assunta Linq, *Principal*
George Liu, *Executive*
EMP: 5
SALES (est): 177.5K **Privately Held**
SIC: 2711 Commercial printing & newspaper publishing combined; newspapers, publishing & printing

(G-10673)
NW CENTER INDUSTRIES 5307
7272 W Marginal Way S (98108-4140)
PHONE.................................206 285-9140
Sarah Case, *Manager*
EMP: 1500 **EST:** 2009
SALES (est): 48.9MM **Privately Held**
SIC: 3999 Manufacturing industries

(G-10674)
NW POLE VAULT CAMPS
7527 27th Ave Ne (98115-4630)
PHONE.................................206 526-0436
Kathy Reilly, *Principal*

GEOGRAPHIC SECTION

Seattle - King County (G-10706)

Timothy Reilly, *Director*
EMP: 3
SALES (est): 279.8K **Privately Held**
SIC: 3272 Burial vaults, concrete or precast terrazzo

(G-10675)
NW PUBLISHING CENTER
11611 Marine View Dr Sw (98146-1825)
PHONE..................206 242-1822
Mike Daigle, *Principal*
EMP: 2 **EST:** 2010
SALES (est): 126.7K **Privately Held**
SIC: 2741 Miscellaneous publishing

(G-10676)
NWFSC
2725 Montlake Blvd E (98112-2013)
PHONE..................206 860-3415
EMP: 2
SALES (est): 233.6K **Privately Held**
SIC: 2399 Fishing nets

(G-10677)
O B WILLIAMS COMPANY
Also Called: William Ob Co Woodwork
1939 1st Ave S (98134-1405)
PHONE..................206 623-2494
David A Wick, *Ch of Bd*
Terry Wick, *Vice Pres*
▼ **EMP:** 30 **EST:** 1889
SQ FT: 38,220
SALES (est): 5.5MM **Privately Held**
WEB: www.obwilliams.com
SIC: 2431 Millwork

(G-10678)
OBJECT PUBLISHING SOFTWARE
4616 25th Ave Ne (98105-4183)
PHONE..................206 414-9440
Tim Hennings, *Principal*
EMP: 2 **EST:** 2010
SALES (est): 112.1K **Privately Held**
SIC: 2741 Miscellaneous publishing

(G-10679)
OBSERVA INC
323 N 46th St Ste B (98103-6310)
PHONE..................206 499-4444
Hugh Holman, *CEO*
Erik Chelstad, *Chief Engr*
EMP: 12 **EST:** 2015
SALES (est): 100.1K **Privately Held**
SIC: 7372 Business oriented computer software

(G-10680)
OCARINA ARENA
2629 E Aloha St (98112-4121)
PHONE..................206 446-5354
EMP: 2 **EST:** 2010
SALES (est): 91.1K **Privately Held**
SIC: 3931 Ocarinas

(G-10681)
OCCASIONAL PUBLISHING INC
2221 Nw 56th St Ste 101 (98107-4057)
PHONE..................877 373-8273
Michael John, *Principal*
EMP: 2
SALES (est): 109.5K **Privately Held**
SIC: 2741 Miscellaneous publishing

(G-10682)
OCEAN BEAUTY SEAFOODS LLC (PA)
1100 W Ewing St (98119-1321)
P.O. Box 70739 (98127-1539)
PHONE..................206 285-6800
Stacey Colvin, *Sales Staff*
Terry Woods, *Director*
Howard Klein,
◆ **EMP:** 150
SQ FT: 200,000
SALES: 438.8MM **Privately Held**
WEB: www.oceanbeauty.com
SIC: 2091 2092 Canned & cured fish & seafoods; fresh or frozen packaged fish

(G-10683)
OCEAN PEACE INC
4201 21st Ave W (98199-1202)
PHONE..................206 282-6100
Michael Faris, *President*
Mikeal Runyon, *Principal*
EMP: 67
SALES (est): 6.2MM **Privately Held**
SIC: 0912 2092 Finfish; fresh or frozen packaged fish

(G-10684)
OCTOBER MIST PUBLISHING
3012 Nw 85th St Apt B (98117-3955)
PHONE..................206 933-1414
EMP: 2
SALES (est): 87.4K **Privately Held**
SIC: 2741 Miscellaneous publishing

(G-10685)
ODYSSEY ENTERPRISES INC
2729 6th Ave S (98134-2101)
PHONE..................206 285-7445
EMP: 200
SALES (corp-wide): 161.8MM **Privately Held**
SIC: 2092 5146 5812 5142 Seafoods, frozen: prepared; seafoods; eating places; packaged frozen goods
PA: Odyssey Enterprises, Inc.
2729 6th Ave S Ste 200
Seattle WA 98134
206 285-7445

(G-10686)
OF THE EARTH
7706 Aurora Ave N (98103-4752)
PHONE..................206 462-7022
Kevin John Graham, *Owner*
◆ **EMP:** 10
SALES: 750K **Privately Held**
WEB: www.custompaper.com
SIC: 2621 Stationery, envelope & tablet papers

(G-10687)
OFTEN ON GLASS
4702 42nd Ave S (98118-1630)
PHONE..................206 725-5306
Patrick Odowd, *Owner*
EMP: 2
SALES (est): 89.4K **Privately Held**
SIC: 3229 Vases, glass

(G-10688)
OIL VINEGAR
900 1st Ave S Ste 204 (98134-1236)
PHONE..................206 285-0517
EMP: 2
SALES (est): 62.3K **Privately Held**
SIC: 2099 Vinegar

(G-10689)
OLD GROWTH NORTHWEST
9518 Sand Point Way Ne (98115-2649)
PHONE..................206 856-6293
Erin Fried, *Principal*
Alexander Haddad, *Exec Dir*
Susan Rees, *Instructor*
Massimo Bardetti,
Brian Langston, *Assistant*
EMP: 2
SALES (est): 105.2K **Privately Held**
SIC: 2731 Books: publishing only

(G-10690)
OLIVE OMG OILS
309 S Cloverdale St C25 (98108-4571)
PHONE..................206 340-4114
EMP: 3
SALES (est): 91.3K **Privately Held**
SIC: 2079 Olive oil

(G-10691)
OLYMPIC FOUNDRY INC (PA)
5200 Airport Way S (98108-1725)
PHONE..................206 764-6200
Scott McLaughlin, *President*
Russell Goodsell, *President*
Kenneth Martin, *Corp Secy*
F Gooding, *Vice Pres*
Michael Stuart, *Admin Sec*
◆ **EMP:** 40
SQ FT: 150,000
SALES (est): 25.6MM **Privately Held**
WEB: www.olympicfoundry.com
SIC: 5051 3366 3365 3325 Steel; castings, rough: iron or steel; copper foundries; aluminum foundries; steel foundries; malleable iron foundries

(G-10692)
OLYMPIC MEDICAL CORP
5900 1st Ave S (98108-3249)
PHONE..................206 767-3500
Jones Jay, *President*
Hawkins James, *Purch Dir*
Murphy Steven, *Treasurer*
Brinne Fisher, *Admin Sec*
▲ **EMP:** 100
SQ FT: 60,000
SALES (est): 19MM
SALES (corp-wide): 530.8MM **Publicly Held**
WEB: www.olymed.com
SIC: 3845 3841 Electromedical equipment; surgical & medical instruments
PA: Natus Medical Incorporated
6701 Koll Center Pkwy # 120
Pleasanton CA 94566
925 223-6700

(G-10693)
OLYMPIC PRINT AND APPAREL
6047 California Ave Sw (98136-1612)
PHONE..................206 402-3642
Sandy Jimenez, *Principal*
EMP: 2
SALES (est): 85.4K **Privately Held**
SIC: 5632 3993 2752 Fur apparel, made to custom order; signs & advertising specialties; commercial printing, lithographic

(G-10694)
OLYMPIC PROTEIN SCIENCES LLC
Also Called: Olympic Protein Technologies
454 N 34th St (98103-8602)
PHONE..................206 849-9811
Michael Wittekind, *CEO*
EMP: 3
SQ FT: 1,000
SALES (est): 135.2K **Privately Held**
SIC: 2834 Solutions, pharmaceutical

(G-10695)
OLYMPIC SYTEMS INC
3800 Aurora Ave N Ste 360 (98103-8721)
PHONE..................206 547-5777
James Beers, *President*
Thomas Goodspeed, *Sales Dir*
EMP: 5
SALES: 2MM **Privately Held**
WEB: www.olysystems.com
SIC: 7372 Business oriented computer software

(G-10696)
OMAGE LABS INC
1601 5th Ave Ste 1100 (98101-3603)
PHONE..................844 662-4326
Corey Salka, *CEO*
Adam Elkington, *Principal*
EMP: 2
SQ FT: 110
SALES (est): 68.4K **Privately Held**
SIC: 7372 7374 8059 8082 Application computer software; data processing & preparation; nursing home, except skilled & intermediate care facility; home health care services

(G-10697)
OMEGA GRAPHICS AND SIGNS LLC
4321 Leary Way Nw (98107-4538)
PHONE..................206 789-5480
Robert Kehoe,
EMP: 8
SQ FT: 1,400
SALES (est): 843.6K **Privately Held**
SIC: 7389 3993 7312 Sign painting & lettering shop; signs & advertising specialties; outdoor advertising services

(G-10698)
OMEROS CORPORATION (PA)
201 Elliott Ave W (98119-4240)
PHONE..................206 676-5000
Timothy M Duffy, *Vice Pres*
Timi Edeki, *Vice Pres*
George A Gaitanaris, *Vice Pres*
Marcia S Kelbon, *Vice Pres*
Daniel G Kirby, *Vice Pres*
EMP: 193
SQ FT: 108,000
SALES: 29.8MM **Publicly Held**
WEB: www.omeros.com
SIC: 2834 Pharmaceutical preparations

(G-10699)
OMNI DEVELOPMENT INC
Also Called: Omni Group
1000 Dexter Ave N Ste 400 (98109-3580)
PHONE..................206 523-4152
Kenneth Case, *CEO*
Molly Reed, *Corp Secy*
Brian Covey, *Manager*
Aaron Cendickson, *Info Tech Mgr*
Andrew Burkhalter, *Software Engr*
EMP: 32
SQ FT: 7,500
SALES (est): 4.1MM **Privately Held**
WEB: www.omnigroup.com
SIC: 7372 Prepackaged software

(G-10700)
ON PURPOSE PUBLISHING
8010 13th Ave Nw (98117-4203)
PHONE..................206 789-9677
Robert Dunaway, *President*
EMP: 2
SALES (est): 133.5K **Privately Held**
SIC: 2741 Miscellaneous publishing

(G-10701)
ONE BUILD INC
814 2nd Ave Ste 500 (98104-1543)
PHONE..................206 801-1675
Dale Robert Sperling, *Principal*
EMP: 4
SALES (est): 451.5K **Privately Held**
SIC: 3441 Building components, structural steel

(G-10702)
ONE EARTH PRESS
105 Nw 75th St (98117-3014)
PHONE..................206 784-1641
Marlin Greene, *Principal*
EMP: 2
SALES (est): 96.7K **Privately Held**
SIC: 2741 Miscellaneous publishing

(G-10703)
ONO CAKES AND DELIGHTS
12724 Lake City Way Ne A3 (98125-4450)
PHONE..................206 257-9046
Carlton Braga, *Principal*
EMP: 4
SALES (est): 230.4K **Privately Held**
SIC: 2051 Bakery: wholesale or wholesale/retail combined

(G-10704)
OOLA INDUSTRIES LLC
Also Called: Oola Distillery
1314 E Union St (98122-4144)
PHONE..................206 709-7909
Alan Jackson, *Managing Dir*
Kirby Kallas-Lewis, *Mng Member*
EMP: 8
SQ FT: 4,500
SALES: 1.2MM **Privately Held**
SIC: 2084 Wines, brandy & brandy spirits

(G-10705)
OPI DOWNHOLE TECHNOLOGIES LLC
2151 N Northlake Way D (98103-9157)
PHONE..................206 557-7032
Rahul Shendure, *Partner*
Balakrishnan Nair, *Partner*
EMP: 3
SALES (est): 219K **Privately Held**
SIC: 3533 Drilling tools for gas, oil or water wells

(G-10706)
OPI WIND TECHNOLOGIES INC
Also Called: Linetica
2151 N Northlake Way D (98103-9157)
PHONE..................206 999-5373
Rahul Shendure, *Chairman*
Balakrishnan Nair, *Bd of Directors*
EMP: 5
SALES (est): 488.5K **Privately Held**
SIC: 3511 8711 Turbines & turbine generator sets; mechanical engineering

Seattle - King County (G-10707) — GEOGRAPHIC SECTION

(G-10707)
OPPENHEIMER CAMERA PDTS INC
7400 3rd Ave S (98108-4143)
PHONE..................................206 467-8666
Martin Oppenheimer, *President*
EMP: 7
SALES (est): 1MM **Privately Held**
SIC: 3861 Motion picture film

(G-10708)
OPTICYTE INC
5731 58th Ave Ne (98105-2019)
PHONE..................................206 696-3957
Kenneth Schenkman, *President*
EMP: 3
SALES (est): 239.6K **Privately Held**
SIC: 3841 Surgical & medical instruments

(G-10709)
OPTIMISM BREWING LLC
909 E Union St (98122-3822)
PHONE..................................206 651-5429
EMP: 10 **EST:** 2013
SALES (est): 1MM **Privately Held**
SIC: 2082 Malt beverages

(G-10710)
ORACLE CORPORATION
1501 4th Ave Ste 1800 (98101-1636)
PHONE..................................206 695-9000
EMP: 2
SALES (corp-wide): 39.5B **Publicly Held**
SIC: 7372 Prepackaged software
PA: Oracle Corporation
500 Oracle Pkwy
Redwood City CA 94065
650 506-7000

(G-10711)
ORCA BAY FOODS LLC
Also Called: Odyssey Foods
206 Sw Michigan St (98106-1908)
PHONE..................................206 762-7364
Theodore Hadley, *General Mgr*
EMP: 395
SALES (corp-wide): 119.7MM **Privately Held**
SIC: 2092 Fish, frozen: prepared
PA: Orca Bay Foods, Llc
2729 6th Ave Ste 200
Seattle WA 98134
206 285-7445

(G-10712)
ORCA COMPOSITES
22 S Idaho St (98134-1119)
PHONE..................................206 782-0660
EMP: 3
SALES (est): 180.6K **Privately Held**
SIC: 2821 Plastics materials & resins

(G-10713)
OREILLY SIGNS
1309a Raven Rd (98105)
PHONE..................................206 623-5135
Richard O'Reilly, *Partner*
EMP: 3
SALES: 200K **Privately Held**
WEB: www.oreillysigns.com
SIC: 3993 Signs, not made in custom sign painting shops

(G-10714)
ORIGAMI INC
Also Called: Times Table
9829 Triton Dr Nw (98117-2544)
PHONE..................................206 784-9133
Mary Brunkow, *President*
Ross Colquhoun, *Vice Pres*
▼ **EMP:** 2
SALES: 50K **Privately Held**
WEB: www.origamiinc.com
SIC: 3499 Furniture parts, metal

(G-10715)
OSCILLA POWER INC (PA)
4240 Gilman Pl W Ste C (98199-1248)
PHONE..................................206 557-7102
Rahul Shendure, *CEO*
Tim Mundon, *Chief Engr*
Andrew Gill, *Engineer*
EMP: 4
SALES: 250K **Privately Held**
SIC: 3621 Motors & generators

(G-10716)
OTOGEAR
9212 45th Ave Ne (98115-3848)
PHONE..................................360 852-0250
Kelly Tremblay, *Principal*
EMP: 2
SALES (est): 89.6K **Privately Held**
SIC: 3599 Industrial machinery

(G-10717)
OUTDOOR RESEARCH LLC
2203 1st Ave S Ste 700 (98134-1424)
PHONE..................................206 467-8197
Dan Nordstrom,
Clark Campbell,
David Mahoney,
Ken Meidell,
Jordan Wand,
▲ **EMP:** 200 **EST:** 1978
SQ FT: 144,050
SALES (est): 39.2MM **Privately Held**
WEB: www.orgear.com
SIC: 2393 2353 2381 3021 Bags & containers, except sleeping bags: textile; hats, caps & millinery; gloves, work: woven or knit, made from purchased materials; gloves, woven or knit: made from purchased materials; mittens, woven or knit: made from purchased materials; gaiters, rubber or rubber soled fabric; traveling bags; first aid, snake bite & burn kits

(G-10718)
OUTDOOR RESEARCH-CANADA INC
2203 1st Ave S Ste 700 (98134-1424)
PHONE..................................206 467-8197
Ron Gregg, *Principal*
Michelle Wardian, *Principal*
▲ **EMP:** 3
SALES (est): 147.3K **Privately Held**
SIC: 2393 Textile bags

(G-10719)
OUTLAW LEATHER LLC
5020 Ohio Ave S (98134-2445)
PHONE..................................206 679-7483
EMP: 2
SALES (est): 207.7K **Privately Held**
SIC: 3111 Leather tanning & finishing

(G-10720)
OVERDUE MEDIA LLC
4819 S Oregon St (98118-1449)
PHONE..................................206 860-2199
William Barnes,
▲ **EMP:** 3
SALES: 100K **Privately Held**
WEB: www.overduemedia.com
SIC: 2731 Books: publishing only

(G-10721)
OVERNIGHT PRTG & GRAPHICS INC
2412 1st Ave S (98134-1422)
PHONE..................................206 621-9412
Peter Yang, *President*
EMP: 5
SQ FT: 1,300
SALES (est): 982.9K **Privately Held**
SIC: 2752 5044 Commercial printing, offset; copying equipment

(G-10722)
OVERSEA CASING COMPANY LLC (PA)
601 S Nevada St (98108-1713)
PHONE..................................206 682-6845
Michael Mayo, *Mng Member*
David Mayo,
◆ **EMP:** 25
SALES (est): 17.9MM **Privately Held**
WEB: www.overseacasing.com
SIC: 5149 2013 Sausage casings; sausage casings, natural

(G-10723)
OVERSEAS SECURITY
12345 Lake City Way Ne # 2052 (98125-5401)
PHONE..................................206 364-6784
Jeffery Cox, *Owner*
EMP: 2
SALES (est): 112.5K **Privately Held**
SIC: 3599 Custom machinery

(G-10724)
OWEN KOTLER SELECTIONS LLC
1400 10th Ave W (98119-3229)
PHONE..................................917 912-0678
Owen Kotler,
EMP: 4
SALES (est): 126K **Privately Held**
SIC: 2084 Wines

(G-10725)
P & M FIBERGLASS COMPANY INC
1403 10th Ave W (98119-3228)
PHONE..................................206 784-1940
Pat McCormick, *President*
Margie McCormick, *Vice Pres*
EMP: 3 **EST:** 1967
SQ FT: 2,500
SALES (est): 170K **Privately Held**
SIC: 3089 Plastic hardware & building products

(G-10726)
PACARC LLC
202 Lake Washington Blvd (98122-6540)
PHONE..................................206 547-4591
Mike Blaskowsky, *General Mgr*
James Allard, *Marketing Staff*
▲ **EMP:** 5
SQ FT: 1,200
SALES (est): 562.9K **Privately Held**
SIC: 3261 Bathroom accessories/fittings, vitreous china or earthenware

(G-10727)
PACIFIC ASIAN ENTERPRISES INC
Also Called: Nordhavn Yachts, Northwest
2601 W Marina Pl Ste S (98199-4331)
PHONE..................................206 223-3624
Don Kuhlmann, *Branch Mgr*
EMP: 2
SALES (corp-wide): 9.3MM **Privately Held**
WEB: www.nordhavn.com
SIC: 3732 Yachts, building & repairing
PA: Pacific Asian Enterprises, Inc.
25001 Dana Dr
Dana Point CA 92629
949 496-4848

(G-10728)
PACIFIC BIOMARKERS INC (PA)
645 Elliott Ave W Ste 300 (98119-3898)
PHONE..................................206 298-0068
Ronald Helm, *CEO*
John P Jensen, *Vice Pres*
Maribeth Raines, *Vice Pres*
EMP: 40
SALES (est): 6MM **Privately Held**
SIC: 8071 8734 3826 8731 Testing laboratories; testing laboratories; calibration & certification; blood testing apparatus; commercial physical research; industrial instrmnts msrmnt display/control process variable

(G-10729)
PACIFIC COAST FEATHER LLC (DH)
1736 4th Ave S Ste B (98134-1512)
PHONE..................................206 624-1057
Stew Bayuk, *Vice Pres*
Alex Blanco, *Vice Pres*
Scott Carlson, *Vice Pres*
Joana Zhang, *Vice Pres*
Pedro Pena, *Plant Mgr*
◆ **EMP:** 150
SALES (est): 291.4MM
SALES (corp-wide): 929.4MM **Privately Held**
WEB: www.pacificcoast.com
SIC: 2392 Cushions & pillows; comforters & quilts: made from purchased materials
HQ: Hollander Sleep Products, Llc
901 W Yamato Rd Ste 250
Boca Raton FL 33431
561 997-6900

(G-10730)
PACIFIC COATINGS INC
9243 Martin Luther King (98118-5314)
PHONE..................................206 722-1413
Gerald Guertin, *President*
Keith Antonius, *Vice Pres*
Karl Eels, *Admin Sec*
EMP: 12
SALES: 1MM **Privately Held**
SIC: 2952 5033 5072 5082 Coating compounds, tar; roofing, siding & insulation; hand tools; power tools & accessories; general construction machinery & equipment

(G-10731)
PACIFIC FISHERMEN INC
5351 24th Ave Nw (98107-4196)
PHONE..................................206 784-2562
Gunnar Iidhuso Jr, *President*
Doug Dixon, *General Mgr*
Ron Van Hoose, *Controller*
Debbie Duback, *Bookkeeper*
EMP: 72
SQ FT: 33,000
SALES (est): 9MM **Privately Held**
WEB: www.pacificfishermen.com
SIC: 3731 Fishing vessels, large: building & repairing

(G-10732)
PACIFIC FSHRMEN SHPYRD ELC LLC
Also Called: Pfi Marine Electric
5351 24th Ave Nw (98107-4122)
PHONE..................................206 784-2562
Ron Van Hoose, *Sales Mgr*
Doug Dixon, *Mng Member*
▲ **EMP:** 70
SALES: 13.6MM **Privately Held**
SIC: 3731 Shipbuilding & repairing

(G-10733)
PACIFIC GEM INC
2107 Elliott Ave Ste 209 (98121-2139)
PHONE..................................206 448-7700
Dave Stone, *President*
Rose Stone, *Vice Pres*
EMP: 2
SQ FT: 1,300
SALES: 1MM **Privately Held**
SIC: 5094 3911 Diamonds (gems); jewelry, precious metal

(G-10734)
PACIFIC MARKET INC (PA)
2401 Elliott Ave Ste 400 (98121-3309)
PHONE..................................206 441-1400
Robert Harris, *President*
Brian Shea, *Treasurer*
◆ **EMP:** 142
SALES (est): 14.6MM **Privately Held**
SIC: 3221 Bottles for packing, bottling & canning: glass

(G-10735)
PACIFIC MARKET INTL LLC (HQ)
Also Called: P M I
2401 Elliott Ave Ste 400 (98121-3309)
PHONE..................................206 441-1400
Robert M Harris Jr,
Steve Fraser,
Rob Harris Jr,
Arnie Prentice,
◆ **EMP:** 142
SQ FT: 22,000
SALES (est): 74.2MM
SALES (corp-wide): 14.6MM **Privately Held**
SIC: 3411 Food & beverage containers
PA: Pacific Market, Inc.
2401 Elliott Ave Ste 400
Seattle WA 98121
206 441-1400

(G-10736)
PACIFIC NORTHWEST
4215 23rd Ave W (98199-1210)
PHONE..................................206 453-3182
Brian Farmer, *Principal*
Christine Clymer, *Office Mgr*
EMP: 8
SALES (est): 975.8K **Privately Held**
SIC: 3444 Sheet metalwork

▲ = Import ▼ = Export ◆ = Import/Export

GEOGRAPHIC SECTION

Seattle - King County (G-10767)

(G-10737)
PACIFIC NORTHWEST NEWSPAPER
101 Elliott Ave W (98119-4236)
PHONE.................................206 448-8125
EMP: 2
SALES (est): 69.2K Privately Held
SIC: 2711 Newspapers, publishing & printing

(G-10738)
PACIFIC PLUMBING SUPPLY CO LLC
Also Called: Master Source
5964 6th Ave S (98108-3302)
PHONE.................................425 251-0604
Tom Heaney, *Branch Mgr*
EMP: 15
SALES (corp-wide): 85.3MM Privately Held
WEB: www.mastersource.biz
SIC: 5074 2499 Plumbing fittings & supplies; kitchen, bathroom & household ware: wood
PA: Pacific Plumbing Supply Co Llc
    7115 W Marginal Way Sw
    Seattle WA 98106
    206 762-5920

(G-10739)
PACIFIC PUBLISHING STUDIO LLC
4518 Sw Edmunds St (98116-4423)
PHONE.................................206 371-5628
Stacie White Vander Pol, *Principal*
EMP: 2 **EST:** 2012
SALES (est): 90.8K Privately Held
SIC: 2741 Miscellaneous publishing

(G-10740)
PACIFIC SHEET METAL INC
1128 Sw Spokane St (98134-1128)
P.O. Box 80583 (98108-0583)
PHONE.................................206 682-5354
William N Zaknich, *President*
Nick Zaknich, *Vice Pres*
EMP: 20 **EST:** 1957
SQ FT: 18,000
SALES (est): 3.4MM Privately Held
SIC: 1761 3444 Roofing contractor; sheet metalwork; sheet metalwork

(G-10741)
PACIFIC STUDIO INC
5311 Shilshole Ave Nw (98107-4021)
PHONE.................................206 783-5226
Al Salm, *CEO*
Malcolm Perkins Jr, *President*
Ruth Brinton, *Vice Pres*
EMP: 100
SQ FT: 38,000
SALES (est): 12.6MM Privately Held
WEB: www.pnta.com
SIC: 3999 Preparation of slides & exhibits

(G-10742)
PACIFICA MARINE INC
4233 W Marginal Way Sw (98106-1211)
PHONE.................................206 764-1646
Bill Patz, *President*
Lita Bass, *Administration*
EMP: 15
SQ FT: 80,000
SALES: 1MM Privately Held
WEB: www.pacifica.cc
SIC: 3743 3713 Train cars & equipment, freight or passenger; railroad car rebuilding; truck & bus bodies

(G-10743)
PACIFICA RESOURCES LLC
4233 W Marginal Way Sw (98106-1211)
P.O. Box 81106 (98108-1106)
PHONE.................................206 764-1646
Bill Patz, *Administration*
EMP: 15
SALES (est): 992K Privately Held
SIC: 3743 Railroad equipment

(G-10744)
PAD PRINTING SERVICES INC
12051 31st Ave Ne (98125-5501)
P.O. Box 82103, Kenmore (98028-0103)
PHONE.................................206 362-4544
Gordon Christensen, *President*
EMP: 5 **EST:** 2000
SALES (est): 440K Privately Held
WEB: www.padprintingservices.com
SIC: 3993 3555 2759 Signs & advertising specialties; printing presses; promotional printing; screen printing

(G-10745)
PAMELA MCALLISTER
723 N 105th St (98133-9217)
PHONE.................................206 783-9534
Universal Restoration, *CEO*
EMP: 2 **EST:** 2017
SALES (est): 73.1K Privately Held
SIC: 2721 Periodicals

(G-10746)
PANGAEA LTD
Also Called: Feathered Friends
119 Yale Ave N (98109-5428)
PHONE.................................206 292-9911
Rob Page, *General Mgr*
EMP: 8
SALES (corp-wide): 6MM Privately Held
WEB: www.featheredfriends.com
SIC: 3999 Down (feathers)
PA: Pangaea, Ltd.
    3314 4th Ave S
    Seattle WA 98134
    206 292-9911

(G-10747)
PAPENHAUSE COMPOSITES INC
9513 Evanston Ave N (98103-3131)
PHONE.................................206 669-3260
Paul Papenhause, *Principal*
EMP: 2
SALES (est): 158.3K Privately Held
SIC: 3732 Boat building & repairing

(G-10748)
PAPER DELIGHTS
2205 N 45th St Ste B (98103-6903)
PHONE.................................206 547-1002
Alicia Olsen, *President*
EMP: 3 **EST:** 2008
SALES (est): 321K Privately Held
SIC: 2771 2678 5947 Greeting cards; stationery products; gift shop

(G-10749)
PAPER PANDUH
2956 S Webster St (98108-3943)
PHONE.................................206 538-0202
Maricris Mende, *Principal*
EMP: 3
SALES (est): 76.2K Privately Held
SIC: 2711 Newspapers

(G-10750)
PAPER STUFFCOM
3134 Elliott Ave (98121-1053)
PHONE.................................206 462-6079
Robert Thornton, *Principal*
EMP: 2
SALES (est): 146.1K Privately Held
SIC: 2679 Paper products, converted

(G-10751)
PARADIGM PUBLISHING NW LLC
4314 6th Ave Nw Unit B (98107-4437)
PHONE.................................206 257-0214
Jason Kono, *Principal*
EMP: 2
SALES (est): 110K Privately Held
SIC: 2741 Miscellaneous publishing

(G-10752)
PARAMOUNT PETROLEUM CORP
20555 Richmond Bch Dr Nw (98177-2461)
PHONE.................................503 273-4700
John Deuschett, *Manager*
EMP: 34
SALES (corp-wide): 10.2B Publicly Held
SIC: 2911 Fractionation products of crude petroleum, hydrocarbons
HQ: Paramount Petroleum Corporation
    14700 Downey Ave
    Paramount CA 90723
    562 531-2060

(G-10753)
PARAMOUNT PETROLEUM CORP
20555 Richmond Bch Dr Nw (98177-2461)
PHONE.................................503 273-4705
John Deuschett, *Branch Mgr*
EMP: 10
SALES (corp-wide): 10.2B Publicly Held
SIC: 2911 Petroleum refining
HQ: Paramount Petroleum Corporation
    14700 Downey Ave
    Paramount CA 90723
    562 531-2060

(G-10754)
PARAMOUNT PETROLEUM CORP
20555 Richmond Bch Dr Nw (98177-2461)
PHONE.................................206 542-3121
EMP: 12
SALES (corp-wide): 10.3B Publicly Held
SIC: 2911 Petroleum Refiner
HQ: Paramount Petroleum Corporation
    14700 Downey Ave
    Paramount CA 90723
    562 531-2060

(G-10755)
PARAVERSAL PUBLISHING LLC
9416 1st Ave Ne Apt 117 (98115-2748)
PHONE.................................206 366-1981
John Johnson, *Bd of Directors*
EMP: 2 **EST:** 2012
SALES (est): 81.2K Privately Held
SIC: 2741 Miscellaneous publishing

(G-10756)
PARIS GOURMET DESSERT
Also Called: Parisian Star
5601 1st Ave S (98108-2404)
PHONE.................................206 767-9097
Pierre Sauvet, *Owner*
EMP: 15
SALES (est): 790K Privately Held
WEB: www.parisianstardesserts.com
SIC: 2024 2053 Non-dairy based frozen desserts; frozen bakery products, except bread

(G-10757)
PARK & MOAZEZ ENTERPRISES INC
Also Called: Minuteman Press
2960 4th Ave S Ste 112 (98134-1203)
PHONE.................................206 464-0100
Farzad Mike Moazez, *President*
Farzad Moazez, *President*
Jim Moazez, *Vice Pres*
EMP: 5
SQ FT: 1,200
SALES (est): 817.6K Privately Held
WEB: www.mmpunion.com
SIC: 2752 Commercial printing, lithographic

(G-10758)
PARK AVENUE CONSTRUCTION INC
1110 Nw 45th St (98107-4626)
PHONE.................................206 783-3693
Charles Stratton, *President*
Christine Stratton, *Vice Pres*
EMP: 13
SQ FT: 6,400
SALES (est): 1.2MM Privately Held
SIC: 2434 Wood kitchen cabinets

(G-10759)
PARK POSTAL LLC
4111 E Madison St Ste 2 (98112-6229)
PHONE.................................206 860-7678
Michael Culwell, *Principal*
Mark Doran, *Principal*
EMP: 2
SALES (est): 251K Privately Held
SIC: 2759 5113 Commercial printing; shipping supplies

(G-10760)
PART WORKS INC
2900 4th Ave S (98134-1915)
P.O. Box 3605 (98124-3605)
PHONE.................................206 632-8900
Katie Parris, *President*
Sandra E Johnson, *Corp Secy*
Larry Farley, *Cust Mgr*
▲ **EMP:** 20
SQ FT: 16,000
SALES: 5.7MM Privately Held
WEB: www.thepartworks.com
SIC: 3432 5084 5074 Faucets & spigots, metal & plastic; pumps & pumping equipment; plumbing fittings & supplies

(G-10761)
PARVIA CORP
800 5th Ave 101-160 (98104-3176)
PHONE.................................206 310-2205
Peter Cyrus, *President*
EMP: 10
SQ FT: 2,000
SALES (est): 650K Privately Held
WEB: www.parvia.com
SIC: 3944 5945 Games, toys & children's vehicles; hobby, toy & game shops

(G-10762)
PASTELERIA DEL CASTILLO
10434 16th Ave Sw (98146-1475)
PHONE.................................206 242-6247
Omar Delrio, *Owner*
Omar Del Rio, *Owner*
EMP: 3
SQ FT: 4,348
SALES (est): 226.2K Privately Held
SIC: 2051 Bread, cake & related products

(G-10763)
PASTERIA LUCCHESE
3004 Nw 59th St (98107-2555)
PHONE.................................206 420-4939
Sara Bristow, *Principal*
EMP: 4 **EST:** 2010
SALES (est): 442K Privately Held
SIC: 3556 Pasta machinery

(G-10764)
PAT FILES
Also Called: Commercial Application Sales
2427 6th Ave S (98134-2024)
PHONE.................................206 405-4370
Pat Files, *Owner*
EMP: 3
SQ FT: 10,000
SALES (est): 260K Privately Held
SIC: 5074 3088 Plumbing & hydronic heating supplies; plastics plumbing fixtures

(G-10765)
PAT-CO INC
Also Called: Cde Software
4515 44th Ave Sw (98116-4116)
PHONE.................................206 937-8927
Patrick Lajko, *President*
Lance Rasmussen, *Vice Pres*
Ray Yokoyama, *Vice Pres*
EMP: 5
SQ FT: 2,000
SALES (est): 786.4K Privately Held
WEB: www.cdesoftware.com
SIC: 7379 7371 7372 Computer related consulting services; computer software systems analysis & design, custom; prepackaged software

(G-10766)
PATH VACCINE SOLUTIONS
2201 Westlake Ave (98121-2778)
P.O. Box 900922 (98109-9715)
PHONE.................................206 285-3500
Steve Davis, *President*
N Regina Rabinovich, *Vice Pres*
Marlow Kee, *Treasurer*
Tom Brewer, *Director*
Doug Holtzman, *Director*
EMP: 4 **EST:** 2005
SALES: 24.7MM
SALES (corp-wide): 289.2MM Privately Held
SIC: 2836 Vaccines
PA: Path
    2201 Westlake Ave Ste 200
    Seattle WA 98121
    206 285-3500

(G-10767)
PATHFINDER WIRELESS CORP
2402 E Newton St (98112-3054)
PHONE.................................206 409-5767
Colby Harper, *CEO*

Seattle - King County (G-10768) GEOGRAPHIC SECTION

EMP: 2
SALES (est): 125.8K **Privately Held**
SIC: 3663 Radio & TV communications equipment

(G-10768)
PATRICIA A WELCH
1122 E Pike St (98122-3916)
PHONE..................206 322-1226
Pat Welch, *Principal*
EMP: 2
SALES (est): 65.4K **Privately Held**
SIC: 2084 Wines, brandy & brandy spirits

(G-10769)
PATRICIA KINSELLA
14100 Westwood Pl Ne (98125-3851)
PHONE..................206 285-5885
Patricia Kinsella, *Principal*
EMP: 2
SALES (est): 199.3K **Privately Held**
SIC: 2519 Household furniture

(G-10770)
PATRICK CLARKE
11345 40th Ave Ne (98125-5722)
PHONE..................206 365-8804
Patrick Clarke, *Principal*
EMP: 2
SALES (est): 85.9K **Privately Held**
SIC: 3571 Electronic computers

(G-10771)
PATROLTAG INC
2800 Western Ave Apt 212 (98121-1354)
PHONE..................650 678-3790
Stephen Hollis, *President*
EMP: 6
SQ FT: 2,000
SALES (est): 733.2K **Privately Held**
SIC: 3699 Security devices

(G-10772)
PAULAS CHOICE LLC
Also Called: Paula's Choice Skincare
705 5th Ave S Ste 200 (98104-4425)
PHONE..................425 988-6068
Paula Begoun, *President*
Shana Storozhev, *Partner*
Janmilly Campbell, *Research*
Michael Aquino, *Accountant*
Debra Rux, *Sales Staff*
▲ **EMP:** 103
SQ FT: 42,647
SALES (est): 58.7MM **Privately Held**
WEB: www.cosmeticscop.com
SIC: 2844 7231 5122 Cosmetic preparations; beauty shops; drugs, proprietaries & sundries

(G-10773)
PAULAS CHOICE HOLDINGS INC (PA)
705 5th Ave S Ste 200 (98104-4425)
PHONE..................425 988-6068
Jeffrey Drazan, *CEO*
EMP: 2
SALES (est): 74.4K **Privately Held**
SIC: 2844 5122 Cosmetic preparations; drugs, proprietaries & sundries

(G-10774)
PD PHARMATECH LLC
135 S Brandon St (98108-2231)
PHONE..................800 452-4682
EMP: 3
SALES (est): 168.7K **Privately Held**
SIC: 2834 Pharmaceutical preparations

(G-10775)
PEACH FUZZER LLC (PA)
1415 10th Ave Ste 7 (98122-3864)
PHONE..................206 453-0339
Akshay Aggarwal, *CEO*
Adam Cecchetti,
Mike Eddington,
EMP: 11
SALES (est): 516K **Privately Held**
SIC: 7372 7371 7379 Prepackaged software; computer software development; computer related consulting services

(G-10776)
PEACH FUZZER LLC
1122 E Pike St Ste 1064 (98122-3916)
PHONE..................844 557-3224
EMP: 5
SALES (est): 359K
SALES (corp-wide): 516K **Privately Held**
SIC: 7372 Prepackaged software
PA: Peach Fuzzer, Llc
  1415 10th Ave Ste 7
  Seattle WA 98122
  206 453-0339

(G-10777)
PEARSON BUSINESS MGT SVCS
1411 4th Ave Ste 1506 (98101-2247)
PHONE..................206 382-1457
Carol Pearson, *President*
EMP: 3
SALES (est): 280K **Privately Held**
WEB: www.pearsonbizgroup.com
SIC: 7372 Business oriented computer software

(G-10778)
PEEKABOO CUPCAKERY
1001 4th Ave Ste 3200 (98154-1003)
PHONE..................206 458-6986
EMP: 4
SALES (est): 301.4K **Privately Held**
SIC: 3331 Primary Copper Producer

(G-10779)
PEEL AND PRESS LLC
6503 California Ave Sw (98136-1899)
PHONE..................206 937-1457
EMP: 7
SALES (est): 273K **Privately Held**
SIC: 2741 Miscellaneous publishing

(G-10780)
PENCILS AND INKS INC
3715 S Angeline St (98118-1709)
PHONE..................206 683-4441
EMP: 2
SALES (est): 101.4K **Privately Held**
SIC: 2893 Printing ink

(G-10781)
PENTHOUSE DRAPERY CLRS & MFRS
4033 16th Ave Sw Ste A (98106-1206)
PHONE..................206 292-8336
Colin Tsuchikawa, *President*
Barbara Tsuchikawa, *Principal*
Trent Tsuchikawa, *Project Mgr*
Amy Post, *Manager*
EMP: 23
SALES (est): 1.8MM **Privately Held**
WEB: www.penthousedrapery.com
SIC: 2391 5719 7216 5023 Draperies, plastic & textile: from purchased materials; venetian blinds; window shades; curtain cleaning & repair; home furnishings

(G-10782)
PEPSI NORTHWEST BEVERAGES LLC
Also Called: Pepsico
2646 Rainier Ave S (98144-5331)
P.O. Box 14417 (98114)
PHONE..................206 326-7487
Keith Reimer, *Branch Mgr*
EMP: 115
SALES (corp-wide): 64.6B **Publicly Held**
SIC: 2086 Soft drinks: packaged in cans, bottles, etc.
HQ: Pepsi Northwest Beverages Llc
  3003 R W Johnson Blvd Sw
  Tumwater WA 98512

(G-10783)
PEPSI-COLA METRO BTLG CO INC
2300 26th Ave S (98144-5339)
PHONE..................206 326-7431
Jason Boyovich, *Opers Mgr*
Keith Kawachi, *Branch Mgr*
Cliff Griffin, *Manager*
EMP: 100
SALES (corp-wide): 64.6B **Publicly Held**
WEB: www.joy-of-cola.com
SIC: 2086 Soft drinks: packaged in cans, bottles, etc.
HQ: Pepsi-Cola Metropolitan Bottling Company, Inc.
  1111 Westchester Ave
  White Plains NY 10604
  914 767-6000

(G-10784)
PEPTIDE SCIENTIFIC USA LTD
Also Called: PSI Scientific
1920 4th Ave Unit 1909 (98101-5119)
PHONE..................718 618-5025
John Ye, *CEO*
Dora Xie, *Partner*
EMP: 10
SALES: 500K **Privately Held**
SIC: 2833 Medicinal chemicals

(G-10785)
PER GIOIA
1101 17th Ave Ste No108 (98122-4668)
PHONE..................206 240-4216
EMP: 3
SALES: 0 **Privately Held**
SIC: 2389 Mfg Apparel/Accessories

(G-10786)
PERFECT COPY & PRINT INC (PA)
111 Broadway E (98102-5711)
PHONE..................206 325-4733
Asif Alvi, *President*
EMP: 5
SQ FT: 1,500
SALES (est): 606.4K **Privately Held**
SIC: 2759 Commercial printing

(G-10787)
PERFORMANCE RADIATOR PCF LLC
2447 6th Ave S (98134-2024)
PHONE..................206 624-2440
Mike Carr, *Branch Mgr*
EMP: 6 **Privately Held**
SIC: 3714 5013 Radiators & radiator shells & cores, motor vehicle; radiators
HQ: Performance Radiator Pacific, L.L.C.
  2447 6th Ave S
  Seattle WA 98134
  800 273-0571

(G-10788)
PERIL PRINTS
2802 32nd Ave S (98144-6112)
PHONE..................323 599-1447
Victoria Molinarolo, *Principal*
EMP: 2 **EST:** 2016
SALES (est): 83.9K **Privately Held**
SIC: 2752 Commercial printing, lithographic

(G-10789)
PERLAGE SYSTEMS INC (PA)
1507 Western Ave Apt 606 (98101-1505)
PHONE..................206 973-7500
Evan Wallace, *President*
▲ **EMP:** 5
SQ FT: 2,000
SALES (est): 1MM **Privately Held**
SIC: 3556 Beverage machinery

(G-10790)
PET/CT IMAGING AT SWDISH CNCER
1221 Madison St Ste 150 (98104-1385)
PHONE..................206 215-6433
Todd Barnett, *Mng Member*
James Dingels, *Mng Member*
Dan Harris, *Mng Member*
David Haseley, *Mng Member*
James Rogers, *Mng Member*
EMP: 10
SALES (est): 1.4MM **Privately Held**
SIC: 3845 Position emission tomography (PET scanner)

(G-10791)
PET/X LLC
8002 39th Ave Ne (98115-4922)
PHONE..................206 715-5743
Paul Kinahan, *Partner*
Lawrence Macdonald, *Partner*
EMP: 3
SALES (est): 221.9K **Privately Held**
SIC: 3841 Diagnostic apparatus, medical

(G-10792)
PGI PUBLICATIONS
10307 Lake City Way Ne (98125-7737)
PHONE..................206 588-2968
EMP: 2 **EST:** 2015
SALES (est): 75.6K **Privately Held**
SIC: 2759 2731 Commercial Printing Books-Publishing/Printing

(G-10793)
PHELPS TIRE CO INC (PA)
3266 Nw Esplanade (98117-2625)
PHONE..................206 447-0169
Norval E Phelps Jr, *President*
▲ **EMP:** 90 **EST:** 1947
SALES (est): 12.5MM **Privately Held**
WEB: www.phelpstire.com
SIC: 5014 5531 7534 3011 Automobile tires & tubes; automotive tires; tire retreading & repair shops; tires & inner tubes

(G-10794)
PHILIPS NORTH AMERICA LLC
2301 5th Ave Ste 200 (98121-1825)
PHONE..................206 664-5000
Chuck Little, *General Mgr*
EMP: 158
SALES (corp-wide): 20.8B **Privately Held**
WEB: www.usa.philips.com
SIC: 3845 Electromedical equipment
HQ: Philips North America Llc
  3000 Minuteman Rd Ms1203
  Andover MA 01810
  978 659-3000

(G-10795)
PHILS CUSTOM BINDERY
309 S Cloverdale St A12 (98108-4568)
PHONE..................206 728-1541
Phil Goldader, *Owner*
EMP: 2
SQ FT: 2,800
SALES (est): 161.2K **Privately Held**
WEB: www.philscustombindery.com
SIC: 2789 Bookbinding & repairing: trade, edition, library, etc.

(G-10796)
PHOENIX PROCESSOR LTD PARTNR
333 1st Ave W (98119-4103)
PHONE..................206 286-8584
David Galloway, *Mng Member*
Robert Czeisler,
Kenneth Davidson,
Bruce Pereya,
Daphne Pereyra,
EMP: 220
SALES (est): 71MM **Privately Held**
SIC: 5149 2092 Groceries & related products; fish, fresh: prepared

(G-10797)
PHOTON FACTORY
4810 Airport Way S (98108-1723)
PHONE..................818 795-6957
Vanessa Molano, *Principal*
EMP: 4
SALES (est): 322.3K **Privately Held**
SIC: 3661 Fiber optics communications equipment

(G-10798)
PHUONG DNG TIMES
6221 39th Ave S (98118-3123)
PHONE..................206 760-9168
Phuong Dong, *Principal*
EMP: 3
SALES (est): 155.3K **Privately Held**
SIC: 2711 Newspapers, publishing & printing

(G-10799)
PICCELL LLC
Also Called: Piccell Wireless
918 S Horton St Ste 901 (98134-1953)
PHONE..................206 780-0478
Brandon Ferrante,
EMP: 2 **EST:** 2003
SALES (est): 190.5K **Privately Held**
SIC: 3663 Receivers, radio communications

▲ = Import ▼ = Export
◆ = Import/Export

GEOGRAPHIC SECTION Seattle - King County (G-10831)

(G-10800)
PICKLE BALL INC
4700 9th Ave Nw (98107-4528)
PHONE 206 632-0119
Doug Smith, *President*
David V Mc Callum, *Vice Pres*
Janet Alonson, *Office Mgr*
▲ **EMP:** 3 **EST:** 1972
SQ FT: 1,700
SALES (est): 420.3K **Privately Held**
WEB: www.pickleball.com
SIC: 3949 Sporting & athletic goods

(G-10801)
PICMONKEY INC
2106 E Union St (98122-2955)
PHONE 206 486-2106
Brian S Terry, *President*
Frits Habermann, *Vice Pres*
Pearl Chan, *CFO*
Charlie Whiton, *Treasurer*
Celeste Sipherd, *VP Finance*
EMP: 13 **EST:** 2012
SQ FT: 950
SALES (est): 1.8MM **Privately Held**
SIC: 7372 Application computer software

(G-10802)
PICOBREW INC
2121 N 35th St Ste 100 (98103-9103)
PHONE 425 503-0132
William Mitchell, *President*
AVI R Geiger, *Vice Pres*
James B Mitchell, *Vice Pres*
Greg White, *Engineer*
Steve Rohrbach, *CFO*
EMP: 6 **EST:** 2014
SALES (est): 1.6MM **Privately Held**
SIC: 3556 Brewers' & maltsters' machinery

(G-10803)
PIECE MIND TOBACCO ACC LLC
12516 Lake City Way Ne (98125-4425)
PHONE 206 588-0216
Quinn Sharpe,
EMP: 2
SALES (est): 197.8K **Privately Held**
SIC: 2131 Smoking tobacco

(G-10804)
PIGN WHISTLE
1234 23rd Ave E (98112-3537)
PHONE 206 782-6044
Celester Gray, *Owner*
EMP: 2
SALES (est): 119.7K **Privately Held**
SIC: 3999 Whistles

(G-10805)
PIKE BREWING COMPANY
Also Called: Pike Pub
1415 1st Ave (98101-2017)
PHONE 206 622-6044
Rich Hamilton, *President*
Drew Gillespie, *General Mgr*
Steve French, *Warehouse Mgr*
Zan McColloch-Lussi, *Corp Comm Staff*
EMP: 43
SQ FT: 15,000
SALES (est): 7.3MM **Privately Held**
WEB: www.pikebrewing.com
SIC: 2082 5813 5812 Beer (alcoholic beverage); tavern (drinking places); eating places

(G-10806)
PIKE PLACE BAGEL BAKERY INC
1525 1st Ave Ste 1 (98101-1548)
PHONE 206 382-4297
Fax: 206 521-9431
EMP: 17
SALES (est): 810K **Privately Held**
SIC: 2051 5461 Retail Bakery

(G-10807)
PIKE STREET PRESS
1510 Alaskan Way (98101-1514)
PHONE 206 971-0120
Sean Brown, *Principal*
EMP: 4
SALES (est): 312.8K **Privately Held**
SIC: 2741 Miscellaneous publishing

(G-10808)
PIN HSIAO & ASSOCIATES LLC
Also Called: Zen Bakery, MA
11752 15th Ave Ne (98125-5026)
PHONE 206 818-0155
Pin Hsiano,
EMP: 15
SALES (corp-wide): 12MM **Privately Held**
SIC: 2051 Bakery: wholesale or wholesale/retail combined
PA: Pin Hsiao & Associates L.L.C.
2535 152nd Ave Ne
Redmond WA 98052
425 637-3357

(G-10809)
PIONEER HUMAN SERVICES (PA)
Also Called: Pioneer Industries
7440 W Marginal Way S (98108-4141)
PHONE 206 768-1990
Karen Lee, *CEO*
Lee Fish, *Ch of Bd*
Charles S Musso Jr, *Ch of Bd*
Anthony Wright, *COO*
Tim Boyer, *Vice Pres*
▲ **EMP:** 75 **EST:** 1962
SQ FT: 50,000
SALES (est): 81.9MM **Privately Held**
WEB: www.pioneerhumanservices.org
SIC: 3444 8331 8322 Sheet metalwork; job training & vocational rehabilitation services; settlement house

(G-10810)
PIONEER HUMAN SERVICES
Also Called: Pioneer Industries
7000 Highland Pkwy Sw (98106-1927)
PHONE 206 762-7737
Dan Hawkins, *General Mgr*
EMP: 200
SALES (corp-wide): 81.9MM **Privately Held**
SIC: 8331 3471 3444 Vocational rehabilitation agency; plating & polishing; sheet metalwork
PA: Pioneer Human Services
7440 W Marginal Way S
Seattle WA 98108
206 768-1990

(G-10811)
PIONEER SQUARE BRANDS INC
Also Called: Brenthaven
321 3rd Ave S Ste 403 (98104-4602)
PHONE 360 733-5608
EMP: 2
SALES (est): 166.4K **Privately Held**
SIC: 3172 Card cases

(G-10812)
PIONEER WOODWORKS COMPANY INC
12337 Lake City Way Ne (98125-5401)
PHONE 206 362-5637
Walter L Meyer, *CEO*
EMP: 5 **EST:** 1976
SQ FT: 3,000
SALES (est): 580K **Privately Held**
SIC: 5712 2511 Custom made furniture, except cabinets; wood household furniture

(G-10813)
PIP MCKAY UNLIMITED LLC
1746 Nw 58th St (98107-3041)
PHONE 206 390-0988
EMP: 2
SALES (est): 101.5K **Privately Held**
SIC: 2752 Commercial printing, offset

(G-10814)
PIPELINEDEALS INC
1008 Western Ave Ste 401 (98104-3622)
PHONE 866 702-7303
Spencer Hogger, *Accounts Exec*
Jon Englund, *Executive*
EMP: 10
SALES (est): 978.2K **Privately Held**
SIC: 7372 Application computer software

(G-10815)
PIVOT CUSTOM METAL FABRICATION
6501 E Marginal Way S C (98108-3221)
PHONE 206 762-3755
EMP: 6
SALES (est): 433.7K **Privately Held**
SIC: 3499 Fabricated metal products

(G-10816)
PIXEL PLANET INC
5208 45th Ave Sw (98136-1106)
PHONE 206 669-7371
David E Jeschke, *President*
EMP: 2
SALES (est): 122.7K **Privately Held**
SIC: 7372 7371 Publishers' computer software; custom computer programming services

(G-10817)
PIXELSAURUS GAMES LLC
1115 Ne 78th St (98115-4307)
PHONE 617 893-7755
Dean Tate, *Principal*
EMP: 2 **EST:** 2013
SALES (est): 98.5K **Privately Held**
SIC: 7372 Prepackaged software

(G-10818)
PIXVANA INC
3621 Stone Way N Unit A (98103-8050)
PHONE 206 910-5747
Forest Key, *CEO*
Jim Eadie, *CFO*
Nicole Bunselmeyer, *VP Sales*
William Hensler, *Officer*
Scott Squires, *Officer*
EMP: 18
SALES (est): 426.3K **Privately Held**
SIC: 7372 Home entertainment computer software

(G-10819)
PIZZICATO PUBLISHING CO
Also Called: David T Stone Consulting
17400 32nd Ave Nw (98155)
PHONE 206 361-0444
EMP: 3
SALES (est): 180K **Privately Held**
SIC: 8748 2731 Business Consulting Services Books-Publishing/Printing

(G-10820)
PJ FINNEY CORPORATION
Also Called: Allegra-Patrick Print Imaging
3243 20th Ave W (98199-2301)
PHONE 206 282-8400
EMP: 10
SQ FT: 4,000
SALES (est): 1.4MM **Privately Held**
SIC: 2752 Lithographic Commercial Printing

(G-10821)
PLAY IMPOSSIBLE CORPORATION
Also Called: Wonderball
111 S Jackson St (98104-3111)
PHONE 206 852-7015
Brian Monnin, *CEO*
EMP: 2 **EST:** 2016
SALES (est): 108.6K **Privately Held**
SIC: 3949 Sporting & athletic goods

(G-10822)
PLEASURE BOAT STUDIO
3710 Sw Barton St (98126-3844)
PHONE 206 962-0460
Lauren Grosskopf, *Principal*
EMP: 2 **EST:** 2017
SALES (est): 85.9K **Privately Held**
SIC: 2741 Miscellaneous publishing

(G-10823)
PLIMP INC
Also Called: Plimp Company, The
605 1st Ave Ste 400 (98104-2224)
PHONE 206 795-3292
James Egan, *CEO*
EMP: 2
SALES (est): 156K **Privately Held**
SIC: 3721 7389 Airships;

(G-10824)
PLUM CREEK NORTHWEST PLYWD INC (DH)
601 Union St Ste 3100 (98101-1374)
PHONE 206 467-3600
Rick R Holley, *President*
▼ **EMP:** 1
SALES (est): 36.6MM
SALES (corp-wide): 7.4B **Publicly Held**
SIC: 2435 2436 Hardwood veneer & plywood; softwood veneer & plywood
HQ: Plum Creek Timberlands, L.P.
601 Union St Ste 3100
Seattle WA 98101
206 467-3600

(G-10825)
PLUM CREEK TIMBERLANDS LP (HQ)
601 Union St Ste 3100 (98101-1374)
PHONE 206 467-3600
Rick Holley, *CEO*
Michael Covey, *Senior VP*
David Lambert, *Senior VP*
James A Kraft, *Vice Pres*
William R Brown, *CFO*
EMP: 10
SQ FT: 20,000
SALES (est): 95.4MM
SALES (corp-wide): 7.4B **Publicly Held**
SIC: 2421 2436 2493 5031 Lumber: rough, sawed or planed; plywood, softwood, fiberboard, other vegetable pulp; lumber, plywood & millwork; plywood; medium density fiberboard
PA: Weyerhaeuser Company
220 Occidental Ave S
Seattle WA 98104
206 539-3000

(G-10826)
PM WEIZENBAUM
115 N 85th St Ste 202 (98103-3674)
PHONE 206 427-4127
EMP: 2
SALES (est): 85.5K **Privately Held**
SIC: 2741 Miscellaneous publishing

(G-10827)
POHLMAN KNOWLES
3824 Sw Morgan St (98126-3063)
PHONE 206 933-7450
Sabrina Knowles, *Partner*
Jenny Pohlman, *Partner*
EMP: 3
SALES (est): 209.4K **Privately Held**
SIC: 8999 3572 Artist; computer storage devices

(G-10828)
POLLUTION CONTROL SYSTEMS CORP
8036 35th Ave Ne (98115-4815)
P.O. Box 15570 (98115-0570)
PHONE 206 523-7220
Richard C Conrad, *President*
EMP: 4
SALES (est): 376.7K **Privately Held**
SIC: 3823 5084 Industrial instrmnts msrmnt display/control process variable; industrial machinery & equipment

(G-10829)
POMUM CELLARS LLC
2334 N 61st St (98103-5739)
PHONE 206 362-9203
Javier Alfonso,
Shylah Alfonso,
EMP: 2
SALES (est): 204.5K **Privately Held**
SIC: 2084 Wine cellars, bonded: engaged in blending wines

(G-10830)
PONDER PRESS
1804 S Charles St (98144-2955)
PHONE 206 861-0448
EMP: 2 **EST:** 2010
SALES (est): 100K **Privately Held**
SIC: 2741 Misc Publishing

(G-10831)
POP POP LLC
14129 Phinney Ave N (98133-6846)
PHONE 206 384-8121

Seattle - King County (G-10832)

(G-10832)
Kjell Connelly, *CEO*
EMP: 2 **EST:** 2013
SALES (est): 114.3K **Privately Held**
SIC: 7372 Application computer software

(G-10832)
POPE JOHN
905 30th Ave S (98144-3206)
PHONE 206 320-0686
John Pope, *Founder*
EMP: 2
SALES (est): 73.1K **Privately Held**
SIC: 2721 Periodicals

(G-10833)
POROS
600 1st Ave Ste 205 (98104-2221)
PHONE 773 504-2908
John Borofka, *CFO*
EMP: 10
SALES (est): 852.2K **Privately Held**
SIC: 3161 Luggage

(G-10834)
PORT BLAKELY COMPANY (PA)
Also Called: Port Lakely Cummunities
1501 4th Ave Ste 2150 (98101-1600)
PHONE 206 624-5810
James E Warjone, *President*
Tim Leypold, *Vice Pres*
EMP: 9
SALES (est): 21.9MM **Privately Held**
SIC: 0811 2421 6531 Tree farm; specialty sawmill products; real estate brokers & agents

(G-10835)
PORTLAND PRESS INCORPORATED
1111 Nw 50th St (98107-5120)
PHONE 206 297-1304
Diane Caillier, *Principal*
EMP: 2 **EST:** 2007
SALES (est): 105.5K **Privately Held**
SIC: 2731 Books: publishing only

(G-10836)
PORTLOCK SMKED SFDS-BLLARD RET
2821 Nw Market St Ste E (98107-5815)
PHONE 206 466-1931
Lo Reichert, *Manager*
EMP: 2
SALES (est): 62.3K **Privately Held**
SIC: 2092 Fresh or frozen packaged fish

(G-10837)
POST ALLEY PRESS
1304 Ne 63rd St (98115-6718)
PHONE 206 522-5963
Barbara Robertson, *Principal*
EMP: 2
SALES (est): 125.4K **Privately Held**
SIC: 2741 Miscellaneous publishing

(G-10838)
POTLUCK PRESS LLC
Also Called: Potluck Pairs
920 S Bayview St (98134-2054)
PHONE 206 328-1300
Patti McKillop, *Mng Member*
▲ **EMP:** 4
SALES (est): 327.1K **Privately Held**
SIC: 5947 2741 Greeting cards; miscellaneous publishing

(G-10839)
POTTER & ASSOCIATES INC
4400 26th Ave W (98199-1276)
PHONE 206 623-8844
Steven Potter, *President*
Stephen Cook, *Vice Pres*
EMP: 4 **EST:** 1957
SQ FT: 28,800
SALES (est): 476.5K **Privately Held**
WEB: www.potterinc.com
SIC: 2752 7336 2761 2759 Commercial printing, offset; commercial art & graphic design; manifold business forms; commercial printing; book printing

(G-10840)
POW INC
Also Called: Spacecraft Collective
1118 Nw Ballard Way (98107-4638)
P.O. Box 33090 (98133-0090)
PHONE 206 366-0224
Dustin Goss, *President*
Alvin Danielson, *Branch Mgr*
EMP: 15
SALES (corp-wide): 2.4MM **Privately Held**
SIC: 3949 Winter sports equipment
PA: Pow, Inc.
4509 Interlake Ave N
Seattle WA 98103
206 366-0224

(G-10841)
POW INC (PA)
Also Called: Pow Gloves
4509 Interlake Ave N (98103-6782)
PHONE 206 366-0224
Greg Danielson, *CEO*
Dustin Goss, *President*
Dan Egan, *Vice Pres*
▲ **EMP:** 8
SALES (est): 2.4MM **Privately Held**
WEB: www.powgloves.com
SIC: 2369 2329 Ski & snow suits: girls' & children's; ski & snow clothing: men's & boys'

(G-10842)
POWDER MONKEY GAMES LLC
1601 2nd Ave Ste 800 (98101-3522)
PHONE 206 501-2340
Shanis Windland, *Vice Pres*
EMP: 2 **EST:** 2013
SQ FT: 4,914
SALES (est): 130K **Privately Held**
SIC: 7372 Prepackaged software

(G-10843)
PRAXAIR INC
4442 27th Ave W (98199-1220)
PHONE 206 632-7138
Alan Lindwall, *Manager*
EMP: 3
SQ FT: 6,670 **Privately Held**
SIC: 2813 Industrial gases
HQ: Praxair, Inc.
10 Riverview Dr
Danbury CT 06810
203 837-2000

(G-10844)
PRAXAIR INC
545 S Lander St (98134-1921)
PHONE 206 264-2881
Joe Weens, *Manager*
EMP: 2 **Privately Held**
SIC: 2813 Industrial gases
HQ: Praxair, Inc.
10 Riverview Dr
Danbury CT 06810
203 837-2000

(G-10845)
PRECEPT BRANDS LLC (PA)
Also Called: Precept Wine
1910 Frview Ave E Ste 400 (98102)
PHONE 206 267-5252
Andrew Browne, *CEO*
Mike Williamson, *President*
Kirk Brewer, *Senior VP*
Lisa Clarkson, *Vice Pres*
Phil Kazanjian, *Vice Pres*
◆ **EMP:** 52
SQ FT: 4,000
SALES (est): 72.6MM **Privately Held**
WEB: www.preceptbrands.com
SIC: 2084 Wines

(G-10846)
PRECISE PRINTING INC
Also Called: Nikko Media
2525 W Commodore Way (98199-1229)
PHONE 206 343-0942
John Teeny, *President*
EMP: 10
SALES (est): 1.3MM **Privately Held**
WEB: www.preciseprint.com
SIC: 2752 Commercial printing, offset

(G-10847)
PRECISE TOOL & GAGE CO INC
1122 3rd Ave (98101-2904)
PHONE 206 623-1120
Steve Drew, *Branch Mgr*
EMP: 2
SALES (est): 161.3K
SALES (corp-wide): 6MM **Privately Held**
SIC: 3599 Machine shop, jobbing & repair
PA: Precise Tool & Gage Co., Inc.
30540 Se 84th St Unit 2
Preston WA 98050
425 222-9567

(G-10848)
PRECISION ART WORKS
1731 Nw 62nd St (98107-2361)
PHONE 206 714-7074
EMP: 2
SALES (est): 149.8K **Privately Held**
SIC: 3999 Framed artwork

(G-10849)
PRECISION BIOMETRICS INC
2303 W Commodore Way # 301 (98199-1560)
PHONE 206 448-3464
David Marcarian, *President*
EMP: 8
SQ FT: 3,250
SALES (est): 3.2MM **Privately Held**
WEB: www.myovision.com
SIC: 3841 Surgical & medical instruments

(G-10850)
PRECISION FABRICATORS LLC
10554 Aurora Ave N (98133-8812)
PHONE 206 362-1195
Charles Ihrig, *Manager*
EMP: 8
SQ FT: 2,921
SALES (est): 1MM
SALES (corp-wide): 625K **Privately Held**
SIC: 3444 Gutters, sheet metal
PA: Precision Fabricators Llc
1202 N 143rd St
Seattle WA
206 362-1195

(G-10851)
PRECISION FLDPOWER SYSTEMS LLC
Also Called: Precision Fluidpower Engrg
10659 Marine View Dr Sw (98146-1672)
PHONE 206 938-2894
Pete Preusser,
EMP: 3
SALES (est): 218K **Privately Held**
SIC: 8748 7389 3594 Business consulting; design, commercial & industrial; pumps, hydraulic power transfer

(G-10852)
PRECISION SHAPES NW LLC
522 W Crockett St (98119-2824)
PHONE 206 605-4396
Susan Locke, *Mng Member*
Michael Ewaliko,
EMP: 3
SALES (est): 363.7K **Privately Held**
SIC: 3547 5091 7371 Rolling mill machinery; surfing equipment & supplies; computer software development

(G-10853)
PRECISION STEEL RULE DIE CO
4526 53rd Ave Sw (98116-3915)
PHONE 206 397-3982
Kim Tien N Vo, *Owner*
EMP: 4
SALES (est): 328.5K **Privately Held**
SIC: 3423 7389 3544 Cutting dies, except metal cutting; metal cutting services; special dies, tools, jigs & fixtures

(G-10854)
PRECISION WELDER AND ENG REPR
4427 Airport Way S (98108-1710)
PHONE 206 382-6227
Dave Krueger, *President*
Wendy Krueger, *Admin Sec*
EMP: 6
SQ FT: 2,400
SALES: 600K **Privately Held**
SIC: 7692 Welding repair

(G-10855)
PREMIERE SOFTWARE
12549 28th Ave Ne (98125-4391)
PHONE 206 399-7495
Rex Yang, *Principal*
EMP: 2
SALES (est): 103.3K **Privately Held**
SIC: 7372 Prepackaged software

(G-10856)
PRESS
7342 10th Ave Nw (98117-4107)
PHONE 206 290-7392
Brett Clifton, *Principal*
EMP: 3
SALES (est): 254.7K **Privately Held**
SIC: 2741 Miscellaneous publishing

(G-10857)
PRESTIGE COPY AND PRINT (PA)
11023 8th Ave Ne (98125-6103)
PHONE 206 365-5770
Rubina Siddiqui, *President*
Jawaid Siddiqui, *Vice Pres*
EMP: 5
SALES (est): 520.9K **Privately Held**
SIC: 2752 7334 2791 2789 Commercial printing, offset; photocopying & duplicating services; typesetting; bookbinding & related work

(G-10858)
PRICEMEDIA INC
Also Called: Outdoors NW
10002 Aurora Ave N Ste 36 (98133-9348)
PHONE 206 418-0747
Carolyn Price, *President*
Greg Price, *Vice Pres*
EMP: 3
SALES: 500K **Privately Held**
WEB: www.pricemedia.com
SIC: 2721 Magazines: publishing only, not printed on site

(G-10859)
PRIMAL SCREENS LLC
6309 24th Ave Nw (98107-2423)
PHONE 206 784-5266
Stephen K Angell, *President*
Sarah Angel,
EMP: 2
SQ FT: 700
SALES (est): 220.6K **Privately Held**
SIC: 2396 7336 Screen printing on fabric articles; graphic arts & related design

(G-10860)
PRINT SERVICES NORTHWEST INC
5616 4th Ave S (98108-2421)
PHONE 206 763-9230
EMP: 5 **EST:** 1969
SQ FT: 5,000
SALES: 580K **Privately Held**
WEB: www.printservicesnw.com
SIC: 2752 7336 2791 Commercial printing, offset; commercial art & graphic design; typesetting

(G-10861)
PRINT SOLUTIONS AND CONSULTING
466 Smith St (98109-2154)
PHONE 206 726-8053
Liz Anderson, *Principal*
EMP: 2
SALES (est): 202.5K **Privately Held**
SIC: 2752 Commercial printing, offset

(G-10862)
PRINT TIME INC
1932 9th Ave (98101-1304)
PHONE 206 682-1000
Luke Hitt, *Opers Staff*
EMP: 12
SALES (est): 1.5MM
SALES (corp-wide): 4MM **Privately Held**
WEB: www.printtime.com
SIC: 2752 Commercial printing, offset

GEOGRAPHIC SECTION

Seattle - King County (G-10894)

PA: Print Time, Inc.
1105 W 24th St
Kansas City MO 64108
816 756-3900

(G-10863)
PRINT WORKS INC
Also Called: Seattle Printworks
711 9th Ave N (98109-4309)
PHONE..................206 623-3512
Brian Thompson, *President*
Brenda Thompson, *Vice Pres*
EMP: 7
SALES (est): 1.4MM **Privately Held**
SIC: 2752 Commercial printing, lithographic

(G-10864)
PRINT24COM USA LP
800 5th Ave (98104-3176)
PHONE..................206 607-0639
EMP: 2 EST: 2017
SALES (est): 104.2K **Privately Held**
SIC: 2759 Commercial printing

(G-10865)
PRISM DESIGNS INC
Also Called: Prism Kite Technology
4214 24th Ave W (98199-1216)
PHONE..................206 838-8682
Mark Reed, *President*
▲ EMP: 7
SALES (est): 1.1MM **Privately Held**
WEB: www.prismkites.com
SIC: 3944 3949 Kites; sporting & athletic goods

(G-10866)
PRISM GRAPHICS INC
7609 5th Ave S (98108-4117)
PHONE..................206 282-1801
Brad Cole, *President*
Dawn Fulmer, *Manager*
EMP: 6
SQ FT: 1,500
SALES (est): 337.3K **Privately Held**
WEB: www.prismvinyl.com
SIC: 3993 Advertising artwork

(G-10867)
PRISM MOTORS INC
Also Called: Prism Energy
703 Ne Northlake Way (98105-6429)
PHONE..................425 503-5415
Derek Gutheil, *CEO*
EMP: 5
SALES (est): 231.2K **Privately Held**
SIC: 3714 7389 Motor vehicle parts & accessories;

(G-10868)
PRO FAB INC
211 S Austin St (98108-4119)
PHONE..................206 762-5149
Mark Hansen, *President*
EMP: 3 EST: 1983
SQ FT: 3,060
SALES (est): 441.5K **Privately Held**
SIC: 3441 Fabricated structural metal

(G-10869)
PRO-LITHO INC
4411 Wallingford Ave N C (98103-7565)
PHONE..................206 547-6462
Gil R Kim, *President*
Jisook Kim, *Vice Pres*
EMP: 8
SQ FT: 8,000
SALES (est): 710K **Privately Held**
SIC: 2752 Commercial printing, lithographic

(G-10870)
PROCESS HEATING COMPANY
2732 3rd Ave S (98134-1983)
P.O. Box 84585 (98124-5885)
PHONE..................206 682-3414
Ron Jay, *CEO*
Rick Jay, *President*
Jackie Jay, *Corp Secy*
EMP: 9 EST: 1945
SQ FT: 3,800
SALES (est): 1.8MM **Privately Held**
WEB: www.processheating.com
SIC: 3567 5084 Electrical furnaces, ovens & heating devices, exc. induction; industrial machinery & equipment

(G-10871)
PROFESSIONAL DESIGNED SEWING
9051 18th Ave Sw (98106-2371)
PHONE..................206 234-5955
Sok Hong, *Owner*
EMP: 8
SALES (est): 907.3K **Privately Held**
SIC: 3639 Sewing equipment

(G-10872)
PROFESSIONAL MKTG GROUP
11416 Rainier Ave S # 18 (98178-3937)
PHONE..................206 322-7303
Sydney Dolder, *Principal*
EMP: 2
SALES (est): 196.6K **Privately Held**
SIC: 3556 Food products machinery

(G-10873)
PROFILE SYSTEMS INC
Also Called: Magnum Print Solutions
5300 4th Ave S (98108-2217)
PHONE..................206 624-7715
Stephen Seavecki, *CEO*
EMP: 12
SQ FT: 3,000
SALES (est): 2.5MM **Privately Held**
WEB: www.magnumlaser.com
SIC: 3861 7378 Toners, prepared photographic (not made in chemical plants); computer & data processing equipment repair/maintenance

(G-10874)
PROJECT SEEZIT INC
Also Called: Rivet & Sway
4111 E Madison St (98112-3241)
PHONE..................415 336-4000
Sarah Bryar, *CEO*
John Lusk, *Chief Mktg Ofcr*
▲ EMP: 2
SALES (est): 269.3K **Privately Held**
SIC: 3851 Ophthalmic goods

(G-10875)
PROLIANCE INTERNATIONAL
7951 2nd Ave S (98108-4204)
PHONE..................206 764-7028
John Scott, *Manager*
EMP: 3
SALES (est): 147.3K **Privately Held**
SIC: 3465 Automotive stampings

(G-10876)
PROTECTIVE COATING CONSULTANTS
Also Called: P C C I
1501 S 92nd Pl Ste A (98108-5103)
P.O. Box 84162 (98124-5462)
PHONE..................206 762-6119
Barney Lubetkin, *President*
Tom Lockwood, *Corp Secy*
Jim Lockwood, *Vice Pres*
Nathan Lubetkin, *Sales Mgr*
EMP: 6
SQ FT: 10,000
SALES (est): 1.1MM **Privately Held**
WEB: www.pcciseattle.com
SIC: 3479 Coating of metals & formed products; painting, coating & hot dipping

(G-10877)
PROTEK-USA LLC
3927 1st Ave Ne Apt 31 (98105-6823)
PHONE..................206 782-8399
F Bert Lerch, *Partner*
EMP: 5
SQ FT: 1,200
SALES (est): 1.5MM **Privately Held**
WEB: www.protek-usa.com
SIC: 3479 1742 Painting, coating & hot dipping; plastering, drywall & insulation

(G-10878)
PROXYGROOVE LLC
Also Called: Pageclean
517 30th Ave E (98112-4204)
PHONE..................415 264-1906

Julius Schorzman,
EMP: 4 EST: 2014
SALES (est): 122.9K **Privately Held**
SIC: 7372 Home entertainment computer software

(G-10879)
PRYDE JOHNSON 1536 LLC
419 Ne 70th St (98115-5481)
PHONE..................206 352-7000
Curt Pryde, *Principal*
EMP: 4
SALES (est): 454.2K **Privately Held**
SIC: 3861 Developers, photographic (not made in chemical plants)

(G-10880)
PS COLORS INC
7006 42nd Ave S (98118-3514)
PHONE..................206 371-1341
EMP: 2 EST: 2015
SALES (est): 100.9K **Privately Held**
SIC: 2759 Screen printing

(G-10881)
PSF INDUSTRIES INC (PA)
65 S Horton St (98134-1824)
PHONE..................800 426-1204
Jeff Brown, *CEO*
Jeffrey Brown, *Principal*
Brian Monk, *Project Engr*
Brien H Harrison, *CFO*
Steve Long, *Sales Engr*
EMP: 50
SQ FT: 40,000
SALES (est): 23.3MM **Privately Held**
WEB: www.psfindustries.com
SIC: 3443 1791 1629 Tanks, standard or custom fabricated; metal plate; structural steel erection; power plant construction

(G-10882)
PUDDLES BARKERY LLC
146 N Canal St Ste 350 (98103-8651)
PHONE..................206 495-3072
EMP: 2
SALES (est): 140.6K **Privately Held**
SIC: 2047 Dog food

(G-10883)
PUGET LITE-PAVERS INC
309 S Cloverdale St C8 (98108-4570)
PHONE..................206 849-7091
Rusty Sproatt, *Principal*
EMP: 4
SALES (est): 227.7K **Privately Held**
SIC: 3531 Pavers

(G-10884)
PUGET SOUND COMMERCE CTR INC (HQ)
1801 16th Ave Sw (98134-1017)
PHONE..................206 623-1635
Frank J Foti, *President*
David R Whitcomb, *COO*
Berger A Dodge, *CFO*
Lon V Leneve, *CFO*
Julie Skirvin, *Admin Sec*
▲ EMP: 75 EST: 1916
SQ FT: 426,833
SALES (est): 109.9MM
SALES (corp-wide): 599.5MM **Privately Held**
WEB: www.toddpacific.com
SIC: 3731 Combat vessels, building & repairing
PA: Vigor Industrial Llc
5555 N Channel Ave # 71
Portland OR 97217
503 247-1777

(G-10885)
PUGET SOUND REPAIR INC
Also Called: PSR
7410 5th Ave S (98108-4112)
P.O. Box 80244 (98108-0244)
PHONE..................506 556-9722
James L Shreve, *President*
Dianne L Shreve, *Corp Secy*
EMP: 9 EST: 1998
SQ FT: 600
SALES (est): 1.5MM **Privately Held**
SIC: 3325 3365 7699 7622 Steel foundries; aluminum foundries; nautical repair services; radio & television repair; boat building & repairing

(G-10886)
PULPO GAMES LLC
4412 2nd Ave Ne (98105-6129)
PHONE..................206 371-6924
Andrew Seavy, *Principal*
EMP: 2
SALES (est): 79K **Privately Held**
SIC: 7372 Educational computer software

(G-10887)
PURE BLUE TECH INC
1200 12th Ave S Ste 1110 (98144-2776)
PHONE..................206 724-5707
Ryan Vogel, *CEO*
EMP: 4
SALES (est): 293.5K **Privately Held**
SIC: 3589 Sewage & water treatment equipment

(G-10888)
PURE DROP
1515 Sw Roxbury St (98106-2840)
PHONE..................425 351-9007
Roberto Murillo, *Principal*
EMP: 2
SALES (est): 122.9K **Privately Held**
SIC: 3589 Water purification equipment, household type

(G-10889)
PURE FIRE INDEPENDENT LLC
310 1st Ave S (98104-2536)
PHONE..................206 218-3297
Mason Wardell, *Principal*
EMP: 2 EST: 2012
SALES (est): 111.6K **Privately Held**
SIC: 3652 Pre-recorded records & tapes

(G-10890)
PURE WATERCRAFT INC
2151 N Northlake Way # 210 (98103-9157)
PHONE..................206 451-0350
Andrew Rebele, *President*
EMP: 5
SALES (est): 489.5K **Privately Held**
SIC: 3089 Plastic boats & other marine equipment

(G-10891)
PURELY TANGIBLE
2827 14th Ave W Apt 1 (98119-2045)
PHONE..................206 301-9999
Doug Andrews, *Owner*
Ross Andrews, *Director*
EMP: 2
SALES (est): 119.4K **Privately Held**
SIC: 2752 Commercial printing, offset

(G-10892)
PUSHSPRING INC
712 N 34th St Ste 201 (98103-8867)
PHONE..................206 455-6128
Karl Stillner, *CEO*
Chris L Kinsman, *Chief*
Patrick Callinan, *Vice Pres*
Carli Visser, *Marketing Staff*
Josie Bolotski, *Director*
EMP: 7
SALES (est): 220.8K **Privately Held**
SIC: 7372 7389 Business oriented computer software;

(G-10893)
PYRAMID BREWERIES INC (DH)
Also Called: Thomas Kemper
91 S Royal Brougham Way (98134-1219)
PHONE..................206 682-8322
George Hancock, *Ch of Bd*
Scott S Barnum, *President*
Martin Kelly, *COO*
Mark House, *VP Opers*
Michael O'Brien, *CFO*
◆ EMP: 81
SALES (est): 74MM **Privately Held**
SIC: 2082 5813 Ale (alcoholic beverage); beer (alcoholic beverage); drinking places
HQ: Independent Brewers United Corporation
431 Pine St Ste G12
Burlington VT 05401
802 862-6114

(G-10894)
PYRAMID BREWERIES INC
1201 1st Ave S (98134-1238)
PHONE..................206 682-3377

Seattle - King County (G-10895)   GEOGRAPHIC SECTION

Teressa Morgan, *Branch Mgr*
EMP: 98 Privately Held
SIC: 2082 Beer (alcoholic beverage)
HQ: Pyramid Breweries Inc.
91 S Royal Brougham Way
Seattle WA 98134
206 682-8322

(G-10895)
PZ WIND DOWN INC
Also Called: Phaserx
410 W Harrison St Ste 300 (98119-4034)
PHONE..................206 805-6300
Steven Gillis, *Ch of Bd*
Robert W Overell, *President*
Gordon Brandt, *Chief Mktg Ofcr*
EMP: 21
SQ FT: 11,291
SALES (est): 664.3K Privately Held
SIC: 2834 Pharmaceutical preparations

(G-10896)
QNC MACHINE INC
3401 17th Ave W (98119)
P.O. Box 99304 (98139-0304)
PHONE..................206 282-5854
Kaz Zawitkowski, *President*
EMP: 2
SQ FT: 1,200
SALES (est): 146.4K Privately Held
SIC: 3599 Machine shop, jobbing & repair

(G-10897)
QORUS SOFTWARE INC
500 Yale Ave N 100 (98109-5680)
PHONE..................844 516-8000
Ray Meirian, *CEO*
David Mead, *Bus Dvlpt Dir*
EMP: 70 **EST:** 2013
SALES (est): 2.4MM
SALES (corp-wide): 3.7MM Privately Held
SIC: 7372 Business oriented computer software
PA: Relate Spin (Pty) Ltd
2nd Floor Corporate Place
Bellville WC 7530

(G-10898)
QUADIENT DATA USA INC
1301 5th Ave Ste 1300 (98101-2645)
PHONE..................206 443-0765
Dale Garrett, *President*
Hugh Rogovy, *Principal*
Fabrice Assous, *Director*
Joseph Bonassar, *Director*
Dennis Lestrange, *Director*
EMP: 60
SALES (est): 11MM
SALES (corp-wide): 38.4MM Privately Held
WEB: www.satorisoftware.com
SIC: 7371 7372 Computer software development; prepackaged software
HQ: Mailroom Holding, Inc
478 Wheelers Farms Rd
Milford CT 06461

(G-10899)
QUAL FAB INC
1705 S 93rd St Ste F11 (98108-5136)
PHONE..................206 762-2117
John M Williams, *President*
John F Williams, *Vice Pres*
Craig Chandler, *Opers Mgr*
Greg Parish, *Supervisor*
Chris Riccitti, *Prgrmr*
EMP: 45 **EST:** 1977
SQ FT: 35,000
SALES (est): 16.3MM Privately Held
WEB: www.qual-fab.com
SIC: 3444 Sheet metal specialties, not stamped

(G-10900)
QUALITY CODE PUBLISHING
8015 15th Ave Nw (98117-3802)
PHONE..................206 216-9500
Nancy Helmer, *CEO*
EMP: 2
SALES (est): 10.5K Privately Held
SIC: 2741 Miscellaneous publishing

(G-10901)
QUALITY COPY AND PRINT LLC
Also Called: Professional Copy 'n' Print
4200 University Way Ne (98105-5807)
PHONE..................206 634-2689
Dhiresh Tewari,
Mohammed Azmath,
EMP: 3 **EST:** 2001
SQ FT: 2,500
SALES (est): 443.5K Privately Held
WEB: www.qcnp.com
SIC: 2752 Commercial printing, offset

(G-10902)
QUALITY PRESS INC
222 S Orcas St (98108-2441)
PHONE..................206 768-2655
John Depasquale, *President*
John Melberg, *Administration*
EMP: 20
SQ FT: 11,000
SALES (est): 4.3MM Privately Held
WEB: www.qualitypress.com
SIC: 2752 2789 2759 Commercial printing, offset; bookbinding & related work; commercial printing

(G-10903)
QUANTUM SAILS
6319 Seaview Ave Nw (98107-2664)
PHONE..................206 634-0636
Bob Pistay, *Owner*
EMP: 2 **EST:** 2007
SQ FT: 2,600
SALES (est): 500K Privately Held
SIC: 3732 5551 Sailboats, building & repairing; sailboats & equipment
PA: Raptor Sails, Inc.
2320 Place Rd
Port Angeles WA
206 842-6840

(G-10904)
QUARRY S/E INC
Also Called: Lakeview Stone and Garden
916 N 143rd St (98133-6911)
PHONE..................206 525-5270
Rebecca Boehm, *Manager*
EMP: 7
SALES (corp-wide): 3.5MM Privately Held
WEB: www.lakeviewstone.com
SIC: 1411 Sandstone, dimension-quarrying
PA: Quarry S/E, Inc.
916 N 143rd St
Seattle WA 98133
206 522-8670

(G-10905)
QUEST SOFTWARE INC
1400 Taylor Ave N Apt 302 (98109-3366)
PHONE..................949 720-1434
EMP: 30
SALES (corp-wide): 1.7B Privately Held
SIC: 7372 Prepackaged software
HQ: Quest Software, Inc.
4 Polaris Way
Aliso Viejo CA 92656
949 754-8000

(G-10906)
QUIRING MONUMENTS INC
Also Called: Memories In Granite
9608 Aurora Ave N (98103-3296)
PHONE..................206 522-8400
David H Quiring, *President*
▲ **EMP:** 44
SQ FT: 30,000
SALES (est): 9.5MM Privately Held
WEB: www.monuments.com
SIC: 5099 5999 3281 Monuments & grave markers; monuments, finished to custom order; cut stone & stone products

(G-10907)
QUMULO INC (PA)
1501 4th Ave Ste 1600 (98101-3613)
PHONE..................206 260-3588
Bill Richter, *CEO*
Justin Doolittle, *Counsel*
Molly Brown, *Vice Pres*
Karim Fanous, *Vice Pres*
Josh Harbert, *Vice Pres*
EMP: 80
SALES (est): 39.9MM Privately Held
SIC: 3572 Computer storage devices

(G-10908)
QWELL PHARMACEUTICALS INC
1000 2nd Ave Ste 3700 (98104-1053)
PHONE..................206 674-3027
Steven Gillis, *Chairman*
EMP: 5
SALES (est): 50K Privately Held
SIC: 2836 Biological products, except diagnostic

(G-10909)
R & B ART GLASS
1813 19th Ave Apt 407 (98122-2859)
PHONE..................206 323-6430
EMP: 2
SALES (est): 128.7K Privately Held
SIC: 3229 Mfg Pressed/Blown Glass

(G-10910)
R & D INDUSTRIES
Also Called: Travel Wrap
2224 1st Ave S (98134-1408)
PHONE..................206 382-1370
Duane Ruud, *Mng Member*
EMP: 2
SALES (est): 100K Privately Held
WEB: www.travelwrap.com
SIC: 3161 Traveling bags

(G-10911)
R R DONNELLEY & SONS COMPANY
5601 6th Ave S Ste 350 (98108-2544)
PHONE..................206 587-0278
Jim Christensen, *Manager*
EMP: 9
SALES (corp-wide): 6.8B Publicly Held
WEB: www.rrdonnelley.com
SIC: 2711 Commercial printing & newspaper publishing combined
PA: R. R. Donnelley & Sons Company
35 W Wacker Dr Ste 3650
Chicago IL 60601
312 326-8000

(G-10912)
RACER MATE INC
3016 Ne Blakeley St (98105-4012)
PHONE..................206 524-7392
EMP: 45
SQ FT: 8,000
SALES (est): 3.6MM
SALES (corp-wide): 16.8MM Privately Held
SIC: 3949 5091 7371 7372 Mfg Sport/Athletic Goods Whol Sporting Goods/Supp Computer Programming Svc Prepackaged Software Svc
PA: Floscan Instrument Company, Inc.
3012 Ne Blakeley St
Seattle WA 98230
206 524-6625

(G-10913)
RAEPOP
6323 Sand Point Way Ne (98115-7914)
PHONE..................206 729-3996
Paul Jackson, *Principal*
EMP: 2
SALES (est): 100.5K Privately Held
SIC: 2741 Miscellaneous publishing

(G-10914)
RAIN CITY WEST PRINTING LLC
8133 16th Ave Sw (98106-1849)
PHONE..................206 767-1151
David Ho, *Bd of Directors*
EMP: 4 **EST:** 2012
SALES (est): 391.4K Privately Held
SIC: 2752 Commercial printing, offset

(G-10915)
RAIN CITY WOOD WORKS LLC
1611 7th Ave W (98119-2918)
PHONE..................206 378-0494
Peter Carey Feichtmeir, *Administration*
EMP: 2
SALES (est): 154.2K Privately Held
SIC: 2431 Millwork

(G-10916)
RAINIER CORP
4536 University Way Ne (98105-4511)
PHONE..................206 280-4666

Aquil Ahmed Mohammed, *Principal*
EMP: 3
SALES (est): 200.1K Privately Held
SIC: 2759 Commercial printing

(G-10917)
RAINIER INDUSTRIES
620 S Industrial Way (98108-5236)
PHONE..................206 622-8219
Judy Cooper, *Principal*
EMP: 3 **EST:** 2007
SALES (est): 245.5K Privately Held
SIC: 3999 Manufacturing industries

(G-10918)
RAM BIG HORN BREWERY-NORTHGATE
401 Ne Northgate Way (98125-6036)
PHONE..................206 364-8000
Gene Juarez, *Principal*
EMP: 4
SALES (est): 306.8K Privately Held
SIC: 2082 Beer (alcoholic beverage)

(G-10919)
RAMSAY SIGNS INC
Also Called: Heath Northwest
727 S 96th St (98108-4922)
PHONE..................206 623-3100
Ken Naas, *Branch Mgr*
Steve Sampson, *Branch Mgr*
EMP: 5
SALES (corp-wide): 10.3MM Privately Held
WEB: www.ramsaysigns.com
SIC: 5046 7359 3993 Signs, electrical; sign rental; signs & advertising specialties
PA: Ramsay Signs, Inc.
9160 Se 74th Ave
Portland OR 97206
503 777-4555

(G-10920)
RANKIN ASSOCIATES
2337 13th Ave E (98102-4018)
PHONE..................206 325-9440
Carolyn Rankin, *President*
EMP: 2
SALES (est): 220K Privately Held
SIC: 7372 Prepackaged software

(G-10921)
RAOSOFT INC
6645 Ne Windermere Rd (98115-7942)
PHONE..................206 523-9278
Catherine McDole RAO, *CEO*
P M RAO, *Ch of Bd*
Sanjay RAO, *Treasurer*
Shanti RAO, *Admin Sec*
EMP: 6
SALES: 48.7K Privately Held
WEB: www.raosoft.com
SIC: 7371 7372 Computer software development; prepackaged software

(G-10922)
RAPP MARINE HP LLC
2260 W Commodore Way (98199-1259)
PHONE..................206 286-8162
Fax: 206 285-9579
▼ **EMP:** 25 **EST:** 2011
SQ FT: 17,000
SALES (est): 6.7MM
SALES (corp-wide): 0 Privately Held
SIC: 3531 Mfg Construction Machinery
HQ: Rapp Marine U.S. Inc.
2260 W Commodore Way
Seattle WA 98199
206 286-8162

(G-10923)
RAPTOR SAILS INC
6319 Seaview Ave Nw (98107-2664)
PHONE..................360 775-6039
▲ **EMP:** 2
SALES (est): 103.7K Privately Held
SIC: 2394 Canvas & related products

(G-10924)
RASTON PUBLISHING LLC
1752 Nw Market St (98107-5264)
PHONE..................206 962-7839
Gail Marie Sexton, *Administration*
EMP: 2
SALES (est): 98.4K Privately Held
SIC: 2741 Miscellaneous publishing

GEOGRAPHIC SECTION
Seattle - King County (G-10956)

(G-10925)
RAUCH INDUSTRIES INC
Also Called: Christopher Radko
Lakeside Ave Ste 200 (98122)
PHONE..................................800 717-2356
Kristin McCave, *Branch Mgr*
EMP: 15
SALES (corp-wide): 200.2MM **Privately Held**
SIC: 3229 Christmas tree ornaments, from glass produced on-site
PA: Rauch Industries, Inc.
 3800a Little Mountain Rd
 Gastonia NC 28056
 704 867-5333

(G-10926)
RAUDA SCALE MODELS INC
Also Called: Models By Rauda Scale Models
13711 Lake City Way Ne (98125-3615)
PHONE..................................206 365-8877
Vija Rauda, *President*
Guanurs Radua, *Admin Sec*
EMP: 10
SQ FT: 20,000
SALES: 500K **Privately Held**
WEB: www.raudascalemodels.com
SIC: 3999 5945 2741 Models, except toy; hobby, toy & game shops; miscellaneous publishing

(G-10927)
RAZORGIRL PRESS
130 Sw 112th St (98146-4328)
PHONE..................................206 290-7990
EMP: 2
SALES (est): 59.2K **Privately Held**
SIC: 2741 Miscellaneous publishing

(G-10928)
RE-MARKS INC
3610 Albion Pl N (98103-7904)
PHONE..................................206 548-1008
Grace Crowley, *President*
Tom Moser, *COO*
Gary Smoot, *Art Dir*
EMP: 10
SALES (est): 1.6MM **Privately Held**
WEB: www.remarks.net
SIC: 3944 Board games, puzzles & models, except electronic

(G-10929)
READ PRODUCTS INC
3615 15th Ave W (98119-1392)
PHONE..................................206 283-2510
Robert C Read, *President*
Charles R Read Jr, *Chairman*
Arlene K Read, *Vice Pres*
Arlene Read, *Human Resources*
EMP: 15
SQ FT: 30,000
SALES (est): 2.7MM **Privately Held**
WEB: www.cuttingboards.com
SIC: 5722 5713 5031 3269 Household appliance stores; floor covering stores; building materials, interior; kitchen & table articles, coarse earthenware

(G-10930)
REALNETWORKS INC (PA)
1501 1st Ave S Ste 600 (98134-1470)
PHONE..................................206 674-2700
Robert Glaser, *Ch of Bd*
William J Patrizio, *President*
Massimiliano Pellegrini, *President*
Jun Lee, *General Mgr*
David Stout, *General Mgr*
▲ **EMP:** 148
SQ FT: 86,000
SALES: 69.5MM **Publicly Held**
WEB: www.real.com
SIC: 7371 7372 Software programming applications; application computer software

(G-10931)
REALTIME INC
Also Called: Realtime Audio
336 Ne 89th St (98115-2941)
PHONE..................................206 523-8050
Philip Mc Caslin, *President*
EMP: 3
SALES (est): 377K **Privately Held**
SIC: 3695 Magnetic & optical recording media

(G-10932)
REALTY SOLUTIONS INC
3435 4th Ave S (98134-1904)
P.O. Box 94123 (98124-6423)
PHONE..................................206 839-1023
John Mackenzie, *President*
EMP: 15
SQ FT: 3,000
SALES (est): 1.4MM **Privately Held**
WEB: www.agentshelper.com
SIC: 3993 Signs & advertising specialties

(G-10933)
RECREATIONAL EQUIPMENT INC
Also Called: Rei
222 Yale Ave N (98109-5429)
PHONE..................................206 223-1944
Kevin Galic, *Owner*
John Sulcs, *Warehouse Mgr*
Tim Runge, *Opers Staff*
Peter Newton, *Design Engr*
Rachel Lictenburg, *Manager*
EMP: 500
SALES (corp-wide): 2.7B **Privately Held**
WEB: www.rei.com
SIC: 3949 7997 5941 5561 Sporting & athletic goods; membership sports & recreation clubs; sporting goods & bicycle shops; recreational vehicle dealers
PA: Recreational Equipment, Inc.
 6750 S 228th St
 Kent WA 98032
 253 395-3780

(G-10934)
RECURSIVE FROG LLC
9222 22nd Ave Sw (98106-2618)
PHONE..................................206 745-2561
Tony Patino, *Owner*
EMP: 2
SALES (est): 90.7K **Privately Held**
SIC: 7372 Application computer software

(G-10935)
RED DEVIL RACEWAY
10000 Lake City Way Ne (98125-7734)
PHONE..................................206 402-6690
Gerald Brott, *Principal*
EMP: 3
SALES (est): 215.1K **Privately Held**
SIC: 3644 Raceways

(G-10936)
RED LETTER PRESS CORP
4710 University Way Ne # 100 (98105-4427)
PHONE..................................206 985-4621
Helen Gilbert, *President*
EMP: 3
SALES (est): 209.4K **Privately Held**
WEB: www.redletterpress.org
SIC: 2731 Books: publishing only

(G-10937)
RED PROPELLER LLC
1605 Boylston Ave Ste 301 (98122-6734)
PHONE..................................206 452-5664
Kevin Jeffries, *Principal*
EMP: 2
SALES (est): 292.3K **Privately Held**
SIC: 3366 Propellers

(G-10938)
RED SEAL GAMES LLC
8057 28th Ave Ne (98115-4639)
PHONE..................................425 922-6500
David Hasle,
Richard Ellis,
EMP: 2
SALES (est): 122K **Privately Held**
SIC: 3944 7389 Electronic games & toys;

(G-10939)
REDBIRD SPORTS INC
4868 Beacon Ave S (98108-1501)
PHONE..................................206 725-7872
Jay Turner, *President*
▲ **EMP:** 12
SQ FT: 7,000
SALES: 1MM **Privately Held**
WEB: www.redbirdsports.com
SIC: 3949 5941 Golf equipment; sporting goods & bicycle shops

(G-10940)
REELWORLD PRODUCTIONS INC (PA)
2214 Queen Anne Ave N (98109-2312)
PHONE..................................206 448-1518
Mike Thomas, *President*
Chris Cline, *Vice Pres*
Victor Lisle, *Production*
Ali Ashik, *Web Dvlpr*
EMP: 7
SALES (est): 934K **Privately Held**
WEB: www.reelworld.com
SIC: 2731 5736 Books: publishing only; sheet music

(G-10941)
REFINED WOODWORKS INC
Also Called: Pearl Woodworks
5701 6th Ave S Ste 121 (98108-2521)
PHONE..................................206 762-2603
Christopher T Forde, *President*
Chris Forde, *President*
EMP: 7
SQ FT: 3,000
SALES (est): 720K **Privately Held**
WEB: www.refined-woodworks.com
SIC: 2434 Wood kitchen cabinets

(G-10942)
REG GRAYS HARBOR LLC (HQ)
1741 1st Ave S (98134-1403)
PHONE..................................206 753-0155
EMP: 20
SALES (est): 9.5MM
SALES (corp-wide): 2.3B **Publicly Held**
SIC: 2819 Chemicals, high purity: refined from technical grade
PA: Renewable Energy Group, Inc.
 416 S Bell Ave
 Ames IA 50010
 515 239-8000

(G-10943)
REGENERATED TEXTILE INDS LLC
8715 Dayton Ave N (98103-3714)
PHONE..................................206 427-9343
Karim Lessard, *President*
Jennifer Henninger, *Opers Staff*
EMP: 5
SALES (est): 177.6K **Privately Held**
SIC: 2299 Fibers, textile: recovery from textile mill waste & rags

(G-10944)
REHEAL LLC
14333 Interlake Ave N (98133-7107)
PHONE..................................206 440-5948
Brandon Bowman, *CEO*
Chris Allan, *COO*
EMP: 2
SALES (est): 95.3K **Privately Held**
SIC: 3842 3826 3841 Orthopedic appliances; analytical instruments; suction therapy apparatus

(G-10945)
REID SIGNS INC
3916 15th Pl W (98119-1628)
PHONE..................................206 547-5487
Greg Reid, *President*
EMP: 4
SALES (est): 360.7K **Privately Held**
WEB: www.reidsigns.com
SIC: 3993 5046 Signs, not made in custom sign painting shops; neon signs; electric signs; displays & cutouts, window & lobby; neon signs

(G-10946)
REJUVENATION INC
Also Called: Rejuve - Seattle
2910 1st Ave S (98134-1859)
PHONE..................................206 382-1901
Chris Migdol, *Branch Mgr*
EMP: 13
SALES (corp-wide): 5.6B **Publicly Held**
WEB: www.rejuvenation.com
SIC: 3648 Lighting equipment
HQ: Rejuvenation Inc.
 2550 Nw Nicolai St
 Portland OR 97210
 888 401-1900

(G-10947)
RENEWABLE ENERGY INC
3601 Fremont Ave N # 216 (98103-2709)
PHONE..................................206 634-3601
Daniel Cawdrey Sr, *President*
EMP: 8
SALES (est): 950K **Privately Held**
SIC: 2869 Industrial organic chemicals

(G-10948)
REPAIR TECHNOLOGY INC
400 S 96th St (98108-4912)
PHONE..................................206 762-6221
Ken Morehead, *President*
Leon Gardner, *General Mgr*
EMP: 15
SQ FT: 15,000
SALES (est): 1.7MM **Privately Held**
SIC: 7699 3471 Industrial machinery & equipment repair; plating & polishing

(G-10949)
REPRODACTYL INC
Also Called: Reproduction Services
6237 3rd Ave Nw (98107-2106)
PHONE..................................206 782-1128
Gretchen Marks, *Principal*
Ken Kucher, *COO*
EMP: 2 **EST:** 2001
SALES (est): 210K **Privately Held**
WEB: www.reprodactyl.com
SIC: 3562 Casters

(G-10950)
RESISTERS
3811 S Horton St (98144-7027)
PHONE..................................206 722-3482
EMP: 3
SALES (est): 132.4K **Privately Held**
SIC: 2711 Newspapers, publishing & printing

(G-10951)
RESOLVE THERAPEUTICS LLC
454 N 34th St (98103-8602)
PHONE..................................208 727-7010
James Posada, *CEO*
EMP: 8
SALES (est): 1MM **Privately Held**
SIC: 2834 Pharmaceutical preparations

(G-10952)
RESONANT SYSTEMS INC
Also Called: Truesonic
1406 Nw 53rd St Ste 2a (98107-3731)
PHONE..................................206 557-4398
Robin Elnga, *CEO*
EMP: 5
SALES (est): 531.9K **Privately Held**
SIC: 3674 Solid state electronic devices

(G-10953)
RESTLESS PRINTS
5518 21st Ave S (98108-2908)
PHONE..................................772 205-9868
Gregory S Hughes, *Owner*
EMP: 2
SALES (est): 111.6K **Privately Held**
SIC: 2752 Commercial printing, lithographic

(G-10954)
RETRODYNE INDUSTRIES LLC
8560 Greenwood Ave N (98103-3614)
PHONE..................................206 906-9762
Thomas J Skewes, *Principal*
EMP: 3
SALES (est): 193.9K **Privately Held**
SIC: 3999 Manufacturing industries

(G-10955)
REVEL BODY
1406 Nw 53rd St Ste 2a (98107-3731)
PHONE..................................206 409-2940
Dan Knodle, *Manager*
EMP: 5
SALES (est): 403K **Privately Held**
SIC: 3634 Massage machines, electric, except for beauty/barber shops

(G-10956)
REVOLUTION INC
3663 1st Ave S (98134-2246)
PHONE..................................206 714-3529
Robert Bass, *President*

Seattle - King County (G-10957) GEOGRAPHIC SECTION

Lance Bass, *Corp Secy*
Jim McCall, *Exec VP*
Christopher Mohn, *Vice Pres*
Deforest Shotwell, *Vice Pres*
EMP: 14
SALES (est): 2.3MM **Privately Held**
WEB: www.revolution8.com
SIC: 2759 Commercial printing

(G-10957)
RFP LLC
11712 5th Ave Ne (98125-4902)
PHONE 206 523-8996
Roger Parks, *Principal*
EMP: 2
SALES (est): 130.8K **Privately Held**
SIC: 2721 Magazines: publishing only, not printed on site

(G-10958)
RGB SODA
1809 15th Ave (98122-2635)
PHONE 206 437-8395
Adam Peters, *Principal*
EMP: 4
SALES (est): 304.9K **Privately Held**
SIC: 2086 Carbonated beverages, nonalcoholic: bottled & canned

(G-10959)
RGB14 LLC
3629b Courtland Pl S (98144-7114)
PHONE 206 818-8207
Ryan Burrows,
EMP: 2
SALES: 60K **Privately Held**
SIC: 7372 7389 Prepackaged software;

(G-10960)
RH APPETIZING INC
Also Called: Chocolopolis
1631 15th Ave W Ste 111 (98119-3071)
PHONE 206 282-0776
Lauren Adler, *Principal*
EMP: 7
SALES (est): 620.9K **Privately Held**
SIC: 2064 2066 Candy & other confectionery products; chocolate

(G-10961)
RICHARD C BUSHER JR
Also Called: Dick Busher Photographics
7042 20th Pl Ne (98115-5712)
PHONE 206 524-6726
Richard C Busher Jr, *Owner*
Ron McLean, *Owner*
EMP: 2
SALES: 150K **Privately Held**
WEB: www.cosgroveweb.com
SIC: 7335 2741 Commercial photography; catalogs: publishing only, not printed on site

(G-10962)
RICHARD SAUNDERS
Also Called: Recognition Unlimited
13716 Lake City Way Ne # 502 (98125-2600)
PHONE 612 861-1061
EMP: 2
SALES (est): 180K **Privately Held**
SIC: 7311 3479 Advertising Agency Coating/Engraving Service

(G-10963)
RICHMARK COMPANY
Also Called: Richmark Label
1110 E Pine St (98122-3987)
P.O. Box 22310 (98122-0310)
PHONE 206 322-8884
William Donner, *President*
EMP: 85
SQ FT: 45,000
SALES (est): 13.1MM **Privately Held**
WEB: www.richmarklabel.com
SIC: 2759 Labels & seals: printing

(G-10964)
RIDEMIND LLC
4215 Whitman Ave N # 201 (98103-7399)
PHONE 206 226-0016
EMP: 2
SALES (est): 120K **Privately Held**
SIC: 3751 Mfg Motorcycles/Bicycles

(G-10965)
RIDES PUBLISHING CO LLC
Also Called: Ample Technologies
2442 Nw Market St Ste 43 (98107-4137)
PHONE 206 789-0827
Ruth Ishihara,
EMP: 8
SALES (est): 791.8K **Privately Held**
WEB: www.amplepower.com
SIC: 2731 Book publishing

(G-10966)
RIVAL IQ CORPORATION
500 Union St Ste 500 # 500 (98101-4047)
PHONE 206 395-8572
John Clark, *CEO*
EMP: 19
SALES (est): 1.6MM **Privately Held**
SIC: 7372 Business oriented computer software

(G-10967)
RK BURK MEG MURCH ARTWORKS
11810 8th Ave Nw (98177-4536)
PHONE 206 954-1297
R Burk, *Manager*
EMP: 2 **EST:** 2017
SALES (est): 85.2K **Privately Held**
SIC: 1382 Oil & gas exploration services

(G-10968)
RK PRINT GROUP
10203 47th Ave Sw Apt C17 (98146-1040)
PHONE 206 972-0874
EMP: 2 **EST:** 2010
SALES (est): 120K **Privately Held**
SIC: 2752 Lithographic Commercial Printing

(G-10969)
RMC INCORPORATED
Also Called: RMC Powder Coating
7951 2nd Ave S (98108-4204)
PHONE 206 243-4831
Kevin Gracey, *President*
Ryan S Gracey, *Vice Pres*
Carolyn Walker, *Admin Sec*
EMP: 30
SQ FT: 7,000
SALES (est): 1.5MM **Privately Held**
SIC: 3479 3531 3728 Coating of metals & formed products; marine related equipment; aircraft parts & equipment

(G-10970)
ROAD RUNNER TRANSPORTATION LLC
4435 S Camano Pl (98118-4626)
PHONE 253 778-3848
Leonard Williams, *Owner*
EMP: 2
SALES (est): 100K **Privately Held**
SIC: 3713 Truck & bus bodies

(G-10971)
ROBERT MADSEN DESIGN INC
5448 Shilshole Ave Nw (98107-4022)
PHONE 206 588-0090
Robert Madsen, *President*
EMP: 2
SALES (est): 200K **Privately Held**
SIC: 2426 2421 8712 Hardwood dimension & flooring mills; sawmills & planing mills, general; architectural services

(G-10972)
ROBERT ROWE
3809 Interlake Ave N (98103-8129)
PHONE 206 632-7997
Robert Rowe, *Owner*
EMP: 6
SALES (est): 380K **Privately Held**
SIC: 7372 Application computer software

(G-10973)
ROBODUB INC
4000 Mason Rd Ste 308c (98195-0001)
PHONE 408 250-5723
Parminder Devsi, *CEO*
EMP: 4
SALES (est): 310.4K **Privately Held**
SIC: 3721 Motorized aircraft

(G-10974)
RODAX SOFTWARE
8734 20th Ave Nw (98117-3526)
PHONE 206 782-3482
John Boyer, *Principal*
Cynthia S Boyer, *Principal*
EMP: 5
SALES (est): 360.4K **Privately Held**
SIC: 7372 Application computer software

(G-10975)
ROERACING SLALOM SKATEBOARDS
3912 W Bertona St (98199-1933)
PHONE 206 371-9710
Gareth Roe, *Partner*
Henry Hester, *Partner*
EMP: 2
SALES (est): 163.2K **Privately Held**
WEB: www.roeslalom.com
SIC: 3949 Skateboards

(G-10976)
ROGERS MACHINERY COMPANY INC
7800 5th Ave S (98108-4398)
PHONE 206 763-2530
Tony Zwiefel, *Materials Mgr*
Dave Debeaux, *Sales Staff*
Tim Kenyon, *Sales Staff*
Mike Proulx, *Branch Mgr*
Bob Mecum, *Manager*
EMP: 24
SQ FT: 13,822
SALES (corp-wide): 69.8MM **Privately Held**
SIC: 3561 3564 5084 7699 Industrial pumps & parts; blowers & fans; industrial machinery & equipment; compressors, except air conditioning; pumps & pumping equipment; compressor repair; pumps & pumping equipment repair; industrial machinery & equipment repair
PA: Rogers Machinery Company, Inc.
14650 Sw 72nd Ave
Portland OR 97224
503 639-0808

(G-10977)
ROMANZOF FISHING COMPANY LLC
Also Called: Baranof Courageous
4502 14th Ave Nw (98107-4618)
PHONE 206 545-9501
Charles Hosmer, *Mng Member*
◆ **EMP:** 14
SALES (est): 2.1MM **Privately Held**
SIC: 2298 Cordage & twine

(G-10978)
RONIN GREEN PUBLISHING
6731 29th Ave S (98108-3791)
PHONE 206 725-2839
Chris Pramas, *Principal*
▲ **EMP:** 4
SALES (est): 412.7K **Privately Held**
SIC: 2741 Miscellaneous publishing

(G-10979)
RONS TRANSMISSION
Also Called: Ron's Transhop
12667 Renton Ave S (98178-3712)
PHONE 206 772-8200
Ronald N Ramolete, *Owner*
EMP: 2
SQ FT: 1,500
SALES: 185K **Privately Held**
SIC: 3714 Motor vehicle transmissions, drive assemblies & parts

(G-10980)
ROOFTOP BREWING COMPANY
1220 W Nickerson St (98119-1325)
PHONE 206 457-8598
Craig Christian, *Principal*
EMP: 3
SALES (est): 304K **Privately Held**
SIC: 2082 Beer (alcoholic beverage)

(G-10981)
ROOMMATE FILTER LLC
2319 W Smith St (98199-3524)
PHONE 863 224-6462
Ryan Black, *CEO*
Ryan Palmer, *Vice Pres*

EMP: 2 **EST:** 2014
SALES (est): 91K **Privately Held**
SIC: 7372 7389 Application computer software;

(G-10982)
ROSS ANDREW MICKEL
Also Called: Precept Wine
1910 Frview Ave E Ste 400 (98102)
PHONE 206 267-5252
Ross Andrew Mickel, *Owner*
EMP: 4
SALES (est): 90.3K **Privately Held**
SIC: 2084 Wines

(G-10983)
ROWPERFECT 3
3954 Ne 115th St (98125-5745)
PHONE 206 331-5319
Carlos Dinares, *Principal*
▲ **EMP:** 2
SALES (est): 191.9K **Privately Held**
SIC: 3699 Countermeasure simulators, electric

(G-10984)
ROY MCMAKIN
Also Called: Big Leaf Manufacturing Company
1128 Poplar Pl S (98144-2834)
PHONE 206 323-0111
Roy McMakin, *Owner*
EMP: 6
SALES (est): 613.5K **Privately Held**
SIC: 2511 Wood household furniture

(G-10985)
ROYAL ALEUTIAN SEAFOODS INC
701 Dexter Ave N Ste 403 (98109-4343)
P.O. Box 97018, Redmond (98073-9718)
PHONE 206 283-6605
Garry Loncon, *CEO*
William Blades, *President*
Dave Keene, *Vice Pres*
▼ **EMP:** 50
SALES (est): 26.1K **Privately Held**
SIC: 2092 Fresh or frozen packaged fish

(G-10986)
ROYAL LINE CABINET CO
700 S Orchard St (98108-3427)
PHONE 206 767-9125
EMP: 2 **EST:** 1969
SALES (est): 130K **Privately Held**
SIC: 2541 Mfg Wood Partitions/Fixtures

(G-10987)
ROYAL VIKING INC
Also Called: Trident Sea Foods
5303 Shilshole Ave Nw (98107-4021)
PHONE 206 783-3818
Charles Bundrant, *President*
Adam Taylor, *Vice Pres*
EMP: 2
SQ FT: 20,000
SALES (est): 267.5K
SALES (corp-wide): 2.3B **Privately Held**
WEB: www.tridentseafoods.com
SIC: 2092 Fresh or frozen packaged fish
PA: Trident Seafoods Corporation
5303 Shilshole Ave Nw
Seattle WA 98107
206 783-3818

(G-10988)
RP 2000 LLC
Also Called: Rainier Precision
13500 Linden Ave N (98133-7538)
P.O. Box 77610 (98177-0610)
PHONE 206 624-8258
Wendy Speck, *Mng Member*
EMP: 5
SQ FT: 17,000
SALES (est): 895.6K **Privately Held**
SIC: 3089 Injection molded finished plastic products; injection molding of plastics

(G-10989)
RR DONNELLEY & SONS COMPANY
Also Called: R R Donnelly Financial
999 3rd Ave Ste 500 (98104-4042)
PHONE 206 389-8900
Pam Fish, *Manager*

▲ = Import ▼ = Export
◆ = Import/Export

GEOGRAPHIC SECTION

Seattle - King County (G-11023)

EMP: 12
SALES (corp-wide): 6.8B **Publicly Held**
WEB: www.rrdonnelley.com
SIC: 2754 2759 Commercial printing, gravure; commercial printing
PA: R. R. Donnelley & Sons Company
  35 W Wacker Dr Ste 3650
  Chicago IL 60601
  312 326-8000

(G-10990)
RRR INC
8549 Greenwood Ave N (98103-3613)
PHONE..................................206 782-9260
Beverly Newey, *Principal*
EMP: 2 **EST:** 2011
SALES (est): 202.8K **Privately Held**
SIC: 3569 General industrial machinery

(G-10991)
RUBYTHROAT PRESS LLC
1325 N Allen Pl Apt 540 (98103-7561)
PHONE..................................206 634-9173
Patricia Weenolsen, *Principal*
EMP: 2
SALES (est): 109.1K **Privately Held**
SIC: 2741 Miscellaneous publishing

(G-10992)
RUDD COMPANY INC
1141 Nw 50th St (98107-5120)
PHONE..................................206 789-1000
Alan M Park, *CEO*
Laurel Jamison, *President*
Anita Lewis, *CFO*
Doug Carroll, *Controller*
Tom Parker, *VP Sales*
▲ **EMP:** 5 **EST:** 1912
SQ FT: 150,000
SALES (est): 2.4MM **Privately Held**
WEB: www.ruddcompany.com
SIC: 2851 Lacquers, varnishes, enamels & other coatings

(G-10993)
RUM RUAY INC
12711 Evanston Ave N (98133-7940)
PHONE..................................206 660-4647
EMP: 2
SALES (est): 156.2K **Privately Held**
SIC: 3799 Transportation equipment

(G-10994)
RUMOR GAMES LLC
1717 1st Ave N (98109-2804)
PHONE..................................585 771-7642
Kevin Tarchenski, *Bd of Directors*
EMP: 2
SALES (est): 100.4K **Privately Held**
SIC: 7372 Home entertainment computer software

(G-10995)
RUNAWAY BIKE INDUSTRIES LLC
4412 Densmore Ave N (98103-7540)
PHONE..................................206 817-1787
Douglas Cottington, *Principal*
EMP: 2
SALES (est): 157.2K **Privately Held**
SIC: 3999 Manufacturing industries

(G-10996)
RUNE INC
107 Spring St (98104-1005)
PHONE..................................425 766-6134
Kamran Zargahi, *Branch Mgr*
EMP: 2
SALES (corp-wide): 430.4K **Privately Held**
SIC: 7372 Application computer software; publishers' computer software
PA: Rune, Inc.
  268 Bush St 2702
  San Francisco CA 94104
  646 660-2284

(G-10997)
RUNWAY LIQUIDATION LLC
Also Called: Bcbg
7907-09 S Parkside (98101)
PHONE..................................262 654-3726
EMP: 2
SALES (corp-wide): 645.5MM **Privately Held**
SIC: 2335 Women's, juniors' & misses' dresses
HQ: Runway Liquidation, Llc
  2761 Fruitland Ave
  Vernon CA 90058
  323 589-2224

(G-10998)
RUNWAY LIQUIDATION LLC
Also Called: Bcbg
12841 Towne Center Dr (98101)
PHONE..................................262 948-7035
EMP: 2
SALES (corp-wide): 645.5MM **Privately Held**
SIC: 2335 Women's, juniors' & misses' dresses
HQ: Runway Liquidation, Llc
  2761 Fruitland Ave
  Vernon CA 90058
  323 589-2224

(G-10999)
RUSSELL LAMAR JACQUET-ACEA
4717 Ballard Ave Nw (98107-4810)
PHONE..................................206 334-2935
Russell Jacquet-Acea, *Principal*
EMP: 2
SALES (est): 101.7K **Privately Held**
SIC: 2741 Miscellaneous publishing

(G-11000)
S F MCKINNON CO INC (PA)
Also Called: McKinnon Furniture Company
1201 Western Ave Ste 100 (98101-2953)
PHONE..................................206 622-4948
Sheila McKinnon, *President*
Theresa Schneider, *Vice Pres*
◆ **EMP:** 9
SQ FT: 5,000
SALES (est): 3.5MM **Privately Held**
SIC: 2511 5712 Wood household furniture; furniture stores

(G-11001)
S J W STUDIOS INC
Also Called: S J W Design
1424 10th Ave (98122-3805)
PHONE..................................206 323-8020
Steve Jensen, *President*
Steven Jensen, *President*
EMP: 10
SQ FT: 9,000
SALES (est): 1.5MM **Privately Held**
WEB: www.sjwstudios.com
SIC: 2679 5023 5999 Wallpaper; decorative home furnishings & supplies; art dealers

(G-11002)
SAFECO FIELD
1250 1st Ave S (98134-1216)
PHONE..................................206 346-4000
Bob Aylward, *Partner*
EMP: 2 **EST:** 2011
SALES (est): 235.9K **Privately Held**
SIC: 2531 Stadium seating

(G-11003)
SAIGON PRINTING
3311 Rainier Ave S (98144-6033)
PHONE..................................206 722-6788
Ha La, *Sales Mgr*
Tan La, *Manager*
EMP: 3
SALES (est): 342.4K **Privately Held**
SIC: 2752 Commercial printing, offset

(G-11004)
SAKAI FOODS AMERICA INC
5506 6th Ave S Ste 103 (98108-2552)
PHONE..................................484 494-4322
▼ **EMP:** 2
SALES (est): 196K **Privately Held**
SIC: 2013 2038 Canned meats (except baby food) from purchased meat; ethnic foods, frozen

(G-11005)
SALISH LLC
1001 Ne Boat St (98105-6708)
PHONE..................................206 375-7270
Jim Long, *Managing Dir*
Jonathan Rentz, *Principal*
EMP: 2
SALES (est): 99.2K **Privately Held**
SIC: 7692 Welding repair

(G-11006)
SALLY AND HARRY SIMMONS
8731 18th Ave Nw (98117-3515)
PHONE..................................206 297-1868
Sally Simmons, *Principal*
EMP: 3
SALES (est): 163.9K **Privately Held**
SIC: 3999 Pet supplies

(G-11007)
SALMON BAY SAND AND GRAVEL CO
5228 Shilshole Ave Nw (98107-4832)
P.O. Box 70328 (98127-0328)
PHONE..................................206 784-1234
Paul L Nerdrum, *President*
Calvin W Nerdrum, *Director*
Paul W Cochran, *Admin Sec*
EMP: 80
SQ FT: 28,000
SALES (est): 24MM **Privately Held**
WEB: www.sbsg.com
SIC: 5211 5032 3273 Sand & gravel; cement; masonry materials & supplies; sand, construction; gravel; concrete mixtures; ready-mixed concrete

(G-11008)
SALMON BAY WOODWORKS
643 Nw 53rd St (98107-3553)
PHONE..................................206 612-3993
Michael Nauman-Montana, *Owner*
EMP: 6
SALES (est): 681.9K **Privately Held**
SIC: 2431 Millwork

(G-11009)
SALT STUDIO
66 Bell St Apt 1 (98121-3615)
PHONE..................................206 784-9652
EMP: 2
SALES (est): 103.8K **Privately Held**
SIC: 2899 Salt

(G-11010)
SAMURAI NOODLE (PA)
606 5th Ave S (98104-3897)
PHONE..................................206 624-9321
Phil Sancken, *President*
EMP: 4
SALES (est): 374.4K **Privately Held**
SIC: 2098 Noodles (e.g. egg, plain & water), dry

(G-11011)
SANDMAIDEN SLEEPWEAR
2112 Nw 70th St (98117-5605)
PHONE..................................206 595-4303
Caleb C Buchanan, *Owner*
Amenda Boyd, *Co-Owner*
EMP: 2
SALES (est): 56K **Privately Held**
SIC: 2389 7389 Disposable garments & accessories;

(G-11012)
SANDRA S BERLIN
914 21st Ave (98122-4759)
PHONE..................................206 612-4126
Sandra S Berlin, *Principal*
EMP: 2
SALES (est): 87.3K **Privately Held**
SIC: 3269 7389 Pottery products;

(G-11013)
SANTOROS BOOKS
7405 Greenwood Ave N (98103-5043)
PHONE..................................206 784-2113
Carol Santoros, *Owner*
EMP: 8
SALES (est): 450.3K **Privately Held**
SIC: 2731 Book publishing

(G-11014)
SARA HUEY PBLCY PROMOTIONS LLC
103 Nw 104th St (98177-4917)
PHONE..................................206 619-0610
EMP: 2

SALES (est): 126.4K **Privately Held**
SIC: 2741 Miscellaneous publishing

(G-11015)
SASQUATCH BOOKS LLC
Also Called: Sasqutch Acqstion Frmerly Name
1904 3rd Ave Ste 710 (98101-1100)
PHONE..................................206 467-4300
Gary Luke, *Mng Member*
▲ **EMP:** 18
SQ FT: 3,000
SALES (est): 5.3MM
SALES (corp-wide): 75.3MM **Privately Held**
WEB: www.sasquatchbooks.com
SIC: 2731 Books: publishing only
HQ: Penguin Random House Llc
  1745 Broadway Frnt 1
  New York NY 10019
  212 782-9000

(G-11016)
SATIN GROUP LLC A
1029 Belmont Ave E # 202 (98102-4430)
PHONE..................................206 228-1364
Albert Shen, *President*
EMP: 2
SALES (est): 155K **Privately Held**
SIC: 2221 Satins

(G-11017)
SAUSAGE SKATEBOARDS
2607 Nw 57th St (98107-3246)
PHONE..................................206 679-3619
Lee Dumas, *Bd of Directors*
EMP: 2 **EST:** 2012
SALES (est): 138K **Privately Held**
SIC: 3949 Skateboards

(G-11018)
SAVAGE INC
6201 15th Ave Nw (98107-2306)
PHONE..................................206 972-8217
Tomi Marsh, *President*
EMP: 2
SALES (est): 111K **Privately Held**
SIC: 2759 Commercial printing

(G-11019)
SAVAGE COLOR LLC
3614 2nd Ave Nw (98107-4911)
PHONE..................................206 632-2866
Mark Malnes, *President*
Dan Pens, *Bookkeeper*
Carlin Kennedy, *Sales Staff*
EMP: 9
SALES (est): 1.1MM **Privately Held**
WEB: www.savagecolor.com
SIC: 2752 Commercial printing, offset

(G-11020)
SAVANG SINE
6464 M Luther King Jr Way (98118)
PHONE..................................206 721-2558
EMP: 2 **EST:** 2005
SALES (est): 110K **Privately Held**
SIC: 3651 Mfg Home Audio/Video Equipment

(G-11021)
SAVOY TRUFFLE
5915 Airport Way S (98108-2714)
PHONE..................................206 762-7411
Ron Morgan, *Owner*
EMP: 4
SALES (est): 186.8K **Privately Held**
SIC: 2051 5461 Bread, cake & related products; bakeries

(G-11022)
SAWDUST SUPPLY
6314 7th Ave S (98108-3439)
PHONE..................................206 622-4321
Milan Moss, *Owner*
EMP: 7 **EST:** 2007
SALES (est): 1MM **Privately Held**
SIC: 2875 5999 Compost; miscellaneous retail stores

(G-11023)
SCARED OF GENRE
4716 S Orcas St (98118-2435)
PHONE..................................206 227-2574
Brad Strain, *Director*
EMP: 2

Seattle - King County (G-11024)

SALES (est): 91.4K **Privately Held**
SIC: 2741 Catalogs: publishing & printing

(G-11024)
SCHATTAUER SAILMAKER CORP
Also Called: Schattauer Sails
6010 Seaview Ave Nw (98107-2657)
PHONE..................................206 783-0173
Axel Schattauer, *President*
Frank Schattauer, *Treasurer*
Helga Schattauer, *Admin Sec*
EMP: 2 EST: 1959
SQ FT: 4,800
SALES (est): 189.3K **Privately Held**
SIC: 2394 5551 Sails: made from purchased materials; sails & equipment

(G-11025)
SCHEDULES DIRECT
8613 42nd Ave S (98118-4521)
PHONE..................................206 701-7800
Robert Eden, *President*
EMP: 2 EST: 2009
SALES (est): 117.8K **Privately Held**
SIC: 2741 Miscellaneous publishing

(G-11026)
SCHILLING CIDER
2722 Mayfair Ave N (98109-1742)
PHONE..................................208 660-4086
Yameen Ali, *Principal*
EMP: 6 EST: 2013
SALES (est): 396.8K **Privately Held**
SIC: 2099 Food preparations

(G-11027)
SCHIPPERS & CREW INC
5309 Shlshl Ave Nw 100 (98107)
PHONE..................................206 782-2325
Bert Schippers, *CEO*
Lynne Ellen Hoverson, *President*
Bert Johan, *Vice Pres*
Dany Touch, *Purch Agent*
David Cardenas, *Engineer*
▲ EMP: 60
SQ FT: 15,000
SALES (est): 16.4MM **Privately Held**
WEB: www.schippers.com
SIC: 3672 Circuit boards, television & radio printed

(G-11028)
SCHOONER EXACT
Also Called: Schooner Exact Brewing Co.
3901 1st Ave S (98134-2236)
PHONE..................................206 432-9734
Heather McClung, *Mng Member*
EMP: 6
SQ FT: 7,200
SALES (est): 755.2K **Privately Held**
SIC: 2082 5182 Beer (alcoholic beverage); liquor

(G-11029)
SCHUMACHER CREATIVE SERVICES
2025 Ne 123rd St (98125-5244)
PHONE..................................206 364-7151
Michael Schumacher, *Owner*
EMP: 3
SALES (est): 248.3K **Privately Held**
WEB: www.engine-swaps.com
SIC: 7336 3694 Commercial art & illustration; engine electrical equipment

(G-11030)
SCHWARTZ BROTHERS RESTAURANTS
619 S Nevada St (98108-1713)
PHONE..................................206 623-3134
Dennis Ford, *Branch Mgr*
EMP: 155
SALES (corp-wide): 38.5MM **Privately Held**
SIC: 2051 Bread, cake & related products
PA: Schwartz Brother's Restaurants
325 118th Ave Se Ste 106
Bellevue WA 98005
425 455-3948

(G-11031)
SCOPE 5 INC
Also Called: Carbon Salon
999 N Northlake Way 225 (98103-3422)
PHONE..................................206 456-5656
Yoram Bernet, *CEO*
David Billstrom, *Principal*
John Daly, *Principal*
Derek Eisel, *Sales Staff*
EMP: 4 EST: 2014
SALES (est): 292.1K **Privately Held**
SIC: 7372 Application computer software

(G-11032)
SCOUGAL RUBBER CORPORATION (PA)
6239 Corson Ave S (98108-3443)
PHONE..................................206 763-2650
Tom Foley, *CEO*
Matt Bowman, *President*
Rob Anderson, *Vice Pres*
Alfredo Shanklin, *Plant Mgr*
Pete Etcheverry, *QC Mgr*
▲ EMP: 100 EST: 1916
SQ FT: 35,000
SALES: 15MM **Privately Held**
WEB: www.scougalrubber.com
SIC: 3069 Molded rubber products

(G-11033)
SCOUT MEDIA INC
150 Nickerson St Ste 300 (98109-1634)
P.O. Box 4129, Hopkins MN (55343-0497)
PHONE..................................206 313-4932
EMP: 30
SALES (est): 3.9MM
SALES (corp-wide): 143.8MM **Privately Held**
SIC: 2741 Internet Publishing And Broadcasting
HQ: North American Membership Group Inc.
915 Mainstreet Ste Ll
Hopkins MN 55343
952 936-9333

(G-11034)
SCRAPPYS BITTERS LLC
13749 Midvale Ave N (98133-7009)
PHONE..................................206 632-7257
Miles Thomas, *President*
EMP: 7
SALES (est): 503.6K **Privately Held**
SIC: 2087 Flavoring extracts & syrups

(G-11035)
SCREENLIFE LLC
315 5th Ave S Ste 600 (98104-2699)
PHONE..................................206 829-0743
David Long, *CEO*
Charles Harper, *President*
Craig Kinzer, *Chairman*
▲ EMP: 80
SALES (est): 7.9MM
SALES (corp-wide): 12.9B **Publicly Held**
WEB: www.screenlifegames.com
SIC: 3944 Games, toys & children's vehicles
HQ: Paramount Pictures Corporation
5555 Melrose Ave
Los Angeles CA 90038
323 956-5000

(G-11036)
SCRIBBLE SKETCH PRESS
1525 Nw 57th St Unit 404 (98107-5630)
PHONE..................................707 364-4072
Emily Cummings, *Principal*
EMP: 2
SALES (est): 86.4K **Privately Held**
SIC: 2741 Miscellaneous publishing

(G-11037)
SEA PAC TRANSPORT SERVICES LLC
3544 W Marginal Way Sw (98106-1010)
PHONE..................................206 763-0339
Paul Kimball, *President*
▲ EMP: 25 EST: 1945
SQ FT: 42,000

SALES (est): 2.7MM **Privately Held**
WEB: www.seapacservice.com
SIC: 4783 3441 4225 4213 Packing goods for shipping; crating goods for shipping; fabricated structural metal; general warehousing & storage; heavy machinery transport

(G-11038)
SEA STORM FISHERIES INC
2727 Alaskan Way Pier 69 (98121-1107)
PHONE..................................206 547-6557
Micheal Haggarty, *President*
Chris Dean, *Manager*
Dale Myer, *Director*
EMP: 25
SALES (est): 839K **Privately Held**
SIC: 0912 2092 Finfish; fresh or frozen packaged fish

(G-11039)
SEA TECHNOLOGY CONSTRUCTION
Also Called: Stcc
309 S Cloverdale St E15 (98108-4568)
PHONE..................................206 282-9158
Jose Zamalloa, *President*
Rob Weaver, *Office Mgr*
EMP: 14
SQ FT: 3,000
SALES: 1.7MM **Privately Held**
WEB: www.seatechnologycompany.com
SIC: 3441 Fabricated structural metal for ships

(G-11040)
SEA TO SOFTWARE LLC
3626 Fremont Ln N Apt 202 (98103-8743)
PHONE..................................206 617-6893
Pavel Sorokin, *Principal*
EMP: 2
SALES (est): 144.6K **Privately Held**
SIC: 7372 Prepackaged software

(G-11041)
SEACAST INC
Also Called: Seacast Investment Castings
207 S Bennett St (98108-2226)
PHONE..................................206 767-5759
Mike Robins, *President*
Keih Semen, *Plant Mgr*
George Rasmussen, *VP Finance*
Keith Stemen, *Manager*
EMP: 40
SQ FT: 28,000
SALES (corp-wide): 41.4MM **Privately Held**
WEB: www.seacast.com
SIC: 3324 8734 3369 Steel investment foundries; testing laboratories; nonferrous foundries
PA: Seacast, Inc.
6130 31st Ave Ne
Tulalip WA 98271
360 653-9388

(G-11042)
SEAFOAM STUDIOS LLC
6519 Cleopatra Pl Nw (98117-5057)
PHONE..................................702 509-4742
Arieh Shapiro, *Partner*
Patrick Flickinger, *Partner*
Mike Schubert, *Partner*
EMP: 2
SALES (est): 95.1K **Privately Held**
SIC: 7372 7389 Home entertainment computer software;

(G-11043)
SEAFREEZE LIMITED PARTNERSHIP
Also Called: Seafreeze Cold Storage
206 Sw Michigan St (98106-1908)
P.O. Box 24978 (98124-0978)
PHONE..................................206 767-7350
Frank Breen, *Managing Prtnr*
Adam Forste, *Partner*
Connie Strain,
▲ EMP: 100
SQ FT: 330,000

SALES (est): 15.7MM
SALES (corp-wide): 33.4MM **Publicly Held**
WEB: www.seafreeze.com
SIC: 2092 4222 Seafoods, fresh: prepared; seafoods, frozen: prepared; warehousing, cold storage or refrigerated
PA: Bay City Capital Llc
750 Battery St Ste 400
San Francisco CA 94111
415 676-3830

(G-11044)
SEAMOBILE INC (PA)
1200 Westlake Ave N (98109-3543)
PHONE..................................206 838-7700
▲ EMP: 8
SALES (est): 14.5MM **Privately Held**
WEB: www.seamobile.com
SIC: 3663 Satellites, communications

(G-11045)
SEATTLE BARREL CO
Also Called: Al's Seattle Barrel
4716 Airport Way S (98108-1721)
PHONE..................................206 622-7218
Louie Sam, *Owner*
▼ EMP: 7
SQ FT: 3,200
SALES (est): 1.7MM **Privately Held**
SIC: 5085 3412 Barrels, new or reconditioned; metal barrels, drums & pails

(G-11046)
SEATTLE BISCUIT COMPANY LLC
6710 35th Ave Nw (98117-6105)
PHONE..................................206 327-2940
Sam Thompson, *Principal*
EMP: 3
SALES (est): 214.7K **Privately Held**
SIC: 2041 Biscuit dough

(G-11047)
SEATTLE BOAT WORKS LLC
2542 Westlake Ave N # 9 (98109-2292)
PHONE..................................206 849-4259
Alex Wilken, *Mng Member*
EMP: 2
SALES (est): 181.8K **Privately Held**
SIC: 3732 Boat building & repairing

(G-11048)
SEATTLE BOILER WORKS INC
500 S Myrtle St (98108-3495)
PHONE..................................206 762-0737
Frank H Hopkins, *President*
Isaac Osborn, *General Mgr*
Frederick J Hopkins, *Corp Secy*
Craig R Hopkins, *Vice Pres*
Don Hanson, *Executive*
▲ EMP: 25
SQ FT: 70,000
SALES: 5MM **Privately Held**
WEB: www.seattleboiler.com
SIC: 3443 Tanks, standard or custom fabricated: metal plate; boiler & boiler shop work; industrial vessels, tanks & containers; heat exchangers, condensers & components

(G-11049)
SEATTLE BUSINESS JOURNAL INC
Also Called: Puget Sound Business Journal
801 2nd Ave Ste 210 (98104-1528)
PHONE..................................206 583-0701
Emory Thomas, *President*
Melissa Leonard, *Accounts Mgr*
Ryan Lambert, *Creative Dir*
EMP: 51
SALES (est): 3.6MM
SALES (corp-wide): 1.4B **Privately Held**
WEB:
www.pugetsoundbusinessjournal.com
SIC: 2711 2721 Newspapers: publishing only, not printed on site; periodicals
HQ: American City Business Journals, Inc.
120 W Morehead St Ste 400
Charlotte NC 28202
704 973-1000

(G-11050)
SEATTLE CASCADES
2610 Western Ave (98121-1376)
PHONE..................................773 387-0502

GEOGRAPHIC SECTION

Seattle - King County (G-11081)

Xtehn Titcomb, *Principal*
Isaac Chamberlain, *Merchandise Mgr*
EMP: 7
SALES (est): 385.7K **Privately Held**
SIC: 3949 Sporting & athletic goods

(G-11051)
SEATTLE CHINESE POST INC
412 Maynard Ave S (98104-2917)
P.O. Box 3468 (98114-3468)
PHONE...................................206 223-0623
Assunta Ng, *Owner*
Jeff Gray, *Vice Pres*
David Levine, *Asst Controller*
Jim Hunt, *Supervisor*
Eric Brockman, *Fmly & Gen Dent*
EMP: 23
SQ FT: 800
SALES (est): 2.3MM **Privately Held**
SIC: 2759 2711 Letterpress printing; newspapers: printing; newspapers

(G-11052)
SEATTLE CIDER COMPANY
4701 Colorado Ave S Ste C (98134-2363)
PHONE...................................206 762-0490
Adam Carlson, *Sales Staff*
Brent Miles, *Manager*
EMP: 12
SALES (est): 2.4MM **Privately Held**
SIC: 2082 Malt beverages

(G-11053)
SEATTLE CREATIVE BRANDS INC
3226 26th Ave W (98199-2824)
PHONE...................................206 782-6548
Theodore Smith, *President*
EMP: 3
SALES (est): 340.4K **Privately Held**
SIC: 3229 Pressed & blown glass

(G-11054)
SEATTLE CUSTOM PLASTICS INC
Also Called: Seattle Plastics
309 S Cloverdale St E7 (98108-4568)
PHONE...................................206 233-0869
Mike Albanese, *President*
EMP: 12
SQ FT: 5,000
SALES (est): 1.7MM **Privately Held**
WEB: www.seattleplastics.com
SIC: 3089 Injection molding of plastics; plastic processing

(G-11055)
SEATTLE DAILY JOURNAL COMMERCE
83 Columbia St Ste 200 (98104-1416)
PHONE...................................206 622-8272
Dennis Brown, *President*
Phil Brown, *Publisher*
Robert Crowley, *Consultant*
EMP: 43
SQ FT: 40,000
SALES (est): 3.1MM **Privately Held**
WEB: www.djc.com
SIC: 2711 2752 Newspapers: publishing only, not printed on site; commercial printing, lithographic

(G-11056)
SEATTLE ENGRAVING CENTER LLC
414 Stewart St (98101-5113)
PHONE...................................206 420-4604
EMP: 2
SALES (est): 73.2K **Privately Held**
SIC: 2759 Currency: engraved

(G-11057)
SEATTLE ESPRESSO MACHINE CORP
Also Called: Slayer Espresso
6133 6th Ave S (98108-3309)
PHONE...................................206 284-7171
Jason Prefontaine, *President*
Fred Baruch, *COO*
Antoinette Trimble, *Accountant*
Brandon King, *Sales Mgr*
Sam Grant, *Sales Staff*
EMP: 5
SQ FT: 1,500

SALES (est): 500K **Privately Held**
SIC: 3845 Electromedical equipment

(G-11058)
SEATTLE GAMECO
5932 18th Ave S (98108-2839)
PHONE...................................206 767-0922
Robert McConaughy, *Owner*
EMP: 2
SALES (est): 56.9K **Privately Held**
SIC: 3944 Board games, puzzles & models, except electronic

(G-11059)
SEATTLE GLASSBLOWING STUDIO
2227 5th Ave (98121-1807)
PHONE...................................206 448-2181
Cliff Goodman, *President*
Terri Sullivan, *Business Mgr*
◆ **EMP:** 20
SQ FT: 3,000
SALES (est): 2.2MM **Privately Held**
WEB: www.seattleglassblowing.com
SIC: 3229 Novelty glassware

(G-11060)
SEATTLE GOLD GRILLS
901 Occidental Ave S (98134-1218)
PHONE...................................206 250-0833
Frederick Bennett Jr, *Owner*
EMP: 5 **Privately Held**
SIC: 3843 3961 Teeth, artificial (not made in dental laboratories); costume jewelry

(G-11061)
SEATTLE GOURMET FOODS INC (PA)
19016 72nd Ave S (98188)
PHONE...................................425 656-9076
David J Taylor, *President*
Thomas Means, *Vice Pres*
Alexis Taylor, *Vice Pres*
Kathleen Taylor, *Director*
▲ **EMP:** 99
SQ FT: 1,000
SALES (est): 50.7MM **Privately Held**
WEB: www.seattlegourmetfoods.com
SIC: 2064 Candy & other confectionery products

(G-11062)
SEATTLE HEAT TREATERS
521 S Holden St (98108-4361)
PHONE...................................206 763-2744
George Chiaro, *President*
Jeff Stover, *Vice Pres*
EMP: 4 **EST:** 1964
SQ FT: 4,000
SALES (est): 667.2K **Privately Held**
SIC: 3398 Metal heat treating

(G-11063)
SEATTLE MACHINE WORKS INC
1511 W Thurman St (98119-1623)
PHONE...................................206 763-2710
Donald Lindblad, *President*
EMP: 9
SALES (est): 819.4K
SALES (corp-wide): 1.7MM **Privately Held**
WEB: www.fvo.com
SIC: 3599 Machine shop, jobbing & repair
PA: Fishing Vessel Owners Marine Way
1511 W Thurman St
Seattle WA 98119
206 282-6421

(G-11064)
SEATTLE METROPOLITAN
509 Olive Way (98101-1720)
PHONE...................................206 957-2234
Nicole Vogel, *President*
Dan Gemmethu, *President*
EMP: 16
SALES (est): 2.8MM **Privately Held**
WEB: www.seattlemet.com
SIC: 2721 Magazines: publishing only, not printed on site

(G-11065)
SEATTLE MUSIC PARTNERS
1425 Broadway 508 (98122-3854)
PHONE...................................206 408-8588
Marlette Buchanan, *Exec Dir*

EMP: 4
SALES (est): 400K **Privately Held**
SIC: 3931 Musical instruments

(G-11066)
SEATTLE NORTHWEST SERVICE CORP
309 S Cloverdale St B11 (98108-4568)
PHONE...................................206 553-9209
Stacey Le, *President*
EMP: 10
SQ FT: 1,200
SALES (est): 622.7K **Privately Held**
SIC: 2393 2353 5136 2311 Bags & containers, except sleeping bags: textile; uniform hats & caps; men's & boys' hats, scarves & gloves; military uniforms, men's & youths': purchased materials; men's & boys' athletic uniforms

(G-11067)
SEATTLE OIL SOLUTION LLC
7915 7th Ave Sw (98106-2102)
PHONE...................................206 375-7575
Gary D Cleaves, *Administration*
EMP: 3 **EST:** 2016
SALES (est): 109K **Privately Held**
SIC: 1311 Crude petroleum & natural gas

(G-11068)
SEATTLE POPCORN COMPANY INC
Also Called: Uncle Woody's Caramel Corn
9320 15th Ave S Ste Cd (98108-5105)
PHONE...................................206 937-1292
Nancy Horiuchi, *President*
EMP: 9 **EST:** 2007
SALES (est): 1.2MM **Privately Held**
SIC: 2064 5145 Popcorn balls or other treated popcorn products; popcorn & supplies

(G-11069)
SEATTLE PRINTWORKS LLC
711 9th Ave N (98109-4309)
PHONE...................................206 623-3512
Rembrandt Murphy, *Principal*
EMP: 3
SALES (est): 92.3K **Privately Held**
SIC: 2752 Commercial printing, lithographic

(G-11070)
SEATTLE PURE EXTRACTS
3810 Arprt Way S Ste 110 (98108)
PHONE...................................206 788-5754
Josh Keeler, *Principal*
EMP: 2 **EST:** 2017
SALES (est): 74.4K **Privately Held**
SIC: 2836 Extracts

(G-11071)
SEATTLE RADIATOR LLC
Also Called: Seattle Radiator Works
5011 Ohio Ave S (98134-2446)
P.O. Box 80036 (98108-0036)
PHONE...................................206 682-5148
Lou White, *Owner*
Debbie White, *Owner*
EMP: 6 **EST:** 1944
SQ FT: 9,000
SALES (est): 775.7K **Privately Held**
SIC: 7539 3714 Radiator repair shop, automotive; motor vehicle parts & accessories

(G-11072)
SEATTLE RANT
4208 University Way Ne (98105-5807)
PHONE...................................206 545-6957
Doug Campbell, *Principal*
EMP: 2
SALES (est): 125.2K **Privately Held**
SIC: 2679 Paper products, converted

(G-11073)
SEATTLE SEWING SOLUTIONS INC
Also Called: Sound Uniform Solutions
270 S Hanford St (98134-1926)
PHONE...................................253 625-7420
Renee Pitra, *CEO*
Jerry Baker, *CFO*
EMP: 45 **EST:** 2017
SQ FT: 2,500

SALES (est): 1.1MM **Privately Held**
SIC: 2389 Uniforms & vestments

(G-11074)
SEATTLE SHIPWORKS LLC
1801 Fairview Ave E # 100 (98102-3717)
PHONE...................................206 763-3133
Matthew Doherty, *Mng Member*
EMP: 100
SQ FT: 5,000
SALES (est): 5MM **Privately Held**
SIC: 3731 Shipbuilding & repairing

(G-11075)
SEATTLE SIGNS & PRINTING
1000 2nd Ave Ste 2000 (98104-3629)
PHONE...................................206 588-5592
EMP: 2
SALES (est): 83.9K **Privately Held**
SIC: 2752 Commercial printing, lithographic

(G-11076)
SEATTLE SOFTWARE CORP
6523 California Ave Sw (98136-1833)
PHONE...................................206 286-7677
Shane G Eckel, *President*
Carmen Smith, *Cust Mgr*
EMP: 2 **EST:** 2010
SALES (est): 205.2K **Privately Held**
SIC: 7372 Prepackaged software

(G-11077)
SEATTLE SPORTS COMPANY (PA)
3217 W Smith St Ste 1 (98199-3261)
PHONE...................................206 782-0773
Mike Moore, *President*
▲ **EMP:** 10
SALES (est): 1.5MM **Privately Held**
WEB: www.seattlesportsco.com
SIC: 3949 Sporting & athletic goods

(G-11078)
SEATTLE STAIR & DESIGN LLC
3810 4th Ave S (98134-2210)
PHONE...................................206 587-5354
Matt Decker, *President*
David Shuler, *Vice Pres*
EMP: 15
SQ FT: 5,000
SALES: 1.8MM **Privately Held**
SIC: 2431 Staircases & stairs, wood

(G-11079)
SEATTLE STUMP GRINDING
321 Mcgraw St (98109-2043)
PHONE...................................206 285-2887
EMP: 2 **EST:** 2001
SALES (est): 130K **Privately Held**
SIC: 3599 0782 Mfg Industrial Machinery Lawn/Garden Services

(G-11080)
SEATTLE TARP CO INC
18449 Cascade Ave S (98188-4714)
PHONE...................................206 285-2819
Donna K Perlatti, *President*
Kay Perlatti, *Corp Secy*
Christopher Perlatti, *Vice Pres*
Robert D Perlatti, *Vice Pres*
Rob Warzyski, *Sales Staff*
EMP: 23
SQ FT: 10,000
SALES: 3MM **Privately Held**
WEB: www.seattletarp.com
SIC: 2394 3315 2298 Tarpaulins, fabric: made from purchased materials; steel wire & related products; cordage & twine

(G-11081)
SEATTLE TIMES COMPANY (HQ)
Also Called: Times Communications Co
1000 Denny Way Ste 501 (98109-5323)
P.O. Box 70 (98111-0070)
PHONE...................................206 464-2111
Frank A Blethen, *Ch of Bd*
Carolyn S Kelly, *President*
Sandy Dunham, *Editor*
Joel Petterson, *Editor*
Alayne Fardella, *COO*
EMP: 200
SQ FT: 310,000

Seattle - King County (G-11082)

SALES (est): 226.3MM **Privately Held**
WEB: www.seattletimes.nwsource.com
SIC: 2711 Newspapers, publishing & printing
PA: Blethen Corporation
1120 John St
Seattle WA 98109
206 464-2471

(G-11082)
SEATTLE WEEKLY LLC
307 3rd Ave S Ste 2002 (98104-1006)
PHONE..................................206 623-0500
Gavin Borchert, *Opers Staff*
Pam Dunning, *Mng Member*
Rick Anderson, *Author*
EMP: 45
SQ FT: 15,000
SALES (est): 2MM
SALES (corp-wide): 269.2MM **Privately Held**
SIC: 2711 Newspapers: publishing only, not printed on site
PA: Voice Media Group, Inc.
969 N Broadway
Denver CO 80203
303 296-7744

(G-11083)
SEATTLE WHEELCHAIR RUGBY
18 W Mercer St Ste 400 (98119-3971)
PHONE..................................360 440-2498
Curt L Chapman, *Principal*
Sonya Neely, *Research*
EMP: 3
SALES (est): 216K **Privately Held**
SIC: 3842 Wheelchairs

(G-11084)
SEATTLE WOOD SIGNS
820 Blanchard St # 1610 (98121-2645)
PHONE..................................425 422-3750
Ashley Vanderwel, *Principal*
EMP: 2
SALES (est): 72.6K **Privately Held**
SIC: 3993 Signs & advertising specialties

(G-11085)
SEAVIEW BOAT YARD INC (PA)
Also Called: Seaview West
6701 Seaview Ave Nw (98117-6099)
PHONE..................................206 783-6550
Philip Riise, *President*
EMP: 50
SQ FT: 1,000
SALES (est): 6.5MM **Privately Held**
WEB: www.seaviewboatyard.com
SIC: 3732 Boat building & repairing

(G-11086)
SEAVIEW BOAT YARD INC
Also Called: Silicle Bay Marina
6701 Seaview Ave Nw (98117-6099)
PHONE..................................206 783-6550
Roland Sando, *Branch Mgr*
EMP: 15
SALES (corp-wide): 6.5MM **Privately Held**
WEB: www.seaviewboatyard.com
SIC: 3732 3731 3441 Boat building & repairing; shipbuilding & repairing; fabricated structural metal
PA: Seaview Boat Yard Inc
6701 Seaview Ave Nw
Seattle WA 98117
206 783-6550

(G-11087)
SEAVIEW BOATYARD WEST INC
6701 Seaview Ave Nw (98117-6099)
PHONE..................................206 783-6550
Phil Riise, *President*
EMP: 6 EST: 2012
SALES (est): 735.5K **Privately Held**
SIC: 3732 Boat building & repairing

(G-11088)
SEELIG FUEL INC
Also Called: Honeywell Authorized Dealer
8523 18th Ave Nw (98117-3645)
PHONE..................................206 789-6434
Kay Seelig, *Principal*
EMP: 5
SALES (est): 453.2K **Privately Held**
SIC: 2869 Fuels

(G-11089)
SENTINEL OFFENDER SERVICES LLC
600 5th Ave Fl 8 (98104-1900)
PHONE..................................206 223-9681
Morgann McClarin, *Branch Mgr*
EMP: 21
SALES (corp-wide): 71.6MM **Privately Held**
SIC: 3822 Building services monitoring controls, automatic
PA: Sentinel Offender Services Llc
1290 N Hancock St Ste 103
Anaheim CA 92807
949 453-1550

(G-11090)
SER PRO INC
11064 1st Ave S (98168-1402)
PHONE..................................206 767-3100
Fax: 206 767-3100
EMP: 5 EST: 1980
SQ FT: 2,500
SALES (est): 300K **Privately Held**
SIC: 3599 3441 3312 Machine Shop Metal Fabrication & Tool & Die Steel

(G-11091)
SERVICE PRINTING CO INC
3837 13th Ave W Ste 106 (98119-1355)
PHONE..................................206 283-6800
Christopher Gianelli, *President*
EMP: 5 EST: 1964
SQ FT: 2,500
SALES: 600K **Privately Held**
WEB: www.serviceprintingco.com
SIC: 2752 Commercial printing, offset

(G-11092)
SERVICE WELDING & MACHINE CO
1435 S Jackson St (98144-2022)
PHONE..................................206 325-1153
Mike Daniels, *President*
EMP: 2
SALES (est): 295.3K **Privately Held**
SIC: 7692 Welding repair

(G-11093)
SEVENTY FRTH ST PRDUCTIONS LLC
350 N 74th St (98103-5026)
PHONE..................................206 781-1447
G Leilani Jacobsen, *Principal*
Peter Kahle,
Albert Sampson,
EMP: 4
SALES (est): 248.9K **Privately Held**
WEB: www.74thstreet.com
SIC: 2731 Books: publishing only

(G-11094)
SHADE SUNGLO & DRAPERY CO
5503 Airport Way S (98108-2202)
P.O. Box 80465 (98108-0465)
PHONE..................................206 767-4561
Larry J Linarelli, *Owner*
EMP: 3
SQ FT: 2,800
SALES: 250K **Privately Held**
SIC: 2391 2591 5719 5714 Draperies, plastic & textile: from purchased materials; window shades; venetian blinds; drapery & upholstery stores

(G-11095)
SHAH SAFARI INC (PA)
Also Called: Raw Edge
14 W Roy St (98119-3828)
PHONE..................................206 282-6122
Rajnikant Shah, *CEO*
Akhil R Shah, *President*
Amit Shah, *Exec VP*
Ashok Shah, *Treasurer*
◆ EMP: 25
SALES (est): 20.3MM **Privately Held**
SIC: 5136 2339 3999 Sportswear, men's & boys'; women's & misses' outerwear; atomizers, toiletry

(G-11096)
SHARPE MIXERS INC
1541 S 92nd Pl Ste A (98108-5116)
P.O. Box 3906 (98124-3906)
PHONE..................................206 767-5660
Jay Dinnison, *President*
Steven Drury, *Vice Pres*
Tiffanie Tatick, *Treasurer*
Nikki Sides, *Manager*
Rick Graham, *Director*
◆ EMP: 30
SQ FT: 15,000
SALES (est): 11.5MM
SALES (corp-wide): 41.9MM **Privately Held**
SIC: 3561 Pumps & pumping equipment
HQ: Hayward Gordon Us, Inc.
1541 S 92nd Pl
Seattle WA 98108
206 767-5660

(G-11097)
SHEAR PRECISION INC
Also Called: Kai Scissors
10859 1st Ave S (98168-1309)
P.O. Box 13671 (98198-1009)
PHONE..................................800 481-4943
James Peterson, *President*
▲ EMP: 2
SALES (est): 154.8K **Privately Held**
SIC: 3421 Scissors, hand

(G-11098)
SHELFBOT CO
1218 3rd Ave Ste 1010 (98101-3290)
PHONE..................................425 679-1421
Bede Jordan, *Principal*
Stefan Kalb, *Principal*
EMP: 2
SALES (est): 64.6K **Privately Held**
SIC: 7372 Application computer software

(G-11099)
SHELFGENIE
5055 38th Ave Ne (98105-3022)
PHONE..................................206 774-0336
EMP: 2
SALES (est): 82.8K **Privately Held**
SIC: 2511 Wood household furniture

(G-11100)
SHERWIN-WILLIAMS COMPANY
13318 Lake City Way Ne (98125-4431)
PHONE..................................206 417-4502
EMP: 2
SALES (corp-wide): 17.5B **Publicly Held**
SIC: 2851 1721 Paints & allied products; residential painting
PA: The Sherwin-Williams Company
101 W Prospect Ave # 1020
Cleveland OH 44115
216 566-2000

(G-11101)
SHIP TO SHORE INC
3456 37th Ave W (98199-1906)
PHONE..................................206 284-0406
Lorraine Betts, *President*
Michael Dubery, *Admin Sec*
▲ EMP: 2
SALES (est): 269.6K **Privately Held**
SIC: 3999 5947 5551 Novelties, bric-a-brac & hobby kits; gift shop; boat dealers

(G-11102)
SHISHKABERRYS L L C
1536 Ne 89th St (98115-3141)
PHONE..................................206 650-3564
Steve G Tuey, *President*
Barbara Armani, *Principal*
EMP: 2
SALES (est): 58.8K **Privately Held**
SIC: 2064 Fruit, chocolate covered (except dates)

(G-11103)
SHRUBBERY LLC
1210 E John St Apt 5 (98102-5835)
PHONE..................................949 690-9834
Rebecca Servoss, *Principal*
EMP: 5 EST: 2015
SALES (est): 360.9K **Privately Held**
SIC: 2087 Flavoring extracts & syrups

(G-11104)
SIDELINE SPORTS INC
1100 Nw Leary Way (98107-5133)
P.O. Box 70274 (98127-0271)
PHONE..................................206 906-9652
EMP: 2
SALES (est): 137.5K **Privately Held**
SIC: 2759 Commercial printing

(G-11105)
SIENNA SOFTWARE INC
11912 Exeter Ave Ne (98125-5938)
PHONE..................................206 306-2752
Marc Coltrera, *President*
EMP: 2
SALES (est): 125.5K **Privately Held**
SIC: 7372 Prepackaged software

(G-11106)
SIGN WIZARD
300 Queen Anne Ave N (98109-4512)
PHONE..................................206 285-9535
Steven Ang, *Owner*
EMP: 3
SALES (est): 196.6K **Privately Held**
SIC: 3993 Signs & advertising specialties

(G-11107)
SIGNAGE
701 Union St (98101-2353)
PHONE..................................206 903-6446
Mark Schulz, *Branch Mgr*
EMP: 2 **Privately Held**
SIC: 5099 3993 Signs, except electric; signs & advertising specialties
PA: Signage
5419 26th Ave Nw
Seattle WA 98107

(G-11108)
SIGNATURE SEAFOODS INC
Also Called: Lucky Buck
4257 24th Ave W (98199-1214)
PHONE..................................206 285-2815
William Orr, *President*
John Kelley, *Vice Pres*
Greg Thomas, *Admin Sec*
◆ EMP: 5
SQ FT: 3,000
SALES (est): 5.2MM
SALES (corp-wide): 4.2MM **Privately Held**
SIC: 2092 Prepared fish or other seafood cakes & sticks; seafoods, fresh: prepared; fish, fresh: prepared
PA: T K O Fisheries Inc
4257 24th Ave W
Seattle WA 98199
206 285-2815

(G-11109)
SIGNS 2C
2913 S Court St (98144-6837)
P.O. Box 18404 (98118-0404)
PHONE..................................206 335-9519
EMP: 2 EST: 2008
SALES (est): 99K **Privately Held**
SIC: 3993 Mfg Signs/Advertising Specialties

(G-11110)
SIGNS OF SEATTLE INC
6263 Ellis Ave S (98108-2735)
PHONE..................................206 292-7446
David Desrochers, *President*
EMP: 2
SALES (est): 495.9K **Privately Held**
SIC: 3993 Signs & advertising specialties

(G-11111)
SIK SCENTS LLC
11818 Military Rd S (98168-1232)
PHONE..................................206 420-4647
Curtis Olsen, *Principal*
EMP: 3
SALES (est): 235.3K **Privately Held**
SIC: 2844 Toilet preparations

(G-11112)
SILKSCREEN COMPANY
Also Called: Silk Screen Company The
6336 6th Ave S (98108-3436)
PHONE..................................206 763-8108
Wander Theizen, *President*
Sergio Dias, *Vice Pres*
EMP: 20

SQ FT: 3,000
SALES (est): 2.2MM **Privately Held**
WEB: www.thesilkscreencompany.com
SIC: 2759 2396 Screen printing; automotive & apparel trimmings

(G-11113)
SILVER MOON WOODWORKS
1709 S Lander St (98144-5131)
PHONE..................................425 753-4476
George Knutson, *Principal*
EMP: 2
SALES (est): 169.2K **Privately Held**
SIC: 2431 Millwork

(G-11114)
SIMPLY AUGMENTED INC
7041 19th Ave Ne (98115-5703)
PHONE..................................206 771-9774
Boaz Ashkenazy, *CEO*
Nicholas Hirsch, *Vice Pres*
EMP: 2
SALES: 1MM **Privately Held**
SIC: 7372 7371 Business oriented computer software; computer software development & applications

(G-11115)
SIMPSON INVESTMENT COMPANY (HQ)
1301 5th Ave Ste 2700 (98101-2675)
PHONE..................................253 272-0158
Douglas Reed, *President*
A Trinkwald, *Principal*
Colin Moseley, *Chairman*
Betsy Stauffer, *Counsel*
Joseph R Breed, *Senior VP*
▲ EMP: 90
SQ FT: 33,000
SALES (est): 173.5MM
SALES (corp-wide): 242.9MM **Privately Held**
SIC: 2621 2611 2421 2431 Paper mills; pulp mills; lumber: rough, sawed or planed; doors, wood; plastics pipe
PA: Kamilche Company
    1301 5th Ave Ste 2700
    Seattle WA 98101
    206 224-5800

(G-11116)
SINGLES GOING STEADY
2219 2nd Ave Ste C (98121-2028)
PHONE..................................206 441-7396
Peter Genest, *Owner*
EMP: 3
SQ FT: 1,500
SALES (est): 256.8K **Privately Held**
WEB: www.singlesgoingsteady.com
SIC: 3652 Pre-recorded records & tapes

(G-11117)
SIRLIN ENTERPRISES
120 Lakeside Ave Ste 110 (98122-6548)
PHONE..................................206 883-7988
Josh Sirlin, *Principal*
EMP: 2
SALES (est): 105.6K **Privately Held**
SIC: 3999 Framed artwork

(G-11118)
SISTAHOLOGY
2011 S Nye Pl (98144-2944)
PHONE..................................206 604-1418
Andrea Brooks, *Principal*
EMP: 2 EST: 2010
SALES (est): 86.3K **Privately Held**
SIC: 2741 Miscellaneous publishing

(G-11119)
SISTER SOULS GLUTEN FREE BKG
2809 Ne 110th St (98125-6740)
PHONE..................................206 909-9054
Lila Richardson, *President*
EMP: 4
SALES (est): 206.5K **Privately Held**
SIC: 2051 Bread, cake & related products

(G-11120)
SITTIN PRETTY DESIGN
4112 50th Ave S (98118-1235)
PHONE..................................206 725-2453
Lamar Van Dyke, *Partner*
EMP: 2

SALES (est): 160K **Privately Held**
SIC: 2499 Seats, toilet

(G-11121)
SITTING ROOM
108 W Roy St (98119-3830)
PHONE..................................206 285-2830
Michael Uetz, *Owner*
EMP: 6
SALES (est): 370K **Privately Held**
SIC: 7372 8741 Prepackaged software; restaurant management

(G-11122)
SIVART SOFTWARE
3035 Ne 94th St (98115-3539)
PHONE..................................206 527-2164
Jon McEwen, *Principal*
EMP: 5
SALES (est): 348.7K **Privately Held**
SIC: 7372 Application computer software

(G-11123)
SIX LLC
1319 Dexter Ave N (98109-3519)
PHONE..................................206 466-5186
Saman Kouretchian, *Mng Member*
EMP: 6
SALES: 300K **Privately Held**
SIC: 7999 2037 7372 Yoga instruction; frozen fruits & vegetables; application computer software

(G-11124)
SK FOOD GROUP INC (HQ)
4600 37th Ave Sw Ste 300 (98126-2720)
PHONE..................................206 935-8100
Steve Stosari, *Principal*
George Paleologou, *Chairman*
David Meares, *Vice Pres*
Tony Dimarco, *Mfg Mgr*
Laurence Leslie, *CFO*
EMP: 19
SQ FT: 41,000
SALES (est): 332.6MM
SALES (corp-wide): 2.2B **Privately Held**
WEB: www.skfoodgroup.com
SIC: 2099 Food preparations
PA: Premium Brands Holdings Corporation
    10991 Shellbridge Way Unit 100
    Richmond BC V6X 3
    604 656-3100

(G-11125)
SKATE LIKE A GIRL
305 Harrison St (98109-4623)
P.O. Box 95902 (98145-2902)
PHONE..................................206 973-8005
Nancy Chang, *Principal*
EMP: 2 EST: 2009
SALES (est): 175.1K **Privately Held**
SIC: 3949 Skateboards

(G-11126)
SKILLET FOOD PRODUCTS LLC
1400 E Union St (98122-4150)
PHONE..................................206 420-7297
Carl Skillet,
Greg Petrillo,
EMP: 6
SALES (est): 541.7K **Privately Held**
SIC: 2099 Food preparations

(G-11127)
SKILLS INC
825 Nw 47th St Ste 46 (98107)
PHONE..................................206 782-6000
Charlie Herris, *Manager*
EMP: 20
SQ FT: 13,469
SALES (corp-wide): 53.6MM **Privately Held**
SIC: 3728 Aircraft parts & equipment
PA: Skills, Inc.
    715 30th St Ne
    Auburn WA 98002
    206 782-6000

(G-11128)
SKT INDUSTRIES
802 Nw 97th St (98117-2211)
PHONE..................................206 633-4461
Scott Carlile, *Principal*
EMP: 2
SALES (est): 124K **Privately Held**
SIC: 3999 Manufacturing industries

(G-11129)
SKT PUBLISHERS INC
Also Called: Northwest Yachting Magazine
7342 15th Ave Nw (98117-5401)
PHONE..................................206 789-8116
Dan Schworer, *Publisher*
L Bruce Hedrick, *Principal*
Dan S Schworer, *Chairman*
Michelle Deasman, *Business Mgr*
Jessica Hoeper, *Advt Staff*
EMP: 7
SQ FT: 1,200
SALES (est): 640K **Privately Held**
WEB: www.nwyachting.com
SIC: 2721 Magazines: publishing & printing

(G-11130)
SKY PRINTING
4151 Fauntleroy Way Sw (98126-2672)
PHONE..................................206 933-5900
EMP: 2
SALES (est): 83.9K **Privately Held**
SIC: 2752 Commercial printing, lithographic

(G-11131)
SKYBREEZE INC
10021 10th Ave Sw (98146-3820)
PHONE..................................206 764-1872
David Steyh, *Principal*
EMP: 2 EST: 2008
SALES (est): 143.9K **Privately Held**
SIC: 3999 Music boxes

(G-11132)
SKYFISH MEDIA LLC
Also Called: Unicorn Booty
1425 Broadway 427 (98122-3854)
PHONE..................................415 779-2132
Nick Vivion,
EMP: 3 EST: 2010
SALES (est): 146.6K **Privately Held**
SIC: 2741

(G-11133)
SKYLINE INTERNATIONAL LLC
4105 Airport Way S (98108-5218)
PHONE..................................206 624-1874
EMP: 32
SALES (corp-wide): 5.7MM **Privately Held**
SIC: 3999 Advertising display products
PA: Skyline International, Llc
    3355 Discovery Rd
    Saint Paul MN 55121
    651 234-6592

(G-11134)
SLAP STICKERS LLC
Also Called: Slaptastick
915 S 96th St Ste A8 (98108-4935)
PHONE..................................971 238-8329
Wesley Rankin, *Mng Member*
EMP: 2
SALES (est): 135K **Privately Held**
SIC: 2741 Art copy: publishing only, not printed on site

(G-11135)
SLAVE TO LATHE
4132 40th Ave Sw (98116-4239)
PHONE..................................206 937-2129
Lawrence J Ferrari, *Owner*
EMP: 2
SALES (est): 90.1K **Privately Held**
SIC: 3541 Lathes

(G-11136)
SLP CREATIVE LLC
Also Called: Seattle Logo Pro
6521 California Ave Sw (98136-1833)
PHONE..................................206 935-5646
David Groves,
EMP: 4
SQ FT: 2,200
SALES (est): 317.9K **Privately Held**
SIC: 2759 Screen printing

(G-11137)
SMALL BUSINESS AUTOMATION
131 Bellevue Ave E # 403 (98102-5528)
PHONE..................................206 324-3820
James AGA, *Principal*
EMP: 2
SALES (est): 155.3K **Privately Held**
SIC: 7372 Prepackaged software

(G-11138)
SMARTPLUG SYSTEMS LLC
2500 Westlake Ave N Ste G (98109-2262)
PHONE..................................206 285-2990
Kristian Wiles,
▲ EMP: 7
SALES (est): 1.3MM **Privately Held**
SIC: 3678 Electronic connectors

(G-11139)
SMITH-BERGER MARINE INC
7915 10th Ave S (98108-4404)
PHONE..................................206 764-4650
Bonnie Warrick, *President*
Kenneth Bullock, *Chairman*
Thomas E Phipps, *Vice Pres*
Simon Jacob, *Project Engr*
Smith Pasero, *Senior Engr*
◆ EMP: 21
SQ FT: 24,000
SALES (est): 5.8MM **Privately Held**
WEB: www.smithberger.com
SIC: 3556 3429 Fish & shellfish processing machinery; marine hardware

(G-11140)
SMMA CANDELARIA INC
701 5th Ave Ste 2150 (98104-7004)
PHONE..................................206 405-2800
Ryoichi Suzuki, *President*
EMP: 3
SALES (est): 203.1K **Privately Held**
SIC: 1081 Metal mining services

(G-11141)
SMUCKWELL INDUSTRIES LLC
1635 34th Ave (98122-3337)
PHONE..................................206 412-3598
Jason Barnwell, *Bd of Directors*
EMP: 2
SALES (est): 134.6K **Privately Held**
SIC: 3999 Manufacturing industries

(G-11142)
SNAP CUSTOM CLOTHING
400 Pine St Ste 230 (98101-1691)
PHONE..................................206 682-0686
Ibad Siddiqui, *Principal*
EMP: 3
SALES (est): 225.9K **Privately Held**
SIC: 2759 Screen printing

(G-11143)
SNAPPY CERAMICS
330 29th Ave (98122-6216)
PHONE..................................206 329-7137
Mathew Patton, *Owner*
EMP: 2
SALES (est): 110.8K **Privately Held**
SIC: 3253 Ceramic wall & floor tile

(G-11144)
SNOW & COMPANY INC
5302 26th Ave Nw (98107-4125)
PHONE..................................206 953-7676
Brett Snow, *President*
EMP: 36
SALES: 4.2MM **Privately Held**
SIC: 7699 3731 3732 Boat repair; shipbuilding & repairing; boat building & repairing

(G-11145)
SNOW & COMPANY INC
4606 Whitman Ave N (98103-6677)
PHONE..................................206 396-8997
Brett C Snow, *President*
Bryan Ford, *Principal*
EMP: 7
SALES: 700K **Privately Held**
SIC: 2399 3731 Flags, fabric; crew boats, building & repairing

(G-11146)
SNOWBRIDGE DISTILLING LLC
909 5th Ave Unit 1604 (98164-2032)
PHONE..................................206 442-1707
Tom Bingman, *Principal*
EMP: 3
SALES (est): 74.8K **Privately Held**
SIC: 2085 Distilled & blended liquors

Seattle - King County (G-11147)

(G-11147)
SOARING HEART LLC (PA)
Also Called: Soaring Heart Natural Bed Co
101 Nickerson St Ste 400 (98109-1620)
PHONE.................................206 282-1717
Michael Schaefer, *President*
Jeff Greenwood, *Manager*
EMP: 11
SQ FT: 3,000
SALES (est): 3.7MM **Privately Held**
WEB: www.soaringheart.com
SIC: 2515 5712 Mattresses & bedsprings; mattresses

(G-11148)
SOARING HEART NATURAL BED CO
41 Dravus St (98109-1667)
PHONE.................................206 257-4158
EMP: 2
SALES (est): 82.7K **Privately Held**
SIC: 5712 2515 Mattresses; mattresses & foundations

(G-11149)
SOCIAL VOTER LABS LLC
936 N 79th St (98103-4714)
PHONE.................................206 981-9225
Ana Jamborcic, *Principal*
EMP: 2
SALES (est): 95.2K **Privately Held**
SIC: 7372 Educational computer software

(G-11150)
SOCIETY43 LLC
720 N 91st St (98103-3812)
P.O. Box 17182 (98127-0882)
PHONE.................................206 327-0778
EMP: 3
SALES (est): 239.7K **Privately Held**
SIC: 3851 Ophthalmic goods

(G-11151)
SOCK MONSTER
1909 N 45th St (98103-6804)
PHONE.................................206 724-0123
Holly Gummelt, *Owner*
EMP: 6 **EST:** 2010
SALES (est): 511K **Privately Held**
SIC: 2252 Socks

(G-11152)
SOFTCHOICE CORPORATION
1144 Eastlake Ave E # 700 (98109-4450)
PHONE.................................206 709-9000
Darrel Frevola, *Manager*
EMP: 3 **Privately Held**
SIC: 7372 Prepackaged software
HQ: Softchoice Corporation
314 W Superior St Ste 400
Chicago IL 60654

(G-11153)
SOL SUNGUARD CORPORATION
6525 15th Ave Nw Ste 125 (98117-5587)
PHONE.................................206 283-0409
Steven N Johnson, *President*
Julie Johnson, *Vice Pres*
◆ **EMP:** 20
SALES (est): 3MM **Privately Held**
WEB: www.solsunguard.com
SIC: 2834 Dermatologicals

(G-11154)
SOLAR SPACE INDUSTRIES INC
701 5th Ave Ste 4620 (98104-7097)
PHONE.................................206 332-9966
Asa Williams, *Principal*
EMP: 3
SALES (est): 142.8K **Privately Held**
SIC: 3999 Manufacturing industries

(G-11155)
SONIC PATCH LLC
4806 Sw Stevens St (98116-2939)
PHONE.................................425 284-6072
EMP: 2 **EST:** 2016
SALES (est): 119.8K **Privately Held**
SIC: 2299 Textile goods

(G-11156)
SONODIAGNOSTICS
5601 32nd Ave Sw (98126-2915)
PHONE.................................206 938-7922
Lisa Marie Still, *Principal*
EMP: 4
SALES (est): 379.6K **Privately Held**
SIC: 3841 Diagnostic apparatus, medical

(G-11157)
SORENSEN MARINE INC
9808 17th Ave Sw (98106-2713)
PHONE.................................206 767-4622
Tim Sorenson, *President*
George Sorenson, *Vice Pres*
EMP: 2
SQ FT: 1,500
SALES: 300K **Privately Held**
SIC: 3732 5551 Boats, fiberglass: building & repairing; motor boat dealers

(G-11158)
SOUND PHARMACEUTICALS INC
4010 Stone Way N Ste 120 (98103-8099)
PHONE.................................206 634-2559
Jonathan Kil MD, *President*
Eric Lynch, *Vice Pres*
James Lagasse, *Research*
Paul Rickey, *CFO*
EMP: 10
SALES (est): 1.7MM **Privately Held**
WEB: www.soundpharmaceuticals.com
SIC: 2834 Drugs acting on the central nervous system & sense organs

(G-11159)
SOUND PROPELLER SERVICES INC
7916 8th Ave S (98108-4300)
PHONE.................................206 788-4202
Clifford Burns, *President*
Terry McKeon, *Vice Pres*
▲ **EMP:** 45
SQ FT: 15,000
SALES (est): 10.1MM **Privately Held**
WEB: www.soundprop.com
SIC: 3366 7699 Propellers; marine propeller repair

(G-11160)
SOUTH PAW SCREENPRINTING
309 S Cloverdale St B30 (98108-4568)
PHONE.................................206 762-2926
Scott Graham, *Partner*
EMP: 2
SALES (est): 142.6K **Privately Held**
SIC: 2759 Screen printing

(G-11161)
SOUTHERN EXPLORATIONS
2600 2nd Ave Apt 2202 (98121-1221)
P.O. Box 70257 (98127-0257)
PHONE.................................206 641-9241
Justin Laycob, *Principal*
EMP: 3
SALES (est): 355.5K **Privately Held**
SIC: 3281 Slate products

(G-11162)
SOUTHPARK FUEL & FOOD
9525 14th Ave S (98108-5047)
PHONE.................................206 762-7550
EMP: 6 **EST:** 2010
SALES (est): 629.4K **Privately Held**
SIC: 2869 Fuels

(G-11163)
SPACE AGE INDUSTRIES LLC
1305 E Denny Way Apt 201 (98122-2504)
PHONE.................................206 992-7731
Christopher Allen Chapin, *Principal*
EMP: 2 **EST:** 2012
SALES (est): 121.2K **Privately Held**
SIC: 3999 Manufacturing industries

(G-11164)
SPACE ROCK IT INC
500 Wall St Apt 1502 (98121-1580)
PHONE.................................206 395-8383
Christopher Rabe, *CEO*
EMP: 5
SALES (est): 276.3K **Privately Held**
SIC: 1731 7373 7376 7372 Computer installation; computer systems analysis & design; computer facilities management; application computer software; computer related consulting services;

(G-11165)
SPACEFLIGHT INDUSTRIES INC (PA)
1505 Westlake Ave N # 600 (98109-6237)
PHONE.................................206 342-9934
Jason Andrews, *President*
Monica Shrestha, *Purch Mgr*
Andrey Smirnov, *Engineer*
John Springmann, *Engineer*
Tom Neary, *CFO*
EMP: 30
SQ FT: 17,000
SALES (est): 20.9MM **Privately Held**
SIC: 3761 8731 3764 Guided missiles & space vehicles, research & development; commercial physical research; guided missile & space vehicle engines, research & devel.

(G-11166)
SPECIALIZED COMPUTING INC
942 N 82nd St (98103-4322)
P.O. Box 31593 (98103-1593)
PHONE.................................206 915-9033
Heath Geremy, *Principal*
EMP: 2
SALES (est): 145.7K **Privately Held**
SIC: 7372 Prepackaged software

(G-11167)
SPEECHACE LLC
2133 5th Ave Apt 406 (98121-2518)
PHONE.................................425 241-3033
Abhishek Gupta, *Principal*
Chun Ho Cheung, *Principal*
EMP: 2 **EST:** 2015
SALES (est): 81.4K **Privately Held**
SIC: 7371 7372 Computer software systems analysis & design, custom; computer software development; educational computer software

(G-11168)
SPIRAL ARTS
901 Nw 49th St (98107-3654)
PHONE.................................206 768-9765
Fred Metz, *Owner*
EMP: 4
SQ FT: 4,000
SALES: 400K **Privately Held**
WEB: www.spiralarts.com
SIC: 3559 Glass making machinery: blowing, molding, forming, etc.

(G-11169)
SPLUNK INC
1730 Minor Ave Ste 900 (98101-1488)
PHONE.................................206 430-5200
Robert Pratt, *Director*
Aaron Lewis, *Administration*
EMP: 7
SALES (corp-wide): 1.8B **Publicly Held**
SIC: 7371 7372 Computer software development; prepackaged software
PA: Splunk Inc.
270 Brannan St
San Francisco CA 94107
415 848-8400

(G-11170)
SPOKESINGER PRINTS
7320 20th Ave Ne (98115-5710)
P.O. Box 15183 (98115-0183)
PHONE.................................206 522-5179
EMP: 2
SALES (est): 150K **Privately Held**
SIC: 2752 Lithographic Commercial Printing

(G-11171)
SPORE INCORPORATED
2101 9th Ave Ste B1 (98121-2742)
P.O. Box 4758 (98194-0758)
PHONE.................................206 624-9573
EMP: 2
SQ FT: 1,200
SALES (est): 339.7K **Privately Held**
WEB: www.sporeinc.com
SIC: 3612 Doorbell transformers, electric

(G-11172)
SPRY PRODUCT DEVELOPMENT LLC
511 Stadium Pl S Apt 382 (98104-7801)
PHONE.................................206 556-1246
Charish Correa,
Nainoa Kuna,
EMP: 2
SALES (est): 97.2K **Privately Held**
SIC: 3634 Vaporizers, electric: household

(G-11173)
SQUONK INDUSTRIES
1015 Ne 72nd St (98115-5640)
PHONE.................................206 250-4355
Ivana Begley, *Principal*
EMP: 2
SALES (est): 95.4K **Privately Held**
SIC: 3999 Manufacturing industries

(G-11174)
STABBERT & ASSOCIATES INC
2629 Nw 54th St Ste W201 (98107-4157)
PHONE.................................206 547-6161
John Parker, *Vice Pres*
Dan Stabbert,
EMP: 150 **EST:** 1981
SALES (est): 11.6MM **Privately Held**
SIC: 3731 4412 Shipbuilding & repairing; deep sea foreign transportation of freight

(G-11175)
STABBERT MRTIME YACHT SHIP LLC
Also Called: Venture Pacific Marine
2629 Nw 54th St Ste 201 (98107-4157)
PHONE.................................206 547-6161
Dan Stabbert, *CEO*
Ron Pauley, *Exec VP*
Rick Bergfeld, *CFO*
EMP: 16
SALES (est): 2.9MM **Privately Held**
SIC: 3731 Cargo vessels, building & repairing

(G-11176)
STABBERT YACHT AND SHIP LLC
2629 Nw 54th St Ste 201 (98107-4157)
PHONE.................................206 547-6161
Dan Stabbert, *President*
Ron Pauley, *Exec VP*
Neal Forde, *Senior VP*
Lindsay Sckorohod, *Vice Pres*
EMP: 40
SQ FT: 15,188
SALES (est): 6.8MM **Privately Held**
SIC: 3731 3732 Shipbuilding & repairing; boat building & repairing

(G-11177)
STACYA SILVERMAN & ASSOCIATES
614 W Mcgraw St Ste 101 (98119-3073)
PHONE.................................206 270-9465
Stacya Silverman, *Principal*
EMP: 2 **EST:** 2007
SALES (est): 41.1K **Privately Held**
SIC: 7231 2844 Unisex hair salons; shaving preparations

(G-11178)
STAGECRAFT INDUSTRIES INC
5503 6th Ave S (98108-2503)
P.O. Box 80191 (98108-0191)
PHONE.................................206 763-8800
Ted Ross, *Branch Mgr*
EMP: 4
SALES (corp-wide): 12.1MM **Privately Held**
SIC: 3999 Stage hardware & equipment, except lighting
PA: Stagecraft Industries, Inc.
5051 N Lagoon Ave
Portland OR 97217
503 286-1600

(G-11179)
STAKANA LLC
Also Called: Stakana Analytics
815 1st Ave Ste 287 (98104-1404)
PHONE.................................206 227-4329
Nick Simonton, *Vice Pres*
Nathaniel Derby,
EMP: 2
SALES (est): 143.1K **Privately Held**
SIC: 2721 Statistical reports (periodicals): publishing & printing

Seattle - King County (G-11212)

(G-11180)
STANDARD STEEL FABG CO INC
8155 1st Ave S (98108-4202)
P.O. Box 80907 (98108-0907)
PHONE..................................206 767-0499
W James Duthie, *CEO*
W Greg Duthie, *President*
Kevin M Duthie, *COO*
EMP: 3
SQ FT: 16,000
SALES (est): 493K **Privately Held**
WEB: www.standardsteelfab.com
SIC: 3441 Fabricated structural metal

(G-11181)
STARBOUND LLC
2157 N Northlake Way (98103-9184)
PHONE..................................206 784-5000
Cary Swasand,
▼ **EMP:** 120
SALES (est): 22.9MM **Privately Held**
SIC: 2092 Fresh or frozen packaged fish

(G-11182)
STARFORM INC
1501 E Madison St Ste 150 (98122-4491)
PHONE..................................206 446-9657
Lou Fasulo, *Principal*
Taylor Daynes, *Principal*
Joshua Rosen, *Principal*
EMP: 5
SALES: 500K **Privately Held**
SIC: 7372 7371 Application computer software; computer software development & applications

(G-11183)
STARLIGHT DESSERTS INC
2001 W Grfield St Bldg 28 (98119)
PHONE..................................206 284-8770
Emily Brune, *President*
EMP: 2
SALES: 250K **Privately Held**
SIC: 2053 Frozen bakery products, except bread

(G-11184)
STARPATH CORPORATION (PA)
Also Called: Starpath School of Navigation
3050 Nw 63rd St (98107-2521)
PHONE..................................206 783-1414
David Burch, *Principal*
EMP: 7
SQ FT: 1,100
SALES: 250K **Privately Held**
SIC: 8299 5942 2721 7371 Educational services; book stores; magazines: publishing & printing; computer software development & applications

(G-11185)
STATELESS LABS LLC
1425 Broadway 20-1524 (98122-3854)
PHONE..................................512 387-3115
Paul Sesar, *Mng Member*
Zachary Hyatt,
EMP: 2
SALES (est): 59.5K **Privately Held**
SIC: 7372 Application computer software

(G-11186)
STEEL ENCOUNTERS INC
Also Called: SEI Northwest
2300 W Commodore Way # 200 (98199-1564)
PHONE..................................206 281-8500
Peter Hatton, *Manager*
EMP: 15
SALES (corp-wide): 45.3MM **Privately Held**
WEB: www.steelencounters.com
SIC: 1791 1761 1793 3441 Structural steel erection; sheet metalwork; glass & glazing work; fabricated structural metal; products of purchased glass
PA: Steel Encounters, Inc.
525 E 300 S
Salt Lake City UT 84102
801 478-8100

(G-11187)
STEELER INC (PA)
10023 Martin Luther King (98178-2078)
PHONE..................................206 725-8500
Matt Surowiecki, *Owner*
William Hitsman, *General Mgr*
Maj Surowiecki, *Corp Secy*
Tony Vallerga, *Maint Spvr*
Randy Atwood, *Purch Agent*
▲ **EMP:** 90
SQ FT: 47,000
SALES (est): 41.7MM **Privately Held**
WEB: www.steeler.com
SIC: 3444 5072 5082 Studs & joists, sheet metal; builders' hardware; miscellaneous fasteners; power handtools; construction & mining machinery

(G-11188)
STEELER CONSTRUCTION SUP LTD
10023 M L King Jr Way S (98178)
PHONE..................................206 725-2500
F Matt Surowiecki, *President*
Don Woodruff, *Controller*
EMP: 20
SQ FT: 40,000
SALES (est): 2.5MM **Privately Held**
SIC: 3444 Sheet metalwork

(G-11189)
STELLA COLOR INC
3131 Elliott Ave Ste 100 (98121-3043)
PHONE..................................206 223-2303
Lynn Krinsky, *President*
▲ **EMP:** 18
SQ FT: 6,000
SALES (est): 2.2MM **Privately Held**
WEB: www.stellacolor.com
SIC: 2752 Commercial printing, lithographic

(G-11190)
STELLR INC
315 5th Ave S Ste 1000 (98104-2682)
PHONE..................................425 312-3798
Alexandra Eikenbary, *CFO*
EMP: 10
SALES (est): 651.8K **Privately Held**
SIC: 7372 Application computer software

(G-11191)
STEMPEL ART AND INDUSTRY LLC
630 W Nickerson St (98119-1512)
PHONE..................................206 718-6562
Thomas Stempel, *Principal*
EMP: 9
SQ FT: 1,800
SALES (est): 454.4K **Privately Held**
SIC: 3229 Pressed & blown glass

(G-11192)
STEPHAN J LESSER WOODWORKING
Also Called: Lesser, Stephan Woodworking
940 Nw 49th St (98107-3653)
P.O. Box 70454 (98127-0454)
PHONE..................................206 782-9463
Stephan Lesser, *Owner*
EMP: 4
SALES: 300K **Privately Held**
SIC: 2431 1799 Millwork; kitchen & bathroom remodeling

(G-11193)
STEWARD PUBLISHING
814 W Emerson St (98119-1417)
PHONE..................................206 283-0077
Norman Edwards, *Owner*
EMP: 3
SALES (est): 181.6K **Privately Held**
SIC: 2721 Periodicals

(G-11194)
STEWART INDUSTRIES INC
16 S Idaho St (98134-1119)
PHONE..................................206 652-9110
Ralph Smith, *President*
EMP: 20
SQ FT: 15,000
SALES (est): 3.3MM **Privately Held**
WEB: www.stewartindustries.net
SIC: 3089 3544 Injection molded finished plastic products; molding primary plastic; special dies & tools

(G-11195)
STICK & SAND TUTORING
6515 44th Ave S (98118-3305)
PHONE..................................206 721-6261
Shelly Lischke, *Principal*
EMP: 2
SALES (est): 85.2K **Privately Held**
SIC: 1442 Construction sand & gravel

(G-11196)
STITCH PUBLICATIONS LLC
1534 45th Ave Sw (98116-1624)
PHONE..................................206 214-5225
Priscilla Knoble, *Principal*
▲ **EMP:** 4 **EST:** 2012
SALES (est): 277.4K **Privately Held**
SIC: 2741 Miscellaneous publishing

(G-11197)
STITCHBLADE LLC
2315 Western Ave Ste 106 (98121-1697)
PHONE..................................206 940-7448
Joe Florence, *Mng Member*
EMP: 2
SALES (est): 100K **Privately Held**
SIC: 2759 Screen printing

(G-11198)
STONE CRAFT LLC
112 S Mead St (98108-2436)
PHONE..................................206 762-3920
Jordan Baldwin,
Jennifer Baldwin,
EMP: 8
SQ FT: 3,000
SALES: 700K **Privately Held**
SIC: 3281 Granite, cut & shaped

(G-11199)
STORK SOFTWARE LLC
5216 Ravenna Ave Ne (98105-3218)
PHONE..................................206 669-0644
EMP: 2
SALES (est): 105.7K **Privately Held**
SIC: 7372 Prepackaged software

(G-11200)
STORYTELLERS INK INC
The Highlands (98133)
P.O. Box 33398 (98133-0398)
PHONE..................................206 365-8265
Malcolm Stamper, *Ch of Bd*
Candace Johnson, *CFO*
EMP: 3
SALES (est): 210K **Privately Held**
WEB: www.storytellers-ink.com
SIC: 2731 Books: publishing only

(G-11201)
STRAIGHT PUBLICATIONS INC
1007 32nd Ave E (98112-3703)
PHONE..................................206 324-0618
Sally Straight, *President*
EMP: 3
SALES (est): 196.3K **Privately Held**
SIC: 2741 Miscellaneous publishing

(G-11202)
STRETCH 22 INC ✪
1913 2nd Ave (98101-1101)
PHONE..................................206 375-3358
Kris Sasaki, *Principal*
EMP: 4 **EST:** 2018
SALES (est): 200K **Privately Held**
SIC: 7991 7372 Physical fitness facilities; application computer software

(G-11203)
STRETCH AND STAPLE
8005 Greenwood Ave N (98103-4228)
PHONE..................................206 607-9277
EMP: 2
SALES (est): 159.7K **Privately Held**
SIC: 2211 Canvas

(G-11204)
STRONGBACK METAL BOATS INC
2442 Nw Market St Ste 473 (98107-4137)
PHONE..................................206 321-9965
Patrick Pitsch, *President*
EMP: 6 **EST:** 2009
SALES (est): 949.4K **Privately Held**
SIC: 3731 Crew boats, building & repairing

(G-11205)
STRUBLE CIDER LLC
1817 E Howell St (98122-2815)
PHONE..................................206 766-0009
John Struble, *Principal*
EMP: 3
SALES (est): 122.1K **Privately Held**
SIC: 2086 Carbonated soft drinks, bottled & canned

(G-11206)
STRYVE INC
1823 Terry Ave Apt 2309 (98101-2410)
PHONE..................................425 802-3832
Akshay Ahooja, *CEO*
Frank Fan, *Principal*
EMP: 5
SALES (est): 128.9K **Privately Held**
SIC: 7372 7389 Application computer software;

(G-11207)
STUDIO FOGLIO LLC
Also Called: Xenophile Books
2400 Nw 80th St Ste 129 (98117-4449)
PHONE..................................206 782-8739
Phil Foglio, *Mng Member*
Kaja Foglio,
◆ **EMP:** 3
SALES (est): 125K **Privately Held**
WEB: www.studiofoglio.com
SIC: 2721 5942 Comic books: publishing only, not printed on site; book stores

(G-11208)
STUDY IN THE USA INC
100 S King St Ste 425 (98104-2894)
PHONE..................................206 622-2075
Peggy Printz, *President*
Wesley Costa, *Opers Staff*
EMP: 5
SQ FT: 1,800
SALES (est): 672.8K **Privately Held**
WEB: www.studyusa.com
SIC: 8748 2741 Publishing consultant; miscellaneous publishing

(G-11209)
SUBSET GAMES LLC
1400 Nw 95th St (98117-2327)
PHONE..................................206 354-4010
Justin MA, *Partner*
Matthew Davis, *Partner*
EMP: 2
SALES: 800K **Privately Held**
SIC: 7372 Application computer software

(G-11210)
SUBSPLASH INC
3257 16th Ave W Ste 200 (98119-7160)
PHONE..................................206 965-8090
Tim Turner, *President*
Gretchen Gelman, *Opers Staff*
Phil Goodman, *Opers Staff*
Chris Hudson, *Sales Staff*
Sarah Thomas, *Sales Staff*
EMP: 30 **EST:** 2006
SALES (est): 5MM **Privately Held**
SIC: 3172 Wallets

(G-11211)
SUDDEN PRINTING INC (PA)
11009 1st Ave S (98168-1401)
PHONE..................................206 243-4444
Cecil Bristol, *President*
Brian Bach, *Vice Pres*
EMP: 20
SQ FT: 13,000
SALES (est): 5.2MM **Privately Held**
WEB: www.suddenprinting.com
SIC: 2752 7334 7331 3993 Commercial printing, offset; photocopying & duplicating services; direct mail advertising services; signs & advertising specialties; typesetting; bookbinding & related work

(G-11212)
SUENOS DE SALSA
12524 Lake City Way Ne (98125-4425)
PHONE..................................206 334-7496
EMP: 2
SALES (est): 77.2K **Privately Held**
SIC: 2099 Dips, except cheese & sour cream based

Seattle - King County (G-11213)

(G-11213)
SUGAR & STAMP
4846 41st Ave Sw (98116-4533)
PHONE..................404 944-1354
Lori Bailey, *Principal*
EMP: 3
SALES (est): 127.4K Privately Held
SIC: 2052 Cookies & crackers

(G-11214)
SUGAR MOUNTAIN LIVESTOCK LLC
Also Called: Mishima Reserve
1725 Westlake Ave N # 200 (98109-3045)
PHONE..................206 322-1644
Kurt Beecher Dammeier, *Mng Member*
EMP: 10
SALES: 5.1K Privately Held
SIC: 2011 Boxed beef from meat slaughtered on site

(G-11215)
SUMITOMO METAL MINING AMERICA (HQ)
701 5th Ave Ste 2150 (98104-7004)
PHONE..................206 405-2800
Norifumi Ushirone, *President*
Ryoichi Suvuki, *President*
Takashi Kuriyama, *Vice Pres*
Ryota Sekine, *Vice Pres*
Katsuya Tanaka, *Vice Pres*
▲ EMP: 4
SALES (est): 141.4MM Privately Held
SIC: 1081 Metal mining services

(G-11216)
SUMITOMO METAL MINING ARIZ INC
701 5th Ave Ste 4800 (98104-7009)
PHONE..................206 405-2800
Ryoisihi Sufuki, *President*
Sato Masaposapo, *Asst Sec*
EMP: 3
SQ FT: 6,000
SALES (est): 329.5K Privately Held
SIC: 1241 Mining services: bituminous
PA: Sumitomo Metal Mining Co., Ltd.
5-11-3, Shimbashi
Minato-Ku TKY 105-0

(G-11217)
SUMMIT CARBON CAPTURE LLC
83 S King St Ste 200 (98104-2875)
PHONE..................206 780-3551
EMP: 2
SALES (est): 130K Privately Held
SIC: 1311 Crude petroleum & natural gas production

(G-11218)
SUN LIQUOR MFG INC
4612 Union Bay Pl Ne (98105-4027)
PHONE..................206 419-5857
EMP: 2
SALES (est): 123.7K Privately Held
SIC: 3999 Manufacturing industries

(G-11219)
SUNFRESH FOODS INC
Also Called: Sunfresh Freezerves
125 S Kenyon St (98108-4207)
PHONE..................206 764-0940
Reed Hadley, *President*
EMP: 6
SQ FT: 6,000
SALES (est): 1.4MM Privately Held
WEB: www.sunfreshjam.com
SIC: 2037 2087 Fruits, quick frozen & cold pack (frozen); syrups, flavoring (except drink)

(G-11220)
SUNRICE LLC
3513 Ne (98105)
PHONE..................206 841-2454
Unju Kim, *Bd of Directors*
EMP: 3 EST: 2008
SALES (est): 130K Privately Held
SIC: 2099 Food preparations

(G-11221)
SUPERGRAPHICS LLC
2201 15th Ave W (98119-2417)
PHONE..................206 284-2201
Kim Magraw, *VP Sales*
Carol Beard,
Jacob Meier, *Graphic Designe*
EMP: 26
SALES: 8MM Privately Held
SIC: 3993 Signs & advertising specialties

(G-11222)
SUPERIOR CUSTOM CONTROL
12544 27th Ave Ne (98125-4310)
PHONE..................206 362-8866
Phyllis Jordan, *President*
EMP: 10
SQ FT: 4,800
SALES (est): 600K Privately Held
SIC: 3613 Switchgear & switchgear accessories

(G-11223)
SUPERIOR IMPRINTS INC
4226 6th Ave S (98108-1701)
PHONE..................206 441-7147
Russ Engle, *President*
Charlene C Engle, *Corp Secy*
Shari Frye, *Office Mgr*
EMP: 15
SQ FT: 4,000
SALES (est): 2MM Privately Held
SIC: 2752 Commercial printing, lithographic

(G-11224)
SUPERIOR RUBBER DIE CO INC
520 S River St (98108-3461)
P.O. Box 80846 (98108-0846)
PHONE..................206 763-2440
William Gabel, *President*
EMP: 4 EST: 1966
SQ FT: 2,500
SALES (est): 290K Privately Held
SIC: 3953 3544 Printing dies, rubber or plastic, for marking machines; special dies, tools, jigs & fixtures

(G-11225)
SUPLARI INC
1525 4th Ave Ste 700 (98101-1640)
PHONE..................425 610-9496
Alberto Sutton, *Senior VP*
Chad Baker, *Vice Pres*
Achim Bassler, *Vice Pres*
EMP: 2
SALES (est): 244.6K Privately Held
SIC: 7372 Business oriented computer software

(G-11226)
SURLY INDUSTRIES
2022 Franklin Ave E B (98102-3517)
PHONE..................206 349-3289
EMP: 2
SALES (est): 82K Privately Held
SIC: 3999 Manufacturing industries

(G-11227)
SURVEY ANALYTICS LLC (PA)
Also Called: Question Pro.com
93 S Jackson St 71641 (98104-2818)
PHONE..................800 326-5570
Andrew Jeavons, *CEO*
Aditya Bhat, *General Mgr*
Rahul Dogra, *Manager*
Manoj Kumar, *Manager*
Vivek Bhaskaran,
EMP: 11
SALES (est): 4.6MM Privately Held
SIC: 7372 Business oriented computer software

(G-11228)
SURVEY ANALYTICS LLC
3518 Fremont Ave N 598 (98103-8814)
PHONE..................800 326-5570
Kevin Battey, *Principal*
EMP: 23
SALES (corp-wide): 4.6MM Privately Held
SIC: 7372 Business oriented computer software
PA: Survey Analytics Llc
93 S Jackson St 71641
Seattle WA 98104
800 326-5570

(G-11229)
SURVIVAL INC
Also Called: School of Survival Specialties
2633 Eastlake Ave E 103 (98102-3231)
PHONE..................206 726-9363
Rick Stewart, *President*
Lee Brillhart, *Shareholder*
EMP: 25
SQ FT: 24,000
SALES (est): 2.7MM Privately Held
SIC: 3842 Clothing, fire resistant & protective; bulletproof vests

(G-11230)
SUSANS CUSTOM EMBRIODERY
2122 Nw 95th St (98117-2425)
PHONE..................206 783-3127
Susan Hopkins, *Principal*
EMP: 2
SALES (est): 89.1K Privately Held
SIC: 2389 Apparel & accessories

(G-11231)
SUSE LLC (DH)
705 5th Ave S Ste 1000 (98104-4450)
PHONE..................206 217-7500
Nils Brauckmann, *CEO*
Thomas Di Giacomo, *President*
Sander Huyts, *COO*
Edwin L Bowman III, *Vice Pres*
Craig Gardner, *Engineer*
EMP: 33
SALES (est): 16.1MM Privately Held
SIC: 7372 Prepackaged software
HQ: Micro Focus (Us), Inc.
700 King Farm Blvd # 125
Rockville MD 20850
301 838-5000

(G-11232)
SUSE LLC
Also Called: Suse Linux
705 5th Ave S Ste 1000 (98104-4450)
PHONE..................206 217-7100
David Golob, *Manager*
EMP: 4 Privately Held
SIC: 7372 Prepackaged software
HQ: Suse Llc
705 5th Ave S Ste 1000
Seattle WA 98104
206 217-7500

(G-11233)
SUTLIFF CANDY & PROMOTIONS CO (PA)
Also Called: Sutliff Candy Co
7710 Aurora Ave N (98103-4752)
PHONE..................206 784-5212
Kristin Wong, *President*
EMP: 5
SQ FT: 2,500
SALES (est): 288.1K Privately Held
SIC: 2064 Candy & other confectionery products

(G-11234)
SUZABELLE
5551 Greenwood Ave N (98103-5816)
PHONE..................206 790-5163
Suzanne Jaberg, *Principal*
EMP: 2 EST: 2011
SALES (est): 136.9K Privately Held
SIC: 3949 Hunting equipment

(G-11235)
SWANTON HILLS PRESS LLC
524 Ne 80th St (98115-4152)
PHONE..................206 972-1205
EMP: 2
SALES (est): 109.9K Privately Held
SIC: 2741 Miscellaneous publishing

(G-11236)
SWEET SANITY
9723 Wallingford Ave N (98103-3525)
PHONE..................425 212-7490
Devin Duvall, *Principal*
EMP: 2
SALES (est): 79.4K Privately Held
SIC: 2051 Bread, cake & related products

(G-11237)
SWIFT INDUSTRIES
1422 20th Ave (98122-2802)
PHONE..................415 608-8227
Martina Brimmer, *President*
EMP: 3 EST: 2011
SALES (est): 149.1K Privately Held
SIC: 2393 Textile bags

(G-11238)
SWIFT TOOL COMPANY INC
7709 5th Ave S (98108-4301)
PHONE..................206 763-9280
Casey Reed, *Branch Mgr*
EMP: 2
SALES (corp-wide): 5.6MM Privately Held
WEB: www.swifttool.com
SIC: 3541 Machine tools, metal cutting: exotic (explosive, etc.)
PA: Swift Tool Company, Inc
1720 Central Ave S
Kent WA 98032
253 854-7777

(G-11239)
SWIFTY PRTG DGITAL IMAGING INC
2001 3rd Ave (98121-2412)
PHONE..................206 441-0800
Ben Nikfard, *President*
Tracy Delosantos, *Vice Pres*
George Nikfard, *Vice Pres*
Dan Hatch, *Accounts Exec*
EMP: 22
SQ FT: 15,000
SALES (est): 2.9MM Privately Held
WEB: www.swiftydi.com
SIC: 2752 2759 Commercial printing, offset; letterpress printing

(G-11240)
SWISSA INC
Also Called: Swissa Jewelers
1905 Queen Anne Ave N # 101 (98109-2500)
PHONE..................206 625-9202
Moti M Swissa, *President*
Moti Swissa, *President*
EMP: 6
SQ FT: 1,600
SALES (est): 1.1MM Privately Held
WEB: www.swissa.com
SIC: 5094 3911 Jewelry; jewelry, precious metal

(G-11241)
SWYPE INC
505 1st Ave S (98104-3284)
PHONE..................206 547-5250
Mike Mc Sherry, *CEO*
Mike McSherry, *President*
George Harrison, *Vice Pres*
Leslie Wyles, *Accountant*
EMP: 80 EST: 2003
SQ FT: 2,000
SALES (est): 6MM Publicly Held
SIC: 3663 7371 Mobile communication equipment; software programming applications
PA: Nuance Communications, Inc.
1 Wayside Rd
Burlington MA 01803

(G-11242)
SYLVIA VANZEE
3050 Magnolia Blvd W (98199-2413)
PHONE..................206 284-2977
EMP: 3
SALES (est): 360K Privately Held
SIC: 5031 2421 Whol Lumber/Plywood/Millwork Sawmill/Planing Mill

(G-11243)
SYNERGY BUSINESS SERVICES INC
1001 4th Ave Ste 3262 (98154-1012)
PHONE..................206 859-6500
Jared Cady, *Vice Pres*
EMP: 23 Privately Held
SIC: 7372 Prepackaged software
PA: Synergy Business Services Inc
2537 S Gessner Rd 228
Houston TX 77063

GEOGRAPHIC SECTION

Seattle - King County (G-11274)

(G-11244)
SYNESSO INC
5610 4th Ave S (98108-2421)
PHONE 206 764-0600
Mark Burnette, *President*
Sandra Schneider, *Admin Sec*
▲ **EMP:** 15
SALES: 816.2K **Privately Held**
WEB: www.synesso.com
SIC: 3589 Coffee brewing equipment

(G-11245)
SYSTEM & APPLICATION ASSOC
6201 15th Ave Nw (98107-2306)
PHONE 206 949-4153
Robert Heald, *Owner*
Ray Levy, *Vice Pres*
EMP: 2 **EST:** 2001
SALES (est): 190K **Privately Held**
WEB: www.saacorp.com
SIC: 7372 Application computer software

(G-11246)
SYSTEM 1 SOFTWARE INC
501 N 34th St (98103-8856)
PHONE 206 548-1633
Alan Morihiro, *Principal*
EMP: 2
SALES (est): 144.1K **Privately Held**
SIC: 7372 Prepackaged software

(G-11247)
T & K CSTM FABRICATION & REPR
Also Called: T & K Fab
112 Sw 119th St (98146-2980)
PHONE 206 242-0197
Thomas Shields, *Owner*
EMP: 2
SALES: 150K **Privately Held**
SIC: 3535 3699 5084 Conveyors & conveying equipment; security control equipment & systems; conveyor systems

(G-11248)
T & TS
7314 28th Ave Sw (98126-3313)
PHONE 206 938-0177
Larry Tamura, *Owner*
EMP: 2
SALES (est): 154.7K **Privately Held**
SIC: 2759 Screen printing

(G-11249)
T K O FISHERIES INC (PA)
4257 24th Ave W (98199-1214)
PHONE 206 285-2815
William R Orr, *President*
John Kelley, *Vice Pres*
EMP: 9 **EST:** 2000
SQ FT: 1,100
SALES: 4.2MM **Privately Held**
SIC: 2092 Prepared fish or other seafood cakes & sticks

(G-11250)
T N W INC
7929 2nd Ave S (98108-4204)
PHONE 206 762-5755
Scott Mc Connell, *President*
EMP: 5
SQ FT: 13,000
SALES (est): 471.9K **Privately Held**
SIC: 2851 Paints & allied products

(G-11251)
T-SHIRT MADNESS SILK SCREEN
945 Nw 51st St (98107-3639)
PHONE 206 427-8720
EMP: 2
SALES (est): 111.3K **Privately Held**
SIC: 2752 Commercial printing, lithographic

(G-11252)
TABLEAU IRELAND LLC (HQ)
1621 N 34th St (98103-9193)
PHONE 206 633-3400
EMP: 2
SALES (est): 56.5K
SALES (corp-wide): 1.1B **Publicly Held**
SIC: 7372 Business oriented computer software

PA: Tableau Software, Inc.
1621 N 34th St
Seattle WA 98103
206 633-3400

(G-11253)
TABLEAU SOFTWARE INC (PA)
1621 N 34th St (98103-9193)
PHONE 206 633-3400
Christian Chabot, *Ch of Bd*
Adam Selipsky, *President*
Shannon St Clair, *Partner*
Damon Fletcher, *CFO*
Elissa Fink, *Chief Mktg Ofcr*
EMP: 148
SALES: 1.1B **Publicly Held**
WEB: www.tableausoftware.com
SIC: 7372 Business oriented computer software

(G-11254)
TACO TRUCK GAMES LLC
911 E Pike St Ste 202 (98122-3852)
PHONE 360 218-4967
Adrian Sotomayor,
EMP: 2
SALES (est): 56.5K **Privately Held**
SIC: 7372 Home entertainment computer software

(G-11255)
TACOMA RUBBER STAMP CO
Also Called: Advanced Marking Systems
5950 6th Ave S (98108-3317)
PHONE 206 728-8888
Jeff Lovely, *Manager*
EMP: 10
SALES (corp-wide): 8.4MM **Privately Held**
WEB: www.tacomarubberstamp.com
SIC: 3953 Marking devices
PA: Tacoma Rubber Stamp Co
919 Market St
Tacoma WA 98402
253 383-5433

(G-11256)
TACOMA SCREW PRODUCTS INC
1121 S Bailey St (98108-2723)
PHONE 206 767-3750
Greg Genereux, *General Mgr*
EMP: 9
SALES (corp-wide): 42.4MM **Privately Held**
WEB: www.tacomascrew.com
SIC: 3451 Screw machine products
PA: Tacoma Screw Products, Inc.
2001 Center St
Tacoma WA 98409
253 572-3444

(G-11257)
TAG MANUFACTURING INC
1201 3rd Ave Ste 3400 (98101-3268)
PHONE 206 359-8440
A Allan Skidmore, *Principal*
EMP: 2
SALES (est): 87.5K **Privately Held**
SIC: 3999 Manufacturing industries

(G-11258)
TAGGART WOODWORKS LLC
2311 N 45th St Ste 365 (98103-6905)
PHONE 206 729-8028
James Sprott, *Principal*
EMP: 4 **EST:** 2010
SALES (est): 259.5K **Privately Held**
SIC: 2431 Millwork

(G-11259)
TAHOMA TECHNOLOGY INC
6040 Palatine Ave N (98103-5351)
PHONE 206 393-0909
Glen Bradburn, *President*
William D Waddington, *Vice Pres*
EMP: 3
SQ FT: 2,200
SALES (est): 369.5K **Privately Held**
WEB: www.tahomatech.com
SIC: 3577 7371 Input/output equipment, computer; custom computer programming services

(G-11260)
TAKOVO LED LIGHTS
8009 7th Ave S (98108-4365)
PHONE 206 330-6862
EMP: 2
SALES (est): 129.9K **Privately Held**
SIC: 3648 Lighting equipment

(G-11261)
TALAERA
1908 8th Ave W (98119-2818)
PHONE 206 229-0631
Anita Anthonj, *CEO*
Mel Macmahon, *Manager*
EMP: 6
SALES (est): 163.7K **Privately Held**
SIC: 7372 Business oriented computer software; educational computer software

(G-11262)
TALGO INC (DH)
1000 2nd Ave Ste 1950 (98104-3616)
PHONE 206 254-7051
Antonio Perez, *President*
Nora Friend, *Vice Pres*
Felix Perez, *Project Mgr*
Miguel Tello, *Purch Mgr*
Eduardo Fernandez, *Engineer*
▲ **EMP:** 44 **EST:** 1994
SALES (est): 5.3MM
SALES (corp-wide): 17.1MM **Privately Held**
WEB: www.talgoamerica.com
SIC: 3743 Train cars & equipment, freight or passenger
HQ: Patentes Talgo Slu
Paseo Tren Talgo 2
Las Rozas De Madrid 28290
916 313-800

(G-11263)
TALK TO TARACOM
4714 Ballard Ave Nw (98107-4850)
PHONE 206 226-2606
Tara Talk To, *Principal*
EMP: 2 **EST:** 2016
SALES (est): 80.3K **Privately Held**
SIC: 2899 Chemical preparations

(G-11264)
TAM INDUSTRIES INC
9420 16th Ave Sw (98106-2824)
PHONE 206 763-6868
Irwin Q Tam, *President*
Luis W Tam, *President*
Diana Tam, *Treasurer*
Pacita Tam, *Admin Sec*
▲ **EMP:** 10
SQ FT: 20,000
SALES (est): 1.5MM **Privately Held**
WEB: www.tamskylights.com
SIC: 3211 5162 5231 Skylight glass; resins; plastics materials; paint, glass & wallpaper

(G-11265)
TANK WISE LLC
5405 W Marginal Way Sw (98106-1518)
PHONE 206 937-3995
Tom Wise, *Mng Member*
EMP: 2
SALES (est): 402.1K **Privately Held**
SIC: 3567 Heating units & devices, industrial: electric

(G-11266)
TAP PLASTICS INC A CAL CORP
710 9th Ave N (98109-4308)
PHONE 206 389-5900
Patrick Bond, *Branch Mgr*
EMP: 4
SALES (corp-wide): 62.3MM **Privately Held**
WEB: www.tapplastics.com
SIC: 3089 Plastic containers, except foam
PA: Tap Plastics, Inc., A California Corporation
3011 Alvarado St Ste A
San Leandro CA 94577
510 357-3755

(G-11267)
TAPENADE INC (PA)
Also Called: Tasting Room, The
1103 Grand Ave (98122-3515)
PHONE 206 325-3051

Lyle L Wilhelmi, *President*
Lysle Wilhelmi, *General Mgr*
Paul Beveridge, *Admin Sec*
EMP: 6
SALES: 800K **Privately Held**
WEB: www.wilridgewinery.com
SIC: 2084 Wines

(G-11268)
TAPESTRY INC
2680 Ne University Vlg St (98105-5023)
PHONE 206 729-5908
Andrea Graham, *Branch Mgr*
EMP: 2
SALES (corp-wide): 5.8B **Publicly Held**
WEB: www.coach.com
SIC: 3171 Handbags, women's
PA: Tapestry, Inc.
10 Hudson Yards
New York NY 10001
212 594-1850

(G-11269)
TAPHANDLES LLC (PA)
1424 4th Ave Ste 201 (98101-4602)
PHONE 206 462-6800
Paul Fichter, *President*
Nicole Bennett, *Project Mgr*
Joyce Luu, *Project Mgr*
Ashley McEneny, *Project Mgr*
Anna Scharer, *Project Mgr*
◆ **EMP:** 22
SQ FT: 5,400
SALES (est): 17.5MM **Privately Held**
WEB: www.taphandles.com
SIC: 2499 3089 8742 Handles, wood; handles, brush or tool: plastic; marketing consulting services

(G-11270)
TASSELS & WINGS PUBLISHING
6208 S Bangor St (98178-2433)
PHONE 206 725-5075
EMP: 3
SALES (est): 97.9K **Privately Held**
SIC: 2731 Books-Publishing/Printing

(G-11271)
TASSO INC
1631 15th Ave W Ste 105 (98119-2792)
PHONE 608 556-7606
Ben Moga, *Ch of Bd*
Erwin Berthier, *Vice Pres*
Ben Casavant, *Vice Pres*
EMP: 2 **EST:** 2011
SALES (est): 284.3K **Privately Held**
SIC: 3841 Diagnostic apparatus, medical

(G-11272)
TASTEBUD FUSION INC
Also Called: Sojo Foods
2025 1st Ave Ste 200 (98121-3124)
PHONE 253 826-8700
EMP: 20
SQ FT: 16,000
SALES (est): 2.2MM **Privately Held**
SIC: 2048 Mfg Prepared Feeds

(G-11273)
TASTING ROOM WINES WASHINGTON
1924 Post Aly (98101-1015)
PHONE 206 770-9463
Jen Doak, *Principal*
EMP: 2
SALES (est): 155.1K **Privately Held**
SIC: 2084 Wines

(G-11274)
TATOOSH DISTILLERY LLC (PA)
Also Called: Tattoosh Distillery & Spirits
309 S Cloverdale St C29 (98108-4571)
PHONE 206 818-0127
Mark Simon, *Mng Member*
Michael Carrosino,
Joseph Eliasen,
Troy Turner,
EMP: 4
SQ FT: 50,000
SALES (est): 456.3K **Privately Held**
SIC: 2084 5182 Brandy & brandy spirits; brandy & brandy spirits

Seattle - King County (G-11275)

(G-11275)
TC GLOBAL INC (PA)
Also Called: Tully's Coffee
2003 Western Ave Ste 660 (98121-2177)
PHONE................................206 233-2070
Scott M Pearson, *President*
Kirk Heinrich, *Vice Pres*
Dana Pratt, *VP Opers*
Catherine M Campbell, *CFO*
Robert Martin, *VP Sales*
▲ **EMP:** 99
SQ FT: 17,800
SALES (est): 98.6MM **Privately Held**
WEB: www.tullys.com
SIC: 5149 2095 Coffee, green or roasted; coffee roasting (except by wholesale grocers)

(G-11276)
TCC PRINTING AND IMAGING INC
616 6th Ave S (98104-2815)
PHONE................................206 622-4050
Michael Crumpacker, *President*
Lidia Hess, *Chairman*
Cathy Powell, *Vice Pres*
Justin Tomajko, *Accounts Mgr*
Pamela Crumpacker, *Marketing Mgr*
EMP: 23 **EST:** 1953
SQ FT: 19,000
SALES (est): 2.9MM **Privately Held**
WEB: www.thecopycompany.com
SIC: 2759 5199 7334 Commercial printing; artists' materials; architects' supplies (non-durable); photocopying & duplicating services

(G-11277)
TECHNICAL & ASSEMBLY SVCS CORP (PA)
Also Called: Tasc
2222 N Pacific St (98103-9127)
PHONE................................206 682-2967
Richard Hirst, *President*
Margaret Hirst, *Vice Pres*
Maggi Hirst, *VP Sales*
Matthew Grzywinski, *Supervisor*
Paula Bauer, *Administration*
EMP: 21
SQ FT: 4,000
SALES: 1.2MM **Privately Held**
WEB: www.tasc-wa.com
SIC: 3672 Printed circuit boards

(G-11278)
TEDDY BEAR PRESS
3703 S Edmunds St Ste 67 (98118-1728)
PHONE................................206 402-6947
Adina Segal, *Principal*
EMP: 2 **EST:** 2011
SALES (est): 122.6K **Privately Held**
SIC: 2741 Miscellaneous publishing

(G-11279)
TEKNOTHERM INC
3941 Leary Way Nw (98107-5041)
P.O. Box 70230 (98127-0230)
PHONE................................206 547-5629
Roar Ellefsen, *CEO*
Jan Roar Ellefsen, *President*
Kristian Ellefsen, *President*
Vladimir Sukharev, *Vice Pres*
Chris Complita, *Sales Staff*
▲ **EMP:** 100
SQ FT: 11,000
SALES: 5.3MM
SALES (corp-wide): 418.9MM **Privately Held**
WEB: www.teknotherm-us.com
SIC: 5078 7623 3585 Refrigeration equipment & supplies; refrigeration repair service; refrigeration equipment, complete
HQ: Teknotherm Marine As
Sorliveien 90/92
Halden 1788
691 909-00

(G-11280)
TELECOMMUNICATION SYSTEMS INC
Also Called: TCS
2401 Elliott Ave Ste 200 (98121-3311)
PHONE................................206 792-2000
John Clark, *Branch Mgr*
EMP: 205
SALES (corp-wide): 570.5MM **Publicly Held**
WEB: www.telecomsys.com
SIC: 4822 3661 Electronic mail; telephone & telegraph apparatus
HQ: Telecommunication Systems, Inc.
275 West St
Annapolis MD 21401
410 263-7616

(G-11281)
TERRASHIELD COATINGS LTD
6505 21st Ave Nw (98117-5745)
PHONE................................206 992-2157
EMP: 2
SALES (est): 122.7K **Privately Held**
SIC: 3479 Metal coating & allied service

(G-11282)
TESTED FIELD SYSTEMS LLC
4014 47th Ave S (98118-1218)
PHONE................................206 453-4851
Tom Field, *President*
Cathleen Bernier, *Vice Pres*
EMP: 2
SALES (est): 306.5K **Privately Held**
SIC: 3821 7371 Physics laboratory apparatus; computer software writing services

(G-11283)
THAW CORPORATION (HQ)
8300 Military Rd S (98108-3951)
PHONE................................206 505-2100
James Cross, *President*
Adam Atwell, *CFO*
Page Temple, *Director*
EMP: 120
SQ FT: 88,400
SALES: 39.3MM
SALES (corp-wide): 2.7B **Privately Held**
WEB: www.rei.com
SIC: 2329 2339 Athletic (warmup, sweat & jogging) suits: men's & boys'; ski & snow clothing: men's & boys'; women's & misses' outerwear; ski jackets & pants: women's, misses' & juniors'
PA: Recreational Equipment, Inc.
6750 S 228th St
Kent WA 98032
253 395-3780

(G-11284)
THC PARTNERS
9369 8th Ave S (98108-4624)
PHONE................................347 459-8450
Allan Abramovitz, *Principal*
EMP: 3
SALES (est): 212.5K **Privately Held**
SIC: 3999

(G-11285)
THE FUEL
2201 E Aloha St (98112-4081)
PHONE................................206 829-8033
Lorraine Ketch, *Principal*
EMP: 3
SALES (est): 205.1K **Privately Held**
SIC: 2869 Fuels

(G-11286)
THE WINDWARD CMMNCATIONS GROUP
504 N 85th St (98103-3721)
PHONE................................206 382-1117
David K Livingston, *Principal*
EMP: 2
SALES (est): 123.9K **Privately Held**
SIC: 2752 Commercial printing, offset

(G-11287)
THEOBALD SOFTWARE INC
2211 Elliott Ave Ste 200 (98121-3622)
PHONE................................425 802-2514
Christoph Schuler, *President*
David Cherry, *Consultant*
EMP: 2 **EST:** 2014
SALES (est): 178.4K **Privately Held**
SIC: 7372 Business oriented computer software

(G-11288)
THERMETRICS LLC
4220 24th Ave W (98199-1216)
PHONE................................206 456-9119
EMP: 1
SALES: 4.2MM
SALES (corp-wide): 8.7MM **Privately Held**
SIC: 3825 Radar testing instruments, electric
PA: Measurement Technology Northwest, Inc.
4220 24th Ave W
Seattle WA 98199
206 634-1308

(G-11289)
THESE TWO GIRLS LLC
Also Called: Rain or Shine Kids
300 Nw 62nd St (98107-2112)
PHONE................................206 200-3620
Heather Correa,
▲ **EMP:** 2
SALES (est): 110K **Privately Held**
SIC: 2369 Girls' & children's outerwear

(G-11290)
THIN DIPPED ALMONDS
115 N 36th St Unit B (98103-8633)
PHONE................................720 231-9196
Brianna Griffith, *Principal*
EMP: 2
SALES (est): 137.7K **Privately Held**
SIC: 2064 Candy & other confectionery products

(G-11291)
THIRD & WALL ART GROUP LLC
3455 Thorndyke Ave W # 102 (98119-1647)
PHONE................................206 443-8425
Amy Clark,
EMP: 11
SALES (est): 343.8K **Privately Held**
SIC: 2741 5999 7999 Art copy & poster publishing; art dealers; art gallery, commercial

(G-11292)
THIRD ARES INDUSTRIES LLC
915 Queen Anne Ave N (98109-5617)
PHONE................................502 592-2463
David Thurman III,
EMP: 2
SALES (est): 127.3K **Privately Held**
SIC: 3999 Manufacturing industries

(G-11293)
THIRTY SECOND STREEET RACCOONS
9518 32nd Ave Ne (98115-2421)
PHONE................................206 526-8169
EMP: 2 **EST:** 2013
SALES (est): 110K **Privately Held**
SIC: 2741 Misc Publishing

(G-11294)
THOE JOHN
2201 Ne 120th St (98125-5254)
PHONE................................206 505-6229
John Thoe, *Principal*
EMP: 2
SALES (est): 198.1K **Privately Held**
SIC: 2511 Wood household furniture

(G-11295)
THOMAS GRANGE HOLDINGS INC
2716 Elliott Ave Apt 603 (98121-3510)
PHONE................................678 921-0499
Lorne Millwood, *President*
EMP: 10
SALES: 3MM **Privately Held**
SIC: 7371 3999 Computer software development; atomizers, toiletry

(G-11296)
THOUGHT OPS LLC
520 Occidental Ave S # 503 (98104-3163)
PHONE................................206 427-0165
Matthew Ployhar, *Principal*
EMP: 2 **EST:** 2014
SALES (est): 144.4K **Privately Held**
SIC: 2752 Commercial printing, lithographic

(G-11297)
THREE BY THREE INC
Also Called: Three By Three Seattle
3668 Albion Pl N (98103-7904)
PHONE................................206 784-5839
Anita Nadelson, *CEO*
Gwen S Weinberg, *President*
Tom Garvey, *General Counsel*
▲ **EMP:** 20
SQ FT: 20,000
SALES (est): 2.5MM **Privately Held**
WEB: www.threebythree.com
SIC: 2789 Binding & repair of books, magazines & pamphlets

(G-11298)
THREEPENNY SOFTWARE LLC
4649 Eastern Ave N (98103-6931)
PHONE................................206 675-1518
Helen Kim, *Owner*
EMP: 2
SALES (est): 117.4K **Privately Held**
WEB: www.threepenny.net
SIC: 7372 7371 Prepackaged software; custom computer programming services

(G-11299)
THRIFTY PAYLESS INC T/A
201 Broadway E (98102-5723)
PHONE................................206 324-7111
Ed Talbot, *Principal*
EMP: 3
SALES (est): 162.1K **Privately Held**
SIC: 2836 Vaccines & other immunizing products

(G-11300)
THRIFTY PAYLESS INC
9000 Rainier Ave S (98118-5017)
PHONE................................206 760-1076
EMP: 3 **EST:** 2011
SALES (est): 167K **Privately Held**
SIC: 2836 Vaccines & other immunizing products

(G-11301)
THRIFTY PAYLESS INC T/A
2603 3rd Ave (98121-1213)
PHONE................................206 441-8790
Jeff Hartshorn, *Principal*
EMP: 3 **EST:** 2011
SALES (est): 156.2K **Privately Held**
SIC: 2836 Vaccines & other immunizing products

(G-11302)
THRIFTY PAYLESS INC T/A
2707 Rainier Ave S (98144-5332)
PHONE................................206 721-5018
Tu Huyng, *Principal*
EMP: 3 **EST:** 2010
SALES (est): 164K **Privately Held**
SIC: 2836 Vaccines & other immunizing products

(G-11303)
TI GOTHAM INC
Also Called: Cozi
413 Pine St Ste 500 (98101-3669)
PHONE................................206 957-8447
Ensley Eikenburg, *Director*
EMP: 584
SALES (corp-wide): 2.2B **Publicly Held**
SIC: 2721 Magazines: publishing only, not printed on site
HQ: Ti Gotham Inc.
225 Liberty St
New York NY 10281
212 522-1212

(G-11304)
TICKET ENVELOPE COMPANY LLC
4401 E Marginal Way S (98134-1116)
PHONE................................206 784-7266
Nancy Barkley, *Project Mgr*
Suzy Koeppe, *Purch Mgr*
George Crabtree, *Manager*
Traci Pryor, *Director*
Petsy Kenney,
EMP: 2
SQ FT: 1,000
SALES (est): 248.2K **Privately Held**
SIC: 2759 Commercial printing

GEOGRAPHIC SECTION
Seattle - King County (G-11336)

(G-11305)
TIG AEROSPACE LLC
1700 Westlake Ave N (98109-3012)
PHONE..................................206 372-6724
Steve Muenzberg, *Manager*
EMP: 2
SALES (est): 91.7K **Privately Held**
SIC: 3812 Search & navigation equipment

(G-11306)
TIGER OAK MEDIA INCORPORATED
1417 4th Ave Ste 600 (98101-2233)
PHONE..................................206 284-1750
John Kueber, *Principal*
EMP: 35 **Privately Held**
WEB: www.seattlemagazine.com
SIC: 2741 2721 Directories: publishing only, not printed on site; magazines: publishing only, not printed on site
PA: Oak Tiger Media Incorporated
900 S 3rd St
Minneapolis MN 55415

(G-11307)
TILOBEN PUBLISHING CO INC
2600 S Jackson St (98144-2402)
PHONE..................................206 323-3070
Joan Owens, *Principal*
EMP: 4
SALES (est): 258.3K **Privately Held**
SIC: 2741 Miscellaneous publishing

(G-11308)
TILRAY INC
2701 Eastlake Ave E 3 (98102-3104)
PHONE..................................206 432-9325
Brendan Kennedy, *President*
EMP: 4
SALES (corp-wide): 21MM **Publicly Held**
SIC: 2833 5122 Medicinals & botanicals; medicinals & botanicals
PA: Tilray, Inc
1100 Maughan Rd
Nanaimo BC
844 845-7291

(G-11309)
TIME PRINTING INC
4411 Wallingford Ave N E (98103-7597)
PHONE..................................206 633-3320
Gil R Kim, *President*
EMP: 6
SALES (est): 660.6K **Privately Held**
SIC: 2752 2759 Commercial printing, lithographic; commercial printing

(G-11310)
TIMOTHY COLMAN
Also Called: Good Nature Publishing Co
6521 23rd Ave Ne (98115-7031)
PHONE..................................800 631-3086
Timothy Colman, *Owner*
EMP: 5
SALES (est): 240K **Privately Held**
WEB: www.goodnaturepublishing.com
SIC: 2741 Art copy & poster publishing

(G-11311)
TIMSHEL WOODWORKING
3511 Interlake Ave N (98103-8915)
PHONE..................................206 466-1054
Tony Kevin, *Principal*
EMP: 2
SALES (est): 75.5K **Privately Held**
SIC: 2431 Millwork

(G-11312)
TIN TABLE
915 E Pine St (98122-3849)
PHONE..................................206 320-8458
Hallie Kuperman, *Owner*
EMP: 3
SALES (est): 218.1K **Privately Held**
SIC: 3356 Tin

(G-11313)
TINYPULSE
18 W Mercer St Ste 100 (98119-3972)
PHONE..................................206 455-9424
EMP: 50
SALES (est): 1.8MM **Privately Held**
SIC: 7372 Prepackaged Software Services

(G-11314)
TITAN CASE INC
233 S Holden St (98108-4359)
PHONE..................................206 935-0566
EMP: 3
SALES (est): 180K **Privately Held**
SIC: 3161 Mfg Luggage

(G-11315)
TLS PRINTING
10331 Aurora Ave N (98133-9227)
PHONE..................................206 522-8289
EMP: 2
SALES (est): 83.9K **Privately Held**
SIC: 2752 Commercial printing, lithographic

(G-11316)
TOASTER LABS INC
2212 Queen Anne Ave N (98109-2312)
PHONE..................................206 368-3178
Any Buckalder, *CEO*
Michel Goffin, *CFO*
Tom Lerner, *Director*
Douglas Rosen, *Director*
EMP: 8 **EST:** 2013
SQ FT: 2,000
SALES: 10MM **Privately Held**
SIC: 3699 Household electrical equipment

(G-11317)
TOKENYO LLC
91 S Jackson St Unit 4581 (98194-9444)
PHONE..................................206 851-7046
Peter Huang, *Manager*
EMP: 2
SALES (est): 110K **Privately Held**
SIC: 7372 Application computer software

(G-11318)
TOM BIHN INC
Also Called: Tom Bihn - Portable Culture
4750 Ohio Ave S A (98134-2326)
PHONE..................................206 652-4123
Darcy Hudgens, *CEO*
Thomas D Bihn, *President*
▲ **EMP:** 60
SQ FT: 4,000
SALES (est): 4.1MM **Privately Held**
WEB: www.tombihn.com
SIC: 2393 5948 Textile bags; luggage & leather goods stores

(G-11319)
TOP TO BOTTOM
9651 15th Ave Sw (98106-2821)
PHONE..................................206 764-7750
Chung Young, *Principal*
EMP: 2 **EST:** 2010
SALES (est): 220.5K **Privately Held**
SIC: 4499 3732 Boat cleaning; boat building & repairing

(G-11320)
TORMENTED ARTIFACTS LTD
9258 9th Ave Nw (98117-2219)
PHONE..................................206 501-8333
Dmitri Arbacauskas, *Principal*
EMP: 2
SALES (est): 63K **Privately Held**
SIC: 2389 Costumes

(G-11321)
TOTALLY BLOWN GLASSWORKS INC
5607 Corson Ave S (98108-2604)
PHONE..................................206 768-8944
Jackie Mendelson, *President*
Dehanna Jones, *Vice Pres*
EMP: 2 **EST:** 1998
SQ FT: 2,600
SALES: 100K **Privately Held**
SIC: 3229 5199 Art, decorative & novelty glassware; glassware, novelty

(G-11322)
TOURMAP COMPANY
1932 1st Ave Ste 625 (98101-2447)
P.O. Box 16253 (98116-0253)
PHONE..................................206 932-2506
Richard D Ingalls, *President*
Marjorie Ingalls, *Corp Secy*
▲ **EMP:** 2
SALES (est): 184.2K **Privately Held**
WEB: www.tourmap.com
SIC: 7389 7336 2741 Mapmaking or drafting, including aerial; commercial art & illustration; miscellaneous publishing

(G-11323)
TOURNITEK INC
730 Bellevue Ave E Apt 5 (98102-6905)
PHONE..................................423 620-5475
Patrick Jacobs, *CEO*
Shahram Aarabi, *President*
EMP: 3
SALES (est): 156.3K **Privately Held**
SIC: 3845 Electromedical equipment

(G-11324)
TRADE PRINTERY LLC
317 S Bennett St (98108-2228)
PHONE..................................206 728-1600
Marna Hanneman, *General Mgr*
Leroy Hanneman,
EMP: 6
SQ FT: 2,000
SALES (est): 941.5K **Privately Held**
SIC: 2752 Commercial printing, offset

(G-11325)
TRADE-MARX SIGN & DISPLAY CORP
818 S Dakota St (98108-5228)
PHONE..................................206 623-7676
Donald P Jarvis, *President*
Harry Tang, *Purchasing*
Donna Rehfeld, *Accounting Mgr*
Kelly Garrett, *Accounts Exec*
Barton Haynes, *Mktg Dir*
EMP: 27 **EST:** 1969
SQ FT: 25,000
SALES: 3.1MM **Privately Held**
WEB: www.trade-marx.com
SIC: 3993 Neon signs; displays, paint process; signs, not made in custom sign painting shops

(G-11326)
TRANE US INC
4408 4th Ave S (98134-2312)
PHONE..................................206 748-0500
Rock Keller, *Manager*
EMP: 3 **Privately Held**
SIC: 3585 Refrigeration & heating equipment
HQ: Trane U.S. Inc.
3600 Pammel Creek Rd
La Crosse WI 54601
608 787-2000

(G-11327)
TRANSMARINE NAVIGATION CORP
9750 3rd Ave Ne Ste 308 (98115-2022)
PHONE..................................206 525-2051
Henry Ko, *President*
Craig Wear, *Branch Mgr*
EMP: 10
SALES (corp-wide): 18.9MM **Privately Held**
SIC: 3795 Tanks & tank components
PA: Transmarine Navigation Corp
301 E Ocean Blvd Ste 590
Long Beach CA 90802
562 951-8260

(G-11328)
TRAVELERS TEA BAR
501 E Pine St (98122-2310)
PHONE..................................206 329-6260
Allen Kornmesser, *Owner*
EMP: 20
SQ FT: 1,700
SALES (est): 472.8K **Privately Held**
SIC: 5812 2099 Indian/Pakistan restaurant; seasonings & spices

(G-11329)
TREJO TREJO INC
409 Ne 70th St (98115-5481)
P.O. Box 596, Bothell (98041-0596)
PHONE..................................425 298-3144
EMP: 2
SALES (est): 90.8K **Privately Held**
SIC: 2064 Candy & other confectionery products

(G-11330)
TRENZI INC
111 S Jackson St (98104-3111)
PHONE..................................206 769-6501
Calder Wong, *CEO*
EMP: 3 **EST:** 2015
SALES (est): 86K **Privately Held**
SIC: 7372 Application computer software

(G-11331)
TREVORS WOOD WORKING LLC
825 Ne Northgate Way (98125-7311)
P.O. Box 31006 (98103-1006)
PHONE..................................206 940-8000
Blake Martin, *Governor*
EMP: 4 **EST:** 2017
SALES (est): 506.4K **Privately Held**
SIC: 2521 2531 Wood office furniture; public building & related furniture; school furniture

(G-11332)
TRI-RYCHE CORPORATION
Also Called: Queensryche Publishing
10751 Densmore Ave N (98133-8943)
PHONE..................................206 363-8070
Neil Sussman, *Principal*
EMP: 2
SALES (est): 119K **Privately Held**
SIC: 2741 Music book & sheet music publishing

(G-11333)
TRIDENT CARROLLTON LLC
5303 Shilshole Ave Nw (98107-4021)
PHONE..................................206 783-3818
EMP: 3
SALES (est): 143.6K **Privately Held**
SIC: 2092 Fresh or frozen packaged fish

(G-11334)
TRIDENT SEAFOODS ASIA INC (HQ)
5303 Shilshole Ave Nw (98107-4000)
PHONE..................................206 783-3818
Chuck Bundrant, *Chairman*
◆ **EMP:** 10
SALES (corp-wide): 2.3B **Privately Held**
WEB: www.tridentseafoods.com
SIC: 2092 5146 5091 0912 Seafoods, frozen: prepared; crabmeat, frozen; fish, frozen: prepared; seafoods; fishing equipment & supplies; finfish
PA: Trident Seafoods Corporation
5303 Shilshole Ave Nw
Seattle WA 98107
206 783-3818

(G-11335)
TRIDENT SEAFOODS CORPORATION (PA)
5303 Shilshole Ave Nw (98107-4000)
P.O. Box 17599 (98127-1269)
PHONE..................................206 783-3818
Joseph Bundrant, *CEO*
John Webby, *General Mgr*
Edd Perry, *Exec VP*
Dave Benson, *Vice Pres*
Jill Bundrant, *Vice Pres*
◆ **EMP:** 350
SQ FT: 80,000
SALES (est): 2.3B **Privately Held**
WEB: www.tridentseafoods.com
SIC: 2092 5091 5146 Seafoods, frozen: prepared; crabmeat, frozen; fish, frozen: prepared; fishing equipment & supplies; seafoods

(G-11336)
TRIDENT SEAFOODS CORPORATION
653 Nw 41st St (98107-5032)
PHONE..................................206 783-3818
EMP: 4
SALES (corp-wide): 2.3B **Privately Held**
SIC: 2092 Seafoods, frozen: prepared; crabmeat, frozen; fish, frozen: prepared
PA: Trident Seafoods Corporation
5303 Shilshole Ave Nw
Seattle WA 98107
206 783-3818

Seattle - King County (G-11337)

(G-11337)
TRILION QUALITY SYSTEMS LLC
500 Mercer St Ste C2 (98109-4654)
PHONE..................267 565-8062
EMP: 41
SALES (corp-wide): 11.9MM **Privately Held**
SIC: 3545 8711 Precision measuring tools; engineering services
PA: Trilion Quality Systems, Llc
651 Park Ave
King Of Prussia PA 19406
215 710-3000

(G-11338)
TRIOSPORTS USA LLC
4040 23rd Ave W (98199-1209)
PHONE..................206 953-2394
Elaine McNabb,
Laura Hauter,
EMP: 2
SALES (est): 133.4K **Privately Held**
SIC: 3861 Cameras & related equipment

(G-11339)
TRIVITRO CORPORATION
150 Nickerson St Ste 107 (98109-1634)
PHONE..................425 251-8340
Christopher H Freas, *President*
Don Freas, *President*
Chris Freas, *Vice Pres*
Maryjean H Freas, *Admin Sec*
▼ EMP: 12
SQ FT: 30,000
SALES (est): 1.1MM **Privately Held**
WEB: www.trivitro.com
SIC: 3231 Products of purchased glass

(G-11340)
TROOP BOY SCOUTS OF AMERICA
41 Dravus St Apt 208 (98109-1662)
PHONE..................206 284-2164
Mike Kunz, *Principal*
EMP: 2
SALES (est): 85.9K **Privately Held**
SIC: 3577 Computer peripheral equipment

(G-11341)
TRUE COLORS INC
1904 3rd Ave (98101-1126)
PHONE..................206 623-2366
Pat McVicker, *President*
EMP: 3
SALES (est): 270K **Privately Held**
SIC: 3915 Jewelers' materials & lapidary work

(G-11342)
TRUE NORTH GEAR LLC
3723 S Hudson St (98118-1919)
P.O. Box 28789 (98118-8789)
PHONE..................206 723-0735
Jacqueline Leclair, *Marketing Mgr*
Alyx Fier,
Steve Missiano,
▲ EMP: 5
SALES: 7MM **Privately Held**
SIC: 3161 Cases, carrying

(G-11343)
TRUE SOL INNOVATIONS INC
8560 Greenwood Ave N (98103-3614)
PHONE..................206 428-7136
Michael J Black, *President*
EMP: 3
SALES (est): 198.3K **Privately Held**
WEB: www.truesol.com
SIC: 3612 Transformers, except electric

(G-11344)
TRYB INC
3817 Ne 82nd St (98115-4917)
PHONE..................206 310-9025
Joseph Debons, *Principal*
EMP: 4
SALES (est): 200K **Privately Held**
SIC: 7372 Application computer software

(G-11345)
TRYSK PRINT SOLUTIONS LLC
2201 3rd Ave Apt 2704 (98121-2007)
PHONE..................877 605-1164
Stephan Martinez, *Founder*

Gene Anthony, *CFO*
Scott Haggerty, *Marketing Staff*
Rob Griswold, *Director*
Daniel White, *Director*
EMP: 4 EST: 2009
SALES (est): 369.3K **Privately Held**
SIC: 2752 Commercial printing, offset

(G-11346)
TSUE CHONG CO INC
Also Called: Rose Brands
800 S Weller St (98104-3014)
PHONE..................206 623-0801
Kenneth Louie, *President*
Tim Louie, *Vice Pres*
Henry Louie, *Treasurer*
▲ EMP: 30 EST: 1917
SQ FT: 35,000
SALES (est): 3.9MM **Privately Held**
SIC: 2098 2052 2099 Noodles (e.g. egg, plain & water), dry; cookies; food preparations

(G-11347)
TULLYS COF ASIA PCF PRTNERS LP
2003 Western Ave Ste 660 (98121-2177)
PHONE..................206 233-2070
Carl W Pennington Sr, *Partner*
EMP: 4
SALES (est): 340K **Privately Held**
SIC: 2095 Roasted coffee

(G-11348)
TUNE INC (PA)
Also Called: Mobile App Tracking
2200 Western Ave Ste 200 (98121-4091)
PHONE..................206 508-1318
Peter Hamilton, *CEO*
Steve Burgess, *President*
Steve McQuade, *President*
Cameron Stewart, *General Mgr*
Crystal Dicarlo, *Vice Pres*
EMP: 227
SALES (est): 18.9MM **Privately Held**
SIC: 7372 Business oriented computer software

(G-11349)
TWARDUS IRON & WIRE WORKS INC
5269 Rainier Ave S (98118-6103)
PHONE..................206 723-8234
Alex Twardus, *President*
Steven Twardus, *Vice Pres*
EMP: 2 EST: 1950
SQ FT: 2,500
SALES (est): 254.4K **Privately Held**
WEB: www.twardus.com
SIC: 3496 Mesh, made from purchased wire

(G-11350)
TWILIGHT SOFTWARE
3217 14th Ave S (98144-6314)
PHONE..................206 228-2037
EMP: 2
SALES (est): 110.6K **Privately Held**
SIC: 7372 Prepackaged software

(G-11351)
TWIRL CAFE
2111 Queen Anne Ave N (98109-2310)
PHONE..................206 283-4552
EMP: 5
SALES: 200K **Privately Held**
SIC: 5812 2051 Eating Place Mfg Bread/Related Products

(G-11352)
TWO BLUE MULES
4806 25th Ave Sw (98106-1318)
PHONE..................206 935-3762
David Belisle, *Owner*
EMP: 4
SALES (est): 419.3K **Privately Held**
SIC: 2599 3425 Furniture & fixtures; saws, hand: metalworking or woodworking

(G-11353)
TWO DOG ISLAND INC
1118 37th Ave E (98112-4432)
PHONE..................206 325-0609
Galen Jefferson, *President*
▲ EMP: 3

SQ FT: 3,500
SALES (est): 750K **Privately Held**
WEB: www.twodogisland.com
SIC: 2339 Sportswear, women's

(G-11354)
TWO MAC INC
Also Called: Scan Marine Equipment
2144 Westlake Ave N Ste D (98109-2486)
PHONE..................206 285-3675
Bruce McElroy, *President*
Doug McElroy, *Vice Pres*
EMP: 3
SQ FT: 1,100
SALES: 1.1MM **Privately Held**
WEB: www.scanmarineusa.com
SIC: 3433 Heating equipment, except electric

(G-11355)
TWO ZERO SIX LLC
920 S Holgate St Ste 103 (98134-1623)
PHONE..................206 557-4384
▲ EMP: 3
SALES (est): 235K **Privately Held**
SIC: 2511 Dining room furniture: wood

(G-11356)
TWOBITBEAR LLC
1905 E Pine St (98122-2827)
PHONE..................206 658-5797
Llewellyn Mason, *CEO*
EMP: 2 EST: 2012
SALES (est): 88.1K **Privately Held**
SIC: 7372 Home entertainment computer software

(G-11357)
TYMLEZ INC
600 1st Ave Ste 441 (98104-2216)
PHONE..................630 215-7878
John Haggard, *President*
EMP: 2
SQ FT: 225
SALES: 425K **Privately Held**
SIC: 7372 Prepackaged software

(G-11358)
U DON LLC
Also Called: Don Noodle Station
1640 12th Ave (98122-2567)
PHONE..................206 466-1471
Tak Krushi, *Mng Member*
EMP: 12
SALES (est): 313.1K **Privately Held**
SIC: 2098 Noodles (e.g. egg, plain & water), dry

(G-11359)
UBI INTERACTIVE INC
1818 Westlake Ave N # 317 (98109-2707)
PHONE..................206 457-2493
EMP: 5
SALES (est): 395.9K **Privately Held**
SIC: 7372 Application computer software

(G-11360)
UKUSH PRINT AND MAIL
2645 S Warsaw St (98108-3706)
PHONE..................206 763-0454
EMP: 2 EST: 2017
SALES (est): 92.3K **Privately Held**
SIC: 2752 Commercial printing, lithographic

(G-11361)
ULIS FAMOUS SAUSAGE INC
1511 Pike Place Market (98101)
PHONE..................206 839-1000
EMP: 2
SALES (est): 22.2K **Privately Held**
SIC: 2013 Sausages And Other Prepared Meats

(G-11362)
ULIS FAMOUS SAUSAGE LLC
1511 Pike Pl (98101-3536)
PHONE..................206 839-1000
Karl Andersson, *QC Mgr*
Uli Lengenberg,
EMP: 5
SALES (est): 584K **Privately Held**
WEB: www.ulisfamoussausage.com
SIC: 2013 Sausages from purchased meat

(G-11363)
ULUWATU
4817 44th Ave S (98118-1809)
PHONE..................206 852-7289
EMP: 2
SALES (est): 130K **Privately Held**
SIC: 3423 Mfg Hand/Edge Tools

(G-11364)
UNAUTHORIZED SCREEN PRINTING
700 Nw 42nd St Ste 105 (98107-4506)
PHONE..................425 224-5602
Steven Teeter, *President*
EMP: 2
SALES (est): 151.3K **Privately Held**
SIC: 2752 Commercial printing, lithographic

(G-11365)
UNAUTHORIZED SCREEN PRINTING
6701 Greenwood Ave N (98103-5225)
PHONE..................425 502-1150
EMP: 2
SALES (est): 83.9K **Privately Held**
SIC: 2752 Commercial printing, lithographic

(G-11366)
UNDEAD LABS LLC
308 Occidental Ave S (98104-3884)
PHONE..................206 452-0590
William Strain,
EMP: 1
SALES (est): 1.1MM
SALES (corp-wide): 110.3B **Publicly Held**
SIC: 7372 Application computer software
PA: Microsoft Corporation
1 Microsoft Way
Redmond WA 98052
425 882-8080

(G-11367)
UNDERGROUND1969 CO
2606 2nd Ave (98121-1212)
PHONE..................747 254-0595
Analise Spensieri, *President*
EMP: 2
SALES (est): 81.8K **Privately Held**
SIC: 2844 Toilet preparations

(G-11368)
UNIGEN INC
3005 1st Ave (98121-1010)
PHONE..................360 486-8200
Ed Cannon, *CEO*
B William Lee, *Chairman*
Wenwen MA, *Vice Pres*
CM Pyo, *CFO*
Sang Shin, *Accounts Mgr*
▲ EMP: 18
SQ FT: 15,000
SALES (est): 4.2MM **Privately Held**
WEB: www.upi1.com
SIC: 2834 Pharmaceutical preparations
PA: Econet, Inc.
3005 1st Ave
Seattle WA 98121

(G-11369)
UNITED ASSOCIATION OF JOURNEYM
Also Called: Sprinkler Fitters Local Un 699
2800 1st Ave Ste 3 (98121-1144)
PHONE..................206 441-0737
Kelly Simmons, *President*
John Allen, *Vice Pres*
EMP: 2
SALES: 2.3MM **Privately Held**
SIC: 3569 Sprinkler systems, fire: automatic

(G-11370)
UNITED ELECTRIC MOTORS INC
1510 Nw 46th St (98107-4709)
PHONE..................206 624-0044
Richard Waller, *President*
Kathleen Waller, *Vice Pres*
EMP: 4
SQ FT: 2,000

GEOGRAPHIC SECTION

Seattle - King County (G-11397)

SALES: 1MM **Privately Held**
SIC: 5063 5999 7694 Motors, electric; motors, electric; electric motor repair

(G-11371)
UNITED MACHINE SHOPS INC
9448 17th Ave Sw (98106-2709)
PHONE..................................206 767-0100
Royal Ruetter, *President*
Gunnar Wiskoff, *Office Mgr*
EMP: 2
SQ FT: 600
SALES (est): 236.1K **Privately Held**
SIC: 3599 Machine shop, jobbing & repair

(G-11372)
UNITED REPROGRAPHICS L L C
Also Called: United Print Signs Graphics
1750 4th Ave S (98134-1502)
PHONE..................................206 382-1177
Brian Sims,
EMP: 32
SQ FT: 10,000
SALES (est): 6MM **Privately Held**
WEB: www.unitedreprographics.com
SIC: 2752 2732 2754 7389 Commercial printing, offset; promotional printing, lithographic; books: printing only; pamphlets: printing & binding, not published on site; color printing, gravure; printers' services: folding, collating

(G-11373)
UNITED STATES BAKERY
Franz Bakery
2006 S Weller St (98144-2237)
P.O. Box 24327 (98124-0327)
PHONE..................................206 726-7535
K Van Emerick, *Controller*
EMP: 650
SALES (corp-wide): 541.5MM **Privately Held**
SIC: 2051 5149 Bakery: wholesale or wholesale/retail combined; bakery products
PA: United States Bakery
315 Ne 10th Ave
Portland OR 97232
503 232-2191

(G-11374)
UNITED STATES BAKERY
Franz Bakery
2901 6th Ave S (98134-2103)
P.O. Box 3664 (98124-3664)
PHONE..................................206 682-2244
Murray R Albers, *CEO*
EMP: 175
SALES (corp-wide): 541.5MM **Privately Held**
SIC: 2051 5149 Bakery: wholesale or wholesale/retail combined; bakery products
PA: United States Bakery
315 Ne 10th Ave
Portland OR 97232
503 232-2191

(G-11375)
UNITED VISUAL COMMS GRP LLC
1750 4th Ave S (98134-1502)
PHONE..................................206 228-5144
Brian Sims,
EMP: 8 **EST:** 2014
SQ FT: 2,000
SALES: 10MM **Privately Held**
SIC: 3993 Signs & advertising specialties

(G-11376)
UNIVERSAL ALLOY CORPORATION
5450 Beach Dr Sw (98136-1046)
PHONE..................................253 350-4079
Dean Mick, *Principal*
EMP: 200
SALES (corp-wide): 121.2MM **Privately Held**
SIC: 3354 Aluminum extruded products
HQ: Universal Alloy Corporation
180 Lamar Haley Pkwy
Canton GA 30114
888 479-7230

(G-11377)
UNIVERSAL REPAIR SHOP INC
1611 Boylston Ave (98122-2217)
P.O. Box 22049 (98122-0049)
PHONE..................................206 322-2726
Robert Schwennsen Jr, *President*
Robert Schwennsen Sr, *President*
Clinton Rost, *Corp Secy*
Florence Schwennsen, *Vice Pres*
EMP: 11
SQ FT: 6,200
SALES (est): 2MM **Privately Held**
WEB: www.universalrepairshop.com
SIC: 3546 7699 Power-driven handtools; hydraulic equipment repair

(G-11378)
UNIVERSE BUILDERS INC
999 3rd Ave Ste 700 (98104-4039)
PHONE..................................206 390-4313
Thomas Riecken, *President*
EMP: 4
SALES (est): 181K **Privately Held**
SIC: 3944 7371 Electronic games & toys; computer software development & applications

(G-11379)
UNIVERSITY OF WASHINGTON
Also Called: Copy Duplicating Service
3900 7th Ave Ne (98195-0004)
P.O. Box 359000 (98195-9000)
PHONE..................................206 543-5680
Eric Mosher, *Branch Mgr*
EMP: 200
SALES (corp-wide): 5.1B **Privately Held**
WEB: www.washington.edu
SIC: 2752 8221 Commercial printing, lithographic; university
PA: University Of Washington Inc
4311 11th Ave Ne Ste 600
Seattle WA 98105
206 543-2100

(G-11380)
UNIVERSITY OF WASHINGTON
Also Called: Computing & Communications
4333 Brooklyn Ave Ne (98195-1016)
P.O. Box 395504 (98195-0001)
PHONE..................................206 543-2565
Mark Emmerc, *Branch Mgr*
EMP: 400
SALES (corp-wide): 5.1B **Privately Held**
WEB: www.washington.edu
SIC: 3999 8221 Honeycomb foundations (beekeepers' supplies); university
PA: University Of Washington Inc
4311 11th Ave Ne Ste 600
Seattle WA 98105
206 543-2100

(G-11381)
UNIVERSITY OF WASHINGTON
Also Called: Journal Fncl Qntitative Analis
115 Lewis Hall (98195-0001)
P.O. Box 353200 (98195-3200)
PHONE..................................206 543-4598
Marty Auvil, *Director*
Thomas Gilbert, *Training Spec*
EMP: 4
SALES (corp-wide): 5.1B **Privately Held**
WEB: www.washington.edu
SIC: 2741 2711 2721 Miscellaneous publishing; newspapers, publishing & printing; periodicals
PA: University Of Washington Inc
4311 11th Ave Ne Ste 600
Seattle WA 98105
206 543-2100

(G-11382)
UNIVERSITY OF WASHINGTON
Also Called: Publications Services
3900 7th Ave Ne (98195-0004)
P.O. Box 359000 (98195-9000)
PHONE..................................206 543-5680
Jean Hayes, *Vice Pres*
Carter Ashley, *Research*
Patricia Lichiello, *Marketing Staff*
Katie Mercurio, *Marketing Staff*
Frank Davis, *Branch Mgr*
EMP: 230

SALES (corp-wide): 5.1B **Privately Held**
WEB: www.washington.edu
SIC: 2752 8221 Commercial printing, lithographic; colleges universities & professional schools
PA: University Of Washington Inc
4311 11th Ave Ne Ste 600
Seattle WA 98105
206 543-2100

(G-11383)
UNIVERSITY OF WASHINGTON
University of Washington Press
1326 5th Ave Ste 555 (98101-2604)
P.O. Box 50096 (98145-5096)
PHONE..................................206 543-4050
John P Soden, *Director*
EMP: 36
SALES (corp-wide): 5.1B **Privately Held**
WEB: www.washington.edu
SIC: 2731 8221 Books: publishing only; university
PA: University Of Washington Inc
4311 11th Ave Ne Ste 600
Seattle WA 98105
206 543-2100

(G-11384)
UNIVERSITY OF WASHINGTON
Also Called: University News and Info Svc
B54 Gerberding Hall (98195-0001)
P.O. Box 351207 (98195-1207)
PHONE..................................206 543-2580
Robert Roseth, *Director*
Linda Dodson, *Admin Asst*
EMP: 13
SALES (corp-wide): 5.1B **Privately Held**
WEB: www.washington.edu
SIC: 2741 8743 2711 Newsletter publishing; public relations services; newspapers
PA: University Of Washington Inc
4311 11th Ave Ne Ste 600
Seattle WA 98105
206 543-2100

(G-11385)
UNIVERSITY REPROGRAPHICS INC
150 Nickerson St Ste 109 (98109-1634)
PHONE..................................206 633-0925
Jeffery Thurston, *President*
EMP: 5
SQ FT: 6,000
SALES: 800K **Privately Held**
WEB: www.universityrepro.com
SIC: 7335 7334 2752 5199 Commercial photography; blueprinting service; commercial printing, offset; architects' supplies (non-durable); bookbinding & related work

(G-11386)
UNIX PACKAGES LLC
Also Called: Sunfreeware
9257 9th Ave Nw (98117-2220)
PHONE..................................206 310-4610
Colin Prior, *Partner*
Steve Christensen, *Co-Owner*
EMP: 5
SALES (est): 417.1K **Privately Held**
SIC: 7371 7372 7373 7378 Software programming applications; prepackaged software; systems engineering, computer related; computer & data processing equipment repair/maintenance

(G-11387)
UPSTART INDUSTRIES LLC
1803 Nw 83rd St (98117-3649)
PHONE..................................206 265-1521
Cory Clark, *Principal*
EMP: 2
SALES (est): 109.6K **Privately Held**
SIC: 3999 Manufacturing industries

(G-11388)
UPTAKE MEDICAL TECHNOLOGY INC (PA)
936 N 34th St Ste 200 (98103-8869)
PHONE..................................206 926-7405
Robert Barry, *President*
Mary Ann Mason, *Accountant*
EMP: 6 **EST:** 2016
SALES: 2MM **Privately Held**
SIC: 3841 Surgical & medical instruments

(G-11389)
URBAN BUGGY LLC
Also Called: Urban Buggy Farm, The
308 22nd Ave S Ste 101 (98144-2260)
P.O. Box 28536 (98118-8536)
PHONE..................................206 743-5727
Dennis Comer, *Mng Member*
EMP: 2
SALES (est): 157.8K **Privately Held**
SIC: 5149 2833 4215 0161 Natural & organic foods; specialty food items; medicinals & botanicals; package delivery, vehicular; parcel delivery, vehicular; vegetables & melons; direct selling establishments

(G-11390)
URBAN FAMILY BREWING CO
4441 26th Ave W (98199-1218)
PHONE..................................206 861-6769
Andy Gundel, *Opers Staff*
EMP: 2
SALES (est): 62.3K **Privately Held**
SIC: 2082 Malt beverages

(G-11391)
URBAN PRESS INC
317 S Bennett St (98108-2228)
PHONE..................................206 325-4060
Patricia Carlisle, *President*
Karen Jensen, *Vice Pres*
EMP: 3
SQ FT: 4,000
SALES: 550K **Privately Held**
WEB: www.urbanpressseattle.com
SIC: 2752 Commercial printing, offset

(G-11392)
US FAB
1801 16th Ave Sw (98134-1017)
PHONE..................................206 623-1635
EMP: 8
SALES (est): 1.5MM **Privately Held**
SIC: 3731 Military ships, building & repairing

(G-11393)
US MILL WORKS LLC
2203 N 59th St (98103-5747)
PHONE..................................206 355-5143
Brad Degrazia, *Principal*
EMP: 2 **EST:** 2012
SALES (est): 189.6K **Privately Held**
SIC: 2431 Millwork

(G-11394)
US STARCRAFT CORPORATION
703 30th Ave Apt B (98122-5066)
PHONE..................................206 762-0607
Karl Mayer, *President*
EMP: 6
SALES (est): 821.6K **Privately Held**
SIC: 3446 Architectural metalwork

(G-11395)
USA PRINTING CORPORATION
Also Called: Seattle Chinese News
2010 Ne 137th St (98125-3338)
PHONE..................................206 682-2423
Shiaoshia Shu, *Branch Mgr*
EMP: 8
SALES (est): 442K
SALES (corp-wide): 2.4MM **Privately Held**
WEB: www.gedn.com
SIC: 2711 2741 Newspapers; miscellaneous publishing
PA: U.S.A. Printing Corporation
11122 Bellaire Blvd
Houston TX 77072
281 498-4310

(G-11396)
UTILIKILTS CO LLC
620 1st Ave (98104-2210)
PHONE..................................206 282-4226
Steven Villegas,
EMP: 16
SQ FT: 3,500
SALES (est): 1.7MM **Privately Held**
SIC: 2325 Men's & boys' trousers & slacks

(G-11397)
UTRIP INC
2101 4th Ave Ste 1020 (98121-2313)
PHONE..................................509 954-9393

Seattle - King County (G-11398) — GEOGRAPHIC SECTION

Gilad Berenstein, *CEO*
EMP: 18
SQ FT: 2,500
SALES (est): 346.8K **Privately Held**
SIC: 7372 Business oriented computer software

(G-11398)
VALENCE SURFACE TECH LLC
Also Called: Mapsco
8135 1st Ave S (98108-4202)
PHONE 206 762-5855
Mary Smith, *President*
EMP: 200
SALES (corp-wide): 103MM **Privately Held**
SIC: 3479 7389 8734 3471 Painting, coating & hot dipping; inspection & testing services; testing laboratories; plating & polishing
PA: Valence Surface Technologies Llc
1790 Hughes Landing Blvd
The Woodlands TX 77380
855 370-5920

(G-11399)
VALIDIGM BIOTECHNOLOGY INC
3417 Evanston Ave N # 327 (98103-8626)
PHONE 415 205-3377
Donna Hines, *Director*
EMP: 2 **EST:** 2012
SALES (est): 172.7K **Privately Held**
SIC: 3699 High-energy particle physics equipment

(G-11400)
VAMPT AMERICA INC (PA)
2212 Queen Anne Ave N (98109-2312)
PHONE 800 508-6149
EMP: 0 **EST:** 2006
SALES (est): 1.9MM **Publicly Held**
SIC: 2082 Producer Of And Distributor Of Ready-To-Drink Flavored Malt Alcoholic Beverages

(G-11401)
VAMPT BEVERAGE USA CORP
2212 Queen Anne Ave N (98109-2312)
PHONE 800 508-6149
EMP: 15 **EST:** 2011
SALES (est): 760K
SALES (corp-wide): 1.9MM **Publicly Held**
SIC: 2082 Producer And Distributor Of Ready-To-Drink Flavored Malt Beverages
PA: Vampt America, Inc.
2212 Queen Anne Ave N
Seattle WA 98109
800 508-6149

(G-11402)
VANA LIFE FOODS LP
98 S Jackson St (98104)
PHONE 347 446-6504
Krishan Walia, *Partner*
EMP: 4 **EST:** 2014
SALES (est): 256K **Privately Held**
SIC: 2099 Food preparations

(G-11403)
VANEX INDUSTRIES LLC
186 35th Ave E (98112-4920)
PHONE 206 860-0455
Jerry Parrish, *Bd of Directors*
EMP: 2 **EST:** 2011
SALES (est): 135.2K **Privately Held**
SIC: 3999 Pet supplies

(G-11404)
VANGUARD PRESS
8300 Greenwood Ave N (98103-4235)
PHONE 206 782-1448
Fax: 206 789-4335
EMP: 2 **EST:** 2008
SALES (est): 100K **Privately Held**
SIC: 2759 Commercial Printing

(G-11405)
VARIETY SHOW STUDIOS LLC
1545 Nw Market St Apt 205 (98107-5350)
PHONE 571 242-1724
Paul Pilone, *Mng Member*
Alfred Janavel,
EMP: 2

SALES: 10K **Privately Held**
SIC: 7372 7389 Application computer software;

(G-11406)
VAUPELL INDUSTRIAL PLAS INC (HQ)
1144 Nw 53rd St (98107-3735)
PHONE 206 784-9050
Joe Jahn, *President*
Kelly Schroeder, *Treasurer*
▲ **EMP:** 410
SALES (est): 175.1MM **Privately Held**
SIC: 3089 Injection molding of plastics

(G-11407)
VAUPELL MOLDING & TOOLING INC (DH)
1144 Nw 53rd St (98107-3735)
PHONE 206 784-9050
Joe Jahn, *President*
Matthew Jennings, *Engineer*
▲ **EMP:** 100
SALES (est): 25.2MM **Privately Held**
SIC: 3089 Injection molding of plastics

(G-11408)
VELOTRON HEAVY INDUSTRIES
3515 Meridian Ave N (98103-9121)
PHONE 206 799-5089
EMP: 2
SALES (est): 115.8K **Privately Held**
SIC: 3999 Mfg Misc Products

(G-11409)
VENDORHAWK INC
12038 70th Pl S (98178-4120)
PHONE 360 903-3744
Patrick Lowndes, *President*
Brian Geihsler, *CTO*
EMP: 2
SALES (est): 176.2K
SALES (corp-wide): 2.6B **Publicly Held**
SIC: 7372 7371 Prepackaged software; software programming applications
PA: Servicenow, Inc.
2225 Lawson Ln
Santa Clara CA 95054
408 501-8550

(G-11410)
VENSPARK INC
2700 4th Ave S (98134-1942)
PHONE 206 588-2756
EMP: 2 **EST:** 2017
SALES (est): 104.1K **Privately Held**
SIC: 3999 6799 ; venture capital companies

(G-11411)
VENTURI HOLDINGS LLC
Also Called: Wright Machine
719 S Monroe St (98108-4352)
PHONE 206 305-0642
Max Zimmerman,
EMP: 6 **EST:** 2015
SALES (est): 483.1K **Privately Held**
SIC: 3599 Machine & other job shop work

(G-11412)
VERALLIA
5801 E Marginal Way S (98134-2413)
PHONE 206 762-0660
Lee Harmon, *President*
EMP: 3
SALES (est): 135.8K **Privately Held**
SIC: 3221 Glass containers

(G-11413)
VERICLOUDS
555 8th Ave (98125)
PHONE 844 532-5332
EMP: 50
SALES (est): 955.3K **Privately Held**
SIC: 7372 Prepackaged Software Services

(G-11414)
VICIS INC
570 Mercer St (98109-4655)
PHONE 206 456-6680
David Marver, *CEO*
Gary Kaplan, *COO*
Bill Osborn, *Vice Pres*
Frank Pietromonaco, *Vice Pres*
Tony Titus, *Vice Pres*

EMP: 47
SQ FT: 10,000
SALES (est): 303.7K **Privately Held**
SIC: 3949 Football equipment & supplies, general

(G-11415)
VIETNAMESE NW NEWSPPR & ANNUAL
Also Called: Vietnamese NW Newsppr & Yellow
6951 M L King Jr Way S (98118)
PHONE 206 722-6984
Kim Pham, *President*
EMP: 10
SALES (est): 779.3K **Privately Held**
SIC: 2759 Commercial printing

(G-11416)
VIEW POINT GLOBAL INC
1700 7th St Ave Ste 110 (98101)
PHONE 206 714-4884
Mario Sanchez, *CEO*
Jack Hale, *President*
Edward Alexander, *Treasurer*
EMP: 10
SALES (est): 1.2MM **Privately Held**
SIC: 2079 Olive oil

(G-11417)
VIGOR FAB LLC
1801 16th Ave Sw (98134-1017)
PHONE 206 623-1635
Art Parker, *Manager*
EMP: 2 **EST:** 2015
SALES (est): 322.4K **Privately Held**
SIC: 3731 Shipbuilding & repairing

(G-11418)
VIGOR MARINE LLC
1801 16th Ave Sw (98134-1017)
PHONE 206 623-1635
Adam Beck, *Branch Mgr*
EMP: 300
SALES (corp-wide): 599.5MM **Privately Held**
SIC: 3731 Shipbuilding & repairing
HQ: Vigor Marine Llc
5555 N Channel Ave # 71
Portland OR 97217
503 247-1804

(G-11419)
VIGOR SHIPYARDS INC
1801 16th Ave Sw (98134-1017)
P.O. Box 3806 (98124-3806)
PHONE 206 623-1635
Frank J Foti, *President*
David R Whitcomb, *COO*
Lon V Leneve, *CFO*
Berger A Dodge, *Treasurer*
Deena Wallis York, *Controller*
▲ **EMP:** 580 **EST:** 1977
SQ FT: 400,000
SALES (est): 104.6MM
SALES (corp-wide): 599.5MM **Privately Held**
WEB: www.toddpacific.com
SIC: 3731 Shipbuilding & repairing
HQ: Puget Sound Commerce Center, Inc.
1801 16th Ave Sw
Seattle WA 98134
206 623-1635

(G-11420)
VIKING FIRE
4710 Ballard Ave Nw (98107-4850)
PHONE 206 715-8052
Steve Anderson, *Owner*
EMP: 2 **EST:** 2009
SALES (est): 109.8K **Privately Held**
SIC: 2899 Fire retardant chemicals

(G-11421)
VINO VERITE
4908 Rainier Ave S Ste C (98118-2893)
PHONE 206 324-0324
Thomas Hajduk, *Bd of Directors*
EMP: 7
SALES (est): 571K **Privately Held**
SIC: 2084 Wines

(G-11422)
VIRTUAL STREAM
9751 43rd Pl Sw (98136-2701)
PHONE 206 938-3886

August Kristoferson, *President*
EMP: 2
SALES (est): 95K **Privately Held**
WEB: www.virtualstream.com
SIC: 5045 3355 Computer software; structural shapes, rolled, aluminum

(G-11423)
VISION LEADERSHIP INC
14306 22nd Ave Ne (98125-3318)
PHONE 206 418-0808
Valdo O Lallemand, *President*
Rob Hyman, *Officer*
EMP: 2
SALES (est): 133.1K **Privately Held**
WEB: www.visionleadership.com
SIC: 8742 3949 Training & development consultant; track & field athletic equipment

(G-11424)
VISION PRESS INC
4018 2nd Ave Nw (98107-4915)
PHONE 206 782-8476
Stan Thomas, *President*
Diane Thomas, *Vice Pres*
EMP: 4
SQ FT: 5,500
SALES (est): 780K **Privately Held**
WEB: www.visionpress.com
SIC: 2752 Commercial printing, offset

(G-11425)
VISTA COPY AND PRINT
12354 15th Ave Ne Ste E (98125-4878)
PHONE 206 715-2011
EMP: 4
SALES (est): 347.3K **Privately Held**
SIC: 2752 Commercial printing, offset

(G-11426)
VISTAPRINT
12545 Phinney Ave N (98133-8051)
PHONE 703 868-1794
Lindsay Koehler, *Principal*
EMP: 2
SALES (est): 97.7K **Privately Held**
SIC: 2752 Commercial printing, lithographic

(G-11427)
VISTAPRINT
3406 18th Ave S (98144-6704)
PHONE 206 973-0324
Michal Bryc, *Principal*
EMP: 2 **EST:** 2010
SALES (est): 147.1K **Privately Held**
SIC: 2752 Commercial printing, lithographic

(G-11428)
VITAL JUICE CO INC
1424 4th Ave Ste 800 (98101-2235)
PHONE 206 258-4203
Edward Balassanian, *CEO*
Olga Longan, *CFO*
EMP: 25
SQ FT: 3,000
SALES (est): 4MM **Privately Held**
SIC: 2033 Vegetable juices: fresh; fruit juices: fresh

(G-11429)
VODKA IS VEGAN LLC
1425 Broadway Ste 474 (98122-3854)
PHONE 206 278-4257
Matt Letten, *Mng Member*
EMP: 2
SALES (est): 62.3K **Privately Held**
SIC: 2085 Vodka (alcoholic beverage)

(G-11430)
VOYAGER RCORDINGS PUBLICATIONS
424 35th Ave (98122-6412)
PHONE 206 323-1112
Vivian Williams, *Owner*
Philip Williams, *Co-Owner*
EMP: 2
SALES: 50K **Privately Held**
WEB: www.voyagerrecords.com
SIC: 2782 Record albums

GEOGRAPHIC SECTION

Seattle - King County (G-11459)

(G-11431)
VULCAN TECHNOLOGIES LLC
505 5th Ave S Ste 900 (98104-3821)
PHONE...................................206 342-2000
Paul Allen,
Paul G Allen,
Susan Drake,
Christopher Purcell,
EMP: 2
SALES (est): 127.7K **Privately Held**
SIC: 7372 Application computer software

(G-11432)
W SYSTEMS
906 14th Ave E (98112-3904)
PHONE...................................425 616-2512
Uwais Khan, *Principal*
EMP: 2
SALES (est): 104.8K **Privately Held**
SIC: 3589 Water treatment equipment, industrial

(G-11433)
WALLBEDS NORTHWEST INC
2801 1st Ave Ste D (98121-1140)
PHONE...................................206 256-1700
Jack Hchuster, *Branch Mgr*
EMP: 2
SALES (corp-wide): 2.1MM **Privately Held**
WEB: www.wallbedsnw.com
SIC: 2515 5712 Sleep furniture; furniture stores
PA: Wallbeds Northwest Inc.
  17646 Ne 65th St
  Redmond WA 98052
  425 284-6692

(G-11434)
WALTS ORGANIC FERT CO INC
2209 W Elmore St (98199-1243)
P.O. Box 31580 (98103-1580)
PHONE...................................206 297-9092
Walter T Benecki, *CEO*
EMP: 3
SALES (est): 388.4K **Privately Held**
WEB: www.waltsorganic.com
SIC: 2873 0782 Fertilizers: natural (organic), except compost; lawn & garden services

(G-11435)
WANDERBACK DISTILLERY LLC
333 W Kinnear Pl (98119-3732)
PHONE...................................206 390-7530
Philip Downer, *Principal*
EMP: 3
SALES (est): 181.2K **Privately Held**
SIC: 2085 Distilled & blended liquors

(G-11436)
WARMINGTON & NORTH CO INC
3408 Densmore Ave N (98103-9030)
PHONE...................................206 324-5043
Todd Warmington, *President*
Julie North, *Principal*
Carter Warmington-Nort, *Manager*
EMP: 10
SQ FT: 1,500
SALES (est): 910K **Privately Held**
WEB: www.warmingtonandnorth.com
SIC: 1751 1542 1521 2522 Cabinet building & installation; commercial & office buildings, renovation & repair; general remodeling, single-family houses; office furniture, except wood

(G-11437)
WASHINGTON BIODIESEL LLC
1730 Nw Greenbrier Way (98177-5325)
PHONE...................................206 297-6101
Daniel Malarkey, *Mng Member*
Jeff Stephens, *Mng Member*
EMP: 2
SQ FT: 1,500
SALES (est): 245.5K **Privately Held**
SIC: 5169 2899 Chemicals & allied products; chemical supplies for foundries

(G-11438)
WASHINGTON CHAIN & SUPPLY INC (DH)
Also Called: Marquip
2901 Utah Ave S (98134-1833)
P.O. Box 3645 (98124-3645)
PHONE...................................206 623-8500
Gabriel Benavidez, *President*
Bert Cehovet, *Corp Secy*
Lance Eggers, *Engineer*
◆ EMP: 33
SQ FT: 80,000
SALES (est): 26MM
SALES (corp-wide): 59MM **Privately Held**
WEB: www.wachain.com
SIC: 5072 5088 5051 3429 Hardware; marine supplies; rope, wire (not insulated); manufactured hardware (general)
HQ: Branford Chain, Inc.
  150 E 58th St Fl 29
  New York NY 10155
  212 644-8600

(G-11439)
WASHINGTON DILY DCSION SVC LLC
7018 19th Ave Nw (98117-5609)
PHONE...................................206 250-1138
Horst H Faust, *President*
EMP: 3
SALES (est): 112.6K **Privately Held**
SIC: 2711 Newspapers, publishing & printing

(G-11440)
WASHINGTON HARDWOODS CO LLC
3257 17th Ave W (98119-1763)
P.O. Box 20, Springfield OR (97477-0086)
PHONE...................................206 283-7574
David Wezea, *Mng Member*
▼ EMP: 30
SQ FT: 40,000
SALES (est): 7MM **Privately Held**
WEB: www.washingtonhardwoods.com
SIC: 2431 Millwork

(G-11441)
WASHINGTON PUBLISHING COMPANY (PA)
2107 Elliott Ave Ste 305 (98121-2159)
PHONE...................................425 562-2245
Steven R Bass, *President*
Roger Honz, *CFO*
EMP: 7
SQ FT: 1,700
SALES (est): 838.4K **Privately Held**
SIC: 2741 Miscellaneous publishing

(G-11442)
WASHINGTON WEB COMPANY INC
Also Called: Consolidated Press
600 S Spokane St (98134-2225)
PHONE...................................206 441-1844
Gary Stone, *President*
Bob Brown, *CFO*
▲ EMP: 145
SQ FT: 38,000
SALES (est): 15MM **Privately Held**
WEB: www.consolidatedpress.com
SIC: 2711 Newspapers, publishing & printing

(G-11443)
WATCHGUARD TECHNOLOGIES INC (PA)
505 5th Ave S Ste 500 (98104-3892)
PHONE...................................206 613-6600
Prakash Panjwani, *CEO*
Demetri Fanourgiakis, *President*
Erik Holverson, *Partner*
Darlene Corrie, *General Mgr*
Alan Chan, *Regional Mgr*
▲ EMP: 200
SQ FT: 100,000
SALES (est): 97.1MM **Privately Held**
WEB: www.watchguard.com
SIC: 7372 Business oriented computer software

(G-11444)
WATER BEETLE USA (PA)
13511 36th Ave Ne (98125-3710)
PHONE...................................702 899-2266
Alison West, *President*
EMP: 2
SALES (est): 1MM **Privately Held**
SIC: 3569 Filters, general line: industrial

(G-11445)
WATERSTONE BRANDS INC
1211 E Denny Way Ste 22b (98122-2516)
PHONE...................................800 579-3644
Harvey Jones, *President*
▲ EMP: 5
SALES (est): 864.6K **Privately Held**
SIC: 2321 Men's & boys' sports & polo shirts

(G-11446)
WE INDUSTRIES LLC
1519 10th Ave W (98119-3230)
PHONE...................................206 853-4505
EMP: 2 EST: 2017
SALES (est): 106.7K **Privately Held**
SIC: 3999 Manufacturing industries

(G-11447)
WELCOME ROAD WINERY
4415 Sw Stevens St (98116-2433)
PHONE...................................206 778-3028
Kristen Dorrity, *Principal*
EMP: 4
SALES (est): 153.6K **Privately Held**
SIC: 2084 Wines

(G-11448)
WELLPEPPER INC
3502 Fremont Ave N (98103-3418)
PHONE...................................206 455-7377
Anne Weiler, *CEO*
Mike Van Snellenberg, *Admin Sec*
EMP: 2 EST: 2013
SALES (est): 185.7K **Privately Held**
SIC: 7372 Business oriented computer software

(G-11449)
WESCOLD INC
Also Called: Western Engineers
4816 15th Ave Nw (98107-4717)
PHONE...................................206 284-5710
Julie Copp, *President*
Bruce P Warren, *Vice Pres*
Lisa Harris, *Director*
Mark Youngren, *Director*
EMP: 25 EST: 1913
SQ FT: 30,000
SALES (est): 8.2MM **Privately Held**
WEB: www.wescold.com
SIC: 5078 5075 7623 3585 Refrigeration equipment & supplies; air conditioning & ventilation equipment & supplies; refrigeration repair service; refrigeration equipment, complete; engineering services

(G-11450)
WEST COAST INSULATION INC
Also Called: West Coast Waterjet
2426 W Commodore Way (98199-1265)
PHONE...................................206 459-2233
J Michael Heckinger, *President*
Kalin Tobin, *Opers Staff*
Kris Glaze, *Prgrmr*
EMP: 3 EST: 1977
SALES: 500K **Privately Held**
SIC: 3296 1742 Fiberglass insulation; insulation, buildings

(G-11451)
WEST SEATTLE BREWING COMPANY
Also Called: West Seattle Brewing Company L
2613 58th Ave Sw (98116-2227)
PHONE...................................206 708-6627
EMP: 6
SALES (est): 181.6K **Privately Held**
SIC: 2082 Malt beverages

(G-11452)
WESTERN FOIL CORPORATION
2900 1st Ave S (98134-1820)
PHONE...................................206 624-3645
Morty Weingarten, *President*
Gary Thon, *Vice Pres*
Marianne L Weingarten, *Treasurer*
Tom Weingarten, *Admin Sec*
EMP: 8
SQ FT: 16,000
SALES (est): 1.3MM **Privately Held**
SIC: 3497 2671 2396 Foil, laminated to paper or other materials; packaging paper & plastics film, coated & laminated; automotive & apparel trimmings

(G-11453)
WESTERN LIME CORP
800 5th Ave (98104-3176)
PHONE...................................604 249-1997
Linda Easterook, *Principal*
▼ EMP: 2
SALES (est): 396.1K **Privately Held**
SIC: 3274 Lime

(G-11454)
WESTERN NEON INC ✪
2902 4th Ave S (98134-1915)
PHONE...................................206 682-7738
EMP: 3 EST: 2018
SALES (est): 135.6K **Privately Held**
SIC: 2813 Neon

(G-11455)
WESTERN OPTICAL CORPORATION
1200 Mercer St (98109-5578)
PHONE...................................206 622-7627
John D'Amico Jr, *President*
Peter J D'Amico, *Corp Secy*
Vincent R Fletcher, *Vice Pres*
EMP: 60
SQ FT: 12,000
SALES: 15MM **Privately Held**
SIC: 5995 3851 5084 5048 Opticians; eyeglasses, prescription; contact lenses, prescription; eyeglasses, lenses & frames; contact lenses; safety equipment; ophthalmic goods; optometric equipment & supplies; lenses, ophthalmic

(G-11456)
WESTERN TOWBOAT COMPANY
617 Nw 40th St (98107-5028)
PHONE...................................206 789-9000
Robert H Shrewsbury Jr, *President*
Robert Shrewsbury II, *General Mgr*
Diane Shrewsbury, *Vice Pres*
Theresa Shrewsbury, *Treasurer*
Jeff Slesinger, *Human Res Mgr*
▲ EMP: 130
SQ FT: 9,000
SALES (est): 22.8MM **Privately Held**
WEB: www.westerntowboat.com
SIC: 4492 3732 Tugboat service; boat building & repairing

(G-11457)
WESTLAND DISTILLERY
2931 1st Ave S (98134-1821)
PHONE...................................206 763-5381
Emerson Lamb, *Principal*
▲ EMP: 16 EST: 2010
SALES (est): 1.9MM **Privately Held**
SIC: 2082 Malt beverages

(G-11458)
WESTWARD SEAFOODS INC
Also Called: West Ward Fishing Co
413 3rd Ave W (98119-4001)
PHONE...................................206 341-9996
Marcos Aldon, *Manager*
EMP: 3 **Privately Held**
SIC: 3732 Fishing boats: lobster, crab, oyster, etc.: small
HQ: Westward Seafoods, Inc.
  3015 112th Ave Ne Ste 100
  Bellevue WA 98004
  206 682-5949

(G-11459)
WEYERHAEUSER COMPANY (PA)
220 Occidental Ave S (98104-3120)
PHONE...................................206 539-3000
Doyle R Simons, *President*
Tim Butcher, *Engineer*
Andrea Thacker, *Accounts Mgr*
Doug Degroot, *Manager*
Steven Lau, *Manager*
◆ EMP: 1000 EST: 1900

(PA)=Parent Co (HQ)=Headquarters (DH)=Div Headquarters
✪ = New Business established in last 2 years

2019 Washington Manufacturers Register

Seattle - King County (G-11460)   GEOGRAPHIC SECTION

SALES: 7.4B Publicly Held
SIC: 2435 2611 0811 1382 Hardwood veneer & plywood; pulp mills; pulp produced from wood base; timber tracts; oil & gas exploration services; real estate investment trusts; timber, cut at logging camp

(G-11460)
WEYERHAEUSER COMPANY
601 Union St Ste 3100 (98101-1374)
PHONE.................................206 467-3600
EMP: 1325
SALES (corp-wide): 7.4B Publicly Held
SIC: 6798 1311 Real estate investment trusts; crude petroleum & natural gas
PA: Weyerhaeuser Company
    220 Occidental Ave S
    Seattle WA 98104
    206 539-3000

(G-11461)
WEYERHAEUSER COMPANY
Also Called: Weyerhaeuser Tech Ctr Div
220 Occidental Ave S (98104-3120)
PHONE.................................253 924-6373
Kim Bekkem, *Analyst*
EMP: 10
SALES (corp-wide): 7.4B Publicly Held
SIC: 2611 Pulp mills
PA: Weyerhaeuser Company
    220 Occidental Ave S
    Seattle WA 98104
    206 539-3000

(G-11462)
WEYERHAEUSER COMPANY
Also Called: Northwest Hardwoods
220 Occidental Ave S (98104-3120)
PHONE.................................425 210-5880
Rob Taylor, *Manager*
EMP: 35
SALES (corp-wide): 7.4B Publicly Held
SIC: 5031 2426 2421 Lumber: rough, dressed & finished; hardwood dimension & flooring mills; lumber: rough, sawed or planed
PA: Weyerhaeuser Company
    220 Occidental Ave S
    Seattle WA 98104
    206 539-3000

(G-11463)
WEYERHAEUSER COMPANY
220 Occidental Ave S (98104-3120)
PHONE.................................253 924-2345
Leslie Hendrix, *Engineer*
Cathy Jordan, *Finance Asst*
Jana Dobb, *Sales Staff*
Kathy Scoggins, *Manager*
Rose Fagler, *Manager*
EMP: 300
SALES (corp-wide): 7.4B Publicly Held
SIC: 2431 Millwork
PA: Weyerhaeuser Company
    220 Occidental Ave S
    Seattle WA 98104
    206 539-3000

(G-11464)
WHATCOUNTS INC
101 Yesler Way Ste 500 (98104-2587)
PHONE.................................206 709-8250
David Geller, *CEO*
Brian Ratzliff, *President*
Daniel Caplin, *Chief Mktg Ofcr*
Bill Donges, *CTO*
Aaron Ling, *Info Tech Dir*
EMP: 34
SALES (est): 3.2MM
SALES (corp-wide): 44.1MM Privately Held
WEB: www.wc4.net
SIC: 7372 Business oriented computer software
HQ: Output Services Group, Inc.
    100 Challenger Rd Ste 303
    Ridgefield Park NJ 07660

(G-11465)
WHEEL
1902 2nd Ave (98101-1155)
P.O. Box 2548 (98111-2548)
PHONE.................................206 956-0334
EMP: 3

SALES (est): 273.3K Privately Held
SIC: 3559 Wheel balancing equipment, automotive

(G-11466)
WHEELCHAIRS FOR NIGERIA
1542 Palm Ave Sw (98116-1732)
PHONE.................................206 932-6129
Mark Stewart, *Principal*
EMP: 2
SALES: 157.2K Privately Held
SIC: 3842 Wheelchairs

(G-11467)
WHEELS UP LLC
Also Called: Kari Gran
1735 Westlake Ave N # 110 (98109-3043)
PHONE.................................206 588-1573
Lisa Strain, *Partner*
Kari Gran, *Partner*
EMP: 3
SALES (est): 217.3K Privately Held
SIC: 3999 Barber & beauty shop equipment

(G-11468)
WHITBYS WHIMSIES
6717 Holly Pl Sw (98136-1741)
PHONE.................................206 937-1312
Georgia Whitby, *Owner*
Allen Whitby, *Co-Owner*
EMP: 2
SALES (est): 84.2K Privately Held
SIC: 3944 Craft & hobby kits & sets

(G-11469)
WHITE CENTER GLASS & UPHL
9443 Delridge Way Sw (98106-2783)
PHONE.................................206 762-8088
Tom McLaughlin, *President*
EMP: 6
SQ FT: 2,500
SALES (est): 580.8K Privately Held
SIC: 3211 Window glass, clear & colored

(G-11470)
WHITEPAGES INC (PA)
1301 5th Ave Ste 1600 (98101-2625)
PHONE.................................206 973-5100
Leigh McMillian, *CEO*
Alex Algard, *Chairman*
Rob Eleveld, *Vice Pres*
Ryan Curvey, *Accounts Exec*
Sergei Akulich, *Manager*
EMP: 63
SALES (est): 10MM Privately Held
WEB: www.w3data.com
SIC: 2741

(G-11471)
WHOOSHH INNOVATIONS INC
2001 W Grfeld St Bldg 156 (98119)
PHONE.................................206 801-3565
Vincent E Bryan III, *CEO*
Janine Bryan, *Vice Pres*
Jim Otten, *Chief Engr*
Ryan Johnson, *Engineer*
Jay Powers, *Executive*
EMP: 11
SALES (est): 2.8MM Privately Held
SIC: 3535 Conveyors & conveying equipment

(G-11472)
WIBOTIC INC
4545 Roosevelt Way Ne # 400 (98105-4721)
P.O. Box 352141 (98195-2141)
PHONE.................................503 484-3930
Benjamin Waters, *CEO*
Josh Pan, *Principal*
Joshua Smith, *Manager*
EMP: 3
SALES (est): 245.6K Privately Held
SIC: 3663 3629 Telemetering equipment, electronic; electronic generation equipment

(G-11473)
WIGFUR PRODUCTIONS
3658 Dayton Ave N Apt 104 (98103-9300)
PHONE.................................206 545-4306
Patty O'Hara, *Principal*
EMP: 2 EST: 2016
SALES (est): 90.8K Privately Held
SIC: 3353 Aluminum sheet, plate & foil

(G-11474)
WILD NOODLE
1615 Sunset Ave Sw (98116-1650)
PHONE.................................206 935-1100
Brian Conte, *Ch of Bd*
EMP: 2
SALES (est): 92.8K Privately Held
SIC: 7372 Educational computer software

(G-11475)
WILD TREE WOODWORKS LLC
1405 E John St Apt 9 (98112-5240)
PHONE.................................206 650-2565
David Geisen, *Principal*
EMP: 2
SALES (est): 72K Privately Held
SIC: 2431 Millwork

(G-11476)
WILLAPA BAY COMPANY INC
Also Called: Safe Ride News
220 Allaha 303 (98109)
P.O. Box 38, Edmonds (98020-0038)
PHONE.................................206 465-5616
Deborah Stewart, *President*
Nancy Beaumont, *COO*
EMP: 2
SALES (est): 180K Privately Held
SIC: 2731 Book publishing

(G-11477)
WILRIDGE WINERY
1924 Post Aly (98101-1015)
PHONE.................................206 770-9463
EMP: 2
SALES (est): 62.3K Privately Held
SIC: 2084 Wines

(G-11478)
WILSON & HAYES INC
1601 Eastlake Ave E (98102-3786)
PHONE.................................206 323-6758
David Reid, *President*
Jeanne Reid, *Corp Secy*
EMP: 8 EST: 1935
SQ FT: 20,000
SALES: 518K Privately Held
SIC: 2599 Ship furniture

(G-11479)
WILSON AND ASSOCIATES NW
Also Called: Wilcor Grounding Systems
4045 7th Ave S (98108-5240)
PHONE.................................206 292-9756
Patricia Wilson, *Ch of Bd*
Susan Wilson, *President*
Chester Wilson Jr, *Vice Pres*
EMP: 10
SQ FT: 20,000
SALES (est): 1.4MM Privately Held
SIC: 3643 3644 Ground clamps (electric wiring devices); electric conduits & fittings

(G-11480)
WILSON MACHINE WORKS INC
1038 Elliott Ave W (98119-3610)
PHONE.................................206 282-7560
Robert D Wilson Jr, *President*
Richard Irvin, *Vice Pres*
EMP: 8
SQ FT: 5,000
SALES: 150K Privately Held
SIC: 3599 Machine shop, jobbing & repair

(G-11481)
WIND PLAY INC
Also Called: Goodwins Kites
8326 24th Ave Nw (98117-4439)
PHONE.................................206 784-0414
Kathy Goodwin, *President*
EMP: 3
SQ FT: 2,700
SALES: 450K Privately Held
WEB: www.gasworksparkkiteshop.com
SIC: 3944 5091 5945 Kites; sporting & recreation goods; kite stores

(G-11482)
WINDORCO SUPPLY INC
1201 Nw 92nd St (98117-3497)
PHONE.................................206 784-9440
Gregory R Staats, *President*
EMP: 7 EST: 1961
SQ FT: 7,000

SALES: 500K Privately Held
WEB: www.windorco.com
SIC: 3442 2431 Storm doors or windows, metal; jalousies, glass, wood frame

(G-11483)
WINDWARD WAYS II LLC
12236 10th Ave Nw (98177-4308)
PHONE.................................206 364-5236
Shelagh Bradley,
Dennis Bradley,
EMP: 2
SALES (est): 163.9K Privately Held
SIC: 3511 7389 Turbines & turbine generator sets;

(G-11484)
WINEBLOCK LLC
4412 31st Ave W (98199-1436)
PHONE.................................877 919-4921
Brenda Kirkpatrick,
EMP: 2
SALES (est): 74.4K Privately Held
SIC: 2834 Lip balms

(G-11485)
WINERYBOUND LLC
80 Vine St Apt 703 (98121-1375)
PHONE.................................206 458-2831
Heather Kelly, *Principal*
EMP: 2
SALES (est): 101.3K Privately Held
SIC: 2084 Wines

(G-11486)
WINES OF SUBSTANCE
Also Called: Charles Smith Wines
1136 S Albro Pl (98108-2774)
PHONE.................................206 745-7456
David Borne, *CEO*
EMP: 10
SALES (corp-wide): 1.4MM Privately Held
SIC: 2084 Wines
PA: Wines Of Substance
    35 S Spokane St
    Walla Walla WA 99362
    509 526-5230

(G-11487)
WINN/DEVON ART GROUP LTD (PA)
6015 6th Ave S (98108-3307)
PHONE.................................604 276-4551
Hal Krieger, *CEO*
▲ EMP: 5
SQ FT: 24,000
SALES (est): 3.1MM Privately Held
WEB: www.winndevon.com
SIC: 2741 Art copy & poster publishing

(G-11488)
WINSOL LABORATORIES INC
1417 Nw 51st St (98107-5188)
PHONE.................................206 782-5500
Lesley W Winney, *President*
Debra Martin, *Vice Pres*
Gary Millard, *Vice Pres*
Elisha Dalman, *Office Mgr*
EMP: 7
SQ FT: 4,200
SALES (est): 1.6MM Privately Held
WEB: www.winsol.com
SIC: 5169 2842 Industrial chemicals; specialty cleaning & sanitation preparations; specialty cleaning preparations; sanitation preparations, disinfectants & deodorants

(G-11489)
WOF PNW POG 1 LLC
601 Union St Ste 630 (98101-2390)
PHONE.................................206 624-2144
Dan Evans, *Partner*
EMP: 4
SQ FT: 600
SALES (est): 156.7K Privately Held
SIC: 2869 Fuels

(G-11490)
WON-DOOR CORPORATION
2141 E Hamlin St (98112-2011)
PHONE.................................206 726-9449
Jim Sheehan, *Manager*
EMP: 2 Privately Held
WEB: www.wondoor.com

GEOGRAPHIC SECTION
Seattle - King County (G-11522)

SIC: 2542 Partitions & fixtures, except wood
PA: Won-Door Corporation
1865 S 3480 W
Salt Lake City UT 84104
801 973-7500

(G-11491)
WOOD-WORKS CABINETRY & DESIGN
401 S Brandon St (98108-2237)
PHONE.....................................206 257-3335
Alfred D Downs, *Administration*
▲ EMP: 3
SALES (est): 123.4K **Privately Held**
SIC: 2434 2511 Wood kitchen cabinets; wood household furniture

(G-11492)
WOODCRAFT SUPPLY LLC
5963 Corson Ave S Ste 120 (98108-2646)
PHONE.....................................206 767-6394
Tom Gibbson, *Manager*
EMP: 10
SALES (corp-wide): 221.9MM **Privately Held**
WEB: www.woodcraft.com
SIC: 5251 3553 3423 Tools, hand; planers, woodworking machines; edge tools for woodworking: augers, bits, gimlets, etc.
PA: Woodcraft Supply, Llc
1177 Rosemar Rd
Parkersburg WV 26105
304 422-5412

(G-11493)
WOOLDRIDGE BOATS INC
1303 S 96th St (98108-5011)
PHONE.....................................206 722-8998
Glen R Wooldridge, *President*
Ann Wooldridge, *Corp Secy*
Steve Boney, *Vice Pres*
Glen Wooldridge, *Manager*
▼ EMP: 15
SQ FT: 16,000
SALES (est): 2.4MM **Privately Held**
WEB: www.wooldridgeboats.com
SIC: 3732 Boat building & repairing

(G-11494)
WORD & RABY LLC
Also Called: Word & Raby Publishing
260 Ne 43rd St (98105-6549)
PHONE.....................................206 795-5267
David Bauman, *Managing Prtnr*
EMP: 2
SALES: 80K **Privately Held**
SIC: 2731 7389 Books: publishing only;

(G-11495)
WORKBENCH PRODUCTIONS LLC
1715 36th Ave S (98144-4958)
PHONE.....................................206 853-3742
Kevin Adams, *Principal*
EMP: 2
SALES (est): 138.2K **Privately Held**
SIC: 2491 Preserving (creosoting) of wood

(G-11496)
WORKHORSE IND
129 N 85th St (98103-3601)
PHONE.....................................206 257-5374
Brennan Coyle, *Principal*
EMP: 3 EST: 2016
SALES (est): 199.2K **Privately Held**
SIC: 2759 Screen printing

(G-11497)
WORKTANK ENTERPRISES LLC
Also Called: Worktank Creative Media
400 E Pine St Ste 301 (98122-2315)
PHONE.....................................206 254-0950
Melinda Partin,
Leslie A Rugaber,
EMP: 27 EST: 2000
SQ FT: 4,000
SALES: 16MM **Privately Held**
WEB: www.worktankseattle.com
SIC: 3823 Digital displays of process variables

(G-11498)
WOUND WOOD TECHNOLOGIES LLC
9131 10th Ave S (98108-4612)
PHONE.....................................206 762-0400
Dean Wilson, *Mng Member*
EMP: 10
SQ FT: 7,000
SALES: 1MM **Privately Held**
SIC: 2426 Bobbin blocks & blanks, wood

(G-11499)
WRIGHT MACHINE INC
719 S Monroe St (98108-4352)
PHONE.....................................206 305-0642
Max Zimmerman, *President*
EMP: 3 EST: 1973
SALES (est): 492.4K **Privately Held**
SIC: 3599 Machine shop, jobbing & repair

(G-11500)
WRY INK PUBLISHING LLC
2400 Nw 80th St (98117-4449)
PHONE.....................................206 714-3178
EMP: 2 EST: 2012
SALES (est): 87K **Privately Held**
SIC: 2741 Misc Publishing

(G-11501)
X MEDIA COMMUNICATIONS
113 Nw 56th St (98107-2024)
PHONE.....................................206 789-6758
Michael Sheldon, *Owner*
Eloise Sheldon, *Owner*
EMP: 2
SALES (est): 102.5K **Privately Held**
WEB: www.xmediacom.com
SIC: 2741 Miscellaneous publishing

(G-11502)
X TRACTED
3423 4th Ave S (98134-1904)
PHONE.....................................206 294-3308
Ryan Abernathy, *Owner*
EMP: 8
SALES (est): 549.3K **Privately Held**
SIC: 2657 Folding paperboard boxes

(G-11503)
XENEX SEATTLE
Also Called: Xenex Group
3600 15th Ave W Ste 201 (98119-1330)
PHONE.....................................206 281-9370
Toll Free:.........................888   -
John Foster, *President*
EMP: 7
SALES (est): 461.8K **Privately Held**
WEB: www.xenexseattle.com
SIC: 7372 Prepackaged software

(G-11504)
XETA TECHNOLOGIES INC
10303 Meridian Ave N # 101 (98133-9483)
PHONE.....................................425 653-4500
Mark Petersen, *Branch Mgr*
EMP: 4
SALES (corp-wide): 5.7B **Publicly Held**
SIC: 3661 Telephones & telephone apparatus
HQ: Xeta Technologies, Inc.
4001 N Rodney Parham Rd
Little Rock AR 72212
800 697-8153

(G-11505)
XTAEROS INC
113 Cherry St Ste 58189 (98104-2205)
PHONE.....................................206 883-4034
Travis Brandt, *President*
EMP: 8
SQ FT: 3,000
SALES (est): 1MM **Privately Held**
SIC: 3731 Offshore supply boats, building & repairing

(G-11506)
YACHT MASTERS NORTHWEST LLC
1341 N Northlake Way # 100 (98103-8995)
PHONE.....................................206 285-3460
Greg Allen,
Robert Houston,
EMP: 22
SALES (est): 2.9MM **Privately Held**
SIC: 3732 Boat building & repairing

(G-11507)
YACHTFISH MARINE INC (PA)
Also Called: Northcoast Yachts
1141 Fairview Ave N (98109-4418)
PHONE.....................................206 623-3233
Stephen Yadvish, *President*
John Barr, *Manager*
▲ EMP: 15
SQ FT: 3,000
SALES (est): 2.6MM **Privately Held**
WEB: www.yachtfishmarine.com
SIC: 3732 5551 Yachts, building & repairing; boat dealers

(G-11508)
YARDARM KNOT INC
2440 W Commodore Way # 200 (98199-1482)
PHONE.....................................206 216-0220
Alan J Chaffee, *President*
Gary Baxter, *Shareholder*
Jay Koetje, *Shareholder*
▼ EMP: 20
SQ FT: 2,500
SALES (est): 3.1MM **Privately Held**
WEB: www.yardarm.net
SIC: 2092 Fish, frozen: prepared; crab-meat, frozen

(G-11509)
YAZDI CORPORATION (PA)
Also Called: Yazdi Imports
1815 N 45th St Ste 208 (98103-6856)
PHONE.....................................425 787-6328
Julia J Garmire, *President*
Steve Garmire, *Accountant*
EMP: 2
SQ FT: 480
SALES: 990K **Privately Held**
SIC: 2331 2335 2337 5621 Women's & misses' blouses & shirts; women's, juniors' & misses' dresses; women's & misses' suits & skirts; women's specialty clothing stores

(G-11510)
YEHUN LLC
Also Called: Marakey Company, The
2729 S Elmwood Pl (98144-3131)
PHONE.....................................425 533-9641
Amen Gibreab, *Mng Member*
Amanda Gibrea,
Eleleta Gibreab,
Lelam Gibreab,
Kanna Teferi,
EMP: 2
SALES: 13K **Privately Held**
SIC: 2759 7336 7389 Screen printing; commercial art & graphic design;

(G-11511)
YIPPIE-PIE-YAY
2625 13th Ave W Apt 405 (98119-2061)
PHONE.....................................206 227-9665
Courtney Rhoades, *Administration*
EMP: 4
SALES (est): 240.9K **Privately Held**
SIC: 2051 Cakes, pies & pastries

(G-11512)
YMS
3635 S Findlay St (98118-2241)
PHONE.....................................206 354-2048
EMP: 5 EST: 2009
SQ FT: 15,000
SALES (est): 400K **Privately Held**
SIC: 2611 5093 Pulp Mill Whol Scrap/Waste Material

(G-11513)
YOULOOKFAB LLC
1600 29th Ave (98122-3206)
PHONE.....................................206 709-9541
Gregory Cox, *Principal*
EMP: 3
SALES (est): 188.5K **Privately Held**
SIC: 2399 Fabricated textile products

(G-11514)
YOUNG CORPORATION
3444 13th Ave Sw (98134-1031)
P.O. Box 3522 (98124-3522)
PHONE.....................................206 623-3274
Allen Browning, *Manager*
EMP: 40
SQ FT: 27,408
SALES (corp-wide): 22.3MM **Privately Held**
WEB: www.youngcorp.com
SIC: 3531 3313 3624 3325 Construction machinery; electrometallurgical products; carbon & graphite products; steel foundries
PA: Young Corporation
3231 Utah Ave S
Seattle WA 98134
206 624-1071

(G-11515)
YOUNG CORPORATION ✪
Also Called: Meltec Division
3444 13th Ave Sw (98134-1031)
PHONE.....................................206 623-3274
Andrea Ortiz, *Engineer*
EMP: 5 EST: 2018
SALES (est): 574.3K **Privately Held**
SIC: 3325 Steel foundries

(G-11516)
YOUNGQUIST BOAT REPAIR
2476 Westlake Ave N Ste D (98109-2263)
PHONE.....................................206 283-9555
Toren B Youngquist, *Owner*
EMP: 2
SQ FT: 4,277
SALES (est): 150K **Privately Held**
SIC: 3732 Boat building & repairing

(G-11517)
Z & Z ART LLC
2440 Western Ave Apt 212 (98121-3301)
PHONE.....................................206 669-3323
Nina Zingale, *Principal*
EMP: 2
SALES (est): 130.4K **Privately Held**
SIC: 2273 Carpets & rugs

(G-11518)
Z2LIVE INC (DH)
1420 5th Ave Ste 1900 (98101-4043)
PHONE.....................................206 890-4996
David Bluhm, *CEO*
EMP: 24
SQ FT: 17,000
SALES (est): 17.7MM
SALES (corp-wide): 7.5B **Publicly Held**
SIC: 7372 Home entertainment computer software
HQ: King.Com(Us), Llc
3100 Ocean Park Blvd
Santa Monica CA 90405
424 744-5697

(G-11519)
ZEBRA PRINT AND COPY
701 5th Ave (98104-7097)
PHONE.....................................206 223-1800
EMP: 2
SALES (est): 206.6K **Privately Held**
SIC: 2752 2711 Commercial printing, offset; job printing & newspaper publishing combined

(G-11520)
ZHURO SOFTWARE LLC
2639 Sw Nevada St (98126-2535)
PHONE.....................................206 607-9073
EMP: 2
SALES (est): 118.5K **Privately Held**
SIC: 7372 Prepackaged Software Services

(G-11521)
ZILLOW GROUP INC (PA)
1301 2nd Ave Fl 31 (98101-0003)
PHONE.....................................206 470-7000
Spencer M Rascoff, *CEO*
Richard N Barton, *Ch of Bd*
Lloyd D Frink, *President*
Paul Levine, *President*
Amy C Bohutinsky, *COO*
EMP: 148
SQ FT: 200,426
SALES: 1.3B **Publicly Held**
SIC: 7372 6531 4813 Business oriented computer software; real estate brokers & agents;

(G-11522)
ZILYN LLC
1323 Boren Ave Apt 603 (98101-3715)
PHONE.....................................360 509-2436
Martin Holladay, *Managing Dir*

EMP: 2 EST: 2014
SALES (est): 86.9K **Privately Held**
SIC: 7372 Application computer software

(G-11523)
ZOMETEK LLC
Also Called: Zometek Decking
616 S Lucile St (98108-2623)
PHONE..................,888 505-7953
Eric Penewell,
▲ EMP: 5
SALES (est): 417.2K **Privately Held**
SIC: 3996 Tile, floor: supported plastic

(G-11524)
ZONAR SYSTEMS INC (PA)
18200 Cascade Ave S # 200 (98188-4728)
PHONE..................206 878-2459
Ian McKerlich, *President*
Chad Maglaque, *Partner*
William Brinton Jr, *Senior VP*
Bill Portin, *Vice Pres*
Charles Garland, *Opers Staff*
◆ EMP: 160
SQ FT: 39,000
SALES (est): 42.8MM **Privately Held**
WEB: www.zonarsys.com
SIC: 3663 3669 Airborne radio communications equipment; intercommunication systems, electric

(G-11525)
ZUBER POLYMERS LLC
3005 Nw Market St A214 (98107-4290)
PHONE..................360 929-7888
EMP: 5
SALES (est): 495K **Privately Held**
SIC: 2822 Ethylene-propylene rubbers, EPDM polymers

(G-11526)
ZUMEDIX LP
3410 47th Ave Ne (98105-5329)
PHONE..................206 618-2848
David Sapestein, *Principal*
Eric Brown, *Principal*
EMP: 2
SALES (est): 122.8K **Privately Held**
SIC: 2834 Pharmaceutical preparations

(G-11527)
ZYMOGENETICS INC (HQ)
1201 Eastlake Ave E (98102-3702)
PHONE..................206 442-6600
Stephen Zaruby, *President*
Jeremy Levin, *Principal*
Jan K Hrstr M, *Senior VP*
David T Bonk, *Vice Pres*
Joseph Campisi Jr, *Vice Pres*
EMP: 113
SALES (est): 27MM
SALES (corp-wide): 22.5B **Publicly Held**
WEB: www.zymogenetics.com
SIC: 2834 8731 Pharmaceutical preparations; commercial physical research
PA: Bristol-Myers Squibb Company
430 E 29th St Fl 14
New York NY 10016
212 546-4000

Seattle
Kitsap County

(G-11528)
MASLACH ART GLASS A CORP
Also Called: Cuneo Furnace
7000 Blue Sky Ln Ne (98110-2623)
P.O. Box 11747 (98110-5747)
PHONE..................206 842-9212
Julia Maslach, *Vice Pres*
EMP: 2
SALES (corp-wide): 600K **Privately Held**
WEB: www.cuneofurnace.com
SIC: 3231 8412 3229 Art glass: made from purchased glass; museums & art galleries; art, decorative & novelty glassware
PA: Maslach Art Glass A Corporation
44 Industrial Way
Greenbrae CA

Seaview
Pacific County

(G-11529)
SPORTSMENS CANNERY (PA)
35th & Pacific Hwy (98644)
P.O. Box 7 (98644-0007)
PHONE..................360 642-2335
Tina Ward, *Owner*
Kevin Ward, *Co-Owner*
EMP: 15 EST: 1943
SALES: 110K **Privately Held**
SIC: 2091 Salmon: packaged in cans, jars, etc.

Sedro Woolley
Skagit County

(G-11530)
ACUNA CEDAR PRODUCTS
7906 Renic Dr (98284-7537)
P.O. Box 127 (98284-0127)
PHONE..................425 359-3224
Shelly Acuna, *Principal*
EMP: 2
SALES (est): 213.4K **Privately Held**
SIC: 2429 Special product sawmills

(G-11531)
ADVANCE SEPTIC TRTMNT SYSTEMS
8000 Parker Rd (98284-8448)
PHONE..................360 856-0550
Dean Hamilton, *President*
De Etta Hamilton, *Corp Secy*
EMP: 2 EST: 1992
SQ FT: 2,000
SALES (est): 267.8K **Privately Held**
WEB: www.advancedsepticsystems.com
SIC: 3589 Sewage & water treatment equipment

(G-11532)
BISSON & ASSOCIATES INC
Also Called: Fly By Night Welding Service
26680 Helmick Rd (98284-8330)
PHONE..................360 856-0434
Darias Bisson, *President*
Kathy Bission, *Vice Pres*
EMP: 2
SALES: 46K **Privately Held**
SIC: 7692 Welding repair

(G-11533)
BP WEST COAST PRODUCTS LLC
830 Moore St (98284-1239)
PHONE..................360 856-5022
EMP: 321
SALES (corp-wide): 298.7B **Privately Held**
SIC: 1311 Crude petroleum production
HQ: Bp West Coast Products Llc
4519 Grandview Rd
Blaine WA 98230
310 549-6204

(G-11534)
BREAST CARE CENTER
2000 Hospital Dr (98284-4327)
PHONE..................360 424-6161
Mark Studley MD, *Principal*
EMP: 12
SALES (est): 952.8K **Privately Held**
SIC: 3845 8071 3842 8011 Electromedical equipment; medical laboratories; surgical appliances & supplies; radiologist

(G-11535)
COKEDALE CREAMERY LLC
26818 Minkler Rd (98284-7936)
PHONE..................360 856-1695
Guy Stratton, *Principal*
EMP: 4
SALES (est): 144.9K **Privately Held**
SIC: 2021 Creamery butter

(G-11536)
DAY CREEK ORGANIC FARMS INC
Also Called: HI Q Compost
1020 Hodgin St (98284-4331)
PHONE..................360 856-4770
Howard D Koozer, *President*
EMP: 9
SALES: 1MM **Privately Held**
SIC: 2824 Organic fibers, noncellulosic

(G-11537)
FIBER MEADOWS ALPACAS LLC
26417 Minkler Rd (98284-7933)
PHONE..................360 856-5740
Dean C Hiestand Jr, *Administration*
EMP: 4
SALES (est): 231.4K **Privately Held**
SIC: 2231 Alpacas, mohair: woven

(G-11538)
FINCO CORP ✪
1310 Heather Ln (98284-1511)
PHONE..................360 854-0772
EMP: 2 EST: 2019
SALES (est): 81.4K **Privately Held**
SIC: 3599 Industrial machinery

(G-11539)
GENERAL MILLS INC
719 Metcalf St (98284-1420)
PHONE..................763 764-7600
Carol Starck, *Branch Mgr*
EMP: 50
SALES (corp-wide): 16.8B **Publicly Held**
WEB: www.generalmills.com
SIC: 2037 2033 2035 2099 Fruits, quick frozen & cold pack (frozen); vegetables, quick frozen & cold pack, excl. potato products; jams, including imitation: packaged in cans, jars, etc.; vegetables: packaged in cans, jars, etc.; pickles, vinegar; food preparations
PA: General Mills, Inc.
1 General Mills Blvd
Minneapolis MN 55426
763 764-7600

(G-11540)
HOW-MAC MANUFACTURING INC
Also Called: Howmac Dmnsional Letters Logos
720 Puget St Ste A (98284-1140)
PHONE..................360 855-2649
Joel Howard, *President*
Shirley McCulley, *Vice Pres*
EMP: 24
SQ FT: 15,000
SALES: 1.1MM **Privately Held**
WEB: www.howmac.com
SIC: 3086 3354 5099 Plastics foam products; aluminum extruded products; signs, except electric

(G-11541)
IMPACT STUDIO
412 Haines St (98284-1161)
PHONE..................425 890-3914
Nick Pringle, *Owner*
EMP: 2
SALES (est): 73.2K **Privately Held**
SIC: 2759 Commercial printing

(G-11542)
J&K ENTERPRISE
11344 Foxfire Ln (98284-7764)
PHONE..................360 854-0020
Jerry Burleson, *Partner*
EMP: 2 EST: 1998
SALES (est): 190K **Privately Held**
SIC: 2451 Mobile homes, personal or private use

(G-11543)
JAN-R CORPORATION (PA)
524 Rhodes Rd (98284-2502)
P.O. Box 708 (98284-0708)
PHONE..................360 856-0836
Neal Rothenbuhler, *President*
Paul Hess, *Treasurer*
Linda Dawson, *Admin Sec*
EMP: 25
SQ FT: 20,000
SALES (est): 4.2MM **Privately Held**
SIC: 3699 Security control equipment & systems

(G-11544)
JANICKI ENERGY
103 N Township St (98284-1243)
PHONE..................360 856-2068
Robert Janicki, *Owner*
EMP: 2
SALES: 100K **Privately Held**
SIC: 2869 Industrial organic chemicals

(G-11545)
JANICKI INDUSTRIES INC
1476 Moore St (98284-7522)
PHONE..................360 856-5143
EMP: 44 **Privately Held**
SIC: 3728 Aircraft assemblies, subassemblies & parts
PA: Janicki Industries, Inc.
719 Metcalf St
Sedro Woolley WA 98284

(G-11546)
JEREMY RIEKEN
2972 Cedar Ln (98284-9509)
PHONE..................360 428-7736
Jeremy Rieken, *Owner*
EMP: 3
SALES (est): 150K **Privately Held**
SIC: 2822 Synthetic rubber

(G-11547)
JETPOINT TECHNOLOGIES INC
500 Metcalf St Ste R2 (98284-1068)
P.O. Box 778 (98284-0778)
PHONE..................360 854-0518
John Swapp, *President*
EMP: 7
SALES (est): 867K **Privately Held**
WEB: www.jetpoint.com
SIC: 3599 Machine shop, jobbing & repair

(G-11548)
JIM JOHNSON & SON TRUCKING LLC
Also Called: Anderson's Logging
7755 Cully Ln (98284-8057)
PHONE..................360 770-5073
Melissa Anderson,
Donald Anderson,
EMP: 11
SALES (est): 981.8K **Privately Held**
SIC: 2411 7389 Timber, cut at logging camp;

(G-11549)
KAPLAN HOMES UNLIMITED LLC
8635 Garden Of Eden Rd (98284-8752)
PHONE..................360 855-1675
Nathan Kaplan,
EMP: 3
SALES: 30K **Privately Held**
SIC: 1521 1629 1751 1721 Single-family housing construction; land preparation construction; carpentry work; painting & paper hanging; forestry services; wood preserving

(G-11550)
LOAN GOAT WOODWORKS
929 Beachley Rd (98284-9304)
PHONE..................360 395-8996
Art Gibbons, *Principal*
EMP: 2
SALES (est): 72K **Privately Held**
SIC: 2431 Millwork

(G-11551)
MORGAN CREEK ENVMTL RSRCES INC
31409 S Skagit Hwy (98284-8612)
PHONE..................360 202-6536
Christine Morgan, *Principal*
EMP: 2
SALES: 235K **Privately Held**
SIC: 3531 Construction machinery

(G-11552)
NIELSEN BROTHERS INC
25046 State Route 20 (98284-8014)
P.O. Box 2789, Bellingham (98227-2789)
PHONE..................360 671-9078

GEOGRAPHIC SECTION

Toll Free:..................................888 -
Robert C Nielsen, *President*
David Nielsen, *Vice Pres*
EMP: 65
SALES (est): 18.6MM **Privately Held**
SIC: 5031 2411 Lumber: rough, dressed & finished; logging

(G-11553)
ONEILS FOUNDRY FORGING METAL &
1386 Moore St (98284-7524)
PHONE..................................360 941-7557
Stan Oneil, *Principal*
EMP: 2
SALES (est): 159.4K **Privately Held**
SIC: 1791 3446 5211 Iron work, structural; railings, bannisters, guards, etc.; made from metal pipe; fencing

(G-11554)
PACIFIC RIM PORTFOLIOS LTD
Also Called: Pacific Rim Forestry
120 Valley Hwy (98284-9549)
PHONE..................................360 595-2854
Bradley J Gorum, *President*
EMP: 22
SALES: 7.8MM **Privately Held**
SIC: 2411 Logging

(G-11555)
PATRIOT LEATHER COMPANY
1543 E Gateway Hts Loop (98284-6401)
PHONE..................................360 393-1392
Skyler Storm, *Principal*
EMP: 2 **EST:** 2017
SALES (est): 137K **Privately Held**
SIC: 3199 Leather goods

(G-11556)
PATRIOT SALES INC
500 Metcalf St Ste L3 (98284-1068)
PHONE..................................360 855-0737
Dick Butler, *President*
Rex Habgood, *Shareholder*
EMP: 17
SQ FT: 18,800
SALES (est): 1.7MM **Privately Held**
SIC: 3648 Street lighting fixtures

(G-11557)
PRINT IT NORTHWEST
7632 Valley View Rd (98284-8114)
PHONE..................................360 840-0807
Wes Tyra, *Principal*
EMP: 2
SALES (est): 83.9K **Privately Held**
SIC: 2752 Commercial printing, lithographic

(G-11558)
PROCTOR FARM ANIMAL REMOVAL
5509 Brookings Rd (98284-8923)
PHONE..................................360 856-1995
Dixey Proctor, *Owner*
EMP: 2
SALES: 250K **Privately Held**
SIC: 0752 2077 Animal specialty services; rendering

(G-11559)
READ E-Z
11510 Panorama Dr (98284-7976)
PHONE..................................360 708-8491
Tess Carroll, *Principal*
EMP: 2 **EST:** 2016
SALES (est): 87.7K **Privately Held**
SIC: 2741 Miscellaneous publishing

(G-11560)
RICHARDSON LOG & LAND CLEARING
5675 Brookings Rd (98284-8924)
PHONE..................................360 631-2107
Scott Richardson, *Principal*
EMP: 3
SALES (est): 213.4K **Privately Held**
SIC: 2411 Logging

(G-11561)
RONALD REX DAIRY FARM
Also Called: Rex, Ron Dairy
26455 Burmaster Rd (98284-9047)
PHONE..................................360 856-0629
Ronald Rex, *Owner*
EMP: 5
SALES (est): 262K **Privately Held**
SIC: 0241 2411 Dairy farms; logging

(G-11562)
ROTHENBUHLER ENGINEERING CO (HQ)
524 Rhodes Rd (98284-2502)
P.O. Box 708 (98284-0708)
PHONE..................................360 856-0836
Neal Rothenbuhler, *President*
Linda Dawson, *Corp Secy*
Kriss Johnson, *Vice Pres*
Darlys Yeager, *Purch Mgr*
Richard Taft, *Engineer*
EMP: 13 **EST:** 1946
SQ FT: 10,000
SALES (est): 4.1MM
SALES (corp-wide): 4.2MM **Privately Held**
WEB: www.rothenbuhlereng.com
SIC: 3663 Marine radio communications equipment; radio broadcasting & communications equipment
PA: Jan-R Corporation
524 Rhodes Rd
Sedro Woolley WA 98284
360 856-0836

(G-11563)
SAXON CONTRACTING LLC
322 Rowland Rd (98284-8075)
PHONE..................................360 595-2854
Heather Schuh, *Mng Member*
EMP: 30
SALES (est): 1.2MM **Privately Held**
SIC: 2411 Logging camps & contractors

(G-11564)
SHEA YOUR LIPS LIP BALM
190 N Murdock St Apt E107 (98284-1076)
PHONE..................................360 856-4803
Kelsi Frederic, *Principal*
EMP: 2
SALES (est): 74.4K **Privately Held**
SIC: 2834 Lip balms

(G-11565)
SIS NORTHWEST INC
500 Metcalf St (98284-1064)
PHONE..................................360 854-0074
John Norton, *Principal*
Brian Ganske, *Exec VP*
EMP: 8 **EST:** 2010
SALES (est): 978.2K **Privately Held**
SIC: 3312 Blast furnaces & steel mills

(G-11566)
SKAGIT CREST VINYRD WINERY LLC
22230 Cully Rd (98284-8734)
PHONE..................................360 630-5176
Rollin Jackson, *Principal*
EMP: 3
SALES (est): 82.6K **Privately Held**
SIC: 2084 Wines

(G-11567)
SKAGIT INDUSTRIAL STEEL INC
Also Called: SIS Northwest
500 Metcalf St Bldg A (98284-1064)
PHONE..................................360 854-0074
EMP: 30
SQ FT: 60,000
SALES (est): 2.7MM **Privately Held**
WEB: www.snelsonco.com
SIC: 1541 1542 3441 Industrial buildings & warehouses; nonresidential construction; fabricated structural metal

(G-11568)
SKAGIT RIVER REMAN COMPANY
8354 S Healy Rd (98284-5032)
PHONE..................................360 826-4344
Chad Findlay, *President*
EMP: 40 **EST:** 2013
SALES: 3MM **Privately Held**
SIC: 2421 Resawing lumber into smaller dimensions; kiln drying of lumber; lumber: rough, sawed or planed; chipper mill

(G-11569)
SMALL PLANET FOODS INC (HQ)
106 Woodworth St (98284-1431)
P.O. Box 429 (98284-0429)
PHONE..................................800 624-4123
Eugene B Kahn, *President*
Laura Calhoun, *Vice Pres*
EMP: 20
SALES (est): 8MM
SALES (corp-wide): 16.8B **Publicly Held**
WEB: www.smallplanetfoods.com
SIC: 2099 5149 Food preparations; natural & organic foods
PA: General Mills, Inc.
1 General Mills Blvd
Minneapolis MN 55426
763 764-7600

(G-11570)
SMELTS SEA MAMMAL EDUCATION LE
1003 Iowa Heights Rd (98284-9574)
PHONE..................................360 303-9338
Richard Riels, *President*
Ann Marie Riels, *Vice Pres*
EMP: 2
SALES (est): 21.1K **Privately Held**
SIC: 8299 3669 Educational services; sirens, electric: vehicle, marine, industrial & air raid

(G-11571)
SMOKEY POINT CONCRETE
Also Called: Skagit Readymix
23315 Gike Rd (98284)
PHONE..................................360 856-0422
Mark Crawford, *President*
EMP: 18
SQ FT: 1,500
SALES (est): 241.1K
SALES (corp-wide): 5.8MM **Privately Held**
WEB: www.skagitreadymix.com
SIC: 3273 Ready-mixed concrete
PA: Smokey Point Concrete, Inc.
23315 Dike Rd
Arlington WA
360 435-5791

(G-11572)
STERN & FAYE
37607 Cape Horn Rd (98284-7790)
P.O. Box 593, Mount Vernon (98273-0593)
PHONE..................................360 770-1967
Jules Remedios Faye, *Principal*
EMP: 2 **EST:** 2013
SALES (est): 137K **Privately Held**
SIC: 2752 Commercial printing, offset

(G-11573)
SUMMER MOON PRODUCTS
32069 Lyman Hamilton Hwy (98284-7913)
PHONE..................................360 826-3157
M Rogers, *Principal*
EMP: 2
SALES (est): 121.4K **Privately Held**
SIC: 3931 Musical instruments

(G-11574)
TALKIE TOOTER
524 Rhodes Rd (98284-2502)
PHONE..................................360 856-0836
Neil Rohenbuhler, *President*
Sedro Woolley, *Engineer*
Paul Hess, *Treasurer*
EMP: 25
SQ FT: 200,000
SALES (est): 958.8K
SALES (corp-wide): 4.2MM **Privately Held**
WEB: www.rothenbuhlereng.com
SIC: 8741 5945 3625 Management services; hobby, toy & game shops; relays & industrial controls
HQ: Rothenbuhler Engineering Co.
524 Rhodes Rd
Sedro Woolley WA 98284
360 856-0836

(G-11575)
TENNESON BROTHERS
Also Called: Skagvale Holsteins
10117 Fruitdale Rd (98284-8200)
PHONE..................................360 856-6242
Mark Carolyn Tenneson, *Partner*
Glen Tenneson, *Partner*
EMP: 2
SALES: 500K **Privately Held**
SIC: 0241 2411 Dairy farms; logging

(G-11576)
TOUSSINT MACHINE AND MFG LLC
307 W State St (98284-1554)
PHONE..................................360 840-0705
Joseph Toussint IV, *Co-Owner*
Vanessa Toussint, *Mng Member*
EMP: 3
SQ FT: 2,400
SALES: 300K **Privately Held**
SIC: 7699 3827 3429 5088 Industrial machinery & equipment repair; microscopes, except electron, proton & corneal; aircraft hardware; aircraft equipment & supplies

(G-11577)
TRUCKVAULT INC (PA)
315 Twnship St Sdro Wlley Sedro Woolley (98284)
P.O. Box 734 (98284-0734)
PHONE..................................360 855-0464
Al Chandler, *CEO*
Martin Pagel, *President*
Patricia Pienta, *Manager*
EMP: 40
SQ FT: 17,000
SALES (est): 7.3MM **Privately Held**
WEB: www.truckvault.com
SIC: 3714 Motor vehicle parts & accessories

(G-11578)
TUCKERS TUFFER COATINGS INC
4667 Humphrey Hill Rd (98284-7636)
PHONE..................................360 707-2168
Toll Free:..................................888 -
Mitchell Tucker, *President*
EMP: 6
SALES (est): 777.9K **Privately Held**
WEB: www.tuckerslinex.com
SIC: 3714 Pickup truck bed liners

(G-11579)
TURN PRO MANUFACTURING
938 Warner St (98284-1849)
PHONE..................................425 220-8767
James Anderson, *Principal*
EMP: 2
SALES (est): 101K **Privately Held**
SIC: 3999 Manufacturing industries

(G-11580)
WHOLE SHEBANG
401 Bennett St (98284-1622)
PHONE..................................360 941-5125
Erica Demming, *Principal*
EMP: 3
SALES (est): 155.5K **Privately Held**
SIC: 2711 Newspapers

(G-11581)
WORKSKIFF INC
500 Metcalf St Ste F1 (98284-1065)
PHONE..................................360 707-5622
George Lundgren, *President*
Steve Perry, *General Mgr*
Jeff Clark, *Principal*
Kay Clark, *Vice Pres*
◆ **EMP:** 8
SQ FT: 12,000
SALES (est): 2.2MM **Privately Held**
WEB: www.workskiff.com
SIC: 3732 Boats, fiberglass: building & repairing

Sekiu
Clallam County

(G-11582)
AL FLETCHER
Also Called: Fletcher Diving
81 Vista Ln (98381-9726)
PHONE..................................360 963-2241
Al Fletcher, *Owner*
Vivian Fletcher, *Manager*
EMP: 3

SALES (est): 150.8K **Privately Held**
SIC: 3731 Shipbuilding & repairing

(G-11583)
PATS WELDING SERVICE
Also Called: Golden Rod Services
13311 Highway 112 (98381-9733)
PHONE..................................360 963-2370
Pat Sherlock, *Owner*
EMP: 2
SALES (est): 142.8K **Privately Held**
SIC: 7692 Welding repair

Selah
Yakima County

(G-11584)
CENTURION PROCESS LLC
307 1/2 S 3rd St Selah (98942)
PHONE..................................509 759-3001
Michael Bauman, *Mng Member*
Tanya Bauman,
EMP: 4
SALES: 50K **Privately Held**
SIC: 7389 1711 3823 3491 Design services; process piping contractor; industrial process control instruments; industrial valves; industrial pumps & parts; mechanical engineering

(G-11585)
CROWN RECOGNITION
681 E Huntzinger Rd (98942-9712)
PHONE..................................509 698-4446
Jeffrey Hartwick, *Administration*
EMP: 2
SALES (est): 148.8K **Privately Held**
SIC: 2499 Trophy bases, wood

(G-11586)
DANIEL CABINETS LLC
Also Called: Built By Daniel
180 Shaw Rd (98942-9759)
PHONE..................................509 949-0855
Daniel Flathers,
EMP: 2
SALES: 350K **Privately Held**
SIC: 2434 Wood kitchen cabinets

(G-11587)
EAKIN ENTERPRISES INC
Also Called: Environmental Technologies
115 S 2nd St Ste B (98942-1321)
PHONE..................................509 698-3200
John Eakin, *President*
EMP: 10
SQ FT: 10,660
SALES (est): 2.2MM **Privately Held**
SIC: 2899 6163 Chemical preparations; mortgage brokers arranging for loans, using money of others

(G-11588)
FRAZIER INDUSTRIAL COMPANY
420 Reitmeier Ln (98942-9546)
PHONE..................................509 698-4100
Nathan Richards, *Manager*
EMP: 2
SALES (corp-wide): 281.2MM **Privately Held**
WEB: www.ecologic.com
SIC: 2542 3441 Pallet racks: except wood; fabricated structural metal
PA: Frazier Industrial Company
91 Fairview Ave
Long Valley NJ 07853
908 876-3001

(G-11589)
GRAHAM PACKAGING COMPANY LP
510 E Naches Ave (98942-9301)
PHONE..................................509 698-4545
Ken Carloson, *Manager*
EMP: 45
SQ FT: 87,360
SALES (corp-wide): 1MM **Privately Held**
WEB: www.grahampackaging.com
SIC: 3089 3085 5085 Plastic containers, except foam; plastics bottles; commercial containers

HQ: Graham Packaging Company, L.P.
700 Indian Springs Dr # 100
Lancaster PA 17601
717 849-8500

(G-11590)
H R MANAGEMENT NORTHWEST
670 Tibbling Rd (98942-9255)
PHONE..................................509 697-5377
Douglas J Southard, *Owner*
EMP: 7
SALES (est): 298.8K **Privately Held**
SIC: 2084 Wines, brandy & brandy spirits

(G-11591)
JAHRS EUROPEAN SAUSAGE & CSTM
160 Ranchette Ln (98942-9525)
PHONE..................................509 697-8904
Pete Jahr, *Owner*
EMP: 2
SALES (est): 111.6K **Privately Held**
SIC: 2011 Sausages from meat slaughtered on site

(G-11592)
JAKES ELECTRICAL SIGN SERVICE
1060 N Wenas Rd Trlr 11 (98942-9768)
PHONE..................................509 901-1012
Jerry Prater, *Principal*
EMP: 2 **EST:** 2012
SALES (est): 152.1K **Privately Held**
SIC: 3993 Signs & advertising specialties

(G-11593)
NUPRO PRODUCTS INC
2234 N Wenas Rd (98942-9536)
P.O. Box 400 (98942-0400)
PHONE..................................509 698-6983
Joan Gieseke, *President*
EMP: 6
SALES: 200K **Privately Held**
SIC: 3334 Aluminum ingots & slabs

(G-11594)
PHOENIX MAPS
1290 N Wenas Rd (98942-9535)
P.O. Box 522 (98942-0522)
PHONE..................................509 697-5059
Craig Russell, *Owner*
Donna Russell, *Co-Owner*
EMP: 2
SALES: 32K **Privately Held**
WEB: www.alittlepeaceofheaven.net
SIC: 2759 Maps: printing

(G-11595)
R & J ORGNAL KETTLEKORN SNACKS
10 Fruitspur Dr (98942-1246)
PHONE..................................509 698-5533
Linda Morse, *Partner*
Rick Morse, *Partner*
EMP: 2
SALES (est): 117.3K **Privately Held**
SIC: 2064 Popcorn balls or other treated popcorn products

(G-11596)
SHAFFER WOODWORKS LLC
211 Rainier Ln (98942-9754)
PHONE..................................509 697-3023
R Shaffer, *Principal*
EMP: 2
SALES (est): 131K **Privately Held**
SIC: 2431 Millwork

(G-11597)
SOUTHARD WINERY
670 Tibbling Rd (98942-9255)
PHONE..................................509 697-3003
Douglas Southard, *Principal*
EMP: 2
SALES (est): 75.4K **Privately Held**
SIC: 2084 Wines

(G-11598)
SUN-RYPE PRODUCTS (USA) INC
1 S Railroad Ave (98942-1401)
P.O. Box 940 (98942-0940)
PHONE..................................509 697-7292

Dave McAnerney, *CEO*
Don Vanderzwaag, *CFO*
EMP: 100
SALES (est): 21.6MM
SALES (corp-wide): 194.9MM **Privately Held**
SIC: 2037 Fruit juice concentrates, frozen
PA: Sun-Rype Products Ltd
1165 Ethel St
Kelowna BC V1Y 2
250 860-7973

(G-11599)
TRAPP INDUSTRIES
491 Buffalo Rd (98942-8622)
PHONE..................................509 895-4282
Robert Trapp, *Principal*
EMP: 2 **EST:** 2011
SALES (est): 117.7K **Privately Held**
SIC: 3999 Manufacturing industries

(G-11600)
TREE TOP INC (PA)
220 E 2nd Ave (98942-1408)
P.O. Box 248 (98942-0248)
PHONE..................................509 697-7251
Tom Hurson, *President*
Craig Green, *Vice Pres*
Cris Hales, *Vice Pres*
Ken Janes, *Vice Pres*
Gary Price, *Vice Pres*
◆ **EMP:** 900 **EST:** 1960
SQ FT: 27,000
SALES: 399.9MM **Privately Held**
WEB: www.treetop.com
SIC: 2033 2034 2037 Fruit juices: packaged in cans, jars, etc.; fruits, dried or dehydrated, except freeze-dried; frozen fruits & vegetables

(G-11601)
TREE TOP INC
220 E 2nd Ave (98942-1408)
P.O. Box 248 (98942-0248)
PHONE..................................509 698-1447
Luz Escobar, *Branch Mgr*
EMP: 95
SALES (corp-wide): 399.9MM **Privately Held**
SIC: 2033 Canned fruits & specialties
PA: Tree Top, Inc.
220 E 2nd Ave
Selah WA 98942
509 697-7251

(G-11602)
TREE TOP INC
Also Called: Ross Packing Co
101 S Railroad Ave (98942-1444)
P.O. Box 248 (98942-0248)
PHONE..................................509 698-1432
Mike Frausto, *Manager*
EMP: 90
SQ FT: 1,850
SALES (corp-wide): 399.9MM **Privately Held**
SIC: 2033 2034 2043 Fruit juices: fresh; fruits, dried or dehydrated, except freeze-dried; cereal breakfast foods
PA: Tree Top, Inc.
220 E 2nd Ave
Selah WA 98942
509 697-7251

(G-11603)
YAKIMA VALLEY PEPSI PAK
201 Merinda Dr (98942-9444)
P.O. Box 821 (98942-0821)
PHONE..................................509 952-0318
Michael Archer, *Principal*
EMP: 3
SALES (est): 146.3K **Privately Held**
SIC: 2086 Soft drinks: packaged in cans, bottles, etc.

Sequim
Clallam County

(G-11604)
A-M SYSTEMS LLC
131 Business Park Loop (98382-8338)
P.O. Box 850, Carlsborg (98324-0850)
PHONE..................................360 683-8300
Arthur Green III,

Mark Latimer,
Robert Latimer,
Whitney Latimer,
◆ **EMP:** 20
SQ FT: 16,000
SALES (est): 4.1MM **Privately Held**
WEB: www.a-msystems.com
SIC: 8731 3845 3841 3842 Commercial physical research; electromedical equipment; surgical & medical instruments; respirators

(G-11605)
ABSOLUTE SOLUTIONS
101 Ritter Rd (98382-8308)
PHONE..................................360 683-4597
EMP: 2
SALES (est): 88.9K **Privately Held**
SIC: 3442 Metal doors, sash & trim

(G-11606)
ADMIRALTY CRANE LLC
504 Taylor Cutoff Rd (98382-8281)
PHONE..................................360 461-2092
EMP: 2
SALES (est): 182.5K **Privately Held**
SIC: 3663 Mfg Radio/Tv Communication Equipment

(G-11607)
ALLFORM WELDING INC
81 Hooker Rd Unit 9 (98382-9122)
P.O. Box 175, Carlsborg (98324-0175)
PHONE..................................360 681-0584
Dan Donovan, *President*
EMP: 6
SALES: 600K **Privately Held**
WEB: www.allformwelding.com
SIC: 3441 Fabricated structural metal

(G-11608)
ALLIED TITANIUM INC
1400 E Washington St (98382-3681)
PHONE..................................302 725-8300
Christopher G Greimes, *CEO*
Gang Tian, *Vice Pres*
Amanda Snell, *Accounts Mgr*
Sean Ferris, *Manager*
EMP: 11
SQ FT: 4,000
SALES (est): 598.7K **Privately Held**
SIC: 3356 Titanium

(G-11609)
ALLPLAY SYSTEMS LLC
170 Havenwood Ln (98382-8880)
P.O. Box 1886 (98382-4332)
PHONE..................................360 808-5925
Danielle Patterson, *General Mgr*
Jeff Hansen, *General Mgr*
EMP: 2
SALES: 100K **Privately Held**
SIC: 3949 Playground equipment

(G-11610)
ALSET CORPORATION
131 Macawa Trl (98382-8177)
PHONE..................................206 335-3700
Gary L Fox, *President*
EMP: 3
SALES: 150K **Privately Held**
SIC: 3643 Current-carrying wiring devices

(G-11611)
ANGELES CONCRETE PRODUCTS INC
1369 Cays Rd (98382-8005)
PHONE..................................360 681-5429
EMP: 2 **EST:** 2014
SALES (est): 70.2K **Privately Held**
SIC: 5261 5211 5032 3273 Lawn & garden supplies; cement; concrete & cinder building products; ready-mixed concrete

(G-11612)
ARLENES KITCHEN
41 Opal Ln (98382-3873)
PHONE..................................208 254-0591
Brittany Huntsman, *Principal*
EMP: 2
SALES (est): 115.9K **Privately Held**
SIC: 3469 Kitchen fixtures & equipment: metal, except cast aluminum

GEOGRAPHIC SECTION

Sequim - Clallam County (G-11646)

(G-11613)
AWNINGS & SUNROOMS DISTINCTION
Also Called: A-Awnings of Distinction
141 Timberline Dr (98382-9238)
PHONE 360 681-2727
Brad Busher, *Owner*
EMP: 3
SALES: 200K **Privately Held**
SIC: 3448 Sunrooms, prefabricated metal

(G-11614)
BAXIS INC
2086 Old Gardiner Rd (98382-8750)
P.O. Box 2445 (98382-4343)
PHONE 360 797-0084
EMP: 3 EST: 2010
SALES (est): 158.9K **Privately Held**
SIC: 2339 Women's & misses' outerwear

(G-11615)
BLUEPENGUIN SOFTWARE INC
1400 W Washington St # 104 (98382-3236)
PHONE 561 459-5393
EMP: 2
SALES: 150K **Privately Held**
SIC: 7372 7371 Prepackaged Software Services Custom Computer Programing

(G-11616)
BOBEK ENTERPRISES
212 Cougar Crest Rd (98382-8447)
P.O. Box 2938 (98382-4351)
PHONE 360 683-8785
Robert S Hanna, *Partner*
Rebecca J Hanna, *Partner*
EMP: 2
SALES: 40K **Privately Held**
SIC: 8748 3674 Business consulting; semiconductors & related devices

(G-11617)
CHEMICAL CLOTH CO
91 River Rd (98382-9701)
PHONE 360 582-9684
Barbara Johnson, *Owner*
Barbara Casterline, *Owner*
EMP: 2
SALES (est): 196.5K **Privately Held**
WEB: www.chemicalcloth.com
SIC: 2299 5949 5085 Carbonized rags; fabric stores piece goods; industrial supplies

(G-11618)
CONACHEN AVIATION
161 Hooker Rd (98382-7249)
PHONE 360 516-7740
James W Conachen, *Owner*
EMP: 4
SALES (est): 179.2K **Privately Held**
SIC: 3721 Aircraft

(G-11619)
COOL RACING OIL
1400 W Washington St (98382-3236)
PHONE 971 235-7611
Steve Danielson, *Principal*
EMP: 2 EST: 2016
SALES (est): 95.7K **Privately Held**
SIC: 1311 Crude petroleum & natural gas

(G-11620)
COPPER CREEK FABRICATIONS LLC
14 Banana Way (98382-9111)
P.O. Box 686, Carlsborg (98324-0686)
PHONE 360 582-9676
Troy Tosland, *Mng Member*
EMP: 3
SALES (est): 286.3K **Privately Held**
SIC: 8641 3444 Civic associations; sheet metalwork; ducts, sheet metal; sheet metal specialties, not stamped

(G-11621)
COPPER RIDGE FABRICATION LLC
214 Wilders Ln (98382-9281)
PHONE 360 582-3898
Troy Tosland, *Mng Member*
EMP: 2
SALES (est): 353.8K **Privately Held**
SIC: 3444 Sheet metalwork

(G-11622)
D&E KUSTOMS LLC
63 Hooker Rd (98382-7934)
P.O. Box 1982 (98382-4334)
PHONE 360 681-0511
Eric Jones,
Daniel D Edwards,
EMP: 3
SALES (est): 290K **Privately Held**
SIC: 3449 Miscellaneous metalwork

(G-11623)
DALE A WEST SPECIALTY WDWKG
92 Dory Rd (98382-9033)
PHONE 360 683-9419
Dale A West, *President*
EMP: 3
SALES: 320K **Privately Held**
SIC: 2511 3732 Wood household furniture; boat building & repairing

(G-11624)
DAVE BEKKEVAR LOGGING & TRCKG
273054 Highway 101 (98382-9616)
PHONE 360 683-3655
Dave Bekkevar, *President*
EMP: 12
SALES: 300K **Privately Held**
SIC: 2411 Logging

(G-11625)
DAVIS SAND & GRAVEL INC
870 Evans Rd (98382-8940)
PHONE 360 683-5680
Dana Davis, *President*
Gloria Davis, *Corp Secy*
EMP: 4 EST: 1960
SQ FT: 300
SALES (est): 525K **Privately Held**
SIC: 1442 Common sand mining; gravel mining

(G-11626)
DER HEINTZELMANN INC
Also Called: Sauer Kraut
152 Windy Way (98382-8318)
PHONE 360 683-4740
Daniel L Heintz, *Principal*
EMP: 3
SALES (est): 118.1K **Privately Held**
SIC: 2711 Newspapers: publishing only, not printed on site

(G-11627)
DMC SATELLITE SYSTEMS INC
70 Timber Rd (98382-9634)
PHONE 360 681-4204
Dieter Moenig, *President*
Birgit Moenig, *Vice Pres*
EMP: 6
SALES (est): 746.1K **Privately Held**
WEB: www.dmcsatellite.com
SIC: 3663 Satellites, communications; marine crafts & supplies

(G-11628)
DOODLEBUGS
138 W Washington St (98382-3336)
P.O. Box 321 (98382-4305)
PHONE 360 683-3154
Victor Brancacio, *President*
Mary Brancacio, *Corp Secy*
Catherine Brancacio, *Vice Pres*
EMP: 6
SQ FT: 2,300
SALES (est): 420K **Privately Held**
SIC: 2782 7359 Scrapbooks; party supplies rental services

(G-11629)
DOUG HOUSE POWDER COATING
503b S 3rd Ave Ste B (98382)
P.O. Box 1274 (98382-4321)
PHONE 360 681-5412
Steven Harwood, *Owner*
EMP: 2
SALES (est): 132K **Privately Held**
SIC: 3479 Coating of metals & formed products

(G-11630)
DUNGENESS VALLEY CREAMERY
876 N Beverage St (98382-3101)
PHONE 360 683-0716
EMP: 3 EST: 2014
SALES (est): 82.6K **Privately Held**
SIC: 2021 Creamery butter

(G-11631)
DWIGHT HOSTVEDT
Also Called: Woodmark Design
303 Sunny View Dr (98382-7283)
PHONE 360 683-2315
Dwight Hostvedt, *Owner*
EMP: 4
SQ FT: 2,000
SALES: 100K **Privately Held**
SIC: 2434 2426 Wood kitchen cabinets; furniture stock & parts, hardwood

(G-11632)
EDDIE ODELL
Also Called: O'Dell Logging
381 Daisy King Rd (98382-8710)
PHONE 360 797-7549
Saula O'Dell, *Owner*
Eddie O'Dell, *Owner*
EMP: 2
SALES (est): 185.6K **Privately Held**
SIC: 2411 Logging camps & contractors

(G-11633)
EVIL ROYS ELIXIRS
209 S Sequim Ave (98382-3805)
PHONE 360 463-6105
EMP: 4
SALES (est): 257.8K **Privately Held**
SIC: 2085 Distilled & blended liquors

(G-11634)
FIRST MILLENNIUM BANK
Also Called: Millennium Financial Group
64 Johnson Creek Rd (98382-9704)
PHONE 360 797-5108
Brandon Salle, *Controller*
EMP: 2
SALES (est): 74.9K **Privately Held**
SIC: 8249 3578 6035 6531 Banking school, training; banking machines; federal savings banks; fiduciary, real estate; national commercial banks; charitable trust management

(G-11635)
FRED HILL MATERIALS
1369 Cays Rd (98382-8005)
PHONE 360 779-4431
Fred Hill, *Owner*
EMP: 12
SALES (est): 784.6K **Privately Held**
SIC: 5032 3273 Brick, stone & related material; ready-mixed concrete

(G-11636)
GLOBAL SCIENTIFIC SYSTEMS
162 River Run Rd (98382-8265)
PHONE 360 504-5100
Jerry Pittman, *President*
Patrick S Pittman, *Vice Pres*
EMP: 7
SQ FT: 4,000
SALES (est): 560K **Privately Held**
WEB: www.globalscientificsystems.com
SIC: 3826 Analytical instruments

(G-11637)
HAASE WOODWORKS
258955 Highway 101 (98382-7423)
PHONE 360 681-2600
Russell Haase, *President*
EMP: 3
SALES (est): 370K **Privately Held**
SIC: 2431 Millwork

(G-11638)
HIGH ENERGY METALS INC
293 Business Park Loop (98382-9423)
PHONE 360 683-6390
Donald J Butler, *President*
David Brasher, *Exec VP*
Mech Watne, *Engineer*
EMP: 10 EST: 1997
SQ FT: 7,000
SALES: 1.8MM **Privately Held**
WEB: www.highenergymetals.com
SIC: 3542 High energy rate metal forming machines

(G-11639)
HOLMES PUBLISHING GROUP LLC
407 S Sequim Ave (98382-4045)
PHONE 360 681-2900
JD Holmes, *Bd of Directors*
EMP: 2
SALES (est): 103.9K **Privately Held**
SIC: 2741 Miscellaneous publishing

(G-11640)
HOWAT FINE WOODWORKING INC
302 Ward Ln (98382-6684)
PHONE 360 681-3451
Jeffrey Howat, *President*
EMP: 3
SALES: 387K **Privately Held**
SIC: 2431 Millwork

(G-11641)
IN GRAPHIC DETAIL LLC
577 W Washington St Ste B (98382-3269)
P.O. Box 1627 (98382-4328)
PHONE 360 582-0002
Larry Perry, *Partner*
Lynda Perry, *Partner*
EMP: 3
SALES: 250K **Privately Held**
SIC: 7336 2759 7334 Graphic arts & related design; commercial printing; photocopying & duplicating services

(G-11642)
J KING FORMULAS INC
686 N Sequim Ave (98382-3148)
P.O. Box 576 (98382-4309)
PHONE 360 683-6908
James King, *President*
Lorna King, *Corp Secy*
EMP: 3
SQ FT: 1,200
SALES: 122K **Privately Held**
SIC: 2844 5122 Hair preparations, including shampoos; drugs, proprietaries & sundries

(G-11643)
JETWEST
335 Riverview Dr (98382-7878)
PHONE 801 223-9149
Paul Reinarz, *President*
EMP: 2
SALES (est): 74.4K **Privately Held**
SIC: 2899 Chemical preparations

(G-11644)
JONES ARMS LLC
63 Hooker Rd (98382-7934)
P.O. Box 1982 (98382-4334)
PHONE 360 681-0511
Sarah Jones, *Vice Pres*
EMP: 5
SQ FT: 2,000
SALES (est): 192.5K **Privately Held**
SIC: 3484 Carbines, 30 mm. & below

(G-11645)
KRISTINE AUMSPACH
517 W Fir St (98382-3210)
PHONE 360 681-4277
Debbie Moore, *Principal*
EMP: 3
SALES (est): 162.6K **Privately Held**
SIC: 2066 Chocolate

(G-11646)
LINCOLN INDUSTRIAL CORP INC
Also Called: Allform Welding
81 Hooker Rd Unit 9 (98382-9122)
PHONE 360 681-0584
EMP: 8
SALES (corp-wide): 4.2MM **Privately Held**
SIC: 3715 7692 Truck trailers; welding repair

Sequim - Clallam County (G-11647)   GEOGRAPHIC SECTION

PA: Lincoln Industrial Corporation, Inc.
4130 Tumwater Truck Rte
Port Angeles WA
360 457-6122

(G-11647)
MARKETECH INTERNATIONAL INC
Also Called: J&S Fabrication
4896 Lost Mountain Rd (98382-7932)
PHONE................................360 379-6707
Beth A Juran, *President*
William Juran, *Vice Pres*
▲ **EMP:** 15
SALES (est): 3.4MM **Privately Held**
WEB: www.mkt-intl.com
SIC: 3441 7389 Fabricated structural metal; grinding, precision: commercial or industrial

(G-11648)
MESA RESOURCES INC
453 Grandview Dr (98382-7872)
PHONE................................360 683-1912
David Soderlind, *President*
EMP: 5
SALES (est): 352.4K **Privately Held**
WEB: www.mesaresources.com
SIC: 2411 Logging

(G-11649)
MUDSLAYER MANUFACTURING LLC
261340 Highway 101 (98382-9248)
PHONE................................360 477-0251
James Laporte, *Bd of Directors*
◆ **EMP:** 8 **EST:** 2009
SALES (est): 1MM **Privately Held**
SIC: 3999 Manufacturing industries

(G-11650)
NATION TO NATION PREMIUM
20 Cedar Hill Ln (98382-8893)
PHONE................................360 731-0330
John Goodwin,
EMP: 2
SALES (est): 250K **Privately Held**
SIC: 2499 Wood products

(G-11651)
NORM STOKEN LOGGING INC
384 Knapp Rd (98382-9653)
PHONE................................360 683-0908
Norm Stoken, *President*
EMP: 5
SALES (est): 421.9K **Privately Held**
SIC: 2411 Logging camps & contractors

(G-11652)
NORTHWEST FENCE CO
31 Pheasant Run Dr (98382-8325)
PHONE................................360 683-4673
Wes Gilbert, *Owner*
EMP: 4
SQ FT: 500
SALES (est): 385K **Privately Held**
SIC: 3446 1799 Fences or posts, ornamental iron or steel; fence construction

(G-11653)
NORTHWEST MEDIA WASHINGTON LP
150 S 5th Ave Ste 2 (98382-2915)
P.O. Box 1207, Port Angeles (98362-0222)
PHONE................................360 681-2390
Jeana Johnson, *Manager*
EMP: 41
SALES (corp-wide): 14.8MM **Privately Held**
SIC: 2711 Commercial printing & newspaper publishing combined; newspapers, publishing & printing
PA: Northwest Media Washington Lp
500 108th Ave Ne
Bellevue WA 98004
425 274-4782

(G-11654)
OAKBRIDGE UNIVERSITY
41 Windmill Ln (98382-8315)
PHONE................................360 681-5233
Thomas Coates, *Principal*
EMP: 4 **EST:** 2014
SALES (est): 256.3K **Privately Held**
SIC: 2741 Miscellaneous publishing

(G-11655)
OLYMPIC VIEW PUBLISHING LLC (PA)
Also Called: Sequim Gazette
147 W Washington St (98382-3372)
P.O. Box 1750 (98382-4330)
PHONE................................360 683-3311
Mike Dashiell, *Department Mgr*
Harmony Liebert, *Department Mgr*
Brown Maloney,
EMP: 30
SQ FT: 5,000
SALES (est): 1.7MM **Privately Held**
WEB: www.sequimgazette.com
SIC: 2711 Newspapers: publishing only, not printed on site

(G-11656)
OMEGA MINISTRIES INC
Also Called: Media Spotlight
21 Petal Ln (98382-3601)
P.O. Box 3640 (98382-5045)
PHONE................................360 477-4180
Albert J Dager, *President*
Hector Tamez, *Vice Pres*
Gerwin McFarland, *Treasurer*
Jean Dager, *Admin Sec*
EMP: 4
SALES (est): 54.3K **Privately Held**
SIC: 2721 Magazines: publishing only, not printed on site

(G-11657)
OSP SLING INC (PA)
Also Called: Olympic Synthetic Products
803 S 3rd Ave (98382-3709)
P.O. Box 1207 (98382-4320)
PHONE................................360 683-4109
Todd Negus, *President*
Kay Glover, *Vice Pres*
Randy Kokrda, *Plant Mgr*
John Glover, *Treasurer*
Jody Negus, *Admin Sec*
EMP: 28
SQ FT: 5,000
SALES (est): 3.1MM **Privately Held**
WEB: www.ospsling.com
SIC: 2399 Belting, fabric: made from purchased materials

(G-11658)
PACIFIC AEROSPACE & ELEC INC
2249 Diamond Point Rd (98382-8663)
PHONE................................360 683-4167
Joe Munn, *Manager*
EMP: 13
SALES (corp-wide): 67.1MM **Privately Held**
SIC: 3365 Aerospace castings, aluminum
HQ: Pacific Aerospace & Electronics, Llc
434 Olds Station Rd
Wenatchee WA 98801

(G-11659)
PENINSULA TANKS INC
1370 Woodcock Rd (98382-7555)
PHONE................................360 683-4714
Rocky Billings, *President*
EMP: 2
SALES (est): 286.8K **Privately Held**
SIC: 3272 1711 Concrete products; septic system construction

(G-11660)
PILE PROTECTORS
206 Lake Of The Hlls Loop (98382-3868)
PHONE................................360 683-3926
William Ellis, *Owner*
EMP: 2
SALES (est): 104.9K **Privately Held**
SIC: 2491 Piles, foundation & marine construction: treated wood

(G-11661)
PRAXAIR DISTRIBUTION INC
Also Called: Praxair Distrubution
302 Clearview Ln (98382-8495)
PHONE................................360 504-2086
EMP: 3 **Privately Held**
SIC: 2813 Industrial gases
HQ: Praxair Distribution, Inc.
10 Riverview Dr
Danbury CT 06810
203 837-2000

(G-11662)
SELLIN STYLE
251 W Old Blyn Hwy (98382-9667)
PHONE................................360 670-5540
Ann Oniel, *Owner*
EMP: 2
SALES (est): 129.3K **Privately Held**
SIC: 2842 Automobile polish

(G-11663)
T & JS MACHINE SHOP
92 Sampson Ct (98382-7803)
PHONE................................360 504-2387
Tom Calonder, *Principal*
EMP: 2
SALES (est): 205.8K **Privately Held**
SIC: 3599 Machine shop, jobbing & repair

(G-11664)
TC NW INC
518 N Sequim Ave (98382-3160)
PHONE................................360 683-6655
Tom Parkwell, *Owner*
EMP: 3
SALES (est): 259.6K **Privately Held**
SIC: 2541 Store fixtures, wood

(G-11665)
THUNDER HILL WINERY LLC
763 Sporseen Rd (98382-7155)
P.O. Box 3790 (98382-5065)
PHONE................................360 681-5209
Pamela Entwistle, *Principal*
EMP: 2
SALES (est): 62.3K **Privately Held**
SIC: 2084 Wines, brandy & brandy spirits

(G-11666)
TIMBER IRON ERECTORS
1329 Taylor Cutoff Rd (98382-8285)
P.O. Box 516, Carlsborg (98324-0516)
PHONE................................360 681-8611
David Richardson, *Owner*
EMP: 4
SALES (est): 332.3K **Privately Held**
SIC: 3462 Iron & steel forgings

(G-11667)
TRIANGLE WELLNESS LLC ●
394 Kirner Rd (98382-9382)
PHONE................................727 773-0054
EMP: 2 **EST:** 2019
SALES (est): 69.9K **Privately Held**
SIC: 3471 Plating & polishing

(G-11668)
US WORKBOATS INC (PA)
60 Airpark Rd (98382-9791)
PHONE................................360 808-2292
Josh S Armstrong, *President*
◆ **EMP:** 2
SQ FT: 25,000
SALES (est): 12MM **Privately Held**
SIC: 3732 5551 Boat building & repairing; boat dealers

(G-11669)
WEST BAY BOAT & MANUFACTURING
1451 W Sequim Bay Rd (98382-8434)
PHONE................................360 683-4066
William Kuss, *President*
Annette Kuss, *Corp Secy*
Jeff Kuss, *Vice Pres*
EMP: 2
SALES (est): 236.6K **Privately Held**
SIC: 3732 5551 Boat building & repairing; motor boat dealers

(G-11670)
WICKED LURES LLC
23 Valley Center Pl (98382-6955)
PHONE................................360 460-6078
James Beasley, *Principal*
EMP: 2 **EST:** 2011
SALES (est): 156.4K **Privately Held**
SIC: 3949 Lures, fishing: artificial

Shaw Island
San Juan County

(G-11671)
NORTHWEST MARINE TECH INC (PA)
Also Called: N M T
976 Ben Nevis Loop (98286-7572)
P.O. Box 427 (98286-0427)
PHONE................................360 468-3375
Guy Thornburgh, *CEO*
Doug Hogue, *Production*
Jaime Smith, *Admin Sec*
EMP: 22 **EST:** 1971
SQ FT: 5,800
SALES (est): 3.5MM **Privately Held**
WEB: www.nmt-inc.com
SIC: 3812 3469 Detection apparatus: electronic/magnetic field, light/heat; metal stampings

Shelton
Mason County

(G-11672)
AAA TREE SERVICE & LOGGING LLC
141 Se Harrier Rd (98584-9255)
PHONE................................360 463-7553
EMP: 2
SALES (est): 81.7K **Privately Held**
SIC: 2411 Logging

(G-11673)
AGATE BACKHOE TRACTOR
41 E Lighthouse Rd (98584-9579)
PHONE................................360 426-7085
Gary G Woolett, *Principal*
EMP: 2
SALES (est): 159.6K **Privately Held**
SIC: 3531 Backhoes

(G-11674)
ALASKA STANDARD MINING INC
4403 W Dayton Airport Rd (98584-8011)
PHONE................................360 432-8797
EMP: 2 **EST:** 2001
SALES (est): 150K **Privately Held**
SIC: 1081 Metal Mining Services

(G-11675)
ALPHA TEST CORPORATION
Also Called: Alphatest
261 W Business Park Loop (98584-8227)
P.O. Box 1791 (98584-5012)
PHONE................................360 462-0201
Patrick Tarzwell, *President*
EMP: 24
SQ FT: 3,200
SALES (est): 4.6MM **Privately Held**
WEB: www.alphatest.com
SIC: 3559 3825 Electronic component making machinery; instruments to measure electricity

(G-11676)
ALTA FOREST PRODUCTS LLC
Also Called: Little Skookum Lumber
708 W State Route 108 (98584-7753)
P.O. Box 1307, Olympia (98507-1307)
PHONE................................360 426-9721
Dick Bored, *Branch Mgr*
EMP: 100 **Privately Held**
WEB: www.welco-skookum.com
SIC: 2421 2448 Sawmills & planing mills, general; wood pallets & skids
HQ: Alta Forest Products Llc
810 Nw Alta Way
Chehalis WA 98532
360 219-0008

(G-11677)
AMPHIBIOUS MARINE INC
3121 Se Kamilche Point Rd (98584-6923)
PHONE................................360 426-3170
William Phillips, *President*
EMP: 5
SQ FT: 3,200

GEOGRAPHIC SECTION

Shelton - Mason County (G-11710)

SALES: 500K **Privately Held**
WEB: www.amphibiousmarine.com
SIC: 3732 Boat building and repairing

(G-11678)
ANDERSON RESOURCES INC
Also Called: Walter Dacon Wines
50 Se Skookum Inlet Rd (98584-8610)
PHONE...................360 426-5913
Lloyd L Anderson Jr, *President*
Ann Anderson, *Admin Sec*
EMP: 4
SQ FT: 2,100
SALES: 343K **Privately Held**
WEB: www.walterdaconwines.com
SIC: 2084 5182 5921 Wines; wine; wine

(G-11679)
ARRIS KOLLMAN TRUCKING INC
Also Called: Little Creek Rock Quarry
951 W Kamilche Ln (98584-7702)
PHONE...................360 532-0351
Kyle Jarmin, *Manager*
EMP: 6
SALES (corp-wide): 7.8MM **Privately Held**
SIC: 1411 Dimension stone
PA: Arris Kollman Trucking Inc
 2421 W 1st St
 Aberdeen WA 98520
 360 532-0351

(G-11680)
ARRO LAST TARGET SYSTEMS
6311 Se Arcadia Rd (98584-8332)
PHONE...................360 427-9512
Daniel Mann, *Owner*
EMP: 3
SALES (est): 160K **Privately Held**
WEB: www.arrolast.com
SIC: 3949 5941 Targets, archery & rifle shooting; sporting goods & bicycle shops

(G-11681)
B PLUS INC
270 Se Nighthawk Pl (98584-7602)
P.O. Box 2368 (98584-5061)
PHONE...................360 426-5038
Blain Burgess, *President*
EMP: 7
SALES (est): 647K **Privately Held**
WEB: www.b-plusinc.com
SIC: 2431 1751 Millwork; cabinet building & installation

(G-11682)
BAYSIDE REDI-MIX
Also Called: Bayshore Sand & Gravel
40 Se Mell Rd (98584-7678)
PHONE...................360 426-4987
Dietz Kadoun, *Owner*
EMP: 6
SQ FT: 240
SALES (est): 504.5K **Privately Held**
SIC: 3273 1442 Ready-mixed concrete; construction sand & gravel

(G-11683)
BENNETT PAINTING
1640 Se Lynch Rd (98584-7222)
PHONE...................360 426-6489
James K Bennett, *Owner*
EMP: 2 EST: 1976
SALES (est): 119.9K **Privately Held**
SIC: 1721 2411 Residential painting; logging

(G-11684)
BLACKSTAR
510 E Mason Lake Rd (98584-9628)
PHONE...................360 426-7470
Cathy M Baze, *Owner*
EMP: 2
SALES: 250K **Privately Held**
SIC: 2396 2759 Tip printing & stamping on fabric; screen printing

(G-11685)
BLASE S GORNY DESIGN INC
3810 W Skokomish Vly Rd (98584-7433)
PHONE...................360 426-5613
EMP: 3
SALES: 180K **Privately Held**
SIC: 2434 Mfg Wood Kitchen Cabinets

(G-11686)
BROTHERS UNITED INC
60 W Business Park Loop (98584-8233)
PHONE...................360 426-3959
Billy S Schauer, *President*
Ronald Braakman, *Sales Staff*
▼ EMP: 16
SQ FT: 1,200
SALES: 7MM **Privately Held**
WEB: www.brothersunited.com
SIC: 5193 3999 Nursery stock; Christmas tree ornaments, except electrical & glass

(G-11687)
BROWNS DAILY GRIND
511 E Aycliffe Dr (98584-8591)
PHONE...................360 556-3525
EMP: 2
SALES (est): 181.6K **Privately Held**
SIC: 3599 Grinding castings for the trade

(G-11688)
CASTLE & COLEMAN LOGGING CO
1800 W Highland Rd (98584-8921)
P.O. Box 1760 (98584-5010)
PHONE...................360 426-0840
Lyle Coleman, *President*
Mike Coleman, *Vice Pres*
Don Gardner, *Treasurer*
EMP: 9
SALES (est): 937.6K **Privately Held**
SIC: 2411 Logging camps & contractors

(G-11689)
CBD OUTREACH
935 E Johns Prairie Rd (98584-1270)
PHONE...................360 426-2000
Dennis Coughlin, *Administration*
EMP: 3
SALES (est): 149.4K **Privately Held**
SIC: 3999

(G-11690)
CENTERPIECE CUSTOMS
604 Dearborn Ave (98584-1526)
PHONE...................360 490-8636
Sam Luedtke, *Owner*
EMP: 2
SALES: 60K **Privately Held**
SIC: 2431 Millwork

(G-11691)
CHAVEZ NOLBERTO
2253 E Johns Prairie Rd (98584-8203)
PHONE...................360 426-9550
Nolberto Chavez, *Principal*
EMP: 3
SALES (est): 159.8K **Privately Held**
SIC: 2411 Logging

(G-11692)
CORRECTIONAL INDUSTRIES
2321 W Dayton Airport Rd (98584-6319)
P.O. Box 900 (98584-0974)
PHONE...................360 427-4613
EMP: 2
SALES (est): 118.5K **Privately Held**
SIC: 3999 Manufacturing industries

(G-11693)
D & H PRINTING
2505 Olympic Hwy N (98584-2974)
PHONE...................360 427-7423
Dale Sherman, *Owner*
Marie Sherman, *Manager*
EMP: 3
SALES: 140K **Privately Held**
SIC: 2759 Commercial printing

(G-11694)
D-WAY TOOLS INC
3661 E Pickering Rd (98584-8885)
PHONE...................360 432-9509
David Schweitzer, *President*
Louise Schweitzer, *Corp Secy*
EMP: 2
SQ FT: 3,300
SALES (est): 275K **Privately Held**
WEB: d-waytools.com
SIC: 2499 Bearings, wood

(G-11695)
DB INDUSTRIES LLC
116 W Rr Ave Ste 108 (98584)
PHONE...................360 432-8239
EMP: 2 EST: 2016
SALES (est): 66.1K **Privately Held**
SIC: 3999 Manufacturing industries

(G-11696)
DENIM DUDS
70 Se Bluff Loop Rd (98584-9347)
PHONE...................360 432-1183
EMP: 2 EST: 2008
SALES (est): 119.6K **Privately Held**
SIC: 2211 Denims

(G-11697)
FRANTZ GLASS GALLERY
Also Called: Frantz Art Glass Gallery
130 W Corporate Rd (98584-1285)
PHONE...................360 426-6712
Mike Frantz, *Owner*
▲ EMP: 12
SALES (est): 981.4K **Privately Held**
SIC: 3229 Pressed & blown glass

(G-11698)
GRAPHIC COMMUNICATIONS
Also Called: Digital Printing
120 S 7th St (98584-3820)
PHONE...................360 426-8628
Cherry Travis, *Branch Mgr*
EMP: 3
SALES (corp-wide): 1.1MM **Privately Held**
WEB: www.gcprint.com
SIC: 2752 Commercial printing, offset
PA: Graphic Communications
 109 Columbia St Nw
 Olympia WA 98501
 360 786-5110

(G-11699)
HEAVENLY GELATO INC
Also Called: Olympic Mountain Ice Cream
301 E Wallace Kneeland (98584-2985)
PHONE...................360 426-0696
Karl Black, *President*
Joel Black, *Vice Pres*
Trail Black, *Vice Pres*
Beth Black, *Admin Sec*
EMP: 12
SQ FT: 3,000
SALES (est): 1.9MM **Privately Held**
WEB: www.olympicmountainicecream.com
SIC: 2024 Ice cream & frozen desserts

(G-11700)
ISLAND CONSTRUCTION
3591 Se Old Olympic Hwy (98584-7733)
PHONE...................360 426-3442
John Ericks,
Joseph Davis,
Squaxin Island Tribe,
▲ EMP: 3
SQ FT: 900
SALES (est): 280K **Privately Held**
SIC: 3851 Frames & parts, eyeglass & spectacle

(G-11701)
ISLAND ENTERPRISES (PA)
Also Called: Kamilche Trading Post
3591 Se Old Olympic Hwy (98584-7733)
PHONE...................360 426-4933
Robert Whitner, *CEO*
EMP: 4 EST: 1961
SALES (est): 18.8MM **Privately Held**
SIC: 5921 5411 2091 Liquor stores; grocery stores; delicatessens; oysters: packaged in cans, jars, etc.

(G-11702)
ISLAND ENTERPRISES
Also Called: Salish Seafoods Company
92 E Chapman Rd (98584-9407)
PHONE...................360 426-4933
Rod Schuffenhauer, *Branch Mgr*
EMP: 29
SALES (corp-wide): 18.8MM **Privately Held**
SIC: 0913 5411 2091 Oysters, dredging or tonging of; delicatessens; oysters: packaged in cans, jars, etc.
PA: Island Enterprises
 3591 Se Old Olympic Hwy
 Shelton WA 98584
 360 426-4933

(G-11703)
ISLAND ENTERPRISES
Also Called: Kamilche Trading Post
W98 Hwy 108 (98584)
PHONE...................360 426-3442
Ryan Johnson, *Branch Mgr*
EMP: 12
SALES (corp-wide): 18.8MM **Privately Held**
SIC: 5921 5411 2091 Liquor stores; delicatessens; oysters: packaged in cans, jars, etc.
PA: Island Enterprises
 3591 Se Old Olympic Hwy
 Shelton WA 98584
 360 426-4933

(G-11704)
JALISCO LLC
Also Called: Jalisco Tortilla Factory
128 E Railroad Ave (98584-1430)
PHONE...................360 432-9397
Mark Velasco,
Medardo Lucero,
Magdalena Velasco,
EMP: 10 EST: 1997
SALES (est): 1.2MM **Privately Held**
SIC: 2096 Tortilla chips

(G-11705)
JIMINI CONSTRUCTION LLC
741 Se Cook Plant Farm Rd (98584-8696)
P.O. Box 2079 (98584-5037)
PHONE...................360 426-9918
Jim Oaks, *President*
EMP: 5
SALES: 800K **Privately Held**
SIC: 1771 2411 Blacktop (asphalt) work; logging

(G-11706)
KENNEDY CREEK QUARRY INC
Also Called: Thurman Enterprises
250 W Hurley Waldrip Rd (98584-7244)
PHONE...................360 426-4743
Jim Thurman, *President*
Todd Fennel, *Admin Sec*
EMP: 10
SALES (est): 1.7MM **Privately Held**
SIC: 1481 2411 Mine & quarry services, nonmetallic minerals; logging camps & contractors

(G-11707)
KNIT ALTERATION & DESIGN
Also Called: Sandy M Serrett
230 Se State Route 3 (98584-9118)
PHONE...................360 426-5078
Sandy M Serrett, *Owner*
EMP: 3
SALES (est): 180K **Privately Held**
WEB: www.knitalteration.com
SIC: 5199 2389 Fabrics, yarns & knit goods; apparel & accessories

(G-11708)
LC WELDING FABRICATION LL
271 Se Craig Rd (98584-9263)
PHONE...................360 359-8853
Leif H Christensen, *Administration*
EMP: 3
SALES (est): 45.2K **Privately Held**
SIC: 7692 Welding repair

(G-11709)
LUND CUSTOM MACHINING INC
110 W Metzler Mill Rd (98584-8926)
PHONE...................360 432-0310
Niels Lund, *President*
Mike Lund, *Vice Pres*
Bruce Lund, *Opers Mgr*
Lee Roy Junkers, *Treasurer*
EMP: 7
SALES: 250K **Privately Held**
SIC: 3599 Machine shop, jobbing & repair

(G-11710)
MANKE LUMBER COMPANY INC
826 Fairmont Ave (98584)
PHONE...................360 426-5536
Dale Hall, *Managing Dir*

Shelton - Mason County (G-11711) — GEOGRAPHIC SECTION

Joel Manke, *Mfg Staff*
Kim Paller, *Administration*
EMP: 8
SQ FT: 1,000
SALES (corp-wide): 97.1MM **Privately Held**
WEB: www.mankelumber.com
SIC: 2421 5211 2411 Sawmills & planing mills, general; planing mill products & lumber; logging
PA: Manke Lumber Company, Inc.
1717 Marine View Dr
Tacoma WA 98422
253 572-6252

(G-11711)
MARTIAN BOAT WORKS
773 W Hurley Waldrip Rd (98584-7704)
PHONE 360 427-8629
EMP: 2
SALES (est): 164.1K **Privately Held**
SIC: 3732 Boatbuilding/Repairing

(G-11712)
MATTHAEIS CAMCO INC
6400 E Agate Rd (98584-7321)
P.O. Box 249, Sweet Home OR (97386-0249)
PHONE 360 426-7900
Steve Vizina, *President*
EMP: 30
SQ FT: 2,300
SALES (est): 7.9MM **Privately Held**
SIC: 5031 2421 2439 Lumber: rough, dressed & finished; sawmills & planing mills, general; structural wood members

(G-11713)
MIKE FRANTZ INC
Also Called: Frantz Bead Company
140 E Hideaway Ln (98584-6932)
PHONE 800 839-6712
Mike Frantz, *President*
▲ **EMP:** 7
SALES: 600K **Privately Held**
SIC: 3961 Costume jewelry

(G-11714)
MILES SAND & GRAVEL COMPANY
3100 W Franklin St (98584)
PHONE 360 427-0946
Jeff Phipps, *Branch Mgr*
EMP: 13
SALES (corp-wide): 88MM **Privately Held**
SIC: 3531 5211 5032 3273 Concrete plants; concrete & cinder block; concrete & cinder block; ready-mixed concrete
PA: Miles Sand & Gravel Company
400 Valley Ave Ne
Puyallup WA 98372
253 833-3705

(G-11715)
MOR-LOG INC
1153 E Agate Rd (98584)
PHONE 360 426-7872
Kevin Morris, *President*
EMP: 5
SALES (est): 411.3K **Privately Held**
SIC: 2411 Logging

(G-11716)
OLYMPIC MANGANESE MINING CO ✪
2631 W Skokomish Vly Rd (98584-7402)
PHONE 360 426-9273
EMP: 2 **EST:** 2018
SALES (est): 66K **Privately Held**
SIC: 1499 Miscellaneous nonmetallic minerals

(G-11717)
OLYMPIC MOUNTAIN MILLWORK LLC
Also Called: O M M C O
822 E Hiawatha Blvd (98584-7892)
PHONE 360 432-2992
Tracy Dyrdal,
Kc Ellison,
Jim Lanman,
EMP: 9
SQ FT: 7,500
SALES (est): 1.3MM **Privately Held**
SIC: 2431 1751 Millwork; cabinet & finish carpentry

(G-11718)
OLYMPIC PANEL PRODUCTS LLC
204 E Railroad Ave (98584-1486)
P.O. Box 60, Boise ID (83707-0060)
PHONE 360 432-5033
Richard Yarbrough,
Gary Weza, *Maintence Staff*
◆ **EMP:** 6
SALES: 1.8MM
SALES (corp-wide): 58.8MM **Privately Held**
WEB: www.olypanel.com
SIC: 2435 Hardwood veneer & plywood
PA: Wood Resources Llc
204 E Railroad Ave
Shelton WA 98584
360 432-5048

(G-11719)
OSHELL DELMONT
1190 E Shelton Springs Rd (98584-9128)
PHONE 360 427-9600
Delmont O'Shell, *Owner*
▲ **EMP:** 2
SQ FT: 1,200
SALES (est): 153.1K **Privately Held**
SIC: 5092 3944 5945 Toys; blocks, toy; toys & games

(G-11720)
PAPERCRAFT COTTAGE
825 W Franklin St (98584-2549)
P.O. Box 377, Union (98592-0377)
PHONE 360 426-1038
Lea Sorley, *Owner*
EMP: 2 **EST:** 2010
SALES (est): 113K **Privately Held**
SIC: 2782 Scrapbooks

(G-11721)
PERFECT REFLECTIONS AUTO BODY
101 W Hulbert Rd (98584-8016)
PHONE 360 426-0805
Robert Rosie, *Owner*
EMP: 5
SALES (est): 350K **Privately Held**
SIC: 3446 7532 7538 Architectural metalwork; top & body repair & paint shops; general automotive repair shops

(G-11722)
PINNACLE NW
500 E Export Rd (98584-4900)
PHONE 360 264-5484
EMP: 2
SALES (est): 54.1K **Privately Held**
SIC: 0139 3999 6531 ; ; real estate agents & managers

(G-11723)
RAINESTREE TIMBER MARKETING
9100 Se Lynch Rd (98584-8657)
P.O. Box 2268 (98584-5054)
PHONE 360 462-6197
EMP: 2
SALES (est): 120K **Privately Held**
SIC: 2411 Logging

(G-11724)
RANDALL CUSTOM LUMBER LTD
3530 Se Arcadia Rd (98584-9328)
PHONE 360 426-8518
Thomas E Randall, *President*
Karen Patrick, *Corp Secy*
EMP: 2
SALES: 90K **Privately Held**
SIC: 2421 Custom sawmill

(G-11725)
RICHARD ANDREWS LOGGING
170 W Metzler Mill Rd (98584-8926)
PHONE 360 426-1096
Richard Andrews, *Owner*
EMP: 2
SALES (est): 161.9K **Privately Held**
SIC: 2411 5541 Logging camps & contractors; gasoline service stations

(G-11726)
RICHARD KNANNLEIN
Also Called: Fiberglass Marine Products
393 Se Dahman Rd (98584-8605)
P.O. Box 657, Auburn (98071-0657)
PHONE 360 426-9757
Richard Knannlein, *Owner*
EMP: 3
SALES: 300K **Privately Held**
SIC: 3732 4493 Boats, fiberglass: building & repairing; marinas

(G-11727)
RIVER ROCK SOFTWARE INC
50 E Blenheim Pl (98584-9612)
PHONE 916 797-6746
Arthur Jordan, *President*
EMP: 4 **EST:** 1998
SALES (est): 360K **Privately Held**
WEB: www.riverrocksoftware.com
SIC: 7372 Prepackaged software

(G-11728)
RYANS MACHINE SHOP
621 E Leeds Dr (98584-8178)
PHONE 360 427-9490
Ryan Chris, *Owner*
EMP: 3
SALES (est): 170K **Privately Held**
SIC: 3599 Machine shop, jobbing & repair

(G-11729)
SALSA MANIA LLC
Also Called: Salso So Fresh
1290 Se Phillips Rd (98584-7614)
P.O. Box 11412, Olympia (98508-1412)
PHONE 360 432-9240
Randall R Milligan,
Joy Milligan,
EMP: 2
SALES (est): 110K **Privately Held**
SIC: 2032 Ethnic foods: canned, jarred, etc.

(G-11730)
SENIOR SERVICES FOR S SOUND
Also Called: Senior Nutrition Department
190 W Sentry Dr (98584-8045)
P.O. Box 1066 (98584-0930)
PHONE 360 426-3697
Debra Del Bosque, *Office Mgr*
Donna Gayda, *Asst Mgr*
EMP: 3
SALES: 95K **Privately Held**
SIC: 2099 8322 Food preparations; senior citizens' center or association

(G-11731)
SHEARER BROTHERS CHIPPING LLC
500 E Millwright Rd (98584-8254)
P.O. Box 2638, Belfair (98528-2638)
PHONE 360 426-6466
Sandy Hanson, *Office Mgr*
Thomas Mario Shearer,
Allen M Shearer,
EMP: 15
SALES (est): 2.9MM **Privately Held**
SIC: 2421 Sawdust, shavings & wood chips; wood chips, produced at mill

(G-11732)
SHELTON PUBLISHING INC
Also Called: Shelton-Mason County Journal
227 W Cota St (98584-2263)
P.O. Box 430 (98584-0430)
PHONE 360 426-4412
Charlie Gay, *President*
EMP: 25 **EST:** 1886
SQ FT: 3,000
SALES (est): 1.2MM **Privately Held**
WEB: www.masoncounty.com
SIC: 2711 2752 Job printing & newspaper publishing combined; commercial printing, lithographic

(G-11733)
SHEPHERDS SOAP CO
790 E Johns Prairie Rd (98584-1265)
PHONE 360 427-7811
Deb Peterson, *Owner*
EMP: 3
SALES (est): 209.1K **Privately Held**
SIC: 2841 Soap & other detergents

(G-11734)
SIERRA PACIFIC INDUSTRIES
204 E Railroad Ave (98584-1486)
PHONE 530 378-8251
EMP: 167
SALES (corp-wide): 1.2B **Privately Held**
SIC: 2421 Lumber: rough, sawed or planed
PA: Sierra Pacific Industries
19794 Riverside Ave
Anderson CA 96007
530 378-8000

(G-11735)
SIMS VIBRATION LABORATORY INC
Also Called: Limbsaver
50 W Rose Nye Way (98584-1206)
PHONE 360 427-6031
Steven Sims, *President*
Alan Lotton, *Vice Pres*
David Smith, *Purch Mgr*
Gary Sims, *Research*
George Clarke, *Sales Executive*
▲ **EMP:** 60
SQ FT: 35,000
SALES (est): 15.7MM **Privately Held**
WEB: www.limbsaver.com
SIC: 3484 Guns (firearms) or gun parts, 30 mm. & below

(G-11736)
STEVE POOL SERVICE INC
320 Se Snider Rd (98584-9332)
PHONE 360 533-0421
Sue Patterson, *President*
Mike Patterson, *Vice Pres*
EMP: 9 **EST:** 1961
SQ FT: 5,440
SALES (est): 1MM **Privately Held**
SIC: 3556 7699 Fish & shellfish processing machinery; industrial machinery & equipment repair

(G-11737)
SUNLIGHT WOODENWORKS INC
876 E Johns Prairie Rd (98584-1267)
PHONE 360 275-5263
Robert Love, *President*
Suzanne Love, *Corp Secy*
EMP: 8
SQ FT: 6,000
SALES (est): 1MM **Privately Held**
SIC: 2521 Cabinets, office: wood

(G-11738)
SUSAN BENNETT
Also Called: Sue's Stitch In Time
927 W Railroad Ave (98584-3847)
PHONE 360 427-6164
Susan Bennett, *Owner*
EMP: 4
SQ FT: 3,500
SALES (est): 179.4K **Privately Held**
SIC: 2395 2311 Quilting & quilting supplies; men's & boys' suits & coats

(G-11739)
TAYLOR MARICULTURE LLC
130 Se Lynch Rd (98584-8615)
PHONE 360 426-6178
Brooke Pearson, *Bd of Directors*
EMP: 4
SALES (est): 241.1K **Privately Held**
SIC: 2092 Fresh or frozen packaged fish

(G-11740)
TAYLOR RESOURCES INC (PA)
130 Se Lynch Rd (98584-8615)
PHONE 360 426-6178
Paul Taylor, *President*
William Taylor, *Vice Pres*
Jeff Pearson, *Treasurer*
◆ **EMP:** 139
SQ FT: 40,000
SALES (est): 7.8MM **Privately Held**
SIC: 0273 2092 Animal aquaculture; fresh or frozen packaged fish

(G-11741)
TAYLOR SHELLFISH COMPANY INC (HQ)
130 Se Lynch Rd (98584-8615)
PHONE 360 426-6178
Jeff Pearson, *President*

GEOGRAPHIC SECTION

Shoreline - King County (G-11772)

Gordon King, *Division Mgr*
William Taylor, *Vice Pres*
Marcelle Taylor, *Project Mgr*
Tom Bettinger, *Sales Dir*
◆ **EMP:** 115 **EST:** 1969
SQ FT: 40,000
SALES (est): 61.5MM
SALES (corp-wide): 62.8MM **Privately Held**
SIC: 2092 2091 Shellfish, fresh: shucked & packed in nonsealed containers; shellfish: packaged in cans, jars, etc.
PA: Taylor United, Inc.
130 Se Lynch Rd
Shelton WA 98584
360 426-6178

(G-11742)
TAYLOR UNITED INC (PA)
130 Se Lynch Rd (98584-8615)
PHONE..................360 426-6178
William Taylor, *President*
Jason Ragan, *Division Mgr*
Jeff Pearson, *Corp Secy*
Paul Taylor, *Vice Pres*
Diane Cooper, *Project Mgr*
EMP: 35 **EST:** 1969
SQ FT: 40,000
SALES (est): 62.8MM **Privately Held**
WEB: www.taylorunited.com
SIC: 5812 2092 2091 0273 Seafood restaurants; shellfish, fresh: shucked & packed in nonsealed containers; shellfish: packaged in cans, jars, etc.; animal aquaculture; timber tracts

(G-11743)
TECHWOOD LLC
121 W Enterprise Rd (98584-2870)
PHONE..................360 427-9616
Emmanovel Piliaris,
Paul Bouska,
Panny Piliaris,
EMP: 60
SQ FT: 23,000
SALES (est): 8.6MM **Privately Held**
SIC: 2431 2435 Millwork; hardwood veneer & plywood

(G-11744)
THERMEDIA CORPORATION
301 E W Kneeland Blvd 2 (98584)
PHONE..................360 427-1877
James Thomas, *President*
Darla Thomas, *Treasurer*
▲ **EMP:** 9
SALES (est): 1MM **Privately Held**
SIC: 2211 Filter cloth, cotton

(G-11745)
TJN PUBLISHING INC
Also Called: Shoppers Weekly, The
2505 Olympic Hwy N # 220 (98584-2974)
PHONE..................360 426-4677
Jeffrey Neely, *President*
Tracy Neely, *Principal*
EMP: 9
SQ FT: 1,300
SALES (est): 425.1K **Privately Held**
WEB: www.shoppersweekly.com
SIC: 2711 6531 Newspapers: publishing only, not printed on site; real estate agents & managers

(G-11746)
TRIPLE C FABRICATORS LLC
3340 E Johns Prairie Rd (98584-1248)
P.O. Box 3009 (98584-4420)
PHONE..................360 868-4125
Robert Santo,
Ronnie Clark,
EMP: 2
SALES (est): 437.1K **Privately Held**
SIC: 3441 Fabricated structural metal

(G-11747)
TRUFAB LLC
410 W Enterprise Rd (98584-2870)
PHONE..................360 229-3028
Don Putvin, *President*
▼ **EMP:** 14
SALES: 2.5MM **Privately Held**
SIC: 3441 Fabricated structural metal

(G-11748)
UNIVERSAL COATINGS LLC
215 Turner Ave Apt A103 (98584-3726)
PHONE..................360 936-2855
Aureliano Estrada, *Principal*
EMP: 2
SALES (est): 119.5K **Privately Held**
SIC: 3479 Metal coating & allied service

(G-11749)
VAN HARTEN
318 Mill St (98584-1400)
PHONE..................360 868-2011
Denis Duggan II, *Administration*
EMP: 2
SALES (est): 81.1K **Privately Held**
SIC: 0139 3999 4212 ; ; local trucking, without storage

(G-11750)
WHISKEY RIDGE MFG INC
21 Adonai Ct (98584-7853)
PHONE..................360 426-6100
David Panchot, *President*
Fred Hewins, *General Mgr*
EMP: 11 **EST:** 1996
SQ FT: 3,000
SALES (est): 1.2MM **Privately Held**
SIC: 3599 Machine shop, jobbing & repair

(G-11751)
WOOD RESOURCES LLC (PA)
204 E Railroad Ave (98584-1486)
P.O. Box 60, Boise ID (83707-0060)
PHONE..................360 432-5048
Richard Yarbrough, *CEO*
Eric Larsen, *Corp Secy*
Edward Fletcher, *CFO*
EMP: 6
SALES (est): 58.8MM **Privately Held**
SIC: 2435 Panels, hardwood plywood

Shoreline
King County

(G-11752)
206 FOODS LLC (PA)
Also Called: Seattle Granola Company
1208 Ne 168th St (98155-5932)
PHONE..................206 387-5881
Emily Dean, *Mng Member*
Gordon Smith, *Manager*
Chris Field,
EMP: 5
SALES (est): 401.6K **Privately Held**
SIC: 2043 Cereal breakfast foods

(G-11753)
A-Z BUSINESS FORMS
17713 15th Ave Ne (98155-3839)
P.O. Box 45288, Tacoma (98448-5288)
PHONE..................206 363-8170
Wayne Alkire, *Owner*
EMP: 4
SALES (est): 260K **Privately Held**
SIC: 2752 5112 Commercial printing, lithographic; business forms

(G-11754)
ALAN R & SARA BALMFORTH
1865 Ne 171st St (98155-6024)
PHONE..................206 363-7349
Alan R Balmforth, *Owner*
Sarah Balmforth, *Partner*
EMP: 2
SALES (est): 90.5K **Privately Held**
SIC: 3931 Musical instruments

(G-11755)
ALASKA FRESH SEAFOODS INC (PA)
17012 Aurora Ave N 200 (98133-5315)
PHONE..................206 285-2412
Ted Otness, *President*
David M Woodruff, *Vice Pres*
Theodore Painter, *Treasurer*
▼ **EMP:** 5 **EST:** 1978
SQ FT: 2,000
SALES (est): 719.8K **Privately Held**
SIC: 2092 Crab meat, fresh: packaged in nonsealed containers; crabmeat, frozen

(G-11756)
ASHER GRAPHICS
Also Called: Asher Printing & Graphics
18025 Meridian Ave N (98133-4642)
PHONE..................206 546-6500
Robin Asher, *Owner*
Tim Asher, *Co-Owner*
EMP: 2
SALES (est): 212.4K **Privately Held**
SIC: 2752 Commercial printing, offset

(G-11757)
AZURE FIRE PUBLISHING
2308 N 149th St (98133-6716)
PHONE..................206 380-2036
Leeland Artra, *Principal*
EMP: 2 **EST:** 2017
SALES (est): 59.2K **Privately Held**
SIC: 2741 Miscellaneous publishing

(G-11758)
B & D ADVERTISING PRTG & SVC
124 Nw 203rd St (98177-2020)
PHONE..................206 542-3262
Lunetta J Dodeward, *Owner*
EMP: 2
SALES (est): 130K **Privately Held**
SIC: 2752 7311 Commercial printing, offset; advertising agencies

(G-11759)
B & D SHEET METAL LLC
17038 Aurora Ave N (98133-5315)
PHONE..................206 533-0350
Ed Devos, *Owner*
Tom Bonfiglio,
EMP: 6
SQ FT: 11,392
SALES (est): 715.7K **Privately Held**
WEB: www.banddsheetmetal.com
SIC: 3444 1761 Sheet metal specialties, not stamped; roofing, siding & sheet metal work

(G-11760)
BENT WHISKER PRESS
1846 N 184th St (98133-4648)
PHONE..................206 914-3556
EMP: 2
SALES (est): 59.2K **Privately Held**
SIC: 2741 Miscellaneous publishing

(G-11761)
BEYOND ZONE INC
816 Ne 152nd St (98155-7026)
P.O. Box 31974, Seattle (98103-0074)
PHONE..................206 363-2147
EMP: 2
SALES (est): 120K **Privately Held**
SIC: 2844 5999 Hair preparations, including shampoos; hair coloring preparations; shampoos, rinses, conditioners: hair; hair care products

(G-11762)
BIODYNAMICS CORPORATION
14739 Aurora Ave N # 100 (98133-6547)
PHONE..................206 526-0205
Edward Rifkin, *President*
David Woodruff, *Vice Pres*
Wade Anderson, *Prdtn Mgr*
▲ **EMP:** 6
SQ FT: 1,500
SALES (est): 490K **Privately Held**
WEB: www.biodyncorp.com
SIC: 3845 8011 Electromedical apparatus; offices & clinics of medical doctors

(G-11763)
BORUCK PRTG & SILK SCREENING
16802 11th Ave Ne (98155-5908)
PHONE..................206 522-8500
Art Boruck, *Owner*
EMP: 5 **EST:** 1969
SQ FT: 5,000
SALES: 375.9K **Privately Held**
WEB: www.garagesalekit.com
SIC: 2752 Commercial printing, lithographic

(G-11764)
CCW LLC ✪
16724 10th Ave Ne (98155-5906)
PHONE..................206 363-4916
EMP: 2 **EST:** 2019
SALES (est): 94.5K **Privately Held**
SIC: 3444 Sheet metalwork

(G-11765)
CITY GRIND WORKS
15541 27th Ave Ne (98155-6438)
PHONE..................206 769-0006
Barry Hansen, *Principal*
EMP: 2
SALES (est): 126.1K **Privately Held**
SIC: 3599 Grinding castings for the trade

(G-11766)
COMPASS NORTHWEST
19302 Palatine Ave N (98133-3809)
P.O. Box 60216, Seattle (98160-0216)
PHONE..................206 546-1178
E L White, *Owner*
EMP: 2
SALES (est): 93.9K **Privately Held**
SIC: 7372 Prepackaged software

(G-11767)
COMPONENT ENGINEERING INC
14739 Aurora Ave N (98133-6547)
PHONE..................206 284-9171
William H Purdy, *President*
EMP: 10
SQ FT: 11,600
SALES (est): 1.1MM **Privately Held**
WEB: www.componentengineering.com
SIC: 3861 Sound recording & reproducing equipment, motion picture

(G-11768)
DIAMONDBACK CONSTRUCTION LLC
14825 Ashworth Ave N (98133-6229)
PHONE..................206 730-1239
David Snell,
Dave Snell,
EMP: 2
SALES (est): 140K **Privately Held**
SIC: 1442 Construction sand & gravel

(G-11769)
DOWNTOWN CLEANERS & TAILORING
Also Called: Magic Cleaner
14701 Aurora Ave N (98133-6547)
PHONE..................206 363-5455
Amir Ali, *Owner*
EMP: 5
SALES (est): 192.3K **Privately Held**
SIC: 7216 2311 Cleaning & dyeing, except rugs; tailored suits & formal jackets

(G-11770)
DRAGON HEAD STUDIOS LLC
14601 9th Ave Ne (98155-7038)
PHONE..................925 813-2881
EMP: 3 **EST:** 2012
SALES (est): 170K **Privately Held**
SIC: 7372 Prepackaged Software Services

(G-11771)
FEDEX OFFICE & PRINT SVCS INC
1145 N 205th St (98133-3206)
PHONE..................206 546-7600
EMP: 20
SALES (corp-wide): 69.6B **Publicly Held**
WEB: www.kinkos.com
SIC: 7334 2752 7336 2791 Photocopying & duplicating services; commercial printing, lithographic; commercial art & graphic design; typesetting
HQ: Fedex Office And Print Services, Inc.
7900 Legacy Dr
Plano TX 75024
800 463-3339

(G-11772)
FLYTES OF FANCY
16003 Meridian Ave N (98133-5839)
PHONE..................206 306-9233
Elizabeth Fye, *Partner*
Maryn Wynne, *Partner*
EMP: 2

Shoreline - King County (G-11773)

SALES (est): 186.9K **Privately Held**
WEB: www.flytesoffancy.com
SIC: 3961 Costume novelties

(G-11773)
FOOD SERVICE EQP REPR INC
20126 Ballinger Way Ne (98155-1117)
P.O. Box 12224, Mill Creek (98082-0224)
PHONE 206 730-2662
Todd L Lachmund, *President*
EMP: 3
SQ FT: 1,500
SALES (est): 500K **Privately Held**
SIC: 3263 1799 Commercial tableware or kitchen articles, fine earthenware; kitchen cabinet installation

(G-11774)
GARRETT PRESS
2122 N 155th St (98133-6046)
PHONE 206 362-1466
Gary Garrett, *Owner*
Ann Garrett, *Owner*
EMP: 2
SALES (est): 160K **Privately Held**
SIC: 2752 Commercial printing, offset

(G-11775)
GREEN TRAILS INC
2416 Nw 201st Ct (98177-2462)
P.O. Box 77734, Seattle (98177-0734)
PHONE 206 546-6277
Alan Coburn, *President*
Gail Coburn, *Vice Pres*
EMP: 5
SALES (est): 409.1K **Privately Held**
SIC: 2741 Maps: publishing & printing

(G-11776)
GREENES TEES LLC
16001 Wallingford Ave N (98133-5833)
PHONE 206 801-7725
EMP: 2 **EST:** 2016
SALES (est): 97.5K **Privately Held**
SIC: 2759 Screen printing

(G-11777)
GT DARTS
19528 Echo Lake Pl N (98133-3628)
PHONE 206 498-9855
Gary Tinder, *President*
EMP: 2 **EST:** 2009
SALES (est): 140.5K **Privately Held**
SIC: 3949 Darts & table sports equipment & supplies

(G-11778)
JOY SPECIALTY METALS LLC
17768 13th Ave Nw (98177-3202)
PHONE 206 542-5161
Michael Joy,
EMP: 3
SALES (est): 339.6K **Privately Held**
WEB: www.joyspecialtymetals.com
SIC: 3449 Miscellaneous metalwork

(G-11779)
KASAGANAAN ENTERPRISE
239 Ne 178th St (98155-3538)
PHONE 206 361-2645
Rodil Deang Alcantara, *President*
EMP: 2
SALES (est): 172K **Privately Held**
SIC: 3061 Medical & surgical rubber tubing (extruded & lathe-cut)

(G-11780)
LABORE INDUSTRIES
1247 N 172nd St (98133-5417)
PHONE 206 533-8709
Joseph Labore, *Principal*
EMP: 2
SALES (est): 143.6K **Privately Held**
SIC: 3999 Manufacturing industries

(G-11781)
LEGITIMENT LIGHT CO
1414 Nw 198th Pl (98177-2762)
PHONE 206 542-3268
EMP: 2
SALES (est): 155.9K **Privately Held**
SIC: 3646 Mfg Commercial Lighting Fixtures

(G-11782)
LIGHTLOOM
19034 12th Ave Ne (98155-2243)
PHONE 206 228-5001
EMP: 2
SALES (est): 150K **Privately Held**
SIC: 3648 Mfg Lighting Equipment

(G-11783)
LITTLE PICTURE PRESS
619 Nw 195th St (98177-2537)
PHONE 206 542-7808
EMP: 2
SALES (est): 120K **Privately Held**
SIC: 2741 Misc Publishing

(G-11784)
MANNS WELDING & TRAILER HITCH
16535 Aurora Ave N (98133-5308)
PHONE 206 542-7434
Robert L Mann, *President*
Mary Mann, *Vice Pres*
Tim Mann, *Manager*
EMP: 6
SQ FT: 2,500
SALES (est): 1.1MM **Privately Held**
SIC: 5561 3715 Recreational vehicle parts & accessories; trailer bodies

(G-11785)
MARMO E GRANITO INC
15545 12th Ave Ne (98155-6225)
PHONE 206 368-0990
Robert Douenhouer, *President*
▲ **EMP:** 8
SALES (est): 978.4K **Privately Held**
WEB: www.marmoegranito.net
SIC: 3281 Granite, cut & shaped

(G-11786)
MASS MEDIA OUTLET CORPORATION
Also Called: Aurora Prints
15200 Aurora Ave N (98133-6138)
PHONE 206 274-8475
Abyaz Mahmud, *President*
Melinda Mahmud, *Vice Pres*
EMP: 2
SALES (est): 272.5K **Privately Held**
SIC: 2752 Commercial printing, lithographic

(G-11787)
MCKEONS FINE WDWKG LLC GC
608 N 165th Pl (98133-5203)
PHONE 206 920-6724
Michael McKeon,
EMP: 2
SALES (est): 147.4K **Privately Held**
SIC: 2431 Millwork

(G-11788)
MEDICAL EQUIPMENT DEV CO LLC
Also Called: B E I Packaging
313 Ne 185th St (98155-2104)
P.O. Box 55095 (98155-0095)
PHONE 206 364-3894
R Larry Bingham, *Mng Member*
Judy Bingham, *Mng Member*
Larry Bingham, *E-Business*
EMP: 3
SQ FT: 1,500
SALES (est): 158.6K **Privately Held**
SIC: 5047 5199 8748 7336 Medical equipment & supplies; packaging materials; foams & rubber; plastics foam; foam rubber; business consulting; package design; corrugated boxes, partitions, display items, sheets & pad

(G-11789)
MINDCASTLE BOOKS INCORPORATED
19833 18th Ave Nw (98177-2204)
PHONE 206 801-7338
Gudrun Geibel Ongman, *President*
James Ongman, *Vice Pres*
EMP: 2 **EST:** 2001
SALES (est): 224.5K **Privately Held**
SIC: 2731 5942 Books: publishing only; book stores

(G-11790)
MSR MARINE & VHCL HTG SYSTEMS
19302 1st Ave Nw (98177-3002)
P.O. Box 33241, Seattle (98133-0241)
PHONE 206 546-5670
Ann L Schimke, *President*
Jim Schimke, *Vice Pres*
John Schimke, *Treasurer*
EMP: 4
SALES (est): 300K **Privately Held**
SIC: 3585 Refrigeration & heating equipment

(G-11791)
MULTIPLE STREAMS MARKETIN
19323 15th Ave Nw (98177-2783)
PHONE 206 650-6769
Terry Roberts, *Principal*
EMP: 2
SALES (est): 98.2K **Privately Held**
SIC: 2741 Miscellaneous publishing

(G-11792)
NEW ROYAL MEAT LLC
Also Called: Oriental Kitchen
18019 Aurora Ave N (98133-4419)
PHONE 206 629-4958
Joanna Nielsen,
▲ **EMP:** 8
SALES (est): 1.5MM **Privately Held**
SIC: 2099 Ready-to-eat meals, salads & sandwiches; salads, fresh or refrigerated

(G-11793)
NICOS WOODWORKING
18804 Midvale Ave N (98133-4030)
PHONE 206 755-8110
Nicolas Margotat, *Principal*
EMP: 2
SALES (est): 149.6K **Privately Held**
SIC: 2431 Millwork

(G-11794)
NORWEGIAN AMERICAN
17713 15th Ave Ne Ste 205 (98155-3839)
PHONE 206 784-4617
Emily Skaftun, *Principal*
EMP: 2
SALES (est): 274.1K **Privately Held**
SIC: 2741 Miscellaneous publishing

(G-11795)
NW ELEMENTS
15527 12th Ave Ne (98155-6225)
PHONE 206 440-9135
EMP: 3 **EST:** 2011
SALES (est): 187.7K **Privately Held**
SIC: 2819 Mfg Industrial Inorganic Chemicals

(G-11796)
O2D SOFTWARE INC
86 Olympic Dr Nw (98177-8008)
P.O. Box 77784, Seattle (98177-0784)
PHONE 206 364-0055
EMP: 2
SALES (est): 140K **Privately Held**
SIC: 7372 Prepackaged Software Services

(G-11797)
OLYMPIC FLY FISHERS
20109 15th Ave Nw (98177-2164)
P.O. Box 148, Edmonds (98020-0148)
PHONE 206 546-2677
Rolf Mogster, *Principal*
EMP: 3
SALES (est): 178.3K **Privately Held**
SIC: 2399 Fishing nets

(G-11798)
ORTECH CONTROLS
14739 Aurora Ave N 120 (98133-6547)
PHONE 206 633-7914
Kenneth Orchard, *Principal*
▲ **EMP:** 8
SALES (est): 742.6K **Privately Held**
WEB: www.ortechcontrols.com
SIC: 3999 Manufacturing industries

(G-11799)
PET ENCLOSURES NORTHWEST
20126 Ballinger Way Ne (98155-1117)
PHONE 425 786-1221
EMP: 2
SALES (est): 118.8K **Privately Held**
SIC: 3444 Metal housings, enclosures, casings & other containers

(G-11800)
PETER BLUE WOODWORKS
715 N 200th St (98133-3101)
PHONE 206 542-4281
Peter J Blue, *Owner*
EMP: 2
SALES (est): 123K **Privately Held**
WEB: www.peterwegner.com
SIC: 2499 Decorative wood & woodwork

(G-11801)
PLANETA WORKS LLC
14709 26th Ave Ne (98155-7404)
PHONE 206 250-4311
Jennifer Planeta, *Manager*
EMP: 6
SALES (est): 266.1K **Privately Held**
SIC: 2426 Hardwood dimension & flooring mills

(G-11802)
POLARITY ELEC
916 N 188th St (98133-3907)
PHONE 206 546-3539
Nathan Hacker, *Principal*
EMP: 2 **EST:** 2007
SALES (est): 271.5K **Privately Held**
SIC: 3699 Electrical equipment & supplies

(G-11803)
PROCOAT LLC
16537 25th Ave Ne (98155-6114)
PHONE 425 252-0070
EMP: 4 **EST:** 2013
SALES (est): 374.8K **Privately Held**
SIC: 2431 Millwork

(G-11804)
PUGET BRIDGE SUPPLY (PA)
Also Called: Gary's Games
2333 N 179th St (98133-5151)
PHONE 206 367-3629
Gary Teachout, *Owner*
EMP: 2
SQ FT: 1,400
SALES (est): 341.4K **Privately Held**
WEB: www.garysgamesandhobbies.com
SIC: 5961 2752 5945 Toys & games (including dolls & models); mail order; cards, lithographed; games (chess, backgammon & other durable games)

(G-11805)
RODNEYS CUSTOM WOODWORK
220 Nw 195th St (98177-2532)
PHONE 206 542-2517
Rodney Soelter, *Owner*
EMP: 10
SQ FT: 8,500
SALES (est): 1MM **Privately Held**
SIC: 2541 Store & office display cases & fixtures

(G-11806)
RULERSMITH INC
14739 Aurora Ave N (98133-6547)
PHONE 360 707-2828
Edward Rifkin, *President*
EMP: 20
SQ FT: 10,000
SALES (est): 2.9MM **Privately Held**
WEB: www.rulersmith.com
SIC: 3083 3423 2759 Plastic finished products, laminated; hand & edge tools; screen printing

(G-11807)
SAMS PRESS INC
17617 Bagley Pl N (98133-5153)
PHONE 425 423-8181
Samuel Goei, *President*
Frances Goei, *Vice Pres*
EMP: 2
SQ FT: 1,000

GEOGRAPHIC SECTION

Silverdale - Kitsap County (G-11840)

SALES (est): 192K **Privately Held**
SIC: 2752 7334 Lithographing on metal; photocopying & duplicating services

(G-11808)
SEATTLE POPS
20111 30th Ave Ne (98155-1527)
P.O. Box 31285, Seattle (98103-1285)
PHONE..................................206 714-1354
Megan Janes, *Administration*
EMP: 5 EST: 2014
SALES (est): 334.6K **Privately Held**
SIC: 2024 Ice cream & frozen desserts

(G-11809)
SENSI SWEETS
14553 Linden Ave N Unit A (98133-6500)
P.O. Box 33021, Seattle (98133-0021)
PHONE..................................206 387-8589
EMP: 2
SALES (est): 106.8K **Privately Held**
SIC: 2064 Candy bars, including chocolate covered bars

(G-11810)
SHIP ELECTRONICS INC
1824 Nw 201st St (98177-2245)
PHONE..................................206 819-3853
Thomas Varne, *President*
Evelyn A Varne, *Admin Sec*
EMP: 8
SALES (est): 960K **Privately Held**
SIC: 3812 3663 Search & navigation equipment; satellites, communications

(G-11811)
SHORELINE CERT
18328 Ashworth Ave N (98133-4523)
PHONE..................................206 533-6500
Troy Cook, *Principal*
EMP: 4 EST: 2012
SALES (est): 295.3K **Privately Held**
SIC: 3711 Fire department vehicles (motor vehicles), assembly of

(G-11812)
SIMPLY SINFUL
20214 5th Ave Nw (98177-2031)
PHONE..................................206 546-4461
E Beaulaurier, *Principal*
EMP: 2
SALES (est): 145.4K **Privately Held**
SIC: 2064 Popcorn balls or other treated popcorn products

(G-11813)
SKYLINE WINDOWS INC (PA)
17240 Ronald Pl N (98133-5401)
PHONE..................................206 542-2147
Kevin Sill, *President*
Anina Sill, *Vice Pres*
EMP: 5
SQ FT: 2,800
SALES (est): 583.8K **Privately Held**
SIC: 3442 Screens, window, metal; metal doors; sash, door or window: metal; window & door frames

(G-11814)
SLEEP AIRE MATTRESS COMPANY (PA)
19022 Aurora Ave N (98133-3915)
PHONE..................................206 546-4195
Myron Pearson, *President*
Armond D Person, *CFO*
EMP: 20 EST: 1952
SQ FT: 25,000
SALES (est): 3.1MM **Privately Held**
WEB: www.sleep-aire.com
SIC: 5712 2515 Mattresses; beds & accessories; mattresses & foundations; sofa beds (convertible sofas)

(G-11815)
SLOWPITCH SOFTBALL ASSOC
19924 Aurora Ave N (98133-3526)
P.O. Box 55577, Seattle (98155-0577)
PHONE..................................206 719-2161
Rod Smith, *Owner*
EMP: 4
SALES (est): 123.6K **Privately Held**
SIC: 2741 Directories: publishing only, not printed on site

(G-11816)
SPECIALTY VETPATH
14810 15th Ave Ne (98155-7126)
PHONE..................................206 453-5691
EMP: 5
SALES (est): 310K **Privately Held**
SIC: 2836 Mfg Biological Products

(G-11817)
SPOONY LUV
2336 N 185th St (98133-4234)
PHONE..................................206 240-8584
Mari Apana, *Principal*
EMP: 2 EST: 2010
SALES (est): 195K **Privately Held**
SIC: 2131 Smoking tobacco

(G-11818)
STEMAR MEDIA GROUP LLC
Also Called: Global Biodefense
17438 10th Ave Ne (98155-5108)
PHONE..................................206 877-3560
Stephanie Lizotte, *President*
EMP: 2
SALES (est): 89.7K **Privately Held**
SIC: 7336 2741 8742 Commercial art & graphic design; ; marketing consulting services

(G-11819)
VBS REACHOUT ADVENTURES
14830 Wallingford Ave N (98133-6620)
PHONE..................................206 365-0860
Anna Van Wechel, *Owner*
Kothra Lidstrom, *Office Mgr*
EMP: 2
SALES (est): 130K **Privately Held**
SIC: 2741 Miscellaneous publishing

(G-11820)
VES COMPANY INC
20416 Richmond Bch Dr Nw (98177-2472)
PHONE..................................206 940-5742
William R Rothman, *President*
EMP: 2
SALES (est): 1.3MM **Privately Held**
WEB: www.vescompany.com
SIC: 5085 3052 Hose, belting & packing; rubber & plastics hose & beltings

(G-11821)
WEST COAST INDUSTRIES INC
Also Called: W C I
14900 Whitman Ave N (98133-6532)
PHONE..................................206 365-7513
Horst H Faust, *President*
Sieglinde Faust, *Vice Pres*
Rob Shaw, *Opers Mgr*
Brad Thompson, *Treasurer*
Rick Heusser, *Sales Executive*
EMP: 25
SQ FT: 10,000
SALES (est): 4.9MM **Privately Held**
WEB: www.coldwork.com
SIC: 3599 Machine shop, jobbing & repair

(G-11822)
WHISTLE WORKWEAR SHORELINE LLC
15240 Aurora Ave N (98133-6124)
PHONE..................................206 364-2253
Del L Deide, *Mng Member*
EMP: 6
SALES (est): 607.4K **Privately Held**
SIC: 3999 Whistles

Silver Creek
Lewis County

(G-11823)
HOWARD & SON EXCAVATING LLC
494 Flynn Rd (98585-9722)
PHONE..................................360 983-3922
Larry W Howard,
Jackie Howard,
EMP: 3
SALES (est): 318.9K **Privately Held**
SIC: 1794 2411 7389 Excavation work; logging;

(G-11824)
KIMS HORSE BLANKETS
2978 Us Highway 12 (98585-9737)
PHONE..................................360 623-9567
EMP: 2
SALES (est): 106.9K **Privately Held**
SIC: 2399 Horse blankets

(G-11825)
SILVERCREEK ICE
Also Called: Silver Creek Ice
2879 Us Highway 12 (98585)
P.O. Box 21 (98585-0021)
PHONE..................................360 985-2385
Greg Poirier, *Owner*
EMP: 2
SQ FT: 2,856
SALES (est): 152.7K **Privately Held**
SIC: 2097 Block ice

Silverdale
Kitsap County

(G-11826)
ARTISTS EDGE INC (PA)
9960 Silverdale Way Nw # 5 (98383-8984)
P.O. Box 206 (98383-0206)
PHONE..................................360 698-3113
William Greenlaw, *President*
EMP: 8
SQ FT: 7,500
SALES (est): 654K **Privately Held**
WEB: www.artistsedge.com
SIC: 2499 5947 Picture & mirror frames, wood; artcraft & carvings

(G-11827)
BAE SYSTEMS TECH SOL SRVC INC
3100 Nw Bucklin Hill Rd (98383-8358)
PHONE..................................360 598-8800
Ed Cornely, *Director*
EMP: 9
SALES (corp-wide): 21.6B **Privately Held**
SIC: 3812 Search & navigation equipment
HQ: Bae Systems Technology Solutions & Services Inc.
520 Gaither Rd
Rockville MD 20850
703 847-5820

(G-11828)
CENTRAL KITSAP FIRE RESCU
5350 Nw Newberry Rd (98383)
PHONE..................................360 447-3575
David Fergus, *Chairman*
EMP: 3
SALES (est): 296.7K **Privately Held**
SIC: 3711 Fire department vehicles (motor vehicles), assembly of

(G-11829)
CREATIVE ADS
1427 Nw Cairo St (98383-8634)
PHONE..................................360 981-1106
EMP: 2
SALES (est): 125.3K **Privately Held**
SIC: 3993 Signs & advertising specialties

(G-11830)
CREEKSIDE CABINET & DESIGN
3276 Nw Plaza Rd Ste 111 (98383-8103)
PHONE..................................360 692-7070
B Moore, *Owner*
EMP: 3
SALES (est): 303.5K **Privately Held**
SIC: 2434 Wood kitchen cabinets

(G-11831)
DEX MEDIA HOLDINGS INC
10049 Kitsap Mall Blvd Nw # 102 (98383-8903)
PHONE..................................360 830-0807
Rod Kendall, *Manager*
EMP: 13
SALES (corp-wide): 1.8B **Privately Held**
WEB: www.qwestdex.com
SIC: 2741 Directories: publishing & printing
PA: Thryv, Inc.
2200 W Airfield Dr
Dfw Airport TX 75261
972 453-7000

(G-11832)
DLA DOCUMENT SERVICES
1100 Hunley Rd Ste 108 (98315-1100)
PHONE..................................360 315-4014
Glenn West, *Director*
EMP: 48 **Publicly Held**
SIC: 2752 9711 Commercial printing, lithographic; national security;
HQ: Dla Document Services
5450 Carlisle Pike Bldg 9
Mechanicsburg PA 17050
717 605-2362

(G-11833)
ELECTRIC BOAT CORPORATION
Escolar Rd T 33 (98315)
PHONE..................................360 598-5115
Emerald Rotando, *Manager*
EMP: 50
SALES (corp-wide): 36.1B **Publicly Held**
SIC: 3731 8711 Submarines, building & repairing; engineering services
HQ: Electric Boat Corporation
75 Eastern Point Rd
Groton CT 06340

(G-11834)
FASTSIGNS
9460 Silverdale Way Nw (98383-8343)
P.O. Box 2102 (98383-2102)
PHONE..................................360 692-1660
Jackie Jones, *Owner*
EMP: 6
SALES (est): 428K **Privately Held**
SIC: 3993 Signs & advertising specialties

(G-11835)
FREEDOMPRINT LLC
4110 Michigan Dr Apt D (98315-9430)
PHONE..................................860 333-2448
Brian Ellis, *Mng Member*
EMP: 2
SALES (est): 91.2K **Privately Held**
SIC: 2752 Commercial printing, lithographic

(G-11836)
GRAVEL
4213 Grayback Cir Apt A (98315-8606)
PHONE..................................360 930-5777
Zachary Gravel, *Principal*
EMP: 2
SALES (est): 66K **Privately Held**
SIC: 1442 Construction sand & gravel

(G-11837)
HOMETOWN BAND
12215 Ridgepoint Cir Nw (98383-9493)
P.O. Box 2343 (98383-2343)
PHONE..................................206 842-2084
Cathy Bisaillon, *Principal*
EMP: 2 EST: 2011
SALES (est): 83K **Privately Held**
SIC: 2741 Music book & sheet music publishing

(G-11838)
INTERSTATE ELECTRONICS CORP
Naval Sub Bangor Rm W201 (98383)
PHONE..................................360 779-3723
Hal Woodward, *Manager*
EMP: 4
SALES (corp-wide): 6.1B **Publicly Held**
WEB: www.iechome.com
SIC: 3825 Test equipment for electronic & electric measurement
HQ: Interstate Electronics Corporation
602 E Vermont Ave
Anaheim CA 92805
714 758-0500

(G-11839)
ISLAND BANKRA CARIBBEAN FOODS
4910 Nw 82nd St (98383-9205)
PHONE..................................360 698-3345
EMP: 2
SALES (est): 75K **Privately Held**
SIC: 2099 Mfg Food Preparations

(G-11840)
J P J 3 LLC
1930 Nw Woodcrest Ct (98383-9531)
PHONE..................................360 697-1084

Silverdale - Kitsap County (G-11841)

Patricia Laschinski,
Jean Braun,
EMP: 3
SALES (est): 193.6K **Privately Held**
SIC: 3792 House trailers, except as permanent dwellings

(G-11841)
KINGS WOK
9960 Silverdale Way Nw # 4 (98383-8984)
PHONE 360 337-2512
Zhang Tongcheng, *Owner*
▲ **EMP:** 5
SALES (est): 480K **Privately Held**
WEB: www.kingswok.com
SIC: 3699 Laser systems & equipment

(G-11842)
KITSAP CUSTOM COATINGS LLC
2251 Nw Bucklin Hill Rd (98383-8303)
P.O. Box 2229 (98383-2229)
PHONE 360 471-3095
EMP: 2
SALES (est): 69.9K **Privately Held**
SIC: 3479 Metal coating & allied service

(G-11843)
LEE FABRICATORS INC
6362 Nw Warehouse Way (98383-6313)
PHONE 360 698-1190
Clyde Penwell, *President*
Arlene Penwell, *Vice Pres*
EMP: 14
SQ FT: 12,000
SALES (est): 2.6MM **Privately Held**
SIC: 3441 3444 Fabricated structural metal; sheet metalwork

(G-11844)
LINE-X SILVERDALE INC
9623 Provost Rd Nw # 101 (98383-9256)
PHONE 360 692-4840
Bruce W Tegge, *President*
Bruce Pegge, *Principal*
EMP: 3
SALES (est): 384.7K **Privately Held**
SIC: 2299 Crash, linen

(G-11845)
LITTLE NICKEL-BREMERTON
3888 Nw Randall Way (98383-7847)
PHONE 360 308-0279
Diane Humble, *Manager*
EMP: 3
SALES (est): 120.7K **Privately Held**
SIC: 2711 Newspapers

(G-11846)
LOCKHEED MARTIN CORPORATION
Naval Base Ktsap Bangor (98315)
P.O. Box 6429 (98315-6429)
PHONE 360 396-8591
Duane McDonnel, *Manager*
EMP: 290 **Publicly Held**
WEB: www.lockheedmartin.com
SIC: 3812 Search & navigation equipment
PA: Lockheed Martin Corporation
6801 Rockledge Dr
Bethesda MD 20817

(G-11847)
LOCKHEED MARTIN CORPORATION
Bangor Nsb Bldg 2000 (98315)
P.O. Box 6026 (98315-6026)
PHONE 360 697-6844
Lockheed Martin, *Branch Mgr*
EMP: 232 **Publicly Held**
SIC: 3812 Search & navigation equipment
PA: Lockheed Martin Corporation
6801 Rockledge Dr
Bethesda MD 20817

(G-11848)
LOGO LOFT INC
1572 Nw Duesenberg Ct (98383-9435)
PHONE 360 394-5638
Sandra L Hunter, *President*
John Hunter, *Vice Pres*
EMP: 5
SQ FT: 2,000
SALES (est): 508.2K **Privately Held**
SIC: 2759 Promotional printing

(G-11849)
MAUGHAN PRSTHETIC ORTHOTIC INC
Also Called: Mpo
9220 Ridgetop Blvd Nw # 110 (98383-8556)
P.O. Box 1546, Graham (98338-1546)
PHONE 360 447-0770
Justin Maughan, *President*
Justin M Maughan, *Principal*
Krysten Eads, *Administration*
EMP: 2
SALES: 750K **Privately Held**
SIC: 3842 Limbs, artificial; prosthetic appliances

(G-11850)
MICHAEL M HENNESSEY
Also Called: Shadetree Engineering
3291 Nw Mount Vintage Way (98383-6001)
PHONE 360 471-3313
Michael M Hennessey, *Owner*
EMP: 3
SALES: 100K **Privately Held**
SIC: 3799 Transportation equipment

(G-11851)
NATURES PROVISION
11273 Kiptree Ln Nw (98383-8818)
PHONE 360 307-0113
Tim Lavoie, *Owner*
EMP: 2
SALES (est): 130.9K **Privately Held**
WEB: www.xylipro.com
SIC: 2892 Explosives

(G-11852)
NORTHROP GRUMMAN SYSTEMS CORP
6401 Skipjack Cir (98315-6400)
P.O. Box 934 (98383-0934)
PHONE 360 315-3976
Mark McMillan, *Engineer*
Aaron Wilson, *Manager*
EMP: 20 **Publicly Held**
WEB: www.sperry.ngc.com
SIC: 3761 3764 Guided missiles & space vehicles, research & development; guided missile & space vehicle propulsion unit parts
HQ: Northrop Grumman Systems Corporation
2980 Fairview Park Dr
Falls Church VA 22042
703 280-2900

(G-11853)
PC NETWORKS INC
Also Called: PC Networks
13825 Crestview Cir Nw (98383-9542)
PHONE 360 362-9684
Veronica Anne Clemmons, *President*
Veronica Clemmons, *President*
Paul Clemmons, *Vice Pres*
EMP: 3
SALES (est): 200K **Privately Held**
WEB: www.pcnetworkswa.com
SIC: 3577 3651 Computer peripheral equipment; household video equipment

(G-11854)
QUALITY HEATING & AC LLC
Also Called: Gas Works
9960 Silverdale Way Nw # 14 (98383-8984)
PHONE 360 613-5614
Fax: 360 692-9858
EMP: 13
SALES (est): 930K **Privately Held**
SIC: 3585 1711 Mfg Refrigeration/Heating Equipment Plumbing/Heating/Air Cond Contractor

(G-11855)
SAGRA INC
5997 Nw Altitude Ln (98383-9035)
PHONE 253 476-1403
Richard Smith, *Principal*
Zeena Smith, *Principal*
◆ **EMP:** 2
SALES (est): 420.3K **Privately Held**
SIC: 3556 Food products machinery

(G-11856)
SEAMIST MARINE LLC
5451 Nw Newberry Hill Rd # 103 (98383-7402)
PHONE 253 583-4151
EMP: 2 **EST:** 2017
SALES (est): 130.4K **Privately Held**
SIC: 3732 Boat building & repairing

(G-11857)
SILVER CITY BREWING CO INC
2799 Nw Myhre Rd (98383-8770)
P.O. Box 3606 (98383-3606)
PHONE 360 698-5879
Roger Houmes, *President*
Steve B Houmes, *Vice Pres*
Gary Winn, *Opers Staff*
Scott W Houmes, *Treasurer*
Jordan Marsh, *Sales Staff*
EMP: 80
SQ FT: 1,100
SALES (est): 9.6MM **Privately Held**
WEB: www.silvercitybrewery.com
SIC: 2082 5813 5812 Malt beverages; bar (drinking places); eating places

(G-11858)
SOUND PUBLISHING INC
Also Called: Northwest Navigator
3888 Nw Randall Way # 100 (98383-7847)
PHONE 360 308-9161
Rob White, *Branch Mgr*
EMP: 2 **Privately Held**
WEB: www.soundpublishing.com
SIC: 2711 Newspapers, publishing & printing; newspapers: publishing only, not printed on site
HQ: Sound Publishing, Inc.
11323 Commando Rd W Main
Everett WA 98204
360 394-5800

(G-11859)
SQUARERIGGER INC
9119 Ridgetop Blvd Nw # 300 (98383-8549)
PHONE 360 698-3562
Edward Cooper, *CEO*
Theda Cooper, *President*
Eldon Wright, *Vice Pres*
Misty Just, *Office Mgr*
EMP: 12
SQ FT: 3,000
SALES (est): 1.5MM **Privately Held**
WEB: www.squarerigger.com
SIC: 7372 7373 Business oriented computer software; computer integrated systems design

(G-11860)
STEDMAN BEE SUPPLIES INC
3763 Nw Anderson Hill Rd (98383-9409)
PHONE 360 692-9453
Al Stedman, *President*
EMP: 2
SALES (est): 211.7K **Privately Held**
SIC: 3999 0291 Honeycomb foundations (beekeepers' supplies); animal specialty farm, general

Silverlake
Cowlitz County

(G-11861)
ADAMS TIMBER SERVICE LLC
119 Rockfish Ct (98645-9753)
P.O. Box 1825, Castle Rock (98611-1825)
PHONE 360 636-7766
Adam Lee, *Principal*
EMP: 2
SALES (est): 253.7K **Privately Held**
SIC: 5211 2411 0811 Lumber products; logging; timber tracts

(G-11862)
ANDERSON FOUNDRY FORGE
4004 Spirit Lake Hwy (98645-9784)
PHONE 360 270-2008
EMP: 3
SALES (est): 200.2K **Privately Held**
SIC: 3325 Steel foundries

(G-11863)
FLAGSTONE WILDLIFE ARTISRTY
169 Flagstone Dr (98645-9749)
PHONE 360 967-2005
EMP: 2 **EST:** 2011
SALES (est): 110K **Privately Held**
SIC: 3281 Mfg Cut Stone/Products

(G-11864)
FORT VANCOUVER BEE LLC
3966 Spirit Lake Hwy (98645-9782)
PHONE 360 274-3396
Jean Costello, *Mng Member*
Robert Costello,
EMP: 2
SALES (est): 200K **Privately Held**
SIC: 3443 Fumigating chambers, metal plate

Skamokawa
Wahkiakum County

(G-11865)
GRIBSKOV GLASSBLOWING
123 Middle Valley Rd (98647-9504)
PHONE 360 795-8419
Kyle Gribskov, *Owner*
EMP: 4
SALES (est): 160K **Privately Held**
SIC: 3229 Glassware, art or decorative

Skykomish
King County

(G-11866)
J&N LAND TRUCKING
63708 197th Pl (98288)
PHONE 360 677-2274
James Land, *Owner*
EMP: 3
SALES: 280K **Privately Held**
SIC: 4213 2411 Contract haulers; logging

(G-11867)
MOORE MFG CO
Also Called: Radioharness.com
71509 Ne Old Cascade Hwy (98288-4922)
P.O. Box 309 (98288-0309)
PHONE 360 677-2442
Timothy D Moore, *Owner*
Tim D Moore, *Owner*
EMP: 2
SQ FT: 1,800
SALES: 49K **Privately Held**
WEB: www.radioharness.com
SIC: 3949 5941 Sporting & athletic goods; sporting goods & bicycle shops

Snohomish
Snohomish County

(G-11868)
A&B QUALITY FINISHERS INC
5712 207th Ave Se (98290-7417)
PHONE 360 805-3500
Doreen Atkinson, *President*
EMP: 2
SQ FT: 1,000
SALES (est): 190K **Privately Held**
WEB: www.adpeonies.com
SIC: 3599 3471 Machine shop, jobbing & repair; cleaning, polishing & finishing

(G-11869)
A1 ELECTRIC MOTOR INC
7019 137th Ave Se (98290-9063)
PHONE 360 568-3409
Lonnie Wolk, *President*
Joe Gregory, *Sales Associate*
EMP: 2
SQ FT: 1,500
SALES: 150K **Privately Held**
SIC: 7694 Electric motor repair

GEOGRAPHIC SECTION

Snohomish - Snohomish County (G-11903)

(G-11870)
ADVANCED CARGO CONTROL LLC
19721 76th Ave Se (98296-5103)
PHONE.................................206 498-5824
Leonce Bienville Jr, *President*
Daniel Humphrey, *Principal*
EMP: 5
SALES (est): 222K **Privately Held**
SIC: 3089 7389 Monofilaments, nontextile;

(G-11871)
ADVANCED WATER SYSTEMS INC
4621 157th Ave Se (98290-9358)
PHONE.................................520 575-6718
Peter Lamm, *CEO*
EMP: 2
SQ FT: 6,000
SALES (est): 77K **Privately Held**
WEB: www.advanced-water.com
SIC: 3589 Water purification equipment, household type; water treatment equipment, industrial

(G-11872)
AIRPORT WELDING & MUFFLER INC
10226 Airport Way (98296)
PHONE.................................360 568-7135
Richard Somerville, *President*
Lou Bars, *Treasurer*
Margaret Somerville, *Treasurer*
EMP: 7
SQ FT: 4,032
SALES (est): 581.2K **Privately Held**
SIC: 7692 7533 Welding repair; muffler shop, sale or repair & installation

(G-11873)
ALIA WINES LLC
12216 185th Ave Se (98290-8679)
PHONE.................................360 794-0421
John R Olsen, *Principal*
EMP: 2
SALES (est): 117.5K **Privately Held**
SIC: 2084 Wines

(G-11874)
ALPHA MFG
12306 185th Ave Se (98290-8679)
PHONE.................................360 794-8573
Tara Schwartze, *Owner*
EMP: 2
SALES (est): 128.7K **Privately Held**
SIC: 3629 Electronic generation equipment

(G-11875)
ARDOR PRINTING LLC ✪
12525 Old Snohomish Mnroe (98290-6512)
PHONE.................................425 786-4361
EMP: 2 **EST:** 2018
SALES (est): 100.1K **Privately Held**
SIC: 2752 Commercial printing, lithographic

(G-11876)
ASI SIGNAGE INNOVATIONS
9910 198th St Se (98296-7913)
PHONE.................................360 668-1636
Cathy Boisseranc, *President*
EMP: 2
SALES (est): 72.6K **Privately Held**
SIC: 3993 Signs & advertising specialties

(G-11877)
BOB JOHNSON WOODWORKING
15405 State St (98296-7020)
PHONE.................................360 668-9456
Bob Johnson, *Owner*
EMP: 3
SALES (est): 342.9K **Privately Held**
SIC: 2431 Millwork

(G-11878)
BOCHANS CUSTOM LEATHER WORK
12703 Seattle Hill Rd (98296-8986)
PHONE.................................425 337-6128
Jean Bochans, *Owner*
EMP: 2

SALES (est): 85.8K **Privately Held**
SIC: 3111 Accessory products, leather

(G-11879)
BOEING ✪
1910 Bickford Ave Ste A (98290-1764)
PHONE.................................360 348-0394
EMP: 2 **EST:** 2019
SALES (est): 86K **Privately Held**
SIC: 3721 Airplanes, fixed or rotary wing

(G-11880)
BOWMANS ELECTRO PAINTING
18114 67th Ave Se (98296-8351)
PHONE.................................360 668-1389
Don Scriver, *Owner*
EMP: 2
SALES (est): 85K **Privately Held**
SIC: 3479 1721 Coating of metals & formed products; painting & paper hanging

(G-11881)
BRAD S WELDING
17430 100th Ave Se (98296-8126)
PHONE.................................360 668-7135
EMP: 3
SALES (est): 41.4K **Privately Held**
SIC: 7692 Welding Repair

(G-11882)
BRADSHAW MACHINE CO
1112 Bonneville Ave (98290-2006)
PHONE.................................425 337-2802
Georgia Bradshaw, *Owner*
Thomas Bradshaw, *Co-Owner*
EMP: 3
SQ FT: 17,200
SALES (est): 78K **Privately Held**
SIC: 3599 Machine shop, jobbing & repair

(G-11883)
BUELER FARMS INC
8626 E Lowell Larimer Rd (98296-5997)
PHONE.................................360 668-5289
Michael Bueler, *President*
EMP: 8
SALES (est): 1MM **Privately Held**
SIC: 0241 2411 Dairy farms; logging

(G-11884)
BUILDERS SAND AND GRAVEL INC
18827 Yew Way (98296-8199)
PHONE.................................425 743-3333
Phil Wathne, *President*
Louise Wathne, *Corp Secy*
EMP: 15
SQ FT: 1,000
SALES (est): 1.6MM **Privately Held**
SIC: 4212 1442 Dump truck haulage; construction sand mining; gravel mining

(G-11885)
CARLSON & FITZWATER LLC
Also Called: Wet Fly
23708 139th Dr Se (98296-5400)
PHONE.................................425 941-4020
Kit Carlson, *Owner*
EMP: 3
SQ FT: 400
SALES: 300K **Privately Held**
SIC: 3949 Flies, fishing; artificial

(G-11886)
CASCADE FAMILY FLYERS
1429 Avenue D (98290-1742)
PHONE.................................425 750-4249
Mark Hanson, *Principal*
EMP: 3
SALES (est): 166.7K **Privately Held**
SIC: 3812 Aircraft/aerospace flight instruments & guidance systems

(G-11887)
CEDAR HOMES OF WASHINGTON INC
23209 131st Ave Se (98296-5420)
PHONE.................................360 668-8242
Mike Flanagan, *President*
Judy Flanagan, *Vice Pres*
EMP: 2

SALES: 400K **Privately Held**
WEB: www.chwi.com
SIC: 5211 1521 2452 Prefabricated buildings; prefabricated single-family house erection; log cabins, prefabricated, wood

(G-11888)
CEMEX CNSTR MTLS PCF LLC
Also Called: Maltby Agg. & Landfill
19000 Yew Way (98296-5061)
PHONE.................................360 486-3557
EMP: 23 **Privately Held**
WEB: www.rinkermaterials.com
SIC: 3271 Concrete block & brick
HQ: Cemex Construction Materials Pacific, Llc
1501 Belvedere Rd
West Palm Beach FL 33406
561 833-5555

(G-11889)
CHAMPOUX VINEYARDS LLC
11306 52nd St Se (98290-5727)
PHONE.................................360 563-1330
Bill Reith, *Administration*
EMP: 2
SALES (est): 147.4K **Privately Held**
SIC: 2084 Wines

(G-11890)
CLEVER FOX EDITING
17410 87th Ave Se Trlr 37 (98296-8005)
PHONE.................................805 910-6938
Chelo Biggerstaff, *Principal*
EMP: 2
SALES (est): 81.6K **Privately Held**
SIC: 2741 Miscellaneous publishing

(G-11891)
COOKIE FAIRY
11607 171st Ave Se (98290-6307)
PHONE.................................360 568-0868
Cheryl Ruhnke, *Principal*
EMP: 2
SALES (est): 62.3K **Privately Held**
SIC: 2051 Bread, cake & related products

(G-11892)
CREATIVE MILLWORK & MOULDING
12606 217th St Se (98296-3903)
PHONE.................................425 343-4799
Dana Strobel, *Owner*
EMP: 2
SALES (est): 170.2K **Privately Held**
SIC: 2431 Millwork

(G-11893)
CRT LESS LETHAL
Also Called: Crt Consulting
13303 68th Ave Se (98296-8659)
PHONE.................................425 337-6875
Rick Wyant, *Owner*
Tom Burns, *Co-Owner*
Chris Myers, *Co-Owner*
EMP: 3
SALES: 20K **Privately Held**
SIC: 3484 Guns (firearms) or gun parts, 30 mm. & below

(G-11894)
CURTIS MANUFACTURING INC
Also Called: TCI Scales
17611 Ok Mill Rd (98290-9633)
P.O. Box 1648 (98291-1648)
PHONE.................................425 353-4384
Joann Britt, *President*
Harry Hawkins, *Mfg Staff*
William C Britt Jr, *Treasurer*
EMP: 15 **EST:** 1972
SALES: 1MM **Privately Held**
SIC: 3596 Industrial scales

(G-11895)
DAWSON-ALLEY LLC
Also Called: Dark Moon Artisan Distillery
1830 Bickford Ave (98290-1749)
PHONE.................................360 217-8244
EMP: 2 **EST:** 2011
SALES (est): 166.9K **Privately Held**
SIC: 2085 Mfg Distilled/Blended Liquor

(G-11896)
DEAL PERCH INC
1020 20th St (98290-1306)
PHONE.................................425 372-8514
Jack Peterson, *CEO*
Arnold Deannunti, *Admin Sec*
EMP: 3
SALES (est): 78.2K **Privately Held**
SIC: 7372 Application computer software

(G-11897)
DEM-BART CHECKERING TOOLS INC
1825 Bickford Ave (98290-1754)
PHONE.................................360 568-7356
Walter Mc Vey, *President*
EMP: 4
SQ FT: 1,200
SALES (est): 461.6K **Privately Held**
WEB: www.dembartco.com
SIC: 3423 2426 3545 Hand & edge tools; gun stocks, wood; machine tool accessories

(G-11898)
DESSERT INDUSTRIES INC
12902 Lost Lake Rd (98296-7802)
PHONE.................................425 487-3244
Patrick C Dessert, *President*
Verna Dessert, *Vice Pres*
EMP: 2
SALES: 295K **Privately Held**
WEB: www.dessertindustries.com
SIC: 1799 3594 7699 Hydraulic equipment, installation & service; fluid power pumps; hydraulic equipment repair

(G-11899)
DICK NITE SPOONS INC
16810 Ok Mill Rd (98290-9622)
P.O. Box 175, Lake Stevens (98258-0175)
PHONE.................................425 377-8448
Richard D Figgins, *President*
EMP: 7 **EST:** 1982
SQ FT: 1,280
SALES (est): 1MM **Privately Held**
WEB: www.dicknite.com
SIC: 5091 3949 Fishing tackle; fishing tackle, general

(G-11900)
DRAPED IN STYLE LLC
7220 203rd St Se (98296-5126)
PHONE.................................425 241-6227
EMP: 4
SALES (est): 213.2K **Privately Held**
SIC: 2431 Windows, wood

(G-11901)
DREAM WORKS MACHINE QUILTING
17701 87th Ave Se (98296-8078)
PHONE.................................360 668-0864
Terise Stroghman, *Treasurer*
EMP: 3
SALES (est): 130K **Privately Held**
SIC: 2395 Quilted fabrics or cloth

(G-11902)
DYNO-TECH MACHINE LLC
Also Called: Critical Precision
17816 Dubuque Rd (98290-8509)
PHONE.................................360 568-7023
Edmund C Holloway,
EMP: 2 **EST:** 1981
SALES: 300K **Privately Held**
SIC: 3599 Machine shop, jobbing & repair

(G-11903)
E T L CORP
Also Called: Swartz Engineering Company
9624 Airport Way (98296-8240)
PHONE.................................360 568-1473
George Swartz, *President*
EMP: 10 **EST:** 1977
SQ FT: 6,000
SALES (est): 710K **Privately Held**
SIC: 3679 Static power supply converters for electronic applications

Snohomish - Snohomish County (G-11904)

(G-11904)
ELANDER PERSSON FINE WDWRK LLC
Also Called: Elander-Persson
9305 156th St Se (98296-7093)
PHONE..................................206 818-2882
Van Elander, *Mng Member*
EMP: 3
SALES (est): 310K **Privately Held**
SIC: 2434 Wood kitchen cabinets

(G-11905)
ENDURANCE COATINGS LLC
10106 205th Ave Se (98290-3226)
PHONE..................................206 234-8793
EMP: 2
SALES (est): 124.7K **Privately Held**
SIC: 3479 Metal coating & allied service

(G-11906)
ET HYDRAULICS LLC
8626 180th St Se Ste B (98296-8003)
PHONE..................................206 718-7372
Everett Taggart, *Mng Member*
EMP: 5 **EST:** 2014
SALES (est): 685K **Privately Held**
SIC: 3714 Hydraulic fluid power pumps for auto steering mechanism; exhaust systems & parts, motor vehicle

(G-11907)
EXTREME NETWORKS INC
18820 71st Ave Se (98296-8350)
PHONE..................................408 579-2800
R Lopez, *Branch Mgr*
EMP: 2 **Publicly Held**
SIC: 3661 Telephone & telegraph apparatus
PA: Extreme Networks, Inc.
6480 Via Del Oro
San Jose CA 95119

(G-11908)
F W B ENTERPRISES INC
Also Called: Electrical Sales & Service
5415 93rd Ave Se (98296-9221)
P.O. Box 1777 (98291-1777)
PHONE..................................425 377-2628
Frank W Barson, *President*
Lucy Harrison, *Vice Pres*
EMP: 2
SQ FT: 3,000
SALES (est): 1MM **Privately Held**
SIC: 5063 7694 Motors, electric; electric motor repair

(G-11909)
FEATHERLITE TRAILERS
3100 Bickford Ave (98290-1762)
PHONE..................................425 334-4045
Bill Smallwood, *Principal*
EMP: 2
SALES (est): 23.9K **Privately Held**
SIC: 3792 5599 Travel trailers & campers; utility trailers

(G-11910)
FOBES DISTRICT WATER & ASSN
Also Called: FOBES DIST WATER ASSN
4520 Bickford Ave (98290-5210)
PHONE..................................425 334-3311
Phil Baldwin, *President*
EMP: 3
SALES: 31.3K **Privately Held**
SIC: 4941 3589 3559 Water supply; sewage & water treatment equipment; special industry machinery

(G-11911)
FRITCH FOREST PRODUCTS INC
18507 Waverly Dr (98296-4827)
PHONE..................................360 668-5838
Eric Fritch, *President*
EMP: 30
SALES (est): 4.7MM **Privately Held**
WEB: www.fritchmill.com
SIC: 2421 Lumber: rough, sawed or planed

(G-11912)
FRITCH MILL INC
18507 Waverly Dr (98296-4827)
PHONE..................................425 481-4157
Bruce Fritch, *President*
Eric Fritch, *Principal*
Tracey Denadel, *CFO*
Meryl Phillips, *Sales Staff*
Grant Weed, *Admin Sec*
EMP: 2 **EST:** 1946
SQ FT: 200
SALES (est): 319.3K **Privately Held**
SIC: 2421 Lumber: rough, sawed or planed

(G-11913)
GLOBAL PACIFIC FOREST PRODUCTS
Also Called: Western Pacific Log Exports
310 Maple Ave (98290-2526)
PHONE..................................360 568-1111
Wayne C Cook, *President*
EMP: 10
SQ FT: 2,000
SALES: 9MM **Privately Held**
SIC: 2411 Logging camps & contractors

(G-11914)
GO MANNA INC
Also Called: Ready Greek Go
7820 167th St Se (98296-6323)
PHONE..................................360 794-7480
Christa Staudacher, *CEO*
Mark Staudacher, *President*
EMP: 2
SALES (est): 114.6K **Privately Held**
SIC: 2026 5149 Yogurt; groceries & related products

(G-11915)
GRAPHICODE INC
1924 Bickford Ave Ste 201 (98290-1753)
PHONE..................................360 282-4888
Paul Wells-Edwards, *Manager*
EMP: 24
SQ FT: 6,000
SALES (est): 1.9MM **Privately Held**
WEB: www.graphicode.com
SIC: 7371 7373 7372 Computer software development; computer integrated systems design; prepackaged software

(G-11916)
GREEN VAULT SYSTEMS LLC
7010 136th Pl Se (98296-7641)
PHONE..................................206 900-2036
Robert Smith, *Principal*
EMP: 3 **EST:** 2016
SALES (est): 110.5K **Privately Held**
SIC: 3272 Burial vaults, concrete or precast terrazzo

(G-11917)
GUNDERSONS CUSTOM WELDING
17224 Tester Rd (98290-6630)
PHONE..................................360 794-6165
Dan Gunderson, *Owner*
EMP: 3
SALES (est): 140K **Privately Held**
SIC: 7692 Welding repair

(G-11918)
GW 42 INC
1208 10th St Ste B (98290-2099)
PHONE..................................360 862-8319
Rebekah Gagnon, *Principal*
EMP: 4
SALES (est): 518.2K **Privately Held**
SIC: 3441 Fabricated structural metal

(G-11919)
HARDWOOD INDUSTRIES INC
20124 Broadway Ave Ste D (98296-7993)
PHONE..................................425 420-1050
Jeff Wirkkala, *Branch Mgr*
EMP: 16
SALES (corp-wide): 26MM **Privately Held**
SIC: 3999 Barber & beauty shop equipment
PA: Hardwood Industries, Inc.
20548 Sw Wildrose Pl
Sherwood OR 97140
503 692-6520

(G-11920)
HEIR WEAR LLC
1422 Ridge Ave (98290-1349)
PHONE..................................425 760-0990
EMP: 2

SALES (est): 83.9K **Privately Held**
SIC: 2752 Commercial printing, lithographic

(G-11921)
HOFFMAN HONEY CO
16921 Butler Rd (98290-6354)
PHONE..................................360 568-5210
Robert D Hoffman, *Owner*
EMP: 2
SALES (est): 114.5K **Privately Held**
SIC: 2099 Honey, strained & bottled

(G-11922)
HORSESHOE GRANGE 965
15802 State Route 9 Se (98296-8758)
PHONE..................................360 668-3939
EMP: 2 **EST:** 2011
SALES (est): 110K **Privately Held**
SIC: 3462 Mfg Iron/Steel Forgings

(G-11923)
HPF MANUFACTURING
20105 Broadway Ave (98296-5149)
PHONE..................................425 486-8031
Wendell Malmberg, *Owner*
EMP: 8
SALES (est): 239.2K **Privately Held**
SIC: 3999 Manufacturing industries

(G-11924)
HT INDUSTRIES LLC
1820 Creswell Rd (98290-7605)
PHONE..................................360 863-2029
Haider Tareen, *Principal*
EMP: 2
SALES (est): 124.5K **Privately Held**
SIC: 3999 Manufacturing industries

(G-11925)
HULETT AND COMPANY
21312 E Lost Lake Rd (98296-6184)
PHONE..................................425 922-5224
Michael Hulett, *Principal*
EMP: 2
SALES (est): 114.4K **Privately Held**
SIC: 3444 7389 Sheet metalwork;

(G-11926)
IMPRESSIONS IN WOOD LLC
917 Avenue A (98290-2031)
PHONE..................................425 444-5324
Kyle Mistretta, *Owner*
EMP: 3
SALES: 150K **Privately Held**
SIC: 2499 Engraved wood products

(G-11927)
IMPULSE CONSTRUCTION & GLASS
1429 Avenue D (98290-1742)
PHONE..................................425 530-7728
Kelly Smothermon, *Principal*
EMP: 2
SALES (est): 114.2K **Privately Held**
SIC: 3211 Construction glass

(G-11928)
JOHNSONS STUMP GRINDING S
5221 S Machias Rd (98290-5517)
PHONE..................................360 334-4832
Lisa Shumaker, *Principal*
EMP: 2
SALES (est): 213.7K **Privately Held**
SIC: 3599 Grinding castings for the trade

(G-11929)
KADI MANUFACTURING
6330 180th St Se (98296-5354)
PHONE..................................360 668-5633
Fax: 360 668-5633
EMP: 3
SALES (corp-wide): 413.3K **Privately Held**
SIC: 3949 2499 Mfg Sporting/Athletic Goods Mfg Wood Products
PA: Kadi Manufacturing
6300 And A Half 180 St
Bothell WA
360 668-5633

(G-11930)
KAYE MAG LLC
915 Harrison Ave Apt A (98290-2268)
PHONE..................................360 668-8989

EMP: 2
SALES (est): 62.9K **Privately Held**
SIC: 2711 Newspapers

(G-11931)
KELLY INDUSTRIES LLC
9909 200th Pl Se (98296-7945)
PHONE..................................206 676-2338
Kelly Quinby, *Bd of Directors*
EMP: 2
SALES (est): 114.4K **Privately Held**
SIC: 3999 Manufacturing industries

(G-11932)
KEMP WEST INC
3800 Sinclair Ave (98290-5305)
PHONE..................................425 334-5572
Kari Hakso, *President*
Gary Johnson, *Executive*
EMP: 62
SQ FT: 6,000
SALES (est): 7.3MM **Privately Held**
WEB: www.kempwest.com
SIC: 1629 3531 1794 Land preparation construction; timber removal; construction machinery; excavation work

(G-11933)
KING ENTERPRISES
Also Called: Comserv
1030 Avenue D Ste 3 (98290-2086)
P.O. Box 328 (98291-0328)
PHONE..................................360 568-1644
Barbara King, *Owner*
Corey King, *Co-Owner*
EMP: 2
SQ FT: 1,450
SALES (est): 234.8K **Privately Held**
SIC: 7334 4822 2759 Photocopying & duplicating services; facsimile transmission services; invitation & stationery printing & engraving

(G-11934)
L & L INK
8329 200th St Se (98296-5124)
PHONE..................................206 605-4561
Lamonica Hummel, *Owner*
EMP: 2
SALES (est): 102.6K **Privately Held**
SIC: 2741 Technical manual & paper publishing

(G-11935)
L CLASEN CORP
Also Called: Ironwood Manufacturing Co.
1102 Bonneville Ave M (98290-2080)
PHONE..................................360 658-1823
Trey Clasen, *President*
Sabrina Clasen, *Corp Secy*
EMP: 8
SQ FT: 6,000
SALES: 1MM **Privately Held**
WEB: www.ironwood-mfg.com
SIC: 7389 2541 1799 Design, commercial & industrial; partitions for floor attachment, prefabricated: wood; table or counter tops, plastic laminated; demountable partition installation; counter top installation

(G-11936)
LAZ TOOL AND MANUFACTURING (PA)
Also Called: Laz Tool & Fabricators
14816 Roosevelt Rd (98290-8821)
PHONE..................................360 568-5749
Peggy Lazzimmerman, *President*
Peggy L Zimmerman, *President*
Debra Northey, *Officer*
EMP: 10 **EST:** 1959
SQ FT: 7,000
SALES (est): 1.7MM **Privately Held**
WEB: www.laztool.com
SIC: 3599 3444 Machine shop, jobbing & repair; sheet metalwork

(G-11937)
LB GAMES INC
Also Called: Find It Games
1429 Ave 376 D (98290)
PHONE..................................360 794-7803
Bob Knight, *President*
▲ **EMP:** 7

GEOGRAPHIC SECTION

Snohomish - Snohomish County (G-11972)

SALES (est): 856.1K **Privately Held**
SIC: 3944 5092 5945 Games, toys & children's vehicles; toy novelties & amusements; children's toys & games, except dolls

(G-11938)
LEADING BEYOND TRADITION LLC
13822 233rd St Se (98296-7849)
PHONE..................................425 275-7665
William Cooper, *Owner*
EMP: 2
SALES: 15K **Privately Held**
WEB: www.leadingbeyondtradition.com
SIC: 8748 8742 2731 8299 Educational consultant; business consultant; textbooks: publishing only, not printed on site; educational services; lecturing services

(G-11939)
LEXINGTON PUBLISHING CO LLC
3619 115th Ave Se (98290-5595)
PHONE..................................425 344-0909
EMP: 2 EST: 2017
SALES (est): 65.1K **Privately Held**
SIC: 2741 Miscellaneous publishing

(G-11940)
LOTH INDUSTRIES INC
6620 E Lowell Larimer Rd (98296-5905)
PHONE..................................425 418-5897
Gavin Loth, *Principal*
EMP: 3
SALES (est): 278.8K **Privately Held**
SIC: 3999 Manufacturing industries

(G-11941)
MACH PUBLISHING COMPANY INC
Also Called: Mukilteo Tribune
127 Avenue C Ste B (98290-2768)
P.O. Box 499 (98291-0499)
PHONE..................................425 258-9396
Dave Mach, *President*
EMP: 16
SQ FT: 3,000
SALES (est): 1MM **Privately Held**
WEB: www.snoho.com
SIC: 2741 2711 Miscellaneous publishing; newspapers

(G-11942)
MACHINE TECHNOLOGY
17111 Newberg Rd (98290-4512)
PHONE..................................425 334-1951
Kelly Chambers, *Owner*
EMP: 2
SALES (est): 84.9K **Privately Held**
SIC: 3589 Service industry machinery

(G-11943)
MARKET PLACE WEEKLY INC
Also Called: Tribune Newspapers
127 Avenue C Ste B (98290-2768)
P.O. Box 499 (98291-0499)
PHONE..................................360 568-4121
David Mach, *President*
Beckey Reed, *General Mgr*
EMP: 12
SALES (est): 749.9K **Privately Held**
SIC: 2711 Newspapers, publishing & printing

(G-11944)
MARY ELLEN MCCAFFREE
Also Called: Politics of The Possible
12919 78th Pl Se (98290-6202)
PHONE..................................253 820-0731
Kenneth McCaffree, *Owner*
Alison McCaffree, *Owner*
Mary Ellen McCaffree, *Owner*
EMP: 2
SALES (est): 67K **Privately Held**
SIC: 2731 Book publishing

(G-11945)
MEDICINES CO
6408 138th Pl Se (98290-5260)
PHONE..................................425 829-2540
EMP: 2
SALES (est): 74.4K **Privately Held**
SIC: 2834 Pharmaceutical preparations

(G-11946)
MERRIMAC ALPACAS
2000 Carlson Rd (98290-4702)
PHONE..................................425 387-7586
Ted Burleson, *Principal*
EMP: 2
SALES (est): 128.5K **Privately Held**
SIC: 2231 Alpacas, mohair: woven

(G-11947)
MIKE LAVALLE INC
Also Called: Killer Paint
1033 Avenue D Ste F (98290-2071)
PHONE..................................360 563-0501
Michael Lavalle, *President*
EMP: 6
SQ FT: 220
SALES (est): 608K **Privately Held**
WEB: www.killerpaint.com
SIC: 3993 Signs, not made in custom sign painting shops

(G-11948)
MORDI SOFTWARE
1211 195th Ave Se (98290-7601)
PHONE..................................425 301-4897
Emmanuel Mordi, *Principal*
EMP: 2
SALES (est): 130.3K **Privately Held**
SIC: 7372 Application computer software

(G-11949)
NANCY BAER
18208 67th Ave Se (98296-5374)
PHONE..................................360 668-0350
Nancy Baer, *Principal*
EMP: 5
SALES (est): 283.6K **Privately Held**
SIC: 2047 Dog food

(G-11950)
NEIL BUTLER
6620 196th St Se (98296-5357)
PHONE..................................360 668-9555
Neil Butler, *Manager*
EMP: 2
SALES (est): 73.4K **Privately Held**
SIC: 7372 Prepackaged software

(G-11951)
NICHOLS BROS STONEWORKS LTD
20209 Broadway Ave (98296-7937)
PHONE..................................360 668-5434
Cameron Nichols, *President*
Douglas Hendel, *Corp Secy*
EMP: 20
SQ FT: 20,000
SALES (est): 3.7MM **Privately Held**
WEB: www.nicholsbros.com
SIC: 3271 3281 5199 Architectural concrete: block, split, fluted, screen, etc.; cut stone & stone products; statuary

(G-11952)
NIGHTMARE INDUSTRIES
Also Called: Nightmare Tactical
19516 Badke Rd (98290-7270)
PHONE..................................425 330-1084
William Clark, *Partner*
EMP: 2
SALES (est): 94.1K **Privately Held**
SIC: 3999 Manufacturing industries

(G-11953)
NORTHWEST NATIVE DESIGNS
18210 59th Ave Se (98296-8342)
P.O. Box 8497, Catalina AZ (85738-0497)
PHONE..................................206 679-5847
Ernie Apodaca, *Owner*
EMP: 2
SALES (est): 83K **Privately Held**
WEB: www.northwestnative.com
SIC: 2392 Household furnishings

(G-11954)
NORTHWEST TECHNICAL SERVICES
8516 200th St Se (98296-7990)
PHONE..................................425 419-4321
Steven Jacks, *President*
EMP: 3
SALES (est): 341.6K **Privately Held**
SIC: 3829 Measuring & controlling devices

(G-11955)
O2COMPOST
312 Maple Ave (98290-3301)
P.O. Box 1026 (98291-1026)
PHONE..................................360 563-6709
Chris Moon, *Sales Staff*
Sherri Maben, *Marketing Staff*
EMP: 2
SALES (est): 74.4K **Privately Held**
SIC: 2875 Compost

(G-11956)
OMEGA SILVERSMITHING INC
9621 164th St Se (98296-7036)
PHONE..................................360 863-6771
Tim Maple, *President*
Del Driskol, *Chairman*
Lu Rae Maple, *Corp Secy*
EMP: 3
SALES (est): 249.9K **Privately Held**
SIC: 3914 3471 7641 7389 Silversmithing; gold plating; antique furniture repair & restoration;

(G-11957)
ONCE AGAIN WOODWORKING
707 10th St (98290-2128)
PHONE..................................425 327-9733
Donald Kite, *Principal*
EMP: 2
SALES (est): 172.9K **Privately Held**
SIC: 2431 Millwork

(G-11958)
OROPEZA WOODWORKS
17828 W Interurban Blvd (98296-5352)
PHONE..................................360 668-0438
Martin Oropeza, *Principal*
EMP: 2 EST: 2009
SALES (est): 230K **Privately Held**
SIC: 2431 Millwork

(G-11959)
OSW EQUIPMENT & REPAIR LLC (PA)
20812 Broadway Ave (98296-7300)
P.O. Box 1651, Woodinville (98072-1651)
PHONE..................................425 483-9863
Jay Denoma, *President*
Stephanie L Denoma, *Admin Sec*
EMP: 80
SALES (est): 12.4MM **Privately Held**
WEB: www.oswequipment.com
SIC: 7692 Welding repair

(G-11960)
PACIFIC NORTHWEST SCALE CO
9007 36th St Se (98290-9239)
PHONE..................................425 259-4720
David Brooks, *President*
Ronald M Brooks, *Owner*
Linda G Brooks, *Corp Secy*
EMP: 4
SQ FT: 4,000
SALES (est): 300K **Privately Held**
SIC: 8734 3596 5046 Testing laboratories; weighing machines & apparatus; scales, except laboratory

(G-11961)
POTRISERS INC
4719 Fobes Rd (98290-5125)
PHONE..................................206 240-5579
Terry Smith, *President*
EMP: 3
SQ FT: 2,000
SALES: 100K **Privately Held**
SIC: 2519 Garden furniture, except wood, metal, stone or concrete

(G-11962)
PROFILER INC
17414 Interurban Blvd (98296-5340)
P.O. Box 12858, Mill Creek (98082-0858)
PHONE..................................360 668-3291
Steve Helms, *President*
Carol Helms, *Corp Secy*
Tony D'Alessio, *Vice Pres*
EMP: 2
SALES: 150K **Privately Held**
WEB: www.pipemastertools.com
SIC: 3423 Hand & edge tools

(G-11963)
PUGET SOUND WOODWORKING LLC
112 Long St (98290-2224)
PHONE..................................360 563-0116
Derrick Burke, *Principal*
EMP: 2 EST: 2010
SALES (est): 190.8K **Privately Held**
SIC: 2431 Millwork

(G-11964)
QUILCEDA CREEK VINTNERS INC
11306 52nd St Se (98290-5727)
PHONE..................................360 568-2389
Alexander Golitzin, *President*
Jeanette Golitzin, *Vice Pres*
EMP: 4
SALES (est): 526.6K **Privately Held**
WEB: www.quilcedacreek.com
SIC: 2084 Wines

(G-11965)
R & R MACHINE
17918 S Spada Rd (98290-6129)
PHONE..................................360 568-4844
Michael Lundeberg, *Owner*
EMP: 6
SALES (est): 360K **Privately Held**
SIC: 3599 Machine shop, jobbing & repair

(G-11966)
R WAYNE INDUSTRIES LLC
20531 129th Ave Se Unit B (98296-5485)
PHONE..................................425 359-0432
Ryan McGrath,
EMP: 2 EST: 2017
SALES (est): 88.9K **Privately Held**
SIC: 3089 Plastics products

(G-11967)
RIVER TOWN DISTILLERS LLC
5614 66th Ave Se (98290-5112)
PHONE..................................425 330-4885
David Hopkins, *Principal*
EMP: 3 EST: 2012
SALES (est): 137.5K **Privately Held**
SIC: 2085 Distilled & blended liquors

(G-11968)
ROMEO AND SYLVIA LLC
16305 Railroad Way (98290-8150)
PHONE..................................425 315-5336
Romeo Gonyea, *Bd of Directors*
EMP: 3
SALES (est): 137.7K **Privately Held**
SIC: 2431 Millwork

(G-11969)
ROUTEC INDUSTRIES LLC
9911 198th St Se (98296-7913)
PHONE..................................206 949-2472
John Bacon, *Principal*
EMP: 3
SALES (est): 280K **Privately Held**
SIC: 3728 Aircraft body assemblies & parts

(G-11970)
SCRAPPY PUNK BREWING LLC
707 Avenue A Apt A205 (98290-2475)
PHONE..................................503 810-1655
EMP: 2
SALES (est): 70.4K **Privately Held**
SIC: 2082 Malt beverages

(G-11971)
SCRUB NOGGINZ LLC
5919 121st St Se (98296-6978)
PHONE..................................425 931-9251
Melinda Summers, *Principal*
EMP: 2
SALES (est): 121.5K **Privately Held**
SIC: 2844 Toilet preparations

(G-11972)
SEA ALASKA INDUSTRIAL ELECTRIC
415 Maple Ave (98290-2527)
PHONE..................................360 568-7624
EMP: 3
SQ FT: 5,000
SALES (est): 864.3K **Privately Held**
SIC: 5063 7694 Motors, electric; electric motor repair

Snohomish - Snohomish County (G-11973)

(G-11973)
SEATTLE SOFTWARE WORKS INC
7710 190th St Se (98296-7949)
PHONE.................................206 226-9263
Peter Samson, *President*
EMP: 4
SALES (est): 167K **Privately Held**
WEB: www.seattleworks.com
SIC: 7372 Prepackaged software

(G-11974)
SELFISH APPAREL AND PRINTING
7710 197th St Se (98296-7941)
PHONE.................................206 450-2725
Sarah Hurst, *Principal*
EMP: 2 **EST:** 2017
SALES (est): 107.4K **Privately Held**
SIC: 2752 Commercial printing, lithographic

(G-11975)
SHACKELFORD VINTNERS
908 Ash Ct (98290-2165)
PHONE.................................425 350-2719
Ron Shackelford, *Principal*
EMP: 3
SALES (est): 75.4K **Privately Held**
SIC: 2084 Wines, brandy & brandy spirits

(G-11976)
SIMPLY SWEET CUPCAKES
1206 1st St (98290-2737)
PHONE.................................360 568-8600
EMP: 2
SALES (est): 71K **Privately Held**
SIC: 2051 Mfg Bread/Related Products

(G-11977)
SKIP ROCK DISTILLERS
104 Avenue C (98290-2741)
PHONE.................................360 862-0272
Ryan Hembree, *Managing Prtnr*
EMP: 2 **EST:** 2010
SALES (est): 138.4K **Privately Held**
SIC: 2085 Distilled & blended liquors

(G-11978)
SNAPDOG PRINTING
815 Avenue D (98290-2334)
PHONE.................................360 217-8172
EMP: 2
SALES (est): 83.9K **Privately Held**
SIC: 2752 Commercial printing, lithographic

(G-11979)
SNO VALLEY MILK LLC
12420 92nd St Se (98290-8433)
PHONE.................................360 410-8888
Jeremy Visser,
EMP: 10
SALES (est): 741.9K **Privately Held**
SIC: 2026 Fluid milk

(G-11980)
SNOGRO
502 Maple Ave (98290-2530)
PHONE.................................360 863-6935
EMP: 2
SALES (est): 222.6K **Privately Held**
SIC: 3524 Mfg Lawn/Garden Equipment

(G-11981)
SNOHOMISH BAKERY & CAF
920 1st St (98290-2907)
PHONE.................................360 568-1682
Andy Papadatos, *Owner*
Ingrid Harten, *Owner*
EMP: 2
SALES (est): 94.7K **Privately Held**
SIC: 5461 2052 Pastries; bakery products, dry

(G-11982)
SNOHOMISH IRON WORKS INC
Also Called: Welding & Machine Shop
1st St & Ave E (98290)
PHONE.................................360 568-2811
Don Gamble, *President*
Jenny J Gamble, *Corp Secy*
Judy Gamble, *Corp Secy*
EMP: 2 **EST:** 1902
SQ FT: 13,000
SALES (est): 203.2K **Privately Held**
WEB: www.weldingmachineshop.com
SIC: 3599 7692 3462 Machine shop, jobbing & repair; welding repair; iron & steel forgings

(G-11983)
SNOHOMISH PUBLISHING COMPANY
605 2nd St (98290-2669)
PHONE.................................206 523-7548
EMP: 25 **EST:** 1892
SQ FT: 15,000
SALES (est): 2.2MM **Privately Held**
SIC: 2731 2759 7331 2789 Book-Publishing/Printing Commercial Printing Direct Mail Ad Svcs

(G-11984)
SNOQUALMIE GOURMET ICE CREAM
21106 86th Ave Se (98296-7904)
PHONE.................................360 668-8535
Shahnaz Bettinger, *President*
Barry Bettinger, *Vice Pres*
EMP: 5
SQ FT: 2,000
SALES (est): 660.3K **Privately Held**
SIC: 5451 2024 Ice cream (packaged); ice cream & frozen desserts

(G-11985)
SNOTOWN EMBROIDERY LLC
6103 61st Ave Se (98290-5124)
PHONE.................................425 446-1681
Kayla Lachapelle, *Principal*
EMP: 2 **EST:** 2015
SALES (est): 83.5K **Privately Held**
SIC: 2395 Embroidery & art needlework

(G-11986)
SPECIALTY PUMP AND PLBG INC
Also Called: Specialty Pump & Well
8425 Fobes Rd (98290-9233)
PHONE.................................425 424-8700
Toby Cyr, *President*
EMP: 9 **EST:** 2009
SQ FT: 2,000
SALES (est): 907.5K **Privately Held**
SIC: 7699 3561 1781 1711 Boiler & heating repair services; pumps, domestic: water or sump; water well servicing; heating systems repair & maintenance; plumbing contractors

(G-11987)
SUBSEA AIR SYSTEMS LLC
2610 Bickford Ave (98290-1760)
PHONE.................................360 563-2400
William Haworth, *Partner*
Wallace Haworth, *Mng Member*
▲ **EMP:** 4
SALES (est): 770.2K **Privately Held**
WEB: www.subseaair.com
SIC: 5088 3724 Aircraft & parts; turbines, aircraft type

(G-11988)
SUNSET MANUFACTURING CORP
2301 159th Ave Se (98290-4750)
PHONE.................................425 239-7416
Allan Potter, *Administration*
EMP: 2
SALES (est): 74.6K **Privately Held**
SIC: 3999 Manufacturing industries

(G-11989)
SWIFT PRINT
10922 Wagner Rd (98290-7281)
PHONE.................................360 805-8509
Kenneth Warren, *Owner*
Mellie Warren, *Co-Owner*
EMP: 2 **EST:** 1969
SALES (est): 95K **Privately Held**
SIC: 2759 Commercial printing

(G-11990)
THERMAL TECHNOLOGIES
13405 27th St Se (98290-9735)
PHONE.................................425 359-8681
EMP: 4
SALES (est): 335.5K **Privately Held**
SIC: 3398 Metal heat treating

(G-11991)
THREE KEES CIDER LLC
22831 Woods Creek Rd (98290-7523)
PHONE.................................425 238-3470
Roger Kee,
Donna Kee,
EMP: 2
SALES (est): 126.6K **Privately Held**
SIC: 2084 7389 Wine cellars, bonded: engaged in blending wines;

(G-11992)
TOBYS TORTILLAS LLC
13709 45th Dr Se (98296-7629)
PHONE.................................425 344-7653
Stephen Greely, *Principal*
EMP: 3 **EST:** 2012
SALES (est): 144.4K **Privately Held**
SIC: 2099 Tortillas, fresh or refrigerated

(G-11993)
TOPSOILS NORTHWEST INC
9010 Marsh Rd (98296-5909)
P.O. Box 1697 (98291-1697)
PHONE.................................425 337-0233
Dennis Thomas, *President*
Donald Thomas, *Corp Secy*
Marvin Thomas, *Vice Pres*
EMP: 11
SALES (est): 1.3MM **Privately Held**
WEB: www.topsoilsnw.com
SIC: 5261 5032 2421 Nurseries; gravel; sawdust & shavings

(G-11994)
TRILLIUM CUSTOM SOFTWARE INC
17127 Ok Mill Rd (98290-9621)
P.O. Box 609, Lake Stevens (98258-0609)
PHONE.................................425 397-8000
Dale Schuppenhauer, *President*
EMP: 4
SALES (est): 279K **Privately Held**
SIC: 7371 2731 Computer software systems analysis & design, custom; book publishing

(G-11995)
UFP WASHINGTON LLC (HQ)
Also Called: Universal Forest Products
12027 3 Lakes Rd (98290-5502)
PHONE.................................360 568-3185
Matthew J Missad, *CEO*
EMP: 70 **EST:** 2009
SQ FT: 90,000
SALES: 14.8MM
SALES (corp-wide): 4.4B **Publicly Held**
SIC: 2448 2441 Pallets, wood; nailed wood boxes & shook
PA: Universal Forest Products, Inc.
2801 E Beltline Ave Ne
Grand Rapids MI 49525
616 364-6161

(G-11996)
VERAX CHEMICAL CO
20102 Broadway Ave (98296-7937)
P.O. Box 803, Bothell (98041-0803)
PHONE.................................360 668-2431
Julie Curkendall, *President*
Sue Copeland, *Corp Secy*
▲ **EMP:** 4 **EST:** 1913
SQ FT: 28,000
SALES (est): 621.8K **Privately Held**
SIC: 2841 2842 Soap: granulated, liquid, cake, flaked or chip; disinfectants, household or industrial plant; cleaning or polishing preparations

(G-11997)
VINTAGE EMBROIDERY
15723 Broadway Ave (98296-7062)
PHONE.................................360 668-1923
EMP: 4 **EST:** 1996
SALES (est): 60K **Privately Held**
SIC: 2395 Pleating/Stitching Services

(G-11998)
WESTERN PRINT SYSTEMS INC
1313 Bonneville Ave # 103 (98290-2089)
PHONE.................................206 794-0045
David Valentine, *Principal*
EMP: 5 **EST:** 2012
SALES (est): 511.8K **Privately Held**
SIC: 2752 Commercial printing, offset

(G-11999)
WHEELS NORTHWEST INC
18930 State Route 9 Se (98296-5308)
PHONE.................................206 909-6735
Gary Ziebell, *Principal*
EMP: 2
SALES (est): 201K **Privately Held**
SIC: 3312 Wheels

(G-12000)
WOOLMAN COATINGS LLC
16227 Railroad Way (98296-8173)
PHONE.................................206 402-2960
Zeb Woolman, *Administration*
EMP: 2 **EST:** 2014
SALES (est): 137.6K **Privately Held**
SIC: 3479 Metal coating & allied service

(G-12001)
WOW MOM CORPORATION
14200 69th Dr Se Unit B3 (98296-6947)
PHONE.................................206 240-4068
Wes Wood, *President*
EMP: 3
SALES (est): 100.7K **Privately Held**
SIC: 2741 Miscellaneous publishing

(G-12002)
ZORZI CORPORATION
Also Called: Antony Architectural Stone
17103 14th St Ne (98290-9644)
P.O. Box 1504 (98291-1504)
PHONE.................................425 334-0160
Roberto Zorzi, *President*
▲ **EMP:** 4
SALES (est): 419.7K **Privately Held**
WEB: www.zorzifamily.com
SIC: 3281 Curbing, granite or stone

(G-12003)
ZTRON LABS INC
6405 158th St Se (98296-4637)
PHONE.................................425 289-8794
EMP: 2 **EST:** 2010
SALES (est): 146.4K **Privately Held**
SIC: 3721 Aircraft

Snoqualmie
King County

(G-12004)
ALVELOGRO INC
35300 Se Center St (98065-9216)
PHONE.................................425 831-1110
Mike O'Keefe, *President*
Snoqu Alvelogro, *Principal*
Tracy O'Keefe, *Vice Pres*
EMP: 3
SALES (est): 329.4K **Privately Held**
SIC: 3843 Dental equipment & supplies

(G-12005)
BC SOFTWARE
35014 Se Curtis Dr (98065-8721)
PHONE.................................425 831-0550
EMP: 2
SALES (est): 140K **Privately Held**
SIC: 7372 Prepackaged Software Services

(G-12006)
BRUNELLO
7708 Center Blvd Se (98065-8993)
PHONE.................................425 888-6800
Ivaylo Yonev, *Principal*
EMP: 4
SALES (est): 384.7K **Privately Held**
SIC: 3421 Table & food cutlery, including butchers'

(G-12007)
COMPASS OUTDOOR ADVENTURES LLC
7724 Melrose Ln Se (98065-8955)
PHONE.................................425 281-0267
Luke Talbott, *Principal*
EMP: 4 **EST:** 2012
SALES: 200K **Privately Held**
SIC: 7032 3949 Sporting & recreational camps; camping equipment & supplies

GEOGRAPHIC SECTION
Snoqualmie - King County (G-12035)

(G-12008)
CONNELLY SKIS INC
7926 Bracken Pl Se (98065-9271)
PHONE..................425 831-1099
Dan Trujillo, *Branch Mgr*
EMP: 5
SALES (corp-wide): 143.8MM **Privately Held**
SIC: 3949 Water skiing equipment & supplies, except skis
HQ: Connelly Skis, Inc.
20621 52nd Ave W
Lynnwood WA 98036
425 775-5416

(G-12009)
DANCE AIR INC
8020 Bracken Pl Se (98065-9257)
PHONE..................425 222-6789
Alan Dance, *President*
EMP: 2
SQ FT: 1,000
SALES (est): 170K **Privately Held**
SIC: 3728 Aircraft parts & equipment

(G-12010)
E W BACHTAL INC
7219 Autumn Ave Se (98065-9796)
PHONE..................425 241-2505
Eric W Bachtal, *Principal*
EMP: 2
SALES (est): 121.5K **Privately Held**
SIC: 7372 Prepackaged software

(G-12011)
EASTSIDE SIGNS
9818 354th Ave Se (98065-9313)
PHONE..................425 888-6764
Tom McCandless, *Owner*
EMP: 2
SQ FT: 2,000
SALES (est): 110K **Privately Held**
WEB: www.eastsidesigns.com
SIC: 3993 Signs, not made in custom sign painting shops

(G-12012)
FA GREEN COMPANY
9742 352nd Ave Se (98065-9222)
PHONE..................425 888-0007
Jeff Green, *Owner*
EMP: 22
SALES (est): 1.2MM **Privately Held**
SIC: 3089 3841 Automotive parts, plastic; surgical & medical instruments

(G-12013)
GLACIER NORTHWEST INC
Also Called: Snoqualmie Sand & Gravel
5601 396th Dr Se (98065-9198)
P.O. Box 492 (98065-0492)
PHONE..................425 888-9795
Ken Johnson, *Manager*
EMP: 50 **Privately Held**
WEB: www.glaciernw.com
SIC: 5211 5032 3273 1442 Lumber & other building materials; brick, stone & related material; ready-mixed concrete; construction sand & gravel
HQ: Glacier Northwest, Inc.
5975 E Marginal Way S
Seattle WA 98134
206 764-3000

(G-12014)
KEYCHAIN SOCIAL LLC
9422 Hancock Ave Se (98065-5014)
PHONE..................425 876-3261
Jordan Bremond,
EMP: 5
SALES (est): 143.5K **Privately Held**
SIC: 2741

(G-12015)
KRISMARK GROUP INC (PA)
8020 Bracken Pl Se (98065-9257)
PHONE..................425 396-0829
Kristy Chamberlain, *President*
Mark Chamberlain, *Exec VP*
EMP: 1
SALES (est): 5.3MM **Privately Held**
SIC: 3812 3728 Search & navigation equipment; aircraft parts & equipment

(G-12016)
LIVING SNOQUALMIE LLC
8816 Venn Ave Se (98065-5007)
PHONE..................425 396-7304
Danna McCall, *Principal*
EMP: 2 **EST:** 2012
SALES (est): 120.5K **Privately Held**
SIC: 2711 Newspapers

(G-12017)
LKD AEROSPACE LLC
Gladiator Technologies
8022 Bracken Pl Se (98065-9257)
PHONE..................425 396-0829
Kristy Chamberlain, *President*
EMP: 10
SALES (corp-wide): 5.3MM **Privately Held**
SIC: 3728 Aircraft parts & equipment
HQ: Lkd Aerospace, Llc
8020 Bracken Pl Se
Snoqualmie WA
425 396-0829

(G-12018)
MICROCONNEX CORPORATION (DH)
34935 Se Douglas St # 110 (98065-9228)
PHONE..................425 396-5707
Paul Henwood, *President*
Sam Ishizaka, *Mfg Staff*
Don Saint, *Purchasing*
Steve Leith, *Engineer*
Wayne Van Zandt, *VP Sls/Mktg*
EMP: 5
SQ FT: 15,000
SALES (est): 1.4MM
SALES (corp-wide): 4.4B **Publicly Held**
WEB: www.microconnex.com
SIC: 3679 8731 Power supplies, all types: static; commercial physical research

(G-12019)
MIX IT UP LLC
36532 Se Woody Creek Ln (98065-8907)
PHONE..................425 396-7345
EMP: 2
SALES (est): 91.3K **Privately Held**
SIC: 3273 Ready-mixed concrete

(G-12020)
MOTION WATER SPORTS INC (HQ)
Also Called: O'Brien Water Sports
7926 Bracken Pl Se (98065-9271)
PHONE..................800 662-7436
Robert Archer, *Ch of Bd*
John Clark, *Corp Secy*
Jeff Bannaster, *Senior VP*
Tony Finn, *Vice Pres*
Pete Surrette, *Vice Pres*
◆ **EMP:** 100
SQ FT: 10,000
SALES (est): 14.7MM
SALES (corp-wide): 143.8MM **Privately Held**
WEB: www.motionwatersports.com
SIC: 3949 Water sports equipment; water skis; windsurfing boards (sailboards) & equipment
PA: Kent Sporting Goods Company, Inc.
433 Park Ave
New London OH 44851
419 929-7021

(G-12021)
RSVP SEATTLE
7829 Center Blvd Se 200 (98065-9096)
PHONE..................425 396-7787
Dave Tropf, *CEO*
EMP: 3
SALES (est): 247.2K **Privately Held**
SIC: 2721 Periodicals

(G-12022)
RUDOLPH TECHNOLOGIES INC
35030 Se Douglas St (98065-9266)
PHONE..................425 396-7002
Robert Dicrosta, *Vice Pres*
Foster Lin, *Engineer*
EMP: 7
SALES (corp-wide): 273.7MM **Publicly Held**
SIC: 3829 Measuring & controlling devices
PA: Rudolph Technologies, Inc.
16 Jonspin Rd
Wilmington MA 01887
978 253-6200

(G-12023)
SIGILLO CELLARS
8353 Meadowbrook Way Se (98065-9588)
PHONE..................206 919-2326
EMP: 4
SALES (est): 330.8K **Privately Held**
SIC: 2084 Wines

(G-12024)
SKILFAB INDUSTRIES INC
8300 Railroad Ave Se (98065)
P.O. Box 1775 (98065-1775)
PHONE..................425 831-5555
Dan McNeely, *President*
Sue Neff, *Corp Secy*
Marianne McNeely, *Vice Pres*
EMP: 8
SQ FT: 10,000
SALES (est): 1MM **Privately Held**
SIC: 3444 Sheet metalwork

(G-12025)
SNOQUALMIE MACHINE WORKS
8890 Railroad Ave Se (98065-9642)
PHONE..................425 888-1464
EMP: 2
SALES (est): 140K **Privately Held**
SIC: 3599 Mfg Industrial Machinery

(G-12026)
SOUND PUBLISHING INC
Also Called: Snoqualmie Valley Record
8124 Falls Ave Se (98065)
PHONE..................425 888-2311
William GA Shaw, *Branch Mgr*
EMP: 6 **Privately Held**
WEB: www.soundpublishing.com
SIC: 2711 Newspapers, publishing & printing
HQ: Sound Publishing, Inc.
11323 Commando Rd W Main
Everett WA 98204
360 394-5800

(G-12027)
SPACELABS HEALTHCARE INC (HQ)
35301 Se Center St (98065-9216)
PHONE..................425 396-3300
Deepak Chopra, *CEO*
Nicholas Ong, *President*
Christopher Kelley, *General Mgr*
Doug Weigel, *General Mgr*
Graeme Millan, *Business Mgr*
▲ **EMP:** 599
SALES (est): 201.4MM
SALES (corp-wide): 1B **Publicly Held**
WEB: www.spacelabshealthcare.com
SIC: 3841 3845 3575 7699 Surgical & medical instruments; ultrasonic medical equipment, except cleaning; patient monitoring apparatus; computer terminals, monitors & components; hospital equipment repair services; computer peripheral equipment repair & maintenance
PA: Osi Systems, Inc.
12525 Chadron Ave
Hawthorne CA 90250
310 978-0516

(G-12028)
SPACELABS HEALTHCARE LLC
35301 Se Center St (98065-9216)
PHONE..................425 396-3300
Deepak Chopra, *CEO*
Kujit Sumar, *President*
Alan Edrick, *CFO*
Patrick Ip, *Treasurer*
Kathleen Callaghan,
EMP: 490
SALES (est): 78.9MM
SALES (corp-wide): 1B **Publicly Held**
SIC: 3841 3845 3575 7699 Surgical & medical instruments; electromedical equipment; patient monitoring apparatus; computer terminals, monitors & components; hospital equipment repair services; computer peripheral equipment repair & maintenance
PA: Osi Systems, Inc.
12525 Chadron Ave
Hawthorne CA 90250
310 978-0516

(G-12029)
SPACELABS HEALTHCARE WASH (HQ)
Also Called: Spacelabs Health Care
35301 Se Center St (98065-9216)
PHONE..................425 396-3300
Deepak Chopra, *CEO*
Eugene Defelice, *President*
Kujit Sumar, *President*
Claudia Bailey III, *Buyer*
Jason Vincent, *Engineer*
◆ **EMP:** 132
SALES (est): 201.4MM
SALES (corp-wide): 1B **Publicly Held**
SIC: 3845 3841 3575 7699 Patient monitoring apparatus; diagnostic apparatus, medical; computer terminals, monitors & components; hospital equipment repair services; computer peripheral equipment repair & maintenance
PA: Osi Systems, Inc.
12525 Chadron Ave
Hawthorne CA 90250
310 978-0516

(G-12030)
SPACELABS HEALTHCARE WASH
Also Called: Statcorp Medical
35301 Se Center St (98065-9216)
PHONE..................425 396-3300
Manoocher Mansouri, *Branch Mgr*
EMP: 35
SALES (corp-wide): 1B **Publicly Held**
WEB: www.statcorp.net
SIC: 3841 Surgical & medical instruments
HQ: Spacelabs Healthcare (Washington), Inc
35301 Se Center St
Snoqualmie WA 98065
425 396-3300

(G-12031)
SQUARE ONE DISTRIBUTION INC (PA)
35214 Se Center St (98065-9279)
PHONE..................425 369-6850
Brian Gardner, *President*
◆ **EMP:** 40
SQ FT: 75,000
SALES (est): 12.1MM **Privately Held**
WEB: www.squareonedistribution.com
SIC: 3949 Water sports equipment

(G-12032)
SUPERHERO STUFFCOM
34401 Se Cochrane St (98065-9474)
PHONE..................425 890-3032
Jon Belzer, *CEO*
EMP: 6
SALES (est): 551.8K **Privately Held**
SIC: 2389 Costumes

(G-12033)
T & G MACHINERY LLC
7226 Thompson Ave Se (98065-9753)
P.O. Box 1082 (98065-1082)
PHONE..................425 396-5939
Gene Rousseau, *Mng Member*
Nicole Rousseau,
EMP: 2
SQ FT: 22,100
SALES (est): 210K **Privately Held**
WEB: www.tngmachinery.com
SIC: 3553 Woodworking machinery

(G-12034)
TRIEX TECHNOLOGIES INC
8030 Bracken Pl Se (98065-9257)
PHONE..................425 363-2239
Tim Wright, *Principal*
EMP: 4
SALES (est): 382.8K **Privately Held**
SIC: 3824 Mechanical & electromechanical counters & devices

(G-12035)
ZETEC INC (HQ)
8226 Bracken Pl Se # 100 (98065-2935)
PHONE..................425 974-2700

Timothy J Winfrey, *Ch of Bd*
Wayne Wilkinson, *President*
Jack Buhsmer, *Vice Pres*
Richard A Davis, *Vice Pres*
David B Liner, *Vice Pres*
▲ **EMP:** 135
SQ FT: 63,276
SALES (est): 23.9MM
SALES (corp-wide): 5.1B **Publicly Held**
SIC: 3829 7389 3825 8734 Measuring & controlling devices; inspection & testing services; instruments to measure electricity; testing laboratories
PA: Roper Technologies, Inc.
6901 Prof Pkwy E Ste 200
Sarasota FL 34240
941 556-2601

Soap Lake
Grant County

(G-12036)
3 CS
Also Called: Cascade Grooming Supplies
19345 Road A.3 Ne (98851-9632)
PHONE.................509 246-1451
Ollie Click, *President*
EMP: 3
SALES (est): 286.4K **Privately Held**
WEB: www.oclick.com
SIC: 3999 Pet supplies

(G-12037)
COULTER CANVAS
19115 Saint Andrews Dr Nw (98851-9704)
PHONE.................509 246-2188
Gerald Coulter, *Principal*
EMP: 2
SALES (est): 107.5K **Privately Held**
SIC: 2394 Canvas & related products

(G-12038)
RECHEADZ LLC
285 State Highway 28 W (98851-9610)
PHONE.................509 406-2230
Ryan Rickard, *CEO*
James Robinson, *COO*
EMP: 2
SALES: 244K **Privately Held**
SIC: 7372 Prepackaged software

South Bend
Pacific County

(G-12039)
BEAR MOUNTIN CUTTERS INC
49 Wilson Ln (98586-9009)
PHONE.................360 875-0035
Douglas O Korevaar, *President*
A S Korevaar, *Vice Pres*
EMP: 4
SALES: 150K **Privately Held**
SIC: 4213 2411 Trucking, except local; logging

(G-12040)
COAST SEAFOODS COMPANY
1200 Robert Bush Dr (98586)
P.O. Box 166 (98586-0166)
PHONE.................360 875-5557
Joe Maita, *President*
EMP: 45
SALES (corp-wide): 70.7MM **Privately Held**
WEB: www.coastseafoods.com
SIC: 5812 2092 0273 Seafood restaurants; fresh or frozen packaged fish; animal aquaculture
HQ: Coast Seafoods Company
1200 Robert Bush Dr
Bellevue WA 98007

(G-12041)
JIM HAMILTON
70 Giles Ln (98586-9002)
P.O. Box 1189 (98586-1189)
PHONE.................360 875-6170
Jim Hamilton, *Principal*
EMP: 5
SALES (est): 377K **Privately Held**
SIC: 2411 Logging camps & contractors

(G-12042)
KARL PLATO
Also Called: Pacific Bow Butts Targets
613 Montana St (98586)
PHONE.................360 875-8289
Karl Plato, *Owner*
EMP: 3
SALES (est): 63.1K **Privately Held**
SIC: 3949 Targets, archery & rifle shooting

(G-12043)
LODESTONE CONSTRUCTION INC
99 Trask Rd (98586-9019)
P.O. Box 308, Bay Center (98527-0308)
PHONE.................360 875-6960
Daniel Bayne, *President*
Ricki Bayne, *Admin Sec*
EMP: 4
SALES (est): 448.3K **Privately Held**
SIC: 2411 1794 Logging; excavation work

(G-12044)
LODESTONE QUARRY INCORPARATED
99 Trask Rd (98586)
PHONE.................360 942-0400
Daniel Bayne, *Principal*
EMP: 5
SALES (est): 190K **Privately Held**
SIC: 1429 7389 Basalt, crushed & broken-quarrying;

(G-12045)
SACRED WATERS FISH COMPANY LLC
228 Bay Center Rd (98586-9016)
PHONE.................503 913-1625
Hugh Ahnatook, *Mng Member*
EMP: 3
SALES (est): 68.6K **Privately Held**
SIC: 2091 Fish, cured

(G-12046)
SOUTH BEND BOAT SHOP
255 W Robert Bush Dr (98586)
PHONE.................360 875-5712
Chris Fosse, *Partner*
Dorwin Fosse, *Partner*
EMP: 2
SQ FT: 4,500
SALES: 500K **Privately Held**
SIC: 3732 Boat building & repairing

(G-12047)
SOUTH BEND PRODUCTS LLC
237 W Robert Bush Dr (98586)
PHONE.................360 875-6570
John Swanes, *Mng Member*
Dean Antich,
EMP: 60
SQ FT: 47,000
SALES (est): 4.9MM **Privately Held**
SIC: 2092 Fresh or frozen packaged fish

(G-12048)
TAYLOR SHELLFISH COMPANY INC
Also Called: Ekone Oyster
378 Bay Center Rd (98586-9014)
PHONE.................360 875-5494
Nick Jambor, *Branch Mgr*
EMP: 45
SALES (corp-wide): 62.8MM **Privately Held**
SIC: 2092 2091 5961 5146 Shellfish, fresh: shucked & packed in nonsealed containers; oysters, preserved & cured; food, mail order; fish & seafoods
HQ: Taylor Shellfish Company, Inc.
130 Se Lynch Rd
Shelton WA 98584
360 426-6178

(G-12049)
THE PACIFIC COUNTY PRESS INC
500 W Robert Bush Dr (98586-9075)
P.O. Box 1236 (98586-1236)
PHONE.................360 875-6805
Loretta Hodgson, *President*
Chris Petrich, *Vice Pres*
EMP: 3
SALES (est): 171.8K **Privately Held**
WEB: www.pacificcountypress.com
SIC: 2711 Newspapers, publishing & printing

South Prairie
Pierce County

(G-12050)
JWB MANUFACTURING LLC
125 Nw Washington St (98385)
PHONE.................253 222-1671
Eric Satterthwaite, *Principal*
EMP: 7
SALES (est): 210.3K **Privately Held**
SIC: 3999 Manufacturing industries

Southworth
Kitsap County

(G-12051)
SOUTHWORTH MARINE SERVICE
11113 Tola Rd Se (98386)
P.O. Box 85 (98386-0085)
PHONE.................360 871-5610
John Hager, *Owner*
EMP: 2
SQ FT: 2,000
SALES: 60K **Privately Held**
SIC: 3732 Boat building & repairing

Spanaway
Pierce County

(G-12052)
A-K PRINTING LLC
18920 Pacific Ave S Ste C (98387-8325)
PHONE.................253 249-7133
EMP: 2
SALES (est): 101.5K **Privately Held**
SIC: 2759 Commercial printing

(G-12053)
ALL COMPOSITE INC
3206 232nd St E (98387-7410)
P.O. Box 4743 (98387-4049)
PHONE.................253 847-5106
EMP: 2
SQ FT: 8,000
SALES: 450K **Privately Held**
SIC: 2821 Plastics materials & resins

(G-12054)
BRADLEY ROBLING
Also Called: Bradley's Fabrication
4704 235th St E (98387-6162)
PHONE.................360 832-6778
Bradley D Robling, *Owner*
Bradley B Robling, *Owner*
EMP: 3
SALES: 268K **Privately Held**
SIC: 3089 1799 Fences, gates & accessories: plastic; fence construction

(G-12055)
CONSTRUCTION PARTS
20718 Mountain Hwy E (98387-8180)
PHONE.................253 271-6133
EMP: 4
SALES (est): 510.3K **Privately Held**
SIC: 3531 Mfg Construction Machinery

(G-12056)
CORALLIE INDUSTRIES
3219 253rd Street Ct E (98387-7074)
PHONE.................253 576-5240
Amanda Fortman, *Principal*
EMP: 2
SALES (est): 84.3K **Privately Held**
SIC: 3999 Manufacturing industries

(G-12057)
FINE PRINT WA LLC
21910 65th Avenue Ct E (98387-5869)
PHONE.................206 859-8469
Jaclyn Oakland, *Principal*
EMP: 2
SALES (est): 83.9K **Privately Held**
SIC: 2752 Commercial printing, lithographic

(G-12058)
FIR LANE MEMORIAL PK & FNRL HM
Also Called: Fir Lane Funeral Home & Mem Pk
924 176th St E (98387-7976)
PHONE.................253 531-6600
Mary Ann Overaa, *President*
Charles H Overaa, *Vice Pres*
Chad Vennes, *Director*
William Walker,
EMP: 10
SALES (est): 690K **Privately Held**
WEB: www.firlane.com
SIC: 6553 7261 2411 Cemeteries, real estate operation; funeral home; logging

(G-12059)
HELICAT LLC
16809 Lakeside Dr S (98387-8948)
PHONE.................253 376-8273
Alex Williamson, *Principal*
EMP: 2
SALES (est): 155.6K **Privately Held**
SIC: 3732 Boat building & repairing

(G-12060)
LONNIE HANSEN
4506 277th Street Ct E (98387-9518)
PHONE.................253 847-4632
Lonnie Hansen, *Principal*
EMP: 2 **EST:** 2010
SALES (est): 120.5K **Privately Held**
SIC: 3545 Tools & accessories for machine tools

(G-12061)
M AND M CABINETS
17318 Yakima Ave S (98387-8911)
PHONE.................253 503-0756
Gary Martinson, *Principal*
EMP: 2 **EST:** 2010
SALES (est): 131.8K **Privately Held**
SIC: 2434 Wood kitchen cabinets

(G-12062)
M B LAPIDARY
19408 Crescent Dr E (98387-8015)
PHONE.................253 271-7515
EMP: 3
SALES (est): 233.9K **Privately Held**
SIC: 3915 Jewelers' materials & lapidary work

(G-12063)
MAVERICK METALWORKS LLC
19906 15th Ave E (98387-1816)
PHONE.................253 345-1590
EMP: 2
SQ FT: 1,800
SALES: 100K **Privately Held**
SIC: 7539 3312 Automotive Repair Blast Furnace-Steel Works

(G-12064)
MCCANN INDUSTRIES LLC
132 162nd St S (98387-8210)
P.O. Box 234, Tenino (98589-0234)
PHONE.................253 537-6919
Debra McCann,
EMP: 7
SQ FT: 3,000
SALES: 500K **Privately Held**
SIC: 3599 5941 Machine shop, jobbing & repair; firearms

(G-12065)
MILITARY TAILS
22021 50th Avenue Ct E (98387-6001)
P.O. Box 5424 (98387-4094)
PHONE.................253 229-2427
Marc Gelinas, *Principal*
EMP: 2
SALES (est): 111.3K **Privately Held**
SIC: 2499 Trophy bases, wood

(G-12066)
MOUNTAINSIDE CABINETS
19627 70th Avenue Ct E (98387-5633)
PHONE.................253 278-8400
Jason Scheidler, *Principal*

GEOGRAPHIC SECTION — Spokane - Spokane County (G-12099)

EMP: 2
SALES (est): 101.2K **Privately Held**
SIC: 2434 Wood kitchen cabinets

(G-12067)
P & M VIDEO LIGHTSOURCE LLC
7228 193rd St E (98387-5247)
PHONE 253 569-0286
Santos Marez, *Mng Member*
Patrick Jones, *Mng Member*
EMP: 2
SALES (est): 120.4K **Privately Held**
SIC: 3661 Fiber optics communications equipment

(G-12068)
QUALITY CREATIONS
7414 202nd Street Ct E (98387-5297)
PHONE 253 732-4082
Robert Wolley, *Owner*
EMP: 2
SALES (est): 113.1K **Privately Held**
SIC: 2511 Wood household furniture

(G-12069)
R & M MANUFACTURING LLC
16909 Park Ave S (98387-8958)
P.O. Box 11 (98387-0011)
PHONE 253 503-0956
Daniel Roberts, *Principal*
EMP: 3
SALES (est): 145.3K **Privately Held**
SIC: 3999 Manufacturing industries

(G-12070)
RAINIER VENEER INC
8220 Eustis Hunt Rd (98387-5330)
P.O. Box 1250, Graham (98338-1250)
PHONE 253 846-0242
Don Rigby Jr, *President*
▲ EMP: 75
SQ FT: 150,000
SALES (est): 20.1MM **Privately Held**
WEB: www.rainierveneer.com
SIC: 2435 2421 Veneer stock, hardwood; kiln drying of lumber

(G-12071)
RFP MANUFACTURING INC
21222 Mountain Hwy E (98387-7536)
P.O. Box 5321 (98387-4088)
PHONE 253 847-3330
Rawlin G McInelly, *President*
EMP: 20
SQ FT: 12,000
SALES (est): 2.3MM **Privately Held**
SIC: 2421 Resawing lumber into smaller dimensions

(G-12072)
ROCKING H WOODWORKING
3624 232nd St E (98387-7411)
PHONE 253 448-7978
Mark Humiston, *Principal*
EMP: 2
SALES (est): 158.6K **Privately Held**
SIC: 2431 Millwork

(G-12073)
SIGN DISTRIBUTORS
Also Called: Redwood Signs By Erl Syverstad
23520 41st Ave E (98387-6907)
PHONE 253 847-2747
Erl Syverstad, *Owner*
EMP: 2
SALES (est): 110K **Privately Held**
WEB: www.sempersigns.com
SIC: 3993 Signs & advertising specialties

(G-12074)
SINBADS CUSTOM PRINTING
17501 11th Ave E (98387-5936)
PHONE 253 232-7367
EMP: 2
SALES (est): 83.9K **Privately Held**
SIC: 2752 Commercial printing, lithographic

(G-12075)
SPARKADOODLE BAKING CO LLC
19710 8th Ave E (98387-8480)
PHONE 253 224-0255
Daniel Sparkmon,
Stephanie Sparkmon,
EMP: 2
SALES (est): 5K **Privately Held**
SIC: 2051 Cakes, pies & pastries

(G-12076)
STELLAR ALPACAS
27810 16th Ave E (98387-9720)
PHONE 253 208-2107
EMP: 2 EST: 2013
SALES (est): 122.2K **Privately Held**
SIC: 2231 Alpacas, mohair: woven

(G-12077)
SUSNEY INCORPORATED
20810 52nd Ave E (98387-6073)
PHONE 253 219-7216
Charlotte S Thomas, *President*
Rodney G Thomas, *Vice Pres*
EMP: 2
SALES (est): 122.2K **Privately Held**
WEB: www.susney.com
SIC: 2731 2721 Book publishing; trade journals: publishing & printing

(G-12078)
TORTILLERIA JALISCO
16911 11th Avenue Ct E (98387-7749)
PHONE 253 536-9532
EMP: 3
SALES (est): 146.8K **Privately Held**
SIC: 2096 Mfg Potato Chips/Snacks

(G-12079)
VIKING CABINETS INC
24215 Mountain Hwy E (98387-7001)
PHONE 253 875-1555
Randy Larson, *President*
Gail Larson, *Vice Pres*
EMP: 14
SQ FT: 11,188
SALES (est): 1.6MM **Privately Held**
SIC: 2434 Wood kitchen cabinets

(G-12080)
WESTCOAST TELEMETRY SPECIALIST
1909 159th Street Ct S (98387-9054)
PHONE 253 536-1351
Gary L Logsdon, *Owner*
EMP: 2
SALES: 35K **Privately Held**
SIC: 3663 Telemetering equipment, electronic

(G-12081)
WHIRLPOOL CORPORATION
19700 38th Ave E (98387-6602)
PHONE 253 875-7100
Michael Ledbetter, *General Mgr*
Blair Child, *Regional Mgr*
Ekta Tandon-Vatsal, *Marketing Staff*
EMP: 50
SALES (corp-wide): 21B **Publicly Held**
SIC: 3633 3585 3632 3639 Household laundry machines, including coin-operated; washing machines, household: including coin-operated; laundry dryers, household or coin-operated; air conditioning units, complete: domestic or industrial; refrigerators, mechanical & absorption: household; freezers, home & farm; dishwashing machines, household; garbage disposal units, household; trash compactors, household; household vacuum cleaners; gas ranges, domestic; electric ranges, domestic; microwave ovens, including portable: household
PA: Whirlpool Corporation
2000 N M 63
Benton Harbor MI 49022
269 923-5000

(G-12082)
ZURIBELLA
20621 74th Ave E (98387-5307)
PHONE 253 227-2988
Tina Asagai, *Principal*
EMP: 3
SALES (est): 138.1K **Privately Held**
SIC: 2053 Cakes, bakery: frozen

Spangle
Spokane County

(G-12083)
195 INDUSTRIES INC
705 E Cameron Rd (99031-9733)
PHONE 509 245-3735
Russell J Emtman, *President*
EMP: 12 EST: 2013
SALES (est): 1.3MM **Privately Held**
SIC: 3999 Atomizers, toiletry

(G-12084)
SANTEES GRANOLA INC
2525 E Spangle Waverly Rd (99031)
P.O. Box 30772, Spokane (99223-3012)
PHONE 509 245-3338
Kelly Santee, *Owner*
EMP: 3
SALES (est): 280.9K **Privately Held**
SIC: 2099 Food preparations

(G-12085)
THOMAS R KEEVY
Rr 1 (99031)
PHONE 509 245-3457
Thomas R Keevy, *Owner*
EMP: 2
SALES (est): 130K **Privately Held**
SIC: 3523 0119 Driers (farm): grain, hay & seed; cereal crop farms

Spokane
Spokane County

(G-12086)
16 CENTS CORP
2006 N Ash St (99205-4208)
PHONE 509 329-1600
Jason McSteen, *Owner*
EMP: 16 EST: 2016
SALES (est): 88.8K **Privately Held**
SIC: 2252 Socks

(G-12087)
360 APPAREL LLC
1811 E Sprague Ave (99202-3118)
PHONE 509 924-5219
William McLendon,
EMP: 2
SALES (est): 195.3K **Privately Held**
SIC: 2759 Commercial printing

(G-12088)
A & J BROKERAGE CO INC
Also Called: A & J Brokerage & Pallet Co
6120 N Julia St (99217-6561)
P.O. Box 6332 (99217-0906)
PHONE 509 483-3003
Steve Shuman, *President*
EMP: 22
SQ FT: 10,000
SALES (est): 2MM **Privately Held**
SIC: 2448 2511 Pallets, wood; bed frames, except water bed frames: wood

(G-12089)
A PLUS PRINTING
1818 W Francis Ave (99205-6834)
PHONE 509 714-5514
EMP: 2
SALES (est): 89.3K **Privately Held**
SIC: 2752 Commercial printing, lithographic

(G-12090)
A QUALITY PAINTING
2614 1/2 N Hamilton St (99207)
PHONE 509 362-2398
EMP: 4
SALES: 30K **Privately Held**
SIC: 2851 Mfg Paints/Allied Products

(G-12091)
A-STAR DISTRIBUTING INC
7614 N Market St (99217-7829)
PHONE 509 467-6809
George Ennis, *President*
▲ EMP: 13
SALES (est): 2.1MM **Privately Held**
SIC: 3465 5075 5013 Body parts, automobile: stamped metal; warm air heating & air conditioning; motor vehicle supplies & new parts

(G-12092)
A1A INC
601 E 3rd Ave (99202-2209)
PHONE 509 455-5000
Kyle Tyrell, *Manager*
EMP: 3
SALES (est): 184.9K **Privately Held**
SIC: 3842 Orthopedic appliances

(G-12093)
AAA SANDBAGS
5027 N Post St (99205-5242)
PHONE 509 979-4029
Charles R Garvin, *Principal*
Charles Garvin, *Principal*
EMP: 2 EST: 2001
SALES (est): 248.2K **Privately Held**
SIC: 2674 Bags: uncoated paper & multiwall

(G-12094)
ABSOLUTE AVIATION SERVICES LLC
8122 W Pilot Dr (99224-5723)
PHONE 509 747-2904
Greg Beason, *CEO*
Chris Martens, *General Mgr*
Randall Julin,
Steven Beckerman, *Clerk*
EMP: 25
SQ FT: 5,600
SALES (est): 5.4MM **Privately Held**
WEB: www.absolute-av.com
SIC: 3728 Aircraft parts & equipment

(G-12095)
ACADIE WOODWORKS
230 S Washington St (99201-4318)
PHONE 509 924-1256
Jennifer Gay, *President*
EMP: 4
SALES (est): 385.2K **Privately Held**
SIC: 2431 Millwork

(G-12096)
ACTION APPAREL WASHINGTON INC
1625 W Broadway Ave (99201-1816)
PHONE 509 328-5861
Kelly S Rasmussen, *Principal*
Matt Biggerstaff, *Cust Mgr*
Kelly Corson, *Office Mgr*
Kelly Rasmussen, *Office Mgr*
EMP: 2
SALES (est): 148.8K **Privately Held**
SIC: 2396 Screen printing on fabric articles

(G-12097)
ACTION SPORTSWEAR & PRINTABLES
1625 W Broadway Ave (99201-1816)
PHONE 509 328-5861
Donald E Rasmussen, *President*
Kelly Corson, *Office Mgr*
EMP: 10
SQ FT: 6,000
SALES (est): 1.3MM **Privately Held**
SIC: 2759 Screen printing

(G-12098)
ADEMCO INC
Also Called: ADI Global Distribution
2680 E Ferry Ave (99202-3810)
PHONE 509 534-7300
EMP: 2
SALES (corp-wide): 4.8B **Publicly Held**
SIC: 5063 3669 3822 Electrical apparatus & equipment; emergency alarms; auto controls regulating residntl & coml environmt & applncs
HQ: Ademco Inc.
1985 Douglas Dr N
Golden Valley MN 55422
800 468-1502

(G-12099)
ADM MILLING CO
1131 E Sprague Ave (99202-2100)
PHONE 509 535-2995

Spokane - Spokane County (G-12100)   GEOGRAPHIC SECTION

Terry Appling, *Opers-Prdtn-Mfg*
EMP: 40
SALES (corp-wide): 64.3B **Publicly Held**
WEB: www.admmilling.com
SIC: 2041 Flour & other grain mill products
HQ: Adm Milling Co.
     8000 W 110th St Ste 300
     Overland Park KS 66210
     913 491-9400

(G-12100)
ADM MILLING CO
2301 E Trent Ave (99202-3867)
PHONE 509 534-2636
Shawn Lindhorst, *Manager*
EMP: 50
SALES (corp-wide): 64.3B **Publicly Held**
WEB: www.admmilling.com
SIC: 2041 Grain mills (except rice)
HQ: Adm Milling Co.
     8000 W 110th St Ste 300
     Overland Park KS 66210
     913 491-9400

(G-12101)
ADM MILLING CO
1131 E Sprague Ave (99202-2100)
PHONE 509 534-2636
G Allen Andreas, *CEO*
EMP: 5
SALES (corp-wide): 64.3B **Publicly Held**
WEB: www.admmilling.com
SIC: 2041 Grain mills (except rice)
HQ: Adm Milling Co.
     8000 W 110th St Ste 300
     Overland Park KS 66210
     913 491-9400

(G-12102)
ADVANCED METAL FABRICATION
1605 E Lyons Ave (99217-7505)
PHONE 509 534-0671
Ben Havens, *President*
EMP: 2
SALES (est): 403K **Privately Held**
SIC: 3444 Sheet metalwork

(G-12103)
AGRASYST INC (PA)
16417 N Napa Ln (99208-8511)
PHONE 509 467-2167
Scott Parrish,
EMP: 10
SALES: 3MM **Privately Held**
WEB: www.agrasyst.com
SIC: 2879 Agricultural disinfectants

(G-12104)
AIR TECH ABATEMENT TECH INC
55 E Lincoln Rd Ste 106 (99208-5647)
PHONE 509 315-4550
Cynthia Falk, *CEO*
Sam Wannamaker, *President*
Jeffrey Robinson, *Vice Pres*
EMP: 22
SALES (est): 1.3MM **Privately Held**
SIC: 3589 Asbestos removal equipment

(G-12105)
AIRCRAFT SOLUTIONS LLC
6095 E Rutter Ave Ste 2 (99212-1419)
PHONE 509 838-8883
Charlie Archer, *General Mgr*
Bill Ifft,
EMP: 8 **EST:** 2012
SALES (est): 988.2K **Privately Held**
SIC: 3812 7699 Aircraft/aerospace flight instruments & guidance systems; aircraft flight instrument repair

(G-12106)
ALL PRINT
8 N Post St (99201-0702)
P.O. Box 15353, Spokane Valley (99215-5353)
PHONE 509 328-9344
EMP: 5
SALES: 150K **Privately Held**
SIC: 2759 Commercial Printing

(G-12107)
ALLIED ENVELOPE COMPANY- BOISE
1515 W College Ave (99201-1917)
PHONE 509 328-9800
Dave Lafferty, *Manager*
EMP: 6
SALES (corp-wide): 3.4MM **Privately Held**
SIC: 2759 Commercial printing
HQ: Allied Envelope Company- Boise
     634 N Five Mile Rd
     Boise ID 83713
     208 377-3676

(G-12108)
AMERICAN ARCHITECTURAL SIGNAGE
916 W 30th Ave (99203-1323)
PHONE 509 624-5842
Dan Fry, *Owner*
EMP: 2
SQ FT: 1,200
SALES: 200K **Privately Held**
SIC: 3993 Signs & advertising specialties

(G-12109)
AMERICAN CORDILLERA MIN CORP
1314 S Grand Blvd 2250 (99202-1174)
PHONE 509 671-9401
Frank H Blair, *President*
Gerald J Frankovich, *Vice Pres*
Dwight Weigelt, *CFO*
EMP: 3
SALES (est): 187.5K **Privately Held**
SIC: 1041 Gold ores mining

(G-12110)
AMERICAN ENGINE & MACHINE INC
5302 N Julia St (99217-6628)
PHONE 509 487-3332
Dennis N Provost, *President*
Tam Provost, *Corp Secy*
EMP: 5
SQ FT: 2,400
SALES (est): 376.6K **Privately Held**
SIC: 3462 Automotive & internal combustion engine forgings

(G-12111)
AMERICAN WEST INDUSTRIES INC
3528 E Desmet Ave (99202-4517)
PHONE 509 535-5040
Aaron McCray, *President*
Jim Killmer, *Vice Pres*
Drew Stewert, *Admin Sec*
EMP: 12
SQ FT: 8,000
SALES: 1.5MM **Privately Held**
WEB: www.awchrome.com
SIC: 7699 3593 Hydraulic equipment repair; fluid power cylinders & actuators

(G-12112)
AMGB INC
Also Called: Frank's Boots
3805 N Market St (99207-5824)
PHONE 509 309-2903
Frank Petrilli, *President*
EMP: 8
SQ FT: 6,000
SALES: 500K **Privately Held**
SIC: 3143 3144 Boots, dress or casual: men's; boots, canvas or leather: women's

(G-12113)
AMMONITE INK
Also Called: Fontanelle
1925 N Ash St (99205-4207)
PHONE 907 227-2719
Randi Madison, *Co-Owner*
Jeffrey Jacobs, *Co-Owner*
EMP: 2
SQ FT: 850
SALES (est): 64K **Privately Held**
SIC: 2396 Fabric printing & stamping

(G-12114)
ANDEAVOR
Also Called: Tesoro
901 E Sharp Ave (99202-1936)
PHONE 509 487-9235
Jerome Stark, *Branch Mgr*
EMP: 5 **Publicly Held**
WEB: www.tesoropetroleum.com
SIC: 1311 Crude petroleum production
HQ: Andeavor Llc
     19100 Ridgewood Pkwy
     San Antonio TX 78259
     210 626-6000

(G-12115)
ARBOR CREST WINERIES & NURSERY (PA)
Also Called: Mielke Orchards
4705 N Fruit Hill Rd (99217-9619)
PHONE 509 927-9463
Marsha Mielke, *President*
James V Loben Sels, *General Mgr*
John Mielke, *Corp Secy*
C Harold Mielke, *Vice Pres*
▲ **EMP:** 12
SQ FT: 1,000
SALES (est): 1.9MM **Privately Held**
SIC: 2084 5813 Wine cellars, bonded: engaged in blending wines; drinking places

(G-12116)
ARBOR CREST WINERIES & NURSERY
4502 E Buckeye Ave (99217-7302)
PHONE 509 489-0588
Christine Zanlobensels, *Opers-Prdtn-Mfg*
EMP: 4
SALES (corp-wide): 1.9MM **Privately Held**
SIC: 2084 Wine cellars, bonded: engaged in blending wines
PA: Arbor Crest Wineries & Nursery Inc
     4705 N Fruit Hill Rd
     Spokane WA 99217
     509 927-9463

(G-12117)
ARCHER-DANIELS-MIDLAND COMPANY
Also Called: ADM
2301 E Trent Ave (99202-3867)
PHONE 509 533-9632
William Parr, *Branch Mgr*
EMP: 6
SALES (corp-wide): 64.3B **Publicly Held**
SIC: 2041 Flour & other grain mill products
PA: Archer-Daniels-Midland Company
     77 W Wacker Dr Ste 4600
     Chicago IL 60601
     312 634-8100

(G-12118)
ARRHYTHMIA SOLUTIONS INC
Also Called: Ep Innnovations
Tapio Ofc Ctr 101b (99202)
P.O. Box 601, Mead (99021-0601)
PHONE 509 389-7366
Steven Parker,
EMP: 2 **EST:** 2014
SQ FT: 500
SALES (est): 198.3K **Privately Held**
SIC: 7372 3841 Educational computer software; surgical & medical instruments

(G-12119)
ARTCRAFT PRINTING CO
310 N Crestline St (99202-3007)
P.O. Box 3203 (99220-3203)
PHONE 509 323-5266
Vincent Erban, *President*
Shawn Mc Adams, *Corp Secy*
EMP: 4
SQ FT: 5,000
SALES (est): 386.6K **Privately Held**
SIC: 2752 Commercial printing, offset

(G-12120)
ASC PROFILES LLC
4111 E Ferry Ave (99202-4649)
PHONE 509 535-0600
Donna Knudsen, *Branch Mgr*
EMP: 30
SQ FT: 16,000 **Privately Held**
WEB: www.ascpacific.com
SIC: 3448 3441 Prefabricated metal buildings; fabricated structural metal
HQ: Asc Profiles Llc
     2110 Enterprise Blvd
     West Sacramento CA 95691
     916 376-2800

(G-12121)
ASEPTIC MANUFACTURING SVCS LLC
1841 W Bridge Ave (99201-1815)
PHONE 509 869-4867
Jeffrey Milligan, *Principal*
EMP: 2
SALES (est): 80.6K **Privately Held**
SIC: 3999 Manufacturing industries

(G-12122)
ASPEN CREEK LOG HOMES
405 W Bellwood Dr Apt 91 (99218-3306)
PHONE 509 590-5541
Judy Ridge, *Manager*
EMP: 2
SALES (est): 86.7K **Privately Held**
SIC: 2452 Prefabricated wood buildings

(G-12123)
ASSOCIATION FOR THE DEVELOPM
Also Called: TIMELESS BOOKS
406 S Coeur Dalene St T (99201-5872)
PHONE 509 838-3575
Dawn Spickler, *President*
EMP: 3
SALES: 124.6K **Privately Held**
WEB: www.yasodhara.org
SIC: 2731 8699 Book publishing; charitable organization

(G-12124)
ATLAS ELECTRIC INC
1203 N Havana St (99202-7003)
P.O. Box 11861, Spokane Valley (99211-1861)
PHONE 509 534-8389
John D Jones, *President*
John K Jones, *Vice Pres*
John Brown, *Sales Staff*
▲ **EMP:** 25
SQ FT: 20,000
SALES (est): 7.6MM **Privately Held**
SIC: 3699 5999 7694 Electrical equipment & supplies; engine & motor equipment & supplies; motors, electric; armature rewinding shops

(G-12125)
ATS
408 S Freya St (99202-5058)
PHONE 509 534-2822
Arzen Tom, *President*
EMP: 2
SALES (est): 143.8K **Privately Held**
SIC: 3841 Surgical & medical instruments

(G-12126)
AUDIOCONTROL INC
1215 E Francis Ave (99208-3646)
PHONE 425 775-8461
Frank Denn, *Manager*
EMP: 10
SALES (corp-wide): 6.4MM **Privately Held**
SIC: 3651 Household audio & video equipment
PA: Audiocontrol Inc.
     22410 70th Ave W Ste 1
     Mountlake Terrace WA 98043
     425 775-8461

(G-12127)
AUGUST SYSTEMS INC
4407 N Div St Ste 300 (99208)
P.O. Box 28125 (99228-8125)
PHONE 509 468-2988
Judy Martin, *Principal*
Alan Nelson, *Opers Staff*
Candice Denigan, *Sales Staff*
Josh Williams, *Software Engr*
Mark Manley, *Technical Staff*
EMP: 20
SALES (est): 1.9MM **Privately Held**
WEB: www.august-systems.com
SIC: 7372 7371 Prepackaged software; custom computer programming services

GEOGRAPHIC SECTION

Spokane - Spokane County (G-12158)

(G-12128)
AUSTIN ELSE LLC
Also Called: Maxamps.com
1015 W Garland Ave (99205-2702)
PHONE..................................888 654-4440
Austin Else, *Principal*
▲ **EMP:** 10
SALES (est): 600K **Privately Held**
WEB: www.maxamps.com
SIC: 3679 5961 5063 3692 Electronic loads & power supplies; ; storage batteries, industrial; primary batteries, dry & wet; dry cell batteries, single or multiple cell

(G-12129)
AUTO WHEEL SALES
3803 N Regal St (99207-5845)
PHONE..................................509 483-4251
Steve Howard, *Owner*
EMP: 4
SALES (est): 320K **Privately Held**
SIC: 3312 Wheels

(G-12130)
AUTOMATED OPTIONS INC
9515 N Div St Ste 105 (99218)
PHONE..................................509 467-9860
Gregory Staples, *President*
Carol Staples, *Manager*
EMP: 4
SALES (est): 321.5K **Privately Held**
WEB: www.aoipro.com
SIC: 7372 Business oriented computer software

(G-12131)
AUTOMOTIVE REPAIR CORPORATION (PA)
Also Called: A R C Manufacturing
314 E Jackson Ave (99207-2132)
P.O. Box 3332 (99220-3332)
PHONE..................................509 244-2730
Susan Fuchs, *President*
Tasha Sheets, *Vice Pres*
Harry Case, *Treasurer*
EMP: 17
SQ FT: 25,000
SALES (est): 1.6MM **Privately Held**
WEB: www.arcmanufacturing.com
SIC: 3559 Automotive related machinery

(G-12132)
AVEDA ENVIRONMENTAL LIFESTYLES
808 W Main Ave Ste 211 (99201-0900)
PHONE..................................509 624-5028
Samantha Gordan, *Manager*
EMP: 3 **Publicly Held**
SIC: 5719 2844 5999 Bath accessories; bath salts; perfumes & colognes
HQ: Aveda Environmental Lifestyles
309 Exton Square Mall
Exton PA

(G-12133)
AVISTA CAPITAL INC (HQ)
201 W North River Dr # 610 (99201-2284)
PHONE..................................509 489-0500
Scott Morris, *President*
Terry Syms, *Vice Pres*
Jon E Eliassen, *CFO*
Ron Peterson, *Treasurer*
Diane Thoren, *Asst Treas*
EMP: 7
SQ FT: 10,000
SALES (est): 22.7MM
SALES (corp-wide): 1.4B **Publicly Held**
SIC: 8742 3674 8731 4911 Public utilities consultant; fuel cells, solid state; energy research; electric services; telephone communication, except radio
PA: Avista Corporation
1411 E Mission Ave
Spokane WA 99202
509 489-0500

(G-12134)
AVISTA CORPORATION (PA)
1411 E Mission Ave (99202-1902)
P.O. Box 3727 (99220-3727)
PHONE..................................509 489-0500
Scott L Morris, *Ch of Bd*
Dennis P Vermillion, *President*
Karen S Feltes, *Senior VP*
Jason R Thackston, *Senior VP*
Kevin J Christie, *Vice Pres*
◆ **EMP:** 900 **EST:** 1889
SALES: 1.4B **Publicly Held**
WEB: www.avistacorp.com
SIC: 4911 4924 3499 Distribution, electric power; generation, electric power; ; natural gas distribution; boxes for packing & shipping, metal

(G-12135)
B & C CUSTOM MANUFACTURING INC
1514 E Riverside Ave (99202-3001)
PHONE..................................509 535-0049
David Burgat, *CEO*
Michael S Carver, *Owner*
Mike C Carver, *Purch Mgr*
EMP: 4
SQ FT: 4,560
SALES (est): 647K **Privately Held**
WEB: www.bccustommfg.com
SIC: 3599 Machine shop, jobbing & repair

(G-12136)
BAKER COMMODITIES INC
Spokane Division
4423 E Hutton Ave (99212-1364)
P.O. Box 11157, Spokane Valley (99211-1157)
PHONE..................................509 535-5435
Joe Jacobson, *General Mgr*
EMP: 25
SALES (corp-wide): 161.3MM **Privately Held**
WEB: www.bakercommodities.com
SIC: 2076 2077 Tallow, vegetable; rendering
PA: Baker Commodities, Inc.
4020 Bandini Blvd
Vernon CA 90058
323 268-2801

(G-12137)
BAKER COMMODITIES INC
4423 E Hutton Ave (99212-1364)
P.O. Box 11157, Spokane Valley (99211-1157)
PHONE..................................509 534-2137
John McCartney, *Branch Mgr*
EMP: 23
SALES (corp-wide): 161.3MM **Privately Held**
WEB: www.bakercommodities.com
SIC: 2077 Tallow rendering, inedible
PA: Baker Commodities, Inc.
4020 Bandini Blvd
Vernon CA 90058
323 268-2801

(G-12138)
BAMONTE A TRNADO CRK PBLCTION
1308 E 29th Ave (99203-3228)
P.O. Box 8625 (99203-0625)
PHONE..................................509 838-7114
Anthony Bamonte, *Owner*
EMP: 2
SALES (est): 87.2K **Privately Held**
WEB: www.tornadocreekpublications.com
SIC: 2731 Textbooks: publishing only, not printed on site

(G-12139)
BARRISTER WINERY
1213 W Railroad Ave (99201-4613)
PHONE..................................509 465-3591
Greg Lipsker, *Principal*
Michael White, *Principal*
Tyler Walters, *Manager*
EMP: 2 **EST:** 2011
SALES (est): 157.9K **Privately Held**
SIC: 2084 Wines

(G-12140)
BATON LABS INC
Also Called: Bli International Div
12402 N Division St Ste 2 (99218-1930)
PHONE..................................509 467-4203
Larry Hayslett, *President*
Beth Hayslett, *Vice Pres*
▲ **EMP:** 8
SALES (est): 1MM **Privately Held**
WEB: www.prioritystart.com
SIC: 3694 Engine electrical equipment

(G-12141)
BCARD INC
108 N Washington St # 500 (99201-5003)
PHONE..................................206 963-5211
Brett Turner, *CEO*
EMP: 2 **EST:** 2015
SALES (est): 110K **Privately Held**
SIC: 7372 Application computer software

(G-12142)
BEANPOP LLC
7301 N Mahr Ct (99208-6233)
PHONE..................................509 499-5322
Karen Parisot, *President*
EMP: 2
SALES: 150K **Privately Held**
SIC: 5641 2361 Children's wear; girls' & children's blouses & shirts

(G-12143)
BEAR INDUSTRIES LLC
2525 E 29th Ave 10b-22 (99223-4855)
PHONE..................................509 981-8618
Blane Hoffman, *Bd of Directors*
EMP: 2 **EST:** 2011
SALES (est): 144.5K **Privately Held**
SIC: 3999 Manufacturing industries

(G-12144)
BELAIR COMPOSITES INC
3715 E Longfellow Ave (99217-6716)
PHONE..................................509 482-0442
Mary Avery, *CEO*
Chris Olson, *President*
David Scott, *Vice Pres*
EMP: 10
SQ FT: 5,000
SALES (est): 1.3MM **Privately Held**
WEB: www.belaircomposites.com
SIC: 3052 3089 3724 Air line or air brake hose, rubber or rubberized fabric; rubber hose; heater hose, rubber; plastic processing; exhaust systems, aircraft

(G-12145)
BERG DEVELOPMENT GROUP LLC
850 E Spokane Falls Blvd (99202-2167)
PHONE..................................509 624-8921
Andrew Barrett,
EMP: 5
SALES (est): 310.4K **Privately Held**
SIC: 2299 Textile goods

(G-12146)
BEYOUTIFUL BATH BOMBS MORE
4750 N Division St (99207-1411)
PHONE..................................509 315-9608
EMP: 2
SALES (est): 110.2K **Privately Held**
SIC: 2844 Bath salts

(G-12147)
BILINGUAL PRESS PUBLISHING CO
Also Called: Laprensa Bilingual
2928 E Nebraska Ave (99208-2317)
P.O. Box 48183 (99228-1183)
PHONE..................................509 483-2523
Maria Gaines Alvarez, *Partner*
Ben Cabillo, *Partner*
Troy Gaines, *Partner*
EMP: 3 **EST:** 1996
SALES (est): 143.3K **Privately Held**
SIC: 2711 Newspapers: publishing only, not printed on site

(G-12148)
BILLET CONNECTION LLC
7320 N Regal St (99217-7847)
PHONE..................................509 467-7584
Michael Cofini, *Administration*
EMP: 4
SALES (est): 386.7K **Privately Held**
SIC: 3714 Motor vehicle parts & accessories

(G-12149)
BILLS HELI ARC WELDING
5311 N Julia St (99217-6628)
PHONE..................................509 489-6160
Dave Weber, *Owner*
EMP: 4 **EST:** 1969
SALES (est): 274.2K **Privately Held**
SIC: 7692 Welding repair

(G-12150)
BL BEST INC
1108 N Freya St (99202-4520)
PHONE..................................509 534-0237
Brian Best, *President*
EMP: 2
SALES (est): 252.6K **Privately Held**
SIC: 5063 5932 7694 Electrical supplies; used merchandise stores; electric motor repair

(G-12151)
BLACK BOX CORPORATION
3707 E Decatur Ave Unit 1 (99217-6552)
PHONE..................................406 522-3944
EMP: 2 **Privately Held**
SIC: 3577 Computer peripheral equipment
HQ: Black Box Corporation
1000 Park Dr
Lawrence PA 15055
724 746-5500

(G-12152)
BLACK BOX CORPORATION
3707 E Decatur Ave Unit 1 (99217-6552)
PHONE..................................406 652-1956
EMP: 2 **Privately Held**
SIC: 3577 Computer peripheral equipment
HQ: Black Box Corporation
1000 Park Dr
Lawrence PA 15055
724 746-5500

(G-12153)
BLACK BOX CORPORATION
3707 E Decatur Ave Unit 1 (99217-6552)
PHONE..................................406 652-1956
EMP: 2 **Privately Held**
SIC: 3577 Computer peripheral equipment
HQ: Black Box Corporation
1000 Park Dr
Lawrence PA 15055
724 746-5500

(G-12154)
BLENDER LLC
Also Called: Photoboxx
152 S Jefferson St # 100 (99201-4524)
PHONE..................................509 210-3373
Michael Fisk, *Mng Member*
Devon Lind,
EMP: 2
SALES (est): 62.4K **Privately Held**
SIC: 3955 Print cartridges for laser & other computer printers

(G-12155)
BLUE OVAL CO
10410 S Sharon Rd (99223-9749)
PHONE..................................509 448-2894
Lou Runje, *Owner*
EMP: 2
SALES (est): 250K **Privately Held**
SIC: 5085 7699 3732 Industrial supplies; boat repair; boat building & repairing

(G-12156)
BMT INDUSTRIES INC
421 W Riverside Ave # 720 (99201-0405)
PHONE..................................509 838-4400
Cynthia Schwartz, *Principal*
EMP: 2
SALES (est): 151.6K **Privately Held**
SIC: 3999 Manufacturing industries

(G-12157)
BON LOGIC CORPORATION
14715 W Lincoln Rd (99224-9392)
PHONE..................................509 991-9643
Bonnie Gow, *President*
EMP: 2
SALES (est): 195.7K **Privately Held**
SIC: 2841 2844 Soap & other detergents; face creams or lotions

(G-12158)
BOTTLING GROUP LLC
4014 E Sprague Ave (99202-4849)
PHONE..................................509 535-0605
Rick Cooper, *Manager*
Tom Dornquast, *Manager*
EMP: 225

Spokane - Spokane County (G-12159)

SALES (corp-wide): 64.6B **Publicly Held**
SIC: 2086 5149 Bottled & canned soft drinks; soft drinks
HQ: Bottling Group, Llc
1111 Westchester Ave
White Plains NY 10604
914 253-2000

(G-12159)
BRADLEYS METAL WORKS INC
12128 S Cheney Spokane Rd (99224)
P.O. Box 91, Marshall (99020-0091)
PHONE.................................509 448-2307
Allison Bradley, *President*
David Bradley, *Vice Pres*
EMP: 5 EST: 1995
SALES: 500K **Privately Held**
SIC: 3561 Industrial pumps & parts

(G-12160)
BRASSFINDERS INC
718 N Crestline St Ste B (99202-2821)
PHONE.................................509 747-7412
Michael Eckel, *President*
EMP: 3
SQ FT: 3,000
SALES: 350K **Privately Held**
WEB: www.brassfinders.com
SIC: 3446 Architectural metalwork

(G-12161)
BURLINGAME STEEL INC
4240 E Alki Ave (99202-4666)
PHONE.................................509 535-3735
Howard Burlingame, *President*
Wanda Blankenship, *Corp Secy*
EMP: 10
SQ FT: 8,000
SALES (est): 1.7MM **Privately Held**
SIC: 3441 Building components, structural steel

(G-12162)
BUSINESS EQUIPMENT CENTER INC (PA)
Also Called: Abadan Reprographics
603 E 2nd Ave (99202-2201)
P.O. Box 224 (99210-0224)
PHONE.................................509 747-2964
Paul Rayburn Jr, *President*
Nadine Rayburn, *Corp Secy*
EMP: 16
SQ FT: 8,784
SALES (est): 4.9MM **Privately Held**
WEB: www.businessequipmentcenter.com
SIC: 5044 7389 7334 2759 Copying equipment; microfilm recording & developing service; photocopying & duplicating services; commercial printing

(G-12163)
BUTTERFIELD CELLARS LLC
Also Called: Winescape
6011 E 32nd Ave (99223-1141)
PHONE.................................509 994-0382
Phillip Butterfield, *Mng Member*
Patricia Butterfield,
Tristan Butterfield,
EMP: 3 EST: 2014
SALES: 60K **Privately Held**
SIC: 2084 7389 Wines;

(G-12164)
BUY MORE CAPS CO
2206 W Weile Ave (99208-4317)
PHONE.................................509 599-2944
EMP: 2 EST: 2010
SALES (est): 112.5K **Privately Held**
SIC: 2759 Screen printing

(G-12165)
C&K ENTERPRIZE LLC
Also Called: Theelectricaldepot.com
4704 S Tampa Dr (99223-7878)
PHONE.................................509 448-2866
Clint Nelson, *President*
EMP: 5 EST: 1985
SALES (est): 330K **Privately Held**
SIC: 3613 Distribution boards, electric

(G-12166)
CA INC
505 W Riverside Ave # 500 (99201-0500)
PHONE.................................509 252-5080
Carol Jenkins, *Branch Mgr*
EMP: 84
SALES (corp-wide): 20.8B **Publicly Held**
WEB: www.cai.com
SIC: 7372 Application computer software
HQ: Ca, Inc.
520 Madison Ave
New York NY 10022
800 225-5224

(G-12167)
CANNONBOT GAMES LLC
906 W 2nd Ave Ste 100 (99201-4540)
PHONE.................................510 473-6871
EMP: 2
SALES (est): 56.5K **Privately Held**
SIC: 7372 Home entertainment computer software

(G-12168)
CAPITAL A PUBLICATIONS LL
1429 E 13th Ave (99202-3535)
PHONE.................................509 279-0832
Ariane Smith, *President*
EMP: 2 EST: 2010
SALES (est): 107.3K **Privately Held**
SIC: 2741 Miscellaneous publishing

(G-12169)
CARLSON MACHINE WORKS INC
3310 E Trent Ave (99202-4413)
P.O. Box 1497, Veradale (99037-1497)
PHONE.................................509 535-0028
Steve Carlson, *President*
Carol Carlson, *Treasurer*
EMP: 5
SQ FT: 4,000
SALES (est): 524.3K **Privately Held**
WEB: www.exactrix.com
SIC: 3599 Machine shop, jobbing & repair

(G-12170)
CARLSON SHEET METAL WORKS INC
3621 E Broadway Ave (99202-4604)
PHONE.................................509 535-4228
Brian Fair, *President*
EMP: 17
SALES (est): 2.7MM **Privately Held**
WEB: www.carlsonsheetmetal.com
SIC: 3444 Sheet metalwork

(G-12171)
CASCADE MARBLE & GRANITE
723 N Napa St (99202-2866)
P.O. Box 122, Marshall (99020-0122)
PHONE.................................509 533-0476
Joe Everman, *President*
EMP: 2
SALES (est): 105.9K **Privately Held**
SIC: 3281 5032 Cut stone & stone products; granite building stone

(G-12172)
CASCADIA SCREEN PRINTING
1605 N River Ridge Blvd 11-201 (99224-5381)
PHONE.................................541 490-7012
Jacob McLean, *Principal*
EMP: 2
SALES (est): 83.9K **Privately Held**
SIC: 2752 Commercial printing, lithographic

(G-12173)
CATERPILLAR INC
9610 W Hallett Rd (99224-9748)
PHONE.................................509 623-4640
Matthew Heberer, *Manager*
EMP: 40
SQ FT: 76,000
SALES (corp-wide): 54.7B **Publicly Held**
WEB: www.cat.com
SIC: 3531 Construction machinery
PA: Caterpillar Inc.
510 Lake Cook Rd Ste 100
Deerfield IL 60015
224 551-4000

(G-12174)
CEE GEES & CO
13415 N Calispel Ct (99208-8733)
P.O. Box 28126 (99228-8126)
PHONE.................................509 465-8231
Gordon Fagras, *Owner*
EMP: 9
SALES (est): 621.8K **Privately Held**
SIC: 3751 Bicycles & related parts

(G-12175)
CENTRAL FABRICATORS INC
1011 E Sharpsburg Ave # 546 (99208-6678)
PHONE.................................509 468-3995
Jerome Schwindt, *President*
EMP: 4
SQ FT: 10,000
SALES (est): 342.2K **Privately Held**
SIC: 3441 Fabricated structural metal

(G-12176)
CENTRAL WASH CORN PRCSSORS INC
427 W 1st Ave (99201-3706)
PHONE.................................509 623-1144
Steve Paulson, *President*
Tom Walters, *Treasurer*
EMP: 5
SALES (est): 699.1K **Privately Held**
SIC: 2046 Corn milling by-products

(G-12177)
CEYLON & CYANIDE
174 S Coeur Dalene St H30 (99201-6481)
PHONE.................................509 638-7772
Leslie Tate, *Principal*
EMP: 2
SALES (est): 74.4K **Privately Held**
SIC: 2819 Cyanides

(G-12178)
CGM IMAGING SERVICES LLC
3509 W Prairie Breeze Ave (99208-7160)
PHONE.................................509 995-6153
Claude Michelsen,
EMP: 2
SALES: 114K **Privately Held**
SIC: 3844 X-ray apparatus & tubes

(G-12179)
CHEVRON CORPORATION
3602 E Sprague Ave (99202-4841)
PHONE.................................509 534-4077
Paula Clark, *CEO*
EMP: 2
SALES (corp-wide): 166.3B **Publicly Held**
SIC: 2911 5411 Petroleum refining; convenience stores
PA: Chevron Corporation
6001 Bollinger Canyon Rd
San Ramon CA 94583
925 842-1000

(G-12180)
CHIWAWA MINES INC
28 E Riverside Ave (99202)
PHONE.................................509 455-8080
EMP: 3 EST: 2011
SALES (est): 120K **Privately Held**
SIC: 3483 Ammunition Except For Small Arms Nec

(G-12181)
CHOPPERS BY KRISS
2914 E Liberty Ave (99207-5754)
PHONE.................................509 570-2737
Kriss Dill, *President*
EMP: 2
SALES (est): 135.4K **Privately Held**
SIC: 3751 Motorcycles & related parts

(G-12182)
CLARK SITE MIX CON SPOKANE LLC
4705 W South Oval Rd (99224-5124)
PHONE.................................509 991-7730
Jim Clark, *President*
EMP: 3
SALES (est): 400.1K **Privately Held**
SIC: 3273 Ready-mixed concrete

(G-12183)
CLEARWATER PAPER CORPORATION (PA)
601 W Riverside Ave # 1100 (99201-0644)
PHONE.................................509 344-5900
Alexander Toeldte, *Ch of Bd*
Linda K Massman, *President*
Michael S Gadd, *Senior VP*
Kari G Moyes, *Senior VP*
Rodney Gonzales, *Vice Pres*
▼ EMP: 180
SALES: 1.7B **Publicly Held**
WEB: www.forestphoto.com
SIC: 2631 2621 Paperboard mills; paper mills

(G-12184)
CLEARWATER PAPER OKLAHOMA
Also Called: Cellu Tissue
601 W Riverside Ave # 1100 (99201-0621)
PHONE.................................405 717-5104
Gordon L Jones, *President*
Linda K Massman, *Vice Pres*
▲ EMP: 8
SALES (est): 1.8MM **Privately Held**
SIC: 2621 Tissue paper

(G-12185)
CLINTRON PUBLISHING INC
Also Called: Fruit Country Magazine
5817 S Magnolia St (99223-8360)
PHONE.................................509 448-9878
Clint Withers, *President*
EMP: 3 EST: 1976
SALES: 300K **Privately Held**
SIC: 2721 Magazines: publishing & printing

(G-12186)
COBALT TRAILER SALES
4620 E Trent Ave (99212-1343)
PHONE.................................509 535-2154
Doyle Whitney, *Sales Mgr*
Luke Stewart, *Manager*
EMP: 2
SALES (est): 99.9K **Privately Held**
SIC: 3312 Blast furnaces & steel mills

(G-12187)
COLLINS AEROSPACE
Also Called: UTC Aerospace Systems
11135 W Westbow Ln (99224-9475)
PHONE.................................509 744-6000
EMP: 3
SALES (est): 69.7K
SALES (corp-wide): 66.5B **Publicly Held**
SIC: 3728 Aircraft parts & equipment
PA: United Technologies Corporation
10 Farm Springs Rd
Farmington CT 06032
860 728-7000

(G-12188)
COLOSSEUM VENTURES LLC
Also Called: Stadium Sports
933 E 3rd Ave (99202-2215)
PHONE.................................509 533-0366
Scott Hoffman, *Mng Member*
EMP: 18
SQ FT: 5,000
SALES (est): 2.2MM **Privately Held**
SIC: 2759 2396 2395 1721 Screen printing; automotive & apparel trimmings; pleating & stitching; interior commercial painting contractor

(G-12189)
COLUMBIA CABINETS LLC
1927 W Maxwell Ave (99201-2833)
PHONE.................................509 325-8995
John Schultz,
EMP: 3 EST: 1948
SQ FT: 4,000
SALES (est): 330K **Privately Held**
SIC: 2521 2434 Cabinets, office: wood; wood kitchen cabinets

(G-12190)
COLUMBIA FURNITURE MFG INC
2821 N Hogan St (99207-4867)
PHONE.................................509 534-7147
John Koppe, *President*
Cindy Koppe, *Corp Secy*
EMP: 10
SQ FT: 9,000
SALES: 400K **Privately Held**
SIC: 5712 2512 Furniture stores; upholstered household furniture

GEOGRAPHIC SECTION

Spokane - Spokane County (G-12220)

(G-12191)
COMMERCE RETAIL SALES INC
Also Called: C R S
1011 E 29th Ave (99203-3221)
P.O. Box 4567 (99220-0567)
PHONE...................509 926-1724
Leon A Frechette, *President*
EMP: 2
SALES: 180K **Privately Held**
WEB: www.asktooltalk.com
SIC: 2759 7389 Publication printing;

(G-12192)
COMMERCIAL CREAMERY CO (PA)
159 S Cedar St (99201-7047)
PHONE...................509 747-4131
Michael Gilmartin, *President*
Earl Gilmartin III, *Exec VP*
Megan G Boell, *Vice Pres*
Jeff White, *Natl Sales Mgr*
Mark Desmond, *Sales Staff*
◆ **EMP:** 53
SQ FT: 20,000
SALES (est): 16.2MM **Privately Held**
WEB: www.cheesepowder.com
SIC: 2023 Powdered milk

(G-12193)
COMMERCIAL CREAMERY CO IDA INC (HQ)
159 S Cedar St (99201-7047)
PHONE...................509 747-4131
Mike Gilmartin, *President*
Michael Gilmartin, *President*
Earl Gilmartin Jr, *Chairman*
Peter Gilmartin, *Corp Secy*
Earl Gilmartin III, *Vice Pres*
EMP: 80
SQ FT: 150,000
SALES (est): 15.3MM
SALES (corp-wide): 16.2MM **Privately Held**
PA: Commercial Creamery Co.
159 S Cedar St
Spokane WA 99201
509 747-4131

(G-12194)
COMP U CHARGE INC
104 N Madelia St (99202-3020)
P.O. Box 3404 (99220-3404)
PHONE...................509 484-1918
Toll Free:......................888 -
Sue Wiley, *President*
Mark Wiley, *Vice Pres*
EMP: 16
SQ FT: 12,000
SALES (est): 2.9MM **Privately Held**
WEB: www.compucharge.com
SIC: 3861 5112 Photographic equipment & supplies; stationery & office supplies

(G-12195)
COMPLETE MUSIC
728 N Hogan St (99202-2833)
P.O. Box 3802 (99220-3802)
PHONE...................509 927-3535
Christian Roseanau, *President*
Crystal Rosenan, *Vice Pres*
EMP: 4
SALES (est): 292.6K **Privately Held**
SIC: 4832 3663 Radio broadcasting stations; mobile communication equipment

(G-12196)
CONCEPT FABRICATION INC
5315 E Union Ave (99212-1320)
P.O. Box 11586, Spokane Valley (99211-1586)
PHONE...................509 534-9235
Randy L Gray, *President*
Daniel W Woodman, *Sales & Mktg St*
▲ **EMP:** 10
SALES (est): 1.4MM **Privately Held**
WEB: www.conceptfabrication.com
SIC: 3053 3086 2821 Packing materials; plastics foam products; plastics materials & resins

(G-12197)
CONCRETE WORKS STATUARY INC
4750 N Division St (99207-1411)
PHONE...................509 922-6168
Curtiss R Grenz, *President*
EMP: 2
SALES (est): 158.6K **Privately Held**
SIC: 3272 Cast stone, concrete

(G-12198)
CONSTANTINE ARMORY LLC
2615 N Cincinnati St # 102 (99207-2703)
PHONE...................509 998-6959
EMP: 3
SALES (est): 121.1K **Privately Held**
SIC: 3489 Mfg Ordnance/Accessories

(G-12199)
CONTINUUM
1611 E Sprague Ave (99202-3114)
PHONE...................509 534-0655
Alan Ross, *Principal*
Alan G Ross, *Principal*
EMP: 2
SALES (est): 109.1K **Privately Held**
SIC: 2759 Commercial printing

(G-12200)
COPY-RITE INC
Also Called: Copy-Rite Printing
1108 W 2nd Ave (99201-4506)
PHONE...................509 624-8503
Marshall Canwell, *President*
EMP: 9
SQ FT: 10,000
SALES (est): 1.2MM **Privately Held**
WEB: www.copyrite.net
SIC: 2752 7334 7331 2759 Commercial printing, offset; photocopying & duplicating services; direct mail advertising services; commercial printing

(G-12201)
COUGAR HILLS LLC
8 N Post St (99201-0702)
PHONE...................509 241-3850
Deborah Kay Hansen, *Branch Mgr*
EMP: 2
SALES (corp-wide): 2.1MM **Privately Held**
SIC: 2084 Wines
PA: Cougar Hills, Llc
50 Frenchtown Rd
Walla Walla WA 99362
509 529-5980

(G-12202)
COUNTRY HARVEST SOUP
33 Av (99223)
PHONE...................509 535-8357
Martin Bos, *Principal*
EMP: 2
SALES (est): 133.9K **Privately Held**
SIC: 2034 Soup mixes

(G-12203)
COUNTRY STONEWARE
803 E Illinois Ave (99207-2636)
PHONE...................509 484-6950
Judith Donley, *Principal*
EMP: 2
SALES (est): 95.5K **Privately Held**
SIC: 3269 Stoneware pottery products

(G-12204)
COWLES PUBLISHING COMPANY (PA)
Also Called: Journal of Business
999 W Riverside Ave (99201-1005)
P.O. Box 2160 (99210-2160)
PHONE...................509 459-5000
William Stacey Cowles, *President*
Rob Curley, *Editor*
Wes Bates, *Sales Staff*
Alisha Merkt, *Supervisor*
Barbara Jones, *Admin Sec*
EMP: 400
SQ FT: 150,000
SALES (est): 128.9MM **Privately Held**
WEB: www.spokesmanreview.com
SIC: 2711 2611 2621 4833 Newspapers, publishing & printing; pulp produced from wood base; newsprint paper; television broadcasting stations

(G-12205)
CRAFTED NORTHWEST DOORS INC
3604 E Rowan Ave (99217-6665)
PHONE...................509 484-3722
Fax: 509 484-3705
EMP: 10 **EST:** 1999
SQ FT: 12,500
SALES (est): 800K **Privately Held**
SIC: 2431 2426 Mfg Millwork Hardwood Dimension/Floor Mill

(G-12206)
CRAFTSMAN CELLARS LLC
3222 W Providence Ave (99205-2251)
PHONE...................509 328-3960
Margle Shelman, *Mng Member*
Greg Shelman,
EMP: 3 **EST:** 2015
SALES (est): 284K **Privately Held**
SIC: 5921 2084 Wine; wines

(G-12207)
CREATIVE INTERACTION LLC
Also Called: Clayfox Pottery
15221 N Shady Slope Rd (99208-9510)
PHONE...................509 466-4612
Jill Smith,
Shawn Smith,
EMP: 2
SALES (est): 153.3K **Privately Held**
WEB: www.creativeinteraction.net
SIC: 3269 Pottery cooking & kitchen articles

(G-12208)
CRESCENT MACHINE WORKS INC
821 N Monroe St (99201-2193)
PHONE...................509 328-2820
Toll Free:......................888 -
Daniel Mengert, *President*
Mark Mengert, *Vice Pres*
EMP: 5 **EST:** 1916
SALES: 500K **Privately Held**
SIC: 7699 3599 7692 Restaurant equipment repair; machine shop, jobbing & repair; welding repair

(G-12209)
CROSS ROADS PRINTING
1204 W Maxwell Ave (99201-2619)
PHONE...................509 328-1627
Carol Nottier, *Owner*
EMP: 2
SALES (est): 131.3K **Privately Held**
SIC: 2752 Commercial printing, lithographic

(G-12210)
CROWN CARRIAGE WORKS INC
5107 E Union Ave (99212-1319)
P.O. Box 11103, Spokane Valley (99211-1103)
PHONE...................509 535-4427
Tim House, *President*
EMP: 4
SQ FT: 10,000
SALES (est): 360K **Privately Held**
SIC: 3441 7538 Fabricated structural metal; general truck repair

(G-12211)
CUMMINS INC
Also Called: Cummins Northwest
11134 W Westbow Ln (99224-9475)
PHONE...................509 455-4411
Corey Chyczewski, *Branch Mgr*
EMP: 40
SALES (corp-wide): 23.7B **Publicly Held**
SIC: 5084 3714 3519 Engines & parts, diesel; motor vehicle parts & accessories; internal combustion engines
PA: Cummins Inc.
500 Jackson St
Columbus IN 47201
812 377-5000

(G-12212)
CUSTOM BILT HOLDINGS LLC
812 N Madelia St (99202-2845)
PHONE...................509 533-1703
Brian Horn, *Manager*
Dale Kemmish, *Manager*
EMP: 8
SALES (corp-wide): 40MM **Privately Held**
SIC: 3334 5033 1761 Slabs (primary), aluminum; roofing, asphalt & sheet metal; gutter & downspout contractor
PA: Custom Bilt Holdings, Llc
3001 Skyway Cir N Ste 160
Irving TX 75038
214 699-4876

(G-12213)
CYNTHIA ROCHLITZER
Also Called: Mobitat Portable Housing Units
10703 N Ritchey Rd (99224-8932)
PHONE...................509 796-4199
Cynthia Rochlitzer, *Owner*
Mark Rochlitzer, *Owner*
EMP: 2
SALES (est): 133.6K **Privately Held**
SIC: 2452 Prefabricated wood buildings

(G-12214)
D-MAC CARPENTRY
4828 N Stevens St (99205-5223)
PHONE...................509 326-6601
David Mc Laughlin, *Owner*
EMP: 2
SALES (est): 156.1K **Privately Held**
SIC: 2511 2434 Wood household furniture; wood kitchen cabinets

(G-12215)
DAILY GRIND UPTOWN
422 W Riverside Ave (99201-0303)
PHONE...................509 448-1281
EMP: 2
SALES (est): 120K **Privately Held**
SIC: 3599 Grinding castings for the trade

(G-12216)
DAIRYLAND ORTHOPEDICS PUBG
1610 S Deer Heights Rd (99224-5191)
PHONE...................509 868-0096
Michle Lynn Souza, *Principal*
EMP: 2
SALES (est): 143.5K **Privately Held**
SIC: 5143 2741 Dairy products, except dried or canned; miscellaneous publishing

(G-12217)
DARIGOLD INC
33 E Francis Ave (99208-1097)
PHONE...................509 489-8600
Duane Dubois, *President*
Rob Horton, *Accounts Mgr*
EMP: 90
SALES (corp-wide): 1.4B **Privately Held**
SIC: 2026 2021 Milk processing (pasteurizing, homogenizing, bottling); creamery butter
HQ: Darigold, Inc.
5601 6th Ave S Ste 300
Seattle WA 98108
206 284-7220

(G-12218)
DASH CONNECTOR TECHNOLOGY INC
3915 E Francis Ave Ste C6 (99217-0500)
PHONE...................509 465-1903
Pete Distel, *President*
EMP: 4
SQ FT: 2,000
SALES (est): 757.1K **Privately Held**
WEB: www.dashconnector.com
SIC: 3678 Electronic connectors

(G-12219)
DAVID BOL
711 W Birchbend Dr (99224-9068)
P.O. Box 2508, Moses Lake (98837-0752)
PHONE...................425 802-0804
David Bol, *Owner*
EMP: 2
SALES (est): 66.6K **Privately Held**
SIC: 2834 Druggists' preparations (pharmaceuticals)

(G-12220)
DAVID OLSON HONEYWELL ARSPC
2810 S Lincoln St (99203-1350)
PHONE...................509 321-7368

Spokane - Spokane County (G-12221)

EMP: 2
SALES (est): 106.8K **Privately Held**
SIC: 3724 Mfg Aircraft Engines/Parts

(G-12221)
DEBBIE MUMM INC
3521 W Horizon Ave (99208-8494)
PHONE.................................509 939-1479
Steve Mumm, *CEO*
EMP: 6
SQ FT: 1,000
SALES (est): 2.1MM **Privately Held**
WEB: www.debbiemumm.com
SIC: 5199 5949 5192 2741 Gifts & novelties; sewing, needlework & piece goods; books, periodicals & newspapers; miscellaneous publishing; book publishing

(G-12222)
DECAL FACTORY
Also Called: Decal Factory, The
421 W Riverside Ave # 400 (99201-2467)
PHONE.................................509 465-8931
Donna Bryant, *President*
Doug Bryant, *Vice Pres*
Dan Williams, *Sales Staff*
EMP: 5
SALES (est): 886.1K **Privately Held**
WEB: www.decalfactory.com
SIC: 5199 3993 2759 5131 Decals; signs & advertising specialties; poster & decal printing & engraving; flags & banners; adhesive papers, labels or tapes: from purchased material; packaging & labeling services

(G-12223)
DEINES AUTOMATION LLC
108 N Washington St # 408 (99201-5003)
PHONE.................................509 230-2369
EMP: 2
SALES (est): 120K **Privately Held**
SIC: 3569 Mfg General Industrial Machinery

(G-12224)
DENTAL X RAY SUPPORT SYSTEMS
3102 E Trent Ave Ste 100 (99202-3800)
PHONE.................................509 279-2061
Jim Jacobson, *Vice Pres*
EMP: 11
SQ FT: 2,000
SALES (est): 1.4MM **Privately Held**
WEB: www.imagemax.us
SIC: 3843 3844 Dental equipment & supplies; X-ray apparatus & tubes

(G-12225)
DESIGN CENTRE
Also Called: Adteck Laser Engraving
3613 E Springfield Ave (99202-4641)
PHONE.................................509 534-6461
Janice Croskrey, *Owner*
EMP: 2
SQ FT: 1,500
SALES: 70K **Privately Held**
SIC: 3993 Signs & advertising specialties

(G-12226)
DESIGNER DECAL INC
1120 E 1st Ave (99202-2104)
PHONE.................................509 535-0267
Gary Russell Orne, *President*
Geoff Whitcomb, *Sales Dir*
EMP: 12
SQ FT: 15,000
SALES: 1.5MM **Privately Held**
SIC: 2759 7336 Decals: printing; art design services

(G-12227)
DIGATRON LLC
120 N Wall St Ste 300 (99201-0639)
PHONE.................................509 467-3128
Jonathan Levin, *Engineer*
Jim R Birch,
Tom Stiritz,
EMP: 32
SQ FT: 14,000
SALES (est): 3.5MM **Privately Held**
WEB: www.digatronusa.com
SIC: 3823 Digital displays of process variables

(G-12228)
DIGITAL COLOR PRESS
8117 N Division St Ste I (99208-5765)
PHONE.................................509 362-1152
Jeff Byrd, *Principal*
EMP: 2
SALES (est): 164.6K **Privately Held**
SIC: 2741 Miscellaneous publishing

(G-12229)
DITTOS PRINT & COPY CENTER INC
2515 E Sprague Ave (99202-3936)
PHONE.................................509 533-0025
Russell Lynn Davis, *President*
Julie Ann Davis, *Vice Pres*
EMP: 14
SALES (est): 1.8MM **Privately Held**
SIC: 2752 Commercial printing, offset

(G-12230)
DOVE PRINTING INC
1227 E Francis Ave (99208-3646)
PHONE.................................509 483-6164
David Dysart, *President*
Teresa Dysart, *Vice Pres*
EMP: 4
SQ FT: 2,000
SALES (est): 531.3K **Privately Held**
SIC: 2752 Commercial printing, offset

(G-12231)
DRAXIS HEALTH INC ✪
3525 N Regal St (99207-5788)
PHONE.................................509 489-5656
EMP: 2 EST: 2018
SALES (est): 86.6K **Privately Held**
SIC: 3841 Surgical & medical instruments

(G-12232)
DRY FLY DISTILLING INC
1003 E Trent Ave Ste 200 (99202-2181)
PHONE.................................509 489-2112
Don Poffenroth, *President*
Kent Fleischmann, *Vice Pres*
EMP: 10
SALES (est): 2MM **Privately Held**
SIC: 2085 Vodka (alcoholic beverage)

(G-12233)
DRY FLY OR DIE
505 W Riverside Ave (99201-0500)
PHONE.................................509 252-5022
EMP: 2
SALES (est): 110K **Privately Held**
SIC: 3544 Special dies & tools

(G-12234)
DYNAMIC FOOD INGREDIENTS CORP
831 E Rockwood Blvd (99203-3540)
PHONE.................................303 459-5908
Benjamin Sykora, *CFO*
EMP: 5
SALES (est): 368.1K **Privately Held**
SIC: 2869 2099 Industrial organic chemicals; food preparations

(G-12235)
E Z LOADER ADJUSTABLE BOAT
717 N Hamilton St (99202-2044)
PHONE.................................509 489-0181
Randy Johnson, *President*
Bill Lang, *Vice Pres*
Garry Potter, *Vice Pres*
Christina Johnson, *Admin Sec*
EMP: 150
SALES: 40MM
SALES (corp-wide): 63.3MM **Privately Held**
SIC: 3799 Boat trailers
PA: E Z Loader Boat Trailers, Inc.
717 N Hamilton St
Spokane WA 99202
574 266-0092

(G-12236)
E Z LOADER BOAT TRAILERS INC (PA)
Also Called: EZ Loder Adjustable Boat Trlrs
717 N Hamilton St (99202-2044)
P.O. Box 3263 (99220-3263)
PHONE.................................574 266-0092

Randy Johnson, *President*
David Osenga, *Vice Pres*
Gary Potter, *Vice Pres*
Gina Maclean, *Transportation*
Jennifer Joy, *Purchasing*
◆ EMP: 105
SQ FT: 160,000
SALES (est): 65.6MM **Privately Held**
WEB: www.ezloader.com
SIC: 3799 Boat trailers

(G-12237)
EAGLE PUMP & EQUIPMENT INC
1310 S Ferrall St (99202-5436)
PHONE.................................509 534-1111
Ron Moffatt, *President*
Michael Moore, *CFO*
EMP: 3
SALES (est): 1.5MM **Privately Held**
SIC: 3594 Fluid power pumps & motors

(G-12238)
EATON AGENCY INC
6626 S Tomaker Ln (99223-6202)
P.O. Box 31415 (99223-3023)
PHONE.................................509 448-6556
EMP: 2
SALES (est): 206.1K **Privately Held**
SIC: 3625 Mfg Relays/Industrial Controls

(G-12239)
ELECTRIC AMP INNVTIONS USA LLC
7702 N Country Homes Blvd (99208-6368)
P.O. Box 164 (99210-0164)
PHONE.................................509 455-7469
Joel C Wheeler,
EMP: 3
SALES (est): 265.5K **Privately Held**
SIC: 3651 Household audio & video equipment

(G-12240)
ELKAY SSP LLC
3200 E Trent Ave (99202-4456)
PHONE.................................509 533-0808
EMP: 3
SALES (corp-wide): 1.2B **Privately Held**
SIC: 3431 Metal sanitary ware
HQ: Elkay Ssp, Llc
421 N Freya St
Spokane WA 99202
509 533-0808

(G-12241)
ELKAY SSP LLC (HQ)
421 N Freya St (99202-4606)
PHONE.................................509 533-0808
Lovon Fausett, *Mng Member*
Jennifer F Fausett,
▲ EMP: 22
SQ FT: 35,000
SALES (est): 10.8MM
SALES (corp-wide): 1.2B **Privately Held**
WEB: www.sspinc.net
SIC: 3431 3444 3599 Metal sanitary ware; sheet metalwork; machine & other job shop work
PA: Elkay Manufacturing Company Inc
2222 Camden Ct
Oak Brook IL 60523
630 574-8484

(G-12242)
EMERALD PHOENIX OIL CO LLC
111 E Lincoln Rd (99208-6901)
PHONE.................................509 466-0555
James Ivers, *Principal*
EMP: 2
SALES (est): 73.3K **Privately Held**
SIC: 1389 Haulage, oil field

(G-12243)
EMMA KNITS INC
Also Called: Abandoned Yarn Online
16 W 18th Ave (99203-2001)
P.O. Box 8093 (99203-0093)
PHONE.................................509 999-8583
Linda Lynn, *President*
EMP: 2
SALES (est): 59.9K **Privately Held**
SIC: 5949 2281 Knitting goods & supplies; knitting yarn, spun

(G-12244)
EMPIRE CREEK EXPLORATION CO
36 W 16th Ave (99203-2119)
PHONE.................................509 747-0996
EMP: 2
SALES (est): 81.9K **Privately Held**
SIC: 1382 Oil & gas exploration services

(G-12245)
EMPIRE LAB AUTOMTN SYSTEMS LLC
2704 N Hogan St Ste 1 (99207-4979)
PHONE.................................509 808-6050
Peter Bean, *General Mgr*
Michael Everett,
EMP: 3
SALES (est): 371.2K **Privately Held**
SIC: 3826 Laser scientific & engineering instruments

(G-12246)
EMPIRE LUMBER CO (PA)
Also Called: Kamiah Mills
14 E Main Ave (99202-1620)
P.O. Box 638, Kamiah ID (83536-0638)
PHONE.................................509 534-0266
David Klaue, *President*
EMP: 6
SQ FT: 1,100
SALES: 13.5MM **Privately Held**
SIC: 2421 Kiln drying of lumber; planing mills; chipper mill

(G-12247)
EMPIRE UPHOLSTERY
4907 N Cannon St (99205-5623)
PHONE.................................509 467-5263
Russell Porter, *Owner*
Jacklyn Porter, *Co-Owner*
EMP: 3
SALES: 55K **Privately Held**
SIC: 2512 Upholstered household furniture

(G-12248)
EQUIPMENT TECHNOLOGY & DESIGN
2201 N Craig Rd Lot 237 (99224-8552)
PHONE.................................509 747-5550
Evelyn Russell, *President*
Janis L Russell, *Vice Pres*
Jonie R Russell, *Engineer*
EMP: 5
SQ FT: 5,600
SALES (est): 942.7K **Privately Held**
SIC: 3613 Control panels, electric

(G-12249)
ERB WOODCRAFT LLC
15111 N Columbus St (99208-9536)
PHONE.................................509 467-1134
Edward Baum, *Principal*
EMP: 2
SALES (est): 142.7K **Privately Held**
SIC: 2511 Wood household furniture

(G-12250)
ERICKSON INC
Also Called: Erickson's Eyes
422 W Riverside Ave # 730 (99201-0305)
PHONE.................................509 747-6148
Kim Erickson, *President*
Leif Erickson, *Vice Pres*
▲ EMP: 3
SQ FT: 900
SALES (est): 443.5K **Privately Held**
WEB: www.ericksons-eyes.com
SIC: 3851 Eyes, glass & plastic

(G-12251)
ESCENT LIGHTING
605 W Spokane Falls Blvd (99201-0807)
PHONE.................................509 838-9028
EMP: 2
SALES (est): 185.6K **Privately Held**
SIC: 3648 Mfg Lighting Equipment

(G-12252)
EWING CONSTRUCTION
701 N Flint Rd (99224-9571)
PHONE.................................509 624-2246
EMP: 2 EST: 1987
SALES (est): 257.1K **Privately Held**
SIC: 1521 2411 Single-Family House Construction Logging

▲ = Import ▼=Export
◆ =Import/Export

GEOGRAPHIC SECTION

Spokane - Spokane County (G-12283)

(G-12253)
FEDERAL EXPRESS CORPORATION
Also Called: Fedex
8404 W Aviation Rd (99224-9537)
PHONE.................................800 463-3339
EMP: 9
SALES (corp-wide): 69.6B **Publicly Held**
SIC: 4215 2741 Package delivery, vehicular; miscellaneous publishing
HQ: Federal Express Corporation
3610 Hacks Cross Rd
Memphis TN 38125
901 369-3600

(G-12254)
FEDEX OFFICE & PRINT SVCS INC
259 W Spokane Falls Blvd (99201-0123)
PHONE.................................509 484-0601
EMP: 22
SALES (corp-wide): 69.6B **Publicly Held**
WEB: www.kinkos.com
SIC: 7334 2752 Photocopying & duplicating services; commercial printing, lithographic
HQ: Fedex Office And Print Services, Inc.
7900 Legacy Dr
Plano TX 75024
800 463-3339

(G-12255)
FESSCO FLEET AND MARINE INC
3025 S Geiger Blvd (99224-5409)
PHONE.................................509 534-5880
Mark Sessler, *President*
Andrea Holdren, *Office Admin*
EMP: 35
SALES (est): 930K **Privately Held**
SIC: 3531 Marine related equipment

(G-12256)
FILE-EZ FOLDER INC
4111 E Mission Ave (99202-4497)
P.O. Box 284 (99210-0284)
PHONE.................................509 534-1044
Laura Lawton, *President*
Laura Lawton Forsyth, *President*
Gary Lawton, *Chairman*
Ray Lawton, *Vice Pres*
EMP: 20 EST: 1964
SQ FT: 25,000
SALES: 3MM **Privately Held**
SIC: 2678 Memorandum books, notebooks & looseleaf filler paper

(G-12257)
FIRST IMPRSSIONS CREATIVE PRTG
1716 E Holyoke Ave Ste D (99217-6007)
P.O. Box 18704 (99228-0704)
PHONE.................................509 483-6822
Robin Cook, *President*
Kenneth Cook, *Vice Pres*
EMP: 3
SALES (est): 386.7K **Privately Held**
SIC: 2752 Commercial printing, offset

(G-12258)
FLANNERY COMERFORD INC
3009 S Mount Vernon St # 4 (99223-4777)
PHONE.................................509 242-5000
James B Comerford, *President*
Michael P Flannery, *Treasurer*
Nora B Comerford, *Admin Sec*
EMP: 6
SQ FT: 1,700
SALES (est): 420K **Privately Held**
SIC: 2491 Poles & pole crossarms, treated wood

(G-12259)
FLSMIDTH INC
3311 E Ferry Ave (99202-4633)
PHONE.................................509 434-8605
EMP: 6
SALES (corp-wide): 2.8B **Privately Held**
SIC: 5084 3532 Conveyor systems; crushers, stationary
HQ: Flsmidth Inc.
16002 Winfield Rd
Fraziers Bottom WV 25082
610 264-6011

(G-12260)
FLY GIRLS AERO COVERS
8812 N Prescott Rd (99208-8899)
PHONE.................................509 466-7794
EMP: 2 EST: 2014
SALES (est): 107.6K **Privately Held**
SIC: 3728 Aircraft parts & equipment

(G-12261)
FOOLS PRAIRIE VINEYARDS LLC
3828 S Skyview Dr (99203-2739)
PHONE.................................509 319-0752
EMP: 2
SALES (est): 85.9K **Privately Held**
SIC: 2084 Wines

(G-12262)
FRANCIS & WALL SHELL
618 W Francis Ave (99205-6428)
PHONE.................................509 467-5493
Bob Beal, *Principal*
EMP: 2
SALES (est): 117.9K **Privately Held**
SIC: 3589 Car washing machinery

(G-12263)
FRED A WIDMAN
6704 S Tomaker Ln (99223-6203)
PHONE.................................509 863-9320
Fred A Widman, *Owner*
EMP: 2
SALES (est): 171.8K **Privately Held**
SIC: 3523 Driers (farm): grain, hay & seed

(G-12264)
FREE BIRTHDAY FUN LLC ✪
10 N Post St Ste 214 (99201-0705)
PHONE.................................509 999-7517
Carrie Pierpoint,
EMP: 3 EST: 2018
SALES (est): 71.1K **Privately Held**
SIC: 7372 Application computer software

(G-12265)
FRENCH QUARTER
1311 W Sprague Ave (99201-4132)
PHONE.................................509 624-5350
EMP: 3
SALES (est): 150K **Privately Held**
SIC: 3131 Mfg Footwear Cut Stock

(G-12266)
G&J DISTRIBUTORS
5329 N Alameda Blvd (99205-6013)
PHONE.................................509 325-2100
Gary Williams, *Owner*
EMP: 2 EST: 1999
SALES (est): 152.2K **Privately Held**
SIC: 3613 Switchgear & switchboard apparatus

(G-12267)
GARLAND PRINTING CO INC
833 W Garland Ave (99205-2818)
PHONE.................................509 327-5556
Mark Sleizer, *President*
EMP: 8 EST: 1953
SQ FT: 5,500
SALES (est): 1.2MM **Privately Held**
WEB: www.garlandprinting.com
SIC: 2761 2759 2752 Manifold business forms; commercial printing; commercial printing, offset

(G-12268)
GENERAL FIRE PRTECTION SYSTEMS
3904 E Trent Ave (99202-4425)
PHONE.................................509 535-4255
Darrell L Siria, *President*
Patricia Siria, *President*
Ken Gormley, *Sales Staff*
EMP: 10
SALES (est): 777.2K
SALES (corp-wide): 9.1MM **Privately Held**
WEB: www.generalfire.com
SIC: 3669 7382 1731 Fire alarm apparatus, electric; fire alarm maintenance & monitoring; fire detection & burglar alarm systems specialization
PA: General Fire Equipment Company
4004 E Trent Ave
Spokane WA
509 535-4255

(G-12269)
GENUINE PARTS COMPANY
Also Called: NAPA Auto Parts
2125 E Francis Ave (99208-2751)
PHONE.................................509 484-4400
Rick Zienert, *Branch Mgr*
EMP: 10
SALES (corp-wide): 18.7B **Publicly Held**
WEB: www.genpt.com
SIC: 3465 5531 Body parts, automobile: stamped metal; automotive parts
PA: Genuine Parts Company
2999 Wildwood Pkwy
Atlanta GA 30339
770 953-1700

(G-12270)
GEODESIC STRUCTURES INC
Also Called: Geodesic Structures Toys
1034 E Overbluff Rd (99203-3449)
P.O. Box 11893, Spokane Valley (99211-1893)
PHONE.................................509 535-0220
EMP: 3
SALES (est): 270K **Privately Held**
SIC: 2452 1541 Mfg Prefabricated Wood Buildings Industrial Building Construction

(G-12271)
GEOLOGIC DRILL EXPLORATIONS
14811 W Coulee Hite Rd (99224-7032)
PHONE.................................509 466-5241
Ritch Gibson, *Principal*
EMP: 7
SALES (est): 828.7K **Privately Held**
SIC: 3541 Drilling & boring machines

(G-12272)
GEPFORD WELDING INC
4003 W 40th Ave (99224-5140)
PHONE.................................509 624-6610
Ronald Gepford, *President*
Tom Gepford, *Vice Pres*
Dorothy Gepford, *Treasurer*
EMP: 3
SALES (est): 299.5K **Privately Held**
SIC: 3441 3443 Fabricated structural metal; metal parts

(G-12273)
GERALD MCCALLUM
Also Called: Mac's Metal
8324 N Regal St (99217-8122)
P.O. Box 6083 (99217-0902)
PHONE.................................509 467-8456
Fax: 509 467-5898
EMP: 5
SALES (est): 300K **Privately Held**
SIC: 3441 3446 Steel Fabrication

(G-12274)
GILL PRINT
6119 S Moran Dr (99223-7224)
PHONE.................................509 535-2521
Kevin Gill, *Owner*
EMP: 4
SALES (est): 237.3K **Privately Held**
SIC: 2752 Commercial printing, lithographic

(G-12275)
GLAMAZON SALON LLC
5130 N Assembly St (99205-6109)
PHONE.................................509 703-7145
Jessica Marburger, *Principal*
EMP: 2
SALES (est): 98.6K **Privately Held**
SIC: 3599 Industrial machinery

(G-12276)
GOLD RESERVE INC (PA)
999 W Riverside Ave # 401 (99201-1005)
PHONE.................................509 623-1500
Rockne J Timm, *CEO*
James H Coleman, *Ch of Bd*
A Douglas Belanger, *President*
Mary E Smith, *Vice Pres*
Douglas Stewart, *VP Bus Dvlpt*
EMP: 5
SALES (est): 1.4MM **Publicly Held**
WEB: www.goldreserveinc.com
SIC: 1041 1044 1481 Gold ores mining; silver ores; mine exploration, nonmetallic minerals; mine development, nonmetallic minerals

(G-12277)
GOLDRICH MINING COMPANY (PA)
2607 Sthast Blvd Ste B211 (99223)
PHONE.................................509 535-7367
William V Schara, *CEO*
William Orchow, *Ch of Bd*
Ted R Sharp, *CFO*
EMP: 15
SALES: 218.7K **Publicly Held**
SIC: 1081 1041 1499 Exploration, metal mining; gold ores; precious stones mining

(G-12278)
GOODRICH CORPORATION
Also Called: Goodrich Aerospace
11135 W Westbow Ln (99224-9475)
P.O. Box 19210 (99219-9210)
PHONE.................................509 744-6000
Duncan Ben, *Manager*
David Beaudry, *Telecom Exec*
Joe Dorosh, *Analyst*
EMP: 45
SALES (corp-wide): 66.5B **Publicly Held**
WEB: www.bfgoodrich.com
SIC: 3728 Aircraft parts & equipment
HQ: Goodrich Corporation
2730 W Tyvola Rd
Charlotte NC 28217
704 423-7000

(G-12279)
GRAVITY LABS INC
3803 S Sherman St (99203-2732)
PHONE.................................509 220-0817
Robbi Katherine Anthony, *CEO*
Patrick McHugh, *COO*
EMP: 2
SALES (est): 56.5K **Privately Held**
SIC: 7372 Application computer software

(G-12280)
GREAT BASIN ENERGIES INC
426 W Sprague Ave Ste 200 (99201)
PHONE.................................509 623-1500
Rockne J Timm, *CEO*
EMP: 4
SALES (est): 169.2K
SALES (corp-wide): 1.4MM **Publicly Held**
WEB: www.goldreserveinc.com
SIC: 1041 Gold ores
PA: Gold Reserve Inc.
999 W Riverside Ave # 401
Spokane WA 99201
509 623-1500

(G-12281)
GREAT HARVEST BREAD CO INC
2530 E 29th Ave (99223-4804)
PHONE.................................509 535-1146
Trevor Plaisted, *President*
Jacque Sanchez, *President*
EMP: 20
SQ FT: 2,000
SALES (est): 952.8K **Privately Held**
SIC: 5461 2051 5812 Bread; bakery: wholesale or wholesale/retail combined; eating places

(G-12282)
GREENCASTLE SOAP & SUPPLY
203 N Stone St (99202-3864)
PHONE.................................509 466-7223
Sandy Tarbox, *Owner*
EMP: 2
SALES: 100K **Privately Held**
WEB: www.greencastlesoap.com
SIC: 2841 Soap: granulated, liquid, cake, flaked or chip

(G-12283)
GREG MICHAEL CELLARS LLC
1213 W Railroad Ave (99201-4613)
PHONE.................................509 465-3591
Greg Lipsker, *Principal*
EMP: 2
SALES (est): 126.9K **Privately Held**
SIC: 2084 Wines

Spokane - Spokane County (G-12284)

(G-12284)
GRIESE ENTERPRISES
2721 E Diamond Ave (99217-6113)
PHONE.....................................509 868-7963
Mike Griese, *Owner*
EMP: 2
SALES (est): 140.7K **Privately Held**
SIC: 3999 Hot tubs

(G-12285)
HACIENDA LAS FLARES
3308 E 11th Ave Apt D313 (99202-5481)
PHONE.....................................208 819-8879
Luis A Vera, *Owner*
EMP: 6
SALES (est): 656K **Privately Held**
SIC: 2899 Flares

(G-12286)
HALLETT CONFECTIONS
Also Called: Hallett Choclat & Treat Fctry
1419 E Holyoke Ave (99217-7523)
PHONE.....................................509 484-6454
Kiity Kane, *Owner*
Kitty Kene, *Owner*
EMP: 10
SQ FT: 5,000
SALES (est): 487.6K **Privately Held**
WEB: www.hallettschocolates.com
SIC: 5441 5145 2064 Confectionery produced for direct sale on the premises; candy; candy & other confectionery products

(G-12287)
HALME CONSTRUCTION INC
8727 W Highway 2 (99224-9424)
PHONE.....................................509 725-4200
Jason Halme, *President*
Steven Halme, *Chairman*
Tyler Halme, *Project Mgr*
Marshall Sampson, *Project Mgr*
Jared Hereford, *Project Engr*
EMP: 40
SALES (est): 10MM **Privately Held**
WEB: www.halmeconstruction.com
SIC: 1623 1629 5084 3272 Water, sewer & utility lines; industrial plant construction; cranes, industrial; tanks, concrete; general contractor, highway & street construction

(G-12288)
HANGER PRSTHETCS & ORTHO INC
514 S Washington St (99204-2620)
PHONE.....................................509 624-3314
Darrell Liston, *Manager*
EMP: 8
SALES (corp-wide): 1B **Publicly Held**
SIC: 3842 Limbs, artificial; orthopedic appliances
HQ: Hanger Prosthetics & Orthotics, Inc.
10910 Domain Dr Ste 300
Austin TX 78758
512 777-3800

(G-12289)
HANSON WORLDWIDE LLC
2425 E Magnesium Rd (99217-5122)
PHONE.....................................509 252-9290
Christopher Wood, *President*
William Hockett,
Yosufi Tyebkhan,
EMP: 53
SALES (est): 17.9MM **Privately Held**
SIC: 3532 3531 Mining machinery; construction machinery

(G-12290)
HASKILL CREEK PUBLISHING
10017 N Stevens Ln (99218-2381)
PHONE.....................................509 467-9439
Dennis Michael Howke, *Principal*
EMP: 2
SALES (est): 93.9K **Privately Held**
SIC: 2741 Miscellaneous publishing

(G-12291)
HEARN BROTHERS PRINTING INC
2105 N Monroe St (99205-4544)
PHONE.....................................509 324-2882
Dale Hearn, *President*
John Hearn, *Vice Pres*
Mark Hearn, *Admin Sec*
EMP: 9
SQ FT: 4,500
SALES (est): 1.3MM **Privately Held**
SIC: 2752 Commercial printing, offset

(G-12292)
HELENA CHEMICAL COMPANY
4802 N Florida St (99217-6707)
PHONE.....................................901 761-0050
Ken Seppa, *Branch Mgr*
EMP: 4 **Privately Held**
SIC: 5191 2819 Chemicals, agricultural; seeds & bulbs; chemicals, high purity: refined from technical grade
HQ: Helena Agri-Enterprises, Llc
255 Schilling Blvd # 300
Collierville TN 38017
901 761-0050

(G-12293)
HERRERA ISAEL GOMEZ
1504 E Illinois Ave (99207-5046)
PHONE.....................................509 270-7022
Isael Herrara, *Owner*
Isael Gomez Herrara, *Owner*
EMP: 2
SALES (est): 110K **Privately Held**
SIC: 3711 Truck tractors for highway use, assembly of

(G-12294)
HIGHLAND QUARRY LLC
5426 N Old Trails Rd (99224-9179)
P.O. Box 2087, Airway Heights (99001-2087)
PHONE.....................................509 624-4136
Michael Evenoff,
Mark Schuetzle,
EMP: 3
SALES (est): 166.1K **Privately Held**
SIC: 5032 1411 Gravel; limestone & marble dimension stone

(G-12295)
HIGHWOOD GLOBAL LP (PA)
2425 E Magnesium Rd (99217-5122)
PHONE.....................................509 655-7711
Kevin Kerr, *Manager*
EMP: 28
SALES: 2MM **Privately Held**
SIC: 3533 Oil field machinery & equipment

(G-12296)
HOME BUILDERS SERVICE COMPANY
Also Called: Security Door and Window Co
1606 E 54th Ln (99223-6375)
PHONE.....................................509 747-1206
W S Melcher, *President*
Randy Melcher, *Treasurer*
EMP: 15
SQ FT: 5,000
SALES (est): 1.5MM **Privately Held**
SIC: 3442 3446 3444 Storm doors or windows, metal; grillwork, ornamental metal; sheet metalwork

(G-12297)
HOME SWEET HOME INDOOR
1517 W Fairway Dr (99218-2921)
PHONE.....................................509 327-9637
Rosa Yates,
Gerry Yates,
Jeff Yates,
EMP: 5
SALES (est): 390.3K **Privately Held**
SIC: 2591 5999 Window blinds; tents

(G-12298)
HOMERS ORNAMENTAL IRON
5806 N A St (99205-7208)
PHONE.....................................509 327-8673
Homer Thomas, *Owner*
EMP: 3
SALES (est): 190.8K **Privately Held**
SIC: 3446 1799 Stairs, staircases, stair treads: prefabricated metal; ornamental metal work

(G-12299)
HUGOS ON HILL
3023 E 28th Ave (99223-4920)
PHONE.....................................509 822-7149
H T Higgins, *Principal*
EMP: 2
SALES (est): 248.2K **Privately Held**
SIC: 3949 Bowling alleys & accessories

(G-12300)
HWY GRIND INC
14607 N Shady Slope Rd (99208-8563)
PHONE.....................................509 710-7704
David Mackey, *Principal*
EMP: 2
SALES (est): 134.5K **Privately Held**
SIC: 3599 Grinding castings for the trade

(G-12301)
HYPROTEK INC
665 N Riverpoint Blvd # 410 (99202-1671)
PHONE.....................................509 343-3121
Patrick Tennican, *President*
Flynn Tennican, *Corp Secy*
Russel Michaelsen, *Vice Pres*
Floyd Phipps, *Vice Pres*
Michael Tennican, *CFO*
EMP: 5
SALES (est): 320K **Privately Held**
WEB: www.hyprotek.com
SIC: 3841 Medical instruments & equipment, blood & bone work

(G-12302)
I M A C (PA)
2525 E 29th Ave Ste 10b (99223-4857)
PHONE.....................................509 747-3607
Lawrence W Johnson, *Owner*
EMP: 3
SQ FT: 2,000
SALES (est): 1.1MM **Privately Held**
WEB: www.imac.net
SIC: 2851 Paint removers

(G-12303)
ILINKLIVE INC
1622 W Pinehill St (99218-2949)
PHONE.....................................509 464-0062
David D Cebert, *President*
David Cebert, *President*
EMP: 4
SALES: 30K **Privately Held**
SIC: 7372 Prepackaged software

(G-12304)
IMPACT HEALTH PUBLISHING
339 E Rockwood Blvd (99202-1139)
PHONE.....................................509 624-2599
Eugene Heyden, *Principal*
EMP: 2 EST: 2010
SALES (est): 106.7K **Privately Held**
SIC: 2741 Miscellaneous publishing

(G-12305)
IMPACT SERVICE CORPORATION
Also Called: I S C
3811 E Francis Ave (99217-6533)
PHONE.....................................509 468-7900
Ken D Warren, *President*
▼ EMP: 21
SALES (est): 8.1MM **Privately Held**
WEB: www.isc-vsi.com
SIC: 5084 7699 5082 3532 Crushing machinery & equipment; industrial machinery & equipment repair; construction & mining machinery; mining machinery

(G-12306)
INDUSTRIAL WELDING CO INC
1203 N Greene St (99202-4454)
PHONE.....................................509 598-2356
Charles Jordan, *President*
Gloria Avery, *Admin Sec*
EMP: 11
SQ FT: 6,000
SALES (est): 1.4MM **Privately Held**
SIC: 7692 3599 3531 Welding repair; machine shop, jobbing & repair; construction machinery

(G-12307)
INLAND EMPIRE PAPER COMPANY
3320 N Argonne Rd (99212-2099)
P.O. Box 11935, Spokane Valley (99211-1935)
PHONE.....................................509 924-1911
Kevin Rasler, *President*
Steve Rector, *Corp Secy*
◆ EMP: 140
SQ FT: 150,000
SALES (est): 59.3MM
SALES (corp-wide): 128.9MM **Privately Held**
WEB: www.iepco.com
SIC: 2621 Newsprint paper
PA: Cowles Publishing Company
999 W Riverside Ave
Spokane WA 99201
509 459-5000

(G-12308)
INLAND EMPIRE RESTEEL
8314 N Regal St (99217-8122)
PHONE.....................................509 863-9870
EMP: 2
SALES (est): 90.8K **Privately Held**
SIC: 3312 Ammonia & liquor, from chemical recovery coke ovens

(G-12309)
INLAND FIXTURES CO INC
2909 N Crestline St (99207-4810)
PHONE.....................................509 487-2759
James E Lewis, *President*
Daryl Marcus, *Vice Pres*
Steve Rasmussion, *Treasurer*
Carol Lewis, *Admin Sec*
EMP: 8
SQ FT: 3,600
SALES (est): 650K **Privately Held**
SIC: 2521 2431 2541 Cabinets, office: wood; millwork; office fixtures, wood

(G-12310)
INLAND NORTHWEST DAIRIES LLC (PA)
33 E Francis Ave (99208-1034)
PHONE.....................................509 489-8600
Arthur Coffey,
EMP: 100
SALES (est): 6.7MM **Privately Held**
WEB: www.inlandnwdairy.com
SIC: 2026 5143 Fluid milk; dairy products, except dried or canned

(G-12311)
INLAND NORTHWEST MFG LLC
7211 S Grove Rd (99224-5839)
PHONE.....................................509 218-7424
Margie Lundberg, *Principal*
EMP: 3
SALES (est): 196K **Privately Held**
SIC: 3999 Manufacturing industries

(G-12312)
INLAND PUBLICATIONS INC
Also Called: Pacific Northwest Inlander
1227 W Summit Pkwy (99201-7003)
PHONE.....................................509 325-0634
Ted McGregor Jr, *President*
Jeanne McGregor, *Corp Secy*
Jeremy McGregor, *Vice Pres*
Tamara McGregor, *Director*
EMP: 32
SQ FT: 1,100
SALES (est): 2MM **Privately Held**
WEB: www.inlander.com
SIC: 2711 Newspapers: publishing only, not printed on site

(G-12313)
INLAND SYNTHETICS
9011 N Farmdale St (99208-9153)
PHONE.....................................509 466-6101
EMP: 2 EST: 2004
SALES (est): 120K **Privately Held**
SIC: 2899 Mfg Chemical Preparations

(G-12314)
INLAND WOODWORKS
12421 E Moffat Rd (99217-1201)
PHONE.....................................509 701-0985
Kenneth Neu, *Principal*
EMP: 3
SALES (est): 377.2K **Privately Held**
SIC: 2431 1799 Staircases, stairs & railings; special trade contractors

(G-12315)
INSTANT AUCTION CO
3307 E 55th Ave (99223-7014)
PHONE.....................................509 448-0279
EMP: 2 EST: 2002

SALES (est): 150K **Privately Held**
SIC: 2752 Lithographic Commercial Printing

(G-12316)
INSTANT OPTION
5009 N Market St (99217-5032)
PHONE.................................509 290-6481
Tamara Stith Weech, *Principal*
EMP: 2
SALES (est): 143.2K **Privately Held**
SIC: 2752 Commercial printing, lithographic

(G-12317)
INSTANT SIGN FACTORY
721 W 2nd Ave (99201-4412)
PHONE.................................509 456-3333
David Nail, *Owner*
Greg Nail, *Production*
EMP: 7
SQ FT: 3,800
SALES (est): 707.5K **Privately Held**
WEB: www.instantsignfactory.com
SIC: 3993 Signs, not made in custom sign painting shops

(G-12318)
INTEGRATED COMPOSITION SYSTEMS
Also Called: I C S
715 E Sprague Ave Ste 75 (99202-2142)
PHONE.................................509 624-5064
Richard W Woodbury, *President*
Alice Woodbury, *Vice Pres*
Suzanne Harris, *Manager*
EMP: 4
SQ FT: 1,035
SALES (est): 440.3K **Privately Held**
SIC: 2791 Typographic composition, for the printing trade

(G-12319)
INTEGRATED DESIGN GROUP INC
2512 W Francis Ave (99205-7012)
P.O. Box 646, Tekoa (99033-0646)
PHONE.................................509 328-4244
Joseph Porie, *President*
William Isbell, *Vice Pres*
EMP: 3 EST: 1997
SQ FT: 900
SALES (est): 250.6K **Privately Held**
SIC: 3663 Radio & TV communications equipment

(G-12320)
INTEGRITY BIOPHARMA SERVICES
10525 N Edna Ln (99218-2646)
PHONE.................................509 474-1381
EMP: 3
SALES (est): 168.2K **Privately Held**
SIC: 2834 Pharmaceutical preparations

(G-12321)
INTELLIPAPER LLC (PA)
2525 E 29th Ave (99223-4855)
PHONE.................................509 343-9410
Andrew Depaula, *CEO*
Victor Pires, *Chairman*
Larry Aamodt,
Jesse Johnson,
Jon Larsell,
EMP: 11 EST: 2009
SALES: 150K **Privately Held**
SIC: 2679 Paper products, converted

(G-12322)
INTERMOUNTAIN MACHINE
5328 N Sycamore St (99217-6678)
PHONE.................................509 482-0431
Pat Rice, *Owner*
EMP: 9
SALES (est): 580K **Privately Held**
WEB: www.intermountainmachine.com
SIC: 3599 Machine shop, jobbing & repair

(G-12323)
INTERNATIONAL GLACE INC
1616 E Lyons Ave (99217-6005)
PHONE.................................503 267-7917
Dan R Indgjerd, *Principal*
Alan Sipole, *VP Sales*
▲ EMP: 3 EST: 2010

SALES (est): 222.5K **Privately Held**
SIC: 2087 Fruits, crushed: for fountain use

(G-12324)
INTERNATIONAL TRADE & TRVL LTD
Also Called: Signs Now
4401 S Glenview Ln (99223-2261)
PHONE.................................509 981-2307
James W Lee, *President*
EMP: 8
SALES: 400K **Privately Held**
SIC: 3993 Signs & advertising specialties

(G-12325)
INTERNTNAL AROSPC COATINGS INC (PA)
5709 W Sunset Hwy Ste 205 (99224-9442)
P.O. Box 19166 (99219-9166)
PHONE.................................509 321-0342
Niall Cunningham, *CEO*
Rodney Friese, *President*
Alan McKee, *CFO*
Scott Olson,
EMP: 95
SQ FT: 7,000
SALES (est): 217.5MM **Privately Held**
WEB: www.associatedpaintersinc.com
SIC: 3721 4581 Motorized aircraft; aircraft maintenance & repair services

(G-12326)
IRONHOUSE ORNAMENTAL
3001 E 34th Ave (99223-4620)
PHONE.................................509 993-7601
Antonio Fino, *Principal*
EMP: 3 EST: 2017
SALES (est): 233.9K **Privately Held**
SIC: 3446 Architectural metalwork

(G-12327)
J N W INC
Also Called: Baldwin Sign Co
6409 N Pittsburg St (99217-7553)
P.O. Box 6819 (99217-0913)
PHONE.................................509 489-9191
Nicol Whipple, *President*
Jon Whipple, *Vice Pres*
▲ EMP: 23
SQ FT: 5,000
SALES (est): 3MM **Privately Held**
WEB: www.baldwinsigns.com
SIC: 3993 3496 7336 Signs, not made in custom sign painting shops; miscellaneous fabricated wire products; graphic arts & related design

(G-12328)
JAN A THOMPSON LCPO
502 E 5th Ave (99202-1313)
PHONE.................................509 241-3820
Jan A Thompson, *Principal*
EMP: 3
SALES (est): 293.5K **Privately Held**
SIC: 3842 Technical aids for the handicapped

(G-12329)
JASON THOMPSON
817 E Longfellow Ave (99207-3122)
PHONE.................................757 867-6494
Jason Thompson, *President*
EMP: 2 EST: 2017
SALES (est): 91.3K **Privately Held**
SIC: 3273 Ready-mixed concrete

(G-12330)
JASPER ENTERPRISES INC
Also Called: Jasper Trucking
10015 N Div St Ste 201 (99218)
PHONE.................................509 549-3664
Tom Cauley, *Manager*
EMP: 3
SALES (corp-wide): 1.3MM **Privately Held**
WEB: www.jasper-inc.com
SIC: 2491 Poles, posts & pilings: treated wood
PA: Jasper Enterprises, Inc.
   23721 N Crescent Rd
   Chattaroy WA 99003
   509 238-6540

(G-12331)
JELD-WEN HOLDING INC
Also Called: VPI
3420 E Ferry Ave (99202-4632)
PHONE.................................509 535-1026
EMP: 200 **Publicly Held**
SIC: 3089 Windows, plastic
PA: Jeld-Wen Holding, Inc.
   2645 Silver Crescent Dr
   Charlotte NC 28273

(G-12332)
JERRY CARTER
Also Called: Quality Machines
3512 E Crown Ave (99217-6666)
PHONE.................................509 487-8294
Jerry Carter, *Owner*
EMP: 8
SQ FT: 2,600
SALES (est): 835.4K **Privately Held**
WEB: www.qualitymachines.com
SIC: 3399 3565 Metal fasteners; packaging machinery

(G-12333)
JETPROP LLC (PA)
6427 E Rutter Ave (99212-1445)
PHONE.................................509 535-4401
Darwin Conrad, *Principal*
EMP: 3
SALES (est): 337.5K **Privately Held**
WEB: www.jetprop.com
SIC: 3721 Research & development on aircraft by the manufacturer

(G-12334)
JEWELRY DESIGN CENTER INC
821 N Division St Ste C (99202-1623)
PHONE.................................509 487-5905
Douglas Toone, *Ch of Bd*
Brian Toone, *President*
EMP: 33
SQ FT: 5,500
SALES (est): 4MM **Privately Held**
WEB: www.jewelrydesigncenter.com
SIC: 5944 3911 Jewelry, precious stones & precious metals; jewelry, precious metal

(G-12335)
JJP ELECTRIC
6826 N Greenwood Blvd (99208-5033)
PHONE.................................509 325-5266
Jeffrey J Piton, *Owner*
EMP: 6
SALES (est): 654.5K **Privately Held**
SIC: 3643 Current-carrying wiring devices

(G-12336)
JO BEE INC
Also Called: Jo Bee Company
816 W Francis Ave Ste 313 (99205-6512)
PHONE.................................509 483-1118
Bill Phares, *President*
EMP: 2
SALES (est): 181.9K **Privately Held**
SIC: 3651 Audio electronic systems

(G-12337)
JOHANNA BEVERAGE COMPANY LLC
5625 W Thorpe Rd (99224-5317)
P.O. Box 272, Flemington NJ (08822-0272)
PHONE.................................509 455-8059
Robert A Facchina,
▲ EMP: 65
SQ FT: 107,946
SALES (est): 16.7MM
SALES (corp-wide): 178.1MM **Privately Held**
WEB: www.johannafoods.com
SIC: 2086 Carbonated beverages, nonalcoholic: bottled & canned
PA: Johanna Foods, Inc.
   20 Johanna Farms Rd
   Flemington NJ 08822
   908 788-2200

(G-12338)
JOHN H WOLF CPA PC
6008 N Washington St (99205-6331)
P.O. Box 30279 (99223-3004)
PHONE.................................509 465-9165
John H Wolf, *President*
EMP: 2

SALES (est): 50K **Privately Held**
WEB: www.cpawolf.com
SIC: 8721 7372 Certified public accountant; prepackaged software

(G-12339)
JOHNSON CONTROLS INC
9718 W Flight Dr (99224-5189)
PHONE.................................509 747-8053
Leanne Turner, *Administration*
EMP: 5 **Privately Held**
SIC: 2531 Seats, automobile
HQ: Johnson Controls, Inc.
   5757 N Green Bay Ave
   Milwaukee WI 53209
   414 524-1200

(G-12340)
JOHNSTON PRINTING INC
159 S Mcclellan St (99201-3619)
PHONE.................................509 892-2055
J Steve Johnston, *President*
Pat Johnston, *Corp Secy*
Chad Johnston, *Vice Pres*
Jason Johnston, *Vice Pres*
EMP: 22
SQ FT: 11,000
SALES (est): 2.6MM **Privately Held**
WEB: www.johnstonprinting.com
SIC: 2752 Commercial printing, lithographic

(G-12341)
JONES AUTOMOTIVE ENGINE INC (PA)
Also Called: Jones Automotive Warehouse
817 N Lincoln St (99201-2124)
PHONE.................................509 838-3625
Robert Jones, *President*
Barbara Jones, *Corp Secy*
EMP: 40
SQ FT: 11,000
SALES (est): 1.4MM **Privately Held**
SIC: 7538 5531 3714 Engine rebuilding: automotive; engine repair, except diesel: automotive; automotive parts; motor vehicle parts & accessories

(G-12342)
JOSEPHINE MINING CORP
601 W Main Ave Ste 600 (99201-0613)
P.O. Box 4006 (99220-0006)
PHONE.................................509 343-3193
Robert L Russell, *President*
EMP: 3
SALES (est): 189.6K **Privately Held**
SIC: 1041 Gold ores mining

(G-12343)
JOURNEYMAN CABINETS INC
2929 E Providence Ave (99207-5840)
PHONE.................................509 483-6864
Paul Ruckhaber, *President*
EMP: 6
SALES (est): 750K **Privately Held**
WEB: www.journeymancabinets.com
SIC: 2541 Cabinets, except refrigerated: show, display, etc.: wood

(G-12344)
JS UNIFORM
33 E Lincoln Rd Ste 203 (99208-5600)
PHONE.................................509 467-8416
Charles T Post, *Owner*
EMP: 3
SALES (est): 150K **Privately Held**
SIC: 5699 7694 Uniforms; electric motor repair

(G-12345)
JUBILANT HOLLISTERSTIER LLC (HQ)
Also Called: Hollister-Stier Laboratories
3525 N Regal St (99207-5788)
P.O. Box 3145 (99220-3145)
PHONE.................................509 482-4945
Marcelo Morales, *CEO*
Curtis L Gingles, *Vice Pres*
Jeffrey K Milligan, *Vice Pres*
Rabindra Sahoo, *Vice Pres*
Richard Freeman, *CFO*
▲ EMP: 265 EST: 1999
SQ FT: 120,000

Spokane - Spokane County (G-12346)

GEOGRAPHIC SECTION

SALES (est): 80.5MM
SALES (corp-wide): 485.2MM **Privately Held**
WEB: www.hollister-stier.com
SIC: 2834 Pharmaceutical preparations
PA: Jubilant Life Sciences Limited
1a, Sector 16a, Institutional Area,
Noida UP 20130
120 436-1000

(G-12346)
JUICY GEMS
1923 W Knox Ave (99205-4147)
PHONE................................425 232-3567
Neal Arsenault, *Principal*
EMP: 2 **EST:** 2017
SALES (est): 93K **Privately Held**
SIC: 3915 Jewelers' materials & lapidary work

(G-12347)
K-L MFG CO INC (PA)
2438 N Ruby St (99207-2156)
PHONE................................509 232-8655
Michael E Doohan, *Ch of Bd*
Joseph M Doohan, *President*
Winifred Doohan, *Vice Pres*
Maura Doohan, *Admin Sec*
▲ **EMP:** 41 **EST:** 1932
SQ FT: 30,000
SALES (est): 12.9MM **Privately Held**
WEB: www.klmfg.com
SIC: 2339 2329 Women's & misses' outerwear; men's & boys' sportswear & athletic clothing

(G-12348)
KALASTAR HOLDINGS INC
1611 E Sprague Ave (99202-3114)
P.O. Box 3267 (99220-3267)
PHONE................................509 534-0655
Alan G Ross, *President*
Stanley Ross, *Chairman*
Kathryn Ross, *Vice Pres*
Benjamin Ross, *Treasurer*
EMP: 25
SQ FT: 37,000
SALES (est): 3.1MM **Privately Held**
WEB: www.rossprint.com
SIC: 2752 Lithographing on metal

(G-12349)
KANNBERG MEDIA CORP
611 E Lakeview Ln (99208-8979)
PHONE................................509 468-4226
Robert Kannberg, *President*
EMP: 2
SALES: 360K **Privately Held**
SIC: 2741 Directories: publishing & printing

(G-12350)
KICHI SYSTEMS LLC
10304 E Upriver Dr (99206-4523)
PHONE................................509 924-7672
Alan Roecks, *Bd of Directors*
EMP: 2
SALES (est): 142.6K **Privately Held**
SIC: 3824 Mechanical & electromechanical counters & devices

(G-12351)
KIDD DEFENSE
901 N Adams St (99201-2050)
PHONE................................509 290-6171
EMP: 3
SALES (est): 207.2K **Privately Held**
SIC: 3812 Defense systems & equipment

(G-12352)
KINDLE EITHAN
Also Called: Hot Shot Slabs
920 S Thor St (99202-5369)
PHONE................................509 558-7023
Ethan Kindle, *Owner*
EMP: 2
SALES (est): 90.8K **Privately Held**
SIC: 3312 Slabs, steel

(G-12353)
KNIPPRATH CELLARS INC
5634 E Commerce Ave (99212-1307)
PHONE................................208 699-3393
▲ **EMP:** 2
SQ FT: 2,944
SALES: 55K **Privately Held**
SIC: 2084 5182 5921 Wines; wine; wine

(G-12354)
KOCH INDUSTRIES INC
4327 N Thor St (99217-7098)
P.O. Box 6226 (99217-0904)
PHONE................................509 487-4560
Scott Blubough, *Branch Mgr*
EMP: 8
SALES (corp-wide): 42.6B **Privately Held**
WEB: www.kochind.com
SIC: 2951 Asphalt paving mixtures & blocks
PA: Koch Industries, Inc.
4111 E 37th St N
Wichita KS 67220
316 828-5500

(G-12355)
KRUEGER SHEET METAL CO (PA)
731 N Superior St (99202-2014)
P.O. Box 2963 (99220-2963)
PHONE................................509 489-0221
Thomas H Brandt, *President*
Alexander E Brandt, *Vice Pres*
Robert A Starkey, *Vice Pres*
David T Brandt, *Admin Sec*
EMP: 80 **EST:** 1948
SQ FT: 25,000
SALES: 28.5MM **Privately Held**
SIC: 1761 3444 Roofing contractor; sheet metalwork; sheet metalwork

(G-12356)
KURT A FLECHEL
1808 S Maple Blvd (99203-1165)
PHONE................................509 953-8358
Kurt A Flechel, *Principal*
EMP: 2
SALES (est): 164.8K **Privately Held**
SIC: 3842 Welders' hoods

(G-12357)
L LAZY CORP
4815 S Perry St (99223-6336)
PHONE................................509 448-3426
Lane Guin, *Principal*
EMP: 2
SALES (est): 62.3K **Privately Held**
SIC: 2095 Roasted coffee

(G-12358)
LAWTON PRINTING INC
4111 E Mission Ave (99202-4497)
P.O. Box 284 (99210-0284)
PHONE................................509 534-1044
Ray Lawton, *Ch of Bd*
Laura Lawton, *President*
Gary Lawton, *Vice Pres*
EMP: 45 **EST:** 1940
SQ FT: 25,000
SALES (est): 9MM **Privately Held**
WEB: www.lawtonprinting.com
SIC: 2752 2759 Commercial printing, offset; publication printing; screen printing

(G-12359)
LAYLAS FUN SOCKS
1314 W Fairview Ave (99205-3436)
PHONE................................509 279-8343
Kevin Whitcomb, *Principal*
EMP: 2
SALES (est): 73.4K **Privately Held**
SIC: 2252 Socks

(G-12360)
LEE FRAME SHOPPE INC
421 W 1st Ave (99201-3706)
PHONE................................509 624-2715
Dick Hughes, *President*
Molly Hughes, *Owner*
EMP: 2
SALES (est): 85.7K **Privately Held**
SIC: 5999 2499 Picture frames, ready made; wood products

(G-12361)
LEONHARDS PICKLES LLC
3407 E Marietta Ave (99217-7145)
PHONE................................509 280-4267
Jeffrey Nett, *Principal*
EMP: 2
SALES (est): 82.9K **Privately Held**
SIC: 2035 Pickled fruits & vegetables

(G-12362)
LIBERTY BUSINESS FORMS INC
3230 E Main Ave (99202-4728)
PHONE................................509 536-0515
Willy Schumacher, *President*
Dwayne Hornbeck, *Plant Mgr*
Chris Johnston, *Engineer*
▲ **EMP:** 52
SQ FT: 23,000
SALES (est): 6.7MM **Privately Held**
WEB: www.libertybf.com
SIC: 2759 5112 Business forms: printing; stationery & office supplies

(G-12363)
LIBERTY PRINT SOLUTIONS
3230 E Main Ave (99202-4728)
PHONE................................509 536-0515
EMP: 2
SALES (est): 83.9K **Privately Held**
SIC: 2752 Commercial printing, lithographic

(G-12364)
LIFESTYLE GRANOLAS INC
944 E 42nd Ave (99203-6202)
PHONE................................509 768-5126
Craig Tate, *President*
Chris Tate, *Vice Pres*
EMP: 5
SALES (est): 333.1K **Privately Held**
SIC: 2064 Granola & muesli, bars & clusters

(G-12365)
LIGHTHOUSE INTERNATIONAL LTD
423 E Cleveland Ave Ste A (99207-2008)
PHONE................................509 466-2502
Bill Dyer, *President*
Darlana Dyer, *Vice Pres*
Nathan Dyer, *Sales Mgr*
EMP: 30
SQ FT: 3,500
SALES (est): 3.4MM **Privately Held**
WEB: www.warm-welcome.com
SIC: 3433 Heating equipment, except electric

(G-12366)
LIMELYTE TECHNOLOGY GROUP INC
28 W 3rd Ave Ste 100 (99201-3654)
PHONE................................509 241-0138
Rob Martinson, *President*
Nomi Martinson, *CTO*
Joel Keener, *Web Dvlpr*
Michael Williams, *Software Engr*
EMP: 3
SALES (est): 313.4K **Privately Held**
SIC: 7372 Application computer software

(G-12367)
LINCOLN DATA INC
10103 N Div St Ste 101 (99218)
PHONE................................509 466-1744
Clifford Hackney, *President*
Donald Hackney, *Vice Pres*
Sherie Hackney, *Vice Pres*
Marie Hackney, *Admin Sec*
EMP: 5
SQ FT: 931
SALES (est): 323.4K **Privately Held**
WEB: www.lincolndata.com
SIC: 7372 Business oriented computer software

(G-12368)
LINDEN VIC B & SONS SIGN ADVG
122 S Lincoln St (99201-3906)
PHONE................................509 624-0663
Chris Linden, *President*
Nick Linden, *Vice Pres*
EMP: 4
SQ FT: 3,900
SALES (est): 450.7K **Privately Held**
WEB: www.lindensigns.com
SIC: 3993 Signs & advertising specialties

(G-12369)
LINNS SERVICE & REMODEL INC
Also Called: Linn's Door Service
9810 S Grove Rd (99224)
P.O. Box 19167 (99219-9167)
PHONE................................509 448-2540
David Linn, *President*
Gaile Linn, *Admin Sec*
EMP: 3
SALES (est): 487.6K **Privately Held**
SIC: 3446 Acoustical suspension systems, metal

(G-12370)
LIQUID BRANDS DISTILLERY LLC
714 N Lee St (99202-2837)
PHONE................................509 413-1885
Richard Clemson,
EMP: 3
SALES (est): 194.1K **Privately Held**
SIC: 2085 Distilled & blended liquors

(G-12371)
LITE-CHECK LLC
301 N Havana St (99202-4725)
PHONE................................509 535-7512
Michael Ceparano, *Accounting Mgr*
Todd Potter, *Sales Staff*
Steven Yrigoyen, *Manager*
Robert M Blair,
▼ **EMP:** 18
SQ FT: 5,000
SALES (est): 4.2MM **Privately Held**
WEB: www.lite-check.com
SIC: 3825 Instruments to measure electricity

(G-12372)
LITE-CHECK FLEET SOLUTIONS INC
301 N Havana St (99202-4725)
PHONE................................509 535-7512
Robert Blair, *President*
EMP: 25
SALES (est): 1.8MM **Privately Held**
SIC: 3825 Digital test equipment, electronic & electrical circuits

(G-12373)
LITHIA MOTORS INC
Also Called: Lithia Chrysler Jeep Dodge Ram
10701 N Newport Hwy (99218-1642)
PHONE................................509 321-7300
Bryan Deboer, *President*
EMP: 2
SALES (corp-wide): 11.8B **Publicly Held**
SIC: 3714 7519 Motor vehicle parts & accessories; recreational vehicle rental
PA: Lithia Motors, Inc.
150 N Bartlett St
Medford OR 97501
541 776-6401

(G-12374)
LONGSHOT OIL LLC
1011 S Jefferson St (99204-3929)
PHONE................................509 455-5924
Glen M Landry, *Principal*
EMP: 2 **EST:** 2010
SALES (est): 194.8K **Privately Held**
SIC: 1382 Oil & gas exploration services

(G-12375)
LOREEN HOME SERVICING
3508 W Walton Ave (99205-1773)
PHONE................................509 325-4290
EMP: 2
SALES (est): 97K **Privately Held**
SIC: 1389 Oil/Gas Field Services

(G-12376)
LYN-TRON INC
6001 S Thomas Mallen Rd (99224-9406)
PHONE................................509 456-4545
Donald E Lynn, *Ch of Bd*
Tyler W Lynn, *President*
Jeffrey Nichols, *Vice Pres*
Mike Quinn, *Vice Pres*
Douglas Smith, *Vice Pres*
EMP: 66
SQ FT: 60,000

GEOGRAPHIC SECTION
Spokane - Spokane County (G-12409)

SALES (est): 15.7MM **Privately Held**
WEB: www.lyntron.com
SIC: 3452 Nuts, metal

(G-12377)
M-TRONIC INC
1620 E Houston Ave # 700 (99217-6040)
PHONE.................................509 484-3572
Vang Moua, *President*
EMP: 5
SQ FT: 2,800
SALES: 50K **Privately Held**
WEB: www.mtronic.net
SIC: 3672 Circuit boards, television & radio printed

(G-12378)
MAGNIFICENT SIGNS INC
2311 W 16th Ave Lot 114 (99224-4439)
PHONE.................................509 468-2794
Michael Glen, *Principal*
EMP: 2
SALES (est): 183.7K **Privately Held**
SIC: 3993 Electric signs

(G-12379)
MAID NATURALLY LLC
3012 N Nevada St Ste 1 (99207-2800)
PHONE.................................509 994-3685
Heather Brown,
Ruthanne Eberly,
EMP: 25
SQ FT: 5,000
SALES (est): 655.8K **Privately Held**
SIC: 7349 2842 Maid services, contract or fee basis; cleaning or polishing preparations

(G-12380)
MAIKA FOODS LLC
304 W Pacific Ave Ste 210 (99201-4320)
PHONE.................................310 893-7050
Diego Vidal, *Mng Member*
▼ **EMP:** 2
SQ FT: 900
SALES: 45K **Privately Held**
SIC: 2033 Vegetables: packaged in cans, jars, etc.

(G-12381)
MARK GRID SIGNS INC
442 W Sinto Ave (99201-2426)
PHONE.................................509 323-0328
Chris Gridley, *Owner*
Michele Gridley, *Admin Sec*
EMP: 3
SALES (est): 338.1K **Privately Held**
SIC: 3993 Electric signs

(G-12382)
MARKETPLACE CELLARS
39 W Pacific Ave (99201-3647)
PHONE.................................509 795-8500
EMP: 4
SALES (est): 83K **Privately Held**
SIC: 2084 Brandy & brandy spirits; wines

(G-12383)
MARLOWE MACHINE INC
2718 N Perry St (99207-4965)
P.O. Box 464, Calder ID (83808-0464)
PHONE.................................509 484-5979
Richard Marlowe, *President*
EMP: 5
SQ FT: 4,800
SALES (est): 299.4K **Privately Held**
SIC: 3599 Machine shop, jobbing & repair

(G-12384)
MARYHILL WINERY
1303 W Summit Pkwy (99201-7033)
PHONE.................................509 443-3832
EMP: 2
SALES (est): 101K **Privately Held**
SIC: 2084 Wines

(G-12385)
MATAMP DISTRIBUTION USA
524 W 7th Ave Apt 606 (99204-2727)
PHONE.................................509 455-7349
Joel Wheeler, *Owner*
EMP: 4
SALES (est): 124.8K **Privately Held**
WEB: www.matamp.com
SIC: 3651 Speaker systems

(G-12386)
MATES SEAL SMART
3523 N Freya St (99217-6911)
P.O. Box 6191 (99217-0903)
PHONE.................................509 489-6346
Tom Nuxoll, *Owner*
EMP: 5
SALES (est): 1.4MM **Privately Held**
SIC: 2952 Asphalt felts & coatings

(G-12387)
MCFARLAND CASCADE HOLDINGS INC
1717 S Rustle St Ste 105 (99224-2065)
P.O. Box 1496, Tacoma (98401-1496)
PHONE.................................800 426-8430
Alton McFarland, *Principal*
EMP: 3
SALES (corp-wide): 1.6B **Privately Held**
SIC: 2491 Wood preserving
HQ: Mcfarland Cascade Holdings, Inc.
1640 E Marc St
Tacoma WA 98421
253 572-3033

(G-12388)
MEDTRONIC INC
327 W 8th Ave Ste 130 (99204-2564)
PHONE.................................509 991-0159
Kelea Rego, *Branch Mgr*
EMP: 3 **Privately Held**
SIC: 3841 Surgical & medical instruments
HQ: Medtronic, Inc.
710 Medtronic Pkwy
Minneapolis MN 55432
763 514-4000

(G-12389)
MEILI MANUFACTURING
Also Called: Meili Truck Top
3511 N Market St (99207-5766)
PHONE.................................509 489-9180
Russ Meili, *Owner*
EMP: 3
SQ FT: 15,000
SALES (est): 337.6K **Privately Held**
WEB: www.meilitrucktops.com
SIC: 3792 5561 Pickup covers, canopies or caps; recreational vehicle dealers

(G-12390)
MERLYN PRODUCTS INC
7500 W Park Dr (99224-5726)
PHONE.................................509 838-7500
Suzanne Evans, *President*
EMP: 11
SQ FT: 21,000
SALES (est): 400K **Privately Held**
WEB: www.merlynproducts.com
SIC: 3724 3728 3721 Aircraft engines & engine parts; aircraft parts & equipment; aircraft

(G-12391)
MERRILL CORP RESOURCE MGT
621 W Mallon Ave Ste 606 (99201-2121)
PHONE.................................509 326-7892
Mark Barranger, *Manager*
EMP: 2
SALES (est): 162K **Privately Held**
SIC: 2759 Commercial printing

(G-12392)
METAL ROLLFORMING SYSTEMS INC
Also Called: Metal Roofing and Siding Sup
4511 N Freya St (99217-6803)
P.O. Box 6246 (99217-0904)
PHONE.................................509 315-8737
Dan McDonald, *President*
EMP: 40
SALES (est): 9.7MM **Privately Held**
SIC: 3444 Sheet metalwork

(G-12393)
METAL SALES MANUFACTURING CORP
2727 E Trent Ave (99202-3852)
P.O. Box 3827 (99220-3827)
PHONE.................................509 536-6000
Jay Mullin, *Branch Mgr*
EMP: 30
SQ FT: 85,000
SALES (corp-wide): 390.6MM **Privately Held**
SIC: 3444 Metal roofing & roof drainage equipment
HQ: Metal Sales Manufacturing Corporation
545 S 3rd St Ste 200
Louisville KY 40202
502 855-4300

(G-12394)
MILLIANNA LLC
905 W Riverside Ave # 608 (99201-1001)
PHONE.................................415 505-8507
Sharmila Persaud, *Co-Owner*
Arianna Brooke, *Co-Owner*
EMP: 2
SALES (est): 165.9K **Privately Held**
SIC: 3961 Costume jewelry

(G-12395)
MINAPSYS SOFTWARE CORP
850 E Spokane Falls Blvd # 121 (99202-2167)
PHONE.................................425 891-1460
Mark Colby, *Principal*
EMP: 2
SALES (est): 100K **Privately Held**
SIC: 7372 Prepackaged software

(G-12396)
MISSOULA ORTHOTICS & PROSTHET
514 S Washington St (99204-2620)
PHONE.................................406 549-0921
Laren Williams, *President*
Karen Williams, *Admin Sec*
EMP: 6
SQ FT: 4,000
SALES (est): 505.7K **Privately Held**
WEB: www.missoulaortho.com
SIC: 3842 Prosthetic appliances

(G-12397)
MODERN TRANSPORT SYSTEMS CORP
4823 E 50th Ave (99223-1504)
PHONE.................................509 443-5031
John Barber, *President*
EMP: 5
SALES (est): 349.4K **Privately Held**
SIC: 3799 Transportation equipment

(G-12398)
MOTOR WORKS INC
1026 N Haven St (99202-6105)
PHONE.................................509 535-9240
Michael R Ulrick, *President*
EMP: 85
SALES (est): 12.9MM **Privately Held**
WEB: www.motorworksengines.com
SIC: 3714 Motor vehicle engines & parts

(G-12399)
MOUNTAIN STTES ELEC CONTRS INC
1220 E 1st Ave (99202-2106)
P.O. Box 4325 (99220-0325)
PHONE.................................509 532-0110
Bruce Farley, *President*
Bruce Carter, *Vice Pres*
Dick Anderson, *Shareholder*
EMP: 50
SQ FT: 5,000
SALES (est): 7MM **Privately Held**
WEB: www.mountainstateselectrical.com
SIC: 1731 3643 General electrical contractor; current-carrying wiring devices

(G-12400)
NABAT PUBLISHING
4210 E Ermina Ave (99217-7271)
PHONE.................................509 869-8707
Bogdan Marish, *Principal*
EMP: 2
SALES (est): 108.4K **Privately Held**
SIC: 2741 Miscellaneous publishing

(G-12401)
NALCO COMPANY LLC
Also Called: Nalco Chemical
421 W Riverside Ave # 770 (99201-0402)
PHONE.................................509 928-7713
Michael Lesniak, *Branch Mgr*
EMP: 2
SALES (corp-wide): 14.6B **Publicly Held**
WEB: www.nalco.com
SIC: 2899 Chemical preparations
HQ: Nalco Company Llc
1601 W Diehl Rd
Naperville IL 60563
630 305-1000

(G-12402)
NATIONAL COLOR GRAPHICS INC
25 W Boone Ave (99201-2307)
PHONE.................................509 326-6464
Harlan Knobel, *President*
Velma A Knobel, *Corp Secy*
EMP: 15
SQ FT: 10,000
SALES: 1.3MM **Privately Held**
SIC: 2752 Color lithography; commercial printing, offset

(G-12403)
NATIONAL MANAGEMENT SOFTWARE
827 W 1st Ave Ste 401 (99201-3904)
PHONE.................................509 327-0192
Dan Womach, *President*
Cathryn Womach, *Vice Pres*
Christina Rohrig, *Manager*
EMP: 25
SALES (est): 250K **Privately Held**
WEB: www.nmsoftware.com
SIC: 7371 7372 Computer software development; prepackaged software

(G-12404)
NEXUS SURGICAL INNOVATIONS
809 W Main Ave Apt 303 (99201-5008)
PHONE.................................509 499-0937
Chris Crago, *President*
EMP: 2
SALES (est): 86.6K **Privately Held**
SIC: 3841 Surgical & medical instruments

(G-12405)
NOODLE EXPRESS
Also Called: Noodle Express Spokane
707 N Sullivan Rd (99201)
PHONE.................................509 927-4117
Chris Seamons, *Owner*
EMP: 14
SALES (est): 990K **Privately Held**
SIC: 2098 5812 Noodles (e.g. egg, plain & water), dry; eating places

(G-12406)
NORDAL DENVER
Also Called: Monrovia Apartments
14 S Oak St (99201-7420)
PHONE.................................509 456-8969
Denver Nordal, *Owner*
EMP: 5
SALES (est): 323.3K **Privately Held**
WEB: www.monroviaapartments.com
SIC: 6513 2511 Apartment building operators; wood household furniture

(G-12407)
NORTH FACE 047
714 W Main Ave (99201-0600)
PHONE.................................509 747-5389
Melanie Cuaresma, *Principal*
EMP: 2
SALES (est): 165K **Privately Held**
SIC: 3949 Camping equipment & supplies

(G-12408)
NORTHERN LIGHTS BREWING CO
1003 E Trent Ave Ste 170 (99202-2185)
PHONE.................................509 242-2739
Mark Irvin, *Owner*
EMP: 8
SALES: 800K **Privately Held**
SIC: 2082 Malt beverages

(G-12409)
NORTHERN LIGHTS SUNRM CREATN L
6211 S Meadowlane Rd (99224-9654)
PHONE.................................509 747-1110
Daniel R Bothmer,
Todd Blund,
Dan Bothmer,

Spokane - Spokane County (G-12410)

EMP: 7
SALES: 380K **Privately Held**
SIC: 3448 Sunrooms, prefabricated metal

(G-12410)
NORTHSTONE INDUSTRIES LLC
Also Called: Northstone Manufacturing
111 W Elcliff Ave (99218-2582)
PHONE.................................509 844-7775
Bradley Ward, *Mng Member*
EMP: 3
SALES (est): 267.3K **Privately Held**
SIC: 3429 3728 3599 3451 Aircraft hardware; aircraft parts & equipment; machine & other job shop work; screw machine products; catalog & mail-order houses

(G-12411)
NORTHWEST BEDDING COMPANY (PA)
Also Called: Spring Craft
4614 S Saint Andrews Ln (99223-4305)
PHONE.................................509 244-3000
Robert L Evanson, *President*
▲ **EMP:** 40 **EST:** 1966
SALES: 10.1MM **Privately Held**
WEB: www.nwbedding.com
SIC: 2515 5712 Mattresses, innerspring or box spring; mattresses

(G-12412)
NORTHWEST BUSINESS STAMP INC
5218 N Market St (99217-6132)
P.O. Box 7350 (99207-0350)
PHONE.................................509 483-0308
Blake Carlson, *President*
Carrie Carlson, *Vice Pres*
EMP: 7
SALES (est): 956.4K **Privately Held**
WEB: www.nbstamp.com
SIC: 3953 Marking devices

(G-12413)
NORTHWEST MONITORING SERVICES
921 N Adams St (99201-2050)
PHONE.................................509 326-6270
Eric Houchin, *Owner*
EMP: 4
SALES (est): 237.6K **Privately Held**
SIC: 3699 Security control equipment & systems

(G-12414)
NORTHWEST SEED & PET INC
7302 N Division St (99208-6528)
PHONE.................................509 484-7387
Lori Hardin, *Manager*
EMP: 15
SALES (est): 378.6K
SALES (corp-wide): 4.8MM **Privately Held**
WEB: www.nwseed.com
SIC: 0782 3999 Garden services; pet supplies
PA: Northwest Seed & Pet Inc
2422 E Sprague Ave
Spokane WA 99202
509 534-0694

(G-12415)
NW SOFTWARE SOLUTIONS
Also Called: Staffready
421 W Main Ave Ste 200 (99201-0660)
PHONE.................................509 252-3550
Mark Coski, *Comptroller*
EMP: 6 **EST:** 2014
SALES (est): 396.5K **Privately Held**
SIC: 7372 Business oriented computer software

(G-12416)
NW SOLAR PROTECTION LLC
10125 N Division St (99218-1306)
PHONE.................................509 294-9878
Darren Reynolds,
EMP: 2
SALES (est): 140K **Privately Held**
SIC: 2396 Automotive & apparel trimmings

(G-12417)
O NEIL INDUSTRIES LLC
827 W 1st Ave Ste 425 (99201-3914)
PHONE.................................509 828-0213
EMP: 2 **EST:** 2017
SALES (est): 68.3K **Privately Held**
SIC: 3999 Manufacturing industries

(G-12418)
ODO
1111 W 1st Ave Ste B (99201-4060)
PHONE.................................303 915-9652
EMP: 3
SALES (est): 90.5K **Privately Held**
SIC: 3999 5813 ; bars & lounges

(G-12419)
OGLE EQUIPMENT CO
6619 N Crestline St (99217-7508)
P.O. Box 7167 (99207-0167)
PHONE.................................509 489-6306
Robert Ogle, *President*
Mary Ogle, *Vice Pres*
EMP: 3
SQ FT: 2,500
SALES (est): 467.7K **Privately Held**
SIC: 3444 Sheet metalwork

(G-12420)
OIL & VINEGAR RETAIL
808 W Main Ave Ste 201 (99201-0900)
PHONE.................................509 838-7115
Fidel Huerta, *Principal*
EMP: 6
SALES (est): 412.6K **Privately Held**
SIC: 2099 Vinegar

(G-12421)
ONEILL STEEL FABRICATION INC
7004 N Altamont St (99217-7644)
PHONE.................................509 467-5309
Dianne Meeks, *President*
EMP: 17
SALES (est): 3.1MM **Privately Held**
WEB: www.oneillsteelfab.com
SIC: 3449 3441 Bars, concrete reinforcing: fabricated steel; fabricated structural metal

(G-12422)
OTIS ELEVATOR INTL INC
510 E North Foothills Dr (99207-2100)
PHONE.................................509 483-7328
Eric Johnson, *Manager*
EMP: 16
SALES (corp-wide): 66.5B **Publicly Held**
WEB: www.otis.com
SIC: 5084 3534 Elevators; elevators & moving stairways
HQ: Otis Elevator Company
1 Carrier Pl
Farmington CT 06032
860 674-3000

(G-12423)
OUTDOOR LEISURE CENTERS
7302 N Palmer Rd (99217-9703)
PHONE.................................509 599-2150
Jory Mollenhauer, *Partner*
EMP: 6
SALES: 100K **Privately Held**
SIC: 3444 Awnings & canopies

(G-12424)
OXALIS GROUP
428 W 27th Ave (99203-1854)
P.O. Box 8051 (99203-0051)
PHONE.................................509 838-3295
Shawn Higgins, *Owner*
Ann Glendening, *Principal*
EMP: 2
SALES (est): 120.4K **Privately Held**
SIC: 2731 5942 Books: publishing & printing; book stores

(G-12425)
OXARC INC
3417 E Springfield Ave (99202-4638)
PHONE.................................509 755-0651
Janna Nelson, *Branch Mgr*
EMP: 32
SALES (corp-wide): 77.9MM **Privately Held**
SIC: 3548 Welding apparatus
PA: Oxarc, Inc.
4003 E Broadway Ave
Spokane WA 99202
509 535-7794

(G-12426)
PACIFIC NW POWDR COATING
Also Called: Evergreen Powder Coatings
17117 E Macmahan Rd (99217-9404)
PHONE.................................509 535-9950
Fax: 509 535-9319
EMP: 10
SQ FT: 15,000
SALES: 1.2MM **Privately Held**
SIC: 3479 3471 Coating/Engraving Service Plating/Polishing Service

(G-12427)
PACIFIC WHOLESALE BANNER & SUP
2823 N Martin St (99207-4843)
PHONE.................................509 487-4189
Steve Decker, *President*
EMP: 4 **EST:** 2001
SQ FT: 5,544
SALES (est): 232K **Privately Held**
SIC: 5999 2051 Banners; bakery, for home service delivery

(G-12428)
PANTROL INC (PA)
3108 E Ferry Ave (99202-3870)
P.O. Box 4387 (99220-0387)
PHONE.................................509 535-9061
Jim Kucera, *President*
Roy Givens, *President*
Jon Gessele, *Engineer*
Jack Marquard, *Manager*
EMP: 18
SQ FT: 25,000
SALES (est): 6.1MM **Privately Held**
WEB: www.pantrol.com
SIC: 3823 3672 Controllers for process variables, all types; panelboard indicators, recorders & controllers: receiver; printed circuit boards

(G-12429)
PAPE MACHINERY INC (PA)
Also Called: John Deere Authorized Dealer
6210 W Rowand Rd (99224-5321)
P.O. Box 19099 (99219-9099)
PHONE.................................509 838-5252
Rodger Spears, *President*
David C Rowand, *Vice Pres*
EMP: 50
SQ FT: 20,000
SALES (est): 25.2MM **Privately Held**
WEB: www.rowand.com
SIC: 5082 3531 Contractors' materials; forestry equipment; construction machinery

(G-12430)
PARKWATER AVIATION INC
5627 E Rutter Ave (99212-1337)
PHONE.................................509 536-1969
Matt McBlair, *Principal*
EMP: 10
SALES (est): 201.1K **Privately Held**
SIC: 4581 3728 Aircraft maintenance & repair services; aircraft training equipment

(G-12431)
PATIT CREEK CELLARS
822 W Sprague Ave (99201-3908)
PHONE.................................509 868-4045
Ed Dudley, *Principal*
EMP: 2
SALES (est): 110.8K **Privately Held**
SIC: 2084 Wines

(G-12432)
PAULS MOBILE WASHING
510 W Dalton Ave (99205-4908)
PHONE.................................509 954-1910
Pavel Bondarenko, *Principal*
EMP: 2 **EST:** 2010
SALES (est): 128.6K **Privately Held**
SIC: 3589 High pressure cleaning equipment

(G-12433)
PAYNESTAKING DETAIL
9412 W Trails Rd (99224-9574)
PHONE.................................509 599-2207
Jeffrey Payne, *Principal*
EMP: 2

SALES (est): 108.7K **Privately Held**
SIC: 1389 Construction, repair & dismantling services

(G-12434)
PEAK INDUSTRIES ◯
7916 W Sunset Hwy (99224-9048)
PHONE.................................509 448-5793
EMP: 2 **EST:** 2018
SALES (est): 134.6K **Privately Held**
SIC: 3999 Manufacturing industries

(G-12435)
PEDAL PUSHERS BIKE RNTL & RPR
2427 E Nebraska Ave (99208-2309)
PHONE.................................208 689-3436
John Kolbe, *Owner*
EMP: 2
SALES (est): 113.8K **Privately Held**
SIC: 3545 Pushers

(G-12436)
PEONE INDUSTRIES
503 E Dave Ct (99208-1210)
P.O. Box 6735 (99217-0912)
PHONE.................................509 443-4710
EMP: 2 **EST:** 2010
SALES (est): 88K **Privately Held**
SIC: 3999 Mfg Misc Products

(G-12437)
PERCEPTION PLASTICS INC
301 W 2nd Ave (99201-4306)
PHONE.................................509 624-5408
Jerry Judd, *President*
EMP: 2
SQ FT: 2,800
SALES: 250K **Privately Held**
SIC: 3069 Hard rubber & molded rubber products

(G-12438)
PETITE CHAT LLC
9910 N Waikiki Rd (99218-2359)
PHONE.................................509 468-2720
Harlow Morgan,
EMP: 4
SALES (est): 266.4K **Privately Held**
SIC: 2051 Bread, cake & related products

(G-12439)
PETNET SOLUTIONS INC
7011 W Flightline Blvd (99224-5721)
PHONE.................................509 455-4178
EMP: 4
SALES (corp-wide): 95B **Privately Held**
SIC: 2835 Radioactive diagnostic substances
HQ: Petnet Solutions, Inc.
810 Innovation Dr
Knoxville TN 37932
865 218-2000

(G-12440)
PHAZR LLC
314 W Mansfield Ave (99205-4730)
PHONE.................................509 329-8306
Noorulden Abduljabar, *Principal*
EMP: 5
SALES (est): 222.6K **Privately Held**
SIC: 3843 3949 5013 5075 Dental equipment & supplies; polo equipment & supplies, general; motor vehicle supplies & new parts; alternators; condensing units, air conditioning; shirts, men's & boys'; paints, varnishes & supplies

(G-12441)
PIECE OF MIND LLC
9303 N Division St Ste A (99218-1253)
PHONE.................................509 868-0850
Justin Wilson, *Mng Member*
EMP: 5
SALES (est): 175.6K **Privately Held**
SIC: 3443 Fabricated plate work (boiler shop)

(G-12442)
PILKINGTON NORTH AMERICA INC
3200 E Trent Ave (99202-4456)
PHONE.................................509 534-4899
Bob Schmidt, *Manager*
Harold Verstrate, *Manager*

GEOGRAPHIC SECTION

Spokane - Spokane County (G-12472)

EMP: 223 **Privately Held**
SIC: 3211 Flat glass
HQ: Pilkington North America, Inc.
  811 Madison Ave Fl 3
  Toledo OH 43604
  419 247-3731

(G-12443)
PISHWACOM
1906 W Wedgewood Ave (99208-7122)
PHONE..............................509 991-8972
Dan Waterbly, *Principal*
EMP: 2
SALES (est): 106K **Privately Held**
SIC: 3559 Special industry machinery

(G-12444)
PITNEY BOWES INC
1313 N Atlantic St Fl 3 (99201-2318)
PHONE..............................509 363-3694
Toll Free:.............................888 -
Billie Corpus, *Branch Mgr*
EMP: 45
SALES (corp-wide): 3.5B **Publicly Held**
SIC: 3579 7359 Postage meters; business machine & electronic equipment rental services
PA: Pitney Bowes Inc.
  3001 Summer St Ste 3
  Stamford CT 06905
  203 356-5000

(G-12445)
PITNEY BOWES INC
200 E 2nd Ave Ste A (99202-1524)
PHONE..............................509 835-1272
Peter Nauditt, *General Mgr*
EMP: 35
SALES (corp-wide): 3.5B **Publicly Held**
SIC: 3579 7359 Postage meters; business machine & electronic equipment rental services
PA: Pitney Bowes Inc.
  3001 Summer St Ste 3
  Stamford CT 06905
  203 356-5000

(G-12446)
PITNEY BOWES INC
313 N Atl St Ste 3000 (99201)
PHONE..............................509 838-0115
Terry Besenyody, *Manager*
EMP: 35
SALES (corp-wide): 3.5B **Publicly Held**
SIC: 3579 7359 Postage meters; business machine & electronic equipment rental services
PA: Pitney Bowes Inc.
  3001 Summer St Ste 3
  Stamford CT 06905
  203 356-5000

(G-12447)
PLESE PRINTING & MARKETING
4201 E Trent Ave (99202-4430)
PHONE..............................509 534-2355
Barbara Neeser, *Business Mgr*
EMP: 3
SALES (est): 31.2K **Privately Held**
SIC: 2752 Commercial printing, offset

(G-12448)
PLESE PRINTING & MARKETING (PA)
Also Called: PIP Printing
4201 E Trent Ave (99202-4430)
PHONE..............................509 534-2355
Kim Plese, *President*
Mark Plese, *Vice Pres*
Josh Burkhardt, *Prdtn Mgr*
Mary Farnsworth, *Sales Associate*
Barbara Neeser, *Info Tech Mgr*
EMP: 12
SQ FT: 10,000
SALES (est): 1.3MM **Privately Held**
SIC: 2752 2791 2789 Commercial printing, offset; typesetting; bookbinding & related work

(G-12449)
POTLATCHDELTIC MFG L L C (HQ)
601 W 1st Ave Ste 1600 (99201-3807)
PHONE..............................509 835-1500
EMP: 2
SALES (est): 6.5MM
SALES (corp-wide): 974.5MM **Publicly Held**
SIC: 2435 Hardwood veneer & plywood
PA: Potlatchdeltic Corporation
  601 W 1st Ave Ste 1600
  Spokane WA 99201
  509 835-1500

(G-12450)
POWER MACHINE SERVICES INC
4105 E Broadway Ave (99202-4530)
PHONE..............................509 536-1721
Ben Zimmerman, *President*
Tim Zimmerman, *Vice Pres*
EMP: 4
SQ FT: 4,000
SALES (est): 430K **Privately Held**
WEB: www.powermachineservice.com
SIC: 3599 Machine shop, jobbing & repair

(G-12451)
POWER PLUS INCORPORATED
7302 N Market St (99217-7823)
PHONE..............................509 489-8308
Rich Gortsema, *Principal*
EMP: 4 **EST:** 2007
SALES (est): 395.9K **Privately Held**
SIC: 3444 Sheet metalwork

(G-12452)
POWERS CANDY AND NUT COMPANY
6061 N Freya St (99217-6542)
P.O. Box 6525 (99217-0909)
PHONE..............................509 489-1955
John G Cooley, *President*
Janice C Cooley, *Vice Pres*
▲ **EMP:** 16
SQ FT: 53,000
SALES: 4MM **Privately Held**
WEB: www.powerscandy.com
SIC: 2064 Candy & other confectionery products

(G-12453)
PRESS
909 S Grand Blvd (99202-1210)
PHONE..............................509 869-2242
Matty Goodwin, *Owner*
EMP: 2
SALES (est): 114K **Privately Held**
SIC: 2741 Miscellaneous publishing

(G-12454)
PRESSWORKS
2717 N Perry St (99207-4966)
PHONE..............................509 462-7627
Larry Dilley, *Principal*
EMP: 13 **EST:** 2007
SALES (est): 1.9MM **Privately Held**
WEB: www.pressworks-ink.com
SIC: 2752 Commercial printing, offset

(G-12455)
PRIMEONE PRODUCTS LLC
6310 S Madelia St (99223-8355)
P.O. Box 30816 (99223-3013)
PHONE..............................509 448-8818
Rocky Rajewski,
EMP: 3
SQ FT: 500
SALES (est): 95.1K **Privately Held**
SIC: 3822 Auto controls regulating residntl & coml environmt & applncs

(G-12456)
PROTO MANUFACTURING INC
5959 N Freya St (99217-6541)
PHONE..............................509 535-9683
John Long, *President*
Joe Sadkowski, *General Mgr*
Sandi Corey, *Info Tech Mgr*
EMP: 60
SQ FT: 36,000
SALES (est): 11.1MM **Privately Held**
WEB: www.proto-mfg.com
SIC: 3444 Sheet metalwork

(G-12457)
PSI LOGISTICS INTL LLC
9 S Washington St Ste 301 (99201-5117)
PHONE..............................855 473-5877
Caleb Ashbeck,

EMP: 2
SQ FT: 800
SALES (est): 496.9K **Privately Held**
SIC: 5113 3537 4212 4789 Shipping supplies; trucks: freight, baggage, etc.: industrial, except mining; steel hauling, local; cargo loading & unloading services

(G-12458)
PUFFIN GLASS
3904 N Division St (99207-1703)
PHONE..............................509 328-0661
Brook Davis, *Partner*
EMP: 2
SALES (est): 120K **Privately Held**
SIC: 8299 3269 Art school, except commercial; smokers' articles, pottery

(G-12459)
PUREHEART
3704 E 5th Ave (99202-5037)
PHONE..............................509 535-2323
Darlene Thompson, *Principal*
EMP: 2
SALES (est): 171.3K **Privately Held**
SIC: 2841 Soap & other detergents

(G-12460)
PURINA MILLS LLC
4714 E Trent Ave (99212)
P.O. Box 11127, Spokane Valley (99211-1127)
PHONE..............................509 534-0594
Ken Rockhill, *Branch Mgr*
EMP: 31
SALES (corp-wide): 10.4B **Privately Held**
WEB: www.purina-mills.com
SIC: 2048 Stock feeds, dry; poultry feeds; feed supplements
HQ: Purina Mills, Llc
  555 Maryvle Univ Dr 200
  Saint Louis MO 63141

(G-12461)
PVC DEBONDING SYSTEMS INC
3102 E Trent Ave Ste 208 (99202-3800)
PHONE..............................866 961-8349
Nancy Sheffield-Tate, *President*
EMP: 2
SALES (est): 140.4K **Privately Held**
SIC: 3088 Plastics plumbing fixtures

(G-12462)
PYROTEK INCORPORATED (PA)
705 W 1st Ave (99201-3909)
PHONE..............................509 926-6212
Allan Roy, *CEO*
Don Ting, *President*
Paul Rieckers, *CFO*
Paul Carlstrom, *Sales Engr*
Beth Winter, *Manager*
▲ **EMP:** 82
SQ FT: 50,000
SALES (est): 592MM **Privately Held**
WEB: www.pyrotek.info
SIC: 3365 Aluminum & aluminum-based alloy castings

(G-12463)
QUAD GROUP INC
Also Called: Quad Labs
1815 S Lewis St (99224-9789)
PHONE..............................509 458-4558
Maria Riegert, *President*
EMP: 10 **EST:** 1972
SQ FT: 21,000
SALES (est): 1.6MM **Privately Held**
WEB: www.quadgroupinc.com
SIC: 3825 8734 Field strength & intensity measuring equipment, electrical; testing laboratories

(G-12464)
R A PEARSON COMPANY (PA)
Also Called: Pearson Packaging Systems
8120 W Sunset Hwy (99224-9770)
PHONE..............................509 838-6226
Michael A Senske, *President*
Richard Daily, *Vice Pres*
Rick Daily, *Vice Pres*
Richard Gardner, *Vice Pres*
Tim Neton, *Opers Mgr*
▲ **EMP:** 193 **EST:** 1955
SQ FT: 110,000

SALES (est): 53.9MM **Privately Held**
WEB: www.pearsonpkg.com
SIC: 3565 Carton packing machines

(G-12465)
R PLUM CORPORATION (PA)
Also Called: Empire Cold Storage
1327 N Oak St (99201-2842)
PHONE..............................509 328-2070
Ronland F Plummer, *President*
Bruce Figy, *Manager*
EMP: 12 **EST:** 1903
SQ FT: 63,000
SALES (est): 2.2MM **Privately Held**
WEB: www.empirecoldstorage.com
SIC: 4222 2097 Warehousing, cold storage or refrigerated; block ice

(G-12466)
RAINBOW RACING SYSTEM INC
814 W Rosewood Ave (99208-4142)
P.O. Box 18310 (99228-0310)
PHONE..............................509 326-5470
Walter Egger, *President*
Heather Rhea, *Sales Staff*
EMP: 15
SQ FT: 3,600
SALES (est): 2.6MM **Privately Held**
WEB: www.rainbowracing.com
SIC: 5961 7336 2759 Mail order house; commercial art & graphic design; commercial printing

(G-12467)
RAMAX PRINTING AND AWARDS
3209 N Argonne Rd (99212-2061)
PHONE..............................509 928-1222
Stanley Soash, *President*
Carol Soash, *Vice Pres*
Maxine Soash, *Admin Sec*
EMP: 3 **EST:** 1961
SQ FT: 2,600
SALES: 200K **Privately Held**
SIC: 2759 2752 3999 2396 Letterpress printing; commercial printing, offset; gold stamping, except books; automotive & apparel trimmings

(G-12468)
RDEAN ENTERPRISES INC
Also Called: Sign Service & Manufacturing
6824 N Market St (99217-7813)
PHONE..............................208 772-8571
Rob Dean, *President*
Kristen Dean, *Corp Secy*
EMP: 11
SALES (est): 1.8MM **Privately Held**
WEB: www.signserv.com
SIC: 3993 1721 Electric signs; painting & paper hanging

(G-12469)
REGAL ROAD WINERY
8224 S Regal Rd (99223-9540)
PHONE..............................509 838-8024
EMP: 2
SALES (est): 82K **Privately Held**
SIC: 2084 Wines

(G-12470)
REIFF INJECTION MOLDING INC
Also Called: Bauer Enterprizes
131 N Pittsburg St (99202-3041)
PHONE..............................509 340-1020
Jim McCall, *President*
J McCall, *Vice Pres*
Marilyn McCall, *Treasurer*
▲ **EMP:** 5
SQ FT: 13,000
SALES: 500K **Privately Held**
WEB: www.reiffmolding.com
SIC: 3089 Molding primary plastic

(G-12471)
REININGER WINERY
824 W Sprague Ave (99201-3908)
PHONE..............................509 242-3190
EMP: 2
SALES (est): 66.3K **Privately Held**
SIC: 2084 Wines

(G-12472)
RESOURCE ASSOCIATES INTL
Also Called: Scada Nexus
11721 N Lancelot Dr (99218-1758)
PHONE..............................509 466-1894

Scott Hamilton, *President*
Patricia Hamilton, *Vice Pres*
EMP: 6
SALES (est): 816.8K **Privately Held**
WEB: www.raiinc.com
SIC: 8711 3823 1731 7389 Consulting engineer; water quality monitoring & control systems; computerized controls installation; meter readers, remote

(G-12473)
RETIRED GORILLA PUBLISHING
1311 S Westcliff Pl # 401 (99224-2028)
PHONE...............................509 474-9345
James A Stinson, *Principal*
EMP: 2
SALES (est): 118.6K **Privately Held**
SIC: 2741 Miscellaneous publishing

(G-12474)
RGZPRINTS
1907 W 3rd Ave (99201-7648)
PHONE...............................208 310-0500
Ashley R Vaughn, *Owner*
EMP: 2
SALES (est): 83.9K **Privately Held**
SIC: 2752 Commercial printing, lithographic

(G-12475)
RISKLENS INC
601 W Main Ave Ste 917 (99201-0613)
PHONE...............................866 936-0191
Steven Tabacek, *CEO*
Nicola Sanna, *Principal*
Dave Sutor, *CFO*
Leslie Yates, *Controller*
EMP: 16
SALES (est): 499.4K **Privately Held**
SIC: 7372 7379 8243 Application computer software; business oriented computer software; computer related consulting services; software training, computer

(G-12476)
RIVER CITY BREWING LLC
121 S Cedar St (99201-6500)
PHONE...............................509 413-2388
Gage Stromberg, *President*
EMP: 7
SALES (est): 210.5K **Privately Held**
SIC: 2082 5813 Beer (alcoholic beverage); beer garden (drinking places)

(G-12477)
RJ JARVIS ENTERPRISES INC
Also Called: R.J. Jarvis Enterprise
3412 E Bismark Ct (99217-6592)
PHONE...............................509 482-0254
Richard Clarence Jarvis, *President*
Jolene S Jarvis, *Admin Sec*
EMP: 45
SQ FT: 152,460
SALES (est): 9.3MM **Privately Held**
WEB: www.rwfab.com
SIC: 3441 3446 Building components, structural steel; architectural metalwork

(G-12478)
ROAST HOUSE LLC
Also Called: Roast Hse From Frm To Cup Mfg
423 E Cleveland Ave Ste C (99207-2008)
PHONE...............................509 995-6500
Deborah Bernard, *Owner*
Jim Haynes, *Owner*
EMP: 3
SALES (est): 97K **Privately Held**
SIC: 2095 Roasted coffee

(G-12479)
ROBERT J PARRY
4108 S Scott St (99203-6255)
PHONE...............................509 456-6204
Robert J Parry, *Owner*
EMP: 2
SALES (est): 95.2K **Privately Held**
SIC: 3569 Assembly machines, non-metalworking

(G-12480)
ROBERT KARL CELLARS LLC
115 W Pacific Ave (99201-3621)
PHONE...............................509 363-1353
Joseph Gunselman, *Principal*
EMP: 4
SALES (est): 312K **Privately Held**
SIC: 2084 Wines

(G-12481)
ROBINSON WINDWORD INC
2503 S Geiger Blvd (99224-5410)
PHONE...............................509 536-1617
Jack Robinson, *President*
Ben Browning, *General Mgr*
▲ **EMP:** 12
SQ FT: 10,000
SALES (est): 1.1MM **Privately Held**
WEB: www.robinsonpostal.com
SIC: 7389 2399 Sewing contractor; banners, made from fabric

(G-12482)
RODS CUSTOM FIBERGLASS INC
2928 N Napa St (99207-4848)
PHONE...............................509 483-2174
Rod Tomsha, *President*
EMP: 2
SALES (est): 150K **Privately Held**
WEB: www.rodscustomfiberglass.com
SIC: 3089 Boats, nonrigid: plastic; heels, boot or shoe: plastic

(G-12483)
ROOTZ
923 E Hoffman Ave (99207-3225)
PHONE...............................509 443-5999
Lenny Volpe, *Owner*
EMP: 3
SALES (est): 251.9K **Privately Held**
SIC: 3524 Lawn & garden tractors & equipment

(G-12484)
ROSS PRINTING NORTHWEST INC
1611 E Sprague Ave (99202-3114)
P.O. Box 3267 (99220-3267)
PHONE...............................509 534-0655
Alan G Ross, *President*
Stanley Ross, *Principal*
EMP: 30
SALES (est): 4.1MM **Privately Held**
SIC: 2752 Commercial printing, offset

(G-12485)
RUMPELTES ENTERPRISES INC
Also Called: Inland PCF Stamp & Mkg Pdts
215 W 2nd Ave (99201-3605)
PHONE...............................509 624-1391
Ned Rumpeltes, *President*
Dan C Rumpeltes, *Corp Secy*
Nancy Rumpeltes, *Vice Pres*
EMP: 40
SQ FT: 17,000
SALES (est): 1.9MM **Privately Held**
SIC: 7389 3953 Sign painting & lettering shop; date stamps, hand: rubber or metal

(G-12486)
RUNWAY LIQUIDATION LLC
Also Called: Bcbg
670 Rising Sun Ln (99218)
PHONE...............................262 253-4000
EMP: 2
SALES (corp-wide): 645.5MM **Privately Held**
SIC: 2335 Women's, juniors' & misses' dresses
HQ: Runway Liquidation, Llc
2761 Fruitland Ave
Vernon CA 90058
323 589-2224

(G-12487)
RUNWAY LIQUIDATION LLC
Also Called: Bcbg
4 Colebrook Ct (99205)
PHONE...............................920 387-3180
EMP: 2
SALES (corp-wide): 645.5MM **Privately Held**
SIC: 2335 Women's, juniors' & misses' dresses
HQ: Runway Liquidation, Llc
2761 Fruitland Ave
Vernon CA 90058
323 589-2224

(G-12488)
RW HOT SHOT SERVICE
202 E Spokane Falls Blvd # 403 (99202-1612)
PHONE...............................509 868-6644
S Schmidt, *Bd of Directors*
EMP: 2
SALES (est): 202.3K **Privately Held**
SIC: 1389 Hot shot service

(G-12489)
S & S ENGINE REMANUFACTURING (PA)
Also Called: Engine Installation Service
1023 N Monroe St (99201-2113)
PHONE...............................509 325-4558
Jeff Johnson, *President*
Linda Johnson, *Corp Secy*
▼ **EMP:** 40
SQ FT: 9,000
SALES (est): 2.9MM **Privately Held**
WEB: www.sandsengines.com
SIC: 7538 3714 Engine rebuilding: automotive; motor vehicle parts & accessories

(G-12490)
S&J ENGINES INC
817 N Lincoln St (99201-2124)
PHONE...............................509 325-4558
Robert L Jones, *Principal*
EMP: 12
SALES (est): 1.5MM **Privately Held**
SIC: 3694 Engine electrical equipment

(G-12491)
S&S NDT LLC
4711 S South Morrill Ct (99223-2236)
P.O. Box 30847 (99223-3014)
PHONE...............................509 688-7996
Steve Siderius, *Administration*
Steven Siderius,
EMP: 2
SALES (est): 148.4K **Privately Held**
SIC: 2899 7389 Magnetic inspection oil or powder; penetrants, inspection; industrial & commercial equipment inspection service

(G-12492)
SAFEGUARD BUS FORMS & SYSTEMS
617 N Helena St (99202-2911)
PHONE...............................800 727-9120
EMP: 2
SALES (est): 83.9K **Privately Held**
SIC: 2752 Commercial printing, lithographic

(G-12493)
SCAFCO CORPORATION (PA)
Also Called: Scafco Steel Stud Mfg
2800 E Main Ave (99202-7004)
P.O. Box 3949 (99220-3949)
PHONE...............................509 343-9000
Lawrence Stone, *Chairman*
Arthur Mell, *Vice Pres*
Greg Lewis, *Plant Mgr*
Andy Sheen, *Foreman/Supr*
Wayde Deatherage, *Mfg Staff*
▼ **EMP:** 120
SALES (est): 160.5MM **Privately Held**
WEB: www.scafco.com
SIC: 3523 5065 6531 3444 Farm machinery & equipment; electronic parts & equipment; real estate managers; sheet metalwork

(G-12494)
SCAFCO CORPORATION
250 N Altamont St (99202-3812)
PHONE...............................509 343-9012
EMP: 12
SALES (corp-wide): 160.5MM **Privately Held**
SIC: 3523 5065 6531 Farm machinery & equipment; electronic parts & equipment; real estate agents & managers
PA: Scafco Corporation
2800 E Main Ave
Spokane WA 99202
509 343-9000

(G-12495)
SEATON ENGINEERING CORPORATION
Also Called: Maxpulse Maxdim
217 W Garden Ct (99208-8764)
PHONE...............................509 290-5919
Jeffery Christensen, *President*
EMP: 3
SALES (est): 200K **Privately Held**
WEB: www.seatoneng.com
SIC: 3728 5088 Aircraft parts & equipment; aircraft equipment & supplies

(G-12496)
SEAYS LAKE CITY MARINE LLC
1617 E Holyoke Ave (99217-7534)
PHONE...............................509 483-1461
Vince Seay, *Mng Member*
Tara Seay,
EMP: 3
SQ FT: 5,000
SALES (est): 281.4K **Privately Held**
SIC: 7694 Motor repair services

(G-12497)
SECURE IT LLC
4022 E Sumac Dr (99223-7849)
PHONE...............................509 992-6190
Kristopher Wise,
EMP: 5 **EST:** 2001
SALES: 1MM **Privately Held**
SIC: 7379 5699 2841 8734 Computer hardware requirements analysis; customized clothing & apparel; soap & other detergents; forensic laboratory; apiary (bee & honey farm)

(G-12498)
SEMGROUP CORPORATION
4327 N Thor St (99217-7098)
P.O. Box 6226 (99217-0904)
PHONE...............................509 487-4560
Charles Koch, *Owner*
EMP: 6
SALES (corp-wide): 2.5B **Publicly Held**
WEB: www.semgrouplp.com
SIC: 4612 5171 2951 Crude petroleum pipelines; petroleum bulk stations & terminals; asphalt paving mixtures & blocks
PA: Semgroup Corporation
6120 S Yale Ave Ste 1500
Tulsa OK 74136
918 524-8100

(G-12499)
SEVEN-K COMPANY
3120 W Kiernan Ave (99205-2241)
PHONE...............................509 863-3429
Vernon Mulford, *Owner*
EMP: 2
SALES (est): 69.7K **Privately Held**
SIC: 3999 Manufacturing industries

(G-12500)
SEVILLA LLC
1203 S Cedar St (99204-4029)
PHONE...............................509 280-8447
Maria Sevilla, *Administration*
EMP: 3 **EST:** 2010
SALES (est): 322.3K **Privately Held**
SIC: 3645 Residential lighting fixtures

(G-12501)
SHAPECUT INDUSTRIES LLC
3410 E Trent Ave (99202-4415)
P.O. Box 190, Usk (99180-0190)
PHONE...............................509 828-3265
Steve Hermann, *Owner*
EMP: 3 **EST:** 2013
SALES (est): 248K **Privately Held**
SIC: 3999 Manufacturing industries

(G-12502)
SHELL ENERGY NORTH AMER US LP
601 W 1st Ave Ste 1700 (99201-3811)
PHONE...............................509 688-6002
EMP: 5
SALES (corp-wide): 388.3B **Privately Held**
SIC: 1311 Crude petroleum & natural gas
HQ: Shell Energy North America (Us), L.P.
1000 Main St
Houston TX 77002

GEOGRAPHIC SECTION
Spokane - Spokane County (G-12533)

(G-12503)
SIGN CORPORATION
Also Called: Inland Sign and Lighting Sign
131 N Altamont St (99202-3803)
PHONE...................509 535-2913
Scott Sherick, *President*
EMP: 10
SALES (est): 1.7MM **Privately Held**
WEB: www.signcorp.com
SIC: 3993 Electric signs

(G-12504)
SIGNS FOR SUCCESS
6824 N Market St (99217-7813)
PHONE...................509 489-4200
Vanessa Bogensberger, *General Mgr*
John Bogensberger, *Principal*
EMP: 4
SQ FT: 5,600
SALES (est): 533K **Privately Held**
WEB: www.signsfs.com
SIC: 7384 3993 Photofinish laboratories; signs & advertising specialties

(G-12505)
SIGNSOUTH
4508 S Regal St (99223-7937)
P.O. Box 30714 (99223-3011)
PHONE...................509 448-4404
Sam Hands, *Principal*
EMP: 2
SALES (est): 162.1K **Privately Held**
SIC: 3993 Electric signs

(G-12506)
SKILSKIN
920 W Riverside Ave (99201-1010)
PHONE...................509 326-6760
EMP: 3
SALES (est): 56.7K
SALES (corp-wide): 3.2MM **Privately Held**
SIC: 8322 3999 Social services for the handicapped; barber & beauty shop equipment
PA: Skils'kin
4004 E Boone Ave
Spokane WA 99202
509 326-6760

(G-12507)
SMOKIN LEGAL ANYWHERE
9301 N Division St Ste A (99218-1254)
PHONE...................509 465-2695
David Phillips, *Owner*
EMP: 2
SALES (est): 200.9K **Privately Held**
SIC: 2131 Smoking tobacco

(G-12508)
SNACKFLASH LLC
6106 E Big Rock Rd (99223-9200)
PHONE...................509 443-0396
Beau Bozett, *Principal*
EMP: 2
SALES (est): 62.3K **Privately Held**
SIC: 2099 Food preparations

(G-12509)
SNEVA MANUFACTURING
1304 W Chelan Ave (99205-3424)
PHONE...................317 496-8935
EMP: 2
SALES (est): 73K **Privately Held**
SIC: 3999 Manufacturing industries

(G-12510)
SONDEREN PACKAGING INC (PA)
Also Called: Sonderen Paper Box
2906 N Crestline St (99207-4809)
P.O. Box 7369 (99207-0369)
PHONE...................509 487-1632
Mark A Sonderen, *President*
EMP: 112
SQ FT: 85,000
SALES (est): 16.5MM **Privately Held**
SIC: 2657 Folding paperboard boxes

(G-12511)
SONDRA L GROCE
Also Called: D & S Small Equipment
9624 N Colfax Rd (99218-1205)
PHONE...................509 467-8788
Sondra L Groce, *Owner*
EMP: 2
SALES: 100K **Privately Held**
SIC: 7699 3546 7629 Lawn mower repair shop; saws & sawing equipment; electrical repair shops

(G-12512)
SOPH-WARE ASSOCIATES INC
1818 W Francis Ave # 250 (99205-6834)
PHONE...................509 467-0668
Ronald C Turner, *President*
Audrey J Turner, *Vice Pres*
EMP: 12
SALES (est): 811.7K **Privately Held**
WEB: www.soph-ware.com
SIC: 7371 2741 Computer software development; miscellaneous publishing

(G-12513)
SPECIALTY ROOFING LLC
2222 E Mallon Ave (99202-3756)
PHONE...................509 534-8372
Mark Simmet, *President*
Rick Simmet, *Corp Secy*
EMP: 7
SQ FT: 700
SALES (est): 803.5K **Privately Held**
SIC: 3444 Metal roofing & roof drainage equipment

(G-12514)
SPILKER PRECAST LLC
4231 E Queen Ave (99217-6615)
P.O. Box 6266 (99217-0905)
PHONE...................509 487-2261
John Darrow, *Project Mgr*
Timothy Spilker,
EMP: 8 **EST:** 1970
SQ FT: 400
SALES (est): 1.2MM **Privately Held**
SIC: 3272 5032 Concrete products, precast; brick, stone & related material

(G-12515)
SPOKANARAMA PUBLISHING
627 W 16th Ave (99203-2130)
PHONE...................509 455-8009
EMP: 2
SALES (est): 62.9K **Privately Held**
SIC: 2711 Newspapers-Publishing/Printing

(G-12516)
SPOKANE ATHORS SELF-PUBLISHERS
2504 W Walton Ave (99205-1569)
PHONE...................509 325-2072
David A McChesney, *Principal*
EMP: 2 **EST:** 2012
SALES (est): 81.4K **Privately Held**
SIC: 2741 Miscellaneous publishing

(G-12517)
SPOKANE DISCOUNT AND BRASS CO
6715 N Division St (99208-3941)
PHONE...................509 467-8063
Steve Waco, *President*
Pamela Waco, *Treasurer*
EMP: 5
SQ FT: 10,000
SALES (est): 805.7K **Privately Held**
SIC: 2542 5947 Office & store showcases & display fixtures; gift shop

(G-12518)
SPOKANE FORKLIFT CNSTR EQP INC
Also Called: Spokaneforklift.com
4907 E Trent Ave (99212-1348)
PHONE...................509 868-5962
Barry Melton, *President*
Tyler Melton, *Sales Staff*
EMP: 4 **EST:** 2007
SQ FT: 3,000
SALES: 750K **Privately Held**
SIC: 7353 7699 3537 Heavy construction equipment rental; aircraft & heavy equipment repair services; forklift trucks

(G-12519)
SPOKANE MACHINERY COMPANY (DH)
Also Called: Spomac
3730 E Trent Ave (99202-4421)
PHONE...................509 535-1654
James Peplinski, *President*
Elaine Peplinski, *Vice Pres*
◆ **EMP:** 10
SQ FT: 60,000
SALES (est): 5.5MM
SALES (corp-wide): 377.3MM **Privately Held**
WEB: www.spomac.com
SIC: 5082 5084 5085 3599 General construction machinery & equipment; industrial machinery & equipment; industrial supplies; machine shop, jobbing & repair
HQ: Modern Machinery Co., Inc.
101 International Dr
Missoula MT 59808
406 523-1100

(G-12520)
SPOKANE PAW PRINTS LLC
3929 N Crestline St (99207-4504)
PHONE...................509 475-6885
Jose Casarez, *Principal*
EMP: 2
SALES (est): 108.8K **Privately Held**
SIC: 2752 Commercial printing, lithographic

(G-12521)
SPOKANE TIN SHEET IR WORKS INC
3807 E Ferry Ave (99202-4627)
PHONE...................509 534-0539
John Pansie, *President*
Kerrie Pansie, *Corp Secy*
Johnny Varecha, *Opers Mgr*
EMP: 15
SQ FT: 12,000
SALES (est): 2.4MM **Privately Held**
WEB: www.spokanetin.com
SIC: 3444 Sheet metalwork

(G-12522)
SPOKANE WILBERT VAULT COMPANY (PA)
Also Called: Wilbert Precast
2215 E Brooklyn Ave (99217-7702)
PHONE...................509 325-4573
Dan T Houk, *President*
Scott Erickson, *Sales Executive*
Kelli Jenson, *Mktg Dir*
Johnny Sanchez, *Office Mgr*
Mike Dooley, *Branch Mgr*
▲ **EMP:** 4 **EST:** 1906
SQ FT: 20,000
SALES: 12MM **Privately Held**
WEB: www.wilbertprecast.com
SIC: 3272 1542 Burial vaults, concrete or precast terrazzo; septic tanks, concrete; tanks, concrete; meter boxes, concrete; mausoleum construction

(G-12523)
SPRAY CENTER ELECTRONICS INC
9721 W Flight Dr (99224-5189)
PHONE...................509 838-2209
Shayne Zielske, *President*
Scott Zielske, *Vice Pres*
Margaret Zielske, *Treasurer*
EMP: 5
SQ FT: 7,200
SALES: 2.3MM **Privately Held**
WEB: www.spraycenter.com
SIC: 5083 3523 5999 Agricultural machinery & equipment; farm machinery & equipment; farm equipment & supplies

(G-12524)
STANDARD DIGITAL PRINT CO INC
256 W Riverside Ave (99201-0118)
PHONE...................509 624-2985
Steven J Lundberg, *President*
Leon Davis, *Vice Pres*
Krista Davis, *Treasurer*
Kathy Lundberg, *Admin Sec*
EMP: 14 **EST:** 1909
SQ FT: 5,000
SALES (est): 2.2MM **Privately Held**
WEB: www.sbprint.com
SIC: 7334 2752 Blueprinting service; commercial printing, lithographic

(G-12525)
STANFORD TECHNOLOGY INC
1010 N Normandie St # 305 (99201-2271)
P.O. Box 1218, Okanogan (98840-1218)
PHONE...................509 638-1191
Arthur E Stanford, *President*
William Stanford, *Vice Pres*
EMP: 4
SQ FT: 1,600
SALES (est): 402.3K **Privately Held**
WEB: www.stanford-technology.com
SIC: 7371 7372 Computer software systems analysis & design, custom; prepackaged software

(G-12526)
STEEL STRUCTURES AMERICA INC
4006 N Division St (99207-1745)
PHONE...................509 590-1230
EMP: 2
SALES (est): 148.8K **Privately Held**
SIC: 3448 Prefabricated metal buildings

(G-12527)
STEELHEAD SPECIALTY MINERALS
1212 N Washington St # 107 (99201-2441)
PHONE...................509 328-5685
Wallace McGregor, *President*
Thomas Menner, *Vice Pres*
EMP: 4
SQ FT: 500
SALES (est): 117.5K **Privately Held**
SIC: 3295 Minerals, ground or treated

(G-12528)
STEPHEN M KRAFT
1311 W Maxine Ct (99208-8837)
PHONE...................509 465-1980
Stephen Kraft, *Principal*
EMP: 2
SALES (est): 184K **Privately Held**
SIC: 2022 Processed cheese

(G-12529)
STEVE CZAKO ASSOCIATES
3025 S Geiger Blvd (99224-5409)
PHONE...................509 624-7018
EMP: 2
SALES (est): 112.6K **Privately Held**
SIC: 2759 Commercial Printing

(G-12530)
STICKER SHOCK SIGNS INC
4023 E Sprague Ave (99202-4848)
P.O. Box 4040 (99220-0040)
PHONE...................509 535-0070
Clarence I Paulsen, *President*
EMP: 3
SALES (est): 455K **Privately Held**
SIC: 3993 Signs & advertising specialties

(G-12531)
STRAIN NIGHT VISION & SECURITY
5709 N Ella St (99212-1628)
PHONE...................509 926-2025
Mark Strain, *Owner*
EMP: 2
SALES (est): 206.1K **Privately Held**
WEB: www.strainsecurity.com
SIC: 3699 Security devices; security control equipment & systems

(G-12532)
SUMMER RRH LLC
Also Called: River Ridge Hardware
2803 W Garland Ave (99205-2376)
PHONE...................509 328-0915
Lawrence J Myers,
Peggy Lusk, *Administration*
EMP: 15 **EST:** 2017
SALES: 1.7MM **Privately Held**
SIC: 5251 7359 2499 Builders' hardware; equipment rental & leasing; picture & mirror frames, wood

(G-12533)
SUPERIOR CRAFTED CABINETS
Also Called: Superior Construction
1612 S Campbell St (99202)
P.O. Box 923, Airway Heights (99001-0923)
PHONE...................509 535-9403

Spokane - Spokane County (G-12534)

Chad Fagerland, *President*
Anna Fagerland, *Treasurer*
EMP: 9
SQ FT: 4,000
SALES: 500K **Privately Held**
SIC: 2434 Wood kitchen cabinets

(G-12534)
SUPERIOR TRAMWAY CO INC
2311 E Main Ave (99202-7002)
PHONE 509 483-6181
James L Ellis, *President*
John Ellis, *Vice Pres*
EMP: 4
SQ FT: 30,000
SALES (est): 583.9K
SALES (corp-wide): 786.6K **Privately Held**
WEB: www.superiortramway.com
SIC: 3799 Ski lifts, tows or gondolas
PA: Aerial Engineering Inc
  15501 N Lantern Ln
  Spokane WA 99208
  509 466-6292

(G-12535)
SURE-FIT SEAT COVERS
1730 W Broadway Ave (99201-1818)
PHONE 509 326-0122
Rick Walsh, *Owner*
EMP: 3
SQ FT: 2,646
SALES (est): 290.5K **Privately Held**
SIC: 3111 Upholstery leather

(G-12536)
SURVIVAL GEAR SYSTEMS
9708 N Nevada St Ste 204 (99216-6012)
PHONE 866 257-2978
Michael Semerad, *Principal*
EMP: 2
SALES (est): 111.6K **Privately Held**
SIC: 5941 2311 2329 5999 Sporting goods & bicycle shops; military uniforms, men's & youths': purchased materials; policemen's uniforms: made from purchased materials; field jackets, military; police supply stores; first aid, snake bite & burn kits

(G-12537)
SUSAN WEINHANDL
Also Called: Patriot Support Services
3310 W Eagles Nest Ln (99208-8760)
PHONE 509 953-4329
Susan Weinhandl, *Owner*
EMP: 2
SALES (est): 141.6K **Privately Held**
SIC: 3715 Truck trailers

(G-12538)
SYNTHIGEN LLC
717 W Sprague Ave # 1600 (99201-3922)
PHONE 208 772-7294
Jed Morris,
Jack Zimmer,
EMP: 7
SALES (est): 409.9K **Privately Held**
SIC: 3599 Industrial machinery

(G-12539)
SYSTEMATIC MACHINERY LLC
13824 E Francis Ave (99217-9674)
PHONE 509 892-0399
David B Shill, *Owner*
Karen Shill,
EMP: 14
SQ FT: 7,000
SALES (est): 1.5MM **Privately Held**
WEB: www.systematicmachinery.com
SIC: 3599 Machine shop, jobbing & repair

(G-12540)
SYTECH INC
3900 E Main Ave (99202-4737)
PHONE 509 924-7797
Scott E Young, *President*
EMP: 35
SQ FT: 50,000
SALES (est): 11.9MM **Privately Held**
SIC: 3444 Sheet metal specialties, not stamped

(G-12541)
T R RIZZUTO PIZZA CRUST INC
3420 E Riverside Ave (99202-4754)
PHONE 509 536-9268
Tony Rizzuto, *President*
Joe Rizzuto, *Vice Pres*
Nancy Frye, *Regl Sales Mgr*
Rebecca Rizzuto, *Admin Sec*
▲ **EMP:** 55
SQ FT: 16,800
SALES (est): 9.5MM **Privately Held**
WEB: www.rizzutofoods.com
SIC: 2045 Pizza doughs, prepared: from purchased flour

(G-12542)
TAI INCORPORATED
501 N Riverpoint Blvd (99202-1659)
PHONE 509 747-6111
M E Agg, *President*
EMP: 2
SALES (est): 158.7K **Privately Held**
SIC: 1081 Metal mining services

(G-12543)
TAINIO BIOLOGICALS INC
4814 S Ben Franklin Ln (99224-5462)
P.O. Box 19185 (99219-9185)
PHONE 509 747-5471
Athena Tainio, *President*
Steve Becker, *Vice Pres*
Dennis Warnecke, *Sales Staff*
Amy Becker, *VP Mktg*
Marc Tainio, *Officer*
▲ **EMP:** 15
SALES: 2MM **Privately Held**
WEB: www.tainio.com
SIC: 2873 Fertilizers: natural (organic), except compost

(G-12544)
TAKEDA PHARMACEUTICALS USA INC
446 W 18th Ave (99203-2009)
PHONE 509 747-5551
Michael Gross, *Principal*
Brian Sherle, *Sales Staff*
EMP: 3 **Privately Held**
SIC: 2834 Pharmaceutical preparations
HQ: Takeda Pharmaceuticals U.S.A., Inc.
  1 Takeda Pkwy
  Deerfield IL 60015
  224 554-6500

(G-12545)
TAMARACK SOFTWARE INC
1616 W Dean Ave (99201-1825)
PHONE 509 329-0456
Mickey Orcutt, *Principal*
Ryan Bleeker, *Chief Engr*
EMP: 2
SQ FT: 698
SALES (est): 129.8K **Privately Held**
SIC: 7372 Business oriented computer software

(G-12546)
TATE HONEY FARM
8900 E Maringo Dr (99212-1827)
PHONE 509 924-6669
Jerome Tate, *Owner*
EMP: 2
SALES (est): 56.4K **Privately Held**
WEB: www.tateshoneyfarm.com
SIC: 0279 3999 Apiary (bee & honey farm); beekeepers' supplies

(G-12547)
TATE TECHNOLOGY INC
3102 E Trent Ave Ste 100 (99202-3800)
PHONE 509 534-2500
Scott Tate, *President*
Susan Mitchell, *Human Resources*
Tim Sayer, *Natl Sales Mgr*
Lee Tate, *Director*
Chase Copeland, *Admin Sec*
EMP: 43
SQ FT: 38,500
SALES (est): 7.2MM **Privately Held**
WEB: www.tatetech.com
SIC: 3679 Electronic circuits

(G-12548)
TECK AMERICAN INCORPORATED (HQ)
501 N Riverpoint Blvd # 300 (99202-1659)
P.O. Box 3087 (99220-3087)
PHONE 509 747-6111
Norman B Keevil, *Ch of Bd*
Mayank M Ashar, *President*
Donald R Lindsay, *President*
Warren S R Seyffert, *Principal*
Takashi Kuriyama, *Exec VP*
▲ **EMP:** 30
SQ FT: 17,000
SALES (est): 731.9MM
SALES (corp-wide): 9.5B **Privately Held**
SIC: 1081 Exploration, metal mining
PA: Teck Resources Limited
  550 Burrard St Suite 3300
  Vancouver BC V6C 0
  604 699-4000

(G-12549)
TECK AMERICAN METAL SALES INC
501 N Riverpoint Blvd (99202-1659)
PHONE 509 747-6111
Phillip Pesek, *CEO*
EMP: 8
SALES (est): 16.2K **Privately Held**
SIC: 3313 Electrometallurgical products

(G-12550)
TECK CO LLC
501 N Riverpoint Blvd (99202-1659)
PHONE 509 747-6111
Magg, *Principal*
EMP: 2
SALES (est): 203.7K **Privately Held**
SIC: 1081 Exploration, metal mining

(G-12551)
TEMPUS CELLARS
8 N Post St Ste 8 # 8 (99201-0702)
PHONE 509 368-9267
EMP: 2
SALES (est): 77.2K **Privately Held**
SIC: 2084 Wines

(G-12552)
TENEFF JEWELRY MFG CO
421 W Riverside Ave # 280 (99201-0402)
P.O. Box 195 (99210-0195)
PHONE 509 747-1038
Steven G Teneff, *CEO*
Mike Sudlow, *President*
EMP: 23
SQ FT: 1,500
SALES (est): 1.4MM **Privately Held**
SIC: 7631 3911 3915 Jewelry repair services; jewelry, precious metal; jewelers' materials & lapidary work

(G-12553)
TESORO CORPORATION
228 S Thor St (99202-4954)
PHONE 509 533-2705
Barry Bassette, *Branch Mgr*
EMP: 9 **Publicly Held**
WEB: www.tesoropetroleum.com
SIC: 1311 Crude petroleum production; natural gas production
HQ: Andeavor Llc
  19100 Ridgewood Pkwy
  San Antonio TX 78259
  210 626-6000

(G-12554)
THE RIFF
215 W Main Ave (99201-0111)
PHONE 509 280-1300
Tyler Youngstrom, *Principal*
EMP: 2
SALES (est): 174.6K **Privately Held**
SIC: 3651 Household audio & video equipment

(G-12555)
THERAPEUTIC DIMENSION INC
Also Called: Rangemaster Shoulder Therapy
319 W Hastings Rd (99218-5012)
PHONE 509 323-9275
Robert Allen, *CEO*
▲ **EMP:** 3
SQ FT: 6,300
SALES (est): 552.6K **Privately Held**
SIC: 5047 3841 Medical equipment & supplies; surgical & medical instruments

(G-12556)
TICONDEROGA ENTERPRISES
5212 N Northwood Dr (99212-1664)
PHONE 509 922-2411
Ethan Allen, *Owner*
EMP: 2
SALES (est): 170K **Privately Held**
SIC: 2721 Periodicals

(G-12557)
TIK TIK GARMENT MANUFACTURING
160 S Cowley St (99202-1553)
PHONE 509 624-0806
Clodall Jacobson, *Owner*
EMP: 10
SQ FT: 1,800
SALES: 120K **Privately Held**
WEB: www.tiktikclothing.com
SIC: 2337 5621 2339 Uniforms, except athletic: women's, misses' & juniors'; women's clothing stores; women's & misses' outerwear

(G-12558)
TIM KROTZER
Also Called: Tri-Form Top Company
10909 N Iroquois Dr (99208-9069)
PHONE 509 487-2704
Tim Krotzer, *Owner*
EMP: 2
SQ FT: 13,000
SALES: 130K **Privately Held**
SIC: 2542 5211 2541 Counters or counter display cases: except wood; lumber & other building materials; wood partitions & fixtures

(G-12559)
TIPKE MANUFACTURING COMPANY
321 N Helena St (99202-2905)
PHONE 509 534-5336
James M Tipke, *President*
Ryan Ford, *Foreman/Supr*
▲ **EMP:** 25
SQ FT: 20,000
SALES (est): 4.8MM **Privately Held**
WEB: www.tipkemfg.com
SIC: 3599 3499 Machine shop, jobbing & repair; wheels: wheelbarrow, stroller, etc.; disc, stamped metal

(G-12560)
TL HOLDINGS INC
Also Called: 509
10424 W Aero Rd Unit G (99224-9405)
PHONE 877 743-3509
Thomas Lee Delanoy, *President*
▲ **EMP:** 16
SALES (est): 2.7MM
SALES (corp-wide): 6B **Publicly Held**
SIC: 3199 Helmets, leather
PA: Polaris Industries Inc.
  2100 Highway 55
  Medina MN 55340
  763 542-0500

(G-12561)
TODD M BEARDEN
226 S Washington St (99201-4318)
PHONE 509 624-2875
Todd M Bearden, *Principal*
EMP: 2
SALES (est): 135.3K **Privately Held**
SIC: 3949 Skateboards

(G-12562)
TOLIYS JIG FABRICATION
2530 E 4th Ave (99202-4023)
PHONE 509 534-2261
Anatoliy Nosov, *Principal*
EMP: 2
SALES (est): 170K **Privately Held**
SIC: 3599 Crankshafts & camshafts, machining

(G-12563)
TORTILLA UNION
808 W Main Ave (99201-2950)
PHONE 509 381-5162

Jayne Blackwell, *Principal*
EMP: 5
SALES (est): 161K **Privately Held**
SIC: 2099 Tortillas, fresh or refrigerated

(G-12564)
TOWER MOUNTAIN PRODUCTS
5721 S Willamette Ln (99223-1661)
PHONE.................................509 448-4000
John Burke, *Principal*
EMP: 3
SALES (est): 156.9K **Privately Held**
SIC: 2051 Bakery: wholesale or wholesale/retail combined

(G-12565)
TOWNSHEND CELLAR INC
1222 N Regal St (99202-3682)
P.O. Box 4067 (99220-0067)
PHONE.................................509 919-3699
Michael Townshend, *Principal*
Brendon Townshend, *Principal*
EMP: 5 **EST:** 2016
SALES (est): 83K **Privately Held**
SIC: 2084 Wines

(G-12566)
TRAVIS PATTERN & FOUNDRY INC (PA)
1413 E Hawthorne Rd (99218-3100)
P.O. Box 6325 (99217-0906)
PHONE.................................509 466-3545
Travis Garske, *President*
Scott Chaffin, *Vice Pres*
Daniel Garske, *Vice Pres*
Gene Johnson, *Project Mgr*
Mary Wright, *Admin Sec*
▲ **EMP:** 500
SQ FT: 360,000
SALES (est): 115.6MM **Privately Held**
SIC: 3523 3369 3313 3321 Irrigation equipment, self-propelled; castings, except die-castings, precision; alloys, additive, except copper: not made in blast furnaces; gray & ductile iron foundries; switches, electronic applications

(G-12567)
TREE OF KINDNESS INC (PA)
Also Called: Tok
1119 W 1st Ave (99201-4005)
P.O. Box 651 (99210-0651)
PHONE.................................509 315-2206
Steven Brian Main, *President*
EMP: 5
SALES (est): 940.6K **Privately Held**
SIC: 2899 Oils & essential oils

(G-12568)
TRESKO MONUMENT INC (PA)
Also Called: Washington Stone
1979 W 5th Ave (99201-5310)
PHONE.................................509 838-3196
John Tresko, *President*
Bill Tresko, *Corp Secy*
Richard Tresko, *Vice Pres*
EMP: 15
SQ FT: 11,000
SALES (est): 1.2MM **Privately Held**
SIC: 3281 Monuments, cut stone (not finishing or lettering only); building stone products

(G-12569)
TRIPLE B CORPORATION
Also Called: Charlie's Produce
3530 E Ferry Ave (99202-4631)
PHONE.................................509 535-7393
Alex Poummer, *General Mgr*
Trevor Magney, *Plant Mgr*
Terry Braithwaite, *Buyer*
Julie Thompson, *Finance Dir*
Karen Hendricks, *Finance Mgr*
EMP: 74
SALES (corp-wide): 366.8MM **Privately Held**
WEB: www.triplebcorp.com
SIC: 5148 2099 Fruits, fresh; vegetables, fresh; salads, fresh or refrigerated; vegetables, peeled for the trade
PA: Triple "b" Corporation
4103 2nd Ave S
Seattle WA 98134
206 625-1412

(G-12570)
TRIUMPH COMPOSITE SYSTEMS INC
1514 S Flint Rd (99224-9447)
P.O. Box 19357 (99219-9357)
PHONE.................................509 623-8536
Patrick Jones, *President*
Chuck Ruchert, *Principal*
Kathleen Sharp, *Principal*
Jonathan Merkel, *Design Engr*
▲ **EMP:** 463
SALES (est): 100.8MM **Publicly Held**
WEB: www.triumphgrp.com
SIC: 3724 3728 Aircraft engines & engine parts; aircraft landing assemblies & brakes
PA: Triumph Group, Inc.
899 Cassatt Rd Ste 210
Berwyn PA 19312

(G-12571)
TRUMARK INDUSTRIES INC
4917 N Penn Ave (99206-4475)
PHONE.................................509 534-0644
Jack Brace, *President*
EMP: 40
SQ FT: 82,000
SALES (est): 6.4MM **Privately Held**
SIC: 5031 2421 2431 Lumber: rough, dressed & finished; cut stock, softwood; millwork

(G-12572)
TTI INC
8704 E Red Oak Dr (99217-9265)
PHONE.................................509 998-9456
EMP: 2
SALES (est): 129.5K **Privately Held**
SIC: 3799 Recreational vehicles

(G-12573)
TTS OLD IRON BREWERY LLC
8707 E Honorof Ln (99223-8336)
PHONE.................................509 847-4393
Travis Thosath, *Principal*
EMP: 4
SALES (est): 91.3K **Privately Held**
SIC: 2082 Malt beverages

(G-12574)
TYPEBEE LTTRPRESS PRNTSHOP LLC
914 S Monroe St (99204-3836)
PHONE.................................509 979-6017
EMP: 2
SALES (est): 83.9K **Privately Held**
SIC: 2752 Commercial printing, lithographic

(G-12575)
UNIFIRE INC
3904 E Trent Ave (99202-4425)
PHONE.................................509 535-7746
Jeffery Schwartz, *CEO*
EMP: 13
SQ FT: 5,000
SALES: 26MM
SALES (corp-wide): 2.3MM **Privately Held**
WEB: www.unifireusa.com
SIC: 3546 3564 5087 Saws & sawing equipment; ventilating fans: industrial or commercial; firefighting equipment
PA: Mission Ready Solutions Inc
750 W Pender St Suite 804
Vancouver BC V6C 2
877 479-7778

(G-12576)
UNINTERRUPTIBLE POWER SYSTEMS
3003 N Crestline St (99207-4702)
PHONE.................................509 327-7722
Toby Willis, *Principal*
EMP: 2
SALES (est): 88.3K **Privately Held**
SIC: 3691 Storage batteries

(G-12577)
UNITED SEATING & MOBILITY LLC
423 E Cleveland Ave (99207-2008)
PHONE.................................509 484-6720
Valerie Eastwood, *Branch Mgr*
EMP: 3
SALES (corp-wide): 3.2B **Privately Held**
SIC: 2531 Stadium seating
HQ: United Seating & Mobility Llc
975 Hornet Dr
Hazelwood MO 63042
800 500-9150

(G-12578)
US POLYCO INC
8914 N Torrey Ln (99208-9167)
PHONE.................................509 413-1006
Thomas Nichols, *Principal*
EMP: 2
SALES (est): 117.4K **Privately Held**
SIC: 2951 Asphalt paving mixtures & blocks

(G-12579)
VALLEYFORD METAL CRAFTERS LLC
6313 E Rutter Ave (99212-1445)
PHONE.................................509 448-5583
Charlie Goldbach, *President*
EMP: 25 **EST:** 1985
SALES (est): 5.2MM **Privately Held**
SIC: 3441 3599 Fabricated structural metal; industrial machinery

(G-12580)
VALUE PLUS
9623 N Indian Trail Rd (99208-9360)
P.O. Box 9928 (99209-0928)
PHONE.................................509 468-0393
Joanne Sandstrom, *Owner*
Ronald Sandstorm, *Owner*
EMP: 2
SALES (est): 135.9K **Privately Held**
SIC: 2677 Envelopes

(G-12581)
VERTICAL LIMITS LLC
4116 W Indian Trail Rd (99208-4905)
PHONE.................................509 294-9878
Amber Reynolds, *Principal*
EMP: 2
SALES (est): 132.1K **Privately Held**
SIC: 2591 Blinds vertical

(G-12582)
VICTORY CIRCLE SIGNS
2212 E Decatur Ave (99208-2734)
PHONE.................................509 489-3083
EMP: 2 **EST:** 2010
SALES (est): 99K **Privately Held**
SIC: 3993 Mfg Signs/Advertising Specialties

(G-12583)
WASHINGTON EQP MFG CO INC (PA)
Also Called: Wemco
5510 W Thorpe Rd (99224-5371)
PHONE.................................509 244-4773
Karma Rouse, *President*
Matt Turner, *Exec VP*
John Rouse, *Vice Pres*
Justin Almeida, *Project Mgr*
Tj Shields, *Purch Mgr*
▲ **EMP:** 40
SQ FT: 18,000
SALES (est): 7.8MM **Privately Held**
WEB: www.wemcoinc.com
SIC: 3531 3535 3599 3523 Aerial work platforms; hydraulic/elec. truck/carrier mounted; bucket type conveyor systems; machine shop, jobbing & repair; farm machinery & equipment; cranes, overhead traveling

(G-12584)
WEAR-TEK INC
8021 W Highway 2 (99224-9019)
PHONE.................................509 747-4139
Bill Reynolds, *President*
Jeff Bailey, *General Mgr*
Robert F Underhill, *Vice Pres*
Jeffrey Bailey, *Treasurer*
Mike Summers, *Natl Sales Mgr*
EMP: 75
SQ FT: 6,000
SALES (est): 12MM **Privately Held**
WEB: www.wear-tek.com
SIC: 3369 3364 3325 3321 Nonferrous foundries; nonferrous die-castings except aluminum; steel foundries; gray & ductile iron foundries

(G-12585)
WESTERN AVIONICS INC
6095 E Rutter Ave Ste 1 (99212-1419)
P.O. Box 11835, Spokane Valley (99211-1835)
PHONE.................................509 534-7371
David Hood, *President*
Barry Huck, *Vice Pres*
EMP: 6
SALES (est): 1.3MM **Privately Held**
WEB: www.pilotsplace.com
SIC: 3721 7622 Aircraft; aircraft radio equipment repair

(G-12586)
WESTERN STATES ASPHALT LLC (HQ)
4327 N Thor St (99217-7098)
PHONE.................................509 487-4560
Chip Ray, *President*
EMP: 14
SALES: 50MM
SALES (corp-wide): 8.5MM **Privately Held**
SIC: 3531 Asphalt plant, including gravel-mix type
PA: Western States Group, Llc
4327 N Thor St
Spokane WA 99217
509 487-4560

(G-12587)
WESTERN STATES GROUP LLC (PA)
4327 N Thor St (99217-7098)
PHONE.................................509 487-4560
David Lynch, *Manager*
EMP: 1
SALES: 8.5MM **Privately Held**
SIC: 6719 Personal holding companies, except banks; asphalt plant, including gravel-mix type

(G-12588)
WESTERN STTES STL FBRCTION INC
1515 E Holyoke Ave (99217-7524)
PHONE.................................509 489-8046
Jesse Price, *President*
EMP: 29 **EST:** 1989
SALES (est): 3.2MM **Privately Held**
SIC: 3312 5051 Tubes, steel & iron; steel

(G-12589)
WHITES BOOTS INC
4002 E Ferry Ave (99202-4646)
PHONE.................................509 535-1875
Gary W March, *President*
▲ **EMP:** 103
SQ FT: 40,000
SALES (est): 15.5MM **Privately Held**
WEB: www.whitesboots.com
SIC: 5661 3143 3144 Men's boots; women's boots; boots, dress or casual: men's; women's footwear, except athletic
HQ: Lacrosse Footwear, Inc.
17634 Ne Airport Way
Portland OR 97230
503 262-0110

(G-12590)
WIESE AND SON INC
4125 W Thorpe Rd (99224-4905)
PHONE.................................509 455-8610
Teri Wiese, *Treasurer*
EMP: 2 **EST:** 2012
SALES (est): 140.9K **Privately Held**
SIC: 3441 Fabricated structural metal

(G-12591)
WILDROSE LTD
Also Called: Wild Rose Graphics
134 N Madelia St (99202-3020)
P.O. Box 3945 (99220-3945)
PHONE.................................509 535-8555
Sherie C Hackney, *President*
Clayton Soliday, *Principal*
Donald D Hackney, *Vice Pres*
Pat Soliday, *Vice Pres*
Ken Kleiner, *Sales Staff*
EMP: 15
SQ FT: 6,150

Spokane - Spokane County (G-12592)

SALES (est): 1.6MM **Privately Held**
SIC: **5699** 5999 3993 2396 Sports apparel; trophies & plaques; signs & advertising specialties; automotive & apparel trimmings; pleating & stitching

(G-12592)
WILFORD NOORDA FOUNDATION
1318 E Nebraska Ave (99208-3469)
PHONE..................................509 487-6832
Steven Hoerner, *Principal*
Donna Hoerner, *Principal*
EMP: 2
SALES (est): 124.8K **Privately Held**
SIC: **3559** Special industry machinery

(G-12593)
WILLIAM LOUIS BECKER
Also Called: Bk Laser Art
3617 S Abbott Rd (99224-5009)
PHONE..................................509 624-3466
William Becker, *Principal*
EMP: 3
SALES (est): 161.8K **Privately Held**
SIC: **2796** Photoengraving plates, linecuts or halftones

(G-12594)
WILSON OIL INC
Also Called: Wilcox & Flegel
220 N Haven St (99202-3824)
PHONE..................................509 536-3550
Donovan Bresco, *Manager*
EMP: 12
SALES (corp-wide): 147.9MM **Privately Held**
SIC: **2992** Lubricating oils & greases
PA: Wilson Oil, Inc.
  95 Panel Way
  Longview WA 98632
  360 575-9222

(G-12595)
YOURCEBA LLC
5123 N Post St (99205-5244)
PHONE..................................509 747-5027
John Temple, *Principal*
EMP: 3
SALES (est): 208.5K **Privately Held**
SIC: **3841** Surgical & medical instruments

Spokane Valley
Spokane County

(G-12596)
A-1 ILLUMINATED SIGN COMPANY
511 N Ella Rd (99212-2855)
PHONE..................................509 534-6134
Delbert Luttrell, *President*
EMP: 10
SQ FT: 5,500
SALES (est): 1MM **Privately Held**
WEB: www.a1illuminated.com
SIC: **3993** Signs & advertising specialties

(G-12597)
AC LAROCCO PIZZA CO
12412 E Desmet Ave # 203 (99216-5082)
PHONE..................................509 924-9113
Clarence Scott, *President*
EMP: 4 EST: 1996
SALES (est): 294.9K **Publicly Held**
WEB: www.aclarocco.com
SIC: **2041** 2038 Pizza mixes; pizza, frozen
PA: Fresh Harvest Products, Inc.
  280 Madison Ave Ste 1005
  New York NY 10016

(G-12598)
ACADIE WOODWORKS INCORPORATED
11319 E Carlisle Ave # 4 (99206-7651)
PHONE..................................509 230-6874
Jonathan Gay, *President*
EMP: 2
SALES (est): 180K **Privately Held**
SIC: **2431** Millwork

(G-12599)
ACCUCON INC
904 N Dyer Rd (99212-1007)
P.O. Box 11342 (99211-1342)
PHONE..................................509 534-4460
Hannalore Rae, *President*
David Rae, *Vice Pres*
EMP: 3
SQ FT: 8,000
SALES: 300K **Privately Held**
WEB: www.accucon.com
SIC: **3535** Conveyors & conveying equipment

(G-12600)
ACT MANUFACTURING INC
10310 E Buckeye Ln (99206-4241)
PHONE..................................509 893-4100
EMP: 2
SALES (est): 173.3K **Privately Held**
SIC: **3999** Manufacturing industries

(G-12601)
AFIRM CONSTRUCTION INC
5423 N Rees Ct (99216-3003)
PHONE..................................509 928-4361
Gary Norton, *Owner*
Kari Norton, *Partner*
EMP: 2
SALES (est): 133.4K **Privately Held**
SIC: **3589** High pressure cleaning equipment

(G-12602)
AG ENERGY SOLUTIONS INC
7921 E Broadway Ave (99212-2740)
PHONE..................................509 343-3156
Philip Appel, *President*
Thomas Weir, *CTO*
EMP: 13
SQ FT: 2,500
SALES: 500K **Privately Held**
SIC: **3533** 8711 Oil & gas field machinery; consulting engineer

(G-12603)
ALACAN SOLATENS
10221 E Montgomery Dr (99206-4240)
PHONE..................................509 462-2310
Alacan Solatens, *Principal*
▲ EMP: 2
SALES (est): 146.6K **Privately Held**
SIC: **3334** Primary aluminum

(G-12604)
ALLIANCE MCH SYSTEMS INTL LLC
Also Called: J & L Industries
5303 E Desmet Ave (99212-0915)
PHONE..................................509 842-5104
Mark Duchesne, *CEO*
Brian Barnes, *Vice Pres*
Steve Ponsness, *Buyer*
Chris Enzler, *Engineer*
Jose Lara, *Engineer*
◆ EMP: 300
SQ FT: 52,000
SALES (est): 117.9MM
SALES (corp-wide): 141.1MM **Privately Held**
WEB: www.jlcompanies.com
SIC: **3554** Corrugating machines, paper; folding machines, paper
PA: H Enterprises International, Inc.
  120 S 6th St Ste 2300
  Minneapolis MN 55402
  612 343-8293

(G-12605)
ALLIANCE PACKAGING LLC
Spokane Packaging
3808 N Sullivan Rd # 21 (99216-1610)
PHONE..................................509 924-7623
Hap Gotzian, *Sales Associate*
Craig Mc Donald, *Manager*
EMP: 70 **Privately Held**
SIC: **2653** 2671 5199 5113 Boxes, corrugated: made from purchased materials; packaging paper & plastics film, coated & laminated; packaging materials; corrugated & solid fiber boxes
HQ: Alliance Packaging, Llc
  1000 Sw 43rd St
  Renton WA 98057
  425 291-3500

(G-12606)
AMBIENT WATER CORPORATION
7721 E Trent Ave (99212-2213)
P.O. Box 119, Liberty Lake (99019-0119)
PHONE..................................509 474-9451
Keith White, *CEO*
Jeff Stockdale, *President*
Michael Wende, *Admin Sec*
EMP: 3
SALES: 40.7K **Privately Held**
SIC: **3589** Water purification equipment, household type

(G-12607)
AMERICAN ALLOY LLC
3808 N Sullivan Rd 11m (99216-1616)
PHONE..................................509 921-5794
Brett Stevens, *General Mgr*
Michael Book, *Mfg Staff*
Pat Hays, *Controller*
Garret Guinn,
EMP: 65
SALES: 7MM **Privately Held**
SIC: **3353** Aluminum sheet & strip

(G-12608)
AMERICAN BOTTLING COMPANY
Also Called: Dr. Pepper
6815 E Mission Ave (99212-1152)
PHONE..................................509 328-6984
Kristi Totten, *Human Res Dir*
Edward Narado, *Branch Mgr*
Eric Merkel, *Manager*
EMP: 70 **Publicly Held**
SIC: **2086** Soft drinks: packaged in cans, bottles, etc.
HQ: The American Bottling Company
  5301 Legacy Dr
  Plano TX 75024

(G-12609)
AMERICAN CNC FABRICATING INC
9922 E Montgomery Dr # 24 (99206-4158)
PHONE..................................509 315-4095
Connor S Nicholas, *Vice Pres*
EMP: 6
SALES (est): 694.9K **Privately Held**
SIC: **3089** Plastic processing

(G-12610)
AMERICAN DRILLING CORP LLC (PA)
19208 E Broadway Ave (99016-8577)
PHONE..................................509 921-7836
Steve Elloway, *President*
Alex M Deeds, *Vice Pres*
Ken Joy, *Opers Staff*
Cassandra Elloway, *CFO*
EMP: 44 EST: 2008
SQ FT: 21,000
SALES (est): 11.8MM **Privately Held**
SIC: **1799** 1481 Core drilling & cutting; mine exploration, nonmetallic minerals

(G-12611)
AMERICAN INNOVATIVE MFG LLC
Also Called: Aim
1419 N Thierman Rd (99212-1125)
PHONE..................................509 244-2730
John Hjaltalin, *Mng Member*
Michael McKinney, *Mng Member*
EMP: 6
SQ FT: 6,000
SALES (est): 678.8K **Privately Held**
SIC: **3999** Barber & beauty shop equipment

(G-12612)
AMERICAN MIN & TUNNELING LLC (PA)
19208 E Broadway Ave (99016-8577)
PHONE..................................509 921-7836
Steve Elloway, *President*
Alex M Deeds, *Vice Pres*
Cassandra Elloway, *CFO*
EMP: 7
SQ FT: 20,000
SALES (est): 1.4MM **Privately Held**
SIC: **1241** 1629 7363 1799 Mine preparation services; preparing shafts or tunnels, anthracite mining; preparing shafts or tunnels, bituminous or lignite mining; land reclamation; engineering help service; hydraulic equipment, installation & service

(G-12613)
AMERICAN MOBILE DRUG TESTING (PA)
Also Called: Drug Free Alliance
10905 E Montgomery Dr # 4 (99206-6606)
PHONE..................................509 921-2730
Peter Lichtnam, *CEO*
Renda Leichtnam, *Administration*
EMP: 8
SALES (est): 559K **Privately Held**
WEB: www.drugfreealliance.com
SIC: **2899**

(G-12614)
AMERICAN RECYCLING CORP
6203 E Mission Ave (99212-1206)
P.O. Box 11337 (99211-1337)
PHONE..................................509 535-4271
Glenn Dart, *Systems Mgr*
EMP: 21
SALES (corp-wide): 41.2MM **Privately Held**
SIC: **7389** 5093 4953 3341 Scrap steel cutting; nonferrous metals scrap; refuse systems; secondary nonferrous metals
HQ: American Recycling Corp
  6203 E Mission Ave
  Spokane Valley WA 99212
  509 535-4271

(G-12615)
AMERICAN SIGN & INDICATOR
1013 S Mariam St (99206-3552)
PHONE..................................509 926-6979
Steve Bishop, *Principal*
EMP: 2
SALES (est): 119.4K **Privately Held**
SIC: **3993** Signs & advertising specialties

(G-12616)
AMERISTAR MEATS INC (HQ)
210 S Mckinnon Rd (99212-0742)
PHONE..................................509 535-2049
Timothy Loveall, *President*
Peter Smith, *Vice Pres*
Steven Twist, *Vice Pres*
EMP: 125
SQ FT: 50,000
SALES (est): 55.9MM
SALES (corp-wide): 4.7B **Privately Held**
WEB: www.spmeats.com
SIC: **5147** 3556 Meats, fresh; meat processing machinery
PA: Services Group Of America, Inc.
  16100 N 71st St Ste 500
  Scottsdale AZ 85254
  480 927-4000

(G-12617)
ANDEAVOR
Also Called: 2go
13819 E Trent Ave (99216-2230)
PHONE..................................509 928-5632
Victor Azar, *Branch Mgr*
EMP: 9 **Publicly Held**
WEB: www.tesoropetroleum.com
SIC: **1311** Crude petroleum production; natural gas production
HQ: Andeavor Llc
  19100 Ridgewood Pkwy
  San Antonio TX 78259
  210 626-6000

(G-12618)
ANDRITZ HYDRO CORP
15708 E Marietta Ln (99216-1828)
PHONE..................................704 943-4343
EMP: 2 EST: 1991
SALES (est): 135.9K **Privately Held**
SIC: **1081** Metal mining exploration & development services

(G-12619)
ANOXPRESS LLC
4910 N Bolivar Rd (99216-1435)
PHONE..................................509 220-2741
Andrey Arnaut, *Owner*

GEOGRAPHIC SECTION

Spokane Valley - Spokane County (G-12649)

EMP: 4
SQ FT: 300
SALES: 800K Privately Held
SIC: 3537 Trucks: freight, baggage, etc.: industrial, except mining

(G-12620)
ANVIL ALLOY
18127 E 8th Ave (99016-8750)
PHONE 509 891-5914
Lonny Benn, *President*
EMP: 2
SALES (est): 176.4K Privately Held
SIC: 7692 Welding repair

(G-12621)
APEX INDUSTRIES INC
3808 N Sullivan Rd 14d (99216-1613)
PHONE 509 928-8450
Matthew S Matthews, *President*
C Gordon Cudney, *Vice Pres*
EMP: 75
SQ FT: 66,000
SALES (est): 11.8MM Privately Held
SIC: 3479 3444 Painting, coating & hot dipping; coating of metals & formed products; coating of metals with plastic or resins; painting of metal products; sheet metalwork

(G-12622)
APOLLO ANTENNA & SALES INC (PA)
Also Called: Apollo Plastics
720 N Fancher Rd (99212-1053)
PHONE 509 534-6972
Steve Mc Donald, *President*
Maercel Roles, *General Mgr*
Mike Orlich, *Vice Pres*
Rob Anselmo, *Accounting Mgr*
EMP: 8
SALES (est): 5.4MM Privately Held
WEB: www.apollospas.com
SIC: 3999 5999 Hot tubs; spas & hot tubs

(G-12623)
APPLE BROOKE LLC
1220 S Marigold St (99037-9629)
PHONE 509 922-0696
EMP: 2
SALES (est): 85.9K Privately Held
SIC: 3571 Mfg Electronic Computers

(G-12624)
ARCHER-DANIELS-MIDLAND COMPANY
Also Called: ADM
3808 N Sullivan Rd Bldg 3 (99216-1608)
PHONE 509 534-2636
Marti Lynch, *Manager*
EMP: 4
SALES (corp-wide): 64.3B Publicly Held
WEB: www.admworld.com
SIC: 2041 5191 Flour & other grain mill products; animal feeds
PA: Archer-Daniels-Midland Company
77 W Wacker Dr Ste 4600
Chicago IL 60601
312 634-8100

(G-12625)
ARK COMMERCIAL ROOFING INC
11505 E Trent Ave (99206-4633)
PHONE 509 443-9300
Wilson Thomas, *President*
Kathleen Wilson, *Corp Secy*
EMP: 12
SQ FT: 1,200
SALES (est): 2.3MM Privately Held
WEB: www.arkcommercialroofing.com
SIC: 1761 3444 Roofing contractor; sheet metalwork

(G-12626)
ASC MACHINE TOOLS INC (PA)
900 N Fancher Rd (99212-1283)
P.O. Box 11619 (99211-1619)
PHONE 509 534-6600
Ray McGriff Jr, *President*
Don Cornell, *General Mgr*
Steve Countryman, *Opers Mgr*
Bob McLellan, *Purch Mgr*
Alishia Thomas, *Buyer*
▲ EMP: 180 EST: 1952

SQ FT: 158,800
SALES (est): 58.2MM Privately Held
WEB: www.ascmt.com
SIC: 3542 3549 3554 Sheet metalworking machines; coilers (metalworking machines); box making machines, paper

(G-12627)
ASH GROVE CEMENT COMPANY
Also Called: Spokane Terminal
1312 N Thierman Rd (99212-1125)
PHONE 509 928-4343
Tim Martin, *Manager*
EMP: 4
SALES (corp-wide): 30.6B Privately Held
WEB: www.ashgrove.com
SIC: 3241 Portland cement
HQ: Ash Grove Cement Company
11011 Cody St Ste 300
Overland Park KS 66210
913 451-8900

(G-12628)
ATLAS SUPPLY INC
12918 E Indiana Ave B (99216-2709)
PHONE 509 924-2417
Marni Sams, *Principal*
EMP: 2
SALES (corp-wide): 4.3B Publicly Held
SIC: 2891 Adhesives & sealants
HQ: Atlas Supply, Inc.
611 S Charlestown St
Seattle WA 98108
206 623-4697

(G-12629)
ATLAS SYSTEMS LLC
6416 E Main Ave (99212-2879)
PHONE 509 535-7775
Bryan W Vanhoff, *Mng Member*
Gary Vanhoff,
EMP: 4
SQ FT: 5,000
SALES (est): 411K Privately Held
WEB: www.atlassystems.net
SIC: 3535 Bulk handling conveyor systems

(G-12630)
ATS INLAND NW LLC (PA)
9507 E Sprague Ave (99206-3616)
PHONE 509 892-1000
William Kissinger, *Mng Member*
Jared Miller, *Software Dev*
Brian Allen,
EMP: 2
SQ FT: 3,000
SALES: 3MM Privately Held
SIC: 3822 Temperature controls, automatic

(G-12631)
AVIAN BALLOON COMPANY
12925 E Riverside Ave (99206-0754)
PHONE 509 928-6847
Forey Walter, *President*
Barbara Walter, *Corp Secy*
Noel Walter, *Vice Pres*
EMP: 6 EST: 1975
SQ FT: 5,000
SALES (est): 784K Privately Held
SIC: 3721 5945 Balloons, hot air (aircraft); hobby, toy & game shops

(G-12632)
AXAMA CORPORATION
2321 N Coleman Rd (99212-1458)
PHONE 509 922-8400
EMP: 6
SQ FT: 5,000
SALES: 75K Privately Held
SIC: 3829 Mfr Computer Aided Plotting Equipment

(G-12633)
AXIOM DRILLING CORP
19208 E Broadway Ave (99016-8577)
PHONE 509 921-7836
Steve Elloway, *CEO*
Alex M Deeds, *President*
Jason W Black, *CFO*
EMP: 10
SALES (est): 596.9K Privately Held
SIC: 1499 Mineral abrasives mining

(G-12634)
AXIS MFG
6010 E Alki Ave (99212-1064)
PHONE 509 368-9895
EMP: 2
SALES (est): 110.8K Privately Held
SIC: 3999 Manufacturing industries

(G-12635)
B G INSTRUMENTS INC
13607 E Trent Ave (99216-1284)
PHONE 509 893-9881
David Wright, *President*
Hannelore Wright, *Vice Pres*
EMP: 8
SQ FT: 3,000
SALES (est): 500K Privately Held
WEB: www.bginstruments.com
SIC: 3577 5112 Printers, computer; plotters, computer; computer & photocopying supplies

(G-12636)
BAREFOOTE CONCRETE INC
2804 S Progress Rd (99037-8301)
PHONE 509 879-3736
Robby Foote, *President*
EMP: 2
SALES (est): 154.3K Privately Held
SIC: 3721 3272 5032 Aircraft; concrete products; concrete building products

(G-12637)
BECKWITH & KUFFEL
11327 E Montgomery Dr # 5 (99206-7624)
PHONE 509 922-5222
Lou Kussel, *President*
EMP: 50 EST: 2010
SALES (est): 2.2MM Privately Held
SIC: 5999 5085 5084 3561 Engine & motor equipment & supplies; gaskets & seals; pumps & pumping equipment; pumps & pumping equipment

(G-12638)
BERG MANUFACTURING INC
6811 E Mission Ave (99212-1152)
PHONE 509 624-8921
Donald Myers, *President*
Craig Dolsby, *Exec VP*
Joseph Herzog, *CFO*
Andrew Barrett, *Exec Dir*
▼ EMP: 150
SQ FT: 130,000
SALES (est): 41.1MM
SALES (corp-wide): 51.6MM Privately Held
SIC: 3449 4731 Miscellaneous metalwork; freight transportation arrangement
PA: Berg Companies Inc.
6811 E Mission Ave
Spokane Valley WA 99212
509 624-8921

(G-12639)
BIMBO BAKERIES USA INC
Also Called: Oro Weat
5424 E Sprague Ave (99212-0823)
PHONE 509 688-3966
Andrea Hilly, *Manager*
EMP: 18 Privately Held
WEB: www.oroweat.com
SIC: 2051 Bakery: wholesale or wholesale/retail combined
HQ: Bimbo Bakeries Usa, Inc
255 Business Center Dr # 200
Horsham PA 19044
215 347-5500

(G-12640)
BIONIC BUILDERS LLC
2423 S Sunrise Rd (99206-3330)
PHONE 509 435-1114
Alexis Bradshaw, *Mng Member*
Mason Bradshaw, *Mng Member*
EMP: 2
SALES (est): 85.2K Privately Held
SIC: 3549 Assembly machines, including robotic

(G-12641)
BIT ELIXIR LLC
11511 E Valleyway Ave (99206-5127)
PHONE 509 842-4121
Quinn Hoener, *Mng Member*
Kris Pockell,

EMP: 2 EST: 2017
SALES: 16K Privately Held
SIC: 7372 7389 Prepackaged software;

(G-12642)
BLACK & DECKER (US) INC
5308 E Sprague Ave (99212-0821)
PHONE 509 535-9252
Bruce Moeller, *Branch Mgr*
EMP: 7
SALES (corp-wide): 13.9B Publicly Held
WEB: www.dewalt.com
SIC: 3546 Power-driven handtools
HQ: Black & Decker (U.S.) Inc.
1000 Stanley Dr
New Britain CT 06053
860 225-5111

(G-12643)
BLUE FALLS USA LP
3808 N Sullivan Rd N4 (99216-1616)
PHONE 509 891-1933
Nell T Jorgensen, *Principal*
◆ EMP: 2
SALES: 284K Privately Held
SIC: 3088 Tubs (bath, shower & laundry), plastic

(G-12644)
BONDARCHUK ANDREY
Also Called: Signs TEC
9923 E 10th Ave (99206-3513)
PHONE 509 290-2525
Andrey Bondarchuk, *Owner*
EMP: 2
SALES (est): 55.7K Privately Held
SIC: 3993 Signs & advertising specialties

(G-12645)
BRIGGS MCH & FABRICATION LLC
5308 E Sharp Ave (99212-0973)
P.O. Box 2988, Spokane (99220-2988)
PHONE 509 535-0125
Peter A Briggs, *President*
Pat Hanson, *Vice Pres*
Pat Hansen, *Financial Exec*
EMP: 15
SQ FT: 12,000
SALES (est): 2.8MM Privately Held
SIC: 3599 3531 Machine shop, jobbing & repair; logging equipment

(G-12646)
BULLET HOLE LLC
11518 E Sprague Ave (99206-5135)
PHONE 509 868-8884
Brad Hess, *Principal*
EMP: 3
SALES (est): 203.9K Privately Held
SIC: 5091 5941 3484 5099 Firearms, sporting; firearms; guns (firearms) or gun parts, 30 mm. & below; firearms & ammunition, except sporting

(G-12647)
BULLHIDE LINER CORP
1511 N Thierman Rd (99212-1178)
PHONE 509 532-9007
Grossman Ronald, *Principal*
EMP: 2
SALES (est): 145.7K Privately Held
SIC: 3479 Metal coating & allied service

(G-12648)
BUMBLEBAR INC
3014 N Flora Rd Ste 4b (99216-1872)
PHONE 509 924-2080
Elizabeth Ward, *President*
Glenn Ward, *Vice Pres*
▲ EMP: 17
SALES (est): 1.3MM Privately Held
WEB: www.bumblebar.com
SIC: 2099 Food preparations

(G-12649)
CAMP TIME INC
3310 N Tschirley Rd (99216-1716)
PHONE 509 928-3051
David Cook, *President*
Isabelle Cook, *Corp Secy*
Doug Cook, *Vice Pres*
Margaret Cook, *Vice Pres*
Richard Cook, *Vice Pres*
EMP: 10
SQ FT: 16,000

Spokane Valley - Spokane County (G-12650) — GEOGRAPHIC SECTION

SALES (est): 670K **Privately Held**
WEB: www.camptime.com
SIC: 2514 Camp furniture: metal

(G-12650)
CANYON CREEK CABINET COMPANY
10221 E Montgomery Dr B (99206-4240)
PHONE 509 921-7807
Bob Novac, *Manager*
EMP: 3
SALES (corp-wide): 44.5MM **Privately Held**
SIC: 2434 2511 2521 Wood kitchen cabinets; wood household furniture; wood office furniture
PA: Canyon Creek Cabinet Company
16726 Tye St Se
Monroe WA 98272
360 348-4600

(G-12651)
CASCADIA SCREEN PRINTING
14208 E Sprague Ave Ste C (99216-2193)
PHONE 509 362-8900
EMP: 2
SALES (est): 83.9K **Privately Held**
SIC: 2752 Commercial printing, lithographic

(G-12652)
CBS OUTDOOR
15320 E Marietta Ave # 2 (99216-1870)
PHONE 509 892-4720
Todd Chaffins, *Principal*
EMP: 2
SALES (est): 260.3K **Privately Held**
SIC: 3993 Signs & advertising specialties

(G-12653)
CELLARS NODLAND
11616 E Montgomery Dr # 69 (99206-7645)
PHONE 509 927-7770
Nodland Cellars, *Owner*
EMP: 2
SALES (est): 113.9K **Privately Held**
SIC: 2084 Wines

(G-12654)
CENTRAL PRE-MIX CONCRETE CO
5111 E Broadway Ave (99212-0928)
P.O. Box 3366, Spokane (99220-3366)
PHONE 509 534-6221
Ricardo Linares, *President*
Paul Franz, *Vice Pres*
Craig Mayfield, *Vice Pres*
Caroll Schoeder, *Controller*
Julie Holcomb, *Human Res Mgr*
EMP: 700 EST: 1930
SQ FT: 10,000
SALES (est): 2.4MM
SALES (corp-wide): 30.6B **Privately Held**
WEB: www.centralpremix.com
SIC: 3273 5032 Ready-mixed concrete; concrete building products; sand, construction; gravel
HQ: Cpm Development Corporation
5111 E Broadway Ave
Spokane Valley WA 99212
509 534-6221

(G-12655)
CHILD EVNGELISM FELLOWSHIP INC
19306 E Dove Cir (99016-9689)
P.O. Box 141646 (99214-1646)
PHONE 509 928-2820
Ray Paulson, *Branch Mgr*
EMP: 41
SALES (corp-wide): 24.4MM **Privately Held**
SIC: 2752 Commercial printing, lithographic
PA: Child Evangelism Fellowship Incorporated
17482 Highway M
Warrenton MO 63383
636 456-4321

(G-12656)
CIENA CORPORATION
12730 E Mirabeau Pkwy # 100 (99216-5105)
PHONE 509 242-9000
Matthew Frey, *Branch Mgr*
EMP: 2 **Publicly Held**
SIC: 3663 Radio & TV communications equipment
PA: Ciena Corporation
7035 Ridge Rd
Hanover MD 21076

(G-12657)
CIRCUIT IMAGING LLC
1420 N Mullan Rd Ste 108 (99206-4333)
PHONE 509 315-3400
Ben Joseph, *Principal*
John Michaelis, *Principal*
Mark Michaelis, *Mng Member*
EMP: 3
SALES (est): 118.7K **Privately Held**
SIC: 3575 Keyboards, computer, office machine

(G-12658)
CLEAR RF LLC
12825 E Mirabeau Pkwy (99216-1617)
PHONE 855 321-9527
Chuck Griep, *Sales Staff*
Tod Byers,
John Miskulin,
Keith Swenson,
Shawn Taylor,
EMP: 10 EST: 2009
SQ FT: 65,000
SALES: 1MM **Privately Held**
SIC: 3699 3357 Pulse amplifiers; communication wire

(G-12659)
CLELAND INVESTMENT LC
Also Called: B C T
11407 E Montgomery Dr (99216-7621)
PHONE 509 326-5898
David R Cleland,
EMP: 14
SQ FT: 5,000
SALES (est): 1.6MM **Privately Held**
WEB: www.bctspokane.com
SIC: 2752 Commercial printing, offset

(G-12660)
COLA COLA ENTERPRISES
9705 E Montgomery Ave (99206-4119)
PHONE 509 921-6229
EMP: 3
SALES (est): 136.7K **Privately Held**
SIC: 2086 Soft drinks: packaged in cans, bottles, etc.

(G-12661)
COLUMBIA ELECTRIC SUPPLY
5818 E Broadway Ave (99212-0925)
PHONE 509 473-9156
EMP: 3
SALES (est): 77.9K **Privately Held**
SIC: 5063 3699 Electrical supplies; electrical equipment & supplies

(G-12662)
COMPONENT TINNING SERVICES INC
Also Called: Ace Production Technologies
3808 N Sullivan Rd 18q (99216-1639)
PHONE 509 315-5840
Roger Cox, *President*
Taylor Cox, *CFO*
▲ EMP: 10
SALES (est): 4.4MM **Privately Held**
WEB: www.ace-protech.com
SIC: 3548 Soldering equipment, except hand soldering irons

(G-12663)
CONOCOPHILLIPS COMPANY
6317 E Sharp Ave (99212-1246)
P.O. Box 11616 (99211-1616)
PHONE 509 536-8417
Paul Gould, *Branch Mgr*
EMP: 19
SALES (corp-wide): 38.7B **Publicly Held**
WEB: www.phillips66.com
SIC: 5541 2911 5171 4612 Filling stations, gasoline; petroleum refining; petroleum bulk stations & terminals; crude petroleum pipelines; refined petroleum pipelines
HQ: Conocophillips Company
925 N Eldridge Pkwy
Houston TX 77079
281 293-1000

(G-12664)
CONSOLIDATED CONTAINER CO LLC
Also Called: Quintex
3808 N Sullivan Rd 8a (99216-1618)
PHONE 509 891-2483
Brian Weiler, *Principal*
EMP: 25
SALES (corp-wide): 14B **Publicly Held**
WEB: www.ccclllc.com
SIC: 3089 Plastic containers, except foam
HQ: Consolidated Container Company, Llc
2500 Windy Ridge Pkwy Se # 1400
Atlanta GA 30339
678 742-4600

(G-12665)
CONSOLIDATED PUMP & SUPPLY
11303 E Montgomery Dr # 4 (99206-7648)
PHONE 509 891-1313
EMP: 3 EST: 2000
SALES (est): 268.7K **Privately Held**
SIC: 3561 Mfg Pumps/Pumping Equipment

(G-12666)
CONTROLFREEK INC
11616 E Montgomery Dr # 4 (99206-6601)
P.O. Box 142192 (99214-2002)
PHONE 509 979-5677
Mandie Snyder, *CFO*
EMP: 5
SALES: 1,000K **Privately Held**
SIC: 3625 Relays & industrial controls

(G-12667)
COUNTRY STORE
5605 E Sprague Ave (99212-0826)
PHONE 509 534-1412
Scott Kaster, *Principal*
EMP: 2
SALES (est): 62.3K **Privately Held**
SIC: 2048 Prepared feeds

(G-12668)
CPM DEVELOPMENT CORPORATION (DH)
Also Called: Inland Asphalt
5111 E Broadway Ave (99212-0928)
P.O. Box 3366, Spokane (99220-3366)
PHONE 509 534-6221
Ricardo Linares, *President*
John Madden, *General Mgr*
Bill Ohlsen, *General Mgr*
Susan Lewis-Devaney, *Vice Pres*
Tameka Lawler, *Research*
EMP: 350
SQ FT: 11,000
SALES (est): 344.9MM
SALES (corp-wide): 30.6B **Privately Held**
SIC: 3273 1771 3272 Ready-mixed concrete; blacktop (asphalt) work; concrete products

(G-12669)
CPM DEVELOPMENT CORPORATION
Also Called: Central Pre-Mix Concrete
5111 E Broadway Ave (99212-0928)
PHONE 509 536-3355
John Madden, *General Mgr*
EMP: 40
SALES (corp-wide): 30.6B **Privately Held**
WEB: www.centralpremix.com
SIC: 3273 Ready-mixed concrete
HQ: Cpm Development Corporation
5111 E Broadway Ave
Spokane Valley WA 99212
509 534-6221

(G-12670)
CRUX SUBSURFACE INC (HQ)
4308 N Barker Rd (99027-9600)
PHONE 509 892-9409
Nick Salisbury, *President*
James H Haddox, *Chairman*
Peter O Brien, *Vice Pres*
Mark Neupert, *Vice Pres*
Scott Tunison, *Vice Pres*
EMP: 100 EST: 1998
SQ FT: 10,000
SALES (est): 23.9MM
SALES (corp-wide): 11.1B **Publicly Held**
WEB: www.cruxsub.com
SIC: 1781 1611 3541 1623 Geothermal drilling; general contractor, highway & street construction; drilling machine tools (metal cutting); electric power line construction
PA: Quanta Services, Inc.
2800 Post Oak Blvd # 2600
Houston TX 77056
713 629-7600

(G-12671)
CRYSTALFONTZ AMERICA INC
12412 E Saltese Ave (99216-0357)
PHONE 509 892-1200
Brent Crosby, *President*
Jean Agte, *COO*
Chris Watson, *Production*
Bob Burger, *CFO*
Janet Crosby, *Shareholder*
◆ EMP: 16
SQ FT: 10,000
SALES: 3MM **Privately Held**
WEB: www.crystalfontz.com
SIC: 5065 3679 Electronic parts & equipment; electronic circuits

(G-12672)
CRYSTALITE INC
3020 N Sullivan Rd Ste E (99216-3106)
PHONE 509 921-9585
Steve Richter, *President*
EMP: 3
SALES (corp-wide): 10.3MM **Privately Held**
WEB: www.crystaliteinc.com
SIC: 3444 Skylights, sheet metal
PA: Crystalite, Inc.
3307 Cedar St
Everett WA 98201
425 259-6000

(G-12673)
CUSTOM WELDING INC
2310 N Marguerite Rd (99212-2323)
PHONE 509 535-0664
Dan Tryon, *CEO*
Barbara Tryon, *Corp Secy*
EMP: 2 EST: 1976
SQ FT: 3,000
SALES: 150K **Privately Held**
SIC: 7692 3443 Welding repair; fuel tanks (oil, gas, etc.): metal plate

(G-12674)
CUT ABOVE ENTERPRISE INC
11413 E Buckeye Ave (99206-6203)
P.O. Box 11355 (99211-1355)
PHONE 509 928-5091
Ted Gay, *President*
Anne Gay, *Vice Pres*
EMP: 10 EST: 2010
SQ FT: 9,000
SALES (est): 1.4MM **Privately Held**
SIC: 7699 3499 Elevators: inspection, service & repair; metal household articles

(G-12675)
CXT INCORPORATED (HQ)
3808 N Sullivan Rd Bldg 7 (99216-1618)
PHONE 509 924-6300
Kevin R Haugh, *President*
John Kasel, *Chairman*
James McCaslin, *Vice Pres*
Roanld D Steiger, *Vice Pres*
A Wolf, *Prdtn Mgr*
▲ EMP: 100
SALES (est): 83.8MM
SALES (corp-wide): 626.9MM **Publicly Held**
WEB: www.cxtinc.com
SIC: 3272 Ties, railroad: concrete; paving materials, prefabricated concrete

▲ = Import ▼ =Export
◆ =Import/Export

GEOGRAPHIC SECTION
Spokane Valley - Spokane County (G-12703)

PA: L. B. Foster Company
415 Holiday Dr Ste 1
Pittsburgh PA 15220
412 928-3400

(G-12676)
CXT INCORPORATED
2420 N Pioneer Ln (99216-1831)
PHONE..................509 921-7878
Dave Millard, *Manager*
EMP: 40
SALES (corp-wide): 626.9MM **Publicly Held**
WEB: www.cxtinc.com
SIC: 3272 Ties, railroad: concrete
HQ: Cxt Incorporated
3808 N Sullivan Rd Bldg 7
Spokane Valley WA 99216
509 924-6300

(G-12677)
DANA-SAAD COMPANY
3808 N Sullivan Rd # 105 (99216-1619)
PHONE..................509 924-6711
Michael H Saad, *Ch of Bd*
William Saad, *President*
Patrick Saad, *Vice Pres*
Scott Simpson, *Admin Sec*
▲ **EMP:** 30 **EST:** 1963
SQ FT: 39,000
SALES (est): 4.8MM **Privately Held**
SIC: 3089 7359 Molding primary plastic; business machine & electronic equipment rental services

(G-12678)
DANIELSON TOOL & DIE
9924 E Jackson Ave (99206-4264)
PHONE..................509 924-5734
Ronald Hill, *President*
Debbie McGhee-Hill, *Admin Sec*
EMP: 30
SQ FT: 5,000
SALES (est): 3.8MM **Privately Held**
WEB: www.danielsontnd.com
SIC: 3544 3545 Special dies & tools; machine tool accessories

(G-12679)
DAYBREAK OIL AND GAS INC (PA)
1101 N Argonne Rd Ste 211 (99212-2699)
PHONE..................509 232-7674
James F Westmoreland, *Ch of Bd*
Bennett W Anderson, *COO*
EMP: 6
SALES: 742.8K **Publicly Held**
WEB: www.daybreakoilandgas.com
SIC: 1311 Crude petroleum & natural gas

(G-12680)
DEGERSTROM CORPORATION
3301 N Sullivan Rd (99216)
PHONE..................509 928-3333
Joan B Degerstrom, *Ch of Bd*
Gary A Craig, *President*
Michael Cannon, *Corp Secy*
James A Fish, *Vice Pres*
Chris C Myers, *Vice Pres*
EMP: 20
SALES (est): 273.4K **Privately Held**
SIC: 2951 5032 1611 Asphalt paving mixtures & blocks; paving materials; surfacing & paving

(G-12681)
DEX MEDIA HOLDINGS INC
Also Called: Qwest
1101 N Argonne Rd Ste 101 (99212-2699)
PHONE..................509 922-1026
Mike Mettam, *Manager*
EMP: 50
SALES (corp-wide): 1.8B **Privately Held**
WEB: www.qwestdex.com
SIC: 2741 Telephone & other directory publishing
PA: Thryv, Inc.
2200 W Airfield Dr
Dfw Airport TX 75261
972 453-7000

(G-12682)
DOORS & MILLWORK INC
2224 N Locust Rd Ste 5 (99216-4211)
PHONE..................509 921-7663
Dave Brady, *President*
Carolyn Brady, *Admin Sec*
EMP: 4
SQ FT: 8,000
SALES (est): 579.9K **Privately Held**
WEB: www.doorsandmillworkinc.com
SIC: 2431 Millwork

(G-12683)
DOTINK LLC
1917 S Union Rd (99206-5724)
PHONE..................509 655-0828
Patrick E Frome,
EMP: 2 **EST:** 2017
SALES (est): 129.9K **Privately Held**
SIC: 2752 Commercial printing, lithographic

(G-12684)
EAGLE LOGGING INC
12401 E Trent Ave (99216-1256)
P.O. Box 30594, Spokane (99223-3009)
PHONE..................509 226-1329
Mike Schmedding, *Principal*
EMP: 6
SALES (est): 384.5K **Privately Held**
SIC: 2411 Logging camps & contractors

(G-12685)
EAGLE SYSTEMS INC
1725 N Dickey Rd (99212-1265)
P.O. Box 11841 (99211-1841)
PHONE..................509 535-8654
Randy Sundquist, *Manager*
EMP: 23 **Privately Held**
WEB: www.eagleis.com
SIC: 3715 7538 Semitrailers for truck tractors; general automotive repair shops
HQ: Eagle Systems, Inc.
230 Grant Rd Ste A1
East Wenatchee WA 98802
509 884-7575

(G-12686)
ECLIPSE TECHNICAL GRAPHICS LLC
3302 N Flora Rd (99216-1739)
PHONE..................509 922-7700
Matthew Sarner, *President*
Bruce Colwell, *Vice Pres*
Mark Tuttle, *Opers Staff*
EMP: 14
SQ FT: 11,000
SALES: 1MM **Privately Held**
WEB: www.eclipseprinting.com
SIC: 2759 Screen printing; decals: printing

(G-12687)
ECOLITE MANUFACTURING CO (PA)
9919 E Montgomery Dr (99206-4123)
P.O. Box 11366 (99211-1366)
PHONE..................509 922-8888
Ron Caferro, *President*
Edward Caferro, *Vice Pres*
Theresa Caferro, *Treasurer*
Raelene Albinson, *Admin Sec*
▲ **EMP:** 81 **EST:** 1970
SQ FT: 33,000
SALES (est): 27.8MM **Privately Held**
WEB: www.ecolite.com
SIC: 3446 3479 Architectural metalwork; coating of metals & formed products

(G-12688)
ECOLITE MANUFACTURING CO
2622 N Woodruff Rd (99206-4138)
PHONE..................509 922-8888
Ron Caferro, *Branch Mgr*
EMP: 92
SALES (corp-wide): 27.8MM **Privately Held**
SIC: 3446 Architectural metalwork
PA: Ecolite Manufacturing Co.
9919 E Montgomery Dr
Spokane Valley WA 99206
509 922-8888

(G-12689)
ECOTECH SERVICES LLC
6310 E Sprague Ave (99212-0839)
PHONE..................509 995-5809
Julie Olsen,
EMP: 2
SQ FT: 400

SALES (est): 171.7K **Privately Held**
SIC: 3621 Generators for gas-electric or oil-electric vehicles

(G-12690)
ELDONS SAUSAGE INC
Also Called: Eltons Sausage and Jerky Sup
3808 N Sullivan Rd (99216-1608)
P.O. Box 422, Kooskia ID (83539-0422)
PHONE..................509 309-3140
Denise R Crites, *President*
Allen W Crites, *Vice Pres*
EMP: 4
SQ FT: 2,400
SALES (est): 340K **Privately Held**
SIC: 2013 Sausages & other prepared meats

(G-12691)
EMMROD FISHING GEAR INC (PA)
2725 S Bolivar Rd (99037-9368)
PHONE..................509 979-2222
Duane Markley, *CEO*
Lance Markley, *President*
Traci Markley, *Treasurer*
EMP: 3
SALES: 350K **Privately Held**
SIC: 3949 7389 Rods & rod parts, fishing;

(G-12692)
ENGLISH SETTER BREWING
15310 E Marietta Ave (99216-1876)
PHONE..................509 413-3663
EMP: 3 **EST:** 2014
SALES (est): 175.8K **Privately Held**
SIC: 2082 Malt liquors

(G-12693)
ENHANCED SOFTWARE PRODUCTS INC
Also Called: E S P
1811 N Hutchinson Rd (99212-2444)
PHONE..................509 534-1514
Kathy Murray, *President*
Shaun Murray, *Vice Pres*
Alexander Ray, *Engineer*
Christy Harmon, *Manager*
EMP: 30
SQ FT: 3,800
SALES (est): 2MM **Privately Held**
WEB: www.espsolution.net
SIC: 7374 7371 7373 7375 Data processing service; custom computer programming services; value-added resellers, computer systems; information retrieval services; prepackaged software

(G-12694)
EVERGREEN FABRICATION INC
4331 E Mission Ave (99212-1313)
P.O. Box 590, Colbert (99005-0590)
PHONE..................509 534-9096
Jeff Foster, *President*
▲ **EMP:** 3
SQ FT: 5,000
SALES: 400K **Privately Held**
SIC: 3444 3446 Sheet metalwork; restaurant sheet metalwork; architectural metalwork

(G-12695)
EVERLASTING SCENTS LLC
8121 E Appleway Blvd (99212-2966)
PHONE..................509 534-4790
Aubrey Hay, *Principal*
EMP: 2
SALES (est): 74.4K **Privately Held**
SIC: 2844 Toilet preparations

(G-12696)
EVERY OCCASION ENGRAVING
2007 N Woodruff Rd (99206-4130)
PHONE..................509 995-9848
Beth Worthy, *Principal*
EMP: 2
SALES (est): 111.9K **Privately Held**
SIC: 2499 Trophy bases, wood

(G-12697)
EXIDE TECHNOLOGIES
9708 E Montgomery Ave D (99206-4213)
PHONE..................509 922-3135
Chuck Wiedmer, *Manager*
EMP: 7

SALES (corp-wide): 2.4B **Privately Held**
WEB: www.exideworld.com
SIC: 3691 3629 Storage batteries; battery chargers, rectifying or nonrotating
PA: Exide Technologies
13000 Deerfield Pkwy # 200
Milton GA 30004
678 566-9000

(G-12698)
FABRICATION & TRUCK EQP INC (PA)
Also Called: Washington Auto Carriage
5301 E Broadway Ave (99212-0905)
P.O. Box 11435 (99211-1435)
PHONE..................509 535-0363
Neil H Robblee, *Ch of Bd*
Cliff King, *President*
Mel Maki, *Vice Pres*
Cindy Cloe, *Executive*
EMP: 18
SQ FT: 12,000
SALES (est): 7MM **Privately Held**
WEB: www.wacnw.com
SIC: 5013 7532 3713 Truck parts & accessories; body shop, trucks; truck bodies (motor vehicles)

(G-12699)
FABTECH PRECISION MFG INC (PA)
16124 E Euclid Ave (99216-1853)
PHONE..................509 534-7660
Marc Groskreutz, *President*
EMP: 20
SQ FT: 10,000
SALES (est): 3.5MM **Privately Held**
WEB: www.fabtech1.com
SIC: 3444 Sheet metal specialties, not stamped

(G-12700)
FEDEX OFFICE & PRINT SVCS INC
212 N Sullivan Rd (99037-8570)
PHONE..................509 922-4929
EMP: 12
SALES (corp-wide): 69.6B **Publicly Held**
WEB: www.kinkos.com
SIC: 7334 2759 Photocopying & duplicating services; commercial printing
HQ: Fedex Office and Print Services, Inc.
7900 Legacy Dr
Plano TX 75024
800 463-3339

(G-12701)
FIBERGLASS TECHNOLOGY INDS INC (HQ)
Also Called: Fiber-Tech Industries
3808 N Sullivan Rd 29c (99216-1615)
PHONE..................509 928-8880
Terry Keegan, *CEO*
Wayne Durnin, *Vice Pres*
Robert Pfiefer, *Vice Pres*
Dale Forrest, *Manager*
▲ **EMP:** 43
SQ FT: 120,000
SALES (est): 11.1MM
SALES (corp-wide): 28.4MM **Privately Held**
SIC: 3089 Panels, building: plastic
PA: Celstar Group Inc
40 N Main St Ste 1730
Dayton OH 45423
937 224-1730

(G-12702)
FIRECRACKER SOFTWARE LLC
17901 E 8th Ave (99016-9759)
PHONE..................509 443-5308
Jason Stock, *Principal*
EMP: 2 **EST:** 2012
SALES (est): 186.3K **Privately Held**
SIC: 7372 Prepackaged software

(G-12703)
FIRST INDEX INC
12610 E Mirabeau Pkwy (99216-1450)
PHONE..................888 535-8583
EMP: 20 **EST:** 1996
SQ FT: 5,000
SALES (est): 1.4MM **Privately Held**
SIC: 2741 Misc Publishing

Spokane Valley - Spokane County (G-12704)

(G-12704)
FLEET FEET SPORTS
13910 E Indiana Ave (99216-6010)
PHONE..................509 309-2174
EMP: 3
SALES (est): 160K **Privately Held**
SIC: 5661 5139 5087 3149 Ret Shoes Whol Footwear Whol Svc Estblshmt Equip Mfg Footwear-Ex Rubber

(G-12705)
FLEXIBLE CONTAINMENT PDTS INC
6811 E Mission Ave (99212-1152)
PHONE..................509 624-8921
Donald Myers, *President*
Craig Dolsby, *Vice Pres*
Joseph Herzog, *CFO*
Andrew Barrett, *Exec Dir*
▼ EMP: 22
SQ FT: 15,000
SALES: 10MM
SALES (corp-wide): 51.6MM **Privately Held**
SIC: 3081 Unsupported plastics film & sheet
PA: Berg Companies Inc.
6811 E Mission Ave
Spokane Valley WA 99212
509 624-8921

(G-12706)
FO BERG COMPANY
6811 E Mission Ave (99212-1152)
PHONE..................509 624-8921
Bryce Ogle, *President*
Lawayna Smith, *Accountant*
EMP: 15
SQ FT: 20,000
SALES (est): 1.8MM **Privately Held**
SIC: 3444 Awnings & canopies

(G-12707)
FOOD EQUIPMENT INTERNATIONAL
14404 E 20th Ct (99037-9472)
PHONE..................509 924-0181
Susan Evans, *President*
Steven Croonquist, *Vice Pres*
EMP: 3
SALES: 1MM **Privately Held**
WEB: www.food-equipment.com
SIC: 5046 5719 3556 Restaurant equipment & supplies; kitchenware; bakery machinery

(G-12708)
FORREST PAINT CO
Also Called: Forrest Tech Ctngs Div of Forr
3808 N Sullivan Rd N17 (99216-1608)
PHONE..................509 924-3785
Ron England, *Branch Mgr*
EMP: 3
SALES (est): 328.9K
SALES (corp-wide): 57.5MM **Privately Held**
WEB: www.forrestpaint.com
SIC: 2851 5198 Paints & paint additives; paints, varnishes & supplies
PA: Forrest Paint Co.
1011 Mckinley St
Eugene OR 97402
541 868-1222

(G-12709)
FREEPRT-MCMRAN EXPLRATION CORP
Also Called: Phelps Dodge
10807 E Montgomery Dr # 3 (99206-4777)
PHONE..................509 928-0704
Greg C Coffin, *General Mgr*
EMP: 6
SALES (corp-wide): 18.6B **Publicly Held**
SIC: 3331 Primary copper
HQ: Freeport-Mcmoran Exploration Corporation
333 N Central Ave
Phoenix AZ 85004

(G-12710)
FREEZE FURNITURE AND MFG CO (PA)
Also Called: FMI
10408 E Buckeye Ln (99206-4200)
PHONE..................509 924-3545
Vern Freeze, *President*
John Freeze, *Vice Pres*
Evelyn Freeze, *Treasurer*
EMP: 14
SQ FT: 25,000
SALES: 1.5MM **Privately Held**
WEB: www.freezefurniture.com
SIC: 2434 2512 2521 2511 Wood kitchen cabinets; upholstered household furniture; wood office furniture; dressers, household: wood

(G-12711)
FUTURE MACHINE & MFG INC
3808 N Sullivan Rd # 124 (99216-1618)
PHONE..................509 891-5600
Bud Dygert, *President*
EMP: 10
SALES (est): 1.3MM **Privately Held**
SIC: 3842 Personal safety equipment

(G-12712)
GALAXY CMPUND SMCONDUCTORS INC
9922 E Montgomery Dr # 7 (99206-4158)
PHONE..................509 892-1114
Mark Furlong, *President*
John Trevethan, *Vice Pres*
Annette Bollaert, *Treasurer*
Gordon Dallas, *Admin Sec*
▲ EMP: 17
SQ FT: 8,000
SALES (est): 2.6MM
SALES (corp-wide): 200.7MM **Privately Held**
WEB: www.galaxywafer.com
SIC: 3674 Integrated circuits, semiconductor networks, etc.
PA: Iqe Plc
Pascal Close
Cardiff S GLAM CF3 0
292 083-9400

(G-12713)
GDANSK INC
5510 E Broadway Ave (99212-0910)
PHONE..................509 279-2034
Steve Danzig, *President*
Mike Jensen, *President*
EMP: 40
SALES (est): 2MM **Privately Held**
WEB: www.cudaapparel.com
SIC: 2759 Commercial printing

(G-12714)
GEN-SET CO
4308 S Darcy Dr (99206-9651)
PHONE..................509 891-8452
Joe Blaylock, *President*
Myrna Blaylock, *Admin Sec*
EMP: 5
SALES: 500K **Privately Held**
WEB: www.gen-setco.com
SIC: 3621 Motors & generators

(G-12715)
GENUS BREWING COMPANY LLC
1018 S Courtney Ln (99037-9256)
PHONE..................509 808-2395
Michele Miller, *Principal*
EMP: 3
SALES (est): 75.4K **Privately Held**
SIC: 2082 Beer (alcoholic beverage)

(G-12716)
GEORGE W WARDEN CO INC
Also Called: Warden Fluid Dynamics
2501 N Farr Ln Ste 2 (99206-4203)
PHONE..................509 534-2880
Ranse Holcomb, *President*
EMP: 5
SALES (corp-wide): 540.1MM **Privately Held**
WEB: www.wfdonline.com
SIC: 3593 5084 Fluid power cylinders, hydraulic or pneumatic; hydraulic systems equipment & supplies
HQ: George W Warden Co, Inc
19810 141st Pl Ne
Woodinville WA 98072
206 545-0230

(G-12717)
GIBSON PERFORMANCE ENGINES
926 N Lake Rd (99212-1048)
PHONE..................509 251-5171
Andrew Gibson, *President*
EMP: 3 EST: 2013
SALES (est): 209K **Privately Held**
SIC: 3599 Machine shop, jobbing & repair

(G-12718)
GIORGIOS FITNESS CENTER
Also Called: Giorgio's Gym
7 N Herald Rd (99206-6853)
PHONE..................509 922-8833
Suzanne Usai, *Owner*
EMP: 3
SQ FT: 1,100
SALES (est): 168.5K **Privately Held**
WEB: www.giorgiosfitness.com
SIC: 7991 3949 Health club; dumbbells & other weightlifting equipment

(G-12719)
GLOBAL MINING
19208 E Broadway Ave (99016-8577)
PHONE..................509 863-9724
Cassandra Ellowey, *Owner*
EMP: 4
SALES (est): 333.4K **Privately Held**
SIC: 3648 Miners' lamps

(G-12720)
GLOBAL PRODUCT DEVELOPMENT
3808 N Sullivan Rd # 105 (99216-1619)
PHONE..................509 487-1155
Stacy Bartolotta, *Principal*
EMP: 2
SALES (est): 202.5K **Privately Held**
SIC: 3546 3545 3544 Power-driven handtools; machine tool accessories; special dies & tools

(G-12721)
GOBERS FUEL OIL INC
Also Called: Gober's Son & Son
11215 E Trent Ave (99206-4630)
PHONE..................509 924-5372
Phillip Gober, *President*
EMP: 10 EST: 1951
SQ FT: 1,200
SALES (est): 1.5MM **Privately Held**
SIC: 1794 7699 2992 Excavation & grading, building construction; septic tank cleaning service; lubricating oils & greases

(G-12722)
GOLDEN STATE FOODS CORP
3808 N Sullivan Rd 33h (99216-1608)
PHONE..................509 928-9055
Larry McGill, *Branch Mgr*
EMP: 5
SALES (corp-wide): 1.3B **Privately Held**
SIC: 5149 5141 2099 Groceries & related products; groceries, general line; food preparations
PA: Golden State Foods Corp.
18301 Von Karman Ave # 1100
Irvine CA 92612
949 247-8000

(G-12723)
GRAPHIC ART PRODUCTIONS INC
Also Called: Fastsigns
11712 E Montgomery Dr (99206-6163)
PHONE..................509 536-3278
Richard Cole, *President*
Dina Cole, *Treasurer*
EMP: 4
SALES: 100K
SALES (corp-wide): 27.1MM **Privately Held**
SIC: 3993 Signs & advertising specialties
PA: Fastsigns International, Inc.
2542 Highlander Way
Carrollton TX 75006
888 285-5935

(G-12724)
GRIFFIN PUBLISHING INC
2210 N Dollar Rd (99212-1459)
PHONE..................509 534-3625
George Griffin, *President*
EMP: 20
SQ FT: 14,380
SALES (est): 2.5MM **Privately Held**
WEB: www.griffinpublishinginc.com
SIC: 2759 Publication printing

(G-12725)
GSI OUTDOORS INC
1023 S Pines Rd (99206-5424)
PHONE..................509 928-9611
Ian James Scott, *President*
Katherine Diane Scott, *Corp Secy*
Don Allen Scott, *Vice Pres*
Tom Hathaway, *Sales Staff*
▲ EMP: 20
SQ FT: 35,000
SALES (est): 3MM **Privately Held**
SIC: 3949 5091 Fishing equipment; sporting & recreation goods

(G-12726)
GT MACHINING
13607 E Trent Ave (99216-1284)
PHONE..................509 922-8395
Greg Thomas, *Owner*
EMP: 2
SALES (est): 162.1K **Privately Held**
SIC: 7692 Automotive welding

(G-12727)
HEIRLOOM CUSTOM CABINETRY
3524 N Eden Rd (99216-1740)
PHONE..................509 370-9012
Bart Moorhead, *President*
Tana M Moorhead, *Vice Pres*
EMP: 2 EST: 2006
SALES (est): 279.3K **Privately Held**
SIC: 2434 Wood kitchen cabinets

(G-12728)
HEIRLOOM WOODWORKS
225 N Ella Rd (99212-2947)
P.O. Box 13642 (99213-3642)
PHONE..................509 315-9275
EMP: 2
SALES (est): 88K **Privately Held**
SIC: 2431 Mfg Millwork

(G-12729)
HELENA SILVER MINES INC
Also Called: Western Continental
905 N Pines Rd Ste A (99206-4900)
PHONE..................509 922-3035
W L Campbell, *President*
▲ EMP: 5
SALES (est): 311.3K **Privately Held**
SIC: 1044 Silver ores

(G-12730)
HOLMAN DRILLING CORPORATION
1609 S Stanley Ln (99212-3268)
PHONE..................509 534-1013
Arnold Holman, *President*
Holly Holman, *Admin Sec*
EMP: 6 EST: 1960
SQ FT: 600
SALES: 500K **Privately Held**
SIC: 1781 1381 Water well servicing; drilling oil & gas wells

(G-12731)
HONEYWELL ELECTRONIC MTLS INC (HQ)
15128 E Euclid Ave (99216-1801)
PHONE..................509 252-2200
David Diggs, *President*
James M Di Stefano, *Vice Pres*
Ezra Eckhardt, *Vice Pres*
John J Tus, *Treasurer*
Scott Jacobson, *Admin Sec*
▲ EMP: 600
SALES (est): 336.5MM
SALES (corp-wide): 41.8B **Publicly Held**
SIC: 3679 3674 3643 Electronic circuits; semiconductors & related devices; current-carrying wiring devices
PA: Honeywell International Inc.
115 Tabor Rd
Morris Plains NJ 07950
973 455-2000

GEOGRAPHIC SECTION

Spokane Valley - Spokane County (G-12759)

(G-12732)
HONEYWELL INTERNATIONAL INC
11401 E Montgomery Dr # 2 (99206-4720)
PHONE.................................509 534-5226
EMP: 673
SALES (corp-wide): 41.8B Publicly Held
SIC: 3724 Aircraft engines & engine parts
PA: Honeywell International Inc.
115 Tabor Rd
Morris Plains NJ 07950
973 455-2000

(G-12733)
HYDRAFAB NORTHWEST INC
3808 N Sullivan Rd 15z (99216-1608)
P.O. Box 15292 (99215-5292)
PHONE.................................509 535-0075
Chris L Henjum, *President*
Jan Grothe, *Marketing Staff*
Darren Hughes, *Manager*
Dale Renfro, *Manager*
Bo Porter, *Supervisor*
EMP: 33
SQ FT: 16,000
SALES (est): 12.1MM Privately Held
SIC: 3441 Fabricated structural metal

(G-12734)
HYDRO-TECH GENERTR REPAIR PLUS (PA)
Also Called: Hydraulics Plus
5507 E Broadway Ave (99212-0909)
PHONE.................................509 536-9464
Loretta L Roberts, *President*
Michelle Madonna, *Office Mgr*
EMP: 11
SALES (est): 2.7MM Privately Held
WEB: www.hydraulicsplusinc.com
SIC: 3599 7699 Machine shop, jobbing & repair; hydraulic equipment repair

(G-12735)
HYPOTHESIS GARDENS LLC
2709 N Felts Ln (99206-4282)
PHONE.................................206 653-6344
Andrew Benton, *Mng Member*
EMP: 2 EST: 2013
SALES (est): 165.2K Privately Held
SIC: 0139 3999 ;

(G-12736)
I-90 EXPRESS FINISHING INC
225 N Ella Rd Bldg B (99212-2947)
PHONE.................................509 922-2297
Toll Free:..................................877 -
Tom Balmes, *President*
EMP: 25
SQ FT: 25,000
SALES (est): 3.1MM Privately Held
SIC: 3479 Coating of metals & formed products

(G-12737)
ICT GROUP INC
2818 N Sullivan Rd (99216-5074)
PHONE.................................408 907-8000
EMP: 2
SALES (est): 88.3K Privately Held
SIC: 3661 Telephone & telegraph apparatus

(G-12738)
INDIANA HARNESS CO
2425 N Vista Rd (99212-2218)
PHONE.................................509 535-3400
Clint McGowan, *President*
Pat McGowan, *Co-Owner*
EMP: 2
SQ FT: 9,600
SALES (est): 181K Privately Held
SIC: 3199 5661 5941 Saddles or parts; shoe stores; men's boots; women's boots; saddlery & equestrian equipment

(G-12739)
INFINETIX CORP
2721 N Van Marter Dr # 3 (99206-6691)
PHONE.................................509 922-5629
Bruce Weyrauch, *President*
Leon Schmidt, *Vice Pres*
Leon Schmitt, *Vice Pres*
Robert Parker, *Engineer*
Peter Van Doren, *Engineer*
EMP: 17
SQ FT: 4,000
SALES (est): 2.2MM Privately Held
WEB: www.infinetix.com
SIC: 8711 3672 8733 7371 Electrical or electronic engineering; circuit boards, television & radio printed; noncommercial research organizations; custom computer programming services

(G-12740)
INFOMINE USA INC
100 N Mullan Rd Ste 102 (99206-6848)
PHONE.................................509 328-8023
Andrew Robertson, *Ch of Bd*
Jennifer Leinart, *President*
Graham Baldwin, *Vice Pres*
EMP: 8
SQ FT: 1,200
SALES (est): 800K Privately Held
SIC: 2731 8711 Books: publishing only; mining engineer

(G-12741)
INLAND COFFEE AND BEVERAGE
9311 E Trent Ave (99206-4217)
P.O. Box 1434, Deer Park (99006-1434)
PHONE.................................509 228-9239
Ruth Vargas Easley, *President*
EMP: 8
SALES (est): 1.3MM Privately Held
SIC: 3589 Coffee brewing equipment

(G-12742)
INLAND EMPIRE BUS SOLUTIONS
11816 E 24th Ave (99206-7033)
P.O. Box 1366, Veradale (99037-1366)
PHONE.................................509 922-7492
Sue Ganderson, *President*
EMP: 2
SALES: 250K Privately Held
SIC: 2761 Manifold business forms

(G-12743)
INLAND EMPIRE PLATING INC
2401 N Eastern Rd (99212-1440)
PHONE.................................509 535-1704
Kevin Middaugh, *President*
Karen Speerstra, *Corp Secy*
EMP: 10
SQ FT: 36,000
SALES: 250.3K Privately Held
SIC: 3471 Plating of metals or formed products

(G-12744)
INLAND MILLWORK
111 N Vista Rd Ste 4d (99212-2960)
PHONE.................................509 481-7765
Joe Mitchell, *Owner*
EMP: 2
SALES (est): 138.5K Privately Held
SIC: 2431 Millwork

(G-12745)
INLAND NW METALLURGICAL SVCS
16203 E Marietta Ln (99216-1838)
PHONE.................................509 922-7663
David Ederer, *Ch of Bd*
Daniel Ederer, *President*
EMP: 17
SQ FT: 11,500
SALES (est): 1.5MM Privately Held
WEB: www.inlandmet.com
SIC: 3398 Metal heat treating

(G-12746)
INTERMOUNTAIN FABRICATORS INC
6014 E Knox Ave (99212-1461)
P.O. Box 11754 (99211-1754)
PHONE.................................509 534-1676
Gary Jones, *President*
EMP: 15
SALES (est): 1.7MM Privately Held
WEB: www.intermtnfab.com
SIC: 3312 3535 3446 3441 Blast furnaces & steel mills; conveyors & conveying equipment; architectural metalwork; fabricated structural metal

(G-12747)
ISAACS INCRDBL FRZ YOGURT LLC
722 S Blake Rd (99216-0880)
PHONE.................................509 928-9497
Connie Piehler,
Stephanie Peihler,
EMP: 2
SALES (est): 159K Privately Held
SIC: 2026 Yogurt

(G-12748)
ITRON INC
12310 E Mirabeau Pkwy # 500 (99216-1280)
PHONE.................................509 924-9900
Frank Monforte, *Vice Pres*
Mary Rennick, *Vice Pres*
Mike Mathis, *Engineer*
Melinda Markowski, *Financial Analy*
Rich Marll, *Human Res Dir*
EMP: 45
SALES (corp-wide): 2.3B Publicly Held
WEB: www.siliconenergy.com
SIC: 3663 3571 Radio & TV communications equipment; electronic computers
PA: Itron, Inc.
2111 N Molter Rd
Liberty Lake WA 99019
509 924-9900

(G-12749)
ITRON MANUFACTURING INC
2818 N Sullivan Rd (99216-5198)
PHONE.................................509 924-9900
Rob Nielson, *President*
Rob Nielsen, *President*
Mike Zimmer, *President*
Stephen Johnson, *Marketing Mgr*
Jim Stokoe, *Manager*
EMP: 32 EST: 1998
SALES (est): 5.9MM
SALES (corp-wide): 2.3B Publicly Held
WEB: www.siliconenergy.com
SIC: 3663 3571 Radio & TV communications equipment; electronic computers
PA: Itron, Inc.
2111 N Molter Rd
Liberty Lake WA 99019
509 924-9900

(G-12750)
J & J PRECISION MACHINE LLC
3808 N Sullivan Rd (99216-1608)
PHONE.................................509 315-9319
Jeff Bordelon, *Mng Member*
EMP: 2
SQ FT: 4,000
SALES: 400K Privately Held
SIC: 3541 3545 Machine tool replacement & repair parts, metal cutting types; machine tool accessories

(G-12751)
JENED INC
Also Called: Elephant Boys, The
12622 E Sprague Ave (99216-0726)
PHONE.................................509 926-6894
Ed Conley, *President*
Curtis Cayer, *Sales Dir*
EMP: 2
SALES (est): 2.2MM Privately Held
SIC: 3799 5551 Boat trailers; motor boat dealers

(G-12752)
JETSEAL INC
10310 E Buckeye Ln Ste 1 (99206-4241)
PHONE.................................509 467-9133
Barnes Vaughn, *President*
Paul Porter, *President*
Rex Reum, *Vice Pres*
Steve Hudlet, *Engineer*
Carlos Macau, *Treasurer*
EMP: 43
SQ FT: 8,400
SALES (est): 9.2MM Publicly Held
WEB: www.jetseal.com
SIC: 3053 Gaskets & sealing devices
PA: Heico Corporation
3000 Taft St
Hollywood FL 33021

(G-12753)
JIM S MACHINING SERVICE INC
Also Called: J M S
9514 E Montgomery Ave # 26 (99206-4140)
PHONE.................................509 926-1868
Jim Werner, *President*
EMP: 2 EST: 1997
SALES (est): 260.5K Privately Held
SIC: 3599 Carnival machines & equipment, amusement park

(G-12754)
JOHNSON CONTROLS
10010 E Knox Ave Ste 100 (99206-4156)
PHONE.................................509 534-6055
Don Piti, *Branch Mgr*
EMP: 40 Privately Held
WEB: www.simplexgrinnell.com
SIC: 3669 Emergency alarms
HQ: Johnson Controls Fire Protection Lp
6600 Congress Ave
Boca Raton FL 33487
561 988-7200

(G-12755)
JP LOGGING LLC
215 S Conklin Rd Apt F34 (99037-0029)
PHONE.................................208 596-7069
EMP: 3
SALES: 50K Privately Held
SIC: 2411 Logging

(G-12756)
JUBILANT HOLLISTERSTIER LLC
3808 N Sullivan Rd N15-101 (99216-1615)
PHONE.................................509 482-3287
Derek Glover, *Manager*
EMP: 2
SALES (corp-wide): 485.2MM Privately Held
SIC: 2834 Pharmaceutical preparations
HQ: Jubilant Hollisterstier Llc
3525 N Regal St
Spokane WA 99207
509 482-4945

(G-12757)
JUST AMERICAN DESSERTS (PA)
213 S University Rd Ste 2 (99206-5364)
PHONE.................................509 927-2253
Eva Roberts, *President*
Tracy Hunter, *Vice Pres*
EMP: 9
SQ FT: 7,102
SALES (est): 800.2K Privately Held
SIC: 5461 2051 Cakes; bread, cake & related products

(G-12758)
K & M UNIBODY WORKS INC
2011 N Park Rd (99212-1269)
PHONE.................................509 922-2083
Jim Miller, *President*
Berney Miller, *Manager*
EMP: 10
SQ FT: 5,200
SALES (est): 1.4MM Privately Held
WEB: www.kmunibodyworks.com
SIC: 3432 7532 7538 Plumbing fixture fittings & trim; top & body repair & paint shops; general automotive repair shops

(G-12759)
K & N ELECTRIC MOTORS INC (PA)
415 N Fancher Rd (99212-1059)
P.O. Box 303, Spokane (99210-0303)
PHONE.................................509 838-8000
Gerald Schmidlkofer, *President*
Robert J Schmidlkofer, *Corp Secy*
John Schmidlkofer, *Vice Pres*
Steven P Schmidlkofer, *Vice Pres*
Luke Olson, *Project Mgr*
▲ EMP: 70
SQ FT: 54,000
SALES (est): 63.7MM Privately Held
WEB: www.kenix.net
SIC: 5063 7694 5999 3621 Motors, electric; electric motor repair; motors, electric; motors & generators

Spokane Valley - Spokane County (G-12760) — GEOGRAPHIC SECTION

(G-12760)
KAISER ALUMINUM FAB PDTS LLC
Trentwood Rolling Mill
15000 E Euclid Ave
P.O. Box 15108, Spokane (99215-5108)
PHONE 509 927-6508
Jack A Hockema, *President*
Chris Anderson, *Safety Mgr*
Michael Mills, *Production*
Paul Ainsworth, *Research*
Robert Rankin, *Engineer*
EMP: 1000
SALES (corp-wide): 1.5B **Publicly Held**
WEB: www.kaisertwd.com
SIC: 3354 Aluminum extruded products
HQ: Kaiser Aluminum Fabricated Products, Llc
27422 Portola Pkwy # 200
Foothill Ranch CA 92610

(G-12761)
KAISER ALUMINUM WASHINGTON LLC
15000 E Euclid Ave (99216)
PHONE 949 614-1740
Larry Dearman, *Plant Mgr*
Jack Butters, *Opers Staff*
Earnestine Hughley, *Production*
Jerry Lema, *Production*
Joshua Moore, *Production*
EMP: 3
SALES (est): 1.1MM
SALES (corp-wide): 1.5B **Publicly Held**
SIC: 1099 Aluminum & beryllium ores mining
PA: Kaiser Aluminum Corporation
27422 Portola Pkwy # 350
Foothill Ranch CA 92610
949 614-1740

(G-12762)
KAISER ALUTEK INC
3401 N Tschirley Rd (99216-1755)
PHONE 509 924-2689
Larry Dearman, *Principal*
EMP: 3
SALES (est): 395.9K **Privately Held**
SIC: 3354 Aluminum extruded products

(G-12763)
KELLER SUPPLY CO
16212 E Marietta Ave (99216-1838)
PHONE 509 922-6388
EMP: 2 **EST:** 2015
SALES (est): 137.8K **Privately Held**
SIC: 3432 Plumbing fixture fittings & trim

(G-12764)
KEMIRA WATER SOLUTIONS INC
Also Called: Kemiron North America
2315 N Sullivan Rd (99216-1811)
PHONE 509 922-2244
Jane Jones, *Branch Mgr*
EMP: 19
SALES (corp-wide): 2.9B **Privately Held**
WEB: www.kemiron.com
SIC: 2899 Water treating compounds
HQ: Kemira Water Solutions, Inc.
1000 Parkwood Cir Se # 500
Atlanta GA 30339
770 436-1542

(G-12765)
KERMIT ANDERSON
Also Called: Star Steel
6303 E Sprague Ave (99212-0838)
PHONE 509 535-2362
Kermit Anderson, *Owner*
EMP: 9 **EST:** 1966
SQ FT: 2,500
SALES (est): 800K **Privately Held**
SIC: 3441 Fabricated structural metal

(G-12766)
KEY TRONIC CORPORATION (PA)
Also Called: KEYTRONICEMS
4424 N Sullivan Rd (99216-1593)
PHONE 509 928-8000
Craig D Gates, *President*
Ed Carter, *General Mgr*
David Surette, *Business Mgr*
Brett Larsen, *Exec VP*
Mike Larsen, *Exec VP*
▲ **EMP:** 50
SALES: 446.3MM **Publicly Held**
WEB: www.keytronic.com
SIC: 3577 Computer peripheral equipment

(G-12767)
KEY TRONIC CORPORATION
3808 N Sullivan Rd (99216-1608)
PHONE 509 928-8000
Sheri Watson Riley, *Branch Mgr*
EMP: 180
SALES (corp-wide): 446.3MM **Publicly Held**
SIC: 3571 Electronic computers
PA: Key Tronic Corporation
4424 N Sullivan Rd
Spokane Valley WA 99216
509 928-8000

(G-12768)
KEY TRONIC CORPORATION
Also Called: Keytronic Ems
11506 E 47th Ave (99206-9474)
PHONE 509 927-5225
Eric Johnson, *Principal*
EMP: 4
SALES (corp-wide): 446.3MM **Publicly Held**
SIC: 3577 Computer peripheral equipment
PA: Key Tronic Corporation
4424 N Sullivan Rd
Spokane Valley WA 99216
509 928-8000

(G-12769)
L B FOSTER COMPANY
3808 N Sullivan Rd Bldg 7 (99216-1618)
PHONE 509 921-8777
Zechariah Rasmussen, *Branch Mgr*
EMP: 8
SALES (corp-wide): 626.9MM **Publicly Held**
SIC: 3251 Brick & structural clay tile
PA: L. B. Foster Company
415 Holiday Dr Ste 1
Pittsburgh PA 15220
412 928-3400

(G-12770)
LAFARGE NORTH AMERICA INC
Also Called: Lafargeholcim
3808 N Sullivan Rd # 15 (99216-1608)
PHONE 509 893-0034
Pat Cunningham, *Manager*
EMP: 5
SALES (corp-wide): 27.6B **Privately Held**
WEB: www.lafargenorthamerica.com
SIC: 3241 3273 Cement, hydraulic; ready-mixed concrete
HQ: Lafarge North America Inc.
8700 W Bryn Mawr Ave
Chicago IL 60631
773 372-1000

(G-12771)
LANE PIERCE PARTNERS INC
Also Called: Cw Products
6326 E Sharp Ave (99212-1274)
PHONE 509 926-1033
Frank Duffy, *President*
Heidi Duffy, *Principal*
EMP: 13
SALES: 1.5MM **Privately Held**
SIC: 2448 5085 5031 Pallets, wood; boxes, crates, etc., other than paper; lumber, plywood & millwork

(G-12772)
LARRY GUTHRIE CO
13411 E 32nd Ave Ste A (99216-0139)
PHONE 509 922-6121
Larry Guthrie, *Owner*
EMP: 4
SQ FT: 86,540
SALES (est): 180K **Privately Held**
SIC: 2511 1542 Storage chests, household: wood; commercial & office building, new construction

(G-12773)
LATAH CREEK WINE CELLARS LTD
13030 E Indiana Ave (99216-1118)
PHONE 509 926-0164
Mike Conway, *President*
Shauna Morgan, *Corp Secy*
Ellena Conway, *Exec VP*
EMP: 4
SQ FT: 6,200
SALES (est): 495.6K **Privately Held**
WEB: www.latahcreek.com
SIC: 2084 5921 Wines; wine

(G-12774)
LITHOGRAPH REPRODUCTION INC
17323 E Trent Ave (99216-1732)
PHONE 509 926-9526
Lloyd Green, *President*
EMP: 8 **EST:** 1959
SQ FT: 3,500
SALES (est): 1.1MM **Privately Held**
SIC: 2752 Commercial printing, offset

(G-12775)
LLOYD INDUSTRIES LLC
3808 N Sullivan Rd 25j (99216-1616)
PHONE 509 468-8691
Tracy Rennaker, *President*
Traci Rennaker, *Vice Pres*
Damen Sager, *Prdtn Mgr*
Paul Lackey, *Facilities Mgr*
Paul Tiffany, *Engineer*
◆ **EMP:** 33
SALES (est): 7.2MM **Privately Held**
WEB: www.lloydpans.com
SIC: 3444 Sheet metalwork

(G-12776)
LOGAN INDUSTRIES INC
3808 N Sull Rd Spok Indu (99216)
PHONE 509 462-7400
Harold Alexander, *President*
Herb Jones, *Vice Pres*
Sandra Rathbun, *Vice Pres*
Walter Roys, *Vice Pres*
Lori Alexander, *Admin Sec*
▲ **EMP:** 63
SQ FT: 60,000
SALES (est): 9.9MM **Privately Held**
WEB: www.loganind.com
SIC: 3679 Harness assemblies for electronic use: wire or cable

(G-12777)
LONGHORN BARBECUE INC (PA)
10420 E Montgomery Dr (99206-4279)
PHONE 509 922-0702
Duke Fette, *President*
David Lehnertz, *Corp Secy*
▼ **EMP:** 155
SQ FT: 20,000
SALES (est): 7.4MM **Privately Held**
WEB: www.longhornbarbecue.com
SIC: 5812 2013 2033 Barbecue restaurant; sausages & other prepared meats; sausages from purchased meat; barbecue sauce: packaged in cans, jars, etc.

(G-12778)
LONGHORN BARBECUE PROD CTR
Also Called: Longhorn Production
10420 E Montgomery Dr (99206-4279)
PHONE 509 922-0702
Walter Fette, *President*
Dave Leonards, *Admin Sec*
EMP: 30 **EST:** 1984
SALES (est): 3.8MM **Privately Held**
SIC: 2013 2035 2011 Smoked meats from purchased meat; pickles, sauces & salad dressings; meat packing plants

(G-12779)
LYNN L REYNOLDS INC
Also Called: Phoenix Company
5405 E Cataldo Ave (99212-0977)
P.O. Box 13099 (99213-3099)
PHONE 509 536-9396
Lynn L Reynolds, *President*
Celie Reynolds, *Corp Secy*
EMP: 9
SALES (est): 1.2MM **Privately Held**
SIC: 3441 Fabricated structural metal

(G-12780)
MACKAY MANUFACTURING INC
10011 E Montgomery Dr (99206-4125)
P.O. Box 11278 (99211-1278)
PHONE 509 922-7742
Mike Mackay, *President*
Bruce Szember, *General Mgr*
Katie Mackay, *Vice Pres*
Gregg Meyer, *Mfg Spvr*
Don Ludington, *QC Mgr*
EMP: 80 **EST:** 1968
SQ FT: 30,000
SALES (est): 18MM **Privately Held**
WEB: www.mackaymfg.com
SIC: 3599 Machine shop, jobbing & repair

(G-12781)
MACKLIN WELDING
15722 E Sprague Ave (99037-8982)
PHONE 509 926-3597
William J Macklin, *Owner*
EMP: 2
SALES (est): 262.5K **Privately Held**
SIC: 5531 7692 Trailer hitches, automotive; welding repair

(G-12782)
MAGIC SATCHEL
916 N Ella Rd Apt 52 (99212-2773)
PHONE 509 342-8914
Tricia Fuller, *Principal*
EMP: 2
SALES (est): 77.4K **Privately Held**
SIC: 3161 Satchels

(G-12783)
MAPP TOOL LLC
11816 E Mnsfeld Ave Ste 3 (99206)
PHONE 509 228-9449
Mitch Alderman,
Pete Plante,
EMP: 3
SALES (est): 240K **Privately Held**
SIC: 3089 Injection molded finished plastic products

(G-12784)
MARLIN WINDOWS INC
5414 E Broadway Ave Ste A (99212-0937)
PHONE 509 535-3015
Gary Westermann, *President*
Steve Downie, *Superintendent*
Lyle Grambo, *Admin Sec*
EMP: 32
SQ FT: 50,000
SALES (est): 4.1MM **Privately Held**
WEB: www.marlinwindows.com
SIC: 3211 2431 Window glass, clear & colored; doors & door parts & trim, wood; windows & window parts & trim, wood

(G-12785)
MCC ENTERPRISES INC
Also Called: M C C Company
1014 N Pines Rd (99206-6707)
PHONE 509 928-9676
John McCormick, *CEO*
Larry D McCormick, *Vice Pres*
Bonnie McCormick, *Admin Sec*
EMP: 4
SQ FT: 36,000
SALES (est): 372.1K **Privately Held**
WEB: www.mcctextiles.com
SIC: 2369 Girls' & children's outerwear

(G-12786)
MCCULLEY INC
Also Called: Norwest Shop Equipment
9507 E 4th Ave (99206-3662)
P.O. Box 96, Newman Lake (99025-0096)
PHONE 509 891-4134
Robert McCulley, *President*
EMP: 6
SALES (est): 845.2K **Privately Held**
WEB: www.mcculley.com
SIC: 3559 Automotive maintenance equipment

(G-12787)
MELCHER MANUFACTURING CO INC
Also Called: Lifetime Pools
1410 N Howe Rd (99212-0944)
PHONE 509 534-9119
Randy Melcher, *Manager*

▲ = Import ▼ = Export
◆ = Import/Export

EMP: 6
SQ FT: 6,231
SALES (corp-wide): 2.8MM **Privately Held**
WEB: www.melcher-ramps.com
SIC: 1799 3272 Swimming pool construction; bathtubs, concrete
PA: Melcher Manufacturing Company, Inc.
6017 E Mission Ave
Spokane Valley WA
509 535-7626

(G-12788)
MICHAELS GEMSTONE TREES
12006 E 8th Ave (99206-5487)
PHONE..................................509 922-2390
Michael Goering, *Owner*
EMP: 4
SALES (est): 193.3K **Privately Held**
SIC: 3299 Architectural sculptures: gypsum, clay, papier mache, etc.

(G-12789)
MIDDCO TOOL & EQUIPMENT INC
2401 N Eastern Rd (99212-1440)
P.O. Box 11978 (99211-1978)
PHONE..................................509 535-1701
Kevin Middaugh, *President*
Karen Speerstra, *Corp Secy*
EMP: 17
SQ FT: 36,000
SALES (est): 2.4MM **Privately Held**
SIC: 3469 Machine parts, stamped or pressed metal

(G-12790)
MILL MAN STEEL INC
11307 E Montgomery Dr (99206-7620)
PHONE..................................909 854-7020
Ken Dumstra, *Manager*
EMP: 11
SALES (corp-wide): 8.4MM **Privately Held**
SIC: 3317 Steel pipe & tubes
PA: Mill Man Steel, Inc.
1441 Wazee St Ste 104
Denver CO 80202
800 748-2928

(G-12791)
MINUTEMAN PRESS
111 N Vista Rd Ste 2d (99212-2960)
PHONE..................................509 435-0863
EMP: 2
SALES (est): 83.9K **Privately Held**
SIC: 2752 Commercial printing, lithographic

(G-12792)
MOCO ENGINEERING & FABRICATION
3212 N Eden Rd (99216-1719)
PHONE..................................509 226-0199
Chuck Moles, *President*
Erik Humble, *President*
EMP: 11
SALES (est): 1.3MM **Privately Held**
WEB: www.mocoeng.com
SIC: 3599 8711 Custom machinery; engineering services

(G-12793)
MONACO ENTERPRISES INC
14820 E Sprague Ave (99216-2191)
P.O. Box 14129 (99214-0129)
PHONE..................................509 926-6277
Eugene A Monaco, *CEO*
EMP: 80
SQ FT: 39,000
SALES: 17.6MM **Privately Held**
WEB: www.monaco.com
SIC: 3669 7373 7382 Emergency alarms; fire alarm apparatus, electric; fire detection systems, electric; computer integrated systems design; security systems services

(G-12794)
MOUNTAIN DOG SIGN COMPANY INC
1620 N Mamer Rd Ste D100 (99216-3753)
PHONE..................................509 891-9999
Marshon Kempf, *President*
Steven Kempf, *Vice Pres*
EMP: 6
SQ FT: 3,600
SALES (est): 827.6K **Privately Held**
SIC: 3993 Electric signs

(G-12795)
MPM TECHNOLOGIES INC (PA)
16201 E Ind Ave Ste 3200 (99216)
PHONE..................................973 599-4416
Daniel Carraway, *Ch of Bd*
Timothy King, *Principal*
Richard KAO, *Principal*
Brian Burrow, *CFO*
EMP: 5
SALES (est): 739.7K **Publicly Held**
SIC: 3564 8711 Air purification equipment; pollution control engineering

(G-12796)
MULTIFAB INC (PA)
3808 N Sullivan Rd Bldg 6 (99216-1618)
PHONE..................................509 924-6631
Timothy B Smith, *President*
Al B Boschma, *COO*
Mike Zumstein, *Branch Mgr*
Mark Katzke, *Consultant*
▲ **EMP:** 145
SQ FT: 120,000
SALES (est): 98.9MM **Privately Held**
WEB: www.multifab-inc.com
SIC: 5085 2542 Fasteners, industrial: nuts, bolts, screws, etc.; staplers & tackers; packing, industrial; partitions & fixtures, except wood; office & store showcases & display fixtures; racks, merchandise display or storage: except wood

(G-12797)
MY CABINETRY
11425 E Trent Ave (99206-4632)
PHONE..................................509 879-0086
Jim Auer, *Owner*
EMP: 4
SALES (est): 361.2K **Privately Held**
SIC: 2434 Wood kitchen cabinets

(G-12798)
N E S ENTERPRISES
1109 N Bessie Rd (99212-2689)
PHONE..................................509 928-9151
Norman Pierce, *Owner*
EMP: 2
SALES (est): 94.1K **Privately Held**
SIC: 3499 Machine bases, metal

(G-12799)
N E W CASTINGS
3808 N Sullivan Rd 8q (99216-2611)
PHONE..................................509 924-6464
Francis Beach, *President*
Gary Beach, *Vice Pres*
Carl Beach, *Treasurer*
EMP: 20
SQ FT: 40,000
SALES: 1.5MM **Privately Held**
WEB: www.travispattern.com
SIC: 3321 Gray iron castings; ductile iron castings

(G-12800)
NA DEGERSTROM INC (PA)
3303 N Sullivan Rd (99216-1676)
P.O. Box 770, Veradale (99037-0770)
PHONE..................................509 928-3333
Christopher Myers, *President*
Michael Cannon, *Corp Secy*
Mike Coleman, *Vice Pres*
Joan B Degerstrom, *Vice Pres*
Chris Myers, *Vice Pres*
EMP: 50 **EST:** 1904
SQ FT: 5,000
SALES: 62MM **Privately Held**
WEB: www.nadinc.com
SIC: 1041 1475 1622 Open pit gold mining; phosphate rock; bridge, tunnel & elevated highway

(G-12801)
NATIONAL BARRICADE & SIGN CO
6602 E Main Ave (99212-0893)
PHONE..................................509 534-2619
Brian Maphis, *President*
Bruce Maphis, *Vice Pres*
Kathy Maphis, *Treasurer*
Haley Mathis, *Sales Mgr*
EMP: 4
SALES (est): 549.3K **Privately Held**
SIC: 3669 Transportation signaling devices

(G-12802)
NELSON BROTHERS INC
3808 N Sullivan Rd 14e (99216-1608)
PHONE..................................509 922-4988
Rod Nelson, *President*
EMP: 12
SQ FT: 20,000
SALES (est): 1.6MM **Privately Held**
SIC: 2541 Store & office display cases & fixtures

(G-12803)
NORCO INC
6102 E Trent Ave (99212-1228)
PHONE..................................509 535-9808
Shaun Blakeman, *Sales/Mktg Mgr*
Terry Sanchez, *Manager*
EMP: 10
SALES (corp-wide): 413MM **Privately Held**
WEB: www.norco-inc.com
SIC: 5084 7692 Welding machinery & equipment; welding repair
PA: Norco, Inc.
1125 W Amity Rd
Boise ID 83705
208 336-1643

(G-12804)
NORDIC TARPS MANUFACTURING
5805 E Sharp Ave Ste C6 (99212-0955)
PHONE..................................509 533-1530
Gerald W Bordwell, *Owner*
EMP: 2
SQ FT: 1,500
SALES (est): 120K **Privately Held**
SIC: 2394 Tarpaulins, fabric: made from purchased materials

(G-12805)
NORTHWEST BIOFUELS
9908 E Holman Rd (99206-9234)
PHONE..................................509 927-4548
Doug Bartlett, *Principal*
EMP: 3 **EST:** 2011
SALES (est): 234K **Privately Held**
SIC: 2869 Fuels

(G-12806)
NORTHWEST LAUNDRY SUPPLY INC
624 N Fancher Rd (99212-1053)
PHONE..................................509 487-4800
Lawrence Hainsworth, *President*
Loren Hainsworth, *Vice Pres*
EMP: 8 **EST:** 1950
SQ FT: 10,000
SALES (est): 910K **Privately Held**
SIC: 3582 Drycleaning equipment & machinery, commercial

(G-12807)
NORTHWEST METAL CRAFT
1311 N Marguerite Rd (99212-2613)
PHONE..................................509 999-5280
John Hopkins, *Owner*
Brenda Hopkins, *Co-Owner*
EMP: 2
SALES (est): 115.6K **Privately Held**
SIC: 2514 1799 7389 Metal household furniture; ornamental metal work;

(G-12808)
NORTHWEST PEA & BEAN COMPANY (HQ)
6109 E Desmet Ave (99212-1254)
P.O. Box 11973 (99211-1973)
PHONE..................................509 534-3821
Fax: 509 534-4350
▼ **EMP:** 13
SQ FT: 67,000
SALES (est): 15.4MM
SALES (corp-wide): 55.2MM **Privately Held**
SIC: 5153 2034 Whol Grain/Field Beans Mfg Dehydrated Fruits/Vegetables
PA: Cooperative Agricultural Producers, Inc.
120 W Fifth St
Rosalia WA 99170
509 523-3032

(G-12809)
NORTHWEST WIRE EDM INC
1620 N Mamer Rd Ste C300 (99216-3725)
PHONE..................................509 893-0885
Forest C Renslow Jr, *President*
EMP: 2
SALES (est): 291K **Privately Held**
WEB: www.northwestwireedm.com
SIC: 3599 Machine shop, jobbing & repair

(G-12810)
NOVA SERVICES
1101 N Fancher Rd Ste 2 (99212-1272)
PHONE..................................509 928-1588
Linda Brennan, *Exec Dir*
EMP: 20
SQ FT: 19,920
SALES: 917.7K **Privately Held**
WEB: www.nova-services.org
SIC: 8331 7361 3699 Vocational rehabilitation agency; employment agencies; electrical equipment & supplies

(G-12811)
NOVA VERTA USA INC
8207 E Trent Ave (99212-2241)
PHONE..................................509 444-7910
Bob Cross, *President*
▲ **EMP:** 8
SQ FT: 15,000
SALES (est): 3.5MM **Privately Held**
WEB: www.novavertausa.com
SIC: 3089 Automotive parts, plastic

(G-12812)
NOVATION INC
2616 N Locust Rd (99206-4371)
PHONE..................................509 922-1912
Fred Le Friec, *President*
EMP: 50
SQ FT: 36,000
SALES (est): 5.6MM **Privately Held**
SIC: 3471 Anodizing (plating) of metals or formed products; electroplating of metals or formed products; coloring & finishing of aluminum or formed products

(G-12813)
NOVELIS CORPORATION
Also Called: Novelis Solatens Tech Ctr
16004 E Euclid Ave (99216-1878)
PHONE..................................509 462-2310
Andrew King, *VP Sales*
Barry Miller, *Manager*
EMP: 20
SALES (corp-wide): 6.4B **Privately Held**
SIC: 3353 Foil, aluminum
HQ: Novelis Corporation
3560 Lenox Rd Ne Ste 2000
Atlanta GA 30326
404 760-4000

(G-12814)
NOXON INC
2921 N University Rd # 3 (99206-4607)
PHONE..................................509 926-0557
Robert Warner, *CEO*
Emory Clark, *VP Sales*
▲ **EMP:** 4
SQ FT: 600
SALES (est): 300K **Privately Held**
SIC: 3541 Machine tools, metal cutting type

(G-12815)
NUT FACTORY INC
Also Called: Premier Packing Company
19425 E Broadway Ave (99016-8578)
P.O. Box 11444 (99211-1444)
PHONE..................................509 926-6666
Gene Cohen, *President*
EMP: 23
SQ FT: 23,000
SALES (est): 4.4MM **Privately Held**
WEB: www.thenutfactory.com
SIC: 2068 2099 5441 Salted & roasted nuts & seeds; food preparations; candy, nut & confectionery stores

Spokane Valley - Spokane County (G-12816)

(G-12816)
OLDCASTLE APG
16310 E Marietta Ln (99216-1837)
PHONE.................509 926-8235
Cliff Anderson, *Principal*
Charlie May, *Vice Pres*
EMP: 9 **EST:** 2010
SALES (est): 1.4MM **Privately Held**
SIC: 3272 Concrete products

(G-12817)
OLDCASTLE MATERIALS INC
Also Called: Central Premix Sakrete
16310 E Marietta Ave (99216-1837)
PHONE.................509 926-8235
Wade Ficklin, *Branch Mgr*
EMP: 100
SALES (corp-wide): 30.6B **Privately Held**
WEB: www.centralpremix.com
SIC: 5032 3273 Concrete mixtures; ready-mixed concrete
HQ: Oldcastle Materials, Inc.
900 Ashwood Pkwy Ste 700
Atlanta GA 30338

(G-12818)
OLDCASTLE MATERIALS INC
922 N Carnahan Rd (99212-0938)
P.O. Box 3366, Spokane (99220-3366)
PHONE.................509 534-6221
EMP: 11
SALES (est): 1.8MM **Privately Held**
SIC: 3273 Ready-mixed concrete

(G-12819)
OMNIMAX INTERNATIONAL INC
Fabral
6207 E Desmet Ave (99212-1203)
PHONE.................509 535-0344
Mitchell B Lewis, *CEO*
EMP: 10
SALES (corp-wide): 861.3MM **Privately Held**
SIC: 3444 Sheet metalwork
HQ: Omnimax International, Inc.
30 Technology Pkwy S # 400
Peachtree Corners GA 30092

(G-12820)
ONE TREE HARD CIDER
9514 E Montgomery Ave (99206-4140)
PHONE.................509 315-9856
EMP: 7
SALES (est): 646.8K **Privately Held**
SIC: 2084 Wines

(G-12821)
OREGON PCF BLDG PDTS EXCH INC
Also Called: Orepac Building Products
15120 E Euclid Ave (99216-1801)
PHONE.................509 892-5555
Glenn Hart, *President*
Lee Daggett, *Corp Secy*
Alan Kirk, *Vice Pres*
Blaine Graham, *Sales Mgr*
John Schweinsberg, *Sales Staff*
▲ **EMP:** 60 **EST:** 1904
SQ FT: 20,000
SALES (est): 16.9MM
SALES (corp-wide): 597.4MM **Privately Held**
SIC: 5031 2431 Door frames, all materials; windows; lumber: rough, dressed & finished; doors & door parts & trim, wood; moldings, wood: unfinished & prefinished
PA: Orepac Holding Company
30170 Sw Ore Pac Ave
Wilsonville OR 97070
503 685-5499

(G-12822)
PACIFIC CONTRACTORS & SUPPLY
Also Called: Pacific Metal Buildings
10815 E 35th Ave (99206-5889)
PHONE.................509 534-4304
Joe Mazzie, *President*
Stephanie Castillo, *Admin Sec*
EMP: 5
SQ FT: 8,000
SALES (est): 666.9K **Privately Held**
SIC: 1521 3448 Single-family housing construction; buildings, portable: prefabricated metal

(G-12823)
PACIFIC NW PRINT FLFLLMENT INC
18001 E Euclid Ave Ste C (99216-1746)
PHONE.................509 242-7857
Chris Ballard, *President*
Christine Ballard, *Treasurer*
EMP: 11
SQ FT: 7,100
SALES: 600K **Privately Held**
SIC: 2752 8742 Commercial printing, lithographic; marketing consulting services

(G-12824)
PALLET PLACE INC
10315 E Buckeye Ln (99206-4287)
P.O. Box 6547, Spokane (99217-0909)
PHONE.................509 484-4889
Keith Carver, *President*
EMP: 9
SALES (est): 1.5MM **Privately Held**
SIC: 2448 Pallets, wood & wood with metal

(G-12825)
PANTHER PRINTING
111 N Vista Rd Ste 2d (99212-2960)
P.O. Box 13232 (99213-3232)
PHONE.................509 344-4600
Robert Atkins, *Principal*
EMP: 5
SALES (est): 440.9K **Privately Held**
SIC: 3069 7334 2759 Medical & laboratory rubber sundries & related products; blueprinting service; commercial printing

(G-12826)
PEDERSONS CUSTOM WOODWORKING
10809 E 26th Ave (99206-7116)
PHONE.................509 981-0720
EMP: 2
SALES (est): 65.4K **Privately Held**
SIC: 2431 Millwork

(G-12827)
PEPSI
Also Called: Pepsico
11016 E Montgomery Dr (99206-6146)
PHONE.................509 536-5585
EMP: 6
SALES (est): 562.8K **Privately Held**
SIC: 2086 Soft drinks: packaged in cans, bottles, etc.

(G-12828)
PERFECTION COATINGS
15720 E 4th Ave Apt M207 (99037-2117)
PHONE.................509 599-2538
EMP: 2
SALES (est): 90.7K **Privately Held**
SIC: 2952 Mfg Asphalt Felts/Coatings

(G-12829)
PLUG POWER INC
15913 E Euclid Ave (99216-1815)
PHONE.................509 228-6694
Michael Rife, *President*
EMP: 13
SALES (corp-wide): 174.6MM **Publicly Held**
SIC: 2679 Fuel cell forms, cardboard: made from purchased material
PA: Plug Power Inc.
968 Albany Shaker Rd
Latham NY 12110
518 782-7700

(G-12830)
PLUG POWER INC
16005 E Euclid Ave Ste F (99216-1861)
PHONE.................509 228-6638
EMP: 4
SALES (corp-wide): 174.6MM **Publicly Held**
SIC: 3629 Electrochemical generators (fuel cells)
PA: Plug Power Inc.
968 Albany Shaker Rd
Latham NY 12110
518 782-7700

(G-12831)
POHL SPRING WORKS INC
6415 E Nixon Ave (99212-1023)
PHONE.................509 466-0904
William Reese, *Vice Pres*
EMP: 10 **EST:** 1915
SQ FT: 14,000
SALES (est): 1.6MM **Privately Held**
WEB: www.pohlsprings.com
SIC: 3493 Coiled flat springs; leaf springs: automobile, locomotive, etc.

(G-12832)
PORT A COVER & MORE INC
16624 E Sprague Ave (99037-8967)
PHONE.................509 928-9264
Greg Walter, *President*
Regina Walter, *Admin Sec*
EMP: 3
SALES (est): 250K **Privately Held**
WEB: www.portacover.com
SIC: 3448 Prefabricated metal buildings

(G-12833)
POWDERTECH INC
10020 E Montgomery Dr (99206-4137)
PHONE.................509 927-0189
EMP: 5
SQ FT: 12,000
SALES (est): 265.5K **Privately Held**
SIC: 3479 Powder Coating On Commercial Equipment

(G-12834)
POWDERTECH MR SHANNON
3808 N Sullivan Rd (99216-1608)
PHONE.................509 927-5804
Shannon Agnew, *Principal*
EMP: 10
SALES (est): 1.1MM **Privately Held**
SIC: 3479 Hot dip coating of metals or formed products

(G-12835)
POWELL INDUSTRIES INC
3808 N Sullivan Rd 3k (99216-1619)
PHONE.................509 922-0463
Kristin Potter, *Branch Mgr*
EMP: 3
SALES (corp-wide): 395.9MM **Publicly Held**
SIC: 3999 Barber & beauty shop equipment
PA: Powell Industries, Inc.
8550 Mosley Rd
Houston TX 77075
713 944-6900

(G-12836)
PRECIOUS METALS MIN & REF CO
2320 S Bolivar Rd (99037-9425)
PHONE.................509 927-2685
Richard W Morris, *Principal*
EMP: 2
SALES (est): 125K **Privately Held**
SIC: 3339 Precious metals

(G-12837)
PRECISION MACHINE SUPPLY
15708 E Marietta Ln (99216-1828)
PHONE.................509 922-1666
EMP: 2
SALES (est): 119.1K **Privately Held**
SIC: 3599 Mfg Industrial Machinery

(G-12838)
PRESTYL USA LLC
9711 E Knox Ave Ste 2 (99206-4207)
PHONE.................509 703-7661
Christine De Mos, *CEO*
Marius De Mos,
Thomas Morrow,
EMP: 3 **EST:** 2011
SALES (est): 388.6K **Privately Held**
SIC: 3567 Radiant heating systems, industrial process

(G-12839)
PRINT CENTER LLC
11808 E Mnsfeld Ave Ste 2 (99206)
PHONE.................509 979-8272
Ruvim Mishin,
Slava Mishin,
EMP: 7
SALES (est): 691.7K **Privately Held**
SIC: 2752 Commercial printing, offset

(G-12840)
PRINT TECH INC
Also Called: Sir Speedy
16508 E Sprague Ave (99037-8908)
PHONE.................509 535-1460
Troy Parker, *President*
Jay Eisenbarth, *Accounts Mgr*
John Nelson, *Sales Staff*
EMP: 5
SQ FT: 6,800
SALES (est): 1.7MM **Privately Held**
SIC: 2752 Commercial printing, lithographic

(G-12841)
PRO CLIP PRODUCTS INC
3517 S Fox St (99206-5924)
PHONE.................509 924-5544
Tom Morris, *President*
Marcia Morris, *Treasurer*
EMP: 2
SALES (est): 145.3K **Privately Held**
WEB: www.pro-clip.com
SIC: 3089 Holders: paper towel, grocery bag, etc.: plastic

(G-12842)
PRO FAB
7505 E Sprague Ave (99212-2932)
PHONE.................509 879-9293
EMP: 2
SALES (est): 50K **Privately Held**
SIC: 3829 Mfg Measuring/Controlling Devices

(G-12843)
PROLAM INDUSTRIES INC
3808 N Sullivan Rd 29c (99216-1608)
PHONE.................509 926-2001
Barbara Poole, *Branch Mgr*
EMP: 7 **Privately Held**
WEB: www.ltionline.net
SIC: 2435 3083 Hardwood plywood, prefinished; laminated plastics plate & sheet
PA: Prolam Industries Inc
1225 Avenue C Ste A
White City OR 97503

(G-12844)
PURCELL SYSTEMS INC (HQ)
16125 E Euclid Ave (99216-1853)
PHONE.................509 755-0341
Lyle Jordan, *President*
Robert Kjelldorff, *President*
Christopher Craig, *General Mgr*
Peter Chase, *Founder*
Danni Peterson, *Business Mgr*
▲ **EMP:** 90
SQ FT: 81,000
SALES (est): 56.7MM
SALES (corp-wide): 2.8B **Publicly Held**
WEB: www.purcellsystems.com
SIC: 2514 Cabinets, radio & television: metal
PA: Enersys
2366 Bernville Rd
Reading PA 19605
610 208-1991

(G-12845)
PURRFECT LOGOS INC
Also Called: A Purrfect Logo, Dva
12018 E 1st Ave (99206-5228)
P.O. Box 141111 (99214-1111)
PHONE.................509 893-2424
Larry E Garner, *President*
Stanley Macdonald, *Treasurer*
EMP: 8
SQ FT: 6,000
SALES (est): 695.6K **Privately Held**
WEB: www.purrfectlogos.com
SIC: 2395 7336 Embroidery & art needlework; silk screen design

(G-12846)
PYROTEK INCORPORATED
9601 E Montgomery Ave (99206-4117)
PHONE.................509 926-6211
Todd Schroeder, *Manager*
EMP: 61

GEOGRAPHIC SECTION
Spokane Valley - Spokane County (G-12873)

SALES (corp-wide): 592MM **Privately Held**
WEB: www.pyrotek.info
SIC: **3229** 3624 3564 3549 Glass fiber products; carbon & graphite products; blowers & fans; metalworking machinery; aluminum extruded products; porcelain electrical supplies
PA: Pyrotek Incorporated
705 W 1st Ave
Spokane WA 99201
509 926-6212

(G-12847)
PYROTEK INCORPORATED
3808 N Sullivan Rd 27k (99216-1622)
PHONE..................................509 921-8766
Don Prince, *Manager*
EMP: 44
SALES (corp-wide): 592MM **Privately Held**
SIC: **3365** Aluminum foundries
PA: Pyrotek Incorporated
705 W 1st Ave
Spokane WA 99201
509 926-6212

(G-12848)
QUARRY TILE COMPANY
Also Called: Precision H2o
6328 E Utah Ave Ste 1 (99212-1400)
PHONE..................................509 536-2812
Sean O'Kesse, *President*
Jed Durbin, *Exec VP*
Tim Ragan, *Vice Pres*
James Thomas Sawyer, *Vice Pres*
Jim Skeie, *Vice Pres*
▲ EMP: 100 EST: 1965
SQ FT: 150,000
SALES (est): 17.1MM **Privately Held**
WEB: www.quarrytile.com
SIC: **3253** Floor tile, ceramic; wall tile, ceramic

(G-12849)
RAH INC
Also Called: Nick's Custom Boots
6510 E Sprague Ave Bldg 1 (99212-1130)
P.O. Box 293, Harrison ID (83833-0293)
PHONE..................................509 482-0943
Dick Hoesly, *President*
EMP: 20
SQ FT: 2,200
SALES (est): 2.4MM **Privately Held**
WEB: www.nicksboots.com
SIC: **5661** 3131 3144 3143 Men's shoes; footwear cut stock; women's footwear, except athletic; men's footwear, except athletic

(G-12850)
RANDL INDUSTRIES INC
3808 N Sullivan Rd 10p (99216-7003)
PHONE..................................509 340-0050
Robert Hagarty, *President*
Nick Hagarty, *Marketing Staff*
▲ EMP: 2 EST: 1999
SALES (est): 371.3K **Privately Held**
WEB: www.randl-inc.com
SIC: **3825** Energy measuring equipment, electrical

(G-12851)
REYES COCA-COLA BOTTLING LLC
9705 E Montgomery Ave (99206-4119)
PHONE..................................509 921-6200
Andy Alverz, *Manager*
EMP: 65
SALES (corp-wide): 713.8MM **Privately Held**
SIC: **2086** Bottled & canned soft drinks
PA: Reyes Coca-Cola Bottling, L.L.C.
3 Park Plz Ste 600
Irvine CA 92614
213 744-8616

(G-12852)
RIGGSAFE SOLUTIONS INC
15908 E 6th Ln (99037-7940)
P.O. Box 52003, Knoxville TN (37950-2003)
PHONE..................................865 266-9989
Connie Riggs, *President*
EMP: 2

SALES (est): 89.3K **Privately Held**
SIC: **2731** Book publishing

(G-12853)
ROAD PRODUCTS INC
Also Called: R P I
12301 E Empire Ave (99216-1231)
P.O. Box 11072 (99211-1072)
PHONE..................................509 922-1206
Denise M Lawless, *President*
EMP: 3
SALES (est): 440K **Privately Held**
SIC: **1611** 2952 Highway & street maintenance; asphalt felts & coatings

(G-12854)
ROCKET BAKERY INC (PA)
4124 N Burns Rd (99216-1351)
PHONE..................................509 462-2345
Jeff Postlewait, *President*
EMP: 8
SALES (est): 1.4MM **Privately Held**
SIC: **5461** 2051 Bread; bread, cake & related products

(G-12855)
ROCKY MOUNTAIN MACHINING
1105 S Glenbrook Ct (99016-9668)
PHONE..................................509 927-8797
Kurt Campbell, *Principal*
EMP: 2
SALES (est): 212.6K **Privately Held**
SIC: **3599** Machine shop, jobbing & repair

(G-12856)
ROGERS MACHINERY COMPANY INC
16615 E Euclid Ave (99216-1825)
PHONE..................................509 922-0556
Mitch Johnson, *Sales & Mktg St*
EMP: 13
SQ FT: 5,045
SALES (corp-wide): 69.8MM **Privately Held**
SIC: **3561** 3564 5084 7699 Industrial pumps & parts; blowers & fans; industrial machinery & equipment; compressors, except air conditioning; pumps & pumping equipment; compressor repair; pumps & pumping equipment repair; industrial machinery & equipment repair
PA: Rogers Machinery Company, Inc.
14650 Sw 72nd Ave
Portland OR 97224
503 639-0808

(G-12857)
S2M ENTERPRISES LLC
2205 N Woodruff Rd Ste 9 (99206-4190)
PHONE..................................509 919-3714
Molly Paridon,
Stephanie Bernards,
Sommer Teague,
EMP: 5
SQ FT: 4,000
SALES (est): 195.8K **Privately Held**
SIC: **2835** In vitro diagnostics

(G-12858)
SATURDAY NIGHT INC
3520 N Eden Rd (99216-1762)
PHONE..................................509 928-5816
Jim Warpenburg, *President*
Kathy Warpenburg, *Corp Secy*
EMP: 10 EST: 1975
SQ FT: 10,000
SALES (est): 1.4MM **Privately Held**
WEB: www.saturdaynightt-shirt.com
SIC: **2752** 5699 2396 7336 Business form & card printing, lithographic; T-shirts, custom printed; screen printing on fabric articles; commercial art & graphic design

(G-12859)
SCHINDLER ELEVATOR CORPORATION
409 N Thierman Rd Ste D (99212-1129)
P.O. Box 13160 (99213-3160)
PHONE..................................509 535-2471
Joe Stumph, *Manager*
EMP: 22
SALES (corp-wide): 10.9B **Privately Held**
WEB: www.us.schindler.com
SIC: **3534** 1796 Elevators & equipment; installing building equipment

HQ: Schindler Elevator Corporation
20 Whippany Rd
Morristown NJ 07960
973 397-6500

(G-12860)
SCHNEIDER ELC BUILDINGS LLC
Also Called: Invensys Environmental Contrls
7222 E Nora Ave (99212-1216)
PHONE..................................509 892-1121
Pat McGahey, *Branch Mgr*
EMP: 10
SALES (corp-wide): 355.8K **Privately Held**
SIC: **3822** 1711 Building services monitoring controls, automatic; mechanical contractor
HQ: Schneider Electric Buildings, Llc
839 N Perryville Rd
Rockford IL 61107
815 381-5000

(G-12861)
SCHOLASTIC INC
3808 N Sullivan Rd 35d (99216-1615)
PHONE..................................509 926-4465
Greg McKim, *Manager*
EMP: 8
SALES (corp-wide): 1.6B **Publicly Held**
WEB: www.scholasticdealer.com
SIC: **2731** Books: publishing only
HQ: Scholastic Inc.
557 Broadway Lbby 1
New York NY 10012
212 343-6100

(G-12862)
SEATON CONCEPTS INC
18405 E Baldwin Ave (99016-9507)
PHONE..................................509 928-0633
William J Seaton, *President*
EMP: 2
SALES (est): 133.6K **Privately Held**
SIC: **3993** Signs & advertising specialties

(G-12863)
SEFCO LLC
15215 E Upland Dr (99216-1347)
PHONE..................................509 921-1121
Steve Ford, *Mng Member*
EMP: 2
SALES (est): 286.9K **Privately Held**
SIC: **3599** Machine shop, jobbing & repair

(G-12864)
SEMGROUP CORP
16710 E Euclid Ave (99216-1821)
PHONE..................................509 921-7089
Dan Walker, *Branch Mgr*
EMP: 5
SALES (corp-wide): 2.5B **Publicly Held**
WEB: www.semgrouplp.com
SIC: **4612** 5171 2951 Crude petroleum pipelines; petroleum bulk stations & terminals; asphalt paving mixtures & blocks
PA: Semgroup Corporation
6120 S Yale Ave Ste 1500
Tulsa OK 74136
918 524-8100

(G-12865)
SERVATRON INC
12825 E Mirabeau Pkwy # 104 (99216-1617)
PHONE..................................509 321-9500
Tod Byers, *President*
John Miskulin, *Vice Pres*
Keith Swenson, *Vice Pres*
Shawn Taylor, *Treasurer*
▲ EMP: 150
SQ FT: 61,000
SALES (est): 45.3MM **Privately Held**
WEB: www.servatron.com
SIC: **3672** 7629 Printed circuit boards; electrical repair shops

(G-12866)
SERVICE PARTNERS LLC
125 N Dyer Rd (99212-0846)
PHONE..................................509 535-4600
Nat Bonanno, *Managing Dir*
Julie Leatherman, *CFO*
Joseph Carrington,
EMP: 52
SQ FT: 2,000

SALES (est): 181K
SALES (corp-wide): 2.3B **Publicly Held**
SIC: **3296** 5033 1742 Mineral wool insulation products; insulation, thermal; insulation, buildings
HQ: Service Partners, Llc
475 N Williamson Blvd
Daytona Beach FL 32114
804 515-7400

(G-12867)
SHADOW WORKS LLC
315 S Dishman Rd (99206-3119)
PHONE..................................509 251-8306
Carl Jessen, *Mng Member*
EMP: 8 EST: 2014
SALES (est): 400K **Privately Held**
SIC: **5122** 2844 Cosmetics; toilet preparations

(G-12868)
SHAMROCK MACHINING INC
5704 E 1st Ave (99212-0750)
PHONE..................................509 534-3031
Marv Wheeler, *President*
Neil Wheeler, *Vice Pres*
EMP: 25
SQ FT: 20,000
SALES (est): 4.3MM **Privately Held**
WEB: www.shamrock-machining.com
SIC: **3599** 5571 7629 Machine shop, jobbing & repair; motorcycle dealers; electrical repair shops

(G-12869)
SHANNON D AGNEW
3808 N Sullivan Rd (99216-1608)
PHONE..................................509 926-6209
Shannon D Agnew, *Principal*
EMP: 2
SALES (est): 130.2K **Privately Held**
SIC: **3479** Metal coating & allied service

(G-12870)
SIDE HUSTLE LLC
1423 N Locust Rd (99206-4019)
PHONE..................................509 435-6773
Dillon Hueser, *Mng Member*
EMP: 3
SALES (est): 127K **Privately Held**
SIC: **2086** 2087 Iced tea & fruit drinks, bottled & canned; beverage bases, concentrates, syrups, powders & mixes

(G-12871)
SIEMENS INDUSTRY INC
1225 N Argonne Rd Ste A (99212-2798)
PHONE..................................509 891-9070
Ron Studebaker, *Branch Mgr*
EMP: 10
SALES (corp-wide): 95B **Privately Held**
WEB: www.sibt.com
SIC: **3829** 8711 5075 5074 Measuring & controlling devices; engineering services; warm air heating & air conditioning; plumbing & hydronic heating supplies
HQ: Siemens Industry, Inc.
1000 Deerfield Pkwy
Buffalo Grove IL 60089
847 215-1000

(G-12872)
SIGN MAN
6323 E Mallon Ave (99212-1040)
PHONE..................................509 535-8181
Jeff Gulliford, *President*
Brenda Gulliford, *Treasurer*
EMP: 3 EST: 1961
SQ FT: 6,000
SALES (est): 300K **Privately Held**
SIC: **3993** Signs, not made in custom sign painting shops

(G-12873)
SIGNS NOW IN PROCESS INC (PA)
10502 E Montgomery Dr # 2 (99206-4273)
PHONE..................................509 928-3467
Elizabeth Ely, *President*
Myong Buster, *Owner*
EMP: 3
SALES (est): 707.6K **Privately Held**
SIC: **3993** Signs & advertising specialties

Spokane Valley - Spokane County (G-12874)

(G-12874)
SJB ENTERPRISES INC (PA)
Also Called: Meineke Discount Mufflers
1013 S Mariam St (99206-3552)
P.O. Box 10544, Spokane (99209-0544)
PHONE 509 926-6979
Steve D Bishop, *President*
EMP: 3
SQ FT: 900
SALES (est): 399.7K **Privately Held**
SIC: 7538 3993 General automotive repair shops; signs & advertising specialties

(G-12875)
SKETCHFORSCHOOLS PUBG INC
2716 N University Rd (99206-4718)
PHONE 877 397-5655
Daniel Finck, *President*
Joanne Finck, *General Mgr*
EMP: 9
SQ FT: 12,000
SALES (est): 1.2MM **Privately Held**
SIC: 2789 Bookbinding & related work

(G-12876)
SMITH & NEPHEW INC
12409 E Mirabeau Pkwy # 10 (99216-5057)
PHONE 509 363-0600
EMP: 50
SALES (corp-wide): 4.9B **Privately Held**
SIC: 3841 Surgical & medical instruments
HQ: Smith & Nephew, Inc.
1450 E Brooks Rd
Memphis TN 38116
901 396-2121

(G-12877)
SMOOTHIE VENTURES LLC
14025 E 26th Ave (99037-9382)
PHONE 509 315-4492
Nick Kiourkas, *Principal*
EMP: 4 **EST:** 2012
SALES (est): 292.3K **Privately Held**
SIC: 2037 Frozen fruits & vegetables

(G-12878)
SNOW PEAK FOREST PRODUCTS INC (PA)
3808 N Sullivan Rd N5 (99216-1616)
PHONE 208 714-4243
James Virgil, *President*
Monya Virgil, *Vice Pres*
EMP: 6
SQ FT: 1,000
SALES (est): 3.1MM **Privately Held**
SIC: 2426 5031 Lumber, hardwood dimension; lumber: rough, dressed & finished

(G-12879)
SOCIETY FOR MINING METALLURGY
12720 E Nora Ave Ste A (99216-1197)
PHONE 509 922-4063
Bernard Kronschnabel, *Principal*
EMP: 2
SALES (est): 66K **Privately Held**
SIC: 1499 Miscellaneous nonmetallic minerals

(G-12880)
SOL LIGHTING INC
16124 E Euclid Ave (99216-1853)
PHONE 509 789-1092
Alan Rubens, *President*
EMP: 2
SALES (est): 278.6K
SALES (corp-wide): 3.5MM **Privately Held**
WEB: www.fabtech1.com
SIC: 3444 5063 Sheet metal specialties, not stamped; lighting fixtures
PA: Fabtech Precision Manufacturing, Inc.
16124 E Euclid Ave
Spokane Valley WA 99216
509 534-7660

(G-12881)
SP HOLDINGS INC
Spokane Packaging
3808 N Sullivan Rd # 21 (99216-1608)
PHONE 509 924-7623
Craig McDonald, *Branch Mgr*
EMP: 45 **Privately Held**
WEB: www.alliancepackaging.net
SIC: 2671 2653 Packaging paper & plastics film, coated & laminated; boxes, corrugated: made from purchased materials
PA: Sp Holdings, Inc.
1000 Sw 43rd St
Renton WA 98057

(G-12882)
SPECIALISTS SEALANT
5610 E Broadway Ave (99212-0940)
PHONE 509 321-0424
EMP: 3
SALES (est): 123.2K **Privately Held**
SIC: 2891 Sealants

(G-12883)
SPOKANE HOUSE OF HOSE INC
5520 E Sprague Ave (99212-0825)
PHONE 509 535-3638
Karen Hayden-Rau, *President*
▲ **EMP:** 38 **EST:** 1967
SQ FT: 80,000
SALES (est): 12.3MM **Privately Held**
WEB: www.spokanehose.com
SIC: 5085 5999 3492 Hose, belting & packing; alarm & safety equipment stores; hose & tube fittings & assemblies, hydraulic/pneumatic

(G-12884)
SPOKANE HYDROGEN HYBRIDS
13714 E 23rd Ct (99216-2802)
PHONE 509 443-5919
EMP: 2 **EST:** 2011
SALES (est): 84K **Privately Held**
SIC: 2813 Mfg Industrial Gases

(G-12885)
SPOKANE INDUSTRIES INC (PA)
Also Called: Spokane Metal Products
3808 N Sullivan Rd Bldg 1 (99216-5065)
P.O. Box 3305, Spokane (99220-3305)
PHONE 509 924-0440
Gregory G Tenold, *President*
Tyrus N Tenold, *Vice Pres*
Ken J Ovnicek, *Purchasing*
Ken Vorhees, *CFO*
▲ **EMP:** 112 **EST:** 1950
SQ FT: 240,000
SALES (est): 55.8MM **Privately Held**
WEB: www.spokaneindustries.com
SIC: 3322 3325 3369 3443 Malleable iron foundries; alloy steel castings, except investment; castings, except die-castings, precision; fabricated plate work (boiler shop)

(G-12886)
SPOKANE INDUSTRIES INC
Spokane Metal Products
3808 N Sullivan Rd Bldg 4 (99216-1608)
P.O. Box 3303, Spokane (99220-3303)
PHONE 509 928-0720
Nathan Datsan, *Branch Mgr*
EMP: 22
SALES (corp-wide): 55.8MM **Privately Held**
WEB: www.spokaneindustries.com
SIC: 3443 3728 Boiler shop products: boilers, smokestacks, steel tanks; aircraft parts & equipment
PA: Spokane Industries, Inc.
3808 N Sullivan Rd Bldg 1
Spokane Valley WA 99216
509 924-0440

(G-12887)
SPOKANE RAIN GUTTER INC
8710 E Sprague Ave (99212-2924)
P.O. Box 141706 (99214-1706)
PHONE 509 922-4880
Chuck Mullenix, *President*
Elaine A Mullenix, *Vice Pres*
EMP: 12
SALES (est): 1.3MM **Privately Held**
WEB: www.spokaneraingutter.com
SIC: 1761 3444 Gutter & downspout contractor; metal roofing & roof drainage equipment

(G-12888)
SPOKANE ROCK PRODUCTS INC (PA)
4418 E 8th Ave (99212-0292)
P.O. Box 1929, Airway Heights (99001-1929)
PHONE 509 244-5421
Steve Robinson, *President*
EMP: 2
SALES (est): 2.5MM **Privately Held**
WEB: www.spokanerock.com
SIC: 1442 Construction sand & gravel

(G-12889)
SPOKANE VALLEY SCREEN PRINTING
12005 E Trent Ave (99206-4638)
P.O. Box 141598 (99214-1598)
PHONE 509 921-0207
Patrick Maguire, *President*
EMP: 9
SALES: 44K **Privately Held**
SIC: 2759 Screen printing

(G-12890)
SPRINGCREST DRAPERY GALLERY
14109 E Sprague Ave Ste 7 (99216-2171)
PHONE 509 928-9269
Michael Doug Cantrell, *Owner*
Doug Cantrell, *Manager*
EMP: 2
SALES (est): 110K **Privately Held**
WEB: www.springcrestco.com
SIC: 2391 Draperies, plastic & textile: from purchased materials

(G-12891)
STEELER INC
Also Called: Steeler Construction Supply
7903 E Harrington Ave (99212-2962)
PHONE 509 926-7403
Scott Towell, *Branch Mgr*
EMP: 4
SALES (corp-wide): 41.7MM **Privately Held**
WEB: www.steeler.com
SIC: 3452 3546 5251 Screws, metal; power-driven handtools; hardware; tools, power
PA: Steeler, Inc.
10023 Martin Luther King
Seattle WA 98178
206 725-8500

(G-12892)
STERLING BUSINESS FORMS INC
13110 E Indiana Ave (99216-2760)
PHONE 509 926-8191
Jim Baily, *Manager*
EMP: 30
SALES (corp-wide): 25.7MM **Privately Held**
SIC: 5112 2761 Business forms; manifold business forms
PA: Sterling Business Forms, Inc.
5300 Crater Lake Ave
Central Point OR 97502
541 858-4022

(G-12893)
STERLING INTERNATIONAL INC
Also Called: Rescue
3808 N Sullivan Rd 16bv (99216-1608)
PHONE 509 926-6766
Rod Schneidmiller, *President*
Jim Oxley, *Vice Pres*
Gerry Simpson, *Vice Pres*
Paul Crooks, *Opers Mgr*
Christine Vierow, *Manager*
◆ **EMP:** 175
SQ FT: 200,000
SALES (est): 20.9MM **Privately Held**
WEB: www.flies.com
SIC: 2671 Plastic film, coated or laminated for packaging

(G-12894)
STIER HOLLISTER SALES
10907 E Marietta Ave 1 (99206-6620)
PHONE 509 892-1188
Marcelo Morales, *President*
Dan Mork, *Manager*
EMP: 5
SALES (est): 690.9K **Privately Held**
SIC: 2834 Pharmaceutical preparations

(G-12895)
SUNRISE MATTRESS COMPANY INC
328 N Fancher Rd (99212-0859)
P.O. Box 1141, Veradale (99037-1141)
PHONE 509 290-5728
Dan Tabish, *President*
EMP: 3
SQ FT: 25,000
SALES (est): 423.6K **Privately Held**
WEB: www.sunrisematt.com
SIC: 2515 Mattresses, containing felt, foam rubber, urethane, etc.; box springs, assembled

(G-12896)
SUPERIOR FLUID POWER INC (PA)
9516 E Montgomery Ave # 19 (99206-4121)
PHONE 509 482-7949
Brad White, *Owner*
EMP: 2
SALES: 200K **Privately Held**
SIC: 5084 7699 3593 Hydraulic systems equipment & supplies; industrial equipment services; fluid power cylinders & actuators

(G-12897)
SUREWOOD CUSTOM CABINETS INC
3808 N Sullivan Rd 11d (99216-1608)
PHONE 509 893-9522
Mike Swanton, *President*
Jay Toews, *Corp Secy*
EMP: 8
SQ FT: 7,500
SALES: 400K **Privately Held**
SIC: 2511 Wood household furniture

(G-12898)
SWIRE PACIFIC HOLDINGS INC
9705 E Montgomery Ave (99206-4119)
PHONE 509 921-6200
EMP: 3 **Privately Held**
SIC: 2086 Bottled & canned soft drinks
HQ: Swire Pacific Holdings Inc.
12634 S 265 W Bldg A
Draper UT 84020
801 816-5300

(G-12899)
T2 SERVICES INC
12205 E Empire Ave (99206-4565)
PHONE 509 893-3666
Tim Fuhrman, *President*
Candice Fuhrman, *Corp Secy*
EMP: 11
SQ FT: 17,000
SALES (est): 1.7MM **Privately Held**
SIC: 3441 3444 Fabricated structural metal; sheet metalwork

(G-12900)
TARGET MEDIA PARTNERS
Also Called: Wheel Base
12510 E Sprague Ave (99216-0755)
P.O. Box 2320, Airway Heights (99001-2320)
PHONE 509 328-5555
Mike Kment, *Manager*
EMP: 200
SALES (corp-wide): 27.7MM **Privately Held**
WEB: www.targetmediapartners.com
SIC: 7313 2741 Newspaper advertising representative; miscellaneous publishing
HQ: Target Media Partners
5200 Lankershim Blvd # 350
North Hollywood CA 91601
323 930-3123

(G-12901)
TARGET SYSTEM TECHNOLOGY INC
14717 E Olympic Ave (99216-1468)
PHONE 509 456-4852
Robert Batty, *President*
EMP: 2

SALES (est): 171.2K **Privately Held**
WEB: www.target-sys-tech.com
SIC: 7372 Prepackaged software

(G-12902)
TAYLOR COMMUNICATIONS INC
9212 E Montgomry Ave 401-5 (99206-4239)
PHONE...................509 747-5872
Randy Countryman, *Branch Mgr*
EMP: 4
SALES (corp-wide): 3.2B **Privately Held**
WEB: www.stdreg.com
SIC: 2761 Manifold business forms
HQ: Taylor Communications, Inc.
 1725 Roe Crest Dr
 North Mankato MN 56003
 507 625-2828

(G-12903)
TECHNIFAB INC
5714 E 1st Ave (99212-0750)
PHONE...................509 534-1022
Frank Schubach, *President*
Leanne Schubach, *Vice Pres*
EMP: 3
SALES (est): 727.5K **Privately Held**
WEB: www.technifab.net
SIC: 3441 Fabricated structural metal

(G-12904)
TEK MANUFACTURING INC
6315 E Alki Ave (99212-1002)
PHONE...................509 921-5424
Molly Keene, *Treasurer*
EMP: 8
SQ FT: 6,000
SALES: 880K **Privately Held**
WEB: www.tekmfg.com
SIC: 3599 Machine shop, jobbing & repair

(G-12905)
THRIFTY PAYLESS INC T/A
1443 N Argonne Rd (99212-2685)
PHONE...................509 928-9121
EMP: 2 **EST: 2010**
SALES (est): 97.5K **Privately Held**
SIC: 2836 Vaccines & other immunizing products

(G-12906)
TIPTOP TIMERS LLC
2225 N Dollar Rd (99212-1413)
PHONE...................509 448-2819
Mark Hutchinson, *Principal*
EMP: 4
SALES (est): 228.8K **Privately Held**
SIC: 3625 Relays & industrial controls

(G-12907)
TNT INDUSTRIES LLC
323 N Flora Rd (99037-9518)
P.O. Box 703, Veradale (99037-0703)
PHONE...................509 279-8011
Timothy Ruebush, *Principal*
EMP: 2
SALES (est): 158.9K **Privately Held**
SIC: 3999 Manufacturing industries

(G-12908)
TOBIN CINEMA SYSTEMS INC
Also Called: Film To Dvd
19415 E Augusta Ln (99016-8427)
PHONE...................509 621-0323
Clive Tobin, *President*
Donna Tobin, *Corp Secy*
EMP: 3
SALES (est): 272.2K **Privately Held**
WEB: www.tobincinemasystems.com
SIC: 3861 Photographic equipment & supplies

(G-12909)
TRA INDUSTRIES INC
3808 N Sullivan Rd Bldg 2 (99216-1608)
PHONE...................509 924-5858
A Folino, *Branch Mgr*
EMP: 14
SALES: 1.5MM
SALES (corp-wide): 88.3MM **Privately Held**
SIC: 3999 Barber & beauty shop equipment

PA: T.R.A. Industries, Inc.
 23800 E Appleway Ave
 Liberty Lake WA 99019
 509 924-5858

(G-12910)
TRANE US INC
10502 E Montgomery Dr # 1 (99206-4273)
PHONE...................509 535-9057
EMP: 10 **Privately Held**
SIC: 3585 Air conditioning equipment, complete
HQ: Trane U.S. Inc.
 3600 Pammel Creek Rd
 La Crosse WI 54601
 608 787-2000

(G-12911)
TRAVIS PATTERN & FOUNDRY INC
3808 N Sullivan Rd Ste 4b (99216-1608)
PHONE...................509 924-6464
EMP: 306
SALES (corp-wide): 115.6MM **Privately Held**
SIC: 3321 Gray iron castings
PA: Travis Pattern & Foundry, Inc.
 1413 E Hawthorne Rd
 Spokane WA 99218
 509 466-3545

(G-12912)
TRI STATES REBAR INC
7208 E Indiana Ave (99212-1287)
PHONE...................509 922-5901
Jack Ilenstine, *President*
Jeff Ilenstine, *Vice Pres*
Janis Ilenstine, *Admin Sec*
EMP: 20
SQ FT: 35,000
SALES (est): 7.8MM **Privately Held**
WEB: www.tristatesrebar.com
SIC: 3449 1791 Miscellaneous metalwork; concrete reinforcement, placing of

(G-12913)
TRIUMPH CORPORATION
1225 N Argonne Rd Ste A (99212-2798)
PHONE...................509 926-7000
EMP: 3
SALES (est): 340K **Privately Held**
SIC: 1241 Mining Services

(G-12914)
TRUE SEALS LLC
1309 N Bradley Rd (99212-1193)
PHONE...................509 385-0300
Craig Dolsby, *Mng Member*
Jim Hemingway,
EMP: 5
SQ FT: 11,200
SALES (est): 1MM **Privately Held**
SIC: 3053 Gaskets, all materials

(G-12915)
TRUSS COMPANY AND BLDG SUP INC
118 S Union Rd (99206-5326)
PHONE...................509 928-0550
EMP: 9
SALES (corp-wide): 22.4MM **Privately Held**
SIC: 2439 Trusses, wooden roof
PA: The Truss Company And Building Supply Inc
 2802 142nd Ave E
 Sumner WA 98390
 253 863-5555

(G-12916)
TWILIGHT BEDDING COMPANY INC
12013 E Trent Ave Ste W2 (99206-4638)
PHONE...................509 926-2333
Paul Defazio, *President*
Nicholas Defazio, *President*
Vincent Defazio, *President*
EMP: 7
SQ FT: 10,000
SALES (est): 1MM **Privately Held**
SIC: 2515 5712 Mattresses & foundations; box springs, assembled; furniture stores

(G-12917)
U DECK IT INC
Also Called: Bullhide Line of The Inland Em
5524 E Cataldo Ave (99212-0913)
PHONE...................509 532-9007
Michael Spring, *President*
Anita L Spring, *Vice Pres*
EMP: 2
SQ FT: 4,990
SALES (est): 180K **Privately Held**
SIC: 3479 Coating of metals & formed products

(G-12918)
U S WAX & POLYMER INC
Also Called: Uswp Manufacuring
17625 E Euclid Ave (99216-1737)
PHONE...................509 922-1069
Thomas A Bove, *President*
Eric Messingale, *Manager*
◆ EMP: 35
SQ FT: 6,000
SALES (est): 7.4MM **Privately Held**
WEB: www.uswaxpolymer.com
SIC: 3061 3089 3544 3599 Mechanical rubber goods; plastic processing; die sets for metal stamping (presses); industrial molds; machine & other job shop work

(G-12919)
ULTRASHRED LLC
Also Called: Ultrashred Sales and Service
409 N Thierman Rd Ste A (99212-1129)
PHONE...................509 244-1894
Doug Ferrante, *Regl Sales Mgr*
Micheal Spiger,
EMP: 9
SALES (est): 1.7MM **Privately Held**
WEB: www.ultrashred.com
SIC: 3589 Shredders, industrial & commercial

(G-12920)
UNITED STATES BAKERY
Franz Bakery
110 N Fancher Rd (99212-0850)
PHONE...................509 535-7726
Barry Ware, *Manager*
EMP: 349
SALES (corp-wide): 541.5MM **Privately Held**
SIC: 2051 5149 Bakery: wholesale or wholesale/retail combined; bakery products
PA: United States Bakery
 315 Ne 10th Ave
 Portland OR 97232
 503 232-2191

(G-12921)
UTEC METALS INC
17305 E Euclid Ave (99216-1743)
PHONE...................509 891-7833
Thomas S Best, *President*
EMP: 7
SQ FT: 8,000
SALES (est): 1MM **Privately Held**
WEB: www.utecmetals.com
SIC: 3599 3398 Machine shop, jobbing & repair; annealing of metal

(G-12922)
VACCINES 2 U
17110 E Daybreak Ln (99016-8767)
PHONE...................509 475-1347
EMP: 3
SALES (est): 128.1K **Privately Held**
SIC: 2836 Vaccines

(G-12923)
VALIN CORPORATION
3808 N Sullivan Rd 18p (99216-1639)
PHONE...................509 924-4914
Dick Floyd, *Opers Staff*
EMP: 7
SALES (corp-wide): 4.3MM **Privately Held**
WEB: www.pacificpowertech.com
SIC: 5085 5084 7699 3568 Valves & fittings; hydraulic systems equipment & supplies; hydraulic equipment repair; power transmission equipment
PA: Valin Corporation
 1941 Ringwood Ave
 San Jose CA 95131
 408 730-9850

(G-12924)
VALLEY INSTANT PRINTING INC
1014 N Pines Rd Ste 118 (99206-6713)
PHONE...................509 924-8040
Jeffrey Weisen, *President*
Debbie Weisen, *Corp Secy*
EMP: 2
SQ FT: 2,500
SALES: 190K **Privately Held**
SIC: 2752 Commercial printing, offset

(G-12925)
VALMONT INDUSTRIES INC
Also Called: Cascade Earth Sciences
12720 E Nora Ave Ste A (99216-1197)
PHONE...................509 921-0290
Dan Burgard, *Manager*
Sara Rodriguez, *Admin Asst*
EMP: 6
SALES (corp-wide): 2.7B **Publicly Held**
WEB: www.valmont.com
SIC: 3441 Fabricated structural metal
PA: Valmont Industries, Inc.
 1 Valmont Plz Ste 500
 Omaha NE 68154
 402 963-1000

(G-12926)
VALON KONE NORTH AMERICA
3808 N Sullivan Rd (99216-1608)
PHONE...................509 434-6436
Charles Kable, *Branch Mgr*
EMP: 3
SALES (corp-wide): 633.7MM **Publicly Held**
SIC: 2499 Mulch, wood & bark
HQ: Valon Kone Oy
 Honkatie 5
 Lohja 08500
 193 606-1

(G-12927)
VANDALEZ INDUSTRIES INC
3020 N Sullivan Rd Ste E (99216-3106)
PHONE...................509 228-9000
EMP: 2
SALES (est): 118.6K **Privately Held**
SIC: 3999 Manufacturing industries

(G-12928)
VANETTEN FINE ART
626 N Best Rd (99216-2089)
PHONE...................509 928-2385
Elizabeth Van Etten, *Owner*
Sheldon Van Etten, *Co-Owner*
EMP: 2
SALES: 15K **Privately Held**
SIC: 8748 5231 7999 2759 Urban planning & consulting services; paint; art gallery, commercial; ready prints

(G-12929)
VERTEK OIS INC
3910 S Union Ct (99206-6345)
PHONE...................425 455-9921
Gale Gibson, *President*
John Rosenoff, *Vice Pres*
EMP: 5
SQ FT: 2,200
SALES (est): 331.9K **Privately Held**
SIC: 7372 7371 Prepackaged software; custom computer programming services

(G-12930)
VESSELS ARCHTCTRAL WOODTURNING
6801 E 3rd Ave (99212-0614)
PHONE...................509 927-0721
Doug Bendewald, *Owner*
EMP: 2
SALES (est): 116.7K **Privately Held**
SIC: 2499 Carved & turned wood

(G-12931)
VIRTUAL EDUCATION SOFTWARE INC
Also Called: Vesi
16201 E Ind Ave Ste 1450 (99216)
PHONE...................509 891-7219
Mick Jackson, *President*
Steve Dahl, *Publisher*
Joan Halverstadt, *Director*
Bryan Wells, *Director*
Jackie Bainbridge, *Representative*
EMP: 11

Spokane Valley - Spokane County (G-12932)

SALES: 1.2MM **Privately Held**
WEB: www.virtualeduc.com
SIC: 7371 8621 7372 Computer software development; education & teacher association; educational computer software

(G-12932)
WAGSTAFF INC (PA)
3910 N Flora Rd (99216-1720)
PHONE.................................509 922-1404
Kevin N Person, *CEO*
Michael O'Grady, *General Mgr*
Olivier Gabis, *Area Mgr*
Manfred Luck, *Area Mgr*
Michael Megaard, *Exec VP*
◆ EMP: 300
SQ FT: 21,000
SALES: 118.7MM **Privately Held**
WEB: www.wagstaff.com
SIC: 3542 3364 Machine tools, metal forming type; nonferrous die-castings except aluminum

(G-12933)
WELD-RITE MFG LLC
3519 N Eden Rd (99216-1729)
PHONE.................................509 927-9353
Terry Fowler,
EMP: 2
SQ FT: 18,000
SALES (est): 230K **Privately Held**
SIC: 3317 Tubes, wrought: welded or lock joint

(G-12934)
WESLEY TODD
Also Called: Cardiac Self Assessment
1605 S Clinton Rd (99216-0420)
PHONE.................................509 926-0344
Wesley Todd, *Owner*
EMP: 2
SALES: 20K **Privately Held**
SIC: 2731 Books: publishing & printing

(G-12935)
WHEELCHAIRS AND MORE LLC
9904 E 50th Ave (99206-9200)
PHONE.................................509 926-9337
Wendy Johnson, *Principal*
EMP: 2
SALES (est): 121.2K **Privately Held**
SIC: 3842 Wheelchairs

(G-12936)
WHEELER INDUSTRIES INC
1118 N Howe Rd (99212-0917)
PHONE.................................509 534-4556
Loyde Wheeler, *President*
Cynthia Wheeler, *Corp Secy*
David A Wheeler, *Vice Pres*
EMP: 23
SQ FT: 33,000
SALES (est): 3.1MM **Privately Held**
WEB: www.wheelerindustries.net
SIC: 3599 Machine shop, jobbing & repair

(G-12937)
WHITE BLOCK CO INC
6219 E Trent Ave (99212-1280)
PHONE.................................509 534-0651
Bruce Corigliano, *President*
Shayne White, *Corp Secy*
Paul White, *Senior VP*
Gary Corigliano, *Vice Pres*
EMP: 25
SQ FT: 1,000
SALES (est): 4.7MM **Privately Held**
SIC: 3272 3271 Concrete products, precast; blocks, concrete or cinder: standard

(G-12938)
WILLIAM REED & ASSOCIATES
5702 E Alki Ave Ste C (99212-0964)
P.O. Box 9164, Spokane (99209-9164)
PHONE.................................509 534-4727
William Reed, *Owner*
EMP: 2
SQ FT: 450
SALES (est): 245.6K **Privately Held**
SIC: 7389 2791 Printing broker; design services; typesetting

(G-12939)
WILSON TOOL & MANUFACTURING CO
2622 N Dartmouth Ln (99206-4276)
P.O. Box 11276 (99211-1276)
PHONE.................................509 928-9441
Jay Adkins, *President*
Roy Dugger, *Vice Pres*
Cindy Dugger, *Treasurer*
Yvonne Adkins, *Admin Sec*
▼ EMP: 12 EST: 1946
SQ FT: 30,000
SALES: 2MM **Privately Held**
WEB: www.wilsonmfgco.com
SIC: 3599 Machine shop, jobbing & repair

(G-12940)
WOODPECKER GRAPHICS
1119 N Bowdish Rd (99206-4907)
PHONE.................................509 481-8406
Robert Tipps, *Owner*
EMP: 2
SALES: 21K **Privately Held**
SIC: 2752 Commercial printing, lithographic

(G-12941)
WORLD WIDE PACKETS INC (HQ)
115 N Sullivan Rd (99037-8533)
P.O. Box 14665 (99214-0665)
PHONE.................................509 242-9000
Dave Curry, *CEO*
Matthew Frey, *CFO*
▲ EMP: 24
SQ FT: 30,000
SALES: 5.5MM **Publicly Held**
WEB: www.worldwidepackets.com
SIC: 3679 Electronic circuits

(G-12942)
WRBQ INC
111 N Vista Rd Ste 1d (99212-2960)
PHONE.................................509 927-7181
Emily W Thiessen, *President*
EMP: 5
SALES (est): 363.4K **Privately Held**
SIC: 2741 Directories: publishing & printing

(G-12943)
WSA-HL INC
16710 E Euclid Ave (99216-1821)
PHONE.................................509 921-7089
David Lynch, *Vice Pres*
EMP: 5
SALES (est): 521.4K **Privately Held**
SIC: 2911 Road materials, bituminous; road oils
PA: Wsa-Hl, Inc.
4327 N Thor St
Spokane WA 99217

(G-12944)
WSF LLC (PA)
Also Called: Western Systems & Fabrication
911 N Thierman Rd (99212-1180)
PHONE.................................509 922-1300
Scott Smits, *Engineer*
Scot Frazer, *Sales Mgr*
Keely Scott, *Office Mgr*
Marc B Torre, *Mng Member*
Heather D Torre,
EMP: 34 EST: 1978
SQ FT: 38,000
SALES (est): 5.7MM **Privately Held**
WEB: www.westernsystem.com
SIC: 3444 Sheet metalwork

(G-12945)
YAGER COMPANY INC
Also Called: Yager Sails & Canvas
9209 E Mission Ave (99206-4056)
P.O. Box 279, Veradale (99037-0279)
PHONE.................................509 922-2772
Don Yager, *Principal*
Mary Yager, *Corp Secy*
EMP: 2
SQ FT: 1,000
SALES: 60K **Privately Held**
WEB: www.yagersails.net
SIC: 2394 5199 5999 Sails: made from purchased materials; canvas products; canvas products

(G-12946)
YOUNIQUE
17417 E Apollo Rd (99016-5065)
PHONE.................................509 842-6908
Heather Cook, *Principal*
EMP: 2
SALES (est): 84.3K **Privately Held**
SIC: 2339 Sportswear, women's

(G-12947)
Z-AXIS PRINTS
6213 E Valleyview Dr (99212-3276)
PHONE.................................509 842-6680
Harvey Jewett, *Principal*
EMP: 2
SALES (est): 100.1K **Privately Held**
SIC: 2752 Commercial printing, lithographic

Sprague
Lincoln County

(G-12948)
J&R HENNINGS INC
2715 E Rehn Rd (99032-9612)
PHONE.................................509 659-0102
Ron Hennings, *President*
EMP: 8
SALES (est): 292.8K **Privately Held**
SIC: 2041 Flour & other grain mill products

(G-12949)
WESTERN PRODUCTS
406 N G St (99032)
PHONE.................................509 994-1288
Al Mootry, *Owner*
EMP: 2
SALES (est): 56K **Privately Held**
SIC: 2842 5999 Laundry cleaning preparations; cleaning equipment & supplies

Springdale
Stevens County

(G-12950)
BRESCH LOGGING
4518 Hidden Rd (99173-5138)
P.O. Box 480 (99173-0480)
PHONE.................................509 258-9620
Fred G Bresch, *Principal*
EMP: 3
SALES (est): 215.9K **Privately Held**
SIC: 2411 Logging camps & contractors

(G-12951)
MONTE WHTZEL CON QARTER CIR HA
4341 Sprngdale Hunters Rd (99173-9713)
PHONE.................................509 220-8449
EMP: 2
SALES (est): 77.4K **Privately Held**
SIC: 3131 Quarters

Stanwood
Island County

(G-12952)
ADVANCED AERO SAFETY INC
1938 Forest Hill Rd (98282-6361)
PHONE.................................360 387-8472
Sherman Hall, *President*
EMP: 2
SALES (est): 220.9K **Privately Held**
WEB: www.safeaero.net
SIC: 3669 5088 3812 Emergency alarms; transportation equipment & supplies; search & navigation equipment

(G-12953)
BODLE DIAMOND INDUSTRIES
656 Chinook Ct (98282-7266)
PHONE.................................360 939-0242
Tom Bodle, *Owner*
EMP: 3
SALES (est): 157.9K **Privately Held**
SIC: 3915 Jewelry soldering for the trade

(G-12954)
CAMANO ISLAND LICENSING
811 N Sunrise Blvd Ste D (98282-8778)
PHONE.................................360 387-4700
Mike Ganz, *Principal*
EMP: 10
SALES (est): 846.8K **Privately Held**
SIC: 3469 Automobile license tags, stamped metal

(G-12955)
INTUITIVE SOFTWARE SOLUTION
908 Sands Ln (98282-6507)
PHONE.................................360 387-2271
Debra Kosky, *President*
EMP: 2 EST: 2001
SALES (est): 143.7K **Privately Held**
SIC: 7372 Prepackaged software

(G-12956)
RECLAIMED WOOD PRODUCTS
724 Halls Hill Rd (98282-7313)
PHONE.................................360 387-1570
Laura Jones, *Partner*
EMP: 2
SALES (est): 91.4K **Privately Held**
SIC: 2511 Wood household furniture

(G-12957)
TEAZER
Also Called: Teazer Hats
1256 Country Club Dr (98282-7602)
PHONE.................................360 387-1737
EMP: 5
SALES: 150K **Privately Held**
SIC: 2253 5136 5137 Knit Outerwear Mills

(G-12958)
WINDEMERE CAMINO ISLAND REALTY
1283 Elger Bay Rd Ste A (98282-8375)
PHONE.................................360 387-3411
Marla Heagle, *President*
EMP: 50
SALES (est): 2.1MM **Privately Held**
SIC: 6531 2411 Real estate brokers & agents; logging

Stanwood
Snohomish County

(G-12959)
AUSTIN SPECIATIES INC
Also Called: Austin Fire and Safety
8212 Hennings Dr (98292-7416)
PHONE.................................360 629-6662
Debbie Shay, *President*
EMP: 2
SALES (est): 200K **Privately Held**
SIC: 5099 3999 7389 Fire extinguishers; fire extinguishers, portable; fire extinguisher servicing

(G-12960)
BBC
8510 Cedarhome Dr (98292-9539)
PHONE.................................360 629-4477
Adrian Biesecker, *Vice Pres*
Laura Biesecker, *CFO*
EMP: 2
SALES (est): 104.2K **Privately Held**
SIC: 3821 Laboratory apparatus & furniture

(G-12961)
BECK MILL CO INC
2105 276th St Nw (98292-9462)
PHONE.................................360 629-4769
Gordy Beck, *President*
EMP: 2 EST: 1968
SALES (est): 206.9K **Privately Held**
SIC: 2421 Lumber: rough, sawed or planed

(G-12962)
BUTCHS BULLDOZING & BACKHOE
Also Called: Butch's Self Loader Hauling
8715 180th St Nw (98292-9580)
PHONE.................................360 652-0473
Robert Hurless, *Owner*
Heather Hurless, *Co-Owner*

▲ = Import ▼=Export
◆ =Import/Export

EMP: 2
SALES: 120K Privately Held
SIC: 2411 Logging

(G-12963)
CAMPBELL & ASSOCIATES INC
Also Called: Bruce Campbell
17410 Marine Dr (98292-6740)
PHONE..............................360 652-9502
Robert Bruce Campbell, *President*
EMP: 2
SALES (est): 84.5K Privately Held
SIC: 8748 2731 Educational consultant; book publishing

(G-12964)
CARDINAL CLEAN
8430 S Lake Ketchum Rd (98292-9793)
PHONE..............................360 629-4399
Diana Logan, *Owner*
Jeff Logan, *Co-Owner*
EMP: 5 **EST:** 2000
SALES (est): 445.9K Privately Held
WEB: www.cardinalclean.com
SIC: 2842 Specialty cleaning preparations; laundry cleaning preparations

(G-12965)
DEL FOX CUSTOM MEATS INC (PA)
Also Called: Del Fox Locker Meats
7229 300th St Nw (98292-9704)
PHONE..............................360 629-3723
Patrick Cairus, *President*
Dawn Cairus, *Vice Pres*
EMP: 6
SALES: 704K Privately Held
SIC: 2011 Meat packing plants

(G-12966)
DIAL ONE TELECOMMUNICATIONS
31310 English Grade Rd (98292-5417)
P.O. Box 873 (98292-0873)
PHONE..............................360 629-2085
Paul Kalmakoff, *President*
Linda Kalmakoff, *Vice Pres*
EMP: 5
SALES: 1MM Privately Held
WEB: www.dialonefiber.com
SIC: 1731 3661 Fiber optic cable installation; fiber optics communications equipment

(G-12967)
DR BIESECKERS LLC
Also Called: Biesecker Body Care
125 316th St Nw (98292-7122)
P.O. Box 741, Mount Vernon (98273-0741)
PHONE..............................360 386-1530
James Biesecker, *CEO*
EMP: 6
SALES: 100K Privately Held
SIC: 2844 2841 2834 Shampoos, rinses, conditioners: hair; face creams or lotions; soap & other detergents; lip balms; ointments

(G-12968)
EARTHEN ALCHEMY
18902 Marine Dr (98292-7807)
P.O. Box 114, Granite Falls (98252-0114)
PHONE..............................360 926-8467
EMP: 2
SALES (est): 139.1K Privately Held
SIC: 3446 Architectural metalwork

(G-12969)
ENERGY ARROW
26910 92nd Ave Nw (98292-5437)
PHONE..............................267 932-7769
Charles Schaar, *Director*
EMP: 5
SALES (est): 129.4K Privately Held
SIC: 7371 7372 Computer software development & applications; publishers' computer software

(G-12970)
FELAMERE VINEYARD LLC
19310 40th Ave Nw (98292-9036)
PHONE..............................360 652-7414
EMP: 2
SALES (est): 76.9K Privately Held
SIC: 2084 Wines

(G-12971)
FOREST LAND SERVICES INC
26700 Pioneer Hwy (98292-5111)
P.O. Box 129 (98292-0129)
PHONE..............................360 652-9044
Jon Buse, *President*
Gayeann Buse, *Vice Pres*
Vonda Buse, *Treasurer*
Gary Buse, *Admin Sec*
EMP: 11
SQ FT: 4,480
SALES (est): 1.3MM Privately Held
SIC: 2411 0782 Logging camps & contractors; lawn & garden services

(G-12972)
FRONTIER MANUFACTURING INC
18303 60th Ave Nw (98292-5601)
PHONE..............................360 652-4046
Michael Davidson, *CEO*
EMP: 6
SALES: 500K Privately Held
SIC: 3999 Manufacturing industries

(G-12973)
FUTURE SOFTWARE SYSTEMS INC
27924 84th Ave Nw (98292-4700)
PHONE..............................360 629-9973
Robert Mitchell, *President*
EMP: 5
SALES (est): 450K Privately Held
SIC: 7372 Prepackaged software

(G-12974)
GIBBONS DRILLING INC
7212 265th St Nw Apt 360 (98292-4607)
PHONE..............................360 671-3040
Robert M Gibbons, *President*
Jo Ann Gibbons, *Treasurer*
EMP: 5
SALES (est): 530K Privately Held
SIC: 1629 2411 Blasting contractor, except building demolition; logging

(G-12975)
GLACIER MOULDINGS LTD
3927 300th St Nw (98292-9670)
PHONE..............................360 629-5313
Dean Maher, *President*
Image Don Pad, *Vice Pres*
Robert Werner, *Treasurer*
Joe Reynolds, *Manager*
Joseph Reynolds, *Admin Sec*
◆ **EMP:** 19
SQ FT: 35,000
SALES (est): 3.1MM Privately Held
SIC: 2493 2431 Reconstituted wood products; millwork

(G-12976)
INTERLOCK INDUSTRIES INC
26910 92nd Ave Nw Pmb 425 (98292-5437)
PHONE..............................360 713-3036
EMP: 8
SALES (est): 857.1K Privately Held
SIC: 3444 Roof deck, sheet metal

(G-12977)
KILIAN & KILIAN ARTISTS
16604 Marine Dr (98292-6777)
PHONE..............................360 654-1799
Michael Kilian, *Owner*
EMP: 2
SALES (est): 96.2K Privately Held
SIC: 3952 Paints for china painting

(G-12978)
MICHAEL P APPLEBY
14227 Evergreen Way (98292-9122)
PHONE..............................360 652-1178
Michael Appleby, *Principal*
EMP: 3
SALES (est): 180.8K Privately Held
SIC: 3571 Personal computers (microcomputers)

(G-12979)
MICHELLE SCHWARTZMAN
Also Called: D & M Enterprises
1722 267th St Nw (98292-9264)
PHONE..............................360 629-5255
Michelle Schwartzman, *Owner*

EMP: 2
SALES (est): 137.1K Privately Held
SIC: 2342 Foundation garments, women's

(G-12980)
MIKES MACHINE
18303 60th Ave Nw (98292-5601)
PHONE..............................360 652-4046
Mike Hurn, *Owner*
EMP: 5 **EST:** 1997
SQ FT: 7,500
SALES: 500K Privately Held
SIC: 3544 Special dies & tools

(G-12981)
MM INDUSTRIES LLC
8530 Cedarhome Dr Ste B (98292-5968)
PHONE..............................360 629-4595
Mike Moffett, *Owner*
EMP: 8
SALES (est): 804.1K Privately Held
SIC: 3999 Manufacturing industries

(G-12982)
NELSCORP INC
18416 40th Ave Nw (98292-6000)
PHONE..............................206 660-6313
Aaron Nelson, *Principal*
EMP: 2
SALES (est): 101.1K Privately Held
SIC: 3599 Industrial machinery

(G-12983)
NORTH STAR COLD STORAGE INC
27100 Pioneer Hwy (98292-6057)
P.O. Box 1359 (98292-1359)
PHONE..............................360 629-9591
John Boggs, *President*
Linda Boggs, *Vice Pres*
EMP: 24
SALES: 5MM
SALES (corp-wide): 30.1MM Privately Held
WEB: www.northstarcoldstorage.com
SIC: 2092 4222 Fresh or frozen packaged fish; storage, frozen or refrigerated goods
PA: Deep Sea Fisheries, Inc.
3900 Railway Ave
Everett WA 98201
425 742-8609

(G-12984)
ONE OIL LOVIN MAMA
27821 70th Ave Nw (98292-9550)
PHONE..............................360 572-4511
Justin Eckelbarger, *Principal*
EMP: 3
SALES (est): 120.1K Privately Held
SIC: 1311 Crude petroleum & natural gas

(G-12985)
PRECISE MACHINING INC
8536 Cedarhome Dr Ste C (98292-5967)
PHONE..............................360 629-0420
Doug Whitney, *President*
EMP: 5
SQ FT: 2,400
SALES (est): 540K Privately Held
WEB: www.precisemachining.com
SIC: 3599 7692 Machine shop, jobbing & repair; welding repair

(G-12986)
PRO FAB INDUSTRIES INC
8130 311th St NW (98292-9705)
PHONE..............................360 629-4642
Tim Reid, *President*
Julie Reid, *Corp Secy*
EMP: 8
SQ FT: 14,280
SALES: 1MM Privately Held
WEB: www.valleyint.com
SIC: 3441 Fabricated structural metal

(G-12987)
PROCESS SOLUTIONS INC
7112 265th St Nw (98292-6293)
PHONE..............................360 629-0910
Todd Busby, *President*
David Crumpley, *Vice Pres*
Greg Schock, *Project Mgr*
Greg McVey, *Engineer*
Mike Schneider, *Engineer*
EMP: 30
SQ FT: 15,000

SALES (est): 7MM Privately Held
WEB: www.processsolutions.com
SIC: 3625 3823 3613 Control equipment, electric; industrial instrmnts msrmnt display/control process variable; switchgear & switchboard apparatus

(G-12988)
PUGET LOGGING & EXCAVATION
28921 64th Ave Nw (98292)
PHONE..............................360 629-0461
Jeffery Lervick, *Owner*
EMP: 2
SALES (est): 162.4K Privately Held
SIC: 2411 1629 1794 Logging; land clearing contractor; excavation work

(G-12989)
RAM-BONE INDUSTRIES LLC
2720 212th St Nw (98292-6895)
P.O. Box 42672, Phoenix AZ (85080-2672)
PHONE..............................360 652-8277
Korrine Gowin, *Principal*
EMP: 2
SALES (est): 116.2K Privately Held
SIC: 3999 Manufacturing industries

(G-12990)
S AND R LOGGING AND CUTTING
18515 75th Ave Nw (98292-6953)
PHONE..............................425 314-7662
Steve Skaglund, *President*
Rhonda Skaglund, *Treasurer*
EMP: 5
SALES (est): 410K Privately Held
SIC: 2411 Logging

(G-12991)
SIMPSON GRAVEL PIT
6610 140th St Nw (98292-4805)
PHONE..............................425 879-1024
EMP: 3
SALES (est): 128.9K Privately Held
SIC: 1442 Construction sand & gravel

(G-12992)
SPOTTER LEVELS LLC
6720 Happy Hollow Rd (98292-9044)
PHONE..............................425 238-5117
Scott Peterson, *Principal*
EMP: 2
SALES (est): 170.4K Privately Held
SIC: 3545 Machine tool accessories

(G-12993)
STANWOOD CUPCAKES LLC
28127 85th Dr Nw (98292-5958)
PHONE..............................360 926-8241
EMP: 4
SALES (est): 239.2K Privately Held
SIC: 2051 Bakery: wholesale or wholesale/retail combined

(G-12994)
STANWOOD REDI-MIX INC
2431 Larson Rd (98292)
P.O. Box 69, Silvana (98287-0069)
PHONE..............................360 652-7777
Kenneth Christoferson Jr, *President*
Brian Christoferson, *Corp Secy*
EMP: 30 **EST:** 1966
SQ FT: 10,000
SALES (est): 6MM Privately Held
WEB: www.stanwoodredi-mix.com
SIC: 3273 5211 Ready-mixed concrete; sand & gravel

(G-12995)
STANWOOD-CAMANO NEWS INC
9005 271st St Nw (98292-5998)
P.O. Box 999 (98292-0999)
PHONE..............................360 629-8066
David Pinkham, *President*
John Dean -Editor, *Principal*
EMP: 30
SQ FT: 3,200
SALES (est): 1.6MM Privately Held
WEB: www.scnews.com
SIC: 2711 5112 7375 2752 Job printing & newspaper publishing combined; office supplies; information retrieval services; commercial printing, lithographic

Stanwood - Snohomish County (G-12996)

(G-12996)
THERMAL PIPE SHIELDS
29020 40th Ave Nw (98292-9488)
P.O. Box 103 (98292-0103)
PHONE..............................425 330-3765
Jeff Heckman, *Owner*
▲ **EMP:** 3
SALES (est): 338.7K **Privately Held**
WEB: www.thermalpipeshieldsinc.com
SIC: 3312 Pipes & tubes

(G-12997)
TOPDOWN INCORPORATED
2691092 Ndavenwste (98292)
PHONE..............................206 920-5566
Tim Schmitt, *President*
EMP: 2 **EST:** 2001
SQ FT: 1,500
SALES (est): 147.8K **Privately Held**
SIC: 3714 Motor vehicle parts & accessories

(G-12998)
TWIN CITY FOODS INC (PA)
10120 269th Pl Nw (98292-4736)
P.O. Box 699 (98292-0699)
PHONE..............................206 515-2400
Roger O Lervick, *President*
John Lervick, *President*
Mark Lervick, *Vice Pres*
Virgil Roehl, *CFO*
◆ **EMP:** 100 **EST:** 1945
SQ FT: 10,000
SALES (est): 213.6MM **Privately Held**
WEB: www.twincityfoods.com
SIC: 2037 Vegetables, quick frozen & cold pack, excl. potato products

(G-12999)
WHISTLE STOP STUDIOS LLC
5919 Happy Hollow Rd (98292-9034)
PHONE..............................360 652-9728
Warren Phillips, *Principal*
EMP: 2
SALES (est): 103.7K **Privately Held**
SIC: 3999 Whistles

(G-13000)
WINTERHALTER INC
5219 220th St Nw (98292-9009)
PHONE..............................360 652-6337
Kurt J Winterhalter, *President*
EMP: 3
SQ FT: 2,400
SALES (est): 311.6K **Privately Held**
SIC: 3731 Fishing vessels, large: building & repairing

Starbuck
Columbia County

(G-13001)
COLUMBIA PULP I LLC
1351 State Hwy 261 (99359)
PHONE..............................509 288-4892
John Begley, *CEO*
Larry Tantalo, *Project Mgr*
Michele McCarthy, *CFO*
EMP: 30 **EST:** 2015
SALES (est): 1.2MM **Privately Held**
SIC: 2611 Pulp mills

Startup
Snohomish County

(G-13002)
MOUNTAIN LOG HOMES INC
Also Called: Cascade Mountain Log Homes
35409 State Rte 2 (98293)
PHONE..............................360 799-0533
EMP: 12
SALES (est): 1.2MM **Privately Held**
SIC: 2452 Mfg Prefabricated Wood Buildings

Stehekin
Chelan County

(G-13003)
JW CUSTOM CONSTRUCTION
200 Stehekin Valley Rd (98852)
P.O. Box 5 (98852-0005)
PHONE..............................509 679-2959
John Wilsey, *Owner*
EMP: 2
SALES (est): 50K **Privately Held**
SIC: 1799 2452 Swimming pool construction; log cabins, prefabricated, wood

Steilacoom
Pierce County

(G-13004)
ELLSWORTH & COMPANY LLC
58 Chapman Loop (98388-1731)
PHONE..............................253 301-2800
Peter Dahlgren,
Don Dahlgren,
Susan Dahlgren,
EMP: 3
SALES (est): 325.6K **Privately Held**
SIC: 2252 Hosiery

(G-13005)
HEARTHLAND PUBLISHING LLC
106 Chinook Ln (98388-1442)
PHONE..............................253 588-2149
Donald Brown, *Principal*
EMP: 2
SALES (est): 70.7K **Privately Held**
SIC: 2741 Miscellaneous publishing

(G-13006)
RANGER PUBLISHING COMPANY INC
Also Called: Winning Times
218 Wilkes St (98388-2122)
P.O. Box 98801, Lakewood (98496-8801)
PHONE..............................253 584-1212
Thomas Swarner, *President*
Joan Swarner, *Vice Pres*
EMP: 14
SALES (est): 925.3K **Privately Held**
WEB: www.weeklyvolcano.com
SIC: 2711 Newspapers: publishing only, not printed on site

Steptoe
Whitman County

(G-13007)
MICRO AG INC
Hwy 195 (99174)
P.O. Box 48 (99174-3048)
PHONE..............................509 397-4278
John Morgan, *President*
EMP: 3
SQ FT: 40,000
SALES (est): 250K **Privately Held**
SIC: 5261 5191 2873 Garden supplies & tools; garden supplies; urea

Stevenson
Skamania County

(G-13008)
ACOUSTIC INFO PROC LAB LLC
110 Ne Cedar St (98648-4217)
PHONE..............................509 427-5374
Kenneth Levy, *Owner*
EMP: 2
SALES (est): 178.3K **Privately Held**
WEB: www.aipl.com
SIC: 3651 Audio electronic systems

(G-13009)
CASCADE COUNTRY CABINS
1080 Sw Briggs St (98648-4405)
PHONE..............................509 427-8515
Benny Sciacca, *Owner*
EMP: 2
SALES (est): 205.6K **Privately Held**
WEB: www.cascadecountrycabins.com
SIC: 2452 1521 Log cabins, prefabricated, wood; single-family housing construction

(G-13010)
CLIFFORD W LEESON INC
Also Called: Stevenson Sports Supply
347 Nw Jefferson Ave (98648-6452)
P.O. Box 1096 (98648-1096)
PHONE..............................509 427-4155
Clifford W Leeson, *President*
EMP: 2
SALES (est): 133.1K **Privately Held**
SIC: 3949 Sporting & athletic goods

(G-13011)
DIGITRON ELECTRONICS LLC
42382 State Route 14 (98648)
PHONE..............................509 427-4005
Ronald Gookin, *President*
Susan Gookin, *Corp Secy*
EMP: 12
SALES (est): 1.6MM **Privately Held**
SIC: 3625 Control equipment, electric

(G-13012)
GREENLEAF PUBLISHING INC
Also Called: Skamania County Pioneer
198 Sw 2nd St (98648)
PHONE..............................509 427-8444
Frank Devaul, *President*
EMP: 5
SALES (est): 262.5K **Privately Held**
SIC: 2711 Newspapers: publishing only, not printed on site

(G-13013)
JESTER AND JUDGE CIDER COMPANY
30 Se Cascade Ave (98648-6282)
PHONE..............................509 651-0381
Carrie Nissen, *COO*
EMP: 20 **EST:** 2015
SALES (est): 1.1MM **Privately Held**
SIC: 2099 Cider, nonalcoholic

(G-13014)
JOHN MEADOWS LOGGING
662 Kelly Henke Rd (98648-6516)
PHONE..............................509 427-4330
John W Meadows, *Owner*
J D Hayes, *Manager*
EMP: 3
SALES (est): 126.7K **Privately Held**
SIC: 2411 Logging camps & contractors

(G-13015)
LDB BEVERAGE COMPANY
30 Se Cascade Ave Spc A (98648-6282)
P.O. Box 1519 (98648-1519)
PHONE..............................509 651-0381
Bruce Nissen, *President*
Carrie Nissen, *Principal*
EMP: 12
SALES (est): 2.3MM **Privately Held**
SIC: 2082 2084 2086 8742 Malt beverage products; wine cellars, bonded: engaged in blending wines; carbonated beverages, nonalcoholic: bottled & canned; food & beverage consultant

(G-13016)
NEXUS LIFE CYCLE MGT LLC
Also Called: Nexus Lcm
25 Sw Ruellen Rd (98648-9100)
PHONE..............................541 400-0765
Joel Battistoni, *Mng Member*
Roch Bertucat, *Mng Member*
Xenia Siorentini, *Mng Member*
EMP: 3
SALES (est): 110K **Privately Held**
SIC: 7372 8742 7371 7373 Business oriented computer software; management information systems consultant; computer software development & applications; value-added resellers, computer systems

(G-13017)
OUT ON A LIMB
240 Sw 2nd St (98648-4226)
P.O. Box 413 (98648-0413)
PHONE..............................360 607-3429
Bonnie Heemeier, *Principal*
EMP: 3
SALES (est): 257.4K **Privately Held**
SIC: 3842 Limbs, artificial

(G-13018)
RIVERMIST LABRADOODLES
212 Sprague Landing Rd (98648-6503)
PHONE..............................509 427-4810
EMP: 2
SALES (est): 72K **Privately Held**
SIC: 3999 Mfg Misc Products

(G-13019)
SILVER STAR INDUSTIES INC
30 Sw Cascade Ave (98648)
PHONE..............................509 427-8800
EMP: 2
SALES (est): 112K **Privately Held**
SIC: 2541 Wood partitions & fixtures

(G-13020)
SS INDUSTRIAL INC
191 S Tucker Rd (98648-6032)
P.O. Box 251, North Bonneville (98639-0251)
PHONE..............................509 427-7836
Steve Simms, *President*
Ramona Simms, *Vice Pres*
EMP: 2
SALES (est): 500K **Privately Held**
WEB: www.ssindustrial.net
SIC: 3441 5084 Fabricated structural metal; industrial machinery & equipment

Sultan
Snohomish County

(G-13021)
ASSOCIATED METALS FABRICATION
122 S Sultan Basin Rd (98294-9625)
PHONE..............................360 793-2422
EMP: 6
SQ FT: 30,000
SALES (est): 47.3K **Privately Held**
SIC: 3441 Steel Fabrication Manufacturer

(G-13022)
DOCUFEED TECHNOLOGIES
32533 Cascade View Dr (98294-7733)
PHONE..............................360 793-2001
Mike Chambers, *Principal*
EMP: 5 **EST:** 2007
SALES (est): 602.7K **Privately Held**
SIC: 3069 Fabricated rubber products

(G-13023)
ERIK DOANE MANUFACTURING
32621 121st St Se (98294-8619)
PHONE..............................360 799-0997
EMP: 2 **EST:** 2009
SALES (est): 79K **Privately Held**
SIC: 3999 Mfg Misc Products

(G-13024)
F A KOENIG & SONS INC
33523 State Route 2 (98294-9619)
P.O. Box 1182 (98294-1182)
PHONE..............................360 793-1711
Darcy Koenig, *President*
Chris Koenig, *Principal*
Bob Koenig, *Vice Pres*
EMP: 6 **EST:** 1968
SQ FT: 11,000
SALES (est): 570K **Privately Held**
SIC: 2421 2411 Kiln drying of lumber; logging camps & contractors

(G-13025)
FLOWER RACING
14110 339th Ave Se (98294-9600)
P.O. Box 504 (98294-0504)
PHONE..............................360 793-2196
James F Flower, *Owner*
EMP: 2
SQ FT: 2,400
SALES: 100K **Privately Held**
SIC: 3542 7699 Machine tools, metal forming type; motorcycle repair service

GEOGRAPHIC SECTION

Sumner - Pierce County (G-13055)

(G-13026)
GRIZZLY MACHINING SOLUTIONS
122 S Sultan Basin Rd (98294-9625)
PHONE.....................406 396-4087
Jeff Davis, *Owner*
EMP: 2 **EST:** 2015
SQ FT: 1,350
SALES (est): 117.1K **Privately Held**
SIC: 3451 3541 Screw machine products; milling machines

(G-13027)
INDUSTRIAL FABRICATION CO
14124 339th Ave Se (98294-9600)
P.O. Box 709 (98294-0709)
PHONE.....................360 793-9001
Bob Bowles, *President*
Steven C Bruce, *Vice Pres*
EMP: 31
SQ FT: 16,000
SALES (est): 7.5MM **Privately Held**
WEB: www.indfabco.com
SIC: 3441 Fabricated structural metal

(G-13028)
L L G MACHINE WORKS
10617 323rd Ave Se (98294)
PHONE.....................360 793-1920
Larry Gilkerson, *Principal*
EMP: 2 **EST:** 2008
SALES (est): 160.8K **Privately Held**
SIC: 3599 Machine shop, jobbing & repair

(G-13029)
MOTORSPORTS
32615 Cascade View Dr B1 (98294-7675)
PHONE.....................360 799-0865
James D Schmitt, *Principal*
EMP: 3
SALES (est): 117.1K **Privately Held**
SIC: 2711 Newspapers, publishing & printing

(G-13030)
NORTH STAR MINING CO INC
903 Dyer Rd (98294-9746)
PHONE.....................360 793-0848
David Kjorsvik, *Principal*
Dave Kjorsvik, *Principal*
EMP: 2
SALES (est): 106.4K **Privately Held**
SIC: 1081 Metal mining exploration & development services

(G-13031)
OUT FOR A WALK
1121 Loves Hill Dr (98294-7633)
PHONE.....................360 793-4419
EMP: 2 **EST:** 2008
SALES (est): 150K **Privately Held**
SIC: 2542 Mfg Partitions/Fixtures-Non-wood

(G-13032)
PAULS CABINETRY
31928 116th St Se (98294-9663)
PHONE.....................425 343-7930
Paul Toutonghi, *President*
EMP: 2
SALES (est): 166.1K **Privately Held**
SIC: 2434 Wood kitchen cabinets

(G-13033)
PROSPECTORS PLUS LLC
1311 Skywall Dr (98294-9624)
P.O. Box 1316, Gold Bar (98251-1316)
PHONE.....................425 750-9290
Brawn Chris, *Mng Member*
Brawn Michelle,
EMP: 2
SALES (est): 229.9K **Privately Held**
SIC: 3669 Metal detectors

(G-13034)
ROMAC INDUSTRIES INC
Also Called: Romac Foundry Division
125 S Sultan Basin Rd (98294-9625)
PHONE.....................425 951-6200
Chris Nichols, *Engineer*
Anna Blau, *Human Res Mgr*
Colin Corcoran, *Sales Staff*
Bart Walker, *Branch Mgr*
EMP: 100
SALES (corp-wide): 82MM **Privately Held**
WEB: www.romacindustries.com
SIC: 3491 3494 3325 Water works valves; valves & pipe fittings; steel foundries
PA: Romac Industries, Inc.
21919 20th Ave Se Ste 100
Bothell WA 98021
425 951-6200

(G-13035)
SH RTS OFF SCREEN PRINTING
403 W Stevens Ave 4/6 (98294-9457)
PHONE.....................425 319-1269
Elizheva Lazella, *Partner*
Jeffery Dwor, *Partner*
EMP: 3
SQ FT: 1,400
SALES (est): 91.1K **Privately Held**
SIC: 2396 Apparel & other linings, except millinery; linings, apparel: made from purchased materials; bindings, cap & hat: made from purchased materials; screen printing on fabric articles

(G-13036)
SHEA EDWARDS FURNITURE LLP
Also Called: Pacific Bay Wooddesign
32615 Cascade View Dr (98294-7675)
PHONE.....................206 898-1992
Corey Shea, *Principal*
EMP: 10
SALES: 750K **Privately Held**
SIC: 2511 Wood household furniture

(G-13037)
SOCAL LIGHTING & SIGN LLC
710 Stratford Pl (98294-7710)
PHONE.....................425 345-5596
EMP: 2
SALES (est): 90.6K **Privately Held**
SIC: 3993 Signs & advertising specialties

(G-13038)
STANDEVER INDUSTRIES LLC
317 Walbrun Rd (98294-7649)
P.O. Box 1368 (98294-1368)
PHONE.....................206 687-9610
Karrie Billingsley, *Bd of Directors*
EMP: 2
SALES (est): 108.9K **Privately Held**
SIC: 3999 Manufacturing industries

(G-13039)
STEVE BOEK MFG (PA)
Also Called: Banners of Every Kind
501 8th St (98294-9775)
PHONE.....................503 257-5056
Steve Boek, *Owner*
EMP: 2
SALES (est): 236.2K **Privately Held**
WEB: www.boeksigns.com
SIC: 3993 Signs & advertising specialties

(G-13040)
STONEHENGE
32604 149th St Se (98294-7670)
PHONE.....................425 879-9574
Frank Duke, *Principal*
EMP: 3
SALES (est): 245.1K **Privately Held**
SIC: 3272 Concrete products

Sumas
Whatcom County

(G-13041)
B & B MANUFACTURING LLC
9314 Swanson Rd (98295-9314)
PHONE.....................360 988-5020
Bernie Mulder, *Owner*
EMP: 3
SALES (est): 233.9K **Privately Held**
SIC: 3999 Manufacturing industries

(G-13042)
CEDARPRIME INC
601 W Front St Ste C (98295-9651)
PHONE.....................360 988-2120
Duncan Davies, *Principal*
EMP: 50
SALES (est): 7.5MM
SALES (corp-wide): 1.6B **Privately Held**
SIC: 2421 Lumber: rough, sawed or planed
PA: Interfor Corporation
1055 Dunsmuir St Suite 3500
Vancouver BC V7X 1
604 689-6800

(G-13043)
DATAPARK LLC
726 Cherry St 100 (98295-9649)
PHONE.....................360 224-2157
John Gyorffy,
EMP: 20
SALES (est): 424.1K **Privately Held**
SIC: 7371 7372 8731 Computer software systems analysis & design, custom; application computer software; computer (hardware) development

(G-13044)
EPL FEED LLC (PA)
411 W Front St (98295-9603)
P.O. Box 39 (98295-0039)
PHONE.....................360 988-5811
Dennis W Elenbaas, *President*
Glen Elenbaas, *Vice Pres*
Richard J Elenbaas, *Admin Sec*
EMP: 35
SALES (est): 4.6MM **Privately Held**
SIC: 2048 5999 Feed concentrates; feed & farm supply

(G-13045)
HOWARD DENSON LOGGING
9088 Kendall Rd (98295-8608)
PHONE.....................360 988-4910
Howard Denson, *Principal*
EMP: 3
SALES (est): 266.4K **Privately Held**
SIC: 2411 Logging camps & contractors

(G-13046)
IKO PACIFIC INC (DH)
850 W Front St (98295-9634)
PHONE.....................360 988-9103
David Koschitzky, *President*
Randy Dalton, *President*
Aubrey Ellis, *Vice Pres*
Lance Greenwood, *Plant Supt*
Ron Healey, *Admin Sec*
◆ **EMP:** 49
SQ FT: 1,000
SALES (est): 17.1MM
SALES (corp-wide): 54.8MM **Privately Held**
SIC: 2952 Asphalt felts & coatings
HQ: Iko Industries Ltd
80 Stafford Dr
Brampton ON L6W 1
905 457-2880

(G-13047)
MAZDAK INTERNATIONAL INC
Also Called: Splitvane Engineers
410 W 3rd St (98295-9699)
P.O. Box 117 (98295-0117)
PHONE.....................360 988-6058
Baha Elsayed Abulnaga, *President*
EMP: 2
SALES (est): 293.7K **Privately Held**
SIC: 8711 3321 Consulting engineer; gray & ductile iron foundries

(G-13048)
MILL FRAME LLC
534 Railroad Ave # 1265 (98295-4000)
PHONE.....................425 599-5992
John Hunter, *President*
Rod Erdos, *Plant Mgr*
Blair Nutting, *VP Sls/Mktg*
Lisa Hodges, *Controller*
Sandy Erdos, *Manager*
EMP: 6
SALES (est): 124.8K
SALES (corp-wide): 2.3MM **Privately Held**
SIC: 2431 Door screens, wood frame
PA: Luxor Industrial Corporation
889 Pender St W Suite 702
Vancouver BC V6C 3
604 684-7929

(G-13049)
MODULAR DRIVEN TECH INC
Also Called: Mdt
726 Cherry St 100 (98295-9649)
PHONE.....................604 393-0800
Maarten V Ruitenburg, *CEO*
George Lainhart, *Director*
EMP: 10 **EST:** 2014
SALES (est): 951.4K **Privately Held**
SIC: 3484 Guns (firearms) or gun parts, 30 mm. & below

(G-13050)
SOCCO INC
Also Called: Socco Forest Products
601 W Front St Ste A (98295-9651)
PHONE.....................360 988-4900
Gary Jones, *President*
Candace Laird, *Controller*
EMP: 14
SQ FT: 40,000
SALES: 3MM **Privately Held**
WEB: www.soccoforest.com
SIC: 2421 Kiln drying of lumber; custom sawmill
PA: National Energy Systems Company
335 Parkplace Ctr Ste 110
Kirkland WA

(G-13051)
SUMAS MT LOG CO
8373 Westergreen Rd (98295-8406)
P.O. Box 296, Everson (98247-0296)
PHONE.....................360 966-4781
Ed Westergreen, *President*
EMP: 2
SALES (est): 184.4K **Privately Held**
SIC: 2411 Logging

(G-13052)
TNT MACHINING LLC
285 Garfield St (98295-9677)
P.O. Box 400 (98295-0400)
PHONE.....................360 988-0274
Aaron Theisen,
Aaron Theisein,
Adam Theisen,
Heidi Theisen,
EMP: 9
SALES: 1.2MM **Privately Held**
SIC: 3714 7389 Motor vehicle parts & accessories;

Sumner
Pierce County

(G-13053)
4EVERGREEN FABRICATORS LLC
1402 Lake Tapps Pkwy E (98391)
PHONE.....................253 691-6752
Travis Hansen,
EMP: 2
SALES (est): 14.1K **Privately Held**
SIC: 3549 Wiredrawing & fabricating machinery & equipment, ex. die

(G-13054)
AIM AEROSPACE SUMNER INC
Also Called: Precision Arospc & Composites
1516 Fryar Ave (98390-1514)
PHONE.....................253 863-7868
Bill Keilman, *General Mgr*
Mark Kinkella, *Production*
Chris Johnson, *Engineer*
Ken Fagan, *Manager*
EMP: 150
SALES (corp-wide): 168.2MM **Privately Held**
SIC: 3728 8711 Aircraft assemblies, sub-assemblies & parts; aviation &/or aeronautical engineering
HQ: Aim Aerospace Sumner, Inc.
1502 20th St Nw
Auburn WA 98001
253 804-3355

(G-13055)
BEAU MAC ENTERPRISES
4100 150th Avenue Ct E (98390-2174)
PHONE.....................253 447-8093
Mike Zimmer, *Owner*
Robert Guhanan, *Owner*

Sumner - Pierce County (G-13056)

EMP: 5
SALES (est): 278.4K **Privately Held**
SIC: 5941 5091 3949 Bait & tackle; fishing equipment & supplies; fishing tackle, general

(G-13056)
BESTFITT GASKET COMPANY INC
3025 142nd Ave E Ste 105 (98390-9576)
PHONE...................253 863-9521
Ray Davis, *President*
Tari Davis Knott, *Vice Pres*
EMP: 3
SALES (est): 444.3K **Privately Held**
SIC: 3069 3053 3264 Hard rubber & molded rubber products; gaskets, all materials; cleats, porcelain

(G-13057)
BROOKS SPORTS INC
2701 142nd Ave E Ste 100 (98390-9636)
PHONE...................253 863-4343
Jim Weber, *President*
EMP: 8
SALES (corp-wide): 225.3B **Publicly Held**
SIC: 3949 Sporting & athletic goods
HQ: Brooks Sports, Inc.
  3400 Stone Way N Ste 500
  Seattle WA 98103
  425 488-3131

(G-13058)
CFI BLUE SKY II LLC
Also Called: Carlson Formetec
14513 32nd St E (98390-8500)
PHONE...................253 627-1903
Raela Guernsey, *President*
Buck Cook,
EMP: 34
SQ FT: 26,000
SALES (est): 7.7MM **Privately Held**
WEB: www.carlsonformetec.com
SIC: 3724 Aircraft engines & engine parts

(G-13059)
COLD LOCKER PROCESSING LLC
2200 140th Ave E Ste 200 (98390-9652)
PHONE...................253 321-3233
Holly Iniguez, *Controller*
Edward Devito,
EMP: 18
SALES (est): 4.4MM **Privately Held**
SIC: 2092 Fresh or frozen packaged fish

(G-13060)
COMPOSITE SOLUTIONS CORP
14810 Puyallup St E # 100 (98390-2404)
PHONE...................253 833-1878
Arthur Sauls, *President*
Clive Rees, *Chief Engr*
Melissa Ricks, *Human Res Dir*
Ken Chien, *VP Mktg*
EMP: 67
SQ FT: 60,000
SALES (est): 19.2MM **Privately Held**
WEB: www.compositesolutions.com
SIC: 3728 5088 Aircraft assemblies, sub-assemblies & parts; aircraft equipment & supplies

(G-13061)
COOPER TIRE & RUBBER COMPANY
3012 142nd Ave E Ste 300 (98390-9673)
PHONE...................253 826-5742
David Schock, *Manager*
EMP: 6
SALES (corp-wide): 2.8B **Publicly Held**
WEB: www.coopertire.com
SIC: 3011 Automobile tires, pneumatic
PA: Cooper Tire & Rubber Company Inc
  701 Lima Ave
  Findlay OH 45840
  419 423-1321

(G-13062)
CUMMINS INC
Also Called: Rental Fleet
1800 Fryar Ave (98390-1529)
PHONE...................425 277-3342
Nick Johnson, *Branch Mgr*
EMP: 5
SALES (corp-wide): 23.7B **Publicly Held**
SIC: 3519 Engines, diesel & semi-diesel or dual-fuel
PA: Cummins Inc.
  500 Jackson St
  Columbus IN 47201
  812 377-5000

(G-13063)
CURTIS MACHINING
21515 112th St E (98391-7801)
P.O. Box 1534, Buckley (98321-1534)
PHONE...................253 862-9256
Curt Satterthwaite, *Owner*
EMP: 4
SALES (est): 315.2K **Privately Held**
SIC: 3599 Machine shop, jobbing & repair

(G-13064)
CUSTOM CRAFT LLC
2920 142nd Ave E Ste 103 (98390-9643)
PHONE...................253 826-5450
Leary Jobe,
Todd Hegstad,
EMP: 33
SALES (est): 3.5MM **Privately Held**
SIC: 3599 2541 Custom machinery; wood partitions & fixtures

(G-13065)
DANZER VENEER AMERICAS INC
3107 142nd Ave E Ste 101 (98390-9610)
PHONE...................253 770-4664
Jason Shade, *Principal*
EMP: 7
SALES (corp-wide): 200.2K **Privately Held**
SIC: 2435 Hardwood veneer & plywood
HQ: Danzer Veneer Americas, Inc.
  119 A I D Dr
  Darlington PA 16115

(G-13066)
DILLANOS COFFEE ROASTERS INC
1607 45th St E (98390-2202)
PHONE...................253 826-1807
Howard Heyer, *President*
David Morris, *Vice Pres*
Tim Lidstrom, *Opers Mgr*
Melissa Huston, *Human Res Mgr*
Carissa Campbell, *Sales Mgr*
◆ **EMP:** 20
SQ FT: 12,000
SALES (est): 10.8MM **Privately Held**
WEB: www.dillanos.com
SIC: 5149 2095 Coffee, green or roasted; roasted coffee

(G-13067)
DURABLE SUPERIOR CASTERS
12620 Valley Ave E (98390-1508)
PHONE...................253 750-0379
EMP: 2
SALES (est): 107.4K **Privately Held**
SIC: 3562 Casters

(G-13068)
ELMO FOKKER INC
1725 Puyallup St Ste 200 (98390-2405)
PHONE...................253 395-2652
EMP: 30
SALES (est): 3.9MM
SALES (corp-wide): 12.7B **Privately Held**
SIC: 3724 Mfg Aircraft Engines/Parts
HQ: Fokker Elmo B.V.
  Aviolandalaan 33
  Hoogerheide
  164 617-000

(G-13069)
ENERSYS
14323 32nd St E (98390-9500)
PHONE...................253 299-0005
John D Craig, *Branch Mgr*
EMP: 15
SALES (corp-wide): 2.8B **Publicly Held**
SIC: 3691 Lead acid batteries (storage batteries)
PA: Enersys
  2366 Bernville Rd
  Reading PA 19605
  610 208-1991

(G-13070)
EVO
3209 West Valley Hwy E # 100 (98390-9000)
PHONE...................866 386-1590
Valerie Woods, *Manager*
EMP: 4
SALES (est): 132.5K **Privately Held**
SIC: 3949 Snow skis

(G-13071)
EXIDE TECHNOLOGIES
2005 Fryar Ave (98390-1523)
PHONE...................253 863-5134
Linda Schalansky, *Branch Mgr*
EMP: 4
SALES (corp-wide): 2.4B **Privately Held**
SIC: 3691 3629 Storage batteries; battery chargers, rectifying or nonrotating
PA: Exide Technologies
  13000 Deerfield Pkwy # 200
  Milton GA 30004
  678 566-9000

(G-13072)
GAFFTECH LLC
3107 142nd Ave E Ste 105 (98390-9610)
PHONE...................844 423-3486
Daniel Kretz,
Jonathan Harkliss,
EMP: 7
SQ FT: 23,000
SALES: 60MM **Privately Held**
SIC: 2241 Slide fastener tapes

(G-13073)
HELLY HANSEN (US) INC (DH)
14218 Stewart Rd Ste 100a (98390-5500)
PHONE...................800 435-5901
Paul Stoneham, *CEO*
Deborah Thayer, *Finance Dir*
▲ **EMP:** 46 **EST:** 1980
SQ FT: 67,000
SALES (est): 334.6MM
SALES (corp-wide): 10.6B **Privately Held**
SIC: 5137 5699 2339 2329 Women's & children's dresses, suits, skirts & blouses; apparel belts, women's & children's; work clothing; marine apparel; raincoats; ski jackets & pants: women's, misses' & juniors'; down-filled coats, jackets & vests: women's & misses'; ski & snow clothing: men's & boys'; men's & boys' leather, wool & down-filled outerwear
HQ: Helly Hansen As
  Munkedamsveien 35
  Oslo 0250
  692 490-00

(G-13074)
HUMAN SCIENCE LLC
Also Called: Hu-SC
13701 24th St E Unit F2 (98390-9681)
P.O. Box 511, Milton (98354-0511)
PHONE...................253 321-6800
Steve Avila, *CEO*
Trevor Shaw, *President*
EMP: 2
SALES (est): 57.1K **Privately Held**
SIC: 2833 2834 Medicinals & botanicals; vitamin, nutrient & hematinic preparations for human use

(G-13075)
J & B IMPORTERS INC
1725 Puyallup St Ste 300 (98390-2405)
PHONE...................253 395-0441
Ben Joannou, *Branch Mgr*
EMP: 3
SALES (corp-wide): 62.3MM **Privately Held**
SIC: 3751 5091 Bicycles & related parts; bicycle equipment & supplies
PA: J & B Importers, Inc.
  11925 Sw 128th St
  Miami FL 33186
  305 238-1866

(G-13076)
K&M STORAGE
Also Called: K & M Steel Storage Buildings
22919 State Route 410 E (98391-3969)
PHONE...................253 862-3515
Mark Plank, *Owner*
EMP: 2
SALES (est): 207.1K **Privately Held**
SIC: 1542 4226 3448 2452 Nonresidential construction; special warehousing & storage; prefabricated metal buildings; prefabricated wood buildings

(G-13077)
KELLER SUPPLY CO
2601 142nd Ave E (98390-9694)
PHONE...................253 863-9271
Barnay Barnhart, *Branch Mgr*
EMP: 5
SQ FT: 77,375
SALES (corp-wide): 327MM **Privately Held**
SIC: 3432 5074 Plumbing fixture fittings & trim; plumbing fittings & supplies
PA: Keller Supply Co
  3209 17th Ave W
  Seattle WA 98119
  206 285-3300

(G-13078)
KEURIG GREEN MOUNTAIN INC
3324 142nd Ave E Ste 200 (98390-9691)
PHONE...................253 447-9100
Matt Koopman, *Branch Mgr*
Brian Potts, *Director*
EMP: 125 **Publicly Held**
SIC: 2095 5499 Roasted coffee; coffee
HQ: Keurig Green Mountain, Inc.
  33 Coffee Ln
  Waterbury VT 05676
  802 244-5621

(G-13079)
LEE R MASON INC
15022 Puyallup St E U103 (98390-2401)
PHONE...................253 863-8666
Lee Radford Mason, *President*
EMP: 6 **EST:** 2012
SALES (est): 294.9K **Privately Held**
SIC: 3281 Curbing, granite or stone

(G-13080)
MAC ARTHUR CO
4504 East Valley Hwy E (98390-9506)
PHONE...................253 863-8830
Todd Volden, *Branch Mgr*
EMP: 25
SALES (corp-wide): 206.5MM **Privately Held**
SIC: 5033 3448 Insulation materials; roofing & siding materials; farm & utility buildings
PA: Mac Arthur Co.
  2400 Wycliff St
  Saint Paul MN 55114
  651 646-2773

(G-13081)
MACHINE REPAIR & DESIGN INC
1710 Fryar Ave Ste 102 (98390-1513)
PHONE...................253 826-6329
Ronald M Tweden, *President*
Todd Tweden, *General Mgr*
L Charlene Tweden, *Admin Sec*
EMP: 10
SQ FT: 9,000
SALES (est): 1.1MM **Privately Held**
WEB: www.mrdinc.com
SIC: 7699 3599 Industrial machinery & equipment repair; machine shop, jobbing & repair

(G-13082)
MACHINE WORKS INC
13701 24th St E Unit D8 (98390-9679)
PHONE...................253 750-0238
Michael Durham, *President*
Peter Pierkarski, *Vice Pres*
Dawn Durham, *Treasurer*
EMP: 5 **EST:** 2017
SQ FT: 4,000
SALES (est): 625K **Privately Held**
SIC: 3555 Type & type making machinery & equipment

(G-13083)
MADRONA STONE LLC
3900 150th Avenue Ct E (98390-2175)
P.O. Box 2186 (98390-0480)
PHONE...................253 750-5064
Philip Jensen, *Principal*
Joshua Hulburt, *Mng Member*

GEOGRAPHIC SECTION

Sumner - Pierce County (G-13110)

EMP: 2
SQ FT: 20,471
SALES: 1MM Privately Held
SIC: 2541 Counter & sink tops

(G-13084)
MANKE LUMBER COMPANY INC
13702 Stewart Rd (98390-9612)
PHONE.................................253 863-4495
Craig McNeal, Branch Mgr
EMP: 90
SALES (corp-wide): 97.1MM Privately Held
WEB: www.mankelumber.com
SIC: 5031 2421 Lumber: rough, dressed & finished; lumber: rough, sawed or planed
PA: Manke Lumber Company, Inc.
1717 Marine View Dr
Tacoma WA 98422
253 572-6252

(G-13085)
MCLANE FOODSERVICE DIST INC
Also Called: Mdm Food Service
4301 West Valley Hwy E # 400 (98390-9713)
PHONE.................................253 891-6943
EMP: 8
SALES (corp-wide): 225.3B Publicly Held
SIC: 3589 Shredders, industrial & commercial
HQ: Mclane Foodservice Distribution, Inc.
2641 Meadowbrook Rd
Rocky Mount NC 27801
252 985-7200

(G-13086)
METALTECH INC
1907 Fryar Ave (98390-1526)
PHONE.................................253 863-7532
Matt Steinman, President
EMP: 30
SALES (est): 9.1MM Privately Held
WEB: www.mtmw.com
SIC: 3444 Sheet metal specialties, not stamped

(G-13087)
NAPS FORMING SYSTEMS
13616 8th St E (98390)
PHONE.................................800 922-2082
Greg Jenks, Branch Mgr
EMP: 5
SALES (corp-wide): 205.2K Privately Held
SIC: 3444 Concrete forms, sheet metal
PA: Nap's Forming Systems
10116 221st Ave E
Bonney Lake WA 98391
253 862-4811

(G-13088)
NEON CONNECTION
20322 73rd St E (98391-6125)
PHONE.................................360 224-3061
Christina McVay, President
EMP: 3
SALES (est): 160K Privately Held
SIC: 3993 Neon signs

(G-13089)
NORTHWEST BAKING LTD PARTNR
Also Called: Pacific Northwest Baking Co
1307 Puyallup St (98390-1602)
P.O. Box 890 (98390-0160)
PHONE.................................253 863-0373
Bill Zimmerman Jr, President
EMP: 53
SQ FT: 43,000
SALES (est): 15.4MM Privately Held
WEB: www.pnwb.com
SIC: 2051 Buns, bread type: fresh or frozen

(G-13090)
ODE PRODUCTS LLC
Also Called: Ode Gutter Products
13701 24th St E Unit F8 (98390-9681)
PHONE.................................253 859-7902
Mark Odekirk, Mng Member
Bill Odekirk,
▲ EMP: 3
SQ FT: 5,300
SALES: 500K Privately Held
SIC: 3444 5211 Gutters, sheet metal; lumber & other building materials

(G-13091)
OMADA INTERNATIONAL LLC (PA)
14513 32nd St E (98390-8500)
PHONE.................................425 242-5400
Jason Wilder, Vice Pres
Jim Hoover,
Doug Fletcher,
Michael Warren,
EMP: 174 EST: 2013
SALES (est): 48.2MM Privately Held
SIC: 3365 Aerospace castings, aluminum

(G-13092)
PACIFIC BAY INC
1016 57th St E Ste 150 (98390-1527)
PHONE.................................253 848-5541
Omri Kathleen, Director
EMP: 2 EST: 2013
SALES (est): 159.6K Privately Held
SIC: 2452 Prefabricated wood buildings

(G-13093)
PACIFIC CREST INDUSTRIES INC
Also Called: Bellmont Cabinet Company
13610 52nd St E Ste 300 (98390-9221)
P.O. Box 2050 (98390-0450)
PHONE.................................253 321-3011
Steven J Bell, President
Casey Bell, COO
Carolyn M Bell, Vice Pres
▲ EMP: 121
SQ FT: 192,000
SALES (est): 23.1MM Privately Held
WEB: www.pacificcrestcabinets.com
SIC: 2434 2499 2517 2521 Wood kitchen cabinets; kitchen, bathroom & household ware: wood; home entertainment unit cabinets, wood; wood office furniture; millwork

(G-13094)
PIN HSIAO & ASSOCIATES LLC
Also Called: Antonina's Bakery
5501 West Valley Hwy E (98390-9218)
P.O. Box 40177, Bellevue (98015-4177)
PHONE.................................253 863-0337
Konstantin Matkovskiy, Plant Mgr
EMP: 35
SALES (corp-wide): 12MM Privately Held
SIC: 2051 Bakery: wholesale or wholesale/retail combined
PA: Pin Hsiao & Associates L.L.C.
2535 152nd Ave Ne
Redmond WA 98052
425 637-3357

(G-13095)
PLYWOOD COMPONENTS INC
Also Called: Pasquier Panel
1510 Puyallup St (98390-2233)
P.O. Box 1170 (98390-0230)
PHONE.................................253 863-6323
Tom Pasquier, President
Stanley Andrews, President
Steve Pasquier, Vice Pres
John Nolen, Admin Sec
EMP: 40
SQ FT: 100,000
SALES (est): 5.3MM Privately Held
WEB: www.plywoodcomponents.com
SIC: 2436 2493 Plywood, softwood; particleboard products

(G-13096)
RMG NUTRITION
Also Called: Herbalife Independent Distr
6323 151st Ave E (98390-2663)
PHONE.................................253 863-7017
REA M Grisham, Owner
Donald L Grisham, Co-Owner
EMP: 2
SALES (est): 110K Privately Held
SIC: 2833 Vitamins, natural or synthetic: bulk, uncompounded

(G-13097)
RONALD WAYNE DAGLEY
Also Called: All Around Fence Company
14323 16th St E (98390-9633)
P.O. Box 1029, Ravensdale (98051-1029)
PHONE.................................253 863-4895
Ronald Wayne Dagley, Owner
EMP: 6
SQ FT: 75,000
SALES (est): 713K Privately Held
SIC: 3446 1799 Fences, gates, posts & flagpoles; fence construction

(G-13098)
SHINING OCEAN INC
1515 Puyallup St (98390-2234)
PHONE.................................253 826-3700
Robert Bleu, Ch of Bd
Lawrence Mulvey, President
Gisela Drake, Prdtn Mgr
Howard Frisk, Treasurer
Cris Hernandez, Human Res Dir
◆ EMP: 134
SQ FT: 95,000
SALES: 35MM
SALES (corp-wide): 598.4MM Privately Held
WEB: www.kanimi.com
SIC: 2092 Crab meat, fresh: packaged in nonsealed containers
HQ: True World Holdings Llc
24 Link Dr Unit D
Rockleigh NJ 07647
201 750-0024

(G-13099)
SIGN RITE
1725 137th Ave E (98390-9637)
PHONE.................................253 447-8997
Steven M Bateman, President
EMP: 2
SALES (est): 116.7K Privately Held
SIC: 3993 Signs & advertising specialties

(G-13100)
SMITHCO MEATS INC
15509 Main St E (98390-2643)
PHONE.................................253 863-5157
Jay Keener, President
Patrick Marshall, General Mgr
Dan Weldon, Sales Staff
EMP: 32
SQ FT: 20,000
SALES (est): 10.7MM Privately Held
SIC: 5142 5147 2013 2011 Meat, frozen: packaged; meats, fresh; sausages & other prepared meats; meat packing plants

(G-13101)
SONOCO PRODUCTS COMPANY
1802 Steele Ave (98390-1606)
P.O. Box 489 (98390-0489)
PHONE.................................206 682-0440
Kishor Jhala, Branch Mgr
EMP: 55
SQ FT: 175,000
SALES (corp-wide): 5.3B Publicly Held
WEB: www.sonoco.com
SIC: 2631 Paperboard mills
PA: Sonoco Products Company
1 N 2nd St
Hartsville SC 29550
843 383-7000

(G-13102)
SSB MANUFACTURING COMPANY
13605 52nd St E Ste 200 (98390-9216)
PHONE.................................253 891-3272
Dan McCallister, Principal
EMP: 109 Privately Held
SIC: 2515 5021 Mattresses, innerspring or box spring; mattresses
HQ: Ssb Manufacturing Company
1 Concourse Pkwy Ste 800
Atlanta GA 30328
770 512-7700

(G-13103)
STAR PIPE LLC
13605 52nd St E Ste 100 (98390-9216)
PHONE.................................253 826-3950
EMP: 6

SALES (corp-wide): 67.8MM Privately Held
WEB: www.starpipeproducts.com
SIC: 3498 Fabricated pipe & fittings
PA: Star Pipe, L.L.C.
4018 Westhollow Pkwy
Houston TX 77082
281 558-3000

(G-13104)
SUPERIOR COATINGS
1325 Bonney Ave Apt 8 (98390-2104)
PHONE.................................253 405-5424
Donny Peters, Administration
EMP: 2 EST: 2017
SALES (est): 89.8K Privately Held
SIC: 3479 Metal coating & allied service

(G-13105)
SURAIN INDUSTRIES INC
Also Called: McConkey Co.
1615 Puyallup St (98390-2203)
P.O. Box 1690 (98390-0369)
PHONE.................................253 863-8111
Derek Moeller, President
EMP: 3
SALES (est): 186.1K Privately Held
SIC: 3089 Flower pots, plastic

(G-13106)
THERMAL SOLUTIONS MFG
14218 Stewart Rd Ste 200b (98390-5501)
PHONE.................................206 764-7028
EMP: 2
SALES (est): 124.1K Privately Held
SIC: 3714 Motor vehicle parts & accessories

(G-13107)
TRUSS COMPANY AND BLDG SUP INC (PA)
2802 142nd Ave E (98390-9615)
P.O. Box 1770 (98390-0380)
PHONE.................................253 863-5555
Roger Helgeson, President
William Matheny, President
Martin D Waiss, President
Kelly Graham, General Mgr
Todd Grogan, General Mgr
EMP: 100
SQ FT: 80,000
SALES (est): 22.4MM Privately Held
WEB: www.thetrussco.com
SIC: 2439 Trusses, wooden roof; trusses, except roof: laminated lumber

(G-13108)
U S FIRE EQUIPMENT LLC
4200 150th Avenue Ct E (98390-2172)
PHONE.................................253 863-1301
Lloyd W Hamilton Jr, CEO
Virginia A Karahuta,
EMP: 13
SALES: 1.7MM Privately Held
WEB: www.usfireequipment.com
SIC: 3713 3569 7389 Truck & bus bodies; firefighting apparatus & related equipment; fire extinguisher servicing

(G-13109)
UPRIGHT POSTS LLC
902 Kincaid Ave (98390-1448)
PHONE.................................253 224-0076
Nathan Coons,
Donald Stambaugh,
Kristina Stambaugh,
Melanie Stambaugh,
Tina Stambaugh,
EMP: 3
SALES (est): 92.1K Privately Held
SIC: 3993 Advertising artwork

(G-13110)
WASHINGTON TRACTOR INC (PA)
Also Called: John Deere Authorized Dealer
2700 136th Avenue Ct E (98390-9228)
PHONE.................................253 863-4436
James Hale, President
Brent Huppert, Director
EMP: 204 EST: 2009

Sumner - Pierce County (G-13111)

SALES (est): 129.6MM **Privately Held**
WEB: washingtontractor.org
SIC: 3523 5083 5261 7699 Farm machinery & equipment; farm & garden machinery; lawnmowers & tractors; farm machinery repair; heavy construction equipment rental

(G-13111)
WESTERN WOOD PRESERVING CO
1310 Zehnder St (98390-1618)
P.O. Box 1250 (98390-0250)
PHONE..................................253 863-8191
EMP: 30
SQ FT: 2,400
SALES (est): 5.7MM **Privately Held**
WEB: www.westernwoodpreserving.com
SIC: 2491 Wood preserving

(G-13112)
WEYERHAEUSER COMPANY
6210 207th Ave E (98391-6106)
PHONE..................................631 863-1117
Steve Rogel, *Manager*
EMP: 117
SALES (corp-wide): 7.4B **Publicly Held**
SIC: 2421 Custom sawmill
PA: Weyerhaeuser Company
220 Occidental Ave S
Seattle WA 98104
206 539-3000

Sunnyside
Yakima County

(G-13113)
BEE JAY SCALES INC
116 N 1st St (98944-1302)
P.O. Box 154 (98944-0154)
PHONE..................................509 837-8280
Arno Johnson, *President*
EMP: 2
SALES (est): 170K **Privately Held**
SIC: 3596 Truck (motor vehicle) scales

(G-13114)
BLACK RIVER SEAL COATING WESLE
7431 Van Belle Rd (98944-9127)
PHONE..................................509 836-0125
EMP: 2
SALES (est): 87.9K **Privately Held**
SIC: 3479 Metal coating & allied service

(G-13115)
CANAM STEEL CORPORATION
2099 Sheller Rd (98944-9808)
PHONE..................................360 329-7048
EMP: 2 **Privately Held**
SIC: 3441 Building components, structural steel
HQ: Canam Steel Corporation
4010 Clay St
Point Of Rocks MD 21777
301 874-5141

(G-13116)
CCO HOLDINGS LLC
401 S 6th St (98944-1411)
PHONE..................................509 643-3364
EMP: 2
SALES (corp-wide): 43.6B **Publicly Held**
SIC: 5064 4841 3663 3651 Electrical appliances, television & radio; cable & other pay television services; radio & TV communications equipment; household audio & video equipment
HQ: Cco Holdings, Llc
400 Atlantic St
Stamford CT 06901
203 905-7801

(G-13117)
COTE BONNEVILLE
2841 Fordyce Rd (98944-9771)
PHONE..................................509 840-4596
Kathy Shiels, *Owner*
▲ EMP: 4
SALES (est): 203.1K **Privately Held**
SIC: 2084 Wines

(G-13118)
CPM DEVELOPMENT CORPORATION
Also Called: Central Pre-Mix Concrete
112 Factory Rd (98944-9757)
PHONE..................................509 837-5171
Troy Holt, *General Mgr*
EMP: 66
SALES (corp-wide): 30.6B **Privately Held**
SIC: 3273 Ready-mixed concrete
HQ: Cpm Development Corporation
5111 E Broadway Ave
Spokane Valley WA 99212
509 534-6221

(G-13119)
CULLENS CUSTOM MEATS
6852 Van Belle Rd (98944-9765)
PHONE..................................509 837-0079
Eric Blankenship, *Principal*
EMP: 3
SQ FT: 4,500
SALES (est): 147.9K **Privately Held**
SIC: 5421 2011 Meat markets, including freezer provisioners; meat packing plants

(G-13120)
DOUBLE DUTCH LLC
351 W Merz Rd (98944-9418)
PHONE..................................509 837-6539
Matthew Van Wingerden,
Michael Van Wingerden,
EMP: 2
SALES (est): 117.6K **Privately Held**
SIC: 0139 3999 2034 ; ; dried & dehydrated vegetables

(G-13121)
DRR FRUIT PRODUCTS CO INC
705 Alexander Rd (98944-8935)
P.O. Box 1014 (98944-3014)
PHONE..................................509 836-2051
Russ Lloyd, *President*
Robert Weaver, *President*
Dave Frank, *Treasurer*
Russell Lloyd, *Shareholder*
EMP: 20
SALES (est): 381.9K **Privately Held**
SIC: 2037 Frozen fruits & vegetables

(G-13122)
DUBRUL VINEYARD LLC
2841 Fordyce Rd (98944-9771)
PHONE..................................509 837-7746
Hugh Shiels, *Principal*
EMP: 2
SALES (est): 105.7K **Privately Held**
SIC: 2084 Wines

(G-13123)
EMMANUEL PALLETS LLC
405 Scoon Rd (98944-1074)
PHONE..................................509 439-0924
Adolfo De La Cruz, *President*
EMP: 3
SALES (est): 119.9K **Privately Held**
SIC: 2448 Wood pallets & skids

(G-13124)
ENTRUST COMMUNITY SERVICES
520 S 7th St (98944-2215)
PHONE..................................509 839-8066
Tom Gaulke, *Director*
Glen Medicraft, *Director*
EMP: 90
SQ FT: 2,700
SALES (est): 3.9MM **Privately Held**
WEB: www.horizon.net
SIC: 8331 3086 7389 7349 Sheltered workshop; packaging & shipping materials, foamed plastic; document & office record destruction; janitorial service, contract basis

(G-13125)
FASHION CORNER
401 S 6th St (98944-1411)
PHONE..................................509 837-7345
Irene Jochen, *Owner*
EMP: 8
SQ FT: 10,000
SALES: 1MM **Privately Held**
SIC: 2335 5621 Wedding gowns & dresses; bridal shops

(G-13126)
GALLO WINERY
2310 Holmason Rd (98944-9222)
PHONE..................................509 947-4520
EMP: 2
SALES (est): 160.1K **Privately Held**
SIC: 2084 Wines

(G-13127)
INNOVATION RESOURCE CENTER
214 S 6th St (98944-1446)
PHONE..................................509 836-2400
Marie E Guerrer, *Principal*
EMP: 2 **EST:** 2011
SALES (est): 72.3K **Privately Held**
SIC: 8093 2899 8322 Alcohol clinic, outpatient; drug clinic, outpatient; ; substance abuse counseling

(G-13128)
J-M MANUFACTURING COMPANY INC
Also Called: JM Eagle
1820 S 1st St (98944-2084)
PHONE..................................509 837-7800
Tom Colton, *Manager*
EMP: 50
SALES (corp-wide): 1B **Privately Held**
WEB: www.pwpipe.com
SIC: 3084 Plastics pipe
PA: J-M Manufacturing Company, Inc.
5200 W Century Blvd
Los Angeles CA 90045
800 621-4404

(G-13129)
JOHN DALRYMPLE
Also Called: Bert's Excavating
1536 S 16th St (98944-2529)
P.O. Box 73 (98944-0073)
PHONE..................................509 837-2117
John Dalrymple, *Owner*
EMP: 3
SALES (est): 340.7K **Privately Held**
SIC: 1794 3272 Excavation work; septic tanks, concrete

(G-13130)
JOHNSON CONCENTRATES INC
310 E Edison Ave (98944-1436)
P.O. Box 955 (98944-0955)
PHONE..................................509 837-4600
◆ EMP: 30
SQ FT: 50,000
SALES (est): 3.4MM **Privately Held**
SIC: 2037 2033 Fruit juice concentrates, frozen; canned fruits & specialties

(G-13131)
JOHNSON FOODS INC
Also Called: Johnson Fruit Cannery
300 Warehouse Ave (98944-1310)
PHONE..................................509 837-4188
Gary Johnson, *Manager*
Gloria Miser, *Manager*
EMP: 25
SALES (corp-wide): 56.2MM **Privately Held**
SIC: 2033 Vegetables: packaged in cans, jars, etc.; maraschino cherries: packaged in cans, jars, etc.
PA: Johnson Foods, Inc.
336 Blaine Ave
Sunnyside WA 98944
509 837-4214

(G-13132)
LENOX INDEPENDENT DEALER
211 Lappin Ave (98944-1014)
PHONE..................................509 837-6400
EMP: 2 **EST:** 2012
SALES (est): 120K **Privately Held**
SIC: 3585 Mfg Refrigeration/Heating Equipment

(G-13133)
MARQUEZ MFG LTD
410 Factory Rd (98944-9193)
P.O. Box 120 (98944-0120)
PHONE..................................509 837-6230
Robert Marquez, *President*
EMP: 20
SQ FT: 10,000
SALES (est): 2.1MM **Privately Held**
SIC: 3715 7539 Semitrailers for truck tractors; trailer repair

(G-13134)
MOUNTAIN VALLEY PRODUCTS INC
Also Called: Valley Processing
108 Blaine Ave (98944-1458)
P.O. Box 246 (98944-0246)
PHONE..................................509 837-8084
Mary Ann Glazner, *Owner*
EMP: 23
SALES (est): 1.1MM **Privately Held**
SIC: 0172 2099 2034 Grapes; food preparations; dehydrated fruits, vegetables, soups

(G-13135)
NATURAL SELECTION FARMS INC
6800 Emerald Rd (98944-9708)
P.O. Box 893 (98944-0893)
PHONE..................................509 837-3501
Ted Durfey, *President*
Pamela Durfey, *Vice Pres*
EMP: 15 **EST:** 1992
SALES (est): 2.4MM **Privately Held**
WEB: www.naturalselectionfarms.com
SIC: 2875 Fertilizers, mixing only

(G-13136)
PALETERIA LANORPEANA
120 Rohman St (98944-1073)
PHONE..................................509 839-5802
Jesse Ramos, *Partner*
EMP: 2
SALES (est): 40K **Privately Held**
SIC: 2024 Ice cream & frozen desserts

(G-13137)
PARR LUMBER COMPANY
525 E South Hill Rd (98944-8449)
P.O. Box 822 (98944-0822)
PHONE..................................509 543-7594
EMP: 9
SALES (corp-wide): 320.2MM **Privately Held**
SIC: 2439 Trusses, wooden roof
PA: Parr Lumber Company
5630 Ne Century Blvd
Hillsboro OR 97124
503 614-2500

(G-13138)
PINATAS TRADEDIA
701 S 11th St (98944-2242)
PHONE..................................509 836-2442
Alberto Mercado, *Owner*
Martha Mercado, *Owner*
EMP: 2
SQ FT: 4,000
SALES (est): 110.6K **Privately Held**
SIC: 2679 Building, insulating & packaging paper

(G-13139)
ROSE TUCKER
Also Called: Tucker's Fruit & Produce
70 Ray Rd (98944-8412)
PHONE..................................509 837-8701
Rose Tucker, *Owner*
Deanna Tucker, *Manager*
Randy Tucker, *Manager*
EMP: 4
SQ FT: 5,000
SALES (est): 199.6K **Privately Held**
SIC: 0175 2084 5431 2033 Deciduous tree fruits; wines; fruit stands or markets; vegetable stands or markets; canned fruits & specialties

(G-13140)
SENECA FOODS CORPORATION
1525 S 4th St (98944-2184)
P.O. Box 357 (98944-0357)
PHONE..................................509 837-3806
Jack Watson, *Manager*
EMP: 250
SALES (corp-wide): 1.2B **Publicly Held**
SIC: 2099 Food preparations
PA: Seneca Foods Corporation
3736 S Main St
Marion NY 14505
315 926-8100

GEOGRAPHIC SECTION

Tacoma - Pierce County (G-13169)

(G-13141)
SHIRAUL LLC
Also Called: Bullet Trailer By Shiraul
410 Factory Rd (98944-9193)
P.O. Box 1060 (98944-3060)
PHONE..................509 837-6230
Shane Aulick, *Mng Member*
Vinc Aulick, *Mng Member*
EMP: 28 **EST:** 2013
SALES: 4.8MM **Privately Held**
SIC: 3537 Truck trailers, used in plants, docks, terminals, etc.

(G-13142)
SNIPES MOUNTAIN BREWING INC
905 Yakima Valley Hwy (98944-1334)
P.O. Box 274 (98944-0274)
PHONE..................509 837-2739
Mary Ann Bliesner, *President*
Kari Bliesner, *Corp Secy*
Gene Bliesner, *Vice Pres*
EMP: 32
SQ FT: 7,406
SALES (est): 4MM **Privately Held**
WEB: www.snipesmountain.com
SIC: 2082 5812 Malt beverages; eating places

(G-13143)
STANDARD NUTRITION COMPANY
105 S 11th St (98944-1517)
PHONE..................509 839-3500
Gene Wiederspohn, *Manager*
EMP: 5
SALES (corp-wide): 34MM **Privately Held**
SIC: 2048 Feed concentrates
PA: Standard Nutrition Company
11823 Arbor St Ste 100
Omaha NE 68144
402 393-3198

(G-13144)
STAR TRANSPORT TRAILERS INC
230 State Rt 241 (98944)
P.O. Box 403 (98944-0403)
PHONE..................509 837-3136
Gene Waller, *President*
Dave Waller, *Vice Pres*
EMP: 10 **EST:** 1960
SQ FT: 20,000
SALES: 2.5MM **Privately Held**
SIC: 3715 3713 Semitrailers for truck tractors; truck bodies (motor vehicles)

(G-13145)
SUNNYSIDE DAILY NEWS INC
Also Called: Daily Sun News
600 S 6th St (98944-2111)
P.O. Box 878 (98944-0878)
PHONE..................509 837-4500
Andrew McNab, *Exec Dir*
Tim Graff, *Director*
EMP: 14 **EST:** 1962
SALES: 1.1MM **Privately Held**
WEB: www.dailysunnews.com
SIC: 2711 Newspapers, publishing & printing

(G-13146)
UPLAND WINERY LLC
3073 Emerald Rd (98944-9459)
PHONE..................509 839-2606
Todd Newhouse,
EMP: 4
SALES (est): 175.6K **Privately Held**
SIC: 2084 Wines

(G-13147)
VALLEY MANUFACTURED HSING INC
1717 S 4th St (98944-9427)
PHONE..................509 839-9409
Arthur Berger, *CEO*
Darin Berger, *President*
Robert Standfill, *Corp Secy*
Gary Males, *Manager*
Arthur Berger Jr, *Shareholder*
EMP: 209
SQ FT: 75,000
SALES (est): 24.5MM **Privately Held**
SIC: 2451 Mobile homes

(G-13148)
VALLEY PROCESSING INC (PA)
108 Blaine Ave (98944-1458)
P.O. Box 246 (98944-0246)
PHONE..................509 837-8084
Mary Ann Bliesner, *President*
Penny Babalya, *QC Mgr*
Tim Collett, *Maintence Staff*
Jay Fanciullo, *Maintence Staff*
◆ **EMP:** 77 **EST:** 1980
SQ FT: 100,000
SALES: 30MM **Privately Held**
WEB: www.valleyprocessing.com
SIC: 2037 Fruit juice concentrates, frozen

Suquamish
Kitsap County

(G-13149)
TO THE T EMBROIDERY
6199 Ne Pine St (98392-9602)
PHONE..................360 509-0156
Tammy Navarro, *Principal*
EMP: 3
SALES (est): 92.7K **Privately Held**
SIC: 2395 Embroidery & art needlework

(G-13150)
WESTECH AEROSOL CORPORATION
26268 Twlve Trees Ln Nw (98392)
PHONE..................206 930-9291
David Carnahan, *CEO*
◆ **EMP:** 35
SQ FT: 12,000
SALES (est): 7MM **Privately Held**
WEB: www.ok2spray.com
SIC: 2891 Adhesives

Tacoma
Pierce County

(G-13151)
21CELLARS
17 North Rd N (98406-7613)
PHONE..................253 353-2317
Philip Coates, *Principal*
EMP: 2
SALES (est): 175K **Privately Held**
SIC: 2084 Wines

(G-13152)
56 THUNDER BATTERIES
5601 S Durango St (98409-2620)
PHONE..................253 267-0059
EMP: 2
SALES (est): 88.3K **Privately Held**
SIC: 3691 Storage batteries

(G-13153)
ABODE SPECIALIST INSPECTION SE
4408 Browns Point Blvd (98422-2042)
P.O. Box 828, Wauna (98395-0828)
PHONE..................253 209-0878
Tony Parent, *Principal*
EMP: 3
SALES (est): 367.8K **Privately Held**
SIC: 3826 Moisture analyzers

(G-13154)
ABOVE & BEYOND UNLIMITED
602 104th St S (98444-5812)
PHONE..................253 921-3535
Curtis Foster, *President*
Suzanne Foster, *Vice Pres*
EMP: 2
SALES (est): 158K **Privately Held**
SIC: 3441 7692 Fabricated structural metal; welding repair

(G-13155)
ABRAHAM INDUSTRIES LLC
Also Called: Green American Transport
820 A St Ste 220 (98402-5221)
PHONE..................509 329-8260
Abraham Kellogg,
EMP: 13
SALES (est): 1.4MM **Privately Held**
SIC: 3999 Atomizers, toiletry

(G-13156)
ACCOUNTING SOFTWARE INC
Also Called: Accounting Software Company
4802 Nassau Ave Ne (98422-4624)
PHONE..................253 952-6040
Doug Jones, *President*
Elizabeth P Jones, *Treasurer*
EMP: 2
SQ FT: 1,000
SALES (est): 204.2K **Privately Held**
WEB: www.acctsoft.com
SIC: 7372 Prepackaged software

(G-13157)
ADDISON CONSTRUCTION SUP INC (PA)
6201 S Adams St (98409-2511)
P.O. Box 9066 (98490-0066)
PHONE..................253 474-0711
Mark J Andrews, *President*
Edwin D Andrews, *President*
Bradley Armour, *Corp Secy*
Mark Andrews, *Vice Pres*
EMP: 52 **EST:** 1979
SALES: 16.8MM **Privately Held**
SIC: 3441 7389 Fabricated structural metal;

(G-13158)
AERO PRECISION LLC (PA)
Also Called: API
2320 Commerce St (98402)
PHONE..................253 272-8188
Scott Dover, *CEO*
Derek Dover, *Foreman/Supr*
Eli Koransky, *Manager*
▼ **EMP:** 44
SQ FT: 20,000
SALES (est): 30MM **Privately Held**
WEB: www.api-cnc.com
SIC: 5941 5099 3484 Firearms; firearms & ammunition, except sporting; shotguns or shotgun parts, 30 mm. & below

(G-13159)
AIRWAY METRICS LLC
6436 East Side Dr Ne S (98422-1107)
PHONE..................206 949-8839
Robert L Horchover,
Robin M Horchover,
EMP: 2
SALES (est): 181.3K **Privately Held**
SIC: 3843 Dental equipment & supplies

(G-13160)
ALASKA METAL RECYCLING CO
1902 Marine View Dr (98422-4108)
PHONE..................907 349-4833
Winifred Newell, *President*
J Chris Alexander, *General Mgr*
EMP: 20
SQ FT: 450
SALES (est): 2.2MM **Privately Held**
WEB: www.alaskametalrecycling.com
SIC: 5093 3341 Ferrous metal scrap & waste; secondary nonferrous metals

(G-13161)
ALCOA INC
2020 Milwaukee Way (98421-2704)
PHONE..................253 272-8413
Nick Cootsona, *Manager*
EMP: 135
SALES (corp-wide): 14B **Publicly Held**
SIC: 3353 Aluminum sheet & strip
PA: Arconic Inc.
390 Park Ave Fl 12
New York NY 10022
212 836-2758

(G-13162)
ALL COLOR SCREEN PRINTING
Also Called: All Color EMB & Screen Prtg
1706 112th St E (98445-3722)
PHONE..................253 536-2822
David C Lane, *President*
EMP: 9
SQ FT: 4,950
SALES (est): 770K **Privately Held**
SIC: 2396 Screen printing on fabric articles

(G-13163)
ALL CS INC
Also Called: Dande Co
5425 South Tacoma Way (98409-4312)
PHONE..................253 474-3434
Tom Chubb, *President*
Chris Chubb, *Corp Secy*
Rosetta Chubb, *Vice Pres*
EMP: 5
SQ FT: 5,000
SALES: 185K **Privately Held**
SIC: 3499 5699 Trophies, metal, except silver; sports apparel

(G-13164)
ALL WOOD CONCEPTS INC (PA)
Also Called: American Woodcraft
11003 A St S (98444-5729)
PHONE..................253 255-6518
Tom Buck, *President*
Larry Buck, *Vice Pres*
Joe Bowman, *Shareholder*
Lori Bowman, *Shareholder*
Ronald Larter, *Shareholder*
EMP: 8
SALES (est): 710.5K **Privately Held**
SIC: 2511 Wood bedroom furniture

(G-13165)
ALLIANCE MFG GROUP LLC (PA)
Also Called: Ebed System
2516 Holgate St (98402-1203)
PHONE..................253 922-3090
Kelsie Herdlevar, *Office Mgr*
Jacob Matthaei,
Brian Haynes,
EMP: 3 **EST:** 2012
SALES: 845.9K **Privately Held**
SIC: 5047 5084 3544 Medical & hospital equipment; machine tools & accessories; special dies & tools

(G-13166)
ALLIANCE STEEL FABRICATION
4516 176th St E (98446-2809)
PHONE..................253 538-7935
Tom Thompson, *President*
Tony Linares, *Purch Mgr*
Jeff Glidewell, *Manager*
EMP: 20
SQ FT: 7,000
SALES (est): 3.9MM **Privately Held**
SIC: 3449 Bars, concrete reinforcing: fabricated steel

(G-13167)
ALPHA AUDIO GROUP INC
19304 38th Ave E Ste 3 (98446-1022)
PHONE..................253 846-1536
Dean Hart, *President*
EMP: 3 **EST:** 1994
SQ FT: 3,000
SALES: 114K **Privately Held**
WEB: www.alphagroupusa.com
SIC: 3652 Compact laser discs, prerecorded

(G-13168)
AMERICAN LIFTING PRODUCTS INC
Also Called: Northwest Wire Rope & Sling Co
1952 Milwaukee Way (98421-2702)
PHONE..................253 572-8981
Shawn Ober, *President*
EMP: 7
SALES (corp-wide): 66.8MM **Privately Held**
SIC: 3315 3499 5051 Steel wire & related products; metal ladders; metals service centers & offices
HQ: American Lifting Products, Inc.
1227 W Lincoln Hwy
Coatesville PA 19320
610 384-1300

(G-13169)
AMERICAS SLEEP COMFORT CENTER
10406 Pacific Ave S (98444-6009)
PHONE..................253 548-8890
EMP: 2 **EST:** 2005
SALES (est): 750K **Privately Held**
SIC: 2515 Mfg Mattresses/Bedsprings

Tacoma - Pierce County (G-13170) — GEOGRAPHIC SECTION

(G-13170)
ANA OVEN
629 St Helens Ave (98402-2333)
PHONE.................................661 878-4277
Felicia Matthews-Springer, *Principal*
EMP: 3 **EST:** 2013
SALES (est): 123.2K **Privately Held**
SIC: 2052 Cookies & crackers

(G-13171)
ANAGRAM PRESS LLC
2911 N 27th St (98407-6309)
PHONE.................................253 310-8770
EMP: 4 **EST:** 2008
SALES (est): 254.5K **Privately Held**
SIC: 2741 Miscellaneous publishing

(G-13172)
ANDREWS FIXTURE COMPANY INC
1720 Puyallup Ave (98421-2616)
PHONE.................................253 627-7481
Kenson Lee, *President*
EMP: 10
SQ FT: 10,000
SALES (est): 1.6MM **Privately Held**
SIC: 2521 2541 2434 Wood office furniture; store fixtures, wood; cabinets, except refrigerated: show, display, etc.: wood; wood kitchen cabinets

(G-13173)
ANTIPODES INC
2725 S Hosmer St (98409-7823)
PHONE.................................253 444-5555
EMP: 7
SALES (corp-wide): 2.1MM **Privately Held**
SIC: 3577 Computer peripheral equipment
PA: Antipodes, Inc
   1801 Center St
   Tacoma WA 98409
   253 444-5555

(G-13174)
ANTIPODES INC (PA)
Also Called: E Z Interface
1801 Center St (98409-7818)
PHONE.................................253 444-5555
Gregory P Kuraspediani, *Ch of Bd*
Chuck Berglund, *President*
EMP: 18
SQ FT: 11,000
SALES (est): 2.1MM **Privately Held**
WEB: www.eazy.com
SIC: 7373 3577 Local area network (LAN) systems integrator; computer peripheral equipment

(G-13175)
ANTIQUE & HEIRLOOM
10418 34th Ave E (98446-2224)
PHONE.................................253 531-6126
Martin Rice, *Principal*
EMP: 2
SALES (est): 163.9K **Privately Held**
SIC: 3599 Machine shop, jobbing & repair

(G-13176)
APOLLONIAN PUBLICATIONS LLC
731 Commerce St (98402-4502)
PHONE.................................206 922-7910
Christy Goodsel, *Branch Mgr*
EMP: 3
SALES: 229.4K
SALES (corp-wide): 410.7K **Privately Held**
SIC: 2741 Miscellaneous publishing
PA: Apollonian Publications Llc
   125 Trade Ct Ste F75
   Mooresville NC 28117
   206 922-7910

(G-13177)
APPLE STREET L L C
3008 43rd St Ne (98422-2368)
PHONE.................................253 988-4120
EMP: 2 **EST:** 2012
SALES (est): 220.7K **Privately Held**
SIC: 3571 Mfg Electronic Computers

(G-13178)
ARCLIN SURFACES LLC
2144 Milwaukee Way (98421-2706)
PHONE.................................253 572-5600
Spencer Miniely, *Plant Mgr*
Scott Godin, *Plant Mgr*
EMP: 33
SQ FT: 136,000 **Privately Held**
SIC: 2821 Plastics materials & resins
HQ: Arclin Surfaces Llc
   1000 Holcomb Wds Pkwy
   Roswell GA 30076
   678 781-4400

(G-13179)
AREA 253 GLASSBLOWING
2514 Holgate St (98402-1203)
PHONE.................................253 779-0101
Patrick Cahill, *Administration*
EMP: 2
SALES (est): 52.9K **Privately Held**
SIC: 3229 Glass tubes & tubing

(G-13180)
ARMOUR MFG & CNSTR INC
4838 S Washington St (98409-2827)
PHONE.................................253 984-1213
Mia Armour-Ottow, *President*
Linda Armour, *Vice Pres*
EMP: 4
SQ FT: 14,000
SALES (est): 579.3K **Privately Held**
SIC: 2449 7699 7692 8748 Rectangular boxes & crates, wood; customizing services; welding repair; testing services; wood pallets & skids; metal barrels, drums & pails

(G-13181)
ART OF SHAVING - FL LLC
4502 S Steele St Ste 923 (98409-7224)
PHONE.................................253 777-0993
EMP: 3
SALES (corp-wide): 66.8B **Publicly Held**
SIC: 5999 2844 3421 5122 Hair care products; toilet preparations; razor blades & razors; razor blades
HQ: The Art Of Shaving - Fl Llc
   6100 Blue Lagoon Dr # 150
   Miami FL 33126

(G-13182)
ARTISAN STONE WOOD WORKS INC
5015 Tok A Lou Ave Ne (98422-1636)
PHONE.................................253 740-7102
Julie Perkins, *Vice Pres*
EMP: 2
SALES (est): 146.9K **Privately Held**
SIC: 2431 Millwork

(G-13183)
ARTS & CRAFTS PRESS INC
2515 South Tacoma Way (98409-7527)
PHONE.................................360 871-7707
Yoshiko Yamamoto, *President*
EMP: 3
SALES (est): 209.5K **Privately Held**
SIC: 2759 Letterpress printing

(G-13184)
ASC PROFILES LLC
Also Called: AEP Span
2141 Milwaukee Way (98421-2705)
PHONE.................................253 383-4955
Jim Holland, *Branch Mgr*
EMP: 40 **Privately Held**
WEB: www.ascpacific.com
SIC: 3448 3441 Prefabricated metal buildings; fabricated structural metal
HQ: Asc Profiles Llc
   2110 Enterprise Blvd
   West Sacramento CA 95691
   916 376-2800

(G-13185)
AUSTIN RESOURCES LLC
5110 184th St E (98446-3731)
PHONE.................................253 472-1703
Walter Austin,
Sharon Austin,
EMP: 20 **EST:** 1997
SQ FT: 18,000
SALES (est): 1.6MM **Privately Held**
SIC: 3519 Internal combustion engines

(G-13186)
AUTOMATED SYSTEMS TACOMA LLC
4110 S Washington St (98409-3099)
PHONE.................................253 475-0200
Dwayne Hummel, *Project Mgr*
Royce Tourtillott, *Chief Engr*
Steven Ng, *Engineer*
Don Hoban, *Mng Member*
Don J Teodoro,
EMP: 50
SQ FT: 60,000
SALES (est): 13.7MM **Privately Held**
WEB: www.ast-inc.com
SIC: 3599 Custom machinery

(G-13187)
AUTOMATIC WILBERT VAULT CO INC (PA)
Also Called: Puget Sound Pre-Cast
2206 121st St E (98445-3661)
P.O. Box 45517 (98448-5517)
PHONE.................................253 531-2656
Glenn C Colbert, *President*
Ken Colbert, *General Mgr*
Alice M Colbert, *Corp Secy*
John Colbert, *Vice Pres*
Steve Hall, *Opers Staff*
EMP: 20
SQ FT: 17,000
SALES (est): 2.7MM **Privately Held**
WEB: www.psprecast.com
SIC: 3272 Burial vaults, concrete or pre-cast terrazzo; concrete products, precast

(G-13188)
BAKER BOYS NORTHWEST LLC
3812 S Wright Ave (98409-3142)
PHONE.................................253 383-3113
Gavin Jury, *Mng Member*
EMP: 5
SQ FT: 4,000
SALES (est): 452.5K **Privately Held**
SIC: 2051 Bread, all types (white, wheat, rye, etc): fresh or frozen

(G-13189)
BARGREEN-ELLINGSON INC (PA)
6626 Tacoma Mall Blvd B (98409-9002)
PHONE.................................253 475-9201
Paul G Ellingson, *President*
Neal Bradley, *General Mgr*
Richard Ellingson, *Vice Pres*
Thomas Murphy, *VP Opers*
Niki Doyle, *Project Mgr*
◆ **EMP:** 95
SQ FT: 88,000
SALES (est): 129.8MM **Privately Held**
SIC: 5046 2541 Restaurant equipment & supplies; store & office display cases & fixtures

(G-13190)
BAYE ENTERPRISES INC
10749 A St S Ste F (98444-6097)
PHONE.................................253 536-2277
Kristina Keller, *President*
EMP: 25
SALES (est): 3.8MM **Privately Held**
SIC: 2441 Cases, wood

(G-13191)
BAYSIDE EMB & SCREENPRINT
Also Called: Bayside Apparel
3003 S Houston St Ste A (98409)
PHONE.................................253 565-1521
Randy Gollinger, *President*
Barbara Gollinger, *Vice Pres*
EMP: 8
SQ FT: 7,500
SALES (est): 915.5K **Privately Held**
WEB: www.baysideapparel.com
SIC: 2395 2261 3999 Embroidery products, except schiffli machine; screen printing of cotton broadwoven fabrics; advertising display products

(G-13192)
BECHRIS INC
7511 S 19th St (98466-3612)
PHONE.................................253 565-0905
Marvin O Christman, *CEO*
Gary M Christman, *President*
Betty Christman, *Corp Secy*
EMP: 2 **EST:** 1962
SALES: 100K **Privately Held**
SIC: 2678 Stationery products

(G-13193)
BELINA INTERIORS INC
Also Called: Belina Woodworks
4540 S Adams St (98409-2907)
PHONE.................................253 474-0276
Paul Birkey, *President*
EMP: 100
SQ FT: 58,000
SALES (est): 18.3MM **Privately Held**
WEB: www.belinainteriors.com
SIC: 2599 2431 2434 2542 Ship furniture; interior & ornamental woodwork & trim; wood kitchen cabinets; partitions & fixtures, except wood; wood office furniture; hardwood veneer & plywood

(G-13194)
BENNETT INDUSTRIES INC (PA)
1160 Thorne Rd (98421-3202)
PHONE.................................253 627-7775
Erwin Kettner, *CEO*
Robert Firch, *General Mgr*
Dave Riddle, *General Mgr*
John C Dimmer, *Treasurer*
EMP: 30
SQ FT: 50,000
SALES (est): 3.9MM **Privately Held**
SIC: 3441 7692 Fabricated structural metal for ships; brazing

(G-13195)
BENNETT INDUSTRIES INC
Also Called: Bennett Machinery
1160 Thorne Rd (98421-3202)
PHONE.................................253 627-7775
George Umruh, *Branch Mgr*
EMP: 30
SQ FT: 7,000
SALES (est): 2.6MM
SALES (corp-wide): 3.9MM **Privately Held**
SIC: 3599 Machine shop, jobbing & repair
PA: Bennett Industries, Inc.
   1160 Thorne Rd
   Tacoma WA 98421
   253 627-7775

(G-13196)
BENT NEEDLE DESIGNS
3405 72nd St E (98443-1209)
PHONE.................................253 531-9440
Michelle Drorbaugh, *Owner*
Michael Drorbaugh, *Co-Owner*
EMP: 2
SALES: 50K **Privately Held**
SIC: 2395 Embroidery products, except schiffli machine; embroidery & art needlework

(G-13197)
BENTSON PRINTING LLC
118 N Tacoma Ave (98403-2632)
PHONE.................................253 272-6563
Tadd Bentson, *Mng Member*
EMP: 4
SQ FT: 4,440
SALES: 500K **Privately Held**
SIC: 2759 2752 Commercial printing; commercial printing, lithographic

(G-13198)
BERRY GLOBAL INC
635 E 15th St (98421-1605)
PHONE.................................253 627-2151
Janet Betner, *Branch Mgr*
EMP: 127 **Publicly Held**
SIC: 3089 Plastic containers, except foam
HQ: Berry Global, Inc.
   101 Oakley St
   Evansville IN 47710
   812 424-2904

(G-13199)
BHS MARKETING LLC
Also Called: Bhs Specialty Chemicals
2001 Thorne Rd (98421-3209)
PHONE.................................208 740-9369
Thomas Fraser, *Branch Mgr*
EMP: 8
SQ FT: 59,500 **Privately Held**
WEB: www.olin.com

▲ = Import ▼ = Export
◆ = Import/Export

GEOGRAPHIC SECTION

Tacoma - Pierce County (G-13228)

SIC: **2819** 2842 Industrial inorganic chemicals; bleaches, household: dry or liquid
HQ: Bhs Marketing, Llc
2320 W Indiana Ave
Salt Lake City UT 84104
801 973-8232

(G-13200)
BIGHORN BREWERY WAREHOUSE
5001 S Washington St (98409-2828)
PHONE..................................253 474-7465
Steve Kirven, *Manager*
EMP: 3 EST: 2008
SALES (est): 168.2K **Privately Held**
SIC: **2082** Beer (alcoholic beverage)

(G-13201)
BIMBO BAKERIES USA INC
5401 6th Ave Ste 321 (98406-2618)
PHONE..................................253 759-2146
Chris Rio, *Manager*
EMP: 4 **Privately Held**
SIC: **2099** Tortillas, fresh or refrigerated
HQ: Bimbo Bakeries Usa, Inc
255 Business Center Dr # 200
Horsham PA 19044
215 347-5500

(G-13202)
BIZ DESIGN & SIGN
10003 40th Ave E (98446-3636)
PHONE..................................253 472-3070
Tahvia Adams, *Principal*
EMP: 3
SALES (est): 292K **Privately Held**
SIC: **3993** Electric signs

(G-13203)
BLACK FLEET BREWING
2313 Martin Luther King (98405-3841)
P.O. Box 5543 (98415-0543)
PHONE..................................425 432-6868
Caitlyn Byce, *Principal*
EMP: 2
SALES (est): 62.3K **Privately Held**
SIC: **2082** Malt beverages

(G-13204)
BLACK MOUSE INC
3835 A St (98418-7816)
PHONE..................................253 677-3491
Jeff Pedersen, *Principal*
EMP: 2 EST: 2011
SALES (est): 106.9K **Privately Held**
SIC: **3999** Manufacturing industries

(G-13205)
BLACKWOOD FIBER CO
4311 S 7th St (98405-1536)
PHONE..................................206 387-3854
Mia Allen, *Principal*
EMP: 2 EST: 2014
SALES (est): 93.4K **Privately Held**
SIC: **2253** T-shirts & tops, knit

(G-13206)
BOOTH & ASSOCIATES
5917 N 46th St (98407-2005)
PHONE..................................253 752-2494
Dean Booth, *Owner*
EMP: 2
SALES: 750K **Privately Held**
SIC: **3552** Dyeing, drying & finishing machinery & equipment

(G-13207)
BRADKEN INC
3021 S Wilkeson St (98409-7857)
PHONE..................................253 475-4600
Lisa Schitoskey, *Controller*
EMP: 314
SQ FT: 404,000 **Privately Held**
SIC: **3325** Alloy steel castings, except investment
HQ: Bradken, Inc.
12200 N Ambassador Dr # 647
Kansas City MO 64163
816 270-0701

(G-13208)
BRADKEN INC
Ideal Machine Division
3611 S Warner St (98409-5722)
P.O. Box 1624, Gig Harbor (98335-3624)
PHONE..................................253 475-3464
Susan Wagner, *Safety Mgr*
Dave Thompson, *Branch Mgr*
EMP: 50 **Privately Held**
SIC: **3441** Fabricated structural metal
HQ: Bradken, Inc.
12200 N Ambassador Dr # 647
Kansas City MO 64163
816 270-0701

(G-13209)
BRADYS SPECIALTIES
Also Called: Brady's Welding
5228 S Mason Ave (98409-1817)
PHONE..................................253 572-3768
Toll Free:..............................888 -
Pete Brady, *Owner*
EMP: 2
SALES: 50K **Privately Held**
SIC: **7692** Welding repair

(G-13210)
BROWN & HALEY (PA)
Also Called: Almond Roca
110 E 26th St (98421-1109)
P.O. Box 1596 (98401-1596)
PHONE..................................253 620-3067
Pierson E Clair III, *President*
Bob Martin, *Vice Pres*
Michael Franklin, *Safety Mgr*
Jason Imbruglio, *Warehouse Mgr*
Richard Ramos, *Warehouse Mgr*
▲ EMP: 200
SQ FT: 85,000
SALES: 6MM **Privately Held**
WEB: www.brown-haley.com
SIC: **2064** 5145 Candy & other confectionery products; candy

(G-13211)
BROWN & HALEY
110 E 26th St (98421-1109)
P.O. Box 1596 (98401-1596)
PHONE..................................253 620-3077
Mark T Haley, *Branch Mgr*
EMP: 200
SALES (corp-wide): 6MM **Privately Held**
SIC: **2064** 2066 Candy & other confectionery products; chocolate & cocoa products
PA: Brown & Haley
110 E 26th St
Tacoma WA 98421
253 620-3067

(G-13212)
BUFFELEN WOODWORKING CO
1901 Taylor Way (98421-4113)
PHONE..................................253 627-1191
David E Erickson, *CEO*
Joseph Guizzetti, *CEO*
Connie Karlson, *Treasurer*
Roger W Gjerstad, *Director*
Paula Levtzow, *Admin Sec*
▲ EMP: 53 EST: 1913
SQ FT: 500,000
SALES (est): 11.7MM **Privately Held**
WEB: www.buffelen.com
SIC: **2431** Doors, wood

(G-13213)
C & H LIGHTING ASSOCIATES INC
3904 118th St E (98446-3412)
P.O. Box 44725 (98448-0725)
PHONE..................................253 531-1270
Howard Wouters, *President*
Clarice Wouters, *Vice Pres*
EMP: 2
SALES (est): 226.3K **Privately Held**
SIC: **3648** 5063 Lighting equipment; lighting fixtures, residential

(G-13214)
C & M COUNTRY CREATIONS
6221 S Stevens St (98409-1647)
PHONE..................................253 535-3327
Cynthia McBride, *Owner*
EMP: 2
SALES (est): 85K **Privately Held**
SIC: **3944** Craft & hobby kits & sets

(G-13215)
CABLECRAFT MOTION CONTROLS LLC
4401 S Orchard St (98466-6619)
PHONE..................................253 475-1080
Ken Stjohn, *General Mgr*
EMP: 85 **Privately Held**
SIC: **3315** 3568 Steel wire & related products; power transmission equipment
PA: Cablecraft Motion Controls Llc
2110 Summit St
New Haven IN 46774

(G-13216)
CAFE LAS AMERICAS
1205 N J St (98403-2129)
PHONE..................................253 272-0644
Ken White, *Owner*
EMP: 2
SALES (est): 100.6K **Privately Held**
SIC: **2095** Coffee, ground: mixed with grain or chicory

(G-13217)
CALHOUN TNKS & SERVCES INC
3320 Lincoln Ave (98421-4003)
PHONE..................................206 870-0802
Gary A Raymond, *President*
EMP: 5 EST: 2013
SALES (est): 495.3K **Privately Held**
SIC: **3443** Fabricated plate work (boiler shop)

(G-13218)
CAMCO INC
633 N Mildred St Ste C (98406-1725)
P.O. Box 249, Sweet Home OR (97386-0249)
PHONE..................................866 856-4826
Dave Komar, *Principal*
EMP: 3
SALES (est): 566.3K **Privately Held**
SIC: **5031** 2421 Lumber: rough, dressed & finished; lumber: rough, sawed or planed

(G-13219)
CANOPY WORLD INC (PA)
Also Called: Canopy World of Seattle
10025 Pacific Ave S (98444-6546)
PHONE..................................253 531-5192
Roy Schaefer, *President*
Eleanor Schaefer, *Corp Secy*
EMP: 5
SQ FT: 12,500
SALES (est): 4.6MM **Privately Held**
WEB: www.canopy-world.com
SIC: **5531** 5013 3792 Truck equipment & parts; truck parts & accessories; travel trailers & campers

(G-13220)
CAPTIVE PLASTICS LLC
635 E 15th St (98421-1605)
PHONE..................................253 627-2151
Tom Kerstetter, *Manager*
EMP: 72 **Publicly Held**
WEB: www.captiveplastics.com
SIC: **3089** Plastic containers, except foam
HQ: Captive Plastics, Llc
101 Oakley St
Evansville IN 47710
812 424-2904

(G-13221)
CARAUSTAR INDUSTRIAL AND CON
808 E 26th St (98421-2108)
PHONE..................................253 627-1197
Mark Lindstrom, *General Mgr*
Dawn Ragan, *Purch Mgr*
EMP: 53
SALES (corp-wide): 3.8B **Publicly Held**
SIC: **2655** 2631 2621 Tubes, fiber or paper: made from purchased material; paperboard mills; paper mills
HQ: Caraustar Industrial And Consumer Products Group Inc
5000 Austell Powder Ste
Austell GA 30106
803 548-5100

(G-13222)
CARAUSTAR INDUSTRIAL AND CON
Also Called: Tacoma Tube Plant
902 E 11th St Ste 300 (98421-3025)
PHONE..................................253 272-1648
Homer Henry, *Branch Mgr*
EMP: 23
SALES (corp-wide): 3.8B **Publicly Held**
SIC: **2679** 2671 2655 Paper products, converted; packaging paper & plastics film, coated & laminated; fiber cans, drums & similar products
HQ: Caraustar Industrial And Consumer Products Group Inc
5000 Austell Powder Ste
Austell GA 30106
803 548-5100

(G-13223)
CARAUSTAR INDUSTRIES INC
Also Called: Protect-A-Board
902 E 11th St Ste 300 (98421-3025)
PHONE..................................253 272-1648
Peter Bohocky, *Prdtn Mgr*
Homer Henry, *Manager*
EMP: 10
SALES (corp-wide): 3.8B **Publicly Held**
WEB: www.caraustar.com
SIC: **2655** Fiber cans, drums & similar products
HQ: Caraustar Industries, Inc.
5000 Austell Powder Sprin
Austell GA 30106
770 948-3101

(G-13224)
CARLSON BROTHERS INC
Also Called: Carlson Brothers Mfg Jewelers
861 S 38th St (98418-5012)
PHONE..................................253 472-9232
Carl L Carlson Jr, *President*
Walletta R Carlson, *Vice Pres*
EMP: 10
SQ FT: 3,000
SALES (est): 1.2MM **Privately Held**
SIC: **3911** 3873 5944 7631 Rings, finger: precious metal; watchcases; jewelry, precious stones & precious metals; jewelry repair services; watch repair

(G-13225)
CARPINITO BROTHERS INC
Also Called: Landscape Bark
2351 Lincoln Ave (98421-3404)
PHONE..................................253 627-3121
Mike Palmer, *Manager*
EMP: 5
SALES (corp-wide): 15.9MM **Privately Held**
WEB: www.carpinito.com
SIC: **2421** Sawmills & planing mills, general
PA: Carpinito Brothers, Inc.
1148 Central Ave N
Kent WA 98032
253 854-5692

(G-13226)
CASCADE CUSTOM JEWELERS
4302 S J St (98418-3701)
PHONE..................................253 535-2121
Barrett Thompson, *Owner*
EMP: 5
SALES: 350K **Privately Held**
SIC: **3911** Jewelry, precious metal

(G-13227)
CASCADE PRINTING COMPANY
3321 S Lawrence St (98409-4712)
PHONE..................................253 472-5500
Mario Menconi, *President*
Jerry McNulty, *Sales Mgr*
EMP: 15 EST: 1965
SQ FT: 14,400
SALES (est): 3.1MM **Privately Held**
WEB: www.cascadeprintmedia.com
SIC: **2752** 2789 Commercial printing, offset; bookbinding & related work

(G-13228)
CASCADES SONOCO INC
4320 95th St Sw Ste C (98499-5955)
PHONE..................................253 584-4295
Greg Hayes, *Manager*
EMP: 21 **Privately Held**

Tacoma - Pierce County (G-13229)

SIC: 2671 2655 2822 2675 Paper coated or laminated for packaging; fiber cans, drums & similar products; synthetic rubber; die-cut paper & board
PA: Cascades Sonoco Us Inc.
170 Cleage Dr
Birmingham AL 35217

(G-13229)
CELEBRITY BAKERY & CAFE
602 E 25th St Ste 2 (98421-2002)
PHONE..................253 627-4773
Sherry Grant, *Principal*
EMP: 3
SALES (est): 144.3K **Privately Held**
SIC: 2051 Bread, cake & related products

(G-13230)
CELLAR DOOR MEDIA LLC
938 Broadway (98402-4405)
PHONE..................253 732-9560
Chris Teitzel, *CEO*
Michael Todd Ostrander, *Principal*
EMP: 2
SALES (est): 163K **Privately Held**
SIC: 7371 7372 Computer software systems analysis & design, custom; computer software development; application computer software; business oriented computer software

(G-13231)
CENTER ELECTRIC INC (PA)
1212 S 30th St (98409-8097)
P.O. Box 111300 (98411-1300)
PHONE..................253 383-4416
Judy Bergin, *General Mgr*
Rick Stegner, *General Mgr*
Jon Carmony, *Corp Secy*
EMP: 18
SQ FT: 15,000
SALES (est): 1.9MM **Privately Held**
WEB: www.centerelectric.com
SIC: 7694 5063 5072 5085 Electric motor repair; motors, electric; hand tools; industrial supplies

(G-13232)
CH MURPHY/CLARK-ULLMAN INC
3113 S Pine St Unit A (98409-4708)
PHONE..................253 475-6566
Annette Cavanaugh, *Office Mgr*
Mike Dolan, *Branch Mgr*
Michael Silleck, *Info Tech Mgr*
EMP: 55
SALES (corp-wide): 14.7MM **Privately Held**
WEB: www.chmcu.com
SIC: 7699 1741 5085 3443 Boiler repair shop; refractory or acid brick masonry; refractory material; fabricated plate work (boiler shop); nonclay refractories; fabricated structural metal
PA: C.H. Murphy/Clark-Ullman, Inc.
5565 N Dolphin St
Portland OR 97217
503 285-5030

(G-13233)
CHANDLER W JEPPSEN ✪
821 S 43rd St (98418-4936)
PHONE..................541 466-0908
EMP: 2 EST: 2019
SALES (est): 81.7K **Privately Held**
SIC: 2411 Logging

(G-13234)
CHRISTOPHER PALLIS INC
1209 N Cedar St (98406-6405)
PHONE..................206 619-4146
Christopher Pallis, *President*
▲ EMP: 5
SQ FT: 2,600
SALES: 500K **Privately Held**
WEB: www.christopherpallis.com
SIC: 3172 Personal leather goods

(G-13235)
CLARO CANDLES
3806 E Portland Ave (98404-4620)
PHONE..................253 678-1173
EMP: 2 EST: 2013
SALES (est): 154.6K **Privately Held**
SIC: 3999 Candles

(G-13236)
CLEARWAY SIGNS
4720 South Tacoma Way (98409-4445)
PHONE..................253 324-1706
John Sevener, *Principal*
EMP: 2
SALES (est): 140.9K **Privately Held**
SIC: 3993 Signs & advertising specialties

(G-13237)
COGENT HOLDINGS-1 LLC
Also Called: Berry Sign Systems
5002 S Washington St (98409-2829)
PHONE..................425 776-8835
Donald Gerould,
EMP: 29
SALES (corp-wide): 2.4MM **Privately Held**
SIC: 3993 Signs & advertising specialties
PA: Cogent Holdings-1, Llc
7400 Hardeson Rd
Everett WA 98203
425 776-8835

(G-13238)
COLE GRAPHIC SOLUTIONS INC
4901 Center St (98409-2363)
PHONE..................253 564-4600
Ed Ogle, *President*
Hannah Magin, *General Mgr*
Stacey A Ogle, *Vice Pres*
Hannah Reese, *Project Mgr*
Jenise Notti, *Bookkeeper*
EMP: 31 EST: 1930
SQ FT: 24,000
SALES (est): 5.4MM **Privately Held**
WEB: www.colescreenprint.com
SIC: 2759 Screen printing

(G-13239)
CONSTANT COMPUTER
919 126th Street Ct E (98445-2915)
PHONE..................253 227-0532
Fang Yang, *Co-Owner*
Anthony Chopkoski, *Co-Owner*
EMP: 2
SALES (est): 144.2K **Privately Held**
SIC: 3571 3672 3674 Electronic computers; printed circuit boards; semiconductors & related devices

(G-13240)
CONTECH SYSTEMS INC (HQ)
3736 South Tacoma Way (98409-3135)
PHONE..................360 332-1718
Horst Aschenbroich, *President*
Ross Dennison, *Vice Pres*
◆ EMP: 5 EST: 1998
SALES (est): 1.1MM
SALES (corp-wide): 6.6MM **Privately Held**
SIC: 3462 3315 Anchors, forged; steel wire & related products
PA: Con-Tech Systems Ltd
8150 River Rd
Delta BC V4G 1
604 946-5571

(G-13241)
CONTOUR COATINGS LLC
4101 N 24th St (98406-4822)
PHONE..................253 830-4994
Joshua Samardick, *Principal*
EMP: 2
SALES (est): 99.5K **Privately Held**
SIC: 3479 Metal coating & allied service

(G-13242)
CORBAN TECH LLC
4533 S 79th St (98409-1011)
PHONE..................253 353-0849
Nick Sseba, *Principal*
EMP: 2
SALES (est): 165.7K **Privately Held**
SIC: 3571 Electronic computers

(G-13243)
CORE TECH LLC
5219 84th St E (98446-5624)
P.O. Box 1614, Sumner (98390-0340)
PHONE..................253 457-3239
Dana Pratt, *Mng Member*
▼ EMP: 2
SALES (est): 43.6K **Privately Held**
SIC: 3728 Aircraft parts & equipment

(G-13244)
CORONA STEEL INC
1701 Bay St (98421-2612)
PHONE..................253 874-4766
John Paulson, *Principal*
EMP: 2
SALES (est): 100K **Privately Held**
SIC: 3446 Ornamental metalwork

(G-13245)
COUNTERPANE INC
10729 A St S (98444-6019)
PHONE..................253 535-0145
Andy Stevens, *Principal*
EMP: 2
SALES: 2MM **Privately Held**
SIC: 3131 Counters

(G-13246)
COWBOYZ
2131 S Sprague Ave (98405-2815)
P.O. Box 18008, Seattle (98118-0008)
PHONE..................206 793-6831
Michael Blackwell, *Principal*
EMP: 5
SALES: 20K **Privately Held**
SIC: 2024 Ice cream & frozen desserts

(G-13247)
COWLITZ ELECTRIC CONSTRUCTION
6811 S C St (98408-6106)
PHONE..................253 355-7163
Brian Smithlin Jr, *Principal*
EMP: 2
SALES (est): 163.8K **Privately Held**
SIC: 3699 1521 Electrical equipment & supplies; single-family housing construction

(G-13248)
CREATIVE CASTING COMPANY
3762 S 60th St Ste A (98409-2504)
PHONE..................253 475-2643
Dennis F Nyland, *Owner*
EMP: 2
SQ FT: 5,000
SALES: 400K **Privately Held**
WEB: www.creativecastingco.com
SIC: 3365 3366 Aluminum & aluminum-based alloy castings; copper foundries

(G-13249)
CROSS CURRENT BREWING
4922 Harbor View Dr (98422-1848)
PHONE..................253 952-2105
EMP: 2
SALES (est): 63.6K **Privately Held**
SIC: 2082 Mfg Malt Beverages

(G-13250)
CUBBY B & FRIENDS
5203 80th St E (98443-2753)
PHONE..................253 537-6266
Judith B Cubby, *Partner*
Judith Scott, *Partner*
EMP: 2
SALES (est): 90.9K **Privately Held**
SIC: 3952 Canvas, prepared on frames: artists'

(G-13251)
CURT ARNESON ENTERPRISES INC
Also Called: Minuteman Press
1111 A St (98402-5003)
PHONE..................253 383-4377
H Curtis Arneson, *President*
Mickie Arneson, *Treasurer*
Jeff Brunson, *Manager*
EMP: 10
SQ FT: 12,500
SALES (est): 1.2MM **Privately Held**
SIC: 2752 Commercial printing, lithographic

(G-13252)
CUTTING EDGE MACHINE & MFG
4428 Gy Rd E (98443)
PHONE..................253 926-8514
Mark Evensen, *Owner*
Lynn Evensen, *Co-Owner*
EMP: 2
SQ FT: 1,152
SALES (est): 149.7K **Privately Held**
WEB: www.latheman.com
SIC: 3541 Lathes, metal cutting & polishing

(G-13253)
DANNYS ELECTRONICS INC
2015 S 96th St Ste 1 (98444-1774)
P.O. Box 44950 (98448-0950)
PHONE..................253 314-5056
Shwan Saber, *Principal*
EMP: 3
SALES (est): 243.1K **Privately Held**
SIC: 5999 3663 2678 4812 Electronic parts & equipment; cameras, television; tablets & pads; cellular telephone services; computers & accessories, secondhand

(G-13254)
DARLING INGREDIENTS INC
Also Called: Darling Pro
2041 Marc Ave (98421-2945)
P.O. Box 1716 (98401-1716)
PHONE..................253 572-3922
Philipp Anderson, *General Mgr*
EMP: 50
SALES (corp-wide): 3.3B **Publicly Held**
WEB: www.darlingii.com
SIC: 2077 Grease rendering, inedible; tallow rendering, inedible; bone meal, except as animal feed; meat meal & tankage, except as animal feed
PA: Darling Ingredients Inc.
5601 N Macarthur Blvd
Irving TX 75038
972 717-0300

(G-13255)
DAVAN COMMUNICATIONS ENTP
3040 44th Ave Ne (98422-2809)
PHONE..................253 517-9300
Leon Walker, *Owner*
EMP: 2
SALES (est): 76.7K **Privately Held**
SIC: 3661 Fiber optics communications equipment

(G-13256)
DEGROOT DESIGNS
4532 E C St (98404-1445)
PHONE..................253 472-7279
Cheryl E Degroot, *Owner*
EMP: 2
SALES (est): 87.8K **Privately Held**
SIC: 3961 Costume jewelry

(G-13257)
DELTA CAMSHAFT INC
2366 Tacoma Ave S (98402-1408)
PHONE..................253 383-4152
Jon Bodwell, *President*
Scott Bennatt, *Corp Secy*
Floyd Hayne, *Vice Pres*
EMP: 9
SQ FT: 8,000
SALES: 1MM **Privately Held**
SIC: 3599 Machine & other job shop work

(G-13258)
DELTA PNTG & PREFINISHING CO
4025 100th St Sw (98499-4309)
PHONE..................253 588-8278
Eric Demark, *President*
EMP: 5
SQ FT: 10,000
SALES: 400K **Privately Held**
SIC: 2431 2435 Millwork; hardwood plywood, prefinished

(G-13259)
DENISE MAYWARD ✪
3820 Nassau Ave Ne (98422-2242)
PHONE..................253 927-0219
Denise Mayward, *Principal*
EMP: 2 EST: 2018
SALES (est): 69.9K **Privately Held**
SIC: 3471 Plating & polishing

GEOGRAPHIC SECTION

Tacoma - Pierce County (G-13291)

(G-13260)
DETEC SYSTEMS LLC
711 St Helens Ave Ste 201 (98402-3731)
P.O. Box 32148, Bellingham (98228-4148)
PHONE..................................253 272-3252
Shaun Katz, *Sales Staff*
Chad Herrick, *Manager*
David Vokey,
Jacqueline Albrecht, *Administration*
EMP: 7
SQ FT: 1,100
SALES (est): 1.1MM **Privately Held**
SIC: 3599 Water leak detectors

(G-13261)
DF INDUSTRIES INC
Also Called: Strictly For Kids
11708 24th Ave E Bldg 6 (98445-5133)
P.O. Box 45406 (98448-5406)
PHONE..................................253 472-0422
Dale Fusch, *President*
EMP: 13
SALES (est): 2.2MM **Privately Held**
SIC: 2531 School furniture

(G-13262)
DIAMOND STORE INC
Also Called: Leroy Jewelers
940 Broadway (98402-4405)
PHONE..................................253 272-3377
Steph Farber, *President*
James Farber, *Vice Pres*
Phyllis Harrison, *Treasurer*
Susan Long, *Admin Sec*
EMP: 5 EST: 1935
SQ FT: 5,000
SALES (est): 730K **Privately Held**
WEB: www.leroyjewelers.com
SIC: 5944 3911 5947 Jewelry, precious stones & precious metals; jewelry, precious metal; gift shop

(G-13263)
DICKSON COMPANY
3315 S Pine St (98409-5718)
PHONE..................................253 472-4489
William B Dickson, *President*
Richard Dickson, *Vice Pres*
Randy Asahara, *Project Mgr*
Greg Linklater, *Project Mgr*
David Dickson, *Treasurer*
EMP: 60
SQ FT: 12,000
SALES: 23MM **Privately Held**
WEB: www.wmdickson.net
SIC: 1795 1799 1623 1611 Demolition, buildings & other structures; asbestos removal & encapsulation; sewer line construction; general contractor, highway & street construction; construction sand & gravel; nonmetallic mineral services

(G-13264)
DML TOOL GRINDING
1602 S Tyler St (98405-1142)
PHONE..................................253 752-3638
Laura J Shirley, *Owner*
Dennis J Shirley, *Owner*
EMP: 2
SALES (est): 128.7K **Privately Held**
SIC: 3599 Machine shop, jobbing & repair

(G-13265)
DRC SPECIALTY VENEERING LLC
4020 S 56th St Ste 103 (98409-2626)
PHONE..................................253 301-0443
Matthew Miller, *Mng Member*
EMP: 4
SALES: 500K **Privately Held**
SIC: 2435 Hardwood veneer & plywood

(G-13266)
DUALOS LLC
917 Pacific Ave Ste 400 (98402-4421)
P.O. Box 24088, Federal Way (98093-1088)
PHONE..................................253 750-5125
Nancy Papineau, *President*
EMP: 9
SALES: 5MM **Privately Held**
SIC: 7319 3825 Coupon distribution; instruments to measure electricity

(G-13267)
DYNEA OVERLAYS INC
2144 Milwaukee Way (98421-2706)
PHONE..................................253 572-5600
Nina Kopola, *Principal*
▲ EMP: 10
SALES (est): 1.2MM **Privately Held**
SIC: 2759 Commercial printing

(G-13268)
E AND S INDUSTRIES LLC
155 133rd St E (98445-1417)
PHONE..................................253 678-1539
Eric Robinson, *Principal*
EMP: 2
SALES (est): 106.8K **Privately Held**
SIC: 3999 Manufacturing industries

(G-13269)
ECOLAB INC
4301 S Pine St Ste 540 (98409-7216)
PHONE..................................253 733-3000
Greg Peelman, *Principal*
EMP: 34
SALES (corp-wide): 14.6B **Publicly Held**
SIC: 2842 Specialty cleaning, polishes & sanitation goods
PA: Ecolab Inc.
1 Ecolab Pl
Saint Paul MN 55102
800 232-6522

(G-13270)
ECONO QUALITY SIGNS INC
16411 22nd Ave E (98445-4517)
P.O. Box 357, Spanaway (98387-0357)
PHONE..................................253 531-3943
Rick Watkins, *President*
Millie Watkins, *Admin Sec*
EMP: 9
SALES: 500K **Privately Held**
SIC: 3993 5046 5031 2434 Signs & advertising specialties; commercial equipment; lumber, plywood & millwork; wood kitchen cabinets

(G-13271)
EDENSAW WOODS LTD
925 E 25th St (98421-2103)
PHONE..................................253 216-1150
James Ferris, *President*
EMP: 9
SALES (est): 1.2MM
SALES (corp-wide): 18.7MM **Privately Held**
SIC: 2435 5031 5211 Hardwood veneer & plywood; building materials, interior; lumber products
PA: Edensaw Woods, Ltd.
211 Seton Rd
Port Townsend WA 98368
800 745-3336

(G-13272)
EDMAN COMPANY
2502 Marine View Dr (98422-3509)
PHONE..................................253 572-5306
F Talmadge Edman, *President*
Mary Edman, *Corp Secy*
▼ EMP: 16
SALES (est): 8.7MM **Privately Held**
SIC: 2421 Wood chips, produced at mill

(G-13273)
EDWARD FISHER
Also Called: Efx Locomotive Services
5503 78th Avenue Ct W (98467-3969)
PHONE..................................253 566-4335
Edward Fisher, *Owner*
EMP: 5
SALES (est): 280K **Privately Held**
SIC: 3743 Train cars & equipment, freight or passenger

(G-13274)
EDWIN ENTERPRISES INC
Also Called: Defiance Forest Products
3401 Lincoln Ave Ste E (98421-4017)
P.O. Box 1696 (98401-1696)
PHONE..................................253 272-7090
Terry Tebb, *President*
Travis Tebb, *President*
▼ EMP: 2
SQ FT: 12,000
SALES (est): 280.5K **Privately Held**
SIC: 2436 2431 2435 2421 Softwood veneer & plywood; millwork; hardwood veneer & plywood; sawmills & planing mills, general

(G-13275)
ELLIPSE MFG INC
16113 7th Avenue Ct E (98445-1058)
PHONE..................................253 653-5554
Todd M Lundberg, *Principal*
EMP: 2
SALES (est): 125.7K **Privately Held**
SIC: 3999 Barber & beauty shop equipment

(G-13276)
EM GLOBAL MANUFACTURING INC
10721 A St S Ste A (98444-6086)
PHONE..................................253 655-5206
Floyd Meredith, *President*
EMP: 2
SALES: 250K **Privately Held**
SIC: 3728 Aircraft parts & equipment

(G-13277)
EMERALD CITY SMOOTHIE
5977 6th Ave (98406-2035)
PHONE..................................253 564-1966
San Harris, *Branch Mgr*
EMP: 5
SALES (corp-wide): 1.1MM **Privately Held**
SIC: 5499 2024 Juices, fruit or vegetable; ice cream & frozen desserts
PA: Emerald City Smoothie
318 Central Way
Kirkland WA 98033
425 739-9349

(G-13278)
EMERALD HOME FURNISHINGS LLC
3025 Pioneer Way E (98443-1602)
PHONE..................................253 922-1400
Joyce Nelson, *Controller*
David Beckmann,
David Beckmann,
◆ EMP: 300
SQ FT: 240,000
SALES (est): 22.2MM **Privately Held**
WEB: www.emeraldhome.com
SIC: 2515 5021 2511 Mattresses & foundations; household furniture; wood household furniture

(G-13279)
ENCORE ANALYTICS LLC
2522 N Proctor St # 368 (98406-5338)
PHONE..................................866 890-4331
Gary W Toop, *Mng Member*
James Price,
EMP: 8 EST: 2009
SALES (est): 702.9K **Privately Held**
SIC: 7372 Application computer software

(G-13280)
EPIC WHEEL AND TIRE INC
7030 South Tacoma Way (98409-3932)
PHONE..................................253 691-1785
Harry Zantkovsky, *CEO*
Rick Greehow, *COO*
EMP: 20
SALES (est): 6MM **Privately Held**
SIC: 3312 1799 Wheels; glass tinting, architectural or automotive

(G-13281)
ERUDITE INC
711 Court A Ste 204 (98402-5228)
PHONE..................................253 272-8542
Joseph Simeone, *Vice Pres*
Richard Schmidtke, *CFO*
EMP: 3
SALES (est): 279.6K **Privately Held**
SIC: 3799 Trailers & trailer equipment

(G-13282)
ETC TACOMA
907 Pacific Ave (98402-4401)
PHONE..................................253 223-5459
Perris Wright, *Administration*
EMP: 3
SALES (est): 126.9K **Privately Held**
SIC: 5136 2371 Men's & boys' clothing; hats, fur

(G-13283)
EVERGREEN CONTROLS LLC
672 E 11th St (98421-2402)
PHONE..................................253 405-3770
John Jackson,
David Davey,
EMP: 2
SQ FT: 85,000
SALES: 25K **Privately Held**
SIC: 3613 Control panels, electric

(G-13284)
EXACTO INC
13826 50th Ave E (98446-4157)
PHONE..................................253 531-5311
Ray Pennington, *President*
Ray Pennington, *President*
EMP: 9
SQ FT: 7,000
SALES (est): 1.2MM **Privately Held**
SIC: 3599 Machine shop, jobbing & repair

(G-13285)
F D COMPANY
Also Called: Doyle Printing Co
1702 112th St E (98445-3722)
PHONE..................................253 531-7087
John Doyle, *Partner*
Jan Farmer, *Partner*
EMP: 5
SQ FT: 1,200
SALES (est): 570.9K **Privately Held**
SIC: 2759 2752 Letterpress printing; commercial printing, offset

(G-13286)
FABLAB LLC
1938 Market St (98402-3108)
PHONE..................................253 426-1267
Steve Tibbitts,
EMP: 2
SALES (est): 290.7K **Privately Held**
SIC: 3699 Laser welding, drilling & cutting equipment

(G-13287)
FAITH DAIRY INC
3509 72nd St E (98443-1210)
PHONE..................................253 531-3398
Fax: 253 539-4198
EMP: 30 EST: 1963
SQ FT: 22,602
SALES (est): 3.7MM **Privately Held**
SIC: 0241 2026 2024 Dairy Farm Mfg Fluid Milk Mfg Ice Cream/Frozen Desert

(G-13288)
FALLEN HERO BRACELETS
16011 3rd Avenue Ct E (98445-1054)
PHONE..................................253 537-1212
Michael Friedmann, *Principal*
EMP: 2 EST: 2016
SALES (est): 94.3K **Privately Held**
SIC: 3961 Bracelets, except precious metal

(G-13289)
FALX GAMES
8823 S I St (98444-4323)
PHONE..................................253 439-9121
Darany Falah, *Partner*
Saleh Falah, *Partner*
EMP: 4 EST: 2012
SALES (est): 197.6K **Privately Held**
SIC: 7372 Application computer software

(G-13290)
FARBER NEWS SERVICE
2322 Sunset Dr W (98466-2812)
PHONE..................................253 565-1131
Stan Farber, *Owner*
EMP: 2
SALES (est): 76.4K **Privately Held**
SIC: 2731 Book publishing

(G-13291)
FARM BREEZE INTERNATIONAL LLC
2602 S 38th St Unit 127 (98409-6665)
PHONE..................................253 365-0542
Carol Ye, *Director*

Tacoma - Pierce County (G-13292)

John Bidart,
EMP: 1
SALES: 10MM **Privately Held**
SIC: 0173 5451 2033 7389 Tree nuts; dairy products stores; fruits & fruit products in cans, jars, etc.;

(G-13292)
FEDEX OFFICE & PRINT SVCS INC
6909 S 19th St Ste A (98466-5529)
PHONE.................................253 565-4882
Melissa Fish, *Manager*
Francine Smith, *Manager*
EMP: 20
SALES (corp-wide): 69.6B **Publicly Held**
WEB: www.kinkos.com
SIC: 7334 5943 2752 Photocopying & duplicating services; stationery stores; commercial printing, lithographic
HQ: Fedex Office And Print Services, Inc.
 7900 Legacy Dr
 Plano TX 75024
 800 463-3339

(G-13293)
FEED COMMODITIES LLC (PA)
2006 E Portland Ave (98421-2712)
PHONE.................................626 799-1196
James D Seley,
EMP: 14
SQ FT: 22,000
SALES: 5MM **Privately Held**
WEB: www.feedcomm.com
SIC: 2048 Prepared feeds

(G-13294)
FIBRO CORPORATION
3101 South Tacoma Way (98409-4717)
PHONE.................................253 503-3568
Paul Zhang, *President*
▲ **EMP:** 8
SALES (est): 1.9MM **Privately Held**
SIC: 2621 Pressed & molded pulp & fiber products; molded pulp products

(G-13295)
FIELDS COMPANY LLC (PA)
Also Called: Atco
2240 Taylor Way (98421-4303)
PHONE.................................253 627-4098
John Fields, *Principal*
Matt Fields, *Sales Staff*
▲ **EMP:** 90
SQ FT: 60,000
SALES (est): 5.9MM **Privately Held**
SIC: 2952 Roofing materials

(G-13296)
FIRCREST PRE-FIT DOOR CO INC
3024 S Mullen St Ste A (98409-2389)
PHONE.................................253 564-6921
Donald P Klemme, *President*
Vicki Thornhill, *Manager*
EMP: 9 **EST:** 1956
SQ FT: 8,000
SALES (est): 690K **Privately Held**
SIC: 2431 Doors, wood

(G-13297)
FITTS INDUSTRIES INC
5640 S Durango St Ste B (98409-2601)
PHONE.................................253 474-0376
Boyd Winker, *Manager*
Fred Nix, *Manager*
EMP: 4
SALES (est): 476.7K
SALES (corp-wide): 10.6MM **Privately Held**
WEB: www.fitts.com
SIC: 2431 Staircases & stairs, wood
PA: Fitts Industries, Inc
 2211 Greensboro Ave
 Tuscaloosa AL 35401
 205 345-5188

(G-13298)
FIVE TOOL FOOD SERVICE LLC
2502 S Tyler St (98405-1051)
PHONE.................................253 761-5621
EMP: 2
SALES (est): 81.4K **Privately Held**
SIC: 3599 Industrial machinery

(G-13299)
FLOOD & ASSOCIATES INC
Also Called: Pillow Products
11010 Pacific Ave S (98444-5738)
P.O. Box 45214 (98448-5214)
PHONE.................................253 531-7305
Thomas J Flood, *President*
Sharon L Flood, *Corp Secy*
EMP: 3
SQ FT: 2,400
SALES: 110K **Privately Held**
SIC: 3842 Orthopedic appliances

(G-13300)
FOOD MASTER (PNW) CORP (PA)
18420 50th Ave E (98446-3758)
PHONE.................................253 846-2600
Michael Ishida, *President*
Koichi Iwasaki, *Principal*
EMP: 50
SALES (est): 11.4MM **Privately Held**
SIC: 2099 Food preparations

(G-13301)
FRED TEBB & SONS INC
1906 E Marc St (98421)
P.O. Box 2235 (98401-2235)
PHONE.................................253 272-4107
Rick Tebb, *President*
John Tebb, *Exec VP*
◆ **EMP:** 70
SQ FT: 2,000
SALES (est): 20.2MM **Privately Held**
SIC: 2421 Specialty sawmill products

(G-13302)
FRONTIER DOOR & CABINET LLC
Also Called: Pacific Door and Molding
11721 Steele St S (98444-1321)
PHONE.................................206 768-2524
Eugene L Kettler, *Mng Member*
Curtis Bjornstad,
William Boyer,
William Edson,
Gabriel Kettler,
EMP: 100
SQ FT: 16,000
SALES (est): 23.1MM **Privately Held**
WEB: www.frontierdoor.com
SIC: 2434 Wood kitchen cabinets

(G-13303)
G M PALLET INC
2102 109th St S (98444-8717)
P.O. Box 755, Puyallup (98371-0068)
PHONE.................................253 435-1040
Matt Shdo, *President*
EMP: 9
SALES (est): 1MM **Privately Held**
SIC: 2448 5031 2449 Pallets, wood; pallets, wood; rectangular boxes & crates, wood

(G-13304)
GARDNER-FIELDS INC
2240 Taylor Way (98421-4303)
PHONE.................................253 627-4098
Raymond Hyer Jr, *President*
Patrick Morelli, *Plant Mgr*
Sandy McArthur, *Human Res Mgr*
Larry Nordi, *Manager*
EMP: 2
SALES (est): 245.6K **Privately Held**
SIC: 2952 Asphalt felts & coatings

(G-13305)
GAYNORS GLASS & RESTORATION
10735 A St S Ste D (98444-6069)
PHONE.................................253 538-2501
Tim Gaynor, *Owner*
EMP: 5
SALES (est): 280K **Privately Held**
SIC: 2869 7536 1793 Industrial organic chemicals; automotive glass replacement shops; glass & glazing work

(G-13306)
GENERAL PLASTICS MFG CO
4910 S Burlington Way (98409-2833)
P.O. Box 9097 (98490-0097)
PHONE.................................253 473-5000
Henry Schatz, *CEO*
Bruce Lind, *President*
Eric Hahn, *Vice Pres*
Kirk Lider, *Vice Pres*
Kyle Riddle, *Production*
◆ **EMP:** 134
SQ FT: 150,000
SALES (est): 52.2MM **Privately Held**
WEB: www.generalplastics.com
SIC: 3086 2821 Plastics foam products; plastics materials & resins

(G-13307)
GEORGIA-PACIFIC LLC
1240 E Alexander Ave (98421-4104)
PHONE.................................253 627-2100
Stephen Ruff, *Manager*
Charlie Garrott, *Manager*
EMP: 98
SALES (corp-wide): 42.6B **Privately Held**
WEB: www.gp.com
SIC: 3275 Wallboard, gypsum
HQ: Georgia-Pacific Llc
 133 Peachtree St Nw
 Atlanta GA 30303
 404 652-4000

(G-13308)
GIG HARBOR BREWING CO
3120 South Tacoma Way (98409-4717)
PHONE.................................253 474-0672
John Fosberg, *Principal*
EMP: 2
SALES (est): 62.3K **Privately Held**
SIC: 2082 Malt beverages

(G-13309)
GINKGO FOREST WINERY
2221 N 30th St (98403-3320)
PHONE.................................253 301-4372
Lois Thiede, *Principal*
EMP: 2
SALES (est): 131.7K **Privately Held**
SIC: 2084 Wines

(G-13310)
GLACIER NORTHWEST INC
Also Called: Hylebos Plant
3601 Taylor Way (98421-4307)
PHONE.................................253 572-7412
Bruce Lanham, *Branch Mgr*
EMP: 40 **Privately Held**
WEB: www.glaciernw.com
SIC: 5032 5211 3241 1442 Concrete & cinder block; concrete & cinder block; cement, hydraulic; construction sand & gravel
HQ: Glacier Northwest, Inc.
 5975 E Marginal Way S
 Seattle WA 98134
 206 764-3000

(G-13311)
GLASS RESTORATION SPECIALISTS
Also Called: Grs
3817 N 16th St (98406-5203)
PHONE.................................253 473-7779
Fax: 253 473-8459
EMP: 40
SQ FT: 10,000
SALES (est): 5.4MM **Privately Held**
SIC: 2816 2842 Mfg Inorganic Pigments Mfg Polish/Sanitation Goods

(G-13312)
GLOBAL MTAL WORKS ERECTORS LLC
1144 Thorne Rd (98421-3202)
PHONE.................................253 572-5363
Karen Howlett, *Mng Member*
Marty Howlett, *Mng Member*
EMP: 40 **EST:** 2012
SALES (est): 3.2MM **Privately Held**
SIC: 3441 3446 Fabricated structural metal; stairs, fire escapes, balconies, railings & ladders

(G-13313)
GLOBE INTERNATIONAL INC (PA)
701 E D St (98421-1811)
P.O. Box 2274 (98401-2274)
PHONE.................................253 383-2584
Calvin D Bamford Jr, *President*
EMP: 2
SQ FT: 3,000
SALES: 1.8MM **Privately Held**
WEB: www.globemachine.com
SIC: 5084 3537 Materials handling machinery; industrial trucks & tractors

(G-13314)
GLOBE MACHINE MANUFACTURING CO (PA)
701 E D St (98421-1811)
P.O. Box 2274 (98401-2274)
PHONE.................................253 383-2584
Calvin D Bamford Jr, *Ch of Bd*
Ronald Jacobsen, *Vice Pres*
Laura E Shane, *Admin Sec*
▲ **EMP:** 250 **EST:** 1917
SQ FT: 100,000
SALES (est): 76.2MM **Privately Held**
SIC: 3553 3537 Woodworking machinery; lift trucks, industrial: fork, platform, straddle, etc.

(G-13315)
GO VENTURES INC
Also Called: Go Industrial Services
719 N Mullen St (98406-3029)
PHONE.................................253 313-4070
Amber Blakeslee, *Principal*
EMP: 2
SALES (est): 95.5K **Privately Held**
SIC: 3537 3569 5084 1799 Industrial trucks & tractors; blast cleaning equipment, dustless; industrial machinery & equipment; cleaning equipment, high pressure, sand or steam; steam cleaning of building exteriors

(G-13316)
GOLDEN APPLE INC
3802 S Warner St (98409-4630)
PHONE.................................253 473-7880
EMP: 2
SALES (est): 93.5K **Privately Held**
SIC: 3571 Mfg Electronic Computers

(G-13317)
GOODMAN CUSTOM FAB
7215 S Alder St (98409-5109)
PHONE.................................253 720-2451
Daniel Goodman, *Principal*
EMP: 2
SALES (est): 132.1K **Privately Held**
SIC: 3441 Fabricated structural metal

(G-13318)
GR SILICATE NANO-
Also Called: Gr Nano Materials
401 E Alex 326 (98421)
PHONE.................................253 267-8781
Vijay Mathur,
EMP: 10
SALES (est): 1.2MM **Privately Held**
SIC: 2869 Industrial organic chemicals

(G-13319)
GRAYMONT WESTERN US INC
Also Called: Continental Lime
1220 E Alexander Ave (98421-4104)
PHONE.................................253 572-7600
Tom Wakefield, *Div Sub Head*
Eric Stover, *Plant Supt*
Keith Hille, *Plant Mgr*
Paul Liner, *Plant Mgr*
Troy Page, *Accounts Mgr*
EMP: 37 **Privately Held**
SIC: 5191 5032 3274 2819 Farm supplies; brick, stone & related material; lime; industrial inorganic chemicals
HQ: Graymont Western Us Inc.
 3950 S 700 E Ste 301
 Salt Lake City UT 84107

(G-13320)
GRAYMONT WESTERN US INC
Also Called: PCC Plant
1220 E Alexander Ave (98421-4104)
PHONE.................................253 572-7600
Moo Han, *Branch Mgr*
EMP: 8 **Privately Held**
SIC: 2819 Calcium compounds & salts, inorganic
HQ: Graymont Western Us Inc.
 3950 S 700 E Ste 301
 Salt Lake City UT 84107

GEOGRAPHIC SECTION

Tacoma - Pierce County (G-13351)

(G-13321)
GREAT NORTHERN HOLDINGS INC (PA)
Also Called: McFarland Cascade
1640 E Marc St (98421)
P.O. Box 1496 (98401-1496)
PHONE.................................253 572-3033
B Corry McFarland, *President*
Greg D McFarland, *Vice Pres*
EMP: 2
SQ FT: 15,000
SALES (est): 885.3K **Privately Held**
SIC: 2491 Wood preserving

(G-13322)
GREAT WHITE SMILE INSTANT
4045 S Park Ave (98418-4916)
PHONE.................................253 255-0456
Marie Elaina Reichle, *Principal*
EMP: 2
SALES (est): 130.2K **Privately Held**
SIC: 2752 Commercial printing, lithographic

(G-13323)
GREEN AIR SUPPLY INC
216 Puyallup Ave S-111 (98421-1114)
PHONE.................................877 427-4361
Thomas Hoare, *President*
Jessse McLaughlin, *Vice Pres*
Chino McLaughlin, *Treasurer*
Browyn Rogers, *Admin Sec*
▲ EMP: 3
SALES (est): 422.8K **Privately Held**
SIC: 3556 Brewers' & maltsters' machinery

(G-13324)
GREEN GLOBAL SOLUTION INC
1310 E 60th St (98404-3528)
P.O. Box 112284 (98411-2284)
PHONE.................................253 202-2304
EMP: 5
SALES (est): 404.1K **Privately Held**
SIC: 2844 Mfg Toilet Preparations

(G-13325)
GREYSLADE
5040 S M St (98408-3507)
PHONE.................................253 332-5985
Frederick Hagedorn, *Principal*
EMP: 3
SALES (est): 228.8K **Privately Held**
SIC: 2836 Culture media

(G-13326)
GRIT CITY GRIND HOUSE LLC
2312 N 8th St Apt A (98403-1068)
PHONE.................................203 898-5627
Robert Boyle,
Taylor Woodrich,
EMP: 2
SALES (est): 141.8K **Privately Held**
SIC: 3599 Grinding castings for the trade

(G-13327)
GROZDI INC
3852 S 31st St (98409-3328)
PHONE.................................253 820-0653
Natasha Grozdeva, *President*
EMP: 4 EST: 2010
SALES (est): 360K **Privately Held**
SIC: 2431 Woodwork, interior & ornamental

(G-13328)
GRUNDFOS CBS INC
Also Called: Paco Pumps By Grundfos
3113 S Pine St Unit C (98409-4708)
PHONE.................................206 433-2600
Peter Hague, *Branch Mgr*
EMP: 14
SALES (corp-wide): 4.1B **Privately Held**
WEB: www.us.grundfos.com
SIC: 3561 7699 5084 Industrial pumps & parts; pumps & pumping equipment repair; pumps & pumping equipment
HQ: Grundfos Cbs Inc.
   902 Koomey Rd
   Brookshire TX 77423
   281 994-2700

(G-13329)
GUILD OF AMERICAN LUTHIERS
8222 S Park Ave (98408-5226)
PHONE.................................253 472-7853
Tim Olsen, *President*
Debra Olsen, *Exec Dir*
EMP: 6
SALES: 365.3K **Privately Held**
WEB: www.luth.org
SIC: 2721 Magazines: publishing & printing

(G-13330)
HANGER ORTHOPEDIC GROUP INC
723 Martin Luther King Jr (98405-4139)
PHONE.................................253 383-4447
Justin Maughon, *Branch Mgr*
EMP: 13
SALES (corp-wide): 1B **Publicly Held**
SIC: 3842 Prosthetic appliances; orthopedic appliances
PA: Hanger, Inc.
   10910 Domain Dr Ste 300
   Austin TX 78758
   512 777-3800

(G-13331)
HARMON BREWING COMPANY L L C (PA)
Also Called: Harmon Pub & Brewery
1938 Pacific Ave (98402-3110)
PHONE.................................253 383-2739
Pat Nagle, *President*
James Tasley, *Vice Pres*
Gary Davis,
Fred Roberson,
EMP: 33
SALES (est): 2.3MM **Privately Held**
WEB: www.harmonbrewingco.com
SIC: 5812 2082 Chicken restaurant; malt beverage products

(G-13332)
HARRIS REBAR SEATTLE INC (PA)
4421 192nd St E (98446-2700)
PHONE.................................253 847-5001
Brian Booth, *President*
Lyall Hadden, *General Mgr*
Steve Gariano, *Project Mgr*
Jeriod Klovas, *Foreman/Supr*
Ken Jarvis, *Manager*
EMP: 22
SQ FT: 24,000
SALES (est): 5.4MM **Privately Held**
SIC: 3441 1791 3449 Fabricated structural metal; structural steel erection; miscellaneous metalwork

(G-13333)
HAWTHORNE HILL
320 E 32nd St Unit 410 (98404-1609)
PHONE.................................253 572-3744
Mike Wickre, *Principal*
EMP: 2
SALES (est): 180K **Privately Held**
SIC: 3537 Cranes, industrial truck

(G-13334)
HELM MANUFACTURING CO LLC
13502 Pacific Ave S (98444-4742)
PHONE.................................253 537-3382
Nancy Lemay, *Mng Member*
Douglas Lemay, *Mng Member*
EMP: 9
SALES (est): 1.2MM **Privately Held**
SIC: 3715 3537 Truck trailers; industrial trucks & tractors

(G-13335)
HERALD CHERAINE PHD
1614 S Mildred St Ste B (98465-1626)
PHONE.................................253 564-1193
Cheraine Herald, *Principal*
EMP: 3
SALES (est): 156.9K **Privately Held**
SIC: 2711 8049 Newspapers, publishing & printing; psychologist, psychotherapist & hypnotist

(G-13336)
HEWITT CABINETS & INTERIORS
3301 S Lawrence St (98409-4712)
PHONE.................................253 272-0404
Ted Harrison, *President*
EMP: 12
SQ FT: 10,000
SALES: 750K **Privately Held**
SIC: 2434 1521 Wood kitchen cabinets; general remodeling, single-family houses

(G-13337)
HIGHROAD PRODUCTS INC
Also Called: Minuteman Press
2941 S 38th St Ste C (98409-5647)
PHONE.................................253 474-9900
Lee Short, *President*
Angie Davidson, *Prdtn Mgr*
EMP: 5
SALES (est): 525.8K **Privately Held**
SIC: 2752 Commercial printing, lithographic

(G-13338)
HOLIDAY ENGINEERING & MFG CO
Also Called: Best Guitars
10718 A St S (98444-6024)
PHONE.................................253 238-0671
Andy Artz, *Owner*
EMP: 2
SALES (est): 199.6K **Privately Held**
WEB: www.hemcoofwa.com
SIC: 3553 Bandsaws, woodworking

(G-13339)
HOLROYD BLOCK COMPANY INC
7216 Lakewood Dr W (98499-7917)
P.O. Box 39009 (98496-3009)
PHONE.................................253 474-8481
John A Holroyd, *Vice Pres*
Andrew Holroyd, *Vice Pres*
David D Nielson, *Vice Pres*
Bill Davis, *Opers Staff*
Margaret M Nielson, *Treasurer*
EMP: 10 EST: 1926
SQ FT: 2,400
SALES (est): 1.4MM **Privately Held**
SIC: 3271 Blocks, concrete or cinder: standard

(G-13340)
HOLROYD COMPANY INC (PA)
7216 Lakewood Dr W (98499-7917)
P.O. Box 39009, Lakewood (98496-3009)
PHONE.................................253 474-0725
Stephen A Nielsen, *President*
Margaret M Nielsen, *President*
Doug Hanson, *General Mgr*
David D Nielsen, *Vice Pres*
Rita Nielsen, *Vice Pres*
EMP: 70
SQ FT: 4,200
SALES (est): 16.7MM **Privately Held**
WEB: www.holroyd.com
SIC: 3273 5032 Ready-mixed concrete; sand, construction; gravel

(G-13341)
HOLROYD COMPANY INC
923 E 26th St (98421-2111)
PHONE.................................253 627-0571
Lisa Holroyd, *Branch Mgr*
EMP: 60
SALES (corp-wide): 16.7MM **Privately Held**
SIC: 3273 Ready-mixed concrete
PA: Holroyd Company, Inc.
   7216 Lakewood Dr W
   Tacoma WA 98499
   253 474-0725

(G-13342)
HOOBER INDUSTRIES INC
716 140th St E (98445-2761)
PHONE.................................253 370-9553
Brett Hoober, *Principal*
EMP: 2 EST: 2016
SALES (est): 126.3K **Privately Held**
SIC: 3999 Manufacturing industries

(G-13343)
HOPP INDUSTRIES
4702 N Cheyenne St (98407-5109)
PHONE.................................253 732-7348
EMP: 2 EST: 2008
SALES (est): 136.7K **Privately Held**
SIC: 3999 Framed artwork

(G-13344)
HOYA OPTICAL LABORATORIES
Also Called: Hoya Vision Care
2330 S 78th St (98409-9051)
P.O. Box 1798 (98401-1798)
PHONE.................................253 475-7809
Ray Knoll, *President*
Lydia Knoll, *Vice Pres*
▲ EMP: 50
SQ FT: 12,000
SALES (est): 7MM **Privately Held**
SIC: 3851 8011 Lenses, ophthalmic; offices & clinics of medical doctors

(G-13345)
I HART LIPSTICK
10311 50th Ave E (98446-5414)
PHONE.................................253 720-7126
Nikkie Hart, *Principal*
EMP: 2
SALES (est): 74.4K **Privately Held**
SIC: 2844 Lipsticks

(G-13346)
IASCO
4808 S Washington St (98409-2827)
PHONE.................................253 474-0497
David Hurd, *Branch Mgr*
EMP: 30
SALES (corp-wide): 7.7MM **Privately Held**
SIC: 3399 Powder, metal
PA: Iasco
   1833 Castenada Dr
   Burlingame CA 94010
   707 252-3522

(G-13347)
IMPERIAL MOTION LLC
Also Called: Clothing
2920 S Steele St (98409-7630)
PHONE.................................253 779-4400
Thomas Tucci, *Mng Member*
Grant Curtis, *Graphic Designe*
Spencer B Goetz,
Stephen Goetz,
Diane Tucci,
▲ EMP: 8
SALES (est): 1.2MM **Privately Held**
SIC: 3161 Clothing & apparel carrying cases

(G-13348)
IMPRESSIVE PRINTING
118 116th St S (98444-5402)
PHONE.................................253 538-2948
Jay Kutchera, *Principal*
EMP: 2
SALES (est): 138.7K **Privately Held**
SIC: 2752 Commercial printing, lithographic

(G-13349)
INTERACTIVE ELECTRONIC SYSTEMS
Also Called: Lift It
1201 Pacific Ave Ste 600 (98402-4384)
PHONE.................................877 543-8698
Tony Branham, *CEO*
Wally Bertram, *Vice Pres*
Chris Erickson, *Vice Pres*
▲ EMP: 38
SQ FT: 10,000
SALES (est): 5MM **Privately Held**
SIC: 3612 Transformers, except electric

(G-13350)
INVENTURE CHEMICAL INC
2244 Port Of Tacoma Rd (98421-3607)
P.O. Box 530, Gig Harbor (98335-0530)
PHONE.................................253 576-1577
Mark Tegen, *CEO*
EMP: 9
SALES: 474K **Privately Held**
SIC: 2869 Industrial organic chemicals

(G-13351)
ISLANDERS
10202 109th Ave Sw (98498-1739)
PHONE.................................253 588-9246
Barbara Quarless, *Owner*
EMP: 3
SALES: 80K **Privately Held**
SIC: 2389 7929 Band uniforms; musicians

Tacoma - Pierce County (G-13352)

(G-13352)
ITEM HOUSE INC (PA)
Also Called: Kristen Blake
2920 S Steele St (98409-7630)
P.O. Box 11267 (98411-0267)
PHONE.................................253 627-7168
Gregory J Davis, *President*
Gail Crandall, *Buyer*
David Wyman, *Admin Sec*
▲ **EMP:** 45
SQ FT: 200,000
SALES (est): 5.9MM **Privately Held**
WEB: www.itemhouse.com
SIC: 2339 Women's & misses' outerwear

(G-13353)
J M MRTNAC SHIPBUILDING CORP
2902 N 27th St (98407-6310)
PHONE.................................253 572-4005
Joe Martinac, *President*
Joseph S Martinac Jr, *President*
Jonathan Platt, *Vice Pres*
▲ **EMP:** 125 **EST:** 1924
SQ FT: 3,000
SALES (est): 16.4MM **Privately Held**
WEB: www.martinacship.com
SIC: 3731 Shipbuilding & repairing

(G-13354)
J R REDING COMPANY INC
3005 Chandler St (98409-7932)
PHONE.................................253 474-0938
John R Reding, *President*
EMP: 8
SQ FT: 15,000
SALES (est): 328.9K **Privately Held**
WEB: www.jrreding.com
SIC: 7641 2441 Furniture refinishing; antique furniture repair & restoration; re-upholstery; cases, wood

(G-13355)
JAMES HARDIE BUILDING PDTS INC
Also Called: James Hardy Building Products
18200 50th Ave E (98446-3735)
PHONE.................................253 847-8700
Scott Hoard, *Manager*
John Harrison, *Technical Staff*
EMP: 100 **Privately Held**
SIC: 5032 3272 2421 Brick, stone & related material; concrete products; sawmills & planing mills, general
HQ: James Hardie Building Products Inc.
231 S La Salle St # 2000
Chicago IL 60604
312 291-5072

(G-13356)
JCI JONES CHEMICALS INC
1919 Marine View Dr (98422-4107)
PHONE.................................253 274-0104
James Groh, *Manager*
EMP: 20
SQ FT: 15,024
SALES (corp-wide): 179MM **Privately Held**
WEB: www.jcichem.com
SIC: 5169 2819 Industrial chemicals; industrial inorganic chemicals
PA: Jci Jones Chemicals, Inc.
1765 Ringling Blvd
Sarasota FL 34236
941 330-1537

(G-13357)
JDKK INVESTMENT GROUP INC
Also Called: Pacific Business Printing
2331 Ross Way (98421-3402)
PHONE.................................253 565-4713
Fax: 253 566-9811
EMP: 4
SALES (est): 420K **Privately Held**
SIC: 2752 Lithographic Commercial Printing

(G-13358)
JESSE ENGINEERING COMPANY (PA)
1840 Marine View Dr (98422-4106)
PHONE.................................253 552-1500
Marty Diklich, *President*
Philip Jesse, *Division Mgr*
Anne Jesse, *Vice Pres*
Darrell Jesse, *Vice Pres*
Pat Moldan, *Admin Sec*
◆ **EMP:** 40
SQ FT: 44,000
SALES (est): 31.5MM **Privately Held**
WEB: www.jesse-wallace.com
SIC: 3441 3542 Fabricated structural metal; bending machines

(G-13359)
JET DOOR LLC
1832 112th St E (98445-3724)
PHONE.................................253 531-2261
Timothy Yokes,
G Edward Knoben,
Jeffrey Zacher,
EMP: 25
SALES (est): 2.5MM **Privately Held**
WEB: www.jetdoorllc.com
SIC: 2431 Millwork

(G-13360)
JHARC INDUSTRIES LLC
1652 S 57th St (98408-2316)
PHONE.................................571 205-5422
Jonathan Nylen, *Principal*
EMP: 2
SALES (est): 135.5K **Privately Held**
SIC: 3999 Manufacturing industries

(G-13361)
JOE FROYO LLC (PA)
914 A St Ste 200 (98402-5108)
PHONE.................................909 204-1301
Brent Hall, *CEO*
Zach Miller, *President*
Patrick McNerthney, *Vice Pres*
Jesse Roberge, *Vice Pres*
EMP: 5
SQ FT: 10,000
SALES (est): 844.3K **Privately Held**
SIC: 2026 5143 Yogurt; yogurt

(G-13362)
JOHNNYS FINE FOODS INC
Also Called: Johnnys Chef Blnded Seasonings
319 E 25th St (98421-1398)
PHONE.................................253 383-4597
John Crabill, *CEO*
Kevin Ruda, *President*
Henry Gumm, *Plant Mgr*
Dan Leadbetter, *CFO*
EMP: 45
SQ FT: 40,000
SALES (est): 17MM **Privately Held**
WEB: www.johnnysfinefoods.com
SIC: 5149 2099 Salad dressing; seasonings: dry mixes

(G-13363)
JOHNSON CANDY CO INC
924 Martin Lthr Kng Jr Wa (98405-4188)
PHONE.................................253 272-8504
Ronald K Johnson, *President*
EMP: 6 **EST:** 1925
SQ FT: 2,800
SALES (est): 528K **Privately Held**
SIC: 2064 5145 5441 Candy & other confectionery products; confectionery; candy, nut & confectionery stores

(G-13364)
JOHNSON COX CO INC
726 Pacific Ave (98402-5208)
PHONE.................................253 272-2238
Ken Creech, *President*
Cynthia Faul, *Vice Pres*
Kay Creech, *Treasurer*
Gary Faul, *Admin Sec*
EMP: 20
SQ FT: 22,500
SALES (est): 2.6MM **Privately Held**
WEB: www.johnsoncox.com
SIC: 2732 2752 Books: printing & binding; pamphlets: printing & binding, not published on site; commercial printing, lithographic

(G-13365)
JOHNSON ENTERPRISES
Also Called: Jj's Draperies
4617 76th St E (98443-2236)
PHONE.................................253 537-8056
John H Johnson, *Owner*
Mary Johnson, *Owner*
EMP: 2
SALES (est): 100K **Privately Held**
SIC: 5023 2591 Window covering parts & accessories; drapery hardware & blinds & shades

(G-13366)
JOHNSON SIGNS OF FEDERAL WAY
1742 Pnte Woodworth Dr Ne (98422-3480)
PHONE.................................253 678-4304
EMP: 2
SALES (est): 61.3K **Privately Held**
SIC: 3993 Signs & advertising specialties

(G-13367)
JOHNSONS MILLWORK INC
2319 South Tacoma Way (98409-7520)
PHONE.................................253 472-5900
Eric Johnson, *President*
EMP: 10
SQ FT: 19,900
SALES (est): 1.2MM **Privately Held**
SIC: 2431 Doors & door parts & trim, wood

(G-13368)
JOSHUA M LENNOX MA
10202 Pcf Ave S Ste 204 (98444)
PHONE.................................253 590-8952
Joshua Lennox, *Principal*
EMP: 2
SALES (est): 79.9K **Privately Held**
SIC: 3585 Refrigeration & heating equipment

(G-13369)
JSG FINE CSTM CBNTRY WDWRK LLC
5904 N 45th St (98407-1902)
PHONE.................................253 906-9043
Sofya Kochubey, *Administration*
EMP: 2 **EST:** 2015
SALES (est): 91.7K **Privately Held**
SIC: 2431 Millwork

(G-13370)
JUNEFALSETTA
12206 47th Ave E (98446-4306)
PHONE.................................253 536-3576
June Falsetta, *Principal*
EMP: 2
SALES (est): 88.3K **Privately Held**
SIC: 3669 Communications equipment

(G-13371)
JWOODWORKING
2918 N 20th St (98406-7004)
PHONE.................................253 229-9581
Justin Webber, *Principal*
EMP: 2 **EST:** 2010
SALES (est): 156.2K **Privately Held**
SIC: 2431 Millwork

(G-13372)
KAMAN FLUID POWER LLC
2909 Pcf Hwy E Ste 103 (98424)
PHONE.................................253 922-5710
Mike Socall, *Manager*
EMP: 4
SALES (corp-wide): 1.8B **Publicly Held**
SIC: 5084 3492 Hydraulic systems equipment & supplies; hose & tube fittings & assemblies, hydraulic/pneumatic
HQ: Kaman Fluid Power, Llc
1 Vision Way
Bloomfield CT 06002
860 243-7100

(G-13373)
KCI COMMERCIAL INC
2407 N 31st St Ste 201 (98407-6439)
P.O. Box 1135 (98401-1135)
PHONE.................................253 475-4363
EMP: 2
SALES (est): 120.3K **Privately Held**
SIC: 2599 Hospital beds

(G-13374)
KEL-TECH PLASTICS INC
Also Called: Keltech
3510 S Pine St (98409-5703)
PHONE.................................253 472-9654
Deanna Keller, *President*
Scott Niels, *Vice Pres*
Rainee Eckhardt, *Assistant*
▲ **EMP:** 40
SQ FT: 13,000
SALES (est): 10.2MM **Privately Held**
WEB: www.keltechplastic.com
SIC: 3089 Thermoformed finished plastic products

(G-13375)
KENS POWDER COATING
10739 A St S B (98444-6063)
PHONE.................................253 539-5845
Alan Cain Jr, *Partner*
EMP: 3 **EST:** 2014
SALES (est): 151.2K **Privately Held**
SIC: 5571 3479 Motorcycle parts & accessories; hot dip coating of metals or formed products

(G-13376)
KINGS KITCHEN LLC
11105 Steele St S # 114 (98444-8700)
PHONE.................................253 212-3623
Kerstin Cobb,
EMP: 2
SALES (est): 123.9K **Privately Held**
SIC: 5812 5031 5021 2521 Eating places; lumber, plywood & millwork; furniture; wood office furniture; wood kitchen cabinets; cut stone & stone products

(G-13377)
KJJ ENTERPRISES INC
Also Called: Fast Sign
2528 S 38th St (98409-7348)
PHONE.................................253 474-6607
Kyle Jones, *President*
Jackie Jones, *Admin Sec*
EMP: 5
SALES (est): 551.6K **Privately Held**
SIC: 3993 Signs & advertising specialties

(G-13378)
KOLIBABA AND ASSOCIATES
3902 N Gove St (98407-4907)
PHONE.................................253 752-0368
EMP: 2
SALES (est): 61.4K **Privately Held**
SIC: 5199 3999 Gifts & novelties; fire extinguishers, portable

(G-13379)
KURTISFACTOR LLC
Also Called: Mfg Precision
2368 Yakima Ave Unit 103 (98405-3873)
PHONE.................................208 863-6180
Brandon Hemingway,
EMP: 3
SALES (est): 33.8K **Privately Held**
SIC: 7389 3724 3761 3711 ; aircraft engines & engine parts; guided missiles & space vehicles; military motor vehicle assembly; shipbuilding & repairing

(G-13380)
L LEATHER LLC
602 108th St S (98444-5602)
PHONE.................................253 733-9196
Kery Anderson, *Principal*
EMP: 2
SALES (est): 119.3K **Privately Held**
SIC: 3199 Leather goods

(G-13381)
LARKIN JEWELERS
2405 N Pearl St Ste 8 (98406-2575)
PHONE.................................253 756-0712
David Ellestad, *Partner*
Tina Ellestad, *Partner*
EMP: 4
SALES (est): 480K **Privately Held**
SIC: 5944 3911 7631 Jewelry stores; jewelry, precious metal; jewelry repair services

(G-13382)
LASER SUPPORT SERVICES INC
3223 148th St E (98446-1569)
PHONE.................................253 531-9008
Errol Hern, *President*
EMP: 2
SALES (est): 140K **Privately Held**
SIC: 3841 Surgical lasers

GEOGRAPHIC SECTION

Tacoma - Pierce County (G-13410)

(G-13383)
LASER WRITING
3016 N Narrows Dr (98407-1562)
PHONE....................253 686-6909
John Leach, *Owner*
EMP: 3
SQ FT: 600
SALES: 90K **Privately Held**
SIC: 2721 7338 Periodicals: publishing & printing; word processing service

(G-13384)
LEGGETT & PLATT INCORPORATED
Also Called: Seattle 0062
440 E 19th St (98421-1501)
PHONE....................801 825-9739
Dean Nelson, *Branch Mgr*
EMP: 4
SALES (corp-wide): 4.2B **Publicly Held**
WEB: www.leggett.com
SIC: 2515 Mattresses & bedsprings
PA: Leggett & Platt, Incorporated
1 Leggett Rd
Carthage MO 64836
417 358-8131

(G-13385)
LEHIGH NORTHWEST CEMENT CO (DH)
2115 N 30th St Ste 202 (98403-3397)
P.O. Box 6979 (98417-0393)
PHONE....................800 752-6794
Jim Derkatch, *President*
Richard Harper, *CFO*
Cindy Brown, *Admin Mgr*
▲ **EMP:** 15
SQ FT: 1,000
SALES (est): 22.5MM
SALES (corp-wide): 20.6B **Privately Held**
SIC: 5032 3241 Cement; portland cement

(G-13386)
LESKAJAN JOHN
Also Called: Tacoma Iron Work
3131 S Lawrence St (98409-4823)
PHONE....................253 539-8018
John Leskajan, *Mng Member*
Mika Leskajan,
EMP: 10
SALES (est): 1MM **Privately Held**
WEB: www.tacomaironwork.com
SIC: 3446 Fences or posts, ornamental iron or steel; gates, ornamental metal; railings, bannisters, guards, etc.: made from metal pipe

(G-13387)
LIFE-GRO INC
4302 S Washington St (98409-2910)
PHONE....................253 682-1669
Denneace Bowen, *President*
Bret Bowen, *Vice Pres*
EMP: 5
SALES (est): 900K **Privately Held**
SIC: 3812 Hydrophones

(G-13388)
LIGHT IT BRIGHT PRODUCTS LLC
7211 S Sheridan Ave (98408-3041)
PHONE....................253 666-2278
Lakreesha Bonds, *President*
Antonio Stinson, *Vice Pres*
Felicia Stinson, *Vice Pres*
Lila Stinson, *Vice Pres*
EMP: 2
SALES: 15K **Privately Held**
SIC: 3646 5063 5719 7389 Commercial indusl & institutional electric lighting fixtures; lighting fixtures, commercial & industrial; lighting, lamps & accessories;

(G-13389)
LOAD CONTROL SYSTEMS INC
Also Called: Tarpx
2407 N 31st St (98407-6439)
P.O. Box 1135 (98401-1135)
PHONE....................253 284-0331
Trevor Colby, *President*
Dan Kinley, *Corp Secy*
Mike Walters, *Vice Pres*
EMP: 3
SQ FT: 1,000

SALES (est): 180K **Privately Held**
SIC: 2221 Nylon broadwoven fabrics

(G-13390)
LUCKS COMPANY (PA)
Also Called: Lucks Food Decorating Company
3003 S Pine St (98409-4793)
PHONE....................253 383-4815
Richard Ellison, *President*
Richard E Ellison, *President*
Dan Elliott, *Senior VP*
John E Lantz, *Vice Pres*
Carl Lucks, *CFO*
▲ **EMP:** 150 **EST:** 1953
SQ FT: 5,500
SALES (est): 35MM **Privately Held**
WEB: www.edibleimage.com
SIC: 2087 Food colorings

(G-13391)
LUCKS COMPANY
Also Called: Food Decorating Division
3003 S Pine St (98409-4793)
PHONE....................253 383-4815
Rick Ellison, *President*
EMP: 120
SALES (corp-wide): 35MM **Privately Held**
WEB: www.edibleimage.com
SIC: 2064 Candy & other confectionery products
PA: The Lucks Company
3003 S Pine St
Tacoma WA 98409
253 383-4815

(G-13392)
LUMIN ART SIGNS INC
4320 S Adams St Ste A (98409-2921)
PHONE....................253 833-2800
David B Bowen, *President*
EMP: 9
SQ FT: 8,000
SALES (est): 600K **Privately Held**
WEB: www.luminartsigns.com
SIC: 3993 Signs, not made in custom sign painting shops; neon signs

(G-13393)
M2 INNOVATIVE CONCEPTS INC
3032 S Cedar St (98409-4830)
PHONE....................253 383-5659
Timothy Hagen, *President*
Kevin C Hagen, *CFO*
EMP: 10
SALES (est): 1.2MM **Privately Held**
WEB: www.m2ic.com
SIC: 3253 Ceramic wall & floor tile

(G-13394)
MAGAWAY FIRE LLC
5810 S Cushman Ave (98408-2346)
P.O. Box 110669 (98411-0669)
PHONE....................253 394-3255
Mike Magaway, *Principal*
Jeff Magaway, *Principal*
EMP: 2
SALES (est): 43.7K **Privately Held**
SIC: 7692 2899 Welding repair; chemical preparations

(G-13395)
MAGNOLIA SIGNS
8218 Pacific Ave Ste 6 (98408-5827)
PHONE....................253 592-5121
Jennifer Heitz, *Principal*
EMP: 2
SALES (est): 72.6K **Privately Held**
SIC: 3993 Signs & advertising specialties

(G-13396)
MAJESTIC AEROTECH INC
401 E 25th St Ste H (98421-1313)
PHONE....................360 528-4142
Jeffrey Roberts, *CEO*
EMP: 10
SALES (est): 1.2MM **Privately Held**
SIC: 3728 Aircraft parts & equipment

(G-13397)
MANKE LUMBER COMPANY INC (PA)
Also Called: Superior Wood Treating
1717 Marine View Dr (98422-4192)
PHONE....................253 572-6252

Charles Manke, *President*
James Manke, *Vice Pres*
Brad Meyer, *Electrical Engi*
Traci Responte, *Human Res Mgr*
Jeffrey James, *Sales Staff*
▲ **EMP:** 300
SQ FT: 7,500
SALES (est): 97.1MM **Privately Held**
WEB: www.mankelumber.com
SIC: 2421 2491 2499 Lumber: rough, sawed or planed; wood preserving: poles & pole crossarms, treated wood; posts, treated wood; flooring, treated wood block; mulch or sawdust products, wood

(G-13398)
MANKE TIMBER COMPANY INC
1717 Marine View Dr (98422-4104)
PHONE....................253 572-9029
Arlene Gomez, *Principal*
EMP: 1
SALES (est): 6.1MM
SALES (corp-wide): 97.1MM **Privately Held**
WEB: www.mankelumber.com
SIC: 2421 Sawmills & planing mills, general
PA: Manke Lumber Company, Inc.
1717 Marine View Dr
Tacoma WA 98422
253 572-6252

(G-13399)
MAPLETEX INC
3401 Lincoln Ave Ste G (98421-4017)
P.O. Box 771 (98401-0771)
PHONE....................253 572-3608
Steven J Geffre, *President*
EMP: 6
SQ FT: 16,000
SALES (est): 1.8MM **Privately Held**
WEB: www.mapletex.com
SIC: 2821 Plasticizer/additive based plastic materials

(G-13400)
MARSHALL MARKETING GROUP INC
Also Called: Sir Speedy
7450 South Tacoma Way B1 (98409-3936)
PHONE....................253 473-0765
James S Brebner, *President*
EMP: 24
SQ FT: 8,000
SALES (est): 4.6MM **Privately Held**
WEB: www.sirspeedy0905.com
SIC: 7334 7336 2752 2791 Photocopying & duplicating services; graphic arts & related design; commercial printing, offset; typesetting; bookbinding & related work

(G-13401)
MATTRESS MAKERS INCORPORATED
Also Called: Custom Comfort
1635 E Portland Ave (98421-2802)
PHONE....................253 984-1730
Ray Burgess, *President*
◆ **EMP:** 12
SQ FT: 36,000
SALES: 1MM **Privately Held**
SIC: 2515 5199 Mattresses, innerspring or box spring; advertising specialties

(G-13402)
MAXX DISTRIBUTION LLC
7431 S Madison St (98409-1000)
PHONE....................888 507-6790
John Gibson,
Mike McHugh,
Kelly Walker,
EMP: 3 **EST:** 2015
SALES (est): 106.9K **Privately Held**
SIC: 3691 Batteries, rechargeable

(G-13403)
MCD TECHNOLOGIES INC
2515 South Tacoma Way (98409-7527)
PHONE....................253 564-2420
Karin M Bolland, *President*
Richard E Magoon, *Exec VP*
▼ **EMP:** 11
SQ FT: 18,000
SALES: 1MM **Privately Held**
WEB: www.mcdtechnologiesinc.com
SIC: 3556 Food products machinery

(G-13404)
MCFARLAND CASCADE HOLDINGS INC (HQ)
1640 E Marc St (98421)
P.O. Box 1496 (98401-1496)
PHONE....................253 572-3033
Brian McManus, *President*
Wayne Wilkeson, *President*
Greg D Mc Farland, *Vice Pres*
Jerry Heemstra, *Admin Sec*
▲ **EMP:** 100
SQ FT: 15,000
SALES (est): 171MM
SALES (corp-wide): 1.6B **Privately Held**
SIC: 2491 6552 6531 Poles & pole crossarms, treated wood; wood products, creosoted; land subdividers & developers, commercial; real estate managers
PA: Stella-Jones Inc
3100 Boul De La Cote-Vertu Bureau 300
Saint-Laurent QC H4R 2
514 934-8666

(G-13405)
MECONI PUB & EATERY
709 Pacific Ave (98402-5207)
PHONE....................253 383-3388
Dave Meconi, *Owner*
EMP: 2
SALES (est): 183K **Privately Held**
WEB: www.tacomapub.com
SIC: 2082 5813 5812 Malt beverages; tavern (drinking places); eating places

(G-13406)
MEDALLION FOODS INC
18420 50th Ave E (98446-3758)
PHONE....................253 846-2600
Masaki Saito, *President*
Tetsu Kitsukawa, *Vice Pres*
Marcello Mancini, *Vice Pres*
Brian Westberg, *Production*
Lynnette Baker, *Buyer*
▲ **EMP:** 60
SQ FT: 77,540
SALES (est): 11.1MM
SALES (corp-wide): 11.4MM **Privately Held**
WEB: www.medallionfoods.com
SIC: 2099 Food preparations
PA: Food Master (Pnw) Corp.
18420 50th Ave E
Tacoma WA 98446
253 846-2600

(G-13407)
MEIER MANUFACTURING
4638 N Pearl St (98407-2926)
PHONE....................253 545-9798
Bailey Meier, *Principal*
EMP: 2
SALES (est): 74.7K **Privately Held**
SIC: 3999 Manufacturing industries

(G-13408)
MERCHANTS METALS LLC
7303 Golden Given Rd E (98404-5564)
PHONE....................253 531-5454
James Hatfield, *Manager*
EMP: 30
SALES (corp-wide): 2.9B **Privately Held**
SIC: 3496 Fencing, made from purchased wire
HQ: Merchants Metals Llc
211 Perimeter Center Pkwy
Atlanta GA 30346
770 741-0306

(G-13409)
METAL MASTER LLC
5620 S Proctor St Ste A (98409-2628)
PHONE....................253 948-7295
Marvin Dekruyf, *Principal*
EMP: 3
SALES (est): 275.1K **Privately Held**
SIC: 3599 Machine shop, jobbing & repair

(G-13410)
MICHAEL BLACKWELL
1429 S Verde St (98405-1148)
PHONE....................253 759-2906
Michael Blackwell, *Partner*
EMP: 2 **EST:** 2016
SALES (est): 85.9K **Privately Held**
SIC: 3571 Electronic computers

Tacoma - Pierce County (G-13411) GEOGRAPHIC SECTION

(G-13411)
MICHAEL ECKLES
4745 Silver Bow Rd Ne (98422-2082)
PHONE.................................253 568-2934
Michael Eckles, *President*
EMP: 3
SALES (est): 98.4K **Privately Held**
SIC: 2038 Frozen specialties

(G-13412)
MICRPRINT INC
11102 25th Ave E Ste D (98445-5309)
PHONE.................................253 539-1103
EMP: 2 EST: 2011
SALES (est): 133.6K **Privately Held**
SIC: 2782 Mfg Blankbooks/Binders

(G-13413)
MIKES LOGGING
12814 19th Avenue Ct S (98444-1234)
P.O. Box 331, Kapowsin (98344-0331)
PHONE.................................360 893-5336
Mike Harwell, *Principal*
EMP: 2
SALES (est): 128.6K **Privately Held**
SIC: 2411 Logging camps & contractors

(G-13414)
MILES SAND & GRAVEL COMPANY
I5 Highway 512 Hwy 512 (98402)
PHONE.................................253 922-9116
Tom Butler, *Manager*
EMP: 25
SALES (est): 1.3MM
SALES (corp-wide): 88MM **Privately Held**
SIC: 3273 Ready-mixed concrete
PA: Miles Sand & Gravel Company
    400 Valley Ave Ne
    Puyallup WA 98372
    253 833-3705

(G-13415)
MILLWORK CABINET SPECIALIST
13006 50th Ave E (98446-4244)
PHONE.................................253 377-4334
Jim Haight, *Owner*
EMP: 5
SALES (est): 250K **Privately Held**
SIC: 2434 Wood kitchen cabinets

(G-13416)
MITCHELL HARDWARE W LINN INC
2675 N Pearl St (98407-2416)
PHONE.................................253 752-2000
EMP: 2 EST: 2017
SALES (est): 75.8K **Privately Held**
SIC: 3429 Manufactured hardware (general)

(G-13417)
MIX
635 St Helens Ave (98402-2304)
PHONE.................................253 383-4327
Brock Leach, *Owner*
EMP: 4
SALES (est): 330.6K **Privately Held**
SIC: 2599 Bar, restaurant & cafeteria furniture

(G-13418)
MODUTECH MARINE INC
2218 Marine View Dr (98422-4183)
PHONE.................................253 272-9319
Darrin Swindahl, *President*
Brian Swindahl, *Chairman*
Elaine S Swindahl, *Corp Secy*
Carl R Swindahl, *Vice Pres*
Bruce House, *Purch Agent*
▲ EMP: 25
SQ FT: 3,000
SALES (est): 6.1MM **Privately Held**
WEB: www.modutechmarine.com
SIC: 3732 Boats, fiberglass: building & repairing

(G-13419)
MOOR INNOVATIVE TECH LLC
4812 64th St E (98443-2345)
PHONE.................................253 343-2216
Timothy Moore, *Principal*
EMP: 2
SALES: 100MM **Privately Held**
SIC: 2326 Work uniforms

(G-13420)
MORNING NEWS TRIBUNE
1950 S State St (98405-2860)
PHONE.................................253 597-8511
Yolanda Bailey, *Principal*
EMP: 3
SALES (est): 152K **Privately Held**
SIC: 2711 Newspapers, publishing & printing

(G-13421)
MOUNTAIN MUESLI LLC
1401 S Sprague Ave # 570 (98405-2967)
PHONE.................................253 426-8092
Christopher Young, *Mng Member*
EMP: 2 EST: 2010
SQ FT: 1,000
SALES: 50K **Privately Held**
SIC: 2043 Cereal breakfast foods

(G-13422)
MR PRINT ONE
2005 Mtn View Ave W (98466-3651)
PHONE.................................253 693-2802
EMP: 2
SALES (est): 83.9K **Privately Held**
SIC: 2752 Commercial printing, lithographic

(G-13423)
MUTUAL MATERIALS COMPANY INC
2201 112th St S (98444-1545)
PHONE.................................253 589-6434
Jim Anderegg, *Branch Mgr*
EMP: 4
SALES (corp-wide): 44.8MM **Privately Held**
SIC: 1741 2421 Retaining wall construction; building & structural materials, wood
PA: Mutual Materials Company
    605 119th Ave Ne
    Bellevue WA 98005
    425 452-2300

(G-13424)
NARROWS BREWING LLP
9007 S 19th St (98466-1819)
PHONE.................................253 327-1400
Matthew J Smith, *Administration*
EMP: 9
SALES (est): 35.7K **Privately Held**
SIC: 2082 Beer (alcoholic beverage)

(G-13425)
NATURAL VENOM ALL STAR
10421 92nd Street Ct Sw (98498-1962)
PHONE.................................253 370-7986
Valerie Wolpert, *Principal*
EMP: 2
SALES (est): 81.8K **Privately Held**
SIC: 2836 Venoms

(G-13426)
NESTER BROTHERS LLC
Also Called: Tommy's Johnson
3008 S 10th St (98405-2525)
PHONE.................................253 320-9405
Thomas Nester,
EMP: 2
SALES (est): 141.9K **Privately Held**
SIC: 2844 Toilet preparations

(G-13427)
NEWS TRBUNE SCHLRSHP FNDATION
1950 S State St (98405-2817)
PHONE.................................253 597-8593
Jerry Allen, *Principal*
EMP: 2
SALES: 0 **Privately Held**
SIC: 2711 Newspapers, publishing & printing

(G-13428)
NICHOLSON ENGINEERING CO INC
680 E 11th St (98421-2402)
P.O. Box 1006 (98401-1006)
PHONE.................................253 272-9167
Bill Nicholson, *President*
EMP: 8
SQ FT: 18,000
SALES: 570K **Privately Held**
SIC: 3599 Machine shop, jobbing & repair

(G-13429)
NORTH STAR GLOVE COMPANY
2916 S Steele St (98409-7630)
P.O. Box 1214 (98401-1214)
PHONE.................................253 627-7107
Robert G Wekell, *President*
Kathryn W Brown, *Vice Pres*
C Thomas Wekell, *Treasurer*
Megan Wekell, *Sales Staff*
Jim Nordgulen, *Supervisor*
EMP: 45
SQ FT: 30,000
SALES (est): 6.4MM **Privately Held**
WEB: www.northstarglove.com
SIC: 3151 2381 5136 Gloves, leather: work; gloves, work: woven or knit, made from purchased materials; gloves, men's & boys'

(G-13430)
NORTHERN FISH PRODUCTS INC (PA)
Also Called: Northern Fish - Old Town
3911 S 56th St (98409-2607)
P.O. Box 9615 (98490-0615)
PHONE.................................253 475-3858
Ross Swanes, *President*
EMP: 39
SQ FT: 10,000
SALES (est): 38.4MM **Privately Held**
WEB: www.northernfish.com
SIC: 5146 2092 Fish, fresh; fish, cured; fresh or frozen packaged fish

(G-13431)
NORTHWEST COMPANY INTL
2000 Taylor Way (98421-4114)
PHONE.................................253 365-6316
EMP: 7 EST: 2009
SALES (est): 997.6K **Privately Held**
SIC: 2741 Miscellaneous publishing

(G-13432)
NORTHWEST HARDWOODS INC (HQ)
1313 Broadway Ste 300 (98402-3427)
PHONE.................................253 568-6800
Tony Rosengarth, *President*
Mikki Pieruccioni, *President*
Jessie Burkett, *Superintendent*
Jeffrey Steed, *Corp Secy*
Darrell Keeling, *COO*
◆ EMP: 1000
SALES (est): 708.5MM **Privately Held**
SIC: 2426 5031 Lumber, hardwood dimension; lumber, plywood & millwork; lumber: rough, dressed & finished

(G-13433)
NORTHWEST HOME DESIGNING INC
6720 Regents Blvd Ste 104 (98466-5400)
PHONE.................................253 584-6309
Loree Lord, *President*
Bob Mickey, *Vice Pres*
April Lordwood, *Treasurer*
Michael Wittig, *Marketing Staff*
April Lordwitig, *Manager*
EMP: 8
SQ FT: 10,000
SALES (est): 754.6K **Privately Held**
WEB: www.nhdinc.com
SIC: 8712 2731 House designer; books: publishing only

(G-13434)
NORTHWEST IMPRESSIONS
5407 South Tacoma Way (98409-4312)
PHONE.................................253 474-1119
Lawrence G Childers, *Owner*
Tanya Asuria, *Manager*
EMP: 3
SQ FT: 2,400
SALES (est): 252.9K **Privately Held**
WEB: www.nwimpressions.com
SIC: 2752 Commercial printing, offset

(G-13435)
NORTHWEST SPORTS PRODUCTS
3702 S Fife St Ste K384 (98409-7360)
PHONE.................................253 576-5958
Mark Langford, *Owner*
EMP: 2
SALES (est): 128.4K **Privately Held**
SIC: 3949 Sporting & athletic goods

(G-13436)
NOVUS COMPOSITES INCORPORATED
Also Called: NC Cyacks
10801 A St S Ste O (98444-5730)
PHONE.................................253 476-8582
Douglas E Searles, *President*
Greg Swenson, *Vice Pres*
Mark Potocki, *Admin Sec*
EMP: 5
SALES (est): 571.3K **Privately Held**
WEB: www.nckayak.com
SIC: 3812 3732 Navigational systems & instruments; fishing boats: lobster, crab, oyster, etc.: small

(G-13437)
NU ELEMENT INC
1201 Pacific Ave Ste 600 (98402-4384)
PHONE.................................206 356-4525
Karen Fleckner, *President*
EMP: 7
SALES (est): 442.9K **Privately Held**
WEB: www.nuelement.com
SIC: 7389 8731 2899 Personal service agents, brokers & bureaus; commercial physical research; fire extinguisher charges; fire retardant chemicals

(G-13438)
NW LOGGING COMPANY
2522 N Proctor St (98406-5338)
PHONE.................................360 226-2691
EMP: 2 EST: 2016
SALES (est): 98K **Privately Held**
SIC: 2411 Logging

(G-13439)
OATRIDGE-EVERGREEN 8A2 JV LLC
2111 S 90th St (98444-1824)
PHONE.................................253 627-3794
John Forslin, *Partner*
Cy Oatridge, *Partner*
EMP: 4 EST: 2017
SALES (est): 95.2K **Privately Held**
SIC: 7382 7373 8741 3669 Security systems services; computer integrated systems design; management services; emergency alarms; guard services

(G-13440)
OBITUARIES AND LEGALS
1950 S State St (98405-2817)
PHONE.................................253 597-8605
Terri Armour, *Principal*
EMP: 2
SALES (est): 87.4K **Privately Held**
SIC: 2711 Newspapers, publishing & printing

(G-13441)
OLD SOLDIER DISTILLERY
309 Puyallup Ave Unit B1 (98421-1314)
PHONE.................................253 223-4306
EMP: 3 EST: 2017
SALES (est): 142.1K **Privately Held**
SIC: 2085 Distilled & blended liquors

(G-13442)
OLYMPIC CASCADE PUBLISHING
Also Called: McClatchy
1950 S State St (98405-2817)
P.O. Box 11000 (98411-0008)
PHONE.................................253 274-7344
EMP: 28
SALES (corp-wide): 807.2MM **Publicly Held**
SIC: 2711 Newspapers, publishing & printing
HQ: Olympic Cascade Publishing Inc
    2100 Q St
    Sacramento CA 95816
    916 321-1000

▲ = Import ▼ = Export
◆ = Import/Export

GEOGRAPHIC SECTION

Tacoma - Pierce County (G-13472)

(G-13443)
OLYMPIC MACHINE & WELDING INC
3115 N 14th St (98406-6413)
PHONE.....................................253 627-8571
Marit Christenson, *President*
Marit Christenson, *President*
Tage C Christnsen, *Vice Pres*
EMP: 9
SALES (est): 1MM **Privately Held**
SIC: 3599 Machine & other job shop work

(G-13444)
OPTIC LED GROW LIGHTS LLC
17923 52nd Ave E Unit A (98446-3705)
PHONE.....................................971 704-2912
Gregory Weston, *Principal*
EMP: 2
SALES (est): 74.9K **Privately Held**
SIC: 3674 Light emitting diodes

(G-13445)
ORBITER INC
13500 Pacific Ave S (98444-4742)
PHONE.....................................253 627-5588
Greg Stewart, *Principal*
EMP: 1
SALES: 1MM **Privately Held**
SIC: 3825 Oscillators, audio & radio frequency (instrument types)

(G-13446)
OREGON GLOVE COMPANY (PA)
Also Called: Western Glove Co
1538 N Cascade Ave (98406-1115)
P.O. Box 558, Lakeview MI (48850-0558)
PHONE.....................................253 475-6733
Shirley Wood, *President*
C Thomas Wekell, *Corp Secy*
Shirley M Wekell, *Vice Pres*
▲ **EMP:** 4 **EST:** 1965
SALES (est): 1.1MM **Privately Held**
WEB: www.oregonglove.com
SIC: 3199 3151 Aprons: welders', blacksmiths', etc.: leather; leather gloves & mittens

(G-13447)
P S NORTHWEST RADIOGRAPHY
1950 S Cedar St Ste B (98405-2315)
PHONE.....................................253 627-3988
Jan Bell, *Manager*
EMP: 2
SALES (corp-wide): 816K **Privately Held**
WEB: www.nwrad.com
SIC: 3844 8011 Radiographic X-ray apparatus & tubes; offices & clinics of medical doctors
PA: P S Northwest Radiography
1515 116th Ave Ne Ste 108
Bellevue WA 98004
425 453-3440

(G-13448)
P&JS WAFFLE DELIGHT
2117 155th St E (98445-5926)
PHONE.....................................510 335-5393
Paige Dimmore, *Owner*
James Meeks, *Co-Owner*
EMP: 2
SALES (est): 109.9K **Privately Held**
SIC: 2038 Waffles, frozen

(G-13449)
PABCO BUILDING PRODUCTS LLC
Also Called: Pabco Roofing Products
1476 Thorne Rd (98421-3204)
PHONE.....................................253 284-1200
Philip Kohl, *VP Sales*
Donna Mims, *Sales Mgr*
Tim Spencer, *Sales Mgr*
Russell Miller, *Sales Staff*
John Corbet, *Branch Mgr*
EMP: 135
SALES (corp-wide): 1.6B **Privately Held**
SIC: 2679 2952 Paper products, converted; asphalt felts & coatings
HQ: Pabco Building Products, Llc
10600 White Rock Rd # 100
Rancho Cordova CA 95670
510 792-1577

(G-13450)
PACIFIC CONTAINER CORP
4101 S 56th St (98409-2698)
PHONE.....................................206 682-1778
John D Kiehl, *President*
Brett Kiehl, *Vice Pres*
Bryan Kiehl, *Opers Staff*
Lorraine Peterson, *Treasurer*
Roger Hanke, *Sales Dir*
EMP: 55
SQ FT: 50,000
SALES (est): 12.6MM **Privately Held**
WEB: www.pccbox.com
SIC: 2653 Boxes, corrugated: made from purchased materials

(G-13451)
PACIFIC INTEGRATED HDLG INC (PA)
10215 Portland Ave E A (98445-3919)
PHONE.....................................253 535-5888
David R Sidor, *CEO*
Michael R Sidor, *President*
Deanna Peterson, *Vice Pres*
◆ **EMP:** 36
SQ FT: 28,000
SALES: 13.9MM **Privately Held**
WEB: www.pacificintegrated.com
SIC: 2542 5084 Office & store showcases & display fixtures; shelving, office & store: except wood; materials handling machinery

(G-13452)
PACIFIC MOUNT INC
4723 S Washington St (98409-2824)
PHONE.....................................253 473-2580
Jane M Richards, *President*
Ed Richards, *CFO*
▲ **EMP:** 12
SQ FT: 5,000
SALES (est): 1.4MM **Privately Held**
WEB: www.pacificmount.com
SIC: 2679 Paperboard products, converted

(G-13453)
PACIFIC PAPER PRODUCTS INC (PA)
4301 S Pine St Ste 92 (98409-7259)
P.O. Box 2055 (98401-2055)
PHONE.....................................253 272-9195
Roger W Molt, *CEO*
Roger A Molt, *President*
▲ **EMP:** 90
SALES (est): 25.2MM **Privately Held**
SIC: 2679 Paper products, converted

(G-13454)
PACIFIC SPORTSWEAR INC
Also Called: Sweats Unlimited
3827 100th St Sw (98499-4420)
PHONE.....................................253 582-4444
Jay Gigandet, *President*
James M Chaffeur, *Treasurer*
EMP: 20
SQ FT: 17,000
SALES (est): 2.4MM **Privately Held**
WEB: www.pacificsportswear.com
SIC: 2262 2396 Screen printing: man-made fiber & silk broadwoven fabrics; automotive & apparel trimmings

(G-13455)
PACIFIC SPORTSWEAR LLC
10731 A St S Ste B (98444-6074)
PHONE.....................................253 582-4444
Mark Winward, *CEO*
Jay Gigandet, *Principal*
▲ **EMP:** 45
SALES (est): 223.6K **Privately Held**
SIC: 5699 2329 2339 Sports apparel; men's & boys' sportswear & athletic clothing; women's & misses' athletic clothing & sportswear

(G-13456)
PAGE EDITORIAL
1950 S State St (98405-2817)
P.O. Box 11000 (98411-0008)
PHONE.....................................253 597-8634
David Seago, *Manager*
EMP: 3
SALES (est): 104.6K **Privately Held**
SIC: 2711 Newspapers

(G-13457)
PALEO PUSHERS LLC
1509 102nd St S (98444-2912)
PHONE.....................................253 539-3848
EMP: 2 **EST:** 2014
SALES (est): 183.5K **Privately Held**
SIC: 3545 Mfg Machine Tool Accessories

(G-13458)
PAR TACOMA LLC (DH)
3001 Marshall Ave (98421-3116)
PHONE.....................................253 383-1651
Cameron Proudfoot, *President*
Thor Nielsen, *CFO*
EMP: 5 **EST:** 2014
SALES (est): 61.7MM
SALES (corp-wide): 3.4B **Publicly Held**
SIC: 2911 Petroleum refining

(G-13459)
PARTNERS IN EMRGNCY PRPREDNESS
1500 Commerce St (98402-3307)
P.O. Box 755, Seattle (98111-0755)
PHONE.....................................509 335-3530
Aaron Collins, *Principal*
EMP: 2
SALES (est): 34.7K **Privately Held**
SIC: 8699 7372 Charitable organization; application computer software

(G-13460)
PATRICIA AVERY (PA)
Also Called: Royal Body Treats
10912 4th Avenue Ct E A103 (98445-1800)
PHONE.....................................206 602-0017
Patricia Avery, *Owner*
EMP: 2
SALES (est): 93.2K **Privately Held**
SIC: 2844 7389 Perfumes & colognes; perfumes, natural or synthetic; suntan lotions & oils; bath salts;

(G-13461)
PAULS CUSTOM CABINETS
2730 90th St E (98445-5846)
PHONE.....................................253 536-6330
Paul Stoehr, *Partner*
Susan Stoehr, *Mng Member*
EMP: 2
SALES (est): 150K **Privately Held**
SIC: 2434 Wood kitchen cabinets

(G-13462)
PENINSULA OPTICAL LAB INC
1901 S Union Ave B1001 (98405-1702)
PHONE.....................................800 540-4640
Blayne Rollman, *President*
Patricia Rollman, *Corp Secy*
EMP: 20
SQ FT: 1,800
SALES (est): 2.8MM
SALES (corp-wide): 1.4MM **Privately Held**
WEB: www.peninsula-optical.com
SIC: 3851 Frames, lenses & parts, eyeglass & spectacle
HQ: Essilor Laboratories Of America, Inc.
13515 N Stemmons Fwy
Dallas TX 75234
972 241-4141

(G-13463)
PEPSICO
2309 Milwaukee Way (98421-2709)
PHONE.....................................253 778-7107
EMP: 5
SALES (est): 390K **Privately Held**
SIC: 2086 Carbonated soft drinks, bottled & canned

(G-13464)
PERFORMANCE RADIATOR PCF LLC
2667 South Tacoma Way (98409-7525)
PHONE.....................................253 472-0586
Tracey Kiekennep, *Manager*
EMP: 26 **Privately Held**
WEB: www.usaradiator.com
SIC: 5013 3714 7539 Radiators; radiators & radiator shells & cores, motor vehicle; automotive repair shops
HQ: Performance Radiator Pacific, L.L.C.
2447 6th Ave S
Seattle WA 98134
800 273-0571

(G-13465)
PERYL PROFESSIONAL TOUCH
Also Called: Canon Chropractic
5216 72nd St E (98443-2722)
P.O. Box 146, Puyallup (98371-0015)
PHONE.....................................253 537-8181
Terry Richardson, *Owner*
EMP: 4
SALES (est): 78.6K **Privately Held**
SIC: 8049 3999 Offices of health practitioner; massage machines, electric: barber & beauty shops

(G-13466)
PLUMB SIGNS INC
909 S 28th St (98409-8106)
PHONE.....................................253 474-6702
Robert C Marston, *President*
EMP: 30
SQ FT: 12,000
SALES (est): 4.3MM **Privately Held**
WEB: www.plumbsigns.com
SIC: 1731 3993 Electrical work; electric signs

(G-13467)
PM INDUSTRIES
2318 Martin Luther King (98405-3840)
PHONE.....................................253 666-8977
EMP: 2 **EST:** 2012
SALES (est): 95K **Privately Held**
SIC: 3999 Manufacturing industries

(G-13468)
PMW CAPITAL INC (HQ)
2102 Eells St (98421-4500)
P.O. Box 1115 (98401-1115)
PHONE.....................................253 272-5119
EMP: 8 **EST:** 2007
SALES (est): 37.2MM
SALES (corp-wide): 195.8MM **Privately Held**
SIC: 3728 3724 Aircraft parts & equipment; aircraft engines & engine parts
PA: Cadence Aerospace, Llc
3150 E Miraloma Ave
Anaheim CA 92806
949 877-3630

(G-13469)
POISON APPLE TACOMA
902 S 7th St Apt 9 (98405-4509)
PHONE.....................................253 304-1874
EMP: 2 **EST:** 2014
SALES (est): 141.2K **Privately Held**
SIC: 3571 Mfg Electronic Computers

(G-13470)
POLYTECH COIL WINDING
4301 N 9th St (98406-4025)
PHONE.....................................253 324-3044
Desmond Policani, *Owner*
EMP: 4
SALES: 120K **Privately Held**
SIC: 3677 Electronic coils, transformers & other inductors

(G-13471)
PORTLAND PRESS INC
2101 Jefferson Ave (98402-1519)
P.O. Box 70856, Seattle (98127-1305)
PHONE.....................................253 274-8883
Dale Chihuly, *President*
▲ **EMP:** 12
SALES (est): 4.9MM
SALES (corp-wide): 19.5MM **Privately Held**
WEB: www.portlandpress.net
SIC: 2721 2731 Periodicals; book publishing
PA: Chihuly, Inc
1111 Nw 50th St
Seattle WA 98107
206 781-8707

(G-13472)
POST INDUS STRESS & DESIGN
Also Called: Post-Industrial Press
5211 S Washington St C (98409-2700)
P.O. Box 7375 (98417-0375)
PHONE.....................................253 572-9782

Tacoma - Pierce County (G-13473)

Skip Jensen, *President*
Marie Jensen, *Treasurer*
EMP: 10
SQ FT: 9,300
SALES (est): 970K **Privately Held**
SIC: 2759 2396 2395 Screen printing; automotive & apparel trimmings; pleating & stitching

(G-13473)
PRAXAIR DISTRIBUTION INC
480 E 19th St (98421-1501)
P.O. Box 3617, Seattle (98124-3617)
PHONE 253 620-1620
Randy Michael, *General Mgr*
Mark Lulich, *Foreman/Supr*
Ed Sijer, *Branch Mgr*
EMP: 40 **Privately Held**
SIC: 2813 5084 5999 Carbon dioxide; dry ice, carbon dioxide (solid); oxygen, compressed or liquefied; welding machinery & equipment; welding supplies
HQ: Praxair Distribution, Inc.
10 Riverview Dr
Danbury CT 06810
203 837-2000

(G-13474)
PRECISION MACHINE WORKS INC
2102 Eells St (98421-4500)
P.O. Box 1115 (98401-1115)
PHONE 253 272-5119
David Baublits, *CEO*
Ken Kelley, *President*
Richard Wood, *Chairman*
Craig McHugh, *Vice Pres*
Bill Helenberg, *CFO*
▲ **EMP:** 165
SQ FT: 80,000
SALES (est): 37.2MM
SALES (corp-wide): 195.8MM **Privately Held**
WEB: www.pmwinc.com
SIC: 3728 3724 Aircraft parts & equipment; aircraft engines & engine parts
HQ: Pmw Capital, Inc.
2102 Eells St
Tacoma WA 98421
253 272-5119

(G-13475)
PRECISION PATTERN
2620 E G St (98421-1907)
PHONE 253 572-4333
Alex Munroe, *Director*
EMP: 2
SALES (est): 85.2K **Privately Held**
SIC: 3543 Industrial patterns

(G-13476)
PREFERRED ORTHOTIC & PROSTHETC (PA)
Also Called: Evergreen Prsthetics Orthotics
1901 S Cedar St Ste 202 (98405-2303)
PHONE 253 572-1282
Timothy O'Neill, *President*
Dee Dee Davis, *Office Mgr*
EMP: 6
SALES: 2MM **Privately Held**
SIC: 3842 Limbs, artificial; orthopedic appliances

(G-13477)
PREMIER MEMORIAL LLC (PA)
Also Called: Centralia Monument
2309 South Tacoma Way (98409-7520)
P.O. Box 112553 (98411-2553)
PHONE 253 472-0369
Effie Stilnovich, *Vice Pres*
Robb Stilnovich,
▲ **EMP:** 24
SQ FT: 6,500
SALES (est): 4.2MM **Privately Held**
WEB: www.premiermemorial.com
SIC: 3272 3281 Monuments & grave markers, except terrazo; cut stone & stone products

(G-13478)
PRINT NW LLC
9914 32nd Ave S (98499-9265)
PHONE 253 284-2300
Steve Andrews, *Plant Mgr*
Lois Heilman, *Opers Staff*
Heather Prince, *Accounting Mgr*

Jenilee Antone, *VP Sales*
Scott Swift, *Accounts Mgr*
EMP: 75 **EST:** 1970
SQ FT: 43,000
SALES (est): 19.7MM **Privately Held**
SIC: 2752 2759 7334 Commercial printing, offset; commercial printing; posters, including billboards: printing; photocopying & duplicating services

(G-13479)
PROFESSIONAL SLEEP SERVICES
Also Called: Blue Mountain Medical
1818 S Union Ave Ste 2b (98405-1953)
PHONE 253 759-2700
Al Tall, *Branch Mgr*
EMP: 2
SALES (corp-wide): 392.2K **Privately Held**
SIC: 2399 5712 Sleeping bags; beds & accessories
PA: Professional Sleep Services, Inc
7320 216th St Sw Ste 30
Edmonds WA 98026
425 673-3773

(G-13480)
PRS GROUP INC
3003 Taylor Way (98421-4309)
PHONE 206 255-7509
Tom Smith, *Vice Pres*
Jay Johnson, *Manager*
EMP: 10
SQ FT: 500
SALES: 3MM **Privately Held**
SIC: 2992 Lubricating oils & greases

(G-13481)
PT DEFIANCE FOOD MART
Also Called: Forge Jackpot
4601 N Pearl St (98407-2925)
PHONE 253 761-5084
Mark Friesn, *Owner*
EMP: 10 **EST:** 2001
SALES (est): 453.4K **Privately Held**
SIC: 1321 Natural gasoline production

(G-13482)
PUGET SOUND RECYCLING
222 107th St S (98444-6010)
PHONE 253 536-2260
Don Bullard, *Owner*
EMP: 4
SQ FT: 3,922
SALES (est): 410K **Privately Held**
WEB: www.pugetsoundplastics.net
SIC: 3559 Recycling machinery

(G-13483)
PW METAL RECOVERY LLC
3522 112th St E (98446-3502)
PHONE 253 537-6301
EMP: 3
SALES (est): 151.9K **Privately Held**
SIC: 3341 Recovery & refining of nonferrous metals

(G-13484)
QUICKPRINT CENTERS LLC
Also Called: Quick Print
11319 Pacific Ave S (98444-5527)
P.O. Box 44457 (98448-0457)
PHONE 253 531-3105
Yvonne Roberts,
EMP: 7
SALES (est): 399.4K **Privately Held**
SIC: 2752 Commercial printing, offset

(G-13485)
QUICKTIN INCORPORATED
2515 Holgate St (98402-1202)
PHONE 253 779-8885
Donna G Sorteberg, *President*
Derrick Hiensburg, *Principal*
EMP: 10
SALES (est): 1.4MM **Privately Held**
SIC: 3444 Sheet metalwork

(G-13486)
QUIKRETE COMPANIES LLC
1420 Port Of Tacoma Rd (98421-3704)
PHONE 253 396-9996
Byron Ehmann, *Plant Mgr*
EMP: 32 **Privately Held**
WEB: www.quikrete.com

SIC: 3272 Dry mixture concrete
HQ: The Quikrete Companies Llc
5 Concourse Pkwy Ste 1900
Atlanta GA 30328
404 634-9100

(G-13487)
R G ROLLIN CO
2702 A St (98402-2803)
PHONE 253 274-0882
Harry Fawcett, *President*
Brett Fawcett, *Manager*
EMP: 4
SALES (est): 564.6K **Privately Held**
WEB: www.rgrsolo.com
SIC: 3625 3429 Marine & navy auxiliary controls; manufactured hardware (general)

(G-13488)
RAIL FX LLC
1002 E F St (98421-1806)
P.O. Box 220, Gig Harbor (98335-0220)
PHONE 206 453-1123
John Moss,
EMP: 2
SALES (est): 88.9K
SALES (corp-wide): 1.5B **Privately Held**
SIC: 3446 2431 Railings, prefabricated metal; stair railings, wood
HQ: Nwi Enterprises, Inc.
7733 Forsyth Blvd Fl 23
Saint Louis MO 63105
314 727-5550

(G-13489)
RAINIER PLYWOOD COMPANY
Also Called: Rainier Richlite
624 E 15th St (98421-1696)
PHONE 253 383-5533
Rodney Baum, *President*
Ted Baum, *Vice Pres*
Patricia Gunning, *Vice Pres*
Richard O'Day, *Vice Pres*
Shawn O'Day, *Vice Pres*
▼ **EMP:** 23
SQ FT: 45,000
SALES (est): 7.9MM **Privately Held**
WEB: www.richlite.com
SIC: 2672 Coated & laminated paper

(G-13490)
RAINIER WOODWORKING CO
3865 Center St (98409-3163)
PHONE 253 272-5210
Fax: 253 848-8796
EMP: 42
SALES (est): 4.7MM **Privately Held**
SIC: 2431 Mfg Millwork

(G-13491)
RAINIER WOODWORKING CO
2615 S 80th St (98409-8401)
PHONE 253 272-5210
Scott Reader, *President*
Dennis Engelhart, *Principal*
EMP: 17
SQ FT: 8,000
SALES (est): 2MM **Privately Held**
WEB: www.rainierwoodworking.com
SIC: 5712 1751 2499 Cabinet work, custom; cabinet & finish carpentry; laundry products, wood

(G-13492)
REAL LOVE CUPCAKES
16023 19th Avenue Ct E (98445-3359)
PHONE 206 849-9688
Ashley Spillane, *Principal*
EMP: 4 **EST:** 2014
SALES (est): 141.8K **Privately Held**
SIC: 2051 Bread, cake & related products

(G-13493)
REDQUARRY LLC
708 Broadway Ste 300a (98402-3761)
P.O. Box 1714 (98401-1714)
PHONE 206 981-5300
Patrick Adrian, *CEO*
Chris Tinsley, *Mng Member*
EMP: 10 **EST:** 2014
SALES (est): 352K **Privately Held**
SIC: 7372 Business oriented computer software

(G-13494)
RENTIEL PRECISION LASER CUTNG
2307 58th Ave Ne (98422-3410)
PHONE 253 297-2823
Stephen Leitner, *Principal*
Steve Leitner,
EMP: 8 **EST:** 2005
SQ FT: 5,000
SALES (est): 1MM **Privately Held**
SIC: 3699 3724 Laser welding, drilling & cutting equipment; aircraft engines & engine parts; exhaust systems, aircraft

(G-13495)
REVALESIO CORPORATION
1202 E D St Ste 101 (98421-1700)
PHONE 253 922-2600
Greg Archambeau, *President*
Mark Huang, *Vice Pres*
EMP: 21
SQ FT: 5,400
SALES (est): 2.5MM **Privately Held**
SIC: 3561 Industrial pumps & parts

(G-13496)
REVCHEM COMPOSITES INC
1132 Thorne Rd (98421-3202)
P.O. Box 333, Bloomington CA (92316-0333)
PHONE 253 305-0303
Marvin Fleck, *Manager*
EMP: 5
SALES (corp-wide): 30.7MM **Privately Held**
WEB: www.revchem.com
SIC: 5033 2221 Fiberglass building materials; fiberglass fabrics
PA: Revchem Composites, Inc.
2720 S Willow Ave B
Bloomington CA 92316
909 877-8477

(G-13497)
REVERSE IMAGE TECHNOLOGIES LLC
3310 View Point Cir Ne (98422-4519)
PHONE 253 219-5345
Fred Holt, *CEO*
Thomas Logan, *President*
Michael McIntosh, *COO*
EMP: 3 **EST:** 2014
SALES (est): 68.4K **Privately Held**
SIC: 7372 Application computer software

(G-13498)
REYES COCA-COLA BOTTLING LLC
2115 116th St S Ste 101 (98444-1421)
PHONE 253 503-4341
EMP: 150
SALES (corp-wide): 713.8MM **Privately Held**
SIC: 2086 Bottled & canned soft drinks
PA: Reyes Coca-Cola Bottling, L.L.C.
3 Park Plz Ste 600
Irvine CA 92614
213 744-8616

(G-13499)
RICHARDS PACKAGING INC
9403 43rd Avenue Ct Sw # 8 (98499-5968)
P.O. Box 11249, Portland OR (97211-0249)
PHONE 253 582-1096
Terry Edwards, *General Mgr*
EMP: 40
SALES (corp-wide): 241.1MM **Privately Held**
WEB: www.richardspackaging.com
SIC: 3085 Plastics bottles
HQ: Richards Packaging, Inc.
2321 Ne Argyle St Ste D
Portland OR 97211
503 290-0000

(G-13500)
ROBERT NICKEL
2207 84th St E (98445-5609)
PHONE 239 565-0450
Robert Nickel, *Principal*
EMP: 3 **EST:** 2012
SALES (est): 220.4K **Privately Held**
SIC: 3356 Nickel

GEOGRAPHIC SECTION

Tacoma - Pierce County (G-13531)

(G-13501)
ROBERTA LOWES
11922 A St S (98444-5141)
PHONE 253 572-1859
Roberta Lowes, *Owner*
EMP: 4
SALES (est): 327.3K **Privately Held**
SIC: 3663 Studio equipment, radio & television broadcasting

(G-13502)
ROGERS TERMINAL AND SHIPPING
550 Dock St (98402-4622)
PHONE 253 572-0146
Arthur Hayes, *Principal*
EMP: 10 **EST:** 2001
SALES (est): 650K **Privately Held**
SIC: 3625 Controls for adjustable speed drives

(G-13503)
RUSSELLS CUSTOM CABINETS INC
5640 S Durango St Ste A (98409-2601)
PHONE 253 473-7883
Steve Russell, *President*
EMP: 9
SQ FT: 9,500
SALES (est): 971.3K **Privately Held**
SIC: 2434 Wood kitchen cabinets

(G-13504)
S & S METAL FABRICATION INC
1551 South Tacoma Way (98409-7916)
PHONE 253 472-4461
Harold Schulz, *President*
Mike Wire, *Vice Pres*
EMP: 19
SQ FT: 15,000
SALES (est): 3.9MM **Privately Held**
WEB: www.schneidersimpson.com
SIC: 3444 Sheet metalwork

(G-13505)
S C JR LLC
12415 40th Ave E (98446-3229)
PHONE 253 539-1097
Thomas Young, *Principal*
EMP: 2
SALES (est): 140.9K **Privately Held**
SIC: 3429 Locks or lock sets

(G-13506)
SAFS INC
629 S Trafton St Apt 2 (98405-3078)
PHONE 253 301-0615
Steven Randall, *President*
◆ **EMP:** 3
SALES (est): 1.6MM **Privately Held**
SIC: 5199 5091 3499 5046 Variety store merchandise; sporting & recreation goods; novelties & specialties, metal; commercial equipment

(G-13507)
SCHILLING GRAPHICS
2340 E 11th St (98421-3303)
PHONE 253 572-8171
Randy Hayes, *President*
EMP: 5
SALES (est): 500K **Privately Held**
WEB: www.seri-prep.com
SIC: 3559 2791 Screening equipment, electric; typesetting

(G-13508)
SCHNITZER STEEL INTERNATIONAL (HQ)
Also Called: M M I International
1902 Marine View Dr (98422-4108)
PHONE 253 572-4000
Si Wooh, *President*
Hy Gim, *Principal*
◆ **EMP:** 4
SALES (est): 23.7MM
SALES (corp-wide): 2.3B **Publicly Held**
SIC: 5093 3341 Ferrous metal scrap & waste; secondary nonferrous metals
PA: Schnitzer Steel Industries, Inc.
299 Sw Clay St Ste 350
Portland OR 97201
503 224-9900

(G-13509)
SCRIBBLY TEES
3901 Military Rd E (98446-3021)
PHONE 517 285-3648
Allison Rook, *Principal*
EMP: 2 **EST:** 2016
SALES (est): 112.1K **Privately Held**
SIC: 2759 Screen printing

(G-13510)
SEAPORT SOUND TERMINAL LLC
4130 E 11th St (98421-4203)
PHONE 253 272-9348
▼ **EMP:** 23
SQ FT: 6,000
SALES (est): 7.9MM
SALES (corp-wide): 1.5B **Privately Held**
WEB: www.soundrefining.com
SIC: 2911 Asphalt or asphaltic materials, made in refineries
PA: Arclight Energy Partners Fund Vi, L.P.
200 Clarendon St Fl 55
Boston MA 02116
617 531-6300

(G-13511)
SEVIERLY GOOD GLUTEN FREE LLC
1401 S Sprague Ave (98405-2967)
PHONE 253 759-5288
Marc Sevier, *Owner*
Maria Sevier, *Owner*
EMP: 2 **EST:** 2009
SALES (est): 125K **Privately Held**
SIC: 2099 Food preparations

(G-13512)
SHEPP ENTERPRISES LLC
Also Called: Uptop Imaging
2602 Westridge Ave W E303 (98466-1881)
PHONE 206 697-0327
Bradley Shepherd, *Principal*
EMP: 2
SALES (est): 146.7K **Privately Held**
SIC: 5731 7389 1382 7311 Consumer electronic equipment; pipeline & power line inspection service; safety inspection service; oil & gas exploration services; advertising agencies

(G-13513)
SIGN-A-RAMA
7610 South Tacoma Way B (98409-3801)
PHONE 253 474-1991
William Jackson, *Owner*
Linda Jackson, *Co-Owner*
EMP: 5 **EST:** 2010
SALES (est): 230K **Privately Held**
SIC: 3993 1799 Signs & advertising specialties; sign installation & maintenance

(G-13514)
SIMPSON TACOMA KRAFT CO LLC
801 E Portland Ave (98421-3098)
PHONE 253 779-6444
EMP: 6
SALES (corp-wide): 14.8B **Publicly Held**
SIC: 2631 Paperboard Mill
HQ: Simpson Tacoma Kraft Company Llc
901 E 11th St
Tacoma WA 98421
253 596-0173

(G-13515)
SMAD WORLD LLC
15917 12th Avenue Ct E (98445-2374)
PHONE 253 536-5460
Michael Lusk,
Robert Martin,
EMP: 2
SALES (est): 96K **Privately Held**
SIC: 3944 7389 Electronic games & toys;

(G-13516)
SOAP ARIA LLC
6529 23rd St Ne (98422-3750)
P.O. Box 94, Nashua NH (03061-0094)
PHONE 206 229-4351
Elizabeth Teichert,
EMP: 2
SALES (est): 159.7K **Privately Held**
SIC: 2844 7389 Toothpastes or powders, dentifrices;

(G-13517)
SONUS-USA INC
1901 S Union Ave B2006 (98405-1802)
PHONE 253 272-3090
Shashi Daniels, *Branch Mgr*
EMP: 3
SALES (corp-wide): 2.6MM **Privately Held**
WEB: www.sonus.com
SIC: 3842 5999 Hearing aids; hearing aids
HQ: Sonus-Usa, Inc.
5000 Cheshire Pkwy N # 1
Plymouth MN 55446

(G-13518)
SOUND GLASS SALES INC (PA)
5501 75th St W (98499-8627)
PHONE 253 473-7477
Warren Willoughby, *President*
Gvido Bars, *Vice Pres*
EMP: 64
SQ FT: 22,000
SALES (est): 17.5MM **Privately Held**
WEB: www.soundglass.com
SIC: 1793 5231 3231 Glass & glazing work; glass; insulating glass: made from purchased glass

(G-13519)
SPANKY BURGER & BREW
601 S Pine St Ste 205 (98405-2793)
PHONE 253 720-3344
EMP: 2
SALES (est): 62.3K **Privately Held**
SIC: 2082 Malt beverages

(G-13520)
SPECIAL EDITION INCORPORATED
Also Called: Dp Printing
315 99th St E (98445-2015)
PHONE 253 537-1836
Leslie White, *President*
Thomas Schumacher, *Corp Secy*
Carol Campbell, *CFO*
EMP: 3
SQ FT: 3,500
SALES (est): 266.2K **Privately Held**
WEB: dpprinting.8k.com
SIC: 2752 Commercial printing, offset

(G-13521)
SPECTRUM HEALTH SYSTEMS INC
1016 S 28th St Fl 3 (98409-8020)
PHONE 253 572-3398
Perry Mowery, *Manager*
EMP: 713
SALES (corp-wide): 74MM **Privately Held**
SIC: 2752 Commercial printing, lithographic
PA: Spectrum Health Systems, Inc.
10 Mechanic St Ste 302
Worcester MA 01608
508 794-5400

(G-13522)
SPEEDY MIX CONCRETE
8836 E D St (98445-2246)
PHONE 253 531-3260
Stanley Clark, *Partner*
EMP: 2
SALES (est): 200K **Privately Held**
SIC: 1771 3273 5211 Concrete work; ready-mixed concrete; lumber & other building materials

(G-13523)
SPIN TEES
6450 Tacoma Mall Blvd (98409-6796)
PHONE 253 301-2047
EMP: 2
SALES (est): 90.7K **Privately Held**
SIC: 2759 Screen printing

(G-13524)
SPINNING HEADS INC
420 E 18th St (98421-1507)
PHONE 253 219-5457
EMP: 4
SALES (est): 50K **Privately Held**
SIC: 2741 Miscellaneous publishing

(G-13525)
STEELER INC
540 E 15th St (98421-1604)
PHONE 253 572-8200
Marcos Cuevaz, *Manager*
EMP: 8
SALES (corp-wide): 41.7MM **Privately Held**
WEB: www.steeler.com
SIC: 3444 5072 Studs & joists, sheet metal; builders' hardware; miscellaneous fasteners; power handtools
PA: Steeler, Inc.
10023 Martin Luther King
Seattle WA 98178
206 725-8500

(G-13526)
STICKERS NORTHWEST
2124 N Steele St (98406-8213)
PHONE 360 731-0255
A Winberg Sandler, *President*
Anthony Winberg Sandler, *President*
EMP: 4
SALES (est): 500K **Privately Held**
SIC: 2759 Screen printing

(G-13527)
STREICH BROS INC
1650 Mar View Dr Ste Main (98422)
PHONE 253 383-1491
Wayne A Streich, *President*
Christine Fisher, *President*
John Streich, *Vice Pres*
Phillip Selmer, *Treasurer*
Wayne Streich, *Treasurer*
EMP: 50
SQ FT: 24,000
SALES (est): 9MM **Privately Held**
WEB: www.streichbros.com
SIC: 3599 7692 1791 Machine shop, jobbing & repair; welding repair; structural steel erection

(G-13528)
STRETCHING CHARTS INC
Also Called: Visual Health Information
11003 A St S (98444-5729)
P.O. Box 44646 (98448-0646)
PHONE 253 536-4922
John E Beaulieu, *President*
Ann C Beaulieu, *Corp Secy*
Tracy Swift, *Mktg Dir*
EMP: 22
SQ FT: 12,000
SALES (est): 2.4MM **Privately Held**
WEB: www.vhikits.com
SIC: 2761 7336 8742 5045 Manifold business forms; chart & graph design; management consulting services; computer software

(G-13529)
SUPER SMOOTHIE
4502 S Steele St Ste 319 (98409-7226)
PHONE 253 671-8883
EMP: 3
SALES (est): 108.1K **Privately Held**
SIC: 2037 Mfg Frozen Fruits/Vegetables

(G-13530)
SUPERLON PLASTICS CO INC
2116 Taylor Way (98421-4398)
PHONE 253 383-4000
Reidar Ilvedson, *President*
Eivor Donahue, *Treasurer*
Sergiy Vasylyshyn, *Manager*
EMP: 15 **EST:** 1969
SQ FT: 41,000
SALES (est): 9.7MM **Privately Held**
WEB: www.superlon.com
SIC: 5074 3084 Pipes & fittings, plastic; plastics pipe

(G-13531)
SUPPLY GUY
10735 A St S Ste A (98444-6072)
P.O. Box 8007, Lacey (98509-8007)
PHONE 253 531-8600
EMP: 7
SALES (est): 310K **Privately Held**
SIC: 1442 Construction Sand/Gravel

Tacoma - Pierce County (G-13532)

(G-13532)
SURE FIT INC
13804 50th Ave E (98446-4157)
PHONE..................253 426-1025
Scott Allan Stephens, *President*
EMP: 6
SALES (est): 887.6K **Privately Held**
SIC: 3339 Precious metals

(G-13533)
SUTTA COMPANY INCORPORATED
2122 Port Of Tacoma Rd (98421-3608)
PHONE..................253 572-2558
Steve Sutta, *Branch Mgr*
EMP: 2
SALES (corp-wide): 15.7MM **Privately Held**
WEB: www.sutta.com
SIC: 2671 Packaging paper & plastics film, coated & laminated
PA: Green Planet 21, Inc.
336 Adeline St
Oakland CA 94607
510 873-8777

(G-13534)
SWIM SCOTT
Also Called: Defense Health Agency
9933 W Hayes St (98431-0001)
P.O. Box 339500 (98433-9500)
PHONE..................253 968-3389
Scott Swim, *Owner*
David Coleman, *Owner*
EMP: 6 **EST:** 2017
SALES (est): 208.1K **Privately Held**
SIC: 3812 Defense systems & equipment

(G-13535)
SWISS ORNAMENTAL IRON
3417 6th Ave (98406-5498)
PHONE..................253 759-6796
Hugh A Mentry, *Owner*
EMP: 4
SQ FT: 2,300
SALES: 400K **Privately Held**
SIC: 3446 1791 Architectural metalwork; structural steel erection

(G-13536)
SYNTHESIS BY JEFFREY BLAND PHD
3414 60th Street Ct E (98443-1574)
PHONE..................253 238-7898
EMP: 2
SALES (est): 121.8K **Privately Held**
SIC: 3825 Mfg Electrical Measuring Instruments

(G-13537)
T D KENNEDY AND ASSOCIATES INC ◊
3404 Pioneer Way E (98443-1604)
PHONE..................253 922-2558
EMP: 2 **EST:** 2019
SALES (est): 62.3K **Privately Held**
SIC: 2096 Potato chips & similar snacks

(G-13538)
T R S INC
Also Called: Tacoma Range Sheet Metal
7717 Portland Ave E (98404-3327)
PHONE..................253 444-1555
Paul Ellingson, *President*
Ken Kessler, *General Mgr*
Rick Ellingson, *Vice Pres*
EMP: 12
SQ FT: 12,000
SALES (est): 790.4K **Privately Held**
SIC: 1761 2542 2541 2434 Sheet metalwork; partitions & fixtures, except wood; wood partitions & fixtures; wood kitchen cabinets; millwork; carpentry work

(G-13539)
T TOWN APPAREL
1934 Market St (98402-3108)
PHONE..................253 471-2960
Brandon Green, *President*
EMP: 5
SALES (est): 439.4K **Privately Held**
SIC: 2759 5621 5949 Screen printing; women's clothing stores; sewing, needlework & piece goods

(G-13540)
TACOMA COMMUNITY BOAT BUILDERS
1120 E D St (98421-1706)
PHONE..................253 720-8227
Paul Birkey, *President*
Peter Hales, *Vice Pres*
Shannon Shea, *Exec Dir*
Wallace Sauby, *Admin Sec*
David Bovee, *Advisor*
EMP: 4 **EST:** 2013
SALES: 72.1K **Privately Held**
SIC: 1521 3069 New construction, single-family houses; life rafts, rubber

(G-13541)
TACOMA FABRICATION LLC
1327 N Fir St (98406-1118)
PHONE..................253 303-1143
Michael Ord, *Principal*
EMP: 2 **EST:** 2015
SALES (est): 72.3K **Privately Held**
SIC: 3499 Fabricated metal products

(G-13542)
TACOMA FIXTURE CO INC
Also Called: Tacoma Cabinet & Fixture Co
1815 E D St (98421-1598)
PHONE..................253 383-5541
Jim Ryan, *President*
Bob Ryan, *Vice Pres*
Earle Fitch, *Plant Mgr*
Erika Lopez, *Purchasing*
EMP: 100 **EST:** 1952
SQ FT: 100,000
SALES (est): 11.1MM **Privately Held**
WEB: www.tacomafixture.com
SIC: 2434 2521 2541 1751 Wood kitchen cabinets; wood office filing cabinets & bookcases; wood partitions & fixtures; carpentry work

(G-13543)
TACOMA GLASS BLOWING STUDIO
114 S 23rd St (98402-2903)
PHONE..................253 383-3499
Mark Sigafoos, *Principal*
Jeannine Sigafoos, *Principal*
EMP: 3
SALES (est): 180K **Privately Held**
SIC: 3229 Pressed & blown glass

(G-13544)
TACOMA LASER CLINIC LLC
112 S 8th St Ste 200 (98402-5294)
PHONE..................253 272-0655
Jessica Valarousky,
EMP: 12
SALES (est): 478.8K **Privately Held**
SIC: 3841 Surgical lasers

(G-13545)
TACOMA NEWS INC
Also Called: News Tribune
1950 S State St (98405-2817)
P.O. Box 11000 (98411-0008)
PHONE..................253 597-8593
Cheryl Dell, *President*
David Zeeck, *Publisher*
EMP: 300
SALES (corp-wide): 807.2MM **Publicly Held**
WEB: www.tacomanews.com
SIC: 2711 Newspapers: publishing only, not printed on site
HQ: Tacoma News Inc
2100 Q St
Sacramento CA 95816
916 321-1846

(G-13546)
TACOMA PRINTING
3711 Center St (98409-3121)
PHONE..................253 470-1454
Don Powell, *Owner*
EMP: 2
SALES (est): 15.5K **Privately Held**
SIC: 2759 Commercial printing

(G-13547)
TACOMA PUBLIC SCHOOLS
Also Called: Printing and Graphics Dept
601 S 8th St (98405-4614)
PHONE..................253 571-1170
Michael McKinlay, *Manager*
EMP: 6
SALES (corp-wide): 495.8MM **Privately Held**
WEB: www.tacoma.k12.wa.us
SIC: 2759 Coupons: printing
PA: Tacoma Public Schools
601 S 8th St
Tacoma WA 98405
253 571-1000

(G-13548)
TACOMA RUBBER STAMP CO (PA)
Also Called: Advance Marking Systems
919 Market St (98402-3604)
P.O. Box 1398 (98401-1398)
PHONE..................253 383-5433
Tim L Lovely, *President*
Jeffrey Lovely, *Vice Pres*
Jackie Clark, *Executive*
EMP: 42
SQ FT: 32,500
SALES (est): 8.4MM **Privately Held**
WEB: www.tacomarubberstamp.com
SIC: 2759 3953 3993 2796 Flexographic printing; marking devices; signs, not made in custom sign painting shops; platemaking services; packaging paper & plastics film, coated & laminated

(G-13549)
TACOMA TENT & AWNING CO INC
Also Called: SIGN LANGUAGE
121 N G St (98403-2299)
PHONE..................253 627-4128
Scott Sutherland, *President*
Mary Hall, *General Mgr*
Mary Kaye Hall, *Controller*
◆ **EMP:** 36
SQ FT: 24,000
SALES: 4MM **Privately Held**
WEB: www.tacomatent.com
SIC: 2394 3993 Tents: made from purchased materials; signs & advertising specialties

(G-13550)
TACOMA TOFU INC
1302 Martin Luther King (98405-3928)
PHONE..................253 627-5085
James Vanwie, *Principal*
▲ **EMP:** 3
SALES (est): 280.2K **Privately Held**
SIC: 2099 Food preparations

(G-13551)
TEAMSTER LOCAL 313
Also Called: Teamsters Union Local 313
220 S 27th St Unit Main (98402-2796)
PHONE..................253 627-0103
J Michael Cserepes, *Corp Secy*
EMP: 7
SALES (est): 769.6K **Privately Held**
SIC: 8631 2411 Labor union; logging

(G-13552)
TECHNICAL TOOLING LLC
1118 E D St (98421-1705)
PHONE..................253 327-1149
Jacob Matthaei, *Mng Member*
EMP: 2
SALES: 500K **Privately Held**
SIC: 2655 Cans, composite: foil-fiber & other: from purchased fiber

(G-13553)
TEODORO FOUNDATION
4110 S Washington St (98409-3009)
PHONE..................253 475-0200
Dave Teodoro, *Principal*
EMP: 3
SALES: 37.5K **Privately Held**
SIC: 3599 Machine shop, jobbing & repair

(G-13554)
TERAS CONSTRUCTION LLC
4516 176th St E (98446-2809)
PHONE..................253 539-2887
Tom Thompson, *Principal*
Christopher Beck,
EMP: 2
SALES (est): 469K **Privately Held**
SIC: 1531 3441 ; fabricated structural metal; dam gates, metal plate; floor posts, adjustable: metal; joists, open web steel: long-span series

(G-13555)
TINPLATE TOYS & TRAINS
743 Broadway (98402-3709)
PHONE..................206 715-8118
EMP: 2
SALES (est): 90.8K **Privately Held**
SIC: 3312 Tinplate

(G-13556)
TOMAR CABINETS
14606 Pacific Ave S Ste B (98444-4602)
PHONE..................253 538-1183
Tom Adams, *Principal*
EMP: 2
SALES (est): 218.4K **Privately Held**
SIC: 2434 Wood kitchen cabinets

(G-13557)
TORAY COMPOSITE MTLS AMER INC (DH)
19002 50th Ave E (98446-3752)
PHONE..................253 846-1777
Moriyuki Onishi, *CEO*
Yasuo Suga, *Ch of Bd*
Greg Clemons, *General Mgr*
Jeff Cross, *General Mgr*
Jeffrey Hawkey, *General Mgr*
◆ **EMP:** 950
SQ FT: 400,000
SALES (est): 228.8MM **Privately Held**
WEB: www.toraycompam.com
SIC: 3624 Carbon & graphite products
HQ: Toray Holding (U.S.A.), Inc.
461 5th Ave Fl 9
New York NY 10017
212 697-8150

(G-13558)
TORCH & REGULATOR REPAIR CO
Also Called: T & R Welding Supplies
2526 Tacoma Ave S (98402-1307)
PHONE..................253 272-0467
Tom Fitzpatrick, *Owner*
EMP: 4
SQ FT: 2,100
SALES (est): 288.8K **Privately Held**
WEB: www.torchandregulator.com
SIC: 7692 Welding repair

(G-13559)
TOTAL FABRICARE LLC
417 99th St E (98445-2017)
PHONE..................206 226-3370
Robert Park,
EMP: 7
SQ FT: 3,492
SALES (est): 460.4K **Privately Held**
SIC: 3582 Pressing machines, commercial laundry & drycleaning

(G-13560)
TOWER INDUSTRIES INC
5721 34th Ave E (98443-1507)
PHONE..................206 760-3022
Gary F Watson, *President*
Joyce Watson, *Vice Pres*
EMP: 10
SQ FT: 15,000
SALES: 945K **Privately Held**
SIC: 2842 Specialty cleaning preparations; polishing preparations & related products; floor waxes; degreasing solvent

(G-13561)
TRACTION CAPITAL PARTNERS INC
2516 Holgate St (98402-1203)
PHONE..................253 922-3090
Jacob Matthaei,
Brian Haynes,
EMP: 4 **EST:** 2016
SALES (est): 243.3K **Privately Held**
SIC: 6726 5047 5084 5999 Investment offices; medical & hospital equipment; machine tools & accessories; medical apparatus & supplies; special dies & tools

GEOGRAPHIC SECTION

Tacoma - Pierce County (G-13591)

(G-13562)
TRIAD COATINGS CORP
14307 7th Ave S (98444-3303)
PHONE..................253 537-4464
Fred L Tobiason, *Principal*
EMP: 2
SALES (est): 99K **Privately Held**
SIC: 3479 Metal coating & allied service

(G-13563)
TRIDENT SEAFOODS CORPORATION
401 E Alexander Ave # 592 (98421-4200)
PHONE..................253 502-5318
McKenzie Morgan, *Purchasing*
Dave Peck, *Purchasing*
Rom Sok, *Purchasing*
Gene Copenspire, *Research*
Mark Schneider, *Branch Mgr*
EMP: 264
SALES (corp-wide): 2.3B **Privately Held**
SIC: 2092 Fresh or frozen packaged fish
PA: Trident Seafoods Corporation
   5303 Shilshole Ave Nw
   Seattle WA 98107
   206 783-3818

(G-13564)
TRIPLE-T DESIGNS INC
4037 S Union Ave (98409-4626)
PHONE..................253 284-9200
Tiffany Spaulding, *President*
▲ EMP: 4
SALES (est): 253.9K **Privately Held**
SIC: 2782 Scrapbooks

(G-13565)
TROGER ENTERPRISES LTD
Also Called: Trogar Awning and Sunscreen Co
1722 Tacoma Ave S (98402-1709)
PHONE..................253 627-8878
Gerhard J Troger, *President*
Christine Troger, *Manager*
EMP: 2
SQ FT: 16,000
SALES: 450K **Privately Held**
SIC: 2394 Awnings, fabric: made from purchased materials

(G-13566)
TUCCI & SONS INC (PA)
4224 Waller Rd E (98443-1099)
PHONE..................253 922-6676
Michael A Tucci, *President*
Jeremy Hopson, *Project Mgr*
Dan Nelson, *Project Mgr*
Matt Pavolka, *Project Mgr*
Timothy F Tucci, *Treasurer*
EMP: 60
SQ FT: 11,000
SALES (est): 38.6MM **Privately Held**
WEB: www.tucciandsons.com
SIC: 1611 2951 General contractor, highway & street construction; asphalt paving mixtures & blocks

(G-13567)
U S SHEET METAL COMPANY INC
1325 South Tacoma Way (98409-8230)
P.O. Box 7969 (98417-0969)
PHONE..................253 272-2444
Fax: 253 572-4911
EMP: 16 EST: 1920
SQ FT: 13,452
SALES: 980K **Privately Held**
SIC: 3444 1761 Mfg Sheet Metalwork Roofing/Siding Contractor

(G-13568)
ULTRA VAN KROME PRDUCTIONS LLC
13125 Spanaway Loop Rd S (98444-1110)
PHONE..................206 859-3459
Georgette Hunter,
Steven Raymays,
EMP: 2
SALES (est): 25K **Privately Held**
SIC: 2741 7389 7922 8999 ; music recording producer; ; agent or manager for entertainers; entertainment promotion; song writers

(G-13569)
UNCORKED CANVAS
711 St Helens Ave Ste 202 (98402-3731)
PHONE..................253 301-1254
Rebekah Slusher, *Principal*
EMP: 2
SALES (est): 106.5K **Privately Held**
SIC: 2211 Canvas

(G-13570)
UNITED IRON WORKS INC
2215 Davis Ct Ne (98422-4535)
PHONE..................206 767-3630
Joseph D'Amico, *President*
Frank Damico, *Purchasing*
Toni Rendoni, *CFO*
EMP: 45
SQ FT: 50,000
SALES (est): 6.5MM **Privately Held**
WEB: www.unitedironwork.com
SIC: 3441 Fabricated structural metal

(G-13571)
UNITED STATES SHEEPSKIN INC
450 Fawcett Ave (98402-2415)
PHONE..................253 627-7114
Herbert Reissner, *President*
Jackie Olson, *General Mgr*
▲ EMP: 15
SQ FT: 12,000
SALES: 1.8MM **Privately Held**
WEB: www.ussheepskin.com
SIC: 5013 2386 5632 2399 Seat covers; garments, sheep-lined; fur apparel; seat covers, automobile

(G-13572)
UNIVERSAL STL FABRICATORS LLC
525 E 15th St (98421-1603)
PHONE..................253 891-4224
Joe Knutson,
EMP: 14
SALES (est): 2.3MM **Privately Held**
SIC: 3441 Fabricated structural metal

(G-13573)
URBAN ACCESSORIES INC
465 E 15th St (98421-1601)
P.O. Box 1171 (98401-1171)
PHONE..................253 572-1112
Karenanne J White, *CEO*
◆ EMP: 49
SQ FT: 20,000
SALES (est): 13.3MM **Privately Held**
WEB: www.urbanaccessories.com
SIC: 3446 Ornamental metalwork

(G-13574)
US OIL & REFINING CO (DH)
3001 Marshall Ave (98421-3116)
P.O. Box 2255 (98401-2255)
PHONE..................253 383-1651
Cameron Proudfoot, *President*
Harvey Van, *Research*
Rupesh S Sansgiri, *Controller*
Steven Ellingsen, *Mktg Coord*
◆ EMP: 160 EST: 1952
SQ FT: 40,000
SALES (est): 61.7MM
SALES (corp-wide): 3.4B **Publicly Held**
WEB: www.usor.com
SIC: 3531 2911 Asphalt plant, including gravel-mix type; gasoline
HQ: Par Tacoma, Llc
   3001 Marshall Ave
   Tacoma WA 98421
   253 383-1651

(G-13575)
VERONE SAUSAGE COMPANY
1456 S Ferdinand Dr (98405-1107)
PHONE..................253 759-7532
Joe Verone, *Owner*
EMP: 2
SALES: 125K **Privately Held**
SIC: 2013 Sausages & other prepared meats

(G-13576)
VIGOR INDUSTRIAL LLC
313 E F St (98421-1821)
PHONE..................253 627-9136
James Marshall, *Branch Mgr*
EMP: 14

SALES (corp-wide): 599.5MM **Privately Held**
SIC: 3731 Shipbuilding & repairing
PA: Vigor Industrial Llc
   5555 N Channel Ave # 71
   Portland OR 97217
   503 247-1777

(G-13577)
VIGOR MARINE LLC
Also Called: Vigor Marine Tacoma
313 E F St (98421-1821)
PHONE..................253 627-9136
EMP: 68
SALES (corp-wide): 599.5MM **Privately Held**
SIC: 3731 Shipbuilding & repairing
HQ: Vigor Marine Llc
   5555 N Channel Ave # 71
   Portland OR 97217
   503 247-1804

(G-13578)
VINO AQUINO TACOMA INC
Also Called: Wine & Labels By Vino Aquino
4417 6th Ave (98406-3501)
PHONE..................253 272-5511
Richard Aquino, *President*
Frank Messina, *Treasurer*
Heather Aquino, *Admin Sec*
EMP: 4 EST: 2001
SALES: 150K **Privately Held**
SIC: 2084 Wines

(G-13579)
VINTAGE ADS
2207 144th St E (98445-3667)
P.O. Box 39713 (98496-3713)
PHONE..................253 278-3297
EMP: 2
SALES (est): 83.9K **Privately Held**
SIC: 2752 Commercial printing, lithographic

(G-13580)
VISIPRINTING
2014 112th St E (98445-3728)
PHONE..................253 565-4713
Ralph Erickson, *Principal*
EMP: 2
SALES (est): 171.8K **Privately Held**
SIC: 2752 Commercial printing, offset

(G-13581)
VISUAL OPTIONS INC
4302 S Washington St C (98409-2910)
PHONE..................253 472-1440
Denneace Bowen, *President*
Bret Bowen, *Treasurer*
EMP: 28
SQ FT: 30,000
SALES (est): 4.5MM **Privately Held**
WEB: www.visualoptions.net
SIC: 2821 Plastics materials & resins

(G-13582)
VITAL FORCE PUBLISHING LLC
5922 16th Street Ct Ne (98422-3475)
PHONE..................253 350-6359
Robert Britten, *Principal*
EMP: 2
SALES (est): 59.2K **Privately Held**
SIC: 2741 Miscellaneous publishing

(G-13583)
VIVASOURCE INC
Also Called: Powder Coating Systems
3131 S Lawrence St (98409-4823)
PHONE..................253 627-3853
Gregg Taylor, *President*
Lynette Bericith, *Office Mgr*
EMP: 20
SQ FT: 18,000
SALES: 800K **Privately Held**
SIC: 3479 Coating of metals & formed products

(G-13584)
VOSE TECHNICAL SYSTEMS INC (PA)
Also Called: Vts
711 Commerce St Ste 12 (98402-4514)
PHONE..................253 272-7273
Deborah Vose, *President*
Gregory A Vose, *COO*
John Wilson, *Exec VP*

Jim Droskinis, *Vice Pres*
Alena Leasure, *Accountant*
▲ EMP: 6
SQ FT: 1,500
SALES (est): 13.9MM **Privately Held**
WEB: www.vtsc.net
SIC: 3721 Autogiros; research & development on aircraft by the manufacturer

(G-13585)
VTS AVIATION LLC
711 Commerce St Ste 12 (98402-4514)
PHONE..................253 272-7273
Greg Vose, *Principal*
Gregory Vose, *COO*
EMP: 3 EST: 2016
SQ FT: 9,000
SALES (est): 148.4K **Privately Held**
SIC: 3728 Roto-blades for helicopters

(G-13586)
WALT RACING LLP
Also Called: Irc
5110 184th St E (98446-3731)
PHONE..................253 847-8221
Walt Austin,
Mike Austin,
EMP: 5
SQ FT: 18,000
SALES: 800K **Privately Held**
WEB: www.waltaustinracing.com
SIC: 3519 Gasoline engines

(G-13587)
WANE FLITCH
701 E 72nd St (98404-1068)
PHONE..................253 414-2783
Jeff Wolff, *Principal*
EMP: 4
SALES (est): 126.9K **Privately Held**
SIC: 2421 Sawdust, shavings & wood chips

(G-13588)
WASHINGTON MSO INC
Also Called: Home Doctor, The
4901 108th St Sw (98499-3724)
P.O. Box 98886, Lakewood (98496-8886)
PHONE..................253 984-7247
Charles Plunkett, *President*
Lena Plunkett, *Vice Pres*
EMP: 18
SQ FT: 8,000
SALES (est): 1.5MM **Privately Held**
SIC: 6321 8011 6311 7372 Accident & health insurance; internal medicine practitioners; life insurance; prepackaged software

(G-13589)
WEB PRESS LLC
701 E D St (98421-1811)
P.O. Box 2274 (98401-2274)
PHONE..................253 620-4747
Tom Loesch, *President*
Rick Guinn, *Opers Mgr*
Gail Sampson, *Sales Staff*
EMP: 50
SALES (est): 3.9MM
SALES (corp-wide): 76.2MM **Privately Held**
SIC: 3555 Printing presses
PA: Globe Machine Manufacturing Company
   701 E D St
   Tacoma WA 98421
   253 383-2584

(G-13590)
WEBGIRL
6406 Fawcett Ave (98408-6223)
PHONE..................253 473-6895
EMP: 2
SALES (est): 86K **Privately Held**
SIC: 3999 Mfg Misc Products

(G-13591)
WELDCO-BEALES MFG CORP
11106 25th Ave E Ste B (98445-5328)
PHONE..................253 383-0180
Doug Schindel, *Ch of Bd*
Wayne Gordon, *Chairman*
Ken Bird, *Vice Pres*
Peter Baumann, *Sales Mgr*
Jim Roche, *Manager*
EMP: 45

Tacoma - Pierce County (G-13592) GEOGRAPHIC SECTION

SQ FT: 40,000
SALES (est): 13.8MM
SALES (corp-wide): 98.3MM **Privately Held**
WEB: www.weldco-beales.com
SIC: 3531 Blades for graders, scrapers, dozers & snow plows; logging equipment
PA: Weldco-Beales Mfg. Alberta Ltd
12155 154 St Nw
Edmonton AB T5V 1
780 454-5244

(G-13592)
WENDY RAWLEY
Also Called: PC Techs & Parts
9918 Portland Ave E (98445-3958)
PHONE...................253 531-6785
Wendy Rawley, *Owner*
EMP: 3
SQ FT: 1,000
SALES (est): 350.4K **Privately Held**
WEB: www.pctechsandparts.com
SIC: 3577 7378 Computer peripheral equipment; computer maintenance & repair

(G-13593)
WESTEC TOOL & PRODUCTIONS INC
6229 S Adams St Ste A (98409-2501)
PHONE...................253 476-3404
Timothy Hopkins, *President*
EMP: 4
SALES (est): 390K **Privately Held**
SIC: 3549 Metalworking machinery

(G-13594)
WESTERN MACHINE WORKS INC
652 E 11th St (98421-2402)
PHONE...................253 627-6538
Andy Nations, *CEO*
James Schmitz, *Vice Pres*
Lauren N Lanter, *CFO*
Michael T Nations, *Admin Sec*
EMP: 15
SQ FT: 14,000
SALES (est): 583K
SALES (corp-wide): 164.7MM **Privately Held**
SIC: 3549 Metalworking machinery
PA: Bearings & Drives, Inc.
607 Lower Poplar St
Macon GA 31201
478 746-7623

(G-13595)
WEYERHAEUSER COMPANY
Also Called: Library
33663 Weyerhaeuser Way S (98477)
PHONE...................253 924-3030
Steven Rogel, *Branch Mgr*
EMP: 300
SALES (corp-wide): 7.4B **Publicly Held**
SIC: 2411 2435 Logging; hardwood veneer & plywood
PA: Weyerhaeuser Company
220 Occidental Ave S
Seattle WA 98104
206 539-3000

(G-13596)
WHATS YOUR SIGN INC
Also Called: Image 360 Tacoma Central
3838 S Warner St (98409-4624)
PHONE...................253 475-7446
Rose Mednick, *President*
Alan Mednick, *Treasurer*
EMP: 8
SQ FT: 4,000
SALES (est): 689.1K **Privately Held**
WEB: www.sbttacoma.com
SIC: 3993 Signs & advertising specialties

(G-13597)
WILSON AIR TECHNOLOGIES INC
5045 Yakima Ave (98408-5727)
PHONE...................253 474-9928
Michael Henrickson, *President*
Michael R Hendrickson, *President*
EMP: 6
SQ FT: 5,000

SALES (est): 610K **Privately Held**
SIC: 1711 3585 Warm air heating & air conditioning contractor; ventilation & duct work contractor; dehumidifiers electric, except portable

(G-13598)
WIMETRICS CORP
711 E 11th St (98421-2403)
PHONE...................253 593-1220
Mike O'Brien, *CEO*
Mike Obrien, *CEO*
EMP: 10
SALES (est): 440.3K **Privately Held**
WEB: www.wimetrics.com
SIC: 7372 Business oriented computer software

(G-13599)
WOODLAND PATTERN INC
5408 S Proctor St (98409-2704)
PHONE...................253 475-3131
Randall Theinert, *President*
Valerie Theinert, *Vice Pres*
EMP: 18
SALES (est): 1.2MM **Privately Held**
SIC: 3543 Industrial patterns

(G-13600)
WOODROCK INC
1515 Dock St Ste 1 (98402-3295)
PHONE...................253 565-6090
Scott Carino, *President*
Douglas Argo, *President*
Anthony Carino, *Exec VP*
Tony Carino, *Exec VP*
EMP: 11
SALES (est): 1.4MM **Privately Held**
SIC: 1389 Oil field services

(G-13601)
WOODWORKING SERVICES
6614 Vickery Ave E (98443-1314)
PHONE...................253 678-7951
Joe Hendershot, *Owner*
EMP: 2 EST: 2013
SALES (est): 178.6K **Privately Held**
SIC: 2431 Millwork

(G-13602)
WORLD TUBE COMPANY
2608 N 15th St (98406-7413)
PHONE...................253 756-6489
Rod Dill, *Principal*
EMP: 2
SALES (est): 155.1K **Privately Held**
SIC: 3671 Vacuum tubes

(G-13603)
X-CEL FEEDS INC
5436 S Washington St (98409-2708)
P.O. Box 9157 (98490-0157)
PHONE...................253 472-5140
John H Wriglesworth, *President*
Robert B Boesch, *Treasurer*
EMP: 25
SQ FT: 20,000
SALES (est): 15MM **Privately Held**
SIC: 5191 2048 Feed; prepared feeds

(G-13604)
YES CABINET & GRAENT
3702 Center St (98409-3122)
PHONE...................253 572-1188
Lin Shufen, *Bd of Directors*
EMP: 4 EST: 2011
SALES (est): 412.4K **Privately Held**
SIC: 2434 Wood kitchen cabinets

(G-13605)
YOUNG ELECTRIC SIGN COMPANY
Also Called: Yesco
7515 Portland Ave E Ste A (98404-3322)
PHONE...................253 722-5753
Clif Mihm, *Branch Mgr*
EMP: 18
SALES (corp-wide): 331.2MM **Privately Held**
SIC: 3993 Electric signs
PA: Young Electric Sign Company Inc
2401 S Foothill Dr
Salt Lake City UT 84109
801 464-4600

(G-13606)
YVONNE ROBERTS
Also Called: Parkland Quick Print
11319 Pacific Ave S (98444-5527)
P.O. Box 44457 (98448-0457)
PHONE...................253 531-3105
Yvonne Roberts, *Owner*
EMP: 7
SQ FT: 3,000
SALES: 660K **Privately Held**
SIC: 2752 7334 Commercial printing, offset; photocopying & duplicating services

(G-13607)
ZIONS RIVER
4602 S 56th St (98409-1705)
PHONE...................253 473-1838
James Sheen, *Pastor*
EMP: 6 EST: 1943
SALES: 475K **Privately Held**
SIC: 8661 7372 Non-denominational church; application computer software

(G-13608)
ZUMAR INDUSTRIES INC (PA)
12015 Steele St S (98444-1300)
P.O. Box 44549 (98448-0549)
PHONE...................253 536-7740
Peter Lemcke, *President*
Jane Bye, *Corp Secy*
Dale Case, *Plant Mgr*
Frank Kroupa, *Project Mgr*
Lee Young, *Finance Dir*
EMP: 63
SQ FT: 33,000
SALES (est): 31.8MM **Privately Held**
WEB: www.zumar.com
SIC: 3993 Signs & advertising specialties

Taholah
Grays Harbor County

(G-13609)
QUINAULT PRIDE SEAFOODS
100 Quinault St (98587)
PHONE...................360 276-4431
Rudy Tsucada, *CEO*
Ellen Heather, *General Mgr*
EMP: 25
SQ FT: 3,600
SALES (est): 2.7MM **Privately Held**
SIC: 2091 5421 5146 2092 Fish, canned & cured; meat & fish markets; fish & seafoods; fresh or frozen packaged fish
PA: Quinault Indian Nation
1214 Aalis Dr
Taholah WA 98587
360 276-0107

Tahuya
Mason County

(G-13610)
G B C ENTERPRISES INC
Also Called: Campbell Enterprises
811 Ne Snowcap Dr (98588-9542)
PHONE...................360 275-3522
Howard T Cherry Jr, *President*
Corie Smock, *Treasurer*
Rene F Cherry, *Admin Sec*
EMP: 8
SALES: 160K **Privately Held**
SIC: 3728 5088 Aircraft assemblies, sub-assemblies & parts; transportation equipment & supplies

Tekoa
Whitman County

(G-13611)
FABRICTN MELTON & PRECISION
223 N Crosby St (99033)
PHONE...................509 284-2620
Clifford Melton, *CEO*
EMP: 2
SALES (est): 231.1K **Privately Held**
SIC: 3499 Metal household articles

Tenino
Thurston County

(G-13612)
ASH LOGGING COMPANY INC
149 N Ritter St (98589)
P.O. Box 757 (98589-0757)
PHONE...................360 264-4367
Judith Logan, *President*
Judy Logan, *Vice Pres*
EMP: 2
SQ FT: 900
SALES (est): 239.4K **Privately Held**
SIC: 2411 Logging camps & contractors

(G-13613)
CASCADIA DYNAMIX LLC
Also Called: Big Foot Extractors
152 Stage St N (98589-9207)
PHONE...................360 584-3044
Thomas Husmann, *Mng Member*
EMP: 1
SQ FT: 4,200
SALES: 3MM **Privately Held**
SIC: 3556 8742 Food products machinery; marketing consulting services

(G-13614)
COUNTER INTUITIVE
13937 Chein Hill Ln Se (98589-9410)
PHONE...................360 264-5150
Todd Wheeler, *Owner*
Chinton Wheeler, *Co-Owner*
EMP: 4
SALES: 300K **Privately Held**
SIC: 2541 Counter & sink tops

(G-13615)
DANIELS WOODWORKS
20148 Tyrell Rd Se (98589-9518)
PHONE...................360 264-7311
EMP: 2
SALES (est): 113.5K **Privately Held**
SIC: 2431 Millwork

(G-13616)
DANZCO INC
1006 143rd Ave Se (98589-9242)
PHONE...................360 264-2141
Kristie Danzer, *President*
Edward Danzer, *CFO*
EMP: 6
SQ FT: 8,000
SALES (est): 700K **Privately Held**
WEB: www.danzcoinc.com
SIC: 3531 Forestry related equipment

(G-13617)
DIVERSIFIED COATINGS LLC
4107 119th Ave Se (98589-9630)
PHONE...................360 264-2099
Eric Blue, *Principal*
EMP: 2
SALES (est): 148.8K **Privately Held**
SIC: 3479 Metal coating & allied service

(G-13618)
ED BOHL
13019 Black Bear Blvd Se (98589-9406)
PHONE...................360 264-5822
Ed Bohl, *Owner*
EMP: 2
SALES (est): 62.3K **Privately Held**
SIC: 2038 Frozen specialties

(G-13619)
JAMES RICHARD SIMPSON ◆
17446 Crowder Rd Se (98589-9366)
PHONE...................509 679-9720
EMP: 2 EST: 2019
SALES (est): 86.7K **Privately Held**
SIC: 2421 Sawmills & planing mills, general

(G-13620)
LANE GIBBONS VINEYARD INC
12035 Gibbons Ln Se (98589-9678)
P.O. Box 7755, Olympia (98507-7755)
PHONE...................360 264-8466
Fred Goldberg, *President*
EMP: 3

SALES (est): 84.7K **Privately Held**
SIC: 0172 2084 Grapes; wines

(G-13621)
M L WOODWORKS
4009 Offut Lake Rd Se (98589-9633)
PHONE...................................360 264-4859
EMP: 2
SALES (est): 198.3K **Privately Held**
SIC: 2431 Mfg Millwork

(G-13622)
ROCKY PRAIRIE ENGRAVING ✪
840 143rd Ave Se (98589-9430)
PHONE...................................360 264-2188
Wayne Ishler, *Principal*
EMP: 2 EST: 2018
SALES (est): 69.9K **Privately Held**
SIC: 3479 Metal coating & allied service

(G-13623)
SANDSTONE DISTILLERY
842 Wright Rd Se (98589-9439)
PHONE...................................360 239-7272
John Boundon, *President*
EMP: 5
SALES (est): 408.5K **Privately Held**
SIC: 2085 Distilled & blended liquors

(G-13624)
SCATTER CREEK WINERY
3442 180th Ave Sw (98589-9762)
P.O. Box 42 (98589-0042)
PHONE...................................360 264-9463
Andrea Keary, *Owner*
Terril Keary, *Co-Owner*
EMP: 2
SALES (est): 54K **Privately Held**
SIC: 2084 Wines

(G-13625)
SYGNET RAIL TECHNOLOGIES LLC
5915 Waldrick Rd Se (98589-9252)
P.O. Box 160, Bend OR (97709-0160)
PHONE...................................360 264-8211
David Swanson, *President*
Eric Munson, *General Mgr*
Ken Michel, *Purch Mgr*
Coby Armstrong, *Manager*
EMP: 7
SALES (est): 1.5MM **Privately Held**
SIC: 3462 Railroad, construction & mining forgings

Thorp
Kittitas County

(G-13626)
ANDERSON MACHINERY INC
2574 Thorp Cemetery Rd (98946-9570)
P.O. Box 190 (98946-0190)
PHONE...................................509 964-2225
John Wheacley Jr, *President*
EMP: 2
SQ FT: 1,892
SALES: 60K **Privately Held**
SIC: 3523 Elevators, farm

(G-13627)
BOGDEN INC
Also Called: Tractorco.com
270 Mission Rd (98946-9577)
PHONE...................................509 964-2008
Mitch Bogden, *CEO*
▲ EMP: 2
SALES (est): 246.2K **Privately Held**
SIC: 3537 Industrial trucks & tractors

(G-13628)
MILL RACE FARM
310 N 2nd St (98946-5902)
PHONE...................................509 964-2473
Adrienne Fields, *Owner*
William Fields, *Co-Owner*
EMP: 2
SALES (est): 74.7K **Privately Held**
SIC: 3999 Soap dispensers

(G-13629)
RECORD PRINTING INC
Also Called: Record Printing Packg & Design
10441 N Thorp Hwy (98946-5903)
P.O. Box 209 (98946-0209)
PHONE...................................509 964-9500
Susan Johnston, *President*
John Karlson, *Vice Pres*
EMP: 13 EST: 1977
SQ FT: 6,000
SALES (est): 2MM **Privately Held**
SIC: 2752 7336 2759 Commercial printing, offset; graphic arts & related design; letterpress printing

Tieton
Yakima County

(G-13630)
FREEDOMWEEDER COMPANY LLC
814 Wisconsin St Ste 444 (98947-9800)
P.O. Box 444 (98947-0444)
PHONE...................................509 673-0014
Johnny Tuttle, *President*
Ed Green, *Manager*
EMP: 4
SQ FT: 400
SALES (est): 264.7K **Privately Held**
SIC: 2879 Pesticides, agricultural or household

(G-13631)
NORMAN LANCASTER BROWN
201 Funkhouser Rd (98947-9663)
PHONE...................................509 678-5980
Norman Brown, *Owner*
Janet Brown, *Principal*
EMP: 2
SALES (est): 91.8K **Privately Held**
SIC: 2426 7389 Carvings, furniture: wood;

Tokeland
Pacific County

(G-13632)
CRABHAWK
3224 Kindred Ave (98590-9733)
PHONE...................................541 921-3593
Bill Paterak, *Principal*
EMP: 2
SALES (est): 111.6K **Privately Held**
SIC: 3949 Fishing equipment

(G-13633)
NELSON CRAB INC
3088 Kindred Ave (98590-9744)
P.O. Box 520 (98590-0520)
PHONE...................................360 267-2911
Kristi Nelson, *President*
Mel Preston, *Corp Secy*
▲ EMP: 30 EST: 1934
SQ FT: 15,000
SALES (est): 3.4MM **Privately Held**
WEB: www.nelsoncrab.com
SIC: 2092 Crab meat, fresh: packaged in nonsealed containers; shrimp, fresh: prepared; fish, fresh: prepared

Toledo
Lewis County

(G-13634)
505 PRINTING
1911 State Route 505 (98591-9634)
PHONE...................................360 864-6510
Betty Mickelsen, *Principal*
EMP: 2
SALES (est): 137.7K **Privately Held**
SIC: 2752 Offset & photolithographic printing

(G-13635)
ALAN GOOD
Also Called: Good Construction Company
265 Rupp Rd (98591-9432)
PHONE...................................360 864-2974
Alan Good, *Owner*
EMP: 15
SALES (est): 1MM **Privately Held**
WEB: www.alangood.com
SIC: 1629 1423 Rock removal; crushed & broken granite

(G-13636)
COMPOSITE AIRCRAFT TECH LLC
148 Skyhawk Dr (98591-8790)
PHONE...................................360 864-6271
Darrell M Peterson, *Manager*
EMP: 2
SALES (est): 251.7K **Privately Held**
SIC: 3721 Aircraft

(G-13637)
DENNIS DAVIS LOGGING CO INC
741 S First St (98591-9421)
PHONE...................................360 864-2548
Dennis Davis, *President*
Vicki Davis, *Corp Secy*
EMP: 10
SQ FT: 1,200
SALES: 1MM **Privately Held**
SIC: 2411 Logging camps & contractors

(G-13638)
FILLA COMPANY LLC
496 Schmit Rd (98591-9506)
PHONE...................................360 864-2531
Roy Filla,
EMP: 3
SALES (est): 168.8K **Privately Held**
SIC: 2411 Logging

(G-13639)
GOOD CRUSHING INC
Also Called: Brown Road Quarry
265 Rupp Rd (98591-9432)
PHONE...................................360 864-2974
Alan Good, *President*
Pamela Good, *Admin Sec*
EMP: 15
SALES (est): 2.4MM **Privately Held**
SIC: 1429 Boulder, crushed & broken-quarrying

(G-13640)
NORTHWEST CONTAINER SVCS INC
104 Smokey Valley Rd (98591)
P.O. Box 427 (98591-0427)
PHONE...................................360 864-2571
David Powell, *President*
Jeff Burns, *Vice Pres*
Heidi Powell, *Treasurer*
EMP: 20
SQ FT: 521,000
SALES (est): 3.6MM **Privately Held**
SIC: 2449 Shipping cases, wood: wirebound

(G-13641)
REICHERT SHAKE & FENCING INC
207 Kangas Rd (98591-9644)
PHONE...................................360 864-6434
Tod Reichert, *President*
Kimberly K Wallace, *Vice Pres*
Sonja R Reichert, *Admin Sec*
EMP: 50
SQ FT: 720
SALES (est): 8.2MM **Privately Held**
SIC: 2499 Fencing, wood

(G-13642)
STANTON
357 Spencer Rd (98591-9217)
P.O. Box 576 (98591-0576)
PHONE...................................360 864-6897
Steve Stan, *Owner*
EMP: 6
SALES (est): 221.1K **Privately Held**
SIC: 2411 Timber, cut at logging camp

(G-13643)
TIGHT LINE INDUSTRIES INC
305 Lone Yew Rd (98591-9427)
PHONE...................................360 751-1621
Jeff Smith, *President*
EMP: 18
SALES (est): 1.2MM **Privately Held**
SIC: 2411 Logging

(G-13644)
TREE MANAGEMENT PLUS INC
Also Called: Tree MGT Plus Seeding Sls
422 Tucker Rd (98591-8651)
PHONE...................................360 978-4305
Tom Fox, *President*
Sherry Fox, *Corp Secy*
John Bull, *Vice Pres*
EMP: 12
SALES: 1.5MM **Privately Held**
SIC: 0851 2411 0783 Forestry services; logging camps & contractors; ornamental shrub & tree services

Tonasket
Okanogan County

(G-13645)
ALPINE SHED LLC
130c Clarkson Mill Rd (98855-9242)
PHONE...................................509 322-0808
Stephen Kresek, *Mng Member*
EMP: 2
SALES (est): 122.5K **Privately Held**
SIC: 3999 Manufacturing industries

(G-13646)
BLUE BIRD INC
215 W 4th St (98855-8600)
P.O. Box 634 (98855-0634)
PHONE...................................509 486-2160
Burt Swallom, *Branch Mgr*
EMP: 14
SALES (corp-wide): 13.6MM **Privately Held**
SIC: 2034 Dehydrated fruits, vegetables, soups
PA: Bird Blue Inc
    10135 Mill Rd
    Peshastin WA 98847
    509 548-1700

(G-13647)
CANVAS CREATIONS
209 Main Rd (98855-9552)
PHONE...................................425 210-5993
Edward Moyer, *Owner*
EMP: 2 EST: 2001
SALES (est): 96.4K **Privately Held**
SIC: 2394 Canvas & related products

(G-13648)
EMPRESS PRINT LLC
4 Ponderosa Dr (98855-9435)
PHONE...................................509 826-5154
Kelsie Kalma, *Principal*
EMP: 2
SALES (est): 83.9K **Privately Held**
SIC: 2752 Commercial printing, lithographic

(G-13649)
HAVILLAH LUMBER
Also Called: Smith Timber
982 Havillah Rd (98855-9404)
P.O. Box 109 (98855-0109)
PHONE...................................509 486-4650
Mikel Smith, *Owner*
Bonnie Smith, *Co-Owner*
EMP: 2
SALES (est): 150K **Privately Held**
SIC: 2411 0851 Logging; fire fighting services, forest

(G-13650)
HAVILLAH SHAKE CO (PA)
521 N Siwash Creek Rd (98855-9461)
PHONE...................................509 486-1467
Phil Baker, *Owner*
EMP: 3
SQ FT: 5,500
SALES (est): 401.6K **Privately Held**
SIC: 2429 2449 5211 2421 Shakes (hand split shingles); shingles, wood: sawed or hand split; wood containers; lumber products; kiln drying of lumber

(G-13651)
INNOVATIVE OUTDOOR PDTS LLC
8 Norway Pine Dr (98855-9433)
P.O. Box 141, Riverside (98849-0141)
PHONE...................................509 826-0219

Tonasket - Okanogan County (G-13652)

Tom Gibbons, *CEO*
EMP: 2 **EST:** 2010
SALES (est): 40K **Privately Held**
SIC: 3949 7389 Fishing tackle, general;

(G-13652)
KRESEK BROTHERS MANUFACTURING
130c Clarkson Mill Rd (98855-9242)
PHONE 509 322-0808
Andrew Kresek, *Partner*
Stephen Kresek, *General Ptnr*
EMP: 2
SALES (est): 153.6K **Privately Held**
SIC: 3999 Barber & beauty shop equipment

(G-13653)
LORZ & LORZ INC
32158 Highway 97 (98855-9245)
PHONE 509 486-2202
Steve Lorz, *President*
EMP: 2
SALES (est): 75K **Privately Held**
SIC: 2411 Logging

(G-13654)
MECHANICAL FUELS TREATMENT LLC
2265b Highway 20 (98855-9624)
PHONE 509 486-1438
Marcia Henneman, *Partner*
Steve Henneman, *General Ptnr*
EMP: 2
SALES: 300K **Privately Held**
SIC: 0291 4212 2411 General farms, primarily animals; lumber (log) trucking, local; logging

(G-13655)
NORTH COUNTRY FOREST RESOURCES
446 Hagood Rd (98855)
PHONE 509 486-2882
Robert Anderson, *Owner*
EMP: 2
SALES (est): 143.5K **Privately Held**
SIC: 2426 0851 Furniture stock & parts, hardwood; timber cruising services

(G-13656)
PACIFIC CALCIUM INCORPORATED
32117 Highway 97 (98855-9245)
PHONE 509 486-1201
Leroy Rothrock, *President*
EMP: 20
SQ FT: 660
SALES (est): 3.9MM **Privately Held**
WEB: www.pirl.com
SIC: 1422 Limestones, ground; chalk, ground or otherwise treated; lime rock, ground

(G-13657)
PINE RIDGE CABINETS
31 Coyote Dr (98855-8912)
PHONE 509 486-0789
Mick Koehn, *Owner*
EMP: 2 **EST:** 2011
SALES (est): 232.8K **Privately Held**
SIC: 2434 Wood kitchen cabinets

(G-13658)
SAWYER & SAWYER INC
8d N State Frontage Rd (98855-9262)
P.O. Box 554 (98855-0554)
PHONE 509 486-1304
Roger Sawyer, *President*
Kristing Sawyer, *Principal*
Kristina Meyers, *Vice Pres*
Ruth Boge, *Treasurer*
EMP: 22
SALES (est): 1.8MM **Privately Held**
SIC: 1422 1429 Crushed & broken limestone; igneous rock, crushed & broken-quarrying

(G-13659)
SPRING CREEK INDUSTRIES INC
35 Sour Dough Creek Rd (98855-9545)
PHONE 509 486-0599
Jim Wheeler, *President*
Shauneen P Wheeler, *Vice Pres*

EMP: 2
SALES (est): 236.1K **Privately Held**
SIC: 3732 Boat building & repairing

(G-13660)
TIMS COUNTRY SAW SHOP
48 N State Frontage Rd (98855-9262)
P.O. Box 749 (98855-0749)
PHONE 509 486-2798
Roberta Gallagher, *Owner*
Timothy Gallagher, *Partner*
EMP: 5
SQ FT: 6,500
SALES: 340K **Privately Held**
SIC: 5084 5251 7538 5699 Chainsaws; chainsaws; engine rebuilding: automotive; work clothing; lawnmowers & tractors; saws & sawing equipment

(G-13661)
TOM BRETZ
Also Called: Apple Valley Machine Shop
2 Tonasket Shop Rd (98855-9297)
PHONE 509 486-2251
Tom Bretz, *Owner*
EMP: 2
SQ FT: 1,920
SALES (est): 228.1K **Privately Held**
SIC: 3599 7692 Machine shop, jobbing & repair; welding repair

(G-13662)
WIZARD WORKS
32156 Highway 97 (98855-9245)
P.O. Box 581 (98855-0581)
PHONE 509 486-2654
Robert Thompson, *Owner*
EMP: 4
SQ FT: 650
SALES (est): 285.7K **Privately Held**
SIC: 3433 1521 Stoves, wood & coal burning; single-family housing construction

Toppenish
Yakima County

(G-13663)
BIOTWINE MANUFACTURING COMPANY
206210 S Division (98948)
P.O. Box 430 (98948-0430)
PHONE 509 865-3340
Tom Sauve, *President*
EMP: 38
SQ FT: 14,000
SALES: 3.2MM **Privately Held**
SIC: 2298 Twine
PA: Fish & Fly Investors
   101 E 2nd Ave
   Toppenish WA 98948

(G-13664)
CPM DEVELOPMENT CORPORATION
Also Called: Central Pre-Mix Concrete
441 E Mcdonald Rd (98948-9533)
PHONE 509 865-2975
Troy Holt, *General Mgr*
EMP: 15
SALES (corp-wide): 30.6B **Privately Held**
WEB: www.centralpremix.com
SIC: 3273 Ready-mixed concrete
HQ: Cpm Development Corporation
   5111 E Broadway Ave
   Spokane Valley WA 99212
   509 534-6221

(G-13665)
D & S ROCK LLC
Also Called: Wapenish Sand & Gravel
680 Olden Way Rd (98948-9598)
P.O. Box 979 (98948-0979)
PHONE 509 877-7400
Josie Long, *Bookkeeper*
Scott Parker,
Alex Long,
EMP: 15 **EST:** 2008
SALES (est): 1.3MM **Privately Held**
SIC: 1442 5032 Construction sand & gravel; concrete building products

(G-13666)
DAUENHAUER MANUFACTURING INC
63351 Us Highway 97 (98948-9434)
PHONE 509 865-3300
Irving Butch Melton, *Manager*
EMP: 3
SALES (corp-wide): 633.3K **Privately Held**
WEB: www.dmfg.com
SIC: 3523 Farm machinery & equipment
PA: Dauenhauer Manufacturing Inc.
   111 5th St
   Santa Rosa CA
   707 546-0577

(G-13667)
FAITHFUL ENTERPRISES INC
931 Buena Way (98948-9370)
PHONE 509 865-7300
EMP: 20
SALES (est): 2.6MM **Privately Held**
SIC: 2611 Pulp Mills, Nsk

(G-13668)
FISH & FLY INVESTORS (PA)
101 E 2nd Ave (98948-1794)
P.O. Box 430 (98948-0430)
PHONE 509 865-3340
Tom Sauve, *Partner*
Macey Wall, *Partner*
Don Weathers, *Partner*
EMP: 3
SALES: 1.2MM **Privately Held**
SIC: 2298 Twine

(G-13669)
FLINT PUBLISHING INC
Also Called: Wapato Independent
16 W 1st Ave (98948-1525)
P.O. Box 511 (98948-0511)
PHONE 509 314-6400
James Flint, *President*
Linda Layman, *General Mgr*
EMP: 8 **EST:** 1905
SQ FT: 10,000
SALES (est): 424K **Privately Held**
SIC: 2711 Job printing & newspaper publishing combined; newspapers: publishing only, not printed on site

(G-13670)
HOPE CHEST CRAFTS
508 W 2nd Ave (98948-1605)
PHONE 509 865-5666
Merlin Peterson, *Owner*
Denice Peterson, *Owner*
EMP: 2
SQ FT: 2,200
SALES (est): 113.1K **Privately Held**
SIC: 5945 2284 5331 5999 Arts & crafts supplies; embroidery thread; variety stores; artificial flowers

(G-13671)
RATHBUN IRON WORKS INC
202 Washington Ave (98948-1563)
PHONE 509 865-3717
James O Rathbun, *President*
Cindy Rathbun, *Vice Pres*
EMP: 3 **EST:** 1968
SQ FT: 4,225
SALES: 290K **Privately Held**
SIC: 7692 5083 Welding repair; agricultural machinery & equipment

(G-13672)
SILGAN CONTAINERS MFG CORP
45 E 3rd Ave (98948-1783)
PHONE 509 865-4125
Paul Kogut, *Branch Mgr*
EMP: 85
SALES (corp-wide): 4.4B **Publicly Held**
WEB: www.silgancontainers.com
SIC: 3411 Metal cans
HQ: Silgan Containers Manufacturing Corporation
   21600 Oxnard St Ste 1600
   Woodland Hills CA 91367

(G-13673)
WASHINGTON AGRICULTURAL DEV
Also Called: St Helens Foods
201 Elmwood Rd (98948-9779)
P.O. Box 832 (98948-0832)
PHONE 509 865-2121
Gayland Pedhirney, *President*
Albert Lawrence, *Senior VP*
EMP: 8
SALES (est): 753.7K **Privately Held**
SIC: 2011 Beef products from beef slaughtered on site

(G-13674)
WASHINGTON BEEF LLC
201 Elmwood Rd (98948-9779)
P.O. Box 832 (98948-0832)
PHONE 509 865-2121
Robert Rebholtz,
▼**EMP:** 670
SALES (est): 126.6MM
SALES (corp-wide): 342.6MM **Privately Held**
SIC: 2011 Beef products from beef slaughtered on site
HQ: Ab Foods Llc
   201 Elmwood Rd
   Toppenish WA 98948
   509 865-2121

(G-13675)
YAKIMA FORKLIFT LLC
890 Rocky Ford Rd (98948-9644)
PHONE 509 985-3568
EMP: 2
SALES (est): 130.2K **Privately Held**
SIC: 3537 Forklift trucks

(G-13676)
YAKIMA VALLEY TEEN MAGAZINE
16 W 1st Ave (98948-1525)
PHONE 509 865-4055
EMP: 3 **EST:** 2008
SALES (est): 160K **Privately Held**
SIC: 2721 Periodicals-Publishing/Printing

Touchet
Walla Walla County

(G-13677)
REA SERVICES INC
105 4th St (99360-9691)
PHONE 509 394-2305
John REA, *President*
EMP: 12
SALES (est): 700K **Privately Held**
SIC: 3523 7699 Trailers & wagons, farm; farm machinery repair

(G-13678)
WEAVER FAMILY WINERY
5223 Detour Rd (99360-9633)
PHONE 509 386-8018
EMP: 4 **EST:** 2014
SALES (est): 135.6K **Privately Held**
SIC: 2084 Wines

Trout Lake
Klickitat County

(G-13679)
JMA PRINTING
4 Greenwood Ct (98650-2012)
P.O. Box 115 (98650-0115)
PHONE 509 395-2145
Morgan Colburn, *Principal*
EMP: 2 **EST:** 2008
SALES (est): 217.5K **Privately Held**
SIC: 2752 Commercial printing, lithographic

(G-13680)
MEADOWROCK ALPACAS
80 Mount Adams Rd (98650-9723)
PHONE 509 395-2266
Barbara Hansen, *Principal*
EMP: 2 **EST:** 2017

GEOGRAPHIC SECTION

SALES (est): 109.6K **Privately Held**
SIC: 2231 Alpacas, mohair: woven

(G-13681)
MOUNT ADAMS LUMBER CO INC
Also Called: Woodruff Aviation Co
10 Church St (98650-3000)
P.O. Box 40 (98650-0040)
PHONE......................................509 395-2122
George Woodruff, *President*
David Woodruff, *Vice Pres*
Diane Paxson, *Admin Sec*
EMP: 2 **EST:** 1975
SALES (est): 240.6K **Privately Held**
SIC: 2411 4522 2421 Logging; flying charter service; sawmills & planing mills, general

(G-13682)
MT ADAMS LUMBER COMPANY INC
10 Church St (98650-3000)
P.O. Box 359 (98650-0359)
PHONE......................................509 395-2131
David Woodruff, *President*
EMP: 5
SALES (est): 230K **Privately Held**
SIC: 4581 2421 1794 4212 Flying field, except those maintained by clubs; sawmills & planing mills, general; excavation work; lumber & timber trucking

(G-13683)
SOUTHSIDE ENTERPRISES INC
40 Binns Rd (98650-9700)
PHONE......................................509 395-2345
Bruce A Schmid, *President*
Wendy Schmid, *Vice Pres*
EMP: 10
SALES (est): 1.3MM **Privately Held**
SIC: 2411 1611 7389 Logging; general contractor, highway & street construction;

(G-13684)
TROUT LAKE FARM LLC (PA)
42 Warner Rd (98650-9727)
P.O. Box 181 (98650-0181)
PHONE......................................509 395-2025
Lloyd Scott, *General Mgr*
◆ **EMP:** 20
SQ FT: 4,000
SALES (est): 5MM **Privately Held**
SIC: 0139 5149 2833 0182 Herb or spice farm; organic & diet foods; medicinals & botanicals; food crops grown under cover

---

Tukwila
King County

(G-13685)
3TAC DISTRIBUTION INC
923 Industry Dr (98188-3413)
PHONE......................................206 257-1552
Edan Gross, *President*
EMP: 2
SALES (est): 149.1K **Privately Held**
SIC: 3991 Brushes for vacuum cleaners, carpet sweepers, etc.

(G-13686)
4 M COMPANY INC
Also Called: Porter Seal Company
15660 Nelson Pl (98188-5506)
PHONE......................................425 227-4100
Vernon L Meyers, *CEO*
Steve Smolinske, *President*
Virginia C Meyers, *Corp Secy*
Jeff Dickinson, *Maintence Staff*
▲ **EMP:** 70
SQ FT: 30,000
SALES (est): 14.6MM **Privately Held**
WEB: www.rainierrubber.com
SIC: 3069 5085 Molded rubber products; seals, industrial

(G-13687)
ADS LLC
Also Called: A D S Environmental Srvs
4455 S 134th Pl (98168-6204)
PHONE......................................206 762-5070
Steve Salyer, *Manager*
EMP: 2

SALES (corp-wide): 2.4B **Publicly Held**
SIC: 8748 3823 Systems analysis & engineering consulting services; flow instruments, industrial process type
HQ: Ads Llc
340 The Bridge St Ste 204
Huntsville AL 35806
256 430-3366

(G-13688)
ADVANCED ROBOTIC VEHICLES INC (PA)
12923 E Marginal Way S (98168-3147)
PHONE......................................206 310-1122
Henry Happel, *President*
Henry Seemann, *CTO*
EMP: 1
SQ FT: 1,000
SALES: 1MM **Privately Held**
WEB: www.arvirobots.com
SIC: 3569 Robots, assembly line: industrial & commercial

(G-13689)
AEROGO INC
1170 Andover Park W (98188-3900)
PHONE......................................206 575-3344
John Massanburg, *President*
Steve Paige, *Vice Pres*
▼ **EMP:** 60 **EST:** 1967
SQ FT: 55,000
SALES: 17.9MM **Privately Held**
WEB: www.aerogo.com
SIC: 3535 5084 Conveyors & conveying equipment; industrial machinery & equipment

(G-13690)
AGALITE SEATTLE (PA)
17830 W Valley Hwy (98188-5532)
PHONE......................................425 656-2626
Bob Miller, *COO*
▲ **EMP:** 2
SALES (est): 231.8K **Privately Held**
SIC: 2392 Shower curtains: made from purchased materials

(G-13691)
APCO NORTHWEST
Also Called: Graphic Systems
4493 S 134th Pl (98168-6204)
PHONE......................................800 815-8028
Todd Liken, *President*
EMP: 10
SALES (est): 600K **Privately Held**
WEB: www.gsisigns.com
SIC: 3993 Signs, not made in custom sign painting shops

(G-13692)
ARROW RELIANCE INC
Also Called: Darwins Natural Pet Products
350 Treck Dr (98188-7604)
PHONE......................................206 324-7387
Gary Tashjian, *CEO*
Jim Bridges, *VP Opers*
EMP: 12
SQ FT: 6,000
SALES (est): 3.4MM **Privately Held**
WEB: www.darwinspet.com
SIC: 2047 2048 Dog & cat food; meat meal & tankage: prepared as animal feed

(G-13693)
AUTOMATED EQUIPMENT COMPANY
Also Called: Automated Gates & Equipment
10847 E Marginal Way S (98168-1931)
PHONE......................................206 767-9080
Jerry Alahadeff, *President*
Judith Alahadeff, *Corp Secy*
Mike Pishue, *Prdtn Mgr*
Christopher Lee, *Production*
EMP: 27
SQ FT: 9,800
SALES (est): 6.2MM
SALES (corp-wide): 81.6MM **Privately Held**
WEB: www.aegates.com
SIC: 3446 Gates, ornamental metal
PA: Diamond Parking Services, Llc
605 1st Ave Ste 600
Seattle WA 98104
206 284-2732

(G-13694)
AVERY WEIGH-TRONIX LLC
Also Called: Weigh Tronix Company Store
808 Industry Dr (98188-3410)
PHONE......................................206 575-1992
Michael Spear, *Manager*
EMP: 8
SALES (corp-wide): 14.7B **Publicly Held**
WEB: www.agscales.com
SIC: 3596 7699 5046 Industrial scales; scale repair service; scales, except laboratory
HQ: Avery Weigh-Tronix, Llc
1000 Armstrong Dr
Fairmont MN 56031
507 238-4461

(G-13695)
BATTERY X-CHANGE & REPAIR INC
Also Called: Blanchard Auto Elc & Fleet Sup
9112 E Marginal Way S (98108-4028)
PHONE......................................206 682-2981
Keith Tugias, *President*
EMP: 6
SALES (corp-wide): 6.8MM **Privately Held**
SIC: 1731 3429 Electrical work; marine hardware
PA: Battery X-Change & Repair Inc
3750 Se Belmont St
Portland OR 97214
503 232-8248

(G-13696)
BELFOR USA GROUP INC
4320 S 131st Pl (98168-3200)
PHONE......................................206 632-0800
Ted Sitterley, *Manager*
EMP: 44
SALES (corp-wide): 1.5B **Privately Held**
SIC: 1799 3999 Post-disaster renovations; wool pulling
HQ: Belfor Usa Group Inc.
185 Oakland Ave Ste 150
Birmingham MI 48009

(G-13697)
BEVERAGE SPECIALIST INC
905 Industry Dr (98188-3413)
P.O. Box 986, Kent (98035-0986)
PHONE......................................206 763-0255
Robert S Burgess, *President*
Linda J Burgess, *Corp Secy*
▲ **EMP:** 20
SALES (est): 6.3MM **Privately Held**
WEB: www.burgessenterprises.net
SIC: 5046 7359 3589 Restaurant equipment & supplies; soda fountain fixtures, except refrigerated; coffee brewing equipment & supplies; equipment rental & leasing; commercial cooking & foodwarming equipment

(G-13698)
BLUE STAR GAS - SEATTLE CO
10802 E Marginal Way S (98168-1932)
PHONE......................................206 762-2583
Jeff Stewart, *President*
EMP: 8 **EST:** 2013
SALES (est): 886.7K
SALES (corp-wide): 37.9MM **Privately Held**
SIC: 2869 Fuels
HQ: Blue Star Gas Co.
880 N Wright Rd
Santa Rosa CA 95407
707 573-3130

(G-13699)
BOEING CHINA INC
7755 E Marginal Way S (98108-4002)
PHONE......................................206 655-2121
Michael Winters, *Principal*
EMP: 2
SALES (est): 315.6K
SALES (corp-wide): 101.1B **Publicly Held**
SIC: 3721 Aircraft
PA: The Boeing Company
100 N Riverside Plz
Chicago IL 60606
312 544-2000

(G-13700)
BOEING COMPANY
9725 E Marginal Way S (98108-4040)
P.O. Box 3707, Seattle (98124-2207)
PHONE......................................206 655-9974
Ron Selvidge, *Project Mgr*
Warren Nedved, *Engineer*
Robert Ormsby, *Manager*
James Schuehle, *Project Leader*
Debra Young, *Technology*
EMP: 20
SALES (corp-wide): 101.1B **Publicly Held**
SIC: 3721 Aircraft
PA: The Boeing Company
100 N Riverside Plz
Chicago IL 60606
312 544-2000

(G-13701)
BOEING COMPANY
7755 E Marginal Way S (98108-4002)
P.O. Box 3707, Seattle (98124-2207)
PHONE......................................206 655-1131
Brett Hendrickx, *Project Mgr*
Karen Qualls, *Project Mgr*
Carol Greetham, *Opers Staff*
Kuljit Singh, *Opers Staff*
Emily Biss, *Production*
EMP: 7200
SALES (corp-wide): 101.1B **Publicly Held**
SIC: 3721 Airplanes, fixed or rotary wing
PA: The Boeing Company
100 N Riverside Plz
Chicago IL 60606
312 544-2000

(G-13702)
BOEING COMPANY
2925 S 112th St (98168-1800)
P.O. Box 3707, Seattle (98124-2207)
PHONE......................................206 544-4524
Gordon Yip, *Treasurer*
Rick Post, *Manager*
Rick N Post, *Manager*
Jennifer Mack, *Director*
EMP: 831
SALES (corp-wide): 101.1B **Publicly Held**
SIC: 3721 Aircraft
PA: The Boeing Company
100 N Riverside Plz
Chicago IL 60606
312 544-2000

(G-13703)
BOEING COMPANY
7755 E Marginal Way S (98108-4002)
PHONE......................................206 655-1131
Dave Bullock, *CFO*
EMP: 1100
SALES (corp-wide): 101.1B **Publicly Held**
SIC: 3721 Aircraft
PA: The Boeing Company
100 N Riverside Plz
Chicago IL 60606
312 544-2000

(G-13704)
BOEING COMPANY
7755 E Marginal Way S (98108-4002)
PHONE......................................206 655-2121
Brian M Woebkenberg, *Exec VP*
Patricia Avery, *Engineer*
Dan Lavallee, *Engineer*
Lori Smith, *Engineer*
Karen Burt, *Marketing Mgr*
EMP: 23
SALES (corp-wide): 101.1B **Publicly Held**
SIC: 3721 Aircraft
PA: The Boeing Company
100 N Riverside Plz
Chicago IL 60606
312 544-2000

(G-13705)
BOEING COMPANY
7775 E Marginal Way S (98108)
PHONE......................................206 544-9246
EMP: 3
SALES (corp-wide): 101.1B **Publicly Held**
SIC: 3721 Aircraft

Tukwila - King County (G-13706)

PA: The Boeing Company
100 N Riverside Plz
Chicago IL 60606
312 544-2000

(G-13706)
BOEING COMPANY INCORPORATED
6840 Fort Dent Way # 250 (98188-8504)
PHONE...............................425 965-4300
Pat Parmley, *Director*
EMP: 35
SALES (est): 5.2MM
SALES (corp-wide): 101.1B **Publicly Held**
SIC: 3721 Aircraft
PA: The Boeing Company
100 N Riverside Plz
Chicago IL 60606
312 544-2000

(G-13707)
BOEING DOMESTIC SALES CORP
7755 E Marginal Way S (98108-4002)
PHONE...............................206 655-2121
James A Bell, *President*
David Jaeger, *Architect*
EMP: 7
SALES (est): 1.1MM
SALES (corp-wide): 101.1B **Publicly Held**
SIC: 3721 3769 Aircraft; guided missile & space vehicle parts & auxiliary equipment
PA: The Boeing Company
100 N Riverside Plz
Chicago IL 60606
312 544-2000

(G-13708)
BOEING OPERATIONS INTL INC (HQ)
7755 E Marginal Way S (98108-4002)
PHONE...............................206 655-2121
Harry Stonecipher, *President*
EMP: 8
SALES (est): 13.4MM
SALES (corp-wide): 101.1B **Publicly Held**
SIC: 3721 Airplanes, fixed or rotary wing
PA: The Boeing Company
100 N Riverside Plz
Chicago IL 60606
312 544-2000

(G-13709)
BORAL RESOURCES LLC
950 Andover Park E Ste 24 (98188-7624)
PHONE...............................206 394-3734
EMP: 6
SALES (corp-wide): 3.1B **Privately Held**
SIC: 3251 Mfg Brick/Structural Tile
HQ: Boral Resources, Llc
10701 S River Front Pkwy
South Jordan UT 84095
801 984-9400

(G-13710)
CAPTIVATING COVERS
12628 Intrurban Ave S # 120 (98168-3319)
PHONE...............................800 975-8198
EMP: 2
SALES (est): 105.6K **Privately Held**
SIC: 2759 Commercial printing

(G-13711)
CENTER FOR ADVANCED
495 Andover Park E (98188-7605)
PHONE...............................253 298-7490
Tom McLaughlin, *Exec Dir*
EMP: 2
SALES: 445K **Privately Held**
SIC: 3999 Manufacturing industries

(G-13712)
CLEARSIGN COMBUSTION CORP
12870 Interurban Ave S (98168-3318)
PHONE...............................206 673-4848
Robert Hoffman, *CEO*
Robert T Hoffman Sr, *Ch of Bd*
Colin Deller, *President*
Joseph Colannino, *Senior VP*
Andrew U Lee, *Senior VP*
EMP: 19

SQ FT: 9,425
SALES: 530K **Privately Held**
SIC: 3823 Industrial process control instruments

(G-13713)
CMX CORPORATION
Also Called: CMX Medical Imaging
6601 S Glacier St (98188-4718)
P.O. Box 58088, Seattle (98138-1088)
PHONE...............................425 656-1269
Roger Van Valey, *President*
Tim Beyer, *Principal*
Fred Prenner, *Vice Pres*
Brian Van Valey, *Vice Pres*
John E Vanvaley, *Vice Pres*
EMP: 44
SQ FT: 45,000
SALES (est): 15.7MM **Privately Held**
SIC: 5047 3861 X-ray film & supplies; developers, photographic (not made in chemical plants)

(G-13714)
COMPUTER HUMAN INTERACTION LLC
16040 Christensen Rd # 110 (98188-2934)
PHONE...............................425 282-6900
Uli CHI, *Mng Member*
Dave Mitchell,
EMP: 22
SALES (est): 2.1MM **Privately Held**
WEB: www.chi-llc.com
SIC: 7372 7371 Prepackaged software; custom computer programming services

(G-13715)
CONSOLIDATED CONTAINER CO LLC
Also Called: Stewart/Walker Company
6545 S Glacier St (98188-4716)
PHONE...............................425 251-0303
Colleen Habenicht, *COO*
Mike Tliston, *Manager*
EMP: 35
SQ FT: 22,000
SALES (corp-wide): 14B **Publicly Held**
WEB: www.ccccllc.com
SIC: 3089 3085 Pallets, plastic; plastics bottles
HQ: Consolidated Container Company, Llc
2500 Windy Ridge Pkwy Se # 1400
Atlanta GA 30339
678 742-4600

(G-13716)
CONTINENTAL MILLS INC (PA)
Also Called: CM
18100 Andover Park W (98188-4703)
P.O. Box 88176, Seattle (98138-2176)
PHONE...............................206 816-7000
John M Heily, *Ch of Bd*
Mark Harris, *Senior VP*
James M Hershberger, *Senior VP*
Michael Meredith, *Senior VP*
Clyde Walker, *Senior VP*
▼ **EMP:** 130 **EST:** 1932
SQ FT: 28,000
SALES (est): 237.6MM **Privately Held**
WEB: www.crustease.com
SIC: 2045 2038 Flours & flour mixes, from purchased flour; breakfasts, frozen & packaged

(G-13717)
CONTROLLED PRODUCTS OF WASH
Also Called: Handley Sales
14520 Interurban Ave S # 150 (98168-4665)
PHONE...............................206 575-2249
Brian Brandli, *Manager*
EMP: 2
SALES (est): 334.7K
SALES (corp-wide): 1.4B **Privately Held**
WEB: www.controlledproducts.com
SIC: 5063 5065 3699 Electrical apparatus & equipment; security control equipment & systems; security devices
HQ: Controlled Products Systems Group, Inc.
5000 Osage St Ste 500
Denver CO 80221
303 333-1141

(G-13718)
CROWN CORK & SEAL USA INC
18340 Segale Park Drive B (98188-4734)
PHONE...............................206 575-4260
Ken Tutin, *Manager*
EMP: 46
SALES (corp-wide): 11.1B **Publicly Held**
WEB: www.crowncork.com
SIC: 3565 3411 Packaging machinery; metal cans
HQ: Crown Cork & Seal Usa, Inc.
770 Township Line Rd # 100
Yardley PA 19067
215 698-5100

(G-13719)
CROWN CORK & SEAL USA INC
18340 Segale Park Drive B (98188-4734)
PHONE...............................206 575-4260
Dave Sellhausen, *Manager*
EMP: 123
SALES (corp-wide): 11.1B **Publicly Held**
WEB: www.crowncork.com
SIC: 3411 Metal cans
HQ: Crown Cork & Seal Usa, Inc.
770 Township Line Rd # 100
Yardley PA 19067
215 698-5100

(G-13720)
CROWN CORK & SEAL USA INC
18340 Segale Park Drive B (98188-4734)
PHONE...............................206 575-4260
David Sellhausen, *Branch Mgr*
EMP: 118
SALES (corp-wide): 11.1B **Publicly Held**
WEB: www.crowncork.com
SIC: 3411 Metal cans
HQ: Crown Cork & Seal Usa, Inc.
770 Township Line Rd # 100
Yardley PA 19067
215 698-5100

(G-13721)
CUMMINS - ALLISON CORP
1012 Industry Dr (98188-4801)
PHONE...............................206 763-3900
Marvin H Mohatt, *Branch Mgr*
EMP: 8
SALES (corp-wide): 383.8MM **Privately Held**
WEB: www.gsb.com
SIC: 5999 5943 5046 3519 Business machines & equipment; office forms & supplies; coin counters; internal combustion engines
PA: Cummins - Allison Corp.
852 Feehanville Dr
Mount Prospect IL 60056
847 759-6403

(G-13722)
CUSTOM GEAR INC
10834 E Marginal Way S (98168-1932)
PHONE...............................206 767-9448
Carl Walker Jr, *President*
Barbara Walker, *Vice Pres*
EMP: 10
SQ FT: 7,750
SALES (est): 1.2MM **Privately Held**
WEB: www.customgear.com
SIC: 3599 3462 Machine shop, jobbing & repair; iron & steel forgings

(G-13723)
DEMATIC CORP
14900 Interurban Ave S (98168-4635)
PHONE...............................206 674-4578
EMP: 527
SALES (corp-wide): 9.1B **Privately Held**
SIC: 3535 Conveyors & conveying equipment
HQ: Dematic Corp.
500 Plymouth Ave Ne
Grand Rapids MI 49505
877 725-7500

(G-13724)
DIPIETRO ENTERPRISES INC
Also Called: Delta Electric Motors
10831 E Marginal Way S (98168-1931)
PHONE...............................206 423-7633
Josephine De Pietro, *President*
Luigi De Pietro, *Vice Pres*
Joseph De Peitro, *Treasurer*
Joseph Di Pietro, *Treasurer*

Michael De Peitro, *Admin Sec*
EMP: 15 **EST:** 1976
SQ FT: 1,850
SALES (est): 4.4MM **Privately Held**
WEB: www.deltaelectricmotors.com
SIC: 7694 Electric motor repair

(G-13725)
DIRECT CONTACT LLC (PA)
575 Andover Park W # 210 (98188-3348)
PHONE...............................425 235-1723
Curt Rothman, *CEO*
EMP: 23
SQ FT: 10,000
SALES (est): 4.3MM **Privately Held**
WEB: www.dciheat.com
SIC: 5075 3585 8711 4939 Air pollution control equipment & supplies; heat exchangers; evaporative condensers, heat transfer equipment; chemical engineering; combination utilities

(G-13726)
DIVISION FIVE INC
Also Called: The Steel Fabrication Co.
6458 S 144th St (98186-4609)
P.O. Box 69676, Seattle (98168-9676)
PHONE...............................206 988-5004
Laurie Hagedorn, *President*
Leslee Van, *President*
James Hagedorn, *Vice Pres*
EMP: 12
SALES (est): 2.3MM **Privately Held**
SIC: 3441 Building components, structural steel

(G-13727)
EASY RIDER CANOE & KAYAK CO
15666 W Valley Hwy (98188-5534)
PHONE...............................425 228-3633
Peter Kaupat, *President*
Mike Gloster, *Managing Dir*
Barbara Kaupat, *Vice Pres*
EMP: 6
SQ FT: 17,000
SALES (est): 865.6K **Privately Held**
WEB: www.easyriderkayaks.com
SIC: 3732 5551 Canoes, building & repairing; kayaks, building & repairing; canoes; kayaks

(G-13728)
ELLIOTT BAY PUBLISHING INC
16040 Christensen Rd # 205 (98188-2966)
PHONE...............................206 283-8144
EMP: 3
SALES (est): 193.3K **Privately Held**
SIC: 2721 Periodicals: publishing & printing

(G-13729)
ENERVANA LLC
869 Industry Dr (98188-3411)
PHONE...............................253 220-8413
Gabriala Brown, *Manager*
EMP: 2
SALES (est): 166.3K **Privately Held**
SIC: 2844 Toilet preparations

(G-13730)
ESP SEATTLE
950 Andover Park E (98188-7624)
PHONE...............................206 388-4800
EMP: 2 **EST:** 2010
SALES (est): 142.4K **Privately Held**
SIC: 3699 Mfg Electrical Equipment/Supplies

(G-13731)
FARWEST PAINT MANUFACTURING CO (PA)
Also Called: Jarvie Paint Division
4522 S 133rd St (98168-3251)
P.O. Box 68726, Seattle (98168-0726)
PHONE...............................206 244-8844
Brian Huber, *CEO*
Paul E Sheehan, *President*
Roberta L Ehli, *Corp Secy*
▼ **EMP:** 18
SALES (est): 4.9MM **Privately Held**
WEB: www.farwestpaint.com
SIC: 2851 5231 Paints & paint additives; paint & painting supplies

GEOGRAPHIC SECTION

Tukwila - King County (G-13756)

(G-13732)
FATIGUE TECHNOLOGY INC (DH)
401 Andover Park E (98188-7605)
PHONE 206 246-2010
Kevin Stein, *President*
Kevin Dooley, *President*
Ruth Beyer, *Vice Pres*
Steven C Blackmore, *Vice Pres*
Shawn R Hagel, *Vice Pres*
◆ **EMP:** 122
SQ FT: 120,000
SALES (est): 35.8MM
SALES (corp-wide): 225.3B **Publicly Held**
WEB: www.tcto2060.com
SIC: 3728 Aircraft parts & equipment
HQ: Precision Castparts Corp.
4650 Sw Mcdam Ave Ste 300
Portland OR 97239
503 946-4800

(G-13733)
FEDEX OFFICE & PRINT SVCS INC
116 Andover Park E (98188-2955)
PHONE 206 244-8884
John Stebbins, *Manager*
EMP: 21
SQ FT: 17,000
SALES (corp-wide): 69.6B **Publicly Held**
WEB: www.kinkos.com
SIC: 7334 2789 2752 Photocopying & duplicating services; bookbinding & related work; commercial printing, lithographic
HQ: Fedex Office And Print Services, Inc.
7900 Legacy Dr
Plano TX 75024
800 463-3339

(G-13734)
FILEONQ INC
832 Industry Dr (98188-3410)
PHONE 206 575-3488
Kim Webley, *President*
EMP: 15
SQ FT: 1,750
SALES: 3.5MM **Privately Held**
WEB: www.fileonq.com
SIC: 7372 Business oriented computer software

(G-13735)
FINE DESIGN INC
16550 W Valley Hwy (98188-5524)
PHONE 425 271-2866
Victor Kostroub, *President*
Yuli Opalvhuk, *Vice Pres*
Troy Taylor, *Accounts Exec*
▲ **EMP:** 20
SQ FT: 5,985
SALES (est): 3.1MM **Privately Held**
SIC: 2759 5999 Commercial printing; trophies & plaques

(G-13736)
FOSSIL GROUP INC
846 Southcenter Mall (98188-2819)
PHONE 206 248-6984
EMP: 2
SALES (corp-wide): 2.5B **Publicly Held**
WEB: www.fossil.com
SIC: 3873 Watches, clocks, watchcases & parts
PA: Fossil Group, Inc.
901 S Central Expy
Richardson TX 75080
972 234-2525

(G-13737)
GE AVIATION SYSTEMS LLC
12600 Interurban Ave S (98168-3317)
PHONE 206 662-2934
Jason Swanson, *Branch Mgr*
EMP: 240
SALES (corp-wide): 121.6B **Publicly Held**
SIC: 3728 3593 Aircraft assemblies, subassemblies & parts; fluid power cylinders & actuators
HQ: Ge Aviation Systems Llc
1 Neumann Way
Cincinnati OH 45215
937 898-9600

(G-13738)
GENTZEN LLC
Also Called: Mastercraft of Seattle
12628 Interurban Ave S (98168-3319)
PHONE 206 768-1297
Mark Gentzen,
Deborah Gentzen,
EMP: 7 **EST:** 2008
SALES (est): 356.4K **Privately Held**
SIC: 2782 Blankbooks & looseleaf binders

(G-13739)
GEO HEISER BODY CO LLC
11210 Tukla Intl Blvd (98168-1945)
PHONE 206 622-7985
Wayne Miller, *Principal*
Simon Castle, *Principal*
George Heiser, *Sales Executive*
Frank Mann, *Technology*
Steven Tran,
EMP: 36
SALES (est): 3.2MM **Privately Held**
SIC: 3713 Truck & bus bodies

(G-13740)
GEOMETRIC
Also Called: Geometric Engrv & Template Co
4036 S 128th St (98168-2574)
PHONE 206 244-2222
Philip Hemenway, *Owner*
EMP: 4
SALES (est): 230.2K **Privately Held**
SIC: 2759 Engraving

(G-13741)
GLOBAL HARVEST FOODS LTD
16000 Christensen Rd # 300 (98188-2931)
P.O. Box 430, Mead (99021-0430)
PHONE 206 957-1350
Edward H Mills, *Manager*
EMP: 4
SALES (corp-wide): 6.2MM **Privately Held**
SIC: 2048 4783 5141 Bird food, prepared; packing & crating; groceries, general line
HQ: Global Harvest Foods, Ltd.
16000 Christensen Rd # 300
Tukwila WA 98188

(G-13742)
GLOBAL HARVEST FOODS LTD (HQ)
16000 Christensen Rd # 300 (98188-2931)
PHONE 206 957-1350
Ed Mills, *Principal*
Todd Hager, *Business Mgr*
Frederick Mills, *Vice Pres*
Steve Haines, *Opers Spvr*
Rod Epps, *Info Tech Dir*
▲ **EMP:** 2
SALES (est): 1.1MM
SALES (corp-wide): 6.2MM **Privately Held**
SIC: 2048 4783 Bird food, prepared; packing & crating
PA: Mills Bros. International, Inc.
16000 Christensen Rd # 300
Tukwila WA 98188
206 957-1350

(G-13743)
HARTUNG GLASS INDUSTRIES (PA)
Also Called: Holcam Shower Doors
3351 E Valley Rd (98188)
PHONE 206 772-7800
John A Holmes, *President*
Rick Wenala, *Vice Pres*
Judy Forcier, *Treasurer*
Nathan Townsend, *Admin Sec*
▲ **EMP:** 68
SQ FT: 46,000
SALES (est): 5.8MM **Privately Held**
WEB: www.holcam.com
SIC: 3231 Doors, glass: made from purchased glass

(G-13744)
HARTUNG GLASS INDUSTRIES
17750 W Valley Hwy (98188-5507)
PHONE 206 772-7800
EMP: 2

SALES (corp-wide): 5.8MM **Privately Held**
SIC: 3231 Doors, glass: made from purchased glass
PA: Hartung Glass Industries
3351 E Valley Rd
Tukwila WA 98188
206 772-7800

(G-13745)
HEATCON INC (PA)
Also Called: Heatcon Composite Systems
480 Andover Park E (98188-7606)
PHONE 206 575-0815
Eric Casterline, *President*
Thomas Lane, *Managing Dir*
Christina Thompson, *Purch Agent*
Jason Rota, *Engineer*
Nicole Rodriguez, *Marketing Mgr*
EMP: 60
SQ FT: 29,500
SALES (est): 28.2MM **Privately Held**
SIC: 5075 3625 4581 Electrical heating equipment; thermostats; control equipment, electric; aircraft maintenance & repair services

(G-13746)
HEATCON COMPOSITE SYSTEMS INC
600 Andover Park E (98188-7610)
PHONE 206 575-1333
EMP: 2
SALES (est): 88.3K **Privately Held**
SIC: 3625 Relays And Industrial Controls, Nsk

(G-13747)
HEATCON COMPOSITE SYSTEMS INC (HQ)
480 Andover Park E (98188-7606)
PHONE 206 575-1333
Eric Casterline, *President*
Howard Banasky, *Chairman*
Pam Miller, *Purch Mgr*
Cindy Brown, *Controller*
Matt Pentland, *Sales Engr*
▲ **EMP:** 59
SQ FT: 43,000
SALES (est): 12.8MM
SALES (corp-wide): 28.2MM **Privately Held**
SIC: 3625 3829 8299 Control equipment, electric; aircraft & motor vehicle measurement equipment; educational services
PA: Heatcon, Inc.
480 Andover Park E
Tukwila WA 98188
206 575-0815

(G-13748)
HEISER GEORGE BODY CO INC
11210 Tukla Intl Blvd (98168-1945)
PHONE 206 622-7985
George G Heiser, *President*
Joyce Heiser, *Treasurer*
Steven Tran,
EMP: 40
SQ FT: 43,000
SALES (est): 5.9MM **Privately Held**
SIC: 7532 7538 3713 Paint shop, automotive; general automotive repair shops; truck bodies & parts

(G-13749)
HNG GROUP LLC
Also Called: HNG Appliances
431 Industry Dr Ste 150 (98188-3562)
PHONE 206 723-6848
Hieu Nguyen,
EMP: 5
SALES (est): 284.3K **Privately Held**
SIC: 3363 7623 Aluminum die-castings; refrigerator repair service

(G-13750)
HUNTINGTON PIER INTERNATIONAL
Also Called: Hpi
4310 S 131st Pl (98168-3200)
PHONE 310 640-8358
Bill Liu, *Branch Mgr*
EMP: 4

SALES (corp-wide): 2.4MM **Privately Held**
WEB: www.hpiemblem.com
SIC: 2395 Embroidery & art needlework
PA: Huntington Pier International
12335 World Trade Dr
San Diego CA 92128
858 618-1798

(G-13751)
IFLOORCOM
1187 Andover Park W (98188-3910)
P.O. Box 88153, Seattle (98138-2153)
PHONE 206 438-3022
Tad Amell, *Principal*
Robert Espinoza, *Store Mgr*
EMP: 2
SALES (est): 120K **Privately Held**
SIC: 2426 Flooring, hardwood

(G-13752)
INDUSTRIAL REVOLUTION INC
5835 Segale Park Drive C (98188-4739)
PHONE 425 285-1111
Keith Jackson, *CEO*
Steven Llorente, *Vice Pres*
Anita Rodgers, *Vice Pres*
Jim Suthers, *Human Res Mgr*
Ken Bathurst, *Sales Mgr*
▲ **EMP:** 21
SQ FT: 15,000
SALES (est): 5.3MM **Privately Held**
WEB: www.industrialrev.com
SIC: 3949 3648 3469 3354 Camping equipment & supplies; lighting equipment; metal stampings; aluminum extruded products; clamps, metal

(G-13753)
INNOVASIAN CUISINE ENTPS INC
116 Andover Park E # 200 (98188-2955)
PHONE 800 324-5140
Takyua Araki, *Ch of Bd*
Mark Phelps, *President*
Dan Peanch, *Vice Pres*
Gerry Niemer, *Engineer*
Dan Peach, *Finance*
EMP: 45 **EST:** 2012
SQ FT: 17,000
SALES: 86.5MM **Privately Held**
SIC: 5149 2013 Specialty food items; frozen meats from purchased meat
HQ: Nichirei Foods Inc.
6-19-20, Tsukiji
Chuo-Ku TKY 104-0

(G-13754)
IRONCLAD COMPANY
Also Called: Transcb-Dot Apprved Desl Tanks
12218 51st Pl S (98178-3432)
P.O. Box 66950, Seattle (98166-0950)
PHONE 206 588-2272
Montaldo Faith, *Principal*
EMP: 6
SALES (est): 663.2K **Privately Held**
SIC: 3443 5172 Fuel tanks (oil, gas, etc.): metal plate; service station supplies, petroleum

(G-13755)
JELD-WEN INC
Jeld-Wen Coatings
1061 Industry Dr (98188-4802)
PHONE 206 574-0986
Ollie Raza, *Manager*
EMP: 12 **Publicly Held**
WEB: www.jeld-wen.com
SIC: 2431 Moldings, wood: unfinished & prefinished
HQ: Jeld-Wen, Inc.
2645 Silver Crescent Dr
Charlotte NC 28273
800 535-3936

(G-13756)
JET SET NORTHWEST INC
9026 E Marginal Way S (98108-4026)
P.O. Box 46164, Seattle (98146-0164)
PHONE 206 762-0434
Mark Laures, *President*
Vickie Laures, *Corp Secy*
Ashley Laures, *Vice Pres*
EMP: 5
SQ FT: 3,200

Tukwila - King County (G-13757)

SALES (est): 450K **Privately Held**
SIC: 3272 Dry mixture concrete

(G-13757)
JFC HOLDING CORPORATION
Also Called: Jorgensen Forge Parent
8531 E Marginal Way S (98108-4018)
PHONE....................206 762-1100
Steven Abelman, *President*
Richards E Clemens, *President*
Joseph Haviv, *Chairman*
Juan Lynch, *Corp Secy*
Robert O Connor, *Vice Pres*
◆ **EMP:** 27
SALES (est): 34.7MM **Privately Held**
SIC: 3462 Iron & steel forgings
PA: Constellations Enterprise Llc
  1775 Logan Ave
  Youngstown OH 44505

(G-13758)
JOES GARAGE LLC
Also Called: Caffe Luca Coffee Roasters
1025 Industry Dr (98188-4802)
PHONE....................206 466-5579
Gregory Gould, *President*
Dawn Hong, *Manager*
EMP: 10
SQ FT: 10,000
SALES (est): 1.7MM **Privately Held**
WEB: www.nwlymphedemacenter.org
SIC: 2095 5499 5149 Coffee roasting (except by wholesale grocers); coffee; coffee & tea; coffee, green or roasted

(G-13759)
JORGENSEN FORGE CORPORATION
8531 E Marginal Way S (98108-4018)
PHONE....................206 762-1100
Mike Jewell, *CEO*
Kevin Haynes, *Director*
◆ **EMP:** 180
SQ FT: 350,000
SALES (est): 52.5MM
SALES (corp-wide): 8.1MM **Privately Held**
WEB: www.jorgensenforge.com
SIC: 3462 Gear & chain forgings
PA: Ce Star Holdings, Llc
  1775 Logan Ave
  Youngstown OH 44505
  800 826-5867

(G-13760)
KAMIYA BIOMEDICAL COMPANY LLC
12779 Gateway Dr S (98168-3308)
PHONE....................206 575-8068
Kohji Kamiya,
▲ **EMP:** 18
SQ FT: 5,000
SALES (est): 3.6MM **Privately Held**
WEB: www.kamiyabiomedical.com
SIC: 2836 2899 2835 Biological products, except diagnostic; chemical preparations; in vitro & in vivo diagnostic substances

(G-13761)
KARCHER DESIGN
Also Called: Izabel Karcher, Owner
1042 Industry Dr (98188-4801)
PHONE....................253 220-8244
Jan Karcher, *Owner*
▲ **EMP:** 80
SALES (est): 6.3MM **Privately Held**
SIC: 3429 Builders' hardware

(G-13762)
KAWNEER COMPANY INC
18235 Olympic Ave S (98188-4722)
PHONE....................253 236-2848
Kendal Mufitt, *Manager*
Stacey Bill, *Director*
EMP: 11
SALES (corp-wide): 14B **Publicly Held**
WEB: www.kawneer.com
SIC: 3442 Metal doors
HQ: Kawneer Company, Inc.
  555 Guthridge Ct
  Norcross GA 30092
  770 449-5555

(G-13763)
KENTICO SOFTWARE LLC
14900 Interurban Ave S (98168-4635)
PHONE....................206 674-4507
EMP: 2
SALES (est): 119.3K **Privately Held**
SIC: 7372 Prepackaged Software Services

(G-13764)
KENWOOD MANUFACTURING INC
1131 Andover Park W (98188-3910)
PHONE....................602 625-4012
LI Su, *Principal*
EMP: 2 **EST:** 2017
SALES (est): 141K **Privately Held**
SIC: 3999 Atomizers, toiletry

(G-13765)
LG HAUSYS AMERICA INC
18290 Olympic Ave S (98188-4721)
PHONE....................425 251-3698
EMP: 4
SALES (corp-wide): 2.5B **Privately Held**
SIC: 2541 Counter & sink tops
HQ: Lg Hausys America Inc.
  900 Cir 75 Pkwy Se # 1500
  Atlanta GA 30339
  678 486-8210

(G-13766)
LITHO DESIGN INC
370 Upland Dr (98188-3801)
PHONE....................206 574-3000
Susan Estep, *President*
EMP: 10
SALES: 1MM **Privately Held**
WEB: www.lithodesign.com
SIC: 2752 Commercial printing, offset

(G-13767)
LNP LLC
Also Called: Lightsnplastics
1059 Andover Park E (98188-7615)
PHONE....................206 467-4556
Royce Honstain, *Principal*
EMP: 7
SALES (est): 982.2K **Privately Held**
SIC: 3089 Injection molding of plastics

(G-13768)
MARY FLEMING
Also Called: Type Cellar
3400 S 150th St (98188-2109)
PHONE....................206 246-4871
Mary Fleming, *Owner*
EMP: 2 **EST:** 1980
SQ FT: 400
SALES: 80K **Privately Held**
SIC: 7336 2791 Graphic arts & related design; linotype composition, for the printing trade

(G-13769)
MEDFORD TECHNOLOGIES INC
345 Andover Park E (98188-7601)
PHONE....................206 963-0589
Daniel S Diederichs, *Administration*
EMP: 3
SALES (est): 315.8K **Privately Held**
SIC: 3993 Signs & advertising specialties

(G-13770)
MERCER TIMBER PRODUCTS LLC
14900 Interurban Ave S (98168-4635)
PHONE....................206 674-4639
David Gandossi,
Richard Short,
Genevieve Stannus,
David Ure,
EMP: 2 **EST:** 2017
SALES (est): 95.4K **Privately Held**
SIC: 2421 Flooring (dressed lumber), softwood

(G-13771)
MERIDIAN VALLEY LABORATORIES
6839 Fort Dent Way # 206 (98188-2502)
PHONE....................206 209-4200
Holly Han, *President*
Jonathan Wright, *Treasurer*
EMP: 5

SALES (est): 390K **Privately Held**
SIC: 8734 3842 Testing laboratories; hydrotherapy equipment

(G-13772)
MFG UNIVERSE CORP
Also Called: Digilite Led
1045 Andover Park E # 105 (98188-7615)
PHONE....................800 883-8779
Paul Koo, *President*
EMP: 5
SQ FT: 5,000
SALES: 2MM **Privately Held**
SIC: 3648 8742 Outdoor lighting equipment; manufacturing management consultant

(G-13773)
MIKE AND LESLIE CORPORATION
Also Called: Cutting Specialists
6400 S 143rd Pl (98168-4606)
PHONE....................206 246-4911
Mike Engsprom, *President*
EMP: 9 **EST:** 1952
SQ FT: 7,500
SALES (est): 1.1MM **Privately Held**
SIC: 3599 Machine shop, jobbing & repair

(G-13774)
N C POWER SYSTEMS CO
Also Called: Caterpillar Authorized Dealer
17900 W Valley Hwy (98188-5533)
PHONE....................425 251-5877
Mary Simon, *Manager*
EMP: 120
SQ FT: 28,580
SALES (corp-wide): 560.8MM **Privately Held**
WEB: www.ncpowersystems.com
SIC: 5082 7699 3714 3519 General construction machinery & equipment; industrial machinery & equipment repair; motor vehicle parts & accessories; internal combustion engines
HQ: N C Power Systems Co.
  17900 W Valley Hwy
  Tukwila WA 98188

(G-13775)
NANOICE
495 Andover Park E (98188-7605)
PHONE....................206 257-3380
EMP: 2 **EST:** 2013
SALES (est): 125K **Privately Held**
SIC: 2097 Manufactured ice

(G-13776)
NESTOR INC
18360 Olympic Ave S (98188-4723)
PHONE....................253 395-0285
Michael C James, *Branch Mgr*
EMP: 76
SALES (corp-wide): 6.3MM **Privately Held**
SIC: 3669 Pedestrian traffic control equipment
PA: Nestor, Inc.
  42 Oriental St Fl 3
  Providence RI 02908
  401 274-5345

(G-13777)
NEWMAN BURROWS LLC
1000 Andover Park E (98188-7632)
PHONE....................206 324-5644
Michael Daigle, *Mng Member*
Gerald Robinson,
EMP: 22 **EST:** 1893
SQ FT: 11,000
SALES (est): 3.4MM **Privately Held**
WEB: www.newman-burrows.com
SIC: 2752 Commercial printing, lithographic

(G-13778)
NIGHT SHIFT LLC
4214 S 137th St (98188-6203)
PHONE....................206 334-2548
Joseph Guanlao, *Principal*
EMP: 3
SALES (est): 76.1K **Privately Held**
SIC: 2711 Newspapers

(G-13779)
NORMED INC (PA)
Also Called: Hart Health
4320 S 131st Pl Ste 160 (98168-3200)
P.O. Box 3644, Seattle (98124-3644)
PHONE....................800 288-8200
Lawrence M Shaw, *President*
Chris Simons, *Purch Mgr*
Liesa Kolonics, *Cust Mgr*
▲ **EMP:** 36
SQ FT: 12,000
SALES (est): 17.3MM **Privately Held**
WEB: www.normed.com
SIC: 5199 3842 5122 6794 First aid supplies; first aid, snake bite & burn kits; pharmaceuticals; franchises, selling or licensing

(G-13780)
NORTHWEST PUBLISHING CTR LLC
14240 Interurban Ave S # 190 (98168-4658)
PHONE....................206 324-5644
Michael Daigle, *CEO*
EMP: 2
SALES (est): 238.9K **Privately Held**
SIC: 2741 Miscellaneous publishing

(G-13781)
NW LAUNDRY SERVICE
6446 S 144th St (98168-4609)
PHONE....................206 242-5500
EMP: 2
SALES (est): 90K **Privately Held**
SIC: 2842 Laundry cleaning preparations

(G-13782)
ODWALLA INC
6440 S 143rd St (98168-4669)
PHONE....................206 242-8519
Brook Carpenter, *Manager*
EMP: 45
SALES (corp-wide): 31.8B **Publicly Held**
WEB: www.odwalla.com
SIC: 2033 Fruit juices: packaged in cans, jars, etc.; vegetable juices: packaged in cans, jars, etc.
HQ: Odwalla, Inc.
  1 Coca Cola Plz Nw
  Atlanta GA 30313
  479 721-6260

(G-13783)
OLYMPUS PRESS INC
3400 S 150th St (98188-2109)
PHONE....................206 242-2700
Frank Vertrees, *President*
Glen Blue, *Corp Secy*
EMP: 30
SQ FT: 20,000
SALES (est): 5.2MM **Privately Held**
WEB: www.olypress.com
SIC: 2752 Commercial printing, offset

(G-13784)
OTIS ELEVATOR COMPANY
3315 S 116th St Ste 149 (98168-3349)
PHONE....................206 285-2285
Doug Johnson, *Principal*
EMP: 6
SALES (corp-wide): 66.5B **Publicly Held**
SIC: 2591 Blinds vertical
HQ: Otis Elevator Company
  1 Carrier Pl
  Farmington CT 06032
  860 674-3000

(G-13785)
P S PLUS SIZES TUKWILA
17580 Southcenter Pkwy (98188-3703)
PHONE....................206 575-3690
EMP: 2 **EST:** 2010
SALES (est): 140K **Privately Held**
SIC: 2899 Mfg Chemical Preparations

(G-13786)
PACCAR INC
8801 E Marginal Way S (98108-4007)
PHONE....................206 764-5400
Dave Sirlin, *General Mgr*
Krista Van Gaver, *Technology*
EMP: 400

GEOGRAPHIC SECTION

Tukwila - King County (G-13812)

SALES (corp-wide): 23.5B **Publicly Held**
WEB: www.paccar.com
SIC: 3711 Truck & tractor truck assembly; truck tractors for highway use, assembly of
PA: Paccar Inc
777 106th Ave Ne
Bellevue WA 98004
425 468-7400

(G-13787)
PACIFIC PROPELLER INTER LLC
1125 Andover Park W (98188-3910)
PHONE..................................206 575-5107
EMP: 2
SALES (est): 76.7K **Privately Held**
SIC: 3366 Propellers

(G-13788)
PACIFIC STRAPPING INC
Also Called: Herculine
2922 S 112th St (98168-1809)
P.O. Box 3715, Seattle (98124-3715)
PHONE..................................206 262-9800
Igor I Bitners, *Ch of Bd*
Sven R Bitners, *President*
Dagmara Bitners, *Corp Secy*
EMP: 13 EST: 1973
SQ FT: 20,000
SALES: 4MM **Privately Held**
WEB: www.pacstrap.com
SIC: 2241 Strapping webs

(G-13789)
PARAGON INDUSTRIES INC (DH)
Also Called: Paragon Pacific Insulation
18270 Segale Park Drive B (98188-4732)
PHONE..................................253 872-0800
Luke De Jardin, *CEO*
Richard J Mitchell, *President*
Robert M Rayner, *President*
Benjamin G Dicarlo, *Admin Sec*
EMP: 38
SQ FT: 75,000
SALES (est): 58.1MM
SALES (corp-wide): 2B **Publicly Held**
SIC: 5033 2679 Insulation materials; building, insulating & packaging paperboard
HQ: Fbm Galaxy, Inc.
1650 Manheim Pike Ste 202
Lancaster PA 17601
717 569-3900

(G-13790)
PARTY CITY CORPORATION
17356 Southcenter Pkwy (98188-3316)
PHONE..................................206 575-0502
Chad Hanni, *Manager*
EMP: 15
SALES (corp-wide): 2.4B **Publicly Held**
WEB: www.partycity.com
SIC: 5947 7299 2759 Party favors; costume rental; invitation & stationery printing & engraving
HQ: Party City Corporation
25 Green Pond Rd Ste 1
Rockaway NJ 07866

(G-13791)
PETER KAUPAT EASY
15666 W Valley Hwy (98188-5534)
P.O. Box 88108, Seattle (98138-2108)
PHONE..................................425 228-3633
Peter Kaupat, *Owner*
EMP: 11
SQ FT: 14,720
SALES (est): 780K **Privately Held**
SIC: 3732 Boat building & repairing

(G-13792)
POP GOURMET LLC
Also Called: P O P
14520 Interurban Ave S D100 (98168-4676)
PHONE..................................425 277-5225
David Israel, *President*
Jerry Hardt, *COO*
▲ EMP: 65 EST: 2010
SQ FT: 30,000
SALES: 7.5MM **Privately Held**
SIC: 2096 Potato chips & similar snacks

(G-13793)
POWELL INDUSTRIES INC
809 Industry Dr (98188-3411)
PHONE..................................206 402-3591
Sandy Powell, *President*
Mike Powell, *Vice Pres*
Sam Hsieh, *Prgrmr*
EMP: 10
SQ FT: 1,000
SALES (est): 2.2MM **Privately Held**
SIC: 3559 Electronic component making machinery

(G-13794)
PRECISION CASTPARTS CORP
3215 S 116th St Ste 109 (98168-1973)
PHONE..................................206 433-2600
Dennis Lord, *Branch Mgr*
EMP: 3
SALES (corp-wide): 225.3B **Publicly Held**
SIC: 3561 Pumps & pumping equipment
HQ: Precision Castparts Corp.
4650 Sw Mcdam Ave Ste 300
Portland OR 97239
503 946-4800

(G-13795)
PROFESSIONAL PLASTICS INC
6233 Segale Park Drive D (98188-4753)
PHONE..................................425 251-4140
EMP: 11
SALES (corp-wide): 121.3MM **Privately Held**
SIC: 2821 Plastics materials & resins
PA: Professional Plastics, Inc.
1810 E Valencia Dr
Fullerton CA 92831
714 446-6500

(G-13796)
PROFESSIONAL PLASTICS INC
6233 Segale Park Drive D (98188-4753)
PHONE..................................253 872-7430
Scott Patton, *Manager*
EMP: 13
SALES (corp-wide): 121.3MM **Privately Held**
WEB: www.professionalplastics.com
SIC: 5162 3089 Plastics materials & basic shapes; plastic processing
PA: Professional Plastics, Inc.
1810 E Valencia Dr
Fullerton CA 92831
714 446-6500

(G-13797)
PROFESSIONAL PLASTICS INC
6233 Segale Park Drive D (98188-4753)
PHONE..................................253 872-7430
David Kietzke, *President*
Dave Keitzke, *General Mgr*
Terry Tewell, *Business Mgr*
Michael Kietzke, *Vice Pres*
Bob Stonack, *Purchasing*
EMP: 16 EST: 1995
SALES (est): 2.5MM **Privately Held**
SIC: 2821 Plastics materials & resins

(G-13798)
PUGET SOUND INNOVATIONS INC
838 Industry Dr (98188-3410)
PHONE..................................206 575-7500
Juan Lozano, *Treasurer*
EMP: 2
SALES: 150K **Privately Held**
SIC: 3842 Surgical appliances & supplies

(G-13799)
PUGET SOUND PATTERN INC
Also Called: Puget Sound Pattern Works
6406 S 143rd St (98168-4626)
PHONE..................................206 439-6810
James Justin, *President*
EMP: 8
SQ FT: 7,200
SALES (est): 1MM **Privately Held**
SIC: 3543 Industrial patterns

(G-13800)
PUGET SOUND TENT & AWNING
18375 Olympic Ave S (98188-4724)
PHONE..................................425 251-9786
Bruce Dickinson, *Sales Executive*
EMP: 2 EST: 2017
SALES (est): 64.5K **Privately Held**
SIC: 2394 Canvas & related products

(G-13801)
RAINIER INDUSTRIES LTD
18375 Olympic Ave S (98188-4724)
PHONE..................................425 251-1800
Scott C Campbell, *President*
Brian Rowinski, *VP Opers*
Andrew King, *VP Finance*
Bruce Dickinson, *VP Sales*
▲ EMP: 140 EST: 1896
SQ FT: 140,000
SALES (est): 30.3MM **Privately Held**
SIC: 2394 3993 Tents: made from purchased materials; signs & advertising specialties

(G-13802)
RAISBECK ENGINEERING INC
4411 S Ryan Way (98178-2021)
PHONE..................................206 723-2000
Peter Greenthal, *CEO*
Lynn Thomas, *President*
Bo Alabic, *Opers Spvr*
Joel Shaw, *Engineer*
Davud Kasparov, *Design Engr*
EMP: 15
SQ FT: 16,000
SALES (est): 3MM **Privately Held**
WEB: www.raisbeck.com
SIC: 3728 8711 3812 Research & dev by manuf., aircraft parts & auxiliary equip; aircraft propellers & associated equipment; engineering services; search & navigation equipment

(G-13803)
RED DOT CORPORATION (PA)
495 Andover Park E (98188-7605)
P.O. Box 58270, Seattle (98138-1270)
PHONE..................................206 151-3840
Nick Janus, *President*
Gary Larry, *Opers Mgr*
Gary Wilson, *Prdtn Mgr*
Andrew Mitzel, *Production*
Brian Kennedy, *Purchasing*
◆ EMP: 310
SQ FT: 250,000
SALES (est): 109.1MM **Privately Held**
WEB: www.rdac.com
SIC: 3714 3585 Heaters, motor vehicle; air conditioning, motor vehicle

(G-13804)
REDI-BAG INC
17100 W Valley Hwy (98188-5555)
PHONE..................................425 251-9841
James Ulrich, *President*
Daniel Ulrich, *Vice Pres*
Coleman Binnie, *Cust Svc Dir*
EMP: 45
SQ FT: 100,000
SALES (est): 10.2MM **Privately Held**
SIC: 3081 Polyvinyl film & sheet

(G-13805)
REISCHLING PRESS INC (PA)
Also Called: RPI
3325 S 116th St Ste 161 (98168-1974)
PHONE..................................206 905-5999
Rick Bellamy, *CEO*
Traci Pichette, *Vice Pres*
Robert Reischling, *Vice Pres*
Dave Barnhart, *Prdtn Mgr*
Dave Gens, *CFO*
EMP: 44
SQ FT: 2,000
SALES (est): 23.9MM **Privately Held**
WEB: www.rpiprint.com
SIC: 2752 Commercial printing, offset

(G-13806)
RELIANCE STEEL & ALUMINUM CO
Bralco Metals
18325 Olympic Ave S (98188-4724)
PHONE..................................253 395-0614
Jim Kinney, *Principal*
EMP: 30
SALES (corp-wide): 11.5B **Publicly Held**
WEB: www.rsac.com
SIC: 3444 5051 Sheet metalwork; metals service centers & offices
PA: Reliance Steel & Aluminum Co.
350 S Grand Ave Ste 5100
Los Angeles CA 90071
213 687-7700

(G-13807)
RIVERS WEST APPAREL INC
1141 Andover Park W (98188-3910)
PHONE..................................425 272-2949
Michael J McGinley, *President*
Bruce Mathias, *Controller*
▲ EMP: 20
SQ FT: 23,000
SALES (est): 2.2MM **Privately Held**
WEB: www.riverswest.com
SIC: 2385 Waterproof outerwear

(G-13808)
RTS PACKAGING LLC
18340 Southcenter Pkwy (98188-8611)
PHONE..................................206 575-0380
Dave Githens, *Manager*
EMP: 7
SALES (corp-wide): 14.8B **Publicly Held**
WEB: www.rtspackaging.com
SIC: 2653 Corrugated & solid fiber boxes
HQ: Rts Packaging, Llc
504 Thrasher St
Norcross GA 30071
800 558-6984

(G-13809)
SAFEWORKS LLC (HQ)
Also Called: Spider
365 Upland Dr (98188-3802)
PHONE..................................206 575-6445
Scott Farrell, *President*
Greg Kennelly, *CFO*
Mike Dubois, *Supervisor*
▲ EMP: 95
SQ FT: 50,000
SALES (est): 108.4MM
SALES (corp-wide): 3B **Privately Held**
WEB: www.safeworks.com
SIC: 3536 3531 3446 5082 Hoists; construction machinery; architectural metalwork; cranes, construction
PA: Brand Industrial Services, Inc.
1325 Cobb Intl Dr Nw A1
Kennesaw GA 30152
678 285-1400

(G-13810)
SAFEWORKS HOLDINGS INC
365 Upland Dr (98188-3802)
PHONE..................................206 575-6445
Scott Farrell, *President*
Greg Kennelly, *CFO*
EMP: 300
SALES (est): 35.9MM **Privately Held**
SIC: 3536 Hoists, cranes & monorails

(G-13811)
SAHALE SNACKS INC
3411 S 120th Pl Ste 100 (98168-5135)
PHONE..................................206 624-7244
Eric Edding, *CEO*
Erika Cottrell, *Vice Pres*
Joelle Simmons, *Vice Pres*
Jerry Hardt, *CFO*
Christi Robertson, *Manager*
EMP: 65
SQ FT: 15,000
SALES (est): 28.1MM
SALES (corp-wide): 7.8B **Publicly Held**
WEB: www.sahalesnacks.com
SIC: 5145 2068 Snack foods; nuts: dried, dehydrated, salted or roasted
PA: The J M Smucker Company
1 Strawberry Ln
Orrville OH 44667
330 682-3000

(G-13812)
SAND CARRIER INC
16217 48th Ave S (98188-2728)
PHONE..................................206 790-6791
Abdi Ali, *Principal*
EMP: 2
SALES (est): 66K **Privately Held**
SIC: 1442 Construction sand & gravel

(PA)=Parent Co (HQ)=Headquarters (DH)=Div Headquarters
✪ = New Business established in last 2 years

Tukwila - King County (G-13813)

(G-13813)
SEA-TAC LIGHTING & CONTRLS LLC (PA)
4439e S 134th Pl (98168-6204)
PHONE 206 575-6865
Joyce Cassidy, *Principal*
Shannon Buckingham, *Project Mgr*
John Borrelli III,
Amanda Lowrance,
Kraig McFarlane,
EMP: 17
SQ FT: 15,000
SALES (est): 2.2MM **Privately Held**
WEB: www.seataclighting.com
SIC: 3699 5063 Electrical equipment & supplies; electrical apparatus & equipment

(G-13814)
SEATTLE BINDERY
6540 S Glacier St Ste 120 (98188-4737)
PHONE 425 656-8210
Milton Vine, *President*
Thomas Alvis, *Production*
Janet Vine, *Admin Sec*
Gary Klinger, *Administration*
EMP: 26 **EST:** 1960
SALES: 1.6MM **Privately Held**
WEB: www.seattlebindery.com
SIC: 2789 Binding only: books, pamphlets, magazines, etc.

(G-13815)
SEATTLE CHOCOLATE COMPANY LLC
1180 Andover Park W (98188-3909)
PHONE 425 264-2800
Kirsty Ellison, *Vice Pres*
Lee Ingrid, *Vice Pres*
Marie McNally, *VP Opers*
Omar Ruiz, *Warehouse Mgr*
Dyjen Collins, *Accounting Mgr*
▲ **EMP:** 50
SQ FT: 60,000
SALES (est): 8.7MM **Privately Held**
WEB: www.seachoco.com
SIC: 2066 Chocolate

(G-13816)
SELECT FLUID POWER USA INC
17300 W Valley Hwy (98188-5512)
PHONE 604 343-1111
Alison Fuller, *Principal*
Andrew Cuckow, *Controller*
Joshua Thomashefsky, *Sales Mgr*
EMP: 3
SALES (est): 134.6K **Privately Held**
SIC: 3492 Control valves, aircraft: hydraulic & pneumatic

(G-13817)
SHASTA BEVERAGES INC
1227 Andover Park E (98188-3956)
PHONE 206 575-0525
Tim Reckard, *Sales/Mktg Mgr*
EMP: 40
SALES (corp-wide): 1B **Publicly Held**
SIC: 2086 5149 Soft drinks: packaged in cans, bottles, etc.; carbonated beverages, nonalcoholic: bottled & canned; soft drinks
HQ: Shasta Beverages, Inc.
  26901 Indl Blvd
  Hayward CA 94545
  954 581-0922

(G-13818)
SHIPCO TRANSPORT INC
14900 Interurban Ave S # 215 (98168-4635)
PHONE 206 444-7447
Claus Jebson, *President*
◆ **EMP:** 6
SALES (est): 789.7K **Privately Held**
SIC: 2441 4731 Shipping cases, wood: nailed or lock corner; freight transportation arrangement

(G-13819)
SIMULAB CORPORATION
13001 48th Ave S (98168-3303)
PHONE 206 297-1260
Christopher Toly, *CEO*
EMP: 43
SQ FT: 10,000
SALES: 4MM **Privately Held**
WEB: www.simulab.com
SIC: 3845 3842 Endoscopic equipment, electromedical; surgical appliances & supplies

(G-13820)
SOUND SCREEN PRINTING INC
3216 S 136th St (98168-3962)
PHONE 206 890-2700
Daniel Blanchette, *Principal*
EMP: 2 **EST:** 2017
SALES (est): 83.9K **Privately Held**
SIC: 2752 Commercial printing, lithographic

(G-13821)
STAR FORGE LLC
Also Called: Jorgensen Forge
8531 E Marginal Way S (98108-4018)
PHONE 206 762-1100
Sandy Denune, *Principal*
EMP: 108 **EST:** 2016
SALES (est): 3.3MM **Privately Held**
SIC: 3462 3463 Gear & chain forgings; aluminum forgings

(G-13822)
STELFAST INC
350 Midland Dr (98188-3807)
PHONE 206 574-3078
EMP: 8
SALES (corp-wide): 155.6MM **Privately Held**
SIC: 3452 Bolts, nuts, rivets & washers
HQ: Stelfast Llc
  22979 Stelfast Pkwy
  Strongsville OH 44149
  440 879-0077

(G-13823)
STRESSWAVE INC
1130 Andover Park E (98188-3903)
P.O. Box 88648, Seattle (98138-2648)
PHONE 253 259-8796
Michael Landy, *President*
Eric Easterbrook, *Exec VP*
EMP: 2 **EST:** 1999
SQ FT: 300
SALES (est): 206.9K **Privately Held**
WEB: www.stress-wave.com
SIC: 3812 Aircraft/aerospace flight instruments & guidance systems

(G-13824)
SUPERIOR CUSTOM CABINETS INC (PA)
Also Called: Superior Cabinets
7120 S 180th St (98188-5536)
P.O. Box 88352, Seattle (98138-2352)
PHONE 425 251-1520
Bob J Dando, *President*
Ryan Desimone, *Sales Staff*
EMP: 25
SQ FT: 2,000
SALES: 4MM **Privately Held**
WEB: www.superiorcabinets.com
SIC: 2434 5211 Wood kitchen cabinets; lumber & other building materials

(G-13825)
SWADDLEDESIGNS LLC
500 Andover Park E (98188-7608)
PHONE 206 971-0426
Jamie Brigham-Knodle, *Opers Mgr*
Lynette Damir,
Jeffrey Damir,
▲ **EMP:** 30
SQ FT: 5,600
SALES: 9.7MM **Privately Held**
WEB: www.swaddledesigns.com
SIC: 2369 2393 Buntings, infants'; rompers: infants'; textile bags

(G-13826)
THERMAL SOLUTIONS MFG INC
400 Industry Dr Ste 160 (98188-3427)
PHONE 800 776-4650
Sandra Ainsworth, *Branch Mgr*
EMP: 3
SALES (corp-wide): 30.1MM **Privately Held**
SIC: 3714 Motor vehicle parts & accessories
PA: Thermal Solutions Manufacturing, Inc.
  15 Century Blvd Ste 102
  Nashville TN 37214
  800 359-9186

(G-13827)
TOUCH MARK PUBLISHING & PRINT
1181 Andover Park W (98188-3910)
PHONE 206 551-0578
Ali Osseiran, *President*
EMP: 4 **EST:** 2009
SALES (est): 340.2K **Privately Held**
SIC: 2752 Commercial printing, lithographic

(G-13828)
TRAFFIC TECH INC
14900 Interurban Ave S # 208 (98168-4635)
PHONE 206 357-1141
EMP: 4
SALES (corp-wide): 214MM **Privately Held**
SIC: 2819 Industrial inorganic chemicals
HQ: Traffic Tech, Inc.
  180 N Michigan Ave # 700
  Chicago IL 60601
  877 383-1167

(G-13829)
TWELVE THIRTY-ONE INCORPORATED
Also Called: Seattle Bindery & Finishing
6540 S Glacier St Ste 120 (98188-4737)
PHONE 425 656-8210
Thomas Alvis, *President*
Janice Alvis, *Treasurer*
EMP: 20 **EST:** 2012
SALES (est): 1.9MM **Privately Held**
SIC: 2789 Binding only: books, pamphlets, magazines, etc.

(G-13830)
TX FINE DESIGNS INC
16550 W Valley Hwy (98188-5524)
PHONE 425 271-2866
Viktor Kostroub, *Manager*
EMP: 4 **Privately Held**
SIC: 7389 2759 Design services; screen printing
PA: Tx Fine Designs, Inc.
  13645 Welch Rd
  Dallas TX 75244

(G-13831)
UTILITIES SERVICE COMPANY INC
12608 E Marginal Way S (98168-2563)
PHONE 206 246-5674
Anthony R Mola, *President*
EMP: 6
SQ FT: 2,400
SALES (est): 620K **Privately Held**
SIC: 1731 5084 7699 3599 Electrical work; industrial machinery & equipment; industrial machinery & equipment repair; machine shop, jobbing & repair

(G-13832)
VALHALLA BREWING AND BEV CO LL
402 Baker Blvd (98188-2905)
PHONE 206 243-6346
Daniel Lee, *Administration*
EMP: 5 **EST:** 2015
SALES (est): 110.5K **Privately Held**
SIC: 2082 Malt beverages

(G-13833)
VERTICAL DIMENSIONS LLC
1115 Andover Park W (98188-3910)
PHONE 206 767-8022
Steven McBride, *President*
Mary McBride, *Owner*
EMP: 7 **EST:** 2000
SQ FT: 20,000
SALES (est): 1.4MM **Privately Held**
WEB: www.verticaldimensions.net
SIC: 3534 Elevators & equipment

(G-13834)
VIA AIRLIFT INC
815 Industry Dr (98188-3411)
PHONE 206 258-6844
Sandeep Phadke, *President*
EMP: 5
SALES (est): 91K **Privately Held**
SIC: 7372 Application computer software

(G-13835)
W B MASON CO INC
18351 Cascade Ave S (98188-4712)
PHONE 888 926-2766
EMP: 40
SALES (corp-wide): 773MM **Privately Held**
SIC: 5943 5712 2752 Office forms & supplies; office furniture; commercial printing, lithographic
PA: W. B. Mason Co., Inc.
  59 Center St
  Brockton MA 02301
  781 794-8800

(G-13836)
WISDOMS MARIONETTES
4509 S 139th St (98168-3262)
PHONE 206 243-6172
Virginia Wisdom, *Owner*
EMP: 3
SALES (est): 174.2K **Privately Held**
SIC: 3999 Puppets & marionettes

(G-13837)
XEROX
435 Minkler Blvd (98188-7619)
PHONE 253 437-4000
EMP: 2
SALES (est): 158K **Privately Held**
SIC: 3577 Mfg Computer Peripheral Equipment

(G-13838)
XETA TECHNOLOGIES INC
3425 S 116th St Ste 101 (98168-1985)
PHONE 425 316-0721
Andrea Kloiber, *Manager*
EMP: 20
SALES (corp-wide): 5.7B **Publicly Held**
WEB: www.xeta.com
SIC: 3661 Telephones & telephone apparatus
HQ: Xeta Technologies, Inc.
  4001 N Rodney Parham Rd
  Little Rock AR 72212
  800 697-8153

(G-13839)
ZIRCONIA INC
4611 S 134th Pl Ste 240 (98168-3214)
PHONE 206 219-9236
Benjamin Cook, *President*
Muralee Balaguru, *CTO*
EMP: 3
SALES (est): 81.8K **Privately Held**
SIC: 2851 Undercoatings, paint

Tulalip
Snohomish County

(G-13840)
CAST 7020 LLC
Also Called: Seacast
6130 31st Ave Ne (98271-7407)
PHONE 401 885-9555
Micheal Robins,
Bert Robins,
EMP: 70
SALES (est): 12.2MM
SALES (corp-wide): 41.4MM **Privately Held**
WEB: www.aicasting.com
SIC: 3324 Steel investment foundries
PA: Seacast, Inc.
  6130 31st Ave Ne
  Tulalip WA 98271
  360 653-9388

(G-13841)
GOODNIGHT WOOD DESIGNS
12528 Marine Dr Ste M158 (98271)
PHONE 360 652-7765
M Bonasera, *Principal*
EMP: 2
SALES (est): 161K **Privately Held**
SIC: 2434 Wood kitchen cabinets

GEOGRAPHIC SECTION
Tumwater - Thurston County (G-13869)

(G-13842)
NET SERVICES LLC
13010 11th Ave Ne (98271-6751)
PHONE..................................360 651-1955
Terri Nunn, *General Mgr*
Daniel R Nunn,
Daniel Nunn,
EMP: 12
SALES (est): 1.9MM **Privately Held**
WEB: www.netservices.com
SIC: 2258 Net & netting products

(G-13843)
SEACAST INC (PA)
Also Called: Seacast Eagle
6130 31st Ave Ne (98271-7407)
PHONE..................................360 653-9388
Michael A Robins, *President*
Bertrand G Robins, *Vice Pres*
Brian Robins, *QC Mgr*
Andy Barnes, *Engineer*
Ty Ueland, *Engineer*
▲ **EMP:** 140
SQ FT: 100,000
SALES (est): 41.4MM **Privately Held**
WEB: www.seacast.com
SIC: 3324 3365 Steel investment foundries; aluminum foundries

(G-13844)
SHADES OF GREEN
917 129th Pl Nw (98271-7056)
P.O. Box 958, Marysville (98270-0958)
PHONE..................................425 387-2335
Jennifer Green, *Owner*
EMP: 2
SALES (est): 130.7K **Privately Held**
SIC: 3645 Lamp & light shades

(G-13845)
THE CREATION STATION INC
2001 71st St Ne (98271-9119)
PHONE..................................425 775-7959
Frank Knight, *President*
EMP: 2
SALES (est): 75K **Privately Held**
WEB: www.creationstationinc.com
SIC: 3944 5943 Craft & hobby kits & sets; school supplies

(G-13846)
VITAL SIGNS MINISTRIES
6118 Mission Beach Rd (98271-9724)
PHONE..................................360 659-2726
EMP: 2 **EST:** 2012
SALES (est): 115.3K **Privately Held**
SIC: 3993 Mfg Signs/Advertising Specialties

Tumtum
Stevens County

(G-13847)
TAILORED SOLUTIONS LLC
Also Called: Tailored Accents
5688 Corkscrew Canyon Rd (99034-9701)
PHONE..................................509 258-4314
Vickie Humbert,
EMP: 2
SALES (est): 155.8K **Privately Held**
SIC: 1799 7389 3089 Spraying contractor, non-agricultural; ; molding primary plastic

---
Tumwater
Thurston County

(G-13848)
ACE RACE PARTS INC
8108 River Dr Se Ste 106 (98501-6813)
PHONE..................................844 223-7243
Richard Whitlinger, *President*
EMP: 5
SALES (est): 202.2K **Privately Held**
SIC: 3751 Motorcycles & related parts

(G-13849)
AGBANGA KARITE LLC
Also Called: Alaffia
8109 River Dr Se B (98501-6871)
P.O. Box 11143, Olympia (98508-1143)
PHONE..................................360 515-9013
Joe Desimone, *Facilities Mgr*
Chris Schmidt, *Purchasing*
Stephen Mulcock, *Human Res Dir*
Andrew Dorf, *Natl Sales Mgr*
Olowo-N'djo Tchala,
▲ **EMP:** 7
SALES (est): 1.2MM **Privately Held**
SIC: 2844 2841 Shampoos, rinses, conditioners: hair; lotions, shaving; soap & other detergents

(G-13850)
ALASKA WHOLESALE HARDWOODS
2442 Mottman Rd Sw (98512-6219)
PHONE..................................360 704-4444
John Christopherson, *Principal*
EMP: 2 **EST:** 2007
SALES (est): 150K **Privately Held**
SIC: 5023 3272 3089 2426 Floor coverings; floor tile, precast terrazzo; floor coverings, plastic; flooring, hardwood

(G-13851)
AMCOR RIGID PACKAGING USA LLC
Also Called: Amcor Rigid Plastics
3025 32nd Ave Sw (98512-6161)
PHONE..................................360 753-4162
Tim Stewart, *Branch Mgr*
EMP: 290 **Privately Held**
WEB: www.slpcamericas.com
SIC: 3089 Plastic containers, except foam
HQ: Amcor Rigid Packaging Usa, Llc
40600 Ann Arbor Rd E # 201
Plymouth MI 48170

(G-13852)
AMERISAFE INC
3006 29th Ave Sw (98512-6101)
PHONE..................................360 943-5634
Martha McLeod, *Principal*
EMP: 8
SALES (est): 1MM **Privately Held**
SIC: 3842 Gloves, safety

(G-13853)
BRINEY SEA DELICACIES INC
Also Called: Briney Sea Delicaseas
715 78th Ave Sw Ste A (98501-5700)
P.O. Box 636, Thompson Falls MT (59873-0636)
PHONE..................................360 956-1797
Jay Garrison, *President*
EMP: 3
SALES (est): 290K **Privately Held**
SIC: 2092 Seafoods, fresh: prepared; seafoods, frozen: prepared

(G-13854)
C T SPECIALTIES
2815 37th Ave Sw Ste 120 (98512-5102)
PHONE..................................360 786-0274
Thomas Craigen, *Owner*
Terry Craigen, *Owner*
EMP: 7
SQ FT: 2,400
SALES (est): 440K **Privately Held**
WEB: www.ctspecialties.com
SIC: 3599 3441 Machine & other job shop work; fabricated structural metal

(G-13855)
CAPITAL INDUSTRIAL INC
2649 R W Johnson Blvd Sw (98512-6110)
PHONE..................................360 786-1890
Janete Colleen Nieman, *Principal*
Alan Nieman, *Principal*
EMP: 2
SALES (est): 86K **Privately Held**
SIC: 3799 Trailers & trailer equipment; automobile trailer chassis

(G-13856)
CAPITAL INDUSTRIAL SUPPLY INC
2649 R W Johnson Blvd Sw (98512-6110)
PHONE..................................360 786-1890
Irene Ann Stephens, *President*
Matt Grinstine, *Principal*
Matt Russell, *Principal*
Rudy Smith, *Principal*
Dirk E Stephens, *Vice Pres*
EMP: 25
SQ FT: 7,000
SALES (est): 10.9MM **Privately Held**
WEB: www.capitalindustrial.com
SIC: 5085 3715 3537 Industrial supplies; truck trailers; trucks, tractors, loaders, carriers & similar equipment

(G-13857)
CAPITOL CITY PRESS INC
2975 37th Ave Sw (98512-8243)
PHONE..................................360 943-3556
Michael McKnight, *President*
Carol Mc Carty, *Vice Pres*
Nick Eisenmann, *Plant Mgr*
Craig Francom, *Project Mgr*
Carrie Johnson, *Project Mgr*
EMP: 46
SQ FT: 25,000
SALES (est): 14.9MM **Privately Held**
WEB: www.capitolcitypress.com
SIC: 2752 Commercial printing, offset

(G-13858)
CARDINAL GLASS INDUSTRIES INC
Also Called: Cardinal Cg
700 Pat Kennedy Way Sw (98501-7249)
PHONE..................................360 956-9002
Steve Nelson, *President*
Jeff Tramel, *Facilities Mgr*
Doug Kimbrough, *Purch Mgr*
Jeremy Underwood, *Purch Agent*
Patty Woods, *Cust Mgr*
EMP: 100
SALES (corp-wide): 1B **Privately Held**
WEB: www.cardinalcorp.com
SIC: 3231 Products of purchased glass
PA: Cardinal Glass Industries Inc
775 Pririe Ctr Dr Ste 200
Eden Prairie MN 55344
952 229-2600

(G-13859)
CH 20 INC
8820 Old Highway 99 Se (98501-5744)
PHONE..................................360 956-9772
Carl Iverson, *CEO*
Tony McNamara, *President*
Karen Hall, *Owner*
EMP: 6 **EST:** 2011
SALES (est): 783.5K **Privately Held**
SIC: 3589 Water treatment equipment, industrial

(G-13860)
CHRISTOPHER ROSS DEWAYNE
Also Called: Standard Environmental Probe
6645 Littlerock Rd Sw (98512-7336)
PHONE..................................360 918-4586
Christopher Ross, *Owner*
EMP: 2
SALES (est): 146.7K **Privately Held**
SIC: 1081 1799 Metal mining exploration & development services; boring for building construction

(G-13861)
CLARK CONTRACT CUTTING INC
6827 Bel Mor Ct Sw (98512-1202)
PHONE..................................360 705-0355
Jeff Clark, *Principal*
EMP: 3
SALES (est): 199.1K **Privately Held**
SIC: 2411 Logging

(G-13862)
COLOR GRPHICS SCRNPRINTING INC
Also Called: Color Grphics Scrnprinting EMB
2540 Crites St Sw (98512-6135)
PHONE..................................360 352-3970
Voshte Gustafson, *President*
Kiley Gustafson, *Admin Sec*
EMP: 16
SQ FT: 22,000
SALES: 2MM **Privately Held**
WEB: www.colorgraphicswa.com
SIC: 2759 2395 3993 Screen printing; emblems, embroidered; signs & advertising specialties

(G-13863)
COLUMBUS SYSTEMS INC (PA)
2945 37th Ave Sw (98512-8243)
PHONE..................................360 943-4165
Mark Gerdts, *President*
EMP: 4 **EST:** 1997
SQ FT: 3,000
SALES (est): 328K **Privately Held**
WEB: www.propane98.com
SIC: 7372 Prepackaged software

(G-13864)
COLUMBUS SYSTEMS INC
855 Trosper Rd Sw (98512-8108)
PHONE..................................360 943-4165
Mark Gerdts, *President*
EMP: 2
SALES (est): 56.5K
SALES (corp-wide): 328K **Privately Held**
SIC: 7372 Prepackaged software
PA: Columbus Systems, Inc.
2945 37th Ave Sw
Tumwater WA 98512
360 943-4165

(G-13865)
CORNER STONE R V CENTER LLC
8500 Old Highway 99 Se A (98501-5739)
PHONE..................................360 704-4441
Jim Elliott Sr,
Jane Elliott,
EMP: 5
SALES (est): 530.4K **Privately Held**
WEB: www.cornerstonervcenter.com
SIC: 3714 Motor vehicle parts & accessories

(G-13866)
CSW INC
7745 Arab Dr Se Unit D (98501-6916)
PHONE..................................360 491-9365
EMP: 5
SALES (est): 450.4K **Privately Held**
SIC: 2431 Mfg Millwork

(G-13867)
CUMMINS INC
Also Called: Cummins Northwest
3300 Mottman Rd Sw (98512-8220)
PHONE..................................360 748-8841
Bryce Hood, *Branch Mgr*
EMP: 20
SALES (corp-wide): 23.7B **Publicly Held**
SIC: 5013 7538 5084 3714 Automotive supplies & parts; truck engine repair, except industrial; engines & parts, diesel; motor vehicle parts & accessories; internal combustion engines
PA: Cummins Inc.
500 Jackson St
Columbus IN 47201
812 377-5000

(G-13868)
CUSTOM SOURCE WOODWORKING INC
Also Called: C S W
7745d Arab Dr Se Unit D (98501-6840)
PHONE..................................360 491-9365
James A Mammina, *President*
Joseph P Wadsworth, *Vice Pres*
Dallas Lemon, *Purch Mgr*
John Fetters, *Treasurer*
Karen Sanders, *Controller*
EMP: 50
SALES (est): 8.2MM **Privately Held**
WEB: www.csw.co
SIC: 2434 Wood kitchen cabinets

(G-13869)
DAPAUL INC (PA)
9300 Kimmie St Sw (98512-9119)
P.O. Box 4094, Olympia (98501-0094)
PHONE..................................360 943-9844
Dan Sandy, *President*
EMP: 21
SQ FT: 5,000
SALES (est): 16.2MM **Privately Held**
SIC: 2421 Wood chips, produced at mill

Tumwater - Thurston County (G-13870)

(G-13870)
DART CONTAINER CORP GEORGIA
600 Israel Rd Se (98501-6413)
PHONE 360 352-7045
Byron Chen, *Manager*
Biyuan Chen, *Director*
EMP: 40
SQ FT: 109,701
SALES (corp-wide): 146.4MM Privately Held
SIC: 3086 2656 Cups & plates, foamed plastic; sanitary food containers
PA: Dart Container Corporation Of Georgia
500 Hogsback Rd
Mason MI 48854
517 676-3800

(G-13871)
DENISE HAASE
Also Called: Haase Logging
5729 Littlerock Rd Sw # 107 (98512-7386)
P.O. Box 136, Tenino (98589-0136)
PHONE 360 264-4680
Dennis Haase, *Owner*
EMP: 3
SALES: 400K Privately Held
SIC: 2411 Logging camps & contractors

(G-13872)
FOREVER POWDER COATING LLC
715 78th Ave Sw Ste 1 (98501-5700)
PHONE 360 786-6345
Jeffrey A Pinard,
EMP: 3
SALES (est): 272.1K Privately Held
SIC: 3479 Coating of metals & formed products

(G-13873)
GENOTHEN HOLDINGS LLC
2948 29th Ave Sw (98512-6194)
PHONE 360 352-3636
Leighann McClintock, *General Mgr*
Terese Dwinal, *Mng Member*
Steve Dwinal,
EMP: 60
SALES (est): 8.8MM Privately Held
SIC: 2521 2531 Wood office furniture; public building & related furniture

(G-13874)
H2O JET INC
1145 85th Ave Se (98501-5708)
PHONE 360 866-7161
Halan Arnold, *President*
Duane Johnson, *President*
Kevin McManus, *Chairman*
John Stanko, *Vice Pres*
Malin Jakobsson, *Treasurer*
▲ **EMP:** 28 **EST:** 1992
SQ FT: 20,000
SALES: 8.7MM
SALES (corp-wide): 162.7MM Privately Held
WEB: www.h2ojetcorp.com
SIC: 3561 7389 Pumps & pumping equipment; metal cutting services
HQ: Shape Technologies Group, Inc.
23500 64th Ave S
Kent WA 98032
253 246-3200

(G-13875)
HANG GLIDING ADVENTURES
884 Anthony Ct Sw (98512-6367)
PHONE 360 357-1460
Grant Nelson, *Owner*
EMP: 2
SALES (est): 173.5K Privately Held
SIC: 3721 Hang gliders

(G-13876)
JACKNUT APPAREL
2320 Mottman Rd Sw # 102 (98512-6232)
PHONE 360 742-3523
Christian Burgess, *Owner*
EMP: 2
SALES (est): 113.9K Privately Held
SIC: 2261 Screen printing of cotton broad-woven fabrics

(G-13877)
JAYTEES MANAGEMENT GROUP LLC ◆
915 Trosper Rd Sw Ste 101 (98512-6972)
PHONE 360 352-0038
EMP: 3 **EST:** 2018
SALES (est): 186.4K Privately Held
SIC: 2759 Screen printing

(G-13878)
JONES COMPANY INC
2840 Black Lake Blvd Sw (98512-5107)
PHONE 360 352-1022
Diana Wall, *President*
Phyllis Thompson, *Vice Pres*
EMP: 6
SALES (est): 305K Privately Held
SIC: 1442 Construction sand & gravel

(G-13879)
JONES QUARRY INC
2840 Black Lake Blvd Sw C (98512-6197)
PHONE 360 352-1022
Diana Wall, *President*
Phyllis Thompson, *Vice Pres*
William Jones, *Shareholder*
EMP: 6 **EST:** 1979
SQ FT: 1,500
SALES (est): 930K Privately Held
SIC: 1429 5999 Boulder, crushed & broken-quarrying; rock & stone specimens

(G-13880)
KINCAID WOODWORKING
3740 Antsen St Sw (98512-6224)
PHONE 518 810-1374
Scott Kincaid, *Principal*
EMP: 2 **EST:** 2017
SALES (est): 82.3K Privately Held
SIC: 2431 Millwork

(G-13881)
KNOT YOUR EVERY DAY CROCHET
7511a Trails End Dr Se (98501-5844)
PHONE 360 791-9154
Kymberli McRostie, *Principal*
EMP: 2
SALES (est): 77K Privately Held
SIC: 2399 Hand woven & crocheted products

(G-13882)
L & E BOTTLING CO INC
3200 Mottman Rd Sw (98512-5658)
P.O. Box 11159, Olympia (98508-1159)
PHONE 360 357-3812
Brian Charneski, *President*
Jack F Charneski, *Chairman*
Luellen Charneski, *Vice Pres*
Kay Charneski, *Treasurer*
Eric Charneski, *Admin Sec*
EMP: 70 **EST:** 1945
SQ FT: 60,000
SALES (est): 12.1MM Privately Held
WEB: www.olypepsi.com
SIC: 2086 Soft drinks: packaged in cans, bottles, etc.

(G-13883)
LEXYS NAILS & SPA
111 Tumwater Blvd Se (98501-6400)
PHONE 360 352-5044
Tina Tran, *General Mgr*
EMP: 3
SALES (est): 53.8K Privately Held
SIC: 7231 2842 Manicurist, pedicurist; wax removers

(G-13884)
LINEX OF OLYMPIA
Also Called: Line-X of Olympia
5403 Capitol Blvd Sw (98501-4422)
PHONE 360 709-0363
Clint Owen, *Owner*
Michelle Lee, *Manager*
EMP: 6
SALES (est): 622.4K Privately Held
SIC: 5531 2851 Automotive accessories; shellac (protective coating)

(G-13885)
LOST SIGNAL LLC
510 N 6th Ave Sw (98512-6427)
PHONE 360 601-2227
Brian Gish,
EMP: 3
SALES (est): 153.7K Privately Held
SIC: 7372 Application computer software

(G-13886)
MAIL IT SIGN IT LLC
4005 Pifer Rd Se (98501-3600)
PHONE 360 515-5198
B David Platt, *Administration*
EMP: 2 **EST:** 2013
SALES (est): 101.4K Privately Held
SIC: 3993 Signs & advertising specialties

(G-13887)
MIKES CUSTOM WELDING
Also Called: Mike's Welding
5211 Joppa St Sw (98512-6734)
PHONE 360 754-3719
Mike Grate, *Owner*
Michelle Grate, *Treasurer*
EMP: 6
SQ FT: 12,000
SALES: 600K Privately Held
SIC: 1799 7353 7692 7389 Exterior cleaning, including sandblasting; heavy construction equipment rental; welding repair; crane & aerial lift service

(G-13888)
MVP ATHLETIC INC
6005 Capitol Blvd Sw (98512-5268)
PHONE 360 915-8715
EMP: 2 **EST:** 2010
SALES (est): 89K Privately Held
SIC: 7999 5941 2759 Amusement/Recreation Services Ret Sporting Goods/Bicycles Commercial Printing

(G-13889)
PARETO-CURVE MARKETING INC
Also Called: Coffee News
6200 Capitol Blvd Se C (98501-5288)
P.O. Box 4008, Olympia (98501-0008)
PHONE 360 357-1000
Daniel Stusser, *President*
Jennifer Templeton, *Office Mgr*
EMP: 5 **EST:** 1996
SALES (est): 675.3K Privately Held
WEB: www.ergotecgroup.com
SIC: 8742 2711 Marketing consulting services; commercial printing & newspaper publishing combined

(G-13890)
PARK PLACE INDUSTRIES
11020 Park Place Ln Se (98501-9416)
PHONE 360 584-9762
David Moore, *Principal*
EMP: 2
SALES (est): 97K Privately Held
SIC: 3999 Manufacturing industries

(G-13891)
PEPSI NORTHWEST BEVERAGES LLC (DH)
3003 R W Johnson Blvd Sw (98512-6173)
PHONE 360 357-9090
Tom Connolly, *General Mgr*
Timothy Howard, *Sales Staff*
Gerald Marsland, *Maintence Staff*
▼ **EMP:** 140
SALES (est): 68.2MM
SALES (corp-wide): 64.6B Publicly Held
SIC: 2086 Soft drinks: packaged in cans, bottles, etc.; carbonated soft drinks, bottled & canned
HQ: Pepsi-Cola Metropolitan Bottling Company, Inc.
1111 Westchester Ave
White Plains NY 10604
914 767-6000

(G-13892)
QUANEX BUILDING PRODUCTS CORP
3003 Sunset Way Se (98501-3400)
PHONE 360 345-1241
EMP: 8 Publicly Held
SIC: 3272 Building materials, except block or brick: concrete
PA: Quanex Building Products Corporation
1800 West Loop S Ste 1500
Houston TX 77027

(G-13893)
RAINBOW CLOUD KOMBUCHA LLC
2915 29th Ave Sw Ste D (98512-6183)
PHONE 253 312-3697
Leland Harmell, *Managing Dir*
Graham Newman, *Sales Mgr*
Matthew Eklund,
EMP: 3
SQ FT: 3,000
SALES (est): 136.9K Privately Held
SIC: 2086 Carbonated beverages, nonalcoholic: bottled & canned

(G-13894)
RCC LOGGING LIMITED
1675 View Point Ct Sw (98512-6357)
PHONE 360 556-8904
Richard Clark, *Principal*
EMP: 2
SALES (est): 160.9K Privately Held
SIC: 2411 Logging

(G-13895)
RUBENSTEINS OLYMPIA
321 Cleveland Ave Se (98501-3348)
PHONE 360 753-9156
EMP: 2
SALES (est): 142.8K Privately Held
SIC: 2273 Carpets & rugs

(G-13896)
SAND PAPER & INK INC
Also Called: Emery Systems
2918 Ferguson St Sw C1 (98512-6186)
PHONE 360 705-0918
Lawrence C Emery, *President*
Larry Emery, *President*
Sandy Emery, *CFO*
EMP: 3
SQ FT: 2,000
SALES (est): 32.6K Privately Held
WEB: www.emerysystems.com
SIC: 2759 8742 7336 2761 Business forms: printing; management consulting services; commercial art & graphic design; manifold business forms

(G-13897)
SIGN SHOP LLC
1381 Linwood Ave Sw (98512-6853)
PHONE 360 352-5926
Ross L Young, *Mng Member*
Joni Merten, *Mng Member*
EMP: 2
SALES (est): 225.9K Privately Held
WEB: www.signshopolympia.com
SIC: 3993 Electric signs

(G-13898)
SOLOY LLC
Also Called: Soloy Aviation Solutions
450 Pat Kennedy Way Sw (98501-7201)
PHONE 360 754-7000
David Stauffer, *CEO*
Elling Halvorson, *Mng Member*
▲ **EMP:** 42
SQ FT: 33,000
SALES (est): 9.1MM Privately Held
WEB: www.soloy.com
SIC: 3728 8711 4581 3721 Aircraft parts & equipment; engineering services; aircraft maintenance & repair services; aircraft

(G-13899)
THOMPSON & CLOUD LLC
4842 Rural Rd Sw Apt 301 (98512-6742)
PHONE 206 218-9991
Claude Ruiter, *Principal*
EMP: 3
SALES (est): 205.8K Privately Held
SIC: 3999 Candles

(G-13900)
TRUSS COMPONENTS OF WASHINGTON
5102 Lambskin St Sw (98512-8012)
PHONE 360 753-0057
Frederick Prosser, *President*
EMP: 35
SQ FT: 8,640 Privately Held
SIC: 2439 Trusses, wooden roof

GEOGRAPHIC SECTION — Union Gap - Yakima County (G-13929)

PA: Truss Components Of Washington Inc
5232 Joppa St Sw
Tumwater WA 98512

(G-13901)
TRUSS COMPONENTS OF WASHINGTON (PA)
Also Called: Truss Companies
5232 Joppa St Sw (98512-6782)
PHONE..................360 753-0057
Frederick Prosser, President
EMP: 30
SQ FT: 700
SALES (est): 5.1MM **Privately Held**
SIC: 2439 Trusses, wooden roof

(G-13902)
TUMWATER EYE CENTER INC
100 Dennis St Sw Ste F (98501-6523)
PHONE..................360 352-6060
Douglas Jeske, President
EMP: 4
SALES (est): 766.8K **Privately Held**
SIC: 8042 3851 Offices & clinics of optometrists; eyeglasses, lenses & frames

(G-13903)
TUMWATER PRINTING
7675 New Market St Sw (98501-5798)
PHONE..................360 943-2204
Allen Walton, Owner
EMP: 11
SALES (est): 1.1MM **Privately Held**
WEB: www.tumwaterprinting.com
SIC: 2752 Commercial printing, offset

(G-13904)
WESTERN SUPERIOR STRUCTURALS
7380 New Market St Sw (98501-6566)
PHONE..................360 943-0339
Tim Howard, President
Mary Maloy, Vice Pres
Vanessa Carver, Treasurer
Laura Howard, Admin Sec
EMP: 17
SQ FT: 6,500
SALES (est): 3.5MM **Privately Held**
SIC: 3441 Building components, structural steel

(G-13905)
WHISLERS INC (PA)
Also Called: Whisler Communications
2875 R W Johnson Blvd Sw (98512-6114)
PHONE..................360 352-8777
L R Whisler, President
J A Whisler, Corp Secy
EMP: 5
SQ FT: 11,300
SALES (est): 600K **Privately Held**
SIC: 5731 3812 Radios, receiver type; antennas, radar or communications

(G-13906)
WINDFALL LUMBER INC
711 Tumwater Blvd Sw D (98501-7254)
PHONE..................360 352-2250
Scott Royer, President
EMP: 20
SQ FT: 25,000
SALES (est): 3.5MM **Privately Held**
SIC: 5712 2521 2421 2493 Cabinet work, custom; wood office furniture; flooring (dressed lumber), softwood; reconstituted wood products; table or counter tops, plastic laminated

(G-13907)
WINSOR FIREFORM LLC
3401 Mottman Rd Sw (98512-6277)
PHONE..................360 786-8200
Bryan R Stockdale, Mng Member
EMP: 20 **EST:** 1998
SALES (est): 2.7MM **Privately Held**
WEB: www.winsorfireform.com
SIC: 3993 7336 Signs & advertising specialties; commercial art & graphic design

(G-13908)
WOOD & SON EARTHWORK & UTILITY
2840 Black Lake Blvd Sw (98512-5107)
P.O. Box 5240, Yelm (98597-5240)
PHONE..................360 352-1022
Michael Wood, Principal
EMP: 11
SALES (est): 1.5MM **Privately Held**
SIC: 1411 Dimension stone

Twisp
Okanogan County

(G-13909)
CASCADE GROWERS LLC ✪
166 Benson Creek Dr (98856-9605)
PHONE..................530 919-3431
EMP: 2 **EST:** 2018
SALES (est): 74.9K **Privately Held**
SIC: 0139 3999 ;

(G-13910)
CASCADE PIPE & FEED SUPPLY
420 E Methow Valley Hwy (98856)
P.O. Box 1327 (98856-1327)
PHONE..................509 997-0720
Julie Palm, President
Julie L Palm, President
Gerald L Palm, Co-Owner
EMP: 6
SALES (est): 1.2MM **Privately Held**
SIC: 5099 5999 5083 5051 Logs, hewn ties, posts & poles; plumbing & heating supplies; lawn & garden machinery & equipment; pipe & tubing, steel; saws & sawing equipment; culverts, sheet metal

(G-13911)
EQPD GEAR LLC
502 Glover St S Bldg 7 (98856-5818)
PHONE..................509 997-2010
Jonathan Baker, President
EMP: 6 **EST:** 2017
SALES (est): 368.5K **Privately Held**
SIC: 3949 Sporting & athletic goods

(G-13912)
LLOYD LOGGING INC
1219 Methow Vly E (98856)
P.O. Box 218 (98856-0218)
PHONE..................509 997-2441
Donald Maples, President
Robert Lloyd Jr, Treasurer
EMP: 10 **EST:** 1953
SQ FT: 500
SALES (est): 1.4MM **Privately Held**
SIC: 1611 4212 1794 1623 General contractor, highway & street construction; local trucking, without storage; excavation work; water, sewer & utility lines; construction sand & gravel

(G-13913)
LLOYD REMSBERG LOGGING
Also Called: Remsberg Trucking
993 Twisp Carlton Rd (98856-9619)
PHONE..................509 997-7362
Lloyd Remsberg, Owner
INA Remsberg, Co-Owner
EMP: 5
SALES (est): 50K **Privately Held**
SIC: 4212 2411 Lumber (log) trucking, local; logging

(G-13914)
METHOW VALLEY INDUSTRIAL LLC
202 Industrial Park Ave (98856)
P.O. Box 978 (98856-0978)
PHONE..................509 997-7777
Leone C Edson, Mng Member
EMP: 2 **EST:** 2002
SQ FT: 4,800
SALES (est): 397.8K **Privately Held**
SIC: 7692 3599 7538 Welding repair; machine shop, jobbing & repair; general automotive repair shops

(G-13915)
METHOW VALLEY PUBLISHING LLC
101 Glover St N (98856)
PHONE..................509 997-7011
Paul Butler,
EMP: 12
SQ FT: 3,000
SALES (est): 572K **Privately Held**
WEB: www.methowvalleynews.com
SIC: 2711 Newspapers

(G-13916)
PHILLIP L REMSBERG
Also Called: Phillip Remsberg Logging
1021 Twisp Carlton Rd (98856)
PHONE..................509 997-3231
Phillip L Remsberg, Owner
Theresa Remsberg, Co-Owner
EMP: 2
SALES: 348K **Privately Held**
SIC: 7389 2411 Log & lumber broker; logging

(G-13917)
WHITE LOGGING LLC
Also Called: Methow Valley Septic
110 Lookout Mnt Rd (98856)
P.O. Box 1250 (98856-1250)
PHONE..................509 997-0279
Erin White, Principal
Tom White,
EMP: 5
SALES: 84K **Privately Held**
SIC: 2411 Logging

Union
Mason County

(G-13918)
POLYVENTURE INTERNATIONAL
3500 E State Route 106 (98592-9515)
PHONE..................360 898-7013
Carl Mease, Principal
EMP: 2 **EST:** 2010
SALES (est): 90.9K **Privately Held**
SIC: 2741 Miscellaneous publishing

Union Gap
Yakima County

(G-13919)
A & B PLASTICS INC
2405 S 3rd Ave (98903-1510)
PHONE..................509 248-9166
Shelia Zirlin, Director
EMP: 2 **EST:** 2011
SALES (est): 143K **Privately Held**
SIC: 3721 Airplanes, fixed or rotary wing

(G-13920)
ATRIUM DOOR AND WIN CO OF NW
3400 Tacoma St (98903-1979)
PHONE..................509 248-4462
Gregory T Faherty, CEO
EMP: 7
SALES (est): 812.6K **Privately Held**
SIC: 3442 Window & door frames

(G-13921)
ATRIUM WINDOWS AND DOOR WASH
3400 Tacoma St (98903-1979)
P.O. Box 10444, Yakima (98909-1444)
PHONE..................509 248-4462
Brent Dobbs, General Mgr
EMP: 320
SQ FT: 77,000
SALES (est): 31.2MM
SALES (corp-wide): 2B **Publicly Held**
WEB: www.bestbuiltinc.com
SIC: 3442 3231 Window & door frames; doors, glass: made from purchased glass
HQ: Atrium Windows And Doors, Inc.
959 Profit Dr
Dallas TX 75247
214 583-1840

(G-13922)
ATRIUM WINDOWS AND DOORS INC
3400 Tacoma St (98903-1979)
P.O. Box 10444, Yakima (98909-1444)
PHONE..................509 248-4462
Kevin Omeara, President
EMP: 235

SALES (corp-wide): 2B **Publicly Held**
SIC: 3442 Metal doors, sash & trim
HQ: Atrium Windows And Doors, Inc.
959 Profit Dr
Dallas TX 75247
214 583-1840

(G-13923)
BIMBO BAKERIES USA INC
1910 Mcnair Ave (98903-4014)
PHONE..................509 469-3707
Dick Staley, Principal
EMP: 15 **Privately Held**
SIC: 2051 Bakery: wholesale or wholesale/retail combined
HQ: Bimbo Bakeries Usa, Inc
255 Business Center Dr # 200
Horsham PA 19044
215 347-5500

(G-13924)
CASCADE INDUS & HYDRAULIC LLC
3315 Main St (98903-1849)
PHONE..................509 452-1752
Cong Huynh,
EMP: 4
SQ FT: 2,000
SALES (est): 685.9K **Privately Held**
SIC: 5251 3566 Pumps & pumping equipment; gears, power transmission, except automotive

(G-13925)
CCS EQUIPMENT INC
1917 S 14th St (98903-1849)
P.O. Box 9974, Yakima (98909-0974)
PHONE..................509 248-4001
EMP: 37
SALES (est): 3.6MM **Privately Held**
SIC: 3523 Mfg Farm Machinery/Equipment

(G-13926)
CLAYTON HOMES INC
2010 Rudkin Rd (98903-4020)
PHONE..................509 452-9228
Silvestre Lozano, Sales Staff
Julie Escamilla, Branch Mgr
EMP: 2
SALES (corp-wide): 225.3B **Publicly Held**
SIC: 2451 Mobile homes
HQ: Clayton Homes, Inc.
5000 Clayton Rd
Maryville TN 37804
865 380-3000

(G-13927)
CREATIVE GARMENT DESIGN & EMB
207 W Court St (98903-1932)
PHONE..................509 457-3482
Marilynn Kendrick, Owner
Marilynee Kendrick, Owner
EMP: 5
SALES: 100K **Privately Held**
WEB: www.creativegd.com
SIC: 2395 Embroidery & art needlework

(G-13928)
EDWARDS EQUIPMENT CO INC
4312 Main St (98903-2116)
PHONE..................509 248-1770
Randy Searl, President
Gerald Searl, Corp Secy
EMP: 11 **EST:** 1947
SQ FT: 7,500
SALES (est): 2.1MM **Privately Held**
WEB: www.edwards-equip.com
SIC: 3523 Farm machinery & equipment

(G-13929)
FARMER BROS CO
Also Called: Farmers Brothers Coffee
2301 S 18th St (98903-1635)
PHONE..................509 457-6031
Barry Mote, Manager
EMP: 6
SALES (corp-wide): 606.5MM **Publicly Held**
WEB: www.farmerbros.com
SIC: 2095 5149 Coffee roasting (except by wholesale grocers); coffee & tea

Union Gap - Yakima County (G-13930) — GEOGRAPHIC SECTION

PA: Farmer Bros. Co.
1912 Farmer Brothers Dr
Northlake TX 76262
888 998-2468

(G-13930)
FINISHING SPECIALIST LLC
1907 S 14th St (98903-1282)
PHONE.................................509 248-5510
John Wingerter, *Owner*
EMP: 4
SALES (est): 364.4K **Privately Held**
SIC: 3479 Coating of metals & formed products

(G-13931)
FREEDOM TRUCK CENTERS INC
Also Called: Yakima Freightliner
1910 Rudkin Rd (98903-4028)
PHONE.................................509 248-9478
Larry Pierson, *Manager*
EMP: 20
SALES (corp-wide): 23.1MM **Privately Held**
WEB: www.freedomfreightliner.net
SIC: 5013 7538 5012 3713 Truck parts & accessories; general automotive repair shops; automobiles & other motor vehicles; truck & bus bodies
PA: Freedom Truck Centers, Inc.
10310 W Westbow Rd
Spokane WA 99224
509 744-0390

(G-13932)
HY-GRADE GLASS INC
2003 S 14th St (98903-1284)
P.O. Box 10027, Yakima (98909-1027)
PHONE.................................509 248-9919
Karl Hendricks, *President*
Jana Hendrix, *Vice Pres*
EMP: 19
SQ FT: 7,200
SALES (est): 3MM **Privately Held**
WEB: www.hygradeglass.com
SIC: 3211 5039 Insulating glass, sealed units; glass construction materials; exterior flat glass: plate or window; interior flat glass: plate or window

(G-13933)
INTERNATIONAL PAPER COMPANY
660 W Ahtanum Rd (98903)
PHONE.................................509 576-3158
EMP: 2
SALES (corp-wide): 22.3B **Publicly Held**
SIC: 2621 Paper Mill
PA: International Paper Company
6400 Poplar Ave
Memphis TN 38197
901 419-9000

(G-13934)
ITEC INC
1602 Rudkin Rd (98901-4030)
PHONE.................................509 452-3672
Jim Lydigsen, *Principal*
EMP: 4
SALES (est): 236.6K **Privately Held**
SIC: 3799 Trailer hitches

(G-13935)
JJS AUTOMOTIVE & AUTO ELC LLC
2626 Rudkin Rd (98903-1633)
PHONE.................................509 248-2622
Juan Alvarez, *Principal*
EMP: 3 **EST:** 2011
SALES (est): 198.4K **Privately Held**
SIC: 7539 3699 Automotive repair shops; electrical equipment & supplies

(G-13936)
KING BROTHERS WOODWORKING INC (PA)
602 W Valley Mall Blvd (98903-1621)
PHONE.................................509 453-4683
EMP: 30 **EST:** 1948
SQ FT: 21,600
SALES (est): 2MM **Privately Held**
SIC: 2431 2541 2434 Mfg Millwork Mfg Wood Partitions/Fixtures Mfg Wood Kitchen Cabinets

(G-13937)
KWIK LOK CORPORATION (HQ)
2712 S 16th Ave (98903-9530)
P.O. Box 9548, Yakima (98909-0548)
PHONE.................................509 248-4770
Jerre H Paxton, *President*
Lorne House, *Corp Secy*
Kohen Kelley, *Marketing Staff*
◆ **EMP:** 105
SQ FT: 66,000
SALES (est): 35.7MM **Privately Held**
SIC: 3565 Packaging machinery

(G-13938)
LAROCK ENTERPRISES INC
Also Called: Eagle Machine
1401 W Pine St (98903-1557)
PHONE.................................509 966-4542
Douglas Larock, *President*
Linda Larock, *Corp Secy*
Robert J Hendry, *Vice Pres*
EMP: 19
SQ FT: 12,800
SALES: 1.5MM **Privately Held**
SIC: 3599 7692 Custom machinery; machine shop, jobbing & repair; welding repair

(G-13939)
M & M FABRICATORS INC
2004 S 14th St (98903-1283)
PHONE.................................509 248-8890
Ron Gillespie, *Owner*
EMP: 2
SALES (est): 170.3K **Privately Held**
SIC: 3444 Sheet metalwork

(G-13940)
MACRO PLASTICS INC
3555 Bay St (98903-1887)
PHONE.................................509 452-1200
Matthew Barnett, *Manager*
EMP: 30
SALES (corp-wide): 573.1MM **Privately Held**
SIC: 3089 3443 2441 Injection molding of plastics; fabricated plate work (boiler shop); nailed wood boxes & shook
HQ: Macro Plastics, Inc.
2250 Huntington Dr
Fairfield CA 94533
707 437-1200

(G-13941)
MAF INDUSTRIES INC
2705 S 16th Ave (98903-9530)
PHONE.................................509 574-8775
Bryan Brown, *Manager*
EMP: 12
SALES (est): 2MM **Privately Held**
WEB: www.mafindustries.com
SIC: 3565 Packing & wrapping machinery
HQ: Maf Industries, Inc.
36470 Highway 99
Traver CA 93673
559 897-2905

(G-13942)
MAGIC METALS INC
3401 Bay St (98903-1886)
PHONE.................................509 453-1690
Garry L Griggs, *President*
Kevin D Griggs, *President*
Brian Warren, *Vice Pres*
Timothy W Lick, *CFO*
Tim Fornshell, *Accounts Mgr*
▼ **EMP:** 168
SQ FT: 102,500
SALES: 30MM **Privately Held**
SIC: 7692 3444 Welding repair; sheet metalwork

(G-13943)
MARTIN FABRICATIONS
2012 Longfibre Rd (98903-1567)
PHONE.................................509 457-8309
Martin Capdeville, *Owner*
EMP: 2
SALES (est): 163.5K **Privately Held**
SIC: 7692 Welding repair

(G-13944)
METALS MCHNING FABRICATORS INC
2004 S 14th St (98903-1283)
P.O. Box 11204, Yakima (98909-2204)
PHONE.................................509 248-8890
Ronald Gillespie, *President*
Byrna Grove, *Corp Secy*
EMP: 15
SQ FT: 2,000
SALES (est): 1.7MM **Privately Held**
WEB: www.mmfabricatorsinc.com
SIC: 3444 3599 Sheet metalwork; machine shop, jobbing & repair

(G-13945)
N A I INC
Also Called: Fab Tek
2603 S 16th Ave (98903-9531)
PHONE.................................509 453-4778
Peggy Cupples, *President*
EMP: 5
SALES: 500K **Privately Held**
SIC: 1761 3399 Sheet metalwork; powder, metal

(G-13946)
NORTHSTAR ATTACHMENTS LLC
3205 Bay St (98903-1881)
P.O. Box 168, Yakima (98907-0168)
PHONE.................................509 453-8271
David C Rankin, *Principal*
EMP: 5
SALES (est): 496.5K **Privately Held**
SIC: 8742 1799 3531 Construction project management consultant; playground construction & equipment installation; construction machinery

(G-13947)
ORCHARD-RITE LIMITED INC
Also Called: Orchard Rite Ld
1615 W Ahtanum Rd (98903-1815)
PHONE.................................509 834-2029
Dennis Hill, *Manager*
EMP: 25
SALES (corp-wide): 28.3MM **Privately Held**
SIC: 3523 3564 Farm machinery & equipment; blowers & fans
PA: Orchard-Rite Limited, Inc.
1702 Englewood Ave
Yakima WA 98902
509 834-2029

(G-13948)
PACKING HOUSE SERVICES INC
Also Called: Red Pearl Systems
1916 S 18th St (98903-3930)
P.O. Box 399, Yakima (98907-0399)
PHONE.................................509 452-5002
Jeff Odman, *President*
Del Odman, *Principal*
Todd Odman, *Vice Pres*
Pat Odman, *Treasurer*
EMP: 8 **EST:** 1980
SALES (est): 1.5MM **Privately Held**
WEB: www.phsweb.com
SIC: 3523 Grading, cleaning, sorting machines, fruit, grain, vegetable

(G-13949)
PARAGON FILMS INC
915 Rose St (98903-1900)
PHONE.................................509 424-3700
Alex Jach, *Manager*
EMP: 23
SALES (corp-wide): 25.4MM **Privately Held**
SIC: 3081 Polyethylene film
PA: Paragon Films, Inc.
3500 W Tacoma St
Broken Arrow OK 74012
918 250-3456

(G-13950)
PEXCO AEROSPACE INC (HQ)
2405 S 3rd Ave (98903-1510)
PHONE.................................509 248-9166
Halle Terrion, *Director*
EMP: 145
SALES (est): 97.9MM
SALES (corp-wide): 3.8B **Publicly Held**
SIC: 3083 Plastic finished products, laminated
PA: Transdigm Group Incorporated
1301 E 9th St Ste 3000
Cleveland OH 44114
216 706-2960

(G-13951)
PRECISION METAL WORKS LLC
2004 S 14th St (98903-1283)
PHONE.................................509 945-8433
Kyle Osborne, *Business Mgr*
EMP: 5
SALES (est): 145.8K **Privately Held**
SIC: 1099 2295 3441 Antimony ore mining; metallizing of fabrics; fabricated structural metal

(G-13952)
RENEGADE POWDER COATING LLC
916 Rose St (98903-1900)
PHONE.................................509 575-4623
Tony Adams,
EMP: 3
SQ FT: 20,000
SALES (est): 539.9K **Privately Held**
SIC: 3312 Coated or plated products

(G-13953)
T E C I INC
Also Called: Independent Trailer & Eqp Co
1602 Rudkin Rd (98901-4030)
PHONE.................................509 452-3672
Michael D Nash, *President*
EMP: 11
SQ FT: 12,000
SALES: 1.1MM **Privately Held**
WEB: www.itec-inc.com
SIC: 3537 Dollies (hand or power trucks), industrial except mining

(G-13954)
THERMOFORMING SYSTEMS LLC
Also Called: T S L
1601 W Pine St (98903-9502)
PHONE.................................509 454-4578
Roger Moore, *Senior VP*
James Naughton, *Mng Member*
Dave Irwin,
◆ **EMP:** 24
SQ FT: 54,900
SALES (est): 8.8MM **Privately Held**
SIC: 3565 3089 Packaging machinery; thermoformed finished plastic products
HQ: Davis-Standard, Llc
1 Extrusion Dr
Pawcatuck CT 06379

(G-13955)
UNITED SALES INC
1917 S 14th St (98903-1282)
P.O. Box 9313, Yakima (98909-0313)
PHONE.................................509 225-0636
Paul Fehrer Sr, *President*
Betty L Fehrer, *Vice Pres*
EMP: 19
SALES (est): 4.7MM **Privately Held**
WEB: www.yakimaquality.com
SIC: 3565 Packaging machinery

(G-13956)
WEYERHAEUSER COMPANY
600 W Ahtanum Rd (98903-1860)
PHONE.................................509 453-4741
Jeff Bickford, *Branch Mgr*
EMP: 150
SALES (corp-wide): 7.4B **Publicly Held**
SIC: 2449 2653 2631 Containers, plywood & veneer wood; corrugated & solid fiber boxes; paperboard mills
PA: Weyerhaeuser Company
220 Occidental Ave S
Seattle WA 98104
206 539-3000

▲ = Import ▼ = Export
◆ = Import/Export

Uniontown
Whitman County

(G-13957)
NEW SAGE BAKERY LLC
111 Montgomery St (99179)
PHONE..................................208 596-5331
Amy Holt, *Partner*
Amy Holt-Stillwaugh, *Partner*
EMP: 6
SALES (est): 493K **Privately Held**
SIC: **2051** 5812 Bakery: wholesale or wholesale/retail combined; coffee shop

University Place
Pierce County

(G-13958)
ALPINE WOODWORKING
7202 35th St W (98466-4421)
PHONE..................................253 565-4560
Rodney W Overland, *Owner*
EMP: 2
SQ FT: 6,500
SALES (est): 181.9K **Privately Held**
SIC: **2434** Wood kitchen cabinets

(G-13959)
AMERICAN METAL SPECIALTIES
7012 27th St W (98466-5215)
PHONE..................................253 272-9344
Paul Stockdale, *President*
Michael C Baker, *President*
EMP: 5
SQ FT: 4,000
SALES (est): 688K **Privately Held**
WEB: www.cablerailings.com
SIC: **3446** Architectural metalwork

(G-13960)
BALLOON MASTERS
5314 66th Avenue Ct W (98467-2232)
PHONE..................................253 566-0201
Jenny Bender, *Owner*
EMP: 2
SALES (est): 110K **Privately Held**
SIC: **3721** Balloons, hot air (aircraft)

(G-13961)
BARRYS WOOD WORKING
7902 27th St W Ste 7a (98466-3431)
PHONE..................................253 312-1585
Chris Hansen, *Owner*
EMP: 2 EST: 1997
SALES (est): 80.7K **Privately Held**
SIC: **2431** Woodwork, interior & ornamental

(G-13962)
CARBIDE ONLINE SALES LLC
4007 Bridgeport Way W F3 (98466-4330)
PHONE..................................253 476-1338
Roger White,
EMP: 5
SQ FT: 600
SALES (est): 305K **Privately Held**
SIC: **5961** 3425 5084 3423 ; saw blades for hand or power saws; drilling bits; metalworking tools (such as drills, taps, dies, files); edge tools for woodworking: augers, bits, gimlets, etc.

(G-13963)
CARBIDE WEB SALES LLC
4007 Bridgeport Way W F4 (98466-4330)
PHONE..................................253 353-2595
EMP: 2
SALES (est): 74.4K **Privately Held**
SIC: **2819** Carbides

(G-13964)
CHAMBERS BAY DISTILLERY
2013 70th Ave W (98466-5540)
PHONE..................................503 819-0542
EMP: 5
SALES (est): 346.9K **Privately Held**
SIC: **2085** Distilled & blended liquors

(G-13965)
CRITCHLOW CUSTOM COATINGS LLC
9733 52nd St W Apt 252 (98467-1210)
PHONE..................................253 651-9675
Douglas Critchlow, *Principal*
EMP: 2
SALES (est): 137.1K **Privately Held**
SIC: **3479** Metal coating & allied service

(G-13966)
EDGE TECHNOLOGIES INC
7350 Cirque Dr W Ste 103 (98467-2241)
PHONE..................................253 383-9181
Gary Hughes, *Principal*
EMP: 4 EST: 2011
SALES (est): 503.6K **Privately Held**
SIC: **3578** Cash registers

(G-13967)
FAB5VENTURES LLC
3800 Bridgeport Way W # 315 (98466-4495)
PHONE..................................425 310-2543
EMP: 2
SALES (est): 107.3K **Privately Held**
SIC: **3999** Manufacturing industries

(G-13968)
FANAPPTIC LLC
2911 Grandview Dr W (98466-2622)
PHONE..................................253 548-7443
Braydon Batungbacal, *Mng Member*
EMP: 2 EST: 2017
SALES (est): 62.1K **Privately Held**
SIC: **7372** Application computer software

(G-13969)
FAST YETI INC
3560 Bridgeport Way W 1b (98466-4446)
PHONE..................................253 573-1877
Linda Brooks Rix, *CEO*
James Miller, *President*
EMP: 9
SQ FT: 2,068
SALES (est): 417.8K **Privately Held**
SIC: **7372** Prepackaged software

(G-13970)
GLOBAL PROFESSIONAL SVCS LLC
Also Called: G P S
5619 54th Avenue Ct W (98467-4812)
PHONE..................................808 682-0404
Katherine B Nesmith,
EMP: 2
SALES: 250K **Privately Held**
SIC: **3993** Signs & advertising specialties

(G-13971)
HOLLAND ORNAMENTAL IRON INC
7026 27th St W (98466-5215)
PHONE..................................253 564-5671
Raymond E Brabham, *Principal*
EMP: 2
SALES (est): 159.7K **Privately Held**
SIC: **3446** Architectural metalwork

(G-13972)
INDEPNDENT DISTR REXALL SHOWCA
8330 34th St W (98466-2525)
PHONE..................................253 565-6595
Marcy McPherson, *Principal*
EMP: 2
SALES (est): 90.8K **Privately Held**
SIC: **3321** Gray & ductile iron foundries

(G-13973)
INK INC
3021 69th Ave W Ste A (98466-5297)
PHONE..................................253 565-4000
David Woodruss, *President*
Mark Bender, *President*
Matt McClain, *Principal*
Terry Lee Bender, *Corp Secy*
EMP: 17
SQ FT: 4,500
SALES: 760.2K **Privately Held**
WEB: www.inkinctacoma.com
SIC: **2261** 2395 2759 2396 Screen printing of cotton broadwoven fabrics; emblems, embroidered; embroidery products, except schiffli machine; commercial printing; automotive & apparel trimmings

(G-13974)
IRRATIONAL HATS N STUFF
2939 Crystal Springs Rd W (98466-2732)
PHONE..................................253 460-5565
Andrea Neill, *Partner*
EMP: 2
SALES (est): 123.1K **Privately Held**
SIC: **2353** Hats & caps

(G-13975)
KRAMER HANDGUN LEATHER INC
3036 68th Ave W (98466-5230)
P.O. Box 112154, Tacoma (98411-2154)
PHONE..................................253 564-6652
Sun Cha Kramer, *President*
Gregory Kramer, *President*
EMP: 12
SQ FT: 2,000
SALES (est): 990K **Privately Held**
WEB: www.kramerleather.com
SIC: **3199** Holsters, leather

(G-13976)
KWIK LOC CORP
7708 47th St W (98466-3025)
PHONE..................................253 564-3574
William Klancke, *Principal*
EMP: 3 EST: 2010
SALES (est): 217.3K **Privately Held**
SIC: **3565** Packaging machinery

(G-13977)
PUREBLISNATURALS
5706 95th Avenue Ct W (98467-1328)
PHONE..................................253 719-2683
Skyler Bosley, *Principal*
EMP: 2
SALES (est): 116.3K **Privately Held**
SIC: **2844** Toilet preparations

(G-13978)
REACH SERVICE LLC ✪
3800 Bridgeprt Way W A4 (98466)
PHONE..................................253 370-6229
EMP: 2 EST: 2019
SALES (est): 86.6K **Privately Held**
SIC: **3843** Dental equipment

(G-13979)
REAL FINE PUBLISHING
5123 57th Avenue Ct W (98467-4804)
PHONE..................................253 318-6553
Chiara Montante, *Principal*
EMP: 2
SALES (est): 62.9K **Privately Held**
SIC: **2711** Newspapers

(G-13980)
RED LOON SOFTWARE
3800 Bridgeport Way W (98466-4495)
PHONE..................................253 353-7963
EMP: 2 EST: 2008
SALES (est): 120K **Privately Held**
SIC: **7372** Prepackaged Software Services

(G-13981)
SOUTH SOUND METAL INC
7406 27th St W Ste 10 (98466-4635)
PHONE..................................253 564-0226
Ted Fick, *President*
Dave Fick, *Vice Pres*
EMP: 3
SQ FT: 1,800
SALES: 900K **Privately Held**
WEB: www.southsoundmetal.com
SIC: **3443** 3841 3714 Metal parts; surgical & medical instruments; motor vehicle parts & accessories
PA: Fick & Associates Inc
  7406 27th St W Ste 5
  University Place WA 98466
  253 565-4703

(G-13982)
TRUNK SHOW
7710 29th St W (98466-4124)
PHONE..................................253 302-4301
Jessica Eugenio, *Owner*
EMP: 3
SALES (est): 300.7K **Privately Held**
SIC: **3161** Trunks

(G-13983)
VECTOR R&D INC (PA)
Also Called: Vector Research & Development
2810 69th Ave W (98466-5286)
PHONE..................................877 883-7455
Brent Bigler, *President*
◆ EMP: 6
SQ FT: 4,000
SALES (est): 8MM **Privately Held**
SIC: **3843** Dental hand instruments

Usk
Pend Oreille County

(G-13984)
HERMANN INTERMOUNTAIN CORP (HQ)
22 Triangle Rd (99180-8717)
P.O. Box 190 (99180-0190)
PHONE..................................509 445-0966
Steven E Hermann, *President*
Linda Hermann, *President*
Sam Hermann, *Treasurer*
Ted Hermann, *Admin Sec*
EMP: 4
SQ FT: 3,500
SALES (est): 613K
SALES (corp-wide): 10.7MM **Privately Held**
SIC: **1442** Construction sand & gravel
PA: Hermann Brothers Logging & Construction, Incorporated
  2095 Blue Mountain Rd
  Port Angeles WA 98362
  360 452-3341

(G-13985)
PONDERAY NEWSPRINT COMPANY
422767 Highway 20 (99180-9717)
PHONE..................................509 445-2133
Myron Johnson, *General Mgr*
Jim Leblanc Sr, *Opers Mgr*
Steve Wood, *Controller*
Dexter Campbell, *Manager*
Robert Grace, *Manager*
◆ EMP: 178
SQ FT: 800,000
SALES (est): 80.7MM **Privately Held**
SIC: **2621** Newsprint paper

Vader
Lewis County

(G-13986)
MOUNTAIN LOOM CO
1339 State Route 506 (98593-9732)
P.O. Box 509 (98593-0509)
PHONE..................................360 295-3856
John Anderson, *Owner*
Joyce Anderson, *Co-Owner*
EMP: 3
SQ FT: 9,000
SALES: 200K **Privately Held**
WEB: www.mtnloom.com
SIC: **3552** Textile machinery

Valley
Stevens County

(G-13987)
AMERICAN EDGE LLC
3211 Beitey Rd (99181-9741)
P.O. Box 130 (99181-0130)
PHONE..................................509 937-4404
Karen D Odle, *CEO*
▼ EMP: 12
SQ FT: 10,000

Valley - Stevens County (G-13988)   GEOGRAPHIC SECTION

SALES: 300K **Privately Held**
SIC: 3728 2399 5131 2393 Aircraft parts & equipment; banners, pennants & flags; flags & banners; bags & containers, except sleeping bags: textile; nets, seines, slings & insulator pads; screen printing on fabric articles

(G-13988)
B & W EXCAVATING & CNSTR
3728 W Jump Off Rd (99181-9627)
PHONE...........................509 937-2028
Ben Burrows, *President*
John Willey, *Vice Pres*
EMP: 3
SALES: 1.2MM **Privately Held**
SIC: 2411 Logging camps & contractors

(G-13989)
CUSTOM VEILS & ACCESSORIES
4137 Hesseltine Rd (99181-9646)
PHONE...........................509 258-7810
Pj Farance-Rabel, *Owner*
EMP: 2
SALES (est): 77.4K **Privately Held**
SIC: 2339 Women's & misses' outerwear

(G-13990)
D E METLOW LOGGING LLC
3586 Waitts Lake Rd (99181-9785)
PHONE...........................509 937-2233
Sheila Klingbeil, *Mng Member*
Darren Metlow, *Mng Member*
EMP: 6 **EST:** 2011
SALES: 440K **Privately Held**
SIC: 2411 Logging

(G-13991)
DTI READY MIX COMPANY
3147 Highway 231 (99181-9636)
PHONE...........................509 937-4683
Brian Gilbert, *Manager*
EMP: 2
SALES (est): 275.2K **Privately Held**
SIC: 3273 Ready-mixed concrete

(G-13992)
KESSLER WOOD PRODUCTS
3171 Bull Dog Creek Rd (99181-9703)
PHONE...........................509 937-2500
Charles Kessler, *Owner*
EMP: 2
SALES (est): 134.1K **Privately Held**
SIC: 2511 Wood bedroom furniture

(G-13993)
LANE MT SILICA CO
3119 Highway 231 (99181-9636)
P.O. Box 127 (99181-0127)
PHONE...........................206 762-7622
Joe H Scates, *Manager*
EMP: 25
SALES (corp-wide): 6.6MM **Privately Held**
SIC: 3295 1446 Minerals, ground or treated; industrial sand
HQ: Lane Mt Silica Co
5427 Ohio Ave S
Seattle WA 98134
206 762-7622

(G-13994)
MTN THREDS AND CLOTHING
4266 Jepsen Rd (99181-9652)
P.O. Box 1250, Chewelah (99109-1250)
PHONE...........................509 258-4443
Kent Morgan, *Owner*
EMP: 3
SALES: 130K **Privately Held**
SIC: 5699 2329 Sports apparel; ski & snow clothing: men's & boys'

(G-13995)
VALLEY FUEL LLC
3080 Highway 231 (99181-9687)
P.O. Box 26 (99181-0026)
PHONE...........................509 937-2230
John Morris, *Principal*
EMP: 7 **EST:** 2009
SALES (est): 753.5K **Privately Held**
SIC: 2869 Fuels

(G-13996)
VALLEY GRAPHICS INC
3091 5th Ave (99181-9657)
PHONE...........................509 937-4055
Laura Moe, *President*
EMP: 4
SALES (est): 394.3K **Privately Held**
SIC: 2396 Screen printing on fabric articles

Valleyford
Spokane County

(G-13997)
JR GRENNAY CO
12208 E Old Palouse Hwy (99036-9576)
P.O. Box 406 (99036-0406)
PHONE...........................509 484-5056
EMP: 3
SALES (est): 47.6K **Privately Held**
SIC: 7699 4499 3732 Repair services; marine surveyors; non-motorized boat, building & repairing

(G-13998)
METAL MEISTER INC
5310 E Stoughton Rd (99036-5009)
PHONE...........................480 845-6717
William Wipf, *President*
Timothy Wipf, *Vice Pres*
EMP: 5
SALES (est): 700.7K **Privately Held**
SIC: 3498 Fabricated pipe & fittings

(G-13999)
OFF ROAD ADDICTION LLC
12013 S Jackson Rd (99023-8511)
PHONE...........................509 999-7824
Barry Sather, *Mng Member*
EMP: 4
SALES (est): 308.1K **Privately Held**
SIC: 3498 Tube fabricating (contract bending & shaping)

Vancouver
Clark County

(G-14000)
1 WILD PRINT
13804 Ne 44th St (98682-6517)
PHONE...........................360 550-1916
Misty Caamal, *Principal*
EMP: 2
SALES (est): 83.9K **Privately Held**
SIC: 2752 Commercial printing, lithographic

(G-14001)
A & J CUSTOM CABINETS INC
2300 E 1st St Ste B (98661)
PHONE...........................360 694-4833
Donald E Sullivan, *President*
EMP: 80
SQ FT: 36,000
SALES (est): 5.9MM **Privately Held**
WEB: www.ajcustomcabinets.com
SIC: 1751 2434 Cabinet building & installation; wood kitchen cabinets

(G-14002)
A A AUTO TOWING
19809 Ne 58th St (98682-9018)
PHONE...........................360 892-2924
Tracey Langley, *Owner*
EMP: 2
SALES (est): 149.8K **Privately Held**
SIC: 3531 7549 Automobile wrecker hoists; automotive maintenance services; towing service, automotive

(G-14003)
A B GRAPHICS
4316 Ne 130th Ave (98682-6417)
PHONE...........................360 566-3666
Georgia Allender, *Principal*
EMP: 3 **EST:** 2001
SALES (est): 233.7K **Privately Held**
SIC: 2759 Commercial printing

(G-14004)
AA WELDING INC
3800 Ne 68th St Ste B2 (98661-1373)
PHONE...........................360 694-4066
Jeff Winkleman, *President*
EMP: 2
SALES (est): 47.7K **Privately Held**
SIC: 7692 Welding repair

(G-14005)
ABSCI LLC
101 E 6th St Ste 300 (98660-3342)
PHONE...........................360 949-1041
Sean McClain, *Mng Member*
V Bryan Lawlis,
EMP: 22 **EST:** 2011
SALES (est): 3.8MM **Privately Held**
SIC: 2836 Biological products, except diagnostic

(G-14006)
ACCENT BY DESIGN
9905 Ne 26th St (98662-7690)
PHONE...........................360 256-6607
EMP: 2
SALES (est): 79K **Privately Held**
SIC: 2397 Mfg Schiffli Embroideries

(G-14007)
ACCURATE MACHINE AND MFG
Also Called: Mellema Manufacturing
2910 Kauffman Ave (98660-2044)
PHONE...........................360 693-4783
Jeremy Holst, *President*
EMP: 8
SQ FT: 5,200
SALES (est): 1.1MM **Privately Held**
WEB: www.mellemamfg.com
SIC: 3599 Machine shop, jobbing & repair

(G-14008)
ADALIS CORPORATION (HQ)
417 Nw 136th St (98685-2955)
PHONE...........................360 574-8828
Traci Jensen, *President*
Patrick Hessini, *President*
Cheryl Ann Reinitz, *Treasurer*
James Clinton Jr McCreary, *Director*
Timothy J Keenan, *Admin Sec*
◆ **EMP:** 20
SQ FT: 6,000
SALES (est): 10.2MM
SALES (corp-wide): 3B **Publicly Held**
WEB: www.adaliscorp.com
SIC: 3086 Packaging & shipping materials, foamed plastic
PA: H.B. Fuller Company
1200 Willow Lake Blvd
Saint Paul MN 55110
651 236-5900

(G-14009)
ADVANCE WELDING INC
1509 Ne 106th St Ste A (98686-5980)
PHONE...........................360 573-1311
Dennis Ledridge, *President*
Henning Pederson, *Vice Pres*
Alf Gergeson, *Admin Sec*
EMP: 12 **EST:** 1964
SQ FT: 11,000
SALES (est): 1.5MM **Privately Held**
WEB: www.advanceweldinginc.com
SIC: 7692 Welding repair

(G-14010)
ADVANCED ENERGY INDUSTRIES INC
Noah Precision
2501 Se Columbia Way # 190 (98661-8045)
PHONE...........................360 759-2713
Tim Kerr, *Manager*
EMP: 9
SALES (corp-wide): 718.8MM **Publicly Held**
WEB: www.advanced-energy.com
SIC: 3674 Semiconductors & related devices
PA: Advanced Energy Industries, Inc.
1625 Sharp Point Dr
Fort Collins CO 80525
970 221-4670

(G-14011)
AGC CWW
11617 Ne 224th Ave (98682-9757)
PHONE...........................360 608-4642
Allan Campbell, *Owner*
EMP: 3
SALES (est): 306.8K **Privately Held**
SIC: 2499 Decorative wood & woodwork

(G-14012)
AGILECORE SOFTWARE LLC
10201 Ne 46th Ave (98686-5996)
PHONE...........................360 910-3140
Paul Burkett,
EMP: 3 **EST:** 2012
SALES: 400K **Privately Held**
SIC: 7372 Prepackaged software

(G-14013)
AIDAPAK SERVICES LLC
14301 Se 1st St (98684-3501)
PHONE...........................360 448-2090
Michael Rodeman,
Randy Murphy,
EMP: 10
SALES (est): 990K **Privately Held**
SIC: 2823 Cellulosic manmade fibers

(G-14014)
AIRTRAN WIRELESS TECHNOLOGIES
1417 Ne 76th St (98665-0464)
PHONE...........................360 430-3179
Forrest Bishop, *President*
EMP: 2 **EST:** 1998
SALES (est): 144.5K **Privately Held**
SIC: 8711 3823 Engineering services; transmitters of process variables, stand. signal conversion

(G-14015)
AJS CUSTOM EMBROIDERY
3303 Ne Minnehaha St D (98663-1499)
P.O. Box 3043, Battle Ground (98604-2929)
PHONE...........................360 993-1987
Alida Young, *Owner*
Gary Young, *Co-Owner*
EMP: 2
SALES: 150K **Privately Held**
WEB: www.ajsembroidery.com
SIC: 2395 Embroidery products, except schiffli machine; embroidery & art needlework

(G-14016)
AL JADID MAGAZINE
11500 Ne 76th St Ste A3 (98662-3901)
PHONE...........................360 936-1765
Martha Macke, *Principal*
EMP: 3
SALES (est): 155.2K **Privately Held**
SIC: 2721 Periodicals

(G-14017)
ALBINA HOLDINGS INC
Also Called: Albina Fuel
1300 W 8th St (98660-3015)
P.O. Box 768 (98666-0768)
PHONE...........................360 696-3408
Bob Davis, *Manager*
EMP: 57
SALES (corp-wide): 51.2MM **Privately Held**
SIC: 3531 Asphalt plant, including gravel-mix type
PA: Albina Holdings, Inc.
801 Main St
Vancouver WA 98660
360 816-8016

(G-14018)
ALDERGROVE LLC
Also Called: Certified Air Safety
600 Se Maritime Ave # 210 (98661-8044)
PHONE...........................360 253-7378
Robert K Sant,
Thomas Stupfel,
EMP: 4
SALES (est): 260K **Privately Held**
WEB: www.certifiedairsafety.com
SIC: 7629 3826 Electrical measuring instrument repair & calibration; environmental testing equipment

Vancouver - Clark County (G-14048)

(G-14019)
ALL CITY PRINT
3714 Main St (98663-2228)
PHONE..................360 718-2448
EMP: 2
SALES (est): 83.9K Privately Held
SIC: 2752 Commercial printing, lithographic

(G-14020)
ALL PRO PRINTER SERVICE LLC
8908 Boulder Ave (98664-2550)
PHONE..................360 818-4592
Adrianna Pfeiffer, Principal
EMP: 4
SALES (est): 332.1K Privately Held
SIC: 2752 Commercial printing, offset

(G-14021)
ALL SOFTWARE TOOLS INC
11001 Ne 80th St (98662-3093)
PHONE..................360 883-2981
Richard Seng, Principal
EMP: 2
SALES (est): 138.8K Privately Held
WEB: www.allsoftwaretools.com
SIC: 7372 Business oriented computer software

(G-14022)
ALLSTAR MAGNETICS LLC
6205 Ne 63rd St (98661-1908)
PHONE..................360 693-0213
Tyee Harpster, President
Donald Burgett, Opers Mgr
Chuck Davidson, Sales Staff
Robert Parr,
▲ EMP: 25
SQ FT: 20,000
SALES (est): 9.1MM Privately Held
WEB: www.allstarmagnetics.com
SIC: 5065 8742 4225 3679 Electronic parts; business consultant; general warehousing & storage; cores, magnetic

(G-14023)
ALPACAS NORTHWEST INC
6421 Ne 171st St (98686-1979)
PHONE..................503 519-7587
EMP: 2
SALES (est): 100.1K Privately Held
SIC: 2231 Alpacas, mohair; woven

(G-14024)
ALPHAWAVE SYSTEMS
26313 Ne 52nd Way (98682-7669)
PHONE..................719 888-9283
Stephen Nahas, Owner
EMP: 4
SALES (est): 89.7K Privately Held
SIC: 7371 7373 7372 7389 Computer software development & applications; computer systems analysis & design; systems integration services; prepackaged software;

(G-14025)
ALSEA VENEER INC
201 Ne Park Plaza Dr # 288 (98684-5808)
PHONE..................360 891-2020
Chester Clark, President
Paul Smud, Corp Secy
Brad Clark, Vice Pres
Rick Prest, Controller
EMP: 3 EST: 1963
SQ FT: 800
SALES: 797K Privately Held
SIC: 2436 2435 2421 Veneer stock, softwood; hardwood veneer & plywood; sawmills & planing mills, general

(G-14026)
AMERICAN BANCARD LLC
Also Called: Alpine Payment Systems
1111 Main St Ste 201 (98660-2958)
PHONE..................360 713-0690
EMP: 35
SALES (corp-wide): 7.7MM Privately Held
SIC: 3578 7389 7374 Automatic teller machines (ATM); credit card service; computer graphics service
PA: American Bancard, Llc
1081 Holland Dr
Boca Raton FL 33487
800 793-3250

(G-14027)
AMERICAN CRAFTWARE LLC
2800 Ne 184th Ave (98682-3727)
PHONE..................360 606-1827
Eugene Ligman, Mng Member
EMP: 2
SALES: 14K Privately Held
SIC: 3423 Hand & edge tools

(G-14028)
AMERON INTERNATIONAL CORP
Ameron Concrete & Steel Pipe
201 Ne Park Plaza Dr # 100 (98684-5808)
PHONE..................909 944-4100
Larry Williams, Principal
EMP: 34
SALES (corp-wide): 8.4B Publicly Held
WEB: www.ameron.com
SIC: 3272 Concrete products, precast
HQ: Ameron International Corporation
7909 Parkwood Circle Dr
Houston TX 77036
713 375-3700

(G-14029)
AMERON INTERNATIONAL CORP
Ameron Concrete & Steel Pipe
201 Ne Park Plaza Dr # 100 (98684-5808)
PHONE..................909 944-4100
Manuel Ramirez, Engineer
David Tantalean, Sales Staff
EMP: 67
SALES (corp-wide): 8.4B Publicly Held
WEB: www.ameron.com
SIC: 3272 3312 5051 Pipe, concrete or lined with concrete; blast furnaces & steel mills; pipe & tubing, steel
HQ: Ameron International Corporation
7909 Parkwood Circle Dr
Houston TX 77036
713 375-3700

(G-14030)
AMERON INTERNATIONAL CORP
Ameron Steel Fabrication
201 Ne Park Plaza Dr # 100 (98684-5808)
PHONE..................909 944-4100
Richard Kaatz, Manager
EMP: 150
SALES (corp-wide): 8.4B Publicly Held
WEB: www.ameron.com
SIC: 3317 Steel pipe & tubes
HQ: Ameron International Corporation
7909 Parkwood Circle Dr
Houston TX 77036
713 375-3700

(G-14031)
AMERON INTERNATIONAL CORP
Ameron Water Transm Group
201 Ne Park Plaza Dr # 100 (98684-5808)
PHONE..................909 944-4100
William M Smith, President
EMP: 40
SALES (corp-wide): 8.4B Publicly Held
WEB: www.ameron.com
SIC: 3272 3317 Concrete products; steel pipe & tubes
HQ: Ameron International Corporation
7909 Parkwood Circle Dr
Houston TX 77036
713 375-3700

(G-14032)
AMFIT INC
3611 Ne 68th St (98661-1371)
PHONE..................360 573-9100
Tony Tadin Jr, CEO
Arjen Sundman, President
John Depalma, Admin Sec
▲ EMP: 35
SQ FT: 30,000
SALES (est): 12.8MM Privately Held
WEB: www.amfit.com
SIC: 5047 3842 Medical & hospital equipment; surgical appliances & supplies

(G-14033)
ANALYTICAL REASERCH CONSULTING
2516 Nw 91st St (98665-6235)
PHONE..................360 573-5700
Karl R Stum, Partner
EMP: 2
SALES (est): 161.3K Privately Held
SIC: 3826 Analytical instruments

(G-14034)
ANDREWS NATION INC
Also Called: Accelerated Postal and Print
9208 Ne Highway 99 # 107 (98665-8986)
PHONE..................360 989-1700
Bryan Andrews, President
Heather A Andrews, Admin Sec
EMP: 4 EST: 2009
SQ FT: 4,000
SALES (est): 204.9K Privately Held
SIC: 2752 5943 7389 Commercial printing, lithographic; stationery stores; mailbox rental & related service

(G-14035)
ANDRITZ IGGESUND TOOLS INC
1108 Ne 146th St Ste E (98685-1412)
PHONE..................360 574-1440
Terry Knight, Manager
EMP: 5
SALES (est): 581.1K
SALES (corp-wide): 570.3K Privately Held
WEB: www.iggesundtools.com
SIC: 3553 Woodworking machinery
HQ: Andritz Iggesund Tools, Inc.
220 Scarlet Blvd
Oldsmar FL 34677
813 855-6902

(G-14036)
ANEWIN LLC
17218 Se 32 St Vancouver (98683)
PHONE..................360 606-5591
Mike Hagan, Mng Member
EMP: 2
SALES: 250K Privately Held
SIC: 3825 7373 Instruments to measure electricity; systems software development services

(G-14037)
ANT LAMP CORP
810 Main Street Vancouver (98660)
PHONE..................360 600-1031
Sultan Weatherspoon, Director
EMP: 3 EST: 2013
SALES (est): 285.9K Privately Held
SIC: 3679 Power supplies, all types: static

(G-14038)
APM GAMES LLC
16407 Ne 83rd St (98682-1530)
PHONE..................512 961-6515
Jonathan Johnson,
Joshua Coulter,
Nathan Hennessy,
Daniel Sgranfetto,
EMP: 4
SALES: 20K Privately Held
SIC: 7371 7372 Computer software development & applications; application computer software

(G-14039)
ARCHETYPE WOODWORKING LLC
9009 Boulder Ave (98664-2551)
PHONE..................360 977-0565
Matthew Phelan, Administration
EMP: 2
SALES (est): 185.4K Privately Held
SIC: 2431 Millwork

(G-14040)
ARGO WEST INC
4200 Nw Fruit Valley Rd (98660-1223)
P.O. Box 61995 (98666-1995)
PHONE..................360 213-1503
Kosta Fassilis, Principal
EMP: 2 EST: 2007
SALES (est): 152K Privately Held
SIC: 3731 Shipbuilding & repairing

(G-14041)
ARIEL TRUSS COMPANY INC
616 Nw 139th St (98685-2521)
PHONE..................360 574-7333
Clarence Holt, President
EMP: 48
SQ FT: 2,500
SALES (est): 5.9MM Privately Held
SIC: 2439 Trusses, wooden roof

(G-14042)
ARTYS DOOR SHOP INC
7200 Ne 40th Ave (98661-1345)
PHONE..................360 695-7898
Arthur Rausch, President
Sheri Rausch, Corp Secy
Jerry Rausch, Vice Pres
EMP: 3
SQ FT: 1,500
SALES (est): 398K Privately Held
SIC: 2431 Doors & door parts & trim, wood

(G-14043)
ASCO MACHINE INC
1900 W 39th St Ste B202 (98660-1221)
PHONE..................360 735-0500
Allan Mannhalter, President
EMP: 49
SQ FT: 5,000
SALES (est): 6.2MM Privately Held
SIC: 3599 Machine shop, jobbing & repair; machine & other job shop work

(G-14044)
ASO INC
500 W 8th St Ste 110 (98660-3019)
PHONE..................360 883-3962
Jim Krause, Principal
EMP: 2 EST: 2011
SALES (est): 230K Privately Held
SIC: 3822 Air flow controllers, air conditioning & refrigeration

(G-14045)
AVAILBLE CREAT SCREEN PRTG EMB
14707 Ne 13th Ct Ste B102 (98685-1447)
PHONE..................360 576-8542
Todd Bingham, Mng Member
EMP: 4 EST: 1989
SQ FT: 2,640
SALES (est): 100K Privately Held
SIC: 2396 2395 Screen printing on fabric articles; pleating & stitching

(G-14046)
AVANTBIO CORPORATION
8013 Ne St Johns Rd Ste E (98665-1090)
P.O. Box 5820, Lynnwood (98046-5820)
PHONE..................360 521-8904
Paul W Cook, President
EMP: 5 EST: 2015
SALES (est): 527.6K Privately Held
SIC: 2834 Pharmaceutical preparations

(G-14047)
AVARIC LETTER PRESS
3514 Ne 155th Ave (98682-8496)
PHONE..................360 836-5993
Aaron Piel, Principal
EMP: 3 EST: 2016
SALES (est): 100.4K Privately Held
SIC: 2711 Newspapers

(G-14048)
AVID HEALTH INC (HQ)
6350 Ne Campus Dr (98661-6877)
PHONE..................360 737-6800
Martin Rifkin, President
Kathryn Jones, Vice Pres
Richard Falconer, Treasurer
▲ EMP: 8
SALES (est): 71.8MM
SALES (corp-wide): 4.1B Publicly Held
SIC: 2833 5122 Vitamins, natural or synthetic: bulk, uncompounded; vitamins & minerals
PA: Church & Dwight Co., Inc.
500 Charles Ewing Blvd
Ewing NJ 08628
609 806-1200

Vancouver - Clark County (G-14049)

(G-14049)
AVOS INC
4207 Ne 94th St (98665-9389)
PHONE................503 713-8404
Slavik P Sova, *Principal*
EMP: 8
SALES (est): 1.2MM **Privately Held**
SIC: 3441 Fabricated structural metal

(G-14050)
B & R BINDERY AND COLLATING
6707 Ne 117th Ave 103e (98662-5515)
PHONE................360 944-0326
Rod Beck, *Owner*
Betty Beck, *Principal*
EMP: 4
SQ FT: 5,000
SALES (est): 170K **Privately Held**
SIC: 2789 Bookbinding & related work

(G-14051)
B KARNES BOOKS INC
10520 Ne 113th Cir (98662-3532)
PHONE................360 828-7132
Barbara Karnes, *CEO*
EMP: 5
SALES (est): 279.6K **Privately Held**
SIC: 2731 Book publishing

(G-14052)
B LINE MFG
13205 Ne 5th Ave (98685-2678)
PHONE................360 718-2158
Ursala Mitchell, *Bd of Directors*
EMP: 2
SALES (est): 112.1K **Privately Held**
SIC: 3999 Barber & beauty shop equipment

(G-14053)
BAGCRAFT
6416 Nw Whitney Rd (98665-7016)
PHONE................360 695-7771
Robert Fike, *Principal*
EMP: 2
SALES (est): 90.7K **Privately Held**
SIC: 2611 Pulp mills

(G-14054)
BAKE WORKS INC
5600 Ne 121st Ave Ste T-1 (98682-6245)
P.O. Box 822373 (98682-0052)
PHONE................360 213-2001
Zachary Fitzgerald, *COO*
EMP: 23
SALES (est): 5MM **Privately Held**
SIC: 2052 Bakery products, dry

(G-14055)
BAR KUSTOM MACHINING INC
1209 Se Nancy Rd (98664-5422)
PHONE................360 892-3016
Allen Trenary, *President*
Ralph Trenary, *Vice Pres*
Barbara Trenary, *Bookkeeper*
EMP: 3
SALES (est): 156.1K **Privately Held**
SIC: 3599 Machine shop, jobbing & repair

(G-14056)
BARBARA KARNES BOOKS INC
10520 Ne 113th Cir (98662-3532)
P.O. Box 822139 (98682-0048)
PHONE................360 828-7132
Barbara Karnes, *CEO*
Jack Karnes, *Vice Pres*
Jacquelyn Karnes, *Vice Pres*
EMP: 5
SALES (est): 503.8K **Privately Held**
SIC: 2731 Book clubs: publishing & printing

(G-14057)
BARBARA SOMERS
Also Called: Somers Automotive Machine
12510 Ne Laurin Rd (98662-1127)
P.O. Box 549, Brush Prairie (98606-0549)
PHONE................360 699-5205
Barbara Somers, *Owner*
Archie C Somers, *Co-Owner*
EMP: 2
SALES: 300K **Privately Held**
SIC: 7694 Rebuilding motors, except automotive

(G-14058)
BEAMING WHITE LLC
1205 Ne 95th St Ste A (98665-8960)
PHONE................360 635-5600
Luis Lajous, *CEO*
Heidi Deishl, *Sales Staff*
Mark Moerman, *Mng Member*
▲ EMP: 41 EST: 2008
SALES (est): 3MM **Privately Held**
SIC: 2844 5999 Oral preparations; cosmetic preparations; toiletries, cosmetics & perfumes

(G-14059)
BEE NATURAL LEATHERCARE LLC
11700 Ne 60th Way Ste 4b (98682-0807)
P.O. Box 820803 (98682-0018)
PHONE................360 891-7178
Paul Kummer, *Principal*
Glenna Kummer,
EMP: 4
SALES: 300K **Privately Held**
WEB: www.beenaturalleather.com
SIC: 2842 Leather dressings & finishes

(G-14060)
BEIGEBLOND INC
909 Main St (98660-3135)
PHONE................360 693-3283
Brett Alldred, *President*
Brett Allred, *President*
Victoria Newblum, *Manager*
EMP: 6
SALES (est): 450K **Privately Held**
WEB: www.beigeblond.com
SIC: 3999 Hair, dressing of, for the trade

(G-14061)
BERGSTROM NUTRITION
1900 W 39th St 106-A (98660-1221)
PHONE................360 693-0601
EMP: 3
SALES (est): 150.1K **Privately Held**
SIC: 2834 Mfg Pharmaceutical Preparations

(G-14062)
BEST CABINET & GRANITE SUP INC
3001 E Fourth Plain Blvd (98661-4661)
PHONE................503 285-1838
Xue Hui Chen, *President*
Xijian Chen, *Admin Sec*
▲ EMP: 4
SQ FT: 2,000
SALES (est): 523K **Privately Held**
SIC: 2434 Wood kitchen cabinets

(G-14063)
BEST CONNECTION LLC
11800 Ne 124th Ave # 22 (98682-1613)
PHONE................360 241-8244
Vitalie Sorbala, *Principal*
EMP: 3
SALES (est): 219.6K **Privately Held**
SIC: 3643 Electric connectors

(G-14064)
BESTWAY INDUSTRIES LLC
10306 Ne 7th St (98664-3857)
PHONE................360 513-2000
Jennifer Brower, *Comp Spec*
Susan D Groth,
EMP: 4
SALES: 100K **Privately Held**
SIC: 3999 Manufacturing industries

(G-14065)
BIEC INTERNATIONAL INC
5100 Nw 140th St (98685-1565)
PHONE................360 750-5791
Arif Humayun, *President*
◆ EMP: 3
SALES (est): 299.3K **Privately Held**
WEB: www.biecint.com
SIC: 3479 Coating of metals & formed products
PA: Bluescope Steel Limited
    L 11 120 Collins St
    Melbourne VIC 3000

(G-14066)
BIG BLOK LLC
17408 Ne 29th St (98682-3631)
PHONE................360 442-0655
Ken Rogers, *General Mgr*
Pam Rogers,
EMP: 2
SALES (est): 226.9K **Privately Held**
SIC: 3089 Plastic containers, except foam

(G-14067)
BIRDSEED
11306 Ne 34th Ct (98686-4376)
PHONE................360 574-7516
EMP: 2 EST: 2001
SALES (est): 140K **Privately Held**
SIC: 3559 Mfg Misc Industry Machinery

(G-14068)
BLEFA KEGS INC
3801 Ne 109th Ave (98682-7779)
PHONE................615 267-1385
EMP: 3
SALES (est): 167.9K
SALES (corp-wide): 2.9B **Privately Held**
SIC: 3412 Metal barrels, drums & pails
HQ: Blefa Gmbh
    Huttenstr. 43
    Kreuztal 57223
    273 277-7400

(G-14069)
BLOKABLE INC
1800 W Fourth Plain Blvd (98660-1367)
PHONE................800 928-6778
Aaron Holm, *CEO*
EMP: 11
SALES (corp-wide): 5MM **Privately Held**
SIC: 2452 Modular homes, prefabricated, wood
PA: Blokable, Inc.
    1136 Poplar Pl S
    Seattle WA 98144
    800 928-6778

(G-14070)
BLUEROSE PROCESSING
5605 Ne 46th St (98661-2914)
PHONE................360 281-7371
EMP: 2
SALES (est): 87.9K **Privately Held**
SIC: 3471 Plating & polishing

(G-14071)
BNC PRINTING
13811 Ne 42nd Ave (98686-1683)
PHONE................503 318-5916
EMP: 2
SALES (est): 151.3K **Privately Held**
SIC: 2752 Commercial printing, offset

(G-14072)
BOARD SHARK LLC
2808 Ne 65th Ave Ste C (98661-6880)
PHONE................503 351-5424
Carl Moehring, *Mng Member*
EMP: 27 EST: 2016
SALES (est): 9MM **Privately Held**
SIC: 3672 5063 Printed circuit boards; electrical apparatus & equipment

(G-14073)
BOAT TOTE
17401 Se 39th St Unit 147 (98683-9488)
PHONE................360 600-1364
Ken Brachman, *Partner*
EMP: 2
SALES (est): 240K **Privately Held**
SIC: 3536 Boat lifts

(G-14074)
BOB NAGEL INC
Also Called: Bennett Paper and Supply
1602 Washington St (98660-2952)
PHONE................503 869-6933
Robert Nagel, *President*
EMP: 10 EST: 2016
SQ FT: 10,000
SALES: 3MM **Privately Held**
SIC: 2621 Paper mills

(G-14075)
BOGGS MANUFACTURING
16414 Ne 32nd St (98682-8670)
PHONE................360 449-3479
EMP: 4 EST: 1988
SALES: 30K **Privately Held**
SIC: 3949 Mfg Sporting/Athletic Goods

(G-14076)
BOISE CASCADE COMPANY
907 W 7th St (98660-3066)
P.O. Box 690 (98666-0690)
PHONE................360 690-7028
Jim Gosnell, *Branch Mgr*
EMP: 100
SALES (corp-wide): 5B **Publicly Held**
SIC: 2621 Paper mills
PA: Boise Cascade Company
    1111 W Jefferson St # 300
    Boise ID 83702
    208 384-6161

(G-14077)
BOISE CASCADE COMPANY
222 Se Park Plaza Dr # 300 (98684)
PHONE................360 891-8787
Dale Young, *Business Mgr*
Peter Meuleveld, *Opers-Prdtn-Mfg*
EMP: 90
SALES (corp-wide): 5B **Publicly Held**
SIC: 2621 Paper mills
PA: Boise Cascade Company
    1111 W Jefferson St # 300
    Boise ID 83702
    208 384-6161

(G-14078)
BOOMERANG EXPRESS LLC
4601 E 18th St Apt 182 (98661-6253)
PHONE................360 449-2173
Heorhiy Zhyryada, *Principal*
EMP: 4
SALES (est): 243.3K **Privately Held**
SIC: 3949 Boomerangs

(G-14079)
BOOMERANG PHYSICAL THERAPY LLC
18414 Ne Garden Dr (98682-3612)
PHONE................360 258-1637
Jennifer Flentke, *Principal*
EMP: 3 EST: 2016
SALES (est): 81.6K **Privately Held**
SIC: 3949 Boomerangs

(G-14080)
BRAINLESS TEES INC
12401 Ne 60th Way A8 (98682-5972)
PHONE................360 608-8417
Adam Funderburg, *Owner*
EMP: 2
SALES (est): 250K **Privately Held**
SIC: 2759 Screen printing

(G-14081)
BRIAN FRIESEN FINE WOODWORKING
3315 Ne 112th Ave (98682-8733)
PHONE................360 314-6427
Brian Andrew Friesen, *Owner*
EMP: 2
SALES (est): 70.7K **Privately Held**
SIC: 2431 Woodwork, interior & ornamental

(G-14082)
BRIDGE CITY PUBLISHING
6117 Kansas St (98661-6921)
PHONE................360 600-0558
Travis Uhlig, *Partner*
Carrie Riley, *Partner*
EMP: 4 EST: 2000
SALES (est): 175.4K **Privately Held**
SIC: 2731 Book publishing

(G-14083)
BRIDGETOWN INDUSTRIES L L
8504 Ne 63rd St (98662-4361)
PHONE................503 953-3580
EMP: 2
SALES (est): 76K **Privately Held**
SIC: 3999 Manufacturing industries

(G-14084)
BRIGHT SIGNS SCREEN PRINTING
10501 Ne Highway 99 (98686-5697)
PHONE................360 695-6444
Dung Tran, *Owner*

GEOGRAPHIC SECTION
Vancouver - Clark County (G-14116)

EMP: 2
SALES (est): 135.8K Privately Held
SIC: 2752 Commercial printing, lithographic

(G-14085)
BRIGHTEN SIGN
5615 Ne 44th St (98661-3281)
PHONE..................360 608-5863
Dung Tran, *Principal*
EMP: 2
SALES (est): 149.1K Privately Held
SIC: 3993 Signs & advertising specialties

(G-14086)
BURGENERS WOODWORKING INC
4809 Nw Fruit Valley Rd (98660-1241)
PHONE..................360 694-9408
Robin Burgener, *President*
EMP: 35
SQ FT: 16,000
SALES (est): 3.8MM Privately Held
WEB: www.burgenerswoodworking.com
SIC: 2521 Cabinets, office: wood

(G-14087)
BUTLER DID IT
2805 Ne 54th St (98663-1944)
PHONE..................360 737-2672
Karen Schimer, *Owner*
EMP: 2
SALES (est): 166K Privately Held
SIC: 2099 Food preparations

(G-14088)
BUZS EQUIPMENT TRAILERS
5815 Ne 78th St (98665-0948)
PHONE..................360 694-9116
Scott A Peck, *President*
Gloria Walck, *Admin Sec*
EMP: 5
SQ FT: 3,200
SALES: 284K Privately Held
SIC: 3799 Trailers & trailer equipment

(G-14089)
CABINET MASTERS INC
7105 Ne 40th Ave Ste E (98661-1349)
PHONE..................360 695-6615
William Flanagan, *President*
Leslie Flanagan, *Vice Pres*
EMP: 8
SQ FT: 9,000
SALES (est): 909.4K Privately Held
SIC: 2599 2434 Cabinets, factory; wood kitchen cabinets

(G-14090)
CALLIDUS SOFTWARE INC
13115 Ne 4th St Ste 115 (98684-5957)
PHONE..................503 579-4484
Leslie J Stretch, *President*
EMP: 15
SALES (corp-wide): 28.2B Privately Held
SIC: 8742 2741 Hospital & health services consultant;
HQ: Callidus Software Inc.
 4140 Dublin Blvd Ste 400
 Dublin CA 94568
 925 251-2200

(G-14091)
CALPORTLAND COMPANY
18606 Se 1st St (98684-7510)
PHONE..................360 892-5100
Greg Delbridge, *Sales Executive*
Chris Parrish, *Branch Mgr*
EMP: 50 Privately Held
SIC: 3273 Ready-mixed concrete
HQ: Calportland Company
 2025 E Financial Way
 Glendora CA 91741
 626 852-6200

(G-14092)
CALVERT COMPANY INC (PA)
218 N V St (98661-7701)
PHONE..................360 693-0971
Douglas Calvert, *President*
Randall Calvert, *Vice Pres*
Brian Oberg, *Vice Pres*
EMP: 60 EST: 1947
SQ FT: 19,000

SALES (est): 9.4MM Privately Held
SIC: 2439 Trusses, wooden roof; arches, laminated lumber; timbers, structural: laminated lumber; trusses, except roof: laminated lumber

(G-14093)
CAMPBELL PET COMPANY (PA)
Also Called: Campbell Enterprises
9606 Ne 126th Ave (98682-2310)
P.O. Box 122, Brush Prairie (98606-0122)
PHONE..................360 892-9786
Samuel S Campbell, *President*
Martha Campbell, *Treasurer*
Sam Leslie, *Sales Staff*
EMP: 14
SQ FT: 6,000
SALES (est): 1.9MM Privately Held
WEB: www.campbellpet.com
SIC: 3199 2221 Dog furnishings: collars, leashes, muzzles, etc.: leather; broadwoven fabric mills, manmade

(G-14094)
CANAM STEEL CORPORATION
Also Called: Sun Steel Canam
312 Se Stnmill Dr Ste 147 (98684)
PHONE..................509 837-7008
Marcus Redmond, *Branch Mgr*
EMP: 200 Privately Held
WEB: www.canamsteel.com
SIC: 3448 3449 3441 Prefabricated metal buildings; miscellaneous metalwork; fabricated structural metal
HQ: Canam Steel Corporation
 4010 Clay St
 Point Of Rocks MD 21777
 301 874-5141

(G-14095)
CANDEO CANDLE FACTORY LLC
18720 Se 21st St (98683-9761)
PHONE..................360 524-2310
Caitlin Marsters, *Principal*
EMP: 2
SALES (est): 164.6K Privately Held
SIC: 3999 Candles

(G-14096)
CANNAMAN
6212 Ne 152nd Ave (98682-5109)
PHONE..................360 597-4850
EMP: 2
SALES (est): 69.4K Privately Held
SIC: 0139 3999 0191 ; ; general farms, primarily crop

(G-14097)
CAPSULE URN LLC
293 Date St (98661-5545)
P.O. Box 1351 (98666-1351)
PHONE..................360 695-2618
Steven Prastka, *Principal*
EMP: 3
SALES (est): 221.3K Privately Held
SIC: 3272 Burial vaults, concrete or pre-cast terrazzo

(G-14098)
CARDINAL ASSOCIATES INC
Also Called: Bergstrom Nutrition
1000 W 8th St (98660-3011)
PHONE..................360 693-1883
James Hughes, *President*
Tim Hammond, *Vice Pres*
Pamela Link, *Vice Pres*
Kelly H Link, *Treasurer*
Roma Bergstrom, *Director*
▲ EMP: 26
SALES (est): 7.7MM Privately Held
WEB: www.cardinalmsm.com
SIC: 2834 Veterinary pharmaceutical preparations; vitamin, nutrient & hematinic preparations for human use

(G-14099)
CAREER DEVELOPMENT SOFTWARE
Also Called: School Company, The
5905 Buena Vista Dr (98661-7111)
P.O. Box 5379 (98668-5379)
PHONE..................360 696-3529
Phillip Mattox, *President*
EMP: 10

SALES (est): 1.2MM Privately Held
SIC: 5045 7372 7812 7371 Computer software; educational computer software; motion picture & video production; custom computer programming services; pre-recorded records & tapes

(G-14100)
CARTECH INDUSTRIES INC
4016 Ne 44th St (98661-3135)
PHONE..................360 693-3616
Gayle Stoddard, *President*
Nelson Stoddard, *Admin Sec*
EMP: 2
SALES (est): 268.8K Privately Held
WEB: www.cartechnw.com
SIC: 3829 8331 Instrument board gauges, automotive: computerized; job training services

(G-14101)
CARTER GAME TESTERS
206 Ne 126th Ave (98684-0858)
PHONE..................360 326-3245
EMP: 2 EST: 2014
SALES (est): 77.7K Privately Held
SIC: 1389 Testing, measuring, surveying & analysis services

(G-14102)
CASCADE APPAREL & EMBROIDERY
16505 Se 1st St Ste H (98684-9586)
PHONE..................360 253-3022
EMP: 3 EST: 2001
SALES (est): 130K Privately Held
SIC: 2395 Pleating/Stitching Services

(G-14103)
CASCADE CANING
5305 E 18th St (98661-6583)
PHONE..................360 258-1738
EMP: 3 EST: 2010
SALES (est): 186.6K Privately Held
SIC: 3565 Canning machinery, food

(G-14104)
CASCADE MEDICAL TECHNOLOGIES
406 Se 131st Ave Ste 205 (98683-4013)
PHONE..................360 896-6944
Larry Foltz, *Principal*
EMP: 2
SALES (est): 217.5K Privately Held
WEB: www.cascademedtech.com
SIC: 7372 Prepackaged software

(G-14105)
CASCADE PAPER CONVERTING INC
7000 Ne 40th Ave Ste B1 (98661-1300)
PHONE..................360 735-1602
Richard Nelson, *President*
Amy Nelson, *Vice Pres*
EMP: 6
SQ FT: 12,000
SALES: 1MM Privately Held
SIC: 2679 Paper products, converted

(G-14106)
CASCADE SPECIALTY HARDWARE
Also Called: Safebar
2910 Kauffman Ave (98660-2044)
PHONE..................360 823-3995
Jeremy Holst, *President*
Lorin Armstrong, *Manager*
EMP: 3
SALES (est): 223.1K Privately Held
SIC: 3261 Vitreous plumbing fixtures

(G-14107)
CASCADE WIRE WORKS LLC
10310 Ne 96th St (98662-2278)
PHONE..................360 904-4412
Jason Pacheco, *Principal*
EMP: 2
SALES (est): 303.2K Privately Held
SIC: 3496 Miscellaneous fabricated wire products

(G-14108)
CASCADE WOODWRIGHTS
3018 Ne Littler Way (98662-7136)
PHONE..................360 771-3908

Layne Carney, *Owner*
EMP: 2
SALES (est): 147K Privately Held
SIC: 2499 Decorative wood & woodwork

(G-14109)
CEBA SYSTEMS LLC
13213 Ne Kerr Rd Ste 110 (98682-4630)
P.O. Box 821978 (98682-0045)
PHONE..................360 891-1823
Ethan Clark,
Annette Clark,
EMP: 2
SALES: 300K Privately Held
SIC: 3545 Machine tool attachments & accessories

(G-14110)
CELLAR 55 INC
1812 Washington St (98660-2664)
PHONE..................360 693-2700
Terry Blake, *President*
Michael Sasse, *Vice Pres*
EMP: 2
SALES (est): 128.8K Privately Held
SIC: 2084 Wine cellars, bonded: engaged in blending wines

(G-14111)
CEMEX MATERIALS LLC
8705 Ne 117th Ave (98662-3247)
PHONE..................360 254-7770
Nancy Alldrin, *Vice Pres*
EMP: 33 Privately Held
WEB: www.rinkermaterials.com
SIC: 3273 Ready-mixed concrete
HQ: Cemex Materials Llc
 1501 Belvedere Rd
 West Palm Beach FL 33406
 561 833-5555

(G-14112)
CHAMPION SPORTS GROUP
1321 Ne 76th St (98665-0400)
PHONE..................360 258-0546
Jesse Villanueva, *Bd of Directors*
EMP: 2
SALES (est): 124.3K Privately Held
SIC: 3949 Sporting & athletic goods

(G-14113)
CHARTER CONTROLS INC
1705 Ne 64th Ave Ste B (98661-6989)
PHONE..................360 695-2161
Charlene Oday, *President*
Curtis Carter, *Vice Pres*
EMP: 12
SALES (est): 4MM Privately Held
SIC: 3625 Relays & industrial controls

(G-14114)
CHEMTRADE CHEMICALS US LLC
2611 W 26th St (98660-1073)
PHONE..................360 693-1379
Rick Butmiller, *Manager*
EMP: 5
SALES (corp-wide): 1.2B Privately Held
SIC: 2819 Aluminum sulfate
HQ: Chemtrade Chemicals Us Llc
 90 E Halsey Rd
 Parsippany NJ 07054

(G-14115)
CHEVY METAL
11812 Ne Highway 99 (98686-4057)
PHONE..................360 694-7295
Rick Severson, *Principal*
EMP: 4
SALES (est): 253K Privately Held
SIC: 3399 Primary metal products

(G-14116)
CHEYENNE LIVESTOCK & PRODUCTS
14712 Ne 13th Ct (98685-1400)
P.O. Box 25, Brush Prairie (98606-0025)
PHONE..................360 256-0293
Sue Silagy, *CEO*
Kim Silagy, *President*
▼ EMP: 15
SQ FT: 10,000
SALES (est): 3.5MM Privately Held
SIC: 3089 Synthetic resin finished products

Vancouver - Clark County (G-14117)

(G-14117)
CHIMCARE VANCOUVER
6715 Ne 63rd St (98661-1980)
PHONE..................360 696-8309
EMP: 2
SALES (est): 74.4K **Privately Held**
SIC: 2842 Specialty cleaning, polishes & sanitation goods

(G-14118)
CHINOOK MECHANICAL LLC
4214 Ne Minnehaha St (98661-1204)
PHONE..................360 947-9035
Tim Wise,
EMP: 5
SALES (est): 393.3K **Privately Held**
SIC: 3498 Fabricated pipe & fittings

(G-14119)
CHRISTENSEN SHIPYARDS LLC
4400 Se Columbia Way (98661-5570)
P.O. Box 11549, Chattanooga TN (37401-2549)
PHONE..................360 831-9800
Henry G Luken,
▲ EMP: 15
SALES (est): 2.7MM **Privately Held**
SIC: 3732 Boat building & repairing

(G-14120)
CLAUDES ACCURATE MACHINING
Also Called: C A M
14413 Ne 10th Ave A112 (98685-1717)
PHONE..................360 546-5840
Claude Jiganie, *Owner*
EMP: 2 EST: 1993
SQ FT: 2,500
SALES (est): 372.6K **Privately Held**
SIC: 3599 Air intake filters, internal combustion engine, except auto; machine shop, jobbing & repair

(G-14121)
CLAUS PAWS ANIMAL HOSPITAL LLC
5819 Ne 162nd Ave (98682-5189)
PHONE..................360 896-7449
Katherine Claus Dvm,
EMP: 13
SALES (est): 452.6K **Privately Held**
WEB: www.clauspaws.com
SIC: 0742 3841 Animal hospital services, pets & other animal specialties; surgical lasers

(G-14122)
CLEAR FOREST PRODUCTS INC
201 Ne Park Plaza Dr # 1 (98684-5808)
PHONE..................360 253-0101
Harvey Hetfeld, *President*
▲ EMP: 2
SALES (est): 147.7K **Privately Held**
SIC: 2421 Lumber: rough, sawed or planed

(G-14123)
CLEVELAND ENTERPRISES INC
3207 Ne 65th St (98663-1455)
PHONE..................360 694-0435
Tim Kane, *President*
Jerry Noack, *Corp Secy*
EMP: 6
SQ FT: 4,050
SALES (est): 841.1K **Privately Held**
SIC: 3441 3444 Fabricated structural metal; sheet metalwork

(G-14124)
CLOTH CREATIONS INC
4700 Ne 128th St (98686-2805)
PHONE..................360 573-7348
Gerald E Matthieu, *President*
EMP: 1
SALES: 1MM **Privately Held**
SIC: 3589 Car washing machinery

(G-14125)
CM CABINETS L L C
10017 Nw 27th Ave (98685-4823)
PHONE..................360 921-3493
Edward James Haynes, *Principal*
EMP: 2
SALES (est): 184.7K **Privately Held**
SIC: 2434 Wood kitchen cabinets

(G-14126)
CO C GRAPHICS
Also Called: Ad Pro
7902 Ne St Johns Rd Ste B (98665-1094)
PHONE..................360 571-8488
Dan Grimes, *Owner*
EMP: 2
SQ FT: 1,200
SALES: 150K **Privately Held**
SIC: 2759 Screen printing

(G-14127)
COASTAL SOFTWARE & CONSULTING
1499 Se Tech Center Pl # 170 (98683-5529)
PHONE..................360 891-6174
Deryk Marien, *President*
EMP: 6
SALES (est): 716.9K **Privately Held**
WEB: www.coastalsoftware.com
SIC: 7372 8748 7371 Business oriented computer software; business consulting; custom computer programming services

(G-14128)
COINSTAR LLC
9000 Ne Highway 99 (98665-8923)
PHONE..................866 733-2693
EMP: 2
SALES (corp-wide): 2B **Privately Held**
SIC: 1311 Crude petroleum & natural gas
HQ: Coinstar, Llc
1800 114th Ave Se
Bellevue WA 98004

(G-14129)
COLUMBIA CASCADE COMPANY
1801 W 20th St (98660-1348)
PHONE..................360 693-8558
Dean Ness, *Superintendent*
EMP: 80
SALES (corp-wide): 12.8MM **Privately Held**
WEB: www.timberform.com
SIC: 2421 3949 Chipper mill; sporting & athletic goods
PA: Columbia Cascade Company
1300 Sw 6th Ave Ste 310
Portland OR 97201
503 223-1157

(G-14130)
COLUMBIA GEM HOUSE INC
Also Called: C G H Imports
12507 Ne 95th St (98682-2463)
P.O. Box 820889 (98682-0020)
PHONE..................360 514-0569
Eric Braunwart, *President*
▲ EMP: 20
SQ FT: 5,000
SALES (est): 5.6MM **Privately Held**
WEB: www.columbiagemhouse.com
SIC: 5094 5944 3911 Precious stones (gems); jewelry; jewelry stores; jewelry, precious metal

(G-14131)
COLUMBIA MACHINE INC (PA)
107 Grand Blvd (98661-7795)
P.O. Box 8950 (98668-8950)
PHONE..................360 694-1501
Fred Neth Jr, *Ch of Bd*
Rick Goode, *President*
Richard Armstrong, *Vice Pres*
Bill Naumann, *Purch Mgr*
Branson Debbie, *Buyer*
◆ EMP: 368 EST: 1937
SQ FT: 300,000
SALES: 69MM **Privately Held**
WEB: www.columbiamachine.com
SIC: 3559 3537 Concrete products machinery; palletizers & depalletizers

(G-14132)
COLUMBIA MACHINE INC
3000 Columbia House Blvd (98661-2965)
PHONE..................360 905-1611
Bob St John, *Principal*
EMP: 5
SALES (corp-wide): 69MM **Privately Held**
SIC: 3559 Concrete products machinery
PA: Columbia Machine, Inc.
107 Grand Blvd
Vancouver WA 98661
360 694-1501

(G-14133)
COLUMBIA MACHINE INC
Turmac
107 Grand Blvd (98661-7795)
P.O. Box 8950 (98668-8950)
PHONE..................360 694-1501
Mike Richard, *Branch Mgr*
EMP: 187
SALES (corp-wide): 69MM **Privately Held**
WEB: www.columbiamachine.com
SIC: 3559 3537 Concrete products machinery; palletizers & depalletizers
PA: Columbia Machine, Inc.
107 Grand Blvd
Vancouver WA 98661
360 694-1501

(G-14134)
COLUMBIA METAL WORKS INC
4200 Nw Fruit Valley Rd (98660-1223)
P.O. Box 61982 (98666-1982)
PHONE..................360 693-5818
George Fassilis, *President*
Areti Fassilis, *Corp Secy*
EMP: 7
SALES (est): 1.1MM **Privately Held**
SIC: 3441 Fabricated structural metal

(G-14135)
COLUMBIA NUTRITIONAL LLC (PA)
6317 Ne 131st Ave 103 (98682-5879)
P.O. Box 820829 (98682-0019)
PHONE..................360 737-9966
Kevin Unger, *CEO*
Russell White, *President*
Greg Seter, *Vice Pres*
Brea Viratos, *Vice Pres*
Kandis White, *Vice Pres*
EMP: 103
SQ FT: 24,000
SALES (est): 88.4MM **Privately Held**
SIC: 2023 Dietary supplements, dairy & non-dairy based

(G-14136)
COLUMBIA OFFICE AND BUS
2300 E 3rd Loop (98661-7723)
PHONE..................360 695-6245
EMP: 2 EST: 2011
SALES (est): 93K **Privately Held**
SIC: 2759 Commercial Printing

(G-14137)
COLUMBIA ROCK & AGGREGATES INC
913 Ne 172nd Ave (98684-9323)
P.O. Box 370, Washougal (98671-0370)
PHONE..................360 892-0510
Ronald M Wamberg, *President*
George Schmid, *Vice Pres*
Patrick Nelson, *Treasurer*
EMP: 18
SQ FT: 2,000
SALES (est): 1.3MM **Privately Held**
SIC: 3295 Minerals, ground or treated

(G-14138)
COLUMBIA SIGN INC
11808 Ne 4th Plain Blvd (98682-5637)
PHONE..................360 696-1919
Tim Owens, *Principal*
EMP: 3
SALES (est): 233.3K **Privately Held**
SIC: 3993 Electric signs

(G-14139)
COLUMBIA/OKURA LLC
301 Grove St Ste A (98661-4944)
PHONE..................360 735-1952
Rick Goode, *President*
▲ EMP: 48
SQ FT: 48,000
SALES: 13.3MM **Privately Held**
WEB: www.columbiaokura.com
SIC: 3537 Palletizers & depalletizers

(G-14140)
COMBUSTION TECHNOLOGY LLC
3307 Ne 109th Ave (98682-7724)
P.O. Box 820845 (98682-0019)
PHONE..................360 253-9600
Melissa Beall, *CFO*
Dave Beall, *Sales Staff*
David Beall,
EMP: 5
SQ FT: 2,500
SALES (est): 1.1MM **Privately Held**
WEB: www.combustion-tech.net
SIC: 3823 Industrial instrmnts msrmnt display/control process variable

(G-14141)
COMEAU LETTERING
11911 Ne 50th Ave (98686-3306)
PHONE..................360 573-2216
Paul A Comeau, *Owner*
Vicki Comeaue, *Principal*
EMP: 2 EST: 1994
SALES (est): 133.7K **Privately Held**
SIC: 2211 2675 7532 Pin stripes, cotton; stencils & lettering materials: die-cut; lettering, automotive

(G-14142)
COMPLETE CONTROLS
9306 Ne 7th St (98664-3322)
PHONE..................360 904-7525
Jim Palmer, *President*
EMP: 3 EST: 2008
SALES (est): 308.5K **Privately Held**
SIC: 3429 Marine hardware

(G-14143)
COMPOUND PHOTONICS US CORP
805 Broadway St Ste 300 (98660-3310)
PHONE..................360 597-3654
Jonathan A Sachs PHD, *Branch Mgr*
EMP: 29
SALES (corp-wide): 3MM **Privately Held**
SIC: 3826 Automatic chemical analyzers
HQ: Compound Photonics U.S. Corporation
300 N 56th St
Chandler AZ 85226

(G-14144)
CONCEPT REALITY INC
7812 Ne 19th Ct (98665-9759)
P.O. Box 65055 (98665-0002)
PHONE..................360 695-3860
Christopher Nunn, *President*
Nancy Nunn, *Vice Pres*
EMP: 10
SQ FT: 5,600
SALES (est): 1.3MM **Privately Held**
WEB: www.conceptreality.com
SIC: 3999 3599 Models, except toy; machine shop, jobbing & repair

(G-14145)
CONCRETE SHOP INC
1702 Ne 99th St (98665-9018)
PHONE..................360 573-5775
Jeff Stevens, *President*
EMP: 15 EST: 1974
SQ FT: 7,500
SALES: 1.2MM **Privately Held**
WEB: www.concreteshopinc.com
SIC: 3272 3271 5032 Concrete products, precast; architectural concrete: block, split, fluted, screen, etc.; concrete building products

(G-14146)
CONEX SAND & GRAVEL
17007 Ne 22nd St (98684-9798)
PHONE..................503 437-0536
Pavel Baranets, *Principal*
EMP: 3
SALES (est): 150K **Privately Held**
SIC: 1442 Construction sand & gravel

(G-14147)
CONSOLIDATED METCO INC (HQ)
Also Called: Conmet
5701 Se Columbia Way (98661-5963)
PHONE..................360 828-2599
Edward J Oeltjen, *President*
John E Waters, *President*

GEOGRAPHIC SECTION

Vancouver - Clark County (G-14177)

Mike Harman, *Vice Pres*
Ruben Roman, *Opers Staff*
Sean McDowell, *Buyer*
◆ **EMP:** 100
SQ FT: 25,000
SALES (est): 705.8MM
SALES (corp-wide): 2.3B **Privately Held**
WEB: www.conmet.com
SIC: 3365 3363 3089 3714 Aluminum & aluminum-based alloy castings; aluminum die-castings; injection molded finished plastic products; fuel systems & parts, motor vehicle; fabricated plate work (boiler shop); hot-rolled iron & steel products
PA: Amsted Industries Incorporated
180 N Stetson Ave # 1800
Chicago IL 60601
312 645-1700

(G-14148)
CONSOLIDATED METCO INC
3301 Se Columbia Way (98661-8098)
PHONE.................360 828-2689
EMP: 11
SALES (corp-wide): 1.3B **Privately Held**
SIC: 3365 3363 Aluminum Foundry Mfg Aluminum Die-Castings
HQ: Consolidated Metco, Inc.
5701 Se Columbia Way
Vancouver WA 98661
360 828-2599

(G-14149)
CONTACEZ LLC
Also Called: Ultimate Intr-Prximal Solution
217 Se 136th Ave Ste 105 (98684-6908)
PHONE.................360 694-1000
Stella Hooja Kim, *President*
Bruce Kyte, *Business Mgr*
Daniel Kim,
Joshua Kim, *Advisor*
◆ **EMP:** 12
SQ FT: 4,000
SALES (est): 1.2MM **Privately Held**
SIC: 3843 Dental equipment & supplies

(G-14150)
CONTOUR COUNTERTOPS INC
Also Called: Superior Counter Tops
5305 Ne 121st Ave Ste 511 (98682-6241)
PHONE.................503 654-2245
Charles Maiwurm, *President*
EMP: 15
SALES (est): 1.6MM
SALES (corp-wide): 6.6MM **Privately Held**
WEB: www.contourcountertops.com
SIC: 2541 2431 Counter & sink tops; millwork
PA: Contour Laminates, Inc.
24602 Pacific Hwy S
Kent WA
253 681-6400

(G-14151)
CONWOOD CONSTRUCTION INC
1701 W 31st St (98660-1281)
PHONE.................360 694-5195
Bryan Chon, *Principal*
▼ **EMP:** 2
SALES (est): 125.2K **Privately Held**
SIC: 2431 Millwork

(G-14152)
CRAVE MAGAZINE
1013 Ne 68th St (98665-0503)
PHONE.................360 991-9332
Robin Steeley, *CEO*
EMP: 2
SALES (est): 14.4K **Privately Held**
SIC: 2721 7313 Magazines: publishing & printing; magazine advertising representative

(G-14153)
CREATING MEMORIES TOGETHER
1612 Ne 128th Ave (98684-5662)
PHONE.................360 944-8393
Kandi Lukowski, *Owner*
Edward Lukowski, *Co-Owner*
EMP: 2

SALES (est): 56.9K **Privately Held**
WEB: www.lukowski-family.com
SIC: 7221 5999 5699 3993 Photographer, still or video; banners; customized clothing & apparel; signs & advertising specialties

(G-14154)
CROSSRADS PRECISION RIFLES LLC
2614 Ne 176th Ave (98684-0749)
PHONE.................360 931-4505
Cheryl Spatz, *Manager*
EMP: 2
SALES (est): 175.9K **Privately Held**
SIC: 3599 Industrial machinery

(G-14155)
CROWN PLATING INC
4221 Ne St Johns Rd Ste G (98661-3343)
PHONE.................360 693-3040
Melinda Tyler-Furniss, *President*
EMP: 2
SQ FT: 3,500
SALES (est): 209.5K **Privately Held**
SIC: 3471 Chromium plating of metals or formed products; electroplating of metals or formed products

(G-14156)
CRYSTAL TRIANGLE PUBLISHING
16210 Se 19th St (98683-4427)
PHONE.................360 546-2497
Donald Hurd, *Owner*
EMP: 2
SALES (est): 104.8K **Privately Held**
SIC: 2741 Miscellaneous publishing

(G-14157)
CSI GROUP LLC
3301 Se Columbia Way 45 (98661-8098)
PHONE.................360 334-5455
Otis Edric, *Principal*
Michael Michaelclellan, *Human Res Mgr*
EMP: 9
SALES (est): 875.4K **Privately Held**
SIC: 2671 Plastic film, coated or laminated for packaging

(G-14158)
CYNS INSANITYS
3320 E 17th St (98661-5322)
PHONE.................360 694-2459
Steven Powers, *Owner*
Cynthia Powers, *Co-Owner*
EMP: 2
SALES (est): 116K **Privately Held**
SIC: 3429 Bicycle racks, automotive

(G-14159)
CYTODYN OPERATIONS INC
1111 Main St Ste 660 (98660-2970)
PHONE.................360 980-8524
Anthony D Caracciolo, *Ch of Bd*
Nader Z Pourhassan, *President*
Brendan Rae, *Senior VP*
Michael D Mulholland, *CFO*
Richard G Pestell, *Chief Mktg Ofcr*
EMP: 6
SQ FT: 1,812
SALES (est): 1.2MM **Privately Held**
SIC: 2834 Pharmaceutical preparations

(G-14160)
D & D CONTROLS INC
3106 Ne 65th St Ststea (98663-1583)
PHONE.................360 695-8931
Brian Morin, *President*
Don Baxter, *Principal*
EMP: 4
SALES (est): 686.2K **Privately Held**
SIC: 3679 8711 Electronic circuits; industrial engineers

(G-14161)
D & G AUTO PARTS
Also Called: Modrall Machine
2504 Ne Stapleton Rd (98661-6542)
PHONE.................360 696-3631
Lynn K Modrall, *Owner*
EMP: 4
SQ FT: 2,160

SALES (est): 220K **Privately Held**
SIC: 3599 5013 5531 Machine shop, jobbing & repair; automotive supplies & parts; automotive parts

(G-14162)
D & K CONCRETE PRODUCTS INC
15008 Ne 15th Ave (98685-1420)
P.O. Box 306, Carson (98610-0306)
PHONE.................360 573-4020
Fred Newman, *President*
Lauren Newman, *Vice Pres*
EMP: 15
SQ FT: 2,500
SALES (est): 1.2MM **Privately Held**
SIC: 3272 Septic tanks, concrete

(G-14163)
D S FABRICATION & DESIGN INC
13504 Ne 84th St Ste 103 (98682-3091)
PHONE.................360 600-9706
Dan Smark, *President*
Krista Smark, *Admin Sec*
EMP: 4
SALES (est): 823K **Privately Held**
SIC: 3448 Prefabricated metal buildings

(G-14164)
DAIRY QUEENS VANCOUVER (PA)
10507 Ne 4th Plain Blvd (98662-5753)
PHONE.................360 256-7302
Barbara Rice, *Owner*
EMP: 50
SALES (est): 907.9K **Privately Held**
SIC: 5812 2023 Ice cream stands or dairy bars; dry, condensed, evaporated dairy products

(G-14165)
DAISY MAIZ LLC
10309 Ne 14th St (98664-4303)
PHONE.................360 718-8288
EMP: 4
SALES (est): 397.4K **Privately Held**
SIC: 2096 Potato chips & similar snacks

(G-14166)
DAN COATS
Also Called: Columbia River Quilting
10805 Ne 44th St (98682-6609)
PHONE.................360 892-2730
Dan Coats, *Owner*
EMP: 2
SALES (est): 110.7K **Privately Held**
WEB: www.columbiariverquilting.com
SIC: 2221 Comforters & quilts, manmade fiber & silk

(G-14167)
DAVIS & WALKER FABRICATION
15017 Ne 24th St (98684-7829)
P.O. Box 820407 (98682-0008)
PHONE.................360 944-0057
Tim Walker, *Partner*
EMP: 2
SALES (est): 121K **Privately Held**
SIC: 3441 Fabricated structural metal

(G-14168)
DAVIS DEVELOPMENT & MFG
9500 Ne 72nd Ave (98665-9399)
PHONE.................360 892-7802
Donald W Davis, *CEO*
Paul Davis, *President*
EMP: 5
SQ FT: 3,900
SALES (est): 721.6K **Privately Held**
SIC: 3589 Commercial cooking & food-warming equipment; swimming pool filter & water conditioning systems

(G-14169)
DCB INDUSTRIES INC
Also Called: Bowers Steel
2451 St Francis Ln (98660-1061)
PHONE.................360 750-0009
Dave Towers, *Branch Mgr*
EMP: 9
SALES (est): 796.7K **Privately Held**
SIC: 3316 Bars, steel, cold finished, from purchased hot-rolled

PA: D.C.B. Industries, Inc.
9702 Se 12th St
Vancouver WA 98664

(G-14170)
DCB INDUSTRIES INC (PA)
Also Called: Bowers Steel
9702 Se 12th St (98664-3631)
PHONE.................360 750-0009
David Bowers, *President*
Larry Bowers, *Corp Secy*
Barbara Bowers, *Manager*
EMP: 8
SQ FT: 25,000
SALES (est): 9.1MM **Privately Held**
SIC: 3449 Bars, concrete reinforcing: fabricated steel

(G-14171)
DECORADO FABRICATION
Also Called: Decorado Thin Brick
15008 Ne 15th Ste B (98686)
PHONE.................360 694-6832
Oscar Corado, *Owner*
EMP: 6 **EST:** 2014
SALES (est): 623K **Privately Held**
SIC: 2436 Softwood veneer & plywood

(G-14172)
DECORATIVE METAL SERVICES INC
3810 H St (98663-2366)
PHONE.................360 695-7052
Margaret Kibbee-Martin, *President*
EMP: 4
SQ FT: 9,000
SALES (est): 599.9K **Privately Held**
WEB: www.decorativemetalservices.com
SIC: 3446 Architectural metalwork

(G-14173)
DEEKAY ESSENTIALS LLC
12407 Nw 49th Ave (98685-1980)
PHONE.................732 809-7284
EMP: 2
SQ FT: 250
SALES (est): 9MM **Privately Held**
SIC: 2087 Mfg Flavor Extracts/Syrup

(G-14174)
DEHAVILLAND ELC AMPLIFIER CO
2401 Ne 148th Ct (98684-7878)
PHONE.................360 891-6570
Kara Chaffee, *Principal*
EMP: 4
SALES (est): 319.9K **Privately Held**
SIC: 3651 Amplifiers: radio, public address or musical instrument

(G-14175)
DENIM FRILLS
10501 Ne Highway 99 # 17 (98686-5698)
PHONE.................360 844-5163
Hazel Dell, *Principal*
EMP: 2
SALES (est): 149.3K **Privately Held**
SIC: 2211 Denims

(G-14176)
DESI TELEPHONE LABELS INC
8100 Ne St Johns Rd A101 (98665-2011)
PHONE.................360 571-0713
Larry Kingsella, *President*
Nathan Silva, *Vice Pres*
EMP: 17
SQ FT: 4,500
SALES (est): 3.5MM **Privately Held**
WEB: www.desi.com
SIC: 2679 2672 7372 Labels, paper: made from purchased material; labels (unprinted), gummed: made from purchased materials; prepackaged software

(G-14177)
DEWILS INDUSTRIES INC (PA)
6307 Ne 127th Ave (98682-5899)
P.O. Box 820568 (98682-0012)
PHONE.................360 892-0300
Tracy S Wilson, *President*
Randal O Wilson, *Vice Pres*
EMP: 120
SALES (est): 17.6MM **Privately Held**
WEB: www.dewils.com
SIC: 2434 Vanities, bathroom: wood

Vancouver - Clark County (G-14178)

(G-14178)
DEWILS INDUSTRIES INC
6307 Ne 127th Ave (98682-5899)
P.O. Box 820568 (98682-0012)
PHONE...................................360 892-0300
Duane Wilson, *President*
EMP: 100
SALES (corp-wide): 17.6MM **Privately Held**
WEB: www.dewils.com
SIC: 2434 Vanities, bathroom: wood
PA: Dewils Industries, Inc.
6307 Ne 127th Ave
Vancouver WA 98682
360 892-0300

(G-14179)
DIGITAL IMAGING SERVICES INC
610 E 40th St (98663-1824)
PHONE...................................360 567-1260
Kevin Brubacher, *President*
EMP: 4
SALES (est): 320.2K **Privately Held**
SIC: 2752 Commercial printing, lithographic

(G-14180)
DILIGENCE GROUP OIL & GAS BIOF
8805 Ne 36th St (98662-7311)
PHONE...................................360 892-0745
EMP: 2
SALES (est): 96.7K **Privately Held**
SIC: 1389 Oil & gas field services

(G-14181)
DIS-TRAN WOOD PRODUCTS LLC
1810 W 39th St (98660-1271)
PHONE...................................360 735-9356
Davie Bryant, *Branch Mgr*
EMP: 6 **Privately Held**
SIC: 2439 Structural wood members
PA: Dis-Tran Packaged Substations, Llc
4725 Highway 28 E
Pineville LA 71360

(G-14182)
DISCOUNT DOORS & MILLWORK LLC
2502 E Fourth Plain Blvd (98661-3965)
PHONE...................................360 687-1942
Kelly Jones,
Shari Jones,
EMP: 4
SALES (est): 555.7K **Privately Held**
SIC: 2431 Millwork

(G-14183)
DIVERSIFIED WELDING WORKS INC
8009 Ne 19th Ct (98665-9750)
PHONE...................................360 576-0929
Monica Binns, *President*
William Binns, *Treasurer*
EMP: 8
SQ FT: 18,000
SALES: 1.1MM **Privately Held**
SIC: 7692 Welding repair

(G-14184)
DIY TECH SHOP LLC
2464 Ne Stapleton Rd # 3 (98661-6695)
PHONE...................................360 258-1519
Servando Nava,
EMP: 3
SALES (est): 243.2K **Privately Held**
SIC: 3559 Plastics working machinery

(G-14185)
DM2 SOFTWARE INC
7700 Ne Greenwood Dr # 200 (98662-6823)
PHONE...................................360 574-6984
Scott Burkard, *CEO*
EMP: 45
SQ FT: 1,600
SALES (est): 5.9MM
SALES (corp-wide): 225.3MM **Publicly Held**
WEB: www.dm2.com
SIC: 7372 Prepackaged software

HQ: Professional Datasolutions, Inc.
4001 Central Pointe Pkwy
Temple TX 76504

(G-14186)
DOUGLAS GREEN
Also Called: Douglas Green & Associates
17413 Se 28th St (98683-3427)
PHONE...................................360 260-9708
Douglas Green, *Owner*
EMP: 6
SALES: 1.1MM **Privately Held**
SIC: 2711 2741 Newspapers, publishing & printing; miscellaneous publishing

(G-14187)
DREAM LINE CABINETS LLC
2700 Ne An 2 F (98661)
PHONE...................................503 841-8575
Sergey Voloshko, *President*
Roman Vasilchuk, *President*
EMP: 5 **EST:** 2011
SALES (est): 518.7K **Privately Held**
SIC: 2531 1751 2434 Public building & related furniture; cabinet & finish carpentry; wood kitchen cabinets

(G-14188)
DRU WOOD
8608 Mt Olympus Ave (98664-2620)
PHONE...................................360 213-7444
Duane Underwood, *Principal*
EMP: 2
SALES (est): 150.3K **Privately Held**
SIC: 2542 Cabinets: show, display or storage: except wood

(G-14189)
DULLUM INDUSTRIES INC
Also Called: Dullum Enterprises
13315 Ne Kerr Rd Ste A (98682-4653)
PHONE...................................360 254-3220
Ronald R Dullum, *President*
Corinne Dullum, *Treasurer*
EMP: 4
SQ FT: 4,000
SALES (est): 479.2K **Privately Held**
SIC: 3599 Machine shop, jobbing & repair

(G-14190)
DUNCANS WOODS
1221 Se Ellsworth Rd # 276 (98664-6299)
PHONE...................................360 604-7140
Duncan Macleod, *Owner*
Duncan McLeod, *Owner*
EMP: 2
SQ FT: 2,216
SALES (est): 110K **Privately Held**
WEB: www.duncanswoods.com
SIC: 2441 Boxes, wood

(G-14191)
DUSTYS MACHINE SHOP
3108a Ne 66th St (98663-1585)
PHONE...................................360 694-6201
Dale Vermire, *Owner*
EMP: 2
SALES: 10K **Privately Held**
SIC: 3599 Machine shop, jobbing & repair

(G-14192)
EAST VANCOUVER VENOM
513 Ne 146th Ct (98684-8004)
PHONE...................................360 518-1658
Catherine Souder, *President*
EMP: 2
SALES (est): 74.4K **Privately Held**
SIC: 2836 Venoms

(G-14193)
ECLAIRE FARM LLC
9604 Ne 126th Ave (98682-2312)
PHONE...................................360 524-9775
Rick Falconer,
EMP: 3 **EST:** 2017
SALES (est): 84.5K **Privately Held**
SIC: 2099 Food preparations

(G-14194)
EFCO CORP
10000 Ne 7th Ave (98685-4599)
PHONE...................................360 566-0300
EMP: 3
SALES (corp-wide): 259.3MM **Privately Held**
SIC: 3444 Mfg Sheet Metalwork

HQ: Efco Corp
1800 Ne Broadway Ave
Des Moines IA 50313
515 266-1141

(G-14195)
EH METAL RECYCLING
8801 Ne 117th Ave (98662-3251)
PHONE...................................360 334-6005
Misty Girod, *Principal*
Joshua Girod, *Manager*
EMP: 2
SALES (est): 120.7K **Privately Held**
SIC: 2611 Pulp mills, mechanical & recycling processing

(G-14196)
EKKO BIOSCIENCE LLC
Also Called: Ekko Health
290 Edwards Ln (98661-5515)
PHONE...................................844 822-9300
Brent Lunde, *Manager*
Glenn Rouse,
Barbara Rouse,
Erinn Rouse,
EMP: 4
SALES (est): 172.3K **Privately Held**
SIC: 2842 7389 Sanitation preparations, disinfectants & deodorants;

(G-14197)
ELECTRIC AVENUE SIGN CO
16005 Ne 12th St (98684-4173)
PHONE...................................360 903-5447
Michael Paginton, *Principal*
EMP: 3
SALES (est): 283.8K **Privately Held**
SIC: 3993 Signs & advertising specialties

(G-14198)
ELEMENT 13 PRECISION LLC
8715 Ne 58th St (98662-5267)
PHONE...................................360 597-3195
Gene Sorenson, *Principal*
EMP: 2 **EST:** 2016
SALES (est): 98.6K **Privately Held**
SIC: 3599 Industrial machinery

(G-14199)
ELGUJI SOFTWARE LLC
3709 Nw 107th St (98685-1549)
PHONE...................................360 450-5022
Bruce Elgort,
Gayle Elgort,
EMP: 2
SALES: 150K **Privately Held**
WEB: www.elguji.com
SIC: 7372 Application computer software

(G-14200)
ELUX INC
18110 Se 34th St Ste 480 (98683-9418)
PHONE...................................360 281-4568
Jong-Jan Lee, *President*
Paul Schuele, *CTO*
EMP: 2 **EST:** 2016
SALES (est): 220.4K **Privately Held**
SIC: 3663 Television monitors

(G-14201)
EMMA DANFORTH
Also Called: Danforth Signs & Carving
12700 Se Angus St (98683-3810)
PHONE...................................360 931-5060
Jeff Danforth, *Owner*
Emma Danforth, *Owner*
EMP: 2
SALES: 30K **Privately Held**
SIC: 2431 Millwork

(G-14202)
ENERGY SAVER PRODUCTS INC
Also Called: Stepsavers
6401 Nw Lincoln Ave (98663-1164)
PHONE...................................888 778-4537
Jennifer Brower, *CEO*
Jerry Brower, *President*
◆ **EMP:** 6
SQ FT: 50,000
SALES (est): 953.7K **Privately Held**
SIC: 2899 Patching plaster, household

(G-14203)
ENVIROLUX ENERGY SYSTEMS LLC
Also Called: Homeland Energy
1304 Ne 154th St Ste 102 (98685-1466)
PHONE...................................800 914-8779
Debbie Grover, *President*
Patricia Gray, *Vice Pres*
Terry Grover,
▲ **EMP:** 6 **EST:** 2008
SALES (est): 1.4MM **Privately Held**
SIC: 1531 3641 3612 3646 ; tubes, electric light; ballasts for lighting fixtures; ceiling systems, luminous

(G-14204)
ENVISION CUSTOM EMB & DESIGNS
6503 E Mill Plain Blvd B (98661-7400)
PHONE...................................360 693-2588
Richard A Griffiths, *Partner*
Linda Griffiths, *Partner*
Richard Griffiths, *Partner*
EMP: 4
SQ FT: 1,000
SALES: 200K **Privately Held**
SIC: 2395 5199 Embroidery products, except schiffli machine; advertising specialties

(G-14205)
ESP SUPPLY COMPANY LLC
3800 Se Columbia Way # 180 (98661-5586)
PHONE...................................503 256-2933
Curtis L Green,
EMP: 15
SALES (est): 2.1MM **Privately Held**
WEB: www.espsupplyonline.com
SIC: 3231 Doors, glass: made from purchased glass

(G-14206)
ESSENTIAL BUILDING TECH LLC
600 Se Maritime Ave # 240 (98661-8044)
PHONE...................................360 573-3200
Scott Conley,
EMP: 7
SALES: 1.4MM **Privately Held**
SIC: 3822 Auto controls regulating residntl & coml environmt & applncs

(G-14207)
ETERNAL COLOR PRINTS
14300 Ne 88th St (98682-2587)
PHONE...................................360 771-9408
Ryan Whittingham, *Owner*
EMP: 2
SALES (est): 125.3K **Privately Held**
SIC: 2752 Commercial printing, lithographic

(G-14208)
EVENT 1 SOFTWARE INC
3305 Main St Ste 19 (98663-2234)
PHONE...................................360 567-3752
Michael Newland, *President*
Heather Harlan, *Opers Mgr*
Heather Hymas, *Opers Mgr*
EMP: 13
SALES (est): 1.1MM **Privately Held**
SIC: 7372 Business oriented computer software

(G-14209)
EVERGREEN PLASTIC CONTAINER
6501 Ne 47th Ave (98661-1315)
PHONE...................................360 828-7174
Helen Nguyen, *CFO*
▲ **EMP:** 15 **EST:** 2007
SQ FT: 50,000
SALES (est): 3.4MM **Privately Held**
SIC: 3085 Plastics bottles
PA: Velendo Inc
6501 Ne 47th Ave
Vancouver WA 98661

(G-14210)
EVERGREEN PROSTHETCS & ORTHOTC
11201 Ne 9th St Ste 100 (98684-5961)
PHONE...................................360 213-2088

▲ = Import ▼ = Export
◆ = Import/Export

Cindy Ottley, *Branch Mgr*
EMP: 12
SALES (corp-wide): 10MM **Privately Held**
SIC: 3842 Prosthetic appliances
PA: Evergreen Prosthetics And Orthotics Llc
862 Se Oak St Ste 2b
Hillsboro OR 97123
503 726-1010

(G-14211)
EVERY WATT MATTERS LLC (PA)
2501 Se Columbia Way # 220 (98661-8038)
PHONE.............................425 985-2171
George Blackstone, *CEO*
Neal Forsthoefel, *COO*
Dwayne Kula,
EMP: 22
SQ FT: 5,000
SALES (est): 9.6MM **Privately Held**
SIC: 3646 Commercial indusl & institutional electric lighting fixtures

(G-14212)
EVERY WATT MATTERS LLC
Also Called: Ewm International
2501 Se Columbia Way # 220 (98661-8038)
PHONE.............................503 221-2113
EMP: 65
SALES (corp-wide): 9.6MM **Privately Held**
SIC: 3646 Commercial indusl & institutional electric lighting fixtures
PA: Every Watt Matters, Llc
2501 Se Columbia Way # 220
Vancouver WA 98661
425 985-2171

(G-14213)
EXCEL DESIGNS INC
6019 Ne 109th Ave (98662-5735)
PHONE.............................360 892-1412
Ron Rucker, *President*
Patricia Rucker, *Corp Secy*
Keneth Willis, *Vice Pres*
EMP: 5
SQ FT: 2,400
SALES: 510K **Privately Held**
WEB: www.exceldesigns.com
SIC: 2395 2759 Embroidery products, except schiffli machine; screen printing

(G-14214)
EXPRESS MESSENGER
3665 Nw 32nd Ave (98660-5004)
PHONE.............................360 992-9999
Kevin Comstock, *Principal*
EMP: 2
SALES (est): 26.4K **Privately Held**
SIC: 2741 Miscellaneous publishing

(G-14215)
EXQUISITECRYSTALS COM LLC
619 Barnes St (98661-3805)
PHONE.............................360 573-6745
John Van Rees,
EMP: 3
SALES (est): 200.5K **Privately Held**
SIC: 5999 7372 Rock & stone specimens; application computer software

(G-14216)
EZR COMMUNICATIONS INC
1709 Daniels St (98660-2501)
PHONE.............................360 936-0070
EMP: 2
SALES (est): 56.5K **Privately Held**
SIC: 7372 Prepackaged Software Services

(G-14217)
FABRICATED PRODUCTS INC
Also Called: Seafab Metals
3201 Nw Lower River Rd (98660-1078)
PHONE.............................360 695-5949
Michael Blasco, *Manager*
Michael Blasko, *Manager*
EMP: 171
SALES (est): 41.4MM
SALES (corp-wide): 4.1B **Privately Held**
SIC: 3441 Fabricated structural metal

HQ: Doe Run Resources Corporation
1801 Park 270 Dr Ste 300
Saint Louis MO 63146
314 453-7100

(G-14218)
FABRICATION ENTERPRISES INC
Also Called: Industrial Machine Services
3105 Ne 65th St Ste B (98663-1482)
PHONE.............................503 240-0878
Rebecca Prentice, *CEO*
David Prevost, *President*
◆ **EMP:** 10
SALES: 1.1MM **Privately Held**
WEB: www.industrialmachineservices.com
SIC: 7692 3599 Welding repair; machine & other job shop work

(G-14219)
FABRICATION PRODUCTS INC
4201 Ne Minnehaha St (98661-1244)
PHONE.............................503 283-3218
Ron Jones, *President*
Marsha M Dee, *Vice Pres*
John Montgomery, *Vice Pres*
Bryan Sword, *Manager*
EMP: 25
SQ FT: 50,000
SALES (est): 8.6MM **Privately Held**
WEB: www.fabproducts.com
SIC: 3441 3312 3531 3444 Fabricated structural metal; structural shapes & pilings, steel; construction machinery; sheet metalwork

(G-14220)
FAIRLIGHT BAKERY INC
5600 Ne 121st Ave Ste T1 (98682-6245)
P.O. Box 822373 (98682-0052)
PHONE.............................360 576-8587
Fax: 360 573-8597
EMP: 15 **EST:** 1998
SQ FT: 6,800
SALES (est): 3.5MM **Privately Held**
SIC: 5149 2051 2052 Whol Groceries Mfg Bread/Related Products Mfg Cookies/Crackers

(G-14221)
FAMILY VALUES MAG CLARK CNTY
10128 Nw 19th Ave (98685-5014)
PHONE.............................360 909-5945
Gary Mott, *Owner*
EMP: 2
SALES (est): 93.8K **Privately Held**
SIC: 7313 2721 Magazine advertising representative; magazines: publishing & printing

(G-14222)
FAR STAR PRODUCTS
Also Called: World Wide Store.com
14805 Ne 39th St (98682-8273)
PHONE.............................360 604-0080
EMP: 2
SALES (est): 10K **Privately Held**
SIC: 5961 3229 7379 7371 Ret Mail-Order House Mfg Pressed/Blown Glass Computer Related Svcs Computer Programming Svc

(G-14223)
FARWEST STEEL FABRICATION CO (HQ)
3703 Nw Gateway Ave (98660-1090)
PHONE.............................800 793-1493
Patrick Eagen, *President*
Wan Koo Huh, *Chairman*
Robert Bronson, *Admin Sec*
EMP: 55
SQ FT: 75,000
SALES (est): 8.6MM
SALES (corp-wide): 530.4MM **Privately Held**
WEB: www.ecklundindustries.com
SIC: 3441 Fabricated structural metal
PA: Farwest Steel Corporation
2000 Henderson Ave
Eugene OR 97403
541 686-2000

(G-14224)
FASTSIGNS
14415 Se Mill Plain Blvd # 1 (98684-3543)
PHONE.............................360 567-3313
Teresa Kung, *Principal*
EMP: 2
SALES (est): 190.3K **Privately Held**
SIC: 3993 Signs & advertising specialties

(G-14225)
FAVORITE DISCOVERY LLC
Also Called: We Are Wild
13301 Se Forest St (98683-6533)
PHONE.............................646 337-3574
Kevin Kim, *Partner*
▲ **EMP:** 3
SQ FT: 2,000
SALES: 2MM **Privately Held**
SIC: 2844 Toilet preparations

(G-14226)
FEDEX OFFICE & PRINT SVCS INC
303 E 15th St (98663-3403)
PHONE.............................360 694-8584
EMP: 10
SALES (corp-wide): 69.6B **Publicly Held**
WEB: www.kinkos.com
SIC: 7334 2789 2752 2672 Photocopying & duplicating services; bookbinding & related work; commercial printing, lithographic; coated & laminated paper
HQ: Fedex Office And Print Services, Inc.
7900 Legacy Dr
Plano TX 75024
800 463-3339

(G-14227)
FERMIUM IT LLC
12209 Ne Fourth Pln (98682-5604)
PHONE.............................541 213-9291
Igor Ivanov, *Mng Member*
Jason Lamb,
EMP: 6 **EST:** 2014
SQ FT: 950
SALES: 225K **Privately Held**
SIC: 3823 Computer interface equipment for industrial process control

(G-14228)
FIFTY FIFTY PRINT
1101 W 34th Way (98660-1464)
PHONE.............................360 936-9516
EMP: 2
SALES (est): 83.9K **Privately Held**
SIC: 2752 Commercial printing, lithographic

(G-14229)
FIFTY FIFTY PRINT CO
3714 Main St (98663-2228)
PHONE.............................360 718-2448
John Hardy, *President*
EMP: 3
SALES (est): 92.3K **Privately Held**
SIC: 2752 Commercial printing, lithographic

(G-14230)
FILTER CLEAN RECYCLING LLC
3311 Ne 101st Ct (98662-7536)
PHONE.............................360 798-1012
Mary Wallace, *Principal*
Douglas Wallace, *Principal*
EMP: 5
SALES (est): 571.4K **Privately Held**
SIC: 7699 3569 5172 1711 Filter cleaning; machinery cleaning; filters; engine fuels & oils; heating & air conditioning contractors

(G-14231)
FIRE LION GLOBAL LLC
3009 Ne 145th St (98686-2250)
PHONE.............................360 901-9828
Tom Reser, *Mng Member*
Treasha Reser,
▲ **EMP:** 4 **EST:** 2004
SALES (est): 736.6K **Privately Held**
SIC: 3586 Measuring & dispensing pumps

(G-14232)
FIRESTONE PACIFIC FOODS INC
4211 Fruit Valley Rd (98660-1280)
P.O. Box 61928 (98666-1928)
PHONE.............................360 695-9484
Stan A Firestone, *President*
Zackary Schmitz, *Senior VP*
Dave Williams, *Vice Pres*
Nick Saletto, *Sales Associate*
Zackary Schmits, *Admin Sec*
◆ **EMP:** 90
SALES (est): 19.1MM **Privately Held**
WEB: www.firestonepacificfoods.com
SIC: 2037 0171 Frozen fruits & vegetables; raspberry farm

(G-14233)
FIRST SILICON DESIGNS LLC
605 Main St (98660-3129)
PHONE.............................303 883-6891
Dave Hollenbeck, *Principal*
EMP: 3
SALES (est): 180.3K **Privately Held**
SIC: 3674 Semiconductors & related devices

(G-14234)
FLEXABILI-TEES
10015 Ne 152nd Ave (98682-1767)
PHONE.............................360 260-3163
Steve Taylor, *President*
Linda Taylor, *Vice Pres*
EMP: 2
SALES: 1MM **Privately Held**
SIC: 2759 5999 7389 Screen printing; banners; sign painting & lettering shop

(G-14235)
FLORENCE L ELLIS
7017 Ne Highway 99 # 106 (98665-0554)
PHONE.............................360 213-2475
Florence Ellis, *Principal*
EMP: 2
SALES (est): 162.3K **Privately Held**
SIC: 7372 Prepackaged software

(G-14236)
FOIL GRAPHICS
Also Called: Www.hotfoilgraphics.com
10511 Ne 45th Ave (98686-5882)
PHONE.............................360 574-9030
Jeff Turner, *Owner*
Kathy Turner, *Owner*
EMP: 2
SALES: 44K **Privately Held**
WEB: www.hotfoilgraphics.com
SIC: 3469 Metal stampings

(G-14237)
FOURPLAY AWD
13806 Ne 49th St Vncouver Vancouver (98682)
PHONE.............................971 706-7646
Erik Renick,
EMP: 2
SALES (est): 58.8K **Privately Held**
SIC: 5699 5999 2211 Customized clothing & apparel; T-shirts, custom printed; sports apparel; banners, flags, decals & posters; apparel & outerwear fabrics, cotton

(G-14238)
FOX COATINGS
411 Ne 112th Cir (98685-3972)
PHONE.............................360 574-7471
Anthony Fox, *Principal*
EMP: 4
SALES (est): 470.3K **Privately Held**
SIC: 3479 Metal coating & allied service

(G-14239)
FRANKLIN AND FRANKLIN COMPANY
Also Called: Northwest Scents
13003 Ne 25th St (98684-6879)
P.O. Box 6271 (98668-6271)
PHONE.............................360 254-4767
Ololade Franklin, *Co-Owner*
Emanuael Franklin, *Co-Owner*
EMP: 2
SALES (est): 70K **Privately Held**
SIC: 2844 Toilet preparations

Vancouver - Clark County (G-14240)

(G-14240)
FRISBEE ENTERPRISES LLC
1518 Se 105th Ct (98664-4783)
PHONE.................................360 991-1662
Mitch Frisbee, *Owner*
EMP: 2
SALES (est): 168.5K **Privately Held**
SIC: 3441 Fabricated structural metal

(G-14241)
FRITO-LAY NORTH AMERICA INC
4808 Nw Fruit Valley Rd (98660-1242)
PHONE.................................360 737-3000
John Munroe, *Branch Mgr*
Rich Wilson, *Manager*
Mike Bach, *Maintence Staff*
EMP: 600
SALES (corp-wide): 64.6B **Publicly Held**
WEB: www.fritolay.com
SIC: 2096 Potato chips & other potato-based snacks
HQ: Frito-Lay North America, Inc.
7701 Legacy Dr
Plano TX 75024

(G-14242)
FRONTIER MTAL FABRICATIONS INC
11218 Ne 66th St Bldg B (98662-5477)
P.O. Box 820890 (98682-0020)
PHONE.................................360 514-0961
Gary Blomdahl, *President*
EMP: 15
SALES (est): 2.2MM **Privately Held**
SIC: 3398 Metal heat treating

(G-14243)
FULL COLOR PRINTING NW
717 Ne 82nd Ave Apt 203 (98664-2050)
PHONE.................................360 721-2110
Nolan Parrett, *Principal*
EMP: 2
SALES (est): 130.1K **Privately Held**
SIC: 2752 Commercial printing, lithographic

(G-14244)
FUSE WELD GRIND
12118 Se Mcgillivray Blvd (98683-6342)
PHONE.................................360 261-2722
Joe Clifton, *Principal*
EMP: 2 **EST:** 2010
SALES (est): 172.4K **Privately Held**
SIC: 3599 Grinding castings for the trade

(G-14245)
G-TECH COMMUNICATIONS INC
13801 Nw 10th Ct Apt A4 (98685-2937)
PHONE.................................503 784-1147
Kenneth W Burns, *Principal*
EMP: 15
SALES (est): 760K **Privately Held**
SIC: 3661 Telephone dialing devices, automatic

(G-14246)
GABRIELLI DISTILLERS
825 Ne 145th Ave (98684-8023)
PHONE.................................503 421-2797
Ralph Gabrielli, *Principal*
EMP: 2
SALES (est): 62.3K **Privately Held**
SIC: 2085 Distilled & blended liquors

(G-14247)
GARRETT SIGN CO INC
811 Harney St (98660-3042)
PHONE.................................360 693-9081
Steve Taylor, *President*
Dana Taylor, *Treasurer*
EMP: 16 **EST:** 1946
SQ FT: 10,000
SALES (est): 2.4MM **Privately Held**
WEB: www.garrettsign.com
SIC: 3993 Neon signs

(G-14248)
GARY L OSTENSON DDS PS
Also Called: East Vancouver Dental Bldg
217 S Morrison Rd (98664-1436)
PHONE.................................360 896-9595
Gary L Ostenson, *President*
Kathy Hunt, *Manager*
EMP: 8
SALES (est): 646.9K **Privately Held**
SIC: 8021 2411 Dentists' office; logging

(G-14249)
GEMS N GOLD
12603 Ne 42nd Ave (98686-3155)
PHONE.................................360 574-5085
Jackson Cooper, *Owner*
EMP: 2
SALES (est): 120K **Privately Held**
SIC: 3911 Jewelry, precious metal

(G-14250)
GENERAL PLASTICS MACHINES
2828 Kauffman Ave (98660-2042)
PHONE.................................360 694-8836
Bob Elder, *President*
Steve Ramage, *Vice Pres*
EMP: 4
SQ FT: 11,400
SALES (est): 551.4K **Privately Held**
WEB: www.gpm-inc.net
SIC: 3559 Plastics working machinery

(G-14251)
GHOST RUNNERS BREWERY
4216 Ne Minnehaha St # 108 (98661-1244)
PHONE.................................360 989-3912
Jeff Seibel, *Partner*
Robert Ziebell, *Partner*
EMP: 2
SALES (est): 200.9K **Privately Held**
SIC: 2082 7389 Beer (alcoholic beverage);

(G-14252)
GILLASPIE MANUFACTURING INC
12800 Ne 95th St (98682-2413)
PHONE.................................360 260-1975
Molly Hayes, *President*
EMP: 11
SQ FT: 9,500
SALES (est): 975.5K **Privately Held**
WEB: www.gillaspiemfg.com
SIC: 3469 Stamping metal for the trade

(G-14253)
GLACIER NORTHWEST INC
Also Called: Snoqualmie Sand & Gravel
2327 W Mill Plain Blvd (98660-1366)
PHONE.................................360 694-9420
EMP: 16 **Privately Held**
SIC: 3273 Ready-mixed concrete
HQ: Glacier Northwest, Inc.
5975 E Marginal Way S
Seattle WA 98134
206 764-3000

(G-14254)
GLACIER NORTHWEST INC
3101 Nw Gateway Ave (98660-1045)
PHONE.................................360 694-1627
EMP: 2 **Privately Held**
SIC: 3273 Ready-mixed concrete
HQ: Glacier Northwest, Inc.
5975 E Marginal Way S
Seattle WA 98134
206 764-3000

(G-14255)
GLACIER NORTHWEST INC
Also Called: Apis
7215 Ne 18th St (98661)
PHONE.................................360 896-8922
Lonnie Allen, *Manager*
EMP: 6 **Privately Held**
WEB: www.glaciernw.com
SIC: 3273 3272 5032 1442 Ready-mixed concrete; concrete products; cement; asphalt mixture; paving materials; construction sand & gravel
HQ: Glacier Northwest, Inc.
5975 E Marginal Way S
Seattle WA 98134
206 764-3000

(G-14256)
GLACIER NORTHWEST INC
18516 Se 1st St (98684-7509)
PHONE.................................360 892-5100
Paul Campbell, *Branch Mgr*
EMP: 35 **Privately Held**
WEB: www.glaciernw.com
SIC: 3273 Ready-mixed concrete
HQ: Glacier Northwest, Inc.
5975 E Marginal Way S
Seattle WA 98134
206 764-3000

(G-14257)
GLEN DIMPLEX AMERICAS COMPANY (HQ)
Also Called: Cadet
2500 W Fourth Plain Blvd (98660-1354)
PHONE.................................360 693-2505
Hutch Johnson, *President*
Ed Otto, *Business Mgr*
Frank Twardoch, *Opers Staff*
Shane Mongelli, *Production*
Oliver Wally, *Senior Buyer*
◆ **EMP:** 120
SALES (est): 24.3MM
SALES (corp-wide): 4.1MM **Privately Held**
WEB: www.cadetco.com
SIC: 3634 Heating units, electric (radiant heat; baseboard or wall
PA: Glen Dimplex Unlimited Company
Old Airport Road
Dublin
185 234-00

(G-14258)
GLOBAL SOLARIUM INC
7402 Ne St Johns Rd B (98665-0619)
PHONE.................................360 695-0313
Roman Sobolewski, *President*
EMP: 6
SALES (est): 1MM **Privately Held**
WEB: www.globalsolariums.com
SIC: 3448 Sunrooms, prefabricated metal

(G-14259)
GLOBAL TECHNICAL STAFFIN
Also Called: Gtsp Global
15640 Ne Fourth Plain Blv (98682-5141)
PHONE.................................512 694-7621
David C Delong,
EMP: 2
SALES (est): 249.6K **Privately Held**
SIC: 3441 Fabricated structural metal

(G-14260)
GNARLY TEES
12416 Nw 36th Ave Ste 2b (98685-2225)
PHONE.................................360 326-3770
EMP: 2
SALES (est): 85.3K **Privately Held**
SIC: 2759 Screen printing

(G-14261)
GRANGER COMPANY
5605 Se Scenic Ln # 301 (98661-0520)
PHONE.................................509 758-9458
Richard A Granger Sr, *CEO*
Richard A Granger Jr, *President*
Mary K Granger, *Admin Sec*
EMP: 20
SALES (est): 2.8MM **Privately Held**
SIC: 2421 Chipper mill

(G-14262)
GRAPHIC CONTROL SYSTEM INC
13215 Se Mill Plain Blvd (98684-6991)
PHONE.................................360 833-9522
Martin Eggiman, *President*
Cindy Eggiman, *Admin Sec*
EMP: 2
SALES (est): 210K **Privately Held**
SIC: 3577 Graphic displays, except graphic terminals

(G-14263)
GRAPHIC PACKAGING INTL LLC
900 Se Tech Center Dr (98683-5515)
PHONE.................................360 896-6486
Terry McElligott, *President*
EMP: 7 **Publicly Held**
SIC: 2631 Container, packaging & boxboard
HQ: Graphic Packaging International, Llc
1500 Riveredge Pkwy # 100
Atlanta GA 30328

(G-14264)
GRATING FABRICATORS INC
3001 Se Columbia Way (98661-8051)
PHONE.................................360 696-0886
Rhonda Abernathy, *President*
Larry Abernathy, *Vice Pres*
EMP: 10
SQ FT: 20,000
SALES: 1MM **Privately Held**
SIC: 3446 Gratings, tread: fabricated metal; gratings, open steel flooring

(G-14265)
GRAYS HARBOR RACEWAY
32 Elma Mccleary Rd (98682)
P.O. Box 821898 (98682-0044)
PHONE.................................360 482-4374
Nikki Gamell, *General Mgr*
EMP: 4
SALES (est): 354.9K **Privately Held**
SIC: 3644 Raceways

(G-14266)
GREAT WESTERN MALTING CO
Also Called: Country Malt
3601 Se Columbia Way (98661-8056)
PHONE.................................360 859-0940
EMP: 5 **Privately Held**
SIC: 2083 Malt
HQ: Great Western Malting Co.
1705 Nw Harborside Dr
Vancouver WA 98660
360 693-3661

(G-14267)
GREAT WESTERN MALTING CO
Also Called: Grain Corp Malt
700 Washington St Ste 508 (98660-3336)
PHONE.................................360 991-0888
EMP: 2 **Privately Held**
SIC: 2083 Malt
HQ: Great Western Malting Co.
1705 Nw Harborside Dr
Vancouver WA 98660
360 693-3661

(G-14268)
GREAT WESTERN MALTING CO (HQ)
1705 Nw Harborside Dr (98660-1026)
P.O. Box 1529 (98668-1529)
PHONE.................................360 693-3661
Mike O'Toole, *President*
Tevis Vance, *Plant Mgr*
Phillip Kurtz, *Project Mgr*
Teala Kaiser, *Warehouse Mgr*
Keith Todd, *Opers Staff*
◆ **EMP:** 75
SALES (est): 50.7MM **Privately Held**
SIC: 2083 Malt

(G-14269)
GREAT WESTERN MALTING CO
Also Called: Country Malt Group
2501 Kotobuki Way (98660)
PHONE.................................360 695-3484
Josh Fuqua, *President*
EMP: 12 **Privately Held**
SIC: 2083 Malt
HQ: Great Western Malting Co.
1705 Nw Harborside Dr
Vancouver WA 98660
360 693-3661

(G-14270)
GREEN LABEL MANUFACTURING INC
5305 Ne 121st Ave (98682-6202)
PHONE.................................954 445-0001
Alexander Shlaen, *President*
EMP: 6
SQ FT: 10,000
SALES: 2.5MM **Privately Held**
SIC: 5087 2674 Vacuum cleaning systems; vacuum cleaner bags: made from purchased materials

(G-14271)
GREEN STAR ENERGIES INC
10000 Ne 7th Ave 100-C (98685-4599)
PHONE.................................360 989-5549
Brandon Toth, *Principal*
EMP: 3
SALES (est): 197.2K **Privately Held**
SIC: 1311 Crude petroleum & natural gas

GEOGRAPHIC SECTION

Vancouver - Clark County (G-14301)

(G-14272)
GREENLIFE INDUSTRIES
414 W 12th St Apt 2 (98660-2864)
P.O. Box 822494 (98682-0054)
PHONE...................................360 566-3984
EMP: 2 EST: 2008
SALES (est): 77K **Privately Held**
SIC: 3999 Mfg Misc Products

(G-14273)
GREENSLEEVES LLC
712 W Mcloughlin Blvd (98660-2414)
PHONE...................................360 606-1934
EMP: 2 EST: 2007
SALES (est): 91.7K **Privately Held**
SIC: 3993 Signs & advertising specialties

(G-14274)
GROUPWARE INCORPORATED
Also Called: Isupport Software
110 E 17th St (98663-3419)
PHONE...................................360 397-1000
Daren Nelson, *CEO*
Ryan Terrell, *Vice Pres*
Jeff Byrne, *Engineer*
Jo Hicks, *Engineer*
Adam Nelson, *Software Dev*
EMP: 30
SALES (est): 4.2MM **Privately Held**
WEB: www.gwi.com
SIC: 7372 Business oriented computer software

(G-14275)
GSL SOLUTIONS INC
2414 Se 125th Ave (98683-3841)
PHONE...................................360 896-5354
Shelton Louie, *President*
Joe Intile, *COO*
Greg Bell, *Project Mgr*
Jason Collins, *Project Mgr*
Robbie Wilbur, *Project Mgr*
EMP: 27
SQ FT: 3,100
SALES: 3.8MM **Privately Held**
WEB: www.gslcorp.com
SIC: 3577 3699 5047 7379 Computer peripheral equipment; electrical equipment & supplies; medical & hospital equipment; computer related consulting services

(G-14276)
GUNDERSONS AUTO LICENSE
Also Called: Heights Auto License
2700 Ne Andresen Rd A6 (98661-7347)
PHONE...................................360 695-2122
Linda Gunderson, *Owner*
EMP: 2 EST: 2001
SALES (est): 112.2K **Privately Held**
SIC: 3469 Automobile license tags, stamped metal

(G-14277)
GUTSY SERVICES LLC
2514 E 26th St (98661-3910)
PHONE...................................503 750-9024
Michael Marchant, *Principal*
EMP: 3 EST: 2015
SALES (est): 87.9K **Privately Held**
SIC: 2711 Newspapers

(G-14278)
H & H WOOD RECYCLERS INC
8401 Ne 117th Ave (98662-3258)
P.O. Box 1855, Battle Ground (98604-1855)
PHONE...................................360 892-2805
Richard Henker, *President*
Pam Henker, *Vice Pres*
EMP: 24
SQ FT: 800
SALES (est): 4.9MM **Privately Held**
SIC: 2875 2421 4953 Compost; fuelwood, from mill waste; refuse systems

(G-14279)
HALDEX BRAKE PRODUCTS CORP
Also Called: Haldex Brake Systems
9116 Ne 130th Ave Ste 106 (98682-2798)
PHONE...................................360 944-3070
Larry Clark, *Manager*
EMP: 4
SALES (corp-wide): 528.7MM **Privately Held**
WEB: www.hbsna.com
SIC: 3714 7538 5169 5015 Motor vehicle brake systems & parts; general automotive repair shops; chemicals & allied products; motor vehicle parts, used; motor vehicle supplies & new parts
HQ: Haldex Brake Products Corporation
10930 N Pomona Ave
Kansas City MO 64153
816 891-2470

(G-14280)
HANGER PROSTHETICS & ORTHO W
505 Ne 87th Ave Ste Ll10 (98664-1988)
PHONE...................................360 256-0026
Tim Zanis, *Manager*
EMP: 6
SALES (corp-wide): 1B **Publicly Held**
SIC: 3842 Surgical appliances & supplies
HQ: Hanger Prosthetics & Orthotics West, Inc.
4155 E La Palma Ave
Anaheim CA 92807
714 961-2112

(G-14281)
HARD NOTCHED CUSTOMS LLC
6615 Ne Highway 99 (98665-8720)
PHONE...................................360 205-3252
Tom Cruise, *Owner*
Matt Cruise, *Manager*
Joel Cruise,
Matthew Cruise,
EMP: 15 EST: 2010
SALES (est): 465.7K **Privately Held**
SIC: 3465 Automotive stampings

(G-14282)
HARDTAIL CHOPPERS INC
1412 Se 83rd Ct (98664-2344)
PHONE...................................360 750-6780
John Grant, *Principal*
EMP: 3
SALES (est): 220.9K **Privately Held**
SIC: 3751 Motorcycles & related parts

(G-14283)
HARLANE CO LLC
2412 Nw 121st Cir (98685-2018)
PHONE...................................404 771-9300
EMP: 3 EST: 2010
SALES (est): 150.7K **Privately Held**
SIC: 3999 Manufacturing industries

(G-14284)
HAROLD TYMER CO INC
Also Called: Tymers Camra Sp Reprographics
8005 Nw 17th Ave (98665-6960)
PHONE...................................360 573-6053
William Tymer, *President*
Linda Tymer, *Treasurer*
EMP: 18
SQ FT: 7,000
SALES (est): 1.2MM **Privately Held**
WEB: www.tymers.com
SIC: 5946 7334 2791 2759 Camera & photographic supply stores; photocopying & duplicating services; blueprinting service; typesetting; commercial printing

(G-14285)
HARRY PRICE
Also Called: Automated Manufacturing Cons
12006 Ne 119th St (98682-1646)
PHONE...................................360 254-5534
Harry F Price, *Owner*
EMP: 4
SQ FT: 4,000
SALES (est): 271.1K **Privately Held**
SIC: 3544 Special dies, tools, jigs & fixtures

(G-14286)
HARVEST FOOD SOLUTIONS
501 Se Clmbia Shrs 900 (98661-8024)
PHONE...................................503 926-6499
Jonathan Dolp, *Principal*
EMP: 9
SALES (est): 1.8MM **Privately Held**
SIC: 7372 Prepackaged software

(G-14287)
HASH INC
10411 Ne 110th Cir (98662-1591)
PHONE...................................360 750-0042
Martin Hash, *President*
Marshall Hash, *President*
Steven Sappington, *Vice Pres*
EMP: 15
SQ FT: 7,500
SALES (est): 1.3MM **Privately Held**
WEB: www.hash.com
SIC: 7371 7372 Computer software development; prepackaged software

(G-14288)
HB FULLER COMPANY
417 Nw 136th St (98685-2955)
PHONE...................................360 574-8828
Joe Renzetti, *Vice Pres*
EMP: 46
SALES (corp-wide): 3B **Publicly Held**
WEB: www.hbfuller.com
SIC: 2891 Adhesives
PA: H.B. Fuller Company
1200 Willow Lake Blvd
Saint Paul MN 55110
651 236-5900

(G-14289)
HCO HOLDING I CORPORATION
Also Called: Henry Roofing Products
4212 Ne 139th Ave (98682-6531)
PHONE...................................503 255-3767
Kenneth Rydman, *Manager*
EMP: 7
SALES (corp-wide): 254.1MM **Privately Held**
WEB: www.henry.com
SIC: 2952 Asphalt felts & coatings
HQ: Hco Holding I Corporation
999 N Pacific Coast Hwy
El Segundo CA 90245
323 583-5000

(G-14290)
HD INTERNATIONAL CORP
Also Called: H D I
5700 Ne 82nd Ave Unit B11 (98662-9430)
PHONE...................................503 997-9325
Steve Wilkerson, *CEO*
Bill Bennett, *Minister*
▲ EMP: 2
SALES (est): 431.9K **Privately Held**
SIC: 5085 3492 Industrial tools; control valves, fluid power: hydraulic & pneumatic

(G-14291)
HEATHEN ESTATE VINEYARDS
9400 Ne 134th St (98662-1123)
PHONE...................................360 768-5199
Lynda Lathrop, *President*
EMP: 2
SALES (est): 73.2K **Privately Held**
SIC: 2084 Wines

(G-14292)
HEAVY METAL BREWING CO LLC
809 Macarthur Blvd (98661-7013)
PHONE...................................503 710-6296
David Miner,
EMP: 5
SALES (est): 204.8K **Privately Held**
SIC: 2082 Beer (alcoholic beverage)

(G-14293)
HENDRICKSON INTERNATIONAL CORP
3301 Se Columbia Way (98661-8098)
PHONE...................................360 906-0222
Jerry Whitman, *Branch Mgr*
EMP: 5
SALES (corp-wide): 916.4MM **Privately Held**
SIC: 3714 Axles, motor vehicle
HQ: Hendrickson International Corporation
840 S Frontage Rd
Woodridge IL 60517
630 874-9700

(G-14294)
HEWLETT-PACKARD COMPANY
Also Called: HP
1115 Se 164th Ave Ste 210 (98683-8556)
PHONE...................................800 325-5372
Mitchell Abrams, *Business Mgr*
Angela Nguyen, *Research*
Robert Wolfington, *Design Engr*
Janel Johnson, *Technology*
Bhaskar Mulakaluri, *Director*
EMP: 115
SALES (est): 19MM **Privately Held**
SIC: 7373 5045 3572 Computer integrated systems design; computers; computer storage devices

(G-14295)
HIGH CALIBER MILL
1321 Ne 76th St Ste 3b (98665-0400)
PHONE...................................360 984-6669
Brandon Hallervik, *President*
Mark Dow, *Admin Sec*
EMP: 25
SQ FT: 1,500
SALES (est): 2.7MM **Privately Held**
SIC: 3536 1541 Cranes, industrial plant; industrial buildings & warehouses

(G-14296)
HIGH-TECH MFG SVCS INC
3105 Ne 65th St Ste B (98663-1482)
PHONE...................................360 696-1611
Brian Smith, *Ch of Bd*
Steve Smith, *President*
EMP: 10
SQ FT: 7,000
SALES: 875K **Privately Held**
WEB: www.htmfg.com
SIC: 3469 Machine parts, stamped or pressed metal

(G-14297)
HIGHLAND MILLING LLC
9901 Ne 7th Ave Ste C247 (98685-4539)
PHONE...................................360 901-8332
Dale Danner, *CEO*
EMP: 2
SALES (corp-wide): 28.9MM **Privately Held**
SIC: 2041 Flour & other grain mill products
HQ: Highland Milling, Llc
161 W 2nd St N
Bancroft ID 83217
208 648-0954

(G-14298)
HIGHWAY SPECIALTIES LLC
1119 Ne 146th St (98685-1404)
PHONE...................................360 823-0511
Kelsey Sullivan, *Office Mgr*
Kim Thatcher, *Mng Member*
EMP: 2
SALES (est): 110.2K **Privately Held**
SIC: 5699 7389 3669 Uniforms & work clothing; flagging service (traffic control); signaling apparatus, electric; pedestrian traffic control equipment

(G-14299)
HISTORIC PHOTOS PRINTS CDS LLC
2814 Washington St (98660-2228)
PHONE...................................360 695-6151
Margaret Byrne, *Principal*
EMP: 2
SALES (est): 128.2K **Privately Held**
SIC: 2752 Commercial printing, lithographic

(G-14300)
HOLCIM (US) INC
1217 W 8th St (98660-3013)
PHONE...................................360 695-9208
Howard Banbruger, *Branch Mgr*
EMP: 3
SALES (corp-wide): 27.6B **Privately Held**
SIC: 3241 Portland cement
HQ: Holcim (Us) Inc.
8700 W Bryn Mawr Ave
Chicago IL 60631
773 372-1000

(G-14301)
HOMEPLATE HEROES
8903 Ne 117th Ave Ste 100 (98662-3282)
PHONE...................................360 798-7974
Christopher Baird, *Partner*
EMP: 3
SALES: 250K **Privately Held**
SIC: 3949 Sporting & athletic goods

Vancouver - Clark County (G-14302)

(G-14302)
HOOD PACKAGING CORPORATION
Also Called: Bemis Paper Packaging Division
1401 W Fourth Plain Blvd (98660-2024)
P.O. Box 1178 (98666-1178)
PHONE..................................360 695-1251
Guy Davis, *Branch Mgr*
Tom Hore, *Manager*
Pascale Malandein, *Manager*
John A Fisher, *Info Tech Dir*
Scott Fraser, *Technology*
EMP: 150 **Privately Held**
WEB: www.bemis.com
SIC: 2674 Bags: uncoated paper & multi-wall
HQ: Hood Packaging Corporation
25 Woodgreen Pl
Madison MS 39110
601 853-7260

(G-14303)
HORSESHOE FALLS LLC
7112 Ne Fairway Ave (98662-3645)
PHONE..................................360 256-0668
Gary English, *Principal*
EMP: 2
SALES (est): 114.3K **Privately Held**
SIC: 3462 Horseshoes

(G-14304)
HOUSE OF RISING BUNS
1804 Nw 119th St Unit 104 (98685-3716)
PHONE..................................360 718-8330
Fred Thomas, *Administration*
EMP: 2
SALES (est): 94.5K **Privately Held**
SIC: 2051 Bread, cake & related products

(G-14305)
HWY 99 AUTO LICENSE
13009 Ne Highway 99 (98686-2741)
PHONE..................................360 573-6226
Sheila Damis, *Owner*
EMP: 6
SALES (est): 300K **Privately Held**
SIC: 3469 Automobile license tags, stamped metal

(G-14306)
HYAK ELECTROWORKS
600 Se 45th Pl (98661-5591)
PHONE..................................360 737-0157
Jim Cramer, *Owner*
EMP: 25
SALES (est): 3.2MM **Privately Held**
SIC: 3699 Electrical equipment & supplies

(G-14307)
HYDRO EXTRUSION NORTH AMER LLC
2001 Kotobuki Way (98660-1351)
PHONE..................................503 802-3000
EMP: 3
SALES (corp-wide): 18.9B **Privately Held**
SIC: 3354 Aluminum extruded products
HQ: Hydro Extrusion North America, Llc
6250 N River Rd
Rosemont IL 60018
877 710-7272

(G-14308)
ILLUMINATION ARTS INC
Also Called: Illumination Arts Pubg Co
13023 Ne Highway 99 (98686-2767)
P.O. Box 1865, Bellevue (98009-1865)
PHONE..................................360 984-5173
John M Thompson, *President*
▲ **EMP:** 6
SQ FT: 2,000
SALES (est): 669.4K **Privately Held**
SIC: 2731 5192 Book publishing; books

(G-14309)
IM3 INC
12414 Ne 95th St (98682-2400)
PHONE..................................360 254-2981
Phillip Bloom, *President*
Dorthoy Bloom, *Vice Pres*
Lehman Bloom, *Vice Pres*
Susan Dollar, *Administration*
▲ **EMP:** 10
SALES (est): 1.6MM **Privately Held**
WEB: www.im3vet.com
SIC: 3843 Dental equipment & supplies

(G-14310)
IMAT INC
Also Called: Implanted Material Technology
12516 Ne 95th St Ste D110 (98682-2463)
PHONE..................................360 256-5600
Tatsuo Nakato, *President*
Daniel Webb, *Vice Pres*
▲ **EMP:** 20
SQ FT: 3,750
SALES (est): 3.9MM **Privately Held**
WEB: www.imatinc.com
SIC: 3679 Electronic circuits

(G-14311)
IMPRINTS NORTHWEST
12209 Ne 4th Plain Blvd (98682-5604)
PHONE..................................360 254-8700
Tom Lundberg, *Principal*
EMP: 3
SALES (est): 215.2K **Privately Held**
SIC: 2752 Commercial printing, lithographic

(G-14312)
INDABA MANAGEMENT COMPANY LLC
Also Called: Indaba Systems
400 E Mill Plain Blvd # 103 (98660-3394)
PHONE..................................360 546-5528
Gary Jones,
EMP: 17
SQ FT: 4,000
SALES (est): 339.3K **Privately Held**
SIC: 5942 7372 5192 Book stores; prepackaged software; books

(G-14313)
INDUSTRIAL PIPE AND VALVE
1501 Ne 106th St (98686-5604)
PHONE..................................360 314-6492
Mike Baker, *President*
EMP: 3
SALES (est): 177.9K **Privately Held**
SIC: 3491 Industrial valves

(G-14314)
INDUSTRIAL SYSTEMS INC
12119 Ne 99th St Ste 2090 (98682-2461)
PHONE..................................503 262-0367
Troy Collison, *President*
Mark Wirfs, *Admin Sec*
EMP: 7
SALES (est): 1.3MM **Privately Held**
SIC: 3625 Electric controls & control accessories, industrial

(G-14315)
INDUSTRIAL SYSTEMS LLC
12119 Ne 99th St Ste 2090 (98682-2461)
PHONE..................................503 262-0367
Troy Collison, *Owner*
EMP: 2
SALES (est): 130.8K **Privately Held**
SIC: 3569 General industrial machinery

(G-14316)
INFLUX LLC
305 Se Chkalov Dr Ste 111 (98683-5263)
PHONE..................................360 200-4323
Ben Richardson, *CEO*
John Danielson, *COO*
EMP: 5
SALES (est): 261.4K **Privately Held**
SIC: 3663 Radio broadcasting & communications equipment

(G-14317)
INSTAFAB COMPANY INC
2424 E 2nd St (98661-7705)
P.O. Box 6129 (98668-6129)
PHONE..................................360 737-8235
Bruce Perkins, *President*
EMP: 33
SQ FT: 18,000
SALES (est): 8.9MM **Privately Held**
SIC: 3441 Fabricated structural metal

(G-14318)
INSTANT IMPRINTS
13521 Se 3rd Way Ste 400 (98684-6909)
PHONE..................................360 694-9711
Jason Beatty, *Principal*
EMP: 4
SALES (est): 467.6K **Privately Held**
SIC: 2752 Commercial printing, offset

(G-14319)
INSTANTIATIONS INC
4412 Se 185th Ct (98683-8292)
PHONE..................................503 770-0861
Michael Taylor, *CEO*
EMP: 10
SALES (est): 916.5K **Privately Held**
SIC: 7372 Prepackaged software

(G-14320)
INSTRUCTIONAL TECHNOLOGIES INC (PA)
14511 Ne 13th Ave Ste 108 (98685-1969)
PHONE..................................360 576-5976
James Voorhees, *CEO*
Laura McMillan, *Vice Pres*
Phaedra Karoy, *Controller*
Mike Flavin, *Sales Dir*
Thom Schoenborn, *VP Mktg*
EMP: 19
SQ FT: 6,500
SALES (est): 4.4MM **Privately Held**
WEB: www.instructiontech.net
SIC: 8299 7372 Educational services; truck driving training; application computer software

(G-14321)
INTELLIGENT TECHNOLOGIES INC
12119 Ne 99th St Ste 2030 (98682-2461)
PHONE..................................360 254-4211
▲ **EMP:** 7
SQ FT: 2,850
SALES: 900K **Privately Held**
WEB: www.it-press.com
SIC: 2731 8742 Book publishing; management consulting services

(G-14322)
INTERNTNAL RHBLTATIVE SCIENCES
Also Called: R S Medical
14001 Se 1st St (98684-3513)
P.O. Box 872650 (98687-2650)
PHONE..................................360 892-0339
Richard Terrell, *President*
Sean Kerr, *Vice Pres*
Randy Murphy, *Vice Pres*
Kimberley Terrell, *Vice Pres*
▲ **EMP:** 75
SQ FT: 120,000
SALES (est): 17.9MM **Privately Held**
WEB: www.rsmedical.com
SIC: 3841 Surgical & medical instruments

(G-14323)
INTERNTONAL GRAPHICS NAMEPLATE
Also Called: I P N
14413 Ne 10th Ave Ste C (98685-1718)
PHONE..................................360 699-4808
Dennis Hanna, *President*
Bob Newcombe, *Vice Pres*
Laurie Hanna, *Treasurer*
Joe Nelson, *Sales Staff*
Jordan Hicks, *Sales Executive*
EMP: 17
SQ FT: 9,000
SALES (est): 2.4MM **Privately Held**
SIC: 3993 Name plates: except engraved, etched, etc.: metal

(G-14324)
IRRIGATION ACCESSORIES CO
Also Called: Iaco
12410 Ne 95th St (98682-2400)
P.O. Box 820118 (98682-0002)
PHONE..................................360 896-9440
Jon Johnston, *President*
EMP: 10
SQ FT: 12,000
SALES (est): 1.8MM **Privately Held**
WEB: www.eiaco.com
SIC: 3523 Irrigation equipment, self-propelled

(G-14325)
ISLA CARMEN LLC
229 E Reserve St Ste 104 (98661-3803)
PHONE..................................360 836-5955
Mark Goracke,
EMP: 3

SALES: 100K **Privately Held**
WEB: www.islacarmen.com
SIC: 3354 Aluminum extruded products

(G-14326)
ISO POLY FILMS INC
3807 Se Hidden Way (98661-8025)
PHONE..................................864 684-8198
Kurt Howard, *Branch Mgr*
EMP: 10 **Privately Held**
SIC: 3081 Unsupported plastics film & sheet
HQ: Iso Poly Films, Inc.
101 Iso Pkwy
Gray Court SC 29645

(G-14327)
ISO-QUIP CORP
418 Ne Repass Rd Ste B1 (98665-8300)
P.O. Box 65190 (98665-0007)
PHONE..................................360 695-4243
David Reinhardt, *President*
EMP: 15
SALES (est): 4.6MM **Privately Held**
WEB: www.isoquip.com
SIC: 3585 Refrigeration equipment, complete

(G-14328)
IVIE BOAT BUILDING
14004 Ne 28th St (98682-8159)
PHONE..................................360 892-2883
Zale Ivie, *Owner*
EMP: 2
SALES (est): 110K **Privately Held**
SIC: 3732 Boat building & repairing

(G-14329)
J & M REPORTS LLC
Also Called: Nada Literature
7402 Ne 58th St (98662-5207)
PHONE..................................360 260-8620
Jules Renaud,
Mary Renaud,
EMP: 3
SALES: 150K **Privately Held**
WEB: www.acudetox.com
SIC: 2721 Periodicals: publishing only

(G-14330)
J & REE FASHIONS
3116 E Mill Plain Blvd (98661-4840)
PHONE..................................360 281-8610
Winner Martha B Fajardo, *Owner*
EMP: 3
SALES (est): 1.7K **Privately Held**
SIC: 2311 Men's & boys' suits & coats

(G-14331)
J LANNING JEWELERS
Also Called: My Jewele
809 Main St (98660-3133)
PHONE..................................360 693-9940
Joe Lanning, *Owner*
EMP: 4
SQ FT: 1,200
SALES: 250K **Privately Held**
SIC: 5944 3911 Jewelry, precious stones & precious metals; jewelry, precious metal

(G-14332)
JAG TECHNOLOGIES
2111 Ne 181st Ave (98684-0765)
PHONE..................................360 910-2933
Jeff Prowell, *President*
EMP: 3
SALES: 78K **Privately Held**
WEB: www.jagtechnologies.net
SIC: 3679 Antennas, receiving

(G-14333)
JAMES CLAY
9208 Ne 156th Ave (98682-3591)
PHONE..................................360 891-8147
James Clay, *Principal*
EMP: 2
SALES (est): 85.9K **Privately Held**
SIC: 3572 Computer storage devices

(G-14334)
JASON C BAILES PLLC
2805 E 26th St (98661-4505)
PHONE..................................360 975-4687
Jason Bailes, *Principal*
EMP: 2 **EST:** 2014

▲ = Import ▼ = Export
◆ = Import/Export

GEOGRAPHIC SECTION
Vancouver - Clark County (G-14364)

SALES (est): 196.2K **Privately Held**
SIC: 3523 Farm machinery & equipment

(G-14335)
JAXJOX INC
10400 Ne 4th St Ste 500 (98660)
PHONE..................................425 324-3017
Stephen Owusu, *Director*
EMP: 7
SQ FT: 1,100
SALES (est): 441.9K **Privately Held**
SIC: 3944 5091 Scooters, children's; fitness equipment & supplies

(G-14336)
JEANNE JOLIVETTE
Also Called: Minuteman Press
12004 Ne 4th Plain Blvd (98682-5564)
PHONE..................................360 750-4447
Jeanne Jolivette, *Owner*
EMP: 7
SQ FT: 1,350
SALES (est): 354.3K **Privately Held**
SIC: 2752 Commercial printing, lithographic

(G-14337)
JERRY GAMIN
Also Called: Henderson Bay Products
12303 Ne 56th St (98682-6476)
PHONE..................................253 884-3075
Jerry Gamin, *Owner*
EMP: 5
SQ FT: 9,000
SALES (est): 453.6K **Privately Held**
WEB: www.hendersonbayproducts.com
SIC: 3599 Machine shop, jobbing & repair

(G-14338)
JOESCAN INC
4510 Ne 68th Dr Unit 124 (98661-1261)
PHONE..................................360 993-0069
Joseph H Nelson, *President*
Jacalyn McGeehan, *Opers Mgr*
David Vainikka, *Electrical Engi*
Joe Scanti, *Manager*
EMP: 4
SQ FT: 4,246
SALES: 1.5MM **Privately Held**
WEB: www.joescan.com
SIC: 3829 Measuring & controlling devices

(G-14339)
JOHNSON CONTROLS INC
14114 Se 35th St (98683-3900)
PHONE..................................360 448-7771
Greg Frick, *Principal*
EMP: 2 **Privately Held**
SIC: 3585 Refrigeration equipment, complete
HQ: Johnson Controls, Inc.
5757 N Green Bay Ave
Milwaukee WI 53209
414 524-1200

(G-14340)
JOINT WAY INTERNATIONAL INC
2500 E 5th St (98661-7718)
PHONE..................................503 286-7781
Huaxin Lou, *President*
Scott Toms, *Vice Pres*
Xiu Fen Gao, *Admin Sec*
▲ EMP: 7
SQ FT: 11,000
SALES (est): 1.6MM **Privately Held**
WEB: www.jointway.com
SIC: 3568 Power transmission equipment

(G-14341)
JOLLY HATCHET GAMES LLC
6410 Ne 144th St (98686-2017)
PHONE..................................360 624-2758
Maria Sullivan,
EMP: 5
SALES: 200K **Privately Held**
SIC: 7372 7389 Home entertainment computer software;

(G-14342)
JR MOORE
Also Called: MSC International
14413 Ne 10th Ave (98685-1717)
PHONE..................................360 607-6128
James R Moore, *Principal*
▲ EMP: 2

(G-14343)
JT MARINE INC
Also Called: J T
2501 Se Hdden Way Vncuver Vancouver (98661)
P.O. Box 61648 (98666-1648)
PHONE..................................360 750-1300
Timo Toristoja, *President*
Cristy Toristoja, *Principal*
Dano Toristoja, *Vice Pres*
EMP: 20
SQ FT: 28,000
SALES (est): 5.2MM **Privately Held**
SIC: 3731 Shipbuilding & repairing

(G-14344)
KASO PLASTICS INC
5720 Ne 121st Ave C (98682-6480)
PHONE..................................360 254-3980
Ralph Miller, *Ch of Bd*
Norm Webb, *Principal*
Craig Ausmus, *Vice Pres*
James C Ausmus, *Vice Pres*
Timothy Bailey, *Vice Pres*
◆ EMP: 96
SQ FT: 45,000
SALES (est): 23.7MM **Privately Held**
WEB: www.kaso.com
SIC: 3089 Injection molding of plastics

(G-14345)
KEY PUBLISHING GROUP LLC
Also Called: Makeup Artist Magazine
12808 Ne 95th St (98682-2413)
PHONE..................................360 882-3488
Larlyn Fitzpatrick, *Controller*
Scott Jones, *Sales Dir*
Heidi Ohara, *Sales Mgr*
Misty Faler, *Cust Mgr*
Grace Mahar, *Sales Staff*
▼ EMP: 17
SALES (est): 2.2MM **Privately Held**
WEB: www.makeupmag.com
SIC: 2741 Miscellaneous publishing

(G-14346)
KGO STONE
229 E Reserve St (98661-3803)
PHONE..................................360 573-0272
Karin Lee Corado, *Owner*
EMP: 10
SALES (est): 1.1MM **Privately Held**
SIC: 3281 Stone, quarrying & processing of own stone products

(G-14347)
KHANS OIL LLC
12113 Ne 4th Plain Blvd (98682-5638)
PHONE..................................360 668-6415
Sohail Khan, *Principal*
EMP: 2
SALES (est): 105.7K **Privately Held**
SIC: 1311 Crude petroleum & natural gas

(G-14348)
KIC LLC
3800 Fruit Valley Rd (98660-1220)
PHONE..................................360 823-4440
Richard Dauch, *CEO*
John Schneider, *President*
Stephen Martin, *Admin Sec*
EMP: 30
SQ FT: 15,500
SALES (est): 8.1MM
SALES (corp-wide): 685.5MM **Privately Held**
SIC: 4214 3715 Local trucking with storage; bus trailers, tractor type
HQ: Accuride Corporation
7140 Office Cir
Evansville IN 47715
812 962-5000

(G-14349)
KIC-N CORP
1308 Nw 41st St (98660-1528)
PHONE..................................360 696-9595
Kay Bushey, *Principal*
EMP: 2 EST: 2012
SALES (est): 200.1K **Privately Held**
SIC: 3714 Motor vehicle parts & accessories

(G-14350)
KINGS OF COATINGS INC
11116 Nw 3rd Ave (98685-3809)
PHONE..................................360 721-0636
Andrew R McKinnon, *Principal*
EMP: 2 EST: 2013
SALES (est): 107.5K **Privately Held**
SIC: 3479 Metal coating & allied service

(G-14351)
KOLORKRAZE
11515 Ne 49th St Ofc (98682-6144)
P.O. Box 820799 (98682-0018)
PHONE..................................360 609-2771
EMP: 3
SALES (est): 247.5K **Privately Held**
SIC: 3993 Signs & advertising specialties

(G-14352)
KOLORKRAZE LLC
4501 Ne 123rd Ave (98682)
PHONE..................................360 609-2771
Judy Covarrubias, *Principal*
EMP: 3
SALES (est): 360.8K **Privately Held**
SIC: 2752 Commercial printing, lithographic

(G-14353)
KONECRANES INC
2903 Ne 109th Ave Ste A (98682-7273)
PHONE..................................503 548-4078
Justin Duncan, *Branch Mgr*
EMP: 2
SALES (corp-wide): 3.6B **Privately Held**
SIC: 3531 Construction machinery
HQ: Konecranes, Inc.
4401 Gateway Blvd
Springfield OH 45502

(G-14354)
KRAMERICA INDUSTRIES LLC
4104 Nw Fir St (98660-1638)
PHONE..................................360 931-9690
Jesse Sawyer, *Principal*
EMP: 3 EST: 2012
SALES (est): 149.5K **Privately Held**
SIC: 3999 Manufacturing industries

(G-14355)
LAFARGE NORTH AMERICA INC
Also Called: Lafargeholcim
1217 W 8th St (98660-3013)
PHONE..................................360 695-9208
Nicholas Stevens, *Terminal Mgr*
EMP: 4
SALES (corp-wide): 27.6B **Privately Held**
WEB: www.lafargenorthamerica.com
SIC: 3241 Cement, hydraulic
HQ: Lafarge North America Inc.
8700 W Bryn Mawr Ave
Chicago IL 60631
773 372-1000

(G-14356)
LAKESIDE INDUSTRIES INC
8705 Ne 117th Ave (98662-3247)
P.O. Box 820465 (98682-0010)
PHONE..................................360 604-1869
Ron Green, *Office Mgr*
EMP: 40
SALES (corp-wide): 326.4MM **Privately Held**
WEB: www.lakesideind.com
SIC: 1611 2951 5032 Highway & street paving contractor; asphalt & asphaltic paving mixtures (not from refineries); gravel
PA: Lakeside Industries, Inc.
6505 226th Pl Se Ste 200
Issaquah WA 98027
425 313-2600

(G-14357)
LAM RESEARCH CORPORATION
222 Ne Park Plaza Dr # 130 (98684-5898)
PHONE..................................360 260-0352
Linda Lamont, *Branch Mgr*
EMP: 86
SALES (corp-wide): 11B **Publicly Held**
WEB: www.lamrc.com
SIC: 3674 Semiconductors & related devices
PA: Lam Research Corporation
4650 Cushing Pkwy
Fremont CA 94538
510 572-0200

(G-14358)
LAPEL SOLUTIONS LLC
11304 Ne 66th St (98662-2407)
PHONE..................................360 597-4958
Larry Lindland, *Mng Member*
EMP: 15
SQ FT: 30,000
SALES (est): 2.9MM **Privately Held**
SIC: 3291 3299 3211 3281 Grinding balls, ceramic; ceramic fiber; ophthalmic glass, flat; cut stone & stone products

(G-14359)
LAPO INC
3001 Se Columbia Way (98661-8051)
PHONE..................................360 314-4546
Opal A Dill, *Admin Sec*
EMP: 2
SALES (est): 88.9K **Privately Held**
SIC: 3291 Abrasive products

(G-14360)
LASER MATERIALS CORPORATION
12706 Ne 95th St Ste 102 (98682-2867)
PHONE..................................360 254-4180
Paul R Collins, *President*
David Collins, *Vice Pres*
EMP: 7
SQ FT: 4,500
SALES (est): 2.5MM **Privately Held**
WEB: www.lasermaterials.com
SIC: 3679 Quartz crystals, for electronic application

(G-14361)
LAST US BAG CO
3000 Columbia House Blvd # 114 (98661-2969)
PHONE..................................360 993-2247
William P Macia, *President*
Al Nyman, *Principal*
Jackie L Nyman, *Principal*
▲ EMP: 7
SQ FT: 7,500
SALES (est): 878.5K **Privately Held**
SIC: 2393 Bags & containers, except sleeping bags: textile

(G-14362)
LAUDA-NOAH LP (HQ)
2501 Se Columbia Way # 140 (98661-8046)
PHONE..................................360 993-1395
Peter Adams, *President*
EMP: 17
SALES (est): 2.4MM
SALES (corp-wide): 92.1MM **Privately Held**
SIC: 3674 Semiconductors & related devices
PA: Lauda Dr. R. Wobser Gmbh & Co. Kg
Pfarrstr. 41-43
Lauda-Konigshofen 97922
934 350-30

(G-14363)
LAUDA-NOAH LP
2501 Se Columbia Way # 140 (98661-8046)
PHONE..................................360 993-1395
Peter Adams,
EMP: 9
SALES (corp-wide): 92.1MM **Privately Held**
SIC: 3674 Semiconductors & related devices
HQ: Lauda-Noah, Lp
2501 Se Columbia Way # 140
Vancouver WA 98661
360 993-1395

(G-14364)
LAUGHLIN INDUSTRIES INC
14511 Ne 10th Ave Ste B (98685-1386)
PHONE..................................360 514-9218
Mike Moran, *Branch Mgr*
EMP: 3
SALES (corp-wide): 12.6MM **Privately Held**
SIC: 3699 Electrical equipment & supplies

Vancouver - Clark County (G-14365)

PA: Laughlin Industries, Inc.
12301 E Marginal Way S
Tukwila WA 98168
206 433-1900

(G-14365)
LAUTERBACH INC
1111 Main St Ste 610 (98660-2978)
PHONE.................360 567-2666
EMP: 2 EST: 2017 **Privately Held**
SIC: 5065 3679 Electronic parts; electronic components

(G-14366)
LAWRENCE ENTERPRISES
Also Called: Cleanaire Systems
1809 Ne 49th St (98663-1370)
PHONE.................360 750-8551
James Lawrence, *Owner*
Judith Lawrence, *Co-Owner*
EMP: 2
SALES (est): 163.8K **Privately Held**
SIC: 3564 Air cleaning systems

(G-14367)
LEADS MANUFACTURING COMPANY
14920 Se Sun Park Ct (98683-8333)
P.O. Box 1562, Lakeside CA (92040-0913)
PHONE.................541 259-1128
Richard Jones, *President*
EMP: 3 EST: 1991
SQ FT: 6,000
SALES (est): 344.6K **Privately Held**
SIC: 3965 Fasteners

(G-14368)
LEAVES IN WIND WOODWORKS LLC
802 Nw 143rd St (98685-1714)
PHONE.................360 574-6750
Thomas Nichols, *Principal*
EMP: 2
SALES (est): 137.1K **Privately Held**
SIC: 2431 Millwork

(G-14369)
LECTENT LLC
Also Called: Keepeez
1101 Ne 144th St Ste 107 (98685-1475)
PHONE.................360 574-7737
Tim Widmer, *Sales Staff*
Edward Cai,
Rick Van Abkoude,
▲ EMP: 80
SQ FT: 10,000
SALES: 100K **Privately Held**
SIC: 3089 5023 Kitchenware, plastic; kitchenware

(G-14370)
LEE SIGNS
7302 Kansas St (98664-1133)
PHONE.................360 750-0689
Michael Lee, *Owner*
EMP: 2 EST: 1987
SALES (est): 157.6K **Privately Held**
SIC: 3993 Signs & advertising specialties

(G-14371)
LENOX CLOTHING LLC
13212 Ne 12th Ave (98685-2741)
PHONE.................360 213-9634
EMP: 2
SALES (est): 109.9K **Privately Held**
SIC: 3585 Mfg Refrigeration/Heating Equipment

(G-14372)
LEVEL 10 FITNESS PRODUCTS LLC
10700 Nw 35th Ave (98685-3576)
PHONE.................503 572-5530
Reginald J Senegal, *Principal*
EMP: 2 EST: 2010
SALES (est): 144.6K **Privately Held**
SIC: 3949 Exercise equipment

(G-14373)
LIEDTKE TOOL AND GAGE INC
3801 Ne 102nd St (98686-5725)
PHONE.................360 694-9573
Gary D Liedtke, *President*
EMP: 3 EST: 1977
SQ FT: 2,500
SALES (est): 260K **Privately Held**
SIC: 3469 Machine parts, stamped or pressed metal

(G-14374)
LIFEPORT INC
12000 Ne 95th St (98682-2448)
PHONE.................360 944-9606
EMP: 2 EST: 2010
SALES (est): 110K **Privately Held**
SIC: 3841 Mfg Surgical/Medical Instruments

(G-14375)
LIGHT EDGE INC (PA)
16703 Se Mcgillivray Blvd (98683-4300)
PHONE.................360 567-1680
David Gerton, *President*
Tony Adams, *Vice Pres*
John Erickson, *CFO*
EMP: 22
SQ FT: 1,000
SALES (est): 2.9MM **Privately Held**
WEB: www.thelightedge.com
SIC: 3646 Commercial indusl & institutional electric lighting fixtures

(G-14376)
LIL SQUIRTZ
303 Ne 135th St (98685-2812)
PHONE.................360 521-9598
Shannon Stewart, *Principal*
EMP: 2
SALES (est): 173.9K **Privately Held**
SIC: 2361 2369 5137 Girls' & children's dresses, blouses & shirts; girls' & children's outerwear; women's & children's clothing

(G-14377)
LINCOLN ELECTRIC COMPANY
705 Se Victory Ave # 220 (98661-8036)
PHONE.................360 693-4712
Wade Pickett, *Manager*
EMP: 15
SALES (corp-wide): 3B **Publicly Held**
WEB: www.subarc-welding.com
SIC: 3548 Welding apparatus
HQ: Lincoln Electric Company
22801 Saint Clair Ave
Cleveland OH 44117
216 481-8100

(G-14378)
LISA APPEL
20113 Ne 80th Way (98682-9770)
P.O. Box 822322 (98682-0051)
PHONE.................360 521-5472
Lisa Appel, *Principal*
EMP: 2
SALES (est): 109K **Privately Held**
SIC: 3571 Personal computers (microputers)

(G-14379)
LJ PRINT GROUP LLC
8019 Ne 13th Ave (98665-9604)
PHONE.................360 852-0914
EMP: 2
SALES (est): 83.9K **Privately Held**
SIC: 2752 Commercial printing, lithographic

(G-14380)
LJRO INC
Also Called: El Tapatio
6202 Nrthast Hwy 99 Ste 8 (98685)
PHONE.................360 693-2443
Lucia Rodriguez, *President*
Jose Rodriguez, *Vice Pres*
Orlando Rodriguez, *Admin Sec*
EMP: 10
SALES (est): 600K **Privately Held**
SIC: 2032 Mexican foods: packaged in cans, jars, etc.

(G-14381)
LOG MAX INC
1114 W Fourth Plain Blvd (98660-2021)
PHONE.................360 699-7300
Stig Linderholm, *President*
Dennis Peil, *Engineer*
Greg Porter, *Treasurer*
▲ EMP: 14
SQ FT: 14,000
SALES (est): 3.3MM **Privately Held**
WEB: www.logmax.com
SIC: 3829 0851 Electrogamma ray loggers; forestry services
HQ: Log Max Ab
Stationsvagen 12
Grangarde 770 1
240 591-100

(G-14382)
LOSTACOS LOCOS
1309 Ne 134th St (98685-2704)
PHONE.................360 573-1327
Stella Avelar, *Owner*
EMP: 3
SALES (est): 192.4K **Privately Held**
SIC: 2099 Food preparations

(G-14383)
LOUISIANA-PACIFIC CORPORATION
16701 Se Mcgillivray Blvd # 200 (98683-3462)
PHONE.................503 821-5001
Jeff Duncan, *COO*
EMP: 14
SALES (corp-wide): 2.8B **Publicly Held**
WEB: www.lpcorp.com
SIC: 2499 Decorative wood & woodwork
PA: Louisiana-Pacific Corporation
414 Union St Ste 2000
Nashville TN 37219
615 986-5600

(G-14384)
LOVING SUPERFOODS LLC
14015 Ne 53rd St (98682-6088)
PHONE.................214 717-3321
Melissa A Cantrelle, *Principal*
EMP: 2
SALES (est): 149.4K **Privately Held**
SIC: 2099 Food preparations

(G-14385)
LUANS LEATHERS
4600 Ne 99th St (98665-9235)
PHONE.................360 546-5050
Luan La Londe, *Owner*
EMP: 2
SALES (est): 134.4K **Privately Held**
SIC: 3199 Leather goods

(G-14386)
LUMBERLINE LASER INC
12119 Ne 99th St Ste 2040 (98682-2500)
P.O. Box 821087 (98682-0025)
PHONE.................360 686-3077
Byron Hatfield, *Vice Pres*
EMP: 3
SQ FT: 1,400
SALES (est): 121.3K **Privately Held**
SIC: 3699 Laser systems & equipment

(G-14387)
LUNA LACTATION
5617 Ne 69th St (98661-1066)
PHONE.................360 693-7616
Melissa Cole, *Principal*
EMP: 3 EST: 2010
SALES (est): 131.3K **Privately Held**
SIC: 2048 Feed supplements

(G-14388)
LYNNSVILLE PRESS PATTERNS
4214 Ne 136th Cir (98686-2618)
PHONE.................360 573-1396
Lynn Stiglich, *Principal*
EMP: 2
SALES (est): 103.6K **Privately Held**
SIC: 2741 Miscellaneous publishing

(G-14389)
M & M MANUFACTURING INC
2208 Laframbois Rd (98660-1119)
PHONE.................360 896-2822
Martin P Schoen, *President*
Marlene Schoen, *Corp Secy*
EMP: 8
SQ FT: 8,000
SALES (est): 951.5K **Privately Held**
SIC: 3599 Machine shop, jobbing & repair

(G-14390)
M C PRINTING
11505 Ne 70th Ave (98686-4627)
PHONE.................360 573-7499
EMP: 2
SALES (est): 83.9K **Privately Held**
SIC: 2752 Commercial Printing, Lithographic

(G-14391)
MACRO MFG LLC
2525 W Firestone Ln (98660-1182)
PHONE.................360 750-3544
EMP: 3
SALES (est): 168K **Privately Held**
SIC: 3999 Manufacturing industries

(G-14392)
MADLYN METAL FAB LLC
Also Called: Jt Metal Fab
2301 Se Hidden Way # 100 (98661-8054)
PHONE.................360 693-1019
Mary Jo Newton, *Office Mgr*
Stacy Toristoja, *Mng Member*
EMP: 30 EST: 2015
SQ FT: 30,000
SALES (est): 1.4MM **Privately Held**
SIC: 3441 Fabricated structural metal

(G-14393)
MAREN-GO SOLUTIONS CORPORATION
13801 Nw 20th Ct (98685-1674)
PHONE.................217 506-2749
Christopher Thobaben, *Owner*
EMP: 3
SALES (est): 123.1K **Privately Held**
SIC: 4522 3571 7375 3812 Air cargo carriers, nonscheduled; minicomputers; remote data base information retrieval; aircraft/aerospace flight instruments & guidance systems; automobile & truck equipment & parts;

(G-14394)
MARKED DEPARTURE POTTERY
3713 Creston Ave (98663-2219)
PHONE.................360 991-5910
EMP: 2
SALES (est): 91K **Privately Held**
SIC: 2759 5719 8999 Commercial Printing, Nec

(G-14395)
MARKON INC
Also Called: Markon Signs & Decals
215 W 12th St Ste 201 (98660-2905)
PHONE.................503 222-3966
Kristine Kemp, *President*
EMP: 3
SQ FT: 2,500
SALES (est): 332.6K **Privately Held**
WEB: www.markonsigns.com
SIC: 7389 7336 2759 Sign painting & lettering shop; silk screen design; commercial printing

(G-14396)
MARKS DESIGN & METALWORKS LLC
4220 Ne Minnehaha St (98661-1244)
PHONE.................360 859-3535
Ryan Marks,
▲ EMP: 80 EST: 2011
SQ FT: 31,660
SALES (est): 24.3MM **Privately Held**
SIC: 3444 Hoppers, sheet metal

(G-14397)
MARKS KEG WASHER
12004 Ne Fourth Pln D (98682-5564)
PHONE.................503 806-4115
Mark N Milroy, *Principal*
EMP: 6
SALES (est): 694.9K **Privately Held**
SIC: 3452 Washers

(G-14398)
MASTER PEACE PRODUCTIONS
5114 Ne St Johns Rd # 18 (98661-2376)
PHONE.................360 600-2736
Scott Hone, *Owner*
EMP: 2 EST: 1998

GEOGRAPHIC SECTION
Vancouver - Clark County (G-14431)

SALES (est): 149.9K **Privately Held**
WEB: www.masterpeaceproductions.com
SIC: 3695 Magnetic & optical recording media

(G-14399)
MATHEMECHANIX
3205 Se Spyglass Dr (98683-3724)
PHONE..................360 944-2029
John L Stewart, *CEO*
EMP: 2
SALES: 1K **Privately Held**
SIC: 2741 Miscellaneous publishing

(G-14400)
MATRIX APPLICATIONS COMPANY (PA)
1000 Se 160th Ave Aa218 (98683-9607)
PHONE..................509 547-7609
Tim E Wright, *Partner*
Catherine E Helten, *Partner*
EMP: 7
SALES (est): 1.3MM **Privately Held**
SIC: 3086 5999 5199 Packaging & shipping materials, foamed plastic; packaging materials: boxes, padding, etc.; packaging materials

(G-14401)
MATRIX APPLICATIONS COMPANY
1000 Se 160th Ave Aa218 (98683-9607)
PHONE..................360 256-2534
EMP: 6
SALES (est): 582.9K
SALES (corp-wide): 1.3MM **Privately Held**
SIC: 3086 Packaging & shipping materials, foamed plastic
PA: Matrix Applications Company
  1000 Se 160th Ave Aa218
  Vancouver WA 98683
  509 547-7609

(G-14402)
MATRIX HEALTH
9700 Ne 126th Ave (98682-2304)
PHONE..................360 816-1200
Steve Kravitz, *Principal*
EMP: 5
SALES (est): 316.3K **Privately Held**
SIC: 5149 2099 Organic & diet foods; food preparations

(G-14403)
MATT HAMMAR QUALITY WOODCRAFTI
3612 Ne 49th St (98661-2526)
PHONE..................360 904-9015
Matt Hammar, *Owner*
EMP: 2
SALES (est): 80.2K **Privately Held**
SIC: 2499 Wood products

(G-14404)
MAYERS CUSTOM MEATS INC
Also Called: Mayer's Custom Curing
12903 Ne 72nd Ave (98686-2915)
PHONE..................360 574-2828
Jeff Mayer, *President*
EMP: 5
SALES (est): 461.3K **Privately Held**
SIC: 5421 2013 Meat markets, including freezer provisioners; sausages & other prepared meats; sausage casings, natural

(G-14405)
MC BAC INC (PA)
Also Called: PIP Printing
1009 Main St (98660-3150)
PHONE..................360 699-4466
Tom Mc Leod, *President*
Gary Bachle, *Vice Pres*
Nancy Mc Leod, *Vice Pres*
Melissa McLeod, *Technician*
EMP: 10
SQ FT: 1,500
SALES (est): 1.5MM **Privately Held**
SIC: 2752 Commercial printing, offset

(G-14406)
MCMULLEN MFG SERVICES
8804 Ne 80th Ct (98662-1726)
PHONE..................360 891-3662
Thomas McMullen, *Principal*
EMP: 2
SALES (est): 155.9K **Privately Held**
SIC: 3999 Manufacturing industries

(G-14407)
MCSTEVENS INC
5600 Ne 88th St (98665-0971)
PHONE..................360 944-5788
Brent P Huston, *President*
Dave Demsky, *Vice Pres*
David Demsky, *Vice Pres*
David A Demsky, *Admin Sec*
▲ **EMP:** 20
SQ FT: 50,000
SALES (est): 4.4MM **Privately Held**
WEB: www.mcstevens.com
SIC: 2066 2087 Cocoa & cocoa products; flavoring extracts & syrups

(G-14408)
MEDIA MATRIX DIGITAL CENTER
6307 Ne St Johns Rd Ste D (98661-1246)
PHONE..................360 693-6455
Becky Conerly, *Owner*
Darren Conerly, *Co-Owner*
EMP: 2
SALES (est): 136K **Privately Held**
WEB: www.mediamatrixdc.com
SIC: 7384 8243 7221 7372 Photograph developing & retouching; data processing schools; photographic studios, portrait; prepackaged software

(G-14409)
MEDWORKS INSTRUMENTS
12911 Nw 25th Ct (98685-2036)
PHONE..................360 597-3754
Cynthia Heise-Swartz, *Owner*
EMP: 4
SALES (est): 160K **Privately Held**
SIC: 3841 7375 Medical instruments & equipment, blood & bone work; remote data base information retrieval

(G-14410)
MERCURY PLASTICS LLC
3807 Se Hidden Way (98661-8025)
PHONE..................360 693-0627
Andrew Teo, *Treasurer*
EMP: 9
SALES (est): 1.6MM **Privately Held**
SIC: 3089 Plastics products

(G-14411)
MERITOR INC
500 Broadway St Ste 310 (98660-3324)
PHONE..................360 737-0175
Ken Santschi, *Principal*
EMP: 157 **Publicly Held**
SIC: 3714 Motor vehicle parts & accessories
PA: Meritor, Inc.
  2135 W Maple Rd
  Troy MI 48084

(G-14412)
MESSER LLC
4715 Ne 78th St (98665-0905)
PHONE..................360 695-1255
Larry Hoose, *Branch Mgr*
EMP: 65
SALES (corp-wide): 1.4B **Privately Held**
SIC: 2813 Nitrogen; oxygen, compressed or liquefied
HQ: Messer Llc
  200 Somerset Corporate
  Bridgewater NJ 08807
  908 464-8100

(G-14413)
MESSER LLC
4715 Ne 78th St (98665-0905)
PHONE..................509 738-6611
Jeff Goddard, *Manager*
EMP: 10
SALES (corp-wide): 1.4B **Privately Held**
SIC: 2813 Industrial gases
HQ: Messer Llc
  200 Somerset Corporate
  Bridgewater NJ 08807
  908 464-8100

(G-14414)
METAL ART BELLS
2211 Nw 116th St (98685-3695)
PHONE..................360 546-2018
Michael W Correll, *Principal*
EMP: 2
SALES (est): 137K **Privately Held**
SIC: 3944 Bells, toy

(G-14415)
METRO COATINGS INC
6608 Kansas St (98661-7427)
PHONE..................360 906-0646
John D Rogge, *President*
Romona Fraser, *Treasurer*
EMP: 15
SALES: 1MM **Privately Held**
SIC: 2851 Lacquers, varnishes, enamels & other coatings

(G-14416)
MEYLE INDUSTRIES LLC
15513 Ne 85th St (98682-9484)
PHONE..................360 250-6114
Benjamin Meyle, *Principal*
EMP: 2 EST: 2017
SALES (est): 97.3K **Privately Held**
SIC: 3999 Manufacturing industries

(G-14417)
MICHAELS STORES INC
16601 Se Mill Plain Blvd (98684-8948)
PHONE..................360 892-4494
Denise Curtis, *Branch Mgr*
EMP: 38
SALES (corp-wide): 5.2B **Publicly Held**
SIC: 3944 5092 5945 Games, toys & children's vehicles; arts & crafts equipment & supplies; hobbies
HQ: Michaels Stores, Inc.
  8000 Bent Branch Dr
  Irving TX 75063
  972 409-1300

(G-14418)
MICRO MOTION INC
11912 Ne 95th St (98682-2396)
PHONE..................360 896-0522
Greg Brunette, *Manager*
EMP: 5
SALES (corp-wide): 17.4B **Publicly Held**
SIC: 3823 Industrial instrmnts msrmnt display/control process variable
HQ: Micro Motion Inc
  7060 Winchester Cir
  Boulder CO 80301
  303 530-8400

(G-14419)
MICROCHIPS SOFTWARE
4115 Ne 115th St (98686-5976)
PHONE..................360 921-8562
Richard or Ruth Chuprinko, *Principal*
EMP: 2
SALES (est): 106.4K **Privately Held**
SIC: 7372 Prepackaged software

(G-14420)
MICROTEMP ELECTRONICS
2716 Ne 168th Ave (98684-9365)
PHONE..................360 256-6789
Robert Read, *Owner*
Anne Read, *Co-Owner*
EMP: 3
SALES: 300K **Privately Held**
SIC: 3679 6794 Electronic circuits; patent owners & lessors

(G-14421)
MINUTEMAN PRESS ✪
7415 Ne Highway 99 # 103 (98665-8889)
PHONE..................360 258-2411
EMP: 2 EST: 2018
SALES (est): 83.9K **Privately Held**
SIC: 2752 Commercial printing, lithographic

(G-14422)
MIXIE MANUFACTURING LLC
1309 Ne 134th St Ste C (98685-2704)
PHONE..................360 696-4943
Randy Questad,
EMP: 6
SALES (est): 581.4K **Privately Held**
SIC: 3089 Plastic containers, except foam

(G-14423)
MOHAWK METAL COMPANY
3825 Ne 68th St (98661-1306)
PHONE..................360 816-0679
David Sheflin, *Branch Mgr*
EMP: 7
SALES (est): 688.6K
SALES (corp-wide): 3.6MM **Privately Held**
SIC: 3441 Fabricated structural metal
PA: Mohawk Metal Company
  30011 Leghorn Ave
  Eugene OR 97402
  541 744-3838

(G-14424)
MOMENTUM GEAR
5601 E 18th St Ste 308 (98661-6889)
PHONE..................360 524-2098
EMP: 2
SALES (est): 33.4K **Privately Held**
SIC: 7999 2389 Physical fitness instruction; apparel for handicapped

(G-14425)
MORRIS PRINTER SOLUTIONS
9505 Ne 8th St (98664-3329)
PHONE..................360 891-3812
EMP: 2
SALES (est): 86.6K **Privately Held**
SIC: 2752 Lithographic Commercial Printing

(G-14426)
MUTUAL MATERIALS COMPANY
10019 Ne 72nd Ave (98686-6040)
PHONE..................360 573-5683
Craig Olson, *Manager*
EMP: 13
SALES (corp-wide): 44.8MM **Privately Held**
SIC: 5211 5032 3272 1741 Concrete & cinder block; concrete & cinder block; concrete products, precast; retaining wall construction
PA: Mutual Materials Company
  605 119th Ave Ne
  Bellevue WA 98005
  425 452-2300

(G-14427)
NATIONAL SIGN SYSTEMS LTD
Also Called: Signs & More
4401 Ne St Johns Rd (98661-2548)
PHONE..................360 699-3055
Carl Green, *Partner*
EMP: 4
SALES (est): 466.1K **Privately Held**
WEB: www.signs-n-more.com
SIC: 3993 Signs, not made in custom sign painting shops

(G-14428)
NATIONWIDE SEC SOLUTIONS INC
6407 Ne 117th Ave (98662-5520)
P.O. Box 821959 (98682-0045)
PHONE..................800 908-8992
Mairin Moore-Cane, *CEO*
EMP: 3
SALES (est): 220.6K **Privately Held**
SIC: 3699 Security control equipment & systems

(G-14429)
NCS POWER INC
5139 Ne 94th Ave Ste F (98662-6195)
PHONE..................360 896-4063
▲ **EMP:** 12
SALES (est): 1.1MM **Privately Held**
SIC: 3648 Mfg Lighting Equipment

(G-14430)
NEUCOR INC
5803 Texas Dr (98661-7156)
PHONE..................866 638-2671
John Fujii, *Principal*
EMP: 2 EST: 2017
SALES (est): 158K **Privately Held**
SIC: 2431 Millwork

(G-14431)
NICOLE LEWIS/NORTHWEST BREAST
14019 Ne 20th Ave Apt 41 (98686-1794)
PHONE..................360 989-0312
Nicole Lewis, *Principal*
EMP: 2

Vancouver - Clark County (G-14432)

SALES (est): 118.1K **Privately Held**
SIC: 2759 Thermography

(G-14432)
NLIGHT INC (PA)
5408 Ne 88th St Ste E (98665-0990)
PHONE..................360 566-4460
Scott Keeney, *Ch of Bd*
Jesse Masnov, *Mfg Mgr*
Nathalie Rajwar, *Mfg Mgr*
Misty Caamal, *Mfg Spvr*
Tom Baertlein, *Opers Staff*
▲ EMP: 424
SQ FT: 122,400
SALES: 191.3MM **Publicly Held**
WEB: www.nlight.net
SIC: 3674 3699 Semiconductors & related devices; laser systems & equipment

(G-14433)
NOORS LURES LLC
7012 Ne 142nd Ct (98682-4641)
PHONE..................360 896-4032
Steve Noorlander, *Principal*
EMP: 2 EST: 2012
SALES (est): 88K **Privately Held**
SIC: 3949 Lures, fishing: artificial

(G-14434)
NORTHWEST DYNAMICS INC
6709 Ne 131st Ave (98682-4918)
PHONE..................360 253-3656
William G Kelly, *President*
EMP: 8
SQ FT: 8,000
SALES: 1.5MM **Privately Held**
SIC: 3728 3492 Aircraft landing assemblies & brakes; brakes, aircraft; valves, hydraulic, aircraft

(G-14435)
NORTHWEST NAPKIN LLC
7016 Ne 40th Ave (98661-1304)
PHONE..................360 571-0051
Bud Bowie,
EMP: 11
SQ FT: 25,000
SALES (est): 2.4MM **Privately Held**
SIC: 2621 Towels, tissues & napkins: paper & stock

(G-14436)
NORTHWEST PIPE COMPANY (PA)
201 Ne Park Plaza Dr # 100 (98684-5874)
PHONE..................360 397-6250
Richard Roman, *Ch of Bd*
Scott Montross, *President*
William Smith, *Exec VP*
Robin Gantt, *CFO*
Aaron Wilkins, *VP Finance*
▲ EMP: 51
SALES: 172.1MM **Publicly Held**
WEB: www.nwpipe.com
SIC: 3443 3317 Industrial vessels, tanks & containers; tanks, standard or custom fabricated: metal plate; vessels, process or storage (from boiler shops): metal plate; welded pipe & tubes

(G-14437)
NORTHWEST PIPE COMPANY
201 Ne Park Plaza Dr # 100 (98684-5874)
PHONE..................801 326-6044
Krista Roberts, *Branch Mgr*
EMP: 13
SQ FT: 51,000
SALES (corp-wide): 172.1MM **Publicly Held**
SIC: 3498 Fabricated pipe & fittings
PA: Northwest Pipe Company
201 Ne Park Plaza Dr # 100
Vancouver WA 98684
360 397-6250

(G-14438)
NORTHWEST PIPE COMPANY
201 Ne Park Plaza Dr # 100 (98684-5874)
PHONE..................303 289-4080
Chuck Cohen, *Branch Mgr*
EMP: 275
SALES (corp-wide): 172.1MM **Publicly Held**
WEB: www.nwpipe.com
SIC: 5051 3312 Pipe & tubing, steel; blast furnaces & steel mills

PA: Northwest Pipe Company
201 Ne Park Plaza Dr # 100
Vancouver WA 98684
360 397-6250

(G-14439)
NORTHWEST PLYWOOD SALES OF ORE
Also Called: Trimac Vancouver
2601 W 26th Ave (98660-1084)
PHONE..................360 750-1561
Mike Webber, *Planning Mgr*
EMP: 13
SALES (corp-wide): 15.5MM **Privately Held**
WEB: www.trimacpanel.com
SIC: 2431 2435 Panel work, wood; hardwood veneer & plywood
PA: Northwest Plywood Sales Of Oregon, Inc
5201 Sw Westgate Dr
Portland OR 97221
503 297-1826

(G-14440)
NORTHWEST REO PRESERVATION LLC
5500 Ne 109th Ct Ste D (98662-6104)
PHONE..................360 521-6761
Joe Spies, *CEO*
EMP: 8
SQ FT: 1,140
SALES (est): 467.3K **Privately Held**
SIC: 1389 Construction, repair & dismantling services

(G-14441)
NORTHWEST SUSHI LLC
5601 E 18th St Ste 208 (98661-6888)
PHONE..................360 878-3464
Hkaw Du Sandawng,
EMP: 5
SQ FT: 500
SALES (est): 164K **Privately Held**
SIC: 2499 Food handling & processing products, wood

(G-14442)
NORTHWEST WALK-IN BATH INC
Also Called: Bathing Solutions
6715 Ne 63rd St Ste 476 (98661-1980)
PHONE..................206 898-2625
Brian Bailey, *President*
EMP: 2
SQ FT: 2,000
SALES (est): 200K **Privately Held**
SIC: 3088 Tubs (bath, shower & laundry), plastic

(G-14443)
NORTHWOOD CABINETS INC
8720 Ne Centerpointe Dr # 217 (98665-1160)
PHONE..................360 314-2446
Ray Koistnen, *Branch Mgr*
EMP: 30
SALES (corp-wide): 3.1MM **Privately Held**
SIC: 2434 Wood kitchen cabinets
PA: Northwood Cabinets, Inc.
1570 Guild Rd
Woodland WA 98674
360 225-1001

(G-14444)
NW MOLD REMOVAL
2815 H St (98663-3051)
PHONE..................360 433-7353
Pete Johnson, *Principal*
EMP: 2
SALES (est): 150.7K **Privately Held**
SIC: 3544 Industrial molds

(G-14445)
NW WOOD HOLDING LLC
Also Called: Fantastic Floor
4818 Ne 142nd St (98686-2212)
PHONE..................360 326-8794
Nathalie Lindsay, *Mng Member*
EMP: 8
SALES (est): 150K **Privately Held**
SIC: 5023 5211 2426 Wood flooring; flooring, wood; hardwood dimension & flooring mills

(G-14446)
OCEAN IN A BOX
4601 Ne 78th St Ste 250 (98665-2908)
PHONE..................360 573-2250
EMP: 2
SALES (est): 131.9K **Privately Held**
SIC: 3999 Mfg Misc Products

(G-14447)
OCTAPHARMA PLASMA
5000 E Fourth Plain Blvd (98661-6584)
PHONE..................360 450-3135
EMP: 2
SALES (est): 74.4K **Privately Held**
SIC: 2836 Plasmas

(G-14448)
OFFROAD OUTPOST
10920 Ne 113th St (98662-2380)
PHONE..................360 910-0021
Cody McCormick, *Principal*
EMP: 2
SALES (est): 95.9K **Privately Held**
SIC: 3714 Motor vehicle parts & accessories

(G-14449)
OLD IRON CLASSICS
6707 Ne 117th Ave 103c (98662-5512)
PHONE..................360 852-8854
Ron Pelz, *Owner*
EMP: 2
SALES (est): 98K **Privately Held**
SIC: 3548 Resistance welders, electric

(G-14450)
OMEGA INDUSTRIES INC (PA)
7304 Ne St Johns Rd (98665-0618)
P.O. Box 65369 (98665-0013)
PHONE..................360 574-9086
Maria Garifalakis, *President*
Isidoros Garifalakis, *Vice Pres*
George Apostolou, *Opers Mgr*
Argyro Apostolou, *Treasurer*
Sophia Kosaris, *Admin Sec*
EMP: 49
SQ FT: 30,000
SALES: 16.2MM **Privately Held**
WEB: www.omega-industries.com
SIC: 7692 3441 Welding repair; fabricated structural metal

(G-14451)
ONBOARD SYSTEMS INTL LLC
13915 Nw 3rd Ct (98685-5701)
PHONE..................360 546-3072
Jason Lemmon, *President*
Jenny Casper, *Admin Sec*
EMP: 40
SQ FT: 20,000
SALES (est): 5.9MM **Privately Held**
WEB: www.onboardsystems.com
SIC: 3728 Aircraft parts & equipment

(G-14452)
ONTARIO SYSTEMS LLC
Also Called: Columbia Ultimate
4400 Ne 77th Ave Ste 100 (98662-6829)
PHONE..................360 256-7358
R Fredhouston, *President*
EMP: 185
SALES (corp-wide): 51.3MM **Privately Held**
SIC: 5045 7372 7373 Computer software; business oriented computer software; systems software development services
PA: Ontario Systems, Llc
1150 W Kilgore Ave
Muncie IN 47305
765 751-7000

(G-14453)
OR SPECIFIC INC
4000 Se Columbia Way (98661-5578)
PHONE..................800 937-7949
Rick Pedigo, *President*
Joel Richter, *CFO*
EMP: 3
SQ FT: 3,000
SALES (est): 295.1K
SALES (corp-wide): 58.3MM **Privately Held**
WEB: www.pedigo-usa.com
SIC: 3842 3841 Drapes, surgical (cotton); operating tables
PA: Pedigo Products, Inc.
4000 Se Columbia Way
Vancouver WA 98661
360 695-3500

(G-14454)
ORANGE HOMES LLC ◆
9208 Ne Highway 99 107-201 (98665-8986)
PHONE..................360 450-4640
EMP: 2 EST: 2019
SALES (est): 83.9K **Privately Held**
SIC: 2752 Commercial printing, lithographic

(G-14455)
ORCHARDS PREGNANCY RESOURCES
Also Called: Options 360 Pregnancy Clinic
221 Ne104th Ave Ste 209 (98664)
PHONE..................360 567-0285
Renee Wooten, *CEO*
Kelly Moys, *President*
EMP: 6
SALES (est): 811.9K **Privately Held**
SIC: 2835 Pregnancy test kits

(G-14456)
OREGON CAM GRINDING INC
5913 Ne 127th Ave Ste 200 (98682-5889)
PHONE..................503 252-5505
Kenneth E Heard, *President*
EMP: 5
SQ FT: 7,500
SALES (est): 752.5K **Privately Held**
WEB: www.oregoncamshaft.com
SIC: 3714 Camshafts, motor vehicle

(G-14457)
ORGANIC CREATIONS
5601 E 18th St Ste 201 (98661-6887)
PHONE..................503 891-0479
Barbara Anne Polzel, *President*
EMP: 8 EST: 2012
SALES (est): 1.1MM **Privately Held**
SIC: 2844 Toilet preparations

(G-14458)
ORTWEIN INTERNATIONAL
7902 Ne St Johns Rd 107b (98665-1032)
PHONE..................503 313-0514
Andrew Ortwein, *President*
EMP: 3
SALES (est): 186.3K **Privately Held**
SIC: 3484 Small arms

(G-14459)
ORYAN INDUSTRIES INC
12711 Ne 95th St (98682-2412)
P.O. Box 1736 (98668-1736)
PHONE..................360 892-0447
Rick Grant, *President*
Sharon Grant, *Vice Pres*
▲ EMP: 20
SQ FT: 18,000
SALES (est): 3.5MM **Privately Held**
WEB: www.oryanindustries.com
SIC: 3646 Commercial indusl & institutional electric lighting fixtures

(G-14460)
OVIVO USA LLC
5139 Ne 94th Ave Ste E (98662-6195)
PHONE..................360 253-3440
Malek Salamor, *Mng Member*
Jaren Leet,
▲ EMP: 220 EST: 2006
SQ FT: 25,000
SALES (est): 28MM
SALES (corp-wide): 501.4K **Privately Held**
WEB: www.christwater.com
SIC: 3823 Water quality monitoring & control systems
HQ: Ovivo Switzerland Ag
Benkenstrasse 262
Witterswil SO 4108
615 551-200

(G-14461)
PAC-PAPER INC
6416 Nw Whitney Rd (98665-7099)
PHONE..................800 223-4981
Robert M Fike, *CEO*
Robert McNally, *President*
Robert Baker, *Opers Mgr*

GEOGRAPHIC SECTION

Vancouver - Clark County (G-14491)

Steve Marks, *CFO*
Tom Skesavage, *Executive*
◆ **EMP:** 140
SQ FT: 150,000
SALES (est): 39.3MM
SALES (corp-wide): 2.9B **Privately Held**
WEB: www.pacpaperinc.com
SIC: 2621 Specialty papers
HQ: Packaging Dynamics Corporation
3900 W 43rd St
Chicago IL 60632
773 254-8000

(G-14462)
PACIFIC APPLIED TECHNOLOGY
1701 Broadway St Ste 392 (98663-3436)
PHONE....................360 693-4292
Vincent H Scott, *President*
Carric Scott, *Vice Pres*
Virginia Scott, *Treasurer*
EMP: 3
SQ FT: 800
SALES (est): 220K **Privately Held**
SIC: 7372 Prepackaged software

(G-14463)
PACIFIC DIE CAST INC
Also Called: Duraguard Products
1304 Ne 154th St Ste 104 (98685-1466)
PHONE....................360 571-9681
Johnie Edens, *President*
EMP: 30
SALES (corp-wide): 11.6MM **Privately Held**
SIC: 3544 Special dies & tools
PA: Pacific Die Cast, Inc.
12802 Commodity Pl
Tampa FL 33626
813 316-2221

(G-14464)
PACIFIC FOUNDATION INC
1400 Columbia St (98660-2966)
PHONE....................360 200-6608
Michael Zeman, *President*
Mike Zeman, *Principal*
Christopher Wrench, *Vice Pres*
▲ **EMP:** 10
SALES: 31.4MM **Privately Held**
SIC: 5082 1629 1799 1741 Wellpoints (drilling equipment); caisson drilling; shoring & underpinning work; core drilling & cutting; foundation building; piles, foundation & marine construction: treated wood

(G-14465)
PACIFIC JEWELERS
Also Called: Pacific Sterling
2313 Main St (98660-2641)
PHONE....................360 693-3410
Norbert Anderson, *Owner*
EMP: 2
SQ FT: 1,300
SALES: 2.5MM **Privately Held**
SIC: 5094 5944 3915 Jewelry; jewelry stores; diamond cutting & polishing

(G-14466)
PACIFIC N W SHEDS BUILDINGS
2009 Ne 117th St (98686-4022)
PHONE....................360 573-7433
EMP: 2
SALES (est): 189K **Privately Held**
SIC: 3448 Prefabricated metal buildings

(G-14467)
PACIFIC NUTRITIONAL INC
6317 Ne 131st Ave Buildb (98682-5879)
P.O. Box 820829 (98682-0019)
PHONE....................360 253-3197
Chris Taylor, *CEO*
Michael Schaeffer, *President*
Pamela Nielson, *Vice Pres*
Ron Golden, *Treasurer*
Mike Crew, *Admin Sec*
EMP: 180
SQ FT: 35,000
SALES (est): 88.4MM **Privately Held**
WEB: www.pacnut.com
SIC: 5122 2099 Vitamins & minerals; food preparations
PA: Columbia Nutritional, Llc
6317 Ne 131st Ave 103
Vancouver WA 98682
360 737-9966

(G-14468)
PACIFIC NW PLATING INC
7001 Ne 40th Ave (98661-1303)
PHONE....................360 735-9000
Anthony Cecilia, *President*
EMP: 12
SALES (est): 1.1MM **Privately Held**
SIC: 3471 Plating of metals or formed products; electroplating of metals or formed products

(G-14469)
PACIFIC POWER GROUP LLC (HQ)
Also Called: Pacific Power Products
805 Broadway St Ste 700 (98660-3301)
PHONE....................360 887-7400
Timothy Price, *President*
Wesley Wilson, *Business Mgr*
Kim Barham, *Project Mgr*
Jim Russell, *Parts Mgr*
John Todd, *Sales Staff*
▲ **EMP:** 80
SQ FT: 20,000
SALES (est): 16.7MM
SALES (corp-wide): 18.1MM **Privately Held**
WEB: www.pacificdda.net
SIC: 5088 3621 5063 3519 Marine propulsion machinery & equipment; motor generator sets; generators; diesel engine rebuilding; engines & parts, diesel
PA: Yaculta Companies, Inc.
805 Broadway St Ste 700
Vancouver WA 98660
360 887-7493

(G-14470)
PACIFIC PRECAST INC
2611 E 5th St (98661-7730)
PHONE....................360 750-0099
Jim Morrison, *CEO*
EMP: 15
SQ FT: 10,000
SALES (est): 1.5MM **Privately Held**
SIC: 3272 Concrete products

(G-14471)
PACIFIC PRECISION MFG
2850 Ne 65th Ave Ste B (98661-6803)
PHONE....................360 737-2938
Bo Ojstersek, *President*
EMP: 2
SALES: 120K **Privately Held**
WEB: www.pacificprecisioninc.com
SIC: 3599 Machine shop, jobbing & repair

(G-14472)
PACIFIC RIM INTERNATIONAL LLC
19120 Se 34th St Ste 105 (98683-1435)
PHONE....................503 781-2394
Hong Qiu,
Yibin Ye,
▲ **EMP:** 5
SALES (est): 820.5K **Privately Held**
SIC: 3799 Trailer hitches

(G-14473)
PACIFIC ROCK PRODUCTS LLC
Also Called: Readymix - Pacrock Portabl R/M
18208 Se 1st St (98684-7506)
PHONE....................360 896-8721
Jim Summers, *Manager*
EMP: 3 **Privately Held**
SIC: 1442 Construction sand & gravel
HQ: Pacific Rock Products, L.L.C.
8705 Ne 117th Ave
Vancouver WA 98662
360 254-7770

(G-14474)
PACIFIC ROCK PRODUCTS LLC (DH)
8705 Ne 117th Ave (98662-3247)
PHONE....................360 254-7770
John Hjaltalin, *Vice Pres*
EMP: 21 **EST:** 2012
SALES (est): 16.8MM **Privately Held**
SIC: 3272 Concrete products
HQ: Cemex, Inc.
10100 Katy Fwy Ste 300
Houston TX 77043
713 650-6200

(G-14475)
PACKAGING CORPORATION AMERICA
Also Called: PCA
222 Ne Park Plaza Dr # 105 (98684-5895)
PHONE....................360 891-8796
EMP: 3
SALES (corp-wide): 7B **Publicly Held**
SIC: 2653 Boxes, corrugated: made from purchased materials
PA: Packaging Corporation Of America
1 N Field Ct
Lake Forest IL 60045
847 482-3000

(G-14476)
PACWEST DENTAL LAB
3513 Ne 158th Ave (98682-7307)
PHONE....................360 635-3976
Corey Fellman, *Owner*
EMP: 2
SALES (est): 62.3K **Privately Held**
SIC: 2099 Food preparations

(G-14477)
PAMAR SYSTEMS INC
1801 D St Ste 7 (98663-3376)
PHONE....................360 992-4120
William R Pratt, *CEO*
EMP: 5
SALES: 750K **Privately Held**
SIC: 5045 7374 7372 Computer software; computer time-sharing; prepackaged software

(G-14478)
PANTHER SYSTEMS NORTHWEST INC
19111 Se 34th St Ste 101 (98683-1449)
PHONE....................360 750-9783
Lawrence Foltz, *President*
▲ **EMP:** 40
SALES (est): 6.5MM **Privately Held**
WEB: www.panthersys.com
SIC: 7372 Prepackaged software

(G-14479)
PARADIGM OPTICS INCORPORATED
9600 Ne 126th Ave # 2540 (98682-2314)
PHONE....................360 573-6500
David Welker, *President*
▼ **EMP:** 6
SQ FT: 4,800
SALES (est): 968.3K **Privately Held**
WEB: www.paradigmoptics.com
SIC: 3827 Optical instruments & lenses

(G-14480)
PARR LUMBER COMPANY
Also Called: Trus-Way Vancouver
3901 Ne 68th St (98661-1372)
PHONE....................360 750-1470
EMP: 2
SALES (corp-wide): 320.2MM **Privately Held**
SIC: 2439 Trusses, wooden roof
PA: Parr Lumber Company
5630 Ne Century Blvd
Hillsboro OR 97124
503 614-2500

(G-14481)
PCB UNIVERSE INC
11818 Se Mill Plain Blvd # 208 (98684-5089)
PHONE....................360 256-7228
Paul C Tsay, *President*
EMP: 6
SALES (est): 820.4K **Privately Held**
SIC: 3672 Printed circuit boards

(G-14482)
PEEL PRODUCTIONS INC
9415 Ne Woodridge St (98664-3167)
PHONE....................360 256-2450
Susan Dubosque, *President*
Douglas Dubosque, *Corp Secy*
▲ **EMP:** 2
SALES (est): 130K **Privately Held**
SIC: 2731 Books: publishing & printing

(G-14483)
PEGLER AUTOMATION INC
10117 Ne 21st St (98664-2907)
PHONE....................503 329-5377
Tim Pegler, *President*
EMP: 3 **EST:** 1998
SQ FT: 4,500
SALES: 1MM **Privately Held**
SIC: 3491 Automatic regulating & control valves

(G-14484)
PERFORMANCE PACKAGING INC
3006 Ne 112th Ave Ste A (98682-7260)
PHONE....................360 737-9966
▲ **EMP:** 26
SQ FT: 12,000
SALES (est): 3.8MM **Privately Held**
SIC: 2834 Mfg Pharmaceutical Preparations

(G-14485)
PERISCOPE SLS & ANALYTICS LLC
2214 Nw 148th St (98685-1014)
PHONE....................503 707-1907
Troy Nolan, *Principal*
EMP: 2
SALES (est): 104.2K **Privately Held**
SIC: 3827 Periscopes

(G-14486)
PETERS INDUSTRIES
6301 Ne 67th St (98661-1527)
PHONE....................360 254-9889
Dan Peters, *Principal*
EMP: 2 **EST:** 2010
SALES (est): 126.5K **Privately Held**
SIC: 3999 Manufacturing industries

(G-14487)
PETROCHEM INSULATION INC
6811 Ne 131st Ave (98682-4993)
PHONE....................360 254-8953
Stephen Louis, *Vice Pres*
Mike Fitzsimmons, *Manager*
EMP: 29
SALES (corp-wide): 2.9B **Privately Held**
WEB: www.petrocheminc.com
SIC: 3443 1742 Industrial vessels, tanks & containers; insulation, buildings
HQ: Petrochem Insulation, Inc.
2300 Clayton Rd Ste 1050
Concord CA 94520
707 644-7455

(G-14488)
PLASTICS NORTHWEST INC
2851 Nw Lower River Rd (98660-1037)
PHONE....................360 823-0505
Michael Martin, *President*
Jenny Yocom, *Controller*
▲ **EMP:** 17
SQ FT: 88,500
SALES: 2.6MM **Privately Held**
WEB: www.plasticsnw.com
SIC: 3089 Injection molding of plastics

(G-14489)
PLATINUM PETS LLC
9604 Ne 126th Ave # 2330 (98682-2312)
PHONE....................360 859-4027
Martin Rifkin, *CEO*
EMP: 12 **EST:** 2016
SALES (est): 398.8K **Privately Held**
SIC: 3999 Pet supplies

(G-14490)
PLUS SIX PUBLISHING
6715 Ne 63rd St (98661-1980)
PHONE....................360 553-2316
Lewis Gerhardt, *Principal*
EMP: 2
SALES (est): 82.4K **Privately Held**
SIC: 2741 Miscellaneous publishing

(G-14491)
POA PHARMA NORTH AMERICA LLC
4400 Ne 77th Ave Ste 275 (98662-6857)
PHONE....................855 416-6826
David Lindsley, *Principal*
EMP: 5 **EST:** 2014

Vancouver - Clark County (G-14492)

SALES (est): 522.6K **Privately Held**
SIC: 2834 Pharmaceutical preparations

(G-14492)
POIZER METAL WORKS
9707 Nw 10th Ave (98665-6410)
PHONE..................360 892-2629
Jay Poizer, *Owner*
EMP: 2 **EST:** 2001
SALES (est): 152.9K **Privately Held**
SIC: 3312 Stainless steel

(G-14493)
POLYMER FOUNDRY INC
1108 Ne 146th St Ste B (98685-1412)
PHONE..................360 574-1617
EMP: 3
SALES (est): 250K **Privately Held**
SIC: 3089 Mfg Plastic Products

(G-14494)
POLYURETHANE SALES & SVC LLC
Also Called: Viper Protective Coatings
20019 Ne 68th St (98682-9090)
P.O. Box 87753 (98687-7753)
PHONE..................360 334-5364
Robert Oleg Pemberton, *Managing Prtnr*
EMP: 1
SQ FT: 1,000
SALES: 1.2MM **Privately Held**
SIC: 2851 Polyurethane coatings

(G-14495)
POWER AND LIGHTING LLC
404 E 25th St (98663-3222)
PHONE..................360 750-0158
Samuel Leone, *Principal*
EMP: 3
SALES (est): 232.2K **Privately Held**
SIC: 3612 Transformers, except electric

(G-14496)
POWERLINK TRANSMISSION CO LLC
754 Officers Row (98661-3845)
PHONE..................360 314-6840
Frederick Buckman, *Principal*
EMP: 3
SALES (est): 253.3K **Privately Held**
SIC: 3568 Power transmission equipment

(G-14497)
PRAXAIR DISTRIBUTION INC
603 Se Victory Ave (98661-8203)
PHONE..................360 694-1338
Chris Leifsen, *Branch Mgr*
EMP: 22 **Privately Held**
SIC: 2813 5084 Industrial gases; industrial machinery & equipment
HQ: Praxair Distribution, Inc.
  10 Riverview Dr
  Danbury CT 06810
  203 837-2000

(G-14498)
PRECAST OLDCASTLE
6500 Nw Whitney Rd (98665-7017)
PHONE..................800 509-6150
EMP: 2 **EST:** 2011
SALES (est): 206.6K **Privately Held**
SIC: 3272 Precast terrazo or concrete products

(G-14499)
PRECISE MANUFACTURING & ENGRG
5600 N Vancouver (98682)
P.O. Box 821048 (98682-0024)
PHONE..................360 604-8742
Richard Jones, *President*
Kelsey French, *General Mgr*
Carrie Cortes, *Purch Mgr*
EMP: 18
SQ FT: 20,000
SALES (est): 5.4MM **Privately Held**
SIC: 3312 Blast furnaces & steel mills

(G-14500)
PRECISION AUTOMATION INC
Also Called: Tiger Stop
12909 Ne 95th St (98682-2426)
PHONE..................360 254-0661
Spencer Dick, *President*
Mary Dick, *Corp Secy*

Norman Gorny, *COO*
Ed Scott, *Info Tech Mgr*
Elaine Mercer, *Admin Asst*
◆ **EMP:** 20
SQ FT: 3,000
SALES (est): 3.3MM **Privately Held**
SIC: 3823 Industrial instrmnts msrmnt display/control process variable

(G-14501)
PRECISION REBAR & ACC INC
1712 Ne 99th St (98665-9018)
PHONE..................360 574-1022
Thomas G Schmaltz, *President*
EMP: 15
SQ FT: 4,000
SALES (est): 3.1MM **Privately Held**
SIC: 3441 Fabricated structural metal

(G-14502)
PRECISION SHEET METAL & HEATIN
1212 Se 181st Ave (98683-7208)
PHONE..................503 939-8600
Braden Hurt, *Principal*
EMP: 2
SALES (est): 296.9K **Privately Held**
SIC: 3444 Sheet metalwork

(G-14503)
PRECISION WELDING & BOAT RES
2422 Ne 172nd Ave (98684-9722)
PHONE..................360 607-3546
Tom Maxfield, *Principal*
EMP: 6
SALES (est): 269.3K **Privately Held**
SIC: 7692 Welding repair

(G-14504)
PRIDE OF THE WEST INC
1610 Markle Ave (98660-2765)
PHONE..................360 694-4976
Douglas Perrone, *President*
Paul Baker, *Vice Pres*
EMP: 4
SQ FT: 10,000
SALES: 1.2MM **Privately Held**
WEB: www.prideofthewest.com
SIC: 2099 7389 Seasonings: dry mixes; packaging & labeling services

(G-14505)
PRIMER SPECIALTIES INC
630 Ne 127th Ave (98684)
PHONE..................360 518-3716
Mark Merrill, *President*
EMP: 4 **EST:** 2013
SALES (est): 411.4K **Privately Held**
SIC: 2851 Paints & allied products

(G-14506)
PRINT & PLAY PRODUCTIONS
1417 Ne 76th St Ste G19 (98665-0486)
PHONE..................503 750-5316
Andrew Tullsen, *Principal*
EMP: 4
SALES (est): 304.4K **Privately Held**
SIC: 2752 Commercial printing, lithographic

(G-14507)
PRINT N SURF
5702 Ne 42nd Ave (98661-1778)
PHONE..................360 693-1710
EMP: 2
SALES (est): 83.9K **Privately Held**
SIC: 2752 Lithographic Commercial Printing

(G-14508)
PRINTGRAPHICS INC
3104 Se 174th Ave (98683-2313)
PHONE..................503 641-8811
Charlie Mc Donald, *President*
EMP: 23
SQ FT: 13,000
SALES (est): 4.4MM **Privately Held**
WEB: www.prntgrfx.com
SIC: 2752 2791 2789 Commercial printing, offset; typesetting; bookbinding & related work

(G-14509)
PRO STAFF ELECTRIC
6109 E 18th St (98661-6970)
PHONE..................360 859-3749
EMP: 2
SALES (est): 157.6K **Privately Held**
SIC: 3699 Mfg Electrical Equipment/Supplies

(G-14510)
PRO TECH INDUSTRIES INC (PA)
14113 Ne 3rd Ct (98685-2975)
P.O. Box 933 (98666-0933)
PHONE..................360 573-6641
Peter Miller, *CEO*
David Wager, *President*
Lisa Grain, *Vice Pres*
Jolene Stephens, *Vice Pres*
Harold B Trumbower, *Vice Pres*
◆ **EMP:** 250
SQ FT: 76,000
SALES (est): 111.1MM **Privately Held**
WEB: www.protech.net
SIC: 3714 Motor vehicle parts & accessories

(G-14511)
PROCEDURE PRODUCTS INC
1801 W Fourth Plain Blvd (98660-1310)
PHONE..................360 693-1832
Richard Bynum, *President*
EMP: 9
SQ FT: 3,200
SALES: 1.8MM **Privately Held**
SIC: 3841 Surgical instruments & apparatus

(G-14512)
PROCEDURE PRODUCTS CORP (PA)
1801 W Fourth Plain Blvd (98660-1310)
PHONE..................360 693-1832
Gayle Everett, *President*
▲ **EMP:** 7
SQ FT: 5,500
SALES (est): 1.3MM **Privately Held**
WEB: www.procedureproducts.com
SIC: 3841 Surgical & medical instruments

(G-14513)
PROTECH COMPOSITES
11700 Ne 60th Way Ste 3b (98682-0808)
PHONE..................360 573-7800
Jeff Olsen, *CEO*
Michelle Fennimore, *Vice Pres*
Sam Olsen, *Director*
EMP: 40
SALES (est): 5.9MM **Privately Held**
SIC: 3552 Carbonizing equipment, wool processing machinery

(G-14514)
PROTO-RPID MCHNING SLTIONS LLC
3010 Se Menlo Dr Apt 20 (98683-5344)
PHONE..................503 744-0358
Huy Duong, *Principal*
EMP: 3 **EST:** 2009
SALES (est): 300.3K **Privately Held**
SIC: 3599 Crankshafts & camshafts, machining

(G-14515)
PULSE ELECTRONICS INC
Pulse Engineering Vancouver
18110 Se 34th St Bldg 2 (98683-9418)
PHONE..................360 944-7551
Laura Chamberlain, *General Mgr*
EMP: 100
SALES (corp-wide): 652.7MM **Privately Held**
WEB: www.pulseeng.com
SIC: 3663 Radio & TV communications equipment
HQ: Pulse Electronics, Inc.
  15255 Innovation Dr # 100
  San Diego CA 92128

(G-14516)
PURE LITE CANDLE PORTLAND I
4115 Nw 118th Cir (98685-3590)
PHONE..................360 909-9499
Kevin Ryan, *Principal*

EMP: 3
SALES (est): 218.3K **Privately Held**
SIC: 3999 Candles

(G-14517)
QUALIDENT DENTAL LAB LLC
5305 E 18th St Ste 100 (98661-8506)
PHONE..................360 695-7411
Scott Alvarez, *Mng Member*
EMP: 40
SQ FT: 3,000
SALES (est): 2MM **Privately Held**
SIC: 3843 8072 Dental equipment & supplies; dental laboratories; denture production

(G-14518)
QUALITY EQUIPMENT SUPPLY INC
4400 Ne 77th Ave Ste 275 (98662-6857)
P.O. Box 467 (98666-0467)
PHONE..................503 544-9779
Lance Garrettson, *President*
Shane McCormick, *Vice Pres*
EMP: 2 **EST:** 2013
SQ FT: 800
SALES (est): 269.3K **Privately Held**
SIC: 2631 3792 3715 Container, packaging & boxboard; camping trailers & chassis; truck trailer chassis

(G-14519)
QUALITY MACHINE
13023 Ne Highway 99 Ste 7 (98686-2699)
P.O. Box 119 (98666-0119)
PHONE..................360 573-8773
Bob Fuller, *Owner*
Donna Fuller, *Co-Owner*
EMP: 5
SQ FT: 4,000
SALES: 300K **Privately Held**
SIC: 3599 Machine shop, jobbing & repair

(G-14520)
QUALITY PALLETS
310 Nw 41st St (98660-1727)
PHONE..................360 773-3973
Angelina Monica Sosa, *Principal*
EMP: 3
SALES (est): 217.3K **Privately Held**
SIC: 2448 Pallets, wood

(G-14521)
QUALITY SALES INC
1304 Ne 154th St Ste 101 (98685-1466)
PHONE..................360 694-3165
Ken Kinghorn, *President*
Mike Lehman, *Vice Pres*
Steve Hughes, *Sales Staff*
Kara Nowland, *Sales Staff*
Ross Watkins, *Sales Associate*
EMP: 14
SALES (est): 2.1MM **Privately Held**
SIC: 3432 Plumbing fixture fittings & trim

(G-14522)
QUALITYLOGIC INC
16700 Ne 12th St (98684-6405)
PHONE..................360 882-0201
Tara Vaughn, *Principal*
EMP: 2
SALES (est): 107.4K **Privately Held**
SIC: 3561 Pumps & pumping equipment

(G-14523)
QUICK COLLECT INC
5500 Ne 107th Ave (98662-6169)
P.O. Box 821330 (98682-0030)
PHONE..................360 256-7888
David Garner, *President*
Jonathan Garner, *Accounts Exec*
Larry Bair, *Admin Sec*
EMP: 33
SALES (est): 2.7MM **Privately Held**
WEB: www.quickcollect.net
SIC: 7372 7322 Prepackaged software; adjustment & collection services

(G-14524)
R & R PLASTICS
3109 Ne 65th St Ste F (98663-1485)
PHONE..................360 694-9573
Robert Wilgus, *Owner*
EMP: 6
SQ FT: 5,000

▲ = Import ▼ =Export
◆ =Import/Export

GEOGRAPHIC SECTION
Vancouver - Clark County (G-14556)

SALES (est): 908.5K **Privately Held**
SIC: 3082 2821 Tubes, unsupported plastic; plastics materials & resins

(G-14525)
R 2 MANUFACTURING INC
3108 Ne 65th St Ste A (98663-1484)
PHONE..................................360 693-5096
Russell Lee Arn, *Principal*
EMP: 5
SALES (est): 689.4K **Privately Held**
WEB: www.uni-dolly.com
SIC: 3559 3533 Automotive maintenance equipment; water well drilling equipment

(G-14526)
R D F PRODUCTS
17706 Ne 72nd St (98682-9122)
PHONE..................................360 253-2181
Alex J Burwasser, *Owner*
EMP: 3
SALES (est): 311.7K **Privately Held**
WEB: www.rdfproducts.com
SIC: 3825 8748 8243 Frequency meters: electrical, mechanical & electronic; systems engineering consultant, ex. computer or professional; software training, computer

(G-14527)
R L WOODWORKS
10012 Ne 142nd Ave (98682-1765)
PHONE..................................360 607-4471
EMP: 2
SALES (est): 161.3K **Privately Held**
SIC: 2431 Millwork

(G-14528)
R&D MACHINE LLC
3109 Ne 65th St Ste B (98663-1485)
PHONE..................................360 694-9573
EMP: 8
SALES (est): 1.2MM **Privately Held**
SIC: 3599 Machine shop, jobbing & repair

(G-14529)
RAC AVIATION SERVICES LLC
508 Ne 139th Ave (98684-7462)
PHONE..................................360 256-6698
Timothy Conroy, *Owner*
EMP: 2
SALES (est): 84K **Privately Held**
SIC: 3721 Aircraft

(G-14530)
RAILPRO OF OREGON INC
14110 Nw 3rd Ct (98685-5704)
PHONE..................................360 213-0958
Jermey Kushner, *CEO*
Thomas Sugeno, *Corp Secy*
Joseph Worklen, *Vice Pres*
EMP: 3
SQ FT: 3,500
SALES (est): 443.9K **Privately Held**
SIC: 3446 3743 Railings, bannisters, guards, etc.: made from metal pipe; railroad equipment

(G-14531)
RALPH DOGGETT
8515 Ne Hazel Dell Ave (98665-8144)
PHONE..................................503 998-5935
Ray Jones, *Principal*
EMP: 2
SALES (est): 104.7K **Privately Held**
SIC: 3577 Computer peripheral equipment

(G-14532)
RAPID PRINT INC
3902 Ne 61st Ave (98661-3252)
PHONE..................................360 695-6400
Ronald E McDonald, *President*
Ron Mc Donald, *President*
EMP: 6
SALES (est): 300K **Privately Held**
WEB: www.rapidprint.com
SIC: 2752 5943 2791 Commercial printing, offset; office forms & supplies; typesetting, computer controlled

(G-14533)
RARING CORPORATION
12007 Ne 95th St (98682-2439)
PHONE..................................360 892-1659
David Raring, *President*
Gonzalo Campos, *COO*

Kathleen M Putek, *Admin Sec*
▼ EMP: 8
SQ FT: 6,000
SALES (est): 2MM **Privately Held**
WEB: www.raringcorp.com
SIC: 3564 Air purification equipment; blowers & fans

(G-14534)
RAW CHEMISTRY LLC
1321 Ne 76th St Ste 3d (98665-0400)
PHONE..................................360 521-2115
Brett Messinger, *Principal*
Ken Messinger, *Manager*
EMP: 6
SALES (est): 267.4K **Privately Held**
SIC: 2844 Perfumes & colognes

(G-14535)
RAWSON WOODCRAFT LLC
109 E 38th St (98663-2214)
PHONE..................................503 650-4383
Jeff Rawson,
EMP: 2
SALES (est): 179.4K **Privately Held**
SIC: 2499 Laundry products, wood

(G-14536)
REALTY SIGN GUYS
17912 Ne 37th St (98682-3735)
PHONE..................................360 909-1540
Cole Grover, *Principal*
EMP: 2 EST: 2009
SALES (est): 91K **Privately Held**
SIC: 3993 Signs & advertising specialties

(G-14537)
RED DOG FABRICATION LLC
1701 W 31st St Bldg C (98660-1281)
P.O. Box 330 (98666-0330)
PHONE..................................360 892-3647
Mark Dunkle, *Project Mgr*
Patrick Kiely,
Heather Glenn,
EMP: 18
SALES (est): 2.1MM **Privately Held**
SIC: 7692 3441 Welding repair; fabricated structural metal

(G-14538)
RED HAT LIGHTING LLC
18508 Ne 73rd St (98682-9623)
PHONE..................................360 624-5773
Jesse Mack, *Principal*
EMP: 2 EST: 2014
SALES (est): 162.5K **Privately Held**
SIC: 3648 Lighting equipment

(G-14539)
REDPOINT INTERNATIONAL INC
9208 Ne Highway 99 107-20 (98665-8986)
PHONE..................................360 573-5957
Ron Merryman, *President*
Valerie Vance, *Vice Pres*
Martin Jackson, *Sales Mgr*
Ron Mes, *Manager*
EMP: 15
SALES (est): 2MM **Privately Held**
SIC: 3841 Surgical & medical instruments

(G-14540)
REFRIGERATION SUPPLIES DISTR
Also Called: Johnson Contrls Authorized Dlr
3217 Ne 112th Ave (98682-7738)
PHONE..................................503 234-4334
Tim O'Omeara, *Enginr/R&D Mgr*
EMP: 8
SALES (corp-wide): 193MM **Privately Held**
WEB: www.rsd-tc.com
SIC: 3585 5078 5075 Refrigeration equipment, complete; refrigerators, commercial (reach-in & walk-in); air conditioning equipment, except room units
PA: Refrigeration Supplies Distributor
26021 Atlantic Ocean Dr
Lake Forest CA 92630
949 380-7878

(G-14541)
REGAL HOMES CONSTRUCTION LLC
9901 Ne 26th St (98662-7690)
PHONE..................................360 606-3486

Daniel Persa, *Principal*
EMP: 2
SALES (est): 185K **Privately Held**
SIC: 1521 2452 New construction, single-family houses; log cabins, prefabricated, wood; modular homes, prefabricated, wood

(G-14542)
REMSING ENTERPRISES
2111 Ne 49th St (98663-1375)
PHONE..................................360 521-8049
David Remsing, *Owner*
EMP: 2 EST: 2009
SALES (est): 140K **Privately Held**
SIC: 2952 Siding materials

(G-14543)
RENAISSANCE LEARNING INC
Also Called: Renaissance Corporate Services
4601 Ne 77th Ave Ste 250 (98662-6736)
PHONE..................................360 944-8996
Glenn R James, *Branch Mgr*
EMP: 55
SALES (corp-wide): 111.3MM **Privately Held**
WEB: www.renlearn.com
SIC: 7372 7371 Educational computer software; computer software development
PA: Renaissance Learning, Inc.
2911 Peach St
Wisconsin Rapids WI 54494
715 424-4242

(G-14544)
RENEWABLE ENRGY CMPS SLTNS LLC
Also Called: Recs
4400 Se Columbia Way (98661-5570)
P.O. Box 823190 (98682-0066)
PHONE..................................360 695-3238
Joe F Foggia,
EMP: 6
SALES (est): 623.6K **Privately Held**
SIC: 3559 Special industry machinery

(G-14545)
REST-A-PHONE CORPORATION
Also Called: Rest-A-Phone ABC Plastics
2801 Nw Lower River Rd (98660-1037)
PHONE..................................503 235-6778
Myrtle Van Dyke-Roth, *President*
EMP: 10 EST: 1946
SQ FT: 8,000
SALES (est): 700K **Privately Held**
WEB: www.restaphone.com
SIC: 3661 Telephones & telephone apparatus

(G-14546)
REST-A-PHONE CORPORATION
2801 Nw Lower River Rd (98660-1037)
PHONE..................................360 750-8686
Douglas J Hall, *President*
EMP: 7
SALES (est): 854K **Privately Held**
SIC: 3661 Telephone & telegraph apparatus

(G-14547)
RESTORE INCORPORATED
12110 Nw 41st Ave (98685-2057)
PHONE..................................360 909-1161
EMP: 3
SALES (est): 232.9K **Privately Held**
SIC: 2992 Mfg Lubricating Oils/Greases

(G-14548)
REVQ INC
12905 Ne 93rd Ave (98662-1189)
PHONE..................................360 260-5710
Bruce Randall, *Principal*
EMP: 3
SALES (est): 209.6K **Privately Held**
WEB: www.revq.com
SIC: 7372 Prepackaged software

(G-14549)
REX PLASTICS INC
12515 Ne 95th St (98682-2463)
PHONE..................................360 892-0366
Rich Clark, *President*
Eric Clark, *Vice Pres*
Toni Schmidt, *Manager*
▼ EMP: 25
SQ FT: 10,000

SALES (est): 4.7MM **Privately Held**
SIC: 3089 3599 Injection molded finished plastic products; machine shop, jobbing & repair

(G-14550)
REYNA MOORE ADVERTISING
18514 Ne 23rd St (98684-0955)
PHONE..................................503 230-9440
Laverne L Moore, *Partner*
Humberto Reyna, *Partner*
EMP: 2
SALES (est): 157.9K **Privately Held**
WEB: www.reynamoore.com
SIC: 7336 3993 Graphic arts & related design; advertising artwork

(G-14551)
REZABEK VINEYARDS LLC
5700 Ne 82nd Ave (98662-9428)
PHONE..................................360 896-0218
EMP: 2 EST: 2015
SALES (est): 105.3K **Privately Held**
SIC: 2084 Wines

(G-14552)
RITZY BATH BOMBS
2727 E Evergreen Blvd N (98661-4900)
PHONE..................................206 499-7336
Shelby Griffith, *Principal*
EMP: 2
SALES (est): 138K **Privately Held**
SIC: 2844 Bath salts

(G-14553)
RJ HYDRAULICS INC
713 W 11th St (98660-3054)
PHONE..................................360 693-4399
Robert Hegewald, *President*
Adam Hegewald, *General Mgr*
Margaret Hegewald, *Treasurer*
EMP: 10
SQ FT: 14,000
SALES (est): 2.6MM **Privately Held**
WEB: www.hydraulics-inc.com
SIC: 7699 5084 3569 3492 Hydraulic equipment repair; hydraulic systems equipment & supplies; filter elements, fluid, hydraulic line; jacks, hydraulic; hose & tube couplings, hydraulic/pneumatic

(G-14554)
RKBA CONCEALMENT
4307 Ne 118th St (98686-5912)
PHONE..................................360 624-3874
Ryan Johnson, *Principal*
EMP: 2
SALES (est): 119.2K **Privately Held**
SIC: 3199 Leather goods

(G-14555)
ROADMASTER INC
6110 Ne 127th Ave (98682-5816)
PHONE..................................360 896-0407
Jerry Miller, *Branch Mgr*
EMP: 5
SALES (corp-wide): 26.6MM **Privately Held**
SIC: 3714 3799 Motor vehicle parts & accessories; recreational vehicles
PA: Roadmaster, Inc.
6110 Ne 127th Ave
Vancouver WA 98682
503 777-1317

(G-14556)
ROADMASTER INC
Flow Chem
1800 W Fourth Plain Blvd # 115 (98660-1367)
PHONE..................................360 735-7575
Jerry Edwards, *President*
EMP: 3
SALES (corp-wide): 26.6MM **Privately Held**
SIC: 3714 2842 Motor vehicle parts & accessories; cleaning or polishing preparations
PA: Roadmaster, Inc.
6110 Ne 127th Ave
Vancouver WA 98682
503 777-1317

Vancouver - Clark County (G-14557) GEOGRAPHIC SECTION

(G-14557)
ROBERT COMEAU
5112 Ne 119th St (98686-3438)
PHONE..................360 573-2241
Robert Comeau, *Owner*
EMP: 3
SALES (est): 284.1K **Privately Held**
SIC: 3561 Pumps & pumping equipment

(G-14558)
ROCKING HORSE RITA CSTM HMES
11077 N Vancouver Way (98660)
PHONE..................360 600-1000
Gil Castaneda, *Principal*
EMP: 2
SALES (est): 146.5K **Privately Held**
SIC: 3944 Rocking horses

(G-14559)
RS MACHINE INC
6133 Ne 63rd St (98661-1906)
PHONE..................360 694-0044
Shane Scales, *President*
EMP: 4
SALES (est): 292.8K **Privately Held**
SIC: 3599 Machine shop, jobbing & repair

(G-14560)
RUBBER & PLASTICS INC
Also Called: R P I
7401 Ne 47th Ave (98661-1327)
PHONE..................503 289-7720
Rodney W Roalsen, *President*
Laura Hoggan, *Vice Pres*
Patrick Oconnor, *Warehouse Mgr*
Karissa Moore, *Sales Staff*
Katie Pearson, *Manager*
▲ **EMP:** 30
SQ FT: 25,000
SALES (est): 8.1MM **Privately Held**
WEB: www.conveyorbelt.com
SIC: 3052 3069 Rubber belting; medical & laboratory rubber sundries & related products

(G-14561)
RYONET CORPORATION
12303 Ne 56th St (98682-6476)
PHONE..................360 576-7188
Ryan Moor, *President*
Rogier Ducloo, *President*
Jared Hoch, *President*
Tyson Stuart, *Warehouse Mgr*
Ashley Metzger, *Purchasing*
◆ **EMP:** 100
SALES (est): 32MM **Privately Held**
WEB: www.ryonetcorp.com
SIC: 2752 Commercial printing, lithographic

(G-14562)
S & W MANUFACTURING INC
7414 Ne 47th Ave (98661-1328)
PHONE..................360 690-8558
Fax: 360 690-4453
EMP: 5
SQ FT: 3,200
SALES: 750K **Privately Held**
SIC: 2448 Mfg Wood Pallets

(G-14563)
S SCOTT & ASSOCIATES LLC
4719 Ne Salmon Creek St (98686-1605)
PHONE..................360 576-4830
Brian Scott, *Principal*
Laura Scott, *Principal*
EMP: 2
SALES (est): 137.8K **Privately Held**
SIC: 3089 3824 3443 0273 Plastics products; fluid meters & counting devices; trash racks, metal plate; animal aquaculture

(G-14564)
SAFETEC COMPLIANCE SYSTEMS INC
7700 Ne Parkway Dr # 125 (98662-6648)
PHONE..................360 567-0280
James Frohlich, *President*
Paul D Bundy, *CFO*
Duane Burkett, *Treasurer*
Martin Wehner, *CTO*
EMP: 62
SQ FT: 12,000
SALES (est): 7.2MM **Privately Held**
WEB: www.safetec.net
SIC: 7372 Business oriented computer software
PA: American Safety And Health Institute, Inc.
1450 Westec Dr
Eugene OR 97402

(G-14565)
SAFETEC SOFTWARE LLC
5512 Ne 109th Ct Ste N (98662-6175)
PHONE..................888 745-8943
Dwayne Burkett, *Principal*
EMP: 2
SALES (est): 169.2K **Privately Held**
SIC: 7372 Business oriented computer software

(G-14566)
SAFETY DEFENSE TECHNOLOGY
1900 Fort Vancouver Way (98663-3500)
PHONE..................360 718-2078
John Hill, *Principal*
EMP: 3
SALES (est): 173.7K **Privately Held**
SIC: 3812 Defense systems & equipment

(G-14567)
SALEM EQUIPMENT INC
2525 W Firestone Ln (98660-1182)
PHONE..................503 581-8411
Ray Brown, *Manager*
EMP: 12
SALES (corp-wide): 12MM **Privately Held**
WEB: www.salem-equipment.com
SIC: 3553 5084 Sawmill machines; sawmill machinery & equipment
PA: Salem Equipment, Inc.
14440 Sw Tltn Shrwd Rd
Sherwood OR 97140
503 581-8411

(G-14568)
SALMON CREEK MACHINE
14503 Nw 56th Ave (98685-1139)
PHONE..................360 573-7958
John Baumann, *Owner*
EMP: 13
SQ FT: 2,500
SALES (est): 1.3MM **Privately Held**
WEB: www.salmoncreekmachine.com
SIC: 3599 Machine shop, jobbing & repair

(G-14569)
SANDYS SIGN & DESIGN
4715 Ne 60th St (98661-1818)
PHONE..................360 693-9229
Sandy Cereghino, *Owner*
EMP: 2
SALES: 120K **Privately Held**
SIC: 3993 Signs & advertising specialties

(G-14570)
SAXCO PACIFIC COAST LLC
3812 Ne 112th Ave 100 (98682-8711)
PHONE..................360 892-3451
Keith L Sachs,
Herbert L Sachs,
▲ **EMP:** 13
SALES (est): 2.9MM **Privately Held**
SIC: 3565 Bottle washing & sterilizing machines

(G-14571)
SCHEFFLER NORTHWEST INC
351 Grand Blvd Ste B (98661-7776)
PHONE..................360 213-2070
EMP: 2
SALES (est): 126.6K **Privately Held**
SIC: 1381 Drilling oil & gas wells

(G-14572)
SCHROEDERS MACHINE WORKS INC
8010 Ne 19th Ct (98665-9751)
PHONE..................360 573-6911
Peter R Schroeder, *CEO*
Kaye Schroeder, *Corp Secy*
EMP: 11 **EST:** 1968
SQ FT: 5,000
SALES: 1.4MM **Privately Held**
SIC: 3599 Machine shop, jobbing & repair

(G-14573)
SCOTT PARRISH
17707 Ne 50th Ave (98686-1855)
PHONE..................360 259-8080
Scott Parrish, *Principal*
EMP: 2
SALES (est): 101K **Privately Held**
SIC: 3269 Lamp bases, pottery

(G-14574)
SCOTTYS ELC MTR & PUMP REPR
Also Called: Scotty's Electric Motor
7917 Ne St Johns Rd (98665-1022)
PHONE..................360 573-9544
Sharon Scott, *President*
EMP: 5
SQ FT: 4,000
SALES (est): 555.5K **Privately Held**
SIC: 7694 Electric motor repair

(G-14575)
SCREEN PRINTING INTERNATIONAL
12303 Ne 56th St (98682-6476)
PHONE..................678 231-9195
EMP: 2 **EST:** 2016
SALES (est): 83.9K **Privately Held**
SIC: 2752 Commercial printing, lithographic

(G-14576)
SE INDUSTRIES LLC
10212 Ne 219th Ave (98682-9728)
PHONE..................360 256-3775
EMP: 2
SALES (est): 81K **Privately Held**
SIC: 3999 Mfg Misc Products

(G-14577)
SEAL DYNAMICS
4609 Nw Lincoln Ave (98663-1767)
PHONE..................503 232-0973
Lance Crosier, *Owner*
EMP: 2
SALES (est): 125.1K **Privately Held**
SIC: 3297 Graphite refractories: carbon bond or ceramic bond

(G-14578)
SECTION MAGAZINE LLC
610 Esther St Ste 200 (98660-3027)
PHONE..................360 694-8571
Casey Wyckoff,
EMP: 2
SALES: 50K **Privately Held**
SIC: 2759 Publication printing

(G-14579)
SEKIDENKO INC
2501 Se Columbia Way # 230 (98661-8038)
PHONE..................360 694-7871
Doug Schatz, *President*
EMP: 23
SALES (est): 3MM
SALES (corp-wide): 718.8MM **Publicly Held**
WEB: www.advanced-energy.com
SIC: 3826 3823 Spectroscopic & other optical properties measuring equipment; industrial instrmnts msrmnt display/control process variable
PA: Advanced Energy Industries, Inc.
1625 Sharp Point Dr
Fort Collins CO 80525
970 221-4670

(G-14580)
SERVICE PARTNERS OF OREGON
5900 Ne 88th St Ste 100 (98665-1901)
PHONE..................360 694-6747
Dorie Bird, *General Mgr*
James R Cole,
▲ **EMP:** 35
SQ FT: 4,400
SALES (est): 4.8MM
SALES (corp-wide): 2.3B **Publicly Held**
WEB: www.service-partners.com
SIC: 5033 5032 3296 Insulation materials; stucco; mineral wool insulation products
HQ: Service Partners, Llc
475 N Williamson Blvd
Daytona Beach FL 32114
804 515-7400

(G-14581)
SHANNOCK TAPESTRY LOOMS
10402 Nw 11th Ave (98665-5111)
P.O. Box 65295 (98665-0010)
PHONE..................360 573-7264
John Shannock, *Owner*
Laura Shannock, *Co-Owner*
EMP: 2
SALES (est): 272.3K **Privately Held**
SIC: 3552 5949 Looms, textile machinery; sewing, needlework & piece goods

(G-14582)
SHILOH PUBLISHING
16406 Ne 35th St (98682-8660)
P.O. Box 100, Woodburn OR (97071-0100)
PHONE..................800 607-6195
Carol Robeson, *Owner*
Dr Jerry Robeson, *Partner*
EMP: 6 **EST:** 1983
SALES (est): 463K **Privately Held**
WEB: www.shilohpublishing.com
SIC: 2731 Books: publishing only

(G-14583)
SHIN-ETSU HANDOTAI AMERICA INC (DH)
Also Called: S E H America
4111 Ne 112th Ave (98682-6776)
P.O. Box 8965 (98668-8965)
PHONE..................360 883-7000
Yashuhiko Saitoh, *President*
Terry Borneman, *Mfg Spvr*
Rodger Donald, *Engineer*
Jess Dyba, *Engineer*
Cason Franklin, *Engineer*
▲ **EMP:** 710
SALES (est): 335.3MM **Privately Held**
SIC: 3674 5065 Wafers (semiconductor devices); semiconductor devices

(G-14584)
SHIRLEY SUNSET
Also Called: Sunset Collections
9014 Ne St Johns Rd # 113 (98665-5806)
PHONE..................360 574-3276
Shirley Sunset, *Owner*
EMP: 4
SALES (est): 226.5K **Privately Held**
WEB: www.shirleyclarke.com
SIC: 2759 2396 Screen printing; automotive & apparel trimmings

(G-14585)
SIGMA DG CORPORATION
5019 Nw 127th St (98685-2151)
PHONE..................360 859-3170
Ashley McWatters, *Principal*
▲ **EMP:** 2 **EST:** 2010
SALES (est): 200.3K **Privately Held**
SIC: 3999 Manufacturing industries

(G-14586)
SIGN BIZ
6206 E 18th St Ste A (98661-6969)
PHONE..................360 750-9175
Dave Forester, *Owner*
EMP: 6
SALES (est): 395.6K **Privately Held**
SIC: 3993 Signs & advertising specialties

(G-14587)
SIGN OF TIMES
5809 Ne 105th Ave (98662-5793)
PHONE..................360 891-9477
Bob Hart, *Owner*
EMP: 2
SQ FT: 1,200
SALES: 75K **Privately Held**
SIC: 3993 Signs & advertising specialties

(G-14588)
SILICON FOREST ELECTRONICS INC
6204 E 18th St (98661-6840)
PHONE..................360 694-2000
Frank Nichols, *President*
Jay Schmidt, *Exec VP*
Ladena Rich, *Buyer*
Bryan Summer, *Buyer*

John Feuerstein, *Engineer*
EMP: 115
SQ FT: 26,000
SALES (est): 39.1MM **Privately Held**
WEB: www.si-forest.com
SIC: 3672 Printed circuit boards

(G-14589)
SIRENS BATH BOMBS
3102 Harney St Apt 4 (98660-2068)
PHONE...................360 852-4938
Dylan Griffith, *Principal*
EMP: 2
SALES (est): 83.9K **Privately Held**
SIC: 2844 Bath salts

(G-14590)
SKINNER COMMUNICATIONS
10214 Ne 65th Ave (98686-7004)
P.O. Box 5284 (98668-5284)
PHONE...................360 980-4906
Karlyn Skinner, *Owner*
EMP: 5
SALES (est): 474.6K **Privately Held**
SIC: 3571 Electronic computers

(G-14591)
SKUNK BROTHERS SPIRITS INC
2201 Ne 94th Ct (98664-2900)
P.O. Box 360, North Bonneville (98639-0360)
PHONE...................360 213-3420
Scott Donoho, *President*
Steven Donoho, *Vice Pres*
Sharlaina Kramer, *Vice Pres*
EMP: 4
SALES (est): 279K **Privately Held**
SIC: 2085 7389 Neutral spirits, except fruit;

(G-14592)
SKYLINE NW INC A WASH COR
7001 Ne 40th Ave (98661-1303)
PHONE...................360 695-6006
EMP: 2
SALES (est): 69.9K **Privately Held**
SIC: 3471 Plating & polishing

(G-14593)
SKYTECH MACHINE INC
10505 Ne Maitland Rd (98686-7028)
PHONE...................360 253-6378
Daniel Savala, *President*
Teri Savala, *Corp Secy*
EMP: 2
SALES: 142K **Privately Held**
WEB: www.skytechmachine.com
SIC: 3569 Assembly machines, non-metal-working

(G-14594)
SLS RUNOUT LLC (DH)
Also Called: National Garden Wholesale
3204 Nw 38th Cir (98660-1327)
PHONE...................360 883-8846
Craig Ryan Hargreaves, *President*
Kim Hargreaves, *Vice Pres*
Kne Hunter, *Vice Pres*
Erik Olsen, *Vice Pres*
Steve Schantin, *Vice Pres*
◆ **EMP:** 80
SALES (est): 52.1MM
SALES (corp-wide): 2.6B **Publicly Held**
SIC: 3524 5191 Lawn & garden equipment; garden supplies
HQ: Hawthorne Hydroponics Llc
  14111 Scottslawn Rd
  Marysville OH 43040
  888 478-6544

(G-14595)
SMAK PLASTICS INC
9116 Ne 130th Ave (98682-2798)
PHONE...................360 882-0410
Jonathan Smalley, *President*
▲ **EMP:** 45
SQ FT: 25,000
SALES (est): 11.3MM **Privately Held**
SIC: 3089 Molding primary plastic; plastic processing

(G-14596)
SMARTRG INC (HQ)
501 Se Columbia Shr (98661-8099)
PHONE...................877 486-6210
Jeff McInnis, *President*
Tim Bennington-Davis, *Vice Pres*
David La Cagnina, *Vice Pres*
Patrick Maloney, *Engineer*
Oleg Buzinover, *CFO*
▲ **EMP:** 29 **EST:** 2012
SALES (est): 9MM
SALES (corp-wide): 529.2MM **Publicly Held**
SIC: 7372 Utility computer software
PA: Adtran, Inc.
  901 Explorer Blvd Nw
  Huntsville AL 35806
  256 963-8000

(G-14597)
SMITH & REILLY INC
3107 Ne 65th St (98663-1483)
PHONE...................360 693-9225
EMP: 3 **EST:** 1984
SQ FT: 1,000
SALES (est): 210K **Privately Held**
SIC: 2082 Brewery

(G-14598)
SOLARWORLD INDUSTRIES AMER LP
Also Called: Siemens Solar Industries
12016 Ne 95th St Ste 720 (98682-2451)
PHONE...................360 944-9251
EMP: 68
SALES (corp-wide): 612.5MM **Privately Held**
SIC: 3674 Mfg Semiconductors/Related Devices
HQ: Solarworld Industries America Lp
  25300 Nw Evergreen Rd
  Hillsboro OR 97124
  805 482-6800

(G-14599)
SOLID SOLUTIONS INC
2700 Ne Burton Rd Ste B (98662-7399)
PHONE...................360 882-9074
Scott Curtis, *President*
Barbara Curtis, *President*
Mark Curtis, *Director*
EMP: 7
SQ FT: 7,000
SALES: 1.6MM **Privately Held**
WEB: www.solidsolutionsinc.com
SIC: 3131 Counters

(G-14600)
SOMATICS LLC
12911 Nw 25th Ct (98685-2036)
PHONE...................847 234-6761
EMP: 4
SALES (est): 200.8K **Privately Held**
SIC: 3845 Electromedical equipment

(G-14601)
SOUND PRODUCT SOLUTIONS LLC
12515 Ne 95th St (98682-2463)
PHONE...................360 553-7898
Rex Clark, *CEO*
Rich Clark, *President*
EMP: 4
SQ FT: 10,000
SALES (est): 381.4K **Privately Held**
SIC: 3651 Loudspeakers, electrodynamic or magnetic

(G-14602)
SPEEDFAB
9305 Ne Highway 99 (98665-8979)
PHONE...................360 571-4093
John Gaynor, *Principal*
EMP: 4
SALES (est): 371.4K **Privately Held**
SIC: 3441 Fabricated structural metal

(G-14603)
SPORTING SYSTEMS CORPORATION
Also Called: Humidity Systems
7415 Ne Highway 99 # 104 (98665-8891)
PHONE...................360 607-0036
Hiedi Lee, *President*
EMP: 2 **EST:** 2015
SALES (est): 279.4K **Privately Held**
SIC: 3822 3585 Humidity controls, air-conditioning types; humidifiers & dehumidifiers

(G-14604)
SPORTS-FAB INC
9505 Ne 84th Ct (98662-3207)
PHONE...................503 408-0920
Bruce Zunker, *President*
EMP: 4
SQ FT: 2,000
SALES (est): 490K **Privately Held**
WEB: www.sportsfab.com
SIC: 3949 Exercise equipment

(G-14605)
SPUTTERTECH INC
12117 Ne 99th St Ste 1920 (98682-2446)
PHONE...................360 253-5944
Christian Smith, *President*
EMP: 7
SALES (est): 856.1K **Privately Held**
SIC: 3674 Semiconductors & related devices

(G-14606)
STAINLESS CABLE & RAILING INC
3315 Nw 112th Ave (98682)
PHONE...................360 314-4288
Eric Reimer, *President*
◆ **EMP:** 9 **EST:** 2008
SALES (est): 1.5MM **Privately Held**
SIC: 3446 Stairs, fire escapes, balconies, railings & ladders

(G-14607)
STAIRCRAFTERS INCORPORATED
712 Ne 157th Ct (98684-8734)
P.O. Box 873606 (98687-3606)
PHONE...................360 882-2772
Ronald Sylwester, *President*
EMP: 2 **EST:** 2007
SALES (est): 190.6K **Privately Held**
SIC: 5211 2431 1799 Lumber & other building materials; staircases, stairs & railings; special trade contractors

(G-14608)
STARDUST MATERIALS LLC
12518 Ne 95th St (98682-2463)
PHONE...................360 260-7399
Jose Gasque, *Engineer*
Elina Tolmacheva, *Engineer*
Kyle Goble, *Electrical Engi*
Crystal Ng, *Marketing Staff*
Bobbie Keith, *Manager*
▲ **EMP:** 7
SQ FT: 8,250
SALES: 2MM **Privately Held**
SIC: 3699 2816 8731 Security control equipment & systems; inorganic pigments; commercial physical research

(G-14609)
STASON ANIMAL HEALTH INC
16821se Mcgllvryblvdst112 # 112 (98683)
PHONE...................360 200-5300
Thomas A Friar, *CEO*
Molly Van Pelt, *General Mgr*
EMP: 5
SALES (est): 340.3K **Privately Held**
SIC: 2834 5199 Veterinary pharmaceutical preparations; pets & pet supplies
PA: Stason Pharmaceuticals, Inc.
  11 Morgan
  Irvine CA 92618

(G-14610)
STEALTH SERVICES & TECHNOLOGY
3315 Ne 112th Ave Ste 57 (98682-8734)
PHONE...................360 882-7211
EMP: 3
SALES (est): 270K **Privately Held**
SIC: 3561 3563 Mfg Pumps/Pumping Equipment Mfg Air/Gas Compressors

(G-14611)
STICK IT PRINT
1000 Grand Blvd (98661-4826)
PHONE...................360 909-6060
EMP: 2 **EST:** 2016
SALES (est): 83.9K **Privately Held**
SIC: 2752 Lithographic Commercial Printing

(G-14612)
STITCHYBOX
305 Se Chkalov Dr 111-195 (98683-5292)
PHONE...................360 450-1089
Liz Westlake, *Principal*
EMP: 2
SALES (est): 106.8K **Privately Held**
SIC: 2395 Embroidery & art needlework

(G-14613)
STONG ENTERPRISES LLC
Also Called: Image360
1720 Ne 64th Ave Ste B (98661-6981)
PHONE...................360 326-4752
Seana Stong,
EMP: 3
SQ FT: 3,000
SALES (est): 282K **Privately Held**
SIC: 3993 7389 5999 Signs & advertising specialties; advertising, promotional & trade show services; banners, flags, decals & posters

(G-14614)
SUBARU OF AMERICA INC
3309 Nw Gateway Ave (98660-1043)
PHONE...................360 737-7630
Jay Orell, *Manager*
EMP: 9 **Privately Held**
SIC: 5511 4213 3714 3711 Automobiles, new & used; trucking, except local; motor vehicle parts & accessories; motor vehicles & car bodies
HQ: Subaru Of America, Inc.
  1 Subaru Dr
  Camden NJ 08103
  856 488-8500

(G-14615)
SUNMODO CORPORATION
14800 Ne 65th St (98682-5916)
PHONE...................360 844-0048
Jun Liu, *President*
Ben Oliver, *Accounts Exec*
Tony Liu, *CTO*
◆ **EMP:** 9
SQ FT: 7,200
SALES: 3.2MM **Privately Held**
SIC: 3441 Fabricated structural metal

(G-14616)
SUNRISE BAGELS & MORE INC
16010 Ne 25th St (98684-8691)
PHONE...................360 254-1012
Bruce Yamamura, *President*
EMP: 15
SQ FT: 3,000
SALES (est): 1.6MM **Privately Held**
SIC: 2051 5812 5719 2052 Bagels, fresh or frozen; coffee shop; delicatessen (eating places); kitchenware; cookies & crackers; bakeries

(G-14617)
SUNRISE WASHINGTON INC
5900 Ne 88th St Ste 119 (98665-1901)
PHONE...................360 574-3512
James Sewell, *Principal*
▲ **EMP:** 5
SALES (est): 690K **Privately Held**
SIC: 2679 Building, insulating & packaging paper

(G-14618)
SUNSHINE EMBROIDERY
1812 Ne 155th Ave (98684-8615)
PHONE...................360 892-1556
Heidi Harvey, *Partner*
Bill Harvey, *Principal*
EMP: 2
SALES: 250K **Privately Held**
SIC: 2395 Embroidery & art needlework

(G-14619)
SUNSTEEL LLC
312 Se Stnmill Dr Ste 147 (98684)
PHONE...................509 836-3078
Blake Hoskisson, *President*
Mike Eckert, *Vice Pres*
Paul Willden, *Vice Pres*
Fred Clingman,
Dan De Boer,
EMP: 35
SALES (est): 7.9MM **Privately Held**
SIC: 3443 Autoclaves, industrial

Vancouver - Clark County (G-14620)

(G-14620)
SUPER H CORPORATION
Also Called: Battle Ground Printing
12403 Ne 60th Way 1d (98682-5972)
P.O. Box 2500, Battle Ground (98604-2500)
PHONE.................................360 687-2824
Michael Harden, *President*
Mikalae E Harden, *Vice Pres*
Mikalae Harden, *Vice Pres*
EMP: 5 **EST:** 2006
SALES (est): 502.6K **Privately Held**
SIC: 2759 Commercial printing

(G-14621)
SURPRISE AL CARE GROUP LLC
5101 Ne 82nd Ave Ste 200 (98662-6343)
PHONE.................................775 746-2200
EMP: 2
SALES (est): 127.3K **Privately Held**
SIC: 3669 Emergency alarms

(G-14622)
SYNDYNE CORPORATION
12109 Ne 95th St (98682-2407)
P.O. Box 820543 (98682-0012)
PHONE.................................360 256-8466
Arthur Young, *President*
Barbara Young, *Vice Pres*
Marcus Young, *Vice Pres*
▲ **EMP:** 9
SQ FT: 3,600
SALES (est): 1.4MM **Privately Held**
WEB: www.syndyne.com
SIC: 3931 Organ parts & materials

(G-14623)
SYSTEMATIC DESIGNS INTL
Also Called: S D I
5305 E 187th St Ste 215 (98661)
PHONE.................................360 944-9890
Jenshih Jessi Niou, *President*
James Wang, *Treasurer*
Jane Niou, *Admin Sec*
EMP: 15
SQ FT: 5,000
SALES (est): 1MM **Privately Held**
SIC: 7371 7372 Computer software development; prepackaged software

(G-14624)
TANDAR CORP
Also Called: A-1 Scales Sales & Service
13911 Nw 3rd Ct Ste 100 (98685-5703)
P.O. Box 29107, Portland OR (97296-9107)
PHONE.................................503 248-0711
John Cassa, *President*
Jeff Walling, *Admin Sec*
EMP: 14
SALES (est): 1.2MM
SALES (corp-wide): 3.1MM **Privately Held**
WEB: www.a-1scale.com
SIC: 5046 7699 3596 Scales, except laboratory; scale repair service; scales & balances, except laboratory
PA: Abm Equipment Company, Inc.
13911 Nw 3rd Ct Ste 100
Vancouver WA 98685
503 248-0079

(G-14625)
TANGO MANUFACTURING INC
1222 W Mcloughlin Blvd (98660-2383)
P.O. Box 569 (98666-0569)
PHONE.................................360 693-7228
Brian Burt, *President*
Kelley Burt, *Vice Pres*
EMP: 5
SQ FT: 5,500
SALES: 750K **Privately Held**
SIC: 3599 Custom machinery

(G-14626)
TAYLOR COMMUNICATIONS INC
1498 Se Tech Center Pl # 110 (98683-9591)
P.O. Box 83, Carrolls (98609-0081)
PHONE.................................360 699-4013
Scott Wheelon, *Branch Mgr*
EMP: 3
SALES (corp-wide): 3.2B **Privately Held**
SIC: 2759 Commercial printing
HQ: Taylor Communications, Inc.
1725 Roe Crest Dr
North Mankato MN 56003
507 625-2828

(G-14627)
TAYLOR TRUCKING LLC
7211 Ne 43rd Ave Ste A (98661-1377)
PHONE.................................360 573-2000
Jerry Nutter,
Jeff Woodside,
EMP: 11
SQ FT: 13,000
SALES: 5MM **Privately Held**
SIC: 4212 1442 Dump truck haulage; sand mining

(G-14628)
TELECOM RESELLER INC
Also Called: Telecom Reseller Monthly
17413 Se 28th St (98683-3427)
PHONE.................................360 260-9708
Doug Green, *Manager*
EMP: 9 **Privately Held**
WEB: www.usernews.com
SIC: 2711 Newspapers
PA: Telecom Reseller, Inc.
3472 Coral Springs Dr
Coral Springs FL

(G-14629)
TEN HATS
5411 E Mill Plain Blvd # 7 (98661-7057)
PHONE.................................702 375-6504
John Urdesich, *Principal*
EMP: 2
SALES (est): 70.9K **Privately Held**
SIC: 2353 Hats, caps & millinery

(G-14630)
TEN TALENTS USA
2910 Se Blairmont Dr (98683-7635)
PHONE.................................360 256-2847
Douglas Beck, *Owner*
EMP: 2 **EST:** 1989
SALES (est): 100.8K **Privately Held**
SIC: 3499 Novelties & giftware, including trophies

(G-14631)
TENNMAX AMERICA INC
7500 Ne St Johns Rd (98665-0612)
PHONE.................................360 567-0707
Jeffery Davis, *President*
Hsien-WEI Tseng, *Principal*
Mansford Pseng, *Vice Pres*
Ray Davis, *Treasurer*
◆ **EMP:** 4
SQ FT: 7,000
SALES (est): 637K **Privately Held**
SIC: 3443 Heat exchangers, condensers & components

(G-14632)
TERRATRENCH USA INC
815 Ne 172nd Ave (98684-9321)
PHONE.................................360 694-0141
Peter Blundell, *CEO*
Jay Harris, *VP Sales*
EMP: 6
SQ FT: 2,000
SALES: 1.1MM
SALES (corp-wide): 186.1K **Privately Held**
SIC: 3531 Entrenching machines
PA: Terrasaw Industries Limited
Level 2, Building 5, 60 Highbrook Drive
Auckland
943 164-00

(G-14633)
TETRA PAK MATERIALS LP
1616 W 31st St (98660-1201)
PHONE.................................360 693-3664
Steve Bean, *Manager*
Enrique Sosa Tribaldos, *Manager*
EMP: 120
SALES (corp-wide): 7.5B **Privately Held**
WEB: www.tetrapak.com
SIC: 2655 2656 Containers, liquid tight fiber: from purchased material; sanitary food containers
HQ: Tetra Pak Materials Lp
101 Corporate Woods Pkwy
Vernon Hills IL 60061
847 955-6000

(G-14634)
THOMPSON LITHO GROUP INC
Also Called: Visions In Print
4018 Ne 112th Ave Ste D9 (98682-5703)
PHONE.................................360 892-7888
Tim Thompson, *President*
EMP: 9
SQ FT: 4,000
SALES (est): 1.4MM **Privately Held**
WEB: www.visionsinprint.com
SIC: 2752 Commercial printing, offset

(G-14635)
TIDEWATER HOLDINGS INC (PA)
6305 Nw Old Lwer River Rd (98660-1021)
P.O. Box 1210 (98666-1210)
PHONE.................................360 693-1491
Robert Curcio, *President*
Bruce Reed, *COO*
Myron Reiseng, *Vice Pres*
Jim McGovern, *CFO*
EMP: 3
SQ FT: 10,000
SALES (est): 52.7MM **Privately Held**
SIC: 4449 3731 River transportation, except on the St. Lawrence Seaway; shipbuilding & repairing

(G-14636)
TIDLAND HYDRAULICS INC
3408 Ne Corbin Rd (98686-2838)
PHONE.................................360 573-6506
John Tidland, *President*
Pat Tidland, *Vice Pres*
EMP: 8
SQ FT: 3,000
SALES (est): 268.1K **Privately Held**
SIC: 3599 8711 Custom machinery; consulting engineer

(G-14637)
TIGERSTOP LLC
12909 Ne 95th St (98682-2426)
PHONE.................................360 254-0661
Rakesh Sridharan, *CEO*
Mathias Forsman, *Sales Staff*
Brenda Hehn, *Sales Staff*
Mike Anderson, *Manager*
Ed Scott, *Info Tech Mgr*
▲ **EMP:** 37
SALES (est): 9.7MM **Privately Held**
WEB: www.tigerstop.com
SIC: 3823 Industrial instrmnts msrmnt display/control process variable

(G-14638)
TIM ANDERS
15816 Ne 36th St (98682-8492)
PHONE.................................360 944-0806
Tim Anders, *Principal*
EMP: 2
SALES (est): 90.1K **Privately Held**
SIC: 3669 Communications equipment

(G-14639)
TIMBERS AT TOWNCENTER
608 Ne 86th St (98665-8142)
PHONE.................................360 433-9627
EMP: 3
SALES (est): 151K **Privately Held**
SIC: 1041 Gold ores

(G-14640)
TIMBERSOFT INC
205 E 11th St Ste 103 (98660-3309)
PHONE.................................360 750-5575
James Durham, *President*
Brian Durham, *Vice Pres*
Shannon Werbowski, *Office Mgr*
Maurice Boers, *Prgrmr*
EMP: 10
SQ FT: 1,300
SALES (est): 1MM **Privately Held**
WEB: www.timbersoft.com
SIC: 7371 7372 Computer software development; application computer software

(G-14641)
TNT SOFTWARE INC
2001 Main St (98660-2673)
P.O. Box 176, Mossyrock (98564-0176)
PHONE.................................360 546-0878
Steve Taylor, *President*
Susie Taylor, *Treasurer*
Brent Skadsen, *Admin Sec*
EMP: 18
SALES (est): 1.8MM **Privately Held**
WEB: www.tntsoftware.com
SIC: 7372 7371 Prepackaged software; custom computer programming services

(G-14642)
TOMS PRFMCE MCH & REPR INC
6707 Ne 117th Ave A (98662-5513)
PHONE.................................360 256-1722
Tom Pinkowsky, *President*
Sherry Pinkowsky, *Corp Secy*
EMP: 6
SALES (est): 500K **Privately Held**
SIC: 3599 7538 Machine shop, jobbing & repair; engine rebuilding: automotive

(G-14643)
TRACKER SAFE LLC
6317 Ne 63rd St (98661-1909)
PHONE.................................360 213-0363
Sean Zern, *Sales Staff*
Luke Boyer,
Zachary Boyer,
▲ **EMP:** 6 **EST:** 2015
SALES (est): 96.3K **Privately Held**
SIC: 3499 5999 Safes & vaults, metal; vaults & safes

(G-14644)
TREK GLOBAL
4400 Ne 77th Ave Ste 275 (98662-6857)
PHONE.................................760 576-5115
Joel Strangeland, *Owner*
EMP: 3 **EST:** 2012
SALES (est): 240.9K **Privately Held**
SIC: 7372 Prepackaged software

(G-14645)
TRI-SHELL CORES SHOP INC
1215 W 19th St (98660-2305)
PHONE.................................360 694-7600
Fax: 360 694-0225
EMP: 10
SALES (est): 610K **Privately Held**
SIC: 3544 Mfg Industrial Patterns

(G-14646)
TRIARII INDUSTRIES LLC
15501 Nw 27th Ct (98685-1609)
PHONE.................................360 314-6091
EMP: 2
SALES (est): 91.6K **Privately Held**
SIC: 3999 Manufacturing industries

(G-14647)
TRITON PRINT AND POUR POOR
8380 Ne Highway 99 (98665-8819)
PHONE.................................360 828-8809
EMP: 6 **EST:** 2014
SALES (est): 321.7K **Privately Held**
SIC: 2752 Commercial printing, lithographic

(G-14648)
TRIXIE PUBLISHING INC
203 Nw 153rd St (98685-1796)
PHONE.................................360 521-8246
Tracey Jackson, *Principal*
EMP: 2
SALES (est): 92.3K **Privately Held**
SIC: 2741 Miscellaneous publishing

(G-14649)
TROBELLA CABINETRY INC
3201 Nw Lower River Rd (98660-1078)
PHONE.................................360 947-2114
Kraig Tront, *President*
Denise Tront, *Vice Pres*
EMP: 30
SALES: 4MM **Privately Held**
SIC: 3553 Cabinet makers' machinery

GEOGRAPHIC SECTION

Vancouver - Clark County (G-14680)

(G-14650)
TRU CUT DIE INC
5906 Ne 41st Ave (98661-1757)
PHONE..................................360 571-7158
Steve Smith, *President*
Gary Sylvester, *President*
EMP: 2
SALES: 250K **Privately Held**
WEB: www.trucutdie.com
SIC: 3544 3364 Dies & die holders for metal cutting, forming, die casting; nonferrous die-castings except aluminum

(G-14651)
TVAN INC
3901 Ne 68th St (98661-1372)
P.O. Box 5005 (98668-5005)
PHONE..................................503 285-2615
Mark S Turner, *President*
Kenneth T Carty, *Corp Secy*
Zach Gaug, *Sales Mgr*
EMP: 100
SALES (est): 15.2MM **Privately Held**
WEB: www.trusway.com
SIC: 2439 Trusses, wooden roof

(G-14652)
TWICE LIGHT INC
6137 Ne 63rd St Vancouver (98661)
P.O. Box 65279 (98665-0010)
PHONE..................................360 573-6101
Lisa J Littleton, *President*
▲ **EMP:** 15
SALES (est): 3.4MM **Privately Held**
SIC: 1731 3645 Electrical work; lamp & light shades

(G-14653)
TWIN OHANA ENTERPRISES LLC (PA)
11011 Ne Burton Rd (98682-7674)
PHONE..................................360 882-8022
Kimberly Newton, *Mng Member*
EMP: 5 **EST:** 2013
SQ FT: 1,000
SALES (est): 831.8K **Privately Held**
SIC: 3634 Vaporizers, electric: household

(G-14654)
TWIN OHANA ENTERPRISES LLC
10501 Ne Highway 99 # 27 (98686-5697)
PHONE..................................360 314-2965
Nikki Prentice, *Branch Mgr*
EMP: 5
SALES (corp-wide): 831.8K **Privately Held**
SIC: 3634 Vaporizers, electric: household
PA: Twin Ohana Enterprises Llc
11011 Ne Burton Rd
Vancouver WA 98682
360 882-8022

(G-14655)
ULTRABLOCK INC
815 Ne 172nd Ave (98684-9321)
PHONE..................................360 694-0141
Peter J Blundell, *President*
EMP: 31
SQ FT: 20,000
SALES: 7.2MM **Privately Held**
SIC: 3272 Concrete products

(G-14656)
US FILTER VANCOUVER
11606 Ne 66th Cir (98662-2408)
PHONE..................................360 892-6977
Greg Bachman, *Manager*
EMP: 2
SALES (est): 201.7K **Privately Held**
SIC: 3569 Filters

(G-14657)
US HOSPITALITY PUBLISHERS INC
1406 Se 164th Ave Ste 200 (98683-9664)
PHONE..................................615 956-0080
EMP: 2
SALES (est): 66.7K **Privately Held**
SIC: 2711 Newspapers

(G-14658)
US WATER SERVICES INC
2700 W Firestone Ln (98660-1181)
PHONE..................................360 695-1270
EMP: 9
SALES (corp-wide): 1.5B **Publicly Held**
SIC: 2899 3589 Water treating compounds; water treatment equipment, industrial
HQ: U.S. Water Services, Inc.
12270 43rd St Ne
Saint Michael MN 55376
763 689-3636

(G-14659)
UTR MANUFACTURING INC
8010 Ne 19th Ct (98665-9751)
PHONE..................................360 901-1435
Shawn Whisenhunt, *President*
EMP: 5
SQ FT: 3,000
SALES (est): 732.7K **Privately Held**
SIC: 3599 Machine shop, jobbing & repair

(G-14660)
VANCOUVER BUSINESS JOURNAL
1251 Officers Row (98661-3854)
PHONE..................................360 695-2442
David Fenton, *President*
EMP: 12
SALES: 600K **Privately Held**
SIC: 2711 7331 Newspapers, publishing & printing; mailing list compilers

(G-14661)
VANCOUVER FOUNDRY COMPANY
1200 W 13th St (98660-2716)
PHONE..................................360 695-3914
Dan Shwartz, *President*
Lisa Runkle, *Controller*
Ray Anderson, *Manager*
EMP: 200
SALES (est): 13.9MM
SALES (corp-wide): 23.8MM **Privately Held**
WEB: www.rentmidwest.com
SIC: 3325 Steel foundries
PA: Varicast, Inc.
1200 W 13th St
Vancouver WA 98660
360 816-7350

(G-14662)
VANCOUVER IRON & STEEL INC
Also Called: Varicast
1200 W 13th St (98660-2716)
PHONE..................................360 695-3914
Dan Swartz, *President*
EMP: 99
SQ FT: 50,000
SALES: 16MM **Privately Held**
SIC: 3325 Steel foundries

(G-14663)
VANCOUVER SIGN CO INC
2600 Ne Andresen Rd # 50 (98661-7353)
PHONE..................................360 693-4773
Bruce Hagensen, *President*
Carmen Stuart, *Business Mgr*
Miriam O Hagensen, *Corp Secy*
Richard Miller, *Vice Pres*
Jeff Mickel, *Accounts Exec*
EMP: 20 **EST:** 1923
SQ FT: 10,000
SALES (est): 3.5MM **Privately Held**
SIC: 3993 7359 1799 Electric signs; neon signs; sign rental; sign installation & maintenance

(G-14664)
VANCOUVER WOODWORKS INC
3000 Ne Andresen Rd A101 (98661-7351)
PHONE..................................360 696-8590
Bruce Lyons, *President*
▲ **EMP:** 7
SQ FT: 6,000
SALES (est): 710K **Privately Held**
WEB: www.vancouverwoodworks.com
SIC: 2519 5712 Lawn & garden furniture, except wood & metal; furniture stores

(G-14665)
VANS INC
8700 Ne Vncvr Mll Dr 25 (98662)
PHONE..................................360 254-3075
Karen Willette, *Branch Mgr*
EMP: 10
SALES (corp-wide): 13.8B **Publicly Held**
SIC: 3021 Protective footwear, rubber or plastic; canvas shoes, rubber soled
HQ: Vans, Inc.
1588 S Coast Dr
Costa Mesa CA 92626
855 909-8267

(G-14666)
VARICAST INC (PA)
Also Called: Vancouver Iron and Steel
1200 W 13th St (98660-2716)
PHONE..................................360 816-7350
Dan R Swartz, *President*
Fred Meikle, *Principal*
John Steadman, *Principal*
Ray Anderson, *VP Opers*
James Gagan, *CFO*
EMP: 100
SQ FT: 50,000
SALES (est): 21.5MM **Privately Held**
SIC: 3325 3321 Alloy steel castings, except investment; ductile iron castings; gray iron castings

(G-14667)
VELENDO INC (PA)
6501 Ne 47th Ave (98661-1315)
PHONE..................................360 828-7174
Vincent Do, *President*
▲ **EMP:** 17
SALES (est): 3.4MM **Privately Held**
SIC: 3085 Plastics bottles

(G-14668)
VERACIOUS PRINTING LLC
11301 Ne 7th St Apt H5 (98684-4936)
PHONE..................................360 823-7395
Angela Valdez, *Principal*
EMP: 2
SALES (est): 83.9K **Privately Held**
SIC: 2752 Commercial printing, lithographic

(G-14669)
VIETNAMESE BAPTIST CHURCH TIN
7814 Ne 20th St (98664-1164)
PHONE..................................360 953-8311
An Nguyen, *Principal*
EMP: 3 **EST:** 2012
SALES (est): 191.8K **Privately Held**
SIC: 3356 Tin

(G-14670)
VIGOR WORKS LLC
3515 Se Columbia Way 48 (98661-8007)
PHONE..................................360 699-1547
Dwight Edwards, *Principal*
EMP: 28
SQ FT: 30,000
SALES (corp-wide): 599.5MM **Privately Held**
WEB: www.oriron.com
SIC: 3441 Fabricated structural metal
HQ: Vigor Works Llc
9700 Se Lawnfield Rd
Clackamas OR 97015
503 653-6300

(G-14671)
VIGOR WORKS LLC
3515 Se Columbia Way (98661-8007)
PHONE..................................360 694-7636
Robert Wise, *Branch Mgr*
EMP: 100
SALES (corp-wide): 599.5MM **Privately Held**
WEB: www.oriron.com
SIC: 3441 Boat & barge sections, prefabricated metal
HQ: Vigor Works Llc
9700 Se Lawnfield Rd
Clackamas OR 97015
503 653-6300

(G-14672)
VIRIDIAN SCIENCES INC
2114 Main St Ste 101 (98660-2674)
P.O. Box 132, Woodland (98674-0200)
PHONE..................................360 719-4451
Justin Dufour, *CEO*
EMP: 8
SALES: 2.5MM **Privately Held**
SIC: 7372 Application computer software

(G-14673)
VIXON CORPORATION
Also Called: Vixon Custom Cabinets
3315 Ne 112th Ave Ste 51 (98682-8700)
PHONE..................................360 607-5817
Viktor Chernichenko, *President*
Roman Chernichenko, *Vice Pres*
Yevgeniy Chernichenko, *Treasurer*
Oleg Chernichenko, *Admin Sec*
EMP: 9
SALES: 36.6K **Privately Held**
SIC: 2434 Wood kitchen cabinets

(G-14674)
VULCAN ORACLE
815 E 20th St (98663-3320)
PHONE..................................360 609-9272
Mark Effinger, *Principal*
EMP: 2
SALES (est): 101.3K **Privately Held**
SIC: 7372 Prepackaged software

(G-14675)
WADDELL WOODWORKING LLC
12323 Ne 39th St (98682-6880)
PHONE..................................503 752-1940
Holly L Waddell, *Principal*
EMP: 2
SALES (est): 152.1K **Privately Held**
SIC: 2431 Millwork

(G-14676)
WAFER RECLAIM SERVICES LLC
Also Called: Wrs Materials
12117 Ne 99th St Ste 1900 (98682-2446)
PHONE..................................360 254-0221
John Sakys, *Principal*
EMP: 3
SALES (est): 321.1K **Privately Held**
SIC: 3674 Semiconductors & related devices

(G-14677)
WARRIOR BROWN PUBLISHING LLC
Also Called: Vancouver Business Journal
1251 Officers Row (98661-3854)
PHONE..................................360 695-2442
EMP: 15
SALES (est): 315.3K **Privately Held**
SIC: 2711 Newspapers-Publishing/Printing

(G-14678)
WASHINGTON CRANE HOIST CO INC
4707 Ne Minnehaha St # 503 (98661-1860)
PHONE..................................360 694-9844
Patrick Keep, *Branch Mgr*
EMP: 7
SALES: 611.3K
SALES (corp-wide): 18.7MM **Privately Held**
SIC: 5084 3536 7389 Materials handling machinery; cranes, industrial plant; crane & aerial lift service
PA: Washington Crane & Hoist Co., Inc.
1334 Thornton Ave Sw
Pacific WA 98047
253 863-6661

(G-14679)
WATERAX CORPORATION
3801 Ne 109th Ave Ste A (98682-7779)
PHONE..................................360 574-1818
Marcello Iacovella, *President*
Raffaele Gerbasi, *Treasurer*
Frederic Lefrancois, *Admin Sec*
▲ **EMP:** 4
SALES (est): 1MM **Privately Held**
SIC: 3561 Pumps & pumping equipment

(G-14680)
WELLONS INC (PA)
2525 W Firestone Ln (98660-1182)
PHONE..................................360 750-3500
Martin Nye, *CEO*
Mike Cantrell, *Vice Pres*
Kenneth Kinsley, *Vice Pres*
Scott Carlson, *Safety Mgr*
Jennifer Rose, *Buyer*
▲ **EMP:** 150
SQ FT: 190,000

Vancouver - Clark County

SALES (est): 110.6MM Privately Held
WEB: www.wellonsusa.com
SIC: 3559 3443 Kilns, lumber; boilers: industrial, power, or marine; bins, prefabricated metal plate

(G-14681)
WELLONS INC
2600 W Firestone Ln (98660-1183)
PHONE 360 750-3500
EMP: 4
SALES (corp-wide): 110.6MM Privately Held
SIC: 3559 Ammunition & explosives, loading machinery
PA: Wellons, Inc.
2525 W Firestone Ln
Vancouver WA 98660
360 750-3500

(G-14682)
WELLONS GROUP INC
2525 W Firestone Ln (98660-1182)
PHONE 360 750-3500
Martin Nye, *CEO*
Robert Moore, *CFO*
Paul Parsons, *Controller*
EMP: 15
SALES (est): 2.2MM Privately Held
WEB: www.wellons.com
SIC: 3443 4931 3553 Fabricated plate work (boiler shop); ; sawmill machines

(G-14683)
WELWATER
2924 Ne 116th Ave (98682-8720)
PHONE 360 909-7970
EMP: 2 **EST:** 2010
SALES (est): 162.1K Privately Held
SIC: 3589 Water treatment equipment, industrial

(G-14684)
WESTERN AEROSPACE & ENGRG LLC
12401 Ne 60th Way Unit A1 (98682-5972)
PHONE 360 253-8282
Michael Armstrong, *Mng Member*
EMP: 2
SALES: 60K Privately Held
SIC: 3728 Aircraft parts & equipment

(G-14685)
WESTERN FOREST PRODUCTS US LLC
Also Called: Dry Kiln, The
4303 Nw Fruit Valley Rd (98660-1224)
P.O. Box 489 (98666-0489)
PHONE 360 735-9700
Jeff Clark, *Branch Mgr*
EMP: 24
SALES (corp-wide): 907.2MM Privately Held
WEB: www.columbiavistacorp.com
SIC: 2421 Kiln drying of lumber
HQ: Western Forest Products Us Llc
18637 Se Evergreen Hwy
Vancouver WA 98683
360 892-0770

(G-14686)
WESTSIDE CONCRETE ACC INC
11412 Ne 76th St (98662-3937)
PHONE 360 892-0203
Martin Russell, *Owner*
Roy Tabor, *Manager*
Bill Walchli, *Manager*
EMP: 4
SQ FT: 1,068 Privately Held
WEB: www.westconacc.com
SIC: 3444 5082 Concrete forms, sheet metal; contractors' materials
PA: Westside Concrete Accessories, Inc.
5800 Se Alexander St A
Hillsboro OR 97123

(G-14687)
WHEEL HAUS MFG INC
1417 Ne 76th St Ste F (98665-0485)
PHONE 360 719-1030
EMP: 2
SALES (est): 49.2K Privately Held
SIC: 3999 Manufacturing industries

(G-14688)
WHIPPLE FALLS INDUSTRIES
Also Called: Wfi Vancouver
15612 Ne 57th Ave (98686-1907)
PHONE 360 573-0863
Tyler Castle, *Owner*
EMP: 3
SALES (est): 60K Privately Held
SIC: 3599 Bellows, industrial: metal

(G-14689)
WHITE CREEK PROJECT LLC
9611 Ne 117th Ave (98662-2403)
PHONE 360 737-9692
Benton Pud,
EMP: 2
SALES (est): 151.9K Privately Held
SIC: 3621 Windmills, electric generating

(G-14690)
WHITE RABBIT VENTURES INC
Also Called: Matrix Roofing
6000 Ne 88th St Ste D102 (98665-0982)
P.O. Box 822440 (98682-0053)
PHONE 360 474-5828
Wendy Marvin, *President*
EMP: 14
SQ FT: 3,500
SALES (est): 1.9MM Privately Held
SIC: 1521 1761 5031 2499 Single-family home remodeling, additions & repairs; roofing contractor; siding contractor; doors & windows; fencing, docks & other outdoor wood structural products

(G-14691)
WIEBOLD & SONS LOGGING INC
10715 Ne 72nd Ave (98686-6048)
PHONE 360 573-2149
George Wiebold, *President*
Harry Wiebold, *Vice Pres*
Doris B Wiebold, *Treasurer*
George D Wiebold, *Admin Sec*
EMP: 4
SALES: 200K Privately Held
SIC: 2411 Logging camps & contractors

(G-14692)
WIEWECK LLC
14314 Nw 8th Ct (98685-1705)
PHONE 360 576-0509
Jonita Harder, *Principal*
EMP: 2
SALES (est): 185.5K Privately Held
SIC: 3999 Candles

(G-14693)
WILDER TECHNOLOGIES LLC
6101 A 18th St (98661)
PHONE 360 859-3041
Paul Deringer, *Managing Prtnr*
Carol Deringer, *Managing Prtnr*
EMP: 8
SQ FT: 3,200
SALES: 4MM Privately Held
SIC: 3643 Electric connectors

(G-14694)
WILLIAM MINNIEAR
Also Called: Minniear Software Support
9503 Ne 82nd Ave (98662-1868)
PHONE 360 254-6764
William Minniear, *Owner*
EMP: 2
SALES (est): 130K Privately Held
SIC: 7372 Prepackaged software

(G-14695)
WILLIAM WILLIS
Also Called: Printing Expressly For You
7212 Ne 58th St (98662-5203)
PHONE 360 885-2045
William Willis, *Owner*
EMP: 4
SALES (est): 290K Privately Held
WEB: www.pefy.net
SIC: 2752 Commercial printing, lithographic

(G-14696)
WISE CHOICE CUSTOM COATINGS
6100 Ne 79th Ave (98662-5996)
PHONE 360 326-3809
Brandon Wise, *Owner*
EMP: 2 **EST:** 2008
SALES (est): 124.1K Privately Held
SIC: 3479 Metal coating & allied service

(G-14697)
WOOBOX LLC
101 E 6th St Ste 220 (98660-3342)
PHONE 360 450-5200
George Decarlo III,
EMP: 2
SALES (est): 154.9K Privately Held
SIC: 7371 7372 8743 Computer software development; application computer software; promotion service

(G-14698)
WOODEN PALLETS RECYCLED
6905 Ne 119th St (98686-3462)
PHONE 360 624-3935
EMP: 4
SALES (est): 160K Privately Held
SIC: 2448 Mfg Wood Pallets/Skids

(G-14699)
WOODLAND WINDOWS & DOORS
11405 Ne 65th Ave (98686-4616)
PHONE 360 260-5466
William Woodland, *Principal*
EMP: 2
SALES (est): 166.5K Privately Held
SIC: 2431 Windows & window parts & trim, wood

(G-14700)
WOOLYS TREE SERVICE INC
5321 Ne 72nd Ave (98661-3624)
PHONE 360 944-7786
Anne Woldrich, *President*
EMP: 2
SALES (est): 126.7K Privately Held
SIC: 0721 2411 Orchard tree & vine services; logging

(G-14701)
X PRODUCTS LLC
1110 W 17th St (98660-2720)
PHONE 971 302-6127
K V Orden, *General Mgr*
EMP: 29
SALES (est): 2.2MM Privately Held
SIC: 3489 7312 Guns or gun parts, over 30 mm.; outdoor advertising services

(G-14702)
Y-VERGE LLC
3100 Se 168th Ave Apt 258 (98683-2123)
PHONE 360 975-9277
Leon Yeh, *Mng Member*
EMP: 3 **EST:** 2016
SALES: 150K Privately Held
SIC: 7372 7389 Prepackaged software;

(G-14703)
YA WE CAN DO THAT
8905 Ne 136th Ave (98682-3059)
PHONE 360 253-5555
Allen Nielson, *Principal*
EMP: 2 **EST:** 2016
SALES (est): 87.2K Privately Held
SIC: 3714 Motor vehicle parts & accessories

(G-14704)
YACULTA COMPANIES INC (PA)
805 Broadway St Ste 700 (98660-3301)
PHONE 360 887-7493
Bart Walker, *President*
EMP: 300
SALES (est): 18.1MM Privately Held
SIC: 3519 Diesel engine rebuilding

(G-14705)
YAINAX MEDICAL LLC
1915 E 5th St Ste C (98661-4286)
PHONE 503 516-7173
Cathy Epley, *Manager*
EMP: 3
SALES (est): 190K Privately Held
SIC: 3841 Surgical instruments & apparatus

(G-14706)
YON LLC
1312 Nw 148th St (98685-1024)
PHONE 360 947-5895
Ki Kim, *Principal*
EMP: 2
SALES (est): 143K Privately Held
SIC: 2844 Toilet preparations

(G-14707)
YVETTE J COOKE
Also Called: Vancouver Button Makers
2403 Nw 148th St (98685-1008)
P.O. Box 726 (98666-0726)
PHONE 360 718-0306
EMP: 2
SALES (est): 80.6K Privately Held
SIC: 3961 7389 Pins (jewelry), except precious metal;

(G-14708)
ZEBRA TRANS LLC
4500 Nicholson Rd Apt E23 (98661-8616)
PHONE 360 993-0451
Vitaliy Derevyanskyy, *Principal*
EMP: 3
SALES (est): 237.1K Privately Held
SIC: 3577 Computer peripheral equipment

(G-14709)
ZIMMEL UNRUH CELLARS LLC
17011 Se 5th St (98684-8406)
PHONE 503 313-2235
Robb Zimmel, *Principal*
Jon Unruh, *CFO*
EMP: 2
SALES (est): 75.4K Privately Held
SIC: 2084 7389 Wines;

(G-14710)
ZOOMNET POSTAL +
7617 Nw 16th Ave (98665-7113)
PHONE 360 719-0973
Jonathan Kiehle, *Principal*
EMP: 4
SALES (est): 412.4K Privately Held
SIC: 3086 Packaging & shipping materials, foamed plastic

Vashon
King County

(G-14711)
BAR CODE LABELS & EQUIPMENT
9619 Sw 156th St (98070-3937)
P.O. Box 2475 (98070-2475)
PHONE 206 567-5577
Robert Blakeslee, *President*
EMP: 3
SALES: 150K Privately Held
WEB: www.bcle.com
SIC: 2759 Labels & seals: printing

(G-14712)
BATHO STUDIOS
17021 115th Ave Sw (98070-4617)
PHONE 503 282-1460
George Batho, *Principal*
EMP: 8
SALES (est): 659.4K Privately Held
SIC: 3231 Art glass: made from purchased glass

(G-14713)
BF AND BF CO
10108 Sw 268th St (98070-8410)
PHONE 206 463-2661
Barry Foster, *Principal*
EMP: 2
SALES (est): 138.4K Privately Held
SIC: 3011 Tires & inner tubes

(G-14714)
BURN MANUFACTURING CO
18850 103rd Ave Sw (98070-5250)
PHONE 331 444-2876
Peter Scott, *CEO*
EMP: 3
SQ FT: 10,000
SALES (est): 358.7K Privately Held
SIC: 3255 Firing oven & accessories, clay

GEOGRAPHIC SECTION

Vashon - King County (G-14746)

(G-14715)
CAMARDA CORPORATION
Also Called: Andrew Will Winery
12526 Sw Bank Rd (98070-4519)
PHONE..................................206 463-9227
Chris Camarda, *President*
Anne Camarda, *Corp Secy*
Celia Winery, *Manager*
EMP: 2
SQ FT: 3,000
SALES (est): 251K **Privately Held**
WEB: www.andrewwill.com
SIC: 2084 Wines

(G-14716)
CASCADE CHALET
Also Called: Precision Carbide Bit Set
9709 Sw Burton Dr (98070-7001)
P.O. Box 13440, Burton (98013-0440)
PHONE..................................206 463-4628
Kevin Strell, *Owner*
▲ EMP: 25
SALES (est): 2.3MM **Privately Held**
WEB: www.squishwear.com
SIC: 3423 7812 Hand & edge tools; motion picture & video production

(G-14717)
CELESTICOMP INC
Also Called: Fir Tree Press
8903 Sw Bayview Dr (98070-7019)
PHONE..................................206 463-9626
Marjorie M Watkins, *President*
EMP: 2 EST: 1998
SALES (est): 100K **Privately Held**
SIC: 2731 Book publishing

(G-14718)
CHAPMAN AUDIO SYSTEMS
18005 Thorsen Rd Sw (98070-4503)
P.O. Box 140 (98070-0140)
PHONE..................................206 463-3008
Stuart Jones, *Owner*
EMP: 3 EST: 1965
SQ FT: 1,000
SALES (est): 290K **Privately Held**
WEB: www.chapmanaudio.com
SIC: 3651 Speaker systems

(G-14719)
CHORAKS SPORTSMANS INN
17611 Vashon Hwy Sw (98070-4682)
PHONE..................................206 463-0940
Paul Chorak, *Owner*
EMP: 3
SALES (est): 191.8K **Privately Held**
SIC: 2253 Lounge, bed & leisurewear

(G-14720)
CRISMAN ROCKING HORSES LLC
4409 Sw Point Robinson Rd (98070-7355)
PHONE..................................206 408-7465
Randee Crisman Blackstone, *Principal*
EMP: 2
SALES (est): 135.6K **Privately Held**
SIC: 3944 Rocking horses

(G-14721)
DELTA PRODUCTION
Also Called: Linguistic Analysis
8832 Sw Dilworth Rd (98070-4304)
P.O. Box 2237 (98070-2237)
PHONE..................................206 567-4373
David Willingham, *Owner*
Elizabeth Freeman, *Owner*
EMP: 2
SALES: 60K **Privately Held**
WEB: www.paradoxa.com
SIC: 2731 Book publishing

(G-14722)
FREDA BRITT PRINTS
16245 Westside Hwy Sw (98070-3721)
P.O. Box 1805 (98070-1805)
PHONE..................................206 409-4701
EMP: 2 EST: 2016
SALES (est): 83.9K **Privately Held**
SIC: 2752 Commercial printing, lithographic

(G-14723)
FRONTIER PUBLICATION INC
Also Called: Bingo Bugle Newspaper Group
19028 Vashon Hwy Sw (98070-5216)
P.O. Box 527 (98070-0527)
PHONE..................................206 463-5656
Tera Snodan, *President*
Tera Snowden, *President*
EMP: 3
SQ FT: 1,800
SALES (est): 308.9K **Privately Held**
WEB: www.bingobugle.com
SIC: 2711 Newspapers, publishing & printing

(G-14724)
INTENTION PUBLISHING CO
20239 77th Pl Sw (98070-6269)
P.O. Box 526 (98070-0526)
PHONE..................................206 463-9777
Loren Forest, *Principal*
EMP: 2
SALES (est): 90.8K **Privately Held**
SIC: 2741 Miscellaneous publishing

(G-14725)
IRENES TILES
18818 Ridge Rd Sw (98070-5412)
P.O. Box 152 (98070-0152)
PHONE..................................206 463-2808
Irene Otis, *Owner*
James Deignan, *Co-Owner*
EMP: 2
SALES: 50K **Privately Held**
WEB: www.irenes-tiles.com
SIC: 3253 5947 5211 Ceramic wall & floor tile; gift, novelty & souvenir shop; automotive tires

(G-14726)
ISONETIC INC
28408 Vashon Hwy Sw (98070-8850)
PHONE..................................800 670-8871
Bobby Kandaswamy, *CEO*
Diana Neuman, *COO*
EMP: 2
SALES (est): 71.1K **Privately Held**
SIC: 7372 8748 7389 Prepackaged software; systems engineering consultant, ex. computer or professional;

(G-14727)
KING COUNTY WASTEWATER TRTMNT
9615 Sw 171st St (98070-4964)
PHONE..................................206 463-0102
Greg Burnham, *Principal*
EMP: 2 EST: 2007
SQ FT: 240
SALES (est): 119.9K **Privately Held**
SIC: 3589 Sewage & water treatment equipment

(G-14728)
KURT TIMMERMEISTER
Also Called: Kurtwood Farms
18409 Beall Rd Sw (98070-5313)
PHONE..................................206 696-0989
Kurt Wood, *President*
EMP: 7
SALES (est): 489.7K **Privately Held**
SIC: 2022 Natural cheese

(G-14729)
KURT TIMMERMEISTER
Also Called: Kurtwood Farms
18409 Beall Rd Sw (98070-5313)
PHONE..................................206 696-0989
Kurt Timmermeister, *Owner*
EMP: 5
SALES (est): 330K **Privately Held**
SIC: 5154 2022 Cattle; processed cheese

(G-14730)
LIGHTMARK PRESS
20729 87th Ave Sw (98070-6223)
P.O. Box 13215, Burton (98013-0215)
PHONE..................................206 463-0831
EMP: 2
SALES (est): 124.7K **Privately Held**
SIC: 2741 Miscellaneous publishing

(G-14731)
M M ENTERPRISES
Also Called: Vashon Island Technology
17635 Vashon Hwy Sw (98070-4682)
P.O. Box 1242 (98070-1242)
PHONE..................................206 463-1927
Matthew Mosteller, *Owner*
EMP: 5
SALES (est): 400K **Privately Held**
SIC: 3571 7378 Electronic computers; computer maintenance & repair

(G-14732)
M SQUARED MANUFACTURING LLC
16622 86th Pl Sw (98070-4309)
P.O. Box 93, Port Orchard (98366-0093)
PHONE..................................206 380-0233
EMP: 2 EST: 2011
SALES (est): 144.9K **Privately Held**
SIC: 3999 Manufacturing industries

(G-14733)
MAURY HILL FARM ENTERPRISES
5912 Sw Point Robinson Rd (98070-7340)
PHONE..................................206 463-6193
Harley Miedema, *Owner*
EMP: 3
SALES (est): 300K **Privately Held**
SIC: 5148 3589 Fresh fruits & vegetables; water treatment equipment, industrial

(G-14734)
MEADOW CREATURE LLC
18850 103rd Ave Sw (98070-5250)
P.O. Box 746 (98070-0746)
PHONE..................................360 329-2250
Bob Powell, *Principal*
EMP: 6 EST: 2010
SALES (est): 567.7K **Privately Held**
SIC: 3423 Hand & edge tools

(G-14735)
MEAT AND NOODLE
20312 Vashon Hwy Sw (98070-6049)
PHONE..................................206 408-7650
EMP: 4 EST: 2014
SALES (est): 175.9K **Privately Held**
SIC: 2098 Noodles (e.g. egg, plain & water), dry

(G-14736)
NICKOLAY PHILIP AND WENDY LLC
Also Called: Virtual Professional Audio
26817 94th Ave Sw (98070-8644)
PHONE..................................206 463-7997
Philip Nickolay,
EMP: 2
SALES (est): 235.9K **Privately Held**
SIC: 3651 Audio electronic systems

(G-14737)
NIELSENS GRAPHIC SERVICE INC
19923 Robinwood Sw (98070-4052)
P.O. Box Q (98070-0379)
PHONE..................................206 463-2430
Jan Nielsens, *President*
EMP: 10
SALES (est): 929.7K **Privately Held**
SIC: 2752 Commercial printing, lithographic

(G-14738)
NORTHWEST SPORTS
117520 Vashon Hwy Sw (98070)
P.O. Box 2298 (98070-2298)
PHONE..................................206 463-5906
David Page, *Principal*
EMP: 2
SALES (est): 130K **Privately Held**
SIC: 5651 3131 Family clothing stores; footwear cut stock

(G-14739)
OLYMPIC INSTRUMENTS INC
16901 Westside Hwy Sw (98070-4405)
PHONE..................................206 463-3604
Kevin Britz, *President*
EMP: 10 EST: 1946
SQ FT: 15,000
SALES (est): 2.1MM **Privately Held**
WEB: www.olympicinstruments.com
SIC: 3829 3499 Measuring & controlling devices; marine horns, compressed air or steam

(G-14740)
PALOUSE WINERY
12431 Vashon Hwy Sw (98070-3303)
PHONE..................................206 567-4994
Linda Kirkish, *President*
George Kirkish, *Owner*
EMP: 2
SALES (est): 136.5K **Privately Held**
SIC: 2084 Wines

(G-14741)
SEATTLE DISTILLING COMPANY
19429 Vashon Hwy Sw (98070-6052)
P.O. Box 2811 (98070-2811)
PHONE..................................206 463-0830
Ishan Dillon, *CEO*
John Joyce, *Vice Pres*
Paco Joyce, *Software Engr*
EMP: 3 EST: 2011
SALES (est): 284.7K **Privately Held**
SIC: 2085 Distilled & blended liquors

(G-14742)
SHELLBACK LTD
6702 Sw 240th St (98070-7244)
PHONE..................................206 463-9054
Thomas Northington, *Owner*
EMP: 2
SALES (est): 150K **Privately Held**
WEB: www.shellbackltd.com
SIC: 2431 Exterior & ornamental woodwork & trim

(G-14743)
SOLIS ORTUS
13309 Sw 270th St (98070-8202)
PHONE..................................206 463-6245
EMP: 2 EST: 2009
SALES (est): 142K **Privately Held**
SIC: 2499 Decorative wood & woodwork

(G-14744)
SOUND PUBLISHING INC
Also Called: Vashon-Mury Island Beachcomber
17141 Vashon Hwy Sw Ste B (98070-4603)
P.O. Box 447 (98070-0447)
PHONE..................................206 463-9195
Daralyn Anderson, *Branch Mgr*
EMP: 10 **Privately Held**
WEB: www.soundpublishing.com
SIC: 2711 2731 Newspapers: publishing only, not printed on site; book publishing
HQ: Sound Publishing, Inc.
  11323 Commando Rd W Main
  Everett WA 98204
  360 394-5800

(G-14745)
SUMMIT BIOFUELS LLC
Also Called: Berry Beautiful
20720 111th Ave Sw (98070-6436)
PHONE..................................206 291-6402
Robert Kommer,
EMP: 2
SALES (est): 223.9K **Privately Held**
SIC: 2869 Fuels

(G-14746)
VASHON TRADING CO LLC
25826 75th Ave Sw (98070-8522)
P.O. Box 2538 (98070-2538)
PHONE..................................206 463-2278
Billie Hendrix, *Mng Member*
Liz Hendrix Maier, *Mng Member*
EMP: 2
SQ FT: 1,500
SALES (est): 136.1K **Privately Held**
WEB: www.vashontrading.com
SIC: 3221 Food containers, glass

Vaughn
Pierce County

(G-14747)
KEY PENINSULA NEWS
17010 S Vaughn Rd Kp N (98394-9705)
P.O. Box 3 (98394-0003)
PHONE..................253 884-4699
Edie Morgan, *Principal*
EMP: 4 **EST:** 2001
SALES (est): 235.2K **Privately Held**
SIC: 2711 Commercial printing & newspaper publishing combined

Veradale
Spokane County

(G-14748)
ANBO MFG INC
Also Called: Anbo Manufacturing
3602 S Adams Rd (99037-9172)
PHONE..................509 684-6559
Chris Newman, *President*
Barbara Anderson, *Vice Pres*
Sue Newman, *Vice Pres*
EMP: 17 **EST:** 1999
SALES: 3.3MM **Privately Held**
WEB: www.anbomanufacturing.com
SIC: 3531 Construction machinery

(G-14749)
C J WARREN & SONS WELL DRLG
Also Called: CJ Warren & Son Drilling
3005 S Best Rd (99037-9399)
PHONE..................509 924-3872
Charles J Warren, *Owner*
EMP: 2
SALES (est): 156.7K **Privately Held**
SIC: 1381 1781 Drilling oil & gas wells; water well drilling

(G-14750)
ROCKY MOUNTAIN CHOCOLATE FCTRY
1330 N Argonne (99037)
PHONE..................509 927-7623
Rachelle Blackwell, *Principal*
EMP: 5
SALES (est): 211.5K **Privately Held**
SIC: 5441 2066 Candy; chocolate candy, solid

(G-14751)
SOFTWARE INGENUITY LLC
4923 S Bellaire Ln (99037-8220)
PHONE..................509 924-0093
H Marc Lewis, *Principal*
EMP: 2
SALES (est): 125K **Privately Held**
SIC: 7372 Business oriented computer software

Waitsburg
Walla Walla County

(G-14752)
COLUBIA AG & MFG
421 Fields Gulch (99361-9643)
PHONE..................509 382-4849
EMP: 2 **EST:** 2008
SALES (est): 75K **Privately Held**
SIC: 3999 Mfg Misc Products

(G-14753)
CRYSTAL BLUE SCREEN PRINTING
Also Called: Blue Crystal Signs Screen Prtg
505 Willard St (99361-9743)
P.O. Box 816 (99361-0816)
PHONE..................509 337-8201
Ken Cole Sr, *President*
Elizabeth Cole, *Corp Secy*
EMP: 2
SALES: 53.8K **Privately Held**
SIC: 5699 2396 Uniforms & work clothing; screen printing on fabric articles

(G-14754)
FERGUSON - GAGNON INDUSTRIES
123 Gallaher Rd (99361-8756)
PHONE..................509 337-6207
Ricky D Ferguson, *Principal*
EMP: 2
SALES (est): 93.6K **Privately Held**
SIC: 3999 Manufacturing industries

(G-14755)
LAHT NEPPUR VENTURES INC (PA)
444 Preston Ave (99361)
PHONE..................509 337-6261
Lee Irwin, *President*
Katie Ruppenthal, *Manager*
EMP: 5
SALES (est): 401.6K **Privately Held**
SIC: 2082 5181 Beer (alcoholic beverage); beer & other fermented malt liquors

(G-14756)
MURPHY NATHANIAL
Also Called: Mary's
184 Murphy St (99361-9796)
PHONE..................509 386-0727
Nathanial Murphy, *Owner*
EMP: 3
SALES (est): 160.2K **Privately Held**
SIC: 2064 Candy & other confectionery products

(G-14757)
TIMES
139 Main St (99361-9703)
P.O. Box 97 (99361-0097)
PHONE..................509 337-6631
Loyal P Baker, *Owner*
Kathy Baker, *Co-Owner*
EMP: 2 **EST:** 1878
SQ FT: 2,500
SALES (est): 225K **Privately Held**
WEB: www.timemagazine.com
SIC: 2711 2752 Newspapers: publishing only, not printed on site; commercial printing, offset

(G-14758)
TOUCHET VALLEY PUBLISHING
139 Main St (99361-9703)
P.O. Box 97 (99361-0097)
PHONE..................509 337-6631
Kenneth S Graham, *Administration*
EMP: 2 **EST:** 2014
SALES (est): 126.4K **Privately Held**
SIC: 2741 Miscellaneous publishing

Walla Walla
Walla Walla County

(G-14759)
ACUFAB INC
455 A St (99362-7403)
PHONE..................509 525-3833
Dwight Seeffanson, *Vice Pres*
EMP: 2
SQ FT: 6,400
SALES: 250K **Privately Held**
WEB: www.acufab.com
SIC: 1791 3446 3444 3443 Structural steel erection; architectural metalwork; sheet metalwork; fabricated plate work (boiler shop); fabricated structural metal

(G-14760)
ADAMANT CELLARS
525 E Cessna Ave (99362-7412)
PHONE..................509 529-4161
Devin Stinger, *Owner*
EMP: 7
SALES (est): 340K **Privately Held**
SIC: 2084 Wines

(G-14761)
AMAVI CELLARS
3796 Peppers Bridge Rd (99362-7007)
PHONE..................509 525-3541
Eric McKibben, *Partner*
Jean-Francois Pellet, *Partner*
Ray Goff, *Mng Member*
▲ **EMP:** 5
SALES (est): 391.2K **Privately Held**
WEB: www.amavicellars.com
SIC: 2084 Wines

(G-14762)
AMCOR RIGID PACKAGING USA LLC
1041 N 15th Ave (99362-1000)
PHONE..................509 525-0230
EMP: 58 **Privately Held**
SIC: 3085 Plastics bottles
HQ: Amcor Rigid Packaging Usa, Llc
40600 Ann Arbor Rd E # 201
Plymouth MI 48170

(G-14763)
ANATOLIY SEMENKO
Also Called: Blaze To Blizzard Htg & Coolg
502 County Road 448 (99362-7160)
PHONE..................509 525-4486
Anatoliy Semenko, *Owner*
EMP: 3
SALES (est): 175K **Privately Held**
SIC: 3585 Refrigeration & heating equipment

(G-14764)
ANNIES TRUNK LLC
120 N Roosevelt St (99362-2535)
PHONE..................509 529-4395
Susan Laabs, *Principal*
EMP: 3
SALES (est): 179.8K **Privately Held**
SIC: 3161 Trunks

(G-14765)
ARDOR CELLARS
202 E Main St (99362-2002)
PHONE..................509 876-8086
Emma Northrop Kubrock, *Principal*
EMP: 4
SALES (est): 156.1K **Privately Held**
SIC: 2084 Wines

(G-14766)
B & B FOODS INC (PA)
499 N Wilbur Ave (99362-2253)
PHONE..................906 493-6962
William L Hepler, *Principal*
EMP: 4 **EST:** 2012
SALES (est): 502.8K **Privately Held**
SIC: 2099 Food preparations

(G-14767)
BALBOA WINERY
Also Called: Eidolon Winery
4169 Peppers Bridge Rd (99362-7135)
PHONE..................509 529-0461
Thomas A Glase, *Owner*
▲ **EMP:** 6
SALES: 1MM **Privately Held**
SIC: 5921 2084 Wine; wines

(G-14768)
BASEL CELLARS ESTATE WINERY
2901 Old Milton Hwy (99362-7156)
PHONE..................509 522-0200
Ryan Sams, *General Mgr*
Becky Brammer, *Manager*
Kennady Funk, *Manager*
▲ **EMP:** 2
SALES (est): 239.2K **Privately Held**
WEB: www.baselcellars.com
SIC: 2084 Wines

(G-14769)
BERGHAN VINEYEARDS
1722 Evergreen St (99362-2532)
PHONE..................509 301-9229
Mike Berghan, *Owner*
EMP: 2 **EST:** 2005
SALES (est): 88.8K **Privately Held**
SIC: 2084 Wines

(G-14770)
BIELER AND SMITH LLC
820 Mill Creek Rd (99362-8415)
PHONE..................509 526-5230
S Charles Biecer, *Manager*
EMP: 2
SALES (est): 84K **Privately Held**
SIC: 2084 Wines

(G-14771)
BIG HOUSE BREWING INC
Also Called: Mill Creek Brew Pub
11 S Palouse St (99362-1925)
PHONE..................509 522-2440
Gary D Johnson, *President*
EMP: 20
SALES (est): 2.5MM **Privately Held**
WEB: www.millcreek-brewpub.com
SIC: 2082 5812 Beer (alcoholic beverage); eating places

(G-14772)
BLUELINE EQUIPMENT CO LLC
Also Called: Kubota Authorized Dealer
902 W Rose St (99362-1766)
PHONE..................509 525-4550
Carroll Adams, *CEO*
EMP: 6
SALES (corp-wide): 18.9MM **Privately Held**
SIC: 3523 5083 Farm machinery & equipment; farm & garden machinery
HQ: Blueline Equipment Co., Llc
1605 E Mead Ave
Yakima WA 98903
509 248-8411

(G-14773)
BONTZU CELLARS
1460 F St (99362-7421)
PHONE..................425 205-3482
EMP: 7
SALES (est): 442.6K **Privately Held**
SIC: 2084 Wines

(G-14774)
BRIGHT CANDIES
Also Called: Bright's Candies & Gifts
11 E Main St (99362-1921)
PHONE..................509 525-5533
Paul Jenes, *Owner*
EMP: 5
SALES (est): 388.1K **Privately Held**
WEB: www.brightscandies.com
SIC: 2064 5441 2096 2066 Candy & other confectionery products; candy; potato chips & similar snacks; chocolate & cocoa products

(G-14775)
BUILDERS FIRSTSOURCE INC
115 N 11th Ave (99362-1759)
PHONE..................509 525-4008
Eric Palmer, *General Mgr*
EMP: 10
SALES (corp-wide): 7.7B **Publicly Held**
WEB: www.hopelumber.com
SIC: 2431 Doors & door parts & trim, wood
PA: Builders Firstsource, Inc.
2001 Bryan St Ste 1600
Dallas TX 75201
214 880-3500

(G-14776)
BUTY WINERY
535 E Cessna Ave (99362-7412)
PHONE..................509 527-0901
Caleb Foster, *Owner*
▲ **EMP:** 4
SQ FT: 7,000
SALES (est): 230K **Privately Held**
WEB: www.butywinery.com
SIC: 2084 Wines

(G-14777)
CADARETTA
315 E Main St (99362-2095)
PHONE..................509 525-1352
▲ **EMP:** 3
SALES (est): 180.9K **Privately Held**
SIC: 2084 Wines

(G-14778)
CANOE RIDGE VINEYARD LLC (PA)
1102 W Cherry St (99362-1746)
PHONE..................509 527-0885
Lita Holmes, *Manager*
Raymond Chadwick,
Sue Bridwell, *Admin Asst*
▲ **EMP:** 15
SQ FT: 21,000

GEOGRAPHIC SECTION

Walla Walla - Walla Walla County (G-14810)

SALES (est): 1.4MM **Privately Held**
WEB: www.canoeridgevineyard.com
SIC: 2084 5182 Wines; wine

(G-14779)
CASTILLO DE FELICIANA
331 Reserve Way (99362-0700)
PHONE..................................541 558-3656
Samuel Castillo, *Mng Member*
Deborah Castillo,
▲ EMP: 6
SALES (est): 646.9K **Privately Held**
SIC: 2084 Wines

(G-14780)
CAVU CELLARS
175 E Aeronca Ave (99362-7418)
PHONE..................................509 540-6352
Jim Waite, *Principal*
EMP: 7 EST: 2009
SALES (est): 573.6K **Privately Held**
SIC: 2084 Wines

(G-14781)
CAYUSE VINEYARDS
17 E Main St (99362-1921)
P.O. Box 1602 (99362-0030)
PHONE..................................509 526-0686
Christopher Baron, *CEO*
Jeanie Inglis, *Manager*
▲ EMP: 3 EST: 1997
SALES (est): 373.3K **Privately Held**
SIC: 2084 Wines

(G-14782)
CHABRE BROS
875 E Tietan St (99362-4530)
PHONE..................................509 629-0342
Kevin Chabre, *Partner*
Travis Chabre, *Partner*
EMP: 2
SALES (est): 96.2K **Privately Held**
SIC: 3952 Lead pencils & art goods

(G-14783)
CHARLES SMITH VINEYARDS LLC
35 S Spokane St (99362-1930)
PHONE..................................509 526-5230
Dana Dibble, *Administration*
EMP: 2
SALES (est): 101.1K **Privately Held**
SIC: 2084 Wines

(G-14784)
CHATEAU ROLLAT WINERY LLC
1793 J B George Rd (99362-7132)
PHONE..................................509 529-4511
Bowin M Lindglen, *Principal*
EMP: 4
SALES (est): 148K **Privately Held**
SIC: 2084 Wines

(G-14785)
CLAY IN MOTION INC
959 Reser Rd (99362-9070)
PHONE..................................509 529-6146
Bob Neher, *President*
Corina Neher, *Vice Pres*
EMP: 10
SALES: 700K **Privately Held**
WEB: www.clayinmotion.com
SIC: 3269 3843 Pottery cooking & kitchen articles; dental equipment & supplies

(G-14786)
CLIFFSTAR LLC
1164 Dell Ave (99362-1053)
PHONE..................................509 522-8608
Shannon McFall, *Manager*
EMP: 60
SALES (corp-wide): 242.1K **Privately Held**
SIC: 2037 2086 Fruit juices; bottled & canned soft drinks
HQ: Cliffstar Llc
1 Cliffstar Dr
Dunkirk NY 14048
716 366-6100

(G-14787)
COCA COLA BOTTLING CO
Also Called: Coca-Cola
155 Avery St (99362-1669)
P.O. Box 794 (99362-0250)
PHONE..................................509 529-0753
Richard R Pelo, *President*
John E Pelo, *Vice Pres*
Dave Lemen, *Engineer*
Andy Colpitts, *Cust Mgr*
Daniel Hieronymus, *Sales Staff*
EMP: 40
SQ FT: 30,000
SALES: 8.5MM **Privately Held**
SIC: 2086 Bottled & canned soft drinks

(G-14788)
COFFEY COMMUNICATIONS INC (PA)
1505 Business One Cir (99362-9421)
PHONE..................................509 525-0101
Alan Coffey, *CEO*
Barbra Coffey, *Ch of Bd*
Jane Coffey, *President*
Caroline Lebedoff, *Editor*
James John, *CFO*
EMP: 145 EST: 1975
SQ FT: 17,000
SALES (est): 15.3MM **Privately Held**
WEB: www.betterhealth.net
SIC: 2731 2741 2721 Books: publishing only; catalogs: publishing only, not printed on site; shopping news: publishing & printing; periodicals

(G-14789)
COLOR PRESS PUBLISHING INC
1425 W Rose St (99362-1645)
P.O. Box 2377, Fallbrook CA (92088-2377)
PHONE..................................509 525-6030
Rob Ferguson, *President*
Daniel F Houghton, *Chairman*
Jim Barrett, *Treasurer*
EMP: 34
SALES (est): 271.4K **Privately Held**
WEB: www.colorpress.com
SIC: 2754 2752 Commercial printing, gravure; commercial printing, lithographic
PA: Hart Research Center
504 E Alvarado St Ste 105
Fallbrook CA 92028

(G-14790)
CORLISS ESTATES
511 N 2nd Ave (99362-1810)
PHONE..................................509 526-4400
Michael J Corliss, *Owner*
▲ EMP: 4
SALES (est): 220K **Privately Held**
SIC: 2084 Wines

(G-14791)
COUGAR HILLS LLC (PA)
Also Called: Cougar Crest Winery
50 Frenchtown Rd (99362-7266)
PHONE..................................509 529-5980
Deborah K Hansen,
EMP: 14
SQ FT: 5,000
SALES: 2.1MM **Privately Held**
WEB: www.cougarcrestwinery.com
SIC: 2084 5182 Wines; wine & distilled beverages

(G-14792)
CRYSTAL CLEAR ICE CO
1005 W Rose St (99362-1767)
PHONE..................................509 525-1042
Walter Cooper, *President*
EMP: 5
SALES (est): 420K **Privately Held**
SIC: 2097 5999 Manufactured ice; ice

(G-14793)
DAVIDS AQUACUT & BUILDERS
3328 E Isaacs Ave (99362-8017)
PHONE..................................509 527-8700
David Aquacut, *Owner*
EMP: 4
SALES: 160K **Privately Held**
SIC: 3441 Fabricated structural metal

(G-14794)
DEBROECK SOLID SURFACE INC
1401 W Pine St (99362-9497)
PHONE..................................509 525-1349
Mark Debroeck, *President*
EMP: 3
SALES (est): 211.6K **Privately Held**
SIC: 3281 Granite, cut & shaped

(G-14795)
DEPARTMENT CRRCTONS WASH STATE
Also Called: Division Correctional Inds
1313 N 13th Ave (99362-8817)
PHONE..................................509 526-6375
Otto Krouse, *Principal*
Jim Cerna, *Executive*
EMP: 435 **Privately Held**
WEB: www.doc1.wa.gov
SIC: 8322 9223 3993 3429 Offender self-help agency; correctional institutions; ; signs & advertising specialties; manufactured hardware (general); men's & boys' work clothing
HQ: Department Of Corrections, Washington State
7345 Linderson Way Sw
Tumwater WA 98501

(G-14796)
DEVONA LLC
1334 School Ave (99362-9345)
P.O. Box 1555 (99362-0029)
PHONE..................................509 520-2524
Molly Abbott, *Mng Member*
John Abbott,
EMP: 8 EST: 2015
SALES (est): 686.8K **Privately Held**
SIC: 2084 Wines

(G-14797)
DLA DOCUMENT SERVICES
201 N 3rd Ave (99362-1876)
PHONE..................................509 527-7231
Tom Holt, *Manager*
EMP: 2 **Publicly Held**
SIC: 2752 9711 Commercial printing, lithographic; national security
HQ: Dla Document Services
5450 Carlisle Pike Bldg 9
Mechanicsburg PA 17050
717 605-2362

(G-14798)
DOUBLEBACK
229 E Main St (99362-2001)
P.O. Box 518 (99362-0220)
PHONE..................................509 525-3334
Jordan Hostetter, *Opers Staff*
Anne Wilcox, *Sales Dir*
Emily Beamer, *Manager*
EMP: 2
SALES (est): 200.1K **Privately Held**
SIC: 2084 Wines

(G-14799)
DUNHAM CELLARS LLC
150 E Boeing Ave (99362-7400)
PHONE..................................509 529-4685
John Blair, *General Mgr*
Jacquie Roach, *Controller*
Barbara Mosher, *Office Mgr*
Dominie Heiser, *Manager*
Michael Dunham,
▲ EMP: 9 EST: 1999
SQ FT: 5,000
SALES (est): 1MM **Privately Held**
WEB: www.dunhamcellars.com
SIC: 2084 Wines

(G-14800)
DUSTED VALLEY
1248 Old Milton Hwy (99362-8174)
PHONE..................................509 525-1337
Chad Johnson, *Principal*
▲ EMP: 9
SALES (est): 811.3K **Privately Held**
SIC: 2084 Wines

(G-14801)
ENCHANTED CELLARS
8052 Old Highway 12 (99362-6203)
PHONE..................................503 970-2244
EMP: 2

SALES (est): 64.4K **Privately Held**
SIC: 2084 Wines, brandy & brandy spirits

(G-14802)
ETCHINGS WALLA WALLA
54 W Rees Ave (99362-1155)
PHONE..................................509 301-3300
Thad Sirmon, *Principal*
EMP: 2
SALES (est): 169.9K **Privately Held**
SIC: 2499 Trophy bases, wood

(G-14803)
EUCON CORPORATION
1326 Dell Ave (99362-1023)
PHONE..................................509 529-6400
Brian Deatley, *Branch Mgr*
EMP: 10
SALES (corp-wide): 83.3MM **Privately Held**
SIC: 3272 Concrete products
PA: Eucon Corporation
4201 Snake River Ave
Lewiston ID 83501
509 533-1615

(G-14804)
FIGGINS FAMILY WINE ESTATES
1875 Foothills Ln (99362-9052)
PHONE..................................509 525-1428
Chris Figgins, *Partner*
▲ EMP: 2
SALES (est): 231.8K **Privately Held**
SIC: 2084 Wines

(G-14805)
FIVE STAR CELLARS INC
840 C St (99362-7423)
PHONE..................................509 527-8400
Sandra Huse, *President*
David Huse, *President*
EMP: 2
SALES (est): 201.6K **Privately Held**
WEB: www.fivestarcellars.com
SIC: 2084 Wines

(G-14806)
FLYING TROUT WINES LLC
1606 Evergreen St (99362-2527)
PHONE..................................509 520-7701
Ashley Trout, *Principal*
EMP: 4
SALES (est): 158.1K **Privately Held**
SIC: 2084 Wines

(G-14807)
FORGERON CELLARS LLC
33 W Birch St (99362-3004)
PHONE..................................509 522-9463
Jeremy Baker, *Mng Member*
Marie Gilla, *Mng Member*
▲ EMP: 8
SALES (est): 400.4K **Privately Held**
WEB: www.forgeroncellars.com
SIC: 2084 Wines; wine; wine

(G-14808)
FORT WALLA WALLA CELLARS LLC
1383 Barleen Dr (99362-9233)
PHONE..................................509 520-1095
James K Moyer,
Clifford Kontos,
EMP: 2
SALES (est): 128.8K **Privately Held**
SIC: 2084 Wines

(G-14809)
FOUNDRY VINEYARDS LLC
1111 Abadie St (99362-1601)
PHONE..................................509 529-0736
Tammie Buchanan, *Opers Staff*
Lisa Anderson, *Sales Staff*
EMP: 7
SALES (est): 592.5K **Privately Held**
SIC: 2084 Wines

(G-14810)
FRED J KIMBALL MACHINE SHOP
2902 Lower Waitsburg Rd (99362-8568)
PHONE..................................509 529-5339
EMP: 3
SALES (est): 206.7K **Privately Held**
SIC: 3599 Mfg Industrial Machinery

Walla Walla - Walla Walla County (G-14811) **GEOGRAPHIC SECTION**

(G-14811)
GIFFORD HIRLINGER WINERY
1450 Stateline Rd (99362-8180)
PHONE..................................509 301-9229
Mike Berghan, *Principal*
EMP: 2
SALES (est): 175.9K Privately Held
SIC: 2084 Wines

(G-14812)
GINO CUNEO CELLARS LLC
18 N 2nd Ave (99362-1802)
PHONE..................................509 876-4738
Gino Cuneo, *Administration*
EMP: 4
SALES (est): 181.1K Privately Held
SIC: 2084 Wines

(G-14813)
GLENCORRIE
8052 Old Highway 12 (99362-6203)
PHONE..................................509 525-2585
EMP: 5
SALES (est): 179.4K Privately Held
SIC: 2084 Mfg Wines/Brandy/Spirits

(G-14814)
GRAB ON GRIPS LLC
350 E Beech Ave (99362-7416)
PHONE..................................509 529-9800
Mike Tillay,
▲ EMP: 12
SQ FT: 25,000
SALES (est): 2.1MM Privately Held
WEB: www.grabongrips.com
SIC: 3069 3086 Grips or handles, rubber; plastics foam products

(G-14815)
GRAMERCY CELLARS
635 N 13th Ave (99362-1769)
PHONE..................................509 876-2427
Greg Harrington, *Owner*
▲ EMP: 11
SALES (est): 1.5MM Privately Held
SIC: 2084 Wines

(G-14816)
GRAPE VISIONS LLC
1248 Old Milton Hwy (99362-8174)
PHONE..................................509 525-1337
Braunel Corey,
EMP: 20 EST: 2010
SALES (est): 1.8MM Privately Held
SIC: 2084 Wines

(G-14817)
GUNPOWDER CREEK LLC
950 Boyer Ave (99362-2314)
PHONE..................................860 502-9202
Caleb Foster, *Principal*
EMP: 2 EST: 2016
SALES (est): 99K Privately Held
SIC: 2892 Gunpowder

(G-14818)
HANATORO WINERY
1793 J B George Rd (99362-7132)
PHONE..................................404 312-5891
Karen Thomson, *General Mgr*
EMP: 4 EST: 2016
SALES (est): 122.1K Privately Held
SIC: 2084 Wines

(G-14819)
HARD ROCK MACHINE WORKS INC
2878 Melrose St (99362-8903)
PHONE..................................509 529-9833
Dan Townsend, *President*
David Young, *Vice Pres*
Kim Townsend, *Admin Sec*
EMP: 4
SQ FT: 6,000
SALES: 500K Privately Held
WEB: www.hardrockhouse.com
SIC: 3599 7699 Machine shop, jobbing & repair; industrial machinery & equipment repair

(G-14820)
HAROLDS POWER VAC INC
Also Called: Harolds Furnace Cleaning
520 Russet Rd (99362-8257)
PHONE..................................509 529-2088
Harold Rahn, *President*
Jeanine Rahn, *Corp Secy*
Dave Rahn, *Vice Pres*
EMP: 3 EST: 1969
SALES: 400K Privately Held
WEB: www.haroldspowervac.com
SIC: 1711 3589 Heating systems repair & maintenance; vacuum cleaners & sweepers, electric: industrial

(G-14821)
IMAGESMART SIGN COMPANY LLC
1365 Dalles Military Rd B (99362-4300)
PHONE..................................509 525-4343
Mark Snow, *President*
Bruce M Curnuck,
EMP: 4
SALES (est): 463.6K Privately Held
WEB: www.imagesmartcreative.com
SIC: 7336 3993 Commercial art & graphic design; signs & advertising specialties

(G-14822)
INGIO/VINBALANCE LLC
6 E Alder St Ste 224 (99362-1938)
PHONE..................................509 522-1621
EMP: 2
SALES (est): 116.9K Privately Held
SIC: 7372 Prepackaged software

(G-14823)
INLAND SAXUM PRINTING LLC
10 N 7th Ave (99362-1865)
P.O. Box 493 (99362-0014)
PHONE..................................509 525-0467
Gail Lane,
EMP: 7
SALES (est): 774.9K Privately Held
SIC: 2752 7334 7336 Commercial printing, offset; photocopying & duplicating services; graphic arts & related design

(G-14824)
INTERSTATE CONCRETE AND ASP CO
Also Called: American Rock Products
1326 Dell Ave (99362-1023)
PHONE..................................509 529-6400
EMP: 2
SALES (corp-wide): 30.6B Privately Held
SIC: 3273 Ready-mixed concrete
HQ: Interstate Concrete And Asphalt Company
8849 W Wyoming Ave
Rathdrum ID 83858
208 765-1144

(G-14825)
ISAACS & ASSOCIATES INC
3380 Isaacs Ave (99362-8017)
PHONE..................................509 529-2286
Scott Morasch, *President*
Kim L Morasch, *Vice Pres*
▲ EMP: 5
SQ FT: 1,450
SALES (est): 1.3MM Privately Held
WEB: www.isaacstech.com
SIC: 5083 3523 Irrigation equipment; irrigation equipment, self-propelled

(G-14826)
ISENHOWER CELLARS
3471 Pranger Rd (99362-7307)
PHONE..................................509 526-7896
Denise Isenhower, *Co-Owner*
Brett Isenhower, *Co-Owner*
▲ EMP: 2
SALES (est): 141.7K Privately Held
WEB: www.isenhowercellars.com
SIC: 2084 Wines

(G-14827)
JB GEORGE LLC
2901 Old Milton Hwy (99362-7156)
PHONE..................................509 522-0200
Gregory Basel, *Principal*
EMP: 7 EST: 2008
SALES (est): 419.5K Privately Held
SIC: 2084 Wines, brandy & brandy spirits

(G-14828)
JEFFREY A JOHNSON
Also Called: Prosthetic & Orthotic Services
919 W Main St (99362-2746)
P.O. Box 662 (99362-0016)
PHONE..................................509 525-8322
Darryl Hogan, *Owner*
Greta Johnson, *Co-Owner*
EMP: 6
SQ FT: 1,600
SALES (est): 531.4K Privately Held
WEB: www.prostheticorthoticservices.com
SIC: 3842 Limbs, artificial; braces, orthopedic

(G-14829)
JLC WINERY
16 N 2nd Ave (99362-1802)
P.O. Box 1093 (99362-0290)
PHONE..................................509 529-1398
EMP: 2
SALES (est): 62.3K Privately Held
SIC: 2084 Wines, brandy & brandy spirits

(G-14830)
K VINTNERS LLC (PA)
Also Called: Charles Smith Wines
820 Mill Creek Rd (99362-8415)
PHONE..................................509 526-5230
David Lawrence, *COO*
Chris Langan, *Sales Staff*
Jackie Hoover, *Marketing Staff*
Charles Smith, *Mng Member*
Michelle McDermott, *Manager*
▲ EMP: 5
SQ FT: 900
SALES: 19.5MM Privately Held
WEB: www.kvintners.com
SIC: 2084 Wines

(G-14831)
K-W CELLARS
1753 Old Milton Hwy (99362-7103)
PHONE..................................509 525-6222
Robert Kinion, *Manager*
EMP: 4
SALES (est): 173.9K Privately Held
SIC: 2084 Wines

(G-14832)
KEY TECHNOLOGY
150 Avery St (99362-4703)
PHONE..................................509 529-2161
EMP: 3
SALES (est): 337.3K
SALES (corp-wide): 118.2MM Publicly Held
SIC: 3827 Mfg Optical Instruments/Lenses
PA: Key Technology, Inc.
150 Avery St
Walla Walla WA 99362
509 529-2161

(G-14833)
KEY TECHNOLOGY INC (DH)
150 Avery St (99362-4703)
PHONE..................................509 529-2161
Michael J Kachmer, *CEO*
John J Ehren, *President*
Craig Reuther, *CFO*
Jeffrey T Siegal, *VP Finance*
◆ EMP: 277
SQ FT: 173,000
SALES (est): 139.9MM
SALES (corp-wide): 873MM Privately Held
WEB: www.foodsorter.com
SIC: 3556 2834 Food products machinery; pharmaceutical preparations

(G-14834)
KEY TECHNOLOGY INC
Symetix
150 Avery St (99362-4703)
PHONE..................................509 529-2161
Claude Key, *Branch Mgr*
EMP: 5
SALES (corp-wide): 873MM Privately Held
WEB: www.foodsorter.com
SIC: 3556 5499 Food products machinery; dietetic foods
HQ: Key Technology, Inc.
150 Avery St
Walla Walla WA 99362
509 529-2161

(G-14835)
LAZER CARTRIDGES PLUS LLC
31 Looking Glass Rd (99362-8645)
P.O. Box 2643 (99362-0333)
PHONE..................................509 529-0200
Dixie Liening,
Nathan Liening,
EMP: 3 EST: 1998
SALES: 1.8MM Privately Held
WEB: www.lazercartridges.com
SIC: 3955 5112 Print cartridges for laser & other computer printers; stationery & office supplies

(G-14836)
LEIGH JAMES CELLARS LLC
425 B St (99362-2265)
P.O. Box 1093 (99362-0290)
PHONE..................................509 529-1398
Lynne A Chamberlain, *Manager*
EMP: 4
SALES (est): 288.3K Privately Held
SIC: 3421 Table & food cutlery, including butchers'

(G-14837)
LEONETTI CELLAR
1875 Foothills Ln (99362-9052)
PHONE..................................509 525-1670
Gary Figgins,
Nancy Figgins,
▲ EMP: 12
SALES (est): 1.7MM Privately Held
SIC: 2084 Wine cellars, bonded: engaged in blending wines; wines

(G-14838)
LOCATI CELLARS LLC
6 W Rose St Ste 102 (99362-1845)
P.O. Box 327 (99362-0009)
PHONE..................................509 529-5871
Michael Locati, *Sales Staff*
Pearl Crain, *Manager*
Penne Locati,
Heath Snider,
EMP: 4
SALES (est): 286.4K Privately Held
SIC: 2084 5182 Wines; wine

(G-14839)
LOWDEN SCHOOLHOUSE CORPORATION
Also Called: L'Ecole No 41
41 Lowden School Rd (99362-6212)
P.O. Box 111, Lowden (99360-0111)
PHONE..................................509 525-0940
Martin L Clubb, *Principal*
Megan Clubb, *Principal*
▲ EMP: 4
SALES (est): 380.9K Privately Held
SIC: 2084 Wines

(G-14840)
MAISON BLEUE WINERY
20 N 2nd Ave (99362-1802)
PHONE..................................509 525-9084
Jon Meuret, *President*
EMP: 2 EST: 2013
SALES (est): 147.5K Privately Held
SIC: 2084 Wines

(G-14841)
MANI PEDI
17 Boyer Ave (99362-2066)
PHONE..................................509 522-6264
Cherish Gladden, *Principal*
EMP: 2
SALES (est): 170.9K Privately Held
SIC: 2844 Manicure preparations

(G-14842)
MARK THOMAS WOODWORKS
1946 Alco Ave (99362-4353)
PHONE..................................505 220-7560
Mark Thomas, *Principal*
EMP: 2
SALES (est): 64.7K Privately Held
SIC: 2431 Millwork

(G-14843)
MICHAEL L WHITE
Also Called: Advanced Sign Concepts
1491 Artesia St (99362-5000)
PHONE..................................509 526-6923
EMP: 2 EST: 1999

▲ = Import ▼ = Export
◆ = Import/Export

GEOGRAPHIC SECTION

Walla Walla - Walla Walla County (G-14875)

SALES: 100K **Privately Held**
SIC: 3993 Mfg Signs/Advertising Specialties

(G-14844)
MILL CREEK WOODWORKING INC
8153 Mill Creek Rd (99362-8493)
PHONE.................509 526-5660
Marcus Coldsmith, *Principal*
EMP: 2 EST: 2012
SALES (est): 126.4K **Privately Held**
SIC: 2431 Millwork

(G-14845)
MINNICK HILLS VINEYARD LL
2415 Middle Waitsburg Rd (99362-8564)
PHONE.................509 525-5076
Laura M Minnick, *Principal*
Laura Minnick, *Principal*
EMP: 2
SALES (est): 90.3K **Privately Held**
SIC: 2084 Wines

(G-14846)
MIRACLES VINTNERS LLC
2753 Vista Ln (99362-9248)
PHONE.................253 606-6202
Gary Brumfield, *Principal*
EMP: 2
SALES (est): 79.6K **Privately Held**
SIC: 2084 Wines

(G-14847)
MPM VINTNERS LLC
Also Called: Artifex Wine Company
1102 Dell Ave (99362-1053)
P.O. Box 2057 (99362-0949)
PHONE.................509 525-2469
Jean-Francois Pellet, *Mng Member*
Norm McKibben,
Rick Middleton,
EMP: 22 EST: 2006
SQ FT: 28,000
SALES (est): 800K **Privately Held**
SIC: 2084 5182 Wine cellars, bonded: engaged in blending wines; wine

(G-14848)
MTD PUBLISHING
1942 Gemstone Dr (99362-8212)
P.O. Box 2722 (99362-0335)
PHONE.................509 525-7289
EMP: 2 EST: 2008
SALES (est): 88K **Privately Held**
SIC: 2741 Misc Publishing

(G-14849)
NANO ARTS LLC
Also Called: Nano Lopez Studios
96 Frontage Rd (99362-8004)
PHONE.................509 525-8531
Scott Riley, *Production*
Adar Lommassen, *Office Mgr*
Bernardo Lopez, *Mng Member*
Mariya Roth,
▼ EMP: 49
SQ FT: 12,000
SALES: 2.8MM **Privately Held**
SIC: 3299 Architectural sculptures: gypsum, clay, papier mache, etc.

(G-14850)
NELSON IRRIGATION CORPORATION
Also Called: Walla Walla Sprinkler Comp
848 Airport Rd (99362-2271)
PHONE.................509 525-7660
Craig Nelson, *President*
Barton Nelson, *Chairman*
Bryan Zessin, *COO*
Charles Harrold, *Vice Pres*
Robert Rupar, *Vice Pres*
◆ EMP: 160
SQ FT: 120,000
SALES (est): 47.5MM **Privately Held**
WEB: www.nelsonirrigation.com
SIC: 3494 5085 3523 Sprinkler systems, field; valves, pistons & fittings; farm machinery & equipment

(G-14851)
NORTHSTAR WINERY
1736 J B George Rd (99362-7132)
PHONE.................509 525-6100
Kathleen Belcher, *Manager*
Laura Minnick, *Manager*
▲ EMP: 5
SALES (est): 360K **Privately Held**
WEB: www.northstarmerlot.com
SIC: 2084 Wines

(G-14852)
OCTAVE VINEYARD LLC
1334 Crystal Ct (99362-8842)
P.O. Box 2851 (99362-0336)
PHONE.................509 876-2530
Dyan Nelson, *Principal*
EMP: 2
SALES (est): 96.8K **Privately Held**
SIC: 2084 Wines, brandy & brandy spirits

(G-14853)
OKANOGAN LABEL & PRINT LTD
13 1/2 E Main St Ste 214b (99362-1950)
PHONE.................250 328-8660
James Parker, *President*
Jay Gougeon, *Vice Pres*
EMP: 17
SQ FT: 1,400
SALES: 3.8MM **Privately Held**
SIC: 2759 3085 Labels & seals: printing; plastics bottles

(G-14854)
PAPINEAU LLC
31 E Main St Ste 216 (99362-1921)
PHONE.................509 301-9074
Madeleine Shero, *Partner*
Sean Boyd, *Partner*
EMP: 2
SALES (est): 119.1K **Privately Held**
SIC: 2084 Wine cellars, bonded: engaged in blending wines

(G-14855)
PEPPER BRIDGE WINERY LLC (PA)
1704 J B George Rd (99362-7132)
PHONE.................509 525-6502
Travis Goff, *Partner*
Norman McKibben,
Eric McKibben,
▲ EMP: 10
SQ FT: 20,000
SALES (est): 883.2K **Privately Held**
WEB: www.pepperbridge.com
SIC: 2084 Wines

(G-14856)
PLUMB CELLARS
39 E Main St (99362-1921)
PHONE.................509 540-5632
Gary Kagels, *Principal*
EMP: 4 EST: 2010
SALES (est): 303.9K **Privately Held**
SIC: 2084 Wines

(G-14857)
PRECISION BEAM & TIMBER INC
2915 Melrose St (99362-9525)
P.O. Box 147 (99362-0003)
PHONE.................509 525-1381
Dirk Fledderjohann, *President*
Tim Rogers, *Vice Pres*
EMP: 9
SALES: 510K **Privately Held**
SIC: 2439 2421 Structural wood members; specialty sawmill products

(G-14858)
RASA VINEYARDS LLC
4122 Power Line Rd (99362-7760)
PHONE.................509 252-0900
Pinto Naravane, *Managing Prtnr*
Rajaram Godbole, *Principal*
◆ EMP: 4
SALES (est): 338.5K **Privately Held**
SIC: 2084 Wine cellars, bonded: engaged in blending wines; wines

(G-14859)
RDL ENTERPRISES INC
Also Called: Rdl Machine
680 N 13th Ave (99362-1782)
PHONE.................509 529-5480
Ronald K Larson, *President*
Dena Larson, *Vice Pres*
EMP: 15
SQ FT: 11,000
SALES: 1.5MM **Privately Held**
WEB: www.rdlmachine.com
SIC: 3599 3949 Machine shop, jobbing & repair; sporting & athletic goods

(G-14860)
REININGER WINERY LLC
5858 Old Highway 12 (99362-7291)
PHONE.................509 522-1994
Ann Tucker, *Manager*
Kelly Tucker, *Manager*
Charles Reininger,
Tracy Reininger,
EMP: 3
SALES (est): 335.1K **Privately Held**
WEB: www.reiningerwinery.com
SIC: 2084 Wines

(G-14861)
ROSE SAVIAH WINERY LLC
Also Called: Saviah Cellars
1979 J B George Rd (99362-7134)
PHONE.................509 522-2181
Richard Funk, *Mng Member*
Anita Funk, *Mng Member*
▲ EMP: 3 EST: 2001
SALES (est): 319.9K **Privately Held**
SIC: 2084 5182 5921 Wines; wine; wine

(G-14862)
ROTIE CELLARS
4 E Main St (99362-1922)
PHONE.................509 529-2011
EMP: 4
SALES (est): 143.1K **Privately Held**
SIC: 2084 Wines

(G-14863)
RUNWAY LIQUIDATION LLC
Also Called: Bcbg
480 W Boughton (99362)
PHONE.................651 275-3251
EMP: 2
SALES (corp-wide): 645.5MM **Privately Held**
SIC: 2335 Women's, juniors' & misses' dresses
HQ: Runway Liquidation, Llc
2761 Fruitland Ave
Vernon CA 90058
323 589-2224

(G-14864)
SAPOLIL CELLARS
15 E Main St (99362-1921)
PHONE.................509 520-5258
Bill Schwerin, *Principal*
EMP: 2
SALES (est): 142.5K **Privately Held**
SIC: 2084 Wines

(G-14865)
SCHAFER WINERY LLC
Also Called: Amaurice Sellers
178 Vineyard Ln (99362-8657)
PHONE.................509 522-5444
Anna Schafer, *Owner*
Nick Schafer, *Managing Prtnr*
Bryan Hill, *Sales Mgr*
EMP: 9 **Privately Held**
SIC: 2084 Wines
PA: Schafer Winery, Llc
4402 E Mercer Way
Mercer Island WA 98040

(G-14866)
SEVEN HILLS WINERY LLC
212 N 3rd Ave (99362-1883)
PHONE.................509 529-7198
Casey McClellan, *CEO*
▲ EMP: 4
SALES (est): 426.5K
SALES (corp-wide): 67.7MM **Publicly Held**
WEB: www.sevenhillswinery.com
SIC: 2084 Wines
PA: Crimson Wine Group, Ltd.
2700 Napa Vly Corp Dr B
Napa CA 94558
800 486-0503

(G-14867)
SEYMOUR TECHNOLOGY LLC
504 S Roosevelt St (99362-3447)
PHONE.................509 522-3473
David Seymour, *Mng Member*
EMP: 4
SALES (est): 565.7K **Privately Held**
SIC: 3679 5065 5999 7389 Electronic circuits; electronic parts; electronic parts & equipment;

(G-14868)
SHAW ESTATE WINES
26 E Main St (99362-1957)
PHONE.................509 876-2459
EMP: 2
SALES (est): 108K **Privately Held**
SIC: 2084 Wines

(G-14869)
SHERIDAN WOODWORKING LLC
2175 Frog Hollow Rd (99362-5023)
PHONE.................509 540-7799
Dan Wocott, *Principal*
EMP: 4
SALES (est): 481K **Privately Held**
SIC: 2431 Millwork

(G-14870)
SMITH CHROME PLATING INC
1012 N 9th Ave (99362-1099)
PHONE.................509 525-0993
John Edwards, *President*
EMP: 6 EST: 1954
SQ FT: 12,000
SALES: 500K **Privately Held**
WEB: www.smithchromeplating.com
SIC: 3471 Chromium plating of metals or formed products; electroplating of metals or formed products

(G-14871)
SOFTWARE PLANNING
6 E Alder St Ste 224 (99362-1938)
PHONE.................509 522-1620
Larry Nelson, *Owner*
EMP: 2
SQ FT: 500
SALES (est): 187.3K **Privately Held**
WEB: www.softwareplanning.com
SIC: 7372 7371 Business oriented computer software; custom computer programming services

(G-14872)
SPRING VALLEY TASTING ROOM
18 N 2nd Ave (99362-1802)
PHONE.................509 525-1506
Kate Elvin, *Manager*
EMP: 2
SALES (est): 142.8K **Privately Held**
SIC: 2084 Wines

(G-14873)
SPRING VALLEY VINEYARD WINERY
1663 Corkrum Rd (99362-8628)
PHONE.................509 337-6043
Dean Derby, *Principal*
EMP: 2
SALES (est): 79.5K **Privately Held**
SIC: 2084 0762 Wines; vineyard management & maintenance services

(G-14874)
STAR PRESS INC
842 Wallowa Dr (99362-9398)
P.O. Box 2173 (99362-0173)
PHONE.................509 525-2425
John Novakovich, *President*
Cora L Novakovich, *Vice Pres*
EMP: 23
SALES: 470K **Privately Held**
SIC: 2741 7389 Miscellaneous publishing;

(G-14875)
SWIRE PACIFIC HOLDINGS INC
Also Called: Coca-Cola
155 Avery St (99362-1669)
PHONE.................509 529-0753
Al Carlson, *Manager*
EMP: 30
SQ FT: 5,000 **Privately Held**
SIC: 2086 5149 Soft drinks: packaged in cans, bottles, etc.; groceries & related products

Walla Walla - Walla Walla County (G-14876) — GEOGRAPHIC SECTION

HQ: Swire Pacific Holdings Inc.
12634 S 265 W Bldg A
Draper UT 84020
801 816-5300

(G-14876)
SWIVEL INC
213 S 4th Ave (99362-2904)
PHONE 509 557-7000
Keith Nerdin, *CEO*
James Pellow, *President*
EMP: 4
SALES (est): 98.3K **Privately Held**
SIC: 7372 Application computer software

(G-14877)
T & K MARTIN FARMS INC
2109 S Wilbur Ave (99362-9048)
PHONE 509 525-4387
Terry Martin, *Principal*
EMP: 3
SALES (est): 301.2K **Privately Held**
SIC: 3931 Guitars & parts, electric & non-electric

(G-14878)
TESLA WINERY TOURS LLC
422 Diamond Gate Rd (99362-5038)
PHONE 509 520-5528
EMP: 2
SALES (est): 78.7K **Privately Held**
SIC: 2084 Wines

(G-14879)
TRANCHE CELLARS LLC
705 Berney Dr (99362-8475)
PHONE 509 526-3500
Mike Neuffer, *Principal*
Joe Soleau, *Natl Sales Mgr*
EMP: 2 EST: 2008
SALES (est): 133.5K **Privately Held**
SIC: 2084 Wine cellars, bonded: engaged in blending wines; wines

(G-14880)
TRIPLE P PRODUCTS INC
Also Called: 123 Printing
2189 Isaacs Ave (99362-2215)
PHONE 509 527-3131
Vernon Bosley, *President*
EMP: 4
SQ FT: 2,500
SALES (est): 481.6K **Privately Held**
SIC: 2752 Commercial printing, offset

(G-14881)
TUNGSTEN CELLARS LLC
704 Beet Rd (99362-7231)
PHONE 509 525-3672
M Scott Wolfram, *Principal*
EMP: 3 EST: 2012
SALES (est): 205.8K **Privately Held**
SIC: 3356 Nonferrous rolling & drawing

(G-14882)
TUURI WINES LLC
Also Called: Dama Wines
45 E Main St (99362-1921)
PHONE 509 525-2299
Dawn Kammer, *Principal*
Mary Derby, *Mng Member*
EMP: 3
SALES (est): 201.7K **Privately Held**
SIC: 2084 Wines

(G-14883)
TUXBITS INC
722 Crestview Pl (99362-4230)
PHONE 302 313-6831
Nicholas Aliabadi, *CEO*
EMP: 3
SALES (est): 96.9K **Privately Held**
SIC: 8748 7372 Systems engineering consultant, ex. computer or professional; application computer software

(G-14884)
UNIBEST INTERNATIONAL LLC
3301 Isaacs Ave (99362-8017)
PHONE 509 525-3370
Mark Riess,
Teri Riess,
EMP: 9
SQ FT: 2,200
SALES (est): 1.4MM **Privately Held**
SIC: 3823 Water quality monitoring & control systems

(G-14885)
VICTOR GUTIERREZ
2316 Garrison St (99362-2685)
PHONE 509 301-4915
Victor Gutierrez, *Principal*
EMP: 2
SALES (est): 108.8K **Privately Held**
SIC: 2084 Wines

(G-14886)
W-4 CONSTRUCTION INC
Also Called: K Diamond Construction
1646 University Dr (99362-2544)
PHONE 509 529-1603
Steve Walker, *President*
Betty Ann Walker, *Corp Secy*
Mike Walker, *Vice Pres*
Ronald Walker, *Vice Pres*
EMP: 12
SQ FT: 3,000
SALES (est): 1.5MM **Privately Held**
WEB: www.greatsouthwestern.com
SIC: 4212 1541 2421 2411 Lumber (log) trucking, local; industrial buildings & warehouses; sawmills & planing mills, general; logging

(G-14887)
WALISER WINERY LLC
1956 J B George Rd (99362-7134)
PHONE 509 522-4206
Thomas J Waliser, *Principal*
EMP: 2 EST: 2001
SALES (est): 130.7K **Privately Held**
SIC: 2084 Wines

(G-14888)
WALLA WALLA ENVIRONMENTAL INC
4 E Rees Ave (99362-1153)
P.O. Box 1298 (99362-0302)
PHONE 509 522-0490
Roger L Corn, *President*
Nancy Sutherland, *Corp Secy*
Cassie Rothstrom, *COO*
Staci Wanichek, *Exec VP*
Ed Brown, *Manager*
EMP: 10 EST: 1982
SQ FT: 25,000
SALES (est): 1.9MM **Privately Held**
WEB: www.e-zerodischarge.com
SIC: 2842 2879 2899 2851 Sanitation preparations, disinfectants & deodorants; insecticides, agricultural or household; chemical preparations; paints & allied products

(G-14889)
WALLA WALLA FARMERS CO OP
928 W Main St (99362-2774)
PHONE 509 529-5750
Michael Potter, *Principal*
EMP: 2
SQ FT: 9,600
SALES (est): 230K **Privately Held**
SIC: 5199 2394 Canvas products; canvas & related products

(G-14890)
WALLA WALLA FOUNDRY INC (PA)
Also Called: Farwest Materials
405 Woodland Ave (99362-1655)
PHONE 509 522-2114
Mark A Anderson, *CEO*
Dylan Farnum, *President*
Dave M Anderson, *COO*
Patricia Anderson, *Vice Pres*
Dave Anderson, *Opers Staff*
◆ EMP: 129
SQ FT: 35,000
SALES: 17.1MM **Privately Held**
WEB: www.wallawallafoundry.com
SIC: 3366 Castings (except die): bronze

(G-14891)
WALLA WALLA FOUNDRY INC
Also Called: Farm West Materials
944 N 9th Ave (99362-1128)
PHONE 509 525-5690
Mark Anderson, *President*
EMP: 2
SALES (corp-wide): 17.1MM **Privately Held**
SIC: 3364 Lead die-castings
PA: Walla Walla Foundry, Inc.
405 Woodland Ave
Walla Walla WA 99362
509 522-2114

(G-14892)
WALLA WALLA GRAVEL & ROCK LLC
1133 Smith Rd (99362-8658)
PHONE 509 301-1050
Rhonda Sasser, *Principal*
EMP: 3
SALES (est): 229.9K **Privately Held**
SIC: 1442 Construction sand & gravel

(G-14893)
WALLA WALLA MOTOR SUPPLY INC
1830 Isaacs Ave (99362-2210)
PHONE 509 525-2940
Terry Camarillo, *President*
EMP: 10
SQ FT: 7,000
SALES (est): 1.4MM **Privately Held**
SIC: 5013 5531 3599 Automotive supplies & parts; automotive parts; automotive accessories; machine shop, jobbing & repair

(G-14894)
WALLA WALLA SWEETS
109 E Main St Ste C (99362-1940)
PHONE 509 522-2255
Jerry Herman, *Principal*
Stephanie Mayer, *Office Mgr*
Frank Mutz, *Manager*
Jeff Cirillo, *Director*
EMP: 4
SALES (est): 426.3K **Privately Held**
SIC: 2353 Baseball caps

(G-14895)
WALLA WALLA UNION BULLETIN
112 S 1st Ave (99362-3011)
P.O. Box 1358 (99362-0306)
PHONE 509 525-3300
Frank A Blethen, *Ch of Bd*
Larry Duthie, *Principal*
Rick Eskil, *Editor*
Annie Eveland, *Editor*
Bret Rankin, *Editor*
EMP: 100 EST: 1868
SALES (est): 531.8K
SALES (corp-wide): 226.3MM **Privately Held**
WEB: www.union-bulletin.com
SIC: 2711 Newspapers
HQ: Seattle Times Company
1000 Denny Way Ste 501
Seattle WA 98109
206 464-2111

(G-14896)
WALLA WALLA VINTNERS LLC
225 Vineyard Ln (99362-8404)
PHONE 509 525-4724
Ally Venneri, *Vice Pres*
Barb Commare, *Marketing Staff*
Gordon Venneri,
▲ EMP: 2
SQ FT: 3,000
SALES (est): 232.8K **Privately Held**
WEB: www.wallawallavintners.com
SIC: 2084 Wines

(G-14897)
WALLA WALLA WINES LLC
Also Called: Three Rivers Winery
5641 Old Highway 12 (99362-6263)
PHONE 509 526-9463
Duane Wollmuth,
Steve Ahler,
Charles Stocking,
▲ EMP: 10
SQ FT: 18,000
SALES (est): 931.1K **Privately Held**
WEB: www.threeriverswinery.com
SIC: 2084 Wines

(G-14898)
WALLS VINEYARDS
1015 W Pine St (99362-1756)
PHONE 509 876-0200
EMP: 2
SALES (est): 101.4K **Privately Held**
SIC: 2084 Wines

(G-14899)
WATERS WINERY LLC
Also Called: Tr Wine
6 W Rose St Ste 103 (99362-1845)
P.O. Box 400 (99362-0011)
PHONE 541 203-0020
Boug Roskelley, *Managing Prtnr*
Buck Blessing, *Managing Prtnr*
Jamie Brown, *General Mgr*
EMP: 4
SALES (est): 330K **Privately Held**
SIC: 2084 Wines

(G-14900)
WE-MAN VETS GOLF INC
Also Called: Veterans Memorial Pro Shop
201 E Rees Ave (99362-1148)
PHONE 509 527-4507
Fax: 509 529-7586
EMP: 20
SQ FT: 1,250
SALES (est): 1.1MM **Privately Held**
SIC: 7992 5941 7999 0782 Ret Golf Equipment & Supplies Provides Golf Lessons Golf Course Maintenance & Restaurant & Lounge

(G-14901)
WHEATLAND ALPACAS
2010 Stovall Rd (99362-7275)
PHONE 509 526-4847
Cecilia McKean, *Owner*
EMP: 2
SALES (est): 111.9K **Privately Held**
SIC: 2231 Alpacas, mohair: woven

(G-14902)
WHITELATCH-HOCH LLC
175 E Aeronca Ave # 202 (99362-7418)
PHONE 509 586-7337
Richmond Hoch, *President*
EMP: 2
SALES (est): 72K **Privately Held**
SIC: 2084 Wines, brandy & brandy spirits

(G-14903)
WILKINSON GROUP LLC
Also Called: Wilkinson Baking Company
2465 Old Milton Hwy (99362-7150)
PHONE 509 529-5800
Janet Wilkinson, *General Mgr*
Ron Wilkinson, *Manager*
▲ EMP: 10 EST: 1998
SALES (est): 570.4K **Privately Held**
SIC: 2051 Bread, cake & related products

(G-14904)
WINERY FULFILLMENT SVCS LLC
1491 W Rose St (99362-1645)
P.O. Box 3266 (99362-0366)
PHONE 509 529-2497
Vickie Stone, *Mng Member*
EMP: 4 EST: 2013
SALES (est): 357.2K **Privately Held**
SIC: 2084 Wines

(G-14905)
WW VILLAGE WINERY
Also Called: Wala Wala Winery
107 S 3rd Ave (99362-2848)
PHONE 509 529-5300
Lynn Clark, *Owner*
Barb Clark, *Co-Owner*
EMP: 3
SALES (est): 129.1K **Privately Held**
SIC: 2084 Wines

(G-14906)
WWVWA
13 1/2 E Main St Ste 214 (99362-1950)
PHONE 509 526-3117
EMP: 2
SALES (est): 71.2K **Privately Held**
SIC: 2084 Wines

GEOGRAPHIC SECTION

(G-14907)
YUMMY DESIGNS LLC
636 Washington St (99362-3255)
P.O. Box 1851 (99362-0035)
PHONE..................................509 525-2072
Laurie Manahan,
Martin Manahan,
EMP: 2
SALES: 100K **Privately Held**
SIC: 8099 3999 Nutrition services; puppets & marionettes

Wallula
Walla Walla County

(G-14908)
BOISE WHITE PAPER LLC
31831 W Highway 12 (99363)
PHONE..................................509 545-3293
Alexander Toeldte, *Manager*
EMP: 37
SALES (corp-wide): 7B **Publicly Held**
SIC: 2621 Paper mills
HQ: Boise White Paper, L.L.C.
1111 W Jefferson St # 200
Boise ID 83702
208 384-7000

(G-14909)
PACKAGING CORPORATION AMERICA
31831 W Highway 12 (99363)
PHONE..................................509 545-3260
Bryan Tinnin, *Purch Mgr*
Ashim Banerje, *Branch Mgr*
EMP: 75
SALES (corp-wide): 7B **Publicly Held**
SIC: 2631 2621 2671 Paperboard mills; paper mills; printing paper; packaging paper & plastics film, coated & laminated; paper coated or laminated for packaging
PA: Packaging Corporation Of America
1 N Field Ct
Lake Forest IL 60045
847 482-3000

(G-14910)
PACKAGING CORPORATION AMERICA
Also Called: PCA
31827 W Highway 12 (99363-0111)
P.O. Box 108 (99363-0108)
PHONE..................................509 545-3202
Katy Conoan, *Branch Mgr*
EMP: 160
SALES (corp-wide): 7B **Publicly Held**
SIC: 2653 Boxes, corrugated: made from purchased materials
PA: Packaging Corporation Of America
1 N Field Ct
Lake Forest IL 60045
847 482-3000

(G-14911)
SPECIALTY MINERALS INC
31829 W Highway 12 (99363)
PHONE..................................509 545-9777
Jeff Scott, *Manager*
EMP: 5 **Publicly Held**
WEB: www.specialtyminerals.com
SIC: 3295 Minerals, ground or treated
HQ: Specialty Minerals Inc.
622 3rd Ave Fl 38
New York NY 10017
212 878-1800

(G-14912)
TYSON FOODS INC
13983 Dodd Rd (99363)
P.O. Box 4239, Pasco (99302-4239)
PHONE..................................509 547-7545
Tony Lang, *General Mgr*
David Tobias, *Human Res Dir*
Jayson Poole, *Manager*
Laurie Garcia, *Manager*
Laurela Johnson, *Director*
EMP: 1500
SALES (corp-wide): 40B **Publicly Held**
SIC: 2011 2013 Meat packing plants; sausages & other prepared meats

PA: Tyson Foods, Inc.
2200 W Don Tyson Pkwy
Springdale AR 72762
479 290-4000

Wapato
Yakima County

(G-14913)
COLUMBIA ASPHALT & GRAVEL INC
377 Parker Bridge Rd (98951-9014)
PHONE..................................509 457-3654
Chad Carlson, *Branch Mgr*
EMP: 3
SALES (corp-wide): 8.6MM **Privately Held**
SIC: 3273 Ready-mixed concrete
PA: Columbia Asphalt & Gravel, Inc.
377 Parker Bridge Rd
Parker WA 98939
509 453-2063

(G-14914)
COMPOSITES CONSOLIDATION COMPA
180 E Jones Rd (98951-1508)
PHONE..................................509 877-2228
Jerry Armstrong, *CEO*
Kim Brazell, *Vice Pres*
Jacqueline Jensen, *Controller*
EMP: 3
SALES (est): 185.1K **Privately Held**
SIC: 3089 3088 3229 Plastic processing; molding primary plastic; hot tubs, plastic or fiberglass; glass fiber products

(G-14915)
COMPOSITES CONSOLIDATION LLC
180 E Jones Rd (98951-1508)
PHONE..................................509 877-2228
Dick Clarke, *President*
Kim Brazell, *CFO*
EMP: 2
SQ FT: 192,500
SALES (est): 163.9K **Privately Held**
SIC: 3089 3229 Synthetic resin finished products; thermoformed finished plastic products; glass fiber products

(G-14916)
GRIEB OPTIMAL WINECRAFTING LLC
Also Called: Treveri Cellars
71 Gangl Rd (98951-9682)
PHONE..................................509 877-0925
Wilson Cecil, *Sales Staff*
Christian Grieb, *Marketing Staff*
Julie Grieb, *Mng Member*
Katie Grieb, *Executive*
▲ **EMP:** 5 **EST:** 2009
SQ FT: 15,000
SALES (est): 697.4K **Privately Held**
WEB: www.trevericellars.com
SIC: 2084 Wines

(G-14917)
KISSLERS MACHINE & FABRICATION
3690 Lateral B Rd (98951-9726)
PHONE..................................509 877-1177
Richard Kissler, *President*
Dick Kissler, *Vice Pres*
EMP: 2
SALES (est): 260.2K **Privately Held**
SIC: 3699 Heat emission operating apparatus

(G-14918)
MASSET WINERY
620 E Parker Heights Rd (98951-9606)
PHONE..................................509 877-6675
Greg Masset, *Owner*
EMP: 2 **EST:** 2001
SALES (est): 125.7K **Privately Held**
SIC: 2084 Wines

(G-14919)
MCCLARIN PLASTICS LLC
Also Called: Amtech
180 E Jones Rd (98951-1508)
PHONE..................................509 877-5950
Doug Christie, *CEO*
Robert Godwin, *Design Engr*
Kim Brazell, *CFO*
Kit Young, *Sales Staff*
Bill Bushbaum, *Mktg Dir*
▲ **EMP:** 330
SALES (est): 38.9MM **Privately Held**
WEB: www.sonomaspas.com
SIC: 3089 3088 3229 Molding primary plastic; plastic processing; hot tubs, plastic or fiberglass; glass fiber products

(G-14920)
MICHAEL PATRICK MATTHEWS
Also Called: Security Alarms Plus
1691 Yakima Valley Hwy (98951-9646)
P.O. Box 9394, Yakima (98909-0394)
PHONE..................................509 457-8799
Michael Patrick Matthews, *Owner*
EMP: 2
SALES (est): 150K **Privately Held**
SIC: 1731 7382 3669 Fire detection & burglar alarm systems specialization; burglar alarm maintenance & monitoring; fire alarm maintenance & monitoring; emergency alarms; burglar alarm apparatus, electric

(G-14921)
NAUMES CONCENTRATES INC
371 Industrial Park Rd (98951-9009)
PHONE..................................509 877-8882
Michael D Naumes, *President*
Susan F Naumes, *Corp Secy*
▼ **EMP:** 40
SQ FT: 31,800
SALES (est): 5.9MM
SALES (corp-wide): 176.8MM **Privately Held**
WEB: www.naumes.com
SIC: 2037 Fruit juices
PA: Naumes, Inc.
2 W Barnett St
Medford OR 97501
541 772-6268

(G-14922)
PACE INTERNATIONAL LLC (DH)
5661 Branch Rd (98951-9768)
PHONE..................................800 936-6750
Roberto Carpentier, *COO*
Adel Freij, *Purchasing*
Daniel Van Pelt, *Purchasing*
Barbara Lommers, *Human Resources*
Chris Heintzman, *Manager*
▲ **EMP:** 5
SQ FT: 11,000
SALES (est): 25.7MM **Privately Held**
WEB: www.paceint.com
SIC: 2899 2873 2879 Water treating compounds; plant foods, mixed: from plants making nitrog. fertilizers; fungicides, herbicides
HQ: Valent Biosciences Llc
870 Technology Way # 100
Libertyville IL 60048
800 323-9597

(G-14923)
PACIFIC VISION ENTERPRISES
621 Coe Rd (98951-9142)
PHONE..................................509 895-4199
Paul Eatman, *Principal*
EMP: 2
SALES (est): 106K **Privately Held**
SIC: 3556 Food products machinery

(G-14924)
PRO WEST MECHANICAL INC
31 Industrial Park Rd (98951-9025)
PHONE..................................509 965-1750
Jason Moore, *President*
Nicole Moore, *Vice Pres*
EMP: 25
SALES (est): 1.2MM **Privately Held**
SIC: 3535 Conveyors & conveying equipment

(G-14925)
RAHR MALTING
5150 Yakima Valley Hwy (98951-9638)
PHONE..................................509 469-0403
EMP: 2
SALES (est): 91.3K **Privately Held**
SIC: 2083 Malt

(G-14926)
SANCHEZ PALLETS LLC
6191 Yakima Valley Hwy (98951-9633)
PHONE..................................509 877-4004
Sanchez Prostero, *Mng Member*
EMP: 9 **EST:** 2001
SALES (est): 1.2MM **Privately Held**
SIC: 2448 Pallets, wood & wood with metal

(G-14927)
VAMCO LTD INC
Also Called: Wind Machine Sales
5250 Yakima Valley Hwy (98951-9677)
PHONE..................................509 877-2138
Doug Stewart, *Branch Mgr*
EMP: 5
SQ FT: 15,000
SALES (corp-wide): 50MM **Privately Held**
SIC: 3523 5083 5999 Cabs, tractors & agricultural machinery; agricultural machinery; farm equipment & supplies
HQ: Vamco Ltd., Inc.
1460 S Mirage Ave
Lindsay CA
559 562-5185

(G-14928)
WAPATO PAWN & TRADE
201 S Wapato Ave (98951-1344)
PHONE..................................509 877-6405
Andrew Cook, *Owner*
▲ **EMP:** 7
SQ FT: 6,875
SALES (est): 500K **Privately Held**
SIC: 5932 3911 Pawnshop; antiques; jewelry, precious metal

Warden
Grant County

(G-14929)
COUNTRY MORNING FARMS INC
Also Called: Gilbert Farms
653 N Fox Rd (98857)
PHONE..................................509 349-2958
Gale Noyes, *General Mgr*
Angie Panbelidef, *Branch Mgr*
EMP: 25
SALES (corp-wide): 4MM **Privately Held**
SIC: 2026 Fluid milk
PA: Country Morning Farms, Inc.
223 N County Rd
Warden WA
509 349-2958

(G-14930)
CUSTOM CHEMICALS CO INC
320 W 1st St (98857-9345)
P.O. Box 547, Moses Lake (98837-0083)
PHONE..................................509 349-7000
Fred Legault, *President*
EMP: 12
SALES: 4MM **Privately Held**
SIC: 7538 2879 General automotive repair shops; agricultural disinfectants

(G-14931)
DAGNER CONSTRUCTION
16735 Out Of Bounds Ln Se (98857-9700)
PHONE..................................509 349-8944
EMP: 2
SALES (est): 84.2K **Privately Held**
SIC: 1389 1521 Oil/Gas Field Services Single-Family House Construction

(G-14932)
LAMB WESTON BSW LLC
1203 Basin St (98857-9475)
PHONE..................................509 349-2210
Andy Bateman,
EMP: 30

SALES (est): 7.5MM **Privately Held**
SIC: 2096 Potato chips & other potato-based snacks

(G-14933)
MONSANTO COMPANY
115 N 1st St (98857-9300)
PHONE..................................509 349-2327
Pete Ortega, *Safety Mgr*
Robert Bainsty, *Manager*
EMP: 20
SALES (corp-wide): 45.3B **Privately Held**
SIC: 2879 Agricultural chemicals
HQ: Monsanto Company
    800 N Lindbergh Blvd
    Saint Louis MO 63167
    314 694-1000

(G-14934)
OCHOA AG UNLIMITED FOODS INC
1203 Basin St (98857-9475)
PHONE..................................509 349-2210
Kevin Weber, *President*
Alan Bird, *Corp Secy*
Bill Weber, *Vice Pres*
EMP: 150
SALES (est): 24.6MM
SALES (corp-wide): 100MM **Privately Held**
SIC: 2037 Potato products, quick frozen & cold pack
PA: Ochoa Ag Unlimited Foods, Inc.
    910 W Main St Ste 248
    Boise ID 83702
    208 343-6882

(G-14935)
OREGON POTATO COMPANY
Also Called: Washington Potato
1900 1st Ave W (98857)
P.O. Box 2248 (98857-2248)
PHONE..................................509 349-8803
Bob Bernard, *Manager*
EMP: 100
SQ FT: 80,000 **Privately Held**
SIC: 2034 Potato products, dried & dehydrated
PA: Oregon Potato Company
    6610 W Court St Ste B
    Pasco WA 99301

(G-14936)
VITERRA USA LLC
1875 W 1st St (98857-9497)
PHONE..................................509 349-8464
Bill Dahl, *Plant Mgr*
EMP: 15
SALES (corp-wide): 205.4B **Privately Held**
SIC: 2079 Vegetable refined oils (except corn oil)
HQ: Viterra Usa Llc
    1550 Utica Ave S Ste 595
    Minneapolis MN 55416
    952 479-2205

(G-14937)
WARDEN WELDING INC
116 N Ash Ave (98857-9337)
P.O. Box 606 (98857-0606)
PHONE..................................509 349-2478
William Mast, *President*
EMP: 4 EST: 1952
SQ FT: 3,200
SALES (est): 375.1K **Privately Held**
SIC: 3599 7692 Machine shop, jobbing & repair; welding repair

(G-14938)
WASHINGTON POTATO COMPANY INC
1900 1st Ave W (98857)
P.O. Box 2248 (98857-2248)
PHONE..................................509 349-8803
Dave Landon, *President*
Frank Tiegs, *Pastor*
Ramona Thomas, *Manager*
Valerie Jorstad, *Admin Sec*
EMP: 100
SQ FT: 5,000
SALES (est): 23.7MM **Privately Held**
SIC: 5149 2099 2034 Groceries & related products; food preparations; dehydrated fruits, vegetables, soups

Washougal
Clark County

(G-14939)
ADVANCED DRAINAGE SYSTEMS INC
627 S 37th St (98671-2803)
PHONE..................................360 835-8523
Harvey F Miller, *Branch Mgr*
EMP: 50
SALES (corp-wide): 1.3B **Publicly Held**
WEB: www.ads-pipe.com
SIC: 3084 Plastics pipe
PA: Advanced Drainage Systems, Inc.
    4640 Trueman Blvd
    Hilliard OH 43026
    614 658-0050

(G-14940)
ADVANCED LASER PRINTER SERVICE
2513 Se 370th Ave (98671-8943)
PHONE..................................360 835-1824
Paul Della Valle, *Principal*
EMP: 2 EST: 2012
SALES (est): 130.2K **Privately Held**
SIC: 2752 Commercial printing, lithographic

(G-14941)
ALLWEATHER WOOD LLC (DH)
815 S 32nd St (98671-2521)
P.O. Box 227 (98671-0227)
PHONE..................................360 835-8547
Harold Osterman,
▼ EMP: 100
SALES (est): 34.2MM
SALES (corp-wide): 81.8MM **Privately Held**
SIC: 2426 Lumber, hardwood dimension

(G-14942)
ANDERSON AROSPC QULTY WLDG LLC
5252 N St (98671-5199)
PHONE..................................360 607-2634
Michael Anderson, *Principal*
EMP: 2
SALES (est): 151.4K **Privately Held**
SIC: 3599 Machine shop, jobbing & repair

(G-14943)
AP INTERPRICES
211 Thuja Narrow Rd (98671-7292)
PHONE..................................360 837-2548
EMP: 2 EST: 2017
SALES (est): 88.9K **Privately Held**
SIC: 3089 Plastics products

(G-14944)
ARTISANAL GOODS NORTHWEST LLC
35902 Se Evergreen Hwy (98671-9752)
PHONE..................................503 803-7228
Jeannine Mills, *Principal*
EMP: 2
SALES (est): 82.9K **Privately Held**
SIC: 2033 Jams, jellies & preserves: packaged in cans, jars, etc.

(G-14945)
BENTRIVER TECH INC
1117 Se Blair Rd (98671-8462)
P.O. Box 873154, Vancouver (98687-3154)
PHONE..................................360 335-1345
Joseph Gallagher, *President*
Alexander Day, *Manager*
EMP: 2 EST: 2009
SALES (est): 410K **Privately Held**
SIC: 3599 Amusement park equipment

(G-14946)
BURNISH LEATHER CO
4413 Addy Loop (98671-2708)
PHONE..................................360 723-8533
Graci Morris, *Principal*
EMP: 2
SALES (est): 106K **Privately Held**
SIC: 3199 Leather goods

(G-14947)
CALVERT COMPANY INC
3559 S Truman Rd (98671-2571)
PHONE..................................360 835-3110
Douglas Calvert, *President*
EMP: 40
SALES (est): 2.7MM
SALES (corp-wide): 9.4MM **Privately Held**
SIC: 2439 Trusses, wooden roof
PA: Calvert Company, Inc.
    218 N V St
    Vancouver WA 98661
    360 693-0971

(G-14948)
COLUMBIA MFG & TECH CTR LLC
750 S 32nd St (98671-2520)
P.O. Box 87548, Vancouver (98687-7548)
PHONE..................................360 835-0922
Gary Phillips, *Principal*
EMP: 3 EST: 2010
SALES (est): 184.3K **Privately Held**
SIC: 8731 3999 Commercial physical research; manufacturing industries

(G-14949)
CORROSION COMPANIES INC
3725 Grant St Ste 2 (98671-2813)
P.O. Box 1199 (98671-0926)
PHONE..................................360 835-2171
Terry Glenn, *President*
EMP: 20 EST: 2005
SALES (est): 3.5MM **Privately Held**
WEB: www.ccifrp.com
SIC: 2821 3564 Plastics materials & resins; blowers & fans

(G-14950)
CURTINS HERITAGE LOGGING INC
3485 I St (98671-1918)
PHONE..................................360 518-5735
EMP: 2 EST: 2007
SALES (est): 145.2K **Privately Held**
SIC: 2411 Logging

(G-14951)
D S FABRICATION & DESIGN INC
3805 S Truman Rd (98671-2582)
PHONE..................................360 210-7526
Dan Smark, *CEO*
Krista Young-Smark, *Principal*
EMP: 2 EST: 2011
SQ FT: 11,000
SALES: 928K **Privately Held**
SIC: 3469 7692 Machine parts, stamped or pressed metal; welding repair

(G-14952)
DONAMO CO
1413 N 20th St (98671-8278)
PHONE..................................360 835-5634
Donald Sagat, *Owner*
EMP: 4
SALES: 100K **Privately Held**
SIC: 3496 Conveyor belts

(G-14953)
ENERGY EFFICIENCY SYSTEMS CORP
2311 G St (98671-1646)
PHONE..................................360 835-7838
W Robert Hougland, *President*
Christopher Powell, *Vice Pres*
EMP: 36
SALES (est): 2.4MM **Privately Held**
SIC: 7371 8731 3714 3621 Computer software development; commercial physical research; electronic research; air conditioner parts, motor vehicle; generating apparatus & parts, electrical; distribution, electric power

(G-14954)
EXPERT IG
534 K St (98671-1029)
PHONE..................................360 335-0555
Tom Lander, *Owner*
EMP: 2
SALES (est): 88.7K **Privately Held**
SIC: 7372 Prepackaged software

(G-14955)
EXTERIOR WOOD INC (HQ)
2685 Index St (98671-2537)
P.O. Box 206 (98671-0206)
PHONE..................................360 835-8561
Dave Perry, *President*
Michael McGran, *General Mgr*
Larry Draper, *Principal*
Jim Driver, *Buyer*
Nancy Bishoprick, *CFO*
▲ EMP: 110
SQ FT: 1,800
SALES (est): 22.5MM
SALES (corp-wide): 1.1B **Privately Held**
WEB: www.exteriorwood.com
SIC: 2491 Wood preserving
PA: Taiga Building Products Ltd
    4710 Kingsway Suite 800
    Burnaby BC V5H 4
    604 438-1471

(G-14956)
FOCAL POINT PLASTICS INC
3925 Grant St (98671-2800)
P.O. Box 99521, Seattle (98139-0521)
PHONE..................................206 282-0433
Douglas Bryant, *President*
Kim Newman, *Accounts Mgr*
EMP: 10
SALES (est): 665.9K **Privately Held**
SIC: 3089 Molding primary plastic; plastic processing

(G-14957)
GREEN FLUSH TECHNOLOGIES LLC
1420 N Columbia Ridge Way (98671-8022)
PHONE..................................360 718-7595
Kyle Earlywine, *General Mgr*
Kenneth G Earlywine,
Kyle R Earlywine,
EMP: 3
SALES (est): 385.8K **Privately Held**
SIC: 2452 Prefabricated wood buildings

(G-14958)
HAGER WORLDWIDE INC
82 Washougal River Rd (98671-2377)
PHONE..................................360 210-5084
Patrick Hager, *Branch Mgr*
EMP: 2
SALES (corp-wide): 3.2MM **Privately Held**
SIC: 3843 Orthodontic appliances
PA: Hager Worldwide, Inc.
    441 19th St Se
    Hickory NC 28602
    800 328-2335

(G-14959)
HYDRA GROUP LLC
5428 J St (98671-5117)
PHONE..................................503 957-0975
Christian Ruddell, *Vice Pres*
Jesse Oliver, *Vice Pres*
EMP: 2 EST: 2015
SALES (est): 129.8K **Privately Held**
SIC: 3357 3679 3694 3714 Automotive wire & cable, except ignition sets: nonferrous; harness assemblies for electronic use: wire or cable; battery cable wiring sets for internal combustion engines; booster (jump-start) cables, automotive; emergency shelters

(G-14960)
IMMERSIVE MEDIA COMPANY
Also Called: IMC
1700 Main St Ste 248 (98671-4127)
PHONE..................................360 609-3419
Myles McGovern, *President*
Amit Chopra, *COO*
Thomas McGovern, *Vice Pres*
Ben Sirofhton, *Vice Pres*
Darren Battersby, *Director*
EMP: 20
SQ FT: 2,500
SALES (est): 1.6MM **Privately Held**
SIC: 8711 7372 3861 Engineering services; prepackaged software; cameras & related equipment

(G-14961)
INTECH ENTERPRISES INC
3825 Grant St (98671-2810)
PHONE..................................360 835-8785

GEOGRAPHIC SECTION
Washougal - Clark County (G-14992)

Tom Cunning, *President*
EMP: 20
SQ FT: 14,200
SALES (est): 3MM **Privately Held**
WEB: www.intechenterprises.com
SIC: 8742 3565 5084 7699 Industrial consultant; packaging machinery; packaging machinery & equipment; industrial machinery & equipment repair

(G-14962)
KEMIRA CHEMICALS INC
1150 S 35th St (98671-2573)
PHONE..................................360 835-8725
Jay Coomes, *Production*
Scott Rosencrance, *Research*
Nayiby Scott, *Research*
Michael Cavallero, *Sales Staff*
Brad Stephens, *Branch Mgr*
EMP: 14
SALES (corp-wide): 2.9B **Privately Held**
SIC: 5169 2899 Industrial chemicals; chemical preparations
HQ: Kemira Chemicals, Inc.
1000 Parkwood Cir Se # 500
Atlanta GA 30339
770 436-1542

(G-14963)
LEGENDARY YACHT INC
2902 Addy St (98671-2629)
PHONE..................................360 835-0342
Stanley Bishoprick, *President*
EMP: 17 **EST:** 1994
SALES (est): 2.6MM **Privately Held**
WEB: www.legendaryyachts.com
SIC: 3732 5551 Yachts, building & repairing; boat dealers

(G-14964)
LV LOGGING
282 Stevens Rd (98671-7404)
PHONE..................................360 837-3144
Victor Erickson, *Manager*
EMP: 2
SALES (est): 140.5K **Privately Held**
SIC: 2411 Logging camps & contractors

(G-14965)
MARY JANE GLASS PRODUCTIONS
477 S 28th St Ste C1 (98671-2565)
PHONE..................................360 844-5914
Brandon Brock, *President*
EMP: 2 **EST:** 2015
SALES (est): 48K **Privately Held**
SIC: 3229 Glass tubes & tubing

(G-14966)
MICRO MACHINING
251 Sneider Barks Rd (98671-7620)
PHONE..................................360 837-3200
Dale Burnham, *Owner*
EMP: 2
SQ FT: 2,400
SALES: 300K **Privately Held**
SIC: 3599 Machine shop, jobbing & repair

(G-14967)
MICRO MACHINING LLC
1213 Ne 314th Ave (98671-9268)
P.O. Box 182 (98671-0182)
PHONE..................................360 835-3200
Joe Bisson, *Principal*
Eve Merklin,
EMP: 5
SALES (est): 826.5K **Privately Held**
WEB: www.micromachiningllc.com
SIC: 3549 Metalworking machinery

(G-14968)
MILLER MANUFACTURING
2930 Ford St (98671-2528)
P.O. Box 843 (98671-0843)
PHONE..................................360 844-5403
EMP: 2
SALES (est): 121.3K **Privately Held**
SIC: 3999 Manufacturing industries

(G-14969)
MILLER MANUFACTURING INC
Also Called: A & M Manufacturing
3720 S Truman Rd (98671-2581)
P.O. Box 843 (98671-0843)
PHONE..................................360 335-1236
Dennis E Miller, *President*
EMP: 10
SALES (est): 319.6K **Privately Held**
SIC: 3553 Sawmill machines

(G-14970)
MT NORWAY FABRICATION LLC
2319 Se 370th Ave (98671-8942)
PHONE..................................360 836-0322
Steven Koch, *Mng Member*
EMP: 3 **EST:** 2014
SALES: 140K **Privately Held**
SIC: 3441 Building components, structural steel

(G-14971)
NATHAN CAPITAL LLC (PA)
750 S 32nd St (98671-2520)
PHONE..................................360 835-1211
Alexander Abelev,
Andrei Mikhailov,
EMP: 2
SQ FT: 10,000
SALES (est): 813.4K **Privately Held**
SIC: 6719 3299 Investment holding companies, except banks; synthetic stones, for gem stones & industrial use

(G-14972)
NORTHWEST ADHESIVES INC
4325 S Lincoln St (98671-2591)
PHONE..................................360 260-1227
Charles E Asbury, *President*
Beverly A Asbury, *Vice Pres*
Bryan Asbury, *Sales Mgr*
Jim Robinson, *Marketing Staff*
▲ **EMP:** 10
SQ FT: 6,000
SALES (est): 2.2MM **Privately Held**
WEB: www.northwestadhesives.com
SIC: 2891 Sealants; adhesives

(G-14973)
NORWESCO INC
3860 Grant St (98671-2809)
PHONE..................................360 835-3021
Tom Smith, *Branch Mgr*
EMP: 10
SALES (corp-wide): 44.1MM **Privately Held**
WEB: www.ncmmolding.com
SIC: 3089 Septic tanks, plastic
PA: Norwesco, Inc.
4365 Steiner St
Saint Bonifacius MN 55375
952 446-1945

(G-14974)
NUTESLA CORPORATION
853 W Y St (98671-7434)
PHONE..................................910 688-3752
James Honeycutt, *President*
Vickie Honeycutt, *Vice Pres*
EMP: 2
SALES (est): 168K **Privately Held**
SIC: 3825 7389 Pulse (signal) generators;

(G-14975)
OLIVE NAVIDIS OIL & VINEGARS
5287 N St (98671-5199)
P.O. Box 909, Camas (98607-0909)
PHONE..................................360 600-9836
Kenneth A Navidi, *President*
EMP: 7
SALES (est): 792K **Privately Held**
SIC: 2099 Vinegar

(G-14976)
ORBIT INDUSTRIES LLC
778 S 27th St (98671-2594)
PHONE..................................360 835-8526
Scott Worral, *General Mgr*
Tom Welinski, *Sales Mgr*
Dorothy Hartman, *Executive*
Robin Curry,
Michael Burnett,
EMP: 25
SQ FT: 15,000
SALES: 3.9MM **Privately Held**
WEB: www.orbitindustries.com
SIC: 3441 Fabricated structural metal

(G-14977)
PENDLETON WOOLEN MILLS INC
2 Pendleton Way (98671-4201)
P.O. Box 145 (98671-0145)
PHONE..................................360 835-2131
Caitlin Taylor, *President*
Charles Bbishop, *Branch Mgr*
EMP: 240
SALES (corp-wide): 151MM **Privately Held**
WEB: www.pendletonusa.com
SIC: 2231 5949 Broadwoven fabric mills, wool; fabric stores piece goods
PA: Pendleton Woolen Mills, Inc.
220 Nw Broadway
Portland OR 97209
503 226-4801

(G-14978)
PHYL MAR SWISS PRODUCTS INC
3136 Evergreen Way (98671-2046)
PHONE..................................360 695-9242
Allan Kor, *President*
EMP: 3
SALES (est): 371.8K **Privately Held**
SIC: 3599 Machine shop, jobbing & repair

(G-14979)
PILLER AIMMCO INC
3925 Grant St (98671-2800)
PHONE..................................360 835-2103
Jason Hannah, *President*
Richard Hannah, *Vice Pres*
Randy Biskeborn, *CFO*
EMP: 65 **EST:** 1963
SQ FT: 50,000
SALES (est): 21.6MM **Privately Held**
WEB: www.pillarplastics.com
SIC: 3089 Injection molding of plastics; molding primary plastic

(G-14980)
PLASTIC FORMING SERVICES LLC
3830 S Truman Rd Ste 2 (98671-2584)
PHONE..................................360 335-9755
Grant Hedblom, *Principal*
EMP: 13
SALES (est): 1.5MM **Privately Held**
SIC: 3089 Injection molding of plastics

(G-14981)
RAM CELLARS LLC
4554 Rolling Meadows Dr (98671-8624)
PHONE..................................360 909-6714
Rodger Marks, *Principal*
EMP: 2
SALES (est): 62.3K **Privately Held**
SIC: 2084 Wines, brandy & brandy spirits

(G-14982)
SAARISWOODWORKING
4019 A Loop (98671-9001)
PHONE..................................360 835-8106
Larry Saari, *Principal*
EMP: 2
SALES (est): 124.7K **Privately Held**
SIC: 2431 Millwork

(G-14983)
SAPPHIRE MATERIALS COMPANY
750 S 32nd St (98671-2520)
P.O. Box 87548, Vancouver (98687-7548)
PHONE..................................360 210-5124
EMP: 3
SALES (est): 229K **Privately Held**
SIC: 3599 Industrial machinery

(G-14984)
SILICON CHEMICAL CORPORATION
750 S 32nd St (98671-2520)
P.O. Box 87548, Vancouver (98687-7548)
PHONE..................................360 210-5124
Gary W Phillips, *President*
Bob Hewitt, *Vice Pres*
Jeff Ericcsen, *Controller*
EMP: 20
SALES (est): 1.9MM **Privately Held**
SIC: 3339 Silicon, pure

(G-14985)
SILVER STAR INDUSTIES INC
Also Called: Silver Star Industries
412 Silver Star Ln (98671-7736)
PHONE..................................360 837-3685
Chris Califf, *Branch Mgr*
EMP: 15
SALES (corp-wide): 15MM **Privately Held**
WEB: www.silverstarcabinets.com
SIC: 2541 Cabinets, except refrigerated: show, display, etc.: wood
PA: Silver Star Industies Inc.
409 Evergreen Dr
North Bonneville WA 98639
509 427-8800

(G-14986)
SILVER STAR STREET RODS
3331 Skye Rd (98671-7410)
PHONE..................................360 837-1250
Harry Wenick, *Owner*
Yona Wenick, *Co-Owner*
EMP: 2
SALES (est): 132.1K **Privately Held**
SIC: 3711 Automobile assembly, including specialty automobiles

(G-14987)
STEEL FAB NW INC
520 S 28th St (98671-2508)
PHONE..................................360 210-7055
Dennis Greenhalgh, *Principal*
EMP: 2 **EST:** 2016
SALES (est): 108.5K **Privately Held**
SIC: 3312 3441 1791 Blast furnaces & steel mills; building components, structural steel; structural steel erection

(G-14988)
SUNSET MOLDING INC
37438 Se Sunset View Rd (98671-6621)
PHONE..................................360 835-3805
Russell Stacks, *President*
Sandra Stacks, *Vice Pres*
EMP: 2
SALES: 100K **Privately Held**
SIC: 3089 Molding primary plastic

(G-14989)
SUPERIOR RV MANUFACTURING
3801 S Truman Rd Ste 4 (98671-2589)
P.O. Box 444 (98671-0444)
PHONE..................................360 693-1398
James Sweet, *President*
Mona Ford, *Shareholder*
Carol Sweet, *Shareholder*
EMP: 9
SQ FT: 4,800
SALES: 1.5MM **Privately Held**
SIC: 3792 Travel trailers & campers

(G-14990)
SWIFT MACHINING INC
4060 S Grant St Ste 109 (98671-2815)
PHONE..................................360 335-8213
Josh Swift, *President*
EMP: 6
SALES: 500K **Privately Held**
SIC: 3469 3545 3599 Machine parts, stamped or pressed metal; milling machine attachments (machine tool accessories); machine shop, jobbing & repair

(G-14991)
TEXTURED FOREST PRODUCTS INC
721 S 28th St (98671-2511)
P.O. Box 125 (98671-0125)
PHONE..................................360 835-2164
Gene Weber, *President*
Mike Weber, *Treasurer*
EMP: 10
SQ FT: 16,000
SALES (est): 1.5MM **Privately Held**
SIC: 2436 Softwood veneer & plywood

(G-14992)
THERASIGMA INC
4060 S Grant St Ste 100 (98671-2815)
PHONE..................................800 423-7172
Jim Klett, *President*
Steve Klett, *Vice Pres*
EMP: 2

Washougal - Clark County (G-14993)

SALES (est): 86.6K **Privately Held**
SIC: **3841** Surgical instruments & apparatus

(G-14993)
TIMBERLINE CONTROLS & MAR INC
421 C St Ste 2b (98671-2169)
PHONE..................................360 335-8598
Donald Leliefeld, *President*
EMP: 15
SALES (est): 3MM **Privately Held**
SIC: **3613** **5063** Time switches, electrical switchgear apparatus; control panels, electric; signaling equipment, electrical

(G-14994)
TJS MECHANICAL CUTTING LLC
161 Bull Ridge Rd (98671-7398)
PHONE..................................360 837-1234
Teazzua Seekins, *Principal*
EMP: 3
SALES (est): 293.9K **Privately Held**
SIC: **2411** Logging

(G-14995)
TRUEGUARD LLC
725 S 32nd St (98671-2519)
P.O. Box 227 (98671-0227)
PHONE..................................360 835-8547
Michael English,
EMP: 6 EST: 2007
SALES (est): 816.3K **Privately Held**
SIC: **2491** Structural lumber & timber, treated wood

(G-14996)
UNITED HOME TECHNOLOGIES LLC
4060 S Grant St Ste 106 (98671-2815)
PHONE..................................360 574-7737
Edward Cai, *President*
Dave George, *Director*
Pete Milcarek, *Business Dir*
EMP: 12
SALES (est): 1.8MM **Privately Held**
SIC: **8711** **3089** Engineering services; plastic kitchenware, tableware & houseware

(G-14997)
US CRYOGENICS INC
1422 E St (98671-1413)
P.O. Box 57 (98671-0057)
PHONE..................................360 835-2475
Mark Hougan, *President*
EMP: 4
SQ FT: 7,000
SALES (est): 1MM **Privately Held**
WEB: www.uscryogenics.com
SIC: **3399** Cryogenic treatment of metal

(G-14998)
WASHOUGAL BASELT ROCK QUA
404 Ne 367th Ave (98671-8815)
P.O. Box 87010, Vancouver (98687-7010)
PHONE..................................360 335-0111
Annmarie Scholes, *Principal*
EMP: 3
SALES (est): 234K **Privately Held**
SIC: **1429** Crushed & broken stone

(G-14999)
WASHOUGAL MANUFACTURING CO
952 W T St (98671-5161)
PHONE..................................360 261-2199
Mitchell Prieto, *Principal*
Pat Santon, *Principal*
EMP: 2
SALES (est): 62.5K **Privately Held**
SIC: **3999** Manufacturing industries

(G-15000)
WEISSERT TOOL & DESIGN INC
540 Washougal River Rd (98671-1502)
PHONE..................................360 835-7256
Jeff Weissert, *President*
Dorothy Weissert, *Treasurer*
EMP: 6
SQ FT: 2,500
SALES (est): 686.1K **Privately Held**
WEB: www.weissert.com
SIC: **3544** Dies, plastics forming

(G-15001)
WHITE MOUNTAINHOUSE
4211 L Cir (98671-8600)
PHONE..................................360 835-5442
Robert White, *Owner*
EMP: 2
SALES (est): 175.7K **Privately Held**
SIC: **3679** Electronic circuits

(G-15002)
WORKHORSE INCORPORATED
711 Ne 332nd Ct (98671-8242)
PHONE..................................360 835-9417
EMP: 2 EST: 1993
SALES (est): 210K **Privately Held**
SIC: **8711** **5084** **3714** Dump Truck Lifting Mechanism

Washtucna
Adams County

(G-15003)
STOESS MANUFACTURING INC
225 North St W (99371-9545)
PHONE..................................509 646-3292
Lloyd A Stoess, *President*
Donna Stoess, *Vice Pres*
Ernest Stoess, *Vice Pres*
EMP: 7
SQ FT: 16,000
SALES (est): 432.3K **Privately Held**
WEB: www.stoess.com
SIC: **3523** Farm machinery & equipment

Waterville
Douglas County

(G-15004)
BAINBRIDGE MANUFACTURING INC
237 W 3rd St (98858-9600)
P.O. Box 487 (98858-0487)
PHONE..................................800 255-4702
Keith A Soderstrom, *President*
Les Childress, *Corp Secy*
David Soderstrom, *Vice Pres*
▲ EMP: 30 EST: 1960
SQ FT: 9,000
SALES (est): 6.4MM **Privately Held**
WEB: www.bainbridgemfg.com
SIC: **3429** Manufactured hardware (general)

(G-15005)
BARNES WELDING INC
1450 Road 3 Nw (98858)
PHONE..................................509 745-8588
Dave Barnes, *President*
Kathy Barnes, *Admin Sec*
EMP: 4 EST: 1970
SALES (est): 727.2K **Privately Held**
WEB: www.barnesweldinginc.com
SIC: **7692** **3599** **7533** **1799** Welding repair; machine shop, jobbing & repair; muffler shop, sale or repair & installation; sandblasting of building exteriors; farm equipment & supplies

Wenatchee
Chelan County

(G-15006)
A & C PALLET SALES
609 Lincoln St (98801-3523)
PHONE..................................509 669-0653
EMP: 4 EST: 2010
SALES (est): 150K **Privately Held**
SIC: **2448** Mfg Wood Pallets/Skids

(G-15007)
ACCOR TECHNOLOGY INC
337 E Penny Rd (98801-8125)
PHONE..................................509 662-0608
Donna Kaysen, *Manager*
EMP: 45
SALES (corp-wide): 8.6MM **Privately Held**
WEB: www.accortechnology.com
SIC: **3494** **3491** Plumbing & heating valves; industrial valves
PA: Accor Technology, Inc
     608 State St S Ste 100
     Kirkland WA 98033
     425 453-5410

(G-15008)
ADVANCED METAL CREATIONS
3565 School St (98801-9005)
PHONE..................................509 662-0335
Richard L Peterson, *Owner*
Ronetta Peterson, *Co-Owner*
EMP: 2
SALES (est): 93.8K **Privately Held**
SIC: **3993** Signs, not made in custom sign painting shops

(G-15009)
APPLE VALLEY PRINTERS
617 Chinook Dr (98801-6235)
PHONE..................................509 679-9592
Victor Horner, *Principal*
EMP: 2
SALES (est): 149.9K **Privately Held**
SIC: **2752** Commercial printing, lithographic

(G-15010)
ATLAS PACIFIC ENGINEERING CO
Sinclair Systems International
2605 Chester Kimm Rd (98801-8116)
PHONE..................................509 665-6911
Scott Harker, *Sales Mgr*
Carolyn J Fair,
EMP: 8
SALES (corp-wide): 93.8MM **Privately Held**
WEB: www.atlaspacific.com
SIC: **2759** **7389** **2671** Decals: printing; packaging & labeling services; packaging paper & plastics film, coated & laminated
HQ: Atlas Pacific Engineering Company
     1 Atlas Ave
     Pueblo CO 81001
     719 948-3040

(G-15011)
BAGDONS INC
760 S Wenatchee Ave (98801-3096)
PHONE..................................509 662-1411
Larry Bagdon, *President*
EMP: 20
SQ FT: 5,000
SALES: 2.5MM **Privately Held**
WEB: www.bagdons.com
SIC: **2541** **2431** **7389** **5031** Cabinets, except refrigerated: show, display, etc.: wood; doors, wood; interior designer; lumber, plywood & millwork; wood kitchen cabinets

(G-15012)
BEAR SIGNS
1422 N Miller St Ste 1 (98801-6702)
PHONE..................................509 888-4477
Dennis L Weddle, *Owner*
EMP: 3
SALES: 140K **Privately Held**
SIC: **3993** Signs, not made in custom sign painting shops

(G-15013)
BIMBO BAKERIES USA INC
1422 N Miller St (98801-6702)
PHONE..................................509 662-4731
Phillip Unterschuetz, *Owner*
EMP: 18 **Privately Held**
SIC: **2051** Bread, cake & related products
HQ: Bimbo Bakeries Usa, Inc
     255 Business Center Dr # 200
     Horsham PA 19044
     215 347-5500

(G-15014)
BIOCOM SYSTEMS INC
Also Called: Aspen Scientific
153 Heather Ln (98801-9644)
PHONE..................................509 241-0505
Brian Lasater, *President*
EMP: 5

SALES: 216K **Privately Held**
SIC: **3679** Hermetic seals for electronic equipment

(G-15015)
CASCADE POWDER COATING LLC
11 Bridge St (98801-3001)
PHONE..................................509 663-9080
Dora Potter,
Josh Potter,
EMP: 9
SQ FT: 5,500
SALES: 800K **Privately Held**
SIC: **3479** Coating of metals & formed products

(G-15016)
CCO HOLDINGS LLC
1050 N Miller St (98801-1512)
PHONE..................................509 293-4177
EMP: 3
SALES (corp-wide): 43.6B **Publicly Held**
SIC: **5064** **4841** **3663** **3651** Electrical appliances, television & radio; cable & other pay television services; radio & TV communications equipment; household audio & video equipment
HQ: Cco Holdings, Llc
     400 Atlantic St
     Stamford CT 06901
     203 905-7801

(G-15017)
CENTRAL DENTAL TECHNICIANS
23 S Wenatchee Ave # 214 (98801-2264)
PHONE..................................509 663-4113
Jim Mooney, *President*
Loretta Mooney, *Treasurer*
EMP: 3
SQ FT: 700
SALES: 192K **Privately Held**
WEB: www.centraldentaltechnicians.com
SIC: **3843** **8072** Dental equipment & supplies; dental laboratories

(G-15018)
CENTRAL WASH MEDIA GROUP LLC
Also Called: Sign Pro of Wenatchee
3 Orondo Ave (98801-2206)
PHONE..................................509 667-8112
Jim Wallace Jr, *Principal*
EMP: 4
SALES (est): 250K **Privately Held**
SIC: **3993** Signs & advertising specialties

(G-15019)
CENTRAL WASHINGTON WTR CTR INC
Also Called: Clearwater Chemical
514 S Wenatchee Ave (98801-3068)
P.O. Box 260 (98807-0260)
PHONE..................................509 663-1177
Michael Salmon, *President*
EMP: 11 EST: 1958
SQ FT: 15,000
SALES (est): 1.4MM **Privately Held**
SIC: **5999** **2899** **5712** Spas & hot tubs; swimming pool chemicals, equipment & supplies; chemical preparations; water treating compounds; outdoor & garden furniture

(G-15020)
CHATEAU FAIRE LE PONT LLC
1 Vinyard Way (98801-8129)
PHONE..................................509 667-9463
John Brazil, *Mng Member*
EMP: 6
SALES (est): 532.4K **Privately Held**
SIC: **2084** Wines

(G-15021)
CHILD EVNGELISM FELLOWSHIP INC
800 Orondo Ave (98801-2704)
PHONE..................................509 662-2320
Sandy Jones, *Director*
EMP: 41
SALES (corp-wide): 24.4MM **Privately Held**
SIC: **2752** Commercial printing, lithographic

GEOGRAPHIC SECTION
Wenatchee - Chelan County (G-15051)

PA: Child Evangelism Fellowship Incorporated
17482 Highway M
Warrenton MO 63383
636 456-4321

(G-15022)
COLUMBIA STAINLESS METAL-FAB
4 E Orondo Ave (98801-2273)
P.O. Box 2983 (98807-2983)
PHONE..................509 662-9078
Alex Gonzales, *President*
Teresa Gonzales, *Admin Sec*
EMP: 3
SALES (est): 475.4K **Privately Held**
SIC: 3444 Sheet metalwork

(G-15023)
COMMERCIAL PRINTING INC
1449 N Wenatchee Ave (98801-1154)
PHONE..................509 663-4772
Mike Tyrrell, *President*
Patty Tyrrell, *Corp Secy*
Shirley Tyrrell, *Vice Pres*
EMP: 14 **EST:** 1966
SQ FT: 7,200
SALES (est): 1.2MM **Privately Held**
SIC: 2752 2759 Commercial printing, offset; letterpress printing

(G-15024)
CPM DEVELOPMENT CORPORATION
Also Called: Central Washington Concrete
1351 S Wenatchee Ave (98801-3756)
P.O. Box 3366, Spokane (99220-3366)
PHONE..................509 663-5141
Troy Holt, *General Mgr*
Kerry Palmer, *Train & Dev Mgr*
EMP: 9
SALES (corp-wide): 30.6B **Privately Held**
SIC: 1611 3273 2951 Surfacing & paving; ready-mixed concrete; asphalt paving mixtures & blocks
HQ: Cpm Development Corporation
5111 E Broadway Ave
Spokane Valley WA 99212
509 534-6221

(G-15025)
DESIGN SALT INC
Also Called: Cocoon
527 Piere St (98801-2053)
PHONE..................509 667-1600
Josef Sturm, *CEO*
Sue Morrison, *General Mgr*
Randy King, *Vice Pres*
▲ **EMP:** 4
SQ FT: 2,000
SALES (est): 376.2K **Privately Held**
SIC: 5091 2399 Sharpeners, sporting goods; sleeping bags

(G-15026)
DOLCO PACKAGING CORP
1121 S Columbia St (98801-6197)
PHONE..................509 662-8415
Don James, *Principal*
Paul Massey, *Safety Mgr*
Amanda McMahon, *Admin Asst*
EMP: 20
SALES (est): 2MM **Privately Held**
SIC: 5999 2621 Farm equipment & supplies; wrapping & packaging papers

(G-15027)
EAST WA BURIAL VAULTS INC
1095 Rue Jolie (98801-9053)
PHONE..................509 662-5684
Greg Diede, *President*
EMP: 2
SALES (est): 147.7K **Privately Held**
SIC: 3281 Burial vaults, stone

(G-15028)
EASY STREET CUSTOM METAL
1119 Easy St (98801-9658)
PHONE..................509 662-1018
Dave Hosking, *Owner*
EMP: 2
SALES (est): 53.2K **Privately Held**
SIC: 3441 Fabricated structural metal

(G-15029)
EL MUNDO COMMUNICATIONS INC
112 N Mission St (98801-2229)
PHONE..................509 663-5737
Gustavo Montoya, *President*
Gabriel Fernandez, *Admin Sec*
EMP: 5
SALES (est): 265.2K **Privately Held**
SIC: 2711 2741 7313 Newspapers: publishing only, not printed on site; miscellaneous publishing; newspaper advertising representative

(G-15030)
FARWELL PRODUCTS INC
1649 N Wenatchee Ave (98801)
P.O. Box 3347 (98807-3347)
PHONE..................509 663-6212
Wendy Baker, *President*
Ben Baker, *Vice Pres*
EMP: 2
SQ FT: 3,000
SALES (est): 308.5K **Privately Held**
WEB: www.farwellproducts.peachhost.com
SIC: 2833 Medicinals & botanicals

(G-15031)
FARWEST IRON WORKS INC
1301 S Columbia St (98801-3710)
PHONE..................509 662-3546
Peter Scovill, *President*
Nicholas Scovill, *Vice Pres*
EMP: 7 **EST:** 1965
SQ FT: 15,000
SALES (est): 594.3K **Privately Held**
SIC: 3441 Fabricated structural metal

(G-15032)
FENCE STORE BY EAGLE VINYL LLC
735 N Wenatchee Ave (98801-2061)
PHONE..................509 860-3603
Alex Lange, *Mng Member*
EMP: 5 **EST:** 2014
SALES (est): 518.1K **Privately Held**
SIC: 3446 Fences or posts, ornamental iron or steel

(G-15033)
FRUIT PACKERS SUPPLY
3907 State Highway 97a (98801-9626)
PHONE..................509 888-3059
EMP: 2
SALES (est): 68.6K **Privately Held**
SIC: 2033 Fruits: packaged in cans, jars, etc.

(G-15034)
GO USA INC
521 S Columbia St (98801-3033)
PHONE..................509 662-3387
Bill Hamilton, *CEO*
Brett Hamilton, *President*
▲ **EMP:** 25
SQ FT: 20,000
SALES (est): 6.5MM **Privately Held**
WEB: www.gousaquality.com
SIC: 5199 5943 5092 2759 Advertising specialties; writing supplies; balloons, novelty; embossing on paper; labels, paper: made from purchased material; embroidery products, except schiffli machine

(G-15035)
GPA EMBROIDERY
22 N Wenatchee Ave (98801-2237)
PHONE..................509 662-1929
Curt Gavin, *Owner*
Curt Gabbin, *Owner*
EMP: 5
SQ FT: 2,500
SALES (est): 180K **Privately Held**
WEB: www.gpaembroidery.com
SIC: 2395 Embroidery & art needlework

(G-15036)
GRAYBEAL SIGNS
1909 N Wenatchee Ave (98801-1053)
PHONE..................509 662-6926
Monte Graybeal, *Owner*
Jennifer Graybeal, *Co-Owner*
EMP: 12
SQ FT: 6,200

SALES (est): 1.2MM **Privately Held**
SIC: 3993 Electric signs

(G-15037)
GRAYS ELECTRIC INC
1183 S Wenatchee Ave (98801-3752)
PHONE..................509 662-6834
Paul K Gray, *President*
Robert A Searles, *Treasurer*
Charlotte A Gray, *Shareholder*
EMP: 5
SQ FT: 2,000
SALES (est): 617.1K **Privately Held**
SIC: 7699 7694 1731 Pumps & pumping equipment repair; electric motor repair; electrical work

(G-15038)
GREGORY DIEDE
Also Called: Eastern Washington Burial Vlt
403 E Peters St (98801-5999)
PHONE..................509 662-1009
Gregory Diede, *Owner*
EMP: 2
SALES (est): 210.3K **Privately Held**
SIC: 3272 Burial vaults, concrete or precast terrazzo

(G-15039)
HOLLAND MACHINE INC
5 Orondo Ave (98801-2206)
P.O. Box 1712 (98807-1712)
PHONE..................509 662-6235
Michael Holland, *President*
Dorothy Holland, *Corp Secy*
Robert Holland, *Vice Pres*
EMP: 6 **EST:** 1900
SQ FT: 8,400
SALES (est): 698.5K **Privately Held**
SIC: 3599 Machine shop, jobbing & repair

(G-15040)
HORIZON PRINTING COMPANY LLC
320 N Emerson Ave Apt 4 (98801-2187)
PHONE..................509 663-8414
Gordon Wentz, *Owner*
EMP: 4
SQ FT: 2,400
SALES: 450K **Privately Held**
SIC: 2752 2759 2761 Commercial printing, offset; letterpress printing; manifold business forms

(G-15041)
KP2 LLC
Also Called: Lawn Rangers
602 Marian Ave (98801-3163)
PHONE..................509 663-4983
Kole Pennington,
Kyle Pennington,
EMP: 7
SALES: 180K **Privately Held**
SIC: 0781 3271 7389 Landscape services; blocks, concrete: landscape or retaining wall;

(G-15042)
LAURELS CROWN LLC
200 Palouse St Ste 202 (98801-2265)
P.O. Box 1945 (98807-1945)
PHONE..................509 860-2510
Laurie Neal, *Managing Prtnr*
EMP: 2
SALES (est): 131.9K **Privately Held**
SIC: 2022 Natural cheese

(G-15043)
LECTRO TEK SERVICES INC
Also Called: Ltsi
1951 S Wenatchee Ave (98801-3822)
P.O. Box 2161 (98807-2161)
PHONE..................509 663-2891
Jim Tarrant, *CEO*
Hugh D Fitzpatrick, *President*
Jurgen M Krehbiel, *Treasurer*
J D Fitzpatrick, *Admin Sec*
EMP: 30 **EST:** 1979
SQ FT: 16,000
SALES (est): 1.7MM **Privately Held**
SIC: 3596 5084 Weighing machines & apparatus; food product manufacturing machinery

(G-15044)
LLP ENTERPRISES LLC
4300 State Highway 97a (98801-9017)
PHONE..................509 423-7580
Lloyd Palm,
EMP: 3
SALES (est): 263.1K **Privately Held**
SIC: 3532 Rock crushing machinery, stationary

(G-15045)
LOLO FOODS
1712 Washington St Apt 3 (98801-6373)
PHONE..................509 860-8021
EMP: 3
SALES (est): 74K **Privately Held**
SIC: 2099 Mfg Food Preparations

(G-15046)
LOVITT MINING COMPANY INC
Also Called: Lovitt Orchards
2698 S Methow St (98801-9428)
PHONE..................509 668-8170
Lorne Brown, *President*
EMP: 5
SALES: 380.6K **Privately Held**
SIC: 0175 6552 1481 Apple orchard; peach orchard; land subdividers & developers, residential; mine exploration, nonmetallic minerals
PA: Grange Gold Corp.
1111 Hastings St W Suite 708
Vancouver BC V6E 2
604 669-3233

(G-15047)
LOVITT RESOURCES INC
2698 S Methow St (98801-9428)
P.O. Box 2479 (98807-2479)
PHONE..................509 668-8170
EMP: 2 **EST:** 2015
SALES (est): 104.3K **Privately Held**
SIC: 1041 Gold ores mining

(G-15048)
M&E MEMORIAL MARKERS INC
920 N Chelan Ave (98801-1507)
PHONE..................509 662-6469
Jerry Zerr, *President*
EMP: 3
SQ FT: 600
SALES (est): 280K **Privately Held**
SIC: 3281 5999 Monument or burial stone, cut & shaped; monuments & tombstones

(G-15049)
MACKS LURES MANUFACTURING CO
55 Lure Ln (98801-4501)
PHONE..................509 667-9202
Ray McPherson, *President*
Bob Schmidt, *Vice Pres*
Don Talbot, *Vice Pres*
Bob Loomis, *Sales Staff*
Kathryn McPherson, *Admin Sec*
▲ **EMP:** 8 **EST:** 1970
SQ FT: 7,000
SALES (est): 832.1K **Privately Held**
WEB: www.mackslure.com
SIC: 3949 5091 Fishing tackle, general; sporting & recreation goods

(G-15050)
MICHAEL B KNUTSON
1515 N Miller St (98801-1562)
PHONE..................509 398-7312
Michael Knutson, *Owner*
Elizabeth Knutson, *Accountant*
EMP: 3
SQ FT: 1,600
SALES (est): 107.5K **Privately Held**
SIC: 1751 2434 2521 2517 Cabinet & finish carpentry; wood kitchen cabinets; wood office filing cabinets & bookcases; filing cabinets (boxes), office: wood; wood television & radio cabinets

(G-15051)
NCW TOWING
29 N Chelan Ave (98801-2219)
PHONE..................509 630-7155
Jeff Wagner, *Principal*
EMP: 2 **EST:** 2011

Wenatchee - Chelan County (G-15052) GEOGRAPHIC SECTION

SALES (est): 228.1K Privately Held
SIC: 3711 Wreckers (tow truck), assembly of

(G-15052)
NOBLE TRUSS & LUMBER INC
355 Malaga Hwy (98801)
PHONE 509 662-1877
Bradley Kronschnabel, *President*
Bradley A Kronschnabel, *President*
EMP: 15
SQ FT: 11,500
SALES: 850K **Privately Held**
SIC: 2439 Trusses, except roof: laminated lumber

(G-15053)
NORTHWEST DOOR AND MILLWORK
1254 Lower Sunnyslope Rd (98801-9611)
PHONE 509 782-4525
Bob Kirk, *President*
EMP: 2
SQ FT: 6,000
SALES (est): 224.7K **Privately Held**
SIC: 5211 2431 Door & window products; doors & door parts & trim, wood

(G-15054)
ORNAMENTAL IRON WORKS INC
4450 2 Canyon Rd (98801)
PHONE 509 662-8294
Randall Smith, *President*
Rennea Smith, *Corp Secy*
EMP: 2
SALES (est): 150K **Privately Held**
SIC: 3446 1751 Architectural metalwork; carpentry work

(G-15055)
ORNELAS LLC
Also Called: Ornelas Contract Services
3635 Ridgeview Blvd (98801-9096)
PHONE 206 388-2267
Ramona Guentzel,
EMP: 6
SALES: 650K **Privately Held**
SIC: 3613 Control panels, electric

(G-15056)
PA&E INTERNATIONAL INC
430 Olds Station Rd (98801-5975)
PHONE 509 667-9600
Peter Statile, *President*
Paul Laud, *Chairman*
Brian Beazer, *Director*
John Raos, *Director*
Richard Detweiler, *Admin Sec*
EMP: 200
SALES (est): 16MM **Privately Held**
SIC: 3643 Current-carrying wiring devices

(G-15057)
PACIFIC AEROSPACE & ELEC INC
430 Olds Station Rd (98801-5975)
PHONE 509 667-9600
Don Right, *CEO*
EMP: 210
SALES (corp-wide): 67.1MM **Privately Held**
SIC: 3679 Hermetic seals for electronic equipment
HQ: Pacific Aerospace & Electronics, Llc
   434 Olds Station Rd
   Wenatchee WA 98801

(G-15058)
PACIFIC AEROSPACE & ELEC INC
Also Called: Souriau
434 Olds Station Rd (98801-5975)
PHONE 855 285-5200
EMP: 6
SALES (corp-wide): 67.1MM **Privately Held**
SIC: 3643 Current-carrying wiring devices
HQ: Pacific Aerospace & Electronics, Llc
   434 Olds Station Rd
   Wenatchee WA 98801

(G-15059)
PACIFIC AEROSPACE & ELEC LLC (HQ)
Also Called: PA&e
434 Olds Station Rd (98801-5975)
PHONE 855 885-5200
William Hubbard, *President*
▼ EMP: 237
SQ FT: 100,000
SALES (est): 41.2MM
SALES (corp-wide): 67.1MM **Privately Held**
WEB: www.pacaero.com
SIC: 3728 3679 3643 Aircraft parts & equipment; electronic circuits; current-carrying wiring devices
PA: Hermetic Solutions Group Inc.
   4000 State Route 66 # 310
   Tinton Falls NJ 07753
   732 722-8780

(G-15060)
PARKER MANUFACTURING LLC
2127a Duncan Rd (98801-1006)
PHONE 509 663-5923
Jayson Parker, *Managing Prtnr*
Terry Parker, *Managing Prtnr*
Lois Parker, *Treasurer*
Terrence R Parker,
EMP: 3 EST: 1960
SQ FT: 60
SALES (est): 410.4K **Privately Held**
SIC: 3441 Fabricated structural metal

(G-15061)
PESANI GENUINE COATINGS LLC
810 Booie Ct Apt A (98801-6855)
PHONE 509 860-3426
EMP: 2
SALES (est): 135.1K **Privately Held**
SIC: 3479 Metal coating & allied service

(G-15062)
PHILLIPPI FRUIT CO INC
Also Called: Twin Peaks Cider House & Dist
1921 5th St (98801-1356)
P.O. Box 2567 (98807-2567)
PHONE 509 662-8522
Greg A Phillippi, *President*
David Phillippi, *Treasurer*
▼ EMP: 50
SQ FT: 9,000
SALES: 2.1MM **Privately Held**
SIC: 0723 2037 Fruit (fresh) packing services; fruit juices

(G-15063)
PHILLIPS 66 COMPANY
116 N Chelan Ave (98801-2222)
PHONE 509 534-5040
EMP: 2
SALES (corp-wide): 114.2B **Publicly Held**
SIC: 2911 Petroleum refining
HQ: Phillips 66 Company
   2331 Citywest Blvd
   Houston TX 77042
   281 293-6600

(G-15064)
PICKLE PAPERS
21 S Wenatchee Ave (98801-2210)
PHONE 509 665-8661
Peggy Nichols, *Owner*
Marnye Nichols, *Partner*
EMP: 2
SQ FT: 900
SALES (est): 211.2K **Privately Held**
SIC: 5943 5947 7299 2759 Stationery stores; gift, novelty & souvenir shop; gift wrapping services; invitation & stationery printing & engraving

(G-15065)
PRECISION WATERJET INC
207 S Columbia St (98801-3028)
PHONE 509 888-7954
Troy Bassett, *President*
EMP: 5
SALES (est): 757.4K **Privately Held**
SIC: 3281 Granite, cut & shaped

(G-15066)
PRESIDENTIAL
3639 Ridgeview Blvd (98801-9096)
PHONE 509 669-1230
EMP: 2
SALES (est): 77.4K **Privately Held**
SIC: 3161 Clothing & apparel carrying cases

(G-15067)
RAAD INDUSTRIES LLC
2001 N Wenatchee Ave H (98801-1079)
PHONE 509 663-8352
Mark Lowe, *General Mgr*
Darrell Anderson,
EMP: 23
SQ FT: 15,000
SALES (est): 3.9MM **Privately Held**
WEB: www.raadindustries.com
SIC: 3469 Machine parts, stamped or pressed metal

(G-15068)
RICH INTERIORS
2131 N Wenatchee Ave (98801-1057)
PHONE 509 665-8000
Rich Irish, *Owner*
EMP: 2
SALES (est): 163.2K **Privately Held**
SIC: 5719 2434 Lighting fixtures; wood kitchen cabinets

(G-15069)
RIDGELINE GRAPHICS INC
34 N Chelan Ave (98801-2220)
PHONE 509 662-6858
John McDarment, *Owner*
EMP: 5
SALES (est): 548.1K **Privately Held**
SIC: 7336 2752 5092 Graphic arts & related design; commercial printing, lithographic; arts & crafts equipment & supplies

(G-15070)
RYAN CUSTOM COATINGS
614 Highland Dr (98801-3445)
PHONE 808 652-9731
Colin Ryan, *Principal*
EMP: 2
SALES (est): 69.9K **Privately Held**
SIC: 3479 Metal coating & allied service

(G-15071)
S&T TRADING & MORE LLC
Also Called: S&T Jewelry
312 N Delaware Ave (98801-2142)
P.O. Box 5323 (98801-5323)
PHONE 509 421-2326
Susan Busk, *Mng Member*
Anthony Fisher,
EMP: 2
SALES (est): 187.2K **Privately Held**
SIC: 5944 7389 3911 Jewelry stores; ; bracelets, precious metal

(G-15072)
SAM KNUTSONS LUMBER CO INC
1415 S Wenatchee Ave B (98801-3797)
P.O. Box 115 (98807-0115)
PHONE 509 662-6183
Sam C Knutson, *President*
Carolyn Knutson, *Corp Secy*
EMP: 2
SALES (est): 308.7K **Privately Held**
SIC: 2434 Wood kitchen cabinets

(G-15073)
SELLAND CONSTRUCTION INC
1285 S Wenatchee Ave (98801-3754)
P.O. Box 119 (98807-0119)
PHONE 509 662-7119
Bradley Selland, *President*
Adam Brizendine, *General Mgr*
Larry Bosworth, *Corp Secy*
Gary D Bates, *Vice Pres*
Glen Broadsword, *Vice Pres*
EMP: 150
SQ FT: 2,500
SALES (est): 51.3MM **Privately Held**
WEB: www.sellandconstruction.com
SIC: 1081 1794 1611 Metal mining services; excavation & grading, building construction; highway & street construction

(G-15074)
SIGN LANGUAGE INTERPRETER & EN
1116 Foothills Ln (98801-1498)
PHONE 509 860-2727
Patricia Mugg, *Principal*
EMP: 2
SALES (est): 72.6K **Privately Held**
SIC: 3993 Signs & advertising specialties

(G-15075)
SMITH CUSTOM WOODWORKING INC
1902 Hideaway Pl (98801-1073)
PHONE 509 670-4634
Jared Smith, *Principal*
EMP: 2 EST: 2012
SALES (est): 272.3K **Privately Held**
SIC: 2431 Millwork

(G-15076)
STEMILT CREEK WINERY
110 N Wenatchee Ave (98801-2239)
PHONE 509 662-3613
Kyle Mathison, *Principal*
EMP: 7
SALES (est): 377.7K **Privately Held**
SIC: 2084 Wines

(G-15077)
STONE MASTERS INC
Also Called: Chim Chmney Fireplace Pool Spa
1604 N Wenatchee Ave (98801-1159)
PHONE 509 667-8833
Paul McNeill, *CEO*
CAM Mc Neill, *President*
Susan McNeill, *Vice Pres*
EMP: 8
SALES (est): 2MM **Privately Held**
WEB: www.ccfps.com
SIC: 5091 3429 Spa equipment & supplies; manufactured hardware (general)

(G-15078)
TARGET MEDIA PARTNERS
Also Called: Ncw Nickel ADS
201 N Mission St (98801-2003)
PHONE 509 662-1405
Kristen Bryant, *Manager*
EMP: 15
SALES (corp-wide): 27.7MM **Privately Held**
WEB: www.targetmediapartners.com
SIC: 2711 7311 2741 Newspapers; advertising agencies; miscellaneous publishing
HQ: Target Media Partners
   5200 Lankershim Blvd # 350
   North Hollywood CA 91601
   323 930-3123

(G-15079)
TEKNI-PLEX INC
1121 S Columbia St (98801-3007)
PHONE 509 663-8541
Shaun McGuire, *Plant Mgr*
Rich Peters, *Manager*
EMP: 150
SQ FT: 5,500
SALES (corp-wide): 1.1B **Privately Held**
WEB: www.dolco.net
SIC: 3081 3086 5199 Packing materials, plastic sheet; packaging & shipping materials, foamed plastic; packaging materials
PA: Tekni-Plex, Inc.
   460 E Swedesford Rd # 3000
   Wayne PA 19087
   484 690-1520

(G-15080)
TELOS WEALTH MANAGEMENT
656 N Miller St (98801-2044)
PHONE 509 664-8844
Sean Gross, *Principal*
EMP: 2
SALES (est): 179.1K **Privately Held**
SIC: 7372 Prepackaged software

(G-15081)
TERRY SIGNS
527 N Wenatchee Ave (98801-2057)
P.O. Box 2711 (98807-2711)
PHONE 509 662-6672
Terrence L Johnson, *Owner*
Karen Johnson, *Co-Owner*

GEOGRAPHIC SECTION

EMP: 2
SQ FT: 4,500
SALES: 100K **Privately Held**
SIC: 7389 3993 Lettering service; sign painting & lettering shop; signs & advertising specialties; neon signs; electric signs

(G-15082)
TREE TOP INC
3981 Chelan Hwy (98801-9626)
P.O. Box 1300 (98807-1300)
PHONE................................509 663-8583
Joe Brooks, *Manager*
EMP: 200
SALES (corp-wide): 399.9MM **Privately Held**
SIC: 2034 2037 2033 Fruits, dried or dehydrated, except freeze-dried; frozen fruits & vegetables; canned fruits & specialties
PA: Tree Top, Inc.
   220 E 2nd Ave
   Selah WA 98942
   509 697-7251

(G-15083)
WASHINGTON STATE APPLE COMM
2900 Euclid Ave (98801-8102)
P.O. Box 18 (98807-0018)
PHONE................................509 663-9600
Fax: 509 662-5824
EMP: 2
SALES (est): 170.2K **Privately Held**
SIC: 3571 Mfg Electronic Computers

(G-15084)
WENATCHEE PETROLEUM CO (PA)
601e N Wenatchee Ave (98801-2059)
P.O. Box 2233 (98807-2233)
PHONE................................509 662-4423
Robert W Ogan, *President*
Greg Ogan, *Vice Pres*
Phil Dormaier, *CFO*
Ross Ogan, *Admin Sec*
EMP: 20
SQ FT: 1,200
SALES: 20.3MM **Privately Held**
WEB: www.enviroyellowpages.com
SIC: 5411 1321 5541 5172 Convenience stores, independent; propane (natural) production; filling stations, gasoline; gasoline

(G-15085)
WENATCHEE VLY BREWING CO LLC
Also Called: Wenatchee Valley Brewery
7 N Worthen St (98801-6140)
PHONE................................509 888-8088
Brie Bass,
Daniel Bass,
Bridget Shae,
Dakota Shae,
EMP: 5
SALES (est): 139.9K **Privately Held**
SIC: 2082 5812 Beer (alcoholic beverage); family restaurants

(G-15086)
WORLD PUBLISHING CO
110 N Wenatchee Ave (98801-2239)
PHONE................................509 884-7575
EMP: 2
SALES (est): 62.9K **Privately Held**
SIC: 2711 Newspapers

(G-15087)
WORLD PUBLISHING COMPANY
Also Called: Wenatchee World
14 N Mission St (98801-2250)
P.O. Box 1511 (98807-1511)
PHONE................................509 663-5161
Rufus Woods, *President*
Barbara Woods, *Vice Pres*
Katherine Woods, *Vice Pres*
Wendy Manhart, *Treasurer*
Gretchin Woods, *Admin Sec*
EMP: 62 EST: 1905
SQ FT: 80,000
SALES (est): 6.3MM **Privately Held**
WEB: www.spiritofwenatchee.org
SIC: 2711 Commercial printing & newspaper publishing combined; newspapers, publishing & printing

Wenatchee
Douglas County

(G-15088)
ALTO GROUP HOLDINGS INC
Also Called: (AN EXPLORATION STAGE COMPANY)
715 13th St Ne (98802-4522)
PHONE................................801 816-2520
Douglas McFarland, *CEO*
Chene Gardner, *Ch of Bd*
EMP: 2
SALES (est): 113.6K **Privately Held**
SIC: 1041 1044 Gold ores; silver ores

(G-15089)
COCA-COLA BTLG CO OF NY INC
3400 5th St Se (98802-9264)
PHONE................................509 886-1136
Kris McGregor, *Branch Mgr*
EMP: 27
SALES (corp-wide): 31.8B **Publicly Held**
SIC: 2086 2087 5149 5499 Soft drinks: packaged in cans, bottles, etc.; flavoring extracts & syrups; soft drinks; beverage stores
HQ: The Coca-Cola Bottling Company Of New York Inc
   2500 Windy Ridge Pkwy Se
   Atlanta GA 30339
   770 989-3000

(G-15090)
CPM DEVELOPMENT CORPORATION
Also Called: Central Washington Concrete
5515 Enterprise Dr (98802-9540)
P.O. Box 190 (98807-0190)
PHONE................................509 886-4853
Troy Holt, *General Mgr*
EMP: 4
SALES (corp-wide): 30.6B **Privately Held**
SIC: 1771 3273 Concrete work; ready-mixed concrete
HQ: Cpm Development Corporation
   5111 E Broadway Ave
   Spokane Valley WA 99212
   509 534-6221

(G-15091)
MIKE SCOTT ORCHARDS & WINERY
3400 10th St Se (98802-9322)
PHONE................................509 787-3538
EMP: 5
SALES (est): 190K **Privately Held**
SIC: 0175 2084 Fruit Tree Orchard Mfg Wines/Brandy/Spirits

(G-15092)
NORTHWEST WHOLESALE INC (PA)
5416 Enterprise Dr (98802-9600)
P.O. Box 1649 (98807-1649)
PHONE................................509 662-3563
Kenneth P Knappert, *President*
Mike Phillips, *Treasurer*
EMP: 52 EST: 1937
SQ FT: 2,100
SALES: 65.7MM **Privately Held**
WEB: www.nwwinc.com
SIC: 5191 3999 Chemicals, agricultural; advertising curtains

West Richland
Benton County

(G-15093)
ALEXANDER GRAPE
4636 W Canal Dr (99353-9501)
PHONE................................509 942-9850
Alexander Brown, *Mng Member*
EMP: 3
SALES (est): 185.5K **Privately Held**
SIC: 2084 Wines

(G-15094)
APRESVIN ENTERPRISES AVE INC
4411 King Dr (99353-9389)
P.O. Box 2, Prosser (99350-0002)
PHONE................................509 967-3045
Ralph E Leber, *President*
EMP: 2
SALES: 100K **Privately Held**
SIC: 2079 Edible fats & oils

(G-15095)
DESERT VIEW MANUFACTURED HOME
6500 Desert View Dr (99353-9700)
PHONE................................509 967-3456
Herb Ganz, *Principal*
EMP: 2
SALES (est): 107.4K **Privately Held**
SIC: 3999 Manufacturing industries

(G-15096)
HOT SOX LLC
1830 S 38th Ave (99353-9010)
P.O. Box 4342 (99353-4005)
PHONE................................509 947-5193
Lynda Edmundson,
EMP: 4
SALES (est): 328.4K **Privately Held**
WEB: www.hotsoxllc.com
SIC: 3999 Manufacturing industries

(G-15097)
JESSY WILKINSON LLC
4956 Spirea Dr (99353-7833)
PHONE................................509 578-1650
Jessy Wilkinson,
EMP: 2 EST: 2015
SALES (est): 95.8K **Privately Held**
SIC: 2741 Technical manual & paper publishing

(G-15098)
METALFAB INC
5302 W Van Giesen St (99353-9305)
PHONE................................509 967-2946
Charles Barnett, *President*
John Springers, *Vice Pres*
Lucas Stevens, *Vice Pres*
Ronne Fletcher, *Treasurer*
EMP: 25 EST: 1958
SQ FT: 14,400
SALES (est): 5.5MM **Privately Held**
SIC: 3441 7692 Fabricated structural metal; welding repair

(G-15099)
MOONSTUFF INC
5420 Fern Loop (99353-9806)
P.O. Box 4885 (99353-4014)
PHONE................................509 947-2981
James Moon, *Manager*
EMP: 2
SALES (est): 92.6K **Privately Held**
SIC: 3999 Manufacturing industries

(G-15100)
SKYLINE SPIRITS WINE WORKS CO
Also Called: Black Heron Spirits
8011 Keene Rd (99353-7203)
P.O. Box 5622 (99353-4027)
PHONE................................509 967-0781
Mark Williams, *President*
EMP: 2
SQ FT: 5,000
SALES (est): 90.8K **Privately Held**
SIC: 2085 2084 Grain alcohol for beverage purposes; cordials, alcoholic; vodka (alcoholic beverage); wine cellars, bonded: engaged in blending wines

(G-15101)
SSC GREEN INC
405 S 54th Ave (99353-8040)
PHONE................................509 967-4753
Jerod O Shelby, *CEO*
Lorraine Shelby, *Finance Mgr*
EMP: 6
SALES (est): 950K **Privately Held**
SIC: 3711 Motor vehicles & car bodies

(G-15102)
SSC NORTH AMERICA LLC
Also Called: Shelby Super Cars
405 S 54th Ave (99353-8040)
P.O. Box 4508 (99353-4008)
PHONE................................509 967-4753
Jerod O Shelby,
EMP: 8
SALES (est): 1MM **Privately Held**
WEB: www.sscautos.com
SIC: 3711 Motor vehicles & car bodies

(G-15103)
VINMOTION WINES LLC
Also Called: Red Mountain Wine Estates
8111 Keene Rd (99353-7202)
PHONE................................509 967-7477
Steven Seallck,
EMP: 5
SALES (est): 366K
SALES (corp-wide): 86.8MM **Privately Held**
SIC: 2084 Wines
PA: Banfi Products Corporation
   1111 Cedar Swamp Rd
   Glen Head NY 11545
   516 626-9200

Westport
Grays Harbor County

(G-15104)
D&L SUMMERS INC
441 N Melbourne St (98595)
PHONE................................360 268-0769
Lewis Summers, *President*
EMP: 3
SALES: 65K **Privately Held**
SIC: 3732 Fishing boats: lobster, crab, oyster, etc.: small

(G-15105)
HALF MOON BAY BAR & GRILL
421 E Neddie Rose Dr (98595)
PHONE................................360 268-9166
Neddie Farington, *CEO*
EMP: 30
SALES (est): 2.2MM **Privately Held**
SIC: 3799 Recreational vehicles

(G-15106)
OCEAN GOLD SEAFOODS INC
1804 N Nyhus St (98595)
P.O. Box 1104 (98595-1104)
PHONE................................360 268-2510
Dennis Rydman, *President*
Greg Shaughnessy, *Vice Pres*
◆ EMP: 150
SQ FT: 12,000
SALES (est): 33.7MM **Privately Held**
SIC: 2092 Fresh or frozen fish or seafood chowders, soups & stews

(G-15107)
WASHINGTON CRAB PRODUCERS INC (HQ)
1980 N Nyhus St (98595)
P.O. Box 1488 (98595-1488)
PHONE................................360 268-9161
Frank D Dulcich, *President*
Bill Weidman, *General Mgr*
Patrick Swope, *Corp Secy*
Bill Wideman, *Executive*
▲ EMP: 3
SQ FT: 2,500
SALES (est): 15.1MM
SALES (corp-wide): 565.9MM **Privately Held**
SIC: 2092 2091 Crab meat, fresh: packaged in nonsealed containers; shrimp, fresh: prepared; shrimp, frozen: prepared; fish, fresh: prepared; shellfish, canned & cured; fish, canned & cured
PA: Dulcich, Inc.
   16797 Se 130th Ave
   Clackamas OR 97015
   503 226-2200

(G-15108)
WESTPORT LLC
1807 N Nyhus St (98595)
PHONE................................360 268-1800
Jennifer Swogger, *Human Res Mgr*

White Salmon - Klickitat County (G-15109)

EMP: 213
SALES (corp-wide): 40.5MM **Privately Held**
SIC: 3732 Yachts, building & repairing
PA: Westport, L.L.C.
637 Marine Dr
Port Angeles WA 98363
360 452-5095

White Salmon
Klickitat County

(G-15109)
A&C LOGGING LLC
964 Snowden Rd (98672-8227)
PHONE...............................509 493-3160
Ralph Barnedt, *Principal*
EMP: 6
SALES (est): 355.1K **Privately Held**
SIC: 2411 Logging camps & contractors

(G-15110)
ANNI DEMI WINERY INC
139 Cooke Rd (98672-8807)
PHONE...............................509 493-2702
Alexander Myszkowski, *Principal*
EMP: 2
SALES (est): 147.4K **Privately Held**
SIC: 2084 Wines, brandy & brandy spirits

(G-15111)
BEARLY LOGGIN
716 Snowden Rd (98672-8224)
PHONE...............................509 493-1706
Nick Browning, *Owner*
EMP: 4
SALES (est): 170K **Privately Held**
SIC: 2411 Logging

(G-15112)
BILL ANDERSON
Also Called: Anderson's Custom Sawing
52 Anderson Rd (98672-8336)
PHONE...............................509 281-0055
Bill Anderson, *Owner*
EMP: 2
SALES: 250K **Privately Held**
SIC: 2411 Logging

(G-15113)
COLUMBIA RIVER MFG INC
799 Highway 141 (98672-8333)
P.O. Box 260, Husum (98623-0260)
PHONE...............................509 493-3460
Ian Vandehey, *Vice Pres*
EMP: 4
SALES: 150K **Privately Held**
SIC: 3999 Manufacturing industries

(G-15114)
DARRELL A TILLOTSON
Also Called: Tillotson Logging Co
855 Nw Loop Rd (98672)
P.O. Box 46 (98672-0046)
PHONE...............................509 493-2376
EMP: 4 **EST:** 1969
SALES (est): 150K **Privately Held**
SIC: 2411 Logging

(G-15115)
FIDELITAD INC
801 Panorama Ct (98672-2175)
P.O. Box 688 (98672-0688)
PHONE...............................509 637-3938
Eric Eugene Edsall, *President*
Alejandro Pita, *Vice Pres*
EMP: 6
SALES: 1.5MM **Privately Held**
SIC: 3812 Radar systems & equipment

(G-15116)
HEAVY METAL FABRICATION
8 Windago Ln (98672-8432)
PHONE...............................509 493-2979
Paul Casal, *Principal*
EMP: 2 **EST:** 2011
SALES (est): 156.8K **Privately Held**
SIC: 3499 Fabricated metal products

(G-15117)
HENRY KEMPTON
9 Forrest Ln (98672-8009)
PHONE...............................509 493-1160
Henry Kempton, *Owner*
EMP: 3
SALES (est): 231.9K **Privately Held**
SIC: 3531 Plows: construction, excavating & grading

(G-15118)
HERB WITHERED
140 Sleepy Hollow Rd (98672-8223)
PHONE...............................509 493-3614
Herb Withered, *Principal*
EMP: 2
SALES (est): 127.2K **Privately Held**
SIC: 2833 Drugs & herbs: grading, grinding & milling

(G-15119)
INNOVATIVE COMPOSITE ENGRG INC
Also Called: Ice
1265 N Main Ave (98672)
PHONE...............................509 493-4484
Steven J Maier, *CEO*
Jim Nicholls, *Engineer*
Wendy Willow, *CFO*
Brian Hull, *Marketing Staff*
EMP: 70
SQ FT: 8,000
SALES (est): 14.2MM **Privately Held**
WEB: www.innovativecomposite.com
SIC: 3083 3624 Laminated plastics plate & sheet; fibers, carbon & graphite

(G-15120)
KNOT HOLE INC
Also Called: My Wooden Treasures
1440 Nw Richards Ln (98672-8733)
PHONE...............................541 806-0950
Ken Browning, *President*
Seth Browning, *Vice Pres*
EMP: 3
SALES (est): 43K **Privately Held**
SIC: 2411 Logging

(G-15121)
KRISTA K THIE
Also Called: Twin Oaks Cnstr & Metalworks
1549 W Jewett Blvd (98672-8928)
P.O. Box 2046 (98672-2046)
PHONE...............................509 493-2626
Krista Thie, *Owner*
Daryl Hoyt, *Owner*
EMP: 5
SALES (est): 395K **Privately Held**
SIC: 1622 0851 3599 Bridge construction; forestry services; machine & other job shop work

(G-15122)
MCCAFFERTY NW LAND DEV LLC
115 Sleepy Hollow Rd (98672-8223)
PHONE...............................509 483-1222
Mitchell McCafferty, *Principal*
Ashlie McCafferty, *Co-Owner*
EMP: 4
SALES (est): 320.3K **Privately Held**
SIC: 3531 Road construction & maintenance machinery

(G-15123)
MOUNTAIN LOGGING INC (PA)
1000 W Jewett Blvd (98672-8922)
P.O. Box 253 (98672-0253)
PHONE...............................509 493-3511
EMP: 30
SQ FT: 3,000
SALES (est): 4.2MM **Privately Held**
SIC: 2411 Logging camps & contractors

(G-15124)
NORTH SPORTS INC (PA)
Also Called: Aquaglide
1 Northshore Dr (98672-8684)
PHONE...............................509 493-4938
David Johnson, *President*
Brian Klouser, *Finance Mgr*
Doug Hopkins, *Sales Mgr*
Peter Arpag, *Sales Staff*
Dan Schwarz, *Sales Staff*
◆ **EMP:** 18
SQ FT: 15,000
SALES: 2MM **Privately Held**
WEB: www.northsports.com
SIC: 3949 Windsurfing boards (sailboards) & equipment

(G-15125)
NORTHWEST PRECISION TOOL INC
799 Highway 141 (98672-8333)
P.O. Box 65178, Vancouver (98665-0006)
PHONE...............................509 493-4044
EMP: 2
SQ FT: 4,600
SALES (est): 120K **Privately Held**
SIC: 3544 3469 Mfg Dies/Tools/Jigs/Fixtures Mfg Metal Stampings

(G-15126)
OLD SCHOOL WOODCRAFTER
145 Se 3rd Rd (98672)
PHONE...............................509 493-4155
David Swann, *Owner*
EMP: 2
SALES (est): 205.5K **Privately Held**
SIC: 2431 Woodwork, interior & ornamental

(G-15127)
PILOT KNOB CONSTRUCTION INC (PA)
160 Nw Simmons Rd (98672-8735)
PHONE...............................509 493-4196
Phoebe Oglesby, *President*
Sammie Oglesby, *Vice Pres*
Robert Todd Oglesby, *Shareholder*
EMP: 3
SALES (est): 832.8K **Privately Held**
SIC: 1629 1081 1611 Land preparation construction; metal mining exploration & development services; overburden removal, metal mining; general contractor, highway & street construction

(G-15128)
SAGETECH CORPORATION
1320 Green Tree Ln (98672-0486)
P.O. Box 1146 (98672-1146)
PHONE...............................509 493-2154
Kelvin Scribner, *CEO*
Caleb Hotchkiss, *Admin Sec*
EMP: 77
SQ FT: 2,940
SALES (est): 2.3MM **Privately Held**
SIC: 3812 Search & navigation equipment

(G-15129)
SAGETECH CORPORATION
292 E Jewett Blvd (98672)
PHONE...............................509 493-1364
Kelvin Scribner, *CEO*
Caleb Hotchkiss, *Admin Sec*
EMP: 77 **EST:** 2017
SALES (est): 2.3MM **Privately Held**
SIC: 3812 Search & navigation equipment

(G-15130)
SAGETECH CORPORATION
156 Ne Church Ave (98672-0238)
P.O. Box 1146 (98672-1146)
PHONE...............................509 493-2113
Kelvin Scribner, *CEO*
Caleb Hotchkiss, *Admin Sec*
EMP: 77
SQ FT: 1,200
SALES (est): 2.1MM **Privately Held**
SIC: 3812 Search & navigation equipment

(G-15131)
SHARON MCILHENNY
Also Called: Lyle Style
235 Bates Rd (98672-8504)
PHONE...............................509 493-9259
Sharon McIlhenny, *Owner*
EMP: 3
SQ FT: 1,500
SALES: 100K **Privately Held**
WEB: www.lylestyle.net
SIC: 2087 2099 Cocktail mixes, nonalcoholic; food preparations

(G-15132)
SIGNS & DESIGNS
1435 Sw Brislawn Loop Rd (98672-8687)
P.O. Box 936 (98672-0936)
PHONE...............................509 493-8350
Melanie Denton, *Principal*
EMP: 3
SALES (est): 269.3K **Privately Held**
SIC: 3993 Signs & advertising specialties

(G-15133)
TAINA HARTMAN STUDIO
121 N Main Ave (98672-1149)
P.O. Box 2183, Clackamas OR (97015-2183)
PHONE...............................541 806-0053
Taina Hartman, *Owner*
EMP: 3
SALES (est): 159.5K **Privately Held**
SIC: 3911 Jewelry, precious metal

(G-15134)
TRIBAL FISHCO LLC
65335 Highway 14 (98672-8690)
PHONE...............................509 493-1104
Virgil Lewis,
EMP: 10
SALES (est): 505.4K **Privately Held**
SIC: 2092 Fresh or frozen packaged fish

(G-15135)
WINDWALKER VINEYARD
133 Wnuk Rd (98672-8428)
PHONE...............................541 490-4011
EMP: 2
SALES (est): 74.4K **Privately Held**
SIC: 2084 Wines

White Swan
Yakima County

(G-15136)
7 ARROWS LOGGING LLC
310 Coburn Rd (98952)
PHONE...............................509 930-8059
Ryan Spencer, *Principal*
EMP: 2
SALES (est): 161.3K **Privately Held**
SIC: 2411 Logging

(G-15137)
DELBERT L WHEELER
Also Called: Wheeler, Delbert L Logging Co
1200 N White Swan Rd (98952)
P.O. Box 237 (98952-0237)
PHONE...............................509 874-2471
Delbert Wheeler, *Owner*
Wheeler Trina, *Sales Executive*
EMP: 50
SALES: 9MM **Privately Held**
SIC: 2411 Logging camps & contractors

(G-15138)
KING MOUNTAIN TOBACCO CO INC
2000 4th Fort Simcoe Rd (98952)
P.O. Box 422 (98952-0422)
PHONE...............................509 874-9935
Delbert Wheeler, *President*
Kamiakin Wheeler, *Treasurer*
EMP: 55
SQ FT: 80
SALES (est): 6.5MM **Privately Held**
SIC: 3999 Tobacco pipes, pipestems & bits

(G-15139)
TIIN-MA LOGGING
61 Medicine Valley Rd (98952)
P.O. Box 458 (98952-0458)
PHONE...............................509 874-2040
Kip Ramsey, *Owner*
EMP: 40
SQ FT: 1,600
SALES (est): 3.7MM **Privately Held**
SIC: 2411 Logging

(G-15140)
YAKAMA NATION
Also Called: Yakama Forest Products
3191 Wesley Rd (98952-9792)
P.O. Box 489 (98952-0489)
PHONE...............................509 874-2901
Jan Jacobson, *Branch Mgr*
EMP: 15 **Privately Held**
SIC: 2436 Plywood, softwood
PA: Yakama Nation
401 4th Rd
Toppenish WA 98948
509 865-5121

▲ = Import ▼ = Export
◆ = Import/Export

GEOGRAPHIC SECTION

Wilbur
Lincoln County

(G-15141)
EMERSON LOGGING CORPORATION
310 Se Spokane St (99185)
P.O. Box 27 (99185-0027)
PHONE.................................509 647-5658
Darryl Emerson, *President*
Maxine Emerson, *Corp Secy*
EMP: 4
SALES: 65K **Privately Held**
SIC: 2411 1629 Logging camps & contractors; earthmoving contractor

(G-15142)
WILBUR REGISTER INC
110 Se Main Ave (99185)
P.O. Box 186 (99185-0186)
PHONE.................................509 647-5551
Frank Stedman, *President*
Kristine Stedman, *Corp Secy*
EMP: 6
SQ FT: 2,600
SALES (est): 470.7K **Privately Held**
SIC: 2711 2752 Newspapers; commercial printing, lithographic

Wilkeson
Pierce County

(G-15143)
COPPER CREEK LOGGING LLC
520 Vine St (98396-0442)
PHONE.................................253 203-5915
Tracy Dow, *Principal*
EMP: 2
SALES (est): 81.7K **Privately Held**
SIC: 2411 Logging

(G-15144)
WILKESON SANDSTONE QUARRY LLC
29115 Quinnon Rd E (98396)
PHONE.................................360 829-0999
Chuck Nelson, *Principal*
▲ **EMP:** 4 **EST:** 2000
SQ FT: 2,000
SALES (est): 377.7K **Privately Held**
SIC: 1411 Sandstone, dimension-quarrying

Winlock
Lewis County

(G-15145)
BDN LOGGING INC
200 Marttala Rd (98596-9730)
PHONE.................................360 785-4119
Brad Naillon, *Principal*
EMP: 3
SALES (est): 242.7K **Privately Held**
SIC: 2411 Logging

(G-15146)
CARDINAL GLASS INDUSTRIES INC
Also Called: Cardinal Fg - Winlock
545 Avery Rd W (98596-9657)
PHONE.................................360 242-4300
Monte Eslinger, *Maint Spvr*
Jeff Jacobson, *Engineer*
Steve Smith, *Branch Mgr*
EMP: 220
SALES (corp-wide): 1B **Privately Held**
WEB: www.cardinalcorp.com
SIC: 3211 Flat glass
PA: Cardinal Glass Industries Inc
775 Pririe Ctr Dr Ste 200
Eden Prairie MN 55344
952 229-2600

(G-15147)
CARDINAL GLASS INDUSTRIES INC
Also Called: Cardinal Fg
545 Avery Rd W (98596-9657)
PHONE.................................360 242-4336
EMP: 116
SALES (corp-wide): 1B **Privately Held**
WEB: www.cardinalcorp.com
SIC: 3231 3211 Insulating glass: made from purchased glass; tempered glass: made from purchased glass; flat glass
PA: Cardinal Glass Industries Inc
775 Pririe Ctr Dr Ste 200
Eden Prairie MN 55344
952 229-2600

(G-15148)
CRAFT INTERNATIONAL OF WASH
307 Nw Kerron St (98596-9472)
PHONE.................................360 785-3606
Janice Beglin, *President*
Hugh Beglin, *President*
Robert Beglin, *Vice Pres*
EMP: 4
SQ FT: 2,500
SALES: 1MM **Privately Held**
SIC: 3944 2298 2284 7389 Craft & hobby kits & sets; cordage & twine; thread mills; packaging & labeling services; packaging materials

(G-15149)
D CREEK TIMBER INC
379 Avery Rd W (98596-9626)
PHONE.................................360 262-3786
Daniel Dunham, *President*
Duane Eastman, *Vice Pres*
Jonathan Dunham, *Treasurer*
EMP: 3
SALES (est): 400K **Privately Held**
SIC: 2411 Logging camps & contractors

(G-15150)
GARY C HORSLEY
Also Called: Horsley Logging & Cnstr Co
1224 Winlock Vader Rd (98596-9509)
P.O. Box 125, Doty (98539-0125)
PHONE.................................360 274-4502
Gary C Horsley, *Owner*
EMP: 8
SALES (est): 330.6K **Privately Held**
SIC: 2411 1611 Logging; general contractor, highway & street construction

(G-15151)
J D MFG
145 Park Rd (98596-9699)
PHONE.................................360 864-8271
Jay Jdouglas, *Principal*
EMP: 2
SALES (est): 123.2K **Privately Held**
SIC: 3999 Manufacturing industries

(G-15152)
JACK H HILL
Also Called: H&H Enterprises
240 Boone Rd (98596)
PHONE.................................360 864-4939
Jack Hill, *Principal*
EMP: 2
SALES (est): 20.8K **Privately Held**
SIC: 2411 1629 Logging; land clearing contractor

(G-15153)
JUSTIN MAINE LOGGING INC
498 Conrad Rd (98596-9746)
PHONE.................................360 262-4105
Justin Maine, *Principal*
EMP: 2
SALES (est): 81.7K **Privately Held**
SIC: 2411 Logging

(G-15154)
MAPEL MILL LLC
Also Called: J & L Tonewoods
450 State Highway 505 (98596-9750)
PHONE.................................360 508-1313
Harold C Kupers III, *Principal*
EMP: 3
SALES (est): 240.1K **Privately Held**
SIC: 2421 Lumber stacking or sticking

(G-15155)
RANDY WOOD
142 Kollock Rd (98596-9510)
PHONE.................................360 295-3648
Randy Wood, *Principal*
EMP: 2
SALES (est): 148.7K **Privately Held**
SIC: 3589 High pressure cleaning equipment

(G-15156)
SHAKERTOWN 1992 INC
1200 Nw Kerron St (98596-9144)
P.O. Box 400 (98596-0400)
PHONE.................................360 785-3501
Scott William Clarke, *President*
Philip Clarke, *Vice Pres*
Brian Gabbard, *Admin Sec*
EMP: 50
SQ FT: 100,000
SALES: 9.2MM
SALES (corp-wide): 207.6K **Privately Held**
SIC: 2429 2421 Shingles, wood: sawed or hand split; shakes (hand split shingles); sawmills & planing mills, general
PA: Green River Log Sales Ltd
6315 Waterbury Rd
Nanaimo BC V9V 1
604 820-3800

(G-15157)
TOTTEN TILEWORKS
200 Se Front St (98596)
P.O. Box 2 (98596-0002)
PHONE.................................360 785-3282
Charles E Totten, *Owner*
EMP: 4
SALES: 140K **Privately Held**
SIC: 3253 Ceramic wall & floor tile

(G-15158)
WASHINGTON HARDWOODS AND
1200 Nw Kerron St Ste 200 (98596-9144)
P.O. Box 400 (98596-0400)
PHONE.................................206 283-7574
John Gaydos, *Principal*
EMP: 10
SALES (est): 1.5MM **Privately Held**
SIC: 5031 2431 Millwork; millwork

Winthrop
Okanogan County

(G-15159)
EMEASURE INC
129 Eastside Chewuch Rd (98862-9736)
P.O. Box 816 (98862-0816)
PHONE.................................844 382-7326
Michael Schuh, *President*
George Merriman, *Chairman*
Dawn Whitmer, *VP Sales*
Robert Crane, *Director*
EMP: 5 **EST:** 2013
SALES (est): 396.6K **Privately Held**
SIC: 3825 Test equipment for electronic & electric measurement

(G-15160)
FERRYBOAT MUSIC LLC
141 Eastside Chewuch Rd (98862-9736)
P.O. Box 22 (98862-0022)
PHONE.................................509 996-3528
Hank Cramer, *Managing Prtnr*
Kit Cramer, *Partner*
EMP: 5
SALES (est): 263.1K **Privately Held**
SIC: 3999 Manufacturing industries

(G-15161)
GOOD SCENTS CO
63 Raven Rd (98862-9127)
P.O. Box 115 (98862-0115)
PHONE.................................509 996-2620
EMP: 2
SALES (est): 96.5K **Privately Held**
SIC: 2841 Mfg Soap/Other Detergents

(G-15162)
JAMES A WRIGHT CNSTR LLC
19108 Francis Ln (98862-9783)
PHONE.................................509 996-3249
James A Wright,
Laura L Wright,
EMP: 7
SALES (est): 574.4K **Privately Held**
SIC: 1794 1711 1442 1623 Excavation work; septic system construction; gravel & pebble mining; water & sewer line construction; aggregate

(G-15163)
METHOW HOUSE WATCH INC
26 Lynx Ln (98862-9807)
PHONE.................................509 996-3332
Derek Van Marter, *Principal*
EMP: 3 **EST:** 2015
SALES (est): 97K **Privately Held**
SIC: 2082 Malt beverages

(G-15164)
RAMS HEAD CONSTRUCTION INC
Also Called: Valley Machine and Fabrication
22 Intercity Airport Rd (98862-9744)
P.O. Box 637 (98862-0637)
PHONE.................................509 997-6962
Ron Perrow, *President*
Chrystal Perrow, *Corp Secy*
EMP: 2
SQ FT: 6,000
SALES: 160K **Privately Held**
SIC: 3541 Machine tool replacement & repair parts, metal cutting types

(G-15165)
TILLER LLC
303 Riverside Ave (98862)
PHONE.................................425 770-0855
Tim Johns,
Peter Polson,
EMP: 9
SALES: 200K **Privately Held**
SIC: 7372 Application computer software

(G-15166)
WINTHROP WOOD WORKS
810 E Side Rd (98862)
PHONE.................................509 996-2037
Cliff Schwab, *Owner*
Joy Schwab, *Co-Owner*
EMP: 2
SALES: 50K **Privately Held**
SIC: 2511 Wood household furniture

Wishram
Klickitat County

(G-15167)
PACIFIC NW AGGREGATES INC
5 Avery Boat Ramp Rd (98673-0800)
P.O. Box 82879, Portland OR (97282-0879)
PHONE.................................509 748-9188
Randall Steed, *President*
Michael Frazier, *CFO*
EMP: 8
SALES (est): 222.6K **Privately Held**
SIC: 1481 Mine & quarry services, non-metallic minerals

Woodinville
King County

(G-15168)
2 WHEEL DYNOWORKS
19501 Woodinville (98072)
PHONE.................................425 398-4335
EMP: 2 **EST:** 2012
SALES (est): 130K **Privately Held**
SIC: 3312 Blast Furnace-Steel Works

(G-15169)
20 CORNERS BREWING LLC
14148 Ne 190th St Ste A (98072-8437)
PHONE.................................800 840-3346
Andrew Davis,
Vern A Olson,
EMP: 12 **EST:** 2015
SALES (est): 1.4MM **Privately Held**
SIC: 2082 Malt beverages

Woodinville - King County (G-15170)

(G-15170)
A TOUCH OF CLASS CREATIONS
14523 165th Pl Ne (98072-9037)
PHONE...................................425 489-3472
Kimberly Berg, *Principal*
EMP: 2
SALES (est): 120.1K **Privately Held**
SIC: 2273 Carpets & rugs

(G-15171)
ADI THERMAL POWER CORP
19495 144th Ave Ne A160 (98072-6406)
PHONE...................................206 484-2879
Fax: 425 424-9062
EMP: 2
SQ FT: 3,500
SALES (est): 250K **Privately Held**
SIC: 3519 Internal combustion engines

(G-15172)
ADVANCED LEAN MFG LLC
17611 128th Pl Ne (98072-8783)
PHONE...................................425 402-8300
Todd Daniel Reams, *Principal*
Wesley Bates,
EMP: 20
SALES (est): 3.4MM **Privately Held**
SIC: 3999 Barber & beauty shop equipment

(G-15173)
AIRNEXION INC
22111 55th Ave Se (98072-8370)
PHONE...................................425 771-5924
James Larsen, *Principal*
EMP: 2
SALES (est): 81.4K **Privately Held**
SIC: 3599 Industrial machinery

(G-15174)
AIRPORT RANCH ESTATES LLC
14450 Woodinville Redmond (98072-9051)
P.O. Box 1248 (98072-1248)
PHONE...................................425 877-1006
Sabrina Bohlman, *Controller*
Mike Miller, *Branch Mgr*
EMP: 2 **Privately Held**
SIC: 2084 Wines
PA: Airport Ranch Estates, L.L.C.
560 Merlot Dr
Prosser WA 99350

(G-15175)
ALTA CELLARS
19501 144th Ave Ne A500 (98072-4404)
PHONE...................................425 424-9218
EMP: 4
SALES (est): 183.8K **Privately Held**
SIC: 2084 Mfg Wines/Brandy/Spirits

(G-15176)
AMAZE GRAPHICS INC
Also Called: Guy Gifter
19510 144th Ave Ne Ste E5 (98072-8429)
PHONE...................................425 481-8877
Mark Mackaman, *President*
Terry A Mackaman, *Vice Pres*
EMP: 5
SQ FT: 7,500
SALES (est): 679.3K **Privately Held**
WEB: www.amazegraphics.com
SIC: 2752 Catalogs, lithographed

(G-15177)
ANDREW M BALDWIN
20130 164th Ave Ne (98072-7044)
PHONE...................................425 481-6245
Andrew M Baldwin, *Owner*
EMP: 2
SALES (est): 180K **Privately Held**
SIC: 2541 Cabinets, except refrigerated: show, display, etc.: wood

(G-15178)
ANDREW ROSS WINERY
14810 Ne 145th St Ste A2 (98072-4555)
PHONE...................................425 487-9463
Ross A Mickel, *Owner*
Alexandra J Mickel, *Owner*
EMP: 4
SALES (est): 200K **Privately Held**
SIC: 2084 Wines

(G-15179)
ANTONY ARCHITECTURAL STONE
6018 234th St Se Ste D (98072-8679)
PHONE...................................425 424-0051
EMP: 6
SALES (est): 527.8K **Privately Held**
SIC: 3281 Mfg Cut Stone/Products

(G-15180)
ARLINGTON ROAD CELLARS
19495 144th Ave Ne A115 (98072-4427)
PHONE...................................425 482-1801
EMP: 2
SQ FT: 1,800
SALES (est): 13.8K **Privately Held**
SIC: 2084 Mfg Wines/Brandy/Spirits

(G-15181)
ASEPTICO INC
8333 216th St Se (98072-8060)
P.O. Box 1548 (98072-1548)
PHONE...................................425 487-3157
Glenn D Kazen, *President*
Bob Giantonio, *Business Mgr*
Eydie Kazen, *Corp Secy*
Stephanie McKelvey, *COO*
Shane Hohnstein, *Vice Pres*
▲ **EMP:** 100
SQ FT: 45,000
SALES (est): 25.8MM **Privately Held**
WEB: www.asepticonails.com
SIC: 3843 3845 Dental equipment; medical cleaning equipment, ultrasonic

(G-15182)
ASPENWOOD CELLARS
19415 219th Ave Ne (98077-7137)
PHONE...................................425 844-2233
Jim Petty, *Owner*
EMP: 3
SALES (est): 250.1K **Privately Held**
SIC: 2084 Wines

(G-15183)
AVENNIA WINERY
18808 142nd Ave Ne Ste 2b (98072-8281)
PHONE...................................425 392-3191
EMP: 2
SALES (est): 100K **Privately Held**
SIC: 2084 Wines

(G-15184)
BAER WINERY LLC
19501 144th Ave Ne F100 (98072-6463)
PHONE...................................425 483-7060
Les Baer,
Lisa Baer,
EMP: 3
SQ FT: 4,500
SALES: 562.1K **Privately Held**
WEB: www.baerwinery.com
SIC: 2084 Wines

(G-15185)
BARRAGE CELLARS LLC
19501 144th Ave Ne E800 (98072-4476)
PHONE...................................425 381-9675
Kevin Correll, *Mng Member*
Jesse Andrews, *Correspondent*
EMP: 2
SQ FT: 2,500
SALES: 300K **Privately Held**
SIC: 2084 Wines

(G-15186)
BEAR CREEK BOATWORKS INC
19909 Ne 151st Pl (98077-7611)
PHONE...................................425 558-4086
David Pollon V, *Principal*
EMP: 3
SALES (est): 260.6K **Privately Held**
SIC: 3732 Boat building & repairing

(G-15187)
BEAVER MACHINE WORKS INC
12602 Ne 178th St Ste A (98072-8702)
PHONE...................................425 402-1032
Rod Brower, *President*
Jeff Brower, *Vice Pres*
Grace Brower, *Treasurer*
Kelli Mack, *Office Mgr*
Marcus Evans, *Supervisor*
▼ **EMP:** 8
SALES (est): 1.3MM **Privately Held**
SIC: 3599 Machine shop, jobbing & repair

(G-15188)
BENSUSSEN DEUTSCH & ASSOC LLC (PA)
Also Called: Bda
15525 Wdnvll Rdmond Rd Ne (98072)
PHONE...................................425 492-6111
Jay Deutsch, *CEO*
Eric Bensussen, *President*
Rob Martin, *COO*
Barry Deutsch, *Exec VP*
Jared Collinge, *CFO*
◆ **EMP:** 275
SQ FT: 112,000
SALES (est): 307MM **Privately Held**
WEB: www.bdainc.com
SIC: 5136 5137 5199 7311 Sportswear, men's & boys'; sportswear, women's & children's; advertising specialties; advertising agencies; games, toys & children's vehicles; electronic games & toys

(G-15189)
BETTER OFF THREADS
15610 Ne Wdnvlle Dvall Rd (98072)
PHONE...................................425 408-1304
April Palmer, *CEO*
EMP: 4 **EST:** 2010
SALES (est): 306.6K **Privately Held**
SIC: 2389 Apparel & accessories

(G-15190)
BHP HOLDINGS INC
Also Called: Biopure Healing Products
18538 142nd Ave Ne (98072-8520)
PHONE...................................425 462-8414
Johanna Dean, *CEO*
EMP: 10
SALES (est): 208.3K **Privately Held**
SIC: 8099 2023 Nutrition services; dietary supplements, dairy & non-dairy based

(G-15191)
BIMBO BAKERIES USA INC
Oroweat Foods
14103 Ne 200th St C (98072-8443)
PHONE...................................425 415-6745
Ken Jacobs, *Manager*
EMP: 20 **Privately Held**
WEB: www.englishmuffin.com
SIC: 2051 Bread, cake & related products
HQ: Bimbo Bakeries Usa, Inc
255 Business Center Dr # 200
Horsham PA 19044
215 347-5500

(G-15192)
BIO-RAD LABORATORIES INC
8415 216th St Se (98072-8008)
PHONE...................................425 498-1933
Beth Evans, *Branch Mgr*
EMP: 473
SALES (corp-wide): 2.2B **Publicly Held**
SIC: 3826 Analytical instruments
PA: Bio-Rad Laboratories, Inc.
1000 Alfred Nobel Dr
Hercules CA 94547
510 724-7000

(G-15193)
BJORKLUND MACHINE & TOOL CO
21828 87th Ave Se Ste D (98072-8054)
P.O. Box 1170, Granite Falls (98252-1170)
PHONE...................................425 892-1092
Steven Bjorklund, *President*
Lois Bjorklund, *Corp Secy*
▲ **EMP:** 6
SQ FT: 5,200
SALES (est): 671.3K **Privately Held**
WEB: www.bjmach.com
SIC: 3599 Machine shop, jobbing & repair

(G-15194)
BKD SOFTWARE
19903 164th Ave Ne (98072-7042)
PHONE...................................425 487-1475
Bruce White, *Principal*
EMP: 2
SALES (est): 152.1K **Privately Held**
SIC: 7372 Prepackaged software

(G-15195)
BOBBY WOLFORD TRUCKING & SALV
Also Called: Bobby Wolford Trucking & Demo
22014 W Bostian Rd (98072-8000)
PHONE...................................425 481-1800
Robert C Wolford, *President*
EMP: 31
SQ FT: 1,800
SALES (est): 13.1MM **Privately Held**
SIC: 2421 1795 4212 Sawdust & shavings; wrecking & demolition work; dump truck haulage

(G-15196)
BOOKWALTER LLC
14810 Ne 145th St Ste B (98072-4555)
PHONE...................................425 488-1983
Nick James, *Manager*
EMP: 2
SALES (est): 95K **Privately Held**
SIC: 2084 Wines

(G-15197)
BRIOTECH INC
19816 141st Pl Ne (98072-8432)
PHONE...................................425 488-4300
Daniel Terry, *Principal*
EMP: 5
SALES (est): 379.6K **Privately Held**
SIC: 2834 Pharmaceutical preparations

(G-15198)
BROVO SPIRITS LLC
18808 142nd Ave Ne Ste 3b (98072-8281)
PHONE...................................206 354-3919
Mhairi Voelsgen, *CEO*
Erin Prochy, *COO*
Peter Weiss, *CFO*
EMP: 4 **EST:** 2011
SALES (est): 320K **Privately Held**
SIC: 2085 Distilled & blended liquors

(G-15199)
BUDGET PRINTING & MAILING
Also Called: All Access Printing & Mail
24024 85th Ave Se (98072-9588)
PHONE...................................253 872-9969
Craig Martin, *Owner*
EMP: 14
SALES (est): 1.1MM **Privately Held**
SIC: 2752 Commercial printing, offset

(G-15200)
BUNNELL FAMILY CELLULAR
19501 144th Ave Ne C800 (98072-6463)
PHONE...................................425 286-2964
EMP: 2 **EST:** 2012
SALES (est): 92K **Privately Held**
SIC: 2084 Wines

(G-15201)
BYTEWARE LLC
Also Called: Main Branch, The
18423 Ne 186th St (98077-6621)
PHONE...................................503 914-8020
Alex Arthur,
David Scott,
EMP: 5
SALES (est): 117.7K **Privately Held**
SIC: 7371 7372 Computer software development; application computer software

(G-15202)
CABINET REFACING OF SEATTLE
22255 Ne Wdnvlle Dvall Rd (98077)
PHONE...................................425 405-7961
Ronald Abel, *Principal*
EMP: 3
SALES (est): 140.2K **Privately Held**
SIC: 2434 Wood kitchen cabinets

(G-15203)
CALLAHAN CELLARS
19501 144th Ave Ne D900 (98072-4422)
PHONE...................................425 877-1842
Brian Callahan, *Exec VP*
EMP: 7
SALES (est): 743.1K **Privately Held**
SIC: 2084 Wines

▲ = Import ▼ = Export
◆ = Import/Export

GEOGRAPHIC SECTION

Woodinville - King County (G-15235)

(G-15204)
CAMPBELL SOUP COMPANY
22505 State Route 9 Se (98072-6010)
PHONE..................................425 415-2000
Katleen Honour, *President*
EMP: 325
SALES (corp-wide): 8.6B **Publicly Held**
WEB: www.campbellsoups.com
SIC: **2032** 2038 2033 2052 Spaghetti: packaged in cans, jars, etc.; frozen specialties; canned fruits & specialties; cookies & crackers; bread, cake & related products; potato chips & similar snacks
PA: Campbell Soup Company
1 Campbell Pl
Camden NJ 08103
856 342-4800

(G-15205)
CARDINAL INDUSTRIAL FINISHES
19230 144th Ave Ne Ste A (98072-4440)
PHONE..................................425 483-5665
Claudio Morales, *Plant Mgr*
Clint Emerson, *Branch Mgr*
EMP: 10
SALES (corp-wide): 78.7MM **Privately Held**
WEB: www.cardinalpaint.com
SIC: **2851** Paints & allied products
PA: Cardinal Industrial Finishes
1329 Potrero Ave
South El Monte CA 91733
626 444-9274

(G-15206)
CARSSOW JOHN
13504 Ne 148th St (98072-4613)
PHONE..................................425 820-7995
John Carssow, *Principal*
EMP: 2
SALES (est): 160K **Privately Held**
SIC: **3843** Enamels, dentists'

(G-15207)
CDI CODING
21828 87th Ave Se Ste A (98072-8054)
PHONE..................................360 653-6337
Scott Dearing, *Manager*
EMP: 2
SALES (est): 148.9K **Privately Held**
SIC: **2851** Polyurethane coatings

(G-15208)
COLUMBIA WINERY
14030 Ne 145th St (98072-6994)
P.O. Box 1248 (98072-1248)
PHONE..................................425 488-2776
Sean Hails, *Principal*
Kristin Back, *Manager*
Shelly Fitzgerald, *Education*
EMP: 16
SALES (est): 2.2MM **Privately Held**
SIC: **2084** Wines

(G-15209)
COMPUTERGEAR INC
19510 144th Ave Ne Ste E5 (98072-8429)
PHONE..................................425 487-3600
Terry Powers, *President*
Mark G Mackaman, *Vice Pres*
EMP: 9
SQ FT: 1,500
SALES (est): 1.3MM **Privately Held**
WEB: www.computergear.com
SIC: **2396** 5961 7336 Fabric printing & stamping; mail order house; silk screen design

(G-15210)
CONIFER SPECIALTIES INC
15500 Woodinville Redmond (98072-6953)
PHONE..................................425 486-3334
Michael Maher, *President*
Andrew Heily, *Corp Secy*
John Heily, *Vice Pres*
◆ EMP: 75
SQ FT: 40,000
SALES (est): 38.1MM **Privately Held**
WEB: www.conifer-inc.com
SIC: **2099** Food preparations

(G-15211)
CONSTELLATION BRANDS INC
14030 Ne 145th St (98072-6994)
PHONE..................................425 482-7300
David Lake, *CTO*
EMP: 2 EST: 2016
SALES (est): 62.3K **Privately Held**
SIC: **2084** Wines, brandy & brandy spirits

(G-15212)
CONTROL SENECA CORPORATION
12810 Ne 178th St Ste 101 (98072-8795)
PHONE..................................425 602-4700
Ted W Kartes, *President*
Gary Wozow, *Vice Pres*
EMP: 47
SQ FT: 40,000
SALES (est): 5.8MM **Privately Held**
WEB: www.controlseneca.com
SIC: **2759** 5112 Letterpress printing; labels & seals: printing; business forms

(G-15213)
CORNERSTONE SOFTWARE SYSTEMS
15310 232nd Ave Ne (98077-5839)
P.O. Box 1087, Duvall (98019-1087)
PHONE..................................425 788-9681
Richard Shell, *Owner*
EMP: 3
SALES (est): 250K **Privately Held**
SIC: **7372** Prepackaged software

(G-15214)
COVINGTON CELLARS
18580 142nd Ave Ne (98072-8520)
PHONE..................................425 806-8636
Susan Anda, *Principal*
▲ EMP: 6
SALES (est): 797.8K **Privately Held**
SIC: **2084** Wines

(G-15215)
CREATIVE MOTION CONTROL INC
15520 Woodinville Redmond (98072-6961)
PHONE..................................425 883-0100
Shawn Lawlor, *President*
Charles Gillam, *COO*
Chuck Cornelius, *Vice Pres*
Chuck Gillam, *Treasurer*
Mark Novaresi, *Admin Sec*
EMP: 31
SALES (est): 7.2MM **Privately Held**
WEB: www.creativemotioncontrol.com
SIC: **3499** Tablets, bronze or other metal

(G-15216)
CREO INDUSTRIAL ARTS LLC
8329 216th St Se (98072-8060)
PHONE..................................425 775-7444
Mark Robertson, *Project Mgr*
Russ Roberts, *Accounts Exec*
Don Toenyan, *Sr Project Mgr*
Jim Storie,
Patrick Angelel,
▲ EMP: 100
SQ FT: 10,000
SALES (est): 17.2MM **Privately Held**
WEB: www.signtechseattle.com
SIC: **3993** Signs, not made in custom sign painting shops

(G-15217)
CUILLIN HILLS WINERY
19495 144th Ave Ne A110 (98072-6406)
PHONE..................................425 402-1907
Derek Desvoigne, *Principal*
EMP: 4 EST: 2007
SALES (est): 284.9K **Privately Held**
SIC: **2084** Wines

(G-15218)
DAMSEL CELLARS
18744 142nd Ave Ne (98072-8523)
PHONE..................................206 465-2433
EMP: 4
SALES (est): 269.5K **Privately Held**
SIC: **2084** Wines

(G-15219)
DANCING ALDER WINERY
19495 144th Ave Ne A115 (98072-6406)
PHONE..................................425 402-6300
EMP: 2
SALES (est): 86.2K **Privately Held**
SIC: **2084** Wines

(G-15220)
DARBY WINERY INC
19501 144th Ave Ne E700 (98072-4478)
PHONE..................................206 954-4700
Gary Oldham, *Principal*
EMP: 8
SALES (est): 535.9K **Privately Held**
SIC: **2084** Wines

(G-15221)
DES VOIGNE MELISSA
14125 Ne 189th St Ste B (98072-6507)
PHONE..................................206 478-2021
Melissa Des Voigne, *Principal*
EMP: 2
SALES (est): 140.5K **Privately Held**
SIC: **2084** Wines

(G-15222)
DESIGNERS HOLDING COMPANY INC
Also Called: Designers Marble
20150 144th Ave Ne (98072-4919)
PHONE..................................425 487-9887
Anthony Warmuth, *President*
EMP: 6
SALES (est): 239.8K **Privately Held**
SIC: **1522** 3281 Remodeling, multi-family dwellings; building stone products

(G-15223)
DESIGNERS MARBLE INC
20150 144th Ave Ne Main (98072-4919)
PHONE..................................425 487-9887
Anthony Warmuth, *President*
Steve Holtzner, *General Mgr*
Leslie Minch, *Admin Sec*
EMP: 7
SQ FT: 5,000
SALES (est): 680K **Privately Held**
WEB: www.designersmarble.com
SIC: **3281** 1743 1799 Marble, building: cut & shaped; tile installation, ceramic; kitchen & bathroom remodeling; cabinets, except custom made: kitchen

(G-15224)
DESTINY SOFTWARE INC
19724 166th Ave Ne (98072-7047)
P.O. Box 827 (98072-0827)
PHONE..................................425 415-1777
Desta Dickinson, *President*
Dean Dickinson, *Vice Pres*
EMP: 6
SALES: 800K **Privately Held**
WEB: www.destinysoftwareinc.com
SIC: **7372** Application computer software

(G-15225)
DEYOUNGS FARM AND GARDEN
13621 Ne 175th St (98072)
PHONE..................................425 483-9600
EMP: 20
SQ FT: 21,000
SALES (est): 2.5MM **Privately Held**
SIC: **2048** 5261 5983 Mfg Prepared Feeds Ret Nursery/Garden Supplies Ret Fuel Oil Dealer

(G-15226)
DISTEFANO WINERY LTD
12280 Ne Woodinville Dr (98072-5722)
P.O. Box 2048 (98072-2048)
PHONE..................................425 487-1648
Mark Newton, *President*
Donna Distefano, *Director*
EMP: 6
SALES (est): 613.6K **Privately Held**
WEB: www.distefanowinery.com
SIC: **2084** Wines

(G-15227)
DISTILLERY SEASPIRITS ✪
16110 Woodinville Redmond (98072-6250)
PHONE..................................360 820-0770
EMP: 2 EST: 2018
SALES (est): 68.6K **Privately Held**
SIC: **2085** Distilled & blended liquors

(G-15228)
DIVISION PIEDMONT DIRECTIONAL
14241 Ne Wdnvlle Duvall (98072)
PHONE..................................425 482-9022
Scott Rothenberg, *President*
EMP: 2
SALES (est): 230.4K **Privately Held**
SIC: **1381** Directional drilling oil & gas wells

(G-15229)
DURAMARK TECHNOLOGIES INC
14102 Ne 189th St Ste 3 (98072-3528)
PHONE..................................206 473-9212
Boe Sacks, *Manager*
EMP: 7 **Privately Held**
SIC: **2752** Decals, lithographed
PA: Duramark Technologies, Inc.
16450 Southpark Dr
Westfield IN 46074

(G-15230)
DYNON AVIONICS INC (PA)
19825 141st Pl Ne (98072-8432)
PHONE..................................425 402-0433
John Q Torode, *Chairman*
Ian Jordan, *Chief*
Kirk Kleinholz, *Sales Mgr*
Mike Schosield, *Mktg Dir*
Drew Plommer, *Manager*
▲ EMP: 59
SQ FT: 6,000
SALES (est): 9.8MM **Privately Held**
WEB: www.dynondevelopment.com
SIC: **3999** 8731 Airplane models, except toy; electronic research

(G-15231)
DYNON INSTRUMENTS INC
19825 141st Pl Ne (98072-8432)
PHONE..................................425 402-0433
▲ EMP: 4
SALES (est): 360K **Privately Held**
SIC: **3825** Mfg Electrical Measuring Instruments

(G-15232)
EASTLAKE MINUTEMAN PRESS
13432 Ne 177th Pl (98072-8772)
PHONE..................................425 402-7900
EMP: 2
SALES (est): 196.1K **Privately Held**
SIC: **2752** Commercial printing, offset

(G-15233)
ED PRINT INC
Also Called: Woodinville Weekly
16932 Woodinville Rdmnd (98072-4561)
P.O. Box 587 (98072-0587)
PHONE..................................425 483-0606
Julie Boselly, *President*
EMP: 10
SALES (est): 594.4K **Privately Held**
SIC: **2711** Commercial printing & newspaper publishing combined; newspapers, publishing & printing

(G-15234)
EKO BRANDS LLC
6029 238th St Se Ste 130 (98072-8682)
PHONE..................................800 833-0622
Chris Legler, *CEO*
Laura Sommers, *President*
▲ EMP: 40
SALES (est): 6MM **Privately Held**
SIC: **2095** Freeze-dried coffee

(G-15235)
EKTOS LLC
17802 134th Ave Ne Ste 12 (98072-8806)
PHONE..................................800 783-0383
Larry Barich, *CEO*
Rustin Barich, *Vice Pres*
Delane Bartoo, *Director*
Ali Kazemian, *Director*
Karen Morea, *Director*
EMP: 6 EST: 2010
SALES (est): 403.5K **Privately Held**
SIC: **3542** 8741 High energy rate metal forming machines; restaurant management

Woodinville - King County (G-15236)

(G-15236)
ENERGY SALES
20205 144th Ave Ne # 216 (98072-4451)
PHONE.................................425 883-2343
Kim Crook, *Manager*
EMP: 13
SQ FT: 1,500
SALES (corp-wide): 6.4MM **Privately Held**
WEB: www.energy-sales.com
SIC: 5063 3691 Batteries, dry cell; storage batteries
PA: Energy Sales Llc
   2030 Ringwood Ave
   San Jose CA 95131
   503 690-9000

(G-15237)
EUROCRAFT HARDWOOD FLOORS LLC
8522 216th St Se (98072-8009)
PHONE.................................425 670-6769
Ioan Duciuc, *Mng Member*
EMP: 3 EST: 2010
SALES (est): 12.8K **Privately Held**
SIC: 2426 Flooring, hardwood

(G-15238)
EVALESCO INC
15510 Woodinville Redmond (98072-6979)
PHONE.................................425 486-5959
Mark Ihrig, *President*
Thomas Bauer, *Vice Pres*
EMP: 6
SALES (est): 329.7K **Privately Held**
SIC: 2084 Wines

(G-15239)
EVERGREEN SALES GROUP INC
18915 142nd Ave Ne # 145 (98072-3538)
PHONE.................................425 368-2000
Patrick Albin, *President*
Mike Boljat, *Sales Staff*
EMP: 3
SALES (est): 306.7K **Privately Held**
SIC: 3999 Manufacturing industries

(G-15240)
EYE OF NEEDLE WINERY
19501 144th Ave Ne (98072-6463)
PHONE.................................425 210-7463
EMP: 2 EST: 2017
SALES (est): 67.3K **Privately Held**
SIC: 2084 Wines

(G-15241)
FATKID MACHINE LLC
19501 144th Ave Ne F400 (98072-6463)
PHONE.................................425 481-5214
Joseph Pearce,
EMP: 3
SALES (est): 264.5K **Privately Held**
SIC: 3599 Machine shop, jobbing & repair

(G-15242)
FINE WOODWORKING
5817 238th St Se Ste 2 (98072-8669)
PHONE.................................425 486-3305
Cathy Johnson, *Owner*
EMP: 7
SALES (est): 769.1K **Privately Held**
SIC: 2431 Moldings, wood: unfinished & prefinished; woodwork, interior & ornamental

(G-15243)
FLOW CONTROL INDUSTRIES INC
18715 141st Ave Ne (98072-6826)
P.O. Box 848 (98072-0848)
PHONE.................................425 483-1297
Tamara Hansen, *President*
Paul Skoglund, *Chairman*
Dale De Preist, *Vice Pres*
Tracy Ballweber, *Treasurer*
Warren Van Gendren, *Admin Sec*
▲ EMP: 20
SQ FT: 25,000
SALES (est): 6.9MM **Privately Held**
WEB: www.flowcontrol.com
SIC: 3491 Industrial valves

(G-15244)
FMJ STORAGE INC
22601 Ne 166th St (98077-7465)
PHONE.................................206 605-1394
John Conklin, *President*
EMP: 2
SQ FT: 1,500
SALES: 2.5MM **Privately Held**
SIC: 3572 Computer storage devices

(G-15245)
FOOTPRINT PROMOTIONS INC (PA)
23128 State Route 9 Se (98072-6012)
P.O. Box 687 (98072-0687)
PHONE.................................425 408-0966
Joseph Lowry, *President*
EMP: 6
SALES (est): 1.1MM **Privately Held**
SIC: 3993 Signs & advertising specialties

(G-15246)
FOR-D INC
15503 Ne 188th Pl (98072-8467)
P.O. Box 100 (98072-0100)
PHONE.................................425 486-1120
Ted Johns, *President*
Dorothy Johns, *Corp Secy*
David Johns, *Vice Pres*
EMP: 2
SQ FT: 6,000
SALES: 200K **Privately Held**
SIC: 3312 Tool & die steel

(G-15247)
FORCE MAJEURE WINERY
18720 142nd Ave Ne (98072-8523)
PHONE.................................425 892-9848
Todd Alexander, *Principal*
EMP: 2
SALES (est): 73.6K **Privately Held**
SIC: 2084 Wines

(G-15248)
FORMOST FUJI CORPORATION (PA)
19211 144th Ave Ne (98072-4370)
P.O. Box 359 (98072-0359)
PHONE.................................425 483-9090
Norm Formo, *President*
Dennis Gunnell, *Vice Pres*
Ken Meyer, *Plant Mgr*
Tom Plesia, *Prdtn Mgr*
Dennis Quinn, *Prdtn Mgr*
▲ EMP: 85
SQ FT: 40,000
SALES (est): 16.2MM **Privately Held**
WEB: www.formostpkg.com
SIC: 3565 Bag opening, filling & closing machines

(G-15249)
FREEFLY SYSTEMS INC
15540 Woodinville Redmond (98072-4508)
PHONE.................................425 485-5500
Tabb Firchau, *President*
Megan Fogel, *Vice Pres*
Hugh Bell, *Director*
▲ EMP: 33 EST: 2011
SQ FT: 22,000
SALES (est): 18MM **Privately Held**
SIC: 3861 Photographic equipment & supplies

(G-15250)
GARDEN FRESH FOODS INC
14316 Ne 203rd St Ste A (98072-8486)
PHONE.................................425 483-5467
Jim Dugdale, *President*
Steve Mc Farland, *President*
EMP: 80
SQ FT: 13,000
SALES (est): 14.4MM **Privately Held**
WEB: www.gardenfreshfoods.com
SIC: 2099 5812 Vegetables, peeled for the trade; eating places

(G-15251)
GENOA CELLARS
19501 144th Ave Ne D700 (98072-6423)
PHONE.................................425 296-9660
EMP: 7
SALES (est): 498.9K **Privately Held**
SIC: 2084 Wines

(G-15252)
GLACIER VIEW WINERY
18340 Ne 143rd Pl (98072-6366)
PHONE.................................206 719-1331
Stephanie Jones, *Principal*
EMP: 2 EST: 2015
SALES (est): 113.5K **Privately Held**
SIC: 2084 Wines

(G-15253)
GOOD NEWS PRINTING & GRAPHICS
Also Called: Web Printing & Bindery
14303 Ne 193rd Pl (98072-8402)
PHONE.................................425 483-2510
Bill McKinstry, *President*
▲ EMP: 5
SQ FT: 8,500
SALES: 1MM **Privately Held**
SIC: 2752 2789 Commercial printing, offset; bookbinding & related work

(G-15254)
GRAPEWORKS DISTILLING LLC
16110 Woodinvle Rdmond Rd (98072-6250)
PHONE.................................425 478-7181
EMP: 3
SALES (est): 193.6K **Privately Held**
SIC: 2085 Distilled & blended liquors

(G-15255)
GRAPHICS PLACE INC
Also Called: Lavalle Printing Services
16130 Woodnvl Redmnd 2 (98072-6231)
P.O. Box 1053 (98072-1053)
PHONE.................................425 486-3323
EMP: 14
SQ FT: 4,000
SALES (est): 1.8MM **Privately Held**
WEB: www.lavalleprinting.com
SIC: 2752 7336 7331 Commercial printing, offset; graphic arts & related design; direct mail advertising services

(G-15256)
GRAY AREA TECHNOLOGIES INC
14241 Ne Wdnvlle Dvall Rd (98072)
PHONE.................................206 370-2545
Rajen Shah, *CEO*
EMP: 5
SALES (est): 497.3K **Privately Held**
WEB: www.grayareatech.com
SIC: 3695 Computer software tape & disks: blank, rigid & floppy

(G-15257)
GRIZZLY PET PRODUCTS LLC
19600 144th Ave Ne (98072-8484)
PHONE.................................425 481-1110
Harald Fisker,
▲ EMP: 4
SQ FT: 7,900
SALES (est): 390K **Privately Held**
WEB: www.grizzlypetproducts.com
SIC: 3999 Pet supplies

(G-15258)
H & S MACHINE
19819 144th Ave Ne (98072-8428)
P.O. Box 1216 (98072-1216)
PHONE.................................425 483-2772
Jerry Schnoebelen, *Partner*
Blake Schnoebelen, *Partner*
Brian Schnoebelen, *Partner*
EMP: 4
SQ FT: 2,400
SALES: 350K **Privately Held**
SIC: 3599 Machine shop, jobbing & repair

(G-15259)
HAMILTONJET INC
14680 Ne N Woodinville (98072-4456)
PHONE.................................206 784-8400
Eric Rothberg, *President*
Paul Webb, *Project Mgr*
Craig Dickison, *Treasurer*
Steve Peake, *Sales Executive*
Frank Davis, *Manager*
▲ EMP: 20 EST: 1976
SQ FT: 20,000
SALES (est): 6.3MM
SALES (corp-wide): 1MM **Privately Held**
WEB: www.hamiltonjet.com
SIC: 5088 3599 Marine crafts & supplies; machine & other job shop work
HQ: C W F Hamilton & Co Limited
   20 Lunns Rd
   Christchurch

(G-15260)
HOLLYWOOD HILL VINEYARDS LLC
14350 160th Pl Ne (98072-6995)
PHONE.................................425 753-0093
Jeff Jernegan, *Principal*
EMP: 2
SALES (est): 190.5K **Privately Held**
SIC: 2084 Wines

(G-15261)
HOME AND TRAVEL SOLUTIONS LLC
Also Called: Bed Voyage
18915 142nd Ave Ne # 230 (98072-8502)
PHONE.................................425 949-8216
Sharon Stuart, *Mng Member*
▲ EMP: 9
SQ FT: 1,500
SALES (est): 1.2MM **Privately Held**
SIC: 2299 Broadwoven fabrics: linen, jute, hemp & ramie; fabrics: linen, jute, hemp, ramie

(G-15262)
HYDRA PLASTICS INC
Also Called: Clearwater Spas
18800 Wdnvlle Snhomish Rd (98072)
PHONE.................................425 483-1877
Tom Herriges, *CEO*
▼ EMP: 40
SQ FT: 70,000
SALES (est): 12MM **Privately Held**
WEB: www.clearwaterspas.com
SIC: 3088 Hot tubs, plastic or fiberglass

(G-15263)
ICON CELLARS
18654 142nd Ave Ne (98072-8521)
PHONE.................................425 242-4230
Jim Garner, *Principal*
EMP: 2
SALES (est): 62.3K **Privately Held**
SIC: 2084 Wines, brandy & brandy spirits

(G-15264)
IMAGINATION FABRICATION
6524 240th St Se (98072-9761)
PHONE.................................425 415-1311
Brian Paulus, *Principal*
EMP: 2
SALES (est): 187.1K **Privately Held**
SIC: 3599 Machine shop, jobbing & repair

(G-15265)
INNOVATECH PDTS & EQP CO INC
19722 144th Ave Ne (98072-8427)
PHONE.................................425 402-1881
David Forrest, *CTO*
EMP: 2
SALES (est): 106K **Privately Held**
SIC: 3559 Special industry machinery

(G-15266)
INTERNATIONAL HOMES CEDAR INC
8330 Maltby Rd Ste B (98072-8003)
P.O. Box 886 (98072-0886)
PHONE.................................360 668-8511
Rodney Robertson, *President*
Thomas Warren, *Vice Pres*
▼ EMP: 12
SQ FT: 2,000
SALES (est): 1.2MM **Privately Held**
SIC: 2452 Prefabricated buildings, wood

(G-15267)
IOLINE CORPORATION
14140 Ne 200th St (98072-8443)
PHONE.................................425 398-8282
Frank Schimicci, *President*
Criag Mathison, *Vice Pres*
◆ EMP: 23
SQ FT: 21,000

SALES (est): 4.5MM **Privately Held**
WEB: www.ioline.com
SIC: **3555** 3552 3577 Printing trades machinery; textile machinery; computer peripheral equipment; plotters, computer

(G-15268)
IOPI MEDICAL LLC
18500 156th Ave Ne # 104 (98072-4459)
PHONE..............................425 549-0139
Erich Luschei,
Tara Hart,
Nancy S Luschei,
EMP: 3
SALES (est): 447.6K **Privately Held**
SIC: **3845** Electromedical equipment

(G-15269)
ISENHOWER CELLARS
15007 Woodnvle Redmnd Rd (98072-6988)
PHONE..............................425 488-2299
EMP: 2
SALES (est): 90.1K **Privately Held**
SIC: **2084** Wines

(G-15270)
J M CELLARS COMPANY
14404 137th Pl Ne (98072-7912)
PHONE..............................425 485-6508
John Bigelow, *President*
Tyler Farnsworth, *Assistant*
EMP: 2
SALES (corp-wide): 658.4K **Privately Held**
WEB: www.jmcellars.com
SIC: **2084** Wines
PA: J M Cellars Company
3329 W Laurelhurst Dr Ne
Seattle WA 98105
206 321-0052

(G-15271)
J-NH WINE GROUP LLC
14710 Wdnvll Rdmond Ne (98072)
P.O. Box 2107 (98072-2107)
PHONE..............................425 481-5502
Mike Januik,
Carolyn Januik,
EMP: 13
SALES (est): 828.7K **Privately Held**
SIC: **2084** Wines

(G-15272)
JANUIK WINERY
14710 Woodinville Rdmnd Ne (98072-6987)
P.O. Box 2107 (98072-2107)
PHONE..............................425 481-5502
Mike Januik, *Partner*
Carolyn Januik, *Partner*
Travis Birse, *Office Mgr*
▲ EMP: 8
SALES (est): 370K **Privately Held**
WEB: www.januikwinery.com
SIC: **2084** Wines

(G-15273)
JAS STEEL FABRICATING (PA)
19450 144th Ave Ne Ste D (98072-6412)
PHONE..............................425 424-2107
Jim Griffith, *Owner*
EMP: 3 EST: 1994
SALES (est): 301.6K **Privately Held**
SIC: **3441** Fabricated structural metal

(G-15274)
JIT MANUFACTURING INC
19240 144th Ave Ne (98072-4370)
PHONE..............................425 487-0672
Lisa Tiffany, *President*
Nicholas Ricard, *Vice Pres*
EMP: 49
SQ FT: 18,500
SALES (est): 6.7MM **Privately Held**
WEB: www.jit-mfg.com
SIC: **3444** Sheet metal specialties, not stamped

(G-15275)
JP TRODDEN DISTILLING LLC
18646 142nd Ave Ne (98072-8521)
PHONE..............................425 286-2756
EMP: 4 EST: 2010
SALES (est): 245.6K **Privately Held**
SIC: **2085** Distilled & blended liquors

(G-15276)
KEMCOR INC
15925 Woodinville Re (98072-4541)
P.O. Box 387 (98072-0387)
PHONE..............................425 488-7400
Mark Kemis, *President*
▲ EMP: 25
SQ FT: 16,000
SALES (est): 4.7MM **Privately Held**
WEB: www.kemcor.com
SIC: **3677** 3357 Electronic coils, transformers & other inductors; nonferrous wiredrawing & insulating

(G-15277)
KEN BOUDREAU INC
Also Called: Coriander Designs
20485 144th Ave Ne (98072-8418)
PHONE..............................425 402-8001
Carly Boudreau, *President*
Dean Root, *General Mgr*
Jose Maldonado, *Purch Agent*
EMP: 52 EST: 1978
SQ FT: 40,000
SALES (est): 9.5MM **Privately Held**
WEB: www.corianderdesigns.com
SIC: **2521** Wood office furniture

(G-15278)
KESTREL VINTNERS
19501 144th Ave Ne (98072-6463)
PHONE..............................425 398-1199
Helen Walker, *Branch Mgr*
EMP: 3
SALES (est): 156.9K
SALES (corp-wide): 1.4MM **Privately Held**
SIC: **2084** Wines
PA: Kestrel Vintners
2890 Lee Rd
Prosser WA 99350
509 786-2675

(G-15279)
KEVIN WHITE WINERY
19501 144th Ave Ne F100 (98072-6463)
PHONE..............................206 992-5746
Kevin White, *Principal*
EMP: 3
SALES (est): 121K **Privately Held**
SIC: **2084** Wines

(G-15280)
KOOWALLA INC
16709 167th Ave Ne (98072-8987)
PHONE..............................206 948-1803
EMP: 2
SALES (est): 126.1K **Privately Held**
SIC: **7372** Prepackaged Software Services

(G-15281)
KUAU TECHNOLOGY LTD
Also Called: Rain Song Graphite Guitars
12604 Ne 178th St (98072-8702)
P.O. Box 834 (98072-0834)
PHONE..............................425 485-7551
John Decker, *Ch of Bd*
Ashvin Coomar, *President*
▲ EMP: 15
SALES (est): 2MM **Privately Held**
SIC: **3931** Guitars & parts, electric & non-electric

(G-15282)
LAB DOOR PRESS
13507 Ne 200th St (98072-8768)
PHONE..............................425 408-0672
EMP: 2
SALES (est): 86K **Privately Held**
SIC: **2741** Misc Publishing

(G-15283)
LANNOYE EMBLEMS INC
15056 225th Ave Ne (98077-5123)
PHONE..............................425 844-8411
Lorri Lannoye, *CEO*
Larry Lannoye, *President*
Susan Lannoye, *Treasurer*
EMP: 3
SALES: 250K **Privately Held**
SIC: **2395** Emblems, embroidered

(G-15284)
LASERMACH INC
19450 144th Ave Ne Ste 7h (98072-6412)
PHONE..............................425 485-3169

Ken Ligot, *President*
Matt Ligot, *Vice Pres*
EMP: 6
SQ FT: 3,200
SALES (est): 802.4K **Privately Held**
WEB: www.lasermach.com
SIC: **3599** Custom machinery

(G-15285)
LAUREN ASHTON CELLARS LLC
19510 144th Ave Ne D12 (98072-8429)
PHONE..............................206 504-8546
Kit Singh, *President*
EMP: 2
SALES (est): 130.6K **Privately Held**
SIC: **2084** Wines

(G-15286)
LAWRENCE CELLARS
19151 144th Ave Ne Ste D (98072-4311)
PHONE..............................425 286-2198
Lawrence Cellars, *Principal*
EMP: 2
SALES (est): 80.6K **Privately Held**
SIC: **2084** Wines

(G-15287)
LEFT FULL RUDDER AEROSPACE LLC
18250 142nd Ave Ne # 327 (98072-4361)
PHONE..............................516 330-0633
EMP: 2
SALES (est): 135.5K **Privately Held**
SIC: **3721** Mfg Aircraft

(G-15288)
LEMOND FITNESS INC
15540 Woodinvlle Redmond (98072)
PHONE..............................425 615-0116
John Post, *President*
◆ EMP: 13
SALES (est): 1.8MM **Privately Held**
WEB: www.lemondfitness.com
SIC: **3949** Exercise equipment; dumbbells & other weightlifting equipment

(G-15289)
LIBERTY SIGN SHOPPE LLC
19495 144th Ave Ne B230 (98072-4432)
PHONE..............................425 482-2811
Shelly Cloyd, *President*
Shelly Fahrenkopf,
EMP: 3
SQ FT: 1,450
SALES (est): 289.4K **Privately Held**
WEB: www.libertysignshoppe.com
SIC: **3993** Signs, not made in custom sign painting shops

(G-15290)
LITHOS CRAFTSMEN INC
16417 210th Ave Ne (98077-7785)
PHONE..............................206 949-9787
Shawn Christopherson, *President*
Sarah Christopherson, *Vice Pres*
EMP: 2
SALES (est): 190K **Privately Held**
SIC: **2752** Commercial printing, lithographic

(G-15291)
LITTLE SUN SOFTWARE LLC
15920 147th Pl Ne (98072-8958)
PHONE..............................425 442-4911
Eric Peterson, *Principal*
EMP: 2 EST: 2012
SALES (est): 150.4K **Privately Held**
SIC: **7372** Prepackaged software

(G-15292)
LOGO UNLTD
19628 144th Ave Ne Ste D (98072-4435)
PHONE..............................425 896-8412
Artem Ionitsa, *Owner*
EMP: 10
SALES: 1MM **Privately Held**
SIC: **2395** 5699 5136 Embroidery products, except schiffli machine; shirts, custom made; shirts, men's & boys'

(G-15293)
LOLLIPOPPASSIONS
18148 Ne 179th St (98072-9636)
PHONE..............................206 617-4217
Tosha Andersen, *Principal*

EMP: 2
SALES (est): 123.3K **Privately Held**
SIC: **2064** Lollipops & other hard candy

(G-15294)
LOUD AUDIO LLC (PA)
16220 Wood Red Rd Ne (98072-9061)
PHONE..............................425 892-6500
Mark Graham, *Mng Member*
Case Kuehn,
◆ EMP: 122
SQ FT: 90,000
SALES (est): 64.9MM **Privately Held**
WEB: www.loudtechinc.com
SIC: **3651** Audio electronic systems

(G-15295)
LOUS WELDING & FABRICATING
Also Called: L W Products Co
8333 219th St Se Ste A (98072-8078)
PHONE..............................425 483-0300
Louis Fairbairn, *President*
Mary Fairbairn, *Vice Pres*
EMP: 10 EST: 1977
SQ FT: 6,000
SALES (est): 1.3MM **Privately Held**
SIC: **3442** 3446 3444 Metal doors; architectural metalwork; sheet metalwork

(G-15296)
LOVE THAT RED WINERY
144th Ave Ne Ste D-100 (98072)
PHONE..............................425 463-9014
EMP: 3
SALES (est): 69.2K **Privately Held**
SIC: **2084** Wine cellars, bonded: engaged in blending wines

(G-15297)
LUCKY DOG EQP INC DBA PET PROS (PA)
19400 144th Ave Ne Ste E (98072-6425)
PHONE..............................425 402-8833
Harvey Peterson, *CEO*
Danny Albrecht, *President*
Trisha Albrecht, *Principal*
Melissa Grosjean, *Manager*
Ernie Green, *Merchandising*
▲ EMP: 47
SALES (est): 7.4MM **Privately Held**
WEB: www.luckydogequip.com
SIC: **5999** 3999 Pet supplies; pet food; pet supplies

(G-15298)
MACS DISCUS
20103 174th Ave Ne (98072-7012)
PHONE..............................425 483-3729
Steve Macdonald, *Principal*
EMP: 4
SALES (est): 315.2K **Privately Held**
SIC: **3949** Sporting & athletic goods

(G-15299)
MAGNADRIVE CORPORATION
14660 Ne North Woodi Way (98072)
PHONE..............................425 487-2881
Gary Macleod, *Ch of Bd*
Marc Weintraub, *Principal*
Zhongwei MA, *Chairman*
John Everhart, *Vice Pres*
Bruce Densmora, *CFO*
▲ EMP: 21
SQ FT: 8,300
SALES (est): 6.4MM **Privately Held**
WEB: www.magnadrive.com
SIC: **3568** 3566 Couplings, shaft: rigid, flexible, universal joint, etc.; speed changers, drives & gears

(G-15300)
MAINE MARKETING INC
Also Called: Marketing Newspaper
13901 Ne 175th St Ste M (98072-8548)
PHONE..............................425 487-9111
Larry L Coffman, *President*
Larry Sivitz, *Chief*
EMP: 2
SALES: 300K **Privately Held**
WEB: www.mainemarketing.com
SIC: **2711** Newspapers, publishing & printing

Woodinville - King County (G-15301) GEOGRAPHIC SECTION

(G-15301)
MARCIN JEWELRY INC
Also Called: Cindi Marsh
14318 196th Ct Ne (98077-7842)
PHONE....................425 883-7884
Marcia Trager, *President*
Marshall Trager, *Vice Pres*
EMP: 17
SALES (est): 1.7MM **Privately Held**
SIC: 3911 Jewelry, precious metal

(G-15302)
MARKET VINEYARDS
14810 Ne 145th St Ste A2 (98072-4555)
PHONE....................425 486-1171
EMP: 3
SALES (est): 158.2K
SALES (corp-wide): 188.7K **Privately Held**
SIC: 2084 Wines
PA: Market Vineyards
 1950 Keene Rd Bldg S
 Richland WA 99352
 509 396-4798

(G-15303)
MARTEDI WINERY
16110 Woodinvlle Redmond (98072)
PHONE....................425 444-2840
John Miglino, *Principal*
EMP: 2
SALES (est): 159.8K **Privately Held**
SIC: 2084 Wines

(G-15304)
MATCH GRADE INDUSTRIES LLC
20632 Ne 169th Pl (98077-7756)
PHONE....................425 949-8110
Frank Shields, *Principal*
EMP: 2
SALES (est): 91.6K **Privately Held**
SIC: 3999 Manufacturing industries

(G-15305)
MATTHEWS CELLARS
16116 140th Pl Ne (98072-6985)
PHONE....................425 487-9810
Matthew Loso, *Owner*
EMP: 3
SALES (est): 230K **Privately Held**
SIC: 2084 7372 Wines; prepackaged software

(G-15306)
MATTHEWS ESTATE LLC
Also Called: Mathews Estate
19495 144th Ave Ne (98072-6406)
PHONE....................425 488-3883
Aryn Morell, *Principal*
EMP: 2
SALES (est): 87.9K **Privately Held**
SIC: 2084 Wines

(G-15307)
MCKENZIE & ADAMS INC
15620 Ne Woodinvl Duvall (98072-5209)
PHONE....................425 672-8668
Linda Adams, *President*
Martyn Adams, *Vice Pres*
EMP: 3
SALES: 1MM **Privately Held**
WEB: www.rufduck.com
SIC: 3111 2385 Shoe leather; raincoats, except vulcanized rubber: purchased materials

(G-15308)
MICHELLE CHATEAU STE
Also Called: CSM Woodinville Estate
14111 Ne 145th St (98072-6981)
PHONE....................425 488-1133
Janet Hedstrom, *Principal*
Kati Hill, *Manager*
Danai Kongkarat, *Director*
Debra McCloskey, *Art Dir*
EMP: 9 **EST:** 2016
SALES (est): 121.5K **Privately Held**
SIC: 2084 Wines

(G-15309)
MICHELLE STE WINE ESTATES LTD (DH)
Also Called: Domaine Ste Michelle
14111 Ne 145th St (98072-6981)
P.O. Box 1976 (98072-1976)
PHONE....................425 488-1133
Theodor P Baseler, *President*
Carole Viney, *President*
David Strathy, *District Mgr*
Margaret Avellar, *Business Mgr*
Holly Beach, *Business Mgr*
◆ **EMP:** 5 **EST:** 1930
SQ FT: 120,000
SALES (est): 43.6MM
SALES (corp-wide): 25.3B **Publicly Held**
WEB: www.columbia-crest.com
SIC: 2084 Wines
HQ: Ust Llc
 6 High Ridge Park Bldg A
 Stamford CT 06905
 203 817-3000

(G-15310)
MICHELLE STE WINE ESTATES LTD
Also Called: Saint Michelle
14111 Ne 145th St (98072-6981)
P.O. Box 1976 (98072-1976)
PHONE....................425 488-1133
Mark Tobin, *Director*
EMP: 12
SALES (corp-wide): 25.3B **Publicly Held**
WEB: www.columbia-crest.com
SIC: 2084 Wines
HQ: Michelle Ste Wine Estates Ltd
 14111 Ne 145th St
 Woodinville WA 98072
 425 488-1133

(G-15311)
MICROSOFT CORPORATION
17814 198th Ave Ne (98077-8854)
PHONE....................425 703-6921
Raghu Kolluru, *Manager*
EMP: 2
SALES (corp-wide): 110.3B **Publicly Held**
SIC: 7372 Prepackaged software
PA: Microsoft Corporation
 1 Microsoft Way
 Redmond WA 98052
 425 882-8080

(G-15312)
MNC SERVICES INC (PA)
Also Called: Winigent
21520 Ne 144th Pl Ste 103 (98077-8678)
PHONE....................425 527-9031
Kalyani Velagapudi, *CEO*
EMP: 8 **EST:** 2004
SQ FT: 400
SALES: 6MM **Privately Held**
SIC: 7379 7372 Computer related consulting services; business oriented computer software

(G-15313)
MOBILE GAME PARTNERS LLC
18459 Ne 196th Pl (98077-8284)
PHONE....................310 926-3932
Adam Flanders, *Founder*
EMP: 2
SALES: 850K **Privately Held**
SIC: 2741 Miscellaneous publishing

(G-15314)
MONSON RANCHES
14450 Woodnvl Rdmnd Rd Ne (98072-9051)
PHONE....................425 488-0200
Arvid Virgil Monson, *Branch Mgr*
EMP: 2
SALES (corp-wide): 4MM **Privately Held**
SIC: 2084 Wines
PA: Monson Ranches
 63615 E Jacobs Rd Ne
 Benton City WA 99320
 509 627-1618

(G-15315)
MORWENSTOW
14125 Ne 189th St (98072-6507)
PHONE....................425 483-0320
EMP: 2
SALES (est): 141K **Privately Held**
SIC: 3999 Manufacturing industries

(G-15316)
MOUNTAIN VIEW INDUSTRIES
18807 Ne 165th St (98072-6118)
PHONE....................425 788-5551
Steve Griffis, *Owner*
Joni Griffis, *Co-Owner*
EMP: 2
SALES (est): 174.4K **Privately Held**
SIC: 3599 Machine shop, jobbing & repair

(G-15317)
NANNETTE LOUISE DAVIS
Also Called: Qivu Graphics
12601 Ne Wdnvlle Dr Ste F (98072)
PHONE....................425 485-5570
Nannette Davis, *Owner*
EMP: 2 **EST:** 2013
SQ FT: 750
SALES (est): 169.1K **Privately Held**
SIC: 2752 7334 7336 7389 Commercial printing, offset; photocopying & duplicating services; commercial art & graphic design; advertising, promotional & trade show services

(G-15318)
NANOICE INC
17280 Woodinville Redmond (98072-9088)
PHONE....................206 257-3380
Craig Rominger, *Principal*
Sandra Hardardottir, *Director*
EMP: 4
SALES (est): 267.3K **Privately Held**
WEB: www.nanoiceusa.com
SIC: 2097 Manufactured ice

(G-15319)
NATIONAL GLASS INDUSTRIES INC (DH)
17030 Wdnvll Rdmond Rd Ne (98072)
PHONE....................425 488-8126
Marty Nixon, *President*
Owen Lubin, *Vice Pres*
▲ **EMP:** 30
SQ FT: 24,000
SALES (est): 4.6MM
SALES (corp-wide): 14MM **Privately Held**
WEB: www.natglass.com
SIC: 3231 Products of purchased glass
HQ: National Glass Ltd
 5744 198 St
 Langley BC V3A 7
 604 530-2311

(G-15320)
NATIONAL INDUS CONCEPTS INC (PA)
Also Called: Nic Global
23518 63rd Ave Se (98072-8664)
PHONE....................425 489-4300
Bridget Brewer, *President*
Michael Ryan, *Vice Pres*
Troy Wood, *Vice Pres*
William King, *Treasurer*
▲ **EMP:** 150
SQ FT: 100,000
SALES (est): 80.2MM **Privately Held**
WEB: www.nicmfg.com
SIC: 3444 Sheet metal specialties, not stamped

(G-15321)
NORDICK MFG CO
16219 Wdnville Redmond Rd (98072)
PHONE....................425 488-2427
Jeff Desotel, *Manager*
EMP: 2
SALES (est): 81.6K **Privately Held**
SIC: 3999 Manufacturing industries

(G-15322)
NORTHWEST WOODWORKS INC
15100 Wdnvll Rdmnd Rd Ne (98072)
PHONE....................425 482-9663
Harrison Mekeel, *President*
Betty-Lou Mekeel, *Corp Secy*
James A Mekeel, *Vice Pres*
EMP: 32
SALES (est): 5.4MM **Privately Held**
WEB: www.nwwi.biz
SIC: 2521 2541 1751 Cabinets, office: wood; wood partitions & fixtures; cabinet & finish carpentry

(G-15323)
NOVALEAF SOFTWARE LLC
23114 76th Ave Se (98072-9541)
PHONE....................425 486-1242
Jeff Swearingen, *Principal*
EMP: 2
SALES (est): 109.1K **Privately Held**
SIC: 7372 Prepackaged software

(G-15324)
NOVELTY HILL WINERY LLC
14710 Woodinville Redmon (98072-6987)
PHONE....................425 481-5502
Carolyn M Januik,
▲ **EMP:** 15
SALES (est): 1.3MM **Privately Held**
SIC: 2084 Wines

(G-15325)
NTA INC
Also Called: Woodinville Printing Company
19806 141st Pl Ne Bldg D (98072-8432)
PHONE....................425 487-2679
Tally Armand, *President*
Neil Armand, *Vice Pres*
Nancy Blosfield, *Project Mgr*
Linda Payton, *Accounts Mgr*
EMP: 7
SALES (est): 1MM **Privately Held**
SIC: 2752 2759 Commercial printing, offset; commercial printing

(G-15326)
OLDFIELD CELLARS LLC
Also Called: Efefte
19730 144th Ave Ne (98072-8427)
PHONE....................425 398-7200
Kevin C Taylor, *Mng Member*
Leslie Rhodes, *Mng Member*
EMP: 2
SALES (est): 180.5K **Privately Held**
SIC: 2084 Wines

(G-15327)
OLIVER HENRY GAMES LLC
18609 Ne 145th Pl (98072-6306)
PHONE....................971 231-9141
Darren Smith,
EMP: 2
SALES: 50K **Privately Held**
SIC: 7372 Home entertainment computer software

(G-15328)
PACIFIC COAST MANUFACTURING
15604 163rd Ave Ne (98072-8934)
PHONE....................425 485-8866
Jeff Armstrong, *President*
EMP: 10
SALES (est): 860K **Privately Held**
SIC: 3843 7389 Orthodontic appliances; sewing contractor

(G-15329)
PACIFIC FRAME SOURCE LLC
21828 87th Ave Se Ste B (98072-8054)
PHONE....................800 292-3202
R Thede,
▲ **EMP:** 2
SALES (est): 191.4K **Privately Held**
SIC: 2499 Picture & mirror frames, wood

(G-15330)
PACIFIC ORTHOTIC LLC
21828 87th Ave Se Ste C1 (98072-8054)
PHONE....................425 486-4292
Eric Stephenson,
EMP: 6 **EST:** 2016
SQ FT: 4,359
SALES (est): 254K **Privately Held**
SIC: 3842 Foot appliances, orthopedic

(G-15331)
PAGE CELLARS
19495 144th Ave Ne B205 (98072-8457)
PHONE....................253 232-9463
Kenneth Nydam, *Principal*
EMP: 2

SALES (est): 107.4K **Privately Held**
SIC: 2084 Wines

(G-15332)
PARAGON SEAFOOD COMPANY
19703 Ne 167th Ct (98077-9485)
P.O. Box 1591 (98072-1591)
PHONE.....................................425 788-6077
Peter Sandvig, *President*
Kathryn Sandvig, *Admin Sec*
▲ EMP: 2
SALES (est): 240K **Privately Held**
WEB: www.paragonseafood.com
SIC: 2092 Fresh or frozen packaged fish

(G-15333)
PASSING TIME WINERY
18808 142nd Ave Ne (98072-8281)
PHONE.....................................425 892-8684
EMP: 2
SALES (est): 80.7K **Privately Held**
SIC: 2084 Wines

(G-15334)
PEPPER BRIDGE WINERY LLC
14810 Ne 145th St Bldg A3 (98072-4555)
PHONE.....................................425 483-7026
EMP: 4
SALES (est): 212.9K **Privately Held**
SALES (corp-wide): 883.2K **Privately Held**
SIC: 2084 5921 Wines; wine
PA: Pepper Bridge Winery, L.L.C.
   1704 J B George Rd
   Walla Walla WA 99362
   509 525-6502

(G-15335)
PLAY VISIONS INC
19180 144th Ave Ne (98072-4371)
PHONE.....................................425 482-2836
Mark Chernick, *CEO*
Webb Nelson, *President*
Jay Keron, *Corp Secy*
◆ EMP: 30
SQ FT: 32,000
SALES (est): 5.1MM **Privately Held**
WEB: www.playvisions.com
SIC: 3944 5092 5199 Games, toys & children's vehicles; toys; gifts & novelties

(G-15336)
PLEXERA LLC
Also Called: Plexera Bioscience
17625 130th Ave Ne (98072-8706)
PHONE.....................................425 368-7410
Robert Mininni,
Jay Smith,
EMP: 8
SALES (est): 1.1MM **Privately Held**
SIC: 3826 Analytical instruments

(G-15337)
PONDERA WINERY LLC
19501 144th Ave Ne B400 (98072-6463)
PHONE.....................................425 486-8500
Dan Howard, *Mng Member*
Pat Howard,
Shane Howard,
EMP: 3
SQ FT: 2,400
SALES (est): 90K **Privately Held**
SIC: 2084 Wines

(G-15338)
POWER CONVERSION INC
19501 144th Ave Ne B1000 (98072-6463)
P.O. Box 1745 (98072-1745)
PHONE.....................................425 487-1337
Asta Hoiland, *President*
Bryan Mee, *Vice Pres*
Patrick Hoiland, *Treasurer*
Vee Hoiland, *Admin Sec*
▲ EMP: 35
SQ FT: 10,000
SALES (est): 7.6MM **Privately Held**
WEB: www.pcimagnetics.com
SIC: 3612 3677 8711 3621 Power & distribution transformers; inductors, electronic; engineering services; motors & generators

(G-15339)
PRECOR INCORPORATED (DH)
Also Called: Precor USA
20031 142nd Ave Ne (98072-8473)
P.O. Box 7202 (98072-4002)
PHONE.....................................425 486-9292
Rob Barker, *President*
Jonathan Dally, *Superintendent*
Greg May, *Vice Pres*
Louis Carlone, *Opers Dir*
John Reinking, *Traffic Mgr*
◆ EMP: 500
SQ FT: 400,000
SALES (est): 190.5MM **Privately Held**
WEB: www.precor.com
SIC: 3949 Exercise equipment; exercising cycles; treadmills
HQ: Amer Sports Oyj
   Konepajankuja 6
   Helsinki 00510
   207 122-500

(G-15340)
PRIMUS INTERNATIONAL INC
6525 240th St Se A (98072-9761)
PHONE.....................................425 318-4500
EMP: 300
SALES (corp-wide): 210.8B **Publicly Held**
SIC: 3728 Mfg Aircraft Parts/Equipment
HQ: Primus International Inc
   610 Bellevue Way Ne # 200
   Bellevue WA 98001
   425 688-0444

(G-15341)
PROCTOR PRODUCTS CO INC
15323 Woodinville Redm (98072-9058)
PHONE.....................................425 398-8800
Maurice Proctor, *President*
Betty Proctor, *Corp Secy*
Harold Rathman, *Vice Pres*
Randy Keen, *Shareholder*
Fred Riehl, *Shareholder*
EMP: 18
SQ FT: 35,000
SALES (est): 4.1MM **Privately Held**
SIC: 3444 3423 Sheet metalwork; hand & edge tools

(G-15342)
PSM HYDRAULICS
21307 87th Ave Se (98072-8001)
PHONE.....................................360 282-4998
Walter J Pisco, *President*
▲ EMP: 45
SALES (est): 8.1MM **Privately Held**
WEB: www.psmcorp.com
SIC: 3531 7699 Cranes; hydraulic equipment repair
HQ: Cascade Corporation
   2201 Ne 201st Ave
   Fairview OR 97024
   503 669-6300

(G-15343)
PSM LLC
21307 87th Ave Se (98072-8001)
PHONE.....................................425 486-1232
Eric Focht, *Accounts Mgr*
Karol Kilpatrick, *Sales Staff*
Duane Lesh, *Manager*
John Cushing,
EMP: 42
SALES (est): 11.9MM **Privately Held**
SIC: 3531 Construction machinery

(G-15344)
PUGET SOUND ANGLERS EDUC
18609 182nd Ave Ne (98077-8224)
PHONE.....................................206 473-1613
Ron Garner, *President*
Ken Kumasawa, *Vice Pres*
David Reese, *Treasurer*
Karl Brackmann,
Steven Chamberlin, *Admin Sec*
EMP: 15
SALES (est): 872.1K **Privately Held**
SIC: 3949 Bait, artificial; fishing

(G-15345)
RED HORSE SIGNS LLC
8607 219th St Se Ste H (98072-4806)
PHONE.....................................425 415-0654
John Hovard, *Owner*
EMP: 9

SALES (est): 1MM **Privately Held**
SIC: 2741 Posters: publishing & printing

(G-15346)
RED SKY WINERY LLC
19495 144th Ave Ne B210 (98072-4429)
PHONE.....................................425 481-9864
Carol Parsons, *Principal*
Dick Mettler, *Transptn Dir*
EMP: 2
SALES (est): 104.3K **Privately Held**
SIC: 2084 Wines

(G-15347)
RELIANCE LLC
14724 173rd Ave Ne (98072-6512)
PHONE.....................................425 481-3030
David Carlson V, *Principal*
EMP: 2
SALES (est): 184.1K **Privately Held**
SIC: 3599 Machine shop, jobbing & repair

(G-15348)
RELIANCE MANUFACTURING CORP
8412 219th St Se (98072-8084)
PHONE.....................................425 481-3030
Patrick Hawes, *President*
Janet Hawes, *Corp Secy*
Carol Hawes, *Vice Pres*
EMP: 32
SALES (est): 7.3MM **Privately Held**
WEB: www.reliance-manufacturing.com
SIC: 3446 Architectural metalwork

(G-15349)
RICTER ENTERPRISES
23128 State Route 9 Se (98072-6012)
PHONE.....................................425 482-5942
EMP: 2
SALES (est): 65.5K **Privately Held**
SIC: 1389 Oil/Gas Field Services

(G-15350)
ROCKY POND WINERY
18725 164th Ave Ne (98072-6475)
P.O. Box 98 (98072-0098)
PHONE.....................................206 550-0938
EMP: 4
SALES (est): 320.6K **Privately Held**
SIC: 2084 Wines

(G-15351)
ROOF TRUSS SUPPLY INC (PA)
Also Called: RTS Lumber
5910 234th St Se (98072-8659)
P.O. Box 532 (98072-0532)
PHONE.....................................425 481-0900
Paul Taylor, *CEO*
David Brown, *President*
Joe Martinez, *Sales Staff*
Ashley Nordstrom, *Manager*
Donny Pietritz, *Technology*
EMP: 118
SQ FT: 5,700
SALES (est): 66.9MM **Privately Held**
SIC: 5031 2439 2431 Lumber, plywood & millwork; trusses, wooden roof; doors & door parts & trim, wood

(G-15352)
SALMON RIVER DESIGN INC
5817 238th St Se Ste 2 (98072-8669)
PHONE.....................................425 503-7987
Anthony Sexson, *President*
EMP: 2
SQ FT: 8,000
SALES (est): 643.6K **Privately Held**
SIC: 2499 Decorative wood & woodwork

(G-15353)
SALTWORKS INC
16240 Wdinvle Redmnd Ne (98072-9061)
PHONE.....................................425 885-7258
Mark Zoske, *President*
Naomi Novotny, *Vice Pres*
Matt Richardson, *Marketing Staff*
◆ EMP: 52
SQ FT: 27,000
SALES (est): 12.1MM **Privately Held**
WEB: www.seasalt.com
SIC: 2099 Food preparations

(G-15354)
SANDPIPER SOFTWARE INC
18448 Ne 199th St (98077-8290)
PHONE.....................................425 788-6175
Robert Furick, *Principal*
Robert P Furick, *Principal*
EMP: 2
SALES (est): 141.2K **Privately Held**
SIC: 7372 Prepackaged software

(G-15355)
SCHIFERL WOODWORKING
19728 Ne 189th St (98077-8847)
PHONE.....................................425 788-3795
EMP: 2 EST: 2011
SALES (est): 150K **Privately Held**
SIC: 2431 Mfg Millwork

(G-15356)
SCHNAPSLEICHE LLC
19151 144th Ave Ne Ste H (98072-4311)
PHONE.....................................425 591-2586
David Groom, *Partner*
Robert Collins, *Partner*
Markus Zimrpcih, *Partner*
EMP: 3
SQ FT: 1,300
SALES (est): 88.2K **Privately Held**
SIC: 2085 Distilled & blended liquors

(G-15357)
SEATTLE AVIONICS INC
Also Called: Seattle Avionics Software
19825 141st Pl Ne (98072-8432)
PHONE.....................................425 806-0249
John Rutter, *President*
EMP: 8
SALES: 1,000K **Privately Held**
WEB: www.seattleavionics.com
SIC: 7372 Business oriented computer software

(G-15358)
SELECTRONIX INCORPORATED
16419 199th Ct Ne (98077-5401)
PHONE.....................................425 788-2979
Jerry Numata, *President*
Kathy Numata, *Admin Sec*
EMP: 2
SALES: 180K **Privately Held**
WEB: www.selectronix.com
SIC: 3823 8711 Industrial process control instruments; electrical or electronic engineering

(G-15359)
SELG AND ASSOCIATES INC
15617 212th Ave Ne (98077-7732)
PHONE.....................................425 487-6059
Jon Anderson, *President*
EMP: 4
SALES (est): 400K **Privately Held**
WEB: www.selgassociates.com
SIC: 3589 3443 Sewage & water treatment equipment; water treatment equipment, industrial; water tanks, metal plate

(G-15360)
SHIELD TECHNOLOGIES LLC
15915 212th Ave Ne (98077-7789)
PHONE.....................................425 844-8055
Todd Folsom, *Mng Member*
Alissa Howell,
Gary Howell,
EMP: 3
SALES (est): 174.3K **Privately Held**
SIC: 7372 Application computer software

(G-15361)
SHYFT ADVANCED MFG LLC
Also Called: Shyft AM
20004 144th Ave Ne (98072-4461)
PHONE.....................................425 398-4009
EMP: 16
SQ FT: 20,000
SALES: 1.6MM **Privately Held**
SIC: 3089 Mfg Plastic Products

(G-15362)
SIENNA TECHNOLOGIES INC
19501 144th Ave Ne F500 (98072-6463)
PHONE.....................................425 485-0756
Ender Savrun, *President*
Canan Savrun, *Vice Pres*
EMP: 15
SQ FT: 7,500

Woodinville - King County (G-15363)

(G-15363)
SIERRA INDUSTRIES INC (PA)
Also Called: Bravo Leasing
19900 144th Ave Ne (98072-4460)
PHONE...................425 487-5200
Roger Collins, *President*
Matt Enany, *Project Mgr*
Andrew Repass, *Project Mgr*
Jeffrey Lilly, *CFO*
Aaron Brown, *Accountant*
EMP: 150
SQ FT: 15,000
SALES (est): 11MM **Privately Held**
WEB: www.sierraconst.com
SIC: 1541 3536 Industrial buildings, new construction; boat lifts

(G-15364)
SITE WELDING SERVICES INC
Also Called: Sws
19561 144th Ave Ne (98072-8424)
P.O. Box 274 (98072-0274)
PHONE...................425 488-2156
John P Hanlon, *President*
▲ **EMP:** 25
SQ FT: 8,000
SALES (est): 3.2MM **Privately Held**
WEB: www.siteweldingservices.com
SIC: 7692 1799 Welding repair; welding on site

(G-15365)
SKOFLO INDUSTRIES INC
14241 Ne 200th St (98072-8444)
P.O. Box 1728 (98072-1728)
PHONE...................425 485-7816
Paul Skoglund, *Principal*
Dale Depriest, *Vice Pres*
Warren Van Genderen, *Treasurer*
Robert Richards, *Admin Sec*
▲ **EMP:** 100
SQ FT: 25,000
SALES (est): 37.9MM **Privately Held**
WEB: www.skoflo.com
SIC: 3592 Valves

(G-15366)
SKYFLIGHT INC
Also Called: Skyflight Mobile
18580 142nd Ave Ne (98072-8520)
P.O. Box 36, Duvall (98019-0036)
PHONE...................425 844-9199
Holly H Zucker, *President*
Peter B Zucker, *Vice Pres*
EMP: 2
SALES: 420K **Privately Held**
WEB: www.skyflightmobiles.com
SIC: 3299 5961 5199 Art goods: plaster of paris, papier mache & scagliola; mail order house; gifts & novelties

(G-15367)
SLEEPING GIANT WINERY LLC
19501 144th Ave Ne (98072-6463)
PHONE...................206 351-0719
Chris Gorman,
EMP: 12
SALES (est): 518.6K **Privately Held**
SIC: 2084 Wines

(G-15368)
SOGGY HAWK SOFTWARE
19711 222nd Ave Ne (98077-6731)
PHONE...................425 246-6555
EMP: 2
SALES (est): 103.7K **Privately Held**
SIC: 7372 Prepackaged software

(G-15369)
SOL STONE WINERY
19151 144th Ave Ne Ste G (98072-4311)
PHONE...................425 417-8483
EMP: 2
SALES (est): 85.9K **Privately Held**
SIC: 2084 Wines

SALES (est): 2.7MM **Privately Held**
WEB: www.siennatech.com
SIC: 2851 2819 3312 3299 Lacquers, varnishes, enamels & other coatings; aluminum compounds; armor plate; ceramic fiber

(G-15370)
SOURCE NORTHWEST INC
Also Called: Source Window Coverings
8329 216th St Se (98072-8060)
P.O. Box 232, Monroe (98272-0232)
PHONE...................360 512-3535
Laron Olson, *President*
Frank Callahan, *Vice Pres*
▲ **EMP:** 62
SQ FT: 40,000
SALES (est): 7MM **Privately Held**
WEB: www.sourcenw.com
SIC: 2591 Drapery hardware & blinds & shades

(G-15371)
SOURCE TEC INC
Also Called: Washington Fire Safety
13110 Ne 177th Pl 148 (98072-5740)
PHONE...................206 972-3172
Bill Ripley, *President*
EMP: 5
SALES (est): 654.4K **Privately Held**
SIC: 3677 Filtration devices, electronic

(G-15372)
SPARKMAN CELLERS
19501 144th Ave Ne (98072-6463)
PHONE...................425 398-1045
Bryan Keay, *General Mgr*
Chris Sparkman, *Principal*
EMP: 3
SALES (est): 189.3K **Privately Held**
SIC: 2084 Wines

(G-15373)
SPECIALTY PDTS ELEC CNSTR LLC
19495 144th Ave Ne A145 (98072-6406)
PHONE...................425 402-8332
Norman Sovold, *Partner*
Stuart Johnson,
Dave Johnson,
EMP: 2
SQ FT: 3,600
SALES (est): 288.6K **Privately Held**
SIC: 3629 3699 Electronic generation equipment; electrical equipment & supplies

(G-15374)
STANBURY ELECTRICAL ENGRG LLC
14125 Ne 189th St (98072-6507)
PHONE...................206 251-8901
C Stanbury, *Principal*
Claire Stanbury, *Facilities Mgr*
Joseph Scheid, *Sales Staff*
Oliver Stanbury, *Mng Member*
▲ **EMP:** 15
SALES (est): 3.1MM **Privately Held**
SIC: 3629 Electronic generation equipment

(G-15375)
STOMANI CELLARS
16120 Woodinville Redmnd (98072-9090)
PHONE...................425 892-8375
EMP: 2
SALES (est): 62.3K **Privately Held**
SIC: 2084 Brandy & brandy spirits

(G-15376)
STONE DRUMS INC
Also Called: Printcore
12601 Ne Wdnvlle Dr Ste F (98072)
PHONE...................425 485-5570
Nannette Davis, *President*
EMP: 2
SQ FT: 750
SALES (est): 233.4K **Privately Held**
WEB: www.theprintcore.com
SIC: 2759 Commercial printing

(G-15377)
STRASSER WOODENWORKS INC
14237 Ne 200th St (98072-8444)
P.O. Box 446 (98072-0446)
PHONE...................425 402-3080
Andrew G Hedreen, *President*
Judy Hedreen, *Opers Mgr*
Megan Robinson, *Purch Mgr*
Joey Villanueva, *Controller*
EMP: 53
SQ FT: 30,000

SALES (est): 10.6MM **Privately Held**
WEB: www.strasserwood.com
SIC: 2434 Vanities, bathroom: wood

(G-15378)
STUSSER MATTSON VENEER INC
Also Called: Stussers Woodworks
19612 144th Ave Ne Ste 1a (98072-4442)
PHONE...................425 485-0963
Steve Stusser, *President*
EMP: 10
SQ FT: 4,000
SALES (est): 886.2K **Privately Held**
SIC: 2435 2439 2436 Panels, hardwood plywood; structural wood members; softwood veneer & plywood

(G-15379)
SUITE CS VINO
12601 Ne Woodinville Dr (98072-8704)
PHONE...................425 949-5006
EMP: 2
SALES (est): 68.6K **Privately Held**
SIC: 2084 Wines, brandy & brandy spirits

(G-15380)
SUMERIAN BREWING CO LLC
15510 Woodinvilleredmond (98072)
PHONE...................425 486-5330
Mark Ihrig, *Principal*
EMP: 6 EST: 2014
SALES (est): 147K **Privately Held**
SIC: 2082 Beer (alcoholic beverage)

(G-15381)
SUNDANCE EQUESTRIAN INDUSTRIES
18221 236th Ave Ne (98077-7522)
PHONE...................425 205-3775
Rory Wade, *Principal*
EMP: 3 EST: 2010
SALES (est): 172.1K **Privately Held**
SIC: 3999 Manufacturing industries

(G-15382)
SUPERIOR STONE MANUFACTURING
18619 Ne Wdnvlle Dvall Rd (98072)
PHONE...................425 931-9303
EMP: 2
SALES (est): 104.6K **Privately Held**
SIC: 3999 Manufacturing industries

(G-15383)
SYNNE CELLARS
16110 Woodinville Redmond (98072-6250)
PHONE...................206 851-2048
EMP: 2
SALES (est): 98.3K **Privately Held**
SIC: 2084 Wines

(G-15384)
T3 PUBLISHING LLC (PA)
Also Called: T3 Custom
14241 Ne Wdnvlle Dvall Rd (98072)
PHONE...................206 650-0535
Kevin Lund,
EMP: 2
SALES (est): 810K **Privately Held**
SIC: 2741 Miscellaneous publishing

(G-15385)
TAC FAB LLC
17024 141st Pl Ne (98072-9209)
PHONE...................206 755-0519
Sawyer Sjolin,
EMP: 2
SALES (est): 158.5K **Privately Held**
SIC: 3446 3441 Architectural metalwork; fabricated structural metal

(G-15386)
TAYLOR METAL INC
5927 234th St Se (98072)
PHONE...................425 485-3003
Keith Bailey, *Branch Mgr*
EMP: 15 **Privately Held**
SIC: 3444 Roof deck, sheet metal; siding, sheet metal
PA: Taylor Metal, Inc.
4566 Ridge Dr Ne
Salem OR 97301

(G-15387)
TENNANT CO
19915 Ne 175th St (98077-5928)
PHONE...................425 788-9711
Wilfred Levasseur, *Principal*
EMP: 2
SALES (est): 156K **Privately Held**
SIC: 3991 Street sweeping brooms, hand or machine

(G-15388)
THERMAL HYDRA PLASTICS LLC
Also Called: Clearwater Spas
18800 Wdnvlle Snhomish Rd (98072)
PHONE...................425 483-1877
Brent Conver, *CEO*
EMP: 60 EST: 2013
SALES (est): 5.2MM **Privately Held**
SIC: 3088 Hot tubs, plastic or fiberglass

(G-15389)
THREE OF CUPS LLC
18808 142nd Ave Ne Ste 4a (98072-8281)
PHONE...................425 286-6657
Leigh Metheny, *Principal*
EMP: 7 EST: 2014
SALES (est): 511K **Privately Held**
SIC: 2084 Wines, brandy & brandy spirits

(G-15390)
TITANIUM INDUSTRIES INC
6018 234th St Se Ste C (98072-8679)
PHONE...................425 481-7700
Brians Saks, *Regional Mgr*
EMP: 3 **Privately Held**
SIC: 3356 Titanium
PA: Titanium Industries, Inc.
18 Green Pond Rd Ste 1
Rockaway NJ 07866

(G-15391)
TORII MOR WINERY LLC
14525 148th Ave Ne (98072-9083)
PHONE...................425 408-0086
Maria Lund, *Principal*
EMP: 3
SALES (corp-wide): 2.2MM **Privately Held**
SIC: 2084 Wines
PA: Torii Mor Winery, Llc
18365 Ne Fairview Dr
Dundee OR 97115
800 839-5004

(G-15392)
TOTEM STEEL INC
6017 234th St Se (98072-8622)
PHONE...................425 483-6276
Jeff Ross, *President*
EMP: 13
SQ FT: 2,500
SALES: 2MM **Privately Held**
SIC: 3441 Building components, structural steel

(G-15393)
TYLOHELO INC
Also Called: Amerec
17683 128th Pl Ne Bldg C (98072-8783)
P.O. Box 2258 (98072-2258)
PHONE...................425 951-1120
Keith Raisenen, *Principal*
EMP: 36
SALES (corp-wide): 23.6MM **Privately Held**
WEB: www.saunatec.com
SIC: 3634 5091 Sauna heaters, electric; spa equipment & supplies
PA: Tylohelo Inc.
575 Cokato St E
Cokato MN 55321
320 286-5584

(G-15394)
ULTIMATE PRODUCT CORP
Also Called: Precision Prototype
20910 Ne 156th St (98077-7726)
PHONE...................425 788-7500
Frank Ward, *President*
Nancy Ward, *Vice Pres*
EMP: 5
SALES: 240K **Privately Held**
SIC: 3544 Special dies, tools, jigs & fixtures

Woodland - Cowlitz County (G-15423)

(G-15395)
UNIVERSAL SHEET METAL INC
14400 Ne N Wodinville Way (98072-6432)
P.O. Box 927 (98072-0927)
PHONE.....................................425 483-8384
Richard W Peterson, *President*
Mildred J Peterson, *Treasurer*
▲ **EMP:** 40
SQ FT: 20,000
SALES (est): 5.7MM Privately Held
WEB: www.universalsheetmetal.com
SIC: 3544 3444 Special dies, tools, jigs & fixtures; sheet metal specialties, not stamped

(G-15396)
UNIVERSITY SWAGING CORPORATION
Also Called: PCC Arostructures Univ Swaging
6525 240th St Se (98072-9761)
PHONE.....................................425 318-4500
EMP: 5
SALES (corp-wide): 225.3B Publicly Held
SIC: 3728 Aircraft parts & equipment
HQ: University Swaging Corporation
  610 Bellevue Way Ne # 200
  Bellevue WA 98004
  425 318-1965

(G-15397)
URBAN CABINETS
19300 144th Ave Ne (98072-4475)
PHONE.....................................425 286-2977
Andrey Oliferovskiy, *Principal*
EMP: 2
SALES (est): 104.5K Privately Held
SIC: 2434 Wood kitchen cabinets

(G-15398)
VALLEY SUPPLY COMPANY (PA)
8310 Maltby Rd (98072-8020)
PHONE.....................................360 217-4400
Jeff Taylor, *Principal*
EMP: 50
SALES (est): 11.9MM Privately Held
SIC: 5251 5031 3211 2421 Pumps & pumping equipment; building materials, exterior; construction glass; building & structural materials, wood

(G-15399)
VENETIAN STONE WORKS LLC
Also Called: Venetian Interiors
16110 Woodinville Redmond (98072-6250)
PHONE.....................................425 486-1234
Prem Gnanarajah, *Mng Member*
▲ **EMP:** 15
SQ FT: 9,000
SALES (est): 2.7MM Privately Held
SIC: 5211 2542 Counter tops; counters or counter display cases; except wood

(G-15400)
VERNON PUBLICATIONS LLC
12437 Ne 173rd Pl (98072-7902)
P.O. Box 970 (98072-0970)
PHONE.....................................425 488-3211
Suzy Sickles, *Sales Mgr*
Trevor Vernon,
Robert E Walters,
EMP: 11 **EST:** 1964
SQ FT: 10,000
SALES (est): 1.2MM Privately Held
WEB: www.vernonpublications.com
SIC: 2721 8748 Magazines: publishing only, not printed on site; trade journals: publishing only, not printed on site; publishing consultant

(G-15401)
VULCAN PRODUCTS COMPANY INC
6210 234th St Se (98072-8658)
PHONE.....................................425 806-6000
Mike Russell, *President*
Homer Kyle, *Manager*
Marie Anne Russell, *Manager*
EMP: 40
SQ FT: 24,000
SALES (est): 10.5MM Privately Held
SIC: 3441 Fabricated structural metal

(G-15402)
WASHINGTON WINE & BEVERAGE CO (PA)
Also Called: Silver Lake Winery
14701 148th Ave Ne (98072-6923)
PHONE.....................................425 485-2437
Salvatore Leone, *President*
Dr Herbert Selipsky, *Admin Sec*
▲ **EMP:** 12
SALES (est): 3.3MM Privately Held
WEB: www.washingtonwine.org
SIC: 2084 5921 Wines; wine & beer

(G-15403)
WESTCO ENGINEERING
Also Called: Westco Lifts
17011 174th Ave Ne (98072-5201)
PHONE.....................................425 481-7271
Ron Williams, *Owner*
EMP: 2
SALES (est): 345K Privately Held
SIC: 8711 3537 3949 Engineering services; tables, lift: hydraulic; trampolines & equipment

(G-15404)
WFTPD INC
Also Called: Texas Imperial Software
23921 57th Ave Se (98072-8661)
PHONE.....................................206 428-1991
Alun Jones, *President*
Deborah Jones, *Admin Sec*
EMP: 2
SALES (est): 160K Privately Held
WEB: www.texis.com
SIC: 7372 7371 Prepackaged software; custom computer programming services

(G-15405)
WINCRAFT INCORPORATED
Also Called: Colore's International
16750 Woodinville Redmond (98072-4554)
PHONE.....................................507 454-5510
EMP: 50
SALES (corp-wide): 170.8MM Privately Held
WEB: www.wincraft.com
SIC: 2399 Banners, made from fabric
PA: Wincraft, Incorporated
  960 E Mark St
  Winona MN 55987
  507 454-5510

(G-15406)
WOODHOUSE FAMILY CELLARS
15500 Wdnville Rdmnd (98072)
PHONE.....................................425 527-0608
Bijal Shah, *Principal*
Erica Abel, *Manager*
EMP: 7
SALES (est): 801.8K Privately Held
SIC: 2084 Wines

(G-15407)
WOODINVILLE SIGNS INC
13317 Ne 175th St Ste Z (98072-6815)
P.O. Box 2595, Lynnwood (98036-2595)
PHONE.....................................425 483-0296
Pat Burghardt, *President*
EMP: 5
SQ FT: 1,200
SALES (est): 390.6K Privately Held
WEB: www.wsigns.com
SIC: 3993 Signs, not made in custom sign painting shops

(G-15408)
WOODINVILLE WHISKEY CO LLC
14509 Wdnvl Red Rd Ne (98072-9092)
PHONE.....................................425 486-1199
Orlin Sorensen, *Principal*
Brett Carlile, *Principal*
EMP: 10
SQ FT: 7,000
SALES: 2MM
SALES (corp-wide): 361.7MM Privately Held
SIC: 2085 Distilled & blended liquors
HQ: Moet Hennessy Usa, Inc.
  85 10th Ave Fl 2
  New York NY 10011
  212 888-7575

(G-15409)
WOODINVILLE WINE CO
17721 132nd Ave Ne (98072-8753)
P.O. Box 2138, Snohomish (98291-2138)
PHONE.....................................425 481-8860
Stacie Doran, *Principal*
Sandra Lee, *Exec Dir*
EMP: 7
SALES (est): 484.4K Privately Held
SIC: 2084 Wines

(G-15410)
WORLD WIDE GOURMET FOODS INC
Also Called: Alaska Smokehouse
21616 87th Ave Se (98072-8017)
PHONE.....................................360 668-9404
Tiffany Andriesen, *Vice Pres*
Jack Praino, *Executive*
▲ **EMP:** 12
SQ FT: 13,000
SALES (est): 2.7MM Privately Held
WEB: www.alaskasmokehouse.com
SIC: 2091 5421 5146 2441 Salmon, smoked; fish markets; fish & seafoods; nailed wood boxes & shook; bread, cake & related products

(G-15411)
WT VINTNERS LLC
14818 Ne 195th St (98072-8496)
PHONE.....................................425 610-9463
Jeff Lindsay Thorsen, *Principal*
EMP: 4 **EST:** 2010
SALES (est): 408.9K Privately Held
SIC: 2084 Wines

(G-15412)
XD VINTNERS
19501 144th Ave Ne C300 (98072-6463)
PHONE.....................................425 210-1554
Michael Lemmieus, *Principal*
EMP: 2 **EST:** 2008
SALES (est): 86.9K Privately Held
SIC: 2084 Wines, brandy & brandy spirits

(G-15413)
YOUNG CORPORATION
Also Called: Woodinvl Fclty McHne Shp/Wrhs
16219 Woodinvlle Redmnd (98072)
P.O. Box 3522, Seattle (98124-3522)
PHONE.....................................425 488-2427
Jeff Desotel, *Branch Mgr*
EMP: 50
SQ FT: 38,106
SALES (corp-wide): 22.3MM Privately Held
WEB: www.youngcorp.com
SIC: 3531 3593 Construction machinery; fluid power cylinders, hydraulic or pneumatic
PA: Young Corporation
  3231 Utah Ave S
  Seattle WA 98134
  206 624-1071

(G-15414)
ZEBRA TECHNICAL SERVICES LLC
17270 Woodinville Redmond (98072-6963)
PHONE.....................................425 485-8700
Tyler Kopet, *Manager*
EMP: 4 **EST:** 2015
SALES (est): 264.5K Privately Held
SIC: 3822 Auto controls regulating residntl & coml environmt & applncs

(G-15415)
ZIPFIZZ CORPORATION
14400 Ne 145th St Ste 201 (98072-5003)
PHONE.....................................425 398-4240
Brian Winn, *CEO*
Jim Ellexson, *Regional Mgr*
Sean Dennis, *District Mgr*
Terry Makowski, *District Mgr*
EMP: 350
SQ FT: 10,000
SALES: 40.5MM Privately Held
SIC: 2087 5122 Powders, drink; vitamins & minerals

Woodland
Cowlitz County

(G-15416)
ADVANCED ELECTRIC SIGNS INC
1550 Down River Dr Ste A (98674-9762)
PHONE.....................................360 225-6826
Stephen C Slack, *President*
Susan Slack, *Corp Secy*
EMP: 9
SQ FT: 8,300
SALES: 560K Privately Held
SIC: 3993 Electric signs; neon signs

(G-15417)
AMERICAN PAPER CONVERTING INC (PA)
1845 Howard Way (98674-9755)
PHONE.....................................360 225-0488
Lydia Work, *President*
Brian Work, *Opers Mgr*
Jim Dority, *Maint Spvr*
Richard Rosentreter, *Controller*
David Stegner, *Sales Mgr*
EMP: 51
SALES (est): 17.4MM Privately Held
WEB: www.americanpaperco.com
SIC: 2679 Paper products, converted

(G-15418)
AMIRAQ CNSLTNTS INC
35709 Nw Fairchild Rd (98674-3722)
PHONE.....................................936 448-1480
Hamid M Salman, *President*
Patt Campbell, *Vice Pres*
EMP: 4
SALES (est): 165.3K Privately Held
SIC: 1389 Oil consultants

(G-15419)
B2R PARTNERS INC (PA)
Also Called: Knife Gate Valves
675 Mitchell Ave (98674-9597)
PHONE.....................................360 225-1230
Jeffrey M Bowman, *President*
▲ **EMP:** 35
SQ FT: 13,000
SALES (est): 6.8MM Privately Held
WEB: www.linedvci.com
SIC: 3491 Industrial valves

(G-15420)
BOON
6262 Green Mountain Rd (98674-8297)
PHONE.....................................360 225-5224
Dale Boon, *Principal*
EMP: 2
SALES (est): 104.9K Privately Held
SIC: 3944 Games, toys & children's vehicles

(G-15421)
BUTTE HILL WINERY & VINYRD LLC
362 Faloma Rd (98674-8315)
PHONE.....................................360 225-6864
Julianne Gilbert, *Principal*
EMP: 2
SALES (est): 62.3K Privately Held
SIC: 2084 Wines, brandy & brandy spirits

(G-15422)
CALPORTLAND COMPANY
1441 Guild Rd (98674-9585)
PHONE.....................................360 892-5100
Bill Parfet, *Branch Mgr*
EMP: 68 Privately Held
SIC: 3273 Ready-mixed concrete
HQ: Calportland Company
  2025 E Financial Way
  Glendora CA 91741
  626 852-6200

(G-15423)
CHILTON LOGGING INC
1760 Down River Dr (98674-9699)
PHONE.....................................360 225-0427
Craig Chilton, *President*
Joe Berry, *General Mgr*
Joey Yake, *Project Mgr*
Shanna Pritchett, *Bookkeeper*

Woodland - Cowlitz County (G-15424)

Stephen Hart, *Manager*
EMP: 45
SALES: 12MM **Privately Held**
WEB: www.chiltonlogging.com
SIC: 2411 Logging camps & contractors

(G-15424)
COLUMBIA PRECAST PRODUCTS LLC
1765 Howard Way (98674-9399)
PHONE..................360 335-8400
Ron Sparks, *Mng Member*
Lon Tweed, *Manager*
EMP: 12
SALES: 2.1MM **Privately Held**
SIC: 3272 3271 Covers, catch basin: concrete; meter boxes, concrete; sewer & manhole block, concrete

(G-15425)
COLUMBIA RIVER CARBONATES (PA)
300 N Pekin Rd (98674-9541)
PHONE..................360 225-6505
Bernie Schockelt, *General Mgr*
Joerg A Bleeck, *General Ptnr*
Connie Wika, *Buyer*
William Robbins, *Engineer*
Brady Wale, *Project Engr*
▲ **EMP:** 63
SQ FT: 44,000
SALES: 50MM **Privately Held**
WEB: www.carbonates.com
SIC: 2819 Calcium compounds & salts, inorganic

(G-15426)
CROWN VALVE & FITTING LLC
1342 Down River Dr Ste 2 (98674-9546)
PHONE..................360 225-0888
Shane Larango,
Melissa Larango,
EMP: 2
SALES (est): 256.5K **Privately Held**
SIC: 3592 Valves

(G-15427)
DIRTWORX ENTERPRISES INC
1260 Atlantic Ave (98674-9405)
PHONE..................360 225-0146
EMP: 2
SALES (est): 211.9K **Privately Held**
SIC: 3537 Trucks, tractors, loaders, carriers & similar equipment

(G-15428)
DZ & FAMILY MACHINE WORKS
400 2nd St (98674)
P.O. Box 487 (98674-0500)
PHONE..................360 225-6261
David Zumstein, *Owner*
EMP: 8
SQ FT: 3,000
SALES: 800K **Privately Held**
SIC: 3599 Machine shop, jobbing & repair

(G-15429)
ENGINEERED PIPING SYSTEMS
1740 Down Rver Dr Ste 200 (98674)
PHONE..................360 225-5302
Ron Carr, *President*
EMP: 4
SALES (est): 600.1K **Privately Held**
SIC: 3053 Gaskets & sealing devices

(G-15430)
EPIC POLYMER SYSTEMS CORP
1901 Schurman Way (98674-9599)
PHONE..................360 225-1496
Greg Fraser, *President*
Chris Fraser, *Vice Pres*
▲ **EMP:** 15
SALES (est): 2.8MM **Privately Held**
SIC: 2821 Plastics materials & resins

(G-15431)
EVENT POWER & LIGHTING INC
Also Called: Mobile Event Systems
170 Lahti Rd (98674-9629)
PHONE..................360 225-3830
Darren Erickson, *President*
Nina Erickson, *Vice Pres*
EMP: 2
SALES (est): 313K **Privately Held**
SIC: 3648 Outdoor lighting equipment

(G-15432)
FLASHCO MANUFACTURING INC
1383 Down River Dr (98674-9546)
PHONE..................360 225-4662
Richard Morrow, *Branch Mgr*
EMP: 9
SALES (est): 1.2MM
SALES (corp-wide): 6.7MM **Privately Held**
WEB: www.flashcomfg.com
SIC: 3356 Lead & lead alloy bars, pipe, plates, shapes, etc.
PA: Flashco Manufacturing, Inc.
150 Todd Rd Ste 400
Santa Rosa CA 95407
707 824-4448

(G-15433)
FOX ARCHITECTURAL SIGNS INC
1800 Nw Lyons Rd (98674-3023)
PHONE..................503 512-8757
Lauren L Fox, *President*
Kori Fox, *Vice Pres*
James D Fox, *Admin Sec*
EMP: 2
SALES (est): 175.9K **Privately Held**
SIC: 3993 8748 Neon signs; business consulting

(G-15434)
GOOD IMPRESSIONS INC
616 Sommerset Rd (98674-8100)
PHONE..................360 225-9080
Terry Richard, *President*
EMP: 2
SALES: 175K **Privately Held**
SIC: 2752 Commercial printing, lithographic

(G-15435)
GREEN MOUNTAIN METALWORKS LLC
40215 Ne 142nd Ave (98674)
PHONE..................360 281-6048
Benjamin Holland, *Principal*
Trevor Beatty, *Principal*
EMP: 2
SALES (est): 236.1K **Privately Held**
SIC: 3441 Fabricated structural metal

(G-15436)
GREERS MOBILE EQUIPMENT REPAIR
3823 Lewis River Rd (98674-8274)
PHONE..................360 901-0373
Curtis Greer, *Principal*
EMP: 2
SALES (est): 223.9K **Privately Held**
SIC: 3537 Industrial trucks & tractors

(G-15437)
GREIF BROTHERS DISTRIBUTION
701 W Scott Ave (98674-9711)
PHONE..................360 225-9995
Mike Larsh, *Principal*
EMP: 2
SALES (est): 155.6K **Privately Held**
SIC: 2655 Fiber cans, drums & similar products

(G-15438)
HAMBURG PRECISION INC
1356 Down River Dr (98674-9546)
P.O. Box 1276, Kalama (98625-1100)
PHONE..................360 225-0212
Fred Hamburg, *President*
▼ **EMP:** 3
SQ FT: 3,600
SALES (est): 336.5K **Privately Held**
SIC: 3599 Machine shop, jobbing & repair

(G-15439)
HAMILTON MATERIALS WASH LLC (PA)
Also Called: Hamilton Drywall Products
295 N Pekin Rd (98674-9586)
PHONE..................360 225-6888
Mark Hamilton,
▲ **EMP:** 60
SALES (est): 60.6MM **Privately Held**
WEB: www.hamiltonnw.com
SIC: 3259 Wall coping, clay

(G-15440)
HENRY PRATT COMPANY LLC
675 Mitchell Ave (98674-9597)
PHONE..................360 225-1230
EMP: 3
SALES (corp-wide): 916MM **Publicly Held**
SIC: 3491 Industrial valves
HQ: Henry Pratt Company, Llc
401 S Highland Ave
Aurora IL 60506
630 844-4000

(G-15441)
HN GOODS & SERVICES LLC
230 Cc St (98674-9446)
PHONE..................360 841-8414
EMP: 2 **EST:** 2012
SALES (est): 110K **Privately Held**
SIC: 3999 Mfg Misc Products

(G-15442)
ILLINOIS TOOL WORKS INC
701 W Scott Ave (98674-9711)
PHONE..................360 225-9995
Mike Larsh, *Manager*
EMP: 25
SALES (corp-wide): 14.7B **Publicly Held**
WEB: www.greif.com
SIC: 2448 Pallets, wood
PA: Illinois Tool Works Inc.
155 Harlem Ave
Glenview IL 60025
847 724-7500

(G-15443)
KRIEGERS STUMP REMOVAL INC
251 Moonridge Rd (98674-9215)
PHONE..................360 225-1703
Pat Hadaller, *President*
Cindy Hadaller, *Vice Pres*
EMP: 2
SALES: 200K **Privately Held**
SIC: 2411 0783 Stumps, wood; ornamental shrub & tree services

(G-15444)
LAMIGLAS INC
1400 Atlantic Ave (98674-9486)
P.O. Box 1000 (98674-1000)
PHONE..................360 225-9436
Richard Posey, *President*
▲ **EMP:** 40
SQ FT: 35,000
SALES (est): 6.5MM **Privately Held**
WEB: www.lamiglas.com
SIC: 3949 3599 Fishing tackle, general; rods & rod parts, fishing; tubing, flexible metallic

(G-15445)
LIFEPORT INC
1660 Heritage St (98674-9581)
PHONE..................360 225-3200
Summer Lopez, *Manager*
EMP: 5 **Publicly Held**
SIC: 3728 Aircraft parts & equipment
HQ: Lifeport, Llc
1610 Heritage St
Woodland WA 98674
360 225-1212

(G-15446)
LIFEPORT INC
Also Called: Lifeport Interiors
1610 Heritage St (98674-9581)
PHONE..................360 225-6690
Jason Darley, *COO*
Diana McClenahan, *Admin Sec*
EMP: 50
SQ FT: 30,000 **Publicly Held**
WEB: www.lifeport.com
SIC: 3728 3711 3714 Aircraft parts & equipment; motor vehicles & car bodies; motor vehicle parts & accessories
HQ: Lifeport, Llc
1610 Heritage St
Woodland WA 98674
360 225-1212

(G-15447)
LIFEPORT LLC (DH)
Also Called: Sikorsky
1610 Heritage St (98674-9581)
PHONE..................360 225-1212
Ken Ward, *President*
Bill St Croix, *Info Tech Mgr*
Jason Darley,
▼ **EMP:** 84
SQ FT: 130,000
SALES (est): 44.2MM **Publicly Held**
WEB: www.lifeport.com
SIC: 3842 3728 Stretchers; aircraft parts & equipment

(G-15448)
MAC CHAIN COMPANY LIMITED
Also Called: Mac Sales Industries
1855 Schurman Way (98674-9598)
PHONE..................800 663-0072
William J Mc Farland, *President*
Tom Hickey, *Vice Pres*
Tom Mc Farland, *Vice Pres*
Victor Mc Farland, *Vice Pres*
Joseph T McFarland, *Vice Pres*
▲ **EMP:** 32
SALES: 16MM
SALES (corp-wide): 18.7MM **Privately Held**
WEB: www.macchain.com
SIC: 3568 Belting, chain
PA: Mac Chain Company Limited
9445 193a St
Surrey BC V4N 4
604 888-1229

(G-15449)
N C I INC
1819 Schurman Way Ste 106 (98674-9579)
PHONE..................360 225-9701
Willard Latimer, *President*
William Latimer, *President*
Cheryl Poppe, *General Mgr*
Lorane Latimer, *Vice Pres*
EMP: 6
SQ FT: 1,000
SALES (est): 329.2K **Privately Held**
SIC: 3489 Rifles, recoiless

(G-15450)
NORTH FORK COMPOSITES LLC
2617 Ne 434th St (98674-2526)
P.O. Box 2223 (98674-0021)
PHONE..................360 225-2211
Alex Maslov,
Jon Bial,
EMP: 12
SALES (est): 1.2MM **Privately Held**
SIC: 3949 Fishing equipment

(G-15451)
NORTHWEST CARBONATE INC
Also Called: Omya
300 N Pekin Rd (98674-9541)
P.O. Box 2350 (98674-0023)
PHONE..................360 225-6505
Joerg A Bleeck, *Principal*
EMP: 29
SALES (est): 2.1MM
SALES (corp-wide): 3.9B **Privately Held**
SIC: 2819 Calcium compounds & salts, inorganic
HQ: Omya Inc.
9987 Carver Rd Ste 300
Blue Ash OH 45242
513 387-4600

(G-15452)
NORTHWEST PET PRODUCTS INC
Also Called: Western Animal Nutrition
350 S Pekin Rd (98674-9534)
P.O. Box 810 (98674-0800)
PHONE..................360 225-8855
William Behnken, *CEO*
Ray Bialick, *Corp Secy*
Sandi Behnken, *Vice Pres*
Ron Haws, *CFO*
Barbara McPeak, *Controller*
▼ **EMP:** 45
SQ FT: 225,000
SALES (est): 13.3MM
SALES (corp-wide): 400MM **Privately Held**
SIC: 2047 Dog food; cat food

PA: American Nutrition, Inc.
2813 Wall Ave
Ogden UT 84401
801 394-3477

(G-15453)
NORTHWOOD CABINETS INC (PA)
1570 Guild Rd (98674-9585)
P.O. Box 2190 (98674-0021)
PHONE..................360 225-1001
Dan Kysar, *President*
Race Koistino, *Principal*
D Kangas, *Vice Pres*
Derrick Kysar, *Admin Sec*
EMP: 25
SALES (est): 3.1MM **Privately Held**
SIC: 2434 Wood kitchen cabinets

(G-15454)
P D M STILLED SERVICE INC
1785 Schurman Way (98674-9584)
PHONE..................360 225-1133
Lloyd Kegney, *President*
EMP: 30
SALES (est): 3.4MM **Privately Held**
SIC: 3443 Stills, pressure: metal plate

(G-15455)
PACIFIC SCREEN PRINTERS
123 Stenerson Rd (98674-9508)
PHONE..................360 225-7771
Brandon White, *Principal*
EMP: 2 EST: 2009
SALES (est): 196.1K **Privately Held**
SIC: 2752 Commercial printing, lithographic

(G-15456)
PACIFIC SEA FOOD CO INC
Also Called: Jakes Crawfish & Seafood
1635 Down River Dr (98674-9544)
PHONE..................360 225-8553
Randy Morrell, *Plant Mgr*
Patrick Swope, *Manager*
EMP: 30
SALES (corp-wide): 565.9MM **Privately Held**
WEB: www.pacificseafoodco.com
SIC: 4222 2092 Warehousing, cold storage or refrigerated; fish, frozen: prepared
HQ: Pacific Seafood - Portland, Llc
16797 Se 130th Ave
Clackamas OR 97015
503 905-4500

(G-15457)
PACIFIC TRIM PANELS INC
1685 Schurman Way (98674-9556)
PHONE..................360 841-8338
William Charles Groth, *Co-Owner*
Marc Groth, *Co-Owner*
EMP: 26
SQ FT: 30,000
SALES: 1.8MM **Privately Held**
SIC: 2436 Panels, softwood plywood

(G-15458)
PERI FORMWORK SYSTEMS INC
1475 Port Way (98674-9583)
PHONE..................360 225-3583
Tom Grose, *Manager*
Lisa Larcom, *Admin Asst*
EMP: 25
SALES (corp-wide): 1.7B **Privately Held**
WEB: www.peri-usa.com
SIC: 3444 Concrete forms, sheet metal
HQ: Peri Formwork Systems, Inc.
7135 Dorsey Run Rd
Elkridge MD 21075
410 712-7225

(G-15459)
PERI-USA
1475 Port Way (98674-9583)
PHONE..................410 712-7225
EMP: 2
SALES (est): 147.3K **Privately Held**
SIC: 3559 Special industry machinery

(G-15460)
PORTCO CORPORATION
Also Called: Portco Packaging
211 5th St (98674-9355)
P.O. Box 2130 (98674-0020)
PHONE..................360 696-1641
Kenton M Wall, *President*
Staci Mocerino, *Manager*
▲ EMP: 10
SQ FT: 112,000
SALES (est): 15.5MM **Privately Held**
WEB: www.portco.com
SIC: 2674 3081 Paper bags: made from purchased materials; packing materials, plastic sheet

(G-15461)
REDWOOD PLASTICS AND RBR CORP
1901 Schurman Way (98674-9599)
PHONE..................360 225-1491
Pat Curley, *Branch Mgr*
EMP: 25
SALES (corp-wide): 8.5MM **Privately Held**
WEB: www.redwoodplastics.com
SIC: 3089 2821 2221 Plastic processing; plastics materials & resins; broadwoven fabric mills, manmade
PA: Redwood Plastics And Rubber Corp.
19695 92a Ave
Langley BC V1M 3
604 607-6000

(G-15462)
RES INDUSTRIES LLC
1555 Down River Dr (98674-9513)
PHONE..................360 225-7955
Rex Wallen, *Principal*
EMP: 1
SALES (est): 137.2K **Privately Held**
SIC: 3999 Manufacturing industries

(G-15463)
RICHARD & MIKE LYNCH
Also Called: Lynch Brothers Construction
17811 Ne Grinnell Rd (98674-3812)
PHONE..................360 263-4078
Richard Lynch, *Partner*
Michael Lynch, *Partner*
EMP: 2
SALES (est): 233.5K **Privately Held**
SIC: 2411 1611 Logging; highway & street construction

(G-15464)
RSG FOREST PRODUCTS INC
410 N Pekin Rd (98674-9530)
PHONE..................360 225-8513
Royce Morrison, *Facilities Mgr*
Bigby Smith, *Branch Mgr*
EMP: 43
SALES (corp-wide): 145.8MM **Privately Held**
SIC: 2421 Sawmills & planing mills, general
PA: Rsg Forest Products Inc
985 Nw 2nd St
Kalama WA 98625
360 673-2825

(G-15465)
SIGNODE INDUSTRIAL GROUP LLC
Also Called: Down River
701 W Scott Ave (98674-9711)
PHONE..................360 225-9995
EMP: 38
SALES (corp-wide): 11.1B **Publicly Held**
SIC: 2679 Paper products, converted
HQ: Signode Industrial Group Llc
3650 W Lake Ave
Glenview IL 60026
847 724-7500

(G-15466)
SONOCO PRODUCTS COMPANY
Also Called: Cascades Sonoco
1620 Down River Dr (98674-9544)
PHONE..................360 225-1500
Ken Puckels, *Manager*
EMP: 85
SALES (corp-wide): 5.3B **Publicly Held**
WEB: www.sonoco.com
SIC: 2631 2671 2653 2655 Paperboard mills; packaging paper & plastics film, coated & laminated; corrugated & solid fiber boxes; fiber cans, drums & similar products
PA: Sonoco Products Company
1 N 2nd St
Hartsville SC 29550
843 383-7000

(G-15467)
SUPERIOR INDUSTRIAL SERVICES A
132 Upland Dr (98674-9296)
PHONE..................360 841-8542
Bart Rierson, *Sales Staff*
Melissa Sassmen, *Mng Member*
Joseph Sassmen,
EMP: 23 EST: 2010
SALES: 1.5MM **Privately Held**
SIC: 7699 7694 7692 Industrial machinery & equipment repair; armature rewinding shops; welding repair

(G-15468)
SWIVLER INC
Also Called: Pacific Screen Printers
123 Stenerson Rd (98674-9508)
PHONE..................360 225-7774
Rick White, *President*
EMP: 20
SALES (est): 724.2K **Privately Held**
SIC: 3953 5199 5621 5611 Screens, textile printing; bags, textile; women's sportswear; clothing, sportswear, men's & boys'

(G-15469)
US NATURAL RESOURCES INC
Also Called: Newnes McGehee A Div of
1981 Schurman Way (98674-9599)
P.O. Box 310 (98674-0300)
PHONE..................360 841-6346
Bruce Johnson, *Manager*
EMP: 23
SALES (est): 4.6MM **Privately Held**
SIC: 3556 Flour mill machinery

(G-15470)
USNR LLC (PA)
Also Called: Kockums Cancar Chip-N-Saw
1981 Schurman Way (98674-9599)
PHONE..................360 225-8267
Richard H Ward, *Principal*
Donald Bechen, *Vice Pres*
Dale Brown, *Vice Pres*
Michael Travis, *Purch Agent*
Kelly Jackman, *Engineer*
◆ EMP: 5
SQ FT: 3,000
SALES (est): 326.8MM **Privately Held**
WEB: www.friedrich.com
SIC: 3585 3553 3625 1221 Air conditioning units, complete: domestic or industrial; sawmill machines; control equipment, electric; strip mining, bituminous; sawmill machinery & equipment

(G-15471)
USNR LLC
Schurman Machine
1981 Schurman Way (98674-9599)
P.O. Box 310 (98674-0300)
PHONE..................360 225-8267
Michael Knerr, *General Mgr*
EMP: 106
SQ FT: 11,000
SALES (corp-wide): 326.8MM **Privately Held**
WEB: www.friedrich.com
SIC: 3553 Sawmill machines
PA: Usnr, Llc
1981 Schurman Way
Woodland WA 98674
360 225-8267

(G-15472)
W B & L MACHINE INC
Also Called: Aimmco
1665 Schurman Way (98674-9556)
PHONE..................360 225-5020
Barry Waatti, *Vice Pres*
Lloyd Booth, *Vice Pres*
Glen Hendrickson, *Vice Pres*
EMP: 24

SALES (est): 1.2MM **Privately Held**
SIC: 3541 Machine tools, metal cutting type

(G-15473)
WD&L MACHINE CO (PA)
Also Called: Aimmco
1665 Schurman Way (98674-9556)
PHONE..................360 225-5020
Barry Watti, *President*
Glen Hendrickson, *President*
Barry Waatti, *Owner*
EMP: 24 EST: 1997
SQ FT: 1,000
SALES (est): 3.9MM **Privately Held**
SIC: 3089 Injection molding of plastics

(G-15474)
WELLS SIGNS MFG & DISTRG
109 Brothers Rd (98674-9294)
PHONE..................360 225-0520
Randy Wells, *President*
EMP: 3
SALES (est): 326.1K **Privately Held**
SIC: 3993 Letters for signs, metal

(G-15475)
WOODLAND PALLET REPAIR LLC
104 Whalen Rd (98674-9531)
PHONE..................360 624-3935
Felipe Betancourt,
Alicia Vazquez,
EMP: 3
SALES (est): 119.9K **Privately Held**
SIC: 2448 Pallets, wood

(G-15476)
WOODLAND PAVING
3730 Old Lewis River Rd (98674-8249)
PHONE..................360 225-8317
Dave Kleeb, *Owner*
EMP: 2
SALES (est): 135.5K **Privately Held**
SIC: 2951 1611 Asphalt paving mixtures & blocks; surfacing & paving

(G-15477)
ZUMSTEIN LOGGING CO (PA)
1801 Ne Hayes Rd (98674-2415)
PHONE..................360 225-7505
Joseph Zumstein, *Owner*
EMP: 3 EST: 1955
SALES (est): 456.5K **Privately Held**
SIC: 2411 Logging camps & contractors

(G-15478)
ZUMSTEIN LOGGING CO
302 E Scott Ave (98674-9413)
PHONE..................253 225-7521
Joel Zumstein, *Branch Mgr*
EMP: 2
SALES (corp-wide): 456.5K **Privately Held**
SIC: 2411 Logging
PA: Zumstein Logging Co
1801 Ne Hayes Rd
Woodland WA 98674
360 225-7505

Woodway
Snohomish County

(G-15479)
DANS STRIPING AND MOLDING INC
23946 W Woodway Ln (98020-5229)
PHONE..................206 533-1495
Paul D Hardan, *Principal*
▲ EMP: 4 EST: 2012
SALES (est): 372.6K **Privately Held**
SIC: 3089 Molding primary plastic

(G-15480)
SAITEK U S A INC
21700 Nootka Rd (98020-4151)
PHONE..................425 672-8748
Philip Blodgett, *Principal*
EMP: 2
SALES (est): 140K **Privately Held**
SIC: 7692 Welding repair

Yacolt
Clark County

(G-15481)
AVIATION INNOVATIONS LLC
35004 Ne 185th Ave (98675-4129)
PHONE.................................360 907-0888
Marci A Aldred, *Principal*
EMP: 3
SALES (est): 295.4K **Privately Held**
SIC: 3728 Aircraft parts & equipment

(G-15482)
GERRYS MACHINE SHOP INC
22218 Ne Steelhead Ln (98675-3108)
PHONE.................................360 686-1108
Gerry Te Hennepe, *President*
Leatha Te Hennepe, *Corp Secy*
EMP: 2 EST: 1965
SALES: 150K **Privately Held**
SIC: 3599 Machine shop, jobbing & repair

(G-15483)
JAMES HOMOLA
Also Called: Northwestern Sheetmetal
36700 Ne Ridgeview Dr (98675-4634)
PHONE.................................360 686-3549
James Homola, *Owner*
Cameo Homola, *Co-Owner*
EMP: 2
SALES (est): 220K **Privately Held**
WEB: www.northwesternsheetmetal.com
SIC: 3444 Sheet metal specialties, not stamped

(G-15484)
KASKI TOM LOGGING & CAT WORK
38220 Ne Rotschy Rd (98675-5309)
PHONE.................................360 247-5707
Thomas Kaski, *Owner*
Sydney Kaski, *Co-Owner*
EMP: 2
SALES: 66K **Privately Held**
SIC: 2411 Logging

(G-15485)
KURT MUONIO CONTRACT CUTTING
23500 Ne Jehnsen Rd (98675-4861)
P.O. Box 543 (98675-0799)
PHONE.................................360 686-1809
Kurt Muonio, *Principal*
EMP: 6
SALES (est): 471.8K **Privately Held**
SIC: 2411 Logging

(G-15486)
LUMBER LINE LASER REPAIR
26407 Ne 356th St (98675-4403)
P.O. Box 274 (98675-0399)
PHONE.................................360 686-3340
Larry Clark, *Owner*
Victoria Clark, *Co-Owner*
Byron Hatfield, *Vice Pres*
EMP: 2
SALES: 300K **Privately Held**
WEB: www.muskoka.com
SIC: 3679 Electronic circuits

(G-15487)
MILLARS ORGANIC WD ROASTED COF
33111 Ne 236th St (98675-9572)
PHONE.................................360 686-3643
EMP: 2
SALES (est): 62.3K **Privately Held**
SIC: 2095 Roasted coffee

(G-15488)
MILLER PURR FECT PRINTS
18904 Ne Lucia Falls Rd (98675-3060)
PHONE.................................360 687-1186
Carol S Miller, *Owner*
EMP: 2
SALES: 40K **Privately Held**
SIC: 2759 Screen printing

(G-15489)
NORTHWEST CABINET HARDWARE
30502 Ne 181st Ave (98675-3037)
PHONE.................................360 281-5869
EMP: 2
SALES (est): 73.4K **Privately Held**
SIC: 3429 Cabinet hardware

(G-15490)
ORIGINAL EXPRESSO MACHINE
33111 Ne 236th St (98675-9572)
PHONE.................................360 686-3643
Todd Millar, *Owner*
▲ EMP: 5
SALES (est): 642.9K **Privately Held**
SIC: 3589 Coffee brewing equipment

(G-15491)
PRECISION TRUCK & EQUIPMENT
33415 Ne Lewisville Hwy (98675-3501)
PHONE.................................360 263-8940
Clarence Goff, *Owner*
EMP: 2
SALES (est): 81K **Privately Held**
SIC: 0191 3537 General farms, primarily crop; trucks, tractors, loaders, carriers & similar equipment

(G-15492)
PRO SAFETY INC
23400 Ne Jehnsen Rd (98675-4825)
P.O. Box 72 (98675-0101)
PHONE.................................360 686-3686
Irvin W Ritola, *President*
EMP: 3
SALES: 500K **Privately Held**
SIC: 3599 Machine shop, jobbing & repair

(G-15493)
SOMERO LOGGING
36800 Ne 233rd Ave (98675-4808)
PHONE.................................360 686-3926
Douglas Somero, *Owner*
EMP: 2
SALES (est): 154.8K **Privately Held**
SIC: 2411 Logging camps & contractors

(G-15494)
WIRTANEN LOGGING INC
30606 Ne 247th Ave (98675-3203)
PHONE.................................360 686-3042
Ed Wirtanen, *President*
EMP: 2
SALES (est): 209K **Privately Held**
WEB: www.wirtanenfarm.org
SIC: 2411 Logging camps & contractors

Yakima
Yakima County

(G-15495)
4 COLOUR INC
513 W Chestnut Ave (98902-3440)
PHONE.................................509 249-0955
Karl Corprun, *President*
EMP: 3
SALES (est): 270K **Privately Held**
WEB: www.4colour.biz
SIC: 2759 Commercial printing

(G-15496)
A & S CONTRACTORS
722 N 32nd Ave (98902-1501)
PHONE.................................509 930-7994
Jose Serrano, *Owner*
EMP: 2
SALES (est): 130K **Privately Held**
SIC: 2451 Mobile homes

(G-15497)
A I S
7603 Richey Rd (98908-4503)
PHONE.................................509 972-2064
Jerry Potts Jr, *Director*
EMP: 2
SALES (est): 100.5K **Privately Held**
SIC: 3931 Musical instruments

(G-15498)
ABBOTTS PRINTING INC
307 S 3rd Ave (98902-3538)
PHONE.................................509 452-8202
Steve Noble, *Branch Mgr*
EMP: 2
SALES (corp-wide): 3MM **Privately Held**
SIC: 2752 Commercial printing, offset
PA: Abbott's Printing, Inc.
500 S 2nd Ave
Yakima WA 98902
509 452-8202

(G-15499)
ABBOTTS PRINTING INC (PA)
500 S 2nd Ave (98902-3591)
PHONE.................................509 452-8202
Steve Noble, *President*
Kathy Noble, *Corp Secy*
EMP: 18 EST: 1949
SQ FT: 14,000
SALES (est): 3MM **Privately Held**
WEB: www.abbottsprinting.com
SIC: 2752 Commercial printing, offset

(G-15500)
ADVANCED AUTOSOUND
4 Ranch Rite Rd (98901-3554)
PHONE.................................509 453-5363
Sam Juarz, *Principal*
EMP: 4
SALES (est): 374.9K **Privately Held**
SIC: 3651 Audio electronic systems

(G-15501)
ADVENTURER LP
3303 W Washington Ave (98903-9320)
PHONE.................................509 895-7064
Tony Basso, *President*
Dave Frampton, *General Mgr*
Norm Bruso, *Purch Mgr*
Greg Tucknies, *Natl Sales Mgr*
Jim Debord, *Sales Staff*
EMP: 125
SALES: 16.2MM **Privately Held**
SIC: 3792 Automobile house trailer chassis

(G-15502)
AGJET LLC
2101 Oak Ave (98903-1268)
PHONE.................................509 654-9449
Ben Wellner, *General Mgr*
EMP: 10
SALES: 1.5MM
SALES (corp-wide): 24.1MM **Privately Held**
SIC: 7373 3535 5084 Systems integration services; belt conveyor systems, general industrial use; conveyor systems
PA: H. R. Spinner Corporation
115 S 1st Ave
Yakima WA 98902
509 453-9111

(G-15503)
AHTANUM CUSTOM MEATS
3105 S 79th Ave (98903-9424)
PHONE.................................509 966-3642
Don Baggarley, *Owner*
EMP: 3
SQ FT: 2,458
SALES (est): 150K **Privately Held**
SIC: 7299 2011 Butcher service, processing only; meat packing plants

(G-15504)
ALL METAL SOLUTIONS
Also Called: AMS Metals
616 S 2nd St (98901-3214)
PHONE.................................509 426-2400
Donald Bruhn, *Owner*
EMP: 3
SALES (est): 185.6K **Privately Held**
SIC: 3443 Metal parts

(G-15505)
ALTERA INC
Also Called: Mother Nature's Wisdom
5808 Summitview Ave Ste A (98908-3095)
PHONE.................................509 901-9292
Barbara Altera, *President*
EMP: 10
SALES (est): 1.1MM **Privately Held**
SIC: 2844 Perfumes & colognes

(G-15506)
AMERICAN CABINET DOORS INC
1002 River Rd Ste 4 (98902-7103)
PHONE.................................509 574-3176
Cory Roybal, *President*
William Luebke, *Corp Secy*
Bruce Roybal, *Vice Pres*
Karla Kuntz, *Office Mgr*
Donielle Roybal, *Admin Sec*
EMP: 10
SALES: 1.6MM **Privately Held**
SIC: 2434 5031 5211 Wood kitchen cabinets; kitchen cabinets; cabinets, kitchen

(G-15507)
AMERICAN EXCELSIOR COMPANY
609 S Front St (98901-3286)
PHONE.................................509 575-5794
Terry A Sadowski, *President*
EMP: 35
SALES (corp-wide): 77.8MM **Privately Held**
SIC: 3086 2821 Carpet & rug cushions, foamed plastic; plastics materials & resins
PA: American Excelsior Company Inc
850 Avenue H E
Arlington TX 76011
817 385-3500

(G-15508)
AMERICAN WOODWORKING SUPPLY
1606 N 1st St (98901-1729)
PHONE.................................509 424-3800
Cory Roybal, *President*
Bruce Roybal, *Vice Pres*
EMP: 3
SALES (est): 105.7K **Privately Held**
SIC: 2431 Millwork

(G-15509)
ANDERSON ROCK DEM PITS II LLC
41 Rocky Top Rd (98908-9560)
PHONE.................................509 965-3621
Ron Anderson, *Mng Member*
EMP: 7
SQ FT: 722
SALES (est): 567.8K **Privately Held**
SIC: 8744 1442 ; construction sand & gravel

(G-15510)
ANTOLIN CELLARS
6004 Glacier Way (98908-2748)
PHONE.................................509 833-5765
Tony Haralson, *Co-Owner*
EMP: 3
SALES (est): 202.1K **Privately Held**
SIC: 2084 Wines

(G-15511)
APEX MACHINING LLC
7610 W Nob Hill Blvd # 200 (98908-1934)
PHONE.................................509 945-0125
Frank Dixon, *President*
EMP: 2 EST: 2009
SALES (est): 241.1K **Privately Held**
SIC: 3599 Machine shop, jobbing & repair

(G-15512)
ARR TECH MANUFACTURING
3801 W Washington Ave (98903-1181)
P.O. Box 10932 (98909-1932)
PHONE.................................509 966-4300
Tad Marquis, *Owner*
Ted Marquis, *Principal*
Kevin Pearson, *Vice Pres*
▲ EMP: 40
SALES (est): 6.3MM **Privately Held**
SIC: 5084 3556 Stackers, industrial; food products machinery

(G-15513)
ARREOLAS AUTO WRECKING
290 Perry Way (98901-9377)
PHONE.................................509 452-0818
Julio Arreola, *Owner*
EMP: 4
SALES (est): 286.8K **Privately Held**
SIC: 3713 Automobile wrecker truck bodies

GEOGRAPHIC SECTION
Yakima - Yakima County (G-15542)

(G-15514)
ARTISTIC CABINETS & MILLWORK
2105 E Mead Ave (98903-3936)
PHONE.................................509 575-4788
Ken Schiffelbein, *Owner*
EMP: 2
SQ FT: 2,400
SALES (est): 166K **Privately Held**
SIC: 2431 1751 Millwork; cabinet building & installation

(G-15515)
ASAP METAL FABRICATORS INC
Also Called: Finish Line Powder Coating
309 S Front St (98901-2855)
PHONE.................................509 469-3572
Penny Schweyen, *Admin Sec*
EMP: 4
SALES (corp-wide): 2.9MM **Privately Held**
WEB: www.asapmetalfab.com
SIC: 3444 Sheet metalwork
PA: A.S.A.P. Metal Fabricators, Inc.
   315 S 3rd Ave
   Yakima WA 98902
   509 453-9143

(G-15516)
ASAP METAL FABRICATORS INC (PA)
Also Called: Finish Line Product Coating
315 S 3rd Ave (98902-3538)
PHONE.................................509 453-9143
Toll Free:.......................888   -
Terance Schweyen, *President*
Terry Schweyen, *President*
Dale Herdon, *Vice Pres*
Karen Herndon, *Treasurer*
Valerie Fisher, *Office Mgr*
EMP: 30
SQ FT: 10,000
SALES: 2.9MM **Privately Held**
WEB: www.asapmetalfab.com
SIC: 3444 Sheet metalwork

(G-15517)
AVOA PUBLISHING LLC
6408 Cowiche Canyon Ln (98908-9492)
PHONE.................................509 594-9778
Joan Franklin, *Principal*
EMP: 4
SALES (est): 187.3K **Privately Held**
SIC: 2741 Miscellaneous publishing

(G-15518)
BELFOR USA GROUP INC
720 N 16th Ave Ste 9 (98902-1885)
PHONE.................................509 453-8551
Gary V Valkeneer, *Manager*
Troy Hughes, *Manager*
EMP: 5
SALES (corp-wide): 1.5B **Privately Held**
SIC: 1799 3999 Post-disaster renovations; wool pulling
HQ: Belfor Usa Group Inc.
   185 Oakland Ave Ste 150
   Birmingham MI 48009

(G-15519)
BERGEN SCREEN PRINT
1418 S 40th Ave (98908-3931)
PHONE.................................509 965-2511
John Steenbergen, *Principal*
EMP: 3
SALES (est): 262.9K **Privately Held**
SIC: 2395 5699 5199 Embroidery products, except schiffli machine; miscellaneous apparel & accessories; advertising specialties

(G-15520)
BIAFLEX PRINTING SOLUTIONS LLC
3207 W Nob Hill Blvd (98902-4960)
PHONE.................................509 895-7076
Rondi Oldham,
EMP: 2
SALES (est): 189.3K **Privately Held**
SIC: 2759 Commercial printing

(G-15521)
BIMBO BAKERIES USA INC
907 S 1st St (98901-3401)
PHONE.................................509 452-6293
EMP: 18
SALES (corp-wide): 13.7B **Privately Held**
SIC: 2051 Mfg Bread/Related Products
HQ: Bimbo Bakeries Usa, Inc
   255 Business Center Dr # 200
   Horsham PA 19044
   215 347-5500

(G-15522)
BLUELINE EQUIPMENT CO LLC (HQ)
1605 E Mead Ave (98903-3918)
P.O. Box 1108, Moxee (98936-1108)
PHONE.................................509 248-8411
Gregg A Marrs, *Mng Member*
Anita L Marrs,
▲ **EMP:** 41
SQ FT: 24,000
SALES (est): 11.5MM **Privately Held**
WEB: www.bluelinemfg.com
SIC: 3523 Farm machinery & equipment
PA: Blueline Mfg. Co.
   1605 E Mead Ave
   Yakima WA 98903
   509 248-8411

(G-15523)
BLUELINE MFG CO (PA)
1605 E Mead Ave (98903-3918)
PHONE.................................509 248-8411
Anita L Marrs, *Principal*
Gregg A Marrs, *Principal*
EMP: 9
SALES (est): 11.5MM **Privately Held**
SIC: 3523 Farm machinery & equipment

(G-15524)
BOWLBYS SPORTING GOODS
Also Called: Bowlby's
129 S 3rd St (98901-2827)
PHONE.................................509 248-8281
Donald Rennie, *Owner*
EMP: 5
SQ FT: 5,500
SALES (est): 160K **Privately Held**
SIC: 3949 7699 5941 5932 Sporting & athletic goods; gun services; firearms; pawnshop

(G-15525)
BUREN SHEET METAL INC
3801 W Washington Ave (98903-1181)
P.O. Box 9039 (98909-0039)
PHONE.................................509 575-1950
Ted Marquis, *CEO*
Kelli Barton, *Vice Pres*
EMP: 30 **EST:** 1936
SQ FT: 30,000
SALES (est): 4.4MM
SALES (corp-wide): 6.3MM **Privately Held**
WEB: www.marq.net
SIC: 3565 Packaging machinery
PA: Viking Packaging Machinery Inc
   3800 W Washington Ave
   Yakima WA 98903
   509 452-7143

(G-15526)
CABINET TECH LLC
106 W Pine St (98902-3556)
P.O. Box 2872 (98907-2872)
PHONE.................................509 575-0180
Jacob Jundt,
Charles Eglyn,
EMP: 3 **EST:** 1990
SALES: 3.2MM
SALES (corp-wide): 13MM **Privately Held**
WEB: www.cabinettech.com
SIC: 2434 Wood kitchen cabinets
PA: Tri-Ply, Inc.
   106 W Pine St
   Yakima WA
   509 453-6581

(G-15527)
CANTERBURYS DENTAL CERAMICS
7900 Easy St (98903-9698)
PHONE.................................509 966-3622
Andrew Canterbury, *President*
EMP: 2
SALES (est): 129.6K **Privately Held**
SIC: 3269 Pottery products

(G-15528)
CARRIER TRANSPORTS INC
1008 N 1st St (98901-1902)
PHONE.................................509 452-0136
Donald Russell, *President*
Valerie Kunz, *Vice Pres*
EMP: 7 **EST:** 1980
SQ FT: 4,000
SALES: 900K **Privately Held**
SIC: 7539 3537 Trailer repair; straddle carriers, mobile

(G-15529)
CASCADE BRUSH COMPANY
725 E Viola Ave (98901)
PHONE.................................509 965-6603
Patrick Stohr, *President*
Deborah Stohr, *Vice Pres*
▲ **EMP:** 2
SALES (est): 23.8K **Privately Held**
SIC: 3991 Brooms & brushes

(G-15530)
CASCADE QUALITY MOLDING INC
2607 Ahtanum Rd (98903-1225)
PHONE.................................509 248-9642
Larry Kraft, *President*
▲ **EMP:** 12
SALES (est): 3MM **Privately Held**
WEB: www.cascadequalitymolding.com
SIC: 3089 3544 Molding primary plastic; special dies, tools, jigs & fixtures

(G-15531)
CASCADE SIGN
1413 River Rd (98902-1326)
PHONE.................................509 945-1578
Fred Mears, *Owner*
EMP: 8
SALES (est): 813.5K **Privately Held**
SIC: 3993 Electric signs

(G-15532)
CITY OF YAKIMA
Also Called: City Yakima Water Trtmnt Plant
6390 Us Highway 12 (98908-9647)
PHONE.................................509 575-6177
Ted Hikel, *Principal*
EMP: 7 **Privately Held**
WEB: www.co.yakima.wa.us
SIC: 3589 9111 Water treatment equipment, industrial; city & town managers' offices
PA: City Of Yakima
   129 N 2nd St
   Yakima WA 98901
   509 575-6070

(G-15533)
CLASSIC PRINTING INC
104 S 5th Ave (98902-3434)
PHONE.................................509 452-1231
Scott Geer, *Owner*
EMP: 6
SQ FT: 4,000
SALES (est): 696.7K **Privately Held**
SIC: 2752 Commercial printing, offset

(G-15534)
CLASSIC WELDING
107 Nob Blvd (98901)
PHONE.................................509 469-8110
Salvador Gonzalez, *Owner*
EMP: 2
SALES (est): 208.4K **Privately Held**
SIC: 7692 Welding repair

(G-15535)
COCA-COLA BOTTLING CO (HQ)
607 E R St (98901-1860)
P.O. Box 2905 (98907-2905)
PHONE.................................509 248-1855
Adam Dolsen, *President*
Ken Willms, *CFO*
EMP: 50
SALES (est): 16.6MM
SALES (corp-wide): 55.1MM **Privately Held**
WEB: www.dolsenleasing.com
SIC: 2086 Bottled & canned soft drinks
PA: The Dolsen Companies
   301 N 3rd St
   Yakima WA 98901
   509 248-2831

(G-15536)
COOPER ELECTRIC MOTOR SVC CO
205 S 4th Ave (98902-3490)
PHONE.................................509 452-9550
Jesse Froehlich, *President*
EMP: 12
SQ FT: 4,300
SALES (est): 880K **Privately Held**
WEB: www.yakimatristatesupply.com
SIC: 7694 Electric motor repair

(G-15537)
CORE PACK LLC
1803 Presson Pl (98903-2200)
PHONE.................................509 426-2511
Patrick Shields, *Principal*
EMP: 3 **EST:** 2017
SALES (est): 376.9K **Privately Held**
SIC: 2611 2631 Pulp mills; paperboard mills

(G-15538)
CORUS ESTATES & VINEYARDS LLC
Also Called: 12th and Maple Winery
1410 Lakeside Ct Ste 109 (98902-7305)
PHONE.................................503 538-7724
Paul Lukas,
EMP: 23
SALES: 3.5MM
SALES (corp-wide): 5.9MM **Privately Held**
WEB: www.winemakersllc.com
SIC: 2084 Wines
PA: Winemakers, L.L.C.
   1410 Lakeside Ct Ste 109
   Yakima WA 98902
   509 853-1000

(G-15539)
CPM DEVELOPMENT CORPORATION
Also Called: Central Pre-Mix Concrete
2000 E Beech St (98901-2147)
P.O. Box 9575 (98909-0575)
PHONE.................................509 248-2041
John Shogren, *Vice Pres*
Tami Cain, *Branch Mgr*
EMP: 100
SQ FT: 1,000
SALES (corp-wide): 30.6B **Privately Held**
WEB: www.centralpremix.com
SIC: 3273 Ready-mixed concrete
HQ: Cpm Development Corporation
   5111 E Broadway Ave
   Spokane Valley WA 99212
   509 534-6221

(G-15540)
CREATIVE CABINET DESIGN
1102 Tieton Dr (98902-3836)
PHONE.................................509 452-2777
Brenda Brown, *Admin Sec*
EMP: 2
SALES (est): 251.9K **Privately Held**
SIC: 2434 Wood kitchen cabinets

(G-15541)
CUB CRAFTERS INC
Also Called: Cubcrafters
1918 S 16th Ave (98903-1212)
PHONE.................................509 248-9491
James R Richmond, *President*
Jennifer Woodard, *Purchasing*
Pete Dougherty, *Research*
Andrew Young, *Design Engr*
Vera Liebert, *Marketing Staff*
▲ **EMP:** 35
SQ FT: 10,000
SALES (est): 10MM **Privately Held**
WEB: www.cubcrafters.com
SIC: 3728 5088 Aircraft parts & equipment; aircraft & parts

(G-15542)
CUB CRAFTERS GROUP LLC
1918 S 16th Ave (98903-1212)
PHONE.................................509 248-9491
Randy Lervold, *President*
EMP: 2
SALES (est): 104.1K **Privately Held**
SIC: 3721 Motorized aircraft

Yakima - Yakima County (G-15543)

(G-15543)
CUB CRAFTERS SERVICES LLC
1920 S 16th Ave (98903-1212)
PHONE..................509 248-1025
Jim Richmond,
EMP: 12
SALES (est): 1.1MM Privately Held
SIC: 3721 Aircraft

(G-15544)
CUGA VEST
140 Leininger Dr (98901-8313)
PHONE..................509 834-8378
EMP: 2
SALES (est): 115.4K Privately Held
SIC: 3949 Sporting & athletic goods

(G-15545)
CUMMINS INC
Also Called: Cummins Northwest
1905 Central Ave (98901-3609)
P.O. Box 9129 (98909-0129)
PHONE..................509 248-9033
Sandra Ihly, Branch Mgr
Cheryl Hamlin, Manager
EMP: 14
SALES (corp-wide): 23.7B Publicly Held
SIC: 5084 7538 3519 Engines & parts, diesel; diesel engine repair: automotive; internal combustion engines
PA: Cummins Inc.
500 Jackson St
Columbus IN 47201
812 377-5000

(G-15546)
CUSTOM TECHNOLOGY CO INC
Also Called: Ctc
460 Mclaughlin Rd (98908-9659)
PHONE..................509 965-3333
Brandon Haley, President
EMP: 15
SQ FT: 12,000
SALES (est): 3.1MM Privately Held
WEB: www.customtechnology.net
SIC: 3523 3444 3535 Irrigation equipment, self-propelled; sheet metalwork; conveyors & conveying equipment

(G-15547)
CUSTOM WIN TNTING GRAPHICS INC
912 E Terrace Heights Way (98901-3057)
PHONE..................509 453-4293
Jake Macias, President
Maria Macias, Senior VP
EMP: 5
SALES (est): 275K Privately Held
SIC: 7549 1742 3993 3081 Glass tinting, automotive; solar reflecting insulation film; signs & advertising specialties; vinyl film & sheet

(G-15548)
CUTWELL PRODUCTS
1119 S 68th Ave (98908-1904)
PHONE..................509 966-1499
Lyle T Roy, Co-Owner
Ann Roy, Co-Owner
▼ EMP: 2 EST: 1940
SALES (est): 102.3K Privately Held
SIC: 3423 Garden & farm tools, including shovels

(G-15549)
DAKOTA CUB
2008 W Washington Ave (98903-1240)
PHONE..................509 453-3412
Todd Braman, Owner
EMP: 2
SALES (est): 203.6K Privately Held
SIC: 3728 Aircraft parts & equipment

(G-15550)
DAUGHTREY MACHINE
544 Breaum Rd (98908-9620)
PHONE..................509 834-9736
Anna Bailey, Principal
EMP: 2
SALES (est): 170.5K Privately Held
SIC: 1381 Drilling water intake wells

(G-15551)
DEAN THOEMKE
Also Called: Pacwest Interiors
581 Old Naches Hwy (98908-8922)
PHONE..................253 640-2232
Dean Thoemke, Principal
EMP: 6
SALES (est): 209K Privately Held
SIC: 2434 1752 5712 3253 Wood kitchen cabinets; vinyl floor tile & sheet installation; cabinets, except custom made: kitchen; ceramic wall & floor tile

(G-15552)
DEANS MEAN PRFMCE COATINGS
3410 Clinton Way (98902-4722)
PHONE..................509 406-4713
Brandon Dean, Principal
EMP: 2
SALES (est): 99K Privately Held
SIC: 3479 Metal coating & allied service

(G-15553)
DESIGN SERVICE CORPORATION
1507 S 9th Ave (98902-5849)
P.O. Box 10385 (98909-1385)
PHONE..................509 248-8531
Greg Anderson, President
John Gange, Vice Pres
Peggy Anderson, Treasurer
EMP: 13
SQ FT: 8,500
SALES (est): 2MM Privately Held
WEB: www.designservicecorp.com
SIC: 3565 Packaging machinery

(G-15554)
DIESEL TECH MACHINING INC
619 W J St (98902-1375)
P.O. Box 9935 (98909-0935)
PHONE..................509 576-8299
Samuel Ramirez Jr, President
EMP: 8
SALES (est): 1MM Privately Held
SIC: 3599 Machine shop, jobbing & repair

(G-15555)
DILBECK TOOLS INC
502 Bittner Rd (98901-8084)
PHONE..................509 452-3405
Rick Dilbeck, Principal
EMP: 2
SALES (est): 209.8K Privately Held
SIC: 3541 Machine tools, metal cutting type

(G-15556)
DOLLAR STRETCHER
501 W Lincoln Ave (98902-2658)
PHONE..................509 895-7744
James Lee, Branch Mgr
EMP: 8
SALES (est): 772.4K Privately Held
SIC: 3842 Stretchers

(G-15557)
DON PANCHO AUTHENTI
Also Called: Don Pancho Mexican Foods
605 E Nob Hill Blvd (98901-3533)
PHONE..................509 575-4489
Elijio Esquivel, Manager
EMP: 20
SALES (corp-wide): 1.7B Privately Held
WEB: www.donpancho.com
SIC: 2099 Food preparations
HQ: Don Pancho Authentic Mexican Foods, Inc.
3060 Industrial Way Ne
Salem OR 97301
503 370-9710

(G-15558)
DOWTY AEROSPACE
2720 W Washington Ave (98903-2513)
PHONE..................509 248-5000
John Ferry, Principal
EMP: 3 EST: 2010
SALES (est): 230.7K Privately Held
SIC: 3728 Aircraft parts & equipment

(G-15559)
DUDE WHERES MY CAR
1306 S 18th St (98901-3643)
PHONE..................509 249-5440
Ken Hays, Principal
EMP: 4 EST: 2010
SALES (est): 440.5K Privately Held
SIC: 3531 Automobile wrecker hoists

(G-15560)
E/STEP SOFTWARE INC
12015 Summitview Rd (98908-9168)
PHONE..................509 853-5000
John Estep, President
Lee Ann Estep, Vice Pres
EMP: 6
SALES (est): 379.9K Privately Held
WEB: www.estepsoftware.com
SIC: 7372 Business oriented computer software

(G-15561)
EAGLE SIGNS LLC
517 Bittner Rd (98901-8084)
PHONE..................509 453-8159
Larry Oliver, Branch Mgr
EMP: 3
SALES (est): 158.5K Privately Held
SIC: 3993 Electric signs
PA: Eagle Signs, Llc
1511 S Keys Rd
Yakima WA 98901

(G-15562)
EAGLE SIGNS LLC (PA)
1511 S Keys Rd (98901-9537)
PHONE..................509 453-5511
Larry Oliver,
EMP: 10
SQ FT: 8,500
SALES: 1MM Privately Held
SIC: 3993 Electric signs; neon signs

(G-15563)
ECS MACHINING INC
651 S 83rd Ave (98908-9765)
PHONE..................509 317-2557
Elmer Noll, President
Janet Noll, Vice Pres
Anita Noll, CFO
Donald Roeber, Manager
EMP: 11
SALES: 500K Privately Held
SIC: 3324 Aerospace investment castings, ferrous

(G-15564)
EMBROIDERY NORTHWEST
1906 W Nob Hill Blvd (98902-5230)
PHONE..................509 248-1186
Steve Gilley, Owner
EMP: 2
SQ FT: 1,800
SALES (est): 105.5K Privately Held
SIC: 2395 Embroidery products, except schiffli machine

(G-15565)
EVERGREEN MCH & FABRICATION
801 E Viola Ave (98903-1733)
P.O. Box 1566 (98907-1566)
PHONE..................509 249-1141
Jason Galloway, President
EMP: 11
SQ FT: 2,880
SALES (est): 1.3MM Privately Held
SIC: 3599 3499 Machine shop, jobbing & repair; aerosol valves, metal

(G-15566)
EVERLASTING PUBLISHING
1301 S 16th Ave (98902-5335)
P.O. Box 1061 (98907-1061)
PHONE..................509 225-9829
Willie F Pride Jr, President
EMP: 2
SALES (est): 114.1K Privately Held
SIC: 2741 Miscellaneous publishing

(G-15567)
FACT MOTORCYCLE TRAINING INC
Also Called: Fact Safety Companies
10 N 10th Ave (98902-3015)
PHONE..................509 248-2373
John Tull, President
EMP: 3
SALES (est): 342.6K Privately Held
SIC: 3714 Sanders, motor vehicle safety

(G-15568)
FBT
210 Keys Rd (98901-2112)
PHONE..................509 457-3484
Floyd J Blinsky, President
EMP: 7
SALES (est): 1.2MM Privately Held
SIC: 3537 Industrial trucks & tractors

(G-15569)
FELDHEGERS MACHINE & WELDING
806 Wilson Ln (98901-3741)
PHONE..................509 452-9213
John Feldheger, Owner
EMP: 9
SALES (est): 580.2K Privately Held
SIC: 3544 Special dies, tools, jigs & fixtures

(G-15570)
FILLIOLS CUSTOM CAB DOORS INC
1606 S 36th Ave (98902-4861)
PHONE..................509 453-8098
EMP: 14
SQ FT: 7,500
SALES (est): 1.3MM Privately Held
SIC: 2521 Mfg Wood Office Furniture

(G-15571)
FISHER BRDCSTG - WASH TV LLC
2801 Terrace Heights Dr (98901-1455)
PHONE..................509 575-0029
EMP: 2 EST: 2016
SALES (est): 97.2K Privately Held
SIC: 3663 Television broadcasting & communications equipment

(G-15572)
FLIP SIGNS
7610 Scenic Dr (98908-1065)
PHONE..................509 965-2822
EMP: 2 EST: 2011
SALES (est): 81K Privately Held
SIC: 3993 Mfg Signs/Advertising Specialties

(G-15573)
FPS MANUFACTURING LLC
1102 N 16th Ave (98902-1350)
PHONE..................509 248-0423
William B Kile IV,
EMP: 3
SALES (est): 230K Privately Held
SIC: 3086 Packaging & shipping materials, foamed plastic

(G-15574)
FRUIT COMMISSION WASH STATE
Also Called: Good Fruit Grower Magazine
105 S 18th St Ste 205 (98901-2176)
PHONE..................509 453-4837
B J Thurlby, President
EMP: 26
SALES: 8.7MM Privately Held
SIC: 2721 9641 Magazines: publishing only, not printed on site;
HQ: Washington State Dept Of Agriculture
1111 Washington St Se
Olympia WA 98501

(G-15575)
GFG PUBLISHING
105 S 18th St Ste 217 (98901-2177)
PHONE..................509 853-3520
Rich Hudgins, Principal
EMP: 10
SALES (est): 375.3K Privately Held
SIC: 2741 Miscellaneous publishing

GEOGRAPHIC SECTION
Yakima - Yakima County (G-15608)

(G-15576)
GILBERT CELLARS LLC
5 N Front St Ste 100 (98901-2630)
P.O. Box 9066 (98909-0066)
PHONE 509 249-9049
Sean Gilbert,
▲ EMP: 8
SALES (est): 1.2MM **Privately Held**
SIC: 5921 2084 5182 Wine; wines; wine

(G-15577)
GROUND PIERCING INC
1101 Industrial Way # 3504 (98903-5109)
PHONE 509 961-8241
Vickie Walther, *President*
EMP: 6
SALES: 950K **Privately Held**
SIC: 3541 Drilling & boring machines

(G-15578)
H F HAUFF CO INC
2921 Sutherland Dr (98903-1891)
PHONE 509 248-0318
Neil Hauff, *President*
Dean Hauff, *Corp Secy*
EMP: 12 **EST:** 1964
SQ FT: 30,000
SALES (est): 2.8MM **Privately Held**
SIC: 3523 Sprayers & spraying machines, agricultural; windmills for pumping water, agricultural

(G-15579)
H R SPINNER CORPORATION (PA)
115 S 1st Ave (98902-3400)
P.O. Box 1361 (98907-1361)
PHONE 509 453-9111
Ed Jewett, *President*
EMP: 25
SQ FT: 5,000
SALES (est): 24.1MM **Privately Held**
WEB: www.hrspinner.com
SIC: 5085 5113 3554 Packing, industrial; boxes, paperboard & disposable plastic; box making machines, paper

(G-15580)
HAHN MANUFACTURING INC
211 Berndt Bluff Rd (98908-8646)
PHONE 509 930-1621
Wayne Hahn, *President*
Jim Bramini, *Vice Pres*
EMP: 2
SQ FT: 4,000
SALES: 300K **Privately Held**
SIC: 3523 7699 Dusters, mechanical: agricultural; agricultural equipment repair services

(G-15581)
HOLM BING
Also Called: Holm Sales
1002 N 6th Ave (98902-1416)
PHONE 509 454-2277
Bing Holm, *Owner*
Paula Holm, *Co-Owner*
Debbie Holm, *Accountant*
EMP: 10
SQ FT: 6,200
SALES (est): 1MM **Privately Held**
SIC: 3993 7336 Signs & advertising specialties; commercial art & graphic design

(G-15582)
HOPS EXTRACT CORP AMERICA
Also Called: Hopstract
305 N 2nd Ave (98902-2626)
PHONE 509 575-6440
L S Gimbel IV, *President*
Adam Gimbel, *Treasurer*
Theresa Reyes, *Sales Staff*
David C Dunham, *Director*
Richard Krueger, *Maintence Staff*
▲ EMP: 10 **EST:** 1963
SQ FT: 44,000
SALES (est): 2.2MM
SALES (corp-wide): 35.1MM **Privately Held**
SIC: 2836 Extracts
PA: S. S. Steiner, Inc.
  725 5th Ave
  New York NY 10022
  212 838-8900

(G-15583)
HOPUNION CBS LLC
227 S Front St (98902)
PHONE 509 574-5124
Jennifer Stevens, *Branch Mgr*
EMP: 3
SALES (est): 186.5K
SALES (corp-wide): 5.7MM **Privately Held**
SIC: 2082 Malt beverages
PA: Hopunion Cbs Llc
  203 Division St
  Yakima WA 98902
  509 453-4792

(G-15584)
HOPUNION CRAFT BREWING SLS LLC
203 Division St (98902-4622)
PHONE 509 457-3200
Bill Bruce, *Owner*
▲ EMP: 6
SALES (est): 391.8K **Privately Held**
SIC: 2082 Beer (alcoholic beverage)

(G-15585)
HORSESHOE COVE CABIN OWNE
284 Sunnyslope Rd (98908-9018)
PHONE 509 966-4087
EMP: 2
SALES (est): 105.6K **Privately Held**
SIC: 3462 Horseshoes

(G-15586)
HOWARD F HARRISON M D
1460 N 16th Ave Ste C (98902-7102)
PHONE 509 575-8307
Howard Harrison, *Chairman*
EMP: 3
SALES (est): 54.1K **Privately Held**
SIC: 8011 7372 Offices & clinics of medical doctors; prepackaged software

(G-15587)
INDUSTRIAL CONTROL GROUP
Also Called: I C G
11808 Bristol Ct (98908-9598)
PHONE 509 965-5967
Ken Kester, *Owner*
EMP: 3
SALES (est): 140K **Privately Held**
SIC: 3672 8748 Printed circuit boards; systems analysis or design

(G-15588)
INDUSTRIAL TECH INTL LLC
2609 Ahtanum Rd (98903-1225)
PHONE 509 248-0959
Dave Darnall,
EMP: 2
SALES (est): 336.9K **Privately Held**
SIC: 3549 Metalworking machinery

(G-15589)
INLAND ALARM LLC
1100 Ahtanum Rd (98903-1203)
PHONE 509 457-6065
Adrian Wathen,
Douglas Barduhn,
EMP: 4
SALES: 120K **Privately Held**
SIC: 3669 Fire alarm apparatus, electric

(G-15590)
INLAND ICE & FUEL INC
Also Called: Artic-Land Ice
100 Division St (98902-4671)
PHONE 509 457-6151
EMP: 8
SQ FT: 2,000
SALES (est): 685.6K **Privately Held**
SIC: 2097 5983 5989 Block ice; ice cubes; fuel oil dealers; coal

(G-15591)
INLINE STEEL FABRICATORS INC
2506 S 26th Ave (98903-1287)
P.O. Box 9396 (98909-0396)
PHONE 509 248-4554
Mike Corn, *President*
EMP: 25
SQ FT: 18,000
SALES (est): 5.7MM **Privately Held**
SIC: 3441 Building components, structural steel

(G-15592)
INSTANT PRESS INC (PA)
Also Called: Printing Plus
601 W Yakima Ave (98902-3364)
PHONE 509 457-6195
Terry Powell, *President*
Barbara Powell, *Corp Secy*
EMP: 15
SQ FT: 1,500
SALES (est): 1.8MM **Privately Held**
WEB: www.instantpressinc.com
SIC: 2752 Commercial printing, offset

(G-15593)
INTELLICARD INC
8902 Tieton Dr (98908-9706)
P.O. Box 8255 (98908-0255)
PHONE 509 965-9266
Linda Seaman, *President*
Mathew Seaman, *Principal*
▲ EMP: 3
SALES (est): 230.1K **Privately Held**
WEB: www.intelli-card.com
SIC: 2731 Pamphlets: publishing only, not printed on site

(G-15594)
J AND J STAINLESS STEEL SVCS
809 S 60th Ave (98908-3559)
PHONE 509 952-4568
EMP: 2 **EST:** 2016
SALES (est): 90.8K **Privately Held**
SIC: 3312 Stainless steel

(G-15595)
J FREITAG ENTERPRISES INC
Also Called: National Barricade of Yakima
401 S 3rd Ave (98902-3540)
PHONE 509 453-4461
James D Freitag, *President*
EMP: 3
SQ FT: 4,000
SALES (est): 280.2K **Privately Held**
SIC: 3993 3499 7359 Signs & advertising specialties; barricades, metal; sign rental

(G-15596)
JB NEUFELD LLC
204 Arthur Blvd (98902-3740)
PHONE 509 945-1887
Ruth Neufeld, *Principal*
EMP: 4
SALES (est): 143.5K **Privately Held**
SIC: 2084 Wines

(G-15597)
JB NEUFELD LLC
2620 Draper Rd (98903-9216)
PHONE 509 895-9979
Justin Eli Neufeld, *Administration*
EMP: 2
SALES (est): 98.5K **Privately Held**
SIC: 2084 Wines

(G-15598)
JB WOODWORKING
2000 Mapleway Rd (98908-8925)
PHONE 509 949-3683
Jon Bishop, *Principal*
EMP: 2
SALES (est): 226.4K **Privately Held**
SIC: 2431 Millwork

(G-15599)
JBS MILLWORK INC
Also Called: Modern Millwork
401 W Washington Ave (98903-1439)
PHONE 509 248-3412
Jeffrey M Wells, *President*
Patrick Holland, *Manager*
EMP: 2
SALES (est): 334.1K **Privately Held**
SIC: 2431 Millwork

(G-15600)
JENNY MAES GLUTEN-FREE GOODIES
730 N 16th Ave Ste 2 (98902-1897)
PHONE 509 833-5096
Jennifer Simmons, *Owner*
EMP: 8 **EST:** 2010
SALES (est): 497.2K **Privately Held**
WEB: www.jennymaes.com
SIC: 2051 Rolls, bread type: fresh or frozen; cakes, pies & pastries

(G-15601)
JEREMY NICHOLS
1118 N 23rd Ave (98902-1217)
PHONE 509 930-6352
EMP: 2
SALES (est): 73.2K **Privately Held**
SIC: 2759 Commercial printing

(G-15602)
JONES DIGITAL PRINTING INC
Also Called: Printworks
3407 Terrace Heights Dr (98901-1411)
PHONE 509 452-8238
Gary Jones, *President*
EMP: 4
SQ FT: 1,890
SALES (est): 381.6K **Privately Held**
WEB: www.print-werks.com
SIC: 3555 Printing presses

(G-15603)
JULIAS LUMBER
12904 Wide Hollow Rd (98908-9142)
PHONE 509 966-0925
Julia Pell, *Owner*
EMP: 2
SALES (est): 92.2K **Privately Held**
SIC: 2499 Picture & mirror frames, wood

(G-15604)
K & L UNLIMITED
14258 Rutherford Rd (98903-9735)
PHONE 509 965-6451
Kevin Bolin, *Owner*
Linda Bolin, *Co-Owner*
EMP: 2
SALES (est): 153.5K **Privately Held**
SIC: 2221 5013 Upholstery fabrics, manmade fiber & silk; body repair or paint shop supplies, automotive

(G-15605)
KANA WINERY
10 S 2nd St (98901-2618)
PHONE 509 453-6611
Palmer Wright, *Owner*
Katherine Goodson, *General Mgr*
▲ EMP: 4
SALES (est): 238K **Privately Held**
WEB: www.kanawinery.com
SIC: 2084 Wines

(G-15606)
KEMPS MACHINE CO
1012 S 96th Ave (98908-9746)
PHONE 509 784-1326
Gregg Kemp, *Owner*
EMP: 10
SALES (est): 1.4MM **Privately Held**
SIC: 3565 5083 Packing & wrapping machinery; agricultural machinery & equipment

(G-15607)
KING SALES & MANUFACTURING CO
Also Called: Kold King
609 N 20th Ave (98902-1840)
PHONE 509 453-1744
Bob Weimer, *President*
EMP: 5
SQ FT: 8,500
SALES (est): 592.5K **Privately Held**
WEB: www.koldking.com
SIC: 3442 Metal doors

(G-15608)
KLC HOLDINGS LTD (PA)
Also Called: Quick Lok
2712 S 16th Ave (98903-9530)
P.O. Box 9548 (98909-0548)
PHONE 509 248-4770
John K Rothenbueler, *President*
Lorne House, *Partner*
Jerre Paxton, *Partner*
Hal Miller, *Treasurer*
Stephanie Paxton Jackson, *Director*
EMP: 15
SQ FT: 30,000

Yakima - Yakima County (G-15609)

SALES (est): 41.6MM **Privately Held**
WEB: www.quicklok.com
SIC: 3556 3565 Food products machinery; packaging machinery

(G-15609)
KORBLU MFG SOLUTIONS LLC
715a E Viola Ave (98901-3731)
PHONE..................................509 930-2010
Kenneth Davis, *Managing Prtnr*
Robert Simpson, *Partner*
EMP: 5
SQ FT: 4,200
SALES (est): 870.7K **Privately Held**
SIC: 2671 Wrapping paper, waterproof or coated

(G-15610)
KTN THERMO DYNAMICS
382 Fromherz Dr (98908-9096)
PHONE..................................509 823-0560
Kyle Nyberg, *Owner*
EMP: 2
SALES (est): 149K **Privately Held**
SIC: 3089 Automotive parts, plastic

(G-15611)
LITTLE SOAP MAKER
302 W Yakima Ave Ste 103 (98902-3416)
PHONE..................................509 972-8504
Julie Brown, *Owner*
EMP: 5
SALES (est): 834.9K **Privately Held**
SIC: 2841 Soap: granulated, liquid, cake, flaked or chip

(G-15612)
LOOKOUT POINT WINERY
16 N 2nd St (98901-2654)
PHONE..................................509 469-4320
EMP: 2
SALES (est): 62.3K **Privately Held**
SIC: 2084 Wines, brandy & brandy spirits

(G-15613)
LYNCH DISTRIBUTING CO
5205 Richey Rd (98908-2813)
PHONE..................................509 248-0880
Herb Lynch, *Owner*
EMP: 15
SALES (est): 1.8MM **Privately Held**
SIC: 5182 5181 5149 2084 Wine; beer & other fermented malt liquors; beverages, except coffee & tea; wines

(G-15614)
MANHASSET SPECIALTY CO INC
3505 Fruitvale Blvd (98902-7322)
P.O. Box 2518 (98907-2518)
PHONE..................................509 248-3810
Daniel Roberts, *President*
Barry Heid, *General Mgr*
Garry Griggs, *Director*
Michael Lizotte, *Director*
▲ EMP: 20
SQ FT: 38,000
SALES (est): 4.2MM **Privately Held**
WEB: www.manhasset-specialty.com
SIC: 3931 Stands, music

(G-15615)
MARQ PACKAGING SYSTEMS INC
3801 W Washington Ave (98903-1181)
P.O. Box 9063 (98909-0063)
PHONE..................................509 966-4300
Theodore Marquis Sr, *Ch of Bd*
Rocky Marquis, *President*
Gw Walker, *Vice Pres*
Ken Olson, *Opers Mgr*
Jeff Condardo, *Purchasing*
EMP: 30
SQ FT: 30,000
SALES (est): 9.8MM **Privately Held**
SIC: 3565 8741 Packaging machinery; management services

(G-15616)
MC ILVANIE MACHINE WORKS INC
12 S 6th Ave (98902-3302)
PHONE..................................509 452-3131
William A Mc Ilvanie, *President*
EMP: 10

SQ FT: 15,000
SALES (est): 852K **Privately Held**
SIC: 3541 3599 Lathes, metal cutting & polishing; machine shop, jobbing & repair

(G-15617)
MEADE WINERY
7909 Englewood Ave (98908-1026)
PHONE..................................509 972-4443
EMP: 2
SALES (est): 76K **Privately Held**
SIC: 2084 Mfg Wines/Brandy/Spirits

(G-15618)
MICHELSEN PACKAGING CO CAL (PA)
202 N 2nd Ave (98902-2625)
P.O. Box 89 (98907-0089)
PHONE..................................509 248-6270
Dan Keck, *President*
Gary Gavin, *Exec VP*
John Kupanoff, *Admin Sec*
▲ EMP: 60
SQ FT: 42,000
SALES (est): 74.6MM **Privately Held**
WEB: www.mpcyak.com
SIC: 5113 2653 Containers, paper & disposable plastic; paper & products, wrapping or coarse; pads, solid fiber: made from purchased materials

(G-15619)
MICHELSEN PACKAGING COMPANY
202 N 2nd Ave (98902-2625)
PHONE..................................509 248-6270
Dan Keck, *President*
Dan Beddeson, *Vice Pres*
Daniel L Beddeson, *Vice Pres*
Glenna Smith, *Human Resources*
Doug Doty, *Sales Staff*
◆ EMP: 150
SALES (est): 34.9MM **Privately Held**
SIC: 2657 5113 Folding paperboard boxes; folding paperboard boxes

(G-15620)
MICKS PEPPOURRI INC
1707 S 74th Ave (98908-2008)
P.O. Box 8324 (98908-0324)
PHONE..................................509 966-2328
Tadd Mick, *President*
Virginia Mick, *Corp Secy*
Rod Mick, *Vice Pres*
EMP: 7
SALES: 869.7K **Privately Held**
WEB: www.micks.com
SIC: 2033 5961 Jellies, edible, including imitation: in cans, jars, etc.; preserves, including imitation: in cans, jars, etc.; catalog & mail-order houses

(G-15621)
MIKRON INDUSTRIES INC
1123 N 6th Ave (98902-1468)
PHONE..................................815 335-2372
Bill Griffiths, *Branch Mgr*
EMP: 10 **Publicly Held**
SIC: 3272 Building materials, except block or brick: concrete
HQ: Mikron Industries, Inc.
2505 Meridian Pkwy # 250
Durham NC 27713
713 961-4600

(G-15622)
MILL LANE WINERY YAKIMA LLC
12302 Marble Rd (98908-9371)
PHONE..................................206 817-5767
Ronald Mehelich,
EMP: 2 EST: 2017
SALES (est): 84.5K **Privately Held**
SIC: 2084 Wines

(G-15623)
MINUTEMAN PRESS INTL INC
1114 W Lincoln Ave (98902-2534)
PHONE..................................509 452-6144
Hal Frantz, *Manager*
EMP: 3
SALES (corp-wide): 23.4MM **Privately Held**
SIC: 2752 Commercial printing, offset

PA: Minuteman Press International, Inc.
61 Executive Blvd
Farmingdale NY 11735
631 249-1370

(G-15624)
MORCANT SOFTWARE
618 S 13th Ave (98902-4321)
PHONE..................................509 225-6807
EMP: 2 EST: 2010
SALES (est): 100K **Privately Held**
SIC: 7372 Prepackaged Software Services

(G-15625)
MOXEE INNOVATIONS CORPORATION
721 E Viola Ave (98901)
PHONE..................................509 575-6322
C F Clark, *Administration*
EMP: 4 EST: 2016
SALES (est): 252.7K **Privately Held**
SIC: 3568 Power transmission equipment

(G-15626)
MULTI MANUFACTURING INC
1120 1/2 N 34th Ave (98902-1010)
P.O. Box 9041 (98909-0041)
PHONE..................................509 452-5628
Wayne M Parkison, *President*
James Darr, *Vice Pres*
Melba Parkison, *Vice Pres*
EMP: 6 EST: 1977
SQ FT: 6,000
SALES (est): 795.6K **Privately Held**
SIC: 3599 Machine shop, jobbing & repair

(G-15627)
NACHES HEIGHTS VINEYARD LLC
Also Called: Naches Heights Vinyrd & Winery
1857 Weikel Rd (98908-8857)
PHONE..................................509 966-4355
Philip R Cline, *Principal*
EMP: 2
SALES: 250K **Privately Held**
SIC: 0762 5182 2084 5921 Vineyard management & maintenance services; wine; wines; wine

(G-15628)
NATURAL NUTRITION MFG LLC
216 S 24th Ave (98902-3737)
PHONE..................................509 966-8849
Franklin L Davis, *Owner*
EMP: 2
SALES (est): 92.8K **Privately Held**
SIC: 3999 Manufacturing industries

(G-15629)
NELSON FARRIER SHOP INC
Also Called: Studio Equus
8805 Meadowbrook Rd (98903-9234)
P.O. Box 8193 (98908-0193)
PHONE..................................509 966-9598
Dennis A Nelson, *President*
EMP: 2
SALES (est): 122.7K **Privately Held**
WEB: www.studioequus.com
SIC: 7699 3269 Horseshoeing; art & ornamental ware, pottery

(G-15630)
NOEL CORPORATION (PA)
Also Called: Pepsico
1001 S 1st St (98901-3403)
P.O. Box 111 (98907-0111)
PHONE..................................509 248-4545
Roger Noel, *President*
Justin Noel, *Vice Pres*
Cindy Zimmerman, *Treasurer*
Ken Persson, *Info Tech Mgr*
Larry Estes, *Admin Sec*
EMP: 125
SQ FT: 40,000
SALES (est): 97MM **Privately Held**
WEB: www.noelcorp.com
SIC: 2086 7389 4212 6512 Soft drinks: packaged in cans, bottles, etc.; interior designer; local trucking, without storage; nonresidential building operators; general warehousing & storage; merchandising machine operators

(G-15631)
NOEL CORPORATION
Also Called: Modern Millwork & Design
401 W Washington Ave (98903-1439)
PHONE..................................509 248-3412
Dennis Key, *Manager*
EMP: 15
SALES (corp-wide): 97MM **Privately Held**
WEB: www.noelcorp.com
SIC: 2431 1542 3253 2273 Millwork; commercial & office buildings, renovation & repair; ceramic wall & floor tile; carpets & rugs
PA: The Noel Corporation
1001 S 1st St
Yakima WA 98901
509 248-4545

(G-15632)
NORTHSTAR ATTACHMENTS LLC
101 Wagon Trail Dr (98901-8060)
P.O. Box 1937 (98907-1937)
PHONE..................................509 452-1651
Ted Bellamy, *General Mgr*
David C Rankin,
Mike Yearout,
▲ EMP: 25
SALES (est): 8.3MM **Privately Held**
WEB: www.rankineqco.com
SIC: 5083 7692 3523 Farm & garden machinery; welding repair; farm machinery & equipment
PA: Rankin Equipment Co.
3205 Bay St
Union Gap WA 98903
509 453-8271

(G-15633)
NORTHWEST BAGGER COMPANY INC
3801 W Washington Ave (98903-1181)
P.O. Box 10932 (98909-1932)
PHONE..................................509 575-1950
Ted Marquis Jr, *President*
Vince Marquis, *Vice Pres*
EMP: 6
SQ FT: 30,000
SALES (est): 707K
SALES (corp-wide): 6.3MM **Privately Held**
WEB: www.marq.net
SIC: 3565 3556 Bag opening, filling & closing machines; food products machinery
PA: Viking Packaging Machinery Inc
3800 W Washington Ave
Yakima WA 98903
509 452-7143

(G-15634)
NORTHWEST DOVETAIL INC
1606 S 36th Ave (98902-4861)
PHONE..................................509 248-2056
John Filliol, *President*
Denise Filliol, *Vice Pres*
EMP: 2
SALES (est): 232.4K **Privately Held**
SIC: 2441 Boxes, wood

(G-15635)
NORTHWEST TILLERS INC
3801 W Washington Ave (98903-1181)
PHONE..................................509 575-1950
Todd Marquis, *President*
Mike Marquis, *Executive*
▲ EMP: 6
SQ FT: 15,000
SALES (est): 1MM
SALES (corp-wide): 6.3MM **Privately Held**
WEB: www.marq.net
SIC: 3524 3523 Rototillers (garden machinery); farm machinery & equipment
PA: Viking Packaging Machinery Inc
3800 W Washington Ave
Yakima WA 98903
509 452-7143

(G-15636)
NOVOLEX SHIELDS LLC
1009 Rock Ave (98902-4629)
P.O. Box 9848 (98909-0848)
PHONE..................................800 541-8630

Stanley Bikulege, *President*
Paul Palmisano, *CFO*
EMP: 500
SQ FT: 400,000
SALES (est): 40.9MM
SALES (corp-wide): 2.9B **Privately Held**
SIC: 3081 Plastic film & sheet
HQ: Novolex Holdings, Llc
 101 E Carolina Ave
 Hartsville SC 29550
 843 857-4800

(G-15637)
NRS SOFTWARE LLC
2301 W Yakima Ave (98902-2872)
PHONE...............................509 969-4769
EMP: 2 **EST:** 2016
SALES (est): 63.8K **Privately Held**
SIC: 7372 Prepackaged software

(G-15638)
OH SNAP PRINTS
411 N 78th Ave (98908-4500)
PHONE...............................509 901-7719
EMP: 2
SALES (est): 83.9K **Privately Held**
SIC: 2752 Lithographic Commercial Printing

(G-15639)
ORCHARD-RITE LIMITED INC (PA)
1702 Englewood Ave (98902-1846)
P.O. Box 9308 (98909-0308)
PHONE...............................509 834-2029
Doug Riddle, *President*
Jim Decoto, *Vice Pres*
George Johnson, *Engineer*
A Scheu, *Shareholder*
L Scheu, *Shareholder*
EMP: 22
SQ FT: 31,000
SALES (est): 28.3MM **Privately Held**
SIC: 3523 Farm machinery & equipment

(G-15640)
PACIFIC NW REPS LLC
7804 W Washington Ave (98902-2505)
PHONE...............................509 823-7008
Scott Herberg, *President*
EMP: 4 **EST:** 2016
SALES (est): 155.2K **Privately Held**
SIC: 5075 5169 3585 5078 Warm air heating equipment & supplies; industrial chemicals; compressors for refrigeration & air conditioning equipment; condensers, refrigeration; commercial refrigeration equipment

(G-15641)
PACKAGING CORPORATION AMERICA
2013 Ahtanum Rd (98903-2328)
PHONE...............................509 575-3689
Chris Gibbs, *Branch Mgr*
EMP: 5
SALES (corp-wide): 7B **Publicly Held**
SIC: 2653 Boxes, corrugated: made from purchased materials
PA: Packaging Corporation Of America
 1 N Field Ct
 Lake Forest IL 60045
 847 482-3000

(G-15642)
PAXTON SALES CORPORATION
108 W Mead Ave (98902-6028)
PHONE...............................509 453-0347
EMP: 10
SQ FT: 16,000
SALES (est): 760K **Privately Held**
SIC: 3599 3429 Mfg Industrial Machinery Mfg Hardware

(G-15643)
PENDOWN SOFTWARE LLC
3205 Folsom Ave Apt 2 (98902-2297)
P.O. Box 360 (98907-0360)
PHONE...............................509 480-8232
Joshua Childers, *Administration*
EMP: 2
SALES (est): 144.9K **Privately Held**
SIC: 7372 Prepackaged software

(G-15644)
PENINSULA PACKAGING LLC
2801 River Rd (98902-1166)
PHONE...............................509 575-5341
George Plummer, *General Mgr*
Joan Williams, *QC Mgr*
Lowell Romfo, *Manager*
EMP: 70
SQ FT: 54,000
SALES (corp-wide): 5.3B **Publicly Held**
SIC: 3089 Plastic containers, except foam
HQ: Peninsula Packaging, Llc
 1030 N Anderson Rd
 Exeter CA 93221
 559 594-6813

(G-15645)
PERFECT PRINTING & SIGNS
212 N 22nd Ave (98902-2427)
PHONE...............................509 786-3811
Donna Barnard, *Owner*
EMP: 6
SQ FT: 5,000
SALES (est): 260K **Privately Held**
SIC: 2759 2752 3993 Commercial printing; commercial printing, offset; signs & advertising specialties

(G-15646)
PICATTI BROTHERS INC (PA)
Also Called: Engineering Division
105 S 3rd Ave (98902-3421)
P.O. Box 9576 (98909-0576)
PHONE...............................509 248-2540
Donald S Picatti, *President*
David J Picatti, *COO*
Michael L Picatti, *Treasurer*
EMP: 95
SQ FT: 20,000
SALES (est): 22.2MM **Privately Held**
SIC: 1731 7694 5063 8711 Electrical work; motor repair services; electrical apparatus & equipment; switches, except electronic; panelboards; electrical or electronic engineering

(G-15647)
PIETY FLATS WINERY
5202 Bitterroot Way (98908-2639)
PHONE...............................509 877-3115
Jim Russi, *Principal*
EMP: 3
SALES (est): 195.5K **Privately Held**
WEB: www.pietyflatswinery.com
SIC: 2084 Wines

(G-15648)
PIONEER PRINTING AND FORMS
10502 Orchard Ave (98908-8011)
PHONE...............................509 248-7393
Larry Becker, *Principal*
EMP: 2
SALES (est): 151.1K **Privately Held**
SIC: 5943 2759 2754 Office forms & supplies; business forms: printing; business forms: gravure printing

(G-15649)
POMONA SERVICE & SUPPLY CO
Also Called: Pomona Packaging Division
2310 Castlevale Rd (98902-1218)
P.O. Box 2733 (98907-2733)
PHONE...............................509 452-7121
John E Muller Jr, *President*
EMP: 9 **EST:** 1964
SQ FT: 7,500
SALES (est): 830K **Privately Held**
SIC: 3535 3565 3556 Conveyors & conveying equipment; packaging machinery; food products machinery

(G-15650)
PRECISION INDUSTRIAL EQUI
1909 Longfibre Rd (98903-1585)
PHONE...............................509 571-1725
Patrick Flumerfelt,
EMP: 2
SALES (est): 188.8K **Privately Held**
SIC: 3569 7699 General industrial machinery; industrial equipment services

(G-15651)
PRECISION MACHINING
14308 Fisk Rd (98908-9525)
PHONE...............................509 972-1986
Steve Fischer, *Owner*
EMP: 2
SALES (est): 186.2K **Privately Held**
SIC: 3599 Machine shop, jobbing & repair

(G-15652)
PRECISION SHEET METAL LLC
522 N 18th Ave (98902-2404)
PHONE...............................509 969-0055
EMP: 2 **EST:** 2013
SALES (est): 110K **Privately Held**
SIC: 3444 Mfg Sheet Metalwork

(G-15653)
PRINT GUYS
101 N 3rd St (98901-2704)
PHONE...............................509 453-6369
EMP: 4 **EST:** 2016
SALES (est): 101.5K **Privately Held**
SIC: 2752 Commercial printing, lithographic

(G-15654)
PRINT GUYS INC (PA)
2802 W Nob Hill Blvd # 2 (98902-4982)
PHONE...............................509 453-6369
David Ackermam, *President*
EMP: 8
SALES (est): 1.1MM **Privately Held**
SIC: 2741 Miscellaneous publishing

(G-15655)
PRO CONTROLS INC
1312 Gordon Rd (98901-1725)
PHONE...............................509 457-3386
Doug Tilton, *President*
Jerry Sanders, *Corp Secy*
EMP: 6
SQ FT: 5,000
SALES (est): 1MM **Privately Held**
WEB: www.proctrl.com
SIC: 3625 5084 Industrial controls: push button, selector switches, pilot; industrial machinery & equipment

(G-15656)
PROFESSIONAL SALES & SERV
250 Thompson Rd (98908-9470)
PHONE...............................509 678-4535
EMP: 9 **EST:** 1998
SALES (est): 1.2MM **Privately Held**
SIC: 3577 Mfg Computer Peripheral Equipment

(G-15657)
PROMPT PRINTERY
313 S 4th Ave (98902-3544)
PHONE...............................509 457-5848
Glenn Klingel, *Owner*
Bruce Scully, *Co-Owner*
EMP: 2 **EST:** 1914
SQ FT: 2,500
SALES (est): 182.3K **Privately Held**
SIC: 2759 2752 Letterpress printing; lithographing on metal

(G-15658)
PRP FINISHING
401 S 51st Ave (98908-3420)
PHONE...............................509 966-0798
Todd Faith, *Principal*
EMP: 2
SALES (est): 141K **Privately Held**
SIC: 5712 5021 2521 7641 Cabinet work, custom; furniture; cabinets, office: wood; furniture repair & maintenance

(G-15659)
RADS AUTO
1602 S 36th Ave (98902-4861)
PHONE...............................509 965-5712
Glen Radke, *Owner*
EMP: 3
SQ FT: 2,104
SALES (est): 170K **Privately Held**
WEB: www.radialauto.com
SIC: 3429 7539 Manufactured hardware (general); automotive repair shops

(G-15660)
REFRIGERATION SUPPLIES DISTR
2 E D St (98901-2370)
PHONE...............................509 452-8689
Michael Biehl, *Branch Mgr*
EMP: 6
SALES (corp-wide): 193MM **Privately Held**
SIC: 5722 5078 3585 Household appliance stores; refrigeration equipment & supplies; refrigeration equipment, complete
PA: Refrigeration Supplies Distributor
 26021 Atlantic Ocean Dr
 Lake Forest CA 92630
 949 380-7878

(G-15661)
RICHARDSON PRECISION MACHINE
732 N 16th Ave Ste 22 (98902-1890)
PHONE...............................509 945-9939
Ron Richardson, *Principal*
EMP: 3
SALES (est): 489.5K **Privately Held**
SIC: 3599 Machine shop, jobbing & repair

(G-15662)
RIDGERUNNERS INC
9007 Scenic Dr (98908-4509)
PHONE...............................509 248-8531
Doug Rohn, *Principal*
EMP: 3
SALES (est): 192.2K **Privately Held**
SIC: 3565 Packaging machinery

(G-15663)
ROLLO TOMASI ENTERPRISES LLC
101 N 5th Ave (98902-2641)
PHONE...............................509 453-9950
Lonnie Eaton,
EMP: 2 **EST:** 2014
SALES (est): 139.8K **Privately Held**
SIC: 2396 Screen printing on fabric articles

(G-15664)
RWC INTERNATIONAL LTD
1509 S 22nd St (98901-9518)
PHONE...............................509 452-5515
Bryan Warren, *Branch Mgr*
Joe Walls, *Manager*
Lana Magee, *Admin Asst*
EMP: 3
SALES (est): 458.4K **Privately Held**
SIC: 5084 7694 7699 Engines & parts, diesel; motor repair services; mobile home repair; industrial truck repair; miscellaneous automotive repair services

(G-15665)
S S STEINER INC
1 W Washington Ave (98903-1543)
P.O. Box 9009 (98909-0009)
PHONE...............................509 453-4731
Paul Merritt, *General Mgr*
Tom Huck, *Branch Mgr*
EMP: 50
SALES (corp-wide): 35.1MM **Privately Held**
SIC: 5159 2087 Hops; flavoring extracts & syrups
PA: S. S. Steiner, Inc.
 725 5th Ave
 New York NY 10022
 212 838-8900

(G-15666)
SATUS NETWORKS LLC
4901 Scenic Dr (98908-2226)
PHONE...............................509 575-8382
Brad Long, *Exec Dir*
EMP: 2
SALES (est): 130K **Privately Held**
SIC: 7372 Application computer software

(G-15667)
SBF PRINTING
313 S 4th Ave (98902-3544)
PHONE...............................509 457-2877
Glenn Klingele, *Owner*
EMP: 2 **EST:** 2013
SALES (est): 94.8K **Privately Held**
SIC: 2759 Commercial printing

Yakima - Yakima County (G-15668)

(G-15668)
SCREEN FX
731 Old Naches Hwy (98908-9036)
PHONE...................509 966-7515
Randy Allen, *Principal*
EMP: 2
SALES (est): 148.4K Privately Held
SIC: 2759 Screen printing

(G-15669)
SEARS TENTS & AWNING
903 S 1st St (98901-3497)
P.O. Box 391 (98907-0391)
PHONE...................509 452-8971
James Sears, *Owner*
EMP: 7
SQ FT: 1,500
SALES (est): 677.6K Privately Held
SIC: 2394 7999 5999 Tents: made from purchased materials; bridge club, non-membership; awnings

(G-15670)
SEATTLE TIMES COMPANY
Also Called: Yakima Herald Republic
114 N 4th St (98901-2707)
P.O. Box 9668 (98909-0668)
PHONE...................509 248-1251
Michael Shepard, *Publisher*
EMP: 190
SQ FT: 65,000
SALES (corp-wide): 226.3MM Privately Held
WEB: www.seattletimes.nwsource.com
SIC: 2711 7313 Newspapers: publishing only, not printed on site; newspaper advertising representative
HQ: Seattle Times Company
 1000 Denny Way Ste 501
 Seattle WA 98109
 206 464-2111

(G-15671)
SENECA FOODS CORPORATION
Also Called: Juice Operations
2418 River Rd (98902-1131)
PHONE...................509 457-1089
Jim Hartshorn, *Principal*
Greg Janson, *Financial Exec*
Robin Koreis, *Human Res Mgr*
EMP: 50
SALES (corp-wide): 1.2B Publicly Held
SIC: 2099 2034 Food preparations; dehydrated fruits, vegetables, soups
PA: Seneca Foods Corporation
 3736 S Main St
 Marion NY 14505
 315 926-8100

(G-15672)
SERVINE SIGN SERVICES LLC
2903 W Yakima Ave (98902-2842)
PHONE...................509 225-7733
EMP: 2
SALES (est): 107.1K Privately Held
SIC: 3993 Signs & advertising specialties

(G-15673)
SHAKER CRAFTSMAN
2908 Fruitvale Blvd (98902-1126)
PHONE...................509 823-4556
EMP: 2
SALES (est): 188.5K Privately Held
SIC: 2511 Wood household furniture

(G-15674)
SHUTTERWORKS LLC
3002 W Viola Ave (98902-4940)
PHONE...................509 731-4619
Chris Brown, *Principal*
EMP: 3 EST: 2015
SALES (est): 220.9K Privately Held
SIC: 3442 Shutters, door or window: metal

(G-15675)
SIGN WORKS
Also Called: Sign Works Custom Concepts
915 W Yakima Ave (98902-3050)
PHONE...................509 248-8235
John Arthur Thompson Jr, *Owner*
EMP: 2
SALES (est): 156.7K Privately Held
SIC: 3993 Electric signs

(G-15676)
SMARTSTART
516 N 20th Ave Ste A (98902-7006)
PHONE...................509 317-2050
Matt Strausz, *Principal*
EMP: 2 EST: 2015
SALES (est): 88.5K Privately Held
SIC: 5084 3694 Conveyor systems; ignition apparatus & distributors

(G-15677)
SMITH AUTO ELECTRIC INC
12 S 3rd Ave (98902-3420)
PHONE...................509 453-8275
James K Thomas, *President*
Jim Thomas, *President*
Dan Jonus, *Principal*
Matt Louis, *Vice Pres*
EMP: 9
SQ FT: 6,000
SALES: 700K Privately Held
WEB: www.smithae.com
SIC: 5013 5531 7539 7694 Automotive supplies & parts; automotive parts; electrical services; armature rewinding shops

(G-15678)
SOLAR GRAPHICS INC
2208 Oak Ave (98903-1269)
PHONE...................509 248-1129
Ken Harris, *President*
Linda Harris, *Corp Secy*
EMP: 5
SQ FT: 13,500
SALES (est): 340K Privately Held
WEB: www.solar-graphics.com
SIC: 2759 7389 Screen printing; sign painting & lettering shop

(G-15679)
SOLUTEC CORP
1208 N 1st St (98901-1906)
PHONE...................509 453-6502
William E Burke, *President*
◆ EMP: 7
SQ FT: 34,000
SALES (est): 1MM Privately Held
WEB: www.soluteccorp.com
SIC: 2879 Agricultural chemicals

(G-15680)
SOUTHARD WINERY
811 W Yakima Ave (98902-3088)
PHONE...................509 452-8626
EMP: 2
SALES (est): 62.3K Privately Held
SIC: 2084 Brandy & brandy spirits

(G-15681)
SPANTON BUSINESS FORMS
3404 Barge St (98902-2741)
PHONE...................509 966-7384
Dan Spanton, *Owner*
EMP: 3
SALES (est): 252.5K Privately Held
WEB: www.signletters.net
SIC: 3993 Signs & advertising specialties

(G-15682)
STARLINE CONSTRUCTION INC
Also Called: S.C.I. Door
1118 N 6th Ave Ste A (98902-1414)
PHONE...................509 575-7955
Toll Free:......................888 -
Chris Klingele, *President*
EMP: 7
SQ FT: 3,200
SALES (est): 1.5MM Privately Held
WEB: www.scidoor.com
SIC: 3442 2431 Garage doors, overhead: metal; garage doors, overhead: wood

(G-15683)
STEPHENS METAL PRODUCTS INC
3209 W Washington Ave (98903-1176)
PHONE...................509 452-4088
Chester Stephen, *President*
Dennis Stephens, *President*
Amy Stephens, *Vice Pres*
Alice Stephens, *Admin Sec*
EMP: 49
SQ FT: 125,000
SALES (est): 12.7MM Privately Held
WEB: www.stephensmetal.com
SIC: 3444 Sheet metal specialties, not stamped

(G-15684)
STRATFORD BOTTLING COMPANY LLC
2800 S 16th Ave (98903-9529)
PHONE...................509 853-3223
EMP: 2
SALES (est): 120K Privately Held
SIC: 2086 Bottled And Canned Soft Drinks, Nsk

(G-15685)
STRIKE ADDICTION LLC
16357 Ahtanum Rd (98903-9760)
PHONE...................206 713-6061
Clint Novak, *Principal*
EMP: 4
SALES (est): 257.4K Privately Held
SIC: 3949 Sporting & athletic goods

(G-15686)
SUMMITVIEW TOOLING INC
12105 Klendon Dr (98908-8044)
PHONE...................509 966-9859
Larry Benjamin, *President*
Lavonne Benjamin, *Corp Secy*
Ron Benjamin, *Vice Pres*
EMP: 2
SALES (est): 249.4K Privately Held
SIC: 3423 3549 3544 Hand & edge tools; metalworking machinery; special dies, tools, jigs & fixtures

(G-15687)
SUN RIVER FOODS INC
308 N 22nd Ave (98902-2429)
PHONE...................509 249-0820
Greg Berndt, *President*
EMP: 15
SALES (est): 1.1MM Privately Held
SIC: 2034 Dried & dehydrated fruits

(G-15688)
SUN VALLEY ENTERPRISES
Also Called: Sun Valley Collision Center
1511 S 1st St (98901-3543)
PHONE...................509 453-1914
Gary Hyndman, *Owner*
EMP: 5
SQ FT: 7,200
SALES (est): 207.6K Privately Held
SIC: 7532 3792 1542 Paint shop, automotive; pickup covers, canopies or caps; commercial & office building, new construction

(G-15689)
SUPERIOR ASPHALT & PAVING CO (PA)
80 Pond Rd (98901-9354)
PHONE...................509 248-6823
A E De Atley Jr, *Ch of Bd*
John Brian Sims, *President*
John F Benson, *Corp Secy*
Bill Hammett, *Vice Pres*
Cevin Ladwig, *Vice Pres*
EMP: 15
SQ FT: 4,500
SALES (est): 29.1MM Privately Held
SIC: 1611 2951 Surfacing & paving; asphalt & asphaltic paving mixtures (not from refineries)

(G-15690)
SUPR CO (HQ)
2000 E Beech St (98901-2147)
PHONE...................509 248-6823
J Brian Sims, *President*
John Benson, *Corp Secy*
Bill Hammett, *Vice Pres*
EMP: 20 EST: 1935
SQ FT: 5,500
SALES (est): 2.4MM Privately Held
SIC: 1611 2951 Highway & street paving contractor; asphalt paving mixtures & blocks

(G-15691)
SURGIMARK INC
1703 Creekside Loop # 110 (98902-4875)
PHONE...................509 965-1911
Richard A Yarger, *President*
Barbara Yarger, *Vice Pres*
EMP: 4
SALES (est): 693.7K Privately Held
WEB: www.surgimark.com
SIC: 3841 Surgical & medical instruments

(G-15692)
SUSAN EAKIN
130 Udell Ln (98908-8845)
PHONE...................509 966-2014
Susan Eakin, *Partner*
EMP: 2
SALES (est): 87.2K Privately Held
SIC: 3711 Motor vehicles & car bodies

(G-15693)
TAHAC LLC (PA)
Also Called: Sonus-USA
3810 Kern Way Ste B (98902-7805)
PHONE...................509 248-0933
James W Thompson, *Owner*
Judy Thompson, *Manager*
Rodney Thompson,
David Oplinger,
▲ EMP: 7
SQ FT: 3,630
SALES (est): 735.2K Privately Held
SIC: 3842 Hearing aids

(G-15694)
TAPENADE INC
Also Called: Wilridge Winery and Vineyard
250 Ehler Rd (98908-9491)
PHONE...................509 966-0686
Raure Kirkland, *Branch Mgr*
EMP: 6 Privately Held
SIC: 5182 2082 Wine; beer (alcoholic beverage)
PA: Tapenade Inc
 1103 Grand Ave
 Seattle WA 98122

(G-15695)
TDAP
312 S Trail Rd (98901)
PHONE...................509 453-3038
Roz Roberts, *Owner*
EMP: 2
SALES (est): 100K Privately Held
SIC: 3089 Plastic boats & other marine equipment

(G-15696)
TRIUMPH ACTUATION SYSTEMS
2808 W Washington Ave (98903-1100)
PHONE...................509 248-5000
Daniel J Crowley, *President*
Jennifer H Allen, *Senior VP*
James F McCabe Jr, *CFO*
Betty Casey, *Office Mgr*
EMP: 273
SALES (est): 17.7MM Publicly Held
SIC: 3728 3724 3812 Aircraft parts & equipment; aircraft engines & engine parts; aircraft control instruments
PA: Triumph Group, Inc.
 899 Cassatt Rd Ste 210
 Berwyn PA 19312

(G-15697)
TUBE ART DISPLAYS INC
2323 W Washington Ave (98903-1230)
PHONE...................509 469-8186
Dave Stubner, *Vice Pres*
Donald Turner, *Purchasing*
Charles Vanmburg, *Branch Mgr*
EMP: 5
SALES (corp-wide): 23.3MM Privately Held
SIC: 3993 Signs & advertising specialties
PA: Tube Art Displays, Inc.
 11715 Se 5th St Ste 200
 Bellevue WA 98005
 206 223-1122

(G-15698)
U-PULL-IT AUTO PARTS INC
14 E Washington Ave (98903-1617)
PHONE...................509 895-7655
Mark Forcum, *President*
Fred Hopp, *Admin Sec*
EMP: 9

SALES (est): 289.4K **Privately Held**
SIC: 5511 3542 5531 Automobiles, new & used; rebuilt machine tools, metal forming types; automobile air conditioning equipment, sale, installation

(G-15699)
UFP WASHINGTON LLC
Also Called: Nepa Pallet and Container
51 N Mitchell Dr (98908-9656)
PHONE..................509 966-4610
Tom Gimble, *Manager*
EMP: 45
SALES (corp-wide): 4.4B **Publicly Held**
SIC: 2448 2441 Pallets, wood; nailed wood boxes & shook
HQ: Ufp Washington, Llc
  12027 3 Lakes Rd
  Snohomish WA 98290
  360 568-3185

(G-15700)
UNDERWOOD FRUIT & WHSE CO LLC (PA)
401 N 1st Ave (98902-2125)
P.O. Box 1588 (98907-1588)
PHONE..................509 457-6177
EMP: 5 EST: 1908
SQ FT: 5,000
SALES (est): 183.7MM **Privately Held**
SIC: 5149 2033 Canned goods: fruit, vegetables, seafood, meats, etc.; fruits & fruit products in cans, jars, etc.

(G-15701)
US DIES INC
315 S 4th Ave (98902-3544)
PHONE..................509 248-0404
Loey Harding, *Branch Mgr*
EMP: 3
SALES (corp-wide): 4.2MM **Privately Held**
WEB: www.pwcdies.com
SIC: 3544 3423 Dies, steel rule; cutting dies, except metal cutting
PA: Us Dies Inc
  1992 Rockefeller Dr # 300
  Ceres CA 95307
  209 664-1402

(G-15702)
US SYNTEC CORPORATION
Also Called: US Syntec
2809 Fruitvale Blvd (98902-1123)
PHONE..................509 452-4476
Steve Agnew, *President*
Terry Ingle, *Corp Secy*
Dave H Putney, *Shareholder*
▲ EMP: 9
SQ FT: 20,000
SALES (est): 1.8MM **Privately Held**
SIC: 2819 Industrial inorganic chemicals

(G-15703)
VIKING PACKAGING MACHINERY (PA)
3800 W Washington Ave (98903)
P.O. Box 9039 (98909-0039)
PHONE..................509 452-7143
Rocky Marquis, *President*
Ted Marquis Jr, *Corp Secy*
Vince Marquis, *Vice Pres*
Dihann Curtis, *CFO*
EMP: 2
SQ FT: 30,000
SALES (est): 6.3MM **Privately Held**
WEB: www.marq.net
SIC: 3564 3565 3444 Dust or fume collecting equipment, industrial; packaging machinery; sheet metalwork

(G-15704)
WASHINGTON TRACTOR INC
Also Called: John Deere
3110 Fruitvale Blvd (98902-1105)
PHONE..................509 452-2880
EMP: 2 EST: 2013
SALES (est): 269.2K **Privately Held**
SIC: 3523 Farm machinery & equipment

(G-15705)
WEBERS RADIATOR SERVICE INC
310 S 3rd Ave (98902-3539)
PHONE..................509 452-3747

Joel Weber, *President*
EMP: 4
SQ FT: 4,000
SALES (est): 400K **Privately Held**
SIC: 7539 7699 3599 Radiator repair shop, automotive; hydraulic equipment repair; flexible metal hose, tubing & bellows

(G-15706)
WEST COAST PLASTICS INC
1110 N 20th Ave (98902-1208)
PHONE..................509 575-0727
Jack D Wans, *President*
Jon Cyr, *Treasurer*
EMP: 4
SQ FT: 7,500
SALES (est): 492.6K **Privately Held**
SIC: 3089 3356 Extruded finished plastic products; nonferrous rolling & drawing

(G-15707)
WHISTLE PIG LLC
1042 Mahoney Rd (98908-8804)
PHONE..................509 949-1584
Jacob Wyles, *Bd of Directors*
EMP: 2
SALES (est): 131.2K **Privately Held**
SIC: 3999 Whistles

(G-15708)
WILBERT SPOKANE VAULT COMPANY
Also Called: Wilbert Precast
2309 S 38th Ave (98903-2501)
PHONE..................509 248-1984
Dan T Houk, *CEO*
Darrin Cary, *COO*
EMP: 35
SALES: 3MM **Privately Held**
SIC: 3272 Concrete products

(G-15709)
WN INC
3271 Mapleway Rd (98908-9688)
PHONE..................509 966-9409
James Wimberley, *Principal*
EMP: 2
SALES (est): 118.2K **Privately Held**
SIC: 2512 Upholstered household furniture

(G-15710)
WRAP PACK INC
1728 Presson Pl (98903-2238)
PHONE..................509 453-2830
Rebecca Kailes, *CEO*
EMP: 17
SALES (est): 3.4MM **Privately Held**
SIC: 2621 Tissue paper

(G-15711)
WYSS LOGGING INC
7601 Wyss Ln (98901-7962)
PHONE..................509 452-5893
Jeff Wyss, *President*
EMP: 20
SQ FT: 2,000
SALES (est): 9MM **Privately Held**
SIC: 2411 Logging camps & contractors

(G-15712)
YAKAMA YOGERT SHACK LLC
110 S 72nd Ave (98908-4600)
PHONE..................509 965-5569
EMP: 3
SALES (est): 140.1K **Privately Held**
SIC: 2026 Yogurt

(G-15713)
YAKIMA CHIEF-HOPUNION LLC (PA)
203 Division St (98902-4622)
PHONE..................509 453-4792
Bill Davidson,
EMP: 4
SALES (est): 1.5MM **Privately Held**
SIC: 2082 Brewers' grain

(G-15714)
YAKIMA GRINDING CO
Also Called: Federated Auto Parts
515 S 2nd St (98901-3294)
PHONE..................509 575-1977
Peter G Pitzer, *President*
John Farr, *Manager*
EMP: 16

SQ FT: 15,000
SALES (est): 2.9MM **Privately Held**
SIC: 5013 7539 5531 3714 Automotive supplies & parts; machine shop, automotive; automotive & home supply stores; motor vehicle parts & accessories

(G-15715)
YAKIMA HERALD REPUBLIC-309
309 S Front St (98901-2855)
PHONE..................509 367-6376
EMP: 3
SALES (est): 104.3K **Privately Held**
SIC: 2711 Newspapers, publishing & printing

(G-15716)
YAKIMA HERALD-REPUBLIC INC
114 N 4th St (98901-2707)
P.O. Box 9668 (98909-0668)
PHONE..................509 452-7355
Bob Brider, *Publisher*
Sam McManis, *Editor*
Aviva Beach, *Credit Mgr*
Juan Barragan, *Advt Staff*
Alison Bath, *Manager*
▲ EMP: 1
SALES (est): 14.9MM
SALES (corp-wide): 226.3MM **Privately Held**
SIC: 2711 7313 Commercial printing & newspaper publishing combined; newspaper advertising representative
HQ: Seattle Times Company
  1000 Denny Way Ste 501
  Seattle WA 98109
  206 464-2111

(G-15717)
YAKIMA TENT & AWNING CO LTD
1015 E Lincoln Ave (98901-2534)
P.O. Box 391 (98907-0391)
PHONE..................509 457-6169
Pamela Hubbard, *President*
Walt Hubbard, *Vice Pres*
▲ EMP: 10
SQ FT: 12,000
SALES (est): 1.2MM **Privately Held**
WEB: www.yakimatent.com
SIC: 2394 2393 Tents: made from purchased materials; tarpaulins, fabric: made from purchased materials; textile bags

(G-15718)
YAKIMA VALLEY CABINETS INC
701 Madison Ave (98902-1319)
PHONE..................509 248-0472
Ronald Olsen, *President*
Ronald D Olsen, *President*
EMP: 8
SQ FT: 3,900
SALES: 450K **Privately Held**
SIC: 2434 5211 Wood kitchen cabinets; cabinets, kitchen

(G-15719)
YAKIMA VALLEY SENIOR TIMES
Also Called: Yakima Valley Publishing
416 S 3rd St (98901-2834)
P.O. Box 2052 (98907-2052)
PHONE..................509 457-4886
Bruce Smith, *President*
EMP: 8
SQ FT: 3,870
SALES (est): 510.6K **Privately Held**
SIC: 2711 2741 Newspapers: publishing only, not printed on site; miscellaneous publishing

(G-15720)
YAKIMA WATER SOLUTIONS LLC
5808 Summitview Ave 71 (98908-3095)
PHONE..................509 941-9607
David Gutierrez,
EMP: 2
SALES (est): 120K **Privately Held**
SIC: 3589 Water treatment equipment, industrial

(G-15721)
YO YAKIMA
2401 S 1st St (98903-1639)
PHONE..................509 426-2925
Karen Sherman, *Owner*
Gary Sherman, *Owner*
EMP: 7
SALES (est): 370.1K **Privately Held**
SIC: 2024 Ice cream, bulk

Yarrow Point
King County

(G-15722)
POWELL SOFTWARE INC
4631 92nd Ave Ne (98004-1336)
PHONE..................425 974-9692
Cyril De Queral, *Governor*
Antoine Faisandier, *Governor*
Jean Pierre Pierre Vimard, *Governor*
EMP: 20
SALES (est): 94.9K **Privately Held**
SIC: 7372 Prepackaged software

(G-15723)
SCC ENTERPRISES LLC
Also Called: Aerial Consultant
9107 Ne 47th St (98004-1251)
PHONE..................425 454-0567
Carol Clement, *President*
Susan Castle,
Carol Klement,
EMP: 2
SQ FT: 200
SALES (est): 220K **Privately Held**
SIC: 7372 Prepackaged software

Yelm
Thurston County

(G-15724)
ABBOTT INDUSTRIES INC
22406 Basin View Ct Se (98597-9009)
PHONE..................360 894-6230
Scott Abbott, *Principal*
EMP: 2
SALES (est): 138.7K **Privately Held**
SIC: 3999 Manufacturing industries

(G-15725)
ADVANCED TECHNOLOGY RESOURCES
11902 Morris Rd Se (98597-9542)
PHONE..................253 229-3415
Richard Montgomery, *President*
April Stanke, *Manager*
EMP: 5
SALES: 226.2K **Privately Held**
SIC: 3559 Semiconductor manufacturing machinery

(G-15726)
AMICK TACTICAL LLC
14726 Lawrence Lake Rd Se (98597-8946)
PHONE..................253 301-7619
Aaron Amick, *Co-Owner*
Cari Amick, *Co-Owner*
EMP: 3
SALES (est): 125.9K **Privately Held**
SIC: 2393 2399 Bags & containers, except sleeping bags: textile; military insignia, textile

(G-15727)
AQUATIC CO
Also Called: Lasco Bathware
801 Northern Pcf Rd Se (98597-8715)
PHONE..................360 458-3900
Bill Kysor, *Branch Mgr*
EMP: 150
SQ FT: 190,000
SALES (corp-wide): 133.8MM **Privately Held**
SIC: 3088 Shower stalls, fiberglass & plastic
HQ: Aquatic Co.
  1700 N Delilah St
  Corona CA 92879

Yelm - Thurston County (G-15728)

GEOGRAPHIC SECTION

(G-15728)
ARG LOGGING LLC
17730 153rd Ave Se (98597-8529)
P.O. Box 5150 (98597-5150)
PHONE...................253 606-5047
Daniel Jameson, *Principal*
EMP: 3
SALES (est): 194.3K **Privately Held**
SIC: 2411 Logging

(G-15729)
BIOSMART TECHNOLOGIES LLC
18324 Cook Rd Se Unit 1 (98597-9673)
PHONE...................360 888-8638
Norma Milton, *President*
Wen Chan, *Administration*
▲ EMP: 2
SALES (est): 184.5K **Privately Held**
SIC: 3585 Heating equipment, complete

(G-15730)
BOSOM CATTLE CO
Also Called: Jenny's Bar and Grill
115 E Yelm Ave (98597)
PHONE...................206 947-0645
Ken Gaylord, *President*
EMP: 14
SALES: 700K **Privately Held**
SIC: 2599 Bar, restaurant & cafeteria furniture

(G-15731)
DAWN WORKMAN LULAROE
Also Called: Lularoe Dawn Workman
14839 99th Way Se (98597-8782)
PHONE...................360 955-1324
Dawn Workman, *Owner*
EMP: 2 EST: 2016
SALES: 120K **Privately Held**
SIC: 2329 5137 Men's & boys' sportswear & athletic clothing; women's & children's outerwear

(G-15732)
DIVERSIFAB LLC
19510 161st Way Se (98597-9142)
P.O. Box 1536 (98597-1536)
PHONE...................253 459-5170
Alex Granger, *Principal*
EMP: 2 EST: 2016
SALES (est): 160.2K **Privately Held**
SIC: 3441 Fabricated structural metal

(G-15733)
FLORY CABINETS LLC
14846 Vail Rd Se (98597-8411)
PHONE...................360 894-2504
Richard Flory, *Managing Prtnr*
Ty Flory, *Partner*
EMP: 3 EST: 1970
SALES: 150K **Privately Held**
WEB: www.socialevents.com
SIC: 2521 2411 Cabinets, office: wood; logging

(G-15734)
FOCUSBLOOM LLC
21526 Hobson Rd Se (98597-9359)
P.O. Box 1220, Rainier (98576-1220)
PHONE...................360 894-2362
Margo Losa,
EMP: 2 EST: 2008
SALES (est): 79K **Privately Held**
SIC: 2711 Newspapers, publishing & printing

(G-15735)
GREEN LEAF FAMILY ESTATES
13241 Zeller Rd Se (98597-9213)
PHONE...................360 894-4945
EMP: 2
SALES (est): 83.5K **Privately Held**
SIC: 0139 3999 6531 ; ; real estate agents & managers

(G-15736)
ITTY BITS PUBLICATIONS
17915 Lawrence Lake Rd Se (98597-9079)
PHONE...................360 894-3288
EMP: 2 EST: 2009
SALES (est): 84K **Privately Held**
SIC: 2741 Misc Publishing

(G-15737)
LAFROMBOISE NEWSPAPERS
Also Called: Nisqually Valley News
118 Prairie Park St (98597)
P.O. Box 597 (98597-0597)
PHONE...................360 458-2681
Kevin Graves, *Manager*
EMP: 12
SQ FT: 1,652
SALES (corp-wide): 13.5MM **Privately Held**
WEB: www.nisquallyvalleyonline.com
SIC: 2711 2741 Newspapers: publishing only, not printed on site; miscellaneous publishing
PA: Lafromboise Newspapers
321 N Pearl St
Centralia WA 98531
360 736-3311

(G-15738)
LORI SHINE (PA)
Also Called: Shine Specialties & Promotions
305 1st St S Unit A (98597-7694)
PHONE...................360 400-6006
Lori Shine, *Owner*
EMP: 4
SALES (est): 445.2K **Privately Held**
SIC: 2752 Commercial printing, lithographic

(G-15739)
M & M COATINGS INC
8618 Glenlea Ct Se (98597-9456)
PHONE...................360 480-6425
Michael Dominguez, *Principal*
EMP: 2
SALES (est): 115.2K **Privately Held**
SIC: 3479 Metal coating & allied service

(G-15740)
MORTON A KIMBALL
13431 Solberg Rd Se (98597-8547)
PHONE...................360 458-5251
Morton A Kimball, *Principal*
EMP: 2
SALES (est): 127.6K **Privately Held**
SIC: 2834 Pharmaceutical preparations

(G-15741)
MOUNTAIN VIEW INDUSTRIES INC
Also Called: Jameson Tree Experts
17730 153rd Ave Se (98597-8529)
P.O. Box 5150 (98597-5150)
PHONE...................360 894-0499
Daniel Jameson, *President*
EMP: 4
SALES (est): 35K **Privately Held**
SIC: 3999 Manufacturing industries

(G-15742)
OYATE RESEARCH & TRAINING CONS
15816 Yelm Terra Way Se (98597-8447)
PHONE...................360 239-2281
EMP: 2
SALES (est): 130K **Privately Held**
SIC: 3599 Mfg Industrial Machinery

(G-15743)
RAINIER DISTILLERS PMB
14469 Lockwood Ln Se (98597-7730)
P.O. Box 7530 (98597-7530)
PHONE...................360 350-9177
EMP: 4 EST: 2011
SALES (est): 271.9K **Privately Held**
SIC: 2085 Distilled & blended liquors

(G-15744)
REMOTE VIEW DAILY LLC
11211 Clark Rd Se (98597-9584)
P.O. Box 1192 (98597-1192)
PHONE...................360 458-5318
EMP: 3
SALES (est): 104.6K **Privately Held**
SIC: 2711 Newspapers, publishing & printing

(G-15745)
SCREW YOU LLC
15826 Lawrence Lake Rd Se (98597-9078)
PHONE...................360 400-3648
Miguel Marlowe, *Principal*
EMP: 2
SALES (est): 87.3K **Privately Held**
SIC: 3599 Industrial machinery

(G-15746)
STEWARTS MARKETS INC
Also Called: McKenna Meats
17821 State Route 507 Se (98597-9654)
PHONE...................360 458-2091
Dorothy Carlson, *President*
Stewart J Carlson, *Vice Pres*
EMP: 20
SQ FT: 4,500
SALES (est): 2.1MM **Privately Held**
SIC: 5421 2011 Meat markets, including freezer provisioners; meat packing plants

(G-15747)
THE UPS STORE INC
1201 E Yelm Ave Ste 400 (98597-8619)
PHONE...................360 400-6245
Kanti Patel, *Manager*
EMP: 5 EST: 2001
SALES (est): 306.2K **Privately Held**
SIC: 7389 3579 Mailbox rental & related service; mailing, letter handling & addressing machines

(G-15748)
TREE OF LIFE ENTERPRISES INC
16100 Lemuria Ln Se (98597-7934)
PHONE...................360 894-6038
Karla Broschinski, *Principal*
EMP: 2 EST: 2009
SALES (est): 118.9K **Privately Held**
SIC: 3999 Beekeepers' supplies

Zillah
Yakima County

(G-15749)
AGATE FIELD VINEYARD
2911 Roza Dr (98953-9082)
PHONE...................509 829-6097
Bob Radke,
EMP: 2
SALES (est): 124.9K **Privately Held**
SIC: 2084 Wines

(G-15750)
BONAIR WINERY INC
500 S Bonair Rd (98953-9245)
PHONE...................509 829-6027
Shirley Puryear, *President*
Gail Puryear, *Exec VP*
EMP: 10
SQ FT: 6,000
SALES (est): 908.1K **Privately Held**
WEB: www.bonairwine.com
SIC: 2084 5182 5921 Wines; wine; wine

(G-15751)
CASTLE ROCK GOAT FARM LLC
13811 Yakima Valley Hwy (98953-9285)
PHONE...................509 961-5613
Cornelis Vandenberg, *President*
EMP: 4
SQ FT: 2,880
SALES (est): 116.1K **Privately Held**
SIC: 2026 Fluid milk

(G-15752)
DAVID P RUSH
131 White Rd (98953-9229)
PHONE...................509 865-5338
David Rush, *Owner*
EMP: 2
SALES (est): 102.3K **Privately Held**
SIC: 2046 Root starch, edible

(G-15753)
DINEEN FAMILY WINE COMPANY LLC
2980 Gilbert Rd (98953-9766)
PHONE...................509 829-6897
Patrick Dineen, *Mng Member*
EMP: 2
SALES (est): 103.9K **Privately Held**
SIC: 2084 Wines

(G-15754)
DKFAB INC
7240 Yakima Valley Hwy (98953-9218)
PHONE...................503 710-2064
Daniel James James Kirsch, *Principal*
EMP: 2
SALES (est): 154.9K **Privately Held**
SIC: 3599 Machine shop, jobbing & repair

(G-15755)
HORIZONS EDGE WINERY
4530 E Zillah Dr (98953-9326)
PHONE...................509 829-6401
David Padgett, *Owner*
Thomas Campbell, *Owner*
EMP: 20
SALES (est): 250K **Privately Held**
SIC: 0172 2084 Grapes; wine cellars, bonded: engaged in blending wines

(G-15756)
HYATT FARM PARTNERSHIP LP
Also Called: Hyatt Vineyards
2020 Gilbert Rd (98953-9766)
PHONE...................509 829-3737
Leland Hyatt, *Partner*
Lynda Hyatt, *Partner*
EMP: 8
SQ FT: 4,800
SALES (est): 430.7K **Privately Held**
SIC: 0762 2084 1794 Vineyard management & maintenance services; wines, brandy & brandy spirits; excavation & grading, building construction

(G-15757)
PARADISOS DEL SOL WINERY INC
3230 Highland Dr (98953-9382)
PHONE...................509 829-9000
Barbara Sherman, *President*
Paul Vandenberg, *Vice Pres*
EMP: 2 EST: 2013
SQ FT: 1,100
SALES: 200K **Privately Held**
SIC: 2084 Wines

(G-15758)
SECURITY ALARMS PLUS INC
7560 Yakima Valley Hwy (98953-9220)
P.O. Box 9394, Yakima (98909-0394)
PHONE...................509 457-8799
Brandon Burwell, *President*
Michael Matthews, *Treasurer*
Tamera Maybee, *Bookkeeper*
EMP: 5
SALES (est): 614.4K **Privately Held**
SIC: 3569 1731 Sprinkler systems, fire: automatic; fire detection & burglar alarm systems specialization

(G-15759)
SOILCRAFT INC (PA)
2300 E Zillah Dr (98953-9645)
PHONE...................509 314-9227
Dwayne Bowman, *President*
Mason Gordon, *Manager*
EMP: 4
SALES: 1.4MM **Privately Held**
SIC: 2873 Fertilizers: natural (organic), except compost

(G-15760)
STADELMAN FRUIT FRENCHMAN
111 Meade St (98953-9419)
PHONE...................509 829-5145
EMP: 2 EST: 2013
SALES (est): 120K **Privately Held**
SIC: 3571 Electronic computers

(G-15761)
TANJULI
4530 E Zillah Dr (98953-9326)
PHONE...................509 829-6401
EMP: 2
SALES (est): 95.2K **Privately Held**
SIC: 2084 Wines

(G-15762)
TWO MOUNTAIN WINERY
2151 Cheyne Rd (98953-9611)
PHONE...................509 829-3900
Ron Schmidt, *Principal*
EMP: 4

SALES (est): 298.5K **Privately Held**
SIC: 2084 Wines

(G-15763)
VANARNAM VINEYARDS
1305 Gilbert Rd (98953-9789)
PHONE...................................360 904-4800
EMP: 2 **EST:** 2015
SALES (est): 105.7K **Privately Held**
SIC: 2084 Wines

(G-15764)
VARSITY SCREEN PRTG & AWARDS
905 Vintage Valley Pkwy (98953-9699)
PHONE...................................509 829-3700
EMP: 2
SALES (est): 83.9K **Privately Held**
SIC: 2752 Commercial printing, lithographic

(G-15765)
WINGARDNER SAND AND GRAVEL
1300 Roza Dr (98953-9043)
PHONE...................................509 480-3847
Walter Allen Wingardner, *Principal*
EMP: 2
SALES (est): 111.9K **Privately Held**
SIC: 1442 Construction sand & gravel

SIC INDEX

Standard Industrial Classification Alphabetical Index

SIC NO	PRODUCT

A

3291 Abrasive Prdts
2891 Adhesives & Sealants
3563 Air & Gas Compressors
3585 Air Conditioning & Heating Eqpt
3721 Aircraft
3724 Aircraft Engines & Engine Parts
3728 Aircraft Parts & Eqpt, NEC
2812 Alkalies & Chlorine
3363 Aluminum Die Castings
3354 Aluminum Extruded Prdts
3365 Aluminum Foundries
3355 Aluminum Rolling & Drawing, NEC
3353 Aluminum Sheet, Plate & Foil
3483 Ammunition, Large
3826 Analytical Instruments
2077 Animal, Marine Fats & Oils
2389 Apparel & Accessories, NEC
3446 Architectural & Ornamental Metal Work
7694 Armature Rewinding Shops
3292 Asbestos products
2952 Asphalt Felts & Coatings
3822 Automatic Temperature Controls
3581 Automatic Vending Machines
3465 Automotive Stampings
2396 Automotive Trimmings, Apparel Findings, Related Prdts

B

2673 Bags: Plastics, Laminated & Coated
2674 Bags: Uncoated Paper & Multiwall
3562 Ball & Roller Bearings
2836 Biological Prdts, Exc Diagnostic Substances
1221 Bituminous Coal & Lignite: Surface Mining
1222 Bituminous Coal: Underground Mining
2782 Blankbooks & Looseleaf Binders
3312 Blast Furnaces, Coke Ovens, Steel & Rolling Mills
3564 Blowers & Fans
3732 Boat Building & Repairing
3452 Bolts, Nuts, Screws, Rivets & Washers
2732 Book Printing, Not Publishing
2789 Bookbinding
2731 Books: Publishing & Printing
3131 Boot & Shoe Cut Stock & Findings
2342 Brassieres, Girdles & Garments
2051 Bread, Bakery Prdts Exc Cookies & Crackers
3251 Brick & Structural Clay Tile
3991 Brooms & Brushes
3995 Burial Caskets
2021 Butter

C

3578 Calculating & Accounting Eqpt
2064 Candy & Confectionery Prdts
2033 Canned Fruits, Vegetables & Preserves
2032 Canned Specialties
2394 Canvas Prdts
3624 Carbon & Graphite Prdts
3955 Carbon Paper & Inked Ribbons
3592 Carburetors, Pistons, Rings & Valves
2273 Carpets & Rugs
2823 Cellulosic Man-Made Fibers
3241 Cement, Hydraulic
3253 Ceramic Tile
2043 Cereal Breakfast Foods
2022 Cheese
1479 Chemical & Fertilizer Mining
2899 Chemical Preparations, NEC
2067 Chewing Gum
2361 Children's & Infants' Dresses & Blouses
3261 China Plumbing Fixtures & Fittings
2066 Chocolate & Cocoa Prdts
2111 Cigarettes
2121 Cigars
3255 Clay Refractories
1459 Clay, Ceramic & Refractory Minerals, NEC
1241 Coal Mining Svcs
3479 Coating & Engraving, NEC
2095 Coffee
3316 Cold Rolled Steel Sheet, Strip & Bars
3582 Commercial Laundry, Dry Clean & Pressing Mchs
2759 Commercial Printing
2754 Commercial Printing: Gravure
2752 Commercial Printing: Lithographic
3646 Commercial, Indl & Institutional Lighting Fixtures
3669 Communications Eqpt, NEC
3577 Computer Peripheral Eqpt, NEC
3572 Computer Storage Devices
3575 Computer Terminals
3271 Concrete Block & Brick
3272 Concrete Prdts
3531 Construction Machinery & Eqpt
1442 Construction Sand & Gravel
2679 Converted Paper Prdts, NEC
3535 Conveyors & Eqpt
2052 Cookies & Crackers
3366 Copper Foundries
1021 Copper Ores
2298 Cordage & Twine
2653 Corrugated & Solid Fiber Boxes
3961 Costume Jewelry & Novelties
2261 Cotton Fabric Finishers
2211 Cotton, Woven Fabric
2074 Cottonseed Oil Mills
1311 Crude Petroleum & Natural Gas
1423 Crushed & Broken Granite
1422 Crushed & Broken Limestone
1429 Crushed & Broken Stone, NEC
3643 Current-Carrying Wiring Devices
2391 Curtains & Draperies
3087 Custom Compounding Of Purchased Plastic Resins
3281 Cut Stone Prdts
3421 Cutlery
2865 Cyclic-Crudes, Intermediates, Dyes & Org Pigments

D

3843 Dental Eqpt & Splys
2835 Diagnostic Substances
2675 Die-Cut Paper & Board
3544 Dies, Tools, Jigs, Fixtures & Indl Molds
1411 Dimension Stone
2047 Dog & Cat Food
3942 Dolls & Stuffed Toys
2591 Drapery Hardware, Window Blinds & Shades
2381 Dress & Work Gloves
2034 Dried Fruits, Vegetables & Soup
1381 Drilling Oil & Gas Wells

E

3263 Earthenware, Whiteware, Table & Kitchen Articles
3634 Electric Household Appliances
3641 Electric Lamps
3694 Electrical Eqpt For Internal Combustion Engines
3629 Electrical Indl Apparatus, NEC
3699 Electrical Machinery, Eqpt & Splys, NEC
3845 Electromedical & Electrotherapeutic Apparatus
3313 Electrometallurgical Prdts
3675 Electronic Capacitors
3677 Electronic Coils & Transformers
3679 Electronic Components, NEC
3571 Electronic Computers
3678 Electronic Connectors
3676 Electronic Resistors
3471 Electroplating, Plating, Polishing, Anodizing & Coloring
3534 Elevators & Moving Stairways
3431 Enameled Iron & Metal Sanitary Ware
2677 Envelopes
2892 Explosives

F

2241 Fabric Mills, Cotton, Wool, Silk & Man-Made
3499 Fabricated Metal Prdts, NEC
3498 Fabricated Pipe & Pipe Fittings
3443 Fabricated Plate Work
3069 Fabricated Rubber Prdts, NEC
3441 Fabricated Structural Steel
2399 Fabricated Textile Prdts, NEC
2295 Fabrics Coated Not Rubberized
2297 Fabrics, Nonwoven
3523 Farm Machinery & Eqpt
3965 Fasteners, Buttons, Needles & Pins
2875 Fertilizers, Mixing Only
2655 Fiber Cans, Tubes & Drums
2091 Fish & Seafoods, Canned & Cured
2092 Fish & Seafoods, Fresh & Frozen
3211 Flat Glass
2087 Flavoring Extracts & Syrups
2045 Flour, Blended & Prepared
2041 Flour, Grain Milling
3824 Fluid Meters & Counters
3593 Fluid Power Cylinders & Actuators
3594 Fluid Power Pumps & Motors
3492 Fluid Power Valves & Hose Fittings
2657 Folding Paperboard Boxes
3556 Food Prdts Machinery
2099 Food Preparations, NEC
3149 Footwear, NEC
2053 Frozen Bakery Prdts
2037 Frozen Fruits, Juices & Vegetables
2038 Frozen Specialties
2371 Fur Goods
2599 Furniture & Fixtures, NEC

G

3944 Games, Toys & Children's Vehicles
3524 Garden, Lawn Tractors & Eqpt
3053 Gaskets, Packing & Sealing Devices
2369 Girls' & Infants' Outerwear, NEC
3221 Glass Containers
3231 Glass Prdts Made Of Purchased Glass
1041 Gold Ores
3321 Gray Iron Foundries
2771 Greeting Card Publishing
3769 Guided Missile/Space Vehicle Parts & Eqpt, NEC
3764 Guided Missile/Space Vehicle Propulsion Units & parts
3761 Guided Missiles & Space Vehicles
2861 Gum & Wood Chemicals
3275 Gypsum Prdts

H

3423 Hand & Edge Tools
3425 Hand Saws & Saw Blades
3171 Handbags & Purses
3429 Hardware, NEC
2426 Hardwood Dimension & Flooring Mills
2435 Hardwood Veneer & Plywood
2353 Hats, Caps & Millinery
3433 Heating Eqpt
3536 Hoists, Cranes & Monorails
2252 Hosiery, Except Women's
2392 House furnishings: Textile
3639 Household Appliances, NEC
3651 Household Audio & Video Eqpt
3631 Household Cooking Eqpt
2519 Household Furniture, NEC
3633 Household Laundry Eqpt
3632 Household Refrigerators & Freezers
3635 Household Vacuum Cleaners

I

2097 Ice
2024 Ice Cream
2819 Indl Inorganic Chemicals, NEC
3823 Indl Instruments For Meas, Display & Control
3569 Indl Machinery & Eqpt, NEC
3567 Indl Process Furnaces & Ovens
3537 Indl Trucks, Tractors, Trailers & Stackers
2813 Industrial Gases
2869 Industrial Organic Chemicals, NEC
3543 Industrial Patterns
1446 Industrial Sand
3491 Industrial Valves
2816 Inorganic Pigments
3825 Instrs For Measuring & Testing Electricity
3519 Internal Combustion Engines, NEC
3462 Iron & Steel Forgings
1011 Iron Ores

J

3915 Jewelers Findings & Lapidary Work
3911 Jewelry: Precious Metal

K

1455 Kaolin & Ball Clay
2253 Knit Outerwear Mills
2254 Knit Underwear Mills
2259 Knitting Mills, NEC

L

3821 Laboratory Apparatus & Furniture
2258 Lace & Warp Knit Fabric Mills
1031 Lead & Zinc Ores
3952 Lead Pencils, Crayons & Artist's Mtrls
2386 Leather & Sheep Lined Clothing
3151 Leather Gloves & Mittens
3199 Leather Goods, NEC
3111 Leather Tanning & Finishing
3648 Lighting Eqpt, NEC
3274 Lime
3996 Linoleum & Hard Surface Floor Coverings, NEC

SIC INDEX

SIC NO	PRODUCT
2085	Liquors, Distilled, Rectified & Blended
2411	Logging
2992	Lubricating Oils & Greases
3161	Luggage

M

SIC NO	PRODUCT
2098	Macaroni, Spaghetti & Noodles
3545	Machine Tool Access
3541	Machine Tools: Cutting
3542	Machine Tools: Forming
3599	Machinery & Eqpt, Indl & Commercial, NEC
3322	Malleable Iron Foundries
2083	Malt
2082	Malt Beverages
2761	Manifold Business Forms
3999	Manufacturing Industries, NEC
3953	Marking Devices
2515	Mattresses & Bedsprings
3829	Measuring & Controlling Devices, NEC
3586	Measuring & Dispensing Pumps
2011	Meat Packing Plants
3568	Mechanical Power Transmission Eqpt, NEC
2833	Medicinal Chemicals & Botanical Prdts
2329	Men's & Boys' Clothing, NEC
2323	Men's & Boys' Neckwear
2325	Men's & Boys' Separate Trousers & Casual Slacks
2321	Men's & Boys' Shirts
2311	Men's & Boys' Suits, Coats & Overcoats
2322	Men's & Boys' Underwear & Nightwear
2326	Men's & Boys' Work Clothing
3143	Men's Footwear, Exc Athletic
3412	Metal Barrels, Drums, Kegs & Pails
3411	Metal Cans
3442	Metal Doors, Sash, Frames, Molding & Trim
3497	Metal Foil & Leaf
3398	Metal Heat Treating
2514	Metal Household Furniture
1081	Metal Mining Svcs
1099	Metal Ores, NEC
3469	Metal Stampings, NEC
3549	Metalworking Machinery, NEC
2026	Milk
2023	Milk, Condensed & Evaporated
2431	Millwork
3296	Mineral Wool
3295	Minerals & Earths: Ground Or Treated
3532	Mining Machinery & Eqpt
3496	Misc Fabricated Wire Prdts
2741	Misc Publishing
3449	Misc Structural Metal Work
1499	Miscellaneous Nonmetallic Mining
2451	Mobile Homes
3061	Molded, Extruded & Lathe-Cut Rubber Mechanical Goods
3716	Motor Homes
3714	Motor Vehicle Parts & Access
3711	Motor Vehicles & Car Bodies
3751	Motorcycles, Bicycles & Parts
3621	Motors & Generators
3931	Musical Instruments

N

SIC NO	PRODUCT
1321	Natural Gas Liquids
2711	Newspapers: Publishing & Printing
2873	Nitrogenous Fertilizers
3297	Nonclay Refractories
3644	Noncurrent-Carrying Wiring Devices
3364	Nonferrous Die Castings, Exc Aluminum
3463	Nonferrous Forgings
3369	Nonferrous Foundries: Castings, NEC
3357	Nonferrous Wire Drawing
3299	Nonmetallic Mineral Prdts, NEC
1481	Nonmetallic Minerals Svcs, Except Fuels

O

SIC NO	PRODUCT
2522	Office Furniture, Except Wood
3579	Office Machines, NEC
1382	Oil & Gas Field Exploration Svcs
1389	Oil & Gas Field Svcs, NEC
3533	Oil Field Machinery & Eqpt
3851	Ophthalmic Goods
3827	Optical Instruments
3489	Ordnance & Access, NEC
3842	Orthopedic, Prosthetic & Surgical Appliances/Splys

P

SIC NO	PRODUCT
3565	Packaging Machinery
2851	Paints, Varnishes, Lacquers, Enamels
2671	Paper Coating & Laminating for Packaging
2672	Paper Coating & Laminating, Exc for Packaging
3554	Paper Inds Machinery
2621	Paper Mills
2631	Paperboard Mills
2542	Partitions & Fixtures, Except Wood
2951	Paving Mixtures & Blocks
3951	Pens & Mechanical Pencils
2844	Perfumes, Cosmetics & Toilet Preparations
2721	Periodicals: Publishing & Printing
3172	Personal Leather Goods
2879	Pesticides & Agricultural Chemicals, NEC
2911	Petroleum Refining
2834	Pharmaceuticals
3652	Phonograph Records & Magnetic Tape
1475	Phosphate Rock
2874	Phosphatic Fertilizers
3861	Photographic Eqpt & Splys
2035	Pickled Fruits, Vegetables, Sauces & Dressings
3085	Plastic Bottles
3086	Plastic Foam Prdts
3083	Plastic Laminated Plate & Sheet
3084	Plastic Pipe
3088	Plastic Plumbing Fixtures
3089	Plastic Prdts
3082	Plastic Unsupported Profile Shapes
3081	Plastic Unsupported Sheet & Film
2821	Plastics, Mtrls & Nonvulcanizable Elastomers
2796	Platemaking & Related Svcs
2395	Pleating & Stitching For The Trade
3432	Plumbing Fixture Fittings & Trim, Brass
3264	Porcelain Electrical Splys
2096	Potato Chips & Similar Prdts
3269	Pottery Prdts, NEC
2015	Poultry Slaughtering, Dressing & Processing
3546	Power Hand Tools
3612	Power, Distribution & Specialty Transformers
3448	Prefabricated Metal Buildings & Cmpnts
2452	Prefabricated Wood Buildings & Cmpnts
7372	Prepackaged Software
2048	Prepared Feeds For Animals & Fowls
3229	Pressed & Blown Glassware, NEC
3692	Primary Batteries: Dry & Wet
3399	Primary Metal Prdts, NEC
3339	Primary Nonferrous Metals, NEC
3334	Primary Production Of Aluminum
3331	Primary Smelting & Refining Of Copper
3672	Printed Circuit Boards
2893	Printing Ink
3555	Printing Trades Machinery & Eqpt
2531	Public Building & Related Furniture
2611	Pulp Mills
3561	Pumps & Pumping Eqpt

R

SIC NO	PRODUCT
3663	Radio & T V Communications, Systs & Eqpt, Broadcast/Studio
3671	Radio & T V Receiving Electron Tubes
3743	Railroad Eqpt
3273	Ready-Mixed Concrete
2493	Reconstituted Wood Prdts
3695	Recording Media
3625	Relays & Indl Controls
3645	Residential Lighting Fixtures
3547	Rolling Mill Machinery & Eqpt
3351	Rolling, Drawing & Extruding Of Copper
3356	Rolling, Drawing-Extruding Of Nonferrous Metals
3021	Rubber & Plastic Footwear
3052	Rubber & Plastic Hose & Belting

S

SIC NO	PRODUCT
2068	Salted & Roasted Nuts & Seeds
2656	Sanitary Food Containers
2676	Sanitary Paper Prdts
2013	Sausages & Meat Prdts
2421	Saw & Planing Mills
3596	Scales & Balances, Exc Laboratory
2397	Schiffli Machine Embroideries
3451	Screw Machine Prdts
3812	Search, Detection, Navigation & Guidance Systs & Instrs
3341	Secondary Smelting & Refining Of Nonferrous Metals
3674	Semiconductors
3589	Service Ind Machines, NEC
2652	Set-Up Paperboard Boxes
3444	Sheet Metal Work
3731	Shipbuilding & Repairing
2079	Shortening, Oils & Margarine
3993	Signs & Advertising Displays
2262	Silk & Man-Made Fabric Finishers
2221	Silk & Man-Made Fiber
1044	Silver Ores
3914	Silverware, Plated & Stainless Steel Ware
3484	Small Arms
3482	Small Arms Ammunition
2841	Soap & Detergents
2086	Soft Drinks
2436	Softwood Veneer & Plywood
2075	Soybean Oil Mills
2842	Spec Cleaning, Polishing & Sanitation Preparations
3559	Special Ind Machinery, NEC
2429	Special Prdt Sawmills, NEC
3566	Speed Changers, Drives & Gears
3949	Sporting & Athletic Goods, NEC
2678	Stationery Prdts
3511	Steam, Gas & Hydraulic Turbines & Engines
3325	Steel Foundries, NEC
3324	Steel Investment Foundries
3317	Steel Pipe & Tubes
3493	Steel Springs, Except Wire
3315	Steel Wire Drawing & Nails & Spikes
3691	Storage Batteries
3259	Structural Clay Prdts, NEC
2439	Structural Wood Members, NEC
2061	Sugar, Cane
3841	Surgical & Medical Instrs & Apparatus
3613	Switchgear & Switchboard Apparatus
2824	Synthetic Organic Fibers, Exc Cellulosic
2822	Synthetic Rubber (Vulcanizable Elastomers)

T

SIC NO	PRODUCT
3795	Tanks & Tank Components
3661	Telephone & Telegraph Apparatus
2393	Textile Bags
2269	Textile Finishers, NEC
2299	Textile Goods, NEC
3552	Textile Machinery
2284	Thread Mills
2296	Tire Cord & Fabric
3011	Tires & Inner Tubes
2131	Tobacco, Chewing & Snuff
3799	Transportation Eqpt, NEC
3792	Travel Trailers & Campers
3713	Truck & Bus Bodies
3715	Truck Trailers
2791	Typesetting

U

SIC NO	PRODUCT
1094	Uranium, Radium & Vanadium Ores

V

SIC NO	PRODUCT
3494	Valves & Pipe Fittings, NEC
2076	Vegetable Oil Mills
3647	Vehicular Lighting Eqpt

W

SIC NO	PRODUCT
3873	Watch & Clock Devices & Parts
2385	Waterproof Outerwear
3548	Welding Apparatus
7692	Welding Repair
2046	Wet Corn Milling
2084	Wine & Brandy
3495	Wire Springs
2331	Women's & Misses' Blouses
2335	Women's & Misses' Dresses
2339	Women's & Misses' Outerwear, NEC
2337	Women's & Misses' Suits, Coats & Skirts
3144	Women's Footwear, Exc Athletic
2341	Women's, Misses' & Children's Underwear & Nightwear
2441	Wood Boxes
2449	Wood Containers, NEC
2511	Wood Household Furniture
2512	Wood Household Furniture, Upholstered
2434	Wood Kitchen Cabinets
2521	Wood Office Furniture
2448	Wood Pallets & Skids
2499	Wood Prdts, NEC
2491	Wood Preserving
2517	Wood T V, Radio, Phono & Sewing Cabinets
2541	Wood, Office & Store Fixtures
3553	Woodworking Machinery
2231	Wool, Woven Fabric

X

SIC NO	PRODUCT
3844	X-ray Apparatus & Tubes

Y

SIC NO	PRODUCT
2281	Yarn Spinning Mills
2282	Yarn Texturizing, Throwing, Twisting & Winding Mills

SIC INDEX

Standard Industrial Classification Numerical Index

SIC NO	PRODUCT

10 metal mining
1011 Iron Ores
1021 Copper Ores
1031 Lead & Zinc Ores
1041 Gold Ores
1044 Silver Ores
1081 Metal Mining Svcs
1094 Uranium, Radium & Vanadium Ores
1099 Metal Ores, NEC

12 coal mining
1221 Bituminous Coal & Lignite: Surface Mining
1222 Bituminous Coal: Underground Mining
1241 Coal Mining Svcs

13 oil and gas extraction
1311 Crude Petroleum & Natural Gas
1321 Natural Gas Liquids
1381 Drilling Oil & Gas Wells
1382 Oil & Gas Field Exploration Svcs
1389 Oil & Gas Field Svcs, NEC

14 mining and quarrying of nonmetallic minerals, except fuels
1411 Dimension Stone
1422 Crushed & Broken Limestone
1423 Crushed & Broken Granite
1429 Crushed & Broken Stone, NEC
1442 Construction Sand & Gravel
1446 Industrial Sand
1455 Kaolin & Ball Clay
1459 Clay, Ceramic & Refractory Minerals, NEC
1475 Phosphate Rock
1479 Chemical & Fertilizer Mining
1481 Nonmetallic Minerals Svcs, Except Fuels
1499 Miscellaneous Nonmetallic Mining

20 food and kindred products
2011 Meat Packing Plants
2013 Sausages & Meat Prdts
2015 Poultry Slaughtering, Dressing & Processing
2021 Butter
2022 Cheese
2023 Milk, Condensed & Evaporated
2024 Ice Cream
2026 Milk
2032 Canned Specialties
2033 Canned Fruits, Vegetables & Preserves
2034 Dried Fruits, Vegetables & Soup
2035 Pickled Fruits, Vegetables, Sauces & Dressings
2037 Frozen Fruits, Juices & Vegetables
2038 Frozen Specialties
2041 Flour, Grain Milling
2043 Cereal Breakfast Foods
2045 Flour, Blended & Prepared
2046 Wet Corn Milling
2047 Dog & Cat Food
2048 Prepared Feeds For Animals & Fowls
2051 Bread, Bakery Prdts Exc Cookies & Crackers
2052 Cookies & Crackers
2053 Frozen Bakery Prdts
2061 Sugar, Cane
2064 Candy & Confectionery Prdts
2066 Chocolate & Cocoa Prdts
2067 Chewing Gum
2068 Salted & Roasted Nuts & Seeds
2074 Cottonseed Oil Mills
2075 Soybean Oil Mills
2076 Vegetable Oil Mills
2077 Animal, Marine Fats & Oils
2079 Shortening, Oils & Margarine
2082 Malt Beverages
2083 Malt
2084 Wine & Brandy
2085 Liquors, Distilled, Rectified & Blended
2086 Soft Drinks
2087 Flavoring Extracts & Syrups
2091 Fish & Seafoods, Canned & Cured
2092 Fish & Seafoods, Fresh & Frozen
2095 Coffee
2096 Potato Chips & Similar Prdts
2097 Ice
2098 Macaroni, Spaghetti & Noodles
2099 Food Preparations, NEC

21 tobacco products
2111 Cigarettes
2121 Cigars
2131 Tobacco, Chewing & Snuff

22 textile mill products
2211 Cotton, Woven Fabric
2221 Silk & Man-Made Fiber
2231 Wool, Woven Fabric
2241 Fabric Mills, Cotton, Wool, Silk & Man-Made
2252 Hosiery, Except Women's
2253 Knit Outerwear Mills
2254 Knit Underwear Mills
2258 Lace & Warp Knit Fabric Mills
2259 Knitting Mills, NEC
2261 Cotton Fabric Finishers
2262 Silk & Man-Made Fabric Finishers
2269 Textile Finishers, NEC
2273 Carpets & Rugs
2281 Yarn Spinning Mills
2282 Yarn Texturizing, Throwing, Twisting & Winding Mills
2284 Thread Mills
2295 Fabrics Coated Not Rubberized
2296 Tire Cord & Fabric
2297 Fabrics, Nonwoven
2298 Cordage & Twine
2299 Textile Goods, NEC

23 apparel and other finished products made from fabrics and similar material
2311 Men's & Boys' Suits, Coats & Overcoats
2321 Men's & Boys' Shirts
2322 Men's & Boys' Underwear & Nightwear
2323 Men's & Boys' Neckwear
2325 Men's & Boys' Separate Trousers & Casual Slacks
2326 Men's & Boys' Work Clothing
2329 Men's & Boys' Clothing, NEC
2331 Women's & Misses' Blouses
2335 Women's & Misses' Dresses
2337 Women's & Misses' Suits, Coats & Skirts
2339 Women's & Misses' Outerwear, NEC
2341 Women's, Misses' & Children's Underwear & Nightwear
2342 Brassieres, Girdles & Garments
2353 Hats, Caps & Millinery
2361 Children's & Infants' Dresses & Blouses
2369 Girls' & Infants' Outerwear, NEC
2371 Fur Goods
2381 Dress & Work Gloves
2385 Waterproof Outerwear
2386 Leather & Sheep Lined Clothing
2389 Apparel & Accessories, NEC
2391 Curtains & Draperies
2392 House furnishings: Textile
2393 Textile Bags
2394 Canvas Prdts
2395 Pleating & Stitching For The Trade
2396 Automotive Trimmings, Apparel Findings, Related Prdts
2397 Schiffli Machine Embroideries
2399 Fabricated Textile Prdts, NEC

24 lumber and wood products, except furniture
2411 Logging
2421 Saw & Planing Mills
2426 Hardwood Dimension & Flooring Mills
2429 Special Prdt Sawmills, NEC
2431 Millwork
2434 Wood Kitchen Cabinets
2435 Hardwood Veneer & Plywood
2436 Softwood Veneer & Plywood
2439 Structural Wood Members, NEC
2441 Wood Boxes
2448 Wood Pallets & Skids
2449 Wood Containers, NEC
2451 Mobile Homes
2452 Prefabricated Wood Buildings & Cmpnts
2491 Wood Preserving
2493 Reconstituted Wood Prdts
2499 Wood Prdts, NEC

25 furniture and fixtures
2511 Wood Household Furniture
2512 Wood Household Furniture, Upholstered
2514 Metal Household Furniture
2515 Mattresses & Bedsprings
2517 Wood T V, Radio, Phono & Sewing Cabinets
2519 Household Furniture, NEC
2521 Wood Office Furniture
2522 Office Furniture, Except Wood
2531 Public Building & Related Furniture
2541 Wood, Office & Store Fixtures
2542 Partitions & Fixtures, Except Wood
2591 Drapery Hardware, Window Blinds & Shades
2599 Furniture & Fixtures, NEC

26 paper and allied products
2611 Pulp Mills
2621 Paper Mills
2631 Paperboard Mills
2652 Set-Up Paperboard Boxes
2653 Corrugated & Solid Fiber Boxes
2655 Fiber Cans, Tubes & Drums
2656 Sanitary Food Containers
2657 Folding Paperboard Boxes
2671 Paper Coating & Laminating for Packaging
2672 Paper Coating & Laminating, Exc for Packaging
2673 Bags: Plastics, Laminated & Coated
2674 Bags: Uncoated Paper & Multiwall
2675 Die-Cut Paper & Board
2676 Sanitary Paper Prdts
2677 Envelopes
2678 Stationery Prdts
2679 Converted Paper Prdts, NEC

27 printing, publishing, and allied industries
2711 Newspapers: Publishing & Printing
2721 Periodicals: Publishing & Printing
2731 Books: Publishing & Printing
2732 Book Printing, Not Publishing
2741 Misc Publishing
2752 Commercial Printing: Lithographic
2754 Commercial Printing: Gravure
2759 Commercial Printing
2761 Manifold Business Forms
2771 Greeting Card Publishing
2782 Blankbooks & Looseleaf Binders
2789 Bookbinding
2791 Typesetting
2796 Platemaking & Related Svcs

28 chemicals and allied products
2812 Alkalies & Chlorine
2813 Industrial Gases
2816 Inorganic Pigments
2819 Indl Inorganic Chemicals, NEC
2821 Plastics, Mtrls & Nonvulcanizable Elastomers
2822 Synthetic Rubber (Vulcanizable Elastomers)
2823 Cellulosic Man-Made Fibers
2824 Synthetic Organic Fibers, Exc Cellulosic
2833 Medicinal Chemicals & Botanical Prdts
2834 Pharmaceuticals
2835 Diagnostic Substances
2836 Biological Prdts, Exc Diagnostic Substances
2841 Soap & Detergents
2842 Spec Cleaning, Polishing & Sanitation Preparations
2844 Perfumes, Cosmetics & Toilet Preparations
2851 Paints, Varnishes, Lacquers, Enamels
2861 Gum & Wood Chemicals
2865 Cyclic-Crudes, Intermediates, Dyes & Org Pigments
2869 Industrial Organic Chemicals, NEC
2873 Nitrogenous Fertilizers
2874 Phosphatic Fertilizers
2875 Fertilizers, Mixing Only
2879 Pesticides & Agricultural Chemicals, NEC
2891 Adhesives & Sealants
2892 Explosives
2893 Printing Ink
2899 Chemical Preparations, NEC

29 petroleum refining and related industries
2911 Petroleum Refining
2951 Paving Mixtures & Blocks
2952 Asphalt Felts & Coatings
2992 Lubricating Oils & Greases

30 rubber and miscellaneous plastics products
3011 Tires & Inner Tubes
3021 Rubber & Plastic Footwear
3052 Rubber & Plastic Hose & Belting
3053 Gaskets, Packing & Sealing Devices
3061 Molded, Extruded & Lathe-Cut Rubber Mechanical Goods
3069 Fabricated Rubber Prdts, NEC
3081 Plastic Unsupported Sheet & Film

SIC INDEX

SIC NO	PRODUCT
3082	Plastic Unsupported Profile Shapes
3083	Plastic Laminated Plate & Sheet
3084	Plastic Pipe
3085	Plastic Bottles
3086	Plastic Foam Prdts
3087	Custom Compounding Of Purchased Plastic Resins
3088	Plastic Plumbing Fixtures
3089	Plastic Prdts

31 leather and leather products

SIC NO	PRODUCT
3111	Leather Tanning & Finishing
3131	Boot & Shoe Cut Stock & Findings
3143	Men's Footwear, Exc Athletic
3144	Women's Footwear, Exc Athletic
3149	Footwear, NEC
3151	Leather Gloves & Mittens
3161	Luggage
3171	Handbags & Purses
3172	Personal Leather Goods
3199	Leather Goods, NEC

32 stone, clay, glass, and concrete products

SIC NO	PRODUCT
3211	Flat Glass
3221	Glass Containers
3229	Pressed & Blown Glassware, NEC
3231	Glass Prdts Made Of Purchased Glass
3241	Cement, Hydraulic
3251	Brick & Structural Clay Tile
3253	Ceramic Tile
3255	Clay Refractories
3259	Structural Clay Prdts, NEC
3261	China Plumbing Fixtures & Fittings
3263	Earthenware, Whiteware, Table & Kitchen Articles
3264	Porcelain Electrical Splys
3269	Pottery Prdts, NEC
3271	Concrete Block & Brick
3272	Concrete Prdts
3273	Ready-Mixed Concrete
3274	Lime
3275	Gypsum Prdts
3281	Cut Stone Prdts
3291	Abrasive Prdts
3292	Asbestos products
3295	Minerals & Earths: Ground Or Treated
3296	Mineral Wool
3297	Nonclay Refractories
3299	Nonmetallic Mineral Prdts, NEC

33 primary metal industries

SIC NO	PRODUCT
3312	Blast Furnaces, Coke Ovens, Steel & Rolling Mills
3313	Electrometallurgical Prdts
3315	Steel Wire Drawing & Nails & Spikes
3316	Cold Rolled Steel Sheet, Strip & Bars
3317	Steel Pipe & Tubes
3321	Gray Iron Foundries
3322	Malleable Iron Foundries
3324	Steel Investment Foundries
3325	Steel Foundries, NEC
3331	Primary Smelting & Refining Of Copper
3334	Primary Production Of Aluminum
3339	Primary Nonferrous Metals, NEC
3341	Secondary Smelting & Refining Of Nonferrous Metals
3351	Rolling, Drawing & Extruding Of Copper
3353	Aluminum Sheet, Plate & Foil
3354	Aluminum Extruded Prdts
3355	Aluminum Rolling & Drawing, NEC
3356	Rolling, Drawing-Extruding Of Nonferrous Metals
3357	Nonferrous Wire Drawing
3363	Aluminum Die Castings
3364	Nonferrous Die Castings, Exc Aluminum
3365	Aluminum Foundries
3366	Copper Foundries
3369	Nonferrous Foundries: Castings, NEC
3398	Metal Heat Treating
3399	Primary Metal Prdts, NEC

34 fabricated metal products, except machinery and transportation equipment

SIC NO	PRODUCT
3411	Metal Cans
3412	Metal Barrels, Drums, Kegs & Pails
3421	Cutlery
3423	Hand & Edge Tools
3425	Hand Saws & Saw Blades
3429	Hardware, NEC
3431	Enameled Iron & Metal Sanitary Ware
3432	Plumbing Fixture Fittings & Trim, Brass
3433	Heating Eqpt
3441	Fabricated Structural Steel
3442	Metal Doors, Sash, Frames, Molding & Trim
3443	Fabricated Plate Work
3444	Sheet Metal Work
3446	Architectural & Ornamental Metal Work
3448	Prefabricated Metal Buildings & Cmpnts
3449	Misc Structural Metal Work
3451	Screw Machine Prdts
3452	Bolts, Nuts, Screws, Rivets & Washers
3462	Iron & Steel Forgings
3463	Nonferrous Forgings
3465	Automotive Stampings
3469	Metal Stampings, NEC
3471	Electroplating, Plating, Polishing, Anodizing & Coloring
3479	Coating & Engraving, NEC
3482	Small Arms Ammunition
3483	Ammunition, Large
3484	Small Arms
3489	Ordnance & Access, NEC
3491	Industrial Valves
3492	Fluid Power Valves & Hose Fittings
3493	Steel Springs, Except Wire
3494	Valves & Pipe Fittings, NEC
3495	Wire Springs
3496	Misc Fabricated Wire Prdts
3497	Metal Foil & Leaf
3498	Fabricated Pipe & Pipe Fittings
3499	Fabricated Metal Prdts, NEC

35 industrial and commercial machinery and computer equipment

SIC NO	PRODUCT
3511	Steam, Gas & Hydraulic Turbines & Engines
3519	Internal Combustion Engines, NEC
3523	Farm Machinery & Eqpt
3524	Garden, Lawn Tractors & Eqpt
3531	Construction Machinery & Eqpt
3532	Mining Machinery & Eqpt
3533	Oil Field Machinery & Eqpt
3534	Elevators & Moving Stairways
3535	Conveyors & Eqpt
3536	Hoists, Cranes & Monorails
3537	Indl Trucks, Tractors, Trailers & Stackers
3541	Machine Tools: Cutting
3542	Machine Tools: Forming
3543	Industrial Patterns
3544	Dies, Tools, Jigs, Fixtures & Indl Molds
3545	Machine Tool Access
3546	Power Hand Tools
3547	Rolling Mill Machinery & Eqpt
3548	Welding Apparatus
3549	Metalworking Machinery, NEC
3552	Textile Machinery
3553	Woodworking Machinery
3554	Paper Inds Machinery
3555	Printing Trades Machinery & Eqpt
3556	Food Prdts Machinery
3559	Special Ind Machinery, NEC
3561	Pumps & Pumping Eqpt
3562	Ball & Roller Bearings
3563	Air & Gas Compressors
3564	Blowers & Fans
3565	Packaging Machinery
3566	Speed Changers, Drives & Gears
3567	Indl Process Furnaces & Ovens
3568	Mechanical Power Transmission Eqpt, NEC
3569	Indl Machinery & Eqpt, NEC
3571	Electronic Computers
3572	Computer Storage Devices
3575	Computer Terminals
3577	Computer Peripheral Eqpt, NEC
3578	Calculating & Accounting Eqpt
3579	Office Machines, NEC
3581	Automatic Vending Machines
3582	Commercial Laundry, Dry Clean & Pressing Mchs
3585	Air Conditioning & Heating Eqpt
3586	Measuring & Dispensing Pumps
3589	Service Ind Machines, NEC
3592	Carburetors, Pistons, Rings & Valves
3593	Fluid Power Cylinders & Actuators
3594	Fluid Power Pumps & Motors
3596	Scales & Balances, Exc Laboratory
3599	Machinery & Eqpt, Indl & Commercial, NEC

36 electronic and other electrical equipment and components, except computer

SIC NO	PRODUCT
3612	Power, Distribution & Specialty Transformers
3613	Switchgear & Switchboard Apparatus
3621	Motors & Generators
3624	Carbon & Graphite Prdts
3625	Relays & Indl Controls
3629	Electrical Indl Apparatus, NEC
3631	Household Cooking Eqpt
3632	Household Refrigerators & Freezers
3633	Household Laundry Eqpt
3634	Electric Household Appliances
3635	Household Vacuum Cleaners
3639	Household Appliances, NEC
3641	Electric Lamps
3643	Current-Carrying Wiring Devices
3644	Noncurrent-Carrying Wiring Devices
3645	Residential Lighting Fixtures
3646	Commercial, Indl & Institutional Lighting Fixtures
3647	Vehicular Lighting Eqpt
3648	Lighting Eqpt, NEC
3651	Household Audio & Video Eqpt
3652	Phonograph Records & Magnetic Tape
3661	Telephone & Telegraph Apparatus
3663	Radio & T V Communications, Systs & Eqpt, Broadcast/Studio
3669	Communications Eqpt, NEC
3671	Radio & T V Receiving Electron Tubes
3672	Printed Circuit Boards
3674	Semiconductors
3675	Electronic Capacitors
3676	Electronic Resistors
3677	Electronic Coils & Transformers
3678	Electronic Connectors
3679	Electronic Components, NEC
3691	Storage Batteries
3692	Primary Batteries: Dry & Wet
3694	Electrical Eqpt For Internal Combustion Engines
3695	Recording Media
3699	Electrical Machinery, Eqpt & Splys, NEC

37 transportation equipment

SIC NO	PRODUCT
3711	Motor Vehicles & Car Bodies
3713	Truck & Bus Bodies
3714	Motor Vehicle Parts & Access
3715	Truck Trailers
3716	Motor Homes
3721	Aircraft
3724	Aircraft Engines & Engine Parts
3728	Aircraft Parts & Eqpt, NEC
3731	Shipbuilding & Repairing
3732	Boat Building & Repairing
3743	Railroad Eqpt
3751	Motorcycles, Bicycles & Parts
3761	Guided Missiles & Space Vehicles
3764	Guided Missile/Space Vehicle Propulsion Units & parts
3769	Guided Missile/Space Vehicle Parts & Eqpt, NEC
3792	Travel Trailers & Campers
3795	Tanks & Tank Components
3799	Transportation Eqpt, NEC

38 measuring, analyzing and controlling instruments; photographic, medical an

SIC NO	PRODUCT
3812	Search, Detection, Navigation & Guidance Systs & Instrs
3821	Laboratory Apparatus & Furniture
3822	Automatic Temperature Controls
3823	Indl Instruments For Meas, Display & Control
3824	Fluid Meters & Counters
3825	Instrs For Measuring & Testing Electricity
3826	Analytical Instruments
3827	Optical Instruments
3829	Measuring & Controlling Devices, NEC
3841	Surgical & Medical Instrs & Apparatus
3842	Orthopedic, Prosthetic & Surgical Appliances/Splys
3843	Dental Eqpt & Splys
3844	X-ray Apparatus & Tubes
3845	Electromedical & Electrotherapeutic Apparatus
3851	Ophthalmic Goods
3861	Photographic Eqpt & Splys
3873	Watch & Clock Devices & Parts

39 miscellaneous manufacturing industries

SIC NO	PRODUCT
3911	Jewelry: Precious Metal
3914	Silverware, Plated & Stainless Steel Ware
3915	Jewelers Findings & Lapidary Work
3931	Musical Instruments
3942	Dolls & Stuffed Toys
3944	Games, Toys & Children's Vehicles
3949	Sporting & Athletic Goods, NEC
3951	Pens & Mechanical Pencils
3952	Lead Pencils, Crayons & Artist's Mtrls
3953	Marking Devices
3955	Carbon Paper & Inked Ribbons
3961	Costume Jewelry & Novelties
3965	Fasteners, Buttons, Needles & Pins
3991	Brooms & Brushes
3993	Signs & Advertising Displays
3995	Burial Caskets
3996	Linoleum & Hard Surface Floor Coverings, NEC
3999	Manufacturing Industries, NEC

73 business services

SIC NO	PRODUCT
7372	Prepackaged Software

76 miscellaneous repair services

SIC NO	PRODUCT
7692	Welding Repair
7694	Armature Rewinding Shops

SIC SECTION

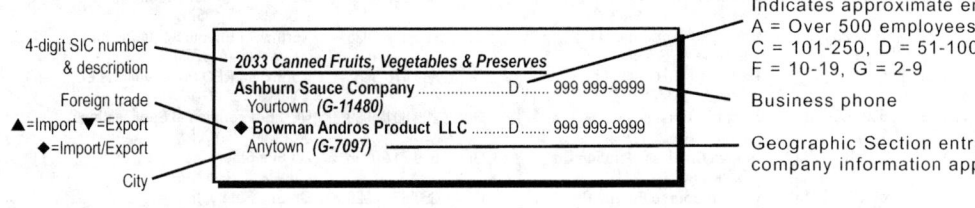

- 4-digit SIC number & description
- Foreign trade
- ▲=Import ▼=Export
- ◆=Import/Export
- City

2033 Canned Fruits, Vegetables & Preserves
Ashburn Sauce Company ....D....... 999 999-9999
Yourtown (G-11480)
◆ Bowman Andros Product LLC ....D....... 999 999-9999
Anytown (G-7097)

Indicates approximate employment figure
A = Over 500 employees, B = 251-500
C = 101-250, D = 51-100, E = 20-50
F = 10-19, G = 2-9

Business phone

Geographic Section entry number where full company information appears.

See footnotes for symbols and codes identification.

- The SIC codes in this section are from the latest Standard Industrial Classification manual published by the U.S. Government's Office of Management and Budget. For more information regarding SICs, see the Explanatory Notes.
- Companies may be listed under multiple classifications.

10 METAL MINING

1011 Iron Ores
Giant Metals Inc ....G...... 206 592-0963
  Seatac (G-9285)

1021 Copper Ores
Silver King Mining & Milling..................G...... 509 445-1406
  Cusick (G-2852)

1031 Lead & Zinc Ores
Lka Gold Incorporated...........................G...... 253 514-6661
  Gig Harbor (G-4133)
Silver King Mining & Milling..................G...... 509 445-1406
  Cusick (G-2852)

1041 Gold Ores
3dx Industries Inc ....G...... 360 244-4339
  Ferndale (G-3808)
Alto Group Holdings Inc......................G...... 801 816-2520
  Wenatchee (G-15088)
American Cordillera Min Corp ....G...... 509 671-9401
  Spokane (G-12109)
Bazooka Gold Mining Co LLC...............G...... 360 202-5953
  Mount Vernon (G-6776)
Boulder Gold LLC ....G...... 425 308-4316
  Everett (G-3399)
Diversified Development Co ....G...... 360 734-1480
  Bellingham (G-1324)
Gold Reserve Inc.................................G...... 509 623-1500
  Spokane (G-12276)
Goldrich Mining Company ....F...... 509 535-7367
  Spokane (G-12277)
Great Basin Energies Inc ....G...... 509 623-1500
  Spokane (G-12280)
Josephine Mining Corp ....G...... 509 343-3193
  Spokane (G-12342)
Kinross Gold Usa Inc............................C...... 509 775-3157
  Republic (G-8959)
Lka Gold Incorporated...........................G...... 253 514-6661
  Gig Harbor (G-4133)
Lovitt Resources Inc............................G...... 509 668-8170
  Wenatchee (G-15047)
NA Degerstrom Inc ....E...... 509 928-3333
  Spokane Valley (G-12800)
Rondys Inc..G...... 425 392-6324
  Issaquah (G-4470)
Timbers At Towncenter ....G...... 360 433-9627
  Vancouver (G-14639)
Walker Goldsmiths ....G...... 360 758-2601
  Bellingham (G-1588)

1044 Silver Ores
3dx Industries Inc ....G...... 360 244-4339
  Ferndale (G-3808)
Alto Group Holdings Inc......................G...... 801 816-2520
  Wenatchee (G-15088)
Gold Reserve Inc.................................G...... 509 623-1500
  Spokane (G-12276)
▲ Helena Silver Mines Inc ....G...... 509 922-3035
  Spokane Valley (G-12729)
Lka Gold Incorporated...........................G...... 253 514-6661
  Gig Harbor (G-4133)
Silver King Mining & Milling..................G...... 509 445-1406
  Cusick (G-2852)

1081 Metal Mining Svcs
Adamera Minerals LLC ....F...... 509 237-7731
  Republic (G-8955)
Alaska Standard Mining Inc ....G...... 360 432-8797
  Shelton (G-11674)
Andritz Hydro Corp..............................G...... 704 943-4343
  Spokane Valley (G-12618)
Boart Longyear...................................G...... 509 926-9575
  Otis Orchards (G-7512)
Cannabis Leaf Incorporated ....G...... 206 430-6250
  Seattle (G-9617)
Ce Metal Fabrication............................F...... 360 673-9663
  Kalama (G-4494)
▲ Chooch Enterprises Inc....................G...... 425 273-4794
  Maple Valley (G-6264)
Christopher Ross Dewayne ....G...... 360 918-4586
  Tumwater (G-13860)
Fam USA Inc ....G...... 509 468-2677
  Nine Mile Falls (G-7074)
Global Metal Technologies LLC............G...... 425 956-3506
  Bellevue (G-928)
Golden Claw Ventures Inc ....G...... 360 927-8276
  Blaine (G-1672)
Goldrich Mining Company ....F...... 509 535-7367
  Spokane (G-12277)
Hart Crowser Inc ....D...... 206 324-9530
  Seattle (G-10145)
Hiett Logging Inc.................................G...... 360 724-5505
  Burlington (G-2164)
High Cascade Incorporated ....G...... 509 763-2195
  Leavenworth (G-5806)
Hunt Family Ltd Partnership ....G...... 509 892-5287
  Greenacres (G-4299)
Hunt Mining Corp................................G...... 509 290-5659
  Liberty Lake (G-5835)
Iron Mountain Quarry LLC ....G...... 425 338-0607
  Bothell (G-1867)
LI3 LLC...G...... 509 332-2109
  Pullman (G-8097)
Mascota Resources Corp.....................G...... 206 818-4799
  Black Diamond (G-1650)
Master Vac LLC ....G...... 253 875-0074
  Graham (G-4231)
North Star Mining Co Inc.....................G...... 360 793-0848
  Sultan (G-13030)
Pilot Knob Construction Inc ....G...... 509 493-4196
  White Salmon (G-15127)
Raz Arthur John..................................F...... 360 518-2665
  Ridgefield (G-9105)
Selland Construction Inc......................C...... 509 662-7119
  Wenatchee (G-15073)
Smma Candelaria Inc...........................G...... 206 405-2800
  Seattle (G-11140)
▲ Sumitomo Metal Mining America......G...... 206 405-2800
  Seattle (G-11215)
Tai Incorporated..................................G...... 509 747-6111
  Spokane (G-12542)
▲ Teck American Incorporated............E...... 509 747-6111
  Spokane (G-12548)
Teck American Incorporated................D...... 509 446-5308
  Metaline Falls (G-6499)
Teck Co LLC ....G...... 509 747-6111
  Spokane (G-12550)
Washington Teck Incorporated............B...... 509 446-4516
  Metaline Falls (G-6500)

1094 Uranium, Radium & Vanadium Ores
Silver King Mining & Milling..................G...... 509 445-1406
  Cusick (G-2852)

1099 Metal Ores, NEC
Kaiser Aluminum Washington LLC ....G...... 949 614-1740
  Spokane Valley (G-12761)
Precision Metal Works LLC..................G...... 509 945-8433
  Union Gap (G-13951)

12 COAL MINING

1221 Bituminous Coal & Lignite: Surface Mining
Coalview Ltd LLC.................................E...... 360 623-7525
  Centralia (G-2394)
Green Mtn Mine Oper Co LLC...............G...... 206 451-7105
  Granite Falls (G-4276)
Morning Sun Inc..................................G...... 253 922-6589
  Lakewood (G-5739)
Pacific Coast Coal Company ....G...... 360 886-1060
  Black Diamond (G-1652)
◆ Usnr LLC..G...... 360 225-8267
  Woodland (G-15470)

1222 Bituminous Coal: Underground Mining
Transalta Centralia Mining LLC ....A...... 360 807-8020
  Centralia (G-2438)

1241 Coal Mining Svcs
American Min & Tunneling LLC.............G...... 509 921-7836
  Spokane Valley (G-12612)
Clowers Corporation ....G...... 206 420-1202
  Lake Forest Park (G-5609)
Groundhog Mines LLC ....G...... 425 609-6901
  Lake Stevens (G-5645)
Hart Crowser Inc ....D...... 206 324-9530
  Seattle (G-10145)
Nika Mines LLC ....G...... 425 609-6901
  Lake Stevens (G-5664)
Procon Min & Tunnelling US Ltd ....F...... 360 685-4253
  Bellingham (G-1506)
Sumitomo Metal Mining Ariz Inc..........G...... 206 405-2800
  Seattle (G-11216)
Triumph Corporation ....G...... 509 926-7000
  Spokane Valley (G-12913)

13 OIL AND GAS EXTRACTION

1311 Crude Petroleum & Natural Gas
Andeavor ....G...... 509 586-2117
  Kennewick (G-4617)
Andeavor ....G...... 509 928-5632
  Spokane Valley (G-12617)
Andeavor ....G...... 360 374-2038
  Forks (G-4008)
Andeavor ....G...... 509 487-9235
  Spokane (G-12114)
Annointed Oil Inc.................................G...... 206 242-6925
  Seattle (G-9405)
BP West Coast Products LLC...............B...... 360 856-5022
  Sedro Woolley (G-11533)
BP West Coast Products LLC...............A...... 360 371-1500
  Blaine (G-1665)
Camwest Inc ....G...... 425 776-7900
  Lynnwood (G-6086)
Coinstar LLC.......................................G...... 866 733-2693
  Vancouver (G-14128)
Cool Racing Oil ....G...... 971 235-7611
  Sequim (G-11619)

13 OIL AND GAS EXTRACTION

Daybreak Oil and Gas Inc..................G........ 509 232-7674
Spokane Valley *(G-12679)*
Dose Oil LLC..................................G........ 954 494-7976
Mill Creek *(G-6508)*
Energy Consulting Services LLC......G........ 701 580-9732
Long Beach *(G-5874)*
Ephrata Oil Change Express............G........ 509 398-8740
Ephrata *(G-3334)*
Grease Heads Lube and Oil LLC......G........ 509 930-3786
East Wenatchee *(G-3017)*
Green Section 30 LLC....................G........ 253 433-4130
Enumclaw *(G-3292)*
Green Star Energies Inc..................G........ 360 989-5549
Vancouver *(G-14271)*
Jackson Oil Anthony Schnell............G........ 253 847-2566
Graham *(G-4227)*
K & S Oil Field Services Inc.............G........ 509 998-5738
Elk *(G-3171)*
Khans Oil LLC................................G........ 360 668-6415
Vancouver *(G-14347)*
Myinterzone....................................G........ 206 679-4566
Seattle *(G-10581)*
One Oil Lovin Mama......................G........ 360 572-4511
Stanwood *(G-12984)*
Pacificorp..G........ 360 827-6467
Chehalis *(G-2520)*
Seattle Oil Solution LLC..................G........ 206 375-7575
Seattle *(G-11067)*
Shell Energy North Amer US LP......G........ 509 688-6002
Spokane *(G-12502)*
Skinny Producing............................G........ 425 443-4552
Bellevue *(G-1135)*
Starry Field Services......................G........ 360 676-7441
Bellingham *(G-1556)*
Summit Carbon Capture LLC...........G........ 206 780-3551
Seattle *(G-11217)*
Tesoro Companies Inc....................D........ 253 896-8700
Federal Way *(G-3794)*
Tesoro Corporation..........................G........ 509 533-2705
Spokane *(G-12553)*
Tesoro Maritime Company................G........ 360 293-3111
Anacortes *(G-176)*
USA Oil LLC..................................G........ 425 226-5555
Renton *(G-8938)*
Weyerhaeuser Company..................A........ 206 467-3600
Seattle *(G-11460)*

1321 Natural Gas Liquids

Emerald Energy Nw LLC..................G........ 425 830-2757
Bothell *(G-1851)*
Prometheus Energy Company..........F........ 425 558-9100
Redmond *(G-8635)*
Prometheus Energy Group Inc.........G........ 425 558-9100
Redmond *(G-8636)*
Pt Defiance Food Mart....................F........ 253 761-5084
Tacoma *(G-13481)*
Wenatchee Petroleum Co.................E........ 509 662-4423
Wenatchee *(G-15084)*

1381 Drilling Oil & Gas Wells

Barker Drilling................................G........ 425 252-4686
Mount Vernon *(G-6774)*
C J Warren & Sons Well Drlg...........G........ 509 924-3872
Veradale *(G-14749)*
Carpenter Drilling LLC....................F........ 509 627-6642
Benton City *(G-1603)*
Dan McMullen Well Drilling.............G........ 707 998-9252
Ethel *(G-3350)*
Daughtrey Machine..........................G........ 509 834-9736
Yakima *(G-15550)*
Directed Technologies Drlg Inc........G........ 800 239-5950
Bremerton *(G-1948)*
Division Piedmont Directional...........G........ 425 482-9022
Woodinville *(G-15228)*
Holman Drilling Corporation.............G........ 509 534-1013
Spokane Valley *(G-12730)*
Malcom Drilling................................G........ 206 623-0776
Seattle *(G-10470)*
Pacific NW Probe & Drlg Inc............G........ 253 651-2477
Puyallup *(G-8218)*
Scheffler Northwest Inc....................G........ 360 213-2070
Vancouver *(G-14571)*
Taylor Drilling Inc............................F........ 360 262-9274
Chehalis *(G-2538)*
Triple A Drilling Inc..........................G........ 509 543-3171
Burbank *(G-2086)*

1382 Oil & Gas Field Exploration Svcs

Access US Oil & Gas Inc..................G........ 206 792-7575
Lacey *(G-5530)*
American Petro Envmtl Svcs LLC....G........ 253 538-5252
Puyallup *(G-8122)*
Blackhawk Synergies Inc..................G........ 509 627-9726
Kennewick *(G-4632)*
Bud Clary Properties LLC................G........ 800 899-1926
Longview *(G-5891)*
Carbon Cycle Crush LLC..................G........ 509 476-3667
Oroville *(G-7462)*
Cascadia Seismic Inc......................G........ 206 801-5999
Bothell *(G-1837)*
Empire Creek Exploration Co..........G........ 509 747-0996
Spokane *(G-12244)*
Ground Source Energy Nw..............G........ 253 852-5926
Kent *(G-4930)*
Longshot Oil LLC............................G........ 509 455-5924
Spokane *(G-12374)*
Radial Energy Inc............................G........ 360 332-0905
Blaine *(G-1700)*
Rk Burk Meg Murch Artworks..........G........ 206 954-1297
Seattle *(G-10967)*
Shepp Enterprises LLC....................G........ 206 697-0327
Tacoma *(G-13512)*
Tucker Garner CA............................G........ 206 236-0856
Mercer Island *(G-6487)*
◆ **Weyerhaeuser Company**..................A........ 206 539-3000
Seattle *(G-11459)*
Xextex Corporation USA..................G........ 425 392-3848
Issaquah *(G-4490)*

1389 Oil & Gas Field Svcs, NEC

Affordable Blackflow Testers............G........ 425 269-9064
Renton *(G-8730)*
Amiraq Cnsltnts Inc..........................G........ 936 448-1480
Woodland *(G-15418)*
Available Backflow Testers..............G........ 425 652-9970
Covington *(G-2820)*
Burnstead Construction Co..............F........ 425 635-1090
Bellevue *(G-831)*
Carter Game Testers........................G........ 360 326-3245
Vancouver *(G-14101)*
Dagner Construction........................G........ 509 349-8944
Warden *(G-14931)*
Dai Environmental Services..............E........ 360 354-1134
Lynden *(G-6012)*
Diligence Group Oil & Gas Biof.......G........ 360 892-0745
Vancouver *(G-14180)*
Dyers Construction & Excav............G........ 903 486-1881
Ocean Park *(G-7181)*
Emerald Phoenix Oil Co Llc..............G........ 509 600-0555
Spokane *(G-12242)*
Firepak Oil and Gas Inds LLC..........G........ 360 679-1747
Oak Harbor *(G-7152)*
First Choice Market Inc....................E........ 360 253-9149
Brush Prairie *(G-2035)*
Foster Surveying Inc........................G........ 503 997-1100
Camas *(G-2253)*
Fox Island Excavation LLC..............G........ 253 677-7291
Fox Island *(G-4020)*
Genesis Wellness............................G........ 425 337-3944
Everett *(G-3494)*
Gibraltar Maint & Cnstr Inc...............G........ 206 365-4440
Redmond *(G-8477)*
Global Fire Response & Safety........G........ 701 774-2022
Kirkland *(G-5349)*
Hammer & Tongs LLC......................G........ 206 526-0549
Seattle *(G-10137)*
Hot Shot Express Inc........................G........ 206 241-5516
Burien *(G-2112)*
Hot Shot Site Dots............................G........ 206 604-8980
Seattle *(G-10185)*
Impact Property Mgnt......................G........ 425 334-6361
Lake Stevens *(G-5647)*
Katerra Inc......................................A........ 650 422-3572
Seattle *(G-10330)*
Lorache Cad/lt Services LLC...........F........ 206 328-4227
Seattle *(G-10442)*
Loreen Home Servicing....................G........ 509 325-4290
Spokane *(G-12375)*
Lyle W Pulling..................................G........ 360 825-6129
Enumclaw *(G-3302)*
M A C I Inc......................................E........ 360 424-7013
Mount Vernon *(G-6808)*
M&S Custom Remodeling................G........ 425 739-0262
Kirkland *(G-5391)*
Madrona Log HM Repr & Care LLC.G........ 360 202-2842
Marysville *(G-6354)*
Master Vac LLC................................G........ 253 875-0074
Graham *(G-4231)*
McLeod Masonry USA Inc................F........ 360 734-4427
Bellingham *(G-1429)*
McLeod Pilot Car & Hot Sht Svc......G........ 360 701-5827
Olympia *(G-7334)*
Murphy JP Construction..................G........ 425 222-7299
Seattle *(G-10571)*
Northwest Envmtl Solutions Inc........G........ 253 241-6213
Puyallup *(G-8205)*
Northwest REO Preservation LLC...G........ 360 521-6761
Vancouver *(G-14440)*
NRC Environmental Services Inc....D........ 206 607-3000
Seattle *(G-10663)*
On Site Safety Inc............................G........ 970 876-1908
Kirkland *(G-5420)*
On-Site Safety Inc............................G........ 701 774-2022
Kirkland *(G-5421)*
Parametrix Inc..................................D........ 206 394-3700
Puyallup *(G-8219)*
Paynestaking Detail..........................G........ 509 599-2207
Spokane *(G-12433)*
Petrogas Lift Tech LLC....................G........ 425 891-7403
Sammamish *(G-9240)*
Praxair Services Inc........................G........ 360 676-8215
Bellingham *(G-1501)*
Precisionhx LLC..............................G........ 509 951-1266
Chattaroy *(G-2451)*
QMS 1 Inc......................................G........ 360 201-7505
Bellingham *(G-1512)*
Ricter Enterprises............................G........ 425 482-5942
Woodinville *(G-15349)*
Rw Hot Shot Service........................G........ 509 868-6644
Spokane *(G-12488)*
S Smith..G........ 425 529-9244
Renton *(G-8901)*
South Sound Contractors LLC..........F........ 360 688-5101
Lacey *(G-5592)*
Superior Energy Services LLC..........E........ 360 733-3030
Bellingham *(G-1564)*
Tube Crazy......................................G........ 206 931-7764
Kirkland *(G-5486)*
Vista Precision Solutions Inc............G........ 908 829-3471
Richland *(G-9050)*
Washigton Field Services Inc..........G........ 253 813-6681
Kent *(G-5206)*
Western Energy Group Inc..............G........ 253 306-4748
Puyallup *(G-8279)*
Woodrock Inc..................................F........ 253 565-6090
Tacoma *(G-13600)*

14 MINING AND QUARRYING OF NONMETALLIC MINERALS, EXCEPT FUELS

1411 Dimension Stone

410 Quarry Dibella Entps Inc............G........ 360 825-7505
Enumclaw *(G-3273)*
Arris Kollman Trucking Inc................G........ 360 532-0351
Shelton *(G-11679)*
Arris Kollman Trucking Inc................E........ 360 532-0351
Aberdeen *(G-2)*
Cadman (rock) Inc............................D........ 425 867-1234
Redmond *(G-8414)*
Cadman Holding Company Inc..........G........ 425 868-1234
Redmond *(G-8415)*
Columbia Granite LLC......................G........ 360 943-4072
Olympia *(G-7253)*
Highland Quarry LLC........................G........ 509 624-4136
Spokane *(G-12294)*
Lavinal Inc..G........ 509 857-2224
Cle Elum *(G-2670)*
Naselle Rock & Asphalt Company....F........ 360 484-3443
Naselle *(G-7017)*
Northwest Lime Co LLC....................G........ 360 815-0304
Ferndale *(G-3877)*
Quarry S/E Inc..................................G........ 206 525-5270
Seattle *(G-10904)*
Urban Stoneworks LLC....................G........ 808 333-6675
Ridgefield *(G-9118)*
▲ **Wilkeson Sandstone Quarry LLC**...G........ 360 829-0999
Wilkeson *(G-15144)*
Wood & Son Earthwork & Utility........F........ 360 352-1022
Tumwater *(G-13908)*

1422 Crushed & Broken Limestone

Clauson Quarry LLC........................G........ 360 599-2731
Maple Falls *(G-6249)*
Hemphill Brothers Inc......................G........ 206 842-0748
Bainbridge Island *(G-639)*
Hemphill Brothers Inc......................G........ 509 732-4481
Northport *(G-7138)*

SIC SECTION   14 MINING AND QUARRYING OF NONMETALLIC MINERALS, EXCEPT FUELS

▲ J A Jack & Sons Inc ....F 206 762-7622
　Seattle (G-10265)
Legacy Vulcan LLC ....E 206 284-7717
　Seattle (G-10400)
Martin Marietta Materials Inc..................F 360 424-3441
　Mount Vernon (G-6810)
Martin Marietta Materials Inc..................G 360 856-5870
　Mount Vernon (G-6811)
Pacific Calcium Incorporated ....E 509 486-1201
　Tonasket (G-13656)
Penny Creek Quarry ....G 360 765-3413
　Quilcene (G-8287)
Pyramid Materials Kitsap Quar................G 360 373-8708
　Bremerton (G-1991)
Rondys Inc..G 425 392-6324
　Issaquah (G-4470)
Sawyer & Sawyer Inc ....E 509 486-1304
　Tonasket (G-13658)

1423 Crushed & Broken Granite

Alan Good..F 360 864-2974
　Toledo (G-13635)

1429 Crushed & Broken Stone, NEC

Amery Rock & Construction Inc..............G 509 365-4122
　Lyle (G-5994)
Beaver Lake Quarry Inc ....G 360 856-5870
　Mount Vernon (G-6778)
County of Pierce ....F 360 893-2844
　Orting (G-7477)
De Rosier Trucking Inc ....E 360 577-1636
　Kelso (G-4523)
Dulin Construction Inc ....F 360 736-9225
　Centralia (G-2399)
Good Crushing Inc..................................F 360 864-2974
　Toledo (G-13639)
H B Q Inc ....G 509 653-1939
　Naches (G-6997)
Hillcar & Fletcher Inc ....G 360 327-3844
　Beaver (G-757)
J L Shrman Excvtg Rock Crshing ....F 509 447-4214
　Newport (G-7059)
Jones Quarry Inc.....................................G 360 352-1022
　Tumwater (G-13879)
Kalama River Road Quarry ....G 360 673-0795
　Kalama (G-4503)
Lodestone Quarry Incorparated ....G 360 942-0400
　South Bend (G-12044)
Manufacturers Mineral Company ....F 425 228-2120
　Renton (G-8847)
Olivine Corp...G 360 733-3332
　Bellingham (G-1479)
Rock Services Inc ....G 360 748-8333
　Chehalis (G-2530)
Rock Services Inc ....G 360 748-8333
　Chehalis (G-2531)
Sawyer & Sawyer Inc ....E 509 486-1304
　Tonasket (G-13658)
Shine Quarry Inc ....F 360 437-2415
　Port Ludlow (G-7775)
Sterling Breen Crushing Inc ....E 360 736-4240
　Centralia (G-2436)
Washougal Baselt Rock Qua ....G 360 335-0411
　Washougal (G-14998)
White Stone Calcium Corp......................G 509 935-0838
　Chewelah (G-2610)
White Stone Calcium Corp......................G 509 738-6571
　Kettle Falls (G-5243)

1442 Construction Sand & Gravel

Anderson Rock Dem Pits II LLC ....G 509 965-3621
　Yakima (G-15509)
Associated Sand Gravel..........................G 425 348-6309
　Gold Bar (G-4185)
Bayside Redi-Mix ....G 360 426-4987
　Shelton (G-11682)
Beans & Rocks LLC................................F 360 942-5414
　Raymond (G-8343)
Bishop-Red Rock Inc...............................G 509 773-5335
　Goldendale (G-4193)
Builders Sand and Gravel Inc ....F 425 743-3333
　Snohomish (G-11884)
Burien Sand and Gravel LLC ....G 206 244-1023
　Burien (G-2094)
Burns Construction Inc ....G 360 957-4183
　Cathlamet (G-2361)
Cadman (rock) Inc...................................D 425 867-1234
　Redmond (G-8414)
Cadman Holding Company Inc...............G 425 868-1234
　Redmond (G-8415)

Chelan Concrete Inc ....F 509 682-2915
　Chelan (G-2549)
Chelan Sand & Gravel LLC ....G 509 682-2569
　Chelan (G-2552)
Conex Sand & Gravel..............................G 503 437-0536
　Vancouver (G-14146)
Connell Sand & Gravel Inc ....E 509 234-3221
　Connell (G-2792)
Connell Sand & Gravel Inc ....F 509 234-3221
　Connell (G-2793)
Cowden Inc..D 360 592-4200
　Bellingham (G-1309)
D & S Rock LLC......................................F 509 877-7400
　Toppenish (G-13665)
Davis Sand & Gravel Inc.........................G 360 683-5680
　Sequim (G-11625)
Diamondback Construction LLC ....G 206 730-1239
　Shoreline (G-11768)
Dickson Company....................................D 253 472-4489
　Tacoma (G-13263)
Doris J Johnson ....G 509 586-3646
　Kennewick (G-4656)
East Valley Sand & Gravel Inc ....G 360 403-7520
　Arlington (G-231)
East Valley Sand and Gravel ....E 360 403-7520
　Arlington (G-232)
Eucon Corporation ....D 509 547-4402
　Pasco (G-7580)
Gary Merlino Cnstr Co Inc......................F 206 763-2134
　Seattle (G-10050)
Gillingham Sand & Gravel Co ....G 509 456-5527
　Cheney (G-2586)
Glacier Northwest Inc ....D 253 912-8500
　Dupont (G-2964)
Glacier Northwest Inc ....E 425 486-3281
　Seattle (G-10076)
Glacier Northwest Inc ....E 253 572-7412
　Tacoma (G-13310)
Glacier Northwest Inc ....G 360 896-8922
　Vancouver (G-14255)
Glacier Northwest Inc ....E 425 888-9795
　Snoqualmie (G-12013)
Gravel..G 360 930-5777
　Silverdale (G-11836)
Gravel Doctor of Washington ....G 509 899-1608
　Ellensburg (G-3205)
Gravel Flat Crop Dusting LLC.................G 509 398-8617
　Ephrata (G-3336)
Gravel Tones Productions Inc ....G 248 202-5757
　Seattle (G-10109)
Gravelroad LLC ....G 760 840-7174
　Seattle (G-10110)
Hermann Intermountain Corp.................G 509 445-0966
　Usk (G-13984)
Hood River Sand Gravel ....G 509 773-0314
　Goldendale (G-4200)
J A Jack & Sons Inc ....F 360 479-4659
　Bremerton (G-1964)
James A Wright Cnstr LLC.....................G 509 996-3249
　Winthrop (G-15162)
Jensen Barton W Inc ....F 360 825-3750
　Enumclaw (G-3297)
Jones Company Inc ....G 360 352-1022
　Tumwater (G-13878)
Konen Rock Crushing Inc ....G 509 382-2768
　Dayton (G-2883)
Krieg Concrete Products Inc ....F 360 675-2727
　Oak Harbor (G-7156)
Lincoln Sand & Gravel.............................G 509 725-4531
　Davenport (G-2875)
Lloyd Enterprises Inc ....D 253 874-6692
　Federal Way (G-3753)
Lloyd Logging Inc ....F 509 997-2441
　Twisp (G-13912)
Lynch Creek Quarry LLC ....G 360 832-4269
　Puyallup (G-8181)
Manufacturers Mineral Company ....F 425 228-2120
　Renton (G-8847)
Miles Sand & Gravel Company ....C 360 757-3121
　Burlington (G-2171)
Mountain Side Sand & Grav Inc ....G 360 701-1241
　Rainier (G-8318)
Mt Baker Stump Grinding & Grav ....G 360 684-1695
　Everson (G-3683)
Neshkaw Sand and Gravel LLC..............G 360 482-0274
　Elma (G-3252)
Northside Sand & Gravel........................G 509 551-5830
　Chattaroy (G-2449)
Northwest Rock Inc................................G 360 533-3050
　Aberdeen (G-25)

Northwest Rock Inc................................G 360 249-2245
　Montesano (G-6651)
Northwest Rock Inc................................G 360 482-3550
　Elma (G-3253)
O L Luther Co ....G 509 837-2527
　Granger (G-4262)
P & R Rock Sand & Gravel......................G 503 278-3512
　Battle Ground (G-727)
Pacific Rock Products LLC.....................G 360 896-8721
　Vancouver (G-14473)
Pipkin-Goodfellow Venture LLC ....G 509 884-2400
　East Wenatchee (G-3029)
Port Orchard Sand & Gravel ....E 360 681-2526
　Port Ludlow (G-7772)
Puget Sound Sand and Grav LLC...........G 360 332-3333
　Blaine (G-1698)
Rainier Gravel..G 206 510-3451
　Enumclaw (G-3316)
Randles Sand & Gravel Inc.....................G 253 531-6800
　Puyallup (G-8234)
Redside Construction LLC......................G 360 297-9557
　Bainbridge Island (G-664)
Ronald Sand & Gravel Inc ....G 509 728-8605
　Ellensburg (G-3223)
Sand Carrier Inc ....G 206 790-6791
　Tukwila (G-13812)
Sea Island Corp......................................F 360 376-4215
　Eastsound (G-3046)
Simpson Gravel Pit ....G 425 879-1024
　Stanwood (G-12991)
Spokane Rock Products Inc ....G 509 244-5421
　Spokane Valley (G-12888)
Stick & Sand Tutoring.............................G 206 721-6261
　Seattle (G-11195)
Stillaquamish Resources LLC ....G 360 474-1999
　Arlington (G-335)
Supply Guy ....G 253 531-8600
　Tacoma (G-13531)
Taylor Trucking LLC ....F 360 573-2000
　Vancouver (G-14627)
Tim Corliss & Son Inc.............................G 360 825-2578
　Enumclaw (G-3324)
Timber Savers Inc ....G 208 799-8748
　Clarkston (G-2652)
Walla Walla Gravel & Rock Llc...............G 509 301-1050
　Walla Walla (G-14892)
Washington Rock Quarries Inc...............F 360 893-7701
　Orting (G-7488)
Wingardner Sand and Gravel..................G 509 480-3847
　Zillah (G-15765)
Winston Quarry Inc.................................G 360 985-0487
　Mossyrock (G-6767)

1446 Industrial Sand

Hemphill Brothers Inc.............................G 206 842-0748
　Bainbridge Island (G-639)
Lane Mt Silica Co ....G 206 762-7622
　Seattle (G-10376)
Lane Mt Silica Co ....E 206 762-7622
　Valley (G-13993)
Reserve Industries Corporation ....G 425 432-1241
　Ravensdale (G-8340)

1455 Kaolin & Ball Clay

J M Huber Corporation ....G 206 762-4263
　Seattle (G-10273)

1459 Clay, Ceramic & Refractory Minerals, NEC

Imerys Minerals California Inc................D 509 787-4575
　Quincy (G-8300)

1475 Phosphate Rock

NA Degerstrom Inc ....E 509 928-3333
　Spokane Valley (G-12800)

1479 Chemical & Fertilizer Mining

Verdesian Life Science US LLC..............F 919 825-1901
　Pasco (G-7648)

1481 Nonmetallic Minerals Svcs, Except Fuels

American Drilling Corp LLC ....E 509 921-7836
　Spokane Valley (G-12610)
Crossroads Group Inc ....G 206 855-3146
　Everett (G-3430)
Dickson Company....................................D 253 472-4489
　Tacoma (G-13263)

French Man Hills Quarry G 509 346-2111
Othello *(G-7496)*
Geocom Resources Inc G 360 392-2898
Bellingham *(G-1357)*
Gold Reserve Inc G 509 623-1500
Spokane *(G-12276)*
Goldmountain Exploration Corp G 360 332-0905
Blaine *(G-1674)*
Hart Crowser Inc D 206 324-9530
Seattle *(G-10145)*
Kennedy Creek Quarry Inc F 360 426-4743
Shelton *(G-11706)*
Lka Gold Incorporated G 253 514-6661
Gig Harbor *(G-4133)*
Lovitt Mining Company Inc G 509 668-8170
Wenatchee *(G-15046)*
Pacific NW Aggregates Inc G 509 748-9188
Wishram *(G-15167)*
Procon Min & Tunnelling US Ltd F 360 685-4253
Bellingham *(G-1506)*

1499 Miscellaneous Nonmetallic Mining

Axiom Drilling Corp F 509 921-7836
Spokane Valley *(G-12633)*
Caesarstone Usa Inc F 425 251-8668
Kent *(G-4834)*
Distribution Northwest Inc G 206 963-6126
Bothell *(G-1846)*
Goldrich Mining Company F 509 535-7367
Spokane *(G-12277)*
Huntmountain Resources Ltd F 509 290-5659
Liberty Lake *(G-5836)*
Olympic Manganese Mining Co G 360 426-9273
Shelton *(G-11716)*
Society For Mining Metallurgy G 509 922-4063
Spokane Valley *(G-12879)*
West Coast Gemstones Inc G 509 522-4851
College Place *(G-2731)*

20 FOOD AND KINDRED PRODUCTS

2011 Meat Packing Plants

Adalbert & Nagy Sausage Co LLC G 206 356-3305
Issaquah *(G-4378)*
Ahtanum Custom Meats G 509 966-3642
Yakima *(G-15503)*
▲ **Beck Pack Systems Inc** E 425 222-9515
Preston *(G-8024)*
BJ & Bobs Farm Butchering G 360 274-4202
Castle Rock *(G-2338)*
Careks Country Custom Meats G 509 276-2237
Deer Park *(G-2895)*
Conagra Fods Clmbia Base Blnds D 509 544-2111
Pasco *(G-7565)*
Crowd Cow Inc G 717 333-0740
Seattle *(G-9756)*
Cullens Custom Meats G 509 837-0079
Sunnyside *(G-13119)*
Del Fox Custom Meats Inc G 360 629-3723
Stanwood *(G-12965)*
Empire Packing D 360 459-3745
Olympia *(G-7276)*
Erickson Custom Meats G 509 962-6099
Ellensburg *(G-3198)*
▲ **Field Roast Grain Meat Co Spc** C 800 311-9797
Seattle *(G-9989)*
Hormel Foods Corporation G 425 635-0109
Bellevue *(G-948)*
Jahrs European Sausage & Cstm G 509 697-8904
Selah *(G-11591)*
Kapowsin Meats Inc F 253 847-1777
Graham *(G-4229)*
Longhorn Barbecue Prod Ctr E 509 922-0702
Spokane Valley *(G-12778)*
Mason Meat Packing Co G 509 447-3788
Newport *(G-7060)*
Matts Custom Meats G 360 414-1073
Kelso *(G-4537)*
Meat & Bread US Inc G 604 819-1728
Seattle *(G-10513)*
Oberto G 425 251-4563
Renton *(G-8862)*
Owens Meats Inc G 509 674-2530
Cle Elum *(G-2674)*
Patriotic Packing G 360 942-3054
Raymond *(G-8357)*
Prime West Beef Co Inc G 360 306-1831
Ferndale *(G-3891)*
Quick Market Inc G 509 653-2268
Naches *(G-7002)*
Rays Custom Cutting G 509 684-5544
Colville *(G-2772)*
Schenk Packing Co Inc E 360 336-2128
Mount Vernon *(G-6834)*
Smithco Meats Inc E 253 863-5157
Sumner *(G-13100)*
Stewarts Markets Inc E 360 458-2091
Yelm *(G-15746)*
Sugar Mountain Livestock LLC F 206 322-1644
Seattle *(G-11214)*
Sundance Beef Intl Inc G 360 224-2333
Ferndale *(G-3909)*
T L C Custom Meats Inc G 509 488-9953
Othello *(G-7507)*
Tyson Foods Inc A 509 547-7545
Wallula *(G-14912)*
Verns Moses Lake Meats Inc F 509 765-5671
Moses Lake *(G-6756)*
Vincent R Taylor G 509 397-3305
Colfax *(G-2722)*
Washington Agricultural Dev G 509 865-2121
Toppenish *(G-13673)*
▼ **Washington Beef LLC** A 509 865-2121
Toppenish *(G-13674)*

2013 Sausages & Meat Prdts

▲ **Bavarian Meat Products Inc** F 206 448-3540
Seattle *(G-9501)*
Bay City Sausage Co Inc G 360 648-2344
Aberdeen *(G-4)*
Bels International Corporation F 206 722-3365
Seattle *(G-9510)*
Black Diamond Smoked Meats G 541 228-2758
Black Diamond *(G-1645)*
BP Marketing G 509 475-7125
Renton *(G-8764)*
Cascioppo Bros Meats Inc F 206 784-6121
Kirkland *(G-5298)*
Crimson Cove LLC G 360 598-2683
Poulsbo *(G-7956)*
Eldons Sausage Inc G 509 309-3140
Spokane Valley *(G-12690)*
▲ **Field Roast Grain Meat Co Spc** C 800 311-9797
Seattle *(G-9989)*
Friday Harbor House of Jerky G 360 207-9652
Friday Harbor *(G-4046)*
Greenleaf Foods Spc E 206 762-5961
Seattle *(G-10120)*
Greenleaf Foods Spc G 206 762-5961
Seattle *(G-10121)*
Hillshire Brands Company D 253 437-3700
Kent *(G-4942)*
Hillshire Brands Company F 253 395-3444
Kent *(G-4943)*
Innovasian Cuisine Entps Inc E 800 324-5140
Tukwila *(G-13753)*
ISC Inc E 253 395-5465
Kent *(G-4961)*
January Company E 253 872-9919
Kent *(G-4964)*
Kings Command Foods LLC C 425 251-6788
Kent *(G-4977)*
▼ **Longhorn Barbecue Inc** C 509 922-0702
Spokane Valley *(G-12777)*
Longhorn Barbecue Prod Ctr E 509 922-0702
Spokane Valley *(G-12778)*
Mayers Custom Meats Inc G 360 574-2828
Vancouver *(G-14404)*
Northwest Sausage & Deli F 360 736-7760
Centralia *(G-2421)*
▲ **Oberto Snacks Inc** C 253 437-6100
Kent *(G-5041)*
◆ **Oversea Casing Company LLC** E 206 682-6845
Seattle *(G-10722)*
▼ **Sakai Foods America Inc** G 484 494-4322
Seattle *(G-11004)*
Smithco Meats Inc E 253 863-5157
Sumner *(G-13100)*
Smoke Plus Cigar G 425 673-1390
Lynnwood *(G-6200)*
Tillamook Country Smoker LLC G 360 456-2640
Olympia *(G-7407)*
Tyson Foods Inc A 509 547-7545
Wallula *(G-14912)*
Ulis Famous Sausage Inc G 206 839-1000
Seattle *(G-11361)*
Ulis Famous Sausage LLC G 206 839-1000
Seattle *(G-11362)*
Verone Sausage Company G 253 759-7532
Tacoma *(G-13575)*
Voise Susage By Schumacher Inc G 509 982-2956
Odessa *(G-7193)*

2015 Poultry Slaughtering, Dressing & Processing

Dynes Farms Inc E 360 757-4025
Burlington *(G-2154)*
Foster Poultry Farms A 360 425-8957
Kelso *(G-4526)*
Jeff Potter G 206 819-4224
Seattle *(G-10289)*
Lues Debeaking G 360 438-9207
Olympia *(G-7326)*
National Food Corporation D 360 653-2904
Arlington *(G-285)*
National Food Corporation F 509 457-4031
Moxee *(G-6883)*
Perdue Foods LLC G 360 748-9466
Chehalis *(G-2523)*
Perdue Foods LLC F 360 398-2911
Lynden *(G-6046)*
Perdue Foods LLC B 360 424-7947
Mount Vernon *(G-6823)*
Salmon Creek Meats G 360 985-7822
Mossyrock *(G-6766)*

2021 Butter

Balleywood Creamery G 206 920-5173
Seattle *(G-9486)*
Cokedale Creamery LLC G 360 856-1695
Sedro Woolley *(G-11535)*
Cosmic Creamery LLC G 425 633-7742
Kirkland *(G-5314)*
Darigold Inc D 425 392-6463
Issaquah *(G-4402)*
Darigold Inc D 509 489-8600
Spokane *(G-12217)*
Dungeness Valley Creamery G 360 683-0716
Sequim *(G-11630)*
Ethos Bakery LLC G 509 942-8799
Richland *(G-8994)*
Ferndale Creamery Co LLC G 360 255-7062
Ferndale *(G-3842)*

2022 Cheese

Annette Kraft G 501 319-5073
Bellingham *(G-1248)*
Appel Farms LLC F 360 384-4996
Ferndale *(G-3815)*
Bfy Food Group LLC G 425 298-5523
Bellevue *(G-816)*
Black Sheep Creamery G 360 520-3397
Seattle *(G-9538)*
◆ **Good Planet Foods LLC** G 425 449-8134
Bellevue *(G-931)*
Joan F Schleh G 360 424-4112
Mount Vernon *(G-6805)*
Kraft G 509 375-2992
Pasco *(G-7597)*
Kraft Foods G 253 395-4237
Kent *(G-4983)*
Kurt Timmermeister G 206 696-0989
Vashon *(G-14728)*
Kurt Timmermeister G 206 696-0989
Vashon *(G-14729)*
Laurels Crown LLC G 509 860-2510
Wenatchee *(G-15042)*
◆ **Northwest Dairy Association** C 206 284-7220
Seattle *(G-10641)*
Nutradried Food Company LLC D 360 366-4567
Ferndale *(G-3880)*
Omicron Investment Corporation G 360 413-7569
Olympia *(G-7361)*
Port Townsend Lcl Mktplc LLC G 360 732-0696
Chimacum *(G-2613)*
Quillisascut Cheese Co G 509 738-2011
Rice *(G-8960)*
Schreiber Foods Inc C 425 286-6598
Bothell *(G-1899)*
Stephen M Kraft G 509 465-1980
Spokane *(G-12528)*
Washington State University D 509 335-4014
Pullman *(G-8113)*
Willapa Hills Cheese LLC G 360 291-3937
Chehalis *(G-2543)*

2023 Milk, Condensed & Evaporated

25 Bits Inc G 206 861-3836
Kent *(G-4747)*

SIC SECTION 20 FOOD AND KINDRED PRODUCTS

Aloe 2000 .... G 206 420-8785
Seattle (G-9385)
Astamed .... G 206 812-0270
Seattle (G-9445)
▲ Astareal Inc .... E 509 855-4370
Moses Lake (G-6680)
Bharat Ratan LLC .... G 206 458-3322
Renton (G-8755)
BHP Holdings Inc .... F 425 462-8414
Woodinville (G-15190)
Cascade Intgrtive Medicine LLC .... G 425 391-5270
Issaquah (G-4390)
Columbia Nutritional LLC .... C 360 737-9966
Vancouver (G-14135)
◆ Commercial Creamery Co .... D 509 747-4131
Spokane (G-12192)
Commercial Creamery Co Ida Inc .... D 509 747-4131
Spokane (G-12193)
Dairy Queens Vancouver .... E 360 256-7302
Vancouver (G-14164)
Deboer Dairy LLC .... E 360 757-2660
Burlington (G-2151)
Emerald City Smoothie .... G 253 826-6664
Bonney Lake (G-1723)
Evolving Nutrition .... F 425 355-5682
Everett (G-3467)
Gariko LLC .... G 509 933-1821
Ellensburg (G-3201)
IMS Corporation .... G 509 687-8116
Chelan (G-2555)
Nestle Usa Inc .... C 425 844-3201
Carnation (G-2296)
◆ Northwest Dairy Association .... C 206 284-7220
Seattle (G-10641)
Pharma Terra Inc .... G 800 215-3957
Mercer Island (G-6479)
Probi Usa Inc .... G 425 883-9518
Redmond (G-8632)
Pure Health Products LLC .... G 360 688-7034
Lacey (G-5579)
Reesman Co .... G 253 564-7997
Fircrest (G-4004)
Summit Lake Labs LLC .... F 509 738-4313
Kettle Falls (G-5241)
Terato Products LLC .... G 425 702-6365
Redmond (G-8689)
Tntgamble Inc .... E 425 883-9518
Redmond (G-8693)
USA Milk Processing LLC .... G 202 657-5399
Olympia (G-7418)
Washington State University .... D 509 335-4014
Pullman (G-8113)

2024 Ice Cream

A J R Enterprises Inc .... G 253 946-1708
Federal Way (G-3711)
Baskin Robbins 1361 .... G 425 226-3113
Renton (G-8751)
Baskin-Robbins .... G 425 793-3544
Bellevue (G-806)
Cherry De Pon .... G 253 277-1907
Covington (G-2823)
Cherry De Pon .... G 425 226-5246
Renton (G-8771)
Cowboyz .... G 206 793-6831
Tacoma (G-13246)
Dina Helmts .... G 509 521-9866
Pasco (G-7577)
Emerald City Smoothie .... G 253 564-1966
Tacoma (G-13277)
Faith Dairy Inc .... E 253 531-3398
Tacoma (G-13287)
Gariko LLC .... G 509 933-1821
Ellensburg (G-3201)
Hain Refrigerated Foods Inc .... F 425 485-2476
Mountlake Terrace (G-6862)
Heavenly Gelato Inc .... F 360 426-0696
Shelton (G-11699)
Jesus Romero .... G 509 545-9551
Pasco (G-7595)
M-K-D Distributors Inc .... C 425 251-0809
Kent (G-4999)
Marias Hawaiian Snow .... G 509 217-1612
Colbert (G-2711)
Megan Nieforth .... G 509 380-6543
Pasco (G-7602)
Molly Moons Homemade Ice Cream ...... G 206 547-5105
Seattle (G-10557)
▲ Mora LLC .... E 206 855-1112
Poulsbo (G-7985)
Nestle Dreyers Ice Cream Co .... D 425 251-0809
Kent (G-5019)
Paleteria Lanorpeana .... G 509 839-5802
Sunnyside (G-13136)
Paris Gourmet Dessert .... F 206 767-9097
Seattle (G-10756)
Revelations Yogurt LLC .... F 425 744-6012
Edmonds (G-3145)
Seattle Pops .... G 206 714-1354
Shoreline (G-11808)
Snoqualmie Gourmet Ice Cream .... G 360 668-8535
Snohomish (G-11984)
Swirl .... G 425 292-0909
North Bend (G-7126)
Tartberry Incorporated .... G 503 295-2700
Battle Ground (G-743)
Transcold Distribution USA Inc .... G 604 519-0600
Kent (G-5189)
Washington State University .... D 509 335-4014
Pullman (G-8113)
Whidbey Island Ice Cream LLC .... G 425 359-6372
Freeland (G-4039)
Yo Gs Gh .... G 253 858-9647
Gig Harbor (G-4177)
Yo Yakima .... G 509 426-2925
Yakima (G-15721)

2026 Milk

Andersen Dairy Inc .... D 360 687-7171
Battle Ground (G-687)
Auburn Dairy Products Inc .... E 253 833-3400
Auburn (G-381)
Berry Nutty .... G 425 265-1680
Everett (G-3386)
Castle Rock Goat Farm LLC .... G 509 961-5613
Zillah (G-15751)
Country Morning Farms Inc .... E 509 349-2958
Warden (G-14929)
Darigold Inc .... D 509 489-8600
Spokane (G-12217)
Darigold Inc .... B 206 722-2655
Seattle (G-9793)
Darigold Inc .... D 425 392-6463
Issaquah (G-4402)
Faith Dairy Inc .... E 253 531-3398
Tacoma (G-13287)
Finnegan Frost .... G 509 572-2477
Richland (G-8997)
Flying Cow Creamery LLC .... G 360 273-1045
Rochester (G-9132)
Froyo Earth .... G 509 888-7201
Chelan (G-2554)
Froyo Fresh .... G 206 447-4599
Seattle (G-10031)
Go Manna Inc .... G 360 794-7480
Snohomish (G-11914)
Harvest House .... G 509 238-6970
Colbert (G-2707)
Houghton Plaza .... G 425 298-4857
Kirkland (G-5360)
Inland Northwest Dairies LLC .... D 509 489-8600
Spokane (G-12310)
Isaacs Incrdbl Frz Yogurt LLC .... G 509 928-9497
Spokane Valley (G-12747)
Joe Froyo LLC .... G 909 204-1301
Tacoma (G-13361)
Lukens Farms Inc .... G 360 366-4151
Custer (G-2856)
◆ Northwest Dairy Association .... C 206 284-7220
Seattle (G-10641)
Smith Brothers Farms Inc .... E 253 852-1000
Kent (G-5135)
Sno Valley Milk LLC .... F 360 410-8888
Snohomish (G-11979)
Wilcox Farms Inc .... F 360 458-6903
Roy (G-9166)
Yakama Yogert Shack LLC .... G 509 965-5569
Yakima (G-15712)

2032 Canned Specialties

Campbell Soup Company .... B 425 415-2000
Woodinville (G-15204)
Effortless Atms LLC .... G 206 456-4130
Seattle (G-9888)
Kastoria Inc .... G 206 633-4170
Seattle (G-10329)
Kraft Heinz Foods Company .... C 800 255-5750
Kent (G-4984)
Ljro Inc .... F 360 693-2443
Vancouver (G-14380)
Salsa Mania LLC .... G 360 432-9240
Shelton (G-11729)
Sheng Mian North America LLC .... G 215 519-5895
Bellevue (G-1128)
Texas Johns .... E 509 659-1402
Ritzville (G-9123)

2033 Canned Fruits, Vegetables & Preserves

Allan Bros Inc .... D 509 653-2625
Naches (G-6993)
Artisanal Goods Northwest LLC .... G 503 803-7228
Washougal (G-14944)
Backyard Bounty Co-Op .... G 360 574-6937
Ridgefield (G-9065)
Blue Cottage Jams .... G 425 836-9580
Redmond (G-8406)
Campbell Soup Company .... B 425 415-2000
Woodinville (G-15204)
Canter-Berry Farms .... G 253 939-2706
Auburn (G-400)
Cindy Lous Artisan Jams .... G 360 873-4178
Marblemount (G-6304)
▲ Coventry Vale Winery Inc .... E 509 882-4100
Grandview (G-4246)
Dairy Export Co Inc .... G 206 284-7220
Seattle (G-9786)
Farm Breeze International LLC .... G 253 365-0542
Tacoma (G-13291)
Fruit Packers Supply .... G 509 888-3059
Wenatchee (G-15033)
G Wolf Enterprises Inc .... G 360 793-2988
Gold Bar (G-4188)
General Mills Inc .... E 763 764-7600
Sedro Woolley (G-11539)
J M Smucker Company .... E 509 882-1530
Grandview (G-4248)
◆ Johnson Concentrates Inc .... E 509 837-4600
Sunnyside (G-13130)
Johnson Foods Inc .... E 509 837-4188
Sunnyside (G-13131)
▼ Longhorn Barbecue Inc .... C 509 922-0702
Spokane Valley (G-12777)
▼ Maika Foods LLC .... G 310 893-7050
Spokane (G-12380)
McNerney Enterprises LLC .... G 206 850-5023
Sammamish (G-9232)
Micks Peppourri Inc .... G 509 966-2328
Yakima (G-15620)
Ocean Spray Cranberries Inc .... D 360 648-2515
Aberdeen (G-26)
Odwalla Inc .... E 206 242-8519
Tukwila (G-13782)
Oly Kraut LLC .... G 360 561-4532
Olympia (G-7352)
Pacific Prepac Inc .... E 360 653-1661
Marysville (G-6366)
Pheasant Brothers LLC .... G 509 539-5899
Benton City (G-1623)
Quincy Fresh Fruit LLC .... F 509 787-7100
Quincy (G-8308)
Rose Tucker .... G 509 837-8701
Sunnyside (G-13139)
Seneca Foods Corporation .... C 509 382-8323
Dayton (G-2884)
Simchuk Karene .... G 509 238-2830
Mead (G-6436)
Snipahs LLC .... G 910 922-4693
Gold Bar (G-4191)
Starvation Alley Socia .... G 503 440-0970
Long Beach (G-5878)
Sugarcrush Hmmade Jams Jellies .... G 253 830-4155
Bonney Lake (G-1741)
◆ Svz USA Washington Inc .... E 509 488-6563
Othello (G-7506)
Tenacious Hgs Jams .... G 360 747-4080
Longview (G-5959)
◆ Tree Top Inc .... A 509 697-7251
Selah (G-11600)
Tree Top Inc .... D 509 782-6809
Cashmere (G-2331)
Tree Top Inc .... D 509 698-1447
Selah (G-11601)
Tree Top Inc .... D 509 698-1432
Selah (G-11602)
Tree Top Inc .... C 509 786-2926
Prosser (G-8069)
Tree Top Inc .... C 509 663-8583
Wenatchee (G-15082)
Underwood Fruit & Whse Co LLC .... G 509 457-6177
Yakima (G-15700)

S I C

Employee Codes: A=Over 500 employees, B=251-500
C=101-250, D=51-100, E=20-50, F=10-19, G=2-9
2019 Washington
Manufacturers Register
533

20 FOOD AND KINDRED PRODUCTS

Vital Juice Co Inc ....E 206 258-4203
　Seattle *(G-11428)*
Welch Foods Inc A Cooperative ....C 509 582-1010
　Kennewick *(G-4744)*
Welch Foods Inc A Cooperative ....E 509 882-1711
　Grandview *(G-4257)*
Welch Foods Inc A Cooperative ....G 509 882-3112
　Grandview *(G-4258)*

2034 Dried Fruits, Vegetables & Soup

◆ Ames International Inc ....D 253 946-4779
　Fife *(G-3932)*
Basic American Inc ....C 509 765-8601
　Moses Lake *(G-6684)*
Basic American Inc ....C 509 765-7807
　Moses Lake *(G-6685)*
Blue Bird Inc ....F 509 486-2160
　Tonasket *(G-13646)*
▲ Cherry Chukar Company ....E 509 786-2055
　Prosser *(G-8032)*
Country Harvest Soup ....G 509 535-8357
　Spokane *(G-12202)*
Dodson Rd Orchard LLC ....D 509 787-3537
　Quincy *(G-8296)*
Double Dutch LLC ....G 509 837-6539
　Sunnyside *(G-13120)*
Fortun Foods Inc ....F 425 827-1977
　Kirkland *(G-5342)*
Lamb Weston Inc ....A 509 547-8851
　Pasco *(G-7598)*
McCain Foods Usa Inc ....A 509 488-9611
　Othello *(G-7502)*
Mountain Valley Products Inc ....E 509 837-8084
　Sunnyside *(G-13134)*
Mutiny Bay Blues LLC ....G 360 678-4315
　Freeland *(G-4033)*
Newly Weds Foods Inc ....D 253 584-9270
　Lakewood *(G-5741)*
▼ Northwest Pea & Bean Company .....F 509 534-3821
　Spokane Valley *(G-12808)*
Oregon Potato Company ....E 509 547-8772
　Pasco *(G-7608)*
Oregon Potato Company ....D 509 349-8803
　Warden *(G-14935)*
▼ Oregon Potato Company ....G 509 545-4545
　Pasco *(G-7609)*
◆ Royal Ridge Frt Cold Stor LLC ....D 509 346-1520
　Royal City *(G-9174)*
Seneca Foods Corporation ....E 509 457-1089
　Yakima *(G-15671)*
Sun River Foods Inc ....F 509 249-0820
　Yakima *(G-15687)*
Tree Top Inc ....C 509 663-8583
　Wenatchee *(G-15082)*
◆ Tree Top Inc ....A 509 697-7251
　Selah *(G-11600)*
Tree Top Inc ....D 509 698-1432
　Selah *(G-11602)*
Washington Potato Company Inc ....D 509 349-8803
　Warden *(G-14938)*
▲ Wyckoff Farms Incorporated ....E 509 882-3934
　Grandview *(G-4259)*

2035 Pickled Fruits, Vegetables, Sauces & Dressings

Blue Bus Cultured Foods LLC ....G 541 399-4141
　Bingen *(G-1633)*
De Marss LLC ....G 425 218-3454
　Bellevue *(G-876)*
Flying Dog Entertainment LLC ....G 206 372-5553
　Kirkland *(G-5340)*
Foster Family Farm ....D 509 543-9330
　Pasco *(G-7582)*
Garden Fresh Gourmet Foods Inc ......C 425 407-6400
　Everett *(G-3491)*
General Mills Inc ....E 763 764-7600
　Sedro Woolley *(G-11539)*
How Pickle Got Out of A Jam ....G 206 940-6532
　Seattle *(G-10187)*
Jud Calvary Inc ....G 708 323-8758
　Redmond *(G-8524)*
▲ Kof Enterprises LLC ....F 206 328-2972
　Seattle *(G-10351)*
Leonhards Pickles LLC ....G 509 280-4267
　Spokane *(G-12361)*
Longhorn Barbecue Prod Ctr ....E 509 922-0702
　Spokane Valley *(G-12778)*
Mad Cat Salsa ....G 360 647-0456
　Bellingham *(G-1419)*

Ocean Spray Cranberries Inc ....D 360 648-2515
　Aberdeen *(G-26)*
▼ Onefarstar LLC ....G 425 999-4894
　Bellevue *(G-1049)*
Rikki Usa Inc ....F 425 881-6881
　Redmond *(G-8651)*
Sheng Mian North America LLC ....G 215 519-5895
　Bellevue *(G-1128)*
Welch Foods Inc A Cooperative ....C 509 582-1010
　Kennewick *(G-4744)*
Wildeberry LLC ....G 360 222-3626
　Greenbank *(G-4311)*
Wm Bolthouse Farms Inc ....G 509 894-4460
　Prosser *(G-8079)*

2037 Frozen Fruits, Juices & Vegetables

Birds Eye Foods Inc ....G 253 833-0255
　Auburn *(G-393)*
◆ Clarks Berry Farm Inc ....E 360 354-1294
　Lynden *(G-6009)*
Cliffstar LLC ....D 509 522-8608
　Walla Walla *(G-14786)*
◆ Crf Frozen Foods LLC ....E 509 542-0018
　Pasco *(G-7570)*
David Lynn Smoothies LLC ....G 907 242-4564
　Redmond *(G-8435)*
Drr Fruit Products Co Inc ....E 509 836-2051
　Sunnyside *(G-13121)*
◆ Firestone Pacific Foods Inc ....D 360 695-9484
　Vancouver *(G-14232)*
Fresh Fruit Juice LLC ....G 206 329-5979
　Seattle *(G-10027)*
General Mills Inc ....E 763 764-7600
　Sedro Woolley *(G-11539)*
Graces Kitchen Inc ....G 425 635-4609
　Bellevue *(G-932)*
Investure - Wa Inc ....D 360 354-6574
　Lynden *(G-6023)*
Jake Maberry Packing Inc ....G 206 366-5411
　Custer *(G-2855)*
◆ Johnson Concentrates Inc ....E 509 837-4600
　Sunnyside *(G-13130)*
JR Simplot Company ....E 509 765-5663
　Othello *(G-7499)*
JR Simplot Company ....E 509 765-3443
　Moses Lake *(G-6719)*
Lamb Weston Inc ....G 509 375-4181
　Richland *(G-9020)*
Lamb Weston Inc ....B 509 735-4651
　Kennewick *(G-4685)*
Lamb Weston Inc ....G 509 713-7200
　Richland *(G-9021)*
Lamb Weston Holdings Inc ....C 509 786-2700
　Prosser *(G-8048)*
Lamb Weston Inc ....A 509 547-8851
　Pasco *(G-7598)*
Lamb Weston Sales Inc ....C 509 735-4651
　Kennewick *(G-4686)*
McCain Foods Usa Inc ....A 509 488-9611
　Othello *(G-7502)*
◆ Milne Fruit Products Inc ....D 509 786-0019
　Prosser *(G-8059)*
National Frozen Foods Corp ....C 360 748-9963
　Chehalis *(G-2516)*
◆ National Frozen Foods Corp ....A 206 322-8900
　Seattle *(G-10588)*
National Frozen Foods Corp ....E 509 766-0793
　Moses Lake *(G-6730)*
▼ Naumes Concentrates Inc ....E 509 877-8882
　Wapato *(G-14921)*
Noon International LLC ....F 206 283-8400
　Seattle *(G-10619)*
Ocean Spray Cranberries Inc ....D 360 648-2515
　Aberdeen *(G-26)*
Ochoa AG Unlimited Foods Inc ....C 509 349-2210
　Warden *(G-14934)*
Pacific Northwest Packers Inc ....E 360 354-0776
　Lynden *(G-6044)*
▼ Phillippi Fruit Co Inc ....E 509 662-8522
　Wenatchee *(G-15062)*
▲ Quincy Foods LLC ....G 509 787-4521
　Quincy *(G-8307)*
◆ Royal Ridge Frt Cold Stor LLC ....D 509 346-1520
　Royal City *(G-9174)*
Seneca Foods Corporation ....C 509 382-8323
　Dayton *(G-2884)*
Six LLC ....G 206 466-5186
　Seattle *(G-11123)*
Smoothie Essentials ....G 360 452-8060
　Port Angeles *(G-7744)*

Smoothie Ventures LLC ....G 509 315-4492
　Spokane Valley *(G-12877)*
Solutions With Innovation ....G 253 872-0783
　Kent *(G-5138)*
Sun-Rype Products (usa) Inc ....D 509 697-7292
　Selah *(G-11598)*
Sunfresh Foods Inc ....G 206 764-0940
　Seattle *(G-11219)*
Sunshine Smoothie Inc ....G 425 497-9211
　Auburn *(G-574)*
Super Smoothie ....G 253 671-8883
　Tacoma *(G-13529)*
Tree Top Inc ....C 509 786-2926
　Prosser *(G-8069)*
Tree Top Inc ....C 509 663-8583
　Wenatchee *(G-15082)*
◆ Tree Top Inc ....A 509 697-7251
　Selah *(G-11600)*
▼ Twin City Foods Inc ....D 206 515-2400
　Stanwood *(G-12998)*
Twin City Foods Inc ....C 509 962-9806
　Ellensburg *(G-3235)*
Twin City Foods Inc ....C 509 346-1483
　Royal City *(G-9177)*
Twin City Foods Inc ....B 509 546-0850
　Pasco *(G-7645)*
Twin City Foods Inc ....B 509 786-2700
　Prosser *(G-8071)*
◆ Valley Processing Inc ....D 509 837-8084
　Sunnyside *(G-13148)*
Washington Fruit & Produce Co ....E 509 932-7981
　Quincy *(G-8310)*
Welch Foods Inc A Cooperative ....G 509 882-3112
　Grandview *(G-4258)*
▲ Willow Wind Organic Farms Inc .....G 509 796-4006
　Ford *(G-4007)*
▲ Wyckoff Farms Incorporated ....E 509 882-3934
　Grandview *(G-4259)*

2038 Frozen Specialties

AC Larocco Pizza Co ....G 509 924-9113
　Spokane Valley *(G-12597)*
Campbell Soup Company ....B 425 415-2000
　Woodinville *(G-15204)*
▼ Continental Mills Inc ....C 206 816-7000
　Tukwila *(G-13716)*
Ed Bohl ....G 360 264-5822
　Tenino *(G-13618)*
Ivars Inc ....E 425 493-1402
　Mukilteo *(G-6945)*
January Company ....E 253 872-9919
　Kent *(G-4964)*
Lamb Weston Inc ....A 509 547-8851
　Pasco *(G-7598)*
Luvo Usa Llc ....G 604 730-0387
　Blaine *(G-1681)*
Man Pies ....G 360 201-4294
　Bellingham *(G-1421)*
McCain Foods Usa Inc ....A 509 488-9611
　Othello *(G-7502)*
Michael Eckles ....G 253 568-2934
　Tacoma *(G-13411)*
National Frozen Foods Corp ....C 360 748-9963
　Chehalis *(G-2516)*
▲ Northwest Frozen LLC ....E 206 388-3551
　Seattle *(G-10645)*
P&Js Waffle Delight ....G 510 335-5393
　Tacoma *(G-13448)*
▼ Sakai Foods America Inc ....G 484 494-4322
　Seattle *(G-11004)*

2041 Flour, Grain Milling

AC Larocco Pizza Co ....G 509 924-9113
　Spokane Valley *(G-12597)*
ADM Milling Co ....E 509 535-2995
　Spokane *(G-12099)*
ADM Milling Co ....E 509 534-2636
　Spokane *(G-12100)*
ADM Milling Co ....F 509 235-6216
　Cheney *(G-2574)*
ADM Milling Co ....G 509 534-2636
　Spokane *(G-12101)*
Archer-Daniels-Midland Company ....G 509 533-9632
　Spokane *(G-12117)*
Archer-Daniels-Midland Company ....F 509 754-5266
　Ephrata *(G-3331)*
Archer-Daniels-Midland Company ....G 509 534-2636
　Spokane Valley *(G-12624)*
Cascade Organic Flour LLC ....F 509 855-7450
　Royal City *(G-9168)*

SIC SECTION 20 FOOD AND KINDRED PRODUCTS

▲ Ener-G Foods Inc .... E 206 767-3928
Seattle *(G-9922)*
Farnworth Group .... G 425 894-8643
Kirkland *(G-5336)*
▲ Field Roast Grain Meat Co Spc .... C 800 311-9797
Seattle *(G-9989)*
Gateway Milling LLC .... G 509 639-2431
Almira *(G-85)*
GF Blends Inc .... G 509 375-0909
Richland *(G-9001)*
Golden Hills Brewing Co .... G 509 389-6253
Airway Heights *(G-53)*
Grain Craft Inc .... D 206 898-3079
Seattle *(G-10104)*
Highland Milling LLC .... G 360 901-8332
Vancouver *(G-14297)*
J&R Hennings Inc .... G 509 659-0102
Sprague *(G-12948)*
Kaniksu Feeds Inc .... G 509 406-1995
Deer Park *(G-2907)*
Kemason Inc .... G 360 757-9947
Burlington *(G-2166)*
Newly Weds Foods Inc .... D 253 584-9270
Lakewood *(G-5741)*
San Gennaro Foods Inc .... F 253 872-1900
Kent *(G-5115)*
Seattle Biscuit Company LLC .... G 206 327-2940
Seattle *(G-11046)*
Todd Imeson .... G 509 397-6570
Colfax *(G-2721)*

2043 Cereal Breakfast Foods

206 Foods LLC .... G 206 387-5881
Shoreline *(G-11752)*
Grain Craft Inc .... D 206 898-3079
Seattle *(G-10104)*
Kellogg Company .... E 253 872-3826
Kent *(G-4974)*
Mountain Muesli LLC .... G 253 426-8092
Tacoma *(G-13421)*
Natures Path Foods USA Inc .... E 360 332-1111
Blaine *(G-1686)*
Natures Path Foods USA Inc .... D 360 603-7200
Blaine *(G-1687)*
Sherpa Foods SPC .... F 425 243-9278
Newcastle *(G-7039)*
Tree Top Inc .... D 509 698-1432
Selah *(G-11602)*
Watford Tanikka .... G 360 499-6327
Lacey *(G-5601)*

2045 Flour, Blended & Prepared

▼ Continental Mills Inc .... C 206 816-7000
Tukwila *(G-13716)*
Continental Mills Inc .... C 206 816-7799
Kent *(G-4864)*
Dawn Food Products Inc .... D 206 763-1711
Seattle *(G-9804)*
Dawn Food Products Inc .... E 206 623-7740
Seattle *(G-9803)*
Gingerbread Factory .... G 509 548-6592
Leavenworth *(G-5803)*
▲ Kof Enterprises LLC .... F 206 328-2972
Seattle *(G-10351)*
Newly Weds Foods Inc .... D 253 584-9270
Lakewood *(G-5741)*
▼ Pizza Blends LLC .... F 800 826-1200
Bellevue *(G-1076)*
▲ T R Rizzuto Pizza Crust Inc .... D 509 536-9268
Spokane *(G-12541)*
Yum Yum Donut Shops Inc .... G 360 423-0150
Longview *(G-5970)*

2046 Wet Corn Milling

Central Wash Corn Prcssors Inc .... G 509 623-1144
Spokane *(G-12176)*
David P Rush .... G 509 865-5338
Zillah *(G-15752)*
Ingredion Incorporated .... G 509 375-1261
Richland *(G-9009)*
Penford Products Co .... E 509 375-1261
Richland *(G-9034)*

2047 Dog & Cat Food

Arrow Reliance Inc .... F 206 324-7387
Tukwila *(G-13692)*
Blue Dog Bakery Group Inc .... F 206 323-6958
Seattle *(G-9547)*
Good Pet Food Inc .... G 310 430-3833
Seattle *(G-10099)*
▲ Himalayan Corporation .... D 425 322-4295
Mukilteo *(G-6934)*
Miss Mags LLC .... G 208 301-0549
Palouse *(G-7545)*
Nancy Baer .... G 360 668-0350
Snohomish *(G-11949)*
Natural Pet Pantry .... G 206 762-5575
Seattle *(G-10593)*
Northwest Farm Food Coop .... E 360 757-4225
Burlington *(G-2175)*
▼ Northwest Pet Products Inc .... E 360 225-8855
Woodland *(G-15452)*
▲ Petforia LLC .... G 425 945-2300
Bellevue *(G-1072)*
Puddles Barkery LLC .... G 206 495-3072
Seattle *(G-10882)*
Wet Noses Natural Dog Treat Co .... E 360 794-7950
Monroe *(G-6636)*

2048 Prepared Feeds For Animals & Fowls

Agrex Inc .... E 509 787-4595
Ephrata *(G-3330)*
Agriaccess Inc .... G 425 806-9356
Bothell *(G-1817)*
Arrow Reliance Inc .... F 206 324-7387
Tukwila *(G-13692)*
Baker Commodities Inc .... D 206 243-4781
Seattle *(G-9478)*
Baker Commodities Inc .... F 509 837-8686
Grandview *(G-4245)*
Bear Inc .... G 253 851-2575
Gig Harbor *(G-4078)*
Bio-Tope Research Inc .... G 509 684-1512
Colville *(G-2739)*
Bio-Tope Research Inc .... G 509 684-1154
Colville *(G-2740)*
Cargill Incorporated .... F 360 757-4012
Burlington *(G-2140)*
Cargill Incorporated .... G 509 854-1035
Granger *(G-4260)*
Cargill Incorporated .... E 360 656-5784
Ferndale *(G-3823)*
Coenzyme-A Technologies Inc .... F 425 438-8586
Lynnwood *(G-6094)*
Cooperative AG Producers Inc .... E 509 523-3032
Rosalia *(G-9154)*
Country Store .... G 509 534-1412
Spokane Valley *(G-12667)*
Deyoungs Farm and Garden .... E 425 483-9600
Woodinville *(G-15225)*
Dr Dons Fishfood LLC .... G 360 533-6620
Aberdeen *(G-8)*
Eh Enterprises Management Inc .... F 206 596-8600
Seattle *(G-9889)*
Elenbaas Company Inc .... E 360 354-3577
Lynden *(G-6014)*
Epl Feed LLC .... G 360 988-5811
Everson *(G-3674)*
Epl Feed LLC .... E 360 988-5811
Sumas *(G-13044)*
Fat-Cat Fish LLC .... E 360 715-1994
Bellingham *(G-1343)*
Feed Commodities LLC .... F 626 799-1196
Tacoma *(G-13293)*
Global Harvest Foods Ltd .... G 509 466-0539
Mead *(G-6428)*
Global Harvest Foods Ltd .... G 206 957-1350
Tukwila *(G-13741)*
▲ Global Harvest Foods Ltd .... G 206 957-1350
Tukwila *(G-13742)*
Grain Craft Inc .... D 206 898-3079
Seattle *(G-10104)*
Iron Horse Hay & Feed .... G 425 432-0636
Maple Valley *(G-6277)*
John McLean Seed Co .... G 509 632-8709
Coulee City *(G-2803)*
Kritter Kookies Ltd .... G 509 233-8414
Loon Lake *(G-5975)*
La Belle Associates Inc .... F 360 671-5122
Bellingham *(G-1400)*
Land OLakes Inc .... F 425 653-4200
Bellevue *(G-976)*
Land OLakes Inc .... F 509 488-5208
Othello *(G-7501)*
Land OLakes Inc .... G 360 592-5115
Everson *(G-3681)*
▲ Lenroc Co .... F 509 754-5266
Ephrata *(G-3341)*
Luna Lactation .... G 360 693-7616
Vancouver *(G-14387)*
Mid-Valley Milling Inc .... G 509 786-1300
Prosser *(G-8056)*
Mmusa Inc .... G 360 306-5383
Lynnwood *(G-6165)*
National Food Corporation .... G 360 435-9207
Arlington *(G-286)*
Pautzke Bait Co Inc .... G 509 925-6154
Ellensburg *(G-3218)*
Purina Animal Nutrition LLC .... G 425 653-4238
Bellevue *(G-1088)*
Purina Mills LLC .... E 509 534-0594
Spokane *(G-12460)*
Quality Liquid Feeds Inc .... G 509 854-2311
Granger *(G-4263)*
Raw Advantage Inc .... G 509 738-3344
Kettle Falls *(G-5240)*
Rietdyks Milling Company .... G 360 887-8874
Ridgefield *(G-9108)*
◆ Sage Hill Northwest Inc .... F 509 269-4966
Mesa *(G-6495)*
Scratch and Peck LLC .... E 360 318-7585
Burlington *(G-2186)*
Seed Factory Northwest Inc .... G 253 395-8813
Kent *(G-5126)*
Standard Nutrition Company .... G 509 839-3500
Sunnyside *(G-13143)*
Tastebud Fusion Inc .... E 253 826-8700
Seattle *(G-11272)*
Thomas Products LLC .... G 253 678-8391
Bellingham *(G-1569)*
Valcom Inc .... G 509 865-5511
Buena *(G-2081)*
Washington Haykingdom Inc .... G 509 925-7000
Ellensburg *(G-3237)*
Wet Noses Natural Dog Treat Co .... E 360 794-7950
Monroe *(G-6636)*
▲ Wolfkill Feed & Fert Corp .... F 360 794-7065
Monroe *(G-6639)*
X-Cel Feeds Inc .... E 253 472-5140
Tacoma *(G-13603)*

2051 Bread, Bakery Prdts Exc Cookies & Crackers

An-Xuyen Bakery Co .... G 253 887-7823
Auburn *(G-375)*
Anjou Bakery and Catering .... G 509 782-4360
Cashmere *(G-2314)*
Anne & Mollys Inc .... D 253 872-8390
Kent *(G-4785)*
Artisan Baking Company .... G 206 240-4713
Seattle *(G-9440)*
Au Gavroche Inc .... G 206 284-8770
Seattle *(G-9461)*
Baked LLC .... G 206 307-4847
Seattle *(G-9477)*
Baker Boys Northwest LLC .... G 253 383-3113
Tacoma *(G-13188)*
Barn Owl Bakery Inc .... G 360 468-3492
Lopez Island *(G-5979)*
Berry Haven LLC .... G 509 521-4902
Pasco *(G-7553)*
Bimbo Bakeries Usa Inc .... F 509 452-6293
Yakima *(G-15521)*
Bimbo Bakeries Usa Inc .... F 509 469-3707
Union Gap *(G-13923)*
Bimbo Bakeries Usa Inc .... F 509 662-4731
Wenatchee *(G-15013)*
Bimbo Bakeries Usa Inc .... E 425 415-6745
Woodinville *(G-15191)*
Bimbo Bakeries Usa Inc .... F 509 688-3966
Spokane Valley *(G-12639)*
Bimbo Bakery USA .... G 425 347-3900
Everett *(G-3388)*
Bread Garden Ltd .... E 253 838-1639
Auburn *(G-396)*
Brown Sugar Baking Company LLC .... G 202 558-8422
Seattle *(G-9590)*
Cake Time Unque Tste Sweet LLC .... G 253 886-9366
Dupont *(G-2956)*
Campbell Soup Company .... B 425 415-2000
Woodinville *(G-15204)*
CCS Baking Co .... G 206 200-5195
Lake Stevens *(G-5637)*
Celebrity Bakery & Cafe .... G 253 627-4773
Tacoma *(G-13229)*
Choukette .... G 206 466-6906
Seattle *(G-9680)*

SIC

20 FOOD AND KINDRED PRODUCTS SIC SECTION

Chuckanut Bay Foods LLC ... E ... 360 380-1908
Blaine (G-1666)
Companion Baking LLC ... G ... 206 856-4080
Seattle (G-9722)
Cookie Fairy ... G ... 360 568-0868
Snohomish (G-11891)
Cupcakes of Auburn ... G ... 253 733-5547
Auburn (G-419)
D & N Farms Partnership ... G ... 509 771-1714
Moses Lake (G-6702)
D Floured LLC ... F ... 206 395-4623
Seattle (G-9781)
Donut Star Inc ... G ... 253 833-2980
Auburn (G-428)
▲ Ener-G Foods Inc ... E ... 206 767-3928
Seattle (G-9922)
Ever Green Donuts ... G ... 425 673-5331
Lynnwood (G-6117)
Fairlight Bakery Inc ... F ... 360 576-8587
Vancouver (G-14220)
Flax 4 Life ... G ... 360 715-1944
Bellingham (G-1349)
Flowers Bkg Co Thomasville Inc ... G ... 253 433-4455
Kent (G-4912)
Fresh Flours ... G ... 206 297-3300
Seattle (G-10026)
Frosty Bay Seafoods LLC ... G ... 360 387-7685
Camano Island (G-2213)
Gais Bakery ... G ... 425 743-2460
Lynnwood (G-6123)
Grand Central Bakery Inc ... D ... 206 768-0320
Seattle (G-10106)
Great Harvest Bread Co Inc ... E ... 509 535-1146
Spokane (G-12281)
Hancocks Bakery ... G ... 425 885-3780
Redmond (G-8487)
Happy Donut ... G ... 253 852-3286
Kent (G-4932)
Henrys Donuts ... G ... 360 653-4044
Marysville (G-6344)
Henrys Donuts ... F ... 425 258-6887
Everett (G-3509)
House of Rising Buns ... G ... 360 718-8330
Vancouver (G-14304)
Itty Bitty Baking Company LLC ... G ... 206 715-6134
Bothell (G-1868)
Jenny Maes Gluten-Free Goodies ... G ... 509 833-5096
Yakima (G-15600)
Just American Desserts ... G ... 509 927-2253
Spokane Valley (G-12757)
Kotelnikov Zinaida ... G ... 206 728-6195
Seattle (G-10357)
Krispy Kreme Doughnuts ... G ... 206 316-7090
Seattle (G-10358)
Kylie BS Pastry Case LLC ... G ... 206 935-6335
Kent (G-4985)
L M Cupcakes LLC ... G ... 425 427-9558
Issaquah (G-4436)
La Waffletz LLC ... G ... 206 432-7548
Federal Way (G-3750)
Lattins Country Cider ... E ... 360 491-7328
Olympia (G-7319)
Laval ... G ... 360 491-8118
Olympia (G-7320)
▲ Lawrence Milner ... G ... 360 860-1924
Seattle (G-10385)
Les Boulangers Associes Inc ... E ... 206 241-9343
Seatac (G-9288)
Lupitas ... G ... 253 838-6132
Federal Way (G-3754)
M and J Distribution ... G ... 360 455-4675
Olympia (G-7327)
Maplehurst Bakeries LLC ... D ... 253 872-7300
Kent (G-5004)
Masons Cheesecake Co LLC ... G ... 206 602-4563
Federal Way (G-3756)
Mc Gavins Bakery ... G ... 360 373-2414
Bremerton (G-1977)
Miss Mfftts Mystcal Cpckes LLC ... G ... 360 890-4403
Olympia (G-7341)
Mount Bakery ... G ... 360 715-2195
Bellingham (G-1445)
New Sage Bakery LLC ... G ... 208 596-5331
Uniontown (G-13957)
Northwest Baking Ltd Partnr ... D ... 253 863-0373
Sumner (G-13089)
Olsons Baking Company LLC ... C ... 425 774-9164
Lynnwood (G-6172)
Ono Cakes and Delights ... G ... 206 257-9046
Seattle (G-10703)
Oroweat ... G ... 253 872-8237
Kent (G-5049)
Pacific Wholesale Banner & Sup ... G ... 509 487-4189
Spokane (G-12427)
Pasteleria Del Castillo ... G ... 206 242-6247
Seattle (G-10762)
Petite Chat LLC ... G ... 509 468-2720
Spokane (G-12438)
Pigs & Angels Inc ... F ... 360 293-4053
Anacortes (G-161)
Pike Place Bagel Bakery Inc ... F ... 206 382-4297
Seattle (G-10806)
Pin Hsiao & Associates LLC ... E ... 253 863-0337
Sumner (G-13094)
Pin Hsiao & Associates LLC ... F ... 206 818-0155
Seattle (G-10808)
Pin Hsiao & Associates LLC ... G ... 425 637-3357
Redmond (G-8622)
Piper 2600 Investments LLC ... G ... 971 409-7596
Ridgefield (G-9102)
Real Love Cupcakes ... G ... 206 849-9688
Tacoma (G-13492)
Rocket Bakery Inc ... G ... 509 462-2345
Spokane Valley (G-12854)
Rolln Dough Ltd ... E ... 206 763-4300
Kent (G-5105)
S & W Management Co Inc ... E ... 425 771-6850
Lynnwood (G-6191)
San Juan Salsa Co ... G ... 360 435-2100
Arlington (G-319)
Savoy Truffle ... G ... 206 762-7411
Seattle (G-11021)
Schwartz Brothers Restaurants ... C ... 206 623-3134
Renton (G-8906)
Schwartz Brothers Restaurants ... C ... 206 623-3134
Seattle (G-11030)
Simply Sweet Cupcakes ... G ... 360 568-8600
Snohomish (G-11976)
Sister Souls Gluten Free Bkg ... G ... 206 909-9054
Seattle (G-11119)
Slays Poulsbo Bakery Inc ... E ... 360 779-2798
Poulsbo (G-8001)
Sparkadoodle Baking Co LLC ... G ... 253 224-0255
Spanaway (G-12075)
Stanwood Cupcakes LLC ... G ... 360 926-8241
Stanwood (G-12993)
Sunrise Bagels & More Inc ... F ... 360 254-1012
Vancouver (G-14616)
Sweet Dahlia Baking LLC ... G ... 206 201-3297
Bainbridge Island (G-675)
Sweet Sanity ... G ... 425 212-7490
Seattle (G-11236)
Taste of Heaven Baking LLC ... G ... 509 786-3657
Prosser (G-8067)
Tower Mountain Products ... G ... 509 448-4000
Spokane (G-12564)
Tree-Top Baking ... G ... 360 720-1937
Clinton (G-2701)
Twirl Cafe ... G ... 206 283-4552
Seattle (G-11351)
United States Bakery ... A ... 206 726-7535
Seattle (G-11373)
United States Bakery ... G ... 509 684-6976
Colville (G-2778)
United States Bakery ... B ... 509 535-7726
Spokane Valley (G-12920)
United States Bakery ... C ... 206 682-2244
Seattle (G-11374)
Watford Tanikka ... G ... 360 499-6327
Lacey (G-5601)
▲ Wilkinson Group LLC ... F ... 509 529-5800
Walla Walla (G-14903)
▲ World Wide Gourmet Foods Inc ... F ... 360 668-9404
Woodinville (G-15410)
Yippie-Pie-Yay ... G ... 206 227-9665
Seattle (G-11511)
Yum Yum Donut Shops Inc ... G ... 360 423-0150
Longview (G-5970)

2052 Cookies & Crackers

Ana Oven ... G ... 661 878-4277
Tacoma (G-13170)
Bake Works Inc ... E ... 360 213-2001
Vancouver (G-14054)
▲ Biscottea Baking Company LLC ... G ... 206 695-2614
Seattle (G-9533)
Bite ME Inc ... E ... 253 244-7194
Lakewood (G-5703)
Brown Sugar Baking Company LLC ... G ... 202 558-8422
Seattle (G-9590)
Campbell Soup Company ... B ... 425 415-2000
Woodinville (G-15204)
▼ Elkins Distribution Inc ... G ... 206 241-0333
Seattle (G-9898)
▲ Ener-G Foods Inc ... E ... 206 767-3928
Seattle (G-9922)
Entenmanns Oroweat Foods ... F ... 360 475-8283
Bremerton (G-1952)
Evas Crackers LLC ... G ... 206 353-5691
Seattle (G-9944)
Fairlight Bakery Inc ... F ... 360 576-8587
Vancouver (G-14220)
Gelatello Inc ... G ... 425 214-1267
Federal Way (G-3740)
Indulge LLC ... G ... 360 589-7226
Richland (G-9008)
▲ Kusher LLC ... G ... 800 445-0655
Fife (G-3963)
Kusina Fillipina ... G ... 206 322-9433
Seattle (G-10365)
▲ Madrona Specialty Foods LLC ... E ... 206 903-0500
Seattle (G-10465)
Nancy Zwieback ... G ... 206 306-0411
Seattle (G-10584)
Pacific NW Cookie Co LLC ... G ... 360 280-4179
Chehalis (G-2519)
Schwartz Brothers Restaurants ... C ... 206 623-3134
Renton (G-8906)
Slays Poulsbo Bakery Inc ... E ... 360 779-2798
Poulsbo (G-8001)
Snohomish Bakery & CAF ... G ... 360 568-1682
Snohomish (G-11981)
Sugar & Stamp ... G ... 404 944-1354
Seattle (G-11213)
▲ Sunne Group Ltd Inc ... G ... 253 839-5240
Federal Way (G-3792)
Sunrise Bagels & More Inc ... F ... 360 254-1012
Vancouver (G-14616)
▲ Tsue Chong Co Inc ... E ... 206 623-0801
Seattle (G-11346)

2053 Frozen Bakery Prdts

Bella Bella Cupcakes LLC ... F ... 253 509-3158
Gig Harbor (G-4079)
Brown Sugar Baking Company LLC ... G ... 202 558-8422
Seattle (G-9590)
Conagra Brands Inc ... C ... 425 251-0761
Kent (G-4861)
Ericka J Thielke ... G ... 206 214-7530
Seattle (G-9937)
Kellis Creations ... G ... 206 371-7130
Lynnwood (G-6147)
Les Boulangers Associes Inc ... E ... 206 241-9343
Seatac (G-9288)
Mondelez Global LLC ... G ... 253 395-4237
Kent (G-5015)
Norstar Specialty Foods Inc ... E ... 206 764-4499
Kent (G-5026)
Olsons Baking Company LLC ... C ... 425 774-9164
Lynnwood (G-6172)
Paris Gourmet Dessert ... F ... 206 767-9097
Seattle (G-10756)
Starlight Desserts Inc ... G ... 206 284-8770
Seattle (G-11183)
Zuribella ... G ... 253 227-2988
Spanaway (G-12082)

2061 Sugar, Cane

Scutters ... G ... 425 350-7480
Renton (G-8907)

2064 Candy & Confectionery Prdts

◆ Ames International Inc ... D ... 253 946-4779
Fife (G-3932)
Apricots & Lollipops ... G ... 509 216-0325
Liberty Lake (G-5826)
B3 Breakfast & Burger Bar ... G ... 425 672-3666
Lynnwood (G-6079)
Baums Candy ... G ... 509 967-9340
Kennewick (G-4628)
▲ Boehms Candies Inc ... E ... 425 392-6652
Issaquah (G-4387)
Bright Candies ... G ... 509 525-5533
Walla Walla (G-14774)
▲ Brown & Haley ... C ... 253 620-3067
Tacoma (G-13210)
Brown & Haley ... C ... 253 620-3077
Tacoma (G-13211)
Brown & Haley ... C ... 253 620-3000
Fife (G-3940)

SIC SECTION 20 FOOD AND KINDRED PRODUCTS

Candy Fix....G....253 770-8242
Orting (G-7475)
Chehalis Mints Co Corp....G....360 736-9899
Centralia (G-2392)
Clarks Country Kitchen....G....509 586-6909
Richland (G-8981)
Cobbs LLC....G....360 302-2692
Olympia (G-7250)
Emerald City Promotions LLC....G....206 271-2880
Mercer Island (G-6461)
Hallett Confections....F....509 484-6454
Spokane (G-12286)
Hershey Company....G....800 468-1714
Bellevue (G-942)
Jackson Yukon....G....206 349-8566
Seattle (G-10278)
Johnson Candy Co Inc....G....253 272-8504
Tacoma (G-13363)
Jonboy Caramels LLC....G....206 850-4225
Seattle (G-10306)
Katies Candies Inc....F....360 748-8967
Chehalis (G-2507)
Killian Korn Inc....G....800 528-7861
Othello (G-7500)
▲ Liberty Orchards Company Inc....D....509 782-4088
Cashmere (G-2326)
Lifestyle Granolas Inc....G....509 768-5126
Spokane (G-12364)
Lollipoppassions....G....206 617-4217
Woodinville (G-15293)
Lucks Company....C....253 383-4815
Tacoma (G-13391)
Moosoo Corporation....G....866 966-6766
Kent (G-5016)
Motovotano LLC....G....206 363-0338
Anacortes (G-148)
Mt Baker Candy Co....G....360 756-0661
Bellingham (G-1446)
Murphy Nathanial....G....509 386-0727
Waitsburg (G-14756)
Nutradried Creations LLP....G....360 332-2101
Blaine (G-1690)
OH Cholocolate LLC....E....206 232-4974
Mercer Island (G-6477)
▲ Powers Candy and Nut Company....F....509 489-1955
Spokane (G-12452)
R & J Orgnal Kettlekorn Snacks....G....509 698-5533
Selah (G-11595)
R & S Roberts Enterprises Inc....F....253 333-7567
Auburn (G-542)
Rh Appetizing Inc....G....206 282-0776
Seattle (G-10960)
▲ Seattle Gourmet Foods Inc....D....425 656-9076
Seattle (G-11061)
Seattle Popcorn Company Inc....G....206 937-1292
Seattle (G-11068)
Sensi Sweets....G....206 387-8589
Shoreline (G-11809)
Shishkaberrys L L C....G....206 650-3564
Seattle (G-11102)
Simply Sinful....G....206 546-4461
Shoreline (G-11812)
Skiers Inc....G....360 663-7777
Enumclaw (G-3320)
Sutliff Candy & Promotions Co....G....206 784-5212
Seattle (G-11233)
Thin Dipped Almonds....G....720 231-9196
Seattle (G-11290)
▲ Totally Chocolate LLC....E....360 332-3900
Blaine (G-1706)
Trejo Trejo Inc....G....425 298-3144
Seattle (G-11329)
Whitehouse Antique & Candy....G....425 486-8453
Bothell (G-1918)

2066 Chocolate & Cocoa Prdts

Adams Place Country Gourmet....G....509 582-8564
Kennewick (G-4611)
◆ Ames International Inc....D....253 946-4779
Fife (G-3932)
Ardezan Chocolate LLC....G....206 244-4440
Seattle (G-9426)
Armoire....G....206 397-4703
Burien (G-2092)
Bright Candies....G....509 525-5533
Walla Walla (G-14774)
Brown & Haley....C....253 620-3077
Tacoma (G-13211)
Chocolate Necessity Inc....G....360 676-0589
Bellingham (G-1296)
Cocoa Future Spc....G....206 877-3347
Seattle (G-9709)
Costellinis LLC....G....877 889-8266
Bellevue (G-866)
▲ Frans Chocolates Ltd....E....206 322-0233
Seattle (G-10022)
Hershey Company....G....800 468-1714
Bellevue (G-942)
Intrigue Chocolates Co....G....206 829-8810
Seattle (G-10253)
Kristine Aumspach....G....360 681-4277
Sequim (G-11645)
▲ McStevens Inc....E....360 944-5788
Vancouver (G-14407)
▲ Progourmet Foods LLC....G....360 769-7420
Port Orchard (G-7843)
R & S Roberts Enterprises Inc....F....253 333-7567
Auburn (G-542)
Rh Appetizing Inc....G....206 282-0776
Seattle (G-10960)
Rocky Mountain Chocolate Fctry....G....509 927-7623
Veradale (G-14750)
▲ Seattle Chocolate Company LLC....E....425 264-2800
Tukwila (G-13815)
Vavako Fine Chocolates....G....425 453-4553
Bellevue (G-1212)
Wax Orchards Inc....G....800 634-6132
Lake Forest Park (G-5627)

2067 Chewing Gum

Wrigley Jr Co....G....408 528-4376
Bothell (G-1923)

2068 Salted & Roasted Nuts & Seeds

◆ Ames International Inc....D....253 946-4779
Fife (G-3932)
Brian Gannon....G....206 782-2276
Seattle (G-9583)
Jud Calvary Inc....G....708 323-8758
Redmond (G-8524)
Nut Factory Inc....E....509 926-6666
Spokane Valley (G-12815)
Sahale Snacks Inc....D....206 624-7244
Tukwila (G-13811)

2074 Cottonseed Oil Mills

Syngenta Seeds Inc....C....509 543-8000
Pasco (G-7636)

2075 Soybean Oil Mills

CHS Inc....F....509 488-9681
Othello (G-7492)
Syngenta Seeds Inc....C....509 543-8000
Pasco (G-7636)

2076 Vegetable Oil Mills

Baker Commodities Inc....E....509 535-5435
Spokane (G-12136)
Syngenta Seeds Inc....C....509 543-8000
Pasco (G-7636)

2077 Animal, Marine Fats & Oils

Baker Commodities Inc....E....509 534-2137
Spokane (G-12137)
Baker Commodities Inc....D....206 243-4781
Seattle (G-9478)
Baker Commodities Inc....F....509 837-8686
Grandview (G-4245)
Baker Commodities Inc....E....509 535-5435
Spokane (G-12136)
Crockers Fish Oil Inc....G....509 787-4983
Quincy (G-8295)
Darling Ingredients Inc....E....253 572-3922
Tacoma (G-13254)
J & S Manufacturing Inc....G....360 384-5553
Ferndale (G-3861)
Ocean Protein LLC....E....360 538-7400
Hoquiam (G-4350)
Powder River Drafting....G....360 679-9859
Oak Harbor (G-7161)
Proctor Farm Animal Removal....G....360 856-1995
Sedro Woolley (G-11558)
Q A R Rendering Services Inc....G....253 847-7220
Graham (G-4236)
Rainier Ranch Inc....G....206 243-2044
Burien (G-2123)
Tri County Dead Stock....G....360 354-3173
Lynden (G-6057)

2079 Shortening, Oils & Margarine

Apresvin Enterprises Ave Inc....G....509 967-3045
West Richland (G-15094)
▲ Barleans Organic Oils LLC....C....360 384-0485
Ferndale (G-3818)
Evergreen Production LLC....G....206 818-5054
Raymond (G-8347)
Hot Oil Company LLC....G....509 338-5678
Seattle (G-10184)
Olive Omg Oils....G....206 340-4114
Seattle (G-10690)
▲ Olive Seattle Oil Co....G....425 740-6055
Mukilteo (G-6959)
View Point Global Inc....F....206 714-4884
Seattle (G-11416)
Viterra USA LLC....F....509 349-8464
Warden (G-14936)

2082 Malt Beverages

20 Corners Brewing LLC....F....800 840-3346
Woodinville (G-15169)
Alpine Brewing Co....G....509 476-9662
Oroville (G-7461)
Ambrew LLC....G....425 774-1717
Edmonds (G-3094)
Aslan Brewing Company LLC....G....360 393-4106
Bellingham (G-1254)
Bad Dog Distillery LLC....G....360 435-3981
Arlington (G-207)
Bastion Brewing Company LLC....G....360 420-8223
Oak Harbor (G-7139)
Bellevue Brewing Company LLC....F....425 497-8686
Bellevue (G-809)
Big House Brewing Inc....E....509 522-2440
Walla Walla (G-14771)
Big Time Brewery Company Inc....E....206 545-4509
Seattle (G-9526)
Bighorn Brewery Warehouse....G....253 474-7465
Tacoma (G-13200)
Black Fleet Brewing....G....425 432-6868
Tacoma (G-13203)
Boundary Bay Brewing Company....E....360 647-5593
Bellingham (G-1281)
Brews Customs....G....253 334-1694
Auburn (G-397)
Brier Brewing LLC....G....206 258-4987
Brier (G-2018)
Brotherhood Brewing Co LLC....G....509 585-6765
Kennewick (G-4634)
Cascade Ales Company....G....360 520-6040
Longview (G-5895)
Cascadia Homebrew....G....360 943-2337
Olympia (G-7247)
Chehalis Brewing Group LLC....G....360 701-7873
Chehalis (G-2483)
Chief Springs Fire & Irons Brw....G....509 382-4677
Dayton (G-2879)
▲ Chuckanut Bay Distillery Inc....G....360 739-0361
Bellingham (G-1297)
Come On Get Hoppy....G....509 276-6288
Nine Mile Falls (G-7069)
Cross Current Brewing....G....253 952-2105
Tacoma (G-13249)
Crucible Brewing Company....G....425 374-7293
Everett (G-3431)
▲ Diamond Knot Brewery Inc....G....425 355-4488
Mukilteo (G-6911)
Diamond Knot Brewing Co Inc....F....425 315-0703
Mukilteo (G-6913)
Diamond Knot Brewing Co Inc....E....425 355-4488
Mukilteo (G-6914)
Dirty Couch LLC....G....203 303-8661
Seattle (G-9835)
Dungeness Brewing Co....G....360 775-1877
Port Angeles (G-7700)
Dwinell LLC....G....312 343-8607
Goldendale (G-4195)
Elliott Bay Brewing Company....E....206 246-4211
Seattle (G-9900)
Elysian Brewing Company Inc....F....206 767-0210
Seattle (G-9907)
▲ Elysian Brewing Company Inc....E....206 860-3977
Seattle (G-9908)
English Setter Brewing....G....509 413-3663
Spokane Valley (G-12692)
Farmstrong LLC....G....360 873-8852
Mount Vernon (G-6795)
Figurehead Brewing Company LLC....G....206 492-7981
Seattle (G-9991)

S I C

20 FOOD AND KINDRED PRODUCTS SIC SECTION

Fish Brewing Co....................F....... 360 943-3650
Olympia *(G-7286)*
Fishtail Pub....................E....... 360 943-3650
Olympia *(G-7287)*
Foggy Noggin Brewing....................G....... 425 486-1070
Bothell *(G-1855)*
Four Generals Brewing....................G....... 425 282-4360
Renton *(G-8803)*
Gb Acquisition Inc....................G....... 206 405-4205
Seattle *(G-10054)*
Genus Brewing Company LLC....................G....... 509 808-2395
Spokane Valley *(G-12715)*
Ghost Runners Brewery....................G....... 360 989-3912
Vancouver *(G-14251)*
Gig Harbor Brewing Co....................G....... 253 474-0672
Tacoma *(G-13308)*
Grains of Wrath Brewery....................G....... 847 727-5100
Camas *(G-2255)*
Great Artisan Beverage LLC....................G....... 425 467-7952
Bellevue *(G-933)*
Green Lake Brewing Company LLC......D....... 206 300-9337
Seattle *(G-10117)*
Half Lion Brewing Company LLC..........G....... 253 561-1115
Auburn *(G-459)*
Harmon Brewing Company L L C..........E....... 253 383-2739
Tacoma *(G-13331)*
Harmon Brewing Company L L C..........F....... 253 853-1585
Gig Harbor *(G-4113)*
Heavy Metal Brewing Co LLC....................G....... 503 710-6296
Vancouver *(G-14292)*
Hilliards Beer LLC....................F....... 206 257-4486
Seattle *(G-10173)*
Holm Brewing Enterpises LLC....................G....... 425 827-9307
Kirkland *(G-5359)*
Hopunion CBS LLC....................G....... 509 574-5124
Yakima *(G-15583)*
▲ **Hopunion Craft Brewing Sls LLC**.....G....... 509 457-3200
Yakima *(G-15584)*
Hoquiam Brewing Co....................G....... 360 637-8252
Hoquiam *(G-4342)*
Ice Harbor Brewing Company....................E....... 509 586-3181
Kennewick *(G-4673)*
Ice Harbor Brewing Company....................E....... 509 545-0927
Kennewick *(G-4674)*
Independent Brewers Untd Corp..........F....... 206 682-8322
Seattle *(G-10222)*
Iron Hop Brewing Co LLC....................G....... 360 421-8138
Monroe *(G-6581)*
Jellyfish Brewing Company....................G....... 206 517-4497
Seattle *(G-10291)*
Joe Nestor....................G....... 509 264-0800
Cashmere *(G-2323)*
Kulshan Brewing Company....................G....... 360 389-5348
Bellingham *(G-1399)*
Lagunitas....................G....... 206 784-2230
Seattle *(G-10373)*
Laht Neppur Ventures Inc....................G....... 509 337-6261
Waitsburg *(G-14755)*
Lantern Brewing LLC....................G....... 206 729-5350
Seattle *(G-10377)*
LDB Beverage Company....................F....... 509 651-0381
Stevenson *(G-13015)*
Ls Brewing Inc....................G....... 425 423-7700
Everett *(G-3541)*
▲ **Mac & Jacks Brewery Inc**....................F....... 425 558-9697
Redmond *(G-8543)*
Maritime Pacific Brewing Co....................F....... 206 782-6181
Seattle *(G-10485)*
McMenamins Inc....................F....... 206 285-4722
Seattle *(G-10510)*
Meconi Pub & Eatery....................G....... 253 383-3388
Tacoma *(G-13405)*
Methow House Watch Inc....................G....... 509 996-3332
Winthrop *(G-15163)*
Mule and Elk Brewing Co LLC....................G....... 206 909-9622
Cle Elum *(G-2672)*
Naan & Brew....................G....... 425 330-3891
Bellingham *(G-1456)*
Narrows Brewing LLP....................G....... 253 327-1400
Tacoma *(G-13424)*
New World Market LP....................G....... 206 653-7754
Federal Way *(G-3761)*
Northern Ales Inc....................G....... 509 738-6913
Kettle Falls *(G-5238)*
Northern Lights Brewing Co....................G....... 509 242-2739
Spokane *(G-12408)*
Northwest Peaks Brewery LLC..........G....... 206 853-0525
Seattle *(G-10649)*
O-Town Brewing LLC....................G....... 360 701-4706
Lacey *(G-5571)*
Optimism Brewing LLC....................F....... 206 651-5429
Seattle *(G-10709)*
Orlison Brewing Co....................G....... 503 894-2917
Airway Heights *(G-59)*
Pike Brewing Company....................E....... 206 622-6044
Seattle *(G-10805)*
Port Townsend Brewing Co....................G....... 360 385-9967
Port Townsend *(G-7908)*
◆ **Pyramid Breweries Inc**....................D....... 206 682-8322
Seattle *(G-10893)*
Pyramid Breweries Inc....................D....... 206 682-3377
Seattle *(G-10894)*
Quiet Giant Brewing Co LLC....................G....... 253 584-8373
Lakewood *(G-5750)*
R Ellersick Brewing Co....................G....... 425 374-7248
Lynnwood *(G-6185)*
Ram Big Horn Brewery-Northgate.........G....... 206 364-8000
Seattle *(G-10918)*
Ram Bighorn Brewery Kent....................G....... 253 520-3881
Kent *(G-5097)*
Rattlesnake Mtn Brewing Co....................E....... 509 783-5747
Richland *(G-9038)*
Rhythm & Brews....................G....... 360 386-9509
Arlington *(G-315)*
River City Brewing LLC....................G....... 509 413-2388
Spokane *(G-12476)*
Riverport Brewing....................G....... 509 758-8889
Clarkston *(G-2646)*
Rooftop Brewing Company....................G....... 206 457-8598
Seattle *(G-10980)*
Roslyn Brewing Co Inc....................G....... 509 649-2232
Roslyn *(G-9156)*
Schooner Exact....................G....... 206 432-9734
Seattle *(G-11028)*
Scrappy Punk Brewing LLC....................G....... 503 810-1655
Snohomish *(G-11970)*
Scuttlebutt Brewing Co LLC....................F....... 425 252-2829
Everett *(G-3606)*
Seattle Cider Company....................F....... 206 762-0490
Seattle *(G-11052)*
Silver City Brewing Co Inc....................D....... 360 698-5879
Silverdale *(G-11857)*
Skye Book & Brew....................G....... 509 382-4677
Dayton *(G-2885)*
Smith & Reilly Inc....................G....... 360 693-9225
Vancouver *(G-14597)*
Snipes Mountain Brewing Inc....................E....... 509 837-2739
Sunnyside *(G-13142)*
Spanky Burger & Brew....................G....... 253 720-3344
Tacoma *(G-13519)*
Sparklehorse LLC....................G....... 253 948-7772
Gig Harbor *(G-4163)*
Stoney Creek Brewing Co LLC....................G....... 425 836-0958
Sammamish *(G-9249)*
Structures Brewing LLC....................G....... 432 770-1540
Bellingham *(G-1561)*
Subdued Brewing LLC....................G....... 360 656-6611
Bellingham *(G-1562)*
Sumerian Brewing Co LLC....................G....... 425 486-5330
Woodinville *(G-15380)*
Tapenade Inc....................G....... 509 966-0686
Yakima *(G-15694)*
Thirsty Crab Brewery LLC....................G....... 360 331-3667
Freeland *(G-4037)*
Tts Old Iron Brewery LLC....................G....... 509 847-4393
Spokane *(G-12573)*
Urban Family Brewing Co....................G....... 206 861-6769
Seattle *(G-11390)*
Valhalla Brewing and Bev Co LL..........G....... 206 243-6346
Tukwila *(G-13832)*
Vampt America Inc....................G....... 800 508-6149
Seattle *(G-11400)*
Vampt Beverage USA Corp....................F....... 800 508-6149
Seattle *(G-11401)*
Wenatchee Vly Brewing Co LLC..........G....... 509 888-8088
Wenatchee *(G-15085)*
West Seattle Brewing Company..........G....... 206 708-6627
Seattle *(G-11451)*
▲ **Westland Distillery**....................F....... 206 763-5381
Seattle *(G-11457)*
Whipsaw Brewing LLC....................F....... 360 463-0436
Ellensburg *(G-3239)*
Whitstran Brewing Company Inc..........G....... 509 786-4922
Prosser *(G-8076)*
Yakima Chief-Hopunion LLC....................G....... 509 453-4792
Yakima *(G-15713)*
▲ **Youngs Market of Washington**..........E....... 206 808-6124
Renton *(G-8953)*

2083 Malt

Great Western Malting Co....................G....... 360 859-0940
Vancouver *(G-14266)*
Great Western Malting Co....................G....... 360 991-0888
Vancouver *(G-14267)*
◆ **Great Western Malting Co**....................D....... 360 693-3661
Vancouver *(G-14268)*
Great Western Malting Co....................F....... 360 695-3484
Vancouver *(G-14269)*
Rahr Malting....................G....... 509 469-0403
Wapato *(G-14925)*
Salish Coast Enterprises LLC....................G....... 360 333-5280
Burlington *(G-2184)*
Salish Post Enterprises LLC....................G....... 360 391-5492
Mount Vernon *(G-6832)*

2084 Wine & Brandy

21cellars....................G....... 253 353-2317
Tacoma *(G-13151)*
37 Cellars....................G....... 509 679-0668
Leavenworth *(G-5793)*
50st Seattle Winery LLC....................G....... 206 409-0994
Chelan *(G-2545)*
Adamant Cellars....................G....... 509 529-4161
Walla Walla *(G-14760)*
Agate Creek Farm....................G....... 360 740-1692
Chehalis *(G-2459)*
Agate Field Vineyard....................G....... 509 829-6097
Zillah *(G-15749)*
Airport Ranch Estates LLC....................F....... 509 786-7401
Prosser *(G-8028)*
Airport Ranch Estates LLC....................G....... 425 877-1006
Woodinville *(G-15174)*
Alexander Grape....................G....... 509 942-9850
West Richland *(G-15093)*
Alexandria Nicole Cellars LLC..........F....... 509 786-3497
Prosser *(G-8029)*
Alia Wines LLC....................G....... 360 794-0421
Snohomish *(G-11873)*
Alpine Wines....................G....... 208 354-9463
Anacortes *(G-98)*
Alta Cellars....................G....... 425 424-9218
Woodinville *(G-15175)*
▲ **Amavi Cellars**....................G....... 509 525-3541
Walla Walla *(G-14761)*
▲ **American Wine Trade Inc**....................E....... 206 357-0607
Seattle *(G-9396)*
American Wine Trade Inc....................F....... 509 588-3155
Benton City *(G-1601)*
Amos Rome Vineyards....................G....... 206 890-4482
Manson *(G-6238)*
Ancient Lake Wine Company LLC........F....... 509 787-2022
Quincy *(G-8288)*
Anderson Resources Inc....................G....... 360 426-5913
Shelton *(G-11678)*
Andrew Ross Winery....................G....... 425 487-9463
Woodinville *(G-15178)*
Anni Demi Winery Inc....................G....... 509 493-2702
White Salmon *(G-15110)*
Antoine Creek Vineyards LLC....................G....... 509 682-4448
Chelan *(G-2547)*
Antolin Cellars....................G....... 509 833-5765
Yakima *(G-15510)*
▲ **Arbor Crest Wineries & Nursery**.......F....... 509 927-9463
Spokane *(G-12115)*
Arbor Crest Wineries & Nursery..........G....... 509 489-0588
Spokane *(G-12116)*
Ardor Cellars....................G....... 509 876-8086
Walla Walla *(G-14765)*
Arlington Road Cellars....................G....... 425 482-1801
Woodinville *(G-15180)*
Ash Hollow Winery LLC....................G....... 509 529-7565
Olympia *(G-7232)*
Aspenwood Cellars....................G....... 425 844-2233
Woodinville *(G-15182)*
Atam Company LLC....................G....... 509 687-4421
Manson *(G-6239)*
Avennia Winery....................G....... 425 392-3191
Woodinville *(G-15183)*
Badger Mountain Inc....................F....... 509 627-4986
Kennewick *(G-4623)*
Badger Mountain Vineyards LLC..........G....... 509 627-4986
Kennewick *(G-4624)*
Baer Winery LLC....................G....... 425 483-7060
Woodinville *(G-15184)*
Bainbrdge Island Wnery Vnyards..........G....... 206 842-9463
Bainbridge Island *(G-612)*
Bainbridge Vineyards LLC....................G....... 206 842-9463
Bainbridge Island *(G-615)*

SIC SECTION
20 FOOD AND KINDRED PRODUCTS

▲ **Balboa Winery** G 509 529-0461 — Walla Walla *(G-14767)*
▲ **Barnard-Griffin Inc** F 509 627-0266 — Richland *(G-8971)*
Barrage Cellars LLC G 425 381-9675 — Woodinville *(G-15185)*
Barrister Winery G 509 465-3591 — Spokane *(G-12139)*
Bartholomew Winery G 206 395-8460 — Seattle *(G-9496)*
Bartholomew Winery Inc F 206 755-5296 — Kennewick *(G-4626)*
Bartholomew Winery Inc G 206 755-5296 — Kennewick *(G-4625)*
Basalt Cellars G 509 758-6442 — Clarkston *(G-2622)*
▲ **Basel Cellars Estate Winery** G 509 522-0200 — Walla Walla *(G-14768)*
Bctld LLC G 206 650-6408 — Seattle *(G-9503)*
Bear Wildfire G 360 379-8915 — Port Townsend *(G-7868)*
Benson Vineyards G 509 687-0313 — Manson *(G-6240)*
Bergdorf Cellars G 509 548-7638 — Leavenworth *(G-5796)*
Berghan Vineyeards G 509 301-9229 — Walla Walla *(G-14769)*
Bertelsen Winery & Tasting Rm G 360 445-2300 — Mount Vernon *(G-6780)*
Bethany Vineyard & Winery G 360 887-3525 — Ridgefield *(G-9067)*
▲ **Betz Cellars LLC** G 425 861-9823 — Redmond *(G-8402)*
Bieler and Smith LLC G 509 526-5230 — Walla Walla *(G-14770)*
Big Derby Distilling Co G 206 504-7604 — Seattle *(G-9522)*
Birchfield Winery G 360 978-6176 — Chehalis *(G-2471)*
Birchfield Winery Inc G 360 280-8998 — Onalaska *(G-7446)*
Blanca Terra Vineyards Inc G 509 588-6082 — Benton City *(G-1602)*
Bonair Winery Inc F 509 829-6027 — Zillah *(G-15750)*
Bontzu Cellars G 425 205-3482 — Walla Walla *(G-14773)*
Bookwalter LLC G 425 488-1983 — Woodinville *(G-15196)*
▲ **Bookwalter Winery LLC** F 509 627-5000 — Richland *(G-8976)*
Bouchard Lake Winery LLC G 425 803-5076 — Kirkland *(G-5296)*
Boulder Estates Winery G 509 628-1209 — Richland *(G-8977)*
Boutique Imports LLC G 206 650-5555 — Seattle *(G-9571)*
Buckmaster Cellars G 509 627-1321 — Richland *(G-8979)*
Bunnell Family Cellar G 509 786-2197 — Prosser *(G-8031)*
Bunnell Family Cellular G 425 286-2964 — Woodinville *(G-15200)*
Butte Hill Winery & Vinyrd LLC G 360 225-6864 — Woodland *(G-15421)*
Butterfield Cellars LLC G 509 994-0382 — Spokane *(G-12163)*
▲ **Buty Winery** G 509 527-0901 — Walla Walla *(G-14776)*
▲ **Cadaretta** G 509 525-1352 — Walla Walla *(G-14777)*
Callahan Cellars G 425 877-1842 — Woodinville *(G-15203)*
Camarda Corporation G 206 463-9227 — Vashon *(G-14715)*
Canoe Ridge Vineyard G 206 267-5252 — Seattle *(G-9619)*
▲ **Canoe Ridge Vineyard LLC** F 509 527-0885 — Walla Walla *(G-14778)*
▲ **Castillo De Feliciana** G 541 558-3656 — Walla Walla *(G-14779)*
Castle Bridge Winery G 425 251-0983 — Renton *(G-8768)*
Cave B Estate Winery G 509 785-3500 — Quincy *(G-8292)*
Cavu Cellars G 509 540-6352 — Walla Walla *(G-14780)*
▲ **Cayuse Vineyards** G 509 526-0686 — Walla Walla *(G-14781)*
Cedar River Cellars G 206 229-2104 — Renton *(G-8769)*
Cedergreen Cellars Inc G 425 827-7244 — Kirkland *(G-5300)*
Cellar 55 Inc G 360 693-2700 — Vancouver *(G-14110)*
Cellars Nodland G 509 927-7770 — Spokane Valley *(G-12653)*
Champoux Vineyards LLC G 360 563-1330 — Snohomish *(G-11889)*
Chandler Reach Vineyard Estate G 509 588-8800 — Benton City *(G-1605)*
Charles Lybecker G 509 687-0555 — Manson *(G-6241)*
Charles Smith Vineyards LLC G 509 526-5230 — Walla Walla *(G-14783)*
Chateau Faire Le Pont LLC G 509 667-9463 — Wenatchee *(G-15020)*
Chateau Plateau Winery Inc G 360 825-2466 — Enumclaw *(G-3281)*
Chateau Rollat Winery LLC G 509 529-4511 — Walla Walla *(G-14784)*
Chelan Estate Winery LLC G 509 682-5454 — Chelan *(G-2550)*
Chelan Vintners G 509 630-8504 — Manson *(G-6242)*
China Bend Vineyards G 509 732-6123 — Kettle Falls *(G-5228)*
Chinook Wines G 509 786-2725 — Prosser *(G-8033)*
Chouette Vineyards LLC G 206 229-5167 — North Bend *(G-7108)*
Cinq Cellars LLC G 206 954-4626 — Redmond *(G-8420)*
▲ **Claar Cellars LLC** G 509 266-4449 — Pasco *(G-7560)*
Cloudlift Cellars G 206 622-2004 — Seattle *(G-9701)*
Clouds Vineyard LLC G 509 830-2785 — Prosser *(G-8034)*
▲ **Col Solare LLP** G 509 588-6806 — Benton City *(G-1607)*
Columbia Cascade Winery Assn G 509 782-3845 — Cashmere *(G-2318)*
Columbia Gorge Winery Inc G 509 365-2900 — Lyle *(G-5995)*
Columbia Winery F 425 488-2776 — Woodinville *(G-15208)*
Confluence Vineyards G 360 887-2343 — Ridgefield *(G-9075)*
Connerlee Vineyards Inc G 509 932-4267 — Sammamish *(G-9199)*
Constellation Brands Inc G 425 482-7300 — Woodinville *(G-15211)*
Copper Mountain Vineyards G 509 476-2762 — Oroville *(G-7463)*
Corkycellars LLC G 425 226-5479 — Renton *(G-8775)*
▲ **Corliss Estates** G 509 526-4400 — Walla Walla *(G-14790)*
Corus Estates & Vineyards LLC G 206 728-9063 — Seattle *(G-9744)*
Corus Estates & Vineyards LLC E 503 538-7724 — Yakima *(G-15538)*
▲ **Cote Bonneville** G 509 840-4596 — Sunnyside *(G-13117)*
Cougar Hills LLC G 425 398-9999 — Redmond *(G-8428)*
Cougar Hills LLC G 509 241-3850 — Spokane *(G-12201)*
Cougar Hills LLC F 509 529-5980 — Walla Walla *(G-14791)*
▲ **Coventry Vale Winery Inc** E 509 882-4100 — Grandview *(G-4246)*
▲ **Covington Cellars** G 425 806-8636 — Woodinville *(G-15214)*
Covington Cellars LLC G 253 347-9463 — Bothell *(G-1844)*
Cox Canyon Vineyards G 206 940-5086 — Ellensburg *(G-3191)*
Coyote Canyon Winery LLC G 509 786-7686 — Prosser *(G-8036)*
Craftsman Cellars LLC G 509 328-3960 — Spokane *(G-12206)*
Cranberry Road Winery G 425 254-8400 — Bonney Lake *(G-1719)*
Crowder Family Winery G 509 834-3270 — Manson *(G-6243)*
Crucible Wines LLC G 206 605-2953 — Seattle *(G-9759)*
Cuillin Hills Winery G 425 402-1907 — Woodinville *(G-15217)*
Damsel Cellars G 206 465-2433 — Woodinville *(G-15218)*
Dancing Alder Winery G 425 402-6300 — Woodinville *(G-15219)*
Darby Winery G 206 954-4700 — Seattle *(G-9792)*
Darby Winery Inc G 206 954-4700 — Woodinville *(G-15220)*
David Loring G 206 772-5004 — Seattle *(G-9799)*
Davis Degrass Enterprises Inc G 360 332-2097 — Blaine *(G-1667)*
Dead Canyon Vineyard LLC G 509 786-2665 — Prosser *(G-8039)*
Delille Cellars Inc G 425 489-0544 — Redmond *(G-8437)*
Delta V Cellars LLC G 425 677-8487 — Issaquah *(G-4405)*
Des Etes Longs Vineyard LLC G 509 430-5488 — Benton City *(G-1609)*
Des Voigne Melissa G 206 478-2021 — Woodinville *(G-15221)*
Desert Wind Vineyard E 509 786-7277 — Prosser *(G-8041)*
Destination Des Moines G 206 824-9462 — Des Moines *(G-2933)*
Devona LLC G 509 520-2524 — Walla Walla *(G-14796)*
Devorah Creek Vinyards G 206 579-8906 — Auburn *(G-425)*
Dineen Family Wine Company LLC G 509 829-6897 — Zillah *(G-15753)*
Distefano Winery Ltd G 425 487-1648 — Woodinville *(G-15226)*
Dodger and Powers Wines G 509 627-4986 — Kennewick *(G-4655)*
Domanico Cellars LLC G 206 465-9406 — Seattle *(G-9845)*
Doubleback G 509 525-3334 — Walla Walla *(G-14798)*
DRM Holdings Inc G 509 338-4699 — Pullman *(G-8089)*
Dubrul Vineyard LLC G 509 837-7746 — Sunnyside *(G-13122)*
▲ **Dunham Cellars LLC** G 509 529-4685 — Walla Walla *(G-14799)*
▲ **Dusted Valley** G 509 525-1337 — Walla Walla *(G-14800)*
Dusty Cellars Winery G 360 387-2171 — Camano Island *(G-2211)*
DVinery G 509 548-7059 — Leavenworth *(G-5798)*
Eagle Creek Winery G 509 548-7059 — Leavenworth *(G-5799)*
Eaton Hill Winery G 509 854-2220 — Granger *(G-4261)*
Efeste G 206 535-6997 — Seattle *(G-9886)*
Eight Bells Winery G 206 294-4131 — Seattle *(G-9890)*
Eleven Winery Inc F 206 780-0905 — Bainbridge Island *(G-628)*
Ellensburg Canyon Winery LLC G 509 933-3523 — Ellensburg *(G-3194)*
Elsom Cellars LLC G 425 298-3082 — Seattle *(G-9905)*
Elsom Cllars Winery 3pp Pnw Hq G 775 848-1771 — Seattle *(G-9906)*
Emory Vineyards LLC G 509 588-2988 — Benton City *(G-1610)*
Enchanted Cellars G 503 970-2244 — Walla Walla *(G-14801)*
Entiat Valley Vineyards LLC G 509 884-1152 — East Wenatchee *(G-3012)*
Epicru Vintners LLC G 206 829-9714 — Seattle *(G-9934)*
Errant Cellars G 509 289-9660 — Quincy *(G-8298)*
Esther Brcques Wnery Vnyrd LLC G 509 476-2861 — Oroville *(G-7465)*
Evalesco Inc G 425 486-5959 — Woodinville *(G-15238)*
Eye of Needle Winery G 425 210-7463 — Woodinville *(G-15240)*
Fall Line Winery LLC G 206 406-4249 — Seattle *(G-9965)*
Farmhand Winery G 509 308-7203 — Kennewick *(G-4665)*

SIC

Employee Codes: A=Over 500 employees, B=251-500
C=101-250, D=51-100, E=20-50, F=10-19, G=2-9
2019 Washington
Manufacturers Register
539

20 FOOD AND KINDRED PRODUCTS SIC SECTION

Felamere Vineyard LLC ....G.... 360 652-7414
Stanwood (G-12970)
Fenette Cellars ....G.... 425 417-6260
Bothell (G-1763)
▲ Fidelitas ....G.... 509 521-1553
Richland (G-8996)
Fidelitas Wines LLC ....G.... 509 588-3469
Benton City (G-1611)
▲ Figgins Family Wine Estates ....G.... 509 525-1428
Walla Walla (G-14804)
▲ Firesteed Corporation ....G.... 503 623-8683
Issaquah (G-4415)
Five Star Cellars Inc ....G.... 509 527-8400
Walla Walla (G-14805)
Fletcher Bay Winery ....G.... 206 780-9463
Bainbridge Island (G-634)
Flying Trout Wines LLC ....G.... 509 520-7701
Walla Walla (G-14806)
Fools Prairie Vineyards LLC ....G.... 509 319-0752
Spokane (G-12261)
Force Majeure Winery ....G.... 425 892-9848
Woodinville (G-15247)
Forgeron Cellars ....G.... 425 908-7683
Redmond (G-8463)
▲ Forgeron Cellars LLC ....G.... 509 522-9463
Walla Walla (G-14807)
Fort Walla Walla Cellars LLC ....G.... 509 520-1095
Walla Walla (G-14808)
Foundry Vineyards LLC ....G.... 509 529-0736
Walla Walla (G-14809)
Fountaine Estates Winery ....G.... 509 972-8123
Naches (G-6996)
Francisco Gomez Vineyard Svcs ....G.... 559 567-7013
Pasco (G-7583)
Frichette Winery ....G.... 509 426-3227
Benton City (G-1612)
Furion Cellars LLC ....G.... 425 314-8922
Everett (G-3489)
Gallo Winery ....G.... 509 947-4520
Sunnyside (G-13126)
Garlic Crush ....G.... 425 968-2539
Redmond (G-8469)
Gary N Lamb ....G.... 360 766-6086
Bow (G-1929)
Generations Winery LLC ....G.... 206 351-0933
Everett (G-3493)
Genoa Cellars ....G.... 425 296-9660
Woodinville (G-15251)
Gifford Hirlinger Winery ....G.... 509 301-9229
Walla Walla (G-14811)
▲ Gilbert Cellars LLC ....G.... 509 249-9049
Yakima (G-15576)
Ginkgo Forest Winery ....G.... 253 301-4372
Tacoma (G-13309)
Ginkgo Forest Winery LLC ....G.... 509 932-0082
Mattawa (G-6406)
Gino Cuneo Cellars LLC ....G.... 509 876-4738
Walla Walla (G-14812)
Glacier Peak Winery ....G.... 360 419-9107
Mount Vernon (G-6799)
Glacier View Winery ....G.... 206 719-1331
Woodinville (G-15252)
Glencorrie ....G.... 509 525-2585
Walla Walla (G-14813)
▲ Goose Ridge LLC ....F.... 509 837-4427
Benton City (G-1613)
Goose Ridge Vineyards LLC ....F.... 509 627-1618
Benton City (G-1614)
▲ Gordon Brothers Cellars Inc ....E.... 509 547-6331
Pasco (G-7588)
Gouger Cellars ....G.... 360 693-2700
Ridgefield (G-9086)
▲ Gramercy Cellars ....F.... 509 876-2427
Walla Walla (G-14815)
Grand Reve Vintners ....G.... 425 892-9848
Carnation (G-2294)
Grape Visions LLC ....E.... 509 525-1337
Walla Walla (G-14816)
Greenwood Cider Co LLC ....G.... 360 961-2902
Seattle (G-10122)
Greg Michael Cellars LLC ....G.... 509 465-3591
Spokane (G-12283)
▲ Grieb Optimal Winecrafting LLC ....G.... 509 877-0925
Wapato (G-14916)
H R Management Northwest ....G.... 509 697-5377
Selah (G-11590)
Hamilton Cellars LLC ....G.... 509 628-8227
Benton City (G-1616)
Hanatoro Winery ....G.... 404 312-5891
Walla Walla (G-14818)
Hard Row To Hoe Vineyards ....G.... 509 687-3000
Manson (G-6244)
Heathen Estate Vineyards ....G.... 360 768-5199
Vancouver (G-14291)
Hestia Cellars ....G.... 425 333-4270
Redmond (G-8492)
Heymann Whinery Etc ....G.... 360 623-1106
Chehalis (G-2502)
Hezel Vineyard and Cellars LLC ....G.... 360 321-4898
Clinton (G-2689)
Hierophant Meadery LLC ....G.... 509 294-0134
Mead (G-6429)
Hightower Cellars ....G.... 509 588-2867
Benton City (G-1617)
▲ Hogue Cellars Ltd ....D.... 509 786-4557
Prosser (G-8042)
Hollywood Hill Vineyards LLC ....G.... 425 753-0093
Woodinville (G-15260)
Holmes Family Winery LLC ....G.... 253 906-6317
Federal Way (G-3743)
Holmes Harbor Cellars LLC ....G.... 360 331-3544
Greenbank (G-4306)
Hoodsport Winery Inc ....G.... 360 877-9894
Hoodsport (G-4325)
Horan Estates Winery ....G.... 509 679-8705
East Wenatchee (G-3020)
Horizons Edge Winery ....E.... 509 829-6401
Zillah (G-15755)
Hyatt Farm Partnership LP ....G.... 509 829-3737
Zillah (G-15756)
Icicle Ridge Winery ....G.... 509 548-7019
Peshastin (G-7663)
Icicle Ridge Winery ....G.... 509 548-7019
Leavenworth (G-5807)
Icon Cellars ....G.... 425 242-4230
Woodinville (G-15263)
Icon Cellars LLC ....G.... 425 223-7300
Sammamish (G-9219)
Isenhower Cellars ....G.... 425 488-2299
Woodinville (G-15269)
▲ Isenhower Cellars ....G.... 509 526-7896
Walla Walla (G-14826)
Island Vintners ....G.... 206 451-4344
Bainbridge Island (G-643)
J As Winery ....G.... 206 409-4841
Sammamish (G-9221)
J M Cellars Company ....G.... 425 485-6508
Woodinville (G-15270)
▲ J M Cellars Company ....G.... 206 321-0052
Seattle (G-10272)
J&S Crushing ....G.... 509 787-3537
Mattawa (G-6409)
J-NH Wine Group LLC ....F.... 425 481-5502
Woodinville (G-15271)
▲ Januik Winery ....G.... 425 481-5502
Woodinville (G-15272)
JB George LLC ....G.... 509 522-0200
Walla Walla (G-14827)
JB Neufeld LLC ....G.... 509 945-1887
Yakima (G-15596)
JB Neufeld LLC ....G.... 509 895-9979
Yakima (G-15597)
Jester Cellars ....G.... 425 785-9217
Redmond (G-8519)
Jlc Winery ....G.... 509 529-1398
Walla Walla (G-14829)
Johnson Ward Winery ....G.... 206 284-2635
Seattle (G-10303)
▲ K Vintners LLC ....G.... 509 526-5230
Walla Walla (G-14830)
K-W Cellars ....G.... 509 525-6222
Walla Walla (G-14831)
▲ Kana Winery ....G.... 509 453-6611
Yakima (G-15605)
Karma Kanyon LLC ....G.... 509 669-5753
Chelan (G-2556)
▲ Kestrel Vintners ....F.... 509 786-2675
Prosser (G-8046)
Kestrel Vintners ....G.... 425 398-1199
Woodinville (G-15278)
Kestrel Vintners ....G.... 509 548-7348
Leavenworth (G-5808)
Kevin W Lantz ....G.... 425 770-2599
Lake Stevens (G-5653)
Kevin White Winery ....G.... 206 992-5746
Woodinville (G-15279)
▲ Kiona Vineyards LLC ....F.... 509 588-6716
Benton City (G-1618)
Klickitat Canyon Winery ....G.... 509 365-2900
Lyle (G-5996)
▲ Knipprath Cellars Inc ....G.... 208 699-3393
Spokane (G-12353)
Knox Cellars Mason Bees ....G.... 360 286-2025
Bremerton (G-1971)
Koi Pond Cellars ....G.... 360 281-2716
Ridgefield (G-9093)
Kristen Rose Winery ....G.... 509 586-4830
Kennewick (G-4684)
La Toscana Bed Brakfast Winery ....G.... 509 548-5448
Cashmere (G-2325)
▼ Lachini Winery ....G.... 503 864-4553
Medina (G-6450)
Lake Chelan Trading Company ....F.... 509 687-9463
Chelan (G-2557)
Lane Gibbons Vineyard Inc ....G.... 360 264-8466
Tenino (G-13620)
Latah Creek Wine Cellars Ltd ....G.... 509 926-0164
Spokane Valley (G-12773)
Laurelhurst Cellars LLC ....G.... 206 992-2875
Seattle (G-10383)
Lauren Ashton Cellars LLC ....G.... 206 504-8546
Woodinville (G-15285)
Lawrence Cellars ....G.... 425 286-2198
Woodinville (G-15286)
Lawrence Cellars LLC ....G.... 509 346-2585
Royal City (G-9171)
Lawrence Fruit Inc ....G.... 509 925-1095
Ellensburg (G-3212)
LDB Beverage Company ....F.... 509 651-0381
Stevenson (G-13015)
Leaf Cellars LLC ....G.... 206 860-6888
Seattle (G-10393)
▲ Leonetti Cellar ....F.... 509 525-1670
Walla Walla (G-14837)
Locati Cellars LLC ....G.... 509 529-5871
Walla Walla (G-14838)
Long Road Winery ....G.... 206 859-7697
Belfair (G-767)
Long Shadows Vintners LLC ....F.... 509 526-0905
Seattle (G-10436)
Lookout Point Winery ....G.... 509 469-4320
Yakima (G-15612)
Lost River Winery LLC ....G.... 509 996-2888
Mazama (G-6414)
Love That Red Winery ....G.... 425 463-9014
Woodinville (G-15296)
▲ Lowden Schoolhouse Corporation ....G.... 509 525-0940
Walla Walla (G-14839)
▲ Lowden Schoolhouse Corporation ....F.... 509 525-0940
Lowden (G-5990)
Lupine Vineyards LLC ....G.... 206 915-5862
Lynnwood (G-6160)
Lynch Distributing Co ....F.... 509 248-0880
Yakima (G-15613)
Madsen Family Cellars ....G.... 360 357-3015
Olympia (G-7329)
Madsen Family Cellars ....G.... 360 339-8371
Olympia (G-7330)
Magdalena Vineyard LLC ....G.... 509 942-4204
Benton City (G-1619)
Maison Bleue Winery ....G.... 509 525-9084
Walla Walla (G-14840)
▲ Mark Anthony Brands Inc ....D.... 206 267-4444
Seattle (G-10486)
Mark Ryan Winery LLC ....F.... 425 481-7070
Kirkland (G-5397)
Market Vineyards ....G.... 509 396-4798
Richland (G-9024)
Market Vineyards ....G.... 425 486-1171
Woodinville (G-15302)
Marketplace Cellars ....G.... 509 795-8500
Spokane (G-12382)
Marshals Winery Inc ....G.... 509 767-4633
Dallesport (G-2864)
Martedi Winery ....G.... 425 444-2840
Woodinville (G-15303)
Martinez and Martinez Winery ....G.... 509 786-2424
Prosser (G-8050)
Martinez Vineyard LLC ....G.... 509 786-2424
Prosser (G-8051)
Maryhill Winery ....G.... 509 443-3832
Spokane (G-12384)
Masset Winery ....G.... 509 877-6675
Wapato (G-14918)
Matthews Cellars ....G.... 425 487-9810
Woodinville (G-15305)
Matthews Estate LLC ....G.... 425 488-3883
Woodinville (G-15306)
McCrea Cellars Inc ....G.... 206 938-8643
Seattle (G-10506)

SIC SECTION 20 FOOD AND KINDRED PRODUCTS

McKinley Springs LLC ....G 509 894-4528
Prosser *(G-8052)*
Meade Winery ....G 509 972-4443
Yakima *(G-15617)*
▲ Mercer Wine Estates LLC ....F 509 786-2097
Prosser *(G-8054)*
Mercer Wine Estates LLC ....F 509 832-2810
Prosser *(G-8055)*
Michelle Chateau Ste ....G 425 488-1133
Woodinville *(G-15308)*
Michelle Ste Wine Estates Ltd ....F 509 875-4227
Paterson *(G-7659)*
◆ Michelle Ste Wine Estates Ltd ....G 425 488-1133
Woodinville *(G-15309)*
Michelle Ste Wine Estates Ltd ....F 509 875-2061
Paterson *(G-7660)*
Michelle Ste Wine Estates Ltd ....F 509 882-3928
Grandview *(G-4253)*
Michelle Ste Wine Estates Ltd ....F 425 488-1133
Woodinville *(G-15310)*
Mike Scott Orchards & Winery ....G 509 787-3538
Wenatchee *(G-15091)*
Milbrandt Vineyards Inc ....F 509 788-0030
Prosser *(G-8057)*
Mill Lane Winery Yakima LLC ....G 206 817-5767
Yakima *(G-15622)*
Minnick Hills Vineyard LL ....G 509 525-5076
Walla Walla *(G-14845)*
Miracles Vintners LLC ....G 253 606-6202
Walla Walla *(G-14846)*
Monson Ranches ....G 425 488-0200
Woodinville *(G-15314)*
Monson Ranches ....E 509 628-3880
Richland *(G-9029)*
Monte Scarlatto Estate Winery ....G 509 531-3081
Benton City *(G-1620)*
Moose Canyon Winery ....G 253 225-1985
Edgewood *(G-3086)*
Mosquito Fleet Winery LLC ....G 360 710-8788
Belfair *(G-768)*
Mpm Vintners LLC ....E 509 525-2469
Walla Walla *(G-14847)*
Naches Heights Vineyard LLC ....G 509 966-4355
Yakima *(G-15627)*
Napeequa Vintners ....G 509 763-1600
Leavenworth *(G-5810)*
Nefarious Cellers ....G 509 682-9505
Chelan *(G-2560)*
New World Market LP ....G 206 653-7754
Federal Way *(G-3761)*
No Grass Winery ....G 509 784-5101
Entiat *(G-3269)*
▲ Northstar Winery ....G 509 525-6100
Walla Walla *(G-14851)*
Northwest Cellars LLC ....F 866 421-9463
Kirkland *(G-5412)*
Nota Bene Cellars Ltd ....G 206 762-5581
Seattle *(G-10657)*
▲ Novelty Hill Winery LLC ....F 425 481-5502
Woodinville *(G-15324)*
Novelty Hill Winery LLC ....G 206 664-2522
Seattle *(G-10660)*
Noviello Vineyards LLC ....G 509 784-0544
Orondo *(G-7458)*
▲ O S Winery LLC ....G 206 243-3427
Mercer Island *(G-6475)*
Oakwood Cellars ....G 509 588-1900
Benton City *(G-1622)*
Octave Vineyard LLC ....G 509 876-2530
Walla Walla *(G-14852)*
Oldfield Cellars LLC ....G 425 398-7200
Woodinville *(G-15326)*
▲ Olsen Estates LLC ....E 509 973-2203
Prosser *(G-8061)*
Olympic Cellars LLC ....G 360 452-0160
Port Angeles *(G-7728)*
One Tree Hard Cider ....G 509 315-9856
Spokane Valley *(G-12820)*
Oola Industries LLC ....G 206 709-7909
Seattle *(G-10704)*
Owen Kotler Selections LLC ....G 917 912-0678
Seattle *(G-10724)*
Page Cellars ....G 253 232-9463
Woodinville *(G-15331)*
Palouse Winery ....G 206 567-4994
Vashon *(G-14740)*
Papineau LLC ....G 509 301-9074
Walla Walla *(G-14854)*
Paradisos Del Sol Winery Inc ....G 509 829-9000
Zillah *(G-15757)*
Pasek Cellars Winery Inc ....G 888 350-9463
Mount Vernon *(G-6822)*
Passing Time Winery ....G 425 892-8684
Woodinville *(G-15333)*
Patit Creek Cellars ....G 509 868-4045
Spokane *(G-12431)*
Patricia A Welch ....G 206 322-1226
Seattle *(G-10768)*
Pepper Bridge Winery LLC ....G 425 483-7026
Woodinville *(G-15334)*
▲ Pepper Bridge Winery LLC ....F 509 525-6502
Walla Walla *(G-14855)*
Piety Flats Winery ....G 509 877-3115
Yakima *(G-15647)*
Plain Cellars LLC ....F 509 548-5412
Leavenworth *(G-5813)*
Pleasant Hill Cellars ....G 206 229-5105
Bonney Lake *(G-1733)*
Pleasant Hill Winery LLC ....G 425 333-6770
Bonney Lake *(G-1734)*
Plumb Cellars ....G 509 540-5632
Walla Walla *(G-14856)*
Pomum Cellars LLC ....G 206 362-9203
Seattle *(G-10829)*
Pondera Winery LLC ....G 425 486-8500
Woodinville *(G-15337)*
Pontin Del Roza Winery ....G 509 786-4449
Prosser *(G-8062)*
Poor Italians Vineyard ....G 360 366-5970
Ferndale *(G-3889)*
Port Townsend Vineyards Winery ....G 360 385-0694
Port Townsend *(G-7917)*
Port Townsend Winery LLC ....G 360 344-8155
Port Townsend *(G-7918)*
◆ Precept Brands LLC ....D 206 267-5252
Seattle *(G-10845)*
Purple Star Winery ....G 509 628-7799
Benton City *(G-1625)*
Quilceda Creek Vintners Inc ....G 360 568-2389
Snohomish *(G-11964)*
Radix Winery ....G 419 283-7924
Richland *(G-9037)*
Rain Shadow Cellars LLC ....G 360 320-3115
Coupeville *(G-2815)*
Ram Cellars LLC ....G 360 909-6714
Washougal *(G-14981)*
◆ Rasa Vineyards LLC ....G 509 252-0900
Walla Walla *(G-14858)*
Red Mntain Amrcn Vntners Alnce ....G 509 588-3155
Benton City *(G-1626)*
Red Sky Winery LLC ....G 425 481-9864
Woodinville *(G-15346)*
Reflection Vineyards LLC ....G 360 904-4800
Ridgefield *(G-9107)*
Regal Road Winery ....G 509 838-8024
Spokane *(G-12469)*
Reininger Winery ....G 509 242-3190
Spokane *(G-12471)*
Reininger Winery LLC ....G 509 522-1994
Walla Walla *(G-14860)*
Rezabek Vineyards LLC ....G 360 896-0218
Vancouver *(G-14551)*
Rickey Canyon Vineyard ....G 206 718-9318
Rice *(G-8961)*
Riveraerie Cellars ....G 509 786-2197
Prosser *(G-8064)*
Riverbend Incorporated ....G 509 460-2886
Benton City *(G-1628)*
Robert Karl Cellars LLC ....G 509 363-1353
Spokane *(G-12480)*
Rockwall Cellars ....G 509 826-0201
OMAK *(G-7443)*
Rocky Pond Winery ....G 206 550-0938
Woodinville *(G-15350)*
Rocky Pond Winery ....G 206 458-9119
Orondo *(G-7460)*
Ros Wine Company LLC ....G 509 301-0627
Prosser *(G-8065)*
▲ Rose Saviah Winery LLC ....G 509 522-2181
Walla Walla *(G-14861)*
Rose Tucker ....G 509 837-8701
Sunnyside *(G-13139)*
Rosebud Ranches ....E 509 932-4617
Mattawa *(G-6412)*
Ross Andrew Mickel ....G 206 267-5252
Seattle *(G-10982)*
Rotie Cellars ....G 509 529-2011
Walla Walla *(G-14862)*
Rusty Grape Vineyard LLC ....G 360 513-9338
Battle Ground *(G-737)*
S&S Industries LLC ....G 360 500-9942
Cashmere *(G-2329)*
Saint Laurent Winery ....G 509 787-3700
Quincy *(G-8309)*
Samson Estates Winery ....G 360 966-4526
Everson *(G-3688)*
Sapolil Cellars ....G 509 520-5258
Walla Walla *(G-14864)*
Scatter Creek Winery ....G 360 264-9463
Tenino *(G-13624)*
Schafer Winery LLC ....G 509 522-5444
Walla Walla *(G-14865)*
Schafer Winery LLC ....F 425 985-7000
Mercer Island *(G-6482)*
▲ Seven Hills Winery LLC ....G 509 529-7198
Walla Walla *(G-14866)*
Shackelford Vintners ....G 425 350-2719
Snohomish *(G-11975)*
Shady Grove Winery LLC ....G 509 767-1400
Dallesport *(G-2865)*
Shaw Estate Wines ....G 509 876-2459
Walla Walla *(G-14868)*
Sigillo Cellars ....G 206 919-2326
Snoqualmie *(G-12023)*
Silent Vineyards Inc ....G 360 692-7497
Bremerton *(G-1999)*
Simpatico Cellars ....G 408 667-9658
Sammamish *(G-9248)*
Skagit Cellars LLC ....G 360 708-2801
Mount Vernon *(G-6837)*
Skagit Crest Vinyrd Winery LLC ....G 360 630-5176
Sedro Woolley *(G-11566)*
Sky River Brewing Inc ....G 360 793-6761
Redmond *(G-8671)*
Sky River Meadery ....F 425 242-3815
Redmond *(G-8672)*
Skyline Spirits Wine Works Co ....G 509 967-0781
West Richland *(G-15100)*
Sleeping Giant Winery LLC ....F 206 351-0719
Woodinville *(G-15367)*
Snoqualmie Vineyards ....E 509 786-2104
Prosser *(G-8066)*
Soaring Suns Properties LLC ....G 509 346-9515
Royal City *(G-9175)*
Sol Stone Winery ....G 425 417-8483
Woodinville *(G-15369)*
Songbird Vineyard LLC ....G 509 318-4044
Benton City *(G-1629)*
Soos Creek Wine Cellars LLC ....G 253 631-8775
Kent *(G-5139)*
Southard Winery ....G 509 697-3003
Selah *(G-11597)*
Southard Winery ....G 509 452-8626
Yakima *(G-15680)*
▲ Sparkman Cellers ....G 425 398-1045
Woodinville *(G-15372)*
Spoiled Dog Winery ....G 360 321-6226
Langley *(G-5786)*
Spring Valley Tasting Room ....G 509 525-1506
Walla Walla *(G-14872)*
Spring Valley Vineyard Winery ....G 509 337-6043
Walla Walla *(G-14873)*
Springboard Winery LLC ....G 509 929-4247
Ellensburg *(G-3227)*
Stavalaura Vinyards ....G 360 887-1476
Ridgefield *(G-9113)*
Stemilt Creek Winery ....G 509 662-3613
Wenatchee *(G-15076)*
Steven Jon Kludt ....F 509 687-4000
Manson *(G-6245)*
Stevens Winery ....G 425 424-9463
Bellevue *(G-1158)*
Stomani Cellars ....G 425 892-8375
Woodinville *(G-15375)*
Stoney Creek Brewing Co LLC ....G 425 836-0958
Sammamish *(G-9249)*
Stottle Winery Tasting Room ....G 360 877-2247
Hoodsport *(G-4326)*
Suite Cs Vino ....G 425 949-5006
Woodinville *(G-15379)*
Sun River Vintners LLC ....G 509 627-3100
Kennewick *(G-4731)*
Sussex Clumber LLC ....G 206 369-3615
Bellevue *(G-1169)*
Swakane Winery ....G 509 881-9688
Raymond *(G-8359)*
Synne Cellars ....G 206 851-2048
Woodinville *(G-15383)*
Tanjuli ....G 509 829-6401
Zillah *(G-15761)*

SIC

Employee Codes: A=Over 500 employees, B=251-500
C=101-250, D=51-100, E=20-50, F=10-19, G=2-9
2019 Washington
Manufacturers Register
541

20 FOOD AND KINDRED PRODUCTS SIC SECTION

Tapenade Inc .... G 206 325-3051
Seattle *(G-11267)*
Tasting Room Wines Washington .... G 206 770-9463
Seattle *(G-11273)*
Tatoosh Distillery LLC .... G 206 818-0127
Seattle *(G-11274)*
Tempus Cellars .... G 509 368-9267
Spokane *(G-12551)*
Terra Vinum LLC .... G 509 628-7799
Kennewick *(G-4732)*
Terra Vinum LLC .... G 509 551-0854
Benton City *(G-1630)*
Tesla Winery Tours LLC .... G 509 520-5528
Walla Walla *(G-14878)*
Thrall & Dodge Winery .... G 509 925-4110
Ellensburg *(G-3231)*
Three Brothers Vineyard A .... G 503 702-5549
Ridgefield *(G-9116)*
Three Kees Cider LLC .... G 425 238-3470
Snohomish *(G-11991)*
Three of Cups LLC .... G 425 286-6657
Woodinville *(G-15389)*
Thunder Hill Winery LLC .... G 360 681-5209
Sequim *(G-11665)*
Tildio Winery LLC .... G 509 687-8463
Manson *(G-6246)*
Tipsy Canyon Winery .... G 425 306-4844
Manson *(G-6247)*
Torii Mor Winery LLC .... G 425 408-0086
Woodinville *(G-15391)*
Townshend Cellar .... G 509 481-5465
Colbert *(G-2712)*
Townshend Cellar Inc .... G 509 919-3699
Spokane *(G-12565)*
Tranche Cellars LLC .... G 509 526-3500
Walla Walla *(G-14879)*
Truthteller Winery .... G 425 985-3568
Redmond *(G-8696)*
Tucannon Cellars .... G 509 545-9588
Benton City *(G-1631)*
Tunnel Hill Winery .... G 509 682-3243
Chelan *(G-2568)*
Tuuri Wines LLC .... G 509 525-2299
Walla Walla *(G-14882)*
Two Mountain Winery .... G 509 829-3900
Zillah *(G-15762)*
Two Winey Bitches Winery .... G 509 796-3600
Ford *(G-4006)*
Upland Winery LLC .... G 509 839-2606
Sunnyside *(G-13146)*
V&C LLC .... F 509 773-1976
Goldendale *(G-4211)*
Vanarnam Vineyards .... G 360 904-4800
Zillah *(G-15763)*
Victor Gutierrez .... G 509 301-4915
Walla Walla *(G-14885)*
Vin Du Lac Winery .... G 509 682-2882
Chelan *(G-2569)*
Vinmotion Wines LLC .... G 509 967-7477
West Richland *(G-15103)*
Vino Aquino Tacoma Inc .... G 253 272-5511
Tacoma *(G-13578)*
Vino Verite .... G 206 324-0324
Seattle *(G-11421)*
Wagging Tails Vineyard .... G 509 847-5287
Chattaroy *(G-2454)*
▲ Wahluke Wine Company Inc .... E 509 932-0030
Mattawa *(G-6413)*
Waliser Winery LLC .... G 509 522-4206
Walla Walla *(G-14887)*
▲ Walla Walla Vintners LLC .... G 509 525-4724
Walla Walla *(G-14896)*
▲ Walla Walla Wines LLC .... F 509 526-9463
Walla Walla *(G-14897)*
Wallfam Inc .... G 509 786-2163
Prosser *(G-8074)*
Walls Vineyards .... G 509 876-0200
Walla Walla *(G-14898)*
Washington Jones Tasting Room .... G 509 787-8108
Quincy *(G-8311)*
▲ Washington Wine & Beverage Co .... F 425 485-2437
Woodinville *(G-15402)*
Waters Winery LLC .... G 541 203-0020
Walla Walla *(G-14899)*
Wautoma Wines LLC .... G 509 378-1163
Richland *(G-9053)*
Waving Tree Vineyard & Winery .... G 509 773-6552
Goldendale *(G-4212)*
Wawawai Canyon Winery .... G 509 338-4916
Pullman *(G-8115)*
Weaver Family Winery .... G 509 386-8018
Touchet *(G-13678)*
Wedge Mountain Winery .... G 509 548-7068
Peshastin *(G-7666)*
Welcome Road Winery .... G 206 778-3028
Seattle *(G-11447)*
Westport Winery Inc .... F 360 648-2224
Aberdeen *(G-40)*
Whidbey Island Vintners .... G 360 331-3544
Greenbank *(G-4310)*
Whidbey Island Vinyard Winery .... G 360 221-2040
Langley *(G-5787)*
White Cellars .... G 425 246-1419
Sammamish *(G-9258)*
White Heron .... G 206 246-5080
Burien *(G-2137)*
Whitelatch-Hoch LLC .... G 509 586-7337
Walla Walla *(G-14902)*
Whitelatch-Hoch LLC .... G 509 956-9311
Kennewick *(G-4745)*
Whitestone Winery Inc .... G 509 636-2001
Creston *(G-2843)*
Whitewall Brewing LLC .... G 360 454-0464
Marysville *(G-6401)*
William Grssie Wine Esttes LLC .... G 913 461-4601
Fall City *(G-3710)*
Willow Crest Winery .... G 509 786-7999
Prosser *(G-8077)*
Wilridge Winery .... G 206 770-9463
Seattle *(G-11477)*
Wind River Cellar .... G 509 493-2324
Husum *(G-4367)*
Windwalker Vineyard .... G 541 490-4011
White Salmon *(G-15135)*
Winery Compliance Northwe .... G 509 528-0905
Richland *(G-9054)*
Winery Fulfillment Svcs LLC .... G 509 529-2497
Walla Walla *(G-14904)*
Winerybound LLC .... G 206 458-2831
Seattle *(G-11485)*
Wines of Substance .... F 206 745-7456
Seattle *(G-11486)*
Wits Cellars .... G 509 786-1311
Prosser *(G-8078)*
Woodhouse Family Cellars .... G 425 527-0608
Woodinville *(G-15406)*
Woodinville Wine Co .... G 425 481-8860
Woodinville *(G-15409)*
Woodward Canyon Winery Inc .... F 509 525-4129
Lowden *(G-5992)*
Wt Vintners LLC .... G 425 610-9463
Woodinville *(G-15411)*
Ww Village Winery .... G 509 529-5300
Walla Walla *(G-14905)*
Wwvwa .... G 509 526-3117
Walla Walla *(G-14906)*
▲ Wyckoff Farms Incorporated .... E 509 882-3934
Grandview *(G-4259)*
Wynoochee River Winery .... G 360 580-4452
Montesano *(G-6666)*
Xd Vintners .... G 425 210-1554
Woodinville *(G-15412)*
Zero One Vintners .... G 206 601-2407
Kent *(G-5221)*
Zero One Vintners .... G 425 242-0735
Kirkland *(G-5500)*
Zimmel Unruh Cellars LLC .... G 503 313-2235
Vancouver *(G-14709)*
Zzaphoria Spirits .... G 206 450-1353
Normandy Park *(G-7100)*

2085 Liquors, Distilled, Rectified & Blended

3 Howls .... G 206 747-8400
Seattle *(G-9321)*
Alaska Distributors Co .... G 206 682-1517
Seattle *(G-9365)*
Bainbridge Organic Distillers .... G 206 842-3184
Bainbridge Island *(G-614)*
Batch 206 Distillery LLC .... G 206 216-2803
Seattle *(G-9500)*
Big Derby Distilling Co .... G 206 504-7604
Seattle *(G-9522)*
Black Magic Beverages LLC .... G 206 632-7257
Seattle *(G-9537)*
Blend Wine Shop .... G 253 884-9688
Lakebay *(G-5688)*
Brovo Spirits LLC .... G 206 354-3919
Woodinville *(G-15198)*
Cadee Distillery LLC .... G 360 969-6041
Clinton *(G-2685)*
Cadee Distillery LLC .... G 360 969-5565
Langley *(G-5772)*
Caudill Bros Distillery .... G 360 460-6172
Port Angeles *(G-7692)*
Caudill Distillery .... G 360 457-0947
Port Angeles *(G-7693)*
Chambers Bay Distillery .... G 503 819-0542
University Place *(G-13964)*
Chehalis Brewing Group LLC .... G 360 628-8259
Olympia *(G-7248)*
Dawson-Alley LLC .... G 360 217-8244
Snohomish *(G-11895)*
Dead Oak Distilling LLC .... G 509 882-2794
Prosser *(G-8040)*
Deception Distilling LLC .... G 360 588-1000
Anacortes *(G-120)*
Delich Distillery .... G 360 552-2282
Belfair *(G-760)*
Distiller LLC .... G 206 659-4759
Kirkland *(G-5321)*
Distillers Way LLC .... G 360 927-8781
Ferndale *(G-3836)*
Distillery A Creative LLC .... G 206 696-0597
Seattle *(G-9836)*
Distillery Loft Events .... G 206 262-1022
Seattle *(G-9837)*
Distillery Provisions LLC .... G 206 861-5350
Seattle *(G-9838)*
Distillery Seaspirits .... G 360 820-0770
Woodinville *(G-15227)*
Double V Distillery .... G 360 666-0716
Battle Ground *(G-699)*
Dry Fly Distilling Inc .... F 509 489-2112
Spokane *(G-12232)*
Evil Roys Elixirs .... G 360 463-6105
Sequim *(G-11633)*
Gabrielli Distillers .... G 503 421-2797
Vancouver *(G-14246)*
Grapeworks Distilling LLC .... G 425 478-7181
Woodinville *(G-15254)*
▲ Heritage Distilling Co Inc .... G 253 509-0008
Gig Harbor *(G-4118)*
Highside Distilling LLC .... G 425 417-9000
Bremerton *(G-1960)*
Its 5 LLC .... G 509 679-9771
Cashmere *(G-2322)*
James Bay Distillers Ltd .... G 703 930-8453
Edmonds *(G-3121)*
JP Trodden Distilling LLC .... G 206 399-6291
Bothell *(G-1871)*
JP Trodden Distilling LLC .... G 425 286-2756
Woodinville *(G-15275)*
Latitude 47 Distillers .... G 206 794-0852
Seattle *(G-10379)*
Liquid Brands Distillery LLC .... G 509 413-1885
Spokane *(G-12370)*
Lynden Liquor Agency 570 .... G 360 354-4744
Lynden *(G-6033)*
▲ Mark Anthony Brands Inc .... D 206 267-4444
Seattle *(G-10486)*
Mastrogiannis Distillery LLC .... G 206 383-2463
Renton *(G-8850)*
Nightside Distillery LLC .... G 253 906-4265
Edgewood *(G-3087)*
Novo Fogo .... G 425 256-2527
Issaquah *(G-4455)*
Old Soldier Distillery .... G 253 223-4306
Tacoma *(G-13441)*
Pursuit Distilling Co .... G 206 406-2263
Enumclaw *(G-3312)*
Rainier Distillers Pmb .... G 360 350-9177
Yelm *(G-15743)*
River Town Distillers LLC .... G 425 330-4885
Snohomish *(G-11967)*
Riversands Distillery .... G 509 492-1015
Kennewick *(G-4719)*
Sandstone Distillery .... G 360 239-7272
Tenino *(G-13623)*
Schnapsleiche LLC .... G 425 591-2586
Woodinville *(G-15356)*
Scratch Distillery LLC .... G 425 673-5541
Lynnwood *(G-6192)*
Scratch Distillery LLC .... G 425 442-7306
Edmonds *(G-3153)*
Seattle Distilling Company .... G 206 463-0830
Vashon *(G-14741)*
Seattle Kombucha Company LLC .... G 425 985-2364
Kent *(G-5122)*
Sidetrack Distillery .... G 206 963-5079
Kent *(G-5130)*

SIC SECTION
20 FOOD AND KINDRED PRODUCTS

Skip Rock Distillers .... G 360 862-0272
  Snohomish *(G-11977)*
Skunk Brothers Spirits Inc .... G 360 213-3420
  Vancouver *(G-14591)*
Skyline Spirits Wine Works Co ..... G 509 967-0781
  West Richland *(G-15100)*
Snowbridge Distilling LLC .... G 206 442-1707
  Seattle *(G-11146)*
Sun Spirits Distillery LLC .... G 509 371-1622
  Richland *(G-9043)*
Tucker Distillery .... G 360 698-7043
  Bremerton *(G-2008)*
Vodka Is Vegan LLC .... G 206 278-4257
  Seattle *(G-11429)*
Wanderback Distillery LLC .... G 206 390-7530
  Seattle *(G-11435)*
White River Distillers LLC .... G 253 219-5100
  Enumclaw *(G-3327)*
Wishkah River Distillery LLC .... G 360 612-4756
  Aberdeen *(G-41)*
Woodinville Whiskey Co LLC .... F 425 486-1199
  Woodinville *(G-15408)*

2086 Soft Drinks

A & W Bottling Company Inc ...... E 425 355-0100
  Everett *(G-3353)*
American Bottling Company .... D 509 328-6984
  Spokane Valley *(G-12608)*
Bottling Group LLC .... C 509 535-0605
  Spokane *(G-12158)*
Cliffstar LLC .... D 509 522-8608
  Walla Walla *(G-14786)*
Coca Cola Bottling Co .... E 509 529-0753
  Walla Walla *(G-14787)*
Coca-Cola Bottling Co .... E 509 248-1855
  Yakima *(G-15535)*
Coca-Cola Bottling Co .... D 509 547-6712
  Pasco *(G-7561)*
Coca-Cola Btlg Co of NY Inc .... E 509 886-1136
  Wenatchee *(G-15089)*
Coca-Cola Company .... F 404 676-0887
  Bellevue *(G-857)*
Coca-Cola Refreshments .... G 425 226-6004
  Renton *(G-8774)*
Cola Cola Enterprises .... G 509 921-6229
  Spokane Valley *(G-12660)*
◆ Concordia Coffee Company Inc ... E 425 453-2800
  Redmond *(G-8422)*
Connelly Company Inc .... G 509 935-6755
  Chewelah *(G-2601)*
Corwin Beverage Co .... D 360 696-0766
  Ridgefield *(G-9076)*
Corwin Beverage Co .... E 360 696-0766
  Ridgefield *(G-9077)*
Custom Bottling Company .... G 509 528-3196
  Benton City *(G-1608)*
Custom Smoothie .... G 206 462-6264
  Seattle *(G-9772)*
Essentia Water Inc .... E 425 402-9555
  Bothell *(G-1761)*
Glacier Water Company LLC .... G 253 876-6500
  Auburn *(G-450)*
Greenland Inc .... F 206 623-2577
  Seattle *(G-10119)*
Harbor Pacific Bottling Inc .... E 360 482-4820
  Elma *(G-3248)*
Hyperfizzics .... G 904 253-5137
  Seattle *(G-10198)*
▲ Johanna Beverage Company LLC .. D 509 455-8059
  Spokane *(G-12337)*
Jones Soda Co .... E 206 624-3357
  Seattle *(G-10307)*
Kombucha Town .... G 360 224-2974
  Bellingham *(G-1398)*
L & E Bottling Co Inc .... D 360 357-3812
  Tumwater *(G-13882)*
LDB Beverage Company .... F 509 651-0381
  Stevenson *(G-13015)*
Noel Corporation .... C 509 248-4545
  Yakima *(G-15630)*
◆ Orca Beverage Inc .... F 425 349-5655
  Mukilteo *(G-6961)*
Pacific Coca Cola Bottling .... G 509 762-6987
  Moses Lake *(G-6734)*
Pepsi .... G 509 536-5585
  Spokane Valley *(G-12827)*
Pepsi Cola 7 Up Bottling Co .... G 360 757-0044
  Burlington *(G-2180)*
Pepsi Cola Bottling Co Pasco .... E 509 545-8585
  Pasco *(G-7615)*

Pepsi Northwest Beverages LLC ..... C 206 326-7487
  Seattle *(G-10782)*
▼ Pepsi Northwest Beverages LLC ... C 360 357-9090
  Tumwater *(G-13891)*
Pepsi-Cola Metro Btlg Co Inc .... D 206 326-7431
  Seattle *(G-10783)*
Pepsico .... G 253 778-7107
  Tacoma *(G-13463)*
Rainbow Cloud Kombucha LLC ...... G 253 312-3697
  Tumwater *(G-13893)*
Refresco Beverages US Inc .... E 509 582-5200
  Kennewick *(G-4717)*
Reyes Coca-Cola Bottling LLC .... C 253 503-4341
  Tacoma *(G-13498)*
Reyes Coca-Cola Bottling LLC .... D 360 475-6528
  Bremerton *(G-1993)*
Reyes Coca-Cola Bottling LLC .... G 509 921-6200
  Spokane Valley *(G-12851)*
Reyes Coca-Cola Bottling LLC .... F 509 762-5480
  Moses Lake *(G-6745)*
Rgb Soda .... G 206 437-8395
  Seattle *(G-10958)*
Richards Packaging Inc .... G 509 545-8690
  Pasco *(G-7623)*
Richardson Bottling Company .... E 253 535-6447
  Puyallup *(G-8237)*
Salish Sea Organic Liqueurs .... G 360 890-4927
  Lacey *(G-5584)*
Scuttlebutt Brewing Co LLC .... F 425 252-2829
  Everett *(G-3606)*
Seven Up Btlg Co Tri Cities .... F 509 547-1660
  Pasco *(G-7627)*
Seven Up Dr Peper Bottling Co .... F 509 547-1660
  Pasco *(G-7628)*
Shasta Beverages Inc .... E 206 575-0525
  Tukwila *(G-13817)*
Shonan Usa Inc .... G 509 453-0757
  Grandview *(G-4255)*
Side Hustle LLC .... G 509 435-6773
  Spokane Valley *(G-12870)*
Stratford Bottling Company LLC ..... G 509 853-3223
  Yakima *(G-15684)*
Struble Cider LLC .... G 206 766-0009
  Seattle *(G-11205)*
Swire Pacific Holdings Inc .... G 509 921-6200
  Spokane Valley *(G-12898)*
Swire Pacific Holdings Inc .... G 425 455-2000
  Bellevue *(G-1172)*
Swire Pacific Holdings Inc .... E 509 529-0753
  Walla Walla *(G-14875)*
▼ Talking Rain Beverage Company ... D 425 222-4900
  Preston *(G-8027)*
Unique Beverage Company LLC ...... G 425 267-0959
  Everett *(G-3643)*
Vs Foods LLC .... F 425 279-8089
  Bellevue *(G-1221)*
Walton Beverage Co .... C 360 380-1660
  Ferndale *(G-3922)*
Yakima Valley Pepsi Pak .... G 509 952-0318
  Selah *(G-11603)*

2087 Flavoring Extracts & Syrups

Allan Bros Inc .... D 509 653-2625
  Naches *(G-6993)*
Callisons Inc .... E 360 748-3316
  Chehalis *(G-2477)*
Coca-Cola Btlg Co of NY Inc .... E 509 886-1136
  Wenatchee *(G-15089)*
Dawn Food Products Inc .... E 206 623-7740
  Seattle *(G-9803)*
Deekay Essentials LLC .... G 732 809-7284
  Vancouver *(G-14173)*
Diamond Knot Brewing Co Inc .... D 425 355-4488
  Mukilteo *(G-6912)*
▲ Eagle Bev & Accessory Pdts LLC ... D 253 867-6134
  Kent *(G-4881)*
Gavriel Jecan .... G 206 332-0993
  Seattle *(G-10053)*
Gourmet Mixes Inc .... G 206 764-6006
  Seattle *(G-10103)*
▲ International Glace Inc .... E 503 267-7917
  Spokane *(G-12323)*
J M Smucker Company .... E 509 882-1530
  Grandview *(G-4248)*
Jet Farms Inc .... F 509 346-2588
  Royal City *(G-9170)*
▲ Lucks Company .... C 253 383-4815
  Tacoma *(G-13390)*
▲ McStevens Inc .... E 360 944-5788
  Vancouver *(G-14407)*

▲ Milne Aseptics LLC .... F 509 786-2240
  Prosser *(G-8058)*
◆ Northwest Naturals LLC .... E 425 885-5252
  Bothell *(G-1781)*
S S Steiner Inc .... E 509 453-4731
  Yakima *(G-15665)*
Scrappys Bitters LLC .... G 206 632-7257
  Seattle *(G-11034)*
Sharon McIlhenny .... G 509 493-9259
  White Salmon *(G-15131)*
Shrubbery LLC .... G 949 690-9834
  Seattle *(G-11103)*
Side Hustle LLC .... G 509 435-6773
  Spokane Valley *(G-12870)*
Simchuk Karene .... G 509 238-2830
  Mead *(G-6436)*
Sunfresh Foods Inc .... G 206 764-0940
  Seattle *(G-11219)*
Tree Top Inc .... D 509 782-6809
  Cashmere *(G-2331)*
Wild Flavors Inc .... G 509 773-4008
  Goldendale *(G-4214)*
Zipfizz Corporation .... B 425 398-4240
  Woodinville *(G-15415)*

2091 Fish & Seafoods, Canned & Cured

▼ Americn-Canadian Fisheries Inc ..... E 360 398-1117
  Bellingham *(G-1246)*
Barleans Fishery Inc .... G 360 384-0325
  Ferndale *(G-3817)*
Bell Buoy Crab Co Inc .... G 360 777-8272
  Chinook *(G-2614)*
Benthic Fishing LLC .... E 253 219-1500
  Bremerton *(G-1938)*
Cape Greig LLC .... G 206 545-9501
  Renton *(G-8767)*
Cauldron Investment Group LLC .... G 360 671-1098
  Bellingham *(G-1293)*
▲ Coast Seafoods Company .... D 360 875-5577
  Bellevue *(G-856)*
Dockside Cannery .... G 360 642-8870
  Ilwaco *(G-4369)*
◆ Dungeness Development Assoc .... E 425 481-0600
  Kirkland *(G-5324)*
Dungeness Development Assoc .... F 360 875-5507
  Seattle *(G-9860)*
Fishers Choice Wild Salmon .... G 360 671-6478
  Bellingham *(G-1346)*
Fishing Vessel St Jude LLC .... G 425 378-0680
  Bellevue *(G-911)*
▼ Glacier Bay Fisheries LLC .... F 206 298-1200
  Seattle *(G-10075)*
◆ Icicle Seafoods Inc .... D 206 282-0988
  Seattle *(G-10200)*
Island Enterprises .... G 360 426-4933
  Shelton *(G-11701)*
Island Enterprises .... E 360 426-4933
  Shelton *(G-11702)*
Island Enterprises .... F 360 426-3442
  Shelton *(G-11703)*
▲ Kasilof Fish Company .... E 360 658-7552
  Everett *(G-3529)*
Maruha Capital Investment Inc ..... F 206 382-0640
  Bellevue *(G-996)*
◆ North Pacific Seafoods Inc .... E 206 726-9900
  Seattle *(G-10626)*
Northwest Smoking & Curing .... G 360 733-3666
  Bellingham *(G-1470)*
Norton Sound Fish Company LLC .. E 206 298-1200
  Seattle *(G-10654)*
◆ Ocean Beauty Seafoods LLC .... C 206 285-6800
  Seattle *(G-10682)*
Pautzke Bait Co Inc .... G 509 925-6154
  Ellensburg *(G-3218)*
Pelican Packers Inc .... F 360 398-8825
  Bellingham *(G-1494)*
◆ Peter Pan Seafoods Inc .... C 206 728-6000
  Bellevue *(G-1071)*
Quinault Pride Seafoods .... G 360 276-4431
  Taholah *(G-13609)*
Sacred Waters Fish Company LLC .. E 503 913-1625
  South Bend *(G-12045)*
Seabear Company .... E 360 293-4661
  Anacortes *(G-165)*
Sportsmens Cannery .... G 360 642-2335
  Seaview *(G-11529)*
Steves Hot Smked Cheese Salmon .. G 360 829-2244
  Buckley *(G-2075)*
Svendsen Brothers Fish Inc .... F 206 767-4258
  Normandy Park *(G-7099)*

Employee Codes: A=Over 500 employees, B=251-500
C=101-250, D=51-100, E=20-50, F=10-19, G=2-9

20 FOOD AND KINDRED PRODUCTS SIC SECTION

Taylor Shellfish Company Inc..............E....... 360 875-5494
South Bend (G-12048)
◆ Taylor Shellfish Company Inc ....C....... 360 426-6178
Shelton (G-11741)
Taylor United Inc....................................E....... 360 426-6178
Shelton (G-11742)
◆ Tri Marine Fishing MGT LLC..............F....... 425 688-1288
Bellevue (G-1199)
▲ Tri-Marine International Inc..............G....... 425 688-1288
Bellevue (G-1200)
▲ Vital Choice Seafood Spc..................E....... 360 325-0104
Bellingham (G-1584)
▲ Washington Crab Producers Inc ......G....... 360 268-9161
Westport (G-15107)
◆ Wfm Select Fish Inc ....F....... 512 542-0676
Bellevue (G-1227)
Wiegardt Bros Inc....................................E....... 360 665-4111
Ocean Park (G-7183)
▲ World Wide Gourmet Foods Inc ......F....... 360 668-9404
Woodinville (G-15410)

2092 Fish & Seafoods, Fresh & Frozen

▼ Alaska Fresh Seafoods Inc ....G....... 206 285-2412
Shoreline (G-11755)
Alaska Seafood Holdings Inc................G....... 360 734-8175
Bellingham (G-1242)
Alaska Star Inc...D....... 206 282-0988
Seattle (G-9366)
Alaska Wathervane Seafoods LLC........G....... 253 582-2580
Lakewood (G-5696)
Alber Seafoods Inc ....G....... 360 642-3773
Seattle (G-9369)
Aleutian Spray Reverse LLC..................G....... 206 784-5000
Seattle (G-9372)
Alyeska Ocean Inc ....E....... 360 293-4677
Anacortes (G-99)
◆ Alyeska Seafoods Inc..........................D....... 206 682-5949
Bellevue (G-785)
◆ American Seafoods Company LLC...D....... 206 448-0300
Seattle (G-9395)
▼ Arctic Fjord Inc.....................................C....... 206 547-6557
Seattle (G-9423)
◆ Arctic Storm Inc...................................E....... 206 547-6557
Seattle (G-9424)
Bay Center Mariculture Co.....................E....... 360 875-6172
Bay Center (G-755)
◆ Bear & Wolf LLC ....F....... 206 281-7777
Seattle (G-9506)
Bell Buoy Crab Co Inc.............................E....... 360 777-8272
Chinook (G-2614)
▼ Big Creek Fisheries LLC ....C....... 425 742-8609
Everett (G-3387)
Blau Oyster Company Inc.......................F....... 360 766-6171
Bow (G-1927)
Blue Sea Fisheries....................................G....... 360 299-0936
Anacortes (G-103)
◆ Bornstein Seafoods Inc ....D....... 360 734-7990
Bellingham (G-1280)
Boundary Fish Company ....E....... 360 332-6715
Blaine (G-1662)
Briney Sea Delicacies Inc........................G....... 360 956-1797
Tumwater (G-13853)
◆ CFC Fish Company LLC ....F....... 253 478-5160
Renton (G-8770)
◆ Clipper Seafoods Ltd ....C....... 206 284-1162
Seattle (G-9697)
Coast Seafoods Company ....E....... 360 875-5557
South Bend (G-12040)
Coastal Star Inc..D....... 206 282-0988
Seattle (G-9706)
Cold Locker Processing LLC...................F....... 253 321-3233
Sumner (G-13059)
Cooke Aquaculture Pacific LLC ....F....... 206 282-0988
Seattle (G-9736)
Cooke Aquaculture Pacific LLC ....G....... 360 293-9448
Anacortes (G-117)
Cooke Seafood Usa Inc...........................G....... 206 282-0988
Seattle (G-9737)
▲ Copper River Smoking Co ....G....... 253 446-0634
Puyallup (G-8137)
Custom Seafood Services Inc ....E....... 360 267-2666
Seattle (G-9771)
D P Clarke..G....... 360 647-8185
Bellingham (G-1317)
Deep Sea Fisheries...................................G....... 206 743-3381
Lynnwood (G-6106)
▲ Dignon Co Inc.......................................G....... 206 448-6677
Lake Forest Park (G-5612)
Dungeness Development Assoc ....F....... 360 875-5507
Seattle (G-9860)
Dutch Harbor Seafoods Ltd ....E....... 425 881-8181
Redmond (G-8444)
E & E Foods Inc..E....... 206 768-8979
Renton (G-8789)
▲ Gallatin International LLC ....G....... 425 557-4356
Issaquah (G-4416)
◆ Gasllc Ltd Liability Company ....C....... 206 441-1990
Seattle (G-10051)
Golden Shamrock Inc...............................G....... 206 282-5825
Seattle (G-10095)
Heckes Clams Inc ....G....... 360 665-4371
Nahcotta (G-7010)
High Tide Seafoods Inc ....E....... 360 452-8488
Port Angeles (G-7710)
Home Port Seafood Inc ....D....... 360 676-4707
Bellingham (G-1372)
◆ Icicle Seafoods Inc ....D....... 206 282-0988
Seattle (G-10200)
▲ Independent Packers Corp ....D....... 206 285-6000
Seattle (G-10223)
Interntional Seafoods Alsk Inc ....G....... 206 284-4830
Lynnwood (G-6141)
Jgc Food Co LLC ....F....... 206 622-0420
Seattle (G-10296)
Julie Cake Fisheries Inc..........................G....... 360 636-3621
Kelso (G-4532)
▼ Kanaway Seafoods Inc ....D....... 425 485-7755
Kenmore (G-4586)
King & Prince Seafood Corp..................E....... 360 733-9090
Bellingham (G-1395)
Kiska Sea Northern LLC.........................G....... 206 784-5000
Seattle (G-10346)
Mike Breckon...G....... 360 380-0622
Ferndale (G-3871)
▲ Nelson Crab Inc.....................................E....... 360 267-2911
Tokeland (G-13633)
▼ New Continent Food USA Inc ....G....... 425 644-6448
Bellevue (G-1026)
Norquest Seafoods Inc.............................D....... 425 349-2563
Everett (G-3553)
▲ Norquest Seafoods Inc.........................E....... 206 281-7022
Seattle (G-10622)
North Star Cold Storage Inc...................E....... 360 629-9591
Stanwood (G-12983)
Northern Fish Products Inc....................E....... 253 475-3858
Tacoma (G-13430)
▲ Northern Wave LLC..............................F....... 206 217-4518
Seattle (G-10633)
◆ Nova Fisheries Inc................................G....... 206 781-2000
Seattle (G-10658)
◆ Ocean Beauty Seafoods LLC ....C....... 206 285-6800
Seattle (G-10682)
◆ Ocean Gold Seafoods Inc....................C....... 360 268-2510
Westport (G-15106)
Ocean Peace Inc ....D....... 206 282-6100
Seattle (G-10683)
Odyssey Enterprises Inc.........................C....... 206 285-7445
Seattle (G-10685)
Orca Bay Foods LLC ....B....... 206 762-7364
Seattle (G-10711)
Orient Food Production...........................G....... 253 926-1389
Fife (G-3976)
Pacific Sea Food Co Inc...........................E....... 360 225-8553
Woodland (G-15456)
▲ Paragon Seafood Company ....G....... 425 788-6077
Woodinville (G-15332)
◆ Peter Pan Seafoods Inc ....C....... 206 728-6000
Bellevue (G-1071)
Phoenix Processor Ltd Partnr ....C....... 206 286-8584
Seattle (G-10796)
Portlock Smked Sfds-Bllard Ret............G....... 206 466-1931
Seattle (G-10836)
Q Sea Specialty Services LLC ....E....... 360 398-9708
Bellingham (G-1511)
Quinault Pride Seafoods ....E....... 360 276-4431
Taholah (G-13609)
▼ Royal Aleutian Seafoods Inc...............E....... 206 283-6605
Seattle (G-10985)
Royal Viking Inc..G....... 206 783-3818
Seattle (G-10987)
Sea Storm Fisheries Inc...........................E....... 206 547-6557
Seattle (G-11038)
◆ Seafood Producers Cooperative.........E....... 360 733-0120
Bellingham (G-1527)
▲ Seafreeze Limited Partnership ....D....... 206 767-7350
Seattle (G-11043)
◆ Shining Ocean Inc ....C....... 253 826-3700
Sumner (G-13098)
◆ Signature Seafoods Inc ....G....... 206 285-2815
Seattle (G-11108)
South Bend Products LLC ....D....... 360 875-6570
South Bend (G-12047)
▼ Starbound LLC......................................C....... 206 784-5000
Seattle (G-11181)
▲ Sugiyo USA Inc.....................................D....... 360 293-0180
Anacortes (G-170)
▼ Swinomish Fish Co Inc........................G....... 360 466-0176
La Conner (G-5526)
T K O Fisheries Inc...................................G....... 206 285-2815
Seattle (G-11249)
Taylor Mariculture LLC...........................G....... 360 426-6178
Shelton (G-11739)
◆ Taylor Resources Inc ....C....... 360 426-6178
Shelton (G-11740)
Taylor Shellfish Company Inc................E....... 360 875-5494
South Bend (G-12048)
◆ Taylor Shellfish Company Inc ....C....... 360 426-6178
Shelton (G-11741)
Taylor United Inc......................................E....... 360 426-6178
Shelton (G-11742)
Toke Point Fisheries Inc..........................G....... 360 753-6917
Olympia (G-7409)
Trader Bay Ltd...D....... 253 884-5249
Lakebay (G-5691)
Tribal Fishco LLC......................................F....... 509 493-1104
White Salmon (G-15134)
Trident Carrollton LLC.............................G....... 206 783-3818
Seattle (G-11333)
◆ Trident Seafoods Asia Inc....................F....... 206 783-3818
Seattle (G-11334)
Trident Seafoods Corporation ....C....... 360 734-8900
Bellingham (G-1575)
Trident Seafoods Corporation ....C....... 425 407-4000
Everett (G-3637)
◆ Trident Seafoods Corporation...........B....... 206 783-3818
Seattle (G-11335)
Trident Seafoods Corporation ....G....... 206 783-3818
Seattle (G-11336)
Trident Seafoods Corporation ....G....... 360 671-0669
Bellingham (G-1576)
Trident Seafoods Corporation ....B....... 360 293-3133
Anacortes (G-180)
Trident Seafoods Corporation ....B....... 253 502-5318
Tacoma (G-13563)
Trident Seafoods Corporation ....B....... 360 740-7816
Chehalis (G-2539)
Trident Seafoods Corporation ....C....... 360 293-7701
Anacortes (G-179)
Trio Machinery Inc ....G....... 360 671-6229
Blaine (G-1707)
▲ Washington Crab Producers Inc ......G....... 360 268-9161
Westport (G-15107)
▼ Westward Seafoods Inc.......................C....... 206 682-5949
Bellevue (G-1225)
Wiegardt Bros Inc......................................E....... 360 665-4111
Ocean Park (G-7183)
▼ Yardarm Knot Inc ....E....... 206 216-0220
Seattle (G-11508)

2095 Coffee

▲ Austin Chase Coffee Inc......................G....... 206 281-8040
Seattle (G-9464)
Bean Collection Coffee Inc ....G....... 206 382-1966
Seattle (G-9505)
Boyd Coffee Company ....G....... 425 744-1394
Lynnwood (G-6085)
Cafe Las Americas.....................................G....... 253 272-0644
Tacoma (G-13216)
▲ Caffe Appassionato Inc ....E....... 206 281-8040
Seattle (G-9605)
Cascade Coffee Inc...................................F....... 425 347-3995
Everett (G-3410)
Chadao Tea Co Inc....................................G....... 206 335-6585
Seattle (G-9664)
Commencement Bay Coffee Co ....G....... 253 851-8259
Gig Harbor (G-4092)
◆ Dillanos Coffee Roasters Inc..............E....... 253 826-1807
Sumner (G-13066)
Distant Lands Trading Co ....G....... 800 758-4437
Renton (G-8784)
▲ Eko Brands LLC.....................................E....... 800 833-0622
Woodinville (G-15234)
Emerald Hills Coffee Inc.........................G....... 800 562-6015
Mukilteo (G-6924)
Farmer Bros Co..G....... 509 457-6031
Union Gap (G-13929)
Farmer Bros Co..E....... 425 881-7030
Redmond (G-8459)
Fidalgo Bay Coffee Inc.............................E....... 360 757-8818
Burlington (G-2158)

SIC SECTION 20 FOOD AND KINDRED PRODUCTS

Fstopcafe LLC .... G 206 842-0335
Bainbridge Island *(G-635)*
▲ Gbjc Inc .... G 360 321-5262
Mukilteo *(G-6927)*
Grounds For Change Inc .... G 360 779-0401
Poulsbo *(G-7964)*
Haley & Bros .... G 253 851-4977
Gig Harbor *(G-4109)*
Hook Line and Espresso .... G 360 691-7095
Granite Falls *(G-4277)*
Java Java Coffee Company Inc .... G 425 432-5261
Maple Valley *(G-6278)*
▲ Java Trading Co LLC .... C 425 917-2920
Renton *(G-8832)*
Joes Garage LLC .... F 206 466-5579
Tukwila *(G-13758)*
Keurig Green Mountain Inc .... C 253 447-9100
Sumner *(G-13078)*
L Lazy Corp .... G 509 448-3426
Spokane *(G-12357)*
Lighthouse Roasters Inc .... F 206 633-4775
Seattle *(G-10418)*
Little Bean Coffee LLC .... G 425 829-8289
Redmond *(G-8535)*
Mark Sholtys .... G 509 930-1725
Moxee *(G-6881)*
Millars Organic WD Roasted Cof .... G 360 686-3643
Yacolt *(G-15487)*
NW Coffee Rosters LLC .... F 360 442-4111
Longview *(G-5939)*
Olympic Crest Coffee Roasters .... G 360 459-5756
Olympia *(G-7357)*
Pioneer Coffee Roasting Co LLC .... G 509 674-4100
Cle Elum *(G-2676)*
Roast House LLC .... G 509 995-6500
Spokane *(G-12478)*
Sirjmr Inc .... E 509 582-2683
Kennewick *(G-4728)*
South Sound Aquaponics LLC .... G 206 510-0408
Federal Way *(G-3789)*
▲ Tc Global Inc .... D 206 233-2070
Seattle *(G-11275)*
Tullys Cof Asia PCF Prtners LP .... G 206 233-2070
Seattle *(G-11347)*

2096 Potato Chips & Similar Prdts

Bright Candies .... G 509 525-5533
Walla Walla *(G-14774)*
Campbell Soup Company .... B 425 415-2000
Woodinville *(G-15204)*
Daisy Maiz LLC .... G 360 718-8288
Vancouver *(G-14165)*
Frito-Lay North America Inc .... A 360 737-3000
Vancouver *(G-14241)*
Gruma Corporation .... C 253 896-4483
Fife *(G-3957)*
Jalisco LLC .... F 360 432-9397
Shelton *(G-11704)*
▼ Kennedy Endeavors Incorporated .... D 253 833-0255
Algona *(G-72)*
La Michoacana .... G 360 658-1635
Marysville *(G-6349)*
Lamb Weston Bsw LLC .... E 509 349-2210
Warden *(G-14932)*
Noahs Ark Foods LLC .... G 509 595-8642
Palouse *(G-7546)*
Old Timers Pork Rinds .... G 509 438-8999
Prosser *(G-8060)*
▲ Pop Gourmet LLC .... D 425 277-5225
Tukwila *(G-13792)*
S & W Management Co Inc .... E 425 771-6850
Lynnwood *(G-6191)*
T D Kennedy and Associates Inc .... G 253 922-2558
Tacoma *(G-13537)*
Tortilleria Jalisco .... G 253 536-9532
Spanaway *(G-12078)*
Watford Tanikka .... G 360 499-6327
Lacey *(G-5601)*

2097 Ice

Airgas Usa LLC .... E 253 872-7000
Kent *(G-4766)*
Allied Grinders Inc .... F 425 493-1313
Mukilteo *(G-6892)*
Articland Ice .... G 509 582-5808
Kennewick *(G-4620)*
Columbia Basin Ice LLC .... E 509 736-9583
Kennewick *(G-4645)*
Crystal Clear Ice Co .... G 509 525-1042
Walla Walla *(G-14792)*
Inland Ice & Fuel Inc .... G 509 457-6151
Yakima *(G-15590)*
Lynden Meat Company LLC .... F 360 354-5227
Lynden *(G-6034)*
Nanoice .... G 206 257-3380
Tukwila *(G-13775)*
Nanoice Inc .... G 206 257-3380
Woodinville *(G-15318)*
R Plum Corporation .... F 509 328-2070
Spokane *(G-12465)*
Silvercreek Ice .... G 360 985-2385
Silver Creek *(G-11825)*

2098 Macaroni, Spaghetti & Noodles

Boom Noodle .... F 425 453-6094
Bellevue *(G-827)*
Boom Noodle Corp Uv .... F 206 525-2675
Seattle *(G-9564)*
▲ Carsos Pasta Company Inc .... E 206 283-8227
Lynnwood *(G-6087)*
Chinese Seafood Noodle LLC .... G 425 877-8856
Bellevue *(G-850)*
Cucina Fresca Inc .... F 206 903-0825
Seattle *(G-9763)*
Dashi Noodle Bar .... G 206 595-1995
Bellingham *(G-1318)*
Hanazono Asian Noodle .... G 360 385-7622
Port Townsend *(G-7887)*
I Love Ramen Japenese Noodle .... G 253 839-1115
Federal Way *(G-3744)*
Love Noodle Inc .... G 425 513-8888
Everett *(G-3540)*
Maninis LLC .... F 206 686-4600
Kent *(G-5003)*
Meat and Noodle .... G 206 408-7650
Vashon *(G-14735)*
Noodle Express .... F 509 927-4117
Spokane *(G-12405)*
Oodles Noodle Bar .... G 425 467-7076
Bellevue *(G-1050)*
Samurai Noodle .... G 206 624-9321
Seattle *(G-11010)*
▲ Tsue Chong Co Inc .... E 206 623-0801
Seattle *(G-11346)*
U Don LLC .... F 206 466-1471
Seattle *(G-11358)*
Youngwol Noodle .... G 253 941-2002
Federal Way *(G-3806)*

2099 Food Preparations, NEC

Anacortes Oil Vinegar Bar LLC .... G 360 293-6410
Anacortes *(G-100)*
Ayurveg Inc .... G 360 863-2457
Gold Bar *(G-4186)*
B & B Foods Inc .... G 906 493-6962
Walla Walla *(G-14766)*
Bad Breath Garlic Co .... G 253 223-1835
Puyallup *(G-8127)*
Basic American Inc .... C 509 765-8601
Moses Lake *(G-6684)*
Bellingham Pasta Company .... F 360 594-6000
Bellingham *(G-1267)*
Bimbo Bakeries Usa Inc .... G 253 759-2146
Tacoma *(G-13201)*
Broussards Creole Foods Inc .... G 253 638-2098
Kent *(G-4824)*
▲ Bumblebar Inc .... F 509 924-2080
Spokane Valley *(G-12648)*
Butler Did It .... G 360 737-2672
Vancouver *(G-14087)*
Cascade Mountain Blends NW LLC .... G 425 275-3344
Lynnwood *(G-6088)*
Central Market Incorporated .... G 509 787-5100
Quincy *(G-8293)*
Cherrys Jubilee .... G 253 862-6751
Lake Tapps *(G-5677)*
◆ Conifer Specialties Inc .... D 425 486-3334
Woodinville *(G-15210)*
Consolidated Food Management .... G 253 589-5654
Lakewood *(G-5708)*
▲ Crunch Pak LLC .... A 509 782-2807
Cashmere *(G-2319)*
Cucina Fresca Inc .... F 206 903-0825
Seattle *(G-9763)*
D A M Salsa LLC .... G 206 527-0300
Seattle *(G-9778)*
Daddy Daughter Diner LLC .... G 425 442-8307
Bothell *(G-1845)*
Damn Good Pepper .... G 206 675-0540
Seattle *(G-9789)*
Dawn Food Products Inc .... E 206 623-7740
Seattle *(G-9803)*
Del Rio Food Processing Corp .... F 206 767-9102
Seattle *(G-9816)*
Desimone Oil and Vinegar Mkt .... G 253 709-5576
Renton *(G-8783)*
Dodson Rd Orchard LLC .... D 509 787-3537
Quincy *(G-8296)*
Don Pancho Authenti .... E 509 575-4489
Yakima *(G-15557)*
Dynamic Food Ingredients Corp .... G 303 459-5908
Spokane *(G-12234)*
Eclaire Farm LLC .... G 360 524-9775
Vancouver *(G-14193)*
El Dorado Tortillas LLC .... G 719 459-2576
Kirkland *(G-5330)*
Ernestinas Tortillas LLC .... G 360 669-0319
Centralia *(G-2400)*
Ethen Foods Inc .... G 206 778-0931
Newcastle *(G-7029)*
Evergreens Salad .... G 206 973-4400
Seattle *(G-9947)*
Factors Group Mfg Inc .... G 360 243-3500
Monroe *(G-6572)*
Fantazimo Food .... G 206 484-8232
Mountlake Terrace *(G-6860)*
Farm To Market Foods LLC .... G 360 708-6103
Burlington *(G-2157)*
Farmer Bros Co .... E 425 881-7030
Redmond *(G-8459)*
Ferris Fun Foods .... G 253 964-2828
Dupont *(G-2963)*
Finas Salsa .... G 360 951-5218
Olympia *(G-7283)*
◆ Flora Inc .... D 360 354-2110
Lynden *(G-6019)*
Food Master (pnw) Corp .... E 253 846-2600
Tacoma *(G-13300)*
For The Love of Spice .... G 253 858-0272
Gig Harbor *(G-4102)*
Fortun Foods Inc .... F 425 827-1977
Kirkland *(G-5342)*
Four Seasons Gourmet Food Proc .... G 847 636-9879
Seattle *(G-10017)*
Freedom Snacks LLC .... G 253 886-1838
Normandy Park *(G-7094)*
Friday Harbor Exports Inc .... G 360 378-6086
Friday Harbor *(G-4045)*
Garden Fresh Foods Inc .... D 425 483-5467
Woodinville *(G-15250)*
Garvey C Maury .... G 425 641-0232
Bellevue *(G-919)*
General Mills Inc .... E 763 764-7600
Sedro Woolley *(G-11539)*
Golden Boy Foods (usa) Inc .... G 360 332-1990
Blaine *(G-1671)*
Golden Nut Company (usa) Inc .... E 360 332-1990
Blaine *(G-1673)*
Golden State Foods Corp .... G 509 928-9055
Spokane Valley *(G-12722)*
Grampas Garlic Salt LLC .... G 425 513-0446
Everett *(G-3504)*
Grand Temple .... G 509 715-7876
Liberty Lake *(G-5833)*
Grandma Ednas .... G 425 200-5435
Marysville *(G-6340)*
Greenland Inc .... F 206 623-2577
Seattle *(G-10119)*
Gruma Corporation .... C 253 896-4483
Fife *(G-3957)*
Guadalupe Foods Inc .... G 360 736-0298
Rochester *(G-9133)*
Guy Chai Inc .... G 360 710-5962
Bremerton *(G-1959)*
Hearthside Usa LLC .... G 206 745-0850
Seatac *(G-9286)*
Hoffman Honey Co .... G 360 568-5210
Snohomish *(G-11921)*
Humming Hemp LLC .... G 503 559-6476
Richland *(G-9007)*
Imagine Food .... G 917 428-4173
Covington *(G-2830)*
Incline Cider Company .... G 503 830-4414
Auburn *(G-475)*
Innovative Freeze Dried Fd LLC .... E 855 836-3233
Ferndale *(G-3857)*
Innovative Solutions Intl .... F 206 365-7200
Mercer Island *(G-6468)*
Island Bankra Caribbean Foods .... G 360 698-3345
Silverdale *(G-11839)*

SIC

Employee Codes: A=Over 500 employees, B=251-500
C=101-250, D=51-100, E=20-50, F=10-19, G=2-9

2019 Washington
Manufacturers Register

545

20 FOOD AND KINDRED PRODUCTS

J&Ds Down Home Entps Inc .... G 206 388-3395
  Seattle *(G-10275)*
January Company .... E 253 872-9919
  Kent *(G-4964)*
Jester and Judge Cider Company .... E 509 651-0381
  Stevenson *(G-13013)*
Jgc Food Co LLC .... F 206 622-0420
  Seattle *(G-10296)*
Johnnys Fine Foods Inc .... E 253 383-4597
  Tacoma *(G-13362)*
Jot Products Co .... G 206 331-6677
  Renton *(G-8833)*
JR Simplot Company .... G 509 765-3443
  Moses Lake *(G-6719)*
JR Simplot Company .... E 509 765-5663
  Othello *(G-7499)*
Jumbo Foods Inc .... C 425 355-1103
  Mukilteo *(G-6946)*
Just Salsa .... G 253 455-4618
  Puyallup *(G-8170)*
▲ Kof Enterprises LLC .... F 206 328-2972
  Seattle *(G-10351)*
Kracker Tortilla Distribution .... G 253 380-2690
  Edgewood *(G-3084)*
La Mexicana Inc .... E 206 763-1488
  Seattle *(G-10368)*
Lamb Weston Holdings Inc .... B 509 234-5511
  Connell *(G-2795)*
Lamb Weston Holdings Inc .... E 509 882-1417
  Prosser *(G-8049)*
Lamb Weston Inc .... A 509 787-3567
  Quincy *(G-8301)*
Lamb Weston Inc .... C 509 875-2423
  Paterson *(G-7658)*
Langes Honey Skep Inc .... G 360 757-1073
  Burlington *(G-2167)*
Larry S Ayre .... G 509 582-8925
  Kennewick *(G-4687)*
Lattins Country Cider .... E 360 491-7328
  Olympia *(G-7319)*
Lolo Foods .... G 509 860-8021
  Wenatchee *(G-15045)*
Lopez Island Chamber Commerce ...... G 360 468-4664
  Olga *(G-7215)*
Lostacos Locos .... G 360 573-1327
  Vancouver *(G-14382)*
Loving Superfoods LLC .... G 214 717-3321
  Vancouver *(G-14384)*
Matrix Health .... G 360 816-1200
  Vancouver *(G-14402)*
McCain Foods Usa Inc .... A 509 488-9611
  Othello *(G-7502)*
▲ Medallion Foods Inc .... D 253 846-2600
  Tacoma *(G-13406)*
Mercer Ranches Inc .... D 509 894-4773
  Prosser *(G-8053)*
Metabolic Global .... G 206 660-7243
  Seattle *(G-10519)*
Miracle Studios .... G 833 728-3233
  Bonney Lake *(G-1729)*
Mountain Valley Products Inc .... E 509 837-8084
  Sunnyside *(G-13134)*
Mustard and Co LLC .... G 734 904-9877
  Seattle *(G-10576)*
My Local Co .... F 360 989-6903
  Seattle *(G-10579)*
National Frozen Foods Corp .... E 509 766-0793
  Moses Lake *(G-6730)*
Natural Matters Inc .... G 206 387-7054
  Seattle *(G-10592)*
▲ New Royal Meat LLC .... G 206 629-4958
  Shoreline *(G-11792)*
▲ Newgem Foods LLC .... F 209 948-1508
  Fife *(G-3973)*
Newly Weds Foods Inc .... D 253 584-9270
  Lakewood *(G-5741)*
Northwest Brewery Works Inc .... G 425 255-0698
  Newcastle *(G-7037)*
Nut Factory Inc .... E 509 926-6666
  Spokane Valley *(G-12815)*
Oil & Vinegar Retail .... G 509 838-7115
  Spokane *(G-12420)*
Oil Vinegar .... G 206 285-0517
  Seattle *(G-10688)*
Olive Navidis Oil & Vinegars .... G 360 600-9836
  Washougal *(G-14975)*
Pacific Nutritional Inc .... C 360 253-3197
  Vancouver *(G-14467)*
Pacific NW Frmrs Coop Inc .... F 509 283-2124
  Fairfield *(G-3697)*

Pacwest Dental Lab .... G 360 635-3976
  Vancouver *(G-14476)*
Passport Food Group LLC .... E 253 520-9299
  Kent *(G-5060)*
▼ Pizza Blends LLC .... F 800 826-1200
  Bellevue *(G-1076)*
Premium World Food Corporation ...... G 206 267-8914
  Renton *(G-8885)*
Pride of The West Inc .... G 360 694-4976
  Vancouver *(G-14504)*
Puget Sound Foods Inc .... F 206 232-2757
  Mercer Island *(G-6481)*
Rallito De Luna .... G 509 488-4272
  Othello *(G-7504)*
Rallito De Luna Tortilla .... G 509 586-8691
  Kennewick *(G-4713)*
Resers Fine Foods Inc .... D 509 543-4911
  Pasco *(G-7622)*
Rich Nature Organic .... G 425 315-7000
  Mukilteo *(G-6973)*
Rojos Famous Inc .... G 206 592-6581
  Normandy Park *(G-7097)*
Roys Salsa LLC .... G 253 514-3767
  Gig Harbor *(G-4157)*
S&L Foods LLC .... G 360 627-7809
  Bremerton *(G-1996)*
Salsa 7 .... G 253 445-6525
  Puyallup *(G-8245)*
Salsa With A Kick .... G 253 820-7622
  Lakewood *(G-5753)*
Salted Vinegar Studios .... G 931 302-0434
  Olympia *(G-7391)*
◆ Saltworks Inc .... D 425 885-7258
  Woodinville *(G-15353)*
Samuel & Company Inc .... G 425 883-1220
  Redmond *(G-8657)*
Santees Granola Inc .... G 509 245-3338
  Spangle *(G-12084)*
Schilling Cider .... G 208 660-4086
  Seattle *(G-11026)*
Schilling Cider LLC .... F 408 390-8754
  Auburn *(G-556)*
▲ Seasalt Superstore LLC .... E 425 249-2331
  Everett *(G-3608)*
Seasoningsnet LLC .... F 253 237-0550
  Kent *(G-5120)*
Seattle Egg Roll Corp .... G 425 226-6256
  Renton *(G-8908)*
Seneca Foods Corporation .... C 509 837-3806
  Sunnyside *(G-13140)*
Seneca Foods Corporation .... E 509 457-1089
  Yakima *(G-15671)*
Senior Services For S Sound .... G 360 426-3697
  Shelton *(G-11730)*
Severly Good Gluten Free LLC .... G 253 759-5288
  Tacoma *(G-13511)*
Sharon McIlhenny .... G 509 493-9259
  White Salmon *(G-15131)*
▲ Sheffield Cider Inc .... G 509 269-4610
  Mesa *(G-6496)*
Sissys Specialty Foods .... G 360 807-4305
  Centralia *(G-2435)*
Sk Food Group Inc .... F 206 935-8100
  Seattle *(G-11124)*
Skagits Best Salsa .... G 360 610-9022
  Mount Vernon *(G-6842)*
Skillet Food Products LLC .... G 206 420-7297
  Seattle *(G-11126)*
Sky Valley Foods Inc .... G 360 805-1430
  Monroe *(G-6620)*
Small Planet Foods Inc .... E 800 624-4123
  Sedro Woolley *(G-11569)*
Snackflash LLC .... G 509 443-0396
  Spokane *(G-12508)*
Spice Hut Corporation .... F 360 671-2800
  Bellingham *(G-1552)*
Suenos De Salsa .... G 206 334-7496
  Seattle *(G-11212)*
▲ Sugimoto Seicha Usa Inc .... G 425 558-5552
  Redmond *(G-8686)*
Sunrice LLC .... G 206 841-2454
  Seattle *(G-11220)*
▲ Tacoma Tofu Inc .... G 253 627-5085
  Tacoma *(G-13550)*
▲ Tacoma Tofu Inc .... G 253 627-5085
  Lakewood *(G-5761)*
Tamu Foods .... G 253 835-1855
  Federal Way *(G-3793)*
Taylor Farms Northwest LLC .... F 206 764-4499
  Kent *(G-5172)*

Tobys Tortillas LLC .... G 425 344-7653
  Snohomish *(G-11992)*
Tortilla Union .... G 509 381-5162
  Spokane *(G-12563)*
Tortilleria Valparaiso .... G 509 542-1340
  Pasco *(G-7642)*
Travelers Tea Bar .... E 206 329-6260
  Seattle *(G-11328)*
Triple b Corporation .... D 509 535-7393
  Spokane *(G-12569)*
▲ Tsue Chong Co Inc .... E 206 623-0801
  Seattle *(G-11346)*
Twin City Foods Inc .... C 509 962-9806
  Ellensburg *(G-3235)*
Twin City Foods Inc .... B 509 786-2700
  Prosser *(G-8071)*
Vana Life Foods LP .... G 347 446-6504
  Seattle *(G-11402)*
Vansh Foods LLC .... G 425 743-1043
  Everett *(G-3646)*
Vinegar & Oil .... G 425 454-8497
  Bellevue *(G-1217)*
Washington Potato Company Inc .... D 509 349-8803
  Warden *(G-14938)*
Waugh Enterprises LLC .... G 360 468-4372
  Lopez Island *(G-5988)*
Zz Inc .... G 360 734-2290
  Bellingham *(G-1598)*

21 TOBACCO PRODUCTS

2111 Cigarettes

Altria .... G 253 922-4267
  Fife *(G-3929)*
BJ II Inc .... G 253 926-8538
  Fife *(G-3939)*
Cigaretto .... G 253 851-2175
  Gig Harbor *(G-4088)*
Cigarland Gig Harbor .... G 253 851-5515
  Gig Harbor *(G-4089)*
Smoke Plus .... G 206 579-3661
  Kent *(G-5137)*
Tobacco City .... G 425 377-1658
  Lake Stevens *(G-5672)*

2121 Cigars

Cigarland Gig Harbor .... G 253 851-5515
  Gig Harbor *(G-4089)*

2131 Tobacco, Chewing & Snuff

Benson Smoke .... G 253 859-6120
  Kent *(G-4813)*
Piece Mind Tobacco ACC LLC ...... G 206 588-0216
  Seattle *(G-10803)*
Smokin Legal Anywhere .... G 509 465-2695
  Spokane *(G-12507)*
Spoony Luv .... G 206 240-8584
  Shoreline *(G-11817)*
Tobacco Station-WA .... G 253 517-5618
  Federal Way *(G-3796)*

22 TEXTILE MILL PRODUCTS

2211 Cotton, Woven Fabric

Barco Inc .... F 425 251-3530
  Kent *(G-4808)*
Billdon LLC .... G 425 736-4316
  Sammamish *(G-9190)*
Canvas .... G 206 829-9858
  Seattle *(G-9620)*
Canvas Traditions .... G 206 313-0223
  Seattle *(G-9622)*
Circa 15 Fabric Studio LLC .... G 425 309-9553
  Anacortes *(G-113)*
▲ Clothworks Textiles Inc .... E 206 762-7886
  Seattle *(G-9698)*
Coffee On Canvas .... G 419 605-2529
  Fircrest *(G-4001)*
Colby Creations Inc .... G 509 234-9736
  Connell *(G-2791)*
Comeau Lettering .... G 360 573-2216
  Vancouver *(G-14141)*
Cookes Canvas & Sewing .... G 360 384-1636
  Ferndale *(G-3833)*
Crimson Canvas Arts .... G 610 235-7605
  Sammamish *(G-9200)*
Denim Dreamz .... G 425 712-1001
  Edmonds *(G-3106)*

SIC SECTION 22 TEXTILE MILL PRODUCTS

Denim Duds ... G ... 360 432-1183
Shelton *(G-11696)*

Denim Frills ... G ... 360 844-5163
Vancouver *(G-14175)*

Fabrications Inc ... G ... 888 808-9878
Mercer Island *(G-6462)*

Fourplay Awd ... G ... 971 706-7646
Vancouver *(G-14237)*

Gaes Draperies ... G ... 360 293-9732
Anacortes *(G-132)*

Glant Textiles Corporation ... E ... 206 725-4444
Seattle *(G-10078)*

Glenbar Alpacas Inc ... G ... 360 574-5428
Ridgefield *(G-9085)*

Hanging Canvas ... G ... 206 937-3525
Seattle *(G-10138)*

Jovipak Corporation ... F ... 206 575-1656
Kent *(G-4971)*

Justus Bag Company Inc ... G ... 509 765-6981
Moses Lake *(G-6720)*

Lady 12 LLC ... G ... 425 218-3080
Redmond *(G-8528)*

Life On Canvas ... G ... 503 470-9474
Auburn *(G-488)*

▲ **Milo & Gabby LLC** ... G ... 206 257-1957
Seattle *(G-10544)*

Nestor Enterprises LLC ... G ... 206 794-4989
Edmonds *(G-3136)*

Northwest Sails & Canvas Inc ... G ... 360 301-3204
Port Townsend *(G-7902)*

Northwest Tarp & Canvas ... G ... 360 296-2321
Bellingham *(G-1472)*

Port Townsend Community ... G ... 360 385-0120
Port Townsend *(G-7909)*

Puget Sound Canvas Uphols ... G ... 206 782-5974
Gold Bar *(G-4190)*

Quilting Fairy LLC ... G ... 253 845-0462
Puyallup *(G-8232)*

Rag Man LLC ... G ... 206 653-7125
Kent *(G-5096)*

Shoreline Custom Canvas & Auto ... G ... 360 874-2702
Port Orchard *(G-7847)*

Stretch and Staple ... G ... 206 607-9277
Seattle *(G-11203)*

▲ **Thermedia Corporation** ... G ... 360 427-1877
Shelton *(G-11744)*

Uncorked Canvas ... G ... 253 301-1254
Tacoma *(G-13569)*

White Cloud Alpacas ... G ... 253 853-6984
Olalla *(G-7212)*

◆ **Wntr Ski Academy LLC** ... G ... 425 829-1384
Kirkland *(G-5495)*

Wright Designs ... G ... 800 866-1245
Renton *(G-8950)*

2221 Silk & Man-Made Fiber

B & C Fiberglass Inc ... G ... 907 842-4767
Bellingham *(G-1255)*

Bedrock Industries Inc ... F ... 206 283-7625
Seattle *(G-9508)*

Breezy Upholstery & Canvas ... G ... 206 545-8538
Seattle *(G-9582)*

Campbell Pet Company ... F ... 360 892-9786
Vancouver *(G-14093)*

Chara Creations ... G ... 360 658-0574
Marysville *(G-6324)*

▲ **Comptex Inc** ... F ... 360 466-5453
La Conner *(G-5522)*

Dan Coats ... G ... 360 892-2730
Vancouver *(G-14166)*

Danalco Inc ... E ... 626 303-4019
Seattle *(G-9790)*

K & L Unlimited ... G ... 509 965-6451
Yakima *(G-15604)*

Load Control Systems Inc ... G ... 253 284-0351
Tacoma *(G-13389)*

Paul Sessions ... G ... 360 265-1658
Bremerton *(G-1987)*

R&D Enterprises ... G ... 360 293-4155
Anacortes *(G-163)*

Redwood Plastics and Rbr Corp ... E ... 360 225-1491
Woodland *(G-15461)*

Revchem Composites Inc ... G ... 253 305-0303
Tacoma *(G-13496)*

Satin Group LLC A ... G ... 206 228-1364
Seattle *(G-11016)*

Squalicum Marine Inc ... G ... 360 733-4353
Bellingham *(G-1554)*

Sunbacker Fiberglass Inc ... G ... 360 794-5547
Monroe *(G-6628)*

◆ **Tactical Tailor Inc** ... D ... 253 984-7854
Lakewood *(G-5762)*

▲ **Tiegrrr Straps Inc** ... G ... 253 520-0303
Kent *(G-5180)*

Warren Hartz ... G ... 360 793-0691
Index *(G-4372)*

Xerium Technologies Inc ... G ... 360 636-0330
Kelso *(G-4561)*

Yong Feng America Inc ... G ... 425 271-8057
Bellevue *(G-1230)*

2231 Wool, Woven Fabric

Alpaca Mentors ... G ... 253 880-6469
Enumclaw *(G-3276)*

Alpaca This LLC ... G ... 425 432-7227
Maple Valley *(G-6256)*

Alpacas Northwest Inc ... G ... 503 519-7587
Vancouver *(G-14023)*

Alpacas of Wintercreek ... G ... 253 332-4026
Auburn *(G-372)*

Alpacas Paradise Pt ... G ... 360 263-2092
Ridgefield *(G-9060)*

Brush Prairie Alpacas ... G ... 360 892-1011
Brush Prairie *(G-2031)*

Cascade Rose Alpacas ... G ... 206 715-6910
Carnation *(G-2291)*

Cusichaca Alpacas ... G ... 360 936-3259
La Center *(G-5503)*

Fiber Meadows Alpacas LLC ... G ... 360 856-5740
Sedro Woolley *(G-11537)*

Meadowrock Alpacas ... G ... 509 395-2266
Trout Lake *(G-13680)*

Merrimac Alpacas ... G ... 425 387-7586
Snohomish *(G-11946)*

Mt Peak Alpacas LLC ... G ... 253 297-4083
Enumclaw *(G-3306)*

Pendleton Woolen Mills Inc ... C ... 360 835-2131
Washougal *(G-14977)*

Peoh Point Alpaca Farm ... G ... 509 674-9120
Cle Elum *(G-2675)*

Rv Alpacas ... G ... 253 431-6747
Rainier *(G-8322)*

Stellar Alpacas ... G ... 253 208-2107
Spanaway *(G-12076)*

Super Suris Alpacas ... G ... 509 475-5110
Mead *(G-6438)*

Wheatland Alpacas ... G ... 509 526-4847
Walla Walla *(G-14901)*

Yangarra Alpacas ... G ... 253 630-5422
Covington *(G-2841)*

2241 Fabric Mills, Cotton, Wool, Silk & Man-Made

▲ **Bridport-Air Carrier Inc** ... E ... 253 872-7205
Kent *(G-4823)*

Gafftech LLC ... G ... 844 423-3486
Sumner *(G-13072)*

H A Milton Corp ... G ... 509 346-1192
Royal City *(G-9169)*

▲ **Mid Mountain Materials Inc** ... E ... 206 762-7600
Seattle *(G-10539)*

Pacific Strapping Inc ... F ... 206 262-9800
Tukwila *(G-13788)*

Ralston Cunningham Associates ... G ... 425 455-0316
Redmond *(G-8645)*

2252 Hosiery, Except Women's

16 Cents Corp ... F ... 509 329-1600
Spokane *(G-12086)*

Ballard Sock Critters ... G ... 206 218-9215
Seattle *(G-9485)*

Danalco Inc ... E ... 626 303-4019
Seattle *(G-9790)*

Ellsworth & Company LLC ... G ... 253 301-2800
Steilacoom *(G-13004)*

Laylas Fun Socks ... G ... 509 279-8343
Spokane *(G-12359)*

OK Sock LLC ... G ... 509 209-6598
Mead *(G-6435)*

Savior Socks Inc ... G ... 360 601-8036
Battle Ground *(G-738)*

Skyline Socks ... G ... 425 454-1323
Bellevue *(G-1137)*

Sock Doctor Com Inc ... G ... 425 223-5173
Bellevue *(G-1144)*

Sock Monster ... G ... 206 724-0123
Seattle *(G-11151)*

Sock Outlet ... E ... 435 787-8888
Issaquah *(G-4477)*

Sock Peddlers ... G ... 253 267-0148
Lakewood *(G-5757)*

Socks In A Box LLC ... G ... 425 533-8316
Kenmore *(G-4606)*

2253 Knit Outerwear Mills

10-20 Services Inc ... G ... 253 503-6000
Lakewood *(G-5692)*

◆ **Ajaxx Design Inc** ... G ... 206 522-4545
Seattle *(G-9363)*

Archivalry ... G ... 206 420-3899
Seattle *(G-9421)*

Bella Tutto Inc ... G ... 425 898-8680
Sammamish *(G-9189)*

Blackwood Fiber Co ... G ... 206 387-3854
Tacoma *(G-13205)*

▲ **Blueseventy LLC** ... G ... 206 547-5273
Seattle *(G-9557)*

Centralia Knitting Mills Inc ... E ... 360 736-3994
Centralia *(G-2390)*

Choraks Sportsmans Inn ... G ... 206 463-0940
Vashon *(G-14719)*

▲ **Freeland Cafe** ... F ... 360 331-9945
Freeland *(G-4028)*

Knitwear Network Inc ... G ... 206 353-1337
Seattle *(G-10347)*

Mix Creations ... G ... 425 392-1123
Issaquah *(G-4450)*

My T-Shirt Source ... G ... 425 746-7447
Bellevue *(G-1022)*

Seatthole Inc ... G ... 360 389-2154
Bellingham *(G-1530)*

Teazer ... G ... 360 387-1737
Stanwood *(G-12957)*

Wapiti Woolies Inc ... G ... 360 663-2268
Enumclaw *(G-3326)*

2254 Knit Underwear Mills

Cheers To Life ... G ... 425 697-2966
Lynnwood *(G-6092)*

Decent Exposures Inc ... F ... 206 364-4540
Seattle *(G-9810)*

Nwd Ink International Inc ... G ... 425 454-0707
Bellevue *(G-1040)*

Pt Shirt ... G ... 360 385-1911
Port Townsend *(G-7920)*

2258 Lace & Warp Knit Fabric Mills

Cascade Nets Inc ... G ... 866 738-8071
Ferndale *(G-3827)*

◆ **Coppertop Enterprises Inc** ... E ... 360 966-9622
Everson *(G-3672)*

Net Services LLC ... F ... 360 651-1955
Tulalip *(G-13842)*

▲ **Pacific Netting Products Inc** ... F ... 360 697-5540
Kingston *(G-5260)*

Pacific Netting Products Inc ... G ... 360 697-5540
Poulsbo *(G-7990)*

2259 Knitting Mills, NEC

Barco Inc ... F ... 425 251-3530
Kent *(G-4808)*

2261 Cotton Fabric Finishers

Bayside EMB & Screenprint ... G ... 253 565-1521
Tacoma *(G-13191)*

◆ **Blue North Trading Company LLC** ... G ... 206 352-9252
Seattle *(G-9553)*

Go Designs ... G ... 206 719-0936
Seattle *(G-10091)*

Ink Inc ... F ... 253 565-4000
University Place *(G-13973)*

Jacknut Apparel ... G ... 360 742-3523
Tumwater *(G-13876)*

Jag Enterprizes Inc ... G ... 509 832-2836
Prosser *(G-8044)*

Jsmd Key Products LLC ... G ... 360 805-4140
Monroe *(G-6583)*

T-Shirts By Design LLC ... G ... 360 293-8898
Anacortes *(G-174)*

2262 Silk & Man-Made Fabric Finishers

Pacific Sportswear Inc ... E ... 253 582-4444
Tacoma *(G-13454)*

Ryno Rollers Inc ... G ... 253 856-0738
Auburn *(G-554)*

S I C

22 TEXTILE MILL PRODUCTS

2269 Textile Finishers, NEC
Traveling Designs .... G 360 695-5887
  Kelso *(G-4557)*

2273 Carpets & Rugs
A Touch of Class Creations .... G 425 489-3472
  Woodinville *(G-15170)*
Aladdin Manufacturing Corp .... E 253 395-3277
  Kent *(G-4767)*
Bentley Mills Inc .... G 206 622-8228
  Seattle *(G-9514)*
Breezy Upholstery & Canvas .... G 206 545-8538
  Seattle *(G-9582)*
Carpet Plus LLC .... G 253 874-0525
  Federal Way *(G-3721)*
Ezion Global Inc .... G 206 446-9476
  Bellevue *(G-906)*
▲ G&S Trading International .... G 253 859-1097
  Kent *(G-4920)*
Howatt Company Inc .... F 425 743-4682
  Mukilteo *(G-6937)*
Le Beau Tapis .... G 360 734-9786
  Bellingham *(G-1404)*
Level 5 Inc .... G 425 260-3440
  Monroe *(G-6592)*
Mat Salleh Satay LLC .... G 206 547-0597
  Seattle *(G-10500)*
Mohawk Esv Inc .... G 253 395-3277
  Kent *(G-5013)*
Mohawk Industries Inc .... G 253 395-3277
  Kent *(G-5014)*
Nielsen Bros & Sons Inc .... G 425 776-9191
  Edmonds *(G-3137)*
Noel Corporation .... F 509 248-3412
  Yakima *(G-15631)*
▲ Out Peak Services Inc .... F 360 255-7282
  Blaine *(G-1691)*
▲ Renaissance Rug Corporation .... G 425 698-1073
  Bellevue *(G-1099)*
Rubensteins Olympia .... G 360 753-9156
  Tumwater *(G-13895)*
▲ Specialty Wipers Inc .... G 425 251-3530
  Kent *(G-5149)*
▲ Spoonk Space Inc .... G 360 392-8067
  Lynden *(G-6054)*
Z & Z Art LLC .... G 206 669-3323
  Seattle *(G-11517)*

2281 Yarn Spinning Mills
Emma Knits Inc .... G 509 999-8583
  Spokane *(G-12243)*
Pinchknitter .... G 360 939-0769
  Camano Island *(G-2221)*

2282 Yarn Texturizing, Throwing, Twisting & Winding Mills
Evrnu Spc .... G 206 466-5269
  Seattle *(G-9950)*
International Carbide Corp .... F 800 422-8665
  Roy *(G-9161)*

2284 Thread Mills
A Good Yarn Shop .... F 360 876-0157
  Port Orchard *(G-7780)*
Action Sports & Locks Inc .... G 360 435-9505
  Arlington *(G-193)*
CNT Technologies Inc .... G 206 522-2256
  Seattle *(G-9702)*
Craft International of Wash .... G 360 785-3606
  Winlock *(G-15148)*
Designs Unlimited .... G 360 792-1372
  Port Orchard *(G-7802)*
Hope Chest Crafts .... G 509 865-5666
  Toppenish *(G-13670)*
Orpilla Santiago .... G 360 876-1976
  Port Orchard *(G-7838)*
▲ Sherri and Brent Wright .... G 360 366-3100
  Ferndale *(G-3904)*

2295 Fabrics Coated Not Rubberized
C&J Industries Inc .... E 253 852-0634
  Kent *(G-4831)*
▲ California Industrial Faciliti .... F 360 863-9333
  Monroe *(G-6562)*
Crown Films LLC .... G 360 757-8880
  Burlington *(G-2149)*
▲ Detro Manufacturing Inc .... G 360 687-9960
  Battle Ground *(G-697)*

♦ Fiber Trends Inc .... G 509 884-8631
  East Wenatchee *(G-3013)*
▲ Mid Mountain Materials Inc .... E 206 762-7600
  Seattle *(G-10539)*
▲ Paneltech Intl Holdings Inc .... F 360 538-1480
  Hoquiam *(G-4354)*
Precision Metal Works LLC .... G 509 945-8433
  Union Gap *(G-13951)*

2296 Tire Cord & Fabric
▲ Bridport-Air Carrier Inc .... E 253 872-7205
  Kent *(G-4823)*

2297 Fabrics, Nonwoven
♦ Warm Products Inc .... E 425 248-2424
  Lynnwood *(G-6221)*

2298 Cordage & Twine
▼ American Edge LLC .... F 509 937-4404
  Valley *(G-13987)*
American Manufacturing Corp .... C 360 384-4669
  Ferndale *(G-3812)*
Biotwine Manufacturing Company .... E 509 865-3340
  Toppenish *(G-13663)*
▲ Bridport-Air Carrier Inc .... E 253 872-7205
  Kent *(G-4823)*
♦ Coppertop Enterprises Inc .... E 360 966-9622
  Everson *(G-3672)*
♦ Cortland Company Inc .... G 360 293-8488
  Anacortes *(G-118)*
Craft International of Wash .... G 360 785-3606
  Winlock *(G-15148)*
▲ Everson Cordage Works LLC .... G 360 966-4613
  Everson *(G-3675)*
Fish & Fly Investors .... G 509 865-3340
  Toppenish *(G-13668)*
▲ Mid Mountain Materials Inc .... E 206 762-7600
  Seattle *(G-10539)*
▲ Noreastern Trawl Systems Inc .... E 206 842-5623
  Bainbridge Island *(G-652)*
Open Water Splicing .... G 360 510-8059
  Ferndale *(G-3881)*
Pnw Select Marketing Group LLC .... G 360 746-8270
  Ferndale *(G-3888)*
♦ Romanzof Fishing Company LLC .... F 206 545-9501
  Seattle *(G-10977)*
♦ Samson Rope Technologies Inc ..... C 360 384-4669
  Ferndale *(G-3896)*
Seattle Tarp Co Inc .... E 206 285-2819
  Seattle *(G-11080)*

2299 Textile Goods, NEC
Berg Development Group LLC .... G 509 624-8921
  Spokane *(G-12145)*
▼ Buffalo Industries LLC .... E 206 682-9900
  Kent *(G-4826)*
Chemical Cloth Co .... G 360 582-9684
  Sequim *(G-11617)*
Garage .... G 425 640-6021
  Lynnwood *(G-6126)*
▲ Home and Travel Solutions LLC ..... G 425 949-8216
  Woodinville *(G-15261)*
▲ Laurelcrest II LLC .... G 206 922-3634
  Seattle *(G-10382)*
Line-X Silverdale Inc .... G 360 692-4840
  Silverdale *(G-11844)*
▲ Mid Mountain Materials Inc .... E 206 762-7600
  Seattle *(G-10539)*
Om LLC Reinstated 2005 .... G 360 821-1802
  Port Townsend *(G-7905)*
Regenerated Textile Inds LLC .... G 206 427-9343
  Seattle *(G-10943)*
Sassy Pillows .... G 425 778-7783
  Edmonds *(G-3151)*
Sonic Patch LLC .... G 425 284-6072
  Seattle *(G-11155)*
Thirteen Sheets LLC .... G 888 676-5270
  Ridgefield *(G-9115)*

23 APPAREL AND OTHER FINISHED PRODUCTS MADE FROM FABRICS AND SIMILAR MATERIAL

2311 Men's & Boys' Suits, Coats & Overcoats
Bellevue Tailors and Formal Wr .... G 425 643-0741
  Bellevue *(G-815)*

Downtown Cleaners & Tailoring .... G 206 363-5455
  Shoreline *(G-11769)*
▲ Formal Wear Inc .... G 425 776-1088
  Lynnwood *(G-6120)*
J & Ree Fashions .... G 360 281-8610
  Vancouver *(G-14330)*
Leo Roux LLC .... G 512 565-3406
  Seattle *(G-10403)*
▲ Locknane Inc .... E 425 493-8300
  Mukilteo *(G-6950)*
Maulcor Inc .... G 773 696-2783
  Seattle *(G-10502)*
♦ Mustang Survival Holdings Inc .... D 360 676-1782
  Bellingham *(G-1453)*
New Uniformity LLC .... G 360 373-2785
  Bremerton *(G-1980)*
Seattle Northwest Service Corp .... F 206 553-9209
  Seattle *(G-11066)*
▼ Steele and Associates Inc .... G 360 297-4555
  Kingston *(G-5264)*
Survival Gear Systems .... G 866 257-2978
  Spokane *(G-12536)*
Susan Bennett .... G 360 427-6164
  Shelton *(G-11738)*

2321 Men's & Boys' Shirts
Arctic Circle Enterprises LLC .... D 253 872-8525
  Kent *(G-4789)*
Nidekken Ltd .... F 425 885-1587
  Redmond *(G-8595)*
▲ Waterstone Brands Inc .... G 800 579-3644
  Seattle *(G-11445)*

2322 Men's & Boys' Underwear & Nightwear
Decent Exposures Inc .... F 206 364-4540
  Seattle *(G-9810)*

2323 Men's & Boys' Neckwear
▲ Formal Wear Inc .... G 425 776-1088
  Lynnwood *(G-6120)*

2325 Men's & Boys' Separate Trousers & Casual Slacks
Caitac USA Corp .... B 360 671-1700
  Bellingham *(G-1287)*
Guess Inc .... E 206 682-7005
  Seattle *(G-10131)*
Nidekken Ltd .... F 425 885-1587
  Redmond *(G-8595)*
Utilikilts Co LLC .... F 206 282-4226
  Seattle *(G-11396)*
V F Services Inc Jansport .... G 425 407-4040
  Everett *(G-3644)*

2326 Men's & Boys' Work Clothing
Buffalo Industries Inc .... G 206 682-9900
  Seattle *(G-9595)*
▲ CC Filson Co .... C 206 624-4437
  Seattle *(G-9649)*
Department Crrctons Wash State .... B 509 526-6375
  Walla Walla *(G-14795)*
Evolution Revolution LLC .... G 623 703-5042
  Leavenworth *(G-5802)*
Fabrications Inc .... G 888 808-9878
  Mercer Island *(G-6462)*
Filson Manufacturing Inc .... G 206 242-9579
  Seattle *(G-9993)*
Kushco .... G 206 772-9333
  Seattle *(G-10363)*
▲ Locknane Inc .... E 425 493-8300
  Mukilteo *(G-6950)*
Maulcor Inc .... G 773 696-2783
  Seattle *(G-10502)*
Misty Mountain Manufacturing .... E 206 763-4055
  Seattle *(G-10548)*
Moor Innovative Tech LLC .... G 253 343-2216
  Tacoma *(G-13419)*
R B Sales .... G 206 870-0741
  Des Moines *(G-2944)*
San Mar Corporation .... C 206 727-3200
  Issaquah *(G-4471)*
▲ Shoot Suit Inc .... G 360 687-3451
  Battle Ground *(G-739)*
Uniform Factory Outl Ariz LLC .... G 360 707-2608
  Burlington *(G-2196)*
Zonecro Llc .... G 760 702-9290
  Bremerton *(G-2014)*

SIC SECTION — 23 APPAREL AND OTHER FINISHED PRODUCTS MADE FROM FABRICS AND SIMILAR MATERIAL

2329 Men's & Boys' Clothing, NEC

▲ CC Filson Co .... C 206 624-4437
  Seattle *(G-9649)*
Cenveo Inc .... G 503 224-7777
  Kent *(G-4848)*
Certified Branching Habit .... G 206 286-9685
  Seattle *(G-9659)*
Chicago Title Insurance Co .... G 509 765-8820
  Moses Lake *(G-6693)*
Dawn Workman Lularoe .... G 360 955-1324
  Yelm *(G-15731)*
▲ DUO Wear Inc .... G 425 251-0760
  Kent *(G-4879)*
Ers Group Inc .... G 360 895-1318
  Port Orchard *(G-7808)*
Ex Officio LLC .... G 206 242-9696
  Seatac *(G-9282)*
▲ Ex Officio LLC .... G 206 283-1471
  Seattle *(G-9951)*
Fashion Sales Inc .... G 206 441-3282
  Seattle *(G-9973)*
▲ Global Sportswear Corporation ..... G 253 813-9788
  Kent *(G-4924)*
◆ Great King of Americas LLC .... G 206 957-0987
  Seattle *(G-10113)*
▲ Guides Chice AP Spcialists LLC .. G 206 931-3838
  Kent *(G-4931)*
▲ Harveys Skin Diving Supplies ...... E 206 824-1114
  Kent *(G-4935)*
▲ Helly Hansen (us) Inc .... E 800 435-5901
  Sumner *(G-13073)*
▲ Helly-Hansen Holdings (u S) .... G 425 378-8700
  Auburn *(G-463)*
Insect Shield LLC .... G 206 624-9307
  Seattle *(G-10241)*
▲ K-L Mfg Co Inc .... E 509 232-8655
  Spokane *(G-12347)*
▲ Locknane Inc .... E 425 493-8300
  Mukilteo *(G-6950)*
McCoy International Ltd .... G 206 284-7734
  Seattle *(G-10505)*
Misho Global LLC .... G 425 829-8881
  Bellevue *(G-1009)*
Mtn Threds and Clothing .... G 509 258-4443
  Valley *(G-13994)*
▲ Pacific Sportswear LLC .... E 253 582-4444
  Tacoma *(G-13455)*
▲ Pow Inc .... G 206 366-0224
  Seattle *(G-10841)*
R B Sales .... G 206 870-0741
  Des Moines *(G-2944)*
▲ Seattle Cotton Works LLC .... F 425 455-8003
  Bellevue *(G-1121)*
Seattle Northwest Service Corp ...... F 206 553-9209
  Seattle *(G-11066)*
▲ Sherpa Adventure Gear LLC .... F 425 251-0760
  Kent *(G-5129)*
Sunrise Identity LLC .... G 425 214-1700
  Bellevue *(G-1167)*
Survival Gear Systems .... G 866 257-2978
  Spokane *(G-12536)*
Thaw Corporation .... C 206 505-2100
  Seattle *(G-11283)*
▲ Thomas Dean & Co LLC .... G 206 355-1009
  Bellevue *(G-1186)*
Tostrz LLC .... G 206 595-3044
  Burien *(G-2133)*
Vf Outdoor LLC .... E 425 455-7349
  Bellevue *(G-1216)*
Vue Internationalk Ltd .... G 206 878-1061
  Seatac *(G-9309)*

2331 Women's & Misses' Blouses

Arctic Circle Enterprises LLC .... D 253 872-8525
  Kent *(G-4789)*
Fashion Sales Inc .... G 206 441-3282
  Seattle *(G-9973)*
Sweet Creek Creations .... G 509 446-2429
  Metaline Falls *(G-6498)*
Yazdi Corporation .... G 425 787-6328
  Seattle *(G-11509)*

2335 Women's & Misses' Dresses

▲ Asabooks Inc .... G 425 885-1889
  Sammamish *(G-9186)*
Central Party & Costume .... G 509 962-3934
  Ellensburg *(G-3189)*
Charlies Coat LLC .... G 206 323-2191
  Seattle *(G-9669)*

Fashion Corner .... G 509 837-7345
  Sunnyside *(G-13125)*
Fern Hollow LLC .... G 360 504-2323
  Poulsbo *(G-7963)*
Happily Ever After .... G 206 226-8814
  Mountlake Terrace *(G-6863)*
Happy Thoughts .... G 360 468-2880
  Lopez Island *(G-5983)*
La Belle Reve LLC .... G 425 454-7772
  Bellevue *(G-974)*
Pacific Coast Bride LLC .... G 360 303-5047
  Bellingham *(G-1484)*
Runway Liquidation LLC .... G 253 474-0610
  Bothell *(G-1788)*
Runway Liquidation LLC .... G 262 253-4000
  Spokane *(G-12486)*
Runway Liquidation LLC .... G 262 654-0726
  Seattle *(G-10997)*
Runway Liquidation LLC .... G 262 948-7035
  Seattle *(G-10998)*
Runway Liquidation LLC .... G 304 325-3603
  Gig Harbor *(G-4158)*
Runway Liquidation LLC .... G 304 645-2799
  Kennewick *(G-4721)*
Runway Liquidation LLC .... G 304 825-6364
  Kennewick *(G-4722)*
Runway Liquidation LLC .... G 304 598-4888
  Kirkland *(G-5454)*
Runway Liquidation LLC .... G 304 748-2055
  Lacey *(G-5582)*
Runway Liquidation LLC .... G 304 636-2020
  Kennewick *(G-4723)*
Runway Liquidation LLC .... G 651 275-3251
  Walla Walla *(G-14863)*
Runway Liquidation LLC .... G 920 387-3180
  Spokane *(G-12487)*
Specialty Stores Inc .... G 206 650-0747
  Bellevue *(G-1151)*
Victorian Hearts .... G 509 926-1425
  Greenacres *(G-4303)*
Weddings Sochic .... G 360 438-6540
  Olympia *(G-7423)*
Yazdi Corporation .... G 425 787-6328
  Seattle *(G-11509)*

2337 Women's & Misses' Suits, Coats & Skirts

Fibrearts Inc .... G 425 432-1454
  Maple Valley *(G-6269)*
Illusion Wear Capes .... G 360 674-2357
  Port Orchard *(G-7815)*
◆ Mustang Survival Holdings Inc .... D 360 676-1782
  Bellingham *(G-1453)*
Tik Tik Garment Manufacturing .... F 509 624-0806
  Spokane *(G-12557)*
Yazdi Corporation .... G 425 787-6328
  Seattle *(G-11509)*

2339 Women's & Misses' Outerwear, NEC

Baxis Inc .... G 360 797-0084
  Sequim *(G-11614)*
Bge Ltd .... F 206 789-2128
  Seattle *(G-9519)*
Certified Branching Habit .... G 206 286-9685
  Seattle *(G-9659)*
▲ Coal Headwear LLC .... F 206 632-1601
  Seattle *(G-9704)*
Crystalli Inc .... G 253 905-6784
  Federal Way *(G-3727)*
Custom Veils & Accessories .... G 509 258-7810
  Valley *(G-13989)*
◆ Derek Andrew Inc .... F 425 453-9888
  Bellevue *(G-877)*
Dogfish Bay Studios LLC .... G 772 335-8711
  Poulsbo *(G-7959)*
Domestique .... G 206 545-3769
  Seattle *(G-9846)*
▲ DUO Wear Inc .... G 425 251-0760
  Kent *(G-4879)*
Ers Group Inc .... G 360 895-1318
  Port Orchard *(G-7808)*
▲ Ex Officio LLC .... G 206 283-1471
  Seattle *(G-9951)*
▲ Harveys Skin Diving Supplies ...... E 206 824-1114
  Kent *(G-4935)*
▲ Helly Hansen (us) Inc .... E 800 435-5901
  Sumner *(G-13073)*
▲ Helly-Hansen Holdings (u S) .... G 425 378-8700
  Auburn *(G-463)*

▲ Item House Inc .... E 253 627-7168
  Tacoma *(G-13352)*
▲ Jumbo Dti Corporation .... F 253 272-9764
  Fife *(G-3961)*
▲ K-L Mfg Co Inc .... E 509 232-8655
  Spokane *(G-12347)*
▲ Locknane Inc .... E 425 493-8300
  Mukilteo *(G-6950)*
Margaret OLeary Inc .... G 206 729-5934
  Seattle *(G-10476)*
◆ Mustang Survival Holdings Inc .... D 360 676-1782
  Bellingham *(G-1453)*
Nuu-Muu LLC .... G 360 223-7151
  Bellingham *(G-1475)*
▲ Pacific Sportswear LLC .... E 253 582-4444
  Tacoma *(G-13455)*
▲ Pkfashions Inc .... G 425 359-6510
  Mill Creek *(G-6520)*
Seattle Pacific Industries .... D 253 872-8822
  Kent *(G-5123)*
◆ Shah Safari Inc .... E 206 282-6122
  Seattle *(G-11095)*
▲ Sherpa Adventure Gear LLC .... F 425 251-0760
  Kent *(G-5129)*
Sunrise Identity LLC .... G 425 214-1700
  Bellevue *(G-1167)*
Thaw Corporation .... C 206 505-2100
  Seattle *(G-11283)*
Tik Tik Garment Manufacturing .... F 509 624-0806
  Spokane *(G-12557)*
▲ Two Dog Island Inc .... G 206 325-0609
  Seattle *(G-11353)*
Younique .... G 509 842-6908
  Spokane Valley *(G-12946)*

2341 Women's, Misses' & Children's Underwear & Nightwear

Country Clothiers .... G 206 632-3319
  Seattle *(G-9747)*
Decent Exposures Inc .... F 206 364-4540
  Seattle *(G-9810)*

2342 Brassieres, Girdles & Garments

Michelle Schwartzman .... G 360 629-5255
  Stanwood *(G-12979)*

2353 Hats, Caps & Millinery

3 Hats .... G 253 606-3474
  Edgewood *(G-3071)*
Arctic Circle Enterprises LLC .... D 253 872-8525
  Kent *(G-4789)*
▲ CC Filson Co .... C 206 624-4437
  Seattle *(G-9649)*
◆ Century 21 Promotions Inc .... E 206 282-8827
  Seattle *(G-9655)*
▲ Coal Headwear LLC .... F 206 632-1601
  Seattle *(G-9704)*
Fuze Create LLC .... G 425 212-8807
  Seattle *(G-10043)*
Grapevine Hats LLC .... G 206 940-3896
  Renton *(G-8810)*
Hatterdashery .... G 206 322-6149
  Seattle *(G-10147)*
Heritage Hats LLC .... G 425 301-2887
  Bellevue *(G-941)*
Irrational Hats N Stuff .... G 253 460-5565
  University Place *(G-13974)*
▲ Kavu Inc .... F 206 456-9305
  Seattle *(G-10332)*
Kushco Clothing LLC .... G 206 772-9333
  Seattle *(G-10364)*
▲ Outdoor Research LLC .... C 206 467-8197
  Seattle *(G-10717)*
Seattle Northwest Service Corp ...... F 206 553-9209
  Seattle *(G-11066)*
Smileys Inc .... F 360 424-7338
  Mount Vernon *(G-6843)*
Suziperi .... G 425 373-1954
  Bellevue *(G-1171)*
Ten Hats .... G 702 375-6504
  Vancouver *(G-14629)*
Tomatesa Enterprises LLC .... G 425 778-6708
  Lynnwood *(G-6211)*
Walla Walla Sweets .... G 509 522-2255
  Walla Walla *(G-14894)*

2361 Children's & Infants' Dresses & Blouses

Beanpop LLC .... G 509 499-5322
  Spokane *(G-12142)*

Employee Codes: A=Over 500 employees, B=251-500
C=101-250, D=51-100, E=20-50, F=10-19, G=2-9

23 APPAREL AND OTHER FINISHED PRODUCTS MADE FROM FABRICS AND SIMILAR MATERIAL — SIC SECTION

Chrysanthemum .... G 206 722-1031
 Seattle *(G-9683)*
Country Clothiers .... G 206 632-3319
 Seattle *(G-9747)*
Lil Squirtz .... G 360 521-9598
 Vancouver *(G-14376)*
Long Construction LLC .... G 360 202-2664
 Anacortes *(G-143)*
Pacific Northwest Wovens LLC .... G 714 392-0634
 Lewis McChord *(G-5821)*

2369 Girls' & Infants' Outerwear, NEC

Country Clothiers .... G 206 632-3319
 Seattle *(G-9747)*
Lil Squirtz .... G 360 521-9598
 Vancouver *(G-14376)*
McC Enterprises Inc .... G 509 928-9676
 Spokane Valley *(G-12785)*
▲ Pow Inc .... G 206 366-0224
 Seattle *(G-10841)*
▲ Swaddledesigns LLC .... E 206 971-0426
 Tukwila *(G-13825)*
▲ These Two Girls Llc .... G 206 200-3620
 Seattle *(G-11289)*

2371 Fur Goods

Etc Tacoma .... G 253 223-5459
 Tacoma *(G-13282)*
Harts Lake Trading Post .... G 360 458-3477
 Roy *(G-9160)*
Noel Inc .... G 206 784-1894
 Seattle *(G-10618)*

2381 Dress & Work Gloves

Blackbirds Nest .... G 509 946-1978
 Richland *(G-8974)*
Brooks Tactical Systems .... F 253 549-2703
 Fox Island *(G-4019)*
Churchill N Mfg Co Inc .... F 360 736-9923
 Centralia *(G-2393)*
Danalco Inc .... E 626 303-4019
 Seattle *(G-9790)*
Maulcor Inc .... G 773 696-2783
 Seattle *(G-10502)*
Mittens By Ann .... G 253 862-1050
 Edgewood *(G-3085)*
Neetas Creations .... G 585 233-1896
 Bellevue *(G-1024)*
North Star Glove Company .... E 253 627-7107
 Tacoma *(G-13429)*
▲ Outdoor Research LLC .... C 206 467-8197
 Seattle *(G-10717)*

2385 Waterproof Outerwear

Advadri LLC .... G 425 228-7558
 Renton *(G-8728)*
Darbonnier Tactical Supply LLC .... G 360 672-0216
 Oak Harbor *(G-7146)*
Fibrearts Inc .... G 425 432-1454
 Maple Valley *(G-6269)*
Florian Design .... G 425 742-7212
 Mill Creek *(G-6511)*
▲ Locknane Inc .... E 425 493-8300
 Mukilteo *(G-6950)*
McKenzie & Adams Inc .... G 425 672-8668
 Woodinville *(G-15307)*
▲ Rivers West Apparel Inc .... E 425 272-2949
 Tukwila *(G-13807)*
Stormy Seas Inc .... F 360 779-4439
 Poulsbo *(G-8005)*
Sweet Creek Creations .... G 509 446-2429
 Metaline Falls *(G-6498)*

2386 Leather & Sheep Lined Clothing

▲ Bigfoot Trading Inc .... G 360 340-7332
 Allyn *(G-81)*
Harts Lake Trading Post .... G 360 458-3477
 Roy *(G-9160)*
▲ United States Sheepskin Inc .... F 253 627-7114
 Tacoma *(G-13571)*

2389 Apparel & Accessories, NEC

Better Off Threads .... G 425 408-1304
 Woodinville *(G-15189)*
▲ Coal Headwear LLC .... F 206 632-1601
 Seattle *(G-9704)*
Costume Atlier Msque Pettycote .... G 360 819-4296
 Olympia *(G-7257)*

Embroidery For Soul .... G 425 319-1269
 Monroe *(G-6568)*
Esquel Apparel Inc .... G 206 223-7338
 Seattle *(G-9941)*
Filson Manufacturing Inc .... G 206 805-3730
 Seatac *(G-9284)*
Inspired .... G 360 504-2590
 Port Angeles *(G-7713)*
Islanders .... G 253 588-9246
 Tacoma *(G-13351)*
Itc USA LLC .... F 206 669-3442
 Seattle *(G-10262)*
Janice Arnold .... G 206 273-8548
 Centralia *(G-2410)*
▲ Kakadu Traders Australia Inc .... F 360 836-5820
 Ridgefield *(G-9091)*
Knit Alteration & Design .... G 360 426-5078
 Shelton *(G-11707)*
Malone Manufacturing LLC .... G 360 366-9964
 Custer *(G-2857)*
Maurices Incorporated .... G 253 845-5577
 Puyallup *(G-8184)*
Momentum Gear .... G 360 524-2098
 Vancouver *(G-14424)*
Morningstar Business Group Inc .... G 509 476-2944
 Oroville *(G-7469)*
▲ Newtown Inc .... F 253 395-9028
 Kent *(G-5022)*
Offerup Inc 844 633-3787
 Bellevue *(G-1043)*
Per Gioia .... G 206 240-4216
 Seattle *(G-10785)*
Sandmaiden Sleepwear .... G 206 595-4303
 Seattle *(G-11011)*
Seattle Sewing Solutions Inc .... E 206 625-7420
 Seattle *(G-11073)*
Seven Twenty Eight CL LLC .... G 206 484-7634
 Hansville *(G-4319)*
South Sound Screen Printing .... G 360 871-4206
 Port Orchard *(G-7851)*
Superhero Stuffcom .... G 425 890-3032
 Snoqualmie *(G-12032)*
Susans Custom Embroidery .... G 206 783-3127
 Seattle *(G-11230)*
Tormented Artifacts Ltd .... G 206 501-8333
 Seattle *(G-11320)*

2391 Curtains & Draperies

American Drpery Blind Crpt Inc .... E 425 793-4477
 Renton *(G-8742)*
American Drpery Blind Crpt Inc .... C 360 676-1121
 Renton *(G-8743)*
Chinook Acoustics Inc .... G 425 307-1976
 Redmond *(G-8418)*
Custom Made Draperies Etc .... G 425 485-2724
 Kenmore *(G-4570)*
Evergreen Textiles .... G 253 852-6565
 Auburn *(G-434)*
Hoss A W & Sons Furn & Mfg .... F 206 522-1229
 Seattle *(G-10182)*
Penthouse Drapery Clrs & Mfrs .... E 206 292-8336
 Seattle *(G-10781)*
Seattle Curtain Mfg Co .... E 206 324-0692
 Mill Creek *(G-6526)*
Shade Sunglo & Drapery Co .... G 206 767-4561
 Seattle *(G-11094)*
Snider Burien Draperies .... G 206 243-3600
 Burien *(G-2129)*
Springcrest Drapery Gallery .... G 509 928-9269
 Spokane Valley *(G-12890)*

2392 House furnishings: Textile

▲ Agalite Seattle .... G 425 656-2626
 Tukwila *(G-13690)*
Alderwood Park .... G 425 774-5266
 Lynnwood *(G-6069)*
Alex Daisley .... G 206 623-5555
 Seattle *(G-9373)*
◆ Anali Incorporated .... F 425 284-1829
 Sammamish *(G-9184)*
▲ Bucky Inc .... E 206 545-8790
 Seattle *(G-9592)*
Buffalo Industries Inc .... G 206 682-9900
 Seattle *(G-9595)*
Corona Decor Company .... F 206 763-1600
 Seattle *(G-9741)*
Dream On Futon Co .... G 360 739-2103
 Bellingham *(G-1325)*
▲ Dutena Blankets .... G 253 581-5715
 Lakewood *(G-5715)*

Edgewalker Woodworks Ltd .... G 360 468-2839
 Lopez Island *(G-5981)*
Fabrications Inc .... G 888 808-9878
 Mercer Island *(G-6462)*
▲ Globalmax Associates Inc .... F 425 392-4848
 Issaquah *(G-4422)*
Glorious Comfort .... G 253 884-1465
 Lakebay *(G-5689)*
Heritage Professional Ldscpg .... G 509 737-8580
 Kennewick *(G-4669)*
Holy Lamb Organics Inc .... G 360 402-5781
 Olympia *(G-7309)*
Jh Marine LLC .... G 425 241-6801
 Kirkland *(G-5373)*
Khann Industries Corp .... G 360 794-1033
 Monroe *(G-6587)*
Laura Townsend-Faber .... G 206 517-5739
 Seattle *(G-10381)*
Malone Manufacturing LLC .... G 360 366-9964
 Custer *(G-2857)*
Northwest Native Designs .... G 206 679-5847
 Snohomish *(G-11953)*
◆ Pacific Coast Feather LLC .... C 206 624-1057
 Seattle *(G-10729)*
Seattle Curtain Mfg Co .... E 206 324-0692
 Mill Creek *(G-6526)*
West Coast Fiber Inc .... F 253 850-5606
 Kent *(G-5210)*

2393 Textile Bags

▼ American Edge LLC .... F 509 937-4404
 Valley *(G-13987)*
AMICK Tactical LLC .... G 253 301-7619
 Yelm *(G-15726)*
Amjay Inc .... G 360 676-1165
 Bellingham *(G-1247)*
▲ Bad Bags Inc .... G 206 722-0916
 Seattle *(G-9476)*
▲ Carry Gear Solutions LLC .... E 206 957-6800
 Seattle *(G-9636)*
▲ International Athletic .... G 360 384-6868
 Ferndale *(G-3860)*
Lammy Industries Inc .... E 206 654-0010
 Seattle *(G-10374)*
▲ Last US Bag Co .... G 360 993-2247
 Vancouver *(G-14361)*
Lk Sewing Co .... G 206 240-9973
 Burien *(G-2118)*
Misty Mountain Manufacturing .... E 206 763-4055
 Seattle *(G-10548)*
Motovotano LLC .... G 206 363-0338
 Anacortes *(G-148)*
▲ Outdoor Research LLC .... C 206 467-8197
 Seattle *(G-10717)*
▲ Outdoor Research-Canada Inc ..... C 206 467-8197
 Seattle *(G-10718)*
▲ Paktek Inc .... E 253 584-4914
 Lakewood *(G-5745)*
Seattle Northwest Service Corp .... F 206 553-9209
 Seattle *(G-11066)*
Seattle Seams .... G 206 251-8231
 Puyallup *(G-8250)*
▲ Sundog LLC .... G 206 313-8871
 Duvall *(G-3002)*
▲ Swaddledesigns LLC .... E 206 971-0426
 Tukwila *(G-13825)*
Swift Industries .... G 415 608-8207
 Seattle *(G-11237)*
▲ Tom Bihn Inc .... D 206 652-4123
 Seattle *(G-11318)*
▲ Yakima Tent & Awning Co Ltd .... F 509 457-6169
 Yakima *(G-15717)*

2394 Canvas Prdts

AGM Fabric Products Inc .... G 253 946-3200
 Federal Way *(G-3713)*
Barrett Enclosures Inc .... G 206 285-8100
 Seattle *(G-9494)*
Bravo Manufacturing Inc .... G 360 817-9124
 Camas *(G-2235)*
▲ Bridport-Air Carrier Inc .... E 253 872-7205
 Kent *(G-4823)*
Bumperchute Co .... G 206 232-8189
 Mercer Island *(G-6457)*
Canvas Creations .... G 425 210-5993
 Tonasket *(G-13647)*
Canvas Man .... G 360 293-2812
 Anacortes *(G-108)*
Canvas Shoppe .... G 360 457-2773
 Port Angeles *(G-7691)*

SIC SECTION

23 APPAREL AND OTHER FINISHED PRODUCTS MADE FROM FABRICS AND SIMILAR MATERIAL

▲ Canvas Supply Co Inc ....E 206 784-0711
  Seattle (G-9621)
Cedar Mountain Spa Covers ....F 253 872-8993
  Kent (G-4844)
Churchill Brothers ....G 360 293-2700
  Everett (G-3417)
▼ Climacover Inc ....G 360 458-1010
  Eatonville (G-3052)
Columbia Tarp Liner & Sup Co ......G 360 577-1834
  Longview (G-5901)
Coulter Canvas ....G 509 246-2188
  Soap Lake (G-12037)
Duane Ruud ....F 206 682-1082
  Seattle (G-9856)
Eastside Tent & Awning Co ....G 425 454-7766
  Bellevue (G-888)
Everett Tent & Awning Inc ....G 425 252-8213
  Everett (G-3464)
Evolution Covers ....G 425 478-2043
  Mill Creek (G-6509)
George Broom Sons Inc ....G 206 282-0800
  Seattle (G-10064)
▲ Hilleberg Inc ....G 425 883-0101
  Redmond (G-8493)
In Canvas ....G 425 355-4102
  Everett (G-3513)
▲ Inland Tarp & Cover Inc ....G 509 766-7024
  Moses Lake (G-6715)
Integrated Systems Design ....G 360 746-0812
  Bellingham (G-1380)
Kvamme Ltd ....G 425 787-1669
  Lynnwood (G-6154)
Nordic Tarps Manufacturing ....G 509 533-1530
  Spokane Valley (G-12804)
Port Townsend Sails Inc ....F 360 385-1640
  Port Townsend (G-7914)
Power Equipment Supply Llc ....G 206 817-5627
  Everett (G-3580)
Puget Sound Tent & Awning ....G 425 251-9786
  Tukwila (G-13800)
▲ Rainier Industries Ltd ....C 425 251-1800
  Tukwila (G-13801)
▲ Raptor Sails Inc ....G 360 775-6039
  Seattle (G-10923)
Rod Carr Sailmaker ....G 425 881-2846
  Redmond (G-8654)
Rush Sails Inc ....G 425 827-9648
  Enumclaw (G-3319)
Schattauer Sailmaker Corp ....G 206 783-0173
  Seattle (G-11024)
Sears Tents & Awning ....G 509 452-8971
  Yakima (G-15669)
Seattle Tarp Co Inc ....E 206 285-2819
  Seattle (G-11080)
Sound Sails ....G 360 385-3881
  Port Townsend (G-7928)
Squalicum Marine Inc ....G 360 733-4353
  Bellingham (G-1554)
◆ Tacoma Tent & Awning Co Inc ...E 253 627-4128
  Tacoma (G-13549)
Troger Enterprises Ltd ....G 253 627-8878
  Tacoma (G-13565)
Walla Walla Farmers Co Op ....G 509 529-5750
  Walla Walla (G-14889)
Washington Tent & Awning Inc ......G 253 581-7177
  Lakewood (G-5765)
Willys Canvas Works ....G 425 923-7810
  Everett (G-3659)
Yager Company Inc ....G 509 922-2772
  Spokane Valley (G-12945)
▲ Yakima Tent & Awning Co Ltd ....F 509 457-6169
  Yakima (G-15717)

2395 Pleating & Stitching For The Trade

AJS Custom Embroidery ....G 360 993-1987
  Vancouver (G-14015)
Allstar Specialty Designs ....G 425 820-0285
  Kirkland (G-5275)
Arctic Circle Enterprises LLC ....D 253 872-8525
  Kent (G-4789)
Arctic Circle Holdings LLC ....G 206 625-9226
  Seattle (G-9422)
Art N Stitches Inc ....G 253 248-1900
  Fife (G-3934)
Autocraft Incorporated ....G 509 926-7002
  Greenacres (G-4295)
Availble Creat Screen Prtg EMB ......G 360 576-8542
  Vancouver (G-14045)
AZ Arts Inc ....F 253 584-8155
  Lakewood (G-5701)

Bayside EMB & Screenprint ....G 253 565-1521
  Tacoma (G-13191)
Bellevue Embroidery ....G 425 646-9191
  Bellevue (G-811)
Bellingham Promotional Pdts ....G 360 676-5416
  Bellingham (G-1268)
Bent Needle Designs ....G 253 531-9440
  Tacoma (G-13196)
Bergen & Company ....F 360 676-7503
  Bellingham (G-1271)
Bergen Screen Print ....G 509 965-2511
  Yakima (G-15519)
Beth Donalley ....G 206 366-8445
  Lake Forest Park (G-5607)
Cachanilla Design ....G 425 207-6396
  Kent (G-4832)
Cascade Apparel & Embroidery ......G 360 253-3022
  Vancouver (G-14102)
Casual Fridays ....G 360 425-8841
  Longview (G-5897)
Casual Fridays Custom E M B ....G 360 425-8841
  Longview (G-5898)
Chings Embroidery ....G 360 613-9861
  Bremerton (G-1942)
Clarks All-Sports Inc ....E 509 684-5069
  Colville (G-2743)
Classic Impressions ....E 206 766-9121
  Seattle (G-9690)
Color Grphics Scrnprinting Inc ....F 360 352-3970
  Tumwater (G-13862)
Colosseum Ventures LLC ....F 509 533-0366
  Spokane (G-12188)
Contract Sew & Repair Inc ....F 253 395-7910
  Kent (G-4865)
Creative Garment Design & EMB .....G 509 457-3482
  Union Gap (G-13927)
Dream Works Machine Quilting ......G 360 668-0864
  Snohomish (G-11901)
Durado Enterprise ....G 509 882-3247
  Grandview (G-4247)
EMB Create Inc ....G 360 384-8072
  Ferndale (G-3808)
▲ Emblems & More X3 ....G 253 248-2400
  Fife (G-3950)
Embroidered Effects LLC ....G 360 380-1928
  Bellingham (G-1334)
Embroidery By Design ....G 509 582-2858
  Kennewick (G-4658)
Embroidery Northwest ....G 509 248-1186
  Yakima (G-15564)
Embroidery Plus LLC ....G 253 630-2616
  Kent (G-4891)
Emerald City Embroidery ....G 253 922-8838
  Milton (G-6534)
Envision Custom EMB & Designs ....G 360 693-2588
  Vancouver (G-14204)
Excel Designs Inc ....G 360 892-1412
  Vancouver (G-14213)
Fashion Embroidery Inc ....G 425 820-7125
  Kirkland (G-5337)
Fast Lane Auto Sports ....G 253 584-3676
  Lakewood (G-5721)
▲ Go Usa Inc ....E 509 662-3387
  Wenatchee (G-15034)
GPA Embroidery ....G 509 662-1929
  Wenatchee (G-15035)
Graphic Apparel ....G 509 525-7630
  College Place (G-2724)
▲ H W Image Works Inc ....G 760 343-3869
  Bellevue (G-935)
Hawkins Lettering ....F 425 481-1938
  Bothell (G-1864)
Hellroaring Company ....G 509 364-3522
  Glenwood (G-4184)
Hull Marigail ....G 425 643-3737
  Bellevue (G-952)
Huntington Pier International ....G 310 640-8358
  Tukwila (G-13750)
Ideal Commercial Uniforms ....G 360 876-1767
  Port Orchard (G-7814)
Ink Inc ....F 253 565-4000
  University Place (G-13973)
J & R Mercantile ....G 425 486-6402
  Kenmore (G-4583)
Jackyes Enterprises Inc ....G 425 355-5997
  Everett (G-3521)
Jmh Enterprises ....G 509 628-2191
  Richland (G-9015)
Jodee Maiorana ....G 509 758-1035
  Clarkston (G-2637)

▲ Johnnie Montice ....G 360 452-6549
  Port Angeles (G-7719)
Julies Designs ....G 206 727-3341
  Issaquah (G-4434)
Lannoye Emblems Inc ....G 425 844-8411
  Woodinville (G-15283)
Larsen Sign Company ....G 253 581-4313
  Lakewood (G-5736)
Little Indian Embroidery ....G 360 414-4165
  Longview (G-5927)
Logo Unltd ....F 425 896-8412
  Woodinville (G-15292)
Material Girls Quilting ....G 360 354-2930
  Lynden (G-6037)
Mr TS Trophies ....G 360 424-9339
  Mount Vernon (G-6815)
Much More Embroidery ....G 360 289-0955
  Ocean Shores (G-7186)
N-Vee Embroidery ....G 425 246-3125
  Kirkland (G-5406)
North Star Embroidery ....G 360 588-0530
  Anacortes (G-155)
Olympic Embroidery ....E 425 413-2848
  Ravensdale (G-8338)
Palouse River Quilts ....G 509 397-2278
  Colfax (G-2720)
Post Indus Stress & Design ....F 253 572-9782
  Tacoma (G-13472)
Prographyx ....G 360 636-1595
  Longview (G-5945)
Purrfect Logos Inc ....G 509 893-2424
  Spokane Valley (G-12845)
Reco Corporate Sportswear Inc ......G 360 354-2134
  Lynden (G-6048)
Red Creek Embroidery LLC ....G 360 956-1792
  Olympia (G-7381)
Sandra Stroup ....G 509 754-0822
  Ephrata (G-3346)
Sew Athletic Jackets and More ....G 253 446-7115
  Puyallup (G-8252)
▲ Sherri and Brent Wright ....G 360 366-3100
  Ferndale (G-3904)
Showcase Specialties Inc ....G 509 547-3344
  Pasco (G-7629)
Snappyduds ....G 206 243-8478
  Burien (G-2128)
Snotown Embroidery LLC ....G 425 446-1681
  Snohomish (G-11985)
Stitchybox ....G 360 450-1089
  Vancouver (G-14612)
Sunshine Embroidery ....G 360 892-1556
  Vancouver (G-14618)
Susan Bennett ....G 360 427-6164
  Shelton (G-11738)
To The T Embroidery ....G 360 509-0156
  Suquamish (G-13149)
Two Harps ....G 425 432-4128
  Maple Valley (G-6295)
Vintage Embroidery ....G 360 668-1923
  Snohomish (G-11997)
Wildrose Ltd ....F 509 535-8555
  Spokane (G-12591)
Williamson Illustration ....G 360 734-5497
  Ferndale (G-3925)

2396 Automotive Trimmings, Apparel Findings, Related Prdts

Action Apparel Washington Inc ....G 509 328-5861
  Spokane (G-12096)
Advantage Precision Graphics ....F 425 285-9787
  Redmond (G-8371)
Alki Sports LLC ....F 206 898-1305
  Redmond (G-8378)
All Color Screen Printing ....G 253 536-2822
  Tacoma (G-13162)
▼ American Edge LLC ....F 509 937-4404
  Valley (G-13987)
Ammonite Ink ....G 907 227-2719
  Spokane (G-12113)
Arctic Circle Enterprises LLC ....D 253 872-8525
  Kent (G-4789)
Arctic Circle Holdings LLC ....G 206 625-9226
  Seattle (G-9422)
Ariel Screenprinting & Design ....G 425 337-1918
  Everett (G-3372)
Availble Creat Screen Prtg EMB ......G 360 576-8542
  Vancouver (G-14045)
Bad Habit Ltd ....G 360 385-3101
  Port Townsend (G-7866)

Employee Codes: A=Over 500 employees, B=251-500
C=101-250, D=51-100, E=20-50, F=10-19, G=2-9

23 APPAREL AND OTHER FINISHED PRODUCTS MADE FROM FABRICS AND SIMILAR MATERIAL SIC SECTION

Blackstar..........G....... 360 426-7470
Shelton *(G-11684)*
▲ **Blanc Industries Inc**..........E....... 360 736-8988
Centralia *(G-2385)*
Brooks Products & Services..........G....... 425 742-4214
Edmonds *(G-3098)*
Budd Bay Embroidery Inc..........F....... 360 709-0483
Olympia *(G-7244)*
Centurion Enterprises..........G....... 509 787-2345
Quincy *(G-8294)*
Classic Impressions..........E....... 206 766-9121
Seattle *(G-9690)*
Colosseum Ventures LLC..........F....... 509 533-0366
Spokane *(G-12188)*
Competitive Edge Athletics..........G....... 206 246-7211
Burien *(G-2098)*
Computergear Inc..........G....... 425 487-3600
Woodinville *(G-15209)*
Countryman Signs Screen Prtrs..........G....... 425 355-1037
Everett *(G-3428)*
Crystal Blue Screen Printing..........G....... 509 337-8201
Waitsburg *(G-14753)*
▲ **D A Graphics Inc**..........G....... 206 760-5886
Seattle *(G-9777)*
Embroidery For Soul..........G....... 425 319-1269
Monroe *(G-6568)*
▲ **Gompf Brackets Inc**..........F....... 425 348-5002
Mukilteo *(G-6929)*
▲ **H W Image Works Inc**..........G....... 760 343-3869
Bellevue *(G-935)*
Hope Moffat..........G....... 401 527-4234
Bainbridge Island *(G-640)*
Ink Inc..........F....... 253 565-4000
University Place *(G-13973)*
▲ **International Athletic**..........G....... 360 384-6868
Ferndale *(G-3860)*
Kitsap Screen Printing LLC..........G....... 360 876-5101
Port Orchard *(G-7824)*
Magna Vis Graphic Impressions..........G....... 509 684-5659
Colville *(G-2764)*
Marysville Printing Inc..........G....... 360 658-9195
Marysville *(G-6357)*
Merrill Corporation..........C....... 360 794-3157
Monroe *(G-6596)*
Moss Green Inc..........F....... 206 285-4020
Seattle *(G-10564)*
▲ **Northwest Designs Ink Inc**..........F....... 425 454-0707
Bellevue *(G-1035)*
NW Solar Protection LLC..........G....... 509 294-9878
Spokane *(G-12416)*
Pacific Sportswear Inc..........E....... 253 582-4444
Tacoma *(G-13454)*
Plastic Sales & Service Inc..........F....... 206 524-8312
Lynnwood *(G-6181)*
Post Indus Stress & Design..........F....... 253 572-9782
Tacoma *(G-13472)*
Primal Screens LLC..........G....... 206 784-5266
Seattle *(G-10859)*
Rainy Day Artistry..........G....... 360 484-3681
Naselle *(G-7019)*
Ramax Printing and Awards..........G....... 509 928-1222
Spokane *(G-12467)*
Rollo Tomasi Enterprises LLC..........G....... 509 453-9950
Yakima *(G-15663)*
Saturday Night Inc..........F....... 509 928-5816
Spokane Valley *(G-12858)*
Screen Print Northwest Inc..........G....... 360 577-1534
Longview *(G-5951)*
Screen Tek Inc..........E....... 509 928-8322
Liberty Lake *(G-5860)*
Sh RTS Off Screen Printing..........G....... 425 319-1269
Sultan *(G-13035)*
Shirley Sunset..........G....... 360 574-3276
Vancouver *(G-14584)*
Shirtbuilders Inc..........G....... 509 765-3885
Moses Lake *(G-6749)*
Silkscreen Company..........E....... 206 763-8108
Seattle *(G-11112)*
Sports N Sorts..........G....... 509 276-6170
Deer Park *(G-2915)*
▲ **Strawberry Kids LLC**..........G....... 425 605-8883
Redmond *(G-8685)*
Sunrise Identity LLC..........G....... 425 214-1700
Bellevue *(G-1167)*
▼ **Trailready Products LLC**..........F....... 425 353-6776
Mount Vernon *(G-6847)*
Tuff TS Connection Screen Prtg..........G....... 253 588-8897
Lakewood *(G-5763)*
Valley Graphics Inc..........G....... 509 937-4055
Valley *(G-13996)*
Vilmas Family Corporation..........G....... 253 941-9008
Federal Way *(G-3801)*
Western Foil Corporation..........G....... 206 624-3645
Seattle *(G-11452)*
Western Graphics Inc..........G....... 206 241-2526
Fife *(G-3998)*
Western Specialties Co..........G....... 425 353-9282
Mukilteo *(G-6991)*
Wildrose Ltd..........F....... 509 535-8555
Spokane *(G-12591)*

2397 Schiffli Machine Embroideries

Accent By Design..........G....... 360 256-6607
Vancouver *(G-14006)*
Chings Embroidery..........G....... 360 613-9861
Bremerton *(G-1942)*
Cruiser Creations..........G....... 360 832-7078
Graham *(G-4222)*

2399 Fabricated Textile Prdts, NEC

3 Lakes Fly Fishing..........G....... 509 675-4200
Kettle Falls *(G-5223)*
Aero Mac Inc..........G....... 425 348-4140
Mukilteo *(G-6890)*
▼ **American Edge LLC**..........F....... 509 937-4404
Valley *(G-13987)*
AMICK Tactical LLC..........G....... 253 301-7619
Yelm *(G-15726)*
Ballenger International LLC..........G....... 970 641-9494
Arlington *(G-209)*
Betty OGuin..........G....... 360 876-0803
Port Orchard *(G-7794)*
Blazing Banners..........G....... 360 756-9990
Bellingham *(G-1275)*
▲ **Bridport-Air Carrier Inc**..........E....... 253 872-7205
Kent *(G-4823)*
Browbandsbydesigncom..........G....... 360 779-9339
Poulsbo *(G-7952)*
Buttonsmith Inc..........G....... 800 789-4364
Carnation *(G-2290)*
Cascade Designs Inc..........E....... 206 505-9500
Seattle *(G-9642)*
Colburn Enterprise..........G....... 509 292-2310
Elk *(G-3169)*
Countryman Signs Screen Prtrs..........G....... 425 355-1037
Everett *(G-3428)*
▲ **Design Salt Inc**..........G....... 509 667-1600
Wenatchee *(G-15025)*
▲ **Diamond Nets Inc**..........E....... 360 354-1319
Everson *(G-3673)*
Direct Hit Golf Flags LLC..........G....... 253 946-6263
Federal Way *(G-3729)*
Factory Trawler Supply Inc..........G....... 206 285-6732
Seattle *(G-9961)*
Hellroaring Company..........G....... 509 364-3522
Glenwood *(G-4184)*
Imc-Innvtive Mktg Cnnction LLC..........G....... 360 895-0178
Port Orchard *(G-7816)*
K&W Enterprises Inc..........G....... 425 255-4316
Renton *(G-8835)*
Kims Horse Blankets..........G....... 360 623-9567
Silver Creek *(G-11824)*
Knot Your Every Day Crochet..........G....... 360 791-9154
Tumwater *(G-13881)*
Lk Sewing Co..........G....... 206 240-9973
Burien *(G-2118)*
Lummi Island Wild Co-Op L L C..........G....... 360 366-8786
Bellingham *(G-1415)*
Misty Mountain Manufacturing..........E....... 206 763-4055
Seattle *(G-10548)*
Nanook Lodge..........G....... 206 200-8233
Seattle *(G-10586)*
Nwfsc..........G....... 206 860-3415
Seattle *(G-10676)*
Olympic Fly Fishers..........G....... 206 546-2677
Shoreline *(G-11797)*
Osp Sling Inc..........E....... 360 683-4109
Sequim *(G-11657)*
Pacific Knight Emblem & Insig..........G....... 206 354-2060
Kent *(G-5052)*
Pics Smartcard Inc..........F....... 800 667-1772
Blaine *(G-1695)*
Pioneer Aerofab Company Inc..........F....... 360 757-4780
Burlington *(G-2181)*
Professional Sleep Services..........G....... 253 759-2700
Tacoma *(G-13479)*
Puget Sound Workshop LLC..........G....... 425 821-7345
Kirkland *(G-5447)*
Recrochetions..........G....... 360 450-8757
Camas *(G-2278)*
Research Nets Incorporated..........G....... 425 821-7345
Redmond *(G-8649)*
Riptide Charters Inc..........G....... 360 815-6568
Blaine *(G-1702)*
Robin Ferris Manufacturing..........G....... 360 757-6804
Burlington *(G-2183)*
▲ **Robinson Windword Inc**..........F....... 509 536-1617
Spokane *(G-12481)*
Sandbox Enterprises LLC..........G....... 360 966-6677
Bellingham *(G-1523)*
▲ **Seattle Cotton Works LLC**..........F....... 425 455-8003
Bellevue *(G-1121)*
Snow & Company Inc..........G....... 206 396-8997
Seattle *(G-11145)*
Ultimate Sheepskin..........G....... 253 677-4384
Graham *(G-4240)*
▲ **United States Sheepskin Inc**..........F....... 253 627-7114
Tacoma *(G-13571)*
Willingham Inc..........F....... 425 432-9867
Maple Valley *(G-6302)*
Wincraft Incorporated..........E....... 507 454-5510
Woodinville *(G-15405)*
Youlookfab LLC..........G....... 206 709-9541
Seattle *(G-11513)*

24 LUMBER AND WOOD PRODUCTS, EXCEPT FURNITURE

2411 Logging

3 X Bar Inc..........G....... 360 274-4502
Castle Rock *(G-2336)*
7 Arrows Logging LLC..........G....... 509 930-8059
White Swan *(G-15136)*
A & RS Logging Inc..........F....... 360 249-4017
Montesano *(G-6641)*
A&C Logging LLC..........G....... 509 493-3160
White Salmon *(G-15109)*
AAA Tree Service & Logging LLC..........G....... 360 463-7553
Shelton *(G-11672)*
Ace Logging Inc..........F....... 360 537-6843
Hoquiam *(G-4327)*
Acorn Tree and Stump Services..........G....... 360 509-0145
Port Gamble *(G-7756)*
Adams Timber Service LLC..........G....... 360 636-7766
Silverlake *(G-11861)*
Aeneas Valley Cnstr & Log..........G....... 206 391-8408
Ravensdale *(G-8328)*
AG Tree Service LLC..........G....... 425 830-8820
Kirkland *(G-5274)*
Ah Logging..........G....... 509 935-4565
Chewelah *(G-2598)*
Ahola Timber Inc..........G....... 360 892-2243
Brush Prairie *(G-2028)*
AK Logging Lumber & Millwork..........G....... 360 461-3764
Port Angeles *(G-7680)*
▼ **Alan Loghry Excavation Inc**..........G....... 360 461-0660
Port Angeles *(G-7681)*
All In Cnstr & Ldscpg LLC..........G....... 360 840-7990
Mount Vernon *(G-6770)*
Allen Bros Diving Logging..........G....... 360 866-3643
Olympia *(G-7222)*
Allways Logging LLC..........G....... 360 893-2724
Graham *(G-4215)*
ALRT Corporation..........D....... 360 592-5300
Everson *(G-3666)*
Altels Logging Inc..........G....... 509 782-5808
Cashmere *(G-2313)*
Amanda Park Services Inc..........G....... 360 288-2230
Amanda Park *(G-87)*
American Forest Lands..........G....... 425 432-5004
Maple Valley *(G-6257)*
American Forest Lands Wash..........G....... 425 358-5235
Maple Valley *(G-6258)*
American Timber Resources LLC..........G....... 360 796-4236
Brinnon *(G-2023)*
Anderson & Middleton Company..........F....... 360 533-2410
Olympia *(G-7225)*
Andrew A Kroiss..........G....... 509 684-4929
Colville *(G-2736)*
Andrew Russell Pond..........G....... 509 690-8509
Colville *(G-2737)*
Arg Logging LLC..........G....... 253 606-5047
Yelm *(G-15728)*
Arthur D Fulford Jr..........G....... 509 826-2225
OMAK *(G-7433)*
Ash Logging Company Inc..........G....... 360 264-4367
Tenino *(G-13612)*
B & B Logging Inc..........G....... 360 247-5237
Amboy *(G-89)*

SIC SECTION
24 LUMBER AND WOOD PRODUCTS, EXCEPT FURNITURE

B & M Logging Inc ... E ... 360 748-6904
Chehalis (G-2468)
B & W Excavating & Cnstr ... G ... 509 937-2028
Valley (G-13988)
B L Logging ... G ... 360 748-8248
Chehalis (G-2469)
B&M Logging Inc ... G ... 360 985-0150
Ethel (G-3348)
Baldwin Logging Incorporated ... G ... 360 520-4484
Salkum (G-9179)
Barry Rankin Logging Inc ... G ... 360 436-1947
Darrington (G-2866)
Basic Homes LLC ... G ... 253 579-2724
Eatonville (G-3050)
Bdn Logging Inc ... G ... 360 785-4119
Winlock (G-15145)
Bear Mountin Cutters Inc ... G ... 360 875-0035
South Bend (G-12039)
Beardslee Logging ... G ... 509 675-2400
Kettle Falls (G-5224)
Bearly Loggin ... G ... 509 493-1706
White Salmon (G-15111)
Bell Creek Contracting Inc ... G ... 360 592-3300
Bellingham (G-1262)
Bennett Painting ... G ... 360 426-6489
Shelton (G-11683)
Bethel Lutheran Church ... G ... 360 892-4231
Brush Prairie (G-2030)
Bill Anderson ... G ... 509 281-0055
White Salmon (G-15112)
Black Lk Bb Camp Cnference Ctr ... F ... 360 539-5337
Olympia (G-7236)
Bme Logging LLC ... G ... 360 931-6797
La Center (G-5502)
Boettcher & Sons Inc ... G ... 360 832-3943
Eatonville (G-3051)
Bradley Heavy Construction ... G ... 360 341-5967
Clinton (G-2684)
Breithaupt Logging Inc ... G ... 360 732-4225
Chimacum (G-2612)
Bremerton Trap & Skeet Club ... G ... 360 674-2438
Port Orchard (G-7796)
Bremmeyer Logging ... E ... 425 432-9310
Ravensdale (G-8332)
Bresch Logging ... G ... 509 258-9620
Springdale (G-12950)
Brian D Ames ... G ... 360 561-5119
Olympia (G-7241)
Brian Martell ... G ... 509 738-3041
Kettle Falls (G-5227)
Brindle Technical Logging Inc ... G ... 360 985-7459
Mossyrock (G-6759)
Brintech Inc ... G ... 360 985-7459
Mossyrock (G-6760)
Brown Lumber Co ... G ... 509 779-4738
Curlew (G-2844)
Bruce & Walter Webster ... G ... 360 697-3975
Poulsbo (G-7953)
Bucks Logging Inc ... G ... 360 985-0758
Ethel (G-3349)
Bueler Farms Inc ... G ... 360 668-5289
Snohomish (G-11883)
Bullfrog Land Co Inc ... G ... 509 223-3055
Loomis (G-5971)
Burgess Logging Inc ... F ... 509 763-3119
Leavenworth (G-5797)
Burya Logging and Trucking Inc ... F ... 509 935-6816
Chewelah (G-2599)
Butchs Bulldozing & Backhoe ... G ... 360 652-0473
Stanwood (G-12962)
C & C Logging LLC ... D ... 360 636-0300
Kelso (G-4519)
C & H Logging Inc ... E ... 509 364-3420
Glenwood (G-4178)
C & J Logging Co Inc ... E ... 360 484-7256
Naselle (G-7012)
C Swanson Logging ... G ... 360 886-0237
Black Diamond (G-1646)
Caribou Creek Logging Inc ... G ... 509 962-6700
Ellensburg (G-3186)
Carl Emil Seastrom ... F ... 509 722-5414
Inchelium (G-4371)
Carlson and Sons Logging Inc ... G ... 360 795-3068
Cathlamet (G-2362)
Carlson Login Inc ... G ... 360 795-3068
Cathlamet (G-2363)
Cascade Tree Service LLC ... G ... 425 241-9326
North Bend (G-7106)
Castle & Coleman Logging Co ... G ... 360 426-0840
Shelton (G-11688)

Chandler W Jeppsen ... G ... 541 466-0908
Tacoma (G-13233)
Charles Washington ... G ... 509 466-9098
Mead (G-6427)
Charlo Timberlands Inc ... G ... 509 447-3671
Newport (G-7055)
Chavez Nolberto ... G ... 360 426-9550
Shelton (G-11691)
Cherry Valley Logging Company ... F ... 206 396-0002
Duvall (G-2981)
Chilton Logging Inc ... E ... 360 225-0427
Woodland (G-15423)
Claquato Farms Inc ... G ... 360 748-6220
Chehalis (G-2484)
Clark Contract Cutting Inc ... G ... 360 705-0355
Tumwater (G-13861)
Clear and Level Logging LLC ... G ... 360 247-5989
Amboy (G-90)
Colburn Timber Inc ... F ... 360 208-4501
Raymond (G-8346)
Colburn Timber Inc ... G ... 360 875-6565
Rainier (G-8312)
Columbia Navigation Inc ... G ... 509 684-4335
Kettle Falls (G-5222)
Copper Creek Logging LLC ... G ... 253 203-5915
Wilkeson (G-15143)
Corporation of The President ... G ... 509 656-2344
Cle Elum (G-2663)
Crawford Enterprises ... G ... 360 866-4972
Olympia (G-7258)
Crw Timber ... G ... 360 425-4858
Longview (G-5905)
Curtins Heritage Logging Inc ... G ... 360 518-5735
Washougal (G-14950)
D & D Logging ... G ... 425 308-2063
Lake Stevens (G-5642)
D Creek Timber Inc ... G ... 360 262-3786
Winlock (G-15149)
D E Metlow Logging LLC ... G ... 509 937-2233
Valley (G-13990)
Dahlquist Logging Inc ... G ... 253 804-9112
Auburn (G-421)
Dale Bradeen Logging ... G ... 509 738-6132
Kettle Falls (G-5230)
Darrell A Tillotson ... G ... 509 493-2376
White Salmon (G-15114)
Dave Bekkevar Logging & Trckg ... F ... 360 683-3655
Sequim (G-11624)
David Littlejohn Logging ... G ... 360 352-5858
Olympia (G-7265)
Deep Creek Logging Inc ... G ... 360 533-2390
Hoquiam (G-4332)
Delbert L Wheeler ... E ... 509 874-2471
White Swan (G-15137)
Deming Log Show Inc ... G ... 360 592-3051
Bellingham (G-1322)
Denise Haase ... G ... 360 264-4680
Tumwater (G-13871)
Dennis Davis Logging Co Inc ... F ... 360 864-2548
Toledo (G-13637)
Derek Mefford ... G ... 360 580-9166
Hoquiam (G-4333)
Diamond Timber Company ... F ... 360 274-7914
Castle Rock (G-2339)
Dills Creek Inc ... G ... 360 826-3841
Hamilton (G-4312)
Don Boehme & Sons Logging ... G ... 360 871-1571
Port Orchard (G-7804)
Don Glaser Logging ... G ... 206 462-9638
Eatonville (G-3053)
Don Larson Logging Inc ... G ... 509 722-6612
Fruitland (G-4065)
Don Painter Logging Inc ... F ... 360 832-3683
Eatonville (G-3054)
Donald R Jacobson ... G ... 360 425-4346
Longview (G-5907)
Donner Logging LLC ... G ... 509 675-2717
Colville (G-2751)
Double a Logging Inc ... F ... 509 476-2907
Oroville (G-7464)
Double D Logging Co Inc ... G ... 360 533-7168
Hoquiam (G-4334)
Dozing & Ditching ... G ... 425 308-2063
Lake Stevens (G-5644)
Drolz Log and Rock Inc ... G ... 360 987-2343
Hoquiam (G-4335)
Duane Bruner Logging Inc ... E ... 360 274-7103
Castle Rock (G-2340)
Dw Cornwall Farms Inc ... G ... 509 291-5011
Fairfield (G-3696)

Eagle Logging Inc ... G ... 509 226-1329
Spokane Valley (G-12684)
Eddie ODell ... G ... 360 797-7549
Sequim (G-11632)
Edward Laurence Pelanconi ... G ... 360 435-2725
Arlington (G-233)
Edwards Logging Co ... F ... 360 457-7330
Port Angeles (G-7702)
Eiger Skyline Inc ... G ... 509 548-6808
Leavenworth (G-5800)
Elder Logging Co ... G ... 360 886-2779
Black Diamond (G-1647)
Elder Logging Inc ... G ... 360 825-7158
Enumclaw (G-3289)
Elk Creek Contractors Inc ... F ... 509 364-3692
Glenwood (G-4179)
Ellensburg Fence Co ... G ... 509 929-4090
Ellensburg (G-3196)
Emerson Logging Corporation ... G ... 509 647-5658
Wilbur (G-15141)
Emery Enterprises ... G ... 360 532-0102
Aberdeen (G-10)
ENB Logging & Construction ... F ... 360 673-2696
Kalama (G-4500)
Endicott Truck & Tractor ... G ... 509 657-3436
Endicott (G-3264)
Engeseth Logging ... F ... 360 327-3391
Beaver (G-756)
Erickson Busheling Inc ... G ... 360 928-3232
Port Angeles (G-7703)
Erickson Logging ... G ... 253 846-2646
Graham (G-4225)
Erickson Logging Inc ... F ... 360 832-8627
Eatonville (G-3056)
Evergreen Fibre Inc ... E ... 360 452-2670
Port Angeles (G-7704)
Evergreen Fibre Inc ... F ... 360 452-3341
Port Angeles (G-7705)
◆ Evergreen Timber Corp ... F ... 206 579-2925
Seattle (G-9946)
Ewing Construction ... G ... 509 624-2246
Spokane (G-12252)
F A Koenig & Sons Inc ... G ... 360 793-1711
Sultan (G-13024)
F and F Excavating and Logging ... G ... 509 637-2551
Glenwood (G-4180)
Fagernes Cutting Inc ... G ... 360 245-3249
Chehalis (G-2496)
Far West Inc ... G ... 360 942-3270
Raymond (G-8348)
Farrer Logging Co ... G ... 509 773-5069
Goldendale (G-4197)
Faubion William J Atty At Law ... G ... 360 795-3367
Cathlamet (G-2366)
Feller Logging Inc ... G ... 509 364-3435
Glenwood (G-4181)
Filla Company LLC ... G ... 360 864-2531
Toledo (G-13638)
Fir Lane Memorial Pk & Fnrl HM ... F ... 253 531-6600
Spanaway (G-12058)
Florek Logging Ltd Inc ... G ... 360 795-8058
Cathlamet (G-2367)
Flory Cabinets LLC ... G ... 360 894-2504
Yelm (G-15733)
Forest Land Services Inc ... F ... 360 652-9044
Stanwood (G-12971)
Forsyth Enterprises ... G ... 360 297-2684
Kingston (G-5252)
Frank Harkness Trckg & Log LLC ... F ... 360 826-6087
Acme (G-42)
Frank Harkness Trckg & Log LLC ... G ... 360 595-2496
Concrete (G-2785)
Frank Swiger Trucking Inc ... G ... 509 258-7226
Ford (G-4005)
Fred B Moe Logging Co ... G ... 360 273-6049
Oakville (G-7174)
Fred Nanamkin ... G ... 509 634-8110
Keller (G-4512)
Fur Tree Forestry ... G ... 360 426-6252
Elma (G-3246)
G&L Horse Logging ... G ... 360 247-5156
Amboy (G-94)
Galivan Logging Inc ... G ... 360 866-1431
Olympia (G-7293)
Gamble Bay Timber ... G ... 360 297-0555
Kingston (G-5253)
Gamble Logging ... G ... 253 857-3294
Gig Harbor (G-4104)
Garkse Logging & Road Bldg LLC ... G ... 360 520-2707
Chehalis (G-2498)

Employee Codes: A=Over 500 employees, B=251-500
C=101-250, D=51-100, E=20-50, F=10-19, G=2-9
2019 Washington
Manufacturers Register
553

24 LUMBER AND WOOD PRODUCTS, EXCEPT FURNITURE SIC SECTION

Gary C Horsley .... G 360 274-4502
Winlock *(G-15150)*
Gary G Guzzie Insurance .... G 509 674-4433
Cle Elum *(G-2668)*
Gary L Ostenson DDS PS .... G 360 896-9595
Vancouver *(G-14248)*
George Anderson Company .... G 425 333-0707
Redmond *(G-8476)*
Gibbons Drilling Inc .... G 360 671-3040
Stanwood *(G-12974)*
Gibson & Son Road Building Inc .... F 509 925-2017
Ellensburg *(G-3202)*
Glenwood Timber Inc .... G 509 364-4158
Glenwood *(G-4182)*
Global Pacific Forest Products .... F 360 568-1111
Snohomish *(G-11913)*
Gould & Sons Logging Inc .... E 360 274-9425
Castle Rock *(G-2343)*
Gould-Sunrise Logging Inc .... F 360 274-8000
Castle Rock *(G-2344)*
Green Diamond Resource Company .... G 360 426-0737
Grapeview *(G-4288)*
Greg Robertson Logging Inc .... G 208 660-3616
Newport *(G-7058)*
Griffiths Inc .... G 360 276-4122
Moclips *(G-6539)*
Gronlund Logging Inc .... G 509 548-5039
Leavenworth *(G-5804)*
H & D Logging Company Inc .... F 509 548-7358
Leavenworth *(G-5805)*
Hadaller Logging Inc .... F 360 425-0602
Kelso *(G-4527)*
Handly & Phillips Logging Inc .... G 360 765-3578
Quilcene *(G-8284)*
Hansen & Spies Logging Inc .... F 509 364-3385
Glenwood *(G-4183)*
Hansen Logging LLC .... E 509 935-4515
Chewelah *(G-2602)*
Harry Wiebold Logging .... G 360 687-2129
Battle Ground *(G-708)*
Haulin Somethin Inc .... G 509 738-4144
Kettle Falls *(G-5232)*
Havillah Lumber .... G 509 486-4650
Tonasket *(G-13649)*
Herbrand Company .... F 253 848-7700
Puyallup *(G-8161)*
Hicks Logging Christmas T .... G 253 208-8914
Olympia *(G-7306)*
Hitchcock Cutting .... G 360 748-7480
Chehalis *(G-2503)*
Ho Stafford Logging .... G 360 853-8816
Rockport *(G-9152)*
Hofstrand Logging Inc .... E 509 968-3197
Ellensburg *(G-3208)*
Holbrook Inc .... E 360 754-9390
Olympia *(G-7307)*
Hood Canal Logging Co Inc .... G 360 275-4676
Belfair *(G-763)*
Horsley Timber & Construction .... G 360 274-7272
Castle Rock *(G-2345)*
Howard & Son Excavating LLC .... G 360 983-3922
Silver Creek *(G-11823)*
Howard Denson Logging .... G 360 988-4910
Sumas *(G-13045)*
Hubster Logging Inc .... G 253 200-7183
Eatonville *(G-3059)*
Hunter Creek Property Ltd .... G 509 675-4949
Hunters *(G-4365)*
Hurworth Logging .... G 360 457-4776
Port Angeles *(G-7712)*
Interfor US Inc .... D 360 575-3600
Longview *(G-5919)*
Islas Cedar LLC .... G 360 590-2176
Hoquiam *(G-4345)*
J & O Timber Falling Inc .... G 360 978-4590
Onalaska *(G-7448)*
J H Holm .... G 360 825-4276
Enumclaw *(G-3295)*
J L & O Enterprises Inc .... G 360 636-5427
Kelso *(G-4530)*
J&M Heavy Cnstr & Log Co LLC .... G 360 747-2735
Port Orchard *(G-7818)*
J&N Land Trucking .... G 360 677-2274
Skykomish *(G-11866)*
Jack H Hill .... G 360 864-4939
Winlock *(G-15152)*
James & Eileen Kaski .... G 360 687-4214
Battle Ground *(G-711)*
James Smith Trucking .... G 360 423-1027
Kelso *(G-4531)*
JB Timberline Logging .... G 360 871-0956
Olalla *(G-7207)*
Jeff Hauenstein Logging .... G 360 826-3490
Concrete *(G-2788)*
Jeffrey Gould .... F 360 274-7914
Castle Rock *(G-2346)*
Jeffrey Hembury .... G 360 535-3737
Belfair *(G-765)*
Jerry Debriae Logging Co Inc .... D 360 795-3309
Cathlamet *(G-2369)*
Jerry Hart & Son Logging .... G 360 871-7037
Port Orchard *(G-7819)*
Jim Davis .... G 360 374-5659
Forks *(G-4010)*
Jim Hamilton .... G 360 875-6170
South Bend *(G-12041)*
Jim Johnson & Son Trucking LLC .... F 360 770-5073
Sedro Woolley *(G-11548)*
Jimini Construction LLC .... G 360 426-9918
Shelton *(G-11705)*
Joe Gordon Logging Inc .... G 360 470-1631
McCleary *(G-6417)*
Joe Zender & Sons Inc .... G 360 599-2064
Deming *(G-2920)*
John Harkness Logging .... F 360 595-2260
Acme *(G-43)*
John Meadows Logging .... G 509 427-4330
Stevenson *(G-13014)*
John Meek Logging .... G 360 491-6976
Olympia *(G-7312)*
Johnson Forestry Contracting .... G 360 484-3311
Naselle *(G-7014)*
Jon Lonning Drywall .... G 253 851-4866
Gig Harbor *(G-4125)*
Jones Logging and Cnstr LLC .... F 509 422-3147
Okanogan *(G-7198)*
Jones Logging LLC .... G 509 732-4511
Colville *(G-2760)*
JP Logging LLC .... G 208 596-7069
Spokane Valley *(G-12755)*
Jrj Inc .... F 360 691-2528
Seattle *(G-10311)*
JSB Logging .... G 360 301-9675
Brinnon *(G-2024)*
Judd Timber Cutting LLC .... G 360 928-9011
Port Angeles *(G-7720)*
Justin Maine Logging Inc .... G 360 262-4105
Winlock *(G-15153)*
K & L Logging .... G 360 273-9916
Rochester *(G-9134)*
Kaski Tom Logging & Cat Work .... G 360 247-5707
Yacolt *(G-15484)*
Kayser Farms .... G 360 274-6277
Castle Rock *(G-2347)*
Kcpk Trucking Inc .... G 360 592-2260
Everson *(G-3680)*
Keith Austin Logging .... G 509 684-8869
Colville *(G-2762)*
Keith Cooper Logging Inc .... G 360 459-3553
Olympia *(G-7315)*
Ken Olson Cutting .... G 360 374-5052
Forks *(G-4011)*
Kennedy Creek Quarry Inc .... F 360 426-4743
Shelton *(G-11706)*
Kenneth Maupin Logging Cnstr .... G 509 442-3484
Ione *(G-4375)*
Kilponen Bros Logging Inc .... G 360 484-7758
Naselle *(G-7015)*
Kiona Creek Timber Inc .... G 360 983-3786
Mossyrock *(G-6762)*
Knoll Tree Care & Logging .... G 253 630-1520
Kent *(G-4981)*
Knot Hole Inc .... G 541 806-0950
White Salmon *(G-15120)*
Knutz Logging & Farming .... G 509 779-4713
Malo *(G-6234)*
Kovash Logging Ltd .... E 360 825-4263
Enumclaw *(G-3299)*
Kriegers Stump Removal Inc .... G 360 225-1703
Woodland *(G-15443)*
Krueger Logging Inc .... G 360 687-5558
Battle Ground *(G-714)*
Krume Logging Excavation .... F 360 274-8667
Castle Rock *(G-2348)*
Kurt Muonio Contract Cutting .... G 360 686-1809
Yacolt *(G-15485)*
LA Excav & Select Log Inc .... G 360 856-4111
Mount Vernon *(G-6806)*
Land Co LLC .... G 360 484-7712
Naselle *(G-7016)*
Leake Logging Inc .... G 509 738-3033
Kettle Falls *(G-5235)*
Leon Wickizer Excavating .... G 253 261-2978
Buckley *(G-2061)*
Levanen Inc .... F 360 687-4314
Battle Ground *(G-715)*
Levanen Lee John .... G 360 687-7478
Battle Ground *(G-716)*
Lewis Cnty Work Opportunities .... E 360 748-9921
Chehalis *(G-2509)*
Liberty Logging Inc .... G 360 423-5454
Kelso *(G-4535)*
Living Waters Logging LLC .... G 360 749-6333
Longview *(G-5928)*
Lloyd Remsberg Logging .... G 509 997-7362
Twisp *(G-13913)*
Lodestone Construction Inc .... G 360 875-6960
South Bend *(G-12043)*
Log Processors Inc .... F 509 773-3043
Goldendale *(G-4202)*
Longview Fibre Ppr & Packg Inc .... D 206 762-7170
Seattle *(G-10437)*
Lorz & Lorz Inc .... G 509 486-2202
Tonasket *(G-13653)*
Lost Creek Logging .... G 509 442-3218
Cusick *(G-2850)*
Loudin Logging LLC .... G 253 691-8679
Eatonville *(G-3061)*
Lv Logging .... G 360 837-3144
Washougal *(G-14964)*
Lynch Creek Quarry LLC .... G 360 832-4269
Eatonville *(G-3062)*
M & M Logging .... G 360 280-5973
McCleary *(G-6418)*
Mac Arthur Land & Timber .... G 509 442-3805
Cusick *(G-2851)*
Macarthur Logging .... G 509 675-8045
Elk *(G-3172)*
Macmillan & Company .... F 360 249-1148
Montesano *(G-6645)*
Macmillan and Company .... E 360 470-1535
Montesano *(G-6646)*
Manastash Logging Inc .... G 206 937-8311
Seattle *(G-10471)*
Manke Lumber Company Inc .... G 360 426-5536
Shelton *(G-11710)*
Mark 3 Logging .... G 360 577-8833
Longview *(G-5931)*
Martin Frank .... G 509 292-2685
Deer Park *(G-2908)*
McClure Ranch .... G 509 634-4685
Nespelem *(G-7022)*
McFadden & Mcfadden Logging .... G 253 847-7695
Graham *(G-4232)*
McKay & Son .... G 360 532-2285
Aberdeen *(G-22)*
McNamee & Sons Logging .... G 509 292-8656
Elk *(G-3173)*
Mechanical Fuels Treatment LLC .... G 509 486-1438
Tonasket *(G-13654)*
Mesa Resources Inc .... G 360 683-1912
Sequim *(G-11648)*
Michael D Worley .... G 509 290-0927
Elk *(G-3174)*
Michellaine Lee Larry Bergsma .... G 360 873-4005
Marblemount *(G-6305)*
Mike Brandeberry .... F 206 524-9656
North Bend *(G-7116)*
Mike Nilles .... G 509 299-3653
Medical Lake *(G-6442)*
Mikes Logging .... G 360 893-5336
Tacoma *(G-13413)*
Miller Shingle Company LLC .... G 360 691-7727
Granite Falls *(G-4281)*
Mischel Bros Logging Inc .... G 360 649-7101
Port Orchard *(G-7829)*
Mitzner Logging .... G 509 422-6834
Okanogan *(G-7200)*
Mnr Logging LLC .... G 360 532-3631
Aberdeen *(G-23)*
Mnr Logging LLC .... G 360 249-2213
Montesano *(G-6648)*
Moerke Family 3 LLC .... G 360 748-8952
Chehalis *(G-2515)*
Monk Logging Inc .... G 509 447-4526
Newport *(G-7061)*
Montes Logging & Firewood .... G 360 943-3181
Olympia *(G-7342)*
Montgomery Law Firm .... G 509 684-2519
Colville *(G-2766)*

SIC SECTION

24 LUMBER AND WOOD PRODUCTS, EXCEPT FURNITURE

Moose Creek Logging Inc ....G....... 360 631-3728
Arlington *(G-282)*

Mor-Log Inc ....G....... 360 426-7872
Shelton *(G-11715)*

Mount Adams Lumber Co Inc ....G....... 509 395-2122
Trout Lake *(G-13681)*

Mountain Logging Inc ....E....... 509 493-3511
White Salmon *(G-15123)*

Mountain Logging Inc ....E....... 509 493-3511
Bingen *(G-1640)*

Mountain Tree Farm Company ....E....... 253 924-2345
Federal Way *(G-3760)*

Mulrony Logging LLC ....G....... 509 261-1549
Goldendale *(G-4204)*

Mulvaney Trucking and Excav ....G....... 509 784-4502
Entiat *(G-3268)*

Mvr Timber Cutting Inc ....F....... 360 459-7409
Olympia *(G-7347)*

NDC Timber Inc ....E....... 360 482-4645
Elma *(G-3251)*

Newport Equipment Entps Inc ....E....... 509 447-4688
Newport *(G-7062)*

Nielsen Brothers Inc ....D....... 360 671-9078
Sedro Woolley *(G-11552)*

Norm Stoken Logging Inc ....G....... 360 683-0908
Sequim *(G-11651)*

North Fork Timber Company Corp ....G....... 360 273-5541
Rochester *(G-9138)*

North Fork Timber Company Corp ....F....... 360 748-8333
Centralia *(G-2420)*

North Fork Timber Company Corp ....G....... 360 748-8333
Chehalis *(G-2517)*

Northman Logging ....G....... 425 870-4727
Granite Falls *(G-4282)*

NW Logging Company ....G....... 360 226-2691
Tacoma *(G-13438)*

Oster Logging Inc ....G....... 425 397-0585
Lake Stevens *(G-5665)*

Pacific Force MGT & Harvest ....G....... 360 484-3854
Naselle *(G-7018)*

Pacific Logging Inc ....E....... 425 334-3600
Marysville *(G-6365)*

Pacific Logging LLC ....G....... 425 508-9150
Lake Stevens *(G-5667)*

Pacific Marine Contractors ....G....... 360 532-2765
Aberdeen *(G-27)*

Pacific Marine Investments ....G....... 360 532-2765
Aberdeen *(G-28)*

Pacific Reign Enterprises ....G....... 360 580-4447
Humptulips *(G-4364)*

Pacific Rim Portfolios Ltd ....E....... 360 595-2854
Sedro Woolley *(G-11554)*

Parker Pacific Inc ....E....... 253 862-9133
Buckley *(G-2066)*

Paul E Sevier ....G....... 360 491-1334
Olympia *(G-7367)*

Perkins Timber LLC ....G....... 360 754-2892
Olympia *(G-7368)*

Petes Logging LLC ....G....... 509 684-6231
Colville *(G-2768)*

Phillip L Remsberg ....G....... 509 997-3231
Twisp *(G-13916)*

Phillips & Reichert Shake Mill ....G....... 360 978-4392
Chehalis *(G-2524)*

Pierson & Son Construction ....G....... 360 642-2796
Long Beach *(G-5877)*

Plaas Timber LLC ....F....... 360 832-2440
Eatonville *(G-3066)*

Pleines Logging Inc ....G....... 360 374-6373
Forks *(G-4015)*

Pope Resources ....G....... 253 851-7009
Gig Harbor *(G-4147)*

Pries Logging ....G....... 360 985-0044
Onalaska *(G-7453)*

Puget Logging & Excavation ....G....... 360 629-0461
Stanwood *(G-12988)*

Puget Sound Logging ....G....... 253 310-5923
Rochester *(G-9139)*

Pursley Logging Co Inc ....G....... 360 274-7297
Castle Rock *(G-2350)*

Quality Logging LLC ....G....... 360 640-1555
Castle Rock *(G-2352)*

Quintana Cutting Inc ....G....... 360 592-5943
Deming *(G-2922)*

R & H Logging & Contract Cutng ....G....... 360 795-3334
Cathlamet *(G-2372)*

R Harper Inc ....G....... 360 985-0806
Mossyrock *(G-6765)*

R L Smith Logging Inc ....F....... 360 943-6540
Olympia *(G-7375)*

R&S Forestry and Cnstr LLC ....G....... 360 436-1771
Arlington *(G-311)*

Rainestree Timber Marketing ....G....... 360 462-6197
Shelton *(G-11723)*

Ramco Mechanical Cutting Ltd ....E....... 360 263-1967
La Center *(G-5513)*

Ramsey Bros Logging Inc ....G....... 253 380-4971
Eatonville *(G-3068)*

Rawson Logging ....G....... 360 829-0474
Buckley *(G-2069)*

Rayfield Oneil Timber Cutters ....G....... 509 925-2061
Ellensburg *(G-3222)*

Rayonier Forest Resources LP ....F....... 360 374-6565
Forks *(G-4017)*

Rayonier Inc ....E....... 425 748-5220
Bellevue *(G-1095)*

Rcc Logging Limited ....G....... 360 556-8904
Tumwater *(G-13894)*

Reano Construction & Logging ....G....... 360 886-1374
Black Diamond *(G-1654)*

Rich Richmond Logging LLC ....E....... 509 935-4833
Chewelah *(G-2606)*

Richard & Mike Lynch ....G....... 360 263-4078
Woodland *(G-15463)*

Richard Andrews Logging ....G....... 360 426-1096
Shelton *(G-11725)*

Richard Meek ....G....... 360 275-4104
Belfair *(G-772)*

Richardson Log & Land Clearing ....G....... 360 631-2107
Sedro Woolley *(G-11560)*

Richardson Logging ....G....... 509 684-4206
Addy *(G-47)*

Richart Company Inc ....G....... 509 935-8857
Chewelah *(G-2607)*

Rick Carlson ....G....... 360 691-4421
Granite Falls *(G-4285)*

Robert E Miller ....G....... 509 485-3032
Oroville *(G-7472)*

Robert Lloyd Zerck ....G....... 509 779-4820
Malo *(G-6235)*

Robert Rogers ....G....... 360 352-9408
Olympia *(G-7387)*

Ronald Brewer ....G....... 360 436-1771
Arlington *(G-317)*

Ronald Rex Dairy Farm ....G....... 360 856-0629
Sedro Woolley *(G-11561)*

Ross Creek Logging Inc ....G....... 509 926-0415
Otis Orchards *(G-7517)*

Rotschy Timber Management ....G....... 360 247-5396
Amboy *(G-96)*

RTS & BBC Inc ....G....... 360 239-1953
Hoquiam *(G-4356)*

Rygaard Logging Inc ....F....... 360 457-4941
Port Angeles *(G-7741)*

S & J Logging Inc ....G....... 360 795-3309
Cathlamet *(G-2374)*

S and R Logging and Cutting ....G....... 425 314-7662
Stanwood *(G-12990)*

S Boone Mechanical Cutting ....G....... 360 748-4293
Chehalis *(G-2534)*

Sam Bickle Logging Inc ....G....... 360 273-5886
Rochester *(G-9140)*

San Poil Logging ....G....... 509 634-8112
Keller *(G-4514)*

Sawtooth Logging ....G....... 360 249-6255
Montesano *(G-6658)*

Saxon Contracting LLC ....E....... 360 595-2854
Sedro Woolley *(G-11563)*

Schaben Logging Inc ....G....... 360 589-9008
Aberdeen *(G-33)*

Schillinger Enterprises Inc ....G....... 360 275-2275
Belfair *(G-774)*

Scotts Home & Roofing Service ....G....... 360 297-7524
Kingston *(G-5263)*

▲ SDS Lumber Co ....C....... 509 493-1444
Bingen *(G-1642)*

Sealaska Timber Corporation ....G....... 360 834-3700
Camas *(G-2281)*

Sevier Logging LLC ....G....... 360 791-5527
Lacey *(G-5586)*

Shipp Construction Inc ....E....... 360 262-0197
Ethel *(G-3351)*

Silver City Timber ....G....... 509 276-5126
Deer Park *(G-2914)*

Skillman Brothers Inc ....G....... 360 866-7083
Olympia *(G-7396)*

Skookum Logging Inc ....F....... 360 532-2186
Aberdeen *(G-36)*

Skyline Logging LLC ....G....... 509 935-7200
Chewelah *(G-2608)*

Smith Logging & Monkey Bus ....G....... 253 857-5900
Olalla *(G-7210)*

Snoqualmie Valley Logging Inc ....G....... 360 794-8205
Monroe *(G-6622)*

Solomon Logging LLC ....G....... 425 292-0745
North Bend *(G-7125)*

Somero Logging ....G....... 360 686-3926
Yacolt *(G-15493)*

Southside Enterprises Inc ....F....... 509 395-2345
Trout Lake *(G-13683)*

Spradlin Rock Products Inc ....G....... 360 532-2994
Hoquiam *(G-4360)*

Stanton ....G....... 360 864-6897
Toledo *(G-13642)*

Steve Hazelwood & Son Trucking ....G....... 253 863-5721
Lake Tapps *(G-5686)*

Stewart & Stewart Law Off PS ....G....... 360 249-4342
Montesano *(G-6659)*

Stewart Logging ....G....... 360 437-2905
Port Ludlow *(G-7779)*

Stewart Logging Inc ....G....... 509 684-6746
Colville *(G-2776)*

Storlie & Graham Cutting Inc ....G....... 509 962-6494
Ellensburg *(G-3228)*

Stormy Mountain Ranch Inc ....G....... 509 687-3295
Chelan *(G-2564)*

Stott Logging Inc ....F....... 360 533-2971
Hoquiam *(G-4361)*

Sumas Mt Log Co ....G....... 360 966-4781
Sumas *(G-13051)*

T & D Gruhn Trucking Inc ....G....... 360 532-1288
Aberdeen *(G-37)*

T & R Log Co ....G....... 509 962-6590
Ellensburg *(G-3229)*

T J Brooks Logging ....G....... 425 220-2263
Camano Island *(G-2225)*

T L Fitzer Logging Inc ....E....... 360 832-4949
Eatonville *(G-3069)*

T&B Logging Inc ....G....... 509 684-4316
Colville *(G-2777)*

Tall Timber Contractoring Inc ....G....... 509 681-1275
Cle Elum *(G-2680)*

Tarbert Logging Inc ....F....... 509 738-6567
Kettle Falls *(G-5242)*

Tc Lumber ....G....... 360 452-2612
Port Angeles *(G-7748)*

Tdb Holdings LLC ....G....... 360 600-5506
La Center *(G-5516)*

Teamster Local 313 ....G....... 253 627-0103
Tacoma *(G-13551)*

Tenneson Brothers ....G....... 360 856-6242
Sedro Woolley *(G-11575)*

Thin Air Logging LLC ....G....... 509 670-8139
Peshastin *(G-7664)*

Thomas L Norman Cnstr & Log ....G....... 253 312-7858
Orting *(G-7487)*

Thomas Tree Svc & Logging ....G....... 360 561-9589
Lacey *(G-5594)*

Tight Line Industries Inc ....F....... 360 751-1621
Toledo *(G-13643)*

Tiin-MA Logging ....E....... 509 874-2040
White Swan *(G-15139)*

Tim Brown Logging Inc ....E....... 360 274-4422
Castle Rock *(G-2353)*

Tj Logging LLC ....G....... 509 826-5203
OMAK *(G-7445)*

Tjs Mechanical Cutting LLC ....G....... 360 837-1234
Washougal *(G-14994)*

Tobin & Riedesel Logging LLC ....E....... 360 482-8127
Elma *(G-3257)*

Tobin and Riedesel Logging LLC ....G....... 360 249-8184
Montesano *(G-6661)*

Tree Management Plus Inc ....F....... 360 978-4305
Toledo *(G-13644)*

Tri-Tex Inc ....E....... 360 274-8511
Castle Rock *(G-2356)*

Triangle C Farms Inc ....G....... 509 682-2189
Chelan *(G-2567)*

Trickinnex Tree Trimming & Fal ....G....... 509 653-1937
Naches *(G-7007)*

Turley Log & Timberland MGT ....G....... 509 239-4523
Cheney *(G-2594)*

Two Horse Logging Inc ....G....... 360 592-5244
Bellingham *(G-1579)*

Van Dyk & Son Logging Inc ....G....... 360 592-5951
Deming *(G-2925)*

Van Dyke Logging Incorporated ....G....... 509 442-3852
Ione *(G-4376)*

W-4 Construction Inc ....F....... 509 529-1603
Walla Walla *(G-14886)*

SIC

Employee Codes: A=Over 500 employees, B=251-500
C=101-250, D=51-100, E=20-50, F=10-19, G=2-9

2019 Washington
Manufacturers Register

555

WA Cutting and Logging ....G....360 520-0464
Ethel *(G-3352)*

Wayne Pond Logging Inc ....G....509 684-8732
Colville *(G-2782)*

West Fork Timber Co LLC ....F....253 383-5871
Lakewood *(G-5766)*

West Pacific Resources Inc ....F....425 210-6427
Arlington *(G-346)*

Westerberg & Associates Inc ....G....509 951-4399
Liberty Lake *(G-5867)*

▼ **Westerlund Log Handlers LLC** ....E....503 325-9877
Naselle *(G-7021)*

Western Land Timber ....E....360 987-2170
Hoquiam *(G-4362)*

Western Timber Inc ....G....360 769-0639
Port Orchard *(G-7857)*

Westlands Resources Corp Inc ....G....360 740-1970
Chehalis *(G-2542)*

Westwood Logging ....G....509 548-7681
Cashmere *(G-2334)*

Weyerhaeuser Company ....C....360 446-2420
Rainier *(G-8323)*

Weyerhaeuser Company ....C....360 274-3058
Castle Rock *(G-2357)*

Weyerhaeuser Company ....G....360 245-3245
Curtis *(G-2849)*

Weyerhaeuser Company ....B....253 924-3030
Tacoma *(G-13595)*

Weyerhaeuser Company ....B....360 425-2150
Longview *(G-5966)*

Weyerhaeuser Company ....C....360 291-3229
Pe Ell *(G-7661)*

◆ **Weyerhaeuser Company** ....A....206 539-3000
Seattle *(G-11459)*

White & Zumstein Inc ....F....360 263-6114
La Center *(G-5519)*

White Logging LLC ....G....509 997-0279
Twisp *(G-13917)*

White River Logging ....F....360 829-1630
Buckley *(G-2080)*

Wiard H Groeneveld ....G....360 793-1638
Monroe *(G-6637)*

Wiebold & Sons Logging Inc ....G....360 573-2149
Vancouver *(G-14691)*

Wiest Logging ....G....360 423-3560
Longview *(G-5969)*

Wilkins Kaiser & Olsen Inc ....C....509 427-5967
Carson *(G-2310)*

Will Logging & Construction ....F....509 223-3560
Loomis *(G-5973)*

Willapa Logging Company Inc ....E....360 875-5670
Raymond *(G-8361)*

Willard Newman ....G....509 442-3265
Ione *(G-4377)*

William Blockley Contracting ....G....360 592-5843
Deming *(G-2926)*

Wilson Operations ....G....360 496-6565
Morton *(G-6674)*

Windemere Camino Island Realty ....E....360 387-3411
Stanwood *(G-12958)*

Wines Company ....G....509 292-8820
Elk *(G-3178)*

Wirtanen Logging Inc ....G....360 686-3042
Yacolt *(G-15494)*

Womsley Logging Company ....G....360 321-5321
Langley *(G-5789)*

Wood Shed Inc ....G....253 405-8890
Pacific *(G-7541)*

Woodland Services Inc ....G....360 652-0412
Arlington *(G-349)*

Woolys Tree Service Inc ....G....360 944-7786
Vancouver *(G-14700)*

Wyss Logging Inc ....E....509 452-5893
Yakima *(G-15711)*

Zender Bros & Wilburn Logging ....G....360 599-2859
Deming *(G-2927)*

Zender Logging Co Inc ....E....360 966-5693
Everson *(G-3694)*

Zepp Resources ....F....360 470-4622
Elma *(G-3260)*

Zercks Logging LLC ....G....509 779-4820
Malo *(G-6236)*

Zumstein Logging Co ....G....360 225-7505
Woodland *(G-15477)*

Zumstein Logging Co ....G....253 225-7521
Woodland *(G-15478)*

2421 Saw & Planing Mills

A JS Custom Portable Sawmilli ....G....425 775-7999
Bothell *(G-1812)*

Ace International Inc ....E....360 736-3937
Centralia *(G-2379)*

▼ **Ace International Inc** ....G....360 736-9999
Centralia *(G-2380)*

Acme Forge ....G....253 217-3801
Auburn *(G-360)*

Allen Logging Co ....E....360 374-6000
Port Angeles *(G-7683)*

Alsea Veneer Inc ....G....360 891-2020
Vancouver *(G-14025)*

◆ **Alta Forest Products LLC** ....E....360 219-0008
Chehalis *(G-2463)*

Alta Forest Products LLC ....B....360 219-0008
Morton *(G-6667)*

Alta Forest Products LLC ....D....360 426-9721
Shelton *(G-11676)*

Alta Forest Products LLC ....G....360 288-2234
Amanda Park *(G-86)*

Artic Timber ....G....360 533-6490
Cosmopolis *(G-2797)*

Beam Machine ....G....425 222-5587
Fall City *(G-3700)*

Beck Mill Co Inc ....G....360 629-4769
Stanwood *(G-12961)*

Bell Lumber & Pole Company ....G....360 445-5565
Conway *(G-2796)*

Bennett Lumber Products Inc ....C....509 758-5558
Clarkston *(G-2623)*

Bennett Lumber Products Inc ....C....208 875-1321
Clarkston *(G-2624)*

Blue North Forest Products LLC ....F....208 935-2547
Seattle *(G-9552)*

Bobby Wolford Trucking & Salv ....E....425 481-1800
Woodinville *(G-15195)*

Brazier Lumber Company Inc ....G....206 441-8184
Mercer Island *(G-6456)*

Builders Firstsource Inc ....E....253 847-2900
Graham *(G-4217)*

Burgess Logging Inc ....F....509 763-3119
Leavenworth *(G-5797)*

▲ **Burke Gibson LLC** ....E....253 735-4444
Auburn *(G-398)*

◆ **Buse Timber & Sales Inc** ....D....425 258-2577
Everett *(G-3404)*

▲ **Butteville Lumber Co** ....E....360 978-6098
Onalaska *(G-7447)*

C Johnson Lumber Company Inc ....G....425 353-4222
Mukilteo *(G-6901)*

Camco Inc ....G....866 856-4826
Tacoma *(G-13218)*

Canfor USA Corporation ....E....360 647-2434
Bellingham *(G-1289)*

Carpinito Brothers Inc ....G....253 627-3121
Tacoma *(G-13225)*

▼ **Cascade Hardwoods LLC** ....C....360 748-3317
Chehalis *(G-2482)*

Cedar Farms LLC ....G....360 779-3575
Poulsbo *(G-7954)*

Cedarprime Inc ....E....360 988-2120
Sumas *(G-13042)*

▲ **Clear Forest Products Inc** ....G....360 253-0101
Vancouver *(G-14122)*

Columbia Cascade Company ....D....360 693-8558
Vancouver *(G-14129)*

Columbia Cedar Inc ....D....509 738-4711
Kettle Falls *(G-5229)*

Columbia Cedar Inc ....G....509 738-4711
Colville *(G-2744)*

▼ **Dahlstrom Lumber Co Inc** ....E....360 533-0448
Hoquiam *(G-4331)*

Dapaul Inc ....E....360 943-9844
Tumwater *(G-13869)*

De Jong Sawdust & Shavings ....F....425 252-1566
Lake Stevens *(G-5643)*

Don Larson Logging Inc ....G....509 722-6612
Fruitland *(G-4065)*

E-Green Building Systems ....G....206 219-9236
Seattle *(G-9867)*

▼ **Edman Company** ....F....253 572-5306
Tacoma *(G-13272)*

▼ **Edwin Enterprises Inc** ....G....253 272-7090
Tacoma *(G-13274)*

Empire Lumber Co ....G....509 534-0266
Spokane *(G-12246)*

Erosion Ctrl Innovations LLC ....G....206 962-9582
Enumclaw *(G-3290)*

F A Koenig & Sons Inc ....G....360 793-1711
Sultan *(G-13024)*

Faye Gear Rhonda ....G....509 380-0950
Pasco *(G-7581)*

◆ **Fred Tebb & Sons Inc** ....D....253 272-4107
Tacoma *(G-13301)*

Fritch Forest Products Inc ....E....360 668-5838
Snohomish *(G-11911)*

Fritch Mill Inc ....G....425 481-4157
Snohomish *(G-11912)*

Full Circle Natural Products ....G....425 337-8844
Everett *(G-3487)*

Granger Company ....E....509 758-9458
Vancouver *(G-14261)*

Great Western Lumber Company ....D....360 966-3061
Everson *(G-3677)*

Green Diamond Resource Company ....G....360 426-0737
Grapeview *(G-4288)*

H & H Wood Recyclers Inc ....E....360 892-2805
Vancouver *(G-14278)*

Hampton Affiliates ....G....360 403-8213
Arlington *(G-246)*

Hampton Dist Companies LLC ....D....360 496-5115
Randle *(G-8325)*

Hampton Lumber Mills Inc ....D....360 474-1504
Arlington *(G-247)*

Havillah Shake Co ....G....509 486-1467
Tonasket *(G-13650)*

Heirloom Quality Modern LLC ....G....206 291-7331
Seattle *(G-10160)*

Hermann Bros Log & Cnstr Inc ....D....360 452-3341
Port Angeles *(G-7709)*

Holbrook Inc ....E....360 754-9390
Olympia *(G-7307)*

Interfor US Inc ....C....360 457-6266
Port Angeles *(G-7714)*

Interfor US Inc ....D....360 575-3600
Longview *(G-5919)*

Interfor US Inc ....E....360 327-3377
Port Angeles *(G-7715)*

James Hardie Building Pdts Inc ....D....253 847-8700
Tacoma *(G-13355)*

James Richard Simpson ....G....509 679-9720
Tenino *(G-13619)*

Jarvis Saw Mill LLC ....G....360 733-7591
Bellingham *(G-1387)*

◆ **Kamilche Company** ....G....206 224-5800
Seattle *(G-10326)*

Ld Forest Inc ....G....360 733-1606
Bellingham *(G-1403)*

Little River Inc ....G....360 532-7490
Hoquiam *(G-4347)*

Local Manufacturing Inc ....F....360 533-0190
Aberdeen *(G-20)*

Longview Fibre Ppr & Packg Inc ....G....509 674-1791
Cle Elum *(G-2671)*

▲ **Manke Lumber Company Inc** ....B....253 572-6252
Tacoma *(G-13397)*

Manke Lumber Company Inc ....G....360 426-5536
Shelton *(G-11710)*

Manke Lumber Company Inc ....D....253 863-4495
Sumner *(G-13084)*

Manke Timber Company Inc ....G....253 572-9029
Tacoma *(G-13398)*

Mapel Mill LLC ....G....360 508-1313
Winlock *(G-15154)*

Matthaeis Camco Inc ....E....360 426-7900
Shelton *(G-11712)*

McClanahan Lumber Inc ....G....360 374-5887
Forks *(G-4012)*

Mercer Timber Products LLC ....G....206 674-4639
Tukwila *(G-13770)*

Merrill & Ring Inc ....E....360 452-2367
Port Angeles *(G-7725)*

Meyer Wells Inc ....E....206 282-0076
Seattle *(G-10525)*

Mhj Wood Works ....G....360 901-8889
Battle Ground *(G-722)*

▲ **Michiels International Inc** ....G....206 365-4060
Kenmore *(G-4592)*

Miller Shingle Company LLC ....G....360 691-7727
Granite Falls *(G-4281)*

Milmor Lumber Manufacturing ....G....253 474-1001
Fircrest *(G-4003)*

Mount Adams Lumber Co Inc ....G....509 395-2122
Trout Lake *(G-13681)*

Mt Adams Lumber Company Inc ....G....509 395-2131
Trout Lake *(G-13682)*

Mutual Materials Company Inc ....G....253 589-6434
Tacoma *(G-13423)*

◆ **Nippon Paper Inds USA Co Ltd** ....G....360 457-4474
Longview *(G-5936)*

North Fork Timber Company Corp ....G....360 273-5541
Rochester *(G-9138)*

SIC SECTION   24 LUMBER AND WOOD PRODUCTS, EXCEPT FURNITURE

North Mason Fiber Company ....G....... 360 275-0228
  Belfair (G-769)
◆ Northern Industrial Inc ....E....... 206 682-2752
  Seattle (G-10631)
NW Fibre LLC ....F....... 360 887-8418
  Morton (G-6671)
Oroville Reman & Reload Inc ....E....... 509 476-2935
  Oroville (G-7471)
Pacific Fibre Products Inc ....D....... 360 577-7112
  Longview (G-5941)
Pacific Northwest Timbers LLC ....G....... 360 379-2792
  Port Townsend (G-7906)
Pacific Topsoils Inc ....E....... 425 337-2700
  Everett (G-3568)
Pat Lydon Saw Mill LLC ....G....... 360 666-0900
  Battle Ground (G-728)
Peterson Manufacturing Co ....F....... 360 425-4170
  Longview (G-5943)
Pleasant Hill Sawmill ....G....... 360 274-7888
  Kelso (G-4542)
Plum Creek Timberlands LP ....F....... 206 467-3600
  Seattle (G-10825)
◆ Port Angeles Hardwood LLC ....G....... 360 452-6041
  Port Angeles (G-7737)
Port Blakely Company ....G....... 206 624-5810
  Seattle (G-10834)
▼ Portac Inc ....F....... 253 922-9900
  Fife (G-3983)
Precision Beam & Timber Inc ....G....... 509 525-1381
  Walla Walla (G-14857)
▲ Rainier Veneer Inc ....D....... 253 846-0242
  Spanaway (G-12070)
Randall Custom Lumber Ltd ....G....... 360 426-8518
  Shelton (G-11724)
Rfp Manufacturing Inc ....E....... 253 847-3330
  Spanaway (G-12071)
Robert Madsen Design Inc ....G....... 206 588-0090
  Seattle (G-10971)
▲ Rsg Forest Products Inc ....C....... 360 673-2825
  Kalama (G-4507)
Rsg Forest Products Inc ....E....... 360 225-8513
  Woodland (G-15464)
Ruff Cuts Custom Sawing LLC ....G....... 360 249-3926
  Montesano (G-6655)
S&L Portable Sawmill LLC ....G....... 360 417-3085
  Port Angeles (G-7742)
Sawarne Lumber Co Ltd ....E....... 360 380-1290
  Ferndale (G-3899)
▲ SDS Lumber Co ....C....... 509 493-1444
  Bingen (G-1642)
Shakertown 1992 Inc ....E....... 360 785-3501
  Winlock (G-15156)
Shearer Brothers Chipping LLC ....F....... 360 426-6466
  Shelton (G-11731)
Sierra Pacific Industries ....C....... 530 378-8251
  Shelton (G-11734)
Sierra Pacific Industries ....C....... 360 532-2323
  Aberdeen (G-34)
Sierra Pacific Industries ....C....... 360 736-5417
  Centralia (G-2433)
Silver City Lumber Inc ....E....... 509 238-6960
  Chattaroy (G-2453)
Simmons Densified Fuels Inc ....G....... 509 453-6008
  Naches (G-7003)
▲ Simpson Investment Company ....D....... 253 272-0158
  Seattle (G-11115)
Skagit River Reman Company ....E....... 360 826-4344
  Sedro Woolley (G-11568)
Smyth Paulenterprises Inc ....G....... 360 598-3262
  Poulsbo (G-8002)
Socco Inc ....F....... 360 988-4900
  Sumas (G-13050)
▼ South Everson Lumber Co Inc ......C....... 360 966-2188
  Everson (G-3689)
Starkenburg Shavings ....G....... 360 734-8818
  Ferndale (G-3907)
Stella-Jones Corporation ....D....... 360 435-2146
  Arlington (G-334)
Sunland Bark and Topsoils Co ....G....... 360 293-7188
  Anacortes (G-172)
Sylvia Vanzee ....G....... 206 284-2977
  Seattle (G-11242)
Thee Legacy Woodshop ....G....... 425 327-0208
  Arlington (G-338)
Topsoils Northwest Inc ....F....... 425 337-0233
  Snohomish (G-11993)
Trumark Industries Inc ....E....... 509 534-0644
  Spokane (G-12571)
Vaagen Bros Lumber Inc ....C....... 509 684-5071
  Colville (G-2779)

Valley Supply Company ....E....... 360 217-4400
  Woodinville (G-15398)
Vandermeer Forest Products Inc ....G....... 360 657-2518
  Marysville (G-6399)
W-4 Construction Inc ....F....... 509 529-1603
  Walla Walla (G-14886)
Wane Flitch ....G....... 253 414-2783
  Tacoma (G-13587)
▲ Washington Alder LLC ....D....... 360 542-1900
  Mount Vernon (G-6854)
Wayne Davidson ....G....... 425 333-4242
  Carnation (G-2302)
Webley Lumber Inc ....G....... 509 684-3980
  Colville (G-2783)
Western Forest Products US LLC ...G....... 360 403-1400
  Arlington (G-348)
Western Forest Products US LLC ...E....... 360 735-9700
  Vancouver (G-14685)
Weyerhaeuser Company ....C....... 360 942-6302
  Raymond (G-8360)
Weyerhaeuser Company ....C....... 360 736-2811
  Centralia (G-2442)
Weyerhaeuser Company ....C....... 360 577-6678
  Longview (G-5967)
Weyerhaeuser Company ....C....... 631 863-1117
  Sumner (G-13112)
Weyerhaeuser Company ....E....... 425 210-5880
  Seattle (G-11462)
Wilkins Kaiser & Olsen Inc ....C....... 509 427-5967
  Carson (G-2310)
Willamette Valley Lumber LLC ....F....... 509 331-0442
  Othello (G-7510)
▼ Willis Enterprises Inc ....G....... 360 273-9266
  Oakville (G-7177)
Windfall Lumber Inc ....E....... 360 352-2250
  Tumwater (G-13906)

2426 Hardwood Dimension & Flooring Mills

Alaska Wholesale Hardwoods ....G....... 360 704-4444
  Tumwater (G-13850)
All Things New LLC ....G....... 253 255-4954
  Lakewood (G-5697)
▼ Allweather Wood LLC ....D....... 360 835-8547
  Washougal (G-14941)
Aurora Hardwood Seattle LLC ....C....... 253 236-8985
  Kent (G-4798)
Bamboo Hardwoods Inc ....G....... 800 607-2414
  Seattle (G-9488)
▲ Bamboo Hardwoods Inc ....E....... 206 264-2414
  Seattle (G-9489)
Bennett Lumber Products Inc ....C....... 208 875-1321
  Clarkston (G-2624)
Carpet Plus LLC ....G....... 253 874-0525
  Federal Way (G-3721)
▼ Cascade Hardwoods LLC ....C....... 360 748-3317
  Chehalis (G-2482)
Child Inc ....G....... 425 775-9076
  Edmonds (G-3100)
Crafted Northwest Doors Inc ....F....... 509 484-3722
  Spokane (G-12205)
Custom Office Design Inc ....F....... 253 735-8777
  Auburn (G-420)
D Ds Hardwood Floors ....G....... 206 726-8808
  Seattle (G-9780)
D S Hardwood Corporation ....G....... 509 369-3442
  Graham (G-4223)
▼ Dahlstrom Lumber Co Inc ....E....... 360 533-0448
  Hoquiam (G-4331)
Dem-Bart Checkering Tools Inc .....G....... 360 568-7356
  Snohomish (G-11897)
Dwight Hostvedt ....G....... 360 683-2315
  Sequim (G-11631)
Eagles Nest ....G....... 360 876-9522
  Port Orchard (G-7806)
Eurocraft Hardwood Floors Llc .....G....... 425 670-6769
  Woodinville (G-15237)
Extreme Hardwood Floors ....G....... 425 985-6735
  Renton (G-8797)
Fredricksons Furn & Cabinets ....G....... 206 782-5310
  Seattle (G-10023)
Grassroots Woodworks LLC ....G....... 360 836-1313
  Bellingham (G-1360)
Great Western Lumber Company ...D....... 360 966-3061
  Everson (G-3677)
Ifloorcom ....G....... 206 438-3022
  Tukwila (G-13751)
JM Ventures Inc ....G....... 206 718-3355
  Bothell (G-1771)
Kelseys Collection Inc ....G....... 206 355-4333
  Lake Forest Park (G-5618)

Macmillan & Company ....F....... 360 249-1148
  Montesano (G-6645)
Nfi Enterprises LLC ....E....... 253 245-5500
  Auburn (G-507)
Norman Lancaster Brown ....G....... 509 678-5980
  Tieton (G-13631)
North Country Forest Resources .....G....... 509 486-2882
  Tonasket (G-13655)
◆ Northwest Hardwoods Inc ....A....... 253 568-6800
  Tacoma (G-13432)
NW Wood Holding LLC ....G....... 360 326-8794
  Vancouver (G-14445)
Planeta Works LLC ....G....... 206 250-4311
  Shoreline (G-11801)
Professional Hardwood Floors ....G....... 425 741-1017
  Mill Creek (G-6521)
Robert Madsen Design Inc ....G....... 206 588-0090
  Seattle (G-10971)
S & S Selden LLC ....G....... 253 922-5700
  Fife (G-3989)
Snow Peak Forest Products Inc ......G....... 208 714-4243
  Spokane Valley (G-12878)
Weyerhaeuser Company ....C....... 360 736-2811
  Centralia (G-2442)
Weyerhaeuser Company ....C....... 360 577-6678
  Longview (G-5967)
Weyerhaeuser Company ....E....... 425 210-5880
  Seattle (G-11462)
Wound Wood Technologies LLC ....F....... 206 762-0400
  Seattle (G-11498)

2429 Special Prdt Sawmills, NEC

Acuna Cedar Products ....G....... 425 359-3224
  Sedro Woolley (G-11530)
Anderson Shake & Shingle Mill ....G....... 360 795-3069
  Cathlamet (G-2359)
Benchmark Barrels LLC ....G....... 360 652-2594
  Arlington (G-212)
Best Shingle Sales Inc ....G....... 360 532-5423
  Hoquiam (G-4329)
Cedarville Shake & Shingle Mil ......G....... 360 715-1856
  Ferndale (G-3829)
Griffiths Inc ....G....... 360 276-4122
  Moclips (G-6539)
Havillah Shake Co ....G....... 509 486-1467
  Tonasket (G-13650)
Hiway 6 Shake & Shingle ....G....... 360 934-5442
  Raymond (G-8354)
Miller Shingle Company LLC ....G....... 360 691-7727
  Granite Falls (G-4281)
N J L Inc ....G....... 360 590-8100
  Ocean Shores (G-7187)
Pacific Reign Enterprises ....G....... 360 580-4447
  Humptulips (G-4364)
Phillips & Reichert Shake Mill ....G....... 360 978-4392
  Chehalis (G-2524)
Shakertown 1992 Inc ....E....... 360 785-3501
  Winlock (G-15156)
Vintage Investments Inc ....G....... 360 293-2596
  Anacortes (G-183)

2431 Millwork

A 1 Doors Inc ....G....... 604 591-1044
  Kent (G-4751)
A and R Cabinets & Wdwkg L L C ...G....... 360 863-8417
  Monroe (G-6541)
Above and Beyond Cnstr LLC ....G....... 509 521-8081
  Kennewick (G-4610)
Acadie Woodworks ....G....... 509 924-1256
  Spokane (G-12095)
Acadie Woodworks Incorporated ....G....... 509 230-6874
  Spokane Valley (G-12598)
Alan and Linda Murray LLC ....G....... 206 527-0841
  Seattle (G-9364)
◆ Alexandria Moulding Inc ....C....... 509 248-2120
  Moxee (G-6874)
Als Custom Woodworking ....G....... 360 354-2407
  Lynden (G-6000)
American Woodworking Supply ......G....... 509 424-3800
  Yakima (G-15508)
Anderson Fine Woods ....G....... 425 422-2753
  Lake Stevens (G-5631)
Anderson Woodworks ....G....... 360 923-2203
  Olympia (G-7226)
Archetype Woodworking LLC ....G....... 360 977-0565
  Vancouver (G-14039)
Argusea Mar Wdwkg & Finshg LLC ...G....... 360 708-9702
  Bow (G-1926)
Artisan Stone Wood Works Inc ....G....... 253 740-7102
  Tacoma (G-13182)

Employee Codes: A=Over 500 employees, B=251-500
C=101-250, D=51-100, E=20-50, F=10-19, G=2-9

Artistic Cabinets & Millwork ....G.... 509 575-4788
Yakima ***(G-15514)***

▲ **Artistic Home & Garden LLC** ....G.... 360 834-7021
Camas ***(G-2229)***

Artys Door Shop Inc ....G.... 360 695-7898
Vancouver ***(G-14042)***

Avn Floor & Mill Work LLC ....G.... 425 345-6071
Everett ***(G-3377)***

B Plus Inc ....G.... 360 426-5038
Shelton ***(G-11681)***

Bagdons Inc ....E.... 509 662-1411
Wenatchee ***(G-15011)***

Bahmiller Woodworks ....G.... 509 929-6300
Ellensburg ***(G-3184)***

Baraa Woodworking ....G.... 360 752-0608
Bellingham ***(G-1257)***

Barmon Door & Plywood Inc ....E.... 425 334-1222
Lake Stevens ***(G-5633)***

Barrys Wood Working ....G.... 253 312-1585
University Place ***(G-13961)***

Bayne Junction Woodworks ....G.... 360 886-8908
Ravensdale ***(G-8331)***

Beaver Lake Woodworks ....G.... 425 391-0661
Sammamish ***(G-9188)***

Belina Interiors Inc ....D.... 253 474-0276
Tacoma ***(G-13193)***

Bellevue Door & Millwork Co ....G.... 425 885-3009
Kirkland ***(G-5290)***

Benchmark Woods ....G.... 360 732-0993
Chimacum ***(G-2611)***

Bernstein Woodworks ....G.... 206 605-1796
Seattle ***(G-9516)***

Blue Heron Woodworks ....G.... 360 766-4475
Bow ***(G-1928)***

Blue Streak Woodworks ....G.... 360 379-0414
Port Townsend ***(G-7869)***

Bob Johnson Woodworking ....G.... 360 668-9456
Snohomish ***(G-11877)***

Bolt Woodworks Corp ....G.... 206 734-5845
Everett ***(G-3398)***

Brad O Connor Woodworking ....G.... 206 302-8424
Seattle ***(G-9575)***

Brian Friesen Fine Woodworking ....G.... 360 314-6427
Vancouver ***(G-14081)***

Budd Bay Homes ....G.... 360 357-6064
Olympia ***(G-7245)***

▲ **Buffelen Woodworking Co** ....D.... 253 627-1191
Tacoma ***(G-13212)***

Builders Firstsource Inc ....F.... 509 525-4008
Walla Walla ***(G-14775)***

Building Specialty Systems ....G.... 425 483-6875
Ellensburg ***(G-3185)***

Bush Woodcraft ....G.... 206 323-2020
Seattle ***(G-9601)***

C & M Woodworks ....G.... 253 503-9440
Graham ***(G-4219)***

Cabin Mill LLC ....G.... 509 235-1808
Cheney ***(G-2579)***

Camelot Treasures ....G.... 360 829-9774
Buckley ***(G-2050)***

▼ **Cams-Usa Inc** ....F.... 253 639-3890
Kent ***(G-4835)***

CDI Custom Design Inc ....E.... 360 650-1150
Bellingham ***(G-1294)***

Centerpiece Customs ....G.... 360 490-8636
Shelton ***(G-11690)***

Chetties Woodworking LLC ....G.... 360 500-9099
Rochester ***(G-9130)***

Chuckanut Woodworks ....G.... 360 724-3129
Burlington ***(G-2143)***

Coastline Woodworking ....G.... 360 678-7572
Coupeville ***(G-2810)***

Colville Wdwkg & Stained GL ....G.... 509 684-7670
Colville ***(G-2748)***

Complete Mllwk Solutions Inc ....G.... 253 875-6769
Federal Way ***(G-3724)***

Conestoga Wood Spc Corp ....G.... 253 437-1320
Kent ***(G-4863)***

Contemporary Woodworks LLC ....G.... 360 897-2162
Orting ***(G-7476)***

Contour Countertops Inc ....F.... 503 654-2245
Vancouver ***(G-14150)***

▼ **Conwood Construction Inc** ....G.... 360 694-5195
Vancouver ***(G-14151)***

Cornerstone Real Property ....G.... 360 455-0862
Olympia ***(G-7256)***

Costom Woodwork ....G.... 425 828-2579
Kirkland ***(G-5315)***

Crafted Northwest Doors Inc ....F.... 509 484-3722
Spokane ***(G-12205)***

Crafty Woodworking ....G.... 425 822-9618
Kirkland ***(G-5316)***

Craig Yamamoto Woodworker LLC ....G.... 206 571-5821
Clinton ***(G-2686)***

Creative Millwork & Moulding ....G.... 425 343-4799
Snohomish ***(G-11892)***

Creative Openings ....G.... 360 671-6420
Bellingham ***(G-1311)***

Crucible NW Woodworks LLC ....G.... 206 661-3545
Seattle ***(G-9758)***

Csw Inc ....G.... 360 491-9365
Tumwater ***(G-13866)***

Curry Custom Cabinets Corp ....G.... 425 315-9355
Mukilteo ***(G-6909)***

Custom Choice Door LLC ....G.... 253 472-0963
Lakewood ***(G-5710)***

Custom Molding Co Inc ....F.... 360 830-0108
Seabeck ***(G-9263)***

Custom Wood Finishes ....G.... 360 468-4383
Lopez Island ***(G-5980)***

Custom Woodworking ....G.... 360 739-3961
Lynden ***(G-6011)***

Cutting Edge Woodworks LLC ....G.... 360 929-5386
Oak Harbor ***(G-7145)***

D & D Millwork Inc ....F.... 800 627-8437
Lynnwood ***(G-6105)***

D Haitre Woodworks LLC ....G.... 360 752-0405
Bellingham ***(G-1316)***

Daniels Woodworks ....G.... 360 264-7311
Tenino ***(G-13615)***

Dave Yocoms Wood Creations ....G.... 425 220-5628
Everett ***(G-3440)***

Delta Pntg & Prefinishing Co ....G.... 253 588-8278
Tacoma ***(G-13258)***

Direys ....G.... 425 788-2026
Duvall ***(G-2983)***

Discount Doors & Millwork LLC ....G.... 360 687-1942
Vancouver ***(G-14182)***

Dkr Wood Working ....G.... 509 943-2273
Richland ***(G-8989)***

Doors & Millwork Inc ....G.... 509 921-7663
Spokane Valley ***(G-12682)***

Draped In Style LLC ....G.... 425 241-6227
Snohomish ***(G-11900)***

Dreamers Woods ....G.... 360 477-5888
Port Angeles ***(G-7698)***

Duncan J Woodworking ....G.... 360 765-0745
Quilcene ***(G-8283)***

▼ **Edwin Enterprises Inc** ....G.... 253 272-7090
Tacoma ***(G-13274)***

▲ **Elochoman Millwork Inc** ....G.... 360 795-3637
Cathlamet ***(G-2365)***

Emma Danforth ....G.... 360 931-5060
Vancouver ***(G-14201)***

Epping-Jordan Fine Wdwkg LLC ....G.... 206 588-2700
Seattle ***(G-9935)***

F Ruckman Enterprises ....E.... 253 531-9132
Puyallup ***(G-8151)***

Fine Woodworking ....G.... 425 486-3305
Woodinville ***(G-15242)***

Finishing Touches ....G.... 425 277-6079
Renton ***(G-8799)***

Fircrest Pre-Fit Door Co Inc ....G.... 253 564-6921
Tacoma ***(G-13296)***

Fitts Industries Inc ....G.... 253 474-0376
Tacoma ***(G-13297)***

Flanagan Woodworks Inc ....G.... 360 221-3352
Langley ***(G-5777)***

Fox Island Woodworks ....G.... 253 549-7019
Fox Island ***(G-4021)***

Frank J Madera ....G.... 253 858-7934
Gig Harbor ***(G-4103)***

G R Plume Co ....F.... 360 384-2800
Ferndale ***(G-3846)***

Garage Sports Woodworking ....G.... 206 433-1645
Burien ***(G-2109)***

Gazebo & Porchworks ....G.... 253 380-0918
Puyallup ***(G-8155)***

Ghl Architectural Millwork LLC ....G.... 206 467-5004
Seattle ***(G-10068)***

◆ **Glacier Mouldings Ltd** ....F.... 360 629-5313
Stanwood ***(G-12975)***

Gnw Corporation ....G.... 425 869-6218
Redmond ***(G-8479)***

Goddard Woodworking Llcpetr Go ....G.... 206 920-8675
Seattle ***(G-10092)***

Great Northwest Industries ....F.... 425 861-9768
Redmond ***(G-8483)***

Grozdi Inc ....G.... 253 820-0653
Tacoma ***(G-13327)***

Haase Woodworks ....G.... 360 681-2600
Sequim ***(G-11637)***

Hacienda Custom Woodwork LLC ....G.... 206 922-9330
Renton ***(G-8816)***

Hacienda Custom Woodwork LLC ....G.... 206 922-9330
Maple Valley ***(G-6272)***

Havens Woodworks & Refinishing ....G.... 360 833-9446
Camas ***(G-2256)***

Heirloom Woodworks ....G.... 509 315-9275
Spokane Valley ***(G-12728)***

Hicks Leathermaking and Wdwkg ....G.... 253 833-8873
Auburn ***(G-465)***

High Country Woodworks ....G.... 360 942-2996
Raymond ***(G-8353)***

Hogan Construction Inc ....G.... 206 290-5553
Kent ***(G-4944)***

Howat Fine Woodworking Inc ....G.... 360 681-3451
Sequim ***(G-11640)***

Hrh Door Corp ....D.... 360 736-7651
Centralia ***(G-2409)***

Hugh Montgomery ....G.... 206 369-9356
Bainbridge Island ***(G-641)***

Independent Woodworks ....G.... 206 239-8577
Seattle ***(G-10224)***

Inland Fixtures Co Inc ....G.... 509 487-2759
Spokane ***(G-12309)***

Inland Millwork ....G.... 509 481-7765
Spokane Valley ***(G-12744)***

Inland Woodworks ....G.... 509 701-0985
Spokane ***(G-12314)***

Interior Construction Spc ....F.... 425 745-8343
Mukilteo ***(G-6944)***

Interior Wdwkg Specialists Inc ....E.... 425 881-1328
Redmond ***(G-8513)***

Island Sash & Door Inc ....F.... 360 331-7752
Freeland ***(G-4031)***

Island Wood Works ....G.... 360 403-7066
Arlington ***(G-258)***

J & K Woodworks ....G.... 425 392-3758
Issaquah ***(G-4433)***

J & R Wood Products Inc ....G.... 360 687-1662
Battle Ground ***(G-710)***

J Wanamaker Cabinetry & Wdwrk ....G.... 206 762-3494
Seattle ***(G-10274)***

Jaks Custom Woodwork ....G.... 425 443-6210
Duvall ***(G-2992)***

Jays Custom Woodworks ....G.... 360 807-0976
Centralia ***(G-2411)***

Jaywick Woodworks LLC ....G.... 206 793-7208
Seattle ***(G-10286)***

JB Woodworking ....G.... 509 949-3683
Yakima ***(G-15598)***

Jbs Millwork Inc ....G.... 509 248-3412
Yakima ***(G-15599)***

Jeld-Wen Inc ....F.... 206 574-0986
Tukwila ***(G-13755)***

Jet Door LLC ....E.... 253 531-2261
Tacoma ***(G-13359)***

Ji Woodwork ....G.... 360 790-4083
Gig Harbor ***(G-4123)***

Jim Lemons Doors & Cabinets ....G.... 360 871-4001
Port Orchard ***(G-7820)***

Johnsons Millwork Inc ....F.... 253 472-5900
Tacoma ***(G-13367)***

Jsg Fine Cstm Cbntry Wdwrk LLC ....G.... 253 906-9043
Tacoma ***(G-13369)***

Jubilee Woodworks LLC ....G.... 206 734-0344
Seattle ***(G-10312)***

JW Woodworks ....G.... 206 719-4229
Federal Way ***(G-3748)***

Jwoodworking ....G.... 253 229-9581
Tacoma ***(G-13371)***

K & S Woodworks LLC ....G.... 360 354-1043
Lynden ***(G-6027)***

Kaci Woodworks LLC ....G.... 206 601-0395
Seattle ***(G-10324)***

◆ **Kamilche Company** ....G.... 206 224-5800
Seattle ***(G-10326)***

Kieu Danh ....G.... 360 548-9649
Marysville ***(G-6347)***

Kincaid Woodworking ....G.... 518 810-1374
Tumwater ***(G-13880)***

King Brothers Woodworking Inc ....E.... 509 453-4683
Union Gap ***(G-13936)***

▲ **Klm Custom Sash LLC** ....G.... 360 403-7400
Arlington ***(G-269)***

Korben Mathis Woodworking Inc ....G.... 360 598-6797
Poulsbo ***(G-7972)***

Kyle O Meara ....G.... 206 874-2626
Federal Way ***(G-3749)***

SIC SECTION | 24 LUMBER AND WOOD PRODUCTS, EXCEPT FURNITURE

L J Smith Inc .... F 253 435-9120
Puyallup *(G-8175)*
Lak Woodworks .... G 253 495-0611
Lakewood *(G-5732)*
Leaves In Wind Woodworks LLC .... G 360 574-6750
Vancouver *(G-14368)*
Left Coast Woodworks LLC .... G 360 790-3188
Centralia *(G-2417)*
Lj Backdoor Inc .... E 206 767-2434
Seattle *(G-10433)*
Loan Goat Woodworks .... G 360 395-8996
Sedro Woolley *(G-11550)*
Lr Woodworking .... G 281 813-1169
Poulsbo *(G-7978)*
Lucky Dog Woodworking .... G 507 218-6767
Okanogan *(G-7199)*
▲ **Lynden Door Inc** .... E 360 354-5676
Lynden *(G-6032)*
M L Woodworks .... G 360 264-4859
Tenino *(G-13621)*
Maizefield Company .... G 360 385-6789
Port Townsend *(G-7896)*
Mark E Padbury .... G 360 376-6200
Eastsound *(G-3039)*
Mark Thomas Woodworks .... G 505 220-7560
Walla Walla *(G-14842)*
Marke Woodworking .... G 360 945-4023
Point Roberts *(G-7669)*
Marlin Windows Inc .... E 509 535-3015
Spokane Valley *(G-12784)*
Master Millwork Inc .... E 253 770-2023
Puyallup *(G-8182)*
McKenna Door and Millwork .... G 360 458-5467
Roy *(G-9162)*
McKeons Fine Wdwkg LLC Gc .... G 206 920-6724
Shoreline *(G-11787)*
Metrie Inc .... E 360 863-1730
Ferndale *(G-3870)*
Miles Woodworking .... G 360 306-3048
Bellingham *(G-1435)*
Milgard Manufacturing Inc .... A 253 922-4341
Fife *(G-3972)*
Mill City Brew Werks .... G 360 210-4761
Camas *(G-2270)*
Mill Creek Woodworking Inc .... G 509 526-5660
Walla Walla *(G-14844)*
Mill Frame LLC .... G 425 599-5992
Sumas *(G-13048)*
Mirror Finish Incorporated .... G 360 384-1710
Ferndale *(G-3872)*
Mitchell Door and Trim Inc .... F 360 874-8901
Port Orchard *(G-7830)*
Modern Art Woodwork LLC .... G 360 303-6054
Ferndale *(G-3874)*
Modern Yacht Joinery .... G 360 928-0214
Port Angeles *(G-7726)*
Monroe Door & Millwork Inc .... F 360 863-9882
Monroe *(G-6598)*
Mountain Springs Building Co .... G 206 550-4380
Bellevue *(G-1017)*
Mystic Woodworking .... G 425 736-1416
Newcastle *(G-7036)*
Neucor Inc .... G 866 638-2671
Vancouver *(G-14430)*
New Touch Woodworking .... G 360 930-1118
Hansville *(G-4316)*
New Whatcom Interiors .... F 360 671-3389
Bellingham *(G-1459)*
Nicos Woodworking .... G 206 755-8110
Shoreline *(G-11793)*
Nissen Woodworks .... G 425 216-3575
North Bend *(G-7117)*
Nk Woodworking LLC .... G 206 257-4395
Seattle *(G-10612)*
Noel Corporation .... F 509 248-3412
Yakima *(G-15631)*
Normandie Woodworks .... G 360 446-0352
Rainier *(G-8319)*
Northwest Custom Podiums Inc .... G 360 830-5858
Seabeck *(G-9269)*
Northwest Door and Millwork .... G 509 782-4525
Wenatchee *(G-15053)*
Northwest Millwork Door Co .... G 360 297-0802
Bainbridge Island *(G-654)*
Northwest Plywood Sales of Ore .... F 360 750-1561
Vancouver *(G-14439)*
Northwest Woodworking LLC .... G 425 488-9597
Kenmore *(G-4594)*
NW Woodworks LLC .... G 206 780-6753
Bainbridge Island *(G-656)*

▼ **O B Williams Company** .... E 206 623-2494
Seattle *(G-10677)*
Oceanus Plastics Inc .... G 360 366-7474
Custer *(G-2858)*
Oka Woodworks Inc .... G 425 221-2573
Sammamish *(G-9239)*
Old Dominion Woodworks .... G 509 684-7931
Colville *(G-2767)*
Old Plank Woodworks .... G 360 455-7366
Olympia *(G-7351)*
Old School Woodcrafter .... G 509 493-4155
White Salmon *(G-15126)*
Old Woodworking Inc .... G 253 770-3650
Puyallup *(G-8209)*
Olsen Cabinet & Millwork .... G 206 242-1188
Seatac *(G-9295)*
Olympic Millwork .... G 360 480-6650
Olympia *(G-7359)*
Olympic Mountain Millwork LLC .... G 360 432-2992
Shelton *(G-11717)*
Once Again Woodworking .... G 425 327-9733
Snohomish *(G-11957)*
Orcas Island Tonewoods .... G 360 376-2747
Olga *(G-7217)*
▲ **Oregon PCF Bldg Pdts Exch Inc** .... D 509 892-5555
Spokane Valley *(G-12821)*
Oropeza Woodworks .... G 360 668-0438
Snohomish *(G-11958)*
Osborne Woodworks .... G 360 428-0245
Mount Vernon *(G-6819)*
Outside In Woodworks LLC .... G 208 403-9067
Port Orchard *(G-7839)*
Overhead Door Corporation .... G 253 520-8008
Fife *(G-3977)*
▲ **Pacific Coast Showcase Inc** .... C 253 445-9000
Puyallup *(G-8216)*
▲ **Pacific Crest Building Pdts** .... F 253 447-7686
Puyallup *(G-8217)*
▲ **Pacific Crest Industries Inc** .... C 253 321-3011
Sumner *(G-13093)*
Pacific Door & Window Inc .... F 360 577-9121
Longview *(G-5940)*
Pan Abode Cedar Homes Inc .... E 425 255-8260
Renton *(G-8874)*
Pcs Mill Work Inc .... E 425 820-5688
Kirkland *(G-5431)*
Pearson Millwork Inc .... F 360 435-9516
Arlington *(G-298)*
Pedersons Custom Woodworking .... G 509 981-0720
Spokane Valley *(G-12826)*
Port Townsend School of Woodwo .... G 303 910-0016
Port Townsend *(G-7915)*
Possession Point Woodworking .... G 360 579-2183
Clinton *(G-2693)*
Precision Customer Woodworking .... G 360 983-3297
Mossyrock *(G-6764)*
Premier Woodworks LLC .... G 509 591-0839
Kennewick *(G-4707)*
Price & Visser Millwork Inc .... F 360 734-7700
Bellingham *(G-1504)*
Pritchard Woodworks LLC .... G 206 755-4503
Hansville *(G-4318)*
Procoat LLC .... G 425 252-0070
Shoreline *(G-11803)*
Puget Sound Wood Windows LLC .... G 425 828-9736
Kirkland *(G-5446)*
Puget Sound Woodworking LLC .... G 360 563-0116
Snohomish *(G-11963)*
Quality Stairs and Woodworking .... G 425 358-4196
Maple Valley *(G-6291)*
Quantum Windows and Doors Inc .... D 425 259-6650
Everett *(G-3591)*
R & R Woodworking Inc .... G 509 279-9345
Medical Lake *(G-6444)*
R L Industries .... F 360 794-1621
Monroe *(G-6611)*
R L Woodworks .... G 360 607-4471
Vancouver *(G-14527)*
R Vision Antq & Restoration .... G 360 280-0328
Olympia *(G-7376)*
Rail Fx LLC .... G 206 453-1123
Tacoma *(G-13488)*
Rain City Wood Works LLC .... G 206 378-0494
Seattle *(G-10915)*
Rain Shadow Woodworks Inc .... G 360 385-6789
Port Townsend *(G-7922)*
Rainier Woodworking Co .... E 253 272-5210
Tacoma *(G-13490)*
Rams Custom Cabinets & Wdwkg .... G 253 952-2551
Federal Way *(G-3775)*

Red Tail Woodworks .... G 360 852-6883
Ridgefield *(G-9106)*
Renaissance Fine Woodworking .... G 509 334-7008
Pullman *(G-8105)*
River Hollow Creations LLC .... G 509 497-1097
Benton City *(G-1627)*
Rocking H Woodworking .... G 253 448-7978
Spanaway *(G-12072)*
Rodocker Woodworks LLC .... G 360 775-1620
Port Angeles *(G-7740)*
Rogers Custom Woodworking .... G 425 757-1799
Renton *(G-8897)*
Romeo and Sylvia LLC .... G 425 315-5336
Snohomish *(G-11968)*
Roof Truss Supply Inc .... C 425 481-0900
Woodinville *(G-15351)*
Rwsd Lumberyard .... G 503 910-9822
Chehalis *(G-2533)*
S G&C Contractor Services LLC .... G 360 671-5121
Bellingham *(G-1520)*
Saariswoodworking .... G 360 835-8106
Washougal *(G-14982)*
Salmon Bay Woodworks .... G 206 612-3993
Seattle *(G-11008)*
▼ **Sauder Mouldings Inc Ferndale** .... C 360 384-4774
Ferndale *(G-3898)*
Schiferl Woodworking .... G 425 788-3795
Woodinville *(G-15355)*
Schober Woodworks .... G 360 595-7519
Bellingham *(G-1526)*
Seattle Stair & Design LLC .... F 206 587-5354
Seattle *(G-11078)*
Shaffer Woodworks LLC .... G 509 697-3023
Selah *(G-11596)*
Shellback Ltd .... G 206 463-9054
Vashon *(G-14742)*
Sheridan Woodworking LLC .... G 509 540-7799
Walla Walla *(G-14869)*
Sign Post Inc .... F 360 671-1343
Bellingham *(G-1533)*
Silver Moon Woodworks .... G 425 753-4476
Seattle *(G-11113)*
Simpson Door Company .... B 360 495-3291
McCleary *(G-6420)*
▲ **Simpson Investment Company** .... D 253 272-0158
Seattle *(G-11115)*
Smith & Valley Gallery .... G 360 766-6230
Bow *(G-1933)*
Smith Custom Woodworking Inc .... G 509 670-4634
Wenatchee *(G-15075)*
Sparrow Woodworks LLC .... G 206 708-5615
Indianola *(G-4373)*
Specialty Woodworking .... G 360 379-1222
Port Townsend *(G-7929)*
Specialty Woodworks .... G 360 670-6280
Port Angeles *(G-7745)*
Spirit In Wood LLC .... G 509 961-3061
Naches *(G-7005)*
Staircrafters Incorporated .... G 360 882-2772
Vancouver *(G-14607)*
Star North Woodworks Inc .... E 360 384-0307
Ferndale *(G-3906)*
Starline Construction Inc .... G 509 575-7955
Yakima *(G-15682)*
Stephan J Lesser Woodworking .... G 206 782-9463
Seattle *(G-11192)*
Stratton Woodworks .... G 425 968-2455
Sammamish *(G-9250)*
Sycamore Woodworks .... G 360 757-4120
Burlington *(G-2192)*
◆ **T & A Supply Company Inc** .... D 206 282-3770
Kent *(G-5166)*
T & A Supply Company Inc .... G 253 872-3682
Kent *(G-5167)*
T R S Inc .... F 253 444-1555
Tacoma *(G-13538)*
Taggart Woodworks LLC .... G 206 729-8028
Seattle *(G-11258)*
Tarpley Woodworking .... G 360 631-1405
Granite Falls *(G-4286)*
Techwood LLC .... D 360 427-9616
Shelton *(G-11743)*
Timshel Woodworking .... G 206 466-1054
Seattle *(G-11311)*
Top Quality Woodworks LLC .... G 509 551-3658
Kennewick *(G-4736)*
Tph Inc DBA Island Wood Works .... G 360 403-7066
Arlington *(G-340)*
Traditional Concepts .... G 253 884-2818
Gig Harbor *(G-4168)*

S I C

Employee Codes: A=Over 500 employees, B=251-500
C=101-250, D=51-100, E=20-50, F=10-19, G=2-9
2019 Washington
Manufacturers Register
559

◆ **Trinity Glass Intl Inc** .... D 800 803-8182
Federal Way *(G-3798)*
Tru Door Inc .... F 509 545-8773
Kennewick *(G-4742)*
Trumark Industries Inc .... E 509 534-0644
Spokane *(G-12571)*
Upper Cut Woodworks LLC .... G 425 785-4817
Redmond *(G-8700)*
US Mill Works LLC .... G 206 355-5143
Seattle *(G-11393)*
Vancouver Door Company Inc .... E 253 845-9581
Puyallup *(G-8272)*
Veritas Custom Woodworks .... G 425 346-5576
Lynnwood *(G-6216)*
Victory Millwork LLC .... E 360 592-6090
Lynden *(G-6060)*
Voiss Wood Products Inc .... G 360 794-1062
Monroe *(G-6635)*
Vrieze & Olson Custom Wdwkg .... F 253 445-9733
Puyallup *(G-8274)*
Waddell Woodworking LLC .... G 503 752-1940
Vancouver *(G-14675)*
Washington Hardwoods and .... F 206 283-7574
Winlock *(G-15158)*
▼ **Washington Hardwoods Co LLC** .... E 206 283-7574
Seattle *(G-11440)*
Wells Ww Millwork LLC .... F 425 405-3252
Everett *(G-3654)*
Weyerhaeuser Company .... B 253 924-2345
Seattle *(G-11463)*
Whites Custom Woodworking LLC .... G 509 582-9474
Kennewick *(G-4746)*
Whitman Cabinets and Wdwkg .... G 360 825-6466
Enumclaw *(G-3329)*
Wild Tree Woodworks LLC .... G 206 650-2565
Seattle *(G-11475)*
Wild Wood Splitting .... G 206 909-8342
Maple Valley *(G-6301)*
Windorco Supply Inc .... G 206 784-9440
Seattle *(G-11482)*
Wojtanowicz Wood Works .... G 253 225-2252
Gig Harbor *(G-4176)*
Wollin Woodworking Inc .... G 360 929-5895
Mount Vernon *(G-6856)*
Wood Creations .... G 360 491-1616
Olympia *(G-7430)*
Wood Works By Rob .... G 206 497-6345
Auburn *(G-601)*
Woodland Windows & Doors .... G 360 260-5466
Vancouver *(G-14699)*
Woodwork Specialties LLC .... G 360 687-5880
Battle Ground *(G-754)*
Woodwork Tattoo and Gallery .... G 360 626-1965
Poulsbo *(G-8022)*
Woodworkers Outpost .... G 253 653-8607
Covington *(G-2840)*
Woodworking Services .... G 253 678-7951
Tacoma *(G-13601)*

2434 Wood Kitchen Cabinets

A & J Custom Cabinets Inc .... D 360 694-4833
Vancouver *(G-14001)*
Acorn Custom Cabinetry Inc .... E 425 235-8366
Renton *(G-8727)*
AE Downs Enterprises Inc .... E 206 295-9831
Kent *(G-4761)*
Alpine Cabinet .... G 509 679-6380
Leavenworth *(G-5794)*
Alpine Woodworking .... G 253 565-4560
University Place *(G-13958)*
American Cabinet Doors Inc .... F 509 574-3176
Yakima *(G-15506)*
Andrews Fixture Company Inc .... F 253 627-7481
Tacoma *(G-13172)*
Arcomm Inc .... G 253 581-9800
Lakewood *(G-5699)*
Aristocratic Cabinets Inc .... D 360 740-0609
Chehalis *(G-2467)*
Aurora Quality Buildings Inc .... G 360 658-9967
Marysville *(G-6314)*
Authentic Woodcraft Inc .... G 253 939-8119
Auburn *(G-383)*
▲ **Avella LLC** .... G 509 217-0347
Liberty Lake *(G-5827)*
Bagdons Inc .... E 509 662-1411
Wenatchee *(G-15011)*
Belina Interiors Inc .... D 253 474-0276
Tacoma *(G-13193)*
Beltecno Inc .... G 360 512-4000
Monroe *(G-6552)*
Benandre LLC .... F 425 298-8635
Arlington *(G-211)*
▲ **Best Cabinet & Granite Sup Inc** .... G 503 285-1838
Vancouver *(G-14062)*
Bilt-Rite Custom Cabinets .... G 360 829-0663
Buckley *(G-2049)*
Blase S Gorny Design Inc .... G 360 426-5613
Shelton *(G-11685)*
Blue Horizon Cabinet Co LLC .... G 509 254-1430
Clarkston *(G-2625)*
Cabinet Aesthetics .... G 808 268-1822
North Bend *(G-7103)*
Cabinet Fx .... G 425 879-6690
Marysville *(G-6319)*
Cabinet Guys .... G 425 344-5882
Everett *(G-3406)*
Cabinet Masters Inc .... G 360 695-6615
Vancouver *(G-14089)*
Cabinet Refacing of Seattle .... G 425 405-7961
Woodinville *(G-15202)*
Cabinet Tech LLC .... G 509 575-0180
Yakima *(G-15526)*
Cabinets & Countertops LLC .... G 206 933-9385
Seattle *(G-9603)*
Cabinets Inc .... G 360 778-1780
Bellingham *(G-1286)*
Caledonia Bay Cabinets Inc .... G 253 905-7368
Federal Way *(G-3720)*
Canyon Creek Cabinet Company .... G 509 921-7807
Spokane Valley *(G-12650)*
Cascade Cabinetry LLC .... G 253 395-6670
Kent *(G-4840)*
CBS Cabinet Center .... G 253 582-8088
Lakewood *(G-5706)*
Cherry Grove Cabinets .... G 360 687-8820
Ridgefield *(G-9071)*
Chets Cabinets .... G 360 659-7500
Marysville *(G-6325)*
Clearwater Cabinet Co .... G 253 853-3644
Gig Harbor *(G-4090)*
CM Cabinets L L C .... G 360 921-3493
Vancouver *(G-14125)*
Colbasia Cabinets Inc .... G 509 765-0718
Moses Lake *(G-6694)*
Columbia Cabinets LLC .... G 509 325-8995
Spokane *(G-12189)*
Columbia Cultured Marble Inc .... G 509 582-5660
Kennewick *(G-4647)*
Copperwood LLC .... G 360 674-3122
Bremerton *(G-1944)*
Covenant Cabinets .... G 425 481-4799
Bothell *(G-1843)*
Creative Cabinet Design .... G 509 452-2777
Yakima *(G-15540)*
Creekside Cabinet & Design .... G 360 692-7070
Silverdale *(G-11830)*
Curry Custom Cabinets Corp .... G 425 315-9355
Mukilteo *(G-6909)*
Custom Cabinet Design .... G 360 679-8729
Oak Harbor *(G-7144)*
Custom Source Woodworking Inc .... E 360 491-9365
Tumwater *(G-13868)*
D and D Trim and Cabinets Inc .... G 360 736-4279
Centralia *(G-2398)*
D-Mac Carpentry .... G 509 326-6601
Spokane *(G-12214)*
Daniel Cabinets LLC .... G 509 949-0855
Selah *(G-11586)*
Days Gone By Cabinetry .... G 425 868-5132
Redmond *(G-8436)*
Dean Powell & Magda Velarde .... G 253 535-4195
Kent *(G-4872)*
Dean Thoemke .... G 253 640-2232
Yakima *(G-15551)*
Designcraft Cabinets Inc .... G 509 758-2160
Clarkston *(G-2631)*
Dewils Industries Inc .... C 360 892-0300
Vancouver *(G-14177)*
Dewils Industries Inc .... D 360 892-0300
Vancouver *(G-14178)*
Dmm Incorporated .... E 360 435-5252
Arlington *(G-229)*
Dogstar Cabinets Inc .... G 509 674-4229
Cle Elum *(G-2665)*
Dream Line Cabinets LLC .... G 503 841-8575
Vancouver *(G-14187)*
DWhittle Shop Inc .... G 509 627-3050
Richland *(G-8990)*
Dwight Hostvedt .... G 360 683-2315
Sequim *(G-11631)*
E & S Custom Cabinets Inc .... E 253 405-2732
Puyallup *(G-8147)*
Eagle Harbor Cabinets LLC .... G 206 317-6942
Bainbridge Island *(G-625)*
Econo Quality Signs Inc .... G 253 531-3943
Tacoma *(G-13270)*
Elander Persson Fine Wdwrk LLC .... G 206 818-2882
Snohomish *(G-11904)*
Elkwood Custom Cabinetry LLC .... G 360 886-1989
Ravensdale *(G-8335)*
Emerald City Cabinet Co LLC .... G 425 429-7887
Mukilteo *(G-6923)*
Encore Cabinets Inc .... F 425 259-0100
Everett *(G-3461)*
Ernest R Howald Inc .... G 360 491-1758
Olympia *(G-7279)*
▲ **Evergreen Granite & Cab Sup** .... G 425 423-9681
Everett *(G-3465)*
EZ Line Cabinets .... G 206 775-2226
Kent *(G-4902)*
F H Sullivan Co Inc .... E 360 442-4222
Kelso *(G-4525)*
F Ruckman Enterprises .... E 253 531-9132
Puyallup *(G-8151)*
Ferguson Woodworking Inc .... G 360 398-1543
Bellingham *(G-1345)*
Ferrier Cabinets .... G 425 788-0230
Duvall *(G-2988)*
Firehouse Custom Cabinets .... G 253 864-4894
Puyallup *(G-8153)*
Freeze Furniture and Mfg Co .... F 509 924-3545
Spokane Valley *(G-12710)*
Frontier Door & Cabinet LLC .... D 206 768-2524
Tacoma *(G-13302)*
Gary R Howe .... G 253 857-5835
Gig Harbor *(G-4105)*
Goodnight Wood Designs .... G 360 652-7765
Tulalip *(G-13841)*
Gordon Becker Construction .... G 425 883-8545
Redmond *(G-8481)*
Great Northwest Industries .... F 425 861-9768
Redmond *(G-8483)*
Green Ndle Cbnets Moldings LLC .... G 206 235-3061
Auburn *(G-456)*
H & E Building Enterprises .... G 253 848-3534
Edgewood *(G-3081)*
Heirloom Custom Cabinetry .... G 509 370-9012
Spokane Valley *(G-12727)*
Heirloom Custom Cabinets Inc .... G 360 354-7851
Lynden *(G-6020)*
Henderson Cabinet Refinishing .... G 206 963-0874
Kenmore *(G-4579)*
Hertco Kitchens LLC .... D 360 380-1100
Ferndale *(G-3851)*
Hewitt Cabinets & Interiors .... F 253 272-0404
Tacoma *(G-13336)*
J M C Cabinets & Interiors .... E 425 258-1204
Everett *(G-3520)*
James Hellar Cabinetry .... G 360 376-5727
Eastsound *(G-3037)*
Jesse Bay Cabinetry .... G 360 417-8122
Port Angeles *(G-7717)*
Jl Cabinet Refacing LLC .... G 253 514-5975
Gig Harbor *(G-4124)*
John Duane King .... G 360 736-6707
Centralia *(G-2412)*
K & M Wdwrkers Port Angles Inc .... G 360 457-9773
Port Angeles *(G-7722)*
Kc Fine Cabinetry .... G 425 359-8491
Monroe *(G-6584)*
Kenco Manufacturing Inc .... G 425 743-1080
Lynnwood *(G-6148)*
King Brothers Woodworking Inc .... E 509 453-4683
Union Gap *(G-13936)*
Kings Kitchen LLC .... G 253 212-3623
Tacoma *(G-13376)*
Kitchen Cabinet and Granite .... G 509 783-9500
Kennewick *(G-4683)*
Kitchens Etc .... G 360 430-4272
Longview *(G-5923)*
Kristines .... G 360 437-0136
Port Ludlow *(G-7769)*
Lb Steele Cabinet Co .... G 360 446-4114
Rainier *(G-8316)*
Legacy Mill and Cabinet LLC .... G 509 440-4884
Kennewick *(G-4689)*
Leon Green Co Fine Woodworking .... G 425 822-8210
Kirkland *(G-5387)*
Lj Backdoor Inc .... E 206 767-2434
Seattle *(G-10433)*

SIC SECTION 24 LUMBER AND WOOD PRODUCTS, EXCEPT FURNITURE

M and M Cabinets ....G.... 253 503-0756
Spanaway (G-12061)
Markay Cabinets Inc ....F.... 360 779-3443
Poulsbo (G-7982)
Master Millwork Inc ....E.... 253 770-2023
Puyallup (G-8182)
Masterbrand Cabinets Inc ....F.... 812 482-2527
Bellevue (G-998)
Michael B Knutson ....G.... 509 398-7312
Wenatchee (G-15050)
Millers Quality Cabinets ....G.... 360 275-4349
Grapeview (G-4289)
Millwork Cabinet Specialist ....G.... 253 377-4334
Tacoma (G-13415)
Morgan Electric & Plumbing Inc ....F.... 206 547-1617
Seattle (G-10562)
Mountainside Cabinets ....G.... 253 278-8400
Spanaway (G-12066)
Murdocks ....G.... 253 858-9697
Gig Harbor (G-4135)
Murphy Runa Inc ....G.... 206 782-2664
Seattle (G-10572)
My Cabinetry ....G.... 509 879-0086
Spokane Valley (G-12797)
Neil Levinson Enterprises ....G.... 425 828-3833
Kirkland (G-5409)
Nelson S Cabinet Installa ....G.... 253 770-3975
Puyallup (G-8198)
North West Cab & Refacing LLC ....G.... 360 415-9999
Bremerton (G-1981)
Northwest Cab & Countertop LLC ....G.... 253 446-7193
Puyallup (G-8201)
Northwest Cabinet & Refacing ....G.... 970 497-8230
Poulsbo (G-7987)
Northwest Cabinetry & Design ....G.... 360 434-0740
Poulsbo (G-7988)
Northwest Custom Cabinets Inc ....F.... 360 757-8788
Burlington (G-2174)
Northwood Cabinets Inc ....E.... 360 314-2446
Vancouver (G-14443)
Northwood Cabinets Inc ....E.... 360 225-1001
Woodland (G-15453)
On The Level Custom Cabinets ....G.... 360 666-9058
La Center (G-5510)
Optima Cabinets ....G.... 509 868-5691
Bremerton (G-1983)
Ovenell Custom Cabinets ....G.... 509 782-3400
Cashmere (G-2328)
Pacific Crest Building Supply ....E.... 360 857-3120
Ridgefield (G-9098)
▲ Pacific Crest Industries Inc ....C.... 253 321-3011
Sumner (G-13093)
Pacific Door & Window Inc ....F.... 360 577-9121
Longview (G-5940)
Paneltech International LLC ....E.... 360 538-1480
Hoquiam (G-4353)
Park Avenue Construction Inc ....F.... 206 783-3693
Seattle (G-10758)
Parr Cabinet Outlet ....G.... 253 926-0505
Fife (G-3978)
Pauls Cabinetry ....G.... 425 343-7930
Sultan (G-13032)
Pauls Custom Cabinets ....G.... 253 536-6330
Tacoma (G-13461)
Peterson Manufacturing Co ....F.... 360 425-4170
Longview (G-5943)
Pine Ridge Cabinets ....G.... 509 486-0789
Tonasket (G-13657)
Precision Custom Cabinets LLC ....F.... 253 397-4240
Auburn (G-534)
R S Manufacturing Inc ....E.... 425 774-1211
Lynnwood (G-6186)
Refined Woodworks Inc ....G.... 206 762-2603
Seattle (G-10941)
Revive Cabinet Closet Pro Llc ....G.... 425 382-0739
Everett (G-3599)
Rich Interiors ....G.... 509 665-8000
Wenatchee (G-15068)
Riverside Cabinet Co Inc ....G.... 360 354-3070
Lynden (G-6049)
Rogers & Associates ....G.... 360 455-1534
Olympia (G-7388)
Ronald G Wahl ....G.... 509 223-3957
Loomis (G-5972)
Room Maker ....G.... 425 432-3324
Maple Valley (G-6292)
Royal Cabinets ....G.... 253 267-5071
Puyallup (G-8239)
Royal Cabinets Inc ....G.... 253 536-6879
Puyallup (G-8240)
Russells Custom Cabinets Inc ....G.... 253 473-7883
Tacoma (G-13503)
Sam Knutsons Lumber Co Inc ....G.... 509 662-6183
Wenatchee (G-15072)
Schwager Design & Construction ....G.... 360 221-8165
Langley (G-5784)
Seaboard Cabinet Company Inc ....F.... 425 776-2000
Lynnwood (G-6193)
Seattle Kitchen Cabinet Inc ....G.... 360 437-1344
Port Ludlow (G-7773)
Sey Mik Cabinets & Millwork ....G.... 360 829-0173
Buckley (G-2071)
▲ Shark Stainless Systems Inc ....G.... 866 960-9779
Kent (G-5128)
Sheldon Custom Cabinets Ltd ....G.... 425 778-0043
Lynnwood (G-6194)
Silvan Craft Inc ....G.... 425 827-7050
Kirkland (G-5462)
Smokey Point Custom Cabinets ....F.... 360 659-6233
Marysville (G-6386)
South Hill Cabinets ....G.... 253 848-2026
Puyallup (G-8255)
Spencer LLC ....G.... 360 805-2500
Monroe (G-6624)
Spencer Cabinetry ....G.... 360 794-8344
Monroe (G-6625)
Spokane Custom Cabinets Inc ....G.... 509 487-8416
Mead (G-6437)
Stonewood Inc ....G.... 425 417-5533
Redmond (G-8683)
Strasser Woodenworks Inc ....D.... 425 402-3080
Woodinville (G-15377)
Superior Crafted Cabinets ....G.... 509 535-9403
Spokane (G-12533)
Superior Custom Cabinets Inc ....E.... 425 251-1520
Tukwila (G-13824)
T R S Inc ....F.... 253 444-1555
Tacoma (G-13538)
Tacoma Fixture Co Inc ....D.... 253 383-5541
Tacoma (G-13542)
Tomar Cabinets ....G.... 253 538-1183
Tacoma (G-13556)
Tonys Custom Cabinets ....G.... 425 444-1086
Kent (G-5181)
Total Building Products LLC ....F.... 360 380-1100
Ferndale (G-3915)
Tri-City Cabinets LLC ....G.... 509 946-5614
Richland (G-9047)
True Custom Cabinetry ....G.... 206 909-4454
Kent (G-5191)
True Custom Cabinetry Inc ....G.... 425 919-1966
Renton (G-8934)
Urban Cabinets ....G.... 425 286-2977
Woodinville (G-15397)
Valley Cabinet Shop Inc ....F.... 509 786-2717
Prosser (G-8072)
Valley Cabinets & More Inc ....G.... 360 428-0916
Mount Vernon (G-6851)
Vanities ....G.... 425 453-5353
Bellevue (G-1211)
Vans Custom Cabinets LLC ....G.... 360 354-5845
Lynden (G-6059)
Veatch Custom Cabinetry LLC ....G.... 425 418-3693
Granite Falls (G-4287)
Viking Cabinets Inc ....F.... 253 875-1555
Spanaway (G-12079)
Vision Woodworks ....G.... 425 432-6772
Maple Valley (G-6297)
Vixon Corporation ....G.... 360 607-5817
Vancouver (G-14673)
▲ Von Grey Custom Cabinets Inc ....G.... 360 679-8641
Oak Harbor (G-7166)
W & S Enterprises ....G.... 253 848-9189
Puyallup (G-8275)
Warners Cabinets ....G.... 425 222-7386
Issaquah (G-4488)
Wells Ww Millwork LLC ....F.... 425 405-3252
Everett (G-3654)
West Coast Laminating LLC ....F.... 253 395-5225
Kent (G-5211)
Western Cabinets ....G.... 253 269-2742
Auburn (G-599)
William H Olson Inc ....G.... 360 249-3691
Olympia (G-7426)
William H Olson Inc ....G.... 360 754-2858
Olympia (G-7427)
Wilsons Custom Cabinets Inc ....G.... 425 334-3522
Lake Stevens (G-5674)
Wood House Custom Cabinets ....G.... 360 293-2890
Anacortes (G-184)
Wood Way Mfg Inc ....G.... 360 366-4854
Blaine (G-1713)
▲ Wood-Works Cabinetry & Design ....G.... 206 257-3335
Seattle (G-11491)
Woodwork Unlimited Inc ....G.... 425 334-5702
Lake Stevens (G-5675)
Woodworks Cnstr & Cabinets ....G.... 253 846-1918
Seatac (G-9310)
Wyndsor Cabinet Group LLC ....G.... 425 775-9828
Edmonds (G-3164)
Yakima Valley Cabinets Inc ....G.... 509 248-0472
Yakima (G-15718)
Yes Cabinet & Graent ....G.... 253 572-1188
Tacoma (G-13604)

2435 Hardwood Veneer & Plywood

Alpac Components Co ....E.... 360 466-2024
La Conner (G-5520)
Alsea Veneer Inc ....G.... 360 891-2020
Vancouver (G-14025)
Belina Interiors Inc ....D.... 253 474-0276
Tacoma (G-13193)
Boise Cascade Company ....D.... 509 738-3200
Kettle Falls (G-5226)
Danzer Veneer Americas Inc ....G.... 253 770-4664
Sumner (G-13065)
Delta Pntg & Prefinishing Co ....G.... 253 588-8278
Tacoma (G-13258)
Dmm Incorporated ....E.... 360 435-5252
Arlington (G-229)
Drc Specialty Veneering LLC ....G.... 253 301-0443
Tacoma (G-13265)
Edensaw Woods Ltd ....G.... 253 216-1150
Tacoma (G-13271)
▼ Edwin Enterprises Inc ....G.... 253 272-7090
Tacoma (G-13274)
Hardel Mutual Plywood Corp ....C.... 360 740-0232
Chehalis (G-2501)
Infinity Building Mtls LLC ....G.... 804 921-0810
Ferndale (G-3856)
◆ Kamilche Company ....G.... 206 224-5800
Seattle (G-10326)
▲ Mt Baker Products Inc ....C.... 360 733-3960
Bellingham (G-1450)
Northwest Plywood Sales of Ore ....F.... 360 750-1561
Vancouver (G-14439)
NW Hardwoods LLC ....G.... 206 784-9369
Mill Creek (G-6518)
◆ Olympic Panel Products LLC ....G.... 360 432-5033
Shelton (G-11718)
▼ Plum Creek Northwest Plywd Inc ....G.... 206 467-3600
Seattle (G-10824)
Potlatchdeltic Mfg L L C ....G.... 509 835-1500
Spokane (G-12449)
Prolam Industries Inc ....G.... 509 926-2001
Spokane Valley (G-12843)
▲ Rainier Veneer Inc ....D.... 253 846-0242
Spanaway (G-12070)
Stusser Mattson Veneer Inc ....F.... 425 485-0963
Woodinville (G-15378)
Techwood LLC ....D.... 360 427-9616
Shelton (G-11743)
Wachtler Inc ....G.... 253 225-1904
Gig Harbor (G-4173)
◆ Weyerhaeuser Company ....A.... 206 539-3000
Seattle (G-11459)
Weyerhaeuser Company ....B.... 253 924-3030
Tacoma (G-13595)
Wood Resources LLC ....G.... 360 432-5048
Shelton (G-11751)

2436 Softwood Veneer & Plywood

Alsea Veneer Inc ....G.... 360 891-2020
Vancouver (G-14025)
Boise Cascade Company ....D.... 509 738-3200
Kettle Falls (G-5226)
Decorado Fabrication ....G.... 360 694-6832
Vancouver (G-14171)
▼ Edwin Enterprises Inc ....G.... 253 272-7090
Tacoma (G-13274)
Erosion Ctrl Innovations LLC ....G.... 206 962-9582
Enumclaw (G-3290)
Hoquiam Plywood Products Inc ....C.... 360 533-3060
Hoquiam (G-4343)
Infinity Building Mtls LLC ....G.... 804 921-0810
Ferndale (G-3856)
Murphy Company ....C.... 360 482-2521
Elma (G-3250)
Pacific Trim Panels Inc ....E.... 360 841-8438
Woodland (G-15457)

S I C

Employee Codes: A=Over 500 employees, B=251-500
C=101-250, D=51-100, E=20-50, F=10-19, G=2-9
2019 Washington
Manufacturers Register
561

▼ **Plum Creek Northwest Plywd Inc** ... G ... 206 467-3600
Seattle *(G-10824)*
Plum Creek Timberlands LP ... F ... 206 467-3600
Seattle *(G-10825)*
Plywood Components Inc ... E ... 253 863-6323
Sumner *(G-13095)*
▲ **SDS Lumber Co** ... C ... 509 493-1444
Bingen *(G-1642)*
Stusser Mattson Veneer Inc ... F ... 425 485-0963
Woodinville *(G-15378)*
Textured Forest Products Inc ... F ... 360 835-2164
Washougal *(G-14991)*
Weyerhaeuser Company ... D ... 360 482-2521
Elma *(G-3259)*
Yakama Nation ... F ... 509 874-2901
White Swan *(G-15140)*

2439 Structural Wood Members, NEC

A & V Investments Inc ... E ... 509 276-5088
Deer Park *(G-2892)*
AAA Truss ... G ... 509 365-2690
Appleton *(G-187)*
Ariel Truss Company Inc ... E ... 360 574-7333
Vancouver *(G-14041)*
Armstrong Lumber Co Inc ... E ... 253 833-6666
Auburn *(G-377)*
Bamboo Hardwoods Inc ... G ... 800 607-2414
Seattle *(G-9488)*
BMC West LLC ... D ... 425 303-0661
Everett *(G-3393)*
BMC West LLC ... E ... 360 943-8050
Lakewood *(G-5704)*
Brooks Manufacturing Co ... E ... 360 733-1700
Bellingham *(G-1283)*
Builders Firstsource Inc ... D ... 509 783-8148
Kennewick *(G-4637)*
Calvert Company Inc ... D ... 360 693-0971
Vancouver *(G-14092)*
Calvert Company Inc ... E ... 360 835-3110
Washougal *(G-14947)*
Canfor USA Corporation ... G ... 360 647-2434
Bellingham *(G-1290)*
Craft Wall of Oregon Inc ... G ... 509 547-2436
Pasco *(G-7569)*
Dis-Tran Wood Products LLC ... G ... 360 735-9356
Vancouver *(G-14181)*
G R Plume Co ... F ... 360 384-2800
Ferndale *(G-3846)*
Louws Truss Inc ... D ... 360 384-9000
Burlington *(G-2169)*
Lumbermens Truss ... E ... 509 627-0495
Richland *(G-9023)*
▲ **Madera Components LLC** ... G ... 800 404-8746
Monroe *(G-6595)*
Matthaeis Camco Inc ... E ... 360 426-7900
Shelton *(G-11712)*
Murphy Company ... C ... 360 482-2521
Elma *(G-3250)*
Noble Truss & Lumber Inc ... F ... 509 662-1877
Wenatchee *(G-15052)*
Parker Lumber Co Inc ... E ... 425 806-7253
Bremerton *(G-1986)*
Parr Lumber Company ... G ... 509 543-7594
Sunnyside *(G-13137)*
Parr Lumber Company ... G ... 360 750-1470
Vancouver *(G-14480)*
Peninsula Truss Co ... G ... 360 297-6026
Kingston *(G-5261)*
Phoenix Truss Corporation ... E ... 509 925-3135
Ellensburg *(G-3220)*
Precision Beam & Timber Inc ... G ... 509 525-1381
Walla Walla *(G-14857)*
Professional Hardwood Floors ... G ... 425 741-1017
Mill Creek *(G-6521)*
Roof Truss Supply Inc ... C ... 425 481-0900
Woodinville *(G-15351)*
Sign Post Inc ... F ... 360 671-1343
Bellingham *(G-1533)*
Stusser Mattson Veneer Inc ... F ... 425 485-0963
Woodinville *(G-15378)*
Summit Components LLC ... G ... 509 750-6629
Royal City *(G-9176)*
Timberline Truss and Sup Inc ... F ... 509 226-0100
Newman Lake *(G-7052)*
Tru-Truss Inc ... E ... 360 491-8024
Lacey *(G-5597)*
Truss Co ... G ... 509 547-2436
Pasco *(G-7644)*
Truss Company and Bldg Sup Inc ... G ... 509 928-0550
Spokane Valley *(G-12915)*
Truss Company and Bldg Sup Inc ... D ... 253 863-5555
Sumner *(G-13107)*
Truss Components of Washington ... E ... 360 753-0057
Tumwater *(G-13900)*
Truss Components of Washington ... E ... 360 753-0057
Tumwater *(G-13901)*
Tvan Inc ... D ... 503 285-2615
Vancouver *(G-14651)*
Vanderpol Building Components ... F ... 360 354-5883
Lynden *(G-6058)*
Weyerhaeuser Company ... D ... 360 482-2521
Elma *(G-3259)*

2441 Wood Boxes

Baye Enterprises Inc ... E ... 253 536-2277
Tacoma *(G-13190)*
Duncans Woods ... G ... 360 604-7140
Vancouver *(G-14190)*
Encased Specialty Mfg LLC ... G ... 509 396-0755
Kennewick *(G-4660)*
Harbor Action Inc ... F ... 360 417-1316
Port Angeles *(G-7708)*
▲ **Industrial Crating & Packing** ... F ... 425 226-9200
Mercer Island *(G-6467)*
J R Reding Company Inc ... G ... 253 474-9938
Tacoma *(G-13354)*
Macro Plastics Inc ... E ... 509 452-1200
Union Gap *(G-13940)*
Mattawa Wood Products Corp ... G ... 509 932-6420
Mattawa *(G-6410)*
Museum Resource LLC ... G ... 206 547-4047
Seatac *(G-9292)*
Northwest Cstm Crating Box Inc ... G ... 253 232-3244
Puyallup *(G-8203)*
Northwest Dovetail Inc ... G ... 509 248-2056
Yakima *(G-15634)*
Oroville Reman & Reload Inc ... E ... 509 476-2935
Oroville *(G-7471)*
Quinault Wood Crafts ... G ... 360 288-2848
Amanda Park *(G-88)*
Shawnee Construction LLC ... G ... 425 430-4232
Renton *(G-8909)*
◆ **Shipco Transport Inc** ... G ... 206 444-7447
Tukwila *(G-13818)*
Ufp Washington LLC ... F ... 509 663-1988
Malaga *(G-6233)*
Ufp Washington LLC ... D ... 360 568-3185
Snohomish *(G-11995)*
Ufp Washington LLC ... E ... 509 966-4610
Yakima *(G-15699)*
Wood Design ... G ... 425 883-8842
Redmond *(G-8717)*
▲ **World Wide Gourmet Foods Inc** ... F ... 360 668-9404
Woodinville *(G-15410)*

2448 Wood Pallets & Skids

A & C Pallet Sales ... G ... 509 669-0653
Wenatchee *(G-15006)*
A & J Brokerage Co Inc ... E ... 509 483-3003
Spokane *(G-12088)*
A 1 Pallets Inc ... E ... 253 395-3119
Kent *(G-4752)*
Alta Forest Products LLC ... D ... 360 426-9721
Shelton *(G-11676)*
Angels Pallets ... G ... 253 426-1770
Lakewood *(G-5698)*
Armour Mfg & Cnstr Inc ... G ... 253 984-1213
Tacoma *(G-13180)*
Ballenger International LLC ... G ... 970 641-9494
Arlington *(G-209)*
Basin Pallett Inc ... F ... 509 765-8083
Moses Lake *(G-6686)*
Bison Fiber Pallet ... G ... 206 291-0778
Des Moines *(G-2930)*
Columbia Pallet LLC ... G ... 509 430-9647
Pasco *(G-7563)*
Ellensburg Pallet ... G ... 509 962-1373
Ellensburg *(G-3197)*
Emmanuel Pallets LLC ... G ... 509 439-0924
Sunnyside *(G-13123)*
F PS Pallet Recycling Inc ... G ... 253 312-7122
Eatonville *(G-3057)*
G M Pallet Inc ... G ... 253 435-1040
Tacoma *(G-13303)*
Girard Management Group LLC ... D ... 253 845-0505
Puyallup *(G-8156)*
Girard Wood Products Inc ... E ... 253 845-0505
Puyallup *(G-8157)*
Girard Wood Products Inc ... D ... 360 482-5151
Elma *(G-3247)*
Illinois Tool Works Inc ... E ... 360 225-9995
Woodland *(G-15442)*
Lane Pierce Partners Inc ... F ... 509 926-1033
Spokane Valley *(G-12771)*
Lewis Cnty Work Opportunities ... E ... 360 748-9921
Chehalis *(G-2509)*
Moberg & Company ... G ... 360 380-5257
Ferndale *(G-3873)*
Once Upon A Pallet ... G ... 360 798-6294
Battle Ground *(G-726)*
Pallet Place Inc ... G ... 509 484-4889
Spokane Valley *(G-12824)*
Pallet Services Inc ... G ... 509 543-3541
Pasco *(G-7612)*
Pallet Services Inc ... G ... 360 424-8171
Burlington *(G-2178)*
Pallet Services Inc ... G ... 360 424-8171
Burlington *(G-2179)*
Pallets Unlimited ... G ... 360 354-1395
Everson *(G-3686)*
Perry Enterprises ... E ... 360 366-5239
Ferndale *(G-3885)*
Pilchuck Pallets Inc ... G ... 425 530-1857
Arlington *(G-302)*
Prime Pallets and Recycling ... G ... 360 410-0238
Blaine *(G-1697)*
Quality Pallets ... G ... 360 773-3973
Vancouver *(G-14520)*
Rcd Timber Inc ... G ... 360 591-9078
Elma *(G-3254)*
Robertson-Ceco II Corporation ... D ... 509 244-5611
Airway Heights *(G-62)*
S & W Manufacturing Inc ... G ... 360 690-8558
Vancouver *(G-14562)*
Sanchez Pallets LLC ... G ... 509 877-4004
Wapato *(G-14926)*
Spinner Wood Products LLC ... G ... 509 653-2222
Naches *(G-7004)*
Standard Pallet Co ... G ... 509 670-0632
Rock Island *(G-9150)*
Tri City Pallets ... G ... 509 543-7500
Pasco *(G-7643)*
Ufp Washington LLC ... F ... 509 663-1988
Malaga *(G-6233)*
Ufp Washington LLC ... D ... 360 568-3185
Snohomish *(G-11995)*
Ufp Washington LLC ... E ... 509 966-4610
Yakima *(G-15699)*
Unicon International Inc ... D ... 253 539-7533
Puyallup *(G-8266)*
Wooden Pallets Recycled ... G ... 360 624-3935
Vancouver *(G-14698)*
Woodland Pallet Repair LLC ... G ... 360 624-3935
Woodland *(G-15475)*
Yancey Pallet Inc ... D ... 509 331-0442
Othello *(G-7511)*

2449 Wood Containers, NEC

Armour Mfg & Cnstr Inc ... G ... 253 984-1213
Tacoma *(G-13180)*
Atomic Crate & Case Inc ... G ... 425 264-0336
Seatac *(G-9273)*
Cedar Grove Wood Specialty ... G ... 360 494-5295
Randle *(G-8324)*
Commercial Crting Box Pckg Inc ... F ... 253 804-8616
Auburn *(G-410)*
Contrary Design ... G ... 253 653-0275
Auburn *(G-415)*
◆ **Fastcap LLC** ... E ... 888 443-3748
Ferndale *(G-3841)*
G M Pallet Inc ... G ... 253 435-1040
Tacoma *(G-13303)*
Havillah Shake Co ... G ... 509 486-1467
Tonasket *(G-13650)*
Howatt Company Inc ... F ... 425 743-4682
Mukilteo *(G-6937)*
Northwest Container Svcs Inc ... E ... 360 864-2571
Toledo *(G-13640)*
Spinner Wood Products LLC ... G ... 509 653-2222
Naches *(G-7004)*
Weyerhaeuser Company ... C ... 509 453-4741
Union Gap *(G-13956)*

2451 Mobile Homes

A & S Contractors ... G ... 509 930-7994
Yakima *(G-15496)*
Aladdin Valley Modular Mfg ... G ... 509 732-6159
Colville *(G-2735)*
Basic Homes LLC ... G ... 253 579-2724
Eatonville *(G-3050)*

Clayton Homes Inc....G.... 509 452-9228
Union Gap (G-13926)
F W Enterprises LLC....G.... 253 439-8090
Buckley (G-2058)
Glen Hidden Mhc LLC....G.... 253 537-9383
Puyallup (G-8159)
J&K Enterprise....G.... 360 854-0020
Sedro Woolley (G-11542)
Lake Samish Terrace Park....G.... 360 671-2741
Bellingham (G-1401)
Mantheys Country Mobile Park....G.... 360 384-5623
Bellingham (G-1422)
▲ Pacific Mat & Coml Flrg LLC....E.... 800 345-6287
Kent (G-5053)
Pacific Mobile Structures Inc....G.... 509 244-8335
Airway Heights (G-60)
Sandy Beach Mobile Villa LLC....G.... 509 255-6222
Liberty Lake (G-5857)
US Builders Team LLC....G.... 425 466-2611
Redmond (G-8701)
Valley Manufactured Hsing Inc....C.... 509 839-9409
Sunnyside (G-13147)
Van Horn Mfd Homes....G.... 253 370-7263
Puyallup (G-8271)

2452 Prefabricated Wood Buildings & Cmpnts

Amish Log Homes....G.... 360 491-4132
Lacey (G-5532)
Archibald Log Homes Inc....G.... 509 782-3703
Cashmere (G-2316)
Armstrong Lumber Co Inc....E.... 253 833-6666
Auburn (G-377)
Aspen Creek Log Homes....G.... 509 590-5541
Spokane (G-12122)
Blokable Inc....G.... 800 928-6778
Seattle (G-9544)
Blokable Inc....F.... 800 928-6778
Vancouver (G-14069)
Cascade Country Cabins....G.... 509 427-8515
Stevenson (G-13009)
Cascade Joinery Inc....F.... 360 527-0119
Ferndale (G-3826)
Cedar Homes of Washington Inc....G.... 360 668-8242
Snohomish (G-11887)
Choice Construction Inc....F.... 360 340-2206
Olalla (G-7205)
Custom Building Services Inc....G.... 509 422-5746
Okanogan (G-7195)
Cynthia Rochlitzer....G.... 509 796-4199
Spokane (G-12213)
Forest View Inc....G.... 360 909-9890
Ridgefield (G-9083)
Geodesic Structures Inc....G.... 509 535-0220
Spokane (G-12270)
Green Flush Technologies LLC....G.... 360 718-7595
Washougal (G-14957)
▼ International Homes Cedar Inc....F.... 360 668-8511
Woodinville (G-15266)
Joom 3d....G.... 413 566-6330
Olympia (G-7314)
JW Custom Construction....G.... 509 679-2959
Stehekin (G-13003)
K&M Storage....G.... 253 862-3515
Sumner (G-13076)
▲ Lindal Cedar Homes Inc....D.... 206 725-0900
Seattle (G-10423)
Mobile Storage Units Inc....G.... 509 276-8220
Deer Park (G-2909)
Modern Building Systems Inc....F.... 800 682-1422
Pacific (G-7532)
Mountain Log Homes Inc....F.... 360 799-0533
Startup (G-13002)
Northwest Modular Service....G.... 253 631-2802
Covington (G-2835)
Pacific Bay Inc....G.... 253 848-5541
Sumner (G-13092)
Pan Abode Cedar Homes Inc....E.... 425 255-8260
Renton (G-8874)
▼ Pan Abode Homes Inc....E.... 425 255-8260
Renton (G-8875)
Protect-A-Cover Inc....G.... 425 408-1072
Kenmore (G-4600)
Regal Homes Construction LLC....G.... 360 606-3486
Vancouver (G-14541)
▲ Seamax Enterprises Inc....F.... 206 323-8886
Puyallup (G-8247)
Shaw Road Development LLC....G.... 253 845-9544
Puyallup (G-8253)
Shire Mountain Log Homes Inc....G.... 360 262-9338
Centralia (G-2432)
Slyfield Enterprises....G.... 509 968-3456
Ellensburg (G-3226)
Smokey Point Log Homes Inc....G.... 360 659-7122
Marysville (G-6387)
Star Lumber LLC....G.... 316 942-2221
Arlington (G-332)
Tropical Sauna....G.... 509 927-7898
Otis Orchards (G-7520)
Vaagen Timbers LLC....G.... 509 684-5071
Colville (G-2780)
West Coast Automation Corp....E.... 509 773-5055
Goldendale (G-4213)
West Coast Laminating LLC....F.... 253 395-5225
Kent (G-5211)
Whitley Evergreen Inc....E.... 360 653-5790
Marysville (G-6402)

2491 Wood Preserving

A-1 Timber Consultants Inc....F.... 360 748-8987
Chehalis (G-2457)
Blue Marine LLC....G.... 253 225-8228
Gig Harbor (G-4082)
Conestoga Wood Spc Corp....G.... 253 437-1320
Kent (G-4863)
▲ Exterior Wood Inc....C.... 360 835-8561
Washougal (G-14955)
Flannery Comerford Inc....G.... 509 242-5000
Spokane (G-12258)
Great Northern Holdings Inc....G.... 253 572-3033
Tacoma (G-13321)
Hamilton Spray....G.... 360 748-9615
Chehalis (G-2500)
Jasper Enterprises Inc....G.... 509 549-3664
Spokane (G-12330)
John Gibb....G.... 360 366-3500
Bellingham (G-1388)
Kaplan Homes Unlimited LLC....G.... 360 855-1675
Sedro Woolley (G-11549)
▲ Manke Lumber Company Inc....B.... 253 572-6252
Tacoma (G-13397)
McCain Timber & Bridge Inc....G.... 360 520-6595
Napavine (G-7011)
McFarland Cascade Holdings Inc....G.... 800 426-8430
Spokane (G-12387)
McFarland Cascade Holdings Inc....G.... 360 273-5541
Rochester (G-9136)
▲ McFarland Cascade Holdings Inc....D.... 253 572-3033
Tacoma (G-13404)
Only Solutions Cabinet Install....G.... 253 848-8358
Puyallup (G-8210)
▲ Pacific Foundation Inc....F.... 360 200-6608
Vancouver (G-14464)
▲ Pacific Western Timbers Inc....F.... 360 674-2700
Port Orchard (G-7841)
Panel Artz....G.... 253 277-1040
Kent (G-5059)
Pile Protectors....G.... 360 683-3926
Sequim (G-11660)
Stampede Forest Products Inc....F.... 509 557-3014
OMAK (G-7444)
Stella-Jones Corporation....D.... 360 435-2146
Arlington (G-334)
▼ Transpac Marinas Inc....G.... 360 293-8888
Anacortes (G-178)
Trueguard LLC....G.... 360 835-8547
Washougal (G-14995)
Virtual Timbers Inc....G.... 509 935-4680
Chewelah (G-2609)
Western Wood Preserving Co....E.... 253 863-8191
Sumner (G-13111)
▲ Wood Care Systems....G.... 425 827-6000
Kirkland (G-5497)
Workbench Productions LLC....G.... 206 853-3742
Seattle (G-11495)

2493 Reconstituted Wood Prdts

Columbia Navigation Inc....G.... 509 684-4335
Kettle Falls (G-5222)
Eleganza Designs Inc....G.... 360 499-2710
Lacey (G-5549)
◆ Glacier Mouldings Ltd....F.... 360 629-5313
Stanwood (G-12975)
Little Nut Inc....G.... 360 327-3394
Beaver (G-758)
▲ Marine Lumber Service Inc....F.... 206 767-4730
Seattle (G-10482)
Northwest Heli Structures....G.... 360 734-1073
Bellingham (G-1467)
PBS Supply Co Inc....F.... 253 395-5550
Kent (G-5063)
Plum Creek Timberlands LP....F.... 206 467-3600
Seattle (G-10825)
Plywood Components Inc....E.... 253 863-6323
Sumner (G-13095)
Windfall Lumber Inc....E.... 360 352-2250
Tumwater (G-13906)

2499 Wood Prdts, NEC

10-20 Services Inc....G.... 253 503-6000
Lakewood (G-5692)
Aayers....G.... 253 872-5108
Kent (G-4753)
AGC Cww....G.... 360 608-4642
Vancouver (G-14011)
Alex Daisley....G.... 206 623-5555
Seattle (G-9373)
Alta Forest Products LLC....G.... 360 426-9721
Chehalis (G-2464)
Alta Forest Products LLC....G.... 800 599-5596
Chehalis (G-2465)
American Dream Homes & Cr....G.... 360 863-9340
Monroe (G-6547)
Aprils Indoor Garden Supplies....G.... 360 537-6850
Hoquiam (G-4328)
Artists Edge Inc....G.... 360 779-2337
Poulsbo (G-7945)
Artists Edge Inc....G.... 360 698-3113
Silverdale (G-11826)
Barbanc....G.... 206 552-0852
Seattle (G-9491)
Bees In Burbs....G.... 425 432-0546
Kent (G-4811)
Book N Brush....G.... 360 748-6221
Chehalis (G-2472)
Cascade Woodwrights....G.... 360 771-3908
Vancouver (G-14108)
CDI Custom Design Inc....E.... 360 650-1150
Bellingham (G-1294)
Cedartone Specialties Inc....C.... 253 852-6628
Kent (G-4845)
Chips & Del Carvings In Wood....G.... 253 858-4751
Gig Harbor (G-4086)
Conagra Foods Specialty Potato....G.... 509 547-8851
Pasco (G-7566)
Creative Wood Sculptures....G.... 360 825-6069
Enumclaw (G-3284)
Crown Recognition....G.... 509 698-4446
Selah (G-11585)
D & D Cedar Stake....G.... 360 435-2254
Arlington (G-226)
D-Way Tools Inc....G.... 360 432-9509
Shelton (G-11694)
▼ Dahlstrom Lumber Co Inc....E.... 360 533-0448
Hoquiam (G-4331)
Dale Butler S Furniture....G.... 509 732-4381
Colville (G-2750)
De Jong Sawdust & Shavings....F.... 425 252-1566
Lake Stevens (G-5643)
DOE Run Studios....G.... 360 765-0935
Quilcene (G-8282)
Donnies Peninsula Sign....G.... 360 642-4512
Ocean Park (G-7180)
Dudleys Fine Engraving....G.... 360 417-9415
Port Angeles (G-7699)
Ek Projects LLC....F.... 360 757-2300
Burlington (G-2155)
Eleganza Designs Inc....G.... 360 499-2710
Lacey (G-5549)
▲ Elite Frames Inc....G.... 360 247-7300
Amboy (G-91)
Erics Woodwork....G.... 206 860-6174
Seattle (G-9938)
Etchings Walla Walla....G.... 509 301-3300
Walla Walla (G-14802)
Everett Bark Supply Inc....G.... 425 353-9024
Everett (G-3463)
Every Occasion Engraving....G.... 509 995-9848
Spokane Valley (G-12696)
Fairwood Commerce Center LLP....G.... 206 903-9200
Issaquah (G-4411)
▲ Ferguson Merchandising LLC....D.... 425 883-2050
Redmond (G-8460)
Foley Sign Company Inc....F.... 206 324-3040
Seattle (G-10011)
Forest Concepts LLC....G.... 253 333-9663
Auburn (G-441)
Frame It Ltd....G.... 206 364-7477
Seattle (G-10019)

S I C

Employee Codes: A=Over 500 employees, B=251-500
C=101-250, D=51-100, E=20-50, F=10-19, G=2-9
2019 Washington
Manufacturers Register
563

Fuze Create LLC ... G ... 425 212-8807
Seattle *(G-10043)*
Garden Expressions ... G ... 360 403-9532
Arlington *(G-239)*
George Kenny School Cainsaw ... G ... 360 275-9570
Allyn *(G-82)*
Goedecke & Goedecke ... G ... 425 481-1153
Bothell *(G-1862)*
Greenhill Lumber Co Inc ... F ... 509 767-0010
Dallesport *(G-2863)*
Grette Custom Woodworking ... G ... 425 392-8584
Issaquah *(G-4424)*
Greywood Manor LLC ... G ... 206 949-1362
Seattle *(G-10124)*
Grizzly Firestarters North ... G ... 360 659-3948
Marysville *(G-6341)*
Grizzly Firestarters North ... G ... 360 652-2100
Mount Vernon *(G-6802)*
Groove Incorporated ... G ... 360 786-9605
Olympia *(G-7300)*
Hd Structures LLC ... G ... 425 327-3931
Marysville *(G-6343)*
Hughes Custom Woodworking Inc ... G ... 509 921-8090
Colbert *(G-2708)*
Impressions In Wood LLC ... G ... 425 444-5324
Snohomish *(G-11926)*
Innovative Manufacturing Inc ... G ... 360 966-7250
Bellingham *(G-1379)*
J L R Design Group Inc ... G ... 206 625-0070
Seattle *(G-10271)*
Julias Lumber ... G ... 509 966-0925
Yakima *(G-15603)*
Kadi Manufacturing ... G ... 360 668-5633
Snohomish *(G-11929)*
Kern Construction Inc ... G ... 360 805-5598
Monroe *(G-6586)*
Lanktree Land Surveying Inc ... F ... 253 653-6423
Kent *(G-4988)*
Larson-Juhl US LLC ... E ... 206 433-6002
Kent *(G-4989)*
Lee Frame Shoppe Inc ... G ... 509 624-2715
Spokane *(G-12360)*
Liteair Aviation Products Inc ... G ... 360 299-6679
Anacortes *(G-142)*
Little Buddies Shanties ... G ... 360 387-0678
Camano Island *(G-2216)*
Louisiana-Pacific Corporation ... F ... 503 821-5001
Vancouver *(G-14383)*
▲ **Manke Lumber Company Inc** ... B ... 253 572-6252
Tacoma *(G-13397)*
Many Endeavors Incorporated ... G ... 360 652-1854
Arlington *(G-273)*
Martin Company ... G ... 360 482-2157
Elma *(G-3249)*
Matt Hammar Quality Woodcrafti ... G ... 360 904-9015
Vancouver *(G-14403)*
Michael Dresdner ... G ... 253 770-1664
Puyallup *(G-8191)*
Michellaine Lee Larry Bergsma ... G ... 360 873-4005
Marblemount *(G-6305)*
Military Tails ... G ... 253 229-2427
Spanaway *(G-12065)*
Mitercraft Inc ... G ... 360 299-9979
Anacortes *(G-147)*
Nation To Nation Premium ... G ... 360 731-0330
Sequim *(G-11650)*
Northwest Dock Systems LLC ... G ... 360 832-2295
Eatonville *(G-3064)*
Northwest Sushi LLC ... G ... 360 878-3464
Vancouver *(G-14441)*
Northwest Wood Products Inc ... G ... 509 738-6190
Kettle Falls *(G-5239)*
Oeser Company ... E ... 360 734-1480
Bellingham *(G-1477)*
OMAK Wood Products LLC ... E ... 360 432-5048
OMAK *(G-7441)*
One Step Ahead Inc ... G ... 425 487-1869
Bothell *(G-1882)*
Orpilla Santiago ... G ... 360 876-1976
Port Orchard *(G-7838)*
◆ **Pacific Coast Evergreen Inc** ... E ... 360 876-2061
Port Orchard *(G-7840)*
▲ **Pacific Crest Industries Inc** ... C ... 253 321-3011
Sumner *(G-13093)*
▲ **Pacific Frame Source LLC** ... G ... 800 292-3202
Woodinville *(G-15329)*
Pacific NW Fine WD Pdts LLC ... G ... 360 275-5397
Belfair *(G-770)*
Pacific Plumbing Supply Co LLC ... F ... 425 251-0604
Seattle *(G-10738)*
◆ **Pacific Woodtech Corporation** ... C ... 360 707-2200
Burlington *(G-2177)*
Peter Blue Woodworks ... G ... 206 542-4281
Shoreline *(G-11800)*
Planned Solutions LLC ... G ... 425 827-4277
Kirkland *(G-5435)*
Prewitt Hardwood Floors Inc ... G ... 360 666-9663
Brush Prairie *(G-2039)*
Rainier Wood Recyclers Inc ... E ... 425 222-0008
Fall City *(G-3707)*
Rainier Woodworking Co ... F ... 253 272-5210
Tacoma *(G-13491)*
Rawson Woodcraft Llc ... G ... 503 650-4383
Vancouver *(G-14535)*
Redwood Subs LLC ... G ... 217 493-9499
Olympia *(G-7382)*
Reichert Shake & Fencing Inc ... E ... 360 864-6434
Toledo *(G-13641)*
Rising Moon Products ... G ... 206 439-0338
Burien *(G-2126)*
▲ **Rsg Forest Products Inc** ... C ... 360 673-2825
Kalama *(G-4507)*
Rustik Kreations ... G ... 509 674-7271
Cle Elum *(G-2678)*
Rwoodsii LLC ... G ... 206 491-9617
Auburn *(G-552)*
Sackman Enterprises ... G ... 509 684-5547
Colville *(G-2774)*
Salmon River Design Inc ... G ... 425 503-7987
Woodinville *(G-15352)*
Silverfeather Creations ... G ... 425 771-9389
Edmonds *(G-3156)*
Sittin Pretty Design ... G ... 206 725-2453
Seattle *(G-11120)*
Slawek Tiles ... G ... 253 529-0823
Auburn *(G-566)*
Solis Ortus ... G ... 206 463-6245
Vashon *(G-14743)*
Spectrum Sign Co Inc ... F ... 253 939-5500
Auburn *(G-570)*
Stitch N Wood ... G ... 360 354-1211
Lynden *(G-6055)*
Summer Rrh LLC ... F ... 509 328-0915
Spokane *(G-12532)*
Sunrisebuswerk ... G ... 360 866-7240
Olympia *(G-7401)*
T Eight Fincing LLC ... G ... 360 794-7369
Monroe *(G-6629)*
◆ **Taphandles LLC** ... E ... 206 462-6800
Seattle *(G-11269)*
Ten Talents ... G ... 360 256-0205
Battle Ground *(G-744)*
▼ **Transpac Marinas Inc** ... G ... 360 293-8888
Anacortes *(G-178)*
Valon Kone North America ... G ... 509 434-6436
Spokane Valley *(G-12926)*
Vertical Visual Solutions ... G ... 425 361-1562
Mountlake Terrace *(G-6873)*
Vessels Archtctral Woodturning ... G ... 509 927-0721
Spokane Valley *(G-12930)*
Village Frame & Gallery ... G ... 206 824-3068
Des Moines *(G-2950)*
Washington Assn of Sheriffs ... E ... 360 438-6618
Lacey *(G-5600)*
Westerly Wood Working ... G ... 360 480-4840
Olympia *(G-7424)*
Whisd Craft ... G ... 253 850-7126
Kent *(G-5215)*
White Rabbit Ventures Inc ... F ... 360 474-5828
Vancouver *(G-14690)*
Williamson Illustration ... G ... 360 734-5497
Ferndale *(G-3925)*
Wood Crafts By Pear Company ... G ... 360 532-6246
Hoquiam *(G-4363)*

25 FURNITURE AND FIXTURES

2511 Wood Household Furniture

A & J Brokerage Co Inc ... E ... 509 483-3003
Spokane *(G-12088)*
All Points East ... G ... 360 863-8971
Monroe *(G-6545)*
All Wood Concepts Inc ... G ... 253 255-6518
Tacoma *(G-13164)*
Arrowood Mini Storage ... G ... 360 769-7400
Port Orchard *(G-7789)*
Barnes Wood Inc ... G ... 360 658-0145
Marysville *(G-6315)*
Beltecno Inc ... G ... 360 512-4000
Monroe *(G-6552)*
Bernard Manufacturing ... F ... 206 242-4017
Burien *(G-2093)*
Bilt-Rite Custom Cabinets ... G ... 360 829-0663
Buckley *(G-2049)*
Briarwood Furniture Ltd Inc ... G ... 425 868-7707
Kingston *(G-5249)*
Brooks Properties ... G ... 360 733-5170
Bellingham *(G-1284)*
Canyon Creek Cabinet Company ... G ... 509 921-7807
Spokane Valley *(G-12650)*
Charles Hanson ... G ... 360 871-2173
Port Orchard *(G-7797)*
Collectible Creations ... G ... 360 613-1799
Bremerton *(G-1943)*
Company K LLC ... G ... 206 632-0509
Seattle *(G-9723)*
D-Mac Carpentry ... G ... 509 326-6601
Spokane *(G-12214)*
Dale A West Specialty Wdwkg ... G ... 360 683-9419
Sequim *(G-11623)*
Dale M Shafman LLC ... G ... 206 499-4408
Seattle *(G-9787)*
David Gray Furnituremaker Inc ... G ... 360 321-4514
Langley *(G-5776)*
David Gulassa & Co Inc ... E ... 206 283-1810
Seattle *(G-9800)*
Deer Creek Cedar Products Inc ... G ... 360 435-4707
Arlington *(G-227)*
Diy Table Legs LLC ... G ... 206 659-8669
Lynnwood *(G-6110)*
Dmm Incorporated ... E ... 360 435-5252
Arlington *(G-229)*
Douglas L Perry ... G ... 253 303-0537
Gig Harbor *(G-4095)*
◆ **Emerald Home Furnishings LLC** ... B ... 253 922-1400
Tacoma *(G-13278)*
Erb Woodcraft LLC ... G ... 509 467-1134
Spokane *(G-12249)*
Ferguson Woodworking Inc ... G ... 360 398-1543
Bellingham *(G-1345)*
Freeze Furniture and Mfg Co ... F ... 509 924-3545
Spokane Valley *(G-12710)*
Furniture By Foss ... G ... 206 783-3626
Seattle *(G-10040)*
Glassique ... G ... 206 963-4400
Seattle *(G-10080)*
Grassroots Woodworks LLC ... G ... 360 836-1313
Bellingham *(G-1360)*
◆ **Greg Aanes Furniture Inc** ... G ... 360 733-9101
Bellingham *(G-1362)*
Heirloom Custom Cabinets Inc ... G ... 360 354-7851
Lynden *(G-6020)*
Henry Products Incorporated ... D ... 206 624-5656
Seattle *(G-10166)*
Jpl Habitability Inc ... F ... 360 377-7660
Bremerton *(G-1967)*
Kessler Wood Products ... G ... 509 937-2500
Valley *(G-13992)*
Kristines ... G ... 360 437-0136
Port Ludlow *(G-7769)*
Larry Guthrie Co ... G ... 509 922-6121
Spokane Valley *(G-12772)*
▼ **Leader Manufacturing Inc** ... E ... 360 895-1184
Port Orchard *(G-7825)*
Lewis Cnty Work Opportunities ... E ... 360 748-9921
Chehalis *(G-2509)*
Maine Cottage Inc ... G ... 866 366-3505
Poulsbo *(G-7981)*
Maywood Shops Inc ... F ... 360 748-9244
Chehalis *(G-2513)*
Modern Classics Inc ... G ... 360 733-6400
Bellingham *(G-1438)*
Nordal Denver ... G ... 509 456-8969
Spokane *(G-12406)*
Petit and Olson ... G ... 206 201-3262
Bainbridge Island *(G-657)*
Pioneer Woodworks Company Inc ... G ... 206 362-5637
Seattle *(G-10812)*
Precision Woodcraft ... G ... 509 276-1362
Deer Park *(G-2913)*
Preston Woodcraft LLC ... G ... 425 749-8074
Issaquah *(G-4460)*
Quality Cabinets Plus Inc ... G ... 360 423-1242
Kelso *(G-4544)*
Quality Creations ... G ... 253 732-4082
Spanaway *(G-12068)*
Reclaimed Wood Products ... G ... 360 387-1570
Stanwood *(G-12956)*
Roy McMakin ... G ... 206 323-0111
Seattle *(G-10984)*

SIC SECTION

25 FURNITURE AND FIXTURES

◆ S F McKinnon Co Inc ....G....... 206 622-4948
   Seattle *(G-11000)*
Shaker Craftsman ....G....... 509 823-4556
   Yakima *(G-15673)*
Shea Edwards Furniture LLP ....F....... 206 898-1992
   Sultan *(G-13036)*
Shelfgenie ....G....... 206 774-0336
   Seattle *(G-11099)*
Ship N Shore ....G....... 360 293-8636
   Anacortes *(G-167)*
▲ Shuttlesystem LLC ....F....... 425 551-1335
   Mount Vernon *(G-6835)*
Simplicity ABC LLC ....G....... 425 250-1186
   Fall City *(G-3708)*
Snow Valley Furniture ....F....... 509 292-8880
   Newport *(G-7066)*
▲ Style Plus LLC ....E....... 206 920-9223
   Renton *(G-8921)*
Surewood Custom Cabinets Inc ....G....... 509 893-9522
   Spokane Valley *(G-12897)*
Thoe John ....G....... 206 505-6229
   Seattle *(G-11294)*
Traditional Heirlooms ....G....... 509 722-2620
   Goldendale *(G-4210)*
▲ Two Zero Six LLC ....G....... 206 557-4384
   Seattle *(G-11355)*
▲ Wallbeds Northwest Inc ....E....... 425 284-6692
   Redmond *(G-8708)*
Whidbey Design Works ....G....... 360 321-8221
   Clinton *(G-2702)*
William Walker Woodworking ....G....... 206 780-5301
   Bainbridge Island *(G-684)*
Winthrop Wood Works ....G....... 509 996-2037
   Winthrop *(G-15166)*
Wintran Trading ....G....... 425 501-7818
   Everett *(G-3660)*
▲ Wood-Works Cabinetry & Design .....G....... 206 257-3335
   Seattle *(G-11491)*
Woodcraft Inc ....G....... 800 225-1153
   Lynnwood *(G-6226)*
Woodcraft Studio ....G....... 404 426-1229
   Bremerton *(G-2013)*
Woodworking Unlimited ....G....... 425 481-7451
   Bothell *(G-1922)*

2512 Wood Household Furniture, Upholstered

Barbara Bogart ....G....... 360 385-0815
   Port Townsend *(G-7867)*
Columbia Furniture Mfg Inc ....F....... 509 534-7147
   Spokane *(G-12190)*
Design Craft Upholstery Inc ....G....... 425 775-7620
   Lynnwood *(G-6107)*
▲ Ecobalanza LLC ....G....... 888 220-6020
   Seattle *(G-9879)*
Empire Upholstery ....G....... 509 467-5263
   Spokane *(G-12247)*
▲ Epoch Design LLC ....F....... 425 284-0880
   Redmond *(G-8452)*
Freeze Furniture and Mfg Co ....F....... 509 924-3545
   Spokane Valley *(G-12710)*
▲ Kaasco Inc ....C....... 425 412-2460
   Mukilteo *(G-6947)*
Maywood Shops Inc ....F....... 360 748-9244
   Chehalis *(G-2513)*
▲ Style Plus LLC ....E....... 206 920-9223
   Renton *(G-8921)*
William Bounds Custom Frames ....G....... 360 404-2002
   Burlington *(G-2202)*
Wn Inc ....G....... 509 966-9409
   Yakima *(G-15709)*

2514 Metal Household Furniture

Alairx LLC ....G....... 425 281-3180
   Carnation *(G-2289)*
Artistic Iron Furniture Mfrs ....F....... 360 398-9351
   Lynden *(G-6002)*
Camp Time Inc ....F....... 509 928-3051
   Spokane Valley *(G-12649)*
David Gulassa & Co Inc ....E....... 206 283-1810
   Seattle *(G-9800)*
Jpl Habitability Inc ....F....... 360 377-7660
   Bremerton *(G-1967)*
Northwest Metal Craft ....G....... 509 999-5280
   Spokane Valley *(G-12807)*
▲ Purcell Systems Inc ....D....... 509 755-0341
   Spokane Valley *(G-12844)*
Schreiner Construction ....G....... 509 525-6205
   College Place *(G-2727)*

2515 Mattresses & Bedsprings

Americas Sleep Comfort Center ....G....... 253 548-8890
   Tacoma *(G-13169)*
Bayshore Office Products Inc ....F....... 360 293-4669
   Anacortes *(G-102)*
▲ Canvas Supply Co Inc ....E....... 206 784-0711
   Seattle *(G-9621)*
▲ Cascade Designs Inc ....B....... 206 505-9500
   Seattle *(G-9640)*
Cascade Manufacturing ....G....... 206 762-3750
   Auburn *(G-402)*
◆ Emerald Home Furnishings LLC .....B....... 253 922-1400
   Tacoma *(G-13278)*
▲ Exomotion LLC ....G....... 206 763-0754
   Seattle *(G-9954)*
Heavenly Mountain Studios ....G....... 360 437-2298
   Port Hadlock *(G-7759)*
Laser Reflections ....G....... 206 818-2940
   Poulsbo *(G-7973)*
Leggett & Platt Incorporated ....G....... 801 825-9739
   Tacoma *(G-13384)*
◆ Mattress Makers Incorporated ....F....... 253 984-1730
   Tacoma *(G-13401)*
▲ Northwest Bedding Company ....E....... 509 244-3000
   Spokane *(G-12411)*
NW Closets ....F....... 253 246-7596
   Kent *(G-5038)*
Paradise Studios ....G....... 360 789-5744
   Kirkland *(G-5428)*
Sealy Mattress Mfg Co Inc ....C....... 360 413-6902
   Lacey *(G-5585)*
Sleep Aire Mattress Company ....E....... 206 546-4195
   Shoreline *(G-11814)*
Sleep Number Corporation ....G....... 360 671-1266
   Bellingham *(G-1543)*
Slumber Ease Mattress Co Inc ....G....... 360 657-1654
   Marysville *(G-6385)*
Soaring Heart LLC ....F....... 206 282-1717
   Seattle *(G-11147)*
Soaring Heart Natural Bed Co ....G....... 206 257-4158
   Seattle *(G-11148)*
Ssb Manufacturing Company ....C....... 253 891-3272
   Sumner *(G-13102)*
Summitclimb Inc ....G....... 360 570-0715
   Longbranch *(G-5880)*
Sunrise Mattress Company Inc ....G....... 509 290-5728
   Spokane Valley *(G-12895)*
Twilight Bedding Company Inc ....G....... 509 926-2333
   Spokane Valley *(G-12916)*
Wallbeds Northwest Inc ....G....... 206 256-1700
   Seattle *(G-11433)*

2517 Wood T V, Radio, Phono & Sewing Cabinets

Acorn Custom Cabinetry Inc ....E....... 425 235-8366
   Renton *(G-8727)*
AE Downs Enterprises Inc ....E....... 206 295-9831
   Kent *(G-4761)*
Lou Hinkley ....G....... 360 312-3604
   Ferndale *(G-3866)*
Markay Cabinets Inc ....F....... 360 779-3443
   Poulsbo *(G-7982)*
Michael B Knutson ....G....... 509 398-7312
   Wenatchee *(G-15050)*
▲ Pacific Crest Industries Inc ....C....... 253 321-3011
   Sumner *(G-13093)*
Seaboard Cabinet Company Inc ....F....... 425 776-2000
   Lynnwood *(G-6193)*
Valley Cabinets & More Inc ....G....... 360 428-0916
   Mount Vernon *(G-6851)*
Wood Way Mfg Inc ....G....... 360 366-4854
   Blaine *(G-1713)*

2519 Household Furniture, NEC

Douglas L Perry ....G....... 253 303-0537
   Gig Harbor *(G-4095)*
◆ Green Store Inc ....G....... 253 939-5757
   Algona *(G-70)*
Kitty Cribs LLC ....G....... 360 312-8102
   Ferndale *(G-3864)*
Meyer Wells Inc ....E....... 206 282-0076
   Seattle *(G-10525)*
Patricia Kinsella ....G....... 206 285-5885
   Seattle *(G-10769)*
Potrisers Inc ....G....... 206 240-5579
   Snohomish *(G-11961)*
Red Rock Creek Inc ....F....... 509 765-1664
   Pullman *(G-8104)*

▲ Vancouver Woodworks Inc ....G....... 360 696-8590
   Vancouver *(G-14664)*
▲ Wallbeds Northwest Inc ....E....... 425 284-6692
   Redmond *(G-8708)*

2521 Wood Office Furniture

AAA Cabinets & Millwork Inc ....F....... 509 484-7152
   Airway Heights *(G-48)*
Acorn Custom Cabinetry Inc ....E....... 425 235-8366
   Renton *(G-8727)*
Andrews Fixture Company Inc ....F....... 253 627-7481
   Tacoma *(G-13172)*
Belina Interiors Inc ....D....... 253 474-0276
   Tacoma *(G-13193)*
Burgeners Woodworking Inc ....E....... 360 694-9408
   Vancouver *(G-14086)*
Canyon Creek Cabinet Company ....G....... 509 921-7807
   Spokane Valley *(G-12650)*
Cedar Mountain Woodwrights ....G....... 509 933-2602
   Ellensburg *(G-3188)*
Columbia Cabinets LLC ....G....... 509 325-8995
   Spokane *(G-12189)*
Contempo Inc ....G....... 509 758-1694
   Clarkston *(G-2627)*
Custom Office Design Inc ....F....... 253 735-8777
   Auburn *(G-420)*
Dogstar Cabinets Inc ....G....... 509 674-4229
   Cle Elum *(G-2665)*
Douglas L Perry ....G....... 253 303-0537
   Gig Harbor *(G-4095)*
Elpis Works Inc ....G....... 206 317-4647
   Everett *(G-3458)*
Family Endurance Corporation ....F....... 253 872-3900
   Kent *(G-4903)*
Filliols Custom Cab Doors Inc ....F....... 509 453-8098
   Yakima *(G-15570)*
Flory Cabinets LLC ....G....... 360 894-2504
   Yelm *(G-15733)*
Fred Misner ....G....... 425 398-7184
   Bothell *(G-1856)*
Freeze Furniture and Mfg Co ....F....... 509 924-3545
   Spokane Valley *(G-12710)*
Furniture By Foss ....G....... 206 783-3626
   Seattle *(G-10040)*
Genothen Holdings LLC ....D....... 360 352-3636
   Tumwater *(G-13873)*
Inland Fixtures Co Inc ....G....... 509 487-2759
   Spokane *(G-12309)*
Interior Environments Inc ....E....... 206 432-8800
   Seattle *(G-10248)*
Johnnystand ....G....... 206 412-2982
   Redmond *(G-8520)*
Jpl Habitability Inc ....F....... 360 377-7660
   Bremerton *(G-1967)*
◆ Kardiel Inc ....G....... 916 999-1050
   Seatac *(G-9287)*
Ken Boudreau Inc ....D....... 425 402-8001
   Woodinville *(G-15277)*
Kings Kitchen LLC ....G....... 253 212-3623
   Tacoma *(G-13376)*
Knoll Inc ....F....... 206 624-0174
   Seattle *(G-10348)*
Kristines ....G....... 360 437-0136
   Port Ludlow *(G-7769)*
Liberty Casework LLC ....G....... 253 651-7891
   Graham *(G-4230)*
Loop Corp ....G....... 206 499-0679
   Seattle *(G-10440)*
Markay Cabinets Inc ....F....... 360 779-3443
   Poulsbo *(G-7982)*
Maywood Shops Inc ....F....... 360 748-9244
   Chehalis *(G-2513)*
Michael B Knutson ....G....... 509 398-7312
   Wenatchee *(G-15050)*
Northwest Woodworks Inc ....E....... 425 482-9663
   Woodinville *(G-15322)*
▲ Pacific Crest Industries Inc ....C....... 253 321-3011
   Sumner *(G-13093)*
Prp Finishing ....G....... 509 966-0798
   Yakima *(G-15658)*
Quality Cabinets Plus Inc ....G....... 360 423-1242
   Kelso *(G-4544)*
R S Manufacturing Inc ....E....... 425 774-1211
   Lynnwood *(G-6186)*
R T London Company ....F....... 360 943-5090
   Lacey *(G-5581)*
Sawbox LLC ....G....... 253 277-0506
   Kent *(G-5117)*
Seaboard Cabinet Company Inc ....F....... 425 776-2000
   Lynnwood *(G-6193)*

25 FURNITURE AND FIXTURES

Smart Office Environments LLC ....G...... 206 730-8871
  Bellevue *(G-1138)*
Solid Visions Inc ....E...... 206 949-4203
  Bothell *(G-1907)*
Sunlight Woodenworks Inc ....G...... 360 275-5263
  Shelton *(G-11737)*
Tacoma Fixture Co Inc ....D...... 253 383-5541
  Tacoma *(G-13542)*
Trevors Wood Working LLC ....G...... 206 940-8000
  Seattle *(G-11331)*
Valley Cabinets & More Inc ....G...... 360 428-0916
  Mount Vernon *(G-6851)*
▲ Watson Furniture Group Inc ....C...... 360 394-1300
  Poulsbo *(G-8019)*
Wells Ww Millwork LLC ....F...... 425 405-3252
  Everett *(G-3654)*
Windfall Lumber Inc ....E...... 360 352-2250
  Tumwater *(G-13906)*

2522 Office Furniture, Except Wood

Artiks Inc ....G...... 206 849-4335
  Redmond *(G-8387)*
CCI Caseworks Inc ....G...... 360 953-9641
  Ridgefield *(G-9070)*
Global Industries Inc ....G...... 425 291-9282
  Renton *(G-8807)*
Jpl Habitability Inc ....F...... 360 377-7660
  Bremerton *(G-1967)*
Kenco Construction Inc ....E...... 206 783-3300
  Seattle *(G-10336)*
Loop Corp ....G...... 206 499-0679
  Seattle *(G-10440)*
Meyer Wells Inc ....E...... 206 282-0076
  Seattle *(G-10525)*
Thermogenesis Group Inc ....F...... 425 999-3550
  Bellevue *(G-1185)*
Warmington & North Co Inc ....F...... 206 324-5043
  Seattle *(G-11436)*

2531 Public Building & Related Furniture

B/E Aerospace Inc ....B...... 425 923-2700
  Everett *(G-3381)*
Bradley Saxton ....G...... 800 643-3512
  Kent *(G-4821)*
Cape Dissapointment State Park ......F...... 360 642-3078
  Ilwaco *(G-4368)*
Df Industries Inc ....F...... 253 472-0422
  Tacoma *(G-13261)*
Douglas L Perry ....G...... 253 303-0537
  Gig Harbor *(G-4095)*
Dream Line Cabinets LLC ....G...... 503 841-8575
  Vancouver *(G-14187)*
▲ Exomotion LLC ....G...... 206 763-0754
  Seattle *(G-9954)*
Federal Way Memorial Field ....G...... 253 945-5575
  Federal Way *(G-3738)*
Genothen Holdings LLC ....D...... 360 352-3636
  Tumwater *(G-13873)*
Johnson Controls Inc ....G...... 509 747-8053
  Spokane *(G-12339)*
S2 Proto Types Inc ....G...... 425 822-0858
  Kirkland *(G-5455)*
Safeco Field ....G...... 206 346-4000
  Seattle *(G-11002)*
Smarte Carte Inc ....G...... 206 431-0844
  Seatac *(G-9306)*
Trevors Wood Working LLC ....G...... 206 940-8000
  Seattle *(G-11331)*
Tri-Way Industries Inc ....D...... 253 859-4585
  Auburn *(G-582)*
United Seating & Mobility LLC ....G...... 509 484-6720
  Spokane *(G-12577)*
Watson Furniture Group Inc ....G...... 360 394-1300
  Poulsbo *(G-8020)*
▲ Watson Furniture Group Inc ....C...... 360 394-1300
  Poulsbo *(G-8019)*

2541 Wood, Office & Store Fixtures

Above and Beyond Cnstr LLC ....G...... 509 521-8081
  Kennewick *(G-4610)*
Andrew M Baldwin ....G...... 425 481-6245
  Woodinville *(G-15177)*
Andrews Fixture Company Inc ....F...... 253 627-7481
  Tacoma *(G-13172)*
Associated Materials LLC ....G...... 425 481-7101
  Fife *(G-3935)*
Bagdons Inc ....E...... 509 662-1411
  Wenatchee *(G-15011)*
◆ Bargreen-Ellingson Inc ....D...... 253 475-9201
  Tacoma *(G-13189)*
Bargreen-Ellingson Inc ....E...... 253 722-2573
  Fife *(G-3937)*
▲ Burke Gibson LLC ....E...... 253 735-4444
  Auburn *(G-398)*
Carlson Custom ....G...... 360 756-0351
  Bellingham *(G-1291)*
Commercial Cabinet Works ....G...... 360 857-3130
  Ridgefield *(G-9074)*
Conestoga Wood Spc Corp ....G...... 253 437-1320
  Kent *(G-4863)*
Contour Countertops Inc ....F...... 503 654-2245
  Vancouver *(G-14150)*
Counter Intuitive ....G...... 360 264-5150
  Tenino *(G-13614)*
Countertops For Less ....G...... 360 306-3921
  Bellingham *(G-1308)*
Custom Craft LLC ....E...... 253 826-5450
  Sumner *(G-13064)*
Display Manufacturing LLC ....G...... 360 653-0990
  Marysville *(G-6330)*
Edgebanding Services Inc ....F...... 866 395-7002
  Kent *(G-4884)*
Ennco Display Systems Inc ....F...... 425 883-1650
  Redmond *(G-8449)*
▲ Epoch Design LLC ....F...... 425 284-0880
  Redmond *(G-8452)*
▲ Gds Direct Countertops Ltd ....G...... 360 312-9688
  Ferndale *(G-3848)*
Higher Plane Cabinetworks ....F...... 360 733-4322
  Bellingham *(G-1370)*
IB Wood Inc ....G...... 253 395-8886
  Kent *(G-4948)*
Imagicorps Inc ....E...... 425 869-0599
  Redmond *(G-8506)*
Inland Fixtures Co Inc ....G...... 509 487-2759
  Spokane *(G-12309)*
Interior Form Tops Inc ....E...... 253 927-8171
  Milton *(G-6535)*
Journeyman Cabinets Inc ....G...... 509 483-6864
  Spokane *(G-12343)*
Kermits Wood Products ....E...... 425 316-6823
  Everett *(G-3530)*
King Brothers Woodworking Inc ....E...... 509 453-4683
  Union Gap *(G-13936)*
L Clasen Corp ....G...... 360 658-1823
  Snohomish *(G-11935)*
Lake Sunset LLC ....G...... 718 683-2269
  Olympia *(G-7317)*
Lakewood Counter Tops Inc ....F...... 253 588-8550
  Lakewood *(G-5733)*
Lg Hausys America Inc ....G...... 425 251-3698
  Tukwila *(G-13765)*
Madrona Stone LLC ....G...... 253 750-5064
  Sumner *(G-13083)*
Nelson Brothers Inc ....F...... 509 922-4988
  Spokane Valley *(G-12802)*
Northwest Building Tech Inc ....E...... 206 767-4012
  Seattle *(G-10638)*
Northwest Woodworks Inc ....E...... 425 482-9663
  Woodinville *(G-15322)*
▲ Pacific Coast Showcase Inc ....C...... 253 445-9000
  Puyallup *(G-8216)*
Passion Works LLC ....G...... 425 260-7777
  Kenmore *(G-4597)*
PBS Supply Co Inc ....F...... 253 395-5550
  Kent *(G-5063)*
Precision Countertops Inc ....E...... 253 867-5317
  Kent *(G-5076)*
Quality Counter ....G...... 425 303-9180
  Everett *(G-5050)*
R S Manufacturing Inc ....E...... 425 774-1211
  Lynnwood *(G-6186)*
Rodneys Custom Woodwork ....F...... 206 542-2517
  Shoreline *(G-11805)*
Room Maker ....G...... 425 432-3324
  Maple Valley *(G-6292)*
Royal Line Cabinet Co ....G...... 206 767-9125
  Seattle *(G-10986)*
Silver Star Industies Inc ....G...... 509 427-8800
  Stevenson *(G-13019)*
Silver Star Industies Inc ....D...... 509 427-8800
  North Bonneville *(G-7133)*
Silver Star Industies Inc ....E...... 509 427-8800
  North Bonneville *(G-7134)*
Silver Star Industies Inc ....F...... 360 837-3685
  Washougal *(G-14985)*
Spacewall West Inc ....G...... 253 852-0203
  Kent *(G-5143)*
Stageplan Inc ....E...... 360 825-2428
  Enumclaw *(G-3322)*
▲ Synsor LLC ....C...... 425 551-1300
  Everett *(G-3624)*
T R S Inc ....F...... 253 444-1555
  Tacoma *(G-13538)*
Tacoma Fixture Co Inc ....D...... 253 383-5541
  Tacoma *(G-13542)*
Tc NW Inc ....G...... 360 683-6655
  Sequim *(G-11664)*
Tim Krotzer ....G...... 509 487-2704
  Spokane *(G-12558)*
Turner Exhibits Inc ....E...... 425 776-4930
  Lynnwood *(G-6214)*
Valley Cabinets & More Inc ....G...... 360 428-0916
  Mount Vernon *(G-6851)*
Vrieze & Olson Custom Wdwkg ....F...... 253 445-9733
  Puyallup *(G-8274)*
West Coast Laminating LLC ....F...... 253 395-5225
  Kent *(G-5211)*
Wilsonart LLC ....E...... 253 833-0551
  Algona *(G-79)*
Windfall Lumber Inc ....E...... 360 352-2250
  Tumwater *(G-13906)*

2542 Partitions & Fixtures, Except Wood

All In Wood ....G...... 360 457-8337
  Port Angeles *(G-7682)*
Aristocratic Cabinets Inc ....D...... 360 740-0609
  Chehalis *(G-2467)*
Belina Interiors Inc ....D...... 253 474-0276
  Tacoma *(G-13193)*
Bfc Architectural Metals Inc ....F...... 206 763-0530
  Seatac *(G-9274)*
Butler Did It ....G...... 360 662-0629
  Bremerton *(G-1941)*
Dru Wood ....G...... 360 213-7444
  Vancouver *(G-14188)*
Ennco Display Systems Inc ....F...... 425 883-1650
  Redmond *(G-8449)*
Frazier Industrial Company ....G...... 509 698-4100
  Selah *(G-11588)*
Higher Plane Cabinetworks ....F...... 360 733-4322
  Bellingham *(G-1370)*
Idx Corporation ....C...... 253 445-9000
  Puyallup *(G-8165)*
Imagicorps Inc ....E...... 425 869-0599
  Redmond *(G-8506)*
Jack Just Enterprises LLC ....G...... 425 836-7755
  Redmond *(G-8518)*
Jpl Habitability Inc ....F...... 360 377-7660
  Bremerton *(G-1967)*
Mail Box & Shipping Center ....G...... 425 869-1448
  Redmond *(G-8546)*
Mail N Beyond ....G...... 425 379-6111
  Everett *(G-3544)*
Mailbox Junction ....G...... 360 658-2445
  Marysville *(G-6355)*
Metal Werks Inc ....F...... 360 651-0300
  Marysville *(G-6359)*
▲ Multifab Inc ....C...... 509 924-6631
  Spokane Valley *(G-12796)*
Museum Resource LLC ....G...... 206 547-4047
  Seatac *(G-9292)*
Northwest Building Tech Inc ....E...... 206 767-4012
  Seattle *(G-10638)*
Obcon Inc ....G...... 253 931-0455
  Auburn *(G-516)*
Out For A Walk ....G...... 360 793-4419
  Sultan *(G-13031)*
Pacific Enviroments Corp ....E...... 408 836-7581
  Kent *(G-5143)*
◆ Pacific Integrated Hdlg Inc ....E...... 253 535-5888
  Tacoma *(G-13451)*
Rack & Maintenance Source LLC ......G...... 509 525-7006
  College Place *(G-2726)*
Souers Manufacturing Inc ....G...... 253 735-2488
  Gig Harbor *(G-4161)*
Spacewall West Inc ....G...... 253 852-0203
  Kent *(G-5143)*
Spokane Discount and Brass Co ....G...... 509 467-8063
  Spokane *(G-12517)*
T R S Inc ....F...... 253 444-1555
  Tacoma *(G-13538)*
Tim Krotzer ....G...... 509 487-2704
  Spokane *(G-12558)*
Tri-Way Industries Inc ....D...... 253 859-4585
  Auburn *(G-582)*
▲ Venetian Stone Works LLC ....F...... 425 486-1234
  Woodinville *(G-15399)*
Won-Door Corporation ....G...... 206 726-9449
  Seattle *(G-11490)*

SIC SECTION

2591 Drapery Hardware, Window Blinds & Shades

Company	Code	Phone
▲ A & I Manufacturing Inc Monroe *(G-6540)*	E	360 805-0858
All Pro Blind Cleaning Repair Auburn *(G-371)*	G	253 804-9497
American Drpery Blind Crpt Inc Renton *(G-8743)*	C	360 676-1121
American Drpery Blind Crpt Inc Renton *(G-8742)*	E	425 793-4477
Blue Home Thermal Imaging LLC Kingston *(G-5248)*	G	360 638-0838
Creative Window Concepts Issaquah *(G-4400)*	G	425 351-2246
Fusion9 Design LLC Camano Island *(G-2214)*	G	360 831-0899
Go Vertical Corporation Seabeck *(G-9264)*	G	360 830-5447
HK Window Fashions Nine Mile Falls *(G-7076)*	G	509 466-4202
Home Sweet Home Indoor Spokane *(G-12297)*	G	509 327-9637
Johnson Enterprises Tacoma *(G-13365)*	G	253 537-8056
Lumenomics Inc Seattle *(G-10451)*	E	206 327-9037
Otis Elevator Company Tukwila *(G-13784)*	G	206 285-2285
Quality Drapery Service Palouse *(G-7547)*	G	509 878-1371
Seattle Curtain Mfg Co Mill Creek *(G-6526)*	E	206 324-0692
Shade Sunglo & Drapery Co Seattle *(G-11094)*	G	206 767-4561
▲ Source Northwest Inc Woodinville *(G-15370)*	D	360 512-3535
Traditional Concepts Gig Harbor *(G-4168)*	G	253 884-2818
▲ Vertical Gardens Northwest LLC Everett *(G-3650)*	G	425 891-7183
Vertical Lift Solutions Port Angeles *(G-7751)*	G	360 928-1126
Vertical Limits LLC Spokane *(G-12581)*	G	509 294-9878
Vertical Technologies Dayton *(G-2888)*	G	509 382-2119
Vertical Welder Port Orchard *(G-7855)*	G	360 265-5457
Vertical Works LLC Cheney *(G-2595)*	G	509 251-0513

2599 Furniture & Fixtures, NEC

Company	Code	Phone
Belina Interiors Inc Tacoma *(G-13193)*	D	253 474-0276
Bosom Cattle Co Yelm *(G-15730)*	F	206 947-0645
Cabinet Masters Inc Vancouver *(G-14089)*	G	360 695-6615
Dingeys LLC Olympia *(G-7271)*	G	360 789-0853
▲ Evolution Technologies USA Ferndale *(G-3839)*	G	360 392-8600
▲ Exomotion LLC Seattle *(G-9954)*	G	206 763-0754
F H Sullivan Co Inc Kelso *(G-4525)*	E	360 442-4222
Foldcraft Co Kent *(G-4915)*	E	253 437-1355
Frankenstein Incorporated Seattle *(G-10021)*	G	206 915-1011
Haun Made LLC Seattle *(G-10150)*	G	253 242-6105
Hot Rods Goldendale *(G-4201)*	G	509 773-7005
International Wood Processors Anacortes *(G-135)*	D	360 299-9996
Judith Ames Furniture Seattle *(G-10313)*	G	206 324-8538
Kci Commercial Inc Tacoma *(G-13373)*	G	253 475-4363
Leigh Interiors Bellevue *(G-980)*	G	206 351-5158
Markay Cabinets Inc Poulsbo *(G-7982)*	F	360 779-3443
Mix Tacoma *(G-13417)*	G	253 383-4327
Nygards Custom Cabinetry Kelso *(G-4540)*	G	360 425-1777
T & A Supply Company Inc Kent *(G-5167)*	G	253 872-3682

Company	Code	Phone
Tri-Way Industries Inc Auburn *(G-582)*	D	253 859-4585
Two Blue Mules Seattle *(G-11352)*	G	206 935-3762
Welco Sales LLC Edmonds *(G-3162)*	G	425 771-9043
Wilson & Hayes Inc Seattle *(G-11478)*	G	206 323-6758

26 PAPER AND ALLIED PRODUCTS

2611 Pulp Mills

Company	Code	Phone
Bagcraft Vancouver *(G-14053)*	G	360 695-7771
Braven Metals LLC Lake Stevens *(G-5635)*	G	206 963-2234
Buddy Shelters LLC Arlington *(G-216)*	G	425 239-8104
Columbia Pulp I LLC Starbuck *(G-13001)*	E	509 288-4892
Core Pack LLC Yakima *(G-15537)*	G	509 426-2511
▼ Cosmo Specialty Fibers Inc Cosmopolis *(G-2799)*	C	360 500-4600
Cowles Publishing Company Spokane *(G-12204)*	B	509 459-5000
Eh Metal Recycling Vancouver *(G-14195)*	G	360 334-6005
Faithful Enterprises Inc Toppenish *(G-13667)*	E	509 865-7300
Fibres International Inc Everett *(G-3471)*	D	425 455-9811
Green Brothers of Seattle LLC Seattle *(G-10115)*	G	303 295-7669
◆ Kamilche Company Seattle *(G-10326)*	G	206 224-5800
Longview Fibre Ppr & Packg Inc Cle Elum *(G-2671)*	G	509 674-1791
Marilyns Recycle Inc Duvall *(G-2995)*	G	425 788-1716
Mint Valley Paper Company Inc Battle Ground *(G-723)*	G	360 931-9055
Nippon Dynawave Packg Co LLC Longview *(G-5935)*	A	360 425-2150
Nippon Paper Inds USA Co Ltd Port Angeles *(G-7727)*	F	360 457-4474
Northwest Cpitl Apprcation Inc Seattle *(G-10640)*	A	206 689-5615
▲ Paneltech Intl Holdings Inc Hoquiam *(G-4354)*	F	360 538-1480
Parberry Inc Bellingham *(G-1491)*	E	360 734-2340
Port Townsend Holdings Co Inc Port Townsend *(G-7911)*	B	360 385-3170
▲ Simpson Investment Company Seattle *(G-11115)*	D	253 272-0158
Sustainable Fiber Tech LLC Renton *(G-8925)*	G	206 818-4130
Weyerhaeuser Company Cosmopolis *(G-2802)*	B	360 532-7110
Weyerhaeuser Company Seattle *(G-11461)*	F	253 924-6373
◆ Weyerhaeuser Company Seattle *(G-11459)*	A	206 539-3000
Yms Seattle *(G-11512)*	G	206 354-2048

2621 Paper Mills

Company	Code	Phone
Alexander Printing Co Inc Everett *(G-3366)*	G	425 252-4212
Avalonphilly LLC Bellevue *(G-800)*	G	800 405-7024
Bella Cupcake Couture LLC Newcastle *(G-7026)*	G	425 260-3224
Bob Nagel Inc Vancouver *(G-14074)*	F	503 869-6933
Boise Cascade Company Vancouver *(G-14076)*	D	360 690-7028
Boise Cascade Company Vancouver *(G-14077)*	D	360 891-8787
Boise White Paper LLC Wallula *(G-14908)*	E	509 545-3293
Butler Design Inc Ferndale *(G-3819)*	G	360 380-1651
Caraustar Industrial and Con Tacoma *(G-13221)*	D	253 627-1197
Cassel Inc Bellevue *(G-841)*	C	206 909-9584
▼ Clearwater Paper Corporation Spokane *(G-12183)*	C	509 344-5900

Company	Code	Phone
▲ Clearwater Paper Oklahoma Spokane *(G-12184)*	G	405 717-5104
Cowles Publishing Company Spokane *(G-12204)*	B	509 459-5000
Crown Paper Group Inc Port Townsend *(G-7875)*	F	360 385-3170
Dcw News Agency Inc Seattle *(G-9807)*	G	206 682-2888
Dj Creations Kettle Falls *(G-5231)*	G	509 738-6200
Dolco Packaging Corp Wenatchee *(G-15026)*	E	509 662-8415
Domtar Paper Company LLC Federal Way *(G-3730)*	B	253 924-2345
▲ Fibro Corporation Tacoma *(G-13294)*	G	253 503-3568
Georgia-Pacific LLC Covington *(G-2828)*	G	253 631-3250
Glenn Waldren Olympia *(G-7297)*	G	360 570-8400
Grays Harbor Paper LLC Renton *(G-8814)*	F	877 548-3424
◆ Inland Empire Paper Company Spokane *(G-12307)*	G	509 924-1911
International Paper Company Union Gap *(G-13933)*	G	509 576-3158
International Paper Company Kent *(G-4957)*	D	253 372-1360
J & H Printing Inc Pullman *(G-8094)*	G	509 332-0782
◆ Kamilche Company Seattle *(G-10326)*	G	206 224-5800
Kimberly-Clark Corporation Bellevue *(G-968)*	F	425 373-5900
LSI Logistic Svc Solutions LLC Puyallup *(G-8180)*	F	253 872-8970
McKinley Paper Company Port Angeles *(G-7724)*	E	360 457-4474
▲ Memory Box Inc Seattle *(G-10515)*	G	206 722-8438
Mint Valley Paper Company Inc Battle Ground *(G-723)*	G	360 931-9055
Nippon Dynawave Packg Co LLC Longview *(G-5935)*	A	360 425-2150
◆ Nippon Paper Inds USA Co Ltd Longview *(G-5936)*	G	360 457-4474
◆ North Pacific Paper Co LLC Longview *(G-5937)*	B	360 636-6400
Northwest Napkin LLC Vancouver *(G-14435)*	F	360 571-0051
NP Paper Company LLC Longview *(G-5938)*	G	360 636-6400
◆ of The Earth Seattle *(G-10686)*	F	206 462-7022
◆ Pac-Paper Inc Vancouver *(G-14461)*	C	800 223-4981
Packaging Corporation America Wallula *(G-14909)*	D	509 545-3260
◆ Ponderay Newsprint Company Usk *(G-13985)*	C	509 445-2133
▲ Simpson Investment Company Seattle *(G-11115)*	D	253 272-0158
Tevada Publishing Inc Kennewick *(G-4734)*	F	509 783-5455
Westrock Company Longview *(G-5965)*	G	360 575-5256
Wrap Pack Inc Yakima *(G-15710)*	F	509 453-2830

2631 Paperboard Mills

Company	Code	Phone
Action Equipment Inc Buckley *(G-2045)*	G	360 897-0890
Adhesive & Packaging Systems Port Orchard *(G-7783)*	G	360 876-9278
Boise Inc Colville *(G-2741)*	G	509 685-9825
Caraustar Industrial and Con Tacoma *(G-13221)*	D	253 627-1197
Caraustar Industries Inc Longview *(G-5894)*	E	360 423-3420
▼ Clearwater Paper Corporation Spokane *(G-12183)*	C	509 344-5900
Core Pack LLC Yakima *(G-15537)*	G	509 426-2511
Excel Packaging Systems Inc Enumclaw *(G-3291)*	G	360 825-7209
Expensive Cardboard Seattle *(G-9956)*	G	214 564-2670
Forged From Cardboard Everett *(G-3482)*	G	425 399-0715

Graphic Packaging Intl Inc....C....425 235-3300
Renton *(G-8812)*
Graphic Packaging Intl LLC....G....360 896-6486
Vancouver *(G-14263)*
Kaddy....G....360 438-3636
Lacey *(G-5562)*
Legacy Creations....G....206 286-1827
Seattle *(G-10399)*
Longview Fibre Ppr & Packg Inc....D....206 762-7170
Seattle *(G-10437)*
Nippon Dynawave Packaging Co....G....360 414-3379
Federal Way *(G-3763)*
Nippon Dynawave Packg Co LLC....A....360 425-2150
Longview *(G-5935)*
Packaging Corporation America....D....509 545-3260
Wallula *(G-14909)*
Pine Canyon Growers LLC....D....509 888-7017
Orondo *(G-7459)*
◆ Port Townsend Paper Corp....B....360 385-3170
Port Townsend *(G-7912)*
Price Container and Packg Corp....G....360 266-5598
Chehalis *(G-2526)*
Quality Equipment Supply Inc....G....503 544-9779
Vancouver *(G-14518)*
▲ Scott Lumber Packaging LLC....F....425 821-2075
Bothell *(G-1790)*
Simpson Tacoma Kraft Co LLC....G....253 779-6444
Tacoma *(G-13514)*
Sonoco Products Company....D....206 682-0440
Sumner *(G-13101)*
Sonoco Products Company....D....360 225-1500
Woodland *(G-15466)*
Weyerhaeuser Company....C....509 453-4741
Union Gap *(G-13956)*

2652 Set-Up Paperboard Boxes

Northwest Paper Box Mfrs Inc....E....206 782-7105
Seatac *(G-9293)*

2653 Corrugated & Solid Fiber Boxes

Alliance Packaging LLC....D....509 924-7623
Spokane Valley *(G-12605)*
Alliance Packaging LLC....C....425 291-3500
Renton *(G-8738)*
▲ Allpak Container LLC....D....425 227-0400
Renton *(G-8739)*
Allpak Container LLC....E....509 535-4112
Renton *(G-8740)*
▲ Applied Applications Intl LLC....F....360 425-7900
Kelso *(G-4516)*
Box Maker Inc....G....425 291-1291
Kent *(G-4820)*
Commercial Crting Box Pckg Inc....F....253 804-8616
Auburn *(G-410)*
Easy Fold Fixtures....F....425 209-0167
Kent *(G-4883)*
Gbc International Bank....G....425 214-8435
Bellevue *(G-921)*
Georgia-Pacific LLC....C....360 491-1310
Olympia *(G-7295)*
Great Little Box Co Inc....G....425 349-4522
Everett *(G-3506)*
Heritage Gbc....G....360 392-8541
Bellingham *(G-1369)*
▲ Industrial Crating & Packing....F....425 226-9200
Mercer Island *(G-6467)*
International Paper Company....C....509 765-0262
Moses Lake *(G-6716)*
Kapstone Seattle....G....206 762-7170
Seattle *(G-10327)*
◆ Longview Fibre Ppr & Packg Inc....A....360 425-1550
Longview *(G-5930)*
Longview Fibre Ppr & Packg Inc....D....206 762-7170
Seattle *(G-10437)*
Medical Equipment Dev Co LLC....G....206 364-3894
Shoreline *(G-11788)*
Menasha Packaging Company LLC....C....425 677-7788
Issaquah *(G-4448)*
▲ Michelsen Packaging Co Cal....D....509 248-6270
Yakima *(G-15618)*
▲ Mystic Ltd....D....425 251-5959
Seattle *(G-10583)*
Orora Packaging Solutions....F....253 796-6200
Kent *(G-5048)*
Pacific Container Corp....D....206 682-1778
Tacoma *(G-13450)*
Packaging Corporation America....G....509 575-3689
Yakima *(G-15641)*
Packaging Corporation America....F....800 223-2307
Algona *(G-73)*
Packaging Corporation America....G....360 891-8796
Vancouver *(G-14475)*
Packaging Corporation America....C....509 545-3202
Wallula *(G-14910)*
Port Townsend Holdings Co Inc....B....360 385-3170
Port Townsend *(G-7911)*
RTS Packaging LLC....G....206 575-0380
Tukwila *(G-13808)*
Sonoco Products Company....D....360 225-1500
Woodland *(G-15466)*
Sp Holdings Inc....E....509 924-7623
Spokane Valley *(G-12881)*
Sp Holdings Inc....C....425 291-3500
Renton *(G-8918)*
▲ Unilode AVI Solution US Inc....F....206 824-7123
Auburn *(G-587)*
Westrock Rkt Company....E....425 885-5851
Redmond *(G-8712)*
Weyerhaeuser Co....G....425 455-1111
Bellevue *(G-1226)*
Weyerhaeuser Company....C....360 491-1200
Olympia *(G-7425)*
Weyerhaeuser Company....C....509 453-4741
Union Gap *(G-13956)*

2655 Fiber Cans, Tubes & Drums

Adaptive Cargo Solutions LLC....F....240 475-6521
Everett *(G-3360)*
Caraustar Industrial and Con....D....253 627-1197
Tacoma *(G-13221)*
Caraustar Industrial and Con....E....253 272-1648
Tacoma *(G-13222)*
Caraustar Industries Inc....F....253 272-1648
Tacoma *(G-13223)*
Cascades Sonoco Inc....E....253 584-4295
Tacoma *(G-13228)*
Greif Brothers Distribution....G....360 225-9995
Woodland *(G-15437)*
JC Global Supply LLC....G....253 275-6093
Kent *(G-4966)*
LP Composites Inc....F....509 493-4447
Bingen *(G-1639)*
▼ Nelson-Ball Paper Products....C....360 423-3420
Longview *(G-5933)*
◆ Olde English Crackers Inc....G....360 715-2972
Bellingham *(G-1478)*
Pac Rite Inc....G....253 833-7071
Puyallup *(G-8215)*
Pacific Paper Tube Inc....F....253 872-7981
Kent *(G-5057)*
▲ Paneltech Intl Holdings Inc....F....360 538-1480
Hoquiam *(G-4354)*
Sonoco Products Company....D....360 225-1500
Woodland *(G-15466)*
Technical Tooling LLC....G....253 327-1149
Tacoma *(G-13552)*
Tetra Pak Materials LP....C....360 693-3664
Vancouver *(G-14633)*

2656 Sanitary Food Containers

Dart Container Corp Georgia....E....360 352-7045
Tumwater *(G-13870)*
▲ Eagle Bev & Accessory Pdts LLC....D....253 867-6134
Kent *(G-4881)*
Nanofiber Tech Inc....G....206 781-9288
Seattle *(G-10585)*
Sheng Mian North America LLC....G....215 519-5895
Bellevue *(G-1128)*
Stark Raving Foods LLC....G....425 361-7640
Everett *(G-3621)*
Tetra Pak Materials LP....C....360 693-3664
Vancouver *(G-14633)*

2657 Folding Paperboard Boxes

Charles Hanson....G....360 871-2173
Port Orchard *(G-7797)*
Decomp....G....360 306-8516
Bellingham *(G-1321)*
Graphic Packaging Intl Inc....C....425 235-3300
Renton *(G-8812)*
◆ Michelsen Packaging Company....C....509 248-6270
Yakima *(G-15619)*
Nippon Dynawave Packg Co LLC....A....360 425-2150
Longview *(G-5935)*
Sonderen Packaging Inc....C....509 487-1632
Spokane *(G-12510)*
▲ Trojan Lithograph Corporation....C....425 873-2200
Renton *(G-8933)*
X Tracted....G....206 294-3308
Seattle *(G-11502)*

2671 Paper Coating & Laminating for Packaging

Adhesive Products Inc....F....206 762-7459
Seattle *(G-9352)*
Alliance Packaging LLC....D....509 924-7623
Spokane Valley *(G-12605)*
▲ Allpak Container LLC....D....425 227-0400
Renton *(G-8739)*
Atlas Pacific Engineering Co....G....509 665-6911
Wenatchee *(G-15010)*
Caraustar Industrial and Con....E....253 272-1648
Tacoma *(G-13222)*
Cascades Sonoco Inc....E....253 584-4295
Tacoma *(G-13228)*
Cassel Inc....C....206 909-9584
Bellevue *(G-841)*
CP Films Custom Printed Films....G....253 261-9404
Kent *(G-4867)*
Csi Group LLC....G....360 334-5455
Vancouver *(G-14157)*
Emerald City Label Inc....F....425 347-3479
Everett *(G-3460)*
Glacier Packaging Inc....F....253 272-4682
Lakewood *(G-5726)*
Hexacomb Corporation....F....253 288-2820
Auburn *(G-464)*
Korblu Mfg Solutions LLC....G....509 930-2010
Yakima *(G-15609)*
Leading Edge Labeling Inc....E....425 821-4137
Redmond *(G-8531)*
Merrill Corporation....C....360 794-3157
Monroe *(G-6596)*
Packaging Corporation America....D....509 545-3260
Wallula *(G-14909)*
Pactiv LLC....D....847 482-2000
Auburn *(G-526)*
◆ Portland Plastics....B....360 887-2230
Ridgefield *(G-9103)*
Sonoco Products Company....D....360 225-1500
Woodland *(G-15466)*
Sp Holdings Inc....E....509 924-7623
Spokane Valley *(G-12881)*
Stafford Press Inc....F....425 861-5856
Redmond *(G-8680)*
◆ Sterling International Inc....C....509 926-6766
Spokane Valley *(G-12893)*
Sutta Company Incorporated....G....253 572-2558
Tacoma *(G-13533)*
Tacoma Rubber Stamp Co....E....253 383-5433
Tacoma *(G-13548)*
▲ Trojan Lithograph Corporation....C....425 873-2200
Renton *(G-8933)*
Western Foil Corporation....G....206 624-3645
Seattle *(G-11452)*

2672 Paper Coating & Laminating, Exc for Packaging

Adhesa-Plate Manufacturing Co....E....206 682-0141
Seattle *(G-9351)*
Adhesive Products Inc....F....206 762-7459
Seattle *(G-9352)*
Avery Dennison Corporation....F....253 872-6993
Kent *(G-4802)*
Caraustar Industries Inc....E....360 423-3420
Longview *(G-5894)*
Decal Factory....G....509 465-8931
Spokane *(G-12222)*
Desi Telephone Labels Inc....F....360 571-0713
Vancouver *(G-14176)*
Fedex Office & Print Svcs Inc....F....360 694-8584
Vancouver *(G-14226)*
Halldata Inc....E....509 588-5080
Benton City *(G-1615)*
Leading Edge Labeling Inc....E....425 821-4137
Redmond *(G-8531)*
Litho-Craft Inc....G....253 872-9161
Kent *(G-4997)*
Northwest Label/Design Inc....E....206 282-5568
Seattle *(G-10646)*
NRG Resources Inc....D....509 588-4786
Benton City *(G-1621)*
Paneltech International LLC....E....360 538-1480
Hoquiam *(G-4353)*
Paneltech Products Inc....E....360 538-1480
Hoquiam *(G-4355)*
Phillips Industrial Supply Inc....F....206 523-0477
Everett *(G-3572)*
▼ Rainier Plywood Company....E....253 383-5533
Tacoma *(G-13489)*

SIC SECTION

27 PRINTING, PUBLISHING, AND ALLIED INDUSTRIES

Westmark Industries Inc ....G..... 425 251-8444
  Kent *(G-5214)*
Wholesale Forms Inc ....G..... 800 826-7095
  Rochester *(G-9145)*

2673 Bags: Plastics, Laminated & Coated

A Well Balanced Home LLC ....G..... 206 280-5532
  Seattle *(G-9327)*
▲ American Plastic Mfg Inc ....F..... 206 763-1055
  Seattle *(G-9394)*
Ampac Packaging LLC ....C..... 253 939-8206
  Auburn *(G-374)*
Chunder Bag ....G..... 253 987-6224
  Renton *(G-8772)*
Elkay Plastics Co Inc ....F..... 425 251-1488
  Kent *(G-4890)*
Envision Inc ....G..... 509 247-5732
  Fairchild Afb *(G-3695)*
◆ Portland Plastics ....B..... 360 887-2230
  Ridgefield *(G-9103)*
▼ STS Trading Co ....G..... 425 830-6368
  Bellevue *(G-1162)*
Top Shelf Closet Inc ....G..... 360 953-1690
  Battle Ground *(G-747)*

2674 Bags: Uncoated Paper & Multiwall

AAA Sandbags ....G..... 509 979-4029
  Spokane *(G-12093)*
Green Label Manufacturing Inc ....G..... 954 445-0001
  Vancouver *(G-14270)*
Hood Packaging Corporation ....C..... 360 695-1251
  Vancouver *(G-14302)*
▲ Portco Corporation ....F..... 360 696-1641
  Woodland *(G-15460)*
▲ Seatac Packaging Mfg Corp ....D..... 253 682-6588
  Puyallup *(G-8248)*

2675 Die-Cut Paper & Board

Arrow International Inc ....D..... 425 407-1475
  Lynnwood *(G-6077)*
Cascades Sonoco Inc ....E..... 253 584-4295
  Tacoma *(G-13228)*
Comeau Lettering ....G..... 360 573-2216
  Vancouver *(G-14141)*
Cowlitz Cont & Diecutting Inc ....F..... 360 577-8748
  Kelso *(G-4521)*
Graphic Impressions Inc ....E..... 253 872-0555
  Kent *(G-4925)*
Nippon Dynawave Packaging Co .....G..... 360 414-3379
  Federal Way *(G-3763)*
Tabs To Go Inc ....G..... 253 854-8227
  Auburn *(G-576)*

2676 Sanitary Paper Prdts

Envision Inc ....G..... 509 247-5732
  Fairchild Afb *(G-3695)*
Feminina Group Inc ....G..... 310 237-5733
  Seattle *(G-9983)*
▲ Five Food Inc ....G..... 509 855-6914
  Moses Lake *(G-6708)*
Georgia-Pacific LLC ....C..... 404 652-4000
  Camas *(G-2254)*
Gerris Dry Bunk ....G..... 509 782-2653
  Cashmere *(G-2320)*
▲ J K Properties Inc ....G..... 360 354-6719
  Lynden *(G-6025)*
Kimberly-Clark Corporation ....F..... 425 373-5900
  Bellevue *(G-968)*
Malone Manufacturing LLC ....G..... 360 366-9964
  Custer *(G-2857)*
Procter & Gamble Company ....C..... 425 313-3511
  Issaquah *(G-4461)*

2677 Envelopes

Cenveo Worldwide Limited ....B..... 206 576-4300
  Kent *(G-4849)*
▲ Direct Connect Group (dcg) LLC ...B..... 206 784-6892
  Seattle *(G-9833)*
Envelope Converting Service ....G..... 206 767-3653
  Seattle *(G-9932)*
Value Plus ....G..... 509 468-0393
  Spokane *(G-12580)*
▲ West Coast Paper Company ....E..... 253 850-1900
  Kent *(G-5212)*

2678 Stationery Prdts

Bechris Inc ....G..... 253 565-0905
  Tacoma *(G-13192)*

Dannys Electronics Inc ....G..... 253 314-5056
  Tacoma *(G-13253)*
File-EZ Folder Inc ....E..... 509 534-1044
  Spokane *(G-12256)*
Paper Delights ....G..... 206 547-1002
  Seattle *(G-10748)*
Ron Hall ....G..... 360 468-2294
  Lopez Island *(G-5986)*
Verzitelle LLC ....G..... 360 829-1628
  Buckley *(G-2079)*

2679 Converted Paper Prdts, NEC

American Paper Converting Inc ....D..... 360 225-0488
  Woodland *(G-15417)*
Caraustar Industrial and Con ....E..... 253 272-1648
  Tacoma *(G-13222)*
Caraustar Industries Inc ....G..... 360 423-3420
  Longview *(G-5894)*
Cascade Paper Converting Inc ....G..... 360 735-1602
  Vancouver *(G-14105)*
Desi Telephone Labels Inc ....F..... 360 571-0713
  Vancouver *(G-14176)*
▲ Go Usa Inc ....E..... 509 662-3387
  Wenatchee *(G-15034)*
Harpo Investment Inc ....F..... 360 532-5516
  Aberdeen *(G-15)*
Intellipaper LLC ....F..... 509 343-9410
  Spokane *(G-12321)*
▲ Label Company Inc ....G..... 206 568-6000
  Seattle *(G-10369)*
Maxcess International Corp ....D..... 360 834-2345
  Camas *(G-2268)*
▲ Merchant Investments Inc ....E..... 425 235-8675
  Kent *(G-5006)*
▼ Nelson-Ball Paper Products ....C..... 360 423-3420
  Longview *(G-5933)*
Northwest Flexo Spc LLC ....G..... 425 776-4315
  Lynnwood *(G-6170)*
▲ Northwest Pioneer Inc ....D..... 253 872-9693
  Kent *(G-5034)*
Pabco Building Products LLC ....C..... 253 284-1200
  Tacoma *(G-13449)*
▲ Pacific Mount Inc ....F..... 253 473-2580
  Tacoma *(G-13452)*
▲ Pacific Paper Products Inc ....D..... 253 272-9195
  Tacoma *(G-13453)*
▲ Paneltech Intl Holdings Inc ....F..... 360 538-1480
  Hoquiam *(G-4354)*
Paper Stuffcom ....G..... 206 462-6079
  Seattle *(G-10750)*
Paragon Industries Inc ....E..... 253 872-0800
  Tukwila *(G-13789)*
Peacetags ....G..... 206 932-8247
  Bellevue *(G-1067)*
Pinatas Tradedia ....G..... 509 836-2442
  Sunnyside *(G-13138)*
Pipe Vlves Fttngs Wrldwide Inc ....G..... 509 991-7191
  Newman Lake *(G-7051)*
Plug Power Inc ....F..... 509 228-6694
  Spokane Valley *(G-12829)*
S J W Studios Inc ....F..... 206 323-8020
  Seattle *(G-11001)*
Seattle Rant ....G..... 206 545-6957
  Seattle *(G-11072)*
Signode Industrial Group LLC ....E..... 360 225-9995
  Woodland *(G-15465)*
Sno King Recycling Inc ....G..... 425 582-2919
  Lynnwood *(G-6201)*
▲ Sunrise Washington Inc ....G..... 360 574-3512
  Vancouver *(G-14617)*
Tabs To Go Inc ....G..... 253 854-8227
  Auburn *(G-576)*
Ultra Paper Co LLC ....G..... 425 443-5505
  Renton *(G-8936)*
Wholesale Forms Inc ....G..... 800 826-7095
  Rochester *(G-9145)*

27 PRINTING, PUBLISHING, AND ALLIED INDUSTRIES

2711 Newspapers: Publishing & Printing

11 Times Creative LLC ....G..... 206 523-2985
  Seattle *(G-9315)*
Advocate Printing ....G..... 360 748-3335
  Chehalis *(G-2458)*
Allied Daily Newspapers Wash ....G..... 360 943-9960
  Olympia *(G-7223)*
Animal People Inc ....G..... 360 579-2505
  Clinton *(G-2683)*

Avaric Letter Press ....G..... 360 836-5993
  Vancouver *(G-14047)*
Beacon Publishing Inc ....F..... 425 347-1711
  Mukilteo *(G-6897)*
Bellingham Business Journal ....G..... 360 647-8805
  Bellingham *(G-1263)*
Bellingham Escape ....G..... 360 519-9213
  Bellingham *(G-1265)*
▲ Big Sky Publishing Co ....F..... 406 587-4491
  Seattle *(G-9525)*
Bilingual Press Publishing Co ....G..... 509 483-2523
  Spokane *(G-12147)*
Blethen Corporation ....G..... 206 464-2471
  Seattle *(G-9541)*
Bob Nelson ....G..... 360 795-3391
  Cathlamet *(G-2360)*
Brian Murphy ....G..... 206 323-8001
  Seattle *(G-9584)*
British Footpaths ....G..... 206 525-2466
  Seattle *(G-9587)*
Budo LLC ....G..... 206 854-1161
  Seattle *(G-9594)*
Business To Business ....G..... 360 748-6848
  Chehalis *(G-2475)*
Buy Monthly Deals ....G..... 360 321-6748
  Langley *(G-5771)*
Cabin Fever Media ....G..... 509 544-2155
  Pasco *(G-7557)*
Camas-Washougal Post-Record ......F..... 360 834-2141
  Camas *(G-2237)*
Cascadia Newspaper Company LLC ...G..... 360 647-8200
  Bellingham *(G-1292)*
Casey Communications Inc ....G..... 206 448-5902
  Seattle *(G-9645)*
Catholic Northwest Progress ....F..... 206 382-4850
  Seattle *(G-9647)*
Chewelah Independent Inc ....G..... 509 935-8422
  Chewelah *(G-2600)*
Chronicle ....E..... 509 826-1110
  OMAK *(G-7436)*
Clyde Hill Publishing LLC ....G..... 425 454-8220
  Clyde Hill *(G-2703)*
Columbia Basin Publishing Co ....D..... 509 765-4561
  Moses Lake *(G-6696)*
Columbia River Reader ....G..... 360 636-6097
  Longview *(G-5900)*
Coordinating Services Inc ....G..... 425 334-8966
  Lake Stevens *(G-5640)*
Courier-Herald ....F..... 360 825-2555
  Enumclaw *(G-3283)*
Cowles Publishing Company ....B..... 509 459-5000
  Spokane *(G-12204)*
Daily Bulletin ....G..... 509 397-3332
  Colfax *(G-2713)*
Daily Conner ....G..... 360 643-0056
  Port Townsend *(G-7876)*
Daily Dessert LLC ....G..... 757 746-7744
  Seattle *(G-9785)*
Daily Ellensburg Record Inc ....E..... 509 925-1414
  Ellensburg *(G-3192)*
Daily Herald Company ....D..... 425 339-3000
  Everett *(G-3437)*
Daily Plant-It ....G..... 425 677-4948
  Issaquah *(G-4401)*
Daily Toils & Troubles ....G..... 360 337-9028
  Poulsbo *(G-7957)*
Deer Park Gazette LLC ....G..... 509 276-7737
  Deer Park *(G-2898)*
Der Heintzelmann Inc ....G..... 360 683-4740
  Sequim *(G-11626)*
Devaul Publishing Inc ....E..... 360 748-3335
  Chehalis *(G-2489)*
Double Up LLC ....G..... 908 398-9088
  Sammamish *(G-9202)*
Douglas Green ....G..... 360 260-9708
  Vancouver *(G-14186)*
Dow Jones & Company Inc ....E..... 253 661-8850
  Federal Way *(G-3731)*
East County Journal ....G..... 360 496-5993
  Morton *(G-6668)*
East Oregonian Publishing Co ....G..... 360 642-8181
  Long Beach *(G-5873)*
East Washingtonian ....G..... 509 843-1313
  Pomeroy *(G-7672)*
Eastern News Inc ....G..... 206 760-9168
  Seattle *(G-9872)*
Eatonville Dispatch Newspaper ....F..... 360 832-4411
  Eatonville *(G-3055)*
Echo Springs Publishing ....G..... 360 417-1346
  Port Angeles *(G-7701)*

Employee Codes: A=Over 500 employees, B=251-500
C=101-250, D=51-100, E=20-50, F=10-19, G=2-9

27 PRINTING, PUBLISHING, AND ALLIED INDUSTRIES SIC SECTION

Ed Print Inc .... F 425 483-0606
Woodinville *(G-15233)*
Edmund Lucy .... G 425 703-4155
Issaquah *(G-4409)*
El Mundo Communications Inc .... G 509 663-5737
Wenatchee *(G-15029)*
Empire Press Co .... G 509 886-8668
East Wenatchee *(G-3011)*
Endex Newspaper LLC .... G 206 322-4194
Seattle *(G-9921)*
Examinercom .... G 206 459-0562
Auburn *(G-437)*
Executive Media Corp .... G 509 933-2993
Ellensburg *(G-3200)*
Facts Newspaper .... G 206 324-0552
Seattle *(G-9962)*
Fanipin Korea Corp .... G 425 218-6555
Mill Creek *(G-6510)*
Ferndale Record Inc .... G 360 384-1411
Ferndale *(G-3844)*
Fishermens News Inc .... G 206 282-7545
Seattle *(G-9999)*
Flint Publishing Inc .... G 509 314-6400
Toppenish *(G-13669)*
Focusbloom LLC .... G 360 894-2362
Yelm *(G-15734)*
Franklin County Graphic .... G 509 234-3181
Connell *(G-2794)*
Frontier Publication Inc .... G 206 463-5656
Vashon *(G-14723)*
Gannett Co Inc .... E 425 391-2530
Bellevue *(G-918)*
Gatehouse Media LLC .... F 360 532-4000
Aberdeen *(G-13)*
Giraffe Project .... G 360 221-7989
Langley *(G-5778)*
Golden Child Inc .... G 206 901-9502
Seattle *(G-10094)*
Goldendale Grapplers .... G 509 314-9975
Goldendale *(G-4198)*
Goldendale Sentinel Inc .... G 509 773-3777
Goldendale *(G-4199)*
▲ **Good News Church** .... G 509 544-0938
Pasco *(G-7587)*
▲ **Grand Image Ltd** .... F 206 624-0444
Seattle *(G-10107)*
Greenleaf Publishing Inc .... G 509 427-8444
Stevenson *(G-13012)*
Gutsy Services LLC .... G 503 750-9024
Vancouver *(G-14277)*
Havre Daily News .... G 206 284-4424
Seattle *(G-10151)*
Hearst Corporation .... C 206 448-8000
Seattle *(G-10157)*
Hearst Seattle Media LLC .... G 206 448-8000
Seattle *(G-10158)*
Herald Cheraine PHD .... G 253 564-1193
Tacoma *(G-13335)*
Herald Classified Want ADS .... G 425 339-3100
Everett *(G-3510)*
Hipple Family Ltd Liability Co .... G 425 432-9696
Covington *(G-2829)*
Hispanic Yellow Pages .... G 206 297-8532
Seattle *(G-10176)*
Horizon of Change .... G 425 355-1712
Everett *(G-3512)*
Horizon Publications Inc .... F 509 276-5043
Deer Park *(G-2905)*
Horvitz Newspapers Inc .... G 425 274-4782
Bellevue *(G-949)*
House Reporter LLC .... G 360 678-4931
Greenbank *(G-4307)*
Index Publishing .... D 206 323-7101
Seattle *(G-10225)*
Inland Publications Inc .... E 509 325-0634
Spokane *(G-12312)*
Inside Real Estate .... G 360 379-0139
Port Townsend *(G-7891)*
International Examiner .... G 206 624-3925
Seattle *(G-10250)*
Investigatewest .... G 206 441-4288
Seattle *(G-10255)*
Issaquah Sammamish Reporter .... G 425 391-0363
Bellevue *(G-963)*
Jason K Miller .... G 360 853-8213
Concrete *(G-2787)*
Jasper Publishing LLC .... G 360 875-8383
Raymond *(G-8355)*
▲ **Joongang USA** .... B 206 365-4000
Edmonds *(G-3126)*
Journal-News Publishing Co .... F 509 754-4636
Ephrata *(G-3339)*
Journal-News Publishing Co .... G 509 725-0101
Davenport *(G-2872)*
Journal-News Publishing Co .... E 509 235-6184
Cheney *(G-2588)*
Katherine Ottaway Dr .... G 360 385-3826
Port Townsend *(G-7894)*
Kaye Mag LLC .... G 360 668-8989
Snohomish *(G-11930)*
Ken Robinson Publications Inc .... G 360 794-7116
Monroe *(G-6585)*
Key Peninsula News .... G 253 884-4699
Vaughn *(G-14747)*
Kingston Community News .... E 360 779-4464
Poulsbo *(G-7970)*
Kitsap Sun .... D 360 792-3350
Bremerton *(G-1970)*
Korea Times Los Angeles Inc .... E 206 622-2229
Seattle *(G-10356)*
Korean Sunday News of Seattle .... G 425 778-6747
Edmonds *(G-3129)*
Lafromboise Newspapers .... D 360 736-3311
Centralia *(G-2415)*
Lafromboise Newspapers .... F 360 807-8716
Centralia *(G-2416)*
Lafromboise Newspapers .... F 360 458-2681
Yelm *(G-15737)*
Lee Enterprises Incorporated .... G 509 783-5555
Kennewick *(G-4688)*
Lee Publications Inc .... F 360 577-2500
Longview *(G-5926)*
Letter & Sphere LLC .... G 206 473-7534
Seattle *(G-10407)*
Lewis Publishing Company Inc .... E 360 354-4444
Lynden *(G-6031)*
Little Nickel-Bremerton .... G 360 308-0279
Silverdale *(G-11845)*
Living Snoqualmie LLC .... G 425 396-7304
Snoqualmie *(G-12016)*
Mach Publishing Company Inc .... F 425 258-9396
Snohomish *(G-11941)*
Maine Marketing Inc .... G 425 487-9111
Woodinville *(G-15300)*
Market Place Weekly Inc .... F 360 568-4121
Snohomish *(G-11943)*
McClatchy Newspapers Inc .... C 509 582-1500
Kennewick *(G-4693)*
McClatchy Newspapers Inc .... C 360 676-2600
Bellingham *(G-1428)*
McClatchy Newspapers Inc .... C 360 754-5400
Olympia *(G-7333)*
Methow Valley Publishing LLC .... F 509 997-7011
Twisp *(G-13915)*
Mid-Columbia Newspaper Pubhs .... G 509 845-5253
Kennewick *(G-4694)*
Morning News Tribune .... G 253 597-8511
Tacoma *(G-13420)*
Motorsports .... G 360 799-0865
Sultan *(G-13029)*
Mukilteo Beacon .... G 425 347-5634
Mukilteo *(G-6954)*
Ncw Media Inc .... G 509 548-5286
Leavenworth *(G-5811)*
Ncw Media Inc .... G 509 782-3781
Cashmere *(G-2327)*
News Trbune Schlrship Fndation .... G 253 597-8593
Tacoma *(G-13427)*
News Tribune The 1950 S .... G 253 841-2481
Puyallup *(G-8199)*
Nguoi Viet Ngay Nay .... G 206 725-8384
Seattle *(G-10606)*
Nickel One Ad Newspaper .... G 360 423-3141
Kennewick *(G-4702)*
Night Shift LLC .... G 206 334-2548
Tukwila *(G-13778)*
North American Post Publishing .... G 206 726-6460
Seattle *(G-10623)*
North Beach Media Inc .... G 360 289-2441
Ocean Shores *(G-7188)*
North Cascades Broadcasting .... G 509 826-0100
OMAK *(G-7439)*
Northern Kittitas Cnty Tribune .... G 509 674-2511
Cle Elum *(G-2673)*
Northsound Shopping .... G 425 258-3455
Everett *(G-3554)*
Northwest Flyer Inc .... G 253 471-9888
Lakewood *(G-5742)*
Northwest Media Washington LP .... E 360 681-2390
Sequim *(G-11653)*
Northwest Media Washington LP .... G 425 274-4782
Bellevue *(G-1036)*
Northwest Parents Media .... F 206 842-8500
Bainbridge Island *(G-655)*
Northwest Prime Time .... G 206 824-8600
Des Moines *(G-2941)*
Northwest Publications Inc .... G 360 379-4080
Port Townsend *(G-7901)*
Northwest Satellite Network .... G 425 885-5986
Bellevue *(G-1037)*
Nw Asian Weekly .... G 206 223-5559
Seattle *(G-10672)*
Obituaries and Legals .... G 253 597-8605
Tacoma *(G-13440)*
Odessa Record .... G 509 982-2632
Odessa *(G-7191)*
OfficeMax North America Inc .... E 360 455-4068
Lacey *(G-5572)*
Olympian Newspaper .... G 360 754-5402
Olympia *(G-7355)*
Olympic Cascade Publishing .... E 253 274-7344
Tacoma *(G-13442)*
Olympic View Publishing LLC .... G 360 374-3311
Forks *(G-4014)*
Olympic View Publishing LLC .... E 360 683-3311
Sequim *(G-11655)*
Orcas Island Growlers .... G 360 927-9265
Bellingham *(G-1481)*
Orcas Memories LLC .... G 650 325-9400
Eastsound *(G-3043)*
Oroville Gazette Inc .... G 509 476-3602
Oroville *(G-7470)*
Pacific Northwest Newspaper .... G 206 448-8125
Seattle *(G-10737)*
Pacific Pilot Services LLC .... G 509 899-0858
Ellensburg *(G-3216)*
Page Editorial .... G 253 597-8634
Tacoma *(G-13456)*
Paper Panduh .... G 206 538-0202
Seattle *(G-10749)*
Pareto-Curve Marketing Inc .... G 360 357-1000
Tumwater *(G-13889)*
Paul Middlewood .... G 425 778-4771
Mountlake Terrace *(G-6866)*
Paul Razore .... G 360 734-4845
Bellingham *(G-1492)*
Penny Savers .... G 360 723-0740
Battle Ground *(G-731)*
Periodico Laraza .... G 253 961-5008
Fife *(G-3979)*
Phuong Dng Times .... G 206 760-9168
Seattle *(G-10798)*
Point Roberts Press Inc .... G 360 945-0413
Blaine *(G-1696)*
Port Townsend Publishing Co .... E 360 385-2900
Port Townsend *(G-7913)*
Prentis Literary LLC .... G 425 260-7753
Kent *(G-5080)*
Prosser Grandview-Publishers .... F 509 786-1711
Prosser *(G-8063)*
R R Donnelley & Sons Company .... G 206 587-0278
Seattle *(G-10911)*
Randomalities .... G 253 954-5704
Puyallup *(G-8235)*
Ranger Publishing Company Inc .... F 253 584-1212
Steilacoom *(G-13006)*
Ranger Publishing Inc .... F 253 964-2680
Dupont *(G-2972)*
Real Fine Publishing .... G 253 318-6553
University Place *(G-13979)*
Remote View Daily LLC .... G 360 458-5318
Yelm *(G-15744)*
Resisters .... G 206 722-3482
Seattle *(G-10950)*
Return My Life LLC .... G 360 584-9799
Olympia *(G-7383)*
Royal Register .... G 509 770-8221
Moses Lake *(G-6746)*
Ruser Publications Inc .... G 509 659-1020
Ritzville *(G-9122)*
S J Olsen Publishing Inc .... F 360 249-3311
Montesano *(G-6656)*
San Juan Islander .... G 360 378-2798
Friday Harbor *(G-4056)*
Seattle Business Journal Inc .... D 206 583-0701
Seattle *(G-11049)*
Seattle Chinese Post Inc .... E 206 223-0623
Seattle *(G-11051)*
Seattle Daily Journal Commerce .... E 206 622-8272
Seattle *(G-11055)*

27 PRINTING, PUBLISHING, AND ALLIED INDUSTRIES

Seattle Times - Marysville ....G....... 360 925-6324
  Marysville *(G-6384)*
Seattle Times Company ....C....... 509 248-1251
  Yakima *(G-15670)*
Seattle Times Company ....C....... 206 464-2111
  Seattle *(G-11081)*
Seattle Times Company ....B....... 425 489-7000
  Bothell *(G-1791)*
Seattle Weekly LLC ....E....... 206 623-0500
  Seattle *(G-11082)*
Shelter Peak Publishing LLC ....G....... 360 460-0751
  Port Townsend *(G-7925)*
Shelton Publishing Inc ....E....... 360 426-4412
  Shelton *(G-11732)*
Shoezandmorecom LLC ....F....... 216 544-1745
  Renton *(G-8911)*
Ski Journal ....G....... 360 752-5559
  Bellingham *(G-1541)*
Snohomish County Bus Jurnl ....G....... 425 339-3000
  Everett *(G-3614)*
Snohomish Publishing Company ....E....... 206 523-7548
  Snohomish *(G-11983)*
Sound Publishing Inc ....G....... 253 437-6000
  Federal Way *(G-3786)*
Sound Publishing Inc ....D....... 360 394-5800
  Everett *(G-3617)*
Sound Publishing Inc ....G....... 253 925-5565
  Federal Way *(G-3787)*
Sound Publishing Inc ....G....... 360 786-6973
  Lacey *(G-5590)*
Sound Publishing Inc ....F....... 360 779-4464
  Poulsbo *(G-8003)*
Sound Publishing Inc ....F....... 206 463-9195
  Vashon *(G-14744)*
Sound Publishing Inc ....G....... 360 308-9161
  Silverdale *(G-11858)*
Sound Publishing Inc ....G....... 360 378-5696
  Friday Harbor *(G-4059)*
Sound Publishing Inc ....G....... 360 376-4500
  Eastsound *(G-3047)*
Sound Publishing Inc ....E....... 360 675-6611
  Coupeville *(G-2818)*
Sound Publishing Inc ....G....... 360 876-4414
  Port Orchard *(G-7850)*
Sound Publishing Inc ....G....... 425 483-3732
  Kirkland *(G-5467)*
Sound Publishing Inc ....E....... 253 872-6600
  Federal Way *(G-3788)*
Sound Publishing Inc ....G....... 425 888-2311
  Snoqualmie *(G-12026)*
Sound Publishing Inc ....G....... 360 825-2555
  Enumclaw *(G-3321)*
Sound Publishing Inc ....F....... 360 659-1300
  Marysville *(G-6389)*
Sound Publishing Inc ....D....... 425 355-0717
  Everett *(G-3618)*
Sound Publishing Holding Inc ....E....... 360 394-5800
  Poulsbo *(G-8004)*
▲ Souz LLC ....G....... 206 428-8332
  Renton *(G-8917)*
Spokanarama Publishing ....G....... 509 455-8009
  Spokane *(G-12515)*
Stanwood-Camano News Inc ....E....... 360 629-8066
  Stanwood *(G-12995)*
Star Publishing Inc ....G....... 509 633-1350
  Grand Coulee *(G-4244)*
Statesman-Examiner Inc ....E....... 509 684-4567
  Colville *(G-2775)*
Statesman-Examiner Inc ....G....... 509 276-5043
  Deer Park *(G-2917)*
Sun News Inc ....E....... 360 659-1300
  Marysville *(G-6391)*
Sun Newspaper Daily ....G....... 360 792-3324
  Bremerton *(G-2004)*
Sunnyside Daily News Inc ....F....... 509 837-4500
  Sunnyside *(G-13145)*
Swing Fly Press LLC ....G....... 616 540-3836
  Pullman *(G-8110)*
Tacoma News Inc ....B....... 253 597-8593
  Tacoma *(G-13545)*
Target Media Partners ....F....... 509 662-1405
  Wenatchee *(G-15078)*
Telecom Reseller Inc ....G....... 360 260-9708
  Vancouver *(G-14628)*
Tex Ware ....G....... 425 337-3696
  Everett *(G-3631)*
The Pacific County Press Inc ....G....... 360 875-6805
  South Bend *(G-12049)*
Times ....G....... 509 337-6631
  Waitsburg *(G-14757)*

Tjn Publishing Inc ....G....... 360 426-4677
  Shelton *(G-11745)*
Touchet Valley News Inc ....G....... 509 382-2221
  Dayton *(G-2887)*
Tri-City Model Railroaders ....G....... 509 987-7000
  Kennewick *(G-4739)*
Tricomp Publishing ....G....... 509 737-8778
  Kennewick *(G-4741)*
University of Washington ....G....... 206 543-4598
  Seattle *(G-11381)*
University of Washington ....F....... 206 543-2580
  Seattle *(G-11384)*
US Hospitality Publishers Inc ....G....... 615 956-0080
  Vancouver *(G-14657)*
USA Printing Corporation ....G....... 206 682-2423
  Seattle *(G-11395)*
Valley Bugler LLC ....G....... 360 414-1246
  Renton *(G-8941)*
Valley Publishing Company Inc .....G....... 509 882-3712
  Grandview *(G-4256)*
Valley Publishing Company Inc .....F....... 509 786-1711
  Prosser *(G-8073)*
Vancouver Business Journal ....F....... 360 695-2442
  Vancouver *(G-14660)*
Walla Walla Union Bulletin ....D....... 509 525-3300
  Walla Walla *(G-14895)*
Warrior Brown Publishing LLC .....F....... 360 695-2442
  Vancouver *(G-14677)*
Washington Dily Dcsion Svc LLC ....G....... 206 250-1138
  Seattle *(G-11439)*
Washington Newspaper Publisher ....G....... 360 515-0974
  Olympia *(G-7422)*
Washington State University ....C....... 509 335-4573
  Pullman *(G-8114)*
▲ Washington Web Company Inc ....C....... 206 441-1844
  Seattle *(G-11442)*
Whatcom Watch Newspaper ....G....... 360 734-6007
  Bellingham *(G-1593)*
Whidbey Examiner LLC ....G....... 360 678-8060
  Coupeville *(G-2819)*
Whole Shebang ....G....... 360 941-5125
  Sedro Woolley *(G-11580)*
Wilbur Register Inc ....G....... 509 647-5551
  Wilbur *(G-15142)*
Woodys Relics ....G....... 360 849-4257
  Cathlamet *(G-2377)*
World Publishing Co ....G....... 509 884-7575
  Wenatchee *(G-15086)*
World Publishing Company ....D....... 509 663-5161
  Wenatchee *(G-15087)*
Wsu Bulletin Office ....F....... 509 335-2857
  Pullman *(G-8116)*
Yakima Herald Republic-309 ....G....... 509 367-6376
  Yakima *(G-15715)*
▲ Yakima Herald-Republic Inc ......G....... 509 452-7355
  Yakima *(G-15716)*
Yakima Valley Senior Times ....G....... 509 457-4886
  Yakima *(G-15719)*
Your Daily Dose LLC ....G....... 360 749-7414
  Castle Rock *(G-2358)*
Zebra Print and Copy ....G....... 206 223-1800
  Seattle *(G-11519)*

2721 Periodicals: Publishing & Printing

Al Jadid Magazine ....G....... 360 936-1765
  Vancouver *(G-14016)*
Alice E Marwick ....G....... 206 329-9565
  Seattle *(G-9376)*
American News Company LLC .....G....... 866 466-7231
  Fife *(G-3930)*
Andrew Hoover ....G....... 425 869-1123
  Bellevue *(G-788)*
Arrow Point Media Inc ....G....... 425 885-3922
  Bellevue *(G-795)*
▲ Artful Dragon Press LLC ....G....... 800 630-1117
  Sammamish *(G-9185)*
Avalonphilly LLC ....G....... 800 405-7024
  Bellevue *(G-800)*
Bellingham Business Journal ....G....... 360 647-8805
  Bellingham *(G-1263)*
Blue Water Publishers LLC ....G....... 360 805-6474
  Monroe *(G-6555)*
Boundless Enterprises Inc ....G....... 206 789-7350
  Seattle *(G-9568)*
Builders Exchange Wash Inc ....F....... 425 743-3244
  Everett *(G-3403)*
C E Publications Inc ....F....... 425 806-5200
  Bothell *(G-1833)*
Charles Cerar ....G....... 425 392-1821
  Issaquah *(G-4392)*

Cleaning Consultants Services ....G....... 206 682-9748
  Seattle *(G-9692)*
Clintron Publishing Inc ....G....... 509 448-9878
  Spokane *(G-12185)*
Coffey Communications Inc ....C....... 509 525-0101
  Walla Walla *(G-14788)*
Community Values Magazine ....G....... 360 459-8292
  Olympia *(G-7254)*
Crave Magazine ....G....... 360 991-9332
  Vancouver *(G-14152)*
Data Shaping Solutions LLC ....G....... 425 837-4767
  Issaquah *(G-4403)*
Eastside Parent ....G....... 206 441-0191
  Seattle *(G-9873)*
Edwin Laird ....G....... 206 587-6537
  Seattle *(G-9885)*
Elliott Bay Publishing Inc ....G....... 206 283-8144
  Tukwila *(G-13728)*
Everything Quarterly LLC ....G....... 425 478-2173
  Lynnwood *(G-6118)*
Family Values Mag Clark Cnty ......G....... 360 909-5945
  Vancouver *(G-14221)*
▲ Fantagraphics Books Inc ....E....... 206 524-1967
  Seattle *(G-9968)*
Fantasy Index Magazines LLC ....G....... 206 527-4444
  Redmond *(G-8457)*
Farm Aquisition RES & MGT LLC ....G....... 425 869-0624
  Redmond *(G-8458)*
◆ Feral House Inc ....G....... 323 666-3311
  Port Townsend *(G-7883)*
Focus Group Inc ....G....... 206 281-1977
  Burien *(G-2108)*
Fruit Commission Wash State ....E....... 509 453-4837
  Yakima *(G-15574)*
Funny Feeling ....G....... 360 671-7386
  Bellingham *(G-1355)*
G A News ....G....... 253 471-9888
  Lakewood *(G-5724)*
Gildeane Group ....G....... 206 362-0336
  Kenmore *(G-4575)*
Grist Magazine Inc ....E....... 206 876-2020
  Seattle *(G-10125)*
Grow Northwest ....G....... 360 398-1155
  Everson *(G-3678)*
Guild of American Luthiers ....G....... 253 472-7853
  Tacoma *(G-13329)*
Hundman Publishing Inc ....G....... 425 742-1214
  Edmonds *(G-3119)*
▲ Iocolor LLP ....G....... 206 223-1845
  Seattle *(G-10257)*
J & M Reports LLC ....G....... 360 260-8620
  Vancouver *(G-14329)*
Journal of Japanese Studies ....G....... 206 543-9302
  Seattle *(G-10308)*
Kent Chamber of Commerce Inc ....G....... 253 854-1770
  Kent *(G-4975)*
▲ Kiowna Publishing Inc ....G....... 509 947-0675
  Moses Lake *(G-6721)*
Laser Writing ....G....... 253 686-6909
  Tacoma *(G-13383)*
Lenswork Publishing ....G....... 360 588-1343
  Anacortes *(G-140)*
Loggers World Publications ....G....... 360 262-3376
  Chehalis *(G-2510)*
Magazine For Gigging Musicians ....G....... 425 503-0421
  Sammamish *(G-9229)*
Magnet Magazine ....G....... 206 977-7696
  Kirkland *(G-5394)*
Master Printing Inc ....G....... 509 684-5869
  Colville *(G-2765)*
Mj Directions LLC ....G....... 425 656-3621
  Seattle *(G-10549)*
My City Wise LLC ....G....... 206 409-0818
  Seattle *(G-10578)*
Naval Magazine Code 4214 ....G....... 360 396-2187
  Port Hadlock *(G-7761)*
Nickel One Ad Newspaper ....G....... 360 423-3141
  Kennewick *(G-4702)*
Northwest Architectural League .....G....... 206 971-5596
  Seattle *(G-10637)*
Northwest Fly Fishing LLC ....G....... 206 667-9359
  Seattle *(G-10644)*
Northwest Horse Source LLC ....G....... 360 332-5579
  Blaine *(G-1688)*
Northwest Runner ....G....... 206 527-5301
  Seattle *(G-10651)*
Nova Graphics ....G....... 509 251-2575
  Newman Lake *(G-7050)*
Omega Ministries Inc ....G....... 360 477-4180
  Sequim *(G-11656)*

Employee Codes: A=Over 500 employees, B=251-500
C=101-250, D=51-100, E=20-50, F=10-19, G=2-9

Paizo Publishing LLC .....G..... 425 289-0060
Redmond (G-8612)
Pamela McAllister .....G..... 206 783-9534
Seattle (G-10745)
Peel David and Associates .....G..... 425 577-8980
Kirkland (G-5432)
Pgri Incorporated .....G..... 425 449-3000
Kirkland (G-5433)
Phillips Publishing Group .....G..... 206 429-2429
Normandy Park (G-7096)
Poetry Northwest .....G..... 425 388-9395
Everett (G-3578)
Pope John .....G..... 206 320-0686
Seattle (G-10832)
▲ Portland Press Inc .....F..... 253 274-8883
Tacoma (G-13471)
Positive Futures Network .....E..... 206 842-0216
Bainbridge Island (G-660)
Powell Publishing Inc .....G..... 360 886-6650
Black Diamond (G-1653)
Pricemedia Inc .....G..... 206 418-0747
Seattle (G-10858)
Pulse Publications Inc .....F..... 360 671-3933
Bellingham (G-1510)
Redmond Communications Inc .....F..... 425 739-4669
Kirkland (G-5451)
Rfp LLC .....G..... 206 523-8996
Seattle (G-10957)
Rsvp Seattle .....G..... 425 396-7787
Snoqualmie (G-12021)
Saco Sales LLC .....G..... 253 922-6349
Fife (G-3991)
Scotsman Guide Media Inc .....G..... 425 485-2282
Bothell (G-1900)
Scotsman Publishing Inc .....E..... 425 485-2282
Bothell (G-1901)
Seattle Business Journal Inc .....D..... 206 583-0701
Seattle (G-11049)
Seattle Metropolitan .....F..... 206 957-2234
Seattle (G-11064)
Seattle Viet Times Inc .....G..... 425 678-8872
Mill Creek (G-6528)
Second Amendment Foundation .....F..... 425 454-7012
Bellevue (G-1122)
Skt Publishers Inc .....G..... 206 789-8116
Seattle (G-11129)
Sound Publishing Inc .....G..... 253 437-6000
Federal Way (G-3786)
Sound Publishing Inc .....G..... 360 786-6973
Lacey (G-5590)
Stakana LLC .....G..... 206 227-4329
Seattle (G-11179)
Starpath Corporation .....G..... 206 783-1414
Seattle (G-11184)
Steward Publishing .....G..... 206 283-0077
Seattle (G-11193)
◆ Studio Foglio LLC .....G..... 206 782-8739
Seattle (G-11207)
Susney Incorporated .....G..... 253 219-7216
Spanaway (G-12077)
Terry and Kathy Loney .....G..... 509 375-4005
College Place (G-2729)
Tl Gotham Inc .....A..... 206 957-8447
Seattle (G-11303)
Ticonderoga Enterprises .....G..... 509 922-2411
Spokane (G-12556)
Tiger Oak Media Incorporated .....E..... 206 284-1750
Seattle (G-11306)
Toonhound Studios LLC .....G..... 214 733-9626
Bothell (G-1909)
Townsend Ltr For Dctors Ptents .....F..... 360 385-6021
Port Townsend (G-7935)
U S Practical Shooting Assn .....F..... 360 855-2245
Burlington (G-2195)
University of Washington .....G..... 206 543-4598
Seattle (G-11381)
Varsity Communications Inc .....F..... 425 412-7070
Lynnwood (G-6215)
Vernon Publications LLC .....F..... 425 488-3211
Woodinville (G-15400)
Washington Assn Bldg Officials .....F..... 360 628-8321
Lacey (G-5599)
Washington Cncil Plice Sheriff .....G..... 360 352-8224
Olympia (G-7420)
Washington Media Services Inc .....G..... 360 754-4543
Olympia (G-7421)
Washington State University .....D..... 509 335-3518
Pullman (G-8112)
Wenatchee Business Journal .....G..... 509 663-6730
Cashmere (G-2332)
White Light Publications LLC .....E..... 206 575-4236
Renton (G-8947)
Yakima Valley Teen Magazine .....G..... 509 865-4055
Toppenish (G-13676)

2731 Books: Publishing & Printing

A H Tom Publishing .....G..... 360 385-2059
Port Townsend (G-7858)
AAA Printing Inc .....E..... 425 454-0156
Bellevue (G-777)
American Printing and Pubg .....G..... 253 395-3349
Kent (G-4779)
Ampersan Press Inc .....G..... 360 379-5187
Port Townsend (G-7861)
Ananse Press .....G..... 206 325-8205
Seattle (G-9402)
Association For The Developm .....G..... 509 838-3575
Spokane (G-12123)
B Karnes Books Inc .....G..... 360 828-7132
Vancouver (G-14051)
Bamonte A Trnado Crk Pblction .....G..... 509 838-7114
Spokane (G-12138)
Barbara Karnes Books Inc .....G..... 360 828-7132
Vancouver (G-14056)
▲ Barker Creek Publishing Inc .....F..... 360 881-0292
Poulsbo (G-7946)
▲ Bergman LLC .....G..... 206 910-0138
Seattle (G-9515)
Bilingual Books Inc .....G..... 206 284-4211
Seattle (G-9527)
Blind Eye Books .....G..... 360 715-9117
Bellingham (G-1276)
◆ Blue Lantern Publishing Inc .....G..... 206 632-7075
Seattle (G-9550)
Blue Lantern Publishing Inc .....G..... 206 447-9229
Seattle (G-9551)
Bonfire Productions Inc .....F..... 425 748-5041
Bellevue (G-825)
Boundless Immigration Inc .....F..... 855 268-6353
Seattle (G-9569)
Bridge City Publishing .....G..... 360 600-0558
Vancouver (G-14082)
Cadwallader and Stern LLC .....G..... 206 931-8018
Seattle (G-9604)
Calico Press LLC .....G..... 206 855-1903
Bainbridge Island (G-619)
Campbell & Associates Inc .....G..... 360 652-9502
Stanwood (G-12963)
▲ Cascade Publications .....G..... 360 638-0404
Hansville (G-4315)
Cascade Publishing Inc .....G..... 206 430-6021
Seattle (G-9643)
Cedarbrook .....G..... 360 354-5770
Lynden (G-6006)
Celesticomp Inc .....G..... 206 463-9626
Vashon (G-14717)
Center For East Asian Studies .....E..... 360 650-3836
Bellingham (G-1295)
Center For The Def Free Entp .....G..... 425 455-5038
Bellevue (G-846)
Center For Touch Drawing .....G..... 360 221-5745
Langley (G-5773)
Cepher Publishing Group LLC .....G..... 406 889-7583
Everett (G-3415)
Cherbo Publishing Group Inc .....F..... 818 783-0040
Lynnwood (G-6093)
Cleaning Consultants Services .....G..... 206 682-9748
Seattle (G-9692)
Clyde Curley .....G..... 360 738-6862
Bellingham (G-1300)
Code Publishing Company Inc .....F..... 206 527-6831
Seattle (G-9710)
Coffey Communications Inc .....C..... 509 525-0101
Walla Walla (G-14788)
▲ Columbia Games Inc .....G..... 360 366-2228
Custer (G-2854)
Committee For Children .....D..... 206 343-1223
Seattle (G-9718)
Contracts Company .....G..... 360 299-9900
Anacortes (G-116)
Crescent Moon Studios Inc .....G..... 509 322-7730
Riverside (G-9124)
D & E Enterprises .....G..... 509 684-6618
Colville (G-2749)
D Powers Consulting .....G..... 360 341-1533
Clinton (G-2688)
Debbie Mumm Inc .....G..... 509 939-1479
Spokane (G-12221)
Deca Stories LLC .....G..... 302 219-0373
Seattle (G-9809)
Delta Production .....G..... 206 567-4373
Vashon (G-14721)
Djangobookscom .....G..... 206 528-9873
Seattle (G-9839)
▲ Documentary Media LLC .....G..... 206 935-9292
Seattle (G-9840)
Double Vision Partners Inc .....G..... 360 378-4331
Friday Harbor (G-4043)
Douglass Hemingway & Co LLC .....G..... 360 299-0420
Anacortes (G-122)
▲ Epicenter Press Inc .....G..... 425 485-6822
Kenmore (G-4571)
Ex Ophidia Press LLC .....G..... 360 385-9966
Bainbridge Island (G-632)
Farber News Service .....G..... 253 565-1131
Tacoma (G-13290)
▲ Feral House Inc .....G..... 323 666-3311
Port Townsend (G-7884)
Filmateria Studios Inc .....G..... 206 938-6791
Seattle (G-9992)
Fine Edge .....G..... 360 299-8500
Anacortes (G-130)
Forest Publications Inc .....G..... 360 609-4400
Camas (G-2252)
H&H Publications LLP .....G..... 360 730-1206
Freeland (G-4029)
Health Research .....F..... 509 843-2385
Pomeroy (G-7673)
Hoffmann Petra .....G..... 360 321-4733
Langley (G-5780)
Homestead Book Co .....G..... 206 782-4532
Seattle (G-10180)
Houstory Publishing LLC .....G..... 877 962-6500
Ferndale (G-3853)
Hundman Publishing Inc .....G..... 425 742-1214
Edmonds (G-3119)
▲ Illumination Arts Inc .....G..... 360 984-5173
Vancouver (G-14308)
Infomine Usa Inc .....G..... 509 328-8023
Spokane Valley (G-12740)
▲ Intellicard Inc .....G..... 509 965-9266
Yakima (G-15593)
▲ Intelligent Technologies Inc .....G..... 360 254-4211
Vancouver (G-14321)
Jerry P Osborne .....G..... 360 385-1200
Port Townsend (G-7893)
Justice Systems Press .....G..... 360 417-8845
Port Angeles (G-7721)
Kathleen M Sole .....G..... 360 297-4650
Kingston (G-5255)
King Northern Inc .....F..... 520 604-6379
Auburn (G-484)
▲ Kiowna Publishing Inc .....G..... 509 947-0675
Moses Lake (G-6721)
Krimsten Publishing LLC .....G..... 509 786-7978
Prosser (G-8047)
Kurt Blume .....G..... 206 371-9337
Seattle (G-10362)
La Mesa Fiction .....G..... 206 459-2664
Kirkland (G-5378)
▲ Latitude Blue Press LLC .....G..... 360 421-1934
Kirkland (G-5383)
Leading Beyond Tradition LLC .....G..... 425 275-7665
Snohomish (G-11938)
Librofm Inc .....G..... 206 730-2463
Seattle (G-10413)
Living Free .....G..... 360 446-3032
Rainier (G-8317)
Lundquist Joegil .....G..... 425 454-5830
Medina (G-6451)
M B G Management Services .....G..... 360 493-0522
Olympia (G-7328)
Mabo Publishers .....G..... 425 746-9934
Bellevue (G-994)
Macgregor Publishing Co .....E..... 800 581-5040
Mount Vernon (G-6809)
Many Rivers Company .....G..... 360 221-1324
Langley (G-5782)
▲ Martingale & Company Inc .....E..... 425 483-3313
Bothell (G-1776)
Mary Ellen McCaffree .....G..... 253 820-0731
Snohomish (G-11944)
Members Club At Aldarra .....G..... 206 232-8580
Mercer Island (G-6473)
Merril Mail Marketing Inc .....G..... 425 454-7009
Bellevue (G-1003)
Mindcastle Books Incorporated .....G..... 206 801-7338
Shoreline (G-11789)
Northlight Communications .....F..... 425 493-1903
Seattle (G-10635)

SIC SECTION — 27 PRINTING, PUBLISHING, AND ALLIED INDUSTRIES

◆ Northstar Investment Co ....G..... 360 297-2460
  Kingston (G-5258)
Northwest Home Designing Inc ....G..... 253 584-6309
  Tacoma (G-13433)
Northwest Press LLC ....G..... 646 926-6427
  Seattle (G-10650)
Old Growth Northwest ....G..... 206 856-6293
  Seattle (G-10689)
Our House Publishing ....G..... 360 676-0428
  Bellingham (G-1482)
▲ Overdue Media LLC ....G..... 206 860-2199
  Seattle (G-10720)
Oxalis Group ....G..... 509 838-3295
  Spokane (G-12424)
P F M Industries Inc ....G..... 425 776-3112
  Edmonds (G-3142)
▲ Paizo Inc ....E..... 425 289-0060
  Redmond (G-8611)
Paper Jam Publishing Co LLP ....G..... 360 376-3200
  Eastsound (G-3044)
Pathfinder Press ....G..... 360 687-4319
  Battle Ground (G-729)
Pe Ell Pub ....G..... 360 291-2707
  Chehalis (G-2522)
▲ Peel Productions Inc ....G..... 360 256-2450
  Vancouver (G-14482)
Pgi Publications ....G..... 206 588-2968
  Seattle (G-10792)
Pizzicato Publishing Co ....G..... 206 361-0444
  Seattle (G-10819)
▲ Portland Press Inc ....F..... 253 274-8883
  Tacoma (G-13471)
Portland Press Incorporated ....G..... 206 297-1304
  Seattle (G-10835)
▲ Premier Agendas Inc ....D..... 360 734-1153
  Bellingham (G-1503)
Process Media Inc ....G..... 323 666-3377
  Port Townsend (G-7919)
Purple Coyote Inc ....G..... 509 754-2488
  Ephrata (G-3345)
Quantum Publishing Service ....G..... 360 734-2906
  Bellingham (G-1513)
Red Letter Press Corp ....G..... 206 985-4621
  Seattle (G-10936)
Reelworld Productions Inc ....G..... 206 448-1518
  Seattle (G-10940)
Refuge Music ....G..... 425 271-4278
  Renton (G-8892)
Rides Publishing Co LLC ....G..... 206 789-0827
  Seattle (G-10965)
Riggsafe Solutions Inc ....G..... 865 266-9989
  Spokane Valley (G-12852)
▲ Ruth Publishing LLC ....G..... 253 351-2375
  Federal Way (G-3779)
▲ Rw Morse Co ....G..... 360 943-8600
  Olympia (G-7390)
Saco Sales LLC ....G..... 253 922-6349
  Fife (G-3991)
Saint Square Publishing ....G..... 360 636-2645
  Longview (G-5950)
San Juan Naturals ....G..... 360 378-2648
  Friday Harbor (G-4058)
Santoros Books ....G..... 206 784-2113
  Seattle (G-11013)
▲ Sasquatch Books LLC ....F..... 206 467-4300
  Seattle (G-11015)
Scholastic Inc ....G..... 509 926-4465
  Spokane Valley (G-12861)
Seventy Frth St Prductions LLC ....G..... 206 781-1447
  Seattle (G-11093)
Shiloh Publishing ....G..... 800 607-6195
  Vancouver (G-14582)
Silver Lake Publishing ....G..... 360 532-0308
  Aberdeen (G-35)
Simply Wonder LLC ....G..... 360 866-2482
  Olympia (G-7395)
Snohomish Publishing Company ....E..... 206 523-7548
  Snohomish (G-11983)
Sound Publishing Inc ....F..... 360 779-4464
  Poulsbo (G-8003)
Sound Publishing Inc ....F..... 206 463-9195
  Vashon (G-14744)
Sound Publishing Inc ....G..... 360 376-4500
  Eastsound (G-3047)
Sound Publishing Inc ....E..... 360 675-6611
  Coupeville (G-2818)
St Helens Press ....G..... 360 687-1717
  Battle Ground (G-741)
Statesman-Examiner Inc ....E..... 509 684-4567
  Colville (G-2775)

Storytellers Ink Inc ....G..... 206 365-8265
  Seattle (G-11200)
Susney Incorporated ....G..... 253 219-7216
  Spanaway (G-12077)
Tassels & Wings Publishing ....G..... 206 725-5075
  Seattle (G-11270)
Test Best International Inc ....F..... 360 650-0671
  Bellingham (G-1567)
Thinking Cap Solutions In ....G..... 360 452-6159
  Port Angeles (G-7749)
Trillium Custom Software Inc ....G..... 425 397-8000
  Snohomish (G-11994)
Turtleback Press ....G..... 360 376-4625
  Eastsound (G-3048)
Two Sylvias Press ....G..... 360 447-8735
  Kingston (G-5266)
University of Washington ....E..... 206 543-4050
  Seattle (G-11383)
Vidor ....G..... 425 827-9967
  Kirkland (G-5489)
Washington State University ....D..... 509 335-3518
  Pullman (G-8112)
Wesley Todd ....G..... 509 926-0344
  Spokane Valley (G-12934)
Westerberg & Associates Inc ....G..... 509 951-4399
  Liberty Lake (G-5867)
Wild River Publishing Inc ....G..... 425 486-3638
  Bothell (G-1920)
Willapa Bay Company Inc ....G..... 206 465-5616
  Seattle (G-11476)
Wine Erna A I D Inc ....G..... 360 332-4888
  Blaine (G-1712)
Word & Raby LLC ....G..... 206 795-5267
  Seattle (G-11494)
Youth With A Mission ....F..... 425 771-1153
  Edmonds (G-3166)

2732 Book Printing, Not Publishing

AAA Printing Inc ....E..... 425 454-0156
  Bellevue (G-777)
American Printing and Pubg ....G..... 253 395-3349
  Kent (G-4779)
Johnson Cox Co Inc ....E..... 253 272-2238
  Tacoma (G-13364)
Literaryroad Com ....G..... 206 909-1672
  Seattle (G-10426)
Potter & Associates Inc ....G..... 206 623-8844
  Seattle (G-10839)
Ps2 Group LLC ....G..... 206 714-3025
  Redmond (G-8638)
Quarto Pubg Group USA Inc ....E..... 425 827-7120
  Bellevue (G-1090)
United Reprographics L L C ....E..... 206 382-1177
  Seattle (G-11372)

2741 Misc Publishing

▲ 1 World Globes & Maps LLC ....G..... 206 781-1400
  Seattle (G-9314)
7 Ocean Express Inc ....G..... 206 250-9239
  Kent (G-4749)
AAA Printing Inc ....E..... 425 454-0156
  Bellevue (G-777)
Aapkispace LLC ....G..... 425 614-6465
  Redmond (G-8366)
Action Pages Consolidated Inc ....E..... 360 848-0870
  Mount Vernon (G-6769)
Afar Interactive Inc ....G..... 425 442-5101
  Seattle (G-9357)
AG Creative Publishing ....G..... 206 375-0934
  Seattle (G-9358)
Alki Press LLC ....G..... 206 854-1148
  Seattle (G-9378)
Alry Publications LLC ....G..... 206 274-8204
  Seattle (G-9389)
Amaral Music ....G..... 206 853-9847
  Kent (G-4775)
Anagram Press LLC ....G..... 253 310-8770
  Tacoma (G-13171)
Anaphora Press ....G..... 360 379-4004
  Port Townsend (G-7862)
Ann Silvers ....G..... 253 853-7049
  Gig Harbor (G-4072)
Anniversary Year Press ....G..... 360 348-7945
  Monroe (G-6550)
Apollonian Publications LLC ....G..... 206 922-7910
  Tacoma (G-13176)
Arbuckle Press ....G..... 206 409-2091
  Bainbridge Island (G-610)
ARS Nova Press Inc DBA ARS Nov ....G..... 206 783-9671
  Seattle (G-9433)

Art On File Inc ....G..... 206 329-9607
  Seattle (G-9438)
Ascap ....G..... 206 324-0561
  Seattle (G-9442)
Atlantis Publications Inc ....G..... 206 497-0894
  Lynnwood (G-6078)
Avoa Publishing LLC ....G..... 509 594-9778
  Yakima (G-15517)
Azure Fire Publishing ....G..... 206 380-2036
  Shoreline (G-11757)
Banana Blossom Press ....G..... 206 719-3887
  Seattle (G-9490)
Barefoot Btnik Pblications LLC ....G..... 360 275-0798
  Allyn (G-80)
Barnard Press ....G..... 253 851-2208
  Gig Harbor (G-4076)
Bayview Publishing LLC ....G..... 425 282-4640
  Renton (G-8752)
Bellingham Business Journal ....G..... 360 647-8805
  Bellingham (G-1263)
Bent Whisker Press ....G..... 206 914-3556
  Shoreline (G-11760)
Bewitching Moon Press ....G..... 206 380-3807
  Auburn (G-392)
Bicycle Quarterly ....G..... 206 789-0424
  Seattle (G-9521)
Big Door Music Publishing ....G..... 206 890-1269
  Edmonds (G-3096)
Billabong Publishing & ME ....G..... 206 391-8300
  Maple Valley (G-6260)
Blue Lantern Publishing Inc ....G..... 206 447-9229
  Seattle (G-9551)
Bluer Skies Publishing LLC ....G..... 813 675-7588
  Gig Harbor (G-4083)
Bonnie Press ....G..... 360 807-4442
  Longview (G-5889)
Bravo Publications Inc ....G..... 206 937-3264
  Seattle (G-9579)
Brecht-Pacific Publishing Inc ....E..... 360 425-4671
  Longview (G-5890)
Brindle Press LLC ....G..... 360 434-3302
  Seattle (G-9586)
Bunny Bear Press ....G..... 425 894-0944
  Redmond (G-8412)
Bunnybud Books ....G..... 360 293-4675
  Anacortes (G-105)
C & C Associates Technologies ....G..... 509 710-4464
  Cheney (G-2578)
Calkins Publishing Company LLC ....G..... 425 836-3548
  Sammamish (G-9195)
Callidus Software Inc ....F..... 503 579-4484
  Vancouver (G-14090)
Cape Point Press LLC ....G..... 206 324-2126
  Seattle (G-9623)
Capital A Publications LL ....G..... 509 279-0832
  Spokane (G-12168)
Cargo Express Inc ....G..... 253 630-7294
  Covington (G-2822)
Carrolls Printing Inc ....G..... 360 345-1399
  Chehalis (G-2481)
Case Enterprises ....G..... 425 827-2056
  Kirkland (G-5299)
Cedar Coast Press ....G..... 206 451-4568
  Bainbridge Island (G-620)
Cellartracker LLC ....G..... 206 601-7226
  Seattle (G-9651)
Cellular Directory Corp ....G..... 425 646-4917
  Bellevue (G-844)
Center For Religious Humanism ....F..... 206 281-2988
  Seattle (G-9653)
Centricity Publishing LLC ....G..... 360 692-6162
  Bellevue (G-847)
Chin Music Press Inc ....G..... 206 457-8752
  Seattle (G-9678)
Choix Publishing ....G..... 425 821-2752
  Kirkland (G-5304)
Chromaworks Corporation ....G..... 206 622-7107
  Seattle (G-9681)
City of Naches ....G..... 509 653-1400
  Naches (G-6995)
Claudja Inc ....G..... 206 842-6303
  Bainbridge Island (G-623)
Clever Fox Editing ....G..... 805 910-6938
  Snohomish (G-11890)
Climate Publishing LLC ....G..... 206 515-1795
  Bellevue (G-855)
Coastal Cruise Guides ....G..... 206 448-4488
  Seattle (G-9705)
Coffey Communications Inc ....C..... 509 525-0101
  Walla Walla (G-14788)

Employee Codes: A=Over 500 employees, B=251-500
C=101-250, D=51-100, E=20-50, F=10-19, G=2-9

27 PRINTING, PUBLISHING, AND ALLIED INDUSTRIES SIC SECTION

Conlan Press Incorporated G 650 267-9651
Bellingham *(G-1302)*
▲ **Constancy Press LLC** G 206 522-7513
Seattle *(G-9731)*
Copbong428 LLC G 206 778-1436
Auburn *(G-416)*
Copper Canyon Press G 360 385-4925
Port Townsend *(G-7872)*
Corvidae Press G 360 379-1934
Port Townsend *(G-7873)*
Counterbalance Poetry G 206 282-2677
Seattle *(G-9746)*
Coyote Hill Press G 951 295-9552
Camano Island *(G-2210)*
Crystal Triangle Publishing G 360 546-2497
Vancouver *(G-14156)*
Cuddletunes Com G 206 284-4991
Seattle *(G-9764)*
Custom Publications Wash LLC G 509 628-3500
Richland *(G-8986)*
D B Express LLC G 509 265-4511
Mesa *(G-6491)*
Dahlia Press G 206 229-0817
Seattle *(G-9784)*
Dairyland Orthopedics Pubg G 509 868-0096
Spokane *(G-12216)*
Dark Coast Press Co G 206 902-0906
Seattle *(G-9794)*
Debbie Mumm Inc G 509 939-1479
Spokane *(G-12221)*
Denny Mountain Media LLC D 425 831-7130
Seattle *(G-9822)*
Dex Media Holdings Inc E 509 922-1026
Spokane Valley *(G-12681)*
Dex Media Holdings Inc F 360 830-0807
Silverdale *(G-11831)*
Different Drummers G 509 216-2098
Liberty Lake *(G-5830)*
Digital Color Press G 509 362-1152
Spokane *(G-12228)*
Digital Product Studio LLC G 206 484-8439
Seattle *(G-9829)*
Dmfrank Publication G 360 446-6113
Rainier *(G-8314)*
Doremus & Fahey Publishing G 253 507-8848
Lakewood *(G-5713)*
Douglas Green G 360 260-9708
Vancouver *(G-14186)*
Dow Publishing LLC G 425 572-6540
Renton *(G-8787)*
Dragondyne Publishing G 206 619-1577
Seatac *(G-9281)*
Dumas Holdings LLC G 425 576-4227
Kirkland *(G-5323)*
Dunsire Printers Inc G 360 532-8791
Aberdeen *(G-9)*
Eagle Harbor Editing G 206 293-4264
Bainbridge Island *(G-626)*
Ed Stephan G 360 733-4781
Bellingham *(G-1330)*
Edgetown Pubg & Productions G 360 626-1242
Poulsbo *(G-7961)*
Edwin Laird G 206 587-6537
Seattle *(G-9885)*
El Mundo Communications Inc G 509 663-5737
Wenatchee *(G-15029)*
Encore Publishing Inc G 206 443-0445
Seattle *(G-9920)*
Equipment Inc G 206 826-9577
Kirkland *(G-5333)*
Equity Publishing G 509 994-0505
Deer Park *(G-2900)*
Evergreen Eye Center Inc Ps F 206 212-2163
Federal Way *(G-3735)*
▲ **Evergreen Pacific Publishing** G 425 493-1451
Mukilteo *(G-6926)*
Evergreen Publications G 360 734-4158
Bellingham *(G-1339)*
Everlasting Publishing G 509 225-9829
Yakima *(G-15566)*
Evil Genius Publishing LLC G 253 929-6710
Auburn *(G-435)*
Express Messenger G 360 992-9999
Vancouver *(G-14214)*
Family Roots Publishing Co LLC G 801 949-7259
Orting *(G-7479)*
Federal Express Corporation G 800 463-3339
Spokane *(G-12253)*
Fenwick Publishing Group Inc G 206 842-3981
Bainbridge Island *(G-633)*
Ferndale Record Inc G 360 384-1411
Ferndale *(G-3844)*
Final State Press LLC G 253 237-2474
Des Moines *(G-2935)*
First Index Inc E 888 535-8583
Spokane Valley *(G-12703)*
Fisher Publications Inc G 206 923-2000
Seattle *(G-9998)*
Flagship Custom Publishing LLC G 310 245-9550
Seattle *(G-10003)*
Flannery Publications LLC G 360 942-0060
Raymond *(G-8349)*
Fly By Night Express Frei G 360 420-0844
Mount Vernon *(G-6797)*
Flying Trout Press G 360 647-5740
Bellingham *(G-1351)*
For Art Sake Inc G 253 858-8087
Gig Harbor *(G-4101)*
Formula Web LLC G 425 835-3259
Bellevue *(G-915)*
Frog Hollow Press L L C G 509 943-3331
Richland *(G-8999)*
Frogchart Press G 206 284-7156
Seattle *(G-10028)*
From Field G 360 446-7689
Rainier *(G-8315)*
Fruhla LLC G 206 633-4652
Seattle *(G-10032)*
Fundamentals Publishing G 509 334-8787
Pullman *(G-8090)*
G B E Publishers Inc G 360 438-5779
Lacey *(G-5551)*
Gagne International LLC G 360 733-9500
Bellingham *(G-1356)*
Gambia Press Union GPU-USA G 425 357-6483
Everett *(G-3490)*
Gannett Co Inc E 425 391-2530
Bellevue *(G-918)*
Garpike Inc F 206 719-7820
Seattle *(G-10048)*
Geekwire LLC F 206 913-7926
Seattle *(G-10057)*
Gemelli Press LLC G 360 420-7721
Seattle *(G-10058)*
Genoa Healthcare Mass LLC G 425 789-3050
Everett *(G-3495)*
Gfg Publishing F 509 853-3520
Yakima *(G-15575)*
Giraffe Family Press G 360 437-8018
Port Ludlow *(G-7766)*
Girandola G 206 289-0523
Seattle *(G-10073)*
Glen Cove Press LLC G 509 318-5934
Richland *(G-9002)*
Global Press G 425 254-9323
Renton *(G-8808)*
Glori Publishing LLC G 425 202-7714
Redmond *(G-8478)*
Goldfinch Press G 206 696-2933
Seattle *(G-10096)*
Goldfish Press G 206 380-4181
Seattle *(G-10097)*
Gorman Publicity G 360 676-9393
Bellingham *(G-1359)*
▲ **Grand Image Ltd** F 206 624-0444
Seattle *(G-10107)*
Grapecity Inc G 425 828-4440
Kirkland *(G-5352)*
Green Trails Inc G 206 546-6277
Shoreline *(G-11775)*
Greybeard Publishing G 360 495-4107
McCleary *(G-6416)*
▲ **Grief Inc** G 253 929-0649
Puyallup *(G-8160)*
Gsf Publications G 206 789-7548
Seattle *(G-10129)*
H Brothers Inc G 206 999-9837
Seattle *(G-10134)*
Hal Burton Publishing & Dist G 360 877-0613
Lilliwaup *(G-5871)*
Halfmoon Publishing LLC G 360 934-5387
Raymond *(G-8352)*
Harrison Gray Publishing LLC G 206 783-5682
Seattle *(G-10144)*
Haskill Creek Publishing G 509 467-9439
Spokane *(G-12290)*
Healing Mountain Pubg Inc G 509 433-4719
East Wenatchee *(G-3019)*
Hearthland Publishing LLC G 253 588-2149
Steilacoom *(G-13005)*
Heiret Publications G 253 852-1254
Kent *(G-4939)*
Hexagon Blue G 425 890-5351
Sammamish *(G-9217)*
Hibu Inc D 425 454-1762
Bellevue *(G-944)*
Higher Age Press G 425 891-9129
Seattle *(G-10171)*
Highway Shoppers G 360 494-7641
Packwood *(G-7543)*
Hollywood Triangle Productions G 323 301-3003
Seattle *(G-10179)*
Holmes Publishing Group LLC G 360 681-2900
Sequim *(G-11639)*
Hometown Band G 206 842-2084
Silverdale *(G-11837)*
Hot Off Press G 253 255-2829
Graham *(G-4226)*
How 2 Publishing LLC G 360 878-9274
Centralia *(G-2408)*
Hoyem Publications Inc G 360 676-0864
Bellingham *(G-1374)*
Hrh Press G 206 781-1279
Seattle *(G-10191)*
Huckleberry Press G 844 344-8344
Davenport *(G-2871)*
Hummingbird Press G 617 921-6502
Seattle *(G-10193)*
Hunt Hosted Solutions G 425 222-0098
Fall City *(G-3702)*
Impact Health Publishing G 509 624-2599
Spokane *(G-12304)*
Imperial Publishing G 800 210-5033
Kirkland *(G-5367)*
Impressions Express Inc G 253 874-2923
Auburn *(G-474)*
Informatica Pubg Group LLC G 480 361-6300
Burien *(G-2113)*
Intention Publishing Co G 206 463-9777
Vashon *(G-14724)*
International Comanche Society G 360 332-2743
Blaine *(G-1676)*
Itty Bits Publications G 360 894-3288
Yelm *(G-15736)*
Jessy Wilkinson LLC G 509 578-1650
West Richland *(G-15097)*
Joyful Noise Publications G 425 774-7078
Edmonds *(G-3127)*
JP Publications G 425 835-0021
Mill Creek *(G-6514)*
Juice & Jam Inc G 206 734-5136
Seattle *(G-10314)*
Jury Verdicts Northwest G 425 487-9848
Burien *(G-2115)*
Jvs Publications LLC G 360 412-0516
Lacey *(G-5561)*
Kannberg Media Corp G 509 468-4226
Spokane *(G-12349)*
▼ **Key Publishing Group LLC** F 360 882-3488
Vancouver *(G-14345)*
Keychain Social LLC G 425 876-3261
Snoqualmie *(G-12014)*
Kingdom Life Publishing G 509 465-0672
Colbert *(G-2710)*
Kirsten Gallery Inc G 206 522-2011
Gig Harbor *(G-4126)*
Kith D Lazelles Nture Phtgrphy G 360 765-3697
Quilcene *(G-8286)*
L & L Ink G 206 605-4561
Snohomish *(G-11934)*
Lab Door Press G 425 408-0672
Woodinville *(G-15282)*
Lafromboise Newspapers F 360 458-2681
Yelm *(G-15737)*
Larson Rv Publishing G 360 733-8576
Bellingham *(G-1402)*
Lawyer Avenue G 425 243-7958
Seattle *(G-10387)*
Lead Cat Press LLC G 206 349-3226
Seattle *(G-10391)*
Lee Enterprises Incorporated G 509 783-5555
Kennewick *(G-4688)*
Leonsdeli Express G 360 863-1998
Buckley *(G-2062)*
Leopona Inc F 206 701-7931
Seattle *(G-10404)*
Lets Play Stella LLC G 206 365-6249
Seattle *(G-10406)*
Lewis and Clark Publishing G 253 631-8712
Kent *(G-4993)*

Lexington Publishing Co LLC ....G....... 425 344-0909
Snohomish ***(G-11939)***
Lexington Publishing Company ....G....... 800 774-1170
Lake Stevens ***(G-5654)***
Life Chronicles ....G....... 253 508-8876
Federal Way ***(G-3752)***
Life Spring Press ....G....... 360 872-8452
Orting ***(G-7484)***
Lifecodex Publishing ....G....... 206 453-0235
Mercer Island ***(G-6471)***
Lifesmart Publication ....G....... 253 851-3169
Gig Harbor ***(G-4132)***
Lightmark Press ....G....... 206 463-0831
Vashon ***(G-14730)***
Liquid Industry LLC ....G....... 206 718-3360
Enumclaw ***(G-3300)***
Literary Fatale ....G....... 425 239-2126
Lynnwood ***(G-6158)***
Litfuse Publicity Group ....G....... 206 947-3743
Seattle ***(G-10427)***
Little Picture Press ....G....... 206 542-7808
Shoreline ***(G-11783)***
Live Music Project ....G....... 206 329-8125
Seattle ***(G-10430)***
▲ **Lone Pine Publishing Inc** ....G....... 253 394-0400
Auburn ***(G-490)***
Low Orbit Publications ....G....... 425 398-0598
Kenmore ***(G-4590)***
Lynnsville Press Patterns ....G....... 360 573-1396
Vancouver ***(G-14388)***
M&L Research Inc ....G....... 877 321-8766
Seattle ***(G-10456)***
Maas Publications LLC ....G....... 425 445-7845
Maple Valley ***(G-6281)***
Macgregor Publishing Co ....E....... 800 581-5040
Mount Vernon ***(G-6809)***
Mach Publishing Company Inc ....F....... 425 258-9396
Snohomish ***(G-11941)***
Mammoth Media Inc ....G....... 206 275-3183
Mercer Island ***(G-6472)***
Markarts Inc ....G....... 425 895-0651
Redmond ***(G-8551)***
Marketech ....G....... 425 391-1886
Sammamish ***(G-9230)***
Marlene Marshall ....G....... 360 733-6479
Bellingham ***(G-1424)***
Martian Publishing LLC ....G....... 425 572-0743
Renton ***(G-8848)***
Math Perspectives ....G....... 360 715-2782
Bellingham ***(G-1426)***
Mathemechanix ....G....... 360 944-2029
Vancouver ***(G-14399)***
Max Monitor & Publications LLC ....G....... 206 280-6489
Seattle ***(G-10504)***
MC Publishing LLC ....G....... 253 678-3105
Puyallup ***(G-8186)***
Mdr Publishing ....G....... 360 691-5908
Granite Falls ***(G-4280)***
Media Directed Inc ....G....... 509 886-5759
East Wenatchee ***(G-3024)***
Mediterranean Express ....G....... 206 860-3989
Seattle ***(G-10514)***
Melange Publishing ....G....... 360 387-2395
Camano Island ***(G-2217)***
Mfml Publishing ....G....... 360 603-6148
Bellingham ***(G-1434)***
Mike Montgomery ....G....... 206 306-4599
Seattle ***(G-10542)***
Mindware Inc ....G....... 425 415-3921
Kenmore ***(G-4593)***
Mitchell Osborne ....G....... 360 379-2427
Port Townsend ***(G-7898)***
Mobile Game Partners LLC ....G....... 310 926-3932
Woodinville ***(G-15313)***
Mogul Express ....G....... 206 386-8070
Seattle ***(G-10556)***
Momma DOT Publishing LLC ....G....... 425 322-3486
Lake Stevens ***(G-5663)***
Mondello Publishing ....G....... 425 775-9695
Lynnwood ***(G-6166)***
Moon Donkey Press LLC ....G....... 425 990-8149
Clyde Hill ***(G-2704)***
Mtd Publishing ....G....... 509 525-7289
Walla Walla ***(G-14848)***
Multiple Streams Marketin ....G....... 206 650-6769
Shoreline ***(G-11791)***
Myyearlook ....G....... 303 523-2468
Port Orchard ***(G-7832)***
Nabat Publishing ....G....... 509 869-8707
Spokane ***(G-12400)***
Natural Wonder Publishing ....G....... 253 905-1583
Puyallup ***(G-8197)***
Naturally NW Publications ....G....... 360 332-1777
Blaine ***(G-1685)***
Netherfield Publishing LLC ....G....... 360 903-8512
Montesano ***(G-6649)***
New Foundation Press ....G....... 509 783-5237
Kennewick ***(G-4701)***
Newsdata LLC ....F....... 206 285-4848
Seattle ***(G-10603)***
Newtonia Publishing LLC ....G....... 206 790-6628
Seattle ***(G-10604)***
Nickel One Ad Newspaper ....G....... 360 423-3141
Kennewick ***(G-4702)***
Non Sequitur Music ....G....... 360 733-7145
Bellingham ***(G-1460)***
Noonday Design ....G....... 253 517-8293
Bonney Lake ***(G-1730)***
Noreah/Brownfield Press LLC ....G....... 360 849-4857
Cathlamet ***(G-2371)***
Normandy Press LLC ....G....... 206 285-2881
Seattle ***(G-10621)***
North Cross Aluminum LLC ....G....... 360 821-1481
Freeland ***(G-4036)***
Northwest Company Intl ....G....... 253 365-6316
Tacoma ***(G-13431)***
Northwest Multiple Listing Svc ....G....... 253 566-2331
Graham ***(G-4234)***
Northwest Publishing Ctr LLC ....G....... 206 324-5644
Tukwila ***(G-13780)***
Norwegian American ....G....... 206 784-4617
Shoreline ***(G-11794)***
Nubble Road Music & Pubg LLC ....G....... 206 283-0696
Seattle ***(G-10665)***
NW Publishing Center ....G....... 206 242-1822
Seattle ***(G-10675)***
Oakbridge University ....G....... 360 681-5233
Sequim ***(G-11654)***
Object Publishing Software ....G....... 206 414-9440
Seattle ***(G-10678)***
Occasional Publishing Inc ....G....... 877 373-8273
Seattle ***(G-10681)***
October Mist Publishing ....G....... 206 933-1414
Seattle ***(G-10684)***
On Purpose Publishing ....G....... 206 789-9677
Seattle ***(G-10700)***
One Earth Press ....G....... 206 784-1641
Seattle ***(G-10702)***
Pacific Publishing Studio LLC ....G....... 206 371-5628
Seattle ***(G-10739)***
Page Last Publishing ....G....... 360 289-4165
Ocean Shores ***(G-7189)***
Panesko Publishing ....G....... 360 748-0505
Chehalis ***(G-2521)***
Paradigm Publishing NW LLC ....G....... 206 257-0214
Seattle ***(G-10751)***
Paraversal Publishing LLC ....G....... 206 366-1981
Seattle ***(G-10755)***
Peel and Press LLC ....G....... 206 937-1457
Seattle ***(G-10779)***
Penchant Press International ....G....... 206 687-2401
Blaine ***(G-1694)***
Peridot Publishing LLC ....G....... 509 242-7752
Liberty Lake ***(G-5853)***
Philos Press ....G....... 360 456-5106
Olympia ***(G-7369)***
Piecemeal Publishing LLC ....G....... 425 432-3043
Maple Valley ***(G-6289)***
Pike Street Press ....G....... 206 971-0120
Seattle ***(G-10807)***
Pink Slug Press ....G....... 206 430-2637
Hansville ***(G-4317)***
Platinum Rail Publications LLC ....G....... 360 658-2485
Marysville ***(G-6369)***
Pleasure Boat Studio ....G....... 206 962-0460
Seattle ***(G-10822)***
Plus Six Publishing ....G....... 360 553-2316
Vancouver ***(G-14490)***
PM Weizenbaum ....G....... 206 427-4127
Seattle ***(G-10826)***
Poetry Posters ....G....... 425 831-5809
North Bend ***(G-7120)***
Point Roberts Press Inc ....G....... 360 945-0413
Blaine ***(G-1696)***
Polyventure International ....G....... 360 898-7013
Union ***(G-13918)***
Ponder Press ....G....... 206 861-0448
Seattle ***(G-10830)***
Post Alley Press ....G....... 206 522-5963
Seattle ***(G-10837)***
▲ **Potluck Press LLC** ....G....... 206 328-1300
Seattle ***(G-10838)***
Powerhuse Brnds Consulting LLC ....G....... 503 317-4925
Ridgefield ***(G-9104)***
Press ....G....... 509 869-2242
Spokane ***(G-12453)***
Press ....G....... 206 290-7392
Seattle ***(G-10856)***
Price Jensen Surveys Inc ....E....... 425 747-4143
Bellevue ***(G-1081)***
Print Guys Inc ....G....... 509 453-6369
Yakima ***(G-15654)***
▲ **Privateer Press Inc** ....E....... 425 643-5900
Bellevue ***(G-1084)***
Promenade Publishing Inc ....G....... 800 342-6947
Burien ***(G-2122)***
Puppy Lunch Press ....G....... 360 651-9957
Arlington ***(G-309)***
Purple Coyote Inc ....G....... 509 754-2488
Ephrata ***(G-3345)***
Quality Code Publishing ....G....... 206 216-9500
Seattle ***(G-10900)***
Raepop ....G....... 206 729-3996
Seattle ***(G-10913)***
Raisy Kinder Publishing ....G....... 360 752-0332
Bellingham ***(G-1514)***
Raphoe Press ....G....... 425 486-5036
Kenmore ***(G-4601)***
Raston Publishing LLC ....G....... 206 962-7839
Seattle ***(G-10924)***
Rauda Scale Models Inc ....F....... 206 365-8877
Seattle ***(G-10926)***
Raven Radio Theater ....G....... 360 943-3206
Olympia ***(G-7378)***
Raya Publishing LLC ....G....... 808 635-5908
Gig Harbor ***(G-4151)***
Razorgirl Press ....G....... 206 290-7990
Seattle ***(G-10927)***
Read E-Z ....G....... 360 708-8491
Sedro Woolley ***(G-11559)***
Red Horse Signs LLC ....G....... 425 415-0654
Woodinville ***(G-15345)***
Redemption Press ....G....... 360 226-3488
Enumclaw ***(G-3317)***
Redmond Communications Inc ....F....... 425 739-4669
Kirkland ***(G-5451)***
Relentless Publishing LLC ....G....... 360 929-7530
Oak Harbor ***(G-7163)***
Retired Gorilla Publishing ....G....... 509 474-9345
Spokane ***(G-12473)***
Richard C Busher Jr ....G....... 206 524-6726
Seattle ***(G-10961)***
▲ **Ronin Green Publishing** ....G....... 206 725-2839
Seattle ***(G-10978)***
Rubythroat Press LLC ....G....... 206 634-9173
Seattle ***(G-10991)***
Russell Lamar Jacquet-Acea ....G....... 206 334-2935
Seattle ***(G-10999)***
San Juan Publishing ....G....... 425 485-2813
Kenmore ***(G-4602)***
Sara Huey Pblcy Promotions LLC ....G....... 206 619-0610
Seattle ***(G-11014)***
Scared of Genre ....G....... 206 227-2574
Seattle ***(G-11023)***
Schedules Direct ....G....... 206 701-7800
Seattle ***(G-11025)***
Scout Media Inc ....E....... 206 313-4932
Seattle ***(G-11033)***
Scribble Sketch Press ....G....... 707 364-4072
Seattle ***(G-11036)***
Seatech Publications Inc ....G....... 360 394-1911
Poulsbo ***(G-7997)***
Serious Biz LLC ....G....... 425 454-1906
Bellevue ***(G-1125)***
Service Surplus & Crafts ....G....... 360 636-0250
Longview ***(G-5952)***
Shamrock & Spike Maul Pubg Co ....G....... 360 734-5778
Bellingham ***(G-1532)***
Sistahology ....G....... 206 604-1418
Seattle ***(G-11118)***
Sitka 2 Publishing LLC ....G....... 425 522-4231
Kirkland ***(G-5464)***
Skagit Publishing ....F....... 360 424-3251
Marblemount ***(G-6307)***
Skyfish Media LLC ....G....... 415 779-2132
Seattle ***(G-11132)***
Slap Stickers LLC ....G....... 971 238-8329
Seattle ***(G-11134)***
Slowpitch Softball Assoc ....G....... 206 719-2161
Shoreline ***(G-11815)***

SIC

Employee Codes: A=Over 500 employees, B=251-500
C=101-250, D=51-100, E=20-50, F=10-19, G=2-9
2019 Washington
Manufacturers Register
575

So You Want To Write ....G.... 760 771-8940
Olympia *(G-7398)*
Soph-Ware Associates Inc ....F.... 509 467-0668
Spokane *(G-12512)*
Sound Publishing Inc ....G.... 253 437-6000
Federal Way *(G-3786)*
Sound Publishing Inc ....G.... 360 786-6973
Lacey *(G-5590)*
Spinning Heads Inc ....G.... 253 219-5457
Tacoma *(G-13524)*
Spokane Athors Self-Publishers ....G.... 509 325-2072
Spokane *(G-12516)*
Star Press Inc ....E.... 509 525-2425
Walla Walla *(G-14874)*
Statewide Pubg - Wash Inc ....F.... 509 734-1186
Kennewick *(G-4730)*
Steck Technical Publications ....G.... 253 630-7279
Kent *(G-5153)*
Stemar Media Group LLC ....G.... 206 877-3560
Shoreline *(G-11818)*
▲ Stitch Publications LLC ....G.... 206 214-5225
Seattle *(G-11196)*
Stover Publishing ....G.... 206 240-2438
Bonney Lake *(G-1740)*
Straight Publications Inc ....G.... 206 324-0618
Seattle *(G-11201)*
Strategic News Service LLC ....F.... 360 378-1023
Friday Harbor *(G-4060)*
Strictly Ic ....G.... 253 941-6611
Kent *(G-5160)*
Study In The USA Inc ....G.... 206 622-2075
Seattle *(G-11208)*
Supermedia LLC ....B.... 425 423-7904
Everett *(G-3623)*
Swanton Hills Press LLC ....G.... 206 972-1205
Seattle *(G-11235)*
T3 Publishing LLC ....G.... 206 650-0535
Woodinville *(G-15384)*
Tagorbi Publishing LLC ....G.... 253 466-3214
Puyallup *(G-8261)*
Target Media Partners ....G.... 509 765-5681
Moses Lake *(G-6752)*
Target Media Partners ....C.... 509 328-5555
Spokane Valley *(G-12900)*
Target Media Partners ....F.... 509 662-1405
Wenatchee *(G-15078)*
Teddy Bear Press ....G.... 206 402-6947
Seattle *(G-11278)*
Tevada Publishing Inc ....F.... 509 783-5455
Kennewick *(G-4734)*
Therapeutae Publishing LLC ....G.... 425 242-1580
Sammamish *(G-9252)*
Third & Wall Art Group LLC ....F.... 206 443-8425
Seattle *(G-11291)*
Thirty Second Streeet Raccoons ....G.... 206 526-8169
Seattle *(G-11293)*
Tiger Oak Media Incorporated ....E.... 206 284-1750
Seattle *(G-11306)*
Tiloben Publishing Co Inc ....G.... 206 323-3070
Seattle *(G-11307)*
Timeline Press LLC ....G.... 425 454-7447
Bellevue *(G-1189)*
Timothy Colman ....G.... 800 631-3086
Seattle *(G-11310)*
Toka Box ....G.... 530 505-1289
Bellevue *(G-1193)*
Top Hat Word & Index ....G.... 520 271-2112
Bellevue *(G-1194)*
Topia Press Ltd ....G.... 360 754-4449
Olympia *(G-7410)*
Touchet Valley Publishing ....G.... 509 337-6631
Waitsburg *(G-14758)*
▲ Tourmap Company ....G.... 206 932-2506
Seattle *(G-11322)*
Transact Communications Inc ....F.... 425 977-2100
Lynnwood *(G-6212)*
Transportation Wash State Dept ....G.... 360 705-7428
Olympia *(G-7413)*
Tri-Ryche Corporation ....G.... 206 363-8070
Seattle *(G-11332)*
Trixie Publishing Inc ....G.... 360 521-8246
Vancouver *(G-14648)*
Tropic Bird LLC ....G.... 360 378-5234
Friday Harbor *(G-4062)*
Trumpeter Public House ....G.... 360 588-4515
Mount Vernon *(G-6849)*
Tumbling Leaf Press ....G.... 425 885-6315
Bellevue *(G-1205)*
Ultra Van Krome Prductions LLC ....G.... 206 859-3459
Tacoma *(G-13568)*
University of Washington ....G.... 206 543-4598
Seattle *(G-11381)*
University of Washington ....F.... 206 543-2580
Seattle *(G-11384)*
USA Printing Corporation ....G.... 206 682-2423
Seattle *(G-11395)*
▲ Valcon Games LLC ....G.... 425 223-4672
Redmond *(G-8702)*
Vanguard Foods ....G.... 206 355-5938
Auburn *(G-591)*
Vbs Reachout Adventures ....G.... 206 365-0860
Shoreline *(G-11819)*
Verizon Communications Inc ....F.... 425 641-5900
Bellevue *(G-1214)*
Veronica Dlndba Gold Star Pubg ....G.... 360 398-2446
Bellingham *(G-1581)*
Veterans Express ....G.... 253 517-3798
Federal Way *(G-3800)*
Viar Visual Communications ....G.... 425 391-8443
Sammamish *(G-9257)*
Visual Communications Dev ....G.... 360 676-8625
Bellingham *(G-1583)*
Vital Force Publishing LLC ....G.... 253 350-6359
Tacoma *(G-13582)*
Viva Publishing ....G.... 360 394-3756
Poulsbo *(G-8018)*
Warrington Publications ....G.... 425 793-9629
Renton *(G-8942)*
Washington Publishing Company ....G.... 425 562-2245
Seattle *(G-11441)*
Washington Publishing Hse LLC ....F.... 425 406-9891
Redmond *(G-8710)*
Westwynd Publishing LLC ....G.... 253 588-3066
Lakewood *(G-5767)*
Whalestooth Publishing ....G.... 360 376-2784
Olga *(G-7220)*
Whidbey Marketplace & News LLC ....G.... 360 682-2341
Oak Harbor *(G-7172)*
White Dog Press ....G.... 800 257-2226
Bainbridge Island *(G-683)*
Whitepages Inc ....D.... 206 973-5100
Seattle *(G-11470)*
▲ Winn/Devon Art Group Ltd ....G.... 604 276-4551
Seattle *(G-11487)*
Within Power Publishing ....G.... 425 241-4214
Newcastle *(G-7042)*
Word Up Publishing ....G.... 253 859-7002
Kent *(G-5218)*
World Trends Holdings LLC ....G.... 559 474-2361
Richland *(G-9055)*
Wow Mom Corporation ....G.... 206 240-4068
Snohomish *(G-12001)*
Wrapper Press ....G.... 425 443-4389
Maple Valley *(G-6303)*
Wrbq Inc ....G.... 509 927-7181
Spokane Valley *(G-12942)*
Wry Ink Publishing LLC ....G.... 206 714-3178
Seattle *(G-11500)*
X Media Communications ....G.... 206 789-6758
Seattle *(G-11501)*
X Press Ink Co ....G.... 253 588-1818
Lakewood *(G-5770)*
Yakima Press Company LLC ....G.... 509 480-0642
Naches *(G-7009)*
Yakima Valley Senior Times ....G.... 509 457-4886
Yakima *(G-15719)*
Yopti LLC ....G.... 347 979-1735
Bellevue *(G-1231)*
You Are Better Publishing ....G.... 425 776-8640
Edmonds *(G-3165)*

2752 Commercial Printing: Lithographic

1 Wild Print ....G.... 360 550-1916
Vancouver *(G-14000)*
3d Mail Results ....G.... 253 859-7310
Kent *(G-4748)*
505 Printing ....G.... 360 864-6510
Toledo *(G-13634)*
A & A Printing Inc ....E.... 206 285-1700
Seattle *(G-9326)*
A & H Printers Inc ....G.... 509 765-0283
Moses Lake *(G-6676)*
A & R Enterprise ....G.... 425 453-0010
Lynnwood *(G-6064)*
A & R Print Services Inc ....G.... 206 321-5263
Buckley *(G-2044)*
A D G Data Systems Inc ....G.... 425 771-7603
Lynnwood *(G-6065)*
A D G Printing ....G.... 425 771-7603
Lynnwood *(G-6066)*
A Plus Printing ....G.... 509 714-5514
Spokane *(G-12089)*
A Printing ....G.... 509 235-5160
Cheney *(G-2572)*
A-K Printing ....G.... 253 391-1784
Maple Valley *(G-6252)*
A-Z Business Forms ....G.... 206 363-8170
Shoreline *(G-11753)*
AAA Printing & Graphics Inc ....F.... 425 454-0156
Bellevue *(G-778)*
Abbotts Printing Inc ....G.... 509 452-8202
Yakima *(G-15498)*
Abbotts Printing Inc ....F.... 509 452-8202
Yakima *(G-15499)*
ABC Printers Inc ....G.... 360 423-6991
Longview *(G-5881)*
ABC Printing Inc ....E.... 360 456-4545
Lacey *(G-5528)*
Abcd Ventures LLC ....G.... 206 686-6089
Black Diamond *(G-1644)*
Abracadabra Printing Inc ....G.... 206 343-9087
Seattle *(G-9334)*
Access Printing Inc ....G.... 425 656-0563
Kent *(G-4756)*
Aceface Printing ....G.... 206 427-2272
Seattle *(G-9341)*
Adam Welch ....G.... 206 329-8697
Seattle *(G-9348)*
Adhesa-Plate Manufacturing Co ....E.... 206 682-0141
Seattle *(G-9351)*
Advanced Laser Printer Service ....G.... 360 835-1824
Washougal *(G-14940)*
Advantage Screen Printing ....G.... 360 425-7343
Longview *(G-5882)*
Airport Prints ....G.... 425 760-2235
Arlington *(G-198)*
All City Print ....G.... 360 718-2448
Vancouver *(G-14019)*
All Pro Printer Service LLC ....G.... 360 818-4592
Vancouver *(G-14020)*
AlphaGraphics ....G.... 206 343-5037
Seattle *(G-9387)*
Alphaprint Inc ....G.... 425 771-1140
Lynnwood *(G-6073)*
Amaze Graphics Inc ....G.... 425 481-8877
Woodinville *(G-15176)*
American Printing and Pubg ....G.... 253 395-3349
Kent *(G-4779)*
▲ Amica Inc ....G.... 253 872-9600
Kent *(G-4780)*
Anacortes Printing ....G.... 360 293-2131
Anacortes *(G-101)*
Andrews Nation Inc ....G.... 360 989-1700
Vancouver *(G-14034)*
Apparel Dude Printing ....G.... 425 283-3051
Redmond *(G-8382)*
Apple Valley Printers ....G.... 509 679-9592
Wenatchee *(G-15009)*
Applied Digital Imaging Inc ....E.... 360 671-9465
Bellingham *(G-1250)*
ARC Document Solutions Inc ....G.... 425 883-1110
Bellevue *(G-792)*
Arch Parent Inc ....A.... 206 664-0217
Burien *(G-2091)*
Arctic Printing & Graphics Inc ....F.... 425 967-0700
Mountlake Terrace *(G-6858)*
Ardor Printing LLC ....G.... 425 786-4361
Snohomish *(G-11875)*
Arrow International Inc ....D.... 425 407-1475
Lynnwood *(G-6077)*
Artcraft Printing Co ....G.... 509 323-5266
Spokane *(G-12119)*
Artillery Graphic Design & SCR ....G.... 360 709-3351
Olympia *(G-7231)*
Asher Graphics ....G.... 206 546-6500
Shoreline *(G-11756)*
Ats ....G.... 360 260-2627
Camas *(G-2230)*
B & B Express Printing ....G.... 509 783-7383
Kennewick *(G-4622)*
B & D Advertising Prtg & Svc ....G.... 206 542-3262
Shoreline *(G-11758)*
B & J Printing Inc ....G.... 360 692-3470
Bremerton *(G-1936)*
B C T Inc ....E.... 206 343-9355
Seattle *(G-9474)*
Ballard Printing ....G.... 206 782-7892
Seattle *(G-9483)*
Bas Inc ....G.... 509 943-2611
Richland *(G-8972)*

SIC SECTION

27 PRINTING, PUBLISHING, AND ALLIED INDUSTRIES

Bastet Screen Printing ...G... 360 880-2717
Seattle ***(G-9499)***
Bay Printing Inc ...G... 360 679-3816
Oak Harbor ***(G-7140)***
Beach Bee Inc ...G... 360 289-2244
Ocean Shores ***(G-7184)***
Belgate Printing & Copy Inc ...F... 425 451-9048
Redmond ***(G-8400)***
Bellevue Printing LLC ...G... 425 558-1862
Bellevue ***(G-814)***
Bellingham Screen Printing ...G... 360 920-0114
Bellingham ***(G-1269)***
Belltown Prtg & Graphics Inc ...G... 206 448-8919
Seattle ***(G-9509)***
Bentson Printing LLC ...G... 253 272-6563
Tacoma ***(G-13197)***
Best Practices Wiki ...G... 206 708-1572
Seattle ***(G-9517)***
Bettendorfs Printing & Design ...G... 509 586-7473
Kennewick ***(G-4630)***
Bigwoods Screen Printing ...G... 253 208-3990
Puyallup ***(G-8131)***
Blanksi LLC ...G... 425 453-1224
Bellevue ***(G-820)***
Blue Print ...G... 425 870-5599
Everett ***(G-3390)***
Blue Prints Plus ...G... 425 888-8815
North Bend ***(G-7102)***
Blue Ribbon Printing ...G... 425 478-7628
Everett ***(G-3391)***
Blue Sky Printing LLC ...G... 360 779-2681
Poulsbo ***(G-7949)***
BNC Printing ...G... 503 318-5916
Vancouver ***(G-14071)***
Bob Nelson ...G... 360 795-3391
Cathlamet ***(G-2360)***
Boruck Prtg & Silk Screening ...G... 206 522-8500
Shoreline ***(G-11763)***
Brands Reco ...G... 360 428-8985
Lynden ***(G-6003)***
Bright Signs Screen Printing ...G... 360 695-6444
Vancouver ***(G-14084)***
Bryan Zippro ...G... 425 881-9780
Redmond ***(G-8411)***
Bte Printing Inc ...G... 360 675-8837
Oak Harbor ***(G-7143)***
Budget Printing & Mailing ...F... 253 872-9969
Woodinville ***(G-15199)***
Budget Printing Center ...G... 509 736-7511
Kennewick ***(G-4636)***
Bulldog Printing LLC ...G... 360 217-7317
Monroe ***(G-6560)***
Cadena Printing ...G... 253 951-7545
Kent ***(G-4833)***
Capitol City Press Inc ...E... 360 943-3556
Tumwater ***(G-13857)***
Carlyle Printing ...G... 360 537-0266
Hoquiam ***(G-4330)***
Carrolls Printing Inc ...G... 360 345-1399
Chehalis ***(G-2481)***
Cascade Printing Company ...F... 253 472-5500
Tacoma ***(G-13227)***
Cascadia Screen Printing ...G... 509 362-8900
Spokane Valley ***(G-12651)***
Cascadia Screen Printing ...G... 541 490-7012
Spokane ***(G-12172)***
Cassandra Watterson ...G... 509 306-0205
Ellensburg ***(G-3187)***
Catholic Printery Inc ...E... 206 767-0660
Seattle ***(G-9648)***
Chameleon Prints ...G... 425 493-3071
Marysville ***(G-6323)***
Chelan Printing ...G... 509 682-5157
Chelan ***(G-2551)***
Child Evngelism Fellowship Inc ...E... 509 662-2320
Wenatchee ***(G-15021)***
Child Evngelism Fellowship Inc ...E... 360 424-1014
Mount Vernon ***(G-6784)***
Child Evngelism Fellowship Inc ...E... 509 928-2820
Spokane Valley ***(G-12655)***
Child Evngelism Fellowship Inc ...E... 425 252-6314
Everett ***(G-3416)***
Clarence H Spargo Jr ...G... 360 532-1505
Aberdeen ***(G-7)***
Clark Office Products Inc ...G... 360 657-2018
Marysville ***(G-6326)***
Classic Printing Inc ...G... 509 452-1231
Yakima ***(G-15533)***
Cleland Investment LC ...F... 509 326-5898
Spokane Valley ***(G-12659)***

Color Art Printing Inc ...G... 206 762-0784
Seattle ***(G-9715)***
Color Press Publishing Inc ...E... 509 525-6030
Walla Walla ***(G-14789)***
Color Printing Systems Inc ...F... 206 763-7704
Burien ***(G-2097)***
Colorgraphics ...G... 206 576-4300
Kent ***(G-4857)***
Columbia Litho Inc ...G... 360 834-4662
Camas ***(G-2239)***
Commercial Printing Inc ...F... 509 663-4772
Wenatchee ***(G-15023)***
Consolidated Press LLC ...E... 206 447-9659
Seattle ***(G-9730)***
Consolidated Press LLC ...D... 253 922-3195
Fife ***(G-3945)***
Coprintco Business Forms Inc ...E... 360 425-1810
Longview ***(G-5902)***
Copy Break ...G... 206 782-7506
Seattle ***(G-9739)***
Copy Co ...G... 206 622-4050
Seattle ***(G-9740)***
Copy Shop ...G... 509 962-2679
Ellensburg ***(G-3190)***
Copy-Rite Inc ...G... 509 624-8503
Spokane ***(G-12200)***
County of King ...E... 206 263-3113
Seattle ***(G-9748)***
Cover ME Screen Printing ...G... 509 552-1940
Clarkston ***(G-2629)***
Cross Roads Printing ...G... 509 328-1627
Spokane ***(G-12209)***
Crown Media & Printing Inc ...G... 509 315-8114
Liberty Lake ***(G-5829)***
Curt Arneson Enterprises Inc ...F... 253 383-4377
Tacoma ***(G-13251)***
Curts Printing ...G... 360 456-3041
Lacey ***(G-5543)***
Custom Printing Company ...G... 206 842-1606
Bainbridge Island ***(G-624)***
Custom Prints NW LLC ...G... 253 225-7725
Gig Harbor ***(G-4093)***
Daruma Graphics ...G... 206 365-5644
Seattle ***(G-9796)***
Deer Park Printing ...G... 509 276-9712
Deer Park ***(G-2899)***
Devaul Publishing Inc ...E... 360 748-3335
Chehalis ***(G-2489)***
Digital Imaging Services Inc ...G... 360 567-1260
Vancouver ***(G-14179)***
Digital Impressions Inc ...G... 206 443-1234
Seattle ***(G-9828)***
▲ **Direct Connect Group (dcg) LLC** ...B... 206 784-6892
Seattle ***(G-9833)***
Dittos Print & Copy Center Inc ...F... 509 533-0025
Spokane ***(G-12229)***
Dl Logos ...G... 360 385-3101
Port Townsend ***(G-7880)***
Dla Document Services ...G... 509 527-7231
Walla Walla ***(G-14797)***
Dla Document Services ...E... 360 315-4014
Silverdale ***(G-11832)***
Dolphin Press Inc ...G... 253 735-1856
Auburn ***(G-427)***
▲ **Domenics Printing Inc** ...G... 425 251-4925
Kent ***(G-4876)***
Donnelley Financial LLC ...F... 206 853-5460
Seattle ***(G-9847)***
Dont Stop Printing ...G... 360 292-8610
Olympia ***(G-7272)***
Dotink LLC ...G... 509 655-0828
Spokane Valley ***(G-12683)***
Dove Printing Inc ...G... 509 483-6164
Spokane ***(G-12230)***
Dr Ventures Inc ...G... 253 874-6583
Federal Way ***(G-3733)***
Dtg Inc ...G... 206 622-4387
Brier ***(G-2019)***
Dumas Holdings LLC ...G... 425 576-4227
Kirkland ***(G-5323)***
Dunsire Printers Inc ...G... 360 532-8791
Aberdeen ***(G-9)***
Duramark Technologies Inc ...G... 206 473-9212
Woodinville ***(G-15229)***
Eagle Harbor Print Co LLC ...G... 970 441-0000
Port Orchard ***(G-7805)***
Eagle Printing Inc ...G... 509 943-2611
Richland ***(G-8991)***
East County Journal ...G... 360 496-5993
Morton ***(G-6668)***

Eastlake Minuteman Press ...G... 425 402-7900
Woodinville ***(G-15232)***
Ecographics Inc ...G... 425 825-1888
Bainbridge Island ***(G-627)***
Edmonds Printing Co Inc ...G... 425 775-7907
Lynnwood ***(G-6112)***
EE Printing LLC ...G... 425 656-1250
Kent ***(G-4885)***
▲ **Emerald City Graphics Inc** ...D... 253 520-2600
Kent ***(G-4892)***
Empress Print LLC ...G... 509 826-5154
Tonasket ***(G-13648)***
Encompass Print Solutions LLC ...G... 425 922-6170
Seattle ***(G-9919)***
ESP Printing Inc ...E... 425 251-6240
Seattle ***(G-9940)***
Esprit Grphic Cmmnications Inc ...F... 509 586-7858
Kennewick ***(G-4662)***
Eternal Color Prints ...G... 360 771-9408
Vancouver ***(G-14207)***
Evergreen Printing & Graphics ...G... 425 338-2900
Everett ***(G-3466)***
Everything Prints ...G... 360 447-8217
Puyallup ***(G-8150)***
Evolution Press Inc ...G... 206 783-5522
Seattle ***(G-9949)***
F D Company ...G... 253 531-7087
Tacoma ***(G-13285)***
Fedex Office & Print Svcs Inc ...E... 509 484-0601
Spokane ***(G-12254)***
Fedex Office & Print Svcs Inc ...E... 253 841-3557
Puyallup ***(G-8152)***
Fedex Office & Print Svcs Inc ...E... 206 546-7600
Shoreline ***(G-11771)***
Fedex Office & Print Svcs Inc ...F... 253 872-5539
Kent ***(G-4906)***
Fedex Office & Print Svcs Inc ...F... 360 694-8584
Vancouver ***(G-14226)***
Fedex Office & Print Svcs Inc ...E... 206 467-1767
Seattle ***(G-9981)***
Fedex Office & Print Svcs Inc ...E... 206 244-8884
Tukwila ***(G-13733)***
Fedex Office & Print Svcs Inc ...E... 253 565-4882
Tacoma ***(G-13292)***
Fedex Office Print & Ship Ctr ...G... 425 641-1174
Bellevue ***(G-909)***
Fedexoffice ...G... 206 467-5885
Seattle ***(G-9982)***
Felony Prints ...G... 509 443-6702
Cheney ***(G-2585)***
Fifty Fifty Print ...G... 360 936-9516
Vancouver ***(G-14228)***
Fifty Fifty Print Co ...G... 360 718-2448
Vancouver ***(G-14229)***
Fine Arts Litho ...G... 360 876-5649
Port Orchard ***(G-7809)***
Fine Print WA LLC ...G... 206 859-8469
Spanaway ***(G-12057)***
Finger Prints of His Grace ...G... 253 514-6150
Gig Harbor ***(G-4099)***
First Imprssions Creative Prtg ...G... 509 483-6822
Spokane ***(G-12257)***
Flake Printing ...G... 425 210-6371
Everett ***(G-3474)***
Footeprints Incorporated ...G... 360 754-8779
Olympia ***(G-7289)***
Footeprints Inc ...G... 360 491-8195
Olympia ***(G-7290)***
Foremost Printing ...G... 206 861-6576
Kent ***(G-4916)***
Forger3d LLC ...G... 425 440-0662
Renton ***(G-8802)***
Four U Printers Inc ...G... 360 671-2032
Bellingham ***(G-1352)***
Fox Printing ...G... 206 595-7055
Edmonds ***(G-3113)***
Freda Britt Prints ...G... 206 409-4701
Vashon ***(G-14722)***
Freedomprint LLC ...G... 860 333-2448
Silverdale ***(G-11835)***
Fremont Printing Co ...G... 206 632-3759
Seattle ***(G-10025)***
Full Color Printing NW ...G... 360 721-2110
Vancouver ***(G-14243)***
Garcia Ink Corp ...G... 425 391-4950
Issaquah ***(G-4417)***
Garland Printing Co Inc ...G... 509 327-5556
Spokane ***(G-12267)***
Garrett Press ...G... 206 362-1466
Shoreline ***(G-11774)***

SIC

Employee Codes: A=Over 500 employees, B=251-500
C=101-250, D=51-100, E=20-50, F=10-19, G=2-9

2019 Washington
Manufacturers Register

577

27 PRINTING, PUBLISHING, AND ALLIED INDUSTRIES SIC SECTION

Gateway Printing Inc G 425 453-3272 Bellevue *(G-920)*
Gill Print G 509 535-2521 Spokane *(G-12274)*
Girlie Press Inc G 206 720-1237 Seattle *(G-10074)*
Good Impressions Inc G 360 225-9080 Woodland *(G-15434)*
▲ **Good News Printing & Graphics** G 425 483-2510 Woodinville *(G-15253)*
GOS Printing Corporation G 253 939-3131 Auburn *(G-454)*
Grandview Screen USA Inc G 360 481-3490 Olympia *(G-7298)*
Graphic Advertising Svcs Inc F 425 688-9980 Richland *(G-9003)*
Graphic Communications G 360 426-8628 Shelton *(G-11698)*
Graphic Communications Inc G 425 251-8680 Renton *(G-8811)*
Graphics Place Inc F 425 486-3323 Woodinville *(G-15255)*
Great White Smile Instant G 253 255-0456 Tacoma *(G-13322)*
Ground Print LLC G 206 852-2622 Maple Valley *(G-6271)*
Hamilton Jan Printing Systems G 425 778-1975 Edmonds *(G-3115)*
Hamilton Printing Systems G 425 778-1936 Edmonds *(G-3117)*
Harbor Graphics Inc G 360 532-1234 Hoquiam *(G-4339)*
Harbor Graphics Inc G 253 858-7909 Gig Harbor *(G-4111)*
Hearn Brothers Printing Inc G 509 324-2882 Spokane *(G-12291)*
Heaton Printing G 360 353-3720 Kelso *(G-4528)*
Heir Wear LLC G 425 760-0990 Snohomish *(G-11920)*
Herff Jones LLC G 425 488-7213 Kenmore *(G-4580)*
Herzog Envelope Inc G 206 618-6765 Redmond *(G-8491)*
Highroad Products Inc G 253 474-9900 Tacoma *(G-13337)*
Hill Print Inc G 425 255-7700 Auburn *(G-467)*
Hilltop Management Inc G 206 933-5900 Seattle *(G-10174)*
Historic Photos Prints Cds LLC G 360 695-6151 Vancouver *(G-14299)*
Hitech Publications Group G 520 378-1155 Lacey *(G-5555)*
Holly Press Inc G 206 623-2444 Seattle *(G-10178)*
Hoof Prints Kitsap G 360 932-3992 Bremerton *(G-1961)*
Hook & Ladder Printing Co LLC G 206 568-0588 Seattle *(G-10181)*
Horizon Printing Company LLC G 509 663-8414 Wenatchee *(G-15040)*
Huskey Printing & Envelop G 206 901-1792 Seattle *(G-10194)*
Im Printing G 206 300-7511 Seattle *(G-10206)*
Images G 509 736-9508 Kennewick *(G-4675)*
Imagine Visual Service LLC G 206 281-5703 Seattle *(G-10208)*
Impression Printing Co Inc G 206 762-6211 Seattle *(G-10216)*
Impressive Printing G 253 538-2948 Tacoma *(G-13348)*
Imprints Northwest G 360 254-8700 Vancouver *(G-14311)*
In An Instant G 206 465-0644 Seattle *(G-10218)*
In An Instant Art LLC G 206 294-3570 Seattle *(G-10219)*
Ink Doctor Printing G 509 237-1644 Ephrata *(G-3338)*
Ink Smiths Screen Printing LLC G 253 446-7126 Puyallup *(G-8168)*
Ink Well Printers Inc G 206 623-1701 Federal Way *(G-3745)*
Inker Prints LLC G 206 499-7379 Seattle *(G-10235)*
Inkwell LLC G 425 277-3655 Renton *(G-8826)*
Inland Saxum Printing LLC G 509 525-0467 Walla Walla *(G-14823)*
Inprint Printing Inc G 509 884-1454 East Wenatchee *(G-3021)*
Instant Access Videocom G 425 273-3496 Newcastle *(G-7031)*
Instant Auction Co G 509 448-0279 Spokane *(G-12315)*
Instant Cheer Illstrations LLC G 206 999-5515 Seattle *(G-10245)*
Instant Gratification LLP G 206 361-2966 Lake Forest Park *(G-5615)*
Instant Imprints G 360 694-9711 Vancouver *(G-14318)*
Instant Option G 509 290-6481 Spokane *(G-12316)*
Instant Press Inc F 509 457-6195 Yakima *(G-15592)*
Insty-Prints G 509 334-4275 Pullman *(G-8092)*
Integrated Print Solutions Inc G 888 716-5666 Everett *(G-3517)*
Iron Street Printing LLC G 360 734-5809 Bellingham *(G-1383)*
Its A Wrap Washington Inc G 425 827-2000 Kirkland *(G-5371)*
J Salgado LLC G 425 367-3188 Marysville *(G-6346)*
Jasper Know Print G 425 486-7147 Bothell *(G-1869)*
Jdkk Investment Group Inc G 253 565-4713 Tacoma *(G-13357)*
Jeanne Jolivette G 360 750-4447 Vancouver *(G-14336)*
Jet City Imaging LLC G 206 447-0600 Seattle *(G-10293)*
Jet City Printing Inc G 425 485-8611 Kenmore *(G-4585)*
Jma Printing G 509 395-2145 Trout Lake *(G-13679)*
Johnson Cox Co Inc E 253 272-2238 Tacoma *(G-13364)*
Johnston Printing Inc E 509 892-2055 Spokane *(G-12340)*
Jomar Holdings Inc G 425 881-7125 Redmond *(G-8521)*
Journal-News Publishing Co F 509 754-4636 Ephrata *(G-3339)*
▲ **K & H Prntrs-Lithographers Inc** D 425 446-3300 Everett *(G-3528)*
K H B Inc G 425 771-0881 Lynnwood *(G-6146)*
Kalastar Holdings Inc E 509 534-0655 Spokane *(G-12348)*
Kennewick Press LLC G 509 491-3801 Kennewick *(G-4682)*
Kewanna Screen Printing Inc G 574 817-0682 Bellingham *(G-1393)*
Kolorkraze LLC G 360 609-2771 Vancouver *(G-14352)*
Kool Change Printing Inc G 360 794-9019 Monroe *(G-6588)*
Kp LLC C 425 204-6355 Renton *(G-8838)*
Kustom Printing Inc F 206 282-8400 Seattle *(G-10366)*
▲ **Kwang Nam Hwang** F 206 433-8811 Burien *(G-2116)*
L & L Printing Inc G 253 848-5546 Puyallup *(G-8174)*
Lakewood Printing Inc F 253 582-6670 Lakewood *(G-5735)*
Lane Chestnut Prints G 206 397-3108 Seattle *(G-10375)*
Laser Printers Plus Inc G 206 786-0107 Bothell *(G-1873)*
Lawton Printing Inc E 509 534-1044 Spokane *(G-12358)*
Leatherback Publishing Inc E 425 822-1202 Kirkland *(G-5385)*
Lewis Publishing Company Inc E 360 354-4444 Lynden *(G-6031)*
Liberty Print Solutions G 509 536-0515 Spokane *(G-12363)*
Lincoln Advertiser G 509 725-8007 Davenport *(G-2874)*
Litho Design Inc F 206 574-3000 Tukwila *(G-13766)*
▲ **Litho Inc** G 206 632-0211 Seattle *(G-10428)*
Litho-Craft Inc G 253 872-9161 Kent *(G-4997)*
Lithograph Reproduction Inc G 509 926-9526 Spokane Valley *(G-12774)*
Lithos Craftsmen Inc G 206 949-9787 Woodinville *(G-15290)*
Lithtex Northwest LLC G 360 424-5945 Mount Vernon *(G-6807)*
Lithtex Northwest LLC F 360 676-1977 Bellingham *(G-1411)*
Livingston Printing Inc F 206 382-1117 Seattle *(G-10431)*
Lj Print Group LLC G 360 852-0914 Vancouver *(G-14379)*
Local Church Publishing G 360 710-8751 Bremerton *(G-1974)*
Logos Church G 425 378-0276 Bellevue *(G-988)*
Lonjina Design and Print G 206 852-6197 Seattle *(G-10438)*
Lori Shine G 360 400-6006 Yelm *(G-15738)*
Lx Packaging & Printing Svc G 206 714-5479 Seattle *(G-10454)*
M C Printing G 360 573-7499 Vancouver *(G-14390)*
Madsam Printing LLC G 425 445-1949 Kirkland *(G-5392)*
Mail Well Envelope G 206 576-4300 Kent *(G-5001)*
Marshall Dt Company F 425 869-2525 Kirkland *(G-5398)*
Marshall Marketing Group Inc E 253 473-0765 Tacoma *(G-13400)*
Martin William Owens G 253 564-5950 Fircrest *(G-4002)*
Marymoor Press Inc G 425 867-9073 Seattle *(G-10495)*
Mass Media Outlet Corporation G 206 274-8475 Shoreline *(G-11786)*
Master Printing Inc G 509 684-5869 Colville *(G-2765)*
Maxart Inc G 425 778-1108 Mountlake Terrace *(G-6864)*
Mc BAC Inc F 360 699-4466 Vancouver *(G-14405)*
McClatchy Newspapers Inc C 360 754-5400 Olympia *(G-7333)*
Merrill Corporation C 360 794-3157 Monroe *(G-6596)*
Metrix Software G 425 361-2415 Edmonds *(G-3134)*
Minute Man Press G 360 738-3539 Bellingham *(G-1436)*
Minuteman Fund of Washington G 253 584-5411 Olympia *(G-7340)*
Minuteman Press G 360 258-2411 Vancouver *(G-14421)*
Minuteman Press G 206 577-9199 Seattle *(G-10547)*
Minuteman Press G 509 435-0863 Spokane Valley *(G-12791)*
Minuteman Press G 360 577-3257 Kelso *(G-4538)*
Minuteman Press Intl Inc G 360 692-3470 Bremerton *(G-1979)*
Minuteman Press Intl Inc G 253 841-3161 Puyallup *(G-8195)*
Minuteman Press Intl Inc G 509 452-6144 Yakima *(G-15623)*
Minuteman Press Renton G 425 251-0781 Renton *(G-8856)*
Morris Printer Solutions G 360 891-3812 Vancouver *(G-14425)*
Mountainview Screen Print G 509 773-6290 Goldendale *(G-4203)*
Mr Print One G 253 693-2802 Tacoma *(G-13422)*
MSC Print House G 206 708-1423 Seattle *(G-10567)*
Nannette Louise Davis G 425 485-5570 Woodinville *(G-15317)*
National Color Graphics Inc F 509 326-6464 Spokane *(G-12402)*
Newman Burrows LLC E 206 324-5644 Tukwila *(G-13777)*
Nielsens Graphic Service Inc F 206 463-2430 Vashon *(G-14737)*
▲ **Norberg Press Inc** G 206 938-3905 Seattle *(G-10620)*

Northwest Executive Corp ..... G 425 883-9010
Redmond *(G-8598)*
Northwest Fine Art Printing ..... G 425 947-1501
Kent *(G-5031)*
Northwest Impressions ..... G 253 474-1119
Tacoma *(G-13434)*
Norwest Business Forms & Sups ..... G 206 938-4387
Seattle *(G-10655)*
Noteadscom Inc ..... G 360 705-4548
Lacey *(G-5569)*
Now Impressions Inc ..... G 425 881-5911
Redmond *(G-8601)*
Nta Inc ..... G 425 487-2679
Woodinville *(G-15325)*
NW Fine Art Printing ..... G 425 947-1539
Redmond *(G-8602)*
OH Snap Prints ..... G 509 901-7719
Yakima *(G-15638)*
Olympic Graphic Arts Inc ..... G 360 374-6020
Forks *(G-4013)*
Olympic Print and Apparel ..... G 206 402-3642
Seattle *(G-10693)*
Olympus Press Inc ..... E 206 242-2700
Tukwila *(G-13783)*
Ooak Prints LLC ..... G 253 886-1539
Buckley *(G-2065)*
Orange Homes LLC ..... G 360 450-4640
Vancouver *(G-14454)*
Out of Woods Printing LLC ..... G 509 447-2590
Newport *(G-7063)*
Overnight Prtg & Graphics Inc ..... G 206 621-9412
Seattle *(G-10721)*
P & Ds IMG-N-That Spcalty Prtg ..... G 509 346-1170
Royal City *(G-9173)*
P and S Print Company LLC ..... G 509 398-6504
Ephrata *(G-3344)*
P I P Printing Inc ..... F 360 456-4742
Olympia *(G-7364)*
Pacific Art Press Inc ..... G 425 778-8095
Lake Stevens *(G-5666)*
Pacific NW Print Flfllment Inc ..... F 509 242-7857
Spokane Valley *(G-12823)*
Pacific Printing Inc ..... G 360 377-0844
Bremerton *(G-1984)*
Pacific Screen Printers ..... G 360 225-7771
Woodland *(G-15455)*
Paradyce Industries Inc ..... G 360 736-4474
Centralia *(G-2423)*
Park & Moazez Enterprises Inc ..... G 206 464-0100
Seattle *(G-10757)*
Pen Print Inc ..... G 360 457-3404
Port Angeles *(G-7735)*
Perfect Press Printing Inc ..... G 425 562-0507
Bellevue *(G-1070)*
Perfect Printing & Signs ..... G 509 786-3811
Yakima *(G-15645)*
Peril Prints ..... G 323 599-1447
Seattle *(G-10788)*
Pickles Printing ..... G 360 456-3230
Olympia *(G-7370)*
Pink Power Printing ..... G 425 295-4324
Maple Valley *(G-6290)*
Pinnacle Printing Foundation ..... G 425 271-7089
Renton *(G-8879)*
PIP Building LLC ..... G 360 961-1702
Ferndale *(G-3887)*
PIP McKay Unlimited LLC ..... G 206 390-0988
Seattle *(G-10813)*
PJ Finney Corporation ..... F 206 282-8400
Seattle *(G-10820)*
Pk Graphics Inc ..... G 425 251-8083
Renton *(G-8881)*
Plese Printing & Marketing ..... G 509 534-2355
Spokane *(G-12447)*
Plese Printing & Marketing ..... F 509 534-2355
Spokane *(G-12448)*
Potter & Associates Inc ..... G 206 623-8844
Seattle *(G-10839)*
Ppcs Inc ..... G 425 883-7464
Redmond *(G-8628)*
Precise Printing Inc ..... F 206 343-0942
Seattle *(G-10846)*
Precision Printing Inc ..... G 360 736-7232
Centralia *(G-2425)*
Pressed In Time Prtg Prmtons L ..... G 253 833-1351
Auburn *(G-536)*
Pressworks ..... F 509 462-7627
Spokane *(G-12454)*
Prestige Copy and Print ..... G 206 365-5770
Seattle *(G-10857)*

Prins Robert P ..... G 360 293-3101
Anacortes *(G-162)*
Prins Williams Analytics LLC ..... G 253 549-0740
Fox Island *(G-4024)*
Print & Copy Factory LLC ..... G 360 738-4931
Bellingham *(G-1505)*
Print & Play Productions ..... G 503 750-5316
Vancouver *(G-14506)*
Print Center LLC ..... G 509 979-8272
Spokane Valley *(G-12839)*
Print Concierge ..... G 206 801-9996
Redmond *(G-8631)*
Print Easy ..... G 800 562-0888
Friday Harbor *(G-4053)*
Print Guys ..... G 509 453-6369
Yakima *(G-15653)*
Print House Inc ..... G 425 742-1434
Everett *(G-3585)*
Print It Northwest ..... G 360 840-0807
Sedro Woolley *(G-11557)*
Print N Surf ..... G 360 693-1710
Vancouver *(G-14507)*
Print NW LLC ..... D 253 284-2300
Tacoma *(G-13478)*
Print Place ..... G 206 878-1380
Des Moines *(G-2943)*
Print Plus Inc ..... G 509 735-6303
Kennewick *(G-4708)*
Print Plus Inc ..... G 509 735-6303
Kennewick *(G-4709)*
Print Pro ..... G 360 807-8716
Centralia *(G-2426)*
Print Rogue LLC ..... G 360 791-0914
Olympia *(G-7372)*
Print Services Northwest Inc ..... G 206 763-9230
Seattle *(G-10860)*
Print Services Northwest Inc ..... G 253 236-8224
Auburn *(G-538)*
Print Solutions and Consulting ..... G 206 726-8053
Seattle *(G-10861)*
Print Stop Inc ..... G 360 354-5100
Lynden *(G-6047)*
Print Tech Inc ..... G 509 535-1460
Spokane Valley *(G-12840)*
Print Time Inc ..... F 206 682-1000
Seattle *(G-10862)*
Print Works Inc ..... G 206 623-3512
Seattle *(G-10863)*
Printcom Inc ..... F 206 763-7600
Burien *(G-2121)*
Printers Bloc ..... G 253 576-6043
Lakewood *(G-5749)*
Printgraphics Inc ..... E 503 641-8811
Vancouver *(G-14508)*
Printing Conexions ..... G 206 383-4516
Bonney Lake *(G-1735)*
Printing Control Services Inc ..... D 206 575-4114
Kent *(G-5082)*
Printing Hope ..... G 253 358-3348
Gig Harbor *(G-4149)*
Printing Ngo LLC ..... G 206 569-8388
Bothell *(G-1890)*
Printing Perfection ..... G 509 843-7455
Pomeroy *(G-7676)*
Printing Services Inc ..... G 253 858-5350
Port Orchard *(G-7842)*
Printing Specialties Press ..... G 509 687-9362
Chelan *(G-2562)*
Printing Unlimited ..... G 360 357-8936
Olympia *(G-7373)*
Printonyx Inc ..... G 360 378-2069
Friday Harbor *(G-4054)*
Printwise Inc ..... F 360 424-5945
Mount Vernon *(G-6826)*
Pro-Litho Inc ..... G 206 547-6462
Seattle *(G-10869)*
Professional Business Svc Inc ..... F 360 352-3000
Olympia *(G-7374)*
Prompt Printery ..... G 509 457-5848
Yakima *(G-15657)*
Puget Bridge Supply ..... G 206 367-3629
Shoreline *(G-11804)*
Punjab Signs & Printing ..... G 425 501-3336
Kent *(G-5089)*
Purely Tangible ..... G 206 301-9999
Seattle *(G-10891)*
Purple Coyote Inc ..... G 509 754-2488
Ephrata *(G-3345)*
Quality Copy and Print LLC ..... G 206 634-2689
Seattle *(G-10901)*

Quality Instant Print ..... G 360 274-0337
Castle Rock *(G-2351)*
Quality Press Inc ..... E 206 768-2655
Seattle *(G-10902)*
Quickprint Centers LLC ..... G 253 531-3105
Tacoma *(G-13484)*
R & R Printing Inc ..... G 206 257-9438
Edgewood *(G-3090)*
Rain City West Printing LLC ..... G 206 767-1151
Seattle *(G-10914)*
Ramax Printing and Awards ..... G 509 928-1222
Spokane *(G-12467)*
Rapid Print Inc ..... G 360 695-6400
Vancouver *(G-14532)*
Record Printing Inc ..... F 509 964-9500
Thorp *(G-13629)*
Refresh Prtg & Promotions LLC ..... G 425 391-3223
Issaquah *(G-4466)*
Reischling Press Inc ..... E 206 905-5999
Tukwila *(G-13805)*
Renton Printery Incorporated ..... G 425 235-1776
Renton *(G-8893)*
Reprographics Inc ..... G 360 423-1237
Longview *(G-5947)*
Restless Prints ..... G 772 205-9868
Seattle *(G-10953)*
Revelation Business Servi ..... G 360 456-1176
Olympia *(G-7384)*
Rgzprints ..... G 208 310-0500
Spokane *(G-12474)*
Richins Printing Inc ..... G 425 776-1800
Edmonds *(G-3147)*
Ridgeline Graphics Inc ..... G 509 662-6858
Wenatchee *(G-15069)*
Ridgewood Industries Inc ..... F 425 774-0170
Edmonds *(G-3148)*
Riley Hopkins Screen Printing ..... G 253 851-9078
Gig Harbor *(G-4155)*
Risque Inc ..... F 360 738-1280
Bellingham *(G-1517)*
Rk Print Group ..... G 206 972-0874
Seattle *(G-10968)*
Ross Printing Northwest Inc ..... E 509 534-0655
Spokane *(G-12484)*
Rotary Offset Press Inc ..... C 253 813-9900
Kent *(G-5107)*
Rss Kennewick ..... G 206 441-9907
Kennewick *(G-4720)*
Ruser Publications Inc ..... G 509 659-1020
Ritzville *(G-9122)*
◆ **Ryonet Corporation** ..... D 360 576-7188
Vancouver *(G-14561)*
Safeguard Bus Forms & Systems ..... G 800 727-9120
Spokane *(G-12492)*
Saigon Printing ..... G 206 722-6788
Seattle *(G-11003)*
Sams Press Inc ..... G 425 423-8181
Shoreline *(G-11807)*
Sanford Art Prints ..... G 509 784-1220
Entiat *(G-3271)*
Saturday Night Inc ..... F 509 928-5816
Spokane Valley *(G-12858)*
Savage Color LLC ..... G 206 632-2866
Seattle *(G-11019)*
Screen Printing International ..... G 678 231-9195
Vancouver *(G-14575)*
Screen Tek Inc ..... E 509 928-8322
Liberty Lake *(G-5860)*
Seattle Custom Printing ..... G 206 268-0443
Seatac *(G-9303)*
Seattle Daily Journal Commerce ..... E 206 622-8272
Seattle *(G-11055)*
Seattle Event Printing ..... G 253 642-6567
Auburn *(G-558)*
Seattle Print House LLC ..... G 503 841-7755
Kent *(G-5125)*
Seattle Printworks LLC ..... G 206 623-3512
Seattle *(G-11069)*
Seattle Signs & Printing ..... G 206 588-5592
Seattle *(G-11075)*
Second Printing Inc ..... G 425 883-2182
Kirkland *(G-5457)*
Selfish Apparel and Printing ..... G 206 450-2725
Snohomish *(G-11974)*
Sensible Horsemanship LLC ..... G 509 292-2475
Elk *(G-3176)*
Service Printing Co Inc ..... G 206 283-6800
Seattle *(G-11091)*
Sharon Rose ..... G 360 341-1898
Clinton *(G-2698)*

Employee Codes: A=Over 500 employees, B=251-500
C=101-250, D=51-100, E=20-50, F=10-19, G=2-9
2019 Washington
Manufacturers Register
579

Shelton Publishing Inc ....E 360 426-4412
Shelton *(G-11732)*
Sign Print 360 LLC ....G 360 578-2476
Kelso *(G-4547)*
Sinbads Custom Printing ....G 253 232-7367
Spanaway *(G-12074)*
Sir Speedy ....G 360 647-7565
Bellingham *(G-1538)*
Sky Printing ....G 206 933-5900
Seattle *(G-11130)*
Sls Development Inc ....G 253 735-0322
Auburn *(G-567)*
Smart Tech 3d Printing ....G 425 614-6451
Renton *(G-8914)*
Snapdog Printing ....G 360 217-8172
Snohomish *(G-11978)*
Snohomish Publishing Company ....E 206 523-7548
Snohomish *(G-11983)*
SOS Printing ....G 360 385-4194
Port Townsend *(G-7927)*
Soterion Co ....G 425 259-8181
Everett *(G-3616)*
Soulier Southbay LLC ....G 360 459-3015
Lacey *(G-5589)*
Sound Screen Printing Inc ....G 206 890-2700
Tukwila *(G-13820)*
Special Edition Incorporated ....G 253 537-1836
Tacoma *(G-13520)*
Spectrum Embroidery & Printing ....G 206 851-9687
Bothell *(G-1796)*
Spectrum Health Systems Inc ....A 253 572-3398
Tacoma *(G-13521)*
Speedy Litho Inc ....G 360 425-3610
Kelso *(G-4550)*
Spokane Paw Prints LLC ....G 509 475-6885
Spokane *(G-12520)*
Spokesinger Prints ....G 206 522-5179
Seattle *(G-11170)*
Spot-On Print & Design Inc ....G 425 558-7768
Bellevue *(G-1154)*
Stafford Press Inc ....F 425 861-5856
Redmond *(G-8680)*
Standard Digital Print Co Inc ....F 509 624-2985
Spokane *(G-12524)*
Stanwood-Camano News Inc ....E 360 629-8066
Stanwood *(G-12995)*
Stat Corporation ....F 425 883-4181
Redmond *(G-8681)*
Statesman-Examiner Inc ....E 509 684-4567
Colville *(G-2775)*
▲ Stella Color Inc ....F 206 223-2303
Seattle *(G-11189)*
Stern & Faye ....G 360 770-1967
Sedro Woolley *(G-11572)*
Stick It Print ....G 360 909-6060
Vancouver *(G-14611)*
Sudden Printing Inc ....E 206 243-4444
Seattle *(G-11211)*
Sun News Inc ....E 360 659-1300
Marysville *(G-6391)*
Sun Printing ....G 253 517-5017
Federal Way *(G-3791)*
Sunshine Prtg & Quick Copy Svc ....G 360 671-0191
Bellingham *(G-1563)*
Superior Imprints Inc ....F 206 441-7147
Seattle *(G-11223)*
Swifty Prtg Dgital Imaging Inc ....E 206 441-0800
Seattle *(G-11239)*
T-Prints LLC ....G 425 780-9380
Kenmore *(G-4609)*
T-Shirt Madness Silk Screen ....G 206 427-8720
Seattle *(G-11251)*
Taylor-Made Printing Inc ....G 253 881-1624
Puyallup *(G-8262)*
Telepress Inc ....E 425 392-1660
Kent *(G-5176)*
The Windward Cmmncations Group ....G 206 382-1117
Seattle *(G-11286)*
Thompson Litho Group Inc ....G 360 892-7888
Vancouver *(G-14634)*
Thought Ops LLC ....G 206 427-0165
Seattle *(G-11296)*
Thunder Specialty Printing ....G 253 921-7647
Puyallup *(G-8263)*
Tiger Press ....G 360 468-3737
Lopez Island *(G-5987)*
Time Printing Inc ....G 206 633-3320
Seattle *(G-11309)*
Times ....G 509 337-6631
Waitsburg *(G-14757)*
Tls Printing ....G 206 522-8289
Seattle *(G-11315)*
Tom & Cheryl McCallaum ....G 360 377-1606
Bremerton *(G-2006)*
Touch Mark Publishing & Print ....G 206 551-0578
Tukwila *(G-13827)*
Touchet Valley News Inc ....G 509 382-2221
Dayton *(G-2887)*
Tracys Print Shop ....G 360 249-5575
Montesano *(G-6662)*
Trade Printery LLC ....G 206 728-1600
Seattle *(G-11324)*
Trade Printery LLC ....G 206 241-3322
Burien *(G-2134)*
Tri-City Tees & Screen Prtg ....G 509 420-6993
Richland *(G-9048)*
Triad Comsural Printing Corp ....F 509 582-1466
Kennewick *(G-4740)*
Tribune Office Supply & Prtg ....G 509 674-2511
Cle Elum *(G-2681)*
Triple P Products Inc ....G 509 527-3131
Walla Walla *(G-14880)*
Triton Print and Pour Poor ....G 360 828-8809
Vancouver *(G-14647)*
▲ Trojan Lithograph Corporation ....C 425 873-2200
Renton *(G-8933)*
Trysk Print Solutions LLC ....G 877 605-1164
Seattle *(G-11345)*
Tumwater Printing ....F 360 943-2204
Tumwater *(G-13903)*
Typebee Lttrpress Prntshop LLC ....G 509 979-6017
Spokane *(G-12574)*
Ukush Print and Mail ....G 206 763-0454
Seattle *(G-11360)*
Unauthorized Screen Printing ....G 425 224-5602
Seattle *(G-11364)*
Unauthorized Screen Printing ....G 425 502-1150
Seattle *(G-11365)*
Unique TS Printing ....G 253 686-3669
Port Orchard *(G-7854)*
United Reprographics L L C ....E 206 382-1177
Seattle *(G-11372)*
University of Washington ....C 206 543-5680
Seattle *(G-11379)*
University of Washington ....C 206 543-5680
Seattle *(G-11382)*
University Reprographics Inc ....G 206 633-0925
Seattle *(G-11385)*
Urban Press Inc ....G 206 325-4060
Seattle *(G-11391)*
V O Printers Inc ....G 360 577-0038
Longview *(G-5962)*
Valley Instant Printing Inc ....G 509 924-8040
Spokane Valley *(G-12924)*
Valley Printing Inc ....G 253 845-0960
Puyallup *(G-8270)*
Valley Publishing Company Inc ....F 509 786-1711
Prosser *(G-8073)*
Van Quill Larry R ....G 360 736-1776
Centralia *(G-2441)*
Varsity Screen Prtg & Awards ....G 509 829-3700
Zillah *(G-15764)*
Veracious Printing LLC ....G 360 823-7395
Vancouver *(G-14668)*
Vessel Printing Studio ....G 360 441-4622
Bellingham *(G-1582)*
Villas Josey ....G 360 405-1944
Bremerton *(G-2010)*
Vintage ADS ....G 253 278-3297
Tacoma *(G-13579)*
Vintage Idaho Prints ....G 509 217-8453
Medical Lake *(G-6445)*
Virtual Imprints LLC ....G 425 998-9994
Bellevue *(G-1219)*
Vision Press Inc ....G 206 782-8476
Seattle *(G-11424)*
Visiprinting ....G 253 565-4713
Tacoma *(G-13580)*
Vista Copy and Print ....G 206 715-2011
Seattle *(G-11425)*
Vistaprint ....G 617 838-2434
Gig Harbor *(G-4172)*
Vistaprint ....G 703 868-1794
Seattle *(G-11426)*
Vistaprint ....G 206 973-0324
Seattle *(G-11427)*
Visual Verve Design Print LLC ....G 509 773-4596
Centerville *(G-2378)*
W B Mason Co Inc ....E 888 926-2766
Tukwila *(G-13835)*
Washington State University ....D 509 335-3518
Pullman *(G-8112)*
Wenatchee Business Journal ....G 509 663-6730
Cashmere *(G-2332)*
Western Business Forms & Sups ....G 503 285-8738
Battle Ground *(G-751)*
Western Print Systems Inc ....G 206 794-0045
Snohomish *(G-11998)*
Wholesale Printers Inc ....E 360 687-5500
Battle Ground *(G-753)*
Wilbur Register Inc ....G 509 647-5551
Wilbur *(G-15142)*
Willapa Printing ....G 360 942-5580
Raymond *(G-8363)*
William Willis ....G 360 885-2045
Vancouver *(G-14695)*
Wilo Inc ....G 425 793-4862
Renton *(G-8948)*
Woitchek Printing LLC ....G 425 869-8212
Redmond *(G-8716)*
Woodpecker Graphics ....G 509 481-8406
Spokane Valley *(G-12940)*
▲ Worldwide Dgital Solutions Inc ....G 425 605-0923
Kirkland *(G-5498)*
Yvonne Roberts ....G 253 531-3105
Tacoma *(G-13606)*
Z-Axis Prints ....G 509 842-6680
Spokane Valley *(G-12947)*
Zebra Print and Copy ....G 206 223-1800
Seattle *(G-11519)*
Zebra Printing ....G 425 656-3700
Kent *(G-5220)*
Zebra Printing Inc ....F 425 462-9775
Bellevue *(G-1233)*
Zkl Printing Company LLC ....G 206 369-6156
Auburn *(G-604)*

2754 Commercial Printing: Gravure

Aesseal Inc ....G 360 414-0118
Longview *(G-5883)*
American Solutions For Bus ....G 509 276-8700
Deer Park *(G-2893)*
Bcwest LLC ....E 206 323-8100
Seattle *(G-9504)*
Citlali Creativo ....G 206 779-5664
Burien *(G-2095)*
Color Press Publishing Inc ....E 509 525-6030
Walla Walla *(G-14789)*
Exone Company ....G 360 286-0556
Bremerton *(G-1953)*
Integrity Press Inc ....G 425 868-3120
Redmond *(G-8511)*
Pioneer Printing and Forms ....G 509 248-7393
Yakima *(G-15648)*
RR Donnelley & Sons Company ....F 206 389-8900
Seattle *(G-10989)*
Sbd Inc ....G 509 545-8845
Pasco *(G-7625)*
United Reprographics L L C ....E 206 382-1177
Seattle *(G-11372)*

2759 Commercial Printing

253 Custom Tees ....G 253 244-7117
Lakewood *(G-5693)*
360 Apparel LLC ....G 509 924-5219
Spokane *(G-12087)*
4 Colour Inc ....G 509 249-0955
Yakima *(G-15495)*
4 Over LLC ....G 818 246-1170
Milton *(G-6531)*
A & J Graphics & Design ....G 206 439-1766
Burien *(G-2087)*
A & R Enterprise ....G 425 453-0010
Lynnwood *(G-6064)*
A and M Impressions LLC ....G 206 595-1111
Burien *(G-2088)*
A B Graphics ....G 360 566-3666
Vancouver *(G-14003)*
A-K Printing LLC ....G 253 249-7133
Spanaway *(G-12052)*
AAA Printing & Graphics Inc ....F 425 454-0156
Bellevue *(G-778)*
Aastha Inc ....G 206 382-4118
Seattle *(G-9331)*
Abadan Repo Graphics ....E 509 946-7697
Richland *(G-8963)*
About Printing and Apparel ....G 360 584-9159
Lacey *(G-5529)*
Abracadabra Printing Inc ....G 206 343-9087
Seattle *(G-9334)*

Absolute Graphix Inc G 425 771-6087 Lynnwood *(G-6067)*
Absolute Sportswear G 206 890-1531 Seattle *(G-9335)*
Action Sports & Locks Inc G 360 435-9505 Arlington *(G-193)*
Action Sportswear & Printables F 509 328-5861 Spokane *(G-12097)*
Adhesa-Plate Manufacturing Co E 206 682-0141 Seattle *(G-9351)*
Advocate Printing G 360 748-3335 Chehalis *(G-2458)*
Aero Safety Graphics Inc G 425 957-0712 Redmond *(G-8372)*
Alexander Printing Co Inc G 425 252-4212 Everett *(G-3366)*
All Print G 509 328-9344 Spokane *(G-12106)*
All Pro Screen Prtg & EMB LLC G 360 438-0304 Lacey *(G-5531)*
Allied Envelope Company- Boise G 509 328-9800 Spokane *(G-12107)*
American Graphic Arts G 425 378-8065 Bellevue *(G-786)*
American Printing and Pubg G 253 395-3349 Kent *(G-4779)*
Angel Screen Printing G 253 872-3040 Kent *(G-4784)*
Apex Marketing Strategy G 360 402-6487 Olympia *(G-7228)*
Apperson Print Management G 425 251-1850 Renton *(G-8747)*
Arctic Circle Enterprises LLC D 253 872-8525 Kent *(G-4789)*
Arrow International Inc B 425 745-3700 Lynnwood *(G-6076)*
Arts & Crafts Press Inc G 360 871-7707 Tacoma *(G-13183)*
ASAP Sign & Design G 360 757-1570 Mount Vernon *(G-6771)*
Atlas Pacific Engineering Co G 509 665-6911 Wenatchee *(G-15010)*
Atomic Screen Printing & EMB E 509 585-2866 Kennewick *(G-4621)*
Awards Etc G 509 758-3537 Clarkston *(G-2621)*
B & B Express Printing G 509 783-7383 Kennewick *(G-4622)*
Badge Boys Awards & Engraving G 360 876-8414 Port Orchard *(G-7792)*
Ballard Outdoor F 206 552-0760 Seattle *(G-9482)*
Bar Code Labels & Equipment G 206 567-5577 Vashon *(G-14711)*
Barking Dog Inc G 425 822-6542 Kirkland *(G-5288)*
Belgate Printing & Copy Inc F 425 451-9048 Redmond *(G-8400)*
Bellevue Fine Art Reprodctn G 425 749-7396 Bellevue *(G-812)*
Bellevue Printing LLC G 425 558-1862 Bellevue *(G-814)*
Bellingham Promotional Pdts G 360 676-5416 Bellingham *(G-1268)*
Bentson Printing LLC G 253 272-6563 Tacoma *(G-13197)*
Bergen & Company F 360 676-7503 Bellingham *(G-1271)*
Biaflex Printing Solutions LLC G 509 895-7076 Yakima *(G-15520)*
Bison Bkbinding Letterpress LP G 360 734-0481 Bellingham *(G-1273)*
Blackstar G 360 426-7470 Shelton *(G-11684)*
Blue Ink G 206 588-0739 Seattle *(G-9549)*
Bob Bracht Llc G 206 678-5168 Lake Forest Park *(G-5608)*
Brainless Tees Inc G 360 608-8417 Vancouver *(G-14080)*
Bras Thermography G 425 677-8430 Issaquah *(G-4388)*
Bremerton Letterpress Co LLC G 360 620-8967 Bremerton *(G-1939)*
Brian E Styke G 360 331-0527 Freeland *(G-4027)*
Brightwork Specialty Printing G 360 930-0218 Poulsbo *(G-7951)*
Bte Printing Inc G 360 675-8837 Oak Harbor *(G-7143)*
Budget Printing Center G 509 736-7511 Kennewick *(G-4636)*
Business Equipment Center Inc F 509 747-2964 Spokane *(G-12162)*
Buy More Caps Co G 509 599-2944 Spokane *(G-12164)*
C S Adventurecorp LLC G 425 679-1172 Ferndale *(G-3821)*
Captivating Covers G 800 975-8198 Tukwila *(G-13710)*
Care Engraving Company G 360 456-0831 Lacey *(G-5539)*
Cascade Printing Direct G 253 661-6213 Federal Way *(G-3722)*
Catholic Printery Inc E 206 767-0660 Seattle *(G-9648)*
Cedar Creek Printing Co G 360 757-7588 Burlington *(G-2142)*
Chelan Printing G 509 682-5157 Chelan *(G-2551)*
Chic Ink G 425 392-3943 Issaquah *(G-4393)*
▼ Choke Shirt Company G 206 624-4444 Seattle *(G-9679)*
▲ City Books Yellow Pages Inc F 805 473-1686 Burlington *(G-2144)*
Clam Digger G 360 299-3444 Anacortes *(G-114)*
Clarence H Spargo Jr G 360 532-1505 Aberdeen *(G-7)*
Classic Impressions E 206 766-9121 Seattle *(G-9690)*
Co C Graphics G 360 571-8488 Vancouver *(G-14126)*
Cole Graphic Solutions Inc E 253 564-4600 Tacoma *(G-13238)*
Color Grphics Scrnprinting Inc F 360 352-3970 Tumwater *(G-13862)*
Colosseum Ventures LLC F 509 533-0366 Spokane *(G-12188)*
Columbia Office and Bus G 360 695-6245 Vancouver *(G-14136)*
Colville Printing LLC G 509 684-5869 Colville *(G-2745)*
Commerce Retail Sales Inc G 509 926-1724 Spokane *(G-12191)*
Commercial Printing Inc F 509 663-4772 Wenatchee *(G-15023)*
Community Networkers LLC G 509 826-5154 OMAK *(G-7437)*
Continuum G 509 534-0655 Spokane *(G-12199)*
Control Seneca Corporation E 425 602-4700 Woodinville *(G-15212)*
Coprintco Business Forms Inc E 360 425-1810 Longview *(G-5902)*
Copy Break G 206 782-7506 Seattle *(G-9739)*
Copy-Rite Inc G 509 624-8503 Spokane *(G-12200)*
Corey Sign & Display Inc G 360 297-5490 Poulsbo *(G-7955)*
Cory A Stemp G 509 491-3847 Kennewick *(G-4650)*
Countryman Signs Screen Prtrs G 425 355-1037 Everett *(G-3428)*
County of Lewis C 360 748-9121 Chehalis *(G-2485)*
Creative Edge Graphics G 253 735-5111 Auburn *(G-418)*
Creative Label Incorporated G 425 821-8810 Kirkland *(G-5317)*
Custom Pressed Tees LLC G 425 264-5909 Renton *(G-8777)*
D & H Printing G 360 427-7423 Shelton *(G-11693)*
D & J Marketing Inc G 360 413-9173 Lacey *(G-5545)*
D & L Screen Printing G 206 781-1977 Seattle *(G-9776)*
▲ D A Graphics Inc G 206 760-5886 Seattle *(G-9777)*
Decal Factory G 509 465-8931 Spokane *(G-12222)*
Delta C Dynamics LLC G 888 704-3626 Kennewick *(G-4653)*
Denrick Tees G 509 429-6675 Riverside *(G-9125)*
Desert Graphics Inc G 509 765-8082 Moses Lake *(G-6704)*
Designer Decal Inc F 509 535-0267 Spokane *(G-12226)*
Designs Unlimited G 360 792-1372 Port Orchard *(G-7802)*
Digital Documents Inc G 509 775-2425 Republic *(G-8956)*
Digital Image G 509 375-6001 Richland *(G-8988)*
Direct Mailing Solutions G 425 739-4568 Lynnwood *(G-6108)*
▲ Diversified Systems Group Inc E 425 947-1500 Redmond *(G-8442)*
Dnlvi Business Solutions G 360 827-5210 Rochester *(G-9131)*
Dreamworks Printing Inc G 425 970-4625 Renton *(G-8788)*
Dunsire Printers Inc G 360 532-8791 Aberdeen *(G-9)*
Duvall Graphics LLC G 425 788-7578 Duvall *(G-2984)*
▲ Dynea Overlays Inc F 253 572-5600 Tacoma *(G-13267)*
E Teez G 425 645-9514 Everett *(G-3450)*
East Washingtonian G 509 843-1313 Pomeroy *(G-7672)*
Eclipse Technical Graphics LLC F 509 922-7700 Spokane Valley *(G-12686)*
Editorial Consultants Inc G 206 329-6499 Seattle *(G-9884)*
Edmonds Athletic Supply Co G 425 778-7322 Lynnwood *(G-6111)*
Eiki Digital Systems Inc G 206 957-2626 Seattle *(G-9891)*
Electronic Imaging Svcs Inc E 253 887-1237 Auburn *(G-432)*
Emerald City Label Inc F 425 347-3479 Everett *(G-3460)*
Enlighting Struck Design LLC G 206 229-9438 Kent *(G-4893)*
Envelopes Unlimited Inc G 425 451-9622 Redmond *(G-8451)*
Environmental Fincl Info Svcs G 206 283-4210 Seattle *(G-9933)*
Ever-Mark LLc G 425 486-7200 Kenmore *(G-4573)*
Excel Designs Inc G 360 892-1412 Vancouver *(G-14213)*
Expressive Promotions G 253 863-4211 Lake Tapps *(G-5678)*
F D Company G 253 531-7087 Tacoma *(G-13285)*
Fedex Office & Print Svcs Inc F 509 922-4929 Spokane Valley *(G-12700)*
Fedex Office & Print Svcs Inc E 206 467-1767 Seattle *(G-9981)*
Fine Arts Litho G 360 876-5649 Port Orchard *(G-7809)*
▲ Fine Design Inc E 425 271-2866 Tukwila *(G-13735)*
◆ Fkc Co Ltd F 360 452-9472 Port Angeles *(G-7706)*
Flexabili-Tees G 360 260-3163 Vancouver *(G-14234)*
Foster Press G 425 334-9317 Everett *(G-3484)*
Funky Screenprint G 509 674-5121 Cle Elum *(G-2667)*
Garjen Corp G 253 862-6140 Bonney Lake *(G-1724)*
Garland Printing Co Inc G 509 327-5556 Spokane *(G-12267)*
Gdansk Inc E 509 279-2034 Spokane Valley *(G-12713)*
Geometric G 206 244-2222 Tukwila *(G-13740)*
Getting Personal Imprinting G 253 302-5566 Lakewood *(G-5725)*
Girlie Press Inc G 206 720-1237 Seattle *(G-10074)*
Global Product Mfg Corp F 425 512-9129 Everett *(G-3501)*
Gnarly Tees G 360 326-3770 Vancouver *(G-14260)*
▲ Go Usa Inc E 509 662-3387 Wenatchee *(G-15034)*
Gordon Gruel G 509 226-1309 Newman Lake *(G-7045)*
Gorilla Screen Printing G 206 621-1728 Seattle *(G-10102)*

Employee Codes: A=Over 500 employees, B=251-500
C=101-250, D=51-100, E=20-50, F=10-19, G=2-9

2019 Washington
Manufacturers Register

581

27 PRINTING, PUBLISHING, AND ALLIED INDUSTRIES — SIC SECTION

Graphic Communications .... F 360 786-5110
  Olympia *(G-7299)*
Graphic Impressions Inc .... E 253 872-0555
  Kent *(G-4925)*
Green Karma Inc .... G 206 786-1988
  Kirkland *(G-5354)*
Greendisk Inc .... G 425 392-8700
  Sammamish *(G-9211)*
Greenes Tees LLC .... G 206 801-7725
  Shoreline *(G-11776)*
Griffin Publishing Inc .... E 509 534-3625
  Spokane Valley *(G-12724)*
Gt Recording .... G 206 783-6911
  Seattle *(G-10130)*
Hamilton Priniting .... G 425 778-1975
  Edmonds *(G-3116)*
Harbor Graphics Inc .... G 360 532-1234
  Hoquiam *(G-4339)*
Harold Tymer Co Inc .... F 360 573-6053
  Vancouver *(G-14284)*
Hemlock Printers USA Inc .... G 206 241-8311
  Seattle *(G-10165)*
Herzog Envelope Inc .... G 206 618-6765
  Redmond *(G-8491)*
Horizon Printing Company LLC ..... G 509 663-8414
  Wenatchee *(G-15040)*
Hs Print Works Difficult .... G 253 251-0045
  Puyallup *(G-8163)*
Hull Marigail .... G 425 643-3737
  Bellevue *(G-952)*
ID Integration Inc .... F 425 438-2533
  Mukilteo *(G-6940)*
ID Label Inc .... F 206 323-8100
  Seattle *(G-10202)*
Ideal Commercial Uniforms .... G 360 876-1767
  Port Orchard *(G-7814)*
Idk Wear .... G 425 346-1904
  Des Moines *(G-2937)*
Impact Studio .... G 425 890-3914
  Sedro Woolley *(G-11541)*
Impression Printing Co Inc .... G 206 762-6211
  Seattle *(G-10216)*
In Graphic Detail LLC .... G 360 582-0002
  Sequim *(G-11641)*
▲ Industrial Screenprint Inc .... G 253 735-5111
  Kent *(G-4951)*
Information Management Tech ..... G 425 322-5078
  Maple Valley *(G-6276)*
Ink Inc .... F 253 565-4000
  University Place *(G-13973)*
Ink Ability .... G 360 342-8174
  Battle Ground *(G-709)*
Ink It Your Way .... G 425 789-1669
  Lake Stevens *(G-5648)*
Inkwell Screenprinting .... G 206 551-1713
  Seattle *(G-10236)*
Integrity Printing LLC .... G 253 841-3161
  Puyallup *(G-8169)*
▲ Intermec Technologies Corp ..... A 425 348-2600
  Lynnwood *(G-6140)*
Invitationinabottlecom .... G 800 489-8048
  Everett *(G-3519)*
Ito Enterprises Inc .... G 425 556-0819
  Redmond *(G-8515)*
James Lund .... G 425 742-9135
  Lynnwood *(G-6143)*
Jaytees Management Group LLC ... G 360 352-0038
  Tumwater *(G-13877)*
Jen Gar Corp .... G 253 862-6140
  Bonney Lake *(G-1727)*
Jeremy Nichols .... G 509 930-6352
  Yakima *(G-15601)*
Jet City Vtg Tees .... G 310 500-0577
  Seattle *(G-10294)*
Jmh Enterprises .... G 509 628-2191
  Richland *(G-9015)*
▲ Johnnie Montice .... G 360 452-6549
  Port Angeles *(G-7719)*
Journal-News Publishing Co .... F 509 754-4636
  Ephrata *(G-3339)*
Journal-News Publishing Co .... G 509 725-0101
  Davenport *(G-2872)*
▲ K Smith Enterprises .... G 425 455-0923
  Bellevue *(G-965)*
KB Hanks Enterprises .... G 425 221-1040
  Renton *(G-8836)*
Kens Engraving Emporium Inc ...... G 360 578-0844
  Longview *(G-5922)*
King Enterprises .... G 360 568-1644
  Snohomish *(G-11933)*

Kool Change Printing Inc .... G 360 794-9019
  Monroe *(G-6588)*
Kp LLC .... C 425 204-6355
  Renton *(G-8838)*
▲ Kwang Nam Hwang .... F 206 433-8811
  Burien *(G-2116)*
L & L Printing Inc .... G 253 848-5546
  Puyallup *(G-8174)*
L & P Screen Printing .... G 253 859-8787
  Kent *(G-4986)*
L&P Screen Printing Inc .... G 253 951-2482
  Auburn *(G-486)*
Label Masters Inc .... G 425 869-2422
  Kent *(G-4987)*
Labels & Lists Inc .... F 425 822-1984
  Bothell *(G-1772)*
Lakeside Gardens .... G 360 483-8889
  Lynden *(G-6030)*
Larrys Screen Printing .... G 425 885-3644
  Bellevue *(G-978)*
Lasting Impressions Inc .... G 360 659-1255
  Marysville *(G-6353)*
Laurel Graphics Fabrication Co .... E 253 872-7617
  Kent *(G-4991)*
Lawton Printing Inc .... E 509 534-1044
  Spokane *(G-12358)*
Legend Data Systems Inc .... F 425 251-1670
  Kent *(G-4992)*
Letterpress Distilling LLC .... G 206 227-4522
  Seattle *(G-10408)*
▲ Liberty Business Forms Inc ...... D 509 536-0515
  Spokane *(G-12362)*
Logo House .... G 206 890-3051
  Seattle *(G-10434)*
Logo Loft Inc .... G 360 394-5638
  Silverdale *(G-11848)*
Lorrand Marketing LLC .... G 360 532-7510
  Aberdeen *(G-21)*
Luckiest Letterpress .... G 425 241-8229
  Bothell *(G-1774)*
Mango Ink .... G 509 990-9085
  Mead *(G-6431)*
Marked Departure Pottery .... G 360 991-5910
  Vancouver *(G-14394)*
Markon Inc .... G 503 222-3966
  Vancouver *(G-14395)*
Martin Business Systems .... G 509 582-3159
  Kennewick *(G-4692)*
Marysville Printing Inc .... G 360 658-9195
  Marysville *(G-6357)*
Masterpress Inc .... E 206 524-1444
  Seattle *(G-10499)*
McClatchy Newspapers Inc .... C 509 582-1500
  Kennewick *(G-4693)*
McMann & Tate Inc .... G 360 676-4396
  Bellingham *(G-1430)*
Mediamax .... G 509 627-2358
  Richland *(G-9026)*
▲ Merchant Investments Inc .... E 425 235-8675
  Kent *(G-5006)*
Merrill Corp Resource MGT .... G 509 326-7892
  Spokane *(G-12391)*
Merrill Corporation .... C 360 794-3157
  Monroe *(G-6596)*
Metrix Create Space .... G 206 357-9406
  Seattle *(G-10524)*
Metrix Software .... G 425 361-2415
  Edmonds *(G-3134)*
Miller Purr Fect Prints .... G 360 687-1186
  Yacolt *(G-15488)*
Moss Green Inc .... F 206 285-4020
  Seattle *(G-10564)*
Mountain Top Inc .... G 360 416-3333
  Mount Vernon *(G-6814)*
Mvp Athletic Inc .... G 360 915-8715
  Tumwater *(G-13888)*
Myseps .... G 858 231-2774
  Port Orchard *(G-7831)*
National Color .... F 206 281-9400
  Seattle *(G-10587)*
Newmata Screen Printing .... G 360 631-7860
  Arlington *(G-288)*
Nicole Lewis/Northwest Breast .... G 360 989-0312
  Vancouver *(G-14431)*
Northern Kittitas Cnty Tribune ..... G 509 674-2511
  Cle Elum *(G-2673)*
Northwest Label/Design Inc .... E 206 282-5568
  Seattle *(G-10646)*
Nova Graphics .... G 206 248-3489
  Seatac *(G-9294)*

NRG Resources Inc .... D 509 588-4786
  Benton City *(G-1621)*
Nta Inc .... G 425 487-2679
  Woodinville *(G-15325)*
NW Wood Box .... G 360 939-2434
  Camano Island *(G-2220)*
Okanogan Label & Print Ltd .... F 250 328-8660
  Walla Walla *(G-14853)*
Omega Printing .... G 425 339-8538
  Everett *(G-3559)*
Oroville Reman & Reload Inc .... E 509 476-2935
  Oroville *(G-7471)*
P G I Publications Inc .... G 425 743-0110
  Everett *(G-3562)*
P I P Printing Inc .... F 360 456-4742
  Olympia *(G-7364)*
Pacific Dealer Services .... G 509 299-7269
  Medical Lake *(G-6443)*
Pacific Labels .... G 360 671-6507
  Bellingham *(G-1486)*
Pad Printing Services Inc .... G 206 362-4544
  Seattle *(G-10744)*
Panther Printing .... G 509 344-4600
  Spokane Valley *(G-12825)*
Paper Muses .... G 425 241-3710
  Maple Valley *(G-6288)*
Pariyatti .... G 360 978-4998
  Onalaska *(G-7452)*
Park Postal LLC .... G 206 860-7678
  Seattle *(G-10759)*
Party City Corporation .... F 206 575-0502
  Tukwila *(G-13790)*
Pcs Laser and Memorial .... G 208 746-1033
  Clarkston *(G-2640)*
Peetz Enterprises .... G 509 276-2608
  Clayton *(G-2659)*
Pen Print Inc .... G 360 457-3404
  Port Angeles *(G-7735)*
Penway Limited Inc .... G 360 435-6445
  Arlington *(G-300)*
Perfect Copy & Print Inc .... G 206 325-4733
  Seattle *(G-10786)*
Perfect Printing & Signs .... G 509 786-3811
  Yakima *(G-15645)*
Pgi Publications .... G 206 588-2968
  Seattle *(G-10792)*
Phoenix Maps .... G 509 697-5059
  Selah *(G-11594)*
Pickle Papers .... G 509 665-8661
  Wenatchee *(G-15064)*
Pioneer Printing and Forms .... G 509 248-7393
  Yakima *(G-15648)*
Plastic Sales & Service Inc .... F 206 524-8312
  Lynnwood *(G-6181)*
Post Indus Stress & Design .... F 253 572-9782
  Tacoma *(G-13472)*
Potter & Associates Inc .... G 206 623-8844
  Seattle *(G-10839)*
Powder-Fab Inc .... E 360 435-0793
  Arlington *(G-303)*
Print NW LLC .... D 253 284-2300
  Tacoma *(G-13478)*
Print Solutions .... G 253 435-1928
  Puyallup *(G-8225)*
Print24com USA LP .... G 206 607-0639
  Seattle *(G-10864)*
Printing Services Inc .... G 253 858-5350
  Port Orchard *(G-7842)*
Printing Washington State Dept ... G 360 407-6013
  Lacey *(G-5578)*
Proforma Crtive Prtg Solutions .... G 360 848-7714
  Mount Vernon *(G-6827)*
Progressive Printing Solutions ..... G 425 867-1296
  Issaquah *(G-4462)*
Proline Printer Services .... G 360 697-2336
  Poulsbo *(G-7992)*
Prompt Printery .... G 509 457-5848
  Yakima *(G-15657)*
PS Colors Inc .... G 206 371-1341
  Seattle *(G-10880)*
Purple Coyote Inc .... G 509 754-2488
  Ephrata *(G-3345)*
Purpletrail .... G 425 292-1811
  Issaquah *(G-4463)*
Quality Press Inc .... E 206 768-2655
  Seattle *(G-10902)*
R P Signs .... G 425 788-6717
  Duvall *(G-2999)*
Rainbow Racing System Inc .... F 509 326-5470
  Spokane *(G-12466)*

Rainier Corp .... G 206 280-4666
Seattle *(G-10916)*
Ramax Printing and Awards .... G 509 928-1222
Spokane *(G-12467)*
Real Time Screen Printinginc .... G 206 818-6346
Des Moines *(G-2945)*
Reco Corporate Sportswear Inc .... G 360 354-2134
Lynden *(G-6048)*
Record Printing Inc .... F 509 964-9500
Thorp *(G-13629)*
Revolution Inc .... F 206 714-3529
Seattle *(G-10956)*
Richmark Company .... D 206 322-8884
Seattle *(G-10963)*
River City Screenprinting .... G 360 428-8985
Mount Vernon *(G-6828)*
Roberta Propst .... G 425 681-9760
Bellevue *(G-1104)*
Ronald Finney .... G 253 857-7635
Olalla *(G-7209)*
RR Donnelley & Sons Company .... F 206 389-8900
Seattle *(G-10989)*
Rulersmith Inc .... E 360 707-2828
Shoreline *(G-11806)*
Saco Sales LLC .... G 253 922-6349
Fife *(G-3991)*
Salish Screenprinting .... G 360 758-2287
Ferndale *(G-3895)*
Sand Paper & Ink Inc .... G 360 705-0918
Tumwater *(G-13896)*
Sandys Nifty Tees .... G 360 861-8669
McCleary *(G-6419)*
Sauther & Assoc Inc .... E 509 922-7828
Liberty Lake *(G-5858)*
Savage Inc .... G 206 972-8217
Seattle *(G-11018)*
Savage Screen .... G 360 321-2040
Clinton *(G-2697)*
Sbd Inc .... G 509 545-8845
Pasco *(G-7625)*
Sbf Printing .... G 509 457-2877
Yakima *(G-15667)*
Scott Wood Associates LLC .... G 253 509-3742
Gig Harbor *(G-4159)*
Screen Fx .... G 509 966-7515
Yakima *(G-15668)*
Screen Printing Northwest Inc .... G 425 303-3381
Everett *(G-3605)*
Screen Tek Inc .... E 509 928-8322
Liberty Lake *(G-5860)*
Scribbly Tees .... G 517 285-3648
Tacoma *(G-13509)*
Seattle Area Tees .... G 425 314-3814
Mukilteo *(G-6976)*
Seattle Chinese Post Inc .... E 206 223-0623
Seattle *(G-11051)*
Seattle Engraving Center LLC .... G 206 420-4604
Seattle *(G-11056)*
Section Magazine LLC .... G 360 694-8571
Vancouver *(G-14578)*
Shirley Sunset .... G 360 574-3276
Vancouver *(G-14584)*
Shirt Image Embroidery .... G 360 870-2837
Hoquiam *(G-4359)*
Shirts Illustrated .... G 425 742-3844
Lynnwood *(G-6195)*
Shirtworks .... G 509 925-3469
Ellensburg *(G-3225)*
Shirtz To Go Inc .... G 206 242-4055
Federal Way *(G-3783)*
Showcase Specialties Inc .... G 509 547-3344
Pasco *(G-7629)*
Shur-Loc Fabric System .... G 360 805-4140
Monroe *(G-6618)*
Sideline Sports Inc .... G 206 906-9652
Seattle *(G-11104)*
Silkscreen Company .... E 206 763-8108
Seattle *(G-11112)*
Skyhawk Press LLC .... G 360 598-2211
Poulsbo *(G-8000)*
Slow Loris Inc .... G 360 588-0321
Anacortes *(G-169)*
Slp Creative LLC .... G 206 935-5646
Seattle *(G-11136)*
Snap Custom Clothing .... G 206 682-0686
Seattle *(G-11142)*
Sno-King Signs .... G 425 775-0594
Edmonds *(G-3158)*
Snohomish Publishing Company .... E 206 523-7548
Snohomish *(G-11983)*
Solar Graphics Inc .... G 509 248-1129
Yakima *(G-15678)*
Sound Publishing Inc .... D 425 355-0717
Everett *(G-3618)*
Soundview Graphics LLC .... G 253 851-2007
Gig Harbor *(G-4162)*
South Paw Screenprinting .... G 206 762-2926
Seattle *(G-11160)*
Specialty Embroidery .... G 509 924-1579
Lacey *(G-5593)*
Spectrum Sign Co Inc .... F 253 939-5500
Auburn *(G-570)*
Spin Tees .... G 360 515-0543
Olympia *(G-7399)*
Spin Tees .... G 253 301-2047
Tacoma *(G-13523)*
Spokane Valley Screen Printing .... G 509 921-0207
Spokane Valley *(G-12889)*
Spring Creek Enterprises .... G 360 876-8884
Port Orchard *(G-7852)*
Stafford Press Inc .... F 425 861-5856
Redmond *(G-8680)*
Star Copy & Reprographics Ctr .... E 360 385-1022
Port Townsend *(G-7931)*
Starshine Products .... G 425 238-9820
Monroe *(G-6627)*
Stat Corporation .... F 425 883-4181
Redmond *(G-8681)*
Stephen L Nelson Inc .... G 425 885-9499
Redmond *(G-8682)*
Steve Czako Associates .... G 509 624-7018
Spokane *(G-12529)*
Stickers Northwest .... G 360 731-0255
Tacoma *(G-13526)*
Stickers Northwest Inc .... G 253 344-1236
Fife *(G-3994)*
Stitchblade LLC .... G 206 940-7448
Seattle *(G-11197)*
Stone Drums Inc .... G 425 485-5570
Woodinville *(G-15376)*
Streamline International .... G 425 392-2350
Issaquah *(G-4483)*
Sun Printing .... G 253 517-5017
Federal Way *(G-3791)*
Super H Corporation .... G 360 687-2824
Vancouver *(G-14620)*
Sweet Tees .... G 253 632-9224
Black Diamond *(G-1656)*
Swift Print .... G 360 805-8509
Snohomish *(G-11989)*
Swifty Prtg Dgital Imaging Inc .... E 206 441-0800
Seattle *(G-11239)*
T & TS .... G 206 938-0177
Seattle *(G-11248)*
T Town Apparel .... G 253 471-2960
Tacoma *(G-13539)*
Tacoma Printing .... G 253 470-1454
Tacoma *(G-13546)*
Tacoma Public Schools .... G 253 571-1170
Tacoma *(G-13547)*
Tacoma Rubber Stamp Co .... E 253 383-5433
Tacoma *(G-13548)*
Taylor Communications Inc .... G 360 699-4013
Vancouver *(G-14626)*
Tc Span America LLC .... F 425 774-3881
Edmonds *(G-3159)*
Tcc Printing and Imaging Inc .... E 206 622-4050
Seattle *(G-11276)*
Theo Coram Corporation .... G 425 774-4731
Brier *(G-2022)*
Thomas Mayer .... G 360 945-0354
Point Roberts *(G-7670)*
Ticket Envelope Company LLC .... G 206 784-7266
Seattle *(G-11304)*
Tiger Press .... G 360 468-3737
Lopez Island *(G-5987)*
Time Printing Inc .... G 206 633-3320
Seattle *(G-11309)*
Touch & Go Tees .... G 253 651-7505
Gig Harbor *(G-4167)*
Touch Color Screen Printing .... G 360 377-5660
Bremerton *(G-2007)*
Touchmark Printing .... G 206 420-4607
Kent *(G-5186)*
Triad Comsural Printing Corp .... F 509 582-1466
Kennewick *(G-4740)*
Twin Cities Printing .... G 360 807-1200
Centralia *(G-2440)*
TX Fine Designs Inc .... G 425 271-2866
Tukwila *(G-13830)*
Typesetter Corporation .... F 425 455-3055
Mercer Island *(G-6488)*
Undershirt Inc .... G 360 740-8048
Chehalis *(G-2541)*
Van Quill Larry R .... G 360 736-1776
Centralia *(G-2441)*
Vanetten Fine Art .... G 509 928-2385
Spokane Valley *(G-12928)*
Vanguard Press .... G 206 782-1448
Seattle *(G-11404)*
Vietnamese NW Newsppr & Annual .... F 206 722-6984
Seattle *(G-11415)*
Vindico Printing and Design .... G 425 329-4739
Lynnwood *(G-6218)*
Vinyl Status .... G 206 601-3598
Bellevue *(G-1218)*
Washington Graphics LLC .... F 425 376-0877
Redmond *(G-8709)*
Washington State University .... F 509 335-2947
Pullman *(G-8111)*
Welco Sales LLC .... G 425 771-9043
Edmonds *(G-3162)*
West Coast Screen Printing .... G 360 581-6466
Aberdeen *(G-39)*
Western Graphics Inc .... G 206 241-2526
Fife *(G-3998)*
Western Typographers Inc .... G 425 967-4700
Lynnwood *(G-6223)*
Wholesale Forms Inc .... G 800 826-7095
Rochester *(G-9145)*
Wide Format Geeks .... G 509 868-2319
Bothell *(G-1919)*
Wild Horse Graphics .... G 425 413-5080
Maple Valley *(G-6300)*
Workhorse Ind .... G 206 257-5374
Seattle *(G-11496)*
Wright Enterprises .... G 360 985-7060
Onalaska *(G-7454)*
Writing Hands .... G 360 893-1606
Orting *(G-7489)*
Yehun LLC .... G 425 533-9641
Seattle *(G-11510)*

2761 Manifold Business Forms

Apperson Inc .... E 206 336-1015
Renton *(G-8746)*
Evergreen Forms Services .... G 425 740-2927
Mukilteo *(G-6925)*
Garland Printing Co Inc .... G 509 327-5556
Spokane *(G-12267)*
Horizon Printing Company LLC .... G 509 663-8414
Wenatchee *(G-15040)*
Inland Empire Bus Solutions .... G 509 922-7492
Spokane Valley *(G-12742)*
Kaye-Smith Enterprises Inc .... C 425 455-0923
Bellevue *(G-967)*
Merrill Corporation .... C 360 794-3157
Monroe *(G-6596)*
Now Impressions Inc .... G 425 881-5911
Redmond *(G-8601)*
Potter & Associates Inc .... G 206 623-8844
Seattle *(G-10839)*
Reynolds and Reynolds Company .... E 425 985-0194
Edmonds *(G-3146)*
Sand Paper & Ink Inc .... G 360 705-0918
Tumwater *(G-13896)*
Sterling Business Forms Inc .... E 509 926-8191
Spokane Valley *(G-12892)*
Stretching Charts Inc .... E 253 536-4922
Tacoma *(G-13528)*
Taylor Communications Inc .... G 509 747-5872
Spokane Valley *(G-12902)*
Wright Business Forms Inc .... E 253 872-0200
Kent *(G-5219)*

2771 Greeting Card Publishing

Alder Grove Distributors .... G 360 423-3138
Longview *(G-5885)*
Blue Lantern Publishing Inc .... G 206 447-9229
Seattle *(G-9551)*
Bookmark Publishing Co .... G 425 562-0909
Bellevue *(G-826)*
▲ **Compendium Incorporated** .... E 206 812-1640
Seattle *(G-9724)*
Emery Burton LLC .... G 206 323-7351
Seattle *(G-9917)*
Ganapati Studios .... G 206 547-2239
Coupeville *(G-2813)*
Gentle Dragon Cards Inc .... G 206 546-3593
Edmonds *(G-3114)*

S I C

Goodall Productions Inc ....G.... 206 722-0544
Seattle *(G-10100)*
Original Hearts ....G.... 253 857-0700
Gig Harbor *(G-4140)*
Paper Delights ....G.... 206 547-1002
Seattle *(G-10748)*
Uncaged Creations LLC ....G.... 509 397-3873
Lacrosse *(G-5604)*

2782 Blankbooks & Looseleaf Binders

All Scrapped Up Inc ....G.... 206 824-3762
Des Moines *(G-2928)*
At Your Service ....G.... 425 348-9129
Everett *(G-3374)*
Automatic Funds Transfer Svcs ....E.... 206 254-0975
Seattle *(G-9467)*
Deluxe ....G.... 360 794-3157
Monroe *(G-6565)*
Doodlebugs ....G.... 360 683-3154
Sequim *(G-11628)*
Finely Finished LLC ....G.... 360 709-0602
Olympia *(G-7284)*
Gentzen LLC ....G.... 206 768-1297
Tukwila *(G-13738)*
Lizzy and Alex Enterprises LLC ....G.... 425 698-1439
Bellevue *(G-987)*
Micrprint Inc ....G.... 253 539-1103
Tacoma *(G-13412)*
Papercraft Cottage ....G.... 360 426-1038
Shelton *(G-11720)*
▲ Quick Quotes Inc ....F.... 360 736-3004
Centralia *(G-2427)*
Trim Seal USA Inc ....G.... 425 867-1522
Redmond *(G-8694)*
▲ Triple-T Designs Inc ....G.... 253 284-9200
Tacoma *(G-13564)*
Voyager Rcordings Publications ....G.... 206 323-1112
Seattle *(G-11430)*

2789 Bookbinding

Armadillo Press Inc ....G.... 425 355-5588
Everett *(G-3373)*
Arsobscura Bk Bnding Rstration ....G.... 206 340-8810
Seattle *(G-9434)*
B & R Bindery and Collating ....G.... 360 944-0326
Vancouver *(G-14050)*
Budget Printing Center ....G.... 509 736-7511
Kennewick *(G-4636)*
Cascade Printing Company ....F.... 253 472-5500
Tacoma *(G-13227)*
Catholic Printery Inc ....E.... 206 767-0660
Seattle *(G-9648)*
Consolidated Press LLC ....E.... 206 447-9659
Seattle *(G-9730)*
Cullen Bindery LLC ....F.... 206 799-6295
Covington *(G-2824)*
Deck Builders ....G.... 360 709-9225
Olympia *(G-7266)*
ESP Printing Inc ....E.... 425 251-6240
Seattle *(G-9940)*
Fedex Office & Print Svcs Inc ....F.... 360 694-8584
Vancouver *(G-14226)*
Fedex Office & Print Svcs Inc ....E.... 206 467-1767
Seattle *(G-9981)*
Fedex Office & Print Svcs Inc ....E.... 206 244-8884
Tukwila *(G-13733)*
Fedex Office & Print Svcs Inc ....E.... 360 647-1114
Bellingham *(G-1344)*
Globe ....G.... 206 527-2480
Seattle *(G-10086)*
▲ Good News Printing & Graphics ....G.... 425 483-2510
Woodinville *(G-15253)*
▲ Karlas Hand Bindery Inc ....E.... 206 405-3350
Seattle *(G-10328)*
Marshall Marketing Group Inc ....E.... 253 473-0765
Tacoma *(G-13400)*
▲ North West Book Oper Co Inc ....G.... 877 591-8608
Bellingham *(G-1465)*
NRG Resources Inc ....D.... 509 588-4786
Benton City *(G-1621)*
Phils Custom Bindery ....G.... 206 728-1541
Seattle *(G-10795)*
Plese Printing & Marketing ....F.... 509 534-2355
Spokane *(G-12448)*
Prestige Copy and Print ....G.... 206 365-5770
Seattle *(G-10857)*
Printgraphics Inc ....E.... 503 641-8811
Vancouver *(G-14508)*
Puget Bindery Inc ....E.... 206 621-8898
Kent *(G-5087)*
Quality Press Inc ....E.... 206 768-2655
Seattle *(G-10902)*
Seattle Bindery ....E.... 425 656-8210
Tukwila *(G-13814)*
Sketchforschools Pubg Inc ....G.... 877 397-5655
Spokane Valley *(G-12875)*
Snohomish Publishing Company ....E.... 206 523-7548
Snohomish *(G-11983)*
SOS Finishing Unlimited Inc ....F.... 425 746-7385
Bellevue *(G-1147)*
Sudden Printing Inc ....E.... 206 243-4444
Seattle *(G-11211)*
▲ Three By Three Inc ....E.... 206 784-5839
Seattle *(G-11297)*
Twelve Thirty-One Incorporated ....E.... 425 656-8210
Tukwila *(G-13829)*
University Reprographics Inc ....G.... 206 633-0925
Seattle *(G-11385)*
Van Quill Larry R ....G.... 360 736-1776
Centralia *(G-2441)*
Watermark Binderies ....G.... 360 379-0186
Port Townsend *(G-7938)*

2791 Typesetting

AAA Printing & Graphics Inc ....F.... 425 454-0156
Bellevue *(G-778)*
Advertising Services Intl LLC ....G.... 206 623-6963
Seattle *(G-9356)*
Catholic Printery Inc ....E.... 206 767-0660
Seattle *(G-9648)*
ESP Printing Inc ....E.... 425 251-6240
Seattle *(G-9940)*
Faithlife Corporation ....C.... 360 685-2300
Bellingham *(G-1342)*
Fedex Office & Print Svcs Inc ....E.... 206 546-7600
Shoreline *(G-11771)*
Foster Press ....G.... 425 334-9317
Everett *(G-3484)*
Graphic Advertising Svcs Inc ....F.... 425 688-9980
Richland *(G-9003)*
Harold Tymer Co Inc ....F.... 360 573-6053
Vancouver *(G-14284)*
Hazelwood Farm LLC ....F.... 425 454-5165
Redmond *(G-8489)*
Integrated Composition Systems ....G.... 509 624-5064
Spokane *(G-12318)*
L G Artworks Inc ....G.... 425 355-9143
Everett *(G-3533)*
Marshall Marketing Group Inc ....E.... 253 473-0765
Tacoma *(G-13400)*
Mary Fleming ....G.... 206 246-4871
Tukwila *(G-13768)*
Olympic Graphic Arts Inc ....G.... 360 374-6020
Forks *(G-4013)*
Pacific Rim Printing Inc ....G.... 360 676-4606
Bellingham *(G-1487)*
Plese Printing & Marketing ....F.... 509 534-2355
Spokane *(G-12448)*
Prestige Copy and Print ....G.... 206 365-5770
Seattle *(G-10857)*
Prime West of Washington Inc ....E.... 360 424-5783
Kent *(G-5081)*
Print Services Northwest Inc ....G.... 206 763-9230
Seattle *(G-10860)*
Printgraphics Inc ....E.... 503 641-8811
Vancouver *(G-14508)*
Rapid Print Inc ....G.... 360 695-6400
Vancouver *(G-14532)*
Schilling Graphics ....G.... 253 572-8171
Tacoma *(G-13507)*
Soulier Southbay LLC ....G.... 360 459-3015
Lacey *(G-5589)*
Sudden Printing Inc ....E.... 206 243-4444
Seattle *(G-11211)*
Typesetter Corporation ....F.... 425 455-3055
Mercer Island *(G-6488)*
V O Printers Inc ....G.... 360 577-0038
Longview *(G-5962)*
Van Quill Larry R ....G.... 360 736-1776
Centralia *(G-2441)*
Washington Media Services Inc ....G.... 360 754-4543
Olympia *(G-7421)*
Wholesale Printers Inc ....E.... 360 687-5500
Battle Ground *(G-753)*
William Reed & Associates ....G.... 509 534-4727
Spokane Valley *(G-12938)*

2796 Platemaking & Related Svcs

Graphic Advertising Svcs Inc ....F.... 425 688-9980
Richland *(G-9003)*
Graphic Impressions Inc ....E.... 253 872-0555
Kent *(G-4925)*
Hazelwood Farm LLC ....F.... 425 454-5165
Redmond *(G-8489)*
Imagine Color Service LLC ....E.... 206 281-5703
Seattle *(G-10207)*
Preflex Digital Prepress Svcs ....F.... 253 583-9100
Lakewood *(G-5747)*
Refocus Laser Engraving-Design ....G.... 541 998-2047
Lynnwood *(G-6188)*
S & G Engraving ....G.... 425 868-4169
Sammamish *(G-9244)*
Sanctuary Corporation ....G.... 360 477-4384
Port Angeles *(G-7743)*
Tacoma Rubber Stamp Co ....E.... 253 383-5433
Tacoma *(G-13548)*
William Louis Becker ....G.... 509 624-3466
Spokane *(G-12593)*

28 CHEMICALS AND ALLIED PRODUCTS

2812 Alkalies & Chlorine

Buckeye International Inc ....G.... 206 575-1185
Seatac *(G-9279)*
Church & Dwight Co Inc ....G.... 253 838-3385
Federal Way *(G-3723)*
Hasa Inc ....E.... 360 578-9300
Longview *(G-5916)*
Solvay Chemicals Inc ....E.... 360 425-1114
Longview *(G-5955)*

2813 Industrial Gases

Air Liquide ....G.... 509 793-9590
Eltopia *(G-3261)*
Air Liquide America LP ....G.... 360 673-1400
Kalama *(G-4491)*
Airgas Usa LLC ....G.... 360 293-6171
Anacortes *(G-97)*
Airgas Usa LLC ....E.... 253 872-7000
Kent *(G-4766)*
Eco Inc ....F.... 206 784-6611
Seattle *(G-9878)*
Helium ....G.... 206 650-4822
Sammamish *(G-9216)*
Helium Advisors ....G.... 425 214-1533
Bellevue *(G-939)*
Helium Development LLC ....G.... 360 550-3322
Port Orchard *(G-7813)*
▲ Homax Group Inc ....E.... 360 733-9029
Bellingham *(G-1371)*
Hydrogen 2o2 LLC ....G.... 704 906-3770
Lake Stevens *(G-5646)*
Hydrogen Fueled Vehicles ....G.... 425 502-7170
Bellevue *(G-953)*
Linde North America Inc ....G.... 360 834-9519
Camas *(G-2264)*
Matheson Tri-Gas Inc ....G.... 253 284-9295
Fife *(G-3969)*
Med-Core Services Inc ....G.... 360 455-5425
Olympia *(G-7337)*
Messer LLC ....D.... 360 695-1255
Vancouver *(G-14412)*
Messer LLC ....F.... 509 738-6611
Vancouver *(G-14413)*
Neon Labs Inc ....G.... 415 854-8795
Seattle *(G-10599)*
Neon Pig LLC ....G.... 509 244-5319
Airway Heights *(G-57)*
Neon Taco ....G.... 323 577-3045
Seattle *(G-10600)*
Noble Gas Neon Company ....G.... 206 708-6290
Seattle *(G-10615)*
Norco Inc ....G.... 509 764-5032
Moses Lake *(G-6731)*
Norco Inc ....G.... 509 754-3518
Ephrata *(G-3343)*
Praxair Inc ....G.... 425 821-2423
Kirkland *(G-5440)*
Praxair Inc ....G.... 360 734-3955
Bellingham *(G-1499)*
Praxair Inc ....G.... 206 632-7138
Seattle *(G-10843)*
Praxair Inc ....G.... 360 733-0971
Bellingham *(G-1500)*
Praxair Inc ....G.... 425 259-0188
Everett *(G-3582)*
Praxair Inc ....F.... 360 371-2900
Ferndale *(G-3890)*

SIC SECTION 28 CHEMICALS AND ALLIED PRODUCTS

Praxair Inc....G....206 264-2881
Seattle *(G-10844)*
Praxair Distribution Inc....E....360 694-1338
Vancouver *(G-14497)*
Praxair Distribution Inc....G....360 504-2086
Sequim *(G-11661)*
Praxair Distribution Inc....E....253 620-1620
Tacoma *(G-13473)*
▲ Rec Silicon Inc....D....509 765-2106
Moses Lake *(G-6741)*
▲ Rosellini Distribution Inc....G....253 867-5648
Kent *(G-5106)*
Ross Metier LLC....G....253 208-8777
Graham *(G-4237)*
Spokane Hydrogen Hybrids....G....509 443-5919
Spokane Valley *(G-12884)*
Vulcan Global LLC....G....509 528-2000
Kennewick *(G-4743)*
We-Man Vets Golf Inc....E....509 527-4507
Walla Walla *(G-14900)*
Western Neon Inc....G....206 682-7738
Seattle *(G-11454)*

2816 Inorganic Pigments

Glass Restoration Specialists....E....253 473-7779
Tacoma *(G-13311)*
▲ Stardust Materials LLC....G....360 260-7399
Vancouver *(G-14608)*

2819 Indl Inorganic Chemicals, NEC

Agrium US Inc....C....509 586-5500
Kennewick *(G-4613)*
Ascensus Specialties LLC....D....360 482-8819
Elma *(G-3240)*
▲ BBC Biochemical Corporation....C....360 542-8400
Mount Vernon *(G-6777)*
Bhs Marketing LLC....G....208 740-9369
Tacoma *(G-13199)*
Carbide Web Sales LLC....G....253 353-2595
University Place *(G-13963)*
Carbon Northwest....G....425 820-0873
Kirkland *(G-5297)*
Ceylon & Cyanide....G....509 638-7772
Spokane *(G-12177)*
Charcoir Corporation....G....213 379-4040
Seattle *(G-9666)*
Chemtrade Chemicals US LLC....G....360 693-1379
Vancouver *(G-14114)*
Chemtrade Chemicals US LLC....E....360 299-1560
Anacortes *(G-111)*
▲ Columbia River Carbonates....D....360 225-6505
Woodland *(G-15425)*
Commercial Chemtech Inc....G....206 932-0841
Seattle *(G-9716)*
Cultured Elements LLC....G....425 442-4595
Cheney *(G-2583)*
Delozier Recovery Services....G....360 385-1258
Port Townsend *(G-7878)*
Element....E....360 682-5649
Oak Harbor *(G-7149)*
Element....G....253 335-8342
Bonney Lake *(G-1722)*
Element....G....425 941-5373
Othello *(G-7494)*
Element 6....G....206 282-0877
Seattle *(G-9895)*
Element 8....G....208 870-8471
Seattle *(G-9896)*
Element Electric LLC....G....360 304-9918
Olympia *(G-7274)*
Element Group Inc....G....206 784-3355
Seattle *(G-9897)*
Elemental Cremation & Burial....G....206 357-1141
Bellevue *(G-893)*
Elements of Iron & Wood LLC....G....360 789-0840
Olympia *(G-7275)*
Energ2 Inc....F....206 465-7243
Seattle *(G-9923)*
Energ2 Technologies Inc....E....206 547-0445
Seattle *(G-9924)*
Excelsior Nanotech Corporation....G....206 898-9477
Bellevue *(G-905)*
Finishing Touch....G....360 391-2108
Camano Island *(G-2212)*
Graymont Western US Inc....G....253 572-7600
Tacoma *(G-13320)*
Graymont Western US Inc....E....253 572-7600
Tacoma *(G-13319)*
Helena Chemical Company....G....901 761-0050
Spokane *(G-12292)*
Hot Yoga Elements....G....360 676-9642
Bellingham *(G-1373)*
Jci Jones Chemicals Inc....E....253 274-0104
Tacoma *(G-13356)*
K2 Carbide....G....425 761-2335
Bellevue *(G-966)*
▲ Lenroc Co....F....509 754-5266
Ephrata *(G-3341)*
Moravek Biochemicals Inc....G....509 375-5124
Richland *(G-9030)*
Northwest Carbonate Inc....E....360 225-6505
Woodland *(G-15451)*
Nouryon Pulp & Prfmce Chem LLC....C....509 765-6400
Moses Lake *(G-6733)*
NW Elements....G....206 440-9135
Shoreline *(G-11795)*
Reg Grays Harbor LLC....E....206 753-0155
Seattle *(G-10942)*
▲ Sandvik Special Metals LLC....C....509 734-4000
Kennewick *(G-4726)*
Sienna Technologies Inc....F....425 485-0756
Woodinville *(G-15362)*
Solvay Chemicals Inc....E....360 425-1114
Longview *(G-5955)*
Structural Diagnostic Services....G....360 647-6681
Bellingham *(G-1560)*
Tessenderlo Kerley Inc....E....509 586-9148
Kennewick *(G-4733)*
Traffic Tech Inc....G....206 357-1141
Tukwila *(G-13828)*
▲ Tyron Global Company....G....360 734-1789
Bellingham *(G-1580)*
▲ US Syntec Corporation....G....509 452-4476
Yakima *(G-15702)*
Vivos Inc....G....509 736-4000
Pasco *(G-7650)*

2821 Plastics, Mtrls & Nonvulcanizable Elastomers

3s Plastics LLC....G....425 747-2827
Bellevue *(G-775)*
A To Z Composites Inc....F....435 680-3762
Bellingham *(G-1236)*
All Composite Inc....G....253 847-5106
Spanaway *(G-12053)*
American Excelsior Company....E....509 575-5794
Yakima *(G-15507)*
Arclin Surfaces LLC....E....253 572-5600
Tacoma *(G-13178)*
Axiall Corporation....D....360 577-3232
Longview *(G-5887)*
Bioguard Research & Dev....G....509 628-0170
Kennewick *(G-4631)*
Columbia Cultured Marble Inc....G....509 582-5660
Kennewick *(G-4647)*
▲ Concept Fabrication Inc....F....509 534-9235
Spokane *(G-12196)*
Corrosion Companies Inc....E....360 835-2171
Washougal *(G-14949)*
Cypress Designs LLC....G....360 384-6572
Bellingham *(G-1314)*
▲ Epic Polymer Systems Corp....F....360 225-1496
Woodland *(G-15430)*
◆ General Plastics Mfg Co....C....253 473-5000
Tacoma *(G-13306)*
High Performance Seals Inc....G....253 218-0123
Auburn *(G-466)*
Honeywell International Inc....A....425 885-3711
Redmond *(G-8500)*
Interplastic Corporation....E....253 872-8067
Kent *(G-4958)*
James Koehnline....G....206 783-6846
Seattle *(G-10282)*
▲ K Rounds LLC....G....206 452-0466
Kent *(G-4972)*
Leggari Products LLC....G....509 727-2979
Pasco *(G-7600)*
Mapletex Inc....G....253 572-3608
Tacoma *(G-13399)*
▲ Microgreen Polymers Inc....E....360 435-7400
Arlington *(G-276)*
Microgreen Polymers Inc....G....360 435-7400
Arlington *(G-277)*
North American Composites Co....G....253 351-9994
Kent *(G-5027)*
▲ Nylatech Incorporated....F....360 966-2838
Everson *(G-3685)*
Orca Composites....G....206 782-0660
Seattle *(G-10712)*
Pexco LLC....C....253 284-8000
Fife *(G-3980)*
Plasticreations Inc....G....425 558-1075
Redmond *(G-8624)*
Polythermics LLC....G....425 823-5568
Kirkland *(G-5438)*
Professional Plastics Inc....F....425 251-4140
Tukwila *(G-13795)*
Professional Plastics Inc....G....714 446-6500
Kent *(G-5084)*
Professional Plastics Inc....F....253 872-7430
Tukwila *(G-13797)*
R & R Plastics....G....360 694-9573
Vancouver *(G-14524)*
Redwood Plastics and Rbr Corp....E....360 225-1491
Woodland *(G-15461)*
Signature Plastics LLC....F....360 366-5044
Custer *(G-2860)*
Tex Enterprises Inc....G....253 939-1660
Auburn *(G-579)*
Visual Options Inc....E....253 472-1440
Tacoma *(G-13581)*
Wilsonart LLC....E....253 833-0551
Algona *(G-79)*
Zila Works LLC....G....425 777-6813
Renton *(G-8954)*

2822 Synthetic Rubber (Vulcanizable Elastomers)

Cascades Sonoco Inc....E....253 584-4295
Tacoma *(G-13228)*
Farley Desighn and Inc....G....425 259-5946
Everett *(G-3470)*
Innovative Technologies Inc....G....425 258-4773
Everett *(G-3516)*
Jeremy Rieken....G....360 428-7736
Sedro Woolley *(G-11546)*
Tex Enterprises Inc....G....253 939-1660
Auburn *(G-579)*
Vennco Rubber Inc....G....360 249-6924
Montesano *(G-6665)*
Zuber Polymers LLC....G....360 929-7888
Seattle *(G-11525)*

2823 Cellulosic Man-Made Fibers

Aidapak Services LLC....F....360 448-2090
Vancouver *(G-14013)*
Spillmasters X LLC....G....360 461-7910
Port Angeles *(G-7746)*

2824 Synthetic Organic Fibers, Exc Cellulosic

Carbitex Inc....G....509 591-9775
Kennewick *(G-4642)*
Day Creek Organic Farms Inc....G....360 856-4770
Sedro Woolley *(G-11536)*
Plastic Sales & Service Inc....F....206 524-8312
Lynnwood *(G-6181)*
▲ Rich Nature Nutraceutical Labs....F....425 493-1885
Mukilteo *(G-6972)*
Tidal Vision Products LLC....F....907 988-8888
Ferndale *(G-3913)*

2833 Medicinal Chemicals & Botanical Prdts

Agro Technic LLC....F....206 669-2446
Bellevue *(G-782)*
Aptevo Biotherapeutics LLC....G....206 838-0500
Seattle *(G-9413)*
▲ Avid Health Inc....G....360 737-6800
Vancouver *(G-14048)*
Awakened Heart....G....360 556-6168
Olympia *(G-7233)*
Blue Moon Marine LLC....G....360 378-2498
Friday Harbor *(G-4041)*
Botanical Blu L L C....G....360 866-8251
Olympia *(G-7240)*
Cloners Market Inc....G....425 218-0440
Everett *(G-3420)*
▲ Econet Inc....E....360 486-8300
Seattle *(G-9880)*
Farwell Products Inc....G....509 663-6212
Wenatchee *(G-15030)*
▲ Glykon Technologies Group LLC....G....510 289-4331
Seattle *(G-10089)*
▲ Heather & Company For Ibs LLC....F....206 264-8069
Kent *(G-4938)*
Herb Withered....G....509 493-3614
White Salmon *(G-15118)*

SIC

Employee Codes: A=Over 500 employees, B=251-500
C=101-250, D=51-100, E=20-50, F=10-19, G=2-9
2019 Washington
Manufacturers Register
585

Human Science LLC G 253 321-6800
Sumner *(G-13074)*
Ian Enterprises LLC G 425 413-0371
Maple Valley *(G-6275)*
Integrity Supplements LLC G 800 210-4863
Bremerton *(G-1962)*
Modulien Inc G 208 874-2219
Pullman *(G-8099)*
Nbty Inc G 425 369-1771
Issaquah *(G-4452)*
▼ **Pacific Coast Cascara Bark Co** G 360 249-3503
Montesano *(G-6652)*
Peptide Scientific USA Ltd F 718 618-5025
Seattle *(G-10784)*
Rmg Nutrition G 253 863-7017
Sumner *(G-13096)*
Tilray Inc G 206 432-9325
Seattle *(G-11308)*
◆ **Trout Lake Farm LLC** E 509 395-2025
Trout Lake *(G-13684)*
Urban Buggy LLC G 206 743-5727
Seattle *(G-11389)*
Worldwide Botanicals Inc G 206 518-1878
Seatac *(G-9311)*

2834 Pharmaceuticals

ABT 360 LLC G 509 592-8144
Pullman *(G-8081)*
Achieve Life Science Inc G 425 686-1500
Bothell *(G-1744)*
Achieve Life Sciences Inc G 425 686-1500
Seattle *(G-9342)*
Adapt Labs Inc G 206 842-2040
Bainbridge Island *(G-606)*
AGC Biologics Inc C 425 485-0280
Bothell *(G-1816)*
Alcide Corporation E 425 882-2555
Redmond *(G-8377)*
Alder Biopharmaceuticals Inc D 425 205-2900
Bothell *(G-1745)*
Aletheia Therapeutics LLC G 206 473-2435
Seattle *(G-9371)*
Alphapharma Inc G 206 413-5122
Renton *(G-8741)*
Alpine Immune Sciences Inc E 206 788-4545
Seattle *(G-9388)*
Altan Inc G 360 331-1595
Greenbank *(G-4304)*
Amgen Inc A 206 265-7504
Seattle *(G-9397)*
Aptevo Therapeutics Inc D 206 838-0500
Seattle *(G-9414)*
Aq Usa Inc G 800 663-8303
Lynden *(G-6001)*
▲ **Aquatic Life Sciences Inc** F 800 283-5292
Ferndale *(G-3816)*
Artemisia Biomedical Inc G 425 444-5619
Newcastle *(G-7024)*
Athira Pharma Inc F 206 221-8112
Seattle *(G-9451)*
Atossa Genetics Inc G 206 325-6086
Seattle *(G-9457)*
Avalyn Pharma Inc F 206 707-0340
Seattle *(G-9469)*
Avantbio Corporation G 360 521-8904
Seattle *(G-9470)*
Avantbio Corporation G 360 521-8904
Vancouver *(G-14046)*
Bausch Health Americas Inc G 425 346-2472
Bothell *(G-1751)*
Bayer Healthcare LLC C 425 245-1392
Lynnwood *(G-6082)*
Bayer Healthcare LLC G 360 886-8182
Ravensdale *(G-8330)*
Bayer Hlthcare Phrmcticals LLC B 862 404-3000
Seattle *(G-9502)*
Bergstrom Nutrition G 360 693-0601
Vancouver *(G-14061)*
Betsy Bells Natyural Solutions G 206 933-1889
Seattle *(G-9518)*
Briotech Inc G 425 488-4300
Woodinville *(G-15197)*
Cardeas Pharma Corporation F 206 973-1026
Seattle *(G-9628)*
▲ **Cardinal Associates Inc** E 360 693-1883
Vancouver *(G-14098)*
Cardinal Health 414 LLC G 206 763-4411
Seattle *(G-9630)*
Cascade Designs Inc G 206 505-9500
Seattle *(G-9641)*
Celgene Corporation D 415 839-7058
Seattle *(G-9650)*
Central Admxture Phrm Svcs Inc E 253 395-8700
Kent *(G-4846)*
Choice Cardiovascular Pllc G 253 229-7003
Gig Harbor *(G-4087)*
CMC Biologics SARI Corp E 425 485-1900
Bothell *(G-1840)*
Cocrystal Pharma Inc F 786 459-1831
Bothell *(G-1756)*
Coronado Biosciences G 206 826-7168
Seattle *(G-9742)*
CTI Biopharma Corp D 206 282-7100
Seattle *(G-9762)*
Cytodyn Operations Inc G 360 980-8524
Vancouver *(G-14159)*
David Bol G 425 802-0804
Spokane *(G-12219)*
Dendreon Corporation B 877 256-4545
Seattle *(G-9820)*
▼ **Dendreon Corporation** C 206 256-4545
Seattle *(G-9821)*
Dr Bieseckers LLC G 360 386-1530
Stanwood *(G-12967)*
Endpoint LLC G 206 780-2905
Bainbridge Island *(G-630)*
Estm Inc G 509 545-0596
Kennewick *(G-4664)*
Faraday Pharmaceuticals Inc G 206 946-1989
Seattle *(G-9971)*
Furtim Therapeutics LLC G 425 273-1035
Seattle *(G-10041)*
Genoa Healthcare LLC G 206 971-9707
Seattle *(G-10061)*
Get Plenish Inc G 425 922-0070
Bellevue *(G-924)*
Gilead Sciences Inc D 206 728-5090
Seattle *(G-10070)*
Glaxosmithkline LLC E 206 755-5725
Bellevue *(G-926)*
Glaxosmithkline LLC E 206 856-5663
Kenmore *(G-4576)*
Grove and Kane Inc G 425 407-3454
Everett *(G-3507)*
Hebert Sam-E LLC G 206 650-4489
Seattle *(G-10159)*
Helix Biomedix Inc G 425 402-8400
Bothell *(G-1865)*
Human Science LLC G 253 321-6800
Sumner *(G-13074)*
Immune Design Corp D 206 682-0645
Seattle *(G-10209)*
Immunex Corporation A 206 551-5169
Seattle *(G-10210)*
Impel Neuropharma Inc G 206 568-1466
Seattle *(G-10211)*
Implicit Bioscience Inc G 650 851-3133
Seattle *(G-10215)*
Indena Usa Inc G 206 340-6140
Seattle *(G-10221)*
Integrity Biopharma Services G 509 474-1481
Spokane *(G-12320)*
▲ **Jubilant Hollisterstier LLC** B 509 482-4945
Spokane *(G-12345)*
Jubilant Hollisterstier LLC G 509 482-3287
Spokane Valley *(G-12756)*
◆ **Key Technology Inc** B 509 529-2161
Walla Walla *(G-14833)*
Kiadis Pharma US Corporation G 585 397-1074
Seattle *(G-10342)*
Kindex Pharmaceuticals Inc G 206 922-2912
Seattle *(G-10344)*
Lyell Immunopharma Inc G 206 909-3809
Seattle *(G-10455)*
Medicines Co G 425 829-2540
Snohomish *(G-11945)*
Medicis Technologies Corp D 425 420-2100
Bothell *(G-1778)*
Miracle Studios G 833 728-3233
Bonney Lake *(G-1729)*
Mk Perrigo Realtor G 425 478-6694
Seattle *(G-10551)*
Morton A Kimball G 360 458-5251
Yelm *(G-15740)*
Neobiotech Global Corporation G 253 732-3573
Auburn *(G-506)*
Nobu Integrative Medicine LLC G 425 363-2970
North Bend *(G-7118)*
◆ **Northwest Natural Products Inc** C 360 737-6800
Ridgefield *(G-9096)*
Novartis Vccnes Dagnostics Inc C 862 778-2100
Seattle *(G-10659)*
▲ **Nutrition Now Inc** D 360 737-6800
Ridgefield *(G-9097)*
Nuun & Company Inc D 206 219-9237
Seattle *(G-10671)*
Oberon Pharma G 206 713-5467
Mercer Island *(G-6476)*
Olympic Protein Sciences LLC G 206 849-9811
Seattle *(G-10694)*
Omeros Corporation C 206 676-5000
Seattle *(G-10698)*
Pd Pharmatech LLC G 800 452-4682
Seattle *(G-10774)*
▲ **Performance Packaging Inc** E 360 737-9966
Vancouver *(G-14484)*
Permesys Inc G 860 961-5367
Bothell *(G-1885)*
Pfizer Inc C 360 701-0799
Lacey *(G-5576)*
Poa Pharma North America LLC G 855 416-6826
Vancouver *(G-14491)*
Promedev LLC G 800 500-8384
Kirkland *(G-5444)*
Pz Wind Down Inc E 206 805-6300
Seattle *(G-10895)*
Rainier Clinical Research Ctr E 425 251-1720
Renton *(G-8891)*
Remeopharma Inc F 206 805-9786
Bainbridge Island *(G-665)*
Resolve Therapeutics LLC G 208 727-7010
Seattle *(G-10951)*
Ross Group of Companies Inc G 800 663-8303
Lynden *(G-6050)*
Sbk Pharma LLC G 425 778-7778
Edmonds *(G-3152)*
Shea Your Lips Lip Balm G 360 856-4803
Sedro Woolley *(G-11564)*
Shilshole Bioscience Inc G 206 459-8341
Sammamish *(G-9247)*
Skinmedica Inc G 760 448-3600
Olympia *(G-7397)*
◆ **Sol Sunguard Corporation** E 206 283-0409
Seattle *(G-11153)*
Sound Pharmaceuticals Inc F 206 634-2559
Seattle *(G-11158)*
Specialized Pharmaceuticals G 253 859-3702
Kent *(G-5147)*
Stason Animal Health Inc G 360 200-5300
Vancouver *(G-14609)*
Stier Hollister Sales G 509 892-1188
Spokane Valley *(G-12894)*
Strong Snax Inc G 360 953-3753
Ridgefield *(G-9114)*
Sunn Pharmaceuticals LLC G 425 835-0418
Mountlake Terrace *(G-6870)*
Takeda Pharmaceuticals USA Inc G 509 747-5551
Spokane *(G-12544)*
Tyson Nutraceuticals Inc G 425 869-1192
Kirkland *(G-5487)*
▲ **Unigen Inc** F 360 486-8200
Seattle *(G-11368)*
US Biopharma Inc G 425 242-0208
Bellevue *(G-1209)*
Vitamin Shoppe Industries Inc G 855 715-8530
Burien *(G-2136)*
Vitamin Shoppe Industries Inc G 855 235-9431
Maple Valley *(G-6298)*
◆ **Western Chemical Incorporated** F 360 384-5898
Ferndale *(G-3923)*
Wineblock LLC G 877 919-4921
Seattle *(G-11484)*
Zumedix LP G 206 618-2848
Seattle *(G-11526)*
Zymogenetics Inc C 206 442-6600
Seattle *(G-11527)*
Zymogenetics Inc G 425 398-9637
Bothell *(G-1925)*

2835 Diagnostic Substances

Abr Inc G 509 334-2968
Pullman *(G-8080)*
Bio-RAD Laboratories Inc C 425 881-8300
Redmond *(G-8403)*
Biotangent Diagnostics LLC G 503 713-3339
Issaquah *(G-4385)*
Cardinal Health 414 LLC G 206 763-4411
Seattle *(G-9630)*
Cell Systems Corporation G 425 823-1010
Kirkland *(G-5301)*

Eurofins Microbiology Labs Inc G 425 686-1996
Bothell *(G-1762)*

Genzyme Corporation D 425 245-1221
Lynnwood *(G-6129)*

Heart Hands Preganacy Care Ctr G 360 532-1104
Hoquiam *(G-4341)*

J J J Farms Inc G 360 398-8641
Bellingham *(G-1386)*

▲ **Kamiya Biomedical Company LLC** F 206 575-8068
Tukwila *(G-13760)*

Kent Laboratories Inc F 360 398-8641
Bellingham *(G-1392)*

Mep Labs LLC G 206 229-2525
Renton *(G-8852)*

Orchards Pregnancy Resources G 360 567-0285
Vancouver *(G-14455)*

Petnet Solutions Inc G 425 656-1640
Kent *(G-5065)*

Petnet Solutions Inc G 509 455-4178
Spokane *(G-12439)*

Photon Biosciences LLC G 509 595-0159
Pullman *(G-8100)*

Prevencio Inc G 425 576-1200
Kirkland *(G-5441)*

S2m Enterprises LLC G 509 919-3714
Spokane Valley *(G-12857)*

2836 Biological Prdts, Exc Diagnostic Substances

Absci LLC E 360 949-1041
Vancouver *(G-14005)*

Advanced Extracts G 360 949-5325
Brush Prairie *(G-2027)*

Alder Biopharmaceuticals Inc D 425 205-2900
Bothell *(G-1745)*

Alpha Biopartners LLC G 405 603-1917
Seattle *(G-9386)*

Amplex Bioresources LLC G 425 285-0628
Bellevue *(G-787)*

Aquabiotics Corporation G 206 842-1708
Bainbridge Island *(G-609)*

Ballard Extracts G 206 499-4476
Seattle *(G-9480)*

Carol Braden Inc G 206 715-9397
Seattle *(G-9635)*

Cascadia Venom Collection G 360 556-3177
Rochester *(G-9129)*

▲ **Chemill Inc** F 425 286-5229
Bothell *(G-1755)*

Chondrex Inc G 425 702-6365
Redmond *(G-8419)*

Csl Plasma Inc G 253 275-2243
Federal Way *(G-3728)*

East Vancouver Venom G 360 518-1658
Vancouver *(G-14192)*

Glycocept Inc G 425 647-7446
Sammamish *(G-9209)*

Greyslade G 253 332-5985
Tacoma *(G-13325)*

Guys Plasma NW LLC G 360 878-9826
Olympia *(G-7301)*

Healionics Corporation G 206 432-9060
Seattle *(G-10155)*

▲ **Hops Extract Corp America** F 509 575-6440
Yakima *(G-15582)*

Immunex Corporation A 206 551-5169
Seattle *(G-10210)*

Immunobioscience Corp G 425 367-4601
Mukilteo *(G-6942)*

Inventprise LLC F 206 858-8472
Redmond *(G-8514)*

Juno Therapeutics Inc E 206 582-1600
Seattle *(G-10317)*

Just Biotherapeutics Inc D 206 651-5094
Seattle *(G-10318)*

▲ **Kamiya Biomedical Company LLC** F 206 575-8068
Tukwila *(G-13760)*

Kc Wheelwright G 206 799-9822
Seattle *(G-10333)*

Natural Venom All Star G 253 370-7986
Tacoma *(G-13425)*

New Culture Media G 206 406-1934
Bothell *(G-1780)*

Octapharma Plasma G 360 450-3135
Vancouver *(G-14447)*

Octapharma Plasma G 253 922-7753
Fife *(G-3975)*

Optimum Extracts G 206 491-9617
Auburn *(G-519)*

Path Vaccine Solutions G 206 285-3500
Seattle *(G-10766)*

Pellets Inc G 360 733-3012
Bellingham *(G-1495)*

Plasma Biolife Services L P G 509 545-3008
Pasco *(G-7617)*

Plasma Steel LLC G 360 801-0444
Bremerton *(G-1988)*

Prorestore Products E 412 264-8340
Burlington *(G-2182)*

Pure Extracts G 509 679-6556
East Wenatchee *(G-3030)*

Qwell Pharmaceuticals Inc G 206 674-3027
Seattle *(G-10908)*

Seattle Genetics Inc B 425 527-4000
Bothell *(G-1902)*

Seattle Genetics Inc G 425 483-1037
Bothell *(G-1903)*

Seattle Pure Extracts G 206 788-5754
Seattle *(G-11070)*

Specialty Vetpath G 206 453-5691
Shoreline *(G-11816)*

Stilly Venom Baseball Club G 360 319-6589
Arlington *(G-336)*

Thrifty Payless Inc T/A G 360 754-8014
Olympia *(G-7405)*

Thrifty Payless Inc T/A G 509 783-1438
Kennewick *(G-4735)*

Thrifty Payless Inc T/A G 509 928-9121
Spokane Valley *(G-12905)*

Thrifty Payless Inc T/A G 360 825-2558
Enumclaw *(G-3323)*

Thrifty Payless Inc T/A G 509 925-4232
Ellensburg *(G-3232)*

Thrifty Payless Inc T/A G 206 324-7111
Seattle *(G-11299)*

Thrifty Payless Inc G 206 760-1076
Seattle *(G-11300)*

Thrifty Payless Inc T/A G 206 441-8790
Seattle *(G-11301)*

Thrifty Payless Inc T/A G 360 332-1616
Blaine *(G-1705)*

Thrifty Payless Inc T/A G 360 794-0943
Monroe *(G-6630)*

Thrifty Payless Inc T/A G 360 457-3456
Port Angeles *(G-7750)*

Thrifty Payless Inc T/A G 206 721-5018
Seattle *(G-11302)*

Thrifty Payless Inc T/A G 360 647-2175
Bellingham *(G-1570)*

Vaccines 2 U G 509 475-1347
Spokane Valley *(G-12922)*

2841 Soap & Detergents

▲ **Agbanga Karite LLC** G 360 515-9013
Tumwater *(G-13849)*

Azure Mountain Botanicals G 425 478-3902
Dayton *(G-2878)*

Birchwood Acres LLC G 360 433-8690
Camas *(G-2232)*

Bon Logic Corporation G 509 991-9643
Spokane *(G-12157)*

Bubbles Bakery G 360 945-1816
Point Roberts *(G-7667)*

Buckeye International Inc G 206 575-1185
Seatac *(G-9279)*

▲ **Church and Dwight** F 360 816-7400
Ridgefield *(G-9072)*

Country Save Products Corp G 360 435-9868
Arlington *(G-223)*

Curlew Country Herbs G 509 779-4941
Curlew *(G-2845)*

Dandelion & Tea LLC G 206 353-2048
Seattle *(G-9791)*

Dave Ledgerwood G 509 843-3677
Pomeroy *(G-7671)*

Diana Thompson G 360 665-0102
Ocean Park *(G-7179)*

Dr Bieseckers LLC G 360 386-1530
Stanwood *(G-12967)*

Earth Soap Company G 425 677-8540
Issaquah *(G-4408)*

Eliza K Trowbridge G 360 376-5152
Olga *(G-7214)*

Good Scents Co G 509 996-2620
Winthrop *(G-15161)*

Greencastle Soap & Supply G 509 466-7223
Spokane *(G-12282)*

Heavenly Soap G 206 349-7982
Monroe *(G-6575)*

Little Soap Maker G 509 972-8504
Yakima *(G-15611)*

Marvin Batcheller G 509 784-7018
Entiat *(G-3267)*

◆ **Olympic Mountain Products Inc** E 253 850-2343
Kent *(G-5044)*

Procter & Gamble Company C 425 313-3511
Issaquah *(G-4461)*

Pureheart G 509 535-2323
Spokane *(G-12459)*

Quail Meadow Creations G 509 685-1429
Colville *(G-2770)*

Samish Bay Soaps & Scents G 360 752-9015
Bellingham *(G-1522)*

Secure It LLC G 509 992-6190
Spokane *(G-12497)*

Shepherds Soap Co G 360 427-7811
Shelton *(G-11733)*

Something For Everybody G 541 805-8495
College Place *(G-2728)*

Townsend Bay Soap Co LLC G 360 379-4140
Port Townsend *(G-7934)*

Venus Laboratories Inc E 360 455-8933
Lacey *(G-5598)*

▲ **Verax Chemical Co** G 360 668-2431
Snohomish *(G-11996)*

Whidbey Island Ntural Pdts Inc G 360 929-2461
Freeland *(G-4040)*

2842 Spec Cleaning, Polishing & Sanitation Preparations

A and V Inc G 425 968-5881
Sammamish *(G-9182)*

Alcide Corporation E 425 882-2555
Redmond *(G-8377)*

Alpine Products Inc G 253 351-9828
Auburn *(G-373)*

Ant Fx International LLC G 253 302-7414
Ferndale *(G-3814)*

Bainbridge Beeswax Works G 206 618-2569
Bainbridge Island *(G-613)*

Bee Natural Leathercare LLC G 360 891-7178
Vancouver *(G-14059)*

Bhs Marketing LLC G 208 740-9369
Tacoma *(G-13199)*

Buckeye International Inc G 206 575-1185
Seatac *(G-9279)*

Cardinal Clean G 360 629-4399
Stanwood *(G-12964)*

Cgt Inc G 253 833-8849
Auburn *(G-405)*

Chimcare Vancouver G 360 696-8309
Vancouver *(G-14117)*

Chimcare West Seattle G 206 673-2203
Seattle *(G-9676)*

Clear-Fx LLC F 800 408-3701
Ferndale *(G-3832)*

Country Save Products Corp G 360 435-9868
Arlington *(G-223)*

Design Hardwood Products Inc G 425 869-0859
Redmond *(G-8440)*

▼ **Discovery Products Corporation** G 877 530-2999
Lynnwood *(G-6109)*

Ecolab Inc E 253 733-3000
Tacoma *(G-13269)*

Ekko Bioscience LLC G 844 822-9300
Vancouver *(G-14196)*

▲ **Faction Ltd** G 360 275-2834
Belfair *(G-762)*

Fir Line Trans & Brake G 509 684-5484
Colville *(G-2752)*

▼ **Formula Corp** E 253 880-0170
Auburn *(G-442)*

Gerris Dry Bunk G 509 782-2653
Cashmere *(G-2320)*

Glass Restoration Specialists E 253 473-7779
Tacoma *(G-13311)*

Globek LLC G 360 627-9714
Bremerton *(G-1958)*

Hassler & Associates Inc G 253 851-3248
Gig Harbor *(G-4115)*

◆ **Jay One Ball** G 360 275-2834
Belfair *(G-764)*

Kepler Absorbents LLC G 844 453-7537
Fife *(G-3962)*

Lexys Nails & Spa G 360 352-5044
Tumwater *(G-13883)*

Maid Naturally LLC E 509 994-3685
Spokane *(G-12379)*

Employee Codes: A=Over 500 employees, B=251-500
C=101-250, D=51-100, E=20-50, F=10-19, G=2-9
2019 Washington
Manufacturers Register
587

28 CHEMICALS AND ALLIED PRODUCTS

▲ Medetech Development Corp ....G...... 425 891-9151
  Bellevue (G-1000)
Northwest Euro LLC ....G...... 206 981-8002
  Seattle (G-10642)
NW Laundry Service ....G...... 206 242-5500
  Tukwila (G-13781)
Olympic Jantr Sup & Svc LLC ....G...... 360 692-0832
  Bremerton (G-1982)
Oxiscience LLC ....G...... 425 777-5488
  Redmond (G-8605)
Pace International LLC ....E...... 800 936-6750
  East Wenatchee (G-3028)
Paramount Chemical Spc Inc ....E...... 425 882-2673
  Redmond (G-8614)
Procter & Gamble Company ....C...... 425 313-3511
  Issaquah (G-4461)
Regency Cleaners LLC ....G...... 206 650-6933
  Burien (G-2125)
Restorfx ....G...... 425 286-5189
  Everett (G-3598)
Restorfx International Inc ....G...... 800 404-4107
  Ferndale (G-3893)
Roadmaster Inc ....G...... 360 735-7575
  Vancouver (G-14556)
Sellin Style ....G...... 360 670-5540
  Sequim (G-11662)
Tower Industries Inc ....F...... 206 760-3022
  Tacoma (G-13560)
◆ United Sorbents Seattle LLC .....E...... 425 656-4440
  Kent (G-5197)
▲ Verax Chemical Co. ....G...... 360 668-2431
  Snohomish (G-11996)
Walla Walla Environmental Inc .....F...... 509 522-0490
  Walla Walla (G-14888)
Waupaca Northwoods LLC ....D...... 509 877-2830
  Parker (G-7550)
▲ Wesmar Company Inc ....D...... 206 783-5344
  Lynnwood (G-6222)
Western Products ....G...... 509 994-1288
  Sprague (G-12949)
Winsol Laboratories Inc ....G...... 206 782-5500
  Seattle (G-11488)

2844 Perfumes, Cosmetics & Toilet Preparations

12 Scents ....G...... 206 588-0314
  Seattle (G-9316)
▲ Agbanga Karite LLC ....G...... 360 515-9013
  Tumwater (G-13849)
▲ All Natural Botanicals Inc ....G...... 253 939-2600
  Kent (G-4771)
Altera Inc ....F...... 509 901-9292
  Yakima (G-15505)
Amera Sales Inc ....G...... 509 735-1531
  Kennewick (G-4615)
▲ Antica Farmacista LLC ....G...... 206 329-3966
  Seattle (G-9406)
Arbordoun ....G...... 360 468-2508
  Lopez Island (G-5978)
Art of Shaving - FI LLC ....G...... 206 737-8370
  Seattle (G-9437)
Art of Shaving - FI LLC ....G...... 253 777-0993
  Tacoma (G-13181)
Aveda Environmental Lifestyles ....G...... 509 624-5028
  Spokane (G-12132)
Basic Topicals LLC ....G...... 206 397-3309
  Seattle (G-9498)
▲ Beaming White LLC ....E...... 360 635-5600
  Vancouver (G-14058)
Beyond Zone Inc ....G...... 206 363-2147
  Shoreline (G-11761)
Beyoutiful Bath Bombs More ....G...... 509 315-9608
  Spokane (G-12146)
Biozn LLC ....G...... 206 388-7865
  Bellevue (G-818)
Bon Logic Corporation ....G...... 509 991-9643
  Spokane (G-12157)
Brown Toes LLC ....G...... 360 873-8407
  Anacortes (G-104)
Butter London LLC ....G...... 206 624-1085
  Seattle (G-9602)
Camille ....G...... 206 284-0407
  Seattle (G-9613)
Chimeras LLC ....G...... 360 754-9217
  Olympia (G-7249)
▲ Creative Collections Co Inc ......E...... 360 866-8840
  Olympia (G-7259)
Crystalwolfe Blends ....G...... 509 217-2132
  Cheney (G-2582)

Dr Bieseckers LLC ....G...... 360 386-1530
  Stanwood (G-12967)
▲ Econet Inc ....E...... 360 486-8300
  Seattle (G-9880)
Emu Emprium Hlthy Alternatives ...G...... 360 269-3459
  Chehalis (G-2492)
Enervana LLC ....G...... 253 220-8413
  Tukwila (G-13729)
Everlasting Scents LLC ....G...... 509 534-4790
  Spokane Valley (G-12695)
Fascinaturals LLC ....G...... 425 954-7151
  Edmonds (G-3111)
Fast Horticultural Services ....G...... 360 393-7057
  Ferndale (G-3840)
▲ Favorite Discovery LLC ....G...... 646 337-3574
  Vancouver (G-14225)
Fiddle and Fern ....G...... 206 898-4165
  Sammamish (G-9206)
Franklin and Franklin Company ....G...... 360 254-4767
  Vancouver (G-14239)
◆ Grace Harvest & Assoc LLC ......F...... 206 973-2363
  Mercer Island (G-6464)
Green Global Solution Inc ....G...... 253 202-2304
  Tacoma (G-13324)
Herbivore Botanicals LLC ....G...... 206 226-5008
  Seattle (G-10167)
▲ Honey House Naturals Inc ......F...... 253 926-8193
  Fife (G-3958)
House of Matriarch Inc ....G...... 425 466-7783
  Bellevue (G-950)
▲ Hydropeptide LLC ....F...... 425 458-1072
  Issaquah (G-4427)
I Hart Lipstick ....G...... 253 720-7126
  Tacoma (G-13345)
▲ Innovative Salon Products Inc ..G...... 360 805-0794
  Monroe (G-6580)
J King Formulas Inc ....G...... 360 683-6908
  Sequim (G-11642)
Jeffrey James LLC ....G...... 562 541-6976
  Seattle (G-10290)
K&G Scents ....G...... 206 380-1831
  Seattle (G-10321)
▲ Koh Gen Do Americas LLC ......G...... 253 267-1769
  Dupont (G-2968)
Kona Gold Corp ....G...... 425 836-0389
  Kirkland (G-5377)
Lch Enterprises ....G...... 253 313-5665
  Gig Harbor (G-4129)
Le Labo ....G...... 206 420-2835
  Seattle (G-10390)
Lipstick Mission ....G...... 360 455-3212
  Lacey (G-5565)
Little Bay Inc ....G...... 646 300-3694
  Seattle (G-10429)
Mani Pedi ....G...... 509 522-6264
  Walla Walla (G-14841)
Marie-Luce Enterprises ....G...... 360 876-7925
  Port Orchard (G-7827)
Maysbeautproductscom ....G...... 253 318-8772
  Auburn (G-493)
▲ Micro Current Technology Inc ..E...... 206 938-5800
  Seattle (G-10530)
Miracle Studios 833 728-3233
  Bonney Lake (G-1729)
Moon Valley Natural Pdts LLC ......G...... 360 595-0500
  Deming (G-2921)
National Hsptlity Rsources LLC ......G...... 360 413-1654
  Olympia (G-7348)
Natural Essences ....G...... 509 820-3242
  Kennewick (G-4699)
Nester Brothers LLC ....G...... 253 320-9405
  Tacoma (G-13426)
Nion Beauty Inc ....G...... 206 228-5988
  Bothell (G-1880)
◆ Olympic Mountain Products Inc ..E...... 253 850-2343
  Kent (G-5044)
Organic Creations ....G...... 503 891-0479
  Vancouver (G-14457)
Patricia Avery ....G...... 206 602-0017
  Tacoma (G-13460)
Paula S Choice ....C...... 425 988-2931
  Kent (G-5062)
▲ Paulas Choice LLC ....C...... 425 988-6068
  Seattle (G-10772)
Paulas Choice Holdings Inc ....G...... 425 988-6068
  Seattle (G-10773)
Polish Nail Spa ....G...... 425 771-1458
  Lynnwood (G-6182)
Procter & Gamble Company ....C...... 425 313-3511
  Issaquah (G-4461)

Pureblisnaturals ....G...... 253 719-2683
  University Place (G-13977)
Quest Products LLC ....F...... 425 451-9876
  Kent (G-5094)
Rainroom Essentials ....G...... 253 988-5889
  Bonney Lake (G-1736)
Raw Chemistry LLC ....G...... 360 521-2115
  Vancouver (G-14534)
▲ Renewalliance Inc ....G...... 425 633-3368
  Bellevue (G-1100)
Resonant Botanicals LLC ....G...... 360 969-5065
  Clinton (G-2694)
Ritzy Bath Bombs ....G...... 206 499-7336
  Vancouver (G-14552)
Scrub Nogginz LLC ....G...... 425 931-9251
  Snohomish (G-11971)
Seattle Pomade Co ....G...... 206 348-3972
  Mill Creek (G-6527)
Shadow Works LLC ....G...... 509 251-8306
  Spokane Valley (G-12867)
Sik Scents LLC ....G...... 206 420-4647
  Seattle (G-11111)
Simply Joyful LLC ....G...... 425 686-5311
  Everett (G-3611)
Sirens Bath Bombs ....G...... 360 852-4938
  Vancouver (G-14589)
Soap Aria LLC ....G...... 206 229-4351
  Tacoma (G-13516)
Stacya Silverman & Associates .....G...... 206 270-9465
  Seattle (G-11177)
Udabomb Bath Bombs ....G...... 509 331-4100
  Othello (G-7508)
Underground1969 Co ....G...... 747 254-0595
  Seattle (G-11175)
Whidbey Island Ntural Pdts Inc ....G...... 360 929-2461
  Freeland (G-4040)
Wisdom Elite LLC ....G...... 806 201-3953
  Lakewood (G-5768)
Yon LLC ....G...... 360 947-5895
  Vancouver (G-14706)

2851 Paints, Varnishes, Lacquers, Enamels

A Quality Painting ....G...... 509 362-2398
  Spokane (G-12090)
Asahipen America Inc ....F...... 206 371-9441
  Seattle (G-9441)
Behr Paint & Stain ....G...... 253 887-9357
  Auburn (G-390)
Behr Process Corporation ....F...... 253 887-8410
  Algona (G-67)
Cardinal Industrial Finishes ....F...... 425 483-5665
  Woodinville (G-15205)
CDI Coding ....G...... 360 653-6437
  Woodinville (G-15207)
Columbia Indus Coatings LLC ......G...... 509 531-7310
  Richland (G-8983)
Curnutt Inc ....G...... 208 520-2598
  Pasco (G-7574)
Dalys Inc ....E...... 425 454-3093
  Seattle (G-9788)
Design Hardwood Products Inc ....F...... 425 869-0859
  Redmond (G-8439)
Dux Technologies Inc ....G...... 206 248-0808
  Burien (G-2103)
▼ Eco Chemical Inc ....F...... 206 448-7930
  Seattle (G-9877)
▼ Farwest Paint Manufacturing Co ..F...... 206 244-8844
  Tukwila (G-13731)
Forrest Paint Co ....G...... 509 924-3785
  Spokane Valley (G-12708)
Forrest Paint Co ....F...... 253 854-6372
  Kent (G-4917)
G C P LLC ....G...... 206 781-1162
  Seattle (G-10045)
Hauge & Hassain Incorporated ....E...... 206 789-8842
  Seattle (G-10149)
▲ Homax Group Inc ....E...... 360 733-9029
  Bellingham (G-1371)
I M A C ....G...... 509 747-3607
  Spokane (G-12302)
▲ Industrial Control Dev Inc ....E...... 360 546-2286
  Ridgefield (G-9090)
International Paint LLC ....F...... 206 763-5884
  Seattle (G-10251)
Jim Suzuki ....G...... 253 804-6070
  Auburn (G-482)
Linex of Olympia ....G...... 360 709-0363
  Tumwater (G-13884)
Mad Label Industries Inc ....G...... 844 623-4897
  Bremerton (G-1976)

SIC SECTION

28 CHEMICALS AND ALLIED PRODUCTS

Metal Finishing Inc .... F 360 659-1971
  Arlington *(G-274)*
Metro Coatings Inc .... F 360 906-0646
  Vancouver *(G-14415)*
◆ Perma-Chink Systems Inc .... F 425 885-6050
  Redmond *(G-8619)*
Polyurethane Sales & Svc LLC .... G 360 334-5364
  Vancouver *(G-14494)*
PPG Industries .... G 253 804-4350
  Auburn *(G-533)*
PPG Industries Inc .... G 425 885-3848
  Redmond *(G-8629)*
Precision Paint .... G 425 235-0340
  Renton *(G-8882)*
Primer Specialties Inc .... G 360 518-3716
  Vancouver *(G-14505)*
Rodda Paint Co .... G 253 283-6581
  Chehalis *(G-2532)*
Rodda Paint Co .... G 360 423-4990
  Longview *(G-5948)*
Rodda Paint Co .... G 360 738-6878
  Bellingham *(G-1519)*
▲ Rudd Company Inc .... G 206 789-1000
  Seattle *(G-10992)*
Sherwin-Williams Company .... G 206 417-4502
  Seattle *(G-11100)*
Sienna Technologies Inc .... F 425 485-0756
  Woodinville *(G-15362)*
◆ Specialty Products Inc .... E 253 588-7101
  Lakewood *(G-5759)*
Stanley Plowing .... G 509 218-2419
  Deer Park *(G-2916)*
T N W Inc .... G 206 762-5755
  Seattle *(G-11250)*
Triple R Enterprises Inc .... G 360 491-1600
  Olympia *(G-7414)*
Wade Sumpter Industries Inc .... G 425 486-9541
  Bothell *(G-1915)*
Wakefield Art .... G 425 260-0257
  Kirkland *(G-5491)*
Walla Walla Environmental Inc .... F 509 522-0490
  Walla Walla *(G-14888)*
▼ Wasser Corp .... G 360 870-3513
  Auburn *(G-594)*
Zirconia Inc .... G 206 219-9236
  Tukwila *(G-13839)*

2861 Gum & Wood Chemicals

Arch Wood Protection Inc .... G 360 673-5099
  Kalama *(G-4492)*
▲ Chemco Acquisition Corporation ..... E 360 366-3500
  Ferndale *(G-3830)*
Kingsford Smith Charles .... G 360 738-6959
  Bellingham *(G-1396)*
RR Products .... G 509 773-5227
  Goldendale *(G-4208)*

2865 Cyclic-Crudes, Intermediates, Dyes & Org Pigments

Botanical Colors LLC .... G 206 518-7073
  Seattle *(G-9566)*
Botanical Colors LLC .... G 206 518-7073
  Seattle *(G-9567)*
Emerald Kalama Chemical LLC .... C 360 673-2550
  Kalama *(G-4499)*
Sunoco .... G 253 872-8500
  Kent *(G-5162)*

2869 Industrial Organic Chemicals, NEC

Agrium US Inc .... C 509 586-5500
  Kennewick *(G-4613)*
Air Products and Chemicals Inc .... G 253 845-4000
  Puyallup *(G-8119)*
Arneson Fuels LLC .... G 425 823-1096
  Kirkland *(G-5280)*
▼ Ascensus Specialties LLC .... D 425 448-1679
  Bellevue *(G-796)*
▲ BBC Biochemical Corporation .... C 360 542-8400
  Mount Vernon *(G-6777)*
Blue Star Gas - Seattle Co .... G 206 762-2583
  Tukwila *(G-13698)*
Clean-Vantage .... G 509 392-2793
  Richland *(G-8982)*
Coulee View Food and Fuel .... G 509 633-2951
  Coulee Dam *(G-2807)*
DFI Mp Eroh LLC .... G 206 499-2687
  Moses Lake *(G-6705)*
Dyna Flow .... G 253 381-9736
  Gig Harbor *(G-4096)*

Dynamic Food Ingredients Corp .... G 303 459-5908
  Spokane *(G-12234)*
Envirosorb Co .... G 425 778-7485
  Edmonds *(G-3109)*
Escape Fuel Game One LLC .... G 425 883-8054
  Redmond *(G-8453)*
Flex Fuel .... G 360 520-9773
  Chehalis *(G-2497)*
Fuel Coffee .... G 206 634-2700
  Seattle *(G-10035)*
Fuel100 LLC .... G 206 898-4904
  Seattle *(G-10036)*
Garrison Fuel Tech .... G 360 739-2634
  Ferndale *(G-3847)*
Gaynors Glass & Restoration .... G 253 538-2501
  Tacoma *(G-13305)*
Gen-X Energy Group Inc .... G 509 547-2447
  Pasco *(G-7585)*
Global Enterprise Intl .... F 303 928-3208
  Kingston *(G-5254)*
GR Silicate Nano .... F 253 267-8781
  Tacoma *(G-13318)*
Hudson Technologies Inc .... G 253 887-7707
  Auburn *(G-468)*
▲ Imperium Renewables Inc .... G 360 532-2387
  Longview *(G-5917)*
▼ International Chem Systems Inc ..... F 253 263-8038
  Gig Harbor *(G-4122)*
Inventure Chemical Inc .... G 253 576-1577
  Tacoma *(G-13350)*
Janicki Energy .... G 360 856-2068
  Sedro Woolley *(G-11544)*
K and M Fuel LLC .... G 509 675-3005
  Colville *(G-2761)*
Kopius Energy Solutions LLC .... G 425 322-2853
  Seattle *(G-10355)*
▲ Manuflaxsterit Llc .... D 360 384-0485
  Ferndale *(G-3867)*
Mileage Maxer LLC .... G 360 550-5809
  Poulsbo *(G-7984)*
◆ Moses Lake Industries Inc .... D 509 762-5336
  Moses Lake *(G-6727)*
Northwest Biofuels .... G 509 927-4548
  Spokane Valley *(G-12805)*
Northwest Innovation Works Ka .... F 360 673-7800
  Kalama *(G-4505)*
Northwestern Fuel Ldscpg Sups .... G 425 743-1550
  Mukilteo *(G-6957)*
Pacific Fuel and Convenience .... G 253 631-8512
  Kent *(G-5051)*
▼ Pan-Pacific Energy Corp .... F 360 673-7800
  Kalama *(G-4506)*
Patroit Fuels LLC .... G 253 507-6256
  Auburn *(G-528)*
Pickens Fuel Corp .... G 206 824-8181
  Seatac *(G-9299)*
Renewable Energy Inc .... G 206 634-3601
  Seattle *(G-10947)*
Romine Fuel Inc .... G 509 476-3610
  Riverside *(G-9126)*
Seelig Fuel Inc .... G 206 789-6434
  Seattle *(G-11088)*
Southpark Fuel & Food .... G 206 762-7550
  Seattle *(G-11162)*
Sovrano Di Ricchezza Group .... G 425 449-8011
  Bellevue *(G-1150)*
Summit Biofuels LLC .... G 206 291-6402
  Vashon *(G-14745)*
Sunoco Inc .... G 253 872-8500
  Kent *(G-5162)*
Tamer Laboratories Inc .... F 206 364-6761
  Lynnwood *(G-6207)*
Tarr Acquisition LLC .... G 253 859-2979
  Auburn *(G-577)*
The Fuel .... G 206 829-8033
  Seattle *(G-11285)*
Tidal Vision Products LLC .... F 907 988-8888
  Ferndale *(G-3913)*
Ultimate Seal LLC .... G 866 567-9149
  Des Moines *(G-2948)*
Valley Fuel LLC .... G 509 937-2230
  Valley *(G-13995)*
Washington Bio-Oils Inc .... G 509 713-3299
  Richland *(G-9051)*
Whole Energy Fuels Corporation .... G 888 600-8611
  Mount Vernon *(G-6855)*
Wof Pnw Pog 1 LLC .... G 206 624-2144
  Seattle *(G-11489)*

2873 Nitrogenous Fertilizers

Agrium US Inc .... C 509 586-5500
  Kennewick *(G-4613)*
Agrium US Inc .... C 509 586-5355
  Kennewick *(G-4614)*
Cenex Supply & Marketing Inc .... G 509 488-5261
  Othello *(G-7491)*
▲ Lenroc Co .... F 509 754-5266
  Ephrata *(G-3341)*
McGregor Company .... G 509 549-3635
  Pomeroy *(G-7675)*
Micraculture LLC .... G 202 838-7645
  Seattle *(G-10528)*
Micro Ag Inc .... G 509 397-4278
  Steptoe *(G-13007)*
Nthree LLC .... G 509 396-2082
  Richland *(G-9031)*
▲ Pace International LLC .... G 800 936-6750
  Wapato *(G-14922)*
Perfect Blend LLC .... E 509 488-5570
  Bellevue *(G-1069)*
Perfect Blend LLC .... G 509 488-5570
  Othello *(G-7503)*
Perfect Blend LLC .... F 509 968-3316
  Ellensburg *(G-3219)*
Soilcraft Inc .... G 509 314-9227
  Zillah *(G-15759)*
▲ Tainio Biologicals Inc .... F 509 747-5471
  Spokane *(G-12543)*
Ultra Yield Micronutrients Inc .... G 509 248-4911
  Moxee *(G-6888)*
Walts Organic Fert Co Inc .... G 206 297-9092
  Seattle *(G-11434)*
Waupaca Northwoods LLC .... D 509 877-2830
  Parker *(G-7550)*
Windtogreen LLC .... G 509 382-4034
  Dayton *(G-2890)*

2874 Phosphatic Fertilizers

JR Simplot Company .... E 509 488-2132
  Othello *(G-7498)*
McGregor Company .... F 509 397-4360
  Colfax *(G-2716)*
Northwest AG Pdts LLC .... E 509 547-8234
  Pasco *(G-7604)*
Soil Science Products LLC .... G 360 876-3734
  Port Orchard *(G-7849)*
Tessenderlo Kerley Inc .... E 509 586-9148
  Kennewick *(G-4733)*

2875 Fertilizers, Mixing Only

Brm Marketing LLC .... G 509 350-5844
  Moses Lake *(G-6688)*
Cedar Grove Composting Inc .... C 425 212-2515
  Everett *(G-3412)*
CHS-Sub Whatcom Inc .... E 360 354-2108
  Lynden *(G-6007)*
CHS-Sub Whatcom Inc .... G 360 966-4193
  Nooksack *(G-7086)*
CHS-Sub Whatcom Inc .... G 360 354-1198
  Lynden *(G-6008)*
CHS-Sub Whatcom Inc .... E 360 966-4782
  Everson *(G-3671)*
Columbia Valley Compost LLC .... G 509 551-7202
  Prosser *(G-8035)*
Compost Manufacturing Alliance .... G 206 755-8309
  Port Orchard *(G-7798)*
Compost Tea By Seaneen .... G 360 678-3288
  Coupeville *(G-2811)*
De Jong Sawdust & Shavings .... F 425 252-1566
  Lake Stevens *(G-5643)*
H & H Wood Recyclers Inc .... E 360 892-2805
  Vancouver *(G-14278)*
Hawaiian Earth Products .... G 808 682-5895
  Seattle *(G-10152)*
Helena Agri-Enterprises LLC .... F 509 549-3566
  Pomeroy *(G-7674)*
JR Simplot Company .... E 509 488-2132
  Othello *(G-7498)*
JR Simplot Company .... F 509 248-5756
  Moxee *(G-6879)*
▲ Kronos Micronutrients LP .... G 509 248-4911
  Moxee *(G-6880)*
L & L Nursery Supply Inc .... E 909 591-0461
  Fife *(G-3964)*
Microbial Magic LLC .... G 360 297-2224
  Poulsbo *(G-7983)*
Natural Selection Farms Inc .... F 509 837-3501
  Sunnyside *(G-13135)*

Employee Codes: A=Over 500 employees, B=251-500
C=101-250, D=51-100, E=20-50, F=10-19, G=2-9

Neilson Organic Compost....G.... 360 983-8125
Mossyrock (G-6763)
Northwest AG Pdts LLC....E.... 509 547-8234
Pasco (G-7604)
Northwest Compost LLC....G.... 509 932-0215
Mattawa (G-6411)
Nutrien AG Solutions Inc....G.... 509 547-9771
Pasco (G-7606)
O2compost....G.... 360 563-6709
Snohomish (G-11955)
Olysunrise Compost Concierge....G.... 360 551-0674
Olympia (G-7360)
Pacific Topsoils Inc....E.... 425 337-2700
Everett (G-3568)
Ronald F Phillips....G.... 360 779-5614
Poulsbo (G-7996)
Sarvel Biofuels Lummi Corp....G.... 360 362-0016
Ferndale (G-3897)
Sawdust Supply....G.... 206 622-4321
Seattle (G-11022)
Sunland Bark and Topsoils Co....G.... 360 293-7188
Anacortes (G-172)
Trinity Farms Inc....G.... 509 968-4107
Ellensburg (G-3234)
▲ Wolfkill Feed & Fert Corp....F.... 360 794-7065
Monroe (G-6639)

2879 Pesticides & Agricultural Chemicals, NEC

Agrasyst Inc....F.... 509 467-2167
Spokane (G-12103)
Agrium US Inc....C.... 509 586-5500
Kennewick (G-4613)
Bw Liberty Inn Dupont....G.... 253 912-8777
Bothell (G-1832)
Custom Chemicals Co Inc....F.... 509 349-7000
Warden (G-14930)
▲ Dow Agroscience....G.... 509 332-3650
Pullman (G-8088)
Dupont Co....G.... 425 260-0257
Kirkland (G-5325)
Dupont De Nemours Inc....G.... 253 212-2278
Dupont (G-2958)
Dupont Delivery LLC....G.... 253 884-2824
Dupont (G-2959)
Dupont Library....G.... 253 548-3326
Dupont (G-2960)
Dupont Pet Sitting & Services....G.... 816 517-7045
Dupont (G-2961)
Dupont Veterinary Center....G.... 253 267-5431
Dupont (G-2962)
Freedomweeder Company LLC....G.... 509 673-0014
Tieton (G-13630)
Helena Chemical Company....G.... 509 539-5761
Moses Lake (G-6714)
▲ Homax Group Inc....E.... 360 733-9029
Bellingham (G-1371)
Home Team Dupont....G.... 253 576-1907
Dupont (G-2966)
Home2 Suites By Hilton Dupont....G.... 253 912-1000
Dupont (G-2967)
JR Simplot Company....F.... 509 248-5756
Moxee (G-6879)
Life Church Dupont....G.... 253 279-1507
Dupont (G-2969)
▲ Matson LLC....E.... 425 888-6212
North Bend (G-7115)
Moms Club of Dupont....G.... 206 209-9048
Dupont (G-2970)
Monsanto....G.... 509 760-0707
Moses Lake (G-6726)
Monsanto Company....E.... 509 349-2327
Warden (G-14933)
Monsanto Company....G.... 509 488-0821
Hatton (G-4322)
Northwest AG Pdts LLC....E.... 509 547-8234
Pasco (G-7604)
Nutrien AG Solutions Inc....G.... 509 547-9771
Pasco (G-7606)
Pace International LLC....F.... 509 877-2830
Parker (G-7549)
▲ Pace International LLC....G.... 800 936-6750
Wapato (G-14922)
Plant Hormones LLC....G.... 253 332-6131
Auburn (G-532)
Plunk LLC....G.... 425 770-1287
Kirkland (G-5436)
R and M Exterminators Inc....E.... 509 239-4411
Cheney (G-2591)
◆ Solutec Corp....G.... 509 453-6502
Yakima (G-15679)
Syngenta Seeds Inc....C.... 509 543-8000
Pasco (G-7636)
▲ Tanada Corporation....G.... 425 396-1050
North Bend (G-7127)
Tidal Vision Products LLC....F.... 907 988-8888
Ferndale (G-3913)
Trax At Dupont Station....G.... 253 503-0693
Dupont (G-2973)
Trax At Dupont Station....G.... 253 912-8729
Dupont (G-2974)
Truhumic Envmtl Solutions LLC....G.... 425 232-6903
Marysville (G-6397)
Walla Walla Environmental Inc....F.... 509 522-0490
Walla Walla (G-14888)
Washington Dupont WA....G.... 253 964-3403
Dupont (G-2975)
Waupaca Northwoods LLC....D.... 509 877-2830
Parker (G-7550)

2891 Adhesives & Sealants

Adhesive Products Inc....F.... 206 762-7459
Seattle (G-9352)
Advanced Adhesive....G.... 360 373-1156
Bremerton (G-1934)
Atacs Products Inc....F.... 206 433-9000
Seattle (G-9449)
Atlas Supply Inc....G.... 509 924-2417
Spokane Valley (G-12628)
▲ Atwood Adhesives Inc....G.... 206 762-7455
Seattle (G-9460)
Blue Seal Inc....G.... 360 568-2098
Lynnwood (G-6084)
Building Envlope Innvtions LLC....G.... 206 985-3788
Seattle (G-9597)
Evans Adhesives Corporation....G.... 614 410-6027
Camas (G-2250)
HB Fuller Company....E.... 360 574-8828
Vancouver (G-14288)
▲ Northwest Adhesives Inc....F.... 360 260-1227
Washougal (G-14972)
Specialists Sealant....G.... 509 321-0424
Spokane Valley (G-12882)
◆ Westech Aerosol Corporation....E.... 206 930-9291
Suquamish (G-13150)
Western Adhesive Solutions....G.... 360 904-5005
Brush Prairie (G-2043)

2892 Explosives

Desparado Cowboy Bullets LLC....G.... 509 382-8926
Dayton (G-2881)
Dyno Nobel Inc....G.... 360 740-0128
Chehalis (G-2491)
Gunpowder Creek LLC....G.... 860 502-9202
Walla Walla (G-14817)
Natures Provision....G.... 360 307-0113
Silverdale (G-11851)

2893 Printing Ink

American Printing and Pubg....G.... 253 395-3349
Kent (G-4779)
Outsmart Office Solutions Inc....G.... 888 688-8154
Mercer Island (G-6478)
Pencils and Inks Inc....G.... 206 683-4441
Seattle (G-10780)
Sunoco Inc....G.... 253 872-8500
Kent (G-5162)

2899 Chemical Preparations, NEC

Adiprene Direct Inc....E.... 425 999-3805
Bellevue (G-781)
American Mobile Drug Testing....G.... 509 921-2730
Spokane Valley (G-12613)
Angstrom Innovations Inc....G.... 425 750-6329
Mountlake Terrace (G-6857)
Aqua-Lift Inc....G.... 253 845-4010
Puyallup (G-8124)
Arch Wood Protection Inc....G.... 360 673-5099
Kalama (G-4492)
▲ Argent Chemical Labs Inc....G.... 425 885-3777
Redmond (G-8385)
Bearded Fellows Elixir LLC....G.... 253 750-3060
Bonney Lake (G-1717)
Beryllium LLC....G.... 206 780-8900
Bainbridge Island (G-617)
Biocontrol Systems Inc....F.... 425 603-1123
Bellevue (G-817)
Buckeye International Inc....G.... 206 575-1185
Seatac (G-9279)
◆ Callisons Inc....E.... 360 412-3340
Lacey (G-5536)
Callisons Inc....F.... 206 545-3900
Seattle (G-9608)
Cartridge World....G.... 509 469-9711
Kennewick (G-4643)
Central Washington Wtr Ctr Inc....F.... 509 663-1177
Wenatchee (G-15019)
Chemtrade Solutions LLC....E.... 360 293-2171
Anacortes (G-112)
Cr Callen LLC....G.... 206 363-7648
Edmonds (G-3102)
Cytec Industries Materials....G.... 425 274-0485
Bellevue (G-871)
Data Quest LLC....G.... 360 568-8708
Everett (G-3439)
Drug Interv Service Amer....G.... 360 299-2700
Anacortes (G-123)
Eakin Enterprises Inc....F.... 509 698-3200
Selah (G-11587)
Eco Tec Inc....G.... 253 884-6804
Gig Harbor (G-4097)
◆ Energy Saver Products Inc....G.... 888 778-4537
Vancouver (G-14202)
▲ Essex Laboratories LLC....G.... 360 740-1770
Chehalis (G-2494)
Fsi Inc....G.... 360 452-9194
Seattle (G-10033)
Gelene Legault....G.... 425 481-5560
Bothell (G-1860)
Gimpy Ninja LLC....G.... 253 282-9943
Gig Harbor (G-4108)
Hacienda Las Flares....G.... 208 819-8879
Spokane (G-12285)
▲ Healthy Pet LP....C.... 360 734-7415
Ferndale (G-3850)
Higher Mind Incense....G.... 541 702-1560
Port Ludlow (G-7767)
Inland Synthetics....G.... 509 466-6101
Spokane (G-12313)
Innovation Resource Center....G.... 509 836-2400
Sunnyside (G-13127)
Integrity Industries Inc....G.... 425 264-9401
Renton (G-8828)
Jetwest....G.... 801 223-9149
Sequim (G-11643)
▲ Kamiya Biomedical Company LLC..F.... 206 575-8068
Tukwila (G-13760)
Kemira Chemicals Inc....F.... 360 835-8725
Washougal (G-14962)
Kemira Water Solutions Inc....F.... 509 922-2244
Spokane Valley (G-12764)
Lachselian Distillery....G.... 206 743-8070
Seattle (G-10370)
Lake City Naturopathic Care In....G.... 509 590-1343
Liberty Lake (G-5842)
Larry Lisk....G.... 425 252-5475
Everett (G-3534)
Life Size 3 D Animal Targ....G.... 206 432-9147
Maple Valley (G-6280)
Lightning Nuggets Inc....F.... 509 725-6211
Davenport (G-2873)
Lonza Inc....G.... 360 673-5099
Kalama (G-4504)
Lumisands Inc....G.... 206 403-7887
Seattle (G-10452)
Mad Concrete Cutting & Coring....G.... 206 367-0263
Lynnwood (G-6161)
Magaway Fire LLC....G.... 253 394-3255
Tacoma (G-13394)
Mercurius Biofuels LLC....G.... 360 941-7207
Ferndale (G-3869)
Nalco Company LLC....G.... 509 928-7713
Spokane (G-12401)
Napalm Racing....G.... 509 991-9759
Chattaroy (G-2448)
▲ Natures Inventory LLC....F.... 425 775-2000
Enumclaw (G-3308)
Network Collaborative 4 LLC....F.... 206 898-5869
Seattle (G-10602)
Northwest Solutions Inc....G.... 360 380-3807
Bellingham (G-1471)
Nu Element Inc....G.... 206 356-4525
Tacoma (G-13437)
Old Salt Merchants LLC....G.... 888 995-7258
Port Townsend (G-7903)
P S Plus Sizes Tukwila....G.... 206 575-3690
Tukwila (G-13785)

SIC SECTION

30 RUBBER AND MISCELLANEOUS PLASTICS PRODUCTS

▲ Pace International LLC ....G....... 800 936-6750
   Wapato *(G-14922)*
Power Punch Distributors LLC............G....... 360 479-0673
   Bremerton *(G-1989)*
S&S NDT LLC ....G....... 509 688-7996
   Spokane *(G-12491)*
Salt Studio ....G....... 206 784-9652
   Seattle *(G-11009)*
Sandbox Enterprises LLC ....G....... 360 966-6677
   Bellingham *(G-1523)*
Spirit of Winds Incense St ....G....... 253 293-2743
   Federal Way *(G-3790)*
Talk To Taracom ....G....... 206 226-2606
   Seattle *(G-11263)*
The Euclid Chemical Company ....G....... 360 848-1202
   Mount Vernon *(G-6846)*
Theo Coram Corporation ....G....... 425 774-4731
   Brier *(G-2022)*
Tidal Vision Products LLC ....F....... 907 988-8888
   Ferndale *(G-3913)*
Tree of Kindness Inc ....G....... 509 315-2206
   Spokane *(G-12567)*
Trondak Inc ....G....... 360 794-8250
   Monroe *(G-6634)*
Truhumic Envmtl Solutions LLC ....G....... 425 232-6903
   Marysville *(G-6397)*
United American Inc ....E....... 360 371-7709
   Blaine *(G-1709)*
US Water Services Inc ....G....... 360 695-1270
   Vancouver *(G-14658)*
Vaportech Solutions LLC ....F....... 888 746-8955
   Everett *(G-3647)*
Viking Fire ....G....... 206 715-8052
   Seattle *(G-11420)*
Walla Walla Environmental Inc ....F....... 509 522-0490
   Walla Walla *(G-14888)*
Walla Walla Valley Mobile LLC ....G....... 509 386-8549
   College Place *(G-2730)*
Washington Biodiesel LLC ....G....... 206 297-6107
   Seattle *(G-11437)*
Xtrudx Technologies Inc ....G....... 206 568-3100
   Auburn *(G-602)*

29 PETROLEUM REFINING AND RELATED INDUSTRIES

2911 Petroleum Refining

AAA Superlubes Inc ....G....... 425 353-4901
   Port Orchard *(G-7781)*
BP America Inc ....A....... 360 371-0373
   Blaine *(G-1663)*
BP Arco Seattle Terminal ....G....... 206 623-4637
   Seattle *(G-9574)*
BP Corporation North Amer Inc ....B....... 360 371-1500
   Blaine *(G-1664)*
Chevron Corporation ....G....... 360 887-8101
   Camas *(G-2238)*
Chevron Corporation ....G....... 509 534-4077
   Spokane *(G-12179)*
Chevron Corporation ....G....... 425 413-8881
   Maple Valley *(G-6263)*
Christine Jamison ....G....... 253 887-1095
   Auburn *(G-406)*
Conocophillips Company ....F....... 509 536-8417
   Spokane Valley *(G-12663)*
Conocophillips Company ....F....... 253 584-0583
   Lakewood *(G-5707)*
Diesel Prfmce Unlimited LLC ....G....... 509 546-9997
   Pasco *(G-7576)*
Doug Skrivan ....G....... 253 584-7323
   Lakewood *(G-5714)*
Dr Dans Alternative Fuel Werks ....G....... 206 783-5728
   Seattle *(G-9851)*
▲ Emerald Services Inc ....C....... 206 430-7795
   Seattle *(G-9913)*
Equilon Enterprises LLC ....B....... 360 293-0800
   Anacortes *(G-126)*
Flotbunker LLC ....G....... 206 354-5205
   Bellevue *(G-913)*
Inlet Petroleum Solvents ....G....... 907 274-3835
   Seattle *(G-10237)*
L Stop-N-Go ....G....... 509 896-6089
   Mabton *(G-6229)*
Pacrim Technologies LLC ....G....... 425 284-7300
   Kirkland *(G-5425)*
Par Tacoma LLC ....G....... 253 383-1651
   Tacoma *(G-13458)*
Paramount Petroleum Corp ....E....... 503 273-4700
   Seattle *(G-10752)*
Paramount Petroleum Corp ....F....... 503 273-4705
   Seattle *(G-10753)*
Paramount Petroleum Corp ....F....... 206 542-3121
   Seattle *(G-10754)*
Phillips 66 Company ....G....... 509 534-5040
   Wenatchee *(G-15063)*
Phillips 66 Company ....D....... 360 384-1011
   Ferndale *(G-3886)*
S&S Transportation Service ....G....... 509 968-9825
   Ellensburg *(G-3224)*
▼ Seaport Sound Terminal LLC ....E....... 253 272-9348
   Tacoma *(G-13510)*
Sinclair Companies ....C....... 360 874-6772
   Port Orchard *(G-7848)*
Specialty Chemical Pdts LLC ....G....... 509 884-4900
   Rock Island *(G-9149)*
Sunoco Inc ....G....... 253 872-8500
   Kent *(G-5162)*
Tesoro Companies Inc ....D....... 253 896-8700
   Federal Way *(G-3794)*
Tesoro Corporation ....E....... 360 293-9119
   Anacortes *(G-175)*
Tesoro Refining & Mktg Co LLC ....G....... 360 293-9119
   Anacortes *(G-177)*
◆ US Oil & Refining Co ....C....... 253 383-1651
   Tacoma *(G-13574)*
Westfall Gooden Sfo Co ....G....... 253 344-1025
   Federal Way *(G-3803)*
Wsa-HI Inc ....G....... 509 921-7089
   Spokane Valley *(G-12943)*

2951 Paving Mixtures & Blocks

▲ Bainter Bainter & Bainter LLC .....G....... 360 267-5521
   Grayland *(G-4292)*
Bayview Composites LLC ....D....... 360 466-4160
   Mount Vernon *(G-6775)*
Clean Lines LLC ....G....... 509 939-2957
   Deer Park *(G-2896)*
CPM Development Corporation ....G....... 509 663-5141
   Wenatchee *(G-15024)*
Degerstrom Corporation ....E....... 509 928-3333
   Spokane Valley *(G-12680)*
Granite Construction Company ....G....... 360 676-2450
   Everson *(G-3676)*
Interstate Asphalt Paving Inc ....G....... 425 318-5008
   Arlington *(G-257)*
Jesse W Palmer ....F....... 509 634-1494
   Keller *(G-4513)*
Karvonen Sand & Gravel Inc ....G....... 360 687-2549
   Battle Ground *(G-712)*
Koch Industries Inc ....G....... 509 487-4560
   Spokane *(G-12354)*
▲ Lakeside Industries Inc ....D....... 425 313-2600
   Issaquah *(G-4437)*
Lakeside Industries Inc ....E....... 360 491-5460
   Olympia *(G-7318)*
Lakeside Industries Inc ....E....... 360 423-6882
   Longview *(G-5925)*
Lakeside Industries Inc ....E....... 360 794-7779
   Monroe *(G-6590)*
Lakeside Industries Inc ....E....... 360 604-1869
   Vancouver *(G-14356)*
Looker & Associates Inc ....E....... 253 210-5200
   Puyallup *(G-8179)*
MA Assoc ....G....... 206 719-1363
   Bothell *(G-1775)*
Michael H Wold Company Inc ....G....... 360 435-6953
   Arlington *(G-275)*
Miles Resources LLC ....C....... 253 383-3585
   Puyallup *(G-8192)*
Mitchell Trucking and Paving ....G....... 509 884-5928
   East Wenatchee *(G-3026)*
Naselle Rock & Asphalt Company ......F....... 360 484-3443
   Naselle *(G-7017)*
Poe Asphalt Paving Inc ....E....... 509 334-6400
   Pullman *(G-8101)*
Semgroup Corp ....G....... 509 921-7089
   Spokane Valley *(G-12864)*
Semgroup Corporation ....G....... 509 487-4560
   Spokane *(G-12498)*
Semmaterials LP ....G....... 509 545-9864
   Pasco *(G-7626)*
Straight Edge Asphalt & Maint ....G....... 206 949-4666
   Burien *(G-2132)*
Superior Asphalt & Paving Co ....F....... 509 248-6823
   Yakima *(G-15689)*
Supr Co ....E....... 509 248-6823
   Yakima *(G-15690)*
Tucci & Sons Inc ....D....... 253 922-6676
   Tacoma *(G-13566)*
Unique Allscapes ....G....... 425 309-6325
   Everett *(G-3642)*
US Polyco Inc ....G....... 509 413-1006
   Spokane *(G-12578)*
Woodland Paving ....G....... 360 225-8317
   Woodland *(G-15476)*
Yk Products LLC ....G....... 425 244-5000
   Everett *(G-3662)*

2952 Asphalt Felts & Coatings

Custom Bilt Holdings LLC ....E....... 253 872-7330
   Lakewood *(G-5709)*
▲ Fields Company LLC ....D....... 253 627-4098
   Tacoma *(G-13295)*
Gardner-Fields Inc ....G....... 253 627-4098
   Tacoma *(G-13304)*
Hco Holding I Corporation ....G....... 503 255-3767
   Vancouver *(G-14289)*
◆ Iko Pacific Inc ....E....... 360 988-9103
   Sumas *(G-13046)*
Johns Manville Corporation ....D....... 800 654-3103
   Kent *(G-4970)*
Mates Seal Smart ....G....... 509 489-6346
   Spokane *(G-12386)*
Metal Sales Manufacturing Corp ....F....... 253 872-5750
   Kent *(G-5007)*
Pabco Building Products LLC ....C....... 253 284-1200
   Tacoma *(G-13449)*
Pacific Coatings Inc ....F....... 206 722-1413
   Seattle *(G-10730)*
Perfection Coatings ....G....... 509 599-2538
   Spokane Valley *(G-12828)*
Remsing Enterprises ....G....... 360 521-8049
   Vancouver *(G-14542)*
Richard Lawson Construction ....E....... 360 378-4313
   Friday Harbor *(G-4055)*
Road Products Inc ....G....... 509 922-1206
   Spokane Valley *(G-12853)*
Seattle Eco Coatings ....G....... 253 539-1113
   Puyallup *(G-8249)*

2992 Lubricating Oils & Greases

◆ Bardahl Manufacturing Corp ....E....... 206 783-4851
   Seattle *(G-9492)*
G and T Renewables ....G....... 206 412-2352
   Seattle *(G-10044)*
Gimpy Ninja LLC ....G....... 253 282-9943
   Gig Harbor *(G-4108)*
Gobers Fuel Oil Inc ....F....... 509 924-5372
   Spokane Valley *(G-12721)*
▲ Interlube International Inc ....G....... 360 332-2132
   Blaine *(G-1675)*
Interlube International Inc ....E....... 360 734-3832
   Bellingham *(G-1381)*
Mobile One Lube Ex Everett ....G....... 425 374-8862
   Everett *(G-3548)*
◆ Mpl Innovations Inc ....G....... 425 398-1310
   Seattle *(G-10566)*
Peninsula Lubricants ....G....... 360 452-8376
   Port Angeles *(G-7736)*
Prs Group Inc ....F....... 206 255-7509
   Tacoma *(G-13480)*
Ray Summerlin ....G....... 253 638-0733
   Kent *(G-5100)*
Restore Incorporated ....G....... 360 909-1161
   Vancouver *(G-14547)*
Wal Med Inc ....G....... 253 845-6633
   Puyallup *(G-8276)*
Wilson Oil Inc ....F....... 509 536-3550
   Spokane *(G-12594)*
Winn Enterprises LLC ....G....... 425 482-6000
   Bothell *(G-1921)*

30 RUBBER AND MISCELLANEOUS PLASTICS PRODUCTS

3011 Tires & Inner Tubes

Bentonfranklin Counties Ian BF ....G....... 509 783-5284
   Kennewick *(G-4629)*
BF and BF Co ....G....... 206 463-2661
   Vashon *(G-14713)*
Cooper Tire & Rubber Company ....G....... 253 826-5742
   Sumner *(G-13061)*
Michelin Mounting Center ....G....... 253 872-0868
   Kent *(G-5010)*
▲ Phelps Tire Co Inc ....D....... 206 447-0169
   Seattle *(G-10793)*
West Worldwide Services Inc ....G....... 509 764-2177
   Moses Lake *(G-6757)*

Employee Codes: A=Over 500 employees, B=251-500
C=101-250, D=51-100, E=20-50, F=10-19, G=2-9

30 RUBBER AND MISCELLANEOUS PLASTICS PRODUCTS

3021 Rubber & Plastic Footwear

AAA Victory Vending Inc .... G 425 235-0378
  Renton (G-8725)
Combat Flip Flops LLC .... G 206 913-9971
  Issaquah (G-4396)
▲ Combat Flip Flops LLC .... G 206 913-9971
  Issaquah (G-4397)
Nike Inc .... G 206 527-3554
  Seattle (G-10609)
Nike Inc .... G 425 747-2848
  Bellevue (G-1031)
▲ Outdoor Research LLC .... C 206 467-8197
  Seattle (G-10717)
Vans Inc .... F 360 254-3075
  Vancouver (G-14665)

3052 Rubber & Plastic Hose & Belting

Aahed Logistics LLC .... G 757 395-7063
  Port Orchard (G-7782)
Belair Composites Inc .... F 509 482-0442
  Spokane (G-12144)
Custom Hydraulic & Machine Inc .... F 253 854-4666
  Kent (G-4868)
▲ Hide-A-Hose Inc .... G 425 750-7636
  Monroe (G-6577)
Lewis-Goetz and Company Inc .... F 206 623-5650
  Kent (G-4994)
Nxedge Inc .... G 425 990-0091
  Bellevue (G-1041)
▲ Rubber & Plastics Inc .... E 503 289-7720
  Vancouver (G-14560)
Ves Company Inc .... G 206 940-5742
  Shoreline (G-11820)

3053 Gaskets, Packing & Sealing Devices

Bestfitt Gasket Company Inc .... G 253 863-9521
  Sumner (G-13056)
Cascade Gasket & Mfg Co Inc .... C 253 854-1800
  Kent (G-4841)
▲ Concept Fabrication Inc .... F 509 534-9235
  Spokane (G-12196)
Engineered Piping Systems .... G 360 225-5302
  Woodland (G-15429)
Jetseal Inc .... E 509 467-9133
  Spokane Valley (G-12752)
Lewis-Goetz and Company Inc .... F 206 623-5650
  Kent (G-4994)
▲ Mid Mountain Materials Inc .... E 206 762-7600
  Seattle (G-10539)
Rembos Hipro .... G 360 492-3100
  Mineral (G-6538)
Scott RI and Associates .... G 253 604-4006
  Puyallup (G-8246)
Seal-Guard Corporation .... G 253 833-7080
  Auburn (G-557)
The O-Ring Store LLC .... G 208 413-6377
  Clarkston (G-2651)
True Seals LLC .... G 509 385-0300
  Spokane Valley (G-12914)

3061 Molded, Extruded & Lathe-Cut Rubber Mechanical Goods

Kasaganaan Enterprise .... G 206 361-2645
  Shoreline (G-11779)
Rogers Rubber Manufacturing .... G 253 845-8374
  Buckley (G-2070)
◆ U S Wax & Polymer Inc .... E 509 922-1069
  Spokane Valley (G-12918)

3069 Fabricated Rubber Prdts, NEC

▲ 4 M Company Inc .... D 425 227-4100
  Tukwila (G-13686)
Assured Independence LLC .... G 425 516-7400
  Issaquah (G-4383)
Bestfitt Gasket Company Inc .... G 253 863-9521
  Sumner (G-13056)
Blackbear Pontoons Fabrication ..... G 206 372-9998
  Montesano (G-6642)
Bowhead Manufacturing Co LLC .... G 206 957-5321
  Seattle (G-9572)
Calendars Northwest LLC .... F 425 454-1145
  Hunts Point (G-4366)
▲ Canflex (usa) Inc .... F 206 282-8233
  Anacortes (G-107)
Cascade Gasket & Mfg Co Inc .... C 253 854-1800
  Kent (G-4841)
▲ Clearsnap Holding Inc .... D 360 293-6634
  Burlington (G-2145)

▲ Creative Collections Co Inc .... E 360 866-8840
  Olympia (G-7259)
Docufeed Technologies .... G 360 793-2001
  Sultan (G-13022)
Entraq Medical .... G 425 495-5143
  Redmond (G-8450)
EZ Lip LLC .... G 425 753-6814
  Renton (G-8798)
▲ Grab On Grips LLC .... F 509 529-9800
  Walla Walla (G-14814)
▲ Harveys Skin Diving Supplies ..... E 206 824-1114
  Kent (G-4935)
Howatt Company Inc .... F 425 743-4682
  Mukilteo (G-6937)
Image Masters Inc .... G 253 939-5868
  Auburn (G-471)
Innocor Foam Technologies LLC ... F 360 575-8844
  Longview (G-5918)
Medilogic Llc .... G 541 991-1006
  Camas (G-2269)
Mustang Survival Inc .... E 360 676-1782
  Bellingham (G-1452)
◆ Mustang Survival Holdings Inc .... D 360 676-1782
  Bellingham (G-1453)
▲ Ovalstrapping Incorporated .... E 360 532-9101
  Hoquiam (G-4352)
Panther Printing .... G 509 344-4600
  Spokane Valley (G-12825)
Perception Plastics Inc .... G 509 624-5408
  Spokane (G-12437)
Proto Technologies Inc .... D 509 891-4747
  Liberty Lake (G-5855)
▲ Rubber & Plastics Inc .... E 503 289-7720
  Vancouver (G-14560)
Rubber Granulators Inc .... G 360 658-7754
  Marysville (G-6380)
Sally Beauty Supply LLC .... G 509 881-2120
  East Wenatchee (G-3032)
Sally Beauty Supply LLC .... G 509 783-7292
  Kennewick (G-4725)
▲ Scougal Rubber Corporation .... D 206 763-2650
  Seattle (G-11032)
Stampadoodle Inc .... G 360 647-9663
  Bellingham (G-1555)
◆ Sterltiech Corporation .... E 253 437-0844
  Kent (G-5156)
Stowe Woodward LLC .... E 360 636-0330
  Kelso (G-4552)
Tacoma Community Boat Builders . G 253 720-8227
  Tacoma (G-13540)
Valmet Inc .... E 253 927-2200
  Federal Way (G-3799)

3081 Plastic Unsupported Sheet & Film

◆ Achilles Usa Inc .... C 425 353-7000
  Everett (G-3357)
Ampac Packaging LLC .... C 253 939-8206
  Auburn (G-374)
Bemis Company Inc .... E 206 632-2246
  Seattle (G-9511)
▲ Cordstrap USA Inc .... G 253 886-5000
  Auburn (G-417)
Custom Win Tnting Graphics Inc .... G 509 453-4293
  Yakima (G-15547)
▼ Flexible Containment Pdts Inc ..... E 509 624-8921
  Spokane Valley (G-12705)
ISO Poly Films Inc .... F 864 684-8198
  Vancouver (G-14326)
▲ Layfield Plastics Incorporated ...... G 425 254-1075
  Renton (G-8841)
Nobelus LLC .... G 800 895-2747
  Seattle (G-10614)
Novolex Shields LLC .... B 800 541-8630
  Yakima (G-15636)
Orbis Rpm LLC .... F 253 333-0606
  Auburn (G-520)
Paragon Films Inc .... E 509 424-3700
  Union Gap (G-13949)
▲ Portco Corporation .... F 360 696-1641
  Woodland (G-15460)
Redi-Bag Inc .... E 425 251-9841
  Tukwila (G-13804)
Tekni-Plex Inc .... C 509 663-8541
  Wenatchee (G-15079)
Wiman Corporation .... G 360 757-8880
  Burlington (G-2204)

3082 Plastic Unsupported Profile Shapes

Envision Manufacturing & Servi ..... G 253 941-1739
  Kent (G-4894)

Extrusion Technology Group Inc .... G 253 583-8283
  Lakewood (G-5720)
Hancor Inc .... E 360 943-3313
  Olympia (G-7302)
Middy Marine Products Inc .... G 425 883-4600
  Redmond (G-8588)
Obcon Inc .... G 253 931-0455
  Auburn (G-516)
Porex Technologies Corporation .... C 253 284-8000
  Fife (G-3982)
R & R Plastics .... G 360 694-9573
  Vancouver (G-14524)

3083 Plastic Laminated Plate & Sheet

Acrylic Concepts Inc .... G 425 881-3603
  Redmond (G-8369)
Angeles Composite Tech Inc .... D 360 452-6776
  Port Angeles (G-7684)
Bridgestone Hosepower LLC .... E 206 767-4670
  Seattle (G-9585)
Dmm Incorporated .... E 360 435-5252
  Arlington (G-229)
◆ Hesco Armor LLC .... E 360 637-6867
  Aberdeen (G-18)
Innovative Composite Engrg Inc .... D 509 493-4484
  White Salmon (G-15119)
Interior Form Tops Inc .... E 253 927-8171
  Milton (G-6535)
Middy Marine Products Inc .... G 425 883-4600
  Redmond (G-8588)
▲ Northwest Laminating Co Inc ...... F 206 789-5536
  Seattle (G-10648)
Pexco Aerospace Inc .... C 509 248-9166
  Union Gap (G-13950)
Prolam Industries Inc .... G 509 926-2001
  Spokane Valley (G-12843)
Rulersmith Inc .... E 360 707-2828
  Shoreline (G-11806)
Sound Manufacturing Inc .... E 253 872-8007
  Kent (G-5141)

3084 Plastic Pipe

Advanced Drainage Systems Inc .... E 360 943-3313
  Olympia (G-7221)
Advanced Drainage Systems Inc ... E 360 835-8523
  Washougal (G-14939)
Cresline-Northwest LLC .... E 360 740-0700
  Chehalis (G-2487)
Ershigs Inc .... F 360 733-2620
  Bellingham (G-1338)
Hancor Inc .... E 360 943-3313
  Olympia (G-7302)
J-M Manufacturing Company Inc ... E 509 837-7800
  Sunnyside (G-13128)
Norma Industries .... G 253 208-1728
  Puyallup (G-8200)
Plactic Services and Products .... E 360 736-5616
  Centralia (G-2424)
▲ Simpson Investment Company .... D 253 272-0158
  Seattle (G-11115)
Superlon Plastics Co Inc .... F 253 383-4000
  Tacoma (G-13530)

3085 Plastic Bottles

Amcor Rigid Packaging Usa LLC .. D 509 525-0230
  Walla Walla (G-14762)
Consolidated Container Co LLC .... E 425 251-0303
  Tukwila (G-13715)
▲ Evergreen Plastic Container .... F 360 828-7174
  Vancouver (G-14209)
Graham Packaging Company LP ... G 509 698-4545
  Selah (G-11589)
▲ Green Willow Trucking Inc .... G 360 687-7171
  Battle Ground (G-705)
Green Willow Trucking Inc .... G 360 687-7171
  Battle Ground (G-706)
Okanogan Label & Print Ltd .... F 250 328-8660
  Walla Walla (G-14853)
Richards Packaging Inc .... E 253 582-1096
  Tacoma (G-13499)
Richards Packaging Inc .... G 253 872-2848
  Auburn (G-547)
▲ Velendo Inc .... F 360 828-7174
  Vancouver (G-14667)

3086 Plastic Foam Prdts

◆ Adalis Corporation .... E 360 574-8828
  Vancouver (G-14008)

592
2019 Washington
Manufacturers Register

SIC SECTION

30 RUBBER AND MISCELLANEOUS PLASTICS PRODUCTS

Alliance Packaging LLC ....C...... 425 291-3500
  Renton *(G-8738)*
American Excelsior Company ....E...... 509 575-5794
  Yakima *(G-15507)*
◆ C4 Enterprises Inc ....E...... 425 347-9200
  Mukilteo *(G-6902)*
▼ Cams-Usa Inc ....F...... 253 639-3890
  Kent *(G-4835)*
▲ Concept Fabrication Inc ....G...... 509 534-9235
  Spokane *(G-12196)*
Cryovac Inc..C...... 509 539-2923
  Prosser *(G-8037)*
Dart Container Corp Georgia ....E...... 360 352-7045
  Tumwater *(G-13870)*
Distribution International Inc ....B...... 425 228-4111
  Renton *(G-8785)*
Entrust Community Services ....D...... 509 839-8066
  Sunnyside *(G-13124)*
▲ Five Food Inc ....G...... 509 855-6914
  Moses Lake *(G-6708)*
Fps Manufacturing LLC ....G...... 509 248-0423
  Yakima *(G-15573)*
Fxi Inc..D...... 253 872-0170
  Kent *(G-4919)*
◆ General Plastics Mfg Co ....C...... 253 473-5000
  Tacoma *(G-13306)*
▲ Grab On Grips LLC ....F...... 509 529-9800
  Walla Walla *(G-14814)*
How-Mac Manufacturing Inc ....E...... 360 855-2649
  Sedro Woolley *(G-11540)*
Innocor Inc...G...... 844 824-9348
  Issaquah *(G-4429)*
J & R Commercial Inc ....G...... 253 639-3890
  Kent *(G-4963)*
JC Global Supply LLC ....G...... 253 275-6093
  Kent *(G-4966)*
Johns Manville Corporation ....D...... 800 654-3103
  Kent *(G-4970)*
▲ Mantec Services Inc ....E...... 206 285-5656
  Seattle *(G-10472)*
Matrix Applications Company ....G...... 509 547-7609
  Vancouver *(G-14400)*
Matrix Applications Company ....G...... 360 256-2534
  Vancouver *(G-14401)*
Mr Ed Floats ....G...... 360 834-3986
  Camas *(G-2272)*
Pac Rite Inc ....G...... 253 833-7071
  Puyallup *(G-8215)*
Pactiv LLC ....D...... 847 482-2000
  Auburn *(G-526)*
Storopack Inc ....F...... 253 872-6844
  Kent *(G-5159)*
Tekni-Plex Inc ....C...... 509 663-8541
  Wenatchee *(G-15079)*
Zoomnet Postal + ...G...... 360 719-0973
  Vancouver *(G-14710)*

3087 Custom Compounding Of Purchased Plastic Resins

Bellwether Gate C LLC ....G...... 360 738-1940
  Bellingham *(G-1270)*
Innovative Technologies Inc ....G...... 425 258-4773
  Everett *(G-3516)*
Polydrop LLC ....G...... 206 601-2191
  Kent *(G-5071)*

3088 Plastic Plumbing Fixtures

Aquatic Co...C...... 360 458-3900
  Yelm *(G-15727)*
◆ Blue Falls Usa LP ....G...... 509 891-1933
  Spokane Valley *(G-12643)*
Columbia Cultured Marble Inc ....G...... 509 582-5660
  Kennewick *(G-4647)*
Composites Consolidation Compa ....G...... 509 877-2228
  Wapato *(G-14914)*
▼ Hydra Plastics Inc..........................E...... 425 483-1877
  Woodinville *(G-15262)*
Maax Hydro Swirl Mfg Co ....D...... 360 734-0616
  Bellingham *(G-1417)*
▲ McClarin Plastics LLC ....B...... 509 877-5950
  Wapato *(G-14919)*
Northwest Walk-In Bath Inc ....G...... 206 898-2625
  Vancouver *(G-14442)*
Pat Files ....G...... 206 405-4370
  Seattle *(G-10764)*
Pvc Debonding Systems Inc ....G...... 866 961-8349
  Spokane *(G-12461)*
Safe Bathtub Inc..................................G...... 509 670-2711
  Entiat *(G-3270)*

Thermal Hydra Plastics LLC ....D...... 425 483-1877
  Woodinville *(G-15388)*

3089 Plastic Prdts

Acrylic Arts & Fabrication ....G...... 360 802-0808
  Enumclaw *(G-3274)*
Adaptive Cargo Solutions LLC ....F...... 240 475-6521
  Everett *(G-3360)*
Advanced Cargo Control LLC ....G...... 206 498-5824
  Snohomish *(G-11870)*
Advanced Plastic & Metal Wldng ....G...... 509 466-1986
  Nine Mile Falls *(G-7067)*
Alaska Wholesale Hardwoods ....G...... 360 704-4444
  Tumwater *(G-13850)*
All Craft Plastics ....G...... 253 887-1768
  Auburn *(G-369)*
Alpine Industries Inc..........................B...... 425 481-7101
  Bothell *(G-1818)*
Alpine Precision Tooling Inc ....G...... 360 474-0547
  Arlington *(G-199)*
▲ Altek Inc..C...... 509 921-0597
  Liberty Lake *(G-5825)*
Amcor Rigid Packaging Usa LLC .....B...... 360 753-4162
  Tumwater *(G-13851)*
American Cnc Fabricating Inc ....G...... 509 315-4095
  Spokane Valley *(G-12609)*
◆ American Nettings & Fabric Inc ....F...... 360 366-2630
  Ferndale *(G-3813)*
American Vinyl Industries Inc ....G...... 253 473-4731
  Fife *(G-3931)*
AP Interprices ....G...... 360 837-2548
  Washougal *(G-14943)*
Applied Finishing Inc ....E...... 425 513-2505
  Mukilteo *(G-6893)*
Artech Sinrud Industries Inc ....G...... 360 435-3520
  Arlington *(G-202)*
Artisan Industries Inc ....F...... 360 474-1282
  Arlington *(G-203)*
▲ Aska Company ....G...... 360 753-4233
  Lacey *(G-5534)*
Avante Technology LLC ....C...... 425 273-4740
  Bellevue *(G-801)*
Avid Products LLC ....G...... 888 271-3616
  Redmond *(G-8394)*
Battery Recycler ....G...... 562 434-4502
  Bellingham *(G-1259)*
Belair Composites Inc ....F...... 509 482-0442
  Spokane *(G-12144)*
Benchmark Injection Molding ....G...... 425 263-9171
  Lynnwood *(G-6083)*
Berry Global Inc ....C...... 253 627-2151
  Tacoma *(G-13198)*
Big Blok LLC ....G...... 360 442-0655
  Vancouver *(G-14066)*
Bite Buddy LLC ....G...... 360 749-4781
  Kelso *(G-4518)*
Blaser Casting Corporation ....E...... 206 767-7800
  Seattle *(G-9539)*
Bradley Robling ....G...... 360 832-6778
  Spanaway *(G-12054)*
▲ Burke Gibson LLC ....E...... 253 735-4444
  Auburn *(G-398)*
Camoflage...G...... 425 744-0764
  Edmonds *(G-3099)*
Captive Plastics LLC ....D...... 253 627-2151
  Tacoma *(G-13220)*
▲ Cascade Designs Inc ....B...... 206 505-9500
  Seattle *(G-9640)*
▲ Cascade Quality Molding Inc ....F...... 509 248-9642
  Yakima *(G-15530)*
Certainteed Corporation ....B...... 253 850-9000
  Auburn *(G-404)*
CFM Consolidated Inc ....F...... 253 922-2700
  Fife *(G-3942)*
▲ CFM Consolidated Inc ....E...... 253 922-2700
  Fife *(G-3943)*
▼ Cheyenne Livestock & Products ....F...... 360 256-0293
  Vancouver *(G-14116)*
▲ Clear Cut Plastics Inc ....G...... 206 545-9131
  Seattle *(G-9694)*
▲ Commercial Plastics Corp ....F...... 206 682-4832
  Seattle *(G-9717)*
Composites Consolidation Compa ....G...... 509 877-2228
  Wapato *(G-14914)*
Composites Consolidation LLC ....G...... 509 877-2228
  Wapato *(G-14915)*
Conrad Manufacturing Co Inc ....F...... 253 852-3420
  Auburn *(G-413)*
Consolidated Container Co LLC ....E...... 425 251-0303
  Tukwila *(G-13715)*

Consolidated Container Co LLC........E...... 509 891-2483
  Spokane Valley *(G-12664)*
◆ Consolidated Metco Inc ....D...... 360 828-2599
  Vancouver *(G-14147)*
Corbitz Ltd ....G...... 206 241-9877
  Burien *(G-2099)*
▲ Dana-Saad Company ....E...... 509 924-6711
  Spokane Valley *(G-12677)*
▲ Dans Striping and Molding Inc .....G...... 206 533-1495
  Woodway *(G-15479)*
Davis Tool Inc.....................................G...... 509 891-5568
  Newman Lake *(G-7044)*
Delestine Designs ....G...... 206 524-6980
  Seattle *(G-9817)*
Desco Plastics LLC............................G...... 360 413-7787
  Olympia *(G-7269)*
Diversified Plastics West Inc ....F...... 360 825-7660
  Enumclaw *(G-3286)*
Dongalen Enterprises Inc..................G...... 253 395-4885
  Kent *(G-4877)*
Dp West...G...... 360 825-7660
  Enumclaw *(G-3287)*
Edt Corp ....G...... 360 574-7294
  Ferndale *(G-3837)*
Elkhart Plastics ....D...... 360 887-2230
  Ridgefield *(G-9080)*
Ershigs Inc ....E...... 360 887-3580
  Ridgefield *(G-9081)*
Ershigs Inc ....F...... 360 733-2620
  Bellingham *(G-1338)*
Exotec ....G...... 425 488-0691
  Kenmore *(G-4574)*
FA Green Company ....E...... 425 888-0007
  Snoqualmie *(G-12012)*
Fabricated Plastics Limited ....G...... 360 527-3430
  Bellingham *(G-1340)*
Fabriform LLC ....E...... 206 587-5303
  Seattle *(G-9960)*
Fabtek Industries Llc ....F...... 360 322-7367
  Arlington *(G-235)*
◆ Fastcap LLC ....E...... 888 443-3748
  Ferndale *(G-3841)*
▲ Fiberglass Technology Inds Inc ...E...... 509 928-8880
  Spokane Valley *(G-12701)*
Finest Accessories Inc ....G...... 425 831-7001
  Preston *(G-8025)*
Focal Point Plastics Inc ....F...... 206 282-0433
  Washougal *(G-14956)*
Fuze Create LLC ....E...... 425 212-8807
  Seattle *(G-10043)*
Garden Bucket LLC ....G...... 425 828-6500
  Kirkland *(G-5346)*
Georges Custom Plastic Inc ....G...... 253 939-1575
  Bonney Lake *(G-1725)*
Gigglydoo LLC ....G...... 425 344-5594
  Ellensburg *(G-3203)*
▲ Globalmax Associates Inc. ....F...... 425 392-4848
  Issaquah *(G-4422)*
◆ Globaltech Plastics LLC ....D...... 253 327-1333
  Fife *(G-3956)*
Go2origins LLC ....G...... 425 413-4134
  Ravensdale *(G-8336)*
Goodwinds LLC ....G...... 206 362-6151
  Mount Vernon *(G-6800)*
Graham Packaging Company LP ....E...... 509 698-4545
  Selah *(G-11589)*
Graves Spray Supply Inc....................G...... 253 854-2660
  Kent *(G-4927)*
Grow Plastics LLC ....G...... 206 954-4564
  Seattle *(G-10128)*
Gutters Inc ....G...... 425 482-2679
  Bothell *(G-1863)*
Intelligent Lids LLC............................G...... 206 920-6484
  Seattle *(G-10247)*
▼ J R Setina Manufacturing Co ....D...... 360 491-6197
  Olympia *(G-7310)*
Jatal Inc...E...... 253 854-0034
  Auburn *(G-478)*
Jeld-Wen Holding Inc ....C...... 509 535-1026
  Spokane *(G-12331)*
Jim Suzuki ....G...... 253 804-6070
  Auburn *(G-482)*
Joseph S Heagney ....G...... 360 631-2982
  Arlington *(G-263)*
Kaenaa Corp ....G...... 425 283-3072
  Sammamish *(G-9225)*
◆ Kaso Plastics Inc ....D...... 360 254-3980
  Vancouver *(G-14344)*
▲ Kel-Tech Plastics Inc ....E...... 253 472-9654
  Tacoma *(G-13374)*

Employee Codes: A=Over 500 employees, B=251-500
C=101-250, D=51-100, E=20-50, F=10-19, G=2-9

Ktn Thermo Dynamics .... G 509 823-0560
Yakima (G-15610)
▲ Lectent LLC .... D 360 574-7737
Vancouver (G-14369)
Legacy Plastics L L C .... G 360 413-7787
Olympia (G-7321)
Lemac Manufacturing Co Inc .... G 360 756-1720
Bellingham (G-1407)
Lnp LLC .... G 206 467-4556
Tukwila (G-13767)
Loomis Plastics Corporation .... E 206 292-0111
Seattle (G-10439)
Lowridge On Site Tech LLC .... G 877 476-8823
Lake Stevens (G-5660)
Lucky Break Wishbone Corp .... G 206 933-8700
Seattle (G-10446)
▲ Lumicor Inc .... D 425 255-4000
Renton (G-8846)
Macro Plastics Inc .... E 509 452-1200
Union Gap (G-13940)
Mapp Tool LLC .... G 509 228-9449
Spokane Valley (G-12783)
Max-Five Importing Company .... G 253 887-8665
Auburn (G-492)
▲ McClarin Plastics LLC .... B 509 877-5950
Wapato (G-14919)
Mercury Plastics LLC .... G 360 693-0627
Vancouver (G-14410)
Michael W Sherer .... G 206 230-8541
Mercer Island (G-6474)
Michellaine Lee Larry Bergsma .... G 360 873-4005
Marblemount (G-6305)
Mico Welding & Machining Inc .... G 509 467-5082
Nine Mile Falls (G-7079)
▲ Milgard Manufacturing Inc .... C 253 922-6030
Fife (G-3971)
Milgard Manufacturing Inc .... A 253 922-4341
Fife (G-3972)
▲ Minds-I Inc .... G 509 252-5725
Liberty Lake (G-5846)
Mixie Manufacturing LLC .... G 360 696-4943
Vancouver (G-14422)
Modular Arts Inc .... G 206 788-4210
Kent (G-5012)
Myco Molding Inc .... F 360 676-9656
Bellingham (G-1454)
New Top Dog LLC .... G 206 817-3395
Bellevue (G-1028)
Norplex Inc .... F 360 736-0727
Centralia (G-2419)
▲ Norplex Inc .... E 253 735-3431
Auburn (G-510)
▲ Northwest Composites Inc .... E 360 653-2211
Marysville (G-6364)
Northwest Inc .... G 360 794-7473
Monroe (G-6602)
Northwest Paper Box Mfrs Inc .... E 206 782-7105
Seatac (G-9293)
▲ Northwest Plastic Tech LLC .... E 206 499-6292
Edmonds (G-3138)
Norwesco Inc .... F 360 835-3021
Washougal (G-14973)
▲ Nova Verta USA Inc .... G 509 444-7910
Spokane Valley (G-12811)
Obcon Inc .... G 253 931-0455
Auburn (G-516)
Oceanus Plastics Inc .... G 360 366-7474
Custer (G-2858)
P & M Fiberglass Company Inc .... G 206 784-1940
Seattle (G-10725)
Pacific Injection Molding .... G 360 733-7466
Bellingham (G-1485)
Peninsula Packaging LLC .... D 509 575-5341
Yakima (G-15644)
Pic Sentry Rail Inc .... G 425 349-3606
Mukilteo (G-6965)
Piller Aimmco Inc .... D 360 835-2103
Washougal (G-14979)
Plastic Forming Services LLC .... F 360 335-9755
Washougal (G-14980)
▲ Plastic Injection Molding Inc .... G 509 375-4260
Richland (G-9035)
▲ Plastics Dynamics Inc .... E 206 762-2164
Kent (G-5067)
▲ Plastics Northwest Inc .... F 360 823-0505
Vancouver (G-14488)
Plexus Manufacturing Inc .... G 425 355-2997
Mukilteo (G-6966)
◆ Polyform US Ltd .... D 253 872-0300
Kent (G-5072)
Polymer Foundry Inc .... G 360 574-1617
Vancouver (G-14493)
Porex Technologies Corporation .... C 253 284-8000
Fife (G-3982)
◆ Portland Plastics .... B 360 887-2230
Ridgefield (G-9103)
Prime Pallets and Recycling .... G 360 410-0238
Blaine (G-1697)
Pro Clip Products Inc .... G 509 924-5544
Spokane Valley (G-12841)
Professional Plastics Inc .... F 253 872-7430
Tukwila (G-13796)
Proto Technologies Inc .... D 509 891-4747
Liberty Lake (G-5855)
Pure Watercraft Inc .... G 206 451-0350
Seattle (G-10890)
R Wayne Industries LLC .... G 425 359-0432
Snohomish (G-11966)
Reality Plastics Inc .... G 360 653-3949
Marysville (G-6377)
Redwood Plastics and Rbr Corp .... E 360 225-1491
Woodland (G-15461)
Reed Composite Solutions LLC .... G 360 637-6867
Aberdeen (G-31)
Reflect-A-Life Inc .... G 253 693-8662
Monroe (G-6614)
▲ Reiff Injection Molding Inc .... G 509 340-1020
Spokane (G-12470)
▼ Rex Plastics Inc .... E 360 892-0366
Vancouver (G-14549)
Rod Thunfield & Custom .... G 253 536-0373
Puyallup (G-8238)
Rods Custom Fiberglass Inc .... G 509 483-2174
Spokane (G-12482)
Rp 2000 LLC .... G 206 624-8258
Seattle (G-10988)
S Scott & Associates LLC .... G 360 576-4830
Vancouver (G-14563)
Saint-Gobain Prfmce Plas Corp .... C 253 466-5400
Puyallup (G-8244)
Seattle Custom Plastics Inc .... F 206 233-0869
Seattle (G-11054)
Sensitech Inc .... E 425 883-7926
Redmond (G-8660)
Sensitech Inc .... C 425 883-7926
Redmond (G-8661)
Shyft Advanced Mfg LLC .... F 425 398-4009
Woodinville (G-15361)
Signature Plastics LLC .... F 360 366-5044
Custer (G-2860)
▲ Sinotechusa Inc .... G 360 566-2880
Ridgefield (G-9111)
Skills For Creative Concepts .... G 360 671-1472
Bellingham (G-1542)
▲ Smak Plastics Inc .... E 360 882-0410
Vancouver (G-14595)
Sound Manufacturing Inc .... E 253 872-8007
Kent (G-5141)
Stewart Industries Inc .... E 206 652-9110
Seattle (G-11194)
▲ Stl International Incorporated .... E 253 840-5252
Buckley (G-2076)
Sully N A Saint-Gobain .... G 253 466-5417
Puyallup (G-8256)
Sunbacker Fiberglass Inc .... G 360 794-5547
Monroe (G-6628)
Sunset Molding Inc .... G 360 835-3805
Washougal (G-14988)
Surain Industries Inc .... G 253 863-8111
Sumner (G-13105)
Tailored Solutions LLC .... G 509 258-4314
Tumtum (G-13847)
Tal Holdings LLC .... G 509 682-1617
Chelan (G-2565)
Tap Plastics Inc A Cal Corp .... G 206 389-5900
Seattle (G-11266)
◆ Taphandles LLC .... E 206 462-6800
Seattle (G-11269)
Tdap .... G 509 453-3038
Yakima (G-15695)
▲ Technical Molded Plastics Inc .... E 425 251-9710
Kent (G-5174)
◆ Thermoforming Systems LLC .... E 509 454-4578
Union Gap (G-13954)
Toolless Plastic Solutions Inc .... E 425 493-1223
Everett (G-3633)
Tri-City Glass Inc .... G 509 586-0454
Kennewick (G-4738)
◆ U S Wax & Polymer Inc .... E 509 922-1069
Spokane Valley (G-12918)
United Home Technologies LLC .... F 360 574-7737
Washougal (G-14996)
Urethane Cast Parts Inc .... G 253 539-4282
Puyallup (G-8268)
Vaporpath Inc .... G 306 208-2747
Bainbridge Island (G-680)
▲ Vaupell Industrial Plas Inc .... B 206 784-9050
Seattle (G-11406)
▲ Vaupell Molding & Tooling Inc .... D 206 784-9050
Seattle (G-11407)
Veva Company LLC .... G 360 687-8550
Battle Ground (G-749)
WD&I Machine Co .... E 360 225-5020
Woodland (G-15473)
West Coast Plastics Inc .... G 509 575-0727
Yakima (G-15706)

31 LEATHER AND LEATHER PRODUCTS

3111 Leather Tanning & Finishing

▼ Aircraft Sheepskin Company .... G 800 874-5747
Ocean Park (G-7178)
Bochans Custom Leather Work .... G 425 337-6128
Snohomish (G-11878)
High Mountain Tannery .... G 509 435-3478
Clayton (G-2658)
McKenzie & Adams Inc .... G 425 672-8668
Woodinville (G-15307)
Obenaufs Online .... G 509 254-3542
Clarkston (G-2639)
Outlaw Leather LLC .... G 206 679-7483
Seattle (G-10719)
Quil Ceda Tanning Co Inc .... G 360 659-1333
Marysville (G-6373)
Sure-Fit Seat Covers .... G 509 326-0122
Spokane (G-12535)
Tidal Vision Products LLC .... F 907 988-8888
Ferndale (G-3913)

3131 Boot & Shoe Cut Stock & Findings

Counterpane Inc .... G 253 535-0145
Tacoma (G-13245)
▲ DBa Euroimport Company Inc .... G 206 763-7303
Seattle (G-9805)
Eagles Eductl Consulting LLC .... G 360 482-6093
Elma (G-3245)
Fence Quarter LLC .... G 800 205-0128
Lynnwood (G-6119)
French Quarter .... G 509 624-5350
Spokane (G-12265)
Irish Acres Foundation Quarter .... G 360 966-4677
Everson (G-3679)
Monte Whtzel Con Qarter Cir Ha .... G 509 220-8449
Springdale (G-12951)
No Quarter LLC .... G 206 412-4311
Kirkland (G-5411)
Northwest Sports .... G 206 463-5906
Vashon (G-14738)
Precision Counter Tech Inc .... G 425 486-8629
Kent (G-5075)
Rah Inc .... E 509 482-0943
Spokane Valley (G-12849)
Solid Solutions Inc .... G 360 882-9074
Vancouver (G-14599)
Sunrise W Quarter Horses LLC .... G 509 780-9426
Clarkston (G-2650)
West Quarter Horses LLC .... G 360 969-0791
Oak Harbor (G-7168)
Windbreak Inc .... G 817 306-9587
Ridgefield (G-9120)

3143 Men's Footwear, Exc Athletic

Amgb Inc .... G 509 309-2903
Spokane (G-12112)
Billdon LLC .... G 425 736-4316
Sammamish (G-9190)
▲ Kulien Shoe Factory .... G 360 736-6943
Centralia (G-2414)
North Star Trading Co LLP .... G 360 341-2953
Clinton (G-2692)
Rah Inc .... E 509 482-0943
Spokane Valley (G-12849)
▲ Snowden Brothers LLC .... G 206 624-1752
Bellevue (G-1142)
▲ Whites Boots Inc .... C 509 535-1875
Spokane (G-12589)

SIC SECTION

3144 Women's Footwear, Exc Athletic

Company	Code	Phone
Amgb Inc	G	509 309-2903
Spokane (G-12112)		
Billdon LLC	G	425 736-4316
Sammamish (G-9190)		
◆ Domino Fashion LLC	G	425 646-0500
Bellevue (G-879)		
▲ Kulien Shoe Factory	G	360 736-6943
Centralia (G-2414)		
North Star Trading Co LLP	G	360 341-2953
Clinton (G-2692)		
Rah Inc	E	509 482-0943
Spokane Valley (G-12849)		
▲ Snowden Brothers LLC	G	206 624-1752
Bellevue (G-1142)		
▲ Whites Boots Inc	C	509 535-1875
Spokane (G-12589)		

3149 Footwear, NEC

Company	Code	Phone
Fleet Feet Sports	G	509 309-2174
Spokane Valley (G-12704)		
No Name Boot Company	G	509 226-1980
Otis Orchards (G-7515)		
Red Wing Brands America Inc	G	651 388-6233
Everett (G-3597)		

3151 Leather Gloves & Mittens

Company	Code	Phone
Churchill N Mfg Co Inc	F	360 736-9923
Centralia (G-2393)		
Darbonnier Tactical Supply LLC	G	360 672-0216
Oak Harbor (G-7146)		
North Star Glove Company	E	253 627-7107
Tacoma (G-13429)		
▲ Oregon Glove Company	G	253 475-6733
Tacoma (G-13446)		

3161 Luggage

Company	Code	Phone
Annies Trunk LLC	G	509 529-4395
Walla Walla (G-14764)		
▲ CC Filson Co	C	206 624-4437
Seattle (G-9649)		
Darbonnier Tactical Supply LLC	G	360 672-0216
Oak Harbor (G-7146)		
Filson Manufacturing Inc	G	206 242-9579
Seattle (G-9993)		
▲ Imperial Motion LLC	G	253 779-4400
Tacoma (G-13347)		
Jeri -Ohs	G	206 722-5918
Seattle (G-10292)		
Lady 12 LLC	G	425 218-3080
Redmond (G-8528)		
Lammy Industries Inc	E	206 654-0010
Seattle (G-10374)		
Magic Satchel	G	509 342-8914
Spokane Valley (G-12782)		
▲ Music Express LLC	G	206 842-6317
Bainbridge Island (G-651)		
Northwest Design & Mfg	G	360 714-8513
Bellingham (G-1466)		
▲ Outdoor Research LLC	C	206 467-8197
Seattle (G-10717)		
▲ Padded Spaces LLC	G	872 222-7767
Lake Stevens (G-5668)		
Poros	F	773 504-2908
Seattle (G-10833)		
Presidential	G	509 669-1230
Wenatchee (G-15066)		
R & D Industries	G	206 382-1370
Seattle (G-10910)		
Resource Accounting Svcs Inc	G	860 608-0457
Port Orchard (G-7846)		
Samsonite LLC	A	253 395-1017
Renton (G-8902)		
Titan Case Inc	G	206 935-0566
Seattle (G-11314)		
▲ True North Gear LLC	G	206 723-0735
Seattle (G-11342)		
Trunk Show	G	253 302-4301
University Place (G-13982)		
Vf Outdoor LLC	E	425 455-7349
Bellevue (G-1216)		

3171 Handbags & Purses

Company	Code	Phone
Alchemy Goods LLC	G	206 484-9469
Seattle (G-9370)		
Colour Coach	G	206 478-6159
Everett (G-3423)		
◆ Domino Fashion LLC	G	425 646-0500
Bellevue (G-879)		
Proshoppers NW	G	206 852-1127
Seatac (G-9300)		
Tapestry Inc	G	206 729-5908
Seattle (G-11268)		

3172 Personal Leather Goods

Company	Code	Phone
▲ Christopher Pallis Inc	G	206 619-4146
Tacoma (G-13234)		
College Portfolios	G	425 427-0126
Sammamish (G-9198)		
Foldz Wallet LLC	G	206 730-6381
Edmonds (G-3112)		
Pioneer Square Brands Inc	G	360 733-5608
Seattle (G-10811)		
Subsplash Inc	E	206 965-8090
Seattle (G-11210)		

3199 Leather Goods, NEC

Company	Code	Phone
5 Shot Leather	G	509 844-3969
Colbert (G-2705)		
Ape Artisan Leather	G	206 399-0967
Seattle (G-9408)		
Burnish Leather Co	G	360 723-8533
Washougal (G-14946)		
Campbell Pet Company	F	360 892-9786
Vancouver (G-14093)		
Ch Leather & Supply	G	360 966-0183
Everson (G-3670)		
Crew Custom Holsters	G	360 270-3588
Longview (G-5904)		
Desert Leathercraft LLC	G	509 392-2589
Richland (G-8987)		
Dog House Leathers	G	206 257-0231
Seattle (G-9841)		
Dolans Dog Doodads LLC	G	206 257-4518
Seattle (G-9844)		
Good Wear Leather Coat Company	G	206 724-6325
Mountlake Terrace (G-6861)		
Hi-Lineleather	G	360 263-7898
La Center (G-5505)		
Indiana Harness Co	G	509 535-3400
Spokane Valley (G-12738)		
Kramer Handgun Leather Inc	F	253 564-6652
University Place (G-13975)		
L Leather LLC	G	253 733-9196
Tacoma (G-13380)		
Luans Leathers	G	360 546-5050
Vancouver (G-14385)		
Nelson Estate	G	206 241-9463
Burien (G-2119)		
▲ Oregon Glove Company	G	253 475-6733
Tacoma (G-13446)		
Patriot Leather Company	G	360 393-1392
Sedro Woolley (G-11555)		
Pioneer Aerofab Company Inc	F	360 757-4780
Burlington (G-2181)		
Reckless Charm	G	253 355-1420
Pullman (G-8103)		
Rkba Concealment	G	360 624-3874
Vancouver (G-14554)		
▲ TI Holdings Inc	F	877 743-3509
Spokane (G-12560)		
Touche Beauty Bar LLC	G	360 972-2345
Olympia (G-7411)		

32 STONE, CLAY, GLASS, AND CONCRETE PRODUCTS

3211 Flat Glass

Company	Code	Phone
Cardinal Glass Industries Inc	C	360 242-4300
Winlock (G-15146)		
Cardinal Glass Industries Inc	D	360 242-4400
Chehalis (G-2479)		
Cardinal Glass Industries Inc	C	360 242-4376
Winlock (G-15147)		
Clear View Auto & Window Glass	G	360 539-5909
Lacey (G-5542)		
Endurance Window Co	G	425 883-1345
Bellevue (G-897)		
Gabrielles Glassworks	G	509 585-9394
Kennewick (G-4666)		
▲ Gaffer Glass USA Limited	G	253 395-3361
Kent (G-4921)		
Glasshape North America LP	G	206 538-5416
Friday Harbor (G-4048)		
Hy-Grade Glass Inc	F	509 248-9919
Union Gap (G-13932)		
Impulse Construction & Glass	G	425 530-7728
Snohomish (G-11927)		
IW International Inc	E	509 735-8411
Kennewick (G-4679)		
KDL Enterprises Inc	E	253 395-3113
Kent (G-4973)		
Lapel Solutions LLC	F	360 597-4958
Vancouver (G-14358)		
Marlin Windows Inc	E	509 535-3015
Spokane Valley (G-12784)		
▲ Northwestern Industries Inc	E	206 285-3140
Seattle (G-10653)		
Pilkington North America Inc	C	509 534-4899
Spokane (G-12442)		
Pilkington North America Inc	F	425 438-8442
Everett (G-3573)		
Pro Tint LLC	G	509 468-8468
Nine Mile Falls (G-7082)		
▲ Snt-Gbain N Vetrotech Amer Inc	G	253 333-7592
Auburn (G-568)		
South Tacoma Glass Specialists	E	253 582-2401
Lakewood (G-5758)		
Sumner Stained Glass Company	G	360 378-2761
Friday Harbor (G-4061)		
Tacoma Glass Manufacturing Inc	E	253 581-7679
Lakewood (G-5760)		
▲ Tam Industries Inc	F	206 763-6868
Seattle (G-11264)		
Valley Supply Company	G	360 217-4400
Woodinville (G-15398)		
White Center Glass & Uphl	G	206 762-8088
Seattle (G-11469)		

3221 Glass Containers

Company	Code	Phone
Adaptive Cargo Solutions LLC	F	240 475-6521
Everett (G-3360)		
Ardagh Glass Inc	A	765 741-7985
Seattle (G-9425)		
Bennu Glass LLC	F	360 524-4970
Kalama (G-4493)		
◆ Pacific Market Inc	C	206 441-1400
Seattle (G-10734)		
Vashon Trading Co LLC	G	206 463-2278
Vashon (G-14746)		
Verallia	G	206 762-0660
Seattle (G-11412)		

3229 Pressed & Blown Glassware, NEC

Company	Code	Phone
Absolute Concreteworks LLC	G	360 297-5055
Port Townsend (G-7859)		
Agile Data Technology Inc	G	206 280-9512
Seattle (G-9359)		
Area 253 Glassblowing	G	253 779-0101
Tacoma (G-13179)		
Benjamin Moore Inc	G	206 329-8607
Seattle (G-9513)		
Blowing Sands	G	206 783-5314
Seattle (G-9545)		
▲ Chihuly Inc	C	206 781-8707
Seattle (G-9675)		
▼ Composite Aquatic Innovations	F	360 403-7707
Arlington (G-221)		
Composites Consolidation Compa	G	509 877-2228
Wapato (G-14914)		
Composites Consolidation LLC	G	509 877-2228
Wapato (G-14915)		
▲ Comptex Inc	F	360 466-5453
La Conner (G-5522)		
◆ Connectzonecom LLC	E	425 212-4400
Lynnwood (G-6097)		
Cq2 Enterprises	G	253 941-4488
Federal Way (G-3726)		
Cultus Bay Tiles Inc	G	360 579-3079
Clinton (G-2687)		
Dennis Nelson	G	360 320-4237
Oak Harbor (G-7148)		
Fantasy Glass Works Inc	G	425 557-6642
Issaquah (G-4412)		
Far Star Products	G	360 604-0080
Vancouver (G-14222)		
▲ Frantz Glass Gallery	F	360 426-6712
Shelton (G-11697)		
Glasshouse Studio	G	206 682-9939
Seattle (G-10079)		
Gribskov Glassblowing	G	360 795-8419
Skamokawa (G-11865)		
▼ Hot Glass Color & Supply	G	206 448-1199
Seattle (G-10183)		
Idea Company	G	253 891-8140
Pacific (G-7530)		
Issaquah Lanscaping Inc	G	425 392-6123
Issaquah (G-4430)		

Employee Codes: A=Over 500 employees, B=251-500
C=101-250, D=51-100, E=20-50, F=10-19, G=2-9

Karen Nichols.....G..... 360 497-2778
Randle (G-8326)
M-Space Inc.....G..... 253 779-0101
Seattle (G-10457)
Martin Blank Studios.....F..... 206 621-9733
Seattle (G-10493)
Mary Jane Glass Productions.....G..... 360 844-5914
Washougal (G-14965)
Maslach Art Glass A Corp.....G..... 206 842-9212
Seattle (G-11528)
▲ McClarin Plastics LLC.....B..... 509 877-5950
Wapato (G-14919)
▲ Mid Mountain Materials Inc.....E..... 206 762-7600
Seattle (G-10539)
Momentum Interactive LLC.....G..... 915 203-5349
Bellingham (G-1440)
Oak Bros Curved Glass.....G..... 253 752-4055
Olympia (G-7349)
Often On Glass.....G..... 206 725-5306
Seattle (G-10687)
Pacific Interconnection LLC.....G..... 425 277-9527
Renton (G-8872)
Pyrotek Incorporated.....D..... 509 926-6211
Spokane Valley (G-12846)
R & B Art Glass.....G..... 206 323-6430
Seattle (G-10909)
Rauch Industries Inc.....F..... 800 717-2356
Seattle (G-10925)
Richards Packaging Inc.....G..... 509 545-8690
Pasco (G-7623)
Sculptures In Glass.....G..... 509 951-3615
Chattaroy (G-2452)
Seattle Creative Brands Inc.....G..... 206 782-6548
Seattle (G-11053)
◆ Seattle Glassblowing Studio.....E..... 206 448-2181
Seattle (G-11059)
Signature Vase.....G..... 253 951-3357
Lacey (G-5588)
Stempel Art and Industry LLC.....G..... 206 718-6562
Seattle (G-11191)
Tacoma Glass Blowing Studio.....G..... 253 383-3499
Tacoma (G-13543)
Totally Blown Glassworks Inc.....G..... 206 768-8944
Seattle (G-11321)
▲ Trimlite LLC.....E..... 425 251-8685
Renton (G-8930)
▲ Trimlite Seattle Inc.....E..... 425 251-8685
Renton (G-8931)
Veteran Awards Inc.....G..... 360 925-6019
Lake Stevens (G-5673)
Walman Optical Company.....E..... 253 872-7137
Kent (G-5205)

3231 Glass Prdts Made Of Purchased Glass

AAA Kartak Co.....G..... 425 844-8555
Everett (G-3355)
Annapurna Glass & Wood Inc.....G..... 206 525-0777
Seattle (G-9404)
Atrium Windows and Door Wash.....B..... 509 248-4462
Union Gap (G-13921)
▲ Bancheros Glass and Etching.....G..... 253 854-4877
Kent (G-4807)
Batho Studios.....G..... 503 282-1460
Vashon (G-14712)
Bedrock Industries Inc.....F..... 206 283-7625
Seattle (G-9508)
Blackwaters Metal.....G..... 425 213-0154
Port Orchard (G-7795)
Cardinal Corp.....G..... 360 242-4400
Chehalis (G-2478)
Cardinal Glass Industries Inc.....C..... 360 242-4336
Winlock (G-15147)
Cardinal Glass Industries Inc.....D..... 360 956-9002
Tumwater (G-13858)
Cardinal Tg.....F..... 360 242-4352
Chehalis (G-2480)
Central Glass Works.....G..... 360 623-1099
Centralia (G-2388)
▲ Charles Parriott.....G..... 206 725-1765
Seattle (G-9668)
Covenant Art Glass Inc.....G..... 425 252-4232
Everett (G-3429)
▲ Crystal Barone.....G..... 206 621-7810
Seattle (G-9760)
David Wight Glass Art Inc.....G..... 360 389-2844
Bellingham (G-1319)
Debbie Zachary.....G..... 253 848-5011
Puyallup (G-8141)
Denny Park Glass Studio LLC.....F..... 206 388-5725
Seattle (G-9823)
Eidos Stained Glass.....G..... 360 468-3577
Lopez Island (G-5982)
ESP Supply Company LLC.....F..... 503 256-2933
Vancouver (G-14205)
Evergreen House Inc.....F..... 425 821-1005
Kirkland (G-5334)
Expressions Glass II.....G..... 206 242-2860
Burien (G-2106)
Fibres International Inc.....E..... 425 455-9811
Everett (G-3472)
Fibres International Inc.....D..... 425 455-9811
Everett (G-3471)
Gary L Jordanger.....G..... 425 271-2617
Renton (G-8805)
Guy Sunglass.....G..... 509 489-2963
Deer Park (G-2904)
▲ Hartung Glass Industries.....D..... 206 772-7800
Tukwila (G-13743)
Hartung Glass Industries.....G..... 206 772-7800
Tukwila (G-13744)
Hexen Glass Studio LLC.....G..... 360 807-4217
Centralia (G-2406)
M7m Investments.....G..... 253 922-2030
Fife (G-3967)
Maslach Art Glass A Corp.....G..... 206 842-9212
Seattle (G-11528)
▲ Matsunami Glass USA Inc.....G..... 360 302-5575
Bellingham (G-1427)
▲ Milestone Products Co.....F..... 425 882-1987
Redmond (G-8589)
Morrison Art Glass Inc.....G..... 360 714-8732
Bellingham (G-1443)
▲ National Glass Industries Inc.....E..... 425 488-8126
Woodinville (G-15319)
▲ Northwestern Industries Inc.....E..... 206 285-3140
Seattle (G-10653)
Oldcastle Buildingenvelope Inc.....D..... 360 816-7777
Battle Ground (G-725)
Opal Art Glass.....G..... 360 532-9268
Cosmopolis (G-2801)
Perry Stained Glass Studio.....G..... 425 392-1600
Issaquah (G-4459)
▼ Real Carriage Door Company.....G..... 253 853-3815
Gig Harbor (G-4152)
Rogue Empire Inc.....F..... 253 857-5300
Gig Harbor (G-4156)
Sandcastle Sandblasting.....G..... 360 354-5087
Lynden (G-6052)
Sound Glass Sales Inc.....D..... 253 473-7477
Tacoma (G-13518)
Steel Encounters Inc.....F..... 206 281-8500
Seattle (G-11186)
▼ Trivitro Corporation.....F..... 425 251-8340
Seattle (G-11339)
Unique Art Glass LLC.....G..... 425 467-5599
Bellevue (G-1207)
Veteran Awards Inc.....G..... 360 925-6019
Lake Stevens (G-5673)
Windowscape Designs.....G..... 360 468-3510
Lopez Island (G-5989)

3241 Cement, Hydraulic

Ash Grove Cement Company.....D..... 206 623-5596
Seattle (G-9443)
Ash Grove Cement Company.....G..... 509 928-4343
Spokane Valley (G-12627)
Calportland Company.....D..... 425 486-3281
Kenmore (G-4568)
Calportland Company.....G..... 206 764-3000
Port Ludlow (G-7764)
Glacier Northwest Inc.....E..... 253 572-7412
Tacoma (G-13310)
Holcim (us) Inc.....G..... 360 695-9208
Vancouver (G-14300)
Lafarge North America Inc.....G..... 360 695-9208
Vancouver (G-14355)
Lafarge North America Inc.....D..... 206 937-8025
Seattle (G-10371)
Lafarge North America Inc.....G..... 509 893-0034
Spokane Valley (G-12770)
Lehigh Northwest Cement Co.....F..... 360 733-6720
Bellingham (G-1405)
▲ Lehigh Northwest Cement Co.....F..... 800 752-6794
Tacoma (G-13385)
Mutual-Target LLC.....E..... 425 452-2300
Bellevue (G-1021)

3251 Brick & Structural Clay Tile

Boral Resources LLC.....G..... 206 394-3734
Tukwila (G-13709)
L B Foster Company.....G..... 509 921-8777
Spokane Valley (G-12769)
Mutual Materials Company.....E..... 509 924-2120
Mica (G-6501)
Ty Enterprises.....G..... 509 826-6597
Riverside (G-9128)

3253 Ceramic Tile

Cultus Bay Tiles Inc.....G..... 360 579-3079
Clinton (G-2687)
Dean Thoemke.....G..... 253 640-2232
Yakima (G-15551)
Florida Tile Inc.....G..... 206 767-9819
Renton (G-8801)
▲ Gary Floyd & Associates LLC.....G..... 253 874-4582
Auburn (G-447)
Gerry Newcomb.....G..... 206 633-0154
Seattle (G-10066)
Irenes Tiles.....G..... 206 463-2808
Vashon (G-14725)
M2 Innovative Concepts Inc.....F..... 253 383-5659
Tacoma (G-13393)
Mosaicsnmore.....G..... 425 273-3216
Lynnwood (G-6167)
Noel Corporation.....F..... 509 248-3412
Yakima (G-15631)
Premium Custom Cnstr LLC.....G..... 503 515-4119
Camas (G-2276)
▲ Quarry Tile Company.....D..... 509 536-2812
Spokane Valley (G-12848)
Snappy Ceramics.....G..... 206 329-7137
Seattle (G-11143)
Totten Tileworks.....G..... 360 785-3282
Winlock (G-15157)

3255 Clay Refractories

Allied Mineral Products Inc.....G..... 360 748-9295
Chehalis (G-2461)
◆ Bricking Solutions.....G..... 360 794-1277
Monroe (G-6558)
Burn Manufacturing Co.....G..... 331 444-2876
Vashon (G-14714)
Harbisonwalker Intl Inc.....E..... 253 872-2552
Kent (G-4933)
Mutual Materials Company.....E..... 509 924-2120
Mica (G-6501)

3259 Structural Clay Prdts, NEC

▲ Hamilton Materials Wash LLC.....D..... 360 225-6888
Woodland (G-15439)

3261 China Plumbing Fixtures & Fittings

Cascade Specialty Hardware.....G..... 360 823-3995
Vancouver (G-14106)
▲ Pacarc LLC.....G..... 206 547-4591
Seattle (G-10726)

3263 Earthenware, Whiteware, Table & Kitchen Articles

Crossing Borders.....G..... 425 466-7680
Bellevue (G-870)
▲ Cuttingboard LLC.....G..... 253 234-7569
Redmond (G-8431)
Food Service Eqp Repr Inc.....G..... 206 730-2662
Shoreline (G-11773)

3264 Porcelain Electrical Splys

Baker Enterprises.....G..... 360 452-1349
Port Angeles (G-7688)
Bestfitt Gasket Company Inc.....G..... 253 863-9521
Sumner (G-13056)
Colorific Porcelain.....G..... 425 743-1591
Lynnwood (G-6096)
Pyrotek Incorporated.....D..... 509 926-6211
Spokane Valley (G-12846)

3269 Pottery Prdts, NEC

Alex Daisley.....G..... 206 623-5555
Seattle (G-9373)
Atlas Ceramic.....G..... 206 280-0041
Seattle (G-9454)
Audrey Josias Ceramics.....G..... 253 862-2365
Buckley (G-2047)
Bodycote Imt Inc.....E..... 360 833-1120
Camas (G-2234)
Canterburys Dental Ceramics.....G..... 509 966-3622
Yakima (G-15527)

Cascadia Stoneware USA In ....G....... 360 595-1171
Deming (G-2918)
Catherine Tomlinson ....G....... 206 789-4405
Seattle (G-9646)
Clay In Motion Inc ....F....... 509 529-6146
Walla Walla (G-14785)
Clayport Pottery ....G....... 425 335-0678
Lake Stevens (G-5638)
Coastal Clayworks ....G....... 315 405-5077
Roy (G-9158)
Cook On Clay ....G....... 360 678-1818
Coupeville (G-2812)
Country Stoneware ....G....... 509 484-6950
Spokane (G-12203)
Creative Interaction LLC ....G....... 509 466-4612
Spokane (G-12207)
Geo Lastomirsky Ceramic A ....G....... 206 782-4695
Seattle (G-10062)
Glazy Daze Ceramics ....G....... 253 770-2979
Puyallup (G-8158)
▲ Gurglepot Inc ....G....... 253 670-6240
Pacific (G-7528)
Handyworks Inc ....G....... 509 299-4918
Medical Lake (G-6441)
Jadeflower Ceramics ....G....... 253 720-6036
Seattle (G-10279)
Jans Ceramics ....G....... 360 425-3540
Longview (G-5920)
Kennedy Creek Pottery ....G....... 360 866-3937
Olympia (G-7316)
Mardie Rees Artist LLC ....G....... 253 279-3244
Gig Harbor (G-4134)
Nelson Farrier Shop Inc ....G....... 509 966-9598
Yakima (G-15629)
Orcas Island Pottery ....G....... 360 376-2813
Eastsound (G-3042)
Puffin Glass ....G....... 509 328-0661
Spokane (G-12458)
Read Products Inc ....F....... 206 283-2510
Seattle (G-10929)
Sandra S Berlin ....G....... 206 612-4126
Seattle (G-11012)
Scott Parrish ....G....... 360 259-8080
Vancouver (G-14573)
T J Pottery ....G....... 253 946-1974
Kent (G-5169)
▲ Washington Pottery Co ....G....... 425 656-7277
Kent (G-5208)

3271 Concrete Block & Brick

Basalite Building Products LLC ....E....... 253 964-5000
Dupont (G-2955)
▲ Cascade Concrete Industries ....F....... 360 757-2900
Burlington (G-2141)
Cemex Cnstr Mtls PCF LLC ....E....... 360 486-3557
Snohomish (G-11888)
Cemex Cnstr Mtls PCF LLC ....E....... 425 355-2111
Lynnwood (G-6091)
Cemex Cnstr Mtls PCF LLC ....G....... 360 474-0173
Arlington (G-218)
Columbia Precast Products LLC ....F....... 360 335-8400
Woodland (G-15424)
Concrete Shop Inc ....F....... 360 573-5775
Vancouver (G-14145)
Eastside Masonry Products Inc ....E....... 425 868-0303
Redmond (G-8445)
Greenland Industries LLC ....G....... 503 841-1835
Port Orchard (G-7811)
Holroyd Block Company Inc ....F....... 253 474-8481
Tacoma (G-13339)
Kelley Blocks LLC ....G....... 253 922-9848
Lake Tapps (G-5680)
Kp2 LLC ....G....... 509 663-4983
Wenatchee (G-15041)
Landsol LLC ....F....... 425 242-5198
Kirkland (G-5382)
Nichols Bros Stoneworks Ltd ....E....... 360 668-5434
Snohomish (G-11951)
Quality Concrete Products ....G....... 509 758-2655
Clarkston (G-2642)
White Block Co Inc ....E....... 509 534-0651
Spokane Valley (G-12937)

3272 Concrete Prdts

Absolute Concreteworks LLC ....G....... 360 297-5055
Port Townsend (G-7859)
▼ Advanced Cement Tech LLC ....G....... 360 332-7060
Blaine (G-1657)
Alaska Wholesale Hardwoods ....G....... 360 704-4444
Tumwater (G-13850)
All About Safes and Vaults ....G....... 570 839-1980
Auburn (G-368)
Altus Industries Inc ....G....... 360 255-7699
Blaine (G-1659)
Ameron International Corp ....E....... 909 944-4100
Vancouver (G-14028)
Ameron International Corp ....D....... 909 944-4100
Vancouver (G-14029)
Ameron International Corp ....E....... 425 258-2616
Everett (G-3369)
Ameron International Corp ....E....... 909 944-4100
Vancouver (G-14031)
Armstrong NW ....G....... 425 251-0353
Kent (G-4791)
Atlas Concrete Products Inc ....F....... 360 736-7642
Centralia (G-2384)
Atlas Construction Spc Co Inc ....E....... 206 283-2000
Seattle (G-9455)
Automatic Wilbert Vault Co Inc ....E....... 253 531-2656
Tacoma (G-13187)
Barefoote Concrete Inc ....G....... 509 879-3736
Spokane Valley (G-12636)
Basalite Building Products LLC ....E....... 253 964-5000
Dupont (G-2955)
Bayview Redi Mix Inc ....E....... 360 533-7372
Aberdeen (G-5)
Bernard Manufacturing ....F....... 206 242-4017
Burien (G-2093)
Bethlehem Construction Inc ....E....... 509 782-1001
Cashmere (G-2317)
Bodes Precast Inc ....F....... 360 354-3912
Everson (G-3668)
Boral Roofing LLC ....E....... 253 581-3666
Lakewood (G-5705)
Builders Firstsource Inc ....E....... 253 847-2900
Graham (G-4217)
Burke Meadow LLC ....G....... 253 439-6092
Auburn (G-399)
C T Sales Inc ....G....... 253 874-8737
Federal Way (G-3719)
▼ Cams-Usa Inc ....F....... 253 639-3890
Kent (G-4835)
Capsule Urn LLC ....G....... 360 695-2618
Vancouver (G-14097)
Cascade Concrete ....G....... 360 354-8901
Lynden (G-6005)
Centralia Box & Vault Co ....G....... 360 736-4757
Centralia (G-2389)
Chelan Concrete Inc ....F....... 509 682-2915
Chelan (G-2549)
Chip Away Bathtub Repair ....G....... 425 246-1306
North Bend (G-7107)
Coffee Vault LLC ....G....... 253 227-5798
Buckley (G-2052)
Columbia Precast Products LLC ....F....... 360 335-8400
Woodland (G-15424)
Concrete Creations ....G....... 509 826-5409
OMAK (G-7438)
Concrete Products Co Ore LLC ....E....... 360 834-3459
Camas (G-2242)
Concrete Products Co Inc ....G....... 253 864-2774
Puyallup (G-8136)
Concrete Shop Inc ....F....... 360 573-5775
Vancouver (G-14145)
Concrete Works Statuary Inc ....G....... 509 922-6168
Spokane (G-12197)
CPM Development Corporation ....B....... 509 534-6221
Spokane Valley (G-12668)
Creative Concrete Concepts ....G....... 425 466-4479
Carnation (G-2292)
Creative Concrete Products LLC ....G....... 360 419-9909
Mount Vernon (G-6786)
Curtiss R Grenz ....E....... 509 893-0317
Greenacres (G-4296)
Custom Concrete Casting Corp ....F....... 425 333-4737
Carnation (G-2293)
▲ Cuz Concrete Products Inc ....E....... 360 435-5531
Arlington (G-224)
Cuz Concrete Products Inc ....G....... 360 435-0769
Arlington (G-225)
▲ Cxt Incorporated ....D....... 509 924-6300
Spokane Valley (G-12675)
Cxt Incorporated ....E....... 509 921-7878
Spokane Valley (G-12676)
D & K Concrete Products Inc ....F....... 360 573-4020
Vancouver (G-14162)
Diamond Concrete Products ....G....... 360 659-6277
Arlington (G-228)
East West General Inc ....G....... 360 673-6404
Kalama (G-4497)
Edgewood Monuments ....G....... 253 561-2498
Puyallup (G-8148)
Eldorado Stone LLC ....E....... 425 349-4107
Everett (G-3453)
Encon United Company ....F....... 360 834-3459
Camas (G-2248)
Eucon Corporation ....F....... 509 529-6400
Walla Walla (G-14803)
Fantasy Sports Vault ....G....... 206 219-9833
Seattle (G-9969)
Fireside Hearth & Home Inc ....F....... 425 251-9447
Kent (G-4907)
Fog Tite Meter Seal Inc ....E....... 206 935-8000
Seattle (G-10010)
Forterra Inc ....G....... 360 943-1600
Olympia (G-7291)
Gary Merlino Cnstr Co Inc ....F....... 206 763-2134
Seattle (G-10050)
Gc Solutions LLC ....G....... 509 243-6030
Asotin (G-352)
Glacier Northwest Inc ....E....... 425 486-3281
Seattle (G-10076)
Glacier Northwest Inc ....G....... 360 896-8922
Vancouver (G-14255)
Green Vault Systems LLC ....G....... 206 900-2036
Snohomish (G-11916)
Gregory Diede ....G....... 509 662-1009
Wenatchee (G-15038)
H2 Pre- Cast Inc ....D....... 509 884-6644
East Wenatchee (G-3018)
Halme Construction Inc ....E....... 509 725-4200
Spokane (G-12287)
Hanson Aggregates LLC ....F....... 360 795-3221
Cathlamet (G-2368)
In Cascade Concrete Industries ....G....... 425 747-0956
Bellevue (G-955)
Inspired Monumental ....G....... 253 468-4835
Gig Harbor (G-4121)
J & R Commercial Inc ....G....... 253 639-3890
Kent (G-4963)
James Hardie Building Pdts Inc ....D....... 253 847-8700
Tacoma (G-13355)
Jet Set Northwest Inc ....G....... 206 762-0434
Tukwila (G-13756)
John Dalrymple ....G....... 509 837-2117
Sunnyside (G-13129)
Krieg Concrete Products Inc ....F....... 360 675-2727
Oak Harbor (G-7156)
Long Septic Services ....E....... 253 852-0550
Lake Stevens (G-5659)
Lopez Redi Mix Inc ....G....... 360 468-2485
Lopez Island (G-5985)
Lynden Precast LLC ....G....... 360 354-8901
Lynden (G-6035)
M 1 Tanks Inc ....G....... 509 766-2914
Moses Lake (G-6722)
Majestic Monument & Stone ....G....... 509 699-8937
Ellensburg (G-3214)
Master Precaster Inc ....G....... 253 770-9119
Puyallup (G-8183)
Melcher Manufacturing Co Inc ....G....... 509 534-9119
Spokane Valley (G-12787)
Mikron Industries Inc ....F....... 815 335-2372
Yakima (G-15621)
Mikron Industries Inc ....C....... 253 854-8020
Kent (G-5011)
▲ Milestone Products Co ....F....... 425 882-1987
Redmond (G-8589)
Monument Wheelworks LLC ....G....... 206 856-9509
Seattle (G-10561)
Monumental Chewelah ....G....... 509 935-6962
Chewelah (G-2604)
Monumental Task ....G....... 509 449-8286
Okanogan (G-7201)
Murdock Roach Inc ....G....... 509 302-1054
Kennewick (G-4697)
Mutual Materials Company ....G....... 425 353-9686
Marysville (G-6362)
Mutual Materials Company ....F....... 360 573-5683
Vancouver (G-14426)
Mutual Materials Company ....G....... 253 838-0803
Auburn (G-502)
Northwest Cascade Inc ....C....... 253 848-2371
Puyallup (G-8202)
Northwest Precast Llc ....E....... 253 770-9119
Puyallup (G-8207)
Novustone LLC ....G....... 206 457-4443
Seattle (G-10661)
NW Pole Vault Camps ....G....... 206 526-0436
Seattle (G-10674)

S I C

Employee Codes: A=Over 500 employees, B=251-500
C=101-250, D=51-100, E=20-50, F=10-19, G=2-9
2019 Washington
Manufacturers Register
597

32 STONE, CLAY, GLASS, AND CONCRETE PRODUCTS

Oldcastle Apg .... G 509 926-8235
  Spokane Valley *(G-12816)*
Oldcastle Precast Inc .... D 253 839-3500
  Auburn *(G-517)*
Ornamental Stone Inc .... G 360 275-4241
  Allyn *(G-84)*
Pacific Precast Inc .... F 360 750-0099
  Vancouver *(G-14470)*
Pacific Rock Products LLC .... E 360 254-7770
  Vancouver *(G-14474)*
Panelsuppliers .... G 253 217-1668
  Pacific *(G-7537)*
Pc2 LLC .... G 360 921-8066
  Battle Ground *(G-730)*
Peninsula Tanks Inc .... G 360 683-4714
  Sequim *(G-11659)*
Phone Vault .... G 360 867-8535
  Ocean Park *(G-7182)*
Pin Foundations Inc .... G 253 858-3844
  Gig Harbor *(G-4145)*
Pioneer Rock & Monument LLC .... G 509 773-4702
  Goldendale *(G-4206)*
Precast By Design Inc .... G 509 292-2988
  Elk *(G-3175)*
Precast Oldcastle .... G 800 509-6150
  Vancouver *(G-14498)*
▲ Premier Memorial LLC .... E 253 472-0369
  Tacoma *(G-13477)*
Quality Concrete Products .... G 509 758-2655
  Clarkston *(G-2642)*
Quality Concrete Products Inc ...... E 425 355-5510
  Mukilteo *(G-6969)*
Quanex Building Products Corp .... G 360 345-1241
  Tumwater *(G-13892)*
Quanex Screens LLC .... F 360 748-9201
  Chehalis *(G-2528)*
Quikrete Companies LLC .... E 253 396-9996
  Tacoma *(G-13486)*
Rada Inc .... G 509 547-7232
  Pasco *(G-7621)*
Rapid Readymix Co .... G 509 493-3153
  Bingen *(G-1641)*
Reese Concrete Products Mfg ...... F 509 586-3704
  Kennewick *(G-4716)*
Rw Precast Inc .... F 253 770-0100
  Puyallup *(G-8242)*
Schneider Drainfield Des .... G 360 758-7353
  Lummi Island *(G-5993)*
Shope Enterprises Inc .... E 253 848-1551
  Puyallup *(G-8254)*
Spilker Precast LLC .... G 509 487-2261
  Spokane *(G-12514)*
Splendid Intl USA Corp .... G 253 813-5692
  Kent *(G-5151)*
▲ Spokane Wilbert Vault Company .. G 509 325-4573
  Spokane *(G-12522)*
Stonehenge .... G 425 879-9574
  Sultan *(G-13040)*
Ultrablock Inc .... E 360 694-0141
  Vancouver *(G-14655)*
Universal Vault of Washington ..... G 360 834-4086
  Camas *(G-2286)*
Up To Grade Concrete Products ... F 253 845-3677
  Puyallup *(G-8267)*
W R Meadows Inc .... G 707 745-6666
  Kent *(G-5204)*
Washington Precast Products ...... G 360 598-1631
  Indianola *(G-4374)*
Western Materials Inc .... D 509 547-3301
  Pasco *(G-7652)*
White Block Co Inc .... E 509 534-0651
  Spokane Valley *(G-12937)*
Wilbert Spokane Vault Company .. E 509 248-1984
  Yakima *(G-15708)*

3273 Ready-Mixed Concrete

A A A Redi Mix II Inc .... F 509 765-1923
  Moses Lake *(G-6677)*
Angeles Concrete Products Inc .... G 360 681-5429
  Sequim *(G-11611)*
Apex Mobile Mix LLC .... G 360 304-8797
  Chehalis *(G-2466)*
Atlas Concrete Products Inc .... F 360 736-7642
  Centralia *(G-2384)*
Bayside Redi-Mix .... G 360 426-4987
  Shelton *(G-11682)*
Bayview Redi Mix Inc .... G 360 875-9993
  Raymond *(G-8342)*
Bayview Redi Mix Inc .... G 360 482-3444
  Elma *(G-3241)*
Bayview Redi Mix Inc .... E 360 533-7372
  Aberdeen *(G-5)*
Best Way Concrete .... G 360 825-5494
  Enumclaw *(G-3279)*
▲ Cadman Inc .... B 425 867-1234
  Redmond *(G-8413)*
Cadman (seattle) Inc .... C 425 316-9100
  Mill Creek *(G-6502)*
Cadman Holding Company Inc ..... G 425 868-1234
  Redmond *(G-8415)*
Calportland .... G 206 764-3000
  Seattle *(G-9609)*
Calportland Company .... G 360 423-8112
  Longview *(G-5893)*
Calportland Company .... D 206 764-3075
  Seattle *(G-9610)*
Calportland Company .... D 360 892-5100
  Woodland *(G-15422)*
Calportland Company .... E 360 892-5100
  Vancouver *(G-14091)*
Calportland Company .... G 253 912-8500
  Dupont *(G-2957)*
Cascade Mobile Mix .... G 253 833-1956
  Graham *(G-4220)*
Case Mix Analysis Inc .... G 206 285-2576
  Seattle *(G-9644)*
Cemex Cnstr Mtls Fla LLC .... G 425 513-6651
  Everett *(G-3413)*
Cemex Cnstr Mtls PCF LLC .... G 425 252-8600
  Everett *(G-3414)*
Cemex Materials LLC .... E 360 254-7770
  Vancouver *(G-14111)*
Central Pre-Mix Concrete Co .... A 509 534-6221
  Spokane Valley *(G-12654)*
Chelan Concrete Inc .... F 509 682-2915
  Chelan *(G-2549)*
Clark Site Mix Con Spokane LLC .. G 509 991-7730
  Spokane *(G-12182)*
Cm2931 LLC .... E 253 447-7537
  Fife *(G-3944)*
Columbia Asphalt & Gravel Inc .... G 509 457-3654
  Wapato *(G-14913)*
Columbia Ready Mix Inc .... D 509 453-2063
  Parker *(G-7548)*
Colville Valley Concrete Corp ...... E 509 684-2534
  Colville *(G-2747)*
Concrete & Aggregate Supply Co ..... G 253 853-2887
  Nine Mile Falls *(G-7070)*
Connell Sand & Gravel Inc .... F 509 545-4066
  Pasco *(G-7567)*
Cowden Inc .... D 360 592-4200
  Bellingham *(G-1309)*
CPM Development Corporation .... D 509 248-2041
  Yakima *(G-15539)*
CPM Development Corporation .... F 509 865-2975
  Toppenish *(G-13664)*
CPM Development Corporation .... B 509 534-6221
  Spokane Valley *(G-12668)*
CPM Development Corporation .... E 509 536-3355
  Spokane Valley *(G-12669)*
CPM Development Corporation .... G 509 932-4525
  Mattawa *(G-6405)*
CPM Development Corporation .... D 509 837-5171
  Sunnyside *(G-13118)*
CPM Development Corporation .... G 509 762-5366
  Moses Lake *(G-6699)*
CPM Development Corporation .... G 509 754-5287
  Ephrata *(G-3332)*
CPM Development Corporation .... G 509 663-5141
  Wenatchee *(G-15024)*
CPM Development Corporation .... G 509 886-4853
  Wenatchee *(G-15090)*
CPM Development Corporation .... G 509 488-2614
  Othello *(G-7493)*
Dinners Ready .... G 425 337-7955
  Mill Creek *(G-6507)*
DTI Ready Mix Company .... G 509 937-4683
  Valley *(G-13991)*
Ferndale Ready-Mix .... F 360 354-1400
  Lynden *(G-6017)*
Ferndale Ready-Mix .... F 360 384-8087
  Ferndale *(G-3843)*
Fred Hill Materials .... F 360 779-4431
  Sequim *(G-11635)*
Gary Merlino Cnstr Co Inc .... F 206 763-2134
  Seattle *(G-10050)*
Gary Merlino Cnstr Co Inc .... B 206 763-9552
  Seattle *(G-10049)*
Glacier Northwest Inc .... G 425 486-3281
  Bothell *(G-1766)*
Glacier Northwest Inc .... F 360 694-9420
  Vancouver *(G-14253)*
Glacier Northwest Inc .... G 360 694-1627
  Vancouver *(G-14254)*
Glacier Northwest Inc .... G 360 896-8922
  Vancouver *(G-14255)*
Glacier Northwest Inc .... F 360 736-1131
  Centralia *(G-2403)*
Glacier Northwest Inc .... E 360 892-5100
  Vancouver *(G-14256)*
Glacier Northwest Inc .... F 206 764-3075
  Seattle *(G-10077)*
Glacier Northwest Inc .... D 253 912-8500
  Dupont *(G-2964)*
Glacier Northwest Inc .... E 425 486-3281
  Seattle *(G-10076)*
Glacier Northwest Inc .... E 425 888-9795
  Snoqualmie *(G-12013)*
Godbey Red-E-Mix Concrete Inc ... G 509 689-2415
  Brewster *(G-2016)*
Hanson Lehigh Inc .... G 425 867-1234
  Issaquah *(G-4425)*
Hardrock Incorporated .... E 360 779-3700
  Poulsbo *(G-7965)*
Holroyd Company Inc .... D 253 474-0725
  Tacoma *(G-13340)*
Holroyd Company Inc .... D 253 627-0571
  Tacoma *(G-13341)*
Holroyd Company Inc .... E 253 474-0725
  Olympia *(G-7308)*
Interstate Concrete and Asp Co ... G 509 375-1021
  Richland *(G-9012)*
Interstate Concrete and Asp Co ... G 509 529-6400
  Walla Walla *(G-14824)*
Interstate Concrete and Asp Co ... G 509 547-2380
  Prosser *(G-8043)*
Interstate Concrete and Asp Co ... G 509 547-2380
  Pasco *(G-7593)*
Jason Thompson .... G 757 867-6494
  Spokane *(G-12329)*
Jerry Nybo Construction Inc .... G 253 691-1797
  Eatonville *(G-3060)*
Krieg Concrete Products Inc .... F 360 675-2727
  Oak Harbor *(G-7156)*
Kubeshs Site Mixed Con Inc .... G 509 684-1381
  Colville *(G-2763)*
Lafarge North America Inc .... G 509 893-0034
  Spokane Valley *(G-12770)*
Lopez Redi Mix Inc .... G 360 468-2485
  Lopez Island *(G-5985)*
Miles Sand & Gravel Company .... B 253 833-3705
  Puyallup *(G-8193)*
Miles Sand & Gravel Company .... C 360 757-3121
  Burlington *(G-2171)*
Miles Sand & Gravel Company .... F 360 435-5511
  Lake Stevens *(G-5661)*
Miles Sand & Gravel Company .... E 253 922-9116
  Tacoma *(G-13414)*
Miles Sand & Gravel Company .... F 360 675-2626
  Oak Harbor *(G-7159)*
Miles Sand & Gravel Company .... E 360 734-1956
  Everson *(G-3682)*
Miles Sand & Gravel Company .... F 360 427-0946
  Shelton *(G-11714)*
Mix It Up LLC .... G 425 396-7345
  Snoqualmie *(G-12019)*
Okanogan Valley Concrete Inc .... G 509 422-3211
  Okanogan *(G-7203)*
Oldcastle Materials Inc .... E 253 872-9466
  Kent *(G-5042)*
Oldcastle Materials Inc .... D 509 926-8235
  Spokane Valley *(G-12817)*
Oldcastle Materials Inc .... F 509 534-6221
  Spokane Valley *(G-12818)*
Rapid Readymix Co .... G 509 773-5919
  Goldendale *(G-4207)*
Rapid Readymix Co .... G 509 493-3153
  Bingen *(G-1641)*
Rempel Bros Concrete Inc .... F 360 678-4622
  Coupeville *(G-2816)*
Richard Lawson Construction ..... E 360 378-4313
  Friday Harbor *(G-4055)*
Salmon Bay Sand and Gravel Co .. D 206 784-1234
  Seattle *(G-11007)*
▼ Samoa Maritime Company .... G 206 246-1182
  Normandy Park *(G-7098)*
Skagit Ready Mix .... G 360 856-0422
  Mount Vernon *(G-6840)*
Smokey Point Concrete .... F 360 856-0422
  Sedro Woolley *(G-11571)*

SIC SECTION

Southwest Concrete Co ....G....... 360 795-8211
  Cathlamet (G-2375)
Specialty Concrete ....G....... 360 577-4555
  Kelso (G-4549)
Speedy Mix Concrete ....G....... 253 531-3260
  Tacoma (G-13522)
Spokane Rock Products Inc ....F....... 509 292-2200
  Elk (G-3177)
Stanwood Redi-Mix Inc ....E....... 360 652-7777
  Stanwood (G-12994)
Stotts Construction Inc ....F....... 509 779-4987
  Curlew (G-2847)
Tillmans Inc ....G....... 509 633-2542
  Coulee Dam (G-2809)
Tim Corliss & Son Inc ....G....... 360 825-2578
  Enumclaw (G-3324)
Two Rivers Sand and Gravel ....G....... 509 763-3280
  Leavenworth (G-5817)
Whyte & Sons Incorporated ....G....... 425 885-3571
  Redmond (G-8713)

3274 Lime

Graymont Western US Inc ....E....... 253 572-7600
  Tacoma (G-13319)
Lime Solutions ....G....... 425 502-7651
  Bellevue (G-984)
▲ Mango and Lime Design LLC ....G....... 425 985-8994
  Redmond (G-8547)
▼ Western Lime Corp ....G....... 604 249-1997
  Seattle (G-11453)

3275 Gypsum Prdts

Certainteed Gypsum Inc ....D....... 425 291-9099
  Kent (G-4850)
Certainteed Gypsum Inc ....C....... 206 763-1441
  Seattle (G-9657)
Certainteed Gypsum Mfg Inc ....A....... 949 282-5300
  Seattle (G-9658)
Georgia-Pacific LLC ....D....... 253 627-2100
  Tacoma (G-13307)
New West Gypsum Inc ....F....... 253 380-1079
  Kent (G-5021)
United States Gypsum Company ....E....... 253 931-6600
  Auburn (G-588)

3281 Cut Stone Prdts

Absolute GM LLC ....E....... 425 814-1011
  Kirkland (G-5267)
Antony Architectural Stone ....G....... 425 424-0051
  Woodinville (G-15179)
Bailey and Bailey Inc ....F....... 253 649-0568
  Gig Harbor (G-4075)
Bedrock Industries Inc ....G....... 206 283-7625
  Seattle (G-9508)
Cascade Marble & Granite ....G....... 509 533-0476
  Spokane (G-12171)
Columbia Cultured Marble Inc ....G....... 509 582-5660
  Kennewick (G-4647)
Columbia Cultured MBL II LLC ....G....... 509 582-5660
  Kennewick (G-4648)
Ddbd Construction ....G....... 253 576-6769
  Bonney Lake (G-1721)
Debroeck Solid Surface Inc ....G....... 509 525-1349
  Walla Walla (G-14794)
Designers Holding Company Inc ....G....... 425 487-9887
  Woodinville (G-15222)
Designers Marble Inc ....G....... 425 487-9887
  Woodinville (G-15223)
Dudley Family Group Inc ....G....... 253 863-9282
  Pacific (G-7525)
East WA Burial Vaults Inc ....G....... 509 662-5684
  Wenatchee (G-15027)
Flagstone ....G....... 425 892-9134
  Bothell (G-1854)
Flagstone Wildlife Artisrty ....G....... 360 967-2005
  Silverlake (G-11863)
Gabrielle England Inc ....G....... 360 956-1017
  Olympia (G-7292)
Gary Merlino Cnstr Co Inc ....F....... 206 763-2134
  Seattle (G-10050)
▲ Homchick Michael Stone Work ....E....... 425 481-2783
  Kenmore (G-4582)
J R Stone Services ....G....... 425 227-8513
  Renton (G-8831)
Kaes Enterprises LLC ....G....... 800 252-5237
  Puyallup (G-8171)
Kgo Stone ....F....... 360 573-0272
  Vancouver (G-14346)
Kings Kitchen LLC ....G....... 253 212-3623
  Tacoma (G-13376)

Koppenberg Enterprises Inc ....F....... 360 793-1600
  Monroe (G-6589)
Lapel Solutions LLC ....F....... 360 597-4958
  Vancouver (G-14358)
Lee R Mason Inc ....G....... 253 863-8666
  Sumner (G-13079)
M&E Memorial Markers Inc ....G....... 509 662-6469
  Wenatchee (G-15048)
Manufacturers Mineral Company ....F....... 425 228-2120
  Renton (G-8847)
▲ Mario & Son Inc ....E....... 509 536-6079
  Liberty Lake (G-5845)
▲ Marmo E Granito Inc ....G....... 206 368-0990
  Shoreline (G-11785)
Nichols Bros Stoneworks Ltd ....E....... 360 668-5434
  Snohomish (G-11951)
Norhtwest Stone Pros ....G....... 206 824-2458
  Kent (G-5025)
Northwest Granite and MBL LLC ....F....... 206 228-6881
  Redmond (G-8599)
Pacific Stone & Tile LLC ....F....... 360 352-3960
  Olympia (G-7365)
Precision Waterjet Inc ....G....... 509 888-7954
  Wenatchee (G-15065)
▲ Premier Memorial LLC ....E....... 253 472-0369
  Tacoma (G-13477)
▲ Quiring Monuments Inc ....E....... 206 522-8400
  Seattle (G-10906)
Rock Bizarre ....G....... 360 275-9742
  Belfair (G-773)
Rock Place ....G....... 425 220-1110
  Marysville (G-6379)
Sandcastle Sandblasting ....G....... 360 354-5087
  Lynden (G-6052)
Savon Caskets and Urns ....G....... 206 390-3797
  Renton (G-8904)
▲ Seaport Tile & Marble Inc ....E....... 425 644-7067
  Bellevue (G-1120)
Service Corp International ....G....... 425 885-2414
  Redmond (G-8663)
Shine Marble Co Inc ....F....... 425 444-5832
  Kenmore (G-4605)
Southern Explorations ....G....... 206 641-9241
  Seattle (G-11161)
Stone Castle Fabrication LLC ....G....... 253 205-8435
  Auburn (G-573)
Stone Craft LLC ....G....... 206 762-3920
  Seattle (G-11198)
Tresko Monument Inc ....F....... 509 838-3196
  Spokane (G-12568)
▲ Zorzi Corporation ....G....... 425 334-0160
  Snohomish (G-12002)

3291 Abrasive Prdts

Blanchard Abrasives ....F....... 360 653-5273
  Marysville (G-6317)
Fresh Impressions By Honey D ....G....... 253 503-7887
  Lakewood (G-5723)
Lapel Solutions LLC ....F....... 360 597-4958
  Vancouver (G-14358)
Lapo Inc ....G....... 360 314-4546
  Vancouver (G-14359)
▲ Mt Baker Powder Coating ....G....... 360 366-3233
  Bellingham (G-1449)
▲ Pro Abrasives Inc ....G....... 360 509-4152
  Bremerton (G-1990)
Radiac Abrasives Inc ....D....... 360 659-6276
  Marysville (G-6374)
Radiac Abrasives Inc ....D....... 360 659-6201
  Marysville (G-6375)
Radiac Abrasives Inc ....D....... 360 659-6201
  Marysville (G-6376)

3292 Asbestos products

A1 Asbestos LLC ....G....... 509 881-0074
  Cashmere (G-2311)
Asbestos Northwest ....G....... 253 941-4343
  Federal Way (G-3717)
Thermal Northwest Inc ....F....... 253 520-8899
  Kent (G-5178)

3295 Minerals & Earths: Ground Or Treated

Columbia Rock & Aggregates Inc ....F....... 360 892-0510
  Vancouver (G-14137)
Imerys Minerals California Inc ....D....... 509 787-4575
  Quincy (G-8300)
Konen Rock Crushing Inc ....G....... 509 382-2768
  Dayton (G-2883)
Lane Mt Silica Co ....E....... 206 762-7622
  Valley (G-13993)

Magic Earth ....G....... 509 738-2801
  Kettle Falls (G-5236)
Manufacturers Mineral Company ....F....... 425 228-2120
  Renton (G-8847)
Puget Sound Surfacers Inc ....G....... 360 374-9590
  Forks (G-4016)
▲ Rec Silicon Inc ....D....... 509 765-2106
  Moses Lake (G-6741)
Specialty Minerals Inc ....G....... 509 545-9777
  Wallula (G-14911)
Steelhead Specialty Minerals ....G....... 509 328-5685
  Spokane (G-12527)

3296 Mineral Wool

Environmental Insul Contg LLC ....E....... 360 647-2532
  Bellingham (G-1336)
Johns Manville Corporation ....D....... 800 654-3103
  Kent (G-4970)
Pmc Inc ....D....... 206 854-2660
  Kent (G-5068)
Service Partners LLC ....D....... 509 535-4600
  Spokane Valley (G-12866)
▲ Service Partners of Oregon ....E....... 360 694-6747
  Vancouver (G-14580)
West Coast Insulation Inc ....G....... 206 459-2233
  Seattle (G-11450)

3297 Nonclay Refractories

Allied Mineral Products Inc ....G....... 360 748-9295
  Chehalis (G-2461)
Aluminum Technologies Inc ....G....... 206 323-6900
  Seattle (G-9390)
CH Murphy/Clark-Ullman Inc ....D....... 253 475-6566
  Tacoma (G-13232)
Industrial Ceramics Inc ....G....... 905 878-2848
  Seattle (G-10230)
Pryor Giggey Co ....G....... 360 647-6021
  Bellingham (G-1508)
Seal Dynamics ....G....... 503 232-0973
  Vancouver (G-14577)

3299 Nonmetallic Mineral Prdts, NEC

Carson/Corbett LLC ....G....... 206 624-8266
  Seattle (G-9638)
Carson/Corbett LLC ....G....... 206 524-9782
  Seattle (G-9639)
Ceradyne Inc ....G....... 206 763-2170
  Seattle (G-9656)
Dugger and Associates Inc ....G....... 425 785-6940
  McCleary (G-6415)
Lapel Solutions LLC ....F....... 360 597-4958
  Vancouver (G-14358)
Mach 2 Arts Inc ....G....... 206 953-0575
  Seattle (G-10458)
Master Stucco Hc ....G....... 425 793-0576
  Renton (G-8849)
Michaels Gemstone Trees ....G....... 509 922-2390
  Spokane Valley (G-12788)
Mihalisin/Walling Studio ....G....... 206 923-1037
  Seattle (G-10541)
▼ Nano Arts LLC ....E....... 509 525-8531
  Walla Walla (G-14849)
Nathan Capital LLC ....G....... 360 835-1211
  Washougal (G-14971)
◆ Perma-Chink Systems Inc ....F....... 425 885-6050
  Redmond (G-8619)
Richard Warrington ....G....... 509 448-8713
  Cheney (G-2592)
San Juan Islands Sculpture Pk ....G....... 360 370-0035
  Friday Harbor (G-4057)
Sienna Technologies Inc ....F....... 425 485-0756
  Woodinville (G-15362)
Skyflight Inc ....G....... 425 844-9199
  Woodinville (G-15366)

33 PRIMARY METAL INDUSTRIES

3312 Blast Furnaces, Coke Ovens, Steel & Rolling Mills

2 Wheel Dynoworks ....G....... 425 398-4335
  Woodinville (G-15168)
Accurate Sheet Metal Inc ....E....... 425 745-6786
  Mukilteo (G-6889)
Ace Galvanizing ....G....... 206 687-7688
  Burien (G-2090)
Advanced All Wheel Drive ....G....... 360 746-8746
  Ferndale (G-3809)
Ameron International Corp ....D....... 909 944-4100
  Vancouver (G-14029)

Employee Codes: A=Over 500 employees, B=251-500
C=101-250, D=51-100, E=20-50, F=10-19, G=2-9

33 PRIMARY METAL INDUSTRIES

Auto Wheel Sales .... G 509 483-4251
  Spokane *(G-12129)*
Boutique On Wheels .... G 425 369-9324
  Sammamish *(G-9192)*
Brooks Steel Fabrication .... G 360 403-9400
  Arlington *(G-215)*
Buyken Metal Products Inc .... E 253 852-0634
  Kent *(G-4827)*
Centralia Supply & Fabrication .... G 360 736-7277
  Centralia *(G-2391)*
Cobalt Trailer Sales .... G 509 535-2154
  Spokane *(G-12186)*
◆ Consolidated Metco Inc .... D 360 828-2599
  Vancouver *(G-14147)*
Cowlitz Fence Co .... G 360 577-6110
  Kelso *(G-4522)*
Epic Wheel and Tire Inc .... E 253 691-1785
  Tacoma *(G-13280)*
Fabrication Products Inc .... E 503 283-3218
  Vancouver *(G-14219)*
Fat Daddys Fabrication LLC .... G 253 677-8005
  Roy *(G-9159)*
For-D Inc .... F 425 486-1120
  Woodinville *(G-15246)*
Franks Custom Wheels .... G 360 333-6887
  Mount Vernon *(G-6798)*
Global Direct Components LLC .... F 253 661-1100
  Federal Way *(G-3741)*
▲ Great Sun Corp .... F 206 329-8027
  Seattle *(G-10114)*
Gundies Inc .... E 360 733-5036
  Bellingham *(G-1364)*
Hci Steel Buildings LLC .... F 360 403-4900
  Arlington *(G-250)*
Inland Empire Resteel .... G 509 863-9870
  Spokane *(G-12308)*
Innotech Metal Designs LLC .... G 360 393-4108
  Bellingham *(G-1378)*
Intermountain Fabricators Inc .... F 509 534-1676
  Spokane Valley *(G-12746)*
J and J Stainless Steel Svcs .... G 509 952-4568
  Yakima *(G-15594)*
K B Alloys .... G 360 371-2312
  Blaine *(G-1677)*
Kindle Eithan .... G 509 558-7023
  Spokane *(G-12352)*
▲ Mad Fiber .... G 206 402-3925
  Seattle *(G-10463)*
Maverick Metalworks LLC .... G 253 345-1590
  Spanaway *(G-12063)*
Metal Masters Northwest Inc .... G 425 775-4481
  Lynnwood *(G-6162)*
Nails On Wheels .... G 253 839-1123
  Auburn *(G-503)*
Northwest Pipe Company .... B 303 289-4080
  Vancouver *(G-14438)*
Nucor Corporation .... C 206 933-2222
  Seattle *(G-10666)*
▲ Nucor Steel Seattle Inc .... C 206 933-2222
  Seattle *(G-10667)*
Pacific Steel Structures LLC .... G 509 921-5835
  Greenacres *(G-4301)*
Poizer Metal Works .... G 360 892-2629
  Vancouver *(G-14492)*
Precise Manufacturing & Engrg .... F 360 604-8742
  Vancouver *(G-14499)*
▲ Puget Sound Steel Co Inc .... E 253 854-3600
  Kent *(G-5088)*
Quality Used Tires and Wheels .... G 253 446-6002
  Puyallup *(G-8231)*
Renegade Powder Coating LLC .... G 509 575-4623
  Union Gap *(G-13952)*
Scott McClure .... G 360 297-7007
  Kingston *(G-5262)*
Ser Pro Inc .... G 206 767-3100
  Seattle *(G-11090)*
Sienna Technologies Inc .... F 425 485-0756
  Woodinville *(G-15362)*
SIS Northwest Inc .... G 360 854-0074
  Sedro Woolley *(G-11565)*
Source Engineering LLC .... E 360 383-5129
  Lynden *(G-6053)*
Steel Fab Nw Inc .... G 360 210-7055
  Washougal *(G-14987)*
Steel Magnolia Inc .... G 360 366-5090
  Blaine *(G-1704)*
Steel Painters Inc .... E 360 425-7720
  Kelso *(G-4551)*
Steelscape LLC .... C 360 673-8200
  Kalama *(G-4510)*

Stephs Custom Sawyering .... G 425 646-8783
  Bellevue *(G-1156)*
▲ Thermal Pipe Shields .... G 425 330-3765
  Stanwood *(G-12996)*
Tinplate Toys & Trains .... G 206 715-8118
  Tacoma *(G-13555)*
Western Sttes Stl Fbrction Inc .... E 509 489-8046
  Spokane *(G-12588)*
Wheels Northwest Inc .... G 206 909-6735
  Snohomish *(G-11999)*

3313 Electrometallurgical Prdts

Teck American Metal Sales Inc .... G 509 747-6111
  Spokane *(G-12549)*
▲ Travis Pattern & Foundry Inc .... B 509 466-3545
  Spokane *(G-12566)*
Young Corporation .... E 206 623-3274
  Seattle *(G-11514)*

3315 Steel Wire Drawing & Nails & Spikes

American Lifting Products Inc .... G 253 572-8981
  Tacoma *(G-13168)*
Cablecraft Motion Controls LLC .... D 253 475-1080
  Tacoma *(G-13215)*
CMC Steel Fabricators Inc .... G 253 833-9060
  Auburn *(G-409)*
◆ Contech Systems Inc .... F 360 332-1718
  Tacoma *(G-13240)*
Davis Wire Corporation .... F 253 872-8910
  Kent *(G-4871)*
Great Gates NW Inc .... G 360 879-5554
  Eatonville *(G-3058)*
ISS (west) Inc .... G 206 470-3754
  Seattle *(G-10261)*
▲ Jaaco Corporation .... G 425 952-4205
  Redmond *(G-8517)*
McBee Metal Fabricators Inc .... G 425 486-1410
  Kenmore *(G-4591)*
Michellaine Lee Larry Bergsma .... G 360 873-4005
  Marblemount *(G-6305)*
Pacific Wire Group Inc .... F 253 249-0249
  Auburn *(G-525)*
Post Tension Cables Inc .... G 425 745-1304
  Everett *(G-3579)*
Quality Fence Builders Inc .... E 253 939-8533
  Auburn *(G-541)*
Safran Elec & Pwr USA LLC .... D 425 407-6700
  Everett *(G-3603)*
Seattle Tarp Co Inc .... E 206 285-2819
  Seattle *(G-11080)*
Suncoast Post-Tension Ltd .... F 360 651-2769
  Marysville *(G-6392)*
Tethers Unlimited Inc .... G 425 486-0100
  Bothell *(G-1800)*
Tree Island Industries Ltd .... E 360 366-0988
  Ferndale *(G-3916)*
Western Wire Works Inc .... E 253 964-6201
  Dupont *(G-2977)*

3316 Cold Rolled Steel Sheet, Strip & Bars

DCB Industries Inc .... G 360 750-0009
  Vancouver *(G-14169)*
Master Roll Manufacturing .... E 425 641-1566
  Bellevue *(G-997)*
▲ Puget Sound Steel Co Inc .... E 253 854-3600
  Kent *(G-5088)*

3317 Steel Pipe & Tubes

Ameron International Corp .... C 909 944-4100
  Vancouver *(G-14030)*
Ameron International Corp .... E 909 944-4100
  Vancouver *(G-14031)*
Bigfoot Pipe & Piling LLC .... G 425 882-1000
  Puyallup *(G-8130)*
Garmire Iron Works Inc .... G 360 651-1001
  Marysville *(G-6339)*
Hanging H Companies LLC .... G 360 899-4638
  Burlington *(G-2160)*
▲ Metal One America Inc .... G 206 223-2273
  Seattle *(G-10520)*
Mill Man Steel Inc .... F 909 854-7020
  Spokane Valley *(G-12790)*
◆ Northwest Pipe Company .... D 360 397-6250
  Vancouver *(G-14436)*
Puget Sound Pipe and Supply Co .... F 509 783-0474
  Kennewick *(G-4711)*
Scot Industries Inc .... D 360 623-1305
  Centralia *(G-2431)*

Weld-Rite Mfg LLC .... G 509 927-9353
  Spokane Valley *(G-12933)*
◆ Western Pneumatic Tube Co LLC ..... E 425 822-8271
  Kirkland *(G-5494)*

3321 Gray Iron Foundries

▲ D & L Foundry Inc .... C 509 765-7952
  Moses Lake *(G-6701)*
Dallesport Foundry Inc .... E 509 767-1183
  Dallesport *(G-2862)*
Ej Usa Inc .... G 360 651-6144
  Marysville *(G-6332)*
▼ H D Fowler Co Inc .... D 425 746-8400
  Bellevue *(G-934)*
Indepndent Distr Rexall Showca .... G 253 565-6595
  University Place *(G-13972)*
Jerry H Hyman .... G 360 479-1724
  Bremerton *(G-1965)*
Mackenzie Spcalty Castings Inc .... E 360 435-5539
  Arlington *(G-271)*
Mazdak International Inc .... G 360 988-6058
  Sumas *(G-13047)*
N E W Castings .... E 509 924-6464
  Spokane Valley *(G-12799)*
Pfc Inc .... G 360 398-8889
  Bellingham *(G-1497)*
Royal Prestige .... G 509 544-0330
  Pasco *(G-7624)*
◆ Specified Fittings LLC .... C 360 398-7700
  Bellingham *(G-1551)*
Travis Pattern & Foundry Inc .... B 509 924-6464
  Spokane Valley *(G-12911)*
▲ Travis Pattern & Foundry Inc .... B 509 466-3545
  Spokane *(G-12566)*
Varicast Inc .... D 360 816-7350
  Vancouver *(G-14666)*
Wear-Tek Inc .... D 509 747-4139
  Spokane *(G-12584)*
Wh International Casting LLC .... G 425 498-7531
  Everett *(G-3658)*
Wh International Casting LLC .... G 562 521-0727
  Moses Lake *(G-6758)*

3322 Malleable Iron Foundries

◆ Olympic Foundry Inc .... E 206 764-6200
  Seattle *(G-10691)*
▲ Spokane Industries Inc .... C 509 924-0440
  Spokane Valley *(G-12885)*

3324 Steel Investment Foundries

Cast 7020 LLC .... D 401 885-9555
  Tulalip *(G-13840)*
Ecs Machining Inc .... F 509 317-2557
  Yakima *(G-15563)*
Elite Aircraft Deburring .... G 360 435-2652
  Arlington *(G-234)*
Gray Mold Company Inc .... F 360 671-5711
  Bellingham *(G-1361)*
Hard Metal Solutions Inc .... F 360 548-8017
  Arlington *(G-249)*
Precision Castparts Corp .... B 425 957-6938
  Bellevue *(G-1080)*
▲ Seacast Inc .... C 360 653-9388
  Tulalip *(G-13843)*
Seacast Inc .... E 206 767-5759
  Seattle *(G-11041)*

3325 Steel Foundries, NEC

Anderson Foundry Forge .... G 360 270-2008
  Silverlake *(G-11862)*
Bradken Inc .... B 253 475-4600
  Tacoma *(G-13207)*
Bradken - Atlas LLC .... D 360 748-6645
  Chehalis *(G-2473)*
Decker Foundry .... G 206 225-9000
  Seattle *(G-9811)*
Jerry H Hyman .... G 360 479-1724
  Bremerton *(G-1965)*
Machstem Inc .... G 801 259-3305
  Nine Mile Falls *(G-7078)*
Mackenzie Spcalty Castings Inc .... E 360 435-5539
  Arlington *(G-271)*
▲ Mt Baker Mining and Mtls LLC .... F 360 595-4445
  Bellingham *(G-1447)*
Mt Baker Mining and Mtls LLC .... F 360 739-7264
  Bellingham *(G-1448)*
North Star Casteel Pdts Inc .... E 206 622-0068
  Seattle *(G-10627)*

SIC SECTION

33 PRIMARY METAL INDUSTRIES

Nucor Corporation .... C 206 933-2222
  Seattle *(G-10666)*
◆ Olympic Foundry Inc .... E 206 764-6200
  Seattle *(G-10691)*
Puget Sound Repair Inc .... G 506 556-9722
  Seattle *(G-10885)*
Roemer Electric Steel Foundry .... E 360 423-1330
  Longview *(G-5949)*
Romac Industries Inc .... D 425 951-6200
  Sultan *(G-13034)*
▲ Spokane Industries Inc .... C 509 924-0440
  Spokane Valley *(G-12885)*
Vancouver Foundry Company .... C 360 695-3914
  Vancouver *(G-14661)*
Vancouver Iron & Steel Inc .... D 360 695-3914
  Vancouver *(G-14662)*
Varicast Inc .... D 360 816-7350
  Vancouver *(G-14666)*
Wear-Tek Inc .... D 509 747-4139
  Spokane *(G-12584)*
Young Corporation .... G 206 623-3274
  Seattle *(G-11515)*
Young Corporation .... E 206 623-3274
  Seattle *(G-11514)*

3331 Primary Smelting & Refining Of Copper

Freeprt-Mcmran Explration Corp .... G 509 928-0704
  Spokane Valley *(G-12709)*
Peekaboo Cupcakery .... G 206 458-6986
  Seattle *(G-10778)*

3334 Primary Production Of Aluminum

▲ Alacan Solatens .... G 509 462-2310
  Spokane Valley *(G-12603)*
AMG Aluminum North America LLC ..... D 509 663-2165
  Malaga *(G-6231)*
Custom Bilt Holdings LLC .... G 509 533-1703
  Spokane *(G-12212)*
Gnr Aerospace Inc .... G 360 652-4040
  Arlington *(G-244)*
◆ Intalco Aluminum LLC .... A 360 384-7061
  Ferndale *(G-3859)*
Kaiser Aluminum Fab Pdts LLC .... D 509 375-0900
  Richland *(G-9016)*
Mavin Mfg Inc .... G 360 663-0354
  Enumclaw *(G-3304)*
Nupro Products Inc .... G 509 698-6963
  Selah *(G-11593)*

3339 Primary Nonferrous Metals, NEC

Fusion Silver .... G 253 740-8117
  Auburn *(G-446)*
▼ Hallmark Refining Corporation .... D 360 428-5880
  Mount Vernon *(G-6803)*
Modumetal Inc .... E 877 632-4242
  Seattle *(G-10555)*
Northwest Alloys Inc .... G 509 935-3300
  Addy *(G-46)*
Precious Metals Min & Ref Co .... G 509 927-2685
  Spokane Valley *(G-12836)*
◆ Rec Silicon Inc .... F 509 793-9000
  Moses Lake *(G-6743)*
▲ Rec Solar Grade Silicon LLC .... C 509 765-2106
  Moses Lake *(G-6744)*
Silicon Chemical Corporation .... E 360 210-5124
  Washougal *(G-14984)*
Sure Fit Inc .... G 253 426-1025
  Tacoma *(G-13532)*

3341 Secondary Smelting & Refining Of Nonferrous Metals

Alaska Metal Recycling Co .... E 907 349-4833
  Tacoma *(G-13160)*
American Recycling Corp .... E 509 535-4271
  Spokane Valley *(G-12614)*
▲ Ecotech Recycling LLC .... E 360 673-3860
  Kalama *(G-4498)*
Fibres International Inc .... D 425 455-9811
  Everett *(G-3471)*
Fran Hunter .... G 253 876-0434
  Port Orchard *(G-7810)*
▼ Hallmark Refining Corporation .... D 360 428-5880
  Mount Vernon *(G-6803)*
Parberry Inc .... E 360 734-2340
  Bellingham *(G-1491)*
Pw Metal Recovery LLC .... G 253 537-6301
  Tacoma *(G-13483)*
◆ Schnitzer Steel International .... G 253 572-4000
  Tacoma *(G-13508)*

Z Recyclers Inc .... F 360 398-2161
  Lynden *(G-6061)*

3351 Rolling, Drawing & Extruding Of Copper

Aria Trading Inc .... G 360 525-0175
  Blaine *(G-1660)*
Kenneth A Edleman .... G 206 524-2814
  Seattle *(G-10337)*

3353 Aluminum Sheet, Plate & Foil

Alcoa Inc .... C 253 272-8413
  Tacoma *(G-13161)*
Alcoa Wenatchee LLC .... B 509 663-9246
  Malaga *(G-6230)*
American Alloy LLC .... D 509 921-5794
  Spokane Valley *(G-12607)*
Ameron International Corp .... C 509 547-3689
  Pasco *(G-7552)*
◆ Chemi-Con Materials Corp .... D 509 762-8788
  Moses Lake *(G-6692)*
Elite Enterprise Co .... G 360 756-0205
  Bellingham *(G-1333)*
Novelis Corporation .... E 509 462-2310
  Spokane Valley *(G-12813)*
Wigfur Productions .... G 206 545-4306
  Seattle *(G-11473)*

3354 Aluminum Extruded Prdts

A & B Fabricators Inc .... G 253 887-0442
  Auburn *(G-355)*
Alaskan Copper Companies Inc .... G 206 623-5800
  Seattle *(G-9368)*
How-Mac Manufacturing Inc .... E 360 855-2649
  Sedro Woolley *(G-11540)*
Hydro Extrusion North Amer LLC .... G 503 802-3000
  Vancouver *(G-14307)*
▲ Industrial Revolution Inc .... E 425 285-1111
  Tukwila *(G-13752)*
Isla Carmen LLC .... G 360 836-5955
  Vancouver *(G-14325)*
Kaiser Aluminum Fab Pdts LLC .... A 509 927-6508
  Spokane Valley *(G-12760)*
Kaiser Aluminum Fab Pdts LLC .... F 509 375-0900
  Richland *(G-9017)*
Kaiser Alutek Inc .... G 509 924-2689
  Spokane Valley *(G-12762)*
Pyrotek Incorporated .... D 509 926-6211
  Spokane Valley *(G-12846)*
Universal Alloy Corporation .... C 253 350-4079
  Seattle *(G-11376)*

3355 Aluminum Rolling & Drawing, NEC

AMG Aluminum North America LLC ..... D 509 663-2165
  Malaga *(G-6231)*
Buddy Shelters LLC .... G 425 239-8104
  Arlington *(G-216)*
Mira Technology .... G 425 678-0183
  Lynnwood *(G-6164)*
Virtual Stream .... G 206 938-3886
  Seattle *(G-11422)*

3356 Rolling, Drawing-Extruding Of Nonferrous Metals

Allied Titanium Inc .... F 302 725-8300
  Sequim *(G-11608)*
Flashco Manufacturing Inc .... G 360 225-4662
  Woodland *(G-15432)*
▲ Interntonal Hearth Melting LLC .... D 509 371-2500
  Richland *(G-9011)*
Jeri -Ohs .... G 206 722-5918
  Seattle *(G-10292)*
Lilly Tin .... F 509 888-8101
  Chelan *(G-2559)*
Nichol Prfmce & Ctrl Automatio .... G 360 961-2833
  Everson *(G-3684)*
Rk Titanium LLC .... G 253 886-1377
  Kent *(G-5103)*
Robert Nickel .... G 239 565-0450
  Tacoma *(G-13500)*
▲ Sandvik Special Metals LLC .... C 509 734-4000
  Kennewick *(G-4726)*
Tin Cup LLC .... G 360 866-1580
  Olympia *(G-7408)*
Tin Table .... E 206 320-8458
  Seattle *(G-11312)*
Titanium Industries Inc .... G 425 481-7700
  Woodinville *(G-15390)*
Tungsten Cellars LLC .... G 509 525-3672
  Walla Walla *(G-14881)*

Vietnamese Baptist Church Tin .... G 360 953-8311
  Vancouver *(G-14669)*
West Coast Plastics Inc .... G 509 575-0727
  Yakima *(G-15706)*

3357 Nonferrous Wire Drawing

Carlisle Interconnect Tech Inc .... G 425 656-5235
  Kent *(G-4837)*
Carlisle Interconnect Tech Inc .... B 425 291-3991
  Kent *(G-4838)*
Clear Rf LLC .... F 855 321-9527
  Spokane Valley *(G-12658)*
Ecco Contractors Incorporated .... G 425 957-1735
  Bellevue *(G-891)*
Hydra Group LLC .... G 503 957-0975
  Washougal *(G-14959)*
▲ Kemcor Inc .... E 425 488-7400
  Woodinville *(G-15276)*
Manta Network Technologies LLC .... G 202 713-0508
  Mukilteo *(G-6952)*
Ruckus Wireless Inc .... G 425 896-6000
  Kirkland *(G-5453)*
Safran Elec & Pwr USA LLC .... D 425 407-6700
  Everett *(G-3603)*
United States Dept of Navy .... C 360 396-2340
  Keyport *(G-5247)*

3363 Aluminum Die Castings

◆ Consolidated Metco Inc .... D 360 828-2599
  Vancouver *(G-14147)*
Consolidated Metco Inc .... F 360 828-2689
  Vancouver *(G-14148)*
Gils Aluminum & Shell Core Sp .... G 206 762-1726
  Seattle *(G-10071)*
HNG Group LLC .... G 206 723-6848
  Tukwila *(G-13749)*

3364 Nonferrous Die Castings, Exc Aluminum

Jerry H Hyman .... G 360 479-1724
  Bremerton *(G-1965)*
Tru Cut Die Inc .... G 360 571-7158
  Vancouver *(G-14650)*
◆ Wagstaff Inc .... B 509 922-1404
  Spokane Valley *(G-12932)*
Walla Walla Foundry Inc .... G 509 525-5690
  Walla Walla *(G-14891)*
Wear-Tek Inc .... D 509 747-4139
  Spokane *(G-12584)*

3365 Aluminum Foundries

Aerofab Industries Inc .... E 360 403-8994
  Arlington *(G-194)*
Bergstrom Foundry Inc .... F 360 532-6981
  Aberdeen *(G-6)*
◆ Consolidated Metco Inc .... D 360 828-2599
  Vancouver *(G-14147)*
Consolidated Metco Inc .... F 360 828-2689
  Vancouver *(G-14148)*
Creative Casting Company .... G 253 475-2643
  Tacoma *(G-13248)*
▼ Frasers Bronze Foundry Inc .... G 877 264-1064
  Marysville *(G-6336)*
Gray Mold Company Inc .... G 360 671-5711
  Bellingham *(G-1361)*
HB Aerospace LLC .... G 425 432-3440
  Hobart *(G-4323)*
Irish Foundry & Mfg Inc .... G 206 623-7147
  Seattle *(G-10259)*
Jerry H Hyman .... G 360 479-1724
  Bremerton *(G-1965)*
▼ Morel Industries Inc .... E 360 691-9722
  Arlington *(G-283)*
◆ Olympic Foundry Inc .... E 206 764-6200
  Seattle *(G-10691)*
Omada International LLC .... C 425 242-5400
  Sumner *(G-13091)*
Pacific Aerospace & Elec Inc .... F 360 683-4167
  Sequim *(G-11658)*
Pentz Design Pattern Fndry Inc .... E 425 788-6490
  Duvall *(G-2997)*
◆ Progressive International Corp .... D 253 850-6111
  Kent *(G-5085)*
Puget Sound Repair Inc .... G 506 556-9722
  Seattle *(G-10885)*
▲ Pyrotek Incorporated .... D 509 926-6212
  Spokane *(G-12462)*
Pyrotek Incorporated .... E 509 921-8766
  Spokane Valley *(G-12847)*

Employee Codes: A=Over 500 employees, B=251-500
C=101-250, D=51-100, E=20-50, F=10-19, G=2-9

33 PRIMARY METAL INDUSTRIES

▲ Seacast Inc .... C 360 653-9388
  Tulalip *(G-13843)*
▲ Senior Operations LLC .... C 360 794-4448
  Monroe *(G-6617)*
Thomas Machine & Foundry Inc ..... D 360 651-9100
  Marysville *(G-6395)*
US Castings LLC .... D 509 784-1001
  Entiat *(G-3272)*

3366 Copper Foundries

Bergstrom Foundry Inc .... F 360 532-6981
  Aberdeen *(G-6)*
Creative Casting Company .... G 253 475-2643
  Tacoma *(G-13248)*
▼ Frasers Bronze Foundry Inc .... G 877 264-1064
  Marysville *(G-6336)*
Fremont Fine Arts Foundry Inc .... G 206 588-6981
  Seattle *(G-10024)*
Garden Expressions .... G 360 403-9532
  Arlington *(G-239)*
Irish Foundry & Mfg Inc .... G 206 623-7147
  Seattle *(G-10259)*
Jerry H Hyman .... G 360 479-1724
  Bremerton *(G-1965)*
▼ Mission Africa .... F 206 850-9155
  Auburn *(G-499)*
▼ Morel Industries Inc .... E 360 691-9722
  Arlington *(G-283)*
▲ North Harbor Propeller .... G 360 299-8266
  Anacortes *(G-152)*
▲ NW Propeller Operations Inc .... G 253 858-5061
  Lakewood *(G-5743)*
◆ Olympic Foundry Inc .... E 206 764-6200
  Seattle *(G-10691)*
▲ Olympic Propeller Company .... G 360 299-8266
  Anacortes *(G-157)*
Pacific Propeller Inter LLC .... G 206 575-5107
  Tukwila *(G-13787)*
Propeller Arprts Pine Feld LLC .... G 425 216-3010
  Everett *(G-3587)*
Rainbow Metals Inc .... G 360 794-3691
  Monroe *(G-6612)*
Red Propeller LLC .... G 206 452-5664
  Seattle *(G-10937)*
S & I Propellers Inc .... G 425 745-1700
  Mukilteo *(G-6974)*
▲ Sound Propeller Services Inc ...... E 206 788-4202
  Seattle *(G-11159)*
◆ Walla Walla Foundry Inc .... C 509 522-2114
  Walla Walla *(G-14890)*

3369 Nonferrous Foundries: Castings, NEC

Aerofab NDT LLC .... G 253 395-8706
  Kent *(G-4762)*
Bergstrom Foundry Inc .... F 360 532-6981
  Aberdeen *(G-6)*
Cashmere Manufacturing LLC .... E 509 888-2141
  East Wenatchee *(G-3009)*
Jerry H Hyman .... G 360 479-1724
  Bremerton *(G-1965)*
Mackenzie Spcalty Castings Inc ..... E 360 435-5539
  Arlington *(G-271)*
North Star Casteel Pdts Inc .... E 206 621-1039
  Seattle *(G-10628)*
Pentz Design Pattern Fndry Inc ...... E 425 788-6490
  Duvall *(G-2997)*
Port Townsend Foundry LLC .... F 360 385-6425
  Port Townsend *(G-7910)*
Precision Castparts Corp .... B 425 957-6938
  Bellevue *(G-1080)*
Precision Technology Corp .... E 360 403-0254
  Arlington *(G-306)*
Roemer Electric Steel Foundry .... E 360 423-1330
  Longview *(G-5949)*
Salish Technology .... G 360 632-4522
  Clinton *(G-2696)*
Seacast Inc .... E 206 767-5759
  Seattle *(G-11041)*
▲ Senior Operations LLC .... C 360 794-4448
  Monroe *(G-6617)*
▲ Spokane Industries Inc .... C 509 924-0440
  Spokane Valley *(G-12885)*
Thomas Machine & Foundry Inc ..... D 360 651-9100
  Marysville *(G-6395)*
Transition Composites Mfg Inc .... G 360 312-1497
  Bellingham *(G-1574)*
▲ Travis Pattern & Foundry Inc .... B 509 466-3545
  Spokane *(G-12566)*
Wear-Tek Inc .... D 509 747-4139
  Spokane *(G-12584)*

3398 Metal Heat Treating

Almet Incorporated .... F 253 852-1690
  Kent *(G-4773)*
Bodycote Imt Inc .... E 360 833-1120
  Camas *(G-2234)*
Cascade Metallurgical Inc .... E 253 838-0477
  Kent *(G-4842)*
Copperheat .... G 360 757-2589
  Burlington *(G-2146)*
Frontier Mtal Fabrications Inc .... F 360 514-0961
  Vancouver *(G-14242)*
Inland NW Metallurgical Svcs .... F 509 922-7663
  Spokane Valley *(G-12745)*
Pacific Metallurgical Inc .... G 206 292-9205
  Kent *(G-5055)*
Seattle Heat Treaters .... G 206 763-2744
  Seattle *(G-11062)*
Team Inc .... E 360 848-0353
  Mount Vernon *(G-6844)*
Team Industrial Services .... G 360 757-2589
  Burlington *(G-2194)*
Thermal Technologies .... G 425 359-8681
  Snohomish *(G-11990)*
Utec Metals Inc .... G 509 891-7833
  Spokane Valley *(G-12921)*

3399 Primary Metal Prdts, NEC

Chevy Metal .... G 360 694-7295
  Vancouver *(G-14115)*
Complex Aerospace LLC .... G 253 886-1323
  Auburn *(G-412)*
Custom Coat .... G 509 542-9431
  Pasco *(G-7575)*
D & D Dividers LLC .... G 360 951-4852
  Centralia *(G-2397)*
Earthbound Corporation .... F 360 863-0722
  Monroe *(G-6567)*
Iasco .... E 253 474-0497
  Tacoma *(G-13346)*
J L Powder Ctg .... G 360 380-3898
  Ferndale *(G-3863)*
Jerry Carter .... G 509 487-8294
  Spokane *(G-12332)*
Meyer Engineered Materials LLC ... G 253 854-6117
  Kent *(G-5009)*
N A I Inc .... G 509 453-4778
  Union Gap *(G-13945)*
Northwest Powder Soultions .... G 253 395-6282
  Kent *(G-5035)*
Smiley Industrial LLC .... G 509 302-8792
  Pasco *(G-7630)*
Sunset Forge LLC .... G 360 201-0160
  Ferndale *(G-3910)*
Twisted Metal LLC .... G 360 966-5309
  Everson *(G-3693)*
US Cryogenics Inc .... G 360 835-2475
  Washougal *(G-14997)*

34 FABRICATED METAL PRODUCTS, EXCEPT MACHINERY AND TRANSPORTATION EQUIPMENT

3411 Metal Cans

Ball .... G 253 854-9950
  Kent *(G-4806)*
Crown Cork & Seal Usa Inc .... C 360 491-4900
  Olympia *(G-7261)*
Crown Cork & Seal Usa Inc .... C 206 575-4260
  Tukwila *(G-13719)*
Crown Cork & Seal Usa Inc .... C 206 575-4260
  Tukwila *(G-13720)*
Crown Cork & Seal Usa Inc .... E 206 575-4260
  Tukwila *(G-13718)*
◆ Pacific Market Intl LLC .... C 206 441-1400
  Seattle *(G-10735)*
Silgan Containers Mfg Corp .... D 509 865-4125
  Toppenish *(G-13672)*
Tin Can Alley .... G 360 353-0773
  Castle Rock *(G-2355)*
Tin Can Diva .... G 253 315-5587
  Enumclaw *(G-3325)*
Tin Can Rocket LLC .... G 206 427-9260
  Maple Valley *(G-6294)*
Xafax Corporation .... G 360 389-5630
  Ferndale *(G-3926)*

3412 Metal Barrels, Drums, Kegs & Pails

Armour Mfg & Cnstr Inc .... G 253 984-1213
  Tacoma *(G-13180)*
Blefa Kegs Inc .... G 615 267-1385
  Vancouver *(G-14068)*
Industrial Container Svcs LLC .... E 206 763-2345
  Seattle *(G-10231)*
Jet City Partners LLC .... G 206 999-0047
  Auburn *(G-479)*
Ocean Cargo Container Inc .... G 253 381-9098
  Gig Harbor *(G-4138)*
Omnifab Inc .... E 253 931-5151
  Auburn *(G-518)*
Scot Industries Inc .... D 360 623-1305
  Centralia *(G-2431)*
▼ Seattle Barrel Co .... G 206 622-7218
  Seattle *(G-11045)*

3421 Cutlery

Art of Shaving - Fl LLC .... G 206 737-8370
  Seattle *(G-9437)*
Art of Shaving - Fl LLC .... G 253 777-0993
  Tacoma *(G-13181)*
▲ Bladegallery Inc .... G 425 889-5980
  Kirkland *(G-5292)*
Brunello .... G 425 888-6800
  Snoqualmie *(G-12006)*
Leigh James Cellars LLC .... G 509 529-1398
  Walla Walla *(G-14836)*
Pacific Hide & Fur Depot .... E 509 545-0688
  Pasco *(G-7611)*
Palace .... G 253 581-0880
  Lakewood *(G-5746)*
Pates Restaurant LLC .... F 253 334-7520
  Federal Way *(G-3769)*
Procter & Gamble Company .... C 425 313-3511
  Issaquah *(G-4461)*
▲ Shear Precision Inc .... G 800 481-4943
  Seattle *(G-11097)*
Skykomish Knife Works .... G 509 763-3117
  Leavenworth *(G-5816)*
◆ Sog Specialty Knives & Tls LLC .... D 425 771-6230
  Lynnwood *(G-6203)*

3423 Hand & Edge Tools

▲ Altos EZ Mat Inc .... G 509 962-9212
  Ellensburg *(G-3181)*
American Craftware LLC .... G 360 606-1827
  Vancouver *(G-14027)*
American Tomahawk Company LLC . G 253 884-1940
  Anderson Island *(G-186)*
Cannon Engineering Solutions ...... G 360 840-6731
  Port Townsend *(G-7871)*
Carbide Online Sales LLC .... G 253 476-1338
  University Place *(G-13962)*
▲ Cascade Chalet .... E 206 463-4628
  Vashon *(G-14716)*
Composite Tooling Innovations ..... G 509 637-3836
  Bingen *(G-1635)*
▼ Cutwell Products .... G 509 966-1499
  Yakima *(G-15548)*
Dem-Bart Checkering Tools Inc ..... G 360 568-7356
  Snohomish *(G-11897)*
Dna Growers LLC .... G 509 793-6606
  Moses Lake *(G-6706)*
Emerald Tool Inc .... G 206 767-5670
  Seattle *(G-9914)*
Garden Expressions .... G 360 403-9532
  Arlington *(G-239)*
Gilt LLC .... G 425 468-4458
  Bellevue *(G-925)*
Hihosilver .... G 509 758-8419
  Clarkston *(G-2635)*
Industrial Automation Inc .... E 206 763-1025
  Seattle *(G-10229)*
International Carbide Corp .... F 800 422-8665
  Roy *(G-9161)*
Jmd Property Preservation .... G 267 713-2277
  Lakewood *(G-5730)*
JMJ Custom Finishes .... G 425 820-4376
  Kirkland *(G-5374)*
K & S Garden .... G 509 476-3287
  Oroville *(G-7468)*
Kestrel Tool .... G 360 468-2103
  Lopez Island *(G-5984)*
Lam-Hammer Inc .... G 509 687-2421
  Chelan *(G-2558)*
Machstem Inc .... G 801 259-3305
  Nine Mile Falls *(G-7078)*

Meadow Creature LLC ......G...... 360 329-2250
Vashon (G-14734)
Pell Industrial LLC ......G...... 425 222-9672
Auburn (G-530)
Picote Solutions Inc......F...... 425 505-0646
Sammamish (G-9241)
Precision Steel Rule Die Co ......G...... 206 397-3982
Seattle (G-10853)
Proctor Products Co Inc......F...... 425 398-8800
Woodinville (G-15341)
Profiler Inc......G...... 360 668-3291
Snohomish (G-11962)
R and D Home and Garden Inc ......G...... 509 826-1730
OMAK (G-7442)
Rulersmith Inc......E...... 360 707-2828
Shoreline (G-11806)
Summitview Tooling Inc......G...... 509 966-9859
Yakima (G-15686)
Uluwatu......G...... 206 852-7289
Seattle (G-11363)
US Dies Inc......G...... 509 248-0404
Yakima (G-15701)
Woodcraft Supply LLC ......F...... 206 767-6394
Seattle (G-11492)

3425 Hand Saws & Saw Blades

Carbide Online Sales LLC......G...... 253 476-1338
University Place (G-13962)
▲ Conclut Inc ......E...... 253 872-3507
Kent (G-4862)
▲ Cut Technologies Usa Inc ......E...... 360 733-0460
Bellingham (G-1313)
Eastside Saw & Sales Inc......E...... 425 454-7627
Bellevue (G-887)
▲ Saw Service Washington Inc ......G...... 360 738-6437
Bellingham (G-1525)
Two Blue Mules......G...... 206 935-3762
Seattle (G-11352)
◆ Www Qualitylacecom......G...... 425 996-0523
Sammamish (G-9260)

3429 Hardware, NEC

▲ A & G Machine Inc......D...... 253 887-8433
Auburn (G-357)
A & G Machine Inc ......G...... 253 887-8433
Auburn (G-358)
Aeroforge Inc......E...... 253 286-2525
Puyallup (G-8117)
Aqua Rec Inc ......G...... 253 826-2561
Bonney Lake (G-1716)
Aqua Rec Inc ......G...... 253 770-9447
Puyallup (G-8123)
Art Brass Aerospace Finshg Inc ......G...... 206 209-3010
Seattle (G-9435)
Automatic Door Solutions LLC......G...... 253 802-0888
Orting (G-7473)
▼ Avia Marine Company......G...... 253 373-1644
Kent (G-4803)
▲ Bainbridge Manufacturing Inc ......E...... 800 255-4702
Waterville (G-15004)
Battery X-Change & Repair Inc......G...... 206 682-2981
Tukwila (G-13695)
▲ Blaser Die Casting Co ......D...... 206 767-7800
Seattle (G-9540)
Bridgestone Hosepower LLC......E...... 206 767-4670
Seattle (G-9585)
Broomflds Wldg Met Fabrication......G...... 206 784-9267
Seattle (G-9589)
Clark Security Products Inc......G...... 206 467-3000
Seattle (G-9689)
Cobra Key Systems LLC ......G...... 509 466-1918
Colbert (G-2706)
Complete Controls......G...... 360 904-7525
Vancouver (G-14142)
Conestoga Wood Spc Corp ......G...... 253 437-1320
Kent (G-4863)
Cyns Insanitys......G...... 360 694-2459
Vancouver (G-14158)
Datrex Inc......G...... 206 762-9070
Seattle (G-9797)
Department Crrctons Wash State......B...... 509 526-6375
Walla Walla (G-14795)
▲ Diamond Tech Innovations Inc ......E...... 360 866-1337
Olympia (G-7270)
Dodge Systems LLC ......G...... 253 405-3967
Lakewood (G-5712)
Dooley Enterprises LLC ......G...... 303 619-7101
Bothell (G-1847)
Dormakaba USA Inc......F...... 253 864-4484
Puyallup (G-8145)
Doug & June Holt......G...... 425 228-6067
Newcastle (G-7028)
Dungeness Gear Works Inc ......E...... 800 548-9743
Arlington (G-230)
Electroimpact Inc......D...... 425 348-8090
Mukilteo (G-6920)
Empire Rubber & Supply Co......F...... 509 547-0026
Pasco (G-7579)
Engineered Products Entps......F...... 253 826-6185
Edgewood (G-3076)
▼ Esterline Technologies Corp ......E...... 425 453-9400
Bellevue (G-902)
Fabrication Technologies LLC......G...... 360 293-3707
Anacortes (G-127)
▲ Harbor Island Supply Corp ......F...... 206 762-1900
Seattle (G-10141)
▲ Heininger Holdings LLC ......G...... 360 756-2411
Bellingham (G-1368)
▲ Industrial Revolution Inc......E...... 425 285-1111
Tukwila (G-13752)
Kaisers Welding & Mfg......G...... 509 738-6855
Kettle Falls (G-5233)
▲ Karcher Design ......D...... 253 220-8244
Tukwila (G-13761)
Lacoto Industries Inc......G...... 360 658-9668
Marysville (G-6350)
◆ Marine Hardware Inc ......E...... 425 883-0651
Redmond (G-8549)
Markey Machinery Co Inc......F...... 206 763-0383
Seattle (G-10490)
Matchlock Clamp Co......G...... 360 262-9942
Chehalis (G-2512)
Mitchell Hardware W Linn Inc......G...... 253 752-2000
Tacoma (G-13416)
Monroe Machined Products Inc......E...... 206 242-4898
Seatac (G-9291)
▲ National Products Inc......C...... 206 763-8361
Seattle (G-10589)
▲ New Found Metals Incorporated ......G...... 360 385-3315
Port Townsend (G-7899)
North Industries Inc......G...... 206 940-0842
Seattle (G-10624)
Northstone Industries LLC......G...... 509 844-7775
Spokane (G-12410)
Northwest Cabinet Hardware......G...... 360 281-5869
Yacolt (G-15489)
Oceanwest Rvm LLC ......G...... 503 569-6969
Lynden (G-6041)
▲ Olympus Lock Inc......E...... 206 362-3290
Lynnwood (G-6173)
▲ Pacific Coast Marine Inds Inc ......D...... 425 743-9550
Lynnwood (G-6177)
Paxton Sales Corporation......F...... 509 453-0397
Yakima (G-15642)
Pcs Mill Work Inc ......E...... 425 820-5688
Kirkland (G-5431)
Power Equipment Supply Llc ......G...... 206 817-5627
Everett (G-3580)
Precision Builders ......G...... 509 882-2232
Grandview (G-4254)
Proctor International LLC......G...... 425 881-7000
Redmond (G-8633)
Pure Safety Group Inc ......G...... 253 854-5877
Kent (G-5090)
R G Rollin Co......G...... 253 274-0882
Tacoma (G-13487)
R&J Industries LLC......G...... 253 466-3627
Puyallup (G-8233)
Rads Auto ......G...... 509 965-5712
Yakima (G-15659)
ROC Racing Inc......G...... 360 658-4353
Marysville (G-6378)
S C Jr LLC......G...... 253 539-1097
Tacoma (G-13505)
Sea Cure Technology Inc ......G...... 360 676-1824
Acme (G-44)
◆ Sea-Dog Corporation ......D...... 425 259-0194
Everett (G-3607)
Sealth Aero Marine Co......E...... 425 481-0727
Mill Creek (G-6525)
Sje Inc ......E...... 360 734-1910
Bellingham (G-1540)
◆ Smith-Berger Marine Inc......E...... 206 764-4650
Seattle (G-11139)
Stone Masters Inc ......G...... 509 667-8833
Wenatchee (G-15077)
Tethers Unlimited Inc......G...... 425 486-0100
Bothell (G-1800)
▲ Titus Tool Company Inc......F...... 206 447-1489
Bellevue (G-1192)
Toussint Machine and Mfg LLC ......G...... 360 840-0705
Sedro Woolley (G-11576)
Tri-City Glass Inc......G...... 509 586-0454
Kennewick (G-4738)
Tri-Way Industries Inc......D...... 253 859-4585
Auburn (G-582)
Triad Products Corporation ......G...... 425 514-8363
Everett (G-3636)
Ultimate Rack Inc......G...... 509 393-3526
East Wenatchee (G-3033)
◆ Washington Chain & Supply Inc ......E...... 206 623-8500
Seattle (G-11438)
White River Fabrication LLC......G...... 253 261-8718
Enumclaw (G-3328)
Zephyrwerks......G...... 360 385-2720
Port Townsend (G-7939)

3431 Enameled Iron & Metal Sanitary Ware

Agdecor......G...... 425 255-2271
Newcastle (G-7023)
Elkay Ssp LLC......G...... 509 533-0808
Spokane (G-12240)
▲ Elkay Ssp LLC......E...... 509 533-0808
Spokane (G-12241)
Familian Northwest Seattle 07......G...... 206 767-7700
Seattle (G-9966)

3432 Plumbing Fixture Fittings & Trim, Brass

Accor Technology Inc......E...... 509 662-0608
East Wenatchee (G-3006)
Desert Rain......G...... 509 545-1900
Burbank (G-2083)
Ferguson......G...... 206 767-7700
Auburn (G-440)
Forever Green Sprinklers......G...... 509 796-2676
Nine Mile Falls (G-7075)
Gordon Exports LLC......G...... 503 313-6544
Redmond (G-8482)
Jl Distribution Ltd ......G...... 206 743-1148
Arlington (G-262)
K & M Unibody Works Inc ......F...... 509 922-2083
Spokane Valley (G-12758)
Keller Supply Co ......G...... 509 922-6388
Spokane Valley (G-12763)
Keller Supply Co ......G...... 253 863-9271
Sumner (G-13077)
Keller Supply Co......F...... 509 925-2400
Ellensburg (G-3210)
Masons Supply Company......G...... 206 883-5550
Seattle (G-10496)
Old & Elegant Distributing ......F...... 425 455-4660
Bellevue (G-1045)
Pac West Sales Inc ......F...... 425 493-9680
Mukilteo (G-6963)
▲ Part Works Inc......E...... 206 632-8900
Seattle (G-10760)
Pipemasters Inc ......G...... 253 377-0717
Gig Harbor (G-4146)
Quality Sales Inc......F...... 360 694-3165
Vancouver (G-14521)
Robs Sprnklr Svc Installation ......G...... 253 581-6491
Lakewood (G-5752)
Tubs To Go Inc......G...... 425 348-7888
Lynnwood (G-6213)

3433 Heating Eqpt

Cleanpwr......G...... 425 334-6100
Lake Stevens (G-5639)
Custom Masonry & Stove Inc ......G...... 206 524-4714
Lake Forest Park (G-5610)
Eclipse Inc......G...... 754 581-1513
Seattle (G-9874)
Fives N Amercn Combustn Inc......E...... 360 659-7432
Marysville (G-6334)
Greenwood Clean Energy Inc......G...... 888 788-3090
Redmond (G-8485)
Hearth & Home Technologies LLC......B...... 509 684-3745
Colville (G-2755)
Home Fire Prest Logs Ltd ......F...... 360 366-2200
Ferndale (G-3852)
Innovative Hearth Products LLC ......D...... 253 735-1100
Auburn (G-477)
J S OWill Inc......G...... 360 226-3637
Enumclaw (G-3296)
Lighthouse International Ltd ......E...... 509 466-2502
Spokane (G-12365)
◆ Marine Hardware Inc ......E...... 425 883-0651
Redmond (G-8549)
North Industries Inc......G...... 206 940-0842
Seattle (G-10624)

S I C

Offset Solar LLC E 866 376-9559
Liberty Lake *(G-5849)*

Pacific Hide & Fur Depot E 509 545-0688
Pasco *(G-7611)*

Paragon Energy Solutions G 425 445-6471
Kirkland *(G-5429)*

▲ **Travis Industries Inc** B 425 609-2500
Mukilteo *(G-6983)*

Two Mac Inc G 206 285-3675
Seattle *(G-11354)*

Wizard Works G 509 486-2654
Tonasket *(G-13662)*

3441 Fabricated Structural Steel

A B Fabricators G 206 763-2600
Auburn *(G-359)*

Aalbu Brothers of Everett Inc G 425 252-9751
Everett *(G-3356)*

ABG G 253 896-1372
Fife *(G-3927)*

Above & Beyond Unlimited G 253 921-3535
Tacoma *(G-13154)*

Abw Technologies Inc C 360 618-4400
Arlington *(G-191)*

Acufab Inc G 509 525-3833
Walla Walla *(G-14759)*

Addison Construction Sup Inc D 253 474-0711
Tacoma *(G-13157)*

Alki Foundry G 206 794-4074
Seattle *(G-9377)*

All Fabrication and Supply LLC G 509 334-1905
Pullman *(G-8083)*

Allform Welding Inc G 360 681-0584
Sequim *(G-11607)*

Allied Steel Fabricators Inc E 425 861-9558
Redmond *(G-8380)*

Alpha Iron LLC E 360 823-1777
Ridgefield *(G-9061)*

American Structures Design Inc G 253 833-4343
Pacific *(G-7522)*

Apex Curb & Turf LLC F 509 758-1543
Clarkston *(G-2620)*

Apex Railing Solutions G 206 452-3281
Seattle *(G-9409)*

Argo Blower & Mfg Co F 206 762-9336
Seattle *(G-9428)*

Artaca Co G 425 398-0122
Kenmore *(G-4565)*

ASC Profiles LLC E 509 535-0600
Spokane *(G-12120)*

ASC Profiles LLC E 253 383-4955
Tacoma *(G-13184)*

Associated Metals Fabrication G 360 793-2422
Sultan *(G-13021)*

Atech Services LLC C 206 453-3182
Seattle *(G-9450)*

Atkore International Group Inc G 253 478-3199
Kent *(G-4796)*

Atwood Fabricating G 425 481-5388
Bothell *(G-1826)*

Automatic Products Mfg Co LLC G 253 395-7173
Kent *(G-4801)*

Avantech Inc D 509 943-6706
Richland *(G-8969)*

Avos Inc G 503 713-8404
Vancouver *(G-14049)*

B & B Parrotts Welding Inc G 360 825-0565
Enumclaw *(G-3277)*

B&B Custom Metals LLC G 425 308-8478
Richland *(G-8970)*

Barreras Precision Fabg LLC G 253 850-6227
Kent *(G-4809)*

Barrett Sheet Metal G 509 886-8708
East Wenatchee *(G-3008)*

Barrys Steve Pool Service LLC G 360 533-0421
Aberdeen *(G-3)*

Bedkers Prtble Wldg Fbrication G 253 581-7077
Lakewood *(G-5702)*

Bennett Industries Inc E 253 627-7775
Tacoma *(G-13194)*

Big C Industries LLC G 844 406-2442
Longview *(G-5888)*

Bmt Metal Fabrication Inc G 509 244-6107
Airway Heights *(G-49)*

Bowman-Morton Mfg & Mch Inc F 206 524-8890
Seattle *(G-9573)*

Bradken Inc E 253 475-3464
Tacoma *(G-13208)*

Broomflds Wldg Met Fabrication G 206 784-9267
Seattle *(G-9589)*

Brown-Mnnplis Tnk-Nrthwest LLC E 360 482-1720
Elma *(G-3243)*

BTS Partners LLC G 253 862-4622
Bonney Lake *(G-1718)*

Burlingame Steel Inc F 509 535-3735
Spokane *(G-12161)*

Buyken Metal Products Inc E 253 852-0634
Kent *(G-4827)*

C & S Welding Inc G 253 520-2095
Kent *(G-4828)*

C J & M Transport Inc F 206 510-8296
Kent *(G-4829)*

C T Specialties G 360 786-0274
Tumwater *(G-13854)*

Cameron Steel Fabrication F 360 403-9400
Arlington *(G-217)*

Can AM Fabrication Inc G 360 653-2245
Marysville *(G-6321)*

Canam Steel Corporation G 360 329-7048
Sunnyside *(G-13115)*

Canam Steel Corporation C 509 837-7008
Vancouver *(G-14094)*

Centerline Fabrication G 509 948-8711
Benton City *(G-1604)*

Centerline Fabricators LLC G 253 922-3226
Fife *(G-3941)*

Central Fabricators Inc G 509 468-3995
Spokane *(G-12175)*

CH Murphy/Clark-Ullman Inc D 253 475-6566
Tacoma *(G-13232)*

Cleveland Enterprises Inc G 360 694-0435
Vancouver *(G-14123)*

Columbia Metal Fab Cnstr Inc G 360 989-0201
Kalama *(G-4496)*

Columbia Metal Works Inc G 360 693-5818
Vancouver *(G-14134)*

Cooper Smithing Co G 253 906-0425
Buckley *(G-2054)*

Cr Enterprises Nw LLC G 425 290-3800
Mukilteo *(G-6908)*

Craftsmen United Inc F 360 379-2500
Port Townsend *(G-7874)*

Crf Metal Works LLC F 509 430-7609
Pasco *(G-7571)*

Crown Carriage Works Inc G 509 535-4427
Spokane *(G-12210)*

Curfman Custom Fabrication LLC G 360 736-7277
Centralia *(G-2396)*

Davids Aquacut & Builders G 509 527-8700
Walla Walla *(G-14793)*

Davis & Walker Fabrication G 360 944-0057
Vancouver *(G-14167)*

Design Construction Heritg Inc G 206 634-1989
Everett *(G-3442)*

Direct Process Metal Fabg G 206 276-6014
Seattle *(G-9834)*

Diversifab LLC G 253 459-5170
Yelm *(G-15732)*

Division Five Inc F 206 988-5004
Tukwila *(G-13726)*

Doug D Froland G 206 932-8433
Seattle *(G-9849)*

Duthie Enterprises Inc E 206 767-3314
Seattle *(G-9862)*

Eastside Welding & Fabrication G 509 765-6434
Moses Lake *(G-6707)*

Easy Street Custom Metal G 509 662-1018
Wenatchee *(G-15028)*

◆ **Edco Inc** E 360 424-6600
Mount Vernon *(G-6792)*

Eridu Designs G 360 247-5980
Amboy *(G-93)*

Eugene P Lamm Jr G 509 460-1240
Richland *(G-8995)*

Excel Manufacturing Inc G 253 939-6446
Auburn *(G-438)*

Expermntal Arcft Met Fbrcation G 360 245-3478
Chehalis *(G-2495)*

Fab-Tech Inc G 360 755-0215
Burlington *(G-2156)*

Fabricated Products Inc C 360 695-5949
Vancouver *(G-14217)*

Fabrication Products Inc E 503 283-3218
Vancouver *(G-14219)*

Fabtech Manufacturing LLC G 509 488-1950
Othello *(G-7495)*

Faqa G 206 362-5916
Seattle *(G-9970)*

Far West Fabricators Inc G 509 453-1663
Moxee *(G-6877)*

Farm Built Fab LLC G 360 213-8458
La Center *(G-5504)*

Farwest Iron Works Inc G 509 662-3546
Wenatchee *(G-15031)*

Farwest Steel Fabrication Co D 800 793-1493
Vancouver *(G-14223)*

Fat Daddys Fabrication LLC G 253 677-8005
Roy *(G-9159)*

Ferrotek Corporation F 360 366-7444
Ferndale *(G-3845)*

Fixture Engineering Inc G 360 671-9052
Bellingham *(G-1347)*

Folsom Industries Inc F 509 921-6602
Greenacres *(G-4298)*

Frazier Industrial Company G 509 698-4100
Selah *(G-11588)*

Frisbee Enterprises LLC G 360 991-1662
Vancouver *(G-14240)*

Frys Welding Inc G
Auburn *(G-445)*

Gepford Welding Inc G 509 624-6610
Spokane *(G-12272)*

Gerald McCallum G 509 467-8456
Spokane *(G-12273)*

Glenns Welding and Mfg Inc E 425 743-2226
Lynnwood *(G-6131)*

Global Incorporated F 206 763-4424
Seattle *(G-10084)*

Global Mtal Works Erectors LLC E 253 572-5363
Tacoma *(G-13312)*

Global Technical Staffin G 512 694-7621
Vancouver *(G-14259)*

▲ **Gompf Brackets Inc** F 425 348-5002
Mukilteo *(G-6929)*

Goodman Custom Fab G 253 720-2451
Tacoma *(G-13317)*

Green Mountain Metalworks LLC G 360 281-6048
Woodland *(G-15435)*

Greenberry Industrial LLC G 360 366-3767
Ferndale *(G-3849)*

Gw 42 Inc G 360 862-8319
Snohomish *(G-11918)*

Harrington Tower Services G 206 760-9191
Seattle *(G-10143)*

Harris Rebar Seattle Inc E 253 847-5001
Tacoma *(G-13332)*

Highlands Welding Repair Inc G 206 283-0080
Seattle *(G-10172)*

Hiline Engrg & Fabrication Inc E 509 943-9043
Richland *(G-9006)*

Hoffman Manufacturing G 509 286-3200
Latah *(G-5791)*

Hydrafab Northwest Inc E 509 535-0075
Spokane Valley *(G-12733)*

Illume G 206 566-5375
Seattle *(G-10205)*

Imsa Steel Corp B 360 673-8200
Kalama *(G-4501)*

Industrial Fabrication Co E 360 793-9001
Sultan *(G-13027)*

Industrial Fbrication Tstg Inc G 360 345-1400
Chehalis *(G-2505)*

Industrial Welding Service G 425 334-2686
Everett *(G-3515)*

Inline Steel Fabricators Inc E 509 248-4554
Yakima *(G-15591)*

Instafab Company Inc E 360 737-8235
Vancouver *(G-14317)*

Integrated Systems Design G 360 746-0812
Bellingham *(G-1380)*

Intermountain Fabricators Inc F 509 534-1676
Spokane Valley *(G-12746)*

Island Riggers Inc G 206 920-3360
Bainbridge Island *(G-642)*

J D Ott Co Inc C 206 749-0777
Seattle *(G-10269)*

J L Brooks Welding Inc F 360 403-9400
Arlington *(G-259)*

Jabez Marpac Construction Jv1 E 253 735-2000
Orting *(G-7483)*

JAS Steel Fabricating G 425 424-2107
Woodinville *(G-15273)*

◆ **Jesse Engineering Company** E 253 552-1500
Tacoma *(G-13358)*

Jet City Partners LLC G 206 999-0047
Auburn *(G-479)*

Jetco Mch & Fabrication LLC F 509 243-8910
Clarkston *(G-2636)*

◆ **Jlt Partners Inc** G 800 325-7513
Kent *(G-4968)*

Johnson Fabrication....G.... 360 874-2679
Port Orchard (G-7821)
Kalispel Tribe of Indians....E.... 509 242-7000
Airway Heights (G-54)
Kermit Anderson....G.... 509 535-2362
Spokane Valley (G-12765)
◆ KY International LLC....G.... 253 373-9602
Covington (G-2831)
Larry Waits Nemesis....G.... 253 863-4444
Lake Tapps (G-5681)
Lee Fabricators Inc....F.... 360 698-1190
Silverdale (G-11843)
Lev Design....G.... 425 417-2758
Seattle (G-10409)
Lynn L Reynolds Inc....G.... 509 536-9396
Spokane Valley (G-12779)
M H R A Corp....G.... 360 978-6878
Onalaska (G-7451)
Machinists Inc....E.... 206 763-0840
Seattle (G-10461)
Madlyn Metal Fab Llc....E.... 360 693-1019
Vancouver (G-14392)
▲ Marketech International Inc....F.... 360 379-6707
Sequim (G-11647)
McVays Mobile Welding LLC....G.... 360 657-0360
Marysville (G-6358)
Metal Solutions LLC....D.... 206 767-5587
Seattle (G-10521)
▲ Metal Works Inc....G.... 509 782-8811
Dryden (G-2953)
Metal Works Northwest....G.... 206 624-4766
Seattle (G-10522)
Metalfab Inc....E.... 509 967-2946
West Richland (G-15098)
Metals Fabrication Company Inc....D.... 509 244-2909
Airway Heights (G-56)
Miller Fabrication Inc....G.... 253 833-5400
Auburn (G-498)
Mohawk Metal Company....G.... 360 816-0679
Vancouver (G-14423)
Monarch Machine and Tl Co Inc....E.... 509 547-7753
Pasco (G-7603)
Morgan Steel & Metal Works....G.... 360 301-6611
Poulsbo (G-7986)
Mt Norway Fabrication LLC....G.... 360 836-0322
Washougal (G-14970)
Naimor Inc....E.... 360 756-9700
Bellingham (G-1457)
Nelson Construction Inc....F.... 253 931-6696
Auburn (G-505)
Newell Corp....F.... 360 435-8955
Arlington (G-287)
Nor-Tech Fabricating LLC....E.... 360 232-0144
Kelso (G-4539)
Northwest Stair and Rail Inc....G.... 425 348-7880
Everett (G-3558)
Nucor Corporation....C.... 206 933-2222
Seattle (G-10666)
Olympic Iron Works....F.... 360 491-2500
Olympia (G-7358)
Omega Industries Inc....E.... 360 574-9086
Vancouver (G-14450)
Omnifab Inc....E.... 253 931-5151
Auburn (G-518)
One Build Inc....G.... 206 801-1675
Seattle (G-10701)
ONeill Steel Fabrication Inc....F.... 509 467-5309
Spokane (G-12421)
Orbit Industries LLC....E.... 360 835-8526
Washougal (G-14976)
Oszman Service Inc....G.... 360 532-4552
Hoquiam (G-4351)
Pacific A Crgo Transf Systems....E.... 253 735-5277
Auburn (G-522)
Pacific Fabricating....G.... 360 588-1078
Anacortes (G-159)
Pacific Northwest Iron LLC....G.... 509 499-0668
Nine Mile Falls (G-7081)
Pacific Northwest Mech LLC....F.... 509 765-9606
Moses Lake (G-6735)
Parker Manufacturing LLC....G.... 509 663-5923
Wenatchee (G-15060)
Parkers Truck & Equipment Repr....G.... 253 833-3696
Pacific (G-7538)
Patriot Jabez Construction JV....G.... 253 293-7100
Auburn (G-527)
Pauley Rodine Inc....G.... 509 773-3200
Goldendale (G-4205)
Pederson Bros Inc....E.... 360 734-9180
Bellingham (G-1493)

Pfc Inc....G.... 360 398-8889
Bellingham (G-1497)
Pinnacle Steel Fabricators....F.... 253 770-1690
Puyallup (G-8223)
Precision Iron Works Inc....E.... 253 887-5555
Pacific (G-7539)
Precision Metal Works LLC....G.... 509 945-8433
Union Gap (G-13951)
Precision Rebar & ACC Inc....F.... 360 574-1022
Vancouver (G-14501)
Pro Fab Inc....G.... 206 762-5149
Seattle (G-10868)
Pro Fab Industries Inc....G.... 360 629-4642
Stanwood (G-12986)
▲ Prometco Inc....F.... 425 486-0759
Bothell (G-1891)
Puget Sound Metal Fabrication....G.... 253 941-7868
Auburn (G-540)
▲ Puget Sound Steel Co Inc....E.... 253 854-3600
Kent (G-5088)
Rainier Building Supply LLC....G.... 206 939-2591
Everett (G-3595)
Ramgen Power Systems LLC....G.... 425 828-4919
Bellevue (G-1094)
Ray Fanns Whispering Pines....G.... 360 384-4750
Custer (G-2859)
Red Dog Fabrication LLC....F.... 360 892-3647
Vancouver (G-14537)
Redmond Wlders Fabricators Inc....E.... 425 222-6330
Issaquah (G-4465)
Reinkes Fabrication Inc....F.... 360 398-2011
Bellingham (G-1515)
Rj Jarvis Enterprises Inc....E.... 509 482-0254
Spokane (G-12477)
S & S Welding Inc....E.... 206 793-9943
Kent (G-5110)
Scotts Sheet Metal....G.... 360 384-3827
Ferndale (G-3902)
Sea Cure Technology Inc....G.... 360 676-1824
Acme (G-44)
▲ Sea Pac Transport Services LLC....E.... 206 763-0339
Seattle (G-11037)
Sea Technology Construction....F.... 206 282-9158
Seattle (G-11039)
Seaview Boat Yard Inc....F.... 206 783-6550
Seattle (G-11086)
Ser Pro Inc....G.... 206 767-3100
Seattle (G-11090)
Skagit Industrial Steel Inc....E.... 360 854-0074
Sedro Woolley (G-11567)
Smileys Inc....F.... 360 424-7338
Mount Vernon (G-6843)
Speedfab....G.... 360 571-4093
Vancouver (G-14602)
Ss Industrial Inc....G.... 509 427-7836
Stevenson (G-13020)
Standard Steel Fabg Co Inc....G.... 206 767-0499
Seattle (G-11180)
Starman Metal Fabrications LLC....G.... 425 235-1431
Renton (G-8919)
Steel Encounters Inc....F.... 206 281-8500
Seattle (G-11186)
Steel Fab Inc....E.... 425 743-9216
Arlington (G-333)
Steel Fab Nw Inc....G.... 360 210-7055
Washougal (G-14987)
▲ Steelhead Communications Inc....E.... 360 829-1330
Buckley (G-2073)
◆ Sunmodo Corporation....G.... 360 844-0048
Vancouver (G-14615)
▲ T Bailey Inc....C.... 360 293-0682
Anacortes (G-173)
T2 Services Inc....F.... 509 893-3666
Spokane Valley (G-12899)
TAC Fab LLC....G.... 206 755-0519
Woodinville (G-15385)
▲ Talco Services LLC....F.... 425 259-0213
Everett (G-3626)
Technifab Inc....G.... 509 534-1022
Spokane Valley (G-12903)
Telegraph Fabrication....G.... 360 739-8170
Ferndale (G-3912)
Teras Construction LLC....G.... 253 539-2887
Tacoma (G-13554)
Three Squared LLC....G.... 206 708-5918
Bellevue (G-1187)
Tl Northwest Corp....F.... 253 445-4104
Puyallup (G-8264)
Totem Steel Inc....F.... 425 483-6276
Woodinville (G-15392)

▼ Transpac Marinas Inc....G.... 360 293-8888
Anacortes (G-178)
Triple C Fabricators LLC....G.... 360 868-4125
Shelton (G-11746)
Triton Holdings Inc....F.... 360 466-4160
Mount Vernon (G-6848)
▼ Trufab LLC....F.... 360 229-3028
Shelton (G-11747)
Twisted Metal LLC....G.... 360 966-5309
Everson (G-3693)
United Iron Works Inc....E.... 206 767-3630
Tacoma (G-13570)
Universal Stl Fabricators LLC....F.... 253 891-4224
Tacoma (G-13572)
Valleyford Metal Crafters LLC....E.... 509 448-5583
Spokane (G-12579)
Valmont Industries Inc....G.... 509 921-0290
Spokane Valley (G-12925)
Vigor Works LLC....E.... 360 699-1547
Vancouver (G-14670)
Vigor Works LLC....D.... 360 694-7636
Vancouver (G-14671)
Vulcan Products Company Inc....E.... 425 806-6000
Woodinville (G-15401)
Wb Mobile Modular Service....G.... 253 952-4630
Edgewood (G-3091)
Weld-Tech Fabrication Inc....G.... 425 591-5912
Rochester (G-9144)
Wenatchee Qlty Wldg Fbrication....F.... 509 782-0807
Cashmere (G-2333)
▲ West Coast Custom Metal Design....G.... 360 738-2884
Bellingham (G-1592)
Western Metal Products LLC....G.... 509 962-4895
Ellensburg (G-3238)
Western Superior Structurals....F.... 360 943-0339
Tumwater (G-13904)
Whodat Towers....G.... 360 786-1984
Centralia (G-2443)
Wiese and Son Inc....G.... 509 455-8610
Spokane (G-12590)

3442 Metal Doors, Sash, Frames, Molding & Trim

A Thrifty Custom Screens....G.... 425 337-2211
Bothell (G-1813)
Absolute Solutions....G.... 360 683-4597
Sequim (G-11605)
All Season Overhead Door....G.... 509 218-8303
Newport (G-7053)
Alpine Industries Inc....B.... 425 481-7101
Bothell (G-1818)
Atrium Door and Win Co of NW....G.... 509 248-4462
Union Gap (G-13920)
Atrium Windows and Door Wash....B.... 509 248-4462
Union Gap (G-13921)
Atrium Windows and Doors Inc....C.... 509 248-4462
Union Gap (G-13922)
Barmon Door & Plywood Inc....E.... 425 334-1222
Lake Stevens (G-5633)
Building Specialty Systems....G.... 425 483-6875
Ellensburg (G-3185)
Ceco Door Products....G.... 253 872-8174
Kent (G-4843)
Certainteed Corporation....B.... 253 850-9000
Auburn (G-404)
Dotson Doors LLC....G.... 253 326-6047
Mount Vernon (G-6791)
Evergreen Construction Spc Inc....F.... 253 288-8455
Auburn (G-433)
Fabtek Industries Llc....F.... 360 322-7367
Arlington (G-235)
Hadley Door & Trim Inc....G.... 360 748-0116
Chehalis (G-2499)
Home Builders Service Company....F.... 509 747-1206
Spokane (G-12296)
Kawneer Company Inc....F.... 253 236-2848
Tukwila (G-13762)
King Sales & Manufacturing Co....G.... 509 453-1744
Yakima (G-15607)
Lakewood Holdings Inc....G.... 253 284-4897
Lakewood (G-5734)
Lous Welding & Fabricating....F.... 425 483-0300
Woodinville (G-15295)
Lundgren Enterprises....G.... 206 789-1122
Seattle (G-10453)
Marine Welding....G.... 360 293-7256
Anacortes (G-145)
▲ Milgard Manufacturing Inc....C.... 253 922-6030
Fife (G-3971)

S I C

Employee Codes: A=Over 500 employees, B=251-500
C=101-250, D=51-100, E=20-50, F=10-19, G=2-9
2019 Washington
Manufacturers Register
605

34 FABRICATED METAL PRODUCTS, EXCEPT MACHINERY AND TRANSPORTATION EQUIPMENT

Milgard Manufacturing Inc ....A...... 253 922-4341
  Fife *(G-3972)*
Novak Windows ....G...... 253 332-4392
  Edgewood *(G-3088)*
Overhead Door Corporation ....G...... 253 520-8008
  Fife *(G-3977)*
Pacific Coast Marine LLC ....D...... 425 743-9550
  Lynnwood *(G-6176)*
▲ Pacific Coast Marine Inds Inc ....D...... 425 743-9550
  Lynnwood *(G-6177)*
S G&C Contractor Services LLC ....G...... 360 671-5121
  Bellingham *(G-1520)*
Seaclear Industries Mfg Inc ....F...... 360 659-2700
  Marysville *(G-6383)*
Shutterpated ....G...... 360 607-9692
  Bothell *(G-1904)*
Shutterworks LLC ....G...... 509 731-4619
  Yakima *(G-15674)*
Skyline Windows Inc ....G...... 206 542-2147
  Shoreline *(G-11813)*
Starline Construction Inc ....G...... 509 575-7955
  Yakima *(G-15682)*
Sun Solutions Inc ....G...... 509 946-7107
  Richland *(G-9042)*
Tru Door Inc ....F...... 509 545-8773
  Kennewick *(G-4742)*
Windorco Supply Inc ....G...... 206 784-9440
  Seattle *(G-11482)*

3443 Fabricated Plate Work

Acufab Inc ....G...... 509 525-3833
  Walla Walla *(G-14759)*
Advanced Fuel Systems ....G...... 425 526-7566
  Fall City *(G-3698)*
Aeronautical Testing Service ....G...... 360 363-4276
  Arlington *(G-196)*
Airlock LLC ....G...... 206 992-3996
  Seattle *(G-9362)*
▲ Alaskan Copper Companies Inc ......B...... 206 623-5800
  Kent *(G-4768)*
Alaskan Copper Companies Inc ....G...... 206 623-5800
  Seattle *(G-9367)*
Alaskan Copper Companies Inc ....E...... 206 623-5800
  Kent *(G-4769)*
▲ Alco Investment Company ....C...... 206 623-5800
  Kent *(G-4770)*
All Metal Solutions ....G...... 509 426-2400
  Yakima *(G-15504)*
Arrow Marine Services Inc ....G...... 360 457-1544
  Port Angeles *(G-7687)*
Arrow Marine Services Inc ....G...... 360 733-7008
  Bellingham *(G-1253)*
Atomic Fabrications LLC ....G...... 206 767-8036
  Seattle *(G-9456)*
Bmt Metal Fabrication Inc ....G...... 509 244-6107
  Airway Heights *(G-49)*
Brown-Mnnplis Tnk-Nrthwest LLC ......E...... 360 482-1720
  Elma *(G-3243)*
Calhoun Tanks and Services ....G...... 253 517-7356
  Milton *(G-6533)*
Calhoun Tnks & Servces Inc ....G...... 206 870-0802
  Tacoma *(G-13217)*
CBI Services LLC ....E...... 425 258-2350
  Everett *(G-3411)*
Centerline Fabricators LLC ....G...... 253 922-3226
  Fife *(G-3941)*
CH Murphy/Clark-Ullman Inc ....D...... 253 475-6566
  Tacoma *(G-13232)*
Coastline Fabricators Inc ....G...... 206 763-5035
  Seattle *(G-9707)*
◆ Consolidated Metco Inc ....D...... 360 828-2599
  Vancouver *(G-14147)*
Contech Engnered Solutions LLC .....F...... 509 244-3694
  Airway Heights *(G-50)*
Contech Engnered Solutions LLC .....F...... 360 357-9735
  Olympia *(G-7255)*
Custom Welding Inc ....G...... 509 535-0664
  Spokane Valley *(G-12673)*
Dep Homes Corporation ....G...... 206 322-1241
  Seattle *(G-9824)*
◆ Edco Inc ....E...... 360 424-6600
  Mount Vernon *(G-6792)*
Efco Corp ....F...... 253 852-3800
  Kent *(G-4886)*
Erickson Tank & Pump LLC ....F...... 509 785-2955
  Quincy *(G-8297)*
▲ Evergreen Cooling Tech Inc ....G...... 360 983-3691
  Mossyrock *(G-6761)*
Fat Daddys Fabrication LLC ....G...... 253 677-8005
  Roy *(G-9159)*

Fort Vancouver Bee LLC ....G...... 360 274-3396
  Silverlake *(G-11864)*
Foss Marine Holdings Inc ....G...... 206 381-5800
  Seattle *(G-10014)*
Gemmells Wldg Fabrication LLC ......G...... 509 547-5200
  Pasco *(G-7584)*
Gepford Welding Inc ....G...... 509 624-6610
  Spokane *(G-12272)*
Global Incorporated ....F...... 206 763-4424
  Seattle *(G-10084)*
Greenberry Industrial LLC ....G...... 360 366-3767
  Ferndale *(G-3849)*
Greer Steel Inc ....E...... 253 581-4100
  Lakewood *(G-5727)*
▼ Hallmark Refining Corporation ......D...... 360 428-5880
  Mount Vernon *(G-6803)*
Hiline Engrg & Fabrication Inc ....E...... 509 943-9043
  Richland *(G-9006)*
Industrial Container Svcs LLC ....E...... 206 763-2345
  Seattle *(G-10231)*
Ironclad Company ....G...... 206 588-2272
  Tukwila *(G-13754)*
Issak Shamso ....G...... 253 457-2964
  Kent *(G-4962)*
Jet City Partners LLC ....G...... 206 999-0047
  Auburn *(G-479)*
Lucky Dumpster ....G...... 360 766-4049
  Bow *(G-1930)*
Macro Plastics Inc ....E...... 509 452-1200
  Union Gap *(G-13940)*
Maintenance Welding Service ....G...... 360 533-4318
  Hoquiam *(G-4348)*
Marine Welding ....G...... 360 293-7256
  Anacortes *(G-145)*
North Industries Inc ....G...... 206 940-0842
  Seattle *(G-10624)*
◆ Northwest Linings & Geo ....E...... 253 872-0244
  Kent *(G-5033)*
▲ Northwest Pipe Company ....D...... 360 397-6250
  Vancouver *(G-14436)*
Nu Way Flume & Equipment Co ....G...... 360 942-3581
  Raymond *(G-8356)*
Omnifab Inc ....E...... 253 931-5151
  Auburn *(G-518)*
P D M Stilled Service Inc ....E...... 360 225-1133
  Woodland *(G-15454)*
Petrochem Insulation Inc ....G...... 360 254-8953
  Vancouver *(G-14487)*
Piece of Mind LLC ....G...... 509 868-0850
  Spokane *(G-12441)*
Psf Industries Inc ....E...... 800 426-1204
  Seattle *(G-10881)*
Quality Fuel Trlr & Tank Inc ....G...... 425 526-7566
  Monroe *(G-6610)*
Rainier Welding Incorporated ....E...... 425 868-1300
  Redmond *(G-8644)*
Ram Piping Industries Inc ....F...... 509 586-0801
  Kennewick *(G-4714)*
Ries Productions LLC ....G...... 360 627-8795
  Bremerton *(G-1994)*
S Scott & Associates LLC ....G...... 360 576-4830
  Vancouver *(G-14563)*
Safran Cabin Inc ....C...... 360 653-2600
  Marysville *(G-6381)*
Seakamp Engineering Inc ....F...... 360 734-2788
  Bellingham *(G-1528)*
▲ Seattle Boiler Works Inc ....E...... 206 762-0737
  Seattle *(G-11048)*
Selg and Associates Inc ....G...... 425 487-6059
  Woodinville *(G-15359)*
South Sound Metal Inc ....G...... 253 564-0226
  University Place *(G-13981)*
Specialty Motors Mfg LLC ....G...... 360 423-9880
  Longview *(G-5956)*
Spokane Industries Inc ....G...... 509 928-0720
  Spokane Valley *(G-12886)*
▲ Spokane Industries Inc ....C...... 509 924-0440
  Spokane Valley *(G-12885)*
Statcodsi Process Systems ....G...... 253 249-7539
  Algona *(G-77)*
Sunsteel LLC ....G...... 509 836-3078
  Vancouver *(G-14619)*
Tech Heavy Industries Inc ....G...... 509 557-8492
  Riverside *(G-9127)*
◆ Tennmax America Inc ....G...... 360 567-0707
  Vancouver *(G-14631)*
Thermal Solar Panels ....G...... 425 445-0244
  Renton *(G-8927)*
◆ Thermaline Inc ....F...... 253 833-7168
  Auburn *(G-580)*

Thurston Co Transfer Station ....E...... 360 459-1901
  Olympia *(G-7406)*
Town Smoke Plus ....G...... 360 456-8234
  Olympia *(G-7412)*
Trunek Enterprises Inc ....F...... 360 734-6860
  Bellingham *(G-1578)*
▲ Wellons Inc ....C...... 360 750-3500
  Vancouver *(G-14680)*
Wellons Group Inc ....F...... 360 750-3500
  Vancouver *(G-14682)*

3444 Sheet Metal Work

5-Star Enterprises Inc ....G...... 360 577-0829
  Kelso *(G-4515)*
A & B Fabricators Inc ....G...... 253 887-0442
  Auburn *(G-355)*
ABC Sheet Metal Inc ....G...... 360 574-4884
  Ridgefield *(G-9058)*
Accra-Fab Inc ....D...... 509 922-3300
  Liberty Lake *(G-5822)*
Accra-Fab Inc ....C...... 509 922-3300
  Liberty Lake *(G-5823)*
Accurate Sheet Metal Inc ....E...... 425 745-6786
  Mukilteo *(G-6889)*
Acufab Inc ....G...... 509 525-3833
  Walla Walla *(G-14759)*
Advanced Metal Fabrication ....G...... 509 534-0671
  Spokane *(G-12102)*
Air Pro Heating & Cooling LLC ....F...... 360 423-9165
  Longview *(G-5884)*
▲ All American Metal Products ....G...... 360 380-6202
  Ferndale *(G-3811)*
Apex Industries Inc ....D...... 509 928-8450
  Spokane Valley *(G-12621)*
Apollo Sheet Metal Inc ....A...... 509 586-1104
  Kennewick *(G-4618)*
▲ Applied Mfg & Engrg Tech Inc ......F...... 253 852-5378
  Edmonds *(G-3095)*
Ark Commercial Roofing Inc ....F...... 509 443-9300
  Spokane Valley *(G-12625)*
ASap Metal Fabricators Inc ....G...... 509 469-3572
  Yakima *(G-15515)*
ASap Metal Fabricators Inc ....G...... 509 453-9143
  Yakima *(G-15516)*
▲ Automated Metal Tech Inc ....F...... 425 895-9733
  Redmond *(G-8390)*
B & D Sheet Metal LLC ....G...... 206 533-0350
  Shoreline *(G-11759)*
B & J Metal Fab ....G...... 360 887-8548
  Ridgefield *(G-9063)*
Bair Construction Inc ....G...... 360 491-2285
  Lacey *(G-5535)*
Ballard Sheet Metal Works Inc ....E...... 206 784-0545
  Seattle *(G-9484)*
Barrys Steve Pool Service LLC ....G...... 360 533-0421
  Aberdeen *(G-3)*
BBH Sheet Metal LLC ....G...... 425 637-0360
  Bellevue *(G-808)*
Bending Solutions Incorporated ....E...... 360 651-2443
  Marysville *(G-6316)*
Bestworth - Rommel Inc ....E...... 360 435-2927
  Arlington *(G-213)*
Brewster Manufacturing Inc ....F...... 509 923-2264
  Brewster *(G-2015)*
Brownfield Manufacturing Inc ....E...... 360 568-0572
  Monroe *(G-6559)*
Buyken Metal Products Inc ....E...... 253 852-0634
  Kent *(G-4827)*
Canopy World Inc ....G...... 206 824-3877
  Des Moines *(G-2932)*
Capital Heating & Cooling Inc ....E...... 360 491-7450
  Lacey *(G-5537)*
Carlson Sheet Metal Works Inc ....F...... 509 535-4228
  Spokane *(G-12170)*
Cascade Pipe & Feed Supply ....G...... 509 997-0720
  Twisp *(G-13910)*
Ccw LLC ....G...... 206 363-4916
  Shoreline *(G-11764)*
CDI Custom Design Inc ....E...... 360 650-1150
  Bellingham *(G-1294)*
▲ Central Fabricators Inc ....F...... 206 633-4762
  Seattle *(G-9654)*
City Sheet Metal Heating & Air ....G...... 253 852-2174
  Auburn *(G-407)*
Cleveland Enterprises Inc ....G...... 360 694-0435
  Vancouver *(G-14123)*
Coastal Manufacturing Inc ....E...... 425 407-0624
  Everett *(G-3421)*
Colored Metal Roofing ....G...... 360 887-4524
  Ridgefield *(G-9073)*

Columbia Stainless Metal-Fab ....G 509 662-9078
Wenatchee *(G-15022)*
Competitive Development & Mfg ....F 360 691-7816
Granite Falls *(G-4269)*
Competitive Development & Mfg ....G 360 691-7816
Granite Falls *(G-4270)*
Copper Creek Fabrications LLC ....G 360 582-9676
Sequim *(G-11620)*
Copper Ridge Fabrication LLC ....G 360 582-3898
Sequim *(G-11621)*
Crystal Distribution Inc ....F 253 736-0016
Fife *(G-3946)*
Crystalite Inc ....E 425 259-6000
Everett *(G-3432)*
Crystalite Inc ....G 509 921-9585
Spokane Valley *(G-12672)*
Crystalite Inc ....E 425 259-6000
Everett *(G-3433)*
Custom Bilt Holdings LLC ....E 253 872-7330
Lakewood *(G-5709)*
Custom Sheet Metal Inc ....G 360 754-5220
Olympia *(G-7262)*
Custom Technology Co Inc ....F 509 965-3333
Yakima *(G-15546)*
David Gulassa & Co Inc ....E 206 283-1810
Seattle *(G-9800)*
Decorative Metal Arts ....G 206 782-4009
Seattle *(G-9812)*
DK Machining LLC ....G 509 991-6110
Nine Mile Falls *(G-7072)*
ECB Corp ....E 425 514-8334
Everett *(G-3451)*
Efco Corp ....G 360 566-0300
Vancouver *(G-14194)*
Efco Corp ....F 253 852-3800
Kent *(G-4886)*
▲ **Elkay Ssp LLC** ....E 509 533-0808
Spokane *(G-12241)*
Ershigs Inc ....F 360 733-2620
Bellingham *(G-1338)*
▲ **Evergreen Fabrication Inc** ....G 509 534-9096
Spokane Valley *(G-12694)*
Evergreen House Inc ....F 425 821-1005
Kirkland *(G-5334)*
▲ **Exact Aerospace Inc** ....E 253 854-1017
Auburn *(G-436)*
Fabrication Products Inc ....E 503 283-3218
Vancouver *(G-14219)*
Fabtech Precision Mfg Inc ....E 509 534-7660
Spokane Valley *(G-12699)*
Farwest Operating LLC ....D 509 453-1663
Moxee *(G-6878)*
First Metals Inc ....G 303 915-2426
Renton *(G-8800)*
FO Berg Company ....F 509 624-8921
Spokane Valley *(G-12706)*
Gaudet Sheetmetal Inc ....G 360 892-5772
Battle Ground *(G-703)*
Gcm North American Arospc LLC ....D 253 872-7488
Algona *(G-69)*
◆ **Gensco Inc** ....C 253 620-8203
Fife *(G-3954)*
Gibraltar Industries Inc ....C 253 926-1600
Fife *(G-3955)*
Glenns Welding and Mfg Inc ....E 425 743-2226
Lynnwood *(G-6131)*
Global Incorporated ....F 206 763-4424
Seattle *(G-10084)*
Gnr Aerospace Inc ....G 360 652-4040
Arlington *(G-244)*
▲ **Gompf Brackets Inc** ....F 425 348-5002
Mukilteo *(G-6929)*
Home Builders Service Company ....F 509 747-1206
Spokane *(G-12296)*
Hulett and Company ....G 425 922-5224
Snohomish *(G-11925)*
Ifh Group West LLC ....G 844 434-9378
Arlington *(G-253)*
Imaginetics Holdings LLC ....G 253 735-0156
Auburn *(G-472)*
Imaginetics LLC ....D 253 735-0156
Auburn *(G-473)*
Independent Chute Company ....G 206 321-8911
Puyallup *(G-8166)*
Interlock Industries Inc ....G 253 872-5750
Kent *(G-4956)*
Interlock Industries Inc ....G 360 713-3036
Stanwood *(G-12976)*
J & E Jensen Inc ....G 253 851-2282
Bremerton *(G-1963)*
J & R Mtlcraft Fabricators Inc ....G 425 254-0392
Renton *(G-8829)*
▼ **J R Setina Manufacturing Co** ....D 360 491-6197
Olympia *(G-7310)*
J S Vail ....G 509 886-8708
East Wenatchee *(G-3022)*
James Homola ....G 360 686-3549
Yacolt *(G-15483)*
Jemco Cmpnents Fabrication Inc ....D 425 827-7611
Kirkland *(G-5372)*
Jet City Partners LLC ....G 206 999-0047
Auburn *(G-479)*
Jit Manufacturing Inc ....E 425 487-0672
Woodinville *(G-15274)*
Jpl Habitability Inc ....F 360 377-7660
Bremerton *(G-1967)*
Kauffmann Industries Inc ....G 425 770-5781
Bothell *(G-1872)*
KDL Enterprises Inc ....E 253 395-3113
Kent *(G-4973)*
Kenneth A Edleman ....G 206 524-2814
Seattle *(G-10337)*
Kingston Mail Center Inc ....G 360 297-2173
Kingston *(G-5256)*
Klw Manufacturing & Design Inc ....F 360 435-6288
Arlington *(G-270)*
Kollmar Incorporated ....E 509 882-3148
Grandview *(G-4250)*
Kollmar Sheet Metal Works Inc ....G 206 283-2330
Seattle *(G-10353)*
Krueger Sheet Metal Co ....D 509 489-0221
Spokane *(G-12355)*
L & E Tubing LLC ....E 425 778-4123
Lynnwood *(G-6155)*
L & M Prcision Fabrication Inc ....E 509 244-5446
Airway Heights *(G-55)*
Laz Tool and Manufacturing ....F 360 568-5749
Snohomish *(G-11936)*
Lee Fabricators Inc ....F 360 698-1190
Silverdale *(G-11843)*
▲ **Lighthouse For The Blind Inc** ....B 206 322-4200
Seattle *(G-10417)*
◆ **Lloyd Industries LLC** ....E 509 468-8691
Spokane Valley *(G-12775)*
Louis Stoffer & Son ....G 360 736-3820
Centralia *(G-2418)*
Lous Welding & Fabricating ....F 425 483-0300
Woodinville *(G-15295)*
Lumenomics Inc ....E 206 327-9037
Seattle *(G-10451)*
M & M Fabricators Inc ....G 509 248-8890
Union Gap *(G-13939)*
▼ **Magic Metals Inc** ....C 509 453-1690
Union Gap *(G-13942)*
Mailboxes Depot ....G 360 651-2651
Arlington *(G-272)*
▲ **Marks Design & Metalworks LLC** ....D 360 859-3535
Vancouver *(G-14396)*
▲ **McKinstry Co LLC** ....B 206 762-3311
Seattle *(G-10509)*
Mechpro Inc ....G 206 445-5230
Auburn *(G-496)*
Metal Mill Corporation ....G 360 262-9080
Chehalis *(G-2514)*
Metal Rollforming Systems Inc ....E 509 315-8737
Spokane *(G-12392)*
Metal Sales Manufacturing Corp ....E 509 536-6000
Spokane *(G-12393)*
Metal Sales Manufacturing Corp ....F 253 872-5750
Kent *(G-5007)*
Metal Smith ....F 509 884-4851
East Wenatchee *(G-3025)*
Metals Fabrication Company Inc ....D 509 244-2909
Airway Heights *(G-56)*
Metals McHning Fabricators Inc ....F 509 248-8890
Union Gap *(G-13944)*
Metals USA Building Pdts LP ....F 425 251-0589
Kent *(G-5008)*
Metaltech Inc ....E 253 863-7532
Sumner *(G-13086)*
Moses Lake Sheet Metal Inc ....E 509 765-1614
Moses Lake *(G-6728)*
▲ **Mutual Industries Inc** ....G 206 767-6647
Seattle *(G-10577)*
Naps Forming Systems ....G 800 922-2082
Sumner *(G-13087)*
▲ **National Indus Concepts Inc** ....C 425 489-4300
Woodinville *(G-15320)*
Noll/Norwesco LLC ....C 253 926-1600
Fife *(G-3974)*
North Industries Inc ....G 206 940-0842
Seattle *(G-10624)*
North Park Heating Company Inc ....F 206 365-1414
Lake Forest Park *(G-5622)*
Northern Mountain Metals LLC ....G 509 226-1957
Newman Lake *(G-7049)*
▼ **Nu-Ray Metal Products Inc** ....F 253 833-8637
Auburn *(G-513)*
▲ **Ode Products LLC** ....G 253 859-7902
Sumner *(G-13090)*
Ogle Equipment Co ....G 509 489-6306
Spokane *(G-12419)*
Olympia Sheet Metal Inc ....E 360 491-1123
Olympia *(G-7354)*
Omnifab Inc ....E 253 931-5151
Auburn *(G-518)*
Omnimax International Inc ....F 509 535-0344
Spokane Valley *(G-12819)*
Optimum Precision Inc ....G 425 778-1455
Lynnwood *(G-6175)*
Orion Industries ....C 253 661-7805
Auburn *(G-521)*
Orion Industries ....C 425 355-1253
Mukilteo *(G-6962)*
Outdoor Leisure Centers ....G 509 599-2150
Spokane *(G-12423)*
P&A Metal Fab Inc ....G 253 435-8947
Puyallup *(G-8213)*
Pacer Design By Sharp Pdts Inc ....F 360 217-8120
Monroe *(G-6603)*
▲ **Pacific Coast Marine Inds Inc** ....D 425 743-9550
Lynnwood *(G-6177)*
▲ **Pacific Metal Fabrication Inc** ....G 253 833-3362
Kent *(G-5054)*
Pacific Northwest ....G 206 453-3182
Seattle *(G-10736)*
Pacific Sheet Metal Inc ....E 206 682-5354
Seattle *(G-10740)*
Palouse Gutters and Cnstr LLC ....G 509 397-0404
Colfax *(G-2719)*
Peninsula Sheet Metal Inc ....G 360 642-2102
Long Beach *(G-5876)*
Peri Formwork Systems Inc ....E 360 225-3583
Woodland *(G-15458)*
Pet Enclosures Northwest ....G 425 786-1221
Shoreline *(G-11799)*
▲ **Pioneer Human Services** ....D 206 768-1990
Seattle *(G-10809)*
Pioneer Human Services ....C 206 762-7737
Seattle *(G-10810)*
Polaris Manufacturing Inc ....E 360 653-7676
Marysville *(G-6370)*
Post All Expressions ....G 509 684-3723
Colville *(G-2769)*
Power Plus Incorporated ....G 509 489-8308
Spokane *(G-12451)*
Precision Fabricators LLC ....G 206 362-1195
Seattle *(G-10850)*
Precision Sheet Metal LLC ....G 509 969-0055
Yakima *(G-15652)*
Precision Sheet Metal & Heatin ....G 503 939-8600
Vancouver *(G-14502)*
Premier Manufacturing Inc ....D 509 927-9860
Liberty Lake *(G-5854)*
Proctor Products Co Inc ....F 425 398-8800
Woodinville *(G-15341)*
Proto Manufacturing Inc ....D 509 535-9683
Spokane *(G-12456)*
Qual Fab Inc ....E 206 762-2117
Seattle *(G-10899)*
Queen City Shtmtl & Roofg Inc ....E 206 623-6020
Kent *(G-5092)*
Quicktin Incorporated ....F 253 779-8885
Tacoma *(G-13485)*
Reliance Steel & Aluminum Co ....E 253 395-0614
Tukwila *(G-13806)*
Rogroc LLC ....G 360 435-6417
Arlington *(G-316)*
Roofing Services Inc ....F 425 347-1146
Mount Vernon *(G-6829)*
▲ **Rozema Boat Works Inc** ....F 360 757-6004
Mount Vernon *(G-6830)*
S & R Sheet Metal Inc ....D 360 425-7020
Kelso *(G-4546)*
S & S Metal Fabrication Inc ....F 253 472-4461
Tacoma *(G-13504)*
▼ **Scafco Corporation** ....C 509 343-9000
Spokane *(G-12493)*
▲ **Sea Lect Products** ....G 253 520-2598
Kent *(G-5118)*

S I C

Employee Codes: A=Over 500 employees, B=251-500 C=101-250, D=51-100, E=20-50, F=10-19, G=2-9
2019 Washington Manufacturers Register
607

Seaport Machine Inc ....F 509 758-2605
Clarkston *(G-2648)*
Sharps Welding & Muffler Ctr ....G 509 452-2101
Moxee *(G-6885)*
▲ Shoemaker Manufacturing Co ....D 509 674-4414
Cle Elum *(G-2679)*
Skilfab Industries Inc ....G 425 831-5555
Snoqualmie *(G-12024)*
Smith Fabrication Inc ....G 253 854-4367
Kent *(G-5136)*
SMK Tri-Cities Inc ....E 509 547-0412
Pasco *(G-7631)*
Sol Lighting Inc ....G 509 789-1092
Spokane Valley *(G-12880)*
▲ Sound Building Supply Inc ....E 425 264-0264
Renton *(G-8916)*
Sound Metal Works Ltd ....F 360 659-0999
Marysville *(G-6388)*
Specialty Roofing LLC ....G 509 534-8372
Spokane *(G-12513)*
Specialty Sheet Metal Inc ....F 253 872-5718
Kent *(G-5148)*
Spiraltec ....G 360 734-7831
Bellingham *(G-1553)*
Spokane Rain Gutter Inc ....F 509 922-4880
Spokane Valley *(G-12887)*
Spokane Tin Sheet Ir Works Inc ....F 509 534-0539
Spokane *(G-12521)*
Star Rentals Inc ....F 509 545-8521
Pasco *(G-7632)*
Steel Fab Inc ....E 425 743-9216
Arlington *(G-333)*
▲ Steeler Inc ....D 206 725-8500
Seattle *(G-11187)*
Steeler Inc ....G 253 572-8200
Tacoma *(G-13525)*
Steeler Construction Sup Ltd ....E 206 725-2500
Seattle *(G-11188)*
Steeltec Supply Inc ....G 253 333-1311
Auburn *(G-572)*
Stephens Metal Products Inc ....E 509 452-4088
Yakima *(G-15683)*
Str8 Sheet Fabrications LLC ....G 425 789-1755
Mukilteo *(G-6980)*
Sytech Inc ....E 509 924-7797
Spokane *(G-12540)*
T N T Enterprises ....G 425 742-8210
Bothell *(G-1908)*
T&C Concepts LLC ....G 253 298-2104
Puyallup *(G-8260)*
T2 Services Inc ....F 509 893-3666
Spokane Valley *(G-12899)*
Taylor Metal Inc ....F 425 485-3003
Woodinville *(G-15386)*
Tl Northwest Corp ....F 253 445-4104
Puyallup *(G-8264)*
Top Notch Manufacturing Co ....G 360 577-9150
Longview *(G-5960)*
Tri-Mechanical Inc ....F 425 391-6016
Bellevue *(G-1201)*
Tri-Way Industries Inc ....D 253 859-4585
Auburn *(G-582)*
Truepoint Metalworks Wldg Inc ....G 360 273-3412
Rochester *(G-9142)*
U S Sheet Metal Company Inc ....F 253 272-2444
Tacoma *(G-13567)*
▲ Universal Sheet Metal Inc ....E 425 483-8384
Woodinville *(G-15395)*
Viking Packaging Machinery ....G 509 452-7143
Yakima *(G-15703)*
▲ West Coast Custom Metal Design ....G 360 738-2884
Bellingham *(G-1592)*
West Coast Manufacturing Inc ....G 208 667-5121
Everett *(G-3655)*
Westside Concrete ACC Inc ....G 360 892-0203
Vancouver *(G-14686)*
Wldg Wilkerson & Fabrication ....G 509 438-9667
Pasco *(G-7655)*
Wsf LLC ....E 509 922-1300
Spokane Valley *(G-12944)*

3446 Architectural & Ornamental Metal Work

A & B Fabricators Inc ....G 253 887-0442
Auburn *(G-355)*
A One Ornamental Iron Works ....G 206 622-4033
Seatac *(G-9271)*
▲ Acoustical Solutions ....G 253 876-0075
Auburn *(G-361)*
Acufab Inc ....G 509 525-3833
Walla Walla *(G-14759)*
◆ AGS Stainless Inc ....F 206 842-9492
Bainbridge Island *(G-607)*
Alabama Metal Industries Corp ....C 253 926-1600
Fife *(G-3928)*
All In Cnstr & Ldscpg LLC ....G 360 840-7990
Mount Vernon *(G-6770)*
All Metal Fab Inc ....F 253 737-5154
Auburn *(G-370)*
Allied Steel Fabricators Inc ....E 425 861-9558
Redmond *(G-8380)*
American Metal Specialties ....G 253 272-9344
University Place *(G-13959)*
American Railworks ....G 425 582-8990
Lynnwood *(G-6075)*
Architect David Vandervort ....G 206 784-1614
Seattle *(G-9420)*
Argent Fabrication LLC ....F 206 438-0068
Seattle *(G-9427)*
Artistic Iron Furniture Mfrs ....F 360 398-9351
Lynden *(G-6002)*
Automated Equipment Company ....E 206 767-9080
Tukwila *(G-13693)*
B K Welding and Fabrication ....G 360 871-0490
Port Orchard *(G-7791)*
Ballard Ornamental Ironworks ....G 206 782-3343
Seattle *(G-9481)*
Benjamin D Schreiner ....G 206 417-4663
Lake Forest Park *(G-5606)*
Bfc Architectural Metals Inc ....F 206 763-0530
Seatac *(G-9274)*
Big C Industries LLC ....G 844 406-2442
Longview *(G-5888)*
Blazen Metal Works ....G 360 897-2053
Orting *(G-7474)*
Brassfinders Inc ....G 509 747-7412
Spokane *(G-12160)*
Buyken Metal Products Inc ....E 253 852-0634
Kent *(G-4827)*
Callison Architecture LLC ....G 206 623-4646
Seattle *(G-9607)*
Click It Picket LLC ....G 253 750-0182
Auburn *(G-408)*
Corona Steel Inc ....G 253 874-4766
Tacoma *(G-13244)*
Creative Metal Concepts LLC ....G 253 230-4933
Bonney Lake *(G-1720)*
Dag Industries Inc ....G 425 228-4962
Renton *(G-8779)*
Decorative Metal Services Inc ....G 360 695-7052
Vancouver *(G-14172)*
Earthen Alchemy ....G 360 926-8467
Stanwood *(G-12968)*
▲ Ecolite Manufacturing Co ....D 509 922-8888
Spokane Valley *(G-12687)*
Ecolite Manufacturing Co ....D 509 922-8888
Spokane Valley *(G-12688)*
European Wrought Iron ....G 509 548-4879
Leavenworth *(G-5801)*
▲ Evergreen Fabrication Inc ....G 509 534-9096
Spokane Valley *(G-12694)*
Fast Flashings LLC ....G 425 827-8367
Seattle *(G-9974)*
Fast Flashings LLC ....G 206 364-3612
Seattle *(G-9975)*
Fence Store By Eagle Vinyl LLC ....G 509 860-3603
Wenatchee *(G-15032)*
Fithian Wldg & Fabrication LLC ....G 206 658-3732
Monroe *(G-6573)*
▲ Forrest Sound Products LLC ....G 425 881-1111
Redmond *(G-8464)*
Garys Garden Gate ....G 360 357-5607
Olympia *(G-7294)*
Gc Solutions LLC ....G 509 243-6030
Asotin *(G-352)*
Gerald McCallum ....G 509 467-8456
Spokane *(G-12273)*
Glenns Welding and Mfg Inc ....E 425 743-2226
Lynnwood *(G-6131)*
Global Mtal Works Erectors LLC ....E 253 572-5363
Tacoma *(G-13312)*
Grating Fabricators Inc ....F 360 696-0886
Vancouver *(G-14264)*
Grating Pacific LLC ....G 253 872-7733
Kent *(G-4926)*
Holland Ornamental Iron Inc ....G 253 564-5671
University Place *(G-13971)*
Home Builders Service Company ....F 509 747-1206
Spokane *(G-12296)*
Homers Ornamental Iron ....G 509 327-8673
Spokane *(G-12298)*
Honolds Ornamental Ironwork ....G 206 779-0668
Langley *(G-5781)*
◆ Inline Design LLC ....F 425 405-5505
Seattle *(G-10238)*
Integrated Stair Systems Inc ....E 360 829-4220
Buckley *(G-2060)*
Intermountain Fabricators Inc ....F 509 534-1676
Spokane Valley *(G-12746)*
Iron Gate Shoppe ....G 360 791-3292
Enumclaw *(G-3294)*
Ironhouse Ornamental ....G 509 993-7601
Spokane *(G-12326)*
J and S Ironworks LLC ....G 509 276-5887
Nine Mile Falls *(G-7077)*
Kitsap Vinyl Deck & Rail LLC ....G 360 830-5959
Seabeck *(G-9266)*
▼ Leader Manufacturing Inc ....E 360 895-1184
Port Orchard *(G-7825)*
Leskajan John ....F 253 539-8018
Tacoma *(G-13386)*
Linns Service & Remodel Inc ....G 509 448-2540
Spokane *(G-12369)*
Little Mexico Ornamental Iron ....G 425 334-1082
Lake Stevens *(G-5658)*
Louisville Ladder ....G 206 762-4888
Seattle *(G-10444)*
Lous Welding & Fabricating ....F 425 483-0300
Woodinville *(G-15295)*
▲ McKinstry Co LLC ....B 206 762-3311
Seattle *(G-10509)*
McNichols Company ....F 253 922-4296
Fife *(G-3970)*
Michael Enterprises Co ....G 253 630-4259
Covington *(G-2833)*
Michellaine Lee Larry Bergsma ....G 360 873-4005
Marblemount *(G-6305)*
▲ Modern Metals LLC ....E 425 405-6994
Everett *(G-3549)*
Mount Baker Fireplace Shop ....G 360 384-3507
Bellingham *(G-1444)*
Northwest Fence Co ....G 360 683-4673
Sequim *(G-11652)*
Oneils Foundry Forging Metal & ....G 360 941-7557
Sedro Woolley *(G-11553)*
Ornamental Iron Specialists ....G 253 630-0328
Kent *(G-5047)*
Ornamental Iron Works Inc ....G 509 662-8294
Wenatchee *(G-15054)*
Perfect Reflections Auto Body ....G 360 426-0805
Shelton *(G-11721)*
Pfc Inc ....G 360 398-8889
Bellingham *(G-1497)*
Premier Sales Northwest Inc ....G 206 763-9857
Federal Way *(G-3773)*
Proweld Fabrication LLC ....G 425 835-6477
Moses Lake *(G-6739)*
Quali Cast Foundry ....G 360 748-6645
Chehalis *(G-2527)*
Rail Fx LLC ....G 206 453-1123
Tacoma *(G-13488)*
Railmakers Northwest ....F 425 259-9236
Everett *(G-3594)*
Railpro of Oregon Inc ....G 360 213-0958
Vancouver *(G-14530)*
Rainier Orna Ir Fbrication Inc ....G 253 833-0101
Auburn *(G-544)*
Reliance Manufacturing Corp ....E 425 481-3030
Woodinville *(G-15348)*
Rescom Railing Systems LLC ....G 853 243-9841
Arlington *(G-314)*
Rj Jarvis Enterprises Inc ....E 509 482-0254
Spokane *(G-12477)*
Ronald Wayne Dagley ....G 253 863-4895
Sumner *(G-13097)*
S & R Spiral LLC ....E 509 747-4723
Davenport *(G-2877)*
S & S Welding Inc ....E 206 793-9943
Kent *(G-5110)*
▲ Safeworks LLC ....D 206 575-6445
Tukwila *(G-13809)*
▲ Shoemaker Manufacturing Co ....D 509 674-4414
Cle Elum *(G-2679)*
Snake River Fence ....G 509 758-7081
Anatone *(G-185)*
◆ Stainless Cable & Railing Inc ....G 360 314-4288
Vancouver *(G-14606)*
Superior Sole Wldg Fabrication ....G 360 653-2565
Marysville *(G-6393)*
Swiss Ornamental Iron ....G 253 759-6796
Tacoma *(G-13535)*

SIC SECTION — 34 FABRICATED METAL PRODUCTS, EXCEPT MACHINERY AND TRANSPORTATION EQUIPMENT

TAC Fab LLC ....G...... 206 755-0519
  Woodinville *(G-15385)*
Twisted Metal LLC ....G...... 360 966-5309
  Everson *(G-3693)*
◆ Urban Accessories Inc ....E...... 253 572-1112
  Tacoma *(G-13573)*
US Starcraft Corporation ....G...... 206 762-0607
  Seattle *(G-11394)*
▲ West Coast Custom Metal Design ....G...... 360 738-2884
  Bellingham *(G-1592)*
Western Clear View Railing ....E...... 253 395-3113
  Kent *(G-5213)*

3448 Prefabricated Metal Buildings & Cmpnts

American Container Homes Inc ....G...... 509 531-3286
  Mead *(G-6424)*
ASC Profiles LLC ....E...... 509 535-0600
  Spokane *(G-12120)*
ASC Profiles LLC ....E...... 253 383-4955
  Tacoma *(G-13184)*
Atomic Fabrications LLC ....G...... 206 767-8036
  Seattle *(G-9456)*
Awnings & Sunrooms Distinction .....G...... 360 681-2727
  Sequim *(G-11613)*
◆ Bellingham Marine Industries ....D...... 360 676-2800
  Bellingham *(G-1266)*
Canam Steel Corporation ....C...... 509 837-7008
  Vancouver *(G-14094)*
D S Fabrication & Design Inc ....G...... 360 600-9706
  Vancouver *(G-14163)*
Evergreen House Inc ....F...... 425 821-1005
  Kirkland *(G-5334)*
▲ Front Panel Express LLC ....F...... 206 768-0602
  Seattle *(G-10029)*
Garco Building Systems Inc ....C...... 509 244-5611
  Airway Heights *(G-52)*
Gimpy Ninja LLC ....G...... 253 282-9943
  Gig Harbor *(G-4108)*
Global Solarium Inc ....G...... 360 695-0313
  Vancouver *(G-14258)*
Grenlar Holdings Inc ....G...... 425 419-4430
  Kenmore *(G-4578)*
▲ Homecare Products Inc ....C...... 253 249-1108
  Algona *(G-71)*
Integrated Systems Design ....G...... 360 746-0812
  Bellingham *(G-1380)*
Joom 3d ....G...... 413 566-6330
  Olympia *(G-7314)*
K&M Storage ....G...... 253 862-3515
  Sumner *(G-13076)*
Latium USA Trading Inc ....G...... 253 850-4530
  Kent *(G-4990)*
Mac Arthur Co ....E...... 253 863-8830
  Sumner *(G-13080)*
Mantle Industries LLC ....F...... 360 332-5276
  Blaine *(G-1683)*
Metal Structures LLC ....G...... 703 628-7808
  Battle Ground *(G-721)*
Northern Lights Sunrm Creatn L ......G...... 509 747-1110
  Spokane *(G-12409)*
Northside Metal Carports LLC ....G...... 360 262-9354
  Chehalis *(G-2518)*
Pacific Contractors & Supply ....G...... 509 534-4304
  Spokane Valley *(G-12822)*
Pacific N W Sheds Buildings ....G...... 360 573-7433
  Vancouver *(G-14466)*
Peninsula Iron ....G...... 253 857-8844
  Gig Harbor *(G-4143)*
Port A Cover & More Inc ....G...... 509 928-9264
  Spokane Valley *(G-12832)*
Robertson-Ceco II Corporation ....D...... 509 244-5611
  Airway Heights *(G-62)*
Shelterlogic Corp ....G...... 253 985-0026
  Lakewood *(G-5755)*
Steel Structures America Inc ....G...... 509 590-1230
  Spokane *(G-12526)*
Vanderpol Building Components ......F...... 360 354-5883
  Lynden *(G-6058)*
Verns Rent It ....G...... 360 458-3302
  Rochester *(G-9143)*
Wazzbizz Inc ....G...... 360 332-5276
  Blaine *(G-1710)*
Welcome Ramp Systems Inc ....G...... 425 754-0489
  Auburn *(G-597)*

3449 Misc Structural Metal Work

ABG ....G...... 253 896-1372
  Fife *(G-3927)*
Alliance Steel Fabrication ....E...... 253 538-7935
  Tacoma *(G-13166)*
Arbon Equipment Corporation ....F...... 253 395-7099
  Kent *(G-4787)*
Arbon Equipment Corporation ....E...... 253 796-0004
  Kent *(G-4788)*
▼ Berg Manufacturing Inc ....C...... 509 624-8921
  Spokane Valley *(G-12638)*
Big C Industries LLC ....G...... 844 406-2442
  Longview *(G-5888)*
Bite-A-Lite LLC ....G...... 360 687-2995
  Battle Ground *(G-693)*
Canam Steel Corporation ....C...... 509 837-7008
  Vancouver *(G-14094)*
CMC Steel Fabricators Inc ....G...... 253 833-9060
  Auburn *(G-409)*
Cutting Edge Manufacturing ....E...... 425 348-0626
  Everett *(G-3434)*
D&E Kustoms LLC ....G...... 360 681-0511
  Sequim *(G-11622)*
Daines Corporation ....G...... 425 212-3169
  Everett *(G-3438)*
DCB Industries Inc ....G...... 360 750-0009
  Vancouver *(G-14170)*
Harris Rebar Seattle Inc ....E...... 253 847-5001
  Tacoma *(G-13332)*
▲ Homecare Products Inc ....C...... 253 249-1108
  Algona *(G-71)*
Jodal Manufacturing ....G...... 206 763-8848
  Seattle *(G-10300)*
Joy Specialty Metals LLC ....G...... 206 542-5161
  Shoreline *(G-11778)*
Katana Industries Inc ....D...... 509 754-5600
  Ephrata *(G-3340)*
Kiln Cart Construction ....G...... 360 319-0414
  Bellingham *(G-1394)*
Knights Welding ....G...... 509 412-1103
  Pasco *(G-7596)*
McVays Mobile Welding LLC ....G...... 360 657-0360
  Marysville *(G-6358)*
Morgan Steel & Metal Works ....G...... 360 301-6611
  Poulsbo *(G-7986)*
▲ National Wirecraft Company Inc ...F...... 360 424-1129
  Mount Vernon *(G-6816)*
Nucor Corporation ....C...... 206 933-2222
  Seattle *(G-10666)*
ONeill Steel Fabrication Inc ....F...... 509 467-5309
  Spokane *(G-12421)*
Pfc Inc ....G...... 360 398-8889
  Bellingham *(G-1497)*
Pickett Spring ....G...... 360 376-6982
  Olga *(G-7218)*
Ries Productions LLC ....G...... 360 627-8795
  Bremerton *(G-1994)*
Titanium Sports Tech LLC ....D...... 509 586-6117
  Pasco *(G-7640)*
Tri States Rebar Inc ....E...... 509 922-5901
  Spokane Valley *(G-12912)*
▲ Ultimate Mtal Fabrications LLC ....F...... 206 356-9666
  Renton *(G-8935)*
Vartan Product Support LLC ....E...... 425 374-8914
  Mukilteo *(G-6988)*
▲ West Coast Custom Metal Design ...G...... 360 738-2884
  Bellingham *(G-1592)*
Western Fabrication Center LLC ......F...... 360 575-1500
  Kelso *(G-4559)*

3451 Screw Machine Prdts

▲ Automatic Products Co Inc ....D...... 253 872-0203
  Kent *(G-4800)*
Ems & Sales LLC ....G...... 253 208-9062
  Renton *(G-8794)*
◆ Fkc Co Ltd ....F...... 360 452-9472
  Port Angeles *(G-7706)*
Go Planit LLC ....G...... 206 227-0660
  Mattawa *(G-6407)*
Grizzly Machining Solutions ....G...... 406 396-4087
  Sultan *(G-13026)*
Jet City Partners LLC ....G...... 206 999-0047
  Auburn *(G-479)*
Jevco International Inc ....F...... 253 858-2605
  Auburn *(G-480)*
Mico Welding & Machining Inc ....G...... 509 467-5082
  Nine Mile Falls *(G-7079)*
Northstone Industries LLC ....G...... 509 844-7775
  Spokane *(G-12410)*
Omnifab Inc ....E...... 253 931-5151
  Auburn *(G-518)*
Roberts Precision Machine Inc ....F...... 360 805-1000
  Monroe *(G-6615)*
Saco Sales ....G...... 253 277-1568
  Kent *(G-5112)*
Tacoma Screw Products Inc ....G...... 253 395-9770
  Kent *(G-5170)*
Tacoma Screw Products Inc ....G...... 206 767-3750
  Seattle *(G-11256)*
Towaco Screw Mch Pdts Co LLC .....G...... 425 481-7100
  Bothell *(G-1910)*

3452 Bolts, Nuts, Screws, Rivets & Washers

Aaron Libolt ....G...... 360 441-0662
  Lynden *(G-5999)*
Closest To The Pin Inc ....G...... 425 820-2297
  Kirkland *(G-5308)*
Go Planit LLC ....G...... 206 227-0660
  Mattawa *(G-6407)*
J & R Mercantile ....G...... 425 486-6402
  Kenmore *(G-4583)*
Karcher North America Inc ....F...... 360 833-1600
  Camas *(G-2260)*
Lyn-Tron Inc ....D...... 509 456-4545
  Spokane *(G-12376)*
Marks Keg Washer ....G...... 503 806-4115
  Vancouver *(G-14397)*
Mico Welding & Machining Inc ....G...... 509 467-5082
  Nine Mile Falls *(G-7079)*
Pin City Wrestling Club ....G...... 425 327-8518
  Lake Stevens *(G-5669)*
Steeler Inc ....G...... 509 926-7403
  Spokane Valley *(G-12891)*
Stelfast Inc ....G...... 206 574-3078
  Tukwila *(G-13822)*
Suncatchers ....G...... 360 293-6360
  Anacortes *(G-171)*
Tree Island Industries Ltd ....E...... 360 366-0988
  Ferndale *(G-3916)*
Waldon Abel Guide Pins LLC ....G...... 509 684-2009
  Colville *(G-2781)*

3462 Iron & Steel Forgings

12th Avenue Iron Inc ....G...... 206 325-0792
  Seattle *(G-9317)*
All American Corporation ....F...... 509 315-9951
  Mead *(G-6423)*
American Engine & Machine Inc .....G...... 509 487-3332
  Spokane *(G-12110)*
◆ Contech Systems Inc ....G...... 360 332-1718
  Tacoma *(G-13240)*
Custom Gear Inc ....F...... 206 767-9448
  Tukwila *(G-13722)*
Electrino Group Inc ....G...... 360 491-9373
  Lacey *(G-5548)*
Forfjord Supply Co ....G...... 206 784-8171
  Seattle *(G-10012)*
Fss Holdings LLC ....G...... 425 820-5455
  Kirkland *(G-5345)*
Hesco Armor Inc ....E...... 360 580-1146
  Aberdeen *(G-17)*
Horseshoe Cove Cabin Owne ....G...... 509 966-4087
  Yakima *(G-15585)*
Horseshoe Falls LLC ....G...... 360 256-0668
  Vancouver *(G-14303)*
Horseshoe Grange 965 ....G...... 360 668-3939
  Snohomish *(G-11922)*
Horseshoe Lake Estates Assn ....G...... 253 851-3514
  Gig Harbor *(G-4120)*
Innotech Metal Designs LLC ....F...... 360 393-4108
  Bellingham *(G-1378)*
▲ Interntonal Hearth Melting LLC ....D...... 509 371-2500
  Richland *(G-9011)*
◆ Jfc Holding Corporation ....E...... 206 762-1100
  Tukwila *(G-13757)*
◆ Jorgensen Forge Corporation ....C...... 206 762-1100
  Tukwila *(G-13759)*
Lister Chain and Forge Inc ....E...... 360 332-4323
  Blaine *(G-1680)*
Peregrine Manufacturing Inc ....G...... 425 673-5600
  Lynnwood *(G-6179)*
Snohomish Iron Works Inc ....G...... 360 568-2811
  Snohomish *(G-11982)*
Star Forge LLC ....C...... 206 762-1100
  Tukwila *(G-13821)*
Sygnet Rail Technologies LLC ....G...... 360 264-8211
  Tenino *(G-13625)*
Timber Iron Erectors ....G...... 360 681-8611
  Sequim *(G-11666)*
TNT Horseshoe Art ....G...... 253 334-7653
  Algona *(G-78)*
Washington State Horseshoe Pit ....G...... 253 735-0213
  Auburn *(G-593)*

Employee Codes: A=Over 500 employees, B=251-500
C=101-250, D=51-100, E=20-50, F=10-19, G=2-9

3463 Nonferrous Forgings

Fix Brothers Inc..........G....... 206 246-5127
Seattle *(G-10002)*
GE Steam Power Inc..........G....... 860 688-1911
Redmond *(G-8470)*
Hayward Gordon Us Inc..........G....... 206 767-5660
Seattle *(G-10153)*
Star Forge LLC..........C....... 206 762-1100
Tukwila *(G-13821)*

3465 Automotive Stampings

▲ A-Star Distributing Inc..........F....... 509 467-6809
Spokane *(G-12091)*
▲ Billy Bob Customs..........G....... 360 637-9147
Elma *(G-3242)*
◆ Capital Industries Inc..........D....... 206 762-8585
Seattle *(G-9624)*
Carburetors Unlimited Inc..........G....... 253 833-4106
Auburn *(G-401)*
Genuine Parts Company..........F....... 509 484-4400
Spokane *(G-12269)*
Hard Notched Customs LLC..........F....... 360 205-3252
Vancouver *(G-14281)*
▼ J R Setina Manufacturing Co..........D....... 360 491-6197
Olympia *(G-7310)*
Joe Constance..........F....... 425 347-8920
Everett *(G-3524)*
Kryki Sports..........G....... 206 660-7359
Seattle *(G-10360)*
Proliance International..........G....... 206 764-7028
Seattle *(G-10875)*
R & A Manufacturing Inc..........G....... 425 228-2109
Renton *(G-8888)*
▲ Shoot Suit Inc..........G....... 360 687-3451
Battle Ground *(G-739)*
T-Zero Racing Inc..........G....... 425 222-5800
Issaquah *(G-4484)*
Zhongtao..........G....... 425 344-9373
Kirkland *(G-5501)*

3469 Metal Stampings, NEC

Arlenes Kitchen..........G....... 208 254-0591
Sequim *(G-11612)*
B & S Enterprises..........G....... 253 859-3605
Auburn *(G-387)*
Battle Ground Auto License..........G....... 360 687-5115
Battle Ground *(G-691)*
Buyken Metal Products Inc..........E....... 253 852-0634
Kent *(G-4827)*
Camano Island Licensing..........F....... 360 387-4700
Stanwood *(G-12954)*
Camas Auto License..........G....... 360 835-2977
Camas *(G-2236)*
◆ Capital Industries Inc..........D....... 206 762-8585
Seattle *(G-9624)*
Coastal Manufacturing Inc..........E....... 425 407-0624
Everett *(G-3421)*
Custom Metal Spinning LLC..........G....... 206 762-2707
Seattle *(G-9768)*
D S Fabrication & Design Inc..........G....... 360 210-7526
Washougal *(G-14951)*
Defensive Driving School Inc..........G....... 425 643-0116
Kirkland *(G-5320)*
Drivers License Examining..........G....... 253 872-2782
Kent *(G-4878)*
Dylan Manufacturing Inc..........F....... 253 333-8260
Auburn *(G-430)*
Fifes Vehicle Vessel..........G....... 253 926-8227
Fife *(G-3952)*
Foil Graphics..........G....... 360 574-9030
Vancouver *(G-14236)*
Gillaspie Manufacturing Inc..........F....... 360 260-1975
Vancouver *(G-14252)*
Glenns Welding and Mfg Inc..........E....... 425 743-2226
Lynnwood *(G-6131)*
▲ Gompf Brackets Inc..........F....... 425 348-5002
Mukilteo *(G-6929)*
Graphic Impressions Inc..........E....... 253 872-0555
Kent *(G-4925)*
Gundersons Auto License..........G....... 360 695-2122
Vancouver *(G-14276)*
▲ H C U Inc..........G....... 425 885-0564
Redmond *(G-8486)*
Hawkbird Auto An Boat Listing..........G....... 360 491-3015
Lacey *(G-5554)*
High-Tech Mfg Svcs Inc..........F....... 360 696-1611
Vancouver *(G-14296)*
Hill Aerosystems Inc..........D....... 360 802-8300
Enumclaw *(G-3293)*
Hwy 99 Auto License..........G....... 360 573-6226
Vancouver *(G-14305)*
Imaginetics Holdings LLC..........G....... 253 735-0156
Auburn *(G-472)*
Imaginetics LLC..........D....... 253 735-0156
Auburn *(G-473)*
▲ Industrial Revolution Inc..........E....... 425 285-1111
Tukwila *(G-13752)*
Lasting Memories..........G....... 509 548-6393
Leavenworth *(G-5809)*
Liedtke Tool and Gage Inc..........G....... 360 694-9573
Vancouver *(G-14373)*
Lumpinee Inc..........F....... 425 497-8383
Redmond *(G-8540)*
Marine Diesel Inc..........G....... 206 767-9594
Seattle *(G-10479)*
Middco Tool & Equipment Inc..........F....... 509 535-1701
Spokane Valley *(G-12789)*
N2 Storage Systems Inc..........G....... 509 981-8097
Mead *(G-6434)*
New Star Technology Inc..........G....... 425 350-7611
Monroe *(G-6601)*
Northwest Marine Tech Inc..........E....... 360 468-3375
Shaw Island *(G-11671)*
Northwest Metal Spinning..........G....... 253 351-8489
Auburn *(G-512)*
Northwest Precision Tool Inc..........G....... 509 493-4044
White Salmon *(G-15125)*
Precision Spring Stamping Corp..........E....... 253 852-6911
Kent *(G-5078)*
Premier Stainless Installers..........G....... 253 370-0521
Puyallup *(G-8224)*
Quality Metal Spinning Co..........G....... 206 242-6751
Seatac *(G-9302)*
Quality On Time Machining Inc..........G....... 360 802-3700
Enumclaw *(G-3314)*
Raad Industries LLC..........E....... 509 663-8352
Wenatchee *(G-15067)*
Skagit Vehicle Licensing Inc..........G....... 360 755-0419
Burlington *(G-2190)*
Sound Spring Inc..........F....... 253 859-9499
Kent *(G-5142)*
Swift Machining Inc..........G....... 360 335-8213
Washougal *(G-14990)*
Vehicle Licensing..........G....... 360 336-9348
Mount Vernon *(G-6852)*
Whitefab..........G....... 253 277-4047
Kent *(G-5216)*

3471 Electroplating, Plating, Polishing, Anodizing & Coloring

A&B Quality Finishers Inc..........G....... 360 805-3500
Snohomish *(G-11868)*
Alloy Polishing Co..........G....... 360 736-2716
Centralia *(G-2382)*
Almet Metal Refinishing..........G....... 206 234-8555
Fall City *(G-3699)*
American Plating..........G....... 360 736-0052
Centralia *(G-2383)*
American Powder Works..........G....... 360 220-3104
Lynnwood *(G-6074)*
Ameristar 124..........G....... 509 783-7518
Kennewick *(G-4616)*
Apex Finishing LLC..........G....... 425 334-6281
Lake Stevens *(G-5632)*
Applied Finishing Inc..........E....... 425 513-2505
Mukilteo *(G-6893)*
Art Brass Aerospace Finshg Inc..........G....... 206 209-3010
Seattle *(G-9435)*
Art Brass Plating Inc..........D....... 206 767-4443
Seattle *(G-9436)*
Artisan Finishing Systems Inc..........G....... 360 658-0686
Marysville *(G-6313)*
▲ Asko Processing Inc..........F....... 206 634-2080
Seattle *(G-9444)*
Asko Processing Inc..........G....... 206 298-9730
Mukilteo *(G-6896)*
Blue Streak Finishers LLC..........D....... 425 347-1944
Everett *(G-3392)*
Bluerose Processing..........G....... 360 281-7371
Vancouver *(G-14070)*
Carl Zapffe Inc..........G....... 206 364-1919
Seattle *(G-9633)*
Complete Deburr Inc..........F....... 253 887-0997
Auburn *(G-411)*
Crown Plating Inc..........G....... 360 693-3040
Vancouver *(G-14155)*
D G Hard Surface LLC..........G....... 206 718-4700
Bellevue *(G-873)*
DCI Metal Finishing LLC..........F....... 425 347-7776
Everett *(G-3441)*
Denise Mayward..........G....... 253 927-0219
Tacoma *(G-13259)*
Design Hardwood Products Inc..........F....... 425 869-0859
Redmond *(G-8439)*
Diamond Polishing Systems..........G....... 253 770-0508
Puyallup *(G-8144)*
Dlm Inc..........F....... 425 348-3204
Mukilteo *(G-6915)*
Electrofinishing Inc..........G....... 253 850-0540
Kent *(G-4888)*
Fc Plating Inc..........G....... 360 679-4665
Oak Harbor *(G-7151)*
Finishing Unlimited Inc..........G....... 425 881-7300
Redmond *(G-8461)*
Friedman Slversmiths Repr Pltg..........G....... 360 752-3119
Bellingham *(G-1354)*
Gamblin Enterprises Inc..........G....... 206 795-3817
Lynnwood *(G-6125)*
Gold Plating Specialist..........G....... 509 582-3430
Kennewick *(G-4668)*
Harrys Radiator Shop Inc..........G....... 509 765-8581
Moses Lake *(G-6713)*
Hytek Finishes Co..........C....... 253 872-7160
Kent *(G-4947)*
Inland Empire Plating Inc..........F....... 509 535-1704
Spokane Valley *(G-12743)*
Ketchum Metal Polishing..........G....... 360 403-8726
Arlington *(G-265)*
▲ Magnetic Penetrant Svcs Co Inc..........D....... 206 762-5855
Seattle *(G-10466)*
Marble Plsg Stone Rstrtion LLC..........G....... 425 564-8284
Federal Way *(G-3755)*
Mastercraft Metal Finishing..........G....... 206 622-6380
Seattle *(G-10498)*
Metal Finishing Inc..........F....... 360 659-1971
Arlington *(G-274)*
Novation Inc..........E....... 509 922-1912
Spokane Valley *(G-12812)*
Omega Silversmithing Inc..........G....... 360 863-6771
Snohomish *(G-11956)*
Pacific NW Plating Inc..........F....... 360 735-9000
Vancouver *(G-14468)*
Pacific NW Powdr Coating..........F....... 509 535-9950
Spokane *(G-12426)*
Pacmet..........G....... 253 854-4241
Kent *(G-5058)*
Pioneer Human Services..........C....... 206 762-7737
Seattle *(G-10810)*
PM Testing Laboratory Inc..........D....... 253 922-1321
Fife *(G-3981)*
Powder Coating Inc..........G....... 425 743-4393
Mukilteo *(G-6967)*
Powder Vision Inc..........G....... 425 222-6363
Preston *(G-8026)*
Pro Finish Inc..........G....... 253 850-9422
Kent *(G-5083)*
◆ Production Plating Inc..........D....... 425 347-4635
Mukilteo *(G-6968)*
Proflections Metal Polishing..........G....... 253 735-6111
Auburn *(G-539)*
Quality Polishing and Plating..........G....... 425 432-5500
Renton *(G-8887)*
Queen City Plating Company Inc..........G....... 425 315-1992
Mukilteo *(G-6970)*
Repair Technology Inc..........F....... 206 762-6221
Seattle *(G-10948)*
Schoeben & Schoeben Inc..........E....... 360 794-1945
Monroe *(G-6616)*
Show Quality Metal Finish..........G....... 206 762-6717
Seatac *(G-9304)*
Show Quality Metal Finishing..........G....... 206 762-6717
Seatac *(G-9305)*
Skyline NW Inc A Wash Cor..........G....... 360 695-6006
Vancouver *(G-14592)*
Smith Chrome Plating Inc..........G....... 509 525-0993
Walla Walla *(G-14870)*
Spokane Galvanizing Inc..........E....... 509 244-4073
Airway Heights *(G-65)*
Triangle Wellness LLC..........G....... 727 773-0054
Sequim *(G-11667)*
▼ Universal Brass Inc..........F....... 253 939-8282
Auburn *(G-589)*
Valence Surface Tech LLC..........C....... 206 762-5855
Seattle *(G-11398)*

3479 Coating & Engraving, NEC

2h Protective Coatings Inc..........G....... 425 346-3306
Lynnwood *(G-6062)*

SIC SECTION 34 FABRICATED METAL PRODUCTS, EXCEPT MACHINERY AND TRANSPORTATION EQUIPMENT

A & S Powder Coating .... G 360 880-2487
Chehalis ***(G-2456)***
Abel Flamespray .... G 360 925-6125
Arlington ***(G-190)***
Ace Galvanizing Inc .... E 206 762-0330
Seattle ***(G-9340)***
▲ Acu-Line Corporation .... G 206 634-1618
Seattle ***(G-9347)***
Advanced Coating Solutions LLC .... G 425 785-0902
Kirkland ***(G-5270)***
Advanced Powder Coating NW .... G 360 398-1460
Bellingham ***(G-1240)***
Advanced Prtctive Coatings LLC .... G 425 818-2820
Kirkland ***(G-5271)***
Alr Specialty Coatings LLC .... G 206 713-2070
Monroe ***(G-6546)***
Ameron International Corp .... C 509 547-3689
Pasco ***(G-7552)***
Apex Industries Inc .... D 509 928-8450
Spokane Valley ***(G-12621)***
Applied Finishing Inc .... E 425 513-2505
Mukilteo ***(G-6893)***
Armor Performance Coating LLC .... G 509 551-1294
Richland ***(G-8967)***
Artisan Finishing Systems Inc .... G 360 658-0686
Marysville ***(G-6313)***
▲ Asko Processing Inc .... F 206 634-2080
Seattle ***(G-9444)***
Awards N More Usa Inc .... G 360 577-3646
Longview ***(G-5886)***
▲ Barrons Specialty Coatings LLC .... G 253 939-2601
Auburn ***(G-389)***
Bay Trophies & Engraving Inc .... G 360 676-0868
Bellingham ***(G-1261)***
Bear Creek Coatings LLC .... G 253 722-4220
Gig Harbor ***(G-4077)***
◆ Biec International Inc .... G 360 750-5791
Vancouver ***(G-14065)***
Black River Seal Coating Wesle .... G 509 836-0125
Sunnyside ***(G-13114)***
Blue Streak Finishers LLC .... D 425 347-1944
Everett ***(G-3392)***
Bowmans Electro Painting .... G 360 668-1389
Snohomish ***(G-11880)***
Bullhide Liner Corp .... G 509 532-9007
Spokane Valley ***(G-12647)***
C and R Coatings LLC .... G 509 949-8515
Moxee ***(G-6876)***
California Coating .... G 609 405-2683
Battle Ground ***(G-694)***
Can AM Coatings .... G 360 386-9692
Marysville ***(G-6320)***
Carls Powder Coating .... G 425 864-7950
North Bend ***(G-7104)***
Cascade Powder Coating LLC .... G 509 663-9080
Wenatchee ***(G-15015)***
Coastal Manufacturing Inc .... E 425 407-0624
Everett ***(G-3421)***
Cobalt Investments LLC .... G 360 691-2298
Granite Falls ***(G-4268)***
Contour Coatings LLC .... G 253 830-4994
Tacoma ***(G-13241)***
Craftwork Coatings .... G 253 508-9358
Puyallup ***(G-8138)***
Critchlow Custom Coatings LLC .... G 253 651-9675
University Place ***(G-13965)***
Cutting Edge Engraving Inc .... G 360 863-2184
Monroe ***(G-6563)***
D & R Quality Coatings Inc .... G 253 209-5441
Orting ***(G-7478)***
Deans Mean Prfmce Coatings .... G 509 406-4713
Yakima ***(G-15552)***
Dimensional Imaging Inc .... G 206 285-0450
Seattle ***(G-9830)***
Diversified Coatings LLC .... G 360 264-2099
Tenino ***(G-13617)***
Dm Coating LLC .... G 509 420-0961
Pasco ***(G-7578)***
DOE Run Studios .... G 360 765-0935
Quilcene ***(G-8282)***
Doug House Powder Coating .... G 360 681-5412
Sequim ***(G-11629)***
Dut Protective Coatings I .... G 253 520-3374
Kent ***(G-4880)***
Dynamic Coatings LLC .... G 360 755-3649
Anacortes ***(G-124)***
▲ Ecolite Manufacturing Co .... D 509 922-8888
Spokane Valley ***(G-12687)***
Eleanor Wiley .... G 360 698-5077
Port Orchard ***(G-7807)***
Electronic Coating Tech Inc .... G 425 265-2212
Everett ***(G-3457)***
Emerald Galvanizing Inc .... G 206 782-8300
Seattle ***(G-9912)***
Endurance Coatings LLC .... G 206 234-8793
Snohomish ***(G-11905)***
Enlighting Struck Design LLC .... G 206 229-9438
Kent ***(G-4893)***
Extreme Indus Coatings LLC .... G 509 991-1773
Airway Heights ***(G-51)***
Farwest Operating LLC .... D 509 453-1663
Moxee ***(G-6878)***
Feller Custom Coatings .... G 360 551-2045
Lakewood ***(G-5722)***
Finishing Specialist LLC .... G 509 248-5510
Union Gap ***(G-13930)***
Flamespray Northwest Inc .... F 206 508-6779
Seattle ***(G-10004)***
Forever Powder Coating LLC .... G 360 786-6345
Tumwater ***(G-13872)***
Fox Coatings .... G 360 574-7471
Vancouver ***(G-14238)***
Franks Custom Coatings LLC .... G 253 973-4361
Puyallup ***(G-8154)***
GM Nameplate Inc .... C 206 284-2201
Seattle ***(G-10090)***
Harrington Trophies .... G 509 943-2593
Richland ***(G-9005)***
Hunnicutts Truck Shop Inc .... G 360 734-9859
Bellingham ***(G-1375)***
I-90 Express Finishing Inc .... E 509 922-2297
Spokane Valley ***(G-12736)***
Imsa Steel Corp .... B 360 673-8200
Kalama ***(G-4501)***
Industrial Coatings .... G 425 742-3415
Lynnwood ***(G-6137)***
Integrity First Coatings LLC .... G 509 619-9983
Pasco ***(G-7592)***
J and T Prtective Coatings LLC .... G 206 498-6147
Seattle ***(G-10266)***
J T Coatings Inc .... G 509 944-1669
Pasco ***(G-7594)***
Jacobs Ladder Painting Inc .... G 425 754-3202
Lake Stevens ***(G-5651)***
Jet City Partners LLC .... G 206 999-0047
Auburn ***(G-479)***
Kens Powder Coating .... G 253 539-5845
Tacoma ***(G-13375)***
Kings of Coatings Inc .... G 360 721-0636
Vancouver ***(G-14350)***
Kitsap Coatings .... G 360 550-3777
Bremerton ***(G-1968)***
Kitsap Custom Coatings LLC .... G 360 471-3095
Silverdale ***(G-11842)***
Kitsap Custom Coatings LLC .... G 360 471-3095
Bremerton ***(G-1969)***
Kitsap Powder Coating LLC .... G 360 297-0015
Poulsbo ***(G-7971)***
Krysaliis LLC .... G 888 579-7254
Blaine ***(G-1679)***
▲ Lazer Trends LLC .... G 253 886-5600
Auburn ***(G-487)***
M & M Coatings Inc .... G 360 480-6425
Yelm ***(G-15739)***
M S I Engineering Corporation .... F 425 827-6797
Kirkland ***(G-5390)***
Mad Custom Coating .... G 360 621-6525
Poulsbo ***(G-7980)***
▲ Magnetic Penetrant Svcs Co Inc .... D 206 762-5855
Seattle ***(G-10466)***
Marysville Awards Inc .... G 360 653-4811
Marysville ***(G-6356)***
Metal Finishing Inc .... F 360 659-1971
Arlington ***(G-274)***
Meticulous Coating Applicators .... G 206 251-3684
Everett ***(G-3547)***
Metron Powdercoating Inc .... G 509 766-1278
Moses Lake ***(G-6725)***
Mr TS Trophies .... G 360 424-9339
Mount Vernon ***(G-6815)***
Multi App Coatings LLC .... G 253 841-1256
Puyallup ***(G-8196)***
No Graf Network Inc .... G 509 531-1334
Kennewick ***(G-4703)***
North PCF Indus Coatings LLC .... G 907 865-8400
Renton ***(G-8859)***
North West Coating & Svcs LLC .... G 360 649-1548
Port Orchard ***(G-7834)***
Olympia Powder Coat .... G 360 570-9100
Olympia ***(G-7353)***
Omnifab Inc .... E 253 931-5151
Auburn ***(G-518)***
Pacific NW Powdr Coating .... F 509 535-9950
Spokane ***(G-12426)***
Pacific Performance Coatings .... G 425 339-5528
Everett ***(G-3565)***
Pacific Powder Coating Inc .... G 360 383-9100
Ferndale ***(G-3882)***
Pats Blue Ribbons & Trophies .... F 360 676-8292
Ferndale ***(G-3884)***
Perfection Powder Coating & FA .... G 253 875-0010
Puyallup ***(G-8221)***
Performance Coatings Inc .... G 253 735-1919
Auburn ***(G-531)***
Pesani Genuine Coatings LLC .... G 509 860-3426
Wenatchee ***(G-15061)***
Powder Coating Inc .... G 425 743-4393
Mukilteo ***(G-6967)***
Powder Vision Inc .... G 425 222-6363
Preston ***(G-8026)***
Powder-Fab Inc .... E 360 435-0793
Arlington ***(G-303)***
Powdertech Inc .... G 509 927-0189
Spokane Valley ***(G-12833)***
Powdertech Mr Shannon .... F 509 927-5804
Spokane Valley ***(G-12834)***
◆ Production Plating Inc .... D 425 347-4635
Mukilteo ***(G-6968)***
Protective Coating Consultants .... G 206 762-6119
Seattle ***(G-10876)***
Protek-USA LLC .... G 206 782-8399
Seattle ***(G-10877)***
Puget Sound Qulty Coatings LLC .... G 253 861-8871
Fife ***(G-3985)***
R and Dee Coatings LLC .... G 509 771-1111
Moses Lake ***(G-6740)***
Richard Saunders .... G 612 861-1061
Seattle ***(G-10962)***
Richardson Coatings LLC .... G 253 861-7611
Morton ***(G-6672)***
Ries Productions LLC .... G 360 627-8795
Bremerton ***(G-1994)***
RMC Incorporated .... E 206 243-4831
Seattle ***(G-10969)***
Rocky Prairie Engraving .... G 360 264-2188
Tenino ***(G-13622)***
Ryan Custom Coatings .... G 808 652-9731
Wenatchee ***(G-15070)***
Sanctuary Corporation .... G 360 477-4384
Port Angeles ***(G-7743)***
Savage Gun Coating .... G 206 485-4125
Kenmore ***(G-4603)***
Schmid Family Engraving LLC .... G 360 491-0997
Olympia ***(G-7392)***
Scott Galvanizing Co Inc .... F 206 783-3100
Arlington ***(G-320)***
Seattle Galvanizing Co Inc .... E 206 783-3100
Arlington ***(G-322)***
Shannon D Agnew .... G 509 926-6209
Spokane Valley ***(G-12869)***
Sitec Coatings .... G 360 840-9979
Lynnwood ***(G-6198)***
Skagit Powder Coating .... G 360 428-0413
Mount Vernon ***(G-6839)***
Skills Inc .... D 206 782-6000
Auburn ***(G-565)***
Solar Guard Coatings Inc .... G 425 413-0545
Maple Valley ***(G-6293)***
Specht Coatings .... G 253 732-5662
Graham ***(G-4239)***
Spokane Galvanizing Inc .... E 509 244-4073
Airway Heights ***(G-65)***
Start 2 Finish Coatings Inc .... G 509 481-8898
Otis Orchards ***(G-7518)***
Steel Painters Inc .... E 360 425-7720
Kelso ***(G-4551)***
▲ Steelscape LLC .... C 360 673-8200
Kalama ***(G-4509)***
Steelscape LLC .... C 360 673-8200
Kalama ***(G-4510)***
Steelscape Washington LLC .... C 360 673-8200
Kalama ***(G-4511)***
Superior Coatings .... G 253 405-5424
Sumner ***(G-13104)***
Terrashield Coatings Ltd .... G 206 992-2157
Seattle ***(G-11281)***
Triad Coatings Corp .... G 253 537-4464
Tacoma ***(G-13562)***
U Deck It Inc .... G 509 532-9007
Spokane Valley ***(G-12917)***

S I C

▼ **Universal Brass Inc** F 253 939-8282
Auburn *(G-589)*
Universal Coatings LLC G 360 936-2855
Shelton *(G-11748)*
Valence Surface Tech LLC C 206 762-5855
Seattle *(G-11398)*
Vivasource Inc E 253 627-3853
Tacoma *(G-13583)*
Wise Choice Custom Coatings G 360 326-3809
Vancouver *(G-14696)*
Woolman Coatings LLC G 206 402-2960
Snohomish *(G-12000)*

3482 Small Arms Ammunition

Eco Cartridge Store G 425 820-3570
Kirkland *(G-5329)*

3483 Ammunition, Large

Chiwawa Mines Inc G 509 455-8080
Spokane *(G-12180)*
Slapshot USA Ltd Liability Co G 360 560-0245
Longview *(G-5954)*

3484 Small Arms

▼ **Aero Precision LLC** E 253 272-8188
Tacoma *(G-13158)*
Blood Eagle Weaponry LLC G 360 929-9567
Oak Harbor *(G-7142)*
Bullet Hole LLC G 509 868-8884
Spokane Valley *(G-12646)*
Crt Less Lethal G 425 337-6875
Snohomish *(G-11893)*
Dayton Traister Co Inc G 360 675-3421
Oak Harbor *(G-7147)*
Defense Sales Intl LLC G 206 999-8684
Renton *(G-8782)*
Go Planit LLC G 206 227-0660
Mattawa *(G-6407)*
Hamilton Equipment G 509 775-3445
Republic *(G-8958)*
Hardened Arms LLC E 425 530-0837
Friday Harbor *(G-4050)*
Jones Arms LLC G 360 681-0511
Sequim *(G-11644)*
L E Wilson Inc G 509 782-1328
Cashmere *(G-2324)*
Lionheart Industries LLC G 888 552-4743
Renton *(G-8845)*
Modular Driven Tech Inc F 604 393-0800
Sumas *(G-13049)*
Okanogan Arms Co LLC G 509 422-4123
Okanogan *(G-7202)*
Olympic Arms Inc D 360 456-3471
Olympia *(G-7356)*
Ortwein International G 503 313-0514
Vancouver *(G-14458)*
▲ **Sims Vibration Laboratory Inc** D 360 427-6031
Shelton *(G-11735)*
Tech Heavy Industries Inc G 509 557-8492
Riverside *(G-9127)*
Wynakos Machine Inc G 360 794-9057
Monroe *(G-6640)*

3489 Ordnance & Access, NEC

Constantine Armory LLC G 509 998-6959
Spokane *(G-12198)*
▲ **Jr Moore** G 360 607-6128
Vancouver *(G-14342)*
N C I Inc G 360 225-9701
Woodland *(G-15449)*
Spec Tech Industries Inc G 360 303-9077
Maple Falls *(G-6251)*
X Products LLC E 971 302-6127
Vancouver *(G-14701)*

3491 Industrial Valves

Accor Technology Inc E 509 662-0608
Wenatchee *(G-15007)*
▲ **B2r Partners Inc** E 360 225-1230
Woodland *(G-15419)*
Centurion Process LLC G 509 759-3001
Selah *(G-11584)*
▲ **Fabricast Valve LLC** F 360 425-0306
Longview *(G-5910)*
▲ **Flow Control Industries Inc** E 425 483-1297
Woodinville *(G-15243)*
Henry Pratt Company LLC G 360 225-1230
Woodland *(G-15440)*
Hilton Acquisition Company LLC F 425 883-7000
Redmond *(G-8494)*
Industrial Pipe and Valve G 360 314-6492
Vancouver *(G-14313)*
Joyson Safety Systems C 509 762-5549
Moses Lake *(G-6718)*
Kilomters To Miles Speedo Exch G 253 872-3839
Kent *(G-4976)*
Michael Chapman G 425 881-0907
Redmond *(G-8556)*
Paramount Supply Co G 360 647-8328
Bellingham *(G-1489)*
Pegler Automation Inc G 503 329-5377
Vancouver *(G-14483)*
Romac Industries Inc D 425 951-6200
Sultan *(G-13034)*
Taurman Distributing & Mfg G 360 330-5886
Centralia *(G-2437)*
Total Home Control G 509 628-1673
Richland *(G-9046)*
Tri-TEC Manufacturing LLC E 425 251-8777
Kent *(G-5190)*

3492 Fluid Power Valves & Hose Fittings

Bridgestone Hosepower LLC E 206 767-4670
Seattle *(G-9585)*
Central Hose and Fittings Inc F 509 547-6460
Pasco *(G-7558)*
Custom Hydraulic & Machine Inc F 253 854-4666
Kent *(G-4868)*
▲ **Hd International Corp** G 503 997-9325
Vancouver *(G-14290)*
Hose Pro G 253 448-1304
Puyallup *(G-8162)*
Hose Shop Inc G 360 757-3776
Burlington *(G-2165)*
Kaman Fluid Power LLC G 253 922-5710
Tacoma *(G-13372)*
Kaman Fluid Power LLC G 360 738-1264
Bellingham *(G-1390)*
Northwest Dynamics Inc G 360 253-3656
Vancouver *(G-14434)*
RJ Hydraulics Inc F 360 693-4399
Vancouver *(G-14553)*
Select Fluid Power USA Inc G 604 343-1111
Tukwila *(G-13816)*
▲ **Spokane House of Hose Inc** E 509 535-3638
Spokane Valley *(G-12883)*

3493 Steel Springs, Except Wire

Pohl Spring Works Inc F 509 466-0904
Spokane Valley *(G-12831)*
Sound Spring Inc F 253 859-9499
Kent *(G-5142)*

3494 Valves & Pipe Fittings, NEC

Accor Technology Inc E 509 662-0608
East Wenatchee *(G-3006)*
Accor Technology Inc E 425 453-5410
Kirkland *(G-5268)*
Accor Technology Inc E 509 662-0608
Wenatchee *(G-15007)*
Aquatronix LLC G 425 881-8600
Redmond *(G-8383)*
Bridgestone Hosepower LLC E 206 767-4670
Seattle *(G-9585)*
C & E Sprinkler G 509 466-2020
Mead *(G-6426)*
Ferguson G 206 767-7700
Auburn *(G-440)*
Go Planit LLC G 206 227-0660
Mattawa *(G-6407)*
Idex Health & Science LLC C 360 679-2528
Oak Harbor *(G-7153)*
Instrument & Valve Services Co E 360 366-3645
Ferndale *(G-3858)*
◆ **Nelson Irrigation Corporation** C 509 525-7660
Walla Walla *(G-14850)*
◆ **Romac Industries Inc** C 425 951-6200
Bothell *(G-1897)*
Romac Industries Inc D 425 951-6200
Sultan *(G-13034)*
Specified Fittings LLC G 360 398-7700
Bellingham *(G-1550)*

3495 Wire Springs

◆ **Airborne Ecs LLC** F 319 538-1051
Port Angeles *(G-7679)*
Sound Spring Inc F 253 859-9499
Kent *(G-5142)*

3496 Misc Fabricated Wire Prdts

Ammeraal Beltech Inc F 510 352-3770
Kent *(G-4781)*
Cascade Wire Works LLC G 360 904-4412
Vancouver *(G-14107)*
CMC Steel Fabricators Inc G 253 833-9060
Auburn *(G-409)*
Columbia Rigging Corporation G 509 545-4657
Pasco *(G-7564)*
Cowlitz River Rigging Inc F 360 425-6720
Longview *(G-5903)*
David L Flink G 253 735-5417
Auburn *(G-423)*
Davis Wire Corporation F 253 872-8910
Kent *(G-4871)*
Donamo Co G 360 835-5634
Washougal *(G-14952)*
Dungeness Gear Works Inc E 800 548-9743
Arlington *(G-230)*
George Broom Sons Inc G 206 282-0800
Seattle *(G-10064)*
Iron Gate Shoppe G 360 791-3292
Enumclaw *(G-3294)*
J K Fabrication Inc G 206 297-7400
Seattle *(G-10270)*
▲ **J N W Inc** E 509 489-9191
Spokane *(G-12327)*
Lulabop Inc G 206 225-0049
Seattle *(G-10448)*
▲ **Majorwire Screen Media** D 253 327-1550
Fife *(G-3968)*
▲ **Mantec Services Inc** E 206 285-5656
Seattle *(G-10472)*
McKay Shrimp & Crab Gear Inc G 360 796-4555
Brinnon *(G-2025)*
Merchants Metals LLC E 253 531-5454
Tacoma *(G-13408)*
Munks Livestock Sling Mfg G 360 293-6581
Anacortes *(G-149)*
▲ **National Wirecraft Company Inc** F 360 424-1129
Mount Vernon *(G-6816)*
▲ **National Wirecraft Company Inc** F 360 424-1129
Mount Vernon *(G-6817)*
Neutek Inc G 206 660-0056
Lynnwood *(G-6169)*
Northwest Belt & Equipment Co G 360 533-7051
Aberdeen *(G-24)*
Pacific Wire Group Inc F 253 249-0249
Auburn *(G-525)*
Quality Fence Builders Inc E 253 939-8533
Auburn *(G-541)*
Silicon & Solar Mfg LLC F 360 703-0701
Longview *(G-5953)*
Smart Cable Company G 253 474-9967
Lakewood *(G-5756)*
Sound Spring Inc F 253 859-9499
Kent *(G-5142)*
Sustain Outdoors Inc G 949 439-4899
Bellevue *(G-1170)*
Twardus Iron & Wire Works Inc G 206 723-8234
Seattle *(G-11349)*
Western Group Pacific G 253 964-6201
Dupont *(G-2976)*

3497 Metal Foil & Leaf

Proto Technologies Inc D 509 891-4747
Liberty Lake *(G-5855)*
Tin Foil Hat Productions G 619 208-5469
Port Orchard *(G-7853)*
Western Foil Corporation G 206 624-3645
Seattle *(G-11452)*

3498 Fabricated Pipe & Pipe Fittings

▲ **Alaskan Copper Companies Inc** B 206 623-5800
Kent *(G-4768)*
Alaskan Copper Companies Inc G 206 623-5800
Seattle *(G-9367)*
Alaskan Copper Companies Inc E 206 623-5800
Kent *(G-4769)*
▲ **Alco Investment Company** C 206 623-5800
Kent *(G-4770)*
Arrow Manufacturing Inc G 253 236-4088
Auburn *(G-378)*
Centerline Fabricators LLC G 253 922-3226
Fife *(G-3941)*
Chinook Mechanical LLC G 360 947-9035
Vancouver *(G-14118)*

35 INDUSTRIAL AND COMMERCIAL MACHINERY AND COMPUTER EQUIPMENT

▲ Fluid Controls and Components .....F 253 922-3226
  Fife (G-3953)
Harris Acquisition IV LLC ....G...... 360 734-3600
  Bellingham (G-1366)
Harris Acquisition IV LLC ....G...... 360 734-3600
  Bellingham (G-1367)
Metal Meister Inc ....G...... 480 845-6717
  Valleyford (G-13998)
Northwest Pipe Company ....F 801 326-6044
  Vancouver (G-14437)
Off Road Addiction LLC ....G...... 509 999-7824
  Valleyford (G-13999)
Offshore Products Inc ....G...... 206 567-5404
  Edmonds (G-3140)
Stans Headers Inc ....F 253 854-5310
  Auburn (G-571)
Star Pipe LLC ....G...... 253 826-3950
  Sumner (G-13103)
Triad Products Corporation ....G...... 425 514-8363
  Everett (G-3636)
▲ University Swaging Corporation ....C...... 425 318-1965
  Bellevue (G-1208)

3499 Fabricated Metal Prdts, NEC

All CS Inc ....G...... 253 474-3434
  Tacoma (G-13163)
American Lifting Products Inc ....G...... 253 572-8981
  Tacoma (G-13168)
▲ Armstrong Magnetics Inc ....G...... 360 647-8438
  Bellingham (G-1252)
▲ Athletic Awards Company Inc ....G...... 206 624-3995
  Seattle (G-9452)
◆ Avista Corporation ....A...... 509 489-0500
  Spokane (G-12134)
Creative Motion Control Inc ....E...... 425 883-0100
  Woodinville (G-15215)
Creon LLC ....G...... 360 318-1559
  Lynden (G-6010)
Custom Fab ....G...... 360 466-1199
  La Conner (G-5523)
Custom Fabrication Tech LLC ....G...... 206 949-0212
  Maple Valley (G-6266)
Cut Above Enterprise Inc ....F 509 928-5091
  Spokane Valley (G-12674)
D&J Custom Metal Fabrication ....G...... 206 242-3238
  Burien (G-2101)
Dylan Manufacturing Inc ....G...... 253 333-8260
  Auburn (G-430)
E R Balaban Custom Fabrication ......G...... 206 883-5030
  Seattle (G-9866)
▲ Elite Frames Inc ....G...... 360 247-7300
  Amboy (G-91)
Evergreen Mch & Fabrication ....F 509 249-1141
  Yakima (G-15565)
Fabrictn Melton & Precision ....G...... 509 284-2620
  Tekoa (G-13611)
Fuze Create LLC ....G...... 425 212-8807
  Seattle (G-10043)
Garden Expressions ....G...... 360 403-9532
  Arlington (G-239)
Heavy Metal Fabrication ....G...... 509 493-2979
  White Salmon (G-15116)
Highlands Welding Repair Inc ....G...... 206 283-0080
  Seattle (G-10172)
Iron Rangers LLC ....G...... 509 891-9355
  Newman Lake (G-7047)
J Freitag Enterprises Inc ....G...... 509 453-4461
  Yakima (G-15595)
Legacy Creations ....G...... 206 286-1827
  Seattle (G-10399)
Marchant Ladders Inc ....G...... 509 882-1912
  Grandview (G-4252)
Mark S Vorobik ....G...... 360 766-6252
  Bow (G-1931)
Married To Metal ....G...... 206 244-2238
  Pacific (G-7531)
Metal Werks Inc ....F 360 651-0300
  Marysville (G-6359)
Metalistics Inc ....G...... 425 348-9377
  Everett (G-3546)
N E S Enterprises ....G...... 509 928-9151
  Spokane Valley (G-12798)
Nipr LLC ....G...... 253 261-6840
  Enumclaw (G-3310)
Northwest Creations ....G...... 253 709-4504
  Kent (G-5030)
Olympic Instruments Inc ....F 206 463-3604
  Vashon (G-14739)
▼ Origami Inc ....G...... 206 784-9133
  Seattle (G-10714)

Pivot Custom Metal Fabrication ....G...... 206 762-3755
  Seattle (G-10815)
Quadradyne Technologies LLC ....G...... 248 342-5977
  Brush Prairie (G-2040)
Ralph A Parise ....G...... 360 387-1794
  Camano Island (G-2223)
Rory Thurrott ....G...... 206 941-7297
  Bainbridge Island (G-668)
SA Consumer Products Inc ....G...... 888 792-4264
  Fife (G-3990)
◆ Safs Inc ....G...... 253 301-0615
  Tacoma (G-13506)
Samson Sports LLC ....F 360 833-2507
  Camas (G-2280)
Spraying Systems Co ....G...... 425 357-6327
  Everett (G-3619)
Steel Fab Inc ....E...... 425 743-9216
  Arlington (G-333)
Tacoma Fabrication LLC ....G...... 253 303-1143
  Tacoma (G-13541)
Ten Talents USA ....G...... 360 256-2847
  Vancouver (G-14630)
Thirtnspades Metal Fabrication ....G...... 425 831-6126
  North Bend (G-7128)
▲ Tipke Manufacturing Company ......E...... 509 534-5336
  Spokane (G-12559)
Tough Outdoor Products LLC ....F 509 621-0034
  Otis Orchards (G-7519)
▲ Tracker Safe LLC ....G...... 360 213-0363
  Vancouver (G-14643)
▼ Universal Brass Inc ....F 253 939-8282
  Auburn (G-589)
Valley Steel & Stone ....G...... 360 378-5758
  Friday Harbor (G-4063)
West Coast Fabrication Inc ....G...... 206 790-1496
  Auburn (G-598)
Winter Mattias ....G...... 206 579-5275
  Monroe (G-6638)

35 INDUSTRIAL AND COMMERCIAL MACHINERY AND COMPUTER EQUIPMENT

3511 Steam, Gas & Hydraulic Turbines & Engines

Airclean Technologies Inc ....F 206 860-4930
  Seattle (G-9360)
Dresser-Rand Company ....F 206 762-7660
  Seattle (G-9855)
◆ Energy Northwest ....G...... 509 585-3677
  Kennewick (G-4661)
General Electric Company ....G...... 253 351-2200
  Auburn (G-448)
Hej LLC ....G...... 425 652-9183
  Seattle (G-10161)
Hydrobee Spc ....G...... 206 491-0945
  Seattle (G-10197)
Opi Wind Technologies Inc ....G...... 206 999-5373
  Seattle (G-10706)
Siemens Gmesa Rnwble Enrgy Inc ...G...... 509 896-5246
  Roosevelt (G-9153)
Steam Engine Metal Art ....G...... 509 302-9941
  Pasco (G-7634)
Supercritical Technologies ....G...... 518 225-3275
  Bremerton (G-2005)
Teladaq LLC ....G...... 661 373-1168
  Everson (G-3691)
Vestas-American Wind Tech Inc ....F 509 382-1800
  Dayton (G-2889)
Windward Ways II LLC ....G...... 206 364-5236
  Seattle (G-11483)

3519 Internal Combustion Engines, NEC

◆ Ade Holding Inc ....D...... 206 789-3600
  Seattle (G-9350)
ADI Thermal Power Corp ....G...... 206 484-2879
  Woodinville (G-15171)
Austin Resources LLC ....E...... 253 472-1703
  Tacoma (G-13185)
Cummins - Allison Corp ....G...... 206 763-3900
  Tukwila (G-13721)
Cummins Inc ....G...... 425 277-5342
  Sumner (G-13062)
Cummins Inc ....G...... 541 276-2561
  Pasco (G-7573)
Cummins Inc ....E...... 509 455-4411
  Spokane (G-12211)

Cummins Inc ....F 509 248-9033
  Yakima (G-15545)
Cummins Inc ....E...... 360 748-8841
  Tumwater (G-13867)
Defbooty LLC ....G...... 800 311-5887
  Chehalis (G-2488)
Eds Automotive and Machine Sp ......G...... 425 355-7268
  Mukilteo (G-6919)
Electrijet Flight Systems Inc ....G...... 509 990-9474
  Liberty Lake (G-5831)
▼ Energy Conversions Inc ....G...... 253 922-6670
  Fife (G-3951)
▲ Eriksen Diesel Repair Inc ....G...... 425 778-8237
  Edmonds (G-3110)
Fairbanks Morse LLC ....F 206 246-8133
  Seatac (G-9283)
◆ Hatch & Kirk Inc ....F 206 783-2766
  Seattle (G-10146)
Hydra-Com Inc ....G...... 253 862-9140
  Pacific (G-7529)
J & M Diesel Inc ....F 425 353-3050
  Lynnwood (G-6142)
Johnson Marine ....G...... 360 437-0467
  Port Ludlow (G-7768)
Man Diesel North America Inc ....G...... 253 479-6800
  Kent (G-5002)
May Mobile Marine Tech ....G...... 360 552-2561
  Port Orchard (G-7828)
Mobile Marine Maintenance ....G...... 360 777-0001
  Chinook (G-2617)
N C Power Systems Co ....C...... 425 251-5877
  Tukwila (G-13774)
◆ Northern Lights Inc ....D...... 206 789-3600
  Seattle (G-10632)
Pacific Power Group LLC ....D...... 360 887-5980
  Ridgefield (G-9100)
▲ Pacific Power Group LLC ....D...... 360 887-7400
  Vancouver (G-14469)
Sje Inc ....E...... 360 734-1910
  Bellingham (G-1540)
US Marine Chemists & Engrg ....G...... 206 200-6912
  Mukilteo (G-6986)
Walt Racing LLP ....G...... 253 847-8221
  Tacoma (G-13586)
Wave Engine Solutions Inc ....G...... 317 554-7201
  Camas (G-2288)
Yaculta Companies Inc ....B...... 360 887-7493
  Vancouver (G-14704)
Yorkston Oil Co ....F 360 734-2201
  Bellingham (G-1597)

3523 Farm Machinery & Eqpt

Adl Cattle Growers LLC ....G...... 509 765-0584
  Moses Lake (G-6678)
AG Engineering & Development ....F 509 582-8900
  Kennewick (G-4612)
AG Enterprise Supply Inc ....F 509 235-2006
  Cheney (G-2575)
Ag Spray Equipment Inc ....E...... 509 488-6631
  Othello (G-7490)
▲ AGCO ....G...... 253 964-2313
  Dupont (G-2954)
Agri-Trac Inc ....G...... 509 265-4327
  Mesa (G-6490)
All Pole Corporation ....F 360 933-1806
  Blaine (G-1658)
Anderson Machinery Inc ....G...... 509 964-2225
  Thorp (G-13626)
Asnw Inc ....F 509 297-4272
  Eltopia (G-3262)
Athletic Cases ....G...... 206 569-8677
  Seattle (G-9453)
Backwoods ....G...... 509 826-0758
  OMAK (G-7434)
Bills Welding & Machine Shop ....G...... 509 334-2222
  Pullman (G-8085)
Blueline Equipment Co LLC ....G...... 509 785-2595
  Quincy (G-8290)
Blueline Equipment Co LLC ....G...... 509 525-4550
  Walla Walla (G-14772)
Blueline Equipment Co LLC ....E...... 509 248-8411
  Moxee (G-6875)
Blueline Equipment Co LLC ....G...... 509 248-8411
  Seattle (G-9556)
▲ Blueline Equipment Co LLC ....E...... 509 248-8411
  Yakima (G-15522)
Blueline Mfg Co ....G...... 509 248-8411
  Yakima (G-15523)
C & V Machinery ....G...... 509 657-3392
  Endicott (G-3263)

Employee Codes: A=Over 500 employees, B=251-500
C=101-250, D=51-100, E=20-50, F=10-19, G=2-9

Callahan Manufacturing Inc ... E ... 509 346-2208 Royal City *(G-9167)*
Case42 ... G ... 509 270-3500 Otis Orchards *(G-7513)*
CCS Equipment Inc ... E ... 509 248-4001 Union Gap *(G-13925)*
Central Machinery Sales Inc ... F ... 509 547-9003 Pasco *(G-7559)*
Craig Fleener ... G ... 509 872-3016 Palouse *(G-7544)*
Custom Technology Co Inc ... F ... 509 965-3333 Yakima *(G-15546)*
◆ Dari-Tech Inc ... E ... 360 354-6900 Lynden *(G-6013)*
Dauenhauer Manufacturing Inc ... G ... 509 865-3300 Toppenish *(G-13666)*
De Kleine Machine Company LLC ... G ... 509 832-1108 Prosser *(G-8038)*
Delaval Inc ... F ... 360 428-1744 Mount Vernon *(G-6788)*
Diamond Blue Manufacturing Co ... E ... 360 428-1744 Mount Vernon *(G-6789)*
Ed Ka Manufacturing Inc ... G ... 509 635-1521 Garfield *(G-4068)*
Edwards Equipment Co Inc ... F ... 509 248-1770 Union Gap *(G-13928)*
EFC Equipment LLC ... G ... 509 713-7230 Richland *(G-8992)*
Eldred Bros Farms LLC ... G ... 360 398-9757 Bellingham *(G-1332)*
Excel Dairy Service Inc ... E ... 360 848-9494 Mount Vernon *(G-6794)*
Fred A Widman ... G ... 509 863-9320 Spokane *(G-12263)*
Frog Creek Co ... G ... 509 276-6467 Deer Park *(G-2903)*
Furford Picker Co ... G ... 360 267-3303 Grayland *(G-4294)*
Gdp Group Ltd Spc ... G ... 253 459-3447 Gig Harbor *(G-4106)*
▲ GP Graders LLC ... F ... 253 239-3727 East Wenatchee *(G-3016)*
Green Hollow Farm Inc ... G ... 509 397-3569 Colfax *(G-2714)*
H F Hauff Co Inc ... F ... 509 248-0318 Yakima *(G-15578)*
Hahn Manufacturing Inc ... G ... 509 930-1621 Yakima *(G-15580)*
Irrigation Accessories Co ... F ... 360 896-9440 Vancouver *(G-14324)*
▲ Isaacs & Associates Inc ... G ... 509 529-2286 Walla Walla *(G-14825)*
Jason C Bailes Pllc ... G ... 360 975-4687 Vancouver *(G-14334)*
Jerrys Iron Works Inc ... G ... 425 788-1467 Duvall *(G-2993)*
K & D Machine LLC ... F ... 509 882-2239 Grandview *(G-4249)*
▼ Kile Machine & Manufacturing ... G ... 509 569-3814 Rosalia *(G-9155)*
▲ Korvan Industries Inc ... D ... 360 354-1500 Lynden *(G-6029)*
Lee H Koehn ... G ... 509 265-4367 Mesa *(G-6494)*
Lower Valley Machine Shop ... F ... 509 882-3881 Grandview *(G-4251)*
Lth Farm Corp ... G ... 509 636-2673 Creston *(G-2842)*
McGregor Company ... F ... 509 397-4360 Colfax *(G-2716)*
Microbial Magic LLC ... G ... 360 297-2224 Poulsbo *(G-7983)*
Mikes Rental Machinery Inc ... E ... 509 925-6126 Ellensburg *(G-3215)*
◆ Nelson Irrigation Corporation ... C ... 509 525-7660 Walla Walla *(G-14850)*
Nicholson Manufacturing Co ... D ... 206 682-2752 Seattle *(G-10607)*
Nolan & Sons Northwest Inc ... G ... 509 658-2604 Naches *(G-7000)*
Norma Industries ... G ... 253 208-1728 Puyallup *(G-8200)*
▲ Northstar Attachments LLC ... E ... 509 452-1651 Yakima *(G-15632)*
▲ Northwest Tillers Inc ... G ... 509 575-1950 Yakima *(G-15635)*
▲ Northwest Wildfoods Co Inc ... G ... 360 757-7940 Burlington *(G-2176)*
Nozzleworks Inc ... G ... 360 668-2548 Bothell *(G-1881)*
Orchard-Rite Limited Inc ... E ... 509 834-2029 Yakima *(G-15639)*
Orchard-Rite Limited Inc ... E ... 509 834-2029 Union Gap *(G-13947)*
Oxbo International Corporation ... G ... 509 544-0362 Pasco *(G-7610)*
Oxbo International Corporation ... D ... 360 354-1500 Lynden *(G-6043)*
Packing House Services Inc ... G ... 509 452-5002 Union Gap *(G-13948)*
Parsons Equipment Inc ... G ... 509 632-5205 Coulee City *(G-2804)*
Perrault Manufacturing Inc ... G ... 509 248-9905 Moxee *(G-6884)*
Prathers Welding & Fabrication ... G ... 509 632-5321 Coulee City *(G-2805)*
R N S Farms Inc ... G ... 509 545-6775 Pasco *(G-7620)*
REA Services Inc ... F ... 509 394-2305 Touchet *(G-13677)*
Reed Farms Inc ... G ... 509 725-4394 Davenport *(G-2876)*
▼ Scafco Corporation ... C ... 509 343-9000 Spokane *(G-12493)*
Scafco Corporation ... F ... 509 343-9012 Spokane *(G-12494)*
Spray Center Electronics Inc ... G ... 509 838-2209 Spokane *(G-12523)*
Stoess Manufacturing Inc ... G ... 509 646-3292 Washtucna *(G-15003)*
Suberizer Inc ... G ... 425 747-8900 Bellevue *(G-1164)*
Thomas R Keevy ... G ... 509 245-3457 Spangle *(G-12085)*
Town of Garfield ... G ... 509 635-1604 Garfield *(G-4069)*
▲ Travis Pattern & Foundry Inc ... B ... 509 466-3545 Spokane *(G-12566)*
Unified Screening & Crushing ... G ... 253 872-6595 Kent *(G-5194)*
US Mower Inc ... F ... 360 757-7555 Burlington *(G-2198)*
Valmont Northwest Inc ... F ... 509 547-1623 Pasco *(G-7647)*
Vamco Ltd Inc ... G ... 509 877-2138 Wapato *(G-14927)*
▲ Van Doren Sales Inc ... D ... 509 886-1837 East Wenatchee *(G-3034)*
▲ Washington Eqp Mfg Co Inc ... E ... 509 244-4773 Spokane *(G-12583)*
Washington Tractor Inc ... G ... 509 452-2880 Yakima *(G-15704)*
Washington Tractor Inc ... C ... 253 863-4436 Sumner *(G-13110)*
Washington Tractor Inc ... E ... 360 533-6393 Aberdeen *(G-38)*
Washington Tractor Inc ... F ... 509 422-3030 Okanogan *(G-7204)*
Wilson Dairy ... G ... 360 736-6001 Rochester *(G-9147)*

3524 Garden, Lawn Tractors & Eqpt

D & M Machine Division Inc ... F ... 360 249-3366 Montesano *(G-6643)*
Garden Guys LLC ... G ... 206 257-4024 Burien *(G-2110)*
▲ Northwest Tillers Inc ... G ... 509 575-1950 Yakima *(G-15635)*
Pacific Topsoils Inc ... E ... 425 337-2700 Everett *(G-3568)*
Rootz ... G ... 509 443-5999 Spokane *(G-12483)*
◆ Sls Runout LLC ... D ... 360 883-8846 Vancouver *(G-14594)*
Snogro ... G ... 360 863-6935 Snohomish *(G-11980)*
US Mower Inc ... F ... 360 757-7555 Burlington *(G-2198)*

3531 Construction Machinery & Eqpt

A A Auto Towing ... G ... 360 892-2924 Vancouver *(G-14002)*
A Millican Crane Service Inc ... G ... 360 779-6723 Poulsbo *(G-7941)*
ABC Water Specialty Inc ... G ... 425 355-9826 Lake Stevens *(G-5629)*
Accurate Surface Grinding ... G ... 206 762-5205 Seattle *(G-9338)*
▲ Acrowood Corporation ... D ... 425 258-3555 Everett *(G-3358)*
Action Materials Inc ... E ... 509 448-9386 Cheney *(G-2573)*
Aerofab Inc ... G ... 253 863-8402 Ravensdale *(G-8329)*
Affordble Trctr Bckhoe Svc LLC ... G ... 360 306-1533 Maple Valley *(G-6253)*
Agate Backhoe Tractor ... G ... 360 426-7085 Shelton *(G-11673)*
Albina Holdings Inc ... D ... 360 696-3408 Vancouver *(G-14017)*
All Seasons Sweeping Service ... G ... 509 782-8015 Cashmere *(G-2312)*
Anbo Mfg Inc ... F ... 509 684-6559 Veradale *(G-14748)*
▼ Anthony Rousseau ... G ... 509 758-8379 Clarkston *(G-2619)*
▲ Armadillo Equipment & Parts ... G ... 360 829-4107 Buckley *(G-2046)*
Asphalt Equipment & Service Co ... E ... 253 939-4150 Auburn *(G-379)*
Austin Jordan Inc ... G ... 253 265-1903 Gig Harbor *(G-4074)*
Bc Pavers Inc ... G ... 425 413-2110 Renton *(G-8753)*
Bizzybee LLC ... G ... 206 707-9417 Seattle *(G-9535)*
Briggs Mch & Fabrication LLC ... F ... 509 535-0125 Spokane Valley *(G-12645)*
Caterpillar Inc ... E ... 509 623-4640 Spokane *(G-12173)*
Caterpillar Inc ... E ... 425 562-2060 Bellevue *(G-842)*
Central Machinery Sales Inc ... F ... 509 547-9003 Pasco *(G-7559)*
Centric Corporation ... F ... 253 833-4342 Auburn *(G-403)*
Cline Rentals LLC ... G ... 206 375-0705 Bothell *(G-1839)*
▲ Concut Inc ... E ... 253 872-3507 Kent *(G-4862)*
Construction Parts ... G ... 253 271-6133 Spanaway *(G-12055)*
Construction Parts LLC ... G ... 253 255-1775 Graham *(G-4221)*
County Public Works ... G ... 509 674-2502 Cle Elum *(G-2664)*
D & M Machine Division Inc ... F ... 360 249-3366 Montesano *(G-6643)*
D W Pape Inc ... G ... 509 586-0522 Kennewick *(G-4652)*
Dandy Digger and Supply Inc ... F ... 360 795-3617 Cathlamet *(G-2364)*
Danzco Inc ... G ... 360 264-2141 Tenino *(G-13616)*
Dude Wheres My Car ... G ... 509 249-5440 Yakima *(G-15559)*
Dyers Construction & Excav ... G ... 903 486-1881 Ocean Park *(G-7181)*
Ed Ka Manufacturing Inc ... G ... 509 635-1521 Garfield *(G-4068)*
▲ Elliot Attachments Inc ... G ... 360 636-2203 Kelso *(G-4524)*
Fabrication Products Inc ... E ... 503 283-3218 Vancouver *(G-14219)*
Fessco Fleet and Marine Inc ... E ... 509 534-5880 Spokane *(G-12255)*
Fluid Power Service Inc ... G ... 360 496-6888 Morton *(G-6669)*
▲ Genie Manufacturing Inc ... A ... 425 881-1800 Redmond *(G-8475)*
Genie Manufacturing Inc ... C ... 509 762-3200 Moses Lake *(G-6712)*
Global Marine Logistics LLC ... E ... 206 854-0201 Kirkland *(G-5350)*
Hansen Fabrication ... G ... 206 283-9181 Seattle *(G-10139)*
Hanson Worldwide LLC ... D ... 509 252-9290 Spokane *(G-12289)*
Hemphill Brothers Inc ... G ... 509 732-4481 Northport *(G-7138)*
Henry Kempton ... G ... 509 493-1160 White Salmon *(G-15117)*
Horseshoe Lake Auto Wreck ... G ... 253 857-3866 Gig Harbor *(G-4119)*
Industrial Welding Co Inc ... F ... 509 598-2356 Spokane *(G-12306)*
International Cnstr Eqp Inc ... G ... 206 764-4787 Seattle *(G-10249)*
Iron Horse Vac LLC ... G ... 509 586-2446 Kennewick *(G-4677)*

SIC SECTION

35 INDUSTRIAL AND COMMERCIAL MACHINERY AND COMPUTER EQUIPMENT

J TS Tractor Work ....G....... 360 263-3016
  La Center (G-5508)
J&L Enterprises Inc ....G....... 360 262-3735
  Onalaska (G-7449)
Joseph Gillum ....G....... 800 624-4578
  Centralia (G-2413)
Junk Car Removal 1 ....G....... 206 369-7832
  Seattle (G-10316)
Kc McCoy Inc ....G....... 360 376-5619
  Eastsound (G-3038)
Kemp West Inc ....D....... 425 334-5572
  Snohomish (G-11932)
Kinematics Marine Eqp Inc ....G....... 360 659-5415
  Marysville (G-6348)
Konecranes Inc ....G....... 503 548-4078
  Vancouver (G-14353)
Les Ware Backhoe ....G....... 425 508-2252
  Monroe (G-6591)
Machine Development Company ....G....... 360 479-4484
  Bremerton (G-1975)
Man Diesel North America Inc ....G....... 253 479-6800
  Kent (G-5002)
Markey Machinery Co Inc ....E....... 206 622-4697
  Seattle (G-10489)
Markey Machinery Co Inc ....F....... 206 763-0383
  Seattle (G-10490)
McCafferty NW Land Dev LLC ....G....... 509 483-1222
  White Salmon (G-15122)
Miles Sand & Gravel Company ....F....... 360 427-0946
  Shelton (G-11714)
Miramac Metals Inc ....F....... 509 483-5331
  Mead (G-6433)
Morgan Creek Envmtl Rsrces Inc ....G....... 360 202-6536
  Sedro Woolley (G-11551)
▲ Morpac Industries Inc ....E....... 253 735-8922
  Pacific (G-7533)
Natural Stone Restorers ....G....... 360 825-3199
  Enumclaw (G-3307)
▲ Naust Marine Usa Inc ....F....... 206 484-5710
  Seattle (G-10595)
◆ Neil F Lampson Inc ....C....... 509 586-0411
  Kennewick (G-4700)
North Hill Resources Inc ....F....... 360 757-1866
  Burlington (G-2173)
Northstar Attachments LLC ....G....... 509 453-8271
  Union Gap (G-13946)
Northwest Equipment Sales Inc ....G....... 253 835-1802
  Federal Way (G-3764)
Pape Machinery Inc ....E....... 509 838-5252
  Spokane (G-12429)
▲ Performance Cnstr Eqp Inc ....G....... 360 794-6220
  Monroe (G-6605)
Plano Bros Paving Inc ....G....... 425 226-8210
  Newcastle (G-7038)
Precisionhx LLC ....G....... 509 951-1266
  Chattaroy (G-2451)
Professional Crane Inspections ....G....... 509 226-5302
  Otis Orchards (G-7516)
▲ PSM Hydraulics ....E....... 360 282-4998
  Woodinville (G-15342)
PSM LLC ....E....... 425 486-1232
  Woodinville (G-15343)
Puget Lite-Pavers Inc ....G....... 206 849-7091
  Seattle (G-10883)
Quality Backhoe Services Inc ....G....... 509 545-0242
  Burbank (G-2085)
Ramsey Company Inc ....G....... 360 748-8918
  Chehalis (G-2529)
▼ Rapp Marine HP LLC ....E....... 206 286-8162
  Seattle (G-10922)
Rios Brick Pavers ....G....... 206 271-3447
  Redmond (G-8652)
RMC Incorporated ....E....... 206 243-4831
  Seattle (G-10969)
Robbins Company ....E....... 253 872-0500
  Kent (G-5104)
▲ Safeworks LLC ....D....... 206 575-6445
  Tukwila (G-13809)
Schermer Construction Inc ....G....... 360 533-5866
  Hoquiam (G-4357)
Steer Straight LLC ....G....... 360 398-6294
  Bellingham (G-1557)
Stella-Jones Corporation ....D....... 360 435-2146
  Arlington (G-334)
Superior Slabjacking Inc ....G....... 425 970-3986
  Renton (G-8924)
Terex Corporation ....F....... 800 536-1800
  Redmond (G-8690)
Terratrench Usa Inc ....G....... 360 694-0141
  Vancouver (G-14632)

Tim Eastman Eqp Repr Wldg LLC ....F....... 360 274-7607
  Castle Rock (G-2354)
TNT Crane & Construction ....G....... 509 682-7711
  Chelan (G-2566)
Track Equipment Company LLC ....G....... 360 201-7881
  Bellingham (G-1573)
▲ Trail Tech Inc ....G....... 360 687-4530
  Battle Ground (G-748)
Twin Peaks ....G....... 509 427-4759
  Carson (G-2309)
Ulrich Trucking Incorporate ....G....... 360 748-0026
  Chehalis (G-2540)
◆ US Oil & Refining Co ....C....... 253 383-1651
  Tacoma (G-13574)
Vetch Construction LLC ....G....... 425 387-3244
  Camano Island (G-2226)
▲ Washington Eqp Mfg Co Inc ....E....... 509 244-4773
  Spokane (G-12583)
▲ Washington Powerscreen Inc ....G....... 253 236-4153
  Kent (G-5209)
Weldco-Beales Mfg Corp ....E....... 253 383-0180
  Tacoma (G-13591)
Western States Asphalt LLC ....F....... 509 487-4560
  Spokane (G-12586)
Western States Asphalt LLC ....G....... 509 545-9864
  Pasco (G-7653)
Western States Group LLC ....G....... 509 487-4560
  Spokane (G-12587)
▲ Willapa Marine Products Inc ....G....... 360 942-2151
  Raymond (G-8362)
Young Corporation ....G....... 206 623-3274
  Seattle (G-11514)
Young Corporation ....E....... 425 488-2427
  Woodinville (G-15413)

3532 Mining Machinery & Eqpt

▲ Armadillo Equipment & Parts ....G....... 360 829-4107
  Buckley (G-2046)
Bedford Industries Inc ....G....... 360 805-9099
  Monroe (G-6551)
▼ Courtright Enterprises Inc ....E....... 509 764-9600
  Moses Lake (G-6698)
Flsmidth Inc ....G....... 509 434-8605
  Spokane (G-12259)
Hanson Worldwide LLC ....D....... 509 252-9290
  Spokane (G-12289)
▼ Impact Service Corporation ....E....... 509 468-7900
  Spokane (G-12305)
Joy Glbal Lngview Oprtions LLC ....G....... 253 588-1726
  Lakewood (G-5731)
LLP Enterprises LLC ....G....... 509 423-7580
  Wenatchee (G-15044)
New Tec LLC ....F....... 509 738-6621
  Kettle Falls (G-5237)
Novex LLC ....G....... 360 296-3467
  Bellingham (G-1473)
▲ Omh Innovations Usa Inc ....G....... 509 264-1129
  Chattaroy (G-2450)
QSP Packers LLC ....G....... 253 770-0315
  Puyallup (G-8230)
Rainier Rigging Inc ....F....... 253 833-4087
  Auburn (G-545)
▲ Ramco Construction Tools Inc .....F....... 253 796-3051
  Kent (G-5098)
Ramco Construction Tools Inc ....G....... 253 796-3051
  Kent (G-5099)
Rebec LLC ....G....... 425 745-4177
  Lynnwood (G-6187)
Thunderbird Pacific Corp ....G....... 425 869-2727
  Redmond (G-8691)
Williams Elite Machining & Mfg ....G....... 253 228-2288
  Rochester (G-9146)
Wittco Separation Systems Inc ....G....... 360 495-3100
  McCleary (G-6421)

3533 Oil Field Machinery & Eqpt

AG Energy Solutions Inc ....F....... 509 343-3156
  Spokane Valley (G-12602)
Airgas Usa LLC ....G....... 360 293-6171
  Anacortes (G-97)
Bayview Pumps ....G....... 360 301-3600
  Nordland (G-7088)
Blue Star Enterprises NW Inc ....F....... 509 946-9388
  Richland (G-8975)
Cameron International Corp ....E....... 425 438-8726
  Everett (G-3409)
Highwood Global LP ....E....... 509 655-7711
  Spokane (G-12295)
Nuovo Parts Inc ....G....... 360 738-1888
  Ferndale (G-3879)

Oil Spills Services Inc ....G....... 425 823-6500
  Kirkland (G-5416)
Opi Downhole Technologies LLC ....G....... 206 557-7032
  Seattle (G-10705)
QSP Packers LLC ....G....... 253 770-0315
  Puyallup (G-8230)
R 2 Manufacturing Inc ....G....... 360 693-5096
  Vancouver (G-14525)
Schell Pump Service ....G....... 509 922-4756
  Greenacres (G-4302)
Technipfmc US Holdings Inc ....G....... 509 925-2500
  Ellensburg (G-3230)
US Mat Systems LLC ....F....... 509 763-4000
  Leavenworth (G-5818)

3534 Elevators & Moving Stairways

Chinook Elevator Solutions ....G....... 425 213-0784
  Kent (G-4851)
J Fillips LLC ....G....... 425 277-1011
  Renton (G-8830)
Olympic Home Modification LLC ....G....... 253 858-9941
  Gig Harbor (G-4139)
Otis Elevator Intl Inc ....F....... 509 483-7328
  Spokane (G-12422)
Schindler Elevator Corporation ....E....... 509 535-2471
  Spokane Valley (G-12859)
Thyssenkrupp Elevator Corp ....E....... 425 828-3110
  Kirkland (G-5482)
Vertical Dimensions LLC ....G....... 206 767-8022
  Tukwila (G-13833)
West Coast Elevator LLC ....G....... 206 878-9378
  Des Moines (G-2951)

3535 Conveyors & Eqpt

A-1 Welding Inc ....F....... 360 671-9414
  Bellingham (G-1237)
Accucon Inc ....G....... 509 534-4460
  Spokane Valley (G-12599)
▼ Aerogo Inc ....D....... 206 575-3344
  Tukwila (G-13689)
Agjet LLC ....F....... 509 654-9449
  Yakima (G-15502)
Atlas Systems LLC ....G....... 509 535-7775
  Spokane Valley (G-12629)
Austin-Mac Inc ....F....... 206 624-7066
  Seattle (G-9465)
▲ Byron Automation LLC ....F....... 509 653-2100
  Naches (G-6994)
Carsoe US Inc ....G....... 206 408-5869
  Seattle (G-9637)
Columbia Chain Belt Inc ....E....... 509 546-2000
  Pasco (G-7562)
Conveyor Works Inc ....G....... 360 829-5378
  Buckley (G-2053)
Custom Technology Co Inc ....F....... 509 965-3333
  Yakima (G-15546)
Dematic Corp ....A....... 206 674-4578
  Tukwila (G-13723)
Easterday Diesel Manufacturing ....G....... 509 269-4577
  Mesa (G-6492)
◆ Edco Inc ....E....... 360 424-6600
  Mount Vernon (G-6792)
Empire Rubber & Supply Co ....F....... 509 547-0026
  Pasco (G-7579)
Fish Transport Systems LLC ....G....... 206 801-3565
  Seattle (G-9997)
Harrah Farm Shop ....G....... 509 848-2941
  Harrah (G-4320)
Intermountain Fabricators Inc ....F....... 509 534-1676
  Spokane Valley (G-12746)
Pomona Service & Supply Co ....G....... 509 452-7121
  Yakima (G-15649)
Pro West Mechanical Inc ....E....... 509 965-1750
  Wapato (G-14924)
Reconveyance Professionals Inc ......G....... 425 257-3038
  Arlington (G-313)
▲ Remcon Equipment Inc ....F....... 509 244-9439
  Airway Heights (G-61)
Source Engineering LLC ....E....... 360 383-5129
  Lynden (G-6053)
T & K Cstm Fabrication & Repr ....G....... 206 242-0197
  Seattle (G-11247)
Tramco Inc ....G....... 425 347-3030
  Everett (G-3635)
▲ Transco Northwest Inc ....E....... 425 251-5422
  Kent (G-5188)
▲ Washington Eqp Mfg Co Inc ....E....... 509 244-4773
  Spokane (G-12583)
Whooshh Innovations Inc ....F....... 206 801-3565
  Seattle (G-11471)

Employee Codes: A=Over 500 employees, B=251-500
C=101-250, D=51-100, E=20-50, F=10-19, G=2-9

35 INDUSTRIAL AND COMMERCIAL MACHINERY AND COMPUTER EQUIPMENT SIC SECTION

3536 Hoists, Cranes & Monorails

A Terex Genie Company ... G ... 800 536-1800
Redmond (G-8365)
Access Equipment LLC ... G ... 360 376-2679
Orcas (G-7455)
Accumar Corporation ... G ... 360 779-7795
Poulsbo (G-7942)
Aqua-Lift Inc ... G ... 253 845-4010
Puyallup (G-8124)
▲ Basta Inc ... E ... 425 641-8911
Bellevue (G-807)
Bmt Metal Fabrication Inc ... G ... 509 244-6107
Airway Heights (G-49)
Boat Tote ... G ... 360 600-1364
Vancouver (G-14073)
Callahan Manufacturing Inc ... E ... 509 346-2208
Royal City (G-9167)
Columbia Rigging Corporation ... G ... 509 545-4657
Pasco (G-7564)
▲ Ederer LLC ... F ... 800 464-1320
Seattle (G-9883)
◆ Genie Holdings Inc ... G ... 425 881-1800
Redmond (G-8471)
◆ Genie Industries Inc ... A ... 425 881-1800
Redmond (G-8472)
Genie Industries Inc ... E ... 425 881-1800
Redmond (G-8473)
Genie Industries Inc ... C ... 254 714-0088
Redmond (G-8474)
Genie Industries Inc ... E ... 425 881-1800
Moses Lake (G-6711)
Genie Industries Inc ... E ... 425 888-4600
North Bend (G-7112)
High Caliber Mill ... E ... 360 984-6669
Vancouver (G-14295)
Knutson Crane ... G ... 509 925-5438
Ellensburg (G-3211)
Konecranes Inc ... F ... 253 872-9696
Kent (G-4982)
Longview Auto Wrecking ... G ... 360 423-9327
Longview (G-5929)
Marine Restoration & Cnstr LLC ... G ... 425 576-8661
Kirkland (G-5396)
Mk20 Inc ... G ... 509 226-5302
Liberty Lake (G-5847)
Nick Jackson Co Inc ... F ... 425 481-1381
Redmond (G-8594)
▼ North Pacific Crane Co LLC ... F ... 206 361-7064
Seattle (G-10625)
▲ Safeworks LLC ... D ... 206 575-6445
Tukwila (G-13809)
Safeworks Holdings Inc ... B ... 206 575-6445
Tukwila (G-13810)
Sierra Industries Inc ... C ... 425 487-5200
Woodinville (G-15363)
Specialty Motors Mfg LLC ... G ... 360 423-9880
Longview (G-5956)
◆ Sunstream Corporation ... E ... 253 395-0500
Kent (G-5163)
Timken Motor & Crane Svcs LLC ... E ... 509 547-1691
Pasco (G-7638)
Vestdavit Inc ... G ... 425 355-4652
Edmonds (G-3160)
Washington Crane Hoist Co Inc ... G ... 360 694-9844
Vancouver (G-14678)
▲ Washington Eqp Mfg Co Inc ... E ... 509 244-4773
Spokane (G-12583)

3537 Indl Trucks, Tractors, Trailers & Stackers

4k Lift Services Inc ... G ... 509 679-9997
East Wenatchee (G-3004)
Anoxpress LLC ... G ... 509 220-2741
Spokane Valley (G-12619)
Arbon Equipment Corporation ... F ... 253 395-7099
Kent (G-4787)
Arbon Equipment Corporation ... E ... 253 796-0004
Kent (G-4788)
Atacs Products Inc ... F ... 206 433-9000
Seattle (G-9449)
▲ Bogden Inc ... G ... 509 964-2008
Thorp (G-13627)
Capital Industrial Supply Inc ... E ... 360 786-1890
Tumwater (G-13856)
Carrier Transports Inc ... G ... 509 452-0136
Yakima (G-15528)
◆ Columbia Machine Inc ... B ... 360 694-1501
Vancouver (G-14131)
Columbia Machine Inc ... C ... 360 694-1501
Vancouver (G-14133)
▲ Columbia/Okura LLC ... E ... 360 735-1952
Vancouver (G-14139)
Conglobal Industries LLC ... D ... 206 624-8180
Seattle (G-9728)
Container Stuffers LLC ... G ... 206 255-3187
Auburn (G-414)
Dirtworx Enterprises Inc ... G ... 360 225-0146
Woodland (G-15427)
Donald R Hollister Trckg Inc ... G ... 360 887-8418
Ridgefield (G-9079)
EMC Electro Mechanical Company ... G ... 206 767-9307
Seattle (G-9910)
Fbt ... G ... 509 457-3484
Yakima (G-15568)
Forklift Training Center Inc - ... G ... 360 515-0696
Lacey (G-5550)
Frys Welding Inc ... G ...
Auburn (G-445)
General Dynamics Ordna ... D ... 509 762-5381
Moses Lake (G-6710)
Gimpy Ninja LLC ... G ... 253 282-9943
Gig Harbor (G-4108)
Globe International Inc ... G ... 253 383-2584
Tacoma (G-13313)
▲ Globe Machine Manufacturing Co ... C ... 253 383-2584
Tacoma (G-13314)
Go Ventures Inc ... G ... 253 313-4070
Tacoma (G-13315)
Greers Mobile Equipment Repair ... G ... 360 901-0373
Woodland (G-15436)
Harbor Action Inc ... F ... 360 417-1316
Port Angeles (G-7708)
Hawthorne Hill ... G ... 253 572-3744
Tacoma (G-13333)
Heavy Duty Transaxle Inc ... G ... 360 794-2021
Monroe (G-6576)
Helm Manufacturing Co LLC ... G ... 253 537-3382
Tacoma (G-13334)
J A Leasing Inc ... G ... 360 380-5290
Ferndale (G-3862)
Jkr Forklift LLC ... G ... 360 275-4811
Belfair (G-766)
Kughler Co Inc ... G ... 206 789-0667
Seattle (G-10361)
▼ Loading Docks Supply LLC ... G ... 360 866-7063
Olympia (G-7324)
Lynns Forklift Service ... G ... 206 979-4272
Bellevue (G-993)
◆ Neil F Lampson Inc ... C ... 509 586-0411
Kennewick (G-4700)
Nicholson Manufacturing Co ... D ... 206 682-2752
Seattle (G-10607)
Paccar Inc ... B ... 425 227-5800
Renton (G-8871)
Paccar Inc ... B ... 425 468-7400
Bellevue (G-1058)
Pf Fishpole Hoists Inc ... G ... 206 767-3887
Renton (G-8878)
◆ Portland Plastics ... B ... 360 887-2230
Ridgefield (G-9103)
Potter-Webster Co ... G ... 360 577-9632
Longview (G-5944)
Precision Truck & Equipment ... G ... 360 263-8940
Yacolt (G-15491)
PSI Logistics Intl LLC ... G ... 855 473-5877
Spokane (G-12457)
Scoggin & Scoggin ... G ... 509 843-1251
Pomeroy (G-7677)
Shiraul LLC ... E ... 509 837-6230
Sunnyside (G-13141)
Spokane Forklift Cnstr Eqp Inc ... G ... 509 868-5962
Spokane (G-12518)
Springbrook Nurs & Trckg Inc ... D ... 360 653-6545
Arlington (G-331)
T E C I Inc ... F ... 509 452-3672
Union Gap (G-13953)
Terex Corporation ... F ... 800 536-1800
Redmond (G-8690)
Trout-Blue Chelan-Magi Inc ... E ... 509 689-2511
Brewster (G-2017)
▲ US Attachments Inc ... F ... 360 501-4484
Kelso (G-4558)
West Columbia Carriers LLC ... G ... 509 488-5000
Othello (G-7509)
Westco Engineering ... G ... 425 481-7271
Woodinville (G-15403)
Woodone-US Corp ... G ... 206 850-0230
Sammamish (G-9259)
Yakima Forklift LLC ... G ... 509 985-3568
Toppenish (G-13675)

3541 Machine Tools: Cutting

3dx Industries Inc ... G ... 360 244-4339
Ferndale (G-3807)
A H Lundberg Inc ... G ... 425 258-4617
Everett (G-3354)
Aem-Network LLC ... G ... 509 946-0813
Richland (G-8966)
Almar Tls & Cutter Grinders Co ... F ... 503 255-2763
Camas (G-2227)
Automated AG Systems LLC ... G ... 813 786-7282
Moses Lake (G-6682)
C N C Repair & Sales Inc ... G ... 408 331-1970
Lynden (G-6004)
Complete Deburr Inc ... F ... 253 887-0997
Auburn (G-411)
Coyote Cleaning Systems Inc ... G ... 425 776-8002
Mukilteo (G-6907)
Crux Subsurface Inc ... D ... 509 892-9409
Spokane Valley (G-12670)
▲ Cut Technologies Metal LLC ... F ... 360 733-0460
Bellingham (G-1312)
Cutting Edge Machine & Mfg ... G ... 253 926-8514
Tacoma (G-13252)
Cw Machine LLC ... G ... 360 829-4171
Buckley (G-2055)
Davincis Workshop LLC ... G ... 206 244-7000
Seatac (G-9280)
Dilbeck Tools Inc ... G ... 509 452-3405
Yakima (G-15555)
First Impressions Co Inc ... G ... 206 372-0361
Kent (G-4908)
Geologic Drill Explorations ... G ... 509 466-5241
Spokane (G-12271)
Grizzly Machining Solutions ... G ... 406 396-4087
Sultan (G-13026)
Ground Piercing Inc ... G ... 509 961-8241
Yakima (G-15577)
J & J Precision Machine LLC ... G ... 509 315-9319
Spokane Valley (G-12750)
Larsen Equipment Design Inc ... G ... 206 789-5121
Seattle (G-10378)
▲ Levetec Surface Prep McHy LLC ... G ... 425 629-8200
Redmond (G-8533)
Lortone Inc ... F ... 425 493-1600
Mukilteo (G-6951)
Maulcor Inc ... G ... 773 696-2783
Seattle (G-10502)
Mc Ilvanie Machine Works Inc ... F ... 509 452-3131
Yakima (G-15616)
Milman Engineering Inc ... G ... 360 273-5080
Rochester (G-9137)
Norwood-Wang Inc ... G ... 206 304-8769
Kent (G-5037)
▲ Noxon Inc ... G ... 509 926-0557
Spokane Valley (G-12814)
Pacific Hide & Fur Depot ... E ... 509 545-0688
Pasco (G-7611)
Q Otm ... F ... 360 802-3700
Enumclaw (G-3313)
R N C Lath & Plaster ... G ... 360 802-0938
Enumclaw (G-3315)
Rams Head Construction Inc ... G ... 509 997-6962
Winthrop (G-15164)
◆ Romac Industries Inc ... C ... 425 951-6200
Bothell (G-1897)
◆ Rottler Manufacturing Company ... E ... 253 872-7050
Kent (G-5108)
S&S Repair ... G ... 360 496-5533
Morton (G-6673)
Serena Inc ... G ... 253 939-6509
Auburn (G-560)
Slave To Lathe ... G ... 206 937-2129
Seattle (G-11135)
▲ South Bend Lathes ... G ... 360 734-1540
Bellingham (G-1548)
Swift Tool Company Inc ... G ... 206 763-9280
Seattle (G-11238)
Tru Square Metal Products Inc ... G ... 253 833-2310
Auburn (G-583)
Universal Refiner Corporation ... G ... 360 249-4415
Montesano (G-6663)
W B & L Machine Inc ... E ... 360 225-5020
Woodland (G-15472)

3542 Machine Tools: Forming

▲ ASC Machine Tools Inc ... C ... 509 534-6600
Spokane Valley (G-12626)
Cincinnati Incorporated ... E ... 425 263-9216
Everett (G-3418)

SIC SECTION

35 INDUSTRIAL AND COMMERCIAL MACHINERY AND COMPUTER EQUIPMENT

Covlet Machine & Design Inc .... F 360 658-1977
   Marysville *(G-6328)*
EDJ Precision Machine Inc .... G 425 745-3937
   Everett *(G-3452)*
Ektos LLC .... G 800 783-0383
   Woodinville *(G-15235)*
Electroimpact Inc .... D 425 348-8090
   Mukilteo *(G-6920)*
Electroimpact Inc .... F 425 348-8090
   Mukilteo *(G-6921)*
◆ Electroimpact Inc .... B 425 348-8090
   Mukilteo *(G-6922)*
Flower Racing .... G 360 793-2196
   Sultan *(G-13025)*
▲ Flux Drive Inc .... F 253 826-9002
   Kent *(G-4914)*
Gemmells Wldg Fabrication LLC .... G 509 547-5200
   Pasco *(G-7584)*
High Energy Metals Inc .... F 360 683-6390
   Sequim *(G-11638)*
J&M Rifle Works .... G 360 985-0445
   Onalaska *(G-7450)*
◆ Jesse Engineering Company .... E 253 552-1500
   Tacoma *(G-13358)*
Metal Frictions Company Inc .... G 425 776-0336
   Edmonds *(G-3133)*
Reed Performance Headers .... G 253 838-7693
   Federal Way *(G-3776)*
Rhino Steel Corporation .... G 425 443-2322
   Kirkland *(G-5452)*
▲ Tonkin Replicas Inc .... E 206 542-6919
   North Bend *(G-7129)*
U-Pull-It Auto Parts Inc .... G 509 895-7655
   Yakima *(G-15698)*
◆ Wagstaff Inc .... B 509 922-1404
   Spokane Valley *(G-12932)*

3543 Industrial Patterns

Aim Aerospace Sumner Inc .... F 253 804-3355
   Auburn *(G-366)*
Continuous Casting Co .... F 206 623-7688
   Seattle *(G-9733)*
Functional Patterns Llc .... G 619 565-3955
   Seattle *(G-10038)*
Gils Aluminum & Shell Core Sp .... G 206 762-1726
   Seattle *(G-10071)*
Model One .... G 206 383-0380
   Seattle *(G-10552)*
Modern Pattern Works Inc .... G 206 762-2227
   Seattle *(G-10554)*
Pattern Integrity LLC .... G 503 752-6018
   Camas *(G-2273)*
Patterns In Nature LLC .... G 360 918-2629
   Olympia *(G-7366)*
Precision Pattern .... G 253 572-4333
   Tacoma *(G-2435)*
Puget Sound Pattern Inc .... G 206 439-6810
   Tukwila *(G-13799)*
Roemer Electric Steel Foundry .... E 360 423-1330
   Longview *(G-5949)*
Woodland Pattern Inc .... F 253 475-3131
   Tacoma *(G-13599)*

3544 Dies, Tools, Jigs, Fixtures & Indl Molds

Advanced Router Technology .... G 360 318-7534
   Ferndale *(G-3810)*
Alliance Mfg Group LLC .... G 253 922-3090
   Tacoma *(G-13165)*
▲ Altek Inc .... C 509 921-0597
   Liberty Lake *(G-5825)*
American Mold Inspection .... G 425 770-4375
   Bainbridge Island *(G-608)*
Ascent Engineering LLC .... G 425 686-7191
   Bothell *(G-1824)*
Bay City Mold Inspection Svcs .... G 415 925-0801
   Olga *(G-7213)*
Boart Longyear .... G 509 926-9575
   Otis Orchards *(G-7512)*
Breedt Prod Tooling Design LLC .... F 253 859-1100
   Kent *(G-4822)*
Buyken Metal Products Inc .... E 253 852-0634
   Kent *(G-4827)*
Capital Tool Co .... G 206 240-7470
   Seattle *(G-9625)*
▲ Cascade Quality Molding Inc .... F 509 248-9642
   Yakima *(G-15530)*
CNA Manufacturing Systems Inc .... G 425 988-3905
   Renton *(G-8773)*
Continuous Casting Co .... F 206 623-7688
   Seattle *(G-9733)*

Daniel E France .... G 360 263-2888
   Ridgefield *(G-9078)*
Danielson Tool & Die .... E 509 924-5734
   Spokane Valley *(G-12678)*
Dry Fly or Die .... G 509 252-5022
   Spokane *(G-12233)*
Feldhegers Machine & Welding .... G 509 452-9213
   Yakima *(G-15569)*
Gilyard Co .... G 509 782-1817
   Cashmere *(G-2321)*
Global Product Development .... G 509 487-1155
   Spokane Valley *(G-12720)*
Graphic Impressions Inc .... E 253 872-0555
   Kent *(G-4925)*
Gray Mold Company Inc .... F 360 671-5711
   Bellingham *(G-1361)*
▲ Gurian Instruments Inc .... G 206 467-7990
   Seattle *(G-10133)*
Harbor Action Inc .... F 360 417-1316
   Port Angeles *(G-7708)*
Harry Price .... G 360 254-5534
   Vancouver *(G-14285)*
Hubbard Jointers Incorporated .... G 509 235-2148
   Cheney *(G-2587)*
Inject Tool & Die Inc .... G 360 679-6160
   Oak Harbor *(G-7154)*
J C Ross Co Inc .... G 206 241-0715
   Seattle *(G-10268)*
Machinists Inc .... F 206 763-0840
   Seattle *(G-10461)*
Mikes Machine .... G 360 652-4046
   Stanwood *(G-12980)*
Modelwerks Inc .... F 206 340-6007
   Seattle *(G-10553)*
Mold Dmage Rmval Pros Lakewood ... G 253 343-0497
   Lakewood *(G-5738)*
New Tech Industries Inc .... E 425 374-3814
   Mukilteo *(G-6955)*
Nicholson Manufacturing Co .... D 206 682-2752
   Seattle *(G-10607)*
Northwest Center .... E 360 403-7330
   Arlington *(G-289)*
Northwest Precision Tool Inc .... G 509 493-4044
   White Salmon *(G-15125)*
NW Mold Removal .... G 360 433-7353
   Vancouver *(G-14444)*
Pacific Die Cast Inc .... E 360 571-9681
   Vancouver *(G-14463)*
Pacific Tool Inc .... D 425 882-1970
   Redmond *(G-8609)*
Precision Steel Rule Die Co .... G 206 397-3982
   Seattle *(G-10853)*
Precision Tooling and Die .... G 253 872-8217
   Renton *(G-8883)*
Proto-Design Inc .... F 425 558-0600
   Redmond *(G-8637)*
Steel Rule Concepts LLC .... G 905 475-0324
   Kent *(G-5154)*
Stewart Industries Inc .... E 206 652-9110
   Seattle *(G-11194)*
Summitview Tooling Inc .... G 509 966-9859
   Yakima *(G-15686)*
Superior Rubber Die Co Inc .... G 206 763-2440
   Seattle *(G-11224)*
Tech Machining Usa LLC .... G 425 754-8221
   Mount Vernon *(G-6845)*
Traction Capital Partners Inc .... G 253 922-3090
   Tacoma *(G-13561)*
Tri-Shell Cores Shop Inc .... F 360 694-7600
   Vancouver *(G-14645)*
Triad Products Corporation .... G 425 514-8363
   Everett *(G-3636)*
Tru Cut Die Inc .... G 360 571-7158
   Vancouver *(G-14650)*
◆ U S Wax & Polymer Inc .... E 509 922-1069
   Spokane Valley *(G-12918)*
Ultimate Product Corp .... G 425 788-7500
   Woodinville *(G-15394)*
▲ Universal Sheet Metal Inc .... G 425 483-8384
   Woodinville *(G-15395)*
US Dies Inc .... G 509 248-0404
   Yakima *(G-15701)*
Weissert Tool & Design Inc .... G 360 835-7256
   Washougal *(G-15000)*
West Coast Automation Corp .... E 509 773-5055
   Goldendale *(G-4213)*
Western Graphics Inc .... G 206 241-2526
   Fife *(G-3998)*

3545 Machine Tool Access

Acf Idea Works Inc .... G 425 335-0958
   Lake Stevens *(G-5630)*
Almar Tls & Cutter Grinders Co .... F 503 255-2763
   Camas *(G-2227)*
Bibbi Co LLC .... G 206 453-4152
   Seattle *(G-9520)*
Bit Pusher LLC .... G 206 457-5242
   Seattle *(G-9534)*
Bogert Aviation Inc .... G 509 736-1513
   Pasco *(G-7554)*
Bridge City Arbors Inc .... G 360 600-3803
   Ridgefield *(G-9069)*
Cannon Lauree .... F 509 627-0505
   Kennewick *(G-4640)*
Ceba Systems LLC .... G 360 891-1823
   Vancouver *(G-14109)*
Chasco LLC .... G 503 803-4675
   Battle Ground *(G-695)*
Cheyenne Scale Co Inc .... G 206 933-7904
   Seattle *(G-9673)*
Cnc Tooling Solutions Inc .... G 425 250-6295
   Kirkland *(G-5309)*
▲ Concut Inc .... E 253 872-3507
   Kent *(G-4862)*
Cutting Tool Control Inc .... F 206 789-7277
   Seattle *(G-9773)*
Danielson Tool & Die .... E 509 924-5734
   Spokane Valley *(G-12678)*
Dem-Bart Checkering Tools Inc .... G 360 568-7356
   Snohomish *(G-11897)*
▲ Digital Control Incorporated .... D 425 251-0701
   Kent *(G-4873)*
East County Machine LLC .... G 360 249-4114
   Montesano *(G-6644)*
Emerald Tool Inc .... G 206 767-5670
   Seattle *(G-9914)*
Fam Waterjet Inc .... G 425 353-6111
   Everett *(G-3469)*
Fostco Inc .... G 509 725-3765
   Davenport *(G-2870)*
Global Product Development .... G 509 487-1155
   Spokane Valley *(G-12720)*
Harris Machine LLC .... G 253 347-6230
   Kent *(G-4934)*
Hexagon Metrology Inc .... G 253 872-2443
   Kent *(G-4940)*
Imaginetics Holdings LLC .... G 253 735-0156
   Auburn *(G-472)*
Imaginetics LLC .... D 253 735-0156
   Auburn *(G-473)*
Innova Mfg LLC .... G 509 946-7461
   Richland *(G-9010)*
International Carbide Corp .... F 800 422-8665
   Roy *(G-9161)*
J & J Precision Machine LLC .... G 509 315-9319
   Spokane Valley *(G-12750)*
Janicki Industries Inc .... B 360 856-5143
   Hamilton *(G-4313)*
Lonnie Hansen .... G 253 847-4632
   Spanaway *(G-12060)*
Manufacturing Technology Inc .... G 206 763-3161
   Seattle *(G-10473)*
Marnis Petal Pushers .... G 360 249-8382
   Montesano *(G-6647)*
▲ Mecadaq Aerospace LLC .... F 714 442-9703
   Kirkland *(G-5399)*
Northwest Carbide Tool & Svc .... G 253 872-7848
   Kent *(G-5029)*
NW Evergreen Products .... G 509 276-7825
   Deer Park *(G-2912)*
◆ Omax Corporation .... C 253 872-2300
   Kent *(G-5045)*
Paleo Pushers LLC .... G 253 539-3848
   Tacoma *(G-13457)*
Pedal Pushers Bike Rntl & RPR .... G 208 689-3436
   Spokane *(G-12435)*
Peregrine Manufacturing Inc .... G 425 673-5600
   Lynnwood *(G-6179)*
Polaris Manufacturing Inc .... E 360 653-7676
   Marysville *(G-6370)*
Precision Spring Stamping Corp .... E 253 852-6911
   Kent *(G-5078)*
Proto-Design Inc .... F 425 558-0600
   Redmond *(G-8637)*
Radiac Abrasives Inc .... D 360 659-6201
   Marysville *(G-6376)*
Spotter Levels LLC .... G 425 238-5117
   Stanwood *(G-12992)*

Employee Codes: A=Over 500 employees, B=251-500 C=101-250, D=51-100, E=20-50, F=10-19, G=2-9

Swift Machining Inc ....G.... 360 335-8213
Washougal (G-14990)
Swiftcarb....G.... 800 227-9876
Kent (G-5164)
Tmf Inc....F.... 360 598-1750
Poulsbo (G-8011)
Trilion Quality Systems LLC ....E.... 267 565-8062
Seattle (G-11337)
Urban Diamond Tools....G.... 206 824-6819
Des Moines (G-2949)
Vanwerven Inc....G.... 360 435-2600
Arlington (G-345)
Wilkins Precision Inc....G.... 253 851-9736
Gig Harbor (G-4175)
▲ Woodstock International Inc....E.... 360 734-3482
Bellingham (G-1596)

3546 Power Hand Tools

Apex Tool Group LLC....C.... 425 226-4491
Renton (G-8745)
Black & Decker (us) Inc....G.... 509 535-9252
Spokane Valley (G-12642)
Black & Decker Corporation....F.... 206 624-4228
Seattle (G-9536)
Blue Water Inc....G.... 509 682-5544
Chelan (G-2548)
Carls Mower and Saw....G.... 360 384-0799
Ferndale (G-3824)
Cascade Pipe & Feed Supply....G.... 509 997-0720
Twisp (G-13910)
Eaton Electric Holdings LLC....D.... 425 271-9237
Renton (G-8791)
Electroimpact Inc....D.... 425 348-8090
Mukilteo (G-6920)
Emerald Tool Inc....G.... 206 767-5670
Seattle (G-9914)
Global Product Development....G.... 509 487-1155
Spokane Valley (G-12720)
Miti LLC....G.... 253 833-9119
Auburn (G-500)
▲ Rousseau Company....E.... 509 758-3954
Clarkston (G-2647)
Shelly Shay....G.... 360 829-2350
Buckley (G-2072)
Sondra L Groce....G.... 509 467-8788
Spokane (G-12511)
Specialty Motors Mfg LLC....G.... 360 423-9880
Longview (G-5956)
Steeler Inc....G.... 509 926-7403
Spokane Valley (G-12891)
Sumner Lawn n Saw LLC....F.... 253 435-9284
Puyallup (G-8257)
Tims Country Saw Shop....G.... 509 486-2798
Tonasket (G-13660)
Unifire Inc....F.... 509 535-7746
Spokane (G-12575)
Universal Repair Shop Inc....F.... 206 322-2726
Seattle (G-11377)

3547 Rolling Mill Machinery & Eqpt

Metal Roofing & Siding Sup Inc....F.... 509 466-6854
Mead (G-6432)
Precision Shapes Nw LLC....G.... 206 605-4396
Seattle (G-10852)

3548 Welding Apparatus

◆ Airborne Ecs LLC....F.... 319 538-1051
Port Angeles (G-7679)
Anvil House LLC....G.... 406 579-3042
Seattle (G-9407)
▲ Component Tinning Services Inc....F.... 509 315-5840
Spokane Valley (G-12662)
▼ Hentec Industries Inc....E.... 509 891-1680
Newman Lake (G-7046)
Lincoln Electric Company....F.... 360 693-4712
Vancouver (G-14377)
Miller Electric Mfg Co....C.... 253 212-5346
Puyallup (G-8194)
Old Iron Classics....G.... 360 852-8854
Vancouver (G-14449)
Oxarc Inc....E.... 509 755-0651
Spokane (G-12425)
Reynold Grey McHining Svcs Inc....G.... 360 385-1167
Port Townsend (G-7924)
Risley Sons Wldg Fbrcation LLC....G.... 509 427-2206
Carson (G-2306)
Salmon Creek Industries Inc....G.... 360 921-5143
La Center (G-5515)
▲ Watts Specialties LLC....F.... 253 848-9288
Puyallup (G-8277)

Wilkerson Weld & Fbrcn Inc....G.... 509 545-3181
Pasco (G-7654)

3549 Metalworking Machinery, NEC

4evergreen Fabricators LLC....G.... 253 691-6752
Sumner (G-13053)
A & M Prcsion Msuring Svcs Inc....F.... 425 432-7554
Kent (G-4750)
▲ ASC Machine Tools Inc....C.... 509 534-6600
Spokane Valley (G-12626)
Bionic Builders LLC....G.... 509 435-1114
Spokane Valley (G-12640)
Industrial Tech Intl LLC....G.... 509 248-0959
Yakima (G-15588)
Micro Machining LLC....G.... 360 835-3200
Washougal (G-14967)
Provail....E.... 206 363-7303
Kent (G-5086)
Pyrotek Incorporated....D.... 509 926-6211
Spokane Valley (G-12846)
◆ Rottler Manufacturing Company....E.... 253 872-7050
Kent (G-5108)
Stelia Aerospace North America....G.... 253 852-4055
Kent (G-5155)
Summitview Tooling Inc....G.... 509 966-9859
Yakima (G-15686)
Trinity Mfg....G.... 360 474-8639
Arlington (G-342)
Westec Tool & Productions Inc....G.... 253 476-3404
Tacoma (G-13593)
Western Machine Works Inc....F.... 253 627-6538
Tacoma (G-13594)

3552 Textile Machinery

Booth & Associates....G.... 253 752-2494
Tacoma (G-13206)
▼ Cosmopolis Specialty Fiber....G.... 360 533-7531
Cosmopolis (G-2800)
Furford Picker....G.... 360 267-3303
Aberdeen (G-12)
Hansencrafts LLC....G.... 360 747-7746
Port Townsend (G-7888)
◆ Ioline Corporation....E.... 425 398-8282
Woodinville (G-15267)
Mountain Loom Co....G.... 360 295-3856
Vader (G-13986)
▲ National Specialties LLC....G.... 253 581-4908
Lakewood (G-5740)
Protech Composites....E.... 360 573-7800
Vancouver (G-14513)
R K I....G.... 360 876-0937
Port Orchard (G-7844)
Shannock Tapestry Looms....G.... 360 573-7264
Vancouver (G-14581)
Vintage Quilting....G.... 253 852-6596
Kent (G-5201)
Windy Acres....G.... 360 491-2177
Olympia (G-7429)

3553 Woodworking Machinery

American Machine Works....G.... 509 968-4415
Ellensburg (G-3182)
Andritz Iggesund Tools Inc....G.... 360 574-1440
Vancouver (G-14035)
▲ Cut Technologies Usa Inc....E.... 360 733-0460
Bellingham (G-1313)
D D M Corporation....G.... 206 282-3422
Seattle (G-9779)
▲ Globe Machine Manufacturing Co....C.... 253 383-2584
Tacoma (G-13314)
Hill Woodworking....G.... 425 488-7943
Kenmore (G-4581)
Holiday Engineering & Mfg Co....G.... 253 238-0671
Tacoma (G-13338)
Miller Manufacturing Inc....F.... 360 335-1236
Washougal (G-14969)
Mt Pickett Woodworking....G.... 360 376-2449
Olga (G-7216)
Multi Score Inc....G.... 206 524-7591
Seattle (G-10568)
New Tec LLC....F.... 509 738-6621
Kettle Falls (G-5237)
Nicholson Manufacturing Co....D.... 206 682-2752
Seattle (G-10607)
Nicholson Manufacturing Co....G.... 206 291-8849
Kent (G-5023)
◆ Northern Industrial Inc....E.... 206 682-2752
Seattle (G-10631)
Salem Equipment Inc....F.... 503 581-8411
Vancouver (G-14567)

Seaport Machine Inc....F.... 509 758-2605
Clarkston (G-2648)
Skidmore & Skidmore Inc....G.... 360 379-6385
Port Townsend (G-7926)
T & G Machinery LLC....G.... 425 396-5939
Snoqualmie (G-12033)
Trobella Cabinetry Inc....E.... 360 947-2114
Vancouver (G-14649)
Usnr LLC....C.... 360 225-8267
Woodland (G-15471)
◆ Usnr LLC....G.... 360 225-8267
Woodland (G-15470)
Wellons Group Inc....F.... 360 750-3500
Vancouver (G-14682)
Woodcraft Supply LLC....F.... 206 767-6394
Seattle (G-11492)
Woodward & White Manufacturing....G.... 253 839-7581
Des Moines (G-2952)

3554 Paper Inds Machinery

A H Lundberg Inc....G.... 425 258-4617
Everett (G-3354)
◆ Alliance Mch Systems Intl LLC....B.... 509 842-5104
Spokane Valley (G-12604)
▲ ASC Machine Tools Inc....C.... 509 534-6600
Spokane Valley (G-12626)
Diane M Young....G.... 310 284-8704
Burien (G-2102)
▲ Enterprises International Inc....G.... 360 533-6222
Hoquiam (G-4336)
H R Spinner Corporation....E.... 509 453-9111
Yakima (G-15579)
Leather Guard Div Int Renovatn....G.... 425 827-4895
Kirkland (G-5384)
▲ Legacy Automation Inc....F.... 360 538-2550
Hoquiam (G-4346)
◆ North Pacific Paper Co LLC....B.... 360 636-6400
Longview (G-5937)
▲ Northwest Paper Converters Inc....F.... 800 681-9748
Ferndale (G-3878)
Simutech International Inc....G.... 360 490-4029
Kirkland (G-5463)
Valmet Inc....G.... 360 753-8831
Olympia (G-7419)

3555 Printing Trades Machinery & Eqpt

Anderson & Vreeland Inc....G.... 419 636-5002
Kent (G-4782)
▲ Applied Mfg & Engrg Tech Inc....F.... 253 852-5378
Edmonds (G-3095)
E H P & Associates Inc....F.... 206 764-3344
Burien (G-2104)
Embodi3d LLC....G.... 425 429-6193
Bellevue (G-894)
▲ Enterprises International Inc....G.... 360 533-6222
Hoquiam (G-4336)
Evergreen Engravers....G.... 253 852-6766
Kent (G-4899)
Exone Company....G.... 253 394-0357
Auburn (G-439)
Green Office Supplies....G.... 408 871-8887
Redmond (G-8484)
Hazelwood Farm LLC....F.... 425 454-5165
Redmond (G-8489)
Heath Graphics LLC....G.... 253 856-1422
Auburn (G-462)
◆ Ioline Corporation....E.... 425 398-8282
Woodinville (G-15267)
Jones Digital Printing Inc....G.... 509 452-8238
Yakima (G-15602)
Machine Works Inc....G.... 253 750-0238
Sumner (G-13082)
▲ Ovalstrapping Incorporated....E.... 360 532-9101
Hoquiam (G-4352)
Pad Printing Services Inc....G.... 206 362-4544
Seattle (G-10744)
Preflex Digital Prepress Svcs....F.... 253 583-9100
Lakewood (G-5747)
Prodeco LLC....G.... 425 827-2573
Kirkland (G-5443)
▼ Scheibler Bros Inc....G.... 509 548-7115
Leavenworth (G-5815)
Sdp Tech Inc....G.... 206 595-3041
Bellevue (G-1118)
Web Press LLC....E.... 253 620-4747
Tacoma (G-13589)

3556 Food Prdts Machinery

Ameristar Meats Inc....C.... 509 535-2049
Spokane Valley (G-12616)

SIC SECTION 35 INDUSTRIAL AND COMMERCIAL MACHINERY AND COMPUTER EQUIPMENT

▲ Arr Tech Manufacturing ......E 509 966-4300
Yakima (G-15512)
B & B Equipment Co Inc ......F 509 786-3838
Prosser (G-8030)
▲ Baader North America ......G 253 333-0422
Auburn (G-388)
◆ Belshaw Bros Inc ......C 206 322-5474
Auburn (G-391)
▲ Bioplex Nutrition Inc ......F 360 332-2101
Blaine (G-1661)
▲ Carnitech US Inc ......G 206 781-1827
Seattle (G-9634)
Cascadia Dynamix LLC ......G 360 584-3044
Tenino (G-13613)
Claudon Inc ......G 425 454-2912
Medina (G-6448)
Coastline Equipment Inc ......E 360 734-8509
Bellingham (G-1301)
Columbia Cove LLC ......G 360 739-7373
Rock Island (G-9148)
Environmental Tech Group ......F 253 804-2507
Pacific (G-7526)
Flodin Inc ......E 509 766-2996
Moses Lake (G-6709)
Food Equipment International ......G 509 924-0181
Spokane Valley (G-12707)
▲ Green Air Supply Inc ......G 877 427-4361
Tacoma (G-13323)
Hobart Corporation ......C 360 893-5554
Orting (G-7480)
Hydro Consulting LLC ......G 509 302-1034
Pasco (G-7591)
Innotech Metal Designs LLC ......F 360 393-4108
Bellingham (G-1378)
ITW Food Equipment Group LLC ......E 360 893-5554
Orting (G-7482)
Jimboneys Malt Mills & More ......G 541 571-1144
Chehalis (G-2506)
JV Designs Inc ......G 509 786-2588
Prosser (G-8045)
▲ Kami Steel US Inc ......F 206 283-9655
Seattle (G-10325)
◆ Key Technology Inc ......B 509 529-2161
Walla Walla (G-14833)
Key Technology Inc ......G 509 529-2161
Walla Walla (G-14834)
Klc Holdings Ltd ......F 509 248-4770
Yakima (G-15608)
▲ Marel Seattle Inc ......D 206 781-1827
Seattle (G-10475)
▼ MCD Technologies Inc ......F 253 564-2420
Tacoma (G-13403)
▲ McKinnon International ......G 206 633-1616
Seattle (G-10508)
Mohr Test and Measurement LLC ......G 888 852-0408
Richland (G-9028)
Mohr Test and Measurement LLC ......E 509 946-0941
Richland (G-9027)
◆ Morice Engineering ......G 360 754-9217
Olympia (G-7343)
◆ Nether Industries Inc ......E 360 825-7940
Enumclaw (G-3309)
North Connection Corp ......G 425 637-7787
Bellevue (G-1034)
Northwest Bagger Company Inc ......G 509 575-1950
Yakima (G-15633)
▲ Nutrifaster Inc ......G 206 767-5054
Seattle (G-10670)
Olympic Distillers LLC ......G 360 920-9645
Port Angeles (G-7729)
Pacific Vision Enterprises ......G 509 895-4199
Wapato (G-14923)
Pasteria Lucchese ......G 206 420-4939
Seattle (G-10763)
Perlage Systems Inc ......G 253 632-0891
Federal Way (G-3770)
▲ Perlage Systems Inc ......G 206 973-7500
Seattle (G-10789)
Picobrew Inc ......G 425 503-0132
Seattle (G-10802)
Plantsplus ......G 360 628-8368
Olympia (G-7371)
Pomona Service & Supply Co ......G 509 452-7121
Yakima (G-15649)
Prater Enterprises Inc ......G 360 893-3620
Graham (G-4235)
▲ Pro Sales Incorporated ......E 253 852-6046
Puyallup (G-8226)
Professional Mktg Group ......G 206 322-7303
Seattle (G-10872)
Roastmasters LLC ......G 425 284-2327
Redmond (G-8653)
Ryco Equipment Inc ......E 425 744-0444
Mountlake Terrace (G-6867)
◆ Sagra Inc ......G 253 476-1403
Silverdale (G-11855)
◆ Smith-Berger Marine Inc ......E 206 764-4650
Seattle (G-11139)
▼ Sonofresco LLC ......G 360 757-2800
Burlington (G-2191)
Star Manufacturing Intl Inc ......C 800 882-6368
Everett (G-3620)
Steve Pool Service Inc ......G 360 533-0421
Shelton (G-11736)
Technipfmc US Holdings Inc ......F 253 853-5060
Gig Harbor (G-4166)
Trader Bay Ltd ......D 253 884-5249
Lakebay (G-5691)
Tramco Inc ......G 425 347-3030
Everett (G-3635)
Tri-State Machinery Inc ......G 509 786-0400
Prosser (G-8070)
US Natural Resources Inc ......E 360 841-6346
Woodland (G-15469)
◆ Wood Stone Corporation ......C 360 650-1111
Bellingham (G-1595)

3559 Special Ind Machinery, NEC

Advanced Technology Resources ......G 253 229-3415
Yelm (G-15725)
Alpha Test Corporation ......E 360 462-0201
Shelton (G-11675)
▼ Aquamira Technologies Inc ......G 360 392-2730
Bellingham (G-1251)
Aritex USA Inc ......G 425 922-3819
Seattle (G-9430)
Arlington Dry Kilns LLC ......F 360 403-3566
Arlington (G-200)
▲ Armadillo Equipment & Parts ......G 360 829-4107
Buckley (G-2046)
Automotive Repair Corporation ......F 509 244-2730
Spokane (G-12131)
Birdseed ......G 360 574-7516
Vancouver (G-14067)
Brandon Company Inc ......G 425 290-5427
Everett (G-3400)
Cedar Recycling Inc ......F 253 863-5353
Pacific (G-7524)
▼ Chemithon Corporation ......E 206 937-9954
Seattle (G-9671)
Chemithon Enterprises Inc ......C 206 937-9954
Seattle (G-9672)
◆ Columbia Machine Inc ......B 360 694-1501
Vancouver (G-14131)
Columbia Machine Inc ......G 360 905-1611
Vancouver (G-14132)
Columbia Machine Inc ......C 360 694-1501
Vancouver (G-14133)
Composite Recycling Tech Ctr ......G 360 819-1204
Port Angeles (G-7694)
Diy Tech Shop LLC ......G 360 258-1519
Vancouver (G-14184)
Dog On It Parks Inc ......G 425 512-8489
Everett (G-3445)
Electro Erosion Specialties ......G 425 251-9440
Renton (G-8792)
Fobes District Water & Assn ......G 425 334-3311
Snohomish (G-11910)
Franklin Machinery ......G 360 581-5079
Aberdeen (G-11)
General Plastics Machines ......G 360 694-8836
Vancouver (G-14250)
Gran Quartz Trading Inc ......G 206 973-7640
Seattle (G-10105)
GTC Innovations LLC ......G 866 241-3149
Renton (G-8815)
Innovatech Pdts & Eqp Co Inc ......G 425 402-1881
Woodinville (G-15265)
Integrated Systems Design ......G 360 746-0812
Bellingham (G-1380)
Joom 3d ......G 413 566-6330
Olympia (G-7314)
Kiln Core Holdings LLC ......G 206 859-1114
Seattle (G-10343)
▼ Lundberg LLC ......E 425 283-5070
Redmond (G-8541)
McCulley Inc ......G 509 891-4134
Spokane Valley (G-12786)
Morley Machine Tool Alignmt Inc ......E 253 926-1515
Milton (G-6536)
Nextrx Corporation ......F 425 402-3485
Bothell (G-1879)
Nite-Hawk Sweepers LLC ......F 253 872-2077
Kent (G-5024)
▲ Northstar Equipment Inc ......F 509 235-9200
Cheney (G-2589)
Ochoa Brothers Inc ......G 509 544-6553
Pasco (G-7607)
▲ Oliver Machinery Company ......G 253 867-0334
Kent (G-5043)
Perco Inc ......G 425 373-1252
Bellevue (G-1068)
Peri-USA ......G 410 712-7225
Woodland (G-15459)
Pishwacom ......G 509 991-8972
Spokane (G-12443)
Powell Industries Inc ......F 206 402-3591
Tukwila (G-13793)
◆ Process Inc ......G 425 401-2000
Bellevue (G-1085)
Puget Sound Recycling ......G 253 536-2260
Tacoma (G-13482)
QSP Packers LLC ......G 253 770-0315
Puyallup (G-8230)
R 2 Manufacturing Inc ......G 360 693-5096
Vancouver (G-14525)
Renewable Enrgy Cmps Sltns LLC ......G 360 695-3238
Vancouver (G-14544)
S & BS Boutique ......G 253 631-2718
Kent (G-5109)
Schilling Graphics ......G 253 572-8171
Tacoma (G-13507)
Skookum Enterprises LLC ......D 360 475-0756
Bremerton (G-2001)
Spiral Arts ......G 206 768-9765
Seattle (G-11168)
▲ Tactical Fabs Inc ......E 360 723-5360
Battle Ground (G-742)
▼ Total Reclaim Incorporated ......C 206 343-7443
Kent (G-5184)
Tru Square Metal Products Inc ......G 253 833-2310
Auburn (G-583)
Unified Scrning Crshing-WA LLC ......G 800 562-1971
Kent (G-5195)
Universal Refiner Corporation ......G 360 249-4415
Montesano (G-6663)
▲ Wellons Inc ......C 360 750-3500
Vancouver (G-14680)
Wellons Inc ......G 360 750-3500
Vancouver (G-14681)
Wheel ......G 206 956-0334
Seattle (G-11465)
Whitten Group International ......F 360 560-3319
Longview (G-5968)
Wilford Noorda Foundation ......G 509 487-6832
Spokane (G-12592)
World Diamonds ......G 425 765-7119
Bellevue (G-1228)
Zepher Inc ......E 509 637-2520
Bingen (G-1643)

3561 Pumps & Pumping Eqpt

2 M Company Inc ......G 509 765-0867
Moses Lake (G-6675)
Aquatech ......G 360 957-5203
Castle Rock (G-2337)
Beckwith & Kuffel ......E 509 922-5222
Spokane Valley (G-12637)
Bradleys Metal Works Inc ......G 509 448-2307
Spokane (G-12159)
Centurion Process LLC ......G 509 759-3001
Selah (G-11584)
Consolidated Pump & Supply ......G 509 891-1313
Spokane Valley (G-12665)
Consolidated Pump & Supply ......G 509 543-7241
Pasco (G-7568)
Erickson Tank & Pump LLC ......F 509 785-2955
Quincy (G-8297)
◆ Flow International Corporation ......B 253 850-3500
Kent (G-4909)
Flow International Corporation ......G 812 590-4922
Kent (G-4910)
Flowserve Corporation ......F 360 573-5211
Ridgefield (G-9082)
Flowserve Corporation ......G 360 676-0702
Bellingham (G-1350)
Grundfos CBS Inc ......F 206 433-2600
Tacoma (G-13328)
▲ H2o Jet Inc ......E 360 866-7161
Tumwater (G-13874)

Employee Codes: A=Over 500 employees, B=251-500
C=101-250, D=51-100, E=20-50, F=10-19, G=2-9
2019 Washington
Manufacturers Register
619

35 INDUSTRIAL AND COMMERCIAL MACHINERY AND COMPUTER EQUIPMENT — SIC SECTION

▼ Hallmark Refining Corporation .... D 360 428-5880
　Mount Vernon *(G-6803)*
HB Jaeger Company LLc .... G 360 707-5958
　Burlington *(G-2161)*
Ingersoll-Rand Company .... C 253 398-3900
　Kent *(G-4953)*
Lufkin Industries LLC .... B 425 295-7676
　Issaquah *(G-4442)*
Mal Inc .... D 360 491-2900
　Olympia *(G-7331)*
Mitchell Lewis & Staver .... G 253 589-2141
　Lakewood *(G-5737)*
Mosesvue LLC .... F 425 644-8501
　Bellevue *(G-1016)*
◆ Omax Corporation .... C 253 872-2300
　Kent *(G-5045)*
Pacific Rim Con Pmpg Eqp Co .... G 425 453-8140
　Bellevue *(G-1060)*
Precision Castparts Corp .... G 206 433-2600
　Tukwila *(G-13794)*
Puyallup Septic Pumping .... G 253 785-6553
　Puyallup *(G-8229)*
Qualitylogic Inc .... G 360 882-0201
　Vancouver *(G-14522)*
Revalesio Corporation .... E 253 922-2600
　Tacoma *(G-13495)*
Robert Comeau .... G 360 573-2241
　Vancouver *(G-14557)*
Rogers Machinery Company Inc .... E 206 763-2530
　Seattle *(G-10976)*
Rogers Machinery Company Inc .... E 360 736-9356
　Centralia *(G-2429)*
Rogers Machinery Company Inc .... F 509 922-0556
　Spokane Valley *(G-12856)*
◆ Sharpe Mixers Inc .... E 206 767-5660
　Seattle *(G-11096)*
▲ Somarakis Inc .... F 360 574-6722
　Kalama *(G-4508)*
Specialty Pump and Plbg Inc .... G 425 424-8700
　Snohomish *(G-11986)*
Stealth Services & Technology .... G 360 882-7211
　Vancouver *(G-14610)*
Thesoftwareworxcom .... G 425 825-3814
　Kirkland *(G-5481)*
▲ Vaughan Co Inc .... C 360 249-4042
　Montesano *(G-6664)*
▲ Waterax Corporation .... G 360 574-1818
　Vancouver *(G-14679)*
Waterra USA Inc .... G 360 738-3366
　Peshastin *(G-7665)*
Western Hydro LLC .... G 509 546-9999
　Pasco *(G-7651)*
Western Hydro LLC .... G 360 428-4704
　Burlington *(G-2200)*

3562 Ball & Roller Bearings

Advanced Caster Corporati .... G 425 821-6574
　Kirkland *(G-5269)*
Durable Superior Casters .... G 253 750-0379
　Sumner *(G-13067)*
Modern Siding LLC .... G 813 484-9498
　Everett *(G-3550)*
Reprodactyl Inc .... G 206 782-1128
　Seattle *(G-10949)*
Richert Lina .... G 206 660-3332
　Camano Island *(G-2224)*

3563 Air & Gas Compressors

Atlas Copco Compressors LLC .... F 425 251-1040
　Kent *(G-4797)*
Atlas Copco Compressors LLC .... G 360 530-2130
　Arlington *(G-204)*
Compressed Air Systems LLC .... G 425 328-0755
　Arlington *(G-222)*
Dresser-Rand Company .... G 425 828-4919
　Bellevue *(G-884)*
I 90 Enterprises Inc .... G 509 988-0380
　Odessa *(G-7190)*
Ingersoll-Rand Company .... E 253 931-8600
　Kent *(G-4952)*
Magnum Venus Products Inc .... D 253 854-2660
　Kent *(G-5000)*
Nordson Select Inc .... E 509 924-4898
　Liberty Lake *(G-5848)*
Northwest Truck & Auto AC .... F 206 242-6034
　Federal Way *(G-3765)*
Ron C England .... G 509 276-9150
　Nine Mile Falls *(G-7083)*
▲ Somarakis Inc .... F 360 574-6722
　Kalama *(G-4508)*

Stealth Services & Technology .... G 360 882-7211
　Vancouver *(G-14610)*
Thermion Inc .... G 360 297-5150
　Poulsbo *(G-8007)*
Thermion Inc .... G 360 692-6469
　Poulsbo *(G-8008)*
Thermion Inc .... G 360 362-1273
　Poulsbo *(G-8009)*
◆ Thermion Inc .... G 360 692-6469
　Poulsbo *(G-8010)*

3564 Blowers & Fans

3 Phase Energy Systems Inc .... F 253 736-2248
　Auburn *(G-354)*
Aaire Particle Control Co Inc .... G 206 767-6692
　Seattle *(G-9330)*
All-Pro Services Ran LLC .... G 425 746-4829
　Redmond *(G-8379)*
Allred Heating Cooling Elc LLC .... F 206 359-2164
　Federal Way *(G-3715)*
American Air Filter Co Inc .... G 253 395-8860
　Kent *(G-4776)*
Argo Blower & Mfg Co .... G 206 762-9336
　Seattle *(G-9428)*
▲ Computer Systems Sales & Svcs .... G 206 979-1731
　Kent *(G-4859)*
Corrosion Companies Inc .... E 360 835-2171
　Washougal *(G-14949)*
Dust Control Technologies Inc .... G 360 256-2479
　Brush Prairie *(G-2033)*
Efficient Dryer Vent Services .... G 360 687-7643
　Battle Ground *(G-700)*
Fsx Equipment Inc .... F 360 691-2999
　Granite Falls *(G-4272)*
Fsx Equipment Inc .... G 360 691-2999
　Granite Falls *(G-4273)*
▼ Higher Power Supplies Inc .... G 425 438-0990
　Mukilteo *(G-6933)*
▲ Injectidry Systems Inc .... G 425 822-3851
　Lynnwood *(G-6138)*
Lawrence Enterprises .... G 360 750-8551
　Vancouver *(G-14366)*
▲ Mechatronics Inc .... G 425 222-5900
　Issaquah *(G-4447)*
Mobile Air Applied Science .... G 206 953-3786
　Bellevue *(G-1012)*
Mpm Technologies Inc .... G 973 599-4416
　Spokane Valley *(G-12795)*
Nidec America Corporation .... G 360 666-2445
　Battle Ground *(G-724)*
Omnitec Design Inc .... F 425 290-3922
　Mukilteo *(G-6960)*
Orchard-Rite Limited Inc .... E 509 834-2029
　Union Gap *(G-13947)*
Pyrotek Incorporated .... G 509 926-6211
　Spokane Valley *(G-12846)*
▼ Raring Corporation .... G 360 892-1659
　Vancouver *(G-14533)*
Rogers Machinery Company Inc .... E 206 763-2530
　Seattle *(G-10976)*
Rogers Machinery Company Inc .... E 360 736-9356
　Centralia *(G-2429)*
Rogers Machinery Company Inc .... F 509 922-0556
　Spokane Valley *(G-12856)*
Unifire Inc .... F 509 535-7746
　Spokane *(G-12575)*
Viking Packaging Machinery .... G 509 452-7143
　Yakima *(G-15703)*
▲ Woodstock International Inc .... E 360 734-3482
　Bellingham *(G-1596)*

3565 Packaging Machinery

Buren Sheet Metal Inc .... E 509 575-1950
　Yakima *(G-15525)*
C & C Packaging Services Inc .... E 425 673-6347
　Camano Island *(G-2208)*
Cascade Caning .... G 360 258-1738
　Vancouver *(G-14103)*
Crown Cork & Seal Usa Inc .... E 206 575-4260
　Tukwila *(G-13718)*
Design Service Corporation .... F 509 248-8531
　Yakima *(G-15553)*
▲ Emerald Automation LLC .... E 509 783-1369
　Kennewick *(G-4659)*
▲ Formost Fuji Corporation .... D 425 483-9090
　Woodinville *(G-15248)*
G & M Machine LLC .... G 509 946-3201
　Richland *(G-9000)*
Intech Enterprises Inc .... E 360 835-8785
　Washougal *(G-14961)*

Jerry Carter .... G 509 487-8294
　Spokane *(G-12332)*
Kemps Machine Co .... F 509 784-1326
　Yakima *(G-15606)*
Klc Holdings Ltd .... F 509 248-4770
　Yakima *(G-15608)*
Kwik Loc Corp .... G 253 564-3574
　University Place *(G-13976)*
◆ Kwik Lok Corporation .... G 509 248-4770
　Union Gap *(G-13937)*
Maf Industries Inc .... F 509 574-8775
　Union Gap *(G-13941)*
Marq Packaging Systems Inc .... E 509 966-4300
　Yakima *(G-15615)*
Northwest Bagger Company Inc .... G 509 575-1950
　Yakima *(G-15633)*
Pomona Service & Supply Co .... G 509 452-7121
　Yakima *(G-15649)*
▲ R A Pearson Company .... G 509 838-6226
　Spokane *(G-12464)*
Ridgerunners Inc .... G 509 248-8531
　Yakima *(G-15662)*
▲ Saxco Pacific Coast LLC .... F 360 892-3451
　Vancouver *(G-14570)*
◆ Thermoforming Systems LLC .... E 509 454-4578
　Union Gap *(G-13954)*
United Sales Inc .... G 509 225-0636
　Union Gap *(G-13955)*
Viking Packaging Machinery .... G 509 452-7143
　Yakima *(G-15703)*

3566 Speed Changers, Drives & Gears

Aahed Logistics LLC .... G 757 395-7063
　Port Orchard *(G-7782)*
Cascade Indus & Hydraulic LLC .... G 509 452-1752
　Union Gap *(G-13924)*
Drive Line Svc of Bellingham .... G 360 734-7828
　Bellingham *(G-1326)*
▲ Magnadrive Corporation .... E 425 487-2881
　Woodinville *(G-15299)*
Peregrine Manufacturing Inc .... G 425 673-5600
　Lynnwood *(G-6179)*
Potter-Webster Co .... G 360 577-9632
　Longview *(G-5944)*
Premier Torque Converter .... G 253 288-2233
　Auburn *(G-535)*

3567 Indl Process Furnaces & Ovens

▼ Advanced Combustn Systems Inc .. E 360 676-6005
　Bellingham *(G-1239)*
Bricor Ceramic Industries .... G 360 377-9197
　Bremerton *(G-1940)*
Ducoterra LLC .... G 360 788-4200
　Bellingham *(G-1327)*
Ets Inc .... F 509 276-2015
　Deer Park *(G-2901)*
▲ King Electrical Mfg Co .... D 206 762-0400
　Seattle *(G-10345)*
Olivine Corp .... G 360 733-3332
　Bellingham *(G-1479)*
Prestyl USA LLC .... G 509 703-7661
　Spokane Valley *(G-12838)*
Process Heating Company .... G 206 682-3414
　Seattle *(G-10870)*
Tank Wise LLC .... G 206 937-3995
　Seattle *(G-11265)*
Team Inc .... E 360 848-0353
　Mount Vernon *(G-6844)*

3568 Mechanical Power Transmission Eqpt, NEC

Aahed Logistics LLC .... G 757 395-7063
　Port Orchard *(G-7782)*
Cablecraft Motion Controls LLC .... D 253 475-1080
　Tacoma *(G-13215)*
Carson NC Inc .... G 509 427-8616
　Carson *(G-2304)*
Gms Procurement LLC .... G 253 852-6552
　Auburn *(G-453)*
Jerry Fry .... G 509 765-4367
　Moses Lake *(G-6717)*
▲ Joint Way International Inc .... G 503 286-7781
　Vancouver *(G-14340)*
▲ Mac Chain Company Limited .... E 800 663-0072
　Woodland *(G-15448)*
▲ Magnadrive Corporation .... E 425 487-2881
　Woodinville *(G-15299)*
Moxee Innovations Corporation .... G 509 575-6322
　Yakima *(G-15625)*

35 INDUSTRIAL AND COMMERCIAL MACHINERY AND COMPUTER EQUIPMENT

Moxee Innovations Corporation .... G 509 575-6322
  Moxee *(G-6882)*
Powerlink Transmission Co LLC .... G 360 314-6840
  Vancouver *(G-14496)*
Snapidle .... G 509 575-6322
  Moxee *(G-6887)*
Tech-Roll Inc .... G 360 371-4321
  Ferndale *(G-3911)*
Valin Corporation .... G 509 924-4914
  Spokane Valley *(G-12923)*

3569 Indl Machinery & Eqpt, NEC

Advance Pattern & Tooling Inc .... G 253 638-0300
  Kent *(G-4760)*
Advanced Robotic Vehicles Inc .... G 206 310-1122
  Tukwila *(G-13688)*
Aerospace Mltxis Machining Inc .... F 253 856-1068
  Kent *(G-4764)*
◆ Algas-Sdi International LLC .... D 206 789-5410
  Seattle *(G-9374)*
Altix North America Inc .... G 425 285-4477
  Redmond *(G-8381)*
▲ American Roof Inc .... F 360 668-3206
  Monroe *(G-6548)*
▲ Armadillo Equipment & Parts .... G 360 829-4107
  Buckley *(G-2046)*
Atkins Machines LLC .... G 253 588-2350
  Lakewood *(G-5700)*
BB Citc LLC .... F 425 776-4950
  Everett *(G-3384)*
Clark Machinery Inc .... G 360 825-1840
  Enumclaw *(G-3282)*
▲ Clarus Technologies LLC .... G 360 671-1514
  Bellingham *(G-1299)*
Cnc Diversified Manufacturing .... G 253 852-6869
  Kent *(G-4854)*
Coates Heater Company Inc .... G 253 872-7256
  Kent *(G-4855)*
Deer Path Industrial Tech .... G 425 391-9223
  Issaquah *(G-4404)*
Deines Automation LLC .... G 509 230-2369
  Spokane *(G-12223)*
▲ Enterprises International Inc .... G 360 533-6222
  Hoquiam *(G-4336)*
Ervin H Tennyson .... G 360 445-2434
  Mount Vernon *(G-6793)*
Evoqua Water Technologies LLC .... G 360 699-7392
  Brush Prairie *(G-2034)*
Filter Clean Recycling LLC .... G 360 798-1012
  Vancouver *(G-14230)*
Fire Def Tech Safety Pdts Inc .... G 509 619-0261
  Richland *(G-8998)*
Flow International Corporation .... B 253 850-3501
  Kent *(G-4911)*
Fourth Corner Wtr Filters LLC .... G 360 296-1647
  Blaine *(G-1670)*
Frencken America Inc .... E 509 924-9777
  Liberty Lake *(G-5832)*
Fsx Incorporated .... G 360 691-2999
  Granite Falls *(G-4274)*
Go Ventures Inc .... G 253 313-4070
  Tacoma *(G-13315)*
Hdc Filters LLC .... G 253 964-0707
  Dupont *(G-2965)*
Highwater Filters .... G 509 685-0933
  Colville *(G-2757)*
Industrial Systems LLC .... G 503 262-0367
  Vancouver *(G-14315)*
Innofresh LLC .... G 206 438-3541
  Seattle *(G-10239)*
Inskiwrx Tool & Machine LLC .... G 425 238-2738
  Arlington *(G-255)*
Kinetic Solutions Intl .... G 503 490-8642
  Ridgefield *(G-9092)*
King Machine LLC .... F 425 743-5464
  Mukilteo *(G-6948)*
▲ Kmt US Holding Company Inc .... G 620 856-2151
  Kent *(G-4980)*
Mal Inc .... D 360 491-2900
  Olympia *(G-7331)*
Membane Solutions Corp .... G 253 487-5134
  Kent *(G-5005)*
Numeric Control LLC .... G 360 269-1497
  Morton *(G-6670)*
NW Filters .... G 253 859-4099
  Kent *(G-5039)*
Oberg Filters LLC .... G 360 403-3222
  Arlington *(G-292)*
Osmonics Inc .... G 425 204-5508
  Renton *(G-8867)*

Pine Filter LLC .... G 360 262-9132
  Chehalis *(G-2525)*
Precision Industrial Equi .... G 509 571-1725
  Yakima *(G-15650)*
Pulsair Systems Inc .... G 425 455-1263
  Kirkland *(G-5448)*
Quantum .... G 509 751-6407
  Clarkston *(G-2643)*
Remember Filtercom .... G 425 359-7905
  Lake Stevens *(G-5671)*
RJ Hydraulics Inc .... F 360 693-4399
  Vancouver *(G-14553)*
Robert J Parry .... G 509 456-6204
  Spokane *(G-12479)*
Rrr Inc .... G 206 782-9260
  Seattle *(G-10990)*
Security Alarms Plus Inc .... G 509 457-8799
  Zillah *(G-15758)*
Skytech Machine Inc .... G 360 253-6378
  Vancouver *(G-14593)*
Sp Indstrial Lubrication A LLC .... G 360 579-2646
  Clinton *(G-2699)*
Specialty Motors Mfg LLC .... G 360 423-9880
  Longview *(G-5956)*
Stevens Holding Company Inc .... G 425 446-4928
  Everett *(G-3622)*
True Machine .... G 425 610-9669
  Ferndale *(G-3919)*
U S Fire Equipment LLC .... F 253 863-1301
  Sumner *(G-13108)*
Unisource Manufacturing Inc .... G 253 854-0541
  Kent *(G-5196)*
United Association of Journeym .... G 206 441-0737
  Seattle *(G-11369)*
US Filter Vancouver .... G 360 892-6977
  Vancouver *(G-14656)*
Vietnam Filter Project .... G 425 772-5401
  Lynnwood *(G-6217)*
Vulcan Global LLC .... G 509 528-2000
  Kennewick *(G-4743)*
Water Beetle USA .... G 702 899-2266
  Seattle *(G-11444)*
Western States Fire Equipment .... G 360 723-0032
  Battle Ground *(G-752)*

3571 Electronic Computers

Adams Apple Cider LLC .... G 509 933-1025
  Ellensburg *(G-3180)*
Allview Services Inc .... G 425 483-6103
  Lynnwood *(G-6072)*
Amy Stevens .... G 206 706-2528
  Seattle *(G-9401)*
Apple Brooke LLC .... G 509 922-0696
  Spokane Valley *(G-12623)*
Apple City Electric LLC .... G 509 782-2334
  Cashmere *(G-2315)*
Apple Earthworks LLC .... G 253 847-3755
  Graham *(G-4216)*
Apple For Hire .... G 206 722-3205
  Seattle *(G-9411)*
Apple of My Pie LLC .... G 509 860-8881
  East Wenatchee *(G-3007)*
Apple Street L L C .... G 253 988-4120
  Tacoma *(G-13177)*
Armstrong & Associates LLC .... G 253 548-6148
  Kennewick *(G-4619)*
Assurware Inc .... G 509 531-8336
  Richland *(G-8968)*
Atomrock Llc .... G 425 281-2371
  Issaquah *(G-4384)*
Audion Laboratory Inc .... G 206 842-5202
  Bainbridge Island *(G-611)*
Bad Apple .... G 360 899-5183
  Mount Vernon *(G-6773)*
Bang & Jack Montgomery .... G 360 403-9444
  Lynnwood *(G-6081)*
Bluefire LLC .... G 206 251-0698
  Issaquah *(G-4386)*
Carburetors Unlimited Inc .... G 253 833-4106
  Auburn *(G-401)*
Chris Barber Apple .... G 360 875-8112
  Raymond *(G-8345)*
Christian Hamilton .... G 360 442-4900
  Longview *(G-5899)*
Constant Computer .... G 253 227-0532
  Tacoma *(G-13239)*
Corban Tech LLC .... G 253 353-0849
  Tacoma *(G-13242)*
County of Asotin .... F 509 758-1668
  Clarkston *(G-2628)*

▲ Cray Inc .... A 206 701-2000
  Seattle *(G-9751)*
Elarm Inc .... G 206 395-9604
  Seattle *(G-9892)*
Electronic Systems Tech Inc .... F 509 735-9092
  Kennewick *(G-4657)*
Engineering Solutions Inc .... F 206 241-9395
  Renton *(G-8795)*
Expert Computer Tech Inc .... G 360 736-7000
  Centralia *(G-2401)*
General Computers Inc .... G 425 405-0588
  Bellevue *(G-923)*
Golden Apple Inc .... G 253 473-7880
  Tacoma *(G-13316)*
Grays Harbor Electronics .... G 360 532-3474
  Hoquiam *(G-4338)*
▲ Gtr Technologies Inc .... F 360 876-2974
  Port Orchard *(G-7812)*
Holowear Ltd .... G 408 759-4656
  Bellevue *(G-947)*
Honeywell International Inc .... C 425 251-9511
  Renton *(G-8821)*
HP Inc .... F 650 857-1501
  Seattle *(G-10190)*
Itron Inc .... E 509 924-9900
  Spokane Valley *(G-12748)*
Itron Manufacturing Inc .... E 509 924-9900
  Spokane Valley *(G-12749)*
James Moore .... G 206 799-0399
  Seattle *(G-10283)*
Key Tronic Corporation .... C 509 928-8000
  Spokane Valley *(G-12767)*
Kingtime LLC .... G 206 375-7422
  Renton *(G-8837)*
Lisa Appel .... G 360 521-5472
  Vancouver *(G-14378)*
M K Hansen Company .... G 509 884-1396
  East Wenatchee *(G-3023)*
M M Enterprises .... G 206 463-1927
  Vashon *(G-14731)*
Maren-Go Solutions Corporation .... G 217 506-2749
  Vancouver *(G-14393)*
Meet Your Price Inc .... G 360 260-2066
  Battle Ground *(G-720)*
Michael Blackwell .... G 253 759-2906
  Tacoma *(G-13410)*
Michael P Appleby .... G 360 652-1178
  Stanwood *(G-12978)*
Micro Standard .... G 425 882-1722
  Redmond *(G-8557)*
Moms Carmel Apples & More LLC .... G 509 515-8153
  Kennewick *(G-4696)*
Monument Apples LLC .... G 509 787-5700
  Quincy *(G-8305)*
P Apple LLC .... G 206 290-9898
  Everett *(G-3561)*
Patrick Clarke .... G 206 365-8804
  Seattle *(G-10770)*
◆ Phytec America LLC .... F 206 780-9047
  Bainbridge Island *(G-658)*
Poison Apple Tacoma .... G 253 304-1874
  Tacoma *(G-13469)*
Rugid Computer .... G 360 866-0909
  Olympia *(G-7389)*
Sammamish .... G 425 295-7300
  Sammamish *(G-9245)*
Sensitronics LLC .... G 360 766-8800
  Bow *(G-1932)*
Skinner Communications .... G 360 980-4906
  Vancouver *(G-14590)*
Sound Services .... G 360 920-3435
  Bellingham *(G-1546)*
Stadelman Fruit Frenchman .... G 509 829-5145
  Zillah *(G-15760)*
Storeanywherecom Inc .... G 425 643-3268
  Bellevue *(G-1159)*
Tablesafe Inc .... D 206 516-6100
  Kirkland *(G-5476)*
Tuigis Tek LLC .... G 360 943-9133
  Olympia *(G-7415)*
Voicelever Inc .... D 425 864-7676
  Redmond *(G-8706)*
Washington State Apple Comm .... G 509 663-9600
  Wenatchee *(G-15083)*
Wenatchee Red Apple Flyers .... G 509 881-7884
  East Wenatchee *(G-3035)*

3572 Computer Storage Devices

Advanced Digital Info Corp .... B 425 881-8004
  Redmond *(G-8370)*

35 INDUSTRIAL AND COMMERCIAL MACHINERY AND COMPUTER EQUIPMENT SIC SECTION

▲ Allsop Inc D 360 734-9090
Bellingham *(G-1244)*
Avere Systems Inc D 425 706-7507
Redmond *(G-8392)*
Benjamin Anderson G 206 228-8174
Seattle *(G-9512)*
Diversified Systems Group Inc G 425 947-1500
Kent *(G-4875)*
E McS2 G 971 295-4641
Port Ludlow *(G-7765)*
EMC Corporation D 206 623-1227
Seattle *(G-9909)*
EMC Corporation F 425 378-9209
Bellevue *(G-895)*
EMC Nursing Services G 425 346-5982
Everett *(G-3459)*
Ergo Design Inc G 360 427-5779
Olympia *(G-7278)*
Expert Computer Tech Inc G 360 736-7000
Centralia *(G-2401)*
Fmj Storage Inc G 206 605-1394
Woodinville *(G-15244)*
Grubstake EMC G 509 775-2041
Republic *(G-8957)*
Hewlett-Packard Company C 800 325-5372
Vancouver *(G-14294)*
▲ Isilon Systems LLC B 206 315-7500
Seattle *(G-10260)*
James Clay G 360 891-8147
Vancouver *(G-14333)*
▲ Jmtek LLC E 425 251-9400
Kent *(G-4969)*
Juntlabs LLC G 253 987-1750
Federal Way *(G-3747)*
▲ Leancode Inc F 425 533-5219
Redmond *(G-8532)*
Mikes Help Key LLC G 360 897-2880
Buckley *(G-2064)*
Optistor Technologies Inc F 425 283-5227
Bellevue *(G-1052)*
Pohlman Knowles G 206 933-7450
Seattle *(G-10827)*
Quantum Corporation D 425 201-1400
Bellevue *(G-1089)*
Quantum Solutions Inc G 360 491-0757
Lacey *(G-5580)*
Qumulo Inc D 206 260-3588
Seattle *(G-10907)*
Rsa The Security EMC G 781 515-5000
Bellevue *(G-1109)*
◆ Synology America Corp F 425 296-3177
Bellevue *(G-1175)*
Valtech G 360 779-6748
Poulsbo *(G-8016)*

3575 Computer Terminals

◆ Ballard Technology Inc D 425 339-0281
Everett *(G-3383)*
Circuit Imaging LLC G 509 315-3400
Spokane Valley *(G-12657)*
Hasco Inc G 425 643-2525
Bellevue *(G-937)*
Igt Global Solutions Corp E 360 412-2140
Lacey *(G-5559)*
Incontrol Systems Corp G 425 424-9707
Everett *(G-3514)*
Leyda Computers G 425 335-1273
Lake Stevens *(G-5655)*
Linare Corp E 425 748-5099
Bellevue *(G-986)*
▲ Spacelabs Healthcare Inc A 425 396-3300
Snoqualmie *(G-12027)*
Spacelabs Healthcare LLC B 425 396-3300
Snoqualmie *(G-12028)*
◆ Spacelabs Healthcare Wash C 425 396-3300
Snoqualmie *(G-12029)*
▲ Touchfire Inc G 425 466-4177
Kent *(G-5185)*

3577 Computer Peripheral Eqpt, NEC

▼ 4m Sigma Corporation G 206 285-9181
Seattle *(G-9322)*
5th Wave Mobile Tech Inc G 425 898-8161
Gig Harbor *(G-4070)*
▲ Allied Telesis Inc C 408 519-8700
Bothell *(G-1746)*
Antipodes Inc G 253 444-5555
Tacoma *(G-13173)*
Antipodes Inc F 253 444-5555
Tacoma *(G-13174)*
Astronics Cstm Ctrl Cncpts Inc D 206 575-0933
Kent *(G-4795)*
Avocent G 425 398-0294
Bothell *(G-1749)*
▲ Avocent Redmond Corp D 425 861-5858
Kirkland *(G-5287)*
AZ Imprint G 360 578-2476
Kelso *(G-4517)*
B G Instruments Inc G 509 893-9881
Spokane Valley *(G-12635)*
Barcode Equipment Recyling Co G 360 393-4232
Bellingham *(G-1258)*
Black Box Corporation G 800 733-0274
Kent *(G-4814)*
Black Box Corporation G 406 522-3944
Spokane *(G-12151)*
Black Box Corporation G 406 652-1956
Spokane *(G-12152)*
Black Box Corporation G 406 652-1956
Spokane *(G-12153)*
Blue Heron Lake Farms Inc G 360 966-5241
Bellingham *(G-1277)*
▲ Byte Brothers E 425 917-8380
Medina *(G-6447)*
Cisco Systems Inc A 206 256-3229
Seattle *(G-9686)*
Cisco Systems Inc G 360 352-3657
Lacey *(G-5541)*
Cisco Systems Inc C 425 468-0800
Bellevue *(G-854)*
Computer Technology Link Corp G 253 872-3608
Kent *(G-4860)*
Copytonix G 503 968-0364
Bellevue *(G-865)*
David G McAlees G 425 641-0318
Bellevue *(G-875)*
Engineering Solutions Inc F 206 241-9395
Renton *(G-8795)*
Enravel Inc G 206 414-8884
Seattle *(G-9928)*
Evans - Hamilton Inc G 206 526-5622
Seattle *(G-9943)*
▲ Exorvision Inc G 206 254-0220
Seattle *(G-9955)*
Fantasy Content G 425 653-2207
Bellevue *(G-907)*
Fox Bay Industries Inc G 253 941-9155
Auburn *(G-443)*
Francis Scientific Inc G 360 687-7019
Battle Ground *(G-702)*
Graphic Control System Inc G 360 833-9522
Vancouver *(G-14262)*
Gsl Solutions Inc E 360 896-5354
Vancouver *(G-14275)*
Intel Corporation F 253 371-1052
Bellevue *(G-959)*
▲ Intermec Inc F 425 348-2600
Lynnwood *(G-6139)*
▲ Intermec Technologies Corp A 425 348-2600
Lynnwood *(G-6140)*
International Bar Coding F 800 661-5570
Oroville *(G-7467)*
◆ Ioline Corporation E 425 398-8282
Woodinville *(G-15267)*
Jaspreet Singh G 253 239-3250
Kent *(G-4965)*
Kemeera Incorporated E 206 582-1062
Seattle *(G-10335)*
▲ Key Tronic Corporation E 509 928-8000
Spokane Valley *(G-12766)*
Key Tronic Corporation G 509 927-5225
Spokane Valley *(G-12768)*
▲ Koolance Inc G 253 249-7669
Auburn *(G-485)*
▲ Leancode Inc F 425 533-5219
Redmond *(G-8532)*
Logitech Inc F 360 817-1200
Camas *(G-2266)*
▲ Lone Ranger LLC E 425 355-7474
Everett *(G-3539)*
Microsoft Corporation A 425 882-8080
Redmond *(G-8580)*
Microstar Laboratories Inc E 425 453-2345
Redmond *(G-8585)*
Microvision Inc C 425 936-6847
Redmond *(G-8587)*
Motek Inc G 206 632-7795
Seattle *(G-10565)*
Netacquire Corporation E 425 821-3100
Kirkland *(G-5410)*
Next Biometrics Inc F 617 510-4086
Bellevue *(G-1029)*
Next Biometrics Inc E 425 406-7055
Bellevue *(G-1030)*
Northwest Hydroprint G 360 249-2220
Montesano *(G-6650)*
▲ Opticon Inc E 425 651-2120
Renton *(G-8865)*
Oroville Reman & Reload Inc E 509 476-2935
Oroville *(G-7471)*
PC Networks Inc G 360 362-9684
Silverdale *(G-11853)*
Professional Sales & Serv G 509 678-4535
Yakima *(G-15656)*
Prologic Engineering Inc D 360 734-9625
Bellingham *(G-1507)*
Prologix LLC G 425 829-8199
Redmond *(G-8634)*
▼ R C Systems Inc G 425 355-3800
Everett *(G-3592)*
Ralph Doggett G 503 998-5935
Vancouver *(G-14531)*
Scitus Tech Solutions LLC G 360 202-9642
Ferndale *(G-3901)*
Signal Interface Group G 425 467-7146
Redmond *(G-8666)*
Smart Cable Company G 253 474-9967
Lakewood *(G-5756)*
Softec Systems Inc G 425 741-2055
Everett *(G-3615)*
Sportsoft Inc G 425 822-4613
Mill Creek *(G-6530)*
Stick It To Violence G 360 758-7488
Bellingham *(G-1559)*
Tahoma Technology Inc G 206 393-0909
Seattle *(G-11259)*
Transport Logistics Inc G 206 824-0667
Seatac *(G-9307)*
Trio Native American Entps LLC G 206 728-8181
Renton *(G-8932)*
Troop Boy Scouts of America G 206 284-2164
Seattle *(G-11340)*
US Micro Pc Inc G 425 462-7300
Bellevue *(G-1210)*
Wendy Rawley G 253 531-6785
Tacoma *(G-13592)*
Xerox G 360 923-8640
Lacey *(G-5602)*
Xerox G 253 437-4000
Tukwila *(G-13837)*
Zebra Trans LLC G 360 993-0451
Vancouver *(G-14708)*

3578 Calculating & Accounting Eqpt

American Bancard LLC E 360 713-0690
Vancouver *(G-14026)*
Burlington Shell G 360 755-0400
Burlington *(G-2138)*
Chevron Kalama F 360 673-2972
Kalama *(G-4495)*
Coinstar Automated Ret Canada G 425 943-8000
Bellevue *(G-858)*
Core Corporation G 425 485-0574
Bothell *(G-1757)*
D S Thermal G 206 789-2271
Seattle *(G-9782)*
Edge Technologies Inc G 253 383-9181
University Place *(G-13966)*
First Millennium Bank G 360 797-5108
Sequim *(G-11634)*
Gene L Henry Inc G 425 392-1485
Issaquah *(G-4418)*
▲ Lone Ranger LLC E 425 355-7474
Everett *(G-3539)*
Posera USA Inc C 206 364-8686
Lynnwood *(G-6183)*
Softec Systems Inc G 425 741-2055
Everett *(G-3615)*

3579 Office Machines, NEC

Abadan Repo Graphics E 509 946-7697
Richland *(G-8963)*
American Postage Scale Corp G 509 299-6144
Medical Lake *(G-6439)*
Democracy Live Inc F 855 655-8683
Seattle *(G-9819)*
▲ Lone Ranger LLC E 425 355-7474
Everett *(G-3539)*
LSI Logistic Svc Solutions LLC F 253 872-8970
Puyallup *(G-8180)*

Peace Arch Business Center ....G....... 360 366-8500 Blaine *(G-1693)*

▲ Pinpoint LLC ....G....... 425 442-4764 Redmond *(G-8623)*

Pitney Bowes Inc ....E....... 509 363-3694 Spokane *(G-12444)*

Pitney Bowes Inc ....E....... 509 835-1272 Spokane *(G-12445)*

Pitney Bowes Inc ....D....... 253 395-8717 Kent *(G-5066)*

Pitney Bowes Inc ....E....... 509 838-0115 Spokane *(G-12446)*

Preferred Business Solutions ....G....... 425 251-1202 Kent *(G-5079)*

◆ Process Inc ....G....... 425 401-2000 Bellevue *(G-1085)*

The UPS Store Inc ....G....... 360 400-6245 Yelm *(G-15747)*

◆ Wizard International Inc ....D....... 425 551-4300 Mukilteo *(G-6992)*

3581 Automatic Vending Machines

B and P Enterprises ....G....... 509 545-9125 Burbank *(G-2082)*

▼ Cardlock Vending Inc ....G....... 888 487-5040 Bothell *(G-1835)*

▲ Cinevend Inc ....G....... 206 388-3784 Seattle *(G-9684)*

Glacier Water Services Inc ....G....... 360 413-7272 Lacey *(G-5553)*

K&M Business Systems Inc ....G....... 425 557-7789 Sammamish *(G-9224)*

3582 Commercial Laundry, Dry Clean & Pressing Mchs

Chauncey and Shirah Bell Inc ....G....... 206 437-7556 Seattle *(G-9670)*

Hoofsbeat Blankets ....G....... 206 390-0016 Monroe *(G-6579)*

◆ Hydramaster LLC ....D....... 425 775-7272 Mukilteo *(G-6938)*

Northwest Laundry Supply Inc ....G....... 509 487-4800 Spokane Valley *(G-12806)*

REM & AES LLC ....G....... 580 284-3410 Puyallup *(G-8236)*

▲ SK&y International LLC ....G....... 253 833-9525 Auburn *(G-564)*

Total Fabricare Llc ....G....... 206 226-3370 Tacoma *(G-13559)*

◆ Ultrasonics International Corp ....G....... 360 676-0056 Ferndale *(G-3921)*

3585 Air Conditioning & Heating Eqpt

Alaska Marine Refrigeration ....F....... 360 871-4414 Port Orchard *(G-7785)*

Anatoliy Semenko ....G....... 509 525-4486 Walla Walla *(G-14763)*

▲ Biosmart Technologies LLC ....G....... 360 888-8638 Yelm *(G-15729)*

Cold Sea Refrigeration Inc ....G....... 360 466-5850 La Conner *(G-5521)*

Custom Mech Solutions Inc ....F....... 206 973-3900 Seattle *(G-9767)*

Direct Contact LLC ....E....... 425 235-1723 Tukwila *(G-13725)*

▲ Dry Air Technology Inc ....F....... 360 755-9176 Burlington *(G-2153)*

Ducoterra LLC ....G....... 360 788-4200 Bellingham *(G-1327)*

Economy Hearth & Home Inc ....G....... 360 692-8709 Bremerton *(G-1950)*

Even Flow Heating A/C & Rfrgn ....G....... 425 381-0400 Lynnwood *(G-6116)*

▲ Frascold USA Corporation ....G....... 855 547-5600 Everett *(G-3485)*

Hoshizaki Western Dist Ctr Inc ....G....... 253 922-8589 Fife *(G-3959)*

Innovative Manufacturing Inc ....G....... 360 966-7250 Bellingham *(G-1379)*

Innovative Thermal Solutions ....G....... 253 830-4550 Edgewood *(G-3082)*

Integrated Marine Systems Inc ....E....... 360 385-0077 Seattle *(G-10246)*

ISO-Quip Corp ....F....... 360 695-4243 Vancouver *(G-14327)*

Johnson Controls Inc ....G....... 360 448-7771 Vancouver *(G-14339)*

Joshua M Lennox MA ....G....... 253 590-8952 Tacoma *(G-13368)*

▲ King Electrical Mfg Co ....D....... 206 762-0400 Seattle *(G-10345)*

Lennox Inc ....G....... 360 970-8954 Olympia *(G-7322)*

Lennox Industries Commeri ....G....... 206 607-1585 Fife *(G-3965)*

Lennox Stores (partsplus) ....G....... 206 607-1818 Fife *(G-3966)*

Lenox Clothing LLC ....G....... 360 213-9634 Vancouver *(G-14371)*

Lenox Independent Dealer ....G....... 509 837-6400 Sunnyside *(G-13132)*

Levington Trane ....G....... 206 352-2453 Seattle *(G-10412)*

Msr Marine & Vhcl Htg Systems ....G....... 206 546-5670 Shoreline *(G-11790)*

Munters Moisture Control Svcs ....G....... 707 863-4189 Auburn *(G-501)*

Pacific NW Reps LLC ....G....... 509 823-7008 Yakima *(G-15640)*

Pepsi Cola Bottling Co Pasco ....E....... 509 248-1313 Pasco *(G-7616)*

Quality Heating & AC LLC ....F....... 360 613-5614 Silverdale *(G-11854)*

◆ Red DOT Corporation ....B....... 206 151-3840 Tukwila *(G-13803)*

Refrigeration Supplies Distr ....G....... 503 234-4334 Vancouver *(G-14540)*

Refrigeration Supplies Distr ....G....... 509 452-8689 Yakima *(G-15660)*

Rob Sullivan ....G....... 425 882-2221 Bellevue *(G-1103)*

Rv Comfort Systems LLC ....G....... 425 408-3140 Bothell *(G-1898)*

Siemens Industry Inc ....G....... 208 883-8330 Issaquah *(G-4474)*

Sporting Systems Corporation ....G....... 360 607-0036 Vancouver *(G-14603)*

▲ Synsor LLC ....C....... 425 551-1300 Everett *(G-3624)*

▲ Teknotherm Inc ....D....... 206 547-5629 Seattle *(G-11279)*

Ten Pin Brewing Company ....G....... 509 750-0396 Moses Lake *(G-6753)*

Trane Company ....E....... 425 455-4148 Bellevue *(G-1196)*

Trane US Inc ....F....... 509 535-9057 Spokane Valley *(G-12910)*

Trane US Inc ....G....... 425 492-2155 Bothell *(G-1802)*

Trane US Inc ....G....... 206 748-0500 Seattle *(G-11326)*

Trane US Inc ....D....... 425 643-4310 Bellevue *(G-1197)*

◆ Usnr LLC ....G....... 360 225-8267 Woodland *(G-15470)*

Wescold Inc ....E....... 206 284-5710 Seattle *(G-11449)*

Whirlpool Corporation ....E....... 253 875-7100 Spanaway *(G-12081)*

Wilson Air Technologies Inc ....G....... 253 474-9928 Tacoma *(G-13597)*

Wsb Sheetmetal Company ....G....... 425 844-2061 Duvall *(G-3003)*

3586 Measuring & Dispensing Pumps

▲ Adamatic Corporation ....G....... 206 322-5474 Auburn *(G-362)*

◆ Belshaw Bros Inc ....C....... 206 322-5474 Auburn *(G-391)*

▲ Fire Lion Global LLC ....G....... 360 901-9828 Vancouver *(G-14231)*

Petroleum Svc & Solutions LLC ....G....... 253 987-5143 Lake Tapps *(G-5684)*

3589 Service Ind Machines, NEC

Advance Septic Trtmnt Systems ....G....... 360 856-0550 Sedro Woolley *(G-11531)*

Advanced Water Systems Inc ....G....... 520 575-6718 Snohomish *(G-11871)*

Afirm Construction Inc ....G....... 509 928-4361 Spokane Valley *(G-12601)*

Air Tech Abatement Tech Inc ....E....... 509 315-4550 Spokane *(G-12104)*

Almeda Cottage Inc ....E....... 206 285-1674 Seattle *(G-9384)*

Always Pure Water Treatment Sy ....G....... 253 631-0294 Kent *(G-4774)*

Ambient Water Corporation ....G....... 509 474-9451 Spokane Valley *(G-12606)*

Aquatic Specialty Services ....G....... 206 275-0694 Seattle *(G-9415)*

Ausclean Technology Inc ....G....... 360 563-9244 Kirkland *(G-5285)*

Basin Nation AG LLC ....G....... 509 289-9030 Quincy *(G-8289)*

▲ Beverage Specialist Inc ....E....... 206 763-0255 Tukwila *(G-13697)*

▼ Bingham Manufacturing Inc ....G....... 360 863-1170 Monroe *(G-6554)*

Capital Hope Innovations Inc ....G....... 360 480-9154 Bellevue *(G-837)*

Capstan Fund ....G....... 206 626-0800 Seattle *(G-9626)*

Cascade Designs Inc ....G....... 206 505-9500 Seattle *(G-9641)*

Cellular To Go Inc ....G....... 253 255-1955 Gig Harbor *(G-4085)*

Ch 2o Inc ....G....... 360 956-9772 Tumwater *(G-13859)*

Ci Support LLC ....G....... 509 586-6090 Kennewick *(G-4644)*

City of Yakima ....G....... 509 575-6177 Yakima *(G-15532)*

▲ Clarus Technologies LLC ....G....... 360 671-1514 Bellingham *(G-1299)*

Clear Water Compliance LLC ....E....... 425 412-5700 Everett *(G-3419)*

Cloth Creations Inc ....G....... 360 573-7348 Vancouver *(G-14124)*

Coffee Catcher LLC ....G....... 202 704-2868 Seattle *(G-9711)*

Compactors Nw ....G....... 206 747-7316 Seattle *(G-9721)*

Creative Concepts ....G....... 425 743-4671 Edmonds *(G-3104)*

Davis Development & Mfg ....G....... 360 892-7802 Vancouver *(G-14168)*

Document MGT Archives LLC ....G....... 360 501-5047 Longview *(G-5906)*

▲ Dri-Eaz Products Inc ....C....... 360 757-7776 Burlington *(G-2152)*

Emerald City Water LLC ....G....... 425 821-0800 Kirkland *(G-5332)*

Endicott Waste Water Treatment ....G....... 509 657-3407 Endicott *(G-3265)*

Endresen Pressure Washing ....G....... 253 858-7743 Gig Harbor *(G-4098)*

Evoqua Water Technologies LLC ....G....... 360 699-7392 Brush Prairie *(G-2034)*

▲ Filtrific Co LLC ....G....... 425 482-6777 Bellevue *(G-910)*

Fobes District Water & Assn ....G....... 425 334-3311 Snohomish *(G-11910)*

Francis & Wall Shell ....G....... 509 467-5493 Spokane *(G-12262)*

Fsx Equipment Inc ....F....... 360 691-2999 Granite Falls *(G-4272)*

Geogenius LLC ....G....... 206 838-8125 Seattle *(G-10063)*

Harolds Power Vac Inc ....G....... 509 529-2088 Walla Walla *(G-14820)*

Health Guard Industries Inc ....G....... 360 474-9298 Arlington *(G-251)*

Healthier Living Products ....G....... 509 582-6346 Pasco *(G-7589)*

Hydroflow Usa LLC ....F....... 425 497-3900 Redmond *(G-8503)*

Inland Coffee and Beverage ....G....... 509 228-9239 Spokane Valley *(G-12741)*

Jerrys Iron Works Inc ....G....... 425 788-1467 Duvall *(G-2993)*

Jts Kettlecorn ....G....... 509 962-2524 Ellensburg *(G-3209)*

Karcher North America Inc ....D....... 360 833-1600 Camas *(G-2261)*

King County Wastewater Trtmnt ....G....... 206 463-0102 Vashon *(G-14727)*

▲ La Marzocco International LLC ....G....... 206 706-9104 Seattle *(G-10367)*

▲ Landa Inc ....D....... 360 833-9100 Camas *(G-2263)*

Legend Brands ....G....... 360 757-7776 Burlington *(G-2168)*

MA & Kt Inc ....G....... 360 321-4019 Freeland *(G-4032)*

Machine Technology ....G....... 425 334-1951 Snohomish *(G-11942)*

Maury Hill Farm Enterprises ....G....... 206 463-6193 Vashon *(G-14733)*

S I C

Employee Codes: A=Over 500 employees, B=251-500 C=101-250, D=51-100, E=20-50, F=10-19, G=2-9

2019 Washington Manufacturers Register

623

35 INDUSTRIAL AND COMMERCIAL MACHINERY AND COMPUTER EQUIPMENT

McLane Foodservice Dist Inc .... G 253 891-6943
  Sumner (G-13085)
Microhaops Inc .... G 206 595-6426
  Seattle (G-10534)
N R G Enterprises Inc .... D 425 556-3993
  Redmond (G-8592)
North Pacific Industrial .... G 425 251-0335
  Issaquah (G-4454)
Northwest Envmtl & Eqp Inc .... G 253 435-5115
  Puyallup (G-8204)
Northwest Water Treatment LLC .... G 360 354-2044
  Lynden (G-6040)
Oiltrap Environmental Pdts Inc .... F 360 943-6495
  Olympia (G-7350)
▲ Original Expresso Machine .... G 360 686-3643
  Yacolt (G-15490)
Pace Solutions Inc .... G 604 520-6211
  Bellingham (G-1483)
Pacific Fluid Solutions Inc .... G 425 432-6535
  Maple Valley (G-6286)
Pauls Mobile Washing .... G 509 954-1910
  Spokane (G-12432)
Pure Blue Tech Inc .... G 206 724-5707
  Seattle (G-10887)
Pure Drop .... G 425 351-9007
  Seattle (G-10888)
▲ Quality Brewing Incorporated .... G 866 268-5953
  Kelso (G-4543)
Quick Cut Inc .... G 360 893-0689
  Orting (G-7486)
Randy Wood .... G 360 295-3648
  Winlock (G-15155)
◆ Rena Ware International Inc .... E 425 881-6171
  Bellevue (G-1098)
Safe Systems Inc .... F 425 251-8662
  Kent (G-5113)
Sapphire Scientific Inc .... E 928 445-3030
  Burlington (G-2185)
Selg and Associates Inc .... G 425 487-6059
  Woodinville (G-15359)
Shredfast Mobile Data Destruct .... E 509 244-7076
  Airway Heights (G-63)
Shredsupply Inc .... G 509 235-3800
  Cheney (G-2593)
Skagit Northwest Holdings Inc .... C 360 757-7776
  Burlington (G-2188)
Stanleys Sanitary Service .... G 360 795-3369
  Cathlamet (G-2376)
Star Manufacturing Intl Inc .... C 800 882-6368
  Everett (G-3620)
Suez Wts Systems Usa Inc .... D 425 828-2400
  Bellevue (G-1165)
▲ Synesso Inc .... F 206 764-0600
  Seattle (G-11244)
Treit Equipment Co Inc .... G 253 549-2399
  Fox Island (G-4026)
Ultrashred LLC .... G 509 244-1894
  Spokane Valley (G-12919)
US Water Services Inc .... G 360 695-1270
  Vancouver (G-14658)
W Systems .... G 425 616-2512
  Seattle (G-11432)
Waterstation Technology LLC .... G 877 475-7717
  Everett (G-3652)
Welwater .... G 360 909-7970
  Vancouver (G-14683)
Yakima Water Solutions LLC .... G 509 941-9607
  Yakima (G-15720)

3592 Carburetors, Pistons, Rings & Valves

4 Valves LLC .... G 360 387-2272
  Camano Island (G-2205)
Crown Valve & Fitting LLC .... G 360 225-0888
  Woodland (G-15426)
▲ Farwest Aircraft Inc .... E 253 568-1707
  Edgewood (G-3078)
Lkq Corporation .... G 800 733-1916
  Bellingham (G-1412)
Mechpro Inc .... G 206 445-5230
  Auburn (G-496)
▲ Skoflo Industries Inc .... D 425 485-7816
  Woodinville (G-15365)
Texas Avenue Associates .... E 425 889-9642
  Bellevue (G-1184)
Valve Adjusters Co Intl .... G 425 322-4241
  Everett (G-3645)

3593 Fluid Power Cylinders & Actuators

American West Industries Inc .... F 509 535-5040
  Spokane (G-12111)
Custom Hydraulic & Machine Inc .... F 253 854-4666
  Kent (G-4868)
GE Aviation Systems LLC .... C 206 662-2934
  Tukwila (G-13737)
George W Warden Co Inc .... G 509 534-2880
  Spokane Valley (G-12716)
▲ Nabtesco Aerospace Inc .... E 425 602-8400
  Kirkland (G-5407)
Parker-Hannifin Corporation .... B 360 802-1039
  Enumclaw (G-3311)
Service Hydraulics Inc .... F 253 351-6010
  Auburn (G-561)
Superior Fluid Power Inc .... G 509 482-7949
  Spokane Valley (G-12896)
Young Corporation .... E 425 488-2427
  Woodinville (G-15413)

3594 Fluid Power Pumps & Motors

◆ Airborne Ecs LLC .... F 319 538-1051
  Port Angeles (G-7679)
Bogert Manufacturing Inc .... F 206 735-2106
  Pasco (G-7556)
Dessert Industries Inc .... G 425 487-3244
  Snohomish (G-11898)
Ditco Inc .... F 253 854-1002
  Kent (G-4874)
Eagle Pump & Equipment Inc .... G 509 534-1111
  Spokane (G-12237)
Environmental Technologies Inc .... F 253 804-2507
  Pacific (G-7527)
Eriks .... G 253 395-4770
  Kent (G-4896)
Parker-Hannifin Corporation .... G 509 764-5430
  Moses Lake (G-6737)
Parker-Hannifin Corporation .... G 509 764-5430
  Moses Lake (G-6738)
Parker-Hannifin Corporation .... G 425 284-2925
  Redmond (G-8616)
Precision Fldpower Systems LLC .... G 206 938-2894
  Seattle (G-10851)
Service Hydraulics Inc .... F 253 351-6010
  Auburn (G-561)
▲ Sound Hydraulics Inc .... G 206 824-7450
  Des Moines (G-2946)

3596 Scales & Balances, Exc Laboratory

Avery Weigh-Tronix LLC .... G 206 575-1992
  Tukwila (G-13694)
Avery Weigh-Tronix LLC .... G 800 903-8823
  Auburn (G-385)
Bee Jay Scales Inc .... G 509 837-8280
  Sunnyside (G-13113)
Creative Microsystems Inc .... F 425 235-4335
  Renton (G-8776)
Curtis Manufacturing Inc .... F 425 353-4384
  Snohomish (G-11894)
Lectro Tek Services Inc .... E 509 663-2891
  Wenatchee (G-15043)
Pacific Northwest Scale Co .... G 425 259-4720
  Snohomish (G-11960)
Pacific Northwest Technology .... G 360 493-8344
  Lacey (G-5574)
Rice Lake Weighing Systems Inc .... E 206 433-0199
  Kent (G-5102)
▲ Solcon Inc .... E 425 222-5963
  Issaquah (G-4480)
Tandar Corp .... F 503 248-0711
  Vancouver (G-14624)
U S Scale Incorporated .... E 253 872-4803
  Kent (G-5193)

3599 Machinery & Eqpt, Indl & Commercial, NEC

3v Precision Machining Inc .... G 253 584-3888
  Lakewood (G-5694)
A & B Machine & Hydraulics .... F 360 532-2580
  Aberdeen (G-1)
A & G Machine .... G 253 887-8433
  Auburn (G-356)
A&B Quality Finishers Inc .... G 360 805-3500
  Snohomish (G-11868)
Accurate Machine and Mfg .... G 360 693-4783
  Vancouver (G-14007)
Accurate Tool & Die .... G 206 277-0234
  Burien (G-2089)
Accurate Tool & Die Inc .... F 206 244-0745
  Seattle (G-9339)
Acro Machining Inc .... G 360 653-1492
  Arlington (G-192)
Acro Machining Inc .... D 360 659-6401
  Marysville (G-6310)
Admiralty Precision LLC .... G 360 344-2212
  Port Townsend (G-7860)
Airnexion Inc .... G 425 771-5924
  Woodinville (G-15173)
All American Spacer Co LLC .... G 509 633-3440
  Grand Coulee (G-4242)
All Seasons Stump Grinding .... G 425 775-7977
  Lynnwood (G-6071)
Allegis Corporation .... G 425 242-6680
  Kent (G-4772)
▲ Altek Inc .... C 509 921-0597
  Liberty Lake (G-5825)
Amazon Tool Shed .... G 206 429-2185
  Normandy Park (G-7090)
Anchor Cnc LLC .... G 360 516-3501
  Poulsbo (G-7943)
Andersen Machine Shop Inc .... G 360 379-1031
  Port Townsend (G-7863)
Anderson Arospc Qulty Wldg LLC .... G 360 607-2634
  Washougal (G-14942)
Angeles Machine Works Inc .... G 360 457-0011
  Port Angeles (G-7685)
Antique & Heirloom .... G 253 531-6126
  Tacoma (G-13175)
Apex Machining LLC .... G 509 945-0125
  Yakima (G-15511)
Aries Efd Lllp .... G 360 710-7093
  Bremerton (G-1935)
Arlington Machine & Welding .... G 360 435-3300
  Arlington (G-201)
Arrow Machining Company Inc .... E 360 659-0342
  Marysville (G-6312)
Asco Machine Inc .... E 360 735-0500
  Vancouver (G-14043)
Asko Processing Inc .... G 206 284-2659
  Mukilteo (G-6895)
Associated Mch Fabrication Inc .... F 253 395-1155
  Auburn (G-380)
Atlas Construction Spc Co Inc .... G 206 283-2000
  Seattle (G-9455)
Automated Systems Tacoma LLC .... E 253 475-0200
  Tacoma (G-13186)
Automatic Products Mfg Co LLC .... G 253 395-7173
  Kent (G-4801)
Automotive Machine Specialties .... G 425 355-0802
  Everett (G-3376)
Axis Cutparts LLC .... G 253 833-5370
  Auburn (G-386)
AZ Precision Mfg LLC .... G 360 441-9008
  Everson (G-3667)
B & B Equipment Co Inc .... F 509 786-3838
  Prosser (G-8030)
B & C Custom Manufacturing Inc .... G 509 535-0049
  Spokane (G-12135)
B & C Manufacturing Inc .... G 425 787-8868
  Everett (G-3379)
B & G Industries Inc .... F 360 802-0363
  Enumclaw (G-3278)
▲ B & G Machine Inc .... E 206 767-6071
  Seattle (G-9473)
B and D Whirlies .... G 360 887-8471
  Ridgefield (G-9064)
B G Bender Inc .... G 253 848-3742
  Puyallup (G-8125)
B M G Industries .... G 425 415-6360
  Arlington (G-206)
B Triplex Inc .... G 360 904-5981
  Battle Ground (G-689)
Bailey Tool Inc .... G 425 745-8427
  Lynnwood (G-6080)
Bair Metal .... G 425 231-1944
  Arlington (G-208)
Baker Manufacturing Inc .... F 253 840-8610
  Puyallup (G-8128)
Bar Kustom Machining Inc .... G 360 892-3016
  Vancouver (G-14055)
Barnes Welding Inc .... G 509 745-8588
  Waterville (G-15005)
Basic Machining & Electronics .... G 509 308-6341
  Kennewick (G-4627)
Batech LLC .... E 253 395-3630
  Kent (G-4810)
Beacon Machine Inc .... G 425 226-8460
  Renton (G-8754)
▼ Beaver Machine Works Inc .... G 425 402-1032
  Woodinville (G-15187)
▲ Bell Machine Inc .... G 425 254-1173
  Kent (G-4812)

35 INDUSTRIAL AND COMMERCIAL MACHINERY AND COMPUTER EQUIPMENT

Bennett Industries Inc ....E 253 627-7775
  Tacoma *(G-13195)*
Bentriver Tech Inc ....G 360 335-1345
  Washougal *(G-14945)*
Bgi Tooling Company ....G 509 684-5556
  Colville *(G-2738)*
Bills Welding & Machine Shop ....G 509 334-2222
  Pullman *(G-8085)*
Birch Equipment Company Inc ....E 360 734-5744
  Bellingham *(G-1272)*
Birdwell Machine LLC ....G 425 881-1916
  Redmond *(G-8404)*
▲ Bjorklund Machine & Tool Co ......G 425 892-1092
  Woodinville *(G-15193)*
Bjorklund Machine and Tool Co ......G 425 949-5761
  Bothell *(G-1830)*
Blackies Grinding Service Inc ....G 253 735-1835
  Auburn *(G-394)*
Blackstone Manufacturing Inc ....G 509 495-1405
  Cheney *(G-2577)*
Blue Heron Group Inc ....F 206 767-2688
  Seattle *(G-9548)*
Bluewater Industries Inc ....F 509 765-4623
  Moses Lake *(G-6687)*
BM Prgrm & Machining Svc Inc .....F 425 743-5373
  Mukilteo *(G-6898)*
Bombora Global LLC ....G 206 617-6996
  Sammamish *(G-9191)*
Bowman-Morton Mfg & Mch Inc ....F 206 524-8890
  Seattle *(G-9573)*
Bradshaw Machine Co ....G 425 337-2802
  Snohomish *(G-11882)*
Bridgeways ....D 425 513-2989
  Everett *(G-3401)*
Briggs Mch & Fabrication LLC ....F 509 535-0125
  Spokane Valley *(G-12645)*
Brockman Machine Works LLC ......F 509 735-1354
  Kennewick *(G-4633)*
Browns Daily Grind ....G 360 556-3525
  Shelton *(G-11687)*
Bullock Machining Co ....G 425 432-8261
  Ravensdale *(G-8333)*
Buried Hatchet Tool Co LLC ....G 253 677-9730
  Seattle *(G-9600)*
Butler Tool & Manufacturing ....G 425 348-7672
  Everett *(G-3405)*
C T Specialties ....G 360 786-0274
  Tumwater *(G-13854)*
Caliber Precision Inc ....G 360 333-7602
  Mount Vernon *(G-6782)*
Camano Mold Inc ....E 360 387-0961
  Camano Island *(G-2209)*
Camco Tool & Prototype Inc ....G 360 966-1106
  Bellingham *(G-1288)*
Cannon Machine Products Inc ....G 509 627-0505
  Kennewick *(G-4641)*
Carlson Machine Works Inc ....G 509 535-0028
  Spokane *(G-12169)*
Cascade Cnc LLC ....G 360 366-2580
  Custer *(G-2853)*
Cascade Hydraulics and Machine ....E 360 423-1082
  Longview *(G-5896)*
Cashmere Manufacturing LLC ....E 509 888-2141
  East Wenatchee *(G-3009)*
Caskey Industrial Supply Co ....G 360 533-6366
  Cosmopolis *(G-2798)*
Catapult Solutions ....G 509 849-2660
  Prescott *(G-8023)*
CD Fabrication ....G 253 273-2005
  Puyallup *(G-8134)*
City Grind Works ....G 206 769-0006
  Shoreline *(G-11765)*
▲ Clarification Techology Inc ....G 425 820-4850
  Kirkland *(G-5307)*
Claudes Accurate Machining ....G 360 546-5840
  Vancouver *(G-14120)*
Coastal Manufacturing Inc ....E 425 407-0624
  Everett *(G-3421)*
Coherent Resources Inc ....F 509 747-3541
  Cheney *(G-2581)*
Collins Machine Inc ....G 206 767-4149
  Seattle *(G-9714)*
Columbia Basin Machine Co Inc ....G 509 765-6212
  Moses Lake *(G-6695)*
Common Tone Arts ....G 206 251-8260
  Seattle *(G-9720)*
Concept Reality Inc ....F 360 695-3860
  Vancouver *(G-14144)*
Config-Systems ....G 360 871-8091
  Port Orchard *(G-7799)*

Corvus and Columba LLC ....G 206 673-7860
  Seattle *(G-9745)*
Cowlitz Valley Machine Inc ....G 360 748-0124
  Chehalis *(G-2486)*
Creative Machining Company ....F 360 855-1981
  Burlington *(G-2148)*
Crescent Machine Works Inc ....G 509 328-2820
  Spokane *(G-12208)*
Crossrads Precision Rifles LLC .....G 360 931-4505
  Vancouver *(G-14154)*
Curtis Machining ....G 253 862-9256
  Sumner *(G-13063)*
Custom Craft LLC ....E 253 826-5450
  Sumner *(G-13064)*
Custom Firescreen Inc ....G 425 821-4800
  Kirkland *(G-5319)*
Custom Gear Inc ....G 206 767-9448
  Tukwila *(G-13722)*
Custom Hydraulic & Machine Inc ....F 253 854-4666
  Kent *(G-4868)*
D & G Auto Parts ....G 360 696-3631
  Vancouver *(G-14161)*
D G Parrott & Son ....G 360 352-8242
  Olympia *(G-7263)*
Dabs Manufacturing & Assembly ....F 253 872-2200
  Kent *(G-4870)*
Daily Grind ....G 253 632-7992
  Buckley *(G-2056)*
Daily Grind Uptown ....G 509 448-1281
  Spokane *(G-12215)*
Dans Machine Works ....G 360 403-0887
  Marysville *(G-6329)*
Dans Tool Truck ....G 509 520-4531
  Dayton *(G-2880)*
Delta Camshaft Inc ....G 253 383-4152
  Tacoma *(G-13257)*
Delta Grind LLC ....G 360 459-8205
  Olympia *(G-7267)*
Dentzel Carousel Co ....G 360 385-1068
  Port Townsend *(G-7879)*
Detec Systems LLC ....G 253 272-3252
  Tacoma *(G-13260)*
Developmental Machine ....G 253 631-6953
  Auburn *(G-424)*
Dg Machine ....G 253 735-1373
  Auburn *(G-426)*
Diebels Welding & Machine ....G 509 422-0457
  Okanogan *(G-7196)*
▼ Diesel America West Inc ....G 360 378-4182
  Friday Harbor *(G-4042)*
Diesel Tech Machining Inc ....G 509 576-8299
  Yakima *(G-15554)*
Dkfab Inc ....G 503 710-2064
  Zillah *(G-15754)*
Dml Tool Grinding ....G 253 752-3638
  Tacoma *(G-13264)*
Dullum Industries Inc ....G 360 254-3220
  Vancouver *(G-14189)*
Dustys Machine Shop ....G 360 694-6201
  Vancouver *(G-14191)*
Dynamic Automotive Distrs ....G 206 725-4474
  Seattle *(G-9864)*
Dyno-Tech Machine LLC ....G 360 568-7023
  Snohomish *(G-11902)*
Dz & Family Machine Works ....G 360 225-6261
  Woodland *(G-15428)*
Ed Ka Manufacturing Inc ....G 509 635-1521
  Garfield *(G-4068)*
◆ Edco Inc ....E 360 424-6600
  Mount Vernon *(G-6792)*
Electro Erosion Specialties ....G 425 251-9440
  Renton *(G-8792)*
Element 13 Precision LLC ....G 360 597-3195
  Vancouver *(G-14198)*
▲ Elkay Ssp LLC ....E 509 533-0808
  Spokane *(G-12241)*
Elliott Bay Holding Co LLC ....G 206 762-6560
  Seattle *(G-9901)*
Evergreen Mch & Fabrication ....F 509 249-1141
  Yakima *(G-15565)*
Exacto Inc ....G 253 531-5311
  Tacoma *(G-13284)*
Fab Shop LLC ....E 253 568-9124
  Edgewood *(G-3077)*
◆ Fabrication Enterprises Inc ....F 503 240-0878
  Vancouver *(G-14218)*
Fabrication Technologies LLC ....G 360 293-3707
  Anacortes *(G-127)*
Far West Machine Inc ....G 509 422-0312
  Malott *(G-6237)*

Farwest Operating LLC ....D 509 453-1663
  Moxee *(G-6878)*
Fatkid Machine LLC ....G 425 481-5214
  Woodinville *(G-15241)*
Finco Corp ....G 360 854-0772
  Sedro Woolley *(G-11538)*
Fishing Vessel Owners Mar Way ....F 206 282-6421
  Seattle *(G-10000)*
Five Tool Food Service LLC ....G 253 761-5621
  Tacoma *(G-13298)*
Fluid Process Engineering LLC ......G 425 868-0899
  Sammamish *(G-9207)*
Fluke Metal Products Inc ....D 425 485-9666
  Bothell *(G-1764)*
Foss Stump Grinding ....G 360 799-2100
  Gold Bar *(G-4187)*
Four-H Machine LLC ....F 425 471-5757
  Anacortes *(G-131)*
Foust Fabrication Co ....G 509 684-3754
  Colville *(G-2753)*
Fred J Kimball Machine Shop ....G 509 529-5339
  Walla Walla *(G-14810)*
Freeman Companies ....G 425 656-1255
  Renton *(G-8804)*
Frontside Grind LLC ....G 206 246-5697
  Seattle *(G-10030)*
Fuhrers Machine LLC ....G 360 533-5517
  Hoquiam *(G-4337)*
Fuse Weld Grind ....G 360 261-2722
  Vancouver *(G-14244)*
G & M Machine LLC ....G 509 946-3201
  Richland *(G-9000)*
G & M Manufacturing Inc ....G 206 281-4039
  Arlington *(G-238)*
G B Machining Inc ....G 253 848-8055
  Edgewood *(G-3079)*
Gem Welding & Fabrication ....G 360 378-5818
  Friday Harbor *(G-4047)*
Gemmells Machine Works Inc ....G 509 382-4159
  Dayton *(G-2882)*
Gerrys Machine Shop Inc ....G 360 686-1108
  Yacolt *(G-15482)*
Gibson Performance Engines ....G 509 251-5171
  Spokane Valley *(G-12717)*
Gilmour Machinery ....G 360 263-5515
  Battle Ground *(G-704)*
Glamazon Salon LLC ....G 509 703-7145
  Spokane *(G-12275)*
Global Machine Works Inc ....E 360 403-8432
  Arlington *(G-243)*
Gms Fabrication ....G 425 677-4573
  Auburn *(G-451)*
Gms Metal Works Inc ....F 253 736-2178
  Auburn *(G-452)*
Go Planit LLC ....G 206 227-0660
  Mattawa *(G-6407)*
Gorleys Precision Machine ....F 360 423-4567
  Longview *(G-5912)*
Grind All Inc ....G 253 854-6117
  Kent *(G-4929)*
Grit City Grind House LLC ....G 203 898-5627
  Tacoma *(G-13326)*
H & S Machine ....G 425 483-2772
  Woodinville *(G-15258)*
Halwest Technologies Inc ....G 509 674-1882
  Cle Elum *(G-2669)*
▼ Hamburg Precision Inc ....G 360 225-0212
  Woodland *(G-15438)*
▲ Hamiltonjet Inc ....E 206 784-8400
  Woodinville *(G-15259)*
Hanson Precision Inc ....G 360 793-0626
  Gold Bar *(G-4189)*
Harbor Island Mch Works Inc ....E 206 682-7637
  Seattle *(G-10140)*
Harbor Machine & Fabricating ....F 360 533-1188
  Hoquiam *(G-4340)*
Hard Rock Machine Works Inc ......G 509 529-9833
  Walla Walla *(G-14819)*
Hardy Engineering & Mfg Inc ....E 253 735-6488
  Auburn *(G-460)*
Heads Up Inc ....G 253 833-4546
  Auburn *(G-461)*
Hensleys Mobile Welding ....G 360 532-1633
  Aberdeen *(G-16)*
High Liftt LLC ....G 425 216-3050
  Mattawa *(G-6408)*
Highland Machine Works ....G 360 263-1216
  La Center *(G-5506)*
Highway Grind Inc ....G 509 466-5061
  Mead *(G-6430)*

Employee Codes: A=Over 500 employees, B=251-500
C=101-250, D=51-100, E=20-50, F=10-19, G=2-9

Hiline Engrg & Fabrication Inc..............E....... 509 943-9043
Richland (G-9006)
Hobart Machined Products Inc.............G....... 425 432-3440
Hobart (G-4324)
Hog Farm Custom Machine...................G....... 509 365-3917
Appleton (G-188)
Holland Machine Inc..............................G....... 509 662-6235
Wenatchee (G-15039)
Homestead Machine...............................G....... 425 228-1851
Renton (G-8818)
Honeycutt Machine Inc.........................E....... 425 493-0525
Mukilteo (G-6935)
Honeycutt Manufacturing LLC..............E....... 425 493-0525
Mukilteo (G-6936)
Horizon Manufacturing Inds Inc...........F....... 360 322-7368
Arlington (G-252)
Huebner Manufacturing.........................G....... 253 630-9600
Auburn (G-469)
Hummingbird Precision Mch Co...........F....... 360 252-2737
Lacey (G-5556)
Hwy Grind Inc...G....... 509 710-7704
Spokane (G-12300)
Hydro-Tech Genertr Repair Plus...........F....... 509 536-9464
Spokane Valley (G-12734)
Hydro-Tech Genertr Repair Plus...........F....... 509 276-2063
Chattaroy (G-2447)
Idl Precision Machining LLC.................E....... 425 315-8080
Mukilteo (G-6941)
Imagination Fabrication........................G....... 425 415-1311
Woodinville (G-15264)
Industrial Repair Service Inc.................G....... 253 395-8852
Kent (G-4950)
Industrial Welding Co Inc.......................F....... 509 598-2356
Spokane (G-12306)
Infinity Fabrication Inc...........................G....... 360 435-7460
Arlington (G-254)
Innova Mfg LLC......................................G....... 509 946-7461
Richland (G-9010)
Inspection Plus..G....... 509 534-9290
Otis Orchards (G-7514)
Intek Manufacturing Inc..........................G....... 253 857-5073
Olalla (G-7206)
Intermountain Machine...........................G....... 509 482-0431
Spokane (G-12322)
Irongate Machine Inc..............................F....... 360 734-4718
Bellingham (G-1384)
Island Custom Machining.......................G....... 360 341-5687
Clinton (G-2690)
J & D Machine & Gear Inc.......................G....... 206 762-3274
Seattle (G-10264)
J & L Machining and More LLC.............G....... 503 317-8284
La Center (G-5507)
▲ **J Newell Corporation**.........................E....... 360 435-8955
Arlington (G-260)
Jadron Tools..G....... 253 862-3908
Lakewood (G-5729)
Jakes Small Mch Fbrication Sp.............G....... 509 286-3690
Latah (G-5792)
Janicki Industries Inc..............................B....... 360 856-5143
Hamilton (G-4313)
JC Manufacturing....................................G....... 206 870-3827
Kent (G-4967)
Jemco Cmpnents Fabrication Inc.........D....... 425 827-7611
Kirkland (G-5372)
Jerry Gamin...G....... 253 884-3075
Vancouver (G-14337)
Jetco Mch & Fabrication LLC................F....... 509 243-8910
Clarkston (G-2636)
Jetpoint Technologies Inc.......................G....... 360 854-0518
Sedro Woolley (G-11547)
Jim s Machining Service Inc...................G....... 509 926-1868
Spokane Valley (G-12753)
Jj Enterprises...G....... 253 862-8854
Lake Tapps (G-5679)
Jodal Manufacturing................................G....... 206 763-8848
Seattle (G-10300)
Joe Constance...F....... 425 347-8920
Everett (G-3524)
Joels Machine Shop................................G....... 509 488-3234
Othello (G-7497)
John M Smith...G....... 360 484-7738
Naselle (G-7013)
Johnsons Machine and Prfmce Sp.......G....... 360 352-4465
Olympia (G-7313)
Johnsons Stump Grinding S...................G....... 360 334-4832
Snohomish (G-11928)
K & D Machine LLC..................................F....... 509 882-2239
Grandview (G-4249)
▲ **K & T Machine Incorporated**.............G....... 425 347-2157
Lynnwood (G-6145)

Kalama Precision Machine.....................G....... 360 673-1255
Kalama (G-4502)
Kenneth Walker..G....... 360 748-7519
Chehalis (G-2508)
Kenworthy Machine..................................G....... 425 788-2131
Duvall (G-2994)
Khan Machine Tool Company Ltd.........G....... 206 784-9694
Lynnwood (G-6149)
Kinematics Marine Eqp Inc....................G....... 360 659-5415
Marysville (G-6348)
King Machine LLC....................................F....... 425 743-5464
Mukilteo (G-6948)
Kjar Industrial...G....... 206 992-7151
Lynnwood (G-6152)
Koch Machine Inc.....................................G....... 206 241-7178
Seattle (G-10350)
▲ **Korvan Industries Inc**..........................D....... 360 354-1500
Lynden (G-6029)
Kraig Green Machining............................G....... 360 275-3732
Bremerton (G-1972)
Krista K Thie..G....... 509 493-2626
White Salmon (G-15121)
Kroll Machine & Supply Inc....................G....... 509 397-4666
Colfax (G-2715)
L & M Prcision Fabrication Inc.............E....... 509 244-5446
Airway Heights (G-55)
L L G Machine Works...............................G....... 360 793-1920
Sultan (G-13028)
Lakota Industries Inc...............................G....... 360 659-5333
Marysville (G-6351)
▲ **Lamiglas Inc**..E....... 360 225-9436
Woodland (G-15444)
Larock Enterprises Inc.............................F....... 509 966-4542
Union Gap (G-13938)
Larsen Machine...G....... 509 545-0346
Pasco (G-7599)
Lasermach Inc...G....... 425 485-3169
Woodinville (G-15284)
Laz Tool and Manufacturing...................F....... 360 568-5749
Snohomish (G-11936)
▲ **Lecoq Machine Work Inc**.....................G....... 206 762-4606
Seattle (G-10397)
Limited Productions Inc...........................G....... 425 635-7489
Bellevue (G-985)
Lindmark Machine Works Inc.................F....... 206 624-0777
Seattle (G-10424)
Locke Precision LLC................................F....... 253 904-8615
Puyallup (G-8178)
Loder Instrument Company Inc.............G....... 425 869-3861
Redmond (G-8536)
Lund Custom Machining Inc...................G....... 360 432-0310
Shelton (G-11709)
Lydens Specialty Machine Llc...............G....... 360 345-1010
Chehalis (G-2511)
M & L Machine Inc.....................................G....... 360 825-4700
Enumclaw (G-3303)
M & M Manufacturing Inc........................G....... 360 896-2822
Vancouver (G-14389)
M E B Manufacturing.................................G....... 425 259-6074
Everett (G-3543)
M3 Machine Inc..G....... 360 778-1427
Bellingham (G-1416)
Machine Repair & Design Inc..................F....... 253 826-6329
Sumner (G-13081)
Machining Technology Inc.......................F....... 253 872-0359
Auburn (G-491)
Machinists Inc..C....... 206 763-0990
Seattle (G-10460)
Machinists Inc..E....... 206 763-0840
Seattle (G-10461)
Machinists Inc..E....... 206 763-1036
Seattle (G-10462)
Mackay Manufacturing Inc......................D....... 509 922-7742
Spokane Valley (G-12780)
Mainland Machinery LLC.........................G....... 360 354-2348
Lynden (G-6036)
Manufacturing & Design Inc...................G....... 425 356-2648
Mukilteo (G-6953)
Maritime Fabrications Inc.......................E....... 360 466-3629
La Conner (G-5524)
Mark Hummel..G....... 425 271-7156
Issaquah (G-4444)
Marlowe Machine Inc................................G....... 509 484-5979
Spokane (G-12383)
Material Inc..G....... 509 633-1740
Grand Coulee (G-4243)
Material Inc..F....... 509 754-4695
Ephrata (G-3342)
Material Inc..G....... 509 787-4585
Quincy (G-8303)

MB Precision Inc..G....... 253 833-1695
Auburn (G-494)
Mc Ilvanie Machine Works Inc................F....... 509 452-3131
Yakima (G-15616)
McCann Industries LLC...........................G....... 253 537-6919
Spanaway (G-12064)
Mechanical Specialties LLC...................G....... 360 273-7604
Olympia (G-7335)
Medical Micro Machining Inc..................G....... 509 397-2276
Colfax (G-2717)
Merlins Workshop LLC............................G....... 206 817-9677
Port Hadlock (G-7760)
Metal Master LLC......................................G....... 253 948-7295
Tacoma (G-13409)
▲ **Metal Works Inc**.....................................G....... 509 782-8811
Dryden (G-2953)
Metals Fabrication Company Inc...........D....... 509 244-2909
Airway Heights (G-56)
Metals McHning Fabricators Inc............F....... 509 248-8890
Union Gap (G-13944)
Methow Valley Industrial LLC.................G....... 509 997-7777
Twisp (G-13914)
Micro Dimension Inc..................................G....... 360 887-0620
Ridgefield (G-9094)
Micro Machining..G....... 360 837-3200
Washougal (G-14966)
Mike and Leslie Corporation...................G....... 206 246-4911
Tukwila (G-13773)
Millard Technical Service........................G....... 253 218-0115
Auburn (G-497)
Milman Engineering Inc...........................G....... 360 273-5080
Rochester (G-9137)
Moco Engineering & Fabrication...........F....... 509 226-0199
Spokane Valley (G-12792)
Monarch Machine and Tl Co Inc............E....... 509 547-7753
Pasco (G-7603)
Monroe Machined Products Inc.............E....... 206 242-4898
Seatac (G-9291)
Monster Concepts Inc..............................G....... 206 706-6730
Seattle (G-10560)
Moonlite Machining Inc............................G....... 360 863-8535
Monroe (G-6599)
Moonlite Machining Inc............................G....... 360 794-6622
Monroe (G-6600)
Morgan Branch Cnc Inc...........................G....... 360 435-7170
Marysville (G-6361)
Mountain View Industries.........................G....... 425 788-5551
Woodinville (G-15316)
Multi Manufacturing Inc............................G....... 509 452-5628
Yakima (G-15626)
Myrle B Foster...G....... 360 733-2509
Bellingham (G-1455)
Nelscorp Inc...G....... 206 660-6313
Stanwood (G-12982)
Neumeier Engineering Inc.......................E....... 253 854-3635
Kent (G-5020)
New Tech Industries Inc..........................E....... 425 374-3814
Mukilteo (G-6955)
Nicholson Engineering Co Inc................G....... 253 272-9167
Tacoma (G-13428)
Nor Prop Inc...E....... 253 939-1200
Auburn (G-508)
North Bend Automotives...........................G....... 425 888-4522
North Bend (G-7119)
North Ridge Machine LLC.......................G....... 509 765-8928
Moses Lake (G-6732)
Northstone Industries LLC.......................G....... 509 844-7775
Spokane (G-12410)
Northway Products Inc.............................E....... 425 493-1127
Mukilteo (G-6956)
Northwest Automatics Inc........................G....... 253 852-9006
Kent (G-5028)
Northwest Center.......................................E....... 360 403-7330
Arlington (G-289)
▲ **Northwest Center**.................................C....... 206 285-9140
Seattle (G-10639)
Northwest Center.......................................E....... 425 355-1855
Everett (G-3557)
Northwest Machine Works.......................G....... 360 435-3600
Arlington (G-290)
Northwest Wire EDM Inc..........................G....... 509 893-0885
Spokane Valley (G-12809)
Northwestern Precision Tool &...............G....... 425 333-5201
Carnation (G-2297)
Nyeberg Machine.......................................G....... 425 235-9675
Renton (G-8861)
Oberg Manufacturing Inc.........................G....... 360 435-8161
Arlington (G-293)
OK Tool & Machine Works........................G....... 360 736-8350
Centralia (G-2422)

SIC SECTION
35 INDUSTRIAL AND COMMERCIAL MACHINERY AND COMPUTER EQUIPMENT

Olympic Machine & Welding Inc ... G ... 253 627-8571
Tacoma ***(G-13443)***
Omak Machine Shop Inc ... G ... 509 826-1030
OMAK ***(G-7440)***
Omega Architectural Pdts Inc ... G ... 425 821-7222
Kirkland ***(G-5417)***
▲ Onamac Industries Inc ... C ... 425 743-6676
Everett ***(G-3560)***
Otogear ... G ... 360 852-0250
Seattle ***(G-10716)***
Overseas Security ... G ... 206 364-6784
Seattle ***(G-10723)***
Oyate Research & Training Cons ... G ... 360 239-2281
Yelm ***(G-15742)***
P & J Machining Inc ... D ... 253 841-0500
Puyallup ***(G-8212)***
P&J Machining Inc ... G ... 253 841-0500
Puyallup ***(G-8214)***
Pacer Design & Manufacturing ... F ... 425 481-5300
Bothell ***(G-1883)***
Pacific Machine Inc ... G ... 253 383-3838
Lakewood ***(G-5744)***
Pacific Precision Mfg ... G ... 360 737-2938
Vancouver ***(G-14471)***
Pacific Tool Inc ... D ... 425 882-1970
Redmond ***(G-8609)***
Pape Machinery Inc ... F ... 360 575-9959
Kelso ***(G-4541)***
Pasco Machine Company ... F ... 509 547-2448
Pasco ***(G-7613)***
Pasco Processing LLC ... D ... 509 544-6700
Pasco ***(G-7614)***
Paul Schurman Machine Inc ... F ... 360 887-3193
Ridgefield ***(G-9101)***
Paxton Sales Corporation ... F ... 509 453-0397
Yakima ***(G-15642)***
Pearce Design ... G ... 425 481-5214
Monroe ***(G-6604)***
Pentz Design Pattern Fndry Inc ... E ... 425 788-6490
Duvall ***(G-2997)***
Peter K Grossman ... G ... 206 824-6626
Renton ***(G-8877)***
Peterson Tools ... G ... 425 870-0137
Marysville ***(G-6368)***
Phyl Mar Swiss Products Inc ... G ... 360 695-9242
Washougal ***(G-14978)***
Plastics West Inc ... G ... 360 538-0115
Aberdeen ***(G-30)***
Power Equipment Supply Llc ... G ... 206 817-5627
Everett ***(G-3580)***
Power Machine Services Inc ... G ... 509 536-1721
Spokane ***(G-12450)***
Powers Machine & Fabrication ... G ... 206 824-9726
Des Moines ***(G-2942)***
Precise Machining Inc ... G ... 360 629-0420
Stanwood ***(G-12985)***
Precise Tool & Gage Co Inc ... G ... 206 623-1120
Seattle ***(G-10847)***
Precision Alias ... G ... 425 222-0744
Fall City ***(G-3706)***
Precision Machine & Mfg ... G ... 360 734-1081
Bellingham ***(G-1502)***
Precision Machine & Tool Inc ... G ... 425 745-6229
Lynnwood ***(G-6184)***
Precision Machine Supply ... G ... 509 922-1666
Spokane Valley ***(G-12837)***
Precision Machine Works ... G ... 253 661-8180
Federal Way ***(G-3771)***
Precision Machining ... G ... 509 972-1986
Yakima ***(G-15651)***
Pro Safety Inc ... G ... 360 686-3686
Yacolt ***(G-15492)***
Progressive Machine Inc ... F ... 509 547-4062
Pasco ***(G-7619)***
Project Machine Inc ... G ... 360 446-2858
Rainier ***(G-8320)***
Proto Technologies Inc ... D ... 509 891-4747
Liberty Lake ***(G-5855)***
Proto-Rpid McHning Sltions LLC ... G ... 503 744-0358
Vancouver ***(G-14514)***
Puget Sound Precision Inc ... F ... 360 297-3939
Poulsbo ***(G-7994)***
Pyramid Grinding ... G ... 425 254-1820
Renton ***(G-8886)***
Qnc Machine Inc ... G ... 206 282-5854
Seattle ***(G-10896)***
Quality Machine ... G ... 360 573-8773
Vancouver ***(G-14519)***
Quality Machine & Hydraulic ... G ... 206 244-5674
Seatac ***(G-9301)***
Quality On Time Machining Inc ... G ... 360 802-3700
Enumclaw ***(G-3314)***
▲ Questech Unlimited ... E ... 360 691-2620
Granite Falls ***(G-4284)***
R & R Machine ... G ... 360 568-4844
Snohomish ***(G-11965)***
R D Wing Co Inc ... F ... 425 821-7222
Kirkland ***(G-5449)***
R&D Machine LLC ... G ... 360 694-9573
Vancouver ***(G-14528)***
Randle Steel & Machine Inc ... G ... 360 497-7477
Randle ***(G-8327)***
Rapid Machine Inc ... G ... 360 435-8135
Arlington ***(G-312)***
Rbk Manufacturing Incorporated ... F ... 253 804-8636
Auburn ***(G-546)***
RDL Enterprises Inc ... F ... 509 529-5480
Walla Walla ***(G-14859)***
Reliance LLC ... G ... 425 481-3030
Woodinville ***(G-15347)***
▼ Rex Plastics Inc ... E ... 360 892-0366
Vancouver ***(G-14549)***
Reynold Grey & Associates ... G ... 360 385-1167
Port Townsend ***(G-7923)***
Richard Ezetta Stump Grinding ... G ... 360 687-8054
Battle Ground ***(G-735)***
Richardson Precision Machine ... G ... 509 945-9939
Yakima ***(G-15661)***
Richmond Systems Inc ... E ... 360 455-8284
Olympia ***(G-7386)***
Rise N Grind ... G ... 360 452-9335
Port Angeles ***(G-7739)***
Rivercrest Holdings LLC ... G ... 360 723-5354
Battle Ground ***(G-736)***
Rjm Corporation ... F ... 253 887-9100
Auburn ***(G-548)***
Roberts Precision Machine Inc ... F ... 360 805-1000
Monroe ***(G-6615)***
Robobear LLC ... G ... 425 453-1391
Bellevue ***(G-1105)***
Rocky Mountain Machining ... G ... 509 927-8797
Spokane Valley ***(G-12855)***
Rogroc LLC ... G ... 360 435-6417
Arlington ***(G-316)***
Rs Machine Inc ... G ... 360 694-0044
Vancouver ***(G-14559)***
Ryan Machine Inc ... E ... 253 854-9000
Auburn ***(G-553)***
Ryans Machine Shop ... G ... 360 427-9490
Shelton ***(G-11728)***
S & H Auto Parts Inc ... G ... 360 354-4468
Lynden ***(G-6051)***
Salmon Creek Machine ... F ... 360 573-7958
Vancouver ***(G-14568)***
Sapphire Materials Company ... G ... 360 210-5124
Washougal ***(G-14983)***
Sarco Precision ... F ... 360 424-0605
Mount Vernon ***(G-6833)***
Schroeders Machine Works Inc ... F ... 360 573-6911
Vancouver ***(G-14572)***
Screw You LLC ... G ... 360 400-3648
Yelm ***(G-15745)***
SDaerospace ... G ... 425 440-9295
Arlington ***(G-321)***
Seal-Guard Corporation ... G ... 253 833-7080
Auburn ***(G-557)***
Seattle Machine Works Inc ... G ... 206 763-2710
Seattle ***(G-11063)***
Seattle Precision Form Inc ... G ... 253 872-8356
Kent ***(G-5124)***
Seattle Stump Grinding ... G ... 206 285-2887
Seattle ***(G-11079)***
Sefco LLC ... G ... 509 921-1121
Spokane Valley ***(G-12863)***
Senior Operations LLC ... B ... 360 435-1119
Arlington ***(G-327)***
Ser Pro Inc ... G ... 206 767-3100
Seattle ***(G-11090)***
Serena Inc ... G ... 253 939-6509
Auburn ***(G-560)***
Shamrock Machining Inc ... E ... 509 534-3031
Spokane Valley ***(G-12868)***
Shareway Industries Inc ... E ... 253 804-0670
Auburn ***(G-562)***
Silver King Mining & Milling ... G ... 509 445-1406
Cusick ***(G-2852)***
Sittauer Industries Inc ... G ... 425 741-1125
Mukilteo ***(G-6977)***
Sno-Mon Stamping Inc ... G ... 360 794-6304
Monroe ***(G-6621)***
Snohomish Iron Works Inc ... G ... 360 568-2811
Snohomish ***(G-11982)***
Snoqualmie Machine Works ... G ... 425 888-1464
Snoqualmie ***(G-12025)***
Sound Machine Products Inc ... F ... 253 872-5876
Kent ***(G-5140)***
Sound Manufacturing Inc ... E ... 253 872-8007
Kent ***(G-5141)***
Southend Machine Inc ... G ... 253 735-1035
Auburn ***(G-569)***
Specialized Machine Works ... G ... 206 715-5901
Kent ***(G-5146)***
◆ Spokane Machinery Company ... F ... 509 535-1654
Spokane ***(G-12519)***
Squires Machine Inc ... G ... 425 672-7101
Lynnwood ***(G-6205)***
Stenerson & Sons ... G ... 360 829-1219
Buckley ***(G-2074)***
Streich Bros Inc ... E ... 253 383-1491
Tacoma ***(G-13527)***
Swift Machining Inc ... G ... 360 335-8213
Washougal ***(G-14990)***
Synthigen LLC ... G ... 208 772-7294
Spokane ***(G-12538)***
Systematic Machinery LLC ... F ... 509 892-0399
Spokane ***(G-12539)***
T & D Machine Inc ... G ... 425 486-8338
Kenmore ***(G-4608)***
T & H Machine Inc ... G ... 253 735-6521
Auburn ***(G-575)***
T & JS Machine Shop ... G ... 360 504-2387
Sequim ***(G-11663)***
T Squared Tools LLC ... G ... 406 260-5232
Bellingham ***(G-1565)***
Tango Manufacturing Inc ... G ... 360 693-7228
Vancouver ***(G-14625)***
Taurus Aerospace Group Inc ... G ... 425 423-6200
Everett ***(G-3627)***
Tech Marine Enterprises Inc ... F ... 206 878-7878
Fife ***(G-3995)***
Tek Manufacturing Inc ... G ... 509 921-5424
Spokane Valley ***(G-12904)***
Teodoro Foundation ... G ... 253 475-0200
Tacoma ***(G-13553)***
Terrys Machine & Mfg Inc ... F ... 425 315-8866
Everett ***(G-3629)***
Thomas Machine & Foundry Inc ... D ... 360 651-9100
Marysville ***(G-6395)***
Three Rivers Industrial Mch ... G ... 360 578-1114
Kelso ***(G-4555)***
Three Sigma Manufacturing Inc ... E ... 253 395-1125
Kent ***(G-5179)***
Tidland Hydraulics Inc ... G ... 360 573-6506
Vancouver ***(G-14636)***
▲ Tipke Manufacturing Company ... E ... 509 534-5336
Spokane ***(G-12559)***
Tk Machine ... G ... 509 946-2363
Richland ***(G-9044)***
Toliys Jig Fabrication ... G ... 509 534-2261
Spokane ***(G-12562)***
Tom Bretz ... G ... 509 486-2251
Tonasket ***(G-13661)***
Toms Prfmce Mch & Repr Inc ... G ... 360 256-1722
Vancouver ***(G-14642)***
Toolcraft Inc ... F ... 360 794-5512
Monroe ***(G-6633)***
Torc Star Bolting Tools LLC ... G ... 334 714-0945
Bellevue ***(G-1195)***
Trinity Manufacturing Inc ... G ... 360 474-8639
Arlington ***(G-341)***
Trulife Inc ... D ... 360 714-9000
Bellingham ***(G-1577)***
Turning Point Machining Inc ... G ... 425 252-7300
Marysville ***(G-6398)***
◆ U S Wax & Polymer Inc ... E ... 509 922-1069
Spokane Valley ***(G-12918)***
Unipar West Inc ... G ... 360 293-5332
Anacortes ***(G-182)***
United Machine Shops Inc ... G ... 206 767-0100
Seattle ***(G-11371)***
United Manufacturing Products ... G ... 425 433-1141
Maple Valley ***(G-6296)***
United Stars Aerospace Inc ... E ... 253 859-4540
Seatac ***(G-9308)***
Universal Plant Services of No ... E ... 360 757-4646
Burlington ***(G-2197)***
Utec Metals Inc ... G ... 509 891-7833
Spokane Valley ***(G-12921)***
Utilities Service Company Inc ... G ... 206 246-5674
Tukwila ***(G-13831)***

SIC

Employee Codes: A=Over 500 employees, B=251-500
C=101-250, D=51-100, E=20-50, F=10-19, G=2-9
2019 Washington
Manufacturers Register
627

Utr Manufacturing Inc......G....... 360 901-1435 Vancouver *(G-14659)*

Valley Automotive Machine......G....... 360 336-9722 Mount Vernon *(G-6850)*

Valley Machine Shop Inc......E....... 425 226-5040 Kent *(G-5199)*

Valleyford Metal Crafters LLC......E....... 509 448-5583 Spokane *(G-12579)*

Venturi Holdings LLC......G....... 206 305-0642 Seattle *(G-11411)*

▲ **Versatile Machining Inc**......G....... 206 855-8296 Bainbridge Island *(G-681)*

Wahoo Fabrication......G....... 360 353-3478 Longview *(G-5963)*

Waite Speciality Mch Work Inc......D....... 360 577-0777 Longview *(G-5964)*

Walla Walla Motor Supply Inc......F....... 509 525-2940 Walla Walla *(G-14893)*

Warden Welding Inc......G....... 509 349-2478 Warden *(G-14937)*

▲ **Washington Eqp Mfg Co Inc**......E....... 509 244-4773 Spokane *(G-12583)*

Webers Radiator Service Inc......G....... 509 452-3747 Yakima *(G-15705)*

Wenatchee Qlty Wldg Fbrication......F....... 509 782-0807 Cashmere *(G-2333)*

West Coast Industries Inc......E....... 206 365-7513 Shoreline *(G-11821)*

Westbay Auto Parts Inc......F....... 360 373-1424 Bremerton *(G-2011)*

Western Industrial Tooling Inc......E....... 425 883-6644 Redmond *(G-8711)*

Westom Tools......G....... 360 355-6741 Kelso *(G-4560)*

▲ **Westwood Precision Inc**......D....... 425 742-7011 Everett *(G-3657)*

Whatzit Machining Inc......G....... 360 378-6874 Friday Harbor *(G-4064)*

Wheeler Industries Inc......E....... 509 534-4556 Spokane Valley *(G-12936)*

Whidbey Auto Parts Inc......G....... 360 675-5946 Oak Harbor *(G-7170)*

Whipple Falls Industries......G....... 360 573-0863 Vancouver *(G-14688)*

Whiskey Ridge Mfg Inc......F....... 360 426-6100 Shelton *(G-11750)*

Whittier Machine & Tool Co......G....... 509 276-7855 Clayton *(G-2660)*

Wilson Machine Works Inc......G....... 206 282-7560 Seattle *(G-11480)*

▼ **Wilson Tool & Manufacturing Co**......F....... 509 928-9441 Spokane Valley *(G-12939)*

Woodford Phoenix Aerospace Mfg......G....... 360 736-9689 Centralia *(G-2444)*

Wright Machine Inc......G....... 206 305-0642 Seattle *(G-11499)*

Wynakos Machine Inc......G....... 360 794-9057 Monroe *(G-6640)*

Z-Machine LLC......G....... 509 991-8628 Chattaroy *(G-2455)*

Zoal & Associates LLC......G....... 425 355-9590 Everett *(G-3663)*

Zombie Tinder......G....... 360 548-3132 Arlington *(G-351)*

36 ELECTRONIC AND OTHER ELECTRICAL EQUIPMENT AND COMPONENTS, EXCEPT COMPUTER

3612 Power, Distribution & Specialty Transformers

ABB Inc......G....... 253 280-9900 Kent *(G-4754)*

Air Mod Inc......G....... 360 895-0910 Port Orchard *(G-7784)*

Electronetics LLC......D....... 425 355-1855 Everett *(G-3456)*

▲ **Envirolux Energy Systems LLC**......G....... 800 914-8779 Vancouver *(G-14203)*

Framatome Inc......F....... 425 250-2775 Redmond *(G-8465)*

▲ **Interactive Electronic Systems**......E....... 877 543-8698 Tacoma *(G-13349)*

Jikopower Inc......F....... 253 678-0074 Auburn *(G-481)*

Maddox Industrial Trans LLC......G....... 360 512-3355 Battle Ground *(G-718)*

New Standard Company Limited......G....... 425 641-5718 Bellevue *(G-1027)*

O-Netics Ltd......G....... 425 823-2279 Kirkland *(G-5415)*

Peoples Solar Inc......G....... 530 217-6020 Curlew *(G-2846)*

Power and Lighting LLC......G....... 360 750-0158 Vancouver *(G-14495)*

▲ **Power Conversion Inc**......E....... 425 487-1337 Woodinville *(G-15338)*

Research Reactr Sfty/Anylst Sv......G....... 509 783-6860 Kennewick *(G-4718)*

Roger Habon......G....... 206 240-0122 Renton *(G-8896)*

Sel Development LLC......F....... 509 332-1890 Pullman *(G-8107)*

Spore Incorporated......G....... 206 624-9573 Seattle *(G-11171)*

Transformer Diagnostic Testing......G....... 425 486-4110 Bothell *(G-1803)*

True Sol Innovations Inc......G....... 206 428-7136 Seattle *(G-11343)*

3613 Switchgear & Switchboard Apparatus

Anderson Electric Controls......E....... 206 575-4444 Kent *(G-4783)*

Applied Power & Control Inc......G....... 425 710-9911 Everett *(G-3370)*

Bluefin Marine LLC......G....... 206 276-4087 Kirkland *(G-5293)*

C&K Enterprize LLC......G....... 509 448-2866 Spokane *(G-12165)*

Cets LLC......G....... 206 992-6993 Seattle *(G-9663)*

Controlled Power Incorporated......E....... 425 485-1778 Bothell *(G-1842)*

Eaton Corporation......F....... 253 833-5021 Auburn *(G-431)*

Eaton Corporation......E....... 425 644-5800 Bellevue *(G-889)*

◆ **Eldec Corporation**......A....... 425 743-1313 Lynnwood *(G-6114)*

Electrical Packaging Co Inc......F....... 425 745-5466 Everett *(G-3455)*

Equipment Technology & Design......G....... 509 747-5550 Spokane *(G-12248)*

Evergreen Controls LLC......G....... 253 405-3770 Tacoma *(G-13283)*

Evs Manufacturing Inc......G....... 360 863-6413 Monroe *(G-6570)*

G&J Distributors......G....... 509 325-2100 Spokane *(G-12266)*

General Electric Company......F....... 253 395-1798 Kent *(G-4922)*

Green-On-Green Energy Inc......G....... 206 701-7321 Auburn *(G-457)*

Heritage Electrical Group Inc......G....... 425 774-7595 Everett *(G-3511)*

Hundred Horse Panels LLC......G....... 509 227-5686 Liberty Lake *(G-5834)*

Ikonika Corp......G....... 253 344-1523 Fife *(G-3960)*

Imco Inc......F....... 360 694-7121 Ridgefield *(G-9089)*

Korry Electronics Co......A....... 425 297-9700 Everett *(G-3532)*

Leach International Corp......G....... 425 519-1826 Bellevue *(G-979)*

Lilibete LLC......G....... 206 407-6890 Kent *(G-4996)*

M & I Systems Inc......G....... 206 547-7899 Everett *(G-3542)*

▲ **Morpac Industries Inc**......E....... 253 735-8922 Pacific *(G-7533)*

Omni Technology......G....... 425 823-9295 Kirkland *(G-5419)*

Ornelas LLC......G....... 206 388-2267 Wenatchee *(G-15055)*

Phoenix Power Control Inc......F....... 360 794-8550 Monroe *(G-6606)*

Polaris Glove & Safety In......G....... 206 789-5887 Redmond *(G-8627)*

Process Solutions Inc......E....... 360 629-0910 Stanwood *(G-12987)*

Superior Custom Control......F....... 206 362-8866 Seattle *(G-11222)*

Timberline Controls & Mar Inc......F....... 360 335-8598 Washougal *(G-14993)*

Timken Motor & Crane Svcs LLC......E....... 509 547-1691 Pasco *(G-7638)*

3621 Motors & Generators

◆ **Airborne Ecs LLC**......F....... 319 538-1051 Port Angeles *(G-7679)*

Automated Controls Inc......G....... 206 246-6499 Auburn *(G-384)*

C H W Enterprises Inc......F....... 360 425-8700 Longview *(G-5892)*

City of Sattle-City Light Dept......E....... 509 446-3083 Metaline Falls *(G-6497)*

Cutsforth Inc......E....... 800 290-6458 Ferndale *(G-3835)*

D Square Energy LLC......F....... 425 888-2882 North Bend *(G-7110)*

Ecotech Services LLC......G....... 509 995-5809 Spokane Valley *(G-12689)*

Electrijet Flight Systems Inc......G....... 509 990-9474 Liberty Lake *(G-5831)*

Energy Efficiency Systems Corp......E....... 360 835-7838 Washougal *(G-14953)*

▲ **Ev Drives**......F....... 360 302-5226 Port Townsend *(G-7882)*

Gen-Set Co......G....... 509 891-8452 Spokane Valley *(G-12714)*

Gen-Tech LLC......G....... 206 634-3399 Seattle *(G-10059)*

Global Emergent Tech LLC......G....... 425 999-9021 Seattle *(G-10083)*

Innovatek Inc......G....... 509 375-1093 Kennewick *(G-4676)*

▲ **K & N Electric Motors Inc**......D....... 509 838-8000 Spokane Valley *(G-12759)*

Kaenaa Corp......G....... 425 283-3072 Sammamish *(G-9225)*

Koma Kulshan Associates......G....... 360 853-8530 Concrete *(G-2789)*

◆ **Marine Engine Repair Co Inc**......E....... 206 286-1817 Seattle *(G-10480)*

Nidec America Corporation......G....... 360 666-2445 Battle Ground *(G-724)*

Nine Mile Power Station......G....... 509 466-5322 Nine Mile Falls *(G-7080)*

Oscilla Power Inc......G....... 206 557-7032 Seattle *(G-10715)*

Pacific Power Group LLC......E....... 360 887-5980 Ridgefield *(G-9099)*

Pacific Power Group LLC......E....... 253 395-9077 Auburn *(G-524)*

▲ **Pacific Power Group LLC**......D....... 360 887-7400 Vancouver *(G-14469)*

Portland Stirling Incorporated......G....... 206 855-0819 Bainbridge Island *(G-659)*

▲ **Power Conversion Inc**......E....... 425 487-1337 Woodinville *(G-15338)*

Renewable Energy Tech Inc......G....... 253 267-1965 Lakewood *(G-5751)*

▲ **Safran**......G....... 425 283-5031 Bellevue *(G-1111)*

Safran Usa Inc......E....... 425 462-8613 Bellevue *(G-1112)*

Seattle Synchro......G....... 206 856-5239 Kirkland *(G-5456)*

Silvergen Inc......G....... 360 732-5091 Port Ludlow *(G-7777)*

Tsunami Products Inc......G....... 509 868-5731 Liberty Lake *(G-5865)*

Viper R/C Solutions Inc......G....... 425 968-5389 Redmond *(G-8705)*

White Creek Project LLC......G....... 360 737-9692 Vancouver *(G-14689)*

3624 Carbon & Graphite Prdts

A To Z Composites Inc......F....... 435 680-3762 Bellingham *(G-1236)*

Hexa Materials LLC......G....... 541 337-3669 Seattle *(G-10168)*

Innovative Composite Engrg Inc......D....... 509 493-4484 White Salmon *(G-15119)*

Pyrotek Incorporated......D....... 509 926-6211 Spokane Valley *(G-12846)*

◆ **Sgl Atomotive Carbn Fibers LLC**......D....... 509 762-4600 Moses Lake *(G-6747)*

▲ **Sgl Composites LLC**......G....... 704 593-5177 Moses Lake *(G-6748)*

◆ **Toray Composite Mtls Amer Inc**......A....... 253 846-1777 Tacoma *(G-13557)*

Transition Composites Mfg Inc......G....... 360 312-1497 Bellingham *(G-1574)*

Young Corporation......E....... 206 623-3274 Seattle *(G-11514)*

SIC SECTION — 36 ELECTRONIC AND OTHER ELECTRICAL EQUIPMENT AND COMPONENTS, EXCEPT COMPUTER

3625 Relays & Indl Controls

Anderson Electric Controls .... E 206 575-4444
  Kent *(G-4783)*
Asphalt Equipment & Service Co .... E 253 939-4150
  Auburn *(G-379)*
Astrake Inc .... G 503 470-4470
  Seattle *(G-9446)*
Automated Controls Inc .... G 206 246-6499
  Auburn *(G-384)*
Automation Modules Inc .... G 253 549-4868
  Fox Island *(G-4018)*
Bunker Hill Diagnostics .... G 206 579-1440
  Renton *(G-8765)*
Camtronics Inc .... G 425 487-0013
  Bothell *(G-1753)*
Ces Enterprises .... G 206 443-1742
  Seattle *(G-9661)*
Charter Controls Inc .... F 360 695-2161
  Vancouver *(G-14113)*
Checkmate Industries Inc .... G 360 691-1753
  Granite Falls *(G-4266)*
Controlfreek Inc .... G 509 979-5677
  Spokane Valley *(G-12666)*
▲ Controls Group The Inc .... G 425 828-4149
  Kirkland *(G-5312)*
Custom Controls Corporation .... F 253 922-5874
  Fife *(G-3947)*
DC Engineering Consulting Inc .... G 360 932-2367
  Rainier *(G-8313)*
Digitron Electronics LLC .... F 509 427-4005
  Stevenson *(G-13011)*
Duren Controls .... G 206 745-4987
  Edmonds *(G-3108)*
Eaton Agency Inc .... G 509 448-6556
  Spokane *(G-12238)*
Eaton Corp .... G 253 375-6013
  Graham *(G-4224)*
Electric Concept Labs Inc .... G 503 244-3000
  Castle Rock *(G-2342)*
Fisher-Rosemount Systems Inc .... G 425 488-4111
  Bothell *(G-1853)*
Heatcon Inc .... D 206 575-0815
  Tukwila *(G-13745)*
Heatcon Composite Systems Inc .... G 206 575-1333
  Tukwila *(G-13746)*
▲ Heatcon Composite Systems Inc ... D 206 575-1333
  Tukwila *(G-13747)*
Industrial Systems Inc .... G 503 262-0367
  Vancouver *(G-14314)*
Ink For You Tattoo .... G 360 649-6972
  Port Orchard *(G-7817)*
J Bozeat & Associates LLC .... G 206 937-5719
  Seattle *(G-10267)*
Liftex .... G 253 395-4458
  Kent *(G-4995)*
Maple Systems Inc .... E 425 745-3229
  Everett *(G-3545)*
Mekltek Engineering & Mfg .... G 360 384-1607
  Ferndale *(G-3868)*
Norgren Gt Development Corp .... C 206 244-1305
  Auburn *(G-509)*
North Coast Electric Company .... F 360 671-1100
  Bellingham *(G-1464)*
P G K Inc .... G 425 432-0945
  Maple Valley *(G-6285)*
Precision Data Technology Inc .... G 425 259-9237
  Everett *(G-3583)*
Pro Controls Inc .... G 509 457-3386
  Yakima *(G-15655)*
Process Solutions Inc .... E 360 629-0910
  Stanwood *(G-12987)*
Prologic Engineering Inc .... D 360 734-9625
  Bellingham *(G-1507)*
R G Rollin Co .... G 253 274-0882
  Tacoma *(G-13487)*
Rockwell Automation Inc .... F 425 519-5109
  Bellevue *(G-1108)*
Rogers Terminal and Shipping .... F 253 572-0146
  Tacoma *(G-13502)*
S & B Inc .... F 425 746-9312
  Bellevue *(G-1110)*
Sayler Custom Controls Inc .... G 360 816-4193
  Centralia *(G-2430)*
Seattle Sound & Vibration .... G 425 497-0660
  Redmond *(G-8658)*
Stoneway Electric Supply Co .... F 253 859-0224
  Kent *(G-5158)*
Systems Engineering Inc .... G 206 633-4972
  Kirkland *(G-5473)*
Talkie Tooter .... E 360 856-0836
  Sedro Woolley *(G-11574)*
Taurus Power and Controls Inc .... G 425 656-4170
  Kent *(G-5171)*
Tiptop Timers LLC .... G 509 448-2819
  Spokane Valley *(G-12906)*
▲ Travis Pattern & Foundry Inc .... B 509 466-3545
  Spokane *(G-12566)*
United Games .... G 360 470-6480
  Oakville *(G-7176)*
◆ Usnr LLC .... G 360 225-8267
  Woodland *(G-15470)*
▼ W H Autopilots Inc .... F 206 780-2175
  Bainbridge Island *(G-682)*

3629 Electrical Indl Apparatus, NEC

All Systems Integrated Inc .... F 253 770-5570
  Puyallup *(G-8121)*
Alpha Mfg .... G 360 794-8573
  Snohomish *(G-11874)*
Ample Power Company LLC .... G 206 789-0827
  Seattle *(G-9400)*
Blue Frog Solar LLC .... G 206 855-5149
  Poulsbo *(G-7948)*
Charge Solutions LLC .... G 425 381-7922
  Sammamish *(G-9196)*
Exide Technologies .... G 509 922-3135
  Spokane Valley *(G-12697)*
Exide Technologies .... G 253 863-5134
  Sumner *(G-13071)*
Industrial Support Service LLC .... G 509 276-5131
  Deer Park *(G-2906)*
Kontak LLC .... G 425 442-5929
  Redmond *(G-8525)*
Lift Av LLC .... G 425 242-7339
  Renton *(G-8843)*
Midnite Solar Inc .... E 360 403-7207
  Arlington *(G-279)*
Plug Power Inc .... G 509 228-6638
  Spokane Valley *(G-12830)*
Quadrep Northwest Inc .... G 425 201-0420
  Bothell *(G-1786)*
Shine Micro Inc .... F 360 437-2503
  Port Ludlow *(G-7774)*
▲ Sinbon Technologies West .... G 425 712-8500
  Lynnwood *(G-6197)*
Specialty Pdts Elec Cnstr LLC .... G 425 402-8332
  Woodinville *(G-15373)*
▲ Stanbury Electrical Engrg LLC ...... F 206 251-8901
  Woodinville *(G-15374)*
Wibotic Inc .... G 503 484-3930
  Seattle *(G-11472)*

3631 Household Cooking Eqpt

Modernchef Inc .... G 425 202-6252
  Bellevue *(G-1013)*
▲ P&M Products Inc .... G 425 939-8349
  Kirkland *(G-5423)*
Sno-Valley Dream Factory LLC .... G 408 888-8183
  North Bend *(G-7124)*
Whirlpool Corporation .... E 253 875-7100
  Spanaway *(G-12081)*

3632 Household Refrigerators & Freezers

Andersons Rebuilding .... G 360 779-5287
  Poulsbo *(G-7944)*
General Electric Company .... G 253 351-2200
  Auburn *(G-448)*
I-90 Express LLC .... G 509 855-6280
  Ephrata *(G-3337)*
Judd & Black Electric Inc .... F 425 258-4557
  Everett *(G-3526)*
Whirlpool Corporation .... E 253 875-7100
  Spanaway *(G-12081)*

3633 Household Laundry Eqpt

Whirlpool Corporation .... E 253 875-7100
  Spanaway *(G-12081)*

3634 Electric Household Appliances

Amhi Inc .... G 425 883-4040
  Kirkland *(G-5278)*
Artistic Talents Styling Salon .... G 360 456-0100
  Lacey *(G-5533)*
Curly Clutch LLC .... G 253 732-3647
  Puyallup *(G-8139)*
Ducoterra LLC .... G 360 788-4200
  Bellingham *(G-1327)*
Esterbrook Inc .... G 509 783-6826
  Kennewick *(G-4663)*
Farmer Bros Co .... E 425 881-7030
  Redmond *(G-8459)*
◆ Glen Dimplex Americas Company ... C 360 693-2505
  Vancouver *(G-14257)*
▲ King Electrical Mfg Co .... D 206 762-0400
  Seattle *(G-10345)*
Magellan Group Ltd .... G 360 332-6868
  Blaine *(G-1682)*
Mavam LLC .... G 360 789-0639
  Seattle *(G-10503)*
Mokajoe Inc .... G 360 714-1953
  Bellingham *(G-1439)*
▲ Nutrifaster Inc .... G 206 767-5054
  Seattle *(G-10670)*
Polar Fusion LLC .... G 206 395-7811
  Kent *(G-5069)*
Precision Appliance Technology .... F 206 960-2467
  Bellevue *(G-1079)*
Revel Body .... G 206 409-2940
  Seattle *(G-10955)*
Spry Product Development LLC .... G 206 556-1246
  Seattle *(G-11172)*
Tml Innovative Products LLC .... F 425 290-3994
  Mukilteo *(G-6982)*
Twin Ohana Enterprises LLC .... G 360 882-8022
  Vancouver *(G-14653)*
Twin Ohana Enterprises LLC .... G 360 314-2965
  Vancouver *(G-14654)*
Tylohelo Inc .... E 425 951-1120
  Woodinville *(G-15393)*
Zippy Pop Inc .... G 855 404-3300
  Blaine *(G-1714)*

3635 Household Vacuum Cleaners

Cleanmaster .... C 425 775-7272
  Mukilteo *(G-6903)*
Dyson Inc .... G 425 968-2456
  Kirkland *(G-5327)*
Hydramaster .... G 425 775-7276
  Lynnwood *(G-6136)*
◆ Hydramaster LLC .... D 425 775-7272
  Mukilteo *(G-6938)*
◆ Rotovac Corporation .... E 425 883-6746
  Redmond *(G-8655)*
Whirlpool Corporation .... E 253 875-7100
  Spanaway *(G-12081)*

3639 Household Appliances, NEC

Applicator Technology Inc .... G 253 859-9501
  Kent *(G-4786)*
Conterra Inc .... F 360 734-2311
  Bellingham *(G-1304)*
Cypress Houseworks LLC .... G 360 676-9778
  Bellingham *(G-1315)*
Daves TV & Appliance Inc .... G 360 293-5129
  Mount Vernon *(G-6787)*
Fredericks Appliance Centers .... E 425 885-0000
  Redmond *(G-8466)*
Judd & Black Electric Inc .... F 425 258-4557
  Everett *(G-3526)*
Natural Machines Inc .... F 206 747-9483
  Seattle *(G-10591)*
Professional Designed Sewing .... G 206 234-5955
  Seattle *(G-10871)*
Whirlpool Corporation .... E 253 875-7100
  Spanaway *(G-12081)*

3641 Electric Lamps

▲ Differential Energy Global Ltd ...... G 360 895-1184
  Port Orchard *(G-7803)*
▲ Envirolux Energy Systems LLC .... G 800 914-8779
  Vancouver *(G-14203)*
Netzero Energy LLC .... G 360 636-5337
  Longview *(G-5934)*
Uv Systems Inc .... G 425 228-9988
  Renton *(G-8939)*

3643 Current-Carrying Wiring Devices

ABB Installation Products Inc .... E 206 548-1595
  Seattle *(G-9332)*
Acacia Controls Inc .... G 253 277-1206
  Kent *(G-4755)*
Alset Corporation .... G 206 335-3700
  Sequim *(G-11610)*
Best Connection LLC .... G 360 241-8244
  Vancouver *(G-14063)*

36 ELECTRONIC AND OTHER ELECTRICAL EQUIPMENT AND COMPONENTS, EXCEPT COMPUTER SIC SECTION

◆ Blue Sea Systems Inc ....E.... 360 738-8230
Bellingham (G-1278)
Bluefin Marine LLC ....G.... 206 276-4087
Kirkland (G-5293)
Carlisle Inc ....A.... 425 251-0700
Kent (G-4836)
Carlyle Holdings Inc ....C.... 425 251-0700
Kent (G-4839)
◆ Fastcap LLC ....E.... 888 443-3748
Ferndale (G-3841)
Gcm North American Arospc LLC ....D.... 253 872-7488
Algona (G-69)
▲ Honeywell Electronic Mtls Inc ....A.... 509 252-2200
Spokane Valley (G-12731)
Jjp Electric ....G.... 509 325-5266
Spokane (G-12335)
Leviton Manufacturing Co Inc ....C.... 425 486-2222
Bothell (G-1874)
Magnix Usa Inc ....G.... 206 304-8129
Redmond (G-8545)
Mountain Sttes Elec Contrs Inc ....E.... 509 532-0110
Spokane (G-12399)
PA&e International Inc ....C.... 509 667-9600
Wenatchee (G-15056)
Pacific Aerospace & Elec Inc ....G.... 855 285-5200
Wenatchee (G-15058)
▼ Pacific Aerospace & Elec LLC ....C.... 855 885-5200
Wenatchee (G-15059)
Safran Usa Inc ....E.... 425 462-8613
Bellevue (G-1112)
Valberg Mfg Inc ....G.... 206 920-1296
Bothell (G-1912)
Wilder Technologies LLC ....G.... 360 859-3041
Vancouver (G-14693)
Wilson and Associates NW ....F.... 206 292-9756
Seattle (G-11479)

3644 Noncurrent-Carrying Wiring Devices

Ephrata Raceway Park LLC ....E.... 509 398-7110
Ephrata (G-3333)
Grays Harbor Raceway ....G.... 360 482-4374
Vancouver (G-14265)
Jpmorgan Chase Bank Nat Assn ....G.... 206 505-1501
Seattle (G-10310)
Pacific Slot Car Raceways LLC ....G.... 253 446-5039
Edgewood (G-3089)
Raceway Electric ....G.... 206 459-5894
Kirkland (G-5450)
Red Devil Raceway ....G.... 206 402-6690
Seattle (G-10935)
Spokane County Raceway ....G.... 509 244-3333
Airway Heights (G-64)
Timezone Raceway Park ....G.... 360 687-5100
Battle Ground (G-746)
Timezone Raceway Park ....G.... 360 450-3730
La Center (G-5517)
Wilson and Associates NW ....F.... 206 292-9756
Seattle (G-11479)

3645 Residential Lighting Fixtures

Get Lit Lighting LLC ....G.... 425 772-1646
Everett (G-3496)
▲ Graypants Inc ....G.... 206 420-3912
Seattle (G-10112)
▲ Howard Lamp Company ....G.... 425 776-7914
Seattle (G-10188)
Michael Ashford Design ....G.... 360 352-0694
Olympia (G-7339)
Patio Plantings ....G.... 253 631-6131
Kent (G-5061)
Rexel Capitol Light ....G.... 425 861-0200
Redmond (G-8650)
Sevilla LLC ....G.... 509 280-8447
Spokane (G-12500)
Shades of Green ....G.... 425 387-2335
Tulalip (G-13844)
Steel Partners Inc ....F.... 360 748-9406
Chehalis (G-2537)
Touch of West ....G.... 509 962-6410
Ellensburg (G-3233)
▲ Twice Light Inc ....F.... 360 573-6101
Vancouver (G-14652)

3646 Commercial, Indl & Institutional Lighting Fixtures

▲ Aleddra Inc ....G.... 425 430-4555
Renton (G-8735)
Aleddra Inc ....G.... 425 430-4555
Renton (G-8736)
Charles Loomis Inc ....F.... 425 823-4560
Kirkland (G-5303)
Dynesco Corporation Inc ....G.... 360 256-0116
Mukilteo (G-6918)
▲ Envirolux Energy Systems LLC ....G.... 800 914-8779
Vancouver (G-14203)
Every Watt Matters LLC ....E.... 425 985-2171
Vancouver (G-14211)
Every Watt Matters LLC ....D.... 503 221-2113
Vancouver (G-14212)
Form Lighting and Controls LLC ....G.... 206 854-8689
Seattle (G-10013)
▲ Graypants Inc ....G.... 206 420-3912
Seattle (G-10112)
I-5 Design Build Inc ....D.... 360 459-3200
Lacey (G-5558)
Iunu Inc ....G.... 253 307-1858
Seattle (G-10263)
Lagoon Conservation LLC ....G.... 253 202-6479
Des Moines (G-2939)
▼ Leader Manufacturing Inc ....E.... 360 895-1184
Port Orchard (G-7825)
Legitiment Light Co ....G.... 206 542-3268
Shoreline (G-11781)
Light Edge Inc ....E.... 360 567-1680
Vancouver (G-14375)
Light It Bright Products LLC ....G.... 253 666-2278
Tacoma (G-13388)
▲ Lightel Technologies Inc ....E.... 425 277-8000
Renton (G-8844)
Lighting Group Northwest Inc ....G.... 206 298-9000
Seattle (G-10419)
▲ Lumenex LLC ....G.... 206 909-3474
Seattle (G-10450)
Netzero Energy LLC ....G.... 360 636-5337
Longview (G-5934)
▲ ORyan Industries Inc ....E.... 360 892-0447
Vancouver (G-14459)
Rexel Capitol Light ....G.... 425 861-0200
Redmond (G-8650)
Roy Pablo ....G.... 425 750-9941
Quil Ceda Village (G-8281)
S3j Elctrnics Acquisition Corp ....G.... 716 206-1309
Mukilteo (G-6975)
Vision X Offroad LLC ....E.... 888 489-9820
Auburn (G-592)
▲ Western Technology Inc ....G.... 360 917-0080
Bremerton (G-2012)

3647 Vehicular Lighting Eqpt

Altus Industries Inc ....G.... 360 255-7699
Blaine (G-1659)
B/E Aerospace Inc ....B.... 425 923-2700
Everett (G-3381)
Idd Aerospace Corp ....C.... 425 885-0617
Redmond (G-8505)
Kent D Bruce ....G.... 360 886-9410
Black Diamond (G-1649)
▲ Klas Technologies LLC ....G.... 360 678-8705
Greenbank (G-4308)
Xenon Arc Inc ....E.... 425 646-1063
Bellevue (G-1229)

3648 Lighting Eqpt, NEC

Avio Corporation ....G.... 425 739-6800
Kirkland (G-5286)
◆ Avtechtyee Inc ....C.... 425 290-3100
Everett (G-3378)
Belfair Garden & Lighting ....G.... 360 275-2130
Belfair (G-759)
C & H Lighting Associates Inc ....G.... 253 531-1270
Tacoma (G-13213)
Christie Lites Seattle LLC ....F.... 206 223-7200
Kent (G-4852)
Deaf Spotlight ....G.... 206 466-4693
Seattle (G-9808)
▲ Eco Safe Technologies LLC ....G.... 360 567-1923
Camas (G-2247)
◆ Electric Mirror LLC ....B.... 425 776-4946
Everett (G-3454)
Emerald City Lighting ....G.... 206 234-8554
Kirkland (G-5331)
Escent Lighting ....G.... 509 838-9028
Spokane (G-12251)
Event Power & Lighting Inc ....G.... 360 225-3830
Woodland (G-15431)
Fishtrap Creek Lighting LLC ....G.... 360 354-7900
Lynden (G-6018)
Global Mining ....G.... 509 863-9724
Spokane Valley (G-12719)
◆ Grakon LLC ....C.... 206 824-6000
Des Moines (G-2936)
▲ Industrial Revolution Inc ....E.... 425 285-1111
Tukwila (G-13752)
Laser Guidance Inc ....G.... 206 679-3909
Redmond (G-8529)
▼ Leader Manufacturing Inc ....E.... 360 895-1184
Port Orchard (G-7825)
Lightloom ....G.... 206 228-5001
Shoreline (G-11782)
Lumenomics Inc ....E.... 206 327-9037
Seattle (G-10451)
Mag Lite Warranty ....G.... 360 398-9798
Bellingham (G-1420)
Mfg Universe Corp ....G.... 800 883-8779
Tukwila (G-13772)
▲ Ncs Power Inc ....F.... 360 896-4063
Vancouver (G-14429)
Netzero Energy LLC ....G.... 360 636-5337
Longview (G-5934)
Nevada Lithium Corp ....G.... 360 318-8352
Lynden (G-6039)
Northwest Outdoor Lighting ....G.... 425 633-6074
Duvall (G-2996)
Nortn Coast Lighting Cash ....G.... 425 454-2122
Bellevue (G-1038)
NW Lighting Solutions LLC ....G.... 253 246-2959
Kent (G-5040)
NW Lighting Solutions LLC ....G.... 253 929-4657
Auburn (G-514)
Pacific Stage Lighting ....G.... 253 248-6344
Gig Harbor (G-4141)
Patriot Sales Inc ....F.... 360 855-0737
Sedro Woolley (G-11556)
Plc-Multipoint Inc ....G.... 425 353-7552
Everett (G-3575)
Quoizel Lighting ....G.... 360 275-5435
Belfair (G-771)
Red Hat Lighting LLC ....G.... 360 624-5773
Vancouver (G-14538)
Rejuvenation Inc ....F.... 206 382-1901
Seattle (G-10946)
Steel Partners Inc ....F.... 360 748-9406
Chehalis (G-2537)
Takovo Led Lights ....G.... 206 330-6862
Seattle (G-11260)
Vleds ....G.... 360 543-5700
Bellingham (G-1586)
Zonecro Llc ....G.... 760 702-9290
Bremerton (G-2014)

3651 Household Audio & Video Eqpt

Acoustic Info Proc Lab LLC ....G.... 509 427-5374
Stevenson (G-13008)
Advanced Autosound ....G.... 509 453-5363
Yakima (G-15500)
Allied Forces Inc ....G.... 360 387-5713
Camano Island (G-2206)
▲ Audiocontrol Inc ....E.... 425 775-8461
Mountlake Terrace (G-6859)
Audiocontrol Inc ....F.... 425 775-8461
Spokane (G-12126)
◆ Bayview Pro Audio Inc ....G.... 360 867-1798
Olympia (G-7235)
Cco Holdings LLC ....G.... 509 293-4177
Wenatchee (G-15016)
Cco Holdings LLC ....G.... 509 643-3364
Sunnyside (G-13116)
Chapman Audio Systems ....G.... 206 463-3008
Vashon (G-14718)
Cloudstream Media Inc ....G.... 858 245-0034
Liberty Lake (G-5828)
Condor Technical Services ....G.... 206 633-5190
Seattle (G-9726)
Couple Power ....G.... 425 641-0278
Bellevue (G-867)
Dehavilland Elc Amplifier Co ....G.... 360 891-6570
Vancouver (G-14174)
Electric AMP Innvtions USA LLC ....G.... 509 455-7469
Spokane (G-12239)
Fusion9 Design LLC ....G.... 360 831-0899
Camano Island (G-2214)
▲ Genesis Advanced Technologies ....F.... 206 762-8383
Seattle (G-10060)
Globo Productions Voiceover ....G.... 206 992-0483
Seattle (G-10087)
Gremlin Inc ....G.... 206 781-4636
Seattle (G-10123)
Half Families Enterprises LLC ....G.... 425 629-3232
Sammamish (G-9213)

SIC SECTION 36 ELECTRONIC AND OTHER ELECTRICAL EQUIPMENT AND COMPONENTS, EXCEPT COMPUTER

High Definition Audio Video ... G ... 360 398-8265 Lynden *(G-6021)*
Impulse Audio Inc ... G ... 206 650-0075 Seattle *(G-10217)*
Innovative Advantage Inc ... G ... 206 910-7528 Redmond *(G-8508)*
Jo Bee Inc ... G ... 509 483-1118 Spokane *(G-12336)*
Lavry Engineering ... G ... 360 598-9757 Poulsbo *(G-7974)*
Leeds Look Listen Inc ... G ... 208 252-6075 Seattle *(G-10398)*
Live Sound & Recording Co LLC ... G ... 425 308-2868 Everett *(G-3537)*
◆ Loud Audio LLC ... C ... 425 892-6500 Woodinville *(G-15294)*
Mackie Designs Inc ... G ... 425 868-0555 Redmond *(G-8544)*
Matamp Distribution USA ... G ... 509 455-7469 Spokane *(G-12385)*
McCauley International Inc ... G ... 253 229-8900 Puyallup *(G-8187)*
▲ McCauley Sound Inc ... E ... 253 848-0363 Puyallup *(G-8188)*
▲ Modwright Instruments Inc ... G ... 360 247-6688 Amboy *(G-95)*
Nepoware Corporation ... G ... 425 802-8821 Medina *(G-6453)*
Nickolay Philip and Wendy LLC ... G ... 206 463-7997 Vashon *(G-14736)*
Padholdr LLC ... G ... 253 447-7328 Bonney Lake *(G-1732)*
▲ Pb Inc ... G ... 206 747-0347 Bellevue *(G-1066)*
PC Networks Inc ... G ... 360 362-9684 Silverdale *(G-11853)*
▼ Playnetwork Inc ... C ... 425 497-8100 Redmond *(G-8626)*
Savang Sine ... G ... 206 721-2558 Seattle *(G-11020)*
Shadow Master ... G ... 253 984-0559 Lakewood *(G-5754)*
▲ Shunyata Research Corporation ... F ... 360 598-9935 Poulsbo *(G-7999)*
Sound Product Solutions LLC ... G ... 360 553-7898 Vancouver *(G-14601)*
The Riff ... G ... 509 280-1300 Spokane *(G-12554)*
▲ U2 Inc ... F ... 360 627-8068 Bremerton *(G-2009)*
▲ Vanatoo LLC ... G ... 206 486-1002 Auburn *(G-590)*
Westek Marketing LLC ... G ... 425 888-1988 Nine Mile Falls *(G-7085)*

3652 Phonograph Records & Magnetic Tape

Alpha Audio Group Inc ... G ... 253 846-1536 Tacoma *(G-13167)*
▲ Arrowdisc LLC ... D ... 253 518-3900 Kent *(G-4792)*
Career Development Software ... F ... 360 696-3529 Vancouver *(G-14099)*
Gt Recording ... G ... 206 783-6911 Seattle *(G-10130)*
Media Holdings LLC ... G ... 503 313-0676 Olympia *(G-7338)*
Pure Fire Independent LLC ... G ... 206 218-3297 Seattle *(G-10889)*
Singles Going Steady ... G ... 206 441-7396 Seattle *(G-11116)*
Soundings of The Planet Inc ... G ... 360 738-9368 Bellingham *(G-1547)*
Soundworks U S A Inc ... G ... 425 882-3344 Lacey *(G-5591)*

3661 Telephone & Telegraph Apparatus

Alaska United Partnership ... G ... 425 741-3350 Lynnwood *(G-6068)*
Atos It Solutions and Svcs Inc ... G ... 425 691-3080 Bellevue *(G-798)*
Avaya Inc ... D ... 425 454-2715 Bellevue *(G-803)*
Avaya Inc ... C ... 425 881-7544 Bellevue *(G-802)*
Bellingham Business Machines ... G ... 360 734-3630 Bellingham *(G-1264)*
Choice Wiring LLC ... G ... 509 588-6185 Benton City *(G-1606)*
Davan Communications Entp ... G ... 253 517-9300 Tacoma *(G-13255)*
Dees Communications Corp ... G ... 425 276-5269 Newcastle *(G-7027)*
Dial One Telecommunications ... G ... 360 629-2085 Stanwood *(G-12966)*
Diversified Northwest Inc ... F ... 425 710-0753 Everett *(G-3444)*
Electronic Systems Tech Inc ... F ... 509 735-9092 Kennewick *(G-4657)*
Extreme Networks Inc ... G ... 408 579-2800 Snohomish *(G-11907)*
G-Tech Communications Inc ... F ... 503 784-1147 Vancouver *(G-14245)*
Green River College ... E ... 253 856-9595 Kent *(G-4928)*
Htc America Innovation Inc ... B ... 425 679-5318 Seattle *(G-10192)*
Ict Group Inc ... G ... 408 907-8000 Spokane Valley *(G-12737)*
John Deely ... G ... 206 527-8218 Seattle *(G-10301)*
Jphotonics Inc ... G ... 206 397-3702 Mercer Island *(G-6469)*
Linc Technology Corporation ... E ... 425 882-2206 Issaquah *(G-4439)*
New Cingular Wireless Svcs Inc ... F ... 425 288-3132 Bothell *(G-1779)*
P & M Video Lightsource LLC ... G ... 253 569-0286 Spanaway *(G-12067)*
Photon Factory ... G ... 818 795-6957 Seattle *(G-10797)*
Planet Headset Inc ... G ... 253 238-0643 Fox Island *(G-4023)*
Powercom Inc ... D ... 425 489-8549 Bothell *(G-1784)*
Proctor International LLC ... G ... 425 881-7000 Redmond *(G-8633)*
Racal Acoustics Inc ... G ... 425 297-9700 Everett *(G-3593)*
Rest-A-Phone Corporation ... F ... 503 235-6778 Vancouver *(G-14545)*
Rest-A-Phone Corporation ... G ... 360 750-8686 Vancouver *(G-14546)*
Ruckus Wireless Inc ... E ... 425 896-6000 Kirkland *(G-5453)*
Siemens AG ... G ... 253 922-4297 Fife *(G-3992)*
Simpleline Inc ... G ... 888 743-7903 Langley *(G-5785)*
Telco Wiring & Repair Inc ... G ... 509 547-4300 Pasco *(G-7637)*
Telecommunication Systems Inc ... C ... 206 792-2000 Seattle *(G-11280)*
▲ Telect Inc ... C ... 509 926-6000 Liberty Lake *(G-5863)*
Xeta Technologies Inc ... G ... 425 653-4500 Seattle *(G-11504)*
Xeta Technologies Inc ... E ... 425 316-0721 Tukwila *(G-13838)*
Xkl LLC ... E ... 425 869-9050 Redmond *(G-8720)*

3663 Radio & T V Communications, Systs & Eqpt, Broadcast/Studio

◆ Aci Communications Inc ... E ... 253 854-9802 Kent *(G-4758)*
Action Communications Inc ... G ... 206 625-1234 Seattle *(G-9344)*
Admiralty Crane LLC ... G ... 360 461-2092 Sequim *(G-11606)*
Airwavz Inc ... G ... 206 696-6649 Renton *(G-8734)*
▼ AR Kalmus Corp ... E ... 425 485-9000 Bothell *(G-1822)*
AR Worldwide ... G ... 425 485-9000 Bothell *(G-1823)*
Astronics Cstm Ctrl Cncpts Inc ... D ... 206 575-0933 Kent *(G-4795)*
Bbtline LLC ... G ... 425 273-3712 Kirkland *(G-5289)*
▲ Behringer Usa Inc ... D ... 425 672-0816 Bothell *(G-1752)*
◆ Bluecosmo Inc ... G ... 877 258-3496 Seattle *(G-9555)*
Boeing Company ... B ... 425 413-3400 Maple Valley *(G-6261)*
Boeing Company ... A ... 206 662-9615 Seatac *(G-9276)*
Boeing Company ... A ... 206 655-1131 Seattle *(G-9563)*
Boeing Company ... A ... 312 544-2000 Everett *(G-3397)*
Cco Holdings LLC ... G ... 509 293-4177 Wenatchee *(G-15016)*
Cco Holdings LLC ... G ... 509 643-3364 Sunnyside *(G-13116)*
Channel Korea ... G ... 425 557-5970 Issaquah *(G-4391)*
Ciena Corporation ... G ... 509 242-9000 Spokane Valley *(G-12656)*
Commscope Technologies LLC ... F ... 425 888-2370 North Bend *(G-7109)*
Complete Music ... G ... 509 927-3535 Spokane *(G-12195)*
Dannys Electronics Inc ... G ... 253 314-5056 Tacoma *(G-13253)*
Differential Networks LLC ... G ... 360 366-8123 Bellingham *(G-1323)*
Diversified Marketing Intl LLC ... G ... 509 585-9377 Kennewick *(G-4654)*
DMC Satellite Systems Inc ... G ... 360 681-4204 Sequim *(G-11627)*
Eln Communications Inc ... G ... 206 256-0420 Seattle *(G-9904)*
Elux Inc ... G ... 360 281-4568 Vancouver *(G-14200)*
Emerging Mkts Cmmnications LLC ... G ... 206 454-8300 Seattle *(G-9916)*
Fisher Brdcstg - Wash TV LLC ... G ... 509 575-0029 Yakima *(G-15571)*
Huawei Device USA Inc ... F ... 425 247-2700 Bellevue *(G-951)*
Influx LLC ... G ... 360 200-4323 Vancouver *(G-14316)*
Integrated Design Group Inc ... G ... 509 328-4244 Spokane *(G-12319)*
Integrated Technologies Inc ... D ... 425 349-2084 Everett *(G-3518)*
Itron Inc ... E ... 509 924-9900 Spokane Valley *(G-12748)*
Itron Manufacturing Inc ... E ... 509 924-9900 Spokane Valley *(G-12749)*
Jeeva Wireless Inc ... G ... 206 214-6177 Seattle *(G-10288)*
Jeffrey Mark Bashe ... G ... 509 684-6925 Colville *(G-2758)*
Katz Media Group Inc ... G ... 206 777-1800 Seattle *(G-10331)*
Kitc Radio Inc ... G ... 360 876-1400 Port Orchard *(G-7823)*
Konnectone LLC ... F ... 425 502-7371 Bellevue *(G-971)*
Kymeta Corporation ... D ... 425 896-3700 Redmond *(G-8526)*
Kymeta Corporation ... D ... 425 896-3700 Redmond *(G-8527)*
Kzbg Big Country 977 ... G ... 509 751-0977 Clarkston *(G-2638)*
Lhc2 Inc ... G ... 509 723-4517 Liberty Lake *(G-5843)*
Loop Devices Inc ... G ... 206 965-9828 Seattle *(G-10441)*
Ludlow Mortgage Inc ... G ... 360 437-1344 Port Ludlow *(G-7770)*
Mahler & Assoc Inc ... G ... 206 365-3800 Lake Forest Park *(G-5620)*
▲ Mary Medina LLC ... G ... 206 719-1730 Medina *(G-6452)*
Meteorcomm LLC ... C ... 253 872-2521 Renton *(G-8853)*
Morad Electronics Corporation ... G ... 206 789-2525 Bellingham *(G-1442)*
Neocific Inc ... G ... 425 451-8278 Bellevue *(G-1025)*
Oak Bay Technologies Inc ... G ... 360 437-0718 Port Ludlow *(G-7771)*
Omohundro Co Kitsap Composites ... D ... 360 519-3047 Port Orchard *(G-7837)*
Oneradio Corporation ... G ... 206 393-2900 Redmond *(G-8603)*
Pacific Tchnical Solutions Inc ... F ... 425 489-5700 Redmond *(G-8608)*
Pathfinder Wireless Corp ... G ... 206 409-5767 Seattle *(G-10767)*
Piccell LLC ... G ... 206 780-0478 Seattle *(G-10799)*
▼ PSI Electronics LLC ... F ... 253 922-7890 Fife *(G-3984)*
Pulse Electronics Inc ... D ... 360 944-7551 Vancouver *(G-14515)*

SIC

Employee Codes: A=Over 500 employees, B=251-500
C=101-250, D=51-100, E=20-50, F=10-19, G=2-9
2019 Washington Manufacturers Register
631

36 ELECTRONIC AND OTHER ELECTRICAL EQUIPMENT AND COMPONENTS, EXCEPT COMPUTER SIC SECTION

Race Horse Studios ....G 206 451-4725
Bainbridge Island *(G-662)*
Reach For Sky Satellite Servic ....G 509 276-9340
Loon Lake *(G-5977)*
Roberta Lowes ....G 253 572-1859
Tacoma *(G-13501)*
Rothenbuhler Engineering Co ....F 360 856-0836
Sedro Woolley *(G-11562)*
Ruckus Wireless Inc ....E 425 896-6000
Kirkland *(G-5453)*
◆ **Sea Com Corporation** ....F 425 771-2182
Mountlake Terrace *(G-6868)*
▲ **Seamobile Inc** ....G 206 838-7700
Seattle *(G-11044)*
▲ **SGC World Inc** ....F 425 746-6310
Bellevue *(G-1126)*
SGC World Inc ....G 425 746-6311
Bellevue *(G-1127)*
Ship Electronics Inc ....G 206 819-3853
Shoreline *(G-11810)*
Skt2 LLC ....G 775 303-3788
Camas *(G-2283)*
Star West Satellite ....G 509 545-4996
Pasco *(G-7633)*
Steppir Comm Systems Inc ....G 425 453-1910
Bellevue *(G-1157)*
Stoothoff Aerospace Inc ....G 360 595-0314
Deming *(G-2924)*
Streambox Inc ....E 206 956-0544
Bellevue *(G-1161)*
Swype Inc ....D 206 547-5250
Seattle *(G-11241)*
▲ **Symetrix Inc** ....E 425 640-3331
Mountlake Terrace *(G-6871)*
Unlimited Possibilities Now ....G 206 930-9100
Bothell *(G-1804)*
Washington State University ....G 509 372-7400
Richland *(G-9052)*
Wave Holdco Corporation ....G 425 576-8200
Kirkland *(G-5493)*
Westcoast Telemetry Specialist ....G 253 536-1351
Spanaway *(G-12080)*
Wibotic Inc ....G 503 484-3930
Seattle *(G-11472)*
Wind Talker Innovations Inc ....G 253 883-3615
Fife *(G-3999)*
Xoceco USA ....G 425 670-3968
Lynnwood *(G-6227)*
Xoceco USA ....G 509 808-2480
Liberty Lake *(G-5869)*
◆ **Zonar Systems Inc** ....C 206 878-2459
Seattle *(G-11524)*

3669 Communications Eqpt, NEC

Ademco Inc ....G 253 872-7128
Kent *(G-4759)*
Ademco Inc ....G 509 534-7300
Spokane *(G-12098)*
Ademco Inc ....G 425 485-3938
Bothell *(G-1815)*
Advanced Aero Safety Inc ....G 360 387-8472
Stanwood *(G-12952)*
Advanced Traffic Products Inc ....F 425 347-6208
Everett *(G-3361)*
Almx-Security Inc ....G 425 485-3801
Kenmore *(G-4564)*
American Digital ....G 800 765-2580
Kirkland *(G-5277)*
B C Traffic ....G 360 895-1000
Port Orchard *(G-7790)*
Electrical Services & SEC Inc ....G 206 276-6629
Kent *(G-4887)*
Fathem LLC ....G 360 403-7418
Arlington *(G-236)*
Fire Protection Inc ....G 206 440-5763
Seattle *(G-9994)*
Foundation International ....G 425 391-1281
Bellevue *(G-916)*
General Fire Prtection Systems ....F 509 535-4255
Spokane *(G-12268)*
Highway Specialties LLC ....G 360 823-0511
Vancouver *(G-14298)*
Inland Alarm LLC ....G 509 457-6065
Yakima *(G-15589)*
J Fillips LLC ....G 425 277-1011
Renton *(G-8830)*
James Wile ....G 360 606-0706
Camas *(G-2259)*
Jay Pathy ....G 425 890-9526
Medina *(G-6449)*
Johnson Controls ....C 206 291-1400
Seattle *(G-10302)*
Johnson Controls ....E 509 534-6055
Spokane Valley *(G-12754)*
Junefalsetta ....G 253 536-3576
Tacoma *(G-13370)*
K & D Services Inc ....G 425 252-0906
Everett *(G-3527)*
Linc Technology Corporation ....E 425 882-2206
Issaquah *(G-4439)*
McCain Inc ....G 760 734-5086
Issaquah *(G-4446)*
Michael Patrick Matthews ....G 509 457-8799
Wapato *(G-14920)*
Monaco Enterprises Inc ....D 509 926-6277
Spokane Valley *(G-12793)*
Motek Inc ....G 206 632-7795
Seattle *(G-10565)*
National Barricade & Sign Co ....G 509 534-2619
Spokane Valley *(G-12801)*
Nestor Inc ....D 253 395-0285
Tukwila *(G-13776)*
Northwest Traffic Control Inc ....G 360 604-5655
Brush Prairie *(G-2038)*
Oatridge-Evergreen 8a2 JV LLC ....G 253 627-3794
Tacoma *(G-13439)*
Orca Information Comm Svs ....G 360 588-1633
Anacortes *(G-158)*
Performnce Fire Protection Inc ....G 253 778-8039
Kent *(G-5064)*
Prospectors Plus LLC ....G 425 750-9290
Sultan *(G-13033)*
Prototek Corp ....F 360 779-1310
Poulsbo *(G-7993)*
Road-Iq LLC ....F 360 733-4151
Bellingham *(G-1518)*
Save Smoke ....G 425 793-5030
Renton *(G-8903)*
SES USA Inc ....G 425 485-3801
Kenmore *(G-4604)*
Smelts Sea Mammal Education Le ....G 360 303-9338
Sedro Woolley *(G-11570)*
Surprise Al Care Group LLC ....G 775 746-2200
Vancouver *(G-14621)*
Tim Anders ....G 360 944-0806
Vancouver *(G-14638)*
Top Notch Manufacturing Co ....G 360 577-9150
Longview *(G-5960)*
Waterfront Solutions Inc ....G 360 348-1874
Edmonds *(G-3161)*
Western Systems Inc ....E 425 438-1133
Everett *(G-3656)*
◆ **Zonar Systems Inc** ....C 206 878-2459
Seattle *(G-11524)*

3671 Radio & T V Receiving Electron Tubes

Ceradyne Inc ....G 206 763-2170
Seattle *(G-9656)*
▲ **Tactical Fabs Inc** ....E 360 723-5360
Battle Ground *(G-742)*
▲ **Tfi Telemark** ....D 360 723-5360
Battle Ground *(G-745)*
World Tube Company ....G 253 756-6489
Tacoma *(G-13602)*

3672 Printed Circuit Boards

Acacia Controls Inc ....G 253 277-1206
Kent *(G-4755)*
▲ **Almax Manufacturing Co** ....G 425 889-8708
Kirkland *(G-5276)*
▲ **Applied Technical Svcs Corp** ....G 425 249-5555
Everett *(G-3371)*
Board Shark LLC ....E 503 351-5424
Vancouver *(G-14072)*
▲ **Circuit Services Worldwide** ....E 425 454-7181
Bellevue *(G-852)*
▲ **Circuit Services Worldwide LLC** ....F 425 454-7181
Bellevue *(G-853)*
Constant Computer ....G 253 227-0532
Tacoma *(G-13239)*
Four Barr Industries ....G 360 659-8182
Marysville *(G-6335)*
I2nnovations LLC ....G 425 298-3143
Sammamish *(G-9218)*
Industrial Control Group ....G 509 965-5967
Yakima *(G-15587)*
Infinetix Corp ....F 509 922-5629
Spokane Valley *(G-12739)*
Jabil Def & Arospc Svcs LLC ....G 206 257-0243
Seattle *(G-10276)*
Jabil Inc ....G 206 257-0243
Seattle *(G-10277)*
M-Tronic Inc ....G 509 484-3572
Spokane *(G-12377)*
Monsoon Solutions Inc ....E 425 378-8081
Bellevue *(G-1014)*
Out of Box Manufacturing LLC ....E 253 214-7448
Renton *(G-8868)*
Pantrol Inc ....F 509 535-9061
Spokane *(G-12428)*
Pcb Universe Inc ....G 360 256-7228
Vancouver *(G-14481)*
Plc-Multipoint Inc ....G 425 353-7552
Everett *(G-3575)*
Printed Circuits Assembly ....C 425 641-7455
Bellevue *(G-1082)*
Printed Circuits Assembly ....C 425 644-7754
Bellevue *(G-1083)*
▲ **Schippers & Crew Inc** ....D 206 782-2325
Seattle *(G-11027)*
▲ **Servatron Inc** ....C 509 321-9500
Spokane Valley *(G-12865)*
Sherman Technical Inds Inc ....G 509 427-8089
Carson *(G-2307)*
Sherman Technical Inds Inc ....G 509 427-8089
Carson *(G-2308)*
Silicon Forest Electronics Inc ....C 360 694-2000
Vancouver *(G-14588)*
Technical & Assembly Svcs Corp ....E 206 682-2967
Seattle *(G-11277)*
White Matter LLC ....G 510 409-0144
Mercer Island *(G-6489)*
Xanfab Inc ....G 206 717-2185
Seatac *(G-9313)*

3674 Semiconductors

Aard Technology LLC ....G 425 785-0682
Sammamish *(G-9183)*
Advanced Energy Industries Inc ....G 360 759-2713
Vancouver *(G-14010)*
Analog Devices Inc ....G 360 834-1900
Camas *(G-2228)*
Applied Multilayers LLC ....G 307 222-0660
Battle Ground *(G-688)*
Applied Precision LLC ....C 425 557-1000
Issaquah *(G-4380)*
Applied Precision Holdings LLC ....C 425 557-1000
Issaquah *(G-4381)*
Arm Inc ....C 425 602-0915
Bellevue *(G-794)*
Arm Inc ....C 408 576-1500
Olympia *(G-7229)*
Asimi ....G 509 766-9641
Moses Lake *(G-6679)*
Automated Tech Solutions LLC ....G 425 999-1297
Maple Valley *(G-6259)*
Avista Capital Inc ....G 509 489-0500
Spokane *(G-12133)*
Blink Device Company LLC ....F 206 708-6043
Seattle *(G-9542)*
Bobek Enterprises ....G 360 683-8785
Sequim *(G-11616)*
Broadcom Corporation ....G 425 748-5076
Bellevue *(G-829)*
Canelle Citron ....G 206 241-4657
Seattle *(G-9616)*
▲ **Conation Technologies LLC** ....G 253 864-8234
Puyallup *(G-8135)*
Constant Computer ....G 253 227-0532
Tacoma *(G-13239)*
Convergent Earned Value Assoc ....G 206 293-6931
Bellevue *(G-864)*
Critical Delivery Service LLC ....G 206 724-3653
Bellevue *(G-868)*
Cypress Microsystems Inc ....F 425 787-4400
Lynnwood *(G-6103)*
Cypress Semiconductor Corp ....F 425 787-4400
Lynnwood *(G-6104)*
▲ **Data I/O Corporation** ....C 425 881-6444
Redmond *(G-8433)*
Dennis Nelson ....G 360 320-4237
Oak Harbor *(G-7148)*
Eaton Corporation ....E 425 644-5800
Bellevue *(G-889)*
Ecorsys Inc ....G 347 282-6888
Seattle *(G-9881)*
Ejimcom ....G 360 459-4785
Lacey *(G-5546)*
◆ **Eldec Corporation** ....A 425 743-1313
Lynnwood *(G-6114)*

SIC SECTION 36 ELECTRONIC AND OTHER ELECTRICAL EQUIPMENT AND COMPONENTS, EXCEPT COMPUTER

First Silicon Designs LLC ......G...... 303 883-6891 Vancouver *(G-14233)*
▲ Galaxy Cmpund Smconductors Inc ......F...... 509 892-1114 Spokane Valley *(G-12712)*
Global Display North Amer Ltd ......G...... 425 698-1938 Bellevue *(G-927)*
Greence Inc ......G...... 360 727-3528 Ridgefield *(G-9087)*
Growlife Inc ......F...... 866 781-5559 Kirkland *(G-5356)*
▲ Hd Pacific Inc ......F...... 425 481-3031 Mukilteo *(G-6931)*
▲ Honeywell Electronic Mtls Inc ......A...... 509 252-2200 Spokane Valley *(G-12731)*
Impinj Inc ......C...... 206 517-5300 Seattle *(G-10212)*
Impinj Inc ......G...... 206 834-1098 Seattle *(G-10213)*
Impinj Inc ......F...... 206 315-4449 Seattle *(G-10214)*
▲ Isilon Systems LLC ......B...... 206 315-7500 Seattle *(G-10260)*
▲ Itekenergy LLC ......D...... 360 647-9531 Bellingham *(G-1385)*
Jet City Electronics Inc ......G...... 206 529-0351 Lake Forest Park *(G-5616)*
Jj 206 LLC ......G...... 206 453-0186 Seattle *(G-10297)*
▲ Jx Crystals Inc ......G...... 425 392-5237 Issaquah *(G-4435)*
Lam Research Corporation ......D...... 360 260-0352 Vancouver *(G-14357)*
Lauda-Noah LP ......F...... 360 993-1395 Vancouver *(G-14362)*
Lauda-Noah LP ......G...... 360 993-1395 Vancouver *(G-14363)*
▼ Leader Manufacturing Inc ......E...... 360 895-1184 Port Orchard *(G-7825)*
Leidos Inc ......E...... 425 267-5600 Lynnwood *(G-6157)*
Leidos Inc ......G...... 360 394-8870 Poulsbo *(G-7975)*
▲ Lightel Technologies Inc ......E...... 425 277-8000 Renton *(G-8844)*
Linear Technology Corporation ......C...... 360 834-1900 Camas *(G-2265)*
Lumotive LLC ......G...... 907 306-6267 Bellevue *(G-992)*
Marketech International Inc ......G...... 360 379-6707 Port Townsend *(G-7897)*
Marvell Semiconductor Inc ......G...... 408 222-2500 Redmond *(G-8552)*
Matrix Visions LLC ......G...... 206 368-3824 Lake Forest Park *(G-5621)*
Mellanox Technologies Inc ......G...... 512 239-8282 Redmond *(G-8555)*
Micrametal Inc ......G...... 206 508-1405 Seattle *(G-10529)*
Micron Technology Inc ......G...... 206 294-7015 Seattle *(G-10535)*
Mips Tech Inc ......G...... 408 610-5900 Bellevue *(G-1008)*
Momentum Interactive LLC ......G...... 915 203-5349 Bellingham *(G-1440)*
Monolithic Power Systems Inc ......G...... 408 826-0600 Seattle *(G-10559)*
▲ Monolithic Power Systems Inc ......C...... 425 296-9956 Kirkland *(G-5405)*
Muscleclub 4 Men ......G...... 206 624-9785 Seattle *(G-10573)*
Nec Corp of America ......G...... 425 373-4400 Bellevue *(G-1023)*
New Age Processors LLC ......G...... 425 656-0174 Renton *(G-8857)*
▲ Nlight Inc ......B...... 360 566-4460 Vancouver *(G-14432)*
Northlight Power LLC ......G...... 206 780-3551 Seattle *(G-10636)*
Nxedge Inc ......G...... 425 990-0091 Bellevue *(G-1041)*
Optic Led Grow Lights LLC ......G...... 971 704-2912 Tacoma *(G-13444)*
Professional Mentors & Pro ......G...... 832 216-9134 Colton *(G-2733)*
▲ Professnl Mntrs & Pro Life Skl ......G...... 832 216-9134 Colton *(G-2734)*
▲ Rec Silicon Inc ......D...... 509 765-2106 Moses Lake *(G-6741)*
Rec Silicon Inc ......G...... 509 793-9015 Moses Lake *(G-6742)*
Resonant Systems Inc ......G...... 206 557-4398 Seattle *(G-10952)*
▲ Shin-Etsu Handotai America Inc ......A...... 360 883-7000 Vancouver *(G-14583)*
Silfab Solar WA Inc ......F...... 360 569-4733 Bellingham *(G-1536)*
Solarworld Industries Amer LP ......D...... 360 944-9251 Vancouver *(G-14598)*
Sputtertech Inc ......G...... 360 253-5944 Vancouver *(G-14605)*
System To Asic Inc ......F...... 425 488-0575 Bothell *(G-1798)*
▲ Tactical Fabs Inc ......E...... 360 723-5360 Battle Ground *(G-742)*
Texas Instruments Inc ......G...... 253 927-0754 Federal Way *(G-3795)*
▲ Tfi Telemark ......D...... 360 723-5360 Battle Ground *(G-745)*
▲ Tsmc Development Inc ......C...... 360 817-3000 Camas *(G-2285)*
Wafer Reclaim Services LLC ......G...... 360 254-0221 Vancouver *(G-14676)*
▲ Wafertech LLC ......A...... 360 817-3000 Camas *(G-2287)*
Wirekat Enterprises ......G...... 425 413-6946 Kent *(G-5217)*
Xkl LLC ......E...... 425 869-9050 Redmond *(G-8720)*
Xnrgi Inc ......G...... 425 272-2703 Bothell *(G-1924)*

3675 Electronic Capacitors

▼ Extreme Capacitor Inc ......G...... 360 878-9749 Olympia *(G-7281)*
Hexa Materials LLC ......G...... 541 337-3669 Seattle *(G-10168)*

3676 Electronic Resistors

First Choice Marketing Inc ......G...... 206 306-1100 Seattle *(G-9996)*
Vishay Precision Group Inc ......G...... 253 872-1910 Kent *(G-5202)*

3677 Electronic Coils & Transformers

AMG Aluminum North America LLC ......D...... 509 663-2165 Malaga *(G-6231)*
▲ Kemcor Inc ......E...... 425 488-7400 Woodinville *(G-15276)*
Polytech Coil Winding ......G...... 253 324-3044 Tacoma *(G-13470)*
▲ Power Conversion Inc ......E...... 425 487-1337 Woodinville *(G-15338)*
Source TEC Inc ......G...... 206 972-3172 Woodinville *(G-15371)*

3678 Electronic Connectors

C&J Offshore Systems LLC ......G...... 360 293-4200 Anacortes *(G-106)*
Cory Siverson ......G...... 425 869-8303 Redmond *(G-8427)*
Dash Connector Technology Inc ......G...... 509 465-1903 Spokane *(G-12218)*
Gravity Square Inc ......G...... 206 524-0063 Seattle *(G-10111)*
▲ Smartplug Systems LLC ......G...... 206 285-2990 Seattle *(G-11138)*

3679 Electronic Components, NEC

Acacia Controls Inc ......G...... 253 277-1206 Kent *(G-4755)*
Aees Inc ......G...... 425 803-2170 Kirkland *(G-5272)*
AFL Ig LLC ......E...... 425 291-4200 Kent *(G-4765)*
▲ Allstar Magnetics LLC ......E...... 360 693-0213 Vancouver *(G-14022)*
Altair Advanced Industries ......E...... 360 756-4900 Bellingham *(G-1245)*
Amx LLC ......C...... 509 235-1464 Cheney *(G-2576)*
Ant Lamp Corp ......G...... 360 600-1031 Vancouver *(G-14037)*
▲ Austin Else LLC ......F...... 888 654-4450 Spokane *(G-12128)*
▲ Behringer Usa Inc ......D...... 425 672-0816 Bothell *(G-1752)*
Bic Inc ......G...... 360 691-1452 Granite Falls *(G-4265)*
Biocom Systems Inc ......G...... 509 241-0505 Wenatchee *(G-15014)*
Black Label Switches ......G...... 360 607-3559 Camas *(G-2233)*
C Quartz Inc ......G...... 360 393-1254 Ferndale *(G-3820)*
Cabi ......G...... 425 413-8772 Renton *(G-8766)*
Carlisle Interconnect Tech Inc ......G...... 425 656-5235 Kent *(G-4837)*
Carlisle Interconnect Tech Inc ......B...... 425 291-3991 Kent *(G-4838)*
▲ Checksum LLC ......E...... 360 435-5510 Arlington *(G-219)*
▲ Crane Electronics Inc ......B...... 425 882-3100 Redmond *(G-8429)*
Crane Electronics Inc ......G...... 425 882-3100 Redmond *(G-8430)*
Creepcocom ......G...... 206 547-7020 Seattle *(G-9752)*
◆ Crystalfontz America Inc ......F...... 509 892-1200 Spokane Valley *(G-12671)*
Custom Interface Inc ......E...... 509 493-8756 Bingen *(G-1636)*
D & D Controls Inc ......G...... 360 695-8931 Vancouver *(G-14160)*
▲ Data I/O Corporation ......C...... 425 881-6444 Redmond *(G-8433)*
David T Mitchell ......G...... 425 227-7111 Renton *(G-8781)*
E T L Corp ......F...... 360 568-1473 Snohomish *(G-11903)*
Eagle Harbor Technologies Inc ......F...... 206 402-5241 Seattle *(G-9868)*
Electronic Prgrm & Design ......G...... 206 767-7262 Seattle *(G-9894)*
Elliott Bay Recording Company ......G...... 206 709-9626 Seattle *(G-9902)*
Emerald City Electronics ......G...... 425 649-1006 Bellevue *(G-896)*
◆ Epson Toyocom Seattle Inc ......F...... 360 200-5537 Longview *(G-5909)*
Ernit LLC ......G...... 425 922-3867 Bellevue *(G-898)*
Evs Manufacturing Inc ......G...... 360 863-6413 Monroe *(G-6570)*
Holmes and Associates ......G...... 360 793-9723 Monroe *(G-6578)*
▲ Honeywell Electronic Mtls Inc ......A...... 509 252-2200 Spokane Valley *(G-12731)*
Hydra Group LLC ......G...... 503 957-0975 Washougal *(G-14959)*
▲ Imat Inc ......E...... 360 256-5600 Vancouver *(G-14310)*
Jag Technologies ......G...... 360 910-2933 Vancouver *(G-14332)*
Jauch Quartz America Inc ......G...... 360 633-7200 Seabeck *(G-9265)*
Krn Services ......G...... 509 366-3431 Richland *(G-9019)*
Laser Materials Corporation ......G...... 360 254-4180 Vancouver *(G-14360)*
Lauterbach Inc ......G...... 360 567-2666 Vancouver *(G-14365)*
Leidos Inc ......E...... 425 267-5600 Lynnwood *(G-6157)*
Leidos Inc ......G...... 360 394-8870 Poulsbo *(G-7975)*
Lhc2 Inc ......G...... 509 723-4517 Liberty Lake *(G-5843)*
▲ Logan Industries Inc ......D...... 509 462-7400 Spokane Valley *(G-12776)*
Lumber Line Laser Repair ......G...... 360 686-3340 Yacolt *(G-15486)*
Mackie Designs Inc ......G...... 425 868-0555 Redmond *(G-8544)*
▲ Mantec Services Inc ......E...... 206 285-5656 Seattle *(G-10472)*
Manufacturing Services Inc ......E...... 509 735-8444 Kennewick *(G-4691)*
Master Switch LLC ......G...... 206 769-9560 Seattle *(G-10497)*
Masterpress Inc ......E...... 206 524-1444 Seattle *(G-10499)*
▲ Micro Current Technology Inc ......E...... 206 938-5288 Seattle *(G-10531)*
Microconnex Corporation ......G...... 425 396-5707 Snoqualmie *(G-12018)*
Microtemp Electronics ......G...... 360 256-6789 Vancouver *(G-14420)*

S I C

Employee Codes: A=Over 500 employees, B=251-500
C=101-250, D=51-100, E=20-50, F=10-19, G=2-9
2019 Washington
Manufacturers Register
633

36 ELECTRONIC AND OTHER ELECTRICAL EQUIPMENT AND COMPONENTS, EXCEPT COMPUTER SIC SECTION

Microvision Inc .... C 425 936-6847
Redmond *(G-8587)*
Misiu Systems LLC .... G 425 402-8700
Bothell *(G-1877)*
▲ **Multisonus Audio Inc** .... G 425 241-1112
Bellingham *(G-1451)*
Nidec America Corporation .... G 360 666-2445
Battle Ground *(G-724)*
Northwest Applied Marine LLC .... G 509 936-4316
Chewelah *(G-2605)*
Omohundro Co Kitsap Composites .... D 360 519-3047
Port Orchard *(G-7837)*
Pacific Aerospace & Elec Inc .... C 509 667-9600
Wenatchee *(G-15057)*
▼ **Pacific Aerospace & Elec LLC** .... C 855 885-5200
Wenatchee *(G-15059)*
▲ **Pacific Custom Cable Inc** .... F 253 373-0800
Auburn *(G-523)*
Paradise Technolgy Inc .... G 253 370-3682
Lakebay *(G-5690)*
Paragon Manufacturing Corp .... E 425 438-0800
Everett *(G-3569)*
Powerguard Corporation .... G 206 764-8882
Kent *(G-5074)*
Pulse Power Solutions LLC .... G 206 369-8277
Bothell *(G-1785)*
▲ **Qualitel Corporation** .... C 425 423-8388
Everett *(G-3589)*
Scrupulous Design .... G 425 788-1812
Duvall *(G-3001)*
Seymour Technology LLC .... G 509 522-3473
Walla Walla *(G-14867)*
Signature Plastics LLC .... F 360 366-5044
Custer *(G-2860)*
◆ **Stargate Inc** .... G 425 251-0701
Kent *(G-5152)*
▲ **Symetrix Inc** .... E 425 640-3331
Mountlake Terrace *(G-6871)*
Tate Technology Inc .... E 509 534-2500
Spokane *(G-12547)*
▲ **Technical Services Inc** .... C 360 675-1322
Oak Harbor *(G-7165)*
Thick Film Technologies Inc .... G 425 347-0919
Everett *(G-3632)*
Vpt Inc .... G 425 353-3010
Bothell *(G-1807)*
Wegners Wire Inc .... G 253 535-0945
Puyallup *(G-8278)*
White Mountainhouse .... G 360 835-5442
Washougal *(G-15001)*
▲ **World Wide Packets Inc** .... E 509 242-9000
Spokane Valley *(G-12941)*
▲ **Xn Technologies Inc** .... D 509 235-2672
Cheney *(G-2596)*

3691 Storage Batteries

56 Thunder Batteries .... G 253 267-0059
Tacoma *(G-13152)*
▲ **Brightvolt Inc** .... D 863 603-7640
Redmond *(G-8409)*
E Power Systems & Battery Inc .... G 253 267-1965
Lakewood *(G-5716)*
East Penn Manufacturing Co .... G 253 983-9622
Lakewood *(G-5718)*
Egis Group LLC .... G 360 768-1211
Bellingham *(G-1331)*
Energy Battery Systems Inc .... G 253 267-1965
Lakewood *(G-5719)*
Energy Sales .... F 425 883-2343
Woodinville *(G-15236)*
Enersys .... F 253 299-0005
Sumner *(G-13069)*
Exide Technologies .... G 509 922-3135
Spokane Valley *(G-12697)*
Exide Technologies .... G 253 863-5134
Sumner *(G-13071)*
Green-On-Green Energy Inc .... G 206 701-7321
Auburn *(G-457)*
Kibbey Battery Service Inc .... G 253 845-9155
Puyallup *(G-8172)*
Maxx Distribution LLC .... G 888 507-6790
Tacoma *(G-13402)*
Megabess Us Inc .... G 425 890-9175
Bellevue *(G-1002)*
Ralph M Eronemo .... G 425 985-1617
Bellevue *(G-1093)*
Unienergy Technologies LLC .... D 425 290-8898
Mukilteo *(G-6985)*
Uninterruptible Power Systems .... G 509 327-7722
Spokane *(G-12576)*

Wli Recycling Inc .... G 253 267-1965
Lakewood *(G-5769)*

3692 Primary Batteries: Dry & Wet

▲ **Austin Else LLC** .... F 888 654-4450
Spokane *(G-12128)*
Khancell Corporation .... G 646 385-7243
Blaine *(G-1678)*
Kibbey Battery Service Inc .... G 253 845-9155
Puyallup *(G-8172)*

3694 Electrical Eqpt For Internal Combustion Engines

▲ **Baton Labs Inc** .... G 509 467-4203
Spokane *(G-12140)*
Hydra Group LLC .... G 503 957-0975
Washougal *(G-14959)*
Jantz Engineering .... G 360 598-2773
Poulsbo *(G-7968)*
Life Safer .... G 800 328-9890
Bremerton *(G-1973)*
Murphy & Dad Inc .... G 360 438-2747
Olympia *(G-7346)*
North PCF Ign Interlock Svc .... G 360 480-4919
Lacey *(G-5567)*
S&J Engines Inc .... F 509 325-4558
Spokane *(G-12490)*
Schumacher Creative Services .... G 206 364-7151
Seattle *(G-11029)*
Smart Start .... G 425 747-4400
Bellevue *(G-1139)*
Smart Start .... G 425 967-5699
Lynnwood *(G-6199)*
Smartstart .... G 509 317-2050
Yakima *(G-15676)*
Washington Ignition Interlock .... G 206 824-6849
Kent *(G-5207)*

3695 Recording Media

Ario Inc .... G 206 852-4877
Seattle *(G-9429)*
Dees Communications Corp .... G 425 276-5269
Newcastle *(G-7027)*
Diversified Systems Group Inc .... G 425 947-1500
Kent *(G-4875)*
Gray Area Technologies Inc .... G 206 370-2545
Woodinville *(G-15256)*
Intermedianet Inc .... F 425 451-3393
Bellevue *(G-960)*
Intrinsyc Software (usa) Inc .... G 604 678-3734
Seattle *(G-10254)*
Jian Wu .... G 425 706-9852
Sammamish *(G-9223)*
Mackichan Software Inc .... F 360 394-6033
Poulsbo *(G-7979)*
Master Peace Productions .... G 360 600-2736
Vancouver *(G-14398)*
Mqs Group LLC .... G 360 956-9114
Olympia *(G-7345)*
Plussoft Inc .... G 425 821-8776
Kirkland *(G-5437)*
Realtime Inc .... G 206 523-8050
Seattle *(G-10931)*

3699 Electrical Machinery, Eqpt & Splys, NEC

Affordable Electronics Inc .... G 425 484-0964
Monroe *(G-6544)*
All Wave Innovations Inc .... G 509 308-7230
Benton City *(G-1600)*
▲ **Apollo Video Technology LLC** .... C 425 483-7100
Bothell *(G-1820)*
▲ **Atlas Electric Inc** .... E 509 534-8389
Spokane *(G-12124)*
▲ **Auroma Technologies Co LLC** .... F 425 582-8674
Everett *(G-3375)*
Automatic Door Solutions LLC .... G 253 802-0888
Orting *(G-7473)*
Battery X-Change & Repair Inc .... G 360 373-2921
Bremerton *(G-1937)*
Bridgeways .... D 425 513-2989
Everett *(G-3401)*
Burke Electric .... G 509 633-8046
Coulee Dam *(G-2806)*
Cartridge Care Inc .... G 360 459-8845
Lacey *(G-5540)*
Cascadia Video Pdts Cvp LLC .... G 509 202-4230
Cheney *(G-2580)*
Cetrestec Inc .... G 206 650-8676
Seattle *(G-9662)*

Clear Rf LLC .... F 855 321-9527
Spokane Valley *(G-12658)*
Columbia Electric Supply .... G 509 473-9156
Spokane Valley *(G-12661)*
Controlled Products of Wash .... G 206 575-2249
Tukwila *(G-13717)*
Cooper Power Systems Inc .... G 206 499-9473
Maple Valley *(G-6265)*
Cowlitz Electric Construction .... G 253 355-7163
Tacoma *(G-13247)*
Darren Mode .... G 509 292-2438
Deer Park *(G-2897)*
Disman Bakner Northwest Inc .... G 425 837-3913
Issaquah *(G-4406)*
Ditco Inc .... F 253 854-1002
Kent *(G-4874)*
E2 Systems LLC .... G 253 284-3707
Lakewood *(G-5717)*
Eaton Hydraulics LLC .... G 360 834-0653
Camas *(G-2245)*
Elmor Inc .... G 206 213-0111
Seattle *(G-9903)*
ESP Seattle .... G 206 388-4800
Tukwila *(G-13730)*
Evelo Inc .... F 877 991-7272
Seattle *(G-9945)*
Fablab LLC .... G 253 426-1267
Tacoma *(G-13286)*
▲ **Frank J Martin Company** .... E 206 523-7665
Lynnwood *(G-6122)*
Graybar Electric Company Inc .... E 425 203-1500
Renton *(G-8813)*
Gsl Solutions Inc .... E 360 896-5354
Vancouver *(G-14275)*
▲ **Helion Energy Inc** .... E 425 332-7463
Redmond *(G-8490)*
Herrington Marine Tech Inc .... G 360 222-3106
Greenbank *(G-4305)*
Hiline Engrg & Fabrication Inc .... E 509 943-9043
Richland *(G-9006)*
Hrh Door Corp .... F 509 575-0832
Kennewick *(G-4672)*
Hunter Fish Enterprises .... G 253 852-8357
Renton *(G-8822)*
▲ **Hy-Security Gate Inc** .... E 253 867-3700
Kent *(G-4945)*
Hyak Electroworks .... E 360 737-0157
Vancouver *(G-14306)*
Interworld Elec Cmpt Inds Inc .... G 425 223-4311
Point Roberts *(G-7668)*
Island Electric .... G 360 293-9275
Anacortes *(G-136)*
Itraq Inc .... G 844 694-8727
Redmond *(G-8516)*
Jan-R Corporation .... E 360 856-0836
Sedro Woolley *(G-11543)*
Jjs Automotive & Auto Elc LLC .... G 509 248-2622
Union Gap *(G-13935)*
JP Innovations LLC .... G 360 805-3124
Monroe *(G-6582)*
Kanon Electric .... G 253 447-7831
Edgewood *(G-3083)*
Kent Enterprises .... G 360 403-0242
Arlington *(G-264)*
Keyking Inc .... G 360 977-7870
Camas *(G-2262)*
▲ **Kings Wok** .... G 360 337-2512
Silverdale *(G-11841)*
Kisslers Machine & Fabrication .... G 509 877-1177
Wapato *(G-14917)*
L3 Systems Inc .... G 425 836-5438
Sammamish *(G-9228)*
Laser Techniques Company LLC .... F 425 885-0607
Redmond *(G-8530)*
Laserfab Inc .... F 509 762-0400
Puyallup *(G-8176)*
Laughlin Industries Inc .... G 360 514-9218
Vancouver *(G-14364)*
Lavry Engineering Inc .... F 206 842-3552
Bainbridge Island *(G-648)*
Lumberline Laser Inc .... G 360 686-3077
Vancouver *(G-14386)*
Malone Electronics .... G 360 687-1034
Battle Ground *(G-719)*
McCoy Electric .... G 360 829-5273
Buckley *(G-2063)*
▲ **Mitsubishi Electric & Elec USA** .... G 425 202-7671
Kirkland *(G-5404)*
▲ **Morpac Industries Inc** .... E 253 735-8922
Pacific *(G-7533)*

N W Sound & Security Tech LLC ....F 360 213-1619
Ridgefield *(G-9095)*
Naimor Inc ....E 360 756-9700
Bellingham *(G-1457)*
Nationwide SEC Solutions Inc ....G 800 908-8992
Vancouver *(G-14428)*
Newton Security Inc ....E 425 251-9494
Renton *(G-8858)*
Next Biometrics Inc ....E 425 406-7055
Bellevue *(G-1030)*
Nextlevel Training LLC ....G 360 933-4640
Ferndale *(G-3876)*
▲ Nlight Inc ....B 360 566-4460
Vancouver *(G-14432)*
Northwest Laser Systems Inc ....G 877 623-1342
Kent *(G-5032)*
Northwest Monitoring Services ....G 509 326-6270
Spokane *(G-12413)*
Nova Services ....E 509 928-1588
Spokane Valley *(G-12810)*
Novanta Inc ....C 425 349-1359
Mukilteo *(G-6958)*
Nuid Inc ....G 360 927-4682
Seattle *(G-10669)*
NW Utility Services LLC ....E 253 891-7802
Pacific *(G-7536)*
Olympic SEC Comm Sys Inc ....G 360 652-1088
Arlington *(G-294)*
Patroltag Inc ....G 650 678-3790
Seattle *(G-10771)*
▲ Pb Inc ....G 206 747-0347
Bellevue *(G-1066)*
▲ PC Open Incorporated ....C 509 777-6736
Liberty Lake *(G-5852)*
▲ Pls Pacific Laser Systems LLC ....D 415 453-5780
Everett *(G-3576)*
Polarity Elec ....G 206 546-3539
Shoreline *(G-11802)*
Power Breaker LLC Seattle ....G 425 286-4276
Monroe *(G-6607)*
Prairie Electric Inc ....D 509 545-1752
Pasco *(G-7618)*
Pro Staff Electric ....G 360 859-3749
Vancouver *(G-14509)*
Provident Electric Inc ....F 509 588-3939
Benton City *(G-1624)*
Quality Fence Builders Inc ....E 253 939-8533
Auburn *(G-541)*
Red Electric ....G 425 670-7035
Mukilteo *(G-6971)*
Rentiel Precision Laser Cutng ....G 253 297-2823
Tacoma *(G-13494)*
▲ Rowperfect 3 ....G 206 331-5319
Seattle *(G-10983)*
Safe Home Security Products ....G 360 384-1239
Ferndale *(G-3894)*
Sea-TAC Lighting & Contrls LLC ....F 206 575-6865
Tukwila *(G-13813)*
Sequoyah Electric ....G 253 520-2064
Kent *(G-5127)*
Siemens ....G 425 507-4380
Bellevue *(G-1130)*
Siemens ....G 425 251-0858
Renton *(G-8912)*
Specialty Pdts Elec Cnstr LLC ....G 425 402-8332
Woodinville *(G-15373)*
Stanley Access Tech LLC ....G 425 493-0482
Mukilteo *(G-6979)*
▲ Stardust Materials LLC ....G 360 260-7399
Vancouver *(G-14608)*
Strain Night Vision & Security ....G 509 926-2025
Spokane *(G-12531)*
T & K Cstm Fabrication & Repr ....G 206 242-0197
Seattle *(G-11247)*
T D Laser Engraving ....G 425 347-6837
Everett *(G-3625)*
Terex Utilities Inc ....E 206 764-5025
Kent *(G-5177)*
Toaster Labs Inc ....G 206 368-3178
Seattle *(G-11316)*
Totem Electric ....G 253 327-1500
Fife *(G-3996)*
United States Electric Corp ....G 360 427-4218
Grapeview *(G-4291)*
Utility Supply Group ....G 360 626-1086
Poulsbo *(G-8014)*
Validigm Biotechnology Inc ....G 415 205-3377
Seattle *(G-11399)*

37 TRANSPORTATION EQUIPMENT

3711 Motor Vehicles & Car Bodies

Andrew McDonald ....G 253 964-5020
Lewis McChord *(G-5819)*
Andyman Online ....G 425 761-5921
Renton *(G-8744)*
Art Morrison Enterprises Inc ....E 253 344-0161
Fife *(G-3933)*
Braun Northwest Inc ....C 800 245-6303
Chehalis *(G-2474)*
Central Kitsap Fire Rescu ....G 360 447-3575
Silverdale *(G-11828)*
County of Lewis ....G 360 494-4123
Packwood *(G-7542)*
Defense Sales Intl LLC ....G 206 999-8684
Renton *(G-8782)*
▲ Eight Star Group of America ....G 206 243-8888
Lynnwood *(G-6113)*
Ferrotek Corporation ....F 360 366-7444
Ferndale *(G-3845)*
Ford Motor Credit Company LLC ....D 425 643-0454
Bellevue *(G-914)*
Herrera Isael Gomez ....G 509 270-7022
Spokane *(G-12293)*
Jamie Kinney ....G 206 953-9302
Seattle *(G-10284)*
Jensen Race Cars ....G 425 745-8000
Lynnwood *(G-6144)*
Kurtisfactor LLC ....G 208 863-6180
Tacoma *(G-13379)*
Lifeport Inc ....E 360 225-6690
Woodland *(G-15446)*
Ncw Towing ....G 509 630-7155
Wenatchee *(G-15051)*
Nite-Hawk Sweepers LLC ....F 253 872-2077
Kent *(G-5024)*
Paccar Inc ....C 425 828-5000
Kirkland *(G-5424)*
Paccar Inc ....C 360 757-5357
Mount Vernon *(G-6820)*
Paccar Inc ....G 206 214-0418
Seatac *(G-9297)*
Paccar Inc ....B 425 468-7400
Bellevue *(G-1058)*
Paccar Inc ....C 425 254-4400
Renton *(G-8870)*
Paccar Inc ....B 425 227-5800
Renton *(G-8871)*
Paccar Inc ....E 425 468-7400
Bellevue *(G-1059)*
Paccar Inc ....B 206 764-5400
Tukwila *(G-13786)*
Patrick Corp ....G 509 925-1300
Ellensburg *(G-3217)*
Paul Parish Limited ....G 509 735-9820
Kennewick *(G-4705)*
Rm Metal Works ....G 253 815-0652
Federal Way *(G-3777)*
Shoreline Cert ....G 206 533-6500
Shoreline *(G-11811)*
▲ Sickspeed Inc ....G 509 833-3768
Moxee *(G-6886)*
Silver Star Street Rods ....G 360 837-1250
Washougal *(G-14986)*
Skagit County Fire Dst 14 ....E 360 724-3451
Burlington *(G-2187)*
SSC Green Inc ....G 509 967-4753
West Richland *(G-15101)*
SSC North America LLC ....G 509 967-4753
West Richland *(G-15102)*
Subaru of America Inc ....G 360 737-7630
Vancouver *(G-14614)*
Susan Eakin ....G 509 966-2014
Yakima *(G-15692)*
Tesla Inc ....G 425 519-8070
Bellevue *(G-1183)*
Tesla Inc ....C 425 453-5021
Bellevue *(G-1182)*
Wildfire Safe LLC ....G 509 670-3816
Cashmere *(G-2335)*

3713 Truck & Bus Bodies

Aalbu Brothers of Everett Inc ....G 425 252-9751
Everett *(G-3356)*
▲ Allied Body Works Inc ....F 206 763-7811
Seattle *(G-9381)*
American Pride Corporation ....F 253 850-1212
Kent *(G-4778)*
Amrep Inc ....G 253 939-6265
Pacific *(G-7523)*
Arreolas Auto Wrecking ....G 509 452-0818
Yakima *(G-15513)*
Auto Body Specialties ....G 360 424-1313
Mount Vernon *(G-6772)*
BTS Exchange LLC ....G 253 859-5450
Kent *(G-4825)*
C & V Machinery ....G 509 657-3392
Endicott *(G-3263)*
◆ Capital Industries Inc ....D 206 762-8585
Seattle *(G-9624)*
Crown Black Car ....G 206 722-7696
Seattle *(G-9757)*
D & H Enterprises ....G 360 374-9500
Forks *(G-4009)*
DMS Motorsports ....G 360 863-3807
Monroe *(G-6566)*
Dougs Diesel Repair ....G 509 665-7480
East Wenatchee *(G-3010)*
Dynamic Utility Services ....G 425 742-1670
Everett *(G-3449)*
Fab Shop LLC ....E 253 568-9124
Edgewood *(G-3077)*
Fabrication & Truck Eqp Inc ....F 509 535-0363
Spokane Valley *(G-12698)*
Freedom Truck Centers Inc ....E 509 248-9478
Union Gap *(G-13931)*
Geo Heiser Body Co LLC ....E 206 622-7985
Tukwila *(G-13739)*
Heiser George Body Co Inc ....E 206 622-7985
Tukwila *(G-13748)*
Imperial Group Mfg Inc ....C 360 748-4201
Chehalis *(G-2504)*
▲ Nelson Truck Equipment Co Inc ....E 253 395-3825
Kent *(G-5018)*
Nelson Truck Equipment Co Inc ....F 206 622-3825
Seattle *(G-10598)*
Norms Truck & Equipment Inc ....F 253 833-8339
Pacific *(G-7535)*
Northend Truck Equipment LLC ....E 360 653-6066
Marysville *(G-6363)*
Paccar Inc ....B 425 468-7400
Bellevue *(G-1058)*
Pacifica Marine Inc ....F 206 764-1646
Seattle *(G-10742)*
Road Runner Transportation LLC ....G 253 778-3848
Seattle *(G-10970)*
Sign Station ....G 360 379-2954
Port Hadlock *(G-7762)*
Star Transport Trailers Inc ....F 509 837-3136
Sunnyside *(G-13144)*
Trivan Truck Body LLC ....D 360 380-0773
Ferndale *(G-3917)*
Trivan Truck Body Texas LLC ....D 254 799-2360
Ferndale *(G-3918)*
Truck Accessories Group LLC ....D 360 736-9991
Centralia *(G-2439)*
U S Fire Equipment LLC ....F 253 863-1301
Sumner *(G-13108)*
▲ Ute Ltd ....G 206 510-8621
Burien *(G-2135)*

3714 Motor Vehicle Parts & Access

Afco Performance Group LLC ....G 360 453-2030
Monroe *(G-6543)*
ARB USA ....G 866 293-9078
Auburn *(G-376)*
Art Morrison Enterprises Inc ....E 253 344-0161
Fife *(G-3933)*
Bic Inc ....G 360 691-1452
Granite Falls *(G-4265)*
Billet Connection Llc ....G 509 467-7584
Spokane *(G-12148)*
▲ Bnb International LLC ....G 425 712-1687
Edmonds *(G-3097)*
Bogert International Inc ....G 509 736-1512
Pasco *(G-7555)*
Brooks Tactical Systems ....F 253 549-2703
Fox Island *(G-4019)*
C & V Machinery ....G 509 657-3392
Endicott *(G-3263)*
◆ Consolidated Metco Inc ....D 360 828-2599
Vancouver *(G-14147)*
Corner Stone R V Center LLC ....G 360 704-4441
Tumwater *(G-13865)*
Cummins Inc ....E 509 455-4411
Spokane *(G-12211)*
Cummins Inc ....E 360 748-8841
Tumwater *(G-13867)*

Employee Codes: A=Over 500 employees, B=251-500
C=101-250, D=51-100, E=20-50, F=10-19, G=2-9
2019 Washington
Manufacturers Register
635

Current Drives LLC.....G..... 206 697-6073
Seattle *(G-9765)*
Delphis Creative Bus Solutions.....G..... 360 689-4063
Gig Harbor *(G-4094)*
Dogfence of North America.....G..... 509 991-0385
Clayton *(G-2657)*
Drive Line Svc of Bellingham.....G..... 360 734-7828
Bellingham *(G-1326)*
Energy Efficiency Systems Corp.....E..... 360 835-7838
Washougal *(G-14953)*
Et Hydraulics LLC.....G..... 206 718-7372
Snohomish *(G-11906)*
Evs Manufacturing Inc.....G..... 360 863-6413
Monroe *(G-6570)*
Fact Motorcycle Training Inc.....G..... 509 248-2373
Yakima *(G-15567)*
▲ **Five Food Inc**.....G..... 509 855-6914
Moses Lake *(G-6708)*
Ford Motor Credit Company LLC.....D..... 425 643-0454
Bellevue *(G-914)*
Genuine Parts Company.....E..... 206 575-8100
Renton *(G-8806)*
Glass Doctor of Wenatchee.....G..... 509 415-3400
East Wenatchee *(G-3014)*
Haldex Brake Products Corp.....G..... 360 944-3070
Vancouver *(G-14279)*
Harris-Ford Inc.....C..... 425 678-0391
Lynnwood *(G-6132)*
Heads Up Inc.....G..... 253 833-4546
Auburn *(G-461)*
▲ **Heininger Holdings LLC**.....G..... 360 756-2411
Bellingham *(G-1368)*
Hendrickson International Corp.....G..... 360 906-0222
Vancouver *(G-14293)*
Hydra Group LLC.....G..... 503 957-0975
Washougal *(G-14959)*
Hytech Power Inc.....F..... 425 890-1180
Redmond *(G-8504)*
Instrument Sales and Svc Inc.....E..... 253 796-5400
Kent *(G-4954)*
Jantz Engineering.....G..... 360 598-2773
Poulsbo *(G-7968)*
Jones Automotive Engine Inc.....E..... 509 838-3625
Spokane *(G-12341)*
Joyson Safety Systems.....C..... 509 762-5549
Moses Lake *(G-6718)*
▲ **Kaper II Inc**.....E..... 360 423-4404
Kelso *(G-4533)*
Kic-N Corp.....G..... 360 696-9595
Vancouver *(G-14349)*
Lifeport Inc.....E..... 360 225-6690
Woodland *(G-15446)*
Lithia Motors Inc.....G..... 509 321-7300
Spokane *(G-12373)*
Luann Ayling.....G..... 509 633-2839
Electric City *(G-3167)*
Makk Motoring LLC.....G..... 509 855-2638
Moses Lake *(G-6723)*
Meritor Inc.....C..... 360 737-0175
Vancouver *(G-14411)*
Metal Frictions Company Inc.....G..... 425 776-0336
Edmonds *(G-3133)*
Model A Wheel Colors.....G..... 206 264-4944
Seatac *(G-9290)*
Motor Works Inc.....D..... 509 535-9240
Spokane *(G-12398)*
N C Power Systems Co.....C..... 425 251-5877
Tukwila *(G-13774)*
Navan Enterprises LLC.....G..... 206 214-6227
Seattle *(G-10596)*
North American Atk Corporation.....E..... 360 733-1916
Bellingham *(G-1463)*
Offroad Outpost.....G..... 360 910-0021
Vancouver *(G-14448)*
Olsons Gaskets.....G..... 360 871-1207
Port Orchard *(G-7836)*
Oregon CAM Grinding Inc.....G..... 503 252-5505
Vancouver *(G-14456)*
▲ **Pacbrake Company**.....G..... 360 332-4717
Blaine *(G-1692)*
Paccar Inc.....C..... 425 828-5000
Kirkland *(G-5424)*
Paccar Inc.....B..... 425 468-7400
Bellevue *(G-1058)*
Pacific Meter & Equipment Inc.....G..... 253 872-3374
Kent *(G-5056)*
Performance Radiator PCF LLC.....G..... 206 624-2440
Seattle *(G-10787)*
Performance Radiator PCF LLC.....E..... 253 472-0586
Tacoma *(G-13464)*
Potter-Webster Co.....G..... 360 577-9632
Longview *(G-5944)*
▲ **Ppr Industries Corporation**.....E..... 360 863-9500
Monroe *(G-6608)*
Precision Airmotive LLC.....G..... 360 403-4803
Arlington *(G-305)*
Precision Driveshaft Inc.....G..... 253 236-5640
Kent *(G-5077)*
Prism Motors Inc.....G..... 425 503-5415
Seattle *(G-10867)*
◆ **Pro Tech Industries Inc**.....C..... 360 573-6641
Vancouver *(G-14510)*
Rebreathers Usa LLC.....G..... 425 789-1255
Everett *(G-3596)*
◆ **Red DOT Corporation**.....B..... 206 151-3840
Tukwila *(G-13803)*
Roadmaster Inc.....G..... 360 896-0407
Vancouver *(G-14555)*
Roadmaster Inc.....G..... 360 735-7575
Vancouver *(G-14556)*
Rons Transmission.....G..... 206 772-8200
Seattle *(G-10979)*
▼ **S & S Engine Remanufacturing**.....E..... 509 325-4558
Spokane *(G-12489)*
Seattle Radiator LLC.....G..... 206 682-5148
Seattle *(G-11071)*
Sje Inc.....E..... 360 734-1910
Bellingham *(G-1540)*
Skagit Transmission Inc.....G..... 360 757-6551
Burlington *(G-2189)*
Skyline Fluid Power Inc.....G..... 509 382-4781
Dayton *(G-2886)*
South Sound Metal Inc.....G..... 253 564-0226
University Place *(G-13981)*
South Tacoma Glass Specialists.....E..... 253 582-2401
Lakewood *(G-5758)*
Subaru of America Inc.....G..... 360 737-7630
Vancouver *(G-14614)*
T3 Technique LLC.....G..... 425 785-0361
Redmond *(G-8687)*
Taylors Marine Center.....G..... 509 633-2945
Electric City *(G-3168)*
Ted Gay.....G..... 425 742-9566
Lynnwood *(G-6209)*
Tesla Inc.....C..... 425 453-5021
Bellevue *(G-1182)*
Thermal Solutions Mfg.....G..... 206 764-7028
Sumner *(G-13106)*
Thermal Solutions Mfg Inc.....G..... 800 776-4650
Tukwila *(G-13826)*
TNT Machining LLC.....G..... 360 988-0274
Sumas *(G-13052)*
Toolcraft Inc.....F..... 360 794-5512
Monroe *(G-6633)*
Topdown Incorporated.....G..... 206 920-5566
Stanwood *(G-12997)*
▲ **Tork Lift International Inc**.....F..... 253 479-0115
Kent *(G-5182)*
Triad Products Corporation.....G..... 425 514-8363
Everett *(G-3636)*
Truckvault Inc.....E..... 360 855-0464
Sedro Woolley *(G-11577)*
Tuckers Tuffer Coatings Inc.....G..... 360 707-2168
Sedro Woolley *(G-11578)*
Ultra Carbon.....G..... 253 922-4266
Lakewood *(G-5764)*
Universal Engine Heater Co.....G..... 509 276-5923
Nine Mile Falls *(G-7084)*
Vehicle Monitor Corporation.....F..... 425 881-5560
Redmond *(G-8703)*
Viper Tactical LLC.....G..... 425 341-0529
Salkum *(G-9181)*
Vulcan Performance.....G..... 360 450-4237
Ridgefield *(G-9119)*
Whidbey Cruzers.....G..... 253 299-6442
Oak Harbor *(G-7171)*
Workhorse Incorporated.....G..... 360 835-9417
Washougal *(G-15002)*
Xtr Off-Road Products.....G..... 208 717-1515
Clarkston *(G-2656)*
Ya We Can Do That.....G..... 360 253-5555
Vancouver *(G-14703)*
Yakima Grinding Co.....F..... 509 575-1977
Yakima *(G-15714)*

3715 Truck Trailers

All Sports School.....G..... 425 747-1511
Issaquah *(G-4379)*
Batp Inc.....G..... 253 677-4706
Edgewood *(G-3072)*
Busby International Inc.....E..... 509 765-1313
Moses Lake *(G-6689)*
Capital Industrial Supply Inc.....E..... 360 786-1890
Tumwater *(G-13856)*
Eagle Systems Inc.....E..... 509 535-8654
Spokane Valley *(G-12685)*
Ed Ka Manufacturing Inc.....G..... 509 635-1521
Garfield *(G-4068)*
Gibbs Trailer Mfg & Repr.....G..... 509 547-8241
Pasco *(G-7586)*
Helm Manufacturing Co LLC.....G..... 253 537-3382
Tacoma *(G-13334)*
Integrated Systems Design.....G..... 360 746-0812
Bellingham *(G-1380)*
Kic LLC.....E..... 360 823-4440
Vancouver *(G-14348)*
Lincoln Industrial Corp Inc.....G..... 360 681-0584
Sequim *(G-11646)*
Manns Welding & Trailer Hitch.....G..... 206 542-7434
Shoreline *(G-11784)*
Marlin Trailers.....G..... 509 345-2316
Marlin *(G-6308)*
Marquez Mfg Ltd.....E..... 509 837-6230
Sunnyside *(G-13133)*
Micahs Custom Works LLC.....G..... 509 665-9631
Malaga *(G-6232)*
Nor E First Response Inc.....G..... 360 738-6467
Bellingham *(G-1461)*
Northwest Services.....G..... 253 922-6475
Puyallup *(G-8208)*
Ocean Cargo Container Inc.....G..... 253 381-9098
Gig Harbor *(G-4138)*
Quality Equipment Supply Inc.....G..... 503 544-9779
Vancouver *(G-14518)*
Quality Fuel Trlr & Tank Inc.....G..... 425 526-7566
Monroe *(G-6610)*
Six Robbles.....G..... 360 398-7173
Bellingham *(G-1539)*
Star Transport Trailers Inc.....F..... 509 837-3136
Sunnyside *(G-13144)*
Susan Weinhandl.....G..... 509 953-4329
Spokane *(G-12537)*

3716 Motor Homes

Redondo Rv Storage & Service.....G..... 253 941-3662
Kent *(G-5101)*

3721 Aircraft

4r Aviation LLC.....G..... 206 336-9415
Seattle *(G-9323)*
A & B Plastics Inc.....G..... 509 248-9166
Union Gap *(G-13919)*
Adrenaline Products LLC.....G..... 503 805-4525
Ridgefield *(G-9059)*
Air Technics.....G..... 425 316-0587
Everett *(G-3364)*
AR Northwest.....G..... 425 485-9000
Bothell *(G-1748)*
Avian Balloon Company.....G..... 509 928-6847
Spokane Valley *(G-12631)*
Balloon Masters.....G..... 253 566-0201
University Place *(G-13960)*
Barefoote Concrete Inc.....G..... 509 879-3736
Spokane Valley *(G-12636)*
Bcb Enterprises LLC.....G..... 360 435-1047
Arlington *(G-210)*
Boeing.....G..... 360 348-0394
Snohomish *(G-11879)*
Boeing Arospc Operations Inc.....G..... 253 773-9906
Puyallup *(G-8132)*
Boeing China Inc.....G..... 206 655-2121
Tukwila *(G-13699)*
Boeing Classic.....G..... 206 381-7804
Seattle *(G-9562)*
Boeing Co.....G..... 206 351-8601
Des Moines *(G-2931)*
▲ **Boeing Commercial Airplane**.....E..... 425 237-2019
Everett *(G-3394)*
Boeing Commercial Airplane.....G..... 206 662-9615
Kent *(G-4817)*
Boeing Commercial Airplanes.....G..... 206 662-9615
Seatac *(G-9275)*
Boeing Company.....B..... 425 413-3400
Maple Valley *(G-6261)*
Boeing Company.....A..... 425 417-5612
Kirkland *(G-5295)*
Boeing Company.....E..... 312 544-2000
Kent *(G-4818)*
Boeing Company.....E..... 206 655-9974
Tukwila *(G-13700)*

SIC SECTION 37 TRANSPORTATION EQUIPMENT

Boeing Company A 425 359-3777
Bothell *(G-1831)*

Boeing Company A 425 493-8267
Mukilteo *(G-6899)*

Boeing Company G 425 266-0616
Mukilteo *(G-6900)*

Boeing Company A 206 662-6863
Renton *(G-8756)*

Boeing Company A 206 655-1131
Tukwila *(G-13701)*

Boeing Company F 312 544-2000
Bellevue *(G-821)*

Boeing Company A 206 766-2770
Renton *(G-8757)*

Boeing Company A 206 662-9615
Seatac *(G-9276)*

Boeing Company G 206 544-2374
Renton *(G-8758)*

Boeing Company E 425 865-6915
Bellevue *(G-822)*

Boeing Company G 253 657-0675
Seatac *(G-9277)*

Boeing Company G 425 407-1400
Everett *(G-3395)*

Boeing Company A 206 655-1131
Seattle *(G-9563)*

Boeing Company G 425 342-2121
Everett *(G-3396)*

Boeing Company G 425 306-8112
Renton *(G-8759)*

Boeing Company A 253 872-5545
Kent *(G-4819)*

Boeing Company A 206 544-4524
Tukwila *(G-13702)*

Boeing Company A 206 655-1131
Tukwila *(G-13703)*

Boeing Company A 312 544-2000
Seatac *(G-9278)*

Boeing Company A 425 865-3308
Bellevue *(G-823)*

Boeing Company A 425 865-3311
Bellevue *(G-824)*

Boeing Company A 253 657-5616
Renton *(G-8761)*

Boeing Company A 206 655-1131
Renton *(G-8762)*

Boeing Company E 206 655-2121
Tukwila *(G-13704)*

Boeing Company G 206 544-9246
Tukwila *(G-13705)*

Boeing Company A 312 544-2000
Everett *(G-3397)*

Boeing Company Incorporated E 425 965-4300
Tukwila *(G-13706)*

Boeing Domestic Sales Corp G 206 655-2121
Tukwila *(G-13707)*

Boeing Employees Flying Assn G 425 271-2332
Renton *(G-8763)*

Boeing Operations Intl Inc G 206 655-2121
Tukwila *(G-13708)*

Cadence Aerospace LLC G 425 353-0405
Everett *(G-3407)*

Carbon Aerospace G 206 697-3832
Seattle *(G-9627)*

Client Service Center G 206 237-0821
Seattle *(G-9696)*

Commet Precision Products G 360 403-7600
Arlington *(G-220)*

Composite Aircraft Tech LLC G 360 864-6271
Toledo *(G-13636)*

Conachen Aviation G 360 516-7740
Sequim *(G-11618)*

Cub Crafters Group LLC G 509 248-9491
Yakima *(G-15542)*

Cub Crafters Services LLC F 509 248-1025
Yakima *(G-15543)*

Droneworks LLC G 253 261-3888
Auburn *(G-429)*

Druid Mountain Drones G 206 321-4771
Puyallup *(G-8146)*

Eaton Corporation G 425 451-4954
Bellevue *(G-890)*

Fairlane Helicopters Inc G 360 398-1015
Lynden *(G-6016)*

Flightways Corporation G 425 747-6903
Bellevue *(G-912)*

Forged Chaos LLC G 360 630-1947
Arlington *(G-237)*

General Aerospace Inc G 425 422-5462
Lynnwood *(G-6127)*

Glacier Aviation Inc F 360 705-3214
Olympia *(G-7296)*

Glasair Aviation LLC G 360 435-8533
Arlington *(G-240)*

▲ Glasair Aviation Usa LLC E 360 435-8533
Arlington *(G-241)*

Grace AVI & Logistics Support G 425 269-9424
Sammamish *(G-9210)*

Hang Gliding Adventures G 360 357-1460
Tumwater *(G-13875)*

Helipower Helicopter Inc G 425 232-0972
Lynnwood *(G-6134)*

Helitrak Inc G 253 857-0890
Gig Harbor *(G-4117)*

Independent Aero Space Svcs G 702 237-9953
Kent *(G-4949)*

Interntnal Arospc Coatings Inc D 509 321-0342
Spokane *(G-12325)*

Jetoptera Inc G 516 456-7609
Edmonds *(G-3123)*

Jetprop LLC G 509 535-4401
Spokane *(G-12333)*

Kenmore Air Harbor Inc D 425 486-3224
Kenmore *(G-4587)*

Kit Planes Northwest G 360 403-0679
Arlington *(G-267)*

Kono Fixed Income Fund 1511 LP F 360 686-7688
Bellevue *(G-972)*

Left Full Rudder Aerospace LLC G 516 330-0633
Woodinville *(G-15287)*

Lehenengo Aerospace Inc G 425 256-1376
Kirkland *(G-5386)*

Lfr Aerospace G 516 330-0633
Kirkland *(G-5388)*

Lockheed Martin Corporation G 360 779-4682
Poulsbo *(G-7976)*

Lockheed Martin Corporation G 360 779-4682
Poulsbo *(G-7977)*

Loki Aerospace Incorporated G 425 361-2353
Brier *(G-2021)*

Mechanical Specilities G 360 273-7604
Olympia *(G-7336)*

Merlyn Products Inc F 509 838-7500
Spokane *(G-12390)*

Monroe Machined Products Inc E 206 242-4898
Seatac *(G-9291)*

▲ Morgan Aerospace LLC F 360 435-9755
Arlington *(G-284)*

Nexus Aerospace G 253 797-0700
Federal Way *(G-3762)*

▲ Northwing Uninsured Ultralight F 509 682-4359
Chelan *(G-2561)*

Pacific Northwest Drone Svcs G 509 679-0863
Lacey *(G-5573)*

Page Aerospace Inc G 425 650-1459
Kirkland *(G-5426)*

Plimp Inc G 206 795-3292
Seattle *(G-10823)*

Pyramis Aerospace LLC G 206 407-3406
Federal Way *(G-3774)*

RAC Aviation Services LLC G 360 256-6698
Vancouver *(G-14529)*

Radian Aerospace Inc G 425 235-1936
Renton *(G-8890)*

Rjh Aerospace NW G 425 394-3775
Cle Elum *(G-2677)*

Robodub Inc G 408 250-5723
Seattle *(G-10973)*

Roy Dintelman G 253 508-9361
Auburn *(G-550)*

Sandy Jo Franks G 206 367-2669
Lake Forest Park *(G-5624)*

Seaplane Landing Area (wa13) G 360 647-7839
Bellingham *(G-1529)*

Seattle Drone Sales Llc G 206 858-2764
Mercer Island *(G-6483)*

Senior Operations LLC G 360 403-2283
Arlington *(G-323)*

Shields Aerospace Services LLC G 425 240-6079
Edmonds *(G-3155)*

Simple Intelligence LLC G 425 418-9803
Pullman *(G-8109)*

Skyidrones LLC G 253 347-7261
Kent *(G-5134)*

Sodexo G 425 656-2860
Renton *(G-8915)*

▲ Soloy LLC E 360 754-7000
Tumwater *(G-13898)*

Spectech Aerospace LLC G 425 286-1101
Bothell *(G-1795)*

Stewarts Hanger 21 Inc G 509 782-3626
Cashmere *(G-2330)*

Sunbird Aerospace G 425 241-8594
Bellevue *(G-1166)*

Thyssenkrupp Materials LLC G 253 239-6023
Auburn *(G-581)*

Topcub Aircraft LLC G 401 209-4756
Arlington *(G-339)*

Triumph Aerostructures LLC G 310 355-3826
Longview *(G-5961)*

Uav Systems Development Corp B 803 767-1351
Moses Lake *(G-6755)*

Up4u Inc G 206 660-8498
Olympia *(G-7417)*

▲ Vectored Solutions Inc G 425 355-8038
Everett *(G-3649)*

▲ Vose Technical Systems Inc G 253 272-7273
Tacoma *(G-13584)*

Western Avionics Inc G 509 534-7371
Spokane *(G-12585)*

X L F Aerospace LLC G 206 592-2249
Seatac *(G-9312)*

Zero Gravity Bldrs Studio LLC G 509 942-8439
Richland *(G-9057)*

Ztron Labs Inc G 425 289-8794
Snohomish *(G-12003)*

3724 Aircraft Engines & Engine Parts

ADI Solar Corporation G 206 484-2879
Monroe *(G-6542)*

Aeroform Inc E 360 403-1919
Arlington *(G-195)*

Associated Aircraft & Mar Svcs G 253 631-3082
Kent *(G-4794)*

Belair Composites Inc F 509 482-0442
Spokane *(G-12144)*

Bspace Corporation G 208 559-7806
Seattle *(G-9591)*

Cascade Arcft Conversions LLC G 509 635-1212
Garfield *(G-4066)*

Cascade Flying Service LLC G 509 635-1212
Garfield *(G-4067)*

CFI Blue Sky II LLC E 253 627-1903
Sumner *(G-13058)*

▲ Coolpc Incorporated G 425 821-6400
Kirkland *(G-5313)*

David Olson Honeywell Arspc G 509 321-7368
Spokane *(G-12220)*

▲ Double D Mfg LLC G 206 954-8099
Marysville *(G-6331)*

Doyon Technical Services LLC G 253 344-5300
Federal Way *(G-3732)*

Elmo Fokker Inc E 253 395-2652
Sumner *(G-13068)*

▲ Exotic Metals Forming Co LLC B 253 220-5900
Kent *(G-4900)*

Falcon Rcnnissance Systems Inc G 360 378-3900
Friday Harbor *(G-4044)*

General Electric Company G 253 351-2200
Auburn *(G-448)*

Gms Procurement LLC G 253 852-6552
Auburn *(G-453)*

Honeywell International Inc B 425 885-3711
Redmond *(G-8496)*

Honeywell International Inc A 509 534-5226
Spokane Valley *(G-12732)*

Honeywell International Inc A 760 339-5592
Renton *(G-8819)*

Honeywell International Inc E 425 921-4598
Lynnwood *(G-6135)*

Honeywell International Inc G 425 413-2453
Maple Valley *(G-6273)*

Honeywell International Inc G 360 253-8100
Mercer Island *(G-6466)*

Honeywell International Inc G 253 966-0203
Lewis Mcchord *(G-5820)*

Honeywell International Inc G 425 885-8944
Redmond *(G-8497)*

Honeywell International Inc D 425 885-3711
Redmond *(G-8498)*

Honeywell International Inc A 425 885-3711
Redmond *(G-8499)*

Honeywell International Inc A 425 885-3711
Redmond *(G-8500)*

Kurtisfactor LLC G 208 863-6180
Tacoma *(G-13379)*

Luma Technologies LLC F 425 643-4000
Bellevue *(G-990)*

Merlyn Products Inc F 509 838-7500
Spokane *(G-12390)*

S I C

Employee Codes: A=Over 500 employees, B=251-500
C=101-250, D=51-100, E=20-50, F=10-19, G=2-9

2019 Washington
Manufacturers Register

637

37 TRANSPORTATION EQUIPMENT SIC SECTION

Mr Rpm LLC....G....360 387-2272
Camano Island *(G-2218)*
Norfil LLC....E....253 863-5888
Pacific *(G-7534)*
Omohundro Co Kitsap Composites....D....360 519-3047
Port Orchard *(G-7837)*
Pmw Capital Inc....G....253 272-5119
Tacoma *(G-13468)*
Precision Airmotive LLC....E....360 659-7348
Marysville *(G-6371)*
▲ **Precision Engines LLC**....D....425 347-2800
Everett *(G-3584)*
▲ **Precision Machine Works Inc**....C....253 272-5119
Tacoma *(G-13474)*
Rentiel Precision Laser Cutng....G....253 297-2823
Tacoma *(G-13494)*
Safran Usa Inc....E....425 462-8613
Bellevue *(G-1112)*
Skein Integrated Systems LLC....D....586 795-2000
Everett *(G-3613)*
▲ **Subsea Air Systems LLC**....G....360 563-2400
Snohomish *(G-11987)*
Tethers Unlimited Inc....G....425 486-0100
Bothell *(G-1800)*
Triumph Actuation Systems....B....509 248-5000
Yakima *(G-15696)*
▲ **Triumph Composite Systems Inc**....B....509 623-8536
Spokane *(G-12570)*
Universal Engine Heater Co....G....509 276-5923
Nine Mile Falls *(G-7084)*

3728 Aircraft Parts & Eqpt, NEC

A & M Prcsion Msuring Svcs Inc....F....425 432-7554
Kent *(G-4750)*
AAA Precise Machine Inc....G....509 375-3268
Benton City *(G-1599)*
Absolute Aviation Services LLC....E....509 747-2904
Spokane *(G-12094)*
▲ **Accra Manufacturing Inc**....D....425 424-1000
Bothell *(G-1814)*
Accurus Aerospace Kent LLC....D....253 872-8541
Kent *(G-4757)*
▲ **Aero Controls Inc**....C....253 269-3000
Auburn *(G-364)*
Aeroacoustics Inc....G....425 438-0215
Everett *(G-3363)*
▲ **Aerocell Corporation**....C....360 653-2211
Marysville *(G-6311)*
Aeroforge Manufacturing Inc....E....253 286-2525
Puyallup *(G-8118)*
Aeroform Inc....E....360 403-1919
Arlington *(G-195)*
Aerojet Rocketdyne Inc....E....425 885-5000
Redmond *(G-8373)*
Aeronautical Testing Service....G....360 363-4276
Arlington *(G-196)*
Aerospace Defense Inc....G....360 548-8017
Arlington *(G-197)*
Aerospace International LLC....G....206 334-7426
Kent *(G-4763)*
▼ **After Market Products Inc**....F....360 825-6500
Enumclaw *(G-3275)*
▲ **Aim Aerospace Inc**....C....425 235-2750
Renton *(G-8732)*
▲ **Aim Aerospace Auburn Inc**....C....253 804-3355
Auburn *(G-365)*
Aim Aerospace Sumner Inc....F....253 804-3355
Auburn *(G-366)*
Aim Aerospace Sumner Inc....C....253 863-7868
Sumner *(G-13054)*
Aim Group USA Inc....C....425 235-2750
Renton *(G-8733)*
Air Metal Fabricators Inc....G....509 923-2274
Pateros *(G-7657)*
◆ **Airborne Ecs LLC**....F....319 538-1051
Port Angeles *(G-7679)*
Aircraft Propulsion Systems....G....425 413-4127
Maple Valley *(G-6254)*
Airworthness Drctive Solutions....G....425 876-9742
Mukilteo *(G-6891)*
Aj Aerospace....G....253 335-7775
Algona *(G-66)*
▼ **American Edge LLC**....F....509 937-4404
Valley *(G-13987)*
Asko Industrial Repair....F....206 284-2659
Mukilteo *(G-6894)*
▲ **Astronics Advncd Electrnc Sys**....A....425 881-1700
Kirkland *(G-5283)*
Astronics Cstm Ctrl Cncpts Inc....D....206 575-0933
Kent *(G-4795)*
Atacs Products Inc....F....206 433-9000
Seattle *(G-9449)*
Aviation Covers Inc....G....360 435-0342
Arlington *(G-205)*
Aviation Innovations LLC....G....360 907-0888
Yacolt *(G-15481)*
▲ **Aviation Partners Inc**....F....206 762-1171
Seattle *(G-9471)*
▲ **Aviation Spares & Svcs Intl Co**....F....425 869-7799
Redmond *(G-8393)*
Avistar Aerospace LLC....G....206 838-6869
Seattle *(G-9472)*
◆ **Avtechtyee Inc**....C....425 290-3100
Everett *(G-3378)*
B/E Aerospace Inc....B....360 657-5197
Everett *(G-3380)*
B/E Aerospace Inc....B....425 923-2700
Everett *(G-3381)*
◆ **Ballard Technology Inc**....D....425 339-0281
Everett *(G-3383)*
Bayview Engineering Inds LLC....G....360 421-2126
Oak Harbor *(G-7141)*
◆ **Blr Aerospace LLc**....E....425 353-6591
Everett *(G-3389)*
▲ **Boeing Commercial Airplane**....E....425 237-2019
Everett *(G-3394)*
Boeing Company....C....253 931-2121
Auburn *(G-395)*
Boeing Company....A....425 865-3311
Bellevue *(G-824)*
Bogert Aviation Inc....G....509 736-1513
Pasco *(G-7554)*
Brooks Tactical Systems....F....253 549-2703
Fox Island *(G-4019)*
Bucher Aerospace Corporation....E....425 355-2202
Everett *(G-3402)*
▲ **C&D Zodiac Inc**....D....360 653-2211
Marysville *(G-6318)*
Cadence Aerospace LLC....F....425 353-0405
Everett *(G-3408)*
Carbon Consultants LLC....E....509 637-2520
Bingen *(G-1634)*
Cascade Aviation Services Inc....E....425 493-1707
Marysville *(G-6322)*
Cashmere Manufacturing LLC....E....509 888-2141
East Wenatchee *(G-3009)*
Center Trade Corporation....G....206 992-2374
Kirkland *(G-5302)*
▲ **Cobalt Enterprises LLC**....D....360 691-2298
Granite Falls *(G-4267)*
Collins Aerospace....G....509 744-6000
Spokane *(G-12187)*
▲ **Compass Aerospace Northwest, I**....D....253 852-9700
Kent *(G-4858)*
Component Products Corporation....F....425 355-6800
Mukilteo *(G-6904)*
Composite Solutions Corp....D....253 833-1878
Sumner *(G-13060)*
▼ **Core Tech LLC**....G....253 457-3239
Tacoma *(G-13243)*
Crane Aerospace Inc....E....425 743-1313
Lynnwood *(G-6100)*
▲ **Cub Crafters Inc**....E....509 248-9491
Yakima *(G-15541)*
Dabs M&A LLC....E....253 872-2200
Kent *(G-4869)*
Dakota Cub....G....509 453-3412
Yakima *(G-15549)*
Dance Air Inc....G....425 222-6789
Snoqualmie *(G-12009)*
Danner Corporation....C....253 833-5333
Auburn *(G-422)*
Defense Sales Intl LLC....G....206 999-8684
Renton *(G-8782)*
Diamond Machine Works Inc....E....206 633-3960
Seattle *(G-9827)*
▲ **Double D Mfg LLC**....G....206 954-8099
Marysville *(G-6331)*
Dowty Aerospace....G....509 248-5000
Yakima *(G-15558)*
Dynamic Safety LLC....G....425 290-9399
Mukilteo *(G-6917)*
◆ **Eldec Corporation**....A....425 743-1313
Lynnwood *(G-6114)*
Ellison Fluid Systems Inc....G....425 271-3220
Renton *(G-8793)*
EM Global Manufacturing Inc....G....253 655-5206
Tacoma *(G-13276)*
Esterline Corporation....G....425 453-9400
Bellevue *(G-899)*
Esterline International Co....G....425 453-9400
Bellevue *(G-901)*
Esterline Technologies Corp....G....253 796-4527
Kent *(G-4897)*
Esterline Technologies Corp....E....425 297-9624
Everett *(G-3462)*
▼ **Esterline Technologies Corp**....E....425 453-9400
Bellevue *(G-902)*
▲ **Exotic Metals Forming Co LLC**....B....253 220-5900
Kent *(G-4900)*
Exotic Metals Forming Co LLC....G....253 395-3710
Kent *(G-4901)*
Fabrication Technologies LLC....G....360 293-3707
Anacortes *(G-127)*
◆ **Fatigue Technology Inc**....C....206 246-2010
Tukwila *(G-13732)*
Fiberdyne Aerospace....G....206 326-8581
Seattle *(G-9987)*
Flight Structures Inc....C....360 651-8537
Everett *(G-3475)*
Fly Girls Aero Covers....G....509 466-7794
Spokane *(G-12260)*
Frisbie Company....G....253 939-0363
Auburn *(G-444)*
G B C Enterprises Inc....G....360 275-3522
Tahuya *(G-13610)*
Gcm North American Arospc LLC....D....253 872-7488
Algona *(G-69)*
GE Aviation Systems LLC....C....206 662-2934
Tukwila *(G-13737)*
Gemini Management Ltd....G....425 739-6800
Kirkland *(G-5347)*
Giddens Aerospace Inc....G....425 353-0405
Everett *(G-3497)*
Giddens Holdings Inc....G....425 353-0405
Everett *(G-3498)*
Giddens Industries Inc....G....425 353-0405
Everett *(G-3499)*
Giddens Industries Inc....C....425 353-0405
Everett *(G-3500)*
Goodrich Aerostructures Integr....G....425 318-9276
Everett *(G-3502)*
Goodrich Corporation....E....425 261-8700
Everett *(G-3503)*
Goodrich Corporation....F....425 822-9851
Kirkland *(G-5351)*
Goodrich Corporation....E....509 744-6000
Spokane *(G-12278)*
Harper Engineering Company....D....425 255-0414
Renton *(G-8817)*
Hexcel Corporation....C....360 757-7212
Burlington *(G-2163)*
Hexcel Corporation....C....253 872-7500
Kent *(G-4941)*
Hirschler Mfg Inc....E....425 827-9384
Kirkland *(G-5358)*
Horizon Flight....G....509 521-4244
Pasco *(G-7590)*
Humbay Health LLC....G....425 922-0200
Kirkland *(G-5363)*
◆ **Hydro Systems USA Inc**....C....253 876-2100
Kent *(G-4946)*
Icarus Aero Components LLC....G....386 299-0529
Kirkland *(G-5366)*
Idd Aerospace Corp....C....425 885-0617
Redmond *(G-8505)*
Intergrated Aerospace LLC....G....360 691-2298
Lake Stevens *(G-5649)*
J C Manufacturing Inc....F....206 824-7650
Des Moines *(G-2938)*
J D Ott Co Inc....C....206 749-0777
Seattle *(G-10269)*
▲ **Jamco America Inc**....C....425 347-4735
Everett *(G-3522)*
Jamco America Inc....G....425 347-4735
Everett *(G-3523)*
Janicki Industries Inc....E....360 856-5143
Sedro Woolley *(G-11545)*
Jet Parts Engineering LLC....E....206 281-0963
Seattle *(G-10295)*
Kira Aviation Services LLC....G....425 361-1060
Lynnwood *(G-6151)*
Klune Industries Inc....C....253 872-7488
Kent *(G-4979)*
Krismark Group Inc....G....425 396-0829
Snoqualmie *(G-12015)*
L & R Industries LLC....G....425 226-2780
Renton *(G-8839)*
▲ **Lamar Technologies LLC**....F....360 651-8869
Marysville *(G-6352)*

37 TRANSPORTATION EQUIPMENT

Landing Gear Work LLC ....G...... 509 884-9546
Renton *(G-8840)*
Lifeport Inc ....G...... 360 225-3200
Woodland *(G-15445)*
Lifeport Inc ....E...... 360 225-6690
Woodland *(G-15446)*
▼ Lifeport LLC ....D...... 360 225-1212
Woodland *(G-15447)*
Lift Solutions Inc ....G...... 360 862-8328
Lake Stevens *(G-5657)*
Linear Controls Inc ....G...... 425 876-9742
Mukilteo *(G-6949)*
Lkd Aerospace LLC ....F...... 425 396-0829
Snoqualmie *(G-12017)*
LMI Aerospace Inc ....G...... 425 293-0340
Everett *(G-3538)*
LMI Aerospace Inc ....C...... 253 288-9379
Auburn *(G-489)*
Longwell Company ....D...... 425 289-0160
Bellevue *(G-989)*
Lrt Inc ....G...... 425 742-0333
Mill Creek *(G-6516)*
▲ Lumicor Inc ....D...... 425 255-4000
Renton *(G-8846)*
Majestic Aerotech Inc ....F...... 360 528-4142
Tacoma *(G-13396)*
Manufacturing Technology Inc .....G...... 206 763-3161
Seattle *(G-10473)*
Marketing Masters Inc ....F...... 425 454-5610
Issaquah *(G-4445)*
Matsushita Avionics Co ....G...... 206 246-6200
Seatac *(G-9289)*
Mechanical Specialties LLC ....G...... 360 273-7604
Olympia *(G-7335)*
Mercer Products & Mfg Co ....G...... 425 742-0333
Mill Creek *(G-6517)*
Merlyn Products Inc ....F...... 509 838-7500
Spokane *(G-12390)*
Micro Aerodynamics Inc ....F...... 360 293-8082
Anacortes *(G-146)*
Morgan Aero Products Inc ....G...... 425 438-9600
Everett *(G-3551)*
▲ Nabtesco Aerospace Inc ....E...... 425 602-8400
Kirkland *(G-5407)*
Northstone Industries LLC ....G...... 509 844-7775
Spokane *(G-12410)*
Northwest Aerospace Tech Inc .....G...... 425 212-5001
Everett *(G-3556)*
Northwest Aerospace Tech Inc .....D...... 425 257-2044
Everett *(G-3555)*
Northwest Dynamics Inc ....G...... 360 253-3656
Vancouver *(G-14434)*
Olympic Aerospace Inc ....G...... 253 835-4984
Federal Way *(G-3767)*
Olympic Areospace Inc ....G...... 253 835-4984
Federal Way *(G-3768)*
Omohundro Co Kitsap Composites ......D...... 360 519-3047
Port Orchard *(G-7837)*
Onboard Systems Intl LLC ....E...... 360 546-3072
Vancouver *(G-14451)*
▼ Pacific Aerospace & Elec LLC ...C...... 855 885-5200
Wenatchee *(G-15059)*
Palomar Products Inc ....G...... 425 453-9400
Bellevue *(G-1061)*
Parkwater Aviation Inc ....F...... 509 536-1969
Spokane *(G-12430)*
Petrichor Industries LLC ....G...... 425 454-8281
Bellevue *(G-1073)*
Plexsys Interface Products Inc .....E...... 360 838-2500
Camas *(G-2275)*
Pmw Capital Inc ....G...... 253 272-5119
Tacoma *(G-13468)*
Pnw Aerospace LLC ....G...... 360 292-0909
Lacey *(G-5577)*
▲ Precision Machine Works Inc ...C...... 253 272-5119
Tacoma *(G-13474)*
▲ Primus Bumstead Manufacturing ......G...... 425 688-0444
Algona *(G-74)*
Primus International ....G...... 425 424-1085
Bothell *(G-1889)*
◆ Primus International Inc ....G...... 425 688-0444
Auburn *(G-537)*
Primus International Inc ....C...... 253 854-2995
Algona *(G-75)*
Primus International Inc ....B...... 425 318-4500
Woodinville *(G-15340)*
Primus International Inc ....C...... 253 876-1500
Algona *(G-76)*
Protium Innovations LLC ....G...... 206 854-8792
Pullman *(G-8102)*

Quality On Time Machining Inc .....G...... 360 802-3700
Enumclaw *(G-3314)*
Quiet Wing Aerospace LLC ....G...... 425 451-8565
Redmond *(G-8640)*
Radioracks Aviation Systems ....G...... 360 651-1200
Lake Stevens *(G-5670)*
Raisbeck Engineering Inc ....F...... 206 723-2000
Tukwila *(G-13802)*
RMC Incorporated ....E...... 206 243-4831
Seattle *(G-10969)*
Roberts Precision Machine Inc .....F...... 360 805-1000
Monroe *(G-6615)*
Routec Industries LLC ....G...... 206 949-2472
Snohomish *(G-11969)*
▲ Royell Manufacturing Inc ....D...... 425 259-9258
Everett *(G-3602)*
RTC Aerospace LLC ....F...... 918 407-0291
Fife *(G-3988)*
Rti Manufacturing Inc ....G...... 360 435-9092
Arlington *(G-318)*
◆ Safran Cabin Bellingham Inc ..C...... 360 738-2005
Bellingham *(G-1521)*
Safran Cabin Inc ....C...... 360 653-2600
Marysville *(G-6381)*
Safran Cabin Inc ....D...... 360 653-2211
Marysville *(G-6382)*
Safran Cabin Inc ....C...... 509 447-4122
Newport *(G-7065)*
Safran Ventilation System Usa .....E...... 425 438-1378
Everett *(G-3604)*
Sakco Precision Inc ....G...... 253 288-9702
Auburn *(G-555)*
Samuel Edwards ....G...... 253 988-0219
Kent *(G-5114)*
Sea West Products Inc ....F...... 253 854-2942
Kent *(G-5119)*
Seaton Engineering Corporation ...G...... 509 290-5919
Spokane *(G-12495)*
▲ Seattle Turbine Inc ....E...... 253 770-7567
Puyallup *(G-8251)*
Senior Operations LLC ....B...... 360 435-1119
Arlington *(G-325)*
Senior Operations LLC ....G...... 360 435-1119
Arlington *(G-326)*
Skills Inc ....E...... 206 782-6000
Seattle *(G-11127)*
▲ Soloy LLC ....E...... 360 754-7000
Tumwater *(G-13898)*
Spartan Industries L L C ....G...... 425 822-2071
Redmond *(G-8677)*
Spearman Corp Kent Division ......F...... 253 236-5980
Kent *(G-5144)*
Spearman Corporation ....E...... 360 651-9281
Kent *(G-5145)*
Spokane Industries Inc ....E...... 509 928-0720
Spokane Valley *(G-12886)*
Stoddard International LLC ....E...... 360 435-6455
Arlington *(G-337)*
Subaru of America Inc ....G...... 425 822-0762
Kirkland *(G-5472)*
Surftech Finishes Co ....G...... 425 453-9400
Bellevue *(G-1168)*
Synchronous Aerospace ....G...... 253 852-9700
Kent *(G-5165)*
Tect Aerospace LLC ....D...... 253 872-7045
Kent *(G-5175)*
Terrys Precision Products LLC .....G...... 425 349-2700
Everett *(G-3630)*
Toolcraft Inc ....F...... 360 794-5512
Monroe *(G-6633)*
Triton Aerospace LLC ....F...... 360 466-4160
La Conner *(G-5527)*
Triumph Actuation Systems ....B...... 509 248-5000
Yakima *(G-15696)*
▲ Triumph Composite Systems Inc ..B...... 509 623-8536
Spokane *(G-12570)*
Triumph Group Inc ....F...... 425 636-9000
Redmond *(G-8695)*
Ttf Aerospace Inc ....C...... 253 736-6300
Auburn *(G-584)*
Tyee Aircraft Inc ....G...... 425 290-3100
Everett *(G-3639)*
Uav Systems Development Corp ...B...... 803 767-1351
Moses Lake *(G-6755)*
Umbra Cuscinetti Incorporated ....D...... 425 405-3500
Everett *(G-3640)*
Universal Aerospace Co Inc ....C...... 360 435-9577
Arlington *(G-344)*
▲ University Swaging Corporation ..C...... 425 318-1965
Bellevue *(G-1208)*

University Swaging Corporation ...G...... 425 318-4500
Woodinville *(G-15396)*
Valley Machine Shop Inc ....E...... 425 226-5040
Kent *(G-5199)*
Vaupell Rapid Solutions ....G...... 206 784-9050
Everett *(G-3648)*
Vts Aviation LLC ....G...... 253 272-7273
Tacoma *(G-13585)*
Waiv Aerospace LLC ....G...... 206 276-2306
Bellevue *(G-1222)*
West Coast Fabrication Inc ....G...... 206 790-1496
Auburn *(G-598)*
West Isle Air Inc ....F...... 425 235-1996
Chelan *(G-2570)*
Western Aerospace & Engrg LLC ..G...... 360 253-8282
Vancouver *(G-14684)*
Wipro Givon Usa Inc ....G...... 425 355-3330
Everett *(G-3661)*
Woodford Phoenix Aerospace Mfg ..G...... 360 736-9689
Centralia *(G-2444)*
Zepher Inc ....E...... 509 637-2520
Bingen *(G-1643)*
Zodiac Aerospace ....G...... 425 791-3302
Everett *(G-3664)*
Zodiac Aerospace ....G...... 425 257-2044
Everett *(G-3665)*
Zodiac Arospc Engineered Mtls ....G...... 360 653-2600
Marysville *(G-6403)*

3731 Shipbuilding & Repairing

Abcd Marine ....G...... 206 527-3428
Seattle *(G-9333)*
Aircraft Cargo Pods ....G...... 509 238-1165
Mead *(G-6422)*
Al Fletcher ....G...... 360 963-2241
Sekiu *(G-11582)*
All Ocean Services LLC ....G...... 206 632-7692
Everett *(G-3367)*
American Flex & Exhaust Pdts ....G...... 206 789-1353
Seattle *(G-9392)*
Argo West Inc ....G...... 360 213-1503
Vancouver *(G-14040)*
Bennett Lumber Products Inc ......C...... 509 758-5558
Clarkston *(G-2623)*
Campbell Maritime Inc ....G...... 206 794-0232
Seattle *(G-9614)*
Cape San Lucas Fishing LP ....E...... 425 688-1288
Bellevue *(G-836)*
Clarus Fluid Intelligence LLC ....E...... 360 671-1514
Bellingham *(G-1298)*
▲ Clarus Technologies LLC ....G...... 360 671-1514
Bellingham *(G-1299)*
Conglobal Industries LLC ....E...... 206 624-8180
Seattle *(G-9727)*
Craft Labor & Support Svcs LLC ..G...... 206 304-4543
Edmonds *(G-3103)*
◆ Dakota Creek Industries Inc ...A...... 360 293-9575
Anacortes *(G-119)*
Daves Mobile Welding LLC ....G...... 360 302-0069
Port Townsend *(G-7877)*
Deep Ocean Expeditions LLC ......G...... 801 390-7025
Seattle *(G-9814)*
Duwamish Marine Services LLC ...G...... 206 870-3027
Seattle *(G-9863)*
Ecm Maritime Services LLC ....G...... 206 780-9980
Seattle *(G-9876)*
Electric Boat Corporation ....E...... 206 598-5115
Silverdale *(G-11833)*
F/V Neahkahnie LLC ....G...... 206 547-6557
Seattle *(G-9958)*
Fabtek Industries Llc ....F...... 360 322-7367
Arlington *(G-235)*
Federal Marine & Def Svcs LLC ...E...... 206 322-5529
Seattle *(G-9958)*
Fishing Vessel Owners Mar Way ..F...... 206 282-6421
Seattle *(G-10000)*
◆ Foss Maritime Company Llc ...D...... 206 281-3800
Seattle *(G-10015)*
Gardner Boat Repair Inc ....G...... 206 784-0854
Seattle *(G-10047)*
General Dynamics Nascco ....G...... 360 373-2845
Bremerton *(G-1956)*
General Steamship Intl Ltd ....G...... 425 329-1040
Lynnwood *(G-6128)*
George G Sharp Inc ....D...... 360 476-8896
Bremerton *(G-1957)*
Guido Perla & Associates Inc ......E...... 206 463-2217
Seattle *(G-10132)*
Hansen Marine Repair & Rigging ..G...... 360 705-1252
Olympia *(G-7303)*

Employee Codes: A=Over 500 employees, B=251-500
C=101-250, D=51-100, E=20-50, F=10-19, G=2-9

2019 Washington Manufacturers Register

37 TRANSPORTATION EQUIPMENT SIC SECTION

Highlands Welding Repair Inc ....G.... 206 283-0080
Seattle *(G-10172)*
J Calman Industries ....G.... 360 398-1932
Lynden *(G-6024)*
▲ J M Mrtnac Shipbuilding Corp ....C.... 253 572-4005
Tacoma *(G-13353)*
Jt Marine Inc ....E.... 360 750-1300
Vancouver *(G-14343)*
Ken Dressler ....G.... 360 765-3131
Quilcene *(G-8285)*
Kurtisfactor LLC ....G.... 208 863-6180
Tacoma *(G-13379)*
Lfs Inc ....E.... 360 734-6825
Bellingham *(G-1408)*
◆ Lfs Inc ....E.... 360 734-3336
Bellingham *(G-1409)*
Lighthouse Envmtl Programs ....G.... 360 579-4489
Coupeville *(G-2814)*
Lovrics Sea Craft Inc ....G.... 360 293-2042
Anacortes *(G-144)*
◆ Marine Fluid Systems Inc ....F.... 206 706-0858
Seattle *(G-10481)*
Mavrik Marine Inc ....D.... 360 296-4051
La Conner *(G-5525)*
Metro Machine Corp ....D.... 360 782-5600
Bremerton *(G-1978)*
Northlake Shipyard Inc ....F.... 206 632-1441
Seattle *(G-10634)*
Npm LLC ....G.... 206 782-8999
Seattle *(G-10662)*
Pac Ship ....G.... 425 622-9030
Everett *(G-3563)*
Pacific Fishermen Inc ....D.... 206 784-2562
Seattle *(G-10731)*
▲ Pacific Fshrmen Shpyrd Elc LLC ....D.... 206 784-2562
Seattle *(G-10732)*
▲ Pacific Pipe & Pump LLC ....F.... 425 640-0376
Mountlake Terrace *(G-6865)*
Pacific Ship Repr Fbrction Inc ....C.... 360 674-2480
Bremerton *(G-1985)*
Pacific Ship Repr Fbrction Inc ....E.... 425 409-5060
Everett *(G-3567)*
Palmer Hayes Offshore ....G.... 253 310-7162
Gig Harbor *(G-4142)*
Pequod Inc ....G.... 425 742-7456
Edmonds *(G-3143)*
Propulsion Controls Engrg ....E.... 425 257-9065
Everett *(G-3588)*
▲ Puget Sound Commerce Ctr Inc ....D.... 206 623-1635
Seattle *(G-10884)*
Puglia Engineering Inc ....C.... 360 647-0080
Bellingham *(G-1509)*
Quilters Heaven LLC ....G.... 800 253-8990
Leavenworth *(G-5814)*
▲ Rozema Boat Works Inc ....F.... 360 757-6004
Mount Vernon *(G-6830)*
Rozema Enterprises Inc ....G.... 360 757-6004
Mount Vernon *(G-6831)*
Seattle Shipworks LLC ....D.... 206 763-3133
Seattle *(G-11074)*
Seaview Boat Yard Inc ....F.... 206 783-6550
Seattle *(G-11086)*
Shipyard LLC ....G.... 360 532-1990
Hoquiam *(G-4358)*
Snow & Company Inc ....E.... 206 953-7676
Seattle *(G-11144)*
Snow & Company Inc ....G.... 206 396-8997
Seattle *(G-11145)*
Stabbert & Associates Inc ....C.... 206 547-6161
Seattle *(G-11174)*
Stabbert Mrtime Yacht Ship LLC ....F.... 206 547-6161
Seattle *(G-11175)*
Stabbert Yacht and Ship LLC ....E.... 206 547-6161
Seattle *(G-11176)*
Stealth Marine ....G.... 509 758-8019
Clarkston *(G-2649)*
Sterling Envmtl Resources ....D.... 360 437-1344
Port Ludlow *(G-7778)*
Strongback Metal Boats Inc ....G.... 206 321-9965
Seattle *(G-11204)*
Technical Marine and Indus LLC ....G.... 206 717-4466
Mountlake Terrace *(G-6872)*
Terry Albracht ....G.... 425 252-2997
Everett *(G-3628)*
Tidewater Holdings Inc ....G.... 360 693-1491
Vancouver *(G-14635)*
Toss Brion Yacht Rigging Inc ....G.... 360 385-1080
Port Townsend *(G-7932)*
Turn Pt Lghthuse Prsrvtion Soc ....G.... 360 376-5246
Orcas *(G-7456)*
▲ University Swaging Corporation ....C.... 425 318-1965
Bellevue *(G-1208)*
US Fab ....G.... 206 623-1635
Seattle *(G-11392)*
Vigor Fab LLC ....G.... 206 623-1635
Seattle *(G-11417)*
Vigor Industrial LLC ....E.... 360 457-8470
Port Angeles *(G-7752)*
Vigor Industrial LLC ....F.... 253 627-9136
Tacoma *(G-13576)*
Vigor Marine LLC ....D.... 253 627-9136
Tacoma *(G-13577)*
Vigor Marine LLC ....B.... 206 623-1635
Seattle *(G-11418)*
▲ Vigor Shipyards Inc ....A.... 206 623-1635
Seattle *(G-11419)*
▲ Washington Marine Repair LLC ....E.... 360 457-8470
Port Angeles *(G-7753)*
Westman Marine Inc ....G.... 360 332-5051
Blaine *(G-1711)*
Winterhalter Inc ....G.... 360 652-6337
Stanwood *(G-13000)*
Xtaeros Inc ....G.... 206 883-4034
Seattle *(G-11505)*

3732 Boat Building & Repairing

Alexander S Service Repair ....G.... 509 773-7010
Goldendale *(G-4192)*
▲ All American Marine Inc ....E.... 360 647-7602
Bellingham *(G-1243)*
All Ocean Services LLC ....G.... 206 632-7692
Everett *(G-3367)*
American Flex & Exhaust Pdts ....G.... 206 789-1353
Seattle *(G-9392)*
Amphibious Marine Inc ....G.... 360 426-3170
Shelton *(G-11677)*
Armstrong Consolidated LLC ....G.... 360 477-7558
Port Townsend *(G-7864)*
Armstrong Marine USA Inc ....D.... 360 457-5752
Port Angeles *(G-7686)*
Arrants Boat Works ....G.... 425 293-4660
Camano Island *(G-2207)*
Auburn Marine ....G.... 253 941-3046
Auburn *(G-382)*
B & J Fiberglass LLC ....G.... 360 398-9342
Bellingham *(G-1256)*
Baycraft Marine Sales Inc ....G.... 253 863-8522
Chehalis *(G-2470)*
Bear Creek Boatworks Inc ....G.... 425 558-4086
Woodinville *(G-15186)*
Better Boats Inc ....F.... 360 797-1244
Port Angeles *(G-7690)*
Bitter End Boatworks ....G.... 360 920-3862
Bellingham *(G-1274)*
Blue Oval Co ....G.... 509 448-2894
Spokane *(G-12155)*
Boat-Tech ....G.... 206 281-9828
Seattle *(G-9559)*
Boatworks Gallery LLC ....G.... 360 626-1284
Poulsbo *(G-7950)*
Boatworks Long Lake ....G.... 509 979-0936
Nine Mile Falls *(G-7068)*
Brunswick Corporation ....D.... 509 769-2142
Clarkston *(G-2626)*
Bushwacker Boats ....G.... 360 969-1648
Burlington *(G-2139)*
C D Boat Works ....G.... 360 942-3669
Raymond *(G-8344)*
▲ Cap Sante International Inc ....E.... 360 293-3145
Anacortes *(G-109)*
Cap Sante Marine Ltd ....E.... 360 293-3145
Anacortes *(G-110)*
Celebration Boatworks ....G.... 206 321-0794
Bothell *(G-1838)*
Chinook Marine Repair Inc ....G.... 360 777-8361
Chinook *(G-2615)*
▲ Christensen Shipyards LLC ....F.... 360 831-9800
Vancouver *(G-14119)*
▲ Commercial Plastics Corp ....F.... 206 682-4832
Seattle *(G-9717)*
Concorde Marine Inc ....G.... 360 755-3471
Anacortes *(G-115)*
Csr Marine Inc ....E.... 206 632-2001
Seattle *(G-9761)*
Custom Fiberglass Mfr ....G.... 360 457-5092
Port Angeles *(G-7696)*
D&L Summers Inc ....G.... 360 268-0769
Westport *(G-15104)*
◆ Dakota Creek Industries Inc ....A.... 360 293-9575
Anacortes *(G-119)*
Dale A West Specialty Wdwkg ....G.... 360 683-9419
Sequim *(G-11623)*
Defiance Boats LLC ....G.... 360 674-7098
Bremerton *(G-1945)*
▼ Defiance Boats LLC ....E.... 360 329-6865
Bremerton *(G-1946)*
▲ Delta Marine Industries Inc ....B.... 206 763-0760
Seattle *(G-9818)*
Devlin Designing Boatbuilders ....G.... 360 866-0164
Seattle *(G-9826)*
Down Island Trading Co ....G.... 360 376-4056
Deer Harbor *(G-2891)*
Duckworth Boat Works Inc ....E.... 509 758-9831
Clarkston *(G-2633)*
Eagle Rock Boat Repair ....G.... 360 391-3219
Anacortes *(G-125)*
Easy Rider Canoe & Kayak Co ....G.... 425 228-3633
Tukwila *(G-13727)*
Edwing Boat Inc ....G.... 360 777-8771
Chinook *(G-2616)*
F/V Native Star ....G.... 360 267-6348
Grayland *(G-4293)*
Fields Fabrication Corporation ....G.... 425 222-5905
Issaquah *(G-4413)*
First Boat Company ....G.... 425 931-9433
Everett *(G-3473)*
First Cabin Yachts Inc ....G.... 206 595-6657
Seattle *(G-9995)*
Fishing Vessel Owners Mar Way ....F.... 206 282-6421
Seattle *(G-10000)*
Fitz Custom Marine ....G.... 253 732-5669
Gig Harbor *(G-4100)*
Fletcher Boats Inc ....G.... 360 452-8430
Port Angeles *(G-7707)*
▲ Fluid Motion LLC ....E.... 253 839-5213
Kent *(G-4913)*
Fv Fast Break ....G.... 360 642-3753
Ilwaco *(G-4370)*
Gig Harbor Boat Works Inc ....G.... 253 851-2126
Gig Harbor *(G-4107)*
Global Marine Specialties Inc ....G.... 206 414-0819
Kent *(G-4923)*
Granite Boatworks Inc ....G.... 360 466-1280
Mount Vernon *(G-6801)*
Grapeview Point ....G.... 360 277-9015
Allyn *(G-83)*
Group 2 Inc ....G.... 206 378-0900
Seattle *(G-10126)*
H F S-Vitek ....G.... 360 293-8054
Anacortes *(G-133)*
Hansen Fabrication ....G.... 206 283-9181
Seattle *(G-10139)*
Hard Drive Marine ....G.... 360 306-8685
Bellingham *(G-1365)*
Haven Boatworks LLC ....G.... 360 385-5727
Port Townsend *(G-7889)*
Haven Boatworks LLC ....F.... 360 385-5727
Port Townsend *(G-7890)*
Helicat LLC ....G.... 253 376-8273
Spanaway *(G-12059)*
Hewes Marine Co Inc ....D.... 509 684-5235
Colville *(G-2756)*
Howard Fabrication ....G.... 360 380-1721
Ferndale *(G-3854)*
▲ Ice Floe LLC ....C.... 360 331-5500
Freeland *(G-4030)*
Ivie Boat Building ....G.... 360 892-2883
Vancouver *(G-14328)*
Jenneth Technologies Inc ....G.... 509 547-8977
Kennewick *(G-4680)*
Jonathan Quinn Barnett Ltd ....G.... 206 322-2152
Seattle *(G-10305)*
Joseph Artese Design ....G.... 206 365-4326
Lake Forest Park *(G-5617)*
Jr Grennay Co ....G.... 509 484-5056
Valleyford *(G-13997)*
Kalhovde Boat Works ....G.... 360 398-1262
Bellingham *(G-1389)*
Kettle River Boat Works LLC ....G.... 509 738-2872
Kettle Falls *(G-5234)*
Kevin Philbin Yacht Detail ....G.... 206 949-0162
Seattle *(G-10339)*
Leclercq Marine Construction ....E.... 206 283-8555
Seattle *(G-10396)*
Lee Shore Boats Inc ....G.... 360 385-1491
Port Townsend *(G-7895)*
Left Coast Composites ....G.... 305 923-4590
Port Angeles *(G-7723)*
Legendary Yacht Inc ....F.... 360 835-0342
Washougal *(G-14963)*

SIC SECTION 37 TRANSPORTATION EQUIPMENT

Level Sky Boatworks .... G 206 789-5655
Seattle *(G-10410)*

Lorelei II Inc .... G 206 783-6045
Seattle *(G-10443)*

Lovrics Sea Craft Inc .... G 360 293-2042
Anacortes *(G-144)*

M & M Craftworks .... G 360 675-9138
Oak Harbor *(G-7157)*

▲ Marine Servicenter Inc .... G 206 323-2405
Seattle *(G-10484)*

Martian Boat Works .... G 360 427-8629
Shelton *(G-11711)*

Martin Boats Inc .... G 360 380-7331
Bellingham *(G-1425)*

Maven Watersports Designs LLC .... G 360 481-2521
Puyallup *(G-8185)*

Mercer Marine Inc .... F 425 641-2090
Fall City *(G-3703)*

Mezich Allegiance Inc .... G 206 782-1767
Seattle *(G-10526)*

Miller & Miller Boatyard Co .... G 206 285-5958
Seattle *(G-10543)*

▲ Modutech Marine Inc .... E 253 272-9319
Tacoma *(G-13418)*

Moe Howard Enterprises Inc .... E 360 538-1622
Hoquiam *(G-4349)*

Nexus Marine Corporation .... G 425 252-8330
Everett *(G-3552)*

Nichols Diversified Inds LLC .... F 360 331-7230
Freeland *(G-4035)*

Nordic Tugs Incorporated .... E 360 757-8847
Burlington *(G-2172)*

Norstar Boats Inc .... G 360 671-3669
Bellingham *(G-1462)*

▲ North Hbr Diesl Yacht Svc Inc .... E 360 293-5551
Anacortes *(G-153)*

North Industries Inc .... G 206 940-0842
Seattle *(G-10624)*

North Island Boat Company Inc .... F 360 293-2565
Anacortes *(G-154)*

Northcoast Yachts Inc .... E 253 383-3803
Seattle *(G-10630)*

Northwest Dock Systems LLC .... G 360 832-2295
Eatonville *(G-3064)*

▲ Northwest Yachts Inc .... G 360 299-0777
Anacortes *(G-156)*

Novus Composites Incorporated .... G 253 476-8582
Tacoma *(G-13436)*

◆ Nucanoe Inc .... F 360 543-9019
Bellingham *(G-1474)*

Oceanus Plastics Inc .... G 360 366-7474
Custer *(G-2858)*

Olympic Outdoor Center .... E 360 297-4659
Port Gamble *(G-7757)*

Outdoor Synergy .... G 360 435-3330
Arlington *(G-296)*

Pacific Asian Enterprises Inc .... G 206 223-3624
Seattle *(G-10727)*

Pacific Ship Repr Fbrction Inc .... C 360 674-2480
Bremerton *(G-1985)*

Pacific Skiffs Nw Inc .... G 360 658-7111
Marysville *(G-6367)*

Palfinger Marine USA Inc .... G 360 299-4585
Anacortes *(G-160)*

Papenhause Composites Inc .... G 206 669-3260
Seattle *(G-10747)*

Passage Inc .... G 425 743-5600
Everett *(G-3570)*

Performance Marine Inc .... F 425 258-9292
Everett *(G-3571)*

Peter Kaupat Easy .... F 425 228-3633
Tukwila *(G-13791)*

Petrzelka Bros Inc .... G 360 424-8095
Mount Vernon *(G-6824)*

Pierres Dock Inc .... G 425 488-8600
Kenmore *(G-4598)*

▲ Pocock Racing Shells Inc .... F 425 438-9048
Everett *(G-3577)*

Port Townsend Sails Inc .... F 360 385-1640
Port Townsend *(G-7914)*

Port Townsend Shipwrights Coop .... E 360 385-6138
Port Townsend *(G-7916)*

Puget Sound Repair Inc .... G 506 556-9722
Seattle *(G-10885)*

Pygmy Boats Inc .... G 360 385-6143
Port Townsend *(G-7921)*

Quantum Sails .... G 206 634-0636
Seattle *(G-10903)*

Raider Boats Inc .... F 509 684-8348
Colville *(G-2771)*

Railmakers Northwest .... F 425 259-9236
Everett *(G-3594)*

Ranger Tugs .... G 360 794-7430
Monroe *(G-6613)*

Redden Marine .... G 206 753-0960
Bellevue *(G-1097)*

▼ Renaissance Marine Group Inc .... D 509 758-9189
Clarkston *(G-2644)*

Richard Knannlein .... G 360 426-9757
Shelton *(G-11726)*

Rjs Marine LLC .... G 509 888-4568
Chelan *(G-2563)*

Rozema Enterprises Inc .... G 360 757-6004
Mount Vernon *(G-6831)*

S Mayton Construction Company .... G 360 532-6138
Aberdeen *(G-32)*

◆ Safe Boats International LLC .... B 360 674-7161
Bremerton *(G-1998)*

▼ San Juan Composites LLC .... E 360 299-3790
Anacortes *(G-164)*

Seamist Marine LLC .... G 253 583-4151
Silverdale *(G-11856)*

Seattle Boat Works LLC .... G 206 849-4259
Seattle *(G-11047)*

Seaview Boat Yard Inc .... E 206 783-6550
Seattle *(G-11085)*

Seaview Boat Yard Inc .... F 206 783-6550
Seattle *(G-11086)*

Seaview Boatyard North Inc .... E 360 676-8282
Bellingham *(G-1531)*

Seaview Boatyard West Inc .... G 206 783-6550
Seattle *(G-11087)*

▲ Sierra Fishers I N C .... G 360 299-1469
Anacortes *(G-168)*

Sifferman & Sifferman .... G 360 426-0714
Grapeview *(G-4290)*

Silver King Mining & Milling .... G 509 445-1406
Cusick *(G-2852)*

Skyline Fisheries LLC .... G 425 583-7259
Arlington *(G-329)*

Skyview Fisheries LLC .... G 425 583-7259
Arlington *(G-330)*

Snow & Company Inc .... E 206 953-7676
Seattle *(G-11144)*

Sorensen Marine Inc .... G 206 767-4622
Seattle *(G-11157)*

South Bend Boat Shop .... G 360 875-5712
South Bend *(G-12046)*

Southworth Marine Service .... G 360 871-5610
Southworth *(G-12051)*

Sp Marine Fabrication LLC .... F 360 813-3600
Bremerton *(G-2002)*

Speedway Marine Inc .... G 360 658-1288
Marysville *(G-6390)*

Spindrift Rowing LLC .... G 360 344-2233
Port Townsend *(G-7930)*

Spring Creek Industries Inc .... G 509 486-0599
Tonasket *(G-13659)*

Stabbert Yacht and Ship LLC .... E 206 547-6161
Seattle *(G-11176)*

Stambaughs Hungry Harbor Entps .... G 360 777-8289
Naselle *(G-7020)*

Sunbacker Fiberglass Inc .... G 360 794-5547
Monroe *(G-6628)*

Time 4 Fun LLC .... G 425 836-5037
Redmond *(G-8692)*

Tony Pecaric .... G 360 398-9885
Lynden *(G-6056)*

Top To Bottom .... G 206 764-7750
Seattle *(G-11319)*

Top To Bottom Inc .... G 360 671-7022
Bellingham *(G-1572)*

Toss Brion Yacht Rigging Inc .... G 360 385-1080
Port Townsend *(G-7932)*

▲ Townsend Bay Marine LLC .... F 360 385-3981
Port Townsend *(G-7933)*

Traditional Boat Works Inc .... G 360 379-6502
Port Townsend *(G-7936)*

▲ University Swaging Corporation .... C 425 318-1965
Bellevue *(G-1208)*

◆ US Workboats Inc .... G 360 808-2292
Sequim *(G-11668)*

▲ Waya Group Inc .... G 877 277-6999
Everett *(G-3653)*

Weldcraft Marine Industries .... C 509 758-9831
Clarkston *(G-2654)*

West Bay Boat & Manufacturing .... G 360 683-4066
Sequim *(G-11669)*

▲ Western Towboat Company .... C 206 789-9000
Seattle *(G-11456)*

Western Yacht Systems Inc .... G 360 384-3648
Ferndale *(G-3924)*

Westport LLC .... C 360 268-1800
Westport *(G-15108)*

Westport LLC .... C 360 452-5095
Port Angeles *(G-7754)*

Westport LLC .... F 360 452-5095
Port Angeles *(G-7755)*

Westward Seafoods Inc .... G 206 341-9996
Seattle *(G-11458)*

▼ William E Munson Company .... D 360 707-2752
Burlington *(G-2203)*

▼ Wooldridge Boats Inc .... F 206 722-8998
Seattle *(G-11493)*

◆ Workskiff Inc .... G 360 707-5622
Sedro Woolley *(G-11581)*

Yacht Masters Northwest LLC .... E 206 285-3460
Seattle *(G-11506)*

Yacht Specialties .... G 360 423-9995
Kelso *(G-4562)*

▲ Yachtfish Marine Inc .... F 206 623-3233
Seattle *(G-11507)*

Youngquist Boat Repair .... G 206 283-9555
Seattle *(G-11516)*

3743 Railroad Eqpt

Edward Fisher .... G 253 566-4335
Tacoma *(G-13273)*

Marine Recuriting .... G 206 763-5050
Seattle *(G-10483)*

Pacifica Marine Inc .... F 206 764-1646
Seattle *(G-10742)*

Pacifica Resources LLC .... F 206 764-1646
Seattle *(G-10743)*

Railpro of Oregon Inc .... G 360 213-0958
Vancouver *(G-14530)*

▲ Talgo Inc .... E 206 254-7051
Seattle *(G-11262)*

▲ Transgoods America Inc .... G 253 661-0440
Federal Way *(G-3797)*

3751 Motorcycles, Bicycles & Parts

Ace of Spades Inc .... G 360 807-6442
Centralia *(G-2381)*

Ace Race Parts Inc .... G 844 223-7223
Tumwater *(G-13848)*

Bgs Cycle Parts .... G 808 368-8122
Battle Ground *(G-692)*

Cee Gees & Co .... G 509 465-8231
Spokane *(G-12174)*

Choppers By Kriss .... G 509 570-2737
Spokane *(G-12181)*

Classic Cycle .... F 206 842-9191
Bainbridge Island *(G-622)*

▲ Clean Republic Sodo LLC .... G 206 682-7499
Seattle *(G-9691)*

DMC Sidecars LLC .... F 360 825-4610
Buckley *(G-2057)*

Elliott Bay Bicycles Inc .... F 206 441-9998
Seattle *(G-9899)*

▲ Focus Designs Inc .... G 360 329-2537
Camas *(G-2251)*

Hardtail Choppers Inc .... G 360 750-6780
Vancouver *(G-14282)*

▲ Heininger Holdings LLC .... G 360 756-2411
Bellingham *(G-1368)*

J & B Importers Inc .... G 253 395-0441
Sumner *(G-13075)*

▲ Lets Ride LLC .... G 253 225-3630
Gig Harbor *(G-4131)*

Liberty Lake Powersports LLC .... G 509 926-5044
Liberty Lake *(G-5844)*

Lt Racing .... G 360 871-2259
Port Orchard *(G-7826)*

▲ Lucky Scooter Parts LLC .... G 425 558-0715
Redmond *(G-8539)*

Metal Frictions Company Inc .... G 425 776-0336
Edmonds *(G-3133)*

▲ Motherwell Products Usa Inc .... G 360 366-2600
Ferndale *(G-3875)*

▲ Pro Wheel Racing Components .... F 360 691-6459
Granite Falls *(G-4283)*

Puget Sound Safety .... G 253 770-8888
Puyallup *(G-8227)*

Ridemind LLC .... G 206 226-0016
Seattle *(G-10964)*

▲ Softride Inc .... G 360 647-7420
Bellingham *(G-1544)*

▲ Volcanic Manufacturing LLC .... G 509 427-8623
North Bonneville *(G-7136)*

S I C

Employee Codes: A=Over 500 employees, B=251-500
C=101-250, D=51-100, E=20-50, F=10-19, G=2-9
2019 Washington Manufacturers Register
641

3761 Guided Missiles & Space Vehicles

▲ Blue Origin LLC ....D 253 872-0411
Kent (G-4815)
Boeing Company ....A 425 865-3311
Bellevue (G-824)
Boeing Company ....A 206 655-1131
Seattle (G-9563)
Bspace Corporation ....G 208 559-7806
Seattle (G-9591)
Kurtisfactor LLC ....G 208 863-6180
Tacoma (G-13379)
Northrop Grumman Systems Corp ....E 360 315-3976
Silverdale (G-11852)
Space Exploration Tech Corp ....A 425 867-9910
Redmond (G-8674)
Space Exploration Tech Corp ....C 425 602-2255
Redmond (G-8675)
Spaceflight Industries Inc ....E 206 342-9934
Seattle (G-11165)

3764 Guided Missile/Space Vehicle Propulsion Units & parts

Atk Manufacturing Inc ....G 951 660-1218
Ridgefield (G-9062)
Boeing Company ....B 425 413-3400
Maple Valley (G-6261)
Bspace Corporation ....G 208 559-7806
Seattle (G-9591)
Electrijet Research Foundation ....G 509 990-9474
Greenacres (G-4297)
General Dynamics Ordna ....D 509 762-5381
Moses Lake (G-6710)
General Dynmics Ots Arospc Inc ....A 425 420-9311
Bothell (G-1765)
Northrop Grumman Systems Corp ....E 360 315-3976
Silverdale (G-11852)
Spaceflight Industries Inc ....E 206 342-9934
Seattle (G-11165)

3769 Guided Missile/Space Vehicle Parts & Eqpt, NEC

▲ Accra Manufacturing Inc ....D 425 424-1000
Bothell (G-1814)
Boeing Domestic Sales Corp ....G 206 655-2121
Tukwila (G-13707)
◆ Eldec Corporation ....A 425 743-1313
Lynnwood (G-6114)
Electroimpact Inc ....D 425 348-8090
Mukilteo (G-6920)
Fabrication Technologies LLC ....G 360 293-3707
Anacortes (G-127)
General Dynamics Ordna ....D 509 762-5381
Moses Lake (G-6710)
Infinity Fabrication Inc ....G 360 435-7460
Arlington (G-254)
Jim Suzuki ....G 253 804-6070
Auburn (G-482)
Neumeier Engineering Inc ....E 253 854-3635
Kent (G-5020)
Omohundro Co Kitsap Composites ....D 360 519-3047
Port Orchard (G-7837)
Primus International Inc ....C 253 876-1500
Algona (G-76)
Tethers Unlimited Inc ....G 425 486-0100
Bothell (G-1800)

3792 Travel Trailers & Campers

Adventurer LP ....C 509 895-7064
Yakima (G-15501)
Alaskan Campers Inc ....G 360 748-6494
Chehalis (G-2460)
Canopy World Inc ....G 253 531-5192
Tacoma (G-13219)
D & R Rv LLC ....F 360 755-3218
Burlington (G-2150)
Featherlite Trailers ....G 425 334-4045
Snohomish (G-11909)
J P J 3 LLC ....G 360 697-1084
Silverdale (G-11840)
Meili Manufacturing ....G 509 489-9180
Spokane (G-12389)
Quality Equipment Supply Inc ....G 503 544-9779
Vancouver (G-14518)
Sun Valley Enterprises ....G 509 453-1914
Yakima (G-15688)
Superior Rv Manufacturing ....G 360 693-1398
Washougal (G-14989)
Truck Accessories Group LLC ....D 360 736-9991
Centralia (G-2439)
▲ Tuff Trailer Inc ....G 360 398-0300
Ferndale (G-3920)

3795 Tanks & Tank Components

D&Topm Inc ....G 425 334-7667
Everett (G-3436)
▲ Regal Tanks USA Inc ....G 360 707-9948
Blaine (G-1701)
Senior Operations LLC ....D 360 435-1116
Arlington (G-324)
Sound Tanks and Cntrs L L C ....G 425 455-2668
Bellevue (G-1149)
Transmarine Navigation Corp ....F 206 525-2051
Seattle (G-11327)

3799 Transportation Eqpt, NEC

Alas Rv ....G 360 676-1515
Bellingham (G-1241)
Blade Cheverlot Rv ....G 360 982-2370
Mount Vernon (G-6781)
Buzs Equipment Trailers ....G 360 694-9116
Vancouver (G-14088)
Capital Industrial Inc ....G 360 786-1890
Tumwater (G-13855)
Chase Race ....G 425 269-5636
Duvall (G-2980)
E Z Loader Adjustable Boat ....C 509 489-0181
Spokane (G-12235)
◆ E Z Loader Boat Trailers Inc ....C 574 266-0092
Spokane (G-12236)
English Racing ....G 360 210-7484
Camas (G-2249)
Erudite Inc ....G 253 272-8542
Tacoma (G-13281)
Frys Welding Inc ....G .....
Auburn (G-445)
Green Synergy ....G 206 779-3324
Ellensburg (G-3206)
Half Moon Bay Bar & Grill ....E 360 268-9166
Westport (G-15105)
Holz Enterprises Inc ....G 360 398-7006
Lynden (G-6022)
Integrated Systems Design ....G 360 746-0812
Bellingham (G-1380)
Itec Inc ....G 509 452-3672
Union Gap (G-13934)
Jened Inc ....G 509 926-6894
Spokane Valley (G-12751)
KMD Invested LLC ....G 425 741-9600
Everett (G-3531)
Michael M Hennessey ....G 360 471-3313
Silverdale (G-11850)
Modern Transport Systems Corp ....G 509 443-5031
Spokane (G-12397)
Mountainview Polaris Inc ....G 509 765-9340
Moses Lake (G-6729)
Pacer Design & Manufacturing ....F 425 481-5300
Bothell (G-1883)
Pacific Coast Tools LLC ....G 360 244-5087
Long Beach (G-5875)
Pacific Engineering & Mfg Co ....G 360 274-8323
Castle Rock (G-2349)
▲ Pacific Rim International LLC ....G 503 781-2394
Vancouver (G-14472)
▲ Powder Keg LLC ....G 509 758-7300
Clarkston (G-2641)
Road-Iq LLC ....F 360 733-4151
Bellingham (G-1518)
Roadmaster Inc ....G 360 896-0407
Vancouver (G-14555)
Rum Ruay Inc ....G 206 660-4647
Seattle (G-10993)
Rvs Express LLC ....G 253 249-7043
Auburn (G-551)
Skandia Northwest Mfg ....G 360 599-2681
Deming (G-2923)
SRP Transport Inc ....G 425 770-3031
Monroe (G-6626)
Ss Trailer Manufacturing ....G 253 750-4724
Bonney Lake (G-1739)
Superior Tramway Co Inc ....G 509 483-6181
Spokane (G-12534)
Tc Motorsports ....G 253 887-0500
Auburn (G-578)
Team Chinook Sales ....G 509 949-0929
Naches (G-7006)
Top Notch Trailer Mfg ....F 360 273-0468
Rochester (G-9141)
TTI Inc ....G 509 998-9456
Spokane (G-12572)
Viper Tactical LLC ....G 425 341-0529
Salkum (G-9181)
◆ Zacklift International Inc ....F 509 674-4426
Cle Elum (G-2682)

38 MEASURING, ANALYZING AND CONTROLLING INSTRUMENTS; PHOTOGRAPHIC, MEDICAL AN

3812 Search, Detection, Navigation & Guidance Systs & Instrs

Aaco Incorporated ....G 206 722-1571
Seattle (G-9329)
Advanced Aero Safety Inc ....G 360 387-8472
Stanwood (G-12952)
Aeries Enterprises LLC ....G 425 739-9997
Kirkland (G-5273)
Aero-Space Port Intl Group Inc ....G 425 264-1000
Renton (G-8729)
▲ Aerocell Corporation ....C 360 653-2211
Marysville (G-6311)
Aeroforge Manufacturing Inc ....E 253 286-2525
Puyallup (G-8118)
◆ Airborne Ecs LLC ....F 319 538-1051
Port Angeles (G-7679)
Aircraft Solutions LLC ....G 509 838-8883
Spokane (G-12105)
Applewhite Aero LLC ....G 206 762-5285
Seattle (G-9412)
Applied Navigation LLC ....G 503 329-3126
Bothell (G-1821)
Argus Defense LLC ....G 206 707-6373
Kent (G-4790)
Auroraview LLC ....F 206 724-5953
Redmond (G-8388)
◆ Avtechtyee Inc ....C 425 290-3100
Everett (G-3378)
B/E Aerospace Inc ....B 360 657-5197
Everett (G-3380)
Bae Systems Controls Inc ....E 607 770-2000
Redmond (G-8396)
Bae Systems Tech Sol Srvc Inc ....G 360 598-8800
Silverdale (G-11827)
◆ Ballard Technology Inc ....D 425 339-0281
Everett (G-3383)
Biosonics Inc ....F 206 782-2211
Seattle (G-9530)
Biosonics Telemetry LP ....G 206 783-9356
Seattle (G-9531)
Boeing Company ....C 206 689-4059
Renton (G-8760)
Boeing Company ....C 253 931-2121
Auburn (G-395)
Boeing Company ....B 425 413-3400
Maple Valley (G-6261)
Bridgeways ....D 425 513-2989
Everett (G-3401)
Brockett Ocean Services Inc ....F 425 869-1834
Redmond (G-8410)
Brooks Tactical Systems ....F 253 549-2703
Fox Island (G-4019)
Burg Criminal & Dui Defense ....G 206 467-3190
Seattle (G-9599)
Cascade Family Flyers ....G 425 750-4249
Snohomish (G-11886)
Ckreed Defense LLC ....G 206 297-2116
Burien (G-2096)
Dabs Manufacturing & Assembly ....F 253 872-2200
Kent (G-4870)
Defensestorm Inc ....G 858 228-1903
Seattle (G-9815)
▲ Digital Control Incorporated ....D 425 251-0701
Kent (G-4873)
Diversified Defense ....G 253 327-0862
Edgewood (G-3075)
Do or Dye Self Defense ....G 253 653-5696
Des Moines (G-2934)
Eaton Corporation ....G 425 451-4954
Bellevue (G-890)
Echodyne Corp ....D 206 713-1216
Kirkland (G-5328)
◆ Eldec Corporation ....A 425 743-1313
Lynnwood (G-6114)
Eldec Corporation ....G 425 882-3100
Redmond (G-8447)

SIC SECTION 38 MEASURING, ANALYZING AND CONTROLLING INSTRUMENTS; PHOTOGRAPHIC, MEDICAL AN

Electrijet Research Foundation............G....... 509 990-9474
Greenacres *(G-4297)*
Electronic Charts Co Inc......................G....... 206 282-4990
Seattle *(G-9893)*
Engine & Aircraft Strategies.................G....... 425 432-2800
Maple Valley *(G-6268)*
Epi Inc..G....... 360 247-5858
Amboy *(G-92)*
Esterline Europe Company LLC............G....... 425 453-9400
Bellevue *(G-900)*
▼ Esterline Technologies Corp............E....... 425 453-9400
Bellevue *(G-902)*
Fidelitad Inc...G....... 509 637-3938
White Salmon *(G-15115)*
Gallivan Gallivan & Omelia....................F....... 206 652-1441
Seattle *(G-10046)*
Gcm North American Arospc LLC.........D....... 253 872-7488
Algona *(G-69)*
General Dynamics Corporation.............E....... 425 885-5010
Duvall *(G-2989)*
Guided Reality Corporation...................G....... 206 856-8819
Bainbridge Island *(G-637)*
Honeywell International Inc..................C....... 425 251-9511
Renton *(G-8820)*
Hydroacoustic Technology Inc.............F....... 206 633-3383
Seattle *(G-10196)*
Idd Aerospace Corp...............................C....... 425 885-0617
Redmond *(G-8505)*
Innov8 Cabin Solutions LLC..................G....... 425 241-8378
Sammamish *(G-9220)*
Iocurrents Inc...G....... 206 494-0099
Seattle *(G-10258)*
Jtc Aerospace LLC.................................G....... 425 869-6812
Redmond *(G-8523)*
Kgr Corporation......................................G....... 360 403-7330
Arlington *(G-266)*
Kidd Defense..G....... 509 290-6171
Spokane *(G-12351)*
King Aerospace Inc................................G....... 360 257-6610
Oak Harbor *(G-7155)*
▲ Kongsberg Underwater Tech Inc......E....... 425 712-1107
Lynnwood *(G-6153)*
Krismark Group Inc................................G....... 425 396-0829
Snoqualmie *(G-12015)*
Lc Logic Defense and Space LLC.........G....... 425 270-5169
Everett *(G-3535)*
Life-Gro Inc...G....... 253 682-1669
Tacoma *(G-13387)*
LMI Aerospace Inc..................................C....... 253 288-9379
Auburn *(G-489)*
Lockheed Martin Corporation...............F....... 425 482-1100
Bothell *(G-1876)*
Lockheed Martin Corporation...............B....... 360 396-8591
Silverdale *(G-11846)*
Lockheed Martin Corporation...............C....... 360 697-6844
Silverdale *(G-11847)*
Maren-Go Solutions Corporation.........G....... 217 506-2749
Vancouver *(G-14393)*
Mintaka Instruments LLC......................G....... 206 783-1414
Seattle *(G-10546)*
▲ Nabtesco Aerospace Inc..................E....... 425 602-8400
Kirkland *(G-5407)*
Nat Seattle Inc..E....... 425 424-3370
Bothell *(G-1878)*
Neumeier Engineering Inc.....................E....... 253 854-3635
Kent *(G-5020)*
Newcore Aviation LLC...........................G....... 509 276-8200
Deer Park *(G-2910)*
Newcore Enterprises LLC.....................G....... 509 276-8200
Deer Park *(G-2911)*
Northwest Marine Tech Inc...................E....... 360 468-3375
Shaw Island *(G-11671)*
Nova-Tech Engineering LP...................G....... 425 245-7000
Bothell *(G-1782)*
Novus Composites Incorporated.........G....... 253 476-8582
Tacoma *(G-13436)*
NW Sextant LLC.....................................G....... 425 746-6475
Bellevue *(G-1039)*
Ocean Instruments Wash LLC..............G....... 425 281-1471
Fall City *(G-3704)*
Omohundro Co Kitsap Composites......D....... 360 519-3047
Port Orchard *(G-7837)*
Pacific Aircraft Modifications...............G....... 360 403-7282
Arlington *(G-297)*
Pacific NW Arospc Aliance....................G....... 425 885-0290
Redmond *(G-8607)*
Pacific Radar Inc.....................................G....... 425 775-0400
Everett *(G-3566)*
Papec..G....... 253 862-6148
Lake Tapps *(G-5683)*

Prototek Corp...F....... 360 779-1310
Poulsbo *(G-7993)*
▼ PSI Electronics LLC..........................F....... 253 922-7890
Fife *(G-3984)*
R Ramjet Inc...G....... 541 312-1648
Seabeck *(G-9270)*
Rainier Defense LLC..............................G....... 253 218-2999
Auburn *(G-543)*
Raisbeck Engineering Inc......................F....... 206 723-2000
Tukwila *(G-13802)*
Random Walk Group LLC.....................G....... 206 724-3621
Olympia *(G-7377)*
Raytheon Company...............................C....... 360 394-3434
Keyport *(G-5244)*
Raytheon Company...............................B....... 360 697-6600
Keyport *(G-5245)*
Raytheon Company...............................C....... 360 394-7559
Keyport *(G-5246)*
Redwood Instrument Co........................G....... 360 446-2860
Rainier *(G-8321)*
Roberts Precision Machine Inc.............F....... 360 805-1000
Monroe *(G-6615)*
Rockwell Collins Inc..............................G....... 425 923-2700
Everett *(G-3600)*
Rockwell Collins Inc..............................E....... 425 492-1400
Bothell *(G-1896)*
Rook Defense LLC.................................G....... 206 518-3593
Auburn *(G-549)*
▲ RTC Aerospace - Fife Div Inc...........D....... 253 922-3806
Fife *(G-3987)*
Safe Defense LLC..................................G....... 509 430-5731
Kennewick *(G-4724)*
Safety Defense Technology...................G....... 360 718-2078
Vancouver *(G-14566)*
Sagetech Corporation...........................D....... 509 493-2154
White Salmon *(G-15128)*
Sagetech Corporation...........................D....... 509 493-1364
White Salmon *(G-15129)*
Sagetech Corporation...........................D....... 509 493-2113
White Salmon *(G-15130)*
Sakco Precision Inc...............................G....... 253 288-9702
Auburn *(G-555)*
Sealth Aero Marine Co...........................E....... 425 481-0727
Mill Creek *(G-6525)*
Sensitronics LLC...................................G....... 360 766-8800
Bow *(G-1932)*
Sensormatic Electronics LLC...............D....... 253 851-6500
Gig Harbor *(G-4160)*
Sequoia Scientific Inc...........................G....... 425 641-0944
Bellevue *(G-1124)*
Ship Electronics Inc...............................G....... 206 819-3853
Shoreline *(G-11810)*
Skookem Aerospace Mfg......................G....... 206 365-8027
Kent *(G-5133)*
Soniq Aerospace LP...............................G....... 253 750-4592
Pacific *(G-7540)*
Sound Metrics Corp................................G....... 425 822-3001
Bellevue *(G-1148)*
Spectralux Corporation..........................D....... 425 285-3000
Redmond *(G-8678)*
◆ Stargate Inc..G....... 425 251-0701
Kent *(G-5152)*
▲ Steppir Antenna Systems Inc............G....... 425 391-1999
Issaquah *(G-4482)*
Strategic Robotic Systems Inc..............G....... 425 285-9229
Redmond *(G-8684)*
Stratodata LLC.......................................G....... 425 623-0094
Carnation *(G-2299)*
Stresswave Inc.......................................G....... 253 259-8796
Tukwila *(G-13823)*
Swim Scott...G....... 253 968-3389
Tacoma *(G-13534)*
Tig Aerospace LLC.................................G....... 206 372-6724
Seattle *(G-11305)*
Tji II LLC..C....... 360 794-4448
Monroe *(G-6632)*
Toolcraft Inc...F....... 360 794-5512
Monroe *(G-6633)*
Triumph Actuation Systems..................B....... 509 248-5000
Yakima *(G-15696)*
Universal Avonics Systems Corp..........C....... 425 821-2800
Redmond *(G-8699)*
Valley Machine Shop Inc.......................E....... 425 226-5040
Kent *(G-5199)*
Volant Aerospace Holdings LLC...........G....... 360 757-2376
Burlington *(G-2199)*
Whislers Inc...G....... 360 352-8777
Tumwater *(G-13905)*
Wolff Defense...G....... 425 284-2000
Kirkland *(G-5496)*

Zodiac Aerospace...................................G....... 360 653-2600
Arlington *(G-350)*
Zultimate Self Defense Studios............G....... 425 688-7888
Bellevue *(G-1235)*

3821 Laboratory Apparatus & Furniture

Atlas Bimetal Labs Inc...........................E....... 360 385-3123
Port Townsend *(G-7865)*
Basis Software Inc.................................G....... 425 861-9390
Redmond *(G-8397)*
BBC..G....... 360 629-4477
Stanwood *(G-12960)*
▲ BBC Biochemical Corporation.........C....... 360 542-8400
Mount Vernon *(G-6777)*
▲ Bmt - Usa LLC...................................E....... 360 863-2252
Monroe *(G-6557)*
Diamond Machine Works Inc................E....... 206 633-3960
Seattle *(G-9827)*
Eden Labs LLC.......................................F....... 888 626-3271
Seattle *(G-9882)*
Loder Instrument Company Inc............G....... 425 869-3861
Redmond *(G-8536)*
Mill Creek Spine Injury Inc PS..............G....... 425 344-6835
Lake Stevens *(G-5662)*
Mobile Air Applied Science...................G....... 206 953-3786
Bellevue *(G-1012)*
Modus Health LLC..................................G....... 703 835-0055
Edmonds *(G-3135)*
Numeric Control LLC.............................G....... 360 269-1497
Morton *(G-6670)*
▲ Pls Pacific Laser Systems LLC........D....... 415 453-5780
Everett *(G-3576)*
Quantum Technology Corp...................G....... 604 222-5539
Blaine *(G-1699)*
Shaker Innovations LLC........................G....... 360 886-1873
Black Diamond *(G-1655)*
Tested Field Systems LLC.....................G....... 206 453-4851
Seattle *(G-11282)*
Tru Line Laser Alignment Inc................G....... 360 371-0552
Blaine *(G-1708)*

3822 Automatic Temperature Controls

A Thousand Hills Inc..............................G....... 360 437-9805
Port Ludlow *(G-7763)*
Ademco Inc..G....... 253 872-7128
Kent *(G-4759)*
Ademco Inc..G....... 509 534-7300
Spokane *(G-12098)*
Ademco Inc..G....... 425 485-3938
Bothell *(G-1815)*
AMP Engineering Services LLC............G....... 480 512-1186
Ellensburg *(G-3183)*
Ample Power Company LLC.................G....... 206 789-0827
Seattle *(G-9400)*
Aso Inc...G....... 360 883-3962
Vancouver *(G-14044)*
Ats Inland Nw LLC.................................G....... 509 892-1000
Spokane Valley *(G-12630)*
Automated Tech Solutions LLC............G....... 425 999-1297
Maple Valley *(G-6259)*
Aynano Technology LLC.......................G....... 208 596-9865
Pullman *(G-8084)*
Branom Operating Company LLC.........E....... 206 762-6050
Seattle *(G-9578)*
▲ Controls Group The Inc....................G....... 425 828-4149
Kirkland *(G-5312)*
Enertec Bas..G....... 360 786-1257
Olympia *(G-7277)*
Engineered Bldg Contrls LLC...............G....... 206 229-7475
Burien *(G-2105)*
Essential Building Tech LLC.................G....... 360 573-3200
Vancouver *(G-14206)*
Golden Harvest Inc................................D....... 360 757-4334
Burlington *(G-2159)*
▲ Index Industries Inc..........................D....... 360 629-5200
Bellingham *(G-1376)*
M K Hansen Company...........................G....... 509 884-1396
East Wenatchee *(G-3023)*
Million Tree Prj For Somalia.................G....... 206 731-9164
Renton *(G-8855)*
Nugent Gis & Environmental Svc.........G....... 206 324-0059
Seattle *(G-10668)*
P & RS Mobile Services Inc...................G....... 425 652-1394
Maple Valley *(G-6284)*
P G K Inc..G....... 425 432-0945
Maple Valley *(G-6285)*
◆ P N D Corporation..............................G....... 425 562-7252
Bellevue *(G-1057)*
Pacific Environmental Inc.....................G....... 760 877-9796
Fall City *(G-3705)*

SIC

Employee Codes: A=Over 500 employees, B=251-500
C=101-250, D=51-100, E=20-50, F=10-19, G=2-9
2019 Washington
Manufacturers Register
643

38 MEASURING, ANALYZING AND CONTROLLING INSTRUMENTS; PHOTOGRAPHIC, MEDICAL AN SIC SECTION

Primeone Products LLC ....G....... 509 448-8818
Spokane *(G-12455)*
Reliable Controls Corp USA ....G....... 250 475-2036
Ferndale *(G-3892)*
Schneider Elc Buildings LLC ....F....... 509 892-1121
Spokane Valley *(G-12860)*
Sentinel Offender Services LLC ....E....... 206 223-9681
Seattle *(G-11089)*
Siemens Industry Inc ....D....... 208 883-8330
Pullman *(G-8108)*
Smart Moves Inc ....G....... 206 842-6575
Bainbridge Island *(G-673)*
Sporting Systems Corporation ....G....... 360 607-0036
Vancouver *(G-14603)*
▲ **Synergistic Technologies Inc** ....G....... 425 822-7777
Bellevue *(G-1174)*
Torrid Marine LLC ....G....... 206 920-9002
Bainbridge Island *(G-679)*
Twintec Inc ....G....... 253 218-0890
Auburn *(G-586)*
Waft Corp ....F....... 425 743-4601
Mukilteo *(G-6990)*
West Coast Stair Company ....G....... 206 406-4927
Renton *(G-8944)*
Zebra Technical Services LLC ....G....... 425 485-8700
Woodinville *(G-15414)*

3823 Indl Instruments For Meas, Display & Control

Academy Infrared Training Inc ....G....... 360 676-1915
Bellingham *(G-1238)*
ADS LLC ....G....... 206 762-5070
Tukwila *(G-13687)*
Airmagnet Inc ....G....... 800 283-5853
Everett *(G-3365)*
Airtran Wireless Technologies ....G....... 360 430-3179
Vancouver *(G-14014)*
Astrake Inc ....G....... 503 470-4470
Seattle *(G-9446)*
Branom Operating Company LLC ....E....... 206 762-6050
Seattle *(G-9578)*
▲ **Cambria Corporation** ....G....... 206 782-8380
Seattle *(G-9612)*
Cape Horn Maintenance Co ....G....... 360 826-9105
Concrete *(G-2784)*
Celestial Monitoring Corp ....G....... 800 477-2506
Lynnwood *(G-6090)*
Centurion Process LLC ....G....... 509 759-3001
Selah *(G-11584)*
Clearsign Combustion Corp ....F....... 206 673-4848
Tukwila *(G-13712)*
Cognex ....G....... 206 448-2343
Seattle *(G-9712)*
Combustion Technology LLC ....G....... 360 253-9600
Vancouver *(G-14140)*
Control Systems America Inc ....G....... 360 210-7475
Camas *(G-2243)*
Control Technology Inc ....G....... 425 823-3878
Kirkland *(G-5311)*
Creative Microsystems Inc ....F....... 425 235-4335
Renton *(G-8776)*
▲ **Data I/O Corporation** ....C....... 425 881-6444
Redmond *(G-8433)*
Digatron LLC ....E....... 509 467-3128
Spokane *(G-12227)*
Digi Resources LLC ....F....... 888 775-3444
Sammamish *(G-9201)*
Dungeness Envmtl Solutions Inc ....G....... 888 481-0326
Everett *(G-3447)*
Dynavest Inc ....E....... 206 728-0777
Seattle *(G-9865)*
Emerson Electric Co ....G....... 360 805-0590
Monroe *(G-6569)*
Emerson Process Management ....G....... 425 391-8565
Sammamish *(G-9204)*
Empire Controls LLC ....G....... 509 795-5615
Chelan *(G-2553)*
Evoqua Water Technologies LLC ....G....... 360 699-7392
Brush Prairie *(G-2034)*
Expert Computer Tech Inc ....G....... 360 736-7000
Centralia *(G-2401)*
Fermium It LLC ....G....... 541 213-9291
Vancouver *(G-14227)*
Fisher-Rosemount Systems Inc ....G....... 425 488-4111
Bothell *(G-1853)*
Fluke Corporation ....F....... 425 446-5600
Everett *(G-3476)*
Fluke Corporation ....E....... 888 993-5853
Everett *(G-3477)*
▲ **Fluke Electronics Corporation** ....A....... 425 347-6100
Everett *(G-3478)*
Fluke Electronics Corporation ....B....... 425 446-5610
Everett *(G-3479)*
Fluke Electronics Corporation ....E....... 888 993-5853
Everett *(G-3481)*
Fortive Corporation ....C....... 425 446-5000
Everett *(G-3483)*
Francis Scientific Inc ....G....... 360 687-7019
Battle Ground *(G-702)*
Geartrology Corporation ....G....... 425 347-1300
Everett *(G-3492)*
General Dynmics Ots Arospc Inc ....A....... 425 420-9311
Bothell *(G-1765)*
Global Fia Inc ....G....... 253 549-2223
Fox Island *(G-4022)*
Hart Systems Inc ....G....... 253 858-8481
Gig Harbor *(G-4114)*
Heckman Inc ....G....... 360 724-4580
Burlington *(G-2162)*
Hexagon Metrology Inc ....G....... 253 872-2443
Kent *(G-4940)*
Idex Health & Science LLC ....C....... 360 679-2528
Oak Harbor *(G-7153)*
Instrumentation Northwest Inc ....E....... 425 822-4434
Kent *(G-4955)*
Krill Systems Inc ....G....... 206 780-2901
Bainbridge Island *(G-647)*
Lee Company ....G....... 425 488-5842
Bothell *(G-1773)*
Lilibete LLC ....G....... 206 407-6890
Kent *(G-4996)*
Mach Transonic LLC ....G....... 206 853-6909
Seattle *(G-10459)*
Marqmetrix Inc ....F....... 206 971-3625
Seattle *(G-10492)*
Micro Motion Inc ....G....... 360 896-0522
Vancouver *(G-14418)*
Mk Optimization and Ctrl LLC ....G....... 509 656-3321
Seattle *(G-10550)*
Mount Fury Co Inc ....G....... 425 391-0747
Issaquah *(G-4451)*
Northwest Envmtl & Eqp Inc ....G....... 253 435-5115
Puyallup *(G-8204)*
Northwest Water Systems Inc ....G....... 360 876-0958
Port Orchard *(G-7835)*
Novex LLC ....G....... 360 296-3467
Bellingham *(G-1473)*
▲ **Ovivo USA LLC** ....C....... 360 253-3440
Vancouver *(G-14460)*
Pacific Biomarkers Inc ....E....... 206 298-0068
Seattle *(G-10728)*
Pantrol Inc ....F....... 509 535-9061
Spokane *(G-12428)*
Pollution Control Systems Corp ....G....... 206 523-7220
Seattle *(G-10828)*
Pra Inc ....F....... 408 743-5300
Arlington *(G-304)*
◆ **Precision Automation Inc** ....E....... 360 254-0661
Vancouver *(G-14500)*
Process Cntrls Instrumentation ....G....... 360 573-4985
Battle Ground *(G-733)*
Process Solutions Inc ....E....... 360 629-0910
Stanwood *(G-12987)*
Quick Pressure LLC ....G....... 206 219-5567
Redmond *(G-8639)*
▼ **R C Systems Inc** ....G....... 425 355-3800
Everett *(G-3592)*
Remote Control Technology Inc ....G....... 425 216-7555
Redmond *(G-8648)*
Resource Associates Intl ....G....... 509 466-1894
Spokane *(G-12472)*
Rosemount Inc ....E....... 206 329-8600
Renton *(G-8898)*
Rosemount Specialty Pdts LLC ....E....... 509 881-2100
East Wenatchee *(G-3031)*
Rosemount Specialty Pdts LLC ....E....... 206 329-8600
Renton *(G-8899)*
S & B Inc ....F....... 425 746-9312
Bellevue *(G-1110)*
Scanivalve Corp ....E....... 509 891-9970
Liberty Lake *(G-5859)*
Sekidenko Inc ....E....... 360 694-7871
Vancouver *(G-14579)*
Selectronix Incorporated ....G....... 425 788-2979
Woodinville *(G-15358)*
Sensitech Inc ....E....... 425 883-7926
Redmond *(G-8660)*
Sensitech Inc ....C....... 425 883-7926
Redmond *(G-8661)*
Showalter Systems Inc ....G....... 206 236-6276
Mercer Island *(G-6484)*
Silicon Designs Inc ....E....... 425 391-8329
Kirkland *(G-5461)*
Slope Indicator Company (inc) ....E....... 425 806-2200
Bothell *(G-1905)*
◆ **Soundnine Inc** ....G....... 206 245-4463
Kirkland *(G-5468)*
▼ **Spectrum Controls Inc** ....D....... 425 462-2087
Bellevue *(G-1153)*
Systems Interface Inc ....E....... 425 481-1225
Mukilteo *(G-6981)*
Technical Systems Inc ....E....... 425 678-4142
Lynnwood *(G-6208)*
▲ **Tigerstop LLC** ....E....... 360 254-0661
Vancouver *(G-14637)*
Unibest International LLC ....G....... 509 525-3370
Walla Walla *(G-14884)*
Valco Instruments Company LP ....G....... 360 697-9199
Poulsbo *(G-8015)*
Vici Metronics Inc ....E....... 360 697-9199
Poulsbo *(G-8017)*
Voltaire Inc ....G....... 425 274-7000
Bellevue *(G-1220)*
Waterline Envirotech Ltd ....G....... 360 676-9635
Bellingham *(G-1590)*
Worktank Enterprises LLC ....E....... 206 254-0950
Seattle *(G-11497)*

3824 Fluid Meters & Counters

Cobalt Utility Products ....G....... 425 823-0708
Kirkland *(G-5310)*
◆ **Eldec Corporation** ....A....... 425 743-1313
Lynnwood *(G-6114)*
Kichi Systems LLC ....G....... 509 924-7672
Spokane *(G-12350)*
S Scott & Associates LLC ....G....... 360 576-4830
Vancouver *(G-14563)*
Triex Technologies Inc ....G....... 425 363-2239
Snoqualmie *(G-12034)*
Wesco Sales Group Inc ....G....... 206 227-5980
Bothell *(G-1916)*

3825 Instrs For Measuring & Testing Electricity

Agilent Technologies Inc ....G....... 425 255-6320
Renton *(G-8731)*
Agilent Technologies Inc ....D....... 509 921-3525
Liberty Lake *(G-5824)*
Ahtna Engineering Services LLC ....D....... 425 864-1695
Seatac *(G-9272)*
Alpha Test Corporation ....E....... 360 462-0201
Shelton *(G-11675)*
Anewin LLC ....G....... 360 606-5591
Vancouver *(G-14036)*
Applied Precision LLC ....C....... 425 557-1000
Issaquah *(G-4380)*
Applied Precision Holdings LLC ....C....... 425 557-1000
Issaquah *(G-4381)*
Astronics Advances Electronic ....G....... 425 895-4622
Kirkland *(G-5282)*
Astronics Corporation ....B....... 425 881-1700
Kirkland *(G-5284)*
Brightwire Networks LLC ....G....... 360 528-6017
Olympia *(G-7242)*
Chase Scientific Co ....G....... 360 221-8455
Langley *(G-5774)*
▼ **Colby Instruments LLC** ....G....... 425 452-8889
Bellevue *(G-859)*
Daniel Oneill ....G....... 509 939-7916
Newman Lake *(G-7043)*
Dualos LLC ....G....... 253 750-5125
Tacoma *(G-13266)*
▲ **Dynon Instruments Inc** ....G....... 425 402-0433
Woodinville *(G-15231)*
Emeasure Inc ....G....... 844 382-7326
Winthrop *(G-15159)*
Esterline Technologies Corp ....F....... 206 281-1312
Seattle *(G-9942)*
Ets-Lindgren Inc ....G....... 425 868-2558
Sammamish *(G-9205)*
▲ **Fluke Electronics Corporation** ....A....... 425 347-6100
Everett *(G-3478)*
Fluke Electronics Corporation ....B....... 425 446-5610
Everett *(G-3479)*
Fluke Electronics Corporation ....B....... 425 446-5858
Everett *(G-3480)*
Fluke Electronics Corporation ....E....... 888 993-5853
Everett *(G-3481)*

38 MEASURING, ANALYZING AND CONTROLLING INSTRUMENTS; PHOTOGRAPHIC, MEDICAL AN

Company	Code	Phone
General Dynmics Ots Arospc Inc Bothell *(G-1765)*	A	425 420-9311
Helldyne Inc Bainbridge Island *(G-638)*	G	206 855-1227
Huntron Inc Mill Creek *(G-6513)*	F	425 743-3171
ID Integration Inc Mukilteo *(G-6940)*	F	425 438-2533
Innovaura Corporation Edmonds *(G-3120)*	G	425 272-2702
Interstate Electronics Corp Silverdale *(G-11838)*	G	360 779-3723
Itron US Gas LLC Liberty Lake *(G-5841)*	G	509 924-9900
KLA Fuels Reductions Chewelah *(G-2603)*	G	509 680-0110
Landis Gyr Kirkland *(G-5381)*	G	425 458-9363
▼ Lite-Check LLC Spokane *(G-12371)*	F	509 535-7512
Lite-Check Fleet Solutions Inc Spokane *(G-12372)*	E	509 535-7512
▲ Metriguard Technologies Inc Pullman *(G-8098)*	E	509 332-7526
Mohr Test and Measurement LLC Richland *(G-9027)*	E	509 946-0941
Nanoport Technologies LLC Friday Harbor *(G-4052)*	G	206 403-1714
North Star High Voltage Corp Bainbridge Island *(G-653)*	G	520 780-9030
Novatech Instruments Inc Lynnwood *(G-6171)*	G	206 284-0704
Novatech Instruments Inc Redmond *(G-8600)*	G	206 301-8986
Nutesla Corporation Washougal *(G-14974)*	G	910 688-3752
Orbiter Inc Tacoma *(G-13445)*	G	253 627-5588
Pacific Engineering & Mfg Co Castle Rock *(G-2349)*	G	360 274-8323
Pacific Wireless Systems LLC Richland *(G-9033)*	G	509 375-3533
Practec LLC Redmond *(G-8630)*	F	425 881-8202
Professional Network Solutions Kennewick *(G-4710)*	G	509 308-0318
Quad Group Inc Spokane *(G-12463)*	F	509 458-4558
R D F Products Vancouver *(G-14526)*	G	360 253-2181
▲ Randl Industries Inc Spokane Valley *(G-12850)*	G	509 340-0050
Schweitzer Engrg Labs Inc Pullman *(G-8106)*	E	509 332-1890
◆ Seattle Safety LLC Auburn *(G-559)*	E	253 395-4321
▼ Sensorlink Corporation Ferndale *(G-3903)*	E	360 380-0592
Siemens Industry Inc Issaquah *(G-4474)*	G	208 883-8330
Signal Hound Inc Battle Ground *(G-740)*	G	360 263-5006
Silicon Designs Inc Kirkland *(G-5461)*	E	425 391-8329
Submeter Solutions Inc Renton *(G-8922)*	G	425 228-6831
Synthesis By Jeffrey Bland PHD Tacoma *(G-13536)*	G	253 238-7898
Thermetrics LLC Seattle *(G-11288)*	G	206 456-9119
Vm Solutions Inc Puyallup *(G-8273)*	F	253 841-2939
▲ Zetec Inc Snoqualmie *(G-12035)*	C	425 974-2700

3826 Analytical Instruments

Company	Code	Phone
Abode Specialist Inspection SE Tacoma *(G-13153)*	G	253 209-0878
Aldergrove LLC Vancouver *(G-14018)*	G	360 253-7378
America West Envmtl Sups Pasco *(G-7551)*	G	509 547-2240
Amnis LLC Seattle *(G-9399)*	E	206 374-7000
Analytical Reaserch Consulting Vancouver *(G-14033)*	G	360 573-5700
Bio-RAD Laboratories Inc Woodinville *(G-15192)*	B	425 498-1933
Bio-RAD Laboratories Inc Redmond *(G-8403)*	C	425 881-8300
Biotangent Diagnostics LLC Issaquah *(G-4385)*	G	503 713-3339
Brooks Rand Inc Seattle *(G-9588)*	G	206 632-6206
Bruker Axs Handheld Inc Kennewick *(G-4635)*	E	509 783-9850
Compound Photonics US Corp Vancouver *(G-14143)*	E	360 597-3654
Customarray Inc Bothell *(G-1758)*	G	425 609-0923
Easyxafs LLC Renton *(G-8790)*	E	208 697-4076
Empire Lab Automtn Systems LLC Spokane *(G-12245)*	G	509 808-6050
Evoqua Water Technologies LLC Brush Prairie *(G-2034)*	G	360 699-7392
Fenologica Biosciences Inc Seattle *(G-9985)*	G	206 726-1200
Fialab Instruments Inc Seattle *(G-9986)*	G	206 258-2290
Full Spectrum Analytics Inc Seattle *(G-10037)*	G	206 729-0775
GE Totten & Associates LLC Seattle *(G-10056)*	G	206 788-0188
Georadar Imaging Sammamish *(G-9208)*	G	425 392-7688
Global Scientific Systems Sequim *(G-11636)*	G	360 504-5100
Hc Laserlign Inc Kent *(G-4936)*	G	253 852-2001
Hummingbird Precision Mch Co Lacey *(G-5556)*	F	360 252-2737
Hummingbird Scientific LLC Lacey *(G-5557)*	F	360 252-2737
Idex Health & Science LLC Oak Harbor *(G-7153)*	C	360 679-2528
Klar Scientific LLC Pullman *(G-8096)*	G	509 330-2103
Metricstory Incorporated Seattle *(G-10523)*	G	206 755-4511
▲ Microbiologique Inc Seattle *(G-10533)*	F	206 714-5275
Pacific Biomarkers Inc Seattle *(G-10728)*	E	206 298-0068
Plexera LLC Woodinville *(G-15336)*	G	425 368-7410
Protac Inc Ellensburg *(G-3221)*	G	509 962-5001
Reheal LLC Seattle *(G-10944)*	G	206 440-5948
Rigaku Americas Corporation Bainbridge Island *(G-666)*	G	206 780-8927
Riverside Scientific Entps Bainbridge Island *(G-667)*	G	206 842-7513
Sekidenko Inc Vancouver *(G-14579)*	E	360 694-7871
Sightman Raymond *(G-8358)*	G	360 934-5886
Spectroglyph LLC Kennewick *(G-4729)*	G	415 793-1242
Viavi Solutions Inc Bothell *(G-1914)*	F	425 398-1298
Viking Industrial Group Inc Battle Ground *(G-750)*	G	360 666-1110

3827 Optical Instruments

Company	Code	Phone
BE Meyers & Co Inc Redmond *(G-8398)*	C	425 881-6648
Eyeon LLC Issaquah *(G-4410)*	G	425 652-9556
Fractal Filters LLC Normandy Park *(G-7093)*	G	206 854-0968
Jan Scientific Inc Seattle *(G-10285)*	G	206 632-1814
Key Technology Walla Walla *(G-14832)*	G	509 529-2161
▲ Lightspeed Design Inc Bellevue *(G-983)*	G	425 637-2818
Luxel Corporation Friday Harbor *(G-4051)*	F	360 378-0064
Nimbus Technologies LLC Seattle *(G-10610)*	G	206 724-5507
Ocular Instruments Inc Bellevue *(G-1042)*	D	425 455-5200
▼ Paradigm Optics Incorporated Vancouver *(G-14479)*	G	360 573-6500
Periscope SIs & Analytics LLC Vancouver *(G-14485)*	G	503 707-1907
Quantum Northwest Inc Liberty Lake *(G-5856)*	G	509 624-9290
R Mathews Optical Works Inc Poulsbo *(G-7995)*	G	360 697-6160
Radiant Vision Systems LLC Redmond *(G-8643)*	C	425 844-0152
Red Periscope Technologie Gig Harbor *(G-4154)*	G	253 851-3968
Refiner49er LLC Brush Prairie *(G-2041)*	G	360 254-0884
Saunders Instruments Inc Bainbridge Island *(G-672)*	G	206 842-6651
Toussint Machine and Mfg LLC Sedro Woolley *(G-11576)*	G	360 840-0705
Usl Technologies LLC Port Townsend *(G-7937)*	G	360 379-0684
Walman Optical Bellevue *(G-1223)*	G	425 462-2576
▲ Westover Scientific Inc Bothell *(G-1917)*	D	425 368-0444

3829 Measuring & Controlling Devices, NEC

Company	Code	Phone
Automated Mechanical Controls Redmond *(G-8389)*	G	425 881-8226
Avac Inc Redmond *(G-8391)*	G	425 869-2822
▲ Avocent Redmond Corp Kirkland *(G-5287)*	D	425 861-5858
Axama Corporation Spokane Valley *(G-12632)*	G	509 922-8400
Basis Software Inc Redmond *(G-8397)*	G	425 861-9390
Beco Inc Redmond *(G-8399)*	G	425 885-2603
Cardinal Health Inc Seattle *(G-9629)*	E	206 763-8500
Cartech Industries Inc Vancouver *(G-14100)*	G	360 693-3616
Chemchek Instruments Inc Richland *(G-8980)*	G	509 943-5000
Custom Sensor Design Inc Lynnwood *(G-6102)*	G	425 778-4980
Dli Engineering Corporation Poulsbo *(G-7958)*	F	206 842-7656
Durham Geo-Enterprises Inc Mukilteo *(G-6916)*	G	770 465-7557
Dyno Resource Corp Issaquah *(G-4407)*	G	425 391-6084
Dynolab Normandy Park *(G-7091)*	G	206 243-8877
Ec/Ndt LLC Federal Way *(G-3734)*	G	253 815-0797
Echo Ultrasonics LLC Bellingham *(G-1328)*	G	360 671-9121
Electrijet Flight Systems Inc Liberty Lake *(G-5831)*	G	509 990-9474
Eustis Co Inc Lynnwood *(G-6115)*	E	425 423-9996
G G Consultants Ridgefield *(G-9084)*	F	541 223-9519
Gillespie Polygraph Lynnwood *(G-6130)*	G	425 775-9015
Gli Interactive LLC Seattle *(G-10082)*	G	206 201-2708
Guardian Interlock Systems Longview *(G-5913)*	G	360 423-4766
Hart Scientific Everett *(G-3508)*	G	425 446-5400
▲ Heatcon Composite Systems Inc Tukwila *(G-13747)*	D	206 575-1333
Hobi Instrument Services LLC Bellevue *(G-946)*	G	425 223-3438
◆ Itron Inc Liberty Lake *(G-5838)*	B	509 924-9900
Itron Brazil II LLC Liberty Lake *(G-5839)*	G	509 924-9900
Itron International Inc Liberty Lake *(G-5840)*	G	866 374-8766
Joescan Inc Vancouver *(G-14338)*	G	360 993-0069
Know Labs Inc Seattle *(G-10349)*	F	206 903-1351
▼ Lawrenson Electronics Co Inc Burien *(G-2117)*	G	206 243-7310
Linda J Mohr Richland *(G-9022)*	G	509 946-0941
▲ Log Max Inc Vancouver *(G-14381)*	F	360 699-7300
Measurement Technology NW Inc Seattle *(G-10512)*	E	206 634-1308
Michael Shaw Federal Way *(G-3758)*	G	206 669-7597

38 MEASURING, ANALYZING AND CONTROLLING INSTRUMENTS; PHOTOGRAPHIC, MEDICAL AN — SIC SECTION

Mindplace Company .... G 360 376-6494
  Eastsound *(G-3040)*
Northwest Metrology LLC .... F 253 853-3183
  Gig Harbor *(G-4136)*
Northwest Technical Services .... G 425 419-4321
  Snohomish *(G-11954)*
Olympic Instruments Inc .... F 206 463-3604
  Vashon *(G-14739)*
Olympus Scientific Solutions .... E 509 735-7550
  Kennewick *(G-4704)*
Physicians Sleep Scoring .... G 360 403-7685
  Arlington *(G-301)*
Pra Inc .... F 408 743-5300
  Arlington *(G-304)*
Precision Data Technology Inc .... G 425 259-9237
  Everett *(G-3583)*
Pro Fab .... G 509 879-9293
  Spokane Valley *(G-12842)*
Puget Sound Breathalyzers .... G 425 359-9515
  Marysville *(G-6372)*
Richard Evans .... G 509 684-1079
  Colville *(G-2773)*
Rjc Enterprises LLC .... F 425 481-3281
  Bothell *(G-1787)*
Rudolph Technologies Inc .... G 425 396-7002
  Snoqualmie *(G-12022)*
◆ Sea-Bird Electronics Inc .... C 425 643-9866
  Bellevue *(G-1119)*
Siemens Industry Inc .... F 509 891-9070
  Spokane Valley *(G-12871)*
▲ Synergistic Technologies Inc .... G 425 822-7777
  Bellevue *(G-1174)*
Team Corporation .... E 360 757-3944
  Burlington *(G-2193)*
◆ Techna NDT LLC .... F 253 872-2415
  Kent *(G-5173)*
Terramar Instruments LLC .... G 425 306-0174
  Carnation *(G-2300)*
Unicon Inc .... G 425 454-2466
  Kirkland *(G-5488)*
United States Dosimetry Tech .... G 509 946-8738
  Richland *(G-9049)*
United Western Tech Corp .... E 509 544-0720
  Pasco *(G-7646)*
Universal Avionics Systems Corp ..... C 425 821-2800
  Redmond *(G-8699)*
Van Essen Instruments Division .... G 520 203-3445
  Mukilteo *(G-6987)*
▲ Zetec Inc .... C 425 974-2700
  Snoqualmie *(G-12035)*

3841 Surgical & Medical Instrs & Apparatus

◆ A-M Systems LLC .... E 360 683-8300
  Sequim *(G-11604)*
American Bnchmark Mch Wrks LLC . G 360 584-9303
  Olympia *(G-7224)*
American Medical Concepts .... G 425 844-2840
  Duvall *(G-2979)*
Aortica Corporation .... G 425 209-0272
  Mercer Island *(G-6454)*
Aqueduct Critical Care Inc .... F 425 984-6090
  Seattle *(G-9416)*
Arrhythmia Solutions Inc .... G 509 389-7366
  Spokane *(G-12118)*
Atossa Genetics Inc .... G 206 325-6086
  Seattle *(G-9457)*
Ats .... G 509 534-2822
  Spokane *(G-12125)*
Bens Precision Instrs Inc .... D 253 883-5040
  Fife *(G-3938)*
Bining Health Inc .... G 604 540-8288
  Seattle *(G-9529)*
▲ Bodypoint Inc .... E 206 405-4555
  Seattle *(G-9560)*
Boston Sceintifics .... G 608 323-3377
  Redmond *(G-8407)*
Btpsurgical LLC .... G 425 657-0805
  Issaquah *(G-4389)*
Cadwell Laboratories Inc .... D 509 735-6481
  Kennewick *(G-4638)*
Capital Instruments Ltd .... G 425 271-3756
  Bellevue *(G-838)*
Cardiac Insight Inc .... F 206 596-2060
  Bellevue *(G-839)*
Cellcyte Genetics Corporation .... G 425 519-3755
  Bellevue *(G-843)*
Cinterion Wireless Modu .... G 630 517-0198
  Issaquah *(G-4394)*
Claus Paws Animal Hospital LLC .... F 360 896-7449
  Vancouver *(G-14121)*

CM Innovations Inc .... G 425 641-0460
  Issaquah *(G-4395)*
Convergent Technology .... G 206 352-5357
  Seattle *(G-9735)*
Cortex Manufacturing Inc .... G 425 334-2277
  Lake Stevens *(G-5641)*
Crh Medical Corporation .... F 425 284-7890
  Kirkland *(G-5318)*
▼ D E Hokanson Inc .... F 425 882-1689
  Bellevue *(G-872)*
Dawling Spay Retractor LLC .... G 360 482-4970
  Elma *(G-3244)*
Draxis Health Inc .... G 509 489-5656
  Spokane *(G-12231)*
Echonous Inc .... E 425 482-6213
  Redmond *(G-8446)*
Ekos Corporation .... G 425 415-3100
  Bothell *(G-1760)*
Ent Solutions Inc .... G 206 769-1735
  Seattle *(G-9929)*
Evergreen Orthpd RES Lab LLC ..... G 425 284-7262
  Kirkland *(G-5335)*
FA Green Company .... E 425 888-0007
  Snoqualmie *(G-12012)*
Fresenius Med Care Hldings Inc ..... D 509 276-7338
  Deer Park *(G-2902)*
Fukuda Denshi Usa Inc .... E 425 881-7737
  Redmond *(G-8467)*
Funeral Directors Research .... G 360 736-7105
  Centralia *(G-2402)*
G Dundas Co Inc .... G 253 631-8008
  Black Diamond *(G-1648)*
Gestsure Technologies Ltd .... G 800 510-2485
  Seattle *(G-10067)*
Ginacor Inc .... F 206 860-1595
  Seattle *(G-10072)*
Harbor Vascular Inc .... G 425 420-6009
  Sammamish *(G-9215)*
Howellcorp .... F 206 954-8011
  Seattle *(G-10189)*
Hyprotek Inc .... G 509 343-3121
  Spokane *(G-12301)*
Impulse Medical Tech Inc .... F 360 829-0400
  Buckley *(G-2059)*
Innovation Associates .... G 206 455-2332
  Bellevue *(G-958)*
▲ Interntnal Rhbltative Sciences .... D 360 892-0339
  Vancouver *(G-14322)*
Isoray Inc .... E 509 375-1202
  Richland *(G-9013)*
Isoray Medical Inc .... E 509 375-1202
  Richland *(G-9014)*
Jointmetrix Medical LLC .... G 425 246-7799
  Seattle *(G-10304)*
Joylux Inc .... G 206 219-6444
  Seattle *(G-10309)*
Karl-Sons LLC .... G 509 627-0152
  Kennewick *(G-4681)*
Kean Center .... G 206 465-4879
  Seattle *(G-10334)*
Kent Laboratories Inc .... F 360 398-8641
  Bellingham *(G-1392)*
Kestra Medical Tech Inc .... G 425 279-8002
  Kirkland *(G-5375)*
Laser Support Services Inc .... G 253 531-9008
  Tacoma *(G-13382)*
Lifeport Inc .... G 360 944-9606
  Vancouver *(G-14374)*
M2 Anesthesia PLLC .... G 206 605-5933
  Lake Tapps *(G-5682)*
Magnolia Medical Tech Inc .... E 206 673-2500
  Seattle *(G-10468)*
Medtronic Inc .... G 509 991-0159
  Spokane *(G-12388)*
Medworks Instruments .... G 360 597-3754
  Vancouver *(G-14409)*
Microsurgical Technology Inc .... F 425 861-4002
  Redmond *(G-8586)*
Mobile Air Applied Science .... G 206 953-3786
  Bellevue *(G-1012)*
▲ Myotronics-Noromed Inc .... F 206 243-4214
  Kent *(G-5017)*
Nexus Surgical Innovations .... G 509 499-0937
  Spokane *(G-12404)*
Novo Contour Inc .... G 425 773-2673
  Edmonds *(G-3139)*
Novuson Surgical Inc .... G 425 481-7165
  Bothell *(G-11388)*
▲ Olympic Medical Corp .... D 206 767-3500
  Seattle *(G-10692)*

Opticyte Inc .... G 206 696-3957
  Seattle *(G-10708)*
or Specific Inc .... G 800 937-7949
  Vancouver *(G-14453)*
▲ Pacific Bioscience Labs Inc .... C 888 525-2747
  Redmond *(G-8606)*
Patcen Healthcare Inc .... G 425 495-5143
  Bellevue *(G-1064)*
Perfint Healthcare Corp USA .... G 425 629-9207
  Redmond *(G-8618)*
Personal Medical Corp .... G 425 497-1044
  Redmond *(G-8620)*
Pet/X LLC .... G 206 715-5743
  Seattle *(G-10791)*
Precision Biometrics Inc .... G 206 448-3464
  Seattle *(G-10849)*
Procedure Products Inc .... G 360 693-1832
  Vancouver *(G-14511)*
▲ Procedure Products Corp .... G 360 693-1832
  Vancouver *(G-14512)*
Quinton Cardiology Systems Inc ..... G 425 556-9761
  Bothell *(G-1893)*
Redpoint International Inc .... F 360 573-5957
  Vancouver *(G-14539)*
Redwood Instrument Co .... G 360 446-2860
  Rainier *(G-8321)*
Reheal LLC .... G 206 440-5948
  Seattle *(G-10944)*
Robert Wickes Od .... G 360 249-3485
  Montesano *(G-6654)*
Sara June Haskin .... G 360 873-4257
  Marblemount *(G-6306)*
Seattle Applied Science Inc .... G 425 773-2673
  Edmonds *(G-3154)*
Sensoria Health Inc .... G 425 533-2928
  Redmond *(G-8662)*
Ship N Shore .... G 360 293-8636
  Anacortes *(G-167)*
Shockwave Medical Inc .... G 425 736-3946
  Newcastle *(G-7040)*
Siemens Med Solutions USA Inc .... C 425 392-9180
  Issaquah *(G-4475)*
Sign Fracture Care Intl .... E 509 371-1107
  Richland *(G-9041)*
Signostics Inc .... F 425 402-0971
  Redmond *(G-8668)*
Smith & Nephew Inc .... E 509 363-0600
  Spokane Valley *(G-12876)*
Sonodiagnostics .... G 206 938-7922
  Seattle *(G-11156)*
South Sound Metal Inc .... G 253 564-0226
  University Place *(G-13981)*
▲ Spacelabs Healthcare Inc .... A 425 396-3300
  Snoqualmie *(G-12027)*
Spacelabs Healthcare LLC .... B 425 396-3300
  Snoqualmie *(G-12028)*
Spacelabs Healthcare Wash .... E 425 396-3300
  Snoqualmie *(G-12030)*
◆ Spacelabs Healthcare Wash .... C 425 396-3300
  Snoqualmie *(G-12029)*
▲ Spio Inc .... G 253 893-0390
  Burien *(G-2130)*
SRS Medical Corp .... F 425 882-1101
  Redmond *(G-8679)*
Stripes Global Inc .... G 800 690-8219
  Bremerton *(G-2003)*
Surgimark Inc .... G 509 965-1911
  Yakima *(G-15691)*
Tacoma Laser Clinic LLC .... F 253 272-0655
  Tacoma *(G-13544)*
Tasso Inc .... G 608 556-7606
  Seattle *(G-11271)*
▲ Therapeutic Dimension Inc .... G 509 323-9275
  Spokane *(G-12555)*
Therasigma Inc .... G 800 423-7172
  Washougal *(G-14992)*
Tissue Regeneration Systems .... G 425 576-4032
  Kirkland *(G-5484)*
Todo Flores Enterprises LLC .... G 206 450-5123
  Renton *(G-8929)*
Triad Products Corporation .... G 425 514-8363
  Everett *(G-3636)*
Trocar Investments .... G 253 851-9206
  Gig Harbor *(G-4170)*
▲ Unfors Raysafe Inc .... E 508 435-5600
  Everett *(G-3641)*
Uptake Medical Technology Inc ...... G 206 926-7405
  Seattle *(G-11388)*
V-Care Health Systems Inc .... G 509 670-9068
  Ellensburg *(G-3236)*

SIC SECTION 38 MEASURING, ANALYZING AND CONTROLLING INSTRUMENTS; PHOTOGRAPHIC, MEDICAL AN

- **Vioguard Inc** ....G....... 425 280-7735 Bothell *(G-1806)*
- **Vioguard LLC** ....F....... 425 406-8009 Kirkland *(G-5490)*
- **Wright Surgical Arts LLC** ....G....... 509 792-1404 Pasco *(G-7656)*
- **Yainax Medical LLC** ....G....... 503 516-7173 Vancouver *(G-14705)*
- **Yourceba LLC** ....G....... 509 747-5027 Spokane *(G-12595)*

3842 Orthopedic, Prosthetic & Surgical Appliances/Splys

- ◆ **A-M Systems LLC** ....E....... 360 683-8300 Sequim *(G-11604)*
- **A1a Inc** ....G....... 509 455-5000 Spokane *(G-12092)*
- **AAA Precise Machine Inc** ....G....... 509 375-3268 Benton City *(G-1599)*
- **All Metal Arts Seattle** ....G....... 206 200-9496 Seattle *(G-9380)*
- **Allnight Wheelchairs** ....G....... 425 774-6814 Edmonds *(G-3093)*
- **Amerisafe Inc** ....G....... 360 943-5634 Tumwater *(G-13852)*
- ▲ **Amfit Inc** ....E....... 360 573-9100 Vancouver *(G-14032)*
- **Andersen Models International** ....G....... 253 952-2135 Milton *(G-6532)*
- **Badger Braces LLC** ....G....... 509 229-3635 Colton *(G-2732)*
- **Breast Care Center** ....F....... 360 424-6161 Sedro Woolley *(G-11534)*
- **Brooks Tactical Systems** ....F....... 253 549-2703 Fox Island *(G-4019)*
- **Buffalo Industries Inc** ....G....... 206 682-9900 Seattle *(G-9595)*
- **Cascade Dafo Inc** ....B....... 360 543-9306 Ferndale *(G-3825)*
- **Cascade Designs Inc** ....E....... 206 505-9500 Seattle *(G-9642)*
- **Cascade Prsthtics Orthtics Inc** ....F....... 360 384-1858 Ferndale *(G-3828)*
- **Cascade Prsthtics Orthtics Inc** ....G....... 360 428-4003 Mount Vernon *(G-6783)*
- **Center For Prosthetic** ....G....... 425 454-4276 Bellevue *(G-845)*
- **Center For Prosthetic** ....F....... 206 328-4276 Seattle *(G-9652)*
- **Coates Innovations LLC** ....G....... 907 617-5801 Kent *(G-4856)*
- **Columbia Basin Prosthetic** ....G....... 509 737-8322 Kennewick *(G-4646)*
- **Contemporary Design Co** ....F....... 360 599-2833 Bellingham *(G-1303)*
- **Control Dynamics Inc** ....E....... 800 738-5004 Everett *(G-3425)*
- **Cornerstone Attache Group Inc** ....G....... 425 577-2713 Redmond *(G-8426)*
- **Cornerstone Prsthtics Orthtics** ....F....... 425 339-2559 Everett *(G-3427)*
- **Cornerstone Prsthtics Orthtics** ....G....... 360 734-0298 Bellingham *(G-1306)*
- **Cox Orthotics Inc** ....G....... 425 493-8015 Mukilteo *(G-6906)*
- **Cresap Orthotics & Prosthetics** ....G....... 509 764-8500 Moses Lake *(G-6700)*
- **Custom Ocular Prosthetics** ....G....... 206 522-4222 Seattle *(G-9770)*
- **Davidson Prosthetics LLC** ....G....... 253 770-6578 Puyallup *(G-8140)*
- **Dolans Dog Doodads LLC** ....G....... 206 257-4518 Seattle *(G-9844)*
- **Dollar Stretcher** ....G....... 509 895-7744 Yakima *(G-15556)*
- **Douglass Certified Prosthetics** ....G....... 206 363-7790 Seattle *(G-9850)*
- **Elite Group Management Corp** ....G....... 253 631-1175 Kent *(G-4889)*
- **Evergreen Circuits LLC** ....G....... 425 382-8412 Duvall *(G-2986)*
- **Evergreen Prosthetcs & Orthotc** ....F....... 360 213-2088 Vancouver *(G-14210)*
- ▲ **Evolution Technologies USA** ....G....... 360 392-8600 Ferndale *(G-3839)*
- ▲ **Exomotion LLC** ....G....... 206 763-0754 Seattle *(G-9954)*
- **Fabtech Systems LLC** ....G....... 425 349-9557 Everett *(G-3468)*
- **Flood & Associates Inc** ....G....... 253 531-7305 Tacoma *(G-13299)*
- **Fox Bay Industries Inc** ....G....... 253 941-9155 Auburn *(G-443)*
- **Future Machine & Mfg Inc** ....F....... 509 891-5600 Spokane Valley *(G-12711)*
- **Hanger Inc** ....G....... 360 423-6049 Longview *(G-5914)*
- **Hanger Orthopedic Group Inc** ....F....... 253 383-4447 Tacoma *(G-13330)*
- **Hanger Prosthetics & Ortho W** ....G....... 360 256-0026 Vancouver *(G-14280)*
- **Hanger Prsthetcs & Ortho Inc** ....G....... 425 451-8831 Bellevue *(G-936)*
- **Hanger Prsthetcs & Ortho Inc** ....G....... 253 372-7478 Gig Harbor *(G-4110)*
- **Hanger Prsthetcs & Ortho Inc** ....G....... 509 624-3314 Spokane *(G-12288)*
- **Hanger Prsthetcs & Ortho Inc** ....F....... 360 423-6049 Longview *(G-5915)*
- **Hanger Prsthetcs & Ortho Inc** ....G....... 509 946-2520 Richland *(G-9004)*
- **Hattingh Holdings Inc** ....E....... 206 323-4040 Seattle *(G-10148)*
- **Hf Acquisition Co LLC** ....E....... 800 331-1984 Mukilteo *(G-6932)*
- **I1 Sensortech Inc** ....F....... 425 372-7811 Kirkland *(G-5365)*
- **Impulse Medical Tech Inc** ....F....... 360 829-0400 Buckley *(G-2059)*
- **Independent Tech Service LLC** ....G....... 253 891-1976 Puyallup *(G-8167)*
- **Integrity Orthotic Laboratory** ....E....... 360 435-0703 Arlington *(G-256)*
- **Intelipedics LLC** ....G....... 509 432-4036 Pullman *(G-8093)*
- **Island Prosthetics & Orthotics** ....G....... 360 331-7070 Clinton *(G-2691)*
- **Jan A Thompson Lcpo** ....G....... 509 241-3820 Spokane *(G-12328)*
- **Jeffrey A Johnson** ....G....... 509 525-8322 Walla Walla *(G-14828)*
- **Joyson Safety Systems** ....C....... 509 762-5549 Moses Lake *(G-6718)*
- **Koolmask Inc** ....F....... 206 886-5248 Bellevue *(G-973)*
- **Kurt A Flechel** ....G....... 509 953-8358 Spokane *(G-12356)*
- ▲ **Lancs Industries Inc** ....E....... 425 823-6634 Kirkland *(G-5380)*
- ▼ **Lifeport LLC** ....D....... 360 225-1212 Woodland *(G-15447)*
- **Maughan Prosthetic Orthotic S** ....G....... 360 338-0284 Olympia *(G-7332)*
- **Maughan Prsthetic Orthotic Inc** ....G....... 360 447-0770 Silverdale *(G-11849)*
- **Medical Pdts For Comfort Inc** ....G....... 360 770-2005 Mount Vernon *(G-6812)*
- **Medline Industries Inc** ....G....... 360 491-0241 Lacey *(G-5566)*
- **Meridian Valley Laboratories** ....G....... 206 209-4200 Tukwila *(G-13771)*
- **Michael D Lynne** ....G....... 800 587-2313 Seattle *(G-10527)*
- **Missoula Orthotics & Prosthet** ....G....... 406 549-0921 Spokane *(G-12396)*
- ▲ **Normed Inc** ....E....... 800 288-8200 Tukwila *(G-13779)*
- **Northwest Podiatric Laboratory** ....D....... 360 332-8411 Blaine *(G-1689)*
- **or Specific Inc** ....G....... 800 937-7949 Vancouver *(G-14453)*
- **Orthocare Innovations LLC** ....F....... 425 771-0797 Edmonds *(G-3141)*
- **Out On A Limb** ....G....... 360 607-3429 Stevenson *(G-13017)*
- **Out On A Limb Enterprises** ....G....... 360 457-8479 Port Angeles *(G-7733)*
- **Out On A Limb Tree Co** ....G....... 206 938-3779 Lake Forest Park *(G-5623)*
- ▲ **Outdoor Research LLC** ....C....... 206 467-8197 Seattle *(G-10717)*
- **Pacific Orthotic LLC** ....G....... 425 417-3742 Issaquah *(G-4457)*
- **Pacific Orthotic LLC** ....G....... 425 486-4292 Woodinville *(G-15330)*
- **Pedologic Orthotics** ....G....... 360 318-3452 Arlington *(G-299)*
- **Perkins Performance** ....G....... 253 389-9669 Puyallup *(G-8222)*
- **Pettibon Bio-Mechanics Inst** ....G....... 360 748-4207 Gig Harbor *(G-4144)*
- **Preferred Orthotic & Prosthetc** ....G....... 253 572-1282 Tacoma *(G-13476)*
- **Preferred Orthotic & Prosthetc** ....G....... 253 838-6726 Federal Way *(G-3772)*
- **Progenica Therapeutics LLC** ....G....... 253 347-7018 Covington *(G-2836)*
- **Progenica Therapeutics LLC** ....G....... 253 347-7018 Covington *(G-2837)*
- **Prosthtic Specialists Wash LLC** ....G....... 425 576-5050 Kirkland *(G-5445)*
- **Puget Sound Innovations Inc** ....G....... 206 575-7500 Tukwila *(G-13798)*
- **RCM Enterprise LLC** ....G....... 888 977-6693 Olympia *(G-7380)*
- **Reheal LLC** ....G....... 206 440-5948 Seattle *(G-10944)*
- **Repcon NW Inc** ....G....... 800 325-8707 Brush Prairie *(G-2042)*
- **Safety Reflection** ....G....... 360 599-1874 Maple Falls *(G-6250)*
- **Saywhatclub** ....G....... 425 486-2667 Bothell *(G-1789)*
- **Seattle Systems** ....G....... 360 598-8916 Poulsbo *(G-7998)*
- **Seattle Wheelchair Rugby** ....G....... 360 440-2498 Seattle *(G-11083)*
- **Simulab Corporation** ....E....... 206 297-1260 Tukwila *(G-13819)*
- **Sonus-Usa Inc** ....G....... 253 272-3090 Tacoma *(G-13517)*
- **Southshore Prsthtics Orthotics** ....G....... 206 440-1811 Kenmore *(G-4607)*
- **Spinal Specialties** ....G....... 253 861-7329 Olympia *(G-7400)*
- **Stuart Orthotics LLC** ....G....... 360 577-3505 Longview *(G-5957)*
- **Sure Trax LLC** ....G....... 360 430-8343 Longview *(G-5958)*
- **Survival Inc** ....E....... 206 726-9363 Seattle *(G-11229)*
- **Survival Gear Systems** ....G....... 866 257-2978 Spokane *(G-12536)*
- ▲ **TAHAc LLC** ....G....... 509 248-0933 Yakima *(G-15693)*
- ▲ **Tisport LLC** ....C....... 509 416-4245 Pasco *(G-7639)*
- **Trulife Inc** ....C....... 360 697-5656 Poulsbo *(G-8012)*
- **Valley Orthopedics Inc** ....G....... 509 922-5040 Liberty Lake *(G-5866)*
- **Van Brynns Wheelchair** ....G....... 360 687-8546 La Center *(G-5518)*
- **Western Wash Safety Conslt** ....G....... 253 815-7920 Federal Way *(G-3802)*
- **Wheelchair Adl Solutions** ....G....... 509 228-8293 Liberty Lake *(G-5868)*
- **Wheelchairs and More LLC** ....G....... 509 926-9337 Spokane Valley *(G-12935)*
- **Wheelchairs For Nigeria** ....G....... 206 932-6129 Seattle *(G-11466)*
- **Wright Surgical Arts LLC** ....G....... 509 792-1404 Pasco *(G-7656)*
- **Yakima Orthtics Prosthetics PC** ....G....... 509 943-8561 Richland *(G-9056)*

3843 Dental Eqpt & Splys

- **Airway Metrics LLC** ....G....... 206 949-8839 Tacoma *(G-13159)*
- **Alvelogro Inc** ....G....... 425 831-1110 Snoqualmie *(G-12004)*
- ▲ **Aseptico Inc** ....D....... 425 487-3157 Woodinville *(G-15181)*
- **Award Dental II LLC** ....G....... 253 520-0100 Kent *(G-4804)*
- **Bellevue Dental Excellence** ....G....... 425 378-1600 Bellevue *(G-810)*
- **Carssow John** ....G....... 425 820-7995 Woodinville *(G-15206)*
- **Center For Dental Implants** ....G....... 509 765-5141 Moses Lake *(G-6690)*
- **Central Dental Technicians** ....G....... 509 663-4113 Wenatchee *(G-15017)*
- **Clay In Motion Inc** ....F....... 509 529-6146 Walla Walla *(G-14785)*
- **Comfort Acrylics Inc** ....G....... 360 834-9218 Camas *(G-2241)*
- ◆ **Contacez LLC** ....F....... 360 694-1000 Vancouver *(G-14149)*

Dental X Ray Support Systems ....F 509 279-2061
Spokane (G-12224)
Ems Dental Designs Inc ....G....... 425 584-7206
Covington (G-2827)
Fairy Floss ....G....... 206 364-3218
Seattle (G-9963)
Fouad Farhat ....G....... 206 628-0404
Seattle (G-10016)
Gator Dental Equip ....G....... 360 770-3502
Concrete (G-2786)
Generations Dental ....G....... 360 379-1591
Port Townsend (G-7886)
Hager Worldwide Inc ....G....... 360 210-5084
Washougal (G-14958)
Hf Acquisition Co LLC ....E....... 800 331-1984
Mukilteo (G-6932)
▲ Im3 Inc ....F....... 360 254-2981
Vancouver (G-14309)
Innovative Dental Tech Inc ....G....... 971 303-5659
Camas (G-2257)
Integrity Dental LLC ....G....... 253 691-7292
Orting (G-7481)
Jerry Brown ....G....... 509 684-3736
Colville (G-2759)
▲ Myotronics-Noromed Inc ....F....... 206 243-4214
Kent (G-5017)
Olympic Peninsula Implants ....G....... 360 385-5121
Port Townsend (G-7904)
Osbourne Square Dental ....G....... 425 225-5757
Mill Creek (G-6519)
Pacific Coast Manufacturing ....F....... 425 485-8866
Woodinville (G-15328)
Pacific Orthodontic Laboratory ....G....... 425 224-4193
Everett (G-3564)
▲ Parts Warehouse Inc ....G....... 360 354-4722
Lynden (G-6045)
▲ Pascal Company Inc ....E....... 425 827-4694
Bellevue (G-1063)
Peaceful Sole ....G....... 425 652-7043
Issaquah (G-4458)
Phazr LLC ....G....... 509 329-8306
Spokane (G-12440)
▼ Philips Oral Healthcare LLC ....A....... 425 487-7000
Bothell (G-1886)
Qualident Dental Lab LLC ....E....... 360 695-7411
Vancouver (G-14517)
Reach Service LLC ....G....... 253 370-6229
University Place (G-13978)
▲ Royal Dental Manufacturing Inc ....D....... 425 743-0988
Everett (G-3601)
Rutillo Chaves ....G....... 425 775-0651
Lynnwood (G-6190)
◆ Sagemax Bioceramics Inc ....E....... 253 214-0389
Federal Way (G-3780)
Seattle Gold Grills ....G....... 206 250-0833
Seattle (G-11060)
Shadewave ....G....... 425 557-7788
Issaquah (G-4473)
Silverdale Orthodontic Lab ....G....... 360 479-5536
Bremerton (G-2000)
Soos Creek Dental ....F....... 253 631-8241
Covington (G-2839)
Sun Rise Dental ....G....... 253 856-3384
Kent (G-5161)
T & S Dental Group Corp ....G....... 714 720-5511
Kent (G-5168)
Taylor Dental Studio ....G....... 360 249-4329
Montesano (G-6660)
◆ Vector R&D Inc ....G....... 877 883-7455
University Place (G-13983)
▲ Westar Medical Products Inc ....F....... 425 290-3945
Arlington (G-347)

3844 X-ray Apparatus & Tubes

Cgm Imaging Services LLC ....G....... 509 995-6153
Spokane (G-12178)
Dental X Ray Support Systems ....F....... 509 279-2061
Spokane (G-12224)
General Electric Company ....C....... 425 557-3022
Issaquah (G-4419)
P S Northwest Radiography ....G....... 253 627-3988
Tacoma (G-13447)
Rigaku Americas Corporation ....G....... 206 780-8927
Bainbridge Island (G-666)

3845 Electromedical & Electrotherapeutic Apparatus

◆ A-M Systems LLC ....E....... 360 683-8300
Sequim (G-11604)
Aqueduct Neurosciences Inc ....G....... 206 661-1538
Seattle (G-9417)
▲ Aseptico Inc ....D....... 425 487-3157
Woodinville (G-15181)
ATL International LLC ....G....... 425 487-7000
Bothell (G-1825)
▲ Biodynamics Corporation ....G....... 206 526-0205
Shoreline (G-11762)
Biolife Solutions Inc ....G....... 425 402-1400
Bothell (G-1827)
Biolife Solutions Inc ....E....... 425 402-1400
Bothell (G-1828)
Blaze Metrics LLC ....G....... 206 972-3890
Quil Ceda Village (G-8280)
Breast Care Center ....F....... 360 424-6161
Sedro Woolley (G-11534)
Cadence Neuroscience Inc ....G....... 425 681-6863
Sammamish (G-9194)
Cadwell Laboratories Inc ....D....... 509 735-6481
Kennewick (G-4638)
▼ Calypso Medical Tech Inc ....C....... 206 254-0600
Seattle (G-9611)
Cardiodynamics Intl Corp ....G....... 208 332-2502
Bothell (G-1834)
Carrot Medical LLC ....F....... 425 318-8089
Bothell (G-1836)
Cerevast Medical Inc ....G....... 425 748-7529
Bothell (G-1754)
Columbia Laser Centers Inc ....G....... 509 529-7711
College Place (G-2723)
Courageous Heart Healing LLC ....G....... 541 517-6222
Seattle (G-9749)
Derma Medical Spa ....G....... 360 350-5321
Olympia (G-7268)
Echo-Sense Inc ....G....... 360 833-9032
Camas (G-2246)
Emergent Detection Inc ....G....... 206 391-4876
Seattle (G-9915)
Emulate Therapeutics Inc ....G....... 206 708-2288
Seattle (G-9918)
Flourish Skin & Laser LLC ....F....... 360 636-1411
Longview (G-5911)
Ftv Business Services LLC ....F....... 425 347-6100
Everett (G-3486)
▲ Fujifilm Sonosite Inc ....B....... 425 951-1200
Bothell (G-1858)
Fujifilm Sonosite Inc ....C....... 425 951-1200
Bothell (G-1859)
General Electric Company ....G....... 253 351-2200
Auburn (G-448)
Impulse Medical Tech Inc ....F....... 360 829-0400
Buckley (G-2059)
Innerscan Inc ....G....... 425 419-7718
Bothell (G-1769)
Innovaura Corporation ....G....... 425 272-2702
Edmonds (G-3120)
Iopi Medical LLC ....G....... 425 549-0139
Woodinville (G-15268)
J & J Engineering Inc ....F....... 360 779-3853
Poulsbo (G-7967)
Lockheed Martin Aculight Corp ....D....... 425 482-1100
Bothell (G-1875)
Medtronic Inc ....F....... 425 867-4000
Redmond (G-8554)
Medtronic Usa Inc ....E....... 425 803-0708
Bellevue (G-1001)
Mind Modulations ....G....... 626 863-7379
Marysville (G-6360)
Mindplace Company ....G....... 360 376-6494
Eastsound (G-3040)
▲ Mindray Medical USA Corp ....E....... 425 881-0361
Redmond (G-8590)
▲ Myotronics-Noromed Inc ....F....... 206 243-4214
Kent (G-5017)
Myovision ....G....... 800 969-6961
Seattle (G-10582)
Natus Medical Incorporated ....F....... 206 767-3500
Seattle (G-10594)
▲ Olympic Medical Corp ....D....... 206 767-3500
Seattle (G-10692)
Palo Alto Health Sciences Inc ....F....... 925 594-8404
Kirkland (G-5427)
Pet/CT Imaging At Swdish Cncer ....F....... 206 215-6433
Seattle (G-10790)
Philips North America LLC ....C....... 206 664-5000
Seattle (G-10794)
◆ Philips Ultrasound Inc ....C....... 800 982-2011
Bothell (G-1887)
Physio-Control Intl Inc ....A....... 425 867-4000
Redmond (G-8621)
Resolute Medical Inc ....G....... 800 750-5784
Bellevue (G-1101)
Seattle Espresso Machine Corp ....G....... 206 284-7171
Seattle (G-11057)
Siemens Med Solutions USA Inc ....C....... 425 392-9180
Issaquah (G-4475)
Simulab Corporation ....E....... 206 297-1260
Tukwila (G-13819)
Solta Medical Inc ....F....... 425 354-1857
Bothell (G-1794)
Somatics LLC ....G....... 847 234-6761
Vancouver (G-14600)
▲ Spacelabs Healthcare Inc ....A....... 425 396-3300
Snoqualmie (G-12027)
Spacelabs Healthcare LLC ....B....... 425 396-3300
Snoqualmie (G-12028)
◆ Spacelabs Healthcare Wash ....C....... 425 396-3300
Snoqualmie (G-12029)
Tiba Medical Inc ....G....... 503 222-1500
Bellevue (G-1188)
Tournitek Inc ....G....... 423 620-5475
Seattle (G-11323)
Ventec Life Systems Inc ....E....... 425 686-1728
Bothell (G-1913)
▲ Verathon Inc ....C....... 425 867-1348
Bothell (G-1805)

3851 Ophthalmic Goods

Capitol Optical Corp ....E....... 360 352-7502
Lacey (G-5538)
▲ Commercial Plastics Corp ....F....... 206 682-4832
Seattle (G-9717)
Council For Edctl Trvl US Amer ....E....... 949 940-1140
Bellingham (G-1307)
East Hill Optometry ....G....... 253 859-0942
Kent (G-4882)
Ellensburg Eye & Cntact Lens C ....G....... 509 925-1000
Ellensburg (G-3195)
Elles Island Spectacle ....G....... 206 715-9475
Bainbridge Island (G-629)
▲ Erickson Inc ....G....... 509 747-6148
Spokane (G-12250)
House of Lashes ....G....... 206 522-5277
Seattle (G-10186)
▲ Hoya Optical Laboratories ....E....... 253 475-7809
Tacoma (G-13344)
▲ Island Construction ....G....... 360 426-3442
Shelton (G-11700)
Market Optical ....G....... 206 448-7739
Seattle (G-10488)
Northwest Eye Design LLC ....G....... 425 823-1861
Kirkland (G-5413)
Peninsula Optical Lab Inc ....E....... 800 540-4640
Tacoma (G-13462)
Prismoid Optical Laboratory ....G....... 360 417-1244
Port Angeles (G-7738)
▲ Project Seezit Inc ....G....... 415 336-4000
Seattle (G-10874)
Society43 LLC ....G....... 206 327-0778
Seattle (G-11150)
Specialized Safety Pdts LLC ....G....... 509 707-0068
Moses Lake (G-6751)
Spectacle Maker ....G....... 425 643-5367
Bellevue (G-1152)
Tumwater Eye Center Inc ....G....... 360 352-6060
Tumwater (G-13902)
United Contact Lens Inc ....G....... 360 474-9577
Arlington (G-343)
Walman Optical Company ....E....... 253 872-7137
Kent (G-5205)
Western Optical Corporation ....D....... 206 622-7627
Seattle (G-11455)

3861 Photographic Eqpt & Splys

Beats4legends ....G....... 253 218-5075
Seattle (G-9507)
▲ Brooke Engrg Photographic Eqp ....F....... 360 638-2591
Hansville (G-4314)
Business Computing Solutions ....G....... 425 644-6174
Bellevue (G-832)
CMX Corporation ....E....... 425 656-1269
Tukwila (G-13713)
Comp U Charge Inc ....F....... 509 484-1918
Spokane (G-12194)
Component Engineering Inc ....F....... 206 284-9171
Shoreline (G-11767)
◆ Contour Inc ....F....... 206 792-5226
Seattle (G-9734)
▲ Express Imaging Systems LLC ....F....... 206 720-1798
Renton (G-8796)

▲ **Freefly Systems Inc** ....E.... 425 485-5500
Woodinville *(G-15249)*
Immersive Media Company ....E.... 360 609-3419
Washougal *(G-14960)*
Indie Flix Inc ....F.... 206 829-9112
Seattle *(G-10226)*
▲ **Lightspeed Design Inc** ....G.... 425 637-2818
Bellevue *(G-983)*
Northwest Video Wall ....G.... 360 403-7773
Arlington *(G-291)*
Oppenheimer Camera Pdts Inc ....G.... 206 467-8666
Seattle *(G-10707)*
Outdoor Specialties LLC ....G.... 425 432-0507
Renton *(G-8869)*
Printers Shopper LLC ....G.... 425 822-7766
Kirkland *(G-5442)*
Profile Systems Inc ....F.... 206 624-7715
Seattle *(G-10873)*
Pryde Johnson 1536 LLC ....G.... 206 352-7000
Seattle *(G-10879)*
Rgd Enterprises Inc ....G.... 360 923-9582
Olympia *(G-7385)*
Silhouette Graphics ....G.... 360 758-4163
Bellingham *(G-1537)*
Stourwater Pictures ....G.... 206 780-6928
Bainbridge Island *(G-674)*
Tarra LLC ....G.... 360 458-4842
Roy *(G-9165)*
Tobin Cinema Systems Inc ....G.... 509 621-0323
Spokane Valley *(G-12908)*
Triosports Usa LLC ....G.... 206 953-2394
Seattle *(G-11338)*
Xerox Corp Xerox Corporat ....G.... 425 947-7046
Redmond *(G-8719)*

3873 Watch & Clock Devices & Parts

Carlson Brothers Inc ....F.... 253 472-9232
Tacoma *(G-13224)*
Fossil Group Inc ....G.... 206 248-6984
Tukwila *(G-13736)*
Kirk Dial of Seattle ....G.... 253 852-5125
Kent *(G-4978)*

39 MISCELLANEOUS MANUFACTURING INDUSTRIES

3911 Jewelry: Precious Metal

A U Cornerstone Inc ....G.... 360 336-5234
Mount Vernon *(G-6768)*
A1 Services ....G.... 509 946-6269
Richland *(G-8962)*
ADI Corporation ....G.... 425 455-4561
Bellevue *(G-780)*
Angelwear ....G.... 206 230-9594
Seattle *(G-9403)*
Astral Holdings Inc ....G.... 206 762-4800
Seattle *(G-9447)*
Brothers Jewelers Inc ....G.... 509 946-7989
Richland *(G-8978)*
Carlson Brothers Inc ....F.... 253 472-9232
Tacoma *(G-13224)*
Cascade Custom Jewelers ....G.... 253 535-2121
Tacoma *(G-13226)*
Cline Manufacturing Jewelers ....G.... 425 673-7979
Edmonds *(G-3101)*
Coin Market LLC ....G.... 425 745-1659
Lynnwood *(G-6095)*
▲ **Columbia Gem House Inc** ....E.... 360 514-0569
Vancouver *(G-14130)*
Daughters of Mary ....G.... 360 943-2186
Olympia *(G-7264)*
Deborah Designs ....G.... 253 848-3274
Puyallup *(G-8142)*
Diamond Store Inc ....G.... 253 272-3377
Tacoma *(G-13262)*
Diamondcraft Jewels ....G.... 509 758-1449
Clarkston *(G-2632)*
DOriginal Jewelers ....G.... 425 454-5559
Bellevue *(G-880)*
Dream It Inc ....G.... 360 379-1070
Port Townsend *(G-7881)*
Dynamic Designs Jewelry Inc ....G.... 425 827-7722
Kirkland *(G-5326)*
▲ **Eastern Merchandise Co Inc** ....G.... 206 448-4466
Seattle *(G-9871)*
Eldorado AG ....G.... 360 491-0394
Lacey *(G-5547)*
Elegantly Yours ....G.... 425 478-2873
Duvall *(G-2985)*
European Creations Inc ....G.... 425 898-0685
Redmond *(G-8454)*
Fairhaven Gold Inc ....G.... 360 733-4667
Bellingham *(G-1341)*
Faris LLC ....G.... 206 992-6453
Seattle *(G-9972)*
Feather and Skull ....G.... 206 227-7951
Seattle *(G-9979)*
Frank Lau Jewelry Inc ....G.... 206 323-6343
Seattle *(G-10020)*
G L Kluh & Sons Jewelers Inc ....F.... 360 491-3530
Lacey *(G-5552)*
Gem East Corporation ....E.... 206 441-1700
Lake Forest Park *(G-5613)*
Gems n Gold ....G.... 360 574-5085
Vancouver *(G-14249)*
Glo Tech Inc ....G.... 360 403-8928
Arlington *(G-242)*
Goedecke & Goedecke ....G.... 425 481-1153
Bothell *(G-1862)*
Gold Mine of Jewelry Inc ....G.... 206 622-3333
Seattle *(G-10093)*
Goldenrod Inc ....G.... 253 840-8114
Edgewood *(G-3080)*
Hartley Jewelers ....G.... 360 754-6161
Olympia *(G-7304)*
Idea Company ....G.... 253 891-8140
Pacific *(G-7530)*
J Lanning Jewelers ....G.... 360 693-9940
Vancouver *(G-14331)*
Jay Lauris & Company Inc ....G.... 206 243-9890
Burien *(G-2114)*
▲ **Jewelry Boutique LLC** ....G.... 360 866-2278
Olympia *(G-7311)*
Jewelry Design Center Inc ....E.... 509 487-5905
Spokane *(G-12334)*
John M Smith ....G.... 360 484-7738
Naselle *(G-7013)*
Kit A Jeweler Designed For You ....G.... 253 851-5546
Gig Harbor *(G-4127)*
Kogita Custom Mfg & Repair ....G.... 425 453-9547
Bellevue *(G-970)*
Larkin Jewelers ....G.... 253 756-0712
Tacoma *(G-13381)*
Marathon N More ....G.... 360 380-5242
Bellingham *(G-1423)*
Marcin Jewelry Inc ....F.... 425 883-7884
Woodinville *(G-15301)*
Norris Techniques ....G.... 360 871-1458
Port Orchard *(G-7833)*
Ofner and Company ....G.... 425 485-0437
Kenmore *(G-4595)*
Originals By Chad Jwly Design ....G.... 360 318-0210
Lynden *(G-6042)*
Pacific Gem Inc ....G.... 206 448-7700
Seattle *(G-10733)*
Pacific Northwest Jewelers ....G.... 509 927-8923
Greenacres *(G-4300)*
Prestige Fine Jewelry ....G.... 206 623-0085
Mount Vernon *(G-6825)*
RC & Co ....G.... 425 774-7511
Mill Creek *(G-6522)*
Robins Jewelers Ltd ....G.... 206 622-4337
Edmonds *(G-3149)*
S&T Trading & More LLC ....G.... 509 421-2326
Wenatchee *(G-15071)*
Sauk Suiattle Indian Tribe Tru ....F.... 360 436-0131
Darrington *(G-2869)*
Swissa Inc ....G.... 206 625-9202
Seattle *(G-11240)*
Taina Hartman Studio ....G.... 541 806-0053
White Salmon *(G-15133)*
Teneff Jewelry Mfg Co ....E.... 509 747-1038
Spokane *(G-12552)*
V S P Jewelry Design Gallery ....G.... 206 367-7310
Lake Forest Park *(G-5626)*
▲ **Wapato Pawn & Trade** ....G.... 509 877-6405
Wapato *(G-14928)*
Zirkus Inc ....G.... 360 385-5478
Port Townsend *(G-7940)*

3914 Silverware, Plated & Stainless Steel Ware

Bardon Inc ....G.... 360 455-1790
Olympia *(G-7234)*
Carl Zapffe Inc ....G.... 206 364-1919
Seattle *(G-9633)*
Friedman Slversmiths Repr Pltg ....G.... 360 752-3119
Bellingham *(G-1354)*
Industrial Design & Eqp Inc ....G.... 360 671-9200
Ferndale *(G-3855)*
John Marshall Metalsmith Inc ....G.... 206 546-5643
Edmonds *(G-3125)*
Mackenzie Spcalty Castings Inc ....E.... 360 435-5539
Arlington *(G-271)*
Omega Silversmithing Inc ....G.... 360 863-6771
Snohomish *(G-11956)*
◆ **Rena Ware International Inc** ....E.... 425 881-6171
Bellevue *(G-1098)*

3915 Jewelers Findings & Lapidary Work

Bodle Diamond Industries ....G.... 360 939-0242
Stanwood *(G-12953)*
Cosmic Resources ....G.... 360 730-8574
Langley *(G-5775)*
▲ **Diamond Tech Innovations Inc** ....E.... 360 866-1337
Olympia *(G-7270)*
Gem Cut Company ....G.... 206 780-0113
Bainbridge Island *(G-636)*
Handmaiden Bead & Jwly Shoppe ....G.... 509 680-5785
Colville *(G-2754)*
John Knutson Lapidary ....G.... 509 653-2111
Naches *(G-6998)*
Juicy Gems ....G.... 425 232-3567
Spokane *(G-12346)*
Le Bijou Corporation ....G.... 206 622-9453
Seattle *(G-10389)*
M B Lapidary ....G.... 253 271-7515
Spanaway *(G-12062)*
Mend ....G.... 949 355-9925
Seattle *(G-10516)*
Nutshell ....G.... 360 438-1054
Lacey *(G-5570)*
Pacific Jewelers ....G.... 360 693-3410
Vancouver *(G-14465)*
Stateside Bead Supply ....G.... 425 644-3448
Bellevue *(G-1155)*
Stockton Cul De Sac ....G.... 253 854-9358
Kent *(G-5157)*
Teneff Jewelry Mfg Co ....E.... 509 747-1038
Spokane *(G-12552)*
True Colors Inc ....G.... 206 623-2366
Seattle *(G-11341)*
Usjade LLC ....G.... 509 535-3411
Otis Orchards *(G-7521)*

3931 Musical Instruments

A I S ....G.... 509 972-2064
Yakima *(G-15497)*
Alan R & Sara Balmforth ....G.... 206 363-7349
Shoreline *(G-11754)*
Arnquist Musical Designs ....G.... 206 420-1639
Seattle *(G-9431)*
Artisan Instruments Inc ....F.... 425 486-6555
Kenmore *(G-4566)*
Big Lloyde ....G.... 509 233-2293
Loon Lake *(G-5974)*
Bowet & Poet Inc ....G.... 360 385-9005
Port Townsend *(G-7870)*
Casey Burns Flutes ....G.... 360 297-4020
Kingston *(G-5250)*
David T Vanzandt Co ....G.... 206 789-7294
Seattle *(G-9801)*
Duncan Macdonald Violins LLC ....G.... 206 352-7219
Seattle *(G-9858)*
▲ **Dusty Strings Co** ....E.... 206 634-1656
Seattle *(G-9861)*
Fluteworks ....G.... 206 729-1903
Seattle *(G-10008)*
Flyingviolin Inc ....G.... 209 595-9709
Olympia *(G-7288)*
Graphite Guitar Systems ....G.... 360 273-7744
Oakville *(G-7175)*
▲ **Gurian Instruments Inc** ....G.... 206 467-7990
Seattle *(G-10133)*
Howling Wolf Drums ....G.... 425 391-2540
Issaquah *(G-4426)*
Intellitouch Communicatons ....G.... 858 457-3300
Liberty Lake *(G-5837)*
Kenmore Violins ....G.... 425 481-5638
Kenmore *(G-4588)*
▲ **Kuau Technology Ltd** ....F.... 425 485-7551
Woodinville *(G-15281)*
L & B Service LLC ....G.... 206 650-4607
Lake Forest Park *(G-5619)*
Mad Ape ....G.... 206 201-3275
Bainbridge Island *(G-649)*
Magical Strings ....G.... 253 857-3716
Olalla *(G-7208)*

S I C

39 MISCELLANEOUS MANUFACTURING INDUSTRIES

▲ Manhasset Specialty Co Inc............E 509 248-3810
  Yakima (G-15614)
Northwest Pipe Organ..........................G 425 432-5039
  Maple Valley (G-6283)
Ocarina Arena......................................G 206 446-5354
  Seattle (G-10680)
Olympic Musical Instrumen ....G 360 779-4620
  Poulsbo (G-7989)
Other Worlds.......................................G 360 459-2323
  Olympia (G-7363)
Pacific Rim Tonewoods Inc................F 360 826-6101
  Concrete (G-2790)
▲ Pacific Rim Tonewoods Inc............F 360 826-6101
  Bellingham (G-1488)
▲ Petosa Accordions Inc...................G 206 632-2700
  Lynnwood (G-6180)
▲ Ray R L Violin Shop LLC...............G 360 570-1085
  Olympia (G-7379)
Rhythmical Steel.................................G 360 263-3141
  La Center (G-5514)
Robert Gee Violins..............................G 425 776-4002
  Lynnwood (G-6189)
Seattle Music Partners ....G 206 408-8588
  Seattle (G-11065)
Sobel Guitars......................................G 505 699-4032
  Ridgefield (G-9112)
Summer Moon Products.....................G 360 826-3157
  Sedro Woolley (G-11573)
▲ Syndyne Corporation......................G 360 256-8466
  Vancouver (G-14622)
T & K Martin Farms Inc......................G 509 525-4387
  Walla Walla (G-14877)
Theo Wanne Mouthpieces Instrs........G 360 392-8416
  Bellingham (G-1568)
▲ TV Jones Inc...................................G 360 930-0418
  Poulsbo (G-8013)
▼ Van Orman Guitars LLC..................G 253 269-8660
  Elma (G-3258)
Windtones LLC....................................G 360 349-9083
  Olympia (G-7428)
Wolfetone Pickups Co........................G 206 417-3548
  Lake Forest Park (G-5628)

3942 Dolls & Stuffed Toys

▲ Brass Key Inc...................................E 866 325-6840
  Maple Valley (G-6262)
▲ Cascade Toy Ltd..............................F 425 888-4600
  North Bend (G-7105)
Dolls By Arlene...................................G 360 687-4321
  Battle Ground (G-698)
One Atta Time Doll Co........................G 360 956-1091
  Olympia (G-7362)
Trans Pac Enterprises Inc..................F 425 688-0037
  Bellevue (G-1198)
Verlindas ....G 253 437-5217
  Kent (G-5200)
Warriners Originals Inc......................G 509 973-2705
  Prosser (G-8075)

3944 Games, Toys & Children's Vehicles

Accurate Models.................................G 253 630-3126
  Renton (G-8726)
Artifactory...G 360 260-2660
  Brush Prairie (G-2029)
◆ Bensussen Deutsch & Assoc LLC...B 425 492-6111
  Woodinville (G-15188)
Boon..G 360 225-5224
  Woodland (G-15420)
▲ Brass Key Inc..................................E 866 325-6840
  Maple Valley (G-6262)
▲ Break From Reality Games LLC.....G 513 884-4940
  Seattle (G-9581)
Bunchgrass Folktoys Inc....................G 509 334-5143
  Pullman (G-8086)
Bungie Inc..G 425 440-6800
  Bellevue (G-830)
C & M Country Creations ....G 253 535-3327
  Tacoma (G-13214)
Craft International of Wash................G 360 785-3606
  Winlock (G-15148)
Creative Dimensions..........................G 360 733-5024
  Bellingham (G-1310)
Crisman Rocking Horses LLC............G 206 408-7465
  Vashon (G-14720)
Dbcs Innovations................................G 206 919-2249
  Seattle (G-9806)
Doug Puzzle..G 425 647-0464
  Bellevue (G-883)
Drachen Design Inc ....G 206 282-4349
  Seattle (G-9853)

Eagle Tree Systems LLC....................G 425 614-0450
  Bellevue (G-886)
Exit Puzzles..G 360 930-9686
  Olympia (G-7280)
Family Treasures................................G 206 282-1194
  Seattle (G-9967)
Flowplay Inc.......................................F 206 903-0457
  Seattle (G-10007)
Freelocalpoker Co..............................G 360 794-5173
  Monroe (G-6574)
Funko Inc...F 425 783-3616
  Everett (G-3488)
Funko Games LLC.............................G 206 547-7155
  Seattle (G-10039)
◆ GAEMS Inc......................................F 855 754-2367
  Redmond (G-8468)
▲ Geospace Products Company Inc....G 206 547-2556
  Seattle (G-10065)
Griptonite Inc......................................C 425 825-6800
  Kirkland (G-5355)
Jaxjox Inc..G 425 324-3017
  Vancouver (G-14335)
▲ Just Think Toys Inc........................G 310 308-5242
  Bainbridge Island (G-645)
▲ Kheper Games Inc..........................F 206 782-2201
  Seattle (G-10341)
Kick Ass Puzzles................................G 425 275-2381
  Lynnwood (G-6150)
Koehler Enterprise Inc.......................G 360 261-0390
  Longview (G-5924)
▲ LB Games Inc..................................G 360 794-7803
  Snohomish (G-11937)
Ljs Plants & Crafts.............................G 253 854-9407
  Kent (G-4998)
Log Cabin Crafts.................................G 425 885-9049
  Redmond (G-8537)
▲ Mamma-Kin LLC..............................G 425 922-9505
  Kirkland (G-5395)
Marninsaylor LLC................................G 307 360-6165
  Seattle (G-10491)
Metal Art Bells....................................G 360 546-2018
  Vancouver (G-14414)
Michaels Stores Inc ....E 360 892-4494
  Vancouver (G-14417)
▲ Milestone Products Co....................F 425 882-1987
  Redmond (G-8589)
Molson Runner Sleds........................G 425 445-2975
  Covington (G-2834)
Nita N Ace LLC....................................G 253 209-4413
  Graham (G-4233)
Novel Inc..E 425 956-3096
  Kirkland (G-5414)
Olive Games Corporation..................G 425 649-1136
  Bellevue (G-1046)
▲ OShell Delmont...............................G 360 427-9600
  Shelton (G-11719)
Oso Railworks Inc..............................G 406 375-7555
  Arlington (G-295)
Panthercorn Studios...........................G 425 501-9717
  Mukilteo (G-6964)
Parvia Corp...F 206 310-2205
  Seattle (G-10761)
Pavel S Puzzles..................................G 425 643-0204
  Bellevue (G-1065)
◆ Play Visions Inc..............................E 425 482-2836
  Woodinville (G-15335)
▲ Prism Designs Inc...........................G 206 838-8682
  Seattle (G-10865)
Puzzle Piece Arts ....G 360 678-3687
  Greenbank (G-4309)
Puzzle Pieces Bookkeeping..............G 360 217-7140
  Monroe (G-6609)
R E B Magnetics.................................G 360 636-4693
  Kelso (G-4545)
RE-Marks Inc......................................F 206 548-1008
  Seattle (G-10928)
Red Seal Games LLC.........................G 425 922-6500
  Seattle (G-10935)
Republic Locomotive Works...............G 360 577-6479
  Cathlamet (G-2373)
Rocking Horse Barns LLC.................G 360 736-5403
  Centralia (G-2428)
Rocking Horse Rita Cstm Hmes........G 360 600-1000
  Vancouver (G-14558)
▲ Screenlife LLC.................................G 206 829-0743
  Seattle (G-11035)
Seattle Gameco...................................G 206 767-0922
  Seattle (G-11058)
▲ Simplyfun LLC.................................E 425 289-0858
  Bellevue (G-1134)

◆ Slingshot Sports LLC.......................F 509 427-4950
  North Bonneville (G-7135)
Smad World LLC.................................G 253 536-5460
  Tacoma (G-13515)
Storybox Studios LLC........................G 206 310-2626
  Mercer Island (G-6486)
T14 Inc..G 425 829-8213
  Kirkland (G-5474)
The Creation Station Inc....................G 425 775-7959
  Tulalip (G-13845)
Tincan Studio LLC..............................G 559 906-3521
  Lynnwood (G-6210)
Tippecanoe Boats Ltd........................G 360 966-7245
  Everson (G-3692)
Touch Sky Kites..................................G 360 459-2063
  Lacey (G-5596)
Tudor Games Inc...............................G 800 914-8836
  Kent (G-5192)
Twopointoh Garmes LLC..................G 360 836-4266
  Anacortes (G-181)
Universe Builders Inc.......................G 206 390-4313
  Seattle (G-11378)
Wargaming Seattle Inc......................G 425 250-0209
  Bellevue (G-1224)
▲ Washington Vg Inc..........................F 425 823-4518
  Kirkland (G-5492)
Whitbys Whimsies..............................G 206 937-1312
  Seattle (G-11468)
Wind Play Inc.....................................G 206 784-0414
  Seattle (G-11481)
▲ Wizards of Coast LLC.....................B 425 226-6500
  Renton (G-8949)
Woodworking Unlimited......................G 425 481-7451
  Bothell (G-1922)

3949 Sporting & Athletic Goods, NEC

Alki Sports LLC...................................F 206 898-1305
  Redmond (G-8378)
Allplay Systems LLC..........................G 360 808-5925
  Sequim (G-11609)
Allsports Cages & Netting LLC..........G 206 933-8987
  Seattle (G-9383)
Amigos Skateboards LLC..................G 901 289-9044
  Seattle (G-9398)
Angela J Bowen & Assoc LLC...........G 360 252-2440
  Olympia (G-7227)
Aqua Rec Inc.....................................G 253 826-2561
  Bonney Lake (G-1716)
Aqua Rec Inc.....................................G 253 770-9447
  Puyallup (G-8123)
Aro-Tek Ltd...G 360 754-2770
  Olympia (G-7230)
Arro Last Target Systems ....G 360 427-9512
  Shelton (G-11680)
B-A-Pro LLC.......................................G 253 861-3634
  Fife (G-3936)
Baden Sports Inc...............................F 253 925-0500
  Renton (G-8750)
Badnasty Paintball..............................G 509 998-0984
  Moses Lake (G-6683)
Baseball Club of Seattle Lllp............A 206 346-4327
  Seattle (G-9497)
Beau Mac Enterprises ....G 253 447-8093
  Sumner (G-13055)
Bikelid LLC..G 206 963-7585
  Medina (G-6446)
Body Builders Gym Equipment..........G 253 631-8274
  Kent (G-4816)
Bodysense Inc....................................G 206 988-1719
  Seattle (G-9561)
Boggs Manufacturing..........................G 360 449-3479
  Vancouver (G-14075)
Boomerang Boxer LLC.......................G 206 227-6569
  Seattle (G-9565)
Boomerang Express LLC...................G 360 449-2173
  Vancouver (G-14078)
Boomerang Physical Therapy LLC ....G 360 258-1637
  Vancouver (G-14079)
Bowlbys Sporting Goods ....G 509 248-8281
  Yakima (G-15524)
Brooks Sports Inc.............................G 253 863-4343
  Sumner (G-13057)
Buoy Wear LLC...................................G 206 899-7926
  Centralia (G-2386)
Carlson & Fitzwater LLC...................G 425 941-4020
  Snohomish (G-11885)
▼ Carter Lift Bag Inc...........................G 360 886-2302
  Enumclaw (G-3280)
▲ Cascade Designs Inc......................B 206 505-9500
  Seattle (G-9640)

Cascade Designs Inc ....G....... 206 505-9500
Seattle *(G-9641)*

Champion Sports Group ....G....... 360 258-0546
Vancouver *(G-14112)*

Chaval Outdoor ....G....... 206 569-0154
Bainbridge Island *(G-621)*

▲ Clean-Shot Archery Inc ....G....... 425 242-5970
Kent *(G-4853)*

Clear Coated ....G....... 425 495-2369
Seattle *(G-9693)*

Clear Your Clutter LLC ....G....... 206 784-1515
Seattle *(G-9695)*

Clifford W Leeson Inc ....G....... 509 427-4155
Stevenson *(G-13010)*

Cloud City Skateboards ....G....... 206 403-1882
Seattle *(G-9699)*

Coaxsher Inc ....E....... 509 663-5148
Chelan Falls *(G-2571)*

Columbia Cascade Company ....D....... 360 693-8558
Vancouver *(G-14129)*

Compass Outdoor Adventures LLC ....G....... 425 281-0267
Snoqualmie *(G-12007)*

Composite Tooling Innovations ....G....... 509 637-3836
Bingen *(G-1635)*

◆ Connelly Skis Inc ....E....... 425 775-5416
Lynnwood *(G-6098)*

Connelly Skis Inc ....G....... 425 831-1099
Snoqualmie *(G-12008)*

Contemporary Design Co ....F....... 360 599-2833
Bellingham *(G-1303)*

◆ Coppertop Enterprises Inc ....E....... 360 966-9622
Everson *(G-3672)*

Crabhawk ....G....... 541 921-3593
Tokeland *(G-13632)*

Cuga Vest ....G....... 509 834-8378
Yakima *(G-15544)*

D & L Outdoor Specialties ....G....... 509 758-5875
Clarkston *(G-2630)*

D & P Products Inc ....G....... 425 551-1380
Everett *(G-3435)*

D Crockett Surfboards ....G....... 425 430-9947
Renton *(G-8778)*

▲ Dashboard Skimboards LLC ....G....... 253 235-1811
Fife *(G-3948)*

▲ Db Skimboards ....F....... 253 235-1811
Fife *(G-3949)*

▲ Diamond Nets Inc ....E....... 360 354-1319
Everson *(G-3673)*

Dick Nite Spoons Inc ....G....... 425 377-8448
Snohomish *(G-11899)*

Digital Anglers LLC ....G....... 206 819-7010
Redmond *(G-8441)*

Direct Hit Golf Flags LLC ....G....... 253 946-6263
Federal Way *(G-3729)*

Dive Xtras ....G....... 425 296-6570
Everett *(G-3443)*

Dyaco Coml & Med N Amer LLC ....G....... 408 966-4239
Bothell *(G-1850)*

Eastern Washington University ....F....... 509 359-6047
Cheney *(G-2584)*

Eccentrixx LLC ....G....... 360 274-4954
Castle Rock *(G-2341)*

Emmrod Fishing Gear Inc ....G....... 509 979-2222
Spokane Valley *(G-12691)*

Eqpd Gear LLC ....G....... 509 997-2010
Twisp *(G-13911)*

Etsoutdoors ....G....... 509 481-3938
Nine Mile Falls *(G-7073)*

Evan Martin Lure Inc ....G....... 425 478-7163
Kenmore *(G-4572)*

Evans Board Shop ....G....... 360 297-4445
Poulsbo *(G-7962)*

Evans Mfg ....G....... 360 332-9505
Blaine *(G-1669)*

Evo ....G....... 866 386-1590
Sumner *(G-13070)*

Fetha Styx Inc ....G....... 360 687-3856
Battle Ground *(G-701)*

Fetha Styx LLC ....G....... 425 242-0014
Kirkland *(G-5338)*

Fortis Manufacturing Inc ....G....... 253 277-3211
Kent *(G-4918)*

Fownes Brothers & Co Inc ....G....... 360 738-3126
Bellingham *(G-1353)*

Freedom Adaptive Systems LLC ....G....... 425 286-9597
Bothell *(G-1857)*

George Gehrkes Gink ....G....... 509 243-4100
Asotin *(G-353)*

Giorgios Fitness Center ....G....... 509 922-8833
Spokane Valley *(G-12718)*

Golden Creek LLC ....G....... 425 830-4343
Issaquah *(G-4423)*

▲ Golfco International Inc ....G....... 425 861-7755
Redmond *(G-8480)*

Goodmans Ski and Sports Inc ....G....... 360 733-8937
Bellingham *(G-1358)*

Grassroots Outdoor LLC ....G....... 425 210-5745
Everett *(G-3505)*

▲ Gsi Outdoors Inc ....E....... 509 928-9611
Spokane Valley *(G-12725)*

Gt Darts ....G....... 206 498-9855
Shoreline *(G-11777)*

H20 Factor ....G....... 425 868-4017
Sammamish *(G-9212)*

Harbour Pointe Golf LLC ....G....... 425 355-6060
Mukilteo *(G-6930)*

Hawks Prairie Golf LLC ....G....... 360 455-8383
Bellevue *(G-938)*

Hemel Board Company ....G....... 206 261-2781
Seattle *(G-10164)*

Homeplate Heroes ....G....... 360 798-7974
Vancouver *(G-14301)*

Hook & Line Fish ....G....... 360 293-0503
Anacortes *(G-134)*

Hugos On Hill ....G....... 509 822-7149
Spokane *(G-12299)*

▲ Ideations Design Inc ....G....... 206 281-0067
Seattle *(G-10203)*

▲ Industrial Revolution Inc ....E....... 425 285-1111
Tukwila *(G-13752)*

Innovative Outdoor Pdts LLC ....G....... 509 826-0219
Tonasket *(G-13651)*

Insect Skateboards Inc ....G....... 206 706-8882
Seattle *(G-10242)*

▲ International Longline Supply ....G....... 360 650-0412
Bellingham *(G-1382)*

▲ Inventist Inc ....G....... 360 833-2357
Camas *(G-2258)*

Island Blueback Inc ....G....... 360 385-0871
Port Townsend *(G-7892)*

Ixia Sports Inc ....G....... 425 417-6454
Issaquah *(G-4432)*

Jesternick Systems LLC ....G....... 509 338-4837
Pullman *(G-8095)*

Jig & Lure ....G....... 360 457-2745
Port Angeles *(G-7718)*

▲ Jumbo Dti Corporation ....F....... 253 272-9764
Fife *(G-3961)*

K&B Custom Rods & Tackle ....G....... 360 354-1945
Lynden *(G-6028)*

◆ K2 Sports LLC ....C....... 206 805-4800
Seattle *(G-10322)*

K2 Sports LLC ....G....... 206 805-4800
Seattle *(G-10323)*

Kadco Tackle Manufacturing ....G....... 253 857-5033
Port Orchard *(G-7822)*

Kadi Manufacturing ....G....... 360 668-5633
Snohomish *(G-11929)*

Karl Plato ....G....... 360 875-8289
South Bend *(G-12042)*

▲ Kc Technology Inc ....G....... 509 933-2312
Auburn *(G-483)*

▲ Lamiglas Inc ....E....... 360 225-9436
Woodland *(G-15444)*

◆ Lemond Fitness Inc ....F....... 425 615-0116
Woodinville *(G-15288)*

Level 10 Fitness Products LLC ....G....... 503 572-5530
Vancouver *(G-14372)*

LP Composites Inc ....F....... 509 493-4447
Bingen *(G-1639)*

Lucky Leaders ....G....... 206 363-2208
Seattle *(G-10447)*

Maax Hydro Swirl Mfg Co ....D....... 360 734-0616
Bellingham *(G-1417)*

▲ Macks Lures Manufacturing Co ....G....... 509 667-9202
Wenatchee *(G-15049)*

Macs Discus ....G....... 425 483-3729
Woodinville *(G-15298)*

Mako Reels Inc ....G....... 360 757-7328
Burlington *(G-2170)*

Makota Co ....G....... 206 226-1843
Edmonds *(G-3132)*

▲ Marco Global Inc ....E....... 206 298-4758
Seattle *(G-10474)*

◆ Marine Cnstr & Design Co ....E....... 206 285-3200
Seattle *(G-10478)*

Maritime Fabrications Inc ....E....... 360 466-3629
La Conner *(G-5524)*

▲ Maverick Sports Medicine Inc ....E....... 425 497-0887
Redmond *(G-8553)*

McKay Shrimp & Crab Gear Inc ....G....... 360 796-4555
Brinnon *(G-2025)*

▲ McNett Corporation ....E....... 360 671-2227
Bellingham *(G-1431)*

Mermaid Bay Enterprises LLC ....G....... 360 312-5522
Bellingham *(G-1433)*

Mervin Manufacturing Inc ....G....... 206 204-7800
Seattle *(G-10517)*

Moore Mfg Co ....G....... 360 677-2442
Skykomish *(G-11867)*

Motion Ducks LLC ....G....... 253 797-0132
Black Diamond *(G-1651)*

◆ Motion Water Sports Inc ....D....... 800 662-7436
Snoqualmie *(G-12020)*

▲ Mustad Longline Inc ....G....... 206 284-4376
Seattle *(G-10575)*

National Banner Supply ....G....... 253 333-7443
Auburn *(G-504)*

New Adventure ....G....... 360 961-4444
Bellingham *(G-1458)*

Nimbus Board Sports LLC ....G....... 360 387-1951
Camano Island *(G-2219)*

Noors Lures LLC ....G....... 360 896-4032
Vancouver *(G-14433)*

North Face 047 ....G....... 509 747-5389
Spokane *(G-12407)*

North Fork Composites LLC ....F....... 360 225-2211
Woodland *(G-15450)*

◆ North Sports Inc ....F....... 509 493-4938
White Salmon *(G-15124)*

▲ Northwest Hygienetics Inc ....G....... 253 529-0294
Auburn *(G-511)*

Northwest Sports Products ....G....... 253 576-5958
Tacoma *(G-13435)*

Noumena LLC ....G....... 206 451-3895
Federal Way *(G-3766)*

▲ Nwt3k Outerwear ....G....... 253 318-2371
Gig Harbor *(G-4137)*

▲ Omega Pacific Inc ....D....... 509 456-0170
Airway Heights *(G-58)*

ORyan Marine LLC ....F....... 425 485-2871
Redmond *(G-8604)*

Pacific Outdoor Products Inc ....F....... 425 432-6000
Maple Valley *(G-6287)*

Par 4 Golf Services ....G....... 360 376-4462
Eastsound *(G-3045)*

Pee Wee Pros Ltd Liability Co ....G....... 206 276-6707
Lynnwood *(G-6178)*

Perch and Play ....G....... 360 393-4925
Bellingham *(G-1496)*

Petrzelka Bros Inc ....G....... 360 424-8095
Mount Vernon *(G-6824)*

Phazr LLC ....G....... 509 329-8306
Spokane *(G-12440)*

▲ Pickle Ball Inc ....G....... 206 632-0119
Seattle *(G-10800)*

Play Impossible Corporation ....G....... 206 852-7015
Seattle *(G-10821)*

▲ Point Wilson Co Inc ....G....... 360 385-7625
Port Townsend *(G-7907)*

Pow Inc ....F....... 206 366-0224
Seattle *(G-10840)*

▲ PR Lifting LLC ....G....... 425 214-4124
Everett *(G-3581)*

◆ Precor Incorporated ....B....... 425 486-9292
Woodinville *(G-15339)*

▲ Prism Designs Inc ....G....... 206 838-8682
Seattle *(G-10865)*

Puget Sound Anglers Educ ....F....... 206 473-1613
Woodinville *(G-15344)*

R & R Rods ....G....... 360 423-7935
Longview *(G-5946)*

R3bar LLC ....G....... 647 296-6265
Redmond *(G-8642)*

Racer Mate Inc ....E....... 206 524-7392
Seattle *(G-10912)*

RDL Enterprises Inc ....F....... 509 529-5480
Walla Walla *(G-14859)*

Recluse LLC ....G....... 253 312-2169
Gig Harbor *(G-4153)*

Recreational Equipment Inc ....B....... 206 223-1944
Seattle *(G-10933)*

▲ Redbird Sports Inc ....F....... 206 725-7872
Seattle *(G-10939)*

Redmond Town Center ....F....... 425 702-9158
Redmond *(G-8646)*

Reeves Cricket Ranch Inc ....F....... 360 966-3300
Everson *(G-3687)*

Retco Inc ....G....... 360 341-1487
Clinton *(G-2695)*

Employee Codes: A=Over 500 employees, B=251-500
C=101-250, D=51-100, E=20-50, F=10-19, G=2-9

2019 Washington
Manufacturers Register

651

39 MISCELLANEOUS MANUFACTURING INDUSTRIES SIC SECTION

Revive A Back Inc....G....360 738-6085
Bellingham *(G-1516)*
Riverside Club....G....509 967-5756
Richland *(G-9039)*
Rj Sports Inc....G....425 227-8777
Renton *(G-8895)*
Roeracing Slalom Skateboards....G....206 371-9710
Seattle *(G-10975)*
Running 26 Inc....G....425 948-6495
Mill Creek *(G-6524)*
Sage Manufacturing Corporation....F....800 952-9827
Bainbridge Island *(G-670)*
Sage Manufacturing Corporation....G....206 842-6608
Bainbridge Island *(G-671)*
Sausage Skateboards....G....206 679-3619
Seattle *(G-11017)*
▲ Schwaldbe North America....G....360 384-6468
Ferndale *(G-3900)*
▲ Seasoft Scuba Inc....G....253 939-5510
Chehalis *(G-2536)*
Seattle Cascades....G....773 387-0502
Seattle *(G-11050)*
Seattle Sport Sciences Inc....F....425 939-0015
Redmond *(G-8659)*
▲ Seattle Sports Company....F....206 782-0773
Seattle *(G-11077)*
Shoreline Poleholders LLC....G....360 659-0826
Arlington *(G-328)*
▲ Silver Horde Fishing Supplies....G....425 778-2640
Lynnwood *(G-6196)*
Sitelines Pk & Playground Pdts....G....425 355-5655
Everett *(G-3612)*
Skate Like A Girl....G....206 973-8005
Seattle *(G-11125)*
◆ Slingshot Sports LLC....F....509 427-4950
North Bonneville *(G-7135)*
SMC Gear....G....360 366-5534
Ferndale *(G-3905)*
Sports-Fab Inc....G....503 408-0920
Vancouver *(G-14604)*
◆ Square One Distribution Inc....E....425 369-6850
Snoqualmie *(G-12031)*
Strike Addiction LLC....G....206 713-6061
Yakima *(G-15685)*
Sturtevants Tennis Shop....G....425 454-6465
Bellevue *(G-1163)*
▲ Sullivan Manufacturing Inc....G....509 545-8000
Pasco *(G-7635)*
Summit Rescue Inc....E....360 366-0221
Ferndale *(G-3908)*
Suzabelle....G....206 790-5163
Seattle *(G-11234)*
Swish....G....425 644-3545
Bellevue *(G-1173)*
Tagline Products LLC....G....360 927-2719
Bellingham *(G-1566)*
Teammates Sports Products LLC....G....206 780-2037
Bainbridge Island *(G-676)*
Teamwest Ltd....G....425 227-8525
Newcastle *(G-7041)*
Tight Group Targets LLC....G....206 227-0201
Renton *(G-8928)*
Todd M Bearden....G....509 624-2875
Spokane *(G-12561)*
Totalwave Fitness LLC....G....509 361-9089
Moses Lake *(G-6754)*
Tweet Promotional Impressions....G....206 660-6074
Auburn *(G-585)*
United Volleyball Supply LLC....F....425 576-8835
Redmond *(G-8698)*
◆ Vectra Fitness Inc....C....425 291-9550
Issaquah *(G-4486)*
Vicis Inc....E....206 456-6680
Seattle *(G-11414)*
Vision Leadership Inc....G....206 418-0808
Seattle *(G-11423)*
Washington Wind Sports Inc....G....360 676-1146
Bellingham *(G-1589)*
West Coast Athletic LLC....G....425 413-9200
Maple Valley *(G-6299)*
Westco Engineering....G....425 481-7271
Woodinville *(G-15403)*
What S Next....G....425 235-1696
Renton *(G-8946)*
Wicked Lures LLC....G....360 460-6078
Sequim *(G-11670)*
World Knives Ltd....G....866 862-5233
Olympia *(G-7431)*
Yakima Bait Co....C....509 854-1311
Granger *(G-4264)*
Zooka....G....425 363-3922
North Bend *(G-7132)*
Zooka Sports Corporation....G....425 861-0111
Redmond *(G-8723)*

3951 Pens & Mechanical Pencils

Djs Pens....G....360 565-0145
Port Angeles *(G-7697)*

3952 Lead Pencils, Crayons & Artist's Mtrls

Alb Framing Gallery & Gift....G....425 432-5505
Maple Valley *(G-6255)*
Biscomb Fleudeliza S (artist)....G....206 842-6417
Bainbridge Island *(G-618)*
Chabre Bros....G....509 629-0342
Walla Walla *(G-14782)*
Color ME House Inc....G....360 742-8646
Olympia *(G-7252)*
Cubby B & Friends....G....253 537-6266
Tacoma *(G-13250)*
Geo Lastomirsky Ceramic A....G....206 782-4695
Seattle *(G-10062)*
Ginny Hardings Equine Classics....G....509 582-7924
Kennewick *(G-4667)*
Grey Gull Ceramics....G....360 321-1582
Langley *(G-5779)*
Kilian & Kilian Artists....G....360 654-1799
Stanwood *(G-12977)*
▲ Milestone Products Co....F....425 882-1987
Redmond *(G-8589)*
▲ Museum Quality Discount Frmng....F....206 624-1057
Seattle *(G-10574)*
PBS Supply Co Inc....F....253 395-5550
Kent *(G-5063)*
Robinsons Inc....G....360 834-0929
Camas *(G-2279)*

3953 Marking Devices

Ace Stamp & Engraving....G....253 582-3322
Lakewood *(G-5695)*
Budget Printing Center....G....509 736-7511
Kennewick *(G-4636)*
Dimensional Products Inc....F....206 352-9065
Seattle *(G-9831)*
Grays Harbor Stamp Works....G....360 533-3830
Aberdeen *(G-14)*
Great Impressions Rbr Stamps....F....360 807-8462
Centralia *(G-2404)*
Jackyes Enterprises Inc....G....425 355-5997
Everett *(G-3521)*
▲ Martronics Corporation....E....360 985-2999
Salkum *(G-9180)*
Northwest Business Stamp Inc....G....509 483-0308
Spokane *(G-12412)*
Peterson Manufacturing Co....F....360 425-4170
Longview *(G-5943)*
Print Plus Inc....G....509 735-6303
Kennewick *(G-4708)*
Rumpeltes Enterprises Inc....E....509 624-1391
Spokane *(G-12485)*
S M Marketing Specialties....G....206 230-0710
Renton *(G-8900)*
Sabine F Price....G....206 780-9211
Bainbridge Island *(G-669)*
Sno King Stamp....G....425 771-9373
Lynnwood *(G-6202)*
Stampadoodle Inc....G....360 647-9663
Bellingham *(G-1555)*
Superior Rubber Die Co Inc....G....206 763-2440
Seattle *(G-11224)*
Swivler Inc....E....360 225-7774
Woodland *(G-15468)*
Symbol Servers....G....360 819-5132
Olympia *(G-7404)*
Tacoma Rubber Stamp Co....F....206 728-8888
Seattle *(G-11255)*
Tacoma Rubber Stamp Co....E....253 383-5433
Tacoma *(G-13548)*

3955 Carbon Paper & Inked Ribbons

Aplus Inkworks....G....206 910-9082
Bothell *(G-1747)*
Blender LLC....G....509 210-3373
Spokane *(G-12154)*
Lazer Cartridges Plus LLC....G....509 529-0200
Walla Walla *(G-14835)*
▲ Olympic Printer Resources Inc....F....360 297-8384
Kingston *(G-5259)*
Rgd Enterprises Inc....G....360 923-9582
Olympia *(G-7385)*

3961 Costume Jewelry & Novelties

Baubles....G....360 647-3857
Bellingham *(G-1260)*
Build-A-Bracelet....G....919 757-1219
Covington *(G-2821)*
▲ Creative Collections Co Inc....E....360 866-8840
Olympia *(G-7259)*
Daughters of Mary....G....360 943-2186
Olympia *(G-7264)*
▲ Deborah Funches Jewelry Design....G....503 381-4017
Camas *(G-2244)*
Degroot Designs....G....253 472-7279
Tacoma *(G-13256)*
Fallen Hero Bracelets....G....253 537-1212
Tacoma *(G-13288)*
Flatter Heights....G....509 238-6192
Chattaroy *(G-2446)*
Flytes of Fancy....G....206 306-9233
Shoreline *(G-11772)*
Gold Impressions....G....509 886-0866
East Wenatchee *(G-3015)*
Infinite Caste....G....206 335-4058
Renton *(G-8825)*
Jane Martin....G....206 842-4569
Bainbridge Island *(G-644)*
Kjs Handcrafted Jewelry....G....425 582-8488
Brier *(G-2020)*
▲ Mike Frantz Inc....G....800 839-6712
Shelton *(G-11713)*
Millianna LLC....G....415 505-8507
Spokane *(G-12394)*
Minnysonoda Corporation....F....360 863-8141
Monroe *(G-6597)*
Nexappeal....G....360 293-5054
Anacortes *(G-151)*
Nora Haugan....G....360 877-0602
Lilliwaup *(G-5872)*
Northwest Family Strands....F....206 779-8997
Seattle *(G-10643)*
Plateau Jewelers Inc....G....425 313-0657
Sammamish *(G-9242)*
Seattle Gold Grills....G....206 250-0833
Seattle *(G-11060)*
Stones By Marie Inc....G....206 643-1520
Renton *(G-8920)*
The McCredy Company....G....509 773-5340
Goldendale *(G-4209)*
Turtleworks....G....425 335-0394
Everett *(G-3638)*
▼ Yue Fon USA Inc....G....206 303-0148
Auburn *(G-603)*
Yvette J Cooke....G....360 718-0306
Vancouver *(G-14707)*

3965 Fasteners, Buttons, Needles & Pins

A & P Fasteners Inc....G....425 486-9562
Kenmore *(G-4563)*
Allspec Fasteners Inc....G....512 263-2593
Everett *(G-3368)*
Bge Ltd....F....206 789-2128
Seattle *(G-9519)*
Buttonsmith Inc....G....800 789-4364
Carnation *(G-2290)*
Centrix Inc....D....253 872-4773
Kent *(G-4847)*
Fastener Training....G....562 400-3009
Olympia *(G-7282)*
Icg Corp....G....425 315-0200
Mukilteo *(G-6939)*
Leads Manufacturing Company....G....541 259-1128
Vancouver *(G-14367)*
Northwest Lcknut Specialty Inc....G....253 604-4860
Puyallup *(G-8206)*
Ralston Cunningham Associates....G....425 455-0316
Redmond *(G-8645)*
YKK (usa) Inc....G....425 277-2503
Renton *(G-8952)*

3991 Brooms & Brushes

3tac Distribution Inc....G....206 257-1552
Tukwila *(G-13685)*
▲ Cascade Brush Company....G....509 965-6603
Yakima *(G-15529)*
Sherwin-Williams Company....G....425 643-8584
Bellevue *(G-1129)*
Tennant Co....G....425 788-9711
Woodinville *(G-15387)*

3993 Signs & Advertising Displays

A-1 Illuminated Sign Company F 509 534-6134
Spokane Valley *(G-12596)*

A-1 Pro Sign G 425 765-8836
Renton *(G-8724)*

Abracadabra Printing Inc G 206 343-9087
Seattle *(G-9334)*

Accent Signs & Engraving Inc G 509 946-8998
Richland *(G-8964)*

Accent Signs Inc G 509 967-7446
Richland *(G-8965)*

Acclaim Sign & Display Partner G 206 706-3900
Seattle *(G-9336)*

Ad One Corp G 253 942-3688
Federal Way *(G-3712)*

Ad Sign Design G 425 259-3000
Everett *(G-3359)*

Ada Signage and Spc Inc G 253 651-1748
Eatonville *(G-3049)*

Adhesa-Plate Manufacturing Co E 206 682-0141
Seattle *(G-9351)*

Advance Sign Design Inc G 206 789-6051
Seattle *(G-9354)*

Advanced Electric Signs Inc G 360 225-6826
Woodland *(G-15416)*

Advanced Metal Creations G 509 662-0335
Wenatchee *(G-15008)*

Advanced Signs LLC G 253 987-5909
Auburn *(G-363)*

Advertising Signs & More G 360 452-7785
Port Angeles *(G-7678)*

Alderwood Signs G 425 744-6555
Lynnwood *(G-6070)*

▲ Allpak Container LLC D 425 227-0400
Renton *(G-8739)*

American Architectural Signage G 509 624-5842
Spokane *(G-12108)*

American Image Displays F 425 556-9511
Port Orchard *(G-7786)*

American Laser Works G 360 871-3738
Port Orchard *(G-7787)*

American Neon Inc F 253 627-7446
Gig Harbor *(G-4071)*

American Sign & Indicator G 509 926-6979
Spokane Valley *(G-12615)*

Amigo Arts LLC G 425 443-5744
Monroe *(G-6549)*

Apco Northwest F 800 815-8028
Tukwila *(G-13691)*

Arrows Sign Servicing LLC G 206 412-4922
Federal Way *(G-3716)*

Artco Sign Co Inc G 206 622-5262
Seattle *(G-9439)*

ASAP Sign & Design G 360 757-1570
Mount Vernon *(G-6771)*

Asi Signage Innovations G 360 668-1636
Snohomish *(G-11876)*

Baby Signs By Laurie Hals G 425 557-6537
Sammamish *(G-9187)*

Bal & Bal 200803466 Inc G 425 481-4900
Everett *(G-3382)*

Balcony Signs & Laminating G 425 454-5500
Bellevue *(G-805)*

Barking Dog Inc G 425 822-6542
Kirkland *(G-5288)*

Bc Signs Inc G 360 835-3570
Camas *(G-2231)*

Bear Signs G 509 888-4477
Wenatchee *(G-15012)*

Bellandi Signs Inc G 253 841-1144
Puyallup *(G-8129)*

Bellevue Instant Sign G 425 451-8218
Redmond *(G-8401)*

Berry Neon Co Inc E 425 776-8835
Everett *(G-3385)*

Birklor LLC G 206 368-7331
Seattle *(G-9532)*

Biz Design & Sign G 253 472-3070
Tacoma *(G-13202)*

▲ Blanc Industries Inc E 360 736-8988
Centralia *(G-2385)*

Blazing Banners G 360 756-9990
Bellingham *(G-1275)*

Blue Water Projects Inc F 206 452-1332
Seattle *(G-9554)*

Bolander Sign Co G 360 943-2447
Olympia *(G-7239)*

Bondarchuk Andrey G 509 290-2525
Spokane Valley *(G-12644)*

Brighten Sign G 360 608-5863
Vancouver *(G-14085)*

Brown & Balsley Sign Co G 360 705-3099
Olympia *(G-7243)*

Budget Signs Inc G 253 473-1760
Fircrest *(G-4000)*

Bullene Sign G 425 260-3311
Seattle *(G-9598)*

Cascade Sign G 509 945-1578
Yakima *(G-15531)*

CBS Outdoor G 509 892-4720
Spokane Valley *(G-12652)*

CDI Custom Design Inc E 360 650-1150
Bellingham *(G-1294)*

Central Wash Media Group LLC G 509 667-8112
Wenatchee *(G-15018)*

Central Washington Sign Co G 509 765-1818
Moses Lake *(G-6691)*

Christine Woodcock G 509 773-4747
Goldendale *(G-4194)*

City Lites Neon Inc G 206 789-4747
Seattle *(G-9687)*

Classic Sign and Graphics G 253 862-8035
Buckley *(G-2051)*

Classic Vinyl LLC G 509 656-3011
Cle Elum *(G-2661)*

Clearway Signs G 253 324-1706
Tacoma *(G-13236)*

Cogent Holdings-1 LLC G 425 776-8835
Everett *(G-3422)*

Cogent Holdings-1 LLC E 425 776-8835
Tacoma *(G-13237)*

Color Grphics Scrnprinting Inc F 360 352-3970
Tumwater *(G-13862)*

Columbia Basin Sign and Ltg G 509 764-8121
Moses Lake *(G-6697)*

Columbia Sign G 360 696-1919
Brush Prairie *(G-2032)*

Columbia Sign Inc G 360 696-1919
Vancouver *(G-14138)*

Colville Sign Co G 509 685-2185
Colville *(G-2746)*

Commercial Displayers G 206 622-8039
Everett *(G-3424)*

▲ Commercial Plastics Corp F 206 682-4832
Seattle *(G-9717)*

Copy Cat Graphics G 360 452-3635
Port Angeles *(G-7695)*

Corwin Scott Thomas Imag G 253 350-6984
Edgewood *(G-3074)*

Cottage Sign Co G 360 312-1565
Ferndale *(G-3834)*

Countryman Signs Screen Prtrs G 425 355-1037
Everett *(G-3428)*

Creating Memories Together G 360 944-8393
Vancouver *(G-14153)*

Creative ADS G 360 981-1106
Silverdale *(G-11829)*

Creative Enterprises Inc G 425 775-7010
Edmonds *(G-3105)*

Creative Imagery G 360 871-6529
Port Orchard *(G-7801)*

▲ Creo Industrial Arts LLC D 425 775-7444
Woodinville *(G-15216)*

Crossroads Sign & Graphic G 425 481-9411
Lynnwood *(G-6101)*

Custom Win Tnting Graphics Inc G 509 453-4293
Yakima *(G-15547)*

▲ D A Graphics Inc G 206 760-5886
Seattle *(G-9777)*

Dancing Clouds LLC G 360 289-0790
Ocean Shores *(G-7185)*

Davis Sign Company Inc G 206 287-9800
Seattle *(G-9802)*

Decal Factory G 509 465-8931
Spokane *(G-12222)*

Dek Enterprises Inc G 360 794-8614
Monroe *(G-6564)*

Department Crrctons Wash State B 509 526-6375
Walla Walla *(G-14795)*

Design Centre G 509 534-6461
Spokane *(G-12225)*

Dick and Janes Spot G 509 925-3224
Ellensburg *(G-3193)*

Dynamic Specialties G 509 447-2755
Newport *(G-7057)*

Eagle Scoreboard Systems G 509 751-7228
Clarkston *(G-2634)*

Eagle Signs LLC G 509 453-8159
Yakima *(G-15561)*

Eagle Signs LLC F 509 453-5511
Yakima *(G-15562)*

Eagles Nest Holding Inc G 206 368-7331
Seattle *(G-9869)*

Eastside Signs G 425 888-6764
Snoqualmie *(G-12011)*

Econo Quality Signs Inc G 253 531-3943
Tacoma *(G-13270)*

Econo Sign of America G 360 739-8480
Bellingham *(G-1329)*

Eden Sign G 360 377-3040
Bremerton *(G-1951)*

Effective Design Studio LLC G 206 328-8989
Seattle *(G-9887)*

Electric Avenue Sign Co G 360 903-5447
Vancouver *(G-14197)*

Elevation Exhibits LLC E 774 696-2549
Redmond *(G-8448)*

Esco Pacific Signs Inc G 360 748-6461
Chehalis *(G-2493)*

Expressions Signs Inc G 425 844-6415
Monroe *(G-6571)*

Fast Sign Man LLC G 360 592-4599
Deming *(G-2919)*

Fast Signs G 253 942-9444
Federal Way *(G-3736)*

Fastsigns G 206 682-2129
Seattle *(G-9977)*

Fastsigns G 425 746-4151
Bellevue *(G-908)*

Fastsigns G 360 567-3313
Vancouver *(G-14224)*

Fastsigns G 206 886-3860
Seattle *(G-9978)*

Fastsigns G 360 692-1660
Silverdale *(G-11834)*

Fastsigns G 206 575-2110
Kent *(G-4904)*

Fastsigns 632 G 206 577-4077
Burien *(G-2107)*

Fastsigns International Inc G 253 835-9450
Federal Way *(G-3737)*

Fastsigns of Auburn G 360 480-1097
Kent *(G-4905)*

Federal Way Sign G 253 529-2011
Federal Way *(G-3739)*

Felts Signs G 360 299-0430
Anacortes *(G-129)*

Flip Signs G 509 965-2822
Yakima *(G-15572)*

Flying Arts Ranch Inc G 509 659-1819
Ritzville *(G-9121)*

Foley Sign Company Inc F 206 324-3040
Seattle *(G-10011)*

Footprint Promotions Inc G 425 408-0966
Woodinville *(G-15245)*

Fox Architectural Signs Inc G 503 512-8757
Woodland *(G-15433)*

Garrett Sign Co Inc F 360 693-9081
Vancouver *(G-14247)*

Gerrard Inc G 253 804-8001
Auburn *(G-449)*

Global Professional Svcs LLC G 808 682-0404
University Place *(G-13970)*

Goodmar Group LLC G 206 622-8204
Seattle *(G-10101)*

▲ Gotagscom LLC G 509 754-2760
Ephrata *(G-3335)*

Grand D Signs G 253 929-9963
Federal Way *(G-3742)*

Graphic Art Productions Inc G 509 536-3278
Spokane Valley *(G-12723)*

Graybeal Signs F 509 662-6926
Wenatchee *(G-15036)*

Great Graphics & Signs Inc F 206 948-9480
Orondo *(G-7457)*

Greensleeves LLC G 360 606-1934
Vancouver *(G-14273)*

Hafa Adai Signs & Graphics LLC G 253 394-0600
Auburn *(G-458)*

HI Tech Signs & Banners G 360 736-6322
Centralia *(G-2407)*

Holm Bing F 509 454-2277
Yakima *(G-15581)*

Home Design Expo G 425 864-6313
Redmond *(G-8495)*

I Concept Signs LLC G 206 658-1158
Seattle *(G-10199)*

I-5 Design Build Inc D 360 459-3200
Lacey *(G-5558)*

Employee Codes: A=Over 500 employees, B=251-500
C=101-250, D=51-100, E=20-50, F=10-19, G=2-9

2019 Washington
Manufacturers Register

653

Image Signs and Design LLC ....G....... 360 533-0133
Hoquiam *(G-4344)*
Imagesmart Sign Company LLC...........G....... 509 525-4343
Walla Walla *(G-14821)*
Imagicorps Inc...E....... 425 869-0599
Redmond *(G-8506)*
In The Zone Promotions.........................G....... 425 246-6313
Issaquah *(G-4428)*
Incentives By Design Inc.......................G....... 206 623-4310
Seattle *(G-10220)*
Indigo Vinylworks LLC............................G....... 425 463-7460
Renton *(G-8823)*
Indigo Vinylworks Llc..............................G....... 425 278-4411
Seattle *(G-10227)*
Industry Sign & Graphics Inc................F....... 253 854-2333
Auburn *(G-476)*
Infinity Sign & Marketing Inc.................G....... 253 539-6771
Lakewood *(G-5728)*
Insignia Sign Inc.......................................F....... 425 917-2109
Renton *(G-8827)*
Instant Sign Factory................................G....... 509 456-3333
Spokane *(G-12317)*
International Trade & Trvl Ltd..............G....... 509 981-2307
Spokane *(G-12324)*
Interntonal Graphics Nameplate...........F....... 360 699-4808
Vancouver *(G-14323)*
Island Dog Sign Company......................F....... 206 381-0661
Duvall *(G-2991)*
Issaquah Signs Inc...................................G....... 425 391-3010
Issaquah *(G-4431)*
J Freitag Enterprises Inc........................G....... 509 453-4461
Yakima *(G-15595)*
▲ **J N W Inc**..E....... 509 489-9191
Spokane *(G-12327)*
Jackson Signs & Graphics......................G....... 360 457-3703
Port Angeles *(G-7716)*
Jakes Electrical Sign Service...............G....... 509 901-1012
Selah *(G-11592)*
James I Manning.......................................G....... 425 774-4275
Edmonds *(G-3122)*
Jamison Signs Inc.....................................G....... 509 226-2000
Newman Lake *(G-7048)*
Jim Manning...G....... 425 774-1964
Edmonds *(G-3124)*
JJ&d Signs Inc...G....... 206 623-3100
Seattle *(G-10298)*
Johnson Signs of Federal Way..............G....... 253 678-4304
Tacoma *(G-13366)*
Jolly Family Corp.......................................G....... 425 438-9350
Everett *(G-3525)*
◆ **Jrotc Dog Tags Inc**................................G....... 509 292-0410
Elk *(G-3170)*
K L Cook Inc..G....... 360 423-0195
Longview *(G-5921)*
King Graphics..G....... 360 423-9781
Kelso *(G-4534)*
Kitsap Business Services Inc.................G....... 360 297-2173
Kingston *(G-5257)*
Kjj Enterprises Inc.....................................G....... 253 474-6607
Tacoma *(G-13377)*
Kolorkraze...G....... 360 609-2771
Vancouver *(G-14351)*
Kts Media Inc..G....... 253 845-0771
Puyallup *(G-8173)*
Landd Ventures Inc...................................G....... 425 775-9709
Lynnwood *(G-6156)*
Larsen Sign Company...............................G....... 253 581-4313
Lakewood *(G-5736)*
▼ **Leader Manufacturing Inc**...................E....... 360 895-1184
Port Orchard *(G-7825)*
Lee Signs...G....... 360 750-0689
Vancouver *(G-14370)*
Lennox Ergonomics & Co........................G....... 253 268-0830
Gig Harbor *(G-4130)*
Lettering Arts..G....... 206 310-6599
Bellevue *(G-982)*
Liberty Sign Shoppe LLC........................G....... 425 482-2811
Woodinville *(G-15289)*
Lid Signs LLC..G....... 206 290-7536
Seattle *(G-10414)*
Lifesigns Plus..G....... 425 330-3710
Lake Stevens *(G-5656)*
Linden Vic B & Sons Sign Advg............G....... 509 624-0663
Spokane *(G-12368)*
LLC Putnam Brothers...............................G....... 509 679-4981
Quincy *(G-8302)*
Loewen Group LLC....................................G....... 425 775-9709
Lynnwood *(G-6159)*
Lonnies Sign Service................................G....... 509 543-7446
Pasco *(G-7601)*
Loomis Plastics Corporation..................E....... 206 292-0111
Seattle *(G-10439)*
Lumin Art Signs Inc..................................G....... 253 833-2800
Tacoma *(G-13392)*
Magic Mountains Services Inc..............G....... 360 830-0634
Seabeck *(G-9268)*
Magnificent Signs Inc..............................G....... 509 468-2794
Spokane *(G-12378)*
Magnolia Signs...G....... 253 592-5121
Tacoma *(G-13395)*
Mail It Sign It LLC......................................G....... 360 515-5198
Tumwater *(G-13886)*
Maple Valley Signs Inc.............................G....... 425 413-1430
Maple Valley *(G-6282)*
Mark Grid Signs Inc...................................G....... 509 323-0328
Spokane *(G-12381)*
Mark Lasting Technology..........................G....... 425 836-4317
Redmond *(G-8550)*
Martin Signs & Fabrication.....................G....... 206 768-5183
Seattle *(G-10494)*
Medford Technologies Inc.......................G....... 206 963-0589
Tukwila *(G-13769)*
Media Incorporated..................................G....... 425 251-5145
Renton *(G-8851)*
Merrill Corporation...................................C....... 360 794-3157
Monroe *(G-6596)*
Messenger Corporation...........................E....... 206 623-4525
Seattle *(G-10518)*
Meyer Sign & Advertising Co..................F....... 360 424-1325
Mount Vernon *(G-6813)*
Michael L White..G....... 509 526-6923
Walla Walla *(G-14843)*
Mike Lavalle Inc..G....... 360 563-0501
Snohomish *(G-11947)*
Misapplied Sciences Inc..........................G....... 425 999-9582
Redmond *(G-8591)*
Mixign Inc..G....... 206 542-8737
Arlington *(G-281)*
Morup Signs Inc..G....... 425 883-6337
Bellevue *(G-1015)*
Mountain Dog Sign Company Inc...........G....... 509 891-9999
Spokane Valley *(G-12794)*
Mustang Signs LLC....................................F....... 509 735-4607
Kennewick *(G-4698)*
National Sign Corporation......................E....... 206 282-0700
Seattle *(G-10590)*
National Sign Systems Ltd.......................G....... 360 699-3055
Vancouver *(G-14427)*
Neon Connection..G....... 360 224-3061
Sumner *(G-13088)*
Neon Electric Sign Co...............................G....... 206 405-4001
Issaquah *(G-4453)*
Neon Moon Longhorned Cattle...............G....... 360 293-2721
Anacortes *(G-150)*
Neon Systems Inc.......................................G....... 425 501-6447
Lynnwood *(G-6168)*
Noble Neon..G....... 206 708-6290
Seattle *(G-10616)*
North West Barricades & Signs..............E....... 206 243-8004
Seattle *(G-10629)*
Nwsignwerxs...G....... 253 217-0053
Auburn *(G-515)*
Olympic Print and Apparel.......................G....... 206 402-3642
Seattle *(G-10693)*
Olysigns..G....... 360 417-5254
Port Angeles *(G-7730)*
OMega Graphics and Signs LLC..............G....... 206 789-5480
Seattle *(G-10697)*
OReilly Signs..G....... 206 623-5135
Seattle *(G-10713)*
Pad Printing Services Inc.........................G....... 206 362-4544
Seattle *(G-10744)*
Patrick E & Patricia M Lydon...................G....... 425 226-3216
Renton *(G-8876)*
Patriot Towing Recovery..........................G....... 360 890-9288
Lacey *(G-5575)*
Patriot Wood LLC..G....... 360 393-7082
Ferndale *(G-3883)*
PDQ Signs..G....... 253 531-8010
Puyallup *(G-8220)*
Peekay Inc..F....... 818 754-1201
Auburn *(G-529)*
Pens By Bill..G....... 509 628-3288
Kennewick *(G-4706)*
Perfect Printing & Signs............................G....... 509 786-3811
Yakima *(G-15645)*
Petroglyph Printing & Signs....................G....... 509 447-2590
Newport *(G-7064)*
Phoenix Sign Company..............................G....... 360 532-1111
Montesano *(G-6653)*
Phoenix Sign Company..............................F....... 360 612-3267
Aberdeen *(G-29)*
Pixelan Works..G....... 425 379-0339
Everett *(G-3574)*
Plumb Signs Inc..E....... 253 474-6702
Tacoma *(G-13466)*
Premium Sign Inc..G....... 253 267-0547
Lakewood *(G-5748)*
Prism Graphics Inc.......................................G....... 206 282-1801
Seattle *(G-10866)*
Quality Sign Service Inc..............................F....... 509 586-0585
Kennewick *(G-4712)*
Quick Signs and Designs............................G....... 253 929-4488
Kent *(G-5095)*
R & R Graphics Inc.......................................G....... 206 406-3604
Renton *(G-8889)*
R E B Magnetics..G....... 360 636-4693
Kelso *(G-4545)*
R P Signs Screenprinting............................G....... 425 788-6717
Duvall *(G-3000)*
▲ **Rainier Industries Ltd**..............................C....... 425 251-1800
Tukwila *(G-13801)*
Rainmaker Signs Inc.....................................G....... 425 861-7446
Bellevue *(G-1091)*
Ramlyn Engraving & Sign Co.....................G....... 206 439-8555
Burien *(G-2124)*
Ramsay Signs Inc..G....... 206 623-3100
Seattle *(G-10919)*
Rdean Enterprises Inc..................................F....... 208 772-8571
Spokane *(G-12468)*
Realty Sign Guys...G....... 360 909-1540
Vancouver *(G-14536)*
Realty Solutions Inc......................................F....... 206 839-1023
Seattle *(G-10932)*
Reid Signs Inc..G....... 206 547-5487
Seattle *(G-10945)*
Reyna Moore Advertising............................G....... 503 230-9440
Vancouver *(G-14550)*
Rnd Sign and Design LLC............................G....... 206 255-1963
Federal Way *(G-3778)*
Ross Metier LLC..G....... 253 208-8777
Graham *(G-4237)*
Roy Pablo..G....... 425 750-9941
Quil Ceda Village *(G-8281)*
Russell Sign Company..................................G....... 425 775-7010
Edmonds *(G-3150)*
Sandis Signs Inc..G....... 253 862-6885
Bonney Lake *(G-1737)*
Sandys Sign & Design...................................G....... 360 693-9229
Vancouver *(G-14569)*
Satellite Sign Design....................................G....... 360 986-0067
Montesano *(G-6657)*
Schurmans Gas & Glass...............................G....... 360 573-3669
Ridgefield *(G-9110)*
Screen Print Northwest Inc.........................G....... 360 577-1534
Longview *(G-5951)*
Screen Tek Inc..E....... 509 928-8322
Liberty Lake *(G-5860)*
Seaton Concepts Inc.....................................G....... 509 928-0633
Spokane Valley *(G-12862)*
Seatons Grove Greenhouse.........................G....... 509 633-0404
Coulee Dam *(G-2808)*
Seattle Engraving LLC..................................G....... 425 212-9797
Everett *(G-3609)*
Seattle Wood Signs..G....... 425 422-3750
Seattle *(G-11084)*
Servine Sign Services LLC..........................G....... 509 225-7733
Yakima *(G-15672)*
Shine On Signs & Graphics Inc...................G....... 253 243-7777
Renton *(G-8910)*
Sign A Rama..G....... 360 915-9207
Lacey *(G-5587)*
Sign Associates Inc.......................................G....... 425 885-6100
Redmond *(G-8664)*
Sign Biz..G....... 360 750-9175
Vancouver *(G-14586)*
Sign By Tommorrow Kent............................G....... 253 872-7844
Kent *(G-5131)*
Sign City Gfx...G....... 253 329-2670
Auburn *(G-563)*
Sign Company...G....... 253 630-6313
Covington *(G-2838)*
Sign Corporation..F....... 509 535-2913
Spokane *(G-12503)*
Sign Crafters Inc...G....... 509 783-8718
Kennewick *(G-4727)*
Sign Department Inc......................................G....... 360 708-3823
Mount Vernon *(G-6836)*
Sign Distributors..G....... 253 847-2747
Spanaway *(G-12073)*

SIC SECTION

39 MISCELLANEOUS MANUFACTURING INDUSTRIES

Sign Guys Inc .... G 253 942-3688
  Federal Way *(G-3784)*
Sign Junkies .... G 360 273-7553
  Olympia *(G-7393)*
Sign Language Interpreter & En ... G 509 860-2727
  Wenatchee *(G-15074)*
Sign Makers Inc .... G 425 828-0688
  Kirkland *(G-5460)*
Sign Man .... G 509 535-8181
  Spokane Valley *(G-12872)*
Sign ME Up Inc .... G 360 271-8070
  Port Ludlow *(G-7776)*
Sign of Times .... G 360 891-9477
  Vancouver *(G-14587)*
Sign Post Inc .... F 360 671-1343
  Bellingham *(G-1533)*
Sign Prints Inc .... G 253 854-7841
  Kent *(G-5132)*
Sign Pro Inc .... G 360 736-6322
  Centralia *(G-2434)*
Sign Pros Inc .... F 425 885-3204
  Redmond *(G-8665)*
Sign Rite .... G 253 447-8997
  Sumner *(G-13099)*
Sign Shop LLC .... G 360 352-5926
  Tumwater *(G-13897)*
Sign Up Sign Co Inc .... G 425 488-9247
  Bothell *(G-1792)*
Sign Wizard .... G 206 285-9535
  Seattle *(G-11106)*
Sign Works .... G 509 248-8235
  Yakima *(G-15675)*
Sign-A-Rama .... G 253 474-1991
  Tacoma *(G-13513)*
Sign-O-Lite .... G 360 746-8651
  Blaine *(G-1703)*
Sign-Tech Elc Ltd Lblty Co .... E 253 922-2146
  Fife *(G-3993)*
Signage .... G 206 903-6446
  Seattle *(G-11107)*
Signdezign LLC .... G 360 709-0505
  Olympia *(G-7394)*
Signfactory .... G 360 833-1515
  Camas *(G-2282)*
Signorama .... G 425 861-9341
  Redmond *(G-8667)*
Signs & Designs .... G 509 493-8350
  White Salmon *(G-15132)*
Signs 2c .... G 206 335-9519
  Seattle *(G-11109)*
Signs By Tomorrow .... G 360 676-7117
  Bellingham *(G-1534)*
Signs For Success .... G 509 489-4200
  Spokane *(G-12504)*
Signs Now In Process Inc .... G 509 928-3467
  Spokane Valley *(G-12873)*
Signs Now of Moses Lake Inc ...... G 509 765-8955
  Moses Lake *(G-6750)*
Signs of Grace .... G 509 488-5081
  Othello *(G-7505)*
Signs of Seattle Inc .... G 206 292-7446
  Seattle *(G-11110)*
Signs Plus Inc .... F 360 671-7165
  Bellingham *(G-1535)*
Signsmart USA .... G 360 578-2476
  Kelso *(G-4548)*
Signsouth .... G 509 448-4404
  Spokane *(G-12505)*
Signworks LLC .... G 206 715-1570
  Bellevue *(G-1131)*
Sjb Enterprises Inc .... G 509 926-6979
  Spokane Valley *(G-12874)*
Skagit City Signs Inc .... G 360 848-8888
  Mount Vernon *(G-6838)*
Skagit Valley Signs .... G 360 755-0356
  Acme *(G-45)*
Sky Signs Inc .... G 425 417-9063
  Renton *(G-8913)*
Slam Signs .... G 253 927-2616
  Federal Way *(G-3785)*
Sno-King Signs .... G 425 775-0594
  Edmonds *(G-3158)*
Socal Lighting & Sign LLC .... G 425 345-5596
  Sultan *(G-13037)*
Spanton Business Forms .... G 509 966-7384
  Yakima *(G-15681)*
Special T Signs & Graphics .... F 360 734-7617
  Bellingham *(G-1549)*
Spectrum Sign Co Inc .... F 253 939-5500
  Auburn *(G-570)*

Speedy Signs .... G 425 771-1700
  Lynnwood *(G-6204)*
Spiller Corporation .... G 206 575-2110
  Kent *(G-5150)*
Spring Creek Enterprises .... G 360 876-8884
  Port Orchard *(G-7852)*
Steve Boek Mfg .... G 503 257-5056
  Sultan *(G-13039)*
Steve Ken Bosman .... G 360 398-7444
  Bellingham *(G-1558)*
Sticker Shock Signs Inc .... G 509 535-0070
  Spokane *(G-12530)*
Stong Enterprises LLC .... G 360 326-4752
  Vancouver *(G-14613)*
Sudden Printing Inc .... E 206 243-4444
  Seattle *(G-11211)*
Supergraphics LLC .... E 206 284-2201
  Seattle *(G-11221)*
Tacoma Rubber Stamp Co .... E 253 383-5433
  Tacoma *(G-13548)*
◆ Tacoma Tent & Awning Co Inc ... E 253 627-4128
  Tacoma *(G-13549)*
Terry Signs .... G 509 662-6672
  Wenatchee *(G-15081)*
Teslavision .... G 425 822-6535
  Kirkland *(G-5479)*
TNT Signs & Design Inc .... G 360 384-3190
  Ferndale *(G-3914)*
TNT Signs Inc .... G 360 438-3800
  Lacey *(G-5595)*
Todd Porter Campbell .... G 253 230-2391
  Buckley *(G-2077)*
Top Notch Manufacturing Co .... G 360 577-9150
  Longview *(G-5960)*
Total Sign Service .... G 253 847-6868
  Eatonville *(G-3070)*
Trade-Marx Sign & Display Corp ... E 206 623-7676
  Seattle *(G-11325)*
Traffic Signs Inc .... G 425 333-6222
  Carnation *(G-2301)*
Tube Art Displays Inc .... G 509 469-8186
  Yakima *(G-15697)*
Tube Art Displays Inc .... E 206 223-1122
  Bellevue *(G-1204)*
United Visual Comms Grp LLC ..... G 206 228-5144
  Seattle *(G-11375)*
Universal Sign and Graphics .... G 253 630-0400
  Kent *(G-5198)*
Upright Posts LLC .... G 253 224-0076
  Sumner *(G-13109)*
US Sign Girl .... G 801 644-1108
  Issaquah *(G-4485)*
US Sign One LLC .... G 253 236-8074
  Puyallup *(G-8269)*
Vancouver Sign Co Inc .... E 360 693-4773
  Vancouver *(G-14663)*
Veva Company LLC .... G 360 687-8550
  Battle Ground *(G-749)*
Viar Visual Communications .... G 425 391-8443
  Sammamish *(G-9257)*
Victory Circle Signs .... G 509 489-3083
  Spokane *(G-12582)*
Vilmas Family Corporation .... G 253 941-9008
  Federal Way *(G-3801)*
Vinyl Lab NW LLC .... G 425 870-8702
  Lynnwood *(G-6219)*
Vital Signs Ministries .... G 360 659-2726
  Tulalip *(G-13846)*
Vital Signs Notary .... G 206 387-6622
  Kent *(G-5203)*
Watsons Wooden Words LLC .... G 253 348-7995
  Bonney Lake *(G-1742)*
Wdk Signs .... G 509 758-0483
  Clarkston *(G-2653)*
Wells Signs Mfg & Distrg .... G 360 225-0520
  Woodland *(G-15474)*
Western Graphics Inc .... G 206 241-2526
  Fife *(G-3998)*
Whats Your Sign Inc .... G 253 475-7446
  Tacoma *(G-13596)*
Whidbey Island Sign Sltons LLC .. G 360 299-0430
  Burlington *(G-2201)*
Whidbey Sign Co .... G 360 720-2015
  Oak Harbor *(G-7173)*
▲ White Signs .... G 425 745-0860
  Lynnwood *(G-6225)*
Wholesale Neon A Division .... G 253 939-0716
  Auburn *(G-600)*
Wildrose Ltd .... F 509 535-8555
  Spokane *(G-12591)*

Winsor Fireform LLC .... E 360 786-8200
  Tumwater *(G-13907)*
Wizz Signs .... G 360 779-3103
  Poulsbo *(G-8021)*
Woodinville Signs Inc .... G 425 483-0296
  Woodinville *(G-15407)*
X Bolt Signs LLC .... G 509 945-6780
  Naches *(G-7008)*
Young Electric Sign Company ...... F 253 722-5753
  Tacoma *(G-13605)*
Young Gun NW .... G 360 996-4275
  Chehalis *(G-2544)*
Youngs Neon Sign Co .... G 253 946-1286
  Federal Way *(G-3805)*
Zumar Industries Inc .... D 253 536-7740
  Tacoma *(G-13608)*

3995 Burial Caskets

▲ Puyallup Casket Company Inc ... G 253 845-1883
  Puyallup *(G-8228)*

3996 Linoleum & Hard Surface Floor Coverings, NEC

Nce Inc .... G 253 884-6255
  Longbranch *(G-5879)*
▲ Seamless Attenuating Tech ...... E 360 748-8711
  Chehalis *(G-2535)*
▲ Zometek LLC .... G 888 505-7953
  Seattle *(G-11523)*

3999 Manufacturing Industries, NEC

195 Industries Inc .... F 509 245-3735
  Spangle *(G-12083)*
206 Industries LLC .... G 206 390-8449
  Seattle *(G-9319)*
2x4 Industries .... G 253 205-0359
  Seattle *(G-9320)*
3 CS .... G 509 246-1451
  Soap Lake *(G-12036)*
613 Industries Inc .... G 612 823-3606
  Seattle *(G-9325)*
99 Smokers Paradise .... G 425 775-8081
  Lynnwood *(G-6063)*
A & S Manufacturing Entps .... G 425 334-6606
  Marysville *(G-6309)*
A 2 Z Mfg LLC .... G 360 398-2126
  Lynden *(G-5998)*
A Path To Avalon .... G 360 403-8884
  Arlington *(G-189)*
Abbott Industries Inc .... G 360 894-6230
  Yelm *(G-15724)*
Abraham Industries LLC .... F 509 329-8260
  Tacoma *(G-13155)*
Ace Anthony Equity MGT LLC ...... F 425 333-6024
  Duvall *(G-2978)*
Act Manufacturing Inc .... G 509 893-4100
  Spokane Valley *(G-12600)*
Advanced Lean Mfg LLC .... E 425 402-8300
  Woodinville *(G-15172)*
▲ Advantac Technologies LLC ..... E 360 217-8500
  Everett *(G-3362)*
AGM Industries Inc .... G 716 256-9470
  Redmond *(G-8375)*
Agrijuana 1 LLC .... G 360 342-8194
  Battle Ground *(G-686)*
Agt Inc .... G 509 935-6140
  Chewelah *(G-2597)*
Alexander Industries LLC .... G 253 686-6066
  Renton *(G-8737)*
All Fur One .... G 206 281-8412
  Seattle *(G-9379)*
Allco Manufacturing Inc .... G 702 616-2081
  Federal Way *(G-3714)*
Alpine Industries LLC .... G 253 261-1500
  Lake Tapps *(G-5676)*
Alpine Shed LLC .... G 509 322-0808
  Tonasket *(G-13645)*
American Innovative Mfg LLC ...... G 509 244-2730
  Spokane Valley *(G-12611)*
American Mfg & Engin .... F 253 520-5865
  Kent *(G-4777)*
Antoine Creek Ranch .... G 509 682-9025
  Chelan *(G-2546)*
Apollo Antenna & Sales Inc .... G 509 534-6972
  Spokane Valley *(G-12622)*
Archer-Daniels-Midland Company ... F 509 754-5266
  Ephrata *(G-3331)*
Aseptic Manufacturing Svcs LLC ... G 509 869-4867
  Spokane *(G-12121)*

Employee Codes: A=Over 500 employees, B=251-500
C=101-250, D=51-100, E=20-50, F=10-19, G=2-9

ATF Mfg LLC G 509 762-2421
Moses Lake *(G-6681)*
Aunt Donnas G 206 519-0143
Raymond *(G-8341)*
Aura Accessories Inc G 208 850-1603
Seattle *(G-9463)*
Austin Speciaties Inc G 360 629-6662
Stanwood *(G-12959)*
AVI Marie Hair Collection LLC G 425 409-9924
Renton *(G-8749)*
▲ Avitech International Corp F 425 885-3863
Redmond *(G-8395)*
Axis Mfg G 509 368-9895
Spokane Valley *(G-12634)*
B & B Manufacturing LLC G 360 988-5020
Sumas *(G-13041)*
B Line Mfg G 360 718-2158
Vancouver *(G-14052)*
Back To Basics Lean Mfg G 253 353-4281
Puyallup *(G-8126)*
Balametrics Inc G 360 452-2842
Port Angeles *(G-7689)*
Balance Construction Inc G 206 364-5555
Lake Forest Park *(G-5605)*
Ballboy LLC G 425 281-9152
North Bend *(G-7101)*
Balros Industries G 206 963-6114
Seattle *(G-9487)*
Bayside EMB & Screenprint G 253 565-1521
Tacoma *(G-13191)*
Bear Industries LLC G 509 981-8618
Spokane *(G-12143)*
Bee Hive Candles Inc G 360 599-9725
Maple Falls *(G-6248)*
Bee Keeper Gordons Gold G 360 202-9523
Mount Vernon *(G-6779)*
Beigeblond Inc G 360 693-3283
Vancouver *(G-14060)*
Belfor USA Group Inc E 206 632-0800
Tukwila *(G-13696)*
Belfor USA Group Inc G 509 453-8551
Yakima *(G-15518)*
Belshire Industries G 360 910-9209
Ridgefield *(G-9066)*
Bering Street Studio LLC G 253 677-4870
Gig Harbor *(G-4080)*
Bestway Industries LLC G 360 513-2000
Vancouver *(G-14064)*
Big C Industries LLC G 360 773-5873
Ridgefield *(G-9068)*
▲ Big Dipper Wax Works G 206 767-7322
Seattle *(G-9523)*
Big Rock Industries G 360 659-3308
Lake Stevens *(G-5634)*
Big Rock Industries LLC G 425 314-8710
Monroe *(G-6553)*
Big Smooth Industries LLC G 206 356-5888
Gig Harbor *(G-4081)*
Bigoni Stiner & Assoc G 253 826-5824
Edgewood *(G-3073)*
▲ Black Dog Industries G 509 946-6400
Richland *(G-8973)*
Black Mouse Inc G 253 677-3491
Tacoma *(G-13204)*
Bloomfield Light Industries G 360 877-5718
Lilliwaup *(G-5870)*
Bmt Industries Inc G 509 838-4400
Spokane *(G-12156)*
Board Systems G 253 307-0166
Roy *(G-9157)*
Boulder Creek Industriescom G 425 879-2322
Arlington *(G-214)*
Brady Worldwide Inc E 800 854-6832
Seattle *(G-9576)*
Brady Worldwide Inc E 206 323-8100
Seattle *(G-9577)*
Bre & Car Industries LLC G 206 268-0204
Seattle *(G-9580)*
Breeze Trees LLC G 808 387-6167
Bellingham *(G-1282)*
Bridgetown Industries L L G 503 953-3580
Vancouver *(G-14083)*
▼ Brothers United Inc F 360 426-3959
Shelton *(G-11686)*
Brushwood Industries Ltd G 509 447-2266
Newport *(G-7054)*
Buck Snort Industries G 509 939-7777
Deer Park *(G-2894)*
Buckley Industries G 425 286-6443
Kenmore *(G-4567)*
Budo Industries LLC G 206 349-8085
Seattle *(G-9593)*
▲ C M F Industries Inc G 425 282-5065
Kent *(G-4830)*
C W Nielsen Manufacturing E 360 748-8835
Chehalis *(G-2476)*
Calib Designs LLC G 206 548-9217
Seattle *(G-9606)*
Candeo Candle Factory LLC G 360 524-2310
Vancouver *(G-14095)*
Cannaman G 360 597-4850
Vancouver *(G-14096)*
Cannon Ball Industries G 206 781-1833
Seattle *(G-9618)*
Cascade Growers LLC G 530 919-3431
Twisp *(G-13909)*
Cascade Ridge Industries G 509 237-1534
Quincy *(G-8291)*
Cbd Outreach G 360 426-2000
Shelton *(G-11689)*
Center For Advanced G 253 298-7490
Tukwila *(G-13711)*
Chambong Industries LLC G 608 335-1882
Seattle *(G-9665)*
Charles Friedman G 206 781-0608
Seattle *(G-9667)*
Christmas Forest E 360 245-3202
Curtis *(G-2848)*
Chrome Industries G 206 682-1343
Seattle *(G-9682)*
Cigarland Gig Harbor G 253 851-5515
Gig Harbor *(G-4089)*
CJ Manufacturing I Inc G 360 543-5297
Ferndale *(G-3831)*
Claro Candles G 253 678-1173
Tacoma *(G-13235)*
Clean As A Whistle G 425 354-9719
Kenmore *(G-4569)*
Cns Industries Inc G 360 424-1624
Mount Vernon *(G-6785)*
Cobblestone Industries LLC G 509 447-4518
Newport *(G-7056)*
Coinforcecom LLC G 253 682-2825
Olympia *(G-7251)*
Colubia AG & Mfg G 509 382-4849
Waitsburg *(G-14752)*
Columbia Manufacturing G 360 210-5124
Camas *(G-2240)*
Columbia Mfg & Tech Ctr LLC G 360 835-0922
Washougal *(G-14948)*
Columbia River Mfg Inc G 509 493-3460
White Salmon *(G-15113)*
Columbia River Mfg Svcs LLC G 801 652-3008
Kennewick *(G-4649)*
Common Industries LLC G 206 963-6649
Seattle *(G-9719)*
Concept Reality Inc F 360 695-3860
Vancouver *(G-14144)*
Conner Industries G 360 261-0265
Kelso *(G-4520)*
Continental Holdings III G 425 502-7055
Seattle *(G-9732)*
Cooper T Kirsch Glass LLC G 206 718-8183
Seattle *(G-9738)*
Cor-Tread LLC G 425 268-6377
Mukilteo *(G-6905)*
Corallie Industries G 253 576-5240
Spanaway *(G-12056)*
Core Training Industries Inc G 206 250-2050
Federal Way *(G-3725)*
Correctional Industries G 360 963-3332
Clallam Bay *(G-2618)*
Correctional Industries G 360 427-4613
Shelton *(G-11692)*
Country Flicker Candle Co G 509 286-3031
Latah *(G-5790)*
Cowin In-Situ Science LLC G 509 392-1329
Richland *(G-8985)*
Crazy J G 360 876-6618
Port Orchard *(G-7800)*
Creative Outlook G 360 607-4013
Battle Ground *(G-696)*
Croix Industries Ltd G 206 528-5555
Seattle *(G-9754)*
Cultured Elements LLC G 425 442-4595
Cheney *(G-2583)*
Curvetec Mfg G 425 760-2844
Mukilteo *(G-6910)*
Custom Mfg Ambassador LLC G 206 963-9853
Seattle *(G-9769)*
Cuzd Industries G 360 742-3126
Lacey *(G-5544)*
CWC Industries LLC A Washingto G 206 528-8090
Seattle *(G-9774)*
D&S Innovative Enterprises G 509 467-2032
Nine Mile Falls *(G-7071)*
Dark Star Candle Company G 206 280-5902
Seattle *(G-9795)*
Db Industries LLC G 360 432-8239
Shelton *(G-11695)*
Decatur Industries Inc G 206 368-3178
Lake Forest Park *(G-5611)*
Deep Cell Industries G 206 909-3858
Seattle *(G-9813)*
Dejay Products LLC G 206 784-8200
Lakewood *(G-5711)*
Denmar Industries Inc G 206 579-9316
Anacortes *(G-121)*
Desert View Manufactured Home G 509 967-3456
West Richland *(G-15095)*
Df Industries Inc G 253 445-7940
Puyallup *(G-8143)*
▲ Digilent Inc F 509 338-3784
Pullman *(G-8087)*
Direct Fire Suppression System G 509 215-0852
Medical Lake *(G-6440)*
Diversified Mfg Techologies G 360 424-9300
Mount Vernon *(G-6790)*
Dk9 Dog Walking G 425 922-4685
Covington *(G-2825)*
Dogsdream Corporation G 425 737-2810
Seattle *(G-9843)*
Dogwood Industries G 425 949-7379
Bothell *(G-1759)*
Don Macintosh G 425 821-1499
Kirkland *(G-5322)*
Double Dutch LLC G 509 837-6539
Sunnyside *(G-13120)*
Dragonfire Candles LLC G 206 851-4235
Everett *(G-3446)*
Drake Industries LLC G 425 672-8266
Edmonds *(G-3107)*
Drama Nine LLP G 206 949-2953
Seattle *(G-9854)*
Duncan Stone LLC G 360 820-0823
Seattle *(G-9859)*
Dunmire Manufacturing G 360 241-9099
Bremerton *(G-1949)*
▲ Dynon Avionics Inc D 425 402-0433
Woodinville *(G-15230)*
E and S Industries LLC G 253 678-1539
Tacoma *(G-13268)*
Eagle Rock Manufacturing Inc G 360 989-0863
Granite Falls *(G-4271)*
Edinger Mfg Inc G 425 413-4008
Ravensdale *(G-8334)*
Element G 425 941-5373
Othello *(G-7494)*
Ellipse Mfg Inc G 253 653-5554
Tacoma *(G-13275)*
Emerald Twist Incorporated G 541 659-2189
Goldendale *(G-4196)*
Enna Products Corporation G 360 306-5369
Bellingham *(G-1335)*
Envision Manufacturing Co G 206 963-7352
Kent *(G-4895)*
Epik Industries G 360 303-6488
Bellingham *(G-1337)*
Erik Doane Manufacturing G 360 799-0997
Sultan *(G-13023)*
Etz Industries LLC G 253 630-2915
Kent *(G-4898)*
Evergreen Sales Group Inc G 425 368-2000
Woodinville *(G-15239)*
Evil Industries G 206 612-3293
Duvall *(G-2987)*
Evo Industries LLC G 717 665-0406
Ellensburg *(G-3199)*
Excel Industries Incorporated G 360 790-3577
Lynden *(G-6015)*
F&S Industries LLC G 206 501-5347
Seattle *(G-9957)*
Fab5ventures LLC G 425 310-2543
University Place *(G-13967)*
Farstad Industries LLC G 360 316-9485
Oak Harbor *(G-7150)*
Fasola Tools G 360 293-9231
Anacortes *(G-128)*
Fenix Industries Inc G 206 695-2582
Seattle *(G-9984)*

Ferguson - Gagnon Industries ... G ... 509 337-6207
Waitsburg *(G-14754)*
Ferryboat Music LLC ... G ... 509 996-3528
Winthrop *(G-15160)*
Fido N-Scratch ... G ... 206 588-2111
Seattle *(G-9988)*
Fire Solutions NW LLC ... G ... 855 876-3473
Bremerton *(G-1954)*
◆ First Strike LLC ... G ... 360 285-4000
Olympia *(G-7285)*
Five Star Industries LLC ... G ... 206 706-2754
Seattle *(G-10001)*
Fortynine Industries ... G ... 253 632-3081
Maple Valley *(G-6270)*
Foxbat Heavy Industries Inc ... G ... 425 890-0410
Port Townsend *(G-7885)*
Fps West Inc ... G ... 206 242-4888
Normandy Park *(G-7092)*
Frame It Ltd ... G ... 206 364-7477
Seattle *(G-10019)*
Frontier Manufacturing Inc ... G ... 360 652-4046
Stanwood *(G-12972)*
Function Works ... G ... 206 219-5636
Oroville *(G-7466)*
Fusion Industries ... G ... 425 703-2867
Bellevue *(G-917)*
Fussy Cloud Puppet Slam ... G ... 206 235-9109
Seattle *(G-10042)*
Fuze Create LLC ... G ... 425 212-8807
Seattle *(G-10043)*
Galaxy Hobby Inc ... G ... 425 670-0454
Lynnwood *(G-6124)*
Gale Industries ... G ... 360 659-7674
Marysville *(G-6338)*
Gale Industries Inc ... G ... 360 479-6271
Bremerton *(G-1955)*
Garvie Industries LLC ... G ... 360 691-1233
Granite Falls *(G-4275)*
Giesbrecht & Sons LLC ... G ... 509 269-4087
Mesa *(G-6493)*
Glassy Baby LLC ... E ... 206 568-7368
Seattle *(G-10081)*
Globodyne Industries Inc ... G ... 425 321-9471
Mukilteo *(G-6928)*
Gman Industries Ltd ... G ... 425 228-2518
Renton *(G-8809)*
▲ Gms Industries Inc ... G ... 425 454-9500
Bellevue *(G-930)*
Gorman Industries ... G ... 509 899-3933
Ellensburg *(G-3204)*
Graymark Industries Inc ... G ... 360 437-5121
Port Hadlock *(G-7758)*
Green Island Growers LLC ... G ... 360 298-0438
Friday Harbor *(G-4049)*
Green Labs LLC ... G ... 360 875-5556
Raymond *(G-8350)*
Green Leaf Family Estates ... G ... 360 894-4945
Yelm *(G-15735)*
Green Valley Management LLC ... G ... 509 830-5240
Mabton *(G-6228)*
Greenfire Candles LLC ... G ... 206 240-9225
Seattle *(G-10118)*
Greenfire Productions ... G ... 360 572-0554
Arlington *(G-245)*
Greenhaven LLC ... G ... 360 436-1420
Darrington *(G-2868)*
Greenlife Industries ... G ... 360 566-3984
Vancouver *(G-14272)*
Greenlite Heavy Industries LLC ... G ... 206 226-3523
Mercer Island *(G-6465)*
Griese Enterprises ... G ... 509 868-7963
Spokane *(G-12284)*
Grigg Farms LLC ... E ... 509 787-3225
Quincy *(G-8299)*
▲ Grizzly Pet Products LLC ... G ... 425 481-1110
Woodinville *(G-15257)*
Halls Drug Center Inc ... E ... 360 736-5000
Centralia *(G-2405)*
Ham Industries ... G ... 360 201-8439
Seattle *(G-10136)*
Haolifts Industries ... G ... 425 836-3968
Sammamish *(G-9214)*
Harbor Steel Fabrication ... G ... 253 858-8804
Gig Harbor *(G-4112)*
Hard Industries Hl ... G ... 360 913-2063
Arlington *(G-248)*
Hardwood Industries Inc ... F ... 425 420-1050
Snohomish *(G-11919)*
Harlane Co LLC ... G ... 404 771-9300
Vancouver *(G-14283)*

Harris Manufacturing Irri ... G ... 509 539-1725
Burbank *(G-2084)*
Harvest Helper ... G ... 360 515-5491
Olympia *(G-7305)*
Hawk International Inc ... G ... 253 851-3444
Gig Harbor *(G-4116)*
Haytools Inc ... G ... 509 933-1102
Ellensburg *(G-3207)*
▲ Healthy Pet LP ... C ... 360 734-7415
Ferndale *(G-3850)*
Heartwarmer Designs ... G ... 253 630-7408
Kent *(G-4937)*
Helm Industries LLC ... G ... 206 419-3973
Seattle *(G-10163)*
Heylo ... G ... 440 522-4674
Seattle *(G-10169)*
Hjalmar Industries Inc ... G ... 360 957-4302
Seattle *(G-10177)*
Hn Goods & Services LLc ... G ... 360 841-8414
Woodland *(G-15441)*
Hodge Industries ... G ... 253 266-6921
Bonney Lake *(G-1726)*
Hollibaugh Manufacturing ... G ... 360 653-8612
Marysville *(G-6345)*
Hoober Industries Inc ... G ... 253 370-9553
Tacoma *(G-13342)*
Hood River Candle Works ... G ... 503 213-4487
Port Angeles *(G-7711)*
Hopp Industries ... G ... 253 732-7348
Tacoma *(G-13343)*
Hot Sox LLC ... G ... 509 947-5193
West Richland *(G-15096)*
Hpf Manufacturing ... G ... 425 486-8031
Snohomish *(G-11923)*
Ht Industries LLC ... G ... 360 863-2029
Snohomish *(G-11924)*
Huney Jun LLC ... G ... 805 903-2011
Peshastin *(G-7662)*
▼ Hydrostraw LLC ... E ... 509 291-6000
Rockford *(G-9151)*
Hypothesis Gardens LLC ... G ... 206 653-6344
Spokane Valley *(G-12735)*
Ideal Industries Intl Inc ... G ... 360 761-9958
Puyallup *(G-8164)*
Infinity Industries LLC ... G ... 425 418-1151
Bothell *(G-1866)*
Inland Northwest Mfg LLC ... G ... 509 218-7424
Spokane *(G-12311)*
Innovate For All Spc ... G ... 425 681-2191
Seattle *(G-10240)*
Insitu Inc ... F ... 509 493-8600
Bingen *(G-1637)*
Insitu Inc ... A ... 509 493-8600
Bingen *(G-1638)*
Insta-Learn By Step Inc ... G ... 425 355-9830
Mukilteo *(G-6943)*
Intelligent Industries LLC ... G ... 206 372-7273
Federal Way *(G-3746)*
Interstate Industries Inc ... G ... 206 387-2364
Kent *(G-4959)*
Interstate Industries Inc ... G ... 425 226-2135
Kent *(G-4960)*
Irondog Industries LLC ... G ... 509 586-0479
Kennewick *(G-4678)*
Isaksen Scale Models ... G ... 425 334-2807
Lake Stevens *(G-5650)*
J & G Industries Inc ... G ... 206 246-3782
Normandy Park *(G-7095)*
J & R Commercial Inc ... G ... 253 639-3890
Kent *(G-4963)*
J D Mfg ... G ... 360 864-8271
Winlock *(G-15151)*
J D Precision Mfg Inc ... G ... 509 496-2607
Colbert *(G-2709)*
J L Innovations Inc ... G ... 425 823-8540
Kenmore *(G-4584)*
Jacks Nasty Candy Company ... G ... 425 418-5282
Arlington *(G-261)*
Jamar Industries LLC ... G ... 206 725-3409
Seattle *(G-10281)*
JD Bargen Industries LLC ... G ... 360 354-5676
Lynden *(G-6026)*
JD Fabrication ... G ... 360 691-4550
Granite Falls *(G-4278)*
Jensen Seed Farm Inc ... G ... 509 896-2312
Bickleton *(G-1632)*
Jett Industries Inc ... G ... 360 649-3840
Bremerton *(G-1966)*
Jharc Industries LLC ... G ... 571 205-5422
Tacoma *(G-13360)*

Jjs Productions LLC ... G ... 360 630-5294
Anacortes *(G-138)*
Jph Industries LLC ... G ... 425 269-8966
Redmond *(G-8522)*
◆ Jrotc Dog Tags Inc ... G ... 509 292-0410
Elk *(G-3170)*
Julias Glows ... G ... 206 722-0411
Seattle *(G-10315)*
JWB Manufacturing LLC ... G ... 253 222-1671
South Prairie *(G-12050)*
K and K Industries LLC ... G ... 425 951-0502
Edmonds *(G-3128)*
K Line Industries LLC ... G ... 425 870-4228
Camano Island *(G-2215)*
K Sports Manufacturing Inc ... G ... 206 251-5211
Renton *(G-8834)*
K Stauffer Manufacturing LLC ... G ... 360 626-1462
Poulsbo *(G-7969)*
K&J Mfg Inc ... G ... 425 503-2174
North Bend *(G-7114)*
Kam Manufacturing ... G ... 360 625-8321
Enumclaw *(G-3298)*
Kason Pet Supply ... G ... 360 886-2306
Maple Valley *(G-6279)*
◆ Katana Industries Inc ... G ... 360 293-0682
Anacortes *(G-139)*
Kelly Industries LLC ... G ... 206 676-2338
Snohomish *(G-11931)*
Kentucky Chrome Industries ... G ... 816 522-1783
Seattle *(G-10338)*
Kenwood Manufacturing Inc ... G ... 602 625-4012
Tukwila *(G-13764)*
Kf Industries LLC ... G ... 360 628-8473
Lacey *(G-5563)*
Kfj Industries LLC ... G ... 425 922-2889
Kirkland *(G-5376)*
King Mountain Tobacco Co Inc ... D ... 509 874-9935
White Swan *(G-15138)*
Klein Joanne Klein Kevin ... G ... 360 435-8615
Arlington *(G-268)*
Knox Cellars ... G ... 425 392-7536
Sammamish *(G-9226)*
Kobelt Manufacturing ... G ... 360 676-2774
Bellingham *(G-1397)*
Koehler Industries Inc ... G ... 360 793-9101
Bellevue *(G-969)*
Kolibaba and Associates ... G ... 253 752-0368
Tacoma *(G-13378)*
Kova Industries LLC ... G ... 360 567-5371
Battle Ground *(G-713)*
Kramerica Industries LLC ... G ... 360 931-9690
Vancouver *(G-14354)*
Kresek Brothers Manufacturing ... G ... 509 322-0808
Tonasket *(G-13652)*
L Rock Industries Inc ... G ... 360 575-8868
Cathlamet *(G-2370)*
Labore Industries ... G ... 206 533-8709
Shoreline *(G-11780)*
Lancs Industries Holdings LLC ... D ... 425 823-6634
Kirkland *(G-5379)*
Landrace Labs ... G ... 360 273-9277
Rochester *(G-9135)*
Landy Corporation ... G ... 253 835-1427
Federal Way *(G-3751)*
Lavender Heart Ltd ... G ... 206 568-4441
Seattle *(G-10384)*
Lawman Industries LLC ... G ... 360 915-7807
Lacey *(G-5564)*
Lazerwood Industries ... G ... 206 650-2367
Seattle *(G-10388)*
Ledford Industries LLC ... G ... 253 446-6508
Puyallup *(G-8177)*
Leeward Industries Inc ... G ... 360 830-0765
Seabeck *(G-9267)*
Leisure Home & Spa ... G ... 360 647-5529
Bellingham *(G-1406)*
Lg Industries LLC ... G ... 425 557-7993
Issaquah *(G-4438)*
Lgk Industries Inc ... G ... 360 299-3140
Anacortes *(G-141)*
Lightbank Studio ... G ... 206 409-0939
Seattle *(G-10416)*
Lighthouse Candles ... G ... 360 671-2598
Bellingham *(G-1410)*
Living Stone Industries Inc ... G ... 425 679-6278
Edmonds *(G-3130)*
Liz Tran ... G ... 206 720-7165
Seattle *(G-10432)*
Lohr Industries ... G ... 360 802-4351
Enumclaw *(G-3301)*

SIC

Lomax Industries LLC ... G ... 206 687-7499
Seattle (G-10435)
Long Life Candles ... G ... 360 866-1127
Olympia (G-7325)
Longhorn Industries ... G ... 509 899-5475
Ellensburg (G-3213)
Looker Industries Inc ... G ... 360 691-1596
Granite Falls (G-4279)
Loth Industries Inc ... G ... 425 418-5897
Snohomish (G-11940)
▲ Lucky Dog Eqp Inc DBA Pet Pros ... E ... 425 402-8833
Woodinville (G-15297)
Luckyhorse Industries ... G ... 206 227-3383
Issaquah (G-4441)
Lunas Custom Puppets ... G ... 360 721-9672
Battle Ground (G-717)
M Squared Manufacturing LLC ... G ... 206 380-0233
Vashon (G-14732)
M&L Industries Inc ... G ... 425 894-7147
Redmond (G-8542)
M24 Industries LLC ... G ... 360 348-3578
Monroe (G-6594)
Macaw Rescue and Santuary ... G ... 425 788-4721
Carnation (G-2295)
Mach 2 Arts Inc ... G ... 206 953-0575
Seattle (G-10458)
Macro Mfg LLC ... G ... 360 750-3544
Vancouver (G-14391)
Madboy Industries ... G ... 206 707-9394
Seattle (G-10464)
Madretierra Candle Company LLC ... G ... 786 374-5913
Kennewick (G-4690)
Malone Industries LLC ... G ... 360 636-1383
Kelso (G-4536)
Match Grade Industries LLC ... G ... 425 949-8110
Woodinville (G-15304)
Mattress Manufacturing Prize ... G ... 509 946-1194
Richland (G-9025)
McDowall Bros Insulation ... G ... 509 762-9530
Moses Lake (G-6724)
McLaren Destiny ... G ... 971 217-5877
La Center (G-5509)
McMullen Mfg Services ... G ... 360 891-3662
Vancouver (G-14406)
McNeeley Mfg ... G ... 206 255-7818
Covington (G-2832)
McNeeley Mfg ... G ... 253 236-4969
Auburn (G-495)
Meadowbrook Manufacturing LLC ... G ... 206 297-1029
Seattle (G-10511)
Meier Manufacturing ... G ... 253 545-9798
Tacoma (G-13407)
Melt Candle Company LLC ... G ... 360 200-0993
Oak Harbor (G-7158)
Menace Industries LLC ... G ... 360 595-4095
Bellingham (G-1432)
Meyle Industries LLC ... G ... 360 250-6114
Vancouver (G-14416)
Michaels Manufacturing ... G ... 253 459-4384
Bonney Lake (G-1728)
Microscan Mfg LLC ... G ... 425 226-5700
Renton (G-8854)
Mid Mountain Materials Inc ... E ... 360 435-9622
Arlington (G-278)
Mill Race Farm ... G ... 509 964-2473
Thorp (G-13628)
Miller Manufacturing ... G ... 360 844-5403
Washougal (G-14968)
Millman Industries LLC ... G ... 425 471-0854
Langley (G-5783)
MJM Manufacturing ... G ... 305 620-2020
Orting (G-7485)
Mjv Mfg ... G ... 509 735-1662
Kennewick (G-4695)
Mk Industries LLC ... G ... 425 922-0139
Bellevue (G-1010)
Mkg Mfg ... G ... 360 398-7518
Bellingham (G-1437)
Mm Industries LLC ... G ... 360 629-4595
Stanwood (G-12981)
Mollys Salads LLC ... G ... 206 512-3075
Seattle (G-10558)
Monkey Wrench Fabrication LLC ... G ... 206 992-8509
Bainbridge Island (G-650)
Moonstuff Inc ... G ... 509 947-2981
West Richland (G-15099)
Moore Manufacturing LLC ... G ... 360 400-3277
Roy (G-9163)
◆ Moore-Clark USA Inc ... E ... 360 425-6715
Longview (G-5932)
Morning Dew Candles ... G ... 206 772-5611
Seattle (G-10563)
Morwenstow ... G ... 425 483-0320
Woodinville (G-15315)
Mount Evergreen Industries ... G ... 360 584-9620
Olympia (G-7344)
Mountain View Industries Inc ... G ... 360 894-0499
Yelm (G-15741)
Mt Baker Manufacturing ... G ... 360 778-1238
Lynden (G-6038)
◆ Mudslayer Manufacturing LLC ... G ... 360 477-0251
Sequim (G-11649)
Mutual Materials ... D ... 425 452-2300
Bellevue (G-1020)
Mybock Manufacturing LLC ... G ... 716 913-4157
Seattle (G-10580)
Natural Nutrition Mfg LLC ... G ... 509 966-8849
Yakima (G-15628)
Neptune Global LLC ... G ... 310 752-9992
Seattle (G-10601)
Nightmare Industries ... G ... 425 330-1084
Snohomish (G-11952)
Nitwit Lice Removal ... G ... 206 327-5782
Seattle (G-10611)
Nordick Mfg Co ... G ... 425 488-2427
Woodinville (G-15321)
▲ Nordkyn Outfitters ... G ... 253 847-4128
Eatonville (G-3063)
Northwest Carbide Tool & Svc ... G ... 253 872-7848
Kent (G-5029)
Northwest Grinding Co LLC ... G ... 509 727-5774
Pasco (G-7605)
Northwest Labor Industries ... G ... 206 388-6135
Seattle (G-10647)
Northwest Marine Inds LLC ... G ... 360 389-5351
Bellingham (G-1468)
Northwest Park Models LLC ... G ... 509 235-2522
Cheney (G-2590)
Northwest Seed & Pet Inc ... F ... 509 484-7387
Spokane (G-12414)
Northwest Territorial Mint LLC ... F ... 253 833-7780
Kent (G-5036)
Northwest Wholesale Inc ... D ... 509 662-3563
Wenatchee (G-15092)
Northwind Industries ... G ... 360 424-6689
Mount Vernon (G-6818)
Nth Degree Inc ... G ... 253 926-6705
Milton (G-6537)
NW Center Industries 5307 ... A ... 206 285-9140
Seattle (G-10673)
NW Hydroponics ... G ... 360 778-3254
Bellingham (G-1476)
O Neil Industries LLC ... G ... 509 828-0213
Spokane (G-12417)
Ocean In A Box ... G ... 360 573-2250
Vancouver (G-14446)
Odo ... G ... 303 915-9652
Spokane (G-12418)
Oe Two Industries LLC ... G ... 425 657-0958
Sammamish (G-9238)
Old Soul Candle Company LLC ... G ... 206 915-0224
Renton (G-8863)
Olympic Home Modification LLC ... G ... 253 858-9941
Gig Harbor (G-4139)
Olympic Manufacturing Inc ... G ... 425 679-6303
Bellevue (G-1048)
▲ Omen Board Industries LLC ... G ... 425 967-3434
Lynnwood (G-6174)
Optimum Extracts ... G ... 206 491-9617
Auburn (G-519)
▲ Orbis Company LLC ... G ... 360 376-4320
Eastsound (G-3041)
Orillia Smoke ... G ... 425 656-1219
Kent (G-5046)
Orion Mfg LLC ... G ... 206 979-5511
Kirkland (G-5422)
▲ Ortech Controls ... G ... 206 633-7914
Shoreline (G-11798)
Orvella Industries Corp ... G ... 206 778-2743
Renton (G-8866)
Otter Creek Industries L L C ... G ... 509 954-3998
Loon Lake (G-5976)
Our Country Beads ... G ... 509 967-3953
Richland (G-9032)
Ozette Industries LLC ... G ... 360 460-4272
Port Angeles (G-7734)
Pacific Grinding ... G ... 208 412-5945
Liberty Lake (G-5850)
Pacific Knight Emblem & Insig ... G ... 206 354-2060
Kent (G-5052)
Pacific Northwest Industries ... G ... 206 841-3144
Seatac (G-9298)
Pacific Sales & Service ... G ... 425 271-9000
Renton (G-8873)
Pacific Spring Mfg Co ... G ... 360 832-3633
Eatonville (G-3065)
Pacific Studio Inc ... D ... 206 783-5226
Seattle (G-10741)
Palmer Industries LLC ... G ... 509 989-1069
Moses Lake (G-6736)
Pam S Bubble Mobile ... G ... 360 630-5511
Mount Vernon (G-6821)
Pangaea Ltd ... G ... 206 292-9911
Seattle (G-10746)
▲ Parasol Enterprises Inc ... G ... 360 733-5579
Bellingham (G-1490)
Park Place Industries ... G ... 360 584-9762
Tumwater (G-13890)
Paul Parish Limited ... G ... 509 735-9820
Kennewick (G-4705)
Paulty Mfg LLC ... G ... 509 470-1791
Leavenworth (G-5812)
Pawpular Companions Bouti ... G ... 509 850-6070
Liberty Lake (G-5851)
Pcs Industries LLC ... G ... 509 406-5852
Naches (G-7001)
Peak Industries ... G ... 509 448-5793
Spokane (G-12434)
Pei Manufacturing LLC ... D ... 360 210-4165
Camas (G-2274)
Pelling Industries Inc ... G ... 206 243-1941
Burien (G-2120)
Pentech Industries LLC ... G ... 360 989-7903
La Center (G-5512)
Peone Industries ... G ... 509 443-4710
Spokane (G-12436)
Peryl Professional Touch ... G ... 253 537-8181
Tacoma (G-13465)
Pet Media Plus LLC ... G ... 360 425-0188
Longview (G-5942)
Peters Industries ... G ... 360 254-9889
Vancouver (G-14486)
Phunnybaggscom ... G ... 253 709-9481
Lake Tapps (G-5685)
Pign Whistle ... G ... 206 782-6044
Seattle (G-10804)
Pinnacle NW ... G ... 360 264-5484
Shelton (G-11722)
Platinum Pets LLC ... F ... 360 859-4027
Vancouver (G-14489)
PM Industries ... G ... 253 666-8977
Tacoma (G-13467)
Polar Fusion LLC ... G ... 206 779-5238
Kent (G-5070)
Polaris Manufacturing Inc ... G ... 206 230-9235
Mercer Island (G-6480)
Poopless In Seattle ... G ... 425 444-6930
North Bend (G-7121)
Porter Etuv Manufacturing Inc ... G ... 360 796-3172
Brinnon (G-2026)
Posh Digs ... G ... 425 286-6245
Bothell (G-1888)
Powell Industries Inc ... G ... 509 922-0463
Spokane Valley (G-12835)
Precision Art Works ... G ... 206 714-7074
Seattle (G-10848)
Precision Industries LLC ... G ... 253 255-3814
Eatonville (G-3067)
Premier Industries ... G ... 253 514-0977
Gig Harbor (G-4148)
Prime Biodiesel ... G ... 360 969-3966
Arlington (G-307)
Pringles Power-Vac Inc ... G ... 509 375-0500
Richland (G-9036)
Pro ARC Industries Inc ... G ... 916 215-7269
Battle Ground (G-732)
Probare Industries LLC ... G ... 206 334-9840
Everett (G-3586)
Prowse Manufacturing Group ... E ... 360 403-8910
Arlington (G-308)
Prudent Products Inc ... G ... 360 445-2556
Oak Harbor (G-7162)
Puppy Stairs ... G ... 360 387-4861
Camano Island (G-2222)
Pure Extracts ... G ... 509 679-6556
East Wenatchee (G-3030)
Pure Lite Candle Portland I ... G ... 360 909-9499
Vancouver (G-14516)
Qr Industries Inc ... G ... 360 435-2840
Arlington (G-310)

39 MISCELLANEOUS MANUFACTURING INDUSTRIES

R & M Manufacturing LLC ....G... 253 503-0956
 Spanaway *(G-12069)*
R-2 Mfg Inc ....G... 360 609-1373
 Battle Ground *(G-734)*
Rainier Industries ....G... 206 622-8219
 Seattle *(G-10917)*
Ram-Bone Industries LLC ....G... 360 652-8277
 Stanwood *(G-12989)*
Ramax Printing and Awards ....G... 509 928-1222
 Spokane *(G-12467)*
Rauda Scale Models Inc ....F... 206 365-8877
 Seattle *(G-10926)*
Rebell Industries ....G... 360 495-4846
 Elma *(G-3255)*
Recall ....G... 253 272-2813
 Fife *(G-3986)*
Red River Industries ....G... 206 992-2446
 Bainbridge Island *(G-663)*
Redd Industries LLC ....G... 509 572-5752
 Kennewick *(G-4715)*
RES Industries LLC ....G... 360 225-7955
 Woodland *(G-15462)*
Retrodyne Industries LLC ....G... 206 906-9762
 Seattle *(G-10954)*
Rh Airport Commerce ....E... 425 454-3030
 Bellevue *(G-1102)*
Rivermist Labradoodles ....G... 509 427-4810
 Stevenson *(G-13018)*
Rmv Industries Inc ....G... 253 297-2556
 Bothell *(G-1895)*
Rock Industries LLC ....G... 206 399-7853
 Bellevue *(G-1106)*
Rt Industries ....G... 253 219-8246
 Puyallup *(G-8241)*
Runaway Bike Industries LLC ....G... 206 817-1787
 Seattle *(G-10995)*
S E Industries LLC ....G... 503 519-2160
 Ridgefield *(G-9109)*
S&S Industries LLC ....G... 360 500-9942
 Puyallup *(G-8243)*
Sabre Blasting Industries LLC ....G... 360 990-2492
 Bremerton *(G-1997)*
Sabre Industries ....G... 253 246-7132
 Kent *(G-5111)*
Sally and Harry Simmons ....G... 206 297-1868
 Seattle *(G-11006)*
Saunders Solutions Inc ....G... 360 678-4788
 Coupeville *(G-2817)*
Savoy Candles LLC ....G... 205 281-9031
 Renton *(G-8905)*
Saw Industries LLC ....G... 360 306-8988
 Bellingham *(G-1524)*
Schachere Industries LLC ....G... 253 235-5205
 Federal Way *(G-3781)*
SE Industries LLC ....G... 360 256-3775
 Vancouver *(G-14576)*
Secondhand Hound ....G... 253 232-9432
 Ruston *(G-9178)*
Seven-K Company ....G... 509 863-3429
 Spokane *(G-12499)*
Shadd Global Industries L ....G... 425 374-3946
 Everett *(G-3610)*
◆ Shah Safari Inc ....E... 206 282-6122
 Seattle *(G-11095)*
▲ Ship To Shore Inc ....G... 206 284-0406
 Seattle *(G-11101)*
▲ Sigma Dg Corporation ....G... 360 859-3170
 Vancouver *(G-14585)*
Silicon Digital Industries Inc ....G... 360 332-1349
 North Bend *(G-7123)*
Sirlin Enterprises ....G... 206 883-7988
 Seattle *(G-11117)*
Skagit Seed Services Inc ....G... 360 466-3191
 Mount Vernon *(G-6841)*
Skilskin ....G... 509 326-6760
 Spokane *(G-12506)*
Skooler Inc ....G... 425 628-5000
 Bellevue *(G-1136)*
Skt Industries ....G... 206 633-4461
 Seattle *(G-11128)*
Skybreeze Inc ....G... 206 764-1872
 Seattle *(G-11131)*
Skyline International LLC ....E... 206 624-1874
 Seattle *(G-11133)*
Sleeping Industries LLC ....G... 360 201-4305
 Edmonds *(G-3157)*
Smiley Dog ....G... 206 903-9631
 Bothell *(G-1906)*

Smj Industries LLC ....G... 425 442-9785
 Bellevue *(G-1140)*
Smuckwell Industries LLC ....G... 206 412-3598
 Seattle *(G-11141)*
Sneva Manufacturing ....G... 317 496-8935
 Spokane *(G-12509)*
Sno River Manufacturing ....G... 425 338-5200
 Mill Creek *(G-6529)*
Soda Pop Miniatures LLC ....G... 425 260-4638
 Issaquah *(G-4478)*
Solar Space Industries Inc ....G... 206 332-9966
 Seattle *(G-11154)*
Sophies Touch ....G... 253 677-1061
 Fox Island *(G-4025)*
Sovereign Manufacturing ....G... 253 318-7180
 Graham *(G-4238)*
Space Age Industries LLC ....G... 206 992-7731
 Seattle *(G-11163)*
Spaz Industries LLC ....G... 206 890-7079
 Mercer Island *(G-6485)*
Spectrum Manufacturing ....G... 509 982-2257
 Odessa *(G-7192)*
Spectyr Industries Corp ....G... 360 863-7720
 Monroe *(G-6623)*
Spinnerrack LLC ....G... 425 268-1084
 Mukilteo *(G-6978)*
Spry Hive Industries ....G... 425 503-9790
 Kirkland *(G-5470)*
Squonk Industries ....G... 206 250-4355
 Seattle *(G-11173)*
Ss Trailer Manufacturing ....G... 253 750-4724
 Bonney Lake *(G-1739)*
Stagecraft Industries Inc ....G... 206 763-8800
 Seattle *(G-11178)*
Standever Industries Llc ....G... 206 687-9610
 Sultan *(G-13038)*
Star Industries Corp Inc ....G... 360 826-3895
 Lyman *(G-5997)*
Stedman Bee Supplies Inc ....G... 360 692-9453
 Silverdale *(G-11860)*
Sun Liquor Mfg Inc ....G... 206 419-5857
 Seattle *(G-11218)*
Sundance Equestrian Industries ....G... 425 205-3775
 Woodinville *(G-15381)*
Sunlight Cottage Industries ....G... 360 321-8302
 Clinton *(G-2700)*
Sunset Manufacturing Corp ....G... 425 239-7416
 Snohomish *(G-11988)*
Super-Keller Industries LLC ....G... 360 459-1059
 Olympia *(G-7402)*
Superfancy Industries ....G... 360 556-9762
 Olympia *(G-7403)*
Superior Stone Manufacturing ....G... 425 931-9303
 Woodinville *(G-15382)*
Superior Stone Manufacturing ....G... 425 312-2968
 Lynnwood *(G-6206)*
Surly Industries ....G... 206 349-3289
 Seattle *(G-11226)*
Sweater Stone Inc ....G... 425 392-2747
 Sammamish *(G-9251)*
Sweeny Industries ....G... 510 701-0384
 Puyallup *(G-8258)*
Sweeny Industries ....G... 253 446-7298
 Puyallup *(G-8259)*
Sweet Creek Creations ....G... 509 446-2429
 Metaline Falls *(G-6498)*
Swift Industries ....G... 360 966-9697
 Nooksack *(G-7087)*
Tag Manufacturing Inc ....G... 206 359-8440
 Seattle *(G-11257)*
Tate Honey Farm ....G... 509 924-6669
 Spokane *(G-12546)*
Taurman Distributing & Mfg ....G... 360 330-5886
 Centralia *(G-2437)*
Techpoint Manufacturing Inc ....G... 425 387-0305
 Marysville *(G-6394)*
Teh Industries LLC ....G... 425 453-1551
 Bellevue *(G-1180)*
Thc Partners ....G... 347 459-8450
 Seattle *(G-11284)*
Thinking Industries Inc. ....G... 206 201-2106
 Bainbridge Island *(G-678)*
Third Ares Industries LLC ....G... 502 592-2463
 Seattle *(G-11292)*
Thomas Grange Holdings Inc ....F... 678 921-0499
 Seattle *(G-11295)*
Thompson & Cloud LLC ....G... 206 218-9991
 Tumwater *(G-13899)*
Thyssenkrupp Elevator Corp ....E... 425 828-3110
 Kirkland *(G-5482)*

Tims Manufacturing Corp ....G... 425 392-2616
 Kirkland *(G-5483)*
Titan Industries USA LLC ....G... 206 466-1300
 Lake Forest Park *(G-5625)*
Titan Mfg ....G... 360 863-1808
 Monroe *(G-6631)*
TNT Industries LLC ....G... 509 279-8011
 Spokane Valley *(G-12907)*
Todays Style ....G... 360 671-4922
 Bellingham *(G-1571)*
Tomar Industries ....G... 509 266-8384
 Pasco *(G-7641)*
Top Left Industries ....G... 360 914-1400
 Marysville *(G-6396)*
TRA Industries Inc ....F... 509 924-5858
 Spokane Valley *(G-12909)*
▲ Traight Industries ....G... 253 630-1489
 Kent *(G-5187)*
Transtech Materials LLC ....G... 425 402-3665
 Bothell *(G-1911)*
Trapp Industries ....G... 509 895-4282
 Selah *(G-11599)*
Tree of Life Enterprises Inc ....G... 360 894-6038
 Yelm *(G-15748)*
Tri Coastal Industries ....G... 425 353-4384
 Mukilteo *(G-6984)*
Tri-Point Industries Inc ....G... 253 514-8890
 Gig Harbor *(G-4169)*
Triarii Industries LLC ....G... 360 314-6099
 Vancouver *(G-14646)*
Turn Pro Manufacturing ....G... 425 220-8767
 Sedro Woolley *(G-11579)*
Ucoinitcom LLC ....G... 253 271-0656
 Puyallup *(G-8265)*
Unique Wreaths ....G... 206 355-2103
 Renton *(G-8937)*
Unisource Manufacturing Inc ....G... 253 854-0541
 Kent *(G-5196)*
United Farms ....F... 253 847-4230
 Graham *(G-4241)*
University of Washington ....B... 206 543-2565
 Seattle *(G-11380)*
Upstart Industries LLC ....G... 206 265-1521
 Seattle *(G-11387)*
Valley Aero Mfg ....G... 206 841-9652
 Renton *(G-8940)*
Van Harten ....G... 360 868-2011
 Shelton *(G-11749)*
Vandalez Industries Inc ....G... 509 228-9000
 Spokane Valley *(G-12927)*
Vanex Industries LLC ....G... 206 860-0455
 Seattle *(G-11403)*
Velotron Heavy Industries ....G... 206 799-5089
 Seattle *(G-11408)*
Venspark Inc ....G... 206 588-2756
 Seattle *(G-11410)*
Vertx Industries LLC ....G... 206 619-1479
 Fall City *(G-3709)*
▲ Vibratrim LLC ....G... 253 238-0675
 Gig Harbor *(G-4171)*
▲ Walflor Industries ....G... 425 766-4161
 Bellingham *(G-1587)*
Washougal Manufacturing Co ....G... 360 261-2199
 Washougal *(G-14999)*
Watermark Art & Framing ....G... 360 871-2906
 Port Orchard *(G-7856)*
Waters Edge Gallery & Framery ....G... 253 858-7449
 Gig Harbor *(G-4174)*
Wax Barn Inc ....F... 425 228-8537
 Renton *(G-8943)*
Wc Manufacturing LLC ....G... 425 890-9709
 Auburn *(G-595)*
We Industries LLC ....G... 206 853-4505
 Seattle *(G-11446)*
Webgirl ....G... 253 473-6895
 Tacoma *(G-13590)*
Weeks Waterjet & Mfg ....G... 206 261-1954
 Auburn *(G-596)*
Wesnip ....G... 360 306-0345
 Bellingham *(G-1591)*
West Coast Fire & Rescue Inc ....G... 253 826-9852
 Lake Tapps *(G-5687)*
West Road Candles ....G... 360 682-5822
 Oak Harbor *(G-7169)*
Westech Industries LLC ....G... 509 751-0401
 Clarkston *(G-2655)*
Whalen Furniture Manufacturing ....G... 425 427-0115
 Issaquah *(G-4489)*
Wheel Haus Mfg Inc ....G... 360 719-1030
 Vancouver *(G-14687)*

Employee Codes: A=Over 500 employees, B=251-500
C=101-250, D=51-100, E=20-50, F=10-19, G=2-9

39 MISCELLANEOUS MANUFACTURING INDUSTRIES SIC SECTION

Wheels Up LLC .... G 206 588-1573
Seattle *(G-11467)*
Whistle Pig LLC .... G 509 949-1584
Yakima *(G-15707)*
Whistle Stop Studios LLC .... G 360 652-9728
Stanwood *(G-12999)*
Whistle Workwear Shoreline LLC .... G 206 364-2253
Shoreline *(G-11822)*
Whitmus Enterprises Inc .... G 509 398-0144
Ephrata *(G-3347)*
Wieweck LLC .... G 360 576-0509
Vancouver *(G-14692)*
Wisdoms Marionettes .... G 206 243-6172
Tukwila *(G-13836)*
Woods Bee Co .... G 360 623-3359
Centralia *(G-2445)*
Wreathe Havoc .... G 206 979-6838
Edmonds *(G-3163)*
▲ **Wychwood Inc** .... G 209 667-8188
Elk *(G-3179)*
Xextex Corporation USA .... G 425 392-3848
Issaquah *(G-4490)*
▲ **Xtreme Pet Products LLC** .... G 206 772-2000
Renton *(G-8951)*
XYZ Manufacturing .... G 206 402-1936
Federal Way *(G-3804)*
Yummy Designs LLC .... G 509 525-2072
Walla Walla *(G-14907)*
Zorn Manufacturing Co .... G 360 456-4747
Lacey *(G-5603)*

73 BUSINESS SERVICES

7372 Prepackaged Software

1strategy LLC .... G 801 824-5660
Bainbridge Island *(G-605)*
2 C Media LLC .... E 206 522-7211
Seattle *(G-9318)*
5 By 5 Software Ventures Ltd .... G 206 779-6234
Seattle *(G-9324)*
7 Grapes Software .... G 425 653-2308
Bellevue *(G-776)*
8stem Inc .... G 360 317-7448
Eastsound *(G-3036)*
8th Shore Inc .... G 425 681-1157
Redmond *(G-8364)*
A & E Systems .... G 509 886-1092
East Wenatchee *(G-3005)*
Aaab Consulting LLC .... G 206 612-7041
Seattle *(G-9328)*
Aav Group .... F 972 834-2750
Bellevue *(G-779)*
Accordent Technologies Inc .... F 310 374-7491
Seattle *(G-9337)*
Accounting Software Inc .... G 253 952-6040
Tacoma *(G-13156)*
Acg Software .... G 425 828-1456
Redmond *(G-8368)*
ACS Technologies Group Inc .... D 843 413-8032
Seattle *(G-9343)*
Activated Content .... G 206 448-3260
Seattle *(G-9345)*
Actively Learn Inc .... G 857 540-6670
Seattle *(G-9346)*
Adaptelligence LLC .... G 509 432-1812
Pullman *(G-8082)*
Add Corporation .... D 206 452-7498
Normandy Park *(G-7089)*
Add Three Inc .... E 206 568-3772
Seattle *(G-9349)*
Adobe Systems Incorporated .... B 206 675-7000
Seattle *(G-9353)*
Advangelists LLC .... G 734 546-4989
Seattle *(G-9355)*
Afar Interactive Inc .... G 425 442-5101
Seattle *(G-9357)*
Agile Advantage Inc .... E 425 629-6361
Redmond *(G-8374)*
Agilecore Software LLC .... G 360 910-3140
Vancouver *(G-14012)*
Aircon Soft .... G 206 851-8476
Seattle *(G-9361)*
Akamai Technologies Inc .... G 206 674-5900
Bellevue *(G-783)*
Alcatel-Lucent USA Inc .... E 425 497-2400
Redmond *(G-8376)*
Algorithmia Inc .... G 415 741-1491
Seattle *(G-9375)*
Alitheon Inc .... F 888 606-7445
Bellevue *(G-784)*
All Software Tools Inc .... G 360 883-2981
Vancouver *(G-14021)*
Alphawave Systems .... G 719 888-9283
Vancouver *(G-14024)*
Amdocs Qpass Inc .... F 206 447-6000
Seattle *(G-9391)*
American Labelmark Company .... E 206 256-0889
Seattle *(G-9393)*
Ann H McCormick PHD .... G 650 451-8020
Leavenworth *(G-5795)*
Antenna Dexterra Inc .... C 425 939-3100
Bothell *(G-1819)*
Apana Inc .... F 360 746-2276
Bellingham *(G-1249)*
APM Games LLC .... G 512 961-6515
Vancouver *(G-14038)*
App Grinder LLC .... G 206 293-9632
Seattle *(G-9410)*
Appagare Software Inc .... G 253 857-4675
Port Orchard *(G-7788)*
Appattach Inc .... G 425 202-5676
Kirkland *(G-5279)*
Appesteem Corporation .... F 240 461-5689
Bellevue *(G-789)*
Appgen Business Software .... G 253 857-9400
Gig Harbor *(G-4073)*
Apptio Inc .... C 866 470-0320
Bellevue *(G-790)*
Arabella Software LLC .... G 206 963-6460
Seattle *(G-9418)*
Arbitrary Software LLC .... G 425 644-7428
Bellevue *(G-791)*
Arcblock Inc .... F 425 442-5101
Bellevue *(G-793)*
Archer USA Inc .... E 206 567-5343
Seattle *(G-9419)*
Archive Solution Providers .... G 425 440-0228
Redmond *(G-8384)*
Arigato LLC .... G 713 492-3858
Issaquah *(G-4382)*
Arrays Software LLC .... G 206 414-8250
Seattle *(G-9432)*
Arrhythmia Solutions Inc .... G 509 389-7366
Spokane *(G-12118)*
ARS Nova Software .... G 425 869-0625
Redmond *(G-8386)*
Ascendance Pole & Aerial Arts .... G 425 256-2246
Renton *(G-8748)*
Ascentis Corporation .... E 425 519-0241
Bellevue *(G-797)*
Assetic Inc .... G 425 658-6603
Kirkland *(G-5281)*
At Once Sales Software Inc .... G 509 845-2453
Seattle *(G-9448)*
Attachmate Corporation .... B 206 217-7100
Seattle *(G-9458)*
Attachmate Intl Sls Corp .... G 206 217-7500
Seattle *(G-9459)*
Auction Edge Inc .... E 206 858-4808
Seattle *(G-9462)*
August Systems Inc .... E 509 468-2988
Spokane *(G-12127)*
Author-It Software Corporation .... F 888 999-1021
Seattle *(G-9466)*
Automated Options Inc .... G 509 467-9860
Spokane *(G-12130)*
Automic Software Inc .... D 425 644-2121
Bellevue *(G-799)*
Avado Inc .... G 415 662-8236
Newcastle *(G-7025)*
Avalara Inc .... D 206 826-4900
Seattle *(G-9468)*
Avidian Technologies Inc .... E 800 399-8980
Bellevue *(G-804)*
Avst Parent LLC .... D 425 951-1600
Bothell *(G-1750)*
Aware Software Inc .... G 206 232-5709
Mercer Island *(G-6455)*
B-Side Software LLC .... G 206 708-6973
Seattle *(G-9475)*
Barking Ant Software LLC .... G 360 281-1118
Battle Ground *(G-690)*
Barn Door Productions .... G 206 780-3535
Bainbridge Island *(G-616)*
Barn2door Inc .... G 206 459-4338
Seattle *(G-9493)*
Barshay Software Inc .... G 206 370-2393
Seattle *(G-9495)*
Battery Informatics Inc .... G 443 534-7671
Poulsbo *(G-7947)*
Bc Software .... G 425 831-0550
Snoqualmie *(G-12005)*
Bcard Inc .... G 206 963-5211
Spokane *(G-12141)*
Bellevue Parent LLC .... G 866 470-0320
Bellevue *(G-813)*
Best Guess Software .... G 360 876-3272
Port Orchard *(G-7793)*
Biblesoft Inc .... F 206 824-0547
Des Moines *(G-2929)*
Big Fish Premium LLC .... F 206 269-3573
Seattle *(G-9524)*
Bill Dibenedetto .... G 206 963-0499
Seattle *(G-9528)*
Bit Elixir LLC .... G 509 842-4121
Spokane Valley *(G-12641)*
Bitpeg Software Inc .... G 509 290-5216
Mead *(G-6425)*
Bittitan Inc .... F 206 428-6030
Kirkland *(G-5291)*
Bittitan Inc .... D 206 428-6030
Bellevue *(G-819)*
Bittium Usa Inc .... G 425 780-4480
Bothell *(G-1829)*
Bizlogr Inc .... G 800 366-4484
Redmond *(G-8405)*
Bkd Software .... G 425 487-1475
Woodinville *(G-15194)*
Blackboard Cyphr Educ Consltng .... G 360 870-8429
Olympia *(G-7237)*
Blockpartygg LLC .... G 206 409-6562
Seattle *(G-9543)*
Blucapp Inc .... F 206 629-8887
Seattle *(G-9546)*
Blue Martini Software .... G 360 754-2207
Olympia *(G-7238)*
Blueberry Meringue Software .... G 425 830-5414
Monroe *(G-6556)*
Bluepenguin Software Inc .... G 561 459-5393
Sequim *(G-11615)*
Bluewave Technologies LLC .... G 800 636-1428
Seattle *(G-9558)*
Bobolink Software .... G 509 684-2800
Kettle Falls *(G-5225)*
Bocada LLC .... E 425 818-4400
Kirkland *(G-5294)*
Bourgeois Bits LLC .... G 434 535-2487
Seattle *(G-9570)*
Brad Pendleton Software LLC .... G 425 898-0309
Sammamish *(G-9193)*
Brak Software Inc .... G 206 280-7157
Bellevue *(G-828)*
Bravura Software LLC .... G 425 881-7305
Redmond *(G-8408)*
Browsereport .... G 206 948-2640
Federal Way *(G-3718)*
Bubbie Bit N Bundle .... G 360 733-8315
Bellingham *(G-1285)*
Budwiz Inc .... G 360 508-2771
Olympia *(G-7246)*
Builder Box LLC .... E 206 778-4753
Seattle *(G-9596)*
Byndl AMC LLC .... E 855 462-9635
Bellevue *(G-833)*
Byteware LLC .... G 503 914-8020
Woodinville *(G-15201)*
C Davis Software Con .... G 847 436-6225
Lake Stevens *(G-5636)*
Ca Inc .... D 509 252-5080
Spokane *(G-12166)*
Ca Inc .... D 425 201-3500
Bellevue *(G-834)*
Cadence Design Systems Inc .... G 425 451-2360
Bellevue *(G-835)*
Cakes Be We .... G 509 460-1399
Kennewick *(G-4639)*
Caminova Inc .... G 206 919-2110
Mill Creek *(G-6503)*
Campusce Corporation .... G 206 686-8003
Seattle *(G-9615)*
▼ **Candela Technologies Inc** .... G 360 380-1618
Ferndale *(G-3822)*
Cannonbot Games LLC .... G 510 473-6871
Spokane *(G-12167)*
Cardswapper LLC .... G 253 549-8600
Gig Harbor *(G-4084)*
Care Zone Inc .... G 888 407-7785
Seattle *(G-9631)*
Care Zone Inc .... E 206 707-9127
Seattle *(G-9632)*

SIC SECTION

73 BUSINESS SERVICES

Career Development Software ... F ... 360 696-3529
Vancouver *(G-14099)*

Cartogram Inc ... E ... 425 628-0395
Bellevue *(G-840)*

Casaba Security LLC ... G ... 888 869-6708
Redmond *(G-8416)*

Cascade Medical Technologies ... G ... 360 896-6944
Vancouver *(G-14104)*

Cascade Software Corp ... G ... 425 558-9017
Redmond *(G-8417)*

CCS Computer Systems Inc ... F ... 425 672-4806
Lynnwood *(G-6089)*

Cellar Door Media LLC ... G ... 253 732-9560
Tacoma *(G-13230)*

Certain Software Inc ... G ... 415 353-5330
Bellevue *(G-848)*

Certifly LLC ... G ... 888 415-9119
Seattle *(G-9660)*

Champlin Technologies LLC ... G ... 425 736-8935
Bellevue *(G-849)*

Chekin MD LLC ... G ... 425 894-9896
Sammamish *(G-9197)*

CHI-Square Labs LLC ... G ... 206 282-8246
Seattle *(G-9674)*

Chiminera LLC ... G ... 401 326-2820
Seattle *(G-9677)*

Chronus Corporation ... F ... 425 629-6327
Bellevue *(G-851)*

Cinematix LLC ... G ... 425 533-1024
Kirkland *(G-5305)*

Circle Systems Inc ... G ... 206 682-3783
Seattle *(G-9685)*

Cirrato Technologies Inc ... G ... 425 999-4500
Kirkland *(G-5306)*

Citrix Systems Inc ... G ... 425 895-4700
Redmond *(G-8421)*

Clario Medical ... G ... 206 315-5410
Seattle *(G-9688)*

Cloudcoreo Inc ... G ... 206 851-0130
Seattle *(G-9700)*

Cnc Software Inc ... G ... 253 858-6677
Gig Harbor *(G-4091)*

Coach Cheetah Inc ... G ... 206 914-8313
Seattle *(G-9703)*

Coastal Software & Consulting ... G ... 360 891-6174
Vancouver *(G-14127)*

Cobalt Group Inc ... B ... 206 269-6363
Seattle *(G-9708)*

Coherent Knowledge Systems LLC ... G ... 206 519-6410
Mercer Island *(G-6458)*

Coinstax LLC ... G ... 206 629-8831
Seattle *(G-9713)*

Columbus Systems Inc ... G ... 360 943-4165
Tumwater *(G-13863)*

Columbus Systems Inc ... G ... 360 943-4165
Tumwater *(G-13864)*

Community Thrift Shop LLC ... G ... 509 438-1302
Richland *(G-8984)*

Company 43 LLC ... G ... 425 269-0430
Bothell *(G-1841)*

Compass Northwest ... G ... 206 546-1178
Shoreline *(G-11766)*

Competentum-Usa Ltd ... F ... 425 996-4201
Issaquah *(G-4398)*

Computer Assisted Message Inc ... F ... 425 392-2496
Issaquah *(G-4399)*

Computer Clinic Northwest Inc ... G ... 360 658-1234
Marysville *(G-6327)*

Computer Connections ... G ... 360 736-2177
Centralia *(G-2395)*

Computer Human Interaction LLC ... E ... 425 282-6900
Tukwila *(G-13714)*

Comscore Inc ... E ... 206 447-1860
Seattle *(G-9725)*

Comtronic Systems LLC ... F ... 509 573-4300
Cle Elum *(G-2662)*

Concur Technologies Inc ... A ... 425 590-5000
Bellevue *(G-860)*

Congruent Software ... G ... 206 301-0553
Seattle *(G-9729)*

Congruent Software (usa) Inc ... D ... 425 460-0172
Bellevue *(G-861)*

Connx Solutions Inc ... E ... 425 519-6600
Redmond *(G-8423)*

Constellation Homebuilder Syst ... G ... 888 723-2222
Redmond *(G-8424)*

Constructivision Inc ... G ... 425 741-4413
Mill Creek *(G-6504)*

Content Master ... G ... 425 274-1970
Bellevue *(G-862)*

Context Reality Inc ... G ... 425 241-5860
Redmond *(G-8425)*

Continental Data Graphics ... G ... 425 562-4050
Bellevue *(G-863)*

Continuum Creative LLC ... G ... 404 985-6648
Mercer Island *(G-6459)*

Conveyor Dynamics Inc ... F ... 360 671-2200
Bellingham *(G-1305)*

Coptracker Inc ... G ... 214 542-2351
Mattawa *(G-6404)*

Cornerstone Software Systems ... G ... 425 788-9681
Woodinville *(G-15213)*

Corporate Vat Management Inc ... G ... 206 292-0300
Seattle *(G-9743)*

Counting Stick Software LLC ... G ... 425 750-1028
Lynnwood *(G-6099)*

Coverity ... G ... 206 467-5967
Seattle *(G-9750)*

Cowlitz River Software Inc ... G ... 253 856-3111
Kent *(G-4866)*

Crema Development LLC ... G ... 360 918-6978
Olympia *(G-7260)*

Crimpd LLC ... G ... 847 436-0433
Seattle *(G-9753)*

Cronus Ventures LLC ... G ... 425 641-4497
Bellevue *(G-869)*

Cross and Crown Church ... G ... 206 498-3551
Seattle *(G-9755)*

Crystal Point Inc ... F ... 425 487-3656
Mill Creek *(G-6505)*

Custom Computer Creat CCC LLC ... G ... 800 295-3381
Seattle *(G-9766)*

Cyrus Biotechnology Inc ... G ... 503 489-8460
Seattle *(G-9775)*

Da Vincis Garage LLC ... G ... 206 579-1333
Seattle *(G-9783)*

Darklight Inc ... G ... 509 940-1818
Redmond *(G-8432)*

Data Enterprises of The NW ... G ... 425 688-8805
Bellevue *(G-874)*

Datapark LLC ... E ... 360 224-2157
Sumas *(G-13043)*

Dauntless Inc ... E ... 206 494-3338
Redmond *(G-8434)*

Dauntless Software Inc ... G ... 206 489-4942
Renton *(G-8780)*

Dave Peck Software Development ... G ... 206 931-7572
Seattle *(G-9798)*

Deal Perch Inc ... G ... 425 372-8514
Snohomish *(G-11896)*

Dealer Info Systems Corp ... D ... 360 733-7610
Bellingham *(G-1320)*

Defsec Solutions LLC ... G ... 855 933-3732
Mill Creek *(G-6506)*

Descartes Biometrics Inc ... G ... 650 743-4435
Blaine *(G-1668)*

Descartes Systems (usa) LLC ... F ... 206 812-7874
Seattle *(G-9825)*

Desema Company ... G ... 425 202-7572
Redmond *(G-8438)*

Desi Telephone Labels Inc ... F ... 360 571-0713
Vancouver *(G-14176)*

Destiny Software Inc ... G ... 425 415-1777
Woodinville *(G-15224)*

Detonator Games LLC ... F ... 206 355-6682
Duvall *(G-2982)*

Digitlis Educatn Solutions Inc ... F ... 360 616-8915
Bremerton *(G-1947)*

Dinesync Inc ... G ... 206 620-2550
Seattle *(G-9832)*

Dining Solutions LLC ... G ... 425 268-6190
Bellevue *(G-878)*

Directeq LLC ... G ... 425 818-9510
Darrington *(G-2867)*

Discovery Tools ... G ... 253 288-1720
Enumclaw *(G-3285)*

▲ Diversified Systems Group Inc ... E ... 425 947-1500
Redmond *(G-8442)*

Dm2 Software Inc ... E ... 360 574-6984
Vancouver *(G-14185)*

Dogfish Software Corporation ... G ... 206 395-9050
Seattle *(G-9842)*

Dojo LLC ... G ... 203 903-0079
Renton *(G-8786)*

Dose Safety Co ... G ... 206 282-7086
Seattle *(G-9848)*

Dose Safety Inc ... G ... 206 276-3385
Redmond *(G-8443)*

DOT Com LLC ... G ... 425 256-2815
Bellevue *(G-881)*

Dot4kids ... G ... 503 884-8838
Olympia *(G-7273)*

Doublebit Software ... G ... 425 503-0692
Bellevue *(G-882)*

Dowling Software Consulta ... G ... 425 489-3026
Bothell *(G-1848)*

Dr Software LLC ... G ... 206 526-1371
Seattle *(G-9852)*

Dragon Head Studios LLC ... G ... 925 813-2881
Shoreline *(G-11770)*

Dreamtones Inc ... G ... 650 265-0576
Bothell *(G-1849)*

Ds-Iq Inc ... D ... 425 974-1400
Bellevue *(G-885)*

Duck Software LLC ... G ... 206 935-9722
Seattle *(G-9857)*

Dumb Luck LLC ... G ... 206 406-1011
Mercer Island *(G-6460)*

Dwaynes Software ... G ... 425 379-7741
Everett *(G-3448)*

Dwight Company LLC ... G ... 360 262-9844
Chehalis *(G-2490)*

Dynamic Software ... G ... 253 630-7026
Covington *(G-2826)*

Dynamic Software Innovations ... G ... 425 432-5313
Maple Valley *(G-6267)*

E B Associates Inc ... G ... 253 709-1433
Enumclaw *(G-3288)*

E L F Software Distributors ... G ... 360 577-6163
Longview *(G-5908)*

E W Bachtal Inc ... G ... 425 241-2505
Snoqualmie *(G-12010)*

E/Step Software Inc ... G ... 509 853-5000
Yakima *(G-15560)*

Eacceleration Corp ... E ... 360 697-9260
Poulsbo *(G-7960)*

Earshot LLC ... G ... 917 822-6074
Seattle *(G-9870)*

Eclipse Technology LLC ... G ... 406 270-6366
Seattle *(G-9875)*

Eduongo Inc ... F ... 206 451-7325
Bellevue *(G-892)*

Electromagnetic Software ... G ... 425 557-4716
Sammamish *(G-9203)*

Elguji Software LLC ... G ... 360 450-5022
Vancouver *(G-14199)*

Elite Athletics Training LLC ... G ... 509 221-1898
Richland *(G-8993)*

Emerald City Software LLC ... G ... 206 321-5252
Seattle *(G-9911)*

Encore Analytics LLC ... G ... 866 890-4331
Tacoma *(G-13279)*

Energsoft Inc ... G ... 425 246-1675
Seattle *(G-9925)*

Energy Arrow ... G ... 267 932-7769
Stanwood *(G-12969)*

Energysavvy Inc ... E ... 206 462-2206
Seattle *(G-9926)*

Engineering ... G ... 360 275-7384
Belfair *(G-761)*

Enhanced Software Products Inc ... E ... 509 534-1514
Spokane Valley *(G-12693)*

Enprecis Inc ... E ... 206 274-0122
Seattle *(G-9927)*

Entirely Inc ... G ... 206 979-9092
Seattle *(G-9930)*

Entropy Killer Software ... G ... 206 526-2488
Seattle *(G-9931)*

Epicore ... G ... 360 659-1986
Marysville *(G-6333)*

Eric Gibbs Software ... G ... 206 784-0741
Seattle *(G-9936)*

Esi Distribution Ltd ... G ... 206 780-9623
Bainbridge Island *(G-631)*

Esoteric Software LLC ... G ... 206 618-3331
Seattle *(G-9939)*

Eternity Software ... G ... 425 486-1622
Bothell *(G-1852)*

Etios Health LLC ... G ... 585 217-1716
Bellevue *(G-903)*

Event 1 Software Inc ... F ... 360 567-3752
Vancouver *(G-14208)*

Everpath Inc ... G ... 206 682-7259
Seattle *(G-9948)*

Exacttarget Inc ... G ... 866 362-4538
Bellevue *(G-904)*

Excelerate Systems LLC ... F ... 425 605-8515
Redmond *(G-8455)*

Exceptionally Smart ... G ... 206 321-0721
Seattle *(G-9952)*

S
I
C

Employee Codes: A=Over 500 employees, B=251-500
C=101-250, D=51-100, E=20-50, F=10-19, G=2-9

2019 Washington
Manufacturers Register

661

73 BUSINESS SERVICES

Exo Labs Inc .... G 206 659-1249
  Seattle *(G-9953)*
Expert Ig .... G 360 335-0555
  Washougal *(G-14954)*
Exquisitecrystals Com LLC .... G 360 573-6787
  Vancouver *(G-14215)*
Ezr Communications Inc .... G 360 936-0070
  Vancouver *(G-14216)*
F5 LLC .... G 425 882-8080
  Redmond *(G-8456)*
F5 Networks Inc .... C 206 272-5555
  Seattle *(G-9959)*
Falconstor Software Inc .... G 206 652-3312
  Seattle *(G-9964)*
Falx Games .... G 253 439-9121
  Tacoma *(G-13289)*
Fanapptic LLC .... G 253 548-7443
  University Place *(G-13968)*
Fast Yeti Inc .... G 253 573-1877
  University Place *(G-13969)*
Fastdataio Inc .... F 888 707-3346
  Seattle *(G-9976)*
Fifth Star Labs LLC .... G 206 369-3956
  Seattle *(G-9990)*
Fileonq Inc .... F 206 575-3488
  Tukwila *(G-13734)*
Financial Management Systems ..... G 425 881-8687
  Issaquah *(G-4414)*
Firecracker Software LLC .... G 509 443-5308
  Spokane Valley *(G-12702)*
Fizikl Inc .... G 360 393-0714
  Bellingham *(G-1348)*
Flexe Inc .... G 855 733-7788
  Seattle *(G-10005)*
Float Technologies LLC .... G 916 947-6646
  Kirkland *(G-5339)*
Florence L Ellis .... G 360 213-2475
  Vancouver *(G-14235)*
Flourish Church Rainier Valley .... G 206 769-7950
  Seattle *(G-10006)*
Fluentpro Software Corporation ...... G 855 358-3688
  Redmond *(G-8462)*
Flying Lab Software LLC .... F 206 272-9815
  Seattle *(G-10009)*
Flying Sofa LLC .... G 206 275-3935
  Mercer Island *(G-6463)*
Followone Inc .... F 206 518-8844
  Kirkland *(G-5341)*
Foof LLC .... G 425 260-8897
  Cle Elum *(G-2666)*
Forword Input Inc .... F 206 227-0191
  Lynnwood *(G-6121)*
Foxfacerabbitfish LLC .... G 206 856-7222
  Seattle *(G-10018)*
Francis Scientific Inc .... G 360 687-7019
  Battle Ground *(G-702)*
Freakn Genius Inc .... G 425 301-4258
  Kirkland *(G-5343)*
Free Birthday Fun LLC .... G 509 999-7517
  Spokane *(G-12264)*
Freemo Inc .... G 425 280-9661
  Kirkland *(G-5344)*
Fti Consulting Tech Sftwr .... D 206 373-6500
  Seattle *(G-10034)*
Fund RR LLC .... G 425 530-7120
  Marysville *(G-6337)*
Future Software Systems Inc .... G 360 629-9973
  Stanwood *(G-12973)*
Gate Technologies LLC .... G 206 229-9947
  North Bend *(G-7111)*
Gatheredtable Inc .... F 206 735-4886
  Seattle *(G-10052)*
GE Healthcare Inc .... B 206 622-9558
  Seattle *(G-10055)*
Gekko Corporation .... G 425 679-9188
  Bellevue *(G-922)*
Gengler Veterinary Svcs Pllc .... F 425 788-2620
  Duvall *(G-2990)*
Ghost Inspector Inc .... G 206 395-3635
  Seattle *(G-10069)*
Ghost Ridge Software Inc .... G 425 646-4822
  Kirkland *(G-5348)*
Girt John .... G 206 399-4977
  Issaquah *(G-4420)*
Glarus Group Inc .... G 425 572-5907
  Newcastle *(G-7030)*
Global Software LLC .... F 425 822-3140
  Bothell *(G-1861)*
Global Software Systems Inc .... G 425 427-8215
  Issaquah *(G-4421)*

Global Studios Consulting LLC ...... E 425 223-5291
  Bellevue *(G-929)*
Global Vision .... G 425 985-9325
  Mill Creek *(G-6512)*
Globalwxdatacom .... G 425 644-4010
  Seattle *(G-10085)*
Globys Inc .... D 206 352-3055
  Seattle *(G-10088)*
Gomotive Inc .... G 206 462-6379
  Seattle *(G-10098)*
Gooseworks Media LLC .... G 425 487-8766
  Kenmore *(G-4577)*
Graphicode Inc .... E 360 282-4888
  Snohomish *(G-11915)*
Gratrack .... G 571 357-4728
  Seattle *(G-10108)*
Gravity Labs Inc .... G 509 220-0817
  Spokane *(G-12279)*
Grcc Student Chapter Saf .... F 253 288-3331
  Auburn *(G-455)*
Greater Intelligence Inc .... G 703 989-2281
  Kirkland *(G-5353)*
Green Hills Software LLC .... G 206 447-1373
  Seattle *(G-10116)*
Grigsby Software Developm .... G 360 942-5240
  Raymond *(G-8351)*
Groupfabric Inc .... G 425 681-2927
  Seattle *(G-10127)*
Groupware Incorporated .... E 360 397-1000
  Vancouver *(G-14274)*
Grove Church .... G 360 386-5760
  Marysville *(G-6342)*
Growfast Software .... G 360 224-5484
  Bellingham *(G-1363)*
Hado Labs LLC .... G 425 891-7124
  Seattle *(G-10135)*
Hahn Software LLC .... G 206 724-4735
  Burien *(G-2111)*
Happy Tab LLC .... G 773 231-8223
  Kirkland *(G-5357)*
Harbinger Knowledge Pdts Inc ...... G 425 861-8400
  Redmond *(G-8488)*
Harmonious Development LLC ...... G 425 248-5794
  Seattle *(G-10142)*
Harvest Food Solutions .... G 503 926-6499
  Vancouver *(G-14286)*
Hash Inc .... F 360 750-0042
  Vancouver *(G-14287)*
Hbsw Inc .... G 217 377-9043
  Lynnwood *(G-6133)*
Headlight Software Inc .... G 206 985-4431
  Seattle *(G-10154)*
Health Guardian Inc .... G 206 999-8153
  Seattle *(G-10156)*
Hearform Software LLC .... G 888 453-8806
  Northport *(G-7137)*
Hearts In Motion Ministries .... G 360 798-0275
  Ridgefield *(G-9088)*
Helcorp Interactive LLC .... G 917 446-8506
  Seattle *(G-10162)*
Hella Shaggy Software LLC .... G 206 533-1468
  Edmonds *(G-3118)*
Her Interactive Inc .... E 425 460-8787
  Bellevue *(G-940)*
HI Baby Software .... G 206 372-8936
  Bellevue *(G-943)*
Hidden Path Entertainment Inc ...... E 425 452-7284
  Bellevue *(G-945)*
High Rise Software Group Inc ...... G 206 290-6087
  Bellevue *(G-10170)*
Hildebrand Consulting .... G 206 465-1729
  Lake Forest Park *(G-5614)*
Hirelytics LLC .... G 843 900-4473
  Seattle *(G-10175)*
Holder Software .... G 509 338-0692
  Pullman *(G-8091)*
Holdiman Software .... G 509 582-5085
  Kennewick *(G-4671)*
Horizon Imaging LLC .... G 509 525-2860
  College Place *(G-2725)*
Horizon Professional Cmpt Svcs ... F 425 883-6588
  Redmond *(G-8501)*
Hough Software Consulting .... G 425 881-2339
  Redmond *(G-8502)*
Howard F Harrison M D .... G 509 575-8307
  Yakima *(G-15586)*
Hoylu Inc .... G 425 269-3299
  Kirkland *(G-5361)*
Hoylu Inc .... G 425 829-2316
  Kirkland *(G-5362)*

Hurkin LLC .... G 425 437-0100
  Maple Valley *(G-6274)*
Hussey Software LLC .... G 206 409-0959
  Seattle *(G-10195)*
Hyperfish Inc .... F 425 332-6567
  Kirkland *(G-5364)*
Icopyright Inc .... G 206 484-8561
  Seattle *(G-10201)*
Ieg7 Inc .... G 206 501-6193
  Auburn *(G-470)*
Ifooddecisionsciences Inc .... E 206 219-3703
  Seattle *(G-10204)*
Ilinklive Inc .... G 509 464-0062
  Spokane *(G-12303)*
Immersive Media Company .... E 360 609-3419
  Washougal *(G-14960)*
Impinj Inc .... C 206 517-5300
  Seattle *(G-10212)*
Imprev Inc .... G 800 809-3356
  Bellevue *(G-954)*
Incremental Systems Corp .... G 425 732-2377
  Bellevue *(G-956)*
Incycle Software Corp .... G 425 880-9200
  Bellevue *(G-957)*
Indaba Management Company LLC ... F 360 546-5528
  Vancouver *(G-14312)*
Indulo Inc .... G 206 383-0373
  Seattle *(G-10228)*
Industrial Generosity Inc .... G 206 336-2268
  Seattle *(G-10232)*
Industrial Software Solutns .... E 425 368-7310
  Bothell *(G-1767)*
Industrial Systems Laboratory .... G 425 226-7585
  Renton *(G-8824)*
Infinity Digital LLC .... G 715 298-3530
  Kelso *(G-4529)*
Infoharvest Inc .... G 206 686-2729
  Seattle *(G-10233)*
Infometrix Inc .... F 425 402-1450
  Bothell *(G-1768)*
Information Builders Inc .... F 206 624-9055
  Seattle *(G-10234)*
Infosoft Solutions Inc .... G 360 738-3060
  Bellingham *(G-1377)*
Ingio/Vinbalance LLC .... G 509 522-1621
  Walla Walla *(G-14822)*
Inner Fence Holdings Inc .... G 888 922-8277
  Redmond *(G-8507)*
Inside Out Medicine Inc .... G 206 920-8959
  Seattle *(G-10243)*
Insightful Corporation .... D 206 283-8802
  Seattle *(G-10244)*
Insights Works Inc .... G 425 577-2206
  Kirkland *(G-5368)*
Insomania Software .... G 425 837-1525
  Redmond *(G-8509)*
Instantiations Inc .... F 503 770-0861
  Vancouver *(G-14319)*
Instructional Technologies Inc ...... F 360 576-5976
  Vancouver *(G-14320)*
Integrated Computer Systems .... F 425 820-6120
  Redmond *(G-8510)*
Intelligenteffects LLC .... G 323 206-0499
  Kirkland *(G-5369)*
Intentionet Inc .... G 206 579-6567
  Redmond *(G-8512)*
Interlocking Software Corp .... G 360 394-5900
  Poulsbo *(G-7966)*
Internet Motors Company .... G 425 654-1154
  Bellevue *(G-961)*
Interworks US LLC .... G 206 934-1074
  Seattle *(G-10252)*
Intradata Inc .... G 425 836-8654
  Newcastle *(G-7032)*
Intuitive Mfg Systems Inc .... D 425 821-0740
  Kirkland *(G-5370)*
Intuitive Software Solution .... G 360 387-2271
  Stanwood *(G-12955)*
Invio Inc .... G 206 915-3563
  Seattle *(G-10256)*
Ipr-Now Inc .... G 425 888-6190
  North Bend *(G-7113)*
Iron Software Development LLC ... G 425 892-2287
  Bothell *(G-1770)*
Iship Inc .... E 425 602-4848
  Bellevue *(G-962)*
Isonetic Inc .... G 800 670-8871
  Vashon *(G-14726)*
Iunu Inc .... G 253 307-1858
  Seattle *(G-10263)*

SIC SECTION
73 BUSINESS SERVICES

J A Ratto Company .... G 206 240-5601
Bellevue *(G-964)*
Jam Developers Inc .... E 206 448-5225
Seattle *(G-10280)*
Jayam Software .... G 425 208-6467
Sammamish *(G-9222)*
Jazzie Software .... G 206 905-7411
Seattle *(G-10287)*
Jima Software Incorporated .... G 206 354-7309
Bothell *(G-1870)*
JM Software .... G 206 453-3544
Seattle *(G-10299)*
John H Wolf CPA PC .... G 509 465-9165
Spokane *(G-12338)*
Jolly Hatchet Games LLC .... G 360 624-2758
Vancouver *(G-14341)*
Justin-Grace Inc .... G 206 992-4292
Seattle *(G-10319)*
Kashoo Cloud Accunting USA Inc .... E 888 520-5274
Bellingham *(G-1391)*
Kennewick Computer Company .... G 509 371-0600
Richland *(G-9018)*
Kentico Software LLC .... G 206 674-4507
Tukwila *(G-13763)*
Keypict .... G 206 522-5201
Seattle *(G-10340)*
Klicktrack Inc .... F 206 557-3223
Bainbridge Island *(G-646)*
Knights Edge Software .... G 425 488-3552
Kenmore *(G-4589)*
Kokako Software .... G 425 922-1115
Seattle *(G-10352)*
Konnekti Incorporated .... G 925 878-5083
Seattle *(G-10354)*
Koowalla Inc .... G 206 948-1803
Woodinville *(G-15280)*
Kragworks Llc .... G 208 871-6413
Naches *(G-6999)*
Krantz News Service Inc .... G 253 857-6590
Gig Harbor *(G-4128)*
Krell Software Inc .... G 425 298-9519
Mill Creek *(G-6515)*
Krill Systems Inc .... G 206 780-2901
Bainbridge Island *(G-647)*
Kronos Incorporated .... E 206 696-1505
Seattle *(G-10359)*
Kuo Software LLC .... G 425 961-0197
Sammamish *(G-9227)*
Lagunamoon Beauty Intl Ltd LLC .... F 480 925-7577
Seattle *(G-10372)*
Lambda Software LLC .... G 425 882-3464
Bellevue *(G-975)*
Laplink Software Inc .... E 425 952-6000
Bellevue *(G-977)*
Laud Social Inc .... G 213 797-0744
Seattle *(G-10380)*
Lawsuite Technologies LLC .... G 206 349-2227
Seattle *(G-10386)*
Ldl- Software Inc .... G 425 652-1473
Renton *(G-8842)*
Leadscorz Inc .... G 206 899-4665
Seattle *(G-10392)*
Leaftail Labs LLC .... G 206 399-4233
Seattle *(G-10394)*
Leavelogic Inc .... G 757 655-3283
Seattle *(G-10395)*
Led Software .... G 206 232-2812
Mercer Island *(G-6470)*
Legal + Plus Software Group .... G 206 286-3600
Newcastle *(G-7033)*
Legal+plus Software Group Inc .... G 206 286-3600
Newcastle *(G-7034)*
Leisure Loyalty Inc .... G 425 223-5102
Bellevue *(G-981)*
Lemmino Inc .... G 571 229-3854
Seattle *(G-10401)*
Lenco Mobile Inc .... D 800 557-4148
Seattle *(G-10402)*
Leviathan Games Inc .... G 206 432-9949
Seattle *(G-10411)*
Life Recovery Solutions Inc .... G 208 771-2161
Olympia *(G-7323)*
Lifter Apps LLC .... G 206 289-0407
Seattle *(G-10415)*
Lightshine Software LLC .... G 425 231-9320
Monroe *(G-6593)*
Lightsmith Consulting LLC .... G 312 953-1193
Seattle *(G-10420)*
Likebright Inc .... G 206 669-2536
Seattle *(G-10421)*

Lill Creates .... G 206 355-4409
Seattle *(G-10422)*
Limelyte Technology Group Inc .... G 509 241-0138
Spokane *(G-12366)*
Lincoln Data Inc .... G 509 466-1744
Spokane *(G-12367)*
Linedata Services .... G 206 545-9522
Seattle *(G-10425)*
Links Business Group LLC .... G 425 961-0565
Issaquah *(G-4440)*
Lionfort Software Inc .... G 425 698-7403
Redmond *(G-8534)*
Little Sun Software LLC .... G 425 442-4911
Woodinville *(G-15291)*
Loki Systems Inc .... G 800 961-5654
Bellingham *(G-1413)*
Loqu8 Inc .... G 650 892-8901
Bellingham *(G-1414)*
Lost City Digital LLC .... G 206 327-4537
Des Moines *(G-2940)*
Lost Signal LLC .... G 360 601-2227
Tumwater *(G-13885)*
Loudscoop Inc .... G 425 391-7159
Redmond *(G-8538)*
Lpr Park LLC .... G 888 884-9507
Seattle *(G-10445)*
Lumatax Inc .... G 206 450-2004
Seattle *(G-10449)*
Lumedx Corporation .... D 425 450-9774
Bellevue *(G-991)*
M I S Construction Software .... G 425 882-3027
Kirkland *(G-5389)*
Mackichan Software Inc .... F 360 394-6033
Poulsbo *(G-7979)*
Maelstrom Interactive .... G 206 841-6071
Kirkland *(G-5393)*
Magnapro Business Systems Inc .... G 206 280-6222
Edmonds *(G-3131)*
Magnolia Desktop Computing LLC .... G 206 282-7161
Seattle *(G-10467)*
Magnum Opus Software & Co .... G 425 227-7712
Newcastle *(G-7035)*
Mainstem Inc .... F 844 623-4084
Seattle *(G-10469)*
Majesco Software Inc .... G 425 242-0327
Bellevue *(G-995)*
Manceps Inc .... G 503 922-1164
Camas *(G-2267)*
Mangoapps Inc .... D 425 274-9950
Issaquah *(G-4443)*
Marcia Hardy .... G 425 880-4460
Redmond *(G-8548)*
Margate Software LLC .... G 206 381-9120
Seattle *(G-10477)*
Mark Muzi .... G 206 523-6954
Seattle *(G-10487)*
Materiant Inc .... E 425 209-1943
Bellevue *(G-999)*
Matersmost Software LLC .... G 425 392-6165
Sammamish *(G-9231)*
Mathsoft Inc .... G 206 283-8802
Seattle *(G-10501)*
Matthews Cellars .... G 425 487-9810
Woodinville *(G-15305)*
McG Health Llc .... E 206 389-5300
Seattle *(G-10507)*
McObject LLC .... F 425 888-8505
Federal Way *(G-3757)*
Media Matrix Digital Center .... G 360 693-6455
Vancouver *(G-14408)*
Mediapro Holdings LLC .... E 425 483-4700
Bothell *(G-1777)*
Medida Health LLC .... G 425 985-5214
Kirkland *(G-5400)*
Mettler Toledo NW .... G 425 774-3510
Lynnwood *(G-6163)*
Mgs Software LLC .... G 253 841-1573
Puyallup *(G-8190)*
Micro Focus Software Inc .... A 206 217-7100
Seattle *(G-10532)*
Microchips Software .... G 360 921-8562
Vancouver *(G-14419)*
Microquill Software Publishing .... G 425 827-7200
Kirkland *(G-5401)*
Microsoft Corporation .... D 509 787-6900
Quincy *(G-8304)*
Microsoft Corporation .... D 425 705-1900
Bellevue *(G-1004)*
Microsoft Corporation .... D 425 705-6218
Redmond *(G-8558)*

Microsoft Corporation .... E 425 706-0040
Redmond *(G-8559)*
Microsoft Corporation .... G 425 281-6768
Sammamish *(G-9233)*
Microsoft Corporation .... G 206 290-9669
Seattle *(G-10536)*
Microsoft Corporation .... G 425 533-6624
Seattle *(G-10537)*
Microsoft Corporation .... G 770 235-8794
Bellevue *(G-1005)*
Microsoft Corporation .... D 425 705-1900
Bellevue *(G-1006)*
Microsoft Corporation .... E 206 724-8130
Kirkland *(G-5402)*
Microsoft Corporation .... E 425 882-8080
Issaquah *(G-4449)*
Microsoft Corporation .... E 425 706-6640
Redmond *(G-8560)*
Microsoft Corporation .... E 425 861-0581
Redmond *(G-8561)*
Microsoft Corporation .... E 425 706-0033
Redmond *(G-8562)*
Microsoft Corporation .... E 425 882-8080
Redmond *(G-8563)*
Microsoft Corporation .... E 360 863-0642
Redmond *(G-8564)*
Microsoft Corporation .... E 425 867-6537
Redmond *(G-8565)*
Microsoft Corporation .... E 206 883-5474
Seattle *(G-10538)*
Microsoft Corporation .... A 425 882-8080
Redmond *(G-8566)*
Microsoft Corporation .... A 425 882-8080
Redmond *(G-8567)*
Microsoft Corporation .... A 425 882-8080
Redmond *(G-8568)*
Microsoft Corporation .... A 425 882-8080
Redmond *(G-8569)*
Microsoft Corporation .... A 425 828-8080
Redmond *(G-8570)*
Microsoft Corporation .... A 425 882-8080
Redmond *(G-8571)*
Microsoft Corporation .... A 425 882-8080
Redmond *(G-8572)*
Microsoft Corporation .... A 425 882-8080
Redmond *(G-8573)*
Microsoft Corporation .... A 425 882-8080
Redmond *(G-8574)*
Microsoft Corporation .... A 425 882-8080
Redmond *(G-8575)*
Microsoft Corporation .... A 425 882-8080
Redmond *(G-8576)*
Microsoft Corporation .... A 425 882-8080
Redmond *(G-8577)*
Microsoft Corporation .... A 425 882-8080
Redmond *(G-8578)*
Microsoft Corporation .... G 425 882-8080
Redmond *(G-8579)*
Microsoft Corporation .... E 425 435-8457
Bellevue *(G-1007)*
Microsoft Corporation .... A 425 882-8080
Redmond *(G-8580)*
Microsoft Corporation .... G 425 633-4929
Sammamish *(G-9234)*
Microsoft Corporation .... G 206 816-0190
Redmond *(G-8581)*
Microsoft Corporation .... E 425 556-9348
Redmond *(G-8582)*
Microsoft Corporation .... G 425 703-6921
Woodinville *(G-15311)*
Microsoft Payments Inc .... F 425 722-0528
Redmond *(G-8583)*
Microsoft Tech Licensing LLC .... G 425 882-8080
Redmond *(G-8584)*
Mighty Ai LLC .... E 425 753-3167
Seattle *(G-10540)*
Mike Houston .... G 425 889-0682
Kirkland *(G-5403)*
Minapsys Software Corp .... G 425 891-1460
Spokane *(G-12395)*
Mindcast Software .... G 425 341-0450
Federal Way *(G-3759)*
Minima Software LLC .... G 206 659-9646
Seattle *(G-10545)*
MNC Services Inc .... G 425 527-9031
Woodinville *(G-15312)*
MNC Services Inc .... G 425 527-9031
Bellevue *(G-1011)*
Mobetize Corp .... G 778 588-5563
Blaine *(G-1684)*

Employee Codes: A=Over 500 employees, B=251-500
C=101-250, D=51-100, E=20-50, F=10-19, G=2-9

Mobimaging LLC....G....859 559-5138
Camas (G-2271)
Modeling Dynamics Inc....G....425 392-2262
Sammamish (G-9235)
Modular Software Systems Inc....G....360 886-8882
Enumclaw (G-3305)
Moneymindersoftware....G....360 255-4300
Bellingham (G-1441)
Morcant Software....G....509 225-6807
Yakima (G-15624)
Mordi Software....G....425 301-4897
Snohomish (G-11948)
Moxie Software Cim Corp....D....425 467-5000
Bellevue (G-1018)
Mscsoftware Corporation....G....855 672-7638
Bellevue (G-1019)
Multico Rating Systems....F....206 357-3928
Seattle (G-10569)
Multimodal Health Inc....G....651 245-2326
Seattle (G-10570)
Mutiny Bay Software LLC....G....360 331-5170
Freeland (G-4034)
National Management Software....E....509 327-0192
Spokane (G-12403)
Navit LLC....G....425 647-3580
Seattle (G-10597)
Nbk Associates Inc....G....216 408-8685
Kirkland (G-5408)
Neil Butler....G....360 668-9555
Snohomish (G-11950)
Newline Software Inc....G....425 442-1126
Redmond (G-8593)
Nextgen Apps Co....G....206 395-6770
Seattle (G-10605)
Nexus Life Cycle MGT LLC....G....541 400-0765
Stevenson (G-13016)
Niftybrick Software....G....206 588-5696
Seattle (G-10608)
Nintendo Software Technology....E....425 497-7500
Redmond (G-8596)
Nintex Usa Inc....D....425 324-2400
Bellevue (G-1032)
Nlpcore LLC....G....206 883-7616
Seattle (G-10613)
Noda Software....G....206 726-1125
Seattle (G-10617)
Noonum Llc....G....425 894-1202
Redmond (G-8597)
Norcom Inc....G....425 868-9973
Sammamish (G-9236)
Norman Langseth....G....425 643-7751
Bellevue (G-1033)
North Sky Games Inc....G....425 283-9634
Sammamish (G-9237)
Northwest Internet....G....509 888-2020
East Wenatchee (G-3027)
Northwest Sftwr Professionals....G....360 734-5747
Bellingham (G-1469)
Northwest Synergistic Software....G....425 271-1491
Renton (G-8860)
▲ Northwest Technologies....G....206 528-5353
Seattle (G-10652)
Nostopsign LLC....G....213 422-1750
Seattle (G-10656)
Novaleaf Software LLC....G....425 486-1242
Woodinville (G-15323)
Nrs Software LLC....G....509 969-4769
Yakima (G-15637)
Nuance Communications Inc....C....781 565-5000
Seattle (G-10664)
NW Software Solutions....G....509 252-3550
Spokane (G-12415)
O2d Software Inc....G....206 364-0055
Shoreline (G-11796)
Observa Inc....F....206 499-4444
Seattle (G-10679)
Office Timeline LLC....E....425 296-9002
Bellevue (G-1044)
Oliver Henry Games LLC....G....971 231-9141
Woodinville (G-15327)
Oltis Software LLC....F....800 557-1780
Bellevue (G-1047)
Olympic Sytems Inc....G....206 547-5777
Seattle (G-10695)
Omage Labs Inc....G....844 662-4326
Seattle (G-10696)
Omega Labs Inc....G....425 296-0886
Kirkland (G-5418)
Omni Development Inc....E....206 523-4152
Seattle (G-10699)
Omnim2m LLC....F....425 278-4090
Issaquah (G-4456)
Ong Innovations LLC....G....253 777-0186
Renton (G-8864)
Onsite Computer Services....G....360 650-1079
Bellingham (G-1480)
Ontario Systems LLC....C....360 256-7358
Vancouver (G-14452)
Open Mobile Solutions Inc....G....206 290-2314
Kenmore (G-4596)
Open Text Inc....E....425 455-6000
Bellevue (G-1051)
Opportunity Interactive Inc....F....206 870-1880
Seatac (G-9296)
Oracle Corporation....G....206 695-9000
Seattle (G-10710)
Oracle Corporation....B....425 945-8200
Bellevue (G-1053)
Oracle Fisheries LLC....G....360 477-9829
Port Angeles (G-7732)
Oracle Hypnosis....G....859 893-8147
Dupont (G-2971)
Oracles of God Ministries....G....425 449-8663
Bellevue (G-1054)
Orderport LLC....F....425 746-2926
Bellevue (G-1055)
Os Nexus Inc....F....425 279-0172
Bellevue (G-1056)
Outbouts LLC....G....253 921-0155
Bonney Lake (G-1731)
Pacific Ally LLC....G....360 760-4266
La Center (G-5511)
Pacific Applied Technology....G....360 693-4292
Vancouver (G-14462)
Pagemark Technology Inc....F....425 444-3735
Redmond (G-8610)
Paladin Data Systems Corp....D....360 779-2400
Poulsbo (G-7991)
Pamar Systems Inc....G....360 992-4120
Vancouver (G-14477)
Panda Dental Software Inc....G....800 517-7716
Bellevue (G-1062)
▲ Panther Systems Northwest Inc....E....360 750-9783
Vancouver (G-14478)
Panthercorn Studios....G....425 501-9717
Mukilteo (G-6964)
Parentasoft LLC....G....425 877-8574
Redmond (G-8615)
Partners In Emrgncy Prpredness....G....509 335-3530
Tacoma (G-13459)
Pat-Co Inc....G....206 937-8927
Seattle (G-10765)
Pateric Software....G....425 814-4949
Kirkland (G-5430)
PC Consulting & Development....G....425 836-0645
Redmond (G-8617)
Peach Fuzzer LLC....F....206 453-0339
Seattle (G-10775)
Peach Fuzzer LLC....G....844 557-3224
Seattle (G-10776)
Pearson Business Mgt Svcs....G....206 382-1457
Seattle (G-10777)
Pendown Software LLC....G....509 480-8232
Yakima (G-15643)
Performance Software Corp....G....425 481-4956
Bothell (G-1884)
Phone Flare Inc....G....425 346-9230
Duvall (G-2998)
Physware Inc....G....562 491-1600
Bellevue (G-1074)
Pl Technologies....G....206 877-3720
Bellevue (G-1075)
Picmonkey Inc....F....206 486-2106
Seattle (G-10801)
Pinnion Inc....F....206 577-3070
Kirkland (G-5434)
Pipelinedeals Inc....F....866 702-7303
Seattle (G-10814)
Pixel Planet Inc....G....206 669-7371
Seattle (G-10816)
Pixelan Software....G....831 222-0339
Bellingham (G-1498)
Pixelsaurus Games LLC....G....617 893-7755
Seattle (G-10817)
Pixotec LLC....G....425 255-0789
Renton (G-8880)
Pixvana Inc....F....206 910-5747
Seattle (G-10818)
Platalytics Inc....E....916 835-9584
Redmond (G-8625)
Point Inside Inc....D....425 590-9522
Bellevue (G-1077)
Pop Pop LLC....G....206 384-8121
Seattle (G-10831)
Portlock Software....G....425 247-0545
Kenmore (G-4599)
Portrait Displays Inc....F....206 420-7514
Edmonds (G-3144)
Posabit Inc....F....903 641-7604
Kirkland (G-5439)
Powder Monkey Games LLC....G....206 501-2340
Seattle (G-10842)
Powell Software Inc....E....425 974-9692
Yarrow Point (G-15722)
Powersoft....G....425 637-8088
Bellevue (G-1078)
Premiere Software....G....206 399-7495
Seattle (G-10855)
Proctor International LLC....G....425 881-7000
Redmond (G-8633)
Professional Practice Systems....F....253 531-8944
Roy (G-9164)
Projul Inc....G....844 776-5853
Ravensdale (G-8339)
Propdocket LLC....G....330 285-6526
Bothell (G-1892)
Provoke Solutions Inc....G....206 792-3680
Bellevue (G-1086)
Proxygroove LLC....G....415 264-1906
Seattle (G-10878)
Prune Hill Software LLC....G....360 834-3067
Camas (G-2277)
Ptc Inc....E....425 455-1930
Bellevue (G-1087)
Pulpo Games LLC....G....206 371-6924
Seattle (G-10886)
Purposeful Software LLC....G....206 855-7927
Bainbridge Island (G-661)
Pushspring Inc....G....206 455-6128
Seattle (G-10892)
Qorus Software Inc....D....844 516-8000
Seattle (G-10897)
Quadient Data USA Inc....D....206 443-0765
Seattle (G-10898)
Quest Integrity Usa LLC....D....253 893-7070
Kent (G-5093)
Quest Software Inc....E....949 720-1434
Seattle (G-10905)
Quick Collect Inc....E....360 256-7888
Vancouver (G-14523)
Qwardo Inc....G....425 753-8865
Redmond (G-8641)
Racer Mate Inc....E....206 524-7392
Seattle (G-10912)
Rainplex Inc....G....253 576-0157
Gig Harbor (G-4150)
Rally Software Development....G....206 266-8408
Bellevue (G-1092)
Rankin Associates....G....206 325-9440
Seattle (G-10920)
Raosoft Inc....G....206 523-9278
Seattle (G-10921)
▲ Realnetworks Inc....C....206 674-2700
Seattle (G-10930)
Recheadz LLC....G....509 406-2230
Soap Lake (G-12038)
Recordpoint Software USA LLC....G....425 245-6235
Bellevue (G-1096)
Recursive Frog LLC....G....206 745-2561
Seattle (G-10934)
Red Loon Software....G....253 353-7963
University Place (G-13980)
Redquarry LLC....F....206 981-5300
Tacoma (G-13493)
Refrelent Software Lab....G....425 898-9657
Sammamish (G-9243)
Reliance Inc....F....615 218-3929
Redmond (G-8647)
Renaissance Learning Inc....D....360 944-8996
Vancouver (G-14543)
Resonant Solutions LLC....G....206 619-7672
Bothell (G-1894)
Retip LLC....G....206 612-5538
Renton (G-8894)
Reverse Image Technologies LLC....G....253 219-5345
Tacoma (G-13497)
Revq Inc....G....360 260-5710
Vancouver (G-14548)
Reynolds and Reynolds Company....E....425 985-0194
Edmonds (G-3146)

Rgb14 LLC G 206 818-8207
Seattle *(G-10959)*
Riggel Productions Limited G 509 758-3209
Clarkston *(G-2645)*
Rimini Software LLC G 425 785-8819
Issaquah *(G-4467)*
Ripley Software G 501 773-5519
Issaquah *(G-4468)*
Risklens Inc F 866 936-0191
Spokane *(G-12475)*
Rival Iq Corporation F 206 395-8572
Seattle *(G-10966)*
River Rock Software Inc G 916 797-6746
Shelton *(G-11727)*
Rleyh Software LLC G 425 837-4643
Issaquah *(G-4469)*
Robert Rowe G 206 632-7997
Seattle *(G-10972)*
Rocket Software G 425 502-9684
Bellevue *(G-1107)*
Rocketcat LLC G 360 204-4037
Bremerton *(G-1995)*
Rodax Software G 206 782-3482
Seattle *(G-10974)*
Rooferpro Software LLC G 425 503-4298
Mill Creek *(G-6523)*
Roommate Filter LLC G 863 224-6462
Seattle *(G-10981)*
Rumor Games LLC G 585 771-7642
Seattle *(G-10994)*
Rune Inc G 425 766-6134
Seattle *(G-10996)*
Rust Proved Software G 206 244-0643
Burien *(G-2127)*
RY Investments Inc G 360 701-1261
Lacey *(G-5583)*
Safetec Compliance Systems Inc D 360 567-0280
Vancouver *(G-14564)*
Safetec Software LLC G 888 745-8943
Vancouver *(G-14565)*
Salesforcecom Inc G 206 701-1755
Bellevue *(G-1113)*
Salire Corporation E 425 284-0679
Redmond *(G-8656)*
Sandpiper Software Inc G 425 788-6175
Woodinville *(G-15354)*
Sansueb Software LLC G 253 630-5208
Kent *(G-5116)*
Sarangsoft LLC G 425 378-3890
Bellevue *(G-1114)*
Sars Corporation F 866 276-7277
Bellevue *(G-1115)*
Satus Networks LLC G 509 575-8382
Yakima *(G-15666)*
Savotta Tech LLC G 425 505-9951
Sammamish *(G-9246)*
Sayitright LLC G 401 682-7630
Oak Harbor *(G-7164)*
Scaleout Software Inc G 503 643-3422
Bellevue *(G-1116)*
SCC Enterprises LLC G 425 454-0567
Yarrow Point *(G-15723)*
Schoolkitcom Inc F 425 454-3373
Bellevue *(G-1117)*
Scope 5 Inc G 206 456-5656
Seattle *(G-11031)*
Sea To Software LLC G 206 617-6893
Seattle *(G-11040)*
Seafoam Studios LLC G 702 509-4742
Seattle *(G-11042)*
Seattle Avionics Inc G 425 806-0249
Woodinville *(G-15357)*
Seattle Software Corp G 206 286-7677
Seattle *(G-11076)*
Seattle Software Works Inc G 206 226-9263
Snohomish *(G-11973)*
Secucred Inc G 508 361-0928
Richland *(G-9040)*
Securitay Inc G 425 392-0203
Issaquah *(G-4472)*
Selah Springs LLC G 206 714-6068
Bellevue *(G-1123)*
Select Selling Inc E 425 895-8959
Kirkland *(G-5458)*
Serious Cybernetics LLC G 646 247-3642
North Bend *(G-7122)*
Servably Inc G 425 216-3333
Kirkland *(G-5459)*
Shared Healthcare Systems Inc E 360 299-4000
Anacortes *(G-166)*

Sharp Synaptics LLC G 253 927-2616
Federal Way *(G-3782)*
Shelfbot Co G 425 679-1421
Seattle *(G-11098)*
Shield Technologies LLC G 425 844-8055
Woodinville *(G-15360)*
Siemens Product Life Mgmt Sftw E 425 507-1900
Issaquah *(G-4476)*
Sienna Software Inc G 206 306-2752
Seattle *(G-11105)*
Simerics Inc F 256 489-1480
Bellevue *(G-1132)*
Simerics Inc F 425 502-9978
Bellevue *(G-1133)*
Simple Agile Corporation G 425 985-1096
Redmond *(G-8669)*
Simply Augmented Inc G 206 771-9774
Seattle *(G-11114)*
Simpos G 360 794-4658
Monroe *(G-6619)*
Sirascom Inc G 425 497-3300
Redmond *(G-8670)*
Sitting Room G 206 285-2830
Seattle *(G-11121)*
Sivart Software G 206 527-2164
Seattle *(G-11122)*
Six LLC G 206 466-5186
Seattle *(G-11123)*
Small Business Automation G 206 324-3820
Seattle *(G-11137)*
Smalldog Net Solutions Inc G 360 376-6056
Olga *(G-7219)*
▲ **Smartrg Inc** E 877 486-6210
Vancouver *(G-14596)*
Snider Software LLC G 206 790-7570
Bellevue *(G-1141)*
Socedo Inc G 206 499-3398
Bellevue *(G-1143)*
Social Voter Labs LLC G 206 981-9225
Seattle *(G-11149)*
Softchoice Corporation G 206 709-9000
Seattle *(G-11152)*
Softresources LLC G 425 216-4030
Kirkland *(G-5465)*
Softsource LLC G 360 676-0999
Bellingham *(G-1545)*
Software AG Usa Inc E 425 519-6600
Redmond *(G-8673)*
Software In 34th St G 425 557-7953
Issaquah *(G-4479)*
Software Ingenuity LLC G 509 924-0093
Veradale *(G-14751)*
Software Planning G 509 522-1620
Walla Walla *(G-14871)*
Soggy Hawk Software G 425 246-6555
Woodinville *(G-15368)*
Soham Inc D 425 445-2125
Bellevue *(G-1145)*
Sola Bothell G 501 487-7652
Bothell *(G-1793)*
Solid Modeling Solutions Inc G 425 246-3943
Bellevue *(G-1146)*
Somerset Software G 425 822-1951
Kirkland *(G-5466)*
Sound Software G 360 375-6375
Blakely Island *(G-1715)*
Source Dynamics Inc G 425 557-3630
Issaquah *(G-4481)*
Space Rock It Inc G 206 395-8383
Seattle *(G-11164)*
Sparkon Inc G 425 273-3904
Redmond *(G-8676)*
Specialized Computing Inc G 206 915-9033
Seattle *(G-11166)*
Specview Corp G 253 853-3199
Gig Harbor *(G-4164)*
Speechace LLC G 425 241-3033
Seattle *(G-11167)*
Splunk Inc G 206 430-5200
Seattle *(G-11169)*
Spry Fox LLC G 425 835-3320
Kirkland *(G-5469)*
Squarerigger Inc F 360 698-3562
Silverdale *(G-11859)*
Squealock Systems Inc G 206 519-4620
Burien *(G-2131)*
Stanford Technology Inc G 509 638-1191
Spokane *(G-12525)*
Starcom Computer Corporation F 425 486-6464
Bothell *(G-1797)*

Starform Inc G 206 446-9657
Seattle *(G-11182)*
Stateless Labs LLC G 512 387-3115
Seattle *(G-11185)*
Stellar Management Inc G 206 724-3973
Mountlake Terrace *(G-6869)*
Stellr Inc F 425 312-3798
Seattle *(G-11190)*
Stork Software LLC G 206 669-0644
Seattle *(G-11199)*
Straightthrough Inc G 425 467-1990
Bellevue *(G-1160)*
Stratagen Systems Inc E 425 821-8454
Kirkland *(G-5471)*
Stretch 22 Inc G 206 375-3358
Seattle *(G-11202)*
Stryve Inc G 425 802-3832
Seattle *(G-11206)*
Subset Games LLC G 206 354-4010
Seattle *(G-11209)*
Suntower Systems F 206 878-0578
Des Moines *(G-2947)*
Suplari Inc G 425 610-9496
Seattle *(G-11225)*
Survey Analytics LLC F 800 326-5570
Seattle *(G-11227)*
Survey Analytics LLC E 800 326-5570
Seattle *(G-11228)*
Suse LLC E 206 217-7500
Seattle *(G-11231)*
Suse LLC G 206 217-7100
Seattle *(G-11232)*
Swivel Inc G 509 557-7000
Walla Walla *(G-14876)*
Synergy Business Services Inc E 206 859-6500
Seattle *(G-11243)*
System & Application Assoc G 206 949-4153
Seattle *(G-11245)*
System 1 Software Inc G 206 548-1633
Seattle *(G-11246)*
Systematic Designs Intl F 360 944-9890
Vancouver *(G-14623)*
T T I Acquisition Corp F 509 358-2036
Liberty Lake *(G-5861)*
Tableau Ireland LLC G 206 633-3400
Seattle *(G-11252)*
Tableau Software Inc F 206 634-5610
Kirkland *(G-5475)*
Tableau Software Inc C 206 633-3400
Seattle *(G-11253)*
Taco Truck Games LLC G 360 218-4967
Seattle *(G-11254)*
Tactuum LLC G 425 941-6958
Bellevue *(G-1176)*
Talaera G 206 229-0631
Seattle *(G-11261)*
Talentwise Inc B 425 974-8863
Bothell *(G-1799)*
Tamarack Software Inc G 509 329-0456
Spokane *(G-12545)*
Tangera Technologies Inc G 425 652-7969
Bellevue *(G-1177)*
Tangible Ventures LLc G 360 818-4000
Bellevue *(G-1178)*
Target System Technology Inc G 509 456-4852
Spokane Valley *(G-12901)*
Teaching 2020 LLC G 253 232-6822
Olalla *(G-7211)*
Team Sport Software LLC G 703 971-2005
Gig Harbor *(G-4165)*
Tecplot Inc E 425 653-1200
Bellevue *(G-1179)*
Ted Gruber Software Inc G 702 735-1980
Kelso *(G-4554)*
Tekoa Software Inc G 509 340-3580
Liberty Lake *(G-5862)*
Tellwise Inc G 425 999-6935
Bellevue *(G-1181)*
Telos Sales Corporation G 425 890-2755
Kirkland *(G-5477)*
Telos Wealth Management G 509 664-8844
Wenatchee *(G-15080)*
Telos3 LLC G 360 900-9274
Poulsbo *(G-8006)*
Telos3 LLC G 360 536-3122
Bainbridge Island *(G-677)*
Telspace LLC E 425 953-2801
Kirkland *(G-5478)*
Tensormake Corporation G 206 659-6139
Redmond *(G-8688)*

Employee Codes: A=Over 500 employees, B=251-500
C=101-250, D=51-100, E=20-50, F=10-19, G=2-9
2019 Washington
Manufacturers Register
665

73 BUSINESS SERVICES

Tenth Generation Software .... G 425 226-1939
  Renton (G-8926)
Tetrachrome Software .... G 425 825-1708
  Kirkland (G-5480)
Theobald Software Inc .... G 425 802-2514
  Seattle (G-11287)
Thinking Man Software Corp .... G 425 313-0607
  Sammamish (G-9253)
Third Wave Software Corp .... G 425 825-9082
  Bothell (G-1801)
Threepenny Software LLC .... G 206 675-1518
  Seattle (G-11298)
Tibco Software Inc .... F 650 846-1000
  Liberty Lake (G-5864)
Tiller LLC .... G 425 770-0855
  Winthrop (G-15165)
Timbersoft Inc .... F 360 750-5575
  Vancouver (G-14640)
Timextender North America .... G 619 813-7625
  Bellevue (G-1190)
Tinman Software .... G 425 417-2142
  Sammamish (G-9254)
Tinman Systems Inc .... G 425 802-9035
  Sammamish (G-9255)
Tinypulse .... E 206 455-9424
  Seattle (G-11313)
Tiptoes Software LLC .... G 650 267-1907
  Bellevue (G-1191)
TNT Software Inc .... F 360 546-0878
  Vancouver (G-14641)
Tokenyo LLC .... G 206 851-7046
  Seattle (G-11317)
Toptec Software LLC .... G 206 331-4420
  Kennewick (G-4737)
Toptec Software LLC .... G 206 331-4420
  Richland (G-9045)
Total Cntrl LLC .... F 425 446-0342
  Everett (G-3634)
Tova Company .... F 800 729-2886
  Freeland (G-4038)
Tracktion Software Corporation .... G 425 273-3376
  Kirkland (G-5485)
Trek Global .... G 760 576-5115
  Vancouver (G-14644)
Trenzi Inc .... G 206 769-6501
  Seattle (G-11330)
Triadd Software Corporation .... G 425 643-3700
  Bellevue (G-1202)
Trick Shot Studios LLC .... G 858 663-7097
  Bellevue (G-1203)
Truegem LLC .... G 360 836-0310
  Camas (G-2284)
Tryb Inc .... G 206 310-9025
  Seattle (G-11344)
Tune Inc .... C 206 508-1318
  Seattle (G-11348)
Tuxbits Inc .... G 302 313-6831
  Walla Walla (G-14883)
Twilight Software .... G 206 228-2037
  Seattle (G-11350)
Twobitbear LLC .... G 206 658-5797
  Seattle (G-11356)
Tyler Technologies Inc .... E 360 852-6696
  Ridgefield (G-9117)
Tyler Technologies Inc .... E 360 352-0922
  Olympia (G-7416)
Tymlez Inc .... G 630 215-7878
  Seattle (G-11357)
Ubi Interactive Inc .... G 206 457-2493
  Seattle (G-11359)
Ultrabac Software Inc .... E 425 644-6000
  Bellevue (G-1206)
Umlaut Software Inc .... G 919 321-8324
  North Bend (G-7130)
Undead Labs LLC .... G 206 452-0590
  Seattle (G-11366)
Underhorse Entertainment Inc .... G 760 216-0164
  Redmond (G-8697)
Unix Packages LLC .... G 206 310-4610
  Seattle (G-11386)
Utrip Inc .... F 509 954-9393
  Seattle (G-11397)
V 4 Software LLC .... G 813 870-6666
  Sammamish (G-9256)
Variety Show Studios LLC .... G 571 242-1724
  Seattle (G-11405)
Vector Blue Services LLC .... F 425 219-2528
  Bellevue (G-1213)
Vendorhawk Inc .... G 360 903-3744
  Seattle (G-11409)

Vergent Software .... G 425 880-4158
  Redmond (G-8704)
Vericlouds .... E 844 532-5332
  Seattle (G-11413)
Versaly Games Inc .... G 425 577-0208
  Issaquah (G-4487)
Vertek Ois Inc .... G 425 455-9921
  Spokane Valley (G-12929)
Verti Technology Group Inc .... G 425 279-1200
  Bellevue (G-1215)
Via Airlift Inc .... G 206 258-6844
  Tukwila (G-13834)
Victory Enterprises LLC .... G 360 420-1161
  Mount Vernon (G-6853)
Vimly Benefit Solutions Inc .... D 425 771-7359
  Mukilteo (G-6989)
Viridian Sciences Inc .... G 360 719-4451
  Vancouver (G-14672)
Virtual Education Software Inc .... F 509 891-7219
  Spokane Valley (G-12931)
Vivid Learning Systems Inc .... D 509 545-1800
  Pasco (G-7649)
Vivonet Incorporated .... G 866 512-2033
  Bellingham (G-1585)
Volometrix Inc .... G 425 706-7507
  Redmond (G-8707)
Vulcan Oracle .... G 360 609-9272
  Vancouver (G-14674)
Vulcan Software LLC .... G 206 407-3057
  Lynnwood (G-6220)
Vulcan Technologies LLC .... G 206 342-2000
  Seattle (G-11431)
Washington Mso Inc .... F 253 984-7247
  Tacoma (G-13588)
Washington Schl Info Proc Coop .... C 425 349-6600
  Everett (G-3651)
▲ Watchguard Technologies Inc .... C 206 613-6600
  Seattle (G-11443)
Wellpepper Inc .... G 206 455-7377
  Seattle (G-11448)
Wftpd Inc .... G 206 428-1991
  Woodinville (G-15404)
Whab Technologies LLC .... G 800 506-2770
  Lynnwood (G-6224)
Whaer Inc .... G 919 946-5720
  Renton (G-8945)
Whatcounts Inc .... E 206 709-8250
  Seattle (G-11464)
Wild Noodle .... G 206 935-1100
  Seattle (G-11474)
Wildcard Properties LLC .... E 425 296-0896
  Redmond (G-8714)
Wildtangent Inc .... D 425 497-4500
  Redmond (G-8715)
William Minniear .... G 360 254-6764
  Vancouver (G-14694)
Wimetrics Corp .... F 253 593-1220
  Tacoma (G-13598)
Winshuttle LLC .... C 425 368-2708
  Bothell (G-1808)
Winshuttle Software Canada Inc .... G 425 368-2708
  Bothell (G-1809)
Wompmobile Inc .... G 888 625-8144
  Bellingham (G-1594)
Woobox LLC .... G 360 450-5200
  Vancouver (G-14697)
Xenex Seattle .... G 206 281-9370
  Seattle (G-11503)
Xensource Inc .... G 425 881-9479
  Redmond (G-8718)
Xeriton Corporation .... E 425 369-2279
  Sammamish (G-9261)
▲ Xmedius America Inc .... E 425 951-1600
  Bothell (G-1810)
Xmedius Buyer LLC .... G 866 368-0400
  Bothell (G-1811)
Y-Verge Llc .... G 360 975-9277
  Vancouver (G-14702)
Z2live Inc .... E 206 890-4996
  Seattle (G-11518)
Zango Inc .... G 425 279-1200
  Bellevue (G-1232)
Zemax LLC .... D 425 305-2800
  Kirkland (G-5499)
Zen Dog Software LLC .... G 425 861-8777
  Bellevue (G-1234)
Zeta Software Inc .... G 503 371-4340
  Redmond (G-8721)
Zhuro Software LLC .... G 206 607-9073
  Seattle (G-11520)

Zillow Group Inc .... C 206 470-7000
  Seattle (G-11521)
Zilyn LLC .... G 360 509-2436
  Seattle (G-11522)
Zions River .... G 253 473-1838
  Tacoma (G-13607)
Zipwire Incorporated .... G 425 591-4924
  Redmond (G-8722)
Zombie Inc .... E 206 623-9655
  Bainbridge Island (G-685)
Zsolutionz LLC .... G 425 502-6970
  Sammamish (G-9262)

76 MISCELLANEOUS REPAIR SERVICES

7692 Welding Repair

A & B Machine & Hydraulics .... F 360 532-2580
  Aberdeen (G-1)
A-1 Welding Inc .... F 360 671-9414
  Bellingham (G-1237)
AA Welding Inc .... G 360 694-4066
  Vancouver (G-14004)
Aalbu Brothers of Everett Inc .... G 425 252-9751
  Everett (G-3356)
Above & Beyond Unlimited .... G 253 921-3535
  Tacoma (G-13154)
Ace Iron Works .... G 206 903-6161
  Redmond (G-8367)
Advance Welding Inc .... F 360 573-1311
  Vancouver (G-14009)
Airport Welding & Muffler Inc ...... G 360 568-7135
  Snohomish (G-11872)
Ajs Welding .... G 253 333-2976
  Auburn (G-367)
All Weather Mobile Welding .... G 509 422-3789
  Okanogan (G-7194)
Allied Technical Services Corp ... F 206 763-3316
  Seattle (G-9382)
Als Wldg Stl Fabrication Inc ...... G 360 740-8020
  Chehalis (G-2462)
Anvil Alloy .... G 509 891-5914
  Spokane Valley (G-12620)
▲ Applied Mfg & Engrg Tech Inc .. F 253 852-5378
  Edmonds (G-3095)
Arlington Machine & Welding ... G 360 435-3300
  Arlington (G-201)
Armour Mfg & Cnstr Inc .... G 253 984-1213
  Tacoma (G-13180)
Assa Abloy AB .... G 253 872-8174
  Kent (G-4793)
Auto Spring Service Inc .... G 253 839-3780
  Kent (G-4799)
B & B Parrotts Welding Inc .... G 253 862-4955
  Buckley (G-2048)
B G Bender Inc .... G 253 848-3742
  Puyallup (G-8125)
B K Welding and Fabrication .. G 360 871-0490
  Port Orchard (G-7791)
Barnes Welding Inc .... G 509 745-8588
  Waterville (G-15005)
Bennett Industries Inc .... E 253 627-7775
  Tacoma (G-13194)
Bills Heli ARC Welding .... G 509 489-6160
  Spokane (G-12149)
Bisson & Associates Inc ...... G 360 856-0434
  Sedro Woolley (G-11532)
Blue Star Welding LLC .... F 360 398-7647
  Bellingham (G-1279)
Bobs Welding & Auto Repair .. G 509 427-5094
  Carson (G-2303)
Brad S Welding .... G 360 668-7135
  Snohomish (G-11881)
Bradys Specialties .... G 253 572-3768
  Tacoma (G-13209)
Brite Light Welding Inc ..... E 253 875-6291
  Puyallup (G-8133)
Broomflds Wldg Met Fabrication .. G 206 784-9267
  Seattle (G-9589)
Bywater Welding .... G 360 794-4618
  Monroe (G-6561)
C & C Mobile Welding LLC .. G 360 879-5623
  Graham (G-4218)
C & C Welding Inc .... G 360 966-4772
  Everson (G-3669)
C & S Welding Inc .... G 253 520-2095
  Kent (G-4828)
C&T Northwest Services .. G 509 680-4890
  Colville (G-2742)

Cannon Engineering Solutions ....G....... 360 840-6731
Port Townsend *(G-7871)*
Classic Welding ....G....... 509 469-8110
Yakima *(G-15534)*
Cook Welding Services ....G....... 425 513-1263
Everett *(G-3426)*
Corbells Portable Welding ....G....... 360 724-4700
Burlington *(G-2147)*
Crescent Machine Works Inc ....G....... 509 328-2820
Spokane *(G-12208)*
Custom Welding ....G....... 206 242-5047
Burien *(G-2100)*
Custom Welding & Orna Ir LLC ....G....... 509 947-8863
Kennewick *(G-4651)*
Custom Welding Inc ....G....... 509 535-0664
Spokane Valley *(G-12673)*
D S Fabrication & Design Inc ....G....... 360 210-7526
Washougal *(G-14951)*
Daves Mobile Welding LLC ....G....... 360 302-0069
Port Townsend *(G-7877)*
Diversified Welding Works Inc ....G....... 360 576-0929
Vancouver *(G-14183)*
EDS Garage & Welding ....G....... 253 845-8741
Puyallup *(G-8149)*
Extreme Indus Coatings LLC ....G....... 509 991-1773
Airway Heights *(G-51)*
◆ Fabrication Enterprises Inc ....F....... 503 240-0878
Vancouver *(G-14218)*
Fabrication Technologies LLC ....G....... 360 293-3707
Anacortes *(G-127)*
Fall City Welding Inc ....G....... 425 222-5105
Fall City *(G-3701)*
Farrenewelding ....G....... 360 941-5571
Mount Vernon *(G-6796)*
Farwest Operating LLC ....D....... 509 453-1663
Moxee *(G-6878)*
Fithian Wldg & Fabrication LLC ....G....... 206 658-3732
Monroe *(G-6573)*
Flying Wrench Svc ....F....... 360 638-0044
Kingston *(G-5251)*
Frys Welding Inc ....G .....
Auburn *(G-445)*
Fuhrers Machine LLC ....G....... 360 533-5517
Hoquiam *(G-4337)*
G E Welding ....G....... 253 653-8869
Algona *(G-68)*
Gem Welding & Fabrication ....G....... 360 378-5818
Friday Harbor *(G-4047)*
Glenns Welding and Mfg Inc ....E....... 425 743-2226
Lynnwood *(G-6131)*
Gorleys Precision Machine ....F....... 360 423-4567
Longview *(G-5912)*
Green River Welding ....G....... 253 632-7551
Ravensdale *(G-8337)*
Gt Machining ....G....... 509 922-8395
Spokane Valley *(G-12726)*
Gundersons Custom Welding ....G....... 360 794-6165
Snohomish *(G-11917)*
Harbor Machine & Fabricating ....F....... 360 533-1188
Hoquiam *(G-4340)*
Harris Metal Fab & Welding ....G....... 360 687-6273
Battle Ground *(G-707)*
High Desert Maintenance Inc ....G....... 509 531-8341
Kennewick *(G-4670)*
Highlands Welding Repair Inc ....G....... 206 283-0080
Seattle *(G-10172)*
Industrial Iron Works ....G....... 509 322-0072
Okanogan *(G-7197)*
Industrial Welding Co Inc ....F....... 509 598-2356
Spokane *(G-12306)*
Integral Fabrications LLC ....G....... 360 831-9353
Lacey *(G-5560)*
Jack E Brossard ....G....... 360 892-7538
Brush Prairie *(G-2036)*
Jason Dunton ....G....... 360 293-7256
Anacortes *(G-137)*
JC Fabworks LLC ....G....... 253 389-5842
Graham *(G-4228)*
Jobsite Stud Welding Inc ....G....... 425 656-9783
Lake Stevens *(G-5652)*
Joe Constance ....F....... 425 347-8920
Everett *(G-3524)*
Kaisers Welding & Mfg ....G....... 509 738-6855
Kettle Falls *(G-5233)*
Knights Welding ....G....... 509 412-1103
Pasco *(G-7596)*
Larock Enterprises Inc ....F....... 509 966-4542
Union Gap *(G-13938)*
Lc Welding Fabrication LL ....G....... 360 359-8853
Shelton *(G-11708)*
Leo Welding Fabrication ....G....... 425 379-5836
Everett *(G-3536)*
Leos Welding & Gab LLC ....G....... 425 343-6920
Seattle *(G-10405)*
Lincoln Industrial Corp Inc ....G....... 360 681-0584
Sequim *(G-11646)*
Lorenz Welding ....G....... 360 384-5258
Ferndale *(G-3865)*
Lower Valley Machine Shop ....F....... 509 882-3881
Grandview *(G-4251)*
Macklin Welding ....G....... 509 926-3597
Spokane Valley *(G-12781)*
Magaway Fire LLC ....G....... 253 394-3255
Tacoma *(G-13394)*
▼ Magic Metals Inc ....C....... 509 453-1690
Union Gap *(G-13942)*
Maintenance Welding Service ....G....... 360 533-4318
Hoquiam *(G-4348)*
Marine Welding ....G....... 360 293-7256
Anacortes *(G-145)*
Martin Fabrications ....G....... 509 457-8309
Union Gap *(G-13943)*
McVays Mobile Welding LLC ....G....... 360 657-0360
Marysville *(G-6358)*
Metal Tech Metalworks Inc ....G....... 253 435-5885
Puyallup *(G-8189)*
▲ Metal Works Inc ....G....... 509 782-8811
Dryden *(G-2953)*
Metalfab Inc ....E....... 509 967-2946
West Richland *(G-15098)*
Methow Valley Industrial LLC ....G....... 509 997-7777
Twisp *(G-13914)*
Michaels Touch ....G....... 509 346-9478
Royal City *(G-9172)*
Mikes Custom Welding ....G....... 360 754-3719
Tumwater *(G-13887)*
Millers Welding ....G....... 360 435-7832
Arlington *(G-280)*
Ne Welding and Fabrication ....G....... 509 549-3982
Colfax *(G-2718)*
Norco Inc ....F....... 509 535-9808
Spokane Valley *(G-12803)*
North Pacific Crane Fab Hyd ....G....... 509 427-4530
Carson *(G-2305)*
North Winds Welding & Met ....G....... 360 379-0487
Port Townsend *(G-7900)*
▲ Northstar Attachments LLC ....E....... 509 452-1651
Yakima *(G-15632)*
Northwest Welding Academy LLC ....G....... 325 574-3212
Oak Harbor *(G-7160)*
Northwest Wldg Fabrication Inc ....G....... 360 338-0923
Lacey *(G-5568)*
Omega Industries Inc ....E....... 360 574-9086
Vancouver *(G-14450)*
One Time Welding ....G....... 360 452-8532
Port Angeles *(G-7731)*
Osw Equipment & Repair LLC ....D....... 425 483-9863
Snohomish *(G-11959)*
Oszman Service Inc ....G....... 360 532-4552
Hoquiam *(G-4351)*
Pats Welding Service ....G....... 360 963-2370
Sekiu *(G-11583)*
Pearls MBL Wldg & Fabrication ....G....... 360 897-9288
Buckley *(G-2067)*
Pioneer Metal Works Inc ....G....... 509 787-4425
Quincy *(G-8306)*
Plastic Sales & Service Inc ....F....... 206 524-8312
Lynnwood *(G-6181)*
Precise Machining Inc ....G....... 360 629-0420
Stanwood *(G-12985)*
Precision Machine & Tool Inc ....G....... 425 745-6229
Lynnwood *(G-6184)*
Precision Welder and Eng Repr ....G....... 206 382-6227
Seattle *(G-10854)*
Precision Welding ....G....... 425 271-7490
Renton *(G-8884)*
Precision Welding & Boat RES ....G....... 360 607-3546
Vancouver *(G-14503)*
Qualls Stud Welding Pdts Inc ....G....... 425 656-9787
Kent *(G-5091)*
Ranier Welding & Fabrication ....G....... 360 829-0445
Buckley *(G-2068)*
Rathbun Iron Works Inc ....G....... 509 865-3717
Toppenish *(G-13671)*
Rdc Enterprises LLC ....G....... 360 265-0723
Port Orchard *(G-7845)*
Ready Weld ....F....... 425 391-4211
Issaquah *(G-4464)*
Red Dog Fabrication LLC ....F....... 360 892-3647
Vancouver *(G-14537)*
Red Goat Fabrication Inc ....G....... 509 240-2896
Lowden *(G-5991)*
Ron & Leos Welding Svcs Inc ....G....... 360 825-1221
Enumclaw *(G-3318)*
Ronald Johnson ....G....... 360 482-4982
Elma *(G-3256)*
S & S Welding & Repair ....G....... 509 657-3340
Endicott *(G-3266)*
Saitek U S A Inc ....G....... 425 672-8748
Woodway *(G-15480)*
Salish LLC ....G....... 206 375-7270
Seattle *(G-11005)*
Scotts Sheet Metal ....G....... 360 384-3827
Ferndale *(G-3902)*
Seattle Welding Inc ....G....... 206 763-0980
Bonney Lake *(G-1738)*
Service Welding & Machine Co ....G....... 206 325-1153
Seattle *(G-11092)*
Sharps Welding & Muffler Ctr ....G....... 509 452-2101
Moxee *(G-6885)*
Shocker Metalshop LLC Welding ....G....... 425 246-5825
Carnation *(G-2298)*
▲ Site Welding Services Inc ....E....... 425 488-2156
Woodinville *(G-15364)*
Snohomish Iron Works Inc ....G....... 360 568-2811
Snohomish *(G-11982)*
Stach Steel Supply ....G....... 509 848-2772
Harrah *(G-4321)*
Steel Fab Inc ....E....... 425 743-9216
Arlington *(G-333)*
Straight Line Industries Inc ....G....... 360 366-0223
Custer *(G-2861)*
Streich Bros Inc ....E....... 253 383-1491
Tacoma *(G-13527)*
Stromski Repair and Welding ....G....... 360 452-1661
Port Angeles *(G-7747)*
Sue A Priebe ....G....... 360 398-7647
Everson *(G-3690)*
Sunset Company LLC ....G....... 425 351-0839
Renton *(G-8923)*
Superior Industrial Services A ....E....... 360 841-8542
Woodland *(G-15467)*
Superior Sole Wldg Fabrication ....G....... 360 653-2565
Marysville *(G-6393)*
Superior Wldg Fabrication LLC ....G....... 360 430-6766
Kelso *(G-4553)*
Synergy Welding Inc ....G....... 360 881-0204
Kingston *(G-5265)*
Tinsley Welding Incorporated ....G....... 509 786-4000
Prosser *(G-8068)*
Tom Bretz ....G....... 509 486-2251
Tonasket *(G-13661)*
Torch & Regulator Repair Co ....G....... 253 272-0467
Tacoma *(G-13558)*
Torklift Central Wldg Kent Inc ....G....... 253 854-1832
Kent *(G-5183)*
Tramweld LLC ....G....... 360 425-1240
Kelso *(G-4556)*
Van Dam Welding Inc ....G....... 360 761-7297
Buckley *(G-2078)*
Warden Welding Inc ....G....... 509 349-2478
Warden *(G-14937)*
Warren Welding ....G....... 425 761-1777
Marysville *(G-6400)*
Washington Iron Works Inc ....F....... 360 679-4868
Oak Harbor *(G-7167)*
Welding By Craig ....G....... 253 307-3936
Edgewood *(G-3092)*
Welding Shop Inc ....G....... 425 888-0911
North Bend *(G-7131)*
Western Equipment Repr & Wldg ....G....... 253 922-8351
Fife *(G-3997)*
Westweld Inc ....G....... 253 862-1107
Bonney Lake *(G-1743)*
Williamson Brock Wldg Mch Sp ....G....... 360 321-3227
Langley *(G-5788)*
Ziglers Welding Shop Inc ....G....... 360 357-6077
Olympia *(G-7432)*

7694 Armature Rewinding Shops

A1 Electric Motor Inc ....G....... 360 568-3409
Snohomish *(G-11869)*
All Electric Motor Service ....G....... 253 845-1938
Puyallup *(G-8120)*
▲ Atlas Electric Inc ....E....... 509 534-8389
Spokane *(G-12124)*
B & B Electric Motors Inc ....G....... 206 763-3538
Kent *(G-4805)*
Ballard Electric ....G....... 800 873-3526
Seattle *(G-9479)*

S I C

Employee Codes: A=Over 500 employees, B=251-500
C=101-250, D=51-100, E=20-50, F=10-19, G=2-9
2019 Washington
Manufacturers Register
667

76 MISCELLANEOUS REPAIR SERVICES

Barbara Somers ....G....... 360 699-5205
  Vancouver *(G-14057)*
Bills Marine Service ....G....... 509 826-5564
  OMAK *(G-7435)*
Bl Best Inc ....G....... 509 534-0237
  Spokane *(G-12150)*
C & R Electric Motor Service ....G....... 360 736-2521
  Centralia *(G-2387)*
Center Electric Inc ....F....... 253 383-4416
  Tacoma *(G-13231)*
Cooper Electric Motor Svc Co ....F....... 509 452-9550
  Yakima *(G-15536)*
Cubbys Elc Mtr & Pump Repr ....G....... 509 544-9317
  Pasco *(G-7572)*
D and D Electric Motor Svc Inc ....G....... 509 762-6136
  Moses Lake *(G-6703)*
Dipietro Enterprises Inc ....F....... 206 423-7633
  Tukwila *(G-13724)*
F W B Enterprises Inc ....G....... 425 377-2628
  Snohomish *(G-11908)*
Grays Electric Inc ....G....... 509 662-6834
  Wenatchee *(G-15037)*

Industrial Electric Co Inc ....G....... 360 424-3239
  Mount Vernon *(G-6804)*
Industrial Electric Service Co ....F....... 360 533-2792
  Aberdeen *(G-19)*
JS Uniform ....G....... 509 467-8416
  Spokane *(G-12344)*
▲ K & N Electric Motors Inc ....D....... 509 838-8000
  Spokane Valley *(G-12759)*
K J M Electric Co Inc ....G....... 206 624-5294
  Seattle *(G-10320)*
M R K Electric ....G....... 360 253-8310
  Brush Prairie *(G-2037)*
Mac & Mac Electric Company ....G....... 360 734-6530
  Bellingham *(G-1418)*
▲ Northwest Paper Converters Inc ...F....... 800 681-9748
  Ferndale *(G-3878)*
Overload Electric Winding Svcs ....G....... 253 848-8900
  Puyallup *(G-8211)*
Panasonic Corp North America ....G....... 425 883-9290
  Redmond *(G-8613)*
Picatti Brothers Inc ....D....... 509 248-2540
  Yakima *(G-15646)*

Poppleton Electric & Mchy Co ....F....... 206 762-9160
  Kent *(G-5073)*
Reds Electric Motors Inc ....G....... 360 377-3903
  Bremerton *(G-1992)*
Rwc International Ltd ....G....... 509 452-5515
  Yakima *(G-15664)*
Scottys Elc Mtr & Pump Repr ....G....... 360 573-9544
  Vancouver *(G-14574)*
Sea Alaska Industrial Electric ....G....... 360 568-7624
  Snohomish *(G-11972)*
Seatac Automotive ....G....... 253 839-0309
  Kent *(G-5121)*
Seays Lake City Marine LLC ....G....... 509 483-1461
  Spokane *(G-12496)*
Smith Auto Electric Inc ....G....... 509 453-8275
  Yakima *(G-15677)*
Superior Industrial Services A ....E....... 360 841-8542
  Woodland *(G-15467)*
Timken Motor & Crane Svcs LLC .....E....... 509 547-1691
  Pasco *(G-7638)*
United Electric Motors Inc ....G....... 206 624-0044
  Seattle *(G-11370)*

ALPHABETIC SECTION

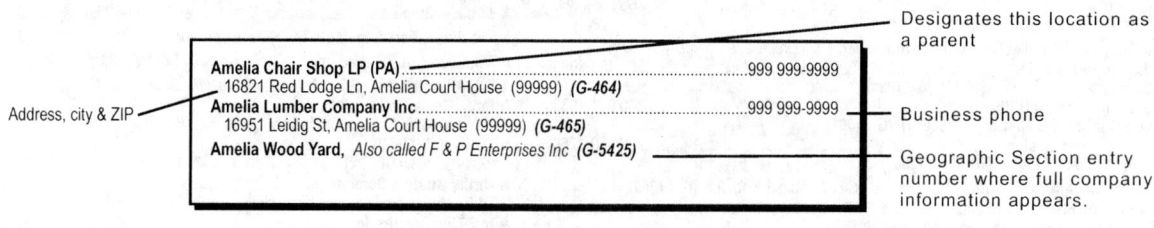

See footnotes for symbols and codes identification.
* Companies listed alphabetically.
* Complete physical or mailing address.

1 Wild Print..360 550-1916
  13804 Ne 44th St Vancouver (98682) *(G-14000)*
1 World Globes & Maps LLC..............................206 781-1400
  1605 S Jackson St Seattle (98144) *(G-9314)*
1-World Globes, Seattle Also called 1 World Globes & Maps LLC *(G-9314)*
10-20 Services Inc...253 503-6000
  10111 South Tacoma Way D5 Lakewood (98499) *(G-5692)*
11 Times Creative LLC....................................206 523-2985
  6609 Woodlawn Ave N Seattle (98103) *(G-9315)*
12 Scents..206 588-0314
  6311 Fauntleroy Way Sw Seattle (98136) *(G-9316)*
123 Printing, Walla Walla Also called Triple P Products Inc *(G-14880)*
12th and Maple Winery, Yakima Also called Corus Estates & Vineyards LLC *(G-15538)*
12th Avenue Iron Inc..206 325-0792
  1423 S Dearborn St Seattle (98144) *(G-9317)*
16 Cents Corp...509 329-1600
  2006 N Ash St Spokane (99205) *(G-12086)*
195 Industries Inc...509 245-3735
  705 E Cameron Rd Spangle (99031) *(G-12083)*
1strategy LLC..801 824-5660
  7250 Ne Bay Hill Rd Bainbridge Island (98110) *(G-605)*
2 C Media LLC..206 522-7211
  10047 38th Ave Ne Seattle (98125) *(G-9318)*
2 M Company Inc...509 765-0867
  1026 W 3rd Ave Moses Lake (98837) *(G-6675)*
2 Wheel Dynoworks...425 398-4335
  19501 Woodinville Woodinville (98072) *(G-15168)*
20 Corners Brewing LLC.................................800 840-3346
  14148 Ne 190th St Ste A Woodinville (98072) *(G-15169)*
206 Foods LLC (PA)...206 387-5881
  1208 Ne 168th St Shoreline (98155) *(G-11752)*
206 Industries LLC..206 390-8449
  1248 Ne 88th St Seattle (98115) *(G-9319)*
21cellars..253 353-2317
  17 North Rd N Tacoma (98406) *(G-13151)*
25 Bits Inc..206 861-3836
  13628 Se 208th St Kent (98042) *(G-4747)*
253 Custom Tees..253 244-7117
  9614 40th Ave Sw Lakewood (98499) *(G-5693)*
2go, Spokane Valley Also called Andeavor *(G-12617)*
2h Protective Coatings Inc..............................425 346-3306
  16824 44th Ave W Lynnwood (98037) *(G-6062)*
2x4 Industries..253 205-0359
  208 Ne 44th St Seattle (98105) *(G-9320)*
3 CS..509 246-1451
  19345 Road A.3 Ne Soap Lake (98851) *(G-12036)*
3 Hats..253 606-3474
  13120 55th St E Edgewood (98372) *(G-3071)*
3 Howls..206 747-8400
  426 S Massachusetts St Seattle (98134) *(G-9321)*
3 Lakes Fly Fishing..509 675-4200
  910 E Riverview Ln Kettle Falls (99141) *(G-5223)*
3 Phase Energy Systems Inc..........................253 736-2248
  3205 C St Ne Auburn (98002) *(G-354)*
3 X Bar Inc..360 274-4502
  1512 Albert Andrson Ln Ne Castle Rock (98611) *(G-2336)*
360 Apparel LLC...509 924-5219
  1811 E Sprague Ave Spokane (99202) *(G-12087)*
37 Cellars...509 679-0668
  1261 Dempsey Rd Leavenworth (98826) *(G-5793)*
3a Guide, Bellingham Also called Marlene Marshall *(G-1424)*
3d Mail Results..253 859-7310
  6205 S 231st St Kent (98032) *(G-4748)*
3dx Industries Inc..360 244-4339
  6920 Salashan Pkwy D101 Ferndale (98248) *(G-3807)*
3dx Industries Inc..360 244-4339
  6920 Salashan Pkwy D101 Ferndale (98248) *(G-3808)*
3s Plastics LLC...425 747-2827
  13620 Ne 20th St Ste H Bellevue (98005) *(G-775)*

3tac Distribution Inc...206 257-1552
  923 Industry Dr Tukwila (98188) *(G-13685)*
3v Precision Machining Inc.............................253 584-3888
  10025 Lakewood Dr Sw H4 Lakewood (98499) *(G-5694)*
4 Colour Inc...509 249-0955
  513 W Chestnut Ave Yakima (98902) *(G-15495)*
4 M Company Inc..425 227-4100
  15660 Nelson Pl Tukwila (98188) *(G-13686)*
4 Over LLC...818 246-1170
  300 Meridian E Milton (98354) *(G-6531)*
4 Valves LLC...360 387-2272
  587 Utsalady Rd Camano Island (98282) *(G-2205)*
410 Quarry Dibella Entps Inc..........................360 825-7505
  718 Griffin Ave Enumclaw (98022) *(G-3273)*
48 Degrees North, Seattle Also called Boundless Enterprises Inc *(G-9568)*
4evergreen Fabricators LLC...........................253 691-6752
  1402 Lake Tapps Pkwy E Sumner (98391) *(G-13053)*
4k Lift Services Inc...509 679-9997
  459 Rock Island Rd East Wenatchee (98802) *(G-3004)*
4m Sigma Corporation.....................................206 285-9181
  1900 W Emerson Pl Ste 208 Seattle (98119) *(G-9322)*
4over, Milton Also called 4 Over LLC *(G-6531)*
4r Aviation LLC..206 336-9415
  14 W Roy St Seattle (98119) *(G-9323)*
5 By 5 Software Ventures Ltd.........................206 779-6234
  8023 18th Ave Ne Seattle (98115) *(G-9324)*
5 Shot Leather...509 844-3969
  18018 N Lidgerwood Ct Colbert (99005) *(G-2705)*
5-Star Enterprises Inc......................................360 577-0829
  513 Colorado St Kelso (98626) *(G-4515)*
505 Printing...360 864-6510
  1911 State Route 505 Toledo (98591) *(G-13634)*
509, Spokane Also called TI Holdings Inc *(G-12560)*
50st Seattle Winery LLC...................................206 409-0994
  3395 Highway 150 Chelan (98816) *(G-2545)*
56 Thunder Batteries..253 267-0059
  5601 S Durango St Tacoma (98409) *(G-13152)*
5th Wave Mobile Tech Inc................................425 898-8161
  4212 Burnham Dr Gig Harbor (98332) *(G-4070)*
613 Industries Inc...612 823-3606
  4726 11th Ave Ne Apt 403 Seattle (98105) *(G-9325)*
7 Arrows Logging LLC....................................509 930-8059
  310 Coburn Rd White Swan (98952) *(G-15136)*
7 Grapes Software..425 653-2308
  480 150th Pl Ne Bellevue (98007) *(G-776)*
7 Ocean Express Inc..206 250-9239
  25617 129th Ave Se Kent (98030) *(G-4749)*
8stem Inc..360 317-7448
  118 Main St Eastsound (98245) *(G-3036)*
8th Shore Inc (PA)...425 681-1157
  4016 148th Ave Ne Redmond (98052) *(G-8364)*
99 Smokers Paradise.......................................425 775-8081
  20829 Highway 99 Lynnwood (98036) *(G-6063)*
A & A Printing Inc...206 285-1700
  222 S Orcas St Seattle (98108) *(G-9326)*
A & B Fabricators Inc......................................253 887-0442
  319 D St Nw Ste 104 Auburn (98001) *(G-355)*
A & B Machine & Hydraulics...........................360 532-2580
  809 E Market St Aberdeen (98520) *(G-1)*
A & B Plastics Inc..509 248-9166
  2405 S 3rd Ave Union Gap (98903) *(G-13919)*
A & C Pallet Sales..509 669-0653
  609 Lincoln St Wenatchee (98801) *(G-15006)*
A & E Systems..509 886-1092
  6350 Batterman Rd East Wenatchee (98802) *(G-3005)*
A & G Machine..253 887-8433
  4132 B Pl Nw Auburn (98001) *(G-356)*
A & G Machine Inc...253 887-8433
  1231 37th St Nw Auburn (98001) *(G-357)*
A & G Machine Inc...253 887-8433
  3520 B St Nw Auburn (98001) *(G-358)*

(PA)=Parent Co (HQ)=Headquarters (DH)=Div Headquarters   2019 Washington Manufacturers Register

A & H Printers Inc 509 765-0283
1030 W Marina Dr Moses Lake (98837) ***(G-6676)***
A & I Manufacturing Inc 360 805-0858
17476 147th St Se Ste E Monroe (98272) ***(G-6540)***
A & J Brokerage & Pallet Co, Spokane *Also called A & J Brokerage Co Inc* ***(G-12088)***
A & J Brokerage Co Inc 509 483-3003
6120 N Julia St Spokane (99217) ***(G-12088)***
A & J Custom Cabinets Inc 360 694-4833
2300 E 1st St Ste B Vancouver (98661) ***(G-14001)***
A & J Graphics & Design 206 439-1766
440 Sw 143rd St Burien (98166) ***(G-2087)***
A & M Manufacturing, Washougal *Also called Miller Manufacturing Inc* ***(G-14969)***
A & M Prcsion Msuring Svcs Inc (PA) 425 432-7554
8320 S 208th St Ste H104 Kent (98032) ***(G-4750)***
A & P Fasteners Inc (PA) 425 486-9562
6824 Ne 154th Ct Kenmore (98028) ***(G-4563)***
A & R Enterprise 425 453-0010
4210 198th St Sw Ste 100 Lynnwood (98036) ***(G-6064)***
A & R Entps A Div A & R PR, Lynnwood *Also called A & R Enterprise* ***(G-6064)***
A & R Print Services Inc 206 321-5263
11312 222nd Avenue Ct E Buckley (98321) ***(G-2044)***
A & RS Logging Inc 360 249-4017
195 Brady Loop Rd E Montesano (98563) ***(G-6641)***
A & S Contractors 509 930-7994
722 N 32nd Ave Yakima (98902) ***(G-15496)***
A & S Manufacturing Entps 425 334-6606
5902 46th St Ne Marysville (98270) ***(G-6309)***
A & S Powder Coating 360 880-2487
185 Keasling Rd Chehalis (98532) ***(G-2456)***
A & V Investments Inc 509 276-5088
2003 E Crawford St Deer Park (99006) ***(G-2892)***
A & W Bottling Company Inc 425 355-0100
7620 Hardeson Rd Everett (98203) ***(G-3353)***
A 1 Doors Inc 604 591-1044
8711 S 222nd St Kent (98031) ***(G-4751)***
A 1 Pallets Inc 253 395-3119
7752 S 259th St Kent (98032) ***(G-4752)***
A 2 Z Mfg LLC 360 398-2126
7157 Guide Meridian Rd A Lynden (98264) ***(G-5998)***
A A A Redi Mix II Inc 509 765-1923
7001 Stratford Rd Ne Moses Lake (98837) ***(G-6677)***
A A Auto Towing 360 892-2924
19809 Ne 58th St Vancouver (98682) ***(G-14002)***
A All-Pro Blind Claning/Repair, Auburn *Also called All Pro Blind Cleaning Repair* ***(G-371)***
A and M Impressions LLC 206 595-1111
12849 9th Ave Sw Burien (98146) ***(G-2088)***
A and R Cabinets & Wdwkg L L C 360 863-8417
22223 Yeager Rd Monroe (98272) ***(G-6541)***
A and V Inc 425 968-5881
20141 Ne 28th Pl Sammamish (98074) ***(G-9182)***
A B Fabricators 206 763-2600
1 30th St Nw Ste 6 Auburn (98001) ***(G-359)***
A B Graphics 360 566-3666
4316 Ne 130th Ave Vancouver (98682) ***(G-14003)***
A C S, Bellingham *Also called Advanced Combustn Systems Inc* ***(G-1239)***
A D G Data Systems Inc 425 771-7603
21021 66th Ave W Lynnwood (98036) ***(G-6065)***
A D G Printing 425 771-7603
19231 36th Ave W Ste D Lynnwood (98036) ***(G-6066)***
A D S Environmental Srvs, Tukwila *Also called ADS LLC* ***(G-13687)***
A E I, Monroe *Also called Affordable Electronics Inc* ***(G-6544)***
A G E L D O R A D O, Lacey *Also called Eldorado AG* ***(G-5547)***
A Good Sign Company, Bellingham *Also called Steve Ken Bosman* ***(G-1558)***
A Good Yarn Shop 360 876-0157
1140 Bethel Ave Ste 101 Port Orchard (98366) ***(G-7780)***
A H Lundberg Inc 425 258-4617
2803 1/2 Hewitt Ave Everett (98201) ***(G-3354)***
A H Tom Publishing 360 385-2059
538 Calhoun St Port Townsend (98368) ***(G-7858)***
A I S 509 972-2064
7603 Richey Rd Yakima (98908) ***(G-15497)***
A J R Enterprises Inc 253 946-1708
29819 5th Ave Sw Federal Way (98023) ***(G-3711)***
A JS Custom Portable Sawmilli 425 775-7999
19304 Filbert Rd Bothell (98012) ***(G-1812)***
A Kroiss Logging & Farming, Colville *Also called Andrew A Kroiss* ***(G-2736)***
A La Francaise Bakery, Kent *Also called Hillshire Brands Company* ***(G-4943)***
A Millican Crane Service Inc 360 779-6723
180 Nw Beaver Rdg Poulsbo (98370) ***(G-7941)***
A O K Manufacturing, Kenmore *Also called Artisan Instruments Inc* ***(G-4566)***
A One Ornamental Iron Works 206 622-4033
19232 39th Ave S Seatac (98188) ***(G-9271)***
A Path To Avalon 360 403-8884
437 N Olympic Ave Ste B Arlington (98223) ***(G-189)***
A Plus Printing 509 714-5514
1818 W Francis Ave Spokane (99205) ***(G-12089)***
A Printing 509 235-5160
27711 S Cheney Spangle Rd Cheney (99004) ***(G-2572)***
A Purrfect Logo, Dva, Spokane Valley *Also called Purrfect Logos Inc* ***(G-12845)***
A Quality Painting 509 362-2398
2614 1/2 N Hamilton St Spokane (99207) ***(G-12090)***
A R C Manufacturing, Spokane *Also called Automotive Repair Corporation* ***(G-12131)***
A S I, Puyallup *Also called All Systems Integrated Inc* ***(G-8121)***
A S M, Mukilteo *Also called Accurate Sheet Metal Inc* ***(G-6889)***
A S M Signs, Port Angeles *Also called Advertising Signs & More* ***(G-7678)***
A T S, Everett *Also called Applied Technical Svcs Corp* ***(G-3371)***
A T S, Arlington *Also called Aeronautical Testing Service* ***(G-196)***
A Terex Genie Company 800 536-1800
18465 Ne 68th St Bldg 17 Redmond (98052) ***(G-8365)***
A Thousand Hills Inc 360 437-9805
103 S Bayview Dr Port Ludlow (98365) ***(G-7763)***
A Thrifty Custom Screens 425 337-2211
22923 Meridian Ave S Bothell (98021) ***(G-1813)***
A To Z Composites Inc 435 680-3762
2321 E Bakerview Rd Ste E Bellingham (98226) ***(G-1236)***
A Touch of Class Creations 425 489-3472
14523 165th Pl Ne Woodinville (98072) ***(G-15170)***
A Touch of Romance, Auburn *Also called Peekay Inc* ***(G-529)***
A U Cornerstone Inc 360 336-5234
401 S 1st St Ste 201 Mount Vernon (98273) ***(G-6768)***
A Well Balanced Home LLC 206 280-5532
24 Roy St 474 Seattle (98109) ***(G-9327)***
A&B Quality Finishers Inc 360 805-3500
5712 207th Ave Se Snohomish (98290) ***(G-11868)***
A&C Logging LLC 509 493-3160
964 Snowden Rd White Salmon (98672) ***(G-15109)***
A-1 Concrete Supplies, Lacey *Also called Bair Construction Inc* ***(G-5535)***
A-1 Illuminated Sign Company 509 534-6134
511 N Ella Rd Spokane Valley (99212) ***(G-12596)***
A-1 Pro Sign 425 765-8836
5024 Ne 23rd St Renton (98059) ***(G-8724)***
A-1 Scales Sales & Service, Vancouver *Also called Tandar Corp* ***(G-14624)***
A-1 Timber Consultants Inc (PA) 360 748-8987
185 Hamilton Rd N Chehalis (98532) ***(G-2457)***
A-1 Welding Inc 360 671-9414
4000 Irongate Rd Bellingham (98226) ***(G-1237)***
A-Awnings of Distinction, Sequim *Also called Awnings & Sunrooms Distinction* ***(G-11613)***
A-K Printing 253 391-1784
27207 Witte Rd Se Maple Valley (98038) ***(G-6252)***
A-K Printing LLC 253 249-7133
18920 Pacific Ave S Ste C Spanaway (98387) ***(G-12052)***
A-M Systems LLC 360 683-8300
131 Business Park Loop Sequim (98382) ***(G-11604)***
A-Star Distributing Inc 509 467-6809
7614 N Market St Spokane (99217) ***(G-12091)***
A-Z Business Forms 206 363-8170
17713 15th Ave Ne Shoreline (98155) ***(G-11753)***
A1 Asbestos LLC 509 881-0074
4113 Mission Creek Rd Cashmere (98815) ***(G-2311)***
A1 Electric Motor Inc 360 568-3409
7019 137th Ave Se Snohomish (98290) ***(G-11869)***
A1 Services 509 946-6269
1617 Hunt Ave Richland (99354) ***(G-8962)***
A1a Inc 509 455-5000
601 E 3rd Ave Spokane (99202) ***(G-12092)***
AA Welding Inc 360 694-4066
3800 Ne 68th St Ste B2 Vancouver (98661) ***(G-14004)***
Aa-Its, Kennewick *Also called Armstrong & Associates LLC* ***(G-4619)***
AAA Cabinets & Millwork Inc 509 484-7152
11403 W 21st Ave Airway Heights (99001) ***(G-48)***
AAA Kartak Co 425 844-8555
13214 4th Ave W Everett (98204) ***(G-3355)***
AAA Precise Machine Inc 509 375-3268
27305 E Ruppert Rd Benton City (99320) ***(G-1599)***
AAA Printing Inc 425 454-0156
1405 132nd Ave Ne Ste 9 Bellevue (98005) ***(G-777)***
AAA Printing & Graphics Inc 425 454-0156
1405 132nd Ave Ne Ste 9 Bellevue (98005) ***(G-778)***
AAA Printing and Graphics, Bellevue *Also called AAA Printing Inc* ***(G-777)***
AAA Readymix, Moses Lake *Also called A A A Redi Mix II Inc* ***(G-6677)***
AAA Sandbags 509 979-4029
5027 N Post St Spokane (99205) ***(G-12093)***
AAA Superlubes Inc 425 353-4901
1860 California Ave Se Port Orchard (98366) ***(G-7781)***
AAA Tree Service & Logging LLC 360 463-7553
141 Se Harrier Rd Shelton (98584) ***(G-11672)***
AAA Truss 509 365-2690
443 Appleton Rd Appleton (98602) ***(G-187)***
AAA Victory Vending Inc 425 235-0378
12824 Se 170th St Renton (98058) ***(G-8725)***
AAA Welding Co, Kent *Also called C & S Welding Inc* ***(G-4828)***
Aaab Consulting LLC 206 612-7041
217 1st Ave S Unit 4003 Seattle (98194) ***(G-9328)***
Aaco Incorporated 206 722-1571
9626 Rainier Ave S Seattle (98118) ***(G-9329)***
Aahed Logistics LLC 757 395-7063
2570 Alaska Ave E Port Orchard (98366) ***(G-7782)***
Aaire Particle Control Co Inc 206 767-6692
420 S 96th St Ste 25 Seattle (98108) ***(G-9330)***
Aalbu Brothers of Everett Inc 425 252-9751
1001 Harborview Ln Everett (98203) ***(G-3356)***

ALPHABETIC SECTION

Aapkispace LLC..425 614-6465
11425 179th Ct Ne Redmond (98052) *(G-8366)*
Aard Technology LLC................................425 785-0682
2816 234th Ave Se Sammamish (98075) *(G-9183)*
Aaron Libolt...360 441-0662
110 Park View Dr Lynden (98264) *(G-5999)*
Aaron's Septic Svc, Olympia Also called *Mal Inc (G-7331)*
Aasc, Grand Coulee Also called *All American Spacer Co LLC (G-4242)*
Aastha Inc..206 382-4118
105 Yesler Way Seattle (98104) *(G-9331)*
Aav Group...972 834-2750
2862 160th Pl Ne Bellevue (98008) *(G-779)*
Aayers...253 872-5108
20119 59th Pl S Ste 102 Kent (98032) *(G-4753)*
Abadan Repo Graphics............................509 946-7697
79 Aaron Dr Ste 100 Richland (99352) *(G-8963)*
Abadan Reprographics, Spokane Also called *Business Equipment Center Inc (G-12162)*
Abandoned Yarn Online, Spokane Also called *Emma Knits Inc (G-12243)*
ABB Inc..253 280-9900
18425 72nd Ave S Kent (98032) *(G-4754)*
ABB Installation Products Inc.................206 548-1595
1101 N Northlake Way # 101 Seattle (98103) *(G-9332)*
Abbott Industries Inc...............................360 894-6230
22406 Basin View Ct Se Yelm (98597) *(G-15724)*
Abbotts Printing Inc................................509 452-8202
307 S 3rd Ave Yakima (98902) *(G-15498)*
Abbotts Printing Inc (PA)........................509 452-8202
500 S 2nd Ave Yakima (98902) *(G-15499)*
ABC Forms, Ellensburg Also called *Cassandra Watterson (G-3187)*
ABC Printers Inc......................................360 423-6991
1291 Industrial Way Longview (98632) *(G-5881)*
ABC Printing Inc......................................360 456-4545
7009 Martin Way E Lacey (98516) *(G-5528)*
ABC Sheet Metal Inc...............................360 574-4884
3714 Nw 166th St Ridgefield (98642) *(G-9058)*
ABC Water Specialty Inc.........................425 355-9826
2918 Cavalero Rd Lake Stevens (98258) *(G-5629)*
Abcd Marine..206 527-3428
346 Nw 89th St Seattle (98117) *(G-9333)*
Abcd Ventures LLC.................................206 686-6089
22541 Se Sawyer Ridge Way Black Diamond (98010) *(G-1644)*
Abel Flamespray.....................................360 925-6125
22627 121st Dr Ne Arlington (98223) *(G-190)*
ABG..253 896-1372
3719 70th Ave E Unit E Fife (98424) *(G-3927)*
Abmw, Olympia Also called *American Bnchmark Mch Wrks LLC (G-7224)*
Abode Specialist Inspection SE.............253 209-0878
4408 Browns Point Blvd Tacoma (98422) *(G-13153)*
About Printing and Apparel...................360 584-9159
5709 Lacey Blvd Se Lacey (98503) *(G-5529)*
Above & Beyond Unlimited....................253 921-3535
602 104th St S Tacoma (98444) *(G-13154)*
Above and Beyond Cnstr LLC................509 521-8081
411 N Underwood St Kennewick (99336) *(G-4610)*
Abr Inc..509 334-2968
425 Nw Albion Dr Pullman (99163) *(G-8080)*
Abracadabra Printing Inc......................206 343-9087
6250 Stanley Ave S Seattle (98108) *(G-9334)*
Abraham Industries LLC......................509 329-8260
820 A St Ste 220 Tacoma (98402) *(G-13155)*
Absci LLC..360 949-1041
101 E 6th St Ste 300 Vancouver (98660) *(G-14005)*
Absolute Aviation Services LLC.........509 747-2904
8122 W Pilot Dr Spokane (99224) *(G-12094)*
Absolute Concrete Colors, Kalama Also called *East West General Inc (G-4497)*
Absolute Concreteworks LLC.............360 297-5055
490 Sunset Blvd Port Townsend (98368) *(G-7859)*
Absolute GM LLC.................................425 814-1011
11809 Ne 116th St Kirkland (98034) *(G-5267)*
Absolute Graphix Inc...........................425 771-6087
19231 36th Ave W Ste F Lynnwood (98036) *(G-6067)*
Absolute Solutions..............................360 683-4597
101 Ritter Rd Sequim (98382) *(G-11605)*
Absolute Sportswear..........................206 890-1531
1900 W Nickerson St # 213 Seattle (98119) *(G-9335)*
ABT 360 LLC.......................................509 592-8144
1615 Ne Eastgate Blvd G1w Pullman (99163) *(G-8081)*
Abw Technologies Inc........................360 618-4400
6720 191st Pl Ne Arlington (98223) *(G-191)*
AC Larocco Pizza Co..........................509 924-9113
12412 E Desmet Ave # 203 Spokane Valley (99216) *(G-12597)*
Acacia Controls Inc............................253 277-1206
1819 Central Ave S Ste 37 Kent (98032) *(G-4755)*
Academy Infrared Thermography, Bellingham Also called *Academy Infrared Training Inc (G-1238)*
Academy Infrared Training Inc..........360 676-1915
702 Kentucky St Ste 720 Bellingham (98225) *(G-1238)*
Acadie Woodworks............................509 924-1256
230 S Washington St Spokane (99201) *(G-12095)*
Acadie Woodworks Incorporated......509 230-6874
11319 E Carlisle Ave # 4 Spokane Valley (99206) *(G-12598)*
Accel Plastics, Auburn Also called *Jatal Inc (G-478)*

Accelerated Postal and Print, Vancouver Also called *Andrews Nation Inc (G-14034)*
Accent By Design................................360 256-6607
9905 Ne 26th St Vancouver (98662) *(G-14006)*
Accent Signs & Engraving Inc...........509 946-8998
72 Wellsian Way Richland (99352) *(G-8964)*
Accent Signs Inc................................509 967-7446
700 S 46th Ave Richland (99353) *(G-8965)*
Access Equipment LLC......................360 376-2679
283 Killebrew Lake Rd Orcas (98280) *(G-7455)*
Access Printing Inc............................425 656-0563
19219 W Valley Hwy M106 Kent (98032) *(G-4756)*
Access US Oil & Gas Inc....................206 792-7575
665 Woodland Sq Loop Se Lacey (98503) *(G-5530)*
Acclaim Sign & Display Partner.........206 706-3900
1149 Nw 52nd St Seattle (98107) *(G-9336)*
Accompany Mobile Technology, Bothell Also called *Antenna Dexterra Inc (G-1819)*
Accor Technology Inc........................509 662-0608
3310 5th St Se East Wenatchee (98802) *(G-3006)*
Accor Technology Inc (PA)...............425 453-5410
608 State St S Ste 100 Kirkland (98033) *(G-5268)*
Accor Technology Inc........................509 662-0608
337 E Penny Rd Wenatchee (98801) *(G-15007)*
Accordent Technologies Inc.............310 374-7491
6905 39th Ave Sw Seattle (98136) *(G-9337)*
Accounting Software Company, Tacoma Also called *Accounting Software Inc (G-13156)*
Accounting Software Inc..................253 952-6040
4802 Nassau Ave Ne Tacoma (98422) *(G-13156)*
Accra Fab, Liberty Lake Also called *Accra-Fab Inc (G-5822)*
Accra Manufacturing Inc.................425 424-1000
17703 15th Ave Se Bothell (98012) *(G-1814)*
Accra-Fab Inc (PA)..........................509 922-3300
23201 E Appleway Ave Liberty Lake (99019) *(G-5822)*
Accra-Fab Inc..................................509 922-3300
23201 E Knox Ave Liberty Lake (99019) *(G-5823)*
Accucon Inc......................................509 534-4460
904 N Dyer Rd Spokane Valley (99212) *(G-12599)*
Accumar Corporation......................360 779-7795
1180 Nw Finn Hill Rd Poulsbo (98370) *(G-7942)*
Accurate Machine and Mfg.............360 693-4783
2910 Kauffman Ave Vancouver (98660) *(G-14007)*
Accurate Models..............................253 630-3126
19214 140th Ave Se Renton (98058) *(G-8726)*
Accurate Sheet Metal Inc................425 745-6786
4301 Russell Rd Mukilteo (98275) *(G-6889)*
Accurate Surface Grinding..............206 762-5205
430 S 96th St Ste 1 Seattle (98108) *(G-9338)*
Accurate Tool & Die........................206 277-0234
15415 Ambaum Blvd Sw Burien (98166) *(G-2089)*
Accurate Tool & Die Inc..................206 244-0745
11291 35th Ave Sw Seattle (98146) *(G-9339)*
Accurus Aerospace Kent LLC.........253 872-8541
5416 S 226th St Kent (98032) *(G-4757)*
Ace Anthony Equity MGT LLC.........425 333-6024
14906 280th Pl Ne Duvall (98019) *(G-2978)*
Ace Galvanizing..............................206 687-7688
16019 3rd Pl S Burien (98148) *(G-2090)*
Ace Galvanizing Inc (PA)................206 762-0330
429 S 96th St Seattle (98108) *(G-9340)*
Ace International Inc......................360 736-3937
1830 Central Blvd Centralia (98531) *(G-2379)*
Ace International Inc (PA)..............360 736-9999
520 N Gold St Centralia (98531) *(G-2380)*
Ace Iron Works................................206 903-6161
1323 Rdmond Fall Cy Rd Ne Redmond (98053) *(G-8367)*
Ace Logging Inc..............................360 537-6843
219 Ocean Beach Rd Hoquiam (98550) *(G-4327)*
Ace of Spades Inc..........................360 807-6442
700 S Tower Ave Centralia (98531) *(G-2381)*
Ace Production Technologies, Spokane Valley Also called *Component Tinning Services Inc (G-12662)*
Ace Race Parts Inc.........................844 223-7223
8108 River Dr Se Ste 106 Tumwater (98501) *(G-13848)*
Ace Stamp & Engraving..................253 582-3322
10510 Bridgeport Way Sw # 6 Lakewood (98499) *(G-5695)*
Aceface Printing............................206 427-2272
4333 Leary Way Nw Seattle (98107) *(G-9341)*
Acf Idea Works Inc.........................425 335-0958
3830 97th Dr Se Lake Stevens (98258) *(G-5630)*
Acg Software.................................425 828-1456
13632 Ne 94th St Redmond (98052) *(G-8368)*
Achieve Life Science Inc...............425 686-1500
19820 North Creek Pkwy # 201 Bothell (98011) *(G-1744)*
Achieve Life Sciences Inc..............425 686-1500
520 Pike St Ste 2250 Seattle (98101) *(G-9342)*
Achilles Inflatable Boats, Everett Also called *Achilles Usa Inc (G-3357)*
Achilles Usa Inc (HQ)....................425 353-7000
1407 80th St Sw Everett (98203) *(G-3357)*
Aci, Arlington Also called *Aviation Covers Inc (G-205)*
Aci Boats, Port Townsend Also called *Armstrong Consolidated LLC (G-7864)*
Aci Communications Inc...............253 854-9802
23307 66th Ave S Kent (98032) *(G-4758)*

(PA)=Parent Co (HQ)=Headquarters (DH)=Div Headquarters

ALPHABETIC SECTION

Acme Forge 253 217-3801
  50 37th St Ne Ste F Auburn (98002) *(G-360)*
Acorn Custom Cabinetry Inc 425 235-8366
  7211 132nd Pl Se Renton (98056) *(G-8727)*
Acorn Tree and Stump Services 360 509-0145
  17-A Hwy 104 Port Gamble (98364) *(G-7756)*
Acoustic Info Proc Lab LLC 509 427-5374
  110 Ne Cedar St Stevenson (98648) *(G-13008)*
Acoustical Solutions 253 876-0075
  420 37th St Nw Ste D Auburn (98001) *(G-361)*
Acro Machining Inc 360 653-1492
  3817 168th St Ne Arlington (98223) *(G-192)*
Acro Machining Inc 360 659-6401
  15303 39th Ave Ne Marysville (98271) *(G-6310)*
Acrowood Corporation 425 258-3555
  4425 S 3rd Ave Everett (98203) *(G-3358)*
Acrylic Arts & Fabrication 360 802-0808
  1462 Blake St Enumclaw (98022) *(G-3274)*
Acrylic Concepts Inc 425 881-3603
  17932 Ne 65th St Redmond (98052) *(G-8369)*
ACS, Ferndale Also called Advanced Router Technology *(G-3810)*
ACS, Everett Also called Adaptive Cargo Solutions LLC *(G-3360)*
ACS Technologies Group Inc 843 413-8032
  1505 Westlake Ave N Seattle (98109) *(G-9343)*
Act Manufacturing Inc 509 893-4100
  10310 E Buckeye Ln Spokane Valley (99206) *(G-12600)*
Acti, Port Angeles Also called Angeles Composite Tech Inc *(G-7684)*
Action Apparel Washington Inc 509 328-5861
  1625 W Broadway Ave Spokane (99201) *(G-12096)*
Action Communications Inc 206 625-1234
  5700 6th Ave S Ste 101 Seattle (98108) *(G-9344)*
Action Equipment Inc 360 897-0890
  12008 238th Ave E Buckley (98321) *(G-2045)*
Action Materials Inc 509 448-9386
  10710 S Cheney Spokane Rd Cheney (99004) *(G-2573)*
Action Pages Consolidated Inc 360 848-0870
  2021 E College Way # 101 Mount Vernon (98273) *(G-6769)*
Action Sports & Locks Inc 360 435-9505
  340 N Olympic Ave Arlington (98223) *(G-193)*
Action Sportswear & Printables 509 328-5861
  1625 W Broadway Ave Spokane (99201) *(G-12097)*
Action West, Longview Also called Top Notch Manufacturing Co *(G-5960)*
Activated Content 206 448-3260
  2125 Western Ave Ste 200 Seattle (98121) *(G-9345)*
Actively Learn Inc 857 540-6670
  220 2nd Ave S Fl 4 Seattle (98104) *(G-9346)*
Acu-Line Chemical Machining, Seattle Also called Acu-Line Corporation *(G-9347)*
Acu-Line Corporation 206 634-1618
  434 N 35th St Seattle (98103) *(G-9347)*
Acufab Inc 509 525-3833
  455 A St Walla Walla (99362) *(G-14759)*
Acuna Cedar Products 425 359-3224
  7906 Renic Dr Sedro Woolley (98284) *(G-11530)*
Ad One Corp 253 942-3688
  30833 Pacific Hwy S Federal Way (98003) *(G-3712)*
Ad Pro, Vancouver Also called Co C Graphics *(G-14126)*
Ad Services, Seattle Also called Advertising Services Intl LLC *(G-9356)*
Ad Sign Design 425 259-3000
  2032 Lombard Ave B Everett (98201) *(G-3359)*
Ada Signage and Spc Inc 253 651-1748
  35511 Etnvlle Cutoff Rd E Eatonville (98328) *(G-3049)*
Adalbert & Nagy Sausage Co LLC 206 356-3305
  13110 244th Ave Se Issaquah (98027) *(G-4378)*
Adalis Corporation (HQ) 360 574-8828
  417 Nw 136th St Vancouver (98685) *(G-14008)*
Adam Welch 206 329-8697
  1740 Melrose Ave Unit 606 Seattle (98122) *(G-9348)*
Adamant Cellars 509 529-4161
  525 E Cessna Ave Walla Walla (99362) *(G-14760)*
Adamatic Corporation 206 322-5474
  814 44th St Nw Ste 103 Auburn (98001) *(G-362)*
Adamera Minerals LLC 509 237-7731
  55 Gold Mountain Rd Republic (99166) *(G-8955)*
Adams Apple Cider LLC 509 933-1025
  221 Canyon Vista Way Ellensburg (98926) *(G-3180)*
Adams Place Country Gourmet 509 582-8564
  193910 E Game Farm Rd Kennewick (99337) *(G-4611)*
Adams Timber Service LLC 360 636-7766
  119 Rockfish Ct Silverlake (98645) *(G-11861)*
Adapt Labs Inc 206 842-2040
  5780 Wimsey Ln Ne Bainbridge Island (98110) *(G-606)*
Adaptelligence Inc 509 432-1812
  525 Nw Aspen Ct Pullman (99163) *(G-8082)*
Adaptive Cargo Solutions LLC 240 475-6521
  11504 Airport Rd Everett (98204) *(G-3360)*
Add Corporation 206 452-7498
  618 Sw 185th St Normandy Park (98166) *(G-7089)*
Add Three Inc 206 568-3772
  500 E Pike St Ste 200a Seattle (98122) *(G-9349)*
Addison Construction Sup Inc (PA) 253 474-0711
  6201 S Adams St Tacoma (98409) *(G-13157)*

Ade Holding Inc (HQ) 206 789-3600
  4420 14th Ave Nw Seattle (98107) *(G-9350)*
Ademco Inc 253 872-7128
  7617 S 180th St Kent (98032) *(G-4759)*
Ademco Inc 509 534-7300
  2680 E Ferry Ave Spokane (99202) *(G-12098)*
Ademco Inc 425 485-3938
  22121 17th Ave Se Ste 103 Bothell (98021) *(G-1815)*
Adhesa-Plate Manufacturing Co 206 682-0141
  4000 7th Ave S Seattle (98108) *(G-9351)*
Adhesive & Packaging Systems 360 876-9278
  12938 Woodside Ln Sw Port Orchard (98367) *(G-7783)*
Adhesive Products Inc 206 762-7459
  945 S Doris St Seattle (98108) *(G-9352)*
ADI Corporation 425 455-4561
  40 Lake Bellevue Dr # 310 Bellevue (98005) *(G-780)*
ADI Global Distribution, Kent Also called Ademco Inc *(G-4759)*
ADI Global Distribution, Spokane Also called Ademco Inc *(G-12098)*
ADI Global Distribution, Bothell Also called Ademco Inc *(G-1815)*
ADI Solar Corporation 206 484-2879
  14815 Chain Lake Rd Ste H Monroe (98272) *(G-6542)*
ADI Thermal Power Corp 206 484-2879
  19495 144th Ave Ne A160 Woodinville (98072) *(G-15171)*
Adic, Redmond Also called Advanced Digital Info Corp *(G-8370)*
Adiprene Direct Inc 425 999-3805
  777 108th Ave Ne Bellevue (98004) *(G-781)*
Adl Cattle Growers LLC 509 765-0584
  6751 Road 16 Ne Moses Lake (98837) *(G-6678)*
ADM, Spokane Also called Archer-Daniels-Midland Company *(G-12117)*
ADM, Ephrata Also called Archer-Daniels-Midland Company *(G-3331)*
ADM, Spokane Valley Also called Archer-Daniels-Midland Company *(G-12624)*
ADM Milling Co 509 535-2995
  1131 E Sprague Ave Spokane (99202) *(G-12099)*
ADM Milling Co 509 534-2636
  2301 E Trent Ave Spokane (99202) *(G-12100)*
ADM Milling Co 509 235-6216
  601 1st St Cheney (99004) *(G-2574)*
ADM Milling Co 509 534-2636
  1131 E Sprague Ave Spokane (99202) *(G-12101)*
Admiralty Crane LLC 360 461-2092
  504 Taylor Cutoff Rd Sequim (98382) *(G-11606)*
Admiralty Precision LLC 360 344-2212
  321 Otto St Port Townsend (98368) *(G-7860)*
Adobe Systems Incorporated 206 675-7000
  801 N 34th St Seattle (98103) *(G-9353)*
Adrenaline Products LLC 503 805-4525
  16003 Ne 25th Ave Ridgefield (98642) *(G-9059)*
ADS LLC 206 762-5070
  4455 S 134th Pl Tukwila (98168) *(G-13687)*
Adsiduous, Redmond Also called Washington Publishing Hse LLC *(G-8710)*
Adteck Laser Engraving, Spokane Also called Design Centre *(G-12225)*
Adult Care Products, Kent Also called Contract Sew & Repair Inc *(G-4865)*
Advadri LLC 425 228-7558
  14127 W Lk Kathleen Dr Se Renton (98059) *(G-8728)*
Advance Marking Systems, Tacoma Also called Tacoma Rubber Stamp Co *(G-13548)*
Advance Pattern & Tooling Inc 253 638-0300
  30218 188th Ave Se Kent (98042) *(G-4760)*
Advance Septic Trtmnt Systems 360 856-0550
  8000 Parker Rd Sedro Woolley (98284) *(G-11531)*
Advance Sign Design Inc 206 789-6051
  6501 6th Ave Nw Seattle (98117) *(G-9354)*
Advance Welding Inc 360 573-1311
  1509 Ne 106th St Ste A Vancouver (98686) *(G-14009)*
Advanced Adhesive 360 373-1156
  1616 Ne Dawn Rd Bremerton (98311) *(G-1934)*
Advanced Aero Safety Inc 360 387-8472
  1938 Forest Hill Rd Stanwood (98282) *(G-12952)*
Advanced All Wheel Drive 360 746-8746
  2869 W 63rd Ln Ferndale (98248) *(G-3809)*
Advanced Autosound 509 453-5363
  4 Ranch Rite Rd Yakima (98901) *(G-15500)*
Advanced Cargo Control LLC 206 498-5824
  19721 76th Ave Se Snohomish (98296) *(G-11870)*
Advanced Caster Corporati 425 821-6574
  8606 Ne 138th St Kirkland (98034) *(G-5269)*
Advanced Cement Tech LLC 360 332-7060
  435 Martin St Ste 2040 Blaine (98230) *(G-1657)*
Advanced Coating Solutions LLC 425 785-0902
  218 Maint St 429 Kirkland (98033) *(G-5270)*
Advanced Combustn Systems Inc 360 676-6005
  1999 Alpine Way Bellingham (98226) *(G-1239)*
Advanced Designs, Everett Also called B & C Manufacturing Inc *(G-3379)*
Advanced Digital Info Corp (HQ) 425 881-8004
  11431 Willows Rd Ne Redmond (98052) *(G-8370)*
Advanced Drainage Systems Inc 360 943-3313
  6001 Belmore St Sw Olympia (98512) *(G-7221)*
Advanced Drainage Systems Inc 360 835-8523
  627 S 37th St Washougal (98671) *(G-14939)*
Advanced Electric Signs Inc 360 225-6826
  1550 Down River Dr Ste A Woodland (98674) *(G-15416)*

Advanced Energy Industries Inc 360 759-2713
2501 Se Columbia Way # 190 Vancouver (98661) *(G-14010)*
Advanced Extracts 360 949-5325
21911 Ne 147th St Brush Prairie (98606) *(G-2027)*
Advanced Fuel Systems, Monroe *Also called Quality Fuel Trlr & Tank Inc (G-6610)*
Advanced Fuel Systems 425 526-7566
29100 Se 43rd Pl Fall City (98024) *(G-3698)*
Advanced Labels NW, Lynnwood *Also called Northwest Flexo Spc LLC (G-6170)*
Advanced Laser Printer Service 360 835-1824
2513 Se 370th Ave Washougal (98671) *(G-14940)*
Advanced Lean Mfg LLC 425 402-8300
17611 128th Pl Ne Woodinville (98072) *(G-15172)*
Advanced Marking Systems, Seattle *Also called Tacoma Rubber Stamp Co (G-11255)*
Advanced Metal Creations 509 662-0335
3565 School St Wenatchee (98801) *(G-15008)*
Advanced Metal Fabrication 509 534-0671
1605 E Lyons Ave Spokane (99217) *(G-12102)*
Advanced Microscopy Group, Bothell *Also called Westover Scientific Inc (G-1917)*
Advanced Plastic & Metal Wldng 509 466-1986
12012 N Landt Farms Ln Nine Mile Falls (99026) *(G-7067)*
Advanced Powder Coating NW 360 398-1460
3910 Spur Ridge Ln Bellingham (98226) *(G-1240)*
Advanced Prtctive Coatings LLC 425 818-2820
10220 Ne Points Dr # 315 Kirkland (98033) *(G-5271)*
Advanced Robotic Vehicles Inc (PA) 206 310-1122
12923 E Marginal Way S Tukwila (98168) *(G-13688)*
Advanced Router Technology 360 318-7534
1355 Pacific Pl Ste 117 Ferndale (98248) *(G-3810)*
Advanced Sign and Light, Auburn *Also called Advanced Signs LLC (G-363)*
Advanced Sign Concepts, Walla Walla *Also called Michael L White (G-14843)*
Advanced Signs LLC 253 987-5909
1 37th St Nw Ste C Auburn (98001) *(G-363)*
Advanced Technology Resources 253 229-3415
11902 Morris Rd Se Yelm (98597) *(G-15725)*
Advanced Traffic Products Inc 425 347-6208
1122 Industry St Ste A Everett (98203) *(G-3361)*
Advanced Water Systems Inc 520 575-6718
4621 157th Ave Se Snohomish (98290) *(G-11871)*
Advangelists LLC (HQ) 734 546-4989
701 5th Ave Fl 75 Seattle (98104) *(G-9355)*
Advantac Technologies LLC 360 217-8500
11504 Airport Rd G Everett (98204) *(G-3362)*
Advantage Precision Graphics 425 285-9787
9474 Redmond Woodinville Redmond (98052) *(G-8371)*
Advantage Screen Printing 360 425-7343
1706 12th Ave Longview (98632) *(G-5882)*
Adventurer LP 509 895-7064
3303 W Washington Ave Yakima (98903) *(G-15501)*
Advertising Services Intl LLC 206 623-6963
10000 Lake City Way Ne Seattle (98125) *(G-9356)*
Advertising Signs & More 360 452-7785
1327 E 1st St Ste A Port Angeles (98362) *(G-7678)*
Advocate Printing 360 748-3335
429 N Market Blvd Chehalis (98532) *(G-2458)*
AE Downs Enterprises Inc 206 295-9831
22227 76th Ave S Kent (98032) *(G-4761)*
Aecs, Port Angeles *Also called Airborne Ecs LLC (G-7679)*
Aees Inc 425 803-2170
4040 Lk Wa Blvd Ne # 150 Kirkland (98033) *(G-5272)*
Aem-Network LLC 509 946-0813
1840 Terminal Dr Richland (99354) *(G-8966)*
Aeneas Valley Cnstr & Log 206 391-8408
27027 316th Ave Se Ravensdale (98051) *(G-8328)*
AEP Span, Tacoma *Also called ASC Profiles LLC (G-13184)*
Aerial Consultant, Yarrow Point *Also called SCC Enterprises LLC (G-15723)*
Aeries Enterprises LLC 425 739-9997
1100 Carillon Pt Kirkland (98033) *(G-5273)*
Aero Controls Inc (PA) 253 269-3000
1610 20th St Nw Auburn (98001) *(G-364)*
Aero Mac Inc 425 348-4140
4602 Chennault Beach Rd D1 Mukilteo (98275) *(G-6890)*
Aero Outdoors, Pasco *Also called Sullivan Manufacturing Inc (G-7635)*
Aero Precision LLC (PA) 253 272-8188
2320 Commerce St Tacoma (98402) *(G-13158)*
Aero Safety Graphics Inc 425 957-0712
6104 208th Ave Ne Redmond (98053) *(G-8372)*
Aero-Space Port Intl Group Inc 425 264-1000
1600 Lind Ave Sw Ste 220 Renton (98057) *(G-8729)*
Aeroacoustics Aircraft Systems, Everett *Also called Aeroacoustics Inc (G-3363)*
Aeroacoustics Inc 425 438-0215
9802 29th Ave W Ste B104 Everett (98204) *(G-3363)*
Aerocell Corporation 360 653-2211
12806 State Ave Marysville (98271) *(G-6311)*
Aerofab Inc 253 863-8402
27924 Se 268th St Ravensdale (98051) *(G-8329)*
Aerofab Industries Inc 360 403-8994
19222 62nd Ave Ne Arlington (98223) *(G-194)*
Aerofab NDT LLC 253 395-8706
8629 S 212th St Kent (98031) *(G-4762)*
Aeroforge Inc (PA) 253 286-2525
609 N Levee Rd Puyallup (98371) *(G-8117)*
Aeroforge Manufacturing Inc 253 286-2525
609 N Levee Rd Puyallup (98371) *(G-8118)*
Aeroform Inc 360 403-1919
19421 59th Ave Ne Arlington (98223) *(G-195)*
Aerogo Inc 206 575-3344
1170 Andover Park W Tukwila (98188) *(G-13689)*
Aerojet Rocketdyne Inc 425 885-5000
11411 139th Pl Ne Redmond (98052) *(G-8373)*
Aeronautical Testing Service 360 363-4276
18820 59th Dr Ne Arlington (98223) *(G-196)*
Aerospace Defense Inc 360 548-8017
17837 59th Ave Ne 11 Arlington (98223) *(G-197)*
Aerospace International LLC 206 334-7426
12329 Se 238th Pl Kent (98031) *(G-4763)*
Aerospace Manufacturing, Kent *Also called Aerospace Mltxis Machining Inc (G-4764)*
Aerospace Manufacturing Tech, Arlington *Also called Senior Operations LLC (G-323)*
Aerospace Mltxis Machining Inc 253 856-1068
7020 Oberto Dr Kent (98032) *(G-4764)*
Aerospace Solutions Intl, Kent *Also called Aerospace International LLC (G-4763)*
Aerostar Engineering, Inc., Puyallup *Also called Aeroforge Manufacturing Inc (G-8118)*
Aerotech Golf Shafts, Bellingham *Also called Mermaid Bay Enterprises LLC (G-1433)*
Aesco, Auburn *Also called Asphalt Equipment & Service Co (G-379)*
Aesseal Inc 360 414-0118
960 Industrial Way Ste 8 Longview (98632) *(G-5883)*
Afar Interactive Inc 425 442-5101
701 5th Ave Ste 3600 Seattle (98104) *(G-9357)*
Afco Performance Group LLC 360 453-2030
101 E Main St Ste 206 Monroe (98272) *(G-6543)*
Affordable Blackflow Testers 425 269-9064
18308 Se 145th St Renton (98059) *(G-8730)*
Affordable Electronics Inc 425 484-0964
16001 234th St Se Monroe (98272) *(G-6544)*
Affordable Ignition Interlock, Kent *Also called Washington Ignition Interlock (G-5207)*
Affordble Trctr Bckhoe Svc LLC 360 306-1533
28819 Se 216th Way Maple Valley (98038) *(G-6253)*
Afirm Construction Inc 509 928-4361
5423 N Rees Ct Spokane Valley (99216) *(G-12601)*
AFL Hyperscale, Kent *Also called AFL Ig LLC (G-4765)*
AFL Ig LLC (HQ) 425 291-4200
8039 S 192nd St Ste 100 Kent (98032) *(G-4765)*
After Market Products Inc 360 825-6500
1751 Garrett St Enumclaw (98022) *(G-3275)*
Afterglowpowercompany.com, Lake Tapps *Also called Phunnybaggscom (G-5685)*
AG Creative Publishing 206 375-0934
1727 14th Ave Apt 10 Seattle (98122) *(G-9358)*
AG Energy Solutions Inc 509 343-3156
7921 E Broadway Ave Spokane Valley (99212) *(G-12602)*
AG Engineering & Development 509 582-8900
1515 E 7th Ave Kennewick (99337) *(G-4612)*
AG Enterprise Supply Inc (PA) 509 235-2006
17005 W State Route 904 Cheney (99004) *(G-2575)*
Ag Spray Equipment Inc 509 488-6631
81 E Pine St Othello (99344) *(G-7490)*
AG Tree Service LLC 425 830-8820
218 Main St Kirkland (98033) *(G-5274)*
AGA Sports, Bellevue *Also called American Graphic Arts (G-786)*
Agalite Seattle (PA) 425 656-2626
17830 W Valley Hwy Tukwila (98188) *(G-13690)*
Agate Backhoe Tractor 360 426-7085
41 E Lighthouse Rd Shelton (98584) *(G-11673)*
Agate Creek Farm 360 740-1692
105 Agate Creek Ln Chehalis (98532) *(G-2459)*
Agate Field Vineyard 509 829-6097
2911 Roza Dr Zillah (98953) *(G-15749)*
Agatecreek Cellars, Chehalis *Also called Agate Creek Farm (G-2459)*
Agbanga Karite LLC 360 515-9013
8109 River Dr Se B Tumwater (98501) *(G-13849)*
AGC Biologics, Bothell *Also called CMC Biologics SARl Corp (G-1840)*
AGC Biologics Inc 425 485-0280
21511 23rd Dr Se Bothell (98021) *(G-1816)*
AGC Cww 360 608-4642
11617 Ne 224th Ave Vancouver (98682) *(G-14011)*
AGCO 253 964-2313
3895 Pioneer Ave Ste 101 Dupont (98327) *(G-2954)*
Agdecor 425 255-2271
6947 Coal Creek Pkwy Se Newcastle (98059) *(G-7023)*
Agile Advantage Inc 425 629-6361
8201 164th Ave Ne Redmond (98052) *(G-8374)*
Agile Data Technology Inc 206 280-9512
2125 Western Ave Ste 488 Seattle (98121) *(G-9359)*
Agile Electrical Solutions, Bothell *Also called Valberg Mfg Inc (G-1912)*
Agilecore Software LLC 360 910-3140
10201 Ne 46th Ave Vancouver (98686) *(G-14012)*
Agilent Technologies Inc 425 255-6320
14410 Se Petrovitsky Rd Renton (98058) *(G-8731)*
Agilent Technologies Inc 509 921-3525
24001 E Mission Ave Liberty Lake (99019) *(G-5824)*
Agjet LLC 509 654-9449
2101 Oak Ave Yakima (98903) *(G-15502)*
AGM Fabric Products Inc 253 946-3200
27721 Pcf Hwy S Ste 101 Federal Way (98003) *(G-3713)*

ALPHABETIC

AGM Industries Inc ALPHABETIC SECTION

AGM Industries Inc ...716 256-9470
2690 152nd Ave Ne # 632 Redmond (98052) ***(G-8375)***
Agrasyst Inc (PA) ...509 467-2167
16417 N Napa Ln Spokane (99208) ***(G-12103)***
Agrex Inc ...509 787-4595
3031 Road E Nw Ephrata (98823) ***(G-3330)***
Agri-Service Northwest, Eltopia *Also called Asnw Inc* ***(G-3262)***
Agri-Trac Inc ...509 265-4327
201 1st Ave Mesa (99343) ***(G-6490)***
Agriaccess Inc ...425 806-9356
4714 175th St Se Bothell (98012) ***(G-1817)***
Agricultural, Ellensburg *Also called Trinity Farms Inc* ***(G-3234)***
Agrijuana 1 LLC ...360 342-8194
1810 Se Commerce Ave Battle Ground (98604) ***(G-686)***
Agrium US Inc ...509 586-5500
227515 E Bowles Rd Kennewick (99337) ***(G-4613)***
Agrium US Inc ...509 586-5355
227108 E Perkins Rd Kennewick (99337) ***(G-4614)***
Agro Technic LLC ...206 669-2446
10708 Main St Apt 403 Bellevue (98004) ***(G-782)***
AGS Stainless Inc ...206 842-9492
7873 Ne Day Rd W Bainbridge Island (98110) ***(G-607)***
Agt Inc ...509 935-6140
Smith Rd Chewelah (99109) ***(G-2597)***
Ah Logging ...509 935-4565
3244 Smola Rd Chewelah (99109) ***(G-2598)***
Ahola Timber Inc ...360 892-2243
15310 Ne Ahola Dr Brush Prairie (98606) ***(G-2028)***
Ahtanum Custom Meats ...509 966-3642
3105 S 79th Ave Yakima (98903) ***(G-15503)***
Ahtna Engineering Services LLC ...425 864-1695
19540 Intl Blvd Ste 201 Seatac (98188) ***(G-9272)***
Aidapak Services LLC ...360 448-2090
14301 Se 1st St Vancouver (98684) ***(G-14013)***
Aim, Spokane Valley *Also called American Innovative Mfg LLC* ***(G-12611)***
Aim Aerospace, Renton *Also called Aim Group USA Inc* ***(G-8733)***
Aim Aerospace Inc ...425 235-2750
705 Sw 7th St Renton (98057) ***(G-8732)***
Aim Aerospace Auburn Inc ...253 804-3355
1502 20th St Nw Auburn (98001) ***(G-365)***
Aim Aerospace Sumner Inc (HQ) ...253 804-3355
1502 20th St Nw Auburn (98001) ***(G-366)***
Aim Aerospace Sumner Inc ...253 863-7868
1516 Fryar Ave Sumner (98390) ***(G-13054)***
Aim Group USA Inc (PA) ...425 235-2750
705 Sw 7th St Renton (98057) ***(G-8733)***
Aimmco, Woodland *Also called WD&I Machine Co* ***(G-15473)***
Aimmco, Woodland *Also called W B & L Machine Inc* ***(G-15472)***
Air Cargo Management Group, Seattle *Also called Edwin Laird* ***(G-9885)***
Air Liquide ...509 793-9590
301 Summit Loop Eltopia (99330) ***(G-3261)***
Air Liquide America LP ...360 673-1400
185 Eastwind Rd Kalama (98625) ***(G-4491)***
Air Metal Fabricators Inc ...509 923-2274
28 Buckhorn Mountain Rd Pateros (98846) ***(G-7657)***
Air Mod Inc ...360 895-0910
11840 Ridge Rim Trl Se Port Orchard (98367) ***(G-7784)***
Air Pro Heating & Cooling LLC ...360 423-9165
967 3rd Ave Ste A Longview (98632) ***(G-5884)***
Air Products and Chemicals Inc ...253 845-4000
1500 39th Ave Se Puyallup (98374) ***(G-8119)***
Air Tech Abatement Tech Inc ...509 315-4550
55 E Lincoln Rd Ste 106 Spokane (99208) ***(G-12104)***
Air Technics ...425 316-0587
12022 39th Dr Se Everett (98208) ***(G-3364)***
Airborne Ecs LLC ...319 538-1051
2007 S O St Port Angeles (98363) ***(G-7679)***
AIRCLEAN ENERGY, Seattle *Also called Airclean Technologies Inc* ***(G-9360)***
Airclean Technologies Inc (PA) ...206 860-4930
4725 W Marginal Way Sw Seattle (98106) ***(G-9360)***
Aircon Soft ...206 851-8476
1925 Ne 143rd St Seattle (98125) ***(G-9361)***
Aircraft Cargo Pods ...509 238-1165
18105 N Sands Rd Mead (99021) ***(G-6422)***
Aircraft Maintenance & Support, Mill Creek *Also called Lrt Inc* ***(G-6516)***
Aircraft Propulsion Systems ...425 413-4127
25316 232nd Ave Se Maple Valley (98038) ***(G-6254)***
Aircraft Sheepskin Company ...800 874-5747
35404 I Pl Ocean Park (98640) ***(G-7178)***
Aircraft Solutions LLC ...509 838-8883
6095 E Rutter Ave Ste 2 Spokane (99212) ***(G-12105)***
Airfield Estates Winery, Prosser *Also called Airport Ranch Estates LLC* ***(G-8028)***
Airgas Usa LLC ...253 872-7000
8008 S 222nd St Kent (98032) ***(G-4766)***
Airgas Usa LLC ...360 293-6171
8581 S Texas Rd Anacortes (98221) ***(G-97)***
Airlock LLC ...206 992-3996
5007 43rd Ave S Seattle (98118) ***(G-9362)***
Airmagnet Inc ...800 283-5853
6920 Seaway Blvd Everett (98203) ***(G-3365)***
Airnexion Inc ...425 771-5924
22111 55th Ave Se Woodinville (98072) ***(G-15173)***
Airport Prints ...425 760-2235
18109 Champions Dr Arlington (98223) ***(G-198)***
Airport Ranch Estates LLC (PA) ...509 786-7401
560 Merlot Dr Prosser (99350) ***(G-8028)***
Airport Ranch Estates LLC ...425 877-1006
14450 Woodinville Redmond Woodinville (98072) ***(G-15174)***
Airport Welding & Muffler Inc ...360 568-7135
10226 Airport Way Snohomish (98296) ***(G-11872)***
Airquip, Nine Mile Falls *Also called Ron C England* ***(G-7083)***
Airtran Wireless Technologies ...360 430-3179
1417 Ne 76th St Vancouver (98665) ***(G-14014)***
Airwavz Inc ...206 696-6649
9628 123rd Ave Se Renton (98056) ***(G-8734)***
Airwavz.tv, Renton *Also called Airwavz Inc* ***(G-8734)***
Airway Metrics LLC ...206 949-8839
6436 East Side Dr Ne S Tacoma (98422) ***(G-13159)***
Airworthness Drctive Solutions ...425 876-9742
9461 53rd Ave W Mukilteo (98275) ***(G-6891)***
Aj Aerospace ...253 335-7775
105 Stanley Ct Algona (98001) ***(G-66)***
Ajaxx 63, Seattle *Also called Ajaxx Design Inc* ***(G-9363)***
Ajaxx Design Inc ...206 522-4545
8917 35th Ave Ne Seattle (98115) ***(G-9363)***
AJS Custom Embroidery ...360 993-1987
3303 Ne Minnehaha St D Vancouver (98663) ***(G-14015)***
Ajs Welding ...253 333-2976
3320 W Valley Hwy N # 108 Auburn (98001) ***(G-367)***
AK Logging Lumber & Millwork ...360 461-3764
4223 S Fey Rd Port Angeles (98363) ***(G-7680)***
Akamai Technologies Inc ...206 674-5900
1100 112th Ave Ne Ste 150 Bellevue (98004) ***(G-783)***
Al Fletcher ...360 963-2241
81 Vista Ln Sekiu (98381) ***(G-11582)***
Al Jadid Magazine ...360 936-1765
11500 Ne 76th St Ste A3 Vancouver (98662) ***(G-14016)***
Al's Custom Welding, Burien *Also called Custom Welding* ***(G-2100)***
Al's Seattle Barrel, Seattle *Also called Seattle Barrel Co* ***(G-11045)***
Alabama Metal Industries Corp ...253 926-1600
3011 70th Ave E Fife (98424) ***(G-3928)***
Alacan Solatens ...509 462-2310
10221 E Montgomery Dr Spokane Valley (99206) ***(G-12603)***
Aladdin Manufacturing Corp ...253 395-3277
23210 71st Pl S Ste 101 Kent (98032) ***(G-4767)***
Aladdin Valley Modular Mfg ...509 732-6159
2211 Gold Field Mine Rd Colville (99114) ***(G-2735)***
Alaffia, Tumwater *Also called Agbanga Karite LLC* ***(G-13849)***
Alairx LLC ...425 281-3180
11126 318th Pl Ne Carnation (98014) ***(G-2289)***
Alan and Linda Murray LLC ...206 527-0841
6319 22nd Ave Ne Seattle (98115) ***(G-9364)***
Alan Good ...360 864-2974
265 Rupp Rd Toledo (98591) ***(G-13635)***
Alan Loghry Excavation Inc ...360 461-0660
1553 Township Line Rd Port Angeles (98362) ***(G-7681)***
Alan R & Sara Balmforth ...206 363-7349
1865 Ne 171st St Shoreline (98155) ***(G-11754)***
Alas Rv ...360 676-1515
4163 Irongate Rd Bellingham (98226) ***(G-1241)***
Alaska Distributors Co ...206 682-1517
1728 4th Ave S Seattle (98134) ***(G-9365)***
Alaska Fresh Seafoods Inc (PA) ...206 285-2412
17012 Aurora Ave N 200 Shoreline (98133) ***(G-11755)***
Alaska General Seafoods, Kenmore *Also called Kanaway Seafoods Inc* ***(G-4586)***
Alaska Marine Refrigeration ...360 871-4414
4390 Cottonwood Dr Se Port Orchard (98366) ***(G-7785)***
Alaska Metal Recycling Co ...907 349-4833
1902 Marine View Dr Tacoma (98422) ***(G-13160)***
Alaska Naturals Pet Products, Bellingham *Also called Trident Seafoods Corporation* ***(G-1576)***
Alaska Pacific Seafood, Seattle *Also called North Pacific Seafoods Inc* ***(G-10626)***
Alaska Seafood Holdings Inc (PA) ...360 734-8175
2825 Roeder Ave Bellingham (98225) ***(G-1242)***
Alaska Smokehouse, Woodinville *Also called World Wide Gourmet Foods Inc* ***(G-15410)***
Alaska Standard Mining Inc ...360 432-8797
4403 W Dayton Airport Rd Shelton (98584) ***(G-11674)***
Alaska Star Inc ...206 282-0988
4019 21st Ave W Ste 200 Seattle (98199) ***(G-9366)***
Alaska United Partnership ...425 741-3350
3721 148th St Sw Lynnwood (98087) ***(G-6068)***
Alaska Wathervane Seafoods LLC ...253 582-2580
3871 Steilacoom Blvd Sw C Lakewood (98499) ***(G-5696)***
Alaska Wholesale Hardwoods ...360 704-4444
2442 Mottman Rd Sw Tumwater (98512) ***(G-13850)***
Alaskan Campers Inc ...360 748-6494
420 Alaskan Way Chehalis (98532) ***(G-2460)***
Alaskan Copper & Brass Co, Kent *Also called Alaskan Copper Companies Inc* ***(G-4768)***
Alaskan Copper & Brass Company, Seattle *Also called Alaskan Copper Companies Inc* ***(G-9368)***
Alaskan Copper Companies Inc (HQ) ...206 623-5800
27402 72nd Ave S Kent (98032) ***(G-4768)***

ALPHABETIC SECTION

Alaskan Copper Companies Inc....................................206 623-5800
628 S Hanford St Seattle (98134) *(G-9367)*
Alaskan Copper Companies Inc....................................206 623-5800
3200 6th Ave S Seattle (98134) *(G-9368)*
Alaskan Copper Companies Inc....................................206 623-5800
27402 72nd Ave S Kent (98032) *(G-4769)*
Alaskan Copper Works, Kent *Also called Alco Investment Company (G-4770)*
Alaskon Copper & Brass Company, Kent *Also called Alaskan Copper Companies Inc (G-4769)*
Alb Framing Gallery & Gift..425 432-5505
20515 292nd Ave Se Maple Valley (98038) *(G-6255)*
Alber Seafoods Inc..360 642-3773
900 1st Ave S Ste 202 Seattle (98134) *(G-9369)*
Albert Zepp Logging, Elma *Also called Zepp Resources (G-3260)*
Albina Fuel, Vancouver *Also called Albina Holdings Inc (G-14017)*
Albina Holdings Inc..360 696-3408
1300 W 8th St Vancouver (98660) *(G-14017)*
Alcatel-Lucent USA Inc..425 497-2400
10675 Willows Rd Ne # 250 Redmond (98052) *(G-8376)*
Alchemy Goods LLC..206 484-9469
1723 1st Ave S Seattle (98134) *(G-9370)*
Alcide Corporation..425 882-2555
8561 154th Ave Ne Redmond (98052) *(G-8377)*
Alco Investment Company (PA).................................206 623-5800
27402 72nd Ave S Kent (98032) *(G-4770)*
Alcoa Inc..253 272-8413
2020 Milwaukee Way Tacoma (98421) *(G-13161)*
Alcoa Intalco Works, Ferndale *Also called Intalco Aluminum LLC (G-3859)*
Alcoa Wenatchee LLC...509 663-9246
6200 Malaga Alcoa Hwy Malaga (98828) *(G-6230)*
Alder Biopharmaceuticals Inc (PA).............................425 205-2900
11804 N Creek Pkwy S Bothell (98011) *(G-1745)*
Alder Grove Distributors...360 423-3138
1559 32nd Ave Longview (98632) *(G-5885)*
Aldergrove LLC..360 253-7378
600 Se Maritime Ave # 210 Vancouver (98661) *(G-14018)*
Alderwood Park..425 774-5266
18031 36th Ave W Lynnwood (98037) *(G-6069)*
Alderwood Signs..425 744-6555
2231 196th St Sw Lynnwood (98036) *(G-6070)*
Aleddra Inc..425 430-4555
2210 Lind Ave Sw Ste 109 Renton (98057) *(G-8735)*
Aleddra Inc..425 430-4555
2210 Lind Ave Sw Ste 109 Renton (98057) *(G-8736)*
Aleddra Led Lighting, Renton *Also called Aleddra Inc (G-8735)*
Aleddra Led Lighting, Renton *Also called Aleddra Inc (G-8736)*
Aletheia Therapeutics LLC......................................206 473-2435
901 Boren Ave Ste 701 Seattle (98104) *(G-9371)*
Aleutian Spray Reverse LLC....................................206 784-5000
2157 N Northlake Way # 210 Seattle (98103) *(G-9372)*
Alex Daisley..206 623-5555
1122 E Pike St Seattle (98122) *(G-9373)*
Alexander Grape..509 942-9850
4636 W Canal Dr West Richland (99353) *(G-15093)*
Alexander Industries LLC..253 686-6066
4033 Ne Sunset Blvd Ste 5 Renton (98056) *(G-8737)*
Alexander Printing Co Inc..425 252-4212
2807 Rockefeller Ave Everett (98201) *(G-3366)*
Alexander S Service Repair....................................509 773-7010
3123 S Columbos Goldendale (98620) *(G-4192)*
Alexandria Moulding Inc (HQ)..................................509 248-2120
101 Grant Way Moxee (98936) *(G-6874)*
Alexandria Nicole Cellars LLC..................................509 786-3497
158422 W Sonova Rd Prosser (99350) *(G-8029)*
Algas-Sdi International LLC.....................................206 789-5410
151 S Michigan St Seattle (98108) *(G-9374)*
Algorithmia Inc..415 741-1491
1925 Post Aly Ste 3c Seattle (98101) *(G-9375)*
Alia Wines LLC..360 794-0421
12216 185th Ave Se Snohomish (98290) *(G-11873)*
Alice E Marwick...206 329-9565
706 Belmont Ave E Apt 203 Seattle (98102) *(G-9376)*
Alitheon Inc..888 606-7445
10900 Ne 8th St Ste 613 Bellevue (98004) *(G-784)*
Alki Foundry...206 794-4074
3600 E Marginal Way S # 11 Seattle (98134) *(G-9377)*
Alki Press LLC..206 854-1148
2420 54th Pl Sw Apt 31 Seattle (98116) *(G-9378)*
Alki Sports LLC (PA)...206 898-1305
16101 Ne 87th St Redmond (98052) *(G-8378)*
All About Safes and Vaults.....................................570 839-1980
1802 A St Se Auburn (98002) *(G-368)*
All Access Printing & Mail, Woodinville *Also called Budget Printing & Mailing (G-15199)*
All American Corporation..509 315-9951
14525 N Newport Hwy Mead (99021) *(G-6423)*
All American Homes, Mead *Also called All American Corporation (G-6423)*
All American Marine Inc...360 647-7602
1010 Hilton Ave Bellingham (98225) *(G-1243)*
All American Metal Finishing, Lynnwood *Also called Gamblin Enterprises Inc (G-6125)*
All American Metal Products...................................360 380-6202
4999 Labounty Dr Ferndale (98248) *(G-3811)*

All American Spacer Co LLC....................................509 633-3440
515 Division St Grand Coulee (99133) *(G-4242)*
All Around Fence Company, Sumner *Also called Ronald Wayne Dagley (G-13097)*
All City Print..360 718-2448
3714 Main St Vancouver (98663) *(G-14019)*
All Color EMB & Screen Prtg, Tacoma *Also called All Color Screen Printing (G-13162)*
All Color Screen Printing..253 536-2822
1706 112th St E Tacoma (98445) *(G-13162)*
All Composite Inc...253 847-5106
3206 232nd St E Spanaway (98387) *(G-12053)*
All Craft Plastics..253 887-1768
12 37th St Nw Ste 12 # 12 Auburn (98001) *(G-369)*
All CS Inc...253 474-3434
5425 South Tacoma Way Tacoma (98409) *(G-13163)*
All Electric Motor Service.......................................253 845-1938
5507 Milwaukee Ave E Puyallup (98372) *(G-8120)*
All Fabrication and Supply LLC.................................509 334-1905
1904 Airport Rd Pullman (99163) *(G-8083)*
All Fur One...206 281-8412
2400 Warren Ave N Seattle (98109) *(G-9379)*
All In Cnstr & Ldscpg LLC.......................................360 840-7990
430 N 30th St Mount Vernon (98273) *(G-6770)*
All In Wood...360 457-8337
845 Shore Rd Port Angeles (98362) *(G-7682)*
All Metal Arts Seattle..206 200-9496
3047 18th Ave S Seattle (98144) *(G-9380)*
All Metal Fab Inc..253 737-5154
1 30th St Nw Ste 6 Auburn (98001) *(G-370)*
All Metal Solutions...509 426-2400
616 S 2nd St Yakima (98901) *(G-15504)*
All Metal Wldg & Fabrication, Onalaska *Also called M H R A Corp (G-7451)*
All Natural Botanicals Inc (PA).................................253 939-2600
835 Central Ave N Kent (98032) *(G-4771)*
All Ocean Services LLC (PA)..................................206 632-7692
1205 Craftsman Way # 100 Everett (98201) *(G-3367)*
All Point Bulletin, Blaine *Also called Point Roberts Press Inc (G-1696)*
All Points East..360 863-8971
21420 189th Ave Se Monroe (98272) *(G-6545)*
All Pole Corporation..360 933-1806
1368 4th St Blaine (98230) *(G-1658)*
All Print...509 328-9344
8 N Post St Spokane (99201) *(G-12106)*
All Pro Blind Cleaning Repair...................................253 804-9497
3716 Auburn Way N Ste 105 Auburn (98002) *(G-371)*
All Pro Printer Service LLC.....................................360 818-4592
8908 Boulder Ave Vancouver (98664) *(G-14020)*
All Pro Screen Prtg & EMB LLC................................360 438-0304
8300 28th Ct Ne Lacey (98516) *(G-5531)*
All Scrapped Up Inc..206 824-3762
23302 17th Pl S Des Moines (98198) *(G-2928)*
All Season Overhead Door.....................................509 218-8303
9261 Coyote Trl Newport (99156) *(G-7053)*
All Seasons Storage & Rentals, Chelan *Also called Blue Water Inc (G-2548)*
All Seasons Stump Grinding...................................425 775-7977
20609 53rd Ave W Lynnwood (98036) *(G-6071)*
All Seasons Sweeping Service.................................509 782-8015
5295 Sunset Hwy Cashmere (98815) *(G-2312)*
All Software Tools Inc...360 883-2981
11001 Ne 80th St Vancouver (98662) *(G-14021)*
All Sports School...425 747-1511
4568 194th Ave Se Issaquah (98027) *(G-4379)*
All Systems Integrated Inc......................................253 770-5570
315 7th St Ne Puyallup (98372) *(G-8121)*
All Things New LLC..253 255-4954
8404 83rd Ave Sw Ste H Lakewood (98498) *(G-5697)*
All Wave Innovations Inc..509 308-7230
45106 N 280 Pr Ne Benton City (99320) *(G-1600)*
All Weather Mobile Welding....................................509 422-3789
1871b Old Highway 97 Okanogan (98840) *(G-7194)*
All Wood Concepts Inc (PA)....................................253 255-6518
11003 A St S Tacoma (98444) *(G-13164)*
All-Pro Services Ran LLC.......................................425 746-4829
16541 Redmond Way 1004c Redmond (98052) *(G-8379)*
Allan Bros Inc...509 653-2625
31 Allan Rd Naches (98937) *(G-6993)*
Allan Brothers, Naches *Also called Allan Bros Inc (G-6993)*
Allco Manufacturing Inc...702 616-2081
31811 Pacific Hwy S Federal Way (98003) *(G-3714)*
Allegis Corporation..425 242-6680
19821 87th Ave S Kent (98031) *(G-4772)*
Allegra-Patrick Print Imaging, Seattle *Also called PJ Finney Corporation (G-10820)*
Allen Bros Diving Logging......................................360 866-3643
8049 Stmboat Island Rd Nw Olympia (98502) *(G-7222)*
Allen Logging Co...360 374-6000
2818 S Cherry St Port Angeles (98362) *(G-7683)*
Allform Welding, Sequim *Also called Lincoln Industrial Corp Inc (G-11646)*
Allform Welding Inc..360 681-0584
81 Hooker Rd Unit 9 Sequim (98382) *(G-11607)*
Alliance Mch Systems Intl LLC.................................509 842-5104
5303 E Desmet Ave Spokane Valley (99212) *(G-12604)*
Alliance Mfg Group LLC (PA)...................................253 922-3090
2516 Holgate St Tacoma (98402) *(G-13165)*

Alliance Packaging LLC ... 509 924-7623
3808 N Sullivan Rd # 21 Spokane Valley (99216) *(G-12605)*

Alliance Packaging LLC ... 425 291-3500
1000 Sw 43rd St Renton (98057) *(G-8738)*

Alliance Steel Fabrication ... 253 538-7935
4516 176th St E Tacoma (98446) *(G-13166)*

Allied Boats, Bremerton Also called Sp Marine Fabrication LLC *(G-2002)*

Allied Body Works Inc ... 206 763-7811
625 S 96th St Seattle (98108) *(G-9381)*

Allied Daily Newspapers Wash ... 360 943-9960
1110 Capitol Way S # 300 Olympia (98501) *(G-7223)*

Allied Envelope Company- Boise ... 509 328-9800
1515 W College Ave Spokane (99201) *(G-12107)*

Allied Forces Inc ... 360 387-5713
1837 Cascade View Dr Camano Island (98282) *(G-2206)*

Allied Grinders Inc (PA) ... 425 493-1313
11431 Cyrus Way Mukilteo (98275) *(G-6892)*

Allied Ice, Mukilteo Also called Allied Grinders Inc *(G-6892)*

Allied Mineral Products Inc ... 360 748-9295
138 Sears Rd Chehalis (98532) *(G-2461)*

Allied Steel Fabricators Inc ... 425 861-9558
4604 148th Ave Ne Redmond (98052) *(G-8380)*

Allied Technical Services Corp ... 206 763-3316
10840 Myers Way S Seattle (98168) *(G-9382)*

Allied Telesis Inc (HQ) ... 408 519-8700
19800 North Creek Pkwy # 100 Bothell (98011) *(G-1746)*

Allied Titanium Inc ... 302 725-8300
1400 E Washington St Sequim (98382) *(G-11608)*

Allnight Wheelchairs ... 425 774-6814
7730 238th Pl Sw Edmonds (98026) *(G-3093)*

Alloy Polishing Co ... 360 736-2716
809 N Tower Ave Centralia (98531) *(G-2382)*

Allpak Container LLC (HQ) ... 425 227-0400
1100 Sw 27th St Renton (98057) *(G-8739)*

Allpak Container LLC ... 509 535-4112
800 Sw 27th St Renton (98057) *(G-8740)*

Allplay Systems LLC ... 360 808-5925
170 Havenwood Ln Sequim (98382) *(G-11609)*

Allred Heating Cooling Elc LLC ... 206 359-2164
1020 Sw 334th St 205 Federal Way (98023) *(G-3715)*

Allsop Inc (PA) ... 360 734-9090
4201 Meridian St Bellingham (98226) *(G-1244)*

Allspec Fasteners Inc ... 512 263-2593
1912 W Mukilteo Blvd Everett (98203) *(G-3368)*

Allsport Polaris, Liberty Lake Also called Liberty Lake Powersports LLC *(G-5844)*

Allsports Cages & Netting LLC ... 206 933-8987
4514 Sw Trenton St Seattle (98136) *(G-9383)*

Allstar Magnetics LLC ... 360 693-0213
6205 Ne 63rd St Vancouver (98661) *(G-14022)*

Allstar Specialty Designs ... 425 820-0285
9308 Ne 126th Pl Kirkland (98034) *(G-5275)*

Allview Services Inc ... 425 483-6101
2215 S Castle Way Lynnwood (98036) *(G-6072)*

Allways Logging LLC ... 360 893-2724
15801 264th St E Graham (98338) *(G-4215)*

Allweather Wood LLC (HQ) ... 360 835-8547
815 S 32nd St Washougal (98671) *(G-14941)*

Almar Tls & Cutter Grinders Co ... 503 255-2763
4859 Nw Lake Rd Camas (98607) *(G-2227)*

Almax Manufacturing Co ... 425 889-8708
903 5th Ave Ste 101 Kirkland (98033) *(G-5276)*

Almax USA, Kirkland Also called Almax Manufacturing Co *(G-5276)*

Almeda Cottage Inc ... 206 285-1674
2400 W Bertona St Seattle (98199) *(G-9384)*

Almet Incorporated ... 253 852-1690
959 5th Ave S Kent (98032) *(G-4773)*

Almet Metal Refinishing ... 206 234-8555
32814 Se 76th St Fall City (98024) *(G-3699)*

Almond Roca, Tacoma Also called Brown & Haley *(G-13210)*

Almx-Security Inc ... 425 485-3801
6527 Ne 192nd Pl Kenmore (98028) *(G-4564)*

Aloe 2000 ... 206 420-8785
10224 Richwood Ave Nw Seattle (98177) *(G-9385)*

Aloe Square, Seattle Also called Aloe 2000 *(G-9385)*

Alpac Components Co ... 360 466-2024
110 Caledonia La Conner (98257) *(G-5520)*

Alpaca Country Shop, Cle Elum Also called Peoh Point Alpaca Farm *(G-2675)*

Alpaca Mentors ... 253 880-6469
30128 Se 402nd St Enumclaw (98022) *(G-3276)*

Alpaca This LLC ... 425 432-7227
23116 244th Ave Se Maple Valley (98038) *(G-6256)*

Alpacas Northwest Inc ... 503 519-7587
6421 Ne 171st St Vancouver (98686) *(G-14023)*

Alpacas of Wintercreek ... 253 332-4026
3302 53rd St Se Auburn (98092) *(G-372)*

Alpacas Paradise Pt ... 360 263-2092
31800 Nw 9th Ave Ridgefield (98642) *(G-9060)*

Alpen Fire Cider, Port Townsend Also called Bear Wildfire *(G-7868)*

Alpha Audio Group Inc ... 253 846-1536
19304 38th Ave E Ste 3 Tacoma (98446) *(G-13167)*

Alpha Biopartners LLC ... 405 603-1917
2308 Eyres Pl W Seattle (98199) *(G-9386)*

Alpha Iron LLC ... 360 823-1777
5823 S 6th Way Ridgefield (98642) *(G-9061)*

Alpha Mfg ... 360 794-8573
12306 185th Ave Se Snohomish (98290) *(G-11874)*

Alpha Test Corporation ... 360 462-0201
261 W Business Park Loop Shelton (98584) *(G-11675)*

AlphaGraphics, Fife Also called Saco Sales LLC *(G-3991)*

AlphaGraphics, Lynnwood Also called Alphaprint Inc *(G-6073)*

AlphaGraphics ... 206 343-5037
3131 Elliott Ave Ste 100 Seattle (98121) *(G-9387)*

Alphapharma Inc ... 206 413-5122
865 Rainier Ave N Renton (98057) *(G-8741)*

Alphaprint Inc ... 425 771-1140
19011 36th Ave W Ste E Lynnwood (98036) *(G-6073)*

Alphase Used Autos, Longview Also called Longview Auto Wrecking *(G-5929)*

Alphatest, Shelton Also called Alpha Test Corporation *(G-11675)*

Alphawave Systems ... 719 888-9283
26313 Ne 52nd Way Vancouver (98682) *(G-14024)*

Alpine Brewing Co ... 509 476-9662
821 14th Ave Oroville (98844) *(G-7461)*

Alpine Cabinet ... 509 679-6380
507 Cedar St Leavenworth (98826) *(G-5794)*

Alpine Immune Sciences Inc (PA) ... 206 788-4545
201 Elliott Ave W Ste 230 Seattle (98119) *(G-9388)*

Alpine Industries Inc ... 425 481-7101
19720 Bothell Everett Hwy Bothell (98012) *(G-1818)*

Alpine Industries LLC ... 253 261-1500
18215 9th St E Ste 110 Lake Tapps (98391) *(G-5676)*

Alpine Payment Systems, Vancouver Also called American Bancard LLC *(G-14026)*

Alpine Precision Tooling Inc ... 360 474-0547
2827 Stanwood Bryant Rd Arlington (98223) *(G-199)*

Alpine Products Inc (PA) ... 253 351-9828
550 3rd St Sw Ste C Auburn (98001) *(G-373)*

Alpine Shed LLC ... 509 322-0808
130c Clarkson Mill Rd Tonasket (98855) *(G-13645)*

Alpine Windows, Bothell Also called Alpine Industries Inc *(G-1818)*

Alpine Wines ... 208 354-9463
1109 29th St Apt 301 Anacortes (98221) *(G-98)*

Alpine Woodworking ... 253 565-4560
7202 35th St W University Place (98466) *(G-13958)*

Alr Specialty Coatings LLC ... 206 713-2070
27008 137th St Se Monroe (98272) *(G-6546)*

ALRT Corporation ... 360 592-5300
4040 Mt Baker Hwy Everson (98247) *(G-3666)*

Alry Publications LLC ... 206 274-8204
1321 Seneca St Apt 2107 Seattle (98101) *(G-9389)*

Als Custom Woodworking ... 360 354-2407
548 E Wiser Lake Rd Lynden (98264) *(G-6000)*

Als Wldg Stl Fabrication Inc ... 360 740-8020
222 Downie Rd Chehalis (98532) *(G-2462)*

Alsea Veneer Inc ... 360 891-2020
201 Ne Park Plaza Dr # 288 Vancouver (98684) *(G-14025)*

Alset Corporation ... 206 335-3700
131 Macawa Trl Sequim (98382) *(G-11610)*

Alside Supply, Fife Also called Associated Materials LLC *(G-3935)*

Alta Cellars ... 425 424-9218
19501 144th Ave Ne A500 Woodinville (98072) *(G-15175)*

Alta Forest Products LLC (HQ) ... 360 219-0008
810 Nw Alta Way Chehalis (98532) *(G-2463)*

Alta Forest Products LLC ... 360 426-9721
810 Nw Liberty Pl Chehalis (98532) *(G-2464)*

Alta Forest Products LLC ... 800 599-5596
714 W Main St Ste A Chehalis (98532) *(G-2465)*

Alta Forest Products LLC ... 360 219-0008
318 State Route 7 Morton (98356) *(G-6667)*

Alta Forest Products LLC ... 360 426-9721
708 W State Route 108 Shelton (98584) *(G-11676)*

Alta Forest Products LLC ... 360 288-2234
7127 Us Hgwy 101 Amanda Park (98526) *(G-86)*

Altair Advanced Industries ... 360 756-4900
3116 Mercer Ave Bellingham (98225) *(G-1245)*

Altan Inc ... 360 331-1595
4605 Honeymoon Bay Rd Greenbank (98253) *(G-4304)*

Altech, Seattle Also called Aluminum Technologies Inc *(G-9390)*

Altek Inc ... 509 921-0597
22819 E Appleway Ave Liberty Lake (99019) *(G-5825)*

Altels Logging Inc ... 509 782-5808
4660 Brisky Canyon Rd Cashmere (98815) *(G-2313)*

Altera Inc ... 509 901-9292
5808 Summitview Ave Ste A Yakima (98908) *(G-15505)*

Altivity Packaging, Renton Also called Graphic Packaging Intl Inc *(G-8812)*

Altix North America Inc ... 425 285-4477
8201 164th Ave Ne Ste 200 Redmond (98052) *(G-8381)*

Alto Group Holdings Inc ... 801 816-2520
715 13th St Ne Wenatchee (98802) *(G-15088)*

Altos EZ Mat Inc ... 509 962-9212
703 N Wenas St Ellensburg (98926) *(G-3181)*

Altria ... 253 922-4267
4512 70th Ave E Fife (98424) *(G-3929)*

Altruen, Seattle Also called Lumenex LLC *(G-10450)*

Altus Industries Inc ... 360 255-7699
435 Martin St Blaine (98230) *(G-1659)*

Aluminum Technologies Inc 206 323-6900
3017 12th Ave S Seattle (98144) *(G-9390)*
Alvelogro Inc 425 831-1110
35300 Se Center St Snoqualmie (98065) *(G-12004)*
Always Pure Water Treatment Sy 253 631-0294
14405 Se 266th St Kent (98042) *(G-4774)*
Alyeska Ocean Inc 360 293-4677
2415 T Ave Ste 208 Anacortes (98221) *(G-99)*
Alyeska Seafoods, Bellevue *Also called Westward Seafoods Inc (G-1225)*
Alyeska Seafoods Inc (HQ) 206 682-5949
3015 112th Ave Ne Ste 100 Bellevue (98004) *(G-785)*
Amanda Park Services Inc 360 288-2230
6095 Us Highway 101 Amanda Park (98526) *(G-87)*
Amaral Music 206 853-9847
10619 Se 261st Pl E201 Kent (98030) *(G-4775)*
Amaroq Technologies, Seattle *Also called Maulcor Inc (G-10502)*
Amaurice Cellars, Mercer Island *Also called Schafer Winery LLC (G-6482)*
Amaurice Sellers, Walla Walla *Also called Schafer Winery LLC (G-14865)*
Amavi Cellars 509 525-3541
3796 Peppers Bridge Rd Walla Walla (99362) *(G-14761)*
Amaze Graphics Inc 425 481-8877
19510 144th Ave Ne Ste E5 Woodinville (98072) *(G-15176)*
Amazon Tool Shed 206 429-2185
19701 1st Pl Sw Normandy Park (98166) *(G-7090)*
Ambient Water Corporation 509 474-9451
7721 E Trent Ave Spokane Valley (99212) *(G-12606)*
Ambrew LLC 425 774-1717
180 W Dayton St Edmonds (98020) *(G-3094)*
Amcor Rigid Packaging Usa LLC 509 525-0230
1041 N 15th Ave Walla Walla (99362) *(G-14762)*
Amcor Rigid Packaging Usa LLC 360 753-4162
3025 32nd Ave Sw Tumwater (98512) *(G-13851)*
Amcor Rigid Plastics, Tumwater *Also called Amcor Rigid Packaging Usa LLC (G-13851)*
Amdocs Qpass Inc 206 447-6000
2211 Elliott Ave Ste 400 Seattle (98121) *(G-9391)*
Amera Cosmetics, Kennewick *Also called Amera Sales Inc (G-4615)*
Amera Sales Inc 509 735-1531
6403 W Rio Grande Ave Kennewick (99336) *(G-4615)*
Amerec, Woodinville *Also called Tylohelo Inc (G-15393)*
America Fiber Optic Technology, Oak Harbor *Also called Dennis Nelson (G-7148)*
America West Envmtl Sups 509 547-2240
3300 E A St Pasco (99301) *(G-7551)*
American Air Filter Co Inc 253 395-8860
22338 68th Ave S Kent (98032) *(G-4776)*
American Alloy LLC 509 921-5794
3808 N Sullivan Rd 11m Spokane Valley (99216) *(G-12607)*
American Architectural Signage 509 624-5842
916 W 30th Ave Spokane (99203) *(G-12108)*
American Bancard LLC 360 713-0690
1111 Main St Ste 201 Vancouver (98660) *(G-14026)*
American Banner & Sign Co, Olympia *Also called Brown & Balsley Sign Co (G-7243)*
American Bnchmark Mch Wrks LLC 360 584-9303
926 Unit A 79th St Se 79 A Olympia (98501) *(G-7224)*
American Bottling Company 509 328-6984
6815 E Mission Ave Spokane Valley (99212) *(G-12608)*
American Brewing Company, Edmonds *Also called Ambrew LLC (G-3094)*
American Cabinet Doors Inc 509 574-3176
1002 River Rd Ste 4 Yakima (98902) *(G-15506)*
American Cnc Fabricating Inc 509 315-4095
9922 E Montgomery Dr # 24 Spokane Valley (99206) *(G-12609)*
American Container Homes Inc 509 531-3286
14525 N Newport Hwy Mead (99021) *(G-6424)*
American Cordillera Min Corp 509 671-9401
1314 S Grand Blvd 2250 Spokane (99202) *(G-12109)*
American Craftware LLC 360 606-1827
2800 Ne 184th Ave Vancouver (98682) *(G-14027)*
American Digital 800 765-2580
8525 120th Ave Ne Ste 301 Kirkland (98033) *(G-5277)*
American Dream Homes & Cr 360 863-9340
17404 147th St Se Ste C Monroe (98272) *(G-6547)*
American Dream Product, Monroe *Also called American Dream Homes & Cr (G-6547)*
American Drilling Corp LLC (PA) 509 921-7836
19208 E Broadway Ave Spokane Valley (99016) *(G-12610)*
American Drpery Blind Crpt Inc 425 793-4477
1040 Thomas Ave Sw Renton (98057) *(G-8742)*
American Drpery Blind Crpt Inc (PA) 360 676-1121
700 S 3rd St Renton (98057) *(G-8743)*
American Edge LLC 509 937-4404
3211 Beitey Rd Valley (99181) *(G-13987)*
American Engine & Machine Inc 509 487-3332
5302 N Julia St Spokane (99217) *(G-12110)*
American Excelsior Company 509 575-5794
609 S Front St Yakima (98901) *(G-15507)*
American Flex & Exhaust Pdts, Seattle *Also called American Flex & Exhaust Pdts (G-9392)*
American Flex & Exhaust Pdts 206 789-1353
1121 Nw 45th St Seattle (98107) *(G-9392)*
American Forest Lands 425 432-5004
24012 Se 276th St Maple Valley (98038) *(G-6257)*
American Forest Lands Wash 425 358-5235
21410 Se 248th St Maple Valley (98038) *(G-6258)*
American Gold Seafoods, Anacortes *Also called Cooke Aquaculture Pacific LLC (G-117)*
American Graphic Arts 425 378-8065
1808 140th Ave Se Bellevue (98005) *(G-786)*
American Group-Samson Division, Ferndale *Also called American Manufacturing Corp (G-3812)*
American Image Displays 425 556-9511
5571 Watauga Beach Dr E Port Orchard (98366) *(G-7786)*
American Innovative Mfg LLC 509 244-2730
1419 N Thierman Rd Spokane Valley (99212) *(G-12611)*
American Kono Group, Bellevue *Also called Kono Fixed Income Fund 1511 LP (G-972)*
American Labelmark Company 206 256-0889
400 E Pine St Ste 325 Seattle (98122) *(G-9393)*
American Laser Works 360 871-3738
1860 California Ave Se Port Orchard (98366) *(G-7787)*
American Lifting Products Inc 253 572-8981
1952 Milwaukee Way Tacoma (98421) *(G-13168)*
American Machine Works 509 968-4415
4621 Rader Rd 1 Ellensburg (98926) *(G-3182)*
American Machines, Goldendale *Also called Pauley Rodine Inc (G-4205)*
American Manufacturing Corp 360 384-4669
2090 Thornton St Ferndale (98248) *(G-3812)*
American Medical Concepts 425 844-2840
28126 Ne 144th St Duvall (98019) *(G-2979)*
American Metal Specialties 253 272-9344
7012 27th St W University Place (98466) *(G-13959)*
American Mfg & Engin 253 520-5865
1513 Central Ave S Ste B Kent (98032) *(G-4777)*
American Min & Tunneling LLC (PA) 509 921-7836
19208 E Broadway Ave Spokane Valley (99016) *(G-12612)*
American Mobile Drug Testing (PA) 509 921-2730
10905 E Montgomery Dr # 4 Spokane Valley (99206) *(G-12613)*
American Mold Inspection 425 770-4375
5884 Ne Eagle Harbor Dr Bainbridge Island (98110) *(G-608)*
American Neon Inc 253 627-7446
10610 Crescent Vly Dr Nw Gig Harbor (98332) *(G-4071)*
American Nettings & Fabric Inc 360 366-2630
2684 Delta Ring Rd Ferndale (98248) *(G-3813)*
American News Company LLC 866 466-7231
3995 70th Ave E Ste B Fife (98424) *(G-3930)*
American Paper Converting Inc (PA) 360 225-0488
1845 Howard Way Woodland (98674) *(G-15417)*
American Petro Envmtl Svcs LLC 253 538-5252
402 Valley Ave Nw Ste 108 Puyallup (98371) *(G-8122)*
American Plastic Mfg Inc 206 763-1055
526 S Monroe St Seattle (98108) *(G-9394)*
American Plating 360 736-0052
524 N Gold St Centralia (98531) *(G-2383)*
American Postage Scale Corp (PA) 509 299-6144
16120 W Silver Lake Rd Medical Lake (99022) *(G-6439)*
American Powder Works 360 220-3104
13127 Beverly Park Rd Lynnwood (98087) *(G-6074)*
American Pride Corporation 253 850-1212
21838 84th Ave S Kent (98032) *(G-4778)*
American Printing, Edmonds *Also called Richins Printing Inc (G-3147)*
American Printing and Pubg 253 395-3349
5844 S 194th St Kent (98032) *(G-4779)*
AMERICAN PRODUCTS, Auburn *Also called Obcon Inc (G-516)*
American Railworks 425 582-8990
13127 Beverly Park Rd Lynnwood (98087) *(G-6075)*
American Recycling Corp 509 535-4271
6203 E Mission Ave Spokane Valley (99212) *(G-12614)*
American Rock Products, Richland *Also called Interstate Concrete and Asp Co (G-9012)*
American Rock Products, Walla Walla *Also called Interstate Concrete and Asp Co (G-14824)*
American Rock Products, Prosser *Also called Interstate Concrete and Asp Co (G-8043)*
American Rock Products, Pasco *Also called Interstate Concrete and Asp Co (G-7593)*
American Roof Inc 360 668-3206
17731 147th St Se Monroe (98272) *(G-6548)*
American Seafoods Company LLC (HQ) 206 448-0300
2025 1st Ave Ste 900 Seattle (98121) *(G-9395)*
American Sign & Indicator 509 926-6979
1013 S Mariam St Spokane Valley (99206) *(G-12615)*
American Solutions For Bus 509 276-8700
5552 S Wallbridge Rd Deer Park (99006) *(G-2893)*
American Spray Technologies, Auburn *Also called Centric Corporation (G-403)*
American Structures Design Inc 253 833-4343
218 Stewart Rd Se Pacific (98047) *(G-7522)*
American Timber Resources LLC 360 796-4236
275 Dogwood Ln Brinnon (98320) *(G-2023)*
American Tomahawk Company LLC 253 884-1940
12224 Wapato Rd Anderson Island (98303) *(G-186)*
American Vinyl Industries Inc 253 473-4731
6310 18th St E Fife (98424) *(G-3931)*
American West Industries Inc 509 535-5040
3528 E Desmet Ave Spokane (99202) *(G-12111)*
American Wine Trade Inc (PA) 206 357-0607
900 Lenora St Apt 103 Seattle (98121) *(G-9396)*
American Wine Trade Inc 509 588-3155
53511 N Sunset Rd Benton City (99320) *(G-1601)*
American Woodcraft, Tacoma *Also called All Wood Concepts Inc (G-13164)*
American Woodworking Supply 509 424-3800
1606 N 1st St Yakima (98901) *(G-15508)*

ALPHABETIC

Americas Sleep Comfort Center 253 548-8890
10406 Pacific Ave S Tacoma (98444) *(G-13169)*
Americn-Canadian Fisheries Inc 360 398-1117
2875 Roeder Ave Ste 8 Bellingham (98225) *(G-1246)*
Amerisafe Inc 360 943-5634
3006 29th Ave Sw Tumwater (98512) *(G-13852)*
Ameristar 124 509 783-7518
2610 W Kennewick Ave Kennewick (99336) *(G-4616)*
Ameristar Meats Inc (HQ) 509 535-2049
210 S Mckinnon Rd Spokane Valley (99212) *(G-12616)*
Ameron International Corp 909 944-4100
201 Ne Park Plaza Dr # 100 Vancouver (98684) *(G-14028)*
Ameron International Corp 509 547-3689
1828 W Lewis St Pasco (99301) *(G-7552)*
Ameron International Corp 909 944-4100
201 Ne Park Plaza Dr # 100 Vancouver (98684) *(G-14029)*
Ameron International Corp 909 944-4100
201 Ne Park Plaza Dr # 100 Vancouver (98684) *(G-14030)*
Ameron International Corp 425 258-2616
1130 W Marine View Dr Everett (98201) *(G-3369)*
Ameron International Corp 909 944-4100
201 Ne Park Plaza Dr # 100 Vancouver (98684) *(G-14031)*
Amery Rock & Construction Inc 509 365-4122
51 Hartland Rd Lyle (98635) *(G-5994)*
Amery Rock and Construction, Lyle *Also called Amery Rock & Construction Inc* *(G-5994)*
Ames International Inc 253 946-4779
4401 Industry Dr E Ste A Fife (98424) *(G-3932)*
Ametech, Edmonds *Also called Applied Mfg & Engrg Tech Inc* *(G-3095)*
Amfit Inc 360 573-9100
3611 Ne 68th St Vancouver (98661) *(G-14032)*
AMG Aluminum North America LLC 509 663-2165
4400 Kawecki Rd Malaga (98828) *(G-6231)*
Amgb Inc 509 309-2903
3805 N Market St Spokane (99207) *(G-12112)*
Amgen Inc 206 265-7504
1201 Amgen Ct W Seattle (98119) *(G-9397)*
Amhi Inc 425 883-4040
11812 Ne 116th St Kirkland (98034) *(G-5278)*
AMI, Milton *Also called Andersen Models International* *(G-6532)*
Amica Inc 253 872-9600
19625 62nd Ave S Ste C110 Kent (98032) *(G-4780)*
AMICK Tactical LLC 253 301-7619
14726 Lawrence Lake Rd Se Yelm (98597) *(G-15726)*
Amigo Arts LLC 425 443-5744
17461 147th St Se Monroe (98272) *(G-6549)*
Amigos Skateboards LLC 901 289-9044
33 S Hanford St Seattle (98134) *(G-9398)*
Amiraq Cnsltnts Inc 936 448-1480
35709 Nw Fairchild Rd Woodland (98674) *(G-15418)*
Amish Log Homes 360 491-4132
6360 Carpenter Rd Se Lacey (98503) *(G-5532)*
Amjay Inc 360 676-1165
1420 N Forest St Bellingham (98225) *(G-1247)*
Amjay Screenprinting, Bellingham *Also called Amjay Inc* *(G-1247)*
Ammeraal Beltech Inc 510 352-3770
6841 S 220th St Ste D Kent (98032) *(G-4781)*
Ammeraal Belting, Kent *Also called Ammeraal Beltech Inc* *(G-4781)*
Ammonite Ink 907 227-2719
1925 N Ash St Spokane (99205) *(G-12113)*
Amnis LLC 206 374-7000
645 Elliott Ave W Ste 100 Seattle (98119) *(G-9399)*
Amos Rome Vineyards 206 890-4482
700 Wapato Lake Rd Manson (98831) *(G-6238)*
AMP Engineering Services LLC 480 512-1186
702 E 7th Ave Ellensburg (98926) *(G-3183)*
Ampac Packaging LLC 253 939-8206
701 A St Ne Auburn (98002) *(G-374)*
Ampersan Press Inc 360 379-5187
750 Lake St Port Townsend (98368) *(G-7861)*
Amphibious Marine Inc 360 426-3170
3121 Se Kamilche Point Rd Shelton (98584) *(G-11677)*
Ample Power Company LLC 206 789-0827
2442 Nw Market St 43 Seattle (98107) *(G-9400)*
Ample Technologies, Seattle *Also called Rides Publishing Co LLC* *(G-10965)*
Amplex Bioresources LLC 425 285-0628
12330 Ne 8th St Ste 101 Bellevue (98005) *(G-787)*
AMR Enviromental Services, Port Orchard *Also called Alaska Marine Refrigeration* *(G-7785)*
Amra Instruments, Centralia *Also called Funeral Directors Research* *(G-2402)*
Amrep Inc 253 939-6265
427 5th Ave Nw Pacific (98047) *(G-7523)*
AMS Metals, Yakima *Also called All Metal Solutions* *(G-15504)*
AMS Offices Solutions, Burien *Also called E H P & Associates Inc* *(G-2104)*
Amsafe Bridport, Kent *Also called Bridport-Air Carrier Inc* *(G-4823)*
Amt Division, Arlington *Also called Senior Operations LLC* *(G-327)*
Amtech, Wapato *Also called McClarin Plastics LLC* *(G-14919)*
Amx LLC 509 235-1464
2416 Cheney Spokane Rd Cheney (99004) *(G-2576)*
Amy Stevens 206 706-2528
6720 11th Ave Nw Seattle (98117) *(G-9401)*
An-Xuyen Bakery Co 253 887-7823
2202 12th Ct Nw Auburn (98001) *(G-375)*
Ana Oven 661 878-4277
629 St Helens Ave Tacoma (98402) *(G-13170)*
Anaco TV & Appliances, Mount Vernon *Also called Daves TV & Appliance Inc* *(G-6787)*
Anacortes Oil Vinegar Bar LLC 360 293-6410
2802 17th St Anacortes (98221) *(G-100)*
Anacortes Printing 360 293-2131
1811 Commercial Ave Anacortes (98221) *(G-101)*
Anagram Press LLC 253 310-8770
2911 N 27th St Tacoma (98407) *(G-13171)*
Anali Incorporated 425 284-1829
20333 Ne 34th Ct Sammamish (98074) *(G-9184)*
Analog Devices Inc 360 834-1900
4200 Nw Pacific Rim Blvd Camas (98607) *(G-2228)*
Analytical Reaserch Consulting 360 573-5700
2516 Nw 91st St Vancouver (98665) *(G-14033)*
Ananse Press 206 325-8205
1504 32nd Ave S Seattle (98144) *(G-9402)*
Anaphora Press 360 379-4004
3110 San Juan Ave Port Townsend (98368) *(G-7862)*
Anatoliy Semenko 509 525-4486
502 County Road 448 Walla Walla (99362) *(G-14763)*
Anbo Manufacturing, Veradale *Also called Anbo Mfg Inc* *(G-14748)*
Anbo Mfg Inc 509 684-6559
3602 S Adams Rd Veradale (99037) *(G-14748)*
Anchor Cnc LLC 360 516-3501
7660 Ne Harbor View Dr Poulsbo (98370) *(G-7943)*
Ancient Lake Wine Company LLC 509 787-2022
795 Beverly Burke Rd N Quincy (98848) *(G-8288)*
Andean Imports, Lynden *Also called Artistic Iron Furniture Mfrs* *(G-6002)*
Andeavor 509 586-2117
22 S Gum St Kennewick (99336) *(G-4617)*
Andeavor 509 928-5632
13819 E Trent Ave Spokane Valley (99216) *(G-12617)*
Andeavor 360 374-2038
171 N Forks Ave Forks (98331) *(G-4008)*
Andeavor 509 487-9235
901 E Sharp Ave Spokane (99202) *(G-12114)*
Andersen Dairy Inc 360 687-7171
305 E Main St Battle Ground (98604) *(G-687)*
Andersen Machine Shop Inc 360 379-1031
2702 Washington St Port Townsend (98368) *(G-7863)*
Andersen Models International 253 952-2135
1302 28th Avenue Ct Milton (98354) *(G-6532)*
Andersen's Plastics, Battle Ground *Also called Green Willow Trucking Inc* *(G-706)*
Anderson & Middleton Company (PA) 360 533-2410
111 Market St Ne Ste 360 Olympia (98501) *(G-7225)*
Anderson & Vreeland Inc 419 636-5002
20206 87th Ave S Kent (98031) *(G-4782)*
Anderson Arospc Qulty Wldg LLC 360 607-2634
5252 N St Washougal (98671) *(G-14942)*
Anderson Controls, Kent *Also called Anderson Electric Controls* *(G-4783)*
Anderson Electric Controls 206 575-4444
8639 S 212th St Kent (98031) *(G-4783)*
Anderson Fine Woods 425 422-2753
2811 121st Ave Se Lake Stevens (98258) *(G-5631)*
Anderson Foundry Forge 360 270-2008
4004 Spirit Lake Hwy Silverlake (98645) *(G-11862)*
Anderson Machinery, Ellensburg *Also called Mikes Rental Machinery Inc* *(G-3215)*
Anderson Machinery Inc 509 964-2225
2574 Thorp Cemetery Rd Thorp (98946) *(G-13626)*
Anderson Resources Inc 360 426-5913
50 Se Skookum Inlet Rd Shelton (98584) *(G-11678)*
Anderson Rock Dem Pits II LLC 509 965-3621
41 Rocky Top Rd Yakima (98908) *(G-15509)*
Anderson Shake & Shingle Mill 360 795-3069
256 E State Route 4 Cathlamet (98612) *(G-2359)*
Anderson Woodworks 360 923-2203
2646 Delphi Rd Sw Olympia (98512) *(G-7226)*
Anderson's Custom Sawing, White Salmon *Also called Bill Anderson* *(G-15112)*
Anderson's Logging, Sedro Woolley *Also called Jim Johnson & Son Trucking LLC* *(G-11548)*
Andersons Rebuilding 360 779-5287
17296 Lemolo Shore Dr Ne Poulsbo (98370) *(G-7944)*
Andrew A Kroiss 509 684-4929
287 Mantz Rickey Rd Colville (99114) *(G-2736)*
Andrew Hoover 425 869-1123
16803 Ne 35th St Bellevue (98008) *(G-788)*
Andrew M Baldwin 425 481-6245
20130 164th Ave Ne Woodinville (98072) *(G-15177)*
Andrew McDonald 253 964-5020
2668 Columbia Ave Apt B Lewis McChord (98433) *(G-5819)*
Andrew Ross Winery 425 487-9463
14810 Ne 145th St Ste A2 Woodinville (98072) *(G-15178)*
Andrew Russell Pond 509 690-8509
285 Corbett Creek Rd Colville (99114) *(G-2737)*
Andrew Will Winery, Vashon *Also called Camarda Corporation* *(G-14715)*
Andrews Fixture Company Inc 253 627-7481
1720 Puyallup Ave Tacoma (98421) *(G-13172)*
Andrews Nation Inc 360 989-1700
9208 Ne Highway 99 # 107 Vancouver (98665) *(G-14034)*
Andritz Hydro Corp 704 943-4343
15708 E Marietta Ln Spokane Valley (99216) *(G-12618)*

Andritz Iggesund Tools Inc....360 574-1440
1108 Ne 146th St Ste E Vancouver (98685) *(G-14035)*
Andy's Food Basket, Battle Ground *Also called Green Willow Trucking Inc (G-705)*
Andyman Online....425 761-5921
4009 Ne 6th Ct Renton (98056) *(G-8744)*
Anewin LLC....360 606-5591
17218 Se 32 St Vancouver Vancouver (98683) *(G-14036)*
Anfield Shop, Poulsbo *Also called Skyhawk Press LLC (G-8000)*
Angel Screen Printing....253 872-3040
8459 S 208th St Kent (98031) *(G-4784)*
Angela J Bowen & Assoc LLC....360 252-2440
2010 Caton Way Sw Ste 203 Olympia (98502) *(G-7227)*
Angeles Composite Tech Inc....360 452-6776
2138 W 18th St Port Angeles (98363) *(G-7684)*
Angeles Concrete Products Inc....360 681-5429
1369 Cays Rd Sequim (98382) *(G-11611)*
Angeles Machine Works Inc....360 457-0011
404 E 2nd St Port Angeles (98362) *(G-7685)*
Angels Pallets....253 426-1770
2520 112th St S Lakewood (98499) *(G-5698)*
Angelwear....206 230-9594
4411 11th Ave S Seattle (98108) *(G-9403)*
Angstrom Innovations Inc....425 750-6329
4103 223rd St Sw Mountlake Terrace (98043) *(G-6857)*
Animal People Inc....360 579-2505
4357 Terra Bella Ln Clinton (98236) *(G-2683)*
Anjou Bakery and Catering....509 782-4360
3898 Old Monitor Rd Cashmere (98815) *(G-2314)*
Ann H McCormick PHD....650 451-8020
10454 Fox Rd Leavenworth (98826) *(G-5795)*
Ann Silvers....253 853-7049
1013 140th Street Ct Nw Gig Harbor (98332) *(G-4072)*
Annapurna Glass & Wood Inc....206 525-0777
4317 Bagley Ave N Seattle (98103) *(G-9404)*
Anne & Mollys Inc....253 872-8390
22330 68th Ave S Kent (98032) *(G-4785)*
Annette Kraft....501 319-5073
1525 Electric Ave Bellingham (98229) *(G-1248)*
Anni Demi Winery Inc....509 493-2702
139 Cooke Rd White Salmon (98672) *(G-15110)*
Annies Trunk LLC....509 529-4395
120 N Roosevelt St Walla Walla (99362) *(G-14764)*
Anniversary Year Press....360 348-7945
15820 291st Ave Se Monroe (98272) *(G-6550)*
Annointed Oil Inc....206 242-6925
12422 8th Ave S Seattle (98168) *(G-9405)*
Anoxpress LLC....509 220-2741
4910 N Bolivar Rd Spokane Valley (99216) *(G-12619)*
Ant Fx International LLC....253 302-7414
2625 Delta Ring Rd Ste 3 Ferndale (98248) *(G-3814)*
Ant Lamp Corp....360 600-1031
810 Main Street Vancouver Vancouver (98660) *(G-14037)*
Antenna Dexterra Inc....425 939-3100
21540 30th Dr Se Ste 230 Bothell (98021) *(G-1819)*
Anthony Rousseau....509 758-8379
1712 13th St Clarkston (99403) *(G-2619)*
Antica Farmacista LLC....206 329-3966
119 Pine St Ste 301 Seattle (98101) *(G-9406)*
Antipodes Inc....253 444-5555
2725 S Hosmer St Tacoma (98409) *(G-13173)*
Antipodes Inc (PA)....253 444-5555
1801 Center St Tacoma (98409) *(G-13174)*
Antique & Heirloom....253 531-6126
10418 34th Ave E Tacoma (98446) *(G-13175)*
Antoine Creek Ranch....509 682-9025
75 Antoine Creek Rd Chelan (98816) *(G-2546)*
Antoine Creek Vineyards LLC....509 682-4448
728 Golf Course Dr Chelan (98816) *(G-2547)*
Antolin Cellars....509 833-5765
6004 Glacier Way Yakima (98908) *(G-15510)*
Antonina's Bakery, Sumner *Also called Pin Hsiao & Associates LLC (G-13094)*
Antonina's Bakery, Redmond *Also called Pin Hsiao & Associates LLC (G-8622)*
Antony Architectural Stone, Snohomish *Also called Zorzi Corporation (G-12002)*
Antony Architectural Stone....425 424-0051
6018 234th St Se Ste D Woodinville (98072) *(G-15179)*
Anvil Alloy....509 891-5914
18127 E 8th Ave Spokane Valley (99016) *(G-12620)*
Anvil House LLC....406 579-3042
6532 57th Ave S Seattle (98118) *(G-9407)*
Aortica Corporation....425 209-0272
6200 Se 27th St Mercer Island (98040) *(G-6454)*
AP Interprices....360 837-2548
211 Thuja Narrow Rd Washougal (98671) *(G-14943)*
Apana Inc (PA)....360 746-2276
4290 Pacific Hwy Unit A Bellingham (98226) *(G-1249)*
Apco Northwest....800 815-8028
4493 S 134th Pl Tukwila (98168) *(G-13691)*
Ape Artisan Leather....206 399-0967
3858 31st Ave W Seattle (98199) *(G-9408)*
Apex Curb & Turf LLC....509 758-1543
1280 Fair St Clarkston (99403) *(G-2620)*
Apex Finishing LLC....425 334-6281
9015 Vernon Rd Ste 3 Lake Stevens (98258) *(G-5632)*
Apex Industries Inc....509 928-8450
3808 N Sullivan Rd 14d Spokane Valley (99216) *(G-12621)*
Apex Machining LLC....509 945-0125
7610 W Nob Hill Blvd # 200 Yakima (98908) *(G-15511)*
Apex Marketing Strategy....360 402-6487
1612 Easthill Pl Nw Olympia (98502) *(G-7228)*
Apex Mobile Mix LLC....360 304-8797
1310 Nw State Ave Chehalis (98532) *(G-2466)*
Apex Railing Solutions....206 452-3281
1505 S 93rd St Ste Bh Seattle (98108) *(G-9409)*
Apex Tool Group LLC....425 226-4491
1020 Thomas Ave Sw Renton (98057) *(G-8745)*
API, Tacoma *Also called Aero Precision LLC (G-13158)*
Apiary Security, Camas *Also called Keyking Inc (G-2262)*
Apis, Vancouver *Also called Glacier Northwest Inc (G-14255)*
Aplus Inkworks....206 910-9082
19604 109th Ct Ne Bothell (98011) *(G-1747)*
APM Games LLC....512 961-6515
16407 Ne 83rd St Vancouver (98682) *(G-14038)*
Apollo Antenna & Sales Inc (PA)....509 534-6972
720 N Fancher Rd Spokane Valley (99212) *(G-12622)*
Apollo Plastics, Spokane Valley *Also called Apollo Antenna & Sales Inc (G-12622)*
Apollo Sheet Metal Inc (PA)....509 586-1104
1201 W Columbia Dr Kennewick (99336) *(G-4618)*
Apollo Video Technology LLC....425 483-7100
24000 35th Ave Se Bothell (98021) *(G-1820)*
Apollonian Publications LLC....206 922-7910
731 Commerce St Tacoma (98402) *(G-13176)*
App Grinder LLC....206 293-9632
5225a 19th Ave Sw Seattle (98106) *(G-9410)*
Appagare Software Inc....253 857-4675
8970 Wyvern Dr Se Port Orchard (98367) *(G-7788)*
Apparel Dude Printing....425 283-3051
13770 Ne 75th Pl Redmond (98052) *(G-8382)*
Appattach Inc....425 202-5676
9704 132nd Ave Ne Kirkland (98033) *(G-5279)*
Appel Farms LLC....360 384-4996
6605a Northwest Dr Ferndale (98248) *(G-3815)*
Apperson Inc....206 336-1015
851 Sw 34th St Renton (98057) *(G-8746)*
Apperson Print Management....425 251-1850
851 Sw 34th St Bldg B Renton (98057) *(G-8747)*
Appesteem Corporation....240 461-5689
655 156th Ave Se Ste 275 Bellevue (98007) *(G-789)*
Appgen Business Software....253 857-9400
3312 Rsdale St Nw Ste 203 Gig Harbor (98335) *(G-4073)*
Apple Brooke LLC....509 922-0696
1220 S Marigold St Spokane Valley (99037) *(G-12623)*
Apple City Electric LLC....509 782-2334
4080 Mission Creek Rd Cashmere (98815) *(G-2315)*
Apple Earthworks LLC....253 847-3755
11708 200th St E Graham (98338) *(G-4216)*
Apple For Hire....206 722-3205
2905 S Dakota St Seattle (98108) *(G-9411)*
Apple of My Pie LLC....509 860-8881
207 Goldcrest St East Wenatchee (98802) *(G-3007)*
Apple Street L L C....253 988-4120
3008 43rd St Ne Tacoma (98422) *(G-13177)*
Apple Valley Machine Shop, Tonasket *Also called Tom Bretz (G-13661)*
Apple Valley Printers....509 679-9592
617 Chinook Dr Wenatchee (98801) *(G-15009)*
Applewhite Aero LLC....206 762-5285
309 S Clvrdle Ste D17 Seattle (98108) *(G-9412)*
Applicator Technology Inc....253 859-9501
24854 116th Ave Se Kent (98030) *(G-4786)*
Applied Applications Intl LLC....360 425-7900
500 Colorado St Kelso (98626) *(G-4516)*
Applied Designs, Bellevue *Also called Hull Marigail (G-952)*
Applied Digital Imaging Inc....360 671-9465
1803 N State St Bellingham (98225) *(G-1250)*
Applied Finishing Inc....425 513-2505
4216 Russell Rd Mukilteo (98275) *(G-6893)*
Applied Mfg & Engrg Tech Inc....253 852-5378
6729 135th Pl Sw Edmonds (98026) *(G-3095)*
Applied Multilayers LLC....307 222-0660
1801 Se Commerce Ave Battle Ground (98604) *(G-688)*
Applied Navigation LLC....503 329-3126
4423 220th St Se Bothell (98021) *(G-1821)*
Applied Power & Control Inc....425 710-9911
12432 Highway 99 Ste 82 Everett (98204) *(G-3370)*
Applied Precision LLC....425 557-1000
1040 12th Ave Nw Issaquah (98027) *(G-4380)*
Applied Precision Holdings LLC....425 557-1000
1040 12th Ave Nw Issaquah (98027) *(G-4381)*
Applied Technical Svcs Corp (PA)....425 249-5555
6300 Merrill Creek Pkwy Everett (98203) *(G-3371)*
Apptio Inc (HQ)....866 470-0320
11100 Ne 8th St Ste 600 Bellevue (98004) *(G-790)*
Apresvin Enterprises Ave Inc....509 967-3045
4411 King Dr West Richland (99353) *(G-15094)*
Apricots & Lollipops....509 216-0325
24013 E Maxwell Ave Liberty Lake (99019) *(G-5826)*

A L P H A B E T I C

Aprils Indoor Garden Supplies 360 537-6850
737 State Route 109 Hoquiam (98550) *(G-4328)*
APS, Medical Lake *Also called American Postage Scale Corp (G-6439)*
Aptevo Biotherapeutics LLC 206 838-0500
2401 4th Ave Ste 1050 Seattle (98121) *(G-9413)*
Aptevo Therapeutics Inc (PA) 206 838-0500
2401 4th Ave Ste 1050 Seattle (98121) *(G-9414)*
Aq Usa Inc 800 663-8303
210 Duffner Dr Ste A Lynden (98264) *(G-6001)*
Aqua Rec Inc 253 826-2561
20880 State Route 410 E Bonney Lake (98391) *(G-1716)*
Aqua Rec Inc 253 770-9447
14019 Meridian E Puyallup (98373) *(G-8123)*
Aqua Seal, Monroe *Also called Trondak Inc (G-6634)*
Aqua-Lift Inc 253 845-4010
7502 116th St E Puyallup (98373) *(G-8124)*
Aquabiotics Corporation 206 842-1708
10750 Arrow Point Dr Ne Bainbridge Island (98110) *(G-609)*
Aquaglide, White Salmon *Also called North Sports Inc (G-15124)*
Aquamira Technologies Inc 360 392-2730
1411 Meador Ave Bellingham (98229) *(G-1251)*
Aquasense, Redmond *Also called Aquatronix LLC (G-8383)*
Aquatech 360 957-5203
198 Newell Rd Castle Rock (98611) *(G-2337)*
Aquatic Co 360 458-3900
801 Northern Pcf Rd Se Yelm (98597) *(G-15727)*
Aquatic Life Sciences Inc (PA) 800 283-5292
1441 W Smith Rd Ferndale (98248) *(G-3816)*
Aquatic Specialty Services 206 275-0694
1605 S 93rd St Ste Ef Seattle (98108) *(G-9415)*
Aquatronix LLC 425 881-8600
16625 Redmond Way M367 Redmond (98052) *(G-8383)*
Aqueduct Critical Care Inc 425 984-6090
1301 5th Ave Ste 3405 Seattle (98101) *(G-9416)*
Aqueduct Neurosciences Inc 206 661-1538
7513 55th Pl Ne Seattle (98115) *(G-9417)*
AR Kalmus Corp 425 485-9000
21222 30th Dr Se Ste 200 Bothell (98021) *(G-1822)*
AR Modular Rs, Bothell *Also called AR Kalmus Corp (G-1822)*
AR Northwest 425 485-9000
11807 N Creek Pkwy S # 109 Bothell (98011) *(G-1748)*
AR Worldwide 425 485-9000
21222 30th Dr Se Ste 200 Bothell (98021) *(G-1823)*
Arabella Software LLC 206 963-6460
1624 42nd Ave E Apt A Seattle (98112) *(G-9418)*
ARB USA 866 293-9078
4810 D St Nw Ste 103 Auburn (98001) *(G-376)*
Arbitrary Software LLC 425 644-7428
15135 Se 46th Way Bellevue (98006) *(G-791)*
Arbon Eqpment Crprtn/Rite-Hite, Kent *Also called Arbon Equipment Corporation (G-4787)*
Arbon Equipment Corporation 253 395-7099
22718 58th Pl S Kent (98032) *(G-4787)*
Arbon Equipment Corporation 253 796-0004
22613 68th Ave S Kent (98032) *(G-4788)*
Arbor Crest Wineries & Nursery (PA) 509 927-9463
4705 N Fruit Hill Rd Spokane (99217) *(G-12115)*
Arbor Crest Wineries & Nursery 509 489-0588
4502 E Buckeye Ave Spokane (99217) *(G-12116)*
Arbordoun 360 468-2508
744 Richardson Rd Lopez Island (98261) *(G-5978)*
Arbuckle Press 206 409-2091
1863 Commodore Ln Nw Bainbridge Island (98110) *(G-610)*
ARC Document Solutions Inc 425 883-1110
1850 130th Ave Ne Bellevue (98005) *(G-792)*
ARCADE, Seattle *Also called Northwest Architectural League (G-10637)*
Arcana Precision Machining, Arlington *Also called Vanwerven Inc (G-345)*
Arcblock Inc 425 442-5101
3150 Richards Rd Ste 130 Bellevue (98005) *(G-793)*
Arch Parent Inc 206 664-0217
158 Sw 148th St Burien (98166) *(G-2091)*
Arch Wood Protection Inc 360 673-5099
532 Hendrickson Dr Kalama (98625) *(G-4492)*
Archer Mobile USA, Seattle *Also called Archer USA Inc (G-9419)*
Archer USA Inc 206 567-5343
2025 1st Ave Ste Garage Seattle (98121) *(G-9419)*
Archer-Daniels-Midland Company 509 533-9632
2301 E Trent Ave Spokane (99202) *(G-12117)*
Archer-Daniels-Midland Company 509 754-5266
16051 Rail Road St Nw Ephrata (98823) *(G-3331)*
Archer-Daniels-Midland Company 509 534-2636
3808 N Sullivan Rd Bldg 3 Spokane Valley (99216) *(G-12624)*
Archetype Woodworking LLC 360 977-0565
9009 Boulder Ave Vancouver (98664) *(G-14039)*
Archibald Log Homes Inc 509 782-3703
7992 Brender Canyon Rd Cashmere (98815) *(G-2316)*
Architect David Vandervort 206 784-1614
2000 Frview Ave E Ste 103 Seattle (98102) *(G-9420)*
Archivalry 206 420-3899
1708 26th Ave E Seattle (98112) *(G-9421)*
Archive Solution Providers 425 440-0228
22822 Ne 58th Pl Redmond (98053) *(G-8384)*
Arclin Surfaces LLC 253 572-5600
2144 Milwaukee Way Tacoma (98421) *(G-13178)*
Arcomm Inc 253 581-9800
4421 98th Street Ct Sw Lakewood (98499) *(G-5699)*
Arctic Circle Enterprises LLC 253 872-8525
19801 87th Ave S Bldg D Kent (98031) *(G-4789)*
Arctic Circle Holdings LLC (HQ) 206 625-9226
419 Occidental Ave S S Seattle (98104) *(G-9422)*
Arctic Fjord Inc 206 547-6557
2727 Alaskan Way Pier 69 Seattle (98121) *(G-9423)*
Arctic Printing & Graphics Inc 425 967-0700
22314 70th Ave W Ste 6 Mountlake Terrace (98043) *(G-6858)*
Arctic Storm Inc 206 547-6557
2727 Alaskan Way Pier 69 Seattle (98121) *(G-9424)*
Ardagh Glass Inc 765 741-7985
5801 E Marginal Way S Seattle (98134) *(G-9425)*
Ardezan Chocolate LLC 206 244-4440
2313 4th Ave N Seattle (98109) *(G-9426)*
Ardor Cellars 509 876-8086
202 E Main St Walla Walla (99362) *(G-14765)*
Ardor Printing LLC 425 786-4361
12525 Old Snohomish Mnroe Snohomish (98290) *(G-11875)*
Area 253 Glassblowing 253 779-0101
2514 Holgate St Tacoma (98402) *(G-13179)*
Arg Logging LLC 253 606-5047
17730 153rd Ave Se Yelm (98597) *(G-15728)*
Argent Chemical Labs Inc (PA) 425 885-3777
8702 152nd Ave Ne Redmond (98052) *(G-8385)*
Argent Fabrication LLC 206 438-0068
1125 Nw 46th St Seattle (98107) *(G-9427)*
Argo Blower & Mfg Co 206 762-9336
5400 E Marginal Way S # 1 Seattle (98134) *(G-9428)*
Argo West Inc 360 213-1503
4200 Nw Fruit Valley Rd Vancouver (98660) *(G-14040)*
Argus Defense LLC 206 707-6373
23402 59th Pl S Kent (98032) *(G-4790)*
Argusea Mar Wdwkg & Finshg LLC 360 708-9702
17608 Samish Heights Rd Bow (98232) *(G-1926)*
Aria Trading Inc 360 525-0175
8105 Birch Bay Square St # 103 Blaine (98230) *(G-1660)*
Ariel Screenprinting & Design 425 337-1918
2128 105th Pl Se Everett (98208) *(G-3372)*
Ariel Truss Company Inc 360 574-7333
616 Nw 139th St Vancouver (98685) *(G-14041)*
Aries Efd Lllp 360 710-7093
2600 Burwell St Bremerton (98312) *(G-1935)*
Arigato LLC 713 492-3858
975 Ne Discovery Dr # 407 Issaquah (98029) *(G-4382)*
Ario Inc 206 852-4877
5333 9th Ave Ne Seattle (98105) *(G-9429)*
Aristocratic Cabinets Inc 360 740-0609
151 Sturdevant Rd Chehalis (98532) *(G-2467)*
Aritex USA Inc 425 922-3819
2101 4th Ave Ste 1370 Seattle (98121) *(G-9430)*
Ark Commercial Roofing Inc 509 443-9300
11505 E Trent Ave Spokane Valley (99206) *(G-12625)*
Arlenes Kitchen 208 254-0591
41 Opal Ln Sequim (98382) *(G-11612)*
Arlington Dry Kilns LLC 360 403-3566
19406 68th Dr Ne Arlington (98223) *(G-200)*
Arlington Machine & Welding 360 435-3300
20621 67th Ave Ne Arlington (98223) *(G-201)*
Arlington Road Cellars 425 482-1801
19495 144th Ave Ne A115 Woodinville (98072) *(G-15180)*
Arm Inc 425 602-0915
915 118th Ave Se 305 Bellevue (98005) *(G-794)*
Arm Inc 408 576-1500
2002 Caton Way Sw Olympia (98502) *(G-7229)*
Armadillo Equipment & Parts 360 829-4107
28120 State Route 410 E D10 Buckley (98321) *(G-2046)*
Armadillo Press Inc 425 355-5588
9609 Belmont Dr Everett (98208) *(G-3373)*
Armoire 206 397-4703
825 Sw 152nd St Burien (98166) *(G-2092)*
Armor Performance Coating LLC 509 551-1294
1857 Bronco Ln Richland (99354) *(G-8967)*
Armour Mfg & Cnstr Inc 253 984-1213
4838 S Washington St Tacoma (98409) *(G-13180)*
Armstrong & Associates LLC 253 548-6148
2528 W 6th Pl Kennewick (99336) *(G-4619)*
Armstrong Building Components, Auburn *Also called Armstrong Lumber Co Inc (G-377)*
Armstrong Consolidated LLC 360 477-7558
2900 Washington St Port Townsend (98368) *(G-7864)*
Armstrong Lumber Co Inc (PA) 253 833-6666
2709 Auburn Way N Auburn (98002) *(G-377)*
Armstrong Magnetics Inc 360 647-8438
700 Sunset Pond Ln Ste 4 Bellingham (98226) *(G-1252)*
Armstrong Marine USA Inc 360 457-5752
151 Octane Ln Port Angeles (98362) *(G-7686)*
Armstrong NW 425 251-0353
18414 80th Ct S Kent (98032) *(G-4791)*
Arneson Fuels LLC 425 823-1096
12117 105th Ave Ne Kirkland (98034) *(G-5280)*

Arnquist Musical Designs 206 420-1639
5700 Ann Arbor Ave Ne Seattle (98105) **(G-9431)**
Aro-Tek Ltd (PA) 360 754-2770
4024 113th Ave Sw Olympia (98512) **(G-7230)**
Arr Tech Manufacturing 509 966-4300
3801 W Washington Ave Yakima (98903) **(G-15512)**
Arrants Boat Works 425 293-4660
2681 Se Camano Dr Camano Island (98282) **(G-2207)**
Arrays Software LLC 206 414-8250
1517 12th Ave Ste 304 Seattle (98122) **(G-9432)**
Arreolas Auto Wrecking 509 452-0818
290 Perry Way Yakima (98901) **(G-15513)**
Arrhythmia Solutions Inc 509 389-7366
Tapio Ofc Ctr 101b Spokane (99202) **(G-12118)**
Arris, Kirkland *Also called Ruckus Wireless Inc* **(G-5453)**
Arris Kollman Trucking Inc 360 532-0351
951 W Kamilche Ln Shelton (98584) **(G-11679)**
Arris Kollman Trucking Inc (PA) 360 532-0351
2421 W 1st St Aberdeen (98520) **(G-2)**
Arro Last Target Systems 360 427-9512
6311 Se Arcadia Rd Shelton (98584) **(G-11680)**
Arrow International Inc 425 745-3700
2807 Lincoln Way Lynnwood (98087) **(G-6076)**
Arrow International Inc 425 407-1475
2807 Lincoln Way Lynnwood (98087) **(G-6077)**
Arrow Machining Company Inc 360 659-0342
7224 44th Ave Ne Marysville (98270) **(G-6312)**
Arrow Manufacturing Inc 253 236-4088
3812 B St Nw Auburn (98001) **(G-378)**
Arrow Marine Services Inc 360 457-1544
830 Boathaven Dr Port Angeles (98362) **(G-7687)**
Arrow Marine Services Inc 360 733-7008
2124 E Bakerview Rd Bellingham (98226) **(G-1253)**
Arrow Point Media Inc 425 885-3922
2810 127th Ave Ne Bellevue (98005) **(G-795)**
Arrow Reliance Inc 206 324-7387
350 Treck Dr Tukwila (98188) **(G-13692)**
Arrowcat Marine, Everett *Also called Waya Group Inc* **(G-3653)**
Arrowdisc LLC 253 518-3900
23008 68th Ave S Kent (98032) **(G-4792)**
Arrowood Mini Storage 360 769-7400
6530 Se Mile Hill Dr Port Orchard (98366) **(G-7789)**
Arrows Sign Servicing LLC 206 412-4922
34809 14th Pl Sw Federal Way (98023) **(G-3716)**
ARS Nova Press Inc DBA ARS Nov 206 783-9671
515 N 62nd St Seattle (98103) **(G-9433)**
ARS Nova Software 425 869-0625
16770 Ne 79th St Ste 201 Redmond (98052) **(G-8386)**
Arsobscura Bk Bnding Rstration 206 340-8810
214 1st Ave S Ste B11 Seattle (98104) **(G-9434)**
Art Brass Aerospace Finshg Inc 206 209-3010
313 S Findlay St Seattle (98108) **(G-9435)**
Art Brass Plating Inc 206 767-4443
313 S Findlay St Seattle (98108) **(G-9436)**
Art Morrison Enterprises Inc 253 344-0161
5301 8th St E Fife (98424) **(G-3933)**
Art N Stitches Inc 253 248-1900
5013 Pacific Hwy E Ste 13 Fife (98424) **(G-3934)**
Art of Shaving - Fl LLC 206 737-8370
600 E Pine St Seattle (98122) **(G-9437)**
Art of Shaving - Fl LLC 253 777-0993
4502 S Steele St Ste 923 Tacoma (98409) **(G-13181)**
Art On File Inc 206 329-9607
1837 E Shelby St Seattle (98112) **(G-9438)**
Art Publishing Direct, Seattle *Also called Kurt Blume* **(G-10362)**
Artaca Co 425 398-0122
8619 Ne 169th St Kenmore (98028) **(G-4565)**
Artco Sign Co Inc 206 622-5262
108 S Brandon St Seattle (98108) **(G-9439)**
Artcraft Printing Co 509 323-5266
310 N Crestline St Spokane (99202) **(G-12119)**
Artech Sinrud Industries Inc 360 435-3520
20350 71st Ave Ne Ste A Arlington (98223) **(G-202)**
Artemisia Biomedical Inc 425 444-5619
7908 127th Ave Se Newcastle (98056) **(G-7024)**
Artful Dragon Press LLC 800 630-1117
22113 Ne 28th Place Samma Sammamish (98074) **(G-9185)**
Arthur D Fulford Jr 509 826-2225
Nichols Rd OMAK (98841) **(G-7433)**
Artic Timber 360 533-6490
42 Lund Rd Cosmopolis (98537) **(G-2797)**
Artic-Land Ice, Yakima *Also called Inland Ice & Fuel Inc* **(G-15590)**
Articland Ice (PA) 509 582-5808
125 N Washington St Kennewick (99336) **(G-4620)**
Artifactory 360 260-2660
19810 Ne Davis Rd Brush Prairie (98606) **(G-2029)**
Artifex Wine Company, Walla Walla *Also called Mpm Vintners LLC* **(G-14847)**
Artiks Inc 206 849-4335
16120 Ne 57th St Redmond (98052) **(G-8387)**
Artillery Graphic Design & SCR 360 709-3351
12305 Littlerock Rd Sw Olympia (98512) **(G-7231)**
Artisan Baking Company 206 240-4713
109 Ne 65th St Seattle (98115) **(G-9440)**
Artisan Finishing Systems Inc 360 658-0686
14219 Smokey Point Blvd # 6 Marysville (98271) **(G-6313)**
Artisan Industries Inc 360 474-1282
19113 63rd Ave Ne Ste 1 Arlington (98223) **(G-203)**
Artisan Instruments Inc 425 486-6555
6450 Ne 183rd St Kenmore (98028) **(G-4566)**
Artisan Machinery, Carnation *Also called Alairx LLC* **(G-2289)**
Artisan Stone Wood Works Inc 253 740-7102
5015 Tok A Lou Ave Ne Tacoma (98422) **(G-13182)**
Artisanal Goods Northwest LLC 503 803-7228
35902 Se Evergreen Hwy Washougal (98671) **(G-14944)**
Artistic Cabinets & Millwork 509 575-4788
2105 E Mead Ave Yakima (98903) **(G-15514)**
Artistic Gardener, Camas *Also called Artistic Home & Garden LLC* **(G-2229)**
Artistic Home & Garden LLC 360 834-7021
550 25th St Camas (98607) **(G-2229)**
Artistic Iron Furniture Mfrs 360 398-9351
6965 Guide Meridian Rd Lynden (98264) **(G-6002)**
Artistic Talents Styling Salon 360 456-0100
5233 Lacey Blvd Se Lacey (98503) **(G-5533)**
Artists Edge Inc 360 779-2337
18723 State Hwy 305 Ne Poulsbo (98370) **(G-7945)**
Artists Edge Inc (PA) 360 698-3113
9960 Silverdale Way Nw # 5 Silverdale (98383) **(G-11826)**
Arts & Crafts Press Inc 360 871-7707
2515 South Tacoma Way Tacoma (98409) **(G-13183)**
Artys Door Shop Inc 360 695-7898
7200 Ne 40th Ave Vancouver (98661) **(G-14042)**
Arvid's Woods, Lynnwood *Also called D & D Millwork Inc* **(G-6105)**
Asabooks Inc 425 885-1889
24233 Se 39th St Sammamish (98029) **(G-9186)**
Asahipen America Inc 206 371-7931
1128 Sw Spokane St Seattle (98134) **(G-9441)**
ASap Metal Fabricators Inc 509 469-3572
309 S Front St Yakima (98901) **(G-15515)**
ASap Metal Fabricators Inc (PA) 509 453-9143
315 S 3rd Ave Yakima (98902) **(G-15516)**
ASAP Sign & Banner, Mount Vernon *Also called ASAP Sign & Design* **(G-6771)**
ASAP Sign & Design 360 757-1570
1202 S 2nd St Ste B Mount Vernon (98273) **(G-6771)**
Asbestos Northwest 253 941-4343
30620 Pacific Hwy S # 103 Federal Way (98003) **(G-3717)**
ASC Machine Tools Inc (PA) 509 534-6600
900 N Fancher Rd Spokane Valley (99212) **(G-12626)**
ASC Profiles LLC 509 535-0600
4111 E Ferry Ave Spokane (99202) **(G-12120)**
ASC Profiles LLC 253 383-4955
2141 Milwaukee Way Tacoma (98421) **(G-13184)**
Ascap 206 324-0561
3206 S Irving St Seattle (98144) **(G-9442)**
Ascendance Pole & Aerial Arts 425 256-2246
724 S 3rd St Ste A Renton (98057) **(G-8748)**
Ascensus Specialties LLC (HQ) 425 448-1679
2821 Northup Way Ste 275 Bellevue (98004) **(G-796)**
Ascensus Specialties LLC 360 482-8819
4800 State Rte 12 Elma (98541) **(G-3240)**
Ascent Engineering LLC 425 686-7191
21540 30th Dr Se Ste 200 Bothell (98021) **(G-1824)**
Ascentis Corporation (PA) 425 519-0241
11040 Main St Ste 101 Bellevue (98004) **(G-797)**
Asco Machine Inc 360 735-0500
1900 W 39th St Ste B202 Vancouver (98660) **(G-14043)**
Aseptic Manufacturing Svcs LLC 509 869-4867
1841 W Bridge Ave Spokane (99201) **(G-12121)**
Aseptico Inc 425 487-3157
8333 216th St Se Woodinville (98072) **(G-15181)**
Ash Grove Cement Company 206 623-5596
3801 E Marginal Way S Seattle (98134) **(G-9443)**
Ash Grove Cement Company 509 928-4343
1312 N Thierman Rd Spokane Valley (99212) **(G-12627)**
Ash Hollow Vineyard, Olympia *Also called Ash Hollow Winery LLC* **(G-7232)**
Ash Hollow Winery LLC 509 529-7565
519 Mission Dr Ne Olympia (98506) **(G-7232)**
Ash Logging Company Inc 360 264-4367
149 N Ritter St Tenino (98589) **(G-13612)**
Asher Graphics 206 546-6500
18025 Meridian Ave N Shoreline (98133) **(G-11756)**
Asher Printing & Graphics, Shoreline *Also called Asher Graphics* **(G-11756)**
Asi Signage Innovations 360 668-1636
9910 198th St Se Snohomish (98296) **(G-11876)**
Asimi 509 766-9641
3322 Road N Ne Moses Lake (98837) **(G-6679)**
Aska Company 360 753-4233
4706 Pacific Ave Se Lacey (98503) **(G-5534)**
Asko Industrial Repair 206 284-2659
12128 Cyrus Way Ste B Mukilteo (98275) **(G-6894)**
Asko Processing Inc (PA) 206 634-2080
434 N 35th St Seattle (98103) **(G-9444)**
Asko Processing Inc 206 284-2659
12128 Cyrus Way Ste B Mukilteo (98275) **(G-6895)**
Asko Processing Inc 206 298-9730
12128 Cyrus Way Ste B Mukilteo (98275) **(G-6896)**

A
L
P
H
A
B
E
T
I
C

Aslan Brewing Company LLC....360 393-4106
1330 N Forest St Bellingham (98225) ***(G-1254)***
Asnw Inc....509 297-4272
12731 Glade North Rd Eltopia (99330) ***(G-3262)***
Aso Inc....360 883-3962
500 W 8th St Ste 110 Vancouver (98660) ***(G-14044)***
Asotin County Jail, Clarkston *Also called County of Asotin* ***(G-2628)***
Aspen Creek Log Homes....509 590-5541
405 W Bellwood Dr Apt 91 Spokane (99218) ***(G-12122)***
Aspen Paint, Seattle *Also called Asahipen America Inc* ***(G-9441)***
Aspen Scientific, Wenatchee *Also called Biocom Systems Inc* ***(G-15014)***
Aspenwood Cellars....425 844-2233
19415 219th Ave Ne Woodinville (98077) ***(G-15182)***
Asphalt Equipment & Service Co....253 939-4150
1531 20th St Nw Auburn (98001) ***(G-379)***
Assa Abloy AB....253 872-8174
20112 72nd Ave S Kent (98032) ***(G-4793)***
Assa Abloy Northwest Svc Ctr, Kent *Also called Assa Abloy AB* ***(G-4793)***
Assetic Inc....425 658-6603
3240 Carillon Pt Kirkland (98033) ***(G-5281)***
Associated Aircraft & Mar Svcs....253 631-3082
17627 Se 292nd Pl Kent (98042) ***(G-4794)***
Associated Materials LLC....425 481-7101
2801 78th Ave E Fife (98424) ***(G-3935)***
Associated Mch Fabrication Inc....253 395-1155
1510 Boundary Blvd # 100 Auburn (98001) ***(G-380)***
Associated Metals Fabrication....360 793-2422
122 S Sultan Basin Rd Sultan (98294) ***(G-13021)***
Associated Sand Gravel....425 348-6309
44000 State Route 2 Gold Bar (98251) ***(G-4185)***
Association For The Developm....509 838-3575
406 S Coeur Dalene St T Spokane (99201) ***(G-12123)***
Assured Independence LLC....425 516-7400
2932 Ne Logan St Issaquah (98029) ***(G-4383)***
Assurware Inc....509 531-8336
497 Winesap Ct Richland (99352) ***(G-8968)***
Astamed....206 812-0270
2200 Alaskan Way Ste 200 Seattle (98121) ***(G-9445)***
Astareal Inc....509 855-4370
7761 Randolph Rd Ne Moses Lake (98837) ***(G-6680)***
Astareal Technologies, Inc., Moses Lake *Also called Astareal Inc* ***(G-6680)***
Astrake Inc....503 470-4470
2137 N 61st St Seattle (98103) ***(G-9446)***
Astral Holdings Inc (HQ)....206 762-4800
5506 6th Ave S Seattle (98108) ***(G-9447)***
Astronics Advances Electronic....425 895-4622
13625 Ne 126th Pl Kirkland (98034) ***(G-5282)***
Astronics Advncd Electrnc Sys....425 881-1700
12950 Willows Rd Ne Kirkland (98034) ***(G-5283)***
Astronics Ballard Technology, Everett *Also called Ballard Technology Inc* ***(G-3383)***
Astronics CCC, Kent *Also called Astronics Cstm Ctrl Cncpts Inc* ***(G-4795)***
Astronics Corporation....425 881-1700
12950 Willows Rd Ne Kirkland (98034) ***(G-5284)***
Astronics Cstm Ctrl Cncpts Inc....206 575-0933
6020 S 190th St Kent (98032) ***(G-4795)***
Astronics-Aes, Kirkland *Also called Astronics Advncd Electrnc Sys* ***(G-5283)***
At Home Publication, Friday Harbor *Also called Double Vision Partners Inc* ***(G-4043)***
At Once Sales Software Inc....509 845-2453
3131 Wstn Ave Ste A486b Seattle (98121) ***(G-9448)***
At Your Service....425 348-9129
10508 Rosewood Ave Everett (98204) ***(G-3374)***
AT&T Wireless, Bothell *Also called New Cingular Wireless Svcs Inc* ***(G-1779)***
At-Spex Lmo Test Solutions, Newman Lake *Also called Daniel Oneill* ***(G-7043)***
Atacs Products Inc....206 433-9000
850 S Cambridge St Seattle (98108) ***(G-9449)***
Atam Company LLC....509 687-4421
148 High Blossom Ln Manson (98831) ***(G-6239)***
Atam Winery, Manson *Also called Atam Company LLC* ***(G-6239)***
Atco, Tacoma *Also called Fields Company LLC* ***(G-13295)***
Atech Services LLC....206 453-3182
4215 23rd Ave W Seattle (98199) ***(G-9450)***
ATF Mfg LLC....509 762-2421
5024 Mcconihe Rd Ne Moses Lake (98837) ***(G-6681)***
Athira Pharma Inc....206 221-8112
4000 Mason Rd Ste 300 Seattle (98195) ***(G-9451)***
Athletic Awards Company Inc....206 624-3995
817 Republican St Seattle (98109) ***(G-9452)***
Athletic Cases....206 569-8677
999 3rd Ave Ste 2525 Seattle (98104) ***(G-9453)***
Athleticsawards.com, Seattle *Also called Athletic Awards Company Inc* ***(G-9452)***
ATI Richland Operations, Richland *Also called Interntonal Hearth Melting LLC* ***(G-9011)***
Atk Manufacturing Inc....951 660-1218
2837 S 10th Way Ridgefield (98642) ***(G-9062)***
Atkins Machines LLC....253 588-2350
10526 Steele St S Ste B Lakewood (98499) ***(G-5700)***
Atkore International Group Inc....253 478-3199
7819 S 206th St Kent (98032) ***(G-4796)***
ATL International LLC....425 487-7000
22100 Bothell Everett Hwy Bothell (98021) ***(G-1825)***
Atlantis Publications Inc....206 497-0894
18120 71st Ave W Lynnwood (98037) ***(G-6078)***
Atlas Bimetal Labs Inc....360 385-3123
305 Glen Cove Rd Port Townsend (98368) ***(G-7865)***
Atlas Ceramic....206 280-0041
8448 17th Ave Sw Seattle (98106) ***(G-9454)***
Atlas Concrete Products Inc....360 736-7642
3031 Harrison Ave Centralia (98531) ***(G-2384)***
Atlas Construction Spc Co Inc....206 283-2000
4044 22nd Ave W Seattle (98199) ***(G-9455)***
Atlas Copco Compressors LLC....425 251-1040
22649 83rd Ave S Kent (98032) ***(G-4797)***
Atlas Copco Compressors LLC....360 530-2130
18930 66th Ave Ne Arlington (98223) ***(G-204)***
Atlas Electric Inc....509 534-8389
1203 N Havana St Spokane (99202) ***(G-12124)***
Atlas Pacific Engineering Co....509 665-6911
2605 Chester Kimm Rd Wenatchee (98801) ***(G-15010)***
Atlas Supply Inc....509 924-2417
12918 E Indiana Ave B Spokane Valley (99216) ***(G-12628)***
Atlas Systems LLC....509 535-7775
6416 E Main Ave Spokane Valley (99212) ***(G-12629)***
Atlas Technologies,, Port Townsend *Also called Atlas Bimetal Labs Inc* ***(G-7865)***
Atm-Plu, Bothell *Also called Core Corporation* ***(G-1757)***
Atomic Crate & Case Inc....425 264-0336
18927 16th Ave S Seatac (98188) ***(G-9273)***
Atomic Fabrications LLC....206 767-8036
1605 S 93rd St Seattle (98108) ***(G-9456)***
Atomic Screen Printing & EMB....509 585-2866
329 W Columbia Dr Kennewick (99336) ***(G-4621)***
Atomic Vinyl Signs & Banners, Kennewick *Also called Atomic Screen Printing & EMB* ***(G-4621)***
Atomrock Llc....425 281-2371
1045 Ridgewood Cir Sw Issaquah (98027) ***(G-4384)***
Atos It Solutions and Svcs Inc....425 691-3080
15400 Se 30th Pl Bellevue (98007) ***(G-798)***
Atossa Genetics Inc (PA)....206 325-6086
107 Spring St Seattle (98104) ***(G-9457)***
Atrium Door and Win Co of NW....509 248-4462
3400 Tacoma St Union Gap (98903) ***(G-13920)***
Atrium Windows and Door Wash....509 248-4462
3400 Tacoma St Union Gap (98903) ***(G-13921)***
Atrium Windows and Doors Inc....509 248-4462
3400 Tacoma St Union Gap (98903) ***(G-13922)***
Ats....509 534-2822
408 S Freya St Spokane (99202) ***(G-12125)***
Ats....360 260-2627
1109 Nw Klickitat Ln Camas (98607) ***(G-2230)***
Ats Inland Nw LLC (PA)....509 892-1000
9507 E Sprague Ave Spokane Valley (99206) ***(G-12630)***
Attachmate Corporation (HQ)....206 217-7100
705 5th Ave S Ste 1000 Seattle (98104) ***(G-9458)***
Attachmate Intl Sls Corp (HQ)....206 217-7500
705 5th Ave S Ste 1000 Seattle (98104) ***(G-9459)***
Attachmate Wrq, Seattle *Also called Attachmate Corporation* ***(G-9458)***
Attbaar Division, Ridgefield *Also called Ershigs Inc* ***(G-9081)***
Attenex, Seattle *Also called Fti Consulting Tech Sftwr* ***(G-10034)***
Atwood Adhesives Inc....206 762-7455
945 S Doris St Seattle (98108) ***(G-9460)***
Atwood Fabricating....425 481-5388
19106 43rd Ave Se Bothell (98012) ***(G-1826)***
Au Gavroche Inc....206 284-8770
2001 W Grfield St Ste C92 Seattle (98119) ***(G-9461)***
Auburn Dairy Products Inc....253 833-3400
702 W Main St Auburn (98001) ***(G-381)***
Auburn Hexacomb Plant, Auburn *Also called Hexacomb Corporation* ***(G-464)***
Auburn Marine....253 941-3046
5506 S 288th St Auburn (98001) ***(G-382)***
Auburn Sign Company, Auburn *Also called Industry Sign & Graphics Inc* ***(G-476)***
Auburn WA 98002, Auburn *Also called Munters Moisture Control Svcs* ***(G-501)***
Auction Edge Inc....206 858-4808
1424 4th Ave Ste 920 Seattle (98101) ***(G-9462)***
Audiocontrol Inc (PA)....425 775-8461
22410 70th Ave W Ste 1 Mountlake Terrace (98043) ***(G-6859)***
Audiocontrol Inc....425 775-8461
1215 E Francis Ave Spokane (99208) ***(G-12126)***
Audion Laboratory Inc....206 842-5202
12903 Manzanita Rd Ne Bainbridge Island (98110) ***(G-611)***
Audioisocket, Seattle *Also called Leopona Inc* ***(G-10404)***
Audrey Josias Ceramics....253 862-2365
23914 66th St E Buckley (98321) ***(G-2047)***
August Systems Inc....509 468-2988
4407 N Div St Ste 300 Spokane (99208) ***(G-12127)***
Aunt Donnas....206 519-0143
1725 Ocean Ave Raymond (98577) ***(G-8341)***
Auntie Anne's, Lynnwood *Also called S & W Management Co Inc* ***(G-6191)***
Aura Accessories Inc (PA)....208 850-1603
714 E Pike St Unit 509s Seattle (98122) ***(G-9463)***
Auroma Technologies Co LLC....425 582-8674
2211 W Casino Rd Ste A Everett (98204) ***(G-3375)***

Aurora Hardwood Seattle LLC 253 236-8985
18630 72nd Ave S Kent (98032) *(G-4798)*
Aurora Prints, Shoreline *Also called Mass Media Outlet Corporation (G-11786)*
Aurora Quality Buildings Inc 360 658-9967
14418 Smokey Point Blvd Marysville (98271) *(G-6314)*
Auroraview LLC (PA) 206 724-5953
8201 164th Ave Ne Ste 200 Redmond (98052) *(G-8388)*
Ausclean Technology Inc 360 563-9244
8554 122nd Ave Ne 244 Kirkland (98033) *(G-5285)*
Austin Chase Coffee, Seattle *Also called Caffe Appassionato Inc (G-9605)*
Austin Chase Coffee Inc (HQ) 206 281-8040
4001 21st Ave W Seattle (98199) *(G-9464)*
Austin Else LLC 888 654-4450
1015 W Garland Ave Spokane (99205) *(G-12128)*
Austin Fire and Safety, Stanwood *Also called Austin Speciaties Inc (G-12959)*
Austin Jordan Inc 253 265-1903
2809 White Cloud Ave Nw Gig Harbor (98335) *(G-4074)*
Austin Resources LLC 253 472-1703
5110 184th St E Tacoma (98446) *(G-13185)*
Austin Speciaties Inc 360 629-6662
8212 Hennings Dr Stanwood (98292) *(G-12959)*
Austin-Mac Inc 206 624-7066
2739 6th Ave S Seattle (98134) *(G-9465)*
Authentic Woodcraft Inc 253 939-8119
2 37th St Nw Auburn (98001) *(G-383)*
Author-It Software Corporation 888 999-1021
1109 1st Ave Ste 500 Seattle (98101) *(G-9466)*
Auto Body Specialties 360 424-1313
2407 Old Highway 99 S Rd # 996 Mount Vernon (98273) *(G-6772)*
Auto Spring Service Inc 253 839-3780
26460 Pacific Hwy S Kent (98032) *(G-4799)*
Auto Wheel Sales 509 483-4251
3803 N Regal St Spokane (99207) *(G-12129)*
Autocraft Incorporated 509 926-7002
525 S Cavalier Ct Greenacres (99016) *(G-4295)*
Automated AG Systems LLC 813 786-7282
145 N Hamilton Rd Moses Lake (98837) *(G-6682)*
Automated Controls Inc 206 246-6499
1531 14th St Nw Ste 4 Auburn (98001) *(G-384)*
Automated Equipment Company 206 767-9080
10847 E Marginal Way S Tukwila (98168) *(G-13693)*
Automated Gates & Equipment, Tukwila *Also called Automated Equipment Company (G-13693)*
Automated Manufacturing Cons, Vancouver *Also called Harry Price (G-14285)*
Automated Mechanical Controls 425 881-8226
9630 153rd Ave Ne Redmond (98052) *(G-8389)*
Automated Metal Tech Inc 425 895-9733
15340 Ne 92nd St Ste C Redmond (98052) *(G-8390)*
Automated Options Inc 509 467-9860
9515 N Div St Ste 105 Spokane (99218) *(G-12130)*
Automated Systems Tacoma LLC 253 475-0200
4110 S Washington St Tacoma (98409) *(G-13186)*
Automated Tech Solutions LLC 425 999-1297
22240 257th Ave Se Maple Valley (98038) *(G-6259)*
Automatic Door Solutions LLC 253 802-0888
19602 153rd Ave E Orting (98360) *(G-7473)*
Automatic Funds Transfer Svcs 206 254-0975
151 S Lander St Ste C Seattle (98134) *(G-9467)*
Automatic Products Co Inc 253 872-0203
5858 S 194th St Kent (98032) *(G-4800)*
Automatic Products Mfg Co LLC 253 395-7173
25329 74th Ave S Kent (98032) *(G-4801)*
Automatic Wilbert Vault Co Inc (PA) 253 531-2656
2206 121st St E Tacoma (98445) *(G-13187)*
Automation Modules Inc 253 549-4868
870 10th Ln Fox Island (98333) *(G-4018)*
Automic Software Inc (HQ) 425 644-2121
14475 Ne 24th St Ste 210 Bellevue (98007) *(G-799)*
Automotive Machine Specialties 425 355-0802
12432 Highway 99 Ste 77 Everett (98204) *(G-3376)*
Automotive Repair Corporation (PA) 509 244-2730
314 E Jackson Ave Spokane (99207) *(G-12131)*
Autopatch, Cheney *Also called Xn Technologies Inc (G-2596)*
Autopatch Group, Cheney *Also called Amx LLC (G-2576)*
Avac Inc 425 869-2822
18350 Redmond Way L Redmond (98052) *(G-8391)*
Avado Inc 415 662-8236
6947 Coal Creek Pkwy Se # 242 Newcastle (98059) *(G-7025)*
Available Backflow Testers 425 652-9970
27732 168th Ave Se Covington (98042) *(G-2820)*
Availble Creat Screen Prtg EMB 360 576-8542
14707 Ne 13th Ct Ste B102 Vancouver (98685) *(G-14045)*
Avalara Inc (PA) 206 826-4900
255 S King St Ste 1800 Seattle (98104) *(G-9468)*
Avalonphilly LLC 800 405-7024
14205 Se 36th St Ste 100 Bellevue (98006) *(G-800)*
Avalyn Pharma Inc (PA) 206 707-0340
701 Pike St Ste 1500 Seattle (98101) *(G-9469)*
Avantbio Corporation 360 521-8904
1011 Ne 103rd St Seattle (98125) *(G-9470)*
Avantbio Corporation 360 521-8904
8013 Ne St Johns Rd Ste E Vancouver (98665) *(G-14046)*
Avante Technology LLC 425 273-4740
17611 Se 46th Pl Bellevue (98006) *(G-801)*
Avantech Inc 509 943-6706
2155 Robertson Dr Richland (99354) *(G-8969)*
Avara Construction, Redmond *Also called Gibraltar Maint & Cnstr Inc (G-8477)*
Avaric Letter Press 360 836-5993
3514 Ne 155th Ave Vancouver (98682) *(G-14047)*
Avaya Inc 425 881-7544
2277 158th Ct Ne Bellevue (98008) *(G-802)*
Avaya Inc 425 454-2715
333 108th Ave Ne Ste 2000 Bellevue (98004) *(G-803)*
Aveda Environmental Lifestyles 509 624-5028
808 W Main Ave Ste 211 Spokane (99201) *(G-12132)*
Avella LLC 509 217-0347
24817 E Liberty Creek Rd Liberty Lake (99019) *(G-5827)*
Avenger USA, Redmond *Also called Levetec Surface Prep McHy LLC (G-8533)*
Avennia Winery 425 392-3191
18808 142nd Ave Ne Ste 2b Woodinville (98072) *(G-15183)*
Avere Systems Inc 425 706-7507
1 Microsoft Way Redmond (98052) *(G-8392)*
Avery Dennison Corporation 253 872-6993
21604 86th Ave S Kent (98031) *(G-4802)*
Avery Weigh-Tronix LLC 206 575-1992
808 Industry Dr Tukwila (98188) *(G-13694)*
Avery Weigh-Tronix LLC 800 903-8823
1720 Pike St Nw Auburn (98001) *(G-385)*
AVI Marie Hair Collection LLC 425 409-9924
2223 Benson Rd S Apt D102 Renton (98055) *(G-8749)*
Avia Marine Company 253 373-1644
1309 Central Ave S Ste E Kent (98032) *(G-4803)*
Avian Balloon Company 509 928-6847
12925 E Riverside Ave Spokane Valley (99216) *(G-12631)*
Aviation Covers Inc 360 435-0342
18712 59th Dr Ne Arlington (98223) *(G-205)*
Aviation Innovations LLC 360 907-0888
35004 Ne 185th Ave Yacolt (98675) *(G-15481)*
Aviation Partners Inc (PA) 206 762-1171
7299 Perimeter Rd S Ste A Seattle (98108) *(G-9471)*
Aviation Spares & Svcs Intl Co (PA) 425 869-7799
8920 152nd Ave Ne Redmond (98052) *(G-8393)*
Avid Health Inc (HQ) 360 737-6800
6350 Ne Campus Dr Vancouver (98661) *(G-14048)*
Avid Products LLC 888 271-3616
18344 Redmond Way Redmond (98052) *(G-8394)*
Avidian Technologies Inc 800 399-8980
14405 Se 36th St Ste 206 Bellevue (98006) *(G-804)*
Avio Corporation 425 739-6800
8525 120th Ave Ne Ste 300 Kirkland (98033) *(G-5286)*
Avio Support, Kirkland *Also called Avio Corporation (G-5286)*
Avista Capital Inc (HQ) 509 489-0500
201 W North River Dr # 610 Spokane (99201) *(G-12133)*
Avista Corporation (PA) 509 489-0500
1411 E Mission Ave Spokane (99202) *(G-12134)*
Avistar Aerospace LLC 206 838-6869
603 Stewart St Ste 1020 Seattle (98101) *(G-9472)*
Avitech International Corp 425 885-3863
15377 Ne 90th St Redmond (98052) *(G-8395)*
Avn Floor & Mill Work LLC 425 345-6071
10124 9th Ave W Apt B106 Everett (98204) *(G-3377)*
Avoa Publishing LLC 509 594-9778
6408 Cowiche Canyon Ln Yakima (98908) *(G-15517)*
Avocent 425 398-0294
18912 North Creek Pkwy Bothell (98011) *(G-1749)*
Avocent Redmond Corp 425 861-5858
11335 Ne 122nd Way # 140 Kirkland (98034) *(G-5287)*
Avos Inc 503 713-8404
4207 Ne 94th St Vancouver (98665) *(G-14049)*
Avst Parent LLC (HQ) 425 951-1600
20000 North Creek Pkwy Bothell (98011) *(G-1750)*
Avtechtyee Inc 425 290-3100
6500 Merrill Creek Pkwy Everett (98203) *(G-3378)*
Awakened Heart 360 556-6168
1213 19th Ave Se Olympia (98501) *(G-7233)*
Award Dental II LLC (PA) 253 520-0100
22430 134th Pl Se Kent (98042) *(G-4804)*
Awards Etc 509 758-3537
2613 20th St Clarkston (99403) *(G-2621)*
Awards N More Usa Inc 360 577-3646
825 Hillcrest Dr Longview (98632) *(G-5886)*
Aware Software Inc 206 232-5709
4534 Ferncroft Rd Mercer Island (98040) *(G-6455)*
Aways Connection, Olympia *Also called Thurston Co Transfer Station (G-7406)*
Awnings & Sunrooms Distinction 360 681-2727
141 Timberline Dr Sequim (98382) *(G-11613)*
Axama Corporation 509 922-8400
2321 N Coleman Rd Spokane Valley (99212) *(G-12632)*
Axiall Corporation 360 577-3232
3541 Industrial Way Longview (98632) *(G-5887)*
Axiom Drilling Corp 509 921-7836
19208 E Broadway Ave Spokane Valley (99016) *(G-12633)*
Axis Cutparts LLC 253 833-5370
226 Pike St Ne Auburn (98002) *(G-386)*

ALPHABETIC

ALPHABETIC SECTION

Axis Mfg 509 368-9895
6010 E Alki Ave Spokane Valley (99212) *(G-12634)*
Aynano Technology LLC 208 596-9865
1805 Nw Ventura Dr Pullman (99163) *(G-8084)*
Ayurveg Inc 360 863-2457
14811 Moonlight Dr Gold Bar (98251) *(G-4186)*
AZ Arts Inc 253 584-8155
9802 40th Ave Sw Lakewood (98499) *(G-5701)*
AZ Imprint 360 578-2476
305 W Main St Ste B Kelso (98626) *(G-4517)*
AZ Precision Mfg LLC 360 441-9008
6872 Mission Rd Everson (98247) *(G-3667)*
Azima Dli, Poulsbo Also called Dli Engineering Corporation *(G-7958)*
Azure Fire Publishing 206 380-2036
2308 N 149th St Shoreline (98133) *(G-11757)*
Azure Mountain Botanicals 425 478-3902
420 E Spring St Dayton (99328) *(G-2878)*
B & B Electric Motors Inc 206 763-3538
22114 68th Ave S Kent (98032) *(G-4805)*
B & B Equipment Co Inc 509 786-3838
County Rte 12 Prosser (99350) *(G-8030)*
B & B Express Printing (PA) 509 783-7383
7519 W Kennewick Ave A Kennewick (99336) *(G-4622)*
B & B Foods Inc (PA) 906 493-6962
499 N Wilbur Ave Walla Walla (99362) *(G-14766)*
B & B Logging Inc 360 247-5237
43901 Ne Protzman Rd Amboy (98601) *(G-89)*
B & B Manufacturing LLC 360 988-5020
9314 Swanson Rd Sumas (98295) *(G-13041)*
B & B Parrotts Welding Inc 253 862-4955
22021 96th St E Buckley (98321) *(G-2048)*
B & B Parrotts Welding Inc 360 825-0565
2401 Cole St Enumclaw (98022) *(G-3277)*
B & B Welding, Buckley Also called B & B Parrotts Welding Inc *(G-2048)*
B & C Custom Manufacturing Inc 509 535-0049
1514 E Riverside Ave Spokane (99202) *(G-12135)*
B & C Fiberglass Inc 907 842-4767
4823 Guide Meridian Bellingham (98226) *(G-1255)*
B & C Manufacturing Inc 425 787-8868
3419 Hayes St Everett (98201) *(G-3379)*
B & D Advertising Prtg & Svc 206 542-3262
124 Nw 203rd St Shoreline (98177) *(G-11758)*
B & D Sheet Metal LLC 206 533-0350
17038 Aurora Ave N Shoreline (98133) *(G-11759)*
B & D Storage, Ridgefield Also called B and D Whirlies *(G-9064)*
B & G Industries Inc 360 802-0363
501 Griffin Ave Enumclaw (98022) *(G-3278)*
B & G Machine Inc (PA) 206 767-6071
6400 Corson Ave S Seattle (98108) *(G-9473)*
B & J Fiberglass LLC 360 398-9342
1005 C St Bellingham (98225) *(G-1256)*
B & J Metal Fab 360 887-8548
31211 Nw Paradise Park Rd Ridgefield (98642) *(G-9063)*
B & J Printing Inc 360 692-3470
187 Ne Conifer Dr Bremerton (98311) *(G-1936)*
B & M Logging Inc 360 748-6904
281 Hamilton Rd N Chehalis (98532) *(G-2468)*
B & R Bindery and Collating 360 944-0326
6707 Ne 117th Ave 103e Vancouver (98662) *(G-14050)*
B & S Enterprises 253 859-3605
4204 Auburn Way N Ste 3 Auburn (98002) *(G-387)*
B & W Excavating & Cnstr 509 937-2028
3728 W Jump Off Rd Valley (99181) *(G-13988)*
B and D Whirlies 360 887-8471
3318 Ne 239th St Ridgefield (98642) *(G-9064)*
B and P Enterprises 509 545-9125
83 Reinken Blvd Burbank (99323) *(G-2082)*
B C T, Spokane Valley Also called Cleland Investment LC *(G-12659)*
B C T Inc 206 343-9355
3433 4th Ave S Seattle (98134) *(G-9474)*
B C Traffic 360 895-1000
2501 Se Mile Hill Dr Port Orchard (98366) *(G-7790)*
B C W, Seattle Also called Bcwest LLC *(G-9504)*
B E I, Seattle Also called Building Envlope Innvtions LLC *(G-9597)*
B E I Packaging, Shoreline Also called Medical Equipment Dev Co LLC *(G-11788)*
B G Bender Inc 253 848-3742
1109 Valley Ave Nw Puyallup (98371) *(G-8125)*
B G Instruments Inc 509 893-9881
13607 E Trent Ave Spokane Valley (99216) *(G-12635)*
B K Welding and Fabrication 360 871-0490
6412 Se Sedgwick Rd Port Orchard (98366) *(G-7791)*
B Karnes Books Inc 360 828-7132
10520 Ne 113th Cir Vancouver (98662) *(G-14051)*
B L Logging 360 748-8248
132 Newaukum Valley Rd Chehalis (98532) *(G-2469)*
B Line Mfg 360 718-2158
13205 Ne 5th Ave Vancouver (98685) *(G-14052)*
B M C Building Materials Ctr, Lakewood Also called BMC West LLC *(G-5704)*
B M G Industries 425 415-6360
19111 61st Ave Ne Unit 2 Arlington (98223) *(G-206)*
B P I Medical, Fife Also called Bens Precision Instrs Inc *(G-3938)*

B Plus Inc 360 426-5038
270 Se Nighthawk Pl Shelton (98584) *(G-11681)*
B Triplex Inc 360 904-5981
24119 Ne 132nd Ave Battle Ground (98604) *(G-689)*
B&B Custom Metals LLC 425 308-8478
2700 Salk Ave Richland (99354) *(G-8970)*
B&M Logging Inc 360 985-0150
1940 Us Highway 12 Ethel (98542) *(G-3348)*
B-A-Pro LLC 253 861-3634
2001 48th Avenue Ct E B Fife (98424) *(G-3936)*
B-Side Software LLC 206 708-6973
620 N 34th St Apt 410 Seattle (98103) *(G-9475)*
B/E Aerospace Inc 360 657-5197
11404 Commando Rd W Everett (98204) *(G-3380)*
B/E Aerospace Inc 425 923-2700
11404 Commando Rd W Everett (98204) *(G-3381)*
B2r Partners Inc (PA) 360 225-1230
675 Mitchell Ave Woodland (98674) *(G-15419)*
B3 Breakfast & Burger Bar 425 672-3666
4027 196th St Sw Lynnwood (98036) *(G-6079)*
Ba Pro Sports Product, Fife Also called B-A-Pro LLC *(G-3936)*
Baader Food Prosessing McHy, Auburn Also called Baader North America *(G-388)*
Baader North America 253 333-0422
1512 Boundary Blvd # 102 Auburn (98001) *(G-388)*
Baby Signs By Laurie Hals 425 557-6537
2801 247th Ave Se Sammamish (98075) *(G-9187)*
Babysakes.com, Bellevue Also called Specialty Stores Inc *(G-1151)*
Back To Basics Lean Mfg 253 353-4281
9101 166th St E Puyallup (98375) *(G-8126)*
Backwoods 509 826-0758
32 Omak River Rd OMAK (98841) *(G-7434)*
Backyard Bounty Co-Op 360 574-6937
809 Nw 164th St Ridgefield (98642) *(G-9065)*
Bad Apple 360 899-5183
2320 N Laventure Rd Mount Vernon (98273) *(G-6773)*
Bad Bags Inc 206 722-0916
5527 56th Ave S Seattle (98118) *(G-9476)*
Bad Breath Garlic Co 253 223-1835
17404 Meridian E Puyallup (98375) *(G-8127)*
Bad Dog Distillery LLC 360 435-3981
19109 63rd Ave Ne Ste 1 Arlington (98223) *(G-207)*
Bad Habit Ltd 360 385-3101
1005 Lawrence St Port Townsend (98368) *(G-7866)*
Baden Sports Inc 253 925-0500
3401 Lind Ave Sw Renton (98057) *(G-8750)*
Badge Boys Awards & Engraving 360 876-8414
3220 Se Puffin Ln Port Orchard (98367) *(G-7792)*
Badger Braces LLC 509 229-3635
502 Steptoe St Colton (99113) *(G-2732)*
Badger Mountain Inc 509 627-4986
1106 N Jurupa St Kennewick (99338) *(G-4623)*
Badger Mountain Vineyards 509 627-4986
110 Jurupa St Kennewick (99338) *(G-4624)*
Badger Mtn Vnyrd Powers Winery, Kennewick Also called Badger Mountain Inc *(G-4623)*
Badnasty Paintball 509 998-0984
11064 Road K Ne Moses Lake (98837) *(G-6683)*
Bae Systems Controls Inc 607 770-2000
8510 154th Ave Ne Redmond (98052) *(G-8396)*
Bae Systems Tech Sol Srvc Inc 360 598-8800
3100 Nw Bucklin Hill Rd Silverdale (98383) *(G-11827)*
Baer Winery LLC 425 483-7060
19501 144th Ave Ne F100 Woodinville (98072) *(G-15184)*
Bagcraft 360 695-7771
6416 Nw Whitney Rd Vancouver (98665) *(G-14053)*
Bagdons Inc 509 662-1411
760 S Wenatchee Ave Wenatchee (98801) *(G-15011)*
Bahmiller Woodworks 509 929-6300
905 W Cascade Ct Unit 56 Ellensburg (98926) *(G-3184)*
Bailey and Bailey Inc 253 649-0568
5246 Olympic Dr Nw 101 Gig Harbor (98335) *(G-4075)*
Bailey Tool & Die, Lynnwood Also called Bailey Tool Inc *(G-6080)*
Bailey Tool Inc 425 745-8427
3605 132nd St Sw Ste 2 Lynnwood (98087) *(G-6080)*
Bainbrdge Island Vnyrds Winery, Bainbridge Island Also called Bainbrdge Island Wnery Vnyards *(G-612)*
Bainbridge Island Wnery Vnyards 206 842-9463
8989 Ne Day Rd E Bainbridge Island (98110) *(G-612)*
Bainbridge Beeswax Works 206 618-2569
280 Wyatt Way Ne Apt B102 Bainbridge Island (98110) *(G-613)*
Bainbridge Manufacturing Inc 800 255-4702
237 W 3rd St Waterville (98858) *(G-15004)*
Bainbridge Organic Distillers 206 842-3184
9727 Coppertop Loop Ne Bainbridge Island (98110) *(G-614)*
Bainbridge Procurement Svcs, Bainbridge Island Also called Hope Moffat *(G-640)*
Bainbridge Vineyards LLC 206 842-9463
8989 Ne Day Rd E Bainbridge Island (98110) *(G-615)*
Bainter Bainter & Bainter LLC 360 267-5521
3079 State Route 105 Grayland (98547) *(G-4292)*
Bair Construction Inc 360 491-2285
8464 30th Ave Ne Lacey (98516) *(G-5535)*
Bair Metal 425 231-1944
13315 103rd Ave Ne Arlington (98223) *(G-208)*

Bait Boy, Clinton *Also called Retco Inc* ***(G-2695)***
Bake Works Inc....360 213-2001
5600 Ne 121st Ave Ste T-1 Vancouver (98682) ***(G-14054)***
Baked LLC....206 307-4847
2604 California Ave Sw Seattle (98116) ***(G-9477)***
Baker Boys Northwest LLC....253 383-3113
3812 S Wright Ave Tacoma (98409) ***(G-13188)***
Baker Cmmdties Inc/Seattle Div, Seattle *Also called Baker Commodities Inc* ***(G-9478)***
Baker Commodities, Ferndale *Also called J & S Manufacturing Inc* ***(G-3861)***
Baker Commodities Inc....509 535-5435
4423 E Hutton Ave Spokane (99212) ***(G-12136)***
Baker Commodities Inc....509 534-2137
4423 E Hutton Ave Spokane (99212) ***(G-12137)***
Baker Commodities Inc....206 243-4781
5795 S 130th Pl Seattle (98178) ***(G-9478)***
Baker Commodities Inc....509 837-8686
150 Bridgeview Rd Fl 1 Grandview (98930) ***(G-4245)***
Baker Enterprises....360 452-1349
172 Snow Ln Port Angeles (98362) ***(G-7688)***
Baker Industries Northwest, Everett *Also called Daines Corporation* ***(G-3438)***
Baker Manufacturing Inc....253 840-8610
11121 Valley Ave E Puyallup (98372) ***(G-8128)***
Bakery Chef Seattle, Kent *Also called Conagra Brands Inc* ***(G-4861)***
Bal & Bal 200803466 Inc....425 481-4900
11630 Arprt Rd Ste B-200 Everett (98204) ***(G-3382)***
Balametrics Inc....360 452-2842
815 S Oak St Port Angeles (98362) ***(G-7689)***
Balance Construction Inc....206 364-5555
17016 32nd Ave Ne Lake Forest Park (98155) ***(G-5605)***
Balboa Winery....509 529-0461
4169 Peppers Bridge Rd Walla Walla (99362) ***(G-14767)***
Balcony Signs & Laminating....425 454-5500
820 102nd Ave Ne Ste 300 Bellevue (98004) ***(G-805)***
Baldwin Logging Incorporated....360 520-4484
124 Jordan Rd Salkum (98582) ***(G-9179)***
Baldwin Sign Co, Spokane *Also called J N W Inc* ***(G-12327)***
Ball....253 854-9950
1220 2nd Ave N Kent (98032) ***(G-4806)***
Ballard Brass, Arlington *Also called Morel Industries Inc* ***(G-283)***
Ballard Electric....800 873-3526
1080 W Ewing St Seattle (98119) ***(G-9479)***
Ballard Extracts....206 499-4476
7741 9th Ave Nw Seattle (98117) ***(G-9480)***
Ballard Ornamental Ironworks....206 782-3343
1510 Nw Ballard Way Seattle (98107) ***(G-9481)***
Ballard Outdoor....206 552-0760
5484 Shilshole Ave Nw Seattle (98107) ***(G-9482)***
Ballard Printing....206 782-7892
1112 Nw Ballard Way Seattle (98107) ***(G-9483)***
Ballard Sheet Metal Works Inc....206 784-0545
4763 Ballard Ave Nw Seattle (98107) ***(G-9484)***
Ballard Smoke Shop, Seattle *Also called Eco Inc* ***(G-9878)***
Ballard Sock Critters....206 218-9215
6537 19th Ave Nw Seattle (98117) ***(G-9485)***
Ballard Technology Inc....425 339-0281
11400 Airport Rd Ste 201 Everett (98204) ***(G-3383)***
Ballboy LLC....425 281-9152
42202 Se 108th St North Bend (98045) ***(G-7101)***
Ballenger International LLC....970 641-9494
25326 133rd Ave Ne Arlington (98223) ***(G-209)***
Balleywood Creamery....206 920-5173
717 Nw 70th St Apt 102 Seattle (98117) ***(G-9486)***
Balloon Masters....253 566-0201
5314 66th Avenue Ct W University Place (98467) ***(G-13960)***
Balros Industries....206 963-6114
1015 Queen Anne Ave N # 102 Seattle (98109) ***(G-9487)***
Bamboo Hardwoods Inc....800 607-2414
6405 Roosevelt Way Ne Seattle (98115) ***(G-9488)***
Bamboo Hardwoods Inc (PA)....206 264-2414
4100 4th Ave S Seattle (98134) ***(G-9489)***
Bamonte A Trnado Crk Pblction....509 838-7114
1308 E 29th Ave Spokane (99203) ***(G-12138)***
Banana Blossom Press....206 719-3887
1805 N 107th St Unit 101 Seattle (98133) ***(G-9490)***
Bancheros Glass and Etching....253 854-4877
22653 83rd Ave S Kent (98032) ***(G-4807)***
Bang & Jack Montgomery....360 403-9444
1826 192nd Pl Sw Lynnwood (98036) ***(G-6081)***
Banner Advertising, Liberty Lake *Also called Sauther & Assoc Inc* ***(G-5858)***
Banners of Every Kind, Sultan *Also called Steve Boek Mfg* ***(G-13039)***
Banquet and Event, Seattle *Also called Bravo Publications Inc* ***(G-9579)***
BANZAI, Seattle *Also called Northwest Frozen LLC* ***(G-10645)***
Bar Code Labels & Equipment....206 567-5577
9619 Sw 156th St Vashon (98070) ***(G-14711)***
Bar Kustom Machining Inc....360 892-3016
1209 Se Nancy Rd Vancouver (98664) ***(G-14055)***
Baraa Woodworking....360 752-0608
1428 Ellis St Bellingham (98225) ***(G-1257)***
Baranof Courageous, Seattle *Also called Romanzof Fishing Company LLC* ***(G-10977)***
Barbanc....206 552-0852
1506 11th Ave Seattle (98122) ***(G-9491)***
Barbara Bogart....360 385-0815
716 Taylor St Port Townsend (98368) ***(G-7867)***
Barbara Karnes Books Inc....360 828-7132
10520 Ne 113th Cir Vancouver (98662) ***(G-14056)***
Barbara Somers....360 699-5205
12510 Ne Laurin Rd Vancouver (98662) ***(G-14057)***
Barco Inc....425 251-3530
7979 S 180th St Kent (98032) ***(G-4808)***
Barco Wiper Supply Co, Kent *Also called Barco Inc* ***(G-4808)***
Barcode Equipment Recyling Co....360 393-4232
1135 Kelly Rd Bellingham (98226) ***(G-1258)***
Bardahl Manufacturing Corp (PA)....206 783-4851
1400 Nw 52nd St Seattle (98107) ***(G-9492)***
Bardon Inc....360 455-1790
512 Seahawk St Se Olympia (98503) ***(G-7234)***
Barefoot Btnik Pblications LLC....360 275-0798
20 E Westlake Pl Allyn (98524) ***(G-80)***
Barefoote Concrete Inc....509 879-3736
2804 S Progress Rd Spokane Valley (99037) ***(G-12636)***
Barf Boutique, The, Seattle *Also called A Well Balanced Home LLC* ***(G-9327)***
Barging In Europe, Lynden *Also called Cedarbrook* ***(G-6006)***
Bargreen-Ellingson Inc (PA)....253 475-9201
6626 Tacoma Mall Blvd B Tacoma (98409) ***(G-13189)***
Bargreen-Ellingson Inc....253 722-2573
2511 70th Ave E Fife (98424) ***(G-3937)***
Barker Creek Publishing Inc....360 881-0292
5686 Ne Minder Rd Ste 205 Poulsbo (98370) ***(G-7946)***
Barker Drilling....425 252-4686
20793 English Rd Mount Vernon (98274) ***(G-6774)***
Barking Ant Software LLC....360 281-1118
1906 Sw 6th St Battle Ground (98604) ***(G-690)***
Barking Dog Inc....425 822-6542
12644 Ne 85th St Kirkland (98033) ***(G-5288)***
Barleans Fishery Inc....360 384-0325
3660 Slater Rd Ferndale (98248) ***(G-3817)***
Barleans Organic Oils LLC....360 384-0485
3660 Slater Rd Ferndale (98248) ***(G-3818)***
Barmon Door & Millwork, Lake Stevens *Also called Barmon Door & Plywood Inc* ***(G-5633)***
Barmon Door & Plywood Inc....425 334-1222
2508 Hartford Dr Lake Stevens (98258) ***(G-5633)***
Barn Door Productions....206 780-3535
9160 Fox Cove Ln Ne Bainbridge Island (98110) ***(G-616)***
Barn Owl Bakery Inc....360 468-3492
108 Grayling Ln Lopez Island (98261) ***(G-5979)***
Barn2door Inc....206 459-4338
3648 Burke Ave N Seattle (98103) ***(G-9493)***
Barnard Griffin Winery, Richland *Also called Barnard-Griffin Inc* ***(G-8971)***
Barnard Press....253 851-2208
14702 33rd Ave Nw Gig Harbor (98332) ***(G-4076)***
Barnard-Griffin Inc....509 627-0266
878 Tulip Ln Richland (99352) ***(G-8971)***
Barnes Welding Inc....509 745-8588
1450 Road 3 Nw Waterville (98858) ***(G-15005)***
Barnes Wood Inc....360 658-0145
1065 Beach Ave Marysville (98270) ***(G-6315)***
Barone Engraving, Seattle *Also called Crystal Barone* ***(G-9760)***
Barrage Cellars LLC....425 381-9675
19501 144th Ave Ne E800 Woodinville (98072) ***(G-15185)***
Barreras Precision Fabg LLC....253 850-6227
8483 S 228th St Kent (98031) ***(G-4809)***
Barrett Enclosures Inc....206 285-8100
12045 Bartlett Ave Ne Seattle (98125) ***(G-9494)***
Barrett Sheet Metal....509 886-8708
435 Rock Island Rd Ste A East Wenatchee (98802) ***(G-3008)***
Barrister Winery....509 465-3591
1213 W Railroad Ave Spokane (99201) ***(G-12139)***
Barrons Specialty Coatings LLC....253 939-2601
215 Clay St Nw Auburn (98001) ***(G-389)***
Barry Rankin Logging Inc....360 436-1947
31710 Crawford Loop Rd Darrington (98241) ***(G-2866)***
Barrys Steve Pool Service LLC....360 533-0421
1604 W Wishkah St Aberdeen (98520) ***(G-3)***
Barrys Wood Working....253 312-1585
7902 27th St W Ste 7a University Place (98466) ***(G-13961)***
Barshay Software Inc....206 370-2393
1916 Pike Pl Ste 12-41 Seattle (98101) ***(G-9495)***
Bartholomew Winery....206 395-8460
3100 Arprt Way S Unit 10 Seattle (98134) ***(G-9496)***
Bartholomew Winery Inc....206 755-5296
10319 W 17th Pl Kennewick (99338) ***(G-4625)***
Bartholomew Winery Inc....206 755-5296
421 E Columbia Dr Bldg B Kennewick (99336) ***(G-4626)***
Bas Inc....509 943-2611
214 Torbett St Ste F Richland (99354) ***(G-8972)***
Basalite Building Products LLC....253 964-5000
3299 International Pl Dupont (98327) ***(G-2955)***
Basalt Cellars....509 758-6442
906 Port Dr Clarkston (99403) ***(G-2622)***
Baseball Club of Seattle Lllp....206 346-4327
1800 4th Ave Seattle (98101) ***(G-9497)***
Basel Cellars Estate Winery....509 522-0200
2901 Old Milton Hwy Walla Walla (99362) ***(G-14768)***

ALPHABETIC

Basic American Inc 509 765-8601
538 Potato Frontage Rd Se Moses Lake (98837) ***(G-6684)***

Basic American Inc 509 765-7807
538 Potato Frontage Rd Se Moses Lake (98837) ***(G-6685)***

Basic American Food, Moses Lake *Also called Basic American Inc* ***(G-6685)***

Basic American Foods, Moses Lake *Also called Basic American Inc* ***(G-6684)***

Basic Homes LLC 253 579-2724
109 Washinton Ave N Eatonville (98328) ***(G-3050)***

Basic Machining & Electronics 509 308-6341
404 E 3rd Ave Kennewick (99336) ***(G-4627)***

Basic Topicals LLC 206 397-3309
1631 15th Ave W Seattle (98119) ***(G-9498)***

Basin Business Journal, Moses Lake *Also called Columbia Basin Publishing Co* ***(G-6696)***

Basin Nation AG LLC 509 289-9030
8858 Road U Nw Quincy (98848) ***(G-8289)***

Basin Pallett Inc 509 765-8083
657 Road N Ne Moses Lake (98837) ***(G-6686)***

Basis Software Inc 425 861-9390
18103 Ne 68th St Ste C100 Redmond (98052) ***(G-8397)***

Baskin Robbins 1361 425 226-3113
520 Rainier Ave S Renton (98057) ***(G-8751)***

Baskin-Robbins, Renton *Also called Baskin Robbins 1361* ***(G-8751)***

Baskin-Robbins 425 793-3544
14618 Se 66th St Bellevue (98006) ***(G-806)***

Basta Inc 425 641-8911
1800 Richards Rd Bellevue (98005) ***(G-807)***

Basta Marine, Bellevue *Also called Basta Inc* ***(G-807)***

Bastet Screen Printing 360 880-2717
1223 Sw Myrtle St Seattle (98106) ***(G-9499)***

Bastion Brewing Company LLC 360 420-8223
2990 Advance Dr Oak Harbor (98277) ***(G-7139)***

Batch 206 Distillery LLC 206 216-2803
1417 Elliott Ave W Seattle (98119) ***(G-9500)***

Batech LLC 253 395-3630
7032 S 196th St Ste A-110 Kent (98032) ***(G-4810)***

Bathing Solutions, Vancouver *Also called Northwest Walk-In Bath Inc* ***(G-14442)***

Batho Studios 503 282-1460
17021 115th Ave Sw Vashon (98070) ***(G-14712)***

Baton Labs Inc 509 467-4203
12402 N Division St Ste 2 Spokane (99218) ***(G-12140)***

Batp Inc 253 677-4706
2917 Meridian Ave E Edgewood (98371) ***(G-3072)***

Battery Informatics Inc 443 534-7671
19491 Willet Ln Ne Poulsbo (98370) ***(G-7947)***

Battery Recycler 562 434-4502
1 Par Ln Bellingham (98229) ***(G-1259)***

Battery X-Change & Repair Inc 360 373-2921
5869 W Werner Rd Bremerton (98312) ***(G-1937)***

Battery X-Change & Repair Inc 206 682-2981
9112 E Marginal Way S Tukwila (98108) ***(G-13695)***

Battle Ground Auto License 360 687-5115
301 W Main St Battle Ground (98604) ***(G-691)***

Battle Ground Printing, Vancouver *Also called Super H Corporation* ***(G-14620)***

Baubles 360 647-3857
937 Sudden Vly Bellingham (98229) ***(G-1260)***

Bauer Enterprizes, Spokane *Also called Reiff Injection Molding Inc* ***(G-12470)***

Baum's House of Chocolate, Kennewick *Also called Baums Candy* ***(G-4628)***

Baums Candy 509 967-9340
513 N Edison St Ste D Kennewick (99336) ***(G-4628)***

Bausch Health Americas Inc 425 346-2472
11720 N Creek Pkwy N Bothell (98011) ***(G-1751)***

Bavarian Meat Products Inc (PA) 206 448-3540
2934 Western Ave Seattle (98121) ***(G-9501)***

Baxis Inc 360 797-0084
2086 Old Gardiner Rd Sequim (98382) ***(G-11614)***

Bay Center Farms, Bay Center *Also called Bay Center Mariculture Co* ***(G-755)***

Bay Center Mariculture Co 360 875-6172
306 Dike Rd Bay Center (98527) ***(G-755)***

Bay City Mold Inspection Svcs 415 925-0801
32 Codfish Ln Olga (98279) ***(G-7213)***

Bay City Sausage Co Inc 360 648-2344
2249 State Route 105 Aberdeen (98520) ***(G-4)***

Bay Printing Inc 360 679-3816
1131 Se Ely St Ste 101 Oak Harbor (98277) ***(G-7140)***

Bay Trophies & Engraving Inc 360 676-0868
524 Ohio St Bellingham (98225) ***(G-1261)***

Baycraft Marine Sales Inc 253 863-8522
554 Sw 18th St Chehalis (98532) ***(G-2470)***

Baye Enterprises Inc 253 536-2277
10749 A St S Ste F Tacoma (98444) ***(G-13190)***

Bayer Healthcare LLC 425 245-1392
2625 162nd St Sw Lynnwood (98087) ***(G-6082)***

Bayer Healthcare LLC 360 886-8182
29335 333rd Ave Se Ravensdale (98051) ***(G-8330)***

Bayer Hlthcare Phrmcticals LLC 862 404-3000
1191 2nd Ave Ste 1200 Seattle (98101) ***(G-9502)***

Bayne Junction Woodworks 360 886-8908
32750 343rd Ave Se Ravensdale (98051) ***(G-8331)***

Bayshore Office Products Inc 360 293-4669
603 Commercial Ave Anacortes (98221) ***(G-102)***

Bayshore Sand & Gravel, Shelton *Also called Bayside Redi-Mix* ***(G-11682)***

Bayside Apparel, Tacoma *Also called Bayside EMB & Screenprint* ***(G-13191)***

Bayside EMB & Screenprint 253 565-1521
3003 S Houston St Ste A Tacoma (98409) ***(G-13191)***

Bayside Redi-Mix 360 426-4987
40 Se Mell Rd Shelton (98584) ***(G-11682)***

Bayview Composites LLC 360 466-4160
13593 Bayview Edison Rd Mount Vernon (98273) ***(G-6775)***

Bayview Engineering Inds LLC 360 421-2126
618 Oak St Ste C Oak Harbor (98277) ***(G-7141)***

Bayview Pro Audio Inc 360 867-1798
630 Oleary St Nw Olympia (98502) ***(G-7235)***

Bayview Publishing LLC 425 282-4640
16409 Se 166th Ter Renton (98058) ***(G-8752)***

Bayview Pumps 360 301-3600
121 Robbins Rd Nordland (98358) ***(G-7088)***

Bayview Redi Mix Inc (PA) 360 533-7372
100 Hagara St Aberdeen (98520) ***(G-5)***

Bayview Redi Mix Inc 360 875-9993
2835 Ocean Ave Raymond (98577) ***(G-8342)***

Bayview Redi Mix Inc 360 482-3444
91 Schouweiler Rd Elma (98541) ***(G-3241)***

Bazooka Gold Mining Co LLC 360 202-5953
17720 Moore Rd Mount Vernon (98273) ***(G-6776)***

BB Citc LLC 425 776-4950
1420 80th St Sw Ste D Everett (98203) ***(G-3384)***

BBC 360 629-4477
8510 Cedarhome Dr Stanwood (98292) ***(G-12960)***

BBC Biochemical Corporation 360 542-8400
409 Eleanor Ln Mount Vernon (98273) ***(G-6777)***

BBH Sheet Metal LLC 425 637-0360
1414 127th Pl Ne Ste 107 Bellevue (98005) ***(G-808)***

Bbtline LLC 425 273-3712
10907 Ne 133rd St Kirkland (98034) ***(G-5289)***

Bc Pavers Inc 425 413-2110
1916 Jones Ave Ne Renton (98056) ***(G-8753)***

Bc Signs Inc 360 835-3570
106 Se Weir St Ste 1 Camas (98607) ***(G-2231)***

Bc Software 425 831-0550
35014 Se Curtis Dr Snoqualmie (98065) ***(G-12005)***

Bcard Inc 206 963-5211
108 N Washington St # 500 Spokane (99201) ***(G-12141)***

Bcb Enterprises LLC 360 435-1047
19220 62nd Ave Ne Arlington (98223) ***(G-210)***

Bcbg, Bothell *Also called Runway Liquidation LLC* ***(G-1788)***

Bcbg, Spokane *Also called Runway Liquidation LLC* ***(G-12486)***

Bcbg, Seattle *Also called Runway Liquidation LLC* ***(G-10997)***

Bcbg, Seattle *Also called Runway Liquidation LLC* ***(G-10998)***

Bcbg, Gig Harbor *Also called Runway Liquidation LLC* ***(G-4158)***

Bcbg, Kennewick *Also called Runway Liquidation LLC* ***(G-4721)***

Bcbg, Kennewick *Also called Runway Liquidation LLC* ***(G-4722)***

Bcbg, Kirkland *Also called Runway Liquidation LLC* ***(G-5454)***

Bcbg, Lacey *Also called Runway Liquidation LLC* ***(G-5582)***

Bcbg, Kennewick *Also called Runway Liquidation LLC* ***(G-4723)***

Bcbg, Walla Walla *Also called Runway Liquidation LLC* ***(G-14863)***

Bcbg, Spokane *Also called Runway Liquidation LLC* ***(G-12487)***

Bctld LLC 206 650-6408
1518 Nw 52nd St Unit Main Seattle (98107) ***(G-9503)***

Bcwest LLC 206 323-8100
2755 Airport Way S Seattle (98134) ***(G-9504)***

Bda, Woodinville *Also called Bensussen Deutsch & Assoc LLC* ***(G-15188)***

Bdn Logging Inc 360 785-4119
200 Marttala Rd Winlock (98596) ***(G-15145)***

BE Meyers & Co Inc (PA) 425 881-6648
9461 Willows Rd Ne # 100 Redmond (98052) ***(G-8398)***

Beach Bee Inc 360 289-2244
698 Ocean Shores Blvd Nw Ocean Shores (98569) ***(G-7184)***

Beacon Machine Inc 425 226-8460
420 Olympia Ave Ne Renton (98056) ***(G-8754)***

Beacon Publishing Inc 425 347-1711
806 5th St Mukilteo (98275) ***(G-6897)***

Beam Machine 425 222-5587
3023 362nd Ave Se Fall City (98024) ***(G-3700)***

Beaming White LLC 360 635-5600
1205 Ne 95th St Ste A Vancouver (98665) ***(G-14058)***

Bean Collection Coffee Inc 206 382-1966
14307 Greenwood Ave N Seattle (98133) ***(G-9505)***

Beanpop LLC 509 499-5322
7301 N Mahr Ct Spokane (99208) ***(G-12142)***

Beans & Rocks LLC (PA) 360 942-5414
60 Hines Valley Rd Raymond (98577) ***(G-8343)***

Bear & Wolf LLC 206 281-7777
4209 21st Ave W Ste 400 Seattle (98199) ***(G-9506)***

Bear & Wolf Salmon Co, Seattle *Also called Bear & Wolf LLC* ***(G-9506)***

Bear Creek Boatworks Inc 425 558-4086
19909 Ne 151st Pl Woodinville (98077) ***(G-15186)***

Bear Creek Coatings LLC 253 722-4220
4212 32nd Avenue Ct Nw Gig Harbor (98335) ***(G-4077)***

Bear Inc 253 851-2575
3120 Harborview Dr Gig Harbor (98335) ***(G-4078)***

Bear Industries LLC 509 981-8618
2525 E 29th Ave 10b-22 Spokane (99223) ***(G-12143)***

Bear Mountin Cutters Inc 360 875-0035
49 Wilson Ln South Bend (98586) *(G-12039)*

Bear Signs 509 888-4477
1422 N Miller St Ste 1 Wenatchee (98801) *(G-15012)*

Bear Wildfire 360 379-8915
220 Pocket Ln Port Townsend (98368) *(G-7868)*

Bearded Fellows Elixir LLC 253 750-3060
18408 100th Street Ct E Bonney Lake (98391) *(G-1717)*

Beards Framing, Seattle *Also called Museum Quality Discount Frmng (G-10574)*

Beardslee Logging 509 675-2400
3200 Hill Loop Rd Kettle Falls (99141) *(G-5224)*

Bearly Loggin 509 493-1706
716 Snowden Rd White Salmon (98672) *(G-15111)*

Beats4legends 253 218-5075
4125 38th Ave S Seattle (98118) *(G-9507)*

Beau Mac Enterprises 253 447-8093
4100 150th Avenue Ct E Sumner (98390) *(G-13055)*

Beaver Lake Quarry, Mount Vernon *Also called Martin Marietta Materials Inc (G-6811)*

Beaver Lake Quarry Inc 360 856-5870
14322 Beaver Lake Rd Mount Vernon (98273) *(G-6778)*

Beaver Lake Woodworks 425 391-0661
1919 E Beaver Lake Dr Se Sammamish (98075) *(G-9188)*

Beaver Machine Works Inc 425 402-1032
12602 Ne 178th St Ste A Woodinville (98072) *(G-15187)*

Bec's Specs, Port Angeles *Also called Prismoid Optical Laboratory (G-7738)*

Bechris Inc 253 565-0905
7511 S 19th St Tacoma (98466) *(G-13192)*

Beck Mill Co Inc 360 629-4769
2105 276th St Nw Stanwood (98292) *(G-12961)*

Beck Pack Systems Inc 425 222-9515
7700 300th Ave Preston (98050) *(G-8024)*

BECker&mayer, Bellevue *Also called Quarto Pubg Group USA Inc (G-1090)*

Beckers Custom Cabinets, Redmond *Also called Gordon Becker Construction (G-8481)*

Beckwith & Kuffel 509 922-5222
11327 E Montgomery Dr # 5 Spokane Valley (99206) *(G-12637)*

Beco Inc 425 885-2603
15715 Ne 56th Way Redmond (98052) *(G-8399)*

Bed Voyage, Woodinville *Also called Home and Travel Solutions LLC (G-15261)*

Bedford Industries Inc 360 805-9099
16726 146th St Se Ste 135 Monroe (98272) *(G-6551)*

Bedkers Prtble Wldg Fbrication 253 581-7077
3802 87th St Sw Lakewood (98499) *(G-5702)*

Bedrock Industries Inc 206 283-7625
4021 13th Ave W Seattle (98119) *(G-9508)*

Bee Hive Candles Inc 360 599-9725
8582 Tilbury Rd Maple Falls (98266) *(G-6248)*

Bee Jay Scales Inc 509 837-8280
116 N 1st St Sunnyside (98944) *(G-13113)*

Bee Keeper Gordons Gold 360 202-9523
17084 Dunbar Rd Mount Vernon (98273) *(G-6779)*

Bee Natural Leathercare LLC 360 891-7178
11700 Ne 60th Way Ste 4b Vancouver (98682) *(G-14059)*

Bees In Burbs 425 432-0546
18911 Se 236th Pl Kent (98042) *(G-4811)*

Behr Paint & Stain 253 887-9337
840 Industry Dr N Ste F Auburn (98001) *(G-390)*

Behr Process Corporation 253 887-8410
840 Industry Dr N Algona (98001) *(G-67)*

Behringer Usa Inc 425 672-0816
18912 North Creek Pkwy # 200 Bothell (98011) *(G-1752)*

BEI, Bellevue *Also called Ultrabac Software Inc (G-1206)*

Beigeblond Inc 360 693-3283
909 Main St Vancouver (98660) *(G-14060)*

Belair Composites Inc 509 482-0442
3715 E Longfellow Ave Spokane (99217) *(G-12144)*

Belfair Garden & Lighting 360 275-2130
24090 Ne State Route 3 F Belfair (98528) *(G-759)*

Belfor USA Group Inc 206 632-0800
4320 S 131st Pl Tukwila (98168) *(G-13696)*

Belfor USA Group Inc 509 453-8551
720 N 16th Ave Ste 9 Yakima (98902) *(G-15518)*

Belgate Printing & Copy Inc 425 451-9048
3817 W Lk Smmmish Pkwy Ne Redmond (98052) *(G-8400)*

Belina Interiors Inc 253 474-0276
4540 S Adams St Tacoma (98409) *(G-13193)*

Belina Woodworks, Tacoma *Also called Belina Interiors Inc (G-13193)*

Bell Buoy Crab Co Inc 360 777-8272
18 Valley St Chinook (98614) *(G-2614)*

Bell Creek Contracting Inc 360 592-3300
3145 Mt Baker Hwy Bellingham (98226) *(G-1262)*

Bell Lumber & Pole Company 360 445-5565
18488 Main St Conway (98238) *(G-2796)*

Bell Machine Inc 425 254-1173
14510 171st Ave Se Kent (98032) *(G-4812)*

Bella Bella Cupcakes LLC 253 509-3158
5515 38th Ave Gig Harbor (98335) *(G-4079)*

Bella Cupcake Couture LLC 425 260-3224
6909 125th Ave Se Newcastle (98056) *(G-7026)*

Bella Tutto Inc 425 898-8680
1100 206th Pl Ne Sammamish (98074) *(G-9189)*

Bellandi Signs Inc 253 841-1144
11515 120th Ave E Puyallup (98374) *(G-8129)*

Belleville Honey Co, Burlington *Also called Langes Honey Skep Inc (G-2167)*

Bellevue Brewing Company LLC 425 497-8686
1820 130th Ave Ne 2 Bellevue (98005) *(G-809)*

Bellevue Dental Excellence 425 378-1600
14700 Ne 8th St Ste 210 Bellevue (98007) *(G-810)*

Bellevue Door & Millwork Co 425 885-3009
12805 141st Ave Ne Kirkland (98034) *(G-5290)*

Bellevue Embroidery 425 646-9191
4035 Factoria Sq Mall Se Bellevue (98006) *(G-811)*

Bellevue Fine Art Reprodctn 425 749-7396
2940 112th Ave Se Bellevue (98004) *(G-812)*

Bellevue Instant Sign 425 451-8218
21903 Ne 18th St Redmond (98074) *(G-8401)*

Bellevue Parent LLC (PA) 866 470-0320
11100 Ne 8th St Ste 600 Bellevue (98004) *(G-813)*

Bellevue Printing LLC (PA) 425 558-1862
1449 130th Ave Ne Bellevue (98005) *(G-814)*

Bellevue Tailors and Formal Wr 425 643-0741
13500 Ne Bel Red Rd # 14 Bellevue (98005) *(G-815)*

Bellingham Business Journal 360 647-8805
1909 Cornwall Ave Bellingham (98225) *(G-1263)*

Bellingham Business Machines (PA) 360 734-3630
205 N Commercial St Bellingham (98225) *(G-1264)*

Bellingham Escape 360 519-9213
1417 Cornwall Ave A101 Bellingham (98225) *(G-1265)*

Bellingham Herald, Bellingham *Also called McClatchy Newspapers Inc (G-1428)*

Bellingham Marine Industries (PA) 360 676-2800
1323 Lincoln St Bellingham (98229) *(G-1266)*

Bellingham Pasta Company 360 594-6000
3125 Mercer Ave Ste 101 Bellingham (98225) *(G-1267)*

Bellingham Promotional Pdts 360 676-5416
2403 James St Bellingham (98225) *(G-1268)*

Bellingham Screen Printing 360 920-0114
4410 Northwest Dr Bellingham (98226) *(G-1269)*

Bellmont Cabinet Company, Sumner *Also called Pacific Crest Industries Inc (G-13093)*

Belltown Prtg & Graphics Inc 206 448-8919
2505 3rd Ave Ste 150 Seattle (98121) *(G-9509)*

Bellwether Gate C LLC 360 738-1940
23 Bellwether Way Bellingham (98225) *(G-1270)*

Bels International Corporation 206 722-3365
29 S Hanford St Seattle (98134) *(G-9510)*

Belshaw Adamatic Bakery Group, Auburn *Also called Belshaw Bros Inc (G-391)*

Belshaw Bros Inc 206 322-5474
814 44th St Nw Ste 103 Auburn (98001) *(G-391)*

Belshire Industries 360 910-9209
27603 Ne 10th Ave Ridgefield (98642) *(G-9066)*

Beltecno Inc 360 512-4000
16726 Tye St Se Monroe (98272) *(G-6552)*

Bemis Company Inc 206 632-2246
256 Ne 50th St Seattle (98105) *(G-9511)*

Bemis Paper Packaging Division, Vancouver *Also called Hood Packaging Corporation (G-14302)*

Ben Franklin Crafts Frames Sp, Redmond *Also called Ferguson Merchandising LLC (G-8460)*

Benandre LLC 425 298-8635
19405 68th Dr Ne Ste B Arlington (98223) *(G-211)*

Benchmark Barrels LLC 360 652-2594
1105 Pioneer Hwy E Arlington (98223) *(G-212)*

Benchmark Injection Molding 425 263-9171
3605 132nd St Sw Ste 1 Lynnwood (98087) *(G-6083)*

Benchmark Woods 360 732-0993
102 Dena Ln Chimacum (98325) *(G-2611)*

Bending Solutions Incorporated 360 651-2443
3815 124th St Ne Marysville (98271) *(G-6316)*

Benjamin Anderson 206 228-8174
4416 47th Ave Sw Seattle (98116) *(G-9512)*

Benjamin D Schreiner 206 417-4663
18245 47th Pl Ne Lake Forest Park (98155) *(G-5606)*

Benjamin Moore Inc 206 329-8607
1213 S King St Seattle (98144) *(G-9513)*

Bennett Industries Inc (PA) 253 627-7775
1160 Thorne Rd Tacoma (98421) *(G-13194)*

Bennett Industries Inc 253 627-7775
1160 Thorne Rd Tacoma (98421) *(G-13195)*

Bennett Lumber Products Inc (PA) 509 758-5558
2050 Wilma Dr Clarkston (99403) *(G-2623)*

Bennett Lumber Products Inc 208 875-1321
1951 Wilma Dr Clarkston (99403) *(G-2624)*

Bennett Machinery, Tacoma *Also called Bennett Industries Inc (G-13195)*

Bennett Painting 360 426-6489
1640 Se Lynch Rd Shelton (98584) *(G-11683)*

Bennett Paper and Supply, Vancouver *Also called Bob Nagel Inc (G-14074)*

Bennu Glass LLC 360 524-4970
2310 N Hendrickson Dr Kalama (98625) *(G-4493)*

Bens Precision Instrs Inc 253 883-5040
5417 12th St E Ste 100 Fife (98424) *(G-3938)*

Benson Smoke 253 859-6120
21006 108th Ave Se Kent (98031) *(G-4813)*

Benson Vineyards 509 687-0313
754 Winesap Ave Manson (98831) *(G-6240)*

Bensussen Deutsch & Assoc LLC (PA) 425 492-6111
15525 Wdnvll Rdmond Rd Ne Woodinville (98072) *(G-15188)*

Bent Needle Designs 253 531-9440
3405 72nd St E Tacoma (98443) ***(G-13196)***

Bent Whisker Press 206 914-3556
1846 N 184th St Shoreline (98133) ***(G-11760)***

Benthic Fishing LLC 253 219-1500
2038 Taft Ave Bremerton (98312) ***(G-1938)***

Bentley Mills Inc 206 622-8228
2424 S Graham St Seattle (98108) ***(G-9514)***

Bentonfranklin Counties Ian BF 509 783-5284
7207 W Deschutes Ave Kennewick (99336) ***(G-4629)***

Bentriver Tech Inc 360 335-1345
1117 Se Blair Rd Washougal (98671) ***(G-14945)***

Bentson Printing LLC 253 272-6563
118 N Tacoma Ave Tacoma (98403) ***(G-13197)***

Beppa, Seattle *Also called Bge Ltd* ***(G-9519)***

Berg Development Group LLC 509 624-8921
850 E Spokane Falls Blvd Spokane (99202) ***(G-12145)***

Berg Manufacturing Inc 509 624-8921
6811 E Mission Ave Spokane Valley (99212) ***(G-12638)***

Bergdorf Cellars 509 548-7638
939 Front St Leavenworth (98826) ***(G-5796)***

Bergen & Company 360 676-7503
4003 Irongate Rd Bellingham (98226) ***(G-1271)***

Bergen Screen Print 509 965-2511
1418 S 40th Ave Yakima (98908) ***(G-15519)***

Berghan Vineyards 509 301-9229
1722 Evergreen St Walla Walla (99362) ***(G-14769)***

Bergman LLC 206 910-0138
733 17th Ave E Seattle (98112) ***(G-9515)***

Bergstrom Foundry Inc 360 532-6981
316 E State St Aberdeen (98520) ***(G-6)***

Bergstrom Nutrition, Vancouver *Also called Cardinal Associates Inc* ***(G-14098)***

Bergstrom Nutrition 360 693-0601
1900 W 39th St 106-A Vancouver (98660) ***(G-14061)***

Bering Street Studio LLC 253 677-4870
5227 Bering St Nw Gig Harbor (98332) ***(G-4080)***

Berlex Biosciences Division, Seattle *Also called Bayer Hlthcare Phrmcticals LLC* ***(G-9502)***

Bernard Manufacturing 206 242-4017
13662 17th Ave Sw Burien (98166) ***(G-2093)***

Bernstein Woodworks 206 605-1796
2916 19th Ave S Seattle (98144) ***(G-9516)***

Berry Beautiful, Vashon *Also called Summit Biofuels LLC* ***(G-14745)***

Berry Garage Door Company, Bellingham *Also called S G&C Contractor Services LLC* ***(G-1520)***

Berry Global Inc 253 627-2151
635 E 15th St Tacoma (98421) ***(G-13198)***

Berry Haven LLC 509 521-4902
3834 Dogwood Rd Pasco (99301) ***(G-7553)***

Berry Neon Co Inc 425 776-8835
7400 Hardeson Rd Everett (98203) ***(G-3385)***

Berry Nutty 425 265-1680
910 Se Everett Mall Way Everett (98208) ***(G-3386)***

Berry Sign Systems, Everett *Also called Cogent Holdings-1 LLC* ***(G-3422)***

Berry Sign Systems, Tacoma *Also called Cogent Holdings-1 LLC* ***(G-13237)***

Berry Signs Systems, Everett *Also called Berry Neon Co Inc* ***(G-3385)***

Bert's Excavating, Sunnyside *Also called John Dalrymple* ***(G-13129)***

Bertelsen Winery & Tasting Rm 360 445-2300
20598 Starbird Rd Mount Vernon (98274) ***(G-6780)***

Beryllium LLC 206 780-8900
7869 Ne Day Rd W Ste 206 Bainbridge Island (98110) ***(G-617)***

Best American Duffel, Seattle *Also called Bad Bags Inc* ***(G-9476)***

Best Cabinet & Granite Sup Inc 503 285-1838
3001 E Fourth Plain Blvd Vancouver (98661) ***(G-14062)***

Best Connection LLC 360 241-8244
11800 Ne 124th Ave # 22 Vancouver (98682) ***(G-14063)***

Best Guess Software 360 876-3272
4306 Pioneer Pl Se Port Orchard (98366) ***(G-7793)***

Best Guitars, Tacoma *Also called Holiday Engineering & Mfg Co* ***(G-13338)***

Best Practices Wiki 206 708-1572
2231 Nw 64th St Seattle (98107) ***(G-9517)***

Best Shingle Sales Inc 360 532-5423
1100 5th St Hoquiam (98550) ***(G-4329)***

Best Way Concrete 360 825-5494
24959 Se 362nd Ln Enumclaw (98022) ***(G-3279)***

Bestfitt Gasket Company Inc 253 863-9521
3025 142nd Ave E Ste 105 Sumner (98390) ***(G-13056)***

Bestway Industries LLC 360 513-2000
10306 Ne 7th St Vancouver (98664) ***(G-14064)***

Bestworth - Rommel Inc 360 435-2927
19818 74th Ave Ne Arlington (98223) ***(G-213)***

Beth Donalley 206 366-8445
18541 35th Ave Ne Lake Forest Park (98155) ***(G-5607)***

Bethany Vineyard & Winery 360 887-3525
4115 Ne 259th St Ridgefield (98642) ***(G-9067)***

Bethel Lutheran Church 360 892-4231
12919 Ne 159th St Brush Prairie (98606) ***(G-2030)***

Bethlehem Construction Inc (PA) 509 782-1001
5505 Titchenal Rd Cashmere (98815) ***(G-2317)***

Betsy Bell Skaklee, Seattle *Also called Betsy Bells Natyural Solutions* ***(G-9518)***

Betsy Bells Natyural Solutions 206 933-1889
4455 51st Ave Sw Seattle (98116) ***(G-9518)***

Bettendorfs Printing & Design 509 586-7473
14 S Benton St Kennewick (99336) ***(G-4630)***

Better Boats Inc 360 797-1244
2271 W Edgewood Dr Port Angeles (98363) ***(G-7690)***

Better Off Threads 425 408-1304
15610 Ne Wdnvlle Dvall Rd Woodinville (98072) ***(G-15189)***

Better Than Good Games, Seattle *Also called App Grinder LLC* ***(G-9410)***

Betty OGuin 360 876-0803
1880 Sidney Ave Port Orchard (98366) ***(G-7794)***

Betz Cellars LLC 425 861-9823
13244 Woodinville Redmond Redmond (98052) ***(G-8402)***

Betz Family Winery, Redmond *Also called Betz Cellars LLC* ***(G-8402)***

Beverage Specialist Inc 206 763-0255
905 Industry Dr Tukwila (98188) ***(G-13697)***

Bewitching Moon Press 206 380-3807
11 3rd St Nw Unit 1111 Auburn (98071) ***(G-392)***

Beyond Zone Inc 206 363-2147
816 Ne 152nd St Shoreline (98155) ***(G-11761)***

Beyoutiful Bath Bombs More 509 315-9608
4750 N Division St Spokane (99207) ***(G-12146)***

BF and BF Co 206 463-2661
10108 Sw 268th St Vashon (98070) ***(G-14713)***

Bfc Architectural Metals Inc 206 763-0530
19034 Des Moines Mem Dr S Seatac (98148) ***(G-9274)***

Bfy Food Group LLC 425 298-5523
1813 115th Ave Ne Bellevue (98004) ***(G-816)***

Bge Ltd 206 789-2128
7700 6th Ave Nw Seattle (98117) ***(G-9519)***

Bgi Tooling Company 509 684-5556
806 Gillette Rd B Colville (99114) ***(G-2738)***

Bgs Cycle Parts 808 368-8122
101 Nw 25th St Battle Ground (98604) ***(G-692)***

Bharat Ratan LLC 206 458-3322
19030 116th Ave Se Renton (98058) ***(G-8755)***

BHP Holdings Inc 425 462-8414
18538 142nd Ave Ne Woodinville (98072) ***(G-15190)***

Bhs Marketing LLC 208 740-9369
2001 Thorne Rd Tacoma (98421) ***(G-13199)***

Bhs Specialty Chemicals, Tacoma *Also called Bhs Marketing LLC* ***(G-13199)***

Bi-Directional Microwave, Kennewick *Also called Diversified Marketing Intl LLC* ***(G-4654)***

Biaflex Printing Solutions LLC 509 895-7076
3207 W Nob Hill Blvd Yakima (98902) ***(G-15520)***

Bibbi Co LLC 206 453-4152
922 Nw 50th St Seattle (98107) ***(G-9520)***

Biblesoft Inc 206 824-0547
22030 7th Ave S Ste 204 Des Moines (98198) ***(G-2929)***

Bic Inc 360 691-1452
10401 Mountain Loop Hwy Granite Falls (98252) ***(G-4265)***

Bickle Land & Timber, Rochester *Also called Sam Bickle Logging Inc* ***(G-9140)***

Bicycle Quarterly 206 789-0424
2116 Western Ave Seattle (98121) ***(G-9521)***

Biec International Inc 360 750-5791
5100 Nw 140th St Vancouver (98685) ***(G-14065)***

Bieler and Smith LLC 509 526-5230
820 Mill Creek Rd Walla Walla (99362) ***(G-14770)***

Biesecker Body Care, Stanwood *Also called Dr Bieseckers LLC* ***(G-12967)***

Big Blok LLC 360 442-0655
17408 Ne 29th St Vancouver (98682) ***(G-14066)***

Big C Industries LLC 360 773-5873
30305 Nw 18th Pl Ridgefield (98642) ***(G-9068)***

Big C Industries LLC 844 406-2442
3339 Washington Way Longview (98632) ***(G-5888)***

Big Creek Fisheries LLC 425 742-8609
3900 Railway Ave Everett (98201) ***(G-3387)***

Big Derby Distilling Co 206 504-7604
1250 Alaskan Way Seattle (98101) ***(G-9522)***

Big Dipper Wax Works 206 767-7322
700 S Orchard St Seattle (98108) ***(G-9523)***

Big Door Music Publishing 206 890-1269
6503 128th Pl Sw Edmonds (98026) ***(G-3096)***

Big Fish Premium LLC 206 269-3573
906 Alaskan Way Ste 700 Seattle (98104) ***(G-9524)***

Big Foot Extractors, Tenino *Also called Cascadia Dynamix LLC* ***(G-13613)***

Big House Brewing Inc 509 522-2440
11 S Palouse St Walla Walla (99362) ***(G-14771)***

Big Leaf Manufacturing Company, Seattle *Also called Roy McMakin* ***(G-10984)***

Big Lloyde 509 233-2293
4044 Pine Meadows Dr Loon Lake (99148) ***(G-5974)***

Big Rock Industries 360 659-3308
10610 115th Ave Ne Lake Stevens (98258) ***(G-5634)***

Big Rock Industries LLC 425 314-8710
17391 Tye St Se Monroe (98272) ***(G-6553)***

Big Salt Bait Tanks, Bremerton *Also called Defiance Boats LLC* ***(G-1946)***

Big Sky Publishing Co (HQ) 406 587-4491
221 1st Ave W Ste 405 Seattle (98119) ***(G-9525)***

Big Smooth Industries LLC 206 356-5888
8611 89th Ave Nw Gig Harbor (98332) ***(G-4081)***

Big Time Brewery & Alehouse, Seattle *Also called Big Time Brewery Company Inc* ***(G-9526)***

Big Time Brewery Company Inc 206 545-4509
4133 University Way Ne Seattle (98105) ***(G-9526)***

Bigfoot Pipe & Piling LLC 425 882-1000
15422 Canyon Rd E Puyallup (98375) ***(G-8130)***

Bigfoot Trading Inc 360 340-7332
140 E Olympic Ct Allyn (98524) ***(G-81)***
Bighorn Brewery Warehouse 253 474-7465
5001 S Washington St Tacoma (98409) ***(G-13200)***
Bigoni Stiner & Assoc 253 826-5824
2722 112th Ave E Edgewood (98372) ***(G-3073)***
Bigwoods Screen Printing 253 208-3990
16203 70th Ave E Puyallup (98375) ***(G-8131)***
Bikelid LLC 206 963-7585
3430 Evergreen Point Rd Medina (98039) ***(G-6446)***
Bilingual Books Inc 206 284-4211
1719 W Nickerson St Seattle (98119) ***(G-9527)***
Bilingual Press Publishing Co 509 483-2523
2928 E Nebraska Ave Spokane (99208) ***(G-12147)***
Bill Anderson 509 281-0055
52 Anderson Rd White Salmon (98672) ***(G-15112)***
Bill Dibenedetto 206 963-0499
620 W Olympic Pl Apt 308 Seattle (98119) ***(G-9528)***
Billabong Publishing & ME 206 391-8300
24405 222nd Ave Se Maple Valley (98038) ***(G-6260)***
Billdon LLC 425 736-4316
22703 Se 18th St Sammamish (98075) ***(G-9190)***
Billet Connection Llc 509 467-7584
7320 N Regal St Spokane (99217) ***(G-12148)***
Bills Heli ARC Welding 509 489-6160
5311 N Julia St Spokane (99217) ***(G-12149)***
Bills Marine Service 509 826-5564
33 Hopfer Rd OMAK (98841) ***(G-7435)***
Bills Welding & Machine Shop 509 334-2222
700 S Grand Ave Pullman (99163) ***(G-8085)***
Billy Bob Customs 360 637-9147
68 Hurd Rd Elma (98541) ***(G-3242)***
Billy Footwear, Sammamish *Also called Billdon LLC* ***(G-9190)***
Billy Sand and Gravel, Arlington *Also called Stillaquamish Resources LLC* ***(G-335)***
Bilt-Rite Custom Cabinets 360 829-0663
152 S River Ave Buckley (98321) ***(G-2049)***
Bimbo Bakeries Usa Inc 509 452-6293
907 S 1st St Yakima (98901) ***(G-15521)***
Bimbo Bakeries Usa Inc 509 469-3707
1910 Mcnair Ave Union Gap (98903) ***(G-13923)***
Bimbo Bakeries Usa Inc 509 662-4731
1422 N Miller St Wenatchee (98801) ***(G-15013)***
Bimbo Bakeries Usa Inc 425 415-6745
14103 Ne 200th St C Woodinville (98072) ***(G-15191)***
Bimbo Bakeries Usa Inc 509 688-3966
5424 E Sprague Ave Spokane Valley (99212) ***(G-12639)***
Bimbo Bakeries Usa Inc 253 759-2146
5401 6th Ave Ste 321 Tacoma (98406) ***(G-13201)***
Bimbo Bakery USA 425 347-3900
909 Se Everett Mall Way E550 Everett (98208) ***(G-3388)***
Bingham Industries, Monroe *Also called Bingham Manufacturing Inc* ***(G-6554)***
Bingham Manufacturing Inc 360 863-1170
17401 147th St Se Ste C Monroe (98272) ***(G-6554)***
Bingo Bugle Newspaper Group, Vashon *Also called Frontier Publication Inc* ***(G-14723)***
Bining Health Inc 604 540-8288
701 5th Ave Ste 5500 Seattle (98104) ***(G-9529)***
Bio-Oregon, Longview *Also called Moore-Clark USA Inc* ***(G-5932)***
Bio-RAD Laboratories Inc 425 498-1933
8415 216th St Se Woodinville (98072) ***(G-15192)***
Bio-RAD Laboratories Inc 425 881-8300
6565 185th Ave Ne Redmond (98052) ***(G-8403)***
Bio-Therapeutic, Seattle *Also called Micro Current Technology Inc* ***(G-10530)***
Bio-Therapeutic, Seattle *Also called Micro Current Technology Inc* ***(G-10531)***
Bio-Tope Research Inc (PA) 509 684-1512
512 Williams Lake Rd Colville (99114) ***(G-2739)***
Bio-Tope Research Inc 509 684-1154
512 Williams Lake Rd Colville (99114) ***(G-2740)***
Biocom Systems Inc 509 241-0505
153 Heather Ln Wenatchee (98801) ***(G-15014)***
Biocontrol Systems Inc 425 603-1123
12822 Se 32nd St Bellevue (98005) ***(G-817)***
Biodynamics Corporation 206 526-0205
14739 Aurora Ave N # 100 Shoreline (98133) ***(G-11762)***
Bioguard Research & Dev 509 628-0170
10815 Cottonwood Dr Kennewick (99338) ***(G-4631)***
Biolife Solutions Inc 425 402-1400
3301 Monte Villa Pkwy Bothell (98021) ***(G-1827)***
Biolife Solutions Inc (PA) 425 402-1400
3303 Monte Villa Pkwy Bothell (98021) ***(G-1828)***
Bionic Builders LLC 509 435-1114
2423 S Sunrise Rd Spokane Valley (99206) ***(G-12640)***
Biooptimal, Bremerton *Also called Integrity Supplements LLC* ***(G-1962)***
Bioplex Nutrition Inc 360 332-2101
2252 Odell St Blaine (98230) ***(G-1661)***
Biopure Healing Products, Woodinville *Also called BHP Holdings Inc* ***(G-15190)***
Biosmart Technologies LLC 360 888-8638
18324 Cook Rd Se Unit 1 Yelm (98597) ***(G-15729)***
Biosonics Inc 206 782-2211
2356 W Commodore Way # 100 Seattle (98199) ***(G-9530)***
Biosonics Telemetry LP 206 783-9356
2356 W Commodore Way # 100 Seattle (98199) ***(G-9531)***
Biotangent Diagnostics LLC 503 713-3339
580 Wilderness Peak Dr Nw Issaquah (98027) ***(G-4385)***
Biotwine Manufacturing Company 509 865-3340
206210 S Division Toppenish (98948) ***(G-13663)***
Biozn LLC 206 388-7865
628 140th Ct Se Apt B207 Bellevue (98007) ***(G-818)***
Birch Equipment Company Inc (PA) 360 734-5744
1619 Kentucky St Bellingham (98229) ***(G-1272)***
Birch Equipment Rental & Sales, Bellingham *Also called Birch Equipment Company Inc* ***(G-1272)***
Birchfield Winery 360 978-6176
242 Kennicott Rd Chehalis (98532) ***(G-2471)***
Birchfield Winery Inc 360 280-8998
921 Middle Fork Rd Onalaska (98570) ***(G-7446)***
Birchiq, Bellevue *Also called Vs Foods LLC* ***(G-1221)***
Birchwood Acres LLC 360 433-8690
3804 Nw Knapp Ln Camas (98607) ***(G-2232)***
Bird's Auto Glass & Body Shop, Electric City *Also called Luann Ayling* ***(G-3167)***
Birdbuffer, Everett *Also called BB Citc LLC* ***(G-3384)***
Birds Eye Foods Inc 253 833-0255
1150 Industry Dr N Ste C Auburn (98001) ***(G-393)***
Birdseed 360 574-7516
11306 Ne 34th Ct Vancouver (98686) ***(G-14067)***
Birdwell Machine LLC 425 881-1916
17445 Ne 70th St Ste 160 Redmond (98052) ***(G-8404)***
Birklor LLC 206 368-7331
12700 Aurora Ave N Ste A Seattle (98133) ***(G-9532)***
Biscomb Fleudeliza S (artist) 206 842-6417
9629 Ne Timberlane Pl Bainbridge Island (98110) ***(G-618)***
Biscomb, William Pl, Bainbridge Island *Also called Biscomb Fleudeliza S (artist)* ***(G-618)***
Biscottea, Seattle *Also called Lawrence Milner* ***(G-10385)***
Biscottea Baking Company LLC 206 695-2614
4209 21st Ave W Ste 400 Seattle (98199) ***(G-9533)***
Bishop-Red Rock Inc 509 773-5335
221 W Main St Goldendale (98620) ***(G-4193)***
Bison Bkbinding Letterpress LP 360 734-0481
112 Grand Ave Bellingham (98225) ***(G-1273)***
Bison Fiber Pallet 206 291-0778
24305 11th Ave S Des Moines (98198) ***(G-2930)***
Bisson & Associates Inc 360 856-0434
26680 Helmick Rd Sedro Woolley (98284) ***(G-11532)***
Bit Elixir LLC 509 842-4121
11511 E Valleyway Ave Spokane Valley (99206) ***(G-12641)***
Bit Pusher LLC 206 457-5242
400 N 34th St Seattle (98103) ***(G-9534)***
Bite Buddy LLC 360 749-4781
1813 S 13th Ave Kelso (98626) ***(G-4518)***
Bite ME Inc 253 244-7194
3827 100th St Sw Ste E Lakewood (98499) ***(G-5703)***
Bite-A-Lite LLC 360 687-2995
22111 Ne 182nd Ave Battle Ground (98604) ***(G-693)***
Bitpeg Software Inc 509 290-5216
14818 N Peone Pines Dr Mead (99021) ***(G-6425)***
Bitter End Boatworks 360 920-3862
3123 Laurelwood Ave Bellingham (98225) ***(G-1274)***
Bittitan Inc 206 428-6030
218 Main St Ste 719 Kirkland (98033) ***(G-5291)***
Bittitan Inc (PA) 206 428-6030
1120 112th Ave Ne Ste 300 Bellevue (98004) ***(G-819)***
Bittium Usa Inc (HQ) 425 780-4480
22722 29th Dr Se Ste 100 Bothell (98021) ***(G-1829)***
Biz Design & Sign 253 472-3070
10003 40th Ave E Tacoma (98446) ***(G-13202)***
Bizlogr Inc 800 366-4484
8201 164th Ave Ne Ste 200 Redmond (98052) ***(G-8405)***
Bizzybee LLC 206 707-9417
4337 15th Ave Ne Apt 712 Seattle (98105) ***(G-9535)***
BJ & Bobs Farm Butchering 360 274-4202
381 Delameter Rd Castle Rock (98611) ***(G-2338)***
BJ II Inc 253 926-8538
1305 Alexander Ave E Fife (98424) ***(G-3939)***
Bjorklund Machine & Tool Co 425 892-1092
21828 87th Ave Se Ste D Woodinville (98072) ***(G-15193)***
Bjorklund Machine and Tool Co 425 949-5761
18831 13th Ave Se Bothell (98012) ***(G-1830)***
Bk Laser Art, Spokane *Also called William Louis Becker* ***(G-12593)***
Bk Welding, Port Orchard *Also called B K Welding and Fabrication* ***(G-7791)***
Bkd Software 425 487-1475
19903 164th Ave Ne Woodinville (98072) ***(G-15194)***
Bl Best Inc 509 534-0237
1108 N Freya St Spokane (99202) ***(G-12150)***
Black & Decker (us) Inc 509 535-9252
5308 E Sprague Ave Spokane Valley (99212) ***(G-12642)***
Black & Decker Corporation 206 624-4228
2100 Airport Way S Seattle (98134) ***(G-9536)***
Black Box Corporation 800 733-0274
6918 S 220th St Kent (98032) ***(G-4814)***
Black Box Corporation 406 522-3944
3707 E Decatur Ave Unit 1 Spokane (99217) ***(G-12151)***
Black Box Corporation 406 652-1956
3707 E Decatur Ave Unit 1 Spokane (99217) ***(G-12152)***

ALPHABETIC

Black Box Corporation ALPHABETIC SECTION

Black Box Corporation....406 652-1956
3707 E Decatur Ave Unit 1 Spokane (99217) *(G-12153)*
Black Diamond Smoked Meats....541 228-2758
35019 257th Ave Se Black Diamond (98010) *(G-1645)*
Black Dog Industries....509 946-6400
2019 Butler Loop Richland (99354) *(G-8973)*
Black Fleet Brewing....425 432-6868
2313 Martin Luther King Tacoma (98405) *(G-13203)*
Black Heron Spirits, West Richland *Also called Skyline Spirits Wine Works Co (G-15100)*
Black Label Switches....360 607-3559
3510 Ne 3rd Ave Camas (98607) *(G-2233)*
Black Lk Bb Camp Cnference Ctr....360 539-5337
6521 Fairview Rd Sw Olympia (98512) *(G-7236)*
Black Magic Beverages LLC....206 632-7257
13749 Midvale Ave N Seattle (98133) *(G-9537)*
Black Mouse Inc....253 677-3491
3835 A St Tacoma (98418) *(G-13204)*
Black River Seal Coating Wesle....509 836-0125
7431 Van Belle Rd Sunnyside (98944) *(G-13114)*
Black Sheep Creamery....360 520-3397
100 4th Ave N Seattle (98109) *(G-9538)*
Blackbear Outdoors, Montesano *Also called Blackbear Pontoons Fabrication (G-6642)*
Blackbear Pontoons Fabrication....206 372-9998
117 Camp Creek Rd Montesano (98563) *(G-6642)*
Blackbirds Nest....509 946-1978
2035 Howell Ave Richland (99354) *(G-8974)*
Blackboard Cyphr Educ Consltng....360 870-8429
1316 Central St Se Olympia (98501) *(G-7237)*
Blackhawk Synergies Inc....509 627-9726
816 S Yolo St Kennewick (99336) *(G-4632)*
Blackies Grinding Service Inc....253 735-1835
3402 C St Ne Ste 211 Auburn (98002) *(G-394)*
Blackstar....360 426-7470
510 E Mason Lake Rd Shelton (98584) *(G-11684)*
Blackstar Industries, Auburn *Also called Jim Suzuki (G-482)*
Blackstone Manufacturing Inc....509 495-1405
530 W 3rd St Cheney (99004) *(G-2577)*
Blackwaters Metal....425 213-0154
8471 Glenwood Rd Sw Port Orchard (98367) *(G-7795)*
Blackwood Fiber Co....206 387-3854
4311 S 7th St Tacoma (98405) *(G-13205)*
Blade Cheverlot Rv....360 982-2370
111 Stewart Rd Mount Vernon (98273) *(G-6781)*
Bladegallery Inc....425 889-5980
107 Central Way Kirkland (98033) *(G-5292)*
Blanc Industries Inc....360 736-8988
3639 Galvin Rd Centralia (98531) *(G-2385)*
Blanca Terra Vineyards Inc....509 588-6082
34715 N Demoss Rd Benton City (99320) *(G-1602)*
Blanchard Abrasives....360 653-5273
13120 State Ave Marysville (98271) *(G-6317)*
Blanchard Auto Elc & Fleet Sup, Tukwila *Also called Battery X-Change & Repair Inc (G-13695)*
Blanksi LLC....425 453-1224
12748 Ne Bel Red Rd Bellevue (98005) *(G-820)*
Blase S Gorny Design Inc....360 426-5613
3810 W Skokomish Vly Rd Shelton (98584) *(G-11685)*
Blaser Casting Corporation....206 767-7800
5700 3rd Ave S Seattle (98108) *(G-9539)*
Blaser Die Casting Co (PA)....206 767-7800
5700 3rd Ave S Seattle (98108) *(G-9540)*
Blau Oyster Company Inc....360 766-6171
11321 Blue Heron Rd Bow (98232) *(G-1927)*
Blaze Metrics LLC....206 972-3890
8825 34th Ave Ne L-190 Quil Ceda Village (98271) *(G-8280)*
Blaze To Blizzard Htg & Coolg, Walla Walla *Also called Anatoliy Semenko (G-14763)*
Blazen Metal Works....360 897-2053
22511 162nd St E Orting (98360) *(G-7474)*
Blazing Banners....360 756-9990
1780 Iowa St Bellingham (98229) *(G-1275)*
Blefa Kegs Inc....615 267-1385
3801 Ne 109th Ave Vancouver (98682) *(G-14068)*
Blend Wine Shop....253 884-9688
8914 Key Peninsula Hwy Nw Lakebay (98349) *(G-5688)*
Blender LLC....509 210-3373
152 S Jefferson St # 100 Spokane (99201) *(G-12154)*
Blethen Corporation (PA)....206 464-2471
1120 John St Seattle (98109) *(G-9541)*
Bli International Div, Spokane *Also called Baton Labs Inc (G-12140)*
Blind Eye Books....360 715-9117
1141 Grant St Bellingham (98225) *(G-1276)*
Blink Device Company LLC....206 708-6043
1530 Westlake Ave N Seattle (98109) *(G-9542)*
Blockable, Seattle *Also called Blokable Inc (G-9544)*
Blockpartygg LLC....206 409-6562
3801 Stone Way N Apt 207 Seattle (98103) *(G-9543)*
Blokable Inc (PA)....800 928-6778
1136 Poplar Pl S Seattle (98144) *(G-9544)*
Blokable Inc....800 928-6778
1800 W Fourth Plain Blvd Vancouver (98660) *(G-14069)*
Blonder Signs, Olympia *Also called Bolander Sign Co (G-7239)*
Blood Eagle Weaponry LLC....360 929-9567
2800 Ne Goldie St Oak Harbor (98277) *(G-7142)*
Bloomfield Light Industries....360 877-5718
40 N Lon Webb Rd Lilliwaup (98555) *(G-5870)*
Blowing Sands....206 783-5314
5805 14th Ave Nw Seattle (98107) *(G-9545)*
Blr Aerospace LLc....425 353-6591
11002 29th Ave W Everett (98204) *(G-3389)*
Blucapp Inc....206 629-8887
6315 Ne Radford Dr # 3412 Seattle (98115) *(G-9546)*
Blue Bird Inc....509 486-2160
215 W 4th St Tonasket (98855) *(G-13646)*
Blue Bus Cultured Foods LLC....541 399-4141
415 W Steuben St Bingen (98605) *(G-1633)*
Blue Cottage Jams....425 836-9580
21701 Ne 73rd Pl Redmond (98053) *(G-8406)*
Blue Crystal Signs Screen Prtg, Waitsburg *Also called Crystal Blue Screen Printing (G-14753)*
Blue Dog Bakery Group Inc....206 323-6958
3302 Fuhrman Ave E # 202 Seattle (98102) *(G-9547)*
Blue Falls Usa LP....509 891-1933
3808 N Sullivan Rd N4 Spokane Valley (99216) *(G-12643)*
Blue Frog Solar LLC....206 855-5149
1015 Ne Hostmark St # 104 Poulsbo (98370) *(G-7948)*
Blue Heron Group Inc....206 767-2688
5211 1st Ave S Seattle (98108) *(G-9548)*
Blue Heron Lake Farms Inc....360 966-5241
2136 E Hemmi Rd Bellingham (98226) *(G-1277)*
Blue Heron Woodworks....360 766-4475
9382 Marshall Rd Bow (98232) *(G-1928)*
Blue Home Thermal Imaging LLC....360 638-0838
33640 Widmark Rd Ne Kingston (98346) *(G-5248)*
Blue Horizon Cabinet Co LLC....509 254-1430
1142 16th Ave Ste B Clarkston (99403) *(G-2625)*
Blue Ink....206 588-0739
13030 Linden Ave N Seattle (98133) *(G-9549)*
Blue J Seed, Bickleton *Also called Jensen Seed Farm Inc (G-1632)*
Blue Lantern Publishing Inc (PA)....206 632-7075
3645 Interlake Ave N Seattle (98103) *(G-9550)*
Blue Lantern Publishing Inc....206 447-9229
3645 Interlake Ave N Seattle (98103) *(G-9551)*
Blue Marine LLC....253 225-8228
11010 Harbor Hill Dr B507 Gig Harbor (98332) *(G-4082)*
Blue Martini Software....360 754-2207
7205 105th Ave Sw Olympia (98512) *(G-7238)*
Blue Moon Marine Botanicals, Friday Harbor *Also called Blue Moon Marine LLC (G-4041)*
Blue Moon Marine LLC....360 378-2498
1945 White Point Rd Friday Harbor (98250) *(G-4041)*
Blue Mountain Medical, Tacoma *Also called Professional Sleep Services (G-13479)*
Blue North Forest Products LLC....208 935-2547
2930 Westlake Ave N # 300 Seattle (98109) *(G-9552)*
Blue North Trading Company LLC....206 352-9252
2940 Westlake Ave N # 302 Seattle (98109) *(G-9553)*
Blue Origin LLC (PA)....253 872-0411
21218 76th Ave S Kent (98032) *(G-4815)*
Blue Oval Co....509 448-2894
10410 S Sharon Rd Spokane (99223) *(G-12155)*
Blue Print....425 870-5599
305 Bedrock Dr Everett (98203) *(G-3390)*
Blue Prints Plus....425 888-8815
301 W North Bend Way North Bend (98045) *(G-7102)*
Blue Ribbon Printing....425 478-7628
12712 Admiralty Way Everett (98204) *(G-3391)*
Blue Sea Fisheries....360 299-0936
12800 Marine Dr Anacortes (98221) *(G-103)*
Blue Sea Systems Inc (HQ)....360 738-8230
4600 Ryzex Way Bellingham (98226) *(G-1278)*
Blue Seal Inc....360 568-2098
15006 35th Ave W Ste A Lynnwood (98087) *(G-6084)*
Blue Sky Printing LLC....360 779-2681
19036 Front St Ne Poulsbo (98370) *(G-7949)*
Blue Star Enterprises NW Inc....509 946-9388
2019 Butler Loop Richland (99354) *(G-8975)*
Blue Star Gas - Seattle Co....206 762-2583
10802 E Marginal Way S Tukwila (98168) *(G-13698)*
Blue Star Welding LLC....360 398-7647
6059 Guide Meridian Bellingham (98226) *(G-1279)*
Blue Streak Finishers LLC....425 347-1944
1520 80th St Sw Ste A Everett (98203) *(G-3392)*
Blue Streak Woodworks....360 379-0414
1039 Jackson St Port Townsend (98368) *(G-7869)*
Blue Water Inc....509 682-5544
611 E Woodin Ave Chelan (98816) *(G-2548)*
Blue Water Projects Inc....206 452-1332
1505 S 93rd St Ste Ba Seattle (98108) *(G-9554)*
Blue Water Publishers LLC....360 805-6474
22727 161st Ave Se Monroe (98272) *(G-6555)*
Blueberry Meringue Software....425 830-5414
16824 Stackpole Rd Monroe (98272) *(G-6556)*
Bluecosmo Inc....877 258-3496
4746 44th Ave Sw Ste 201 Seattle (98116) *(G-9555)*
Bluecsmo Stllite Cmmunications, Seattle *Also called Bluecosmo Inc (G-9555)*

Bluefin Marine LLC 206 276-4087
7429 Ne 129th St Kirkland (98034) ***(G-5293)***
Bluefire LLC 206 251-0698
16231 266th Ave Se Issaquah (98027) ***(G-4386)***
Blueline Equipment Co LLC 509 785-2595
603 Frontage Rd Quincy (98848) ***(G-8290)***
Blueline Equipment Co LLC 509 525-4550
902 W Rose St Walla Walla (99362) ***(G-14772)***
Blueline Equipment Co LLC 509 248-8411
105 N Spokane St Moxee (98936) ***(G-6875)***
Blueline Equipment Co LLC 509 248-8411
105 S Spokane St Seattle (98134) ***(G-9556)***
Blueline Equipment Co LLC (HQ) 509 248-8411
1605 E Mead Ave Yakima (98903) ***(G-15522)***
Blueline Mfg Co (PA) 509 248-8411
1605 E Mead Ave Yakima (98903) ***(G-15523)***
Bluepenguin Software Inc 561 459-5393
1400 W Washington St # 104 Sequim (98382) ***(G-11615)***
Bluephone, Sammamish *Also called Xeriton Corporation* ***(G-9261)***
Bluer Skies Publishing LLC 813 675-7588
11400 Olympus Way C104 Gig Harbor (98332) ***(G-4083)***
Bluerose Processing 360 281-7371
5605 Ne 46th St Vancouver (98661) ***(G-14070)***
Blueseventy LLC 206 547-5273
118 Nw Canal St Ste A Seattle (98107) ***(G-9557)***
Bluewater Industries Inc 509 765-4623
3283 Bell Rd Ne Moses Lake (98837) ***(G-6687)***
Bluewave Technologies LLC 800 636-1428
1546 Nw 56th St Ste 564 Seattle (98107) ***(G-9558)***
BM Prgrm & Machining Svc Inc 425 743-5373
11620 49th Pl W Mukilteo (98275) ***(G-6898)***
BMC West LLC 425 303-0661
3200 35th Ave Ne Everett (98201) ***(G-3393)***
BMC West LLC 360 943-8050
9721 40th Ave Sw Lakewood (98499) ***(G-5704)***
BMC West Truss Plant, Everett *Also called BMC West LLC* ***(G-3393)***
Bme Logging LLC 360 931-6797
32214 Ne 82nd Ave La Center (98629) ***(G-5502)***
Bmt - Usa LLC 360 863-2252
14532 169th Dr Se Ste 142 Monroe (98272) ***(G-6557)***
Bmt Industries Inc 509 838-4400
421 W Riverside Ave # 720 Spokane (99201) ***(G-12156)***
Bmt Metal Fabrication Inc 509 244-6107
2700 S Hayden Rd Airway Heights (99001) ***(G-49)***
Bmt USA, Monroe *Also called Bmt - Usa LLC* ***(G-6557)***
Bnb International LLC 425 712-1687
110 W Dayton St Ste 205 Edmonds (98020) ***(G-3097)***
BNC Printing 503 318-5916
13811 Ne 42nd Ave Vancouver (98686) ***(G-14071)***
Board Shark LLC 503 351-5424
2808 Ne 65th Ave Ste C Vancouver (98661) ***(G-14072)***
Board Systems 253 307-0166
8611 312th St S Roy (98580) ***(G-9157)***
Boart Longyear 509 926-9575
21312 E Gilbert Ave Otis Orchards (99027) ***(G-7512)***
Boat Tote 360 600-1364
17401 Se 39th St Unit 147 Vancouver (98683) ***(G-14073)***
Boat-Tech 206 281-9828
600 W Nickerson St Seattle (98119) ***(G-9559)***
Boatworks Gallery LLC 360 626-1284
1563 Archway Ct Poulsbo (98370) ***(G-7950)***
Boatworks Long Lake 509 979-0936
323 E Shore Rd Nine Mile Falls (99026) ***(G-7068)***
Bob Bracht Llc 206 678-5168
16522 37th Ave Ne Lake Forest Park (98155) ***(G-5608)***
Bob Johnson Woodworking 360 668-9456
15405 State St Snohomish (98296) ***(G-11877)***
Bob Nagel Inc 503 869-6933
1602 Washington St Vancouver (98660) ***(G-14074)***
Bob Nelson 360 795-3391
77 Main St Cathlamet (98612) ***(G-2360)***
Bobby Wolford Trucking & Demo, Woodinville *Also called Bobby Wolford Trucking & Salv* ***(G-15195)***
Bobby Wolford Trucking & Salv 425 481-1800
22014 W Bostian Rd Woodinville (98072) ***(G-15195)***
Bobek Enterprises 360 683-8785
212 Cougar Crest Rd Sequim (98382) ***(G-11616)***
Bobolink Software 509 684-2800
1723 Mountain Garden Way Kettle Falls (99141) ***(G-5225)***
Bobs Welding & Auto Repair 509 427-5094
91 Callahan Rd Carson (98610) ***(G-2303)***
Bocada LLC 425 818-4400
5555 Lakeview Dr Ste 201 Kirkland (98033) ***(G-5294)***
Bochans Custom Leather Work 425 337-6128
12703 Seattle Hill Rd Snohomish (98296) ***(G-11878)***
Bodes Precast Inc 360 354-3912
1861 E Pole Rd Everson (98247) ***(G-3668)***
Bodle Diamond Industries 360 939-0242
656 Chinook Ct Stanwood (98282) ***(G-12953)***
Body Builders Gym Equipment 253 631-8274
12003 Se 248th St Kent (98030) ***(G-4816)***
Bodycote Hot Isostatic Prsg, Camas *Also called Bodycote Imt Inc* ***(G-2234)***
Bodycote Imt Inc 360 833-1120
4605 Nw Pacific Rim Blvd Camas (98607) ***(G-2234)***
Bodypoint Inc 206 405-4555
558 1st Ave S Ste 300 Seattle (98104) ***(G-9560)***
Bodysense Inc (PA) 206 988-1719
4000 Sw 104th St Seattle (98146) ***(G-9561)***
Boehms Candies Inc 425 392-6652
255 Ne Gilman Blvd Issaquah (98027) ***(G-4387)***
Boeing 360 348-0394
1910 Bickford Ave Ste A Snohomish (98290) ***(G-11879)***
Boeing Arospc Operations Inc 253 773-9906
12901 133rd Ave E Puyallup (98374) ***(G-8132)***
Boeing China Inc 206 655-2121
7755 E Marginal Way S Tukwila (98108) ***(G-13699)***
Boeing Classic 206 381-7804
800 Occidental Ave S Seattle (98134) ***(G-9562)***
Boeing Co 206 351-8601
519 S 214th St Des Moines (98198) ***(G-2931)***
Boeing Commercial Airplane 425 237-2019
3003 W Casino Rd Everett (98204) ***(G-3394)***
Boeing Commercial Airplane 206 662-9615
8118 S 208th St Kent (98032) ***(G-4817)***
Boeing Commercial Airplanes 206 662-9615
2201 S 142nd St Seatac (98168) ***(G-9275)***
Boeing Company 425 413-3400
25215 Se 184th St Maple Valley (98038) ***(G-6261)***
Boeing Company 425 417-5612
12605 94th Ave Ne Kirkland (98034) ***(G-5295)***
Boeing Company 312 544-2000
18-01 Bldg 2nd Kent (98032) ***(G-4818)***
Boeing Company 206 655-9974
9725 E Marginal Way S Tukwila (98108) ***(G-13700)***
Boeing Company 425 359-3777
16211 40th Ave Se Bothell (98012) ***(G-1831)***
Boeing Company 425 493-8267
8630 53rd Pl W Mukilteo (98275) ***(G-6899)***
Boeing Company 425 266-0616
8415 Paine Field Blvd Mukilteo (98275) ***(G-6900)***
Boeing Company 206 662-6863
700 S Renton Village Pl Renton (98057) ***(G-8756)***
Boeing Company 206 655-1131
7755 E Marginal Way S Tukwila (98108) ***(G-13701)***
Boeing Company 312 544-2000
2810 160th Ave Se Bellevue (98008) ***(G-821)***
Boeing Company 206 766-2770
1901 Oakesdale Ave Sw Renton (98057) ***(G-8757)***
Boeing Company 206 662-9615
2201 S 142nd St W10 Seatac (98168) ***(G-9276)***
Boeing Company 206 544-2374
555 Monster Rd Sw Renton (98057) ***(G-8758)***
Boeing Company 425 865-6915
3365 160th Ave Se 3307 Bellevue (98008) ***(G-822)***
Boeing Company 253 657-0675
2141 S 211th St Seatac (98198) ***(G-9277)***
Boeing Company 425 407-1400
6200 23rd Dr W Everett (98203) ***(G-3395)***
Boeing Company 206 655-1131
7701 14th Ave S Seattle (98108) ***(G-9563)***
Boeing Company 425 342-2121
3003 W Casino Rd Everett (98204) ***(G-3396)***
Boeing Company 425 306-8112
800 N 6th St Renton (98057) ***(G-8759)***
Boeing Company 253 872-5545
20403 68th Ave S Kent (98032) ***(G-4819)***
Boeing Company 253 931-2121
700 15th St Sw Auburn (98001) ***(G-395)***
Boeing Company 206 544-4524
2925 S 112th St Tukwila (98168) ***(G-13702)***
Boeing Company 206 655-1131
7755 E Marginal Way S Tukwila (98108) ***(G-13703)***
Boeing Company 206 689-4059
800 Logan Ave N Renton (98055) ***(G-8760)***
Boeing Company 312 544-2000
17930 International Blvd Seatac (98188) ***(G-9278)***
Boeing Company 425 865-3308
3076 160th Ave Se Bellevue (98008) ***(G-823)***
Boeing Company 425 865-3311
3265 160th Ave Se Bellevue (98008) ***(G-824)***
Boeing Company 253 657-5616
801 Sw 41st St Renton (98055) ***(G-8761)***
Boeing Company 206 655-1131
635 Park Ave N Bldg 101 Renton (98057) ***(G-8762)***
Boeing Company 206 655-2121
7755 E Marginal Way S Tukwila (98108) ***(G-13704)***
Boeing Company 206 544-9246
7775 E Marginal Way S Tukwila (98108) ***(G-13705)***
Boeing Company 312 544-2000
2600 94th St Sw Everett (98204) ***(G-3397)***
Boeing Company Incorporated 425 965-4300
6840 Fort Dent Way # 250 Tukwila (98188) ***(G-13706)***
Boeing Domestic Sales Corp 206 655-2121
7755 E Marginal Way S Tukwila (98108) ***(G-13707)***
Boeing Employees Flying Assn 425 271-2332
840 W Perimeter Rd Renton (98057) ***(G-8763)***

ALPHABETIC

Boeing Operations Intl Inc (HQ)

ALPHABETIC SECTION

Boeing Operations Intl Inc (HQ) 206 655-2121
   7755 E Marginal Way S Tukwila (98108) *(G-13708)*
Boettcher & Sons Inc 360 832-3943
   186 Dow Ridge Dr N Eatonville (98328) *(G-3051)*
Bogden Inc 509 964-2008
   270 Mission Rd Thorp (98946) *(G-13627)*
Bogert Aviation Inc 509 736-1513
   3606 N Swallow Ave # 100 Pasco (99301) *(G-7554)*
Bogert International Inc 509 736-1512
   3606 N Swallow Ave # 300 Pasco (99301) *(G-7555)*
Bogert Manufacturing Inc 509 735-2106
   3606 N Swallow Ave # 200 Pasco (99301) *(G-7556)*
Boggs Manufacturing 360 449-3479
   16414 Ne 32nd St Vancouver (98682) *(G-14075)*
Boise Cascade Company 360 690-7028
   907 W 7th St Vancouver (98660) *(G-14076)*
Boise Cascade Company 360 891-8787
   222 Se Park Plaza Dr # 300 Vancouver (98684) *(G-14077)*
Boise Cascade Company 509 738-3200
   1274 S Boise Rd Kettle Falls (99141) *(G-5226)*
Boise Inc 509 685-9825
   634 Highway 395 S Colville (99114) *(G-2741)*
Boise White Paper LLC 509 545-3293
   31831 W Highway 12 Wallula (99363) *(G-14908)*
Bolander Sign Co 360 943-2447
   1311 4th Ave E Olympia (98506) *(G-7239)*
Bolar's Custom Meat Cutting, Castle Rock Also called BJ & Bobs Farm Butchering *(G-2338)*
Bolt Woodworks Corp 206 734-5845
   3010 Everett Ave Unit A Everett (98201) *(G-3398)*
Bombora Global LLC 206 617-6996
   4825 240th Ave Se Sammamish (98029) *(G-9191)*
Bon Logic Corporation 509 991-9643
   14715 W Lincoln Rd Spokane (99224) *(G-12157)*
Bonair Winery Inc 509 829-6027
   500 S Bonair Rd Zillah (98953) *(G-15750)*
Bondarchuk Andrey 509 290-2525
   9923 E 10th Ave Spokane Valley (99206) *(G-12644)*
Bonfire Productions Inc 425 748-5041
   2018 156th Ave Ne Bellevue (98007) *(G-825)*
Bonneylk/Sumner Courier-Herald, Enumclaw Also called Sound Publishing Inc *(G-3321)*
Bonnie Press 360 807-4442
   115 Crown Point Rd Longview (98632) *(G-5889)*
Bonnies Best Bet Batter, Camano Island Also called Frosty Bay Seafoods LLC *(G-2213)*
Bontzu Cellars 425 205-3482
   1460 F St Walla Walla (99362) *(G-14773)*
Book N Brush 360 748-6221
   518 N Market Blvd Chehalis (98532) *(G-2472)*
Bookmark Publishing Co 425 562-0909
   15928 Se 41st Pl Bellevue (98006) *(G-826)*
Bookwalter LLC 425 488-1983
   14810 Ne 145th St Ste B Woodinville (98072) *(G-15196)*
Bookwalter Winery LLC 509 627-5000
   894 Tulip Ln Richland (99352) *(G-8976)*
Boom Noodle 425 453-6094
   504 Bellevue Sq Bellevue (98004) *(G-827)*
Boom Noodle Corp Uv 206 525-2675
   2675 Ne Village Ln Seattle (98105) *(G-9564)*
Boomerang Boxer LLC 206 227-6569
   468a Ne Thornton Pl Seattle (98125) *(G-9565)*
Boomerang Express LLC 360 449-2173
   4601 E 18th St Apt 182 Vancouver (98661) *(G-14078)*
Boomerang Physical Therapy LLC 360 258-1637
   18414 Ne Garden Dr Vancouver (98682) *(G-14079)*
Boon 360 225-5224
   6262 Green Mountain Rd Woodland (98674) *(G-15420)*
Booth & Associates 253 752-2494
   5917 N 46th St Tacoma (98407) *(G-13206)*
Bop Filters, Kirkland Also called Lancs Industries Holdings LLC *(G-5379)*
Boral Resources LLC 206 394-3734
   950 Andover Park E Ste 24 Tukwila (98188) *(G-13709)*
Boral Roofing LLC 253 581-3666
   10920 Steele St S Lakewood (98499) *(G-5705)*
Bornstein Seafoods Inc (PA) 360 734-7990
   1001 Hilton Ave Bellingham (98225) *(G-1280)*
Boruck Prtg & Silk Screening 206 522-8500
   16802 11th Ave Ne Shoreline (98155) *(G-11763)*
Bosom Cattle Co 206 947-0645
   115 E Yelm Ave Yelm (98597) *(G-15730)*
Boston Sceintifics 608 323-3377
   6645 185th Ave Ne Redmond (98052) *(G-8407)*
Botanical Blu L L C 360 866-8251
   3749 36th Loop Nw Olympia (98502) *(G-7240)*
Botanical Colors LLC 206 518-7073
   4020 Leary Way Nw Ste 300 Seattle (98107) *(G-9566)*
Botanical Colors LLC 206 518-7073
   10550 Phinney Ave N Seattle (98133) *(G-9567)*
Bothell Rprter Knmore Reporter, Kirkland Also called Sound Publishing Inc *(G-5467)*
Bottling Group LLC 509 535-0605
   4014 E Sprague Ave Spokane (99202) *(G-12158)*
Bouchard Lake Winery LLC 425 803-5076
   12205 Ne 64th St Kirkland (98033) *(G-5296)*
Boulder Creek Industriescom 425 879-2322
   31124 Boulder Creek Dr Arlington (98223) *(G-214)*

Boulder Estates Winery 509 628-1209
   336 Broadmoor St Richland (99352) *(G-8977)*
Boulder Gold LLC 425 308-4316
   2824 110th St Se Everett (98208) *(G-3399)*
Boundary Bay Brewery & Bistro, Bellingham Also called Boundary Bay Brewing Company *(G-1281)*
Boundary Bay Brewing Company 360 647-5593
   1107 Railroad Ave Bellingham (98225) *(G-1281)*
Boundary Creek Majestic, Ione Also called Van Dyke Logging Incorporated *(G-4376)*
Boundary Fish Company 360 332-6715
   223 Sigurdson Ave Blaine (98230) *(G-1662)*
Boundary Power House, Metaline Falls Also called City of Sattle-City Light Dept *(G-6497)*
Boundless Enterprises Inc 206 789-7350
   6327 Seaview Ave Nw Seattle (98107) *(G-9568)*
Boundless Immigration Inc 855 268-6353
   240 2nd Ave S Ste 300 Seattle (98104) *(G-9569)*
Bourgeois Bits LLC 434 535-2487
   3417 Evanston Ave N # 313 Seattle (98103) *(G-9570)*
Boutique Imports LLC 206 650-5555
   8530 20th Ave Nw Seattle (98117) *(G-9571)*
Boutique On Wheels 425 369-9324
   2837 234th Ave Se Sammamish (98075) *(G-9192)*
Bowers Steel, Vancouver Also called DCB Industries Inc *(G-14169)*
Bowers Steel, Vancouver Also called DCB Industries Inc *(G-14170)*
Bowet & Poet Inc 360 385-9005
   5445 Kuhn St Port Townsend (98368) *(G-7870)*
Bowhead Manufacturing Co LLC 206 957-5321
   1011 Sw Kickwat Ste 104 Seattle (98134) *(G-9572)*
Bowlby's, Yakima Also called Bowlbys Sporting Goods *(G-15524)*
Bowlbys Sporting Goods 509 248-8281
   129 S 3rd St Yakima (98901) *(G-15524)*
Bowman-Morton Mfg & Mch Inc 206 524-8890
   7500 W Marginal Way S Seattle (98108) *(G-9573)*
Bowmans Electro Painting 360 668-1389
   18114 67th Ave Se Snohomish (98296) *(G-11880)*
Box Maker Inc 425 291-1291
   6230 S 190th St Kent (98032) *(G-4820)*
Boyd Coffee Company 425 744-1394
   21009 63rd Ave W Lynnwood (98036) *(G-6085)*
Bozeman Daily Chronicle, Seattle Also called Big Sky Publishing Co *(G-9525)*
BP America Inc 360 371-0373
   4519 Grandview Rd Blaine (98230) *(G-1663)*
BP Arco Seattle Terminal 206 623-4637
   1652 Sw Lander St Seattle (98134) *(G-9574)*
BP Corporation North Amer Inc 360 371-1500
   4519 Grandview Rd Blaine (98230) *(G-1664)*
BP Logistics, Seattle Also called BP Arco Seattle Terminal *(G-9574)*
BP Marketing 509 475-7125
   1200 N 27th Pl Renton (98056) *(G-8764)*
BP West Coast Products, Blaine Also called BP Corporation North Amer Inc *(G-1664)*
BP West Coast Products LLC 360 856-5022
   830 Moore St Sedro Woolley (98284) *(G-11533)*
BP West Coast Products LLC 360 371-1500
   4519 Grandview Rd Blaine (98230) *(G-1665)*
Bpb Gypsum, Kent Also called Certainteed Gypsum Inc *(G-4850)*
Bpb Gypsum, Seattle Also called Certainteed Gypsum Inc *(G-9657)*
Bpb Gypsum Inc, Seattle Also called Certainteed Gypsum Mfg Inc *(G-9658)*
Brad O Connor Woodworking 206 302-8424
   4022 52nd Ave Sw Seattle (98116) *(G-9575)*
Brad Pendleton Software LLC 425 898-0309
   23402 Ne 23rd St Sammamish (98074) *(G-9193)*
Brad S Welding 360 668-7135
   17430 100th Ave Se Snohomish (98296) *(G-11881)*
Bradken Inc 253 475-4600
   3021 S Wilkeson St Tacoma (98409) *(G-13207)*
Bradken Inc 253 475-3464
   3611 S Warner St Tacoma (98409) *(G-13208)*
Bradken - Atlas LLC 360 748-6645
   109 Sears Rd Chehalis (98532) *(G-2473)*
Bradley Heavy Construction 360 341-5967
   6992 Holst Rd Clinton (98236) *(G-2684)*
Bradley Robling 360 832-6778
   4704 235th St E Spanaway (98387) *(G-12054)*
Bradley Saxton 800 643-3512
   6718 S 216th St Kent (98032) *(G-4821)*
Bradley's Fabrication, Spanaway Also called Bradley Robling *(G-12054)*
Bradleys Metal Works Inc 509 448-2307
   12128 S Cheney Spokane Rd Spokane (99224) *(G-12159)*
Bradshaw Machine Co 425 337-2802
   1112 Bonneville Ave Snohomish (98290) *(G-11882)*
Brady Worldwide Inc 800 854-6832
   100 S Massachusetts St Seattle (98134) *(G-9576)*
Brady Worldwide Inc 206 323-8100
   1560 1st Ave S Seattle (98134) *(G-9577)*
Brady's Welding, Tacoma Also called Bradys Specialties *(G-13209)*
Bradys Specialties 253 572-3768
   5228 S Mason Ave Tacoma (98409) *(G-13209)*
Brainless Tees Inc 360 608-8417
   12401 Ne 60th Way A8 Vancouver (98682) *(G-14080)*

Brak Software Inc...206 280-7157
15280 Ne 15th Pl Apt A Bellevue (98007) *(G-828)*
Brandeberry Logging, North Bend *Also called Mike Brandeberry (G-7116)*
Brandon Company Inc...425 290-5427
12708 Alexander Rd Everett (98204) *(G-3400)*
Brands Reco...360 428-8985
211 Grover St Lynden (98264) *(G-6003)*
Branom Instrument Co., Seattle *Also called Branom Operating Company LLC (G-9578)*
Branom Operating Company LLC...206 762-6050
5500 4th Ave S Seattle (98108) *(G-9578)*
Bras Thermography...425 677-8430
317 Nw Gilman Blvd Issaquah (98027) *(G-4388)*
Brass Key Inc...866 325-6840
24418 Se 177th St Maple Valley (98038) *(G-6262)*
Brassfinders Inc...509 747-7412
718 N Crestline St Ste B Spokane (99202) *(G-12160)*
Braun Northwest Inc...800 245-6303
150 Northstar Rd Chehalis (98532) *(G-2474)*
Braven Metals LLC...206 963-2234
2315 N Machias Rd Lake Stevens (98258) *(G-5635)*
Bravo Leasing, Woodinville *Also called Sierra Industries Inc (G-15363)*
Bravo Manufacturing Inc...360 817-9124
26401 Ne Brunner Rd Camas (98607) *(G-2235)*
Bravo Publications Inc...206 937-3264
4817 California Ave Sw Seattle (98116) *(G-9579)*
Bravura Software LLC...425 881-7305
6763 191st Pl Ne Redmond (98052) *(G-8408)*
Brazier Lumber Company Inc...206 441-8184
8444 N Mercer Way Mercer Island (98040) *(G-6456)*
Bre & Car Industries LLC...206 268-0204
924 S 117th Ct Seattle (98168) *(G-9580)*
Bread Garden Ltd...253 838-1639
15522 Se Lake Holm Rd Auburn (98092) *(G-396)*
Break From Reality Games LLC...513 884-4940
3273 Sw Avalon Way Unit A Seattle (98126) *(G-9581)*
Breast Care Center...360 424-6161
2000 Hospital Dr Sedro Woolley (98284) *(G-11534)*
Brecht-Pacific Publishing Inc...360 425-4671
884 11th Ave Longview (98632) *(G-5890)*
Breedt Prod Tooling Design LLC...253 859-1100
811 1st Ave S Kent (98032) *(G-4822)*
Breeze Trees LLC...808 387-6167
4845 Guide Meridian Bellingham (98226) *(G-1282)*
Breezy Upholstery & Canvas...206 545-8538
23 Dravus St Seattle (98109) *(G-9582)*
Breithaupt Logging Inc...360 732-4225
425 Whispering Cedars Ln Chimacum (98325) *(G-2612)*
Bremerton Letterpress Co LLC...360 620-8967
423 Pacific Ave Ste 103 Bremerton (98337) *(G-1939)*
Bremerton Trap & Skeet Club...360 674-2438
4956 State Highway 3 Sw Port Orchard (98367) *(G-7796)*
Bremmeyer Logging (PA)...425 432-9310
27034 Se Kent Kangley Rd Ravensdale (98051) *(G-8332)*
Brenthaven, Seattle *Also called Pioneer Square Brands Inc (G-10811)*
Bresch Logging...509 258-9620
4518 Hidden Rd Springdale (99173) *(G-12950)*
Brew Express, Kelso *Also called Quality Brewing Incorporated (G-4543)*
Brews Customs...253 334-1694
4515 S 362nd St Auburn (98001) *(G-397)*
Brewster Manufacturing Inc...509 923-2264
62 Bailey Way Brewster (98812) *(G-2015)*
Brian D Ames...360 561-5119
7424 Puget Beach Rd Ne Olympia (98516) *(G-7241)*
Brian E Styke...360 331-0527
1861 Lancaster Rd Freeland (98249) *(G-4027)*
Brian Friesen Fine Woodworking...360 314-6427
3315 Ne 112th Ave Vancouver (98682) *(G-14081)*
Brian Gannon...206 782-2276
7757 16th Ave Nw Seattle (98117) *(G-9583)*
Brian Martell...509 738-3041
2 Baxter Ln Kettle Falls (99141) *(G-5227)*
Brian Murphy...206 323-8001
2023 E Roy St Seattle (98112) *(G-9584)*
Briarwood Furniture Ltd Inc...425 868-7707
28680 State Hwy 104 Ne Kingston (98346) *(G-5249)*
Bricking Solutions...360 794-1277
1144 Village Way Monroe (98272) *(G-6558)*
Bricor Ceramic Industries...360 377-9197
2591 Ne Cecilia Ln Bremerton (98310) *(G-1940)*
Bridge City Arbors Inc...360 600-3803
18708 Nw 61st Ave Ridgefield (98642) *(G-9069)*
Bridge City Publishing...360 600-0558
6117 Kansas St Vancouver (98661) *(G-14082)*
Bridgestone Hosepower LLC...206 767-4670
5979 4th Ave S Seattle (98108) *(G-9585)*
Bridgetown Industries L L...503 953-3580
8504 Ne 63rd St Vancouver (98662) *(G-14083)*
Bridgeways...425 513-2989
5801 23rd Dr W Ste 104 Everett (98203) *(G-3401)*
Bridport-Air Carrier Inc (HQ)...253 872-7205
1819 Central Ave S # 109 Kent (98032) *(G-4823)*
Brier Brewing LLC...206 258-4987
3501 217th Pl Sw Brier (98036) *(G-2018)*
Briggs Mch & Fabrication LLC...509 535-0125
5308 E Sharp Ave Spokane Valley (99212) *(G-12645)*
Bright Candies...509 525-5533
11 E Main St Walla Walla (99362) *(G-14774)*
Bright Signs Screen Printing...360 695-6444
10501 Ne Highway 99 Vancouver (98686) *(G-14084)*
Bright's Candies & Gifts, Walla Walla *Also called Bright Candies (G-14774)*
Brighten Sign...360 608-5863
5615 Ne 44th St Vancouver (98661) *(G-14085)*
Brightvolt Inc (PA)...863 603-7640
8201 164th Ave Ne Ste 325 Redmond (98052) *(G-8409)*
Brightwire Networks LLC...360 528-6017
2102 Carriage St Sw Ste J Olympia (98502) *(G-7242)*
Brightwork Specialty Printing...360 930-0218
2046 Nw Tregaten Ln Poulsbo (98370) *(G-7951)*
Brim Press, Burien *Also called Kwang Nam Hwang (G-2116)*
Brindle Press LLC...360 434-3302
117 E Louisa St Seattle (98102) *(G-9586)*
Brindle Technical Logging Inc...360 985-7459
451 Winston Creek Rd Mossyrock (98564) *(G-6759)*
Briney Sea Delicacies Inc...360 956-1797
715 78th Ave Sw Ste A Tumwater (98501) *(G-13853)*
Briney Sea Delicaseas, Tumwater *Also called Briney Sea Delicacies Inc (G-13853)*
Brintech Inc...360 985-7459
451 Winston Creek Rd Mossyrock (98564) *(G-6760)*
Brion Toss Rigging, Port Townsend *Also called Toss Brion Yacht Rigging Inc (G-7932)*
Briotech Inc...425 488-4300
19816 141st Pl Ne Woodinville (98072) *(G-15197)*
Brite Light Welding Inc...253 875-6291
5526 184th St E Ste G Puyallup (98375) *(G-8133)*
Brite Light Wldg Frabrication, Puyallup *Also called Brite Light Welding Inc (G-8133)*
British Footpaths...206 525-2466
9521 45th Ave Ne Seattle (98115) *(G-9587)*
Brm Marketing LLC...509 350-5844
1045 E June Dr Moses Lake (98837) *(G-6688)*
Broadcom Corporation...425 748-5076
2018 156th Ave Ne Bellevue (98007) *(G-829)*
Broadview Farms, Burlington *Also called Dynes Farms Inc (G-2154)*
Brockett Ocean Services Inc...425 869-1834
17455 Ne 67th Ct Ste 120 Redmond (98052) *(G-8410)*
Brockman Machine Works LLC...509 735-1354
6820 W Deschutes Ave Kennewick (99336) *(G-4633)*
Brooke Engrg Photographic Eqp...360 638-2591
37567 Vista Key Dr Ne Hansville (98340) *(G-4314)*
Brooke International, Hansville *Also called Brooke Engrg Photographic Eqp (G-4314)*
Brooks Industries, Fox Island *Also called Brooks Tactical Systems (G-4019)*
Brooks Manufacturing Co...360 733-1700
2120 Pacific St Bellingham (98229) *(G-1283)*
Brooks Products & Services...425 742-4214
6417 146th St Sw Edmonds (98026) *(G-3098)*
Brooks Properties (PA)...360 733-5170
2120 Pacific St Bellingham (98229) *(G-1284)*
Brooks Rand Inc...206 632-6206
4415 6th Ave Nw Seattle (98107) *(G-9588)*
Brooks Rand Instruments, Seattle *Also called Brooks Rand Inc (G-9588)*
Brooks Sports Inc...253 863-4343
2701 142nd Ave E Ste 100 Sumner (98390) *(G-13057)*
Brooks Steel Fabrication...360 403-9400
19320 63rd Ave Ne Arlington (98223) *(G-215)*
Brooks Tactical Systems...253 549-2703
865 9th Ave Fox Island (98333) *(G-4019)*
Broomfelds Mar Exhaust Seattle, Seattle *Also called Broomflds Wldg Met Fabrication (G-9589)*
Broomflds Wldg Met Fabrication...206 784-9267
5104 Ballard Ave Nw Seattle (98107) *(G-9589)*
Brotherhood Brewing Co LLC...509 585-6765
107 W 48th Ave Kennewick (99337) *(G-4634)*
Brothers Jewelers Inc...509 946-7989
430 Grge Wash Way Ste 102 Richland (99352) *(G-8978)*
Brothers United Inc...360 426-3959
60 W Business Park Loop Shelton (98584) *(G-11686)*
Broussards Creole Foods Inc...253 638-2098
23915 135th Pl Se Kent (98042) *(G-4824)*
Brovo Spirits LLC...206 354-3919
18808 142nd Ave Ne Ste 3b Woodinville (98072) *(G-15198)*
Browbandsbydesigncom...360 779-9339
2823 Ne Cedar Creek Way Poulsbo (98370) *(G-7952)*
Brown & Balsley Sign Co...360 705-3099
1927 State Ave Ne Olympia (98506) *(G-7243)*
Brown & Haley (PA)...253 620-3067
110 E 26th St Tacoma (98421) *(G-13210)*
Brown & Haley...253 620-3077
110 E 26th St Tacoma (98421) *(G-13211)*
Brown & Haley...253 620-3000
3501 Industry Dr E Ste D Fife (98424) *(G-3940)*
Brown Bear Car Wash, Lakewood *Also called Conocophillips Company (G-5707)*
Brown Lumber Co...509 779-4738
983 Customs Rd Curlew (99118) *(G-2844)*
Brown Road Quarry, Toledo *Also called Good Crushing Inc (G-13639)*
Brown Sugar Baking Company LLC...202 558-8422
308 22nd Ave S Ste 101 Seattle (98144) *(G-9590)*

ALPHABETIC

Brown Toes LLC ALPHABETIC SECTION

Brown Toes LLC 360 873-8407
2020 27th Pl Anacortes (98221) *(G-104)*
Brown-Mnnplis Tnk-Nrthwest LLC 360 482-1720
100 Tower Blvd Ste 99 Elma (98541) *(G-3243)*
Brownfield Manufacturing Inc 360 568-0572
16705 Tye St Se Monroe (98272) *(G-6559)*
Browns Daily Grind 360 556-3525
511 E Aycliffe Dr Shelton (98584) *(G-11687)*
Browsereport 206 948-2640
28908 6th Ave S Federal Way (98003) *(G-3718)*
Bruce & Walter Webster 360 697-3975
6009 Ne Gunderson Rd Poulsbo (98370) *(G-7953)*
Bruce Campbell, Stanwood *Also called Campbell & Associates Inc* *(G-12963)*
Bruker Axs Handheld Inc 509 783-9850
415 N Quay St Kennewick (99336) *(G-4635)*
Bruker Elemental, Kennewick *Also called Bruker Axs Handheld Inc* *(G-4635)*
Brunello 425 888-6800
7708 Center Blvd Se Snoqualmie (98065) *(G-12006)*
Brunswick Corporation 509 769-2142
1401 Bridge St Clarkston (99403) *(G-2626)*
Brush Prairie Alpacas 360 892-1011
19000 Ne 139th St Brush Prairie (98606) *(G-2031)*
Brushwood Industries Ltd 509 447-2266
102 Levitch Rd Newport (99156) *(G-7054)*
Bryan Zippro 425 881-9780
9943 181st Ave Ne Redmond (98052) *(G-8411)*
BSI, Marysville *Also called Bending Solutions Incorporated* *(G-6316)*
Bspace Corporation (PA) 208 559-7806
500 Yale Ave N 105 Seattle (98109) *(G-9591)*
Bte Printing Inc 360 675-8837
1330 Sw Barlow St Ste 1 Oak Harbor (98277) *(G-7143)*
Btpsurgical LLC 425 657-0805
24218 Se 42nd Pl Issaquah (98029) *(G-4389)*
BTS Exchange LLC 253 859-5450
1213 4th Ave N Kent (98032) *(G-4825)*
BTS Partners LLC 253 862-4622
7413 Vandermark Rd E Bonney Lake (98391) *(G-1718)*
Bubbie Bit N Bundle 360 733-8315
5 Flower Ct Bellingham (98229) *(G-1285)*
Bubbles Bakery 360 945-1816
1981 Wellington Rd Point Roberts (98281) *(G-7667)*
Bucher Aerospace Corporation 425 355-2202
1310 Industry St Ste 100 Everett (98203) *(G-3402)*
Buck Snort Industries 509 939-7777
21516 N Felspar Rd Deer Park (99006) *(G-2894)*
Buckeye Cleaning Center, Seatac *Also called Buckeye International Inc* *(G-9279)*
Buckeye International Inc 206 575-1185
18902 13th Pl S Seatac (98148) *(G-9279)*
Buckley Industries 425 286-6443
7238 Ne 147th Pl Kenmore (98028) *(G-4567)*
Buckmaster Cellars 509 627-1321
1600 Brantingham Rd Richland (99352) *(G-8979)*
Bucks Logging Inc 360 985-0758
2160 Us Highway 12 Ethel (98542) *(G-3349)*
Bucky Inc 206 545-8790
6700 Riverside Dr Seattle (98188) *(G-9592)*
Bud Clary Properties LLC 800 899-1926
1030 Commerce Ave Longview (98632) *(G-5891)*
Budd Bay Embroidery Inc 360 709-0483
6906 Martin Way E Olympia (98516) *(G-7244)*
Budd Bay Homes 360 357-6064
7029 Boston Harbor Rd Ne Olympia (98506) *(G-7245)*
Buddy Building Systems, Arlington *Also called Buddy Shelters LLC* *(G-216)*
Buddy Shelters LLC 425 239-8104
17829 59th Ave Ne Unit 13 Arlington (98223) *(G-216)*
Budget Printing & Mailing 253 872-9969
24024 85th Ave Se Woodinville (98072) *(G-15199)*
Budget Printing Center 509 736-7511
7010 W Okanogan Pl Kennewick (99336) *(G-4636)*
Budget Signs Inc 253 473-1760
1021 Fairway Dr Fircrest (98466) *(G-4000)*
Budgetbanners.com, Fircrest *Also called Budget Signs Inc* *(G-4000)*
Budo Industries LLC 206 349-8085
2727 34th Ave S Seattle (98144) *(G-9593)*
Budo LLC 206 854-1161
6212 Woodlawn Ave N Seattle (98103) *(G-9594)*
Budwiz Inc 360 508-2771
921 Lkrdge Way Sw Ste 301 Olympia (98502) *(G-7246)*
Bueler Farms Inc 360 668-5289
8626 E Lowell Larimer Rd Snohomish (98296) *(G-11883)*
Buffalo Industries Inc 206 682-9900
99 S Spokane St Seattle (98134) *(G-9595)*
Buffalo Industries LLC (PA) 206 682-9900
7979 S 180th St Kent (98032) *(G-4826)*
Buffelen Woodworking Co 253 627-1191
1901 Taylor Way Tacoma (98421) *(G-13212)*
Build-A-Bracelet 919 757-1219
29780 214th Ave Se Covington (98042) *(G-2821)*
Builder Box LLC 206 778-4753
4025 Delridge Way Sw # 210 Seattle (98106) *(G-9596)*
Builders Exchange Wash Inc 425 743-3244
2607 Wetmore Ave Everett (98201) *(G-3403)*
Builders Firstsource Inc 253 847-2900
20810 Meridian Ave E Graham (98338) *(G-4217)*
Builders Firstsource Inc 509 525-4008
115 N 11th Ave Walla Walla (99362) *(G-14775)*
Builders Firstsource Inc 509 783-8148
3919 W Clearwater Ave Kennewick (99336) *(G-4637)*
Builders Lumber-Truss Division, Richland *Also called Lumbermens Truss* *(G-9023)*
Builders Sand and Gravel Inc 425 743-3333
18827 Yew Way Snohomish (98296) *(G-11884)*
Building Automation Systems, Olympia *Also called Enertec Bas* *(G-7277)*
Building Envlope Innvtions LLC 206 985-3788
1115 N 97th St Seattle (98103) *(G-9597)*
Building Specialty Systems (PA) 425 483-6875
106 W Joanna Pl Ellensburg (98926) *(G-3185)*
Built By Daniel, Selah *Also called Daniel Cabinets LLC* *(G-11586)*
Bulldog Printing LLC 360 217-7317
10528 Friar Creek Rd Monroe (98272) *(G-6560)*
Bullene Sign 425 260-3311
2801 1st Ave Apt 1005 Seattle (98121) *(G-9598)*
Bullet Hole LLC 509 868-8884
11518 E Sprague Ave Spokane Valley (99206) *(G-12646)*
Bullet Trailer By Shiraul, Sunnyside *Also called Shiraul LLC* *(G-13141)*
Bulletin Office, Pullman *Also called Washington State University* *(G-8111)*
Bullfrog Land Co Inc 509 223-3055
1930 Loomis Oroville Rd Loomis (98827) *(G-5971)*
Bullhide Line of The Inland Em, Spokane Valley *Also called U Deck It Inc* *(G-12917)*
Bullhide Liner Corp 509 532-9007
1511 N Thierman Rd Spokane Valley (99212) *(G-12647)*
Bullock Machining Co 425 432-8261
26212 244th Ave Se Ravensdale (98051) *(G-8333)*
Bumblebar Inc 509 924-2080
3014 N Flora Rd Ste 4b Spokane Valley (99216) *(G-12648)*
Bumperchute Co 206 232-8189
8815 Se 74th Pl Mercer Island (98040) *(G-6457)*
Bunchgrass Folktoys Inc 509 334-5143
835 Se Spring St Pullman (99163) *(G-8086)*
Bungie Inc (PA) 425 440-6800
550 106th Ave Ne Ste 207 Bellevue (98004) *(G-830)*
Bungie Studios, Bellevue *Also called Bungie Inc* *(G-830)*
Bunker Hill Diagnostics 206 579-1440
718 S 38th Ct Renton (98055) *(G-8765)*
Bunnell Family Cellar 509 786-2197
548 Cabernet Ct Prosser (99350) *(G-8031)*
Bunnell Family Cellular 425 286-2964
19501 144th Ave Ne C800 Woodinville (98072) *(G-15200)*
Bunny Bear Press 425 894-0944
11667 168th Ct Ne Redmond (98052) *(G-8412)*
Bunnybud Books 360 293-4675
2308 24th St Anacortes (98221) *(G-105)*
Buoy Wear LLC 206 899-7926
3833 Cooks Hill Rd Centralia (98531) *(G-2386)*
Buren Sheet Metal Inc 509 575-1950
3801 W Washington Ave Yakima (98903) *(G-15525)*
Burg Criminal & Dui Defense 206 467-3190
720 3rd Ave Ste 2015 Seattle (98104) *(G-9599)*
Burgeners Woodworking Inc 360 694-9408
4809 Nw Fruit Valley Rd Vancouver (98660) *(G-14086)*
Burgess Logging Inc 509 763-3119
18600 River Rd Leavenworth (98826) *(G-5797)*
Buried Hatchet Tool Co LLC 253 677-9730
1310 N Menford Pl Seattle (98103) *(G-9600)*
Burien Sand and Gravel LLC 206 244-1023
818 Sw 142nd St Burien (98166) *(G-2094)*
Burke Electric 509 633-8046
102 Stevens Ave Coulee Dam (99116) *(G-2806)*
Burke Gibson LLC (PA) 253 735-4444
702 3rd St Sw Auburn (98001) *(G-398)*
Burke Meadow LLC 253 439-6092
3416 B St Nw Ste B Auburn (98001) *(G-399)*
Burlingame Steel Inc 509 535-3735
4240 E Alki Ave Spokane (99202) *(G-12161)*
Burlington Shell 360 755-0400
575 S Burlington Blvd Burlington (98233) *(G-2138)*
Burn Manufacturing Co 331 444-2876
18850 103rd Ave Sw Vashon (98070) *(G-14714)*
Burnish Leather Co 360 723-8533
4413 Addy Loop Washougal (98671) *(G-14946)*
Burns Construction Inc 360 957-4183
770 Elochoman Valley Rd Cathlamet (98612) *(G-2361)*
Burnstead Construction Co 425 635-1090
324 102nd Ave Se Ofc Bellevue (98004) *(G-831)*
Burya Logging and Trucking Inc 509 935-6816
310 E King Ave Chewelah (99109) *(G-2599)*
Busby International Inc 509 765-1313
12600 Road 3 Ne Moses Lake (98837) *(G-6689)*
Buse Timber & Sales Inc 425 258-2577
3812 28th Pl Ne Everett (98201) *(G-3404)*
Bush Woodcraft 206 323-2020
841 Rainier Ave S Seattle (98144) *(G-9601)*
Bush Woodcraft Shoji Doors, Seattle *Also called Bush Woodcraft* *(G-9601)*
Bushwacker Boats 360 969-1648
11095 Jensen Ln Burlington (98233) *(G-2139)*

Bushwhackers Brushcutting, Eastsound *Also called Kc McCoy Inc* ***(G-3038)***

Business Computing Solutions 425 644-6174
5832 155th Ave Se Bellevue (98006) ***(G-832)***

Business Equipment Center Inc (PA) 509 747-2964
603 E 2nd Ave Spokane (99202) ***(G-12162)***

Business Pulse, Bellingham *Also called Pulse Publications Inc* ***(G-1510)***

Business To Business 360 748-6848
433 N Market Blvd Chehalis (98532) ***(G-2475)***

Butch's Self Loader Hauling, Stanwood *Also called Butchs Bulldozing & Backhoe* ***(G-12962)***

Butchs Bulldozing & Backhoe 360 652-0473
8715 180th St Nw Stanwood (98292) ***(G-12962)***

Butler Design Inc 360 380-1651
7072 Kickerville Rd Ferndale (98248) ***(G-3819)***

Butler Did It 360 737-2672
2805 Ne 54th St Vancouver (98663) ***(G-14087)***

Butler Did It 360 662-0629
3851 Ne Campus Ln Bremerton (98311) ***(G-1941)***

Butler Tool & Manufacturing 425 348-7672
12322 Highway 99 Ste 92 Everett (98204) ***(G-3405)***

Butler Tools, Everett *Also called Butler Tool & Manufacturing* ***(G-3405)***

Butte Hill Winery & Vinyrd LLC 360 225-6864
362 Faloma Rd Woodland (98674) ***(G-15421)***

Butter London LLC 206 624-1085
2401 Utah Ave S Ste 320 Seattle (98134) ***(G-9602)***

Butterfield Cellars LLC 509 994-0382
6011 E 32nd Ave Spokane (99223) ***(G-12163)***

Butteville Lumber Co 360 978-6098
1680 Hwy 508 Onalaska (98570) ***(G-7447)***

Buttonsmith Inc 800 789-4364
31722 E Eugene St Unit 9 Carnation (98014) ***(G-2290)***

Buty Winery 509 527-0901
535 E Cessna Ave Walla Walla (99362) ***(G-14776)***

Buy Monthly Deals 360 321-6748
4357 Peaceful Pl Langley (98260) ***(G-5771)***

Buy More Caps Co 509 599-2944
2206 W Weile Ave Spokane (99208) ***(G-12164)***

Buyken Metal Products, Kent *Also called C&J Industries Inc* ***(G-4831)***

Buyken Metal Products Inc 253 852-0634
1216 4th Ave N Kent (98032) ***(G-4827)***

Buzs Equipment Trailers 360 694-9116
5815 Ne 78th St Vancouver (98665) ***(G-14088)***

Bw Liberty Inn Dupont 253 912-8777
18205 3rd Dr Se Bothell (98012) ***(G-1832)***

Byndl AMC LLC 855 462-9635
13555 Se 36th St Ste 270 Bellevue (98006) ***(G-833)***

Byron Automation LLC 509 653-2100
70 Locust Ln Naches (98937) ***(G-6994)***

Byron Enterprises, Pasco *Also called Oxbo International Corporation* ***(G-7610)***

Byte Brothers 425 917-8380
1004 84th Ave Ne Medina (98039) ***(G-6447)***

Byteware LLC 503 914-8020
18423 Ne 186th St Woodinville (98077) ***(G-15201)***

Bywater Welding 360 794-4618
12115 Wagner Rd Monroe (98272) ***(G-6561)***

C & C Associates Technologies 509 710-4464
11112 S Spotted Rd Cheney (99004) ***(G-2578)***

C & C Logging LLC 360 636-0300
2207 Talley Way Kelso (98626) ***(G-4519)***

C & C Meats, Seattle *Also called Custom Seafood Services Inc* ***(G-9771)***

C & C Mobile Welding LLC 360 879-5623
31206 129th Ave E Graham (98338) ***(G-4218)***

C & C Packaging Services Inc 425 673-6347
1851 Se Camano Dr Camano Island (98282) ***(G-2208)***

C & C Welding Inc 360 966-4772
8716 Trapline Rd Everson (98247) ***(G-3669)***

C & E Sprinkler 509 466-2020
4911 E Greenleaf Ave Mead (99021) ***(G-6426)***

C & H Lighting Associates Inc 253 531-1270
3904 118th St E Tacoma (98446) ***(G-13213)***

C & H Logging Inc 509 364-3420
105 Trout Lake Hwy Glenwood (98619) ***(G-4178)***

C & J Logging Co Inc 360 484-7256
800 State Route 4 Naselle (98638) ***(G-7012)***

C & K General Contractors, Inchelium *Also called Carl Emil Seastrom* ***(G-4371)***

C & M Country Creations 253 535-3327
6221 S Stevens St Tacoma (98409) ***(G-13214)***

C & M Woodworks 253 503-9440
25606 69th Ave E Graham (98338) ***(G-4219)***

C & R Electric Motor Service 360 736-2521
820 N Tower Ave Centralia (98531) ***(G-2387)***

C & S Welding Inc 253 520-2095
22610 85th Pl S Kent (98031) ***(G-4828)***

C & V Machinery 509 657-3392
1562 Swent Rd Endicott (99125) ***(G-3263)***

C A M, Vancouver *Also called Claudes Accurate Machining* ***(G-14120)***

C A P S, Kent *Also called Central Admxture Phrm Svcs Inc* ***(G-4846)***

C and R Coatings LLC 509 949-8515
5260 State Route 24 Moxee (98936) ***(G-6876)***

C D Boat Works 360 942-3669
1001 Harrison Ave Raymond (98577) ***(G-8344)***

C D I, Bellingham *Also called Conveyor Dynamics Inc* ***(G-1305)***

C Davis Software Con 847 436-6225
9004 1st Pl Se Lake Stevens (98258) ***(G-5636)***

C E Publications Inc 425 806-5200
18323 Bothell Everett Hwy # 310 Bothell (98012) ***(G-1833)***

C E Weekly, Bothell *Also called C E Publications Inc* ***(G-1833)***

C G H Imports, Vancouver *Also called Columbia Gem House Inc* ***(G-14130)***

C H S, Othello *Also called CHS Inc* ***(G-7492)***

C H W Enterprises Inc 360 425-8700
1341 Industrial Way Longview (98632) ***(G-5892)***

C J & M Transport Inc 206 510-8296
27430 72nd Ave S Kent (98032) ***(G-4829)***

C J Warren & Sons Well Drlg 509 924-3872
3005 S Best Rd Veradale (99037) ***(G-14749)***

C Johnson Lumber Company Inc 425 353-4222
610 Possession View Ln Mukilteo (98275) ***(G-6901)***

C M F Industries Inc 425 282-5065
20614 84th Ave S Kent (98032) ***(G-4830)***

C N C Repair & Sales Inc 408 331-1970
1770 Front St Ste 142 Lynden (98264) ***(G-6004)***

C P O, Seattle *Also called Center For Prosthetic* ***(G-9652)***

C Quartz Inc 360 393-1254
5863 Portal Way Unit 104 Ferndale (98248) ***(G-3820)***

C R S, Spokane *Also called Commerce Retail Sales Inc* ***(G-12191)***

C S Adventurecorp LLC 425 679-1172
6470 Portal Manor Dr Ferndale (98248) ***(G-3821)***

C S L, Auburn *Also called Container Stuffers LLC* ***(G-414)***

C S W, Tumwater *Also called Custom Source Woodworking Inc* ***(G-13868)***

C Swanson Logging 360 886-0237
29228 218th Pl Se Black Diamond (98010) ***(G-1646)***

C T Sales Inc 253 874-8737
37405 Pacific Hwy S Federal Way (98003) ***(G-3719)***

C T Specialties 360 786-0274
2815 37th Ave Sw Ste 120 Tumwater (98512) ***(G-13854)***

C V L, Duvall *Also called Cherry Valley Logging Company* ***(G-2981)***

C W Nielsen Manufacturing 360 748-8835
225 Nw Cascade Ave Chehalis (98532) ***(G-2476)***

C&D Zodiac Inc 360 653-2211
12810 State Ave Marysville (98271) ***(G-6318)***

C&J Industries Inc 253 852-0634
1216 4th Ave N Kent (98032) ***(G-4831)***

C&J Offshore Systems LLC 360 293-4200
9117 Molly Ln Ste 110 Anacortes (98221) ***(G-106)***

C&K Enterprize LLC 509 448-2866
4704 S Tampa Dr Spokane (99223) ***(G-12165)***

C&T Northwest Services 509 680-4890
1159 Orin Rice Rd Colville (99114) ***(G-2742)***

C-Quarts, Ferndale *Also called C Quartz Inc* ***(G-3820)***

C4 Enterprises Inc 425 347-9200
4605 116th St Sw Mukilteo (98275) ***(G-6902)***

Ca Inc 509 252-5080
505 W Riverside Ave # 500 Spokane (99201) ***(G-12166)***

Ca Inc 425 201-3500
14475 Ne 24th St Ste 210 Bellevue (98007) ***(G-834)***

Cabi 425 413-8772
17525 190th Ave Se Renton (98058) ***(G-8766)***

Cabin Fever Media 509 544-2155
1736 N 21st Ave Pasco (99301) ***(G-7557)***

Cabin Mill LLC 509 235-1808
20321 W Sterling Rd Cheney (99004) ***(G-2579)***

Cabinet Aesthetics 808 268-1822
13827 436th Ave Se North Bend (98045) ***(G-7103)***

Cabinet Fx 425 879-6690
6516 66th St Ne Marysville (98270) ***(G-6319)***

Cabinet Guys 425 344-5882
10802 40th Ave Se Everett (98208) ***(G-3406)***

Cabinet Masters Inc 360 695-6615
7105 Ne 40th Ave Ste E Vancouver (98661) ***(G-14089)***

Cabinet Refacing of Seattle 425 405-7961
22255 Ne Wdnvlle Dvall Rd Woodinville (98077) ***(G-15202)***

Cabinet Tech LLC 509 575-0180
106 W Pine St Yakima (98902) ***(G-15526)***

Cabinets & Countertops LLC 206 933-9385
3030 64th Ave Sw Seattle (98116) ***(G-9603)***

Cabinets Inc 360 778-1780
2225 Old Lakeway Dr Bellingham (98229) ***(G-1286)***

Cablecraft Motion Controls LLC 253 475-1080
4401 S Orchard St Tacoma (98466) ***(G-13215)***

Cachanilla Design 425 207-6396
21110 84th Ave S Ste 202 Kent (98032) ***(G-4832)***

Cadaretta 509 525-1352
315 E Main St Walla Walla (99362) ***(G-14777)***

Cadee Distillery LLC 360 969-6041
8912 Hwy 525 Clinton (98236) ***(G-2685)***

Cadee Distillery LLC 360 969-5565
12 De Bruyn Ave Langley (98260) ***(G-5772)***

Cadena Printing 253 951-7545
27120 121st Pl Se Kent (98030) ***(G-4833)***

Cadence, Seattle *Also called Leaf Cellars LLC* ***(G-10393)***

Cadence Aerospace LLC 425 353-0405
2300 Merrill Creek Pkwy Everett (98203) ***(G-3407)***

Cadence Aerospace LLC 425 353-0405
2600 94th St Sw Ste 150 Everett (98204) ***(G-3408)***

Cadence Design Systems Inc ALPHABETIC SECTION

Cadence Design Systems Inc.....425 451-2360
320 120th Ave Ne Ste B103 Bellevue (98005) ***(G-835)***
Cadence Neuroscience Inc.....425 681-6863
2036 223rd Pl Ne Sammamish (98074) ***(G-9194)***
Cadet, Vancouver *Also called Glen Dimplex Americas Company* ***(G-14257)***
Cadman Inc (HQ).....425 867-1234
7554 185th Ave Ne Ste 100 Redmond (98052) ***(G-8413)***
Cadman (rock) Inc (HQ).....425 867-1234
18816 Ne 80th St Redmond (98052) ***(G-8414)***
Cadman (seattle) Inc.....425 316-9100
18427 Bothell Everett Hwy Mill Creek (98012) ***(G-6502)***
Cadman Administration, Redmond *Also called Cadman Inc* ***(G-8413)***
Cadman Holding Company Inc.....425 868-1234
7735 178th Pl Ne Redmond (98052) ***(G-8415)***
Cadwallader and Stern LLC.....206 931-8018
1122 E Pike St Seattle (98122) ***(G-9604)***
Cadwell Laboratories Inc.....509 735-6481
909 N Kellogg St Kennewick (99336) ***(G-4638)***
Caesar Stone, Kent *Also called Caesarstone Usa Inc* ***(G-4834)***
Caesarstone Usa Inc.....425 251-8668
7832 S 198th St Kent (98032) ***(G-4834)***
Cafe Las Americas.....253 272-0644
1205 N J St Tacoma (98403) ***(G-13216)***
Caffe Appassionato Inc (PA).....206 281-8040
4001 21st Ave W Seattle (98199) ***(G-9605)***
Caffe Luca Coffee Roasters, Tukwila *Also called Joes Garage LLC* ***(G-13758)***
Caffe Lusso, Redmond *Also called Roastmasters LLC* ***(G-8653)***
Caitac USA Corp.....360 671-1700
205 W Smith Rd Bellingham (98226) ***(G-1287)***
Cake Time Unique Sweet, Dupont *Also called Cake Time Unque Tste Sweet LLC* ***(G-2956)***
Cake Time Unque Tste Sweet LLC.....253 886-9366
1649 Palisade Blvd Dupont (98327) ***(G-2956)***
Cakes Be We.....509 460-1399
2625 W Bruneau Pl Kennewick (99336) ***(G-4639)***
Caledonia Bay Cabinets Inc.....253 905-7368
34251 18th Pl S Federal Way (98003) ***(G-3720)***
Calendars Northwest LLC (PA).....425 454-1145
8314 Hunts Point Pl Hunts Point (98004) ***(G-4366)***
Calhoun Tanks and Services.....253 517-7356
301 Porter Way Milton (98354) ***(G-6533)***
Calhoun Tnks & Servces Inc.....206 870-0802
3320 Lincoln Ave Tacoma (98421) ***(G-13217)***
Calib Designs LLC.....206 548-9217
4225 Francis Ave N Apt A Seattle (98103) ***(G-9606)***
Caliber Precision Inc.....360 333-7602
1824 Railroad Ave Mount Vernon (98273) ***(G-6782)***
Calico Press LLC.....206 855-1903
13700 Sunrise Dr Ne Bainbridge Island (98110) ***(G-619)***
California Coating.....609 405-2683
1801 Se Commerce Ave Battle Ground (98604) ***(G-694)***
California Industrial Faciliti.....360 863-9333
13960 179th Ave Se Monroe (98272) ***(G-6562)***
Calkins Publishing Company LLC.....425 836-3548
2125 Sahalee Dr E Smmmishe Sammamish (98074) ***(G-9195)***
Callahan Cellars.....425 877-1842
19501 144th Ave Ne D900 Woodinville (98072) ***(G-15203)***
Callahan Manufacturing Inc.....509 346-2208
219 Balsom St Royal City (99357) ***(G-9167)***
Callidus Software Inc.....503 579-4484
13115 Ne 4th St Ste 115 Vancouver (98684) ***(G-14090)***
Calling Crane Publishing, Olympia *Also called Raven Radio Theater* ***(G-7378)***
Callison Architecture LLC.....206 623-4646
1420 5th Ave Ste 2400 Seattle (98101) ***(G-9607)***
Callisons Inc (PA).....360 412-3340
2400 Callison Rd Ne Lacey (98516) ***(G-5536)***
Callisons Inc.....206 545-3900
520 Pike St Ste 2500 Seattle (98101) ***(G-9608)***
Callisons Inc.....360 748-3316
799 N National Ave Chehalis (98532) ***(G-2477)***
Calportland.....206 764-3000
5975 E Marginal Way S Seattle (98134) ***(G-9609)***
Calportland Company.....253 912-8500
4301 Pioneer Ave Dupont (98327) ***(G-2957)***
Calportland Company.....360 423-8112
1100 3rd Ave Longview (98632) ***(G-5893)***
Calportland Company.....425 486-3281
6423 Ne 175th St Kenmore (98028) ***(G-4568)***
Calportland Company.....206 764-3075
5900 W Marginal Way Sw Seattle (98106) ***(G-9610)***
Calportland Company.....360 892-5100
1441 Guild Rd Woodland (98674) ***(G-15422)***
Calportland Company.....206 764-3000
360 Quarry Rd Port Ludlow (98365) ***(G-7764)***
Calportland Company.....360 892-5100
18606 Se 1st St Vancouver (98684) ***(G-14091)***
Calson Industries, Kent *Also called Eagle Bev & Accessory Pdts LLC* ***(G-4881)***
Calvert Company Inc (PA).....360 693-0971
218 N V St Vancouver (98661) ***(G-14092)***
Calvert Company Inc.....360 835-3110
3559 S Truman Rd Washougal (98671) ***(G-14947)***
Calypso Medical Tech Inc.....206 254-0600
2101 4th Ave Ste 500 Seattle (98121) ***(G-9611)***
Camano Island Licensing.....360 387-4700
811 N Sunrise Blvd Ste D Stanwood (98282) ***(G-12954)***
Camano Mold Inc.....360 387-0961
122 Ne Camano Dr Camano Island (98282) ***(G-2209)***
Camarda Corporation.....206 463-9227
12526 Sw Bank Rd Vashon (98070) ***(G-14715)***
Camas Auto License.....360 835-2977
3252 3rd Ave Lacamas Ctr Camas (98607) ***(G-2236)***
Camas Division, Camas *Also called Karcher North America Inc* ***(G-2261)***
Camas-Washougal Post-Record.....360 834-2141
425 Ne 4th Ave Camas (98607) ***(G-2237)***
Cambria Corporation.....206 782-8380
1328 N 128th St Seattle (98133) ***(G-9612)***
Camco Inc.....866 856-4826
633 N Mildred St Ste C Tacoma (98406) ***(G-13218)***
Camco Tool & Prototype Inc.....360 966-1106
5395 Everson Goshen Rd Bellingham (98226) ***(G-1288)***
Camelot Treasures.....360 829-9774
12722 State Route 165 E Buckley (98321) ***(G-2050)***
Cameron International Corp.....425 438-8726
834 80th St Sw Ste 300 Everett (98203) ***(G-3409)***
Cameron Steel Fabrication.....360 403-9400
19320 63rd Ave Ne Arlington (98223) ***(G-217)***
Camille.....206 284-0407
2333 W Plymouth St Apt 1 Seattle (98199) ***(G-9613)***
Caminova Inc.....206 919-2110
15325 34th Dr Se Mill Creek (98012) ***(G-6503)***
Camoflage.....425 744-0764
5812 159th St Sw Edmonds (98026) ***(G-3099)***
Camp Time Inc.....509 928-3051
3310 N Tschirley Rd Spokane Valley (99216) ***(G-12649)***
Campbell & Associates Inc.....360 652-9502
17410 Marine Dr Stanwood (98292) ***(G-12963)***
Campbell Enterprises, Vancouver *Also called Campbell Pet Company* ***(G-14093)***
Campbell Enterprises, Tahuya *Also called G B C Enterprises Inc* ***(G-13610)***
Campbell Maritime Inc.....206 794-0232
1515 Fairview Ave E Seattle (98102) ***(G-9614)***
Campbell Pet Company (PA).....360 892-9786
9606 Ne 126th Ave Vancouver (98682) ***(G-14093)***
Campbell Soup Company.....425 415-2000
22505 State Route 9 Se Woodinville (98072) ***(G-15204)***
Campusce Corporation.....206 686-8003
1201 3rd Ave Ste 1580 Seattle (98101) ***(G-9615)***
Cams-USA, Kent *Also called J & R Commercial Inc* ***(G-4963)***
Cams-Usa Inc.....253 639-3890
30245 148th Ave Se Kent (98042) ***(G-4835)***
Camss Shelters, Monroe *Also called California Industrial Faciliti* ***(G-6562)***
Camtronics Inc.....425 487-0013
18230 130th Pl Ne Bothell (98011) ***(G-1753)***
Camwest Inc.....425 776-7900
2228 133rd St Sw Lynnwood (98087) ***(G-6086)***
Can AM Coatings.....360 386-9692
1110 5th St Marysville (98270) ***(G-6320)***
Can AM Fabrication Inc.....360 653-2245
4803 56th Pl Ne Marysville (98270) ***(G-6321)***
Canam Steel Corporation.....360 329-7048
2099 Sheller Rd Sunnyside (98944) ***(G-13115)***
Canam Steel Corporation.....509 837-7008
312 Se Stnmill Dr Ste 147 Vancouver (98684) ***(G-14094)***
Candela Technologies Inc.....360 380-1618
2417 Main St Ste 201 Ferndale (98248) ***(G-3822)***
Candeo Candle Factory LLC.....360 524-2310
18720 Se 21st St Vancouver (98683) ***(G-14095)***
Candy Fix.....253 770-8242
14414 133rd Street Ct E Orting (98360) ***(G-7475)***
Canelle Citron.....206 241-4657
10438 40th Ave Sw Seattle (98146) ***(G-9616)***
Canflex (usa) Inc.....206 282-8233
412 30th St Anacortes (98221) ***(G-107)***
Canfor USA Corporation (HQ).....360 647-2434
4395 Curtis Rd Bellingham (98226) ***(G-1289)***
Canfor USA Corporation.....360 647-2434
4395 Curtis Rd Bellingham (98226) ***(G-1290)***
Cannabis Leaf Incorporated.....206 430-6250
4500 9th Ave Ne Seattle (98105) ***(G-9617)***
Cannaman.....360 597-4850
6212 Ne 152nd Ave Vancouver (98682) ***(G-14096)***
Cannon Ball Industries.....206 781-1833
3411 Nw 59th St Seattle (98107) ***(G-9618)***
Cannon Engineering Solutions.....360 840-6731
1463 W Uncas Rd Port Townsend (98368) ***(G-7871)***
Cannon Lauree.....509 627-0505
1204 S Clodfelter Rd Kennewick (99338) ***(G-4640)***
Cannon Machine Products Inc.....509 627-0505
1204 S Clodfelter Rd Kennewick (99338) ***(G-4641)***
Cannonbot Games LLC.....510 473-6871
906 W 2nd Ave Ste 100 Spokane (99201) ***(G-12167)***
Canoe Ridge Vineyard.....206 267-5252
1910 Frview Ave E Ste 400 Seattle (98102) ***(G-9619)***
Canoe Ridge Vineyard LLC (PA).....509 527-0885
1102 W Cherry St Walla Walla (99362) ***(G-14778)***
Canon Chropractic, Tacoma *Also called Peryl Professional Touch* ***(G-13465)***

Canopy World Inc (PA).....253 531-5192
10025 Pacific Ave S Tacoma (98444) ***(G-13219)***
Canopy World Inc.....206 824-3877
22820 Pacific Hwy S Des Moines (98198) ***(G-2932)***
Canopy World of Seattle, Tacoma *Also called Canopy World Inc* ***(G-13219)***
Canter-Berry Farms.....253 939-2706
19102 Se Green Valley Rd Auburn (98092) ***(G-400)***
Canterburys Dental Ceramics.....509 966-3622
7900 Easy St Yakima (98903) ***(G-15527)***
Canvas.....206 829-9858
600 Elliott Ave W Seattle (98119) ***(G-9620)***
Canvas Creations.....425 210-5993
209 Main Rd Tonasket (98855) ***(G-13647)***
Canvas Man.....360 293-2812
401 34th St Ste B Anacortes (98221) ***(G-108)***
Canvas Shoppe.....360 457-2773
255650 Highway 101 Port Angeles (98362) ***(G-7691)***
Canvas Supply Co Inc.....206 784-0711
4711 Ballard Ave Nw Seattle (98107) ***(G-9621)***
Canvas Traditions.....206 313-0223
5267 Shilshole Ave Nw # 106 Seattle (98107) ***(G-9622)***
Canyon Creek Cabinet Company.....509 921-7807
10221 E Montgomery Dr B Spokane Valley (99206) ***(G-12650)***
Cap Sante International Inc (PA).....360 293-3145
2915 W Ave Anacortes (98221) ***(G-109)***
Cap Sante Marine Ltd (PA).....360 293-3145
2915 W Ave Anacortes (98221) ***(G-110)***
Cap Supplies, Puyallup *Also called R&J Industries LLC* ***(G-8233)***
Cape Dissapointment State Park.....360 642-3078
Loop Robert Gray Dr Ilwaco (98624) ***(G-4368)***
Cape Greig LLC.....206 545-9501
900 Powell Ave Sw Renton (98057) ***(G-8767)***
Cape Horn Maintenance Co.....360 826-9105
7849 Fir St Concrete (98237) ***(G-2784)***
Cape Point Press LLC.....206 324-2126
7406 Latona Ave Ne Unit B Seattle (98115) ***(G-9623)***
Cape San Lucas Fishing LP.....425 688-1288
10500 Ne 8th St Ste 1888 Bellevue (98004) ***(G-836)***
Capital A Publications LL.....509 279-0832
1429 E 13th Ave Spokane (99202) ***(G-12168)***
Capital Heating & Cooling Inc.....360 491-7450
1218 Carpenter Rd Se Lacey (98503) ***(G-5537)***
Capital Hope Innovations Inc.....360 480-9154
60 Skagit Ky Bellevue (98006) ***(G-837)***
Capital Industrial Inc.....360 786-1890
2649 R W Johnson Blvd Sw Tumwater (98512) ***(G-13855)***
Capital Industrial Supply Inc.....360 786-1890
2649 R W Johnson Blvd Sw Tumwater (98512) ***(G-13856)***
Capital Industries Inc.....206 762-8585
5801 3rd Ave S Seattle (98108) ***(G-9624)***
Capital Instruments Ltd.....425 271-3756
6210 Lake Wash Blvd Se Bellevue (98006) ***(G-838)***
Capital Tool Co.....206 240-7470
91 S Royal Brougham Way Seattle (98134) ***(G-9625)***
Capitol City Press Inc.....360 943-3556
2975 37th Ave Sw Tumwater (98512) ***(G-13857)***
Capitol Optical Corp.....360 352-7502
8719 Commerce Place Dr Ne D Lacey (98516) ***(G-5538)***
Capstan Fund.....206 626-0800
800 5th Ave Ste 4100 Seattle (98104) ***(G-9626)***
Capsule Urn LLC.....360 695-2618
293 Date St Vancouver (98661) ***(G-14097)***
Captain T'S, Port Angeles *Also called Johnnie Montice* ***(G-7719)***
Captivating Covers.....800 975-8198
12628 Intrurban Ave S # 120 Tukwila (98168) ***(G-13710)***
Captive Plastics LLC.....253 627-2151
635 E 15th St Tacoma (98421) ***(G-13220)***
Captive Spirits, Seattle *Also called Bctld LLC* ***(G-9503)***
Caraustar Industrial and Con.....253 627-1197
808 E 26th St Tacoma (98421) ***(G-13221)***
Caraustar Industrial and Con.....253 272-1648
902 E 11th St Ste 300 Tacoma (98421) ***(G-13222)***
Caraustar Industries Inc.....253 272-1648
902 E 11th St Ste 300 Tacoma (98421) ***(G-13223)***
Caraustar Industries Inc.....360 423-3420
620 11th Ave Longview (98632) ***(G-5894)***
Caravel Gourmet, Everett *Also called Seasalt Superstore LLC* ***(G-3608)***
Carbide Online Sales LLC.....253 476-1338
4007 Bridgeport Way W F3 University Place (98466) ***(G-13962)***
Carbide Web Sales LLC.....253 353-2595
4007 Bridgeport Way W F4 University Place (98466) ***(G-13963)***
Carbitex Inc.....509 591-9775
1426 E 3rd Ave Bldg B Kennewick (99337) ***(G-4642)***
Carbon Aerospace.....206 697-3832
1318 Nw Woodbine Way Seattle (98177) ***(G-9627)***
Carbon Consultants LLC.....509 637-2520
310 S Larch St Bingen (98605) ***(G-1634)***
Carbon Cycle Crush LLC.....509 476-3667
224 Appleway Ave Oroville (98844) ***(G-7462)***
Carbon Northwest.....425 820-0873
7422 Ne 120th Pl Kirkland (98034) ***(G-5297)***
Carbon Salon, Seattle *Also called Scope 5 Inc* ***(G-11031)***
Carbs Unlimited, Auburn *Also called Carburetors Unlimited Inc* ***(G-401)***
Carburetors Unlimited Inc (PA).....253 833-4106
727 22nd St Ne Auburn (98002) ***(G-401)***
Cardeas Pharma Corporation.....206 973-1026
2025 1st Ave Ste 1200 Seattle (98121) ***(G-9628)***
Cardiac Insight Inc.....206 596-2060
2375 130th Ave Ne Ste 101 Bellevue (98005) ***(G-839)***
Cardiac Self Assessment, Spokane Valley *Also called Wesley Todd* ***(G-12934)***
Cardinal Associates Inc.....360 693-1883
1000 W 8th St Vancouver (98660) ***(G-14098)***
Cardinal Cg, Tumwater *Also called Cardinal Glass Industries Inc* ***(G-13858)***
Cardinal Clean.....360 629-4399
8430 S Lake Ketchum Rd Stanwood (98292) ***(G-12964)***
Cardinal Corp.....360 242-4400
214 Downie Rd Chehalis (98532) ***(G-2478)***
Cardinal Fg, Winlock *Also called Cardinal Glass Industries Inc* ***(G-15147)***
Cardinal Fg - Winlock, Winlock *Also called Cardinal Glass Industries Inc* ***(G-15146)***
Cardinal Glass Industries Inc.....360 242-4300
545 Avery Rd W Winlock (98596) ***(G-15146)***
Cardinal Glass Industries Inc.....360 242-4336
545 Avery Rd W Winlock (98596) ***(G-15147)***
Cardinal Glass Industries Inc.....360 242-4400
214 Downie Rd Chehalis (98532) ***(G-2479)***
Cardinal Glass Industries Inc.....360 956-9002
700 Pat Kennedy Way Sw Tumwater (98501) ***(G-13858)***
Cardinal Health Inc.....206 763-8500
421 S Michigan St Seattle (98108) ***(G-9629)***
Cardinal Health 414 LLC.....206 763-4411
5030 1st Ave S Ste 110 Seattle (98134) ***(G-9630)***
Cardinal Industrial Finishes.....425 483-5665
19230 144th Ave Ne Ste A Woodinville (98072) ***(G-15205)***
Cardinal Tg.....360 242-4352
214 Downie Rd Chehalis (98532) ***(G-2480)***
Cardiodynamics Intl Corp.....208 332-2502
21919 30th Dr Se Bothell (98021) ***(G-1834)***
Cardlock Vending Inc.....888 487-5040
3922 148th St Se Ste 105 Bothell (98012) ***(G-1835)***
Cardswapper LLC.....253 549-8600
925 34th Ave Nw Gig Harbor (98335) ***(G-4084)***
Care Engraving Company.....360 456-0831
2131 Agate Ct Se Lacey (98503) ***(G-5539)***
Care Zone Inc.....888 407-7785
1463 E Republican St Seattle (98112) ***(G-9631)***
Care Zone Inc.....206 707-9127
1520 Bellevue Ave Ste 202 Seattle (98122) ***(G-9632)***
Career Development Software.....360 696-3529
5905 Buena Vista Dr Vancouver (98661) ***(G-14099)***
Careks Country Custom Meats.....509 276-2237
3125 W Findley Rd Deer Park (99006) ***(G-2895)***
Carezone, Seattle *Also called Care Zone Inc* ***(G-9632)***
Cargill Incorporated.....360 757-4012
16939 State Route 20 Burlington (98233) ***(G-2140)***
Cargill Incorporated.....509 854-1035
700 Ruehl Way Granger (98932) ***(G-4260)***
Cargill Incorporated.....360 656-5784
5744 3rd Ave Ferndale (98248) ***(G-3823)***
Cargo Express Inc.....253 630-7294
15657 Se 272nd St Covington (98042) ***(G-2822)***
Caribou Creek Logging Inc.....509 962-6700
1921 Riverbottom Rd Ellensburg (98926) ***(G-3186)***
Carl Emil Seastrom.....509 722-5414
190 Kewa Meteor Rd Inchelium (99138) ***(G-4371)***
Carl Zapffe Inc (PA).....206 364-1919
12004 Aurora Ave N Seattle (98133) ***(G-9633)***
Carl' S Mower and Saw, Ferndale *Also called Carls Mower and Saw* ***(G-3824)***
Carlisle Inc.....425 251-0700
7911 S 188th St Ste 100 Kent (98032) ***(G-4836)***
Carlisle Interconnect Tech, Kent *Also called Carlisle Inc* ***(G-4836)***
Carlisle Interconnect Tech Inc.....425 656-5235
24023 104th Ave Se Kent (98030) ***(G-4837)***
Carlisle Interconnect Tech Inc.....425 291-3991
7911 S 188th St Ste 100 Kent (98032) ***(G-4838)***
Carls Mower and Saw.....360 384-0799
6209 Portal Way Ferndale (98248) ***(G-3824)***
Carls Powder Coating.....425 864-7950
46722 Se 161st St North Bend (98045) ***(G-7104)***
Carlson & Fitzwater LLC.....425 941-4020
23708 139th Dr Se Snohomish (98296) ***(G-11885)***
Carlson and Sons Logging Inc.....360 795-3068
1010 Beaver Creek Rd Cathlamet (98612) ***(G-2362)***
Carlson Brothers Inc.....253 472-9232
861 S 38th St Tacoma (98418) ***(G-13224)***
Carlson Brothers Mfg Jewelers, Tacoma *Also called Carlson Brothers Inc* ***(G-13224)***
Carlson Custom.....360 756-0351
1351 Olympic Way Bellingham (98225) ***(G-1291)***
Carlson Formetec, Sumner *Also called CFI Blue Sky II LLC* ***(G-13058)***
Carlson Login Inc.....360 795-3068
1010 Beaver Creek Rd Cathlamet (98612) ***(G-2363)***
Carlson Machine Works Inc.....509 535-0028
3310 E Trent Ave Spokane (99202) ***(G-12169)***
Carlson Sheet Metal Works Inc.....509 535-4228
3621 E Broadway Ave Spokane (99202) ***(G-12170)***

ALPHABETIC

(PA)=Parent Co (HQ)=Headquarters (DH)=Div Headquarters
2019 Washington Manufacturers Register
697

Carlyle Holdings Inc (HQ)...425 251-0700
7911 S 188th St Ste 100 Kent (98032) ***(G-4839)***
Carlyle Printing...360 537-0266
511 M St Hoquiam (98550) ***(G-4330)***
Carnitech US Inc...206 781-1827
1112 Nw Leary Way Seattle (98107) ***(G-9634)***
Carol Braden Inc...206 715-9397
2224 E Miller St Seattle (98112) ***(G-9635)***
Carpenter Drilling LLC...509 627-6642
7 S Goose Gap Rd Benton City (99320) ***(G-1603)***
Carpet Plus LLC...253 874-0525
34515 16th Ave S Federal Way (98003) ***(G-3721)***
Carpinito Brothers Inc...253 627-3121
2351 Lincoln Ave Tacoma (98421) ***(G-13225)***
Carquest Auto Parts, Lynden *Also called S & H Auto Parts Inc* ***(G-6051)***
Carrier Transports Inc...509 452-0136
1008 N 1st St Yakima (98901) ***(G-15528)***
Carrolls Printing Inc...360 345-1399
1976 S Market Blvd Chehalis (98532) ***(G-2481)***
Carrot Medical LLC...425 318-8089
22122 20th Ave Se Ste 166 Bothell (98021) ***(G-1836)***
Carry Gear Solutions LLC...206 957-6800
2125 Western Ave Ste 300 Seattle (98121) ***(G-9636)***
Carsoe US Inc...206 408-5869
1112 Nw Leary Way Seattle (98107) ***(G-9637)***
Carson NC Inc...509 427-8616
91 Cloverdale Ave Carson (98610) ***(G-2304)***
Carson/Corbett LLC...206 624-8266
2010 Airport Way S Seattle (98134) ***(G-9638)***
Carson/Corbett LLC (PA)...206 524-9782
1531 Ne 89th St Seattle (98115) ***(G-9639)***
Carsos Pasta Company Inc...206 283-8227
5530 208th St Sw Lynnwood (98036) ***(G-6087)***
Carssow John...425 820-7995
13504 Ne 148th St Woodinville (98072) ***(G-15206)***
Cartech Industries Inc...360 693-3616
4016 Ne 44th St Vancouver (98661) ***(G-14100)***
Carter Bag Co, Enumclaw *Also called Carter Lift Bag Inc* ***(G-3280)***
Carter Game Testers...360 326-3245
206 Ne 126th Ave Vancouver (98684) ***(G-14101)***
Carter Lift Bag Inc...360 886-2302
29500 Se Green Riv Enumclaw (98022) ***(G-3280)***
Cartogram Inc...425 628-0395
10400 Ne 4th St Ste 500 Bellevue (98004) ***(G-840)***
Cartridge Care Inc...360 459-8845
1314 Lebanon St Se Lacey (98503) ***(G-5540)***
Cartridge World...509 469-9711
1360 N Louisiana St Ste B Kennewick (99336) ***(G-4643)***
Casaba Security LLC...888 869-6708
16625 Redmond Way Ste M Redmond (98052) ***(G-8416)***
Cascade Ales Company...360 520-6040
3621 Oak St Longview (98632) ***(G-5895)***
Cascade Apparel & Embroidery...360 253-3022
16505 Se 1st St Ste H Vancouver (98684) ***(G-14102)***
Cascade Arcft Conversions LLC...509 635-1212
903 Grinnell Rd Garfield (99130) ***(G-4066)***
Cascade Aviation Services Inc...425 493-1707
15318 39th Ave Ne Marysville (98271) ***(G-6322)***
Cascade Brush Company...509 965-6603
725 E Viola Ave Yakima (98901) ***(G-15529)***
Cascade Cabinetry LLC...253 395-6670
19411 66th Ave S Kent (98032) ***(G-4840)***
Cascade Cabinets, Marysville *Also called Smokey Point Custom Cabinets* ***(G-6386)***
Cascade Caning...360 258-1738
5305 E 18th St Vancouver (98661) ***(G-14103)***
Cascade Chalet...206 463-4628
9709 Sw Burton Dr Vashon (98070) ***(G-14716)***
Cascade Cnc LLC...360 366-2580
2772 Birch Bay Lynden Rd Custer (98240) ***(G-2853)***
Cascade Coffee Inc (HQ)...425 347-3995
1525 75th St Sw Ste 100 Everett (98203) ***(G-3410)***
Cascade Concrete...360 354-8901
8987 Jasmine Ln Lynden (98264) ***(G-6005)***
Cascade Concrete Industries...360 757-2900
1912 S Burlington Blvd Burlington (98233) ***(G-2141)***
Cascade Country Cabins...509 427-8515
1080 Sw Briggs St Stevenson (98648) ***(G-13009)***
Cascade Custom Jewelers...253 535-2121
4302 S J St Tacoma (98418) ***(G-13226)***
Cascade Dafo Inc...360 543-9306
1360 Sunset Ave Ferndale (98248) ***(G-3825)***
Cascade Designs Inc (PA)...206 505-9500
4000 1st Ave S Seattle (98134) ***(G-9640)***
Cascade Designs Inc...206 505-9500
3800 1st Ave S Seattle (98134) ***(G-9641)***
Cascade Designs Inc...206 505-9500
4000 1st Ave S Seattle (98134) ***(G-9642)***
Cascade Earth Sciences, Spokane Valley *Also called Valmont Industries Inc* ***(G-12925)***
Cascade Family Flyers...425 750-4249
1429 Avenue D Snohomish (98290) ***(G-11886)***
Cascade Flying Service LLC...509 635-1212
903 Grinnell Rd Garfield (99130) ***(G-4067)***
Cascade Gasket & Mfg Co Inc...253 854-1800
8825 S 228th St Kent (98031) ***(G-4841)***
Cascade Grooming Supplies, Soap Lake *Also called 3 CS* ***(G-12036)***
Cascade Growers LLC...530 919-3431
166 Benson Creek Dr Twisp (98856) ***(G-13909)***
Cascade Hardwoods LLC...360 748-3317
158 Ribelin Rd Chehalis (98532) ***(G-2482)***
Cascade Hydraulics and Machine...360 423-1082
420 Industrial Way Longview (98632) ***(G-5896)***
Cascade Ice Sparkling Water, Everett *Also called Unique Beverage Company LLC* ***(G-3643)***
Cascade Indus & Hydraulic LLC...509 452-1752
3315 Main St Union Gap (98903) ***(G-13924)***
Cascade Intgrtive Medicine LLC...425 391-5270
450 Nw Gilman Blvd # 201 Issaquah (98027) ***(G-4390)***
Cascade Joinery Inc...360 527-0119
1349 Pacific Pl Ste 103 Ferndale (98248) ***(G-3826)***
Cascade Manufacturing...206 762-3750
1124 29th St Nw Auburn (98001) ***(G-402)***
Cascade Marble & Granite...509 533-0476
723 N Napa St Spokane (99202) ***(G-12171)***
Cascade Medical Technologies...360 896-6944
406 Se 131st Ave Ste 205 Vancouver (98683) ***(G-14104)***
Cascade Metallurgical Inc...253 838-0477
21213 76th Ave S Kent (98032) ***(G-4842)***
Cascade Microphones, Olympia *Also called Bayview Pro Audio Inc* ***(G-7235)***
Cascade Mobile Mix (PA)...253 833-1956
6723 304th St E Graham (98338) ***(G-4220)***
Cascade Mobile Mix Concrete, Graham *Also called Cascade Mobile Mix* ***(G-4220)***
Cascade Mountain Blends NW LLC...425 275-3344
4320 196th St Sw Ste B Lynnwood (98036) ***(G-6088)***
Cascade Mountain Log Homes, Startup *Also called Mountain Log Homes Inc* ***(G-13002)***
Cascade Nets Inc...866 738-8071
2138 Buchanan Loop Ferndale (98248) ***(G-3827)***
Cascade Organic Farms, Royal City *Also called Cascade Organic Flour LLC* ***(G-9168)***
Cascade Organic Flour LLC...509 855-7450
310 Camelia St Ne Royal City (99357) ***(G-9168)***
Cascade Paper Converting Inc...360 735-1602
7000 Ne 40th Ave Ste B1 Vancouver (98661) ***(G-14105)***
Cascade Pipe & Feed Supply...509 997-0720
420 E Methow Valley Hwy Twisp (98856) ***(G-13910)***
Cascade Plastics, Fife *Also called CFM Consolidated Inc* ***(G-3943)***
Cascade Powder Coating LLC...509 663-9080
11 Bridge St Wenatchee (98801) ***(G-15015)***
Cascade Printing Company...253 472-5500
3321 S Lawrence St Tacoma (98409) ***(G-13227)***
Cascade Printing Direct...253 661-6213
1505 S 356th St Ste 110 Federal Way (98003) ***(G-3722)***
Cascade Prosthetic & Orthotics, Mount Vernon *Also called Cascade Prsthtics Orthtics Inc* ***(G-6783)***
Cascade Prsthtics Orthtics Inc (PA)...360 384-1858
1360 Sunset Ave Ferndale (98248) ***(G-3828)***
Cascade Prsthtics Orthtics Inc...360 428-4003
17670 Dunbar Rd Mount Vernon (98273) ***(G-6783)***
Cascade Publications...360 638-0404
40503 Skunk Bay Rd Ne Hansville (98340) ***(G-4315)***
Cascade Publishing Inc...206 430-6021
1546 Nw 56th St Ste 495 Seattle (98107) ***(G-9643)***
Cascade Quality Molding Inc...509 248-9642
2607 Ahtanum Rd Yakima (98903) ***(G-15530)***
Cascade Ridge Industries...509 237-1534
3559 Road K Nw Quincy (98848) ***(G-8291)***
Cascade Rose Alpacas...206 715-6910
1826 324th Ave Ne Carnation (98014) ***(G-2291)***
Cascade Seafoods, Bellingham *Also called King & Prince Seafood Corp* ***(G-1395)***
Cascade Sign...509 945-1578
1413 River Rd Yakima (98902) ***(G-15531)***
Cascade Software Corp...425 558-9017
11874 175th Pl Ne Redmond (98052) ***(G-8417)***
Cascade Specialty Hardware...360 823-3995
2910 Kauffman Ave Vancouver (98660) ***(G-14106)***
Cascade Toy Ltd (PA)...425 888-4600
10405 428th Ave Se North Bend (98045) ***(G-7105)***
Cascade Tree Service LLC...425 241-9326
915 Snoqualm Pl North Bend (98045) ***(G-7106)***
Cascade Wire Works LLC...360 904-4412
10310 Ne 96th St Vancouver (98662) ***(G-14107)***
Cascade Woodwrights...360 771-3908
3018 Ne Littler Way Vancouver (98662) ***(G-14108)***
Cascades Sonoco, Woodland *Also called Sonoco Products Company* ***(G-15466)***
Cascades Sonoco Inc...253 584-4295
4320 95th St Sw Ste C Tacoma (98499) ***(G-13228)***
Cascadia Dynamix LLC...360 584-3044
152 Stage St N Tenino (98589) ***(G-13613)***
Cascadia Homebrew...360 943-2337
211 4th Ave E Olympia (98501) ***(G-7247)***
Cascadia Newspaper Company LLC...360 647-8200
115 W Magnolia St Ste 210 Bellingham (98225) ***(G-1292)***
Cascadia Screen Printing...509 362-8900
14208 E Sprague Ave Ste C Spokane Valley (99216) ***(G-12651)***
Cascadia Screen Printing...541 490-7012
1605 N River Ridge Blvd 11-201 Spokane (99224) ***(G-12172)***

Cascadia Seismic Inc.....206 801-5999
1322 238th Pl Sw Bothell (98021) *(G-1837)*
Cascadia Stoneware USA In.....360 595-1171
5651 Strand Rd Deming (98244) *(G-2918)*
Cascadia Venom Collection.....360 556-3177
13831 Littlerock Rd Sw Rochester (98579) *(G-9129)*
Cascadia Video Pdts Cvp LLC.....509 202-4230
1321 2nd St Cheney (99004) *(G-2580)*
Cascadia Weekly, Bellingham *Also called Cascadia Newspaper Company LLC (G-1292)*
Cascading Waterscapes, Mount Vernon *Also called Ervin H Tennyson (G-6793)*
Cascioppo Bros Italian Mt Mkt, Kirkland *Also called Cascioppo Bros Meats Inc (G-5298)*
Cascioppo Bros Meats Inc.....206 784-6121
13613 Ne 126th Pl Ste 310 Kirkland (98034) *(G-5298)*
Case Enterprises.....425 827-2056
12201 Ne 70th St Kirkland (98033) *(G-5299)*
Case Mix Analysis Inc.....206 285-2576
200 W Thomas St Ste 150 Seattle (98119) *(G-9644)*
Case42.....509 270-3500
22606 E Heroy Ave Otis Orchards (99027) *(G-7513)*
Casey Burns Flutes.....360 297-4020
9962 Ne Shrty Campbell Rd Kingston (98346) *(G-5250)*
Casey Communications Inc.....206 448-5902
800 5th Ave Ste 4100 Seattle (98104) *(G-9645)*
Casey Publications, Seattle *Also called Casey Communications Inc (G-9645)*
Cashmere Manufacturing LLC.....509 888-2141
3759 Airport Way East Wenatchee (98802) *(G-3009)*
Cashmere Valley Record, Leavenworth *Also called Ncw Media Inc (G-5811)*
Cashmere Valley Record, Cashmere *Also called Ncw Media Inc (G-2327)*
Caskey Industrial Supply Co.....360 533-6366
1608 1st St Cosmopolis (98537) *(G-2798)*
Cassandra Watterson.....509 306-0205
1411 Alford Rd Ellensburg (98926) *(G-3187)*
Cassel Inc.....206 909-9584
1404 140th Pl Ne Bellevue (98007) *(G-841)*
Cast 7020 LLC.....401 885-9555
6130 31st Ave Ne Tulalip (98271) *(G-13840)*
Castillo De Feliciana.....541 558-3656
331 Reserve Way Walla Walla (99362) *(G-14779)*
Castle & Coleman Logging Co.....360 426-0840
1800 W Highland Rd Shelton (98584) *(G-11688)*
Castle Bridge Winery.....425 251-0983
18706 137th Ct Se Renton (98058) *(G-8768)*
Castle Rock Goat Farm LLC.....509 961-5613
13811 Yakima Valley Hwy Zillah (98953) *(G-15751)*
Casual Fridays.....360 425-8841
3232 Nebraska St Longview (98632) *(G-5897)*
Casual Fridays Custom E M B.....360 425-8841
3232 Nebraska St Longview (98632) *(G-5898)*
Catapult Solutions.....509 849-2660
1070 Sharp Rd Prescott (99348) *(G-8023)*
Caterpillar Authorized Dealer, Tukwila *Also called N C Power Systems Co (G-13774)*
Caterpillar Inc.....509 623-4640
9610 W Hallett Rd Spokane (99224) *(G-12173)*
Caterpillar Inc.....425 562-2060
3535 Factoria Blvd Se # 350 Bellevue (98006) *(G-842)*
Catherine Tomlinson.....206 789-4405
7729 31st Ave Nw Seattle (98117) *(G-9646)*
Catholic Northwest Progress.....206 382-4850
710 9th Ave Seattle (98104) *(G-9647)*
Catholic Printery Inc.....206 767-0660
6327 W Marginal Way Sw Seattle (98106) *(G-9648)*
Caudill Bros Distillery.....360 460-6172
125 Motor Ave Port Angeles (98362) *(G-7692)*
Caudill Distillery.....360 457-0947
1329 W 10th St Port Angeles (98363) *(G-7693)*
Cauldron Broths, Bellingham *Also called Cauldron Investment Group LLC (G-1293)*
Cauldron Investment Group LLC.....360 671-1098
4201 Meridian St Ste 105 Bellingham (98226) *(G-1293)*
Cave B Estate Winery.....509 785-3500
344 Silica Rd Nw Quincy (98848) *(G-8292)*
Cavu Cellars.....509 540-6352
175 E Aeronca Ave Walla Walla (99362) *(G-14780)*
Cayuse Vineyards.....509 526-0686
17 E Main St Walla Walla (99362) *(G-14781)*
Cbd Outreach.....360 426-2000
935 E Johns Prairie Rd Shelton (98584) *(G-11689)*
Cbf, Lake Forest Park *Also called Beth Donalley (G-5607)*
CBI Services LLC.....425 258-2350
5500 S 1st Ave Everett (98203) *(G-3411)*
CBS Cabinet Center.....253 582-8088
4425 100th St Sw Ste B Lakewood (98499) *(G-5706)*
CBS Outdoor.....509 892-4720
15320 E Marietta Ave # 2 Spokane Valley (99216) *(G-12652)*
CC Filson Co (HQ).....206 624-4437
1741 1st Ave S Seattle (98134) *(G-9649)*
Ccfab, Centralia *Also called Curfman Custom Fabrication LLC (G-2396)*
CCI Caseworks Inc.....360 953-9641
7509 S 5th St Ste 109 Ridgefield (98642) *(G-9070)*
Cco Holdings LLC.....509 293-4177
1050 N Miller St Wenatchee (98801) *(G-15016)*
Cco Holdings LLC.....509 643-3364
401 S 6th St Sunnyside (98944) *(G-13116)*
CCS Baking Co.....206 200-5195
8416 25th St Ne Lake Stevens (98258) *(G-5637)*
CCS Computer Systems Inc.....425 672-4806
2100 196th St Sw Ste 112 Lynnwood (98036) *(G-6089)*
CCS Equipment Inc.....509 248-4001
1917 S 14th St Union Gap (98903) *(G-13925)*
CCS Lock & Key, Seattle *Also called Cleaning Consultants Services (G-9692)*
Ccw LLC.....206 363-4916
16724 10th Ave Ne Shoreline (98155) *(G-11764)*
CD Fabrication.....253 273-2005
11914 119th Ave E Puyallup (98374) *(G-8134)*
Cde Software, Seattle *Also called Pat-Co Inc (G-10765)*
CDI, Fife *Also called Crystal Distribution Inc (G-3946)*
CDI Coding.....360 653-6437
21828 87th Ave Se Ste A Woodinville (98072) *(G-15207)*
CDI Custom Design Inc.....360 650-1150
2123 Grant St Bellingham (98225) *(G-1294)*
CDM, Granite Falls *Also called Competitive Development & Mfg (G-4270)*
Cds, Bellevue *Also called Critical Delivery Service LLC (G-868)*
Ce Metal Fabrication.....360 673-9663
2632 N Hendrickson Dr Kalama (98625) *(G-4494)*
Ceba Systems LLC.....360 891-1823
13213 Ne Kerr Rd Ste 110 Vancouver (98682) *(G-14109)*
Ceco Door Products.....253 872-8174
7230 S 227th Pl Kent (98032) *(G-4843)*
Cedar Coast Press.....206 451-4568
12168 Sunrise Dr Ne Bainbridge Island (98110) *(G-620)*
Cedar Creek Printing Co.....360 757-7588
105 Cedar St Burlington (98233) *(G-2142)*
Cedar Farms LLC.....360 779-3575
17582 Noll Rd Ne Poulsbo (98370) *(G-7954)*
Cedar Grove Composting Inc.....425 212-2515
3620 36th Pl Ne Everett (98201) *(G-3412)*
Cedar Grove Wood Specialty.....360 494-5295
109 Cedar Grove Rd Randle (98377) *(G-8324)*
Cedar Homes of Washington Inc.....360 668-8242
23209 131st Ave Se Snohomish (98296) *(G-11887)*
Cedar Mountain Spa Cover Mfg, Kent *Also called Cedar Mountain Spa Covers (G-4844)*
Cedar Mountain Spa Covers (PA).....253 872-8993
22717 72nd Ave S Ste 105 Kent (98032) *(G-4844)*
Cedar Mountain Woodwrights.....509 933-2602
309 S Railroad Ave Ellensburg (98926) *(G-3188)*
Cedar Recycling Inc.....253 863-5353
411 West Valley Hwy S Pacific (98047) *(G-7524)*
Cedar River Cellars.....206 229-2104
2525 Ferndale Ave Ne Renton (98056) *(G-8769)*
Cedarbrook.....360 354-5770
145 E Cedar Dr Lynden (98264) *(G-6006)*
Cedarprime Inc.....360 988-2120
601 W Front St Ste C Sumas (98295) *(G-13042)*
Cedartone Specialties Inc.....253 852-6628
26843 51st Pl S Kent (98032) *(G-4845)*
Cedarville Shake & Shingle Mil.....360 715-1856
3353 Breslin Ln Ferndale (98248) *(G-3829)*
Cedergreen Cellars Inc.....425 827-7244
11315 Ne 65th St Kirkland (98033) *(G-5300)*
Cee Gees & Co.....509 465-8231
13415 N Calispel Ct Spokane (99208) *(G-12174)*
Celebration Boatworks.....206 321-0794
114 240th St Se Bothell (98021) *(G-1838)*
Celebrity Bakery & Cafe.....253 627-4773
602 E 25th St Ste 2 Tacoma (98421) *(G-13229)*
Celestial Monitoring Corp.....800 477-2506
2100 196th St Sw Ste 109 Lynnwood (98036) *(G-6090)*
Celesticomp Inc.....206 463-9626
8903 Sw Bayview Dr Vashon (98070) *(G-14717)*
Celgene Corporation.....415 839-7058
1616 Eastlake Ave E S Seattle (98102) *(G-9650)*
Cell Systems Corporation.....425 823-1010
12815 Ne 124th St Ste A Kirkland (98034) *(G-5301)*
Cellar 55 Inc.....360 693-2700
1812 Washington St Vancouver (98660) *(G-14110)*
Cellar Door Media LLC.....253 732-9560
938 Broadway Tacoma (98402) *(G-13230)*
Cellars Nodland.....509 927-7770
11616 E Montgomery Dr # 69 Spokane Valley (99206) *(G-12653)*
Cellartracker LLC.....206 601-7226
1535 9th Ave W Seattle (98119) *(G-9651)*
Cellcyte Genetics Corporation.....425 519-3755
14205 Se 36th St Ste 100 Bellevue (98006) *(G-843)*
Cellu Tissue, Spokane *Also called Clearwater Paper Oklahoma (G-12184)*
Cellular Directory Corp.....425 646-4917
1611 116th Ave Ne Bellevue (98004) *(G-844)*
Cellular To Go Inc.....253 255-1955
9724 90th Ave Nw Gig Harbor (98332) *(G-4085)*
Cemex Cnstr Mtls Fla LLC.....425 513-6651
6300 Glenwood Ave Everett (98203) *(G-3413)*
Cemex Cnstr Mtls PCF LLC.....360 486-3557
19000 Yew Way Snohomish (98296) *(G-11888)*
Cemex Cnstr Mtls PCF LLC.....425 252-8600
222 W Marine View Dr Everett (98201) *(G-3414)*

(PA)=Parent Co (HQ)=Headquarters (DH)=Div Headquarters
2019 Washington
Manufacturers Register
699

Cemex Cnstr Mtls PCF LLC....425 355-2111
20700 44th Ave W Ste 240 Lynnwood (98036) *(G-6091)*
Cemex Cnstr Mtls PCF LLC....360 474-0173
23605 State Route 9 Ne Arlington (98223) *(G-218)*
Cemex Materials LLC....360 254-7770
8705 Ne 117th Ave Vancouver (98662) *(G-14111)*
Cenex Supply & Marketing Inc....509 488-5261
528 S Booker Rd Othello (99344) *(G-7491)*
Center Electric Inc (PA)....253 383-4416
1212 S 30th St Tacoma (98409) *(G-13231)*
Center For Advanced....253 298-7490
495 Andover Park E Tukwila (98188) *(G-13711)*
Center For Dental Implants....509 765-5141
1308 S Pioneer Way Moses Lake (98837) *(G-6690)*
Center For East Asian Studies....360 650-3836
516 High St Bellingham (98225) *(G-1295)*
Center For Prosthetic....425 454-4276
1231 116th Ave Ne Ste 725 Bellevue (98004) *(G-845)*
Center For Prosthetic (PA)....206 328-4276
411 12th Ave Ste 200 Seattle (98122) *(G-9652)*
Center For Religious Humanism....206 281-2988
3307 3rd Ave W Seattle (98119) *(G-9653)*
Center For The Def Free Entp....425 455-5038
12500 Ne 10th Pl Bellevue (98005) *(G-846)*
Center For Touch Drawing....360 221-5745
628 1st St Langley (98260) *(G-5773)*
Center Trade Corporation....206 992-2374
5400 Carillon Pt Fl 4 Kirkland (98033) *(G-5302)*
Centerline Fabrication....509 948-8711
45219 E Red Mountain Rd Benton City (99320) *(G-1604)*
Centerline Fabricators LLC....253 922-3226
5912 15th St E Fife (98424) *(G-3941)*
Centerpiece Customs....360 490-8636
604 Dearborn Ave Shelton (98584) *(G-11690)*
Central Admxture Phrm Svcs Inc....253 395-8700
7044 S 220th St Kent (98032) *(G-4846)*
Central Dental Technicians....509 663-4113
23 S Wenatchee Ave # 214 Wenatchee (98801) *(G-15017)*
Central Fabricators Inc....206 633-4762
4758 Ballard Ave Nw Seattle (98107) *(G-9654)*
Central Fabricators Inc....509 468-3995
1011 E Sharpsburg Ave # 546 Spokane (99208) *(G-12175)*
Central Ferry, Pomeroy *Also called Helena Agri-Enterprises LLC (G-7674)*
Central Glass Works....360 623-1099
109 W Main St Centralia (98531) *(G-2388)*
Central Hose and Fittings Inc....509 547-6460
2214 N 4th Ave Pasco (99301) *(G-7558)*
Central Kitsap Fire Rescu....360 447-3575
5350 Nw Newberry Rd Silverdale (98383) *(G-11828)*
Central Machinery Sales Inc....509 547-9003
1802 E James St Pasco (99301) *(G-7559)*
Central Market Incorporated....509 787-5100
726 Central Ave S Quincy (98848) *(G-8293)*
Central Party & Costume....509 962-3934
203 W 7th Ave Ellensburg (98926) *(G-3189)*
Central Pre-Mix Concrete, Yakima *Also called CPM Development Corporation (G-15539)*
Central Pre-Mix Concrete, Toppenish *Also called CPM Development Corporation (G-13664)*
Central Pre-Mix Concrete, Spokane Valley *Also called CPM Development Corporation (G-12669)*
Central Pre-Mix Concrete, Mattawa *Also called CPM Development Corporation (G-6405)*
Central Pre-Mix Concrete, Sunnyside *Also called CPM Development Corporation (G-13118)*
Central Pre-Mix Concrete Co....509 534-6221
5111 E Broadway Ave Spokane Valley (99212) *(G-12654)*
Central Premix Sakrete, Spokane Valley *Also called Oldcastle Materials Inc (G-12817)*
Central Wash Corn Prcssors Inc....509 623-1144
427 W 1st Ave Spokane (99201) *(G-12176)*
Central Wash Media Group LLC....509 667-8112
3 Orondo Ave Wenatchee (98801) *(G-15018)*
Central Washington Concrete, Moses Lake *Also called CPM Development Corporation (G-6699)*
Central Washington Concrete, Ephrata *Also called CPM Development Corporation (G-3332)*
Central Washington Concrete, Wenatchee *Also called CPM Development Corporation (G-15024)*
Central Washington Concrete, Wenatchee *Also called CPM Development Corporation (G-15090)*
Central Washington Concrete, Othello *Also called CPM Development Corporation (G-7493)*
Central Washington Sign Co....509 765-1818
10158 Kinder Rd Ne Moses Lake (98837) *(G-6691)*
Central Washington Wtr Ctr Inc....509 663-1177
514 S Wenatchee Ave Wenatchee (98801) *(G-15019)*
Centralia Box & Vault Co....360 736-4757
705 State St Centralia (98531) *(G-2389)*
Centralia Knitting Mills Inc....360 736-3994
1002 W Main St Centralia (98531) *(G-2390)*
Centralia Monument, Tacoma *Also called Premier Memorial LLC (G-13477)*
Centralia Supply & Fabrication....360 736-7277
901 W Main St Centralia (98531) *(G-2391)*
Centric Corporation....253 833-4342
1420 20th St Nw Ste A Auburn (98001) *(G-403)*
Centricity Publishing LLC....360 692-6162
305 108th Ave Ne Ste 200 Bellevue (98004) *(G-847)*
Centrix Inc....253 872-4773
1022 W Valley Hwy Kent (98032) *(G-4847)*
Centurion Enterprises....509 787-2345
107 D St Sw Quincy (98848) *(G-8294)*
Centurion Process LLC....509 759-3001
307 1/2 S 3rd St Selah Selah (98942) *(G-11584)*
Century 21 Promotions Inc (PA)....206 282-8827
2601 W Commodore Way Seattle (98199) *(G-9655)*
Cenveo Inc....503 224-7777
6520 S 190th St Ste 100 Kent (98032) *(G-4848)*
Cenveo Worldwide Limited....206 576-4300
6520 S 190th St Ste 100 Kent (98032) *(G-4849)*
Cepher Publishing Group LLC....406 889-7583
1523 132nd St Se C-350 Everett (98208) *(G-3415)*
Ceradyne Inc....206 763-2170
6701 6th Ave S Seattle (98108) *(G-9656)*
Cerevast Medical Inc....425 748-7529
12100 Ne 195th St Ste 150 Bothell (98011) *(G-1754)*
Certain Software Inc....415 353-5330
11061 Ne 2nd St Ste 107 Bellevue (98004) *(G-848)*
Certainteed Corporation....253 850-9000
5001 D St Nw Auburn (98001) *(G-404)*
Certainteed Gypsum Inc....425 291-9099
8655 S 187th St Kent (98031) *(G-4850)*
Certainteed Gypsum Inc....206 763-1441
5931 E Marginal Way S Seattle (98134) *(G-9657)*
Certainteed Gypsum Mfg Inc....949 282-5300
5931 E Marginal Way S Seattle (98134) *(G-9658)*
Certified Air Safety, Vancouver *Also called Aldergrove LLC (G-14018)*
Certified Branching Habit....206 286-9685
8821 Renton Ave S Seattle (98118) *(G-9659)*
Certified Jeans, Seattle *Also called Certified Branching Habit (G-9659)*
Certifly LLC....888 415-9119
24 Roy St Ste 169 Seattle (98109) *(G-9660)*
Ces Enterprises....206 443-1742
1428 10th Ave Seattle (98122) *(G-9661)*
Cetacean Research Technology, Seattle *Also called Cetrestec Inc (G-9662)*
Cetrestec Inc....206 650-8676
7021 6th Ave Nw Seattle (98117) *(G-9662)*
Cets LLC....206 992-6993
1441 N Northlake Way # 214 Seattle (98103) *(G-9663)*
Cetusa, Bellingham *Also called Council For Edctl Trvl US Amer (G-1307)*
Ceylon & Cyanide....509 638-7772
174 S Coeur Dalene St H30 Spokane (99201) *(G-12177)*
CFC Fish Company LLC....253 478-5160
900 Powell Ave Sw Renton (98057) *(G-8770)*
CFI Blue Sky II LLC....253 627-1903
14513 32nd St E Sumner (98390) *(G-13058)*
CFM, Lakewood *Also called Consolidated Food Management (G-5708)*
CFM Consolidated Inc....253 922-2700
7213 45th Street Ct E Fife (98424) *(G-3942)*
CFM Consolidated Inc....253 922-2700
7009 45th Street Ct E Fife (98424) *(G-3943)*
Cgm Imaging Services LLC....509 995-6153
3509 W Prairie Breeze Ave Spokane (99208) *(G-12178)*
Cgt Inc....253 833-8849
1402 20th St Nw Ste 7 Auburn (98001) *(G-405)*
Ch 2o Inc....360 956-9772
8820 Old Highway 99 Se Tumwater (98501) *(G-13859)*
Ch Leather & Supply....360 966-0183
7602 Nooksack Rd Everson (98247) *(G-3670)*
CH Murphy/Clark-Ullman Inc....253 475-6566
3113 S Pine St Unit A Tacoma (98409) *(G-13232)*
Chabre Bros....509 629-0342
875 E Tietan St Walla Walla (99362) *(G-14782)*
Chadao Tea Co Inc....206 335-6585
3700 Corliss Ave N Seattle (98103) *(G-9664)*
Chain Stitchery, Ephrata *Also called Sandra Stroup (G-3346)*
Chambers Bay Distillery....503 819-0542
2013 70th Ave W University Place (98466) *(G-13964)*
Chambong Industries LLC....608 335-1882
358 29th Ave Seattle (98122) *(G-9665)*
Chameleon Prints....425 493-3071
5008 60th Ave Ne Marysville (98270) *(G-6323)*
Champion Sports Group....360 258-0546
1321 Ne 76th St Vancouver (98665) *(G-14112)*
Champlin Technologies LLC....425 736-8935
5722 155th Ave Se Bellevue (98006) *(G-849)*
Champoux Vineyards LLC....360 563-1330
11306 52nd St Se Snohomish (98290) *(G-11889)*
Chandler Reach Vineyard Estate (PA)....509 588-8800
9506 W Chandler Rd Benton City (99320) *(G-1605)*
Chandler W Jeppsen....541 466-0908
821 S 43rd St Tacoma (98418) *(G-13233)*
Channel Korea....425 557-5970
22525 Se 64th Pl Ste 200 Issaquah (98027) *(G-4391)*
Chaos Graphics, Kent *Also called Universal Sign and Graphics (G-5198)*
Chapman Audio Systems....206 463-3008
18005 Thorsen Rd Sw Vashon (98070) *(G-14718)*

ALPHABETIC SECTION

Chara Creations 360 658-0574
  5810 74th St Ne A Marysville (98270) *(G-6324)*
Charcoir Corporation 213 379-4040
  3537 Sw Rose St Seattle (98126) *(G-9666)*
Charge Solutions LLC 425 381-7922
  24630 Se 24th St Sammamish (98075) *(G-9196)*
Charles Cerar 425 392-1821
  630 Sw Ellerwood St Issaquah (98027) *(G-4392)*
Charles Friedman 206 781-0608
  2841 Nw 70th St Seattle (98117) *(G-9667)*
Charles Hanson 360 871-2173
  8043 E Seaview Dr Port Orchard (98366) *(G-7797)*
Charles Loomis Inc 425 823-4560
  11828 Ne 112th St Kirkland (98033) *(G-5303)*
Charles Lybecker 509 687-0555
  2478 Totem Pole Rd Manson (98831) *(G-6241)*
Charles Parriott 206 725-1765
  3918 S Ferdinand St Seattle (98118) *(G-9668)*
Charles Smith Vineyards LLC 509 526-5230
  35 S Spokane St Walla Walla (99362) *(G-14783)*
Charles Smith Wines, Seattle *Also called Wines of Substance* *(G-11486)*
Charles Smith Wines, Walla Walla *Also called K Vintners LLC* *(G-14830)*
Charles Washington 509 466-9098
  15010 N Neptune Ln Mead (99021) *(G-6427)*
Charlie's Produce, Spokane *Also called Triple b Corporation* *(G-12569)*
Charlies Coat LLC 206 323-2191
  735 35th Ave Seattle (98122) *(G-9669)*
Charlo Timberlands Inc 509 447-3671
  Pend Oreille River Homes Newport (99156) *(G-7055)*
Charter Controls Inc 360 695-2161
  1705 Ne 64th Ave Ste B Vancouver (98661) *(G-14113)*
Chasco LLC 503 803-4675
  419 Sw 13th Cir Battle Ground (98604) *(G-695)*
Chase Race 425 269-5636
  16809 W Snqlmie Vly Rd Ne Duvall (98019) *(G-2980)*
Chase Scientific Co 360 221-8455
  5619 Winona Ln Langley (98260) *(G-5774)*
Chateau Faire Le Pont LLC 509 667-9463
  1 Vinyard Way Wenatchee (98801) *(G-15020)*
Chateau Plateau Winery Inc 360 825-2466
  28925 Se 416th St Enumclaw (98022) *(G-3281)*
Chateau Rollat Winery LLC 509 529-4511
  1793 J B George Rd Walla Walla (99362) *(G-14784)*
Chauncey and Shirah Bell Inc 206 437-7556
  6212 39th Ave Ne Seattle (98115) *(G-9670)*
Chaval Outdoor 206 569-0154
  7720 Springridge Rd Ne Bainbridge Island (98110) *(G-621)*
Chavez Nolberto 360 426-9550
  2253 E Johns Prairie Rd Shelton (98584) *(G-11691)*
Checkmate Industries Inc 360 691-1753
  8810 147th Ave Ne Granite Falls (98252) *(G-4266)*
Checksum LLC 360 435-5510
  6120 195th St Ne Arlington (98223) *(G-219)*
Cheers To Life 425 697-2966
  20722 33rd Ave W Lynnwood (98036) *(G-6092)*
Chehalis Brewing Group LLC 360 628-8259
  222 Capitol Way N Ste 111 Olympia (98501) *(G-7248)*
Chehalis Brewing Group LLC 360 701-7873
  173 Beam Rd Chehalis (98532) *(G-2483)*
Chehalis Mints Co Corp 360 736-9899
  2677 Little Hanaford Rd Centralia (98531) *(G-2392)*
Chekin MD LLC 425 894-9896
  722 210th Pl Se Sammamish (98074) *(G-9197)*
Chelan Concrete Inc 509 682-2915
  23300 State Rte 97a Chelan (98816) *(G-2549)*
Chelan Estate Winery LLC (PA) 509 682-5454
  755 S Lakeshore Rd Chelan (98816) *(G-2550)*
Chelan Printing 509 682-5157
  234 Highway 150 Chelan (98816) *(G-2551)*
Chelan Sand & Gravel LLC 509 682-2569
  879 Howard Flats Rd Chelan (98816) *(G-2552)*
Chelan Seaplanes, Chelan *Also called West Isle Air Inc* *(G-2570)*
Chelan Vintners 509 630-8504
  121 Furey Ave Manson (98831) *(G-6242)*
Chelanmagi, Brewster *Also called Trout-Blue Chelan-Magi Inc* *(G-2017)*
Chemchek Instruments Inc 509 943-5000
  1845 Terminal Dr Ste 101 Richland (99354) *(G-8980)*
Chemco Acquisition Corporation 360 366-3500
  4191 Grandview Rd Ferndale (98248) *(G-3830)*
Chemi-Con Materials Corp 509 762-8788
  9053 Graham St Ne Moses Lake (98837) *(G-6692)*
Chemical Cloth Co 360 582-9684
  91 River Rd Sequim (98382) *(G-11617)*
Chemill Inc 425 286-5229
  15113 98th Ct Ne Bothell (98011) *(G-1755)*
Chemithon Corporation (HQ) 206 937-9954
  5430 W Marginal Way Sw Seattle (98106) *(G-9671)*
Chemithon Enterprises Inc (PA) 206 937-9954
  5430 W Marginal Way Sw Seattle (98106) *(G-9672)*
Chemtrade Chemicals US LLC 360 693-1379
  2611 W 26th St Vancouver (98660) *(G-14114)*
Chemtrade Chemicals US LLC 360 299-1560
  8579 N Texas Rd Anacortes (98221) *(G-111)*
Chemtrade Solutions LLC 360 293-2171
  8579 N Texas Rd Anacortes (98221) *(G-112)*
Cheney Free Press, Cheney *Also called Journal-News Publishing Co* *(G-2588)*
Chep Aerospace US Inc., Auburn *Also called Unilode AVI Solution US Inc* *(G-587)*
Cherbo Publishing Group Inc 818 783-0040
  20006 Cedar Valley Rd # 101 Lynnwood (98036) *(G-6093)*
Cherry Chukar Company (PA) 509 786-2055
  320 Wine Country Rd Prosser (99350) *(G-8032)*
Cherry De Pon 253 277-1907
  17327 Se 270th Pl Ste 101 Covington (98042) *(G-2823)*
Cherry De Pon (PA) 425 226-5246
  365 S Grady Way Renton (98057) *(G-8771)*
Cherry Grove Cabinets 360 687-8820
  22107 Ne 41st Ct Ridgefield (98642) *(G-9071)*
Cherry Valley Logging Company 206 396-0002
  30002 Ne Cherry Valley Rd Duvall (98019) *(G-2981)*
Cherrys Jubilee 253 862-6751
  3618 Deer Island Dr E Lake Tapps (98391) *(G-5677)*
Chets Cabinets 360 659-7500
  7728 47th Ave Ne Marysville (98270) *(G-6325)*
Chetties Woodworking LLC 360 500-9099
  5939 184th Ln Sw Rochester (98579) *(G-9130)*
Chevron Corporation 360 887-8101
  1605 Nw 6th Ave Camas (98607) *(G-2238)*
Chevron Corporation 509 534-4077
  3602 E Sprague Ave Spokane (99202) *(G-12179)*
Chevron Corporation 425 413-8881
  27201 216th Ave Se Maple Valley (98038) *(G-6263)*
Chevron Kalama 360 673-2972
  344 Ne Frontage Rd Kalama (98625) *(G-4495)*
Chevy Metal 360 694-7295
  11812 Ne Highway 99 Vancouver (98686) *(G-14115)*
Chewelah Independent Inc 509 935-8422
  401 S Park St Chewelah (99109) *(G-2600)*
Cheyenne Livestock & Products 360 256-0293
  14712 Ne 13th Ct Vancouver (98685) *(G-14116)*
Cheyenne Scale Co Inc 206 933-7904
  1613 Sw 114th St Seattle (98146) *(G-9673)*
CHI-Square Labs LLC 206 282-8246
  2107 W Barrett St Seattle (98199) *(G-9674)*
Chic Ink 425 392-3943
  4709 240th Ave Se Issaquah (98029) *(G-4393)*
Chicago Title Insurance Co 509 765-8820
  1025 S Pioneer Way Ste C Moses Lake (98837) *(G-6693)*
Chief Springs Fire & Irons Brw 509 382-4677
  148 E Main St Dayton (99328) *(G-2879)*
Chihuly Inc (PA) 206 781-8707
  1111 Nw 50th St Seattle (98107) *(G-9675)*
Child Evngelism Fellowship Inc 509 662-2320
  800 Orondo Ave Wenatchee (98801) *(G-15021)*
Child Evngelism Fellowship Inc 360 424-1014
  1404 Riverside Dr Ste B Mount Vernon (98273) *(G-6784)*
Child Evngelism Fellowship Inc 509 928-2820
  19306 E Dove Cir Spokane Valley (99016) *(G-12655)*
Child Evngelism Fellowship Inc 425 252-6314
  1832 Walnut St Everett (98201) *(G-3416)*
Child Inc 425 775-9076
  7425 Olympic View Dr Edmonds (98026) *(G-3100)*
Chilton Logging Inc 360 225-0427
  1760 Down River Dr Woodland (98674) *(G-15423)*
Chim Chmney Fireplace Pool Spa, Wenatchee *Also called Stone Masters Inc* *(G-15077)*
Chimacum Valley Dairy, Chimacum *Also called Port Townsend Lcl Mktplc LLC* *(G-2613)*
Chimcare Vancouver 360 696-8309
  6715 Ne 63rd St Vancouver (98661) *(G-14117)*
Chimcare West Seattle 206 673-2203
  4742 42nd Ave Sw Seattle (98116) *(G-9676)*
Chimeras LLC 360 754-9217
  8120 Delphi Rd Sw Olympia (98512) *(G-7249)*
Chiminera LLC 401 326-2820
  5023 16th Ave Ne Seattle (98105) *(G-9677)*
Chin Music Press Inc 206 457-8752
  2621 24th Ave W Seattle (98199) *(G-9678)*
China Bend Vineyards 509 732-6123
  3751 Vineyard Way Kettle Falls (99141) *(G-5228)*
Chinese Seafood Noodle LLC 425 877-8856
  12211 Ne 5th St Apt A301 Bellevue (98005) *(G-850)*
Chings Embroidery 360 613-9861
  7277 Sunset Ave Ne Bremerton (98311) *(G-1942)*
Chinook Acoustics Inc 425 307-1976
  14842 Ne 95th St Redmond (98052) *(G-8418)*
Chinook Elevator Solutions 425 213-0784
  824 3rd Ave N Kent (98032) *(G-4851)*
Chinook Marine Repair Inc 360 777-8361
  785 State Route 101 Chinook (98614) *(G-2615)*
Chinook Mechanical LLC 360 947-9035
  4214 Ne Minnehaha St Vancouver (98661) *(G-14118)*
Chinook Wines 509 786-2725
  220 Wittkopf Loop Prosser (99350) *(G-8033)*
Chip Away Bathtub Repair 425 246-1306
  46533 Se 156th Pl North Bend (98045) *(G-7107)*
Chip Pros, Seattle *Also called Navan Enterprises LLC* *(G-10596)*
Chips & Del Carvings In Wood 253 858-4751
  10014 135th St Nw Gig Harbor (98329) *(G-4086)*

Chiwawa Mines Inc 509 455-8080
28 E Riverside Ave Spokane (99202) *(G-12180)*
Chocolate Chocolate, Blaine *Also called Totally Chocolate LLC (G-1706)*
Chocolate Necessities, Bellingham *Also called Chocolate Necessity Inc (G-1296)*
Chocolate Necessity Inc (PA) 360 676-0589
4600 Guide Meridian # 109 Bellingham (98226) *(G-1296)*
Chocolopolis, Seattle *Also called Rh Appetizing Inc (G-10960)*
Choice Cardiovascular Pllc 253 229-7003
4423 Point Fosdick Dr Nw # 300 Gig Harbor (98335) *(G-4087)*
Choice Communications, Benton City *Also called Choice Wiring LLC (G-1606)*
Choice Construction Inc 360 340-2206
8139 Se Millihanna Rd Olalla (98359) *(G-7205)*
Choice Dental Laboratory, Kent *Also called T & S Dental Group Corp (G-5168)*
Choice Wiring LLC 509 588-6185
55911 N Thomas Rd Benton City (99320) *(G-1606)*
Choix Publishing 425 821-2752
12635 93rd Pl Ne Kirkland (98034) *(G-5304)*
Choke Shirt Company 206 624-4444
920 S Holgate St Ste 109 Seattle (98134) *(G-9679)*
Chondrex Inc 425 702-6365
2607 151st Pl Ne Redmond (98052) *(G-8419)*
Chooch Enterprises Inc 425 273-4794
20002 Se 236th St Maple Valley (98038) *(G-6264)*
Choppers By Kriss 509 570-2737
2914 E Liberty Ave Spokane (99207) *(G-12181)*
Choraks Sportsmans Inn 206 463-0940
17611 Vashon Hwy Sw Vashon (98070) *(G-14719)*
Chouette Vineyards LLC 206 229-5167
42311 Se 141st St North Bend (98045) *(G-7108)*
Choukette 206 466-6906
5028 Wilson Ave S Seattle (98118) *(G-9680)*
Chris Barber Apple 360 875-8112
2101 Henkle St Raymond (98577) *(G-8345)*
Christensen Net Works, Everson *Also called Coppertop Enterprises Inc (G-3672)*
Christensen Shipyards LLC 360 831-9800
4400 Se Columbia Way Vancouver (98661) *(G-14119)*
Christian Hamilton 360 442-4900
3376 Olive Way Longview (98632) *(G-5899)*
Christie Lites Seattle LLC 206 223-7200
7815 S 208th St Ste 101 Kent (98032) *(G-4852)*
Christine Hemp, Port Townsend *Also called Bowet & Poet Inc (G-7870)*
Christine Jamison 253 887-1095
403 D St Se Auburn (98002) *(G-406)*
Christine Woodcock 509 773-4747
377 Ekone Rd Goldendale (98620) *(G-4194)*
Christmas Forest 360 245-3202
445 Beaver Creek Rd Curtis (98538) *(G-2848)*
Christopher Pallis Inc 206 619-4146
1209 N Cedar St Tacoma (98406) *(G-13234)*
Christopher Radko, Seattle *Also called Rauch Industries Inc (G-10925)*
Christopher Ross Dewayne 360 918-4586
6645 Littlerock Rd Sw Tumwater (98512) *(G-13860)*
Chromaworks Corporation 206 622-7107
4240 Gilman Pl W Ste A Seattle (98199) *(G-9681)*
Chrome Industries 206 682-1343
1117 1st Ave Seattle (98101) *(G-9682)*
Chronicle 509 826-1110
618 Okoma Dr OMAK (98841) *(G-7436)*
Chronus Corporation 425 629-6327
15395 Se 30th Pl Ste 140 Bellevue (98007) *(G-851)*
Chrysanthemum 206 722-1031
4820 Rainier Ave S Seattle (98118) *(G-9683)*
Chrysanthemum Literary Society, Seattle *Also called Goldfish Press (G-10097)*
CHS Inc 509 488-9681
1296 S Broadway Ave Othello (99344) *(G-7492)*
CHS-Sub Whatcom Inc (HQ) 360 354-2108
402 Main St Lynden (98264) *(G-6007)*
CHS-Sub Whatcom Inc 360 966-4193
106 Nooksack Ave Nooksack (98276) *(G-7086)*
CHS-Sub Whatcom Inc 360 354-1198
300 Main St Lynden (98264) *(G-6008)*
CHS-Sub Whatcom Inc 360 966-4782
102 Nooksack Ave Everson (98276) *(G-3671)*
Chuckanut Bay Distillery Inc 360 739-0361
1115 Railroad Ave Bellingham (98225) *(G-1297)*
Chuckanut Bay Foods LLC 360 380-1908
1649 Boblett St Blaine (98230) *(G-1666)*
Chuckanut Woodworks 360 724-3129
2822 Old Highway 99 N Rd Burlington (98233) *(G-2143)*
Chukar Cherry, Prosser *Also called Cherry Chukar Company (G-8032)*
Chunder Bag 253 987-6224
18116 W Lake Desire Dr Se Renton (98058) *(G-8772)*
Church & Dwight Co Inc 253 838-3385
350 S 333rd St Ste 102 Federal Way (98003) *(G-3723)*
Church and Dwight 360 816-7400
10 S 56th Pl Ridgefield (98642) *(G-9072)*
Churchill Brothers 360 293-2700
1130 W Mar View Dr Ste C Everett (98201) *(G-3417)*
Churchill N Mfg Co Inc 360 736-9923
544 N Pearl St Centralia (98531) *(G-2393)*
Ci Shred, Kennewick *Also called Ci Support LLC (G-4644)*
Ci Support LLC 509 586-6090
900 S Dayton St Kennewick (99336) *(G-4644)*
Ciena Corporation 509 242-9000
12730 E Mirabeau Pkwy # 100 Spokane Valley (99216) *(G-12656)*
Cigaretto 253 851-2175
5500 Olympic Dr Ste A107 Gig Harbor (98335) *(G-4088)*
Cigarland Gig Harbor 253 851-5515
4949 Borgen Blvd Gig Harbor (98332) *(G-4089)*
Cincinnati Incorporated 425 263-9216
2210 Hewitt Ave Ste 201 Everett (98201) *(G-3418)*
Cindi Marsh, Woodinville *Also called Marcin Jewelry Inc (G-15301)*
Cindy Lous Artisan Jams 360 873-4178
61363 State Route 20 Marblemount (98267) *(G-6304)*
Cinematix LLC 425 533-1024
11332 Ne 122nd Way # 100 Kirkland (98034) *(G-5305)*
Cinevend Inc 206 388-3784
3518 Fremont Ave N # 580 Seattle (98103) *(G-9684)*
Cinq Cellars LLC 206 954-4626
21407 Ne Union Hill Rd Redmond (98053) *(G-8420)*
Cinterion Wireless Modu 630 517-0198
22010 Se 51st St Issaquah (98029) *(G-4394)*
Circa 15 Fabric Studio LLC 425 309-9553
2117 18th St Anacortes (98221) *(G-113)*
Circle F Enterprises, Bellingham *Also called Myrle B Foster (G-1455)*
Circle K, Kent *Also called Pacific Fuel and Convenience (G-5051)*
Circle Systems Inc 206 682-3783
1001 4th Ave Ste 3200 Seattle (98154) *(G-9685)*
Circuit Imaging LLC 509 315-3400
1420 N Mullan Rd Ste 108 Spokane Valley (99206) *(G-12657)*
Circuit Services Worldwide 425 454-7181
10 148th Ave Ne Ste 101 Bellevue (98007) *(G-852)*
Circuit Services Worldwide LLC 425 454-7181
10 148th Ave Ne Ste 101 Bellevue (98007) *(G-853)*
Circulation Department, Camas *Also called Camas-Washougal Post-Record (G-2237)*
Cirrato Technologies Inc 425 999-4500
5400 Carillon Pt Fl 4 Kirkland (98033) *(G-5306)*
Cisco Systems Inc 206 256-3229
2901 3rd Ave Ste 600 Seattle (98121) *(G-9686)*
Cisco Systems Inc 360 352-3657
4160 6th Ave Se Ste 203 Lacey (98503) *(G-5541)*
Cisco Systems Inc 425 468-0800
500 108th Ave Ne Ste 500 # 500 Bellevue (98004) *(G-854)*
Citlali Creativo 206 779-5664
14441 Ambaum Blvd Sw A Burien (98166) *(G-2095)*
Citrix Systems Inc 425 895-4700
15809 Bear Creek Pkwy Redmond (98052) *(G-8421)*
City Books Yellow Pages Inc 805 473-1686
1415 Pacific Dr Burlington (98233) *(G-2144)*
City Grind Works 206 769-0006
15541 27th Ave Ne Shoreline (98155) *(G-11765)*
City Lights Sign Company, Seattle *Also called City Lites Neon Inc (G-9687)*
City Lites Neon Inc 206 789-4747
902 Nw 49th St Seattle (98107) *(G-9687)*
City of Naches 509 653-1400
10237 Us Highway 12 Naches (98937) *(G-6995)*
City of Sattle-City Light Dept 509 446-3083
10382 Boundary Rd Metaline Falls (99153) *(G-6497)*
City of Yakima 509 575-6177
6390 Us Highway 12 Yakima (98908) *(G-15532)*
City Sheet Metal Heating & Air 253 852-2174
4202 Auburn Way N Ste 8 Auburn (98002) *(G-407)*
City Yakima Water Trtmnt Plant, Yakima *Also called City of Yakima (G-15532)*
CJ Manufacturing I Inc 360 543-5297
7050 Portal Way Ste 140 Ferndale (98248) *(G-3831)*
CJ Warren & Son Drilling, Veradale *Also called C J Warren & Sons Well Drlg (G-14749)*
Ckreed Defense LLC 206 297-2116
16637 10th Ave Sw Burien (98166) *(G-2096)*
Claar Cellars LLC 509 266-4449
1081 Glenwood Rd Pasco (99301) *(G-7560)*
Clam Digger 360 299-3444
1811 Commercial Ave Anacortes (98221) *(G-114)*
Claquato Farms Inc 360 748-6220
272 Highway 603 Chehalis (98532) *(G-2484)*
Clarence H Spargo Jr 360 532-1505
607 W Wishkah St Aberdeen (98520) *(G-7)*
Clarification Techology Inc 425 820-4850
9805 Ne 116th St Ste A200 Kirkland (98034) *(G-5307)*
Clario Medical 206 315-5410
2033 6th Ave Ste 333 Seattle (98121) *(G-9688)*
Clarisonic, Redmond *Also called Pacific Bioscience Labs Inc (G-8606)*
Clark Contract Cutting Inc 360 705-0355
6827 Bel Mor Ct Sw Tumwater (98512) *(G-13861)*
Clark Machinery Inc 360 825-1840
36923 249th Ave Se Enumclaw (98022) *(G-3282)*
Clark Office Products Inc 360 657-2018
12407 48th Dr Ne Marysville (98271) *(G-6326)*
Clark Security Products Inc 206 467-3000
2760 4th Ave S Seattle (98134) *(G-9689)*
Clark Site Mix Con Spokane LLC 509 991-7730
4705 W South Oval Rd Spokane (99224) *(G-12182)*
Clarks All-Sports Inc 509 684-5069
557 S Main St Colville (99114) *(G-2743)*

Clarks Berry Farm Inc (PA) 360 354-1294
632 Birch Bay Lynden Rd Lynden (98264) ***(G-6009)***
Clarks Country Kitchen 509 586-6909
84104 N Harrington Rd Richland (99353) ***(G-8981)***
Claro Candles 253 678-1173
3806 E Portland Ave Tacoma (98404) ***(G-13235)***
Clarus Fluid Intelligence LLC (HQ) 360 671-1514
3145 Mercer Ave Ste 104 Bellingham (98225) ***(G-1298)***
Clarus Technologies LLC (HQ) 360 671-1514
2015 Alpine Way Ste C Bellingham (98226) ***(G-1299)***
Classic Cycle 206 842-9191
740 Winslow Way E Bainbridge Island (98110) ***(G-622)***
Classic Impressions 206 766-9121
5800 Corson Ave S Seattle (98108) ***(G-9690)***
Classic Printing Inc 509 452-1231
104 S 5th Ave Yakima (98902) ***(G-15533)***
Classic Sign and Graphics 253 862-8035
8221 256th Ave E Buckley (98321) ***(G-2051)***
Classic Vinyl LLC 509 656-3011
50 Pioneer Trl Cle Elum (98922) ***(G-2661)***
Classic Welding 509 469-8110
107 Nob Blvd Yakima (98901) ***(G-15534)***
Claudes Accurate Machining 360 546-5840
14413 Ne 10th Ave A112 Vancouver (98685) ***(G-14120)***
Claudja Inc 206 842-6303
11493 Blue Heron Ln Ne Bainbridge Island (98110) ***(G-623)***
Claudon Inc 425 454-2912
935 88th Ave Ne Medina (98039) ***(G-6448)***
Claus Paws Animal Hospital LLC 360 896-7449
5819 Ne 162nd Ave Vancouver (98682) ***(G-14121)***
Clauson Lime, Maple Falls *Also called Clauson Quarry LLC* ***(G-6249)***
Clauson Quarry LLC 360 599-2731
8899 Silver Lake Rd Maple Falls (98266) ***(G-6249)***
Clay In Motion Inc 509 529-6146
959 Reser Rd Walla Walla (99362) ***(G-14785)***
Clayfox Pottery, Spokane *Also called Creative Interaction LLC* ***(G-12207)***
Clayport Pottery 425 335-0678
11710 60th St Ne Lake Stevens (98258) ***(G-5638)***
Clayton Homes Inc 509 452-9228
2010 Rudkin Rd Union Gap (98903) ***(G-13926)***
Clean As A Whistle 425 354-9719
16638 Juanita Dr Ne 101g Kenmore (98028) ***(G-4569)***
Clean Lines LLC 509 939-2957
4865 W Csberg Brroughs Rd Deer Park (99006) ***(G-2896)***
Clean Republic Sodo LLC 206 682-7499
920 S Holgate St Ste 106 Seattle (98134) ***(G-9691)***
Clean-Shot Archery Inc 425 242-5970
6849 S 220th St Kent (98032) ***(G-4853)***
Clean-Vantage 509 392-2793
3100 Willow Pointe Dr Richland (99354) ***(G-8982)***
Cleanaire Systems, Vancouver *Also called Lawrence Enterprises* ***(G-14366)***
Cleaning Consultants Services 206 682-9748
3693 E Marginal Way S Seattle (98134) ***(G-9692)***
Cleanmaster 425 775-7272
11015 47th Ave W Mukilteo (98275) ***(G-6903)***
Cleanpwr 425 334-6100
930 Sunnyside Blvd Lake Stevens (98258) ***(G-5639)***
Clear and Level Logging LLC 360 247-5989
24319 Ne 426th St Amboy (98601) ***(G-90)***
Clear Coated 425 495-2369
1006 15th Ave E Apt 2 Seattle (98112) ***(G-9693)***
Clear Cut Plastics Inc 206 545-9131
507 N 36th St Seattle (98103) ***(G-9694)***
Clear Forest Products Inc 360 253-0101
201 Ne Park Plaza Dr # 1 Vancouver (98684) ***(G-14122)***
Clear Fx International, Ferndale *Also called Clear-Fx LLC* ***(G-3832)***
Clear Rf LLC 855 321-9527
12825 E Mirabeau Pkwy Spokane Valley (99216) ***(G-12658)***
Clear View Auto & Window Glass 360 539-5909
4207 Pacific Ave Se Lacey (98503) ***(G-5542)***
Clear Water Compliance LLC 425 412-5700
2525 W Casino Rd Ste 7a Everett (98204) ***(G-3419)***
Clear Water Services, Everett *Also called Clear Water Compliance LLC* ***(G-3419)***
Clear Your Clutter LLC 206 784-1515
618 Nw 87th St Seattle (98117) ***(G-9695)***
Clear-Fx LLC 800 408-3701
2625 Delta Ring Rd Ste 3 Ferndale (98248) ***(G-3832)***
Clearsign Combustion Corp 206 673-4848
12870 Interurban Ave S Tukwila (98168) ***(G-13712)***
Clearsnap Holding Inc (PA) 360 293-6634
15218 Josh Wilson Rd Burlington (98233) ***(G-2145)***
Clearwater Cabinet Co 253 853-3644
6869 Kimball Dr Gig Harbor (98335) ***(G-4090)***
Clearwater Chemical, Wenatchee *Also called Central Washington Wtr Ctr Inc* ***(G-15019)***
Clearwater Paper Corporation (PA) 509 344-5900
601 W Riverside Ave # 1100 Spokane (99201) ***(G-12183)***
Clearwater Paper Oklahoma 405 717-5104
601 W Riverside Ave # 1100 Spokane (99201) ***(G-12184)***
Clearwater Spas, Woodinville *Also called Hydra Plastics Inc* ***(G-15262)***
Clearwater Spas, Woodinville *Also called Thermal Hydra Plastics LLC* ***(G-15388)***
Clearway Signs 253 324-1706
4720 South Tacoma Way Tacoma (98409) ***(G-13236)***
Cleland Investment LC 509 326-5898
11407 E Montgomery Dr Spokane Valley (99206) ***(G-12659)***
Cleveland Enterprises Inc 360 694-0435
3207 Ne 65th St Vancouver (98663) ***(G-14123)***
Clever Fox Editing 805 910-6938
17410 87th Ave Se Trlr 37 Snohomish (98296) ***(G-11890)***
Click It Picket LLC 253 750-0182
1402 Lake Tappspkwyse 1 Auburn (98092) ***(G-408)***
Client Service Center 206 237-0821
6333 1st Ave S Seattle (98108) ***(G-9696)***
Clifford W Leeson Inc 509 427-4155
347 Nw Jefferson Ave Stevenson (98648) ***(G-13010)***
Cliffstar LLC 509 522-8608
1164 Dell Ave Walla Walla (99362) ***(G-14786)***
Climacover Inc 360 458-1010
44128 Nsqually Ridge Dr E Eatonville (98328) ***(G-3052)***
Climate Publishing LLC 206 515-1795
15317 Se 49th Pl Bellevue (98006) ***(G-855)***
Cline Custom Jewelers, Edmonds *Also called Cline Manufacturing Jewelers* ***(G-3101)***
Cline Manufacturing Jewelers 425 673-7979
105 5th Ave S Edmonds (98020) ***(G-3101)***
Cline Rentals LLC 206 375-0705
21424 1st Ave W Bothell (98021) ***(G-1839)***
Clintron Publishing Inc 509 448-9878
5817 S Magnolia St Spokane (99223) ***(G-12185)***
Clipper Seafoods Ltd 206 284-1162
641 W Ewing St Seattle (98119) ***(G-9697)***
Cloes Blue Book, Marysville *Also called Clark Office Products Inc* ***(G-6326)***
Cloners Market Inc 425 218-0440
9817 28th Dr Se Everett (98208) ***(G-3420)***
Closest To The Pin Inc 425 820-2297
11605 Ne 116th St Kirkland (98034) ***(G-5308)***
Cloth Creations Inc 360 573-7348
4700 Ne 128th St Vancouver (98686) ***(G-14124)***
Clothing, Tacoma *Also called Imperial Motion LLC* ***(G-13347)***
Clothworks Textiles Inc 206 762-7886
6301 W Marginal Way Sw Seattle (98106) ***(G-9698)***
Cloud City Skateboards 206 403-1882
3270 California Ave Sw Seattle (98116) ***(G-9699)***
Cloudcoreo Inc 206 851-0130
2727 Fairview Ave E # 15 Seattle (98102) ***(G-9700)***
Cloudlift Cellars 206 622-2004
312 S Lucile St Seattle (98108) ***(G-9701)***
Clouds Vineyard LLC 509 830-2785
160589 W Sonova Rd Prosser (99350) ***(G-8034)***
Cloudstream Media Inc (PA) 858 245-0034
24402 E 3rd Ave Liberty Lake (99019) ***(G-5828)***
Clowers Corporation 206 420-1202
16160 41st Ave Ne Lake Forest Park (98155) ***(G-5609)***
Clyde Curley 360 738-6862
2112 J St Bellingham (98225) ***(G-1300)***
Clyde Hill Publishing LLC 425 454-8220
2011 89th Ave Ne Clyde Hill (98004) ***(G-2703)***
CM, Tukwila *Also called Continental Mills Inc* ***(G-13716)***
CM Cabinets L L C 360 921-3493
10017 Nw 27th Ave Vancouver (98685) ***(G-14125)***
CM Innovations Inc 425 641-0460
1062 Ne High St Ste 8 Issaquah (98029) ***(G-4395)***
Cm2931 LLC 253 447-7537
4179 70th Ave E Ste B Fife (98424) ***(G-3944)***
CMC, Bonney Lake *Also called Creative Metal Concepts LLC* ***(G-1720)***
CMC Biologics SARI Corp (HQ) 425 485-1900
21511 23rd Dr Se Bothell (98021) ***(G-1840)***
CMC Steel Fabricators Inc 253 833-9060
2306 B St Nw Auburn (98001) ***(G-409)***
CMH, Olympia *Also called Color ME House Inc* ***(G-7252)***
CMS, Seattle *Also called Custom Mech Solutions Inc* ***(G-9767)***
CMX Corporation 425 656-1269
6601 S Glacier St Tukwila (98188) ***(G-13713)***
CMX Medical Imaging, Tukwila *Also called CMX Corporation* ***(G-13713)***
CNA Manufacturing Systems Inc 425 988-3905
230 S Tobin St Renton (98057) ***(G-8773)***
Cnc Diversified Manufacturing 253 852-6869
311 Railroad Ave S Kent (98032) ***(G-4854)***
Cnc Plasma Cutting, Newman Lake *Also called Northern Mountain Metals LLC* ***(G-7049)***
Cnc Software Inc 253 858-6677
5717 Wollochet Dr Nw 2a Gig Harbor (98335) ***(G-4091)***
Cnc Tooling Solutions Inc 425 250-6295
13820 116th Pl Ne Kirkland (98034) ***(G-5309)***
Cns Industries Inc 360 424-1624
4301 Apache Dr Mount Vernon (98273) ***(G-6785)***
CNT Technologies Inc 206 522-2256
4216 Ne 70th St Seattle (98115) ***(G-9702)***
Co C Graphics 360 571-8488
7902 Ne St Johns Rd Ste B Vancouver (98665) ***(G-14126)***
Coa, Lynnwood *Also called Coenzyme-A Technologies Inc* ***(G-6094)***
Coach Cheetah Inc 206 914-8313
1711 12th Ave Ste 1090 Seattle (98122) ***(G-9703)***
Coal Headwear LLC 206 632-1601
4917 14th Ave Nw Seattle (98107) ***(G-9704)***
Coalview Ltd LLC 360 623-7525
1044 Big Hanaford Rd Centralia (98531) ***(G-2394)***

ALPHABETIC

Coast Seafoods Company 360 875-5557
1200 Robert Bush Dr South Bend (98586) ***(G-12040)***
Coast Seafoods Company (HQ) 360 875-5577
1200 Robert Bush Dr Bellevue (98007) ***(G-856)***
Coastal Clayworks 315 405-5077
33121 82nd Ave S Roy (98580) ***(G-9158)***
Coastal Cruise Guides 206 448-4488
3828 26th Ave W Seattle (98199) ***(G-9705)***
Coastal Cruise Tour Guides, Seattle *Also called Coastal Cruise Guides* ***(G-9705)***
Coastal Manufacturing Inc 425 407-0624
6700 Hardeson Rd Ste 103 Everett (98203) ***(G-3421)***
Coastal Software & Consulting 360 891-6174
1499 Se Tech Center Pl # 170 Vancouver (98683) ***(G-14127)***
Coastal Star Inc 206 282-0988
4019 21st Ave W Ste 200 Seattle (98199) ***(G-9706)***
Coastline Equipment Inc 360 734-8509
2235 E Bakerview Rd Bellingham (98226) ***(G-1301)***
Coastline Fabricators Inc (PA) 206 763-5035
8151 Occidental Ave S Seattle (98108) ***(G-9707)***
Coastline Woodworking 360 678-7572
926 Blockhouse Rd Coupeville (98239) ***(G-2810)***
Coates Heater Company Inc 253 872-7256
840 5th Ave S Kent (98032) ***(G-4855)***
Coates Innovations LLC 907 617-5801
14607 Se 267th St Kent (98042) ***(G-4856)***
Coaxsher Inc 509 663-5148
50 Chestnut St Chelan Falls (98817) ***(G-2571)***
Cobalt Enterprises LLC (PA) 360 691-2298
10913 Mountain Loop Hwy Granite Falls (98252) ***(G-4267)***
Cobalt Finishing, Granite Falls *Also called Cobalt Investments LLC* ***(G-4268)***
Cobalt Group Inc (HQ) 206 269-6363
605 5th Ave S Ste 800 Seattle (98104) ***(G-9708)***
Cobalt Investments LLC 360 691-2298
10917 Mountain Loop Hwy Granite Falls (98252) ***(G-4268)***
Cobalt Trailer Sales 509 535-2154
4620 E Trent Ave Spokane (99212) ***(G-12186)***
Cobalt Utility Products 425 823-0708
8711 Ne 119th St Kirkland (98034) ***(G-5310)***
Cobblestone Industries LLC 509 447-4518
1066 Coyote Trl Newport (99156) ***(G-7056)***
Cobbs LLC 360 302-2692
313 5th Ave Se Ste C Olympia (98501) ***(G-7250)***
Cobra Key Systems LLC 509 466-1918
21912 N Saddle Mtn Ln Colbert (99005) ***(G-2706)***
Coca Cola Bottling Co 509 529-0753
155 Avery St Walla Walla (99362) ***(G-14787)***
Coca-Cola, Walla Walla *Also called Coca Cola Bottling Co* ***(G-14787)***
Coca-Cola, Moses Lake *Also called Pacific Coca Cola Bottling* ***(G-6734)***
Coca-Cola, Walla Walla *Also called Swire Pacific Holdings Inc* ***(G-14875)***
Coca-Cola Bottling Co (HQ) 509 248-1855
607 E R St Yakima (98901) ***(G-15535)***
Coca-Cola Bottling Co 509 547-6712
1225 Road 34 Pasco (99301) ***(G-7561)***
Coca-Cola Btlg Co of NY Inc 509 886-1136
3400 5th St Se Wenatchee (98802) ***(G-15089)***
Coca-Cola Company 404 676-0887
915 118th Ave Se Ste 300 Bellevue (98005) ***(G-857)***
Coca-Cola Refreshments 425 226-6004
300 Sw 27th St Renton (98057) ***(G-8774)***
Coco Mats N More, Blaine *Also called Out Peak Services Inc* ***(G-1691)***
Cocoa Future Spc 206 877-3347
3422 19th Ave S Seattle (98144) ***(G-9709)***
Cocoon, Wenatchee *Also called Design Salt Inc* ***(G-15025)***
Cocrystal Pharma Inc (PA) 786 459-1831
19805 North Creek Pkwy Bothell (98011) ***(G-1756)***
Code 3, Quincy *Also called Centurion Enterprises* ***(G-8294)***
Code Publishing Company Inc 206 527-6831
9410 Roosevelt Way Ne Seattle (98115) ***(G-9710)***
Coenzyme A Technologies, Lynnwood *Also called Mmusa Inc* ***(G-6165)***
Coenzyme-A Technologies Inc 425 438-8586
12512 Beverly Park Rd B1 Lynnwood (98087) ***(G-6094)***
Coffee Catcher LLC 202 704-2868
9516 Palatine Ave N Seattle (98103) ***(G-9711)***
Coffee News, Tumwater *Also called Pareto-Curve Marketing Inc* ***(G-13889)***
Coffee On Canvas 419 605-2529
1003 Laurel Ct Fircrest (98466) ***(G-4001)***
Coffee Vault LLC 253 227-5798
23220 Smner Buckley Hwy E Buckley (98321) ***(G-2052)***
Coffey Communications Inc (PA) 509 525-0101
1505 Business One Cir Walla Walla (99362) ***(G-14788)***
Cogenix, Seattle *Also called Jam Developers Inc* ***(G-10280)***
Cogent Holdings-1 LLC (PA) 425 776-8835
7400 Hardeson Rd Everett (98203) ***(G-3422)***
Cogent Holdings-1 LLC 425 776-8835
5002 S Washington St Tacoma (98409) ***(G-13237)***
Cognex 206 448-2343
2001 6th Ave Seattle (98121) ***(G-9712)***
Coherent Knowledge Systems LLC 206 519-6410
5 Wembley Ln Mercer Island (98040) ***(G-6458)***
Coherent Resources Inc 509 747-3541
12102 S Andrus Rd Cheney (99004) ***(G-2581)***
Coin Market LLC 425 745-1659
1120 164th St Sw Ste J Lynnwood (98087) ***(G-6095)***
Coinforcecom LLC 253 682-2825
9111 Yelm Hwy Se Olympia (98513) ***(G-7251)***
Coinstar LLC 866 733-2693
9000 Ne Highway 99 Vancouver (98665) ***(G-14128)***
Coinstar Automated Ret Canada 425 943-8000
1800 114th Ave Se Bellevue (98004) ***(G-858)***
Coinstax LLC 206 629-8831
1700 Westlake Ave N # 200 Seattle (98109) ***(G-9713)***
Cokedale Creamery LLC 360 856-1695
26818 Minkler Rd Sedro Woolley (98284) ***(G-11535)***
Col Solare LLP (PA) 509 588-6806
50207 Antinori Rd Benton City (99320) ***(G-1607)***
Col Solare Winery, Benton City *Also called Col Solare LLP* ***(G-1607)***
Cola Cola Enterprises 509 921-6229
9705 E Montgomery Ave Spokane Valley (99206) ***(G-12660)***
Colbasia Cabinets Inc 509 765-0718
1228 E Wheeler Rd B Moses Lake (98837) ***(G-6694)***
Colburn Enterprise 509 292-2310
14310 E Blanchard Rd Elk (99009) ***(G-3169)***
Colburn Timber Inc 360 208-4501
1262 Sr6 Raymond (98577) ***(G-8346)***
Colburn Timber Inc 360 875-6565
115 Rainier Estates Ct Se Rainier (98576) ***(G-8312)***
Colby Creations Inc 509 234-9736
449 E Edison Connell (99326) ***(G-2791)***
Colby Instruments LLC 425 452-8889
15375 Se 30th Pl Ste 320 Bellevue (98007) ***(G-859)***
Cold Locker Processing LLC 253 321-3233
2200 140th Ave E Ste 200 Sumner (98390) ***(G-13059)***
Cold Sea Refrigeration Inc 360 466-5850
758 Tillamuk Dr La Conner (98257) ***(G-5521)***
Cole Graphic Solutions Inc 253 564-4600
4901 Center St Tacoma (98409) ***(G-13238)***
Colfax Meat Packing Plant, Colfax *Also called Vincent R Taylor* ***(G-2722)***
Collectible Creations 360 613-1799
8604 Payne Ln Nw Bremerton (98311) ***(G-1943)***
College Portfolios 425 427-0126
26301 Se 31st St Sammamish (98075) ***(G-9198)***
Collins Aerospace 509 744-6000
11135 W Westbow Ln Spokane (99224) ***(G-12187)***
Collins Machine Inc 206 767-4149
1429 S Cloverdale St Seattle (98108) ***(G-9714)***
Colman's Fishing Supply, Auburn *Also called Northwest Hygienetics Inc* ***(G-511)***
Colonial Heirlooms Manchester, Port Orchard *Also called Charles Hanson* ***(G-7797)***
Color Art Press, Seattle *Also called Color Art Printing Inc* ***(G-9715)***
Color Art Printing Inc 206 762-0784
9451 Delridge Way Sw Seattle (98106) ***(G-9715)***
Color Grphics Scrnprinting EMB, Tumwater *Also called Color Grphics Scrnprinting Inc* ***(G-13862)***
Color Grphics Scrnprinting Inc 360 352-3970
2540 Crites St Sw Tumwater (98512) ***(G-13862)***
Color ME Frugal, Everett *Also called At Your Service* ***(G-3374)***
Color ME House Inc 360 742-8646
1801 East Bay Dr Ne Apt J Olympia (98506) ***(G-7252)***
Color One, Seattle *Also called Chromaworks Corporation* ***(G-9681)***
Color Press Publishing Inc 509 525-6030
1425 W Rose St Walla Walla (99362) ***(G-14789)***
Color Printing Systems Inc 206 763-7704
15106 10th Ave Sw Burien (98166) ***(G-2097)***
Colore's International, Woodinville *Also called Wincraft Incorporated* ***(G-15405)***
Colored Metal Roofing 360 887-4524
30515 Nw Paradise Park Rd Ridgefield (98642) ***(G-9073)***
Colorgraphics 206 576-4300
6520 S 190th St Ste 100 Kent (98032) ***(G-4857)***
Colorific Porcelain 425 743-1591
6329 176th St Sw Lynnwood (98037) ***(G-6096)***
Colosseum Ventures LLC 509 533-0366
933 E 3rd Ave Spokane (99202) ***(G-12188)***
Colour Coach 206 478-6159
2026 Rucker Ave Apt B Everett (98201) ***(G-3423)***
Colubia AG & Mfg 509 382-4849
421 Fields Gulch Waitsburg (99361) ***(G-14752)***
Columbia Asphalt & Gravel Inc 509 457-3654
377 Parker Bridge Rd Wapato (98951) ***(G-14913)***
Columbia Basin Ice LLC 509 736-9583
6300 W Deschutes Ave A106 Kennewick (99336) ***(G-4645)***
Columbia Basin Machine Co Inc 509 765-6212
612 W 3rd Ave Moses Lake (98837) ***(G-6695)***
Columbia Basin Prosthetic 509 737-8322
2624a W Deschutes Ave A Kennewick (99336) ***(G-4646)***
Columbia Basin Publishing Co 509 765-4561
813 W 3rd Ave Moses Lake (98837) ***(G-6696)***
Columbia Basin Sign and Ltg 509 764-8121
320 S Alder St Moses Lake (98837) ***(G-6697)***
Columbia Cabinets LLC 509 325-8995
1927 W Maxwell Ave Spokane (99201) ***(G-12189)***
Columbia Cascade Company 360 693-8558
1801 W 20th St Vancouver (98660) ***(G-14129)***
Columbia Cascade Winery Assn 509 782-3845
301 Angier Ave 3b Cashmere (98815) ***(G-2318)***

Columbia Cedar Inc (PA)..........509 738-4711
24419 Highway 395 N Kettle Falls (99141) ***(G-5229)***
Columbia Cedar Inc..........509 738-4711
634 Highway 395 S Colville (99114) ***(G-2744)***
Columbia Chain Belt Inc..........509 546-2000
308 E B Cir Pasco (99301) ***(G-7562)***
Columbia Cove LLC..........360 739-7373
1805 Columbia Cove Ln S Rock Island (98850) ***(G-9148)***
Columbia Crest Winery, Paterson *Also called Michelle Ste Wine Estates Ltd* ***(G-7659)***
Columbia Cultured Marble Inc..........509 582-5660
1601 S Washington St Kennewick (99337) ***(G-4647)***
Columbia Cultured MBL II LLC..........509 582-5660
1601 1/2 S Washington St Kennewick (99337) ***(G-4648)***
Columbia Electric Supply..........509 473-9156
5818 E Broadway Ave Spokane Valley (99212) ***(G-12661)***
Columbia Furniture Mfg Inc..........509 534-7147
2821 N Hogan St Spokane (99207) ***(G-12190)***
Columbia Games Inc..........360 366-2228
3190 Haynie Rd Custer (98240) ***(G-2854)***
Columbia Gem House Inc..........360 514-0569
12507 Ne 95th St Vancouver (98682) ***(G-14130)***
Columbia Gorge Winery Inc..........509 365-2900
6 Lyle Snowden Rd Lyle (98635) ***(G-5995)***
Columbia Granite LLC..........360 943-4072
5209 Boulevard Ext Rd Se Olympia (98501) ***(G-7253)***
Columbia Indus Coatings LLC..........509 531-7310
1212 Columbia Park Trl Richland (99352) ***(G-8983)***
Columbia Laser Centers Inc..........509 529-7711
108 Sw 9th St College Place (99324) ***(G-2723)***
Columbia Litho Inc..........360 834-4662
302 Ne 6th Ave Camas (98607) ***(G-2239)***
Columbia Litho Prtg & Imaging, Camas *Also called Columbia Litho Inc* ***(G-2239)***
Columbia Machine Inc (PA)..........360 694-1501
107 Grand Blvd Vancouver (98661) ***(G-14131)***
Columbia Machine Inc..........360 905-1611
3000 Columbia House Blvd Vancouver (98661) ***(G-14132)***
Columbia Machine Inc..........360 694-1501
107 Grand Blvd Vancouver (98661) ***(G-14133)***
Columbia Manufacturing..........360 210-5124
330 Ne 5th Ave Camas (98607) ***(G-2240)***
Columbia Metal Fab Cnstr Inc..........360 989-0201
1265 Nw 3rd St Kalama (98625) ***(G-4496)***
Columbia Metal Works Inc..........360 693-5818
4200 Nw Fruit Valley Rd Vancouver (98660) ***(G-14134)***
Columbia Mfg & Tech Ctr LLC..........360 835-0922
750 S 32nd St Washougal (98671) ***(G-14948)***
Columbia Navigation Inc..........509 684-4335
365 2nd Ave Kettle Falls (99160) ***(G-5222)***
Columbia Nutritional LLC (PA)..........360 737-9966
6317 Ne 131st Ave 103 Vancouver (98682) ***(G-14135)***
Columbia Office and Bus..........360 695-6245
2300 E 3rd Loop Vancouver (98661) ***(G-14136)***
Columbia Pallet LLC..........509 430-9647
1651 Se Road 33 Pasco (99301) ***(G-7563)***
Columbia Precast Products LLC..........360 335-8400
1765 Howard Way Woodland (98674) ***(G-15424)***
Columbia Pulp I LLC..........509 288-4892
1351 State Hwy 261 Starbuck (99359) ***(G-13001)***
Columbia Ready Mix Inc..........509 453-2063
371 Parker Ridge Rd Parker (98939) ***(G-7548)***
Columbia Rigging Corporation..........509 545-4657
2407 E A St Pasco (99301) ***(G-7564)***
Columbia River Carbonates (PA)..........360 225-6505
300 N Pekin Rd Woodland (98674) ***(G-15425)***
Columbia River Mfg Inc..........509 493-3460
799 Highway 141 White Salmon (98672) ***(G-15113)***
Columbia River Mfg Svcs LLC..........801 652-3008
1030 N Center Pkwy Kennewick (99336) ***(G-4649)***
Columbia River Quilting, Vancouver *Also called Dan Coats* ***(G-14166)***
Columbia River Reader..........360 636-6097
1333 14th Ave Longview (98632) ***(G-5900)***
Columbia Rock & Aggregates Inc..........360 892-0510
913 Ne 172nd Ave Vancouver (98684) ***(G-14137)***
Columbia Sign..........360 696-1919
12003 Ne 121st St Brush Prairie (98606) ***(G-2032)***
Columbia Sign Inc..........360 696-1919
11808 Ne 4th Plain Blvd Vancouver (98682) ***(G-14138)***
Columbia Stainless Metal-Fab..........509 662-9078
4 E Orondo Ave Wenatchee (98801) ***(G-15022)***
Columbia Tarp Liner & Sup Co..........360 577-1834
3048 Lindsey Dr Longview (98632) ***(G-5901)***
Columbia Ultimate, Vancouver *Also called Ontario Systems LLC* ***(G-14452)***
Columbia Valley Compost LLC..........509 551-7202
251 S Wamba Rd Prosser (99350) ***(G-8035)***
Columbia Winery..........425 488-2776
14030 Ne 145th St Woodinville (98072) ***(G-15208)***
Columbia/Okura LLC..........360 735-1952
301 Grove St Ste A Vancouver (98661) ***(G-14139)***
Columbus Systems Inc (PA)..........360 943-4165
2945 37th Ave Sw Tumwater (98512) ***(G-13863)***
Columbus Systems Inc..........360 943-4165
855 Trosper Rd Sw Tumwater (98512) ***(G-13864)***
Colville Printing LLC..........509 684-5869
511 S Main St Colville (99114) ***(G-2745)***
Colville Sign Co..........509 685-2185
153 N Wynne St Colville (99114) ***(G-2746)***
Colville Valley Concrete Corp..........509 684-2534
1175 E 3rd Ave Colville (99114) ***(G-2747)***
Colville Wdwkg & Stained GL..........509 684-7670
115 S Main St Colville (99114) ***(G-2748)***
Combat Flip Flops LLC..........206 913-9971
280 Ne Birch St Issaquah (98027) ***(G-4396)***
Combat Flip Flops LLC..........206 913-9971
1422 Nw Gilman Blvd Ste 2 Issaquah (98027) ***(G-4397)***
Combustion Technology LLC..........360 253-9600
3307 Ne 109th Ave Vancouver (98682) ***(G-14140)***
Come On Get Hoppy..........509 276-6288
6431 Lakeview Dr Nine Mile Falls (99026) ***(G-7069)***
Comeau Lettering..........360 573-2216
11911 Ne 50th Ave Vancouver (98686) ***(G-14141)***
Comfort Acrylics Inc..........360 834-9218
2103 Ne 272nd Ave Camas (98607) ***(G-2241)***
Comfort Design Windows & Doors, Lakewood *Also called Lakewood Holdings Inc* ***(G-5734)***
Commencement Bay Coffee Co..........253 851-8259
8626 Dogwood Ln Nw Gig Harbor (98332) ***(G-4092)***
Commerce Retail Sales Inc..........509 926-1724
1011 E 29th Ave Spokane (99203) ***(G-12191)***
Commercial Application Sales, Seattle *Also called Pat Files* ***(G-10764)***
Commercial Cabinet Works..........360 857-3130
5901 S 11th St Ridgefield (98642) ***(G-9074)***
Commercial Chemtech Inc..........206 932-0841
309 S Cloverdale St D5 Seattle (98108) ***(G-9716)***
Commercial Creamery Co (PA)..........509 747-4131
159 S Cedar St Spokane (99201) ***(G-12192)***
Commercial Creamery Co Ida Inc (HQ)..........509 747-4131
159 S Cedar St Spokane (99201) ***(G-12193)***
Commercial Crting Box Pckg Inc..........253 804-8616
1445 R St Nw Auburn (98001) ***(G-410)***
Commercial Displayers..........206 622-8039
2916 100th St Sw Ste E Everett (98204) ***(G-3424)***
Commercial Fabric Mfg, Seattle *Also called Duane Ruud* ***(G-9856)***
Commercial Plastics Corp..........206 682-4832
3414 4th Ave S Seattle (98134) ***(G-9717)***
Commercial Printing Inc..........509 663-4772
1449 N Wenatchee Ave Wenatchee (98801) ***(G-15023)***
Commercial Service & Repair, Everett *Also called Terry Albracht* ***(G-3628)***
Commet Precision Products..........360 403-7600
15328 State Route 530 Ne Arlington (98223) ***(G-220)***
Committee For Children..........206 343-1223
2815 2nd Ave Ste 400 Seattle (98121) ***(G-9718)***
Common Ground Pottery, Medical Lake *Also called Handyworks Inc* ***(G-6441)***
Common Industries LLC..........206 963-6649
6548 Palatine Ave N Seattle (98103) ***(G-9719)***
Common Tone Arts..........206 251-8260
3827 Meridian Ave N Seattle (98103) ***(G-9720)***
Commscope Technologies LLC..........425 888-2370
1546 Boalch Ave Nw Ste 60 North Bend (98045) ***(G-7109)***
Community Networkers LLC..........509 826-5154
208 S Main St OMAK (98841) ***(G-7437)***
Community Thrift Shop LLC..........509 438-1302
395 Wright Ave Richland (99352) ***(G-8984)***
Community Values Magazine..........360 459-8292
3619 Owl Ln Ne Olympia (98516) ***(G-7254)***
Comp U Charge Inc..........509 484-1918
104 N Madelia St Spokane (99202) ***(G-12194)***
Compactors Nw..........206 747-7316
7345 9th Ave Nw Seattle (98117) ***(G-9721)***
Companion Baking LLC..........206 856-4080
4411 42nd Ave Sw Seattle (98116) ***(G-9722)***
Company 43 LLC..........425 269-0430
24016 21st Ave W Bothell (98021) ***(G-1841)***
Company K LLC..........206 632-0509
620 Nw 44th St Seattle (98107) ***(G-9723)***
Compass Aerospace Northwest, I..........253 852-9700
821 3rd Ave S Kent (98032) ***(G-4858)***
Compass Northwest..........206 546-1178
19302 Palatine Ave N Shoreline (98133) ***(G-11766)***
Compass Outdoor Adventures LLC..........425 281-0267
7724 Melrose Ln Se Snoqualmie (98065) ***(G-12007)***
Compass Productions, Seattle *Also called Cascade Publishing Inc* ***(G-9643)***
Compendium Incorporated (PA)..........206 812-1640
2100 N Pacific St Seattle (98103) ***(G-9724)***
Competentum-Usa Ltd..........425 996-4201
1495 Nw Gilman Blvd # 14 Issaquah (98027) ***(G-4398)***
Competitive Development & Mfg..........360 691-7816
19403 63rd Ave Ne Granite Falls (98252) ***(G-4269)***
Competitive Development & Mfg..........360 691-7816
10905 Mountain Loop Hwy Granite Falls (98252) ***(G-4270)***
Competitive Edge Athletics..........206 246-7211
14443 Ambaum Blvd Sw Burien (98166) ***(G-2098)***
Complete Access, Buckley *Also called Integrated Stair Systems Inc* ***(G-2060)***
Complete Controls..........360 904-7525
9306 Ne 7th St Vancouver (98664) ***(G-14142)***

ALPHABETIC

Complete Deburr Inc 253 887-0997
20 37th St Ne Ste 5 Auburn (98002) *(G-411)*
Complete Mllwk Solutions Inc 253 875-6769
33615 1st Way S Ste A Federal Way (98003) *(G-3724)*
Complete Music 509 927-3535
728 N Hogan St Spokane (99202) *(G-12195)*
Complex Aerospace LLC 253 886-1323
3665 C St Ne Auburn (98002) *(G-412)*
Complex Machining, Auburn *Also called Complex Aerospace LLC (G-412)*
Compliance Industries, Renton *Also called Patrick E & Patricia M Lydon (G-8876)*
Component Engineering Inc 206 284-9171
14739 Aurora Ave N Shoreline (98133) *(G-11767)*
Component Products Corporation 425 355-6800
11623 Cyrus Way Mukilteo (98275) *(G-6904)*
Component Tinning Services Inc 509 315-5840
3808 N Sullivan Rd 18q Spokane Valley (99216) *(G-12662)*
Composite Aircraft Tech LLC 360 864-6271
148 Skyhawk Dr Toledo (98591) *(G-13636)*
Composite Aquatic Innovations 360 403-7707
20405 69th Ave Ne Arlington (98223) *(G-221)*
Composite Recycling Tech Ctr 360 819-1204
2220 W 18th St Port Angeles (98363) *(G-7694)*
Composite Solutions Corp 253 833-1878
14810 Puyallup St E # 100 Sumner (98390) *(G-13060)*
Composite Tooling Innovations 509 637-3836
1211 E Bingen Point Way Bingen (98605) *(G-1635)*
Composites Consolidation Compa 509 877-2228
180 E Jones Rd Wapato (98951) *(G-14914)*
Composites Consolidation LLC 509 877-2228
180 E Jones Rd Wapato (98951) *(G-14915)*
Compost Manufacturing Alliance 206 755-8309
1771 Vista Rama Dr E Port Orchard (98366) *(G-7798)*
Compost Tea By Seaneen 360 678-3288
107 S Main St Ste A103 Coupeville (98239) *(G-2811)*
Compound Photonics US Corp 360 597-3654
805 Broadway St Ste 300 Vancouver (98660) *(G-14143)*
Compressed Air Systems LLC 425 328-0755
19009 61st Ave Ne Unit 5 Arlington (98223) *(G-222)*
Comptex Inc 360 466-5453
125 Sherman St La Conner (98257) *(G-5522)*
Computer Assisted Message Inc 425 392-2496
400 Jasmine Pl Nw Issaquah (98027) *(G-4399)*
Computer Clinic Northwest Inc 360 658-1234
1239 State Ave Marysville (98270) *(G-6327)*
Computer Connections 360 736-2177
213 E Main St Centralia (98531) *(G-2395)*
Computer Enhancement, Mercer Island *Also called Led Software (G-6470)*
Computer Human Interaction LLC 425 282-6900
16040 Christensen Rd # 110 Tukwila (98188) *(G-13714)*
Computer Systems Sales & Svcs 206 979-1731
12946 Se Kent Kangley Rd # 300 Kent (98030) *(G-4859)*
Computer Technology Link Corp 253 872-3608
22409 72nd Ave S Kent (98032) *(G-4860)*
Computergear Inc 425 487-3600
19510 144th Ave Ne Ste E5 Woodinville (98072) *(G-15209)*
Computing & Communications, Seattle *Also called University of Washington (G-11380)*
Comscore Inc 206 447-1860
316 Occidental Ave S # 200 Seattle (98104) *(G-9725)*
Comserv, Snohomish *Also called King Enterprises (G-11933)*
Comtronic Systems LLC 509 573-4300
110 E 2nd St Cle Elum (98922) *(G-2662)*
Conachen Aviation 360 516-7740
161 Hooker Rd Sequim (98382) *(G-11618)*
Conagra Brands Inc 425 251-0761
6320 S 190th St Kent (98032) *(G-4861)*
Conagra Fods Clmbia Base Blnds 509 544-2111
3330 Travel Plaza Way Pasco (99301) *(G-7565)*
Conagra Foods Specialty Potato 509 547-8851
960 N Glade Rd Pasco (99301) *(G-7566)*
Conagra Foods-Lamb Weston, Pasco *Also called Conagra Fods Clmbia Base Blnds (G-7565)*
Conagsco, Nine Mile Falls *Also called Concrete & Aggregate Supply Co (G-7070)*
Conation Technologies LLC 253 864-8234
101 S Meridian Ste B Puyallup (98371) *(G-8135)*
Concept Fabrication Inc 509 534-9235
5315 E Union Ave Spokane (99212) *(G-12196)*
Concept Reality Inc 360 695-3860
7812 Ne 19th Ct Vancouver (98665) *(G-14144)*
Concorde Marine Inc 360 755-3471
310 34th St Anacortes (98221) *(G-115)*
Concordia Coffee Company Inc 425 453-2800
6812 185th Ave Ne Redmond (98052) *(G-8422)*
Concordia Coffee Systems, Redmond *Also called Concordia Coffee Company Inc (G-8422)*
Concrete & Aggregate Supply Co 253 853-2887
6533 Long Lake Dr Nine Mile Falls (99026) *(G-7070)*
Concrete Creations 509 826-5409
64 Danker Cutoff OMAK (98841) *(G-7438)*
Concrete Nor'west, Lake Stevens *Also called Miles Sand & Gravel Company (G-5661)*
Concrete Nor'west, Everson *Also called Miles Sand & Gravel Company (G-3682)*
Concrete Nor'west Division, Puyallup *Also called Miles Sand & Gravel Company (G-8193)*
Concrete Norwest, Oak Harbor *Also called Miles Sand & Gravel Company (G-7159)*
Concrete Norwest Division, Burlington *Also called Miles Sand & Gravel Company (G-2171)*
Concrete Products Co Ore LLC 360 834-3459
1615 Se 6th Ave Camas (98607) *(G-2242)*
Concrete Products Inc 253 864-2774
5415 189th St E Puyallup (98375) *(G-8136)*
Concrete Shop Inc 360 573-5775
1702 Ne 99th St Vancouver (98665) *(G-14145)*
Concrete Works, Greenacres *Also called Curtiss R Grenz (G-4296)*
Concrete Works Statuary Inc 509 922-6168
4750 N Division St Spokane (99207) *(G-12197)*
Concur Technologies Inc (HQ) 425 590-5000
601 108th Ave Ne Ste 1000 Bellevue (98004) *(G-860)*
Concut Diamond Products, Kent *Also called Concut Inc (G-4862)*
Concut Inc (HQ) 253 872-3507
6815 S 220th St Kent (98032) *(G-4862)*
Condor Electronics, Seattle *Also called Condor Technical Services (G-9726)*
Condor Technical Services 206 633-5190
10007 Aurora Ave N Seattle (98133) *(G-9726)*
Conestoga Wood Spc Corp 253 437-1320
6122 S 228th St Kent (98032) *(G-4863)*
Conex Sand & Gravel 503 437-0536
17007 Ne 22nd St Vancouver (98684) *(G-14146)*
Config-Systems 360 871-8091
9481 Se Miller Creek Rd Port Orchard (98367) *(G-7799)*
Confluence Vineyards 360 887-2343
19111 Nw 67th Ave Ridgefield (98642) *(G-9075)*
Conglobal Industries LLC 206 624-8180
1818 S 93rd St Seattle (98108) *(G-9727)*
Conglobal Industries LLC 206 624-8180
1 S Idaho St Seattle (98134) *(G-9728)*
Congruent Software 206 301-0553
1001 W Howe St Seattle (98119) *(G-9729)*
Congruent Software (usa) Inc 425 460-0172
4205 148th Ave Ne Ste 100 Bellevue (98007) *(G-861)*
Conifer Specialties Inc 425 486-3334
15500 Woodinville Redmond Woodinville (98072) *(G-15210)*
Conlan Press Incorporated 650 267-9651
1050 Larrabee Ave Ste 104 Bellingham (98225) *(G-1302)*
Conmet, Vancouver *Also called Consolidated Metco Inc (G-14147)*
Connectzonecom LLC 425 212-4400
5030 208th St Sw Ste B Lynnwood (98036) *(G-6097)*
Connell Sand & Gravel Inc 509 545-4066
6220 N Burlington St Pasco (99301) *(G-7567)*
Connell Sand & Gravel Inc 509 234-3221
200 W Date St Connell (99326) *(G-2792)*
Connell Sand & Gravel Inc (PA) 509 234-3221
200 W Date St Connell (99326) *(G-2793)*
Connelly Company Inc 509 935-6755
1767 Highway 395 S Chewelah (99109) *(G-2601)*
Connelly Skis Inc (HQ) 425 775-5416
20621 52nd Ave W Lynnwood (98036) *(G-6098)*
Connelly Skis Inc 425 831-1099
7926 Bracken Pl Se Snoqualmie (98065) *(G-12008)*
Conner Industries 360 261-0265
1390 Mount Pleasant Rd Kelso (98626) *(G-4520)*
Connerlee Vineyards Inc 509 932-4267
22913 Se 25th Pl Sammamish (98075) *(G-9199)*
Connx Solutions, Redmond *Also called Software AG Usa Inc (G-8673)*
Connx Solutions Inc 425 519-6600
2039 152nd Ave Ne Redmond (98052) *(G-8423)*
Conocophillips Company 509 536-8417
6317 E Sharp Ave Spokane Valley (99212) *(G-12663)*
Conocophillips Company 253 584-0583
10913 Bridgeport Way Sw Lakewood (98499) *(G-5707)*
Conrad Manufacturing Co Inc 253 852-3420
4156 B Pl Nw Auburn (98001) *(G-413)*
Consolidated Container Co LLC 425 251-0303
6545 S Glacier St Tukwila (98188) *(G-13715)*
Consolidated Container Co LLC 509 891-2483
3808 N Sullivan Rd 8a Spokane Valley (99216) *(G-12664)*
Consolidated Food Management 253 589-5654
4500 Steilacoom Blvd Sw Lakewood (98499) *(G-5708)*
Consolidated Metco Inc (HQ) 360 828-2599
5701 Se Columbia Way Vancouver (98661) *(G-14147)*
Consolidated Metco Inc 360 828-2689
3301 Se Columbia Way Vancouver (98661) *(G-14148)*
Consolidated Press, Seattle *Also called Washington Web Company Inc (G-11442)*
Consolidated Press LLC (PA) 206 447-9659
600 S Spokane St Seattle (98134) *(G-9730)*
Consolidated Press LLC 253 922-3195
2521 Pacific Hwy E Ste A Fife (98424) *(G-3945)*
Consolidated Pump & Supply 509 891-1313
11303 E Montgomery Dr # 4 Spokane Valley (99206) *(G-12665)*
Consolidated Pump & Supply 509 543-7241
2305 N Capitol Ave Pasco (99301) *(G-7568)*
Constance Machine, Everett *Also called Joe Constance (G-3524)*
Constancy Press LLC 206 522-7513
4532 48th Ave Ne Seattle (98105) *(G-9731)*
Constant Computer 253 227-0532
919 126th Street Ct E Tacoma (98445) *(G-13239)*
Constantine Armory LLC 509 998-6959
2615 N Cincinnati St # 102 Spokane (99207) *(G-12198)*

Constellation Brands Inc 425 482-7300
14030 Ne 145th St Woodinville (98072) *(G-15211)*
Constellation Homebuilder Syst 888 723-2222
8343 154th Ave Ne Ste 200 Redmond (98052) *(G-8424)*
Construction Parts 253 271-6133
20718 Mountain Hwy E Spanaway (98387) *(G-12055)*
Construction Parts LLC 253 255-1775
25302 Meridian Ave E Graham (98338) *(G-4221)*
Construction Unlimited Inc of, Seattle *Also called Lj Backdoor Inc (G-10433)*
Constructivision Inc 425 741-4413
17010 9th Ave Se Mill Creek (98012) *(G-6504)*
Contacez LLC 360 694-1000
217 Se 136th Ave Ste 105 Vancouver (98684) *(G-14149)*
Container Stuffers LLC 206 255-3187
12126 Se 284th St Auburn (98092) *(G-414)*
Containers Division, Olympia *Also called Weyerhaeuser Company (G-7425)*
Contech Engnered Solutions LLC 509 244-3694
2823 S Craig Rd Airway Heights (99001) *(G-50)*
Contech Engnered Solutions LLC 360 357-9735
606 Columbia St Nw # 210 Olympia (98501) *(G-7255)*
Contech Systems Inc (HQ) 360 332-1718
3736 South Tacoma Way Tacoma (98409) *(G-13240)*
Contempo Inc 509 758-1694
1390 Fair St Clarkston (99403) *(G-2627)*
Contemporary Design Co 360 599-2833
4201 Meridian St Ste 101 Bellingham (98226) *(G-1303)*
Contemporary Woodworks LLC 360 897-2162
15619 223rd Ave E Orting (98360) *(G-7476)*
Content Master 425 274-1970
14335 Ne 24th St Ste 205 Bellevue (98007) *(G-862)*
Conterra Inc 360 734-2311
1600 Kentucky St Ste A3 Bellingham (98229) *(G-1304)*
Context Reality Inc 425 241-5860
8040 161st Ave Ne 225 Redmond (98052) *(G-8425)*
Context Vr, Redmond *Also called Context Reality Inc (G-8425)*
Continental Brass, Seattle *Also called Blaser Die Casting Co (G-9540)*
Continental Data Graphics 425 562-4050
3245 146th Pl Se Ste 270 Bellevue (98007) *(G-863)*
Continental Holdings III 425 502-7055
480 S Kenyon St Seattle (98108) *(G-9732)*
Continental Lime, Tacoma *Also called Graymont Western US Inc (G-13319)*
Continental Mills Inc (PA) 206 816-7000
18100 Andover Park W Tukwila (98188) *(G-13716)*
Continental Mills Inc 206 816-7799
7851 S 192nd St Kent (98032) *(G-4864)*
Continuous Casting Co 206 623-7688
2724 6th Pl S Seattle (98134) *(G-9733)*
Continuum 509 534-0655
1611 E Sprague Ave Spokane (99202) *(G-12199)*
Continuum Creative LLC 404 985-6648
2760 76th Ave Se Apt 406 Mercer Island (98040) *(G-6459)*
Contour Inc 206 792-5226
3131 Western Ave Ste 410 Seattle (98121) *(G-9734)*
Contour Coatings LLC 253 830-4994
4101 N 24th St Tacoma (98406) *(G-13241)*
Contour Countertops Inc 503 654-2245
5305 Ne 121st Ave Ste 511 Vancouver (98682) *(G-14150)*
Contract Sew & Repair Inc 253 395-7910
23001 54th Ave S Kent (98032) *(G-4865)*
Contractor Equipment Rental, Everett *Also called Passage Inc (G-3570)*
Contracts Company 360 299-9900
2201 Highland Dr Anacortes (98221) *(G-116)*
Contrary Design 253 653-0275
35821 Military Rd S Auburn (98001) *(G-415)*
Control Dynamics Inc 800 738-5004
21 E Marine View Dr Ste G Everett (98201) *(G-3425)*
Control Seneca Corporation 425 602-4700
12810 Ne 178th St Ste 101 Woodinville (98072) *(G-15212)*
Control Systems America Inc 360 210-7475
2027 Nw Sierra Ln Camas (98607) *(G-2243)*
Control Technology Inc 425 823-3878
12817 Ne 126th Pl Kirkland (98034) *(G-5311)*
Controlfreek Inc 509 979-5677
11616 E Montgomery Dr # 4 Spokane Valley (99206) *(G-12666)*
Controlled Power Incorporated 425 485-1778
17909 Bothell Everett Hwy # 102 Bothell (98012) *(G-1842)*
Controlled Products of Wash 206 575-2249
14520 Interurban Ave S # 150 Tukwila (98168) *(G-13717)*
Controls Group The Inc 425 828-4149
10518 Ne 68th St Ste 103 Kirkland (98033) *(G-5312)*
Convergent Earned Value Assoc 206 293-6931
13606 Se 43rd Pl Bellevue (98006) *(G-864)*
Convergent Technology 206 352-5357
2646 Magnolia Blvd W Seattle (98199) *(G-9735)*
Conveying Solutions, Buckley *Also called Conveyor Works Inc (G-2053)*
Conveyor Dynamics Inc 360 671-2200
3633 Alderwood Ave Bellingham (98225) *(G-1305)*
Conveyor Works Inc 360 829-5378
11012 254th Ave E Buckley (98321) *(G-2053)*
Conwood Construction Inc 360 694-5195
1701 W 31st St Vancouver (98660) *(G-14151)*

Cook On Clay 360 678-1818
19762 State Route 20 Coupeville (98239) *(G-2812)*
Cook Welding Services 425 513-1263
2626 119th St Sw Ste A1 Everett (98204) *(G-3426)*
Cooke Aquaculture Pacific LLC (HQ) 206 282-0988
4019 21st Ave W Ste 300 Seattle (98199) *(G-9736)*
Cooke Aquaculture Pacific LLC 360 293-9448
1201 11th St Anacortes (98221) *(G-117)*
Cooke Seafood Usa Inc 206 282-0988
4207 9th Ave Nw Seattle (98107) *(G-9737)*
Cookes Canvas & Sewing 360 384-1636
5040 Pacific Hwy Ferndale (98248) *(G-3833)*
Cookie Fairy 360 568-0868
11607 171st Ave Se Snohomish (98290) *(G-11891)*
Cool Racing Oil 971 235-7611
1400 W Washington St Sequim (98382) *(G-11619)*
Cooler Guys, Kirkland *Also called Coolpc Incorporated (G-5313)*
Coolest Graphics, Kent *Also called Access Printing Inc (G-4756)*
Coolpc Incorporated 425 821-6400
11630 Slater Ave Ne Ste 6 Kirkland (98034) *(G-5313)*
Cooper Electric Motor Svc Co 509 452-9550
205 S 4th Ave Yakima (98902) *(G-15536)*
Cooper Power Systems Inc 206 499-9473
26733 227th Ave Se Maple Valley (98038) *(G-6265)*
Cooper Smithing Co 253 906-0425
12610 Mundy Loss Rd Buckley (98321) *(G-2054)*
Cooper T Kirsch Glass LLC 206 718-8183
3821 Beach Dr Sw Apt 202 Seattle (98116) *(G-9738)*
Cooper Tire & Rubber Company 253 826-5742
3012 142nd Ave E Ste 300 Sumner (98390) *(G-13061)*
Cooperative AG Producers Inc (PA) 509 523-3032
120 W Fifth St Rosalia (99170) *(G-9154)*
Coordinating Services Inc 425 334-8966
621 State Route 9 Ne Lake Stevens (98258) *(G-5640)*
Copbong428 LLC 206 778-1436
3724 S 316th St Auburn (98001) *(G-416)*
Copper Canyon Press 360 385-4925
Fort Worden State Park Port Townsend (98368) *(G-7872)*
Copper Creek Fabrications LLC 360 582-9676
14 Banana Way Sequim (98382) *(G-11620)*
Copper Creek Logging LLC 253 203-5915
520 Vine St Wilkeson (98396) *(G-15143)*
Copper Mountain Vineyards 509 476-2762
33349c Us Highway 97 Oroville (98844) *(G-7463)*
Copper Ridge Fabrication LLC 360 582-3898
214 Wilders Ln Sequim (98382) *(G-11621)*
Copper River Smoking Co 253 446-0634
240 15th St Se Puyallup (98372) *(G-8137)*
Copperheat 360 757-2589
11837 Watertank Rd Burlington (98233) *(G-2146)*
Coppertop Enterprises Inc (PA) 360 966-9622
401 Lincoln St Ste 102 Everson (98247) *(G-3672)*
Copperwood LLC 360 674-3122
5765 Imperial Way Sw Bremerton (98312) *(G-1944)*
Copperworks Distilling Co, Seattle *Also called Big Derby Distilling Co (G-9522)*
Coprintco Business Forms Inc 360 425-1810
1146 15th Ave Ste 100 Longview (98632) *(G-5902)*
Coptracker Inc 214 542-2351
26619 Road U Sw Mattawa (99349) *(G-6404)*
Copy & Print Store, Mount Vernon *Also called Mountain Top Inc (G-6814)*
Copy Break 206 782-7506
7725 24th Ave Nw Seattle (98117) *(G-9739)*
Copy Cat Graphics 360 452-3635
3234 E Highway 101 Port Angeles (98362) *(G-7695)*
Copy Center 6, Lacey *Also called Printing Washington State Dept (G-5578)*
Copy Co 206 622-4050
616 6th Ave S Seattle (98104) *(G-9740)*
Copy Duplicating Service, Seattle *Also called University of Washington (G-11379)*
Copy Shop 509 962-2679
724 E University Way Ellensburg (98926) *(G-3190)*
Copy Source, Bellingham *Also called Risque Inc (G-1517)*
Copy-Rite Inc 509 624-8503
1108 W 2nd Ave Spokane (99201) *(G-12200)*
Copy-Rite Printing, Spokane *Also called Copy-Rite Inc (G-12200)*
Copytonix 503 968-0364
14432 Se Eastgate Way # 300 Bellevue (98007) *(G-865)*
Cor-Tread LLC 425 268-6377
4493 Russell Rd Ste H Mukilteo (98275) *(G-6905)*
Corallie Industries 253 576-5240
3219 253rd Street Ct E Spanaway (98387) *(G-12056)*
Corban Tech LLC 253 353-0849
4533 S 79th St Tacoma (98409) *(G-13242)*
Corbells Portable Welding 360 724-4700
2161 Old Highway 99 N Rd Burlington (98233) *(G-2147)*
Corbitz Ltd 206 241-9877
16428 12th Ave Sw Burien (98166) *(G-2099)*
Cordova, Kirkland *Also called Wntr Ski Academy LLC (G-5495)*
Cordstrap USA Inc 253 886-5000
2200 W Valley Hwy N # 110 Auburn (98001) *(G-417)*
Core Corporation 425 485-0574
8812 Ne 189th Pl Bothell (98011) *(G-1757)*

A L P H A B E T I C

Core Pack LLC 509 426-2511
1803 Presson Pl Yakima (98903) ***(G-15537)***
Core Tech LLC 253 457-3239
5219 84th St E Tacoma (98446) ***(G-13243)***
Core Training Industries Inc 206 250-2050
103 S 297th Pl Federal Way (98003) ***(G-3725)***
Corey Sign & Display Inc 360 297-5490
5654 Ne Minder Rd Ste 101 Poulsbo (98370) ***(G-7955)***
Corezyn, Kent *Also called Interplastic Corporation* ***(G-4958)***
Coriander Designs, Woodinville *Also called Ken Boudreau Inc* ***(G-15277)***
Corkycellars LLC 425 226-5479
14518 Se 142nd St Renton (98059) ***(G-8775)***
Corliss Estates 509 526-4400
511 N 2nd Ave Walla Walla (99362) ***(G-14790)***
Corliss Redi-Mix, Enumclaw *Also called Tim Corliss & Son Inc* ***(G-3324)***
Corner Stone R V Center LLC 360 704-4441
8500 Old Highway 99 Se A Tumwater (98501) ***(G-13865)***
Cornerstone Attache Group Inc 425 577-2713
15127 Ne 24th St Ste 185 Redmond (98052) ***(G-8426)***
Cornerstone Prsthtics Orthtics (PA) 425 339-2559
1300 44th St Se Everett (98203) ***(G-3427)***
Cornerstone Prsthtics Orthtics 360 734-0298
3106 Northwest Ave Bellingham (98225) ***(G-1306)***
Cornerstone Real Property 360 455-0862
4731 Center Ln Ne Olympia (98516) ***(G-7256)***
Cornerstone Software Systems 425 788-9681
15310 232nd Ave Ne Woodinville (98077) ***(G-15213)***
Corona Decor Company 206 763-1600
6133 6th Ave S Seattle (98108) ***(G-9741)***
Corona Steel Inc 253 874-4766
1701 Bay St Tacoma (98421) ***(G-13244)***
Coronado Biosciences 206 826-7168
1700 7th Ave Seattle (98101) ***(G-9742)***
Corporate Vat Management Inc 206 292-0300
122 S Jackson St Ste 330 Seattle (98104) ***(G-9743)***
Corporation of The President 509 656-2344
3551 Hundley Rd Cle Elum (98922) ***(G-2663)***
Correctional Industries 360 963-3332
1830 Eagle Crest Way Clallam Bay (98326) ***(G-2618)***
Correctional Industries 360 427-4613
2321 W Dayton Airport Rd Shelton (98584) ***(G-11692)***
Corrosion Companies Inc 360 835-2171
3725 Grant St Ste 2 Washougal (98671) ***(G-14949)***
Cortex Manufacturing Inc 425 334-2277
421 S Davies Rd Lake Stevens (98258) ***(G-5641)***
Cortland Company Inc 360 293-8488
1012 2nd St Anacortes (98221) ***(G-118)***
Corus Estates & Vineyards LLC (HQ) 206 728-9063
1910 Frview Ave E Ste 500 Seattle (98102) ***(G-9744)***
Corus Estates & Vineyards LLC 503 538-7724
1410 Lakeside Ct Ste 109 Yakima (98902) ***(G-15538)***
Corvidae Press 360 379-1934
403 U St Port Townsend (98368) ***(G-7873)***
Corvus and Columba LLC 206 673-7860
177 Western Ave W Seattle (98119) ***(G-9745)***
Corwin Beverage Co (PA) 360 696-0766
219 S Timm Rd Ridgefield (98642) ***(G-9076)***
Corwin Beverage Co 360 696-0766
219 S Timm Rd Ridgefield (98642) ***(G-9077)***
Corwin Scott Thomas Imag 253 350-6984
422 106th Avenue Ct E Edgewood (98372) ***(G-3074)***
Cory A Stemp 509 491-3847
222 W Kennewick Ave Kennewick (99336) ***(G-4650)***
Cory Siverson 425 869-8303
18398 Redmond Way Redmond (98052) ***(G-8427)***
Cosalish Design & Lighting, Quil Ceda Village *Also called Roy Pablo* ***(G-8281)***
Cosmic Creamery LLC 425 633-7742
8218 126th Ave Ne Apt E34 Kirkland (98033) ***(G-5314)***
Cosmic Resources 360 730-8574
3939 Saratoga Rd Langley (98260) ***(G-5775)***
Cosmo Specialty Fibers Inc 360 500-4600
1701 1st St Cosmopolis (98537) ***(G-2799)***
Cosmopolis Specialty Fiber 360 533-7531
1701 1st St Cosmopolis (98537) ***(G-2800)***
Cost Center, Redmond *Also called Parker-Hannifin Corporation* ***(G-8616)***
Costellinis LLC 877 889-8266
14150 Ne 20th St 341 Bellevue (98007) ***(G-866)***
Costom Woodwork 425 828-2579
1312 3rd St Kirkland (98033) ***(G-5315)***
Costume Atlier Msque Pettycote 360 819-4296
620 Legion Way Se Olympia (98501) ***(G-7257)***
Cote Bonneville 509 840-4596
2841 Fordyce Rd Sunnyside (98944) ***(G-13117)***
Cottage Sign Co 360 312-1565
6193 Hamilton Ave Ferndale (98248) ***(G-3834)***
Cougar Crest Winery, Walla Walla *Also called Cougar Hills LLC* ***(G-14791)***
Cougar Hills LLC 425 398-9999
14366 Woodnvll Redmond Ne Redmond (98052) ***(G-8428)***
Cougar Hills LLC 509 241-3850
8 N Post St Spokane (99201) ***(G-12201)***
Cougar Hills LLC (PA) 509 529-5980
50 Frenchtown Rd Walla Walla (99362) ***(G-14791)***
Coulee Dam Concrete, Coulee Dam *Also called Tillmans Inc* ***(G-2809)***
Coulee View Food and Fuel 509 633-2951
2 Okanogan Ave Coulee Dam (99116) ***(G-2807)***
Coulter Canvas 509 246-2188
19115 Saint Andrews Dr Nw Soap Lake (98851) ***(G-12037)***
Council For Edctl Trvl US Amer 949 940-1140
220 W Champion St Ste 260 Bellingham (98225) ***(G-1307)***
Counter Intuitive 360 264-5150
13937 Chein Hill Ln Se Tenino (98589) ***(G-13614)***
Counter Stone, Bonney Lake *Also called Ddbd Construction* ***(G-1721)***
Counterbalance Poetry 206 282-2677
2040 13th Ave W Apt 26 Seattle (98119) ***(G-9746)***
Counterpane Inc 253 535-0145
10729 A St S Tacoma (98444) ***(G-13245)***
Countertops For Less 360 306-3921
4781 Guide Meridian Bellingham (98226) ***(G-1308)***
Counting Stick Software LLC 425 750-1028
15015 29th Ave W Lynnwood (98087) ***(G-6099)***
Country Clothiers 206 632-3319
3817 Aurora Ave N Seattle (98103) ***(G-9747)***
Country Flicker Candle Co 509 286-3031
20411 E Wheeler Rd Latah (99018) ***(G-5790)***
Country Harvest Soup 509 535-8357
33 Av Spokane (99223) ***(G-12202)***
Country Malt, Vancouver *Also called Great Western Malting Co* ***(G-14266)***
Country Malt Group, Vancouver *Also called Great Western Malting Co* ***(G-14269)***
Country Morning Farms Inc 509 349-2958
653 N Fox Rd Warden (98857) ***(G-14929)***
Country Save Products Corp 360 435-9868
19704 60th Ave Ne Arlington (98223) ***(G-223)***
Country Stoneware 509 484-6950
803 E Illinois Ave Spokane (99207) ***(G-12203)***
Country Store 509 534-1412
5605 E Sprague Ave Spokane Valley (99212) ***(G-12667)***
Countryman Signs Screen Prtrs 425 355-1037
5615 Broadway Everett (98203) ***(G-3428)***
Countryman Signs/Screen Prtrs, Everett *Also called Countryman Signs Screen Prtrs* ***(G-3428)***
County of Asotin 509 758-1668
838 5th St Clarkston (99403) ***(G-2628)***
County of King 206 263-3113
821 2nd Ave Ste 1100 Seattle (98104) ***(G-9748)***
County of Lewis 360 748-9121
351 Nw North St Chehalis (98532) ***(G-2485)***
County of Lewis 360 494-4123
12953 Us Highway 12 Packwood (98361) ***(G-7542)***
County of Pierce 360 893-2844
20520 162nd Ave Orting (98360) ***(G-7477)***
County Public Works 509 674-2502
1009 E 3rd St Cle Elum (98922) ***(G-2664)***
Couple Power 425 641-0278
2503 158th Ave Se Bellevue (98008) ***(G-867)***
Courageous Heart Healing LLC 541 517-6222
7901 Delridge Way Sw 22d Seattle (98106) ***(G-9749)***
Courier-Herald 360 825-2555
1186 Myrtle Ave Enumclaw (98022) ***(G-3283)***
Courtright Enterprises Inc 509 764-9600
3385 Road M.2 Ne Ste 6 Moses Lake (98837) ***(G-6698)***
Covenant Art Glass Inc 425 252-4232
3232 Broadway Everett (98201) ***(G-3429)***
Covenant Cabinets 425 481-4799
21819 49th Ave Se Bothell (98021) ***(G-1843)***
Coventry Vale Winery Inc 509 882-4100
160602 Evans Rd Grandview (98930) ***(G-4246)***
Cover ME Screen Printing 509 552-1940
1801 13th St Clarkston (99403) ***(G-2629)***
Coverity 206 467-5967
701 5th Ave Seattle (98104) ***(G-9750)***
Covington Cellars 425 806-8636
18580 142nd Ave Ne Woodinville (98072) ***(G-15214)***
Covington Cellars LLC 253 347-9463
21219 45th Ave Se Bothell (98021) ***(G-1844)***
Covington Signs, Maple Valley *Also called Maple Valley Signs Inc* ***(G-6282)***
Covlet Machine & Design Inc 360 658-1977
13115 41st Ave Ne Marysville (98271) ***(G-6328)***
Cowboyz 206 793-6831
2131 S Sprague Ave Tacoma (98405) ***(G-13246)***
Cowden Inc 360 592-4200
3463 Cedarville Rd Bellingham (98226) ***(G-1309)***
Cowden Gravel & Ready Mix, Bellingham *Also called Cowden Inc* ***(G-1309)***
Cowin In-Situ Science LLC 509 392-1329
2500 George Washington Richland (99354) ***(G-8985)***
Cowles Publishing Company (PA) 509 459-5000
999 W Riverside Ave Spokane (99201) ***(G-12204)***
Cowlitz Cont & Diecutting Inc 360 577-8748
2228 Talley Way Kelso (98626) ***(G-4521)***
Cowlitz Electric Construction 253 355-7163
6811 S C St Tacoma (98408) ***(G-13247)***
Cowlitz Fence Co 360 577-6110
2401 Talley Way Ste B Kelso (98626) ***(G-4522)***
Cowlitz River Rigging Inc 360 425-6720
1540 Industrial Way Longview (98632) ***(G-5903)***

ALPHABETIC SECTION

Cowlitz River Software Inc 253 856-3111
1851 Central Pl S Ste 118 Kent (98030) *(G-4866)*
Cowlitz Valley Machine Inc 360 748-0124
126 Northstar Rd Chehalis (98532) *(G-2486)*
Cox Canyon Vineyards 206 940-5086
221 Canyon Vista Way Ellensburg (98926) *(G-3191)*
Cox Orthotics Inc 425 493-8015
4400 Chennault Beach Rd Mukilteo (98275) *(G-6906)*
Coyote Canyon Winery LLC 509 786-7686
80 Mckinley Springs Rd Prosser (99350) *(G-8036)*
Coyote Cleaning Systems Inc 425 776-8002
4208 Russell Rd Ste J Mukilteo (98275) *(G-6907)*
Coyote Hill Press 951 295-9552
930 Cambell Dr Camano Island (98282) *(G-2210)*
Cozi, Seattle *Also called TI Gotham Inc (G-11303)*
CP Films Custom Printed Films 253 261-9404
26910 140th Ave Se Kent (98042) *(G-4867)*
CPM Development Corporation 509 248-2041
2000 E Beech St Yakima (98901) *(G-15539)*
CPM Development Corporation 509 762-5366
5278 Hwy 17 N Moses Lake (98837) *(G-6699)*
CPM Development Corporation 509 865-2975
441 E Mcdonald Rd Toppenish (98948) *(G-13664)*
CPM Development Corporation (HQ) 509 534-6221
5111 E Broadway Ave Spokane Valley (99212) *(G-12668)*
CPM Development Corporation 509 754-5287
2651 Hwy 282 W Ephrata (98823) *(G-3332)*
CPM Development Corporation 509 663-5141
1351 S Wenatchee Ave Wenatchee (98801) *(G-15024)*
CPM Development Corporation 509 536-3355
5111 E Broadway Ave Spokane Valley (99212) *(G-12669)*
CPM Development Corporation 509 886-4853
5515 Enterprise Dr Wenatchee (98802) *(G-15090)*
CPM Development Corporation 509 488-2614
804 E Broadway Ave Othello (99344) *(G-7493)*
CPM Development Corporation 509 932-4525
31002 Hwy 243 S Mattawa (99349) *(G-6405)*
CPM Development Corporation 509 837-5171
112 Factory Rd Sunnyside (98944) *(G-13118)*
Cpo, Bellevue *Also called Center For Prosthetic (G-845)*
Cq2 Enterprises 253 941-4488
29618 Marine View Dr Sw Federal Way (98023) *(G-3726)*
Cr Callen LLC 206 363-7648
17231 76th Ave W Edmonds (98026) *(G-3102)*
Cr Enterprises Nw LLC 425 290-3800
4617 Chennault Beach Rd Mukilteo (98275) *(G-6908)*
Crabhawk 541 921-3593
3224 Kindred Ave Tokeland (98590) *(G-13632)*
Craft International of Wash 360 785-3606
307 Nw Kerron St Winlock (98596) *(G-15148)*
Craft Labor & Support Svcs LLC (PA) 206 304-4543
7636 230th St Sw Apt B Edmonds (98026) *(G-3103)*
Craft Wall of Oregon Inc 509 547-2436
2090 Crane Ave Pasco (99301) *(G-7569)*
Crafted Northwest Doors Inc 509 484-3722
3604 E Rowan Ave Spokane (99217) *(G-12205)*
Craftsman Cellars LLC 509 328-3960
3222 W Providence Ave Spokane (99205) *(G-12206)*
Craftsmen United Inc 360 379-2500
3109 Jefferson St Port Townsend (98368) *(G-7874)*
Craftwork Coatings 253 508-9358
11803 130th Avenue Ct E Puyallup (98374) *(G-8138)*
Craftworks, Seattle *Also called Gb Acquisition Inc (G-10054)*
Crafty Woodworking 425 822-9618
9234 128th Ave Ne Kirkland (98033) *(G-5316)*
Craig Craft Powder Coating, Mukilteo *Also called Powder Coating Inc (G-6967)*
Craig Fleener 509 872-3016
2722 Lawson Rd Palouse (99161) *(G-7544)*
Craig Yamamoto Woodworker LLC 206 571-5821
7598 Hamilton Ln Clinton (98236) *(G-2686)*
Cranberry Road Winery 425 254-8400
19524 100th St E Bonney Lake (98391) *(G-1719)*
Crane Aerospace Inc 425 743-1313
16706 13th Ave W Lynnwood (98037) *(G-6100)*
Crane Aerospace & Electronics, Lynnwood *Also called Eldec Corporation (G-6114)*
Crane Aerospace & Electronics, Redmond *Also called Eldec Corporation (G-8447)*
Crane Electronics Inc (HQ) 425 882-3100
10301 Willows Rd Ne Redmond (98052) *(G-8429)*
Crane Electronics Inc 425 882-3100
10301 Willows Rd Ne Redmond (98052) *(G-8430)*
Crane Pro Services, Kent *Also called Konecranes Inc (G-4982)*
Crave Magazine 360 991-9332
1013 Ne 68th St Vancouver (98665) *(G-14152)*
Crawford Enterprises 360 866-4972
2204 Westwind Dr Nw Olympia (98502) *(G-7258)*
Cray Inc (PA) 206 701-2000
901 5th Ave Ste 1000 Seattle (98164) *(G-9751)*
Crazy J 360 876-6618
4452 Sw Hunter Ln Port Orchard (98367) *(G-7800)*
Creating Memories Together 360 944-8393
1612 Ne 128th Ave Vancouver (98684) *(G-14153)*

Creative ADS 360 981-1106
1427 Nw Cairo St Silverdale (98383) *(G-11829)*
Creative Cabinet Design 509 452-2777
1102 Tieton Dr Yakima (98902) *(G-15540)*
Creative Casting Company 253 475-2643
3762 S 60th St Ste A Tacoma (98409) *(G-13248)*
Creative Collections Co Inc 360 866-8840
1633 Kaiser Rd Nw Olympia (98502) *(G-7259)*
Creative Concepts 425 743-4671
6615 Marine View Dr Edmonds (98026) *(G-3104)*
Creative Concrete Concepts 425 466-4479
8718 Ames Lake Carnation Carnation (98014) *(G-2292)*
Creative Concrete Products LLC 360 419-9909
115 Lind St Mount Vernon (98273) *(G-6786)*
Creative Dimensions 360 733-5024
500 N State St Apt 201 Bellingham (98225) *(G-1310)*
Creative Edge Graphics 253 735-5111
3002 B St Nw Auburn (98001) *(G-418)*
Creative Enterprises Inc 425 775-7010
21104 70th Ave W Edmonds (98026) *(G-3105)*
Creative Garment Design & EMB 509 457-3482
207 W Court St Union Gap (98903) *(G-13927)*
Creative Imagery 360 871-6529
7347 E Collins Rd Port Orchard (98366) *(G-7801)*
Creative Interaction LLC 509 466-4612
15221 N Shady Slope Rd Spokane (99208) *(G-12207)*
Creative Label Incorporated 425 821-8810
18005 Ne 68th St Kirkland (98034) *(G-5317)*
Creative Machining Company 360 855-1981
15846 Preston Pl Burlington (98233) *(G-2148)*
Creative Metal Concepts LLC 253 230-4933
17106 116th St E Bonney Lake (98391) *(G-1720)*
Creative Microsystems Inc 425 235-4335
15224 Se Rnton Issquah Rd Renton (98059) *(G-8776)*
Creative Millwork & Moulding 425 343-4799
12606 217th St Se Snohomish (98296) *(G-11892)*
Creative Motion Control Inc 425 883-0100
15520 Woodinville Redmond Woodinville (98072) *(G-15215)*
Creative Openings 360 671-6420
929 N State St Bellingham (98225) *(G-1311)*
Creative Outlook 360 607-4013
18603 Ne 85th Ave Battle Ground (98604) *(G-696)*
Creative Window Concepts 425 351-2246
2920 200th Ave Se Issaquah (98075) *(G-4400)*
Creative Wood Sculptures 360 825-6069
28801 Se 480th St Enumclaw (98022) *(G-3284)*
Creekside Cabinet & Design 360 692-7070
3276 Nw Plaza Rd Ste 111 Silverdale (98383) *(G-11830)*
Creepcocom 206 547-7020
4504 Woodlawn Ave N Apt 1 Seattle (98103) *(G-9752)*
Crema Development LLC 360 918-6978
3834 Starling Dr Nw Olympia (98502) *(G-7260)*
Creo Industrial Arts LLC 425 775-7444
8329 216th St Se Woodinville (98072) *(G-15216)*
Creon LLC 360 318-1559
7358 Lankhaar Rd Lynden (98264) *(G-6010)*
Cresap Orthotics & Prosthetics 509 764-8500
835 E Colonial Ave Ste 10 Moses Lake (98837) *(G-6700)*
Crescent Machine Works Inc 509 328-2820
821 N Monroe St Spokane (99201) *(G-12208)*
Crescent Moon Studios Inc 509 322-7730
780 Tunk Creek Rd Riverside (98849) *(G-9124)*
Cresline-Northwest LLC 360 740-0700
223 Maurin Rd Chehalis (98532) *(G-2487)*
Crew Custom Holsters 360 270-3588
2824 Fir St Longview (98632) *(G-5904)*
Crf Frozen Foods LLC 509 542-0018
1825 N Commercial Ave Pasco (99301) *(G-7570)*
Crf Metal Works LLC 509 430-7609
3120 Travel Plaza Way Pasco (99301) *(G-7571)*
Crh Medical Corporation 425 284-7890
4040 Lake Washington Blvd Kirkland (98033) *(G-5318)*
Crh O'Regan System, Kirkland *Also called Crh Medical Corporation (G-5318)*
Crimpd LLC 847 436-0433
9321 57th Ave S Seattle (98118) *(G-9753)*
Crimson Canvas Arts 610 235-7605
4207 254th Pl Se Sammamish (98029) *(G-9200)*
Crimson Cove LLC 360 598-2683
22273 Stottlemeyer Rd Ne Poulsbo (98370) *(G-7956)*
Crisman Rocking Horses LLC 206 408-7465
4409 Sw Point Robinson Rd Vashon (98070) *(G-14720)*
Critchlow Custom Coatings LLC 253 651-9675
9733 52nd St W Apt 252 University Place (98467) *(G-13965)*
Critical Delivery Service LLC 206 724-3653
4957 Lakemont Blvd Se C4-104 Bellevue (98006) *(G-868)*
Critical Precision, Snohomish *Also called Dyno-Tech Machine LLC (G-11902)*
Crockers Fish Oil Inc 509 787-4983
214 6th Ave Ne Quincy (98848) *(G-8295)*
Croix Industries Ltd 206 528-5555
4306 3rd Ave Nw Seattle (98107) *(G-9754)*
Cronus Ventures LLC 425 641-4497
16834 Se 58th Pl Bellevue (98006) *(G-869)*

Cross and Crown Church 206 498-3551
4554 12th Ave Ne Seattle (98105) *(G-9755)*
Cross Current Brewing 253 952-2105
4922 Harbor View Dr Tacoma (98422) *(G-13249)*
Cross Roads Printing 509 328-1627
1204 W Maxwell Ave Spokane (99201) *(G-12209)*
Crossing Borders 425 466-7680
2901 167th Ave Ne Bellevue (98008) *(G-870)*
Crossrads Precision Rifles LLC 360 931-4505
2614 Ne 176th Ave Vancouver (98684) *(G-14154)*
Crossroads Export, Everett Also called Crossroads Group Inc *(G-3430)*
Crossroads Group Inc 206 855-3146
12618 Alexander Rd Everett (98204) *(G-3430)*
Crossroads Sign & Graphic 425 481-9411
16406 7th Pl W Lynnwood (98037) *(G-6101)*
Crowd Cow Inc 717 333-0740
801 3rd Ave Ste 325 Seattle (98104) *(G-9756)*
Crowder Family Winery 509 834-3270
546 Klate Rd Manson (98831) *(G-6243)*
Crown Black Car 206 722-7696
715 4th Ave N Apt 36 Seattle (98109) *(G-9757)*
Crown Carriage Works Inc 509 535-4427
5107 E Union Ave Spokane (99212) *(G-12210)*
Crown Cork & Seal Usa Inc 360 491-4900
1202 Fones Rd Se Olympia (98501) *(G-7261)*
Crown Cork & Seal Usa Inc 206 575-4260
18340 Segale Park Drive B Tukwila (98188) *(G-13718)*
Crown Cork & Seal Usa Inc 206 575-4260
18340 Segale Park Drive B Tukwila (98188) *(G-13719)*
Crown Cork & Seal Usa Inc 206 575-4260
18340 Segale Park Drive B Tukwila (98188) *(G-13720)*
Crown Films LLC 360 757-8880
527 N Hill Blvd Burlington (98233) *(G-2149)*
Crown Media & Printing Inc 509 315-8114
24222 E Pinehurst Ln Liberty Lake (99019) *(G-5829)*
Crown Paper Group Inc (PA) 360 385-3170
100 Mill Rd Port Townsend (98368) *(G-7875)*
Crown Plating Inc 360 693-3040
4221 Ne St Johns Rd Ste G Vancouver (98661) *(G-14155)*
Crown Recognition 509 698-4446
681 E Huntzinger Rd Selah (98942) *(G-11585)*
Crown Valve & Fitting LLC 360 225-0888
1342 Down River Dr Ste 2 Woodland (98674) *(G-15426)*
Crt Consulting, Snohomish Also called Crt Less Lethal *(G-11893)*
Crt Less Lethal 425 337-6875
13303 68th Ave Se Snohomish (98296) *(G-11893)*
Crucible Brewing Company 425 374-7293
909 Se Everett Mall Way Everett (98208) *(G-3431)*
Crucible NW Woodworks LLC 206 661-3545
3933 S Edmunds St Seattle (98118) *(G-9758)*
Crucible Wines LLC 206 605-2953
4434 Sw 101st St Seattle (98146) *(G-9759)*
Cruiser Creations 360 832-7078
23607 80th Avenue Ct E Graham (98338) *(G-4222)*
Crunch Pak LLC (PA) 509 782-2807
300 Sunset Hwy Cashmere (98815) *(G-2319)*
Crux Medical Innovations, Issaquah Also called CM Innovations Inc *(G-4395)*
Crux Subsurface Inc (HQ) 509 892-9409
4308 N Barker Rd Spokane Valley (99027) *(G-12670)*
Crw Timber 360 425-4858
540 22nd Ave Longview (98632) *(G-5905)*
Cryovac Inc 509 539-2923
170202 W Apricot Rd Prosser (99350) *(G-8037)*
Crystal Barone 206 621-7810
1907 4th Ave Seattle (98101) *(G-9760)*
Crystal Blue Screen Printing 509 337-8201
505 Willard St Waitsburg (99361) *(G-14753)*
Crystal Clear Ice Co 509 525-1042
1005 W Rose St Walla Walla (99362) *(G-14792)*
Crystal Distribution Inc 253 736-0016
7218 45th Street Ct E # 104 Fife (98424) *(G-3946)*
Crystal Point Inc 425 487-3656
15833 Mill Creek Blvd Mill Creek (98082) *(G-6505)*
Crystal Triangle Publishing 360 546-2497
16210 Se 19th St Vancouver (98683) *(G-14156)*
Crystalfontz America Inc 509 892-1200
12412 E Saltese Ave Spokane Valley (99216) *(G-12671)*
Crystalite Inc (PA) 425 259-6000
3307 Cedar St Everett (98201) *(G-3432)*
Crystalite Inc 509 921-9585
3020 N Sullivan Rd Ste E Spokane Valley (99216) *(G-12672)*
Crystalite Inc 425 259-6000
3307 Cedar St Everett (98201) *(G-3433)*
Crystalli Inc (PA) 253 905-6784
405 Sw 347th St Federal Way (98023) *(G-3727)*
Crystalwolfe Blends 509 217-2132
1320 3rd St Apt 9 Cheney (99004) *(G-2582)*
Csi Group LLC 360 334-5455
3301 Se Columbia Way 45 Vancouver (98661) *(G-14157)*
Csl Plasma Inc 253 275-2243
2200 S 314th St Federal Way (98003) *(G-3728)*
CSM Woodinville Estate, Woodinville Also called Michelle Chateau Ste *(G-15308)*

Csr Marine Inc 206 632-2001
4701 Shilshole Ave Nw Seattle (98107) *(G-9761)*
Csssi, Kent Also called Computer Systems Sales & Svcs *(G-4859)*
Csw Inc 360 491-9365
7745 Arab Dr Se Unit D Tumwater (98501) *(G-13866)*
Ctc, Yakima Also called Custom Technology Co Inc *(G-15546)*
CTI Biopharma Corp (PA) 206 282-7100
3101 Western Ave Ste 800 Seattle (98121) *(G-9762)*
Ctl, Kent Also called Computer Technology Link Corp *(G-4860)*
Cub Crafters Inc 509 248-9491
1918 S 16th Ave Yakima (98903) *(G-15541)*
Cub Crafters Group LLC 509 248-9491
1918 S 16th Ave Yakima (98903) *(G-15542)*
Cub Crafters Services LLC 509 248-1025
1920 S 16th Ave Yakima (98903) *(G-15543)*
Cubby B & Friends 253 537-6266
5203 80th St E Tacoma (98443) *(G-13250)*
Cubbys Elc Mtr & Pump Repr 509 544-9317
1716 W A St Pasco (99301) *(G-7572)*
Cubcrafters, Yakima Also called Cub Crafters Inc *(G-15541)*
Cucina Fresca Inc 206 903-0825
8300 Military Rd S # 120 Seattle (98108) *(G-9763)*
Cuddletunes Com 206 284-4991
2508 Lorentz Pl N Seattle (98109) *(G-9764)*
Cuga Vest 509 834-8378
140 Leininger Dr Yakima (98901) *(G-15544)*
Cuillin Hills Winery 425 402-1907
19495 144th Ave Ne A110 Woodinville (98072) *(G-15217)*
Culinary Arts, Kirkland Also called Farnworth Group *(G-5336)*
Culinary Co., Bellevue Also called Bfy Food Group LLC *(G-816)*
Cullen Bindery Inc 206 799-6295
20504 Se 269th St Covington (98042) *(G-2824)*
Cullens Custom Meats 509 837-0079
6852 Van Belle Rd Sunnyside (98944) *(G-13119)*
Cultural Diversity At Work Onl, Kenmore Also called Gildeane Group *(G-4575)*
Cultured Elements LLC 425 442-4595
13120 W Meadow Lake Rd Cheney (99004) *(G-2583)*
Cultus Bay Tiles Inc 360 579-3079
7712 Hellman Rd Clinton (98236) *(G-2687)*
Cummins - Allison Corp 206 763-3900
1012 Industry Dr Tukwila (98188) *(G-13721)*
Cummins Inc 541 276-2561
1708 E James St Pasco (99301) *(G-7573)*
Cummins Inc 509 455-4411
11134 W Westbow Ln Spokane (99224) *(G-12211)*
Cummins Inc 425 277-5342
1800 Fryar Ave Sumner (98390) *(G-13062)*
Cummins Inc 360 748-8841
3300 Mottman Rd Sw Tumwater (98512) *(G-13867)*
Cummins Inc 509 248-9033
1905 Central Ave Yakima (98901) *(G-15545)*
Cummins Northwest, Pasco Also called Cummins Inc *(G-7573)*
Cummins Northwest, Spokane Also called Cummins Inc *(G-12211)*
Cummins Northwest, Tumwater Also called Cummins Inc *(G-13867)*
Cummins Northwest, Yakima Also called Cummins Inc *(G-15545)*
Cuneo Furnace, Seattle Also called Maslach Art Glass A Corp *(G-11528)*
Cupcakes of Auburn 253 733-5547
33928 42nd Ave S Auburn (98001) *(G-419)*
Curfman Custom Fabrication LLC 360 736-7277
901 W Main St Centralia (98531) *(G-2396)*
Curlew Country Body Luxuries, Curlew Also called Curlew Country Herbs *(G-2845)*
Curlew Country Herbs 509 779-4941
396 Customs Rd Curlew (99118) *(G-2845)*
Curly Clutch LLC 253 732-3647
7110 121st Street Ct E Puyallup (98373) *(G-8139)*
Curnutt Inc 208 520-2550
8607 Packard Dr Pasco (99301) *(G-7574)*
Current Drives LLC 206 697-6073
2622 Nw Market St Ste B Seattle (98107) *(G-9765)*
Curry Custom Cabinets Corp 425 315-9355
4408 Chennault Beach Rd B Mukilteo (98275) *(G-6909)*
Curt Arneson Enterprises Inc 253 383-4377
1111 A St Tacoma (98402) *(G-13251)*
Curtins Heritage Logging Inc 360 518-5735
3485 I St Washougal (98671) *(G-14950)*
Curtis Machining 253 862-9256
21515 112th St E Sumner (98391) *(G-13063)*
Curtis Manufacturing Inc 425 353-4384
17611 Ok Mill Rd Snohomish (98290) *(G-11894)*
Curtis Pole Yard, Curtis Also called Weyerhaeuser Company *(G-2849)*
Curtiss R Grenz 509 893-0317
2620 S Corbin Cir Greenacres (99016) *(G-4296)*
Curts Printing 360 456-3041
1613 Diamond Loop Se Lacey (98503) *(G-5543)*
Curvetec Mfg 425 760-2844
4433 Russell Rd Ste 112 Mukilteo (98275) *(G-6910)*
Cusichaca Alpacas 360 936-3259
33404 Ne 24th Ave La Center (98629) *(G-5503)*
Custom and Production Woodwork, Quilcene Also called DOE Run Studios *(G-8282)*

Custom Bilt Holdings LLC 253 872-7330
2418 104th Street Ct S G Lakewood (98499) ***(G-5709)***
Custom Bilt Holdings LLC 509 533-1703
812 N Madelia St Spokane (99202) ***(G-12212)***
Custom Bottling Company 509 528-3196
8203 W Corral Creek Rd Nw Benton City (99320) ***(G-1608)***
Custom Building Services Inc 509 422-5746
22525 Highway 20 Okanogan (98840) ***(G-7195)***
Custom Cabinet Design 360 679-8729
632 Erin Park Rd Oak Harbor (98277) ***(G-7144)***
Custom Chemicals Co Inc 509 349-7000
320 W 1st St Warden (98857) ***(G-14930)***
Custom Choice Door LLC 253 472-0963
8607 Durango St Sw Ste B Lakewood (98499) ***(G-5710)***
Custom Coat 509 542-9431
927 S Lindsay St Pasco (99301) ***(G-7575)***
Custom Comfort, Tacoma *Also called Mattress Makers Incorporated* ***(G-13401)***
Custom Computer Creat CCC LLC 800 295-3381
5260 University Way Ne # 501 Seattle (98105) ***(G-9766)***
Custom Concrete Casting Corp 425 333-4737
3660 Tolt Ave Carnation (98014) ***(G-2293)***
Custom Controls Corporation 253 922-5874
4630 16th St E Ste B24 Fife (98424) ***(G-3947)***
Custom Craft LLC 253 826-5450
2920 142nd Ave E Ste 103 Sumner (98390) ***(G-13064)***
Custom Cusions and Foam, Bellingham *Also called Dream On Futon Co* ***(G-1325)***
Custom Electric & Controls, Fife *Also called Custom Controls Corporation* ***(G-3947)***
Custom Fab 360 466-1199
65 Kalama Pl La Conner (98257) ***(G-5523)***
Custom Fabrication Tech LLC 206 949-0212
24712 234th Way Se Maple Valley (98038) ***(G-6266)***
Custom Fiberglass Mfr 360 457-5092
4107 Newell Rd Port Angeles (98363) ***(G-7696)***
Custom Firescreen Inc 425 821-4800
12700 Ne 124th St Ste 15 Kirkland (98034) ***(G-5319)***
Custom Gear Inc 206 767-9448
10834 E Marginal Way S Tukwila (98168) ***(G-13722)***
Custom Hats & Apparel, Seattle *Also called Kushco Clothing LLC* ***(G-10364)***
Custom Hats and Apparels, Seattle *Also called Kushco* ***(G-10363)***
Custom Hydraulic & Machine Inc 253 854-4666
22911 86th Ave S Kent (98031) ***(G-4868)***
Custom Interface Inc 509 493-8756
410 S Larch St Bingen (98605) ***(G-1636)***
Custom Machine, Kent *Also called Custom Hydraulic & Machine Inc* ***(G-4868)***
Custom Made Draperies Etc 425 485-2724
7524 Ne 175th St Ste 4 Kenmore (98028) ***(G-4570)***
Custom Masonry & Stove Inc 206 524-4714
17824 28th Ave Ne Lake Forest Park (98155) ***(G-5610)***
Custom Mech Solutions Inc 206 973-3900
2810 Eastlake Ave E Seattle (98102) ***(G-9767)***
Custom Metal Spinning LLC 206 762-2707
9330 15th Ave S Ste Dc Seattle (98108) ***(G-9768)***
Custom Mfg Ambassador LLC 206 963-9853
1422 E Union St Apt 304 Seattle (98122) ***(G-9769)***
Custom Molding Co Inc 360 830-0108
14812 Nw Eagles View Dr Seabeck (98380) ***(G-9263)***
Custom Ocular Prosthetics 206 522-4222
10212 5th Ave Ne Ste 210 Seattle (98125) ***(G-9770)***
Custom Office Design Inc 253 735-8777
61 30th St Nw Ste E Auburn (98001) ***(G-420)***
Custom Pressed Tees LLC 425 264-5909
617 S 3rd St Ste B Renton (98057) ***(G-8777)***
Custom Printing Company 206 842-1606
921 Hildebrand Ln Ne # 111 Bainbridge Island (98110) ***(G-624)***
Custom Prints NW LLC 253 225-7725
13627 131st Street Ct Nw Gig Harbor (98329) ***(G-4093)***
Custom Publications Wash LLC 509 628-3500
1950 Keene Rd Bldg M Richland (99352) ***(G-8986)***
Custom Seafood Services Inc 360 267-2666
1818 Westlake Ave N # 302 Seattle (98109) ***(G-9771)***
Custom Sensor Design Inc 425 778-4980
2006 196th St Sw Ste 102 Lynnwood (98036) ***(G-6102)***
Custom Sheet Metal Inc 360 754-5220
3231 46th Ave Ne Olympia (98506) ***(G-7262)***
Custom Smoothie 206 462-6264
808 2nd Ave Seattle (98104) ***(G-9772)***
Custom Source Woodworking Inc 360 491-9365
7745d Arab Dr Se Unit D Tumwater (98501) ***(G-13868)***
Custom Technology Co Inc 509 965-3333
460 Mclaughlin Rd Yakima (98908) ***(G-15546)***
Custom Veils & Accessories 509 258-7810
4137 Hesseltine Rd Valley (99181) ***(G-13989)***
Custom Welding 206 242-5047
14622 9th Ave Sw Burien (98166) ***(G-2100)***
Custom Welding & Orna Ir LLC 509 947-8863
118 N Gum St Kennewick (99336) ***(G-4651)***
Custom Welding Inc 509 535-0664
2310 N Marguerite Rd Spokane Valley (99212) ***(G-12673)***
Custom Win Tnting Graphics Inc 509 453-4293
912 E Terrace Heights Way Yakima (98901) ***(G-15547)***
Custom Wood Finishes 360 468-4383
4559 Center Rd Lopez Island (98261) ***(G-5980)***
Custom Woodworking 360 739-3961
6867 Vail Dr Lynden (98264) ***(G-6011)***
Customarray Inc 425 609-0923
18916 North Creek Pkwy # 115 Bothell (98011) ***(G-1758)***
Cut Above Enterprise Inc 509 928-5091
11413 E Buckeye Ave Spokane Valley (99206) ***(G-12674)***
Cut Technologies Metal LLC 360 733-0460
3254 Bennett Dr Bellingham (98225) ***(G-1312)***
Cut Technologies Usa Inc (HQ) 360 733-0460
3254 Bennett Dr Bellingham (98225) ***(G-1313)***
Cutsforth Inc (PA) 800 290-6458
5160 Industrial Pl # 101 Ferndale (98248) ***(G-3835)***
Cutters Point Coffee, Gig Harbor *Also called Haley & Bros* ***(G-4109)***
Cutting Edge Engraving Inc 360 863-2184
12621 251st Ave Se Monroe (98272) ***(G-6563)***
Cutting Edge Machine & Mfg 253 926-8514
4428 Gy Rd E Tacoma (98443) ***(G-13252)***
Cutting Edge Manufacturing 425 348-0626
3101 111th St Sw Ste L Everett (98204) ***(G-3434)***
Cutting Edge Woodworks LLC 360 929-5386
1141 Balda Rd Oak Harbor (98277) ***(G-7145)***
Cutting Specialists, Tukwila *Also called Mike and Leslie Corporation* ***(G-13773)***
Cutting Tool Control Inc 206 789-7277
1411 Nw 51st St Seattle (98107) ***(G-9773)***
Cuttingboard LLC 253 234-7569
2739 152nd Ave Ne Redmond (98052) ***(G-8431)***
Cutwell Products 509 966-1499
1119 S 68th Ave Yakima (98908) ***(G-15548)***
Cuz Concrete Products Inc (PA) 360 435-5531
19604 67th Ave Ne Arlington (98223) ***(G-224)***
Cuz Concrete Products Inc 360 435-0769
19521 63rd Ave Ne Arlington (98223) ***(G-225)***
Cuz Septice Service, Arlington *Also called Cuz Concrete Products Inc* ***(G-224)***
Cuzd Industries 360 742-3126
5707 Lacey Blvd Se Lacey (98503) ***(G-5544)***
Cvm, Chehalis *Also called Cowlitz Valley Machine Inc* ***(G-2486)***
Cw Machine LLC 360 829-4171
28120 State Route 410 E B8 Buckley (98321) ***(G-2055)***
Cw Products, Spokane Valley *Also called Lane Pierce Partners Inc* ***(G-12771)***
CWC Industries LLC A Washingto 206 528-8090
7918 Aurora Ave N Seattle (98103) ***(G-9774)***
Cxt Incorporated (HQ) 509 924-6300
3808 N Sullivan Rd Bldg 7 Spokane Valley (99216) ***(G-12675)***
Cxt Incorporated 509 921-7878
2420 N Pioneer Ln Spokane Valley (99216) ***(G-12676)***
Cylinder Division, Enumclaw *Also called Parker-Hannifin Corporation* ***(G-3311)***
Cyns Insanitys 360 694-2459
3320 E 17th St Vancouver (98661) ***(G-14158)***
Cynthia Rochlitzer 509 796-4199
10703 N Ritchey Rd Spokane (99224) ***(G-12213)***
Cypress Designs LLC 360 384-6572
220 Mckenzie Ave Bellingham (98225) ***(G-1314)***
Cypress Houseworks LLC 360 676-9778
511 Cypress Rd Bellingham (98225) ***(G-1315)***
Cypress Microsystems Inc 425 787-4400
2700 162nd St Sw Bldg D Lynnwood (98087) ***(G-6103)***
Cypress Semi Conductor, Lynnwood *Also called Cypress Microsystems Inc* ***(G-6103)***
Cypress Semiconductor Corp 425 787-4400
2700 162nd St Sw Bldg D Lynnwood (98087) ***(G-6104)***
Cyrus Biotechnology Inc 503 489-8460
500 Union St Ste 320 Seattle (98101) ***(G-9775)***
Cytec Industries Materials 425 274-0485
10900 Ne 8th St Bellevue (98004) ***(G-871)***
Cytodyn Operations Inc 360 980-8524
1111 Main St Ste 660 Vancouver (98660) ***(G-14159)***
D & D Cedar Stake 360 435-2254
17632 Jordan Rd Arlington (98223) ***(G-226)***
D & D Controls Inc 360 695-8931
3106 Ne 65th St Ststea Vancouver (98663) ***(G-14160)***
D & D Dividers LLC 360 951-4852
530 N Gold St Centralia (98531) ***(G-2397)***
D & D Logging 425 308-2063
4528 116th Ave Ne Lake Stevens (98258) ***(G-5642)***
D & D Millwork Inc 800 627-8437
19420 21st Ave W Lynnwood (98036) ***(G-6105)***
D & E Enterprises 509 684-6618
938 Kitt Narcisse Rd Colville (99114) ***(G-2749)***
D & G Auto Parts 360 696-3631
2504 Ne Stapleton Rd Vancouver (98661) ***(G-14161)***
D & H Enterprises 360 374-9500
442 Ski Dr Forks (98331) ***(G-4009)***
D & H Printing 360 427-7423
2505 Olympic Hwy N Shelton (98584) ***(G-11693)***
D & J Marketing Inc 360 413-9173
4108 Kyro Rd Se Lacey (98503) ***(G-5545)***
D & K Concrete Products Inc 360 573-4020
15008 Ne 15th Ave Vancouver (98685) ***(G-14162)***
D & L Foundry Inc 509 765-7952
12970 Road 3 Ne Moses Lake (98837) ***(G-6701)***
D & L Outdoor Specialties 509 758-5875
2480 19th St Clarkston (99403) ***(G-2630)***

ALPHABETIC

(PA)=Parent Co (HQ)=Headquarters (DH)=Div Headquarters
2019 Washington
Manufacturers Register
711

D & L Screen Printing........206 781-1977
9047 12th Ave Nw Seattle (98117) ***(G-9776)***
D & M Enterprises, Stanwood *Also called Michelle Schwartzman* ***(G-12979)***
D & M Machine Division Inc........360 249-3366
12 Monte Brady Rd Montesano (98563) ***(G-6643)***
D & N Farms Partnership........509 771-1714
137 Fairmont Ln Moses Lake (98837) ***(G-6702)***
D & P Products Inc........425 551-1380
1310 Industry St Ste 200 Everett (98203) ***(G-3435)***
D & R Quality Coatings Inc........253 209-5441
401 Brown Way Se Orting (98360) ***(G-7478)***
D & R Rv LLC........360 755-3218
1757 Walton Dr Burlington (98233) ***(G-2150)***
D & S Rock LLC........509 877-7400
680 Olden Way Rd Toppenish (98948) ***(G-13665)***
D & S Small Equipment, Spokane *Also called Sondra L Groce* ***(G-12511)***
D A Graphics Inc........206 760-5886
1902 Occidental Ave S Seattle (98134) ***(G-9777)***
D A M Salsa LLC........206 527-0300
7533 21st Ave Ne Seattle (98115) ***(G-9778)***
D and D Electric Motor Svc Inc........509 762-6136
4320 Airway Dr Ne Moses Lake (98837) ***(G-6703)***
D and D Trim and Cabinets Inc........360 736-4279
153 Mcatee Rd Centralia (98531) ***(G-2398)***
D B C Paving, Grayland *Also called Bainter Bainter & Bainter LLC* ***(G-4292)***
D B Express LLC........509 265-4511
220 Park Ave Mesa (99343) ***(G-6491)***
D Creek Timber Inc........360 262-3786
379 Avery Rd W Winlock (98596) ***(G-15149)***
D Crockett Surfboards........425 430-9947
16916 155th Pl Se Renton (98058) ***(G-8778)***
D D M Corporation........206 282-3422
2657 20th Ave W Seattle (98199) ***(G-9779)***
D Ds Hardwood Floors........206 726-8808
7009 Covello Dr S Seattle (98108) ***(G-9780)***
D E Hokanson Inc........425 882-1689
12840 Ne 21st Pl Ste B Bellevue (98005) ***(G-872)***
D E Metlow Logging LLC........509 937-2233
3586 Waitts Lake Rd Valley (99181) ***(G-13990)***
D E N, Bellevue *Also called Data Enterprises of The NW* ***(G-874)***
D Floured LLC........206 395-4623
518 15th Ave E Seattle (98112) ***(G-9781)***
D G Hard Surface LLC........206 718-4700
1839 Killarney Way Bellevue (98004) ***(G-873)***
D G Parrott & Son........360 352-8242
209 Thurston Ave Ne Olympia (98501) ***(G-7263)***
D Haitre Woodworks LLC........360 752-0405
1651 Mt Baker Hwy Bellingham (98226) ***(G-1316)***
D M I, East Wenatchee *Also called Media Directed Inc* ***(G-3024)***
D P Clarke........360 647-8185
1225 E Sunset Dr Ste 727 Bellingham (98226) ***(G-1317)***
D Powers Consulting........360 341-1533
6513 Spencer Ln Clinton (98236) ***(G-2688)***
D S Fabrication & Design Inc........360 210-7526
3805 S Truman Rd Washougal (98671) ***(G-14951)***
D S Fabrication & Design Inc........360 600-9706
13504 Ne 84th St Ste 103 Vancouver (98682) ***(G-14163)***
D S Hardwood Corporation........509 369-3442
4706 247th Street Ct E Graham (98338) ***(G-4223)***
D S Thermal........206 789-2271
632 Nw 77th St Seattle (98117) ***(G-9782)***
D Square Energy LLC........425 888-2882
201 W North Bend Way North Bend (98045) ***(G-7110)***
D W Pape Inc........509 586-0522
722 N Hartford St Kennewick (99336) ***(G-4652)***
D&D RC Hobbies, Moses Lake *Also called D and D Electric Motor Svc Inc* ***(G-6703)***
D&E Kustoms LLC........360 681-0511
63 Hooker Rd Sequim (98382) ***(G-11622)***
D&J Custom Metal Fabrication........206 242-3238
11615 12th Ave S Burien (98168) ***(G-2101)***
D&L Summers Inc........360 268-0769
441 N Melbourne St Westport (98595) ***(G-15104)***
D&S Innovative Enterprises........509 467-2032
15819 N Inch Rd Nine Mile Falls (99026) ***(G-7071)***
D&Topm Inc........425 334-7667
11422 20 St Se Everett (98205) ***(G-3436)***
D-Mac Carpentry........509 326-6601
4828 N Stevens St Spokane (99205) ***(G-12214)***
D-Way Tools Inc........360 432-9509
3661 E Pickering Rd Shelton (98584) ***(G-11694)***
D3 Skis, Auburn *Also called Kc Technology Inc* ***(G-483)***
Da Vincis Garage LLC........206 579-1333
1301 Spring St Apt 10b Seattle (98104) ***(G-9783)***
Dabs M&A LLC........253 872-2200
8622 S 228th St Kent (98031) ***(G-4869)***
Dabs Manufacturing & Assembly, Kent *Also called Dabs M&A LLC* ***(G-4869)***
Dabs Manufacturing & Assembly........253 872-2200
8622 S 228th St Kent (98031) ***(G-4870)***
Daddy Daughter Diner LLC........425 442-8307
21322 Damson Rd Bothell (98021) ***(G-1845)***
Dadoes, Kirkland *Also called Nbk Associates Inc* ***(G-5408)***
Daedalus Cabinets, Ferndale *Also called Lou Hinkley* ***(G-3866)***
Dag Industries Inc........425 228-4962
5210 Ne 23rd Ct Renton (98059) ***(G-8779)***
Dagner Construction........509 349-8944
16735 Out Of Bounds Ln Se Warden (98857) ***(G-14931)***
Dahlia Press........206 229-0817
7910 16th Ave Sw Seattle (98106) ***(G-9784)***
Dahlquist Logging Inc........253 804-9112
31831 102nd Ave Se Auburn (98092) ***(G-421)***
Dahlstrom Lumber Co Inc........360 533-0448
1131 Airport Way Hoquiam (98550) ***(G-4331)***
Dai Environmental Services........360 354-1134
752 Loomis Trail Rd Lynden (98264) ***(G-6012)***
Daily Bulletin........509 397-3332
211 N Main St Colfax (99111) ***(G-2713)***
Daily Conner........360 643-0056
250 Madison St Port Townsend (98368) ***(G-7876)***
Daily Crave Espresso, Moxee *Also called Mark Sholtys* ***(G-6881)***
Daily Dessert LLC........757 746-7744
4550 38th Ave Sw Apt 612 Seattle (98126) ***(G-9785)***
Daily Ellensburg Record Inc........509 925-1414
401 N Main St Ellensburg (98926) ***(G-3192)***
Daily Grind........253 632-7992
11017 223rd Avenue Ct E Buckley (98321) ***(G-2056)***
Daily Grind Uptown........509 448-1281
422 W Riverside Ave Spokane (99201) ***(G-12215)***
Daily Herald Company (HQ)........425 339-3000
1800 41st St Ste 300 Everett (98203) ***(G-3437)***
Daily News, Longview *Also called Lee Publications Inc* ***(G-5926)***
Daily Plant-It........425 677-4948
10603 Issquah Hbart Rd Se Issaquah (98027) ***(G-4401)***
Daily Record, The, Ellensburg *Also called Daily Ellensburg Record Inc* ***(G-3192)***
Daily Sun News, Sunnyside *Also called Sunnyside Daily News Inc* ***(G-13145)***
Daily Toils & Troubles........360 337-9028
18657 State Hwy 305 Ne Poulsbo (98370) ***(G-7957)***
Daily World, Aberdeen *Also called Gatehouse Media LLC* ***(G-13)***
Daines Corporation........425 212-3169
12428 Highway 99 Ste 56 Everett (98204) ***(G-3438)***
Dairy Export Co Inc (HQ)........206 284-7220
635 Elliott Ave W Seattle (98119) ***(G-9786)***
Dairy Queens Vancouver (PA)........360 256-7302
10507 Ne 4th Plain Blvd Vancouver (98662) ***(G-14164)***
Dairyland Orthopedics Pubg........509 868-0096
1610 S Deer Heights Rd Spokane (99224) ***(G-12216)***
Daisy Maiz LLC........360 718-8288
10309 Ne 14th St Vancouver (98664) ***(G-14165)***
Dakota Creek Industries Inc........360 293-9575
820 4th St Anacortes (98221) ***(G-119)***
Dakota Cub........509 453-3412
2008 W Washington Ave Yakima (98903) ***(G-15549)***
Dale A West Specialty Wdwkg........360 683-9419
92 Dory Rd Sequim (98382) ***(G-11623)***
Dale Bradeen Logging........509 738-6132
3934 Highway 20 E Kettle Falls (99141) ***(G-5230)***
Dale Butler S Furniture........509 732-4381
2829 Aladdin Rd Colville (99114) ***(G-2750)***
Dale M Shafman LLC........206 499-4408
1762 Airport Way S Ste B Seattle (98134) ***(G-9787)***
Dallesport Foundry Inc........509 767-1183
102 Parallel Ave Dallesport (98617) ***(G-2862)***
Daly's Wood Finishing Products, Seattle *Also called Dalys Inc* ***(G-9788)***
Dalys Inc (PA)........425 454-3093
3525 Stone Way N Seattle (98103) ***(G-9788)***
Dama Wines, Walla Walla *Also called Tuuri Wines LLC* ***(G-14882)***
Damar Aero Systems, Monroe *Also called Senior Operations LLC* ***(G-6617)***
Damar Machine, Monroe *Also called Tji II LLC* ***(G-6632)***
Damn Good Pepper........206 675-0540
567 John St Seattle (98109) ***(G-9789)***
Damsel Cellars........206 465-2433
18744 142nd Ave Ne Woodinville (98072) ***(G-15218)***
Dan Coats........360 892-2730
10805 Ne 44th St Vancouver (98682) ***(G-14166)***
Dan McMullen Well Drilling........707 998-9252
119 Oyler Way Ethel (98542) ***(G-3350)***
Dana-Saad Company........509 924-6711
3808 N Sullivan Rd # 105 Spokane Valley (99216) ***(G-12677)***
Danalco Inc........626 303-4019
11721 Fremont Ave N Seattle (98133) ***(G-9790)***
Dance Air Inc........425 222-6789
8020 Bracken Pl Se Snoqualmie (98065) ***(G-12009)***
Dancing Alder Winery........425 402-6300
19495 144th Ave Ne A115 Woodinville (98072) ***(G-15219)***
Dancing Clouds LLC........360 289-0790
540 Meadow Ave Ne Ocean Shores (98569) ***(G-7185)***
Dande Co, Tacoma *Also called All CS Inc* ***(G-13163)***
Dandelion & Tea LLC........206 353-2048
1500 Sw Myrtle St Seattle (98106) ***(G-9791)***
Dandy Digger and Supply Inc........360 795-3617
244 W State Route 4 Cathlamet (98612) ***(G-2364)***
Danforth Signs & Carving, Vancouver *Also called Emma Danforth* ***(G-14201)***
Daniel Cabinets LLC........509 949-0855
180 Shaw Rd Selah (98942) ***(G-11586)***

Daniel E France..360 263-2888
30111 Ne Timmen Rd Ridgefield (98642) *(G-9078)*
Daniel Oneill..509 939-7916
14318 N Meadow Ln Newman Lake (99025) *(G-7043)*
Daniels Woodworks..360 264-7311
20148 Tyrell Rd Se Tenino (98589) *(G-13615)*
Danielson Tool & Die..509 924-5734
9924 E Jackson Ave Spokane Valley (99206) *(G-12678)*
Danner Corporation (PA)..................................253 833-5333
307 Oravetz Pl Se Auburn (98092) *(G-422)*
Dannys Electronics Inc...................................253 314-5056
2015 S 96th St Ste 1 Tacoma (98444) *(G-13253)*
Dans Machine Works...360 403-0887
13305 41st Ave Ne Marysville (98271) *(G-6329)*
Dans Striping and Molding Inc........................206 533-1495
23946 W Woodway Ln Woodway (98020) *(G-15479)*
Dans Tool Truck..509 520-4531
108 Johnson Hollow Dayton (99328) *(G-2880)*
Danzco Inc...360 264-2141
1006 143rd Ave Se Tenino (98589) *(G-13616)*
Danzer Veneer Americas Inc............................253 770-4664
3107 142nd Ave E Ste 101 Sumner (98390) *(G-13065)*
Daoust & Daoust, Kirkland *Also called Tyson Nutraceuticals Inc (G-5487)*
Dapaul Inc (PA)..360 943-9844
9300 Kimmie St Sw Tumwater (98512) *(G-13869)*
Darbonnier Tactical Supply LLC (PA).............360 672-0216
951 Ne 21st Ct Oak Harbor (98277) *(G-7146)*
Darby Winery...206 954-4700
9615 57th Ave S Seattle (98118) *(G-9792)*
Darby Winery Inc...206 954-4700
19501 144th Ave Ne E700 Woodinville (98072) *(G-15220)*
Dari-Tech Inc...360 354-6900
8540 Benson Rd Lynden (98264) *(G-6013)*
Darigold Inc...425 392-6463
611 Front St N Issaquah (98027) *(G-4402)*
Darigold Inc...509 489-8600
33 E Francis Ave Spokane (99208) *(G-12217)*
Darigold Inc...206 722-2655
1130 Rainier Ave S Seattle (98144) *(G-9793)*
Darigold Farms, Issaquah *Also called Darigold Inc (G-4402)*
Dark Coast Press Co..206 902-0906
1433 Nw 64th St Apt 306 Seattle (98107) *(G-9794)*
Dark Moon Artisan Distillery, Snohomish *Also called Dawson-Alley LLC (G-11895)*
Dark Star Candle Company..............................206 280-5902
10035 9th Ave Sw Seattle (98146) *(G-9795)*
Darklight Inc (PA)..509 940-1818
8201 164th Ave Ne Redmond (98052) *(G-8432)*
Darling Ingredients Inc...................................253 572-3922
2041 Marc Ave Tacoma (98421) *(G-13254)*
Darling Pro, Tacoma *Also called Darling Ingredients Inc (G-13254)*
Darrell A Tillotson..509 493-2376
855 Nw Loop Rd White Salmon (98672) *(G-15114)*
Darren Mode..509 292-2438
3711 E Deer Park Milan Rd Deer Park (99006) *(G-2897)*
Dart Container Corp Georgia...........................360 352-7045
600 Israel Rd Se Tumwater (98501) *(G-13870)*
Daruma Graphics..206 365-5644
11325 Pinehurst Way Ne Seattle (98125) *(G-9796)*
Darwins Natural Pet Products, Tukwila *Also called Arrow Reliance Inc (G-13692)*
Dash Connector Technology Inc....................509 465-1903
3915 E Francis Ave Ste C6 Spokane (99217) *(G-12218)*
Dashboard Skimboards LLC............................253 235-1811
2519 Pacific Hwy E Ste B Fife (98424) *(G-3948)*
Dashi Noodle Bar..206 595-1995
1900 Dakin St Bellingham (98229) *(G-1318)*
Data Enterprises of The NW............................425 688-8805
9 Lake Bellevue Dr # 205 Bellevue (98005) *(G-874)*
Data I/O Corporation (PA)...............................425 881-6444
6645 185th Ave Ne Ste 100 Redmond (98052) *(G-8433)*
Data Quest LLC...360 568-8708
1010 Se Everett Mall Way # 203 Everett (98208) *(G-3439)*
Data Shaping Solutions LLC...........................425 837-4767
2428 35th Ave Ne Issaquah (98029) *(G-4403)*
Data-Linc Group, Issaquah *Also called Linc Technology Corporation (G-4439)*
Datapark LLC..360 224-2157
726 Cherry St 100 Sumas (98295) *(G-13043)*
Datrex Inc..206 762-9070
309 S Cloverdale St Seattle (98108) *(G-9797)*
Dauenhauer Manufacturing Inc.....................509 865-3300
63351 Us Highway 97 Toppenish (98948) *(G-13666)*
Daughters of Mary..360 943-2186
1921 Parkwood Dr Se Olympia (98501) *(G-7264)*
Daughtrey Machine...509 834-9736
544 Breaum Rd Yakima (98908) *(G-15550)*
Dauntless Inc..206 494-3338
8355 165th Ave Ne Redmond (98052) *(G-8434)*
Dauntless Software Inc...................................206 489-4942
4702 Ne 1st Pl Renton (98059) *(G-8780)*
Davan Communications Entp.........................253 517-9300
3040 44th Ave Ne Tacoma (98422) *(G-13255)*
Dave Bekkevar Logging & Trckg....................360 683-3655
273054 Highway 101 Sequim (98382) *(G-11624)*

Dave Ledgerwood..509 843-3677
61 Hutchens Hill Rd Pomeroy (99347) *(G-7671)*
Dave Peck Software Development..................206 931-7572
2901 Ne Blakeley St Apt 5 Seattle (98105) *(G-9798)*
Dave Yocoms Wood Creations........................425 220-5628
4121 119th St Se Everett (98208) *(G-3440)*
Davenport Times, Davenport *Also called Journal-News Publishing Co (G-2872)*
Daves Mobile Welding LLC.............................360 302-0069
304 10th St Bldg 4 Port Townsend (98368) *(G-7877)*
Daves TV & Appliance Inc................................360 293-5129
230 Belmont Ter Mount Vernon (98274) *(G-6787)*
David Loring..206 772-5004
10434 Forest Ave S Seattle (98178) *(G-9799)*
David Bol...425 802-0804
711 W Birchbend Dr Spokane (99224) *(G-12219)*
David G McAlees..425 641-0318
17425 Se 46th Pl Bellevue (98006) *(G-875)*
David Gray Furnituremaker Inc......................360 321-4514
5227 Crawford Rd Langley (98260) *(G-5776)*
David Gulassa & Co Inc....................................206 283-1810
6 Dravus St Seattle (98109) *(G-9800)*
David L Flink...253 735-5417
19229 Se Aubrn Blck Diamn Auburn (98092) *(G-423)*
David Littlejohn Logging.................................360 352-5858
11946 Case Rd Sw Olympia (98512) *(G-7265)*
David Lynn Smoothies LLC..............................907 242-4564
16717 Redmond Way Redmond (98052) *(G-8435)*
David Olson Honeywell Arspc.........................509 321-7368
2810 S Lincoln St Spokane (99203) *(G-12220)*
David P Rush..509 865-5338
131 White Rd Zillah (98953) *(G-15752)*
David T Mitchell..425 227-7111
14229 143rd Ave Se Renton (98059) *(G-8781)*
David T Stone Consulting, Seattle *Also called Pizzicato Publishing Co (G-10819)*
David T Vanzandt Co...206 789-7294
1119 Nw 60th St Seattle (98107) *(G-9801)*
David Wight Glass Art Inc................................360 389-2844
2111 Lincoln St 102 Bellingham (98225) *(G-1319)*
Davids Aquacut & Builders.............................509 527-8700
3328 E Isaacs Ave Walla Walla (99362) *(G-14793)*
Davidson Prosthetics LLC.............................253 770-6578
11919 Canyon Rd E Puyallup (98373) *(G-8140)*
Davidson's Sawmill, Carnation *Also called Wayne Davidson (G-2302)*
Davincis Workshop LLC...................................206 244-7000
18040 Des Moines Mem Dr S Seatac (98148) *(G-9280)*
Davis & Walker Fabrication............................360 944-0057
15017 Ne 24th St Vancouver (98684) *(G-14167)*
Davis Degrass Enterprises Inc.......................360 332-2097
1625 Boblett St Blaine (98230) *(G-1667)*
Davis Development & Mfg................................360 892-7802
9500 Ne 72nd Ave Vancouver (98665) *(G-14168)*
Davis Sand & Gravel Inc..................................360 683-5680
870 Evans Rd Sequim (98382) *(G-11625)*
Davis Sign Company Inc..................................206 287-9800
4025 7th Ave S Seattle (98108) *(G-9802)*
Davis Tool Inc..509 891-5568
6309 N Harvard Rd Newman Lake (99025) *(G-7044)*
Davis Wire Corporation...................................253 872-8910
19411 80th Ave S Kent (98032) *(G-4871)*
Dawling Spay Retractor LLC...........................360 482-4970
44 Butler Mill Rd Elma (98541) *(G-3244)*
Dawn Food Products Inc................................206 623-7740
1001 John St Ste 101 Seattle (98109) *(G-9803)*
Dawn Food Products Inc................................206 763-1711
6901 Fox Ave S Seattle (98108) *(G-9804)*
Dawn Workman Lularoe...................................360 955-1324
14839 99th Way Se Yelm (98597) *(G-15731)*
Dawson-Alley LLC...360 217-8244
1830 Bickford Ave Snohomish (98290) *(G-11895)*
Day Creek Organic Farms Inc........................360 856-4770
1020 Hodgin St Sedro Woolley (98284) *(G-11536)*
Daybreak Oil and Gas Inc (PA).....................509 232-7674
1101 N Argonne Rd Ste 211 Spokane Valley (99212) *(G-12679)*
Days Gone By Cabinetry..................................425 868-5132
6305 252nd Pl Ne Redmond (98053) *(G-8436)*
Dayton Chronicle, Dayton *Also called Touchet Valley News Inc (G-2887)*
Dayton Traister Co Inc.....................................360 675-3421
4778 Monkey Hill Rd Oak Harbor (98277) *(G-7147)*
Db Industries LLC...360 432-8239
116 W Rr Ave Ste 108 Shelton (98584) *(G-11695)*
Db Skimboards..253 235-1811
2519 Pacific Hwy E Ste B Fife (98424) *(G-3949)*
DBa Euroimport Company Inc.........................206 763-7303
309 S Cloverdale St E10 Seattle (98108) *(G-9805)*
Dbcs Innovations..206 919-2249
6558 43rd Ave Ne Seattle (98115) *(G-9806)*
DC Engineering Consulting Inc......................360 932-2367
15946 Woodbrook Ln Se Rainier (98576) *(G-8313)*
DCB Industries Inc..360 750-0009
2451 St Francis Ln Vancouver (98660) *(G-14169)*
DCB Industries Inc (PA).................................360 750-0009
9702 Se 12th St Vancouver (98664) *(G-14170)*
DCG ONE, Seattle *Also called Direct Connect Group (dcg) LLC (G-9833)*

DCI Metal Finishing LLC 425 347-7776
6700 Hardeson Rd Ste 101 Everett (98203) *(G-3441)*

Dct, Brush Prairie *Also called Dust Control Technologies Inc* *(G-2033)*

Dcw News Agency Inc 206 682-2888
501 S Jackson St Ste 303 Seattle (98104) *(G-9807)*

Ddbd Construction 253 576-6769
12421 200th Avenue Ct E Bonney Lake (98391) *(G-1721)*

De Jong Sawdust & Shavings 425 252-1566
3413 Old Hartford Rd Lake Stevens (98258) *(G-5643)*

De Kleine Machine Company LLC 509 832-1108
209 Sw San Juan Ct Prosser (99350) *(G-8038)*

De Marss LLC 425 218-3454
1300 114th Ave Se Ste 220 Bellevue (98004) *(G-876)*

De Rosier Trucking Inc 360 577-1636
3627 Pleasant Hill Rd Kelso (98626) *(G-4523)*

Dead Canyon Vineyard LLC 509 786-2665
31902 N Crosby Rd Prosser (99350) *(G-8039)*

Dead Oak Distilling LLC 509 882-2794
172006 Dogwood Pr Nw Prosser (99350) *(G-8040)*

Deaf Spotlight 206 466-4693
404 E Harrison St Apt 204 Seattle (98102) *(G-9808)*

Deal Perch Inc 425 372-8514
1020 20th St Snohomish (98290) *(G-11896)*

Dealer Info Systems Corp (HQ) 360 733-7610
1315 Cornwall Ave Bellingham (98225) *(G-1320)*

Dealer Net, Edmonds *Also called Reynolds and Reynolds Company* *(G-3146)*

Dean Powell & Magda Velarde 253 535-4195
25848 33rd Ave S Kent (98032) *(G-4872)*

Dean Thoemke 253 640-2232
581 Old Naches Hwy Yakima (98908) *(G-15551)*

Deans Mean Prfmce Coatings 509 406-4713
3410 Clinton Way Yakima (98902) *(G-15552)*

Debbie Mumm Inc 509 939-1479
3521 W Horizon Ave Spokane (99208) *(G-12221)*

Debbie Zachary 253 848-5011
1210 22nd St Se Puyallup (98372) *(G-8141)*

Deboer Dairy LLC 360 757-2660
8426 District Line Rd Burlington (98233) *(G-2151)*

Deborah Designs 253 848-3274
1910 28th Avenue Ct Sw Puyallup (98373) *(G-8142)*

Deborah Funches Jewelry Design 503 381-4017
19322 Se 33rd St Camas (98607) *(G-2244)*

Debroeck Solid Surface Inc 509 525-1349
1401 W Pine St Walla Walla (99362) *(G-14794)*

Deca Stories LLC 302 219-0373
3247 S Edmunds St Seattle (98118) *(G-9809)*

Decal Factory 509 465-8931
421 W Riverside Ave # 400 Spokane (99201) *(G-12222)*

Decal Factory, The, Spokane *Also called Decal Factory* *(G-12222)*

Decatur Industries Inc 206 368-3178
19536 44th Ave Ne Lake Forest Park (98155) *(G-5611)*

Decent Exposures Inc 206 364-4540
12554 Lake City Way Ne Seattle (98125) *(G-9810)*

Deception Distilling LLC 360 588-1000
9946 Padilla Heights Rd Anacortes (98221) *(G-120)*

Deck Builders 360 709-9225
5641 Maytown Rd Sw Olympia (98512) *(G-7266)*

Decker Foundry 206 225-9000
2654 Sw 112th St Seattle (98146) *(G-9811)*

Decomp 360 306-8516
2205 Queen St Bellingham (98229) *(G-1321)*

Decorado Fabrication 360 694-6832
15008 Ne 15th Ste B Vancouver (98686) *(G-14171)*

Decorado Thin Brick, Vancouver *Also called Decorado Fabrication* *(G-14171)*

Decorative Metal Arts 206 782-4009
45 S Spokane St Seattle (98134) *(G-9812)*

Decorative Metal Services Inc 360 695-7052
3810 H St Vancouver (98663) *(G-14172)*

Deekay Essentials LLC 732 809-7284
12407 Nw 49th Ave Vancouver (98685) *(G-14173)*

Deep Cell Industries 206 909-3858
111 S Jackson St Seattle (98104) *(G-9813)*

Deep Creek Logging Inc 360 533-2390
1847 E Hoquiam Rd Hoquiam (98550) *(G-4332)*

Deep Ocean Expeditions LLC 801 390-7025
4601 Shilshole Ave Nw Seattle (98107) *(G-9814)*

Deep Roots Foods, Lacey *Also called Watford Tanikka* *(G-5601)*

Deep Sea Fisheries 206 743-3381
15030 Highway 99 Lynnwood (98087) *(G-6106)*

Deer Creek Cedar Products Inc 360 435-4707
22422 State Route 530 Ne Arlington (98223) *(G-227)*

Deer Harbor Boat Works, Deer Harbor *Also called Down Island Trading Co* *(G-2891)*

Deer Park Gazette LLC 509 276-7737
5011 W Dahl Rd Deer Park (99006) *(G-2898)*

Deer Park Printing 509 276-9712
220 N Main St Deer Park (99006) *(G-2899)*

Deer Park Tribune, Deer Park *Also called Horizon Publications Inc* *(G-2905)*

Deer Path Industrial Tech 425 391-9223
14236 246th Pl Se Issaquah (98027) *(G-4404)*

Dees Communications Corp 425 276-5269
14221 Se 78th Way Newcastle (98059) *(G-7027)*

Defbooty LLC 800 311-5887
127 Springbrook Dr Chehalis (98532) *(G-2488)*

Defense Health Agency, Tacoma *Also called Swim Scott* *(G-13534)*

Defense Sales Intl LLC 206 999-8684
1934 Shattuck Ave S Renton (98055) *(G-8782)*

Defensestorm Inc 858 228-1903
710 2nd Ave Ste 310 Seattle (98104) *(G-9815)*

Defensive Driving School Inc (PA) 425 643-0116
10505 Ne 38th Pl Bldg 9 Kirkland (98033) *(G-5320)*

Defiance Boats LLC 360 674-7098
5120 Sw Nixon Loop Bremerton (98312) *(G-1945)*

Defiance Boats LLC 360 329-6865
7510 Bree Dr Bremerton (98312) *(G-1946)*

Defiance Forest Products, Tacoma *Also called Edwin Enterprises Inc* *(G-13274)*

Deflector Marine Rudder, Naselle *Also called Stambaughs Hungry Harbor Entps* *(G-7020)*

Defsec Solutions LLC 855 933-3732
914 164th St Se Ste B12 Mill Creek (98012) *(G-6506)*

Degerstrom Corporation 509 928-3333
3301 N Sullivan Rd Spokane Valley (99216) *(G-12680)*

Degroot Designs 253 472-7279
4532 E C St Tacoma (98404) *(G-13256)*

Dehavilland Elc Amplifier Co 360 891-6570
2401 Ne 148th Ct Vancouver (98684) *(G-14174)*

Deines Automation LLC 509 230-2369
108 N Washington St # 408 Spokane (99201) *(G-12223)*

Dejay Products LLC 206 784-8200
8016 Durango St Sw Ste B6 Lakewood (98499) *(G-5711)*

Dek Enterprises Inc 360 794-8614
17288 Beaton Rd Se Monroe (98272) *(G-6564)*

Del Fox Custom Meats Inc (PA) 360 629-3723
7229 300th St Nw Stanwood (98292) *(G-12965)*

Del Fox Locker Meats, Stanwood *Also called Del Fox Custom Meats Inc* *(G-12965)*

Del Rio Food Processing Corp 206 767-9102
9808 16th Ave Sw Seattle (98106) *(G-9816)*

Del-Rio Grocery Store, Seattle *Also called Del Rio Food Processing Corp* *(G-9816)*

Delaval Inc 360 428-1744
3709 Old Highway 99 S Rd Mount Vernon (98273) *(G-6788)*

Delaware Supply, Olympia *Also called Loading Docks Supply LLC* *(G-7324)*

Delbert L Wheeler 509 874-2471
1200 N White Swan Rd White Swan (98952) *(G-15137)*

Delestine Designs 206 524-6980
4024 Ne 57th St Seattle (98105) *(G-9817)*

Delich Distillery 360 552-2282
2590 Ne Old Belfair Hwy Belfair (98528) *(G-760)*

Delightful Treat Distributors, Federal Way *Also called A J R Enterprises Inc* *(G-3711)*

Delille Cellars Inc 425 489-0544
14208 Wdnvlle Rdmnd Rd Ne Redmond (98052) *(G-8437)*

Delozier Recovery Services 360 385-1258
211 Taylor St Ste 37 Port Townsend (98368) *(G-7878)*

Delphis Creative Bus Solutions 360 689-4063
3421 42nd Ave Nw Gig Harbor (98335) *(G-4094)*

Delta C Dynamics LLC 888 704-3626
2839 W Kennewick Ave Kennewick (99336) *(G-4653)*

Delta Camshaft Inc 253 383-4152
2366 Tacoma Ave S Tacoma (98402) *(G-13257)*

Delta Electric Motors, Tukwila *Also called Dipietro Enterprises Inc* *(G-13724)*

Delta Grind LLC 360 459-8205
9105 Martin Way E Olympia (98516) *(G-7267)*

Delta Industries, Kelso *Also called Three Rivers Industrial Mch* *(G-4555)*

Delta Marine Industries Inc 206 763-0760
1608 S 96th St Seattle (98108) *(G-9818)*

Delta Pntg & Prefinishing Co 253 588-8278
4025 100th St Sw Tacoma (98499) *(G-13258)*

Delta Production 206 567-4373
8832 Sw Dilworth Rd Vashon (98070) *(G-14721)*

Delta V Cellars LLC 425 677-8487
1050 1st Pl Se Issaquah (98027) *(G-4405)*

Deluxe 360 794-3157
14640 172nd Dr Se Monroe (98272) *(G-6565)*

Dem-Bart Checkering Tools Inc 360 568-7356
1825 Bickford Ave Snohomish (98290) *(G-11897)*

Dematic Corp 206 674-4578
14900 Interurban Ave S Tukwila (98168) *(G-13723)*

Deming Log Show Inc 360 592-3051
3295 Cedarville Rd Bellingham (98226) *(G-1322)*

Demitris Blody Mary Seasonings, Seattle *Also called Gourmet Mixes Inc* *(G-10103)*

Democracy Live Inc (PA) 855 655-8683
2900 Ne Blakeley St Ste B Seattle (98105) *(G-9819)*

Dendreon Corporation 877 256-4545
1208 Eastlake Ave E Seattle (98102) *(G-9820)*

Dendreon Corporation (HQ) 206 256-4545
1208 Eastlake Ave E Seattle (98102) *(G-9821)*

Denim Dreamz 425 712-1001
19214 80th Ave W Edmonds (98026) *(G-3106)*

Denim Duds 360 432-1183
70 Se Bluff Loop Rd Shelton (98584) *(G-11696)*

Denim Frills 360 844-5163
10501 Ne Highway 99 # 17 Vancouver (98686) *(G-14175)*

Denise Haase 360 264-4680
5729 Littlerock Rd Sw # 107 Tumwater (98512) *(G-13871)*

Denise Mayward 253 927-0219
3820 Nassau Ave Ne Tacoma (98422) *(G-13259)*

Denmar Industries Inc 206 579-9316
5314 Sunset Ave Anacortes (98221) **(G-121)**
Dennis Davis Logging Co Inc 360 864-2548
741 S First St Toledo (98591) **(G-13637)**
Dennis Nelson 360 320-4237
695 Maplewood Loop Oak Harbor (98277) **(G-7148)**
Denny Mountain Media LLC 425 831-7130
1300 N Northlake Way # 200 Seattle (98103) **(G-9822)**
Denny Park Glass Studio LLC 206 388-5725
818 John St Seattle (98109) **(G-9823)**
Denrick Tees 509 429-6675
514 Chewiliken Valley Rd Riverside (98849) **(G-9125)**
Dental X Ray Support Systems 509 279-2061
3102 E Trent Ave Ste 100 Spokane (99202) **(G-12224)**
Dentzel Carousel Co 360 385-1068
843 53rd St Port Townsend (98368) **(G-7879)**
Dep Homes Corporation 206 322-1241
800 23rd Ave S Seattle (98144) **(G-9824)**
Department Community Services, Chehalis *Also called County of Lewis* **(G-2485)**
Department Crrctons Wash State 509 526-6375
1313 N 13th Ave Walla Walla (99362) **(G-14795)**
Der Heintzelmann Inc 360 683-4740
152 Windy Way Sequim (98382) **(G-11626)**
Derek Andrew Inc (PA) 425 453-9888
6232 160th Ave Se Bellevue (98006) **(G-877)**
Derek Mefford 360 580-9166
2221 E Hoquiam Rd Hoquiam (98550) **(G-4333)**
Derma Medical Spa 360 350-5321
3025 Limited Ln Nw Olympia (98502) **(G-7268)**
Des Etes Longs Vineyard LLC 509 430-5488
34821 N 114 Pr Nw Benton City (99320) **(G-1609)**
Des Voigne Melissa 206 478-2021
14125 Ne 189th St Ste B Woodinville (98072) **(G-15221)**
Descartes Biometrics Inc 650 743-4435
9131 Great Blue Heron Ln Blaine (98230) **(G-1668)**
Descartes Systems (usa) LLC 206 812-7874
2014 E Madison St Ste 400 Seattle (98122) **(G-9825)**
Desco Plastics LLC 360 413-7787
7235 40th Ct Ne Olympia (98516) **(G-7269)**
Desema Company 425 202-7572
7241 185th Ave Ne # 2222 Redmond (98073) **(G-8438)**
Desert Graphics Inc 509 765-8082
1626 W Broadway Ave Ste A Moses Lake (98837) **(G-6704)**
Desert Leathercraft LLC 509 392-2589
2532 Banyon St Richland (99352) **(G-8987)**
Desert Rain 509 545-1900
304 Tuttle Ln Burbank (99323) **(G-2083)**
Desert View Manufactured Home 509 967-3456
6500 Desert View Dr West Richland (99353) **(G-15095)**
Desert Wind Vineyard 509 786-7277
2258 Wine Country Rd Prosser (99350) **(G-8041)**
Desi Telephone Labels Inc 360 571-0713
8100 Ne St Johns Rd A101 Vancouver (98665) **(G-14176)**
Design Centre 509 534-6461
3613 E Springfield Ave Spokane (99202) **(G-12225)**
Design Construction Heritg Inc 206 634-1989
1302 125th Pl Sw Everett (98204) **(G-3442)**
Design Craft Upholstery Inc 425 775-7620
19704 Cypress Way Lynnwood (98036) **(G-6107)**
Design Hardwood Products Inc (PA) 425 869-0859
15060 Ne 95th St Redmond (98052) **(G-8439)**
Design Hardwood Products Inc 425 869-0859
15050 Ne 95th St Redmond (98052) **(G-8440)**
Design Salt Inc 509 667-1600
527 Piere St Wenatchee (98801) **(G-15025)**
Design Service Corporation 509 248-8531
1507 S 9th Ave Yakima (98902) **(G-15553)**
Designcraft Cabinets Inc 509 758-2160
1710 13th St Clarkston (99403) **(G-2631)**
Designer Decal Inc 509 535-0267
1120 E 1st Ave Spokane (99202) **(G-12226)**
Designers Holding Company Inc 425 487-9887
20150 144th Ave Ne Woodinville (98072) **(G-15222)**
Designers Marble, Woodinville *Also called Designers Holding Company Inc* **(G-15222)**
Designers Marble Inc 425 487-9887
20150 144th Ave Ne Main Woodinville (98072) **(G-15223)**
Designs Unlimited 360 792-1372
5384 E Collins Rd Port Orchard (98366) **(G-7802)**
Desimone Oil and Vinegar Mkt 253 709-5576
20134 Se 192nd St Renton (98058) **(G-8783)**
Desparado Cowboy Bullets LLC 509 382-8926
2 Port Way Dayton (99328) **(G-2881)**
Dessert Industries Inc 425 487-3244
12902 Lost Lake Rd Snohomish (98296) **(G-11898)**
Destination Des Moines 206 824-9462
22511 Marine View Dr S Des Moines (98198) **(G-2933)**
Destiny Dawn Spirituality, La Center *Also called McLaren Destiny* **(G-5509)**
Destiny Software Inc 425 415-1777
19724 166th Ave Ne Woodinville (98072) **(G-15224)**
Detec Systems LLC 253 272-3252
711 St Helens Ave Ste 201 Tacoma (98402) **(G-13260)**
Detonator Games LLC 206 355-6682
20241 296th Ave Ne Duvall (98019) **(G-2982)**
Detro Manufacturing Inc 360 687-9960
1721 Se Grace Ave Ste E Battle Ground (98604) **(G-697)**
Devaul Publishing Inc 360 748-3335
429 N Market Blvd Chehalis (98532) **(G-2489)**
Developmental Machine 253 631-6953
16205 Se Auburn Black Dia Auburn (98092) **(G-424)**
Devlin Designing Boatbuilders 360 866-0164
3010 37th Ave Sw Seattle (98126) **(G-9826)**
Devona LLC 509 520-2524
1334 School Ave Walla Walla (99362) **(G-14796)**
Devorah Creek Vinyards 206 579-8906
37901 183rd Ave Se Auburn (98092) **(G-425)**
Dewils Industries Inc (PA) 360 892-0300
6307 Ne 127th Ave Vancouver (98682) **(G-14177)**
Dewils Industries Inc 360 892-0300
6307 Ne 127th Ave Vancouver (98682) **(G-14178)**
Dex Media Holdings Inc 509 922-1026
1101 N Argonne Rd Ste 101 Spokane Valley (99212) **(G-12681)**
Dex Media Holdings Inc 360 830-0807
10049 Kitsap Mall Blvd Nw # 102 Silverdale (98383) **(G-11831)**
Deyoungs Farm and Garden 425 483-9600
13621 Ne 175th St Woodinville (98072) **(G-15225)**
Df Industries Inc 253 472-0422
11708 24th Ave E Bldg 6 Tacoma (98445) **(G-13261)**
Df Industries Inc 253 445-7940
16802 116th Avenue Ct E Puyallup (98374) **(G-8143)**
DFI Mp Eroh LLC 206 499-2687
13583 Wheeler Rd Ne Ste D Moses Lake (98837) **(G-6705)**
Dg Machine 253 735-1373
3240 B St Nw Ste B Auburn (98001) **(G-426)**
Dia Avalon Philly, Bellevue *Also called Avalonphilly LLC* **(G-800)**
Diagraph of The Northwest, Kent *Also called Westmark Industries Inc* **(G-5214)**
Dial One Telecommunications 360 629-2085
31310 English Grade Rd Stanwood (98292) **(G-12966)**
Diamond B Constructors, Bellingham *Also called Harris Acquisition IV LLC* **(G-1367)**
Diamond Blue Manufacturing Co 360 428-1744
3709 Old Highway 99 S Rd Mount Vernon (98273) **(G-6789)**
Diamond Concrete Products 360 659-6277
19405 63rd Ave Ne Arlington (98223) **(G-228)**
Diamond Craft Jeweler's, Clarkston *Also called Diamondcraft Jewels* **(G-2632)**
Diamond Knot Brewery Inc 425 355-4488
621 Front St Mukilteo (98275) **(G-6911)**
Diamond Knot Brewing Co Inc (PA) 425 355-4488
4602 Chennault Beach Rd B2 Mukilteo (98275) **(G-6912)**
Diamond Knot Brewing Co Inc 425 315-0703
4602 Chennault Beach Rd B2 Mukilteo (98275) **(G-6913)**
Diamond Knot Brewing Co Inc 425 355-4488
621 Front St Mukilteo (98275) **(G-6914)**
Diamond Knot Craft Brewing, Mukilteo *Also called Diamond Knot Brewing Co Inc* **(G-6912)**
Diamond Knot Craft Brewing, Mukilteo *Also called Diamond Knot Brewing Co Inc* **(G-6913)**
Diamond Machine Works Inc 206 633-3960
2122 W Elmore St Seattle (98199) **(G-9827)**
Diamond Nets Inc 360 354-1319
1064 E Pole Rd Everson (98247) **(G-3673)**
Diamond Pier, Gig Harbor *Also called Pin Foundations Inc* **(G-4145)**
Diamond Polishing Systems 253 770-0508
8801 Canyon Rd E Puyallup (98371) **(G-8144)**
Diamond Store Inc 253 272-3377
940 Broadway Tacoma (98402) **(G-13262)**
Diamond Tech Innovations Inc 360 866-1337
1043 Kaiser Rd Sw Olympia (98512) **(G-7270)**
Diamond Timber Company 360 274-7914
450 Toutle River Rd Castle Rock (98611) **(G-2339)**
Diamondback Construction LLC 206 730-1239
14825 Ashworth Ave N Shoreline (98133) **(G-11768)**
Diamondcraft Jewels 509 758-1449
1327 Commercial Way Clarkston (99403) **(G-2632)**
Diana Thompson 360 665-0102
34704 T Ln Ocean Park (98640) **(G-7179)**
Diane Foods, Fife *Also called Gruma Corporation* **(G-3957)**
Diane M Young 310 284-8704
239 Sw 138th St Burien (98166) **(G-2102)**
Dick and Janes Spot 509 925-3224
101 N Pearl St Ellensburg (98926) **(G-3193)**
Dick and Janes Spot Fine Arts, Ellensburg *Also called Dick and Janes Spot* **(G-3193)**
Dick Busher Photographics, Seattle *Also called Richard C Busher Jr* **(G-10961)**
Dick Nite Spoons Inc 425 377-8448
16810 Ok Mill Rd Snohomish (98290) **(G-11899)**
Dickson Company 253 472-4489
3315 S Pine St Tacoma (98409) **(G-13263)**
Diebels Welding & Machine 509 422-0457
269 Conconully Rd Okanogan (98840) **(G-7196)**
Diesel America West Inc 360 378-4182
92 Little Rd Friday Harbor (98250) **(G-4042)**
Diesel Prfmce Unlimited LLC 509 546-9997
6804 Franklin Rd Pasco (99301) **(G-7576)**
Diesel Tech Machining Inc 509 576-8299
619 W J St Yakima (98902) **(G-15554)**
Different Drummers 509 216-2098
320 N Mitchell Dr Liberty Lake (99019) **(G-5830)**
Differential Energy Global Ltd 360 895-1184
1540 Leader Intl Dr Port Orchard (98367) **(G-7803)**

ALPHABETIC

Differential Networks LLC 360 366-8123
2229 Grant St Bellingham (98225) *(G-1323)*

Digatron LLC 509 467-3128
120 N Wall St Ste 300 Spokane (99201) *(G-12227)*

Digi Resources LLC 888 775-3444
4115 205th Ave Se Sammamish (98075) *(G-9201)*

Digicopy N Print, Seattle Also called Digital Impressions Inc *(G-9828)*

Digilent Inc (HQ) 509 338-3784
1300 Ne Henley Ct Ste 3 Pullman (99163) *(G-8087)*

Digilite Led, Tukwila Also called Mfg Universe Corp *(G-13772)*

Digital Anglers LLC 206 819-7010
16708 Ne 103rd Pl Redmond (98052) *(G-8441)*

Digital Color Press 509 362-1152
8117 N Division St Ste I Spokane (99208) *(G-12228)*

Digital Control Incorporated (PA) 425 251-0701
19625 62nd Ave S Ste B103 Kent (98032) *(G-4873)*

Digital Documents Inc 509 775-2425
771 S Keller St Republic (99166) *(G-8956)*

Digital Image 509 375-6001
2950 George Washington Wa Richland (99354) *(G-8988)*

Digital Imaging Services Inc 360 567-1260
610 E 40th St Vancouver (98663) *(G-14179)*

Digital Impressions Inc 206 443-1234
9 Denny Way Seattle (98109) *(G-9828)*

Digital Print Services, Kent Also called Domenics Printing Inc *(G-4876)*

Digital Printing, Shelton Also called Graphic Communications *(G-11698)*

Digital Product Studio LLC 206 484-8439
8332 Mary Ave Nw Seattle (98117) *(G-9829)*

Digital Threads, Ferndale Also called Sherri and Brent Wright *(G-3904)*

Digitlis Educatn Solutions Inc 360 616-8915
817 Pacific Ave Bremerton (98337) *(G-1947)*

Digitron Electronics LLC 509 427-4005
42892 State Route 14 Stevenson (98648) *(G-13011)*

Dignon Co Inc (PA) 206 448-6677
17851 29th Ave Ne Lake Forest Park (98155) *(G-5612)*

Dilbeck Tools Inc 509 452-3405
502 Bittner Rd Yakima (98901) *(G-15555)*

Diligence Group Oil & Gas Biof 360 892-0745
8805 Ne 36th St Vancouver (98662) *(G-14180)*

Dillanos Coffee Roasters Inc 253 826-1807
1607 45th St E Sumner (98390) *(G-13066)*

Dills Creek Inc 360 826-3841
821 First St Hamilton (98255) *(G-4312)*

Dimensional Imaging Inc 206 285-0450
1475 Elliott Ave W Seattle (98119) *(G-9830)*

Dimensional Products Inc (PA) 206 352-9065
1467 Elliott Ave W Seattle (98119) *(G-9831)*

Dina Helmts 509 521-9866
7904 Wrigley Dr Pasco (99301) *(G-7577)*

Dineen Family Wine Company LLC 509 829-6897
2980 Gilbert Rd Zillah (98953) *(G-15753)*

Dinesync Inc 206 620-2550
999 3rd Ave Ste 700 Seattle (98104) *(G-9832)*

Dingeys LLC 360 789-0853
700 Capitol Way S Olympia (98501) *(G-7271)*

Dining Solutions LLC 425 268-6190
217 165th Ave Ne Bellevue (98008) *(G-878)*

Dinners Ready 425 337-7955
2932 143rd St Se Mill Creek (98012) *(G-6507)*

Dipietro Enterprises Inc 206 423-7633
10831 E Marginal Way S Tukwila (98168) *(G-13724)*

Direct Connect Group (dcg) LLC (PA) 206 784-6892
4401 E Marginal Way S Seattle (98134) *(G-9833)*

Direct Contact LLC (PA) 425 235-1723
575 Andover Park W # 210 Tukwila (98188) *(G-13725)*

Direct Fire Suppression System 509 215-0852
620 N Grant Ave Medical Lake (99022) *(G-6440)*

Direct Hit Golf Flags LLC 253 946-6263
308 Sw 294th Pl Federal Way (98023) *(G-3729)*

Direct Mailing Solutions 425 739-4568
21021 66th Ave W Lynnwood (98036) *(G-6108)*

Direct Process Metal Fabg 206 276-6014
154 N 35th St Apt 103 Seattle (98103) *(G-9834)*

Directed Technologies Drlg Inc (PA) 800 239-5950
3476 W Belfair Valley Rd Bremerton (98312) *(G-1948)*

Directeq LLC 425 818-9510
25207 480th Dr Ne Darrington (98241) *(G-2867)*

Directions On Microsoft, Kirkland Also called Redmond Communications Inc *(G-5451)*

Direys 425 788-2026
32811 Ne 134th St Duvall (98019) *(G-2983)*

Dirtworx Enterprises Inc 360 225-0146
1260 Atlantic Ave Woodland (98674) *(G-15427)*

Dirty Couch LLC (PA) 203 303-8661
Nw 46th St Seattle (98107) *(G-9835)*

Dis-Tran Wood Products LLC 360 735-9356
1810 W 39th St Vancouver (98660) *(G-14181)*

Discount Doors & Millwork LLC 360 687-1942
2502 E Fourth Plain Blvd Vancouver (98661) *(G-14182)*

Discount Fence, Marblemount Also called Michellaine Lee Larry Bergsma *(G-6305)*

Discovery Products Corporation 877 530-2999
13619 Mukilteo Speedway Lynnwood (98087) *(G-6109)*

Discovery Tools 253 288-1720
20921 Se 403rd St Enumclaw (98022) *(G-3285)*

Disman Bakner Northwest Inc 425 837-3913
2243 275th Ct Se Issaquah (98075) *(G-4406)*

Display Manufacturing LLC 360 653-0990
3803 136th St Ne Marysville (98271) *(G-6330)*

Display Mfg, Marysville Also called Display Manufacturing LLC *(G-6330)*

Distant Lands Coffee, Renton Also called Java Trading Co LLC *(G-8832)*

Distant Lands Trading Co 800 758-4437
801 Houser Way N Renton (98057) *(G-8784)*

Distefano Winery Ltd 425 487-1648
12280 Ne Woodinville Dr Woodinville (98072) *(G-15226)*

Distiller LLC 206 659-4759
10510 Northup Way Ste 300 Kirkland (98033) *(G-5321)*

Distillers Way LLC 360 927-8781
5235 Industrial Pl Ferndale (98248) *(G-3836)*

Distillery A Creative LLC 206 696-0597
317 Nw 50th St Seattle (98107) *(G-9836)*

Distillery Loft Events 206 262-1022
1735 Westlake Ave N Seattle (98109) *(G-9837)*

Distillery Provisions LLC 206 861-5350
3257 25th Ave W Seattle (98199) *(G-9838)*

Distillery Seaspirits 360 820-0770
16110 Woodinville Redmond Woodinville (98072) *(G-15227)*

Distribution International Inc 425 228-4111
700 Powell Ave Sw Renton (98057) *(G-8785)*

Distribution Northwest Inc 206 963-6126
22508 31st Ave Se Bothell (98021) *(G-1846)*

Ditch Witch of Washington, Kennewick Also called D W Pape Inc *(G-4652)*

Ditco Inc 253 854-1002
106 E Titus St Kent (98032) *(G-4874)*

Dittos Print & Copy Center Inc 509 533-0025
2515 E Sprague Ave Spokane (99202) *(G-12229)*

Dive Xtras 425 296-6570
11520 Airport Rd Everett (98204) *(G-3443)*

Diversifab LLC 253 459-5170
19510 161st Way Se Yelm (98597) *(G-15732)*

Diversified Coatings LLC 360 264-2099
4107 119th Ave Se Tenino (98589) *(G-13617)*

Diversified Defense 253 327-0862
10710 48th St E Unit A Edgewood (98372) *(G-3075)*

Diversified Development Co 360 734-1480
730 Marine Dr Bellingham (98225) *(G-1324)*

Diversified Marketing Intl LLC 509 585-9377
1807 S Garfield St Kennewick (99337) *(G-4654)*

Diversified Mfg Techologies 360 424-9300
1817 Railroad Ave Bldg A Mount Vernon (98273) *(G-6790)*

Diversified Northwest Inc (PA) 425 710-0753
2941 Chestnut St Everett (98201) *(G-3444)*

Diversified Plastics West Inc 360 825-7660
2551 Cole St Ste E Enumclaw (98022) *(G-3286)*

Diversified Systems Group Inc 425 947-1500
26601 79th Ave S Kent (98032) *(G-4875)*

Diversified Systems Group Inc 425 947-1500
8700 148th Ave Ne Redmond (98052) *(G-8442)*

Diversified Welding Works Inc 360 576-0929
8009 Ne 19th Ct Vancouver (98665) *(G-14183)*

Division Correctional Inds, Walla Walla Also called Department Crrctons Wash State *(G-14795)*

Division Five Inc 206 988-5004
6458 S 144th St Tukwila (98168) *(G-13726)*

Division of Avtechtyee, Inc., Everett Also called Tyee Aircraft Inc *(G-3639)*

Division of Hydramaster, Mukilteo Also called Cleanmaster *(G-6903)*

Division Piedmont Directional 425 482-9022
14241 Ne Wdnvlle Duvall Woodinville (98072) *(G-15228)*

Diy Table Legs LLC 206 659-8669
20927 13th Pl W Lynnwood (98036) *(G-6110)*

Diy Tech Shop LLC 360 258-1519
2464 Ne Stapleton Rd # 3 Vancouver (98661) *(G-14184)*

Dj Creations 509 738-6200
815 W Old Kettle Rd Kettle Falls (99141) *(G-5231)*

Djangobookscom 206 528-9873
4002 Ne 45th St Seattle (98105) *(G-9839)*

Djs Pens 360 565-0145
3013 Obrien Rd Port Angeles (98362) *(G-7697)*

DK Machining LLC 509 991-6110
11325 W Meadowview Ln Nine Mile Falls (99026) *(G-7072)*

DK Precision Machine, Marysville Also called Kieu Danh *(G-6347)*

Dk9 Dog Walking 425 922-4685
17017 Se 263rd St Covington (98042) *(G-2825)*

Dkfab Inc 503 710-2064
7240 Yakima Valley Hwy Zillah (98953) *(G-15754)*

Dkr Wood Working 509 943-2273
1639 April Loop Richland (99354) *(G-8989)*

Dl Logos 360 385-3101
275 Otto St Ste A Port Townsend (98368) *(G-7880)*

Dla Document Services 509 527-7231
201 N 3rd Ave Walla Walla (99362) *(G-14797)*

Dla Document Services 360 315-4014
1100 Hunley Rd Ste 108 Silverdale (98315) *(G-11832)*

Dli Engineering Corporation 206 842-7656
1050 Ne Hostmark St # 101 Poulsbo (98370) *(G-7958)*

Dlm Inc ... 425 348-3204
9800 Harbour Pl Ste 114 Mukilteo (98275) ***(G-6915)***
Dm Coating LLC ... 509 420-0961
804 W Marie St Pasco (99301) ***(G-7578)***
Dm2 Software Inc ... 360 574-6984
7700 Ne Greenwood Dr # 200 Vancouver (98662) ***(G-14185)***
DMC Satellite Systems Inc ... 360 681-4204
70 Timber Rd Sequim (98382) ***(G-11627)***
DMC Sidecars LLC ... 360 825-4610
15616 Crbnado S Pririe Rd Buckley (98321) ***(G-2057)***
Dmfrank Publication ... 360 446-6113
404 California Ave N Rainier (98576) ***(G-8314)***
Dml Tool Grinding ... 253 752-3638
1602 S Tyler St Tacoma (98405) ***(G-13264)***
Dmm Incorporated ... 360 435-5252
7419 204th St Ne Arlington (98223) ***(G-229)***
DMS Motorsports ... 360 863-3807
17461 147th St Se Monroe (98272) ***(G-6566)***
DMW & Marine Repair, Port Townsend *Also called Daves Mobile Welding LLC* ***(G-7877)***
Dna Growers LLC ... 509 793-6606
16833 Road 8 Ne Moses Lake (98837) ***(G-6706)***
Dnlvi Business Solutions ... 360 827-5210
7838 195th Ave Sw Rochester (98579) ***(G-9131)***
Do It Best, Bremerton *Also called Parker Lumber Co Inc* ***(G-1986)***
Do or Dye Self Defense ... 253 653-5696
26431 7th Ave S Des Moines (98198) ***(G-2934)***
Dockside Cannery ... 360 642-8870
Port Of Ilwaco Ilwaco (98624) ***(G-4369)***
Docudriven, La Center *Also called Pacific Ally LLC* ***(G-5511)***
Docufeed Technologies ... 360 793-2001
32533 Cascade View Dr Sultan (98294) ***(G-13022)***
Document MGT Archives LLC ... 360 501-5047
1021 Columbia Blvd Longview (98632) ***(G-5906)***
Documentary Media LLC ... 206 935-9292
3250 41st Ave Sw Seattle (98116) ***(G-9840)***
Dodge Systems LLC ... 253 405-3967
2710 104th Street Ct S A Lakewood (98499) ***(G-5712)***
Dodger and Powers Wines ... 509 627-4986
1106 N Jurupa St Kennewick (99338) ***(G-4655)***
Dodson Rd Orchard LLC ... 509 787-3537
903 A St Se Quincy (98848) ***(G-8296)***
DOE Run Studios ... 360 765-0935
13th Doe Run Rd Quilcene (98376) ***(G-8282)***
Dog & Pony Brewing Company, Cashmere *Also called Joe Nestor* ***(G-2323)***
Dog House Leathers ... 206 257-0231
715 E Pike St Seattle (98122) ***(G-9841)***
Dog On It Parks Inc ... 425 512-8489
4818 Evergreen Way Ste B Everett (98203) ***(G-3445)***
Dogfence of North America ... 509 991-0385
4608 Williams Valley Rd Clayton (99110) ***(G-2657)***
Dogfish Bay Studios LLC ... 772 335-8711
18062 Viking Way Nw Poulsbo (98370) ***(G-7959)***
Dogfish Software Corporation ... 206 395-9050
216 1st Ave S Ste 200 Seattle (98104) ***(G-9842)***
Doggy Delirious, Monroe *Also called Wet Noses Natural Dog Treat Co* ***(G-6636)***
Dogsdream Corporation ... 425 737-2810
8408 Aurora Ave N Seattle (98103) ***(G-9843)***
Dogstar Cabinets Inc ... 509 674-4229
2040 Ley Rd Cle Elum (98922) ***(G-2665)***
Dogwood Industries ... 425 949-7379
10037 Main St Bothell (98011) ***(G-1759)***
Dojo LLC ... 203 903-0079
15627 Se 178th St Renton (98058) ***(G-8786)***
Dolans Dog Doodads LLC ... 206 257-4518
10808 Myers Way S Seattle (98168) ***(G-9844)***
Dolco Packaging Corp ... 509 662-8415
1121 S Columbia St Wenatchee (98801) ***(G-15026)***
Dollar Stretcher ... 509 895-7744
501 W Lincoln Ave Yakima (98902) ***(G-15556)***
Dolls By Arlene ... 360 687-4321
19616 Ne 163rd Ave Battle Ground (98604) ***(G-698)***
Dolphin Press Inc ... 253 735-1856
17828 Se Lake Holm Rd Auburn (98092) ***(G-427)***
Domaine Ste Michelle, Woodinville *Also called Michelle Ste Wine Estates Ltd* ***(G-15309)***
Domanico Cellars LLC ... 206 465-9406
1403 Dexter Ave N Seattle (98109) ***(G-9845)***
Domenics Printing Inc ... 425 251-4925
1819 Central Ave S Ste 80 Kent (98032) ***(G-4876)***
Domestique ... 206 545-3769
6560 5th Pl S Seattle (98108) ***(G-9846)***
Domino Fashion LLC ... 425 646-0500
2042 Bellevue Sq Bellevue (98004) ***(G-879)***
Domtar Paper Company LLC ... 253 924-2345
33663 Weyerhaeuser Way S Federal Way (98001) ***(G-3730)***
Don Boehme & Sons Logging ... 360 871-1571
7084 Se King Rd Port Orchard (98367) ***(G-7804)***
Don Glaser Logging ... 206 462-9638
8707 366th St E Eatonville (98328) ***(G-3053)***
Don Larson Logging Inc ... 509 722-6612
5900b Larson Ln Fruitland (99129) ***(G-4065)***
Don Macintosh ... 425 821-1499
14422 87th Ave Ne Kirkland (98034) ***(G-5322)***
Don Noodle Station, Seattle *Also called U Don LLC* ***(G-11358)***
Don Painter Logging Inc ... 360 832-3683
410 Madison Ave N Eatonville (98328) ***(G-3054)***
Don Pancho Authenti ... 509 575-4489
605 E Nob Hill Blvd Yakima (98901) ***(G-15557)***
Don Pancho Mexican Foods, Yakima *Also called Don Pancho Authenti* ***(G-15557)***
Don's Printery, Colville *Also called Post All Expressions* ***(G-2769)***
Donald R Hollister Trckg Inc ... 360 887-8418
1912 Ne 279th St Ridgefield (98642) ***(G-9079)***
Donald R Jacobson ... 360 425-4346
2525 Germany Creek Rd Longview (98632) ***(G-5907)***
Donamo Co ... 360 835-5634
1413 N 20th St Washougal (98671) ***(G-14952)***
Dongalen Enterprises Inc ... 253 395-4885
22435 68th Ave S Kent (98032) ***(G-4877)***
Donnelley Financial LLC ... 206 853-5460
999 3rd Ave Ste 1500 Seattle (98104) ***(G-9847)***
Donner Logging LLC ... 509 675-2717
740d Arden Butte Rd Colville (99114) ***(G-2751)***
Donnies Peninsula Sign ... 360 642-4512
35504 J Pl Ocean Park (98640) ***(G-7180)***
Dont Stop Printing ... 360 292-8610
1803 Cameo Ct Nw Olympia (98502) ***(G-7272)***
Donut House, Anacortes *Also called Pigs & Angels Inc* ***(G-161)***
Donut Star Inc ... 253 833-2980
914 Auburn Way S Auburn (98002) ***(G-428)***
Doodlebugs ... 360 683-3154
138 W Washington St Sequim (98382) ***(G-11628)***
Dooley Enterprises LLC (PA) ... 303 619-7101
416 228th St Sw Apt G102 Bothell (98021) ***(G-1847)***
Doors & Millwork Inc ... 509 921-7663
2224 N Locust Rd Ste 5 Spokane Valley (99206) ***(G-12682)***
Doremus & Fahey Publishing ... 253 507-8848
12414 Glenwood Ave Sw Lakewood (98499) ***(G-5713)***
DOriginal Jewelers ... 425 454-5559
885 Bellevue Way Ne Bellevue (98004) ***(G-880)***
Doris J Johnson ... 509 586-3646
739 S Tacoma Pl Kennewick (99336) ***(G-4656)***
Dormakaba USA Inc ... 253 864-4484
6319 112th St E Ste 102 Puyallup (98373) ***(G-8145)***
Dose Oil LLC ... 954 494-7976
2302 140th Pl Se Mill Creek (98012) ***(G-6508)***
Dose Safety Co ... 206 282-7086
2925 28th Ave W Seattle (98199) ***(G-9848)***
Dose Safety Inc ... 206 276-3385
17904 Ne 26th St Redmond (98052) ***(G-8443)***
DOT Com LLC ... 425 256-2815
4 102nd Ave Ne Ste 300 Bellevue (98004) ***(G-881)***
Dot4kids ... 503 884-8838
1925 54th Ln Se Olympia (98501) ***(G-7273)***
Dotink LLC ... 509 655-0828
1917 S Union Rd Spokane Valley (99206) ***(G-12683)***
Dotson Doors LLC ... 253 326-6047
3012 Withers Pl Mount Vernon (98274) ***(G-6791)***
Double a Logging Inc ... 509 476-2907
10 Verbeck Rd Oroville (98844) ***(G-7464)***
Double D Logging Co Inc ... 360 533-7168
612 L St Hoquiam (98550) ***(G-4334)***
Double D Mfg LLC ... 206 954-8099
3710b 136th St Ne Marysville (98271) ***(G-6331)***
Double Dutch LLC ... 509 837-6539
351 W Merz Rd Sunnyside (98944) ***(G-13120)***
Double Up LLC ... 908 398-9088
22626 Ne Inglewood Hill R Sammamish (98074) ***(G-9202)***
Double V Distillery ... 360 666-0716
1315 Se Grace Ave Battle Ground (98604) ***(G-699)***
Double Vision Partners Inc ... 360 378-4331
276 Salmonberry Ln Friday Harbor (98250) ***(G-4043)***
Doubleback ... 509 525-3334
229 E Main St Walla Walla (99362) ***(G-14798)***
Doublebit Software ... 425 503-0692
3635 130th Ave Ne Bellevue (98005) ***(G-882)***
Doug & June Holt ... 425 228-6067
12769 Se 73rd Pl Newcastle (98056) ***(G-7028)***
Doug D Froland ... 206 932-8433
10600 8th Ave S Seattle (98168) ***(G-9849)***
Doug House Powder Coating ... 360 681-5412
503b S 3rd Ave Ste B Sequim (98382) ***(G-11629)***
Doug Puzzle ... 425 647-0464
3620 130th Ave Ne Bellevue (98005) ***(G-883)***
Doug Skrivan ... 253 584-7323
10914 93rd Ave Sw Lakewood (98498) ***(G-5714)***
Douglas Green ... 360 260-9708
17413 Se 28th St Vancouver (98683) ***(G-14186)***
Douglas Green & Associates, Vancouver *Also called Douglas Green* ***(G-14186)***
Douglas L Perry ... 253 303-0537
9614 Starlet Ln Nw Gig Harbor (98335) ***(G-4095)***
Douglass Hemingway & Co LLC ... 360 299-0420
13589 Clayton Ln Anacortes (98221) ***(G-122)***
Douglass Certified Prosthetics ... 206 363-7790
10740 Meridian Ave N G2 Seattle (98133) ***(G-9850)***
Dougs Diesel Repair ... 509 665-7480
3703 N Clemons St East Wenatchee (98802) ***(G-3010)***

ALPHABETIC

Dove Printing Inc ... 509 483-6164
1227 E Francis Ave Spokane (99208) ***(G-12230)***
Dow Agroscience ... 509 332-3650
2001 Country Club Rd Pullman (99163) ***(G-8088)***
Dow Jones & Company Inc ... 253 661-8850
600 S 334th St Federal Way (98003) ***(G-3731)***
Dow Publishing LLC ... 425 572-6540
1210 N 42nd Pl Renton (98056) ***(G-8787)***
Dowling Software Consulta ... 425 489-3026
23311 22nd Dr Se Bothell (98021) ***(G-1848)***
Down Island Trading Co ... 360 376-4056
155 Channel Rd Deer Harbor (98243) ***(G-2891)***
Down River, Woodland *Also called Signode Industrial Group LLC* ***(G-15465)***
Downtown Cleaners & Tailoring ... 206 363-5455
14701 Aurora Ave N Shoreline (98133) ***(G-11769)***
Dowty Aerospace ... 509 248-5000
2720 W Washington Ave Yakima (98903) ***(G-15558)***
Doyle Printing Co, Tacoma *Also called F D Company* ***(G-13285)***
Doyon Technical Services LLC ... 253 344-5300
33810 Weyerhaeuser Way S Federal Way (98001) ***(G-3732)***
Dozing & Ditching ... 425 308-2063
4528 116th Ave Ne Lake Stevens (98258) ***(G-5644)***
Dp Printing, Tacoma *Also called Special Edition Incorporated* ***(G-13520)***
Dp West, Enumclaw *Also called Diversified Plastics West Inc* ***(G-3286)***
Dp West ... 360 825-7660
2551 Cole St Enumclaw (98022) ***(G-3287)***
Dr Bieseckers LLC ... 360 386-1530
125 316th St Nw Stanwood (98292) ***(G-12967)***
Dr Dan Bio Diesel, Seattle *Also called Dr Dans Alternative Fuel Werks* ***(G-9851)***
Dr Dans Alternative Fuel Werks ... 206 783-5728
912 Nw 50th St Seattle (98107) ***(G-9851)***
Dr Dons Fishfood LLC ... 360 533-6620
320 W Market St Aberdeen (98520) ***(G-8)***
Dr Software LLC ... 206 526-1371
5123 47th Ave Ne Seattle (98105) ***(G-9852)***
Dr Ventures Inc ... 253 874-6583
1911 Sw Campus Dr Federal Way (98023) ***(G-3733)***
Dr. Pepper, Spokane Valley *Also called American Bottling Company* ***(G-12608)***
Drachen Design Inc ... 206 282-4349
3131 Western Ave Ste 321 Seattle (98121) ***(G-9853)***
Drachen Foundation, Seattle *Also called Drachen Design Inc* ***(G-9853)***
Dragon Head Studios LLC ... 925 813-2881
14601 9th Ave Ne Shoreline (98155) ***(G-11770)***
Dragondyne Publishing ... 206 619-1577
13625 26th Pl S Seatac (98168) ***(G-9281)***
Dragonfire Candles LLC ... 206 851-4235
911 93rd St Se Everett (98208) ***(G-3446)***
Drake Industries LLC ... 425 672-8266
17742 Talbot Rd Edmonds (98026) ***(G-3107)***
Drama Nine LLP ... 206 949-2953
531 Malden Ave E Seattle (98112) ***(G-9854)***
Draped In Style LLC ... 425 241-6227
7220 203rd St Se Snohomish (98296) ***(G-11900)***
Draper Valley Farms, Mount Vernon *Also called Perdue Foods LLC* ***(G-6823)***
Draper Valley Farms, Chehalis *Also called Perdue Foods LLC* ***(G-2523)***
Draxis Health Inc ... 509 489-5656
3525 N Regal St Spokane (99207) ***(G-12231)***
Drc Specialty Veneering LLC ... 253 301-0443
4020 S 56th St Ste 103 Tacoma (98409) ***(G-13265)***
Dream It Inc (PA) ... 360 379-1070
818 Corona St Port Townsend (98368) ***(G-7881)***
Dream Line Cabinets LLC ... 503 841-8575
2700 Ne An 2 F Vancouver (98661) ***(G-14187)***
Dream On Futon Co ... 360 739-2103
2020 Franklin St Ste 108 Bellingham (98225) ***(G-1325)***
Dream Works Machine Quilting ... 360 668-0864
17701 87th Ave Se Snohomish (98296) ***(G-11901)***
Dreamchasers Rv of Burlington, Burlington *Also called D & R Rv LLC* ***(G-2150)***
Dreamers Woods (PA) ... 360 477-5888
102 Holly Hill Rd Port Angeles (98363) ***(G-7698)***
Dreamtones Inc ... 650 265-0576
21209 40th Dr Se Bothell (98021) ***(G-1849)***
Dreamworks Printing Inc ... 425 970-4625
1250 Sw 43rd St Renton (98057) ***(G-8788)***
Dresser-Rand Company ... 425 828-4919
11808 Northup Way W190 Bellevue (98005) ***(G-884)***
Dresser-Rand Company ... 206 762-7660
225 S Lucile St Seattle (98108) ***(G-9855)***
Dreyer's Grand Ice Cream, Kent *Also called Nestle Dreyers Ice Cream Co* ***(G-5019)***
Dreyers Grand Ice Cream NW, Kent *Also called M-K-D Distributors Inc* ***(G-4999)***
Dri-Eaz Products Inc (HQ) ... 360 757-7776
15180 Josh Wilson Rd Burlington (98233) ***(G-2152)***
Drive Line Service Bellingham, Bellingham *Also called Drive Line Svc of Bellingham* ***(G-1326)***
Drive Line Svc of Bellingham ... 360 734-7828
2008 Humboldt St Bellingham (98225) ***(G-1326)***
Drivers License Examining ... 253 872-2782
25410 74th Ave S Kent (98032) ***(G-4878)***
Driveways By Interstate Paving, Arlington *Also called Interstate Asphalt Paving Inc* ***(G-257)***

DRM Holdings Inc ... 509 338-4699
1300 Ne Henley Ct Pullman (99163) ***(G-8089)***
Drolz Log and Rock Inc ... 360 987-2343
95 Bowes Rd Hoquiam (98550) ***(G-4335)***
Drolz Logging & Rock, Hoquiam *Also called Drolz Log and Rock Inc* ***(G-4335)***
Droneworks LLC ... 253 261-3888
29832 42nd Ave S Auburn (98001) ***(G-429)***
Drr Fruit Products Co Inc ... 509 836-2051
705 Alexander Rd Sunnyside (98944) ***(G-13121)***
Dru Wood ... 360 213-7444
8608 Mt Olympus Ave Vancouver (98664) ***(G-14188)***
Drug Free Alliance, Spokane Valley *Also called American Mobile Drug Testing* ***(G-12613)***
Drug Interv Service Amer ... 360 299-2700
9080 S March Point Rd A4 Anacortes (98221) ***(G-123)***
Druid Mountain Drones ... 206 321-4771
2121 5th Ave Nw Puyallup (98371) ***(G-8146)***
Dry Air Technology Inc ... 360 755-9176
1387 Pacific Dr Burlington (98233) ***(G-2153)***
Dry Fly Distilling Inc ... 509 489-2112
1003 E Trent Ave Ste 200 Spokane (99202) ***(G-12232)***
Dry Fly or Die ... 509 252-5022
505 W Riverside Ave Spokane (99201) ***(G-12233)***
Dry Kiln, The, Vancouver *Also called Western Forest Products US LLC* ***(G-14685)***
Ds-Iq Inc ... 425 974-1400
3326 160th Ave Se Ste 200 Bellevue (98008) ***(G-885)***
Dtd, Bremerton *Also called Directed Technologies Drlg Inc* ***(G-1948)***
Dtg Inc ... 206 622-4387
2805 223rd Pl Sw Brier (98036) ***(G-2019)***
Dti Exact, Olympia *Also called Diamond Tech Innovations Inc* ***(G-7270)***
DTI Ready Mix Company ... 509 937-4683
3147 Highway 231 Valley (99181) ***(G-13991)***
Dts, Oak Harbor *Also called Darbonnier Tactical Supply LLC* ***(G-7146)***
Dualos LLC ... 253 750-5125
917 Pacific Ave Ste 400 Tacoma (98402) ***(G-13266)***
Duane Bruner Logging Inc ... 360 274-7103
1176 Chapman Rd Castle Rock (98611) ***(G-2340)***
Duane Ruud ... 206 682-1082
2223 Occidental Ave S Seattle (98134) ***(G-9856)***
Dubrul Vineyard LLC ... 509 837-7746
2841 Fordyce Rd Sunnyside (98944) ***(G-13122)***
Duck Software LLC ... 206 935-9722
5626 42nd Ave Sw Seattle (98136) ***(G-9857)***
Duckworth, Clarkston *Also called Renaissance Marine Group Inc* ***(G-2644)***
Duckworth Boat Works Inc ... 509 758-9831
1061 16th Ave Clarkston (99403) ***(G-2633)***
Ducoterra LLC (PA) ... 360 788-4200
1645 Jills Ct Ste 108 Bellingham (98226) ***(G-1327)***
Dude Wheres My Car ... 509 249-5440
1306 S 18th St Yakima (98901) ***(G-15559)***
Dudley Family Group Inc ... 253 863-9282
1350 Thornton Ave Sw B Pacific (98047) ***(G-7525)***
Dudleys Fine Engraving ... 360 417-9415
918 E 8th St Port Angeles (98362) ***(G-7699)***
Dugger and Associates Inc ... 425 785-6940
336 E Beck St McCleary (98557) ***(G-6415)***
Dulin Construction Inc ... 360 736-9225
3300 Galvin Rd Centralia (98531) ***(G-2399)***
Dullum Enterprises, Vancouver *Also called Dullum Industries Inc* ***(G-14189)***
Dullum Industries Inc ... 360 254-3220
13315 Ne Kerr Rd Ste A Vancouver (98682) ***(G-14189)***
Dumas Holdings LLC ... 425 576-4227
5400 Carillon Pt Kirkland (98033) ***(G-5323)***
Dumb Luck LLC ... 206 406-1011
8333 Se 68th St Mercer Island (98040) ***(G-6460)***
Duncan J Woodworking ... 360 765-0745
50 Cemetary Rd Quilcene (98376) ***(G-8283)***
Duncan Macdonald Violins LLC ... 206 352-7219
2 W Smith St Seattle (98119) ***(G-9858)***
Duncan Stone LLC ... 360 820-0823
7331 21st Ave Nw Seattle (98117) ***(G-9859)***
Duncans Woods ... 360 604-7140
1221 Se Ellsworth Rd # 276 Vancouver (98664) ***(G-14190)***
Dungeness Brewing Co ... 360 775-1877
4017 S Mount Angeles Rd Port Angeles (98362) ***(G-7700)***
Dungeness Development Assoc (PA) ... 425 481-0600
11805 N Creek Pkwy S Kirkland (98034) ***(G-5324)***
Dungeness Development Assoc ... 360 875-5507
2288 W Commodore Way # 205 Seattle (98199) ***(G-9860)***
Dungeness Envmtl Solutions Inc ... 888 481-0326
909 Se Everett Mall Way Everett (98208) ***(G-3447)***
Dungeness Gear Works Inc ... 800 548-9743
18021 59th Ave Ne Arlington (98223) ***(G-230)***
Dungeness Valley Creamery ... 360 683-0716
876 N Beverage St Sequim (98382) ***(G-11630)***
Dunham Cellars LLC ... 509 529-4685
150 E Boeing Ave Walla Walla (99362) ***(G-14799)***
Dunmire Manufacturing ... 360 241-9099
8468 Kaster Dr Ne Bremerton (98311) ***(G-1949)***
Dunsire Printers Inc ... 360 532-8791
122 W Wishkah St Aberdeen (98520) ***(G-9)***
Duntons SEC Systms/Marine Wldg, Anacortes *Also called Jason Dunton* ***(G-137)***

DUO Wear Inc....425 251-0760
7857 S 180th St Kent (98032) *(G-4879)*
Dupont Co....425 260-0257
11203 100th Ave Ne Kirkland (98033) *(G-5325)*
Dupont De Nemours Inc....253 212-2278
1495 Wilmington Dr Dupont (98327) *(G-2958)*
Dupont Delivery LLC....253 884-2824
707 Penniman St Dupont (98327) *(G-2959)*
Dupont Library....253 548-3326
1540 Wilmington Dr Dupont (98327) *(G-2960)*
Dupont Pet Sitting & Services....816 517-7045
1726 Brown Ave Dupont (98327) *(G-2961)*
Dupont Veterinary Center....253 267-5431
1525 Wilmington Dr Dupont (98327) *(G-2962)*
Durable Superior Casters....253 750-0379
12620 Valley Ave E Sumner (98390) *(G-13067)*
Durado Enterprise....509 882-3247
201 Walnut Ln Grandview (98930) *(G-4247)*
Duraguard Products, Vancouver *Also called Pacific Die Cast Inc (G-14463)*
Duramark Technologies Inc....206 473-9212
14102 Ne 189th St Ste 3 Woodinville (98072) *(G-15229)*
Duren Controls....206 745-4987
14328 Beverly Park Rd Edmonds (98026) *(G-3108)*
Durham Geo-Enterprises Inc....770 465-7557
12123 Harbour Reach Dr Mukilteo (98275) *(G-6916)*
Dust Control Technologies Inc....360 256-2479
16121 Ne 119th St Brush Prairie (98606) *(G-2033)*
Dusted Valley....509 525-1337
1248 Old Milton Hwy Walla Walla (99362) *(G-14800)*
Dusty Cellars Winery....360 387-2171
529 Michael Way Camano Island (98282) *(G-2211)*
Dusty Shelf, Randle *Also called Karen Nichols (G-8326)*
Dusty Strings Co (PA)....206 634-1656
3450 16th Ave W Ste 200 Seattle (98119) *(G-9861)*
Dustys Machine Shop....360 694-6201
3108a Ne 66th St Vancouver (98663) *(G-14191)*
Dut Protective Coatings I....253 520-3374
1215 2nd Ave N Kent (98032) *(G-4880)*
Dutch Harbor Seafoods Ltd....425 881-8181
15400 Ne 90th St Ste 200 Redmond (98052) *(G-8444)*
Dutena Blankets....253 581-0312
9122 South Tacoma Way # 102 Lakewood (98499) *(G-5715)*
Duthie Enterprises Inc....206 767-3314
8155 1st Ave S Seattle (98108) *(G-9862)*
Duvall Graphics LLC....425 788-7578
14524 Main St Ne Ste 111 Duvall (98019) *(G-2984)*
Duvall Veterinary Hospital, Duvall *Also called Gengler Veterinary Svcs Pllc (G-2990)*
Duwamish Marine Services LLC....206 870-3027
5600 W Marginal Way Sw Seattle (98106) *(G-9863)*
Dux Technologies Inc....206 248-0808
13838 1st Ave S Ste C Burien (98168) *(G-2103)*
DVinery....509 548-7059
617 Front St Leavenworth (98826) *(G-5798)*
Dw Cornwall Farms Inc....509 291-5011
21706 S Sands Rd Fairfield (99012) *(G-3696)*
Dwaynes Software....425 379-7741
15225 49th Ave Se Everett (98208) *(G-3448)*
DWhittle Shop Inc....509 627-3050
4322 S 47th Ave Richland (99353) *(G-8990)*
Dwight Company LLC....360 262-9844
414 Hewitt Rd Chehalis (98532) *(G-2490)*
Dwight Hostvedt....360 683-2315
303 Sunny View Dr Sequim (98382) *(G-11631)*
Dwinell LLC....312 343-8607
206 W Broadway St Goldendale (98620) *(G-4195)*
Dwinell Country Ales, Goldendale *Also called Dwinell LLC (G-4195)*
Dyaco Coml & Med N Amer LLC....408 966-4239
18303 Bothell Everett Hwy # 210 Bothell (98012) *(G-1850)*
Dyer's Firefighter Cnstr, Ocean Park *Also called Dyers Construction & Excav (G-7181)*
Dyers Construction & Excav....903 486-1881
23621 Birch Ln Ocean Park (98640) *(G-7181)*
Dylan Aerospace, Auburn *Also called Dylan Manufacturing Inc (G-430)*
Dylan Manufacturing Inc....253 333-8260
1702 Pike St Nw Ste 1 Auburn (98001) *(G-430)*
Dyna Flow....253 381-9736
3110 Judson St Gig Harbor (98335) *(G-4096)*
Dynamic Automotive Distrs....206 725-4474
7269 Rainier Ave S Seattle (98118) *(G-9864)*
Dynamic Coatings LLC....360 755-3649
4113 Kingsway Anacortes (98221) *(G-124)*
Dynamic Designs Jewelry Inc....425 827-7722
11711 Ne 67th Pl Kirkland (98033) *(G-5326)*
Dynamic Energy Solutions, Longview *Also called Netzero Energy LLC (G-5934)*
Dynamic Food Ingredients, Moses Lake *Also called DFI Mp Eroh LLC (G-6705)*
Dynamic Food Ingredients Corp....303 459-5908
831 E Rockwood Blvd Spokane (99203) *(G-12234)*
Dynamic Safety LLC....425 290-9399
9700 Harbour Pl Ste 218 Mukilteo (98275) *(G-6917)*
Dynamic Software....253 630-7026
18403 Se Wax Rd Covington (98042) *(G-2826)*
Dynamic Software Innovations....425 432-5313
22949 Se 280th Pl Maple Valley (98038) *(G-6267)*
Dynamic Specialties....509 447-2755
442 City View Ln Newport (99156) *(G-7057)*
Dynamic Utility Services....425 742-1670
13726 1st Pl W Everett (98208) *(G-3449)*
Dynavest Inc....206 728-0777
2201 3rd Ave Apt 2604 Seattle (98121) *(G-9865)*
Dynea Overlays Inc....253 572-5600
2144 Milwaukee Way Tacoma (98421) *(G-13267)*
Dynes Farms Inc (PA)....360 757-4025
1145 S Anacortes St Burlington (98233) *(G-2154)*
Dynesco Corporation Inc (PA)....360 256-0116
12242 Championship Cir Mukilteo (98275) *(G-6918)*
Dynesco Lighting Services, Mukilteo *Also called Dynesco Corporation Inc (G-6918)*
Dyno Nobel Inc....360 740-0128
1516 Bunker Creek Rd Chehalis (98532) *(G-2491)*
Dyno Resource Corp....425 391-6084
26429 Se 152nd St Issaquah (98027) *(G-4407)*
Dyno-Tech Machine LLC....360 568-7023
17816 Dubuque Rd Snohomish (98290) *(G-11902)*
Dynolab....206 243-8877
643 Sw Normandy Rd Normandy Park (98166) *(G-7091)*
Dynon Avionics Inc (PA)....425 402-0433
19825 141st Pl Ne Woodinville (98072) *(G-15230)*
Dynon Instruments Inc....425 402-0433
19825 141st Pl Ne Woodinville (98072) *(G-15231)*
Dyson Inc....425 968-2456
12815 Ne 124th St Ste N Kirkland (98034) *(G-5327)*
Dz & Family Machine Works....360 225-6261
400 2nd St Woodland (98674) *(G-15428)*
E & E Foods Inc (PA)....206 768-8979
900 Powell Ave Sw Renton (98057) *(G-8789)*
E & S Custom Cabinets Inc....253 405-2732
1204 39th Ave Sw Puyallup (98373) *(G-8147)*
E and S Industries LLC....253 678-1539
155 133rd St E Tacoma (98445) *(G-13268)*
E B Associates Inc....253 709-1433
1446 Lafromboise St Enumclaw (98022) *(G-3288)*
E C S, Seattle *Also called Envelope Converting Service (G-9932)*
E H P & Associates Inc....206 764-3344
15106 10th Ave Sw Burien (98166) *(G-2104)*
E L F Software Distributors....360 577-6163
156 Monticello Dr Longview (98632) *(G-5908)*
E McS2....971 295-4641
53 Keller Ln Port Ludlow (98365) *(G-7765)*
E N B Logging, Kalama *Also called ENB Logging & Construction (G-4500)*
E P A D, Seattle *Also called Electronic Prgrm & Design (G-9894)*
E P E, Edgewood *Also called Engineered Products Entps (G-3076)*
E Power Systems & Battery Inc....253 267-1965
10321 Lakeview Ave Sw Lakewood (98499) *(G-5716)*
E R Balaban Custom Fabrication....206 883-5030
411 W Republican St Seattle (98119) *(G-9866)*
E S I, Bainbridge Island *Also called Esi Distribution Ltd (G-631)*
E S P, Spokane Valley *Also called Enhanced Software Products Inc (G-12693)*
E S P Complete Printing Svc, Seattle *Also called ESP Printing Inc (G-9940)*
E T L Corp....360 568-1473
9624 Airport Way Snohomish (98296) *(G-11903)*
E Teez....425 645-9514
1520 112th St Sw Everett (98204) *(G-3450)*
E W Bachtal Inc....425 241-2505
7219 Autumn Ave Se Snoqualmie (98065) *(G-12010)*
E Z Interface, Tacoma *Also called Antipodes Inc (G-13174)*
E Z Loader Adjustable Boat....509 489-0181
717 N Hamilton St Spokane (99202) *(G-12235)*
E Z Loader Boat Trailers Inc (PA)....574 266-0092
717 N Hamilton St Spokane (99202) *(G-12236)*
E-Green Building Systems....206 219-9236
8421 32nd Ave Sw Seattle (98126) *(G-9867)*
E/Step Software Inc....509 853-5000
12015 Summitview Rd Yakima (98908) *(G-15560)*
E2 Systems LLC....253 284-3707
3006 96th St S Lakewood (98499) *(G-5717)*
Eacceleration Corp (PA)....360 697-9260
1050 Ne Hostmark St # 210 Poulsbo (98370) *(G-7960)*
Eagle Bev & Accessory Pdts LLC....253 867-6134
19220 64th Ave S Kent (98032) *(G-4881)*
Eagle Cliffs Distilery, Longview *Also called Koehler Enterprise Inc (G-5924)*
Eagle Creek Winery....509 548-7059
10037 Eagle Creek Rd Leavenworth (98826) *(G-5799)*
Eagle Harbor Cabinets LLC....206 317-6942
9445 Ne Business Park Ln Bainbridge Island (98110) *(G-625)*
Eagle Harbor Editing....206 293-4264
200 High School Rd Ne # 112 Bainbridge Island (98110) *(G-626)*
Eagle Harbor Print Co LLC....970 441-0000
9676 Glenwood Rd Sw Port Orchard (98367) *(G-7805)*
Eagle Harbor Technologies Inc....206 402-5241
169 Western Ave W Ste 263 Seattle (98119) *(G-9868)*
Eagle Ins, Redmond *Also called Jomar Holdings Inc (G-8521)*
Eagle Logging Inc....509 226-1329
12401 E Trent Ave Spokane Valley (99216) *(G-12684)*
Eagle Machine, Union Gap *Also called Larock Enterprises Inc (G-13938)*
Eagle Print, Redmond *Also called Northwest Executive Corp (G-8598)*

A
L
P
H
A
B
E
T
I
C

Eagle Printing Inc 509 943-2611
214 Torbett St Ste F Richland (99354) ***(G-8991)***
Eagle Prtg & Graphic Design, Richland *Also called Eagle Printing Inc **(G-8991)***
Eagle Pump & Equipment Inc 509 534-1111
1310 S Ferrall St Spokane (99202) ***(G-12237)***
Eagle Rock Boat Repair 360 391-3219
1315 Florida Ave Anacortes (98221) ***(G-125)***
Eagle Rock Manufacturing Inc 360 989-0863
12815 Mountain Loop Hwy Granite Falls (98252) ***(G-4271)***
Eagle Scoreboard Systems 509 751-7228
3871 Swallows Nest Ct Clarkston (99403) ***(G-2634)***
Eagle Signs LLC 509 453-8159
517 Bittner Rd Yakima (98901) ***(G-15561)***
Eagle Signs LLC (PA) 509 453-5511
1511 S Keys Rd Yakima (98901) ***(G-15562)***
Eagle Systems Inc 509 535-8654
1725 N Dickey Rd Spokane Valley (99212) ***(G-12685)***
Eagle Tree Systems LLC 425 614-0450
4957 Lakemont Blvd Se Bellevue (98006) ***(G-886)***
Eagles Eductl Consulting LLC 360 482-6093
69 Raspberry Rd Elma (98541) ***(G-3245)***
Eagles Nest 360 876-9522
14423 Glenwood Rd Sw Port Orchard (98367) ***(G-7806)***
Eagles Nest Holding Inc 206 368-7331
12700 Aurora Ave N Seattle (98133) ***(G-9869)***
Eakin Enterprises Inc 509 698-3200
115 S 2nd St Ste B Selah (98942) ***(G-11587)***
Earshot LLC 917 822-6074
1517 12th Ave Ste 101 Seattle (98122) ***(G-9870)***
Earth Soap Company 425 677-8540
24759 Se 56th St Issaquah (98029) ***(G-4408)***
Earthbound Corporation 360 863-0722
17361 Tye St Se Monroe (98272) ***(G-6567)***
Earthen Alchemy 360 926-8467
18902 Marine Dr Stanwood (98292) ***(G-12968)***
East and Nest, Edmonds *Also called Nestor Enterprises LLC **(G-3136)***
East County Journal 360 496-5993
278 Main St Morton (98356) ***(G-6668)***
East County Machine LLC 360 249-4114
426 S Fleet St Montesano (98563) ***(G-6644)***
East Hill Optometry 253 859-0942
11120 Se Kent Kangley Rd Kent (98030) ***(G-4882)***
East Oregonian Publishing Co 360 642-8181
205 Bolstad Ave Ste Long Beach (98631) ***(G-5873)***
East Penn Manufacturing Co 253 983-9622
10803 South Tacoma Way Lakewood (98499) ***(G-5718)***
East Point Seafood, Kirkland *Also called Dungeness Development Assoc **(G-5324)***
East Point Seafood, Seattle *Also called Dungeness Development Assoc **(G-9860)***
East Valley Sand & Gravel Inc 360 403-7520
5802 Cemetery Rd Arlington (98223) ***(G-231)***
East Valley Sand and Gravel 360 403-7520
5802 Cemetery Rd Arlington (98223) ***(G-232)***
East Vancouver Dental Bldg, Vancouver *Also called Gary L Ostenson DDS PS **(G-14248)***
East Vancouver Venom 360 518-1658
513 Ne 146th Ct Vancouver (98684) ***(G-14192)***
East WA Burial Vaults Inc 509 662-5684
1095 Rue Jolie Wenatchee (98801) ***(G-15027)***
East Washingtonian 509 843-1313
933 Highway 12 W Pomeroy (99347) ***(G-7672)***
East West General Inc 360 673-6404
1265 Hendrickson Dr Kalama (98625) ***(G-4497)***
Easterday Diesel Manufacturing 509 269-4577
51 Bellflower Rd Mesa (99343) ***(G-6492)***
Eastern Merchandise Co Inc 206 448-4466
2701 2nd Ave Seattle (98121) ***(G-9871)***
Eastern News Inc 206 760-9168
6221 39th Ave S Seattle (98118) ***(G-9872)***
Eastern Washington Burial Vlt, Wenatchee *Also called Gregory Diede **(G-15038)***
Eastern Washington University 509 359-6047
207 Physcial Educatn Bldg Cheney (99004) ***(G-2584)***
Eastlake Minuteman Press 425 402-7900
13432 Ne 177th Pl Woodinville (98072) ***(G-15232)***
Eastside Masonry Products Inc 425 868-0303
19015 Ne 80th St Redmond (98052) ***(G-8445)***
Eastside Parent 206 441-0191
1530 Westlake Ave N # 600 Seattle (98109) ***(G-9873)***
Eastside Saw & Sales Inc 425 454-7627
12880 Ne Bel Red Rd Ste 1 Bellevue (98005) ***(G-887)***
Eastside Signs 425 888-6764
9818 354th Ave Se Snoqualmie (98065) ***(G-12011)***
Eastside Tent & Awning Co 425 454-7766
12880 Ne Bel Red Rd Ste 2 Bellevue (98005) ***(G-888)***
Eastside Welding & Fabrication 509 765-6434
10828 Road 5.2 Ne Moses Lake (98837) ***(G-6707)***
Easy Fold Fixtures 425 209-0167
19219 W Valley Hwy M110 Kent (98032) ***(G-4883)***
Easy Rider Canoe & Kayak Co 425 228-3633
15666 W Valley Hwy Tukwila (98188) ***(G-13727)***
Easy Street Custom Metal 509 662-1018
1119 Easy St Wenatchee (98801) ***(G-15028)***
Easyxafs LLC 208 697-4076
879 Rainier Ave N A103 Renton (98057) ***(G-8790)***
Eaton Agency Inc 509 448-6556
6626 S Tomaker Ln Spokane (99223) ***(G-12238)***
Eaton Corp 253 375-6013
5211 292nd St E Graham (98338) ***(G-4224)***
Eaton Corporation 425 644-5800
13205 Se 30th St Ste 101 Bellevue (98005) ***(G-889)***
Eaton Corporation 253 833-5021
1604 15th St Sw Ste 114 Auburn (98001) ***(G-431)***
Eaton Corporation 425 451-4954
1300 114th Ave Se Ste 208 Bellevue (98004) ***(G-890)***
Eaton Creek Tree Farm, Olympia *Also called Paul E Sevier **(G-7367)***
Eaton Electric Holdings LLC 425 271-9237
1020 Thomas Ave Sw Renton (98057) ***(G-8791)***
Eaton Hill Winery 509 854-2220
530 Gurley Rd Granger (98932) ***(G-4261)***
Eaton Hydraulics LLC 360 834-0653
7780 Ne Lessard Rd Camas (98607) ***(G-2245)***
Eatonville Dispatch Newspaper 360 832-4411
133 Mashell Ave N Eatonville (98328) ***(G-3055)***
Ebed System, Tacoma *Also called Alliance Mfg Group LLC **(G-13165)***
Ec/Ndt LLC 253 815-0797
1020 S 344th St Ste 214 Federal Way (98003) ***(G-3734)***
ECB Corp 425 514-8334
1515 75th St Sw Everett (98203) ***(G-3451)***
Eccentrixx LLC 360 274-4954
2626 Hazel Dell Rd Castle Rock (98611) ***(G-2341)***
Ecco Contractors Incorporated 425 957-1735
3803 138th Ave Se Bellevue (98006) ***(G-891)***
Echo Springs Publishing 360 417-1346
1503 E 3rd St Port Angeles (98362) ***(G-7701)***
Echo Ultrasonics LLC 360 671-9121
774 Marine Dr Bellingham (98225) ***(G-1328)***
Echo-Sense Inc 360 833-9032
2005 Se 192nd Ave Camas (98607) ***(G-2246)***
Echodyne Corp 206 713-1216
12112 115th Ave Ne Ste A Kirkland (98034) ***(G-5328)***
Echonous Inc 425 482-6213
8310 154th Ave Ne Ste 200 Redmond (98052) ***(G-8446)***
Eckler Mountain Sawmill, Pasco *Also called Faye Gear Rhonda **(G-7581)***
Eclaire Farm LLC 360 524-9775
9604 Ne 126th Ave Vancouver (98682) ***(G-14193)***
Eclipse Inc 754 581-1513
1005 E Roy St Apt 12 Seattle (98102) ***(G-9874)***
Eclipse Technical Graphics LLC 509 922-7700
3302 N Flora Rd Spokane Valley (99216) ***(G-12686)***
Eclipse Technology LLC 406 270-6366
219 1st Ave S Ste 400 Seattle (98104) ***(G-9875)***
Ecm Maritime Services LLC 206 780-9980
603 Stewart St Ste 803 Seattle (98101) ***(G-9876)***
Eco Cartridge Store 425 820-3570
11316 Ne 124th St Kirkland (98034) ***(G-5329)***
Eco Chemical Inc (PA) 206 448-7930
6600 Ursula Pl S Seattle (98108) ***(G-9877)***
Eco Inc 206 784-6611
5439 Ballard Ave Nw Seattle (98107) ***(G-9878)***
Eco Safe Technologies LLC 360 567-1923
4600 Nw Camas Meadows Dr Camas (98607) ***(G-2247)***
Eco Tec Inc 253 884-6804
18617 108th St Ct Kpn Gig Harbor (98329) ***(G-4097)***
Eco-Vac, Freeland *Also called MA & Kt Inc **(G-4032)***
Ecobalanza LLC 888 220-6020
4919 17th Ave Nw Seattle (98107) ***(G-9879)***
Ecographcs Envrmnt- Frindly PR, Bainbridge Island *Also called Ecographics Inc **(G-627)***
Ecographics Inc 425 825-1888
164 Grow Ave Nw Bainbridge Island (98110) ***(G-627)***
Ecolab Inc 253 733-3000
4301 S Pine St Ste 540 Tacoma (98409) ***(G-13269)***
Ecolite Manufacturing Co (PA) 509 922-8888
9919 E Montgomery Dr Spokane Valley (99206) ***(G-12687)***
Ecolite Manufacturing Co 509 922-8888
2622 N Woodruff Rd Spokane Valley (99206) ***(G-12688)***
Econet Inc (PA) 360 486-8300
3005 1st Ave Seattle (98121) ***(G-9880)***
Econo Box, Renton *Also called Sp Holdings Inc **(G-8918)***
Econo Quality Signs Inc 253 531-3943
16411 22nd Ave E Tacoma (98445) ***(G-13270)***
Econo Sign of America 360 739-8480
2006 James St Bellingham (98225) ***(G-1329)***
Economy Hearth & Home Inc 360 692-8709
8753 State Highway 303 Ne Bremerton (98311) ***(G-1950)***
Ecorsys Inc 347 282-6888
5000 22nd Ave Ne Seattle (98105) ***(G-9881)***
Ecosafe Lighting, Camas *Also called Eco Safe Technologies LLC **(G-2247)***
Ecotech Recycling LLC 360 673-3860
2601 N Hendrickson Dr A Kalama (98625) ***(G-4498)***
Ecotech Services LLC 509 995-5809
6310 E Sprague Ave Spokane Valley (99212) ***(G-12689)***
Ecs Machining Inc 509 317-2557
651 S 83rd Ave Yakima (98908) ***(G-15563)***
Ed Bohl 360 264-5822
13019 Black Bear Blvd Se Tenino (98589) ***(G-13618)***

Ed Ka Manufacturing Inc 509 635-1521
213 E Main St Garfield (99130) *(G-4068)*
Ed Print Inc 425 483-0606
16932 Woodinville Rdmnd Woodinville (98072) *(G-15233)*
Ed Stephan 360 733-4781
523 13th St Bellingham (98225) *(G-1330)*
Ed's Automotive & Machine Shop, Mukilteo *Also called Eds Automotive and Machine Sp (G-6919)*
Edco Inc 360 424-6600
14508 Ovenell Rd Mount Vernon (98273) *(G-6792)*
Eddie ODell 360 797-7549
381 Daisy King Rd Sequim (98382) *(G-11632)*
Eddyline Kayaks, Burlington *Also called Ek Projects LLC (G-2155)*
Edelweiss Chalet, Issaquah *Also called Boehms Candies Inc (G-4387)*
Eden Labs LLC 888 626-3271
309 S Cloverdale St D10 Seattle (98108) *(G-9882)*
Eden Sign 360 377-3040
2923 Wheaton Way Bremerton (98310) *(G-1951)*
Edensaw Woods Ltd 253 216-1150
925 E 25th St Tacoma (98421) *(G-13271)*
Ederer LLC (HQ) 800 464-1320
3701 S Norfolk St Ste A Seattle (98118) *(G-9883)*
Edge Technologies Inc 253 383-9181
7350 Cirque Dr W Ste 103 University Place (98467) *(G-13966)*
Edgebanding Services Inc 866 395-7002
6876 S 220th St Kent (98032) *(G-4884)*
Edgetown Pubg & Productions 360 626-1242
19657 Front St Ne Apt 1 Poulsbo (98370) *(G-7961)*
Edgewalker Woodworks Ltd 360 468-2839
653 Shark Reef Rd Lopez Island (98261) *(G-5981)*
Edgewood Monuments 253 561-2498
111 W Meeker Puyallup (98371) *(G-8148)*
Edinger Mfg Inc 425 413-4008
24705 Se Summit Landsbrg Ravensdale (98051) *(G-8334)*
Editorial Consultants Inc 206 329-6499
911 E Allison St Seattle (98102) *(G-9884)*
EDJ Precision Machine Inc 425 745-3937
13317 Ash Way B-1 Everett (98204) *(G-3452)*
Edman Company 253 572-5306
2502 Marine View Dr Tacoma (98422) *(G-13272)*
Edmonds Athletic Supply Co 425 778-7322
20815 67th Ave W Ste 102 Lynnwood (98036) *(G-6111)*
Edmonds Printing Co Inc 425 775-7907
6715 210th St Sw Ste C Lynnwood (98036) *(G-6112)*
Edmund Lucy 425 703-4155
1205 Oakcreek Pl Nw Issaquah (98027) *(G-4409)*
Eds Automotive and Machine Sp 425 355-7268
8622 44th Ave W Mukilteo (98275) *(G-6919)*
EDS Garage & Welding 253 845-8741
10813 Valley Ave E Puyallup (98372) *(G-8149)*
Edt Corp 360 574-7294
5345 Labounty Dr Ferndale (98248) *(G-3837)*
Education Office, Gig Harbor *Also called Cnc Software Inc (G-4091)*
Eduongo Inc 206 451-7325
14205 Se 36th St Ste 100 Bellevue (98006) *(G-892)*
Edward Fisher 253 566-4335
5503 78th Avenue Ct W Tacoma (98467) *(G-13273)*
Edward Laurence Pelanconi 360 435-2725
24216 115th Ave Ne Arlington (98223) *(G-233)*
Edwards Equipment Co Inc 509 248-1770
4312 Main St Union Gap (98903) *(G-13928)*
Edwards Logging Co 360 457-7330
2019 E Maddock Rd Port Angeles (98362) *(G-7702)*
Edwin Enterprises Inc 253 272-7090
3401 Lincoln Ave Ste E Tacoma (98421) *(G-13274)*
Edwin Laird 206 587-6537
2033 6th Ave Ste 830 Seattle (98121) *(G-9885)*
Edwing Boat Inc 360 777-8771
Corner Of 4th And Hwy 101 Chinook (98614) *(G-2616)*
EE Printing LLC 425 656-1250
8258 S 192nd St Kent (98032) *(G-4885)*
Ef Print Copy Center, Duvall *Also called Duvall Graphics LLC (G-2984)*
EFC Equipment LLC 509 713-7230
2155 Stevens Dr Richland (99354) *(G-8992)*
EFC Equipment Feed and Pet, Richland *Also called EFC Equipment LLC (G-8992)*
Efco Corp 253 852-3800
1004 3rd Ave S Kent (98032) *(G-4886)*
Efco Corp 360 566-0300
10000 Ne 7th Ave Vancouver (98685) *(G-14194)*
Efefte, Woodinville *Also called Oldfield Cellars LLC (G-15326)*
Efeste 206 535-6997
1730 1st Ave S Seattle (98134) *(G-9886)*
Effective Design Studio LLC 206 328-8989
1932 1st Ave Ste 605 Seattle (98101) *(G-9887)*
Efficient Dryer Vent Services 360 687-7643
25218 Ne Berlin Rd Battle Ground (98604) *(G-700)*
Effortless Atms LLC 206 456-4130
219 E Garfield St Apt 212 Seattle (98102) *(G-9888)*
Efis, Seattle *Also called Environmental Fincl Info Svcs (G-9933)*
Efx Locomotive Services, Tacoma *Also called Edward Fisher (G-13273)*
Egis Group LLC 360 768-1211
3135 Mercer Ave Ste 102 Bellingham (98225) *(G-1331)*
Egis Mobile Electric, Bellingham *Also called Egis Group LLC (G-1331)*
Eh Enterprises Management Inc (PA) 206 596-8600
3922 6th Ave S Seattle (98108) *(G-9889)*
Eh Metal Recycling 360 334-6005
8801 Ne 117th Ave Vancouver (98662) *(G-14195)*
Eidolon Winery, Walla Walla *Also called Balboa Winery (G-14767)*
Eidos Stained Glass 360 468-3577
242 Raven Hill Rd Lopez Island (98261) *(G-5982)*
Eigen Wireless, Liberty Lake *Also called Lhc2 Inc (G-5843)*
Eiger Skyline Inc 509 548-6808
5332 Old Bluett Rd Leavenworth (98826) *(G-5800)*
Eight Bells Winery 206 294-4131
6213 Roosevelt Way Ne B Seattle (98115) *(G-9890)*
Eight Star Group of America 206 243-8888
17725 11th Pl W Lynnwood (98037) *(G-6113)*
Eiki Digital Systems Inc 206 957-2626
5701 6th Ave S Seattle (98108) *(G-9891)*
Ej Usa Inc 360 651-6144
13127 State Ave Marysville (98271) *(G-6332)*
Ejimcom 360 459-4785
833 Westminster Ct Ne Lacey (98516) *(G-5546)*
Ek Projects LLC 360 757-2300
11977 Westar Ln Burlington (98233) *(G-2155)*
Ekko Bioscience LLC 844 822-9300
290 Edwards Ln Vancouver (98661) *(G-14196)*
Ekko Health, Vancouver *Also called Ekko Bioscience LLC (G-14196)*
Eko Brands LLC 800 833-0622
6029 238th St Se Ste 130 Woodinville (98072) *(G-15234)*
Ekone Oyster, South Bend *Also called Taylor Shellfish Company Inc (G-12048)*
Ekos Corporation 425 415-3100
11911 N Creek Pkwy S Bothell (98011) *(G-1760)*
Ektos LLC 800 783-0383
17802 134th Ave Ne Ste 12 Woodinville (98072) *(G-15235)*
El Dorado Tortillas LLC 719 459-2576
11842 Ne 112th St Kirkland (98033) *(G-5330)*
El Mundo Communications Inc 509 663-5737
112 N Mission St Wenatchee (98801) *(G-15029)*
El Tapatio, Vancouver *Also called Ljro Inc (G-14380)*
Elander Persson Fine Wdwrk LLC 206 818-2882
9305 156th St Se Snohomish (98296) *(G-11904)*
Elander-Persson, Snohomish *Also called Elander Persson Fine Wdwrk LLC (G-11904)*
Elarm Inc 206 395-9604
3114 15th Ave S Seattle (98144) *(G-9892)*
Eldec Corporation (HQ) 425 743-1313
16700 13th Ave W Lynnwood (98037) *(G-6114)*
Eldec Corporation 425 882-3100
10301 Willows Rd Ne Redmond (98052) *(G-8447)*
Elder Logging Co 360 886-2779
33214 293rd Ave Se Black Diamond (98010) *(G-1647)*
Elder Logging Inc 360 825-7158
1614 Cole St Enumclaw (98022) *(G-3289)*
Elder, Daniel, Camano Island *Also called Finishing Touch (G-2212)*
Eldons Sausage Inc 509 309-3140
3808 N Sullivan Rd Spokane Valley (99216) *(G-12690)*
Eldorado AG 360 491-0394
5707 Lacey Blvd Se # 100 Lacey (98503) *(G-5547)*
Eldorado Stone LLC 425 349-4107
1200 Industry St Ste 100 Everett (98203) *(G-3453)*
Eldred Bros Farms LLC 360 398-9757
317 W Laurel Rd Bellingham (98226) *(G-1332)*
Eleanor Wiley 360 698-5077
9992 Fairview Lake Rd Sw Port Orchard (98367) *(G-7807)*
Electric AMP Innvtions USA LLC 509 455-7469
7702 N Country Homes Blvd Spokane (99208) *(G-12239)*
Electric Avenue Sign Co 360 903-5447
16005 Ne 12th St Vancouver (98684) *(G-14197)*
Electric Boat Corporation 360 598-5115
Escolar Rd T 33 Silverdale (98315) *(G-11833)*
Electric Concept Labs Inc 503 244-3000
102 Chapman Rd Castle Rock (98611) *(G-2342)*
Electric Mirror LLC 425 776-4946
6101 Assod Blvd Ste 101 Everett (98203) *(G-3454)*
Electrical Packaging Co Inc 425 745-5466
11627 Airport Rd Ste L Everett (98204) *(G-3455)*
Electrical Sales & Service, Snohomish *Also called F W B Enterprises Inc (G-11908)*
Electrical Services & SEC Inc 206 276-6629
2408 S 272nd St Kent (98032) *(G-4887)*
Electrijet Flight Systems Inc 509 990-9474
23403 E Mission Ave Ste 2 Liberty Lake (99019) *(G-5831)*
Electrijet Research Foundation 509 990-9474
2812 S Steen Ln Greenacres (99016) *(G-4297)*
Electrino Group Inc 360 491-9373
4401 37th Ave Se Unit 14 Lacey (98503) *(G-5548)*
Electro Erosion Specialties 425 251-9440
242 Sw 43rd St Renton (98057) *(G-8792)*
Electrode Store, The, Buckley *Also called Impulse Medical Tech Inc (G-2059)*
Electrofinishing Inc 253 850-0540
22630 88th Ave S Ste A Kent (98031) *(G-4888)*
Electroimpact Inc 425 348-8090
4413 Chennault Beach Rd Mukilteo (98275) *(G-6920)*
Electroimpact Inc 425 348-8090
4630 Chennault Beach Rd F Mukilteo (98275) *(G-6921)*

ALPHABETIC

Electroimpact Inc (PA) 425 348-8090
4413 Chennault Beach Rd Mukilteo (98275) ***(G-6922)***
Electromagnetic Software 425 557-4716
3206 218th Ave Se Sammamish (98075) ***(G-9203)***
Electronetics, Everett *Also called Northwest Center* ***(G-3557)***
Electronetics LLC 425 355-1855
1320 75th St Sw Everett (98203) ***(G-3456)***
Electronic Charts Co Inc 206 282-4990
4241 21st Ave W Ste 107 Seattle (98199) ***(G-9893)***
Electronic Coating Tech Inc 425 265-2212
2615 W Casino Rd Ste 5g Everett (98204) ***(G-3457)***
Electronic Imaging Svcs Inc 253 887-1237
1220 37th St Nw Auburn (98001) ***(G-432)***
Electronic Prgrm & Design 206 767-7262
7114 17th Ave Sw Seattle (98106) ***(G-9894)***
Electronic Systems Tech Inc 509 735-9092
415 N Quay St Ste B1 Kennewick (99336) ***(G-4657)***
Elegantly Yours 425 478-2873
28000 Ne 142nd Pl Duvall (98019) ***(G-2985)***
Eleganza Designs Inc 360 499-2710
7127 Bailey St Se Lacey (98513) ***(G-5549)***
Element 360 682-5649
656 Se Bayshore Dr Oak Harbor (98277) ***(G-7149)***
Element 253 335-8342
18120 85th St E Bonney Lake (98391) ***(G-1722)***
Element 425 941-5373
1199 W Cunningham Rd Othello (99344) ***(G-7494)***
Element 13 Precision LLC 360 597-3195
8715 Ne 58th St Vancouver (98662) ***(G-14198)***
Element 6 ....206 282-0877
2562 Thorndyke Ave W # 301 Seattle (98199) ***(G-9895)***
Element 8 ....208 870-8471
2717 Western Ave Apt 6010 Seattle (98121) ***(G-9896)***
Element Electric LLC 360 304-9918
629 Hawks Glen Dr Se Olympia (98513) ***(G-7274)***
Element Group Inc 206 784-3355
6506 Sycamore Ave Nw Seattle (98117) ***(G-9897)***
Elemental Cremation & Burial 206 357-1141
2105 112th Ave Ne Ste 100 Bellevue (98004) ***(G-893)***
Elements of Iron & Wood LLC 360 789-0840
4525 72nd Ave Ne Olympia (98516) ***(G-7275)***
Elenbaas Company Inc (PA) 360 354-3577
421 Birch Bay Lynden Rd Lynden (98264) ***(G-6014)***
Elephant Boys, The, Spokane Valley *Also called Jened Inc* ***(G-12751)***
Elevation Exhibits LLC 774 696-2549
8117 166th Ave Ne Redmond (98052) ***(G-8448)***
Eleven Winery Inc 206 780-0905
7671 Ne Day Rd W Bainbridge Island (98110) ***(G-628)***
Elguji Software LLC 360 450-5022
3709 Nw 107th St Vancouver (98685) ***(G-14199)***
Elite Aircraft Deburring 360 435-2652
19221 63rd Ave Ne Ste 4 Arlington (98223) ***(G-234)***
Elite Athletics Training LLC 509 221-1898
1221 Columbia Park Trl Richland (99352) ***(G-8993)***
Elite Enterprise Co 360 756-0205
1349 Lowe Ave Bellingham (98229) ***(G-1333)***
Elite Frames Inc 360 247-7300
16807 Ne Grantham Rd Amboy (98601) ***(G-91)***
Elite Group Ballistics, Kent *Also called Elite Group Management Corp* ***(G-4889)***
Elite Group Management Corp 253 631-1175
14200 Se 272nd St F203 Kent (98042) ***(G-4889)***
Eliza K Trowbridge 360 376-5152
53 4th St Olga (98279) ***(G-7214)***
Elk Creek Contractors Inc 509 364-3692
25 Dean Ln Glenwood (98619) ***(G-4179)***
Elkay Plastics Co Inc 425 251-1488
6425 S 224th St Kent (98032) ***(G-4890)***
Elkay Ssp LLC 509 533-0808
3200 E Trent Ave Spokane (99202) ***(G-12240)***
Elkay Ssp LLC (HQ) 509 533-0808
421 N Freya St Spokane (99202) ***(G-12241)***
Elkhart Plastics 360 887-2230
6111 S 6th Way Ridgefield (98642) ***(G-9080)***
Elkins Distribution Inc 206 241-0333
12602 1st Ave S Seattle (98168) ***(G-9898)***
Elkwood Custom Cabinetry LLC 360 886-1989
32022 Se Rtreat Knsket Rd Ravensdale (98051) ***(G-8335)***
Ellensburg Canyon Winery LLC 509 933-3523
221 Canyon Vista Way Ellensburg (98926) ***(G-3194)***
Ellensburg Eye & Cntact Lens C 509 925-1000
2201 W Dolarway Rd Ste 2 Ellensburg (98926) ***(G-3195)***
Ellensburg Fence Co 509 929-4090
2603 W Willis Rd Ellensburg (98926) ***(G-3196)***
Ellensburg Pallet 509 962-1373
208 S Willow St Ellensburg (98926) ***(G-3197)***
Elles Island Spectacle 206 715-9475
4688 Lynwood Center Rd Ne # 113 Bainbridge Island (98110) ***(G-629)***
Elliot Attachments Inc 360 636-2203
244 Milwaukee Pl Unit 2 Kelso (98626) ***(G-4524)***
Elliott Bay Bicycles Inc 206 441-9998
2116 Western Ave Seattle (98121) ***(G-9899)***
Elliott Bay Brewery & Pub, Seattle *Also called Elliott Bay Brewing Company* ***(G-9900)***
Elliott Bay Brewing Company 206 246-4211
4720 California Ave Sw Seattle (98116) ***(G-9900)***
Elliott Bay Holding Co LLC 206 762-6560
7500 W Marginal Way S Seattle (98108) ***(G-9901)***
Elliott Bay Industries, Seattle *Also called Elliott Bay Holding Co LLC* ***(G-9901)***
Elliott Bay Publishing Inc 206 283-8144
16040 Christensen Rd # 205 Tukwila (98188) ***(G-13728)***
Elliott Bay Recording Company 206 709-9626
932 12th Ave Seattle (98122) ***(G-9902)***
Ellipse Mfg Inc 253 653-5554
16113 7th Avenue Ct E Tacoma (98445) ***(G-13275)***
Ellison Fluid Systems Inc 425 271-3220
350 Airport Way Renton (98057) ***(G-8793)***
Ellsworth & Company LLC 253 301-2800
58 Chapman Loop Steilacoom (98388) ***(G-13004)***
Elmo Fokker Inc 253 395-2652
1725 Puyallup St Ste 200 Sumner (98390) ***(G-13068)***
Elmor Inc 206 213-0111
2300 W Elmore St Seattle (98199) ***(G-9903)***
Eln Communications Inc 206 256-0420
814 6th Ave S Seattle (98134) ***(G-9904)***
Elochoman Millwork Inc 360 795-3637
23 Boege Rd Cathlamet (98612) ***(G-2365)***
Elpac, Everett *Also called Electrical Packaging Co Inc* ***(G-3455)***
Elpis Works Inc 206 317-4647
3011 Grand Ave Everett (98201) ***(G-3458)***
Elsom Cellars LLC 425 298-3082
3023 Fauntleroy Ave Sw Seattle (98126) ***(G-9905)***
Elsom Cllars Winery 3pp Pnw Hq 775 848-1771
2960 4th Ave S Seattle (98134) ***(G-9906)***
Eltons Sausage and Jerky Sup, Spokane Valley *Also called Eldons Sausage Inc* ***(G-12690)***
Elux Inc 360 281-4568
18110 Se 34th St Ste 480 Vancouver (98683) ***(G-14200)***
Elysian Brewing Company Inc 206 767-0210
5510 Airport Way S Seattle (98108) ***(G-9907)***
Elysian Brewing Company Inc (HQ) 206 860-3977
6010 Airport Way S Seattle (98108) ***(G-9908)***
EM Global Manufacturing Inc 253 655-5206
10721 A St S Ste A Tacoma (98444) ***(G-13276)***
EMB Create Inc 360 384-8072
4958 Pacific Hwy Ferndale (98248) ***(G-3838)***
Emblems & More X3 ....253 248-2400
1401 52nd Ave E Fife (98424) ***(G-3950)***
Embodi3d LLC (PA) 425 429-6193
1010 185th Ave Ne Bellevue (98008) ***(G-894)***
Embroidered Effects LLC 360 380-1928
1273 Sunset Ave Bellingham (98226) ***(G-1334)***
Embroidery By Design 509 582-2858
3705 S Dennis St Kennewick (99337) ***(G-4658)***
Embroidery For Soul 425 319-1269
18600 State Route 2 Ste A Monroe (98272) ***(G-6568)***
Embroidery Northwest 509 248-1186
1906 W Nob Hill Blvd Yakima (98902) ***(G-15564)***
Embroidery Plus LLC 253 630-2616
15022 Se 282nd Pl Kent (98042) ***(G-4891)***
EMC Corporation 206 623-1227
505 1st Ave S Ste 600 Seattle (98104) ***(G-9909)***
EMC Corporation 425 378-9209
15500 Se 30th Pl Ste 200 Bellevue (98007) ***(G-895)***
EMC Electro Mechanical Company 206 767-9307
5002 2nd Ave S Seattle (98134) ***(G-9910)***
EMC Isilon, Seattle *Also called Isilon Systems LLC* ***(G-10260)***
EMC Nursing Services 425 346-5982
5532 148th St Se Everett (98208) ***(G-3459)***
Emc2, Bellevue *Also called EMC Corporation* ***(G-895)***
Emeasure Inc 844 382-7326
129 Eastside Chewuch Rd Winthrop (98862) ***(G-15159)***
Emerald Automation LLC 509 783-1369
9228 W Clearwater Dr Kennewick (99336) ***(G-4659)***
Emerald Brake and Muffler, Kent *Also called Auto Spring Service Inc* ***(G-4799)***
Emerald City Cabinet Co LLC 425 429-7887
11417 Cyrus Way Mukilteo (98275) ***(G-6923)***
Emerald City Electronics 425 649-1006
17280 Ne 8th St Apt B Bellevue (98008) ***(G-896)***
Emerald City Embroidery 253 922-8838
509 22nd Avenue Ct Milton (98354) ***(G-6534)***
Emerald City Graphics Inc 253 520-2600
23328 66th Ave S Kent (98032) ***(G-4892)***
Emerald City Label Inc 425 347-3479
834 80th St Sw Ste 100 Everett (98203) ***(G-3460)***
Emerald City Lighting 206 234-8554
12613 Ne 112th Pl Kirkland (98033) ***(G-5331)***
Emerald City Promotions LLC 206 271-2880
2741 72nd Ave Se Mercer Island (98040) ***(G-6461)***
Emerald City Smoothie 253 826-6664
20075 State Route 410 E Bonney Lake (98391) ***(G-1723)***
Emerald City Smoothie 253 564-1966
5977 6th Ave Tacoma (98406) ***(G-13277)***
Emerald City Software LLC 206 321-5252
1234 Nw 118th St Seattle (98177) ***(G-9911)***
Emerald City Water LLC 425 821-0800
10925 81st Pl Ne Kirkland (98034) ***(G-5332)***

Emerald Energy Nw LLC 425 830-2757
17505 7th Ave W Bothell (98012) ***(G-1851)***
Emerald Galvanizing Inc 206 782-8300
621 Nw 41st St Seattle (98107) ***(G-9912)***
Emerald Hills Coffee, Mukilteo *Also called Jumbo Foods Inc* ***(G-6946)***
Emerald Hills Coffee Inc 800 562-6015
11502 Cyrus Way Mukilteo (98275) ***(G-6924)***
Emerald Home Furnishings LLC 253 922-1400
3025 Pioneer Way E Tacoma (98443) ***(G-13278)***
Emerald Kalama Chemical LLC 360 673-2550
1296 3rd St Nw Kalama (98625) ***(G-4499)***
Emerald Performance Materials, Kalama *Also called Emerald Kalama Chemical LLC* ***(G-4499)***
Emerald Phoenix Oil Co Llc 509 466-0555
111 E Lincoln Rd Spokane (99208) ***(G-12242)***
Emerald Recycling, Seattle *Also called Emerald Services Inc* ***(G-9913)***
Emerald Services Inc (HQ) 206 430-7795
6851 E Marginal Way S Seattle (98108) ***(G-9913)***
Emerald Sweets, Chehalis *Also called Katies Candies Inc* ***(G-2507)***
Emerald Tool Inc 206 767-5670
8009 7th Ave S Seattle (98108) ***(G-9914)***
Emerald Twist Incorporated 541 659-2189
459 Brentwood Rd Goldendale (98620) ***(G-4196)***
Emergent Detection Inc 206 391-4876
3656 Whitman Ave N Seattle (98103) ***(G-9915)***
Emerging Mkts Cmmnications LLC 206 454-8300
101 Stewart St Ste 800 Seattle (98101) ***(G-9916)***
Emerson Electric Co 360 805-0590
115 W Main St Monroe (98272) ***(G-6569)***
Emerson Logging Corporation 509 647-5658
310 Se Spokane St Wilbur (99185) ***(G-15141)***
Emerson Process Management 425 391-8565
3911 240th Pl Se Sammamish (98029) ***(G-9204)***
Emery Burton LLC 206 323-7351
1534 1st Ave S Seattle (98134) ***(G-9917)***
Emery Enterprises 360 532-0102
2004 Westport Rd Aberdeen (98520) ***(G-10)***
Emery Systems, Tumwater *Also called Sand Paper & Ink Inc* ***(G-13896)***
Emery's Auto Sales & Service, Aberdeen *Also called Emery Enterprises* ***(G-10)***
Emfco, Kent *Also called Exotic Metals Forming Co LLC* ***(G-4900)***
Emily's Chocolate, Fife *Also called Ames International Inc* ***(G-3932)***
Emma Danforth 360 931-5060
12700 Se Angus St Vancouver (98683) ***(G-14201)***
Emma Knits Inc 509 999-8583
16 W 18th Ave Spokane (99203) ***(G-12243)***
Emmanuel Pallets LLC 509 439-0924
405 Scoon Rd Sunnyside (98944) ***(G-13123)***
Emmrod Fishing Gear Inc (PA) 509 979-2222
2725 S Bolivar Rd Spokane Valley (99037) ***(G-12691)***
Emory Vineyards LLC 509 588-2988
18809 E 583 Pr Ne Benton City (99320) ***(G-1610)***
Empire Cold Storage, Spokane *Also called R Plum Corporation* ***(G-12465)***
Empire Controls LLC 509 795-5615
101 Gala Ave Chelan (98816) ***(G-2553)***
Empire Creek Exploration Co 509 747-0996
36 W 16th Ave Spokane (99203) ***(G-12244)***
Empire Lab Automtn Systems LLC 509 808-6050
2704 N Hogan St Ste 1 Spokane (99207) ***(G-12245)***
Empire Lumber Co (PA) 509 534-0266
14 E Main Ave Spokane (99202) ***(G-12246)***
Empire Packing 360 459-3745
7430 32nd Ave Ne Olympia (98516) ***(G-7276)***
Empire Press Co 509 886-8668
832 Valley Mall Pkwy D East Wenatchee (98802) ***(G-3011)***
Empire Rubber & Supply Co 509 547-0026
1428 W A St Pasco (99301) ***(G-7579)***
Empire Upholstery 509 467-5263
4907 N Cannon St Spokane (99205) ***(G-12247)***
Empress Print LLC 509 826-5154
4 Ponderosa Dr Tonasket (98855) ***(G-13648)***
Ems & Sales LLC 253 208-9062
12221 164th Ave Se Renton (98059) ***(G-8794)***
Ems Dental Designs Inc 425 584-7206
18529 Se 244th Pl Covington (98042) ***(G-2827)***
Emu Emprium Hlthy Alternatives 360 269-3459
3512 Jackson Hwy Chehalis (98532) ***(G-2492)***
Emulate Therapeutics Inc 206 708-2288
24 Roy St Ste 437 Seattle (98109) ***(G-9918)***
ENB Logging & Construction 360 673-2696
1743 Cloverdale Rd Kalama (98625) ***(G-4500)***
Encased Presentation, Kennewick *Also called Encased Specialty Mfg LLC* ***(G-4660)***
Encased Specialty Mfg LLC 509 396-0755
4605 S Toro Ct Kennewick (99338) ***(G-4660)***
Enchanted Cellars 503 970-2244
8052 Old Highway 12 Walla Walla (99362) ***(G-14801)***
Encompass Print Solutions LLC 425 922-6170
309 S Cloverdale St C38 Seattle (98108) ***(G-9919)***
Encon United Company 360 834-3459
1615 Se 6th Ave Camas (98607) ***(G-2248)***
Encore Analytics LLC 866 890-4331
2522 N Proctor St # 368 Tacoma (98406) ***(G-13279)***
Encore Cabinets Inc 425 259-0100
2115 39th St Everett (98201) ***(G-3461)***
Encore Media Group, Seattle *Also called Encore Publishing Inc* ***(G-9920)***
Encore Publishing Inc 206 443-0445
87 Wall St Seattle (98121) ***(G-9920)***
Endex Newspaper LLC 206 322-4194
1535 11th Ave Fl 3 Seattle (98122) ***(G-9921)***
Endicott Truck & Tractor 509 657-3436
Po Box 46a Endicott (99125) ***(G-3264)***
Endicott Waste Water Treatment 509 657-3407
102 Margin St Endicott (99125) ***(G-3265)***
Endpoint LLC 206 780-2905
7470 Ne Manual Rd Bainbridge Island (98110) ***(G-630)***
Endresen Pressure Washing 253 858-7743
9111 66th Ave Nw Trlr 124 Gig Harbor (98332) ***(G-4098)***
Endurance Coatings LLC 206 234-8793
10106 205th Ave Se Snohomish (98290) ***(G-11905)***
Endurance Window Co 425 883-1345
2810 131st Pl Ne Bellevue (98005) ***(G-897)***
Ener-G Foods Inc (PA) 206 767-3928
5960 1st Ave S Seattle (98108) ***(G-9922)***
Energ2 Inc 206 465-7243
100 Ne Northlake Way Seattle (98105) ***(G-9923)***
Energ2 Technologies Inc 206 547-0445
100 Ne Northlake Way Seattle (98105) ***(G-9924)***
Energsoft Inc 425 246-1675
701 17th Ave Apt 201 Seattle (98122) ***(G-9925)***
Energy Arrow 267 932-7769
26910 92nd Ave Nw Stanwood (98292) ***(G-12969)***
Energy Battery Systems Inc 253 267-1965
10321 Lakeview Ave Sw Lakewood (98499) ***(G-5719)***
Energy Consulting Services LLC 701 580-9732
1504 196th St Long Beach (98631) ***(G-5874)***
Energy Conversions Inc 253 922-6670
6411 Pacific Hwy E Fife (98424) ***(G-3951)***
Energy Efficiency Systems Corp 360 835-7838
2311 G St Washougal (98671) ***(G-14953)***
Energy Northwest 509 585-3677
92308 S Nine Canyon Rd Kennewick (99337) ***(G-4661)***
Energy Sales 425 883-2343
20205 144th Ave Ne # 216 Woodinville (98072) ***(G-15236)***
Energy Saver Products Inc 888 778-4537
6401 Nw Lincoln Ave Vancouver (98663) ***(G-14202)***
Energy Technology Systems, Deer Park *Also called Ets Inc* ***(G-2901)***
Energysavvy Inc 206 462-2206
506 2nd Ave Ste 1900 Seattle (98104) ***(G-9926)***
Enersys 253 299-0005
14323 32nd St E Sumner (98390) ***(G-13069)***
Enertec Bas 360 786-1257
628 Plymouth St Sw Olympia (98502) ***(G-7277)***
Enervana LLC 253 220-8413
869 Industry Dr Tukwila (98188) ***(G-13729)***
Engeseth Logging 360 327-3391
183 W Lake Pleasant Rd Beaver (98305) ***(G-756)***
Engine & Aircraft Strategies 425 432-2800
22129 234th Ave Se Maple Valley (98038) ***(G-6268)***
Engine Installation Service, Spokane *Also called S & S Engine Remanufacturing* ***(G-12489)***
Engineered Bldg Contrls LLC 206 229-7475
1834 Sw 152nd St Burien (98166) ***(G-2105)***
Engineered Materials, Marysville *Also called Safran Cabin Inc* ***(G-6381)***
Engineered Piping Systems 360 225-5302
1740 Down Rver Dr Ste 200 Woodland (98674) ***(G-15429)***
Engineered Products Entps 253 826-6185
12723 53rd Street Ct E Edgewood (98372) ***(G-3076)***
Engineering 360 275-7384
210 Ne Cherokee Beach Rd Belfair (98528) ***(G-761)***
Engineering Division, Yakima *Also called Picatti Brothers Inc* ***(G-15646)***
Engineering Publications, Olympia *Also called Transportation Wash State Dept* ***(G-7413)***
Engineering Software Appl, Belfair *Also called Engineering* ***(G-761)***
Engineering Solutions Inc 206 241-9395
1201 Monster Rd Sw # 240 Renton (98057) ***(G-8795)***
English Racing 360 210-7484
24514 Ne Dresser Rd Camas (98607) ***(G-2249)***
English Setter Brewing 509 413-3663
15310 E Marietta Ave Spokane Valley (99216) ***(G-12692)***
Enhanced Software Products Inc 509 534-1514
1811 N Hutchinson Rd Spokane Valley (99212) ***(G-12693)***
Enlighting Struck Design LLC 206 229-9438
146 Washington Ave N Kent (98032) ***(G-4893)***
Enna Products Corporation 360 306-5369
1602 Carolina St Ste B3 Bellingham (98229) ***(G-1335)***
Ennco Display Systems Inc 425 883-1650
6975 176th Ave Ne Ste 350 Redmond (98052) ***(G-8449)***
Enprecis Inc (PA) 206 274-0122
111 S Jackson St Ste 400 Seattle (98104) ***(G-9927)***
Enravel Inc 206 414-8884
3014 Nw 75th St Seattle (98117) ***(G-9928)***
Ensign Ranch, Cle Elum *Also called Corporation of The President* ***(G-2663)***
Ent Solutions Inc 206 769-1735
118 Sw 116th St Unit D13 Seattle (98146) ***(G-9929)***
Entenmanns Oroweat Foods 360 475-8283
5887 State Highway 303 Ne Bremerton (98311) ***(G-1952)***

A
L
P
H
A
B
E
T
I
C

Enterprises International Inc (PA) — 360 533-6222
　Blaine & Firman Sts Hoquiam (98550) *(G-4336)*

Entiat Valley Vineyards LLC — 509 884-1152
　406 23rd St Ne East Wenatchee (98802) *(G-3012)*

Entirely Inc — 206 979-9092
　505 Broadway E Unit 123 Seattle (98102) *(G-9930)*

Entraq Medical — 425 495-5143
　11898 178th Pl Ne Redmond (98052) *(G-8450)*

Entropy Killer Software — 206 526-2488
　4222 Meridian Ave N Seattle (98103) *(G-9931)*

Entrust Community Services — 509 839-8066
　520 S 7th St Sunnyside (98944) *(G-13124)*

Enumclaw Herald, Enumclaw Also called Courier-Herald *(G-3283)*

Envelope Converting Service — 206 767-3653
　6603 Ursula Pl S Seattle (98108) *(G-9932)*

Envelopes Unlimited Inc — 425 451-9622
　7114 180th Ave Ne B107 Redmond (98052) *(G-8451)*

Envirolux Energy Systems LLC — 800 914-8779
　1304 Ne 154th St Ste 102 Vancouver (98685) *(G-14203)*

Environmental Chem Solutions, Gig Harbor Also called International Chem Systems Inc *(G-4122)*

Environmental Fincl Info Svcs — 206 283-4210
　2832 Magnolia Blvd W Seattle (98199) *(G-9933)*

Environmental Insul Contg LLC — 360 647-2532
　3003 Bennett Dr Bellingham (98225) *(G-1336)*

Environmental Tech Group — 253 804-2507
　201 Frontage Rd N Pacific (98047) *(G-7526)*

Environmental Technologies, Selah Also called Eakin Enterprises Inc *(G-11587)*

Environmental Technologies Inc — 253 804-2507
　201 Frontage Rd N Ste C Pacific (98047) *(G-7527)*

Envirosorb Co — 425 778-7485
　8128 187th St Sw Edmonds (98026) *(G-3109)*

Envision Inc — 509 247-5732
　610 N Depot Ave Fairchild Afb (99011) *(G-3695)*

Envision Custom EMB & Designs — 360 693-2588
　6503 E Mill Plain Blvd B Vancouver (98661) *(G-14204)*

Envision Express, Fairchild Afb Also called Envision Inc *(G-3695)*

Envision Manufacturing & Servi — 253 941-1739
　25326 39th Pl S Kent (98032) *(G-4894)*

Envision Manufacturing Co — 206 963-7352
　1104 4th Ave N Kent (98032) *(G-4895)*

Ep Innnovations, Spokane Also called Arrhythmia Solutions Inc *(G-12118)*

Ephrata Auto Parts, Ephrata Also called Material Inc *(G-3342)*

Ephrata Raceway Park LLC — 509 398-7110
　14156 Rd B3nw Nw Ephrata (98823) *(G-3333)*

Epi Inc — 360 247-5858
　40300 Ne 169th Ave Amboy (98601) *(G-92)*

Epic Polymer Systems Corp — 360 225-1496
　1901 Schurman Way Woodland (98674) *(G-15430)*

Epic Wheel and Tire Inc — 253 691-1785
　7030 South Tacoma Way Tacoma (98409) *(G-13280)*

Epicenter Press Inc — 425 485-6822
　6524 Ne 181st St Ste 2 Kenmore (98028) *(G-4571)*

Epicore — 360 659-1986
　11127 47th Ave Ne Marysville (98271) *(G-6333)*

Epicru Vintners LLC — 206 829-9714
　4501 2nd Ave Nw Seattle (98107) *(G-9934)*

Epicurean Edge, Kirkland Also called Bladegallery Inc *(G-5292)*

Epik Industries — 360 303-6488
　753 E Smith Rd Bellingham (98226) *(G-1337)*

Epl Feed LLC — 360 988-5811
　5996 Lawrence Rd Everson (98247) *(G-3674)*

Epl Feed LLC (PA) — 360 988-5811
　411 W Front St Sumas (98295) *(G-13044)*

Epoch Design LLC (PA) — 425 284-0880
　17617 Ne 65th St Unit 2 Redmond (98052) *(G-8452)*

Epping-Jordan Fine Wdwkg LLC — 206 588-2700
　4721 W Roberts Way Seattle (98199) *(G-9935)*

Eprhata Oil Change Express — 509 398-8740
　1254 Basin St Sw Ephrata (98823) *(G-3334)*

Epson Toyocom Seattle Inc — 360 200-5537
　1850 Prudential Blvd Longview (98632) *(G-5909)*

Eqpd Gear LLC — 509 997-2010
　502 Glover St S Bldg 7 Twisp (98856) *(G-13911)*

Equilon Enterprises LLC — 360 293-0800
　8505 S Texas Rd Anacortes (98221) *(G-126)*

Equipment Division, Colfax Also called McGregor Company *(G-2716)*

Equipment Inc — 206 826-9577
　218 Main St Ste 730 Kirkland (98033) *(G-5333)*

Equipment Technology & Design — 509 747-5550
　2201 N Craig Rd Lot 237 Spokane (99224) *(G-12248)*

Equity Publishing — 509 994-0505
　4910 W Dahl Rd Deer Park (99006) *(G-2900)*

Erb Woodcraft LLC — 509 467-1134
　15111 N Columbus St Spokane (99208) *(G-12249)*

Ergo Design Inc (PA) — 360 427-5779
　3441 93rd Ave Sw Olympia (98512) *(G-7278)*

Eric Gibbs Software — 206 784-0741
　2918 Nw Esplanade Seattle (98117) *(G-9936)*

Eric The Closet Guy, Kenmore Also called Passion Works LLC *(G-4597)*

Ericka J Thielke — 206 214-7530
　6816 17th Ave Ne Seattle (98115) *(G-9937)*

Erickson Busheling Inc — 360 928-3232
　964 Freshwater Bay Rd Port Angeles (98363) *(G-7703)*

Erickson Custom Meats — 509 962-6099
　1840 Clarke Rd Ellensburg (98926) *(G-3198)*

Erickson Inc — 509 747-6148
　422 W Riverside Ave # 730 Spokane (99201) *(G-12250)*

Erickson Labs Northwest, Kirkland Also called Northwest Eye Design LLC *(G-5413)*

Erickson Logging — 253 846-2646
　21806 103rd Avenue Ct E # 104 Graham (98338) *(G-4225)*

Erickson Logging Inc — 360 832-8627
　41306 90th Ave E Eatonville (98328) *(G-3056)*

Erickson Tank & Pump LLC — 509 785-2955
　800 Road P.5 Sw Quincy (98848) *(G-8297)*

Erickson's Eyes, Spokane Also called Erickson Inc *(G-12250)*

Erickson, Erick R, Quincy Also called Erickson Tank & Pump LLC *(G-8297)*

Erics Woodwork — 206 860-6174
　141 Nw 80th St Seattle (98117) *(G-9938)*

Eridu Designs — 360 247-5980
　17005 Ne Grantham Rd Amboy (98601) *(G-93)*

Erik Doane Manufacturing — 360 799-0997
　32621 121st St Se Sultan (98294) *(G-13023)*

Eriks — 253 395-4770
　7748 S 200th St Kent (98032) *(G-4896)*

Eriksen Diesel Repair Inc — 425 778-8237
　7724 222nd St Sw Edmonds (98026) *(G-3110)*

Ernest R Howald Inc — 360 491-1758
　1645 Marvin Rd Se Olympia (98503) *(G-7279)*

Ernestinas Tortillas LLC — 360 669-0319
　1649 Kresky Ave Centralia (98531) *(G-2400)*

Ernit LLC — 425 922-3867
　2515 140th Ave Ne Bellevue (98005) *(G-898)*

Eros Comix, Seattle Also called Fantagraphics Books Inc *(G-9968)*

Erosion Ctrl Innovations LLC — 206 962-9582
　31002 Se Enumclaw Enumclaw (98022) *(G-3290)*

Errant Cellars — 509 289-9660
　303 N St Sw Quincy (98848) *(G-8298)*

Ers Group Inc — 360 895-1318
　10201 Horizon Ln Se Ste A Port Orchard (98367) *(G-7808)*

Ershigs Inc (HQ) — 360 733-2620
　742 Marine Dr Bellingham (98225) *(G-1338)*

Ershigs Inc — 360 887-3580
　5985 S 6th Way Ridgefield (98642) *(G-9081)*

Erudite Inc — 253 272-8542
　711 Court A Ste 204 Tacoma (98402) *(G-13281)*

Ervin H Tennyson — 360 445-2434
　100 E Washington St Mount Vernon (98273) *(G-6793)*

Escape Fuel Game One LLC — 425 883-8054
　9660 173rd Pl Ne Redmond (98052) *(G-8453)*

Escent Lighting — 509 838-9028
　605 W Spokane Falls Blvd Spokane (99201) *(G-12251)*

Esco Pacific Signs Inc — 360 748-6461
　627 Nw Middle St Chehalis (98532) *(G-2493)*

Esi Distribution Ltd — 206 780-9623
　330 Madison Ave S Ste 203 Bainbridge Island (98110) *(G-631)*

Esin Games, Seattle Also called Exceptionally Smart *(G-9952)*

Esoteric Software LLC — 206 618-3331
　4011 23rd Ave Sw Seattle (98106) *(G-9939)*

ESP Printing Inc — 425 251-6240
　4700 9th Ave Nw Seattle (98107) *(G-9940)*

ESP Seattle — 206 388-4800
　950 Andover Park E Tukwila (98188) *(G-13730)*

ESP Supply Company LLC — 503 256-2933
　3800 Se Columbia Way # 180 Vancouver (98661) *(G-14205)*

Espi's Sausage & Tocino Co, Seattle Also called Bels International Corporation *(G-9510)*

Esprit Grphic Cmmnications Inc — 509 586-7858
　110 N Cascade St Kennewick (99336) *(G-4662)*

Esquel Apparel Inc — 206 223-7338
　1109 1st Ave Ste 204 Seattle (98101) *(G-9941)*

Essentia Water Inc — 425 402-9555
　18911 North Creek Pkwy # 150 Bothell (98011) *(G-1761)*

Essential Building Tech LLC — 360 573-3200
　600 Se Maritime Ave # 240 Vancouver (98661) *(G-14206)*

Esses Cascara Bark, Montesano Also called Pacific Coast Cascara Bark Co *(G-6652)*

Essex Laboratories LLC — 360 740-1770
　115 Klein Rd Chehalis (98532) *(G-2494)*

Essex Labs, Chehalis Also called Essex Laboratories LLC *(G-2494)*

Estate Iron Work, Lake Forest Park Also called Benjamin D Schreiner *(G-5606)*

Esteem Wireless Modems, Kennewick Also called Electronic Systems Tech Inc *(G-4657)*

Esterbrook Inc — 509 783-6826
　3311 W Clearwater Ave B110 Kennewick (99336) *(G-4663)*

Esterline, Kent Also called Hytek Finishes Co *(G-4947)*

Esterline Corporation — 425 453-9400
　500 108th Ave Ne Ste 1500 Bellevue (98004) *(G-899)*

Esterline Ctrl Systems-Korry, Everett Also called Esterline Technologies Corp *(G-3462)*

Esterline Europe Company LLC — 425 453-9400
　500 108th Ave Ne Ste 1500 Bellevue (98004) *(G-900)*

Esterline International Co — 425 453-9400
　500 108th Ave Ne Ste 1500 Bellevue (98004) *(G-901)*

Esterline Technologies Corp — 253 796-4527
　8127 S 216th St Kent (98032) *(G-4897)*

ALPHABETIC SECTION — Evolution Revolution LLC

Esterline Technologies Corp 425 297-9624
11910 Beverly Park Rd Everett (98204) *(G-3462)*

Esterline Technologies Corp (HQ) 425 453-9400
500 108th Ave Ne Ste 1500 Bellevue (98004) *(G-902)*

Esterline Technologies Corp 206 281-1312
901 Dexter Ave N Seattle (98109) *(G-9942)*

Esther Brcques Wnery Vnyrd LLC 509 476-2861
38 Swanson Mill Rd Oroville (98844) *(G-7465)*

Estm Inc 509 545-0596
133 N Ely St Ste C1 Kennewick (99336) *(G-4664)*

Et Hydraulics LLC 206 718-7372
8626 180th St Se Ste B Snohomish (98296) *(G-11906)*

Etc Tacoma 253 223-5459
907 Pacific Ave Tacoma (98402) *(G-13282)*

Etchings Walla Walla 509 301-3300
54 W Rees Ave Walla Walla (99362) *(G-14802)*

Eternal Color Prints 360 771-9408
14300 Ne 88th St Vancouver (98682) *(G-14207)*

Eternity Software 425 486-1622
20415 Bothell Everett Hwy Bothell (98012) *(G-1852)*

Ethen Foods Inc 206 778-0931
8612 137th Ave Se Newcastle (98059) *(G-7029)*

Ethos Bakery LLC 509 942-8799
2150 Keene Rd Richland (99352) *(G-8994)*

Etios Health LLC 585 217-1716
12701 Ne 9th Pl Apt D110 Bellevue (98005) *(G-903)*

Ets Inc 509 276-2015
859 S Main St Deer Park (99006) *(G-2901)*

Ets-Lindgren Inc 425 868-2558
22117 Ne 10th Pl Sammamish (98074) *(G-9205)*

Etsoutdoors 509 481-3938
21223 W Four Mound Rd Nine Mile Falls (99026) *(G-7073)*

Etz Industries LLC 253 630-2915
24103 138th Ave Se Kent (98042) *(G-4898)*

Eucon Corporation 509 529-6400
1326 Dell Ave Walla Walla (99362) *(G-14803)*

Eucon Corporation 509 547-4402
3300 E A St Pasco (99301) *(G-7580)*

Eugene P Lamm Jr 509 460-1240
807 Snow Ave Richland (99352) *(G-8995)*

Eureka Pet Food, Seattle *Also called Good Pet Food Inc (G-10099)*

Euro Amport, Federal Way *Also called Sunne Group Ltd Inc (G-3792)*

Eurocraft Hardwood Floors Llc 425 670-6769
8522 216th St Se Woodinville (98072) *(G-15237)*

Eurofins Microbiology Labs Inc 425 686-1996
11720 N Creek Pkwy N Bothell (98011) *(G-1762)*

European Creations Inc 425 898-0685
24243 Ne Vine Maple Way Redmond (98053) *(G-8454)*

European Wrought Iron 509 548-4879
9351 E Leavenworth Rd Leavenworth (98826) *(G-5801)*

Eustis Co Inc 425 423-9996
12407b Mukilteo Speedway Lynnwood (98087) *(G-6115)*

Ev Drives 360 302-5226
1240 W Sims Way Port Townsend (98368) *(G-7882)*

Evalesco Inc 425 486-5959
15510 Woodinville Redmond Woodinville (98072) *(G-15238)*

Evan Martin Lure Inc 425 478-7163
16308 Inglewood Rd Ne Kenmore (98028) *(G-4572)*

Evans & Assoc, Colville *Also called Richard Evans (G-2773)*

Evans - Hamilton Inc 206 526-5622
4608 Union Bay Pl Ne Seattle (98105) *(G-9943)*

Evans Adhesives Corporation 614 410-6027
28303 Ne 50th St Camas (98607) *(G-2250)*

Evans Board Shop 360 297-4445
2037 Ne Templar Ln Poulsbo (98370) *(G-7962)*

Evans Mfg 360 332-9505
9606 Valley View Rd Blaine (98230) *(G-1669)*

Evas Crackers LLC 206 353-5691
1137 22nd Ave E Seattle (98112) *(G-9944)*

Evelo Electric Bicycle Company, Seattle *Also called Evelo Inc (G-9945)*

Evelo Inc 877 991-7272
1411 34th Ave Seattle (98122) *(G-9945)*

Even Flow Heating A/C & Rfrgn 425 381-0400
17317 38th Ave W Lynnwood (98037) *(G-6116)*

Event 1 Software Inc 360 567-3752
3305 Main St Ste 19 Vancouver (98663) *(G-14208)*

Event Power & Lighting Inc 360 225-3830
170 Lahti Rd Woodland (98674) *(G-15431)*

Ever Green Donuts 425 673-5331
20101 44th Ave W Ste F Lynnwood (98036) *(G-6117)*

Ever-Mark LLc 425 486-7200
7330 Ne Bothell Way 202 Kenmore (98028) *(G-4573)*

Everett Bark Supply Inc 425 353-9024
11715 Highway 99 Everett (98204) *(G-3463)*

Everett Press, Everett *Also called Sound Publishing Inc (G-3618)*

Everett Print, Everett *Also called Integrated Print Solutions Inc (G-3517)*

Everett Tent & Awning Inc 425 252-8213
1625 E Mar View Dr Ste 1 Everett (98201) *(G-3464)*

Everett/Kitsap Press, Everett *Also called Sound Publishing Inc (G-3617)*

Evergreen Circuits LLC 425 382-8412
14023 284th Cir Ne Duvall (98019) *(G-2986)*

Evergreen Construction Spc Inc 253 288-8455
1410 37th St Nw Ste A Auburn (98001) *(G-433)*

Evergreen Controls LLC 253 405-3770
672 E 11th St Tacoma (98421) *(G-13283)*

Evergreen Cooling Tech Inc (PA) 360 983-3691
148-33 Bear Ridge Rd Mossyrock (98564) *(G-6761)*

Evergreen Copy Service, Everett *Also called Evergreen Printing & Graphics (G-3466)*

Evergreen Engravers 253 852-6766
1819 Central Ave S Ste 24 Kent (98032) *(G-4899)*

Evergreen Eye Center Inc Ps 206 212-2163
716 S 348th St Federal Way (98003) *(G-3735)*

Evergreen Fabrication Inc 509 534-9096
4331 E Mission Ave Spokane Valley (99212) *(G-12694)*

Evergreen Fibre Inc 360 452-2670
404 Eclipse West Dr Port Angeles (98363) *(G-7704)*

Evergreen Fibre Inc (HQ) 360 452-3341
2095 Blue Mountain Rd Port Angeles (98362) *(G-7705)*

Evergreen Forms Services 425 740-2927
9800 Harbour Pl Ste 202 Mukilteo (98275) *(G-6925)*

Evergreen Granite & Cab Sup 425 423-9681
8701 Evergreen Way Ste B Everett (98208) *(G-3465)*

Evergreen Herbal, Seattle *Also called Eh Enterprises Management Inc (G-9889)*

Evergreen Hill Design, Arlington *Also called Oso Railworks Inc (G-295)*

Evergreen House Inc 425 821-1005
13645 Ne 126th Pl Kirkland (98034) *(G-5334)*

Evergreen Mch & Fabrication 509 249-1141
801 E Viola Ave Yakima (98901) *(G-15565)*

Evergreen Orthpd RES Lab LLC 425 284-7262
11317 Ne 120th St Kirkland (98034) *(G-5335)*

Evergreen Pacific Publishing 425 493-1451
4204 Russell Rd Ste M Mukilteo (98275) *(G-6926)*

Evergreen Plastic Container 360 828-7174
6501 Ne 47th Ave Vancouver (98661) *(G-14209)*

Evergreen Powder Coatings, Spokane *Also called Pacific NW Powdr Coating (G-12426)*

Evergreen Print Solutions, Mukilteo *Also called Evergreen Forms Services (G-6925)*

Evergreen Printing & Graphics 425 338-2900
10530 19th Ave Se Ste 103 Everett (98208) *(G-3466)*

Evergreen Production LLC 206 818-5054
2870 Ocean Ave Bldg 1 Raymond (98577) *(G-8347)*

Evergreen Products Division, Parker *Also called Pace International LLC (G-7549)*

Evergreen Prosthetcs & Orthotc 360 213-2088
11201 Ne 9th St Ste 100 Vancouver (98684) *(G-14210)*

Evergreen Prsthetics Orthotics, Tacoma *Also called Preferred Orthotic & Prosthetc (G-13476)*

Evergreen Publications 360 734-4158
1443 Lahti Dr Bellingham (98226) *(G-1339)*

Evergreen Sales Group Inc 425 368-2000
18915 142nd Ave Ne # 145 Woodinville (98072) *(G-15239)*

Evergreen Studios, Olympia *Also called Michael Ashford Design (G-7339)*

Evergreen Textiles 253 852-6565
4226 S 280th St Auburn (98001) *(G-434)*

Evergreen Timber Corp 206 579-2925
8823 Renton Ave S Ste 2 Seattle (98118) *(G-9946)*

Evergreen Truss & Supply, Deer Park *Also called A & V Investments Inc (G-2892)*

Evergreens Salad 206 973-4400
823 3rd Ave Seattle (98104) *(G-9947)*

Everlasting Publishing 509 225-9829
1301 S 16th Ave Yakima (98902) *(G-15566)*

Everlasting Scents LLC 509 534-4790
8121 E Appleway Blvd Spokane Valley (99212) *(G-12695)*

Everpath Inc 206 682-7259
720 Olive Way Ste 700 Seattle (98101) *(G-9948)*

Everson Cordage Works LLC 360 966-4613
7180 Everson Goshen Rd Everson (98247) *(G-3675)*

Every Occasion Engraving 509 995-9848
2007 N Woodruff Rd Spokane Valley (99206) *(G-12696)*

Every Watt Matters LLC (PA) 425 985-2171
2501 Se Columbia Way # 220 Vancouver (98661) *(G-14211)*

Every Watt Matters LLC 503 221-2113
2501 Se Columbia Way # 220 Vancouver (98661) *(G-14212)*

Everything Prints 360 447-8217
15301 76th Avenue Ct E Puyallup (98375) *(G-8150)*

Everything Quarterly LLC 425 478-2173
2901 211th St Sw Lynnwood (98036) *(G-6118)*

Evil Genius Publishing LLC 253 929-6710
1411 59th St Se Auburn (98092) *(G-435)*

Evil Industries 206 612-3293
31920 Ne Big Rock Rd Duvall (98019) *(G-2987)*

Evil Roys Elixirs 360 463-6105
209 S Sequim Ave Sequim (98382) *(G-11633)*

Evluma, Renton *Also called Express Imaging Systems LLC (G-8796)*

Evo 866 386-1590
3209 West Valley Hwy E # 100 Sumner (98390) *(G-13070)*

Evo Industries LLC 717 665-0406
2172 Fairview Rd Ellensburg (98926) *(G-3199)*

Evolution Covers 425 478-2043
4109 161st St Se Mill Creek (98012) *(G-6509)*

Evolution Press Inc 206 783-5522
2525 W Commodore Way Seattle (98199) *(G-9949)*

Evolution Revolution LLC 623 703-5042
22584 Meadow Creek Rd Leavenworth (98826) *(G-5802)*

Evolution Technologies USA....360 392-8600
2657 Delta Ring Rd Ferndale (98248) ***(G-3839)***
Evolving Nutrition....425 355-5682
9800 Harbour Pl Ste 208 Everett (98203) ***(G-3467)***
Evoqua Water Technologies LLC....360 699-7392
15403 Ne Caples Rd Brush Prairie (98606) ***(G-2034)***
Evrnu Spc....206 466-5269
3200 1st Ave S Ste 200 Seattle (98134) ***(G-9950)***
Evs Manufacturing Inc....360 863-6413
14253 169th Dr Se Ste 799 Monroe (98272) ***(G-6570)***
Ewing Construction....509 624-2246
701 N Flint Rd Spokane (99224) ***(G-12252)***
Ewm International, Vancouver *Also called Every Watt Matters LLC* ***(G-14212)***
Ex Officio LLC (HQ)....206 283-1471
4202 6th Ave S Unit Main Seattle (98108) ***(G-9951)***
Ex Officio LLC....206 242-9696
17801 International Blvd Seatac (98158) ***(G-9282)***
Ex Ophidia Press LLC....360 385-9966
220 Parfitt Way Sw # 111 Bainbridge Island (98110) ***(G-632)***
Exact Aerospace Inc....253 854-1017
3104 C St Ne Ste 200 Auburn (98002) ***(G-436)***
Exacto Inc....253 531-5311
13826 50th Ave E Tacoma (98446) ***(G-13284)***
Exacttarget Inc....866 362-4538
601 108th Ave Ne Ste 1580 Bellevue (98004) ***(G-904)***
Examiner The, Coupeville *Also called Whidbey Examiner LLC* ***(G-2819)***
Examinercom....206 459-0562
14426 Se Auburn Blck Diam Auburn (98092) ***(G-437)***
Excel Dairy Service Inc (PA)....360 848-9494
2725 Old Highway 99 S Rd Mount Vernon (98273) ***(G-6794)***
Excel Designs Inc....360 892-1412
6019 Ne 109th Ave Vancouver (98662) ***(G-14213)***
Excel Industries Incorporated....360 790-3577
1400 Yarrow Ct Lynden (98264) ***(G-6015)***
Excel Manufacturing Inc....253 939-6446
120 37th St Ne Auburn (98002) ***(G-438)***
Excel Packaging Systems Inc....360 825-7209
3214 Wynalda Dr Enumclaw (98022) ***(G-3291)***
Excelerate Systems LLC....425 605-8515
2205 152nd Ave Ne Redmond (98052) ***(G-8455)***
Excell Aerofab, Arlington *Also called Aerofab Industries Inc* ***(G-194)***
Excelsior Nanotech Corporation....206 898-9477
2023 120th Ave Ne Bellevue (98005) ***(G-905)***
Exceptionally Smart....206 321-0721
500 Union St Ste 420 Seattle (98101) ***(G-9952)***
Executive Media Corp....509 933-2993
701 N Anderson St Ellensburg (98926) ***(G-3200)***
Exide Technologies....509 922-3135
9708 E Montgomery Ave D Spokane Valley (99206) ***(G-12697)***
Exide Technologies....253 863-5134
2005 Fryar Ave Sumner (98390) ***(G-13071)***
Exit Puzzles....360 930-9686
109 State Ave Ne Olympia (98501) ***(G-7280)***
Exo Labs Inc....206 659-1249
3131 Wstn Ave Ste M325 Seattle (98121) ***(G-9953)***
Exomotion LLC....206 763-0754
7936 Exodental Ave S Seattle (98108) ***(G-9954)***
Exone Company....253 394-0357
1307 W Valley Hwy N # 104 Auburn (98001) ***(G-439)***
Exone Company....360 286-0556
252 Wilkes Ave Bremerton (98312) ***(G-1953)***
Exorvision Inc....206 254-0220
3417 Evanston Ave N # 402 Seattle (98103) ***(G-9955)***
Exotec....425 488-0691
15974 82nd Pl Ne Kenmore (98028) ***(G-4574)***
Exotic Metals Forming Co LLC (PA)....253 220-5900
5411 S 226th St Kent (98032) ***(G-4900)***
Exotic Metals Forming Co LLC....253 395-3710
6020 S 226th St Kent (98032) ***(G-4901)***
Expensive Cardboard....214 564-2670
2401 Sw Brandon St # 208 Seattle (98106) ***(G-9956)***
Expermntal Arcft Met Fbrcation....360 245-3478
693 Curtis Hill Rd Chehalis (98532) ***(G-2495)***
Expert Computer Tech Inc....360 736-7000
1600 S Gold St Ste 4 Centralia (98531) ***(G-2401)***
Expert Ig....360 335-0555
534 K St Washougal (98671) ***(G-14954)***
Express Imaging Systems LLC....206 720-1798
3600 Lind Ave Sw Ste 140 Renton (98057) ***(G-8796)***
Express Messenger....360 992-9999
3665 Nw 32nd Ave Vancouver (98660) ***(G-14214)***
Expressions Glass II....206 242-2860
648 Sw 152nd St Burien (98166) ***(G-2106)***
Expressions Signs Inc....425 844-6415
17201 Beaton Rd Se Monroe (98272) ***(G-6571)***
Expressive Promotions....253 863-4211
17505 51st Street Ct E Lake Tapps (98391) ***(G-5678)***
Exquisitecrystals Com LLC....360 573-6787
619 Barnes St Vancouver (98661) ***(G-14215)***
Exterior Wood Inc (HQ)....360 835-8561
2685 Index St Washougal (98671) ***(G-14955)***
Extreme Capacitor Inc....360 878-9749
1835 Cedarbury Ln Sw Olympia (98512) ***(G-7281)***
Extreme Hardwood Floors....425 985-6735
12611 177th Pl Se Renton (98059) ***(G-8797)***
Extreme Indus Coatings LLC....509 991-1773
11319 W Willow Ln Airway Heights (99001) ***(G-51)***
Extreme Networks Inc....408 579-2800
18820 71st Ave Se Snohomish (98296) ***(G-11907)***
Extrusion Technology Group Inc....253 583-8283
2411 104th Street Ct S Lakewood (98499) ***(G-5720)***
Eye of Needle Winery....425 210-7463
19501 144th Ave Ne Woodinville (98072) ***(G-15240)***
Eyeon LLC....425 652-9556
20603 Se 136th St Issaquah (98027) ***(G-4410)***
EZ Grill, Kirkland *Also called P&M Products Inc* ***(G-5423)***
EZ Line Cabinets....206 775-2226
26433 104th Ave Se D302 Kent (98030) ***(G-4902)***
EZ Lip LLC....425 753-6814
2218 Se 2nd Pl Renton (98056) ***(G-8798)***
EZ Loder Adjustable Boat Trlrs, Spokane *Also called E Z Loader Boat Trailers Inc* ***(G-12236)***
Ez-Access, Algona *Also called Homecare Products Inc* ***(G-71)***
Ezion Global Inc....206 446-9476
16434 Se 35th St Bellevue (98008) ***(G-906)***
Ezr Communications Inc....360 936-0070
1709 Daniels St Vancouver (98660) ***(G-14216)***
F A Koenig & Sons Inc....360 793-1711
33523 State Route 2 Sultan (98294) ***(G-13024)***
F and F Excavating and Logging....509 637-2551
1816 Bz Glenwood Hwy Glenwood (98619) ***(G-4180)***
F D Company....253 531-7087
1702 112th St E Tacoma (98445) ***(G-13285)***
F H Sullivan Co Inc....360 442-4222
2219 Talley Way Kelso (98626) ***(G-4525)***
F PS Pallet Recycling Inc....253 312-7122
7020 Ohop Valley Rd E Eatonville (98328) ***(G-3057)***
F Ruckman Enterprises....253 531-9132
14002 Canyon Rd E Puyallup (98373) ***(G-8151)***
F S I Mechanical, Battle Ground *Also called Francis Scientific Inc* ***(G-702)***
F V Alyeska, Redmond *Also called Dutch Harbor Seafoods Ltd* ***(G-8444)***
F W B Enterprises Inc....425 377-2628
5415 93rd Ave Se Snohomish (98290) ***(G-11908)***
F W Enterprises LLC....253 439-8090
9610 226th Avenue Ct E Buckley (98321) ***(G-2058)***
F&S Industries LLC....206 501-5347
1416 N 50th St Seattle (98103) ***(G-9957)***
F/V Native Star....360 267-6348
1174 Wood Ln Grayland (98547) ***(G-4293)***
F/V Neahkahnie LLC....206 547-6557
2727 Alaskan Way Pier 69 Seattle (98121) ***(G-9958)***
F5 LLC....425 882-8080
1 Microsoft Way Redmond (98052) ***(G-8456)***
F5 Networks Inc (PA)....206 272-5555
401 Elliott Ave W Ste 500 Seattle (98119) ***(G-9959)***
FA Green Company....425 888-0007
9742 352nd Ave Se Snoqualmie (98065) ***(G-12012)***
Fab Shop LLC....253 568-9124
10315 16th St E Edgewood (98372) ***(G-3077)***
Fab Shop, The, Edgewood *Also called Fab Shop LLC* ***(G-3077)***
Fab Tek, Union Gap *Also called N A I Inc* ***(G-13945)***
Fab-Tech Inc....360 755-0215
9587 Green Rd Burlington (98233) ***(G-2156)***
Fab5ventures LLC....425 310-2543
3800 Bridgeport Way W # 315 University Place (98466) ***(G-13967)***
Fablab LLC....253 426-1267
1938 Market St Tacoma (98402) ***(G-13286)***
Fabricast Valve LLC....360 425-0306
1061 Industrial Way Longview (98632) ***(G-5910)***
Fabricated Plastics Limited....360 527-3430
742 Marine Dr Bellingham (98225) ***(G-1340)***
Fabricated Products Inc....360 695-5949
3201 Nw Lower River Rd Vancouver (98660) ***(G-14217)***
Fabrication & Truck Eqp Inc (PA)....509 535-0363
5301 E Broadway Ave Spokane Valley (99212) ***(G-12698)***
Fabrication Enterprises Inc....503 240-0878
3105 Ne 65th St Ste B Vancouver (98663) ***(G-14218)***
Fabrication Products Inc....503 283-3218
4201 Ne Minnehaha St Vancouver (98661) ***(G-14219)***
Fabrication Technologies LLC....360 293-3707
12729 Quantum Ln Unit 17 Anacortes (98221) ***(G-127)***
Fabrications Inc....888 808-9878
3010 77th Ave Se Ste 107 Mercer Island (98040) ***(G-6462)***
Fabrictn Melton & Precision....509 284-2620
223 N Crosby St Tekoa (99033) ***(G-13611)***
Fabriform LLC....206 587-5303
3300 Airport Way S Seattle (98134) ***(G-9960)***
Fabtech Manufacturing LLC....509 488-1950
1787 S Broadway Ave Othello (99344) ***(G-7495)***
Fabtech Precision Mfg Inc (PA)....509 534-7660
16124 E Euclid Ave Spokane Valley (99216) ***(G-12699)***
Fabtech Systems LLC....425 349-9557
3304 Hill Ave Everett (98201) ***(G-3468)***
Fabtek, Anacortes *Also called Fabrication Technologies LLC* ***(G-127)***
Fabtek Industries Llc....360 322-7367
6011 199th St Ne Arlington (98223) ***(G-235)***

Fact Motorcycle Training Inc 509 248-2373
10 N 10th Ave Yakima (98902) *(G-15567)*
Fact Safety Companies, Yakima *Also called Fact Motorcycle Training Inc (G-15567)*
Faction Ltd 360 275-2834
23632 Ne State Route 3 Belfair (98528) *(G-762)*
Faction Industries, Belfair *Also called Faction Ltd (G-762)*
Factors Group Mfg Inc 360 243-3500
14224 167th Ave Se Monroe (98272) *(G-6572)*
Factory Direct Windows, Fife *Also called American Vinyl Industries Inc (G-3931)*
Factory Trawler Supply Inc (PA) 206 285-6732
4257 24th Ave W Seattle (98199) *(G-9961)*
Facts Newspaper 206 324-0552
1112 34th Ave Seattle (98122) *(G-9962)*
Fagernes Cutting Inc 360 245-3249
219 Aust Rd Chehalis (98532) *(G-2496)*
Fahrenheit Headwear, Seattle *Also called Century 21 Promotions Inc (G-9655)*
Fairbanks Morse LLC 206 246-8133
18926 13th Pl S Seatac (98148) *(G-9283)*
Fairbanks Morse Engine, Seatac *Also called Fairbanks Morse LLC (G-9283)*
Fairhaven Gold Inc 360 733-4667
1302 12th St Bellingham (98225) *(G-1341)*
Fairhaven Shipyard, Bellingham *Also called Puglia Engineering Inc (G-1509)*
Fairlane Helicopters Inc 360 398-1015
284 Pollman Cir Lynden (98264) *(G-6016)*
Fairlight Bakery Inc 360 576-8587
5600 Ne 121st Ave Ste T1 Vancouver (98682) *(G-14220)*
Fairview Equipment, La Center *Also called Ramco Mechanical Cutting Ltd (G-5513)*
Fairwood Commerce Center LLP 206 903-9200
20728 Se 119th St Issaquah (98027) *(G-4411)*
Fairy Floss 206 364-3218
13728 Interlake Ave N Seattle (98133) *(G-9963)*
Faith Dairy Inc 253 531-3398
3509 72nd St E Tacoma (98443) *(G-13287)*
Faithful Enterprises Inc 509 865-7300
931 Buena Way Toppenish (98948) *(G-13667)*
Faithlife Corporation 360 685-2300
1313 Commercial St Bellingham (98225) *(G-1342)*
Falcon Rcnnissance Systems Inc 360 378-3900
72 Airport Circle Dr Friday Harbor (98250) *(G-4044)*
Falconstor Software Inc 206 652-3312
601 Union St Seattle (98101) *(G-9964)*
Fall City Welding Inc 425 222-5105
33623 Se 43rd St Fall City (98024) *(G-3701)*
Fall Line Winery LLC 206 406-4249
2960 4th Ave S Ste 107 Seattle (98134) *(G-9965)*
Fallen Hero Bracelets 253 537-1212
16011 3rd Avenue Ct E Tacoma (98445) *(G-13288)*
Falx Games 253 439-9121
8823 S I St Tacoma (98444) *(G-13289)*
Fam USA Inc 509 468-2677
18324 N West Shore Rd Nine Mile Falls (99026) *(G-7074)*
Fam Waterjet Inc 425 353-6111
12310 Highway 99 Ste 114 Everett (98204) *(G-3469)*
Familian Northwest Seattle 07 206 767-7700
7115 W Marginal Way Sw Seattle (98106) *(G-9966)*
Family Endurance Corporation 253 872-3900
8805 S 190th St Kent (98031) *(G-4903)*
Family Roots Publishing Co LLC 801 949-7259
220 Bridge St Sw Ste 2 Orting (98360) *(G-7479)*
Family Treasures 206 282-1194
909 2nd Ave N Apt 301 Seattle (98109) *(G-9967)*
Family Values Mag Clark Cnty 360 909-5945
10128 Nw 19th Ave Vancouver (98685) *(G-14221)*
Fanapptic LLC 253 548-7443
2911 Grandview Dr W University Place (98466) *(G-13968)*
Fanipin Korea Corp 425 218-6555
2320 162nd St Se Mill Creek (98012) *(G-6510)*
Fantagraphics Books Inc (PA) 206 524-1967
7563 Lake City Way Ne Seattle (98115) *(G-9968)*
Fantastic Floor, Vancouver *Also called NW Wood Holding LLC (G-14445)*
Fantasy Content 425 653-2207
912 142nd Ave Se Bellevue (98007) *(G-907)*
Fantasy Football Index, Redmond *Also called Fantasy Index Magazines LLC (G-8457)*
Fantasy Glass Works Inc 425 557-6642
7932 Rnton Issaquah Rd Se Issaquah (98027) *(G-4412)*
Fantasy Index Magazines LLC 206 527-4444
12524 177th Ave Ne Redmond (98052) *(G-8457)*
Fantasy Sports Vault 206 219-9833
3210 California Ave Sw Seattle (98116) *(G-9969)*
Fantazimo Food 206 484-8232
7102 229th Pl Sw Mountlake Terrace (98043) *(G-6860)*
Faqa 206 362-5916
1725 Ne 115th St Seattle (98125) *(G-9970)*
Far Star Products 360 604-0080
14805 Ne 39th St Vancouver (98682) *(G-14222)*
Far West Fabricators Inc 509 453-1663
7537 Postma Rd Moxee (98936) *(G-6877)*
Far West Inc 360 942-3270
401 Monohon Landing Rd Raymond (98577) *(G-8348)*
Far West Machine Inc 509 422-0312
21 Three Devils Rd Malott (98829) *(G-6237)*
Fara Haven Organic Flour Mill, Burlington *Also called Kemason Inc (G-2166)*
Faraday Pharmaceuticals Inc 206 946-1989
1616 Eastlake Ave E # 560 Seattle (98102) *(G-9971)*
Farber News Service 253 565-1131
2322 Sunset Dr W Tacoma (98466) *(G-13290)*
Faris LLC 206 992-6453
2233 15th Ave W Seattle (98119) *(G-9972)*
Farley Desighn and Inc 425 259-5946
327 42nd St Sw Everett (98203) *(G-3470)*
Farm Aquisition RES & MGT LLC 425 869-0624
13651 Woodinville Rdmnd Redmond (98052) *(G-8458)*
Farm Breeze International LLC 253 365-0542
2602 S 38th St Unit 127 Tacoma (98409) *(G-13291)*
Farm Built Fab LLC 360 213-8458
216 Ne 349th St La Center (98629) *(G-5504)*
Farm To Market Foods LLC 360 708-6103
11141 View Ridge Dr Burlington (98233) *(G-2157)*
Farm West Materials, Walla Walla *Also called Walla Walla Foundry Inc (G-14891)*
Farma Tech International, North Bend *Also called Tanada Corporation (G-7127)*
Farmer Bros Co 509 457-6031
2301 S 18th St Union Gap (98903) *(G-13929)*
Farmer Bros Co 425 881-7030
8660 Willows Rd Ne Redmond (98052) *(G-8459)*
Farmer Brother's Coffee, Redmond *Also called Farmer Bros Co (G-8459)*
Farmers Brothers Coffee, Union Gap *Also called Farmer Bros Co (G-13929)*
Farmhand Winery 509 308-7203
8101 W 10th Ave Kennewick (99336) *(G-4665)*
Farmstrong LLC 360 873-8852
110 Stewart Rd Mount Vernon (98273) *(G-6795)*
Farmstrong Brewing Co., Mount Vernon *Also called Farmstrong LLC (G-6795)*
Farnworth Group 425 894-8643
8707 123rd Ln Ne Kirkland (98033) *(G-5336)*
Farrenewelding 360 941-5571
22128 State Route 9 # 89 Mount Vernon (98274) *(G-6796)*
Farrer Logging Co 509 773-5069
3275 Highway 142 Goldendale (98620) *(G-4197)*
Farstad Industries LLC 360 316-9485
796 Gun Club Rd Oak Harbor (98277) *(G-7150)*
Farwell Products Inc 509 663-6212
1649 N Wenatchee Ave Wenatchee (98801) *(G-15030)*
Farwest Aircraft Inc 253 568-1707
1415 Meridian Ave E Edgewood (98371) *(G-3078)*
Farwest Iron Works Inc 509 662-3546
1301 S Columbia St Wenatchee (98801) *(G-15031)*
Farwest Materials, Walla Walla *Also called Walla Walla Foundry Inc (G-14890)*
Farwest Operating LLC 509 453-1663
7537 Postma Rd Moxee (98936) *(G-6878)*
Farwest Paint Manufacturing Co (PA) 206 244-8844
4522 S 133rd St Tukwila (98168) *(G-13731)*
Farwest Steel Fabrication Co (HQ) 800 793-1493
3703 Nw Gateway Ave Vancouver (98660) *(G-14223)*
Fascinaturals LLC 425 954-7151
23632 Highway 99 F107 Edmonds (98026) *(G-3111)*
Fashion Corner 509 837-7345
401 S 6th St Sunnyside (98944) *(G-13125)*
Fashion Embroidery Inc 425 820-7125
13625 Ne 126th Pl Ste 430 Kirkland (98034) *(G-5337)*
Fashion Sales Inc 206 441-3282
2617 2nd Ave Ste B Seattle (98121) *(G-9973)*
Fasola Tools 360 293-9231
1405 20th St Anacortes (98221) *(G-128)*
Fast Flashings LLC 425 827-8367
13760 32nd Ave Ne Seattle (98125) *(G-9974)*
Fast Flashings LLC (PA) 206 364-3612
13760 32nd Ave Ne Seattle (98125) *(G-9975)*
Fast Horticultural Services 360 393-7057
3106 Thornton Rd Ferndale (98248) *(G-3840)*
Fast Lane Auto Sports 253 584-3676
8328 South Tacoma Way Lakewood (98499) *(G-5721)*
Fast Sign, Tacoma *Also called Kjj Enterprises Inc (G-13377)*
Fast Sign Man LLC 360 592-4599
5131 Mosquito Lake Rd Deming (98244) *(G-2919)*
Fast Signs 253 942-9444
34930 Enchanted Pkwy S # 170 Federal Way (98003) *(G-3736)*
Fast Yeti Inc 253 573-1877
3560 Bridgeport Way W 1b University Place (98466) *(G-13969)*
Fastcap LLC 888 443-3748
5016 Pacific Hwy Ferndale (98248) *(G-3841)*
Fastdataio Inc 888 707-3346
601 Union St Seattle (98101) *(G-9976)*
Fastener Training 562 400-3009
10111 Tilley Rd S Olympia (98512) *(G-7282)*
Fastsigns, Lacey *Also called TNT Signs Inc (G-5595)*
Fastsigns, Federal Way *Also called Fast Signs (G-3736)*
Fastsigns, Kirkland *Also called Barking Dog Inc (G-5288)*
Fastsigns, Lynnwood *Also called Landd Ventures Inc (G-6156)*
Fastsigns, Seattle *Also called Birklor LLC (G-9532)*
Fastsigns, Auburn *Also called Hafa Adai Signs & Graphics LLC (G-458)*
Fastsigns, Lynnwood *Also called Loewen Group LLC (G-6159)*
Fastsigns, Everett *Also called Jolly Family Corp (G-3525)*
Fastsigns, Spokane Valley *Also called Graphic Art Productions Inc (G-12723)*

ALPHABETIC

Fastsigns, Seattle ALPHABETIC SECTION

Fastsigns, Seattle *Also called Eagles Nest Holding Inc* ***(G-9869)***
Fastsigns.....206 682-2129
1515 9th Ave Ste 4 Seattle (98101) ***(G-9977)***
Fastsigns.....425 746-4151
13279 Ne 20th St Bellevue (98005) ***(G-908)***
Fastsigns.....360 567-3313
14415 Se Mill Plain Blvd # 1 Vancouver (98684) ***(G-14224)***
Fastsigns.....206 886-3860
4721 University Way Ne Seattle (98105) ***(G-9978)***
Fastsigns.....360 692-1660
9460 Silverdale Way Nw Silverdale (98383) ***(G-11834)***
Fastsigns.....206 575-2110
7825 S 180th St Kent (98032) ***(G-4904)***
Fastsigns 632.....206 577-4077
922 Sw 151st St Burien (98166) ***(G-2107)***
Fastsigns International Inc.....253 835-9450
34930 Encntd Pkwy S # 170 Federal Way (98003) ***(G-3737)***
Fastsigns of Auburn.....360 480-1097
9912 S 244th St Kent (98030) ***(G-4905)***
Fat Daddys Fabrication LLC.....253 677-8005
28014 14th Ave E Roy (98580) ***(G-9159)***
Fat-Cat Fish LLC.....360 715-1994
6069 Hannegan Rd Bellingham (98226) ***(G-1343)***
Fathem LLC.....360 403-7418
7212 Harrow Pl Arlington (98223) ***(G-236)***
Fatigue Technology Inc (HQ).....206 246-2010
401 Andover Park E Tukwila (98188) ***(G-13732)***
Fatkid Machine LLC.....425 481-5214
19501 144th Ave Ne F400 Woodinville (98072) ***(G-15241)***
Faubion William J Atty At Law.....360 795-3367
260 Una St Cathlamet (98612) ***(G-2366)***
Favorite Discovery LLC.....646 337-3574
13301 Se Forest St Vancouver (98683) ***(G-14225)***
Faye Gear Rhonda.....509 380-0950
3711 Antigua Dr Pasco (99301) ***(G-7581)***
Fbt.....509 457-3484
210 Keys Rd Yakima (98901) ***(G-15568)***
Fc Plating Inc.....360 679-4665
321 E Henni Rd Oak Harbor (98277) ***(G-7151)***
Feather and Skull.....206 227-7951
317 Nw 41st St Apt 208 Seattle (98107) ***(G-9979)***
Feathered Friends, Seattle *Also called Pangaea Ltd* ***(G-10746)***
Featherlite Trailers.....425 334-4045
3100 Bickford Ave Snohomish (98290) ***(G-11909)***
Federal Express Corporation.....800 463-3339
8404 W Aviation Rd Spokane (99224) ***(G-12253)***
Federal Marine & Def Svcs LLC (PA).....206 322-5529
8000 5th Ave S Seattle (98108) ***(G-9980)***
Federal Way Memorial Field.....253 945-5575
1300 S 308th St Federal Way (98003) ***(G-3738)***
Federal Way Mirror, Federal Way *Also called Sound Publishing Inc* ***(G-3787)***
Federal Way Sand & Gravel, Federal Way *Also called Lloyd Enterprises Inc* ***(G-3753)***
Federal Way Sign.....253 529-2011
34205 18th Pl S Federal Way (98003) ***(G-3739)***
Federated Auto Parts, Yakima *Also called Yakima Grinding Co* ***(G-15714)***
Federated Auto Parts, Colfax *Also called Kroll Machine & Supply Inc* ***(G-2715)***
Fedex, Spokane *Also called Federal Express Corporation* ***(G-12253)***
Fedex Office & Print Svcs Inc.....253 872-5539
5901 S 226th St Kent (98032) ***(G-4906)***
Fedex Office & Print Svcs Inc.....509 922-4929
212 N Sullivan Rd Spokane Valley (99037) ***(G-12700)***
Fedex Office & Print Svcs Inc.....360 647-1114
501 E Holly St Bellingham (98225) ***(G-1344)***
Fedex Office & Print Svcs Inc.....509 484-0601
259 W Spokane Falls Blvd Spokane (99201) ***(G-12254)***
Fedex Office & Print Svcs Inc.....360 694-8584
303 E 15th St Vancouver (98663) ***(G-14226)***
Fedex Office & Print Svcs Inc.....206 467-1767
735 Pike St Ste 11 Seattle (98101) ***(G-9981)***
Fedex Office & Print Svcs Inc.....206 244-8884
116 Andover Park E Tukwila (98188) ***(G-13733)***
Fedex Office & Print Svcs Inc.....253 841-3557
101 37th Ave Se Ste B Puyallup (98374) ***(G-8152)***
Fedex Office & Print Svcs Inc.....206 546-7600
1145 N 205th St Shoreline (98133) ***(G-11771)***
Fedex Office & Print Svcs Inc.....253 565-4882
6909 S 19th St Ste A Tacoma (98466) ***(G-13292)***
Fedex Office Print & Ship Ctr.....425 641-1174
3632 Factoria Blvd Se Bellevue (98006) ***(G-909)***
Fedexoffice.....206 467-5885
1400 6th Ave Seattle (98101) ***(G-9982)***
Feed Commodities LLC (PA).....626 799-1196
2006 E Portland Ave Tacoma (98421) ***(G-13293)***
Felamere Vineyard LLC.....360 652-7414
19310 40th Ave Nw Stanwood (98292) ***(G-12970)***
Feldhegers Machine & Welding.....509 452-9213
806 Wilson Ln Yakima (98901) ***(G-15569)***
Feller Custom Coatings.....360 551-2045
6352 School St Sw Lakewood (98499) ***(G-5722)***
Feller Logging Inc.....509 364-3435
1788 Bz Glenwood Hwy Glenwood (98619) ***(G-4181)***
Felony Prints.....509 443-6702
4708 W Pinto Rd Cheney (99004) ***(G-2585)***
Felts Signs.....360 299-0430
8142 S March Point Rd Anacortes (98221) ***(G-129)***
Feminina Group Inc.....310 237-5733
85 S Atlantic St Ste 203 Seattle (98134) ***(G-9983)***
Fence Quarter LLC.....800 205-0128
16824 44th Ave W Ste 130 Lynnwood (98037) ***(G-6119)***
Fence Store By Eagle Vinyl LLC.....509 860-3603
735 N Wenatchee Ave Wenatchee (98801) ***(G-15032)***
Fenette Cellars.....425 417-6260
20412 123rd Ave Ne Bothell (98011) ***(G-1763)***
Fenix Industries Inc.....206 695-2582
11552 6th Ave Nw Seattle (98177) ***(G-9984)***
Fenologica Biosciences Inc.....206 726-1200
720 Broadway Seattle (98122) ***(G-9985)***
Fenwick Publishing Group Inc.....206 842-3981
3147 Point White Dr Ne # 100 Bainbridge Island (98110) ***(G-633)***
Feral House Inc.....323 666-3311
1240 W Sims Way Ste 124 Port Townsend (98368) ***(G-7883)***
Feral House Inc.....323 666-3311
1240 W Sims Way Ste 124 Port Townsend (98368) ***(G-7884)***
Ferdinand's, Pullman *Also called Washington State University* ***(G-8113)***
Ferguson.....206 767-7700
401 Lund Rd Auburn (98001) ***(G-440)***
Ferguson - Gagnon Industries.....509 337-6207
123 Gallaher Rd Waitsburg (99361) ***(G-14754)***
Ferguson Merchandising LLC (PA).....425 883-2050
15756 Redmond Way Redmond (98052) ***(G-8460)***
Ferguson Woodworking Inc.....360 398-1543
5978 Guide Meridian Bellingham (98226) ***(G-1345)***
Fermium It LLC.....541 213-9291
12209 Ne Fourth Pln Vancouver (98682) ***(G-14227)***
Fern Hollow LLC.....360 504-2323
20726 State Highway 305 N Poulsbo (98370) ***(G-7963)***
Fern's Feature Pens Doll Molds, Longview *Also called Jans Ceramics* ***(G-5920)***
Ferndale Creamery Co LLC.....360 255-7062
2780 Aldergrove Rd Ferndale (98248) ***(G-3842)***
Ferndale Ready-Mix (PA).....360 354-1400
144 River Rd Lynden (98264) ***(G-6017)***
Ferndale Ready-Mix.....360 384-8087
5271 Creighton Rd Ferndale (98248) ***(G-3843)***
Ferndale Record Inc.....360 384-1411
2004 Main St Ferndale (98248) ***(G-3844)***
Ferrier Cabinets.....425 788-0230
20014 312th Ave Ne Duvall (98019) ***(G-2988)***
Ferris Fun Foods.....253 964-2828
18524 190th St Sw Dupont (98327) ***(G-2963)***
Ferrotek Corporation.....360 366-7444
7135 Delta Line Rd Ferndale (98248) ***(G-3845)***
Ferryboat Music LLC.....509 996-3528
141 Eastside Chewuch Rd Winthrop (98862) ***(G-15160)***
Fessco Fleet and Marine Inc.....509 534-5880
3025 S Geiger Blvd Spokane (99224) ***(G-12255)***
Fetha Styx Inc.....360 687-3856
6719 Ne 219th St B Battle Ground (98604) ***(G-701)***
Fetha Styx LLC.....425 242-0014
6825 122nd Ave Ne Kirkland (98033) ***(G-5338)***
Fetha Styx Custom Fishing Rods, Kirkland *Also called Fetha Styx LLC* ***(G-5338)***
Fh Sullivan Company, Kelso *Also called F H Sullivan Co Inc* ***(G-4525)***
Fialab Instruments Inc.....206 258-2290
2151 N Northlake Way # 100 Seattle (98103) ***(G-9986)***
Fiber Meadows Alpacas LLC.....360 856-5740
26417 Minkler Rd Sedro Woolley (98284) ***(G-11537)***
Fiber Trends Inc.....509 884-8631
301 2nd St Se East Wenatchee (98802) ***(G-3013)***
Fiber-Tech Industries, Spokane Valley *Also called Fiberglass Technology Inds Inc* ***(G-12701)***
Fiberdyne Aerospace.....206 326-8581
1222 S Angelo St Ste A Seattle (98108) ***(G-9987)***
Fiberglass Marine Products, Shelton *Also called Richard Knannlein* ***(G-11726)***
Fiberglass Technology Inds Inc (HQ).....509 928-8880
3808 N Sullivan Rd 29c Spokane Valley (99216) ***(G-12701)***
Fibrearts Inc.....425 432-1454
19709 Maxwell Rd Se Maple Valley (98038) ***(G-6269)***
Fibres Internation Recycling, Everett *Also called Fibres International Inc* ***(G-3471)***
Fibres International Inc.....425 455-9811
2600 94th St Sw Ste 100 Everett (98204) ***(G-3471)***
Fibres International Inc.....425 455-9811
2600 94th St Sw 100 Everett (98204) ***(G-3472)***
Fibro Corporation.....253 503-3568
3101 South Tacoma Way Tacoma (98409) ***(G-13294)***
Fidalgo Bay Coffee Inc (PA).....360 757-8818
856 N Hill Blvd Burlington (98233) ***(G-2158)***
Fidalgo Bay Roasting, Burlington *Also called Fidalgo Bay Coffee Inc* ***(G-2158)***
Fiddle and Fern.....206 898-4165
3010 278th Ct Se Sammamish (98075) ***(G-9206)***
Fidelitad Inc.....509 637-3938
801 Panorama Ct White Salmon (98672) ***(G-15115)***
Fidelitas.....509 521-1553
318 Wellhouse Loop Richland (99352) ***(G-8996)***
Fidelitas Wines LLC.....509 588-3469
51810 N Sunset Rd Benton City (99320) ***(G-1611)***

ALPHABETIC SECTION

Fka Interpoint, Redmond

Fido N-Scratch 206 588-2111
   5012 41st Ave Sw Seattle (98136) *(G-9988)*
Field Roast Grain Meat Co Spc 800 311-9797
   3901 7th Ave S Seattle (98108) *(G-9989)*
Fields Company LLC (PA) 253 627-4098
   2240 Taylor Way Tacoma (98421) *(G-13295)*
Fields Fabrication Corporation 425 222-5905
   11138 Upper Preston Rd Se Issaquah (98027) *(G-4413)*
Fifes Vehicle Vessel 253 926-8227
   4905 Pacific Hwy E Ste 2a Fife (98424) *(G-3952)*
Fifth Star Labs LLC 206 369-3956
   626 Randolph Pl Seattle (98122) *(G-9990)*
Fifty Fifty Print 360 936-9516
   1101 W 34th Way Vancouver (98660) *(G-14228)*
Fifty Fifty Print Co 360 718-2448
   3714 Main St Vancouver (98663) *(G-14229)*
Figgins Family Wine Estates 509 525-1428
   1875 Foothills Ln Walla Walla (99362) *(G-14804)*
Figurehead Brewing Company LLC 206 492-7981
   1710 Nw 61st St Seattle (98107) *(G-9991)*
File-EZ Folder Inc 509 534-1044
   4111 E Mission Ave Spokane (99202) *(G-12256)*
Fileonq Inc 206 575-3488
   832 Industry Dr Tukwila (98188) *(G-13734)*
Filla Company LLC 360 864-2531
   496 Schmit Rd Toledo (98591) *(G-13638)*
Filliols Custom Cab Doors Inc 509 453-8098
   1606 S 36th Ave Yakima (98902) *(G-15570)*
Film To Dvd, Spokane Valley Also called Tobin Cinema Systems Inc *(G-12908)*
Filmateria Studios Inc 206 938-6791
   3440 California Ave Sw Seattle (98116) *(G-9992)*
Filson Manufacturing Inc 206 805-3730
   18923 16th Ave S Seatac (98188) *(G-9284)*
Filson Manufacturing Inc 206 242-9579
   1741 1st Ave S Seattle (98134) *(G-9993)*
Filter Clean Recycling LLC 360 798-1012
   3311 Ne 101st Ct Vancouver (98662) *(G-14230)*
Filter Corp, The, Kirkland Also called Clarification Techology Inc *(G-5307)*
Filtrific Co LLC 425 482-6777
   13280 Ne Spring Blvd # 101 Bellevue (98005) *(G-910)*
Filtrona Extrusion Tacoma, Fife Also called Porex Technologies Corporation *(G-3982)*
Final State Press LLC 253 237-2474
   1913 S 262nd Pl Ste 101 Des Moines (98198) *(G-2935)*
Financial Management Systems 425 881-8687
   1420 Nw Gilman Blvd # 2729 Issaquah (98027) *(G-4414)*
Finas Salsa 360 951-5218
   3509 Autumnwood Ct Se Olympia (98501) *(G-7283)*
Finco Corp 360 854-0772
   1310 Heather Ln Sedro Woolley (98284) *(G-11538)*
Find It Games, Snohomish Also called LB Games Inc *(G-11937)*
Fine Arts Litho 360 876-5649
   1014 Bay St Ste 6 Port Orchard (98366) *(G-7809)*
Fine Design Inc 425 271-2866
   16550 W Valley Hwy Tukwila (98188) *(G-13735)*
Fine Edge 360 299-8500
   14004 Biz Point Ln Anacortes (98221) *(G-130)*
Fine Print WA LLC 206 859-8469
   21910 65th Avenue Ct E Spanaway (98387) *(G-12057)*
Fine Woodworking 425 486-3305
   5817 238th St Se Ste 2 Woodinville (98072) *(G-15242)*
Finely Finished LLC 360 709-0602
   3534 49th Ave Sw Olympia (98512) *(G-7284)*
Finest Accessories Inc 425 831-7001
   30545 Se 84th St Rm 5 Preston (98050) *(G-8025)*
Finger Prints of His Grace 253 514-6150
   13621 11th Ave Nw Gig Harbor (98332) *(G-4099)*
Finish Line Powder Coating, Yakima Also called ASap Metal Fabricators Inc *(G-15515)*
Finish Line Product Coating, Yakima Also called ASap Metal Fabricators Inc *(G-15516)*
Finishing Specialist LLC 509 248-5510
   1907 S 14th St Union Gap (98903) *(G-13930)*
Finishing Touch 360 391-2108
   1498 Arrowhead Rd Camano Island (98282) *(G-2212)*
Finishing Touches 425 277-6079
   17832 W Lake Desire Dr Se Renton (98058) *(G-8799)*
Finishing Unlimited Inc 425 881-7300
   9165 151st Ave Ne Redmond (98052) *(G-8461)*
Finnegan Frost 509 572-2477
   2150 Keene Rd Richland (99352) *(G-8997)*
Fir Lane Funeral Home & Mem Pk, Spanaway Also called Fir Lane Memorial Pk & Fnrl HM *(G-12058)*
Fir Lane Memorial Pk & Fnrl HM 253 531-6600
   924 176th St E Spanaway (98387) *(G-12058)*
Fir Line Trans & Brake 509 684-5484
   374 Gold Creek Loop Rd Colville (99114) *(G-2752)*
Fir Tree Press, Vashon Also called Celesticomp Inc *(G-14717)*
Fircrest Pre-Fit Door Co Inc 253 564-6921
   3024 S Mullen St Ste A Tacoma (98409) *(G-13296)*
Fire Def Tech Safety Pdts Inc 509 619-0261
   1588 Sagewood St Richland (99352) *(G-8998)*
Fire Lion Global LLC 360 901-9828
   3009 Ne 145th St Vancouver (98686) *(G-14231)*
Fire Protection Inc 206 440-5763
   12045 31st Ave Ne Seattle (98125) *(G-9994)*
Fire Solutions NW LLC 855 876-3473
   1100 Wheaton Way Ste B Bremerton (98310) *(G-1954)*
Firecracker Software LLC 509 443-5308
   17901 E 8th Ave Spokane Valley (99016) *(G-12702)*
Firehouse Custom Cabinets 253 864-4894
   12603 146th St E Puyallup (98374) *(G-8153)*
Firepak Oil and Gas Inds LLC 360 679-1747
   164 Nw Jib St Oak Harbor (98277) *(G-7152)*
Fireside Hearth & Home Inc (PA) 425 251-9447
   21402 84th Ave S Kent (98032) *(G-4907)*
Firesite, Heart & Home, Bonney Lake Also called Aqua Rec Inc *(G-1716)*
Firesteed Cellars, Issaquah Also called Firesteed Corporation *(G-4415)*
Firesteed Corporation (PA) 503 623-8683
   375 1st Pl Nw Issaquah (98027) *(G-4415)*
Firestone Pacific Foods Inc 360 695-9484
   4211 Fruit Valley Rd Vancouver (98660) *(G-14232)*
First Boat Company 425 931-9433
   615 80th St Sw Everett (98203) *(G-3473)*
First Cabin Yachts Inc 206 595-6657
   3221 W Elmore St Seattle (98199) *(G-9995)*
First Choice Market Inc 360 253-9149
   16105 Ne 182nd Ave Brush Prairie (98606) *(G-2035)*
First Choice Marketing Inc 206 306-1100
   10355 Sand Point Way Ne Seattle (98125) *(G-9996)*
First Impressions Co Inc 206 372-0361
   25818 117th Pl Se Kent (98030) *(G-4908)*
First Imprssions Creative Prtg 509 483-6822
   1716 E Holyoke Ave Ste D Spokane (99217) *(G-12257)*
First Index Inc 888 535-8583
   12610 E Mirabeau Pkwy Spokane Valley (99216) *(G-12703)*
First Metal and Supply, Renton Also called First Metals Inc *(G-8800)*
First Metals Inc 303 915-2426
   430 Olympia Ave Ne Renton (98056) *(G-8800)*
First Millennium Bank 360 797-5108
   64 Johnson Creek Rd Sequim (98382) *(G-11634)*
First Silicon Designs LLC 303 883-6891
   605 Main St Vancouver (98660) *(G-14233)*
First Strike LLC 360 285-4000
   924 Capitol Way S Ste 105 Olympia (98501) *(G-7285)*
Fish & Fly Investors (PA) 509 865-3340
   101 E 2nd Ave Toppenish (98948) *(G-13668)*
Fish Brewing Co (HQ) 360 943-3650
   515 Jefferson St Se Olympia (98501) *(G-7286)*
Fish Tale Ales, Olympia Also called Fish Brewing Co *(G-7286)*
Fish Transport Systems LLC 206 801-3565
   2001 W Grfeld St Bldg 156 Seattle (98119) *(G-9997)*
Fisher Brdcstg - Wash TV LLC 509 575-0029
   2801 Terrace Heights Dr Yakima (98901) *(G-15571)*
Fisher Publications Inc 206 923-2000
   8803 42nd Ave Sw Seattle (98136) *(G-9998)*
Fisher-Rosemount Systems Inc 425 488-4111
   1916 220th St Se Ste 101 Bothell (98021) *(G-1853)*
Fishermens News Inc 206 282-7545
   2201 W Commodore Way Seattle (98199) *(G-9999)*
Fishers Choice Wild Salmon 360 671-6478
   1081 Sudden Vly Bellingham (98229) *(G-1346)*
Fishing Vessel Owners Mar Way (PA) 206 282-6421
   1511 W Thurman St Seattle (98119) *(G-10000)*
Fishing Vessel St Jude LLC 425 378-0680
   11628 Se 48th St Bellevue (98006) *(G-911)*
Fishtail Pub 360 943-3650
   515 Jefferson St Se Olympia (98501) *(G-7287)*
Fishtrap Creek Lighting LLC 360 354-7900
   307 19th St Lynden (98264) *(G-6018)*
Fithian Wldg & Fabrication LLC 206 658-3732
   21407 179th Pl Se Monroe (98272) *(G-6573)*
Fittersweet, Seattle Also called Ericka J Thielke *(G-9937)*
Fittings, Seattle Also called Bridgestone Hosepower LLC *(G-9585)*
Fitts Industries Inc 253 474-0376
   5640 S Durango St Ste B Tacoma (98409) *(G-13297)*
Fitz Custom Marine 253 732-5669
   163 Maple Ln Nw Gig Harbor (98335) *(G-4100)*
Five Food Inc 509 855-6914
   2801 W Broadway Ave Moses Lake (98837) *(G-6708)*
Five Star Cellars Inc 509 527-8400
   840 C St Walla Walla (99362) *(G-14805)*
Five Star Industries LLC 206 706-2754
   2440 W Commodore Way # 201 Seattle (98199) *(G-10001)*
Five Star Rv, Everett Also called KMD Invested LLC *(G-3531)*
Five Tool Food Service LLC 253 761-5621
   2502 S Tyler St Tacoma (98405) *(G-13298)*
Fives N Amercn Combustn Inc 360 659-7432
   6912 77th Ave Ne Marysville (98270) *(G-6334)*
Fix Brothers Inc 206 246-5127
   1332 Sw 113th St Seattle (98146) *(G-10002)*
Fixture Engineering Inc 360 671-9052
   1600 Kentucky St A5 Bellingham (98229) *(G-1347)*
Fizikl Inc 360 393-0714
   114 Park Pl Bellingham (98226) *(G-1348)*
Fka Interpoint, Redmond Also called Crane Electronics Inc *(G-8429)*

(PA)=Parent Co (HQ)=Headquarters (DH)=Div Headquarters

Fkc Co Ltd...360 452-9472
2708 W 18th St Port Angeles (98363) *(G-7706)*
Flagship Custom Publishing LLC...310 245-9550
1416 Nw 46th St Seattle (98107) *(G-10003)*
Flagstone...425 892-9134
18123 34th Dr Se Bothell (98012) *(G-1854)*
Flagstone Wildlife Artisrty...360 967-2005
169 Flagstone Dr Silverlake (98645) *(G-11863)*
Flake Printing...425 210-6371
4729 View Dr Everett (98203) *(G-3474)*
Flamespray Northwest Inc...206 508-6779
250 S Chicago St Seattle (98108) *(G-10004)*
Flanagan Woodworks Inc...360 221-3352
5180 Nighthawk Rd Langley (98260) *(G-5777)*
Flannery Comerford Inc...509 242-5000
3009 S Mount Vernon St # 4 Spokane (99223) *(G-12258)*
Flannery Publications LLC...360 942-0060
168 Stauffer Rd Raymond (98577) *(G-8349)*
Flashco Manufacturing Inc...360 225-4662
1383 Down River Dr Woodland (98674) *(G-15432)*
Flatter Heights...509 238-6192
30009 N Elk Chattaroy Rd Chattaroy (99003) *(G-2446)*
Flax 4 Life...360 715-1944
468 W Horton Rd Bellingham (98226) *(G-1349)*
Fleet Feet Sports...509 309-2174
13910 E Indiana Ave Spokane Valley (99216) *(G-12704)*
Fleet Sheets, Ridgefield *Also called Thirteen Sheets LLC (G-9115)*
Fletcher Bay Winery...206 780-9463
8765 Battle Point Dr Ne Bainbridge Island (98110) *(G-634)*
Fletcher Boats Inc...360 452-8430
292 Wellman Rd Port Angeles (98363) *(G-7707)*
Fletcher Diving, Sekiu *Also called Al Fletcher (G-11582)*
Flex Fuel...360 520-9773
79 Sw 10th St Chehalis (98532) *(G-2497)*
Flex-A-Lite Consolidated, Fife *Also called CFM Consolidated Inc (G-3942)*
Flexabili-Tees...360 260-3163
10015 Ne 152nd Ave Vancouver (98682) *(G-14234)*
Flexe Inc...855 733-7788
83 S King St Ste 600 Seattle (98104) *(G-10005)*
Flexible Containment Pdts Inc...509 624-8921
6811 E Mission Ave Spokane Valley (99212) *(G-12705)*
Flight Structures, Everett *Also called B/E Aerospace Inc (G-3380)*
Flight Structures Inc...360 651-8537
11404 Commando Rd W Ste C Everett (98204) *(G-3475)*
Flightways Corporation...425 747-6903
5827 167th Ave Se Bellevue (98006) *(G-912)*
Flint Publishing Inc...509 314-6400
16 W 1st Ave Toppenish (98948) *(G-13669)*
Flip Signs...509 965-2822
7610 Scenic Dr Yakima (98908) *(G-15572)*
Flitelite, Bellingham *Also called Momentum Interactive LLC (G-1440)*
Float Technologies LLC...916 947-6646
790 6th St S Ste 100 Kirkland (98033) *(G-5339)*
Flodin Inc...509 766-2996
13624 N Frontage Rd E Moses Lake (98837) *(G-6709)*
Flood & Associates Inc...253 531-7305
11010 Pacific Ave S Tacoma (98444) *(G-13299)*
Flora Inc...360 354-2110
805 E Badger Rd Lynden (98264) *(G-6019)*
Florek Logging Ltd Inc...360 795-8058
911 Elochoman Valley Rd Cathlamet (98612) *(G-2367)*
Florence L Ellis...360 213-2475
7017 Ne Highway 99 # 106 Vancouver (98665) *(G-14235)*
Florian Design...425 742-7212
16212 Bothell Everett Hwy Mill Creek (98012) *(G-6511)*
Florida Tile Inc...206 767-9819
1012 Sw 41st St Renton (98057) *(G-8801)*
Florida Tile 73, Renton *Also called Florida Tile Inc (G-8801)*
Flory Cabinets LLC...360 894-2504
14846 Vail Rd Se Yelm (98597) *(G-15733)*
Flotbunker LLC...206 354-5205
13750 Ne 34th Pl Bellevue (98005) *(G-913)*
Flourish Church Rainier Valley...206 769-7950
5231 39th Ave S Apt 212 Seattle (98118) *(G-10006)*
Flourish Skin & Laser LLC (PA)...360 636-1411
625 9th Ave Ste 230 Longview (98632) *(G-5911)*
Flow Control Industries Inc...425 483-1297
18715 141st Ave Ne Woodinville (98072) *(G-15243)*
Flow International Corporation (HQ)...253 850-3500
23500 64th Ave S Kent (98032) *(G-4909)*
Flow International Corporation...812 590-4922
22165 68th Ave S Kent (98032) *(G-4910)*
Flow International Corporation...253 850-3501
23430 64th Ave S Kent (98032) *(G-4911)*
Flow Robotic Systems, Kent *Also called Flow International Corporation (G-4911)*
Flower Racing...360 793-2196
14110 339th Ave Se Sultan (98294) *(G-13025)*
Flowers Bkg Co Thomasville Inc...253 433-4455
7817 S 210th St Kent (98032) *(G-4912)*
Flowplay Inc...206 903-0457
1008 Western Ave Ste 300 Seattle (98104) *(G-10007)*
Flowserve Corporation...360 573-5211
7075 S 5th St Ridgefield (98642) *(G-9082)*
Flowserve Corporation...360 676-0702
1305 Fraser St Ste 108 Bellingham (98229) *(G-1350)*
Flsmidth Inc...509 434-8605
3311 E Ferry Ave Spokane (99202) *(G-12259)*
Fluentpro Software Corporation...855 358-3688
8201 164th Ave Ne Ste 200 Redmond (98052) *(G-8462)*
Fluid Controls and Components (PA)...253 922-3226
5909 12th St E Fife (98424) *(G-3953)*
Fluid Motion LLC...253 839-5213
25802 Pacific Hwy S Kent (98032) *(G-4913)*
Fluid Power Service Inc...360 496-6888
102 Crumb Rd 33 Morton (98356) *(G-6669)*
Fluid Process Engineering LLC...425 868-0899
22931 Ne 27th Pl Sammamish (98074) *(G-9207)*
Fluke Corporation...425 446-5600
9025 Evergreen Way Everett (98204) *(G-3476)*
Fluke Corporation...888 993-5853
1420 75th St Sw Everett (98203) *(G-3477)*
Fluke Electronics Corporation (HQ)...425 347-6100
6920 Seaway Blvd Everett (98203) *(G-3478)*
Fluke Electronics Corporation...425 446-5610
6920 Seaway Blvd Everett (98203) *(G-3479)*
Fluke Electronics Corporation...425 446-5858
9028 Evergreen Way Everett (98204) *(G-3480)*
Fluke Electronics Corporation...888 993-5853
1420 75th St Sw Everett (98203) *(G-3481)*
Fluke Metal Products Inc...425 485-9666
10223 Woodinville Dr Bothell (98011) *(G-1764)*
Fluke Networks, Everett *Also called Fluke Electronics Corporation (G-3479)*
Fluke Networks, Everett *Also called Fluke Electronics Corporation (G-3480)*
Fluke Networks, Everett *Also called Fluke Electronics Corporation (G-3481)*
Fluke Service Center, Everett *Also called Fluke Corporation (G-3477)*
Fluteworks...206 729-1903
1029 Ne 69th St Seattle (98115) *(G-10008)*
Flux Drive Inc...253 826-9002
23412 68th Ave S Kent (98032) *(G-4914)*
Fly By Night Express Frei...360 420-0844
1910 Forest Dr Mount Vernon (98273) *(G-6797)*
Fly By Night Welding Service, Sedro Woolley *Also called Bisson & Associates Inc (G-11532)*
Fly Girls Aero Covers...509 466-7794
8812 N Prescott Rd Spokane (99208) *(G-12260)*
Flying Arts Ranch Inc...509 659-1819
106 N Washington St Ritzville (99169) *(G-9121)*
Flying Cow Creamery LLC...360 273-1045
209 Hyppa Rd E Rochester (98579) *(G-9132)*
Flying Dog Entertainment LLC...206 372-5553
13911 121st Ave Ne Kirkland (98034) *(G-5340)*
Flying Lab Software LLC...206 272-9815
1905 Queen Anne Ave N # 300 Seattle (98109) *(G-10009)*
Flying Sofa LLC...206 275-3935
6040 86th Ave Se Mercer Island (98040) *(G-6463)*
Flying Trout Press...360 647-5740
3712 Lahti Ct Bellingham (98226) *(G-1351)*
Flying Trout Wines LLC...509 520-7701
1606 Evergreen St Walla Walla (99362) *(G-14806)*
Flying Wrench Services, Kingston *Also called Flying Wrench Svc (G-5251)*
Flying Wrench Svc...360 638-0044
31516 Commercial Ave Ne Kingston (98346) *(G-5251)*
Flyingviolin Inc...209 595-9709
8648 Fenwick Loop Se Olympia (98513) *(G-7288)*
Flytes of Fancy...206 306-9233
16003 Meridian Ave N Shoreline (98133) *(G-11772)*
FMI, Spokane Valley *Also called Freeze Furniture and Mfg Co (G-12710)*
Fmj Storage Inc...206 605-1394
22601 Ne 166th St Woodinville (98077) *(G-15244)*
FO Berg Company...509 624-8921
6811 E Mission Ave Spokane Valley (99212) *(G-12706)*
Foam Graphics, Lakewood *Also called Larsen Sign Company (G-5736)*
Foamex, Kent *Also called Fxi Inc (G-4919)*
FOBES DIST WATER ASSN, Snohomish *Also called Fobes District Water & Assn (G-11910)*
Fobes District Water & Assn...425 334-3311
4520 Bickford Ave Snohomish (98290) *(G-11910)*
Focal Point Plastics Inc...206 282-0433
3925 Grant St Washougal (98671) *(G-14956)*
Focus Designs Inc...360 329-2537
4032 Se 199th Ave Camas (98607) *(G-2251)*
Focus Group Inc...206 281-1977
2201 Sw 152nd St Ste 3 Burien (98166) *(G-2108)*
Focusbloom LLC...360 894-2362
21526 Hobson Rd Se Yelm (98597) *(G-15734)*
Fog Tite Meter Seal Inc...206 935-8000
4819 W Marginal Way Sw Seattle (98106) *(G-10010)*
Fog Tite Meter Seal Co, Seattle *Also called Fog Tite Meter Seal Inc (G-10010)*
Foggy Noggin Brewing...425 486-1070
22329 53rd Ave Se Bothell (98021) *(G-1855)*
Foil Graphics...360 574-9030
10511 Ne 45th Ave Vancouver (98686) *(G-14236)*
Foldcraft Co...253 437-1355
8311 S 200th St Kent (98032) *(G-4915)*

Foldz Wallet LLC.......206 730-6381
111 Sunset Ave N Ste 104 Edmonds (98020) ***(G-3112)***
Foley Sign Company Inc.......206 324-3040
572 Mercer St Seattle (98109) ***(G-10011)***
Followone Inc.......206 518-8844
8512 122nd Ave Ne Ste 300 Kirkland (98033) ***(G-5341)***
Followone.com, Kirkland *Also called Followone Inc* ***(G-5341)***
Folsom Industries Inc.......509 921-6602
4015 S Conklin Rd Greenacres (99016) ***(G-4298)***
Folsom Manufacturing, Greenacres *Also called Folsom Industries Inc* ***(G-4298)***
Fontanelle, Spokane *Also called Ammonite Ink* ***(G-12113)***
Food Decorating Division, Tacoma *Also called Lucks Company* ***(G-13391)***
Food Equipment International.......509 924-0181
14404 E 20th Ct Spokane Valley (99037) ***(G-12707)***
Food For Tots Publishing, Mercer Island *Also called Mammoth Media Inc* ***(G-6472)***
Food Group, Othello *Also called JR Simplot Company* ***(G-7499)***
Food Master (pnw) Corp (PA).......253 846-2600
18420 50th Ave E Tacoma (98446) ***(G-13300)***
Food Service Eqp Repr Inc.......206 730-2662
20126 Ballinger Way Ne Shoreline (98155) ***(G-11773)***
Foof LLC.......425 260-8897
131 Spirea Ct Cle Elum (98922) ***(G-2666)***
Fools Prairie Vineyards LLC.......509 319-0752
3828 S Skyview Dr Spokane (99203) ***(G-12261)***
Footeprints Incorporated.......360 754-8779
1025 Black Lake Blvd Sw Olympia (98502) ***(G-7289)***
Footeprints Inc.......360 491-8195
4404 Martin Way E Ste 2 Olympia (98516) ***(G-7290)***
Footprint Promotions Inc (PA).......425 408-0966
23128 State Route 9 Se Woodinville (98072) ***(G-15245)***
For Art Sake Inc.......253 858-8087
3155 Harborview Dr Gig Harbor (98335) ***(G-4101)***
For The Love of Spice.......253 858-0272
3104 Harborview Dr Gig Harbor (98335) ***(G-4102)***
For-D Inc.......425 486-1120
15503 Ne 188th Pl Woodinville (98072) ***(G-15246)***
Force Majeure Winery.......425 892-9848
18720 142nd Ave Ne Woodinville (98072) ***(G-15247)***
Ford Motor Credit Company LLC.......425 643-0454
13555 Se 36th St Ste 350 Bellevue (98006) ***(G-914)***
Foremost Printing.......206 861-6576
21411 100th Ave Se Kent (98031) ***(G-4916)***
Forest Concepts LLC.......253 333-9663
3320 W Valley Hwy N # 110 Auburn (98001) ***(G-441)***
Forest Land Services Inc.......360 652-9044
26700 Pioneer Hwy Stanwood (98292) ***(G-12971)***
Forest Publications Inc.......360 609-4400
1430 Nw Whitman St Camas (98607) ***(G-2252)***
Forest View Inc.......360 909-9890
607 Ne 224th Cir Ridgefield (98642) ***(G-9083)***
Forever Green Sprinklers.......509 796-2676
20727 N Calhoun Ln Nine Mile Falls (99026) ***(G-7075)***
Forever Powder Coating LLC.......360 786-6345
715 78th Ave Sw Ste 1 Tumwater (98501) ***(G-13872)***
Forfjord Supply Co.......206 784-8171
9015 Dibble Ave Nw Seattle (98117) ***(G-10012)***
Forge Jackpot, Tacoma *Also called Pt Defiance Food Mart* ***(G-13481)***
Forged Chaos LLC.......360 630-1947
18530 Hawksview Dr Arlington (98223) ***(G-237)***
Forged From Cardboard.......425 399-0715
13810 Cascadian Way Everett (98208) ***(G-3482)***
Forger3d LLC.......425 440-0662
821 Dayton Ave Ne Renton (98056) ***(G-8802)***
Forgeron Cellars.......425 908-7683
14344 Woodinville Redmond Redmond (98052) ***(G-8463)***
Forgeron Cellars LLC.......509 522-9463
33 W Birch St Walla Walla (99362) ***(G-14807)***
Forklift Training Center Inc -.......360 515-0696
8830 Tallon Ln Ne Lacey (98516) ***(G-5550)***
Forks Forum-Peninsula Herald, Forks *Also called Olympic View Publishing LLC* ***(G-4014)***
Form Lighting and Controls LLC.......206 854-8689
1601 5th Ave Seattle (98101) ***(G-10013)***
Formal Wear Inc.......425 776-1088
19231 36th Ave W Ste P Lynnwood (98036) ***(G-6120)***
Formost Fuji Corporation (PA).......425 483-9090
19211 144th Ave Ne Woodinville (98072) ***(G-15248)***
Formula Corp.......253 880-0170
4432 C St Ne Auburn (98002) ***(G-442)***
Formula Web LLC.......425 835-3259
6745 161st Ave Se Unit B Bellevue (98006) ***(G-915)***
Forrest Paint Co.......509 924-3785
3808 N Sullivan Rd N17 Spokane Valley (99216) ***(G-12708)***
Forrest Paint Co.......253 854-6372
1741 Central Ave S Kent (98032) ***(G-4917)***
Forrest Sound Products LLC.......425 881-1111
15115 Ne 90th St 4a Redmond (98052) ***(G-8464)***
Forrest Tech Ctngs Div of Forr, Spokane Valley *Also called Forrest Paint Co* ***(G-12708)***
Forsyth Enterprises.......360 297-2684
25770 Miller Bay Rd Ne Kingston (98346) ***(G-5252)***
Fort Vancouver Bee LLC.......360 274-3396
3966 Spirit Lake Hwy Silverlake (98645) ***(G-11864)***
Fort Walla Walla Cellars LLC.......509 520-1095
1383 Barleen Dr Walla Walla (99362) ***(G-14808)***
Forterra Inc.......360 943-1600
1414 Cherry St Se Olympia (98501) ***(G-7291)***
Fortis Manufacturing Inc.......253 277-3211
6823 S 220th St Kent (98032) ***(G-4918)***
Fortive Corporation (PA).......425 446-5000
6920 Seaway Blvd Everett (98203) ***(G-3483)***
Fortun Foods Inc.......425 827-1977
6513 132nd Ave Ne Ste 394 Kirkland (98033) ***(G-5342)***
Fortuns Finshg Sauces & Soups, Kirkland *Also called Fortun Foods Inc* ***(G-5342)***
Fortynine Industries.......253 632-3081
24712 197th Ave Se Maple Valley (98038) ***(G-6270)***
Forword Input Inc.......206 227-0191
20615 36th Pl W Lynnwood (98036) ***(G-6121)***
Foss Furniture, Seattle *Also called Furniture By Foss* ***(G-10040)***
Foss Marine Holdings Inc.......206 381-5800
450 Alaskan Way S Ste 706 Seattle (98104) ***(G-10014)***
Foss Maritime Company Llc (HQ).......206 281-3800
450 Alaskan Way S Ste 706 Seattle (98104) ***(G-10015)***
Foss Stump Grinding.......360 799-2100
16023 419th Ave Se Gold Bar (98251) ***(G-4187)***
Fossil Group Inc.......206 248-6984
846 Southcenter Mall Tukwila (98188) ***(G-13736)***
Fostco Inc.......509 725-3765
705 Marshall St Davenport (99122) ***(G-2870)***
Foster Family Farm.......509 543-9330
11006 W Court St Pasco (99301) ***(G-7582)***
Foster Poultry Farms.......360 425-8957
1700 S 13th Ave Kelso (98626) ***(G-4526)***
Foster Press.......425 334-9317
430 91st Ave Ne Ste 3 Everett (98205) ***(G-3484)***
Foster Surveying Inc.......503 997-1100
3517 Se 198th Ave Camas (98607) ***(G-2253)***
Fouad Farhat.......206 628-0404
720 Olive Way Ste 810 Seattle (98101) ***(G-10016)***
Foundation International.......425 391-1281
15786 Ne 25th Pl Bellevue (98008) ***(G-916)***
Foundry, Arlington *Also called Mackenzie Spcalty Castings Inc* ***(G-271)***
Foundry Vineyards LLC.......509 529-0736
1111 Abadie St Walla Walla (99362) ***(G-14809)***
Fountaine Estates Winery.......509 972-8123
151 Rowe Hill Dr Naches (98937) ***(G-6996)***
Four Barr Industries.......360 659-8182
4124 134th St Ne Marysville (98271) ***(G-6335)***
Four Generals Brewing.......425 282-4360
229 Wells Ave S Renton (98057) ***(G-8803)***
Four Seasons Gourmet Food Proc.......847 636-9879
10325 Aurora Ave N Seattle (98133) ***(G-10017)***
Four U Printers Inc.......360 671-2032
1704 N State St Bellingham (98225) ***(G-1352)***
Four-H Machine LLC.......425 471-5757
9056 N Texas Rd Anacortes (98221) ***(G-131)***
Fourplay Awd.......971 706-7646
13806 Ne 49th St Vncouver Vancouver Vancouver (98682) ***(G-14237)***
Fourth Corner Wtr Filters LLC.......360 296-1647
4382 Lateener Ln Blaine (98230) ***(G-1670)***
Foust Fabrication Co.......509 684-3754
1159 Orin Rice Rd Colville (99114) ***(G-2753)***
Fownes Brothers & Co Inc.......360 738-3126
100 Pine St Ste 202 Bellingham (98225) ***(G-1353)***
Fox Architectural Signs Inc.......503 512-8757
1800 Nw Lyons Rd Woodland (98674) ***(G-15433)***
Fox Bay Industries Inc.......253 941-9155
4150 B Pl Nw Ste 101 Auburn (98001) ***(G-443)***
Fox Coatings.......360 574-7471
411 Ne 112th Cir Vancouver (98685) ***(G-14238)***
Fox Island Excavation LLC.......253 677-7291
1101 Island Blvd Fox Island (98333) ***(G-4020)***
Fox Island Woodworks.......253 549-7019
1323 Mowitsh Dr Fox Island (98333) ***(G-4021)***
Fox Printing.......206 595-7055
5705 156th St Sw Edmonds (98026) ***(G-3113)***
Foxbat Heavy Industries Inc.......425 890-0410
886 55th St Port Townsend (98368) ***(G-7885)***
Foxfacerabbitfish LLC.......206 856-7222
1403 S Hanford St Seattle (98144) ***(G-10018)***
Fps Manufacturing LLC.......509 248-0423
1102 N 16th Ave Yakima (98902) ***(G-15573)***
Fps West Inc.......206 242-4888
17020 Sylvester Rd Sw Normandy Park (98166) ***(G-7092)***
Fractal Filters LLC.......206 854-0968
1126 Sw 168th St Normandy Park (98166) ***(G-7093)***
Framatome Inc.......425 250-2775
10865 Willows Rd Ne Redmond (98052) ***(G-8465)***
Frame It Ltd.......206 364-7477
539 Ne Northgate Way F Seattle (98125) ***(G-10019)***
Fran Hunter.......253 876-0434
15384 Glenwood Rd Sw Port Orchard (98367) ***(G-7810)***
France Special Tools, Ridgefield *Also called Daniel E France* ***(G-9078)***
Francis & Wall Shell.......509 467-5493
618 W Francis Ave Spokane (99205) ***(G-12262)***

ALPHABETIC

Francis Scientific Inc 360 687-7019
  22906 Ne 152nd Ave Battle Ground (98604) (G-702)
Francisco Gomez Vineyard Svcs 559 567-7013
  712 W Park St Pasco (99301) (G-7583)
Frank Harkness Trckg & Log LLC (PA) 360 826-6087
  5226 Turkington Rd Acme (98220) (G-42)
Frank Harkness Trckg & Log LLC 360 595-2496
  39394 State Route 20 Concrete (98237) (G-2785)
Frank J Madera 253 858-7934
  2606 120th Street Ct Nw Gig Harbor (98332) (G-4103)
Frank J Martin Company 206 523-7665
  18424 Highway 99 Lynnwood (98037) (G-6122)
Frank Lau Jewelry Inc 206 323-6343
  1010 E Miller St Seattle (98102) (G-10020)
Frank Swiger Trucking Inc 509 258-7226
  5243 Ford Wellpinit Rd Ford (99013) (G-4005)
Frank's Boots, Spokane Also called Amgb Inc (G-12112)
Frankenstein Incorporated 206 915-1011
  2563 24th Ave W Seattle (98199) (G-10021)
Franklin and Franklin Company 360 254-4767
  13003 Ne 25th St Vancouver (98684) (G-14239)
Franklin County Graphic 509 234-3181
  346 S Columbia St Connell (99326) (G-2794)
Franklin Machinery 360 581-5079
  212 Fairway Dr Aberdeen (98520) (G-11)
Franks Custom Coatings LLC 253 973-4361
  9105 118th St E Puyallup (98373) (G-8154)
Franks Custom Wheels 360 333-6887
  1221 Riverside Dr Mount Vernon (98273) (G-6798)
Frans Chocolates Ltd (PA) 206 322-0233
  5900 Airport Way S Seattle (98108) (G-10022)
Frantz Art Glass Gallery, Shelton Also called Frantz Glass Gallery (G-11697)
Frantz Bead Company, Shelton Also called Mike Frantz Inc (G-11713)
Frantz Glass Gallery 360 426-6712
  130 W Corporate Rd Shelton (98584) (G-11697)
Franz Bakery, Colville Also called United States Bakery (G-2778)
Frascold USA Corporation 855 547-5600
  5901 23rd Dr W Ste 101 Everett (98203) (G-3485)
Frasers Bronze Foundry Inc 877 264-1064
  5625 48th Dr Ne Apt D Marysville (98270) (G-6336)
Frazier Industrial Company 509 698-4100
  420 Reitmeier Ln Selah (98942) (G-11588)
Freakn Genius Inc 425 301-4258
  14152 77th Ave Ne Kirkland (98034) (G-5343)
Fred A Widman 509 863-9320
  6704 S Tomaker Ln Spokane (99223) (G-12263)
Fred B Moe Logging Co 360 273-6049
  110 Elma Gate Rd E Oakville (98568) (G-7174)
Fred Hill Materials 360 779-4431
  1369 Cays Rd Sequim (98382) (G-11635)
Fred J Kimball Machine Shop 509 529-5339
  2902 Lower Waitsburg Rd Walla Walla (99362) (G-14810)
Fred Misner 425 398-7184
  22410 35th Ave Se Bothell (98021) (G-1856)
Fred Nanamkin 509 634-8110
  11960 S Highway 21 Keller (99140) (G-4512)
Fred Tebb & Sons Inc 253 272-4107
  1906 E Marc St Tacoma (98421) (G-13301)
Freda Britt Prints 206 409-4701
  16245 Westside Hwy Sw Vashon (98070) (G-14722)
Fredericks Appliance Centers 425 885-0000
  7509 159th Pl Ne Redmond (98052) (G-8466)
Fredricksons Furn & Cabinets 206 782-5310
  8307 22nd Ave Nw Seattle (98117) (G-10023)
Free Birthday Fun LLC 509 999-7517
  10 N Post St Ste 214 Spokane (99201) (G-12264)
Freedom Adaptive Systems LLC 425 286-9597
  21021 49th Ave Se Bothell (98021) (G-1857)
Freedom Metal, Bonney Lake Also called BTS Partners LLC (G-1718)
Freedom Snacks LLC 253 886-1838
  19803 1st Ave S Ste 103 Normandy Park (98148) (G-7094)
Freedom Truck Centers Inc 509 248-9478
  1910 Rudkin Rd Union Gap (98903) (G-13931)
Freedomprint LLC 860 333-2448
  4110 Michigan Dr Apt D Silverdale (98315) (G-11835)
Freedomweeder Company LLC 509 673-0014
  814 Wisconsin St Ste 444 Tieton (98947) (G-13630)
Freefly Systems Inc 425 485-5500
  15540 Woodinville Redmond Woodinville (98072) (G-15249)
Freeland Cafe 360 331-9945
  Main St Freeland (98249) (G-4028)
Freelocalpoker Co 360 794-5173
  319 S Blakeley St Monroe (98272) (G-6574)
Freeman Companies 425 656-1255
  1030 Sw 34th St Ste D Renton (98057) (G-8804)
Freemo Inc 425 280-9661
  5019 112th Ave Ne Apt B Kirkland (98033) (G-5344)
Freeprt-Mcmran Explration Corp 509 928-0704
  10807 E Montgomery Dr # 3 Spokane Valley (99206) (G-12709)
Freeze Furniture and Mfg Co (PA) 509 924-3545
  10408 E Buckeye Ln Spokane Valley (99206) (G-12710)
Freeze Pack, Pasco Also called Oregon Potato Company (G-7608)

Fremont Brewing Co., Seattle Also called Green Lake Brewing Company LLC (G-10117)
Fremont Fine Arts Foundry Inc 206 588-6981
  154 N 35th St Apt 203 Seattle (98103) (G-10024)
Fremont Foundry, Seattle Also called Fremont Fine Arts Foundry Inc (G-10024)
Fremont Printing Co 206 632-3759
  3504 Fremont Ave N Seattle (98103) (G-10025)
French Man Hills Quarry 509 346-2111
  9498 Road H Se Othello (99344) (G-7496)
French Quarter 509 624-5350
  1311 W Sprague Ave Spokane (99201) (G-12265)
Frencken America Inc 509 924-9777
  22924 E Appleway Ave Liberty Lake (99019) (G-5832)
Fresenius Med Care Hldings Inc 509 276-7338
  822 S Main St Deer Park (99006) (G-2902)
Fresh Flours 206 297-3300
  6015 Phinney Ave N Seattle (98103) (G-10026)
Fresh Fruit Juice LLC 206 329-5979
  1043 S Jackson St Seattle (98104) (G-10027)
Fresh Impressions By Honey D 253 503-7887
  7520 John Dower Rd W Lakewood (98499) (G-5723)
Fresh Northwest Design, Gig Harbor Also called Rogue Empire Inc (G-4156)
Frichette Winery 509 426-3227
  39412 N Sunset Rd Benton City (99320) (G-1612)
Friday Harbor Exports Inc 360 378-6086
  343 Vista Way Friday Harbor (98250) (G-4045)
Friday Harbor House of Jerky 360 207-9652
  260 Spring St Ste 7 Friday Harbor (98250) (G-4046)
Friedman SIversmiths Repr Pltg 360 752-3119
  1323 Euclid Ave Bellingham (98229) (G-1354)
Friends of The Inside Passage, Anacortes Also called Douglass Hemingway & Co LLC (G-122)
Frisbee Enterprises LLC 360 991-1662
  1518 Se 105th Ct Vancouver (98664) (G-14240)
Frisbie Company 253 939-0363
  101 F St Nw Auburn (98001) (G-444)
Fritch Forest Products Inc 360 668-5838
  18507 Waverly Dr Snohomish (98296) (G-11911)
Fritch Mill Inc 425 481-4157
  18507 Waverly Dr Snohomish (98296) (G-11912)
Frito-Lay North America Inc 360 737-3000
  4808 Nw Fruit Valley Rd Vancouver (98660) (G-14241)
Frog Creek Co 509 276-6467
  4896 N Williams Valley Rd Deer Park (99006) (G-2903)
Frog Hollow Press L L C 509 943-3331
  1111 Jadwin Ave Richland (99352) (G-8999)
Frogchart Press 206 284-7156
  41 Dravus St Apt 205 Seattle (98109) (G-10028)
Froland Marine Fab, Seattle Also called Doug D Froland (G-9849)
From Field 360 446-7689
  16909 Rivendale Ln Se Rainier (98576) (G-8315)
Front Panel Express LLC 206 768-0602
  5959 Corson Ave S Ste I Seattle (98108) (G-10029)
Frontier Door & Cabinet LLC 206 768-2524
  11721 Steele St S Tacoma (98444) (G-13302)
Frontier Manufacturing Inc 360 652-4046
  18303 60th Ave Nw Stanwood (98292) (G-12972)
Frontier Mtal Fabrications Inc 360 514-0961
  11218 Ne 66th St Bldg B Vancouver (98662) (G-14242)
Frontier Publication Inc 206 463-5656
  19028 Vashon Hwy Sw Vashon (98070) (G-14723)
Frontside Grind LLC 206 246-5697
  12000 Des Moines Mem Dr S Seattle (98168) (G-10030)
Frosty Bay Seafoods LLC 360 387-7685
  285 Driftwood Shores Rd Camano Island (98282) (G-2213)
Froyo Earth 509 888-7201
  246 W Manson Hwy Chelan (98816) (G-2554)
Froyo Fresh 206 447-4599
  701 5th Ave Ste 106 Seattle (98104) (G-10031)
Fruhla LLC 206 633-4652
  4033 Wallingford Ave N Seattle (98103) (G-10032)
Fruit Commission Wash State 509 453-4837
  105 S 18th St Ste 205 Yakima (98901) (G-15574)
Fruit Country Magazine, Spokane Also called Clintron Publishing Inc (G-12185)
Fruit Packers Supply 509 888-3059
  3907 State Highway 97a Wenatchee (98801) (G-15033)
Frys Welding Inc ....
  3240 B St Nw Ste C Auburn (98001) (G-445)
Fsi Inc 360 452-9194
  4601 6th Ave S Seattle (98108) (G-10033)
Fss Holdings LLC 425 820-5455
  13600 Ne 126th Pl Ste D Kirkland (98034) (G-5345)
Fstopcafe LLC 206 842-0335
  5200 Ne Forest Glade Ln Bainbridge Island (98110) (G-635)
Fsx Equipment Inc (PA) 360 691-2999
  10404 Mountain Loop Hwy Granite Falls (98252) (G-4272)
Fsx Equipment Inc 360 691-2999
  10909a Mountain Loop Hwy Granite Falls (98252) (G-4273)
Fsx Incorporated 360 691-2999
  10404 Mountain Loop Hwy Granite Falls (98252) (G-4274)
Fti Consulting Tech Sftwr 206 373-6500
  1111 3rd Ave Seattle (98101) (G-10034)

Ftv Business Services LLC 425 347-6100
6920 Seaway Blvd Everett (98203) *(G-3486)*
Fuego, Hunts Point *Also called Calendars Northwest LLC (G-4366)*
Fuel Coffee (PA) 206 634-2700
1705 N 45th St Seattle (98103) *(G-10035)*
Fuel100 LLC 206 898-4904
2624 E Aloha St Seattle (98112) *(G-10036)*
Fuhrers Machine LLC 360 533-5517
309 10th St Hoquiam (98550) *(G-4337)*
Fuji Heavy Industries, Kirkland *Also called Subaru of America Inc (G-5472)*
Fujifilm Sonosite Inc (HQ) 425 951-1200
21919 30th Dr Se Bothell (98021) *(G-1858)*
Fujifilm Sonosite Inc 425 951-1200
22011 30th Dr Se Bothell (98021) *(G-1859)*
Fukuda Denshi Usa Inc 425 881-7737
17725 Ne 65th St Ste C Redmond (98052) *(G-8467)*
Fulford Logging, OMAK *Also called Arthur D Fulford Jr (G-7433)*
Full Circle Natural Products 425 337-8844
5429 Lowell Larimer Rd Everett (98208) *(G-3487)*
Full Color Printing NW 360 721-2110
717 Ne 82nd Ave Apt 203 Vancouver (98664) *(G-14243)*
Full Spectrum Analytics Inc 206 729-0775
22525 Se 64th Pl Seattle (98115) *(G-10037)*
Fume and Smoke Extraction, Granite Falls *Also called Fsx Incorporated (G-4274)*
Function Works 206 219-5636
1872 Chesaw Rd Oroville (98844) *(G-7466)*
Functional Patterns Llc 619 565-3955
2820 Elliott Ave Seattle (98121) *(G-10038)*
Fund RR LLC 425 530-7120
6502 55th Dr Ne Marysville (98270) *(G-6337)*
Fundamentals Publishing 509 334-8787
1335 Sw Lost Trail Dr Pullman (99163) *(G-8090)*
Funeral Directors Research 360 736-7105
623 N Tower Ave Centralia (98531) *(G-2402)*
Funko Inc (PA) 425 783-3616
2802 Wetmore Ave Ste 100 Everett (98201) *(G-3488)*
Funko Games LLC (HQ) 206 547-7155
5030 Roosevelt Way Ne Seattle (98105) *(G-10039)*
Funky Screenprint 509 674-5121
205 E 1st St Cle Elum (98922) *(G-2667)*
Funny Feeling 360 671-7386
3620 Irongate Rd Bellingham (98226) *(G-1355)*
Fur Tree Forestry 360 426-6252
1701 W Ford Loop Rd Elma (98541) *(G-3246)*
Furford Picker 360 267-3303
283 Newskah Rd Aberdeen (98520) *(G-12)*
Furford Picker Co 360 267-3303
2395 State Route 105 Grayland (98547) *(G-4294)*
Furion Cellars LLC 425 314-8922
2832 102nd Pl Se Everett (98208) *(G-3489)*
Furniture By Foss 206 783-3626
811 Nw 47th St Seattle (98107) *(G-10040)*
Furtim Therapeutics LLC 425 273-1035
4000 Mason Rd Ste 304 Seattle (98105) *(G-10041)*
Fuse Weld Grind 360 261-2722
12118 Se Mcgillivray Blvd Vancouver (98683) *(G-14244)*
Fusion Industries 425 703-2867
17106 Ne 31st Pl Bellevue (98008) *(G-917)*
Fusion Silver 253 740-8117
1402 Auburn Way N Auburn (98002) *(G-446)*
Fusion9 Design LLC 360 831-0899
263 Grandview Ave Camano Island (98282) *(G-2214)*
Fussy Cloud Puppet Slam 206 235-9109
925 14th Ave Apt 1 Seattle (98122) *(G-10042)*
Futon Factory, Redmond *Also called Epoch Design LLC (G-8452)*
Future Machine & Mfg Inc 509 891-5600
3808 N Sullivan Rd # 124 Spokane Valley (99216) *(G-12711)*
Future Software Systems Inc 360 629-9973
27924 84th Ave Nw Stanwood (98292) *(G-12973)*
Fuze Create LLC 425 212-8807
10423 3rd Ave S Seattle (98168) *(G-10043)*
Fv Fast Break 360 642-3753
314 Eliza Ave Ilwaco (98624) *(G-4370)*
Fvo In Seattle, Seattle *Also called Fishing Vessel Owners Mar Way (G-10000)*
Fxi Inc 253 872-0170
19635 78th Ave S Kent (98032) *(G-4919)*
G & M Machine LLC 509 946-3201
205 Wellsian Way Richland (99352) *(G-9000)*
G & M Manufacturing Inc 206 281-4039
19009 61st Ave Ne Unit 2 Arlington (98223) *(G-238)*
G A News 253 471-9888
11120 Gravelly Lake Dr Sw # 7 Lakewood (98499) *(G-5724)*
G and T Renewables 206 412-2352
12619 2nd Ave S Seattle (98168) *(G-10044)*
G B C Enterprises Inc 360 275-3522
811 Ne Snowcap Dr Tahuya (98588) *(G-13610)*
G B E Publishers Inc 360 438-5779
2030 Cardinal Ln Se Lacey (98503) *(G-5551)*
G B Machining Inc 253 848-8055
4415 102nd Ave E Edgewood (98371) *(G-3079)*
G C P LLC 206 781-1162
958 N 127th St Seattle (98133) *(G-10045)*
G C P Manufacturing, Seattle *Also called G C P LLC (G-10045)*
G Dundas Co Inc 253 631-8008
24301 Roberts Dr Ste A Black Diamond (98010) *(G-1648)*
G E Welding 253 653-8869
402 Milwaukee Blvd S Algona (98001) *(G-68)*
G G Consultants 541 223-9519
5604 Nw 234th St Ridgefield (98642) *(G-9084)*
G L Kluh & Sons Jewelers Inc (PA) 360 491-3530
810 Sleater Kinney Rd Se A Lacey (98503) *(G-5552)*
G M K, Newman Lake *Also called Gordon Gruel (G-7045)*
G M Pallet Inc 253 435-1040
2102 109th St S Tacoma (98444) *(G-13303)*
G P S, University Place *Also called Global Professional Svcs LLC (G-13970)*
G R Plume Co 360 384-2800
1373 W Smith Rd Ferndale (98248) *(G-3846)*
G Wolf Enterprises Inc 360 793-2988
14811 Moonlight Dr Gold Bar (98251) *(G-4188)*
G&J Distributors 509 325-2100
5329 N Alameda Blvd Spokane (99205) *(G-12266)*
G&L Horse Logging 360 247-5156
39815 Ne Gerber Mckee Rd Amboy (98601) *(G-94)*
G&S Trading International 253 859-1097
11201 Se 272nd Pl Kent (98030) *(G-4920)*
G-Tech Communications Inc 503 784-1147
13801 Nw 10th Ct Apt A4 Vancouver (98685) *(G-14245)*
Gabrielle England Inc 360 956-1017
1520 Woodard Ct Nw Olympia (98502) *(G-7292)*
Gabrielles Glassworks 509 585-9394
4102 S Green St Kennewick (99337) *(G-4666)*
Gabrielli Distillers 503 421-2797
825 Ne 145th Ave Vancouver (98684) *(G-14246)*
GAEMS Inc 855 754-2367
2517 152nd Ave Ne Bldg 16 Redmond (98052) *(G-8468)*
Gaes Draperies 360 293-9732
5048 Sharpe Rd Anacortes (98221) *(G-132)*
Gaffer Glass USA Limited 253 395-3361
19622 70th Ave S Ste 4 Kent (98032) *(G-4921)*
Gafftech LLC 844 423-3486
3107 142nd Ave E Ste 105 Sumner (98390) *(G-13072)*
Gagne International LLC 360 733-9500
4237 Cedar Hills Ct Bellingham (98229) *(G-1356)*
Gais Bakery 425 743-2460
430 164th St Sw Lynnwood (98087) *(G-6123)*
Galaxy Cmpund Smconductors Inc 509 892-1114
9922 E Montgomery Dr # 7 Spokane Valley (99206) *(G-12712)*
Galaxy Hobby Inc 425 670-0454
19332 60th Ave W Lynnwood (98036) *(G-6124)*
Gale Industries 360 659-7674
13520 45th Ave Ne Marysville (98271) *(G-6338)*
Gale Industries Inc 360 479-6271
4843 Auto Center Way Bremerton (98312) *(G-1955)*
Galivan Logging Inc 360 866-1431
2138 Overhulse Rd Nw Olympia (98502) *(G-7293)*
Gallatin International LLC 425 557-4356
22525 Se 64th Pl Ste 244 Issaquah (98027) *(G-4416)*
Gallivan Gallivan & Omelia (PA) 206 652-1441
1511 3rd Ave Ste 910 Seattle (98101) *(G-10046)*
Gallo Winery 509 947-4520
2310 Holmason Rd Sunnyside (98944) *(G-13126)*
Gambia Press Union GPU-USA 425 357-6483
2017 124th Pl Se Everett (98208) *(G-3490)*
Gamble Bay Timber 360 297-0555
26131 Bond Rd Ne Kingston (98346) *(G-5253)*
Gamble Logging 253 857-3294
11203 70th Ave Nw Gig Harbor (98332) *(G-4104)*
Gamblin Enterprises Inc 206 795-3817
5609 176th St Sw Lynnwood (98037) *(G-6125)*
Ganapati Studios 206 547-2239
2671 Libbey Rd Coupeville (98239) *(G-2813)*
Gannett Co, Olympia *Also called Olympian Newspaper (G-7355)*
Gannett Co Inc 425 391-2530
13810 Se Gateway 110 Bellevue (98005) *(G-918)*
Garage 425 640-6021
3000 184th St Sw Ste 230 Lynnwood (98037) *(G-6126)*
Garage Sports Woodworking 206 433-1645
12233 22nd Ave S Burien (98168) *(G-2109)*
Garcia Ink Corp 425 391-4950
180 Ne Juniper St Issaquah (98027) *(G-4417)*
Garco Building Systems, Airway Heights *Also called Robertson-Ceco II Corporation (G-62)*
Garco Building Systems Inc 509 244-5611
2714 S Garfield Rd Airway Heights (99001) *(G-52)*
Garden Bucket LLC 425 828-6500
512 6th St S Ste 201 Kirkland (98033) *(G-5346)*
Garden Expressions 360 403-9532
22627 State Route 530 Ne Arlington (98223) *(G-239)*
Garden Fresh Foods Inc 425 483-5467
14316 Ne 203rd St Ste A Woodinville (98072) *(G-15250)*
Garden Fresh Gourmet Foods Inc 425 407-6400
1200 Merrill Creek Pkwy Everett (98203) *(G-3491)*
Garden Guys LLC 206 257-4024
17824 1st Ave S Burien (98148) *(G-2110)*
Gardner Boat Repair Inc 206 784-0854
2442 Nw Market St Ste 404 Seattle (98107) *(G-10047)*

ALPHABETIC

(PA)=Parent Co (HQ)=Headquarters (DH)=Div Headquarters
2019 Washington
Manufacturers Register
733

Gardner-Fields Inc 253 627-4098
2240 Taylor Way Tacoma (98421) ***(G-13304)***
Gariko LLC 509 933-1821
1708 W University Way Ellensburg (98926) ***(G-3201)***
Garjen Corp 253 862-6140
19017 68th St E Bonney Lake (98391) ***(G-1724)***
Garkse Logging & Road Bldg LLC 360 520-2707
330a Brockway Rd Chehalis (98532) ***(G-2498)***
Garland Printing Co Inc 509 327-5556
833 W Garland Ave Spokane (99205) ***(G-12267)***
Garlic Crush 425 968-2539
16095 Cleveland St Redmond (98052) ***(G-8469)***
Garlic It, Bellevue *Also called Onefarstar LLC* ***(G-1049)***
Garmire Iron Works Inc 360 651-1001
5620 48th Dr Ne Marysville (98270) ***(G-6339)***
Garpike Inc 206 719-7820
1947 Broadway E Seattle (98102) ***(G-10048)***
Garrett Press 206 362-1466
2122 N 155th St Shoreline (98133) ***(G-11774)***
Garrett Sign Co Inc 360 693-9081
811 Harney St Vancouver (98660) ***(G-14247)***
Garrison Fuel Tech 360 739-2634
5897 Aspen Ave Ferndale (98248) ***(G-3847)***
Garvey C Maury 425 641-0232
15019 Ne 14th St Bellevue (98007) ***(G-919)***
Garvie Industries LLC 360 691-1233
13105 E Loop View Dr Granite Falls (98252) ***(G-4275)***
Gary C Horsley 360 274-4502
1224 Winlock Vader Rd Winlock (98596) ***(G-15150)***
Gary Floyd & Associates LLC 253 874-4582
34731 14th Pl Sw Auburn (98023) ***(G-447)***
Gary G Guzzie Insurance 509 674-4433
216 N Pennsylvania Ave Cle Elum (98922) ***(G-2668)***
Gary Howe Construction, Gig Harbor *Also called Gary R Howe* ***(G-4105)***
Gary L Jordanger 425 271-2617
2301 Ne 28th St Renton (98056) ***(G-8805)***
Gary L Ostenson DDS PS 360 896-9595
217 S Morrison Rd Vancouver (98664) ***(G-14248)***
Gary Merlino Cnstr Co Inc (PA) 206 763-9552
9125 10th Ave S Seattle (98108) ***(G-10049)***
Gary Merlino Cnstr Co Inc 206 763-2134
9216 8th Ave S Seattle (98108) ***(G-10050)***
Gary N Lamb 360 766-6086
10990 Samish Island Rd Bow (98232) ***(G-1929)***
Gary R Howe 253 857-5835
6512 117th Street Ct Nw Gig Harbor (98332) ***(G-4105)***
Gary's Games, Shoreline *Also called Puget Bridge Supply* ***(G-11804)***
Garys Garden Gate 360 357-5607
1900 93rd Ave Sw Olympia (98512) ***(G-7294)***
Gas N' Glass, Ridgefield *Also called Schurmans Gas & Glass* ***(G-9110)***
Gas Works, Silverdale *Also called Quality Heating & AC LLC* ***(G-11854)***
Gasllc Ltd Liability Company 206 441-1990
2200 Alaskan Way Ste 420 Seattle (98121) ***(G-10051)***
Gate Technologies LLC 206 229-9947
825 Ne 6th St North Bend (98045) ***(G-7111)***
Gatehouse Media LLC 360 532-4000
315 S Michigan St Aberdeen (98520) ***(G-13)***
Gateway Milling LLC 509 639-2431
506 N Rail Rd Almira (99103) ***(G-85)***
Gateway Printing Inc 425 453-3272
1470 127th Pl Ne Bellevue (98005) ***(G-920)***
Gatheredtable Inc 206 735-4886
506 2nd Ave Ste 2300 Seattle (98104) ***(G-10052)***
Gator Dental Equip 360 770-3502
7576 Skagit View Dr Concrete (98237) ***(G-2786)***
Gator Dental Repair Services, Concrete *Also called Gator Dental Equip* ***(G-2786)***
Gaudet Sheetmetal Inc 360 892-5772
19207 Ne Erion Rd Battle Ground (98604) ***(G-703)***
Gavco, Kent *Also called Family Endurance Corporation* ***(G-4903)***
Gavriel Jecan 206 332-0993
1944 1st Ave S Seattle (98134) ***(G-10053)***
Gaynors Glass & Restoration 253 538-2501
10735 A St S Ste D Tacoma (98444) ***(G-13305)***
Gazebo & Porch Works, Puyallup *Also called Gazebo & Porchworks* ***(G-8155)***
Gazebo & Porchworks 253 380-0918
728 9th Ave Sw Puyallup (98371) ***(G-8155)***
Gb Acquisition Inc 206 405-4205
600 Pine St Ste 401 Seattle (98101) ***(G-10054)***
Gbc International Bank 425 214-8435
500 108th Ave Ne Ste 1770 Bellevue (98004) ***(G-921)***
Gbjc Inc 360 321-5262
10809 47th Ave W A Mukilteo (98275) ***(G-6927)***
Gc Solutions LLC 509 243-6030
110 2nd St Asotin (99402) ***(G-352)***
Gcm North American Arospc LLC 253 872-7488
701 Milwaukee Ave N Algona (98001) ***(G-69)***
Gdansk Inc 509 279-2034
5510 E Broadway Ave Spokane Valley (99212) ***(G-12713)***
Gdp Group Ltd Spc 253 459-3447
6610 78th Avenue Ct Nw Gig Harbor (98335) ***(G-4106)***
Gds Direct Countertops Ltd 360 312-9688
5506 Nielsen Ave Ste D Ferndale (98248) ***(G-3848)***
GE Aviation Systems LLC 206 662-2934
12600 Interurban Ave S Tukwila (98168) ***(G-13737)***
GE Healthcare Inc 206 622-9558
925 4th Ave Ste 400 Seattle (98104) ***(G-10055)***
GE Steam Power Inc 860 688-1911
10865 Willows Rd Ne Redmond (98052) ***(G-8470)***
GE Totten & Associates LLC 206 788-0188
514 N 86th St Seattle (98103) ***(G-10056)***
Geartrology Corporation 425 347-1300
3101 111th St Sw Ste A Everett (98204) ***(G-3492)***
Gebetto's Rising Moon Products, Burien *Also called Rising Moon Products* ***(G-2126)***
Geekwire LLC (PA) 206 913-7926
123 Nw 36th St Ste 203 Seattle (98107) ***(G-10057)***
Gekko Corporation 425 679-9188
12400 Se 38th St # 40542 Bellevue (98015) ***(G-922)***
Gelatello Inc 425 214-1267
1902 S Commons Ste A Federal Way (98003) ***(G-3740)***
Gelene Legault 425 481-5560
21922 8th Pl W Bothell (98021) ***(G-1860)***
Gem Cut Company 206 780-0113
5780 Ne Crystal Ln Bainbridge Island (98110) ***(G-636)***
Gem East Corporation 206 441-1700
5418 Ne 200th Pl Lake Forest Park (98155) ***(G-5613)***
Gem Welding & Fabrication 360 378-5818
64 Miner Ln Friday Harbor (98250) ***(G-4047)***
Gemelli Press LLC 360 420-7721
9600 Stone Ave N Seattle (98103) ***(G-10058)***
Gemini Management Ltd 425 739-6800
8525 120th Ave Ne Kirkland (98033) ***(G-5347)***
Gemmell's Diving Services, Dayton *Also called Gemmells Machine Works Inc* ***(G-2882)***
Gemmells Machine Works Inc 509 382-4159
3 Port Way Dayton (99328) ***(G-2882)***
Gemmells Wldg Fabrication LLC 509 547-5200
505 S 26th Ave Pasco (99301) ***(G-7584)***
Gems n Gold 360 574-5085
12603 Ne 42nd Ave Vancouver (98686) ***(G-14249)***
Gen-Set Co 509 891-8452
4308 S Darcy Dr Spokane Valley (99206) ***(G-12714)***
Gen-Tech LLC 206 634-3399
250 Nw 39th St Ste 5 Seattle (98107) ***(G-10059)***
Gen-X Energy Group Inc 509 547-2447
2705 Saint Andrews Loop B Pasco (99301) ***(G-7585)***
Gene L Henry Inc 425 392-1485
1175 Nw Gilman Blvd B16 Issaquah (98027) ***(G-4418)***
General Aerospace Inc 425 422-5462
7127 196th St Sw Ste 201 Lynnwood (98036) ***(G-6127)***
General Chemical, Anacortes *Also called Chemtrade Chemicals US LLC* ***(G-111)***
General Computers Inc 425 405-0588
15613 Ne 1st Pl Bellevue (98008) ***(G-923)***
General Dynamics Corporation 425 885-5010
26802 Ne Virginia St Duvall (98019) ***(G-2989)***
General Dynamics Nascco 360 373-2845
6000 W Werner Rd Bremerton (98312) ***(G-1956)***
General Dynamics Ordna 509 762-5381
9256 Randolph Rd Ne Moses Lake (98837) ***(G-6710)***
General Dynamics Ots Seattle, Bothell *Also called General Dynmics Ots Arospc Inc* ***(G-1765)***
General Dynmics Ots Arospc Inc (HQ) 425 420-9311
11714 N Creek Pkwy N # 200 Bothell (98011) ***(G-1765)***
General Electric Company 425 557-3022
1605 Nw Sammamish Rd # 110 Issaquah (98027) ***(G-4419)***
General Electric Company 253 395-1798
6925 S 194th St Kent (98032) ***(G-4922)***
General Electric Company 253 351-2200
2202 Perimeter Rd Ste 107 Auburn (98001) ***(G-448)***
General Fire Prtection Systems 509 535-4255
3904 E Trent Ave Spokane (99202) ***(G-12268)***
General Mills Inc 763 764-7600
719 Metcalf St Sedro Woolley (98284) ***(G-11539)***
General Plastics Machines 360 694-8836
2828 Kauffman Ave Vancouver (98660) ***(G-14250)***
General Plastics Mfg Co 253 473-5000
4910 S Burlington Way Tacoma (98409) ***(G-13306)***
General Steamship Intl Ltd 425 329-1040
19020 33rd Ave W Ste 365 Lynnwood (98036) ***(G-6128)***
Generations Dental 360 379-1591
642 Harrison St Port Townsend (98368) ***(G-7886)***
Generations Winery LLC 206 351-0933
2001 120th Pl Se 3-303 Everett (98208) ***(G-3493)***
Genesis Advanced Technologies 206 762-8383
654 S Lucile St Seattle (98108) ***(G-10060)***
Genesis Wellness 425 337-3944
10604 26th Dr Se Everett (98208) ***(G-3494)***
Gengler Veterinary Svcs Pllc 425 788-2620
26415 Ne Valley St Duvall (98019) ***(G-2990)***
Genie Holdings Inc (HQ) 425 881-1800
18340 Ne 76th St Redmond (98052) ***(G-8471)***
Genie Industries Inc (HQ) 425 881-1800
18340 Ne 76th St Redmond (98052) ***(G-8472)***
Genie Industries Inc 425 881-1800
18700 Ne 65th St Redmond (98052) ***(G-8473)***
Genie Industries Inc 254 714-0088
6464 185th Ave Ne Ste 200 Redmond (98052) ***(G-8474)***

Genie Industries Inc 425 881-1800
8987 Graham St Ne Moses Lake (98837) *(G-6711)*
Genie Industries Inc 425 888-4600
47020 Se 144th St North Bend (98045) *(G-7112)*
Genie Manufacturing Inc (HQ) 425 881-1800
18340 Ne 76th St Redmond (98052) *(G-8475)*
Genie Manufacturing Inc 509 762-3200
8987 Graham St Ne D5820 Moses Lake (98837) *(G-6712)*
Genie Pro Sales Center, Fife *Also called Overhead Door Corporation (G-3977)*
Genie, A Terex Company, Redmond *Also called Genie Holdings Inc (G-8471)*
Genneve, Seattle *Also called Feminina Group Inc (G-9983)*
Genoa 5, Everett *Also called Genoa Healthcare Mass LLC (G-3495)*
Genoa Cellars 425 296-9660
19501 144th Ave Ne D700 Woodinville (98072) *(G-15251)*
Genoa Healthcare LLC 206 971-9707
3639 Martin L King Jr Way Seattle (98144) *(G-10061)*
Genoa Healthcare Mass LLC 425 789-3050
3322 Broadway Ste 230 Everett (98201) *(G-3495)*
Genothen Holdings LLC 360 352-3636
2948 29th Ave Sw Tumwater (98512) *(G-13873)*
Gensco Inc (PA) 253 620-8203
4402 20th St E Fife (98424) *(G-3954)*
Gentle Dragon Cards Inc 206 546-3593
18603 76th Ave W Ste 104 Edmonds (98026) *(G-3114)*
Gentzen LLC 206 768-1297
12628 Interurban Ave S Tukwila (98168) *(G-13738)*
Genuine Parts Company 509 484-4400
2125 E Francis Ave Spokane (99208) *(G-12269)*
Genuine Parts Company 206 575-8100
907 Thomas Ave Sw Renton (98057) *(G-8806)*
Genus Brewing Company LLC 509 808-2395
1018 S Courtney Ln Spokane Valley (99037) *(G-12715)*
Genzyme Corporation 425 245-1221
2625 162nd St Sw Lynnwood (98087) *(G-6129)*
Geo Heiser Body Co LLC 206 622-7985
11210 Tukla Intl Blvd Tukwila (98168) *(G-13739)*
Geo Lastomirsky Ceramic A 206 782-4695
4203 4th Ave Nw Seattle (98107) *(G-10062)*
Geocom Resources Inc 360 392-2898
114 W Magnolia St Ste 143 Bellingham (98225) *(G-1357)*
Geodesic Structures Inc 509 535-0220
1034 E Overbluff Rd Spokane (99203) *(G-12270)*
Geodesic Structures Toys, Spokane *Also called Geodesic Structures Inc (G-12270)*
Geogenius LLC 206 838-8125
1501 4th Ave Ste 301 Seattle (98101) *(G-10063)*
Geologic Drill Explorations 509 466-5241
14811 W Coulee Hite Rd Spokane (99224) *(G-12271)*
Geometric 206 244-2222
4036 S 128th St Tukwila (98168) *(G-13740)*
Geometric Engrv & Template Co, Tukwila *Also called Geometric (G-13740)*
Georadar Imaging 425 392-7688
21418 E Main St Sammamish (98074) *(G-9208)*
George Anderson Company 425 333-0707
4821 272nd Ave Ne Redmond (98053) *(G-8476)*
George Broom Sons Inc 206 282-0800
2440 W Commodore Way # 100 Seattle (98199) *(G-10064)*
George G Sharp Inc 360 476-8896
2450 Wycoff Way Bldg 550 Bremerton (98314) *(G-1957)*
George Gehrkes Gink 509 243-4100
16186 Snake River Rd Asotin (99402) *(G-353)*
George Ghrkes Fly Fishing Pdts, Asotin *Also called George Gehrkes Gink (G-353)*
George Kenny School Cainsaw 360 275-9570
18351 E State Route 3 Allyn (98524) *(G-82)*
George Schuster, Seattle *Also called Marine Lumber Service Inc (G-10482)*
George W Warden Co Inc 509 534-2880
2501 N Farr Ln Ste 2 Spokane Valley (99206) *(G-12716)*
Georges Custom Plastic Inc 253 939-1575
14607 215th Ave E Bonney Lake (98391) *(G-1725)*
Georgia-Pacific LLC 253 627-2100
1240 E Alexander Ave Tacoma (98421) *(G-13307)*
Georgia-Pacific LLC 360 491-1310
1203 Fones Rd Se Olympia (98501) *(G-7295)*
Georgia-Pacific LLC 404 652-4000
401 Ne Adams St Camas (98607) *(G-2254)*
Georgia-Pacific LLC 253 631-3250
16720 Se 271st St Ste 205 Covington (98042) *(G-2828)*
Geospace International, Seattle *Also called Geospace Products Company Inc (G-10065)*
Geospace Products Company Inc 206 547-2556
3931 Leary Way Nw Seattle (98107) *(G-10065)*
Gepford Welding Inc 509 624-6610
4003 W 40th Ave Spokane (99224) *(G-12272)*
Gerald McCallum 509 467-8456
8324 N Regal St Spokane (99217) *(G-12273)*
Gerrard Inc 253 804-8001
1320 26th St Nw Ste 1 Auburn (98001) *(G-449)*
Gerris Dry Bunk 509 782-2653
3264 Mission Creek Rd Cashmere (98815) *(G-2320)*
Gerry Newcomb 206 633-0154
3511 Interlake Ave N Seattle (98103) *(G-10066)*
Gerrys Machine Shop Inc 360 686-1108
22218 Ne Steelhead Ln Yacolt (98675) *(G-15482)*
Gestsure Technologies Ltd 800 510-2485
2200 Alaskan Way Seattle (98121) *(G-10067)*
Get Lit Lighting LLC 425 772-1646
9931 40th Pl Se Everett (98205) *(G-3496)*
Get Plenish Inc 425 922-0070
2020 124th Ave Ne Bellevue (98005) *(G-924)*
Getting Personal Imprinting 253 302-5566
4021 100th St Sw Ste B Lakewood (98499) *(G-5725)*
GF Blends Inc 509 375-0909
2151 Henderson Loop Richland (99354) *(G-9001)*
Gfg Publishing 509 853-3520
105 S 18th St Ste 217 Yakima (98901) *(G-15575)*
GG&o, Seattle *Also called Gallivan Gallivan & Omelia (G-10046)*
Gh, Burlington *Also called Golden Harvest Inc (G-2159)*
Ghl Architectural Millwork LLC 206 467-5004
1938 Occidental Ave S Seattle (98134) *(G-10068)*
Ghost Inspector Inc 206 395-3635
1601 5th Ave Ste 1100 Seattle (98101) *(G-10069)*
Ghost Ridge Software Inc 425 646-4822
5510 Lakeview Dr Apt D Kirkland (98033) *(G-5348)*
Ghost Runners Brewery 360 989-3912
4216 Ne Minnehaha St # 108 Vancouver (98661) *(G-14251)*
Giant Metals Inc 206 592-0963
19280 11th Pl S Apt 3 Seatac (98148) *(G-9285)*
Giant Nickel Want ADS, Kennewick *Also called Tevada Publishing Inc (G-4734)*
Giant Resources Co., Seatac *Also called Giant Metals Inc (G-9285)*
Gibbons Drilling Inc 360 671-3040
7212 265th St Nw Apt 360 Stanwood (98292) *(G-12974)*
Gibbs Trailer Mfg & Repr 509 547-8241
320 S Main Ave Pasco (99301) *(G-7586)*
Gibraltar Industries Inc 253 926-1600
3011 70th Ave E Fife (98424) *(G-3955)*
Gibraltar Maint & Cnstr Inc 206 365-4440
15341 Ne 90th St S Redmond (98052) *(G-8477)*
Gibson & Son Excavation, Ellensburg *Also called Gibson & Son Road Building Inc (G-3202)*
Gibson & Son Road Building Inc 509 925-2017
1221 S Thorp Hwy Ellensburg (98926) *(G-3202)*
Gibson Performance Engines 509 251-5171
926 N Lake Rd Spokane Valley (99212) *(G-12717)*
Giddens Aerospace Inc 425 353-0405
2600 94th St Sw 150 Everett (98204) *(G-3497)*
Giddens Holdings Inc (HQ) 425 353-0405
2600 94th St Sw Ste 150 Everett (98204) *(G-3498)*
Giddens Industries Inc 425 353-0405
2300 Merrill Creek Pkwy Everett (98203) *(G-3499)*
Giddens Industries Inc (HQ) 425 353-0405
2600 94th St Sw Ste 150 Everett (98204) *(G-3500)*
Giesbrecht & Sons LLC 509 269-4087
1061 Hollingsworth Rd Mesa (99343) *(G-6493)*
Gifford Hirlinger Winery 509 301-9229
1450 Stateline Rd Walla Walla (99362) *(G-14811)*
Gig Harbor Boat Works Inc 253 851-2126
9905 Peacock Hill Ave Gig Harbor (98332) *(G-4107)*
Gig Harbor Brewing Co 253 474-0672
3120 South Tacoma Way Tacoma (98409) *(G-13308)*
Gigglydoo LLC 425 344-5594
907 N Hibbs Rd Ellensburg (98926) *(G-3203)*
Gilbert Cellars LLC 509 249-9049
5 N Front St Ste 100 Yakima (98901) *(G-15576)*
Gilbert Farms, Warden *Also called Country Morning Farms Inc (G-14929)*
Gildeane Group 206 362-0336
6015 Ne 205th St Kenmore (98028) *(G-4575)*
Gilead Sciences Inc 206 728-5090
2107 E Republican St Seattle (98112) *(G-10070)*
Gill Print 509 535-2521
6119 S Moran Dr Spokane (99223) *(G-12274)*
Gillaspie Manufacturing Inc 360 260-1975
12800 Ne 95th St Vancouver (98682) *(G-14252)*
Gillespie Polygraph 425 775-9015
16825 48th Ave W Ste 218 Lynnwood (98037) *(G-6130)*
Gillingham Sand & Gravel Co 509 456-5527
9701 W Champion Ln Cheney (99004) *(G-2586)*
Gilmour Machinery 360 263-5515
14812 Ne 379th St Battle Ground (98604) *(G-704)*
Gils Aluminum & Shell Core Sp 206 762-1726
533 S Holden St Seattle (98108) *(G-10071)*
Gilt LLC 425 468-4458
115 Bellevue Sq Bellevue (98004) *(G-925)*
Gilyard Co 509 782-1817
107 Railroad Ave Cashmere (98815) *(G-2321)*
Gilyard Home Furnishings, Cashmere *Also called Gilyard Co (G-2321)*
Gimpy Ninja LLC 253 282-9943
7107 40th St Nw Gig Harbor (98335) *(G-4108)*
Ginacor Inc 206 860-1595
513 31st Ave Seattle (98122) *(G-10072)*
Gingerbread Factory 509 548-6592
828 Commercial St Leavenworth (98826) *(G-5803)*
Ginkco Distillery, Mattawa *Also called Ginkgo Forest Winery LLC (G-6406)*
Ginkgo Forest Winery 253 301-4372
2221 N 30th St Tacoma (98403) *(G-13309)*
Ginkgo Forest Winery LLC 509 932-0082
22561 Rd T27 Sw Mattawa (99349) *(G-6406)*

Ginny Hardings Equine Classics 509 582-7924
228710 E Lechelt Rd Kennewick (99337) **(G-4667)**
Gino Cuneo Cellars LLC 509 876-4738
18 N 2nd Ave Walla Walla (99362) **(G-14812)**
Giorgio's Gym, Spokane Valley *Also called Giorgios Fitness Center* **(G-12718)**
Giorgios Fitness Center 509 922-8833
7 N Herald Rd Spokane Valley (99206) **(G-12718)**
Giraffe Family Press 360 437-8018
45 Jackson Ln Port Ludlow (98365) **(G-7766)**
Giraffe Project 360 221-7989
197 2nd St Ste A Langley (98260) **(G-5778)**
Girandola 206 289-0523
A-242 14419 Grnwood Ave N Greenwood Seattle (98133) **(G-10073)**
Girandola Center, Seattle *Also called Girandola* **(G-10073)**
Girard Management Group LLC 253 845-0505
802 E Main Puyallup (98372) **(G-8156)**
Girard Wood Products Inc (PA) 253 845-0505
802 E Main Puyallup (98372) **(G-8157)**
Girard Wood Products Inc 360 482-5151
10 Bear Rd Elma (98541) **(G-3247)**
Girlie Press Inc 206 720-1237
1658 21st Ave Seattle (98122) **(G-10074)**
Girt John 206 399-4977
4629 191st Ave Se Issaquah (98027) **(G-4420)**
Gitf Card Network, Ridgefield *Also called Powerhuse Brnds Consulting LLC* **(G-9104)**
Glacier Aviation Inc (PA) 360 705-3214
7645 Old Hwy 99 Se Olympia (98501) **(G-7296)**
Glacier Bay Fisheries LLC 206 298-1200
1200 Westlake Ave N # 900 Seattle (98109) **(G-10075)**
Glacier Jet Center, Olympia *Also called Glacier Aviation Inc* **(G-7296)**
Glacier Mouldings Ltd 360 629-5313
3927 300th St Nw Stanwood (98292) **(G-12975)**
Glacier Northwest Inc 253 912-8500
4301 Pioneer Ave Dupont (98327) **(G-2964)**
Glacier Northwest Inc 425 486-3281
6423 Ne 175th St Bothell (98028) **(G-1766)**
Glacier Northwest Inc 253 572-7412
3601 Taylor Way Tacoma (98421) **(G-13310)**
Glacier Northwest Inc 360 694-9420
2327 W Mill Plain Blvd Vancouver (98660) **(G-14253)**
Glacier Northwest Inc 360 694-1627
3101 Nw Gateway Ave Vancouver (98660) **(G-14254)**
Glacier Northwest Inc 360 896-8922
7215 Ne 18th St Vancouver (98661) **(G-14255)**
Glacier Northwest Inc 360 736-1131
305 E Summa St Centralia (98531) **(G-2403)**
Glacier Northwest Inc 425 486-3281
6423 175th St Ne Seattle (98155) **(G-10076)**
Glacier Northwest Inc 360 892-5100
18516 Se 1st St Vancouver (98684) **(G-14256)**
Glacier Northwest Inc 206 764-3075
5900 W Marginal Way Sw Seattle (98106) **(G-10077)**
Glacier Northwest Inc 425 888-9795
5601 396th Dr Se Snoqualmie (98065) **(G-12013)**
Glacier Packaging Inc 253 272-4682
9403 43rd Avenue Ct Sw Lakewood (98499) **(G-5726)**
Glacier Peak Winery 360 419-9107
13821 Best Rd Mount Vernon (98273) **(G-6799)**
Glacier View Winery 206 719-1331
18340 Ne 143rd Pl Woodinville (98072) **(G-15252)**
Glacier Water Company LLC 253 876-6500
1002 15th St Sw Ste 100 Auburn (98001) **(G-450)**
Glacier Water Services Inc 360 413-7272
6290 Gravel Ln Ne Lacey (98516) **(G-5553)**
Glamazon Salon LLC 509 703-7145
5130 N Assembly St Spokane (99205) **(G-12275)**
Glant Textiles Corporation (PA) 206 725-4444
3031 S Walden St Ste 102 Seattle (98144) **(G-10078)**
Glarus Group Inc 425 572-5907
6947 Coal Creek Pkwy Se Newcastle (98059) **(G-7030)**
Glasair Aviation LLC 360 435-8533
18530 59th Dr Ne Arlington (98223) **(G-240)**
Glasair Aviation Usa LLC (HQ) 360 435-8533
18530 59th Dr Ne Arlington (98223) **(G-241)**
Glasrail, Mukilteo *Also called Pic Sentry Rail Inc* **(G-6965)**
Glass Doctor of Wenatchee 509 415-3400
435b Rock Island Rd East Wenatchee (98802) **(G-3014)**
Glass House Studio, Seattle *Also called Glasshouse Studio* **(G-10079)**
Glass Restoration Specialists 253 473-7779
3817 N 16th St Tacoma (98406) **(G-13311)**
Glasshape North America LP 206 538-5416
175 2nd St N Friday Harbor (98250) **(G-4048)**
Glasshouse Studio 206 682-9939
311 Occidental Ave S Seattle (98104) **(G-10079)**
Glassique 206 963-4400
10509 Aurora Ave N Seattle (98133) **(G-10080)**
Glassy Baby LLC (PA) 206 568-7368
3406 E Union St Seattle (98122) **(G-10081)**
Glaxosmithkline LLC 206 755-5725
5494 170th Pl Se Bellevue (98006) **(G-926)**
Glaxosmithkline LLC 206 856-5663
18707 63rd Ave Ne Kenmore (98028) **(G-4576)**
Glazy Daze Ceramics 253 770-2979
6814 96th St E Puyallup (98371) **(G-8158)**
Glen Cove Press LLC 509 318-5934
456 Palm Dr Richland (99352) **(G-9002)**
Glen Dimplex Americas Company (HQ) 360 693-2505
2500 W Fourth Plain Blvd Vancouver (98660) **(G-14257)**
Glen Hidden Mhc LLC 253 537-9383
15616 76th Ave E Puyallup (98375) **(G-8159)**
Glenbar Alpacas Inc 360 574-5428
20801 Ne 50th Ave Ridgefield (98642) **(G-9085)**
Glencorrie 509 525-2585
8052 Old Highway 12 Walla Walla (99362) **(G-14813)**
Glenn Waldren 360 570-8400
2612 Yelm Hwy Se Ste D Olympia (98501) **(G-7297)**
Glenn's Welding & R V Supply, Lynnwood *Also called Glenns Welding and Mfg Inc* **(G-6131)**
Glenns Welding and Mfg Inc 425 743-2226
15330 Meadow Rd Lynnwood (98087) **(G-6131)**
Glenwood Timber Inc 509 364-4158
9 Pine Vista Rd Glenwood (98619) **(G-4182)**
Gli Interactive LLC (PA) 206 201-2708
304 Alaskan Way S Ste 302 Seattle (98104) **(G-10082)**
Glo Tech Inc 360 403-8928
19705 A 60th Ave Ne Ste 3 Arlington (98223) **(G-242)**
Global Biodefense, Shoreline *Also called Stemar Media Group LLC* **(G-11818)**
Global Direct Components LLC 253 661-1100
1820 S 341st Pl Federal Way (98003) **(G-3741)**
Global Display North Amer Ltd 425 698-1938
14925 Se Allen Rd Bellevue (98006) **(G-927)**
Global Emergent Tech LLC 425 999-9021
318 17th Ave S Seattle (98144) **(G-10083)**
Global Enterprise Intl 303 928-3208
26257 Montera Loop Ne Kingston (98346) **(G-5254)**
Global Fia Inc (PA) 253 549-2223
684 6th Ave Fox Island (98333) **(G-4022)**
Global Fire Response & Safety 701 774-2022
1100 Carillon Pt Kirkland (98033) **(G-5349)**
Global Fulfillment, Seattle *Also called Karlas Hand Bindery Inc* **(G-10328)**
Global Harvest Foods Ltd 509 466-0539
3116 E Graves Rd Ste 300 Mead (99021) **(G-6428)**
Global Harvest Foods Ltd 206 957-1350
16000 Christensen Rd # 300 Tukwila (98188) **(G-13741)**
Global Harvest Foods Ltd (HQ) 206 957-1350
16000 Christensen Rd # 300 Tukwila (98188) **(G-13742)**
Global Harvest of Colorado, Mead *Also called Global Harvest Foods Ltd* **(G-6428)**
Global Incorporated 206 763-4424
7619 5th Ave S Seattle (98108) **(G-10084)**
Global Industries Inc 425 291-9282
820 Sw 34th St Ste A Renton (98057) **(G-8807)**
Global Inflight Products, Redmond *Also called Aviation Spares & Svcs Intl Co* **(G-8393)**
Global Machine Works Inc 360 403-8432
19130 59th Dr Ne Arlington (98223) **(G-243)**
Global Marine Logistics LLC 206 854-0201
12638 Ne 70th St Kirkland (98033) **(G-5350)**
Global Marine Specialties Inc 206 414-0819
12932 Se Kent Kangley Rd Kent (98030) **(G-4923)**
Global Metal Technologies LLC (PA) 425 956-3506
10500 Ne 8th St Ste 1920 Bellevue (98004) **(G-928)**
Global Mining 509 863-9724
19208 E Broadway Ave Spokane Valley (99016) **(G-12719)**
Global Mtal Works Erectors LLC 253 572-5363
1144 Thorne Rd Tacoma (98421) **(G-13312)**
Global Pacific Forest Products 360 568-1111
310 Maple Ave Snohomish (98290) **(G-11913)**
Global Press 425 254-9323
927 Harrington Ave Ne Renton (98056) **(G-8808)**
Global Product Development 509 487-1155
3808 N Sullivan Rd # 105 Spokane Valley (99216) **(G-12720)**
Global Product Mfg Corp 425 512-9129
12322 Highway 99 Ste 98 Everett (98204) **(G-3501)**
Global Professional Svcs LLC 808 682-0404
5619 54th Avenue Ct W University Place (98467) **(G-13970)**
Global Scientific Systems 360 504-5100
162 River Run Rd Sequim (98382) **(G-11636)**
Global Software LLC 425 822-3140
22522 29th Dr Se Ste 202 Bothell (98021) **(G-1861)**
Global Software Systems Inc 425 427-8215
23349 Se 51st Pl Issaquah (98029) **(G-4421)**
Global Solarium Inc 360 695-0313
7402 Ne St Johns Rd B Vancouver (98665) **(G-14258)**
Global Sportswear Corporation 253 813-9788
19122 84th Ave S Ste A Kent (98032) **(G-4924)**
Global Studios Consulting LLC 425 223-5291
16301 Ne 8th St Ste 224 Bellevue (98008) **(G-929)**
Global Technical Staffin 512 694-7621
15640 Ne Fourth Plain Blv Vancouver (98682) **(G-14259)**
Global Venture, Kent *Also called Merchant Investments Inc* **(G-5006)**
Global Vision 425 985-9325
4307 147th Pl Se Mill Creek (98012) **(G-6512)**
Globalmax Associates Inc 425 392-4848
1672202 25th Pl Ne Issaquah (98027) **(G-4422)**
Globaltech Plastics LLC 253 327-1333
5555 8th St E Fife (98424) **(G-3956)**

Globalwxdatacom 425 644-4010
4119 Sw Kenyon St Seattle (98136) *(G-10085)*
Globe 206 527-2480
5220 University Way Ne B Seattle (98105) *(G-10086)*
Globe Books The, Seattle *Also called Globe (G-10086)*
Globe International Inc (PA) 253 383-2584
701 E D St Tacoma (98421) *(G-13313)*
Globe Machine Manufacturing Co (PA) 253 383-2584
701 E D St Tacoma (98421) *(G-13314)*
Globek LLC 360 627-9714
130 Tweed Ln Nw Ste 2 Bremerton (98312) *(G-1958)*
Globo Productions Voiceover 206 992-0483
575 Highland Dr Seattle (98109) *(G-10087)*
Globodyne Industries Inc 425 321-9471
4679 Arbors Cir Mukilteo (98275) *(G-6928)*
Globys Inc (PA) 206 352-3055
705 5th Ave S Ste 700 Seattle (98104) *(G-10088)*
Glori Publishing LLC 425 202-7714
18612 Ne 25th St Redmond (98052) *(G-8478)*
Glorious Comfort 253 884-1465
14820 38th Street Kp S Lakebay (98349) *(G-5689)*
Glycocept Inc 425 647-7446
300 211th Pl Se Sammamish (98074) *(G-9209)*
Glykon Technologies Group LLC 510 289-4331
24 Roy St Ste 401 Seattle (98109) *(G-10089)*
GM Nameplate Inc 206 284-2201
2201 15th Ave W Seattle (98119) *(G-10090)*
Gman Industries Ltd 425 228-2518
18530 Se 145th St Renton (98059) *(G-8809)*
Gms Fabrication 425 677-4573
1320 26th St Nw Ste 12 Auburn (98001) *(G-451)*
Gms Industries Inc 425 454-9500
2000 124th Ave Ne B105 Bellevue (98005) *(G-930)*
Gms Metal Works Inc 253 736-2178
1427 20th St Nw Auburn (98001) *(G-452)*
Gms Procurement LLC 253 852-6552
1427 20th St Nw Auburn (98001) *(G-453)*
Gnarly Garlic Dip, Puyallup *Also called Bad Breath Garlic Co (G-8127)*
Gnarly Tees 360 326-3770
12416 Nw 36th Ave Ste 2b Vancouver (98685) *(G-14260)*
Gnr Aerospace Inc 360 652-4040
17723 3rd Ave Ne Arlington (98223) *(G-244)*
Gnw Corporation 425 869-6218
15333 Ne 92nd St Redmond (98052) *(G-8479)*
Go Designs 206 719-0936
3417 21st Ave W Seattle (98199) *(G-10091)*
Go Industrial Services, Tacoma *Also called Go Ventures Inc (G-13315)*
Go Manna Inc 360 794-7480
7820 167th St Se Snohomish (98296) *(G-11914)*
Go Planit LLC 206 227-0660
415 Airport Way Sw Mattawa (99349) *(G-6407)*
Go Usa Inc 509 662-3387
521 S Columbia St Wenatchee (98801) *(G-15034)*
Go Ventures Inc 253 313-4070
719 N Mullen St Tacoma (98406) *(G-13315)*
Go Vertical Corporation 360 830-5447
14881 Nw Goeske Ln Seabeck (98380) *(G-9264)*
Go2origins LLC 425 413-4134
29232 305th Ct Se Ravensdale (98051) *(G-8336)*
Gober's Son & Son, Spokane Valley *Also called Gobers Fuel Oil Inc (G-12721)*
Gobers Fuel Oil Inc 509 924-5372
11215 E Trent Ave Spokane Valley (99206) *(G-12721)*
Godbey Ready Mixed, Chelan *Also called Chelan Concrete Inc (G-2549)*
Godbey Red-E-Mix Concrete Inc 509 689-2415
505 Sw Ansil St Brewster (98812) *(G-2016)*
Goddard Woodworking Llcpetr Go 206 920-8675
3645 36th Ave S Seattle (98144) *(G-10092)*
Goedecke & Goedecke 425 481-1153
128 224th St Se Bothell (98021) *(G-1862)*
Gold Impressions 509 886-0866
1417 Easthills Ter East Wenatchee (98802) *(G-3015)*
Gold Mine Jewelry, Seattle *Also called Gold Mine of Jewelry Inc (G-10093)*
Gold Mine of Jewelry Inc 206 622-3333
1405 1st Ave Seattle (98101) *(G-10093)*
Gold Plating Specialist 509 582-3430
600 W Entiat Ave Kennewick (99336) *(G-4668)*
Gold Reserve Inc (PA) 509 623-1500
999 W Riverside Ave # 401 Spokane (99201) *(G-12276)*
Golden Alaska Seafoods, Seattle *Also called Gasllc Ltd Liability Company (G-10051)*
Golden Apple Inc 253 473-7880
3802 S Warner St Tacoma (98409) *(G-13316)*
Golden Boy Foods (usa) Inc 360 332-1990
1555 Odell St Blaine (98230) *(G-1671)*
Golden Child Inc 206 901-9502
2829 Sw 106th St Seattle (98146) *(G-10094)*
Golden Claw Ventures Inc 360 927-8276
810 Peace Portal Dr Blaine (98230) *(G-1672)*
Golden Creek LLC 425 830-4343
17321 270th Ave Se Issaquah (98027) *(G-4423)*
Golden Graphics Sign Co, Goldendale *Also called Christine Woodcock (G-4194)*
Golden Harvest Inc (PA) 360 757-4334
11944 Westar Ln Burlington (98233) *(G-2159)*
Golden Hills Brewing Co 509 389-6253
12921 W 17th Ave Airway Heights (99001) *(G-53)*
Golden Nut Company (usa) Inc 360 332-1990
1555 Odell St Blaine (98230) *(G-1673)*
Golden Rod Services, Sekiu *Also called Pats Welding Service (G-11583)*
Golden Shamrock Inc 206 282-5825
4005 20th Ave W Ste 218 Seattle (98199) *(G-10095)*
Golden State Foods Corp 509 928-9055
3808 N Sullivan Rd 33h Spokane Valley (99216) *(G-12722)*
Goldendale Grapplers 509 314-9975
111 Rimrock Rd Goldendale (98620) *(G-4198)*
Goldendale Sentinel Inc 509 773-3777
117 W Main St Goldendale (98620) *(G-4199)*
Goldenrod Inc 253 840-8114
2121 Meridian Ave E Ste 5 Edgewood (98371) *(G-3080)*
Goldenrod Jewelry, Edgewood *Also called Goldenrod Inc (G-3080)*
Goldfinch Press 206 696-2933
2308 N 62nd St Seattle (98103) *(G-10096)*
Goldfish Press 206 380-4181
4545 42nd Ave Sw Apt 211 Seattle (98116) *(G-10097)*
Goldmountain Exploration Corp 360 332-0905
225 Marine Dr Ste 210 Blaine (98230) *(G-1674)*
Goldrich Mining Company (PA) 509 535-7367
2607 Sthast Blvd Ste B211 Spokane (99223) *(G-12277)*
Golfco International Inc 425 861-7755
18009 Ne 76th St Redmond (98052) *(G-8480)*
Gomotive Inc 206 462-6379
1501 4th Ave Ste 550 Seattle (98101) *(G-10098)*
Gompf Brackets Inc (PA) 425 348-5002
12426 Mukilteo Speedway Mukilteo (98275) *(G-6929)*
Good Construction Company, Toledo *Also called Alan Good (G-13635)*
Good Crushing Inc 360 864-2974
265 Rupp Rd Toledo (98591) *(G-13639)*
Good Fruit Grower Magazine, Yakima *Also called Fruit Commission Wash State (G-15574)*
Good Impressions Inc 360 225-9080
616 Sommerset Rd Woodland (98674) *(G-15434)*
Good Nature Publishing Co, Seattle *Also called Timothy Colman (G-11310)*
Good News Church 509 544-0938
3203 W Sylvester St Pasco (99301) *(G-7587)*
Good News Printing & Graphics 425 483-2510
14303 Ne 193rd Pl Woodinville (98072) *(G-15253)*
Good Pet Food Inc 310 430-3833
214 1st Ave S Ste G7 Seattle (98104) *(G-10099)*
Good Planet Foods LLC 425 449-8134
1813 115th Ave Ne Bellevue (98004) *(G-931)*
Good Scents Co 509 996-2620
63 Raven Rd Winthrop (98862) *(G-15161)*
Good Wear Leather Coat Company 206 724-6325
5703 215th Pl Sw Mountlake Terrace (98043) *(G-6861)*
Goodall Productions Inc 206 722-0544
5018 8th Ave Ne Seattle (98105) *(G-10100)*
Goodman Custom Fab 253 720-2451
7215 S Alder St Tacoma (98409) *(G-13317)*
Goodmans Ski and Sports Inc 360 733-8937
602 W Lake Samish Dr Bellingham (98229) *(G-1358)*
Goodmar Group LLC 206 622-8204
1117b Nw 54th St Seattle (98107) *(G-10101)*
Goodnight Wood Designs 360 652-7765
12528 Marine Dr Ste M158 Tulalip (98271) *(G-13841)*
Goodrich Aerospace, Spokane *Also called Goodrich Corporation (G-12278)*
Goodrich Aerostructures Integr 425 318-9276
2615 94th St Sw Everett (98204) *(G-3502)*
Goodrich Corporation 425 261-8700
2701 94th St Sw Everett (98204) *(G-3503)*
Goodrich Corporation 425 822-9851
4020 Lake Wash Blvd Ne Kirkland (98033) *(G-5351)*
Goodrich Corporation 509 744-6000
11135 W Westbow Ln Spokane (99224) *(G-12278)*
Goodrich Landing Gear, Everett *Also called Goodrich Corporation (G-3503)*
Goodwinds LLC 206 362-6151
1829 Railroad Ave Mount Vernon (98273) *(G-6800)*
Goodwins Kites, Seattle *Also called Wind Play Inc (G-11481)*
Goose Rdge Est Vneyards Winery, Benton City *Also called Goose Ridge Vineyards LLC (G-1614)*
Goose Ridge LLC 509 837-4427
63615 E Jacobs Rd Ne Benton City (99320) *(G-1613)*
Goose Ridge Vineyards, Benton City *Also called Goose Ridge LLC (G-1613)*
Goose Ridge Vineyards LLC 509 627-1618
63615 E Jacobs Rd Ne Benton City (99320) *(G-1614)*
Gooseworks Media LLC 425 487-8766
8016 Ne 152nd Ct Kenmore (98028) *(G-4577)*
Gordon Becker Construction 425 883-8545
8535 152nd Ave Ne Redmond (98052) *(G-8481)*
Gordon Brothers Cellars Inc 509 547-6331
671 Levey Rd Pasco (99301) *(G-7588)*
Gordon Exports LLC 503 313-6544
15912 Ne 41st St Redmond (98052) *(G-8482)*
Gordon Gruel 509 226-1309
25720 E Princeton Ave Newman Lake (99025) *(G-7045)*
Gorilla Screen Printing 206 621-1728
2232c 1st Ave S Seattle (98134) *(G-10102)*

ALPHABETIC

Gorleys Precision Machine.......360 423-4567
2302 Lee Ave Longview (98632) ***(G-5912)***
Gorman Industries.......509 899-3933
2214 W Dry Creek Rd Ellensburg (98926) ***(G-3204)***
Gorman Publicity.......360 676-9393
1011 Queen St Bellingham (98229) ***(G-1359)***
GOS Printing Corporation.......253 939-3131
1433 W Valley Hwy N Auburn (98001) ***(G-454)***
Gosanko Chocolate Art, Auburn *Also called R & S Roberts Enterprises Inc* ***(G-542)***
Gotagscom LLC.......509 754-2760
55 Alder St Nw Ste B1 Ephrata (98823) ***(G-3335)***
Gouger Cellars.......360 693-2700
26506 Ne 10th Ave Ridgefield (98642) ***(G-9086)***
Gould & Sons Logging Inc.......360 274-9425
1627 Tower Rd Castle Rock (98611) ***(G-2343)***
Gould-Sunrise Logging Inc.......360 274-8000
1036 Huntington Ave S Castle Rock (98611) ***(G-2344)***
Gourmet Display, Kent *Also called Plastics Dynamics Inc* ***(G-5067)***
Gourmet Mixes Inc.......206 764-6006
8230 5th Ave S Ste A Seattle (98108) ***(G-10103)***
Goworld Display, Bellevue *Also called Global Display North Amer Ltd* ***(G-927)***
GP Graders LLC.......253 239-3727
3721 Airport Way East Wenatchee (98802) ***(G-3016)***
GPA, Seattle *Also called Guido Perla & Associates Inc* ***(G-10132)***
GPA Embroidery.......509 662-1929
22 N Wenatchee Ave Wenatchee (98801) ***(G-15035)***
Gr Nano Materials, Tacoma *Also called GR Silicate Nano-* ***(G-13318)***
GR Silicate Nano-.......253 267-8781
401 E Alex 326 Tacoma (98421) ***(G-13318)***
Grab On Grips LLC.......509 529-9800
350 E Beech Ave Walla Walla (99362) ***(G-14814)***
Grace AVI & Logistics Support.......425 269-9424
21402 Se 16th Pl Sammamish (98075) ***(G-9210)***
Grace Harbor Farms, Custer *Also called Lukens Farms Inc* ***(G-2856)***
Grace Harvest & Assoc LLC.......206 973-2363
8245 Se 36th St Mercer Island (98040) ***(G-6464)***
Graces Kitchen Inc.......425 635-4609
225 108th Ave Ne Ste 570 Bellevue (98004) ***(G-932)***
Grad Products, Kenmore *Also called Herff Jones LLC* ***(G-4580)***
Grafika Korps, Ritzville *Also called Flying Arts Ranch Inc* ***(G-9121)***
Graham Packaging Company LP.......509 698-4545
510 E Naches Ave Selah (98942) ***(G-11589)***
Grain Corp Malt, Vancouver *Also called Great Western Malting Co* ***(G-14267)***
Grain Craft Inc.......206 898-3079
3235 16th Ave Sw Seattle (98134) ***(G-10104)***
Grains of Wrath Brewery.......847 727-5100
337 Ne 4th Ave Camas (98607) ***(G-2255)***
Grakon LLC (PA).......206 824-6000
1911 S 218th St Des Moines (98198) ***(G-2936)***
Gram Lumber Company, Kalama *Also called Rsg Forest Products Inc* ***(G-4507)***
Gramercy Cellars.......509 876-2427
635 N 13th Ave Walla Walla (99362) ***(G-14815)***
Grampas Garlic Salt LLC.......425 513-0446
820 Cady Rd Apt J102 Everett (98203) ***(G-3504)***
Gran Quartz Trading Inc.......206 973-7640
6001 6th Ave S Seattle (98108) ***(G-10105)***
Grand Central Bakery Inc (PA).......206 768-0320
21 S Nevada St Seattle (98134) ***(G-10106)***
Grand Central Baking Company, Seattle *Also called Grand Central Bakery Inc* ***(G-10106)***
Grand D Signs.......253 929-9963
1082 S 316th St Federal Way (98003) ***(G-3742)***
Grand Image Ltd (PA).......206 624-0444
4730 Ohio Ave S Seattle (98134) ***(G-10107)***
Grand Reve Vintners.......425 892-9848
404 289th Pl Ne Carnation (98014) ***(G-2294)***
Grand Temple.......509 715-7876
618 S Liberty Cir Liberty Lake (99019) ***(G-5833)***
Grandma Ednas.......425 200-5435
9214 State Ave Marysville (98270) ***(G-6340)***
Grandview Plant, Grandview *Also called Welch Foods Inc A Cooperative* ***(G-4257)***
Grandview Printing, Grandview *Also called Valley Publishing Company Inc* ***(G-4256)***
Grandview Screen USA Inc.......360 481-3490
2121 Crestline Blvd Nw Olympia (98502) ***(G-7298)***
Grandview Winery, Grandview *Also called Michelle Ste Wine Estates Ltd* ***(G-4253)***
Granger Company.......509 758-9458
5605 Se Scenic Ln # 301 Vancouver (98661) ***(G-14261)***
Granite Boatworks Inc.......360 466-1280
11071 Josh Green Ln # 105 Mount Vernon (98273) ***(G-6801)***
Granite Construction Company.......360 676-2450
7017 Everson Goshen Rd Everson (98247) ***(G-3676)***
Grant County Journal, Ephrata *Also called Journal-News Publishing Co* ***(G-3339)***
Grape Visions LLC.......509 525-1337
1248 Old Milton Hwy Walla Walla (99362) ***(G-14816)***
Grapecity Inc.......425 828-4440
401 Parkplace Ctr Ste 411 Kirkland (98033) ***(G-5352)***
Grapeview Point.......360 277-9015
81 E Grapeview Point Rd Allyn (98524) ***(G-83)***
Grapevine Hats LLC.......206 940-3896
10815 Se 184th Ln Renton (98055) ***(G-8810)***
Grapeworks Distilling LLC.......425 478-7181
16110 Woodinvle Rdmond Rd Woodinville (98072) ***(G-15254)***
Graphcomm Services, Point Roberts *Also called Thomas Mayer* ***(G-7670)***
Graphic Advertising Svcs Inc.......425 688-9980
3120 River Park Dr Richland (99354) ***(G-9003)***
Graphic Apparel.......509 525-7630
860 Ne Rose St College Place (99324) ***(G-2724)***
Graphic Art Productions Inc.......509 536-3278
11712 E Montgomery Dr Spokane Valley (99206) ***(G-12723)***
Graphic Communications.......360 426-8628
120 S 7th St Shelton (98584) ***(G-11698)***
Graphic Communications (PA).......360 786-5110
109 Columbia St Nw Olympia (98501) ***(G-7299)***
Graphic Communications Inc.......425 251-8680
4208 Lind Ave Sw Renton (98057) ***(G-8811)***
Graphic Control System Inc.......360 833-9522
13215 Se Mill Plain Blvd Vancouver (98684) ***(G-14262)***
Graphic Fx, Auburn *Also called Sign City Gfx* ***(G-563)***
Graphic Impressions Inc.......253 872-0555
7908 S 228th St Kent (98032) ***(G-4925)***
Graphic Packaging Intl Inc.......425 235-3300
601 Monster Rd Sw Renton (98057) ***(G-8812)***
Graphic Packaging Intl LLC.......360 896-6486
900 Se Tech Center Dr Vancouver (98683) ***(G-14263)***
Graphic Sheet Packaging, Renton *Also called Alliance Packaging LLC* ***(G-8738)***
Graphic Systems, Tukwila *Also called Apco Northwest* ***(G-13691)***
Graphicode Inc.......360 282-4888
1924 Bickford Ave Ste 201 Snohomish (98290) ***(G-11915)***
Graphics Place Inc.......425 486-3323
16130 Woodnvl Redmnd 2 Woodinville (98072) ***(G-15255)***
Graphite Guitar Systems.......360 273-7744
13043 195th Ave Sw Oakville (98568) ***(G-7175)***
Grassroots Outdoor LLC.......425 210-5745
500 Se Everett Mall Way Everett (98208) ***(G-3505)***
Grassroots Woodworks LLC.......360 836-1313
5879 Milwaukee Rd Bellingham (98226) ***(G-1360)***
Grating Fabricators Inc.......360 696-0886
3001 Se Columbia Way Vancouver (98661) ***(G-14264)***
Grating Pacific LLC.......253 872-7733
19411 66th Ave S Kent (98032) ***(G-4926)***
Gratrack.......571 357-4728
901 Occidental Ave S Seattle (98134) ***(G-10108)***
Gravel.......360 930-5777
4213 Grayback Cir Apt A Silverdale (98315) ***(G-11836)***
Gravel Doctor of Washington.......509 899-1608
421 Biltmore Dr Ellensburg (98926) ***(G-3205)***
Gravel Flat Crop Dusting LLC.......509 398-8617
155 D St Ne Ephrata (98823) ***(G-3336)***
Gravel Tones Productions Inc.......248 202-5757
1236 3rd Ave N Seattle (98109) ***(G-10109)***
Gravelroad LLC.......760 840-7174
1124 Nw 57th St Seattle (98107) ***(G-10110)***
Graves Spray Supply Inc.......253 854-2660
1862 Ives Ave Kent (98032) ***(G-4927)***
Gravity Labs Inc.......509 220-0817
3803 S Sherman St Spokane (99203) ***(G-12279)***
Gravity Square Inc.......206 524-0063
5041 46th Ave Ne Seattle (98105) ***(G-10111)***
Gray Area Technologies Inc.......206 370-2545
14241 Ne Wdnvlle Dvall Rd Woodinville (98072) ***(G-15256)***
Gray Mold Company Inc.......360 671-5711
3870 Mustang Way Ste 101 Bellingham (98226) ***(G-1361)***
Graybar Electric Company Inc.......425 203-1500
300 Sw 27th St Ste B Renton (98057) ***(G-8813)***
Graybeal Signs.......509 662-6926
1909 N Wenatchee Ave Wenatchee (98801) ***(G-15036)***
Graymark Industries Inc.......360 437-5121
3655 Oak Bay Rd Port Hadlock (98339) ***(G-7758)***
Graymont Western US Inc.......253 572-7600
1220 E Alexander Ave Tacoma (98421) ***(G-13319)***
Graymont Western US Inc.......253 572-7600
1220 E Alexander Ave Tacoma (98421) ***(G-13320)***
Graypants Inc.......206 420-3912
3220 1st Ave S Ste 400 Seattle (98134) ***(G-10112)***
Grays Electric Inc.......509 662-6834
1183 S Wenatchee Ave Wenatchee (98801) ***(G-15037)***
Grays Harbor Cabinet, Olympia *Also called William H Olson Inc* ***(G-7426)***
Grays Harbor Electronics.......360 532-3474
2614 Simpson Ave Hoquiam (98550) ***(G-4338)***
Grays Harbor Paper LLC.......877 548-3424
451 Sw 10th St Ste 107 Renton (98057) ***(G-8814)***
Grays Harbor Raceway.......360 482-4374
32 Elma Mccleary Rd Vancouver (98682) ***(G-14265)***
Grays Harbor Stamp Works.......360 533-3830
110 N G St Aberdeen (98520) ***(G-14)***
Grcc Student Chapter Saf.......253 288-3331
12401 Se 320th St Auburn (98092) ***(G-455)***
Grd Vintners, Royal City *Also called Lawrence Cellars LLC* ***(G-9171)***
Grease Heads Lube and Oil LLC.......509 930-3786
1130 N Baker Ave East Wenatchee (98802) ***(G-3017)***
Great American Bagel, The, Kent *Also called Rolln Dough Ltd* ***(G-5105)***

Great Artisan Beverage LLC 425 467-7952
11400 Se 8th St Ste 300 Bellevue (98004) *(G-933)*
Great Basin Energies Inc 509 623-1500
426 W Sprague Ave Ste 200 Spokane (99201) *(G-12280)*
Great Gates NW Inc 360 879-5554
33911 Tanwax Ct E Eatonville (98328) *(G-3058)*
Great Graphics & Signs Inc 206 948-9480
33 Kyms Way Orondo (98843) *(G-7457)*
Great Harvest Bread Co Inc 509 535-1146
2530 E 29th Ave Spokane (99223) *(G-12281)*
Great Impressions Rbr Stamps 360 807-8462
220 W Center St Centralia (98531) *(G-2404)*
Great King of Americas LLC 206 957-0987
2701 1st Ave Ste 310 Seattle (98121) *(G-10113)*
Great Little Box Co Inc 425 349-4522
1500 Industry St Ste 100 Everett (98203) *(G-3506)*
Great Northern Holdings Inc (PA) 253 572-3033
1640 E Marc St Tacoma (98421) *(G-13321)*
Great Northwest Industries 425 861-9768
5421 157th Dr Ne Redmond (98052) *(G-8483)*
Great NW Storm Screen Door Co, Redmond *Also called Great Northwest Industries (G-8483)*
Great Sun Corp 206 329-8027
5930 1st Ave S Seattle (98108) *(G-10114)*
Great Western Lumber Company 360 966-3061
7636 Goodwin Rd Everson (98247) *(G-3677)*
Great Western Malting Co 360 859-0940
3601 Se Columbia Way Vancouver (98661) *(G-14266)*
Great Western Malting Co 360 991-0888
700 Washington St Ste 508 Vancouver (98660) *(G-14267)*
Great Western Malting Co (HQ) 360 693-3661
1705 Nw Harborside Dr Vancouver (98660) *(G-14268)*
Great Western Malting Co 360 695-3484
2501 Kotobuki Way Vancouver (98660) *(G-14269)*
Great White Smile Instant 253 255-0456
4045 S Park Ave Tacoma (98418) *(G-13322)*
Greater Intelligence Inc (PA) 703 989-2281
6710 108th Ave Ne Ste 354 Kirkland (98033) *(G-5353)*
Greek Gods, Mountlake Terrace *Also called Hain Refrigerated Foods Inc (G-6862)*
Green Air Supply Inc 877 427-4361
216 Puyallup Ave S-111 Tacoma (98421) *(G-13323)*
Green American Transport, Tacoma *Also called Abraham Industries LLC (G-13155)*
Green Brothers of Seattle LLC 303 295-7669
603 Stewart St Ste 616 Seattle (98101) *(G-10115)*
Green Diamond Resource Company 360 426-0737
1050 E Mason Lake Dr W Grapeview (98546) *(G-4288)*
Green Flush Technologies LLC 360 718-7595
1420 N Columbia Ridge Way Washougal (98671) *(G-14957)*
Green Global Solution Inc 253 202-2304
1310 E 60th St Tacoma (98404) *(G-13324)*
Green Hills Software LLC 206 447-1373
800 5th Ave Ste 4100 Seattle (98104) *(G-10116)*
Green Hollow Farm Inc 509 397-3569
361 Roberts Rd Colfax (99111) *(G-2714)*
Green Island Growers LLC 360 298-0438
142 Pemberton Pl Friday Harbor (98250) *(G-4049)*
Green Karma Inc 206 786-1988
8124 Ne 122nd Pl Kirkland (98034) *(G-5354)*
Green Label Manufacturing Inc 954 445-0001
5305 Ne 121st Ave Vancouver (98682) *(G-14270)*
Green Labs LLC 360 875-5556
45 Raymond South Bend Rd Raymond (98577) *(G-8350)*
Green Lake Brewing Company LLC 206 300-9337
3409 Woodland Park Ave N Seattle (98103) *(G-10117)*
Green Leaf Family Estates 360 894-4945
13241 Zeller Rd Se Yelm (98597) *(G-15735)*
Green Mountain Metalworks LLC 360 281-6048
40215 Ne 142nd Ave Woodland (98674) *(G-15435)*
Green Mtn Mine Oper Co LLC 206 451-7105
26709 Mountain Loop Hwy Granite Falls (98252) *(G-4276)*
Green Ndle Cbnets Moldings LLC 206 235-3061
31040 133rd Ave Se Auburn (98092) *(G-456)*
Green Office Supplies 408 871-8887
704 228th Ave Ne Redmond (98074) *(G-8484)*
Green River College 253 856-9595
417 Ramsay Way Ste 112 Kent (98032) *(G-4928)*
Green River Welding 253 632-7551
33830 Se Grn Rvr Hdwrks R Ravensdale (98051) *(G-8337)*
Green Section 30 LLC 253 433-4130
36000 Enumclaw Franklin R Enumclaw (98022) *(G-3292)*
Green Star Energies Inc 360 989-5549
10000 Ne 7th Ave 100-C Vancouver (98685) *(G-14271)*
Green Store Inc 253 939-5757
100 10th Ave N Algona (98001) *(G-70)*
Green Synergy 206 779-3324
1508 N B St Apt 1304 Ellensburg (98926) *(G-3206)*
Green Trails Inc 206 546-6277
2416 Nw 201st Ct Shoreline (98177) *(G-11775)*
Green Valley Management LLC 509 830-5240
101 Green Valley Rd Ste A Mabton (98935) *(G-6228)*
Green Vault Systems LLC 206 900-2036
7010 136th Pl Se Snohomish (98296) *(G-11916)*
Green Willow Trucking Inc (PA) 360 687-7171
305 E Main St Battle Ground (98604) *(G-705)*
Green Willow Trucking Inc 360 687-7171
305 E Main St Battle Ground (98604) *(G-706)*
Green-On-Green Energy Inc 206 701-7321
3205 C St Ne Auburn (98002) *(G-457)*
Greenberry Industrial LLC 360 366-3767
6980 Salashan Pkwy Ferndale (98248) *(G-3849)*
Greencastle Soap & Supply 509 466-7223
203 N Stone St Spokane (99202) *(G-12282)*
Greence Inc 360 727-3528
2 S 56th Pl Ridgefield (98642) *(G-9087)*
Greendisk Inc 425 392-8700
4404 211th Ct Ne Sammamish (98074) *(G-9211)*
Greenes Tees LLC 206 801-7725
16001 Wallingford Ave N Shoreline (98133) *(G-11776)*
Greenfire Candles LLC 206 240-9225
4302 Greenwood Ave N Seattle (98103) *(G-10118)*
Greenfire Productions 360 572-0554
17831 59th Ave Ne Arlington (98223) *(G-245)*
Greenhaven LLC 360 436-1420
1311 Ne State Rte 530 Darrington (98241) *(G-2868)*
Greenhill Lumber Co Inc 509 767-0010
134 Tidyman Rd Dallesport (98617) *(G-2863)*
Greenland Inc 206 623-2577
815 S Weller St Ste 103 Seattle (98104) *(G-10119)*
Greenland Industries LLC 503 841-1835
2327 Se Sedgwick Rd Port Orchard (98366) *(G-7811)*
Greenleaf Foods Spc 206 762-5961
4011 6th Ave S Seattle (98108) *(G-10120)*
Greenleaf Foods Spc 206 762-5961
3901 7th Ave S Seattle (98108) *(G-10121)*
Greenleaf Publishing Inc 509 427-8444
198 Sw 2nd St Stevenson (98648) *(G-13012)*
Greenlife Industries 360 566-3984
414 W 12th St Apt 2 Vancouver (98660) *(G-14272)*
Greenlite Heavy Industries LLC 206 226-3523
6801 96th Ave Se Mercer Island (98040) *(G-6465)*
Greensleeves LLC 360 606-1934
712 W Mcloughlin Blvd Vancouver (98660) *(G-14273)*
Greenwood Cider Co LLC 360 961-2902
10015 Lake Cy Way Ne 10 Seattle (98125) *(G-10122)*
Greenwood Clean Energy Inc (PA) 888 788-3090
7114 180th Ave Ne B101 Redmond (98052) *(G-8485)*
Greer Steel Inc 253 581-4100
3117 107th St S Lakewood (98499) *(G-5727)*
Greers Mobile Equipment Repair 360 901-0373
3823 Lewis River Rd Woodland (98674) *(G-15436)*
Greg Aanes Furniture Inc 360 733-9101
2109 Queen St Bellingham (98229) *(G-1362)*
Greg Michael Cellars LLC 509 465-3591
1213 W Railroad Ave Spokane (99201) *(G-12283)*
Greg Robertson Logging Inc 208 660-3616
322 S Washington Ave Newport (99156) *(G-7058)*
Greg's Graphic & Printing Co, Olympia *Also called Graphic Communications (G-7299)*
Gregory Diede 509 662-1009
403 E Peters St Wenatchee (98801) *(G-15038)*
Greif Brothers Distribution 360 225-9995
701 W Scott Ave Woodland (98674) *(G-15437)*
Gremlin Inc 206 781-4636
4233 21st Ave W Fl 2 Seattle (98199) *(G-10123)*
Grenlar Construction, Kenmore *Also called Grenlar Holdings Inc (G-4578)*
Grenlar Holdings Inc 425 419-4430
16636 Simonds Rd Ne Kenmore (98028) *(G-4578)*
Grette Custom Woodworking 425 392-8584
27022 Se 162nd Pl Issaquah (98027) *(G-4424)*
Grey Gull Ceramics 360 321-1582
5177 Blacktail Ln Langley (98260) *(G-5779)*
Greybeard Publishing 360 495-4107
1125 W Simpson Ave McCleary (98557) *(G-6416)*
Greyslade 253 332-5985
5040 S M St Tacoma (98408) *(G-13325)*
Greywood Manor LLC 206 949-1362
11833 3rd Ave S Seattle (98168) *(G-10124)*
Gribskov Glassblowing 360 795-8419
123 Middle Valley Rd Skamokawa (98647) *(G-11865)*
Grieb Optimal Winecrafting LLC 509 877-0925
71 Gangl Rd Wapato (98951) *(G-14916)*
Grief Inc 253 929-0649
4227 S Meridian Ste C-363 Puyallup (98373) *(G-8160)*
Grief Store, The, Puyallup *Also called Grief Inc (G-8160)*
Griese Enterprises 509 868-7963
2721 E Diamond Ave Spokane (99217) *(G-12284)*
Griffin Publishing Inc 509 534-3625
2210 N Dollar Rd Spokane Valley (99212) *(G-12724)*
Griffiths Inc 360 276-4122
208 Otis Ave Moclips (98562) *(G-6539)*
Grigg Farms LLC (PA) 509 787-3225
12139 Road 6 Nw Quincy (98848) *(G-8299)*
Grigsby Software Developm 360 942-5240
656 Barnhart St Ste C Raymond (98577) *(G-8351)*
Grind All Inc 253 854-6117
22638 85th Pl S Kent (98031) *(G-4929)*
Grind-All, Kent *Also called Meyer Engineered Materials LLC (G-5009)*

ALPHABETIC

Griptonite Inc ALPHABETIC SECTION

Griptonite Inc ...425 825-6800
12421 Willows Rd Ne # 200 Kirkland (98034) ***(G-5355)***
Grist Magazine Inc ...206 876-2020
1201 Western Ave Ste 410 Seattle (98101) ***(G-10125)***
Grit City Grind House LLC ...203 898-5627
2312 N 8th St Apt A Tacoma (98403) ***(G-13326)***
Grizzly Firestarters North ...360 659-3948
10310 State Ave Marysville (98271) ***(G-6341)***
Grizzly Firestarters North (PA) ...360 652-2100
35177 Deer Creek Rd Mount Vernon (98274) ***(G-6802)***
Grizzly Machining Solutions ...406 396-4087
122 S Sultan Basin Rd Sultan (98294) ***(G-13026)***
Grizzly Pet Products LLC ...425 481-1110
19600 144th Ave Ne Woodinville (98072) ***(G-15257)***
Gronlund Logging Inc ...509 548-5039
236 Mine St Leavenworth (98826) ***(G-5804)***
Groove Incorporated ...360 786-9605
6715 Martin Way E Olympia (98516) ***(G-7300)***
Ground Piercing Inc ...509 961-8241
1101 Industrial Way # 3504 Yakima (98903) ***(G-15577)***
Ground Print LLC ...206 852-2622
21310 Se 271st Pl Maple Valley (98038) ***(G-6271)***
Ground Source Energy Nw ...253 852-5926
10600 Se 212th St Kent (98031) ***(G-4930)***
Groundhog Mines LLC ...425 609-6901
1825 S Lake Stevens Rd Lake Stevens (98258) ***(G-5645)***
Grounds For Change Inc ...360 779-0401
15773 Gorge Ln Ne Ste 204 Poulsbo (98370) ***(G-7964)***
Group 2 Inc ...206 378-0900
4442 27th Ave W Seattle (98199) ***(G-10126)***
Groupfabric Inc ...425 681-2927
819 Virginia St Unit 3007 Seattle (98101) ***(G-10127)***
Groupware Incorporated ...360 397-1000
110 E 17th St Vancouver (98663) ***(G-14274)***
Grove and Kane Inc ...425 407-3454
520 128th St Sw Ste A6 Everett (98204) ***(G-3507)***
Grove Church ...360 386-5760
4705 Grove St Marysville (98270) ***(G-6342)***
Grow Northwest ...360 398-1155
7399 Goodwin Rd Everson (98247) ***(G-3678)***
Grow Plastics LLC ...206 954-4564
7734 15th Ave Ne Seattle (98115) ***(G-10128)***
Growfast Software ...360 224-5484
2300 Taylor Ave Apt 8 Bellingham (98225) ***(G-1363)***
Growlife Inc (PA) ...866 781-5559
5400 Carillon Pt Kirkland (98033) ***(G-5356)***
Grozdi Inc ...253 820-0653
3852 S 31st St Tacoma (98409) ***(G-13327)***
Grs, Tacoma *Also called Glass Restoration Specialists* ***(G-13311)***
Grubstake EMC ...509 775-2041
13 Pine Grove St Republic (99166) ***(G-8957)***
Gruma Corporation ...253 896-4483
6611 Valley Ave E Fife (98424) ***(G-3957)***
Grundfos CBS Inc ...206 433-2600
3113 S Pine St Unit C Tacoma (98409) ***(G-13328)***
Gsf Publications ...206 789-7548
3507 Nw 60th St Seattle (98107) ***(G-10129)***
Gsi Outdoors Inc ...509 928-9611
1023 S Pines Rd Spokane Valley (99206) ***(G-12725)***
Gsl Solutions Inc ...360 896-5354
2414 Se 125th Ave Vancouver (98683) ***(G-14275)***
Gt Darts ...206 498-9855
19528 Echo Lake Pl N Shoreline (98133) ***(G-11777)***
Gt Machining ...509 922-8395
13607 E Trent Ave Spokane Valley (99216) ***(G-12726)***
Gt Recording ...206 783-6911
9921 Aurora Ave N Seattle (98103) ***(G-10130)***
GTC Innovations LLC ...866 241-3149
14201 Se Petrovitsky Rd A3 Renton (98058) ***(G-8815)***
Gtr Technologies Inc ...360 876-2974
1420 Lumsden Rd Port Orchard (98367) ***(G-7812)***
Gtsp Global, Vancouver *Also called Global Technical Staffin* ***(G-14259)***
Guadalupe Foods Inc ...360 736-0298
12231 Independence Rd Sw Rochester (98579) ***(G-9133)***
Guardian Interlock Systems ...360 423-4766
560 Industrial Way Longview (98632) ***(G-5913)***
Guess Inc ...206 682-7005
600 Pine St Ste 220 Seattle (98101) ***(G-10131)***
Guide & Classified, Chehalis *Also called Devaul Publishing Inc* ***(G-2489)***
Guided Reality Corporation ...206 856-8819
9764 Ne Pine St Bainbridge Island (98110) ***(G-637)***
Guides Chice AP Spcialists LLC ...206 931-3838
18930 Se 236th Pl Kent (98042) ***(G-4931)***
Guido Perla & Associates Inc ...206 463-2217
701 5th Ave Ste 1200 Seattle (98104) ***(G-10132)***
Guild of American Luthiers ...253 472-7853
8222 S Park Ave Tacoma (98408) ***(G-13329)***
Gullassa, Seattle *Also called David Gulassa & Co Inc* ***(G-9800)***
Gundersons Auto License ...360 695-2122
2700 Ne Andresen Rd A6 Vancouver (98661) ***(G-14276)***
Gundersons Custom Welding ...360 794-6165
17224 Tester Rd Snohomish (98290) ***(G-11917)***
Gundie's Auto & Truck Wrecking, Bellingham *Also called Gundies Inc* ***(G-1364)***
Gundies Inc (PA) ...360 733-5036
1283 Mt Baker Hwy Bellingham (98226) ***(G-1364)***
Gunpowder Creek LLC ...860 502-9202
950 Boyer Ave Walla Walla (99362) ***(G-14817)***
Gurglepot Inc ...253 670-6240
120 County Line Rd 101 Pacific (98047) ***(G-7528)***
Gurian Instruments Inc ...206 467-7990
5350 30th Ave Nw Ste H Seattle (98107) ***(G-10133)***
Gutsy Services LLC ...503 750-9024
2514 E 26th St Vancouver (98661) ***(G-14277)***
Gutters Inc ...425 482-2679
23815 23rd Ave W Bothell (98021) ***(G-1863)***
Guy Bennett Lumber Co, Clarkston *Also called Bennett Lumber Products Inc* ***(G-2623)***
Guy Chai Inc ...360 710-5962
5885 State Highway 303 Ne Bremerton (98311) ***(G-1959)***
Guy Gifter, Woodinville *Also called Amaze Graphics Inc* ***(G-15176)***
Guy Sunglass ...509 489-2963
39402 N Locher Rd Deer Park (99006) ***(G-2904)***
Guys Plasma NW LLC ...360 878-9826
9611 Summerfield Loop Se Olympia (98513) ***(G-7301)***
Gw 42 Inc ...360 862-8319
1208 10th St Ste B Snohomish (98290) ***(G-11918)***
Gwenies Ckies Hmemade Goodness, Pasco *Also called Berry Haven LLC* ***(G-7553)***
H & D Logging Company Inc ...509 548-7358
11797 Chumstick Hwy Leavenworth (98826) ***(G-5805)***
H & E Building Enterprises ...253 848-3534
10318 32nd St E Edgewood (98372) ***(G-3081)***
H & E Custom Cabinets, Edgewood *Also called H & E Building Enterprises* ***(G-3081)***
H & H Wood Recyclers Inc ...360 892-2805
8401 Ne 117th Ave Vancouver (98662) ***(G-14278)***
H & S Machine ...425 483-2772
19819 144th Ave Ne Woodinville (98072) ***(G-15258)***
H A Milton Corp ...509 346-1192
2140 Road 12 Sw Royal City (99357) ***(G-9169)***
H B Q Inc ...509 653-1939
3001 State Rte 410 Naches (98937) ***(G-6997)***
H Brothers Inc ...206 999-9837
1425 Broadway 480 Seattle (98122) ***(G-10134)***
H C U Inc ...425 885-0564
15362 Ne 96th Pl Redmond (98052) ***(G-8486)***
H D Fowler Co Inc (PA) ...425 746-8400
13440 Se 30th St Bellevue (98005) ***(G-934)***
H D I, Vancouver *Also called Hd International Corp* ***(G-14290)***
H Enterprises, Longview *Also called Christian Hamilton* ***(G-5899)***
H F Hauff Co Inc ...509 248-0318
2921 Sutherland Dr Yakima (98903) ***(G-15578)***
H F S-Vitek ...360 293-8054
301 30th St Anacortes (98221) ***(G-133)***
H R C Refining, Mount Vernon *Also called Hallmark Refining Corporation* ***(G-6803)***
H R Management Northwest ...509 697-5377
670 Tibbling Rd Selah (98942) ***(G-11590)***
H R Spinner Corporation (PA) ...509 453-9111
115 S 1st Ave Yakima (98902) ***(G-15579)***
H W Image Works Inc ...760 343-3869
811 141st Pl Se Bellevue (98007) ***(G-935)***
H&H Enterprises, Winlock *Also called Jack H Hill* ***(G-15152)***
H&H Publications LLP ...360 730-1206
4160 Beach Dr Freeland (98249) ***(G-4029)***
H&N Electric, Pasco *Also called Timken Motor & Crane Svcs LLC* ***(G-7638)***
H/H Estates Reserve, Prosser *Also called Coyote Canyon Winery LLC* ***(G-8036)***
H2 Pre- Cast Inc ...509 884-6644
3835 N Clemons St East Wenatchee (98802) ***(G-3018)***
H20 Factor ...425 868-4017
1340 229th Pl Ne Sammamish (98074) ***(G-9212)***
H2o Jet Inc ...360 866-7161
1145 85th Ave Se Tumwater (98501) ***(G-13874)***
Haase Logging, Tumwater *Also called Denise Haase* ***(G-13871)***
Haase Woodworks ...360 681-2600
258955 Highway 101 Sequim (98382) ***(G-11637)***
Hacienda Custom Woodwork LLC ...206 922-9330
17226 120th Ter Se Renton (98058) ***(G-8816)***
Hacienda Custom Woodwork LLC ...206 922-9330
23213 239th Pl Se Maple Valley (98038) ***(G-6272)***
Hacienda Las Flares ...208 819-8879
3308 E 11th Ave Apt D313 Spokane (99202) ***(G-12285)***
Hadaller Logging Inc ...360 425-0602
1290 Walnut St Kelso (98626) ***(G-4527)***
Hadley Door & Trim Inc ...360 748-0116
915 Nw State Ave Chehalis (98532) ***(G-2499)***
Hado Labs LLC ...425 891-7124
5604 28th Ave Nw Seattle (98107) ***(G-10135)***
Hafa Adai Signs & Graphics LLC ...253 394-0600
1835 Auburn Way N Ste B Auburn (98002) ***(G-458)***
Hager Worldwide Inc ...360 210-5084
82 Washougal River Rd Washougal (98671) ***(G-14958)***
Hahn Manufacturing Inc ...509 930-1621
211 Berndt Bluff Rd Yakima (98908) ***(G-15580)***
Hahn Software LLC ...206 724-4735
2419 Sw 149th St Burien (98166) ***(G-2111)***
Hain Refrigerated Foods Inc ...425 485-2476
21707 66th Ave W Mountlake Terrace (98043) ***(G-6862)***

Hal Burton Publishing & Dist 360 877-0613
61 N Picnic Dr Lilliwaup (98555) ***(G-5871)***
Haldex Brake Products Corp 360 944-3070
9116 Ne 130th Ave Ste 106 Vancouver (98682) ***(G-14279)***
Haldex Brake Systems, Vancouver *Also called Haldex Brake Products Corp* ***(G-14279)***
Haley & Bros 253 851-4977
4909 33rd Avenue Ct Nw Gig Harbor (98335) ***(G-4109)***
Half Families Enterprises LLC 425 629-3232
20910 Ne 17th St Sammamish (98074) ***(G-9213)***
Half Lion Brewing Company LLC 253 561-1115
5123 Nathan Loop Se Auburn (98092) ***(G-459)***
Half Moon Bay Bar & Grill 360 268-9166
421 E Neddie Rose Dr Westport (98595) ***(G-15105)***
Halfmoon Publishing LLC 360 934-5387
105 Half Moon Creek Rd Raymond (98577) ***(G-8352)***
Halldata Inc 509 588-5080
1580 Dale Ave Benton City (99320) ***(G-1615)***
Hallett Choclat & Treat Fctry, Spokane *Also called Hallett Confections* ***(G-12286)***
Hallett Confections 509 484-6454
1419 E Holyoke Ave Spokane (99217) ***(G-12286)***
Hallmark Refining Corporation 360 428-5880
1016 Dale Ln Mount Vernon (98274) ***(G-6803)***
Halls Drug Center Inc 360 736-5000
505 S Tower Ave A Centralia (98531) ***(G-2405)***
Halls Medical Center Pharmacy, Centralia *Also called Halls Drug Center Inc* ***(G-2405)***
Halme Construction Inc 509 725-4200
8727 W Highway 2 Spokane (99224) ***(G-12287)***
Halwest Technologies Inc 509 674-1882
107 Owens Rd Cle Elum (98922) ***(G-2669)***
Ham Industries 360 201-8439
303 Nw 97th St Seattle (98117) ***(G-10136)***
Hamburg Precision Inc 360 225-0212
1356 Down River Dr Woodland (98674) ***(G-15438)***
Hamilton Cellars LLC 509 628-8227
55410 N Sunset Rd Benton City (99320) ***(G-1616)***
Hamilton Drywall Products, Woodland *Also called Hamilton Materials Wash LLC* ***(G-15439)***
Hamilton Equipment 509 775-3445
148 N Portland St Republic (99166) ***(G-8958)***
Hamilton Jan Printing Systems 425 778-1975
120 W Dayton St Ste C8 Edmonds (98020) ***(G-3115)***
Hamilton Materials Wash LLC (PA) 360 225-6888
295 N Pekin Rd Woodland (98674) ***(G-15439)***
Hamilton Priniting 425 778-1975
120 W Dayton St Ste C8 Edmonds (98020) ***(G-3116)***
Hamilton Printing Systems 425 778-1936
22314 97th Ave W Edmonds (98020) ***(G-3117)***
Hamilton Spray 360 748-9615
1316 Nw River St Chehalis (98532) ***(G-2500)***
Hamiltonjet Inc 206 784-8400
14680 Ne N Woodinville Woodinville (98072) ***(G-15259)***
Hammer & Tongs LLC 206 526-0549
1500 N 100th St Seattle (98133) ***(G-10137)***
Hampton Affiliates 360 403-8213
19406 68th Dr Ne Arlington (98223) ***(G-246)***
Hampton Dist Companies LLC 360 496-5115
10166 Us Highway 12 Randle (98377) ***(G-8325)***
Hampton Lumber Cowlitz, Randle *Also called Hampton Dist Companies LLC* ***(G-8325)***
Hampton Lumber Mills Inc 360 474-1504
19406 68th Dr Ne A Arlington (98223) ***(G-247)***
Hanatoro Winery 404 312-5891
1793 J B George Rd Walla Walla (99362) ***(G-14818)***
Hanazono Asian Noodle 360 385-7622
225 Taylor St Fl 1 Port Townsend (98368) ***(G-7887)***
Hancocks Bakery 425 885-3780
16150 Ne 85th St Ste 105 Redmond (98052) ***(G-8487)***
Hancor, Olympia *Also called Advanced Drainage Systems Inc* ***(G-7221)***
Hancor Inc 360 943-3313
6001 Belmore St Sw Olympia (98512) ***(G-7302)***
Handley Sales, Tukwila *Also called Controlled Products of Wash* ***(G-13717)***
Handly & Phillips Logging Inc 360 765-3578
Camelot Rd Quilcene (98376) ***(G-8284)***
Handmaiden Bead & Jwly Shoppe 509 680-5785
162 S Main St Colville (99114) ***(G-2754)***
Handyworks Inc 509 299-4918
405 E Fellows St Medical Lake (99022) ***(G-6441)***
Hang Gliding Adventures 360 357-1460
884 Anthony Ct Sw Tumwater (98512) ***(G-13875)***
Hang-UPS, Buckley *Also called Stl International Incorporated* ***(G-2076)***
Hanger Inc 360 423-6049
1516 Hudson St Ste 105 Longview (98632) ***(G-5914)***
Hanger Clinic, Longview *Also called Hanger Inc* ***(G-5914)***
Hanger Clinic, Gig Harbor *Also called Hanger Prsthetcs & Ortho Inc* ***(G-4110)***
Hanger Orthopedic Group Inc 253 383-4447
723 Martin Luther King Jr Tacoma (98405) ***(G-13330)***
Hanger Prosthetics & Ortho W 360 256-0026
505 Ne 87th Ave Ste Ll10 Vancouver (98664) ***(G-14280)***
Hanger Prsthetcs & Ortho Inc 425 451-8831
616 120th Ave Ne Ste 111 Bellevue (98005) ***(G-936)***
Hanger Prsthetcs & Ortho Inc 253 372-7478
3555 Erickson St Gig Harbor (98335) ***(G-4110)***
Hanger Prsthetcs & Ortho Inc 509 624-3314
514 S Washington St Spokane (99204) ***(G-12288)***
Hanger Prsthetcs & Ortho Inc 360 423-6049
1516 Hudson St Ste 105 Longview (98632) ***(G-5915)***
Hanger Prsthetcs & Ortho Inc 509 946-2520
949 Stevens Dr Richland (99352) ***(G-9004)***
Hanging Canvas 206 937-3525
1027 California Ln Sw Seattle (98116) ***(G-10138)***
Hanging H Companies LLC 360 899-4638
1912 S Burlington Blvd Burlington (98233) ***(G-2160)***
Hanging H Company, Burlington *Also called Hanging H Companies LLC* ***(G-2160)***
Hansen & Spies Logging Inc 509 364-3385
18 Pine Vista Rd Glenwood (98619) ***(G-4183)***
Hansen Fabrication 206 283-9181
4254 23rd Ave W Seattle (98199) ***(G-10139)***
Hansen Logging LLC 509 935-4515
2464 Quarry Browns Lk Rd Chewelah (99109) ***(G-2602)***
Hansen Marine Repair & Rigging 360 705-1252
4433 61st Ave Ne Olympia (98516) ***(G-7303)***
Hansencrafts LLC 360 747-7746
710 E Pk Ave Port Twnsend Port Townsend (98368) ***(G-7888)***
Hanson Aggregates LLC 360 795-3221
273 W State Route 4 Cathlamet (98612) ***(G-2368)***
Hanson Ding Pacific, Mukilteo *Also called Hd Pacific Inc* ***(G-6931)***
Hanson Lehigh Inc 425 867-1234
6600 230th Ave Se Issaquah (98027) ***(G-4425)***
Hanson Precision Inc 360 793-0626
41729 164th St Se Gold Bar (98251) ***(G-4189)***
Hanson Worldwide LLC 509 252-9290
2425 E Magnesium Rd Spokane (99217) ***(G-12289)***
Hanz Extremity Wear, Seattle *Also called Danalco Inc* ***(G-9790)***
Haolifts Industries 425 836-3968
221 259th Ave Ne Sammamish (98074) ***(G-9214)***
Happily Ever After 206 226-8814
23508 65th Pl W Mountlake Terrace (98043) ***(G-6863)***
Happy Donut 253 852-3286
10214 Se 240th St Ste A Kent (98031) ***(G-4932)***
Happy Tab LLC 773 231-8223
319 7th Ln S Kirkland (98033) ***(G-5357)***
Happy Thoughts 360 468-2880
12 Dolphin Ln Lopez Island (98261) ***(G-5983)***
Harbinger Knowledge Pdts Inc 425 861-8400
16770 Ne 79th St Ste 100 Redmond (98052) ***(G-8488)***
Harbisonwalker Intl Inc 253 872-2552
20408 87th Ave S I Kent (98031) ***(G-4933)***
Harbor Action Inc 360 417-1316
166 Alice Rd Port Angeles (98363) ***(G-7708)***
Harbor Cabinet, Olympia *Also called William H Olson Inc* ***(G-7427)***
Harbor Graphics Inc 360 532-1234
608 8th St Hoquiam (98550) ***(G-4339)***
Harbor Graphics Inc 253 858-7909
3123 56th St Nw Ste 3 Gig Harbor (98335) ***(G-4111)***
Harbor Island Mch Works Inc 206 682-7637
3431 11th Ave Sw Seattle (98134) ***(G-10140)***
Harbor Island Supply Corp 206 762-1900
230 S Chicago St Seattle (98108) ***(G-10141)***
Harbor Machine & Fabricating 360 533-1188
710 30th St Hoquiam (98550) ***(G-4340)***
Harbor Pacific Bottling Inc (PA) 360 482-4820
50 Schouweiler Tract Rd E Elma (98541) ***(G-3248)***
Harbor Steel Fabrication 253 858-8804
5926 Sehmel Dr Nw Gig Harbor (98332) ***(G-4112)***
Harbor Vascular Inc 425 420-6009
22445 Se 31st Pl Sammamish (98075) ***(G-9215)***
Harbour Pointe Golf LLC 425 355-6060
11817 Harbour Pointe Blvd Mukilteo (98275) ***(G-6930)***
Harbour Pointe Golf Assn, Mukilteo *Also called Harbour Pointe Golf LLC* ***(G-6930)***
Harchery Division, Lynden *Also called Perdue Foods LLC* ***(G-6046)***
Hard Drive Marine 360 306-8685
3620 Irongate Rd Bellingham (98226) ***(G-1365)***
Hard Industries Hl 360 913-2063
7226 Eaglefield Dr Arlington (98223) ***(G-248)***
Hard Metal Solutions Inc 360 548-8017
17837 59th Ave Ne 11 Arlington (98223) ***(G-249)***
Hard Notched Customs LLC 360 205-3252
6615 Ne Highway 99 Vancouver (98665) ***(G-14281)***
Hard Rock Machine Works Inc 509 529-9833
2878 Melrose St Walla Walla (99362) ***(G-14819)***
Hard Row To Hoe Vineyards 509 687-3000
300 Ivan Morse Rd Manson (98831) ***(G-6244)***
Hardel Builders Center, Chehalis *Also called Hardel Mutual Plywood Corp* ***(G-2501)***
Hardel Mutual Plywood Corp (PA) 360 740-0232
143 Maurin Rd Chehalis (98532) ***(G-2501)***
Hardened Arms LLC 425 530-0837
515 Tucker Ave Friday Harbor (98250) ***(G-4050)***
Hardrock Incorporated 360 779-3700
17672 Widme Rd Poulsbo (98370) ***(G-7965)***
Hardsuit Labs, Seattle *Also called Builder Box LLC* ***(G-9596)***
Hardtail Choppers Inc 360 750-6780
1412 Se 83rd Ct Vancouver (98664) ***(G-14282)***
Hardwood Industries Inc 425 420-1050
20124 Broadway Ave Ste D Snohomish (98296) ***(G-11919)***
Hardy Engineering & Mfg Inc 253 735-6488
120 37th St Ne Auburn (98002) ***(G-460)***

Harlane Co LLC...404 771-9300
2412 Nw 121st Cir Vancouver (98685) ***(G-14283)***
Harmon Brewing Company L L C (PA)...253 383-2739
1938 Pacific Ave Tacoma (98402) ***(G-13331)***
Harmon Brewing Company L L C...253 853-1585
1208 26th Ave Nw Gig Harbor (98335) ***(G-4113)***
Harmon Pub & Brewery, Tacoma *Also called Harmon Brewing Company L L C* ***(G-13331)***
Harmonious Development LLC...425 248-5794
4548 20th Ave Ne Apt 203 Seattle (98105) ***(G-10142)***
Harmony Soapworks, Ocean Park *Also called Diana Thompson* ***(G-7179)***
Harold Tymer Co Inc...360 573-6053
8005 Nw 17th Ave Vancouver (98665) ***(G-14284)***
Harolds Furnace Cleaning, Walla Walla *Also called Harolds Power Vac Inc* ***(G-14820)***
Harolds Power Vac Inc...509 529-2088
520 Russet Rd Walla Walla (99362) ***(G-14820)***
Harper Engineering Company...425 255-0414
700 Sw 7th St Renton (98057) ***(G-8817)***
Harpo Investment Inc...360 532-5516
2421 Port Industrial Rd Aberdeen (98520) ***(G-15)***
Harrah Farm Shop...509 848-2941
3959 Harrah Rd Harrah (98933) ***(G-4320)***
Harrington Tower Services...206 760-9191
3515 S Ferdinand St Seattle (98118) ***(G-10143)***
Harrington Trophies...509 943-2593
717 Jadwin Ave Richland (99352) ***(G-9005)***
Harris Acquisition IV LLC (HQ)...360 734-3600
3436 Airport Dr Bellingham (98226) ***(G-1366)***
Harris Acquisition IV LLC...360 734-3600
3436 Airport Dr Bellingham (98226) ***(G-1367)***
Harris Isuzu, Lynnwood *Also called Harris-Ford Inc* ***(G-6132)***
Harris Machine LLC...253 347-6230
1819 Central Ave S Ste 12 Kent (98032) ***(G-4934)***
Harris Manufacturing Irri...509 539-1725
1257 Hanson Loop C Burbank (99323) ***(G-2084)***
Harris Metal Fab & Welding...360 687-6273
19217 Ne 219th St Battle Ground (98604) ***(G-707)***
Harris Rebar Seattle Inc (PA)...253 847-5001
4421 192nd St E Tacoma (98446) ***(G-13332)***
Harris-Ford Inc (PA)...425 678-0391
20006 64th Ave W Lynnwood (98036) ***(G-6132)***
Harrison Gray Publishing LLC...206 783-5682
5801 Phinney Ave N # 403 Seattle (98103) ***(G-10144)***
Harry Price...360 254-5534
12006 Ne 119th St Vancouver (98682) ***(G-14285)***
Harry Wiebold Logging...360 687-2129
7801 Ne 279th St Battle Ground (98604) ***(G-708)***
Harrys Radiator Shop Inc...509 765-8581
607 E Broadway Ave Moses Lake (98837) ***(G-6713)***
Hart Crowser Inc (PA)...206 324-9530
3131 Elliott Ave Ste 600 Seattle (98121) ***(G-10145)***
Hart Health, Tukwila *Also called Normed Inc* ***(G-13779)***
Hart Scientific...425 446-5400
6920 Seaway Blvd Everett (98203) ***(G-3508)***
Hart Systems Inc...253 858-8481
4911 71st Street Ct Nw Gig Harbor (98335) ***(G-4114)***
Hartley Co, Olympia *Also called Hartley Jewelers* ***(G-7304)***
Hartley Jewelers...360 754-6161
6640 Klein St Nw Olympia (98502) ***(G-7304)***
Harts Lake Furrier, Roy *Also called Harts Lake Trading Post* ***(G-9160)***
Harts Lake Trading Post...360 458-3477
35816 58th Ave S Roy (98580) ***(G-9160)***
Hartung Glass Industries (PA)...206 772-7800
3351 E Valley Rd Tukwila (98188) ***(G-13743)***
Hartung Glass Industries...206 772-7800
17750 W Valley Hwy Tukwila (98188) ***(G-13744)***
Harvest Food Solutions...503 926-6499
501 Se Clmbia Shrs 900 Vancouver (98661) ***(G-14286)***
Harvest Helper...360 515-5491
2747 Pacific Ave Se Olympia (98501) ***(G-7305)***
Harvest House...509 238-6970
9919 E Greenbluff Rd Colbert (99005) ***(G-2707)***
Harvest Timber Company, Longbranch *Also called Nce Inc* ***(G-5879)***
Harvest Time Fruit & Produce, Beaver *Also called Little Nut Inc* ***(G-758)***
Harveys Skin Diving Supplies...206 824-1114
2505 S 252nd St Kent (98032) ***(G-4935)***
Hasa Inc...360 578-9300
3539 Industrial Way Longview (98632) ***(G-5916)***
Hasco Inc...425 643-2525
6335 163rd Pl Se Bellevue (98006) ***(G-937)***
Hash Inc...360 750-0042
10411 Ne 110th Cir Vancouver (98662) ***(G-14287)***
Haskill Creek Publishing...509 467-9439
10017 N Stevens Ln Spokane (99218) ***(G-12290)***
Hasse & Company, Port Townsend *Also called Port Townsend Sails Inc* ***(G-7914)***
Hassler & Associates Inc...253 851-3248
12408 Tanager Dr Nw Gig Harbor (98332) ***(G-4115)***
Hatch & Kirk Inc (PA)...206 783-2766
927 Nw 50th St Seattle (98107) ***(G-10146)***
Hatterdashery...206 322-6149
1862 E Shelby St Seattle (98112) ***(G-10147)***
Hattingh Holdings Inc...206 323-4040
600 Broadway Ste 190 Seattle (98122) ***(G-10148)***
Hauge & Hassain Incorporated...206 789-8842
1140 Nw 46th St Seattle (98107) ***(G-10149)***
Haulin Somethin Inc...509 738-4144
2084 Northprt Flat Crk Rd Kettle Falls (99141) ***(G-5232)***
Haun Made LLC...253 242-6105
16 S Michigan St Ste A Seattle (98108) ***(G-10150)***
Haunted Quigit Sound, Port Orchard *Also called Illusion Wear Capes* ***(G-7815)***
Haven Boatworks LLC...360 385-5727
305 8th St Port Townsend (98368) ***(G-7889)***
Haven Boatworks LLC (PA)...360 385-5727
305 8th St Port Townsend (98368) ***(G-7890)***
Havens Woodworks & Refinishing...360 833-9446
407 Se Everett Rd Camas (98607) ***(G-2256)***
Havillah Lumber...509 486-4650
982 Havillah Rd Tonasket (98855) ***(G-13649)***
Havillah Road Printing, OMAK *Also called Community Networkers LLC* ***(G-7437)***
Havillah Shake Co (PA)...509 486-1467
521 N Siwash Creek Rd Tonasket (98855) ***(G-13650)***
Havre Daily News (HQ)...206 284-4424
221 1st Ave W Ste 405 Seattle (98119) ***(G-10151)***
Hawaiian Earth Products...808 682-5895
7343 E Marginal Way S Seattle (98108) ***(G-10152)***
Hawk International Inc...253 851-3444
10421 Burnham Dr Nw Ste 3 Gig Harbor (98332) ***(G-4116)***
Hawk's Superior Rock, Raymond *Also called Beans & Rocks LLC* ***(G-8343)***
Hawkbird Auto An Boat Listing...360 491-3015
1401 Marvin Rd Ne Ste 105 Lacey (98516) ***(G-5554)***
Hawkins Lettering...425 481-1938
18303 Bothell Everett Hwy # 120 Bothell (98012) ***(G-1864)***
Hawkins Lettering EMB Mfg, Bothell *Also called Hawkins Lettering* ***(G-1864)***
Hawks Prairie Golf LLC...360 455-8383
1416 112th Ave Ne Bellevue (98004) ***(G-938)***
Hawks Prrie Auto Boat Lcensing, Lacey *Also called Hawkbird Auto An Boat Listing* ***(G-5554)***
Hawthorne Hill...253 572-3744
320 E 32nd St Unit 410 Tacoma (98404) ***(G-13333)***
Hays Div, Bothell *Also called Romac Industries Inc* ***(G-1897)***
Haytools Inc...509 933-1102
1003 S Ruby St Ellensburg (98926) ***(G-3207)***
Hayward Gordon Us Inc (HQ)...206 767-5660
1541 S 92nd Pl Seattle (98108) ***(G-10153)***
Hazelwood Farm LLC...425 454-5165
14831 Ne 87th St Redmond (98052) ***(G-8489)***
HB Aerospace LLC...425 432-3440
28819 Se 208th St Hobart (98025) ***(G-4323)***
HB Fuller Company...360 574-8828
417 Nw 136th St Vancouver (98685) ***(G-14288)***
HB Jaeger Company LLc...360 707-5958
1687 Port Dr Burlington (98233) ***(G-2161)***
Hbsw Inc...217 377-9043
200 147th Pl Se Lynnwood (98087) ***(G-6133)***
Hc Laserlign Inc...253 852-2001
10842 Se 208th St Ste 531 Kent (98031) ***(G-4936)***
Hci Steel Buildings LLC...360 403-4900
17833 59th Ave Ne Ste C Arlington (98223) ***(G-250)***
Hco Holding I Corporation...503 255-3767
4212 Ne 139th Ave Vancouver (98682) ***(G-14289)***
Hd International Corp...503 997-9325
5700 Ne 82nd Ave Unit B11 Vancouver (98662) ***(G-14290)***
Hd Pacific Inc (PA)...425 481-3031
4606 107th St Sw Mukilteo (98275) ***(G-6931)***
Hd Structures LLC...425 327-3931
6922 69th Pl Ne Marysville (98270) ***(G-6343)***
Hdc Filters LLC...253 964-0707
1939 Ogden Ave Dupont (98327) ***(G-2965)***
Headlight Software Inc...206 985-4431
2143 N 64th St Seattle (98103) ***(G-10154)***
Heads Up Inc...253 833-4546
1320 26th St Nw Ste 8 Auburn (98001) ***(G-461)***
Headsets Connect, Langley *Also called Simpleline Inc* ***(G-5785)***
Healing Mountain Pubg Inc...509 433-4719
430 Elva Way East Wenatchee (98802) ***(G-3019)***
Healionics Corporation...206 432-9060
2121 N 35th St Seattle (98103) ***(G-10155)***
Health Guard Industries Inc...360 474-9298
25713 70th Ave Ne Arlington (98223) ***(G-251)***
Health Guardian Inc...206 999-8153
3216 Magnolia Blvd W Seattle (98199) ***(G-10156)***
Health Research...509 843-2385
62 7th St Pomeroy (99347) ***(G-7673)***
Healthfirst, Mukilteo *Also called Hf Acquisition Co LLC* ***(G-6932)***
Healthier Living Products...509 582-6346
9315 Chapel Hill Blvd F6101 Pasco (99301) ***(G-7589)***
Healthwind Horizon, Redmond *Also called Horizon Professional Cmpt Svcs* ***(G-8501)***
Healthy Pet LP...360 734-7415
6960 Salashan Pkwy Ferndale (98248) ***(G-3850)***
Healthy Pet BB&T Johson Square, Ferndale *Also called Healthy Pet LP* ***(G-3850)***
Hearform Software LLC...888 453-8806
3339 Highway 25 N Lot 44 Northport (99157) ***(G-7137)***
Hearn Brothers Printing Inc...509 324-2882
2105 N Monroe St Spokane (99205) ***(G-12291)***
Hearst Corporation...206 448-8000
101 Elliott Ave W Seattle (98119) ***(G-10157)***

Hearst Seattle Media LLC 206 448-8000
2901 3rd Ave Ste 120 Seattle (98121) ***(G-10158)***
Heart Hands Preganacy Care Ctr 360 532-1104
2638 Simpson Ave Hoquiam (98550) ***(G-4341)***
Hearth & Home Technologies LLC 509 684-3745
1445 North Highway Colville (99114) ***(G-2755)***
Hearthland Publishing LLC 253 588-2149
106 Chinook Ln Steilacoom (98388) ***(G-13005)***
Hearthside Usa LLC 206 745-0850
2231 S 208th St Ste D Seatac (98198) ***(G-9286)***
Hearts In Motion Ministries 360 798-0275
309 Ne 189th St Ridgefield (98642) ***(G-9088)***
Heartwarmer Designs 253 630-7408
12018 Se 219th Ct Kent (98031) ***(G-4937)***
Heatcon Inc (PA) 206 575-0815
480 Andover Park E Tukwila (98188) ***(G-13745)***
Heatcon Composite Systems, Tukwila *Also called Heatcon Inc* ***(G-13745)***
Heatcon Composite Systems Inc 206 575-1333
600 Andover Park E Tukwila (98188) ***(G-13746)***
Heatcon Composite Systems Inc (HQ) 206 575-1333
480 Andover Park E Tukwila (98188) ***(G-13747)***
Heath Graphics LLC 253 856-1422
1720 Pike St Nw Auburn (98001) ***(G-462)***
Heath Northwest, Seattle *Also called JJ&d Signs Inc* ***(G-10298)***
Heath Northwest, Seattle *Also called Ramsay Signs Inc* ***(G-10919)***
Heathen Estate Vineyards 360 768-5199
9400 Ne 134th St Vancouver (98662) ***(G-14291)***
Heather & Company For Ibs LLC 206 264-8069
19203 78th Ave S Kent (98032) ***(G-4938)***
Heather's Tummy Care, Kent *Also called Heather & Company For Ibs LLC* ***(G-4938)***
Heaton Printing 360 353-3720
3829 Pleasant Hill Rd Kelso (98626) ***(G-4528)***
Heavenly Gelato Inc 360 426-0696
301 E Wallace Kneeland Shelton (98584) ***(G-11699)***
Heavenly Mountain Studios 360 437-2298
26 Leighbrook Ln Port Hadlock (98365) ***(G-7759)***
Heavenly Soap 206 349-7982
115 3/4 W Main St Monroe (98272) ***(G-6575)***
Heavy Duty Transaxle Inc 360 794-2021
16891 146th St Se Monroe (98272) ***(G-6576)***
Heavy Metal Brewing Co LLC 503 710-6296
809 Macarthur Blvd Vancouver (98661) ***(G-14292)***
Heavy Metal Fabrication 509 493-2979
8 Windago Ln White Salmon (98672) ***(G-15116)***
Hebert Sam-E LLC 206 650-4489
427 Bellevue Ave E # 301 Seattle (98102) ***(G-10159)***
Heckes Clams Inc 360 665-4371
28107 Sandridge Rd Nahcotta (98637) ***(G-7010)***
Heckes Oyster Co, Nahcotta *Also called Heckes Clams Inc* ***(G-7010)***
Heckman Inc 360 724-4580
5803 Jennifer Ln Burlington (98233) ***(G-2162)***
Hedges Cellars, Benton City *Also called American Wine Trade Inc* ***(G-1601)***
Hedges Family Estate, Seattle *Also called American Wine Trade Inc* ***(G-9396)***
Heights Auto License, Vancouver *Also called Gundersons Auto License* ***(G-14276)***
Heights of Meydenbauer, The, Bellevue *Also called Burnstead Construction Co* ***(G-831)***
Heininger Automotive, Bellingham *Also called Heininger Holdings LLC* ***(G-1368)***
Heininger Holdings LLC 360 756-2411
2222 Queen St Bellingham (98229) ***(G-1368)***
Heir Wear LLC 425 760-0990
1422 Ridge Ave Snohomish (98290) ***(G-11920)***
Heiret Publications 253 852-1254
20845 102nd Ave Se Kent (98031) ***(G-4939)***
Heirloom Custom Cabinetry 509 370-9012
3524 N Eden Rd Spokane Valley (99216) ***(G-12727)***
Heirloom Custom Cabinets Inc 360 354-7851
406 E Wiser Lake Rd Lynden (98264) ***(G-6020)***
Heirloom Quality Modern LLC 206 291-7331
2409 E Pine St Seattle (98122) ***(G-10160)***
Heirloom Woodworks 509 315-9275
225 N Ella Rd Spokane Valley (99212) ***(G-12728)***
Heiser George Body Co Inc 206 622-7985
11210 Tukla Intl Blvd Tukwila (98168) ***(G-13748)***
Hej LLC 425 652-9183
2414 Sw Andover St D201 Seattle (98106) ***(G-10161)***
Helcorp Interactive LLC 917 446-8506
606 W Galer St Seattle (98119) ***(G-10162)***
Helen Ficalora, Olympia *Also called Jewelry Boutique LLC* ***(G-7311)***
Helena Agri-Enterprises LLC 509 549-3566
82 Central Ferry Rd Pomeroy (99347) ***(G-7674)***
Helena Chemical Company 509 539-5761
9519 Vernal Ave Se Moses Lake (98837) ***(G-6714)***
Helena Chemical Company 901 761-0050
4802 N Florida St Spokane (99217) ***(G-12292)***
Helena Silver Mines Inc 509 922-3035
905 N Pines Rd Ste A Spokane Valley (99206) ***(G-12729)***
Helicat LLC 253 376-8273
16809 Lakeside Dr S Spanaway (98387) ***(G-12059)***
Helion Energy Inc 425 332-7463
8210 154th Ave Ne Ste 100 Redmond (98052) ***(G-8490)***
Helipower Helicopter Inc 425 232-0972
3822 134th Pl Sw Lynnwood (98087) ***(G-6134)***
Helitrak Inc 253 857-0890
1620 26th Ave Nw Ste A Gig Harbor (98335) ***(G-4117)***
Helium 206 650-4822
21728 Se 3rd Pl Sammamish (98074) ***(G-9216)***
Helium Advisors 425 214-1533
11820 Northup Way E101 Bellevue (98005) ***(G-939)***
Helium Development LLC 360 550-3322
3043 Se Travera Dr Port Orchard (98366) ***(G-7813)***
Helix Biomedix Inc 425 402-8400
22121 17th Ave Se Ste 112 Bothell (98021) ***(G-1865)***
Hella Shaggy Software LLC 206 533-1468
10505 Nottingham Rd Edmonds (98020) ***(G-3118)***
Helldyne Inc 206 855-1227
750 Ericksen Ave Ne # 103 Bainbridge Island (98110) ***(G-638)***
Hellroaring Company 509 364-3522
17 Ladiges Rd Glenwood (98619) ***(G-4184)***
Helly Hansen (us) Inc (HQ) 800 435-5901
14218 Stewart Rd Ste 100a Sumner (98390) ***(G-13073)***
Helly-Hansen Holdings (u S) (HQ) 425 378-8700
3703 I St Nw Unit Main Auburn (98001) ***(G-463)***
Helm Industries LLC 206 419-3973
550 Ne Ravenna Blvd Apt 5 Seattle (98115) ***(G-10163)***
Helm Manufacturing Co LLC 253 537-3382
13502 Pacific Ave S Tacoma (98444) ***(G-13334)***
Hemel Board Company 206 261-2781
224 Pontius Ave N Apt 510 Seattle (98109) ***(G-10164)***
Hemlock Printers USA Inc 206 241-8311
318 1st Ave S Ste 300 Seattle (98104) ***(G-10165)***
Hemphill Brothers Inc (PA) 206 842-0748
375 Ericksen Ave Ne Bainbridge Island (98110) ***(G-639)***
Hemphill Brothers Inc 509 732-4481
4183 Wright Rd Northport (99157) ***(G-7138)***
Henderson Bay Products, Vancouver *Also called Jerry Gamin* ***(G-14337)***
Henderson Cabinet Refinishing 206 963-0874
7825 Ne 192nd St Kenmore (98028) ***(G-4579)***
Hendrickson Farms, Marysville *Also called Pacific Prepac Inc* ***(G-6366)***
Hendrickson International Corp 360 906-0222
3301 Se Columbia Way Vancouver (98661) ***(G-14293)***
Henry Kempton 509 493-1160
9 Forrest Ln White Salmon (98672) ***(G-15117)***
Henry Pratt Company LLC 360 225-1230
675 Mitchell Ave Woodland (98674) ***(G-15440)***
Henry Products Incorporated 206 624-5656
4632 Ohio Ave S Seattle (98134) ***(G-10166)***
Henry Roofing Products, Vancouver *Also called Hco Holding I Corporation* ***(G-14289)***
Henrybuilt, Seattle *Also called Henry Products Incorporated* ***(G-10166)***
Henrys Donuts 425 258-6887
2515 Broadway Everett (98201) ***(G-3509)***
Henrys Donuts 360 653-4044
1289 State Ave Ste A Marysville (98270) ***(G-6344)***
Hensleys Mobile Welding 360 532-1633
35 Frosty Way Aberdeen (98520) ***(G-16)***
Hentec Industries Inc 509 891-1680
25517 E Kildea Rd Newman Lake (99025) ***(G-7046)***
Her Interactive Inc 425 460-8787
325 118th Ave Se Ste 209 Bellevue (98005) ***(G-940)***
Herald Cheraine PHD 253 564-1193
1614 S Mildred St Ste B Tacoma (98465) ***(G-13335)***
Herald Classified Want ADS 425 339-3100
1213 California St Everett (98201) ***(G-3510)***
Herb Withered 509 493-3614
140 Sleepy Hollow Rd White Salmon (98672) ***(G-15118)***
Herbalife Independent Distr, Sumner *Also called Rmg Nutrition* ***(G-13096)***
Herbivore Botanicals LLC 206 226-5008
1620 N 45th St Apt 205 Seattle (98103) ***(G-10167)***
Herbrand Company 253 848-7700
315 39th Ave Sw Ste 6 Puyallup (98373) ***(G-8161)***
Herbrand-Mcgowan Timber, Puyallup *Also called Herbrand Company* ***(G-8161)***
Herculine, Tukwila *Also called Pacific Strapping Inc* ***(G-13788)***
Herff Jones LLC 425 488-7213
6134 Ne Bothell Way Kenmore (98028) ***(G-4580)***
Heritage Distilling Co Inc 253 509-0008
3207 57th Street Ct Nw Gig Harbor (98335) ***(G-4118)***
Heritage Electrical Group Inc 425 774-7595
2516 W Marine View Dr Everett (98201) ***(G-3511)***
Heritage Gbc 360 392-8541
3715 Irongate Rd Bellingham (98226) ***(G-1369)***
Heritage Hats LLC 425 301-2887
9518 Se 15th St Bellevue (98004) ***(G-941)***
Heritage Home Accents & Floral, Kennewick *Also called Heritage Professional Ldscpg* ***(G-4669)***
Heritage Marine Electrical, Everett *Also called Heritage Electrical Group Inc* ***(G-3511)***
Heritage Professional Ldscpg 509 737-8580
1350 N Louisiana St Kennewick (99336) ***(G-4669)***
Herman Brothers Log & Cnstr, Port Angeles *Also called Evergreen Fibre Inc* ***(G-7704)***
Hermann Bros Log & Cnstr Inc (PA) 360 452-3341
2095 Blue Mountain Rd Port Angeles (98362) ***(G-7709)***
Hermann Intermountain Corp (HQ) 509 445-0966
22 Triangle Rd Usk (99180) ***(G-13984)***
Heron Creek Press, Langley *Also called Hoffmann Petra* ***(G-5780)***

ALPHABETIC

Herrera Isael Gomez....509 270-7022
1504 E Illinois Ave Spokane (99207) ***(G-12293)***
Herrington Marine Tech Inc....360 222-3106
959 Vashon St Greenbank (98253) ***(G-4305)***
Hershey Company....800 468-1714
15137 Se 66th St Bellevue (98006) ***(G-942)***
Hertco Kitchens LLC....360 380-1100
1810 Scout Pl Ferndale (98248) ***(G-3851)***
Herzog Envelope Inc....206 618-6765
17644 Ne 65th St Redmond (98052) ***(G-8491)***
Hesco Armor, Aberdeen *Also called Reed Composite Solutions LLC* ***(G-31)***
Hesco Armor Inc....360 580-1146
2210 Port Industrial Rd B Aberdeen (98520) ***(G-17)***
Hesco Armor LLC....360 637-6867
2210 Port Industrial Rd B Aberdeen (98520) ***(G-18)***
Hestia Cellars....425 333-4270
28335 Ne Quail Creek Dr Redmond (98053) ***(G-8492)***
Hewes Marine Co Inc....509 684-5235
2600 North Highway Colville (99114) ***(G-2756)***
Hewescraft, Colville *Also called Hewes Marine Co Inc* ***(G-2756)***
Hewitt Cabinets & Interiors....253 272-0404
3301 S Lawrence St Tacoma (98409) ***(G-13336)***
Hewlett-Packard Company....800 325-5372
1115 Se 164th Ave Ste 210 Vancouver (98683) ***(G-14294)***
Hexa Materials LLC....541 337-3669
707 N 64th St Seattle (98103) ***(G-10168)***
Hexacomb Corporation....253 288-2820
2820 B St Nw Ste 111 Auburn (98001) ***(G-464)***
Hexagon Blue....425 890-5351
19301 Se 16th St Sammamish (98075) ***(G-9217)***
Hexagon Metrology Inc....253 872-2443
19625 62nd Ave S Kent (98032) ***(G-4940)***
Hexcel Corporation....360 757-7212
15062 Steele Rd Burlington (98233) ***(G-2163)***
Hexcel Corporation....253 872-7500
19819 84th Ave S Kent (98032) ***(G-4941)***
Hexen Glass Studio LLC....360 807-4217
21631 Oregon Trl Centralia (98531) ***(G-2406)***
Heylo....440 522-4674
145 S Horton St Ste 100 Seattle (98134) ***(G-10169)***
Heymann Whinery Etc....360 623-1106
731 Sw 21st St Chehalis (98532) ***(G-2502)***
Hezel Vineyard and Cellars LLC....360 321-4898
6164 Countner Ct Clinton (98236) ***(G-2689)***
Hf Acquisition Co LLC....800 331-1984
11629 49th Pl W Mukilteo (98275) ***(G-6932)***
HFS Conveyors, Harrah *Also called Harrah Farm Shop* ***(G-4320)***
HI Baby Software....206 372-8936
16600 Se 17th St Bellevue (98008) ***(G-943)***
HI Q Compost, Sedro Woolley *Also called Day Creek Organic Farms Inc* ***(G-11536)***
HI Tech Signs & Banners....360 736-6322
1616 S Gold St Ste 10 Centralia (98531) ***(G-2407)***
Hi-Lineleather....360 263-7898
12013 Ne 368th St La Center (98629) ***(G-5505)***
Hibu Inc....425 454-1762
601 108th Ave Ne Ste 1810 Bellevue (98004) ***(G-944)***
Hicks Leathermaking and Wdwkg....253 833-8873
721 19th St Se Auburn (98002) ***(G-465)***
Hicks Logging Christmas T....253 208-8914
3721 Fuller Ln Se Olympia (98501) ***(G-7306)***
Hidden Acres, Mead *Also called Simchuk Karene* ***(G-6436)***
Hidden Path Entertainment Inc....425 452-7284
1407 116th Ave Ne Ste 100 Bellevue (98004) ***(G-945)***
Hide-A-Hose Inc....425 750-7636
14490 167th Ave Se C Monroe (98272) ***(G-6577)***
Hierophant Meadery LLC....509 294-0134
16602 N Day Mt Spokane Rd Mead (99021) ***(G-6429)***
Hiett Logging Inc....360 724-5505
2540 Old Hwy 99n Rd Burlington (98233) ***(G-2164)***
High Caliber Mill....360 984-6669
1321 Ne 76th St Ste 3b Vancouver (98665) ***(G-14295)***
High Cascade Incorporated....509 763-2195
12285 Allen Rd Leavenworth (98826) ***(G-5806)***
High Country Woodworks....360 942-2996
122 S Fork Rd Raymond (98577) ***(G-8353)***
High Definition Audio Video....360 398-8265
7029 Guide Meridian Rd Lynden (98264) ***(G-6021)***
High Desert Maintenance Inc....509 531-8341
525 E Bruneau Ave Kennewick (99336) ***(G-4670)***
High Energy Metals Inc....360 683-6390
293 Business Park Loop Sequim (98382) ***(G-11638)***
High Liftt LLC....425 216-3050
415 Airport Way Sw Mattawa (99349) ***(G-6408)***
High Mountain Tannery....509 435-3478
4847 Whittier Rd Clayton (99110) ***(G-2658)***
High Performance Seals Inc....253 218-0123
3902 W Valley Hwy N # 200 Auburn (98001) ***(G-466)***
High Rise Software Group Inc....206 290-6087
3859 Beach Dr Sw Seattle (98116) ***(G-10170)***
High Tide Seafoods Inc....360 452-8488
808 Marine Dr Port Angeles (98363) ***(G-7710)***
High-Tech Mfg Svcs Inc....360 696-1611
3105 Ne 65th St Ste B Vancouver (98663) ***(G-14296)***
Higher Age Press....425 891-9129
5222 University Way Ne 304a Seattle (98105) ***(G-10171)***
Higher Mind Incense....541 702-1560
3871 Larson Lake Rd Port Ludlow (98365) ***(G-7767)***
Higher Plane Cabinetworks....360 733-4322
1905 Division St Bellingham (98226) ***(G-1370)***
Higher Power Supplies Inc....425 438-0990
9700 Harbour Pl Ste 128 Mukilteo (98275) ***(G-6933)***
Highland Machine Works....360 263-1216
5405 Ne 399th St La Center (98629) ***(G-5506)***
Highland Milling LLC....360 901-8332
9901 Ne 7th Ave Ste C247 Vancouver (98685) ***(G-14297)***
Highland Quarry LLC....509 624-4136
5426 N Old Trails Rd Spokane (99224) ***(G-12294)***
Highlands Welding Repair Inc (PA)....206 283-0080
2001 W Garfield St Seattle (98119) ***(G-10172)***
Highroad Products Inc....253 474-9900
2941 S 38th St Ste C Tacoma (98409) ***(G-13337)***
Highside Distilling LLC....425 417-9000
7766 Chico Way Nw Bremerton (98312) ***(G-1960)***
Hightower Cellars....509 588-2867
19418 E 583 Pr Ne Benton City (99320) ***(G-1617)***
Highwater Filters....509 685-0933
325 S Alder St Colville (99114) ***(G-2757)***
Highway Grind Inc....509 466-5061
14009 N Newport Hwy Mead (99021) ***(G-6430)***
Highway Shoppers....360 494-7641
12975 Us Highway 12 Packwood (98361) ***(G-7543)***
Highway Specialties LLC....360 823-0511
1119 Ne 146th St Vancouver (98685) ***(G-14298)***
Highwood Global LP (PA)....509 655-7711
2425 E Magnesium Rd Spokane (99217) ***(G-12295)***
Hihosilver....509 758-8419
911 6th St Clarkston (99403) ***(G-2635)***
Hildebrand Consulting....206 465-1729
20215 41st Pl Ne Lake Forest Park (98155) ***(G-5614)***
Hiline Engrg & Fabrication Inc....509 943-9043
2105 Aviator St Richland (99354) ***(G-9006)***
Hill Aerosystems Inc....360 802-8300
911 Battersby Ave Enumclaw (98022) ***(G-3293)***
Hill Print Inc....425 255-7700
32 G St Nw Ste A Auburn (98001) ***(G-467)***
Hill Woodworking....425 488-7943
6869 Ne 153rd Pl Kenmore (98028) ***(G-4581)***
Hillcar & Fletcher Inc....360 327-3844
621 E Lake Pleasant Rd Beaver (98305) ***(G-757)***
Hilleberg Inc....425 883-0101
14790 Ne 95th St Redmond (98052) ***(G-8493)***
Hilleberg The Tentmaker, Redmond *Also called Hilleberg Inc* ***(G-8493)***
Hilliards Beer LLC....206 257-4486
6711 1st Ave Nw Seattle (98117) ***(G-10173)***
Hillshire Brands Company....253 437-3700
20230 70th Ave S Kent (98032) ***(G-4942)***
Hillshire Brands Company....253 395-3444
20360 70th Ave S Kent (98032) ***(G-4943)***
Hilltop Management Inc....206 933-5900
4151 Fauntleroy Way Sw Seattle (98126) ***(G-10174)***
Hilton Acquisition Company LLC....425 883-7000
14520 Ne 91st St Redmond (98052) ***(G-8494)***
Himalayan Corporation....425 322-4295
4480 Chennault Beach Rd Mukilteo (98275) ***(G-6934)***
Himalayan Dog Chew, Mukilteo *Also called Himalayan Corporation* ***(G-6934)***
Hinzerling Winery, Prosser *Also called Wallfam Inc* ***(G-8074)***
Hipple Family Ltd Liability Co....425 432-9696
26909 206th Ave Se Covington (98042) ***(G-2829)***
Hirelytics LLC....843 900-4473
1828 25th Ave Unit B Seattle (98122) ***(G-10175)***
Hirschler Mfg Inc....425 827-9384
915 6th St S Kirkland (98033) ***(G-5358)***
Hispanic Yellow Pages....206 297-8532
324 Nw 47th St Seattle (98107) ***(G-10176)***
Histandard, Bremerton *Also called Machine Development Company* ***(G-1975)***
Historic Photos Prints Cds LLC....360 695-6151
2814 Washington St Vancouver (98660) ***(G-14299)***
Hitchcock Cutting....360 748-7480
678 Logan Hill Rd Chehalis (98532) ***(G-2503)***
Hitech Publications Group....520 378-1155
5005 22nd Ave Se Lacey (98503) ***(G-5555)***
Hiway 6 Shake & Shingle....360 934-5442
2868 State Route 6 Raymond (98577) ***(G-8354)***
Hjalmar Industries Inc....360 957-4302
1535 Nw Ballard Way Seattle (98107) ***(G-10177)***
HK Window Fashions....509 466-4202
8814 N Abrey L White Pkwy Nine Mile Falls (99026) ***(G-7076)***
Hn Goods & Services LLc....360 841-8414
230 Cc St Woodland (98674) ***(G-15441)***
HNG Appliances, Tukwila *Also called HNG Group LLC* ***(G-13749)***
HNG Group LLC....206 723-6848
431 Industry Dr Ste 150 Tukwila (98188) ***(G-13749)***
Ho Stafford Logging....360 853-8816
52748 Main St Rockport (98283) ***(G-9152)***
Hobart Corporation....360 893-5554
19220 State Route 162 E Orting (98360) ***(G-7480)***

Hobart Machined Products Inc (PA) 425 432-3440
28819 Se 208th St Hobart (98025) ***(G-4324)***
Hobi Instrument Services LLC 425 223-3438
4626 143rd Ave Se Bellevue (98006) ***(G-946)***
Hobi Services, Bellevue *Also called Hobi Instrument Services LLC* ***(G-946)***
Hodge Industries 253 266-6921
19609 126th St E Bonney Lake (98391) ***(G-1726)***
Hoffman Honey Co 360 568-5210
16921 Butler Rd Snohomish (98290) ***(G-11921)***
Hoffman Manufacturing 509 286-3200
602 W Spring Valley Rd Latah (99018) ***(G-5791)***
Hoffmann Petra 360 321-4733
5088 Lakeside Dr Langley (98260) ***(G-5780)***
Hofstrand Logging Inc 509 968-3197
11333 Vantage Hwy Ellensburg (98926) ***(G-3208)***
Hog Farm Custom Machine 509 365-3917
12 Chuckwagon Rd Appleton (98602) ***(G-188)***
Hogan Construction Inc 206 290-5553
28621 183rd Ct Se Kent (98042) ***(G-4944)***
Hogue Cellars Ltd 509 786-4557
3090 Wittkopf Loop Prosser (99350) ***(G-8042)***
Hoistpartsnow, Orcas *Also called Access Equipment LLC* ***(G-7455)***
Hokubei Hochi, Seattle *Also called North American Post Publishing* ***(G-10623)***
Holbrook Inc (PA) 360 754-9390
1576 Marine Dr Ne Olympia (98501) ***(G-7307)***
Holbrook Logging Sort Yard, Olympia *Also called Holbrook Inc* ***(G-7307)***
Holcam Shower Doors, Tukwila *Also called Hartung Glass Industries* ***(G-13743)***
Holcim (us) Inc 360 695-9208
1217 W 8th St Vancouver (98660) ***(G-14300)***
Holder Software 509 338-0692
525 Nw Aspen Ct Pullman (99163) ***(G-8091)***
Holdiman Software 509 582-5085
105 N Mayfield St Kennewick (99336) ***(G-4671)***
Holiday Engineering & Mfg Co 253 238-0671
10718 A St S Tacoma (98444) ***(G-13338)***
Holland Machine Inc 509 662-6235
5 Orondo Ave Wenatchee (98801) ***(G-15039)***
Holland Ornamental Iron Inc 253 564-5671
7026 27th St W University Place (98466) ***(G-13971)***
Hollibaugh Manufacturing 360 653-8612
12524 54th Ave Ne Marysville (98271) ***(G-6345)***
Hollister-Stier Laboratories, Spokane *Also called Jubilant Hollisterstier LLC* ***(G-12345)***
Holly Press Inc 206 623-2444
115 Warren Ave N Apt 110 Seattle (98109) ***(G-10178)***
Hollywood Hill Vineyards LLC 425 753-0093
14350 160th Pl Ne Woodinville (98072) ***(G-15260)***
Hollywood Triangle Productions 323 301-3003
1301 1st Ave Apt 709 Seattle (98101) ***(G-10179)***
Holm Bing 509 454-2277
1002 N 6th Ave Yakima (98902) ***(G-15581)***
Holm Brewing Enterpises LLC 425 827-9307
11701 Ne 73rd St Kirkland (98033) ***(G-5359)***
Holm Sales, Yakima *Also called Holm Bing* ***(G-15581)***
Holman Drilling Corporation 509 534-1013
1609 S Stanley Ln Spokane Valley (99212) ***(G-12730)***
Holmes and Associates 360 793-9723
19916 Old Owen Rd 177 Monroe (98272) ***(G-6578)***
Holmes Family Winery LLC 253 906-6317
1625 S 374th Ct Federal Way (98003) ***(G-3743)***
Holmes Harbor Cellars LLC 360 331-3544
4591 Honeymoon Bay Rd Greenbank (98253) ***(G-4306)***
Holmes Publishing Group LLC 360 681-2900
407 S Sequim Ave Sequim (98382) ***(G-11639)***
Holowear Ltd 408 759-4656
11400 Se 8th St Ste 260 Bellevue (98004) ***(G-947)***
Holroyd Block Company Inc 253 474-8481
7216 Lakewood Dr W Tacoma (98499) ***(G-13339)***
Holroyd Company Inc (PA) 253 474-0725
7216 Lakewood Dr W Tacoma (98499) ***(G-13340)***
Holroyd Company Inc 253 627-0571
923 E 26th St Tacoma (98421) ***(G-13341)***
Holroyd Company Inc 253 474-0725
828 Old Pacific Hwy Se Olympia (98513) ***(G-7308)***
Holy Lamb Organics Inc 360 402-5781
4431 Boston Harbor Rd Ne Olympia (98506) ***(G-7309)***
Holz Enterprises Inc 360 398-7006
6226 Chasteen Rd Lynden (98264) ***(G-6022)***
Holz Racing Products, Lynden *Also called Holz Enterprises Inc* ***(G-6022)***
Homax Group Inc 360 733-9029
1835 Barkley Blvd Ste 101 Bellingham (98226) ***(G-1371)***
Homchick Michael Stone Work 425 481-2783
6834 Ne 175th St Kenmore (98028) ***(G-4582)***
Home and Travel Solutions LLC 425 949-8216
18915 142nd Ave Ne # 230 Woodinville (98072) ***(G-15261)***
Home Builders Service Company 509 747-1206
1606 E 54th Ln Spokane (99223) ***(G-12296)***
Home Design Expo 425 864-6313
18425 Ne 95th St Unit 195 Redmond (98052) ***(G-8495)***
Home Doctor, The, Tacoma *Also called Washington Mso Inc* ***(G-13588)***
Home Energy Japan, Seattle *Also called Hej LLC* ***(G-10161)***
Home Fire Prest Logs Ltd 360 366-2200
6925 Salashan Pkwy Ferndale (98248) ***(G-3852)***
Home Port Seafood Inc 360 676-4707
2875 Roeder Ave Ste 11 Bellingham (98225) ***(G-1372)***
Home Sweet Home Indoor 509 327-9637
1517 W Fairway Dr Spokane (99218) ***(G-12297)***
Home Team Dupont 253 576-1907
2705 Macarthur St Dupont (98327) ***(G-2966)***
Home2 Suites By Hilton Dupont 253 912-1000
600 Station Dr Dupont (98327) ***(G-2967)***
Homecare Products Inc (PA) 253 249-1108
700 Milwaukee Ave N Algona (98001) ***(G-71)***
Homeland Energy, Vancouver *Also called Envirolux Energy Systems LLC* ***(G-14203)***
Homeplate Heroes 360 798-7974
8903 Ne 117th Ave Ste 100 Vancouver (98662) ***(G-14301)***
Homers Ornamental Iron 509 327-8673
5806 N A St Spokane (99205) ***(G-12298)***
Homestead Book Co 206 782-4532
6101 22nd Ave Nw Seattle (98107) ***(G-10180)***
Homestead Machine 425 228-1851
15025 Se 116th St Renton (98059) ***(G-8818)***
Hometown Band 206 842-2084
12215 Ridgepoint Cir Nw Silverdale (98383) ***(G-11837)***
Honest Jack, Seattle *Also called Dynamic Automotive Distrs* ***(G-9864)***
Honey House Naturals Inc 253 926-8193
7704 48th St E Fife (98424) ***(G-3958)***
Honeybuckets, Puyallup *Also called Northwest Cascade Inc* ***(G-8202)***
Honeycutt Machine Inc 425 493-0525
12402 Evergreen Dr Mukilteo (98275) ***(G-6935)***
Honeycutt Manufacturing LLC 425 493-0525
12402 Evergreen Dr Mukilteo (98275) ***(G-6936)***
Honeywell Authorized Dealer, Seattle *Also called Seelig Fuel Inc* ***(G-11088)***
Honeywell Authorized Dealer, Longview *Also called Air Pro Heating & Cooling LLC* ***(G-5884)***
Honeywell Authorized Dealer, Olympia *Also called Olympia Sheet Metal Inc* ***(G-7354)***
Honeywell Electronic Mtls Inc (HQ) 509 252-2200
15128 E Euclid Ave Spokane Valley (99216) ***(G-12731)***
Honeywell International Inc 425 885-3711
15001 Ne 36th St Redmond (98052) ***(G-8496)***
Honeywell International Inc 509 534-5226
11401 E Montgomery Dr # 2 Spokane Valley (99206) ***(G-12732)***
Honeywell International Inc 760 339-5592
4150 Lind Ave Sw Renton (98057) ***(G-8819)***
Honeywell International Inc 425 921-4598
16201 25th Ave W Lynnwood (98087) ***(G-6135)***
Honeywell International Inc 425 413-2453
27438 236th Pl Se Maple Valley (98038) ***(G-6273)***
Honeywell International Inc 360 253-8100
9555 Se 36th St Mercer Island (98040) ***(G-6466)***
Honeywell International Inc 253 966-0203
Rainier Dr Lewis Mcchord (98433) ***(G-5820)***
Honeywell International Inc 425 251-9511
4150 Lind Ave Sw Renton (98057) ***(G-8820)***
Honeywell International Inc 425 885-8944
15001 Ne 36th St Redmond (98052) ***(G-8497)***
Honeywell International Inc 425 251-9511
4150 Lind Ave Sw Renton (98057) ***(G-8821)***
Honeywell International Inc 425 885-3711
15001 Ne 36th St Redmond (98052) ***(G-8498)***
Honeywell International Inc 425 885-3711
6670 185th Ave Ne Redmond (98052) ***(G-8499)***
Honeywell International Inc 425 885-3711
15001 Ne 36th St Redmond (98052) ***(G-8500)***
Honolds Ornamental Ironwork 206 779-0668
2635 Dreamland Ln Langley (98260) ***(G-5781)***
Hoober Industries Inc 253 370-9553
716 140th St E Tacoma (98445) ***(G-13342)***
Hood Canal Logging Co Inc 360 275-4676
510 Ne Alder Creek Ln Belfair (98528) ***(G-763)***
Hood Packaging Corporation 360 695-1251
1401 W Fourth Plain Blvd Vancouver (98660) ***(G-14302)***
Hood River Candle Works 503 213-4487
413 Hillstrom Rd Port Angeles (98363) ***(G-7711)***
Hood River Sand Gravel 509 773-0314
1030 W Broadway St Goldendale (98620) ***(G-4200)***
Hoodsport Winery Inc 360 877-9894
23501 N Us Highway 101 Hoodsport (98548) ***(G-4325)***
Hoof Prints Kitsap 360 932-3992
5100 Hart St Nw Bremerton (98311) ***(G-1961)***
Hoofsbeat Blankets 206 390-0016
220 N Woods St Monroe (98272) ***(G-6579)***
Hook & Ladder Printing Co LLC 206 568-0588
2229 Waverly Way E Seattle (98112) ***(G-10181)***
Hook & Line Fish 360 293-0503
15599 Yokeko Dr Anacortes (98221) ***(G-134)***
Hook Line and Espresso 360 691-7095
208 W Stanley St Granite Falls (98252) ***(G-4277)***
Hoonah Cold Storage, Lake Forest Park *Also called Dignon Co Inc* ***(G-5612)***
Hope Chest Crafts 509 865-5666
508 W 2nd Ave Toppenish (98948) ***(G-13670)***
Hope Moffat 401 527-4234
407 Madison Ave N Ste 240 Bainbridge Island (98110) ***(G-640)***
Hopp Industries 253 732-7348
4702 N Cheyenne St Tacoma (98407) ***(G-13343)***

A L P H A B E T I C

(PA)=Parent Co (HQ)=Headquarters (DH)=Div Headquarters
2019 Washington Manufacturers Register
745

Hops Extract Corp America 509 575-6440
305 N 2nd Ave Yakima (98902) *(G-15582)*
Hopstract, Yakima *Also called Hops Extract Corp America (G-15582)*
Hopunion CBS LLC 509 574-5124
227 S Front St Yakima (98902) *(G-15583)*
Hopunion Craft Brewing Sls LLC 509 457-3200
203 Division St Yakima (98902) *(G-15584)*
Hoquiam Brewing Co 360 637-8252
526 8th St Hoquiam (98550) *(G-4342)*
Hoquiam Plywood Products Inc 360 533-3060
1000 Woodlawn Ave Hoquiam (98550) *(G-4343)*
Horan Estates Winery 509 679-8705
431 19th St Ne East Wenatchee (98802) *(G-3020)*
Hores Source, Blaine *Also called Northwest Horse Source LLC (G-1688)*
Horizon Flight 509 521-4244
20 Piekarski Rd Pasco (99301) *(G-7590)*
Horizon Imaging LLC 509 525-2860
29 Sw 9th St College Place (99324) *(G-2725)*
Horizon Manufacturing Inds Inc 360 322-7368
17925 59th Ave Ne Arlington (98223) *(G-252)*
Horizon of Change 425 355-1712
6328 W Beech St Everett (98203) *(G-3512)*
Horizon Printing Company LLC 509 663-8414
320 N Emerson Ave Apt 4 Wenatchee (98801) *(G-15040)*
Horizon Professional Cmpt Svcs 425 883-6588
8410 154th Ave Ne Redmond (98052) *(G-8501)*
Horizon Publications Inc 509 276-5043
104 N Main St Deer Park (99006) *(G-2905)*
Horizons Edge Winery 509 829-6401
4530 E Zillah Dr Zillah (98953) *(G-15755)*
Hormel Foods Corporation 425 635-0109
320 120th Ave Ne Ste 210 Bellevue (98005) *(G-948)*
Horseshoe Bend Quarry, Naches *Also called H B Q Inc (G-6997)*
Horseshoe Cove Cabin Owne 509 966-4087
284 Sunnyslope Rd Yakima (98908) *(G-15585)*
Horseshoe Falls LLC 360 256-0668
7112 Ne Fairway Ave Vancouver (98662) *(G-14303)*
Horseshoe Grange 965 360 668-3939
15802 State Route 9 Se Snohomish (98296) *(G-11922)*
Horseshoe Lake Auto Wreck 253 857-3866
9401 State Route 302 Nw Gig Harbor (98329) *(G-4119)*
Horseshoe Lake Estates Assn 253 851-3514
9216 147th Street Ct Nw Gig Harbor (98329) *(G-4120)*
Horsley Logging & Cnstr Co, Winlock *Also called Gary C Horsley (G-15150)*
Horsley Timber & Construction 360 274-7272
684 Melton Rd Castle Rock (98611) *(G-2345)*
Horvitz Newspapers Inc 425 274-4782
500 108th Ave Ne Ste 1750 Bellevue (98004) *(G-949)*
Hose Pro 253 448-1304
12424 80th Ave E Puyallup (98373) *(G-8162)*
Hose Shop Inc 360 757-3776
856 S Alder St Burlington (98233) *(G-2165)*
Hoshizaki Western Dist Ctr Inc 253 922-8589
7214 26th St E Ste 103 Fife (98424) *(G-3959)*
Hoss A W & Sons Furn & Mfg 206 522-1229
9221 Roosevelt Way Ne Seattle (98115) *(G-10182)*
Hot Glass Color & Supply 206 448-1199
2225 5th Ave Seattle (98121) *(G-10183)*
Hot Off Press 253 255-2829
13510 Kapowsin Hwy E Graham (98338) *(G-4226)*
Hot Off The Press, Redmond *Also called Woitchek Printing LLC (G-8716)*
Hot Oil Company LLC 509 338-5678
1428 Queen Anne Ave N Seattle (98109) *(G-10184)*
Hot Rods 509 773-7005
105 W Main St Goldendale (98620) *(G-4201)*
Hot Shot Express Inc 206 241-5516
19034 7th Ave S Burien (98148) *(G-2112)*
Hot Shot Site Dots 206 604-8980
3032 Sw Charlestown St Seattle (98126) *(G-10185)*
Hot Shot Slabs, Spokane *Also called Kindle Eithan (G-12352)*
Hot Sox LLC 509 947-5193
1830 S 38th Ave West Richland (99353) *(G-15096)*
Hot Wire Direct, Clarkston *Also called Anthony Rousseau (G-2619)*
Hot Yoga Elements 360 676-9642
1308 Meador Ave Ste 103 Bellingham (98229) *(G-1373)*
Hough Software Consulting 425 881-2339
8820 166th Ave Ne Redmond (98052) *(G-8502)*
Houghton Plaza 425 298-4857
935 6th St S Kirkland (98033) *(G-5360)*
House of Bee, Kent *Also called Passport Food Group LLC (G-5060)*
House of Lashes 206 522-5277
10522 Lake City Way Ne C104 Seattle (98125) *(G-10186)*
House of Matriarch Inc 425 466-7783
11000 Ne 10th St Apt 170 Bellevue (98004) *(G-950)*
House of Rising Buns 360 718-8330
1804 Nw 119th St Unit 104 Vancouver (98685) *(G-14304)*
House Reporter LLC 360 678-4931
2674 Harbor Estates Rd Greenbank (98253) *(G-4307)*
Houstory Publishing LLC 877 962-6500
6161 Glacier Pl Ferndale (98248) *(G-3853)*
How 2 Publishing LLC 360 878-9274
1634 S Scheuber Rd Centralia (98531) *(G-2408)*
How Pickle Got Out of A Jam 206 940-6532
821 20th Ave S Seattle (98144) *(G-10187)*
How-Mac Manufacturing Inc 360 855-2649
720 Puget St Ste A Sedro Woolley (98284) *(G-11540)*
Howard & Son Excavating LLC 360 983-3922
494 Flynn Rd Silver Creek (98585) *(G-11823)*
Howard Denson Logging 360 988-4910
9088 Kendall Rd Sumas (98295) *(G-13045)*
Howard F Harrison M D 509 575-8307
1460 N 16th Ave Ste C Yakima (98902) *(G-15586)*
Howard Fabrication 360 380-1721
6968 Dahlberg Rd Ferndale (98248) *(G-3854)*
Howard Lamp Company 425 776-7914
1912 N 45th St Seattle (98103) *(G-10188)*
Howard Security System, Anacortes *Also called Marine Welding (G-145)*
Howat Fine Woodworking Inc 360 681-3451
302 Ward Ln Sequim (98382) *(G-11640)*
Howatt Company Inc 425 743-4682
12212 Cyrus Way Mukilteo (98275) *(G-6937)*
Howell Creations, Renton *Also called Shawnee Construction LLC (G-8909)*
Howellcorp 206 954-8011
1200 Westlake Ave N Ste 1 Seattle (98109) *(G-10189)*
Howling Wolf Drums 425 391-2540
24834 Se Mirrormont Way Issaquah (98027) *(G-4426)*
Howmac Dmnsional Letters Logos, Sedro Woolley *Also called How-Mac Manufacturing Inc (G-11540)*
Hoya Optical Laboratories 253 475-7809
2330 S 78th St Tacoma (98409) *(G-13344)*
Hoya Vision Care, Tacoma *Also called Hoya Optical Laboratories (G-13344)*
Hoyem Publications Inc 360 676-0864
229 Middlefield Rd Bellingham (98225) *(G-1374)*
Hoylu Inc (PA) 425 269-3299
720 4th Ave Ste 220 Kirkland (98033) *(G-5361)*
Hoylu Inc 425 829-2316
7624 116th Ave Ne Kirkland (98033) *(G-5362)*
HP, Vancouver *Also called Hewlett-Packard Company (G-14294)*
HP Inc 650 857-1501
2401 4th Ave Ste 500 Seattle (98121) *(G-10190)*
Hpf Manufacturing 425 486-8031
20105 Broadway Ave Snohomish (98296) *(G-11923)*
Hpi, Tukwila *Also called Huntington Pier International (G-13750)*
Hrh Door Corp 360 736-7651
2001 Industrial Dr Centralia (98531) *(G-2409)*
Hrh Door Corp 509 575-0832
440 N Quay St Kennewick (99336) *(G-4672)*
Hrh Press 206 781-1279
6521 Greenwood Ave N Seattle (98103) *(G-10191)*
Hs Print Works Difficult 253 251-0045
9918 162nd Street Ct E # 13 Puyallup (98375) *(G-8163)*
Ht Industries LLC 360 863-2029
1820 Creswell Rd Snohomish (98290) *(G-11924)*
Htc America Innovation Inc 425 679-5318
308 Occidental Ave S # 300 Seattle (98104) *(G-10192)*
Hu-SC, Sumner *Also called Human Science LLC (G-13074)*
Huawei Device USA Inc 425 247-2700
15375 Se 30th Pl Ste 280 Bellevue (98007) *(G-951)*
Hub Gig Harbor, Gig Harbor *Also called Harmon Brewing Company L L C (G-4113)*
Hubbard Jointers Incorporated 509 235-2148
19606 S Cheney Plaza Rd Cheney (99004) *(G-2587)*
Hubster Logging Inc 253 200-7183
4325 Chrstensen Muck Rd E Eatonville (98328) *(G-3059)*
Huckleberry Press 844 344-8344
38291 State Route 25 N Davenport (99122) *(G-2871)*
Hudson Tech Company, Auburn *Also called Hudson Technologies Inc (G-468)*
Hudson Technologies Inc 253 887-7707
1320 26th St Nw Ste 9 Auburn (98001) *(G-468)*
Huebner Manufacturing 253 630-9600
30660 168th Ave Se Auburn (98092) *(G-469)*
Hugh Montgomery 206 369-9356
7869 Fletcher Bay Rd Ne Bainbridge Island (98110) *(G-641)*
Hughes Custom Woodworking Inc 509 921-8090
1705 W Monroe Rd Colbert (99005) *(G-2708)*
Hugos On Hill 509 822-7149
3023 E 28th Ave Spokane (99223) *(G-12299)*
Hulett and Company 425 922-5224
21312 E Lost Lake Rd Snohomish (98296) *(G-11925)*
Hull Marigail 425 643-3737
4222 181st Ave Se Ne90th Bellevue (98008) *(G-952)*
Human Science LLC 253 321-6800
13701 24th St E Unit F2 Sumner (98390) *(G-13074)*
Humbay Health LLC 425 922-0200
5729 Lakeview Dr Kirkland (98033) *(G-5363)*
Humidity Systems, Vancouver *Also called Sporting Systems Corporation (G-14603)*
Humming Hemp LLC 503 559-6476
723 The Parkway Richland (99352) *(G-9007)*
Hummingbird Precision Mch Co 360 252-2737
2610 Willamette Dr Ne A Lacey (98516) *(G-5556)*
Hummingbird Press 617 921-6502
10113 Radford Ave Nw Seattle (98177) *(G-10193)*
Hummingbird Scientific, Lacey *Also called Hummingbird Precision Mch Co (G-5556)*

ALPHABETIC SECTION Idaho Lime, Issaquah

Hummingbird Scientific LLC 360 252-2737
2610 Willamette Dr Ne A Lacey (98516) ***(G-5557)***
Hundman Publishing Inc 425 742-1214
5115 Monticello Dr Edmonds (98026) ***(G-3119)***
Hundred Horse Panels LLC 509 227-5686
23305 E Knox Ave Bldg B Liberty Lake (99019) ***(G-5834)***
Huney Jun LLC 805 903-2011
10090 Main St 3 Peshastin (98847) ***(G-7662)***
Hungrygen Church, Pasco *Also called Good News Church* ***(G-7587)***
Hunnicutts Truck Shop Inc 360 734-9859
3910 Bakerview Spur Bellingham (98226) ***(G-1375)***
Hunt Family Ltd Partnership 509 892-5287
6425 S Chapman Rd Greenacres (99016) ***(G-4299)***
Hunt Hosted Solutions 425 222-0098
5600 329th Ave Se Fall City (98024) ***(G-3702)***
Hunt Interactive, Fall City *Also called Hunt Hosted Solutions* ***(G-3702)***
Hunt Mining Corp 509 290-5659
23800 E Appleway Ave Liberty Lake (99019) ***(G-5835)***
Hunter Creek Property Ltd 509 675-4949
6447 Springdale Hunter Rd Hunters (99137) ***(G-4365)***
Hunter Fish Enterprises 253 852-8357
19808 144th Pl Se Renton (98058) ***(G-8822)***
Huntington Pier International 310 640-8358
4310 S 131st Pl Tukwila (98168) ***(G-13750)***
Huntmountain Resources Ltd 509 290-5659
1611 N Molter Rd Ste 201 Liberty Lake (99019) ***(G-5836)***
Huntron Inc 425 743-3171
15720 Main St Ste 100 Mill Creek (98012) ***(G-6513)***
Huntron Instruments, Mill Creek *Also called Huntron Inc* ***(G-6513)***
Hurkin LLC 425 437-0100
25500 212th Pl Se Maple Valley (98038) ***(G-6274)***
Hurkin Software, Maple Valley *Also called Hurkin LLC* ***(G-6274)***
Hurrican Hut A Trpcl Sno Dlr, Pasco *Also called Dina Helmts* ***(G-7577)***
Hurworth Logging 360 457-4776
713 Gasman Rd Port Angeles (98362) ***(G-7712)***
Huskey Printing & Envelop 206 901-1792
11405 10th Ave Sw Seattle (98146) ***(G-10194)***
Hussey Software LLC 206 409-0959
7465 Corliss Ave N Seattle (98103) ***(G-10195)***
Hwy 99 Auto License 360 573-6226
13009 Ne Highway 99 Vancouver (98686) ***(G-14305)***
Hwy Grind Inc 509 710-7704
14607 N Shady Slope Rd Spokane (99208) ***(G-12300)***
Hy-Grade Glass Inc 509 248-9919
2003 S 14th St Union Gap (98903) ***(G-13932)***
Hy-Security Gate Inc 253 867-3700
6705 S 209th St Ste 101 Kent (98032) ***(G-4945)***
Hyak Electroworks 360 737-0157
600 Se 45th Pl Vancouver (98661) ***(G-14306)***
Hyatt Farm Partnership LP 509 829-3737
2020 Gilbert Rd Zillah (98953) ***(G-15756)***
Hyatt Vineyards, Zillah *Also called Hyatt Farm Partnership LP* ***(G-15756)***
Hydra Group LLC 503 957-0975
5428 J St Washougal (98671) ***(G-14959)***
Hydra Plastics Inc 425 483-1877
18800 Wdnvlle Snhomish Rd Woodinville (98072) ***(G-15262)***
Hydra-Com Inc 253 862-9140
136 Stewart Rd Se Bldg 2 Pacific (98047) ***(G-7529)***
Hydrafab Northwest Inc 509 535-0075
3808 N Sullivan Rd 15z Spokane Valley (99216) ***(G-12733)***
Hydramaster 425 775-7276
6323 204th St Sw Lynnwood (98036) ***(G-6136)***
Hydramaster LLC (HQ) 425 775-7272
11015 47th Ave W Mukilteo (98275) ***(G-6938)***
Hydramaster North America Inc, Mukilteo *Also called Hydramaster LLC* ***(G-6938)***
Hydraulics Plus, Spokane Valley *Also called Hydro-Tech Genertr Repair Plus* ***(G-12734)***
Hydro Consulting LLC 509 302-1034
615 S Oregon Ave Pasco (99301) ***(G-7591)***
Hydro Excavation / Vac Truck, Chattaroy *Also called Precisionhx LLC* ***(G-2451)***
Hydro Extrusion North Amer LLC 503 802-3000
2001 Kotobuki Way Vancouver (98660) ***(G-14307)***
Hydro Precision Aero, Kent *Also called Hydro Systems USA Inc* ***(G-4946)***
Hydro Systems USA Inc 253 876-2100
7028 S 204th St Kent (98032) ***(G-4946)***
Hydro-Tech Genertr Repair Plus (PA) 509 536-9464
5507 E Broadway Ave Spokane Valley (99212) ***(G-12734)***
Hydro-Tech Genertr Repair Plus 509 276-2063
1004 E Owens Rd Chattaroy (99003) ***(G-2447)***
Hydroacoustic Technology Inc 206 633-3383
715 Ne Northlake Way Seattle (98105) ***(G-10196)***
Hydrobee Spc 206 491-0945
5534 30th Ave Ne Seattle (98105) ***(G-10197)***
Hydroflow Usa LLC 425 497-3900
15301 Ne 90th St Redmond (98052) ***(G-8503)***
Hydrogen 2o2 LLC 704 906-3770
16410 84th St Ne Lake Stevens (98258) ***(G-5646)***
Hydrogen Fueled Vehicles 425 502-7170
118 156th Ave Se Bellevue (98007) ***(G-953)***
Hydropeptide LLC 425 458-1072
295 Ne Gilman Blvd # 201 Issaquah (98027) ***(G-4427)***
Hydrostraw LLC (PA) 509 291-6000
22110 S Sr 27 Rockford (99030) ***(G-9151)***

Hylebos Plant, Tacoma *Also called Glacier Northwest Inc* ***(G-13310)***
Hyperfish Inc 425 332-6567
3410 Carillon Pt Kirkland (98033) ***(G-5364)***
Hyperfizzics 904 253-5137
3948 S Brandon St B Seattle (98118) ***(G-10198)***
Hypothesis Gardens LLC 206 653-6344
2709 N Felts Ln Spokane Valley (99206) ***(G-12735)***
Hyprotek Inc 509 343-3121
665 N Riverpoint Blvd # 410 Spokane (99202) ***(G-12301)***
Hysecurity, Kent *Also called Hy-Security Gate Inc* ***(G-4945)***
Hytech Power Inc 425 890-1180
15340 Ne 92nd St Ste D Redmond (98052) ***(G-8504)***
Hytek Finishes Co 253 872-7160
8127 S 216th St Kent (98032) ***(G-4947)***
I 90 Enterprises Inc 509 988-0380
8 S 5th St Odessa (99159) ***(G-7190)***
I A Rugby.com, Ferndale *Also called International Athletic* ***(G-3860)***
I C E, Seattle *Also called International Cnstr Eqp Inc* ***(G-10249)***
I C G, Yakima *Also called Industrial Control Group* ***(G-15587)***
I C S, Mukilteo *Also called Interior Construction Spc* ***(G-6944)***
I C S, Spokane *Also called Integrated Composition Systems* ***(G-12318)***
I C S, Seattle *Also called Industrial Container Svcs LLC* ***(G-10231)***
I C S Support, Redmond *Also called Integrated Computer Systems* ***(G-8510)***
I Concept Signs LLC 206 658-1158
700 S Orchard St Seattle (98108) ***(G-10199)***
I D T, Camas *Also called Innovative Dental Tech Inc* ***(G-2257)***
I Hart Lipstick 253 720-7126
10311 50th Ave E Tacoma (98446) ***(G-13345)***
I Love Ramen Japenese Noodle 253 839-1115
31254 Pacific Hwy S Federal Way (98003) ***(G-3744)***
I M A C (PA) 509 747-3607
2525 E 29th Ave Ste 10b Spokane (99223) ***(G-12302)***
I P Callison & Sons, Chehalis *Also called Callisons Inc* ***(G-2477)***
I P N, Vancouver *Also called Interntonal Graphics Nameplate* ***(G-14323)***
I S C, Spokane *Also called Impact Service Corporation* ***(G-12305)***
I-5 Design and Manufacture, Lacey *Also called I-5 Design Build Inc* ***(G-5558)***
I-5 Design Build Inc 360 459-3200
8751 Commerce Place Dr Ne Lacey (98516) ***(G-5558)***
I-90 Express Finishing Inc 509 922-2297
225 N Ella Rd Bldg B Spokane Valley (99212) ***(G-12736)***
I-90 Express LLC 509 855-6280
256 Basin St Nw Ste B Ephrata (98823) ***(G-3337)***
I. P. Callison & Sons Division, Lacey *Also called Callisons Inc* ***(G-5536)***
I1 Biometrics, Kirkland *Also called I1 Sensortech Inc* ***(G-5365)***
I1 Sensortech Inc 425 372-7811
12020 113th Ave Ne Kirkland (98034) ***(G-5365)***
I2nnovations LLC 425 298-3143
3020 Issaqh Pine Lk Rd Se Sammamish (98075) ***(G-9218)***
Iaco, Vancouver *Also called Irrigation Accessories Co* ***(G-14324)***
Ian Enterprises LLC 425 413-0371
25918 234th Ave Se Maple Valley (98038) ***(G-6275)***
Iasco 253 474-0497
4808 S Washington St Tacoma (98409) ***(G-13346)***
IB Wood Inc 253 395-8886
22414 72nd Ave S Kent (98032) ***(G-4948)***
Icarus Aero Components LLC 386 299-0529
11818 97th Ln Ne Kirkland (98034) ***(G-5366)***
Icd High Performance Coating, Ridgefield *Also called Industrial Control Dev Inc* ***(G-9090)***
Ice, White Salmon *Also called Innovative Composite Engrg Inc* ***(G-15119)***
Ice Floe LLC 360 331-5500
5400 Cameron Rd Freeland (98249) ***(G-4030)***
Ice Harbor Brewing Company 509 586-3181
350 Clover Island Dr Kennewick (99336) ***(G-4673)***
Ice Harbor Brewing Company (PA) 509 545-0927
206 N Benton St Ste C Kennewick (99336) ***(G-4674)***
Icg Corp 425 315-0200
4403 Russell Rd Ste 116 Mukilteo (98275) ***(G-6939)***
Icicle Ridge Winery (PA) 509 548-7019
8977 North Rd Peshastin (98847) ***(G-7663)***
Icicle Ridge Winery 509 548-7019
821 Front St Leavenworth (98826) ***(G-5807)***
Icicle Seafoods, Seattle *Also called Cooke Aquaculture Pacific LLC* ***(G-9736)***
Icicle Seafoods Inc (HQ) 206 282-0988
4019 21st Ave W Ste 300 Seattle (98199) ***(G-10200)***
Icon Cellars 425 242-4230
18654 142nd Ave Ne Woodinville (98072) ***(G-15263)***
Icon Cellars LLC 425 223-7300
21821 Ne 30th Pl Sammamish (98074) ***(G-9219)***
Icopyright Inc 206 484-8561
4742 42nd Ave Sw 615 Seattle (98116) ***(G-10201)***
Ict Group Inc 408 907-8000
2818 N Sullivan Rd Spokane Valley (99216) ***(G-12737)***
ID Integration, Mukilteo *Also called ID Integration Inc* ***(G-6940)***
ID Integration Inc (PA) 425 438-2533
13024 Beverly Park Rd # 104 Mukilteo (98275) ***(G-6940)***
ID Label Inc 206 323-8100
3250 Arprt Way S Ste 410 Seattle (98134) ***(G-10202)***
ID Superstore, Blaine *Also called Pics Smartcard Inc* ***(G-1695)***
Idaho Lime, Issaquah *Also called Rondys Inc* ***(G-4470)***

ALPHABETIC

(PA)=Parent Co (HQ)=Headquarters (DH)=Div Headquarters
2019 Washington Manufacturers Register
747

Idd Aerospace Corp 425 885-0617
18225 Ne 76th St Redmond (98052) ***(G-8505)***
Idea Company 253 891-8140
743 Valentine Ave Se Pacific (98047) ***(G-7530)***
Ideal Commercial Uniforms 360 876-1767
1008 Bethel Ave Ste C Port Orchard (98366) ***(G-7814)***
Ideal Industries Intl Inc 360 761-9958
17914 93rd Ave E Puyallup (98375) ***(G-8164)***
Ideations Design Inc 206 281-0067
4214 24th Ave W Seattle (98199) ***(G-10203)***
Identities Green Printing, Prosser *Also called Jag Enterprizes Inc* ***(G-8044)***
Idex Health & Science LLC 360 679-2528
619 Oak St Oak Harbor (98277) ***(G-7153)***
Idk Wear 425 346-1904
20426 5th Ave S Des Moines (98198) ***(G-2937)***
Idl Precision Machining LLC 425 315-8080
11600 49th Pl W Ste A Mukilteo (98275) ***(G-6941)***
Idx, Puyallup *Also called Pacific Coast Showcase Inc* ***(G-8216)***
Idx Corporation 253 445-9000
1601 Industrial Park Way # 101 Puyallup (98371) ***(G-8165)***
Idx Seattle, Puyallup *Also called Idx Corporation* ***(G-8165)***
Ieg7 Inc 206 501-6193
5213 Wesley Ave Se Auburn (98092) ***(G-470)***
Ifh Group West LLC 844 434-9378
17301 51st Ave Ne Arlington (98223) ***(G-253)***
Ifloorcom 206 438-3022
1187 Andover Park W Tukwila (98188) ***(G-13751)***
Ifooddecisionsciences Inc 206 219-3703
500 Yale Ave N Fl 1 Seattle (98109) ***(G-10204)***
Igt Global Solutions Corp 360 412-2140
7860 29th Ave Ne Ste B Lacey (98516) ***(G-5559)***
Iko Pacific Inc (HQ) 360 988-9103
850 W Front St Sumas (98295) ***(G-13046)***
Ikonika Corp 253 344-1523
5013 Pcf Hwy E Unit 14 Fife (98424) ***(G-3960)***
Ilinklive Inc 509 464-0062
1622 W Pinehill Rd Spokane (99218) ***(G-12303)***
Illinois Tool Works Inc 360 225-9995
701 W Scott Ave Woodland (98674) ***(G-15442)***
Illume 206 566-5375
4878 Beacon Ave S Seattle (98108) ***(G-10205)***
Illumination Arts Inc 360 984-5173
13023 Ne Highway 99 Vancouver (98686) ***(G-14308)***
Illumination Arts Pubg Co, Vancouver *Also called Illumination Arts Inc* ***(G-14308)***
Illusion Wear Capes 360 674-2357
6101 Sunnyslope Rd Sw Port Orchard (98367) ***(G-7815)***
Illustrated Illusions, Lynden *Also called Sandcastle Sandblasting* ***(G-6052)***
Ilovesalmon.com, Everett *Also called Kasilof Fish Company* ***(G-3529)***
Im Printing 206 300-7511
1800 Federal Ave E Seattle (98102) ***(G-10206)***
Im3 Inc 360 254-2981
12414 Ne 95th St Vancouver (98682) ***(G-14309)***
Image 360 Tacoma Central, Tacoma *Also called Whats Your Sign Inc* ***(G-13596)***
Image Craft Signs & Graphics, Auburn *Also called Gerrard Inc* ***(G-449)***
Image East, Mercer Island *Also called Typesetter Corporation* ***(G-6488)***
Image Masters Inc 253 939-5868
819 14th St Ne Auburn (98002) ***(G-471)***
Image Signs and Design LLC 360 533-0133
718 28th St Ste A Hoquiam (98550) ***(G-4344)***
Image360, Vancouver *Also called Stong Enterprises LLC* ***(G-14613)***
Image360-Burlington, WA, Burlington *Also called Whidbey Island Sign Sltons LLC* ***(G-2201)***
Images 509 736-9508
2527 W Kennewick Ave # 106 Kennewick (99336) ***(G-4675)***
Imagesmart Sign Company LLC 509 525-4343
1365 Dalles Military Rd B Walla Walla (99362) ***(G-14821)***
Imagicorps Inc 425 869-0599
10500 231st Way Ne Redmond (98053) ***(G-8506)***
Imagination Fabrication 425 415-1311
6524 240th St Se Woodinville (98072) ***(G-15264)***
Imagination Technologies, Bellevue *Also called Mips Tech Inc* ***(G-1008)***
Imagine Color Service LLC 206 281-5703
4215 21st Ave W Ste 100 Seattle (98199) ***(G-10207)***
Imagine Food 917 428-4173
25816 163rd Ave Se Covington (98042) ***(G-2830)***
Imagine Visual Service LLC 206 281-5703
4215 21st Ave W Ste 100 Seattle (98199) ***(G-10208)***
Imaginetics Holdings LLC (PA) 253 735-0156
3410 A St Se Auburn (98002) ***(G-472)***
Imaginetics LLC 253 735-0156
3410 A St Se Auburn (98002) ***(G-473)***
Imat Inc 360 256-5600
12516 Ne 95th St Ste D110 Vancouver (98682) ***(G-14310)***
IMC, Washougal *Also called Immersive Media Company* ***(G-14960)***
Imc-Innvtive Mktg Cnnction LLC 360 895-0178
3377 Bethel Rd Se Ste 107 Port Orchard (98366) ***(G-7816)***
Imco Inc 360 694-7121
15812 Ne 10th Ave Ridgefield (98642) ***(G-9089)***
Imerys Minerals California Inc 509 787-4575
16419 Road 10.5 Nw Quincy (98848) ***(G-8300)***
Immersive Media Company 360 609-3419
1700 Main St Ste 248 Washougal (98671) ***(G-14960)***
Immune Design Corp (PA) 206 682-0645
1616 Eastlake Ave E Seattle (98102) ***(G-10209)***
Immunex Corporation 206 551-5169
51 University St Seattle (98101) ***(G-10210)***
Immunobioscience Corp 425 367-4601
12121 Harbour Rch Dr 11 Mukilteo (98275) ***(G-6942)***
IMOVR, Bellevue *Also called Thermogenesis Group Inc* ***(G-1185)***
Impact Health Publishing 509 624-2599
339 E Rockwood Blvd Spokane (99202) ***(G-12304)***
Impact Property Mgnt 425 334-6361
9506 4th St Ne Ste 101 Lake Stevens (98258) ***(G-5647)***
Impact Service Corporation 509 468-7900
3811 E Francis Ave Spokane (99217) ***(G-12305)***
Impact Studio 425 890-3914
412 Haines St Sedro Woolley (98284) ***(G-11541)***
Impel Biopharmaceuticals, Seattle *Also called Impel Neuropharma Inc* ***(G-10211)***
Impel Neuropharma Inc 206 568-1466
201 Elliott Ave W Ste 260 Seattle (98119) ***(G-10211)***
Imperial Fabricating, Chehalis *Also called Imperial Group Mfg Inc* ***(G-2504)***
Imperial Group Mfg Inc 360 748-4201
206 Maurin Rd Chehalis (98532) ***(G-2504)***
Imperial Motion LLC 253 779-4400
2920 S Steele St Tacoma (98409) ***(G-13347)***
Imperial Publishing 800 210-5033
8112 Ne 131st St Kirkland (98034) ***(G-5367)***
Imperium Renewables Inc (HQ) 360 532-2387
821 3rd Ave Longview (98632) ***(G-5917)***
Impinj Inc (PA) 206 517-5300
400 Frview Ave N Ste 1200 Seattle (98109) ***(G-10212)***
Impinj Inc 206 834-1098
716 N 34th St Seattle (98103) ***(G-10213)***
Impinj Inc 206 315-4449
400 Fairview Ave N # 1200 Seattle (98109) ***(G-10214)***
Implanted Material Technology, Vancouver *Also called Imat Inc* ***(G-14310)***
Implicit Bioscience Inc 650 851-3133
1600 E Jefferson St # 505 Seattle (98122) ***(G-10215)***
Impression Printing Co Inc 206 762-6211
222 S Lucile St Seattle (98108) ***(G-10216)***
Impressions Express Inc 253 874-2923
32010 42nd Pl Sw Auburn (98023) ***(G-474)***
Impressions In Wood LLC 425 444-5324
917 Avenue A Snohomish (98290) ***(G-11926)***
Impressive Printing 253 538-2948
118 116th St S Tacoma (98444) ***(G-13348)***
Imprev Inc 800 809-3356
11400 Se 8th St Ste 450 Bellevue (98004) ***(G-954)***
Imprint, Seattle *Also called Stitchblade LLC* ***(G-11197)***
Imprints Northwest 360 254-8700
12209 Ne 4th Plain Blvd Vancouver (98682) ***(G-14311)***
Impulse Audio Inc 206 650-0075
9911 37th Ave Sw Seattle (98126) ***(G-10217)***
Impulse Construction & Glass 425 530-7728
1429 Avenue D Snohomish (98290) ***(G-11927)***
Impulse Medical Tech Inc 360 829-0400
159 W Mason Ave Buckley (98321) ***(G-2059)***
IMS Corporation 509 687-8116
104 Jacob Pl Chelan (98816) ***(G-2555)***
Imsa Steel Corp 360 673-8200
222 W Kalama River Rd Kalama (98625) ***(G-4501)***
In An Instant 206 465-0644
5438 35th Ave Sw Seattle (98126) ***(G-10218)***
In An Instant Art LLC 206 294-3570
1941 1st Ave S Ste 2g Seattle (98134) ***(G-10219)***
In Canvas 425 355-4102
12428 Highway 99 Ste 46 Everett (98204) ***(G-3513)***
In Cascade Concrete Industries 425 747-0956
127 Bellevue Way Se # 100 Bellevue (98004) ***(G-955)***
In Graphic Detail LLC 360 582-0002
577 W Washington St Ste B Sequim (98382) ***(G-11641)***
In The Zone Promotions 425 246-6313
25722 Se Tiger Mtn Rd Issaquah (98027) ***(G-4428)***
Incentives By Design Inc 206 623-4310
1920 Occidental Ave S A Seattle (98134) ***(G-10220)***
Incline Cider Company 503 830-4414
4402 D St Nw Auburn (98001) ***(G-475)***
Incontrol Systems Corp 425 424-9707
216 Heather Rd Everett (98203) ***(G-3514)***
Incremental Systems Corp 425 732-2377
3380 146th Pl Se Ste 107 Bellevue (98007) ***(G-956)***
Incsys, Bellevue *Also called Incremental Systems Corp* ***(G-956)***
Incycle Software Corp 425 880-9200
Eastside Offc Ctr 1420 # 14205 Bellevue (98006) ***(G-957)***
Indaba Management Company LLC 360 546-5528
400 E Mill Plain Blvd # 103 Vancouver (98660) ***(G-14312)***
Indaba Systems, Vancouver *Also called Indaba Management Company LLC* ***(G-14312)***
Indeco, Ferndale *Also called Industrial Design & Eqp Inc* ***(G-3855)***
Indena Usa Inc 206 340-6140
601 Union St Ste 330 Seattle (98101) ***(G-10221)***
Independence Printing, Centralia *Also called Van Quill Larry R* ***(G-2441)***
Independent Aero Space Svcs 702 237-9953
25051 128th Pl Se Kent (98030) ***(G-4949)***

Independent Brewers Untd Corp 206 682-8322
91 S Royal Brougham Way Seattle (98134) **(G-10222)**
Independent Chute Company 206 321-8911
6113 176th St E Bldg B Puyallup (98375) **(G-8166)**
Independent Commerce, Auburn *Also called Pacific Custom Cable Inc* **(G-523)**
Independent Company, Puyallup *Also called Independent Chute Company* **(G-8166)**
Independent Dealer Accessories, Kent *Also called BTS Exchange LLC* **(G-4825)**
Independent Packers Corp 206 285-6000
2001 W Grfeld St Ste C102 Seattle (98119) **(G-10223)**
Independent Tech Service LLC 253 891-1976
9918 162nd Street Ct E # 1 Puyallup (98375) **(G-8167)**
Independent Trailer & Eqp Co, Union Gap *Also called T E C I Inc* **(G-13953)**
Independent Woodworks 206 239-8577
4546 45th Ave Sw Seattle (98116) **(G-10224)**
Indepndent Distr Rexall Showca 253 565-6595
8330 34th St W University Place (98466) **(G-13972)**
Index Industries Inc 360 629-5200
300 Harris Ave Bellingham (98225) **(G-1376)**
Index Publishing (PA) 206 323-7101
1535 11th Ave Ste 300 Seattle (98122) **(G-10225)**
Index Sensors & Controls, Bellingham *Also called Index Industries Inc* **(G-1376)**
Indian Popcorn, Kent *Also called Moosoo Corporation* **(G-5016)**
Indiana Harness Co 509 535-3400
2425 N Vista Rd Spokane Valley (99212) **(G-12738)**
Indie Flix Inc 206 829-9112
4314 E Madison St Seattle (98112) **(G-10226)**
Indigo Vinylworks LLC 425 463-7460
12828 Se 161st St Renton (98058) **(G-8823)**
Indigo Vinylworks Llc 425 278-4411
309 S Cloverdale St B4 Seattle (98108) **(G-10227)**
Indulge LLC 360 589-7226
219 Ontario Ct Richland (99352) **(G-9008)**
Indulo Inc 206 383-0373
100 20th Ave E Apt 10 Seattle (98112) **(G-10228)**
Industrial Automation Inc 206 763-1025
1421 S 93rd St Seattle (98108) **(G-10229)**
Industrial Ceramics Inc 905 878-2848
815 1st Ave Seattle (98104) **(G-10230)**
Industrial Coatings 425 742-3415
2831 156th St Sw Lynnwood (98087) **(G-6137)**
Industrial Container Svcs LLC 206 763-2345
7152 1st Ave S Seattle (98108) **(G-10231)**
Industrial Containers Div, Mercer Island *Also called Industrial Crating & Packing* **(G-6467)**
Industrial Control Dev Inc 360 546-2286
7350 S Union Ridge Pkwy Ridgefield (98642) **(G-9090)**
Industrial Control Group 509 965-5967
11808 Bristol Ct Yakima (98908) **(G-15587)**
Industrial Crating & Packing 425 226-9200
4821 84th Ave Se Mercer Island (98040) **(G-6467)**
Industrial Design & Eqp Inc 360 671-9200
1518 Slater Rd Ferndale (98248) **(G-3855)**
Industrial Electric Co Inc 360 424-3239
1120 W Division St Mount Vernon (98273) **(G-6804)**
Industrial Electric Service Co 360 533-2792
2100 Industrial Rd Aberdeen (98520) **(G-19)**
Industrial Fabrication Co 360 793-9001
14124 339th Ave Se Sultan (98294) **(G-13027)**
Industrial Fans Direct, Mukilteo *Also called Higher Power Supplies Inc* **(G-6933)**
Industrial Fbrication Tstg Inc 360 345-1400
138 Chase Rd Chehalis (98532) **(G-2505)**
Industrial Generosity Inc 206 336-2268
159 S Jackson St Ste 200 Seattle (98104) **(G-10232)**
Industrial Iron Works 509 322-0072
1871 Old Highway 97 Okanogan (98840) **(G-7197)**
Industrial Machine Services, Vancouver *Also called Fabrication Enterprises Inc* **(G-14218)**
Industrial Maintenance & Cnstr, Mount Vernon *Also called M A C I Inc* **(G-6808)**
Industrial Pipe and Valve 360 314-6492
1501 Ne 106th St Vancouver (98686) **(G-14313)**
Industrial Repair Service Inc 253 395-8852
7016 S 196th St Kent (98032) **(G-4950)**
Industrial Revolution Inc 425 285-1111
5835 Segale Park Drive C Tukwila (98188) **(G-13752)**
Industrial Screenprint Inc 253 735-5111
1505 Central Ave S Kent (98032) **(G-4951)**
Industrial Software Solutns 425 368-7310
19909 120th Ave Ne Ste 10 Bothell (98011) **(G-1767)**
Industrial Support Service LLC 509 276-5131
5579 W Mcknzie Woolard Rd Deer Park (99006) **(G-2906)**
Industrial Systems Inc 503 262-0367
12119 Ne 99th St Ste 2090 Vancouver (98682) **(G-14314)**
Industrial Systems Laboratory 425 226-7585
58 Logan Ave S Renton (98057) **(G-8824)**
Industrial Systems LLC 503 262-0367
12119 Ne 99th St Ste 2090 Vancouver (98682) **(G-14315)**
Industrial Tech Intl LLC 509 248-0959
2609 Ahtanum Rd Yakima (98903) **(G-15588)**
Industrial Welding Co Inc 509 598-2356
1203 N Greene St Spokane (99202) **(G-12306)**
Industrial Welding Service 425 334-2686
3425 103rd Pl Se Everett (98208) **(G-3515)**
Industry Sign & Graphics Inc 253 854-2333
4208 Auburn Way N Ste 1 Auburn (98002) **(G-476)**
Infinetix Corp 509 922-5629
2721 N Van Marter Dr # 3 Spokane Valley (99206) **(G-12739)**
Infinite Caste 206 335-4058
3800 Ne Sunset Blvd Renton (98056) **(G-8825)**
Infinity Building Mtls LLC 804 921-0810
4084 Saltspring Dr Ferndale (98248) **(G-3856)**
Infinity Digital LLC 715 298-3530
233 Lasalle Dr Kelso (98626) **(G-4529)**
Infinity Fabrication Inc 360 435-7460
19225 62nd Ave Ne Arlington (98223) **(G-254)**
Infinity Industries LLC 425 418-1151
16520 North Rd Apt D205 Bothell (98012) **(G-1866)**
Infinity Sign & Marketing Inc 253 539-6771
10025 South Tacoma Way H4 Lakewood (98499) **(G-5728)**
Inflation Systems, Moses Lake *Also called Joyson Safety Systems* **(G-6718)**
Influx LLC 360 200-4323
305 Se Chkalov Dr Ste 111 Vancouver (98683) **(G-14316)**
Infoharvest Inc 206 686-2729
8238 15th Ave Ne Seattle (98115) **(G-10233)**
Infometrix Inc 425 402-1450
11807 N Creek Pkwy S # 111 Bothell (98011) **(G-1768)**
Infomine Usa Inc 509 328-8023
100 N Mullan Rd Ste 102 Spokane Valley (99206) **(G-12740)**
Informatica Pubg Group LLC 480 361-6300
15410 Maplewild Ave Sw Burien (98166) **(G-2113)**
Information Builders Inc 206 624-9055
1420 5th Ave Ste 3250 Seattle (98101) **(G-10234)**
Information Management Tech 425 322-5078
2082 Se 213th St Maple Valley (98038) **(G-6276)**
Infosoft Solutions Inc 360 738-3060
229 Jerome St Bellingham (98229) **(G-1377)**
Ingersoll-Rand Company 253 931-8600
20121 72nd Ave S Kent (98032) **(G-4952)**
Ingersoll-Rand Company 253 398-3900
20017 72nd Ave S Kent (98032) **(G-4953)**
Ingio/Vinbalance LLC 509 522-1621
6 E Alder St Ste 224 Walla Walla (99362) **(G-14822)**
Ingredion Incorporated 509 375-1261
216 University Dr Richland (99354) **(G-9009)**
Inhance, Bothell *Also called JM Ventures Inc* **(G-1771)**
Inject Tool & Die Inc 360 679-6160
657 Oak St Oak Harbor (98277) **(G-7154)**
Injectidry Systems Inc 425 822-3851
3223 164th St Sw Ste N Lynnwood (98087) **(G-6138)**
Ink Inc 253 565-4000
3021 69th Ave W Ste A University Place (98466) **(G-13973)**
Ink Ability 360 342-8174
717 W Main St Ste 120 Battle Ground (98604) **(G-709)**
Ink Doctor Printing 509 237-1644
303 Patrick Rd Ephrata (98823) **(G-3338)**
Ink For You Tattoo 360 649-6972
3590 Westminster Dr Se Port Orchard (98366) **(G-7817)**
Ink It Your Way 425 789-1669
10827 27th St Se Lake Stevens (98258) **(G-5648)**
Ink Smiths Screen Printing LLC 253 446-7126
312 N Meridian Puyallup (98371) **(G-8168)**
Ink Well Printers Inc 206 623-1701
2423 S 304th St Federal Way (98003) **(G-3745)**
Inker Prints LLC 206 499-7379
210 S Mead St Seattle (98108) **(G-10235)**
Inkwell LLC (PA) 425 277-3655
709 S 32nd St Renton (98055) **(G-8826)**
Inkwell Property Management, Renton *Also called Inkwell LLC* **(G-8826)**
Inkwell Screenprinting 206 551-1713
1055 S Director St Seattle (98108) **(G-10236)**
Inland Alarm LLC 509 457-6065
1100 Ahtanum Rd Yakima (98903) **(G-15589)**
Inland Asphalt, Spokane Valley *Also called CPM Development Corporation* **(G-12668)**
Inland Coffee and Beverage 509 228-9239
9311 E Trent Ave Spokane Valley (99206) **(G-12741)**
Inland Empire Bus Solutions 509 922-7492
11816 E 24th Ave Spokane Valley (99206) **(G-12742)**
Inland Empire Paper Company 509 924-1911
3320 N Argonne Rd Spokane (99212) **(G-12307)**
Inland Empire Plating Inc 509 535-1704
2401 N Eastern Rd Spokane Valley (99212) **(G-12743)**
Inland Empire Resteel 509 863-9870
8314 N Regal St Spokane (99217) **(G-12308)**
Inland Fixtures Co Inc 509 487-2759
2909 N Crestline St Spokane (99207) **(G-12309)**
Inland Ice, Kennewick *Also called Articland Ice* **(G-4620)**
Inland Ice & Fuel Inc 509 457-6151
100 Division St Yakima (98902) **(G-15590)**
Inland Millwork 509 481-7765
111 N Vista Rd Ste 4d Spokane Valley (99212) **(G-12744)**
Inland Northwest Dairies LLC (PA) 509 489-8600
33 E Francis Ave Spokane (99208) **(G-12310)**
Inland Northwest Mfg LLC 509 218-7424
7211 S Grove Rd Spokane (99224) **(G-12311)**
Inland NW Metallurgical Svcs 509 922-7663
16203 E Marietta Ln Spokane Valley (99216) **(G-12745)**
Inland PCF Stamp & Mkg Pdts, Spokane *Also called Rumpeltes Enterprises Inc* **(G-12485)**

ALPHABETIC

Inland Publications Inc 509 325-0634
1227 W Summit Pkwy Spokane (99201) *(G-12312)*
Inland Saxum Printing LLC 509 525-0467
10 N 7th Ave Walla Walla (99362) *(G-14823)*
Inland Sign and Lighting Sign, Spokane *Also called Sign Corporation (G-12503)*
Inland Synthetics 509 466-6101
9011 N Farmdale St Spokane (99208) *(G-12313)*
Inland Tarp & Cover Inc 509 766-7024
4172 N Frontage Rd E Moses Lake (98837) *(G-6715)*
Inland Woodworks 509 701-0985
12421 E Moffat Rd Spokane (99217) *(G-12314)*
Inlet Petroleum Solvents 907 274-3835
1191 2nd Ave Ste 1800 Seattle (98101) *(G-10237)*
Inline Design LLC (PA) 425 405-5505
1420 Terry Ave Unit 2304 Seattle (98101) *(G-10238)*
Inline Steel Fabricators Inc 509 248-4554
2506 S 26th Ave Yakima (98903) *(G-15591)*
Inner Fence Holdings Inc 888 922-8277
16701 Ne 80th St Ste 204 Redmond (98052) *(G-8507)*
Innerscan Inc 425 419-7718
17401 102nd Ave Ne Bothell (98011) *(G-1769)*
Innocor Inc 844 824-9348
1180 Nw Maple St Issaquah (98027) *(G-4429)*
Innocor Foam Technologies LLC 360 575-8844
1205 Prudential Blvd Longview (98632) *(G-5918)*
Innofresh LLC 206 438-3541
2707 33rd Ave S Seattle (98144) *(G-10239)*
Innotech Metal Designs LLC 360 393-4108
5971 Gide Mrdian Bllngham Bellingham (98226) *(G-1378)*
Innotech Process Equipment, Bellingham *Also called Innotech Metal Designs LLC (G-1378)*
Innov8 Cabin Solutions LLC 425 241-8378
24212 Se 21st St Sammamish (98075) *(G-9220)*
Innova Mfg LLC 509 946-7461
1840 Terminal Dr Richland (99354) *(G-9010)*
Innova Precision Machining Mfg, Richland *Also called Innova Mfg LLC (G-9010)*
Innovasian Cuisine Entps Inc 800 324-5140
116 Andover Park E # 200 Tukwila (98188) *(G-13753)*
Innovate For All Spc 425 681-2191
4000 1st Ave S Seattle (98134) *(G-10240)*
Innovatech Pdts & Eqp Co Inc 425 402-1881
19722 144th Ave Ne Woodinville (98072) *(G-15265)*
Innovatek Inc 509 375-1093
3806 W 40th Pl Kennewick (99337) *(G-4676)*
Innovation Associates 206 455-2332
400 112th Ave Ne Bellevue (98004) *(G-958)*
Innovation Resource Center 509 836-2400
214 S 6th St Sunnyside (98944) *(G-13127)*
Innovative Advantage Inc 206 910-7528
15353 Ne 90th St Redmond (98052) *(G-8508)*
Innovative Composite Engrg Inc 509 493-4484
1265 N Main Ave White Salmon (98672) *(G-15119)*
Innovative Dental Tech Inc 971 303-5659
2005 Se 192nd Ave Camas (98607) *(G-2257)*
Innovative Freeze Dried Fd LLC 855 836-3233
6025 Portal Way Ferndale (98248) *(G-3857)*
Innovative Hearth Products LLC 253 735-1100
1502 14th St Nw Auburn (98001) *(G-477)*
Innovative Manufacturing Inc 360 966-7250
2118 E Hemmi Rd Bellingham (98226) *(G-1379)*
Innovative Outdoor Pdts LLC 509 826-0219
8 Norway Pine Dr Tonasket (98855) *(G-13651)*
Innovative Salon Products Inc 360 805-0794
154 Village Ct Ste 172 Monroe (98272) *(G-6580)*
Innovative Solutions Intl 206 365-7200
8441 Se 68th St Ste 312 Mercer Island (98040) *(G-6468)*
Innovative Technologies Inc 425 258-4773
21 E Marine View Dr Ste C Everett (98201) *(G-3516)*
Innovative Thermal Solutions 253 830-4550
12201 23rd St E Edgewood (98372) *(G-3082)*
Innovaura Corporation 425 272-2702
7418 Soundview Dr Edmonds (98026) *(G-3120)*
Inprint Printing Inc 509 884-1454
962 Valley Mall Pkwy East Wenatchee (98802) *(G-3021)*
Insect Shield LLC 206 624-9307
3201 1st Ave S Ste 350 Seattle (98134) *(G-10241)*
Insect Skateboards Inc 206 706-8882
7536 Dibble Ave Nw Seattle (98117) *(G-10242)*
Inside Golf Newspaper, Port Townsend *Also called Northwest Publications Inc (G-7901)*
Inside Out Medicine Inc 206 920-8959
2026 N 77th St Seattle (98103) *(G-10243)*
Inside Real Estate 360 379-0139
151 Windship Dr Port Townsend (98368) *(G-7891)*
Insightful Corporation (HQ) 206 283-8802
1700 Westlake Ave N # 500 Seattle (98109) *(G-10244)*
Insights Works Inc 425 577-2206
14408 118th Ave Ne Kirkland (98034) *(G-5368)*
Insignia Sign Inc 425 917-2109
325 Burnett Ave N Renton (98057) *(G-8827)*
Insitu Inc 509 493-8600
901 E Bingen Point Way Bingen (98605) *(G-1637)*
Insitu Inc (HQ) 509 493-8600
118 Columbia River Way Bingen (98605) *(G-1638)*
Inskiwrx Tool & Machine LLC 425 238-2738
12121 99th Ave Ne Arlington (98223) *(G-255)*
Insomania Software 425 837-1525
11758 175th Pl Ne Redmond (98052) *(G-8509)*
Inspection Plus 509 534-9290
21312 E Gilbert Ave Otis Orchards (99027) *(G-7514)*
Inspired 360 504-2590
124 W 1st St Ste B Port Angeles (98362) *(G-7713)*
Inspired Monumental 253 468-4835
1620 60th Avenue Ct Nw Gig Harbor (98335) *(G-4121)*
Insta-Learn By Step Inc 425 355-9830
11324 Mukilteo Spdwy # 4 Mukilteo (98275) *(G-6943)*
Instafab Company Inc 360 737-8235
2424 E 2nd St Vancouver (98661) *(G-14317)*
Instant Access Videocom 425 273-3496
12814 Se 80th Way Newcastle (98056) *(G-7031)*
Instant Auction Co 509 448-0279
3307 E 55th Ave Spokane (99223) *(G-12315)*
Instant Cheer Illstrations LLC 206 999-5515
3844 Ne 85th St Seattle (98115) *(G-10245)*
Instant Gratification LLP 206 361-2966
20266 37th Ave Ne Lake Forest Park (98155) *(G-5615)*
Instant Imprints 360 694-9711
13521 Se 3rd Way Ste 400 Vancouver (98684) *(G-14318)*
Instant Option 509 290-6481
5009 N Market St Spokane (99217) *(G-12316)*
Instant Press Inc (PA) 509 457-6195
601 W Yakima Ave Yakima (98902) *(G-15592)*
Instant Sign Factory 509 456-3333
721 W 2nd Ave Spokane (99201) *(G-12317)*
Instantiations Inc 503 770-0861
4412 Se 185th Ct Vancouver (98683) *(G-14319)*
Instructional Technologies Inc (PA) 360 576-5976
14511 Ne 13th Ave Ste 108 Vancouver (98685) *(G-14320)*
Instrument & Valve Services Co 360 366-3645
6920 Salashan Pkwy E208 Ferndale (98248) *(G-3858)*
Instrument Sales and Svc Inc 253 796-5400
7051 S 234th St Kent (98032) *(G-4954)*
Instrumentation Northwest Inc 425 822-4434
19026 72nd Ave S Kent (98032) *(G-4955)*
Insty-Prints 509 334-4275
1652 S Grand Ave Pullman (99163) *(G-8092)*
Intalco Aluminum LLC 360 384-7061
4050 Mountain View Rd Ferndale (98248) *(G-3859)*
Intec, Everett *Also called Integrated Technologies Inc (G-3518)*
Intech Enterprises Inc 360 835-8785
3825 Grant St Washougal (98671) *(G-14961)*
Integral Fabrications LLC 360 831-9353
1420 Marvin Rd Ne Lacey (98516) *(G-5560)*
Integrated Composition Systems 509 624-5064
715 E Sprague Ave Ste 75 Spokane (99202) *(G-12318)*
Integrated Computer Systems 425 820-6120
8541 154th Ave Ne Redmond (98052) *(G-8510)*
Integrated Design Group Inc 509 328-4244
2512 W Francis Ave Spokane (99205) *(G-12319)*
Integrated Marine Systems Inc 360 385-0077
4816 15th Ave Nw Seattle (98107) *(G-10246)*
Integrated Print Solutions Inc 888 716-5666
2215 37th St Everett (98201) *(G-3517)*
Integrated Stair Systems Inc 360 829-4220
1345 Ryan Rd Buckley (98321) *(G-2060)*
Integrated Systems Design 360 746-0812
3924 Irongate Rd Ste B Bellingham (98226) *(G-1380)*
Integrated Technologies Inc 425 349-2084
1910 Merrill Creek Pkwy Everett (98203) *(G-3518)*
Integrity Biopharma Services 509 474-1481
10525 N Edna Ln Spokane (99218) *(G-12320)*
Integrity Dental LLC 253 691-7292
15605 196th St E Orting (98360) *(G-7481)*
Integrity First Coatings LLC 509 619-9983
6405 Chapel Hill Blvd D202 Pasco (99301) *(G-7592)*
Integrity Industries Inc 425 264-9401
2210 Lind Ave Sw Ste 109 Renton (98057) *(G-8828)*
Integrity Orthotic Laboratory 360 435-0703
19113 63rd Ave Ne Ste 4 Arlington (98223) *(G-256)*
Integrity Orthotics, Arlington *Also called Integrity Orthotic Laboratory (G-256)*
Integrity Press Inc 425 868-3120
1211 210th Ave Ne Redmond (98074) *(G-8511)*
Integrity Printing LLC 253 841-3161
2102 E Main Ste 111 Puyallup (98372) *(G-8169)*
Integrity Supplements LLC 800 210-4863
2620 Ne Strand Rd Bremerton (98311) *(G-1962)*
Intek Manufacturing Inc 253 857-5073
3257 Se Gliding Hawk Way Olalla (98359) *(G-7206)*
Intel Corporation 253 371-1052
2700 156th Ave Ne Ste 300 Bellevue (98007) *(G-959)*
Intelipedics LLC 509 432-4036
725 Nw Charlotte St Pullman (99163) *(G-8093)*
Intellicard Inc 509 965-9266
8902 Tieton Dr Yakima (98908) *(G-15593)*
Intelligent Industries LLC 206 372-7273
1900 Sw Campus Dr Federal Way (98023) *(G-3746)*

Intelligent Lids LLC 206 920-6484
505 Bdwy Way S Unit 457 Seattle (98102) ***(G-10247)***
Intelligent Technologies Inc 360 254-4211
12119 Ne 99th St Ste 2030 Vancouver (98682) ***(G-14321)***
Intelligenteffects LLC 323 206-0499
4315 Lake Washington Blvd Kirkland (98033) ***(G-5369)***
Intellipaper LLC (PA) 509 343-9410
2525 E 29th Ave Spokane (99223) ***(G-12321)***
Intellitouch Communicatons 858 457-3300
24310 E 3rd Ave Liberty Lake (99019) ***(G-5837)***
Intention Publishing Co 206 463-9777
20239 77th Pl Sw Vashon (98070) ***(G-14724)***
Intentionet Inc 206 579-6567
16625 Redmond Way M241 Redmond (98052) ***(G-8512)***
Interactive Electronic Systems 877 543-8698
1201 Pacific Ave Ste 600 Tacoma (98402) ***(G-13349)***
Interfor US Inc 360 575-3600
540 3rd Ave Longview (98632) ***(G-5919)***
Interfor US Inc 360 457-6266
243701 W Highway 101 Port Angeles (98363) ***(G-7714)***
Interfor US Inc 360 327-3377
243701 W Highway 101 Port Angeles (98363) ***(G-7715)***
Intergrated Aerospace LLC 360 691-2298
3316 Old Hartford Rd Lake Stevens (98258) ***(G-5649)***
Interior Art & Frame, Kirkland *Also called Its A Wrap Washington Inc* ***(G-5371)***
Interior Construction Spc 425 745-8343
11527 Cyrus Way Ste 1 Mukilteo (98275) ***(G-6944)***
Interior Environments Inc 206 432-8800
3450 4th Ave S Seattle (98134) ***(G-10248)***
Interior Form Tops Inc 253 927-8171
1420 Meridian E Ste 5 Milton (98354) ***(G-6535)***
Interior Wdwkg Specialists Inc 425 881-1328
15337 Ne 92nd St Redmond (98052) ***(G-8513)***
Interiors Renovation, Kirkland *Also called Leather Guard Div Int Renovatn* ***(G-5384)***
Interlock Industries Inc 253 872-5750
20213 84th Ave S Kent (98032) ***(G-4956)***
Interlock Industries Inc 360 713-3036
26910 92nd Ave Nw Pmb 425 Stanwood (98292) ***(G-12976)***
Interlocking Software Corp 360 394-5900
19472 Powder Hill Pl Ne Poulsbo (98370) ***(G-7966)***
Interlube International Inc 360 332-2132
170 3rd St Blaine (98230) ***(G-1675)***
Interlube International Inc 360 734-3832
801 Harris Ave 1 Bellingham (98225) ***(G-1381)***
Intermec Inc (HQ) 425 348-2600
16201 25th Ave W Lynnwood (98087) ***(G-6139)***
Intermec Technologies Corp (HQ) 425 348-2600
16201 25th Ave W Lynnwood (98087) ***(G-6140)***
Intermedianet Inc 425 451-3393
3310 146th Pl Se Bellevue (98007) ***(G-960)***
Intermountain Fabricators Inc 509 534-1676
6014 E Knox Ave Spokane Valley (99212) ***(G-12746)***
Intermountain Machine 509 482-0431
5328 N Sycamore St Spokane (99217) ***(G-12322)***
Intermountain West Intl, Kennewick *Also called IW International Inc* ***(G-4679)***
International Athletic 360 384-6868
2044 Main St Ferndale (98248) ***(G-3860)***
International Bar Coding 800 661-5570
441 11th Ave Oroville (98844) ***(G-7467)***
International Carbide Corp 800 422-8665
32022 8th Ave S Roy (98580) ***(G-9161)***
International Chem Systems Inc 253 263-8038
3006 Judson St Ste 201 Gig Harbor (98335) ***(G-4122)***
International Cnstr Eqp Inc 206 764-4787
8101 Occidental Ave S Seattle (98108) ***(G-10249)***
International Comanche Society 360 332-2743
925 Ludwick Ave Blaine (98230) ***(G-1676)***
International Examiner 206 624-3925
409 Maynard Ave S Ste 203 Seattle (98104) ***(G-10250)***
International Glace Inc 503 267-7917
1616 E Lyons Ave Spokane (99217) ***(G-12323)***
International Homes Cedar Inc 360 668-8511
8330 Maltby Rd Ste B Woodinville (98072) ***(G-15266)***
International Longline Supply 360 650-0412
2207 Valencia St Ste 103 Bellingham (98229) ***(G-1382)***
International Paint LLC 206 763-5884
1621 S 92nd Pl Seattle (98108) ***(G-10251)***
International Paper Company 509 576-3158
660 W Ahtanum Rd Union Gap (98903) ***(G-13933)***
International Paper Company 509 765-0262
13594 Wheeler Rd Ne Moses Lake (98837) ***(G-6716)***
International Paper Company 253 372-1360
1225 6th Ave N Kent (98032) ***(G-4957)***
International Trade & Trvl Ltd 509 981-2307
4401 S Glenview Ln Spokane (99223) ***(G-12324)***
International Wood Processors 360 299-9996
2802 17th St Anacortes (98221) ***(G-135)***
Internet Motors Company 425 654-1154
2018 156th Ave Ne Ste 100 Bellevue (98007) ***(G-961)***
Interntional Seafoods Alsk Inc 206 284-4830
3500 188th St Sw Ste 502 Lynnwood (98037) ***(G-6141)***
Interntnal Arospc Coatings Inc (PA) 509 321-0342
5709 W Sunset Hwy Ste 205 Spokane (99224) ***(G-12325)***
Interntnal Rhbltative Sciences 360 892-0339
14001 Se 1st St Vancouver (98684) ***(G-14322)***
Interntonal Graphics Nameplate 360 699-4808
14413 Ne 10th Ave Ste C Vancouver (98685) ***(G-14323)***
Interntonal Hearth Melting LLC 509 371-2500
3101 Kingsgate Way Richland (99354) ***(G-9011)***
Interplastic Corporation 253 872-8067
22237 76th Ave S Kent (98032) ***(G-4958)***
Interstate Asphalt Paving Inc 425 318-5008
16821 Smokey Point Blvd Arlington (98223) ***(G-257)***
Interstate Concrete and Asp Co 509 375-1021
2590 Hagen Rd Richland (99354) ***(G-9012)***
Interstate Concrete and Asp Co 509 529-6400
1326 Dell Ave Walla Walla (99362) ***(G-14824)***
Interstate Concrete and Asp Co 509 547-2380
2505 Dump Rd Prosser (99350) ***(G-8043)***
Interstate Concrete and Asp Co 509 547-2380
11919 Harris Rd Pasco (99301) ***(G-7593)***
Interstate Electronics Corp 360 779-3723
Naval Sub Bangor Rm W201 Silverdale (98383) ***(G-11838)***
Interstate Industries Inc 206 387-2364
1217 4th Ave N Ste 103 Kent (98032) ***(G-4959)***
Interstate Industries Inc 425 226-2135
8320 S 259th St Kent (98030) ***(G-4960)***
Interstate Plastics, Kent *Also called Dongalen Enterprises Inc* ***(G-4877)***
Interworks US LLC 206 934-1074
6075 California Ave Sw Seattle (98136) ***(G-10252)***
Interworld Elec Cmpt Inds Inc 425 223-4311
1480 Gulf Rd Ste 837 Point Roberts (98281) ***(G-7668)***
Intradata Inc 425 836-8654
6947 Coal Creek Pkwy Se # 17 Newcastle (98059) ***(G-7032)***
Intrigue Chocolates Co 206 829-8810
76 S Washington St Seattle (98104) ***(G-10253)***
Intrinsyc Software (usa) Inc 604 678-3734
600 University St # 3600 Seattle (98101) ***(G-10254)***
Intuitive Mfg Systems Inc (HQ) 425 821-0740
12131 113th Ave Ne # 200 Kirkland (98034) ***(G-5370)***
Intuitive Software Solution 360 387-2271
908 Sands Ln Stanwood (98282) ***(G-12955)***
Invensys Environmental Contrls, Spokane Valley *Also called Schneider Elc Buildings LLC* ***(G-12860)***
Inventist Inc 360 833-2357
1821 Nw 8th Ave Camas (98607) ***(G-2258)***
Inventprise LLC 206 858-8472
18133 Ne 68th St Ste D150 Redmond (98052) ***(G-8514)***
Inventure Chemical Inc 253 576-1577
2244 Port Of Tacoma Rd Tacoma (98421) ***(G-13350)***
Investigatewest 206 441-4288
401 Mercer St Seattle (98109) ***(G-10255)***
Investure - Wa Inc 360 354-6574
1270 E Badger Rd Lynden (98264) ***(G-6023)***
Invio Inc 206 915-3563
325 Harvard Ave E Apt 200 Seattle (98102) ***(G-10256)***
Invio Clinical, Seattle *Also called Invio Inc* ***(G-10256)***
Invitationinabottlecom 800 489-8048
12330 43rd Dr Se Everett (98208) ***(G-3519)***
Inw, Kent *Also called Instrumentation Northwest Inc* ***(G-4955)***
Iocolor LLP 206 223-1845
929 N 130th St Ste 8 Seattle (98133) ***(G-10257)***
Iocurrents Inc 206 494-0099
159 Western Ave W Seattle (98119) ***(G-10258)***
Ioline Corporation 425 398-8282
14140 Ne 200th St Woodinville (98072) ***(G-15267)***
Iopi Medical LLC 425 549-0139
18500 156th Ave Ne # 104 Woodinville (98072) ***(G-15268)***
Ipr-Now Inc 425 888-6190
45839 Se 137th St North Bend (98045) ***(G-7113)***
Irc, Tacoma *Also called Walt Racing LLP* ***(G-13586)***
Irenes Tiles 206 463-2808
18818 Ridge Rd Sw Vashon (98070) ***(G-14725)***
Irish Acres Foundation Quarter 360 966-4677
2422 E Badger Rd Everson (98247) ***(G-3679)***
Irish Foundry & Mfg Inc 206 623-7147
45 S Spokane St Seattle (98134) ***(G-10259)***
Iron Gate Machine, Bellingham *Also called Irongate Machine Inc* ***(G-1384)***
Iron Gate Shoppe 360 791-3292
1108 Loraine St Enumclaw (98022) ***(G-3294)***
Iron Hop Brewing Co LLC 360 421-8138
19639 141st Pl Se Monroe (98272) ***(G-6581)***
Iron Horse Hay & Feed 425 432-0636
19435 244th Ave Se Maple Valley (98038) ***(G-6277)***
Iron Horse Vac LLC 509 586-2446
1915 S Oak St Kennewick (99337) ***(G-4677)***
Iron Mountain Quarry LLC (PA) 425 338-0607
22121 17th Ave Se Ste 117 Bothell (98021) ***(G-1867)***
Iron Rangers LLC 509 891-9355
8401 N Haye Ln Newman Lake (99025) ***(G-7047)***
Iron Software Development LLC 425 892-2287
15730 116th Ave Ne 110b Bothell (98011) ***(G-1770)***
Iron Street Printing LLC 360 734-5809
1421 N Forest St Bellingham (98225) ***(G-1383)***

ALPHABETIC

Ironclad Company — ALPHABETIC SECTION

Ironclad Company 206 588-2272
　12218 51st Pl S Tukwila (98178) *(G-13754)*
Irondog Industries LLC 509 586-0479
　819 W 25th Ave Kennewick (99337) *(G-4678)*
Ironfire Design & Fabrication, Kirkland Also called Fss Holdings LLC *(G-5345)*
Irongate Machine Inc 360 734-4718
　4030 Irongate Rd Bellingham (98226) *(G-1384)*
Ironhouse Ornamental 509 993-7601
　3001 E 34th Ave Spokane (99223) *(G-12326)*
Ironwood Manufacturing Co., Snohomish Also called L Clasen Corp *(G-11935)*
Irrational Hats N Stuff 253 460-5565
　2939 Crystal Springs Rd W University Place (98466) *(G-13974)*
Irrigation Accessories Co 360 896-9440
　12410 Ne 95th St Vancouver (98682) *(G-14324)*
Isaacs & Associates Inc 509 529-2286
　3380 Isaacs Ave Walla Walla (99362) *(G-14825)*
Isaacs Incrdbl Frz Yogurt LLC 509 928-9497
　722 S Blake Rd Spokane Valley (99216) *(G-12747)*
Isaksen Scale Models 425 334-2807
　7419 25th St Ne Lake Stevens (98258) *(G-5650)*
ISC Inc 253 395-5465
　8222 S 228th St Kent (98032) *(G-4961)*
Isenhower Cellars 425 488-2299
　15007 Woodnvle Redmnd Rd Woodinville (98072) *(G-15269)*
Isenhower Cellars 509 526-7896
　3471 Pranger Rd Walla Walla (99362) *(G-14826)*
Isernio Sausage Company, Kent Also called ISC Inc *(G-4961)*
Iship Inc 425 602-4848
　3545 Factoria Blvd Se # 100 Bellevue (98006) *(G-962)*
Isilon Systems LLC 206 315-7500
　505 1st Ave S Seattle (98104) *(G-10260)*
Isla Carmen LLC 360 836-5955
　229 E Reserve St Ste 104 Vancouver (98661) *(G-14325)*
Island Bankra Caribbean Foods 360 698-3345
　4910 Nw 82nd St Silverdale (98383) *(G-11839)*
Island Blueback Inc 360 385-0871
　220 Lincoln St Port Townsend (98368) *(G-7892)*
Island Construction 360 426-3442
　3591 Se Old Olympic Hwy Shelton (98584) *(G-11700)*
Island Custom Machining 360 341-5687
　7206 Heggenes Rd Clinton (98236) *(G-2690)*
Island Dog Sign Company 206 381-0661
　14432 320th Ave Ne Duvall (98019) *(G-2991)*
Island Electric 360 293-9275
　13574 Tibbles Ln Anacortes (98221) *(G-136)*
Island Enterprises (PA) 360 426-4933
　3591 Se Old Olympic Hwy Shelton (98584) *(G-11701)*
Island Enterprises 360 426-4933
　92 E Chapman Rd Shelton (98584) *(G-11702)*
Island Enterprises 360 426-3442
　W98 Hwy 108 Shelton (98584) *(G-11703)*
Island Prosthetics & Orthotics 360 331-7070
　6921 High Point Dr Clinton (98236) *(G-2691)*
Island Riggers Inc 206 920-3360
　8955 Woodbank Dr Ne Bainbridge Island (98110) *(G-642)*
Island Sash & Door Inc 360 331-7752
　18181 D State Rte 525 Freeland (98249) *(G-4031)*
Island Sounder, Eastsound Also called Sound Publishing Inc *(G-3047)*
Island Thyme Herbs and Flowers, Olga Also called Eliza K Trowbridge *(G-7214)*
Island Vintners 206 451-4344
　450 Winslow Way E Bainbridge Island (98110) *(G-643)*
Island Wood Works 360 403-7066
　6011 199th St Ne Arlington (98223) *(G-258)*
Islanders 253 588-9246
　10202 109th Ave Sw Tacoma (98498) *(G-13351)*
Islas Cedar LLC 360 590-2176
　56 Blacktail Ln Hoquiam (98550) *(G-4345)*
ISO Poly Films Inc 864 684-8198
　3807 Se Hidden Way Vancouver (98661) *(G-14326)*
ISO-Quip Corp 360 695-4243
　418 Ne Repass Rd Ste B1 Vancouver (98665) *(G-14327)*
Isonetic Inc 800 670-8871
　28408 Vashon Hwy Sw Vashon (98070) *(G-14726)*
Isoray Inc (PA) 509 375-1202
　350 Hills St Ste 106 Richland (99354) *(G-9013)*
Isoray Medical Inc 509 375-1202
　350 Hills St Ste 106 Richland (99354) *(G-9014)*
ISS (west) Inc 206 470-3754
　801 2nd Ave Ste 1108 Seattle (98104) *(G-10261)*
Issak Shamso 253 457-2964
　25122 117th Ct Se Kent (98030) *(G-4962)*
Issaquah Lanscaping Inc 425 392-6123
　45 1st Pl Nw Issaquah (98027) *(G-4430)*
Issaquah Sammamish Reporter 425 391-0363
　2700 Richards Rd Ste 201 Bellevue (98005) *(G-963)*
Issaquah Signs Inc 425 391-3010
　60 Nw Gilman Blvd Ste C Issaquah (98027) *(G-4431)*
Isupport Software, Vancouver Also called Groupware Incorporated *(G-14274)*
It's 5 Oclock Somewhere Dist, Cashmere Also called Its 5 LLC *(G-2322)*
Itali Lambertini, Port Townsend Also called Dream It Inc *(G-7881)*
Itc, Seattle Also called Independent Packers Corp *(G-10223)*

Itc USA LLC 206 669-3442
　603 Stewart St Ste 200 Seattle (98101) *(G-10262)*
Itec Inc 509 452-3672
　1602 Rudkin Rd Union Gap (98901) *(G-13934)*
Itek Energy, Bellingham Also called Itekenergy LLC *(G-1385)*
Itekenergy LLC 360 647-9531
　3886 Hammer Dr Bellingham (98226) *(G-1385)*
ITEL Terminals of Seattle, Seattle Also called Conglobal Industries LLC *(G-9727)*
Item House Inc (PA) 253 627-7168
　2920 S Steele St Tacoma (98409) *(G-13352)*
Ito Enterprises Inc 425 556-0819
　17717 Ne 108th Way Redmond (98052) *(G-8515)*
Itraq Inc 844 694-8727
　8201 164th Ave Ne Ste 200 Redmond (98052) *(G-8516)*
Itron Inc (PA) 509 924-9900
　2111 N Molter Rd Liberty Lake (99019) *(G-5838)*
Itron Inc 509 924-9900
　12310 E Mirabeau Pkwy # 500 Spokane Valley (99216) *(G-12748)*
Itron Brazil II LLC 509 924-9900
　2111 N Molter Rd Liberty Lake (99019) *(G-5839)*
Itron International Inc 866 374-8766
　2111 N Molter Rd Liberty Lake (99019) *(G-5840)*
Itron Manufacturing Inc. 509 924-9900
　2818 N Sullivan Rd Spokane Valley (99216) *(G-12749)*
Itron US Gas LLC 509 924-9900
　2111 N Molter Rd Liberty Lake (99019) *(G-5841)*
Its 5 LLC 509 679-9771
　207 Mission Ave Cashmere (98815) *(G-2322)*
Its A Wrap Washington Inc 425 827-2000
　11004 Ne 68th St Apt 913 Kirkland (98033) *(G-5371)*
Itty Bits Publications 360 894-3288
　17915 Lawrence Lake Rd Se Yelm (98597) *(G-15736)*
Itty Bitty Baking Company LLC 206 715-6134
　24023 4th Pl W Bothell (98021) *(G-1868)*
ITW Food Equipment Group LLC 360 893-5554
　19220 State Rd 162 E Orting (98360) *(G-7482)*
Iunu Inc 253 307-1858
　558 1st Ave S Ste 100 Seattle (98104) *(G-10263)*
Ivar's Commissary, Mukilteo Also called Ivars Inc *(G-6945)*
Ivars Inc 425 493-1402
　11777 Cyrus Way Mukilteo (98275) *(G-6945)*
Ivie Boat Building 360 892-2883
　14004 Ne 28th St Vancouver (98682) *(G-14328)*
IW International Inc 509 735-8411
　9304 W Clearwater Dr A Kennewick (99336) *(G-4679)*
Iway Software, Seattle Also called Information Builders Inc *(G-10234)*
Ixia Sports Inc 425 417-6454
　1420 Nw Gilman Blvd Issaquah (98027) *(G-4432)*
Izabel Karcher, Owner, Tukwila Also called Karcher Design *(G-13761)*
J & B Importers Inc 253 395-0441
　1725 Puyallup St Ste 300 Sumner (98390) *(G-13075)*
J & B Log Stackers, Centralia Also called Joseph Gillum *(G-2413)*
J & D Machine & Gear Inc 206 762-3274
　624 S Findlay St Seattle (98108) *(G-10264)*
J & E Jensen Inc 253 851-2282
　6608 Kitsap Way Ste 4 Bremerton (98312) *(G-1963)*
J & G Industries Inc 206 246-3782
　18124 Riviera Pl Sw Normandy Park (98166) *(G-7095)*
J & H Printing Inc 509 332-0782
　223 E Main St Pullman (99163) *(G-8094)*
J & J Engineering Inc 360 779-3853
　22797 Holgar Ct Ne Poulsbo (98370) *(G-7967)*
J & J Precision Machine LLC 509 315-9319
　3808 N Sullivan Rd Spokane Valley (99216) *(G-12750)*
J & J Wood Products, Naches Also called Spinner Wood Products LLC *(G-7004)*
J & K Woodworks 425 392-3758
　391 Sw Forest Dr Issaquah (98027) *(G-4433)*
J & L Company, Olympia Also called Creative Collections Co Inc *(G-7259)*
J & L Industries, Spokane Valley Also called Alliance Mch Systems Intl LLC *(G-12604)*
J & L Machining and More LLC 503 317-8284
　1352 E 14th Cir La Center (98629) *(G-5507)*
J & L Tonewoods, Winlock Also called Mapel Mill LLC *(G-15154)*
J & M Diesel Inc 425 353-3050
　3418 121st St Sw Lynnwood (98087) *(G-6142)*
J & M Reports LLC 360 260-8620
　7402 Ne 58th St Vancouver (98662) *(G-14329)*
J & O Timber Falling Inc 360 978-4590
　116 Cattle Dr Onalaska (98570) *(G-7448)*
J & R Commercial Inc 253 639-3890
　30245 148th Ave Se Kent (98042) *(G-4963)*
J & R Mercantile 425 486-6402
　18815 56th Ave Ne Kenmore (98028) *(G-4583)*
J & R Mtlcraft Fabricators Inc 425 254-0392
　1220 N 5th St Renton (98057) *(G-8829)*
J & R Wood Products Inc 360 687-1662
　10519 Ne 314th St Battle Ground (98604) *(G-710)*
J & Ree Fashions 360 281-8610
　3116 E Mill Plain Blvd Vancouver (98661) *(G-14330)*
J & S Manufacturing Inc 360 384-5553
　1508 Slater Rd Ferndale (98248) *(G-3861)*
J A Jack & Sons Inc (HQ) 206 762-7622
　5427 Ohio Ave S Seattle (98134) *(G-10265)*

J A Jack & Sons Inc....360 479-4659
5902 W Sherman Heights Rd Bremerton (98312) ***(G-1964)***
J A Leasing Inc....360 380-5290
6067 Portal Way Ferndale (98248) ***(G-3862)***
J A Ratto Company....206 240-5601
16715 Se 14th St Bellevue (98008) ***(G-964)***
J and J Stainless Steel Svcs....509 952-4568
809 S 60th Ave Yakima (98908) ***(G-15594)***
J and S Ironworks LLC....509 276-5887
6398 Highway 291 Nine Mile Falls (99026) ***(G-7077)***
J and T Prtective Coatings LLC....206 498-6147
8823 41st Ave Sw Seattle (98136) ***(G-10266)***
J Arnold Felt, Centralia *Also called Janice Arnold* ***(G-2410)***
J As Winery....206 409-4841
25435 Se 42nd St Sammamish (98029) ***(G-9221)***
J B Creations, Port Orchard *Also called Betty OGuin* ***(G-7794)***
J Bookwalter Wines, Richland *Also called Bookwalter Winery LLC* ***(G-8976)***
J Bozeat & Associates LLC....206 937-5719
7333 California Ave Sw Seattle (98136) ***(G-10267)***
J C Manufacturing Inc....206 824-7650
22507 1/2 Mar View Dr S Des Moines (98198) ***(G-2938)***
J C Ross Co Inc....206 241-0715
10846 Myers Way S Seattle (98168) ***(G-10268)***
J Calman Industries....360 398-1932
176 W King Tut Rd Lynden (98264) ***(G-6024)***
J Churchill Glove Co, Centralia *Also called Churchill N Mfg Co Inc* ***(G-2393)***
J D Mfg....360 864-8271
145 Park Rd Winlock (98596) ***(G-15151)***
J D Ott Co Inc....206 749-0777
2244 6th Ave S Seattle (98134) ***(G-10269)***
J D Precision Mfg Inc....509 496-2607
10524 E Ruff Ln Colbert (99005) ***(G-2709)***
J Fillips LLC....425 277-1011
3405 Se 7th St Renton (98058) ***(G-8830)***
J Freitag Enterprises Inc....509 453-4461
401 S 3rd Ave Yakima (98902) ***(G-15595)***
J H Holm....360 825-4276
46909 286th Ave Se Enumclaw (98022) ***(G-3295)***
J J J Farms Inc....360 398-8641
777 Jorgensen Pl Bellingham (98226) ***(G-1386)***
J K Fabrication Inc....206 297-7400
3101 W Commodore Way Seattle (98199) ***(G-10270)***
J K Properties Inc....360 354-6719
1309 Woodfield Dr Lynden (98264) ***(G-6025)***
J King Formulas Inc....360 683-6908
686 N Sequim Ave Sequim (98382) ***(G-11642)***
J L & O Enterprises Inc....360 636-5427
2632 Mt Brynion Rd Kelso (98626) ***(G-4530)***
J L Brooks Welding Inc....360 403-9400
19320 63rd Ave Ne Arlington (98223) ***(G-259)***
J L Innovations Inc....425 823-8540
17511 68th Ave Ne Ste 2 Kenmore (98028) ***(G-4584)***
J L Powder Ctg....360 380-3898
6585 Vista Dr Ferndale (98248) ***(G-3863)***
J L R Design Group Inc....206 625-0070
557 Roy St Ste 175a Seattle (98109) ***(G-10271)***
J L Shrman Excvtg Rock Crshing....509 447-4214
1512 Ashenfelter Bay Rd Newport (99156) ***(G-7059)***
J Lanning Jewelers....360 693-9940
809 Main St Vancouver (98660) ***(G-14331)***
J M C Cabinets & Interiors....425 258-1204
3224 Mcdougall Ave Everett (98201) ***(G-3520)***
J M Cellars Company....425 485-6508
14404 137th Pl Ne Woodinville (98072) ***(G-15270)***
J M Cellars Company (PA)....206 321-0052
3329 W Laurelhurst Dr Ne Seattle (98105) ***(G-10272)***
J M Huber Corporation....206 762-4263
5427 Ohio Ave S Seattle (98134) ***(G-10273)***
J M Mrtnac Shipbuilding Corp....253 572-4005
2902 N 27th St Tacoma (98407) ***(G-13353)***
J M S, Spokane Valley *Also called Jim s Machining Service Inc* ***(G-12753)***
J M Smucker Company....509 882-1530
100 Forsell Rd Grandview (98930) ***(G-4248)***
J N W Inc....509 489-9191
6409 N Pittsburg St Spokane (99217) ***(G-12327)***
J Newell Corporation....360 435-8955
6922 204th St Ne Arlington (98223) ***(G-260)***
J P J 3 LLC....360 697-1084
1930 Nw Woodcrest Ct Silverdale (98383) ***(G-11840)***
J R Reding Company Inc....253 474-9938
3005 Chandler St Tacoma (98409) ***(G-13354)***
J R Setina Manufacturing Co....360 491-6197
2926 Yelm Hwy Se Olympia (98501) ***(G-7310)***
J R Stone Services....425 227-8513
12244 155th Ave Se Renton (98059) ***(G-8831)***
J S OWill Inc....360 226-3637
553 Roosevelt Ave Ste 203 Enumclaw (98022) ***(G-3296)***
J S Vail....509 886-8708
435 Rock Island Rd A East Wenatchee (98802) ***(G-3022)***
J Salgado LLC....425 367-3188
9701 35th Ave Ne Marysville (98270) ***(G-6346)***
J T, Vancouver *Also called Jt Marine Inc* ***(G-14343)***
J T Coatings Inc....509 944-1669
4510 Saint Paul Ct Pasco (99301) ***(G-7594)***
J TS Tractor Work....360 263-3016
35808 Ne 84th Ave La Center (98629) ***(G-5508)***
J Wanamaker Cabinetry & Wdwrk....206 762-3494
430 S 96th St Seattle (98108) ***(G-10274)***
J&Ds Down Home Entps Inc....206 388-3395
309 S Cloverdale St A13 Seattle (98108) ***(G-10275)***
J&K Enterprise....360 854-0020
11344 Foxfire Ln Sedro Woolley (98284) ***(G-11542)***
J&L Enterprises Inc....360 262-3735
635 Middle Fork Rd Onalaska (98570) ***(G-7449)***
J&M Heavy Cnstr & Log Co LLC....360 747-2735
14385 Wild Tree Ave Se Port Orchard (98367) ***(G-7818)***
J&M Rifle Works....360 985-0445
704 Burnt Ridge Rd Onalaska (98570) ***(G-7450)***
J&N Land Trucking....360 677-2274
63708 197th Pl Skykomish (98288) ***(G-11866)***
J&R Hennings Inc....509 659-0102
2715 E Rehn Rd Sprague (99032) ***(G-12948)***
J&R Mercantile, Kenmore *Also called J & R Mercantile* ***(G-4583)***
J&S Crushing....509 787-3537
22132 Road T 7 Sw 7 T Mattawa (99349) ***(G-6409)***
J&S Fabrication, Sequim *Also called Marketech International Inc* ***(G-11647)***
J-M Manufacturing Company Inc....509 837-7800
1820 S 1st St Sunnyside (98944) ***(G-13128)***
J-NH Wine Group LLC....425 481-5502
14710 Wdnvll Rdmond Rd Ne Woodinville (98072) ***(G-15271)***
Jaaco Corporation....425 952-4205
18080 Ne 68th St Ste C130 Redmond (98052) ***(G-8517)***
Jabez Marpac Construction Jv1....253 735-2000
13322 142nd Ave E Orting (98360) ***(G-7483)***
Jabil Def & Arospc Svcs LLC....206 257-0243
135 S Brandon St Seattle (98108) ***(G-10276)***
Jabil Inc....206 257-0243
135 S Brandon St Seattle (98108) ***(G-10277)***
Jack E Brossard....360 892-7538
16206 Ne 170th Ave Brush Prairie (98606) ***(G-2036)***
Jack H Hill....360 864-4939
240 Boone Rd Winlock (98596) ***(G-15152)***
Jack Just Enterprises LLC....425 836-7755
23515 Ne Novelt Redmond (98053) ***(G-8518)***
Jacknut Apparel....360 742-3523
2320 Mottman Rd Sw # 102 Tumwater (98512) ***(G-13876)***
Jacks Nasty Candy Company....425 418-5282
19221 63rd Ave Ne Ste 1 Arlington (98223) ***(G-261)***
Jackson Oil Anthony Schnell....253 847-2566
19914 90th Avenue Ct E Graham (98338) ***(G-4227)***
Jackson Signs & Graphics....360 457-3703
472 Mount Pleasant Rd Port Angeles (98362) ***(G-7716)***
Jackson Yukon....206 349-8566
3429 Airport Way S Seattle (98134) ***(G-10278)***
Jackson's Signs & Art Studio, Port Angeles *Also called Jackson Signs & Graphics* ***(G-7716)***
Jackyes Enterprises Inc....425 355-5997
2604 119th St Sw Everett (98204) ***(G-3521)***
Jacobs Ladder Painting Inc....425 754-3202
11304 Vernon Rd Lake Stevens (98258) ***(G-5651)***
Jacobson Logging, Longview *Also called Donald R Jacobson* ***(G-5907)***
Jadeflower Ceramics....253 720-6036
5025 22nd Ave Ne Seattle (98105) ***(G-10279)***
Jadron Tools....253 862-3908
8211 118th Street Ct Sw Lakewood (98498) ***(G-5729)***
Jag Enterprizes Inc....509 832-2836
154008 W Johnson Rd Prosser (99350) ***(G-8044)***
Jag Technologies....360 910-2933
2111 Ne 181st Ave Vancouver (98684) ***(G-14332)***
Jahrs European Sausage & Cstm....509 697-8904
160 Ranchette Ln Selah (98942) ***(G-11591)***
Jake Maberry Packing Inc....206 366-5411
8143 Sunrise Rd Custer (98240) ***(G-2855)***
Jakes Crawfish & Seafood, Woodland *Also called Pacific Sea Food Co Inc* ***(G-15456)***
Jakes Electrical Sign Service....509 901-1012
1060 N Wenas Rd Trlr 11 Selah (98942) ***(G-11592)***
Jakes Small Mch Fbrication Sp....509 286-3690
150 E Coplen St Latah (99018) ***(G-5792)***
Jaks Custom Woodwork....425 443-6210
17516 W Snoqualmie Riv Duvall (98019) ***(G-2992)***
Jalisco LLC....360 432-9397
128 E Railroad Ave Shelton (98584) ***(G-11704)***
Jalisco Tortilla Factory, Shelton *Also called Jalisco LLC* ***(G-11704)***
Jam Developers Inc....206 448-5225
2101 4th Ave Ste 1530 Seattle (98121) ***(G-10280)***
Jamar Industries LLC....206 725-3409
6014 21st Ave S Seattle (98108) ***(G-10281)***
Jamco America Inc (HQ)....425 347-4735
1018 80th St Sw Everett (98203) ***(G-3522)***
Jamco America Inc....425 347-4735
720 80th St Sw Bldg A Everett (98203) ***(G-3523)***
James & Eileen Kaski....360 687-4214
22011 Ne 212th Ave Battle Ground (98604) ***(G-711)***
James A Wright Cnstr LLC....509 996-3249
19108 Francis Ln Winthrop (98862) ***(G-15162)***

ALPHABETIC

(PA)=Parent Co (HQ)=Headquarters (DH)=Div Headquarters
2019 Washington
Manufacturers Register
753

James Bay Distillers Ltd 703 930-8453
10016 Edmonds Way C313 Edmonds (98020) ***(G-3121)***
James Clay 360 891-8147
9208 Ne 156th Ave Vancouver (98682) ***(G-14333)***
James Hardie Building Pdts Inc 253 847-8700
18200 50th Ave E Tacoma (98446) ***(G-13355)***
James Hardy Building Products, Tacoma *Also called James Hardie Building Pdts Inc* ***(G-13355)***
James Hellar Cabinetry 360 376-5727
564 Eastman Rd Eastsound (98245) ***(G-3037)***
James Homola 360 686-3549
36700 Ne Ridgeview Dr Yacolt (98675) ***(G-15483)***
James I Manning 425 774-4275
9003 220th St Sw Edmonds (98026) ***(G-3122)***
James Koehnline 206 783-6846
2405 Nw 67th St Unit 303 Seattle (98117) ***(G-10282)***
James Lund 425 742-9135
1804 142nd St Sw Lynnwood (98087) ***(G-6143)***
James Moore 206 799-0399
726 N 46th St Seattle (98103) ***(G-10283)***
James Richard Simpson 509 679-9720
17446 Crowder Rd Se Tenino (98589) ***(G-13619)***
James Smith Trucking 360 423-1027
1404 Rose Valley Rd Kelso (98626) ***(G-4531)***
James Wile 360 606-0706
28201 Se 7th St Camas (98607) ***(G-2259)***
Jameson Tree Experts, Yelm *Also called Mountain View Industries Inc* ***(G-15741)***
Jamie Kinney 206 953-9302
3620 Burke Ave N Apt 1 Seattle (98103) ***(G-10284)***
Jamison Signs Inc 509 226-2000
25211 E Trent Ave Newman Lake (99025) ***(G-7048)***
Jan A Thompson Lcpo 509 241-3820
502 E 5th Ave Spokane (99202) ***(G-12328)***
Jan Scientific Inc 206 632-1814
4726 11th Ave Ne Ste 101 Seattle (98105) ***(G-10285)***
Jan-R Corporation (PA) 360 856-0836
524 Rhodes Rd Sedro Woolley (98284) ***(G-11543)***
Jane Martin 206 842-4569
3636 Crystal Sprng Dr Ne Bainbridge Island (98110) ***(G-644)***
Janice Arnold 360 273-8548
20604 Grand Mound Way Sw Centralia (98531) ***(G-2410)***
Janicki Energy 360 856-2068
103 N Township St Sedro Woolley (98284) ***(G-11544)***
Janicki Industries Inc 360 856-5143
1476 Moore St Sedro Woolley (98284) ***(G-11545)***
Janicki Industries Inc 360 856-5143
34240 State Route 20 Hamilton (98255) ***(G-4313)***
Jans Ceramics 360 425-3540
1223 Commerce Ave Longview (98632) ***(G-5920)***
Jansi, Seattle *Also called Jan Scientific Inc* ***(G-10285)***
Jantz Engineering 360 598-2773
20555 Pugh Rd Ne Poulsbo (98370) ***(G-7968)***
January Company 253 872-9919
5851 S 194th St Kent (98032) ***(G-4964)***
Januik Winery 425 481-5502
14710 Woodinvile Rdmnd Ne Woodinville (98072) ***(G-15272)***
Jarvie Paint Division, Tukwila *Also called Farwest Paint Manufacturing Co* ***(G-13731)***
Jarvis Saw Mill LLC 360 733-7591
317 Chuckanut Point Rd Bellingham (98229) ***(G-1387)***
JAS Steel Fabricating (PA) 425 424-2107
19450 144th Ave Ne Ste D Woodinville (98072) ***(G-15273)***
Jasmine Bakery, Auburn *Also called Bread Garden Ltd* ***(G-396)***
Jason C Bailes Pllc 360 975-4687
2805 E 26th St Vancouver (98661) ***(G-14334)***
Jason Dunton 360 293-7256
13784 Redtail Ridge Ln Anacortes (98221) ***(G-137)***
Jason K Miller 360 853-8213
7674 Cedar Park Concrete (98237) ***(G-2787)***
Jason Thompson 757 867-6494
817 E Longfellow Ave Spokane (99207) ***(G-12329)***
Jasper Enterprises Inc 509 549-3664
10015 N Div St Ste 201 Spokane (99218) ***(G-12330)***
Jasper Know Print 425 486-7147
830 216th St Sw Bothell (98021) ***(G-1869)***
Jasper Publishing LLC 360 875-8383
168 Stauffer Rd Raymond (98577) ***(G-8355)***
Jasper Trucking, Spokane *Also called Jasper Enterprises Inc* ***(G-12330)***
Jaspreet Singh 253 239-3250
11827 Se 266th Pl Kent (98030) ***(G-4965)***
Jatal Inc (PA) 253 854-0034
4146 B Pl Nw Auburn (98001) ***(G-478)***
Jauch Quartz America Inc 360 633-7200
14601 Nw Arabian Way Seabeck (98380) ***(G-9265)***
Java Java Coffee Company Inc (PA) 425 432-5261
23130 224th Pl Se Ste 101 Maple Valley (98038) ***(G-6278)***
Java Trading Co LLC 425 917-2920
801 Houser Way N Renton (98057) ***(G-8832)***
Jaxjox Inc 425 324-3017
10400 Ne 4th St Ste 500 Vancouver (98660) ***(G-14335)***
Jay Lauris & Company Inc 206 243-9890
920 Sw 152nd St Ste 102 Burien (98166) ***(G-2114)***
Jay Lauris Jewelry, Burien *Also called Jay Lauris & Company Inc* ***(G-2114)***
Jay One Ball 360 275-2834
23632 Ne State Route 3 Belfair (98528) ***(G-764)***
Jay Pathy 425 890-9526
2455 80th Ave Ne Medina (98039) ***(G-6449)***
Jayam Software 425 208-6467
21324 Se 3rd St Sammamish (98074) ***(G-9222)***
Jays Custom Woodworks 360 807-0976
2614 Eureka Ave Centralia (98531) ***(G-2411)***
Jaytees Management Group LLC 360 352-0038
915 Trosper Rd Sw Ste 101 Tumwater (98512) ***(G-13877)***
Jaywick Woodworks LLC 206 793-7208
5551 16th Ave S Seattle (98108) ***(G-10286)***
Jazzie Software 206 905-7411
4815 Calif Ave Sw Apt 210 Seattle (98116) ***(G-10287)***
JB George LLC 509 522-0200
2901 Old Milton Hwy Walla Walla (99362) ***(G-14827)***
JB Neufeld LLC 509 945-1887
204 Arthur Blvd Yakima (98902) ***(G-15596)***
JB Neufeld LLC 509 895-9979
2620 Draper Rd Yakima (98903) ***(G-15597)***
JB Timberline Logging 360 871-0956
11501 Se Black Rd Olalla (98359) ***(G-7207)***
JB Woodworking 509 949-3683
2000 Mapleway Rd Yakima (98908) ***(G-15598)***
Jbm Press, Ferndale *Also called C S Adventurecorp LLC* ***(G-3821)***
Jbs Millwork Inc 509 248-3412
401 W Washington Ave Yakima (98903) ***(G-15599)***
JC Fabworks LLC 253 389-5842
23214 145th Avenue Ct E Graham (98338) ***(G-4228)***
JC Global Supply LLC 253 275-6093
25223 132nd Pl Se Kent (98042) ***(G-4966)***
JC Manufacturing 206 870-3827
23454 30th Ave S Kent (98032) ***(G-4967)***
Jci Jones Chemicals Inc 253 274-0104
1919 Marine View Dr Tacoma (98422) ***(G-13356)***
JD Bargen Industries LLC 360 354-5676
2077 Main St Lynden (98264) ***(G-6026)***
JD Fabrication 360 691-4550
11307 Mountain Loop Hwy Granite Falls (98252) ***(G-4278)***
Jdkk Investment Group Inc 253 565-4713
2331 Ross Way Tacoma (98421) ***(G-13357)***
Jdsu, Bothell *Also called Viavi Solutions Inc* ***(G-1914)***
Jeanne Jolivette 360 750-4447
12004 Ne 4th Plain Blvd Vancouver (98682) ***(G-14336)***
Jeeva Wireless Inc 206 214-6177
4000 Mason Rd Ste 300 Seattle (98195) ***(G-10288)***
Jeff Hauenstein Logging 360 826-3490
38423 State Route 20 Concrete (98237) ***(G-2788)***
Jeff Potter 206 819-4224
6207 Linden Ave N Apt 1 Seattle (98103) ***(G-10289)***
Jeffrey A Johnson 509 525-8322
919 W Main St Walla Walla (99362) ***(G-14828)***
Jeffrey Gould 360 274-7914
450 Toutle River Rd Castle Rock (98611) ***(G-2346)***
Jeffrey Hembury 360 535-3737
90 E Goldfinch Ln Belfair (98528) ***(G-765)***
Jeffrey James Botanical, Seattle *Also called Jeffrey James LLC* ***(G-10290)***
Jeffrey James LLC 562 541-6976
201 Mcgraw St Seattle (98109) ***(G-10290)***
Jeffrey Lee Redington, Ferndale *Also called True Machine* ***(G-3919)***
Jeffrey Mark Bashe 509 684-6925
156 N Main St Colville (99114) ***(G-2758)***
Jeld-Wen Inc 206 574-0986
1061 Industry Dr Tukwila (98188) ***(G-13755)***
Jeld-Wen Holding Inc 509 535-1026
3420 E Ferry Ave Spokane (99202) ***(G-12331)***
Jellyfish Brewing Company 206 517-4497
7566 Roosevelt Way Ne Seattle (98115) ***(G-10291)***
Jemco Cmpnents Fabrication Inc 425 827-7611
603 5th Pl S Kirkland (98033) ***(G-5372)***
Jen Gar Corp 253 862-6140
19017 68th St E Bonney Lake (98391) ***(G-1727)***
Jened Inc 509 926-6894
12622 E Sprague Ave Spokane Valley (99216) ***(G-12751)***
Jenneth Technologies Inc 509 547-8977
4408 W 7th Ave Kennewick (99336) ***(G-4680)***
Jenny Maes Gluten-Free Goodies 509 833-5096
730 N 16th Ave Ste 2 Yakima (98902) ***(G-15600)***
Jenny's Bar and Grill, Yelm *Also called Bosom Cattle Co* ***(G-15730)***
Jensen Barton W Inc 360 825-3750
548 Dickson Ave Enumclaw (98022) ***(G-3297)***
Jensen Lee, Seattle *Also called Misty Mountain Manufacturing* ***(G-10548)***
Jensen Race Cars 425 745-8000
15032 Highway 99 Lynnwood (98087) ***(G-6144)***
Jensen Sand & Gravel, Enumclaw *Also called Jensen Barton W Inc* ***(G-3297)***
Jensen Seed Farm Inc 509 896-2312
255 Ferguson Rd Bickleton (99322) ***(G-1632)***
Jerden Records, Lacey *Also called Soundworks U S A Inc* ***(G-5591)***
Jeremy Nichols 509 930-6352
1118 N 23rd Ave Yakima (98902) ***(G-15601)***
Jeremy Rieken 360 428-7736
2972 Cedar Ln Sedro Woolley (98284) ***(G-11546)***

Jeri -Ohs 206 722-5918
10420 65th Ave S Seattle (98178) *(G-10292)*
Jerry Brown 509 684-3736
181 E 1st Ave Colville (99114) *(G-2759)*
Jerry Carter 509 487-8294
3512 E Crown Ave Spokane (99217) *(G-12332)*
Jerry Debriae Logging Co Inc 360 795-3309
45 Elochoman Valley Rd Cathlamet (98612) *(G-2369)*
Jerry Fry 509 765-4367
830 E Broadway Ave Moses Lake (98837) *(G-6717)*
Jerry Gamin 253 884-3075
12303 Ne 56th St Vancouver (98682) *(G-14337)*
Jerry H Hyman 360 479-1724
3237 Birch Ave Bremerton (98310) *(G-1965)*
Jerry Hart & Son Logging 360 871-7037
4028 Stohlton Rd Se Port Orchard (98366) *(G-7819)*
Jerry Nybo Construction Inc (PA) 253 691-1797
7420 320th St E Eatonville (98328) *(G-3060)*
Jerry P Osborne 360 385-1200
918 Holcomb St Port Townsend (98368) *(G-7893)*
Jerrys Iron Works Inc (PA) 425 788-1467
16015 Main St Ne Duvall (98019) *(G-2993)*
Jesse Bay Cabinetry 360 417-8122
175 S Bayview Ave Unit 21 Port Angeles (98362) *(G-7717)*
Jesse Engineering Company (PA) 253 552-1500
1840 Marine View Dr Tacoma (98422) *(G-13358)*
Jesse W Palmer 509 634-1494
115 Frosty Meadows Rd Keller (99140) *(G-4513)*
Jessy Wilkinson LLC 509 578-1650
4956 Spirea Dr West Richland (99353) *(G-15097)*
Jester and Judge Cider Company 509 651-0381
30 Se Cascade Ave Stevenson (98648) *(G-13013)*
Jester Built, Monroe *Also called Winter Mattias* *(G-6638)*
Jester Cellars 425 785-9217
7581 Old Redmond Rd Apt 1 Redmond (98052) *(G-8519)*
Jesternick Systems LLC 509 338-4837
1520 Sw Casey Ct Pullman (99163) *(G-8095)*
Jesus Romero 509 545-9551
202 W Lewis St Pasco (99301) *(G-7595)*
Jet City Electronics Inc 206 529-0351
17709 Beach Dr Ne Lake Forest Park (98155) *(G-5616)*
Jet City Imaging LLC 206 447-0600
6501 E Marginal Way S B Seattle (98108) *(G-10293)*
Jet City Partners LLC (PA) 206 999-0047
22 42nd St Nw Ste B Auburn (98001) *(G-479)*
Jet City Printing Inc 425 485-8611
6134 Ne Bothell Way Kenmore (98028) *(G-4585)*
Jet City Vtg Tees 310 500-0577
5122 S Dawson St Seattle (98118) *(G-10294)*
Jet Door LLC 253 531-2261
1832 112th St E Tacoma (98445) *(G-13359)*
Jet Farms Inc 509 346-2588
5314 Road 13.9 Sw Royal City (99357) *(G-9170)*
Jet Parts Engineering LLC 206 281-0963
4772 Ohio Ave S Seattle (98134) *(G-10295)*
Jet Set Northwest Inc 206 762-0434
9026 E Marginal Way S Tukwila (98108) *(G-13756)*
Jetco Mch & Fabrication LLC 509 243-8910
3610 Riverside Dr Clarkston (99403) *(G-2636)*
Jetoptera Inc 516 456-7609
144 Railroad Ave Ste 100 Edmonds (98020) *(G-3123)*
Jetpoint Technologies Inc 360 854-0518
500 Metcalf St Ste R2 Sedro Woolley (98284) *(G-11547)*
Jetprop LLC (PA) 509 535-4401
6427 E Rutter Ave Spokane (99212) *(G-12333)*
Jetseal Inc 509 467-9133
10310 E Buckeye Ln Ste 1 Spokane Valley (99206) *(G-12752)*
Jett Industries Inc 360 649-3840
4635 Marine Drive Pl Bremerton (98312) *(G-1966)*
Jetwest 801 223-9149
335 Riverview Dr Sequim (98382) *(G-11643)*
Jevco International Inc 253 858-2605
1320 26th St Nw Ste 13 Auburn (98001) *(G-480)*
Jewelry Boutique LLC (PA) 360 866-2278
6753 Bellevista Pl Nw Olympia (98502) *(G-7311)*
Jewelry Design Center Inc 509 487-5905
821 N Division St Ste C Spokane (99202) *(G-12334)*
Jfc Holding Corporation 206 762-1100
8531 E Marginal Way S Tukwila (98108) *(G-13757)*
Jgc Food Co LLC (HQ) 206 622-0420
1425 4th Ave Ste 420 Seattle (98101) *(G-10296)*
Jh Marine LLC 425 241-6801
109 2nd St S Apt 435 Kirkland (98033) *(G-5373)*
Jharc Industries LLC 571 205-5422
1652 S 57th St Tacoma (98408) *(G-13360)*
Ji Woodwork 360 790-4083
3227 76th Ave Nw Gig Harbor (98335) *(G-4123)*
Jian Wu 425 706-9852
23121 Ne 19th Dr Sammamish (98074) *(G-9223)*
Jig & Lure 360 457-2745
826 Marine Dr Port Angeles (98363) *(G-7718)*
Jikopower Inc 253 678-0074
3205 C St Ne At Las Auburn (98002) *(G-481)*
Jim Davis 360 374-5659
370 Evergreen Loop Forks (98331) *(G-4010)*
Jim Hamilton 360 875-6170
70 Giles Ln South Bend (98586) *(G-12041)*
Jim Johnson & Son Trucking LLC 360 770-5073
7755 Cully Ln Sedro Woolley (98284) *(G-11548)*
Jim Lemons Doors & Cabinets 360 871-4001
205 Bethel Ave Port Orchard (98366) *(G-7820)*
Jim Manning 425 774-1964
9003 220th St Sw Edmonds (98026) *(G-3124)*
Jim Manning & Associates, Edmonds *Also called Jim Manning* *(G-3124)*
Jim s Machining Service Inc 509 926-1868
9514 E Montgomery Ave # 26 Spokane Valley (99206) *(G-12753)*
Jim Suzuki 253 804-6070
1 30th St Nw Ste 4 Auburn (98001) *(G-482)*
Jima Software Incorporated 206 354-7309
4426 216th Pl Se Bothell (98021) *(G-1870)*
Jimboneys Malt Mills & More 541 571-1144
435 Nw Center St Chehalis (98532) *(G-2506)*
Jimini Construction LLC 360 426-9918
741 Se Cook Plant Farm Rd Shelton (98584) *(G-11705)*
Jit Manufacturing Inc 425 487-0672
19240 144th Ave Ne Woodinville (98072) *(G-15274)*
Jj 206 LLC (PA) 206 453-0186
2228 1st Ave Ste B Seattle (98121) *(G-10297)*
Jj Enterprises 253 862-8854
21320 Snag Island Dr E Lake Tapps (98391) *(G-5679)*
JJ&d Signs Inc 206 623-3100
727 S 96th St Seattle (98108) *(G-10298)*
Jj's Draperies, Tacoma *Also called Johnson Enterprises* *(G-13365)*
Jjp Electric 509 325-5266
6826 N Greenwood Blvd Spokane (99208) *(G-12335)*
Jjs Automotive & Auto Elc LLC 509 248-2622
2626 Rudkin Rd Union Gap (98903) *(G-13935)*
Jjs Productions LLC 360 630-5294
12729 Quantum Ln Ste 20 Anacortes (98221) *(G-138)*
Jkr Forklift LLC 360 275-4811
580 Ne Matthew Dr Belfair (98528) *(G-766)*
Jl Cabinet Refacing LLC 253 514-5975
3227 76th Ave Nw Gig Harbor (98335) *(G-4124)*
Jl Distribution Ltd (PA) 206 743-1148
17631 80th Dr Ne Arlington (98223) *(G-262)*
Jlc Winery 509 529-1398
16 N 2nd Ave Walla Walla (99362) *(G-14829)*
Jlt Partners Inc (PA) 800 325-7513
25811 74th Ave S Kent (98032) *(G-4968)*
JM Eagle, Sunnyside *Also called J-M Manufacturing Company Inc* *(G-13128)*
JM Software 206 453-3544
3413 Nw 57th St Seattle (98107) *(G-10299)*
JM Ventures Inc 206 718-3355
10328 Ne 201st Pl Bothell (98011) *(G-1771)*
Jma Printing 509 395-2145
4 Greenwood Ct Trout Lake (98650) *(G-13679)*
Jmd Property Preservation 267 713-2277
9710 Forest Ave Sw Lakewood (98498) *(G-5730)*
Jmh Enterprises 509 628-2191
127 Meadow Hills Dr Richland (99352) *(G-9015)*
Jmh Promotions, Richland *Also called Jmh Enterprises* *(G-9015)*
JMJ Custom Finishes 425 820-4376
8432 Ne 131st Pl Kirkland (98034) *(G-5374)*
Jmtek LLC 425 251-9400
25426 74th Ave S Kent (98032) *(G-4969)*
Jnb, Bellevue *Also called Ezion Global Inc* *(G-906)*
Jo Bee Company, Spokane *Also called Jo Bee Inc* *(G-12336)*
Jo Bee Inc 509 483-1118
816 W Francis Ave Ste 313 Spokane (99205) *(G-12336)*
Joan F Schleh 360 424-4112
17198 Dunbar Rd Mount Vernon (98273) *(G-6805)*
Jobfindersites, Seattle *Also called M&L Research Inc* *(G-10456)*
Jobsite Stud Welding Inc 425 656-9783
3302 Old Hartford Rd Lake Stevens (98258) *(G-5652)*
Jodal Manufacturing 206 763-8848
1410 Sw 102nd St Seattle (98146) *(G-10300)*
Jodee Maiorana 509 758-1035
704 24th Ave Clarkston (99403) *(G-2637)*
Joe Constance 425 347-8920
1410 80th St Sw Ste F Everett (98203) *(G-3524)*
Joe Froyo LLC (PA) 909 204-1301
914 A St Ste 200 Tacoma (98402) *(G-13361)*
Joe Gordon Logging Inc 360 470-1631
194 State Route 108 McCleary (98557) *(G-6417)*
Joe Nestor 509 264-0800
5427 Binder Rd Cashmere (98815) *(G-2323)*
Joe Thomas Supply, OMAK *Also called Backwoods* *(G-7434)*
Joe Zender & Sons Inc 360 599-2064
6272 Mt Baker Hwy Deming (98244) *(G-2920)*
Joels Machine Shop 509 488-3234
1980 S Broadway Ave Othello (99344) *(G-7497)*
Joes Garage LLC 206 466-5579
1025 Industry Dr Tukwila (98188) *(G-13758)*
Joescan Inc 360 993-0069
4510 Ne 68th Dr Unit 124 Vancouver (98661) *(G-14338)*

ALPHABETIC

Johanna Beverage Company LLC 509 455-8059
5625 W Thorpe Rd Spokane (99224) *(G-12337)*
John Dalrymple 509 837-2117
1536 S 16th St Sunnyside (98944) *(G-13129)*
John Deely 206 527-8218
7047 19th Ave Ne Seattle (98115) *(G-10301)*
John Deere, Yakima *Also called Washington Tractor Inc (G-15704)*
John Deere Authorized Dealer, Spokane *Also called Pape Machinery Inc (G-12429)*
John Deere Authorized Dealer, Sumner *Also called Washington Tractor Inc (G-13110)*
John Deere Authorized Dealer, Aberdeen *Also called Washington Tractor Inc (G-38)*
John Deere Authorized Dealer, Kelso *Also called Pape Machinery Inc (G-4541)*
John Deere Authorized Dealer, Port Townsend *Also called Haven Boatworks LLC (G-7890)*
John Duane King 360 736-6707
1127 N Tower Ave Centralia (98531) *(G-2412)*
John Gibb 360 366-3500
5214 Guide Meridian Bellingham (98226) *(G-1388)*
John Girt & Associates, Issaquah *Also called Girt John (G-4420)*
John H Wolf CPA PC 509 465-9165
6008 N Washington St Spokane (99205) *(G-12338)*
John Harkness Logging 360 595-2260
421 Valley Hwy Acme (98220) *(G-43)*
John Knutson Lapidary 509 653-2111
13731 Old Naches Hwy Naches (98937) *(G-6998)*
John M Smith 360 484-7738
17 Torppa Rd Naselle (98638) *(G-7013)*
John Marshall Metalsmith Inc 206 546-5643
23312 Robin Hood Dr Edmonds (98020) *(G-3125)*
John McLean Seed Co 509 632-8709
9516 State Route 17 N Coulee City (99115) *(G-2803)*
John Meadows Logging 509 427-4330
662 Kelly Henke Rd Stevenson (98648) *(G-13014)*
John Meek Logging 360 491-6976
3748 80th Ave Se Olympia (98501) *(G-7312)*
Johnnie Montice 360 452-6549
114 E Front St Port Angeles (98362) *(G-7719)*
Johnnys Chef Blnded Seasonings, Tacoma *Also called Johnnys Fine Foods Inc (G-13362)*
Johnnys Fine Foods Inc 253 383-4597
319 E 25th St Tacoma (98421) *(G-13362)*
Johnnystand 206 412-2982
26462 Ne 53rd St Redmond (98053) *(G-8520)*
Johns Manville Corporation 800 654-3103
21234 76th Ave S Kent (98032) *(G-4970)*
Johnson Cams, Onalaska *Also called J&M Rifle Works (G-7450)*
Johnson Candy Co Inc 253 272-8504
924 Martin Lthr Kng Jr Wa Tacoma (98405) *(G-13363)*
Johnson Concentrates Inc 509 837-4600
310 E Edison Ave Sunnyside (98944) *(G-13130)*
Johnson Contrls Authorized Dlr, Vancouver *Also called Refrigeration Supplies Distr (G-14540)*
Johnson Controls 206 291-1400
9520 10th Ave S Ste 100 Seattle (98108) *(G-10302)*
Johnson Controls 509 534-6055
10010 E Knox Ave Ste 100 Spokane Valley (99206) *(G-12754)*
Johnson Controls Inc 360 448-7771
14114 Se 35th St Vancouver (98683) *(G-14339)*
Johnson Controls Inc 509 747-8053
9718 W Flight Dr Spokane (99224) *(G-12339)*
Johnson Cox Co Inc 253 272-2238
726 Pacific Ave Tacoma (98402) *(G-13364)*
Johnson Enterprises 253 537-8056
4617 76th St E Tacoma (98443) *(G-13365)*
Johnson Fabrication 360 874-2679
3041 Anderson Hill Rd Sw Port Orchard (98367) *(G-7821)*
Johnson Foods Inc 509 837-4188
300 Warehouse Ave Sunnyside (98944) *(G-13131)*
Johnson Forestry Contracting 360 484-3311
1192 State Route 4 Naselle (98638) *(G-7014)*
Johnson Fruit Cannery, Sunnyside *Also called Johnson Foods Inc (G-13131)*
Johnson Marine 360 437-0467
291 Mats View Rd Port Ludlow (98365) *(G-7768)*
Johnson Signs of Federal Way 253 678-4304
1742 Pnte Woodworth Dr Ne Tacoma (98422) *(G-13366)*
Johnson Ward Winery 206 284-2635
1445 Elliott Ave W Seattle (98119) *(G-10303)*
Johnsons Machine and Prfmce Sp 360 352-4465
1510 93rd Ave Sw Olympia (98512) *(G-7313)*
Johnsons Millwork Inc 253 472-5900
2319 South Tacoma Way Tacoma (98409) *(G-13367)*
Johnsons Stump Grinding S 360 334-4832
5221 S Machias Rd Snohomish (98290) *(G-11928)*
Johnston Printing Inc 509 892-2055
159 S Mcclellan St Spokane (99201) *(G-12340)*
Joint Way International Inc 503 286-7781
2500 E 5th St Vancouver (98661) *(G-14340)*
Jointmetrix Medical LLC 425 246-7799
4111 E Madison St Ste 68 Seattle (98112) *(G-10304)*
Jolly Family Corp (PA) 425 438-9350
2802 Colby Ave Everett (98201) *(G-3525)*
Jolly Hatchet Games LLC 360 624-2758
6410 Ne 144th St Vancouver (98686) *(G-14341)*
Jolly Roger Seafoods, Ocean Park *Also called Wiegardt Bros Inc (G-7183)*
Jomar Holdings Inc 425 881-7125
16541 Redmond Way Redmond (98052) *(G-8521)*
Jon Lonning Drywall 253 851-4866
14620 94th Ave Nw Gig Harbor (98329) *(G-4125)*
Jonathan Quinn Barnett Ltd 206 322-2152
116 Vine St Seattle (98121) *(G-10305)*
Jonboy Caramels LLC 206 850-4225
4900 9th Ave Nw Ste 100 Seattle (98107) *(G-10306)*
Jones Arms LLC 360 681-0511
63 Hooker Rd Sequim (98382) *(G-11644)*
Jones Automotive Engine Inc (PA) 509 838-3625
817 N Lincoln St Spokane (99201) *(G-12341)*
Jones Automotive Warehouse, Spokane *Also called Jones Automotive Engine Inc (G-12341)*
Jones Company Inc 360 352-1022
2840 Black Lake Blvd Sw Tumwater (98512) *(G-13878)*
Jones Digital Printing Inc 509 452-8238
3407 Terrace Heights Dr Yakima (98901) *(G-15602)*
Jones Logging and Cnstr LLC 509 422-3147
17 Jones Rd Okanogan (98840) *(G-7198)*
Jones Logging LLC 509 732-4511
2117a Lotze Creek Rd Colville (99114) *(G-2760)*
Jones Produce Dehy, Quincy *Also called Dodson Rd Orchard LLC (G-8296)*
Jones Quarry Inc 360 352-1022
2840 Black Lake Blvd Sw C Tumwater (98512) *(G-13879)*
Jones Soda Co 206 624-3357
66 S Hanford St Ste 150 Seattle (98134) *(G-10307)*
Joom 3d 413 566-6330
7636 Rixie St Se Olympia (98501) *(G-7314)*
Joongang USA 206 365-4000
22727 Highway 99 Ste 204 Edmonds (98026) *(G-3126)*
Jorgensen Forge, Tukwila *Also called Star Forge LLC (G-13821)*
Jorgensen Forge Corporation 206 762-1100
8531 E Marginal Way S Tukwila (98108) *(G-13759)*
Jorgensen Forge Parent, Tukwila *Also called Jfc Holding Corporation (G-13757)*
Joseph Artese Design 206 365-4326
16003 34th Ave Ne Lake Forest Park (98155) *(G-5617)*
Joseph Gillum (PA) 800 624-4578
1010 W Reynolds Ave Centralia (98531) *(G-2413)*
Joseph S Heagney 360 631-2982
1213 278th St Ne Arlington (98223) *(G-263)*
Josephine Mining Corp 509 343-3193
601 W Main Ave Ste 600 Spokane (99201) *(G-12342)*
Joshua M Lennox MA 253 590-8952
10202 Pcf Ave S Ste 204 Tacoma (98444) *(G-13368)*
Jot Products Co 206 331-6677
130 Main Ave S Apt 404 Renton (98057) *(G-8833)*
Journal Fncl Qntitative Analis, Seattle *Also called University of Washington (G-11381)*
Journal of Business, Spokane *Also called Cowles Publishing Company (G-12204)*
Journal of Japanese Studies 206 543-9302
University Of Washington Seattle (98195) *(G-10308)*
JOURNAL OF THE ARTS & RELIGION, Seattle *Also called Center For Religious Humanism (G-9653)*
Journal of The San Juans, Friday Harbor *Also called Sound Publishing Inc (G-4059)*
Journal-News Publishing Co (PA) 509 754-4636
29 Alder St Sw Ephrata (98823) *(G-3339)*
Journal-News Publishing Co 509 725-0101
506 Morgan St Davenport (99122) *(G-2872)*
Journal-News Publishing Co 509 235-6184
1616 W 1st St Cheney (99004) *(G-2588)*
Journeyman Cabinets Inc 509 483-6864
2929 E Providence Ave Spokane (99207) *(G-12343)*
Jovipak Corporation 206 575-1656
19625 62nd Ave S Ste C101 Kent (98032) *(G-4971)*
Joy Glbal Lngview Oprtions LLC 253 588-1726
3107 106th St S Ste 105 Lakewood (98499) *(G-5731)*
Joy Specialty Metals LLC 206 542-5161
17768 13th Ave Nw Shoreline (98177) *(G-11778)*
Joyful Noise Publications 425 774-7078
22506 92nd Ave W Edmonds (98020) *(G-3127)*
Joylux Inc 206 219-6444
1430 34th Ave Seattle (98122) *(G-10309)*
Joyson Safety Systems 509 762-5549
9138 Randolph Rd Ne Moses Lake (98837) *(G-6718)*
JP Innovations LLC 360 805-3124
101 E Main St Ste 207 Monroe (98272) *(G-6582)*
JP Logging LLC 208 596-7069
215 S Conklin Rd Apt F34 Spokane Valley (99037) *(G-12755)*
JP Publications 425 835-0021
16212 Bothell Everett Hwy Mill Creek (98012) *(G-6514)*
JP Trodden Distilling LLC 206 399-6291
3122 218th St Se Bothell (98021) *(G-1871)*
JP Trodden Distilling LLC 425 286-2756
18646 142nd Ave Ne Woodinville (98072) *(G-15275)*
Jph Industries LLC 425 269-8966
14820 Redmond Way Redmond (98052) *(G-8522)*
Jphotonics Inc 206 397-3702
5041 W Mercer Way Mercer Island (98040) *(G-6469)*
Jpl Habitability Inc 360 377-7660
112 Shore Dr Bremerton (98310) *(G-1967)*
Jpmorgan Chase Bank Nat Assn 206 505-1501
20 Mercer St Seattle (98109) *(G-10310)*

ALPHABETIC SECTION — K2 Carbide

Jr Grennay Co 509 484-5056
12208 E Old Palouse Hwy Valleyford (99036) *(G-13997)*

Jr Moore 360 607-6128
14413 Ne 10th Ave Vancouver (98685) *(G-14342)*

JR Simplot Company 509 765-3443
14124 Wheeler Rd Ne Moses Lake (98837) *(G-6719)*

JR Simplot Company 509 248-5756
7528 Postma Rd Moxee (98936) *(G-6879)*

JR Simplot Company 509 488-2132
531 S Booker Rd Othello (99344) *(G-7498)*

JR Simplot Company 509 765-5663
1200 N Broadway Ave Othello (99344) *(G-7499)*

Jrj Inc 360 691-2528
9517 35th Ave Ne 1a Seattle (98115) *(G-10311)*

Jrotc Dog Tags Inc 509 292-0410
11906 E Dolly Ln Elk (99009) *(G-3170)*

Jrotc.com, Elk *Also called Jrotc Dog Tags Inc (G-3170)*

JS Uniform 509 467-8416
33 E Lincoln Rd Ste 203 Spokane (99208) *(G-12344)*

JSB Logging 360 301-9675
61 Elk Ct W Brinnon (98320) *(G-2024)*

Jsg Fine Cstm Cbntry Wdwrk LLC 253 906-9043
5904 N 45th St Tacoma (98407) *(G-13369)*

Jsmd Key Products LLC 360 805-4140
14517 Fryelands Blvd Se Monroe (98272) *(G-6583)*

Jt Marine Inc 360 750-1300
2501 Se Hdden Way Vncuver Vancouver (98661) *(G-14343)*

Jt Metal Fab, Vancouver *Also called Madlyn Metal Fab Llc (G-14392)*

Jtc Aerospace LLC 425 869-6812
10018 184th Ave Ne Redmond (98052) *(G-8523)*

Jts Kettlecorn 509 962-2524
520 Blazing Sky Ln Ellensburg (98926) *(G-3209)*

Jubilant Hollisterstier LLC (HQ) 509 482-4945
3525 N Regal St Spokane (99207) *(G-12345)*

Jubilant Hollisterstier LLC 509 482-3287
3808 N Sullivan Rd N15-101 Spokane Valley (99216) *(G-12756)*

Jubilee Woodworks LLC 206 734-0344
832 16th Ave Seattle (98122) *(G-10312)*

Jud Calvary Inc 708 323-8758
10309 155th Pl Ne Redmond (98052) *(G-8524)*

Judd & Black Electric Inc 425 258-4557
2808 Maple St Everett (98201) *(G-3526)*

Judd Black Applnce-Service Ctr, Everett *Also called Judd & Black Electric Inc (G-3526)*

Judd Timber Cutting LLC 360 928-9011
1283 Crescent Beach Rd Port Angeles (98363) *(G-7720)*

Judith Ames Furniture 206 324-8538
2118 E Olive St Seattle (98122) *(G-10313)*

Juice & Jam Inc 206 734-5136
520 Pike St Ste 1440 Seattle (98101) *(G-10314)*

Juice and Jam, Seattle *Also called Juice & Jam Inc (G-10314)*

Juice Operations, Prosser *Also called Tree Top Inc (G-8069)*

Juice Operations, Yakima *Also called Seneca Foods Corporation (G-15671)*

Juicy Gems 425 232-3567
1923 W Knox Ave Spokane (99205) *(G-12346)*

Juju Joints, Seattle *Also called Jj 206 LLC (G-10297)*

Julian RAD Software, Seattle *Also called Aircon Soft (G-9361)*

Julias Glows 206 722-0411
11602 59th Ave S Seattle (98178) *(G-10315)*

Julias Lumber 509 966-0925
12904 Wide Hollow Rd Yakima (98908) *(G-15603)*

Julie Cake Fisheries Inc 360 636-3621
124 Trapper Ln Kelso (98626) *(G-4532)*

Julies Designs 206 727-3341
30500 Se 79th St Issaquah (98027) *(G-4434)*

Jumbo Dti Corporation 253 272-9764
2909 Pcf Hwy E Ste 101 Fife (98424) *(G-3961)*

Jumbo Foods Inc 425 355-1103
11502 Cyrus Way Mukilteo (98275) *(G-6946)*

Junefalsetta 253 536-3576
12206 47th Ave E Tacoma (98446) *(G-13370)*

Junk Car Removal 1 .... 206 369-7832
5903 11th Ave Nw Seattle (98107) *(G-10316)*

Juno Therapeutics Inc (HQ) 206 582-1600
400 Dexter Ave N Ste 1200 Seattle (98109) *(G-10317)*

Juntlabs LLC 253 987-1750
416 Sw 353rd St Federal Way (98023) *(G-3747)*

Jury Verdicts Northwest 425 487-9848
13258 1st Ave S Ste B Burien (98168) *(G-2115)*

Just American Desserts (PA) 509 927-2253
213 S University Rd Ste 2 Spokane Valley (99206) *(G-12757)*

Just Biotherapeutics Inc 206 651-5094
401 Terry Ave N Seattle (98109) *(G-10318)*

Just Salsa 253 455-4618
6328 121st Street Ct E Puyallup (98373) *(G-8170)*

Just Think Toys Inc 310 308-5242
13507 Chatri Pl Ne Bainbridge Island (98110) *(G-645)*

Justice Systems Press 360 417-8845
32 Chessie Ln Port Angeles (98362) *(G-7721)*

Justin Maine Logging Inc 360 262-4105
498 Conrad Rd Winlock (98596) *(G-15153)*

Justin-Grace Inc 206 992-4292
7950 Seward Park Ave S Seattle (98118) *(G-10319)*

Justus Bag Company Inc 509 765-6981
1312 W Broadway Ave Moses Lake (98837) *(G-6720)*

JV Designs Inc 509 786-2588
1520 Meade Ave Prosser (99350) *(G-8045)*

Jvs Publications LLC 360 412-0516
5320 Marvin Rd Ne Lacey (98516) *(G-5561)*

JW Custom Construction 509 679-2959
200 Stehekin Valley Rd Stehekin (98852) *(G-13003)*

JW Woodworks 206 719-4229
32408 2nd Ave Sw Federal Way (98023) *(G-3748)*

JWB Manufacturing LLC 253 222-1671
125 Nw Washington St South Prairie (98385) *(G-12050)*

Jwoodworking 253 229-9581
2918 N 20th St Tacoma (98406) *(G-13371)*

JWP Construction, Keller *Also called Jesse W Palmer (G-4513)*

Jx Crystals Inc 425 392-5237
1105 12th Ave Nw Ste A2 Issaquah (98027) *(G-4435)*

K & D Machine LLC 509 882-2239
4651 N County Line Rd Grandview (98930) *(G-4249)*

K & D Services Inc (HQ) 425 252-0906
2702 Oakes Ave Everett (98201) *(G-3527)*

K & H Intgrted Print Solutions, Everett *Also called K & H Prntrs-Lithographers Inc (G-3528)*

K & H Prntrs-Lithographers Inc 425 446-3300
7720 Hardeson Rd Ste A Everett (98203) *(G-3528)*

K & L Logging 360 273-9916
12935 Taylor Rd Sw Rochester (98579) *(G-9134)*

K & L Unlimited 509 965-6451
14258 Rutherford Rd Yakima (98903) *(G-15604)*

K & M Steel Storage Buildings, Sumner *Also called K&M Storage (G-13076)*

K & M Unibody Works Inc 509 922-2083
2011 N Park Rd Spokane Valley (99212) *(G-12758)*

K & M Wdwrkers Port Angles Inc 360 457-9773
1619 S Butler St Port Angeles (98363) *(G-7722)*

K & M Woodworkers Port Angeles, Port Angeles *Also called K & M Wdwrkers Port Angles Inc (G-7722)*

K & N Electric Motors Inc (PA) 509 838-8000
415 N Fancher Rd Spokane Valley (99212) *(G-12759)*

K & S Garden 509 476-3287
2101 Highland Dr Oroville (98844) *(G-7468)*

K & S Oil Field Services Inc 509 998-5738
4504 E Elk To Highway Rd Elk (99009) *(G-3171)*

K & S Woodworks LLC 360 354-1043
9641 Benson Rd Lynden (98264) *(G-6027)*

K & T Machine Incorporated 425 347-2157
12315 Mukilteo Speedway H Lynnwood (98087) *(G-6145)*

K and D Asso, Pomeroy *Also called Dave Ledgerwood (G-7671)*

K and K Industries LLC 425 951-0502
172 Sunset Ave Edmonds (98020) *(G-3128)*

K and M Fuel LLC 509 675-3005
370 Knapp Rd Colville (99114) *(G-2761)*

K B Alloys 360 371-2312
8615 Semiahmoo Dr Blaine (98230) *(G-1677)*

K Diamond Construction, Walla Walla *Also called W-4 Construction Inc (G-14886)*

K H B Inc 425 771-0881
5010 194th St Sw Lynnwood (98036) *(G-6146)*

K J M Electric Co Inc 206 624-5294
521 S Monroe St Seattle (98108) *(G-10320)*

K L Cook Inc 360 423-0195
1317 15th Ave Longview (98632) *(G-5921)*

K Line Industries LLC 425 870-4228
298 Echo Ridge Way Camano Island (98282) *(G-2215)*

K O M W AM, OMAK *Also called North Cascades Broadcasting (G-7439)*

K Rounds LLC 206 452-0466
115 E Willis St Kent (98032) *(G-4972)*

K Smith Enterprises 425 455-0923
700 112th Ave Ne Ste 302 Bellevue (98004) *(G-965)*

K Sports Manufacturing Inc 206 251-5211
5501 Ne 1st Pl Renton (98059) *(G-8834)*

K Stauffer Manufacturing LLC 360 626-1462
18082 Miss Ellis Loop Ne Poulsbo (98370) *(G-7969)*

K Vintners LLC (PA) 509 526-5230
820 Mill Creek Rd Walla Walla (99362) *(G-14830)*

K&B Custom Rods & Tackle 360 354-1945
821 Garden Dr Lynden (98264) *(G-6028)*

K&G Scents 206 380-1831
11433 70th Pl S Seattle (98178) *(G-10321)*

K&J Mfg Inc 425 503-2174
1001 Riverside Dr Se North Bend (98045) *(G-7114)*

K&K Industries, Bellingham *Also called Naimor Inc (G-1457)*

K&M Business Systems Inc 425 557-7789
1603 248th Ave Se Sammamish (98075) *(G-9224)*

K&M Storage 253 862-3515
22919 State Route 410 E Sumner (98391) *(G-13076)*

K&W Enterprises Inc 425 255-4316
2433 Jones Ave Ne Renton (98056) *(G-8835)*

K-L Mfg Co Inc (PA) 509 232-8655
2438 N Ruby St Spokane (99207) *(G-12347)*

K-W Cellars 509 525-6222
1753 Old Milton Hwy Walla Walla (99362) *(G-14831)*

K2 Carbide 425 761-2335
1330 177th Ave Ne Bellevue (98008) *(G-966)*

K2 Sports LLC (PA) 206 805-4800
413 Pine St Ste 300 Seattle (98101) ***(G-10322)***

K2 Sports LLC 206 805-4800
4501 6th Ave S Seattle (98108) ***(G-10323)***

K2 Sports USA, Seattle *Also called K2 Sports LLC* ***(G-10322)***

Kaas Tailored, Mukilteo *Also called Kaasco Inc* ***(G-6947)***

Kaasco Inc 425 412-2460
13000 Beverly Park Rd A Mukilteo (98275) ***(G-6947)***

Kaci Woodworks LLC 206 601-0395
4225 Francis Ave N Apt B Seattle (98103) ***(G-10324)***

Kadco Tackle Manufacturing 253 857-5033
10634 Woodchuck Ln Se Port Orchard (98367) ***(G-7822)***

Kaddy 360 438-3636
9327 Classic Dr Ne Lacey (98516) ***(G-5562)***

Kadi Manufacturing 360 668-5633
6330 180th St Se Snohomish (98296) ***(G-11929)***

Kaenaa Corp 425 283-3072
2337 237th Pl Ne Sammamish (98074) ***(G-9225)***

Kaes Enterprises LLC 800 252-5237
16707 129th Avenue Ct E Puyallup (98374) ***(G-8171)***

Kaffeologie, Seattle *Also called Coffee Catcher LLC* ***(G-9711)***

KAGWERKS, Camas *Also called Skt2 LLC* ***(G-2283)***

Kai Scissors, Seattle *Also called Shear Precision Inc* ***(G-11097)***

Kaiser Aluminum Fab Pdts LLC 509 927-6508
15000 E Euclid Ave Spokane Valley (99216) ***(G-12760)***

Kaiser Aluminum Fab Pdts LLC 509 375-0900
2425 Stevens Dr Richland (99354) ***(G-9016)***

Kaiser Aluminum Fab Pdts LLC 509 375-0900
2425 Stevens Dr Richland (99354) ***(G-9017)***

Kaiser Aluminum Washington LLC 949 614-1740
15000 E Euclid Ave Spokane Valley (99216) ***(G-12761)***

Kaiser Alutek Inc 509 924-2689
3401 N Tschirley Rd Spokane Valley (99216) ***(G-12762)***

Kaisers Welding & Mfg 509 738-6855
410 Larch St Kettle Falls (99141) ***(G-5233)***

Kakadu Traders Australia Inc 360 836-5820
17217 Nw 61st Ave Ridgefield (98642) ***(G-9091)***

Kalama Precision Machine 360 673-1255
1629 S Cloverdale Rd Kalama (98625) ***(G-4502)***

Kalama River Road Quarry 360 673-0795
460 Kalama River Rd Kalama (98625) ***(G-4503)***

Kalastar Holdings Inc 509 534-0655
1611 E Sprague Ave Spokane (99202) ***(G-12348)***

Kalhovde Boat Works 360 398-1262
4855 N King Mountain Rd Bellingham (98226) ***(G-1389)***

Kalispel Tribe of Indians 509 242-7000
100 N Hayford Rd Airway Heights (99001) ***(G-54)***

Kam Manufacturing 360 625-8321
2551 Cole St Enumclaw (98022) ***(G-3298)***

Kaman Fluid Power LLC 253 922-5710
2909 Pcf Hwy E Ste 103 Tacoma (98424) ***(G-13372)***

Kaman Fluid Power LLC 360 738-1264
4125 Bakerview Spur Ste C Bellingham (98226) ***(G-1390)***

Kami Steel US Inc 206 283-9655
2001 W Grfeld St Ste C110 Seattle (98119) ***(G-10325)***

Kami Tech, Seattle *Also called Kami Steel US Inc* ***(G-10325)***

Kamiah Mills, Spokane *Also called Empire Lumber Co* ***(G-12246)***

Kamilche Company (PA) 206 224-5800
1301 5th Ave Ste 2700 Seattle (98101) ***(G-10326)***

Kamilche Trading Post, Shelton *Also called Island Enterprises* ***(G-11701)***

Kamilche Trading Post, Shelton *Also called Island Enterprises* ***(G-11703)***

Kamiya Biomedical Company LLC 206 575-8068
12779 Gateway Dr S Tukwila (98168) ***(G-13760)***

Kana Winery 509 453-6611
10 S 2nd St Yakima (98901) ***(G-15605)***

Kanaway Seafoods Inc (HQ) 425 485-7755
6425 Ne 175th St Kenmore (98028) ***(G-4586)***

Kaniksu Feeds Inc 509 406-1995
39124 N Sherman Rd Deer Park (99006) ***(G-2907)***

Kannberg Media Corp 509 468-4226
611 E Lakeview Ln Spokane (99208) ***(G-12349)***

Kanon Electric 253 447-7831
1018 122nd Ave E Edgewood (98372) ***(G-3083)***

Kaper II Inc 360 423-4404
2212 Parrott Way Kelso (98626) ***(G-4533)***

Kaplan Homes Unlimited LLC 360 855-1675
8635 Garden Of Eden Rd Sedro Woolley (98284) ***(G-11549)***

Kapowsin Meats Inc 253 847-1777
29401 118th Ave E Graham (98338) ***(G-4229)***

Kapstone, Longview *Also called Longview Fibre Ppr & Packg Inc* ***(G-5930)***

Kapstone Seattle 206 762-7170
5901 E Marginal Way S Seattle (98134) ***(G-10327)***

Karcher Design 253 220-8244
1042 Industry Dr Tukwila (98188) ***(G-13761)***

Karcher North America Inc 360 833-1600
4275 Nw Pacific Rim Blvd Camas (98607) ***(G-2260)***

Karcher North America Inc 360 833-1600
4275 Nw Pacific Rim Blvd Camas (98607) ***(G-2261)***

Kardiel Inc 916 999-1050
2021 S 208th St Seatac (98198) ***(G-9287)***

Karen Nichols 360 497-2778
995 Peters Rd Randle (98377) ***(G-8326)***

Kari Gran, Seattle *Also called Wheels Up LLC* ***(G-11467)***

Karl Entenmann Cpo, Federal Way *Also called Preferred Orthotic & Prosthetc* ***(G-3772)***

Karl Plato 360 875-8289
613 Montana St South Bend (98586) ***(G-12042)***

Karl Ronald Fredrickson, Seattle *Also called Fredricksons Furn & Cabinets* ***(G-10023)***

Karl-Sons LLC 509 627-0152
28409 Country Meadows Ln Kennewick (99338) ***(G-4681)***

Karlas Hand Bindery Inc 206 405-3350
4 S Idaho St Seattle (98134) ***(G-10328)***

Karlene, Lynden *Also called Tony Pecaric* ***(G-6056)***

Karma Kanyon LLC 509 669-5753
1681 S Lakeshore Rd Chelan (98816) ***(G-2556)***

Karma Vineyards, Chelan *Also called Karma Kanyon LLC* ***(G-2556)***

Karvonen Sand & Gravel Inc 360 687-2549
21310 Ne 87th Ave Battle Ground (98604) ***(G-712)***

Kasaganaan Enterprise 206 361-2645
239 Ne 178th St Shoreline (98155) ***(G-11779)***

Kashoo Cloud Accunting USA Inc 888 520-5274
1210 Lakeview St Bellingham (98229) ***(G-1391)***

Kasilof Fish Company 360 658-7552
1930 Merrill Creek Pkwy B Everett (98203) ***(G-3529)***

Kaski Constuction, Battle Ground *Also called James & Eileen Kaski* ***(G-711)***

Kaski Tom Logging & Cat Work 360 247-5707
38220 Ne Rotschy Rd Yacolt (98675) ***(G-15484)***

Kaso Plastics Inc 360 254-3980
5720 Ne 121st Ave C Vancouver (98682) ***(G-14344)***

Kason Pet Supply 360 886-2306
27203 216th Ave Se Ste 8 Maple Valley (98038) ***(G-6279)***

Kastoria Inc 206 633-4170
4420 Burke Ave N Seattle (98103) ***(G-10329)***

Katana Industries Inc 509 754-5600
1980 Fairchild Ave Ephrata (98823) ***(G-3340)***

Katana Industries Inc 360 293-0682
12441 Bartholomew Rd Anacortes (98221) ***(G-139)***

Katerra Inc 650 422-3572
901 5th Ave Ste 3210 Seattle (98164) ***(G-10330)***

Katharsis, Seatac *Also called Worldwide Botanicals Inc* ***(G-9311)***

Katherine Ottaway Dr 360 385-3826
2120 Lawrence St Port Townsend (98368) ***(G-7894)***

Kathleen M Sole 360 297-4650
12835 Ne Marine View Dr Kingston (98346) ***(G-5255)***

Katies Candies Inc (PA) 360 748-8967
26 Se Spring St Chehalis (98532) ***(G-2507)***

Katz Media Group Inc 206 777-1800
701 5th Ave Ste 4200 Seattle (98104) ***(G-10331)***

Katz Television Group, Seattle *Also called Katz Media Group Inc* ***(G-10331)***

Kauffmann Industries Inc 425 770-5781
17903 Bothell Everett Hwy Bothell (98012) ***(G-1872)***

Kavu Inc (PA) 206 456-9305
1515 Nw 51st St Seattle (98107) ***(G-10332)***

Kavu World, Seattle *Also called Kavu Inc* ***(G-10332)***

Kawneer Company Inc 253 236-2848
18235 Olympic Ave S Tukwila (98188) ***(G-13762)***

Kaye Mag LLC 360 668-8989
915 Harrison Ave Apt A Snohomish (98290) ***(G-11930)***

Kaye-Smith Enterprises Inc (PA) 425 455-0923
700 112th Ave Ne Ste 302 Bellevue (98004) ***(G-967)***

Kayser Farms 360 274-6277
615 Monahan Rd Castle Rock (98611) ***(G-2347)***

Kayser, Melvin L, Castle Rock *Also called Kayser Farms* ***(G-2347)***

KB Hanks Enterprises 425 221-1040
524 Olympia Ave Se Renton (98058) ***(G-8836)***

Kc Fine Cabinetry 425 359-8491
11718 Wagner Rd Monroe (98272) ***(G-6584)***

Kc McCoy Inc 360 376-5619
5290 Olga Rd Eastsound (98245) ***(G-3038)***

Kc Technology Inc 509 933-2312
3526 B St Nw Ste 101 Auburn (98001) ***(G-483)***

Kc Wheelwright 206 799-9822
2258 15th Ave W Seattle (98119) ***(G-10333)***

Kci, Seattle *Also called Kenco Construction Inc* ***(G-10336)***

Kci Commercial Inc 253 475-4363
2407 N 31st St Ste 201 Tacoma (98407) ***(G-13373)***

Kcpk Trucking Inc 360 592-2260
4076 Mt Baker Hwy Everson (98247) ***(G-3680)***

KDL Enterprises Inc 253 395-3113
7818 S 194th St Kent (98032) ***(G-4973)***

Kean Center 206 465-4879
811 1st Ave Ste 475 Seattle (98104) ***(G-10334)***

Keepeez, Vancouver *Also called Lectent LLC* ***(G-14369)***

Keepers Admrlty Head Lghthouse, Coupeville *Also called Lighthouse Envmtl Programs* ***(G-2814)***

Keith Austin Logging 509 684-8869
1622 Clugston Onion Crk Colville (99114) ***(G-2762)***

Keith Cooper Logging Inc 360 459-3553
3846 Mari Ln Se Olympia (98513) ***(G-7315)***

Kel-Tech Plastics Inc 253 472-9654
3510 S Pine St Tacoma (98409) ***(G-13374)***

Keller Supply Co 509 922-6388
16212 E Marietta Ave Spokane Valley (99216) ***(G-12763)***

Keller Supply Co ... 509 925-2400
2060 Vantage Hwy Ste 26 Ellensburg (98926) ***(G-3210)***
Keller Supply Co ... 253 863-9271
2601 142nd Ave E Sumner (98390) ***(G-13077)***
Kelley Blocks LLC ... 253 922-9848
17810 17th St E Lake Tapps (98391) ***(G-5680)***
Kellis Creations ... 206 371-7130
3404 132nd St Sw Lynnwood (98087) ***(G-6147)***
Kellogg Company ... 253 872-3826
21229 72nd Ave S Kent (98032) ***(G-4974)***
Kelly Industries LLC ... 206 676-2338
9909 200th Pl Se Snohomish (98296) ***(G-11931)***
Kelseys Collection Inc ... 206 355-4333
3010 Ne 193rd St Lake Forest Park (98155) ***(G-5618)***
Keltech, Tacoma *Also called Kel-Tech Plastics Inc* ***(G-13374)***
Kemason Inc ... 360 757-9947
808 N Hill Blvd Burlington (98233) ***(G-2166)***
Kemcor Inc ... 425 488-7400
15925 Woodinville Re Woodinville (98072) ***(G-15276)***
Kemeera Incorporated ... 206 582-1062
4302 Stone Way N Seattle (98103) ***(G-10335)***
Kemira Chemicals Inc ... 360 835-8725
1150 S 35th St Washougal (98671) ***(G-14962)***
Kemira Water Solutions Inc ... 509 922-2244
2315 N Sullivan Rd Spokane Valley (99216) ***(G-12764)***
Kemiron North America, Spokane Valley *Also called Kemira Water Solutions Inc* ***(G-12764)***
Kemp West Inc ... 425 334-5572
3800 Sinclair Ave Snohomish (98290) ***(G-11932)***
Kemps Machine Co ... 509 784-1326
1012 S 96th Ave Yakima (98908) ***(G-15606)***
Ken Boudreau Inc ... 425 402-8001
20485 144th Ave Ne Woodinville (98072) ***(G-15277)***
Ken Dressler ... 360 765-3131
1731 Linger Longer Rd Quilcene (98376) ***(G-8285)***
Ken Olson Cutting ... 360 374-5052
1441 Merchants Rd Forks (98331) ***(G-4011)***
Ken Robinson Publications Inc ... 360 794-7116
125 E Main St Ste 202 Monroe (98272) ***(G-6585)***
Kenco Cabinet and Fixture Mfg, Lynnwood *Also called Kenco Manufacturing Inc* ***(G-6148)***
Kenco Construction Inc (PA) ... 206 783-3300
101 Nickerson St Ste 330 Seattle (98109) ***(G-10336)***
Kenco Manufacturing Inc (PA) ... 425 743-1080
13614 Manor Way Lynnwood (98087) ***(G-6148)***
Kenmore Air Harbor Inc (PA) ... 425 486-3224
6321 Ne 175th St Kenmore (98028) ***(G-4587)***
Kenmore Air Seaplanes, Kenmore *Also called Kenmore Air Harbor Inc* ***(G-4587)***
Kenmore Pre-Mix, Seattle *Also called Glacier Northwest Inc* ***(G-10076)***
Kenmore Violins ... 425 481-5638
7330 Ne Bothell Way # 201 Kenmore (98028) ***(G-4588)***
Kennedy Creek Pottery ... 360 866-3937
12320 Summit Lake Rd Nw Olympia (98502) ***(G-7316)***
Kennedy Creek Quarry Inc ... 360 426-4743
250 W Hurley Waldrip Rd Shelton (98584) ***(G-11706)***
Kennedy Endeavors Incorporated (HQ) ... 253 833-0255
1150 Industry Dr N Ste C Algona (98001) ***(G-72)***
Kenneth A Edleman ... 206 524-2814
9422 Roosevelt Way Ne Seattle (98115) ***(G-10337)***
Kenneth Maupin Logging Cnstr ... 509 442-3484
Roy Maupin Rd 1 Ione (99139) ***(G-4375)***
Kenneth Walker ... 360 748-7519
249 Chilvers Rd Chehalis (98532) ***(G-2508)***
Kennewick Computer Company ... 509 371-0600
2290 Robertson Dr Richland (99354) ***(G-9018)***
Kennewick Press LLC ... 509 491-3801
7201 W Clearwater Ave Kennewick (99336) ***(G-4682)***
Kens Engraving Emporium Inc ... 360 578-0844
1165 Commerce Ave Longview (98632) ***(G-5922)***
Kens Powder Coating ... 253 539-5845
10739 A St S B Tacoma (98444) ***(G-13375)***
Kent Chamber of Commerce Inc ... 253 854-1770
524 W Meeker St Ste 1 Kent (98032) ***(G-4975)***
Kent D Bruce ... 360 886-9410
22543 Se 313th Pl Black Diamond (98010) ***(G-1649)***
Kent Enterprises ... 360 403-0242
222 N Gifford Ave Arlington (98223) ***(G-264)***
Kent Laboratories Inc ... 360 398-8641
777 Jorgensen Pl Bellingham (98226) ***(G-1392)***
Kent Reporter, Federal Way *Also called Sound Publishing Inc* ***(G-3788)***
Kentico Software LLC ... 206 674-4507
14900 Interurban Ave S Tukwila (98168) ***(G-13763)***
Kentucky Chrome Industries ... 816 522-1783
3245 31st Ave W Seattle (98199) ***(G-10338)***
Kenwood Manufacturing Inc ... 602 625-4012
1131 Andover Park W Tukwila (98188) ***(G-13764)***
Kenworthy Machine ... 425 788-2131
30330 Ne 172nd St Duvall (98019) ***(G-2994)***
Kepler Absorbents LLC (PA) ... 844 453-7537
6808 26th St E Fife (98424) ***(G-3962)***
Kermit Anderson ... 509 535-2362
6303 E Sprague Ave Spokane Valley (99212) ***(G-12765)***
Kermits Wood Products ... 425 316-6823
13724 51st Dr Se Everett (98208) ***(G-3530)***
Kern Construction Inc ... 360 805-5598
21616 230th St Se Monroe (98272) ***(G-6586)***
Kessler Wood Products ... 509 937-2500
3171 Bull Dog Creek Rd Valley (99181) ***(G-13992)***
Kestra Medical Tech Inc ... 425 279-8002
3933 Lake Washington Blvd Kirkland (98033) ***(G-5375)***
Kestrel Tool ... 360 468-2103
180 Snowberry Ln Lopez Island (98261) ***(G-5984)***
Kestrel Vintners (PA) ... 509 786-2675
2890 Lee Rd Prosser (99350) ***(G-8046)***
Kestrel Vintners ... 425 398-1199
19501 144th Ave Ne Woodinville (98072) ***(G-15278)***
Kestrel Vintners ... 509 548-7348
843 Front St Ste B1 Leavenworth (98826) ***(G-5808)***
Ketchum Metal Polishing ... 360 403-8726
216 E 2nd St Ste A Arlington (98223) ***(G-265)***
Kettle Corn Machine, Gig Harbor *Also called Cellular To Go Inc* ***(G-4085)***
Kettle River Boat Works LLC ... 509 738-2872
1190 W Old Kettle Rd Kettle Falls (99141) ***(G-5234)***
Kettle River Operations, Republic *Also called Kinross Gold Usa Inc* ***(G-8959)***
Keurig Green Mountain Inc ... 253 447-9100
3324 142nd Ave E Ste 200 Sumner (98390) ***(G-13078)***
Kevin Philbin Yacht Detail ... 206 949-0162
2842 Nw 67th St Seattle (98117) ***(G-10339)***
Kevin W Lantz ... 425 770-2599
3001 S Lake Stevens Rd Lake Stevens (98258) ***(G-5653)***
Kevin White Winery ... 206 992-5746
19501 144th Ave Ne F100 Woodinville (98072) ***(G-15279)***
Kewanna Screen Printing Inc ... 574 817-0682
130 S 46th St Bellingham (98229) ***(G-1393)***
Key Peninsula News ... 253 884-4699
17010 S Vaughn Rd Kp N Vaughn (98394) ***(G-14747)***
Key Publishing Group LLC ... 360 882-3488
12808 Ne 95th St Vancouver (98682) ***(G-14345)***
Key Technology ... 509 529-2161
150 Avery St Walla Walla (99362) ***(G-14832)***
Key Technology Inc (HQ) ... 509 529-2161
150 Avery St Walla Walla (99362) ***(G-14833)***
Key Technology Inc ... 509 529-2161
150 Avery St Walla Walla (99362) ***(G-14834)***
Key Tronic Corporation (PA) ... 509 928-8000
4424 N Sullivan Rd Spokane Valley (99216) ***(G-12766)***
Key Tronic Corporation ... 509 928-8000
3808 N Sullivan Rd Spokane Valley (99216) ***(G-12767)***
Key Tronic Corporation ... 509 927-5225
11506 E 47th Ave Spokane Valley (99206) ***(G-12768)***
Keychain Social LLC ... 425 876-3261
9422 Hancock Ave Se Snoqualmie (98065) ***(G-12014)***
Keyking Inc ... 360 977-7870
2005 Se 192nd Ave Camas (98607) ***(G-2262)***
Keypict ... 206 522-5201
6507 57th Ave Ne Seattle (98115) ***(G-10340)***
Keytronic Ems, Spokane Valley *Also called Key Tronic Corporation* ***(G-12768)***
KEYTRONICEMS, Spokane Valley *Also called Key Tronic Corporation* ***(G-12766)***
Kf Industries LLC ... 360 628-8473
1123 Sleater Kinney Rd Se Lacey (98503) ***(G-5563)***
Kfj Industries LLC ... 425 922-2889
9133 126th Ave Ne Kirkland (98033) ***(G-5376)***
Kgo Stone ... 360 573-0272
229 E Reserve St Vancouver (98661) ***(G-14346)***
Kgr Corporation ... 360 403-7330
19003 59th Dr Ne Arlington (98223) ***(G-266)***
Khan Machine Tool Company Ltd ... 206 784-9694
19510 21st Ave W Ste B Lynnwood (98036) ***(G-6149)***
Khancell Corporation ... 646 385-7243
1685 H St Blaine (98230) ***(G-1678)***
Khann Industries Corp ... 360 794-1033
1138 Village Way Monroe (98272) ***(G-6587)***
Khans Oil LLC ... 360 668-6415
12113 Ne 4th Plain Blvd Vancouver (98682) ***(G-14347)***
Kheper Games Inc ... 206 782-2201
440 S Holgate St Seattle (98134) ***(G-10341)***
Kiadis Pharma US Corporation ... 585 397-1074
1812 10th Ave E Seattle (98102) ***(G-10342)***
Kibbey Battery Service Inc ... 253 845-9155
2906 E Main Puyallup (98372) ***(G-8172)***
Kic LLC ... 360 823-4440
3800 Fruit Valley Rd Vancouver (98660) ***(G-14348)***
Kic-N Corp ... 360 696-9595
1308 Nw 41st St Vancouver (98660) ***(G-14349)***
Kichi Systems LLC ... 509 924-7672
10304 E Upriver Dr Spokane (99206) ***(G-12350)***
Kick Ass Puzzles ... 425 275-2381
3807 Serene Way Lynnwood (98087) ***(G-6150)***
Kidd Defense ... 509 290-6171
901 N Adams St Spokane (99201) ***(G-12351)***
Kieu Danh ... 360 548-9649
3707 124th St Ne Ste 6 Marysville (98271) ***(G-6347)***
Kile Machine & Manufacturing ... 509 569-3814
401 Squires Rd Rosalia (99170) ***(G-9155)***
Kilian & Kilian Artists ... 360 654-1799
16604 Marine Dr Stanwood (98292) ***(G-12977)***
Killer Paint, Snohomish *Also called Mike Lavalle Inc* ***(G-11947)***

ALPHABETIC

Killian Korn Inc 800 528-7861
1615 E Catalpa St Othello (99344) ***(G-7500)***
Kiln Cart Construction 360 319-0414
5590 Knight Rd Bellingham (98226) ***(G-1394)***
Kiln Core Holdings LLC 206 859-1114
601 Union St Ste 4950 Seattle (98101) ***(G-10343)***
Kiln Kart Fabrication, Bellingham *Also called Kiln Cart Construction* ***(G-1394)***
Kilomters To Miles Speedo Exch 253 872-3839
21218 76th Ave S Kent (98032) ***(G-4976)***
Kilponen Bros Logging Inc 360 484-7758
9 Cougar Park Ln Naselle (98638) ***(G-7015)***
Kimberly-Clark Corporation 425 373-5900
15500 Se 30th Pl Ste 202 Bellevue (98007) ***(G-968)***
Kims Horse Blankets 360 623-9567
2978 Us Highway 12 Silver Creek (98585) ***(G-11824)***
Kincaid Woodworking 518 810-1374
3740 Antsen St Sw Tumwater (98512) ***(G-13880)***
Kindex Pharmaceuticals Inc 206 922-2912
800 5th Ave Ste 4100 Seattle (98104) ***(G-10344)***
Kindle Eithan 509 558-7023
920 S Thor St Spokane (99202) ***(G-12352)***
Kinematics Marine Eqp Inc 360 659-5415
5625 48th Dr Ne Ste B Marysville (98270) ***(G-6348)***
Kinetic Solutions Intl 503 490-8642
7509 S 5th St Ste 110 Ridgefield (98642) ***(G-9092)***
King & Prince Seafood Corp 360 733-9090
710 Squalicum Way Bellingham (98225) ***(G-1395)***
King Aerospace Inc 360 257-6610
3690 N Ranger St Oak Harbor (98278) ***(G-7155)***
King Brothers Woodworking Inc (PA) 509 453-4683
602 W Valley Mall Blvd Union Gap (98903) ***(G-13936)***
King County Wastewater Trtmnt 206 463-0102
9615 Sw 171st St Vashon (98070) ***(G-14727)***
King Electrical Mfg Co 206 762-0400
9131 10th Ave S Seattle (98108) ***(G-10345)***
King Enterprises 360 568-1644
1030 Avenue D Ste 3 Snohomish (98290) ***(G-11933)***
King Graphics 360 423-9781
1906 Westside Hwy Kelso (98626) ***(G-4534)***
King Machine LLC 425 743-5464
11710 Cyrus Way Mukilteo (98275) ***(G-6948)***
King Mountain Tobacco Co Inc 509 874-9935
2000 4th Fort Simcoe Rd White Swan (98952) ***(G-15138)***
King Northern Inc 520 604-6379
32115 105th Pl Se A104 Auburn (98092) ***(G-484)***
King Northern Publishing, Auburn *Also called King Northern Inc* ***(G-484)***
King Sales & Manufacturing Co 509 453-1744
609 N 20th Ave Yakima (98902) ***(G-15607)***
King's Oriental Foods, Seattle *Also called Kof Enterprises LLC* ***(G-10351)***
Kingdom Life Publishing 509 465-0672
21816 Buckeye Lake Ln Colbert (99005) ***(G-2710)***
Kings Command Foods LLC (HQ) 425 251-6788
7622 S 188th St Kent (98032) ***(G-4977)***
Kings Kitchen LLC 253 212-3623
11105 Steele St S # 114 Tacoma (98444) ***(G-13376)***
Kings of Coatings Inc 360 721-0636
11116 Nw 3rd Ave Vancouver (98685) ***(G-14350)***
Kings Quality Cabinets, Centralia *Also called John Duane King* ***(G-2412)***
Kings Wok 360 337-2512
9960 Silverdale Way Nw # 4 Silverdale (98383) ***(G-11841)***
Kingsford Smith Charles 360 738-6959
4312 Cordero Dr Bellingham (98229) ***(G-1396)***
Kingston Community News 360 779-4464
19351 8th Ave Ne Ste 205 Poulsbo (98370) ***(G-7970)***
Kingston Mail & Print, Kingston *Also called Kingston Mail Center Inc* ***(G-5256)***
Kingston Mail and Print, Kingston *Also called Kitsap Business Services Inc* ***(G-5257)***
Kingston Mail Center Inc 360 297-2173
8202 Ne Stat Hwy 104 10 Kingston (98346) ***(G-5256)***
Kingtime LLC 206 375-7422
4112 Ne 24th St Renton (98059) ***(G-8837)***
Kinross Gold Usa Inc 509 775-3157
363 Fish Hatchery Rd Republic (99166) ***(G-8959)***
Kiona Creek Timber Inc 360 983-3786
105 Caytee Cv Mossyrock (98564) ***(G-6762)***
Kiona Vineyards LLC 509 588-6716
44612 N Sunset Rd Benton City (99320) ***(G-1618)***
Kiowna Publishing Inc 509 947-0675
390 Dream St Se Moses Lake (98837) ***(G-6721)***
Kira Aviation Services LLC 425 361-1060
4208 198th St Sw Ste 104c Lynnwood (98036) ***(G-6151)***
Kira Operations Support, Lynnwood *Also called Kira Aviation Services LLC* ***(G-6151)***
Kirk Dial of Seattle 253 852-5125
112 Central Ave N Kent (98032) ***(G-4978)***
Kirsten Gallery Inc 206 522-2011
6921 120th St Nw Gig Harbor (98332) ***(G-4126)***
Kiska Sea Northern LLC 206 784-5000
2157 N Northlake Way # 210 Seattle (98103) ***(G-10346)***
Kisslers Machine & Fabrication 509 877-1177
3690 Lateral B Rd Wapato (98951) ***(G-14917)***
Kit A Jeweler Designed For You 253 851-5546
3104 Harborview Dr Gig Harbor (98335) ***(G-4127)***
Kit Planes Northwest 360 403-0679
2359 E Mores Trail Dr Arlington (98223) ***(G-267)***
Kitc Radio Inc 360 876-1400
1700 Se Mile Hill Dr # 243 Port Orchard (98366) ***(G-7823)***
Kitchen Cabinet and Granite 509 783-9500
7903 W Grandridge Blvd Kennewick (99336) ***(G-4683)***
Kitchens Etc 360 430-4272
904 12th Ave Longview (98632) ***(G-5923)***
Kith D Lazelles Nture Phtgrphy 360 765-3697
1634 Toandos Rd Quilcene (98376) ***(G-8286)***
Kitsap Business Services Inc 360 297-2173
8202 Ne State Hwy Kingston (98346) ***(G-5257)***
Kitsap Coatings 360 550-3777
2501 N Wycoff Ave Bremerton (98312) ***(G-1968)***
Kitsap Custom Coatings LLC 360 471-3095
2251 Nw Bucklin Hill Rd Silverdale (98383) ***(G-11842)***
Kitsap Custom Coatings LLC 360 471-3095
6801 Holland Rd Nw Bremerton (98311) ***(G-1969)***
Kitsap Powder Coating LLC 360 297-0015
5734 Ne Minder Rd Bldg B Poulsbo (98370) ***(G-7971)***
Kitsap Reclamation & Materials, Bremerton *Also called J A Jack & Sons Inc* ***(G-1964)***
Kitsap Screen Printing LLC 360 876-5101
3995 Bethel Rd Se Ste 4 Port Orchard (98366) ***(G-7824)***
Kitsap Screen Prtg Embroderry, Port Orchard *Also called Kitsap Screen Printing LLC* ***(G-7824)***
Kitsap Sun 360 792-3350
545 5th St Bremerton (98337) ***(G-1970)***
Kitsap Vinyl Deck & Rail LLC 360 830-5959
15712 Nw Hite Center Rd Seabeck (98380) ***(G-9266)***
Kittitas Public Works, Cle Elum *Also called County Public Works* ***(G-2664)***
Kitty Cribs LLC 360 312-8102
1245 W Axton Rd Ferndale (98248) ***(G-3864)***
Kjar Industrial 206 992-7151
6320 208th St Sw Lynnwood (98036) ***(G-6152)***
Kjj Enterprises Inc 253 474-6607
2528 S 38th St Tacoma (98409) ***(G-13377)***
Kjs Handcrafted Jewelry 425 582-8488
22148 34th Ave W Brier (98036) ***(G-2020)***
KLA Fuels Reductions 509 680-0110
206 W Franklin Ave Chewelah (99109) ***(G-2603)***
Klar Scientific LLC 509 330-2103
790 Se Sherwood Ct Pullman (99163) ***(G-8096)***
Klas Technologies LLC 360 678-8705
959 Vashon St Greenbank (98253) ***(G-4308)***
Klc Holdings Ltd (PA) 509 248-4770
2712 S 16th Ave Yakima (98903) ***(G-15608)***
Klein Joanne Klein Kevin 360 435-8615
2121 236th St Ne Arlington (98223) ***(G-268)***
Klickitat Canyon Winery 509 365-2900
6 Lyle Snowden Rd Lyle (98635) ***(G-5996)***
Klicktrack Inc 206 557-3223
9727 Coppertop Loop Ne # 202 Bainbridge Island (98110) ***(G-646)***
Klm Custom Sash LLC 360 403-7400
19011 62nd Ave Ne Unit 1 Arlington (98223) ***(G-269)***
Kluh Jewelers, Lacey *Also called G L Kluh & Sons Jewelers Inc* ***(G-5552)***
Klune Aerospace, Algona *Also called Gcm North American Arospc LLC* ***(G-69)***
Klune Industries Inc 253 872-7488
21719 84th Ave S Kent (98032) ***(G-4979)***
Klw Manufacturing & Design Inc 360 435-6288
17739 59th Ave Ne Arlington (98223) ***(G-270)***
Klw Nameplate, Arlington *Also called Klw Manufacturing & Design Inc* ***(G-270)***
KMD Invested LLC 425 741-9600
13200 Highway 99 Everett (98204) ***(G-3531)***
Kmt US Holding Company Inc (HQ) 620 856-2151
23500 64th Ave S Kent (98032) ***(G-4980)***
Knife Gate Valves, Woodland *Also called B2r Partners Inc* ***(G-15419)***
Knights Edge Software 425 488-3552
15356 Juanita Dr Ne Kenmore (98028) ***(G-4589)***
Knights Welding 509 412-1103
1718 W A St Pasco (99301) ***(G-7596)***
Knipprath Cellars Inc 208 699-3393
5634 E Commerce Ave Spokane (99212) ***(G-12353)***
Knit Alteration & Design 360 426-5078
230 Se State Route 3 Shelton (98584) ***(G-11707)***
Knitwear Network Inc 206 353-1337
1507 30th Ave S Lowr Seattle (98144) ***(G-10347)***
Knoll Inc 206 624-0174
1200 5th Ave Ste 2000 Seattle (98101) ***(G-10348)***
Knoll Tree Care & Logging 253 630-1520
27029 167th Pl Se Kent (98042) ***(G-4981)***
Knot Hole Inc 541 806-0950
1440 Nw Richards Ln White Salmon (98672) ***(G-15120)***
Knot Your Every Day Crochet 360 791-9154
7511a Trails End Dr Se Tumwater (98501) ***(G-13881)***
Know Labs Inc (PA) 206 903-1351
500 Union St Ste 810 Seattle (98101) ***(G-10349)***
Knox Cellars 425 392-7536
4601 244th Pl Se Sammamish (98029) ***(G-9226)***
Knox Cellars Mason Bees 360 286-2025
7075 Corfu Blvd Ne Bremerton (98311) ***(G-1971)***
Knox Cellars Nativ Pollinators, Sammamish *Also called Knox Cellars* ***(G-9226)***
Kns Information Services, Gig Harbor *Also called Krantz News Service Inc* ***(G-4128)***

ALPHABETIC SECTION
Kurt A Flechel

Knutson Crane.....509 925-5438
6402 Manastash Rd Ellensburg (98926) *(G-3211)*
Knutz Logging & Farming.....509 779-4713
1940 N Saint Peters Crk Malo (99150) *(G-6234)*
Kobelt Manufacturing.....360 676-2774
700 Coho Way Bellingham (98225) *(G-1397)*
Koch Industries Inc.....509 487-4560
4327 N Thor St Spokane (99217) *(G-12354)*
Koch Machine Inc.....206 241-7178
10623 16th Ave Sw Seattle (98146) *(G-10350)*
Kockums Cancar Chip-N-Saw, Woodland *Also called Usnr LLC (G-15470)*
Kodiak Seafood, Lynnwood *Also called Interntional Seafoods Alsk Inc (G-6141)*
Koehler Enterprise Inc.....360 261-0390
160 Whitewater Rd Longview (98632) *(G-5924)*
Koehler Industries Inc.....360 793-9101
2625 166th Ave Se Bellevue (98008) *(G-969)*
Kof Enterprises LLC.....206 328-2972
1328 S Weller St Seattle (98144) *(G-10351)*
Kogita Custom Mfg & Repair.....425 453-9547
9 Lake Bellevue Dr # 115 Bellevue (98005) *(G-970)*
Kogita Jewelry, Bellevue *Also called Kogita Custom Mfg & Repair (G-970)*
Koh Gen Do Americas LLC.....253 267-1769
2620 Williamson Pl # 133 Dupont (98327) *(G-2968)*
Koi Pond Cellars.....360 281-2716
24211 Ne 41st Ave Ridgefield (98642) *(G-9093)*
Kokako Software.....425 922-1115
1409 N 41st St Seattle (98103) *(G-10352)*
Kold King, Yakima *Also called King Sales & Manufacturing Co (G-15607)*
Kolibaba and Associates.....253 752-0368
3902 N Gove St Tacoma (98407) *(G-13378)*
Kollmar Incorporated.....509 882-3148
410 O I E Grandview (98930) *(G-4250)*
Kollmar Sheet Metal Works Inc.....206 283-2330
941 S Nebraska St Seattle (98108) *(G-10353)*
Kolorkraze.....360 609-2771
11515 Ne 49th St Ofc Vancouver (98682) *(G-14351)*
Kolorkraze LLC.....360 609-2771
4501 Ne 123rd Ave Vancouver (98682) *(G-14352)*
Koma Kulshan Associates.....360 853-8530
44710 Baker Lake Rd Concrete (98237) *(G-2789)*
Kombucha Town.....360 224-2974
1155 N State St Ste 603 Bellingham (98225) *(G-1398)*
Kona Gold Corp.....425 836-0389
18388 Redmond Fall Cy Rd Kirkland (98033) *(G-5377)*
Konecranes Inc.....253 872-9696
8735 S 212th St Kent (98031) *(G-4982)*
Konecranes Inc.....503 548-4078
2903 Ne 109th Ave Ste A Vancouver (98682) *(G-14353)*
Konen Rock Crushing Inc.....509 382-2768
910 N Touchet Rd Dayton (99328) *(G-2883)*
Kongsberg Underwater Tech Inc.....425 712-1107
19210 33rd Ave W Ste B Lynnwood (98036) *(G-6153)*
Konnectone LLC.....425 502-7371
40 Lake Bellevue Dr # 350 Bellevue (98005) *(G-971)*
Konnekti Incorporated.....925 878-5083
2621 2nd Ave Unit 1001 Seattle (98121) *(G-10354)*
Kono Fixed Income Fund 1511 LP.....360 686-7688
15566 Se 5th Ct Bellevue (98007) *(G-972)*
Kontak LLC.....425 442-5929
21311 Ne 101st Ct Redmond (98053) *(G-8525)*
Kool Change Printing Inc.....360 794-9019
220 N Woods St Monroe (98272) *(G-6588)*
Koolance Inc.....253 249-7669
2840 W Valley Hwy N # 101 Auburn (98001) *(G-485)*
Koolmask Inc.....206 886-5248
777 108th Ave Ne Ste 2000 Bellevue (98004) *(G-973)*
Koowalla Inc.....206 948-1803
16709 167th Ave Ne Woodinville (98072) *(G-15280)*
Kopius Energy Solutions LLC.....425 322-2853
8837 39th Ave Sw Seattle (98136) *(G-10355)*
Koppenberg Enterprises Inc.....360 793-1600
14751 N Kelsey St Ste 105 Monroe (98272) *(G-6589)*
Korben Mathis Woodworking Inc.....360 598-6797
3081 Ne Lincoln Rd Poulsbo (98370) *(G-7972)*
Korblu Mfg Solutions LLC.....509 930-2010
715a E Viola Ave Yakima (98901) *(G-15609)*
Korea Central Daily News, Edmonds *Also called Joongang USA (G-3126)*
Korea Times Los Angeles Inc.....206 622-2229
12532 Aurora Ave N Seattle (98133) *(G-10356)*
Korean Sunday News of Seattle.....425 778-6747
22727 Highway 99 Edmonds (98026) *(G-3129)*
Korean Times, Seattle *Also called Korea Times Los Angeles Inc (G-10356)*
Korry Electronics Co (HQ).....425 297-9700
11910 Beverly Park Rd Everett (98204) *(G-3532)*
Korvan Industries Inc.....360 354-1500
270 Birch Bay Lynden Rd Lynden (98264) *(G-6029)*
Kotelnikov Zinaida.....206 728-6195
1908 Pike Pl Seattle (98101) *(G-10357)*
Kova Industries LLC.....360 567-5371
27120 Ne 220th Ave Battle Ground (98604) *(G-713)*
Kovash Logging Ltd.....360 825-4263
43804 284th Ave Se Enumclaw (98022) *(G-3299)*

Kp LLC.....425 204-6355
555 Monster Rd Sw Renton (98057) *(G-8838)*
Kp2 LLC.....509 663-4983
602 Marian Ave Wenatchee (98801) *(G-15041)*
Kracker Tortilla Distribution.....253 380-2690
916 118th Avenue Ct E Edgewood (98372) *(G-3084)*
Kraft.....509 375-2992
4171 Alder Rd Pasco (99301) *(G-7597)*
Kraft Foods.....253 395-4237
19032 62nd Ave S Kent (98032) *(G-4983)*
Kraft Heinz Foods Company.....800 255-5750
26401 79th Ave S Kent (98032) *(G-4984)*
Kragworks Llc.....208 871-6413
26 Orchard St Naches (98937) *(G-6999)*
Kraig Green Machining.....360 275-3732
5244 Minard Rd W Bremerton (98312) *(G-1972)*
Kramer Handgun Leather Inc.....253 564-6652
3036 68th Ave W University Place (98466) *(G-13975)*
Kramerica Industries LLC.....360 931-9690
4104 Nw Fir St Vancouver (98660) *(G-14354)*
Krantz News Service Inc.....253 857-6590
15407 41st Ave Nw Gig Harbor (98332) *(G-4128)*
Krell Software Inc.....425 298-9519
1805 Village Green Dr # 24 Mill Creek (98012) *(G-6515)*
Kresek Brothers Manufacturing.....509 322-0808
130c Clarkson Mill Rd Tonasket (98855) *(G-13652)*
Krieg Concrete Products Inc.....360 675-2727
35717 State Route 20 Oak Harbor (98277) *(G-7156)*
Kriegers Stump Removal Inc.....360 225-1703
251 Moonridge Rd Woodland (98674) *(G-15443)*
Krill Systems Inc.....206 780-2901
175 Parfitt Way Sw Bainbridge Island (98110) *(G-647)*
Krimsten Publishing LLC (PA).....509 786-7978
65 W Old Inland Empire Prosser (99350) *(G-8047)*
Krismark Group Inc (PA).....425 396-0829
8020 Bracken Pl Se Snoqualmie (98065) *(G-12015)*
Krispy Kreme Doughnuts.....206 316-7090
12505 Aurora Ave N Seattle (98133) *(G-10358)*
Krista K Thie.....509 493-2626
1549 W Jewett Blvd White Salmon (98672) *(G-15121)*
Kristen Blake, Tacoma *Also called Item House Inc (G-13352)*
Kristen Rose Winery.....509 586-4830
109 E 27th Ave Kennewick (99337) *(G-4684)*
Kristine Aumspach.....360 681-4277
517 W Fir St Sequim (98382) *(G-11645)*
Kristines.....360 437-0136
7251 Oak Bay Rd Port Ludlow (98365) *(G-7769)*
Kritter Kookies Ltd.....509 233-8414
4106 Gardenspot Rd Loon Lake (99148) *(G-5975)*
Krn Services.....509 366-3431
1761 George Wash Way 28 Richland (99354) *(G-9019)*
Kroll Machine & Supply Inc.....509 397-4666
602 N Main St Colfax (99111) *(G-2715)*
Kronos Incorporated.....206 696-1505
701 5th Ave Ste 4200 Seattle (98104) *(G-10359)*
Kronos Micronutrients LP.....509 248-4911
213 W Moxee Ave Moxee (98936) *(G-6880)*
Kronos Northwest, Seattle *Also called Kronos Incorporated (G-10359)*
Krueger Logging Inc.....360 687-5558
20300 Ne 279th St Battle Ground (98604) *(G-714)*
Krueger Sheet Metal Co (PA).....509 489-0221
731 N Superior St Spokane (99202) *(G-12355)*
Krume Logging Excavation.....360 274-8667
501 Kroll Rd Castle Rock (98611) *(G-2348)*
Krw Specialties, Kent *Also called PBS Supply Co Inc (G-5063)*
Kryki Sports.....206 660-7359
200 W Comstock St Apt 202 Seattle (98119) *(G-10360)*
Krysaliis LLC.....888 579-7254
288 Martin St Blaine (98230) *(G-1679)*
Ktn Thermo Dynamics.....509 823-0560
382 Fromherz Dr Yakima (98908) *(G-15610)*
Ktnw Channel 31, Richland *Also called Washington State University (G-9052)*
Kts Media Inc.....253 845-0771
15309 88th Avenue Ct E Puyallup (98375) *(G-8173)*
Kuau Technology Ltd.....425 485-7551
12604 Ne 178th St Woodinville (98072) *(G-15281)*
Kubeshs Site Mixed Con Inc.....509 684-1381
476 Williams Lake Rd Colville (99114) *(G-2763)*
Kubota Authorized Dealer, Quincy *Also called Blueline Equipment Co LLC (G-8290)*
Kubota Authorized Dealer, Walla Walla *Also called Blueline Equipment Co LLC (G-14772)*
Kughler Co Inc.....206 789-0667
4601 Shilshole Ave Nw Main Seattle (98107) *(G-10361)*
Kuki Collection, Moses Lake *Also called Five Food Inc (G-6708)*
Kulien Handmade Shoes, Centralia *Also called Kulien Shoe Factory (G-2414)*
Kulien Shoe Factory.....360 736-6943
611 N Tower Ave Centralia (98531) *(G-2414)*
Kulshan Brewing Company (PA).....360 389-5348
1538 Kentucky St Bellingham (98229) *(G-1399)*
Kuo Software LLC.....425 961-0197
27906 Se 24th Way Sammamish (98075) *(G-9227)*
Kurt A Flechel.....509 953-8358
1808 S Maple Blvd Spokane (99203) *(G-12356)*

ALPHABETIC

Kurt Blume — ALPHABETIC SECTION

Kurt Blume 206 371-9337
   511 N 73rd St Seattle (98103) *(G-10362)*
Kurt Muonio Contract Cutting 360 686-1809
   23500 Ne Jehnsen Rd Yacolt (98675) *(G-15485)*
Kurt Timmermeister 206 696-0989
   18409 Beall Rd Sw Vashon (98070) *(G-14728)*
Kurt Timmermeister 206 696-0989
   18409 Beall Rd Sw Vashon (98070) *(G-14729)*
Kurtisfactor LLC 208 863-6180
   2368 Yakima Ave Unit 103 Tacoma (98405) *(G-13379)*
Kurtwood Farms, Vashon *Also called Kurt Timmermeister* *(G-14728)*
Kurtwood Farms, Vashon *Also called Kurt Timmermeister* *(G-14729)*
Kushco 206 772-9333
   11431 Rainier Ave S Seattle (98178) *(G-10363)*
Kushco Clothing LLC 206 772-9333
   11431 Rainier Ave S Seattle (98178) *(G-10364)*
Kusher Bakery, Fife *Also called Kusher LLC* *(G-3963)*
Kusher LLC 800 445-0655
   7214 26th St E Ste 102 Fife (98424) *(G-3963)*
Kusina Filipina Rest & Bky, Seattle *Also called Kusina Fillipina* *(G-10365)*
Kusina Fillipina 206 322-9433
   7612 S 135th St Seattle (98178) *(G-10365)*
Kustom Printing Inc 206 282-8400
   3243 20th Ave W Seattle (98199) *(G-10366)*
Kvamme Ltd 425 787-1669
   15806 Highway 99 Ste 1 Lynnwood (98087) *(G-6154)*
Kwang Nam Hwang 206 433-8811
   446 Sw 153rd St Burien (98166) *(G-2116)*
Kwik Loc Corp 253 564-3574
   7708 47th St W University Place (98466) *(G-13976)*
Kwik Lok Corporation (HQ) 509 248-4770
   2712 S 16th Ave Union Gap (98903) *(G-13937)*
KY International LLC 253 373-9602
   13330 Se 252nd St Covington (98042) *(G-2831)*
Kyle O Meara 206 874-2626
   3857 Sw 339th St Federal Way (98023) *(G-3749)*
Kylie BS Pastry Case LLC 206 935-6335
   11124 Se 272nd Pl Kent (98030) *(G-4985)*
Kymeta Corporation (PA) 425 896-3700
   12277 134th Ct Ne Ste 100 Redmond (98052) *(G-8526)*
Kymeta Corporation 425 896-3700
   12277 134th Ct Ne Ste 100 Redmond (98052) *(G-8527)*
Kz Packaging, Centralia *Also called D & D Dividers LLC* *(G-2397)*
Kzbg Big Country 977 .... 509 751-0977
   2470 Appleside Blvd Clarkston (99403) *(G-2638)*
L & B Service LLC 206 650-4607
   4209 Ne 169th Ct Lake Forest Park (98155) *(G-5619)*
L & E Bottling Co Inc 360 357-3812
   3200 Mottman Rd Sw Tumwater (98512) *(G-13882)*
L & E Tubing LLC 425 778-4123
   5820 188th St Sw Ste D Lynnwood (98037) *(G-6155)*
L & L Ink 206 605-4561
   8329 200th St Se Snohomish (98296) *(G-11934)*
L & L Nursery Supply Inc 909 591-0461
   2507 Frank Albert Rd E # 130 Fife (98424) *(G-3964)*
L & L Printing Inc 253 848-5546
   1430 E Main Ste E Puyallup (98372) *(G-8174)*
L & M Prcision Fabrication Inc 509 244-5446
   13026 W Mcfarlane Rd D14 Airway Heights (99001) *(G-55)*
L & P Screen Printing 253 859-8787
   3420 S 271st St Kent (98032) *(G-4986)*
L & R Industries LLC 425 226-2780
   11876 Se 160th St Renton (98058) *(G-8839)*
L B Foster Company 509 921-8777
   3808 N Sullivan Rd Bldg 7 Spokane Valley (99216) *(G-12769)*
L C I, Mukilteo *Also called Linear Controls Inc* *(G-6949)*
L Clasen Corp 360 658-1823
   1102 Bonneville Ave M Snohomish (98290) *(G-11935)*
L E Wilson Inc 509 782-1328
   404 Pioneer Ave Cashmere (98815) *(G-2324)*
L Ecole N 41 Street, Lowden *Also called Lowden Schoolhouse Corporation* *(G-5990)*
L G Artworks Inc 425 355-9143
   12124 1st Ave Se Everett (98208) *(G-3533)*
L J Smith Inc 253 435-9120
   1212 Valley Ave Nw 300 Puyallup (98371) *(G-8175)*
L L G Machine Works 360 793-1920
   10617 323rd Ave Se Sultan (98294) *(G-13028)*
L L Nursery Supply, Fife *Also called L & L Nursery Supply Inc* *(G-3964)*
L Lazy Corp 509 448-3426
   4815 S Perry St Spokane (99223) *(G-12357)*
L Leather LLC 253 733-9196
   602 108th St S Tacoma (98444) *(G-13380)*
L M Cupcakes LLC 425 427-9558
   250 1st Ave Ne Issaquah (98027) *(G-4436)*
L Rock Industries Inc 360 575-8868
   1902 E State Route 4 Cathlamet (98612) *(G-2370)*
L S I, Puyallup *Also called LSI Logistic Svc Solutions LLC* *(G-8180)*
L Stop-N-Go 509 896-6089
   330 South St Mabton (98935) *(G-6229)*
L W Products Co, Woodinville *Also called Lous Welding & Fabricating* *(G-15295)*
L&P Screen Printing Inc 253 951-2482
   1720 Pike St Nw Ste 6 Auburn (98001) *(G-486)*

L'Ecole No 41, Walla Walla *Also called Lowden Schoolhouse Corporation* *(G-14839)*
L3 Systems Inc 425 836-5438
   21401 Se 37th St Sammamish (98075) *(G-9228)*
La Belle Associates Inc 360 671-5122
   4100 Marblemount Ln Bellingham (98226) *(G-1400)*
La Belle Reve LLC 425 454-7772
   10630 Ne 8th St Ste 4 Bellevue (98004) *(G-974)*
La Belle Reve Bridal, Bellevue *Also called La Belle Reve LLC* *(G-974)*
La Conner Maritime Service, La Conner *Also called Maritime Fabrications Inc* *(G-5524)*
La Cutting Products, Bellingham *Also called Saw Service Washington Inc* *(G-1525)*
LA Excav & Select Log Inc 360 856-4111
   13361 Teak Ln Mount Vernon (98273) *(G-6806)*
La Excavation, Mount Vernon *Also called LA Excav & Select Log Inc* *(G-6806)*
La Jalpita, Pasco *Also called Jesus Romero* *(G-7595)*
La Marzocco International LLC 206 706-9104
   1553 Nw Ballard Way Seattle (98107) *(G-10367)*
La Mesa Fiction 206 459-2664
   6619 132nd Ave Ne Kirkland (98033) *(G-5378)*
La Mexicana Inc (PA) 206 763-1488
   10020 14th Ave Sw Seattle (98146) *(G-10368)*
La Michoacana 360 658-1635
   1511 3rd St Marysville (98270) *(G-6349)*
La Panzanella, Seattle *Also called Madrona Specialty Foods LLC* *(G-10465)*
La Toscana Bed Brakfast Winery 509 548-5448
   9020 Foster Rd Cashmere (98815) *(G-2325)*
La Waffletz LLC 206 432-7548
   2429 S 273rd Pl Apt 234 Federal Way (98003) *(G-3750)*
Lab Door Press 425 408-0672
   13507 Ne 200th St Woodinville (98072) *(G-15282)*
Label Company Inc 206 568-6000
   430 S 96th St Ste 8 Seattle (98108) *(G-10369)*
Label Masters Inc 425 869-2422
   22261 68th Ave S Kent (98032) *(G-4987)*
Labelmaster Software, Seattle *Also called American Labelmark Company* *(G-9393)*
Labels & Lists Inc 425 822-1984
   18912 North Creek Pkwy # 201 Bothell (98011) *(G-1772)*
Labels International, Everett *Also called Global Product Mfg Corp* *(G-3501)*
Labels Plus, Everett *Also called Phillips Industrial Supply Inc* *(G-3572)*
Labinal, Inc., Everett *Also called Safran Elec & Pwr USA LLC* *(G-3603)*
Labore Industries 206 533-8709
   1247 N 172nd St Shoreline (98133) *(G-11780)*
Lachini Winery (PA) 503 864-4553
   7720 Ne 24th St Medina (98039) *(G-6450)*
Lachselian Distillery 206 743-8070
   1712 1st Ave S Seattle (98134) *(G-10370)*
Lacoto Industries Inc 360 658-9668
   7610 80th Ave Ne Marysville (98270) *(G-6350)*
Lady 12 LLC 425 218-3080
   27928 Ne 5th St Redmond (98053) *(G-8528)*
Lafarge & Egge, Lynnwood *Also called L & E Tubing LLC* *(G-6155)*
Lafarge North America Inc 360 695-9208
   1217 W 8th St Vancouver (98660) *(G-14355)*
Lafarge North America Inc 206 937-8025
   5400 W Marginal Way Sw Seattle (98106) *(G-10371)*
Lafarge North America Inc 509 893-0034
   3808 N Sullivan Rd # 15 Spokane Valley (99216) *(G-12770)*
Lafargeholcim, Vancouver *Also called Lafarge North America Inc* *(G-14355)*
Lafargeholcim, Spokane Valley *Also called Lafarge North America Inc* *(G-12770)*
Lafromboise Newspapers (PA) 360 736-3311
   321 N Pearl St Centralia (98531) *(G-2415)*
Lafromboise Newspapers 360 807-8716
   3802 Galvin Rd Centralia (98531) *(G-2416)*
Lafromboise Newspapers 360 458-2681
   118 Prairie Park St Yelm (98597) *(G-15737)*
Lagoon Conservation LLC 253 202-6479
   28200 9th Ave S Des Moines (98198) *(G-2939)*
Lagunamoon Beauty Intl Ltd LLC 480 925-7577
   12345 Lake City Way Ne Seattle (98125) *(G-10372)*
Lagunitas 206 784-2230
   1550 Nw 49th St Seattle (98107) *(G-10373)*
Laht Neppur Ventures Inc (PA) 509 337-6261
   444 Preston Ave Waitsburg (99361) *(G-14755)*
Lai, Hoquiam *Also called Legacy Automation Inc* *(G-4346)*
Lak Woodworks 253 495-0611
   9827 Wildwood Ave Sw Lakewood (98498) *(G-5732)*
Lake Chelan Trading Company 509 687-9463
   3519 Highway 150 Chelan (98816) *(G-2557)*
Lake Chelan Winery, Chelan *Also called Lake Chelan Trading Company* *(G-2557)*
Lake City Naturopathic Care In 509 590-1343
   21950 E Country Vista Dr # 600 Liberty Lake (99019) *(G-5842)*
Lake Missuola Wine, Blaine *Also called Davis Degrass Enterprises Inc* *(G-1667)*
Lake Plating, Moses Lake *Also called Harrys Radiator Shop Inc* *(G-6713)*
Lake Samish Terrace Park 360 671-2741
   921 Autumn Ln Bellingham (98229) *(G-1401)*
Lake Sunset LLC 718 683-2269
   1816 Lenox Ct Nw Olympia (98502) *(G-7317)*
Lakeside Gardens 360 483-8889
   130 Misty Waters Ln Lynden (98264) *(G-6030)*
Lakeside Industries Inc (PA) 425 313-2600
   6505 226th Pl Se Ste 200 Issaquah (98027) *(G-4437)*

Lakeside Industries Inc 360 491-5460
11125 Durgin Rd Se Olympia (98513) *(G-7318)*
Lakeside Industries Inc 360 423-6882
500 Tennant Way Longview (98632) *(G-5925)*
Lakeside Industries Inc 360 794-7779
14282 Galaxy Way Monroe (98272) *(G-6590)*
Lakeside Industries Inc 360 604-1869
8705 Ne 117th Ave Vancouver (98662) *(G-14356)*
Lakeview Stone and Garden, Seattle *Also called Quarry S/E Inc (G-10904)*
Lakewood Counter Tops Inc 253 588-8550
10513 Lakeview Ave Sw Lakewood (98499) *(G-5733)*
Lakewood Holdings Inc 253 284-4897
11101 South Tacoma Way B Lakewood (98499) *(G-5734)*
Lakewood Printing Inc 253 582-6670
9625 Gravelly Lake Dr Sw Lakewood (98499) *(G-5735)*
Lakota Industries Inc 360 659-5333
4001 132nd Pl Ne Marysville (98271) *(G-6351)*
Lam Research Corporation 360 260-0352
222 Ne Park Plaza Dr # 130 Vancouver (98684) *(G-14357)*
Lam-Hammer Inc 509 687-2421
7560 Chelan Ridge Rd Chelan (98816) *(G-2558)*
Lamar Technologies LLC 360 651-8869
14900 40th Ave Ne Marysville (98271) *(G-6352)*
Lamb Weston Inc 509 375-4181
2013 Saint St Richland (99354) *(G-9020)*
Lamb Weston Inc 509 735-4651
8701 W Gage Blvd Kennewick (99336) *(G-4685)*
Lamb Weston Inc 509 713-7200
2005 Saint St Richland (99354) *(G-9021)*
Lamb Weston Bsw LLC 509 349-2210
1203 Basin St Warden (98857) *(G-14932)*
Lamb Weston Holdings Inc 509 234-5511
811 W Gum St Connell (99326) *(G-2795)*
Lamb Weston Holdings Inc 509 786-2700
506 6th St Prosser (99350) *(G-8048)*
Lamb Weston Holdings Inc 509 882-1417
1125 Sheridan Ave Prosser (99350) *(G-8049)*
Lamb Weston Inc 509 787-3567
1005 E St Sw Quincy (98848) *(G-8301)*
Lamb Weston Inc 509 547-8851
960 N Glade Rd Pasco (99301) *(G-7598)*
Lamb Weston Inc 509 875-2423
187107 S Watts Rd Paterson (99345) *(G-7658)*
Lamb Weston Sales Inc 509 735-4651
8701 W Gage Blvd Kennewick (99336) *(G-4686)*
Lambda Software LLC 425 882-3464
16814 Ne 33rd St Bellevue (98008) *(G-975)*
Lamby Nursery Collection, Lynden *Also called J K Properties Inc (G-6025)*
Lamexicana Tortilla Factory, Seattle *Also called La Mexicana Inc (G-10368)*
Lamiglas Inc 360 225-9436
1400 Atlantic Ave Woodland (98674) *(G-15444)*
Lammy Industries Inc 206 654-0010
25 S Hanford St Seattle (98134) *(G-10374)*
Lancs Industries Holdings LLC 425 823-6634
12704 Ne 124th St Ste 36 Kirkland (98034) *(G-5379)*
Lancs Industries Inc (PA) 425 823-6634
12704 Ne 124th St Ste 36 Kirkland (98034) *(G-5380)*
Land Co LLC 360 484-7712
172 Knappton Rd Naselle (98638) *(G-7016)*
Land OLakes Inc 425 653-4200
3605 132nd Ave Se Ste 402 Bellevue (98006) *(G-976)*
Land OLakes Inc 509 488-5208
449 W Mcmanomon Rd Othello (99344) *(G-7501)*
Land OLakes Inc 360 592-5115
5996 Lawrence Rd Everson (98247) *(G-3681)*
Landa Inc 360 833-9100
4275 Nw Pacific Rim Blvd Camas (98607) *(G-2263)*
Landd Ventures Inc 425 775-9709
2921 Alderwood Mall Blvd # 104 Lynnwood (98036) *(G-6156)*
Landing Gear Work LLC 509 884-9546
295 E Perimeter Rd Renton (98057) *(G-8840)*
Landis Gyr 425 458-9363
11425 Ne 120th St Kirkland (98034) *(G-5381)*
Landrace Labs 360 273-9277
5845 192nd Ave Sw Rochester (98579) *(G-9135)*
Landredi, Eatonville *Also called Basic Homes LLC (G-3050)*
Landsburg In Orora North Amer, Kent *Also called Orora Packaging Solutions (G-5048)*
Landscape Bark, Tacoma *Also called Carpinito Brothers Inc (G-13225)*
Landsol LLC 425 242-5198
11447 120th Ave Ne # 300 Kirkland (98033) *(G-5382)*
Landy Corporation 253 835-1427
835 Sw 347th Pl Federal Way (98023) *(G-3751)*
Lane Chestnut Prints 206 397-3108
10001 49th Ave Ne Seattle (98125) *(G-10375)*
Lane Gibbons Vineyard Inc 360 264-8466
12035 Gibbons Ln Se Tenino (98589) *(G-13620)*
Lane Mt Silica Co (HQ) 206 762-7622
5427 Ohio Ave S Seattle (98134) *(G-10376)*
Lane Mt Silica Co 206 762-7622
3119 Highway 231 Valley (99181) *(G-13993)*
Lane Pierce Partners Inc 509 926-1033
6326 E Sharp Ave Spokane Valley (99212) *(G-12771)*
Lang Mfg Division, Everett *Also called Star Manufacturing Intl Inc (G-3620)*
Langes Honey Skep Inc 360 757-1073
18898 Dahlstedt Rd Burlington (98233) *(G-2167)*
Lanktree Equipment and Supply, Kent *Also called Lanktree Land Surveying Inc (G-4988)*
Lanktree Land Surveying Inc 253 653-6423
25510 74th Ave S Kent (98032) *(G-4988)*
Lannoye Emblems Inc 425 844-8411
15056 225th Ave Ne Woodinville (98077) *(G-15283)*
Lantern Brewing LLC 206 729-5350
938 N 95th St Seattle (98103) *(G-10377)*
Lantz Cellars, Lake Stevens *Also called Kevin W Lantz (G-5653)*
Lapel Solutions LLC 360 597-4958
11304 Ne 66th St Vancouver (98662) *(G-14358)*
Laplink Software Inc 425 952-6000
600 108th Ave Ne Ste 610 Bellevue (98004) *(G-977)*
Lapo Inc 360 314-4546
3001 Se Columbia Way Vancouver (98661) *(G-14359)*
Laprensa Bilingual, Spokane *Also called Bilingual Press Publishing Co (G-12147)*
Larkin Jewelers 253 756-0712
2405 N Pearl St Ste 8 Tacoma (98406) *(G-13381)*
Larock Enterprises Inc 509 966-4542
1401 W Pine St Union Gap (98903) *(G-13938)*
Larry Guthrie Co 509 922-6121
13411 E 32nd Ave Ste A Spokane Valley (99216) *(G-12772)*
Larry Harvitz, Bellevue *Also called Larrys Screen Printing (G-978)*
Larry Lisk 425 252-5475
4220 Terrace Dr Everett (98203) *(G-3534)*
Larry S Ayre 509 582-8925
37304 S Lemon Dr Kennewick (99337) *(G-4687)*
Larry Waits Nemesis 253 863-4444
405 202nd Ave E Lake Tapps (98391) *(G-5681)*
Larrys Screen Printing 425 885-3644
3225 134th Ln Ne Bellevue (98005) *(G-978)*
Larsen Equipment Design Inc 206 789-5121
1117 Nw 52nd St Seattle (98107) *(G-10378)*
Larsen Machine 509 545-0346
914 S Maitland Ave Pasco (99301) *(G-7599)*
Larsen Sign Company 253 581-4313
9411 Lakeview Ave Sw Lakewood (98499) *(G-5736)*
Larson Rv Publishing 360 733-8576
1020 E Bakerview Rd Bellingham (98226) *(G-1402)*
Larson-Juhl US LLC 206 433-6002
18401 72nd Ave S Kent (98032) *(G-4989)*
Lasco Bathware, Yelm *Also called Aquatic Co (G-15727)*
Laser Cutting Northwest, Auburn *Also called Pacific A Crgo Transf Systems (G-522)*
Laser Guidance Inc 206 679-3909
14746 Ne 95th St Redmond (98052) *(G-8529)*
Laser Materials Corporation 360 254-4180
12706 Ne 95th St Ste 102 Vancouver (98682) *(G-14360)*
Laser One, Olympia *Also called Rgd Enterprises Inc (G-7385)*
Laser Printers Plus Inc 206 786-0107
18029 25th Dr Se Bothell (98012) *(G-1873)*
Laser Reflections 206 818-2940
18800 Front St Ne Poulsbo (98370) *(G-7973)*
Laser Support Services Inc 253 531-9008
3223 148th St E Tacoma (98446) *(G-13382)*
Laser Techniques Company LLC 425 885-0607
11431 Willows Rd Ne # 100 Redmond (98052) *(G-8530)*
Laser Writing 253 686-6909
3016 N Narrows Dr Tacoma (98407) *(G-13383)*
Laserfab Inc (PA) 509 762-0400
5406 184th St E Ste D Puyallup (98375) *(G-8176)*
Lasermach Inc 425 485-3169
19450 144th Ave Ne Ste 7h Woodinville (98072) *(G-15284)*
Last US Bag Co 360 993-2247
3000 Columbia House Blvd # 114 Vancouver (98661) *(G-14361)*
Lasting Impressions Inc 360 659-1255
1423 6th St Marysville (98270) *(G-6353)*
Lasting Memories 509 548-6393
110 Park Ave Leavenworth (98826) *(G-5809)*
Latah Creek Wine Cellars Ltd 509 926-0164
13030 E Indiana Ave Spokane Valley (99216) *(G-12773)*
Latitude 47 Distillers 206 794-0852
2801 1st Ave Apt 1005 Seattle (98121) *(G-10379)*
Latitude Blue Press LLC 360 421-1934
109 2nd St S Apt 433 Kirkland (98033) *(G-5383)*
Latium USA Trading Inc 253 850-4530
7041 S 234th St Kent (98032) *(G-4990)*
Lattins Country Cider 360 491-7328
9402 Rich Rd Se Olympia (98501) *(G-7319)*
Laud Social Inc 213 797-0744
1802 11th Ave Seattle (98122) *(G-10380)*
Lauda-Noah LP (HQ) 360 993-1395
2501 Se Columbia Way # 140 Vancouver (98661) *(G-14362)*
Lauda-Noah LP 360 993-1395
2501 Se Columbia Way # 140 Vancouver (98661) *(G-14363)*
Laughing Elephant, Seattle *Also called Blue Lantern Publishing Inc (G-9551)*
Laughlin Industries Inc 360 514-9218
14511 Ne 10th Ave Ste B Vancouver (98685) *(G-14364)*
Laura Townsend-Faber 206 517-5739
5730 Ne 60th St Seattle (98115) *(G-10381)*

ALPHABETIC

Laurel Graphics Fabrication Co — ALPHABETIC SECTION

Laurel Graphics Fabrication Co 253 872-7617
 22417 76th Ave S Kent (98032) *(G-4991)*
Laurelcrest II LLC (PA) 206 922-3634
 12033 12th Ave Nw Seattle (98177) *(G-10382)*
Laurelhurst Cellars LLC 206 992-2875
 3935 9th Ave S Seattle (98108) *(G-10383)*
Laurels Crown LLC 509 860-2510
 200 Palouse St Ste 202 Wenatchee (98801) *(G-15042)*
Lauren Ashton Cellars LLC 206 504-8546
 19510 144th Ave Ne D12 Woodinville (98072) *(G-15285)*
Lauterbach Inc 360 567-2666
 1111 Main St Ste 610 Vancouver (98660) *(G-14365)*
Laval 360 491-8118
 4802 31st Ave Se Olympia (98503) *(G-7320)*
Lavalle Printing Services, Woodinville Also called Graphics Place Inc *(G-15255)*
Lavender Heart Ltd (PA) 206 568-4441
 3212 Cascadia Ave S Seattle (98144) *(G-10384)*
Lavinal Inc 509 857-2224
 22732 Hwy 97 Cle Elum (98922) *(G-2670)*
Lavry Engineering 360 598-9757
 15775 George Ln Ne Poulsbo (98370) *(G-7974)*
Lavry Engineering Inc 206 842-3552
 945 Hildebrand Ln Ne # 110 Bainbridge Island (98110) *(G-648)*
Lawman Industries LLC 360 915-7807
 2629 Reinhardt Ln Ne O Lacey (98516) *(G-5564)*
Lawn Rangers, Wenatchee Also called Kp2 LLC *(G-15041)*
Lawrence Cellars 425 286-2198
 19151 144th Ave Ne Ste D Woodinville (98072) *(G-15286)*
Lawrence Cellars LLC 509 346-2585
 13000 Road D Sw Royal City (99357) *(G-9171)*
Lawrence Electronic Company, Burien Also called Lawrenson Electronics Co Inc *(G-2117)*
Lawrence Enterprises 360 750-8551
 1809 Ne 49th St Vancouver (98663) *(G-14366)*
Lawrence Fruit Inc 509 925-1095
 311 N Pearl St Ellensburg (98926) *(G-3212)*
Lawrence Milner 360 860-1924
 3020 W Garfield St Seattle (98199) *(G-10385)*
Lawrenson Electronics Co Inc 206 243-7310
 14636 Ambaum Blvd Sw Burien (98166) *(G-2117)*
Lawsuite Technologies LLC 206 349-2227
 506 2nd Ave Ste 1400 Seattle (98104) *(G-10386)*
Lawton Printing Inc 509 534-1044
 4111 E Mission Ave Spokane (99202) *(G-12358)*
Lawyer Avenue 425 243-7958
 4701 Sw Admiral Way Seattle (98116) *(G-10387)*
Layfield Plastics Incorporated 425 254-1075
 4001 Oakesdale Ave Sw Renton (98057) *(G-8841)*
Laylas Fun Socks 509 279-8343
 1314 W Fairview Ave Spokane (99205) *(G-12359)*
Laz Tool & Fabricators, Snohomish Also called Laz Tool and Manufacturing *(G-11936)*
Laz Tool and Manufacturing (PA) 360 568-5749
 14816 Roosevelt Rd Snohomish (98290) *(G-11936)*
Lazer Cartridges Plus LLC 509 529-0200
 31 Looking Glass Rd Walla Walla (99362) *(G-14835)*
Lazer Trends LLC 253 886-5600
 3902 W Valley Hwy N # 104 Auburn (98001) *(G-487)*
Lazerquick Printing, Brier Also called Dtg Inc *(G-2019)*
Lazerwood Industries 206 650-2367
 1103 E Pike St Seattle (98122) *(G-10388)*
Lazy Boy Brewing Co, Everett Also called Ls Brewing Inc *(G-3541)*
LB Games Inc 360 794-7803
 1429 Ave 376 D Snohomish (98290) *(G-11937)*
Lb Steele Cabinet Co 360 446-4114
 12935 Reo Rd Se Rainier (98576) *(G-8316)*
Lc Logic Defense and Space LLC 425 270-5169
 1818 101st Pl Sw Everett (98204) *(G-3535)*
Lc Welding Fabrication LL 360 359-8853
 271 Se Craig Rd Shelton (98584) *(G-11708)*
Lch Enterprises 253 313-5665
 5315 Point Fosdick Dr Nw B Gig Harbor (98335) *(G-4129)*
Ld Forest Inc 360 733-1606
 1964 N Springfield Ct Bellingham (98229) *(G-1403)*
LDB Beverage Company 509 651-0381
 30 Se Cascade Ave Spc A Stevenson (98648) *(G-13015)*
Ldl- Software Inc 425 652-1473
 5129 Ne 4th Ct Renton (98059) *(G-8842)*
Le Beau Tapis 360 734-9786
 819 14th St Bellingham (98225) *(G-1404)*
Le Bijou Corporation 206 622-9453
 1424 4th Ave Ste 712 Seattle (98101) *(G-10389)*
Le Chateau Winery, Kennewick Also called Whitelatch-Hoch LLC *(G-4745)*
Le Labo 206 420-2835
 921 E Pine St Seattle (98122) *(G-10390)*
Leach International Corp 425 519-1826
 500 108th Ave Ne Bellevue (98004) *(G-979)*
Lead Cat Press LLC 206 349-3226
 1200 Boylston Ave Apt 302 Seattle (98101) *(G-10391)*
Leader Manufacturing Inc 360 895-1184
 1540 Leader Intl Dr Port Orchard (98367) *(G-7825)*
Leader, The, Port Townsend Also called Port Townsend Publishing Co *(G-7913)*
Leading Beyond Tradition LLC 425 275-7665
 13822 233rd St Se Snohomish (98296) *(G-11938)*
Leading Edge Labeling Inc 425 821-4137
 14612 Ne 91st St Redmond (98052) *(G-8531)*
Leads Manufacturing Company 541 259-1128
 14920 Se Sun Park Ct Vancouver (98683) *(G-14367)*
Leadscorz Inc 206 899-4665
 10 Harrison St Ste 311 Seattle (98109) *(G-10392)*
Leaf Cellars LLC 206 860-6888
 9320 15th Ave S Ste Cf Seattle (98108) *(G-10393)*
Leaftail Labs LLC 206 399-4233
 1417 Nw 54th St Ste 337 Seattle (98107) *(G-10394)*
Leake Logging Inc 509 738-3033
 883b Vanasse Rd Kettle Falls (99141) *(G-5235)*
Leancode Inc 425 533-5219
 8511 154th Ave Ne Redmond (98052) *(G-8532)*
Leather Guard Div Int Renovatn 425 827-4895
 11246 Ne 87th St Kirkland (98033) *(G-5384)*
Leatherback Publishing Inc 425 822-1202
 681 7th Ave Kirkland (98033) *(G-5385)*
Leavelogic Inc 757 655-3283
 2008a California Ave Sw Seattle (98116) *(G-10395)*
Leaves In Wind Woodworks LLC 360 574-6750
 802 Nw 143rd St Vancouver (98685) *(G-14368)*
Leclercq Marine Construction 206 283-8555
 1080 W Ewing St Seattle (98119) *(G-10396)*
Lecoq Machine Work Inc 206 762-4606
 1605 S 93rd St Ste G2 Seattle (98108) *(G-10397)*
Lectent LLC 360 574-7737
 1101 Ne 144th St Ste 107 Vancouver (98685) *(G-14369)*
Lectro Tek Services Inc 509 663-2891
 1951 S Wenatchee Ave Wenatchee (98801) *(G-15043)*
Led Software 206 232-2812
 7515 86th Ave Se Mercer Island (98040) *(G-6470)*
Ledford Industries LLC 253 446-6508
 16126 Meridian Ave Puyallup (98375) *(G-8177)*
Lee Company 425 488-5842
 19125 North Creek Pkwy # 120 Bothell (98011) *(G-1773)*
Lee Enterprises Incorporated 509 783-5555
 3321 W Kennewick Ave # 190 Kennewick (99336) *(G-4688)*
Lee Fabricators Inc 360 698-1190
 6362 Nw Warehouse Way Silverdale (98383) *(G-11843)*
Lee Frame Shoppe Inc 509 624-2715
 421 W 1st Ave Spokane (99201) *(G-12360)*
Lee H Koehn 509 265-4367
 2671 Colonial Rd Mesa (99343) *(G-6494)*
Lee Publications Inc 360 577-2500
 770 11th Ave Longview (98632) *(G-5926)*
Lee R Mason Inc 253 863-8666
 15022 Puyallup St E U103 Sumner (98390) *(G-13079)*
Lee Shore Boats, Port Angeles Also called Better Boats Inc *(G-7690)*
Lee Shore Boats Inc 360 385-1491
 950 30th St Port Townsend (98368) *(G-7895)*
Lee Signs 360 750-0689
 7302 Kansas St Vancouver (98664) *(G-14370)*
Leeds Look Listen Inc 208 252-6075
 1300 N Northlake Way # 200 Seattle (98103) *(G-10398)*
Leeward Industries Inc 360 830-0765
 8475 Leeward Ave Nw Seabeck (98380) *(G-9267)*
Left Coast Composites 305 923-4590
 60 Montrose Pl Port Angeles (98362) *(G-7723)*
Left Coast Woodworks LLC 360 790-3188
 21344 Old Highway 99 Sw Centralia (98531) *(G-2417)*
Left Full Rudder Aerospace LLC 516 330-0633
 18250 142nd Ave Ne # 327 Woodinville (98072) *(G-15287)*
Legacy Automation Inc 360 538-2550
 206 Firman Ave Ste P Hoquiam (98550) *(G-4346)*
Legacy Creations 206 286-1827
 903 W Newell St Seattle (98119) *(G-10399)*
Legacy Mill and Cabinet LLC 509 440-4884
 6855 W Clearwater Ave Kennewick (99336) *(G-4689)*
Legacy Plastics L L C 360 413-7787
 7235 40th Ct Ne Olympia (98516) *(G-7321)*
Legacy Vulcan LLC 206 284-7717
 5915 Delridge Way Sw Seattle (98106) *(G-10400)*
Legal + Plus Software Group 206 286-3600
 6947 Coal Creek Pkwy Se Newcastle (98059) *(G-7033)*
Legal Plus, Newcastle Also called Legal + Plus Software Group *(G-7033)*
Legal+plus Software Group Inc 206 286-3600
 6947 Coal Creek Pkwy Se # 35 Newcastle (98059) *(G-7034)*
Legend Brands, Burlington Also called Sapphire Scientific Inc *(G-2185)*
Legend Brands, Burlington Also called Skagit Northwest Holdings Inc *(G-2188)*
Legend Brands 360 757-7776
 15180 Josh Wilson Rd Burlington (98233) *(G-2168)*
Legend Data Systems Inc 425 251-1670
 18024 72nd Ave S Kent (98032) *(G-4992)*
Legend ID, Kent Also called Legend Data Systems Inc *(G-4992)*
Legendary Yacht Inc 360 835-0342
 2902 Addy St Washougal (98671) *(G-14963)*
Leggari Products LLC 509 727-2979
 3105 E Ainsworth Ave Warehouse Pasco (99301) *(G-7600)*
Leggett & Platt Incorporated 801 825-9739
 440 E 19th St Tacoma (98421) *(G-13384)*
Legitiment Light Co 206 542-3268
 1414 Nw 198th Pl Shoreline (98177) *(G-11781)*

Lehenengo Aerospace Inc 425 256-1376
1312 4th St Kirkland (98033) **(G-5386)**
Lehigh Hanson, Mill Creek *Also called Cadman (seattle) Inc* **(G-6502)**
Lehigh Northwest Cement Co (HQ) 800 752-6794
2115 N 30th St Ste 202 Tacoma (98403) **(G-13385)**
Lehigh Northwest Cement Co 360 733-6720
741 Marine Dr Bellingham (98225) **(G-1405)**
Leidos Inc 425 267-5600
12424 Beverly Park Rd A2 Lynnwood (98087) **(G-6157)**
Leidos Inc 360 394-8870
26279 Twelv Trees Ln Nw Poulsbo (98370) **(G-7975)**
Leigh Interiors 206 351-5158
13300 Se 30th St Ste 101 Bellevue (98005) **(G-980)**
Leigh James Cellars LLC 509 529-1398
425 B St Walla Walla (99362) **(G-14836)**
Leisure Home & Spa 360 647-5529
1813 Dakin St Bellingham (98229) **(G-1406)**
Leisure Loyalty Inc 425 223-5102
2019 Killarney Way Bellevue (98004) **(G-981)**
Lemac Manufacturing Co Inc 360 756-1720
3890 Hammer Dr Bellingham (98226) **(G-1407)**
Lemmino Inc 571 229-3854
6520 29th Ave Sw Seattle (98126) **(G-10401)**
Lemond Fitness Inc 425 615-0116
15540 Woodinvlle Redmond Woodinville (98072) **(G-15288)**
Lenco Mobile Inc 800 557-4148
2025 1st Ave Ste 320 Seattle (98121) **(G-10402)**
Lennox, Auburn *Also called Innovative Hearth Products LLC* **(G-477)**
Lennox Ergonomics & Co 253 268-0830
4203 74th Avenue Ct Nw Gig Harbor (98335) **(G-4130)**
Lennox Inc 360 970-8954
2302 Harrison Ave Nw Olympia (98502) **(G-7322)**
Lennox Industries Commeri 206 607-1585
2105 70th Ave E Ste 300 Fife (98424) **(G-3965)**
Lennox Stores (partsplus) 206 607-1818
2105 70th Ave E Ste 100 Fife (98424) **(G-3966)**
Lenox Clothing LLC 360 213-9634
13212 Ne 12th Ave Vancouver (98685) **(G-14371)**
Lenox Independent Dealer 509 837-6400
211 Lappin Ave Sunnyside (98944) **(G-13132)**
Lenroc Co 509 754-5266
16051 Railroad Ave Ephrata (98823) **(G-3341)**
Lenswork Publishing 360 588-1343
1101 8th St Ste C Anacortes (98221) **(G-140)**
Leo Roux LLC 512 565-3406
9016 38th Ave Sw Seattle (98126) **(G-10403)**
Leo Welding Fabrication 425 379-5836
9502 36th Ave Se Everett (98208) **(G-3536)**
Leon Green Co Fine Woodworking 425 822-8210
11130 117th Pl Ne Kirkland (98033) **(G-5387)**
Leon Wickizer Excavating 253 261-2978
26513 112th St E Buckley (98321) **(G-2061)**
Leonards Metal, Auburn *Also called LMI Aerospace Inc* **(G-489)**
Leonetti Cellar 509 525-1670
1875 Foothills Ln Walla Walla (99362) **(G-14837)**
Leonhards Pickles LLC 509 280-4267
3407 E Marietta Ave Spokane (99217) **(G-12361)**
Leonsdeli Express 360 863-1998
27909 Hwy 410 E Buckley (98321) **(G-2062)**
Leony's Cellars, Cashmere *Also called S&S Industries LLC* **(G-2329)**
Leopona Inc 206 701-7931
3518 Fremont Ave N 400 Seattle (98103) **(G-10404)**
Leos Welding & Gab LLC 425 343-6920
4451 26th Ave W Seattle (98199) **(G-10405)**
Leroy Jewelers, Tacoma *Also called Diamond Store Inc* **(G-13262)**
Les Boulangers Associes Inc 206 241-9343
18842 13th Pl S Seatac (98148) **(G-9288)**
Les Ware Backhoe 425 508-2252
11923 Bollenbaugh Hill Rd Monroe (98272) **(G-6591)**
Leskajan John 253 539-8018
3131 S Lawrence St Tacoma (98409) **(G-13386)**
Lesser, Stephan Woodworking, Seattle *Also called Stephan J Lesser Woodworking* **(G-11192)**
Lets Play Stella LLC 206 365-6249
14045 24th Ave Ne Seattle (98125) **(G-10406)**
Lets Ride LLC 253 225-3630
5114 Point Fosdick Dr Nw Gig Harbor (98335) **(G-4131)**
Letter & Sphere LLC 206 473-7534
2415 Ne 65th St Seattle (98115) **(G-10407)**
Lettering Arts 206 310-6599
10885 Ne 4th St Ste 1400 Bellevue (98004) **(G-982)**
Letterpress Distilling LLC 206 227-4522
85 S Atlantic St Seattle (98134) **(G-10408)**
Lev Design 425 417-2758
1818 Westlake Ave N Ste 1 Seattle (98109) **(G-10409)**
Levanen Inc 360 687-4314
24209 Ne 53rd Ave Battle Ground (98604) **(G-715)**
Levanen Lee John 360 687-7478
1906 Se 25th St Battle Ground (98604) **(G-716)**
Level 10 Fitness Products LLC 503 572-5530
10700 Nw 35th Ave Vancouver (98685) **(G-14372)**
Level 5 Inc 425 260-3440
12430 Wagner Rd Monroe (98272) **(G-6592)**
Level Sky Boatworks 206 789-5655
9718 21st Ave Nw Seattle (98117) **(G-10410)**
Levetec Surface Prep McHy LLC 425 629-8200
20245 Ne Redmond Fall Cty Redmond (98053) **(G-8533)**
Leviathan Games Inc 206 432-9949
524 Ne 96th Pl Seattle (98115) **(G-10411)**
Levington Trane 206 352-2453
3401 W Government Way Seattle (98199) **(G-10412)**
Leviton Manufacturing Co Inc 425 486-2222
2222 222nd St Se Bothell (98021) **(G-1874)**
Lewis and Clark Publishing 253 631-8712
13203 Se 233rd St Kent (98042) **(G-4993)**
Lewis Cnty Work Opportunities 360 748-9921
122 Sears Rd Chehalis (98532) **(G-2509)**
Lewis County Fire Dst No 10, Packwood *Also called County of Lewis* **(G-7542)**
Lewis Publishing Company Inc 360 354-4444
113 6th St Lynden (98264) **(G-6031)**
Lewis-Goetz and Company Inc 206 623-5650
7748 S 200th St Kent (98032) **(G-4994)**
Lexington Publishing Co LLC 425 344-0909
3619 115th Ave Se Snohomish (98290) **(G-11939)**
Lexington Publishing Company 800 774-1170
1614 113th Dr Se Lake Stevens (98258) **(G-5654)**
Lexys Nails & Spa 360 352-5044
111 Tumwater Blvd Se Tumwater (98501) **(G-13883)**
Leyda Computers 425 335-1273
11103 22nd Pl Ne Lake Stevens (98258) **(G-5655)**
Lfr Aerospace 516 330-0633
9735 Ne 138th Pl Kirkland (98034) **(G-5388)**
Lfs Inc 360 734-6825
901 Harris Ave Bellingham (98225) **(G-1408)**
Lfs Inc (HQ) 360 734-3336
851 Coho Way Ste 200 Bellingham (98225) **(G-1409)**
Lfs Sports & Specialty Netting, Bellingham *Also called Lfs Inc* **(G-1408)**
Lg Hausys America Inc 425 251-3698
18290 Olympic Ave S Tukwila (98188) **(G-13765)**
Lg Industries LLC 425 557-7993
60 Nw Gilman Blvd Ste D Issaquah (98027) **(G-4438)**
Lgk Industries Inc 360 299-3140
6646 Ivy St Anacortes (98221) **(G-141)**
Lhc2 Inc 509 723-4517
23326 E 2nd Ave Liberty Lake (99019) **(G-5843)**
Liberty Business Forms Inc 509 536-0515
3230 E Main Ave Spokane (99202) **(G-12362)**
Liberty Casework LLC 253 651-7891
22510 152nd Ave E Graham (98338) **(G-4230)**
Liberty Lake Powersports LLC 509 926-5044
19505 E Broadway Ave Liberty Lake (99016) **(G-5844)**
Liberty Logging Inc 360 423-5454
142 Westminster Dr Kelso (98626) **(G-4535)**
Liberty Orchards Company Inc 509 782-4088
117 Mission Ave Cashmere (98815) **(G-2326)**
Liberty Print Solutions 509 536-0515
3230 E Main Ave Spokane (99202) **(G-12363)**
Liberty Sign Shoppe LLC 425 482-2811
19495 144th Ave Ne B230 Woodinville (98072) **(G-15289)**
Library, Tacoma *Also called Weyerhaeuser Company* **(G-13595)**
Librofm Inc 206 730-2463
4533 Ne 55th St C Seattle (98105) **(G-10413)**
Lid Signs LLC 206 290-7536
8915 27th Ave Ne Seattle (98115) **(G-10414)**
Liedtke Tool and Gage Inc 360 694-9573
3801 Ne 102nd St Vancouver (98686) **(G-14373)**
Life Chronicles 253 508-8876
30918 20th Ave Sw Apt B Federal Way (98023) **(G-3752)**
Life Church Dupont 253 279-1507
1315 Rowan Ct Dupont (98327) **(G-2969)**
Life On Canvas 503 470-9474
4816 O Ct Ne Auburn (98002) **(G-488)**
Life Recovery Solutions Inc 208 771-2161
711 Capitol Way S Ste 204 Olympia (98501) **(G-7323)**
Life Safer 800 328-9890
5883 State Highway 303 Ne # 202 Bremerton (98311) **(G-1973)**
Life Size 3 D Animal Targ 206 432-9147
24803 Se 208th St Maple Valley (98038) **(G-6280)**
Life Spring Press 360 872-8452
207 Michell Ln Ne Orting (98360) **(G-7484)**
Life-Gro Inc 253 682-1669
4302 S Washington St Tacoma (98409) **(G-13387)**
Lifecodex Publishing 206 453-0235
7221 87th Ave Se Mercer Island (98040) **(G-6471)**
Lifeport Inc 360 225-3200
1660 Heritage St Woodland (98674) **(G-15445)**
Lifeport Inc 360 225-6690
1610 Heritage St Woodland (98674) **(G-15446)**
Lifeport LLC (HQ) 360 225-1212
1610 Heritage St Woodland (98674) **(G-15447)**
Lifeport Inc 360 944-9606
12000 Ne 95th St Vancouver (98682) **(G-14374)**
Lifeport Interiors, Woodland *Also called Lifeport Inc* **(G-15446)**

A L P H A B E T I C

Lifesigns Plus 425 330-3710
10024 38th Pl Se Lake Stevens (98258) ***(G-5656)***
Lifesmart Publication 253 851-3169
12913 50th Avenue Ct Nw Gig Harbor (98332) ***(G-4132)***
Lifestyle Granolas Inc 509 768-5126
944 E 42nd Ave Spokane (99203) ***(G-12364)***
Lifetime Pools, Spokane Valley *Also called Melcher Manufacturing Co Inc* ***(G-12787)***
Lift Av LLC 425 242-7339
1533 Ilwaco Ave Ne Renton (98059) ***(G-8843)***
Lift It, Tacoma *Also called Interactive Electronic Systems* ***(G-13349)***
Lift Solutions Inc 360 862-8328
1806 S Lake Stevens Rd Lake Stevens (98258) ***(G-5657)***
Lifter Apps LLC 206 289-0407
6312 Calif Ave Sw Apt 409 Seattle (98136) ***(G-10415)***
Liftex 253 395-4458
19632 70th Ave S Ste 1 Kent (98032) ***(G-4995)***
Light Edge Inc (PA) 360 567-1680
16703 Se Mcgillivray Blvd Vancouver (98683) ***(G-14375)***
Light It Bright Products LLC 253 666-2278
7211 S Sheridan Ave Tacoma (98408) ***(G-13388)***
Lightbank Studio 206 409-0939
2200 N Pacific St Seattle (98103) ***(G-10416)***
Lightel Technologies Inc 425 277-8000
2210 Lind Ave Sw Ste 100 Renton (98057) ***(G-8844)***
Lighthouse Candles 360 671-2598
2114 King St Bellingham (98225) ***(G-1410)***
Lighthouse Envmtl Programs 360 579-4489
1280 Engle Rd Coupeville (98239) ***(G-2814)***
Lighthouse For The Blind Inc (PA) 206 322-4200
2501 S Plum St Seattle (98144) ***(G-10417)***
Lighthouse International Ltd 509 466-2502
423 E Cleveland Ave Ste A Spokane (99207) ***(G-12365)***
Lighthouse Roasters Inc 206 633-4775
400 N 43rd St Seattle (98103) ***(G-10418)***
Lighting Group Northwest Inc 206 298-9000
5700 6th Ave S Ste 215 Seattle (98108) ***(G-10419)***
Lighting Ridge Investments, Port Angeles *Also called Olympic Cellars LLC* ***(G-7728)***
Lightloom 206 228-5001
19034 12th Ave Ne Shoreline (98155) ***(G-11782)***
Lightmark Press 206 463-0831
20729 87th Ave Sw Vashon (98070) ***(G-14730)***
Lightning Nuggets Inc 509 725-6211
604 Logan St Davenport (99122) ***(G-2873)***
Lightshine Software LLC 425 231-9320
22305 230th St Se Monroe (98272) ***(G-6593)***
Lightsmith Consulting LLC 312 953-1193
10100 4th Ave Nw Seattle (98177) ***(G-10420)***
Lightsnplastics, Tukwila *Also called Lnp LLC* ***(G-13767)***
Lightspeed Design Inc 425 637-2818
1611 116th Ave Ne Ste 112 Bellevue (98004) ***(G-983)***
Likebright Inc 206 669-2536
122 Nw 36th St Seattle (98107) ***(G-10421)***
Lil Squirtz 360 521-9598
303 Ne 135th St Vancouver (98685) ***(G-14376)***
Lilibete LLC 206 407-6890
23044 148th Ave Se Ste 10 Kent (98042) ***(G-4996)***
Lill Creates 206 355-4409
6234 33rd Ave Ne Seattle (98115) ***(G-10422)***
Lilly Tin 509 888-8101
229 E Woodin Ave Chelan (98816) ***(G-2559)***
Limbsaver, Shelton *Also called Sims Vibration Laboratory Inc* ***(G-11735)***
Lime Solutions 425 502-7651
11322 Se 60th St Bellevue (98006) ***(G-984)***
Limelyte Technology Group Inc 509 241-0138
28 W 3rd Ave Ste 100 Spokane (99201) ***(G-12366)***
Limited Productions Inc 425 635-7489
13404 Se 32nd St Bellevue (98005) ***(G-985)***
Linare Corp 425 748-5099
2018 156th Ave Ne Bellevue (98007) ***(G-986)***
Linc Technology Corporation 425 882-2206
1125 12th Ave Nw Ste B2 Issaquah (98027) ***(G-4439)***
Lincoln Advertiser 509 725-8007
701 12th St Davenport (99122) ***(G-2874)***
Lincoln Advertiser The, Davenport *Also called Lincoln Advertiser* ***(G-2874)***
Lincoln Data Inc 509 466-1744
10103 N Div St Ste 101 Spokane (99218) ***(G-12367)***
Lincoln Electric Company 360 693-4712
705 Se Victory Ave # 220 Vancouver (98661) ***(G-14377)***
Lincoln Industrial Corp Inc 360 681-0584
81 Hooker Rd Unit 9 Sequim (98382) ***(G-11646)***
Lincoln Sand & Gravel 509 725-4531
35031 Indian Creek Rd N Davenport (99122) ***(G-2875)***
Linda J Mohr (PA) 509 946-0941
1440 Agnes St Richland (99352) ***(G-9022)***
Lindal Building Products, Seattle *Also called Lindal Cedar Homes Inc* ***(G-10423)***
Lindal Cedar Homes Inc (PA) 206 725-0900
4300 S 104th Pl Seattle (98178) ***(G-10423)***
Linde North America Inc 360 834-9519
5509 Nw Parker St Camas (98607) ***(G-2264)***
Linden Vic B & Sons Sign Advg 509 624-0663
122 S Lincoln St Spokane (99201) ***(G-12368)***
Lindmark Machine Works Inc 206 624-0777
3626 E Marginal Way S Seattle (98134) ***(G-10424)***
Line X Custom Bed Liners, Lynnwood *Also called Ted Gay* ***(G-6209)***
Line-X of Olympia, Tumwater *Also called Linex of Olympia* ***(G-13884)***
Line-X Silverdale Inc 360 692-4840
9623 Provost Rd Nw # 101 Silverdale (98383) ***(G-11844)***
Linear Controls Inc 425 876-9742
9461 53rd Ave W Mukilteo (98275) ***(G-6949)***
Linear Technology Corporation 360 834-1900
4200 Nw Pacific Rim Blvd Camas (98607) ***(G-2265)***
Linedata Capital Stream, Seattle *Also called Linedata Services* ***(G-10425)***
Linedata Services 206 545-9522
501 N 34th St Ste 301 Seattle (98103) ***(G-10425)***
Linetica, Seattle *Also called Opi Wind Technologies Inc* ***(G-10706)***
Linex of Olympia 360 709-0363
5403 Capitol Blvd Sw Tumwater (98501) ***(G-13884)***
Linguistic Analysis, Vashon *Also called Delta Production* ***(G-14721)***
Links Business Group LLC 425 961-0565
700 Nw Gilman Blvd Issaquah (98027) ***(G-4440)***
Linn's Door Service, Spokane *Also called Linns Service & Remodel Inc* ***(G-12369)***
Linns Service & Remodel Inc 509 448-2540
9810 S Grove Rd Spokane (99224) ***(G-12369)***
Lionfort Software Inc 425 698-7403
18570 Ne 58th Ct K1081 Redmond (98052) ***(G-8534)***
Lionheart Industries LLC 888 552-4743
14138 204th Ave Se Renton (98059) ***(G-8845)***
Lipstick Mission 360 455-3212
9510 Bentley Ct Ne Lacey (98516) ***(G-5565)***
Liquid Brands Distillery LLC 509 413-1885
714 N Lee St Spokane (99202) ***(G-12370)***
Liquid Industry LLC 206 718-3360
19311 Se 416th St Enumclaw (98022) ***(G-3300)***
Lisa Appel 360 521-5472
20113 Ne 80th Way Vancouver (98682) ***(G-14378)***
Lister Chain and Forge Inc 360 332-4323
3810 Loomis Trail Rd Blaine (98230) ***(G-1680)***
Lite-Check LLC 509 535-7512
301 N Havana St Spokane (99202) ***(G-12371)***
Lite-Check Fleet Solutions Inc 509 535-7512
301 N Havana St Spokane (99202) ***(G-12372)***
Liteair Aviation Products Inc 360 299-6679
7001 Palm Ln Anacortes (98221) ***(G-142)***
Literacy Unlmited Publications, Medina *Also called Lundquist Joegil* ***(G-6451)***
Literary Fatale 425 239-2126
4627 192nd St Sw Lynnwood (98036) ***(G-6158)***
Literaryroad Com 206 909-1672
6523 California Ave Sw Seattle (98136) ***(G-10426)***
Litfuse Publicity Group 206 947-3743
1311 12th Ave S Apt C102 Seattle (98144) ***(G-10427)***
Lithia Chrysler Jeep Dodge Ram, Spokane *Also called Lithia Motors Inc* ***(G-12373)***
Lithia Motors Inc 509 321-7300
10701 N Newport Hwy Spokane (99218) ***(G-12373)***
Litho Design Inc 206 574-3000
370 Upland Dr Tukwila (98188) ***(G-13766)***
Litho Inc 206 632-0211
348 Nw 54th St Seattle (98107) ***(G-10428)***
Litho-Craft Inc 253 872-9161
7820 S 228th St Kent (98032) ***(G-4997)***
Lithograph Reproduction Inc 509 926-9526
17323 E Trent Ave Spokane Valley (99216) ***(G-12774)***
Lithos Craftsmen Inc 206 949-9787
16417 210th Ave Ne Woodinville (98077) ***(G-15290)***
Lithtex Northwest LLC 360 424-5945
2226 Market St Mount Vernon (98273) ***(G-6807)***
Lithtex Northwest LLC (PA) 360 676-1977
2000 Kentucky St Bellingham (98229) ***(G-1411)***
Little Bay Inc 646 300-3694
2701 Eastlake Ave E 3 Seattle (98102) ***(G-10429)***
Little Bean Coffee LLC 425 829-8289
11924 158th Ave Ne Redmond (98052) ***(G-8535)***
Little Buddies Shanties 360 387-0678
958 Haven Pl Camano Island (98282) ***(G-2216)***
Little Creek Rock Quarry, Shelton *Also called Arris Kollman Trucking Inc* ***(G-11679)***
Little Hoquiam Shipyard, Hoquiam *Also called Moe Howard Enterprises Inc* ***(G-4349)***
Little Indian Embroidery 360 414-4165
527 Coal Creek Rd Longview (98632) ***(G-5927)***
Little Mexico Ornamental Iron 425 334-1082
3509 139th Ave Ne Lake Stevens (98258) ***(G-5658)***
Little Nickel Classifieds, Federal Way *Also called Sound Publishing Inc* ***(G-3786)***
Little Nickel Classifieds, Lacey *Also called Sound Publishing Inc* ***(G-5590)***
Little Nickel-Bremerton 360 308-0279
3888 Nw Randall Way Silverdale (98383) ***(G-11845)***
Little Nut Inc 360 327-3394
11 Magnolia Rd Beaver (98305) ***(G-758)***
Little Picture Press 206 542-7808
619 Nw 195th St Shoreline (98177) ***(G-11783)***
Little River Inc 360 532-7490
92 Us Highway 101 Hoquiam (98550) ***(G-4347)***
Little Skookum Lumber, Shelton *Also called Alta Forest Products LLC* ***(G-11676)***
Little Soap Maker 509 972-8504
302 W Yakima Ave Ste 103 Yakima (98902) ***(G-15611)***

Little Sun Software LLC 425 442-4911
15920 147th Pl Ne Woodinville (98072) ***(G-15291)***
Live Music Project 206 329-8125
2019 Fairview Ave E Seattle (98102) ***(G-10430)***
Live Sound & Recording Co LLC 425 308-2868
9815 31st Ave Se Everett (98208) ***(G-3537)***
Living Free 360 446-3032
13144 Horizon Pionr Rd Se Rainier (98576) ***(G-8317)***
Living Free Press, Rainier *Also called Living Free* ***(G-8317)***
Living From Vision, Camano Island *Also called Allied Forces Inc* ***(G-2206)***
Living Snoqualmie LLC 425 396-7304
8816 Venn Ave Se Snoqualmie (98065) ***(G-12016)***
Living Stone Industries Inc 425 679-6278
22812 90th Ave W Edmonds (98026) ***(G-3130)***
Living Waters Logging LLC 360 749-6333
921 Hudson St Longview (98632) ***(G-5928)***
Livingston Printing Inc 206 382-1117
504 N 85th St Seattle (98103) ***(G-10431)***
Liz Tran 206 720-7165
940 26th Ave Seattle (98122) ***(G-10432)***
Lizzy and Alex Enterprises LLC 425 698-1439
10700 Ne 4th St Unit 802 Bellevue (98004) ***(G-987)***
Lj Backdoor Inc 206 767-2434
10033 13th Ave Sw Seattle (98146) ***(G-10433)***
Lj Print Group LLC 360 852-0914
8019 Ne 13th Ave Vancouver (98665) ***(G-14379)***
Ljro Inc 360 693-2443
6202 Nrthast Hwy 99 Ste 8 Vancouver (98685) ***(G-14380)***
Ljs Plants & Crafts 253 854-9407
21622 105th Pl Se Kent (98031) ***(G-4998)***
Lk Sewing Co 206 240-9973
15849 6th Ave Sw Burien (98166) ***(G-2118)***
Lka Gold Incorporated (PA) 253 514-6661
3724 47th Street Ct Nw Gig Harbor (98335) ***(G-4133)***
Lkd Aerospace LLC 425 396-0829
8022 Bracken Pl Se Snoqualmie (98065) ***(G-12017)***
Lkq Bellingham, Bellingham *Also called Lkq Corporation* ***(G-1412)***
Lkq Corporation 800 733-1916
2020 E Bakerview Rd Bellingham (98226) ***(G-1412)***
Ll3 LLC 509 332-2109
801 Rose Creek Rd Pullman (99163) ***(G-8097)***
LLC Putnam Brothers 509 679-4981
16995 Frenchman Hills Rd Quincy (98848) ***(G-8302)***
Lloyd Enterprises Inc (PA) 253 874-6692
34667 Pacific Hwy S Federal Way (98003) ***(G-3753)***
Lloyd Industries LLC 509 468-8691
3808 N Sullivan Rd 25j Spokane Valley (99216) ***(G-12775)***
Lloyd Logging Inc 509 997-2441
1219 Methow Vly E Twisp (98856) ***(G-13912)***
Lloyd Remsberg Logging 509 997-7362
993 Twisp Carlton Rd Twisp (98856) ***(G-13913)***
LLP Enterprises LLC 509 423-7580
4300 State Highway 97a Wenatchee (98801) ***(G-15044)***
LMI Aerospace Inc 425 293-0340
1910 Merrill Crekk Pkwy Everett (98203) ***(G-3538)***
LMI Aerospace Inc 253 288-9379
101 Western Ave Auburn (98001) ***(G-489)***
Lmp, Seattle *Also called Live Music Project* ***(G-10430)***
Lnp LLC 206 467-4556
1059 Andover Park E Tukwila (98188) ***(G-13767)***
Load Control Systems Inc 253 284-0351
2407 N 31st St Tacoma (98407) ***(G-13389)***
Loading Docks Supply LLC 360 866-7063
5405 Keating Rd Nw Olympia (98502) ***(G-7324)***
Loan Goat Woodworks 360 395-8996
929 Beachley Rd Sedro Woolley (98284) ***(G-11550)***
Local Church Publishing 360 710-8751
1127 Poindexter Ave Bremerton (98312) ***(G-1974)***
Local Manufacturing Inc 360 533-0190
2421 Port Industrial Rd Aberdeen (98520) ***(G-20)***
Locati Cellars LLC 509 529-5871
6 W Rose St Ste 102 Walla Walla (99362) ***(G-14838)***
Locke Precision LLC 253 904-8615
14119 Pioneer Way E Ste B Puyallup (98372) ***(G-8178)***
Lockheed Martin Aculight Corp 425 482-1100
22121 20th Ave Se Bothell (98021) ***(G-1875)***
Lockheed Martin Corporation 360 779-4682
40 Trailers Poulsbo (98370) ***(G-7976)***
Lockheed Martin Corporation 360 779-4682
40 Trailers Poulsbo (98370) ***(G-7977)***
Lockheed Martin Corporation 425 482-1100
22121 20th Ave Se Bothell (98021) ***(G-1876)***
Lockheed Martin Corporation 360 396-8591
Naval Base Ktsap Bangor Silverdale (98315) ***(G-11846)***
Lockheed Martin Corporation 360 697-6844
Bangor Nsb Bldg 2000 Silverdale (98315) ***(G-11847)***
Locknane Inc 425 493-8300
11417 Cyrus Way Ste 3 Mukilteo (98275) ***(G-6950)***
Loder Instrument Company Inc 425 869-3861
15143 Ne 90th St Redmond (98052) ***(G-8536)***
Lodestone Construction Inc 360 875-6960
99 Trask Rd South Bend (98586) ***(G-12043)***
Lodestone Quarry Incorparated 360 942-0400
99 Trask Rd South Bend (98586) ***(G-12044)***
Lodi Water Co, Chewelah *Also called Connelly Company Inc* ***(G-2601)***
Loewen Group LLC 425 775-9709
2921 Alderwood Mall Blvd # 104 Lynnwood (98036) ***(G-6159)***
Lof Service Center, Everett *Also called Pilkington North America Inc* ***(G-3573)***
Log Cabin Crafts 425 885-9049
9114 171st Ave Ne Redmond (98052) ***(G-8537)***
Log Max Inc 360 699-7300
1114 W Fourth Plain Blvd Vancouver (98660) ***(G-14381)***
Log Processors Inc 509 773-3043
2020 Glenwood Hwy Goldendale (98620) ***(G-4202)***
Logan Industries Inc 509 462-7400
3808 N Sull Rd Spok Indu Spokane Valley (99216) ***(G-12776)***
Loggers World Publications 360 262-3376
4206 Jackson Hwy Chehalis (98532) ***(G-2510)***
Logitech Inc 360 817-1200
4700 Nw Camas Meadows Dr Camas (98607) ***(G-2266)***
Logix, Kirkland *Also called Controls Group The Inc* ***(G-5312)***
Logo House 206 890-3051
2507 S Orcas St Seattle (98108) ***(G-10434)***
Logo Loft Inc 360 394-5638
1572 Nw Duesenberg Ct Silverdale (98383) ***(G-11848)***
Logo Unltd 425 896-8412
19628 144th Ave Ne Ste D Woodinville (98072) ***(G-15292)***
Logos Bible Software, Bellingham *Also called Faithlife Corporation* ***(G-1342)***
Logos Church 425 378-0276
14683 Ne 16th St Bellevue (98007) ***(G-988)***
Lohr Industries 360 802-4351
27644 Se 401st St Enumclaw (98022) ***(G-3301)***
Loki Aerospace Incorporated 425 361-2353
2827 232nd St Sw Brier (98036) ***(G-2021)***
Loki Systems Inc 800 961-5654
119 N Coml St Ste 190 Bellingham (98225) ***(G-1413)***
Lol/Purina Feed, Bellevue *Also called Purina Animal Nutrition LLC* ***(G-1088)***
Lollipoppassions 206 617-4217
18148 Ne 179th St Woodinville (98072) ***(G-15293)***
Lolo Foods 509 860-8021
1712 Washington St Apt 3 Wenatchee (98801) ***(G-15045)***
Loma Hair Care, Monroe *Also called Innovative Salon Products Inc* ***(G-6580)***
Lomax Industries LLC 206 687-7499
1700 Summit Ave Apt 201 Seattle (98122) ***(G-10435)***
Lone Pine Publishing Inc 253 394-0400
1808 B St Nw Ste 140 Auburn (98001) ***(G-490)***
Lone Ranger LLC 425 355-7474
11512 Airport Rd Ste 1 Everett (98204) ***(G-3539)***
Lone Rock Contracting, Keller *Also called Fred Nanamkin* ***(G-4512)***
Lone Star Northwest, Dupont *Also called Glacier Northwest Inc* ***(G-2964)***
Long Construction LLC 360 202-2664
13760 Seaview Way Anacortes (98221) ***(G-143)***
Long Life Bees Wax Candles, Olympia *Also called Long Life Candles* ***(G-7325)***
Long Life Candles 360 866-1127
810 Oleary St Nw Olympia (98502) ***(G-7325)***
Long Road Winery 206 859-7697
550 Ne Lake Ridge Dr Belfair (98528) ***(G-767)***
Long Septic Services 253 852-0550
2910 Old Hartford Rd Lake Stevens (98258) ***(G-5659)***
Long Shadows Vintners LLC (PA) 509 526-0905
3861 1st Ave S C Seattle (98134) ***(G-10436)***
Longacre Racing Products, Monroe *Also called Afco Performance Group LLC* ***(G-6543)***
Longhorn Barbecue Inc (PA) 509 922-0702
10420 E Montgomery Dr Spokane Valley (99206) ***(G-12777)***
Longhorn Barbecue Prod Ctr 509 922-0702
10420 E Montgomery Dr Spokane Valley (99206) ***(G-12778)***
Longhorn Industries 509 899-5475
705 N Cle Elum St Ellensburg (98926) ***(G-3213)***
Longhorn Production, Spokane Valley *Also called Longhorn Barbecue Prod Ctr* ***(G-12778)***
Longshot Oil LLC 509 455-5924
1011 S Jefferson St Spokane (99204) ***(G-12374)***
Longview Auto Wrecking 360 423-9327
2001 38th Ave Longview (98632) ***(G-5929)***
Longview Fibre Ppr & Packg Inc (HQ) 360 425-1550
300 Fibre Way Longview (98632) ***(G-5930)***
Longview Fibre Ppr & Packg Inc 206 762-7170
5901 E Marginal Way S Seattle (98134) ***(G-10437)***
Longview Fibre Ppr & Packg Inc 509 674-1791
300 S Bullfrog Rd Cle Elum (98922) ***(G-2671)***
Longwell Company 425 289-0160
1215 120th Ave Ne Ste 204 Bellevue (98005) ***(G-989)***
Lonjina Design and Print 206 852-6197
3817 Sw 105th St Seattle (98146) ***(G-10438)***
Lonnie Hansen 253 847-4632
4506 277th Street Ct E Spanaway (98387) ***(G-12060)***
Lonnies Sign Service 509 543-7446
1900 W A St Pasco (99301) ***(G-7601)***
Lonza Inc 360 673-5099
532 Hendrickson Dr Kalama (98625) ***(G-4504)***
Looker & Associates Inc 253 210-5200
5625 189th St E Puyallup (98375) ***(G-8179)***
Looker Industries Inc 360 691-1596
7111 210th Dr Ne Granite Falls (98252) ***(G-4279)***

ALPHABETIC

Lookout Point Winery ALPHABETIC SECTION

Lookout Point Winery ... 509 469-4320
16 N 2nd St Yakima (98901) ***(G-15612)***
Loomis Plastics Corporation ... 206 292-0111
3931 1st Ave S Seattle (98134) ***(G-10439)***
Loop Corp ... 206 499-0679
568 1st Ave S Seattle (98104) ***(G-10440)***
Loop Devices Inc ... 206 965-9828
113 Cherry St Ste 70880 Seattle (98104) ***(G-10441)***
Lopez Island Chamber Commerce ... 360 468-4664
532 Point Lawrence Rd Olga (98279) ***(G-7215)***
Lopez Redi Mix Inc ... 360 468-2485
2969 Fisherman Bay Rd Lopez Island (98261) ***(G-5985)***
Lopi, Mukilteo *Also called Travis Industries Inc* ***(G-6983)***
Loqu8 Inc ... 650 892-8901
1200 Harris Ave Ste 413 Bellingham (98225) ***(G-1414)***
Lorache Cad/It Services LLC ... 206 328-4227
11707 87th Ave S Aofc Seattle (98178) ***(G-10442)***
Loreen Home Servicing ... 509 325-4290
3508 W Walton Ave Spokane (99205) ***(G-12375)***
Lorelei II Inc ... 206 783-6045
2944 Nw Esplanade Seattle (98117) ***(G-10443)***
Lorenz Welding ... 360 384-5258
2248 Aldergrove Rd Ferndale (98248) ***(G-3865)***
Lori Shine (PA) ... 360 400-6006
305 1st St S Unit A Yelm (98597) ***(G-15738)***
Lorrand Marketing LLC ... 360 532-7510
2301 Simpson Ave Aberdeen (98520) ***(G-21)***
Lorric Logging, Granite Falls *Also called Rick Carlson* ***(G-4285)***
Lortone Inc ... 425 493-1600
12130 Cyrus Way Mukilteo (98275) ***(G-6951)***
Lorz & Lorz Inc ... 509 486-2202
32158 Highway 97 Tonasket (98855) ***(G-13653)***
Lost City Digital LLC ... 206 327-4537
26016 11th Pl S Des Moines (98198) ***(G-2940)***
Lost Creek Logging ... 509 442-3218
396875 Highway 20 Cusick (99119) ***(G-2850)***
Lost River Winery LLC (PA) ... 509 996-2888
699 Lost River Rd Mazama (98833) ***(G-6414)***
Lost Signal LLC ... 360 601-2227
510 N 6th Ave Sw Tumwater (98512) ***(G-13885)***
Lostacos Locos ... 360 573-1327
1309 Ne 134th St Vancouver (98685) ***(G-14382)***
Loth Industries Inc ... 425 418-5897
6620 E Lowell Larimer Rd Snohomish (98296) ***(G-11940)***
Lou Hinkley ... 360 312-3604
7060 Portal Way Ste 120 Ferndale (98248) ***(G-3866)***
Loud Audio LLC (PA) ... 425 892-6500
16220 Wood Red Rd Ne Woodinville (98072) ***(G-15294)***
Loudin Logging LLC ... 253 691-8679
8807 321st Street Ct E Eatonville (98328) ***(G-3061)***
Loudscoop Inc ... 425 391-7159
4018 173rd Ct Ne Redmond (98052) ***(G-8538)***
Louis Stoffer & Son ... 360 736-3820
1410 Harrison Ave Centralia (98531) ***(G-2418)***
Louisiana-Pacific Corporation ... 503 821-5001
16701 Se Mcgillivray Blvd # 200 Vancouver (98683) ***(G-14383)***
Louisville Ladder ... 206 762-4888
920 S Doris St Seattle (98108) ***(G-10444)***
Lous Welding & Fabricating ... 425 483-0300
8333 219th St Se Ste A Woodinville (98072) ***(G-15295)***
Louws Truss Inc ... 360 384-9000
1010 S Spruce St Burlington (98233) ***(G-2169)***
Love Noodle Inc ... 425 513-8888
7815 Evergreen Way Ste 2 Everett (98203) ***(G-3540)***
Love That Red Winery ... 425 463-9014
144th Ave Ne Ste D-100 Woodinville (98072) ***(G-15296)***
Loving Superfoods LLC ... 214 717-3321
14015 Ne 53rd St Vancouver (98682) ***(G-14384)***
Lovitt Mining Company Inc ... 509 668-8170
2698 S Methow St Wenatchee (98801) ***(G-15046)***
Lovitt Orchards, Wenatchee *Also called Lovitt Mining Company Inc* ***(G-15046)***
Lovitt Resources Inc ... 509 668-8170
2698 S Methow St Wenatchee (98801) ***(G-15047)***
Lovrics Sea Craft Inc ... 360 293-2042
3022 Oakes Ave Anacortes (98221) ***(G-144)***
Low Orbit Publications ... 425 398-0598
5605 Ne 184th St Kenmore (98028) ***(G-4590)***
Lowden Schoolhouse Corporation ... 509 525-0940
41 Lowden School Rd Walla Walla (99362) ***(G-14839)***
Lowden Schoolhouse Corporation ... 509 525-0940
41 Lowden School Rd Lowden (99360) ***(G-5990)***
Lower Valley Machine Shop ... 509 882-3881
104 W 5th St Grandview (98930) ***(G-4251)***
Lowridge On Site Tech LLC ... 877 476-8823
1925 N Machias Rd Lake Stevens (98258) ***(G-5660)***
LP Composites Inc ... 509 493-4447
314 W Steuben St Bingen (98605) ***(G-1639)***
Lpr Park LLC ... 888 884-9507
1601 5th Ave Ste 1100 Seattle (98101) ***(G-10445)***
Lr Woodworking ... 281 813-1169
5686 Ne Minder Rd Ste 101 Poulsbo (98370) ***(G-7978)***
Lrt Inc (PA) ... 425 742-0333
15712 Mill Creek Blvd # 1 Mill Creek (98012) ***(G-6516)***
Ls Brewing Inc ... 425 423-7700
715 100th St Se Ste A1 Everett (98208) ***(G-3541)***
LSI Logistic Svc Solutions LLC ... 253 872-8970
4326 86th Ave E Puyallup (98371) ***(G-8180)***
Lt Racing ... 360 871-2259
6487 Knight Dr Se Port Orchard (98367) ***(G-7826)***
Ltc, Redmond *Also called Laser Techniques Company LLC* ***(G-8530)***
Lth Farm Corp ... 509 636-2673
23526 S Rd 2 E Creston (99117) ***(G-2842)***
Ltsi, Wenatchee *Also called Lectro Tek Services Inc* ***(G-15043)***
Luann Ayling ... 509 633-2839
37 W Coulee Blvd Electric City (99123) ***(G-3167)***
Luans Leathers ... 360 546-5050
4600 Ne 99th St Vancouver (98665) ***(G-14385)***
Lucid Technologies, Mountlake Terrace *Also called Symetrix Inc* ***(G-6871)***
Luckiest Letterpress ... 425 241-8229
15031 93rd Pl Ne Bothell (98011) ***(G-1774)***
Lucks Company (PA) ... 253 383-4815
3003 S Pine St Tacoma (98409) ***(G-13390)***
Lucks Company ... 253 383-4815
3003 S Pine St Tacoma (98409) ***(G-13391)***
Lucks Food Decorating Company, Tacoma *Also called Lucks Company* ***(G-13390)***
Lucky Break Wishbone Corp ... 206 933-8700
4400 Sw Roxbury Pl Seattle (98136) ***(G-10446)***
Lucky Buck, Seattle *Also called Signature Seafoods Inc* ***(G-11108)***
Lucky Dog Eqp Inc DBA Pet Pros (PA) ... 425 402-8833
19400 144th Ave Ne Ste E Woodinville (98072) ***(G-15297)***
Lucky Dog Woodworking ... 507 218-6767
421 Cameron Lake Loop Rd Okanogan (98840) ***(G-7199)***
Lucky Dumpster ... 360 766-4049
14011 Mactaggart Ave Bow (98232) ***(G-1930)***
Lucky Ice Cream Company, Pasco *Also called Megan Nieforth* ***(G-7602)***
Lucky Leaders ... 206 363-2208
12039 Palatine Ave N Seattle (98133) ***(G-10447)***
Lucky Scooter Parts LLC ... 425 558-0715
6855 176th Ave Ne B-235 Redmond (98052) ***(G-8539)***
Luckyhorse Industries ... 206 227-3383
18848 Se 42nd St Issaquah (98027) ***(G-4441)***
Ludlow Mortgage Inc ... 360 437-1344
7446 Oak Bay Rd Port Ludlow (98365) ***(G-7770)***
Lues Debeaking ... 360 438-9207
4114 Fir Tree Rd Se Olympia (98501) ***(G-7326)***
Lufkin Industries LLC ... 425 295-7676
1595 Nw Gilman Blvd Ste 7 Issaquah (98027) ***(G-4442)***
Lukens Farms Inc ... 360 366-4151
2347 Birch Bay Lynden Rd Custer (98240) ***(G-2856)***
Lulabop Inc ... 206 225-0049
7920 1/2 Seward Pk Ave S Seattle (98118) ***(G-10448)***
Lularoe Dawn Workman, Yelm *Also called Dawn Workman Lularoe* ***(G-15731)***
Lum, Arthur B Od, Kent *Also called East Hill Optometry* ***(G-4882)***
Luma Technologies LLC ... 425 643-4000
13226 Se 30th St Ste B3 Bellevue (98005) ***(G-990)***
Lumatax Inc ... 206 450-2004
240 2nd Ave S Ste 300 Seattle (98104) ***(G-10449)***
Lumatech, Bellevue *Also called Luma Technologies LLC* ***(G-990)***
Lumber Line Laser Repair ... 360 686-3340
26407 Ne 356th St Yacolt (98675) ***(G-15486)***
Lumberline Laser Inc ... 360 686-3077
12119 Ne 99th St Ste 2040 Vancouver (98682) ***(G-14386)***
Lumbermens Truss ... 509 627-0495
4213 S 47th Ave Richland (99353) ***(G-9023)***
Lumedx Corporation ... 425 450-9774
110 110th Ave Ne Ste 475 Bellevue (98004) ***(G-991)***
Lumenex LLC ... 206 909-3474
317 32nd Ave Seattle (98122) ***(G-10450)***
Lumenomics Inc (PA) ... 206 327-9037
500 Mercer St C2 Seattle (98109) ***(G-10451)***
Lumicor Inc ... 425 255-4000
1400 Monster Rd Sw Ste A Renton (98057) ***(G-8846)***
Lumin Art Signs Inc ... 253 833-2800
4320 S Adams St Ste A Tacoma (98409) ***(G-13392)***
Lumisands Inc ... 206 403-7887
800 Ne 42nd St Apt 303 Seattle (98105) ***(G-10452)***
Lummi Fisheries Supplies, Bellingham *Also called Lfs Inc* ***(G-1409)***
Lummi Island Wild Co-Op L L C ... 360 366-8786
3131 Mercer Ave Ste 105 Bellingham (98225) ***(G-1415)***
Lumotive LLC ... 907 306-6267
10885 Ne 4th St Ste 250 Bellevue (98004) ***(G-992)***
Lumpinee Inc ... 425 497-8383
8900 161st Ave Ne Redmond (98052) ***(G-8540)***
Luna Lactation ... 360 693-7616
5617 Ne 69th St Vancouver (98661) ***(G-14387)***
Lunas Custom Puppets ... 360 721-9672
812 Sw 4th Ave Battle Ground (98604) ***(G-717)***
Lund Custom Machining Inc ... 360 432-0310
110 W Metzler Mill Rd Shelton (98584) ***(G-11709)***
Lundberg LLC ... 425 283-5070
8271 154th Ave Ne 250 Redmond (98052) ***(G-8541)***
Lundberg, A H Inc Engineers, Everett *Also called A H Lundberg Inc* ***(G-3354)***
Lundgren Enterprises ... 206 789-1122
2442 Nw Market St Seattle (98107) ***(G-10453)***

ALPHABETIC SECTION

Lundquist Joegil 425 454-5830
8621 Ne 6th St Medina (98039) *(G-6451)*

Lupine Vineyards LLC 206 915-5862
18020 67th Ave W Lynnwood (98037) *(G-6160)*

Lupitas 253 838-6132
2124 Sw 336th St Federal Way (98023) *(G-3754)*

Luvo Usa Llc 604 730-0387
250 H St Blaine (98230) *(G-1681)*

Luxel Corporation 360 378-0064
60 Saltspring Dr Friday Harbor (98250) *(G-4051)*

Lv Logging 360 837-3144
282 Stevens Rd Washougal (98671) *(G-14964)*

Lx Packaging & Printing Svc 206 714-5479
9108 35th Ave Ne Seattle (98115) *(G-10454)*

Lydens Specialty Machine Llc 360 345-1010
161 Hamilton Rd N Chehalis (98532) *(G-2511)*

Lyell Immunopharma Inc 206 909-3809
500 Fairview Ave N # 200 Seattle (98109) *(G-10455)*

Lyle Style, White Salmon *Also called Sharon McIlhenny (G-15131)*

Lyle W Pulling 360 825-6129
1805 Lafromboise St Enumclaw (98022) *(G-3302)*

Lyn-Tron Inc 509 456-4545
6001 S Thomas Mallen Rd Spokane (99224) *(G-12376)*

Lynch Brothers Construction, Woodland *Also called Richard & Mike Lynch (G-15463)*

Lynch Creek Quarry LLC 360 832-4269
14115 419th St E Eatonville (98328) *(G-3062)*

Lynch Creek Quarry LLC (PA) 360 832-4269
19209 Canyon Rd E Puyallup (98375) *(G-8181)*

Lynch Distributing Co 509 248-0880
5205 Richey Rd Yakima (98908) *(G-15613)*

Lynden Door, Lynden *Also called JD Bargen Industries LLC (G-6026)*

Lynden Door Inc (PA) 360 354-5676
2077 Main St Lynden (98264) *(G-6032)*

Lynden Liquor Agency 570 .... 360 354-4744
610 Front St Lynden (98264) *(G-6033)*

Lynden Meat Company LLC 360 354-5227
1936 Front St Lynden (98264) *(G-6034)*

Lynden Precast LLC 360 354-8901
8987 Jasmine Ln Lynden (98264) *(G-6035)*

Lynden Tribune Print and Pubg, Lynden *Also called Lewis Publishing Company Inc (G-6031)*

Lynn L Reynolds Inc 509 536-9396
5405 E Cataldo Ave Spokane Valley (99212) *(G-12779)*

Lynns Forklift Service 206 979-4272
305 158th Pl Se Bellevue (98008) *(G-993)*

Lynnsville Press Patterns 360 573-1396
4214 Ne 136th Cir Vancouver (98686) *(G-14388)*

M & I Systems Inc 206 547-7899
2936 Colby Ave Everett (98201) *(G-3542)*

M & L Machine Inc (PA) 360 825-4700
355 Rainier Ave Enumclaw (98022) *(G-3303)*

M & M Coatings Inc 360 480-6425
8618 Glenlea Ct Se Yelm (98597) *(G-15739)*

M & M Craftworks 360 675-9138
687 Maplewood Loop Oak Harbor (98277) *(G-7157)*

M & M Fabricators Inc 509 248-8890
2004 S 14th St Union Gap (98903) *(G-13939)*

M & M Logging 360 280-5973
828 Mox Chehalis Rd McCleary (98557) *(G-6418)*

M & M Manufacturing Inc 360 896-2822
2208 Laframbois Rd Vancouver (98660) *(G-14389)*

M 1 Tanks Inc 509 766-2914
13058 N Frontage Rd E Moses Lake (98837) *(G-6722)*

M A C I Inc 360 424-7013
2525 Old Highway 99 S Rd Mount Vernon (98273) *(G-6808)*

M and J Distribution 360 455-4675
5847 Braywood Ln Se Olympia (98513) *(G-7327)*

M and M Cabinets 253 503-0756
17318 Yakima Ave S Spanaway (98387) *(G-12061)*

M B G Management Services 360 493-0522
3521 Hollywood Dr Ne Olympia (98516) *(G-7328)*

M B Lapidary 253 271-7515
19408 Crescent Dr E Spanaway (98387) *(G-12062)*

M C C Company, Spokane Valley *Also called McC Enterprises Inc (G-12785)*

M C Printing 360 573-7499
11505 Ne 70th Ave Vancouver (98686) *(G-14390)*

M E B Manufacturing 425 259-6074
3410 Everett Ave Everett (98201) *(G-3543)*

M H R A Corp 360 978-6878
156 Moonridge Ln Onalaska (98570) *(G-7451)*

M I S Construction Software 425 882-3027
11319 Ne 120th St Kirkland (98034) *(G-5389)*

M K Hansen Company 509 884-1396
2216 Fancher Blvd East Wenatchee (98802) *(G-3023)*

M L Woodworks 360 264-4859
4009 Offut Lake Rd Se Tenino (98589) *(G-13621)*

M M Enterprises 206 463-1927
17635 Vashon Hwy Sw Vashon (98070) *(G-14731)*

M M I International, Tacoma *Also called Schnitzer Steel International (G-13508)*

M R K Electric 360 253-8310
14000 Ne 195th Ave Brush Prairie (98606) *(G-2037)*

M S I Commerce, Bonney Lake *Also called Miracle Studios (G-1729)*

M S I Engineering Corporation 425 827-6797
603 5th Pl S Kirkland (98033) *(G-5390)*

M Squared Manufacturing LLC 206 380-0233
16622 86th Pl Sw Vashon (98070) *(G-14732)*

M&E Memorial Markers Inc 509 662-6469
920 N Chelan Ave Wenatchee (98801) *(G-15048)*

M&L Industries Inc 425 894-7147
4401 268th Ave Ne Redmond (98053) *(G-8542)*

M&L Research Inc 877 321-8766
4701 Sw Admiral Way Ste 4 Seattle (98116) *(G-10456)*

M&M Grinding, Seattle *Also called J C Ross Co Inc (G-10268)*

M&S Custom Remodeling 425 739-0262
12821 Ne 108th Pl Kirkland (98033) *(G-5391)*

M-K-D Distributors Inc 425 251-0809
18404 72nd Ave S Kent (98032) *(G-4999)*

M-Space Inc 253 779-0101
2727 39th Ave Sw Seattle (98116) *(G-10457)*

M-Tronic Inc 509 484-3572
1620 E Houston Ave # 700 Spokane (99217) *(G-12377)*

M2 Anesthesia PLLC 206 605-5933
20704 Snag Island Dr E Lake Tapps (98391) *(G-5682)*

M2 Innovative Concepts Inc 253 383-5659
3032 S Cedar St Tacoma (98409) *(G-13393)*

M24 Industries LLC 360 348-3578
21030 151st Ave Se Monroe (98272) *(G-6594)*

M3, Seattle *Also called Messenger Corporation (G-10518)*

M3 Machine Inc 360 778-1427
4290 Pacific Hwy Bellingham (98226) *(G-1416)*

M7m Investments 253 922-2030
1010 54th Ave E Fife (98424) *(G-3967)*

MA & Kt Inc 360 321-4019
5586 Double Bluff Rd Freeland (98249) *(G-4032)*

MA Assoc 206 719-1363
15519 65th Pl Ne Bothell (98028) *(G-1775)*

Maas Publications LLC 425 445-7845
23419 Se 250th Pl Maple Valley (98038) *(G-6281)*

Maax Hydro Swirl Mfg Co 360 734-0616
2150 Division St Bellingham (98226) *(G-1417)*

Mabo Publishers 425 746-9934
16053 Ne 8th St Apt 303 Bellevue (98008) *(G-994)*

Mac & Jacks Brewery Inc 425 558-9697
17825 Ne 65th St Redmond (98052) *(G-8543)*

Mac & Mac Electric Company 360 734-6530
1410 Iowa St Bellingham (98229) *(G-1418)*

Mac Arthur Co 253 863-8830
4504 East Valley Hwy E Sumner (98390) *(G-13080)*

Mac Arthur Land & Timber 509 442-3805
398892 Highway 20 Cusick (99119) *(G-2851)*

Mac Chain Company Limited 800 663-0072
1855 Schurman Way Woodland (98674) *(G-15448)*

Mac Flynn, Riverside *Also called Crescent Moon Studios Inc (G-9124)*

Mac Plaque Awards, Kirkland *Also called Don Macintosh (G-5322)*

Mac Sales Industries, Woodland *Also called Mac Chain Company Limited (G-15448)*

Mac's Metal, Spokane *Also called Gerald McCallum (G-12273)*

Macarthur Logging 509 675-8045
39510 N Madison Rd Elk (99009) *(G-3172)*

Macaw Rescue and Santuary 425 788-4721
34032 Ne Lake Joy Rd Carnation (98014) *(G-2295)*

Macgregor Publishing Co 800 581-5040
1100 Roosevelt Ave Ste B Mount Vernon (98273) *(G-6809)*

Mach 2 Arts Inc 206 953-0575
914 Nw 50th St Seattle (98107) *(G-10458)*

Mach Publishing Company Inc 425 258-9396
127 Avenue C Ste B Snohomish (98290) *(G-11941)*

Mach Transonic LLC 206 853-6909
5520 31st Ave Ne Seattle (98105) *(G-10459)*

Machine & Fabrication Inds, Kent *Also called Batech LLC (G-4810)*

Machine Development Company 360 479-4484
3360 Old Sawmill Pl Nw Bremerton (98312) *(G-1975)*

Machine Repair & Design Inc 253 826-6329
1710 Fryar Ave Ste 102 Sumner (98390) *(G-13081)*

Machine Technology 425 334-1951
17111 Newberg Rd Snohomish (98290) *(G-11942)*

Machine Works Inc 253 750-0238
13701 24th St E Unit D8 Sumner (98390) *(G-13082)*

Machining Technology Inc 253 872-0359
4340 B St Nw Auburn (98001) *(G-491)*

Machinists Inc (PA) 206 763-0990
7600 5th Ave S Seattle (98108) *(G-10460)*

Machinists Inc 206 763-0840
509 S Austin St Seattle (98108) *(G-10461)*

Machinists Inc 206 763-1036
8201 7th Ave S Seattle (98108) *(G-10462)*

Machstem Inc 801 259-3305
12611 W Greenfield Rd Nine Mile Falls (99026) *(G-7078)*

Machstem International, Nine Mile Falls *Also called Machstem Inc (G-7078)*

Mackay Manufacturing Inc 509 922-7742
10011 E Montgomery Dr Spokane Valley (99206) *(G-12780)*

Mackenzie Spcalty Castings Inc 360 435-5539
19430 63rd Ave Ne Arlington (98223) *(G-271)*

Mackichan Software Inc (PA) 360 394-6033
19689 7th Ave Ne 183238 Poulsbo (98370) *(G-7979)*

Mackie Designs Inc 425 868-0555
25121 Ne 67th Pl Redmond (98053) ***(G-8544)***
Macklin Welding 509 926-3597
15722 E Sprague Ave Spokane Valley (99037) ***(G-12781)***
Macks Lures Manufacturing Co 509 667-9202
55 Lure Ln Wenatchee (98801) ***(G-15049)***
Macmillan & Company 360 249-1148
511 N Main St Montesano (98563) ***(G-6645)***
Macmillan and Company 360 470-1535
33 Sylvia Ridge Ln Montesano (98563) ***(G-6646)***
Macro Mfg LLC 360 750-3544
2525 W Firestone Ln Vancouver (98660) ***(G-14391)***
Macro Plastics Inc 509 452-1200
3555 Bay St Union Gap (98903) ***(G-13940)***
Macs Discus 425 483-3729
20103 174th Ave Ne Woodinville (98072) ***(G-15298)***
Mad Ape 206 201-3275
9720 Coppertop Loop Ne # 203 Bainbridge Island (98110) ***(G-649)***
Mad Cat Salsa 360 647-0456
1 Granite Cir Bellingham (98229) ***(G-1419)***
Mad Concrete Cutting & Coring 206 367-0263
4320196st Sw B Pmb 1424 Lynnwood (98036) ***(G-6161)***
Mad Custom Coating, Bremerton *Also called Mad Label Industries Inc* ***(G-1976)***
Mad Custom Coating 360 621-6525
22239 Big Valley Rd Ne Poulsbo (98370) ***(G-7980)***
Mad Fiber 206 402-3925
1604 N 34th St Seattle (98103) ***(G-10463)***
Mad Label Industries Inc 844 623-4897
5800 W Werner Rd Ste A Bremerton (98312) ***(G-1976)***
Madboy Industries 206 707-9394
902 1st Ave S Seattle (98134) ***(G-10464)***
Maddox Industrial Trans LLC 360 512-3355
1500 Se Commerce Ave Battle Ground (98604) ***(G-718)***
Made In Washington, Anacortes *Also called Seabear Company* ***(G-165)***
Madera Components LLC 800 404-8746
17146 Beaton Rd Se Ste 4 Monroe (98272) ***(G-6595)***
Madera Woodworking, Gig Harbor *Also called Frank J Madera* ***(G-4103)***
Madlyn Metal Fab Llc 360 693-1019
2301 Se Hidden Way # 100 Vancouver (98661) ***(G-14392)***
Madretierra Candle Company LLC 786 374-5913
2922 Brian Ln Kennewick (99338) ***(G-4690)***
Madrona Log HM Repr & Care LLC 360 202-2842
5609 71st Ave Ne Marysville (98270) ***(G-6354)***
Madrona Specialty Foods LLC (PA) 206 903-0500
18300 Cascade Ave S # 260 Seattle (98188) ***(G-10465)***
Madrona Stone LLC 253 750-5064
3900 150th Avenue Ct E Sumner (98390) ***(G-13083)***
Madsam Printing LLC 425 445-1949
12700 Ne 124th St Kirkland (98034) ***(G-5392)***
Madsen Family Cellars 360 357-3015
1916 Allegro Dr Se Olympia (98501) ***(G-7329)***
Madsen Family Cellars 360 339-8371
2633 Reinhardt Ln Ne D Olympia (98516) ***(G-7330)***
Maelstrom Interactive 206 841-6071
10501 Ne 114th Ln Kirkland (98033) ***(G-5393)***
Maf Industries Inc 509 574-8775
2705 S 16th Ave Union Gap (98903) ***(G-13941)***
Mag Lite Warranty 360 398-9798
5060 Zander Dr Bellingham (98226) ***(G-1420)***
Maga Talk 1400, Port Orchard *Also called Kitc Radio Inc* ***(G-7823)***
Magaway Fire LLC 253 394-3255
5810 S Cushman Ave Tacoma (98408) ***(G-13394)***
Magazine For Gigging Musicans 425 503-0421
23629 Ne 7th Ct Sammamish (98074) ***(G-9229)***
Magdalena Vineyard LLC 509 942-4204
53222 N Sunset Rd Benton City (99320) ***(G-1619)***
Magellan Groul, Blaine *Also called Magellan Group Ltd* ***(G-1682)***
Magellan Group Ltd 360 332-6868
225 Marine Dr Ste 300 Blaine (98230) ***(G-1682)***
Magic Cleaner, Shoreline *Also called Downtown Cleaners & Tailoring* ***(G-11769)***
Magic Earth 509 738-2801
80 Martin Creek Dr Kettle Falls (99141) ***(G-5236)***
Magic Metals Inc 509 453-1690
3401 Bay St Union Gap (98903) ***(G-13942)***
Magic Mountains Services Inc 360 830-0634
10078 Brush Arbor Ln Nw Seabeck (98380) ***(G-9268)***
Magic Satchel 509 342-8914
916 N Ella Rd Apt 52 Spokane Valley (99212) ***(G-12782)***
Magical Strings 253 857-3716
9052 Se Willock Rd Olalla (98359) ***(G-7208)***
Magicare Services, Mukilteo *Also called Dlm Inc* ***(G-6915)***
Magna Vis Graphic Impressions 509 684-5659
1355 Kegel Way Colville (99114) ***(G-2764)***
Magnadrive Corporation 425 487-2881
14660 Ne North Woodi Way Woodinville (98072) ***(G-15299)***
Magnapro Business Systems Inc 206 280-6222
8515 224th St Sw Edmonds (98026) ***(G-3131)***
Magnet Magazine 206 977-7696
11319 Ne 103rd St Kirkland (98033) ***(G-5394)***
Magnetic Penetrant Svcs Co Inc 206 762-5855
8135 1st Ave S Seattle (98108) ***(G-10466)***
Magnificent Signs Inc 509 468-2794
2311 W 16th Ave Lot 114 Spokane (99224) ***(G-12378)***
Magnix Usa Inc 206 304-8129
6724 185th Ave Ne Redmond (98052) ***(G-8545)***
Magnolia Desktop Computing LLC 206 282-7161
2549 34th Ave W Seattle (98199) ***(G-10467)***
Magnolia Medical Tech Inc 206 673-2500
200 W Mercer St Ste 500 Seattle (98119) ***(G-10468)***
Magnolia Signs 253 592-5121
8218 Pacific Ave Ste 6 Tacoma (98408) ***(G-13395)***
Magnum Opus Software & Co 425 227-7712
8021 128th Ave Se Newcastle (98056) ***(G-7035)***
Magnum Print Solutions, Seattle *Also called Profile Systems Inc* ***(G-10873)***
Magnum Venus Products, Kent *Also called Magnum Venus Products Inc* ***(G-5000)***
Magnum Venus Products Inc 253 854-2660
1862 Ives Ave Kent (98032) ***(G-5000)***
Mahler & Assoc Inc 206 365-3800
3322 Ne 200th Ct Lake Forest Park (98155) ***(G-5620)***
Maid Naturally LLC 509 994-3685
3012 N Nevada St Ste 1 Spokane (99207) ***(G-12379)***
Maika Foods LLC 310 893-7050
304 W Pacific Ave Ste 210 Spokane (99201) ***(G-12380)***
Mail Box & Shipping Center 425 869-1448
8040 161st Ave Ne Redmond (98052) ***(G-8546)***
Mail Box & Shipping Center The, Redmond *Also called Mail Box & Shipping Center* ***(G-8546)***
Mail Box Junction, Marysville *Also called Mailbox Junction* ***(G-6355)***
Mail It Sign It LLC 360 515-5198
4005 Pifer Rd Se Tumwater (98501) ***(G-13886)***
Mail N Beyond 425 379-6111
5714 134th Pl Se Ste A18 Everett (98208) ***(G-3544)***
Mail Well Envelope 206 576-4300
6520 S 190th St Ste 100 Kent (98032) ***(G-5001)***
Mailbox Depot, Arlington *Also called Mailboxes Depot* ***(G-272)***
Mailbox Junction 360 658-2445
1242 State Ave Ste I Marysville (98270) ***(G-6355)***
Mailboxes Depot 360 651-2651
3405 172nd St Ne Ste 5 Arlington (98223) ***(G-272)***
Main Branch, The, Woodinville *Also called Byteware LLC* ***(G-15201)***
Maine Cottage Inc 866 366-3505
15771 Gorge Ln Ne Ste 202 Poulsbo (98370) ***(G-7981)***
Maine Marketing Inc 425 487-9111
13901 Ne 175th St Ste M Woodinville (98072) ***(G-15300)***
Mainland Machinery LLC 360 354-2348
9458 Depot Rd Lynden (98264) ***(G-6036)***
Mainstem Inc 844 623-4084
612 S Lucile St Seattle (98108) ***(G-10469)***
Maintenance Welding Service 360 533-4318
17 Fairfield Acres Rd Hoquiam (98550) ***(G-4348)***
Maison Bleue Winery 509 525-9084
20 N 2nd Ave Walla Walla (99362) ***(G-14840)***
Maizefield Company 360 385-6789
203 Frederick St Port Townsend (98368) ***(G-7896)***
Maizefield Mantels, Port Townsend *Also called Maizefield Company* ***(G-7896)***
Majesco Software Inc 425 242-0327
14420 Ne 35th St Apt I2 Bellevue (98007) ***(G-995)***
Majestic Aerotech Inc 360 528-4142
401 E 25th St Ste H Tacoma (98421) ***(G-13396)***
Majestic Monument & Stone 509 699-8937
214 Hanson Rd Ellensburg (98926) ***(G-3214)***
Majorwire Screen Media 253 327-1550
7110 26th St E Fife (98424) ***(G-3968)***
Makeup Artist Magazine, Vancouver *Also called Key Publishing Group LLC* ***(G-14345)***
Makk Motoring LLC 509 855-2638
10766 Road 9 Ne Moses Lake (98837) ***(G-6723)***
Mako Reels Inc 360 757-7328
11777 Watertank Rd Burlington (98233) ***(G-2170)***
Makota Co 206 226-1843
303 5th Ave S Ste 209 Edmonds (98020) ***(G-3132)***
Mal Inc 360 491-2900
7225 Pacific Ave Se Olympia (98503) ***(G-7331)***
Malcom Drilling 206 623-0776
100 S King St Seattle (98104) ***(G-10470)***
Malone Electronics 360 687-1034
24702 Ne 228th Cir Battle Ground (98604) ***(G-719)***
Malone Industries LLC 360 636-1383
838 Carroll Rd Kelso (98626) ***(G-4536)***
Malone Manufacturing LLC 360 366-9964
3023 W 75th St Custer (98240) ***(G-2857)***
Maltby Agg. & Landfill, Snohomish *Also called Cemex Cnstr Mtls PCF LLC* ***(G-11888)***
Mama Jo's Gourmet Sauce, Redmond *Also called Jud Calvary Inc* ***(G-8524)***
Mamma-Kin LLC 425 922-9505
9009 Ne 117th Pl Kirkland (98034) ***(G-5395)***
Mammoth Media Inc 206 275-3183
7650 Se 27th St Unit 307 Mercer Island (98040) ***(G-6472)***
Man Diesel Interval, Kent *Also called Man Diesel North America Inc* ***(G-5002)***
Man Diesel North America Inc 253 479-6800
6608 S 211th St Ste 101 Kent (98032) ***(G-5002)***
Man Pies 360 201-4294
1215 Railroad Ave Bellingham (98225) ***(G-1421)***
Manastash Logging Inc 206 937-8311
2314 Alki Ave Sw Seattle (98116) ***(G-10471)***

ALPHABETIC SECTION

Manceps Inc 503 922-1164
416 Ne Dallas St Ste 209 Camas (98607) *(G-2267)*
Mango and Lime Design LLC 425 985-8994
9117 151st Ave Ne Redmond (98052) *(G-8547)*
Mango Ink 509 990-9085
4601 E Pineglen Rd Mead (99021) *(G-6431)*
Mangoapps Inc 425 274-9950
1495 11th Ave Nw Issaquah (98027) *(G-4443)*
Manhasset Specialty Co Inc 509 248-3810
3505 Fruitvale Blvd Yakima (98902) *(G-15614)*
Mani Pedi 509 522-6264
17 Boyer Ave Walla Walla (99362) *(G-14841)*
Maninis LLC 206 686-4600
22408 72nd Ave S Kent (98032) *(G-5003)*
Manke Lumber Company Inc (PA) 253 572-6252
1717 Marine View Dr Tacoma (98422) *(G-13397)*
Manke Lumber Company Inc 360 426-5536
826 Fairmont Ave Shelton (98584) *(G-11710)*
Manke Lumber Company Inc 253 863-4495
13702 Stewart Rd Sumner (98390) *(G-13084)*
Manke Timber Company Inc 253 572-9029
1717 Marine View Dr Tacoma (98422) *(G-13398)*
Manns Welding & Trailer Hitch 206 542-7434
16535 Aurora Ave N Shoreline (98133) *(G-11784)*
Manta Network Technologies LLC 202 713-0508
12172 Wilmington Way Mukilteo (98275) *(G-6952)*
Mantec Services Inc (PA) 206 285-5656
4400 24th Ave W Seattle (98199) *(G-10472)*
Mantheys Country Mobile Park 360 384-5623
838 W Axton Rd Trlr 31 Bellingham (98226) *(G-1422)*
Mantle Industries LLC 360 332-5276
1100c Yew Ave Blaine (98230) *(G-1683)*
Manufacturers Mineral Company 425 228-2120
1215 Monster Rd Sw Renton (98057) *(G-8847)*
Manufacturing & Design Inc 425 356-2648
4420 Russell Rd Ste A Mukilteo (98275) *(G-6953)*
Manufacturing Services Inc 509 735-8444
1023 N Kellogg St Kennewick (99336) *(G-4691)*
Manufacturing Technology Inc 206 763-3161
7709 5th Ave S Seattle (98108) *(G-10473)*
Manuflaxsterit Llc 360 384-0485
3660 Slater Rd Ferndale (98248) *(G-3867)*
Many Endeavors Incorporated 360 652-1854
232 158th St Nw Arlington (98223) *(G-273)*
Many Rivers Company 360 221-1324
221 2nd St Bldg 13 Langley (98260) *(G-5782)*
Mapel Mill LLC 360 508-1313
450 State Highway 505 Winlock (98596) *(G-15154)*
Maple Systems Inc 425 745-3229
808 134th St Sw Ste 120 Everett (98204) *(G-3545)*
Maple Valley Signs Inc 425 413-1430
23220 Maple Valley Hwy Maple Valley (98038) *(G-6282)*
Maplehurst Bakeries LLC 253 872-7300
21331 88th Pl S Kent (98031) *(G-5004)*
Mapletex Inc 253 572-3608
3401 Lincoln Ave Ste G Tacoma (98421) *(G-13399)*
Mapp Tool LLC 509 228-9449
11816 E Mnsfeld Ave Ste 3 Spokane Valley (99206) *(G-12783)*
Mapsco, Seattle *Also called Magnetic Penetrant Svcs Co Inc (G-10466)*
Mapsco, Seattle *Also called Valence Surface Tech LLC (G-11398)*
Marakey Company, The, Seattle *Also called Yehun LLC (G-11510)*
Marathon N More 360 380-5242
4152 Meridian St Ste 105 Bellingham (98226) *(G-1423)*
Marble Plsg Stone Rstrtion LLC 425 564-8284
32749 6th Ave Sw Federal Way (98023) *(G-3755)*
Marchant Ladders Inc 509 882-1912
1311 W Wine Country Rd Grandview (98930) *(G-4252)*
Marcia Hardy 425 880-4460
3458 W Ames Lake Dr Ne Redmond (98053) *(G-8548)*
Marcin Jewelry Inc 425 883-7884
14318 196th Ct Ne Woodinville (98077) *(G-15301)*
Marco Global Inc 206 298-4758
4242 22nd Ave W Seattle (98199) *(G-10474)*
Mardie Rees Artist LLC 253 279-3244
13515 82nd Ave Nw Gig Harbor (98329) *(G-4134)*
Marel Seattle Inc 206 781-1827
2001 W Garfield St C106 Seattle (98119) *(G-10475)*
Maren-Go Solutions Corporation 217 506-2749
13801 Nw 20th Ct Vancouver (98685) *(G-14393)*
Margaret OLeary Inc 206 729-5934
2609 Ne Village Ln Seattle (98105) *(G-10476)*
Margate Software LLC 206 381-9120
809 Olive Way Apt 1903 Seattle (98101) *(G-10477)*
Marias Hawaiian Snow 509 217-1612
507 E Cooper Ln Colbert (99005) *(G-2711)*
Marie-Luce Enterprises 360 876-7925
840 Prospect St Port Orchard (98366) *(G-7827)*
Marijuana Venture Magazine, Seattle *Also called Mj Directions LLC (G-10549)*
Marilyns Recycle Inc 425 788-1716
18525 W Snoqualmie Riv Duvall (98019) *(G-2995)*
Marine Cnstr & Design Co (PA) 206 285-3200
4259 22nd Ave W Seattle (98199) *(G-10478)*
Marine Diesel Inc 206 767-9594
9448 17th Ave Sw Unit B1 Seattle (98106) *(G-10479)*
Marine Engine Repair Co Inc 206 286-1817
2400 W Commodore Way Seattle (98199) *(G-10480)*
Marine Fluid Systems Inc 206 706-0858
801 Nw 42nd St Ste 202 Seattle (98107) *(G-10481)*
Marine Hardware Inc (PA) 425 883-0651
14560 Ne 91st St Redmond (98052) *(G-8549)*
Marine Lumber Service Inc 206 767-4730
525 S Chicago St Seattle (98108) *(G-10482)*
Marine Recruiting 206 763-5050
4735 E Marginal Way S # 1238 Seattle (98134) *(G-10483)*
Marine Restoration & Cnstr LLC 425 576-8661
6116 114th Ave Ne Kirkland (98033) *(G-5396)*
Marine Servicenter Inc 206 323-2405
2442 Westlake Ave N Seattle (98109) *(G-10484)*
Marine Technical Services, Bellingham *Also called Superior Energy Services LLC (G-1564)*
Marine Welding 360 293-7256
13784 Redtail Ridge Ln Anacortes (98221) *(G-145)*
Mario & Son Inc 509 536-6079
2750 Eagle Ln Liberty Lake (99019) *(G-5845)*
Maritime Fabrications Inc (PA) 360 466-3629
920 Pearl Jensen Way La Conner (98257) *(G-5524)*
Maritime Pacific Brewing Co 206 782-6181
1111 Nw Ballard Way Seattle (98107) *(G-10485)*
Mark 3 Logging 360 577-8833
2151 Delaware St Longview (98632) *(G-5931)*
Mark Anthony Brands Inc 206 267-4444
316 1st Ave S Seattle (98104) *(G-10486)*
Mark E Padbury 360 376-6200
17 Jensen Rd Eastsound (98245) *(G-3039)*
Mark Grid Signs Inc 509 323-0328
442 W Sinto Ave Spokane (99201) *(G-12381)*
Mark Hummel 425 271-7156
19434 Se 118th St Issaquah (98027) *(G-4444)*
Mark II Safety, Oak Harbor *Also called Dayton Traister Co Inc (G-7147)*
Mark Lasting Technology 425 836-4317
5310 240th Ave Ne Redmond (98053) *(G-8550)*
Mark Muzi 206 523-6954
6027 Ne 57th St Seattle (98105) *(G-10487)*
Mark Padbury Construction, Eastsound *Also called Mark E Padbury (G-3039)*
Mark Ryan Winery LLC (PA) 425 481-7070
11025 117th Pl Ne Kirkland (98033) *(G-5397)*
Mark S Vorobik 360 766-6252
6496 Bayview Edison Rd Bow (98232) *(G-1931)*
Mark Sholtys 509 930-1725
4809 Beauchene Rd Moxee (98936) *(G-6881)*
Mark Thmpson Mscal Vntrloqists, Redmond *Also called Markarts Inc (G-8551)*
Mark Thomas Woodworks 505 220-7560
1946 Alco Ave Walla Walla (99362) *(G-14842)*
Markarts Inc 425 895-0651
13821 181st Ln Ne Redmond (98052) *(G-8551)*
Markay Cabinets Inc. 360 779-3443
24950 Stottlemeyer Rd Ne Poulsbo (98370) *(G-7982)*
Marke Woodworking 360 945-4023
1528 Panorama Dr Point Roberts (98281) *(G-7669)*
Marked Departure Pottery 360 991-5910
3713 Creston Ave Vancouver (98663) *(G-14394)*
Market Optical (PA) 206 448-7739
1906 Pike Pl Ste 8 Seattle (98101) *(G-10488)*
Market Place Weekly Inc 360 568-4121
127 Avenue C Ste B Snohomish (98290) *(G-11943)*
Market Spice, Redmond *Also called Samuel & Company Inc (G-8657)*
Market Vineyards (PA) 509 396-4798
1950 Keene Rd Bldg S Richland (99352) *(G-9024)*
Market Vineyards 425 486-1171
14810 Ne 145th St Ste A2 Woodinville (98072) *(G-15302)*
Market Wear, Bothell *Also called Goedecke & Goedecke (G-1862)*
Marketech 425 391-1886
558 241st Ln Se Sammamish (98074) *(G-9230)*
Marketech International Inc 360 379-6707
4896 Lost Mountain Rd Sequim (98382) *(G-11647)*
Marketech International Inc 360 379-6707
11 Westridge Ct Port Townsend (98368) *(G-7897)*
Marketing Masters Inc 425 454-5610
1871 Nw Gilman Blvd Issaquah (98027) *(G-4445)*
Marketing Newspaper, Woodinville *Also called Maine Marketing Inc (G-15300)*
Marketplace Cellars 509 795-8500
39 W Pacific Ave Spokane (99201) *(G-12382)*
Markey Machinery Co Inc (PA) 206 622-4697
7266 8th Ave S Seattle (98108) *(G-10489)*
Markey Machinery Co Inc 206 763-0383
7266 8th Ave S Seattle (98108) *(G-10490)*
Markey Machinery Co-Plant No 2, Seattle *Also called Markey Machinery Co Inc (G-10490)*
Markon Inc 503 222-3966
215 W 12th St Ste 201 Vancouver (98660) *(G-14395)*
Markon Signs & Decals, Vancouver *Also called Markon Inc (G-14395)*
Marks Design & Metalworks LLC 360 859-3535
4220 Ne Minnehaha St Vancouver (98661) *(G-14396)*
Marks Keg Washer 503 806-4115
12004 Ne Fourth Pln D Vancouver (98682) *(G-14397)*

Marlene Marshall 360 733-6479
1430 Mt Baker Hwy Bellingham (98226) ***(G-1424)***
Marley Natural, Seattle *Also called Little Bay Inc* ***(G-10429)***
Marlin Trailers 509 345-2316
22955 Road 22 Ne Marlin (98832) ***(G-6308)***
Marlin Windows Inc 509 535-3015
5414 E Broadway Ave Ste A Spokane Valley (99212) ***(G-12784)***
Marlowe Machine Inc 509 484-5979
2718 N Perry St Spokane (99207) ***(G-12383)***
Marmo E Granito Inc 206 368-0990
15545 12th Ave Ne Shoreline (98155) ***(G-11785)***
Marmot, Seattle *Also called Ex Officio LLC* ***(G-9951)***
Marninsaylor LLC 307 360-6165
2400 S Hill St Apt 1 Seattle (98144) ***(G-10491)***
Marnis Petal Pushers 360 249-8382
114 S Main St Montesano (98563) ***(G-6647)***
Marq Packaging Systems Inc 509 966-4300
3801 W Washington Ave Yakima (98903) ***(G-15615)***
Marqmetrix Inc 206 971-3625
2157 N Northlake Way # 240 Seattle (98103) ***(G-10492)***
Marquez Mfg Ltd 509 837-6230
410 Factory Rd Sunnyside (98944) ***(G-13133)***
Marquip, Seattle *Also called Washington Chain & Supply Inc* ***(G-11438)***
Married To Metal 206 244-2238
1563 Thornton Ave Sw D Pacific (98047) ***(G-7531)***
Marshall Dt Company 425 869-2525
13600 Ne 126th Pl Ste B Kirkland (98034) ***(G-5398)***
Marshall Marketing Group Inc 253 473-0765
7450 South Tacoma Way B1 Tacoma (98409) ***(G-13400)***
Marshals Winery Inc 509 767-4633
150 Oak Creek Rd Dallesport (98617) ***(G-2864)***
Marson & Marson Lumber, Chelan *Also called Tal Holdings LLC* ***(G-2565)***
Martedi Winery 425 444-2840
16110 Woodinvlle Redmond Woodinville (98072) ***(G-15303)***
Martell & Martell, Kettle Falls *Also called Brian Martell* ***(G-5227)***
Martian Boat Works 360 427-8629
773 W Hurley Waldrip Rd Shelton (98584) ***(G-11711)***
Martian Publishing LLC 425 572-0743
5320 Ne 17th Pl Renton (98059) ***(G-8848)***
Martin Blank Studios 206 621-9733
4407 6th Ave Nw Seattle (98107) ***(G-10493)***
Martin Boats Inc 360 380-7331
5415 Bel West Dr Bellingham (98226) ***(G-1425)***
Martin Business Systems 509 582-3159
1010 E 23rd Ave Bldg B Kennewick (99337) ***(G-4692)***
Martin Company 360 482-2157
4733 State Rte 12 Elma (98541) ***(G-3249)***
Martin Fabrications 509 457-8309
2012 Longfibre Rd Union Gap (98903) ***(G-13943)***
Martin Frank 509 292-2685
35414 N Findley Rd Deer Park (99006) ***(G-2908)***
Martin Marietta Materials Inc 360 424-3441
20411 E Hickox Rd Mount Vernon (98274) ***(G-6810)***
Martin Marietta Materials Inc 360 856-5870
14322 Beaver Lake Rd Mount Vernon (98273) ***(G-6811)***
Martin Metal, Bainbridge Island *Also called Jane Martin* ***(G-644)***
Martin Signs & Fabrication 206 768-5183
122 S Mead St Seattle (98108) ***(G-10494)***
Martin William Owens 253 564-5950
1320 Alameda Ave Ste B Fircrest (98466) ***(G-4002)***
Martinez and Martinez Winery 509 786-2424
357 Port Ave Ste C Prosser (99350) ***(G-8050)***
Martinez Vineyard LLC 509 786-2424
1919 Miller Ave Prosser (99350) ***(G-8051)***
Martingale & Company Inc 425 483-3313
19021 120th Ave Ne # 102 Bothell (98011) ***(G-1776)***
Martronics Corporation 360 985-2999
500 Wilcox Rd Salkum (98582) ***(G-9180)***
Maruha Capital Investment Inc (HQ) 206 382-0640
3015 112th Ave Ne Ste 100 Bellevue (98004) ***(G-996)***
Marvell Semiconductor Inc 408 222-2500
10545 Willows Rd Ne Redmond (98052) ***(G-8552)***
Marvin Batcheller 509 784-7018
16981 Casey Ln Entiat (98822) ***(G-3267)***
Mary Ellen McCaffree 253 820-0731
12919 78th Pl Se Snohomish (98290) ***(G-11944)***
Mary Fleming 206 246-4871
3400 S 150th St Tukwila (98188) ***(G-13768)***
Mary Jane Glass Productions 360 844-5914
477 S 28th St Ste C1 Washougal (98671) ***(G-14965)***
Mary Medina LLC 206 719-1730
7835 Ne 14th St Medina (98039) ***(G-6452)***
Mary's, Waitsburg *Also called Murphy Nathanial* ***(G-14756)***
Maryhill Winery, Goldendale *Also called V&C LLC* ***(G-4211)***
Maryhill Winery 509 443-3832
1303 W Summit Pkwy Spokane (99201) ***(G-12384)***
Marymoor Press Inc 425 867-9073
7577 S Laurel St Seattle (98178) ***(G-10495)***
Marysville Awards Inc 360 653-4811
1826 4th St Ste 101 Marysville (98270) ***(G-6356)***
Marysville Globe, Marysville *Also called Sun News Inc* ***(G-6391)***
Marysville Globe, Marysville *Also called Sound Publishing Inc* ***(G-6389)***
Marysville Printing Inc 360 658-9195
1509 6th St Marysville (98270) ***(G-6357)***
Mascota Resources Corp 206 818-4799
29409 232nd Ave Se Black Diamond (98010) ***(G-1650)***
Maslach Art Glass A Corp 206 842-9212
7000 Blue Sky Ln Ne Seattle (98110) ***(G-11528)***
Mason Lake Recreation Area, Grapeview *Also called Green Diamond Resource Company* ***(G-4288)***
Mason Marine Repair, Grapeview *Also called Sifferman & Sifferman* ***(G-4290)***
Mason Meat Packing Co 509 447-3788
1871 Green Rd Newport (99156) ***(G-7060)***
Masons Cheesecake Co LLC 206 602-4563
32801 26th Ave Sw Federal Way (98023) ***(G-3756)***
Masons Supply Company 206 883-5550
5210 1st Ave S Seattle (98108) ***(G-10496)***
Mass Media Outlet Corporation 206 274-8475
15200 Aurora Ave N Shoreline (98133) ***(G-11786)***
Masset Winery 509 877-6675
620 E Parker Heights Rd Wapato (98951) ***(G-14918)***
Master Garden Products, Algona *Also called Green Store Inc* ***(G-70)***
Master Machining & Mfg, Airway Heights *Also called Metals Fabrication Company Inc* ***(G-56)***
Master Millwork Inc 253 770-2023
11603 Canyon Rd E Puyallup (98373) ***(G-8182)***
Master Peace Productions 360 600-2736
5114 Ne St Johns Rd # 18 Vancouver (98661) ***(G-14398)***
Master Precaster Inc 253 770-9119
212 10th St Se Puyallup (98372) ***(G-8183)***
Master Printing Inc 509 684-5869
511 S Main St Colville (99114) ***(G-2765)***
Master Roll Manufacturer, Bellevue *Also called Master Roll Manufacturing* ***(G-997)***
Master Roll Manufacturing 425 641-1566
14023 Ne 8th St Bellevue (98007) ***(G-997)***
Master Source, Seattle *Also called Pacific Plumbing Supply Co LLC* ***(G-10738)***
Master Stucco Hc 425 793-0576
15228 Se 176th Pl Renton (98058) ***(G-8849)***
Master Switch LLC 206 769-9560
1929 42nd Ave E Seattle (98112) ***(G-10497)***
Master Vac LLC 253 875-0074
28002 138th Ave E Graham (98338) ***(G-4231)***
Masterbrand Cabinets Inc 812 482-2527
13433 Ne 20th St Ste O Bellevue (98005) ***(G-998)***
Mastercraft Metal Finishing 206 622-6380
1175 Harrison St Seattle (98109) ***(G-10498)***
Mastercraft of Seattle, Tukwila *Also called Gentzen LLC* ***(G-13738)***
Masterpress Inc 206 524-1444
10717 Midvale Ave N Seattle (98133) ***(G-10499)***
Mastrogiannis Distillery LLC 206 383-2463
123 Vashon Ct Ne Renton (98059) ***(G-8850)***
Mat Salleh Satay LLC 206 547-0597
1711 N 45th St Seattle (98103) ***(G-10500)***
Matamp Distribution USA 509 455-7469
524 W 7th Ave Apt 606 Spokane (99204) ***(G-12385)***
Match Grade Industries LLC 425 949-8110
20632 Ne 169th Pl Woodinville (98077) ***(G-15304)***
Matchlock Clamp Co 360 262-9942
1423 Highway 603 Chehalis (98532) ***(G-2512)***
Material Girls Quilting 360 354-2930
1124 Birch Bay Lynden Rd Lynden (98264) ***(G-6037)***
Material Inc (PA) 509 754-4695
1050 Basin St Sw Ephrata (98823) ***(G-3342)***
Material Inc 509 633-1740
141 Spokane Way Grand Coulee (99133) ***(G-4243)***
Material Inc 509 787-4585
305 F St Se Quincy (98848) ***(G-8303)***
Materiant Inc 425 209-1943
777 108th Ave Ne Ste 1750 Bellevue (98004) ***(G-999)***
Matersmost Software LLC 425 392-6165
1312 270th Way Se Sammamish (98075) ***(G-9231)***
Mates Seal Smart 509 489-6346
3523 N Freya St Spokane (99217) ***(G-12386)***
Math Perspectives 360 715-2782
134 Prince Ave Ste H Bellingham (98226) ***(G-1426)***
Mathemechanix 360 944-2029
3205 Se Spyglass Dr Vancouver (98683) ***(G-14399)***
Matheson Tri-Gas Inc 253 284-9295
510 53rd Ave E Fife (98424) ***(G-3969)***
Mathews Estate, Woodinville *Also called Matthews Estate LLC* ***(G-15306)***
Mathsoft Inc 206 283-8802
1700 Westlake Ave N # 500 Seattle (98109) ***(G-10501)***
Matrix Applications Company (PA) 509 547-7609
1000 Se 160th Ave Aa218 Vancouver (98683) ***(G-14400)***
Matrix Applications Company 360 256-2534
1000 Se 160th Ave Aa218 Vancouver (98683) ***(G-14401)***
Matrix Health 360 816-1200
9700 Ne 126th Ave Vancouver (98682) ***(G-14402)***
Matrix Roofing, Vancouver *Also called White Rabbit Ventures Inc* ***(G-14690)***
Matrix Visions LLC 206 368-3824
20302 44th Ave Ne Lake Forest Park (98155) ***(G-5621)***
Matson LLC 425 888-6212
45620 Se N Bend Way North Bend (98045) ***(G-7115)***
Matsunami Glass USA Inc 360 302-5575
1971 Midway Ln Ste K Bellingham (98226) ***(G-1427)***

Matsushita Avionics Co 206 246-6200
18601 28th Ave S Ste 108 Seatac (98158) **(G-9289)**
Matt Hammar Quality Woodcrafti 360 904-9015
3612 Ne 49th St Vancouver (98661) **(G-14403)**
Mattawa Wood Products Corp 509 932-6420
23961 Road T.2 Sw Mattawa (99349) **(G-6410)**
Matthaeis Camco Inc 360 426-7900
6400 E Agate Rd Shelton (98584) **(G-11712)**
Matthews Cellars 425 487-9810
16116 140th Pl Ne Woodinville (98072) **(G-15305)**
Matthews Estate LLC 425 488-3883
19495 144th Ave Ne Woodinville (98072) **(G-15306)**
Mattress Makers Incorporated 253 984-1730
1635 E Portland Ave Tacoma (98421) **(G-13401)**
Mattress Manufacturing Prize 509 946-1194
1910 Butler Loop Richland (99354) **(G-9025)**
Matts Custom Meats 360 414-1073
705 N Maple Hill Rd Kelso (98626) **(G-4537)**
Maughan Prosthetic Orthotic S 360 338-0284
208 Lilly Rd Ne Ste A Olympia (98506) **(G-7332)**
Maughan Prsthetic Orthotic Inc 360 447-0770
9220 Ridgetop Blvd Nw # 110 Silverdale (98383) **(G-11849)**
Maulcor Inc 773 696-2783
2906 S Jackson St Seattle (98144) **(G-10502)**
Maurices Incorporated 253 845-5577
3500 S Meridian Puyallup (98373) **(G-8184)**
Maury Hill Farm Enterprises 206 463-6193
5912 Sw Point Robinson Rd Vashon (98070) **(G-14733)**
Mavam Espresso, Seattle *Also called Mavam LLC* **(G-10503)**
Mavam LLC 360 789-0639
309 S Cloverdale St D7 Seattle (98108) **(G-10503)**
Maven Watersports Designs LLC 360 481-2521
18203 73rd Ave E Puyallup (98375) **(G-8185)**
Maverick International, Everett *Also called Lone Ranger LLC* **(G-3539)**
Maverick Metalworks LLC 253 345-1590
19906 15th Ave E Spanaway (98387) **(G-12063)**
Maverick Sports Medicine Inc 425 497-0887
18080 Ne 68th St Ste A150 Redmond (98052) **(G-8553)**
Mavin Mfg Inc 360 663-0354
58722 Lumpy Ln E Enumclaw (98022) **(G-3304)**
Mavrik Marine Inc 360 296-4051
780 Pearl Jensen Way La Conner (98257) **(G-5525)**
Max Monitor & Publications LLC 206 280-6489
3121 W Government Way Seattle (98199) **(G-10504)**
Max-Five Importing Company 253 887-8665
11001 Se 291st St Auburn (98092) **(G-492)**
Maxamps.com, Spokane *Also called Austin Else LLC* **(G-12128)**
Maxart Inc 425 778-1108
22410 70th Ave W Ste 12 Mountlake Terrace (98043) **(G-6864)**
Maxcess International Corp 360 834-2345
2305 Se 8th Ave Camas (98607) **(G-2268)**
Maxpulse Maxdim, Spokane *Also called Seaton Engineering Corporation* **(G-12495)**
Maxx Distribution LLC 888 507-6790
7431 S Madison St Tacoma (98409) **(G-13402)**
May Mobile Marine Tech 360 552-2561
13440 Reindeer Ln Sw Port Orchard (98367) **(G-7828)**
Mayer's Custom Curing, Vancouver *Also called Mayers Custom Meats Inc* **(G-14404)**
Mayers Custom Meats Inc 360 574-2828
12903 Ne 72nd Ave Vancouver (98686) **(G-14404)**
Maysbeautproductscom 253 318-8772
1425 N St Ne Auburn (98002) **(G-493)**
Maywood Shops Inc 360 748-9244
465 Nw Prindle St Chehalis (98532) **(G-2513)**
Mazdak International Inc 360 988-6058
410 W 3rd St Sumas (98295) **(G-13047)**
MB Precision Inc 253 833-1695
328 37th St Nw Ste D Auburn (98001) **(G-494)**
Mc BAC Inc (PA) 360 699-4466
1009 Main St Vancouver (98660) **(G-14405)**
Mc Gavins Bakery 360 373-2414
619 N Callow Ave Bremerton (98312) **(G-1977)**
Mc Ilvanie Machine Works Inc 509 452-3131
12 S 6th Ave Yakima (98902) **(G-15616)**
Mc Menamins Pub, Seattle *Also called McMenamins Inc* **(G-10510)**
MC Publishing LLC 253 678-3105
16818 86th Ave E Puyallup (98375) **(G-8186)**
McBee Metal Fabricators Inc 425 486-1410
20117 73rd Ave Ne Kenmore (98028) **(G-4591)**
McC Enterprises Inc 509 928-9676
1014 N Pines Rd Spokane Valley (99206) **(G-12785)**
McCafferty NW Land Dev LLC 509 483-1222
115 Sleepy Hollow Rd White Salmon (98672) **(G-15122)**
McCain Inc 760 734-5086
8172 304th Ave Se Issaquah (98027) **(G-4446)**
McCain Foods Usa Inc 509 488-9611
100 Lee St Othello (99344) **(G-7502)**
McCain Timber & Bridge Inc 360 520-6595
205 Ruger Ln Napavine (98532) **(G-7011)**
McCann Industries LLC 253 537-6919
132 162nd St S Spanaway (98387) **(G-12064)**
McCauley International Inc 253 229-8900
12408 138th Street Ct E Puyallup (98374) **(G-8187)**
McCauley Sound Inc 253 848-0363
16607 Meridian E Puyallup (98375) **(G-8188)**
McClanahan Lumber Inc 360 374-5887
188421 Hwy 101 S Forks (98331) **(G-4012)**
McClarin Plastics LLC 509 877-5950
180 E Jones Rd Wapato (98951) **(G-14919)**
McClatchy, Tacoma *Also called Olympic Cascade Publishing* **(G-13442)**
McClatchy Newspapers Inc 509 582-1500
333 W Canal Dr Kennewick (99336) **(G-4693)**
McClatchy Newspapers Inc 360 676-2600
1155 N State St Bellingham (98225) **(G-1428)**
McClatchy Newspapers Inc 360 754-5400
522 Franklin St Se Olympia (98501) **(G-7333)**
McClure Ranch 509 634-4685
21 N Star Rd Nespelem (99155) **(G-7022)**
McConkey Co., Sumner *Also called Surain Industries Inc* **(G-13105)**
McCoy Electric 360 829-5273
27609 96th St E Buckley (98321) **(G-2063)**
McCoy International Ltd 206 284-7734
4241 21st Ave W Ste 300 Seattle (98199) **(G-10505)**
McCrea Cellars Inc 206 938-8643
7533 34th Ave Sw Seattle (98126) **(G-10506)**
McCulley Inc 509 891-4134
9507 E 4th Ave Spokane Valley (99206) **(G-12786)**
MCD Technologies Inc 253 564-2420
2515 South Tacoma Way Tacoma (98409) **(G-13403)**
McDowall & Son Construction, Moses Lake *Also called McDowall Bros Insulation* **(G-6724)**
McDowall Bros Insulation 509 762-9530
4896 Mcconihe Rd Ne Moses Lake (98837) **(G-6724)**
McFadden & Mcfadden Logging 253 847-7695
29910 Webster Rd E Graham (98338) **(G-4232)**
McFarland Cascade, Tacoma *Also called Great Northern Holdings Inc* **(G-13321)**
McFarland Cascade Holdings Inc 800 426-8430
1717 S Rustle St Ste 105 Spokane (99224) **(G-12387)**
McFarland Cascade Holdings Inc 360 273-5541
18146 Dallas St Sw Rochester (98579) **(G-9136)**
McFarland Cascade Holdings Inc (HQ) 253 572-3033
1640 E Marc St Tacoma (98421) **(G-13404)**
McG Health Llc (HQ) 206 389-5300
901 5th Ave Ste 2000 Seattle (98164) **(G-10507)**
McGregor Company 509 397-4360
28232 Endicott Rd Colfax (99111) **(G-2716)**
McGregor Company 509 549-3635
601 Central Ferry Rd Pomeroy (99347) **(G-7675)**
McKay & Son 360 532-2285
960 Rice St Aberdeen (98520) **(G-22)**
McKay Shrimp & Crab Gear Inc 360 796-4555
306362 Us Highway 101 Brinnon (98320) **(G-2025)**
McKenna Door and Millwork 360 458-5467
35009 46th Ave S Roy (98580) **(G-9162)**
McKenna Meats, Yelm *Also called Stewarts Markets Inc* **(G-15746)**
McKenzie & Adams Inc 425 672-8668
15620 Ne Woodinvl Duvall Woodinville (98072) **(G-15307)**
McKeons Fine Wdwkg LLC Gc 206 920-6724
608 N 165th Pl Shoreline (98133) **(G-11787)**
McKinley Paper Company 360 457-4474
1815 Marine Dr Port Angeles (98363) **(G-7724)**
McKinley Springs LLC 509 894-4528
1201 Alderdale Rd Prosser (99350) **(G-8052)**
McKinnon Furniture Company, Seattle *Also called S F McKinnon Co Inc* **(G-11000)**
McKinnon International 206 633-1616
1101 N Northlake Way # 7 Seattle (98103) **(G-10508)**
McKinstry Co LLC (PA) 206 762-3311
5005 3rd Ave S Seattle (98134) **(G-10509)**
McLane Foodservice Dist Inc 253 891-6943
4301 West Valley Hwy E # 400 Sumner (98390) **(G-13085)**
McLaren Destiny 971 217-5877
116 W 10th St La Center (98629) **(G-5509)**
McLeod Masonry USA Inc 360 734-4427
38ab Sound Way Bellingham (98227) **(G-1429)**
McLeod Pilot Car & Hot Sht Svc 360 701-5827
6430 Guerin St Sw Olympia (98512) **(G-7334)**
McMann & Tate Inc 360 676-4396
831 Reveille St Bellingham (98229) **(G-1430)**
McMenamins Inc 206 285-4722
200 Roy St Ste 105 Seattle (98109) **(G-10510)**
McMullen Mfg Services 360 891-3662
8804 Ne 80th Ct Vancouver (98662) **(G-14406)**
McNamee & Sons Logging 509 292-8656
10310 E Bridges Rd Elk (99009) **(G-3173)**
McNeeley Mfg 206 255-7818
24634 185th Pl Se Covington (98042) **(G-2832)**
McNeeley Mfg 253 236-4969
4202 Auburn Way N Auburn (98002) **(G-495)**
McNerney Enterprises LLC 206 850-5023
253 E Lk Smmmish Pkwy Se Sammamish (98074) **(G-9232)**
McNett Corporation 360 671-2227
1411 Meador Ave Bellingham (98229) **(G-1431)**
McNichols Company 253 922-4296
3400 Industry Dr E Ste B Fife (98424) **(G-3970)**
McObject LLC (PA) 425 888-8505
33309 1st Way S Ste A208 Federal Way (98003) **(G-3757)**

ALPHABETIC

McStevens Inc 360 944-5788
5600 Ne 88th St Vancouver (98665) *(G-14407)*
McVays Mobile Welding LLC 360 657-0360
4100 134th St Ne Marysville (98271) *(G-6358)*
MD Manufacturing, Entiat *Also called Marvin Batcheller (G-3267)*
Mdm Food Service, Sumner *Also called McLane Foodservice Dist Inc (G-13085)*
Mdr Publishing 360 691-5908
501 Eagle View Dr Granite Falls (98252) *(G-4280)*
Mdt, Sumas *Also called Modular Driven Tech Inc (G-13049)*
Mdtoolbox, Kennewick *Also called Toptec Software LLC (G-4737)*
Mdtoolbox, Richland *Also called Toptec Software LLC (G-9045)*
Meade Winery 509 972-4443
7909 Englewood Ave Yakima (98908) *(G-15617)*
Meadow Burke, Auburn *Also called Burke Meadow LLC (G-399)*
Meadow Creature LLC 360 329-2250
18850 103rd Ave Sw Vashon (98070) *(G-14734)*
Meadowbrook Manufacturing LLC 206 297-1029
4025 Leary Way Nw Seattle (98107) *(G-10511)*
Meadowrock Alpacas 509 395-2266
80 Mount Adams Rd Trout Lake (98650) *(G-13680)*
Meals On Wire, Bellevue *Also called Dining Solutions LLC (G-878)*
Measurement Technology NW Inc (PA) 206 634-1308
4220 24th Ave W Seattle (98199) *(G-10512)*
Meat & Bread US Inc 604 819-1728
1201 10th Ave Seattle (98122) *(G-10513)*
Meat and Noodle 206 408-7650
20312 Vashon Hwy Sw Vashon (98070) *(G-14735)*
Meca Aerospace, Kirkland *Also called Mecadaq Aerospace LLC (G-5399)*
Mecadaq Aerospace LLC 714 442-9703
915 6th St S Kirkland (98033) *(G-5399)*
Mechanical Fuels Treatment LLC 509 486-1438
2265b Highway 20 Tonasket (98855) *(G-13654)*
Mechanical Specialties LLC 360 273-7604
1000 85th Ave Se Olympia (98501) *(G-7335)*
Mechanical Specilities 360 273-7604
975 85th Ave Se Olympia (98501) *(G-7336)*
Mechatronics Inc (PA) 425 222-5900
8152 304th Ave Se Issaquah (98027) *(G-4447)*
Mechpro Inc 206 445-5230
1320 26th St Nw Ste 4 Auburn (98001) *(G-496)*
Meconi Pub & Eatery 253 383-3388
709 Pacific Ave Tacoma (98402) *(G-13405)*
Med Products Comfort, Mount Vernon *Also called Medical Pdts For Comfort Inc (G-6812)*
Med-Core Services Inc 360 455-5425
6706 Martin Way E Ste 1 Olympia (98516) *(G-7337)*
Meda Nova, Ellensburg *Also called Gigglydoo LLC (G-3203)*
Medallic Art Company, Kent *Also called Northwest Territorial Mint LLC (G-5036)*
Medallion Foods Inc 253 846-2600
18420 50th Ave E Tacoma (98446) *(G-13406)*
Medetech Development Corp 425 891-9151
2023 120th Ave Ne Bellevue (98005) *(G-1000)*
Medford Technologies Inc 206 963-0589
345 Andover Park E Tukwila (98188) *(G-13769)*
Media Direct, Olympia *Also called Media Holdings LLC (G-7338)*
Media Directed Inc (PA) 509 886-5759
1150 N Grover Ave East Wenatchee (98802) *(G-3024)*
Media Holdings LLC 503 313-0676
3130 Madrona Beach Rd Nw Olympia (98502) *(G-7338)*
Media Inc Sign Manufacturing, Renton *Also called Media Incorporated (G-8851)*
Media Incorporated 425 251-5145
16508 164th Pl Se Renton (98058) *(G-8851)*
Media Matrix Digital Center 360 693-6455
6307 Ne St Johns Rd Ste D Vancouver (98661) *(G-14408)*
Media Spotlight, Sequim *Also called Omega Ministries Inc (G-11656)*
Mediamax 509 627-2358
213 Ontario Ct Richland (99352) *(G-9026)*
Mediapro Holdings LLC 425 483-4700
20021 120th Ave Ne # 102 Bothell (98011) *(G-1777)*
Medical Equipment Dev Co LLC 206 364-3894
313 Ne 185th St Shoreline (98155) *(G-11788)*
Medical Micro Machining Inc 509 397-2276
1115 N Clay St Colfax (99111) *(G-2717)*
Medical Pdts For Comfort Inc 360 770-2005
2301 Martin Rd Mount Vernon (98273) *(G-6812)*
Medicines Co 425 829-2540
6408 138th Pl Se Snohomish (98296) *(G-11945)*
Medicis Technologies Corp 425 420-2100
11818 N Creek Pkwy N Bothell (98011) *(G-1778)*
Medida Health LLC 425 985-5214
6126 130th Ave Ne Kirkland (98033) *(G-5400)*
Medilogic Llc 541 991-1006
3424 Nw Lacamas Ln Camas (98607) *(G-2269)*
Mediterranean Express 206 860-3989
1417 Broadway Seattle (98122) *(G-10514)*
Medline Industries Inc 360 491-0241
3770 Hogum Bay Rd Ne Lacey (98516) *(G-5566)*
Medtronic Inc 509 991-0159
327 W 8th Ave Ste 130 Spokane (99204) *(G-12388)*
Medtronic Inc 425 867-4000
11811 Willows Rd Ne Redmond (98052) *(G-8554)*

Medtronic Usa Inc 425 803-0708
4030 Lake Wash Blvd Ste C Bellevue (98006) *(G-1001)*
Medworks Instruments 360 597-3754
12911 Nw 25th Ct Vancouver (98685) *(G-14409)*
Meet Your Price Inc 360 260-2066
8419 Ne 154th Cir Battle Ground (98604) *(G-720)*
Mefford and Sons Logging, Hoquiam *Also called Derek Mefford (G-4333)*
Megabess Us Inc 425 890-9175
10801 Main St Ste 100 Bellevue (98004) *(G-1002)*
Megan Nieforth 509 380-6543
5011 Sinai Dr Pasco (99301) *(G-7602)*
Meier Manufacturing 253 545-9798
4638 N Pearl St Tacoma (98407) *(G-13407)*
Meili Manufacturing 509 489-9180
3511 N Market St Spokane (99207) *(G-12389)*
Meili Truck Top, Spokane *Also called Meili Manufacturing (G-12389)*
Mein Street, Bellevue *Also called Sheng Mian North America LLC (G-1128)*
Meineke Discount Mufflers, Spokane Valley *Also called Sjb Enterprises Inc (G-12874)*
Mekltek Engineering & Mfg 360 384-1607
6229 Aldrich Rd Ferndale (98248) *(G-3868)*
Melange Publishing 360 387-2395
832 Margie Ann Dr Camano Island (98282) *(G-2217)*
Melbrook Equipment, Bellingham *Also called Brooks Properties (G-1284)*
Melcher Manufacturing Co Inc 509 534-9119
1410 N Howe Rd Spokane Valley (99212) *(G-12787)*
Mellanox Technologies Inc 512 239-8282
8648 154th Ave Ne Redmond (98052) *(G-8555)*
Mellema Manufacturing, Vancouver *Also called Accurate Machine and Mfg (G-14007)*
Melt Candle Company LLC 360 200-0993
1022 Diane Ave Oak Harbor (98277) *(G-7158)*
Meltec Division, Seattle *Also called Young Corporation (G-11515)*
Membane Solutions Corp 253 487-5134
20021 80th Ave S Kent (98032) *(G-5005)*
Members Club At Aldarra 206 232-8580
3853 Island Crest Way Mercer Island (98040) *(G-6473)*
Memories In Granite, Seattle *Also called Quiring Monuments Inc (G-10906)*
Memory Box Inc 206 722-8438
10232 63rd Ave S Seattle (98178) *(G-10515)*
Menace Industries LLC 360 595-4095
3617 Illinois Ln Bellingham (98226) *(G-1432)*
Menasha Packaging Company LLC 425 677-7788
22530 Se 64th Pl Ste 210 Issaquah (98027) *(G-4448)*
Mend 949 355-9925
4117 34th Ave S Seattle (98118) *(G-10516)*
Mep Labs LLC 206 229-2525
1513 Dayton Ct Ne Renton (98056) *(G-8852)*
Mer Equipment, Seattle *Also called Marine Engine Repair Co Inc (G-10480)*
Mercer Estate Winery, Prosser *Also called Mercer Wine Estates LLC (G-8055)*
Mercer Marine Inc 425 641-2090
3911 Lake Wash Blvd Se Fall City (98024) *(G-3703)*
Mercer Products & Mfg Co (HQ) 425 742-0333
15712 Mill Creek Blvd Mill Creek (98012) *(G-6517)*
Mercer Ranch Imperial, Prosser *Also called Mercer Ranches Inc (G-8053)*
Mercer Ranches Inc (PA) 509 894-4773
46 Sonova Rd Prosser (99350) *(G-8053)*
Mercer Timber Products LLC 206 674-4639
14900 Interurban Ave S Tukwila (98168) *(G-13770)*
Mercer Wine Estates LLC (PA) 509 786-2097
3100 Lee Rd Prosser (99350) *(G-8054)*
Mercer Wine Estates LLC 509 832-2810
32302 N Mcdonald Rd Prosser (99350) *(G-8055)*
Merchant Investments Inc 425 235-8675
7412 S 262nd St Kent (98032) *(G-5006)*
Merchants Metals LLC 253 531-5454
7303 Golden Given Rd E Tacoma (98404) *(G-13408)*
Mercurius Biofuels LLC 360 941-7207
3190 Bay Rd Ferndale (98248) *(G-3869)*
Mercury Plastics LLC 360 693-0627
3807 Se Hidden Way Vancouver (98661) *(G-14410)*
Meridian Scale Service, Kent *Also called U S Scale Incorporated (G-5193)*
Meridian Valley Laboratories 206 209-4200
6839 Fort Dent Way # 206 Tukwila (98188) *(G-13771)*
Meritor Inc 360 737-0175
500 Broadway St Ste 310 Vancouver (98660) *(G-14411)*
Merlins Workshop LLC 206 817-9677
251 Brighton St Port Hadlock (98339) *(G-7760)*
Merlyn Products Inc 509 838-7500
7500 W Park Dr Spokane (99224) *(G-12390)*
Mermaid Bay Enterprises LLC 360 312-5522
1971 Midway Ln Ste J Bellingham (98226) *(G-1433)*
Merrie & Macs, Sammamish *Also called McNerney Enterprises LLC (G-9232)*
Merril Associates, Bellevue *Also called Merril Mail Marketing Inc (G-1003)*
Merril Mail Marketing Inc 425 454-7009
12500 Ne 10th Pl Bellevue (98005) *(G-1003)*
Merrill & Ring Inc 360 452-2367
813 E 8th St Port Angeles (98362) *(G-7725)*
Merrill Corp Resource MGT 509 326-7892
621 W Mallon Ave Ste 606 Spokane (99201) *(G-12391)*
Merrill Corporation 360 794-3157
14640 172nd Dr Se Monroe (98272) *(G-6596)*

Merrimac Alpacas..........425 387-7586
2000 Carlson Rd Snohomish (98290) ***(G-11946)***
Merry Cellars, Pullman *Also called DRM Holdings Inc* ***(G-8089)***
Mervin Manufacturing Inc..........206 204-7800
3400 Stone Way N Ste 200 Seattle (98103) ***(G-10517)***
Mesa Resources Inc..........360 683-1912
453 Grandview Dr Sequim (98382) ***(G-11648)***
Messenger Corporation..........206 623-4525
37 S Hudson St Seattle (98134) ***(G-10518)***
Messer LLC..........360 695-1255
4715 Ne 78th St Vancouver (98665) ***(G-14412)***
Messer LLC..........509 738-6611
4715 Ne 78th St Vancouver (98665) ***(G-14413)***
Metabolic Global..........206 660-7243
4214 Stone Way N Seattle (98103) ***(G-10519)***
Metal Art Bells..........360 546-2018
2211 Nw 116th St Vancouver (98685) ***(G-14414)***
Metal Building Products, Kent *Also called Latium USA Trading Inc* ***(G-4990)***
Metal Finishing Inc..........360 659-1971
18640 59th Dr Ne Arlington (98223) ***(G-274)***
Metal Frictions Company Inc..........425 776-0336
650 Birch St Edmonds (98020) ***(G-3133)***
Metal Master LLC..........253 948-7295
5620 S Proctor St Ste A Tacoma (98409) ***(G-13409)***
Metal Masters Northwest Inc..........425 775-4481
20926 63rd Ave W Ste A Lynnwood (98036) ***(G-6162)***
Metal Meister Inc..........480 845-6717
5310 E Stoughton Rd Valleyford (99036) ***(G-13998)***
Metal Mill Corporation..........360 262-9080
146 Estep Rd Chehalis (98532) ***(G-2514)***
Metal Motion, Arlington *Also called Kgr Corporation* ***(G-266)***
Metal Motion, Arlington *Also called Northwest Center* ***(G-289)***
Metal One America Inc..........206 223-2273
1201 3rd Ave Ste 3700 Seattle (98101) ***(G-10520)***
Metal Rollforming Systems Inc..........509 315-8737
4511 N Freya St Spokane (99217) ***(G-12392)***
Metal Roofing & Siding Sup Inc..........509 466-6854
13906 N Newport Hwy Mead (99021) ***(G-6432)***
Metal Roofing and Siding Sup, Spokane *Also called Metal Rollforming Systems Inc* ***(G-12392)***
Metal Sales Manufacturing Corp..........509 536-6000
2727 E Trent Ave Spokane (99202) ***(G-12393)***
Metal Sales Manufacturing Corp..........253 872-5750
20213 84th Ave S Kent (98032) ***(G-5007)***
Metal Smith..........509 884-4851
450 Rock Island Rd East Wenatchee (98802) ***(G-3025)***
Metal Solutions LLC..........206 767-5587
5212 6th Ave S Seattle (98108) ***(G-10521)***
Metal Structures LLC..........703 628-7808
8707 Ne 279th St Battle Ground (98604) ***(G-721)***
Metal Tech, Monroe *Also called Schoeben & Schoeben Inc* ***(G-6616)***
Metal Tech Metalworks Inc..........253 435-5885
9918 162nd Street Ct E Puyallup (98375) ***(G-8189)***
Metal Werks Inc..........360 651-0300
5625 47th Ave Ne Ste D Marysville (98270) ***(G-6359)***
Metal Works Inc..........509 782-8811
8611 Frontage Rd Dryden (98821) ***(G-2953)***
Metal Works Northwest..........206 624-4766
3834 4th Ave S Seattle (98134) ***(G-10522)***
Metalfab Inc..........509 967-2946
5302 W Van Giesen St West Richland (99353) ***(G-15098)***
Metalistics Inc..........425 348-9377
2626 119th St Sw Ste B4 Everett (98204) ***(G-3546)***
Metals Fabrication Company Inc..........509 244-2909
2524 S Hayford Rd Airway Heights (99001) ***(G-56)***
Metals McHning Fabricators Inc..........509 248-8890
2004 S 14th St Union Gap (98903) ***(G-13944)***
Metals USA Building Pdts LP..........425 251-0589
7041 S 234th St D Kent (98032) ***(G-5008)***
Metaltech Inc..........253 863-7532
1907 Fryar Ave Sumner (98390) ***(G-13086)***
Meteorcomm LLC..........253 872-2521
1201 Sw 7th St Renton (98057) ***(G-8853)***
Methow House Watch Inc..........509 996-3332
26 Lynx Ln Winthrop (98862) ***(G-15163)***
Methow Valley Industrial LLC..........509 997-7777
202 Industrial Park Ave Twisp (98856) ***(G-13914)***
Methow Valley Publishing LLC..........509 997-7011
101 Glover St N Twisp (98856) ***(G-13915)***
Methow Valley Septic, Twisp *Also called White Logging LLC* ***(G-13917)***
Meticulous Coating Applicators..........206 251-3684
4834 W Glenhaven Dr Everett (98203) ***(G-3547)***
Metricstory Incorporated..........206 755-4511
12302 Sand Point Way Ne Seattle (98125) ***(G-10523)***
Metrie Inc..........360 863-1730
5575 Nordic Pl Ferndale (98248) ***(G-3870)***
Metriguard Technologies Inc..........509 332-7526
2465 Ne Hopkins Ct Pullman (99163) ***(G-8098)***
Metrix Create Space..........206 357-9406
623 Broadway E Seattle (98102) ***(G-10524)***
Metrix Software..........425 361-2415
123 4th Ave N Edmonds (98020) ***(G-3134)***
Metro Coatings Inc..........360 906-0646
6608 Kansas St Vancouver (98661) ***(G-14415)***
Metro Machine Corp..........360 782-5600
423 Pacific Ave Ste 200 Bremerton (98337) ***(G-1978)***
Metron Powdercoating Inc..........509 766-1278
2000 Wheeler Rd Ne Moses Lake (98837) ***(G-6725)***
Mettler Toledo NW..........425 774-3510
6911 216th St Sw Ste B Lynnwood (98036) ***(G-6163)***
Meyer Engineered Materials LLC..........253 854-6117
22638 85th Pl S Kent (98031) ***(G-5009)***
Meyer Sign & Advertising Co..........360 424-1325
2608 Old Highway 99 S Rd Mount Vernon (98273) ***(G-6813)***
Meyer Wells Inc..........206 282-0076
421 3rd Ave W Seattle (98119) ***(G-10525)***
Meyle Industries LLC..........360 250-6114
15513 Ne 85th St Vancouver (98682) ***(G-14416)***
Mezich Allegiance Inc..........206 782-1767
1445 Nw 56th St Seattle (98107) ***(G-10526)***
Mfg Precision, Tacoma *Also called Kurtisfactor LLC* ***(G-13379)***
Mfg Tech, Seattle *Also called Manufacturing Technology Inc* ***(G-10473)***
Mfg Universe Corp..........800 883-8779
1045 Andover Park E # 105 Tukwila (98188) ***(G-13772)***
Mfml Publishing..........360 603-6148
1400 12th St Apt 908 Bellingham (98225) ***(G-1434)***
Mgs Software LLC..........253 841-1573
14415 115th Avenue Ct E Puyallup (98374) ***(G-8190)***
Mhj Wood Works..........360 901-8889
28017 Ne 132nd Ave Battle Ground (98604) ***(G-722)***
Mic, Moxee *Also called Moxee Innovations Corporation* ***(G-6882)***
Micahs Custom Works LLC..........509 665-9631
56 Hurds River Ranch Ln Malaga (98828) ***(G-6232)***
Michael Ashford Design..........360 352-0694
6543 Alpine Dr Sw Olympia (98512) ***(G-7339)***
Michael B Knutson..........509 398-7312
1515 N Miller St Wenatchee (98801) ***(G-15050)***
Michael Blackwell..........253 759-2906
1429 S Verde St Tacoma (98405) ***(G-13410)***
Michael Chapman..........425 881-0907
8500 148th Ave Ne Redmond (98052) ***(G-8556)***
Michael D Lynne..........800 587-2313
624 S Lander St Ste 20d Seattle (98134) ***(G-10527)***
Michael D Worley..........509 290-0927
5410 E Eloika Ln Elk (99009) ***(G-3174)***
Michael Dresdner..........253 770-1664
3303 28th St Se Puyallup (98374) ***(G-8191)***
Michael Eckles..........253 568-2934
4745 Silver Bow Rd Ne Tacoma (98422) ***(G-13411)***
Michael Enterprises Co..........253 630-4259
26420 180th Ave Se Covington (98042) ***(G-2833)***
Michael H Wold Company Inc..........360 435-6953
24325 131st Ave Ne Arlington (98223) ***(G-275)***
Michael Homchick Stoneworks, Kenmore *Also called Homchick Michael Stone Work* ***(G-4582)***
Michael L White..........509 526-6923
1491 Artesia St Walla Walla (99362) ***(G-14843)***
Michael M Hennessey..........360 471-3313
3291 Nw Mount Vintage Way Silverdale (98383) ***(G-11850)***
Michael P Appleby..........360 652-1178
14227 Evergreen Way Stanwood (98292) ***(G-12978)***
Michael Patrick Matthews..........509 457-8799
1691 Yakima Valley Hwy Wapato (98951) ***(G-14920)***
Michael Shaw..........206 669-7597
29811 5th Ave Sw Federal Way (98023) ***(G-3758)***
Michael W Sherer..........206 230-8541
4741 Fernridge Ln Mercer Island (98040) ***(G-6474)***
Michaels Gemstone Trees..........509 922-2390
12006 E 8th Ave Spokane Valley (99206) ***(G-12788)***
Michaels Manufacturing..........253 459-4384
7731 184th Ave E Bonney Lake (98391) ***(G-1728)***
Michaels Stores Inc..........360 892-4494
16601 Se Mill Plain Blvd Vancouver (98684) ***(G-14417)***
Michaels Touch..........509 346-9478
14041 Crook Loop Sw Royal City (99357) ***(G-9172)***
Michelin Mounting Center..........253 872-0868
20840 84th Ave S Kent (98032) ***(G-5010)***
Michellaine Lee Larry Bergsma..........360 873-4005
7349 Ranger Station Rd Marblemount (98267) ***(G-6305)***
Michelle Chateau Ste..........425 488-1133
14111 Ne 145th St Woodinville (98072) ***(G-15308)***
Michelle Schwartzman..........360 629-5255
1722 267th St Nw Stanwood (98292) ***(G-12979)***
Michelle Ste Wine Estates Ltd..........509 875-4227
178810 Hwy 221 Paterson (99345) ***(G-7659)***
Michelle Ste Wine Estates Ltd (HQ)..........425 488-1133
14111 Ne 145th St Woodinville (98072) ***(G-15309)***
Michelle Ste Wine Estates Ltd..........509 875-2061
Hwy 221 Columbia Crest Dr Paterson (99345) ***(G-7660)***
Michelle Ste Wine Estates Ltd..........509 882-3928
205 W 5th St Grandview (98930) ***(G-4253)***
Michelle Ste Wine Estates Ltd..........425 488-1133
14111 Ne 145th St Woodinville (98072) ***(G-15310)***
Michelsen Packaging Co Cal (PA)..........509 248-6270
202 N 2nd Ave Yakima (98902) ***(G-15618)***

ALPHABETIC

Michelsen Packaging Company 509 248-6270
202 N 2nd Ave Yakima (98902) *(G-15619)*
Michiels International Inc (PA) 206 365-4060
5701 Ne Bothell Way Ste 2 Kenmore (98028) *(G-4592)*
Micks Peppourri Inc 509 966-2328
1707 S 74th Ave Yakima (98908) *(G-15620)*
Mico Welding & Machining Inc 509 467-5082
16332 N Saddlewood Rd Nine Mile Falls (99026) *(G-7079)*
Micraculture LLC 202 838-7645
4608 1st Ave Ne Seattle (98105) *(G-10528)*
Micrametal Inc 206 508-1405
810 Nw 45th St Seattle (98107) *(G-10529)*
Micro Aero Dynamics, Anacortes Also called Micro Aerodynamics Inc *(G-146)*
Micro Aerodynamics Inc 360 293-8082
4000 Airport Rd Ste D Anacortes (98221) *(G-146)*
Micro Ag Inc 509 397-4278
Hwy 195 Steptoe (99174) *(G-13007)*
Micro Current Technology Inc 206 938-5800
2244 1st Ave S Seattle (98134) *(G-10530)*
Micro Current Technology Inc 206 938-5288
4822 California Ave Sw Seattle (98116) *(G-10531)*
Micro Data Bus Forms & Prtg, Olympia Also called Glenn Waldren *(G-7297)*
Micro Dimension Inc 360 887-0620
5617 S 6th Way Ridgefield (98642) *(G-9094)*
Micro Electronics, Ferndale Also called Mekltek Engineering & Mfg *(G-3868)*
Micro Focus Software Inc 206 217-7100
705 5th Ave S Ste 1000 Seattle (98104) *(G-10532)*
Micro Machining 360 837-3200
251 Sneider Barks Rd Washougal (98671) *(G-14966)*
Micro Machining LLC 360 835-3200
1213 Ne 314th Ave Washougal (98671) *(G-14967)*
Micro Motion Inc 360 896-0522
11912 Ne 95th St Vancouver (98682) *(G-14418)*
Micro Standard 425 882-1722
18133 Ne 68th St Redmond (98052) *(G-8557)*
Microbial Magic LLC 360 297-2224
19689 7th Ave Ne Poulsbo (98370) *(G-7983)*
Microbiologique Inc (PA) 206 714-5275
8315 Lake City Way Ne Seattle (98115) *(G-10533)*
Microchips Software 360 921-8562
4115 Ne 115th St Vancouver (98686) *(G-14419)*
Microconnex Corporation (HQ) 425 396-5707
34935 Se Douglas St # 110 Snoqualmie (98065) *(G-12018)*
Microfoils Co., Arlington Also called Joseph S Heagney *(G-263)*
Microgreen Polymers Inc 360 435-7400
7220 201st St Ne Arlington (98223) *(G-276)*
Microgreen Polymers Inc 360 435-7400
17735 59th Ave Ne Arlington (98223) *(G-277)*
Microhaops Inc 206 595-6426
8041 Stroud Ave N Seattle (98103) *(G-10534)*
Micron Technology Inc 206 294-7015
506 2nd Ave Seattle (98104) *(G-10535)*
Microquill Software Publishing 425 827-7200
10512 Ne 68th St Ste 101 Kirkland (98033) *(G-5401)*
Microscan Mfg LLC 425 226-5700
700 Sw 39th St Renton (98057) *(G-8854)*
Microsoft Corporation 509 787-6900
501 Port Industrial Way Quincy (98848) *(G-8304)*
Microsoft Corporation 425 705-1900
205 108th Ave Ne Ste 400 Bellevue (98004) *(G-1004)*
Microsoft Corporation 425 705-6218
4200 150th Ave Ne Redmond (98052) *(G-8558)*
Microsoft Corporation 425 706-0040
15563 Ne 31st St Redmond (98052) *(G-8559)*
Microsoft Corporation 425 281-6768
23436 Ne 6th Pl Sammamish (98074) *(G-9233)*
Microsoft Corporation 206 290-9669
200 W Thomas St Ste 300 Seattle (98119) *(G-10536)*
Microsoft Corporation 425 533-6624
562 1st Ave S Ste 400 Seattle (98104) *(G-10537)*
Microsoft Corporation 770 235-8794
143 129th Ave Ne Bellevue (98005) *(G-1005)*
Microsoft Corporation 425 705-1900
11025 Ne 8th St Bellevue (98004) *(G-1006)*
Microsoft Corporation 206 724-8130
434 Kirkland Way Kirkland (98033) *(G-5402)*
Microsoft Corporation 425 882-8080
21930 Se 51st Pl Issaquah (98029) *(G-4449)*
Microsoft Corporation 425 706-6640
15010 Ne 36th St Redmond (98052) *(G-8560)*
Microsoft Corporation 425 861-0581
15120 Ne 40th St Redmond (98052) *(G-8561)*
Microsoft Corporation 425 706-0033
16070 Ne 36th Way Bldg 33 Redmond (98052) *(G-8562)*
Microsoft Corporation 425 882-8080
3009 157th Pl Ne Redmond (98052) *(G-8563)*
Microsoft Corporation 360 863-0642
3925 159th Ave Ne Redmond (98052) *(G-8564)*
Microsoft Corporation 425 867-6537
5000 148th Ave Ne Ste 100 Redmond (98052) *(G-8565)*
Microsoft Corporation 206 883-5474
320 Westlake Ave N Seattle (98109) *(G-10538)*
Microsoft Corporation 425 882-8080
3635 156th Ave Ne Bldg 11 Redmond (98052) *(G-8566)*
Microsoft Corporation 425 882-8080
15050 Ne 36th St Bldg 110 Redmond (98052) *(G-8567)*
Microsoft Corporation 425 882-8080
15220 Ne 40th St Redmond (98052) *(G-8568)*
Microsoft Corporation 425 882-8080
3801 Ne 39th St Bldg 17 Redmond (98052) *(G-8569)*
Microsoft Corporation 425 828-8080
4350 150th Ave Ne Redmond (98052) *(G-8570)*
Microsoft Corporation 425 882-8080
3600 159th Ave Ne Bldg 16 Redmond (98052) *(G-8571)*
Microsoft Corporation 425 882-8080
4650 154th Pl Ne Bldg 85 Redmond (98052) *(G-8572)*
Microsoft Corporation 425 882-8080
3860 Ne 39th St Bldg 18 Redmond (98052) *(G-8573)*
Microsoft Corporation 425 882-8080
3925 Ne 39th St Bldg 21 Redmond (98052) *(G-8574)*
Microsoft Corporation 425 882-8080
3600 156th Ave Ne Bldg 24 Redmond (98052) *(G-8575)*
Microsoft Corporation 425 882-8080
4900 154th Pl Ne Bldg 86 Redmond (98052) *(G-8576)*
Microsoft Corporation 425 882-8080
4001 156th Ave Ne Bldg 50 Redmond (98052) *(G-8577)*
Microsoft Corporation 425 882-8080
4500 154th Pl Ne Bldg 84 Redmond (98052) *(G-8578)*
Microsoft Corporation 425 882-8080
15595 Ne 36th St Bldg 44 Redmond (98052) *(G-8579)*
Microsoft Corporation 425 435-8457
11111 Ne 8th St Bellevue (98004) *(G-1007)*
Microsoft Corporation (PA) 425 882-8080
1 Microsoft Way Redmond (98052) *(G-8580)*
Microsoft Corporation 425 633-4929
20542 Ne 26th St Sammamish (98074) *(G-9234)*
Microsoft Corporation 206 816-0190
22836 Ne 84th Pl Redmond (98053) *(G-8581)*
Microsoft Corporation 425 556-9348
17760 Ne 67th Ct Redmond (98052) *(G-8582)*
Microsoft Corporation 425 703-6921
17814 198th Ave Ne Woodinville (98077) *(G-15311)*
Microsoft Payments Inc 425 722-0528
1 Microsoft Way Redmond (98052) *(G-8583)*
Microsoft Tech Licensing LLC 425 882-8080
1 Microsoft Way Redmond (98052) *(G-8584)*
Microstar Instruments, Redmond Also called Microstar Laboratories Inc *(G-8585)*
Microstar Laboratories Inc (PA) 425 453-2345
16310 Ne 85th St Ste 201 Redmond (98052) *(G-8585)*
Microsurgical Technology Inc 425 861-4002
8415 154th Ave Ne Redmond (98052) *(G-8586)*
Microtemp Electronics 360 256-6789
2716 Ne 168th Ave Vancouver (98684) *(G-14420)*
Microvision Inc 425 936-6847
6244 185th Ave Ne Ste 100 Redmond (98052) *(G-8587)*
Micrprint Inc 253 539-1103
11102 25th Ave E Ste D Tacoma (98445) *(G-13412)*
Mid Mountain Materials Inc 360 435-9622
18825 67th Ave Ne Arlington (98223) *(G-278)*
Mid Mountain Materials Inc (PA) 206 762-7600
5602 2nd Ave S Seattle (98108) *(G-10539)*
Mid-Columbia Newspaper Pubhs 509 845-5253
9228 W Clearwater Dr Kennewick (99336) *(G-4694)*
Mid-Valley Milling Inc 509 786-1300
N Hinzerling Rd Prosser (99350) *(G-8056)*
Middco Tool & Equipment Inc 509 535-1701
2401 N Eastern Rd Spokane Valley (99212) *(G-12789)*
Middle Forth Temper Cutt, Deming Also called Quintana Cutting Inc *(G-2922)*
Middy Marine Products Inc 425 883-4600
9320 151st Ave Ne Redmond (98052) *(G-8588)*
Middy Plastic Products, Redmond Also called Middy Marine Products Inc *(G-8588)*
Midnite Solar Inc 360 403-7207
17722 67th Ave Ne Unit C Arlington (98223) *(G-279)*
Midnite Sun Printing, Bremerton Also called Villas Josey *(G-2010)*
Mielke Orchards, Spokane Also called Arbor Crest Wineries & Nursery *(G-12115)*
Mighty Ai LLC 425 753-3167
1411 4th Ave Ste 1100 Seattle (98101) *(G-10540)*
Mihalisin/Walling Studio 206 923-1037
4418 Sw College St Seattle (98116) *(G-10541)*
Mike and Leslie Corporation 206 246-4911
6400 S 143rd Pl Tukwila (98168) *(G-13773)*
Mike Brandeberry 206 524-9656
980 Mountain View Blvd Se North Bend (98045) *(G-7116)*
Mike Breckon 360 380-0622
2722 Douglas Rd Ferndale (98248) *(G-3871)*
Mike Frantz Inc 800 839-6712
140 E Hideaway Ln Shelton (98584) *(G-11713)*
Mike Houston 425 889-0682
950 18th Ave W Kirkland (98033) *(G-5403)*
Mike Lavalle Inc 360 563-0501
1033 Avenue D Ste F Snohomish (98290) *(G-11947)*
Mike Montgomery 206 306-4599
1820 Minor Ave Apt 419 Seattle (98101) *(G-10542)*
Mike Nilles 509 299-3653
7302 S Ladd Rd Medical Lake (99022) *(G-6442)*

ALPHABETIC SECTION
Minuteman Press Intl Inc

Mike Scott Orchards & Winery ... 509 787-3538
3400 10th St Se Wenatchee (98802) ***(G-15091)***
Mike's Hard Lemonade, Seattle *Also called Mark Anthony Brands Inc* ***(G-10486)***
Mike's Welding, Tumwater *Also called Mikes Custom Welding* ***(G-13887)***
Mikes Custom Welding ... 360 754-3719
5211 Joppa St Sw Tumwater (98512) ***(G-13887)***
Mikes Help Key LLC ... 360 897-2880
23218 124th St E Buckley (98321) ***(G-2064)***
Mikes Logging ... 360 893-5336
12814 19th Avenue Ct S Tacoma (98444) ***(G-13413)***
Mikes Machine ... 360 652-4046
18303 60th Ave Nw Stanwood (98292) ***(G-12980)***
Mikes Rental Machinery Inc ... 509 925-6126
501 S Main St Ellensburg (98926) ***(G-3215)***
Mikron Industries Inc ... 815 335-2372
1123 N 6th Ave Yakima (98902) ***(G-15621)***
Mikron Industries Inc ... 253 854-8020
1034 6th Ave N Kent (98032) ***(G-5011)***
Milbrandt Vineyards Inc ... 509 788-0030
508 Cabernet Ct Prosser (99350) ***(G-8057)***
Mileage Maxer LLC ... 360 550-5809
23787 Montecarlo Pl Nw Poulsbo (98370) ***(G-7984)***
Miles Resources LLC ... 253 383-3585
400 Valley Ave Ne Puyallup (98372) ***(G-8192)***
Miles Sand & Gravel Company (PA) ... 253 833-3705
400 Valley Ave Ne Puyallup (98372) ***(G-8193)***
Miles Sand & Gravel Company ... 360 757-3121
663 Pease Rd Burlington (98233) ***(G-2171)***
Miles Sand & Gravel Company ... 360 435-5511
15415 84th St Ne Lake Stevens (98258) ***(G-5661)***
Miles Sand & Gravel Company ... 360 427-0946
3100 W Franklin St Shelton (98584) ***(G-11714)***
Miles Sand & Gravel Company ... 253 922-9116
I5 Highway 512 Hwy 512 Tacoma (98402) ***(G-13414)***
Miles Sand & Gravel Company ... 360 675-2626
3199 N Oak Harbor Rd Oak Harbor (98277) ***(G-7159)***
Miles Sand & Gravel Company ... 360 734-1956
6513 Siper Rd Everson (98247) ***(G-3682)***
Miles Woodworking ... 360 306-3048
1305 Cornwall Ave Bellingham (98225) ***(G-1435)***
Milestone Products Co ... 425 882-1987
15127 Ne 24th St Ste 332 Redmond (98052) ***(G-8589)***
Milgard Manufacturing Inc (HQ) ... 253 922-6030
1010 54th Ave E Fife (98424) ***(G-3971)***
Milgard Manufacturing Inc ... 253 922-4341
2935 70th Ave E Fife (98424) ***(G-3972)***
Milgard Mfg, Fife *Also called M7m Investments* ***(G-3967)***
Milgard Pultrusion, Fife *Also called Milgard Manufacturing Inc* ***(G-3972)***
Milgard Windows, Fife *Also called Milgard Manufacturing Inc* ***(G-3971)***
Military Displays Online, Colbert *Also called Hughes Custom Woodworking Inc* ***(G-2708)***
Military Tails ... 253 229-2427
22021 50th Avenue Ct E Spanaway (98387) ***(G-12065)***
Mill City Brew Werks ... 360 210-4761
325 Ne Cedar St Camas (98607) ***(G-2270)***
Mill Creek Brew Pub, Walla Walla *Also called Big House Brewing Inc* ***(G-14771)***
Mill Creek Spine Injury Inc PS ... 425 344-6835
1112 76th Ave Ne Lake Stevens (98258) ***(G-5662)***
Mill Creek Woodworking Inc ... 509 526-5660
8153 Mill Creek Rd Walla Walla (99362) ***(G-14844)***
Mill Frame LLC ... 425 599-5992
534 Railroad Ave # 1265 Sumas (98295) ***(G-13048)***
Mill Lane Winery Yakima LLC ... 206 817-5767
12302 Marble Rd Yakima (98908) ***(G-15622)***
Mill Man Steel Inc ... 909 854-7020
11307 E Montgomery Dr Spokane Valley (99206) ***(G-12790)***
Mill Race Farm ... 509 964-2473
310 N 2nd St Thorp (98946) ***(G-13628)***
Millard Technical Service ... 253 218-0115
3635 C St Ne Auburn (98002) ***(G-497)***
Millars Organic WD Roasted Cof ... 360 686-3643
33111 Ne 236th St Yacolt (98675) ***(G-15487)***
Millennium Financial Group, Sequim *Also called First Millennium Bank* ***(G-11634)***
Miller & Miller Boatyard Co ... 206 285-5958
2700 W Commodore Way B Seattle (98199) ***(G-10543)***
Miller & Sons Logging, Oroville *Also called Robert E Miller* ***(G-7472)***
Miller Bay Excavating, Poulsbo *Also called Bruce & Walter Webster* ***(G-7953)***
Miller Electric Mfg Co ... 253 212-5346
7102 98th Street Ct E Puyallup (98373) ***(G-8194)***
Miller Fabrication Inc ... 253 833-5400
1435 R St Nw Auburn (98001) ***(G-498)***
Miller Lumber Manufacturing, Fircrest *Also called Milmor Lumber Manufacturing* ***(G-4003)***
Miller Manufacturing ... 360 844-5403
2930 Ford St Washougal (98671) ***(G-14968)***
Miller Manufacturing Inc ... 360 335-1236
3720 S Truman Rd Washougal (98671) ***(G-14969)***
Miller Purr Fect Prints ... 360 687-1186
18904 Ne Lucia Falls Rd Yacolt (98675) ***(G-15488)***
Miller Shingle Company LLC ... 360 691-7727
20820 Gun Club Rd Granite Falls (98252) ***(G-4281)***
Miller Studio, Kent *Also called Industrial Screenprint Inc* ***(G-4951)***
Miller, Kenneth D, Blaine *Also called Steel Magnolia Inc* ***(G-1704)***

Millers Quality Cabinets ... 360 275-4349
110 E Pirates Dr Grapeview (98546) ***(G-4289)***
Millers Welding ... 360 435-7832
15521 Jordan Rd Arlington (98223) ***(G-280)***
Millianna LLC ... 415 505-8507
905 W Riverside Ave # 608 Spokane (99201) ***(G-12394)***
Million Tree Prj For Somalia ... 206 731-9164
2223 Smithers Ave S Renton (98055) ***(G-8855)***
Millman Industries LLC ... 425 471-0854
2104 Millman Rd Langley (98260) ***(G-5783)***
Millwork Cabinet Specialist ... 253 377-4334
13006 50th Ave E Tacoma (98446) ***(G-13415)***
Millwork Concepts, Monroe *Also called R L Industries* ***(G-6611)***
Milman Engineering Inc ... 360 273-5080
19207 Guava St Sw Rochester (98579) ***(G-9137)***
Milmor Lumber Manufacturing ... 253 474-1001
4520 Orchard St W Fircrest (98466) ***(G-4003)***
Milne Aseptics LLC ... 509 786-2240
804 Bennett Ave Prosser (99350) ***(G-8058)***
Milne Fruit Products Inc ... 509 786-0019
804 Bennett Ave Prosser (99350) ***(G-8059)***
Milne Microdried, Grandview *Also called Wyckoff Farms Incorporated* ***(G-4259)***
Milo & Gabby LLC ... 206 257-1957
8721 Golden Gardens Dr Nw Seattle (98117) ***(G-10544)***
Minapsys Software Corp ... 425 891-1460
850 E Spokane Falls Blvd # 121 Spokane (99202) ***(G-12395)***
Mind Modulations ... 626 863-7379
8507 78th Ave Ne Marysville (98270) ***(G-6360)***
Mindcast Software ... 425 341-0450
33530 1st Way S Ste 102 Federal Way (98003) ***(G-3759)***
Mindcastle Books Incorporated ... 206 801-7338
19833 18th Ave Nw Shoreline (98177) ***(G-11789)***
Mindmods, Marysville *Also called Mind Modulations* ***(G-6360)***
Mindplace Company ... 360 376-6494
374 N Beach Rd Ste 2b Eastsound (98245) ***(G-3040)***
Mindray Medical USA Corp ... 425 881-0361
8620 154th Ave Ne 130 Redmond (98052) ***(G-8590)***
Mindray North America, Redmond *Also called Mindray Medical USA Corp* ***(G-8590)***
Minds-I Inc ... 509 252-5725
22819 E Appleway Ave Liberty Lake (99019) ***(G-5846)***
Mindware Inc ... 425 415-3921
15435 86th Ave Ne Kenmore (98028) ***(G-4593)***
Minima Software LLC ... 206 659-9646
1629 Harvard Ave Apt 512 Seattle (98122) ***(G-10545)***
Minnick Hills Vineyard LL ... 509 525-5076
2415 Middle Waitsburg Rd Walla Walla (99362) ***(G-14845)***
Minniear Software Support, Vancouver *Also called William Minniear* ***(G-14694)***
Minnysonoda Corporation ... 360 863-8141
14428 167th Ave Se Monroe (98272) ***(G-6597)***
Mint Valley Paper Company Inc ... 360 931-9055
8813 Ne 244th St Battle Ground (98604) ***(G-723)***
Mintaka Instruments LLC ... 206 783-1414
3050 Nw 63rd St Seattle (98107) ***(G-10546)***
Minute Man Press ... 360 738-3539
1616 Cornwall Ave Ste 121 Bellingham (98225) ***(G-1436)***
Minuteman, Redmond *Also called Ppcs Inc* ***(G-8628)***
Minuteman Fund of Washington ... 253 584-5411
3521 17th Way Se Olympia (98501) ***(G-7340)***
Minuteman Press, Bellevue *Also called Bellevue Printing LLC* ***(G-814)***
Minuteman Press, Renton *Also called Wilo Inc* ***(G-8948)***
Minuteman Press, Vancouver *Also called Jeanne Jolivette* ***(G-14336)***
Minuteman Press, Kennewick *Also called Kennewick Press LLC* ***(G-4682)***
Minuteman Press, Bremerton *Also called B & J Printing Inc* ***(G-1936)***
Minuteman Press, Richland *Also called Bas Inc* ***(G-8972)***
Minuteman Press, Issaquah *Also called Garcia Ink Corp* ***(G-4417)***
Minuteman Press, Auburn *Also called Sls Development Inc* ***(G-567)***
Minuteman Press, Seattle *Also called Belltown Prtg & Graphics Inc* ***(G-9509)***
Minuteman Press, Tacoma *Also called Curt Arneson Enterprises Inc* ***(G-13251)***
Minuteman Press, Tacoma *Also called Highroad Products Inc* ***(G-13337)***
Minuteman Press, Everett *Also called Soterion Co* ***(G-3616)***
Minuteman Press, Olympia *Also called Footeprints Inc* ***(G-7290)***
Minuteman Press, Olympia *Also called Footeprints Incorporated* ***(G-7289)***
Minuteman Press, Seattle *Also called Park & Moazez Enterprises Inc* ***(G-10757)***
Minuteman Press, Bellingham *Also called Minute Man Press* ***(G-1436)***
Minuteman Press ... 360 258-2411
7415 Ne Highway 99 # 103 Vancouver (98665) ***(G-14421)***
Minuteman Press ... 206 577-9199
10300 Greenwood Ave N Seattle (98133) ***(G-10547)***
Minuteman Press ... 509 435-0863
111 N Vista Rd Ste 2d Spokane Valley (99212) ***(G-12791)***
Minuteman Press ... 360 577-3257
402 W Main St Kelso (98626) ***(G-4538)***
Minuteman Press Intl Inc ... 360 692-3470
187 Ne Conifer Dr Bremerton (98311) ***(G-1979)***
Minuteman Press Intl Inc ... 253 841-3161
2102 E Main Ste 111 Puyallup (98372) ***(G-8195)***
Minuteman Press Intl Inc ... 509 452-6144
1114 W Lincoln Ave Yakima (98902) ***(G-15623)***

ALPHABETIC

Minuteman Press Renton 425 251-0781
1120 Sw 16th St Ste 1a Renton (98057) ***(G-8856)***
Mips Tech Inc 408 610-5900
12737 Ne Bel Red Rd # 100 Bellevue (98005) ***(G-1008)***
Mira Technology 425 678-0183
20833 67th Ave W Ste 101 Lynnwood (98036) ***(G-6164)***
Miracle Studios 833 728-3233
17120 Orting Rd N Bonney Lake (98391) ***(G-1729)***
Miracles Vintners LLC 253 606-6202
2753 Vista Ln Walla Walla (99362) ***(G-14846)***
Miramac Metals Inc 509 483-5331
13906 N Newport Hwy Mead (99021) ***(G-6433)***
Mirror Finish Incorporated 360 384-1710
2508 Brown Rd Ferndale (98248) ***(G-3872)***
Misapplied Sciences Inc 425 999-9582
16128 Ne 87th St Redmond (98052) ***(G-8591)***
Mischel Bros Logging Inc 360 649-7101
1933 Sw Berry Lake Rd Port Orchard (98367) ***(G-7829)***
Mishima Reserve, Seattle *Also called Sugar Mountain Livestock LLC* ***(G-11214)***
Misho Global LLC 425 829-8881
14028 Ne Bel Red Rd Bellevue (98007) ***(G-1009)***
Misiu Systems LLC 425 402-8700
3808 209th Pl Se Bothell (98021) ***(G-1877)***
Miss Mags LLC 208 301-0549
100 W Church St Palouse (99161) ***(G-7545)***
Miss Mfftts Mystcal Cpckes LLC 360 890-4403
625 Black Lake Blvd Sw Olympia (98502) ***(G-7341)***
Mission Africa 206 850-9155
1020 30th St Ne Auburn (98002) ***(G-499)***
Missoula Orthotics & Prosthet 406 549-0921
514 S Washington St Spokane (99204) ***(G-12396)***
Misty Mountain Manufacturing 206 763-4055
6264 Stanley Ave S Seattle (98108) ***(G-10548)***
Mitchell Door & Trim, Port Orchard *Also called Mitchell Door and Trim Inc* ***(G-7830)***
Mitchell Door and Trim Inc 360 874-8901
3812 Bancroft Rd E Port Orchard (98366) ***(G-7830)***
Mitchell Hardware W Linn Inc 253 752-2000
2675 N Pearl St Tacoma (98407) ***(G-13416)***
Mitchell Lewis & Staver 253 589-2141
2624 112th St S Ste D3 Lakewood (98499) ***(G-5737)***
Mitchell Osborne 360 379-2427
321 Cherry St Port Townsend (98368) ***(G-7898)***
Mitchell Osborne Photography, Port Townsend *Also called Mitchell Osborne* ***(G-7898)***
Mitchell Technologies, Renton *Also called David T Mitchell* ***(G-8781)***
Mitchell Trucking & Paving, East Wenatchee *Also called Mitchell Trucking and Paving* ***(G-3026)***
Mitchell Trucking and Paving 509 884-5928
3223 Nw Alan Ave East Wenatchee (98802) ***(G-3026)***
Mitercraft Inc 360 299-9979
5126 Guemes Island Rd Anacortes (98221) ***(G-147)***
Miti LLC 253 833-9119
3902 W Valley Hwy N # 306 Auburn (98001) ***(G-500)***
Mitsubishi Electric & Elec USA 425 202-7671
127 10th St S Kirkland (98033) ***(G-5404)***
Mittens By Ann 253 862-1050
4018 Caldwell Rd E Edgewood (98372) ***(G-3085)***
Mitzner Logging 509 422-6834
22585 Highway 20 Okanogan (98840) ***(G-7200)***
Mitzner Logging and Cattle, Okanogan *Also called Mitzner Logging* ***(G-7200)***
Mix 253 383-4327
635 St Helens Ave Tacoma (98402) ***(G-13417)***
Mix Creations 425 392-1123
20524 Se 26th St Issaquah (98075) ***(G-4450)***
Mix It Up LLC 425 396-7345
36532 Se Woody Creek Ln Snoqualmie (98065) ***(G-12019)***
Mixie Manufacturing LLC 360 696-4943
1309 Ne 134th St Ste C Vancouver (98685) ***(G-14422)***
Mixign Inc 206 542-8737
12101 Huckleberry Ln Arlington (98223) ***(G-281)***
Mj Directions LLC 425 656-3621
4000 Airport Way S Seattle (98108) ***(G-10549)***
MJM Manufacturing 305 620-2020
19105 205th St E Orting (98360) ***(G-7485)***
Mjv Mfg 509 735-1662
1920 S Taft St Kennewick (99338) ***(G-4695)***
Mk Industries LLC 425 922-0139
13336 Se 52nd St Bellevue (98006) ***(G-1010)***
Mk Machining, Issaquah *Also called Mark Hummel* ***(G-4444)***
Mk Optimization and Ctrl LLC 509 656-3321
3645 Ashworth Ave N Seattle (98103) ***(G-10550)***
Mk Perrigo Realtor 425 478-6694
1112 19th Ave E Seattle (98112) ***(G-10551)***
Mk20 Inc 509 226-5302
25025 E Appleway Ave Liberty Lake (99019) ***(G-5847)***
Mkg Mfg 360 398-7518
292 Kelly Rd Bellingham (98226) ***(G-1437)***
Mm Industries LLC 360 629-4595
8530 Cedarhome Dr Ste B Stanwood (98292) ***(G-12981)***
Mmusa Inc 360 306-5383
12512 Beverly Park Rd 15-16 Lynnwood (98087) ***(G-6165)***
MNC Services Inc (PA) 425 527-9031
21520 Ne 144th Pl Ste 103 Woodinville (98077) ***(G-15312)***
MNC Services Inc 425 527-9031
13701 Ne Bel Red Rd Bellevue (98005) ***(G-1011)***
Mnr Logging LLC 360 532-3631
6918 Grange Rd Aberdeen (98520) ***(G-23)***
Mnr Logging LLC 360 249-2213
330 W Pioneer Ave Montesano (98563) ***(G-6648)***
Moberg & Company 360 380-5257
6726 Northwest Dr Ferndale (98248) ***(G-3873)***
Mobetize Corp 778 588-5563
8150 Birch Bay Square St # 205 Blaine (98230) ***(G-1684)***
Mobile Air Applied Science 206 953-3786
14 168th Ave Ne Bellevue (98008) ***(G-1012)***
Mobile App Tracking, Seattle *Also called Tune Inc* ***(G-11348)***
Mobile Event Systems, Woodland *Also called Event Power & Lighting Inc* ***(G-15431)***
Mobile Game Partners LLC 310 926-3932
18459 Ne 196th Pl Woodinville (98077) ***(G-15313)***
Mobile Marine Maintenance 360 777-0001
10a Prince St E Chinook (98614) ***(G-2617)***
Mobile One Lube Ex Everett 425 374-8862
2411 Broadway Everett (98201) ***(G-3548)***
Mobile Storage Units Inc 509 276-8220
2927 W Owens Rd Deer Park (99006) ***(G-2909)***
Mobimaging LLC 859 559-5138
4019 Nw Jasmine St Camas (98607) ***(G-2271)***
Mobitat Portable Housing Units, Spokane *Also called Cynthia Rochlitzer* ***(G-12213)***
Moco Engineering & Fabrication 509 226-0199
3212 N Eden Rd Spokane Valley (99216) ***(G-12792)***
Model A Wheel Colors 206 264-4944
1400 S 192nd St Seatac (98148) ***(G-9290)***
Model One 206 383-0380
1817 N 49th St Seattle (98103) ***(G-10552)***
Modeling Dynamics Inc 425 392-2262
2721 226th Ave Se Sammamish (98075) ***(G-9235)***
Models By Rauda Scale Models, Seattle *Also called Rauda Scale Models Inc* ***(G-10926)***
Modelwerks Inc 206 340-6007
655 S Andover St Seattle (98108) ***(G-10553)***
Modern Art Woodwork LLC 360 303-6054
6036 N Star Rd Ferndale (98248) ***(G-3874)***
Modern Building Systems Inc 800 682-1422
1550 Thornton Ave Sw Pacific (98047) ***(G-7532)***
Modern Classics Inc 360 733-6400
1788 Midway Ln Bellingham (98226) ***(G-1438)***
Modern Coach, Seattle *Also called Modern Pattern Works Inc* ***(G-10554)***
Modern Metals LLC 425 405-6994
13317 Ash Way Ste A1 Everett (98204) ***(G-3549)***
Modern Millwork, Yakima *Also called Jbs Millwork Inc* ***(G-15599)***
Modern Millwork & Design, Yakima *Also called Noel Corporation* ***(G-15631)***
Modern Pattern Works Inc 206 762-2227
255 S Austin St Seattle (98108) ***(G-10554)***
Modern Siding LLC 813 484-9498
12322 Highway 99 Ste 214 Everett (98204) ***(G-3550)***
Modern Transport Systems Corp 509 443-5031
4823 E 50th Ave Spokane (99223) ***(G-12397)***
Modern Yacht Joinery 360 928-0214
1023 King St Port Angeles (98363) ***(G-7726)***
Modernchef Inc 425 202-6252
10400 Ne 4th St Ste 500 Bellevue (98004) ***(G-1013)***
Modrall Machine, Vancouver *Also called D & G Auto Parts* ***(G-14161)***
Modular Arts Inc 206 788-4210
8207 S 192nd St Kent (98032) ***(G-5012)***
Modular Driven Tech Inc 604 393-0800
726 Cherry St 100 Sumas (98295) ***(G-13049)***
Modular Software Systems Inc 360 886-8882
33628 Se 348th St Enumclaw (98022) ***(G-3305)***
Modulien Inc 208 874-2219
255 Se Dexter St Pullman (99163) ***(G-8099)***
Modumetal Inc (PA) 877 632-4242
1443 N Northlake Way Seattle (98103) ***(G-10555)***
Modus Health LLC 703 835-0055
123 2nd Ave S Ste 220 Edmonds (98020) ***(G-3135)***
Modutech Marine Inc 253 272-9319
2218 Marine View Dr Tacoma (98422) ***(G-13418)***
Modwright Instruments Inc 360 247-6688
21919 Ne 399th St Amboy (98601) ***(G-95)***
Moe Howard Enterprises Inc 360 538-1622
825 Queen Ave Hoquiam (98550) ***(G-4349)***
Moerke Family 3 LLC 360 748-8952
493 Cousins Rd Chehalis (98532) ***(G-2515)***
Mogul Express 206 386-8070
701 5th Ave Ste 5800 Seattle (98104) ***(G-10556)***
Mohawk Esv Inc 253 395-3277
23210 71st Pl S Kent (98032) ***(G-5013)***
Mohawk Industries Inc 253 395-3277
23210 71st Pl S Ste 101 Kent (98032) ***(G-5014)***
Mohawk Metal Company 360 816-0679
3825 Ne 68th St Vancouver (98661) ***(G-14423)***
Mohr & Associates, Richland *Also called Linda J Mohr* ***(G-9022)***
Mohr Test and Measurement LLC (HQ) 509 946-0941
2105 Henderson Loop Richland (99354) ***(G-9027)***
Mohr Test and Measurement LLC 888 852-0408
1440 Agnes St Richland (99352) ***(G-9028)***

Mokajoe Inc 360 714-1953
1050 Larrabee Ave Ste 104 Bellingham (98225) *(G-1439)*
Mold Dmage Rmval Pros Lakewood 253 343-0497
14902 Union Ave Sw Ste C Lakewood (98498) *(G-5738)*
Molly Moons Homemade Ice Cream (PA) 206 547-5105
1622 N 45th St Seattle (98103) *(G-10557)*
Mollys Salads LLC 206 512-3075
4636 E Marginal Way S Seattle (98134) *(G-10558)*
Molson Runner Sleds 425 445-2975
17515 Se 257th St Covington (98042) *(G-2834)*
Momentum Gear 360 524-2098
5601 E 18th St Ste 308 Vancouver (98661) *(G-14424)*
Momentum Interactive LLC 915 203-5349
1201 Birch Falls Dr Bellingham (98229) *(G-1440)*
Momentum Lighting, Mukilteo *Also called S3j Elctrnics Acquisition Corp (G-6975)*
Momma DOT Publishing LLC 425 322-3486
11632 18th St Se Lake Stevens (98258) *(G-5663)*
Moms Carmel Apples & More LLC 509 515-8153
5610 W Clearwater Ave Kennewick (99336) *(G-4696)*
Moms Club of Dupont 206 209-9048
2390 Simmons St Unit A Dupont (98327) *(G-2970)*
Monaco Enterprises Inc 509 926-6277
14820 E Sprague Ave Spokane Valley (99216) *(G-12793)*
Monarch Machine and Tl Co Inc 509 547-7753
410 S Oregon Ave Pasco (99301) *(G-7603)*
Monarch Metals, Pasco *Also called Monarch Machine and Tl Co Inc (G-7603)*
Mondelez Global LLC 253 395-4237
19032 62nd Ave S Kent (98032) *(G-5015)*
Mondello Publishing 425 775-9695
3929 205th Pl Sw Lynnwood (98036) *(G-6166)*
Moneymindersoftware 360 255-4300
3111 Newmarket St Ste 106 Bellingham (98226) *(G-1441)*
Monk Logging Inc 509 447-4526
547 Quail Loop Newport (99156) *(G-7061)*
Monkey Wrench Fabrication LLC 206 992-8509
9392 Ne Wardwell Rd Bainbridge Island (98110) *(G-650)*
Monolithic Power Systems Inc 408 826-0600
101 Elliott Ave W Ste 500 Seattle (98119) *(G-10559)*
Monolithic Power Systems Inc (PA) 425 296-9956
4040 Lake Wash Blvd Ne Kirkland (98033) *(G-5405)*
Monroe Door & Millwork Inc 360 863-9882
17350 Tye St Se Monroe (98272) *(G-6598)*
Monroe Machined Products Inc 206 242-4898
1422 S 192nd St Seatac (98148) *(G-9291)*
Monroe Monitor, Monroe *Also called Ken Robinson Publications Inc (G-6585)*
Monrovia Apartments, Spokane *Also called Nordal Denver (G-12406)*
Monsanto 509 760-0707
912 S Dahlia Dr Moses Lake (98837) *(G-6726)*
Monsanto Company 509 349-2327
115 N 1st St Warden (98857) *(G-14933)*
Monsanto Company 509 488-0821
776 S Booker Rd Hatton (99344) *(G-4322)*
Monson Ranches 425 488-0200
14450 Woodnvl Rdmnd Rd Ne Woodinville (98072) *(G-15314)*
Monson Ranches 509 628-3880
16304 Dallas Rd Richland (99352) *(G-9029)*
Monsoon Solutions Inc 425 378-8081
2405 140th Ave Ne A115 Bellevue (98005) *(G-1014)*
Monster Concepts Inc 206 706-6730
1406 Nw 53rd St Ste 1a Seattle (98107) *(G-10560)*
Monte Scarlatto Estate Winery 509 531-3081
28719 E Sr 224 Ne Benton City (99320) *(G-1620)*
Monte Whtzel Con Qarter Cir Ha 509 220-8449
4341 Sprngdale Hunters Rd Springdale (99173) *(G-12951)*
Montes Logging & Firewood 360 943-3181
7607 Kmrlyn Prairie Ln Se Olympia (98513) *(G-7342)*
Montesano Vidette, Montesano *Also called S J Olsen Publishing Inc (G-6656)*
Montesano Vision Center, Montesano *Also called Robert Wickes Od (G-6654)*
Montgomery Law Firm 509 684-2519
287 E Astor Ave Colville (99114) *(G-2766)*
Montgomery, Chris, Colville *Also called Montgomery Law Firm (G-2766)*
Monument Apples LLC 509 787-5700
13762 Road 11 Nw Quincy (98848) *(G-8305)*
Monument Wheelworks LLC 206 856-9509
335 Nw 49th St Seattle (98107) *(G-10561)*
Monumental Chewelah 509 935-6962
401 S Park St Chewelah (99109) *(G-2604)*
Monumental Task 509 449-8286
1033 7th Ave S Okanogan (98840) *(G-7201)*
Moon Cheese, Ferndale *Also called Nutradried Food Company LLC (G-3880)*
Moon Donkey Press LLC 425 990-8149
3015 92nd Pl Ne Clyde Hill (98004) *(G-2704)*
Moon Valley Natural Pdts LLC 360 595-0500
3288 Valley Hwy Deming (98244) *(G-2921)*
Moon Valley Organics, Deming *Also called Moon Valley Natural Pdts LLC (G-2921)*
Moonlite Machining Inc 360 863-8535
508 Powell St Monroe (98272) *(G-6599)*
Moonlite Machining Inc 360 794-6622
17700 147th St Se Ste H Monroe (98272) *(G-6600)*
Moonstuff Inc 509 947-2981
5420 Fern Loop West Richland (99353) *(G-15099)*
Moor Innovative Tech LLC 253 343-2216
4812 64th St E Tacoma (98443) *(G-13419)*
Moore Manufacturing LLC 360 400-3277
38513 Allen Rd S Roy (98580) *(G-9163)*
Moore Mfg Co 360 677-2442
71509 Ne Old Cascade Hwy Skykomish (98288) *(G-11867)*
Moore-Clark USA Inc (HQ) 360 425-6715
1140 Industrial Way Longview (98632) *(G-5932)*
Moose Canyon Winery 253 225-1985
9813 36th St E Edgewood (98371) *(G-3086)*
Moose Creek Logging Inc 360 631-3728
39209 State Route 530 Ne Arlington (98223) *(G-282)*
Moosoo Corporation 866 966-6766
7818 S 212th St Ste A110 Kent (98032) *(G-5016)*
Mor-Log Inc 360 426-7872
1153 E Agate Rd Shelton (98584) *(G-11715)*
Mora LLC 206 855-1112
22195 Viking Ave Nw C Poulsbo (98370) *(G-7985)*
Mora Iced Creamery, Poulsbo *Also called Mora LLC (G-7985)*
Morad Antenna, Bellingham *Also called Morad Electronics Corporation (G-1442)*
Morad Electronics Corporation 206 789-2525
3125 Mercer Ave Ste 106 Bellingham (98225) *(G-1442)*
Moravek Biochemicals Inc 509 375-5124
2770 Salk Ave Richland (99354) *(G-9030)*
Morcant Software 509 225-6807
618 S 13th Ave Yakima (98902) *(G-15624)*
Mordi Software 425 301-4897
1211 195th Ave Se Snohomish (98290) *(G-11948)*
Morel Industries Inc 360 691-9722
17735 59th Ave Ne Arlington (98223) *(G-283)*
Morgan Aero Products Inc 425 438-9600
1450 80th St Sw Everett (98203) *(G-3551)*
Morgan Aerospace LLC 360 435-9755
17713 48th Dr Ne Arlington (98223) *(G-284)*
Morgan Branch Cnc Inc 360 435-7170
3923 88th St Ne Ste Q Marysville (98270) *(G-6361)*
Morgan Creek Envmtl Rsrces Inc 360 202-6536
31409 S Skagit Hwy Sedro Woolley (98284) *(G-11551)*
Morgan Electric & Plumbing Inc 206 547-1617
3627 Stone Way N Seattle (98103) *(G-10562)*
Morgan Steel & Metal Works 360 301-6611
170 Nw Beaver Rdg Poulsbo (98370) *(G-7986)*
Morice Engineering 360 754-9217
8120 Delphi Rd Sw Olympia (98512) *(G-7343)*
Morley Machine Tool Algnmt Inc 253 926-1515
800 Fife Way Milton (98354) *(G-6536)*
Morning Dew Candles 206 772-5611
10802 Lake Ridge Dr S Seattle (98178) *(G-10563)*
Morning News Tribune 253 597-8511
1950 S State St Tacoma (98405) *(G-13420)*
Morning Sun Inc 253 922-6589
10828 Gravelly Lake Dr Sw # 212 Lakewood (98499) *(G-5739)*
Morningstar Business Group Inc 509 476-2944
3 814 Central Ave Oroville (98844) *(G-7469)*
Morpac Industries Inc (PA) 253 735-8922
117 Frontage Rd N Ste A Pacific (98047) *(G-7533)*
Morris Magnets, Monroe *Also called Minnysonoda Corporation (G-6597)*
Morris Printer Solutions 360 891-3812
9505 Ne 8th St Vancouver (98664) *(G-14425)*
Morrison Art Glass Inc 360 714-8732
2111 Lincoln St Bellingham (98225) *(G-1443)*
Morton A Kimball 360 458-5251
13431 Solberg Rd Se Yelm (98597) *(G-15740)*
Morup Signs Inc 425 883-6337
12824 Ne 14th Pl Bellevue (98005) *(G-1015)*
Morwenstow 425 483-0320
14125 Ne 189th St Woodinville (98072) *(G-15315)*
Mosaicsnmore 425 273-3216
614 Logan Rd Lynnwood (98036) *(G-6167)*
Moses Lake Industries Inc (HQ) 509 762-5336
8248 Randolph Rd Ne Moses Lake (98837) *(G-6727)*
Moses Lake Sheet Metal Inc 509 765-1614
1130 E Wheeler Rd Moses Lake (98837) *(G-6728)*
Mosesvue LLC 425 644-8501
12020 Se 32nd St Ste 2 Bellevue (98005) *(G-1016)*
Mosquito Fleet Winery LLC 360 710-8788
21 Ne Old Belfair Hwy Belfair (98528) *(G-768)*
Moss Green Inc 206 285-4020
3635 Thorndyke Ave W B Seattle (98119) *(G-10564)*
Mostly Muffins, Kent *Also called Anne & Mollys Inc (G-4785)*
Motek Inc 206 632-7795
1849 N 53rd St Seattle (98103) *(G-10565)*
Mother Nature's Wisdom, Yakima *Also called Altera Inc (G-15505)*
Motherwell Products Usa Inc 360 366-2600
7074 Portal Way Ste 140 Ferndale (98248) *(G-3875)*
Motion Ducks LLC 253 797-0132
25811 Lawson St Black Diamond (98010) *(G-1651)*
Motion Water Sports Inc (HQ) 800 662-7436
7926 Bracken Pl Se Snoqualmie (98065) *(G-12020)*
Motion Workshop, Seattle *Also called Gli Interactive LLC (G-10082)*
Motor Works Inc 509 535-9240
1026 N Haven St Spokane (99202) *(G-12398)*

ALPHABETIC

Motorsports ALPHABETIC SECTION

Motorsports...360 799-0865
32615 Cascade View Dr B1 Sultan (98294) ***(G-13029)***
Motovotano LLC...206 363-0338
12756 Quantum Ln 8-30 Anacortes (98221) ***(G-148)***
Mount Adams Lumber Co Inc...509 395-2122
10 Church St Trout Lake (98650) ***(G-13681)***
Mount Baker Fireplace Shop...360 384-3507
1273 Sunset Ave Bellingham (98226) ***(G-1444)***
Mount Bakery...360 715-2195
308 W Champion St Ste C Bellingham (98225) ***(G-1445)***
Mount Evergreen Industries...360 584-9620
4200 Boston Harbor Rd Ne Olympia (98506) ***(G-7344)***
Mount Fury Co Inc...425 391-0747
1592 Nw Maple St Issaquah (98027) ***(G-4451)***
Mount Vernon Electric Mtr Svcs, Mount Vernon *Also called Industrial Electric Co Inc* ***(G-6804)***
Mountain Dog Sign Company Inc...509 891-9999
1620 N Mamer Rd Ste D100 Spokane Valley (99216) ***(G-12794)***
Mountain Log Homes Inc...360 799-0533
35409 State Rte 2 Startup (98293) ***(G-13002)***
Mountain Logging Inc (PA)...509 493-3511
1000 W Jewett Blvd White Salmon (98672) ***(G-15123)***
Mountain Logging Inc...509 493-3511
715 E Steuben St Bingen (98605) ***(G-1640)***
Mountain Loom Co...360 295-3856
1339 State Route 506 Vader (98593) ***(G-13986)***
Mountain Loop Country Store, Darrington *Also called Sauk Suiattle Indian Tribe Tru* ***(G-2869)***
Mountain Mist, Puyallup *Also called Richardson Bottling Company* ***(G-8237)***
Mountain Muesli LLC...253 426-8092
1401 S Sprague Ave # 570 Tacoma (98405) ***(G-13421)***
Mountain Side Sand & Grav LLC...360 701-1241
307 Binghampton St Se Rainier (98576) ***(G-8318)***
Mountain Springs Building Co...206 550-4380
409 161st Pl Se Bellevue (98008) ***(G-1017)***
Mountain Springs Millwork, Bellevue *Also called Mountain Springs Building Co* ***(G-1017)***
Mountain Sttes Elec Contrs Inc...509 532-0110
1220 E 1st Ave Spokane (99202) ***(G-12399)***
Mountain Top Inc...360 416-3333
1726 Riverside Dr Mount Vernon (98273) ***(G-6814)***
Mountain Tree Farm Company...253 924-2345
2515 S 336th St Federal Way (98001) ***(G-3760)***
Mountain Valley Products Inc...509 837-8084
108 Blaine Ave Sunnyside (98944) ***(G-13134)***
Mountain View Industries...425 788-5551
18807 Ne 165th St Woodinville (98072) ***(G-15316)***
Mountain View Industries Inc...360 894-0499
17730 153rd Ave Se Yelm (98597) ***(G-15741)***
Mountainside Cabinets...253 278-8400
19627 70th Avenue Ct E Spanaway (98387) ***(G-12066)***
Mountainview Polaris Inc...509 765-9340
507 E 3rd Ave Moses Lake (98837) ***(G-6729)***
Mountainview Screen Print...509 773-6290
3255 Highway 142 Goldendale (98620) ***(G-4203)***
Moxee Innovations Corporation...509 575-6322
721 E Viola Ave Yakima (98901) ***(G-15625)***
Moxee Innovations Corporation...509 575-6322
207b W Charron Rd Moxee (98936) ***(G-6882)***
Moxie Software Cim Corp...425 467-5000
15 Lake Bellevue Dr # 200 Bellevue (98005) ***(G-1018)***
Mp Industrial, Auburn *Also called Miti LLC* ***(G-500)***
Mpl Innovations Inc (PA)...425 398-1310
2505 2nd Ave Seattle (98121) ***(G-10566)***
Mpm Technologies Inc (PA)...973 599-4416
16201 E Ind Ave Ste 3200 Spokane Valley (99216) ***(G-12795)***
Mpm Vintners LLC...509 525-2469
1102 Dell Ave Walla Walla (99362) ***(G-14847)***
Mpo, Silverdale *Also called Maughan Prsthetic Orthotic Inc* ***(G-11849)***
Mqs Group LLC...360 956-9114
301 18th Ave Se Olympia (98501) ***(G-7345)***
Mr Ed Floats...360 834-3986
4001 Se Crown Rd Camas (98607) ***(G-2272)***
Mr Print One...253 693-2802
2005 Mtn View Ave W Tacoma (98466) ***(G-13422)***
Mr Rpm LLC...360 387-2272
587 Utsalady Rd Camano Island (98282) ***(G-2218)***
Mr TS Trophies...360 424-9339
17691 State Route 536 Mount Vernon (98273) ***(G-6815)***
MSC International, Vancouver *Also called Jr Moore* ***(G-14342)***
MSC Print House...206 708-1423
3300 Wallingford Ave N Seattle (98103) ***(G-10567)***
Mscsoftware Corporation...855 672-7638
150 120th Ave Ne Ste 310 Bellevue (98005) ***(G-1019)***
MSI, Kirkland *Also called M S I Engineering Corporation* ***(G-5390)***
Msr Global Health, Seattle *Also called Cascade Designs Inc* ***(G-9641)***
Msr Marine & Vhcl Htg Systems...206 546-5670
19302 1st Ave Nw Shoreline (98177) ***(G-11790)***
MST, Redmond *Also called Microsurgical Technology Inc* ***(G-8586)***
Mt Adams Lumber Company Inc...509 395-2131
10 Church St Trout Lake (98650) ***(G-13682)***
Mt Baker Candy Co...360 756-0661
1 Bellis Fair Pkwy # 434 Bellingham (98226) ***(G-1446)***
Mt Baker Manufacturing...360 778-1238
1689 Aaron Dr Lynden (98264) ***(G-6038)***
Mt Baker Mining and Mtls LLC (PA)...360 595-4445
5421 Guide Meridian C Bellingham (98226) ***(G-1447)***
Mt Baker Mining and Mtls LLC...360 739-7264
5421 Guide Meridian C Bellingham (98226) ***(G-1448)***
Mt Baker Plywood, Bellingham *Also called Mt Baker Products Inc* ***(G-1450)***
Mt Baker Powder Coating...360 366-3233
2023 Grant St Bellingham (98225) ***(G-1449)***
Mt Baker Products Inc...360 733-3960
2929 Roeder Ave Bellingham (98225) ***(G-1450)***
Mt Baker Stump Grinding & Grav...360 684-1695
501 Shuksan Way Everson (98247) ***(G-3683)***
Mt Norway Fabrication LLC...360 836-0322
2319 Se 370th Ave Washougal (98671) ***(G-14970)***
Mt Peak Alpacas LLC...253 297-4083
47921 284th Ave Se Enumclaw (98022) ***(G-3306)***
Mt Pickett Woodworking...360 376-2449
517 Picketts Ln Olga (98279) ***(G-7216)***
Mt. Adams Forest Pdts & Svcs, Glenwood *Also called Hansen & Spies Logging Inc* ***(G-4183)***
Mtd Publishing...509 525-7289
1942 Gemstone Dr Walla Walla (99362) ***(G-14848)***
Mtn Satellite Communications, Seattle *Also called Emerging Mkts Cmmnications LLC* ***(G-9916)***
Mtn Threds and Clothing...509 258-4443
4266 Jepsen Rd Valley (99181) ***(G-13994)***
Much More Embroidery...360 289-0955
643 E Chance A La Mer Ne Ocean Shores (98569) ***(G-7186)***
Mudslayer Manufacturing LLC...360 477-0251
261340 Highway 101 Sequim (98382) ***(G-11649)***
Mugs and More, Pacific *Also called Idea Company* ***(G-7530)***
Mukilteo Beacon...425 347-5634
806 5th St Mukilteo (98275) ***(G-6954)***
Mukilteo Coffee Company, Mukilteo *Also called Gbjc Inc* ***(G-6927)***
Mukilteo Tribune, Snohomish *Also called Mach Publishing Company Inc* ***(G-11941)***
Mule and Elk Brewing Co LLC...206 909-9622
418 E 1st St Ste 7 Cle Elum (98922) ***(G-2672)***
Mulrony Logging LLC...509 261-1549
192 Horseshoe Bend Rd Goldendale (98620) ***(G-4204)***
Multi App Coatings LLC...253 841-1256
9801 126th St E Puyallup (98373) ***(G-8196)***
Multi Manufacturing Inc...509 452-5628
1120 1/2 N 34th Ave Yakima (98902) ***(G-15626)***
Multi Score Inc...206 524-7591
10327 44th Ave Ne Seattle (98125) ***(G-10568)***
Multi Score Manufacturing, Seattle *Also called Multi Score Inc* ***(G-10568)***
Multico Rating Systems...206 357-3928
610 12th Ave E Seattle (98102) ***(G-10569)***
Multifab Inc (PA)...509 924-6631
3808 N Sullivan Rd Bldg 6 Spokane Valley (99216) ***(G-12796)***
Multimodal Health Inc...651 245-2326
13 10 Mainor Ave 502 Seattle (98101) ***(G-10570)***
Multisonus Audio Inc...425 241-1112
295 Kelly Rd Bellingham (98226) ***(G-1451)***
Multliple Streams Marketin...206 650-6769
19323 15th Ave Nw Shoreline (98177) ***(G-11791)***
Mulvaney Trucking and Excav...509 784-4502
5980 Entiat River Rd Entiat (98822) ***(G-3268)***
Munks Livestock Sling Mfg...360 293-6581
9578 Marchs Point Rd Anacortes (98221) ***(G-149)***
Munson Boats, Burlington *Also called William E Munson Company* ***(G-2203)***
Munson Ranches, Richland *Also called Monson Ranches* ***(G-9029)***
Munters Moisture Control Svcs...707 863-4189
301 30th St Ne Ste 118 Auburn (98002) ***(G-501)***
Murdock Roach Inc...509 302-1054
4708 W 4th Ct Kennewick (99336) ***(G-4697)***
Murdocks...253 858-9697
5501 90th Ave Nw Gig Harbor (98335) ***(G-4135)***
Murphy Nathanial...509 386-0727
184 Murphy St Waitsburg (99361) ***(G-14756)***
Murphy & Dad Inc...360 438-2747
3480 Martin Way E Olympia (98506) ***(G-7346)***
Murphy Company...360 482-2521
505 Elma Mccleary Rd Elma (98541) ***(G-3250)***
Murphy JP Construction...425 222-7299
8430 Fauntleroy Pl Sw Seattle (98136) ***(G-10571)***
Murphy Plywood, Elma *Also called Murphy Company* ***(G-3250)***
Murphy Runa Inc...206 782-2664
5416 Shilshole Ave Nw Seattle (98107) ***(G-10572)***
Muscleclub 4 Men...206 624-9785
1806 8th Ave Apt 214 Seattle (98101) ***(G-10573)***
Museum Quality Discount Frmng (PA)...206 624-1057
1964 4th Ave S Seattle (98134) ***(G-10574)***
Museum Resource LLC...206 547-4047
19102 Des Moines Mem Dr S Seatac (98148) ***(G-9292)***
Music Express LLC...206 842-6317
321 High School Rd Ne D3 Bainbridge Island (98110) ***(G-651)***
Mustad Longline Inc...206 284-4376
4240 Gilman Pl W Ste B Seattle (98199) ***(G-10575)***

Mustang Sign Group, Kennewick *Also called Mustang Signs LLC* ***(G-4698)***
Mustang Signs LLC 509 735-4607
10379 W Clearwater Ave Kennewick (99336) ***(G-4698)***
Mustang Survival Inc 360 676-1782
1215 Old Fairhaven Pkwy Bellingham (98225) ***(G-1452)***
Mustang Survival Holdings Inc 360 676-1782
3870 Mustang Way Ste 101 Bellingham (98226) ***(G-1453)***
Mustard and Co LLC 734 904-9877
4501 Shilshole Ave Nw # 205 Seattle (98107) ***(G-10576)***
Mutiny Bay Blues LLC 360 678-4315
5578 Mutiny Bay Rd Freeland (98249) ***(G-4033)***
Mutiny Bay Software LLC 360 331-5170
5645 Carie Ln Freeland (98249) ***(G-4034)***
Mutual Industries Inc 206 767-6647
9832 17th Ave Sw Ste Es Seattle (98106) ***(G-10577)***
Mutual Materials 425 452-2300
605 119th Ave Ne Bellevue (98005) ***(G-1020)***
Mutual Materials Company 253 838-0803
1357 W Valley Hwy N Auburn (98001) ***(G-502)***
Mutual Materials Company 360 573-5683
10019 Ne 72nd Ave Vancouver (98686) ***(G-14426)***
Mutual Materials Company 509 924-2120
10627 S Highway 27 Mica (99023) ***(G-6501)***
Mutual Materials Company 425 353-9686
1410 Grove St Marysville (98270) ***(G-6362)***
Mutual Materials Company Inc 253 589-6434
2201 112th St S Tacoma (98444) ***(G-13423)***
Mutual-Target LLC (PA) 425 452-2300
605 119th Ave Ne Bellevue (98005) ***(G-1021)***
Mvp Athletic Inc 360 915-8715
6005 Capitol Blvd Sw Tumwater (98501) ***(G-13888)***
Mvr Timber Cutting Inc 360 459-7409
12028 Dream St Sw Olympia (98512) ***(G-7347)***
Mxs, Seattle *Also called Mach Transonic LLC* ***(G-10459)***
My Cabinetry 509 879-0086
11425 E Trent Ave Spokane Valley (99206) ***(G-12797)***
My City Wise LLC 206 409-0818
7724 35th Ave Ne # 15528 Seattle (98115) ***(G-10578)***
My Jewele, Vancouver *Also called J Lanning Jewelers* ***(G-14331)***
My Local Co 360 989-6903
8328 Earl Ave Nw Seattle (98117) ***(G-10579)***
My Local Honey, Seattle *Also called My Local Co* ***(G-10579)***
My T-Shirt Source 425 746-7447
13257 Ne 20th St Bellevue (98005) ***(G-1022)***
My Wooden Treasures, White Salmon *Also called Knot Hole Inc* ***(G-15120)***
Mybock Manufacturing LLC 716 913-4157
3515 Sw Ocean View Dr # 106 Seattle (98146) ***(G-10580)***
Myco Molding Inc 360 676-9656
1650 Jills Ct Bellingham (98226) ***(G-1454)***
Myinterzone 206 679-4566
9735 8th Ave Nw Seattle (98117) ***(G-10581)***
Myo-Tronics, Kent *Also called Myotronics-Noromed Inc* ***(G-5017)***
Myotronics-Noromed Inc 206 243-4214
5870 S 194th St Kent (98032) ***(G-5017)***
Myovision 800 969-6961
13545 Erickson Pl Ne S Seattle (98125) ***(G-10582)***
Myrle B Foster 360 733-2509
2399 Mt Baker Hwy Bellingham (98226) ***(G-1455)***
Myseps 858 231-2774
7312 Mccrmick Wods Dr Sw Port Orchard (98367) ***(G-7831)***
Mystic Ltd 425 251-5959
301 Sw 27th St Seattle (98101) ***(G-10583)***
Mystic Woodworking 425 736-1416
11428 Se 82nd St Newcastle (98056) ***(G-7036)***
Myyearlook 303 523-2468
6749 Se Skycrest Ln Port Orchard (98366) ***(G-7832)***
N A I Inc 509 453-4778
2603 S 16th Ave Union Gap (98903) ***(G-13945)***
N A P Chemical, Pasco *Also called Northwest AG Pdts LLC* ***(G-7604)***
N C I Inc 360 225-9701
1819 Schurman Way Ste 106 Woodland (98674) ***(G-15449)***
N C Power Systems Co 425 251-5877
17900 W Valley Hwy Tukwila (98188) ***(G-13774)***
N E S, Puyallup *Also called Northwest Envmtl Solutions Inc* ***(G-8205)***
N E S Enterprises 509 928-9151
1109 N Bessie Rd Spokane Valley (99212) ***(G-12798)***
N E W Castings 509 924-6464
3808 N Sullivan Rd 8q Spokane Valley (99216) ***(G-12799)***
N J L Inc 360 590-8100
779 Cardinal Ave Ne Ocean Shores (98569) ***(G-7187)***
N L Enterprises, Kirkland *Also called Neil Levinson Enterprises* ***(G-5409)***
N M T, Shaw Island *Also called Northwest Marine Tech Inc* ***(G-11671)***
N P I, Seattle *Also called National Products Inc* ***(G-10589)***
N R G Barriers, Kent *Also called Johns Manville Corporation* ***(G-4970)***
N R G Enterprises Inc 425 556-3993
10826 183rd Ave Ne Redmond (98052) ***(G-8592)***
N W Sound & Security Tech LLC 360 213-1619
16315 Ne Union Rd Ridgefield (98642) ***(G-9095)***
N-Vee Embroidery 425 246-3125
14428 75th Ave Ne Kirkland (98034) ***(G-5406)***
N.everett Asphalt Materials, Everett *Also called Cemex Cnstr Mtls PCF LLC* ***(G-3414)***
N2 Storage Systems Inc 509 981-8097
4227 E Chris Ct Mead (99021) ***(G-6434)***
NA Degerstrom Inc (PA) 509 928-3333
3303 N Sullivan Rd Spokane Valley (99216) ***(G-12800)***
Naan & Brew 425 330-3891
200 E Maple St Apt 101 Bellingham (98225) ***(G-1456)***
Nabat Publishing 509 869-8707
4210 E Ermina Ave Spokane (99217) ***(G-12400)***
Nabisco, Kent *Also called Mondelez Global LLC* ***(G-5015)***
Nabtesco Aerospace Inc 425 602-8400
12413 Willows Rd Ne Kirkland (98034) ***(G-5407)***
Naches Heights Vineyard LLC 509 966-4355
1857 Weikel Rd Yakima (98908) ***(G-15627)***
Naches Heights Vinyrd & Winery, Yakima *Also called Naches Heights Vineyard LLC* ***(G-15627)***
Nada Literature, Vancouver *Also called J & M Reports LLC* ***(G-14329)***
Nails On Wheels 253 839-1123
5416 S 296th Ct Auburn (98001) ***(G-503)***
Naimor Inc 360 756-9700
2025 Masonry Way Bellingham (98226) ***(G-1457)***
Naked Prosthetics, Olympia *Also called RCM Enterprise LLC* ***(G-7380)***
Nalco Chemical, Spokane *Also called Nalco Company LLC* ***(G-12401)***
Nalco Company LLC 509 928-7713
421 W Riverside Ave # 770 Spokane (99201) ***(G-12401)***
Nancy Baer 360 668-0350
18208 67th Ave Se Snohomish (98296) ***(G-11949)***
Nancy Zwieback 206 306-0411
643 Nw 114th Pl Seattle (98177) ***(G-10584)***
Nannette Louise Davis 425 485-5570
12601 Ne Wdnvlle Dr Ste F Woodinville (98072) ***(G-15317)***
Nano Arts LLC 509 525-8531
96 Frontage Rd Walla Walla (99362) ***(G-14849)***
Nano Lopez Studios, Walla Walla *Also called Nano Arts LLC* ***(G-14849)***
Nanofiber Tech Inc 206 781-9288
1420 5th Ave Ste 2200 Seattle (98101) ***(G-10585)***
Nanoice 206 257-3380
495 Andover Park E Tukwila (98188) ***(G-13775)***
Nanoice Inc 206 257-3380
17280 Woodinville Redmond Woodinville (98072) ***(G-15318)***
Nanook Lodge 206 200-8233
1900 W Nickerson St Seattle (98119) ***(G-10586)***
Nanoport Technologies LLC 206 403-1714
300 Cessna Ave Friday Harbor (98250) ***(G-4052)***
NAPA Auto Parts, Oak Harbor *Also called Whidbey Auto Parts Inc* ***(G-7170)***
NAPA Auto Parts, Spokane *Also called Genuine Parts Company* ***(G-12269)***
Napalm Racing 509 991-9759
27915 N Perry Rd Chattaroy (99003) ***(G-2448)***
Napeequa Vintners 509 763-1600
18820 Beaver Valley Rd Leavenworth (98826) ***(G-5810)***
Naps Forming Systems 800 922-2082
13616 8th St E Sumner (98390) ***(G-13087)***
Narrows Brewing LLP 253 327-1400
9007 S 19th St Tacoma (98466) ***(G-13424)***
Naselle Machine, Naselle *Also called John M Smith* ***(G-7013)***
Naselle Rock & Asphalt Company (PA) 360 484-3443
50 Crusher Ln Naselle (98638) ***(G-7017)***
Nat Seattle Inc 425 424-3370
22125 17th Ave Se Ste 107 Bothell (98021) ***(G-1878)***
Nathan Capital LLC (PA) 360 835-1211
750 S 32nd St Washougal (98671) ***(G-14971)***
Nation To Nation Premium 360 731-0330
20 Cedar Hill Ln Sequim (98382) ***(G-11650)***
National Banner Supply 253 333-7443
4204 Auburn Way N Ste 4 Auburn (98002) ***(G-504)***
National Barricade & Sign Co 509 534-2619
6602 E Main Ave Spokane Valley (99212) ***(G-12801)***
National Barricade of Yakima, Yakima *Also called J Freitag Enterprises Inc* ***(G-15595)***
National Color 206 281-9400
769 Hayes St Ste 101 Seattle (98109) ***(G-10587)***
National Color Graphics Inc 509 326-6464
25 W Boone Ave Spokane (99201) ***(G-12402)***
National Feed, Arlington *Also called National Food Corporation* ***(G-286)***
National Food Corporation 509 457-4031
1752 Deering Off Rd Moxee (98936) ***(G-6883)***
National Food Corporation 360 653-2904
16900 51st Ave Ne Arlington (98223) ***(G-285)***
National Food Corporation 360 435-9207
6524 180th St Ne Arlington (98223) ***(G-286)***
National Frozen Foods Corp 360 748-9963
436 Nw State Ave Chehalis (98532) ***(G-2516)***
National Frozen Foods Corp (PA) 206 322-8900
1600 Frview Ave E Ste 200 Seattle (98102) ***(G-10588)***
National Frozen Foods Corp 509 766-0793
14406 Road 3 Se Moses Lake (98837) ***(G-6730)***
National Garden Wholesale, Vancouver *Also called Sls Runout LLC* ***(G-14594)***
National Glass Industries Inc (HQ) 425 488-8126
17030 Wdnvll Rdmond Rd Ne Woodinville (98072) ***(G-15319)***
National Hsptlity Rsources LLC 360 413-1654
1242 Milbanke Dr Se Olympia (98513) ***(G-7348)***
National Indus Concepts Inc (PA) 425 489-4300
23518 63rd Ave Se Woodinville (98072) ***(G-15320)***

National Interad, Seattle *Also called Cobalt Group Inc* ***(G-9708)***
National Management Software.....509 327-0192
827 W 1st Ave Ste 401 Spokane (99201) ***(G-12403)***
National Products Inc (PA).....206 763-8361
8410 Dallas Ave S Seattle (98108) ***(G-10589)***
National Sign Corporation (PA).....206 282-0700
1255 Westlake Ave N Seattle (98109) ***(G-10590)***
National Sign Systems Ltd.....360 699-3055
4401 Ne St Johns Rd Vancouver (98661) ***(G-14427)***
National Specialties LLC.....253 581-4908
12829 Pacific Hwy Sw Lakewood (98499) ***(G-5740)***
National Wirecraft Company Inc.....360 424-1129
1012 W Division St Mount Vernon (98273) ***(G-6816)***
National Wirecraft Company Inc.....360 424-1129
1012 W Division St Mount Vernon (98273) ***(G-6817)***
Nationwide SEC Solutions Inc.....800 908-8992
6407 Ne 117th Ave Vancouver (98662) ***(G-14428)***
Natural Essences.....509 820-3242
210506 E 193 Pr Se Kennewick (99337) ***(G-4699)***
Natural Machines Inc.....206 747-9483
925 4th Ave Ste 2900 Seattle (98104) ***(G-10591)***
Natural Matters Inc.....206 387-7054
3451 24th Ave W Apt 522 Seattle (98199) ***(G-10592)***
Natural Nutrition Mfg LLC.....509 966-8849
216 S 24th Ave Yakima (98902) ***(G-15628)***
Natural Pet Pantry.....206 762-5575
309 S Cloverdale St Seattle (98108) ***(G-10593)***
Natural Selection Farms Inc.....509 837-3501
6800 Emerald Rd Sunnyside (98944) ***(G-13135)***
Natural Stone Restorers.....360 825-3199
29227 Se 374th St Enumclaw (98022) ***(G-3307)***
Natural Venom All Star.....253 370-7986
10421 92nd Street Ct Sw Tacoma (98498) ***(G-13425)***
Natural Wonder Publishing.....253 905-1583
10710 Rampart Dr E Puyallup (98374) ***(G-8197)***
Naturally NW Publications.....360 332-1777
225 Marine Dr Ste 200 Blaine (98230) ***(G-1685)***
Natures Inventory LLC.....425 775-2000
2551 Cole St Ste S Enumclaw (98022) ***(G-3308)***
Natures Path Foods USA Inc.....360 332-1111
2220 Natures Path Way Blaine (98230) ***(G-1686)***
Natures Path Foods USA Inc.....360 603-7200
2220 Natures Path Way Blaine (98230) ***(G-1687)***
Natures Provision.....360 307-0113
11273 Kiptree Ln Nw Silverdale (98383) ***(G-11851)***
Natus Medical Incorporated.....206 767-3500
5900 1st Ave S Seattle (98108) ***(G-10594)***
Naumes Concentrates Inc.....509 877-8882
371 Industrial Park Rd Wapato (98951) ***(G-14921)***
Naust Marine Usa Inc.....206 484-5710
4816 15th Ave Nw Seattle (98107) ***(G-10595)***
Naval Magazine Code 4214.....360 396-2187
100 Indn Island Annex Rd Port Hadlock (98339) ***(G-7761)***
Navan Enterprises LLC.....206 214-6227
8224 16th Ave Ne Seattle (98115) ***(G-10596)***
Navit LLC.....425 647-3580
500 Yale Ave N Ste 400 Seattle (98109) ***(G-10597)***
Navy Castings, Bremerton *Also called Jerry H Hyman* ***(G-1965)***
Nbk Associates Inc.....216 408-8685
6472 Ne 135th Pl Kirkland (98034) ***(G-5408)***
Nbty Inc.....425 369-1771
22526 Se 64th Pl Issaquah (98027) ***(G-4452)***
NC Cyacks, Tacoma *Also called Novus Composites Incorporated* ***(G-13436)***
Nce Inc.....253 884-6255
5005 Mahncke Rd Sw Longbranch (98351) ***(G-5879)***
Ncs Power Inc.....360 896-4063
5139 Ne 94th Ave Ste F Vancouver (98662) ***(G-14429)***
Ncw Media Inc (PA).....509 548-5286
215 14th St Leavenworth (98826) ***(G-5811)***
Ncw Media Inc.....509 782-3781
201 Cottage Ave Cashmere (98815) ***(G-2327)***
Ncw Nickel ADS, Wenatchee *Also called Target Media Partners* ***(G-15078)***
Ncw Towing.....509 630-7155
29 N Chelan Ave Wenatchee (98801) ***(G-15051)***
NDC Timber Inc.....360 482-4645
357 Cloquallum Rd Elma (98541) ***(G-3251)***
Ne Welding and Fabrication.....509 549-3982
127752 State Route 26 Colfax (99111) ***(G-2718)***
Nec Corp of America.....425 373-4400
14335 Ne 24th St Bellevue (98007) ***(G-1023)***
Neetas Creations.....585 233-1896
1275 140th Pl Ne Bellevue (98007) ***(G-1024)***
Nefarious Cellers.....509 682-9505
495 S Lakeshore Rd Chelan (98816) ***(G-2560)***
Neil Butler.....360 668-9555
6620 196th St Se Snohomish (98296) ***(G-11950)***
Neil F Lampson Inc (PA).....509 586-0411
607 E Columbia Dr Kennewick (99336) ***(G-4700)***
Neil Levinson Enterprises.....425 828-3833
11631 Ne 95th St Kirkland (98033) ***(G-5409)***
Neil Pryde Sails, Enumclaw *Also called Rush Sails Inc* ***(G-3319)***
Neilson Organic Compost.....360 983-8125
195 Wilson Rd Mossyrock (98564) ***(G-6763)***
Nelscorp Inc.....206 660-6313
18416 40th Ave Nw Stanwood (98292) ***(G-12982)***
Nelson Brothers Inc.....509 922-4988
3808 N Sullivan Rd 14e Spokane Valley (99216) ***(G-12802)***
Nelson Construction Inc.....253 931-6696
1 37th St Nw Ste G Auburn (98001) ***(G-505)***
Nelson Crab Inc.....360 267-2911
3088 Kindred Ave Tokeland (98590) ***(G-13633)***
Nelson Estate.....206 241-9463
16349 Maplewild Ave Sw Burien (98166) ***(G-2119)***
Nelson Estate Vineyards, Burien *Also called Nelson Estate* ***(G-2119)***
Nelson Farrier Shop Inc.....509 966-9598
8805 Meadowbrook Rd Yakima (98903) ***(G-15629)***
Nelson Irrigation Corporation.....509 525-7660
848 Airport Rd Walla Walla (99362) ***(G-14850)***
Nelson S Cabinet Installa.....253 770-3975
2210 27th Ave Se Puyallup (98374) ***(G-8198)***
Nelson Truck Equipment Co Inc (PA).....253 395-3825
20063 84th Ave S Kent (98032) ***(G-5018)***
Nelson Truck Equipment Co Inc.....206 622-3825
14325 Aurora Ave N Seattle (98133) ***(G-10598)***
Nelson, Carol Ea, Centralia *Also called Computer Connections* ***(G-2395)***
Nelson-Ball Paper Products.....360 423-3420
620 11th Ave Longview (98632) ***(G-5933)***
Nemesis Metal Fabrication Repr, Lake Tapps *Also called Larry Waits Nemesis* ***(G-5681)***
Neobiotech Global Corporation.....253 732-3573
1 30th St Nw Unit 9 Auburn (98001) ***(G-506)***
Neocific Inc.....425 451-8278
1750 112th Ave Ne D161 Bellevue (98004) ***(G-1025)***
Neon Connection.....360 224-3061
20322 73rd St E Sumner (98391) ***(G-13088)***
Neon Electric Sign Co.....206 405-4001
23834 Se 111th St Issaquah (98027) ***(G-4453)***
Neon Labs Inc.....415 854-8795
5511 28th Ave Nw Seattle (98107) ***(G-10599)***
Neon Moon Longhorned Cattle.....360 293-2721
6099 State Route 20 Anacortes (98221) ***(G-150)***
Neon Pig LLC.....509 244-5319
13108 W 6th Ave Airway Heights (99001) ***(G-57)***
Neon Systems Inc.....425 501-6447
1729 143rd Pl Sw Lynnwood (98087) ***(G-6168)***
Neon Taco.....323 577-3045
209 Broadway E Seattle (98102) ***(G-10600)***
Nepa Pallet and Container, Malaga *Also called Ufp Washington LLC* ***(G-6233)***
Nepa Pallet and Container, Yakima *Also called Ufp Washington LLC* ***(G-15699)***
Neposmart, Medina *Also called Nepoware Corporation* ***(G-6453)***
Nepoware Corporation.....425 802-8821
2647 79th Ave Ne Medina (98039) ***(G-6453)***
Neptune Global LLC.....310 752-9992
2124 3rd Ave Ste 201 Seattle (98121) ***(G-10601)***
Neptune Industries, Seattle *Also called Neptune Global LLC* ***(G-10601)***
Neshkaw Sand and Gravel LLC.....360 482-0274
290 W Lillie Rd Elma (98541) ***(G-3252)***
Nester Brothers LLC.....253 320-9405
3008 S 10th St Tacoma (98405) ***(G-13426)***
Nestle Dreyers Ice Cream Co.....425 251-0809
18404 72nd Ave S Kent (98032) ***(G-5019)***
Nestle Regional Training Ctr, Carnation *Also called Nestle Usa Inc* ***(G-2296)***
Nestle Usa Inc.....425 844-3201
28901 Ne Carnation Frm Rd Carnation (98014) ***(G-2296)***
Nestor Inc.....253 395-0285
18360 Olympic Ave S Tukwila (98188) ***(G-13776)***
Nestor Enterprises LLC.....206 794-4989
22620 95th Pl W Edmonds (98020) ***(G-3136)***
Net Services LLC.....360 651-1955
13010 11th Ave Ne Tulalip (98271) ***(G-13842)***
Net Systems, Bainbridge Island *Also called Noreastern Trawl Systems Inc* ***(G-652)***
Netacquire Corporation.....425 821-3100
12000 115th Ave Ne Kirkland (98034) ***(G-5410)***
Nether Industries Inc.....360 825-7940
1633 Commerce St Enumclaw (98022) ***(G-3309)***
Netherfield Publishing LLC.....360 903-8512
409 N River St Montesano (98563) ***(G-6649)***
Network Collaborative 4 LLC.....206 898-5869
3601 Fremont Ave N # 314 Seattle (98103) ***(G-10602)***
Netzero Energy LLC.....360 636-5337
1339 Commerce Ave Ste 314 Longview (98632) ***(G-5934)***
Neucor Inc.....866 638-2671
5803 Texas Dr Vancouver (98661) ***(G-14430)***
Neumeier Engineering Inc.....253 854-3635
22610 88th Ave S Kent (98031) ***(G-5020)***
Neutek Inc.....206 660-0056
5214 201st Pl Sw Lynnwood (98036) ***(G-6169)***
Nevada Lithium Corp.....360 318-8352
9443 Axlund Rd Lynden (98264) ***(G-6039)***
Nevic, Castle Rock *Also called Electric Concept Labs Inc* ***(G-2342)***
New Adventure.....360 961-4444
2511 Queen St Bellingham (98226) ***(G-1458)***
New Age Processors LLC.....425 656-0174
200 Sw 34th St Renton (98057) ***(G-8857)***
New Cingular Wireless Svcs Inc.....425 288-3132
18517 126th Ave Ne Bothell (98011) ***(G-1779)***

New Continent Food USA Inc 425 644-6448
15320 Se 46th Way Bellevue (98006) **(G-1026)**
New Culture Media 206 406-1934
15515 J Woodinville Ne Bothell (98011) **(G-1780)**
New Found Metals Incorporated 360 385-3315
240 Airport Rd Port Townsend (98368) **(G-7899)**
New Foundation Press 509 783-5237
114 Vista Way Kennewick (99336) **(G-4701)**
New Memorial Direct, Gig Harbor *Also called Bailey and Bailey Inc* **(G-4075)**
New Royal Meat LLC 206 629-4958
18019 Aurora Ave N Shoreline (98133) **(G-11792)**
New Sage Bakery LLC 208 596-5331
111 Montgomery St Uniontown (99179) **(G-13957)**
New Standard Company Limited 425 641-5718
14670 Ne 8th St Ste 108 Bellevue (98007) **(G-1027)**
New Star Technology Inc 425 350-7611
17461 147th St Se Ste 6a Monroe (98272) **(G-6601)**
New Tec LLC 509 738-6621
970 Highway 395 N Kettle Falls (99141) **(G-5237)**
New Tech Industries Inc 425 374-3814
7911 44th Ave W Mukilteo (98275) **(G-6955)**
New Top Dog LLC 206 817-3395
5089 119th Ave Se Bellevue (98006) **(G-1028)**
New Touch Woodworking 360 930-1118
6331 Ne Ponderosa Blvd Hansville (98340) **(G-4316)**
New Uniformity LLC 360 373-2785
330 N Callow Ave Bremerton (98312) **(G-1980)**
New West Gypsum Inc 253 380-1079
8657 S 190th St Kent (98031) **(G-5021)**
New West Gypsum USA, Kent *Also called New West Gypsum Inc* **(G-5021)**
New Whatcom Interiors 360 671-3389
1123 Railroad Ave Bellingham (98225) **(G-1459)**
New World Market LP 206 653-7754
2200 S 320th St Ste 1b Federal Way (98003) **(G-3761)**
Newark Paperboard Products, Longview *Also called Nelson-Ball Paper Products* **(G-5933)**
Newcore Aerospace, Deer Park *Also called Newcore Aviation LLC* **(G-2910)**
Newcore Aviation LLC 509 276-8200
110 W Crawford St Deer Park (99006) **(G-2910)**
Newcore Enterprises LLC (PA) 509 276-8200
110 W Crawford St Deer Park (99006) **(G-2911)**
Newell Corp 360 435-8955
6922 204th St Ne Arlington (98223) **(G-287)**
Newell Machine & Repair, Arlington *Also called J Newell Corporation* **(G-260)**
Newgem Foods LLC 209 948-1508
3600 Industry Dr E Ste A Fife (98424) **(G-3973)**
Newline Software Inc 425 442-1126
8201 164th Ave Ne Ste 320 Redmond (98052) **(G-8593)**
Newly Weds Foods Inc 253 584-9270
4421 98th Street Ct Sw C Lakewood (98499) **(G-5741)**
Newman Burrows LLC 206 324-5644
1000 Andover Park E Tukwila (98188) **(G-13777)**
Newmata Screen Printing 360 631-7860
17908 11th Ave Ne Arlington (98223) **(G-288)**
Newnes McGehee A Div of, Woodland *Also called US Natural Resources Inc* **(G-15469)**
Newport Equipment Entps Inc 509 447-4688
328772 Highway 2 Newport (99156) **(G-7062)**
News Trbune Schlrship Fndation 253 597-8593
1950 S State St Tacoma (98405) **(G-13427)**
News Tribune, Tacoma *Also called Tacoma News Inc* **(G-13545)**
News Tribune The 1950 S 253 841-2481
822 E Main Puyallup (98372) **(G-8199)**
Newsdata LLC (HQ) 206 285-4848
4241 21st Ave W Ste 306 Seattle (98199) **(G-10603)**
Newtec, Kettle Falls *Also called New Tec LLC* **(G-5237)**
Newton Security Inc 425 251-9494
443 Sw 41st St Renton (98057) **(G-8858)**
Newtonia Publishing LLC 206 790-6628
2201 3rd Ave Apt 2201 # 2201 Seattle (98121) **(G-10604)**
Newtown Inc 253 395-9028
23001 54th Ave S Kent (98032) **(G-5022)**
Nexappeal 360 293-5054
4060 S Del Mar Dr Anacortes (98221) **(G-151)**
Next Biometrics Inc 617 510-4086
10900 Ne 4th St Bellevue (98004) **(G-1029)**
Next Biometrics Inc 425 406-7055
1100 112th Ave Ne Ste 340 Bellevue (98004) **(G-1030)**
Nextgen Apps Co 206 395-6770
111 W Prospect St Seattle (98119) **(G-10605)**
Nextlevel Training LLC 360 933-4640
5160 Industrial Pl # 101 Ferndale (98248) **(G-3876)**
Nextrx Corporation 425 402-3485
21312 30th Dr Se 101 Bothell (98021) **(G-1879)**
Nexus Aerospace 253 797-0700
4034 S 329th St Federal Way (98001) **(G-3762)**
Nexus Lcm, Stevenson *Also called Nexus Life Cycle MGT LLC* **(G-13016)**
Nexus Life Cycle MGT LLC 541 400-0765
25 Sw Ruellen Rd Stevenson (98648) **(G-13016)**
Nexus Marine Corporation 425 252-8330
3816 Railway Ave Everett (98201) **(G-3552)**
Nexus Surgical Innovations 509 499-0937
809 W Main Ave Apt 303 Spokane (99201) **(G-12404)**

Nfi Enterprises LLC 253 245-5500
2536 Auburn Way N Auburn (98002) **(G-507)**
Nguoi Viet Ngay Nay 206 725-8384
7101 Mlk Jr Way S Seattle (98118) **(G-10606)**
Nhthree LLC 509 396-2082
1161 Viewmoor Ct Richland (99352) **(G-9031)**
Nic Global, Woodinville *Also called National Indus Concepts Inc* **(G-15320)**
Nichol Prfmce & Ctrl Automatio 360 961-2833
5649 Smith Creek Rd Everson (98247) **(G-3684)**
Nichols Bros Stoneworks Ltd 360 668-5434
20209 Broadway Ave Snohomish (98296) **(G-11951)**
Nichols Brothers Boat Builders, Freeland *Also called Ice Floe LLC* **(G-4030)**
Nichols Diversified Inds LLC 360 331-7230
1957 Lancaster Rd Freeland (98249) **(G-4035)**
Nicholson Engineering Co Inc 253 272-9167
680 E 11th St Tacoma (98421) **(G-13428)**
Nicholson Manufacturing, Seattle *Also called Northern Industrial Inc* **(G-10631)**
Nicholson Manufacturing Co (HQ) 206 682-2752
200 S Orcas St Seattle (98108) **(G-10607)**
Nicholson Manufacturing Co 206 291-8849
8300 S 206th St Kent (98032) **(G-5023)**
Nick Jackson Co Inc 425 481-1381
17725 Ne 65th St Ste A110 Redmond (98052) **(G-8594)**
Nick's Custom Boots, Spokane Valley *Also called Rah Inc* **(G-12849)**
Nickel Ads-Fournier Newspaper, Prosser *Also called Valley Publishing Company Inc* **(G-8073)**
Nickel One Ad Newspaper (PA) 360 423-3141
501 S Volland St Kennewick (99336) **(G-4702)**
Nickel Saver, Moses Lake *Also called Target Media Partners* **(G-6752)**
Nickel The, Kennewick *Also called Nickel One Ad Newspaper* **(G-4702)**
Nickolay Philip and Wendy LLC 206 463-7997
26817 94th Ave Sw Vashon (98070) **(G-14736)**
Nicole Lewis/Northwest Breast 360 989-0312
14019 Ne 20th Ave Apt 41 Vancouver (98686) **(G-14431)**
Nicos Woodworking 206 755-8110
18804 Midvale Ave N Shoreline (98133) **(G-11793)**
Nidec America Corporation 360 666-2445
318 E Main St 202 Battle Ground (98604) **(G-724)**
Nidekken Ltd 425 885-1587
18348 Redmond Way Redmond (98052) **(G-8595)**
Nielsen Bros & Sons Inc 425 776-9191
8130 240th St Sw Edmonds (98026) **(G-3137)**
Nielsen Bros Rugs & Carpets, Edmonds *Also called Nielsen Bros & Sons Inc* **(G-3137)**
Nielsen Brothers Inc 360 671-9078
25046 State Route 20 Sedro Woolley (98284) **(G-11552)**
Nielsens Graphic Service Inc 206 463-2430
19923 Robinwood Rd Sw Vashon (98070) **(G-14737)**
Niftybrick Software 206 588-5696
1807 E Pike St Unit C Seattle (98122) **(G-10608)**
Night Shift LLC 206 334-2548
4214 S 137th St Tukwila (98168) **(G-13778)**
Nightmare Industries 425 330-1084
19516 Badke Rd Snohomish (98290) **(G-11952)**
Nightmare Tactical, Snohomish *Also called Nightmare Industries* **(G-11952)**
Nightside Distillery LLC 253 906-4265
2908 Meridian Ave E # 116 Edgewood (98371) **(G-3087)**
Nika Mines LLC 425 609-6901
1825 S Lake Stevens Rd Lake Stevens (98258) **(G-5664)**
Nike Inc 206 527-3554
2649 Ne 46th St Seattle (98105) **(G-10609)**
Nike Inc 425 747-2848
4026 Factoria Sq Mall Se Bellevue (98006) **(G-1031)**
Nikko Media, Seattle *Also called Precise Printing Inc* **(G-10846)**
Nimbus Board Sports LLC 360 387-1951
1551 Bonnie Ln Camano Island (98282) **(G-2219)**
Nimbus Technologies LLC 206 724-5507
4348 9th Ave Ne Apt 101 Seattle (98105) **(G-10610)**
Nine Mile Power Station 509 466-5322
9602 W Old Charles Rd Nine Mile Falls (99026) **(G-7080)**
Nine Seeds, Seattle *Also called Chauncey and Shirah Bell Inc* **(G-9670)**
Nintendo Software Technology 425 497-7500
5001 150th Ave Ne Redmond (98052) **(G-8596)**
Nintex Usa Inc (HQ) 425 324-2400
10800 Ne 8th St Ste 400 Bellevue (98004) **(G-1032)**
Nion Beauty Inc 206 228-5988
4424 185th St Se Bothell (98012) **(G-1880)**
Nippon Dynawave Packaging Co 360 414-3379
32001 32nd Ave S Ste 310 Federal Way (98001) **(G-3763)**
Nippon Dynawave Packaging Co., Longview *Also called Nippon Dynawave Packg Co LLC* **(G-5935)**
Nippon Dynawave Packg Co LLC (HQ) 360 425-2150
3401 Industrial Way Longview (98632) **(G-5935)**
Nippon Paper Inds USA Co Ltd (HQ) 360 457-4474
3401 Industrial Way Longview (98632) **(G-5936)**
Nippon Paper Inds USA Co Ltd 360 457-4474
1902 Marine Dr Port Angeles (98363) **(G-7727)**
Nipr LLC 253 261-6840
47614 260th Ave Se Enumclaw (98022) **(G-3310)**
Nisqualley Valley News, Centralia *Also called Lafromboise Newspapers* **(G-2415)**
Nisqually Valley News, Yelm *Also called Lafromboise Newspapers* **(G-15737)**

ALPHABETIC

(PA)=Parent Co (HQ)=Headquarters (DH)=Div Headquarters
2019 Washington Manufacturers Register 783

Nissen Woodworks 425 216-3575
46325 Se 140th St North Bend (98045) *(G-7117)*
Nita N Ace LLC 253 209-4413
22509 152nd Ave E Graham (98338) *(G-4233)*
Nite-Hawk Sweepers LLC 253 872-2077
19713 58th Pl S Kent (98032) *(G-5024)*
Nitwit Lice Removal 206 327-5782
12551 1st Ave Nw Seattle (98177) *(G-10611)*
Nk Woodworking LLC (PA) 206 257-4395
1605 S 93rd St Ste Eg3 Seattle (98108) *(G-10612)*
Nlight Inc (PA) 360 566-4460
5408 Ne 88th St Ste E Vancouver (98665) *(G-14432)*
Nlpcore LLC 206 883-7616
921 N 82nd St Seattle (98103) *(G-10613)*
No Graf Network Inc 509 531-1334
8524 W Gage Blvd Kennewick (99336) *(G-4703)*
No Grass Winery 509 784-5101
6701 Entiat River Rd Entiat (98822) *(G-3269)*
No Name Boot Company 509 226-1980
4213 N Starr Rd Otis Orchards (99027) *(G-7515)*
No Quarter LLC 206 412-4311
11250 Kirkland Way # 103 Kirkland (98033) *(G-5411)*
Noahs Ark Foods LLC 509 595-8642
330 E Harrison St Palouse (99161) *(G-7546)*
Nobelus LLC 800 895-2747
1414 S Director St Seattle (98108) *(G-10614)*
Noble Gas Neon Company 206 708-6290
11435 Rainier Ave S Seattle (98178) *(G-10615)*
Noble Neon 206 708-6290
11435 Rainier Ave S Seattle (98178) *(G-10616)*
Noble Truss & Lumber Inc 509 662-1877
355 Malaga Hwy Wenatchee (98801) *(G-15052)*
Nobu Integrative Medicine LLC 425 363-2970
301 W North Bend Way # 104 North Bend (98045) *(G-7118)*
Noda Software 206 726-1125
170 Melrose Ave E Seattle (98102) *(G-10617)*
Noel Corporation (PA) 509 248-4545
1001 S 1st St Yakima (98901) *(G-15630)*
Noel Corporation 509 248-3412
401 W Washington Ave Yakima (98903) *(G-15631)*
Noel Inc 206 784-1894
7359 23rd Ave Nw Seattle (98117) *(G-10618)*
Nolan & Sons Northwest Inc 509 658-2604
281 Deer View Ln Naches (98937) *(G-7000)*
Noll/Norwesco LLC 253 926-1600
3011 70th Ave E Fife (98424) *(G-3974)*
Non Sequitur Music 360 733-7145
2112 Ontario St Bellingham (98229) *(G-1460)*
Non Sequitur Music Publishing, Bellingham *Also called Non Sequitur Music* *(G-1460)*
Noodle Express 509 927-4117
707 N Sullivan Rd Spokane (99201) *(G-12405)*
Noodle Express Spokane, Spokane *Also called Noodle Express* *(G-12405)*
Noon International LLC 206 283-8400
5506 6th Ave S Ste 101 Seattle (98108) *(G-10619)*
Noonday Design 253 517-8293
17813 110th Pl E Bonney Lake (98391) *(G-1730)*
Noonum Llc 425 894-1202
6449 191st Pl Ne Redmond (98052) *(G-8597)*
Noors Lures LLC 360 896-4032
7012 Ne 142nd Ct Vancouver (98682) *(G-14433)*
Nor E First Response Inc 360 738-6467
1975 Midway Ln Ste J Bellingham (98226) *(G-1461)*
Nor Prop Inc 253 939-1200
3220 B St Se Auburn (98002) *(G-508)*
Nor-Tech Fabricating LLC 360 232-0144
2510 Talley Way Kelso (98626) *(G-4539)*
Nora Enterprises, Lilliwaup *Also called Nora Haugan* *(G-5872)*
Nora Haugan 360 877-0602
950 N Colony Surf Dr Lilliwaup (98555) *(G-5872)*
Norberg Press Inc 206 938-3905
4700 42nd Ave Sw Ste 160 Seattle (98116) *(G-10620)*
Norco Inc 509 764-5032
2757 Road N Ne Moses Lake (98837) *(G-6731)*
Norco Inc 509 535-9808
6102 E Trent Ave Spokane Valley (99212) *(G-12803)*
Norco Inc 509 754-3518
276 Enterprise St Se Ephrata (98823) *(G-3343)*
Norcom Inc 425 868-9973
24608 Ne 3rd Pl Sammamish (98074) *(G-9236)*
Nordal Denver 509 456-8969
14 S Oak St Spokane (99201) *(G-12406)*
Nordhavn Yachts, Northwest, Seattle *Also called Pacific Asian Enterprises Inc* *(G-10727)*
Nordic Tarps Manufacturing 509 533-1530
5805 E Sharp Ave Ste C6 Spokane Valley (99212) *(G-12804)*
Nordic Tugs Incorporated 360 757-8847
11367 Higgins Airport Way Burlington (98233) *(G-2172)*
Nordick Mfg Co 425 488-2427
16219 Wdnville Redmond Rd Woodinville (98072) *(G-15321)*
Nordkyn Outfitters 253 847-4128
5903 316th St E Eatonville (98328) *(G-3063)*
Nordson Select Inc 509 924-4898
22425 E Appleway Ave Fl 1 Liberty Lake (99019) *(G-5848)*
Noreah/Brownfield Press LLC 360 849-4857
361 E Birnie Slough Rd Cathlamet (98612) *(G-2371)*
Noreastern Trawl Systems Inc (HQ) 206 842-5623
7910 Ne Day Rd W Bainbridge Island (98110) *(G-652)*
Norfil LLC 253 863-5888
1335 Valentine Ave Se Pacific (98047) *(G-7534)*
Norgren Gt Development Corp 206 244-1305
425 C St Nw Ste 100 Auburn (98001) *(G-509)*
Norhtwest Stone Pros 206 824-2458
3922 S 241st St Kent (98032) *(G-5025)*
Norm Stoken Logging Inc 360 683-0908
384 Knapp Rd Sequim (98382) *(G-11651)*
Norma Industries 253 208-1728
133 23rd St Se Puyallup (98372) *(G-8200)*
Norman Lancaster Brown 509 678-5980
201 Funkhouser Rd Tieton (98947) *(G-13631)*
Norman Langseth 425 643-7751
4666 172nd Pl Se Bellevue (98006) *(G-1033)*
Normandie Woodworks 360 446-0352
10915 128th Ave Se Rainier (98576) *(G-8319)*
Normandy Press LLC 206 285-2881
1616 11th Ave W Seattle (98119) *(G-10621)*
Normed Inc (PA) 800 288-8200
4320 S 131st Pl Ste 160 Tukwila (98168) *(G-13779)*
Norms Truck & Equipment Inc 253 833-8339
361 Roy Rd Sw Pacific (98047) *(G-7535)*
Norpac, Longview *Also called North Pacific Paper Co LLC* *(G-5937)*
Norplex Inc 360 736-0727
1703 Lum Rd Centralia (98531) *(G-2419)*
Norplex Inc (PA) 253 735-3431
111 3rd St Nw Bldg C Auburn (98001) *(G-510)*
Norquest Seafoods Inc 425 349-2563
1930 Merrill Creek Pkwy B Everett (98203) *(G-3553)*
Norquest Seafoods Inc (HQ) 206 281-7022
5303 Shilshole Ave Nw Seattle (98107) *(G-10622)*
Norris Techniques 360 871-1458
1528 Puget Dr E Port Orchard (98366) *(G-7833)*
Norstar Boats Inc 360 671-3669
1366 Roy Rd Bellingham (98229) *(G-1462)*
Norstar Specialty Foods Inc 206 764-4499
8030 S 228th St Kent (98032) *(G-5026)*
Nortec, Port Orchard *Also called Norris Techniques* *(G-7833)*
North American Atk Corporation 360 733-1916
2020 E Bakerview Rd Bellingham (98226) *(G-1463)*
North American Composites Co 253 351-9994
22239 76th Ave S Kent (98032) *(G-5027)*
North American Post Publishing 206 726-6460
519 6th Ave S Ste 200 Seattle (98104) *(G-10623)*
North Bch Prtg & Scrapbooking, Ocean Shores *Also called Beach Bee Inc* *(G-7184)*
North Beach Media Inc 360 289-2441
668 Ocean Shores Blvd Nw Ocean Shores (98569) *(G-7188)*
North Bend Automotives 425 888-4522
43306 Se North Bend Way North Bend (98045) *(G-7119)*
North Cascades Broadcasting 509 826-0100
320 Emery Dr OMAK (98841) *(G-7439)*
North Central Cabinets, Loomis *Also called Ronald G Wahl* *(G-5972)*
North Coast Electric Company 360 671-1100
1836 Racine St Bellingham (98229) *(G-1464)*
North Coast News, The, Ocean Shores *Also called North Beach Media Inc* *(G-7188)*
North Connection Corp 425 637-7787
1400 112th Ave Se Ste 100 Bellevue (98004) *(G-1034)*
North Country Forest Resources 509 486-2882
446 Hagood Rd Tonasket (98855) *(G-13655)*
North Cross Aluminum LLC 360 821-1481
4964 Mutiny Bay Rd Freeland (98249) *(G-4036)*
North Face 047 509 747-5389
714 W Main Ave Spokane (99201) *(G-12407)*
North Face 49, The, Bellevue *Also called Vf Outdoor LLC* *(G-1216)*
North Fork Composites LLC 360 225-2211
2617 Ne 434th St Woodland (98674) *(G-15450)*
North Fork Timber Company Corp 360 273-5541
18146 Dallas St Sw Rochester (98579) *(G-9138)*
North Fork Timber Company Corp (PA) 360 748-8333
417 W Main St Ste C Centralia (98531) *(G-2420)*
North Fork Timber Company Corp 360 748-8333
258 Hamilton Rd Chehalis (98532) *(G-2517)*
North Fork Timber Shop, Chehalis *Also called North Fork Timber Company Corp* *(G-2517)*
North Harbor Propeller 360 299-8266
401 34th St Ste A Anacortes (98221) *(G-152)*
North Hbr Diesl Yacht Svc Inc 360 293-5551
720 30th St Anacortes (98221) *(G-153)*
North Hill Resources Inc 360 757-1866
657 N Hill Blvd Burlington (98233) *(G-2173)*
North Industries Inc 206 940-0842
10826 Glen Acres Dr S Seattle (98168) *(G-10624)*
North Island Boat Company Inc 360 293-2565
1910 Skyline Way Anacortes (98221) *(G-154)*
North Kitsap Herald, Poulsbo *Also called Sound Publishing Inc* *(G-8003)*
North Mason Fiber Company 360 275-0228
431 Ne Log Yard Rd Belfair (98528) *(G-769)*
North Pacific Crane Co LLC (PA) 206 361-7064
10734 Lake City Way Ne Seattle (98125) *(G-10625)*

North Pacific Crane Fab Hyd 509 427-4530
1132 Old State Rd Carson (98610) *(G-2305)*
North Pacific Industrial 425 251-0335
457 1st Ave Nw Issaquah (98027) *(G-4454)*
North Pacific Paper Co LLC 360 636-6400
3001 Industrial Way Longview (98632) *(G-5937)*
North Pacific Seafoods Inc (HQ) 206 726-9900
4 Nickerson St Ste 400 Seattle (98109) *(G-10626)*
North Park Heating Company Inc 206 365-1414
19204 Ballinger Way Ne Lake Forest Park (98155) *(G-5622)*
North PCF Ign Interlock Svc 360 480-4919
2633 Willamette Dr Ne G Lacey (98516) *(G-5567)*
North PCF Indus Coatings LLC 907 865-8400
2900 Lind Ave Sw Ste B Renton (98057) *(G-8859)*
North Ridge Machine LLC 509 765-8928
9531 Beacon Rd Ne Moses Lake (98837) *(G-6732)*
North Sky Games Inc 425 283-9634
3741 246th Ave Se Sammamish (98029) *(G-9237)*
North Sports Inc (PA) 509 493-4938
1 Northshore Dr White Salmon (98672) *(G-15124)*
North Star Casteel Pdts Inc (PA) 206 622-0068
820 S Bradford St Seattle (98108) *(G-10627)*
North Star Casteel Pdts Inc 206 621-1039
3401 Colorado Ave S Seattle (98134) *(G-10628)*
North Star Cold Storage Inc 360 629-9591
27100 Pioneer Hwy Stanwood (98292) *(G-12983)*
North Star Embroidery 360 588-0530
718 Commercial Ave Anacortes (98221) *(G-155)*
North Star Glove Company 253 627-7107
2916 S Steele St Tacoma (98409) *(G-13429)*
North Star High Voltage Corp 520 780-9030
5610 Rose Loop Ne Bainbridge Island (98110) *(G-653)*
North Star Mining Co Inc 360 793-0848
903 Dyer Rd Sultan (98294) *(G-13030)*
North Star Trading Co LLP 360 341-2953
11247 State Route 525 Clinton (98236) *(G-2692)*
North West Barricades & Signs 206 243-8004
11229 16th Ave Sw Seattle (98146) *(G-10629)*
North West Book Oper Co Inc 877 591-8608
782 Marine Dr Bellingham (98225) *(G-1465)*
North West Cab & Refacing LLC 360 415-9999
2518 E 16th St Bremerton (98310) *(G-1981)*
North West Coating & Svcs LLC 360 649-1548
2745 Mckinley Pl Se Port Orchard (98366) *(G-7834)*
North West Flagging, Seattle *Also called North West Barricades & Signs* *(G-10629)*
North Winds Welding & Met 360 379-0487
13576 Airport Cutoff Rd Port Townsend (98368) *(G-7900)*
North Woods Productions, Olalla *Also called Ronald Finney* *(G-7209)*
Northcoast Yachts, Seattle *Also called Yachtfish Marine Inc* *(G-11507)*
Northcoast Yachts Inc 253 383-3803
1141 Fairview Ave N Seattle (98109) *(G-10630)*
Northend Truck Equipment LLC 360 653-6066
14919 40th Ave Ne Marysville (98271) *(G-6363)*
Northern Ales Inc 509 738-6913
325 W 3rd Ave Kettle Falls (99141) *(G-5238)*
Northern Fish - Old Town, Tacoma *Also called Northern Fish Products Inc* *(G-13430)*
Northern Fish Products Inc (PA) 253 475-3858
3911 S 56th St Tacoma (98409) *(G-13430)*
Northern Industrial Inc (PA) 206 682-2752
200 S Orcas St Seattle (98108) *(G-10631)*
Northern Kittitas Cnty Tribune 509 674-2511
807 W Davis St Cle Elum (98922) *(G-2673)*
Northern Land Management, Seattle *Also called Jrj Inc* *(G-10311)*
Northern Light, Blaine *Also called Naturally NW Publications* *(G-1685)*
Northern Lights Inc (HQ) 206 789-3600
4420 14th Ave Nw Seattle (98107) *(G-10632)*
Northern Lights Brewing Co 509 242-2739
1003 E Trent Ave Ste 170 Spokane (99202) *(G-12408)*
Northern Lights Sunrm Creatn L 509 747-1110
6211 S Meadowlane Rd Spokane (99224) *(G-12409)*
Northern Mountain Metals LLC 509 226-1957
25323 E Eddy Ln Newman Lake (99025) *(G-7049)*
Northern Sky Games, Sammamish *Also called North Sky Games Inc* *(G-9237)*
Northern Wave LLC 206 217-4518
1818 Westlake Ave N # 420 Seattle (98109) *(G-10633)*
Northern Wave Seafood, Seattle *Also called Northern Wave LLC* *(G-10633)*
Northlake Shipyard Inc 206 632-1441
1441 N Northlake Way # 100 Seattle (98103) *(G-10634)*
Northlight Communications 425 493-1903
11395 5th Ave Ne Seattle (98125) *(G-10635)*
Northlight Power LLC 206 780-3551
83 S King St Ste 200 Seattle (98104) *(G-10636)*
Northman Logging 425 870-4727
3608 233rd Ave Ne Granite Falls (98252) *(G-4282)*
Northport Limestone, Bainbridge Island *Also called Hemphill Brothers Inc* *(G-639)*
Northport Limestone, Northport *Also called Hemphill Brothers Inc* *(G-7138)*
Northrop Grumman Systems Corp 360 315-3976
6401 Skipjack Cir Silverdale (98315) *(G-11852)*
Northside Metal Carports LLC 360 262-9354
110 Avery Rd E Chehalis (98532) *(G-2518)*
Northside Sand & Gravel 509 551-5830
32704 N Hwy 2 Chattaroy (99003) *(G-2449)*
Northsound Shopping 425 258-3455
1213 California St Everett (98201) *(G-3554)*
Northstar Attachments LLC 509 452-1651
101 Wagon Trail Dr Yakima (98901) *(G-15632)*
Northstar Attachments LLC 509 453-8271
3205 Bay St Union Gap (98903) *(G-13946)*
Northstar Equipment Inc 509 235-9200
1341 W 1st St Cheney (99004) *(G-2589)*
Northstar Investment Co 360 297-2260
25923 Washington Blvd Ne Kingston (98346) *(G-5258)*
Northstar Winery 509 525-6100
1736 J B George Rd Walla Walla (99362) *(G-14851)*
Northstar Woodworks, Ferndale *Also called Star North Woodworks Inc* *(G-3906)*
Northstone Industries LLC 509 844-7775
111 W Elcliff Ave Spokane (99218) *(G-12410)*
Northstone Manufacturing, Spokane *Also called Northstone Industries LLC* *(G-12410)*
Northway Prdcts/Mthers Contrls, Mukilteo *Also called Northway Products Inc* *(G-6956)*
Northway Products Inc 425 493-1127
11027 47th Ave W Mukilteo (98275) *(G-6956)*
Northwest - Everett Landsale, Everett *Also called Cemex Cnstr Mtls Fla LLC* *(G-3413)*
Northwest - Lynnwood Office, Lynnwood *Also called Cemex Cnstr Mtls PCF LLC* *(G-6091)*
Northwest Adhesives Inc 360 260-1227
4325 S Lincoln St Washougal (98671) *(G-14972)*
Northwest Aerospace Tech Inc (PA) 425 257-2044
415 Riverside Rd Everett (98201) *(G-3555)*
Northwest Aerospace Tech Inc 425 212-5001
2922 Chestnut St Everett (98201) *(G-3556)*
Northwest AG Pdts LLC 509 547-8234
821 S Chestnut Ave Pasco (99301) *(G-7604)*
Northwest Air Conditioning, Federal Way *Also called Northwest Truck & Auto AC* *(G-3765)*
Northwest Alloys Inc 509 935-3300
1560a Marble Vly Basin Rd Addy (99101) *(G-46)*
Northwest Applied Marine LLC 509 936-4316
3376 Cottonwood Creek Rd Chewelah (99109) *(G-2605)*
Northwest Architectural League 206 971-5596
1201 Alaskan Way Ste 200 Seattle (98101) *(G-10637)*
Northwest Automatics Inc 253 852-9006
25219 74th Ave S Kent (98032) *(G-5028)*
Northwest Bagger Company Inc 509 575-1950
3801 W Washington Ave Yakima (98903) *(G-15633)*
Northwest Baking Ltd Partnr 253 863-0373
1307 Puyallup St Sumner (98390) *(G-13089)*
Northwest Bedding Company (PA) 509 244-3000
4614 S Saint Andrews Ln Spokane (99223) *(G-12411)*
Northwest Belt & Equipment Co 360 533-7051
2011 W 6th St Aberdeen (98520) *(G-24)*
Northwest Biofuels 509 927-4548
9908 E Holman Rd Spokane Valley (99206) *(G-12805)*
Northwest Brewery Works Inc 425 255-0698
7757 142nd Way Se Newcastle (98059) *(G-7037)*
Northwest Building Tech Inc 206 767-4012
215 S Austin St Seattle (98108) *(G-10638)*
Northwest Business Stamp Inc 509 483-0308
5218 N Market St Spokane (99217) *(G-12412)*
Northwest Cab & Countertop LLC 253 446-7193
14611 Meridian E Ste A Puyallup (98375) *(G-8201)*
Northwest Cabinet & Refacing 970 497-8230
22407 Foss Rd Ne Poulsbo (98370) *(G-7987)*
Northwest Cabinet Hardware 360 281-5869
30502 Ne 181st Ave Yacolt (98675) *(G-15489)*
Northwest Cabinetry & Design 360 434-0740
1975 Ne Laurie Vei Loop Poulsbo (98370) *(G-7988)*
Northwest Carbide Tool & Svc 253 872-7848
1120 4th Ave N Kent (98032) *(G-5029)*
Northwest Carbonate Inc 360 225-6505
300 N Pekin Rd Woodland (98674) *(G-15451)*
Northwest Cars & Trucks Mag, Renton *Also called White Light Publications LLC* *(G-8947)*
Northwest Cascade Inc (PA) 253 848-2371
10412 John Bananola Way E Puyallup (98374) *(G-8202)*
Northwest Cellars LLC (PA) 866 421-9463
11909 124th Ave Ne Kirkland (98034) *(G-5412)*
Northwest Center (PA) 206 285-9140
7272 W Marginal Way S Seattle (98108) *(G-10639)*
Northwest Center 360 403-7330
19003 59th Dr Ne Arlington (98223) *(G-289)*
Northwest Center 425 355-1855
1320 75th St Sw Everett (98203) *(G-3557)*
Northwest Company Intl 253 365-6316
2000 Taylor Way Tacoma (98421) *(G-13431)*
Northwest Composites Inc (PA) 360 653-2211
12810 State Ave Marysville (98271) *(G-6364)*
Northwest Compost LLC 509 932-0215
26395 Road U Sw Mattawa (99349) *(G-6411)*
Northwest Container Svcs Inc 360 864-2571
104 Smokey Valley Rd Toledo (98591) *(G-13640)*
Northwest Cpitl Apprcation Inc (PA) 206 689-5615
1200 Westlake Ave N # 310 Seattle (98109) *(G-10640)*
Northwest Creations 253 709-4504
13106 Se 234th St Kent (98031) *(G-5030)*
Northwest Cstm Crating Box Inc 253 232-3244
10227 139th Street Ct E C2 Puyallup (98374) *(G-8203)*

ALPHABETIC

Northwest Custom Cabinets Inc 360 757-8788
15609 Peterson Rd Ste C Burlington (98233) *(G-2174)*
Northwest Custom Podiums Inc 360 830-5858
667 Wyatt Ln W Seabeck (98380) *(G-9269)*
Northwest Dairy Association (PA) 206 284-7220
5601 6th Ave S Ste 300 Seattle (98108) *(G-10641)*
Northwest Design & Mfg 360 714-8513
1801 Franklin St Bellingham (98225) *(G-1466)*
Northwest Designs Ink Inc (PA) 425 454-0707
13456 Se 27th Pl Ste 200 Bellevue (98005) *(G-1035)*
Northwest Dock Systems LLC 360 832-2295
795 State Route 161 N Eatonville (98328) *(G-3064)*
Northwest Door and Millwork 509 782-4525
1254 Lower Sunnyslope Rd Wenatchee (98801) *(G-15053)*
Northwest Dovetail Inc 509 248-2056
1606 S 36th Ave Yakima (98902) *(G-15634)*
Northwest Dynamics Inc 360 253-3656
6709 Ne 131st Ave Vancouver (98682) *(G-14434)*
Northwest Egg Sales, Moxee *Also called National Food Corporation (G-6883)*
Northwest Enterprises, Lynnwood *Also called James Lund (G-6143)*
Northwest Envmtl & Eqp Inc 253 435-5115
2319 E Pioneer Ste B Puyallup (98372) *(G-8204)*
Northwest Envmtl Solutions Inc 253 241-6213
15021 136th Ave E Puyallup (98374) *(G-8205)*
Northwest Equipment Sales Inc 253 835-1802
2011 S 341st Pl Federal Way (98003) *(G-3764)*
Northwest Euro LLC 206 981-8002
2620 W Commodore Way B Seattle (98199) *(G-10642)*
Northwest Executive Corp (PA) 425 883-9010
8108 138th Ave Ne Redmond (98052) *(G-8598)*
Northwest Eye Design LLC 425 823-1861
12911 120th Ave Ne C10 Kirkland (98034) *(G-5413)*
Northwest Family Strands 206 779-8997
14337 Interlake Ave N Seattle (98133) *(G-10643)*
Northwest Farm Food Coop 360 757-4225
1370 S Anacortes St Burlington (98233) *(G-2175)*
Northwest Fence Co 360 683-4673
31 Pheasant Run Dr Sequim (98382) *(G-11652)*
Northwest Fiberglass, Kennewick *Also called Jenneth Technologies Inc (G-4680)*
Northwest Fine Art Printing 425 947-1501
26601 79th Ave S Kent (98032) *(G-5031)*
Northwest Flexo Spc LLC 425 776-4315
2100 196th St Sw Ste 131 Lynnwood (98036) *(G-6170)*
Northwest Fly Fishing LLC 206 667-9359
600 1st Ave Ste 202a Seattle (98104) *(G-10644)*
Northwest Flyer Inc 253 471-9888
5611 76th St W Lakewood (98499) *(G-5742)*
Northwest Frozen LLC 206 388-3551
3623 6th Ave S Ste 200 Seattle (98134) *(G-10645)*
Northwest Granite and MBL LLC 206 228-6881
9289 151st Ave Ne Redmond (98052) *(G-8599)*
Northwest Grinding Co LLC 509 727-5774
1125 E Spokane St Pasco (99301) *(G-7605)*
Northwest Hardwoods, Seattle *Also called Weyerhaeuser Company (G-11462)*
Northwest Hardwoods Inc (HQ) 253 568-6800
1313 Broadway Ste 300 Tacoma (98402) *(G-13432)*
Northwest Heli Structures 360 734-1073
3911 Spur Ridge Ln Bellingham (98226) *(G-1467)*
Northwest Home Designing Inc 253 584-6309
6720 Regents Blvd Ste 104 Tacoma (98466) *(G-13433)*
Northwest Horse Source LLC 360 332-5579
4435 Boblett Rd Blaine (98230) *(G-1688)*
Northwest Hydroprint 360 249-2220
305 W Arland Ave Montesano (98563) *(G-6650)*
Northwest Hygienetics Inc 253 529-0294
29903 43rd Ave S Auburn (98001) *(G-511)*
Northwest Impressions 253 474-1119
5407 South Tacoma Way Tacoma (98409) *(G-13434)*
Northwest Inc 360 794-7473
17461 147th St Se Ste 15 Monroe (98272) *(G-6602)*
Northwest Innovation Works, Kalama *Also called Pan-Pacific Energy Corp (G-4506)*
Northwest Innovation Works Ka 360 673-7800
380 W Marine Dr Kalama (98625) *(G-4505)*
Northwest Internet 509 888-2020
343 Grant Rd East Wenatchee (98802) *(G-3027)*
Northwest Jewelers, Lake Forest Park *Also called Gem East Corporation (G-5613)*
Northwest Label/Design Inc 206 282-5568
3225 20th Ave W Seattle (98199) *(G-10646)*
Northwest Labor Industries 206 388-6135
6204 Latona Ave Ne Seattle (98115) *(G-10647)*
Northwest Laminating Co Inc (PA) 206 789-5536
1136 Nw 51st St Seattle (98107) *(G-10648)*
Northwest Laser Systems Inc 877 623-1342
19219 68th Ave S Ste M105 Kent (98032) *(G-5032)*
Northwest Laundry Supply Inc 509 487-4800
624 N Fancher Rd Spokane Valley (99212) *(G-12806)*
Northwest Lcknut Specialty Inc 253 604-4860
2323 7th St Se Apt R102 Puyallup (98374) *(G-8206)*
Northwest Lime Co LLC 360 815-0304
6175 Aldrich Rd Ferndale (98248) *(G-3877)*
Northwest Linings & Geo 253 872-0244
20824 77th Ave S Kent (98032) *(G-5033)*
Northwest Machine Works 360 435-3600
20611 67th Ave Ne Ste B Arlington (98223) *(G-290)*
Northwest Marine Inds LLC 360 389-5351
809 Harris Ave Bldg 6 Bellingham (98225) *(G-1468)*
Northwest Marine Supplies, Gig Harbor *Also called Hassler & Associates Inc (G-4115)*
Northwest Marine Tech Inc (PA) 360 468-3375
976 Ben Nevis Loop Shaw Island (98286) *(G-11671)*
Northwest Media Washington LP 360 681-2390
150 S 5th Ave Ste 2 Sequim (98382) *(G-11653)*
Northwest Media Washington LP (PA) 425 274-4782
500 108th Ave Ne Bellevue (98004) *(G-1036)*
Northwest Metal Craft 509 999-5280
1311 N Marguerite Rd Spokane Valley (99212) *(G-12807)*
Northwest Metal Spinning 253 351-8489
5521 Duncan Ave Se Auburn (98092) *(G-512)*
Northwest Metrology LLC 253 853-3183
5715 Wollochet Dr Nw Gig Harbor (98335) *(G-4136)*
Northwest Millwork Door Co 360 297-0802
611 Park Ave Ne Bainbridge Island (98110) *(G-654)*
Northwest Modular Service 253 631-2802
16817 Se 264th St Covington (98042) *(G-2835)*
Northwest Monitoring Services 509 326-6270
921 N Adams St Spokane (99201) *(G-12413)*
Northwest Multiple Listing Svc 253 566-2331
19510 104th Ave E Graham (98338) *(G-4234)*
Northwest Napkin LLC 360 571-0051
7016 Ne 40th Ave Vancouver (98661) *(G-14435)*
Northwest Native Designs 206 679-5847
18210 59th Ave Se Snohomish (98296) *(G-11953)*
Northwest Natural Products Inc 360 737-6800
10 S 56th Pl Ridgefield (98642) *(G-9096)*
Northwest Naturals LLC 425 885-5252
11805 N Creek Pkwy S # 104 Bothell (98011) *(G-1781)*
Northwest Navigator, Silverdale *Also called Sound Publishing Inc (G-11858)*
Northwest Outdoor Lighting 425 633-6074
26813 Ne Beadonhall St Duvall (98019) *(G-2996)*
Northwest Paper Box Mfrs Inc 206 782-7105
855 S 192nd St Ste 100 Seatac (98148) *(G-9293)*
Northwest Paper Converters Inc 800 681-9748
5441 Labounty Dr Ferndale (98248) *(G-3878)*
Northwest Parents Media 206 842-8500
5671 Ward Ave Ne Bainbridge Island (98110) *(G-655)*
Northwest Park Models LLC 509 235-2522
18607 W Williams Lake Rd Cheney (99004) *(G-2590)*
Northwest Pea & Bean Company, Rosalia *Also called Cooperative AG Producers Inc (G-9154)*
Northwest Pea & Bean Company (HQ) 509 534-3821
6109 E Desmet Ave Spokane Valley (99212) *(G-12808)*
Northwest Peaks Brewery LLC 206 853-0525
4912 17th Ave Nw Ste B Seattle (98107) *(G-10649)*
Northwest Pet Products Inc 360 225-8855
350 S Pekin Rd Woodland (98674) *(G-15452)*
Northwest Pioneer Inc (PA) 253 872-9693
6006 S 228th St Kent (98032) *(G-5034)*
Northwest Pipe Company (PA) 360 397-6250
201 Ne Park Plaza Dr # 100 Vancouver (98684) *(G-14436)*
Northwest Pipe Company 801 326-6044
201 Ne Park Plaza Dr # 100 Vancouver (98684) *(G-14437)*
Northwest Pipe Company 303 289-4080
201 Ne Park Plaza Dr # 100 Vancouver (98684) *(G-14438)*
Northwest Pipe Organ 425 432-5039
22808 253rd Ave Se Maple Valley (98038) *(G-6283)*
Northwest Plastic Tech LLC (PA) 206 499-6292
10308 242nd Pl Sw Edmonds (98020) *(G-3138)*
Northwest Plywood Sales of Ore 360 750-1561
2601 W 26th Ave Vancouver (98660) *(G-14439)*
Northwest Podiatric Laboratory 360 332-8411
1091 Fir Ave Blaine (98230) *(G-1689)*
Northwest Powder Soultions 253 395-6282
7818 S 194th St Kent (98032) *(G-5035)*
Northwest Precast Llc 253 770-9119
212 10th St Se Puyallup (98372) *(G-8207)*
Northwest Precision Tool Inc 509 493-4044
799 Highway 141 White Salmon (98672) *(G-15125)*
Northwest Press LLC 646 926-6427
2621 E Madison St Seattle (98112) *(G-10650)*
Northwest Prime Time 206 824-8600
22712 10th Ave S Des Moines (98198) *(G-2941)*
Northwest Processing, Olympia *Also called Empire Packing (G-7276)*
Northwest Prosthetic, Seattle *Also called Hattingh Holdings Inc (G-10148)*
Northwest Publications Inc 360 379-4080
460 Dennis Blvd Port Townsend (98368) *(G-7901)*
Northwest Publishing Ctr LLC 206 324-5644
14240 Interurban Ave S # 190 Tukwila (98168) *(G-13780)*
Northwest REO Preservation LLC 360 521-6761
5500 Ne 109th Ct Ste D Vancouver (98662) *(G-14440)*
Northwest Rock Inc (PA) 360 533-3050
642 Newskah Rd Aberdeen (98520) *(G-25)*
Northwest Rock Inc 360 249-2245
155 Wynooche Rd W Montesano (98563) *(G-6651)*
Northwest Rock Inc 360 482-3550
55 Schouweiler Rd Elma (98541) *(G-3253)*

Northwest Runner ... 206 527-5301
6310 Ne 74th St Ste 217e Seattle (98115) ***(G-10651)***
Northwest Sails & Canvas Inc ... 360 301-3204
1238 Blaine St Port Townsend (98368) ***(G-7902)***
Northwest Satellite Network ... 425 885-5986
3400 134th Ave Ne Bellevue (98005) ***(G-1037)***
Northwest Sausage & Deli ... 360 736-7760
5945 Prather Rd Sw Centralia (98531) ***(G-2421)***
Northwest Scents, Vancouver *Also called Franklin and Franklin Company* ***(G-14239)***
Northwest Seed & Pet Inc ... 509 484-7387
7302 N Division St Spokane (99208) ***(G-12414)***
Northwest Services ... 253 922-6475
2019 86th Avenue Ct E Puyallup (98371) ***(G-8208)***
Northwest Sftwr Professionals ... 360 734-5747
3851 Britton Rd Bellingham (98226) ***(G-1469)***
Northwest Smoking & Curing ... 360 733-3666
4600 Guide Meridian # 100 Bellingham (98226) ***(G-1470)***
Northwest Snow & Ice Equipment, Cashmere *Also called All Seasons Sweeping Service* ***(G-2312)***
Northwest Solutions Inc ... 360 380-3807
5381 Waschke Rd Bellingham (98226) ***(G-1471)***
Northwest Sports ... 206 463-5906
117520 Vashon Hwy Sw Vashon (98070) ***(G-14738)***
Northwest Sports Products ... 253 576-5958
3702 S Fife St Ste K384 Tacoma (98409) ***(G-13435)***
Northwest Stair and Rail Inc ... 425 348-7880
12322 Highway 99 Ste 100 Everett (98204) ***(G-3558)***
Northwest Sushi LLC ... 360 878-3464
5601 E 18th St Ste 208 Vancouver (98661) ***(G-14441)***
Northwest Synergistic Software ... 425 271-1491
14024 W Lk Kathleen Dr Se Renton (98059) ***(G-8860)***
Northwest Tarp & Canvas ... 360 296-2321
3334 Granada Way Bellingham (98225) ***(G-1472)***
Northwest Technical Services ... 425 419-4321
8516 200th St Se Snohomish (98296) ***(G-11954)***
Northwest Technologies ... 206 528-5353
5415 Ne 55th St Seattle (98105) ***(G-10652)***
Northwest Territorial Mint LLC ... 253 833-7780
841 Central Ave N Ste 200 Kent (98032) ***(G-5036)***
Northwest Tillers Inc ... 509 575-1950
3801 W Washington Ave Yakima (98903) ***(G-15635)***
Northwest Traffic Control Inc ... 360 604-5655
16818 Ne Maddox Ct Brush Prairie (98606) ***(G-2038)***
Northwest Truck & Auto AC ... 206 242-6034
30014 5th Ave Sw Federal Way (98023) ***(G-3765)***
Northwest Video Wall ... 360 403-7773
3011 252nd St Ne Arlington (98223) ***(G-291)***
Northwest Walk-In Bath Inc ... 206 898-2625
6715 Ne 63rd St Ste 476 Vancouver (98661) ***(G-14442)***
Northwest Water Systems Inc ... 360 876-0958
7245 Bethel Burley Rd Se Port Orchard (98367) ***(G-7835)***
Northwest Water Treatment LLC ... 360 354-2044
8600 Bender Rd Lynden (98264) ***(G-6040)***
Northwest Welding Academy LLC ... 325 574-3212
1233 Nw Elwha St 2 Oak Harbor (98277) ***(G-7160)***
Northwest Wholesale Inc (PA) ... 509 662-3563
5416 Enterprise Dr Wenatchee (98802) ***(G-15092)***
Northwest Wholesale Signs, Monroe *Also called Expressions Signs Inc* ***(G-6571)***
Northwest Wildfoods Co Inc ... 360 757-7940
12535 Pulver Rd Burlington (98233) ***(G-2176)***
Northwest Wire EDM Inc ... 509 893-0885
1620 N Mamer Rd Ste C300 Spokane Valley (99216) ***(G-12809)***
Northwest Wire Rope & Sling Co, Tacoma *Also called American Lifting Products Inc* ***(G-13168)***
Northwest Wldg Fabrication Inc ... 360 338-0923
3900 12th Ave Se Ste A Lacey (98503) ***(G-5568)***
Northwest Wood Design, Seattle *Also called Dale M Shafman LLC* ***(G-9787)***
Northwest Wood Products Inc ... 509 738-6190
850 W Old Kettle Rd Kettle Falls (99141) ***(G-5239)***
Northwest Woodworking LLC ... 425 488-9597
8003 Ne 151st Ct Kenmore (98028) ***(G-4594)***
Northwest Woodworks Inc ... 425 482-9663
15100 Wdnvll Rdmnd Rd Ne Woodinville (98072) ***(G-15322)***
Northwest Yachting Magazine, Seattle *Also called Skt Publishers Inc* ***(G-11129)***
Northwest Yachts Inc ... 360 299-0777
2415 T Ave Ste 207 Anacortes (98221) ***(G-156)***
Northwestern Fuel Ldscpg Sups ... 425 743-1550
4493 Russell Rd Ste A Mukilteo (98275) ***(G-6957)***
Northwestern Industries Inc (HQ) ... 206 285-3140
2500 W Jameson St Seattle (98199) ***(G-10653)***
Northwestern Precision Tool & ... 425 333-5201
31910 E Entwistle St Carnation (98014) ***(G-2297)***
Northwestern Sheetmetal, Yacolt *Also called James Homola* ***(G-15483)***
Northwind Industries ... 360 424-6689
4417 Landmark Dr Mount Vernon (98274) ***(G-6818)***
Northwing Uninsured Ultralight ... 509 682-4359
103 Gala Ave Chelan (98816) ***(G-2561)***
Northwing Uum, Chelan *Also called Northwing Uninsured Ultralight* ***(G-2561)***
Northwood Cabinets Inc ... 360 314-2446
8720 Ne Centerpointe Dr # 217 Vancouver (98665) ***(G-14443)***
Northwood Cabinets Inc (PA) ... 360 225-1001
1570 Guild Rd Woodland (98674) ***(G-15453)***
Nortn Coast Lighting Cash ... 425 454-2122
1034 116th Ave Ne Bellevue (98004) ***(G-1038)***
Norton Sound Fish Company LLC ... 206 298-1200
1200 Westlake Ave N # 900 Seattle (98109) ***(G-10654)***
Norwegian American ... 206 784-4617
17713 15th Ave Ne Ste 205 Shoreline (98155) ***(G-11794)***
Norwesco, Fife *Also called Gibraltar Industries Inc* ***(G-3955)***
Norwesco Inc ... 360 835-3021
3860 Grant St Washougal (98671) ***(G-14973)***
Norwest Business Forms & Sups ... 206 938-4387
3836 Sw Orchard St Seattle (98126) ***(G-10655)***
Norwest Shop Equipment, Spokane Valley *Also called McCulley Inc* ***(G-12786)***
Norwood-Wang Inc ... 206 304-8769
1522 Central Ave S Kent (98032) ***(G-5037)***
Nostopsign LLC ... 213 422-1750
1200 E Pike St Unit 215 Seattle (98122) ***(G-10656)***
Nota Bene Cellars Ltd ... 206 762-5581
9320 15th Ave S Seattle (98108) ***(G-10657)***
Noteadscom Inc ... 360 705-4548
3900 12th Ave Se Lacey (98503) ***(G-5569)***
Noumena LLC ... 206 451-3895
1010 S 312th St Federal Way (98003) ***(G-3766)***
Nouryon Pulp & Prfmce Chem LLC ... 509 765-6400
2701 Road N Ne Moses Lake (98837) ***(G-6733)***
Nova Fisheries Inc ... 206 781-2000
2532 Yale Ave E Seattle (98102) ***(G-10658)***
Nova Fisheries & Market Coop, Seattle *Also called Nova Fisheries Inc* ***(G-10658)***
Nova Graphics ... 509 251-2575
5715 N Malta St Newman Lake (99025) ***(G-7050)***
Nova Graphics ... 206 248-3489
14427 26th Ave S Seatac (98168) ***(G-9294)***
Nova Services ... 509 928-1588
1101 N Fancher Rd Ste 2 Spokane Valley (99212) ***(G-12810)***
Nova Verta USA Inc ... 509 444-7910
8207 E Trent Ave Spokane Valley (99212) ***(G-12811)***
Nova-Tech Engineering LP ... 425 245-7000
19909 120th Ave Ne Bothell (98011) ***(G-1782)***
Novak Windows ... 253 332-4392
11907 18th St E Edgewood (98372) ***(G-3088)***
Novaks Continuous Met Gutters, Bremerton *Also called J & E Jensen Inc* ***(G-1963)***
Novaleaf Software LLC ... 425 486-1242
23114 76th Ave Se Woodinville (98072) ***(G-15323)***
Novanta Inc ... 425 349-1359
4600 Campus Pl Mukilteo (98275) ***(G-6958)***
Novartis Vccnes Dagnostics Inc ... 862 778-2100
201 Elliott Ave W Ste 150 Seattle (98119) ***(G-10659)***
Novatech Instruments Inc ... 206 284-0704
4210 198th St Sw Ste 204 Lynnwood (98036) ***(G-6171)***
Novatech Instruments Inc ... 206 301-8986
12207 184th Ave Ne Redmond (98052) ***(G-8600)***
Novation Inc ... 509 922-1912
2616 N Locust Rd Spokane Valley (99206) ***(G-12812)***
Novel Inc ... 425 956-3096
4020 Lake Washington Blvd Kirkland (98033) ***(G-5414)***
Novelis Corporation ... 509 462-2310
16004 E Euclid Ave Spokane Valley (99216) ***(G-12813)***
Novelis Solatens Tech Ctr, Spokane Valley *Also called Novelis Corporation* ***(G-12813)***
Novell, Seattle *Also called Micro Focus Software Inc* ***(G-10532)***
Novelty Hill Winery LLC ... 425 481-5502
14710 Woodinville Redmon Woodinville (98072) ***(G-15324)***
Novelty Hill Winery LLC ... 206 664-2522
1000 2nd Ave Ste 3700 Seattle (98104) ***(G-10660)***
Novex LLC ... 360 296-3467
1313 E Maple St Ste 201 Bellingham (98225) ***(G-1473)***
Noviello Vineyards LLC ... 509 784-0544
272 Vineyard Dr Orondo (98843) ***(G-7458)***
Novo Contour Inc ... 425 773-2673
7015 147th St Sw Edmonds (98026) ***(G-3139)***
Novo Fogo ... 425 256-2527
13217 255th Ave Se Issaquah (98027) ***(G-4455)***
Novolex Shields LLC ... 800 541-8630
1009 Rock Ave Yakima (98902) ***(G-15636)***
Novus Composites Incorporated ... 253 476-8582
10801 A St S Ste O Tacoma (98444) ***(G-13436)***
Novuson Surgical Inc ... 425 481-7165
11824 N Creek Pkwy N # 103 Bothell (98011) ***(G-1783)***
Novustone LLC ... 206 457-4443
3100 Airport Way S # 71 Seattle (98134) ***(G-10661)***
Now & Again, Bothell *Also called Whitehouse Antique & Candy* ***(G-1918)***
Now Impressions Inc ... 425 881-5911
7126 180th Ave Ne C104 Redmond (98052) ***(G-8601)***
Noxon Inc ... 509 926-0557
2921 N University Rd # 3 Spokane Valley (99206) ***(G-12814)***
Nozzleworks Inc (PA) ... 360 668-2548
3812 209th St Se Bothell (98021) ***(G-1881)***
NP Paper Company LLC (HQ) ... 360 636-6400
3001 Industrial Way Longview (98632) ***(G-5938)***
Npm LLC ... 206 782-8999
1080 W Ewing Pl Ste D Seattle (98119) ***(G-10662)***
NRC Environmental Services Inc ... 206 607-3000
9520 10th Ave S Ste 150 Seattle (98108) ***(G-10663)***

ALPHABETIC

NRG Resources Inc 509 588-4786
733 9th St Benton City (99320) ***(G-1621)***
Nrs Software LLC 509 969-4769
2301 W Yakima Ave Yakima (98902) ***(G-15637)***
Nta Inc 425 487-2679
19806 141st Pl Ne Bldg D Woodinville (98072) ***(G-15325)***
Nth Degree Inc 253 926-6705
1009 Xavier St Milton (98354) ***(G-6537)***
Nu Driveways, Mount Vernon *Also called Creative Concrete Products LLC* ***(G-6786)***
Nu Element Inc 206 356-4525
1201 Pacific Ave Ste 600 Tacoma (98402) ***(G-13437)***
Nu Way Flume & Equipment Co (PA) 360 942-3581
161 Elkhorn Rd Raymond (98577) ***(G-8356)***
Nu-Ray Metal Products Inc (PA) 253 833-8637
1234 37th St Nw Auburn (98001) ***(G-513)***
Nu-Ray Metals, Auburn *Also called Nu-Ray Metal Products Inc* ***(G-513)***
Nuance Communications Inc 781 565-5000
821 2nd Ave Ste 1200 Seattle (98104) ***(G-10664)***
Nubble Road Music & Pubg LLC 206 283-0696
8712 18th Ave Nw Seattle (98117) ***(G-10665)***
Nucanoe Inc 360 543-9019
2125 Humboldt St Bellingham (98225) ***(G-1474)***
Nucor Corporation 206 933-2222
2424 Sw Andover St Seattle (98106) ***(G-10666)***
Nucor Steel Bar Mills Group, Seattle *Also called Nucor Steel Seattle Inc* ***(G-10667)***
Nucor Steel Seattle Inc (HQ) 206 933-2222
2424 Sw Andover St Seattle (98106) ***(G-10667)***
Nuflours, Seattle *Also called D Floured LLC* ***(G-9781)***
Nugent Gis & Environmental Svc 206 324-0059
1925 7th Ave W Seattle (98119) ***(G-10668)***
Nuid Inc 360 927-4682
5111 Latona Ave Ne Seattle (98105) ***(G-10669)***
Numeric Control LLC 360 269-1497
204 2nd St Morton (98356) ***(G-6670)***
Nuovo Parts Inc 360 738-1888
1465 Slater Rd Ferndale (98248) ***(G-3879)***
Nupro Products Inc 509 698-6983
2234 N Wenas Rd Selah (98942) ***(G-11593)***
Nut Factory Inc 509 926-6666
19425 E Broadway Ave Spokane Valley (99016) ***(G-12815)***
Nutesla Corporation 910 688-3752
853 W Y St Washougal (98671) ***(G-14974)***
Nutraceutix, Redmond *Also called Probi Usa Inc* ***(G-8632)***
Nutraceutix, Redmond *Also called Tntgamble Inc* ***(G-8693)***
Nutradried Creations LLP 360 332-2101
2252 Odell St Blaine (98230) ***(G-1690)***
Nutradried Food Company LLC 360 366-4567
6920 Salashan Pkwy D111 Ferndale (98248) ***(G-3880)***
Nutrien AG Solutions Inc 509 547-9771
3486 N Glade Rd Pasco (99301) ***(G-7606)***
Nutrifaster Inc 206 767-5054
209 S Bennett St Seattle (98108) ***(G-10670)***
Nutrition Now Inc 360 737-6800
10 S 56th Pl Ridgefield (98642) ***(G-9097)***
Nutshell 360 438-1054
4748 Lakeshore Ln Se Lacey (98513) ***(G-5570)***
Nuu-Muu LLC 360 223-7151
1715 Ellis St Ste 102 Bellingham (98225) ***(G-1475)***
Nuun & Company Inc 206 219-9237
800 Maynard Ave S Ste 102 Seattle (98134) ***(G-10671)***
Nw Asian Weekly 206 223-5559
412 Maynard Ave S Seattle (98104) ***(G-10672)***
NW Center Industries 5307 206 285-9140
7272 W Marginal Way S Seattle (98108) ***(G-10673)***
NW Closets 253 246-7596
22024 68th Ave S Kent (98032) ***(G-5038)***
NW Coffee Rosters LLC 360 442-4111
1335 14th Ave Longview (98632) ***(G-5939)***
NW Contractor Services, Puyallup *Also called Northwest Envmtl & Eqp Inc* ***(G-8204)***
NW Design Center, Lakewood *Also called Arcomm Inc* ***(G-5699)***
NW Elements 206 440-9135
15527 12th Ave Ne Shoreline (98155) ***(G-11795)***
NW Evergreen Products 509 276-7825
6410 W Groove Ln Deer Park (99006) ***(G-2912)***
NW Fibre LLC 360 887-8418
324 Davis Lake Rd Morton (98356) ***(G-6671)***
NW Filters 253 859-4099
5525 S 231st Pl Kent (98032) ***(G-5039)***
NW Fine Art Printing 425 947-1539
8700 148th Ave Ne Redmond (98052) ***(G-8602)***
NW Hardwoods LLC 206 784-9369
13423 39th Dr Se Mill Creek (98012) ***(G-6518)***
NW Hydroponics 360 778-3254
5655 Guide Meridian Bellingham (98226) ***(G-1476)***
NW Laundry Service 206 242-5500
6446 S 144th St Tukwila (98168) ***(G-13781)***
NW Lighting Solutions LLC 253 246-2959
1819 Central Ave S # 126 Kent (98032) ***(G-5040)***
NW Lighting Solutions LLC 253 929-4657
201 Auburn Way N Ste C Auburn (98002) ***(G-514)***
NW Logging Company 360 226-2691
2522 N Proctor St Tacoma (98406) ***(G-13438)***
NW Marine Industries Nmi, Bellingham *Also called Northwest Marine Inds LLC* ***(G-1468)***
NW Mold Removal 360 433-7353
2815 H St Vancouver (98663) ***(G-14444)***
NW Pole Vault Camps 206 526-0436
7527 27th Ave Ne Seattle (98115) ***(G-10674)***
NW Propeller Operations Inc 253 858-5061
10902 25th Ave S Lakewood (98499) ***(G-5743)***
NW Publishing Center 206 242-1822
11611 Marine View Dr Sw Seattle (98146) ***(G-10675)***
NW Sextant LLC 425 746-6475
4675 144th Pl Se Bellevue (98006) ***(G-1039)***
NW Software Solutions 509 252-3550
421 W Main Ave Ste 200 Spokane (99201) ***(G-12415)***
NW Solar Protection LLC 509 294-9878
10125 N Division St Spokane (99218) ***(G-12416)***
NW Sound & Security Tech, Ridgefield *Also called N W Sound & Security Tech LLC* ***(G-9095)***
NW Utility Services LLC 253 891-7802
228 Frontage Rd S Ste A Pacific (98047) ***(G-7536)***
NW Wood Box 360 939-2434
1244 Moore Rd Ste I2 Camano Island (98282) ***(G-2220)***
NW Wood Holding LLC 360 326-8794
4818 Ne 142nd St Vancouver (98686) ***(G-14445)***
NW Woodworks LLC 206 780-6753
9636 Ne Timberlane Pl Bainbridge Island (98110) ***(G-656)***
Nwd Ink International Inc 425 454-0707
1 Lake Bellevue Dr Bellevue (98005) ***(G-1040)***
Nwfsc 206 860-3415
2725 Montlake Blvd E Seattle (98112) ***(G-10676)***
Nwsignwerxs 253 217-0053
3414 A St Se Auburn (98002) ***(G-515)***
Nwt3k Outerwear 253 318-2371
14919 118th Ave Nw Gig Harbor (98329) ***(G-4137)***
Nxedge Inc 425 990-0091
10900 Ne 8th St Ste 1525 Bellevue (98004) ***(G-1041)***
Nyeberg Machine 425 235-9675
17022 Se 136th St Renton (98059) ***(G-8861)***
Nygards Custom Cabinetry 360 425-1777
1602 Pacific Ave N Ste B Kelso (98626) ***(G-4540)***
Nylatech Incorporated (PA) 360 966-2838
223 W Main St Everson (98247) ***(G-3685)***
O B Williams Company 206 623-2494
1939 1st Ave S Seattle (98134) ***(G-10677)***
O L Luther Co 509 837-2527
2901 Beam Rd Granger (98932) ***(G-4262)***
O M M C O, Shelton *Also called Olympic Mountain Millwork LLC* ***(G-11717)***
O Neil Industries LLC 509 828-0213
827 W 1st Ave Ste 425 Spokane (99201) ***(G-12417)***
O Ryan Water Sports Ski School, Redmond *Also called ORyan Marine LLC* ***(G-8604)***
O S Winery LLC 206 243-3427
6743 80th Ave Se Mercer Island (98040) ***(G-6475)***
O'Brien Water Sports, Snoqualmie *Also called Motion Water Sports Inc* ***(G-12020)***
O'Dell Logging, Sequim *Also called Eddie ODell* ***(G-11632)***
O-Netics Ltd 425 823-2279
14144 76th Pl Ne Kirkland (98034) ***(G-5415)***
O-Town Brewing LLC 360 701-4706
4414 Montclair Dr Se Lacey (98503) ***(G-5571)***
O2compost 360 563-6709
312 Maple Ave Snohomish (98290) ***(G-11955)***
O2d Software Inc 206 364-0055
86 Olympic Dr Nw Shoreline (98177) ***(G-11796)***
Oak Bay Technologies Inc 360 437-0718
521 Verner Ave Port Ludlow (98365) ***(G-7771)***
Oak Bros Curved Glass 253 752-4055
7510 Fair Oaks Rd Se Olympia (98513) ***(G-7349)***
Oak Brothers, Olympia *Also called Oak Bros Curved Glass* ***(G-7349)***
Oakbridge University 360 681-5233
41 Windmill Ln Sequim (98382) ***(G-11654)***
Oakwood Cellars 509 588-1900
12911 E Sr 224 Ne Benton City (99320) ***(G-1622)***
Oatridge-Evergreen 8a2 JV LLC 253 627-3794
2111 S 90th St Tacoma (98444) ***(G-13439)***
Obcon Inc 253 931-0455
1802 Pike St Nw Ste C Auburn (98001) ***(G-516)***
Obenaufs Online 509 254-3542
1440 7th St Clarkston (99403) ***(G-2639)***
Oberg Filters LLC 360 403-3222
17118 112th Ave Ne Arlington (98223) ***(G-292)***
Oberg International, Monroe *Also called Bedford Industries Inc* ***(G-6551)***
Oberg Manufacturing Inc 360 435-8161
17118 112th Ave Ne Arlington (98223) ***(G-293)***
Oberg Race Products, Arlington *Also called Oberg Manufacturing Inc* ***(G-293)***
Oberon Pharma 206 713-5467
8339 Se 57th St Mercer Island (98040) ***(G-6476)***
Oberto 425 251-4563
101 Sw 41st St Ste D Renton (98057) ***(G-8862)***
Oberto Snacks Inc (HQ) 253 437-6100
7060 Oberto Dr Kent (98032) ***(G-5041)***
Obituaries and Legals 253 597-8605
1950 S State St Tacoma (98405) ***(G-13440)***
Object Publishing Software 206 414-9440
4616 25th Ave Ne Seattle (98105) ***(G-10678)***

Observa Inc 206 499-4444
323 N 46th St Ste B Seattle (98103) ***(G-10679)***
Ocarina Arena 206 446-5354
2629 E Aloha St Seattle (98112) ***(G-10680)***
Occasional Publishing Inc 877 373-8273
2221 Nw 56th St Ste 101 Seattle (98107) ***(G-10681)***
Ocean Beauty Seafoods LLC (PA) 206 285-6800
1100 W Ewing St Seattle (98119) ***(G-10682)***
Ocean Cargo Container Inc 253 381-9098
3111 Harborview Dr Gig Harbor (98335) ***(G-4138)***
Ocean Gold Seafoods Inc 360 268-2510
1804 N Nyhus St Westport (98595) ***(G-15106)***
Ocean In A Box 360 573-2250
4601 Ne 78th St Ste 250 Vancouver (98665) ***(G-14446)***
Ocean Instruments Wash LLC 425 281-1471
32617 Se 44th St Fall City (98024) ***(G-3704)***
Ocean Instruments, Inc., Fall City *Also called Ocean Instruments Wash LLC* ***(G-3704)***
Ocean Peace Inc 206 282-6100
4201 21st Ave W Seattle (98199) ***(G-10683)***
Ocean Protein LLC 360 538-7400
518 22nd St Hoquiam (98550) ***(G-4350)***
Ocean Spray Cranberries Inc 360 648-2515
1480 State Route 105 Aberdeen (98520) ***(G-26)***
Oceanus Plastics Inc 360 366-7474
2445 Salashan Loop Custer (98240) ***(G-2858)***
Oceanwest Rvm LLC 503 569-6969
1205 E Badger Rd Lynden (98264) ***(G-6041)***
OCG, Bothell *Also called Unlimited Possibilities Now* ***(G-1804)***
Ochoa AG Unlimited Foods Inc 509 349-2210
1203 Basin St Warden (98857) ***(G-14934)***
Ochoa Brothers Inc 509 544-6553
812 S Myrtle Ave Pasco (99301) ***(G-7607)***
Octapharma Plasma 360 450-3135
5000 E Fourth Plain Blvd Vancouver (98661) ***(G-14447)***
Octapharma Plasma 253 922-7753
5306 Pacific Hwy E Ste D Fife (98424) ***(G-3975)***
Octave Vineyard LLC 509 876-2530
1334 Crystal Ct Walla Walla (99362) ***(G-14852)***
October Mist Publishing 206 933-1414
3012 Nw 85th St Apt B Seattle (98117) ***(G-10684)***
Ocular Instruments Inc 425 455-5200
2255 116th Ave Ne Bellevue (98004) ***(G-1042)***
Ode Gutter Products, Sumner *Also called Ode Products LLC* ***(G-13090)***
Ode Products LLC 253 859-7902
13701 24th St E Unit F8 Sumner (98390) ***(G-13090)***
Odessa Record 509 982-2632
1 W 1st Ave Odessa (99159) ***(G-7191)***
Odo 303 915-9652
1111 W 1st Ave Ste B Spokane (99201) ***(G-12418)***
Odwalla Inc 206 242-8519
6440 S 143rd St Tukwila (98168) ***(G-13782)***
Odyssey Enterprises Inc 206 285-7445
2729 6th Ave S Seattle (98134) ***(G-10685)***
Odyssey Foods, Seattle *Also called Orca Bay Foods LLC* ***(G-10711)***
Oe Two Industries LLC 425 657-0958
3211 216th Ct Se Sammamish (98075) ***(G-9238)***
Oeser Company 360 734-1480
730 Marine Dr Bellingham (98225) ***(G-1477)***
of The Earth 206 462-7022
7706 Aurora Ave N Seattle (98103) ***(G-10686)***
Off Road Addiction LLC 509 999-7824
12013 S Jackson Rd Valleyford (99023) ***(G-13999)***
Offerup Inc 844 633-3787
227 Bellevue Way Ne 57 Bellevue (98004) ***(G-1043)***
Office Timeline LLC 425 296-9002
1400 112th Ave Se Ste 100 Bellevue (98004) ***(G-1044)***
OfficeMax North America Inc 360 455-4068
1200 Marvin Rd Ne Lacey (98516) ***(G-5572)***
Offroad Outpost 360 910-0021
10920 Ne 113th St Vancouver (98662) ***(G-14448)***
Offset Solar LLC 866 376-9559
2111 N Molter Rd Liberty Lake (99019) ***(G-5849)***
Offshore Products Inc 206 567-5404
7905 192nd Pl Sw Edmonds (98026) ***(G-3140)***
Ofner and Company 425 485-0437
8037 Ne 169th St Kenmore (98028) ***(G-4595)***
Often On Glass 206 725-5306
4702 42nd Ave S Seattle (98118) ***(G-10687)***
Ogle Equipment Co 509 489-6306
6619 N Crestline St Spokane (99217) ***(G-12419)***
OH Boy Oberto, Kent *Also called Oberto Snacks Inc* ***(G-5041)***
OH Cholocolate LLC 206 232-4974
2703 76th Ave Se Mercer Island (98040) ***(G-6477)***
OH Snap Prints 509 901-7719
411 N 78th Ave Yakima (98908) ***(G-15638)***
Oil & Vinegar Retail 509 838-7115
808 W Main Ave Ste 201 Spokane (99201) ***(G-12420)***
Oil Spills Services Inc 425 823-6500
12422 68th Ave Ne Kirkland (98034) ***(G-5416)***
Oil Vinegar 206 285-0517
900 1st Ave S Ste 204 Seattle (98134) ***(G-10688)***
Oiltrap Environmental Pdts Inc 360 943-6495
8904 Kimmie St Sw Olympia (98512) ***(G-7350)***
OK Sock LLC 509 209-6598
4815 E Patricia Rd Mead (99021) ***(G-6435)***
OK Tool & Machine Works 360 736-8350
2122 Seminary Hill Rd Centralia (98531) ***(G-2422)***
Oka Woodworks Inc 425 221-2573
22840 Ne 26th St Sammamish (98074) ***(G-9239)***
Okanogan Arms Co LLC 509 422-4123
105 W Oak St Okanogan Wa Okanogan (98840) ***(G-7202)***
Okanogan Chronicle, OMAK *Also called Chronicle* ***(G-7436)***
Okanogan Label & Print Ltd 250 328-8660
13 1/2 E Main St Ste 214b Walla Walla (99362) ***(G-14853)***
Okanogan Valley Concrete Inc 509 422-3211
2145 Elmway Okanogan (98840) ***(G-7203)***
Okanogan Vly Gazette Tribune, Oroville *Also called Oroville Gazette Inc* ***(G-7470)***
Old & Elegant Distributing 425 455-4660
10203 Main St Bellevue (98004) ***(G-1045)***
Old Dominion Woodworks 509 684-7931
760 Hardenbrook Rd Colville (99114) ***(G-2767)***
Old Growth Northwest 206 856-6293
9518 Sand Point Way Ne Seattle (98115) ***(G-10689)***
Old Iron Classics 360 852-8854
6707 Ne 117th Ave 103c Vancouver (98662) ***(G-14449)***
Old Plank Woodworks 360 455-7366
3141 60th Loop Se Olympia (98501) ***(G-7351)***
Old Salt Merchants LLC 888 995-7258
30 E Rhododendron Dr Port Townsend (98368) ***(G-7903)***
Old School Woodcrafter 509 493-4155
145 Se 3rd Rd White Salmon (98672) ***(G-15126)***
Old Soldier Distillery 253 223-4306
309 Puyallup Ave Unit B1 Tacoma (98421) ***(G-13441)***
Old Soul Candle Company LLC 206 915-0224
11903 Se 165th St Renton (98058) ***(G-8863)***
Old Timers Pork Rinds 509 438-8999
129901 W Hanks Rd Prosser (99350) ***(G-8060)***
Old Woodworking Inc 253 770-3650
2203 Inter Ave Ste D Puyallup (98372) ***(G-8209)***
Old World Cone, Seattle *Also called Elkins Distribution Inc* ***(G-9898)***
Oldcastle Apg 509 926-8235
16310 E Marietta Ln Spokane Valley (99216) ***(G-12816)***
Oldcastle Buildingenvelope Inc 360 816-7777
1611 Se Commerce Ave Battle Ground (98604) ***(G-725)***
Oldcastle Materials Inc 509 926-8235
16310 E Marietta Ave Spokane Valley (99216) ***(G-12817)***
Oldcastle Materials Inc 253 872-9466
20609 77th Ave S Kent (98032) ***(G-5042)***
Oldcastle Materials Inc 509 534-6221
922 N Carnahan Rd Spokane Valley (99212) ***(G-12818)***
Oldcastle Precast Inc 253 839-3500
2808 A St Se Auburn (98002) ***(G-517)***
Olde English Crackers Inc 360 715-2972
4071 Hannegan Rd Ste S Bellingham (98226) ***(G-1478)***
Oldfield Cellars LLC 425 398-7200
19730 144th Ave Ne Woodinville (98072) ***(G-15326)***
Olive Games Corporation 425 649-1136
14205 Se 36th St Ste 100 Bellevue (98006) ***(G-1046)***
Olive Navidis Oil & Vinegars 360 600-9836
5287 N St Washougal (98671) ***(G-14975)***
Olive Omg Oils 206 340-4114
309 S Cloverdale St C25 Seattle (98108) ***(G-10690)***
Olive Seattle Oil Co 425 740-6055
10317 Marine View Dr Mukilteo (98275) ***(G-6959)***
Oliver Henry Games LLC 971 231-9141
18609 Ne 145th Pl Woodinville (98072) ***(G-15327)***
Oliver Machinery Company 253 867-0334
6902 S 194th St Kent (98032) ***(G-5043)***
Olivine Corp 360 733-3332
928 Thomas Rd Bellingham (98226) ***(G-1479)***
Olsen Cabinet & Millwork 206 242-1188
12860 23rd Ave S Seatac (98168) ***(G-9295)***
Olsen Estates LLC 509 973-2203
46002 N District Line Rd Prosser (99350) ***(G-8061)***
Olsons Baking Company LLC 425 774-9164
6414 204th St Sw Ste 100 Lynnwood (98036) ***(G-6172)***
Olsons Gaskets 360 871-1207
3059 Opdal Rd E Port Orchard (98366) ***(G-7836)***
Oltis Software LLC 800 557-1780
10900 Ne 4th St Ste 1450 Bellevue (98004) ***(G-1047)***
Oly Kraut LLC 360 561-4532
2300 Friendly Grove Rd Ne Olympia (98506) ***(G-7352)***
Olymipa Copy and Printing, Olympia *Also called Professional Business Svc Inc* ***(G-7374)***
Olympia Powder Coat 360 570-9100
1015 85th Ave Se Olympia (98501) ***(G-7353)***
Olympia Sheet Metal Inc 360 491-1123
7635 Betti Ln Ne Olympia (98516) ***(G-7354)***
Olympian, Olympia *Also called McClatchy Newspapers Inc* ***(G-7333)***
Olympian Newspaper 360 754-5402
11 Duffel St Ne Olympia (98506) ***(G-7355)***
Olympic Aerospace Inc 253 835-4984
34210 9th Ave S Ste 116 Federal Way (98003) ***(G-3767)***
Olympic Areospace Inc 253 835-4984
34729 5th Ave Sw Federal Way (98023) ***(G-3768)***
Olympic Arms Inc 360 456-3471
624 Old Pacific Hwy Se Olympia (98513) ***(G-7356)***

A L P H A B E T I C

Olympic Brake Supply, Renton *Also called Genuine Parts Company* ***(G-8806)***
Olympic Cascade Publishing 253 274-7344
1950 S State St Tacoma (98405) ***(G-13442)***
Olympic Cellars LLC 360 452-0160
255410 Highway 101 Port Angeles (98362) ***(G-7728)***
Olympic Crest Coffee Roasters 360 459-5756
5800 Pacific Ave Se Olympia (98503) ***(G-7357)***
Olympic Distillers LLC 360 920-9645
356 Freshwater Bay Rd Port Angeles (98363) ***(G-7729)***
Olympic Embroidery 425 413-2848
28815 Se 258th St Ravensdale (98051) ***(G-8338)***
Olympic Fly Fishers 206 546-2677
20109 15th Ave Nw Shoreline (98177) ***(G-11797)***
Olympic Foundry Inc (PA) 206 764-6200
5200 Airport Way S Seattle (98108) ***(G-10691)***
Olympic Graphic Arts Inc 360 374-6020
640 S Forks Ave Forks (98331) ***(G-4013)***
Olympic Home Modification LLC 253 858-9941
4700 Point Fosdick Dr Nw Gig Harbor (98335) ***(G-4139)***
Olympic Instruments Inc 206 463-3604
16901 Westside Hwy Sw Vashon (98070) ***(G-14739)***
Olympic Iron Works 360 491-2500
3105 Marvin Rd Ne Olympia (98516) ***(G-7358)***
Olympic Jantr Sup & Svc LLC 360 692-0832
7604 Ne Tyee Ct Bremerton (98311) ***(G-1982)***
Olympic Kayak Co, Port Gamble *Also called Olympic Outdoor Center* ***(G-7757)***
Olympic Machine & Welding Inc 253 627-8571
3115 N 14th St Tacoma (98406) ***(G-13443)***
Olympic Manganese Mining Co 360 426-9273
2631 W Skokomish Vly Rd Shelton (98584) ***(G-11716)***
Olympic Manufacturing Inc 425 679-6303
12121 Northup Way Ste 107 Bellevue (98005) ***(G-1048)***
Olympic Medical, Seattle *Also called Natus Medical Incorporated* ***(G-10594)***
Olympic Medical Corp 206 767-3500
5900 1st Ave S Seattle (98108) ***(G-10692)***
Olympic Millwork 360 480-6650
1521 Thomas St Nw Olympia (98502) ***(G-7359)***
Olympic Mountain Ice Cream, Shelton *Also called Heavenly Gelato Inc* ***(G-11699)***
Olympic Mountain Millwork LLC 360 432-2992
822 E Hiawatha Blvd Shelton (98584) ***(G-11717)***
Olympic Mountain Products Inc 253 850-2343
8655 S 208th St Kent (98031) ***(G-5044)***
Olympic Musical Instrumen 360 779-4620
23022 Miller Bay Rd Ne Poulsbo (98370) ***(G-7989)***
Olympic Outdoor Center 360 297-4659
32379 Rainier Ave Ne Port Gamble (98364) ***(G-7757)***
Olympic Panel Products LLC 360 432-5033
204 E Railroad Ave Shelton (98584) ***(G-11718)***
Olympic Peninsula Implants 360 385-5121
1119 Lawrence St Port Townsend (98368) ***(G-7904)***
Olympic Print and Apparel 206 402-3642
6047 California Ave Sw Seattle (98136) ***(G-10693)***
Olympic Printer Resources Inc 360 297-8384
26127 Calvary Ln Ne # 200 Kingston (98346) ***(G-5259)***
Olympic Propeller Company 360 299-8266
8142 S March Point Rd Anacortes (98221) ***(G-157)***
Olympic Protein Sciences LLC 206 849-9811
454 N 34th St Seattle (98103) ***(G-10694)***
Olympic Protein Technologies, Seattle *Also called Olympic Protein Sciences LLC* ***(G-10694)***
Olympic SEC Comm Sys Inc 360 652-1088
19009 62nd Ave Ne Arlington (98223) ***(G-294)***
Olympic Synthetic Products, Sequim *Also called Osp Sling Inc* ***(G-11657)***
Olympic Sytems Inc 206 547-5777
3800 Aurora Ave N Ste 360 Seattle (98103) ***(G-10695)***
Olympic Technology Resources, Kingston *Also called Olympic Printer Resources Inc* ***(G-5259)***
Olympic View Publishing LLC 360 374-3311
490 S Forks Ave Forks (98331) ***(G-4014)***
Olympic View Publishing LLC (PA) 360 683-3311
147 W Washington St Sequim (98382) ***(G-11655)***
Olympus Lock Inc 206 362-3290
18424 Highway 99 Lynnwood (98037) ***(G-6173)***
Olympus Press Inc 206 242-2700
3400 S 150th St Tukwila (98188) ***(G-13783)***
Olympus Scientific Solutions (HQ) 509 735-7550
421 N Quay St Kennewick (99336) ***(G-4704)***
Olysigns 360 417-5254
12 Findley Rd Port Angeles (98362) ***(G-7730)***
Olysunrise Compost Concierge 360 551-0674
206 Lilly Rd Ne Apt L10 Olympia (98506) ***(G-7360)***
Om LLC Reinstated 2005 ....360 821-1802
60 Huckleberry Pl Port Townsend (98368) ***(G-7905)***
Omada International LLC (PA) 425 242-5400
14513 32nd St E Sumner (98390) ***(G-13091)***
Omage Labs Inc 844 662-4326
1601 5th Ave Ste 1100 Seattle (98101) ***(G-10696)***
Omak Machine Shop Inc 509 826-1030
505 Okoma Dr OMAK (98841) ***(G-7440)***
OMAK Wood Products LLC 360 432-5048
1100 E 8th Ave OMAK (98841) ***(G-7441)***
Omax Corporation 253 872-2300
21409 72nd Ave S Kent (98032) ***(G-5045)***
Omega Aerospace Products, Kirkland *Also called Omega Architectural Pdts Inc* ***(G-5417)***
Omega Architectural Pdts Inc (PA) 425 821-7222
517 6th St S Kirkland (98033) ***(G-5417)***
OMega Graphics and Signs LLC 206 789-5480
4321 Leary Way Nw Seattle (98107) ***(G-10697)***
Omega Industries Inc (PA) 360 574-9086
7304 Ne St Johns Rd Vancouver (98665) ***(G-14450)***
Omega Labs Inc 425 296-0886
10916 101st Pl Ne Kirkland (98033) ***(G-5418)***
Omega Ministries Inc 360 477-4180
21 Petal Ln Sequim (98382) ***(G-11656)***
Omega Pacific Inc 509 456-0170
11427 W 21st Ave Airway Heights (99001) ***(G-58)***
Omega Printing 425 339-8538
2110 Broadway Ste A Everett (98201) ***(G-3559)***
Omega Silversmithing Inc 360 863-6771
9621 164th St Se Snohomish (98296) ***(G-11956)***
Omen Board Industries LLC 425 967-3434
5001 208th St Sw Ste 102 Lynnwood (98036) ***(G-6174)***
Omeros Corporation (PA) 206 676-5000
201 Elliott Ave W Seattle (98119) ***(G-10698)***
Omh Innovations Usa Inc 509 264-1129
30627 N Hardesty Rd Chattaroy (99003) ***(G-2450)***
Omh Proscreen, Chattaroy *Also called Omh Innovations Usa Inc* ***(G-2450)***
Omicron Investment Corporation (PA) 360 413-7569
6736 78th Ave Ne Olympia (98516) ***(G-7361)***
Omni Development Inc 206 523-4152
1000 Dexter Ave N Ste 400 Seattle (98109) ***(G-10699)***
Omni Duct Systems, Everett *Also called ECB Corp* ***(G-3451)***
Omni Group, Seattle *Also called Omni Development Inc* ***(G-10699)***
Omni Technology 425 823-9295
7427 Ne 144th Pl Kirkland (98034) ***(G-5419)***
Omnifab Inc 253 931-5151
1316 W Main St Auburn (98001) ***(G-518)***
Omnim2m LLC 425 278-4090
4826 194th Ave Se Issaquah (98027) ***(G-4456)***
Omnimax International Inc 509 535-0344
6207 E Desmet Ave Spokane Valley (99212) ***(G-12819)***
Omnitec Design Inc 425 290-3922
4640 Campus Pl Ste 100 Mukilteo (98275) ***(G-6960)***
Omohundro Co Kitsap Composites 360 519-3047
1525 Vivian Ct Port Orchard (98367) ***(G-7837)***
Omya, Woodland *Also called Northwest Carbonate Inc* ***(G-15451)***
On Purpose Publishing 206 789-9677
8010 13th Ave Nw Seattle (98117) ***(G-10700)***
On Site Safety Inc 970 876-1908
1100 Carillon Pt Kirkland (98033) ***(G-5420)***
On The Level Custom Cabinets 360 666-9058
9217 Ne 316th St La Center (98629) ***(G-5510)***
On-Site Safety Inc 701 774-2022
1100 Carillon Pt Kirkland (98033) ***(G-5421)***
Onamac Industries Inc 425 743-6676
6300 Merrill Creek Pkwy B200 Everett (98203) ***(G-3560)***
Onamac Machine Works, Everett *Also called Onamac Industries Inc* ***(G-3560)***
Onboard Systems Intl LLC 360 546-3072
13915 Nw 3rd Ct Vancouver (98685) ***(G-14451)***
Once Again Woodworking 425 327-9733
707 10th St Snohomish (98290) ***(G-11957)***
Once Upon A Pallet 360 798-6294
29011 Ne 164th Ave Battle Ground (98604) ***(G-726)***
One Atta Time Doll Co 360 956-1091
6519 Lazy St Sw Olympia (98512) ***(G-7362)***
One Build Inc 206 801-1675
814 2nd Ave Ste 500 Seattle (98104) ***(G-10701)***
One Earth Press 206 784-1641
105 Nw 75th St Seattle (98117) ***(G-10702)***
One Oil Lovin Mama 360 572-4511
27821 70th Ave Nw Stanwood (98292) ***(G-12984)***
One Step Ahead Inc 425 487-1869
1517 183rd St Se Ste 3 Bothell (98012) ***(G-1882)***
One Time Welding 360 452-8532
2917 W Edgewood Dr Port Angeles (98363) ***(G-7731)***
One Tree Hard Cider 509 315-9856
9514 E Montgomery Ave Spokane Valley (99206) ***(G-12820)***
Oneclick.ai, Redmond *Also called Tensormake Corporation* ***(G-8688)***
Onefarstar LLC 425 999-4894
411 165th Ave Se Bellevue (98008) ***(G-1049)***
ONeill Steel Fabrication Inc 509 467-5309
7004 N Altamont St Spokane (99217) ***(G-12421)***
Oneils Foundry Forging Metal & 360 941-7557
1386 Moore St Sedro Woolley (98284) ***(G-11553)***
Oneradio Corporation 206 393-2900
15330 Ne 66th Ct Redmond (98052) ***(G-8603)***
Ong Innovations LLC 253 777-0186
14201 Se Petrovitsky Rd Renton (98058) ***(G-8864)***
Only Solutions Cabinet Install 253 848-8358
12517 164th St E Puyallup (98374) ***(G-8210)***
Ono Cakes and Delights 206 257-9046
12724 Lake City Way Ne A3 Seattle (98125) ***(G-10703)***
Onsite Computer Services 360 650-1079
220 W Champion St Ste 260 Bellingham (98225) ***(G-1480)***

Ontario Systems LLC 360 256-7358
4400 Ne 77th Ave Ste 100 Vancouver (98662) ***(G-14452)***
Ooak Prints LLC 253 886-1539
719 Main St Buckley (98321) ***(G-2065)***
Oodles Noodle Bar 425 467-7076
437 108th Ave Ne Bellevue (98004) ***(G-1050)***
Oola Distillery, Seattle *Also called Oola Industries LLC* ***(G-10704)***
Oola Industries LLC 206 709-7909
1314 E Union St Seattle (98122) ***(G-10704)***
Op-Air Engineering, Kent *Also called Samuel Edwards* ***(G-5114)***
Opal Art Glass 360 532-9268
1232 1st St Cosmopolis (98537) ***(G-2801)***
Open Mobile Solutions Inc 206 290-2314
6442 Ne 192nd Pl Kenmore (98028) ***(G-4596)***
Open Text Inc 425 455-6000
301 116th Ave Se Ste 500 Bellevue (98004) ***(G-1051)***
Open Water Splicing 360 510-8059
5867 Portal Way Unit 103 Ferndale (98248) ***(G-3881)***
Openeye, Liberty Lake *Also called PC Open Incorporated* ***(G-5852)***
Operativ, Kirkland *Also called Evergreen Orthpd RES Lab LLC* ***(G-5335)***
Opi Downhole Technologies LLC 206 557-7032
2151 N Northlake Way D Seattle (98103) ***(G-10705)***
Opi Wind Technologies Inc 206 999-5373
2151 N Northlake Way D Seattle (98103) ***(G-10706)***
Oppenheimer Camera Pdts Inc 206 467-8666
7400 3rd Ave S Seattle (98108) ***(G-10707)***
Opportunity Interactive Inc 206 870-1880
19604 Intl Blvd Ste 101 Seatac (98188) ***(G-9296)***
Opti, Blaine *Also called Interlube International Inc* ***(G-1675)***
Optic Led Grow Lights LLC 971 704-2912
17923 52nd Ave E Unit A Tacoma (98446) ***(G-13444)***
Opticon Inc 425 651-2120
2220 Lind Ave Sw Ste 100 Renton (98057) ***(G-8865)***
Opticyte Inc 206 696-3957
5731 58th Ave Ne Seattle (98105) ***(G-10708)***
Optima Cabinets 509 868-5691
121 N Wycoff Ave Bremerton (98312) ***(G-1983)***
Optimism Brewing LLC 206 651-5429
909 E Union St Seattle (98122) ***(G-10709)***
Optimum Extracts 206 491-9617
3402 C St Ne Ste 109 Auburn (98002) ***(G-519)***
Optimum Precision Inc 425 778-1455
6324 202nd St Sw Lynnwood (98036) ***(G-6175)***
Options 360 Pregnancy Clinic, Vancouver *Also called Orchards Pregnancy Resources* ***(G-14455)***
Optistor Technologies Inc 425 283-5227
11900 Ne 1st St Ste 300 Bellevue (98005) ***(G-1052)***
Opto, Roy *Also called Professional Practice Systems* ***(G-9164)***
or Specific Inc 800 937-7949
4000 Se Columbia Way Vancouver (98661) ***(G-14453)***
Oracle Corporation 206 695-9000
1501 4th Ave Ste 1800 Seattle (98101) ***(G-10710)***
Oracle Corporation 425 945-8200
411 108th Ave Ne Ste 900 Bellevue (98004) ***(G-1053)***
Oracle Fisheries LLC 360 477-9829
1485 Deer Park Rd Port Angeles (98362) ***(G-7732)***
Oracle Hypnosis 859 893-8147
3098 Mcallister St Dupont (98327) ***(G-2971)***
Oracles of God Ministries 425 449-8663
1810 108th Ave Se Apt 12 Bellevue (98004) ***(G-1054)***
Oracoat, Kent *Also called Quest Products LLC* ***(G-5094)***
Orange Homes LLC 360 450-4640
9208 Ne Highway 99 107-201 Vancouver (98665) ***(G-14454)***
Orbis Company LLC 360 376-4320
663 Gafford Ln Eastsound (98245) ***(G-3041)***
Orbis Rpm LLC 253 333-0606
2302 B St Nw Ste 102 Auburn (98001) ***(G-520)***
Orbis World Globes, Eastsound *Also called Orbis Company LLC* ***(G-3041)***
Orbit Industries LLC 360 835-8526
778 S 27th St Washougal (98671) ***(G-14976)***
Orbiter Inc 253 627-5588
13500 Pacific Ave S Tacoma (98444) ***(G-13445)***
Orca Bay Foods LLC 206 762-7364
206 Sw Michigan St Seattle (98106) ***(G-10711)***
Orca Beverage Inc 425 349-5655
11903 Cyrus Way Ste 5 Mukilteo (98275) ***(G-6961)***
Orca Composites 206 782-0660
22 S Idaho St Seattle (98134) ***(G-10712)***
Orca Information Comm Svs 360 588-1633
715 Commercial Ave Anacortes (98221) ***(G-158)***
Orca Marine Cooling Systems, Bellingham *Also called Trunek Enterprises Inc* ***(G-1578)***
Orcas Island Growlers 360 927-9265
4505 Glen Meadows Pl Bellingham (98226) ***(G-1481)***
Orcas Island Pottery 360 376-2813
338 Old Pottery Rd Eastsound (98245) ***(G-3042)***
Orcas Island Tonewoods 360 376-2747
679 Roehls Hill Rd Olga (98279) ***(G-7217)***
Orcas Memories LLC 650 325-9400
2200 Buck Mountain Rd Eastsound (98245) ***(G-3043)***
Orchard Rite Ld, Union Gap *Also called Orchard-Rite Limited Inc* ***(G-13947)***
Orchard-Rite Limited Inc (PA) 509 834-2029
1702 Englewood Ave Yakima (98902) ***(G-15639)***
Orchard-Rite Limited Inc 509 834-2029
1615 W Ahtanum Rd Union Gap (98903) ***(G-13947)***
Orchards Pregnancy Resources 360 567-0285
221 Ne104th Ave Ste 209 Vancouver (98664) ***(G-14455)***
Orderport LLC 425 746-2926
5806a 119th Ave Se 102 Bellevue (98006) ***(G-1055)***
Oregon CAM Grinding Inc 503 252-5505
5913 Ne 127th Ave Ste 200 Vancouver (98682) ***(G-14456)***
Oregon Division-Raw Materials, Rainier *Also called Weyerhaeuser Company* ***(G-8323)***
Oregon Glove Company (PA) 253 475-6733
1538 N Cascade Ave Tacoma (98406) ***(G-13446)***
Oregon PCF Bldg Pdts Exch Inc 509 892-5555
15120 E Euclid Ave Spokane Valley (99216) ***(G-12821)***
Oregon Potato Company 509 547-8772
400 Commercial Ave Pasco (99301) ***(G-7608)***
Oregon Potato Company 509 349-8803
1900 1st Ave W Warden (98857) ***(G-14935)***
Oregon Potato Company (PA) 509 545-4545
6610 W Court St Ste B Pasco (99301) ***(G-7609)***
OReilly Signs 206 623-5135
1309a Raven Rd Seattle (98105) ***(G-10713)***
Orepac Building Products, Spokane Valley *Also called Oregon PCF Bldg Pdts Exch Inc* ***(G-12821)***
Organic Creations 503 891-0479
5601 E 18th St Ste 201 Vancouver (98661) ***(G-14457)***
Orient Food Production 253 926-1389
1494 46th Ave E Fife (98424) ***(G-3976)***
Orient Seafood Production, Fife *Also called Orient Food Production* ***(G-3976)***
Oriental Kitchen, Shoreline *Also called New Royal Meat LLC* ***(G-11792)***
Origami Inc 206 784-9133
9829 Triton Dr Nw Seattle (98117) ***(G-10714)***
Origin Distribution, Fife *Also called Db Skimboards* ***(G-3949)***
Original Expresso Machine 360 686-3643
33111 Ne 236th St Yacolt (98675) ***(G-15490)***
Original Hearts 253 857-0700
1114 138th St Nw Gig Harbor (98332) ***(G-4140)***
Originals By Chad Jwly Design 360 318-0210
521 Front St Ste 101 Lynden (98264) ***(G-6042)***
Orillia Smoke 425 656-1219
18111 E Valley Hwy D102 Kent (98032) ***(G-5046)***
Orion Industries (PA) 253 661-7805
1590 A St Ne Auburn (98002) ***(G-521)***
Orion Industries 425 355-1253
13008 Beverly Park Rd Mukilteo (98275) ***(G-6962)***
Orion Mfg LLC 206 979-5511
210 10th St Apt 6 Kirkland (98033) ***(G-5422)***
Orlison Brewing Co 503 894-2917
12921 W 17th Ave Airway Heights (99001) ***(G-59)***
Orlison Brewing Company, Airway Heights *Also called Golden Hills Brewing Co* ***(G-53)***
Ornamental Iron Specialists 253 630-0328
27221 135th Ave Se Kent (98042) ***(G-5047)***
Ornamental Iron Works Inc 509 662-8294
4450 2 Canyon Rd Wenatchee (98801) ***(G-15054)***
Ornamental Stone Inc 360 275-4241
101 E North Bay Rd Allyn (98524) ***(G-84)***
Ornelas Contract Services, Wenatchee *Also called Ornelas LLC* ***(G-15055)***
Ornelas LLC 206 388-2267
3635 Ridgeview Blvd Wenatchee (98801) ***(G-15055)***
Oro Weat, Spokane Valley *Also called Bimbo Bakeries Usa Inc* ***(G-12639)***
Oropeza Woodworks 360 668-0438
17828 W Interurban Blvd Snohomish (98296) ***(G-11958)***
Orora Packaging Solutions 253 796-6200
20208 72nd Ave S Kent (98032) ***(G-5048)***
Oroville Gazette Inc 509 476-3602
1420 Main St Oroville (98844) ***(G-7470)***
Oroville Reman & Reload Inc 509 476-2935
301 9th St Oroville (98844) ***(G-7471)***
Oroweat 253 872-8237
7054 S 220th St Kent (98032) ***(G-5049)***
Orpilla Santiago 360 876-1976
3161 Se Villa Carmel Dr Port Orchard (98366) ***(G-7838)***
Ortech Controls 206 633-7914
14739 Aurora Ave N 120 Shoreline (98133) ***(G-11798)***
Orthocare Innovations LLC (PA) 425 771-0797
123 2nd Ave S Ste 220 Edmonds (98020) ***(G-3141)***
Ortwein International 503 313-0514
7902 Ne St Johns Rd 107b Vancouver (98665) ***(G-14458)***
Orvella Industries Corp 206 778-2743
1055 Blaine Ave Ne Unit C Renton (98056) ***(G-8866)***
ORyan Industries Inc 360 892-0447
12711 Ne 95th St Vancouver (98682) ***(G-14459)***
ORyan Marine LLC 425 485-2871
9045 Willows Rd Ne Redmond (98052) ***(G-8604)***
Os Nexus Inc 425 279-0172
11711 Se 8th St Ste 305 Bellevue (98005) ***(G-1056)***
Osborne Enterprises, Port Townsend *Also called Jerry P Osborne* ***(G-7893)***
Osborne Woodworks 360 428-0245
13848 Avon Allen Rd Mount Vernon (98273) ***(G-6819)***
Osbourne Square Dental 425 225-5757
13209 44th Ave Se 201 Mill Creek (98012) ***(G-6519)***

ALPHABETIC

Oscilla Power Inc (PA)....206 557-7032
4240 Gilman Pl W Ste C Seattle (98199) *(G-10715)*
OShell Delmont....360 427-9600
1190 E Shelton Springs Rd Shelton (98584) *(G-11719)*
Osmonics Inc....425 204-5508
16814 163rd Pl Se Renton (98058) *(G-8867)*
Osnexus Corporation, Bellevue *Also called Os Nexus Inc (G-1056)*
Oso Railworks Inc (PA)....406 375-7555
31328 N Brooks Creek Rd Arlington (98223) *(G-295)*
Osp Sling Inc (PA)....360 683-4109
803 S 3rd Ave Sequim (98382) *(G-11657)*
Oster Logging Inc....425 397-0585
1205 N Machias Rd Lake Stevens (98258) *(G-5665)*
Osw Equipment & Repair LLC (PA)....425 483-9863
20812 Broadway Ave Snohomish (98296) *(G-11959)*
Oszman Service Inc....360 532-4552
2202 Bay Ave Hoquiam (98550) *(G-4351)*
Other Worlds....360 459-2323
3921 Shincke Rd Ne Olympia (98506) *(G-7363)*
Otis Elevator Company....206 285-2285
3315 S 116th St Ste 149 Tukwila (98168) *(G-13784)*
Otis Elevator Intl Inc....509 483-7328
510 E North Foothills Dr Spokane (99207) *(G-12422)*
Otogear....360 852-0250
9212 45th Ave Ne Seattle (98115) *(G-10716)*
Otter Creek Industries L L C....509 954-3998
4578 E Deer Lake Rd A Loon Lake (99148) *(G-5976)*
Our Country Beads....509 967-3953
302 N 62nd Ave Richland (99353) *(G-9032)*
Our House Publishing....360 676-0428
2511 G St Bellingham (98225) *(G-1482)*
Out For A Walk....360 793-4419
1121 Loves Hill Dr Sultan (98294) *(G-13031)*
Out of Box Manufacturing LLC....253 214-7448
1600 Sw 43rd St Ste 200 Renton (98057) *(G-8868)*
Out of Woods Printing LLC....509 447-2590
300 W 2nd St Newport (99156) *(G-7063)*
Out On A Limb....360 607-3429
240 Sw 2nd St Stevenson (98648) *(G-13017)*
Out On A Limb Enterprises....360 457-8479
430 W 5th St Port Angeles (98362) *(G-7733)*
Out On A Limb Tree Co....206 938-3779
17576 Ballinger Way Ne Lake Forest Park (98155) *(G-5623)*
Out Peak Services Inc....360 255-7282
104 4th St Blaine (98230) *(G-1691)*
Outbouts LLC....253 921-0155
11012 Canyon Rd E Ste 8p Bonney Lake (98391) *(G-1731)*
Outdoor Leisure Centers....509 599-2150
7302 N Palmer Rd Spokane (99217) *(G-12423)*
Outdoor Research LLC....206 467-8197
2203 1st Ave S Ste 700 Seattle (98134) *(G-10717)*
Outdoor Research-Canada Inc....206 467-8197
2203 1st Ave S Ste 700 Seattle (98134) *(G-10718)*
Outdoor Specialties LLC....425 432-0507
17886 W Spring Lake Dr Se Renton (98058) *(G-8869)*
Outdoor Synergy....360 435-3330
17833 59th Ave Ne Arlington (98223) *(G-296)*
Outdoors NW, Seattle *Also called Pricemedia Inc (G-10858)*
Outlaw Leather LLC....206 679-7483
5020 Ohio Ave S Seattle (98134) *(G-10719)*
Outside In Woodworks LLC....208 403-9067
1470 Se Vallair Ct Port Orchard (98366) *(G-7839)*
Outsmart Office Solutions Inc....888 688-8154
7683 Se 27th St Ste 185 Mercer Island (98040) *(G-6478)*
Outsource Communication, Bonney Lake *Also called Garjen Corp (G-1724)*
Oval International Division, Hoquiam *Also called Ovalstrapping Incorporated (G-4352)*
Ovalstrapping Incorporated (HQ)....360 532-9101
206 Firman Ave Hoquiam (98550) *(G-4352)*
Ovenell Custom Cabinets....509 782-3400
305 Mission Ave Cashmere (98815) *(G-2328)*
Overdue Media LLC....206 860-2199
4819 S Oregon St Seattle (98118) *(G-10720)*
Overhead Door Corporation....253 520-8008
2505 F Albert Rd E B127 Fife (98424) *(G-3977)*
Overload Electric Winding Svcs....253 848-8900
6119 56th Avenue Ct E Puyallup (98371) *(G-8211)*
Overnight Prtg & Graphics Inc....206 621-9412
2412 1st Ave S Seattle (98134) *(G-10721)*
Oversea Casing Company LLC (PA)....206 682-6845
601 S Nevada St Seattle (98108) *(G-10722)*
Overseas Security....206 364-6784
12345 Lake City Way Ne # 2052 Seattle (98125) *(G-10723)*
Ovivo USA LLC....360 253-3440
5139 Ne 94th Ave Ste E Vancouver (98662) *(G-14460)*
Owen Kotler Selections LLC....917 912-0678
1400 10th Ave W Seattle (98119) *(G-10724)*
Owens Meats Inc....509 674-2530
502 E 1st St Cle Elum (98922) *(G-2674)*
Owens Press, Fircrest *Also called Martin William Owens (G-4002)*
Oxalis Group....509 838-3295
428 W 27th Ave Spokane (99203) *(G-12424)*
Oxarc Inc....509 755-0651
3417 E Springfield Ave Spokane (99202) *(G-12425)*
Oxbo International Corporation....509 544-0362
815 N Oregon Ave Pasco (99301) *(G-7610)*
Oxbo International Corporation....360 354-1500
270 Birch Bay Lynden Rd Lynden (98264) *(G-6043)*
Oxiscience LLC....425 777-5488
17455 Ne 67th Ct Ste 100 Redmond (98052) *(G-8605)*
Oyate Research & Training Cons....360 239-2281
15816 Yelm Terra Way Se Yelm (98597) *(G-15742)*
Ozbolt Storer, Marylou, Maple Valley *Also called Fibrearts Inc (G-6269)*
Ozette Industries LLC....360 460-4272
133 Doyle Rd Port Angeles (98363) *(G-7734)*
P & Ds IMG-N-That Spcalty Prtg....509 346-1170
10805 Road 13.5 Sw Royal City (99357) *(G-9173)*
P & G Timber, Quilcene *Also called Handly & Phillips Logging Inc (G-8284)*
P & J Machining Inc....253 841-0500
2601 Inter Ave Puyallup (98372) *(G-8212)*
P & M Fiberglass Company Inc....206 784-1940
1403 10th Ave W Seattle (98119) *(G-10725)*
P & M Video Lightsource LLC....253 569-0286
7228 193rd St E Spanaway (98387) *(G-12067)*
P & R Rock Sand & Gravel....503 278-3512
713 Nw 21st St Battle Ground (98604) *(G-727)*
P & R'S Mobile Charpening, Maple Valley *Also called P & RS Mobile Services Inc (G-6284)*
P & RS Mobile Services Inc....425 652-1394
22616 Se 283rd St Maple Valley (98038) *(G-6284)*
P and S Print Company LLC....509 398-6504
56 C St Nw Ephrata (98823) *(G-3344)*
P Apple LLC....206 290-9898
7007 Beverly Blvd Everett (98203) *(G-3561)*
P C C I, Seattle *Also called Protective Coating Consultants (G-10876)*
P D M Stilled Service Inc....360 225-1133
1785 Schurman Way Woodland (98674) *(G-15454)*
P E T Net Solution, Kent *Also called Petnet Solutions Inc (G-5065)*
P F M Industries Inc....425 776-3112
111 Sunset Ave N Edmonds (98020) *(G-3142)*
P G I Publications Inc....425 743-0110
13410 Highway 99 Ste 205 Everett (98204) *(G-3562)*
P G K Inc....425 432-0945
23030 244th Ave Se Maple Valley (98038) *(G-6285)*
P I P Printing Inc....360 456-4742
3530 Martin Way E Olympia (98506) *(G-7364)*
P L C, Everett *Also called Plc-Multipoint Inc (G-3575)*
P M C, Lynnwood *Also called Pacific Coast Marine Inds Inc (G-6177)*
P M I, Seattle *Also called Pacific Market Intl LLC (G-10735)*
P N D Corporation....425 562-7252
14320 Ne 21st St Ste 6 Bellevue (98007) *(G-1057)*
P O P, Tukwila *Also called Pop Gourmet LLC (G-13792)*
P S Northwest Radiography....253 627-3988
1950 S Cedar St Ste B Tacoma (98405) *(G-13447)*
P S Plus Sizes Tukwila....206 575-3690
17580 Southcenter Pkwy Tukwila (98188) *(G-13785)*
P S S Rubber Stamps, Kennewick *Also called Print Plus Inc (G-4709)*
P T C, Everett *Also called Post Tension Cables Inc (G-3579)*
P&A Metal Fab Inc....253 435-8947
1629 28th St Se Puyallup (98372) *(G-8213)*
P&J Machining Inc....253 841-0500
2607 Inter Ave Puyallup (98372) *(G-8214)*
P&Js Waffle Delight....510 335-5393
2117 155th St E Tacoma (98445) *(G-13448)*
P&M Products Inc....425 939-8349
6619 132nd Ave Ne Ste 206 Kirkland (98033) *(G-5423)*
PA&e, Wenatchee *Also called Pacific Aerospace & Elec LLC (G-15059)*
PA&e International Inc....509 667-9600
430 Olds Station Rd Wenatchee (98801) *(G-15056)*
Pabco Building Products LLC....253 284-1200
1476 Thorne Rd Tacoma (98421) *(G-13449)*
Pabco Roofing Products, Tacoma *Also called Pabco Building Products LLC (G-13449)*
Pac Dry Ice, Kent *Also called Rosellini Distribution Inc (G-5106)*
Pac Rite Inc....253 833-7071
418 Valley Ave Nw Ste 105 Puyallup (98371) *(G-8215)*
Pac Ship....425 622-9030
2000 W Marine View Dr Everett (98207) *(G-3563)*
Pac West Sales Inc....425 493-9680
11112 47th Ave W Mukilteo (98275) *(G-6963)*
Pac-Paper Inc....800 223-4981
6416 Nw Whitney Rd Vancouver (98665) *(G-14461)*
Pac/Gro and Associates, Seattle *Also called National Frozen Foods Corp (G-10588)*
Pacarc LLC....206 547-4591
202 Lake Washington Blvd Seattle (98122) *(G-10726)*
Pacbrake Company....360 332-4717
1670 Grant Ave Blaine (98230) *(G-1692)*
Paccar Inc....425 828-5000
10630 Ne 38th Pl Kirkland (98033) *(G-5424)*
Paccar Inc....360 757-5357
12479 Farm To Market Rd Mount Vernon (98273) *(G-6820)*
Paccar Inc....206 214-0418
1500 S 184th St Seatac (98158) *(G-9297)*
Paccar Inc (PA)....425 468-7400
777 106th Ave Ne Bellevue (98004) *(G-1058)*

Paccar Inc.......425 254-4400
750 Houser Way N Renton (98057) ***(G-8870)***
Paccar Inc.......425 227-5800
1601 N 8th St Renton (98057) ***(G-8871)***
Paccar Inc.......425 468-7400
777 106th Ave Ne Bellevue (98004) ***(G-1059)***
Paccar Inc.......206 764-5400
8801 E Marginal Way S Tukwila (98108) ***(G-13786)***
Paccar Seatac, Seatac *Also called Paccar Inc* ***(G-9297)***
Pace International LLC (HQ).......800 936-6750
5661 Branch Rd Wapato (98951) ***(G-14922)***
Pace International LLC.......800 936-6750
3765 N Clemons St Unit 6 East Wenatchee (98802) ***(G-3028)***
Pace International LLC.......509 877-2830
N Track Rd Parker (98939) ***(G-7549)***
Pace Solutions Inc.......604 520-6211
3888 Sound Way Bellingham (98226) ***(G-1483)***
Pacer Design & Manufacturing.......425 481-5300
19315 Bothell Everett Hwy Bothell (98012) ***(G-1883)***
Pacer Design By Sharp Pdts Inc.......360 217-8120
17072 Tye St Se Ste 195 Monroe (98272) ***(G-6603)***
Pacific A Crgo Transf Systems.......253 735-5277
3205 C St Ne Auburn (98002) ***(G-522)***
Pacific Aerospace & Elec Inc.......509 667-9600
430 Olds Station Rd Wenatchee (98801) ***(G-15057)***
Pacific Aerospace & Elec Inc.......855 285-5200
434 Olds Station Rd Wenatchee (98801) ***(G-15058)***
Pacific Aerospace & Elec Inc.......360 683-4167
2249 Diamond Point Rd Sequim (98382) ***(G-11658)***
Pacific Aerospace & Elec LLC (HQ).......855 885-5200
434 Olds Station Rd Wenatchee (98801) ***(G-15059)***
Pacific Aircraft Modifications.......360 403-7282
1304 Stanwood Bryant Rd Arlington (98223) ***(G-297)***
Pacific Ally LLC.......360 760-4266
419 E Cedar Ave Ste A201 La Center (98629) ***(G-5511)***
Pacific Applied Technology.......360 693-4292
1701 Broadway St Ste 392 Vancouver (98663) ***(G-14462)***
Pacific Art Press Inc.......425 778-8095
10730 Vernon Rd Lake Stevens (98258) ***(G-5666)***
Pacific Asian Enterprises Inc.......206 223-3624
2601 W Marina Pl Ste S Seattle (98199) ***(G-10727)***
Pacific Bay Inc.......253 848-5541
1016 57th St E Ste 150 Sumner (98390) ***(G-13092)***
Pacific Bay Wooddesign, Sultan *Also called Shea Edwards Furniture LLP* ***(G-13036)***
Pacific Biomarkers Inc (PA).......206 298-0068
645 Elliott Ave W Ste 300 Seattle (98119) ***(G-10728)***
Pacific Bioscience Labs Inc.......888 525-2747
17425 Ne Union Hill Rd # 150 Redmond (98052) ***(G-8606)***
Pacific Boats, Marysville *Also called Pacific Skiffs Nw Inc* ***(G-6367)***
Pacific Bow Butts Targets, South Bend *Also called Karl Plato* ***(G-12042)***
Pacific Business Printing, Tacoma *Also called Jdkk Investment Group Inc* ***(G-13357)***
Pacific Calcium Incorporated.......509 486-1201
32117 Highway 97 Tonasket (98855) ***(G-13656)***
Pacific Coast Bride LLC.......360 303-5047
1521 Cornwall Ave Bellingham (98225) ***(G-1484)***
Pacific Coast Cascara Bark Co.......360 249-3503
520 W Pioneer Ave Montesano (98563) ***(G-6652)***
Pacific Coast Coal Company.......360 886-1060
30700 Black Diamond Black Diamond (98010) ***(G-1652)***
Pacific Coast Evergreen Inc (PA).......360 876-2061
5158 Bethel Rd Se Port Orchard (98367) ***(G-7840)***
Pacific Coast Feather LLC (HQ).......206 624-1057
1736 4th Ave S Ste B Seattle (98134) ***(G-10729)***
Pacific Coast Manufacturing.......425 485-8866
15604 163rd Ave Ne Woodinville (98072) ***(G-15328)***
Pacific Coast Marine LLC.......425 743-9550
16531 13th Ave W Ste A106 Lynnwood (98037) ***(G-6176)***
Pacific Coast Marine Inds Inc.......425 743-9550
16531 13th Ave W Ste A106 Lynnwood (98037) ***(G-6177)***
Pacific Coast Showcase Inc.......253 445-9000
1601 Industrial Park Way # 101 Puyallup (98371) ***(G-8216)***
Pacific Coast Tools LLC.......360 244-5087
1306 197th St Long Beach (98631) ***(G-5875)***
Pacific Coatings Inc.......206 722-1413
9243 Martin Luther King Seattle (98118) ***(G-10730)***
Pacific Coca Cola Bottling.......509 762-6987
5803 Patton Blvd Ne Moses Lake (98837) ***(G-6734)***
Pacific Container Corp.......206 682-1778
4101 S 56th St Tacoma (98409) ***(G-13450)***
Pacific Contractors & Supply.......509 534-4304
10815 E 35th Ave Spokane Valley (99206) ***(G-12822)***
Pacific Crest Building Pdts.......253 447-7686
4227 S Meridian Ste C114 Puyallup (98373) ***(G-8217)***
Pacific Crest Building Supply.......360 857-3120
5901 S 11th St Ridgefield (98642) ***(G-9098)***
Pacific Crest Custom Cabinetry, Ridgefield *Also called Pacific Crest Building Supply* ***(G-9098)***
Pacific Crest Industries Inc.......253 321-3011
13610 52nd St E Ste 300 Sumner (98390) ***(G-13093)***
Pacific Custom Cable Inc.......253 373-0800
4170 B Pl Nw Auburn (98001) ***(G-523)***
Pacific Dealer Services.......509 299-7269
6315 S Brooks Rd Medical Lake (99022) ***(G-6443)***
Pacific Die Cast Inc.......360 571-9681
1304 Ne 154th St Ste 104 Vancouver (98685) ***(G-14463)***
Pacific Door & Window Inc.......360 577-9121
1041 Columbia Blvd Longview (98632) ***(G-5940)***
Pacific Door and Molding, Tacoma *Also called Frontier Door & Cabinet LLC* ***(G-13302)***
Pacific Egg Products, Arlington *Also called National Food Corporation* ***(G-285)***
Pacific Engineering & Mfg Co.......360 274-8323
317 Sandy Bend Rd Castle Rock (98611) ***(G-2349)***
Pacific Enviroments Corp.......408 836-7581
25331 33rd Pl S Kent (98032) ***(G-5050)***
Pacific Environmental Inc.......760 877-9796
29100 Se 43rd Pl Fall City (98024) ***(G-3705)***
Pacific Fabricating.......360 588-1078
2900 T Ave Ste E Anacortes (98221) ***(G-159)***
Pacific Fast Mail, Edmonds *Also called P F M Industries Inc* ***(G-3142)***
Pacific Fibre Products Inc (PA).......360 577-7112
20 Fibre Way Longview (98632) ***(G-5941)***
Pacific Fishermen Inc.......206 784-2562
5351 24th Ave Nw Seattle (98107) ***(G-10731)***
Pacific Fluid Solutions Inc.......425 432-6535
25005 234th Pl Se Maple Valley (98038) ***(G-6286)***
Pacific Force MGT & Harvest.......360 484-3854
213 Knappton Rd Ste A Naselle (98638) ***(G-7018)***
Pacific Foundation Inc.......360 200-6608
1400 Columbia St Vancouver (98660) ***(G-14464)***
Pacific Frame Source LLC.......800 292-3202
21828 87th Ave Se Ste B Woodinville (98072) ***(G-15329)***
Pacific Fshrmen Shpyrd Elc LLC.......206 784-2562
5351 24th Ave Nw Seattle (98107) ***(G-10732)***
Pacific Fuel and Convenience.......253 631-8512
13122 Se 240th St Kent (98031) ***(G-5051)***
Pacific Gem Inc.......206 448-7700
2107 Elliott Ave Ste 209 Seattle (98121) ***(G-10733)***
Pacific Grinding.......208 412-5945
2100 N Winrock St Liberty Lake (99019) ***(G-5850)***
Pacific Hide & Fur Depot.......509 545-0688
925 N Oregon Ave Pasco (99301) ***(G-7611)***
Pacific Injection Molding.......360 733-7466
122 Ohio St Ste 105 Bellingham (98225) ***(G-1485)***
Pacific Integrated Hdlg Inc (PA).......253 535-5888
10215 Portland Ave E A Tacoma (98445) ***(G-13451)***
Pacific Interconnection LLC.......425 277-9527
1022 N 33rd Pl Renton (98056) ***(G-8872)***
Pacific Jewelers.......360 693-3410
2313 Main St Vancouver (98660) ***(G-14465)***
Pacific Knight Emblem & Insig.......206 354-2060
11358 Se 211th Ln Apt 39 Kent (98031) ***(G-5052)***
Pacific Labels.......360 671-6507
1602 Carolina St Ste D10 Bellingham (98229) ***(G-1486)***
Pacific Logging Inc.......425 334-3600
3603 136th St Ne Marysville (98271) ***(G-6365)***
Pacific Logging LLC.......425 508-9150
8425 123rd Ave Ne Lake Stevens (98258) ***(G-5667)***
Pacific Machine Inc.......253 383-3838
8601 38th Ave Sw Lakewood (98499) ***(G-5744)***
Pacific Marine Contractors.......360 532-2765
207 S Chehalis St Aberdeen (98520) ***(G-27)***
Pacific Marine Investments.......360 532-2765
2118 Morgan St Aberdeen (98520) ***(G-28)***
Pacific Market Inc (PA).......206 441-1400
2401 Elliott Ave Ste 400 Seattle (98121) ***(G-10734)***
Pacific Market Intl LLC (HQ).......206 441-1400
2401 Elliott Ave Ste 400 Seattle (98121) ***(G-10735)***
Pacific Mat & Coml Flrg LLC.......800 345-6287
18414 80th Ct S Kent (98032) ***(G-5053)***
Pacific Mat Co, Kent *Also called T & A Supply Company Inc* ***(G-5167)***
Pacific Metal Buildings, Spokane Valley *Also called Pacific Contractors & Supply* ***(G-12822)***
Pacific Metal Fabrication Inc.......253 833-3362
833 1st Ave S Kent (98032) ***(G-5054)***
Pacific Metallurgical Inc.......206 292-9205
925 5th Ave S Kent (98032) ***(G-5055)***
Pacific Meter & Equipment Inc.......253 872-3374
8001 S 222nd St Kent (98032) ***(G-5056)***
Pacific Mobile Structures Inc.......509 244-8335
10920 W Sunset Hwy Airway Heights (99001) ***(G-60)***
Pacific Mount Inc.......253 473-2580
4723 S Washington St Tacoma (98409) ***(G-13452)***
Pacific N W Sheds Buildings.......360 573-7433
2009 Ne 117th St Vancouver (98686) ***(G-14466)***
Pacific Netting Products Inc.......360 697-5540
25993 United Rd Ne Kingston (98346) ***(G-5260)***
Pacific Netting Products Inc.......360 697-5540
3203 Ne Totten Rd Ste D Poulsbo (98370) ***(G-7990)***
Pacific Northwest.......206 453-3182
4215 23rd Ave W Seattle (98199) ***(G-10736)***
Pacific Northwest Baking Co, Sumner *Also called Northwest Baking Ltd Partnr* ***(G-13089)***
Pacific Northwest Drone Svcs.......509 679-0863
5445 Balustrade Blvd Se Lacey (98513) ***(G-5573)***
Pacific Northwest Industries.......206 841-3144
21414 30th Ave S Seatac (98198) ***(G-9298)***

Pacific Northwest Inlander, Spokane *Also called Inland Publications Inc* ***(G-12312)***
Pacific Northwest Iron LLC....509 499-0668
6196 Moriah Dr Nine Mile Falls (99026) ***(G-7081)***
Pacific Northwest Jewelers....509 927-8923
3925 S Conklin Rd Greenacres (99016) ***(G-4300)***
Pacific Northwest Mech LLC....509 765-9606
1740 W Pheasant St Moses Lake (98837) ***(G-6735)***
Pacific Northwest Newspaper....206 448-8125
101 Elliott Ave W Seattle (98119) ***(G-10737)***
Pacific Northwest Packers Inc....360 354-0776
9900 Hammer Rd Lynden (98264) ***(G-6044)***
Pacific Northwest Scale Co....425 259-4720
9007 36th St Se Snohomish (98290) ***(G-11960)***
Pacific Northwest Technology....360 493-8344
8294 28th Ct Ne Ste 500 Lacey (98516) ***(G-5574)***
Pacific Northwest Timbers LLC....360 379-2792
130 Seton Rd Port Townsend (98368) ***(G-7906)***
Pacific Northwest Wire Works, Dupont *Also called Western Wire Works Inc* ***(G-2977)***
Pacific Northwest Wovens LLC....714 392-0634
2659 S 5th St Lewis McChord (98433) ***(G-5821)***
Pacific Nutritional Inc....360 253-3197
6317 Ne 131st Ave Buildb Vancouver (98682) ***(G-14467)***
Pacific NW Aggregates Inc....509 748-9188
5 Avery Boat Ramp Rd Wishram (98673) ***(G-15167)***
Pacific NW Arospc Aliance....425 885-0290
16911 Ne 95th St Redmond (98052) ***(G-8607)***
Pacific NW Cookie Co LLC....360 280-4179
219 Frogner Rd Chehalis (98532) ***(G-2519)***
Pacific NW Fine WD Pdts LLC....360 275-5397
100 E Nahum Ln Belfair (98528) ***(G-770)***
Pacific NW Frmrs Coop Inc....509 283-2124
102 S Railroad Ave Fairfield (99012) ***(G-3697)***
Pacific NW Met Fabricators, Seattle *Also called Atech Services LLC* ***(G-9450)***
Pacific NW Plating Inc....360 735-9000
7001 Ne 40th Ave Vancouver (98661) ***(G-14468)***
Pacific NW Powdr Coating....509 535-9950
17117 E Macmahan Rd Spokane (99217) ***(G-12426)***
Pacific NW Print Flfllment Inc....509 242-7857
18001 E Euclid Ave Ste C Spokane Valley (99216) ***(G-12823)***
Pacific NW Probe & Drlg Inc....253 651-2477
7613 188th Street Ct E Puyallup (98375) ***(G-8218)***
Pacific NW Reps LLC....509 823-7008
7804 W Washington Ave Yakima (98903) ***(G-15640)***
Pacific Orthodontic Laboratory....425 224-4193
10830 19th Ave Se Ste D Everett (98208) ***(G-3564)***
Pacific Orthotic LLC....425 417-3742
1527 Sycamore Dr Se Issaquah (98027) ***(G-4457)***
Pacific Orthotic LLC....425 486-4292
21828 87th Ave Se Ste C1 Woodinville (98072) ***(G-15330)***
Pacific Outdoor Products Inc....425 432-6000
22415 Se 231st St Maple Valley (98038) ***(G-6287)***
Pacific Paper Products Inc (PA)....253 272-9195
4301 S Pine St Ste 92 Tacoma (98409) ***(G-13453)***
Pacific Paper Tube Inc....253 872-7981
7850 S 196th St Kent (98032) ***(G-5057)***
Pacific Performance Coatings....425 339-5528
2815 W Marine View Dr Everett (98201) ***(G-3565)***
Pacific Pilot Services LLC....509 899-0858
43 Red Mountain Dr Ellensburg (98926) ***(G-3216)***
Pacific Pipe & Pump LLC....425 640-0376
24121 56th Ave W Mountlake Terrace (98043) ***(G-6865)***
Pacific Plumbing Supply Co LLC....425 251-0604
5964 6th Ave S Seattle (98108) ***(G-10738)***
Pacific Powder Coating Inc....360 383-9100
7072 Portal Way Ste 110 Ferndale (98248) ***(G-3882)***
Pacific Power Group LLC (HQ)....360 887-7400
805 Broadway St Ste 700 Vancouver (98660) ***(G-14469)***
Pacific Power Group LLC....360 887-5980
6100 S 6th Way Ridgefield (98642) ***(G-9099)***
Pacific Power Group LLC....360 887-5980
6100 S 6th Way Ridgefield (98642) ***(G-9100)***
Pacific Power Group LLC....253 395-9077
1221 29th St Nw Ste D Auburn (98001) ***(G-524)***
Pacific Power Products, Vancouver *Also called Pacific Power Group LLC* ***(G-14469)***
Pacific Power Products, Ridgefield *Also called Pacific Power Group LLC* ***(G-9099)***
Pacific Power Products, Ridgefield *Also called Pacific Power Group LLC* ***(G-9100)***
Pacific Power Products, Auburn *Also called Pacific Power Group LLC* ***(G-524)***
Pacific Precast Inc....360 750-0099
2611 E 5th St Vancouver (98661) ***(G-14470)***
Pacific Precision Mfg....360 737-2938
2850 Ne 65th Ave Ste B Vancouver (98661) ***(G-14471)***
Pacific Prepac Inc....360 653-1661
3925 134th St Ne Marysville (98271) ***(G-6366)***
Pacific Printing, Bellingham *Also called Pacific Rim Printing Inc* ***(G-1487)***
Pacific Printing Inc....360 377-0844
3930 Burwell St Bremerton (98312) ***(G-1984)***
Pacific Propeller Inter LLC....206 575-5107
1125 Andover Park W Tukwila (98188) ***(G-13787)***
Pacific Publishing Studio LLC....206 371-5628
4518 Sw Edmunds St Seattle (98116) ***(G-10739)***
Pacific Quarry, Mount Vernon *Also called Martin Marietta Materials Inc* ***(G-6810)***
Pacific Radar Inc....425 775-0400
12310 Highway 99 Ste 132 Everett (98204) ***(G-3566)***
Pacific Reign Enterprises....360 580-4447
5403 Us Highway 101 Humptulips (98552) ***(G-4364)***
Pacific Rim Con Pmpg Eqp Co....425 453-8140
3241 110th Ave Se Bellevue (98004) ***(G-1060)***
Pacific Rim Equipment, Bellevue *Also called Pacific Rim Con Pmpg Eqp Co* ***(G-1060)***
Pacific Rim Forestry, Sedro Woolley *Also called Pacific Rim Portfolios Ltd* ***(G-11554)***
Pacific Rim International LLC....503 781-2394
19120 Se 34th St Ste 105 Vancouver (98683) ***(G-14472)***
Pacific Rim Portfolios Ltd....360 595-2854
120 Valley Hwy Sedro Woolley (98284) ***(G-11554)***
Pacific Rim Printing Inc....360 676-4606
22 Southern Ct Bellingham (98229) ***(G-1487)***
Pacific Rim Tonewoods Inc....360 826-6101
38511 State Route 20 Concrete (98237) ***(G-2790)***
Pacific Rim Tonewoods Inc (PA)....360 826-6101
619 15th St Bellingham (98225) ***(G-1488)***
Pacific Rock Products LLC....360 896-8721
18208 Se 1st St Vancouver (98684) ***(G-14473)***
Pacific Rock Products LLC (HQ)....360 254-7770
8705 Ne 117th Ave Vancouver (98662) ***(G-14474)***
Pacific Sales & Service....425 271-9000
17701 108th Ave Se 1010 Renton (98055) ***(G-8873)***
Pacific Screen Printers, Woodland *Also called Swivler Inc* ***(G-15468)***
Pacific Screen Printers....360 225-7771
123 Stenerson Rd Woodland (98674) ***(G-15455)***
Pacific Sea Food Co Inc....360 225-8553
1635 Down River Dr Woodland (98674) ***(G-15456)***
Pacific Sheet Metal Inc....206 682-5354
1128 Sw Spokane St Seattle (98134) ***(G-10740)***
Pacific Ship Repr Fbrction Inc....425 409-5060
13228 4th Ave W Ste A Everett (98204) ***(G-3567)***
Pacific Ship Repr Fbrction Inc....360 674-2480
8390 Sw Barney White Rd Bremerton (98312) ***(G-1985)***
Pacific Skiffs Nw Inc....360 658-7111
5611 48th Dr Ne Ste 5 Marysville (98270) ***(G-6367)***
Pacific Slot Car Raceways LLC....253 446-5039
2908 Meridian Ave E # 104 Edgewood (98371) ***(G-3089)***
Pacific Sportswear Inc....253 582-4444
3827 100th St Sw Tacoma (98499) ***(G-13454)***
Pacific Sportswear LLC....253 582-4444
10731 A St S Ste B Tacoma (98444) ***(G-13455)***
Pacific Spring Mfg Co....360 832-3633
1607 434th St E Eatonville (98328) ***(G-3065)***
Pacific Stage Lighting....253 248-6344
15504 131st Avenue Ct Nw Gig Harbor (98329) ***(G-4141)***
Pacific Star Seafoods, Renton *Also called E & E Foods Inc* ***(G-8789)***
Pacific Steel, Pasco *Also called Pacific Hide & Fur Depot* ***(G-7611)***
Pacific Steel Structures LLC....509 921-5835
19814 E Pheasant Dr Greenacres (99016) ***(G-4301)***
Pacific Sterling, Vancouver *Also called Pacific Jewelers* ***(G-14465)***
Pacific Stone & Tile LLC....360 352-3960
2770 Mottman Rd Sw Ste A Olympia (98512) ***(G-7365)***
Pacific Strapping Inc....206 262-9800
2922 S 112th St Tukwila (98168) ***(G-13788)***
Pacific Studio Inc....206 783-5226
5311 Shilshole Ave Nw Seattle (98107) ***(G-10741)***
Pacific Tchnical Solutions Inc....425 489-5700
16541 Redmond Way 364 Redmond (98052) ***(G-8608)***
Pacific Tool Inc....425 882-1970
15235 Ne 92nd St Redmond (98052) ***(G-8609)***
Pacific Topsoils Inc (PA)....425 337-2700
805 80th St Sw Everett (98203) ***(G-3568)***
Pacific Trim Panels Inc....360 841-8438
1685 Schurman Way Woodland (98674) ***(G-15457)***
Pacific Vision Enterprises....509 895-4199
621 Coe Rd Wapato (98951) ***(G-14923)***
Pacific Western Timbers Inc....360 674-2700
5555 Cruiser Loop Sw Port Orchard (98367) ***(G-7841)***
Pacific Wholesale Banner & Sup....509 487-4189
2823 N Martin St Spokane (99207) ***(G-12427)***
Pacific Wire Group Inc....253 249-0249
2201 R St Nw Auburn (98001) ***(G-525)***
Pacific Wire Products, Auburn *Also called Pacific Wire Group Inc* ***(G-525)***
Pacific Wireless Systems LLC....509 375-3533
135 Patton St Richland (99354) ***(G-9033)***
Pacific Woodtech Corporation....360 707-2200
1850 Park Ln Burlington (98233) ***(G-2177)***
Pacifica Marine Inc....206 764-1646
4233 W Marginal Way Sw Seattle (98106) ***(G-10742)***
Pacifica Resources LLC....206 764-1646
4233 W Marginal Way Sw Seattle (98106) ***(G-10743)***
Pacificorp....360 827-6467
1813 Bishop Rd Chehalis (98532) ***(G-2520)***
Packaging Corporation America....509 545-3260
31831 W Highway 12 Wallula (99363) ***(G-14909)***
Packaging Corporation America....509 575-3689
2013 Ahtanum Rd Yakima (98903) ***(G-15641)***
Packaging Corporation America....800 223-2307
501 10th Ave N Algona (98001) ***(G-73)***

Packaging Corporation America 360 891-8796
222 Ne Park Plaza Dr # 105 Vancouver (98684) ***(G-14475)***
Packaging Corporation America 509 545-3202
31827 W Highway 12 Wallula (99363) ***(G-14910)***
Packing House Services Inc 509 452-5002
1916 S 18th St Union Gap (98903) ***(G-13948)***
Pacmet 253 854-4241
1205 5th Ave S Kent (98032) ***(G-5058)***
Paco Pumps By Grundfos, Tacoma *Also called Grundfos CBS Inc* ***(G-13328)***
Pacrim Technologies LLC 425 284-7300
11321 Ne 120th St Bldg W Kirkland (98034) ***(G-5425)***
PACTIV CORPORATION, Auburn *Also called Pactiv LLC* ***(G-526)***
Pactiv LLC 847 482-2000
2820 B St Nw Ste 109 Auburn (98001) ***(G-526)***
Pacwest Dental Lab 360 635-3976
3513 Ne 158th Ave Vancouver (98682) ***(G-14476)***
Pacwest Interiors, Yakima *Also called Dean Thoemke* ***(G-15551)***
Pad Printing Services Inc 206 362-4544
12051 31st Ave Ne Seattle (98125) ***(G-10744)***
Padded Spaces LLC 872 222-7767
2104 82nd Dr Ne Lake Stevens (98258) ***(G-5668)***
Padholdr LLC 253 447-7328
7518 185th Ave E Bonney Lake (98391) ***(G-1732)***
Page Aerospace Inc 425 650-1459
4020 Lake Wash Blvd Ne Kirkland (98033) ***(G-5426)***
Page Cellars 253 232-9463
19495 144th Ave Ne B205 Woodinville (98072) ***(G-15331)***
Page Editorial 253 597-8634
1950 S State St Tacoma (98405) ***(G-13456)***
Page Last Publishing 360 289-4165
100 Ocean Shores Blvd Nw Ocean Shores (98569) ***(G-7189)***
Pageclean, Seattle *Also called Proxygroove LLC* ***(G-10878)***
Pagemark Technology Inc 425 444-3735
17317 Ne 129th St Redmond (98052) ***(G-8610)***
Paizo Inc 425 289-0060
7120 185th Ave Ne Ste 120 Redmond (98052) ***(G-8611)***
Paizo Publishing LLC 425 289-0060
7120 185th Ave Ne Ste 120 Redmond (98052) ***(G-8612)***
Paktek Inc 253 584-4914
7307 82nd Street Ct Sw Lakewood (98498) ***(G-5745)***
Palace 253 581-0880
8718 South Tacoma Way A1 Lakewood (98499) ***(G-5746)***
Paladin Data Systems Corp 360 779-2400
19362 Powder Hill Pl Ne Poulsbo (98370) ***(G-7991)***
Paleo Pushers LLC 253 539-3848
1509 102nd St S Tacoma (98444) ***(G-13457)***
Paleteria Lanorpeana 509 839-5802
120 Rohman St Sunnyside (98944) ***(G-13136)***
Palfinger Marine USA Inc 360 299-4585
2415 T Ave Ste 204 Anacortes (98221) ***(G-160)***
Pallet Place Inc 509 484-4889
10315 E Buckeye Ln Spokane Valley (99206) ***(G-12824)***
Pallet Services Inc 509 543-3541
1430 N Glade Rd Pasco (99301) ***(G-7612)***
Pallet Services Inc (PA) 360 424-8171
201 E Fairhaven Ave Burlington (98233) ***(G-2178)***
Pallet Services Inc (PA) 360 424-8171
201 E Fairhaven Ave Burlington (98233) ***(G-2179)***
Pallets Unlimited 360 354-1395
2007 Hampton Rd Everson (98247) ***(G-3686)***
Palmer Hayes Offshore 253 310-7162
7419 Rosedale St Nw Gig Harbor (98335) ***(G-4142)***
Palmer Industries LLC 509 989-1069
11835 Chris Dr Ne Moses Lake (98837) ***(G-6736)***
Palo Alto Health Sciences Inc 925 594-8404
12020 113th Ave Ne Kirkland (98034) ***(G-5427)***
Palomar Products Inc 425 453-9400
500 108th Ave Ne Bellevue (98004) ***(G-1061)***
Palouse Gutters and Cnstr LLC 509 397-0404
1009 S Lake St Colfax (99111) ***(G-2719)***
Palouse River Quilts 509 397-2278
101 S Main St Colfax (99111) ***(G-2720)***
Palouse Winery 206 567-4994
12431 Vashon Hwy Sw Vashon (98070) ***(G-14740)***
Pam S Bubble Mobile 360 630-5511
17027 Lake View Blvd Mount Vernon (98274) ***(G-6821)***
Pamar Systems Inc 360 992-4120
1801 D St Ste 7 Vancouver (98663) ***(G-14477)***
Pamela McAllister 206 783-9534
723 N 105th St Seattle (98133) ***(G-10745)***
Pan Abode Cedar Homes Inc 425 255-8260
1100 Maple Ave Sw Renton (98057) ***(G-8874)***
Pan Abode Homes Inc 425 255-8260
1100 Maple Ave Sw Renton (98057) ***(G-8875)***
Pan-Pacific Energy Corp 360 673-7800
380 W Marine Dr Kalama (98625) ***(G-4506)***
Panasonic Avionics, Seatac *Also called Matsushita Avionics Co* ***(G-9289)***
Panasonic Corp North America 425 883-9290
15317 Ne 90th St Redmond (98052) ***(G-8613)***
Panasonic Ind Dev Sales Co Div, Redmond *Also called Panasonic Corp North America* ***(G-8613)***
Panda Dental Software Inc 800 517-7716
14205 Se 36th St Ste 100 Bellevue (98006) ***(G-1062)***
Panel Artz 253 277-1040
20462 84th Ave S Kent (98032) ***(G-5059)***
Panelsuppliers 253 217-1668
116 2nd Ave Se Pacific (98047) ***(G-7537)***
Paneltech International LLC 360 538-1480
2999 John Stevens Way Hoquiam (98550) ***(G-4353)***
Paneltech Intl Holdings Inc (HQ) 360 538-1480
2999 John Stevens Way Hoquiam (98550) ***(G-4354)***
Paneltech Products Inc 360 538-1480
2999 John Stevens Way Hoquiam (98550) ***(G-4355)***
Panesko Publishing 360 748-0505
222 Se Spring St Chehalis (98532) ***(G-2521)***
Pangaea Ltd 206 292-9911
119 Yale Ave N Seattle (98109) ***(G-10746)***
Panorama Ice Company, Colville *Also called Rays Custom Cutting* ***(G-2772)***
Panther Printing 509 344-4600
111 N Vista Rd Ste 2d Spokane Valley (99212) ***(G-12825)***
Panther Systems Northwest Inc 360 750-9783
19111 Se 34th St Ste 101 Vancouver (98683) ***(G-14478)***
Panthercorn Publishing, Mukilteo *Also called Panthercorn Studios* ***(G-6964)***
Panthercorn Studios 425 501-9717
12199 Village Center Pl # 103 Mukilteo (98275) ***(G-6964)***
Pantrol Inc (PA) 509 535-9061
3108 E Ferry Ave Spokane (99202) ***(G-12428)***
Pape Machinery Inc (PA) 509 838-5252
6210 W Rowand Rd Spokane (99224) ***(G-12429)***
Pape Machinery Inc 360 575-9959
2504 Talley Way Kelso (98626) ***(G-4541)***
Papec 253 862-6148
18310 17th St E Lake Tapps (98391) ***(G-5683)***
Papenhause Composites Inc 206 669-3260
9513 Evanston Ave N Seattle (98103) ***(G-10747)***
Paper Delights 206 547-1002
2205 N 45th St Ste B Seattle (98103) ***(G-10748)***
Paper Jam Publishing Co LLP 360 376-3200
10 Madrona St Eastsound (98245) ***(G-3044)***
Paper Muses 425 241-3710
26216 Se 230th St Maple Valley (98038) ***(G-6288)***
Paper Panduh 206 538-0202
2956 S Webster St Seattle (98108) ***(G-10749)***
Paper Scissors On The Rock, Lopez Island *Also called Ron Hall* ***(G-5986)***
Paper Stuffcom 206 462-6079
3134 Elliott Ave Seattle (98121) ***(G-10750)***
Papercraft Cottage 360 426-1038
825 W Franklin St Shelton (98584) ***(G-11720)***
Papineau LLC 509 301-9074
31 E Main St Ste 216 Walla Walla (99362) ***(G-14854)***
Par 4 Golf Services 360 376-4462
112 Discovery Way Eastsound (98245) ***(G-3045)***
Par Tacoma LLC (HQ) 253 383-1651
3001 Marshall Ave Tacoma (98421) ***(G-13458)***
Paradigm Optics Incorporated 360 573-6500
9600 Ne 126th Ave # 2540 Vancouver (98682) ***(G-14479)***
Paradigm Publishing NW LLC 206 257-0214
4314 6th Ave Nw Unit B Seattle (98107) ***(G-10751)***
Paradise Studios 360 789-5744
11410 Ne 124th St Kirkland (98034) ***(G-5428)***
Paradise Technolgy Inc 253 370-3682
5715 151st Avenue Ct Nw Lakebay (98349) ***(G-5690)***
Paradisos Del Sol Winery Inc 509 829-9000
3230 Highland Dr Zillah (98953) ***(G-15757)***
Paradyce Industries Inc 360 736-4474
411 E Union St Centralia (98531) ***(G-2423)***
Paragon Energy Solutions 425 445-6471
5511 105th Ave Ne Kirkland (98033) ***(G-5429)***
Paragon Films Inc 509 424-3700
915 Rose St Union Gap (98903) ***(G-13949)***
Paragon Industries Inc (HQ) 253 872-0800
18270 Segale Park Drive B Tukwila (98188) ***(G-13789)***
Paragon Manufacturing Corp 425 438-0800
2615 W Casino Rd Ste 4c Everett (98204) ***(G-3569)***
Paragon Pacific Insulation, Tukwila *Also called Paragon Industries Inc* ***(G-13789)***
Paragon Seafood Company 425 788-6077
19703 Ne 167th Ct Woodinville (98077) ***(G-15332)***
Parametrix Inc (PA) 206 394-3700
1019 39th Ave Se Ste 100 Puyallup (98374) ***(G-8219)***
Paramount Chemical Spc Inc 425 882-2673
14762 Ne 95th St Redmond (98052) ***(G-8614)***
Paramount Petroleum Corp 503 273-4700
20555 Richmond Bch Dr Nw Seattle (98177) ***(G-10752)***
Paramount Petroleum Corp 503 273-4705
20555 Richmond Bch Dr Nw Seattle (98177) ***(G-10753)***
Paramount Petroleum Corp 206 542-3121
20555 Richmond Bch Dr Nw Seattle (98177) ***(G-10754)***
Paramount Supply Co 360 647-8328
2230 Midway Ln Bellingham (98226) ***(G-1489)***
Parasol Enterprises Inc 360 733-5579
3221 Cherrywood Ave Bellingham (98225) ***(G-1490)***
Paraversal Publishing LLC 206 366-1981
9416 1st Ave Ne Apt 117 Seattle (98115) ***(G-10755)***

ALPHABETIC

Parberry Inc (PA) 360 734-2340
1419 C St Bellingham (98225) ***(G-1491)***
Parberry Iron & Metal, Bellingham *Also called Parberry Inc* ***(G-1491)***
Parent Is Nppon Ppr Inds Japan, Longview *Also called Nippon Paper Inds USA Co Ltd* ***(G-5936)***
Parentasoft LLC 425 877-8574
8201 164th Ave Ne Ste 200 Redmond (98052) ***(G-8615)***
Pareto-Curve Marketing Inc 360 357-1000
6200 Capitol Blvd Se C Tumwater (98501) ***(G-13889)***
Paris Gourmet Dessert 206 767-9097
5601 1st Ave S Seattle (98108) ***(G-10756)***
Parisian Star, Seattle *Also called Paris Gourmet Dessert* ***(G-10756)***
Pariyatti 360 978-4998
867 Larmon Rd Onalaska (98570) ***(G-7452)***
PARIYATTI BOOKSTORE, Onalaska *Also called Pariyatti* ***(G-7452)***
Park & Moazez Enterprises Inc 206 464-0100
2960 4th Ave S Ste 112 Seattle (98134) ***(G-10757)***
Park Avenue Construction Inc 206 783-3693
1110 Nw 45th St Seattle (98107) ***(G-10758)***
Park Place Industries 360 584-9762
11020 Park Place Ln Se Tumwater (98501) ***(G-13890)***
Park Postal LLC 206 860-7678
4111 E Madison St Ste 2 Seattle (98112) ***(G-10759)***
Parker Lumber Co Inc (PA) 425 806-7253
4119 Wheaton Way Bremerton (98310) ***(G-1986)***
Parker Manufacturing LLC 509 663-5923
2127a Duncan Rd Wenatchee (98801) ***(G-15060)***
Parker Pacific Inc 253 862-9133
27120 112th St E Buckley (98321) ***(G-2066)***
Parker Store, The, Bellingham *Also called Kaman Fluid Power LLC* ***(G-1390)***
Parker Truck, Pacific *Also called Parkers Truck & Equipment Repr* ***(G-7538)***
Parker-Hannifin Corporation 509 764-5430
5803 Patton Blvd Ne Ste E Moses Lake (98837) ***(G-6737)***
Parker-Hannifin Corporation 360 802-1039
225 Battersby Ave Enumclaw (98022) ***(G-3311)***
Parker-Hannifin Corporation 509 764-5430
5803 Patton Blvd Ne Moses Lake (98837) ***(G-6738)***
Parker-Hannifin Corporation 425 284-2925
14690 Ne 9th St Ste 104 Redmond (98052) ***(G-8616)***
Parkers Truck & Equipment Repr 253 833-3696
116 Frontage Rd N Pacific (98047) ***(G-7538)***
Parkland Quick Print, Tacoma *Also called Yvonne Roberts* ***(G-13606)***
Parkwater Aviation Inc 509 536-1969
5627 E Rutter Ave Spokane (99212) ***(G-12430)***
Parr Cabinet Outlet 253 926-0505
3500 20th St E Ste A Fife (98424) ***(G-3978)***
Parr Lumber, Fife *Also called Parr Cabinet Outlet* ***(G-3978)***
Parr Lumber Company 509 543-7594
525 E South Hill Rd Sunnyside (98944) ***(G-13137)***
Parr Lumber Company 360 750-1470
3901 Ne 68th St Vancouver (98661) ***(G-14480)***
Parrott D G Son McHnsts Mnfact, Olympia *Also called D G Parrott & Son* ***(G-7263)***
Parsons Equipment Inc 509 632-5205
302 N 2nd St Coulee City (99115) ***(G-2804)***
Part Works Inc 206 632-8900
2900 4th Ave S Seattle (98134) ***(G-10760)***
Partners In Emrgncy Prpredness 509 335-3530
1500 Commerce St Tacoma (98402) ***(G-13459)***
Parts Warehouse Inc 360 354-4722
309 Judson Street Aly Lynden (98264) ***(G-6045)***
Party City Corporation 206 575-0502
17356 Southcenter Pkwy Tukwila (98188) ***(G-13790)***
Parvia Corp 206 310-2205
800 5th Ave 101-160 Seattle (98104) ***(G-10761)***
Pascal Company Inc 425 827-4694
2929 Northup Way Bellevue (98004) ***(G-1063)***
Pasco International, Bellevue *Also called Pascal Company Inc* ***(G-1063)***
Pasco Machine Company 509 547-2448
518 W Columbia St Pasco (99301) ***(G-7613)***
Pasco Potato Processing, Pasco *Also called Resers Fine Foods Inc* ***(G-7622)***
Pasco Processing LLC 509 544-6700
5815 N Industrial Way Pasco (99301) ***(G-7614)***
Pasco Silk Screeners, Pasco *Also called Showcase Specialties Inc* ***(G-7629)***
Pasek Cellars Winery Inc 888 350-9463
2629 Old Hwy 99 S Ste B Mount Vernon (98273) ***(G-6822)***
Pasquier Panel, Sumner *Also called Plywood Components Inc* ***(G-13095)***
Passage Inc 425 743-5600
1720 75th St Sw Everett (98203) ***(G-3570)***
Passing Time Winery 425 892-8684
18808 142nd Ave Ne Woodinville (98072) ***(G-15333)***
Passion Works LLC 425 260-7777
6830 Ne Bothell Way Kenmore (98028) ***(G-4597)***
Passport Food Group LLC 253 520-9299
6931 S 234th St Kent (98032) ***(G-5060)***
Pasteleria Del Castillo 206 242-6247
10434 16th Ave Sw Seattle (98146) ***(G-10762)***
Pasteria Lucchese 206 420-4939
3004 Nw 59th St Seattle (98107) ***(G-10763)***
Pat Files 206 405-4370
2427 6th Ave S Seattle (98134) ***(G-10764)***
Pat Lydon Saw Mill LLC 360 666-0900
23907 Ne 72nd Ave Battle Ground (98604) ***(G-728)***
Pat-Co Inc 206 937-8927
4515 44th Ave Sw Seattle (98116) ***(G-10765)***
Patcen Healthcare Inc 425 495-5143
3600 136th Pl Se Ste 300 Bellevue (98006) ***(G-1064)***
Pateric Software 425 814-4949
13029 Ne 126th Pl Kirkland (98034) ***(G-5430)***
Pates Restaurant LLC 253 334-7520
222 Sw 293rd St Federal Way (98023) ***(G-3769)***
Path Vaccine Solutions 206 285-3500
2201 Westlake Ave Seattle (98121) ***(G-10766)***
Pathfinder Press 360 687-4319
25224 Ne Jolma Rd Battle Ground (98604) ***(G-729)***
Pathfinder Wireless Corp 206 409-5767
2402 E Newton St Seattle (98112) ***(G-10767)***
Patio Plantings 253 631-6131
12810 Se 245th St Kent (98030) ***(G-5061)***
Patit Creek Cellars 509 868-4045
822 W Sprague Ave Spokane (99201) ***(G-12431)***
Patricia A Welch 206 322-1226
1122 E Pike St Seattle (98122) ***(G-10768)***
Patricia Avery (PA) 206 602-0017
10912 4th Avenue Ct E A103 Tacoma (98445) ***(G-13460)***
Patricia Kinsella 206 285-5885
14100 Westwood Pl Ne Seattle (98125) ***(G-10769)***
Patrick Clarke 206 365-8804
11345 40th Ave Ne Seattle (98125) ***(G-10770)***
Patrick Corp 509 925-1300
1043 W University Way Ellensburg (98926) ***(G-3217)***
Patrick E & Patricia M Lydon 425 226-3216
14521 164th Pl Se Renton (98059) ***(G-8876)***
Patriot Jabez Construction JV 253 293-7100
710 A St Nw Auburn (98001) ***(G-527)***
Patriot Leather Company 360 393-1392
1543 E Gateway Hts Loop Sedro Woolley (98284) ***(G-11555)***
Patriot Sales Inc 360 855-0737
500 Metcalf St Ste L3 Sedro Woolley (98284) ***(G-11556)***
Patriot Steel & Supply, Okanogan *Also called Diebels Welding & Machine* ***(G-7196)***
Patriot Support Services, Spokane *Also called Susan Weinhandl* ***(G-12537)***
Patriot Towing Recovery 360 890-9288
5868 Pacific Ave Se Ste B Lacey (98503) ***(G-5575)***
Patriot Wood LLC 360 393-7082
4122 Stuart Cir Ferndale (98248) ***(G-3883)***
Patriotic Packing 360 942-3054
1649 Larson Rd Raymond (98577) ***(G-8357)***
Patroit Fuels LLC 253 507-6256
13410 Se 294th Pl Auburn (98092) ***(G-528)***
Patroltag Inc 650 678-3790
2800 Western Ave Apt 212 Seattle (98121) ***(G-10771)***
Pats Blue Ribbons & Trophies 360 676-8292
6738 Family Hill Ln Ferndale (98248) ***(G-3884)***
Pats Welding Service 360 963-2370
13311 Highway 112 Sekiu (98381) ***(G-11583)***
Pattern Integrity LLC 503 752-6018
2144 Nw 22nd Ave Camas (98607) ***(G-2273)***
Patterns In Nature LLC 360 918-2629
1826 Arbutus St Ne Olympia (98506) ***(G-7366)***
Paul E Sevier 360 491-1334
9721 Yelm Hwy Se Olympia (98513) ***(G-7367)***
Paul Middlewood 425 778-4771
21315 52nd Ave W Apt G144 Mountlake Terrace (98043) ***(G-6866)***
Paul Parish Limited 509 735-9820
4806 S Reed St Kennewick (99337) ***(G-4705)***
Paul Razore 360 734-4845
1009 Marine Dr Bellingham (98225) ***(G-1492)***
Paul Schurman Machine Inc 360 887-3193
23201 Ne 10th Ave Ridgefield (98642) ***(G-9101)***
Paul Sessions 360 265-1658
13842 Kloshi Ct Nw Bremerton (98312) ***(G-1987)***
Paula S Choice 425 988-2931
23215 66th Ave S Kent (98032) ***(G-5062)***
Paula's Choice Skincare, Seattle *Also called Paulas Choice LLC* ***(G-10772)***
Paulas Choice LLC 425 988-6068
705 5th Ave S Ste 200 Seattle (98104) ***(G-10772)***
Paulas Choice Holdings Inc (PA) 425 988-6068
705 5th Ave S Ste 200 Seattle (98104) ***(G-10773)***
Pauley Rodine Inc (PA) 509 773-3200
405 S Columbus Ave Goldendale (98620) ***(G-4205)***
Pauls Cabinetry 425 343-7930
31928 116th St Se Sultan (98294) ***(G-13032)***
Pauls Custom Cabinets 253 536-6330
2730 90th St E Tacoma (98445) ***(G-13461)***
Pauls Mobile Washing 509 954-1910
510 W Dalton Ave Spokane (99205) ***(G-12432)***
Paulty Mfg LLC 509 470-1791
960 Us Highway 2 # 1037 Leavenworth (98826) ***(G-5812)***
Pautzke Bait Co Inc 509 925-6154
800 N Prospect St Ellensburg (98926) ***(G-3218)***
Pavel S Puzzles 425 643-0204
4414 173rd Ave Se Bellevue (98006) ***(G-1065)***
Pawpular Companions Bouti 509 850-6070
21950 E Country Vista Dr # 100 Liberty Lake (99019) ***(G-5851)***

Paxton Sales Corporation 509 453-0397
108 W Mead Ave Yakima (98902) *(G-15642)*
Payment Innovators, Bellevue *Also called PI Technologies (G-1075)*
Paynestaking Detail 509 599-2207
9412 W Trails Rd Spokane (99224) *(G-12433)*
Pb Inc 206 747-0347
1269 120th Ave Ne Bellevue (98005) *(G-1066)*
Pbi, Mount Vernon *Also called Petrzelka Bros Inc (G-6824)*
PBS Supply Co Inc 253 395-5550
7013 S 216th St Kent (98032) *(G-5063)*
PC Consulting & Development 425 836-0645
25819 Ne 25th St Redmond (98053) *(G-8617)*
PC Networks, Silverdale *Also called PC Networks Inc (G-11853)*
PC Networks Inc 360 362-9684
13825 Crestview Cir Nw Silverdale (98383) *(G-11853)*
PC Open Incorporated 509 777-6736
23221 E Knox Ave Liberty Lake (99019) *(G-5852)*
PC Techs & Parts, Tacoma *Also called Wendy Rawley (G-13592)*
Pc2 LLC 360 921-8066
30748 Ne Lewisville Hwy Battle Ground (98604) *(G-730)*
PCA, Algona *Also called Packaging Corporation America (G-73)*
PCA, Vancouver *Also called Packaging Corporation America (G-14475)*
PCA, Wallula *Also called Packaging Corporation America (G-14910)*
Pcb Universe Inc 360 256-7228
11818 Se Mill Plain Blvd # 208 Vancouver (98684) *(G-14481)*
PCC Aerostructures, Auburn *Also called Primus International Inc (G-537)*
PCC Arostructures Univ Swaging, Woodinville *Also called University Swaging Corporation (G-15396)*
PCC Plant, Tacoma *Also called Graymont Western US Inc (G-13320)*
Pcs Industries LLC 509 406-5852
6401 State Route 410 Naches (98937) *(G-7001)*
Pcs Laser and Memorial 208 746-1033
403 Diagonal St Clarkston (99403) *(G-2640)*
Pcs Mill Work Inc (PA) 425 820-5688
116 Slater St Ste 9 Kirkland (98033) *(G-5431)*
Pd Pharmatech LLC 800 452-4682
135 S Brandon St Seattle (98108) *(G-10774)*
Pdi Tooling 2000, Redmond *Also called Proto-Design Inc (G-8637)*
PDQ Signs 253 531-8010
13702 Dana Ln E Puyallup (98373) *(G-8220)*
Pe Ell Pub 360 291-2707
211 W Main St Chehalis (98532) *(G-2522)*
Peace Arch Business Center 360 366-8500
8105 Birch Bay Square St # 103 Blaine (98230) *(G-1693)*
Peaceful Sole 425 652-7043
320 Newport Way Nw Issaquah (98027) *(G-4458)*
Peacetags 206 932-8247
305 Bellevue Way Ne Bellevue (98004) *(G-1067)*
Peach Fuzzer LLC (PA) 206 453-0339
1415 10th Ave Ste 7 Seattle (98122) *(G-10775)*
Peach Fuzzer LLC 844 557-3224
1122 E Pike St Ste 1064 Seattle (98122) *(G-10776)*
Peak Industries 509 448-5793
7916 W Sunset Hwy Spokane (99224) *(G-12434)*
Pearce Design 425 481-5214
14512 167th Ave Se Monroe (98272) *(G-6604)*
Pearl Woodworks, Seattle *Also called Refined Woodworks Inc (G-10941)*
Pearls MBL Wldg & Fabrication 360 897-9288
12617 231st Ave E Buckley (98321) *(G-2067)*
Pearson Business Mgt Svcs 206 382-1457
1411 4th Ave Ste 1506 Seattle (98101) *(G-10777)*
Pearson Millwork Inc 360 435-9516
19311 59th Ave Ne Arlington (98223) *(G-298)*
Pearson Packaging Systems, Spokane *Also called R A Pearson Company (G-12464)*
Pebblebee, Bellevue *Also called Pb Inc (G-1066)*
Pedag USA, Seattle *Also called DBa Euroimport Company Inc (G-9805)*
Pedal Pushers Bike Rntl & RPR 208 689-3436
2427 E Nebraska Ave Spokane (99208) *(G-12435)*
Pederson Bros Inc 360 734-9180
3974 Bakerview Spur Bellingham (98226) *(G-1493)*
Pedersons Custom Woodworking 509 981-0720
10809 E 26th Ave Spokane Valley (99206) *(G-12826)*
Pedologic Orthotics 360 318-3452
6206 275th St Ne Arlington (98223) *(G-299)*
Pee Wee Pros Ltd Liability Co 206 276-6707
12925 Beverly Park Rd Lynnwood (98087) *(G-6178)*
Peekaboo Cupcakery 206 458-6986
1001 4th Ave Ste 3200 Seattle (98154) *(G-10778)*
Peekay Inc 818 754-1201
901 W Main St Ste A Auburn (98001) *(G-529)*
Peel and Press LLC 206 937-1457
6503 California Ave Sw Seattle (98136) *(G-10779)*
Peel David and Associates 425 577-8980
631 8th Ave Kirkland (98033) *(G-5432)*
Peel Productions Inc 360 256-2450
9415 Ne Woodridge St Vancouver (98664) *(G-14482)*
Peetz Enterprises 509 276-2608
4968 Mason Rd Clayton (99110) *(G-2659)*
Pegler Automation Inc 503 329-5377
10117 Ne 21st St Vancouver (98664) *(G-14483)*
Pei Manufacturing LLC 360 210-4165
2848 Nw 11th Ave Camas (98607) *(G-2274)*
Pelican Packers Inc 360 398-8825
6069 Hannegan Rd Bellingham (98226) *(G-1494)*
Pell Industrial LLC 425 222-9672
1812 B St Nw Ste 110 Auburn (98001) *(G-530)*
Pellets Inc 360 733-3012
1481 Island View Dr Bellingham (98225) *(G-1495)*
Pelling Industries Inc 206 243-1941
13206 3rd Ave S Burien (98168) *(G-2120)*
Pemco, Castle Rock *Also called Pacific Engineering & Mfg Co (G-2349)*
Pen Print Inc 360 457-3404
230 E 1st St Ste A Port Angeles (98362) *(G-7735)*
Penchant Press International 206 687-2401
7572 Birch Bay Dr Ste 7 Blaine (98230) *(G-1694)*
Pencils and Inks Inc 206 683-4441
3715 S Angeline St Seattle (98118) *(G-10780)*
Pend Oreille Mine, Metaline Falls *Also called Teck American Incorporated (G-6499)*
Pendleton Woolen Mills Inc 360 835-2131
2 Pendleton Way Washougal (98671) *(G-14977)*
Pendown Software LLC 509 480-8232
3205 Folsom Ave Apt 2 Yakima (98902) *(G-15643)*
Penford Products Co 509 375-1261
216 1st St Richland (99354) *(G-9034)*
Peninsula Daily News, Bellevue *Also called Northwest Media Washington LP (G-1036)*
Peninsula Iron 253 857-8844
11020 State Route 302 Nw Gig Harbor (98329) *(G-4143)*
Peninsula Lubricants 360 452-8376
1230 W 17th St Port Angeles (98363) *(G-7736)*
Peninsula Optical Lab Inc 800 540-4640
1901 S Union Ave B1001 Tacoma (98405) *(G-13462)*
Peninsula Packaging LLC 509 575-5341
2801 River Rd Yakima (98902) *(G-15644)*
Peninsula Sheet Metal Inc 360 642-2102
312 6th St Ne Long Beach (98631) *(G-5876)*
Peninsula Tanks Inc 360 683-4714
1370 Woodcock Rd Sequim (98382) *(G-11659)*
Peninsula Truss Co 360 297-6026
26343 Bond Rd Ne Unit A-1 Kingston (98346) *(G-5261)*
Penny Creek Quarry 360 765-3413
450 Penny Creek Rd Quilcene (98376) *(G-8287)*
Penny Savers 360 723-0740
1507 Ne 17th Ave Battle Ground (98604) *(G-731)*
Pens By Bill 509 628-3288
34115 Cantera St Kennewick (99338) *(G-4706)*
Pentech Industries LLC 360 989-7903
36806 Ne Holling Ave La Center (98629) *(G-5512)*
Penthouse Drapery Clrs & Mfrs 206 292-8336
4033 16th Ave Sw Ste A Seattle (98106) *(G-10781)*
Pentz Design Pattern Fndry Inc 425 788-6490
14823 Main St Ne Duvall (98019) *(G-2997)*
Penway Limited Inc 360 435-6445
18931 59th Ave Ne Unit 1 Arlington (98223) *(G-300)*
Peoh Point Alpaca Farm 509 674-9120
691 Upper Peoh Point Rd Cle Elum (98922) *(G-2675)*
Peone Industries 509 443-4710
503 E Dave Ct Spokane (99208) *(G-12436)*
Peoples Solar Inc 530 217-6020
787 Customs Rd Curlew (99118) *(G-2846)*
Pepper Bridge Winery LLC 425 483-7026
14810 Ne 145th St Bldg A3 Woodinville (98072) *(G-15334)*
Pepper Bridge Winery LLC (PA) 509 525-6502
1704 J B George Rd Walla Walla (99362) *(G-14855)*
Pepperdogz, Bellevue *Also called Petforia LLC (G-1072)*
Pepsi 509 536-5585
11016 E Montgomery Dr Spokane Valley (99206) *(G-12827)*
Pepsi Cola 7 Up Bottling Co 360 757-0044
1946 Park Ln Burlington (98233) *(G-2180)*
Pepsi Cola Bottling Co Pasco (HQ) 509 545-8585
2525 W Hopkins St Pasco (99301) *(G-7615)*
Pepsi Cola Bottling Co Pasco 509 248-1313
2525 W Hopkins St Pasco (99301) *(G-7616)*
Pepsi Cola Btlg Co Vancouver, Ridgefield *Also called Corwin Beverage Co (G-9076)*
Pepsi Northwest Beverages LLC 206 326-7487
2646 Rainier Ave S Seattle (98144) *(G-10782)*
Pepsi Northwest Beverages LLC (HQ) 360 357-9090
3003 R W Johnson Blvd Sw Tumwater (98512) *(G-13891)*
Pepsi-Cola, Pasco *Also called Pepsi Cola Bottling Co Pasco (G-7615)*
Pepsi-Cola, Burlington *Also called Pepsi Cola 7 Up Bottling Co (G-2180)*
Pepsi-Cola, Pasco *Also called Pepsi Cola Bottling Co Pasco (G-7616)*
Pepsi-Cola Metro Btlg Co Inc 206 326-7431
2300 26th Ave S Seattle (98144) *(G-10783)*
Pepsico, Spokane Valley *Also called Pepsi (G-12827)*
Pepsico, Yakima *Also called Noel Corporation (G-15630)*
Pepsico, Ridgefield *Also called Corwin Beverage Co (G-9077)*
Pepsico, Seattle *Also called Pepsi Northwest Beverages LLC (G-10782)*
Pepsico 253 778-7107
2309 Milwaukee Way Tacoma (98421) *(G-13463)*
Peptide Scientific USA Ltd 718 618-5025
1920 4th Ave Unit 1909 Seattle (98101) *(G-10784)*

ALPHABETIC

(PA)=Parent Co (HQ)=Headquarters (DH)=Div Headquarters
2019 Washington Manufacturers Register
797

Pequod Inc — 425 742-7456
7215 156th St Sw Edmonds (98026) *(G-3143)*

Per Gioia — 206 240-4216
1101 17th Ave Ste No108 Seattle (98122) *(G-10785)*

Perception Plastics Inc — 509 624-5408
301 W 2nd Ave Spokane (99201) *(G-12437)*

Perch and Play — 360 393-4925
1707 N State St Bellingham (98225) *(G-1496)*

Perco Inc — 425 373-1252
24 Lopez Ky Bellevue (98006) *(G-1068)*

Perdue Foods LLC — 360 424-7947
1000 Jason Ln Mount Vernon (98273) *(G-6823)*

Perdue Foods LLC — 360 748-9466
575 W Main St Chehalis (98532) *(G-2523)*

Perdue Foods LLC — 360 398-2911
6323 Guide Meridian Rd Lynden (98264) *(G-6046)*

Peregrine Manufacturing Inc — 425 673-5600
19504 24th Ave W Ste 105 Lynnwood (98036) *(G-6179)*

Perfect Blend LLC — 509 968-3316
8270 Tjossem Rd Ellensburg (98926) *(G-3219)*

Perfect Blend LLC (PA) — 509 488-5570
10900 Ne 8th St Ste 615 Bellevue (98304) *(G-1069)*

Perfect Blend LLC — 509 488-5570
771 Kulm Rd Othello (99344) *(G-7503)*

Perfect Copy & Print Inc (PA) — 206 325-4733
111 Broadway E Seattle (98102) *(G-10786)*

Perfect Press Printing Inc — 425 562-0507
1910 132nd Ave Ne Ste 10 Bellevue (98005) *(G-1070)*

Perfect Printing & Signs — 509 786-3811
212 N 22nd Ave Yakima (98902) *(G-15645)*

Perfect Reflections Auto Body — 360 426-0805
101 W Hulbert Rd Shelton (98584) *(G-11721)*

Perfection Coatings — 509 599-2538
15720 E 4th Ave Apt M207 Spokane Valley (99037) *(G-12828)*

Perfection Powder Coating & FA — 253 875-0010
5402 184th St E Ste D Puyallup (98375) *(G-8221)*

Perfint Healthcare Corp USA — 425 629-9207
8201 164th Ave Ne Ste 200 Redmond (98052) *(G-8618)*

Performance Cnstr Eqp Inc — 360 794-6220
7522 Woods Creek Rd Monroe (98272) *(G-6605)*

Performance Coatings Inc — 253 735-1919
60 37th St Ne Ste A Auburn (98002) *(G-531)*

Performance Marine Inc — 425 258-9292
930 W Marine View Dr Everett (98201) *(G-3571)*

Performance Packaging Inc — 360 737-9966
3006 Ne 112th Ave Ste A Vancouver (98682) *(G-14484)*

Performance Radiator PCF LLC — 206 624-2440
2447 6th Ave S Seattle (98134) *(G-10787)*

Performance Radiator PCF LLC — 253 472-0586
2667 South Tacoma Way Tacoma (98409) *(G-13464)*

Performance Software Corp — 425 481-4956
21520 30th Dr Se Bothell (98021) *(G-1884)*

Performnce Fire Protection Inc — 253 778-8039
15322 Se 240th St Kent (98042) *(G-5064)*

Peri Formwork Systems Inc — 360 225-3583
1475 Port Way Woodland (98674) *(G-15458)*

Peri-USA — 410 712-7225
1475 Port Way Woodland (98674) *(G-15459)*

Peridot Publishing LLC — 509 242-7752
2310 N Molter Rd Ste 309 Liberty Lake (99019) *(G-5853)*

Peril Prints — 323 599-1447
2802 32nd Ave S Seattle (98144) *(G-10788)*

Periodico Laraza — 253 961-5008
4505 Pacific Hwy E Ste 2 Fife (98424) *(G-3979)*

Periscope Sls & Analytics LLC — 503 707-1907
2214 Nw 148th St Vancouver (98685) *(G-14485)*

Perkins Lonnie Tmbr & Lnd Clng, Olympia Also called Perkins Timber LLC *(G-7368)*

Perkins Performance — 253 389-9669
11203 Benston Dr E # 110 Puyallup (98372) *(G-8222)*

Perkins Timber LLC — 360 754-2892
4125 Dent Rd Sw Olympia (98512) *(G-7368)*

Perlage Systems Inc — 253 632-0891
1020 S 344th St Federal Way (98003) *(G-3770)*

Perlage Systems Inc (PA) — 206 973-7500
1507 Western Ave Apt 606 Seattle (98101) *(G-10789)*

Perma-Chink Systems Inc (PA) — 425 885-6050
17635 Ne 67th Ct Redmond (98052) *(G-8619)*

Permesys Inc — 860 961-5367
18719 36th Dr Se Bothell (98012) *(G-1885)*

Perrault Manufacturing Inc — 509 248-9905
5700 Beauchene Rd Moxee (98936) *(G-6884)*

Perry Enterprises — 360 366-5239
7200 Delta Line Rd Ste B Ferndale (98248) *(G-3885)*

Perry Pallets, Ferndale Also called Perry Enterprises *(G-3885)*

Perry Stained Glass Studio — 425 392-1600
470 Front St N Ste 3 Issaquah (98027) *(G-4459)*

Personal Medical Corp — 425 497-1044
8672 154th Ave Ne Redmond (98052) *(G-8620)*

Peryl Professional Touch — 253 537-8181
5216 72nd St E Tacoma (98443) *(G-13465)*

Pesani Genuine Coatings LLC — 509 860-3426
810 Booie Ct Apt A Wenatchee (98801) *(G-15061)*

Pet Enclosures Northwest — 425 786-1221
20126 Ballinger Way Ne Shoreline (98155) *(G-11799)*

Pet Media Plus LLC — 360 425-0188
1502 9th Ave Longview (98632) *(G-5942)*

Pet/CT Imaging At Swdish Cncer — 206 215-6433
1221 Madison St Ste 150 Seattle (98104) *(G-10790)*

Pet/X LLC — 206 715-5743
8002 39th Ave Ne Seattle (98115) *(G-10791)*

Peter Blue Woodworks — 206 542-4281
715 N 200th St Shoreline (98133) *(G-11800)*

Peter K Grossman — 206 824-6626
240 Sw 43rd St Renton (98057) *(G-8877)*

Peter Kaupat Easy — 425 228-3633
15666 W Valley Hwy Tukwila (98188) *(G-13791)*

Peter Pan Seafoods Inc (HQ) — 206 728-6000
3015 112th Ave Ne Ste 100 Bellevue (98004) *(G-1071)*

Peters Industries — 360 254-9889
6301 Ne 67th St Vancouver (98661) *(G-14486)*

Peterson Manufacturing Co — 360 425-4170
1005 California Way Longview (98632) *(G-5943)*

Peterson Tools — 425 870-0137
4414 128th Pl Ne Marysville (98271) *(G-6368)*

Petes Logging LLC — 509 684-6231
344 E Birch Ave Ste 102 Colville (99114) *(G-2768)*

Petforia LLC — 425 945-2300
4957 Lakemont Blvd Se C4271 Bellevue (98006) *(G-1072)*

Petit and Olson — 206 201-3262
150 Winslow Way E Bainbridge Island (98110) *(G-657)*

Petite Chat LLC — 509 468-2720
9910 N Waikiki Rd Spokane (99218) *(G-12438)*

Petnet Solutions Inc — 425 656-1640
7048 S 188th St Bldg 1 Kent (98032) *(G-5065)*

Petnet Solutions Inc — 509 455-4178
7011 W Flightline Blvd Spokane (99224) *(G-12439)*

Petosa Accordions Inc — 206 632-2700
19503 56th Ave W Ste B Lynnwood (98036) *(G-6180)*

Petrichor Industries LLC (PA) — 425 454-8281
400 112th Ave Ne Ste 335 Bellevue (98004) *(G-1073)*

Petrochem Insulation Inc — 360 254-8953
6811 Ne 131st Ave Vancouver (98682) *(G-14487)*

Petrogas Lift Tech LLC — 425 891-7403
2317 Sahalee Dr E Sammamish (98074) *(G-9240)*

Petroglyph Printing & Signs — 509 447-2590
300 W 2nd St Newport (99156) *(G-7064)*

Petroleum Svc & Solutions LLC — 253 987-5143
416 196th Ave E Lake Tapps (98391) *(G-5684)*

Petrzelka Bros Inc — 360 424-8095
2320 Cedar Ct Mount Vernon (98273) *(G-6824)*

Pettibon Bio-Mechanics Inst (PA) — 360 748-4207
3208 50th Street Ct Nw 102b Gig Harbor (98335) *(G-4144)*

Pexco Aerospace Inc (HQ) — 509 248-9166
2405 S 3rd Ave Union Gap (98903) *(G-13950)*

Pexco LLC — 253 284-8000
3110 70th Ave E Fife (98424) *(G-3980)*

Pf Fishpole Hoists Inc — 206 767-3887
238 Sw 43rd St Renton (98057) *(G-8878)*

Pf Industries, Port Angeles Also called Harbor Action Inc *(G-7708)*

Pfc Inc — 360 398-8889
5421 Guide Meridian Bellingham (98226) *(G-1497)*

Pfi Marine Electric, Seattle Also called Pacific Fshrmen Shpyrd Elc LLC *(G-10732)*

Pfizer Inc — 360 701-0799
9018 Campus Glen Dr Ne Lacey (98516) *(G-5576)*

Pg Woodworks, Gig Harbor Also called Douglas L Perry *(G-4095)*

Pgi Publications — 206 588-2968
10307 Lake City Way Ne Seattle (98125) *(G-10792)*

Pgri Incorporated — 425 449-3000
218 Main St Ste 203 Kirkland (98033) *(G-5433)*

Pharma Terra Inc — 800 215-3957
3440 W Mercer Way Mercer Island (98040) *(G-6479)*

Phaserx, Seattle Also called Pz Wind Down Inc *(G-10895)*

Phazr LLC — 509 329-8306
314 W Mansfield Ave Spokane (99205) *(G-12440)*

Pheasant Brothers LLC — 509 539-5899
1560 Ne 11th St Benton City (99320) *(G-1623)*

Phelps Dodge, Spokane Valley Also called Freeprt-Mcmran Explration Corp *(G-12709)*

Phelps Tire Co Inc (PA) — 206 447-0169
3266 Nw Esplanade Seattle (98117) *(G-10793)*

Philips Medical Systems, Bothell Also called Philips Ultrasound Inc *(G-1887)*

Philips North America LLC — 206 664-5000
2301 5th Ave Ste 200 Seattle (98121) *(G-10794)*

Philips Oral Healthcare LLC — 425 487-7000
22100 Bothell Everett Hwy Bothell (98021) *(G-1886)*

Philips Ultrasound Inc (HQ) — 800 982-2011
22100 Bothell Everett Hwy Bothell (98021) *(G-1887)*

Phillip L Remsberg — 509 997-3231
1021 Twisp Carlton Rd Twisp (98856) *(G-13916)*

Phillip Remsberg Logging, Twisp Also called Phillip L Remsberg *(G-13916)*

Phillippi Fruit Co Inc — 509 662-8522
1921 5th St Wenatchee (98801) *(G-15062)*

Phillips & Reichert Shake Mill — 360 978-4392
1383 Nw State Ave Chehalis (98532) *(G-2524)*

Phillips 66 Company ... 509 534-5040
116 N Chelan Ave Wenatchee (98801) ***(G-15063)***
Phillips 66 Company ... 360 384-1011
3901 Unick Rd Ferndale (98248) ***(G-3886)***
Phillips Industrial Supply Inc ... 206 523-0477
2407 106th St Sw Everett (98204) ***(G-3572)***
Phillips Publishing Group ... 206 429-2429
19679 Marine View Dr Sw Normandy Park (98166) ***(G-7096)***
Philos Press ... 360 456-5106
8038a N Bcntnnial Loop Se Olympia (98503) ***(G-7369)***
Phils Custom Bindery ... 206 728-1541
309 S Cloverdale St A12 Seattle (98108) ***(G-10795)***
Phoenix Company, Spokane Valley *Also called Lynn L Reynolds Inc* ***(G-12779)***
Phoenix Dragon Limited, Port Angeles *Also called Sanctuary Corporation* ***(G-7743)***
Phoenix Equipment Co, Redmond *Also called Genie Industries Inc* ***(G-8474)***
Phoenix Maps ... 509 697-5059
1290 N Wenas Rd Selah (98942) ***(G-11594)***
Phoenix Power Control Inc ... 360 794-8550
16778 146th St Se Ste 190 Monroe (98272) ***(G-6606)***
Phoenix Processor Ltd Partnr ... 206 286-8584
333 1st Ave W Seattle (98119) ***(G-10796)***
Phoenix Sign Company ... 360 532-1111
112 Clemons Rd Montesano (98563) ***(G-6653)***
Phoenix Sign Company ... 360 612-3267
16 Horizon Ln Aberdeen (98520) ***(G-29)***
Phoenix Truss Corporation ... 509 925-3135
2015 Hwy Old 10 Ellensburg (98926) ***(G-3220)***
Phone Flare Inc ... 425 346-9230
14023 284th Cir Ne Duvall (98019) ***(G-2998)***
Phone Vault ... 360 867-8535
22516 Pacific Way Ocean Park (98640) ***(G-7182)***
Photoboxx, Spokane *Also called Blender LLC* ***(G-12154)***
Photon Biosciences LLC ... 509 595-0159
445 S Grand Ave Pullman (99163) ***(G-8100)***
Photon Factory ... 818 795-6957
4810 Airport Way S Seattle (98108) ***(G-10797)***
Photonics-Usa, Bothell *Also called Dooley Enterprises LLC* ***(G-1847)***
Phunnybaggscom ... 253 709-9481
2702 181st Ave E Lake Tapps (98391) ***(G-5685)***
Phuong Dng Times ... 206 760-9168
6221 39th Ave S Seattle (98118) ***(G-10798)***
Phyl Mar Swiss Products Inc ... 360 695-9242
3136 Evergreen Way Washougal (98671) ***(G-14978)***
Physicians Sleep Scoring ... 360 403-7685
28830 Kunde Rd Arlington (98223) ***(G-301)***
Physio-Control Intl Inc ... 425 867-4000
11811 Willows Rd Ne Redmond (98052) ***(G-8621)***
Physware Inc ... 562 491-1600
600 108th Ave Ne Ste 1035 Bellevue (98004) ***(G-1074)***
Phytec America LLC ... 206 780-9047
203 Parfitt Way Sw G100 Bainbridge Island (98110) ***(G-658)***
PI Biologique, Seattle *Also called Microbiologique Inc* ***(G-10533)***
PI Technologies ... 206 877-3720
2018 156th Ave Ne Bellevue (98007) ***(G-1075)***
Pic Sentry Rail Inc ... 425 349-3606
4215a Russell Rd Ste A Mukilteo (98275) ***(G-6965)***
Picatti Brothers Inc (PA) ... 509 248-2540
105 S 3rd Ave Yakima (98902) ***(G-15646)***
Piccell LLC ... 206 780-0478
918 S Horton St Ste 901 Seattle (98134) ***(G-10799)***
Piccell Wireless, Seattle *Also called Piccell LLC* ***(G-10799)***
Pickens Fuel Corp ... 206 824-8181
19425 28th Ave S Seatac (98188) ***(G-9299)***
Pickett Spring ... 360 376-6982
Hc 172 Olga (98279) ***(G-7218)***
Pickle Ball Inc ... 206 632-0119
4700 9th Ave Nw Seattle (98107) ***(G-10800)***
Pickle Papers ... 509 665-8661
21 S Wenatchee Ave Wenatchee (98801) ***(G-15064)***
Pickles Printing ... 360 456-3230
5046 Viewridge Dr Se Olympia (98501) ***(G-7370)***
Picmonkey Inc ... 206 486-2106
2106 E Union St Seattle (98122) ***(G-10801)***
Picobrew Inc ... 425 503-0132
2121 N 35th St Ste 100 Seattle (98103) ***(G-10802)***
Picote Solutions Inc ... 425 505-0646
20810 Se 18th Pl Sammamish (98075) ***(G-9241)***
Pics Smartcard Inc ... 800 667-1772
250 H St Ste 510 Blaine (98230) ***(G-1695)***
Piece Mind Tobacco ACC LLC ... 206 588-0216
12516 Lake City Way Ne Seattle (98125) ***(G-10803)***
Piece of Mind LLC ... 509 868-0850
9303 N Division St Ste A Spokane (99218) ***(G-12441)***
Piecemeal Publishing LLC ... 425 432-3043
26547 222nd Ave Se Maple Valley (98038) ***(G-6289)***
Pierce County River Imprv, Orting *Also called County of Pierce* ***(G-7477)***
Pierres Dock Inc ... 425 488-8600
7504 Ne 175th St Ste 8 Kenmore (98028) ***(G-4598)***
Pierres Polaris, Kenmore *Also called Pierres Dock Inc* ***(G-4598)***
Pierside Promotions, Kingston *Also called Northstar Investment Co* ***(G-5258)***
Pierson & Son Construction ... 360 642-2796
18000 Sandridge Rd Long Beach (98631) ***(G-5877)***
Piety Flats Winery ... 509 877-3115
5202 Bitterroot Way Yakima (98908) ***(G-15647)***
Pign Whistle ... 206 782-6044
1234 23rd Ave E Seattle (98112) ***(G-10804)***
Pigs & Angels Inc ... 360 293-4053
2719 Commercial Ave Anacortes (98221) ***(G-161)***
Pike Brewing Company ... 206 622-6044
1415 1st Ave Seattle (98101) ***(G-10805)***
Pike Place Bagel Bakery Inc ... 206 382-4297
1525 1st Ave Ste 1 Seattle (98101) ***(G-10806)***
Pike Pub, Seattle *Also called Pike Brewing Company* ***(G-10805)***
Pike Street Press ... 206 971-0120
1510 Alaskan Way Seattle (98101) ***(G-10807)***
Pilchuck Pallets Inc ... 425 530-1857
17811 25th Dr Nw Arlington (98223) ***(G-302)***
Pile Protectors ... 360 683-3926
206 Lake Of The Hlls Loop Sequim (98382) ***(G-11660)***
Pilkington North America Inc ... 509 534-4899
3200 E Trent Ave Spokane (99202) ***(G-12442)***
Pilkington North America Inc ... 425 438-8442
10315 Airport Rd 101 Everett (98204) ***(G-3573)***
Piller Aimmco Inc ... 360 835-2103
3925 Grant St Washougal (98671) ***(G-14979)***
Pillow Products, Tacoma *Also called Flood & Associates Inc* ***(G-13299)***
Pilot Knob Construction Inc (PA) ... 509 493-4196
160 Nw Simmons Rd White Salmon (98672) ***(G-15127)***
Pin City Wrestling Club ... 425 327-8518
13101 20th St Ne Lake Stevens (98258) ***(G-5669)***
Pin Foundations Inc ... 253 858-3844
5114 Point Fosdick Dr Nw E60 Gig Harbor (98335) ***(G-4145)***
Pin Hsiao & Associates LLC ... 253 863-0337
5501 West Valley Hwy E Sumner (98390) ***(G-13094)***
Pin Hsiao & Associates LLC ... 206 818-0155
11752 15th Ave Ne Seattle (98125) ***(G-10808)***
Pin Hsiao & Associates LLC (PA) ... 425 637-3357
2535 152nd Ave Ne Redmond (98052) ***(G-8622)***
Pinatas Tradedia ... 509 836-2442
701 S 11th St Sunnyside (98944) ***(G-13138)***
Pinchknitter ... 360 939-0769
880 Saratoga Way Camano Island (98282) ***(G-2221)***
Pine Canyon Growers LLC ... 509 888-7017
8 Orondo Loop Rd Orondo (98843) ***(G-7459)***
Pine Filter LLC ... 360 262-9132
232 Middle Fork Rd Chehalis (98532) ***(G-2525)***
Pine Ridge Cabinets ... 509 486-0789
31 Coyote Dr Tonasket (98855) ***(G-13657)***
Pink Power Printing ... 425 295-4324
23149 Se 184th St Maple Valley (98038) ***(G-6290)***
Pink Slug Press ... 206 430-2637
5454 Birch Ct Ne Hansville (98340) ***(G-4317)***
Pinnacle NW ... 360 264-5484
500 E Export Rd Shelton (98584) ***(G-11722)***
Pinnacle Printing Foundation ... 425 271-7089
13613 Se 188th St Renton (98058) ***(G-8879)***
Pinnacle Steel Fabricators ... 253 770-1690
14021 Pioneer Way E Puyallup (98372) ***(G-8223)***
Pinnion Inc ... 206 577-3070
821 Kirkland Ave Ste 100 Kirkland (98033) ***(G-5434)***
Pinpoint LLC ... 425 442-4764
16541 Redmond Way Ste 170 Redmond (98052) ***(G-8623)***
Pioneer Aerofab Company Inc ... 360 757-4780
15259 Flightline Rd Burlington (98233) ***(G-2181)***
Pioneer Coffee Roasting Co LLC (PA) ... 509 674-4100
121 N Pennsylvania Ave Cle Elum (98922) ***(G-2676)***
Pioneer Human Services (PA) ... 206 768-1990
7440 W Marginal Way S Seattle (98108) ***(G-10809)***
Pioneer Human Services ... 206 762-7737
7000 Highland Pkwy Sw Seattle (98106) ***(G-10810)***
Pioneer Industries, Seattle *Also called Pioneer Human Services* ***(G-10809)***
Pioneer Industries, Seattle *Also called Pioneer Human Services* ***(G-10810)***
Pioneer Manufacturing, Arlington *Also called Dmm Incorporated* ***(G-229)***
Pioneer Metal Works Inc ... 509 787-4425
512 F St Se Quincy (98848) ***(G-8306)***
Pioneer Packaging, Kent *Also called Northwest Pioneer Inc* ***(G-5034)***
Pioneer Printing and Forms ... 509 248-7393
10502 Orchard Ave Yakima (98908) ***(G-15648)***
Pioneer Rock & Monument LLC ... 509 773-4702
201 Crafton Rd Goldendale (98620) ***(G-4206)***
Pioneer Square Brands Inc ... 360 733-5608
321 3rd Ave S Ste 403 Seattle (98104) ***(G-10811)***
Pioneer Woodworks Company Inc ... 206 362-5637
12337 Lake City Way Ne Seattle (98125) ***(G-10812)***
PIP Building LLC ... 360 961-1702
3777 Brown Rd Ferndale (98248) ***(G-3887)***
PIP McKay Unlimited LLC ... 206 390-0988
1746 Nw 58th St Seattle (98107) ***(G-10813)***
PIP Printing, Vancouver *Also called Mc BAC Inc* ***(G-14405)***
PIP Printing, Olympia *Also called P I P Printing Inc* ***(G-7364)***
PIP Printing, Seattle *Also called Daruma Graphics* ***(G-9796)***
PIP Printing, Spokane *Also called Plese Printing & Marketing* ***(G-12448)***
Pipe Vlves Fttngs Wrldwide Inc ... 509 991-7191
21319 E Harvard Vistas Ln Newman Lake (99025) ***(G-7051)***

ALPHABETIC

Pipelinedeals Inc 866 702-7303
1008 Western Ave Ste 401 Seattle (98104) ***(G-10814)***
Pipemasters Inc 253 377-0717
15807 130th Ave Nw Gig Harbor (98329) ***(G-4146)***
Piper 2600 Investments LLC 971 409-7596
2600 Nw 329th St Ridgefield (98642) ***(G-9102)***
Pipkin-Goodfellow Venture LLC 509 884-2400
4801 Contractors Dr East Wenatchee (98802) ***(G-3029)***
Pishwacom 509 991-8972
1906 W Wedgewood Ave Spokane (99208) ***(G-12443)***
Pit Bull Fabrication, Richland *Also called Eugene P Lamm Jr* ***(G-8995)***
Pitney Bowes Inc 509 363-3694
1313 N Atlantic St Fl 3 Spokane (99201) ***(G-12444)***
Pitney Bowes Inc 509 835-1272
200 E 2nd Ave Ste A Spokane (99202) ***(G-12445)***
Pitney Bowes Inc 253 395-8717
19005 64th Ave S Ste 175 Kent (98032) ***(G-5066)***
Pitney Bowes Inc 509 838-0115
313 N Atl St Ste 3000 Spokane (99201) ***(G-12446)***
Pivot Custom Metal Fabrication 206 762-3755
6501 E Marginal Way S C Seattle (98108) ***(G-10815)***
Pixel Planet Inc 206 669-7371
5208 45th Ave Sw Seattle (98136) ***(G-10816)***
Pixelan Software 831 222-0339
2950 Newmarket St Ste 101 Bellingham (98226) ***(G-1498)***
Pixelan Works 425 379-0339
3427 104th Pl Se Everett (98208) ***(G-3574)***
Pixelsaurus Games LLC 617 893-7755
1115 Ne 78th St Seattle (98115) ***(G-10817)***
Pixotec LLC 425 255-0789
15917 Se Fairwood Blvd Renton (98058) ***(G-8880)***
Pixvana Inc 206 910-5747
3621 Stone Way N Unit A Seattle (98103) ***(G-10818)***
Pizza Blends LLC (HQ) 800 826-1200
400 112th Ave Ne Ste 350 Bellevue (98004) ***(G-1076)***
Pizza Blends, Inc., Bellevue *Also called Pizza Blends LLC* ***(G-1076)***
Pizzicato Publishing Co 206 361-0444
17400 32nd Ave Nw Seattle (98155) ***(G-10819)***
PJ Finney Corporation 206 282-8400
3243 20th Ave W Seattle (98199) ***(G-10820)***
Pk Graphics Inc 425 251-8083
1120 Sw 16th St Ste 1a Renton (98057) ***(G-8881)***
Pkfashions Inc 425 359-6510
13300 Bothell Everett Hwy # 628 Mill Creek (98012) ***(G-6520)***
Plaas Timber LLC 360 832-2440
41427 Orville Rd E Eatonville (98328) ***(G-3066)***
Plactic Services and Products 360 736-5616
3500 Northpark Dr Centralia (98531) ***(G-2424)***
Plain Cellars LLC 509 548-5412
18749 Alpine Acres Rd Leavenworth (98826) ***(G-5813)***
Planet Headset Inc 253 238-0643
811 Enati Way Fox Island (98333) ***(G-4023)***
Planeta Works LLC 206 250-4311
14709 26th Ave Ne Shoreline (98155) ***(G-11801)***
Planned Solutions LLC 425 827-4277
807 Lake St S Kirkland (98033) ***(G-5435)***
Plano Bros Paving Inc (PA) 425 226-8210
9219 Coal Creek Pkwy Se Newcastle (98059) ***(G-7038)***
Plant Hormones LLC 253 332-6131
4272 S 290th St Auburn (98001) ***(G-532)***
Plantsplus 360 628-8368
2244 65th Ln Nw Olympia (98502) ***(G-7371)***
Plasma Biolife Services L P 509 545-3008
7430 Wrigley Dr Pasco (99301) ***(G-7617)***
Plasma Steel LLC 360 801-0444
1415 Madrona Point Dr Bremerton (98312) ***(G-1988)***
Plastic Fabrication, Bellingham *Also called Pfc Inc* ***(G-1497)***
Plastic Forming Services LLC 360 335-9755
3830 S Truman Rd Ste 2 Washougal (98671) ***(G-14980)***
Plastic Injection Molding Inc 509 375-4260
2695 Battelle Blvd Richland (99354) ***(G-9035)***
Plastic Sales & Service Inc 206 524-8312
5522 208th St Sw Lynnwood (98036) ***(G-6181)***
Plasticreations Inc 425 558-1075
16541 Redmond Way Redmond (98052) ***(G-8624)***
Plastics Dynamics Inc 206 762-2164
6004 S 190th St Ste 102 Kent (98032) ***(G-5067)***
Plastics Northwest Inc 360 823-0505
2851 Nw Lower River Rd Vancouver (98660) ***(G-14488)***
Plastics West Inc 360 538-0115
400 W Curtis St Aberdeen (98520) ***(G-30)***
Platalytics Inc 916 835-9584
6128 145th Ct Ne Redmond (98052) ***(G-8625)***
Plateau Jewelers Inc 425 313-0657
2830 228th Ave Se Ste B Sammamish (98075) ***(G-9242)***
Platform Solutions Sector, Redmond *Also called Bae Systems Controls Inc* ***(G-8396)***
Platinum Pets LLC 360 859-4027
9604 Ne 126th Ave # 2330 Vancouver (98682) ***(G-14489)***
Platinum Rail Publications LLC 360 658-2485
5811 75th Ave Ne Marysville (98270) ***(G-6369)***
Play Impossible Corporation 206 852-7015
111 S Jackson St Seattle (98104) ***(G-10821)***
Play It Again Sports 10280, Renton *Also called Rj Sports Inc* ***(G-8895)***
Play Visions Inc 425 482-2836
19180 144th Ave Ne Woodinville (98072) ***(G-15335)***
Playnetwork Inc (HQ) 425 497-8100
8727 148th Ave Ne Redmond (98052) ***(G-8626)***
Plc-Multipoint Inc 425 353-7552
3101 111th St Sw Ste F Everett (98204) ***(G-3575)***
Pleasant Hill Cellars 206 229-5105
14509 189th Avenue Ct E Bonney Lake (98391) ***(G-1733)***
Pleasant Hill Sawmill 360 274-7888
5412 Pleasant Hill Rd Kelso (98626) ***(G-4542)***
Pleasant Hill Winery LLC 425 333-6770
14509 189th Avenue Ct E Bonney Lake (98391) ***(G-1734)***
Pleasure Boat Studio 206 962-0460
3710 Sw Barton St Seattle (98126) ***(G-10822)***
Pleines Logging Inc 360 374-6373
1755 Bogachiel Way Forks (98331) ***(G-4015)***
Plese Printing & Marketing 509 534-2355
4201 E Trent Ave Spokane (99202) ***(G-12447)***
Plese Printing & Marketing (PA) 509 534-2355
4201 E Trent Ave Spokane (99202) ***(G-12448)***
Plexera LLC 425 368-7410
17625 130th Ave Ne Woodinville (98072) ***(G-15336)***
Plexera Bioscience, Woodinville *Also called Plexera LLC* ***(G-15336)***
Plexsys Interface Products Inc (PA) 360 838-2500
4900 Nw Camas Meadows Dr Camas (98607) ***(G-2275)***
Plexus Manufacturing Inc 425 355-2997
4416 Russell Rd Mukilteo (98275) ***(G-6966)***
Plimp Company, The, Seattle *Also called Plimp Inc* ***(G-10823)***
Plimp Inc 206 795-3292
605 1st Ave Ste 400 Seattle (98104) ***(G-10823)***
Pls Pacific Laser Systems LLC 415 453-5780
6920 Seaway Blvd Everett (98203) ***(G-3576)***
Pls Pole Yard, Rochester *Also called North Fork Timber Company Corp* ***(G-9138)***
Pls Pole Yard, Centralia *Also called North Fork Timber Company Corp* ***(G-2420)***
Plug Power Inc 509 228-6694
15913 E Euclid Ave Spokane Valley (99216) ***(G-12829)***
Plug Power Inc 509 228-6638
16005 E Euclid Ave Ste F Spokane Valley (99216) ***(G-12830)***
Plugable Technologies, Redmond *Also called Leancode Inc* ***(G-8532)***
Plum Creek Northwest Plywd Inc (HQ) 206 467-3600
601 Union St Ste 3100 Seattle (98101) ***(G-10824)***
Plum Creek Timberlands LP (HQ) 206 467-3600
601 Union St Ste 3100 Seattle (98101) ***(G-10825)***
Plumb Cellars 509 540-5632
39 E Main St Walla Walla (99362) ***(G-14856)***
Plumb Signs Inc 253 474-6702
909 S 28th St Tacoma (98409) ***(G-13466)***
Plunk LLC 425 770-1287
4313 106th Pl Ne Kirkland (98033) ***(G-5436)***
Plus Six Publishing 360 553-2316
6715 Ne 63rd St Vancouver (98661) ***(G-14490)***
Plussoft Inc 425 821-8776
11637 Ne 148th Ct Kirkland (98034) ***(G-5437)***
Plywood Components Inc 253 863-6323
1510 Puyallup St Sumner (98390) ***(G-13095)***
PM Industries 253 666-8977
2318 Martin Luther King Tacoma (98405) ***(G-13467)***
PM Testing Laboratory Inc 253 922-1321
3921 Pacific Hwy E Fife (98424) ***(G-3981)***
PM Weizenbaum 206 427-4127
115 N 85th St Ste 202 Seattle (98103) ***(G-10826)***
Pmc Inc 206 854-2660
1862 Ives Ave Kent (98032) ***(G-5068)***
Pmw Capital Inc (HQ) 253 272-5119
2102 Eells St Tacoma (98421) ***(G-13468)***
Pnj, Greenacres *Also called Pacific Northwest Jewelers* ***(G-4300)***
Pnw Aerospace LLC 360 292-0909
5709 Lacey Blvd Se # 202 Lacey (98503) ***(G-5577)***
Pnw Select Marketing Group LLC 360 746-8270
1855 Main St Ferndale (98248) ***(G-3888)***
Poa Pharma North America LLC 855 416-6826
4400 Ne 77th Ave Ste 275 Vancouver (98662) ***(G-14491)***
Pocock Racing Shells Inc 425 438-9048
615 80th St Sw Everett (98203) ***(G-3577)***
Poe Asphalt Paving Inc 509 334-6400
5991 Sr 270 Pullman (99163) ***(G-8101)***
Poetry Northwest 425 388-9395
2000 Tower St Everett (98201) ***(G-3578)***
Poetry Posters 425 831-5809
224 Ne 6th St North Bend (98045) ***(G-7120)***
Pohl Spring Works Inc 509 466-0904
6415 E Nixon Ave Spokane Valley (99212) ***(G-12831)***
Pohlman Knowles 206 933-7450
3824 Sw Morgan St Seattle (98126) ***(G-10827)***
Point Inside Inc 425 590-9522
500 108th Ave Ne Ste 520 Bellevue (98004) ***(G-1077)***
Point Roberts Press Inc 360 945-0413
225 Marine Dr Ste 200 Blaine (98230) ***(G-1696)***
Point Wilson Co Inc 360 385-7625
131 Cape George Dr Port Townsend (98368) ***(G-7907)***
Poison Apple Tacoma 253 304-1874
902 S 7th St Apt 9 Tacoma (98405) ***(G-13469)***

ALPHABETIC SECTION
Powdertech Mr Shannon

Poizer Metal Works 360 892-2629
9707 Nw 10th Ave Vancouver (98665) ***(G-14492)***
Polar Fusion LLC 206 395-7811
10605 Se 240th St Kent (98031) ***(G-5069)***
Polar Fusion LLC (PA) 206 779-5238
2737 72nd Ave S Ste 106 Kent (98030) ***(G-5070)***
Polar Graphics, Kent *Also called Arctic Circle Enterprises LLC* ***(G-4789)***
Polaris Glove & Safety In 206 789-5887
309 Nw 88st Redmond (98073) ***(G-8627)***
Polaris Machining, Marysville *Also called Polaris Manufacturing Inc* ***(G-6370)***
Polaris Manufacturing Inc 360 653-7676
103 Cedar Ave Marysville (98270) ***(G-6370)***
Polaris Manufacturing Inc 206 230-9235
3816 Greenbrier Ln Mercer Island (98040) ***(G-6480)***
Polarity Elec 206 546-3539
916 N 188th St Shoreline (98133) ***(G-11802)***
Polenta, Kent *Also called San Gennaro Foods Inc* ***(G-5115)***
Polish Nail Spa 425 771-1458
20101 44th Ave W Ste A Lynnwood (98036) ***(G-6182)***
Politics of The Possible, Snohomish *Also called Mary Ellen McCaffree* ***(G-11944)***
Pollution Control Systems Corp 206 523-7220
8036 35th Ave Ne Seattle (98115) ***(G-10828)***
Polydrop LLC 206 601-2191
22431 76th Ave S Kent (98032) ***(G-5071)***
Polyform US Ltd 253 872-0300
7030 S 224th St Kent (98032) ***(G-5072)***
Polymer Foundry Inc 360 574-1617
1108 Ne 146th St Ste B Vancouver (98685) ***(G-14493)***
Polytech Coil Winding 253 324-3044
4301 N 9th St Tacoma (98406) ***(G-13470)***
Polythermics LLC 425 823-5568
11628 73rd Pl Ne Kirkland (98034) ***(G-5438)***
Polyurethane Sales & Svc LLC 360 334-5364
20019 Ne 68th St Vancouver (98682) ***(G-14494)***
Polyventure International 360 898-7013
3500 E State Route 106 Union (98592) ***(G-13918)***
Pomona Packaging Division, Yakima *Also called Pomona Service & Supply Co* ***(G-15649)***
Pomona Service & Supply Co 509 452-7121
2310 Castlevale Rd Yakima (98902) ***(G-15649)***
Pomum Cellars LLC 206 362-9203
2334 N 61st St Seattle (98103) ***(G-10829)***
Ponder Press 206 861-0448
1804 S Charles St Seattle (98144) ***(G-10830)***
Pondera Winery LLC 425 486-8500
19501 144th Ave Ne B400 Woodinville (98072) ***(G-15337)***
Ponderay Newsprint Company 509 445-2133
422767 Highway 20 Usk (99180) ***(G-13985)***
Pontin Del Roza Winery 509 786-4449
35502 N Hinzerling Rd Prosser (99350) ***(G-8062)***
Pontin Farms, Prosser *Also called Pontin Del Roza Winery* ***(G-8062)***
Poopless In Seattle 425 444-6930
817 Pickett Ave Ne North Bend (98045) ***(G-7121)***
Poor Italians Vineyard 360 366-5970
7110 Valley View Rd Ferndale (98248) ***(G-3889)***
Pop Gourmet LLC 425 277-5225
14520 Interurban Ave S D100 Tukwila (98168) ***(G-13792)***
Pop Pop LLC 206 384-8121
14129 Phinney Ave N Seattle (98133) ***(G-10831)***
Pope John 206 320-0686
905 30th Ave S Seattle (98144) ***(G-10832)***
Pope Resources 253 851-7009
4423 Point Fosdick Dr Nw Gig Harbor (98335) ***(G-4147)***
Poppleton Electric & Mchy Co 206 762-9160
24831 110th Pl Se Kent (98030) ***(G-5073)***
Poppystamps, Seattle *Also called Memory Box Inc* ***(G-10515)***
Porex Technologies Corporation 253 284-8000
3110 70th Ave E Fife (98424) ***(G-3982)***
Poros 773 504-2908
600 1st Ave Ste 205 Seattle (98104) ***(G-10833)***
Port A Cover & More Inc 509 928-9264
16624 E Sprague Ave Spokane Valley (99037) ***(G-12832)***
Port Angeles Hardwood LLC 360 452-6041
333 Eclipse Ind Pkwy Port Angeles (98363) ***(G-7737)***
Port Blakely Company (PA) 206 624-5810
1501 4th Ave Ste 2150 Seattle (98101) ***(G-10834)***
Port Chatham Smoked Seafood, Everett *Also called Trident Seafoods Corporation* ***(G-3637)***
Port Chatham Smoked Seafood's, Everett *Also called Norquest Seafoods Inc* ***(G-3553)***
Port Lakely Cummunities, Seattle *Also called Port Blakely Company* ***(G-10834)***
Port Orchard Independent, Port Orchard *Also called Sound Publishing Inc* ***(G-7850)***
Port Orchard Sand & Gravel 360 681-2526
9868 State Route 104 Port Ludlow (98365) ***(G-7772)***
Port Townsend Brewing Co 360 385-9967
330 10th St Ste C Port Townsend (98368) ***(G-7908)***
Port Townsend Community 360 385-0120
1101 Cherry St Port Townsend (98368) ***(G-7909)***
Port Townsend Foundry LLC 360 385-6425
251 Otto St Port Townsend (98368) ***(G-7910)***
Port Townsend Holdings Co Inc (HQ) 360 385-3170
100 Mill Rd Port Townsend (98368) ***(G-7911)***
Port Townsend Lcl Mktplc LLC 360 732-0696
3383 W Valley Rd Chimacum (98325) ***(G-2613)***
Port Townsend Paper Corp (HQ) 360 385-3170
100 Mill Rd Port Townsend (98368) ***(G-7912)***
Port Townsend Publishing Co 360 385-2900
226 Adams St Port Townsend (98368) ***(G-7913)***
Port Townsend Sails Inc 360 385-1640
315 Jackson St Port Townsend (98368) ***(G-7914)***
Port Townsend School of Woodwo 303 910-0016
200 Battery Way Port Townsend (98368) ***(G-7915)***
Port Townsend Shipwrights Coop 360 385-6138
919 Haines Pl Port Townsend (98368) ***(G-7916)***
Port Townsend Vineyards Winery 360 385-0694
1812 Fir St Port Townsend (98368) ***(G-7917)***
Port Townsend Winery LLC 360 344-8155
2640 W Sims Way Port Townsend (98368) ***(G-7918)***
Portable Baptistry, Lynnwood *Also called Tubs To Go Inc* ***(G-6213)***
Portac Inc 253 922-9900
3600 Port Of Tacoma Rd # 302 Fife (98424) ***(G-3983)***
Portco Corporation 360 696-1641
211 5th St Woodland (98674) ***(G-15460)***
Portco Packaging, Woodland *Also called Portco Corporation* ***(G-15460)***
Porter Etuv Manufacturing Inc 360 796-3172
235 Salmon St Brinnon (98320) ***(G-2026)***
Porter Seal Company, Tukwila *Also called 4 M Company Inc* ***(G-13686)***
Portland Plastics 360 887-2230
6111 S 6th Way Ridgefield (98642) ***(G-9103)***
Portland Press Inc 253 274-8883
2101 Jefferson Ave Tacoma (98402) ***(G-13471)***
Portland Press Incorporated 206 297-1304
1111 Nw 50th St Seattle (98107) ***(G-10835)***
Portland Stirling Incorporated 206 855-0819
9208 Ne Valley Rd Bainbridge Island (98110) ***(G-659)***
Portlock Smked Sfds-Bllard Ret 206 466-1931
2821 Nw Market St Ste E Seattle (98107) ***(G-10836)***
Portlock Software 425 247-0545
20002 73rd Ave Ne Kenmore (98028) ***(G-4599)***
Portrait Displays Inc 206 420-7514
123 2nd Ave S Ste 200 Edmonds (98020) ***(G-3144)***
Posabit Inc 903 641-7604
1128 8th St Kirkland (98033) ***(G-5439)***
Posera USA Inc (PA) 206 364-8686
6016 204th St Sw Ste A Lynnwood (98036) ***(G-6183)***
Posh Digs 425 286-6245
17326 31st Dr Se Bothell (98012) ***(G-1888)***
Posh Speakers Systems, Bremerton *Also called U2 Inc* ***(G-2009)***
Positive Futures Network 206 842-0216
284 Madrona Way Ne # 116 Bainbridge Island (98110) ***(G-660)***
Positive Software Compan, Richland *Also called Kennewick Computer Company* ***(G-9018)***
Possession Point Woodworking 360 579-2183
7927 Blakely Ave Clinton (98236) ***(G-2693)***
Post All Expressions 509 684-3723
166 Buena Vista Dr B Colville (99114) ***(G-2769)***
Post Alley Press 206 522-5963
1304 Ne 63rd St Seattle (98115) ***(G-10837)***
Post Indus Stress & Design 253 572-9782
5211 S Washington St C Tacoma (98409) ***(G-13472)***
Post Tension Cables Inc (PA) 425 745-1304
10127 9th Ave W Everett (98204) ***(G-3579)***
Post-Industrial Press, Tacoma *Also called Post Indus Stress & Design* ***(G-13472)***
Potlatchdeltic Mfg L L C (HQ) 509 835-1500
601 W 1st Ave Ste 1600 Spokane (99201) ***(G-12449)***
Potluck Pairs, Seattle *Also called Potluck Press LLC* ***(G-10838)***
Potluck Press LLC 206 328-1300
920 S Bayview St Seattle (98134) ***(G-10838)***
Potrisers Inc 206 240-5579
4719 Fobes Rd Snohomish (98290) ***(G-11961)***
Potter & Associates Inc 206 623-8844
4400 26th Ave W Seattle (98199) ***(G-10839)***
Potter-Webster Co 360 577-9632
1110 Columbia Blvd Ste A Longview (98632) ***(G-5944)***
Poulsbo Bake Shop, Poulsbo *Also called Slays Poulsbo Bakery Inc* ***(G-8001)***
Pow Inc 206 366-0224
1118 Nw Ballard Way Seattle (98107) ***(G-10840)***
Pow Inc (PA) 206 366-0224
4509 Interlake Ave N Seattle (98103) ***(G-10841)***
Pow Gloves, Seattle *Also called Pow Inc* ***(G-10841)***
Powder Coating Inc 425 743-4393
11324 Mukilteo Speedway # 7 Mukilteo (98275) ***(G-6967)***
Powder Coating Systems, Tacoma *Also called Vivasource Inc* ***(G-13583)***
Powder Keg LLC 509 758-7300
1329 Setlow Ct Clarkston (99403) ***(G-2641)***
Powder Monkey Games LLC 206 501-2340
1601 2nd Ave Ste 800 Seattle (98101) ***(G-10842)***
Powder River Drafting 360 679-9859
1788 Conifer Ln Oak Harbor (98277) ***(G-7161)***
Powder Vision Inc 425 222-6363
8110 304th Ave Se Preston (98050) ***(G-8026)***
Powder-Fab Inc 360 435-0793
19224 62nd Ave Ne Ste 2 Arlington (98223) ***(G-303)***
Powdertech Inc 509 927-0189
10020 E Montgomery Dr Spokane Valley (99206) ***(G-12833)***
Powdertech Mr Shannon 509 927-5804
3808 N Sullivan Rd Spokane Valley (99216) ***(G-12834)***

ALPHABETIC

Powell Industries Inc — 509 922-0463
3808 N Sullivan Rd 3k Spokane Valley (99216) *(G-12835)*

Powell Industries Inc — 206 402-3591
809 Industry Dr Tukwila (98188) *(G-13793)*

Powell Publishing Inc — 360 886-6650
29103 218th Pl Se Black Diamond (98010) *(G-1653)*

Powell Software Inc — 425 974-9692
4631 92nd Ave Ne Yarrow Point (98004) *(G-15722)*

Power and Lighting LLC — 360 750-0158
404 E 25th St Vancouver (98663) *(G-14495)*

Power Breaker LLC Seattle — 425 286-4276
15153 175th Ave Se Monroe (98272) *(G-6607)*

Power Conversion Inc — 425 487-1337
19501 144th Ave Ne B1000 Woodinville (98072) *(G-15338)*

Power Equipment Supply Llc — 206 817-5627
1307 38th St Unit 6 Everett (98201) *(G-3580)*

Power Machine Services Inc — 509 536-1721
4105 E Broadway Ave Spokane (99202) *(G-12450)*

Power Plus Incorporated — 509 489-8308
7302 N Market St Spokane (99217) *(G-12451)*

Power Punch Distributors LLC (PA) — 360 479-0673
1700 W Sunn Fjord Ln L210 Bremerton (98312) *(G-1989)*

Powercom Inc (PA) — 425 489-8549
11824 N Creek Pkwy N S Bothell (98011) *(G-1784)*

Powerguard Corporation — 206 764-8882
6506 S 209th St Ste 200 Kent (98032) *(G-5074)*

Powerhuse Brnds Consulting LLC — 503 317-4925
17007 Ne 30th Ave Ridgefield (98642) *(G-9104)*

Powerlink Transmission Co LLC — 360 314-6840
754 Officers Row Vancouver (98661) *(G-14496)*

Powers Candy and Nut Company — 509 489-1955
6061 N Freya St Spokane (99217) *(G-12452)*

Powers Machine & Fabrication — 206 824-9726
919 S 222nd St Des Moines (98198) *(G-2942)*

Powersoft — 425 637-8088
777 108th Ave Ne Ste 1650 Bellevue (98004) *(G-1078)*

Ppcs Inc — 425 883-7464
16292 Redmond Way Redmond (98052) *(G-8628)*

PPG Industries — 253 804-4350
1220 37th St Nw Ste 104 Auburn (98001) *(G-533)*

PPG Industries Inc — 425 885-3848
9135 Willows Rd Ne Redmond (98052) *(G-8629)*

Ppr Industries Corporation — 360 863-9500
17045 Tye St Se Monroe (98272) *(G-6608)*

PR Lifting LLC — 425 214-4124
3010 Everett Ave Unit A Everett (98201) *(G-3581)*

Pra Inc — 408 743-5300
4821 226th Pl Ne Arlington (98223) *(G-304)*

Practec LLC — 425 881-8202
17625 Ne 65th St Ste 125 Redmond (98052) *(G-8630)*

Practical Trauma, Seattle Also called Michael D Lynne *(G-10527)*

Prairie Electric Inc — 509 545-1752
6931 Road 76 Pasco (99301) *(G-7618)*

Prater Enterprises Inc — 360 893-3620
26619 122nd Ave E Graham (98338) *(G-4235)*

Prathers Welding & Fabrication — 509 632-5321
10668 Highway 2 E Coulee City (99115) *(G-2805)*

Praxair Inc — 425 821-2423
11216 120th Ave Ne Kirkland (98033) *(G-5440)*

Praxair Inc — 360 734-3955
4215 Britton Rd Bellingham (98226) *(G-1499)*

Praxair Inc — 206 632-7138
4442 27th Ave W Seattle (98199) *(G-10843)*

Praxair Inc — 360 733-0971
430 Ohio St Ste A Bellingham (98225) *(G-1500)*

Praxair Inc — 425 259-0188
1111 Hewitt Ave Everett (98201) *(G-3582)*

Praxair Inc — 360 371-2900
4466 Aldergrove Rd Ferndale (98248) *(G-3890)*

Praxair Inc — 206 264-2881
545 S Lander St Seattle (98134) *(G-10844)*

Praxair Distribution Inc — 360 694-1338
603 Se Victory Ave Vancouver (98661) *(G-14497)*

Praxair Distribution Inc — 360 504-2086
302 Clearview Ln Sequim (98382) *(G-11661)*

Praxair Distribution Inc — 253 620-1620
480 E 19th St Tacoma (98421) *(G-13473)*

Praxair Distrubution, Sequim Also called Praxair Distribution Inc *(G-11661)*

Praxair Services Inc — 360 676-8215
4115 Strider Loop Rd Bellingham (98226) *(G-1501)*

Precast By Design Inc — 509 292-2988
133 Allen Rd Elk (99009) *(G-3175)*

Precast Oldcastle — 800 509-6150
6500 Nw Whitney Rd Vancouver (98665) *(G-14498)*

Precept Brands LLC (PA) — 206 267-5252
1910 Frview Ave E Ste 400 Seattle (98102) *(G-10845)*

Precept Wine, Seattle Also called Ross Andrew Mickel *(G-10982)*

Precept Wine, Seattle Also called Canoe Ridge Vineyard *(G-9619)*

Precept Wine, Seattle Also called Precept Brands LLC *(G-10845)*

Precious Metals Min & Ref Co — 509 927-2685
2320 S Bolivar Rd Spokane Valley (99037) *(G-12836)*

Precise Machining Inc — 360 629-0420
8536 Cedarhome Dr Ste C Stanwood (98292) *(G-12985)*

Precise Manufacturing & Engrg — 360 604-8742
5600 N Vancouver Vancouver (98682) *(G-14499)*

Precise Printing Inc — 206 343-0942
2525 W Commodore Way Seattle (98199) *(G-10846)*

Precise Tool & Gage Co Inc — 206 623-1120
1122 3rd Ave Seattle (98101) *(G-10847)*

Precision, Monroe Also called Ppr Industries Corporation *(G-6608)*

Precision Airmotive LLC — 360 403-4803
17716 48th Dr Ne Arlington (98223) *(G-305)*

Precision Airmotive LLC — 360 659-7348
14800 40th Ave Ne Marysville (98271) *(G-6371)*

Precision Alias — 425 222-0744
30211 Se 40th St Fall City (98024) *(G-3706)*

Precision Appliance Technology — 206 960-2467
10400 Ne 4th St Bellevue (98004) *(G-1079)*

Precision Arospc & Composites, Sumner Also called Aim Aerospace Sumner Inc *(G-13054)*

Precision Art Works — 206 714-7074
1731 Nw 62nd St Seattle (98107) *(G-10848)*

Precision Automation Inc — 360 254-0661
12909 Ne 95th St Vancouver (98682) *(G-14500)*

Precision Beam & Timber Inc — 509 525-1381
2915 Melrose St Walla Walla (99362) *(G-14857)*

Precision Biometrics Inc — 206 448-3464
2303 W Commodore Way # 301 Seattle (98199) *(G-10849)*

Precision Builders — 509 882-2232
901 W Robinson Rd Grandview (98930) *(G-4254)*

Precision Carbide Bit Set, Vashon Also called Cascade Chalet *(G-14716)*

Precision Castparts Corp — 206 433-2600
3215 S 116th St Ste 109 Tukwila (98168) *(G-13794)*

Precision Castparts Corp — 425 957-6938
915 118th Ave Se Ste 320 Bellevue (98005) *(G-1080)*

Precision Chain Saw, Buckley Also called Shelly Shay *(G-2072)*

Precision Counter Tech Inc — 425 486-8629
6409 S 194th St Kent (98032) *(G-5075)*

Precision Countertops Inc — 253 867-5317
20866 89th Ave S Bldg Q Kent (98031) *(G-5076)*

Precision Custom Cabinets LLC — 253 397-4240
3705 Auburn Way N Auburn (98002) *(G-534)*

Precision Customer Woodworking — 360 983-3297
180 Mossyrock Rd W Mossyrock (98564) *(G-6764)*

Precision Data Technology Inc — 425 259-9237
3409 Mcdougall Ave # 107 Everett (98201) *(G-3583)*

Precision Driveshaft Inc — 253 236-5640
20835 102nd Pl Se Kent (98031) *(G-5077)*

Precision Engines LLC — 425 347-2800
1523 132nd St Se Ste C Everett (98208) *(G-3584)*

Precision Fabricators LLC — 206 362-1195
10554 Aurora Ave N Seattle (98133) *(G-10850)*

Precision Fldpower Systems LLC — 206 938-2894
10659 Marine View Dr Sw Seattle (98146) *(G-10851)*

Precision Fluidpower Engrg, Seattle Also called Precision Fldpower Systems LLC *(G-10851)*

Precision H2o, Spokane Valley Also called Quarry Tile Company *(G-12848)*

Precision Industrial Equi — 509 571-1725
1909 Longfibre Rd Yakima (98903) *(G-15650)*

Precision Industries LLC — 253 255-3814
33915 Tanwax Ct E Eatonville (98328) *(G-3067)*

Precision Iron Works Inc — 253 887-5555
102 Frontage Rd S Pacific (98047) *(G-7539)*

Precision Machine & Mfg — 360 734-1081
733 Van Wyck Rd Bellingham (98226) *(G-1502)*

Precision Machine & Tool Inc — 425 745-6229
2813 148th St Sw Lynnwood (98087) *(G-6184)*

Precision Machine Supply — 509 922-1666
15708 E Marietta Ln Spokane Valley (99216) *(G-12837)*

Precision Machine Works — 253 661-8180
401 Sw 322nd St Federal Way (98023) *(G-3771)*

Precision Machine Works Inc — 253 272-5119
2102 Eells St Tacoma (98421) *(G-13474)*

Precision Machining — 509 972-1986
14308 Fisk Rd Yakima (98908) *(G-15651)*

Precision Metal Works LLC — 509 945-8433
2004 S 14th St Union Gap (98903) *(G-13951)*

Precision Paint — 425 235-0340
14248 Se Fairwood Blvd Renton (98058) *(G-8882)*

Precision Pattern — 253 572-4333
2620 E G St Tacoma (98421) *(G-13475)*

Precision Press, Redmond Also called Stat Corporation *(G-8681)*

Precision Printing Inc — 360 736-7232
1624 Kresky Ave Centralia (98531) *(G-2425)*

Precision Prototype, Woodinville Also called Ultimate Product Corp *(G-15394)*

Precision Rebar & ACC Inc — 360 574-1022
1712 Ne 99th St Vancouver (98665) *(G-14501)*

Precision Shapes Nw LLC — 206 605-4396
522 W Crockett St Seattle (98119) *(G-10852)*

Precision Sheet Metal LLC — 509 969-0055
522 N 18th Ave Yakima (98902) *(G-15652)*

Precision Sheet Metal & Heatin — 503 939-8600
1212 Se 181st Ave Vancouver (98683) *(G-14502)*

Precision Spring Stamping Corp — 253 852-6911
22617 85th Pl S Kent (98031) *(G-5078)*

Precision Steel Rule Die Co — 206 397-3982
4526 53rd Ave Sw Seattle (98116) *(G-10853)*

ALPHABETIC SECTION
Printcore, Woodinville

Precision Technology Corp....360 403-0254
18640 59th Dr Ne Arlington (98223) ***(G-306)***

Precision Tooling and Die....253 872-8217
800 Sw 27th St Renton (98057) ***(G-8883)***

Precision Truck & Equipment....360 263-8940
33415 Ne Lewisville Hwy Yacolt (98675) ***(G-15491)***

Precision Waterjet Inc....509 888-7954
207 S Columbia St Wenatchee (98801) ***(G-15065)***

Precision Welder and Eng Repr....206 382-6227
4427 Airport Way S Seattle (98108) ***(G-10854)***

Precision Welding....425 271-7490
2213 Aberdeen Ave Ne Renton (98056) ***(G-8884)***

Precision Welding & Boat RES....360 607-3546
2422 Ne 172nd Ave Vancouver (98684) ***(G-14503)***

Precision Woodcraft....509 276-1362
5192 S Swenson Rd Deer Park (99006) ***(G-2913)***

Precisionhx LLC....509 951-1266
11528 E Antler Rd Chattaroy (99003) ***(G-2451)***

Precor Incorporated (HQ)....425 486-9292
20031 142nd Ave Ne Woodinville (98072) ***(G-15339)***

Precor USA, Woodinville *Also called Precor Incorporated* ***(G-15339)***

Preferred Business Solutions....425 251-1202
7691 S 180th St Kent (98032) ***(G-5079)***

Preferred Orthotic & Prosthetc....253 838-6726
34709 9th Ave S Ste A100 Federal Way (98003) ***(G-3772)***

Preferred Orthotic & Prosthetc (PA)....253 572-1282
1901 S Cedar St Ste 202 Tacoma (98405) ***(G-13476)***

Preflex Digital Prepress Svcs....253 583-9100
4620 95th St Sw Ste B Lakewood (98499) ***(G-5747)***

Premier Agendas Inc (HQ)....360 734-1153
400 Sequoia Dr Ste 200 Bellingham (98226) ***(G-1503)***

Premier Industries....253 514-0977
11126 Vipond Dr Nw Gig Harbor (98329) ***(G-4148)***

Premier Manufacturing Inc....509 927-9860
1711 N Madson St Liberty Lake (99019) ***(G-5854)***

Premier Memorial LLC (PA)....253 472-0369
2309 South Tacoma Way Tacoma (98409) ***(G-13477)***

Premier Packing Company, Spokane Valley *Also called Nut Factory Inc* ***(G-12815)***

Premier Sales Northwest Inc....206 763-9857
1505 S 356th St Ste 104 Federal Way (98003) ***(G-3773)***

Premier School Agendas, Bellingham *Also called Premier Agendas Inc* ***(G-1503)***

Premier Stainless Installers....253 370-0521
8719 178th Street Ct E Puyallup (98375) ***(G-8224)***

Premier Torque Converter....253 288-2233
12561 Se Green Valley Rd Auburn (98092) ***(G-535)***

Premier Woodworks LLC....509 591-0839
100 W Canal Dr Kennewick (99336) ***(G-4707)***

Premiere Software....206 399-7495
12549 28th Ave Ne Seattle (98125) ***(G-10855)***

Premium Custom Cnstr LLC....503 515-4119
915 Ne 36th Ave Camas (98607) ***(G-2276)***

Premium Sign Inc....253 267-0547
8203 South Tacoma Way Lakewood (98499) ***(G-5748)***

Premium World Food Corporation....206 267-8914
1672 Lake Youngs Way Se Renton (98058) ***(G-8885)***

Prentis Literary LLC....425 260-7753
25322 36th Pl S Kent (98032) ***(G-5080)***

Presidential....509 669-1230
3639 Ridgeview Blvd Wenatchee (98801) ***(G-15066)***

Press....509 869-2242
909 S Grand Blvd Spokane (99202) ***(G-12453)***

Press....206 290-7392
7342 10th Ave Nw Seattle (98117) ***(G-10856)***

Pressco Products, Kent *Also called Precision Spring Stamping Corp* ***(G-5078)***

Pressed In Time Prtg Prmtons L....253 833-1351
1356 32nd Pl Ne Auburn (98002) ***(G-536)***

Pressworks....509 462-7627
2717 N Perry St Spokane (99207) ***(G-12454)***

Prestige Copy and Print (PA)....206 365-5770
11023 8th Ave Ne Seattle (98125) ***(G-10857)***

Prestige Fine Jewelry....206 623-0085
3601 Mohawk Dr Mount Vernon (98273) ***(G-6825)***

Prestine Environmental, Lynnwood *Also called Rebec LLC* ***(G-6187)***

Preston Woodcraft LLC....425 749-8074
23514 Se 137th St Issaquah (98027) ***(G-4460)***

Prestyl USA LLC....509 703-7661
9711 E Knox Ave Ste 2 Spokane Valley (99206) ***(G-12838)***

Prevencio Inc....425 576-1200
11335 Ne 122nd Way # 105 Kirkland (98034) ***(G-5441)***

Prewitt Hardwood Floors Inc....360 666-9663
14607 Ne 170th St Brush Prairie (98606) ***(G-2039)***

Price & Visser Millwork Inc....360 734-7700
2536 Valencia St Bellingham (98226) ***(G-1504)***

Price Container and Packg Corp....360 266-5598
153 Sturdevant Rd Chehalis (98532) ***(G-2526)***

Price Jensen Surveys Inc....425 747-4143
16645 Se 16th St Bellevue (98008) ***(G-1081)***

Pricemedia Inc....206 418-0747
10002 Aurora Ave N Ste 36 Seattle (98133) ***(G-10858)***

Pride of The West Inc....360 694-4976
1610 Markle Ave Vancouver (98660) ***(G-14504)***

Pries Logging....360 985-0044
561 Burnt Ridge Rd Onalaska (98570) ***(G-7453)***

Primal Screens LLC....206 784-5266
6309 24th Ave Nw Seattle (98107) ***(G-10859)***

Prime Biodiesel....360 969-3966
16821 Smokey P Arlington (98223) ***(G-307)***

Prime Pallets and Recycling....360 410-0238
9409 Delta Line Rd Blaine (98230) ***(G-1697)***

Prime West Beef Co Inc....360 306-1831
7060 Portal Way Ste 140 Ferndale (98248) ***(G-3891)***

Prime West of Washington Inc....360 424-5783
1819 Central Ave S Ste 80 Kent (98032) ***(G-5081)***

Primeone Products LLC....509 448-8818
6310 S Madelia St Spokane (99223) ***(G-12455)***

Primer Specialties Inc....360 518-3716
630 Ne 127th Ave Vancouver (98684) ***(G-14505)***

Primus Bumstead Manufacturing....425 688-0444
4502 B St Nw Algona (98001) ***(G-74)***

Primus International....425 424-1085
17703 15th Ave Se Bothell (98012) ***(G-1889)***

Primus International Inc (HQ)....425 688-0444
610 Bllvue Way Ne Ste 200 Auburn (98001) ***(G-537)***

Primus International Inc....253 854-2995
701 Milwaukee Ave N Algona (98001) ***(G-75)***

Primus International Inc....425 318-4500
6525 240th St Se A Woodinville (98072) ***(G-15340)***

Primus International Inc....253 876-1500
701 Milwaukee Ave N Algona (98001) ***(G-76)***

Pringles Power-Vac Inc....509 375-0500
2395 Robertson Dr Richland (99354) ***(G-9036)***

Prins Robert P....360 293-3101
1213 24th St Anacortes (98221) ***(G-162)***

Prins Williams Analytics LLC....253 549-0740
363 North Shore Blvd Fox Island (98333) ***(G-4024)***

Print & Copy Factory LLC....360 738-4931
4025 Irongate Rd Bellingham (98226) ***(G-1505)***

Print & Play Productions....503 750-5316
1417 Ne 76th St Ste G19 Vancouver (98665) ***(G-14506)***

Print Center LLC....509 979-8272
11808 E Mnsfeld Ave Ste 2 Spokane Valley (99206) ***(G-12839)***

Print Concierge....206 801-9996
7241 185th Ave Ne Redmond (98073) ***(G-8631)***

Print Easy....800 562-0888
158 Channel Heights Way Friday Harbor (98250) ***(G-4053)***

Print Guys....509 453-6369
101 N 3rd St Yakima (98901) ***(G-15653)***

Print Guys Inc (PA)....509 453-6369
2802 W Nob Hill Blvd # 2 Yakima (98902) ***(G-15654)***

Print House Inc....425 742-1434
3101 111th St Sw Ste A Everett (98204) ***(G-3585)***

Print It Northwest....360 840-0807
7632 Valley View Rd Sedro Woolley (98284) ***(G-11557)***

Print Mart, Renton *Also called Pk Graphics Inc* ***(G-8881)***

Print N Surf....360 693-1710
5702 Ne 42nd Ave Vancouver (98661) ***(G-14507)***

Print NW LLC....253 284-2300
9914 32nd Ave S Tacoma (98499) ***(G-13478)***

Print Place....206 878-1380
22207 7th Ave S Ste 2 Des Moines (98198) ***(G-2943)***

Print Place, The, Des Moines *Also called Print Place* ***(G-2943)***

Print Plus Inc....509 735-6303
2514 W Kennewick Ave Kennewick (99336) ***(G-4708)***

Print Plus Inc (PA)....509 735-6303
2514 W Kennewick Ave Kennewick (99336) ***(G-4709)***

Print Pro....360 807-8716
3802 Galvin Rd Centralia (98531) ***(G-2426)***

Print Rogue LLC....360 791-0914
1280 Partridge Dr Nw Olympia (98502) ***(G-7372)***

Print Services Northwest Inc....206 763-9230
5616 4th Ave S Seattle (98108) ***(G-10860)***

Print Services Northwest Inc....253 236-8224
4040 Auburn Way N Ste 3 Auburn (98002) ***(G-538)***

Print Shop The, Centralia *Also called Paradyce Industries Inc* ***(G-2423)***

Print Solutions....253 435-1928
10213 139th Street Ct E B2 Puyallup (98374) ***(G-8225)***

Print Solutions and Consulting....206 726-8053
466 Smith St Seattle (98109) ***(G-10861)***

Print Stop Inc....360 354-5100
514 Front St Lynden (98264) ***(G-6047)***

Print Streams, Mount Vernon *Also called Printwise Inc* ***(G-6826)***

Print Tech Inc....509 535-1460
16508 E Sprague Ave Spokane Valley (99037) ***(G-12840)***

Print Time Inc....206 682-1000
1932 9th Ave Seattle (98101) ***(G-10862)***

Print Wearhouse, The, Kennewick *Also called Cory A Stemp* ***(G-4650)***

Print Works Inc....206 623-3512
711 9th Ave N Seattle (98109) ***(G-10863)***

Print24com USA LP....206 607-0639
800 5th Ave Seattle (98104) ***(G-10864)***

Printco, Auburn *Also called Hill Print Inc* ***(G-467)***

Printcom Inc....206 763-7600
1000 Sw 149th St Burien (98166) ***(G-2121)***

Printcore, Woodinville *Also called Stone Drums Inc* ***(G-15376)***

ALPHABETIC

Printed Circuits Assembly — 425 641-7455
13205 Se 30th St Bellevue (98005) *(G-1082)*

Printed Circuits Assembly (PA) — 425 644-7754
13221 Se 26th St Ste E Bellevue (98005) *(G-1083)*

Printers Bloc — 253 576-6043
9814 Wildwood Ave Sw Lakewood (98498) *(G-5749)*

Printers Shopper LLC — 425 822-7766
12832 Ne 70th Pl Kirkland (98033) *(G-5442)*

Printgraphics Inc — 503 641-8811
3104 Se 174th Ave Vancouver (98683) *(G-14508)*

Printing and Graphics Dept, Tacoma Also called Tacoma Public Schools *(G-13547)*

Printing Conexions — 206 383-4516
7237 Vandermark Rd E Bonney Lake (98391) *(G-1735)*

Printing Control Graphics, Kent Also called Printing Control Services Inc *(G-5082)*

Printing Control Services Inc — 206 575-4114
23328 66th Ave S Kent (98032) *(G-5082)*

Printing Dept, Seattle Also called County of King *(G-9748)*

Printing Expressly For You, Vancouver Also called William Willis *(G-14695)*

Printing For You, Bellingham Also called Four U Printers Inc *(G-1352)*

Printing Hope — 253 358-3348
4918 38th Ave Nw Gig Harbor (98335) *(G-4149)*

Printing Ngo LLC — 206 569-8388
18008 Bothell Everett Hwy E Bothell (98012) *(G-1890)*

Printing Perfection — 509 843-7455
836 W Main St Pomeroy (99347) *(G-7676)*

Printing Plus, Yakima Also called Instant Press Inc *(G-15592)*

Printing Plus, Mountlake Terrace Also called Maxart Inc *(G-6864)*

Printing Services Inc — 253 858-5350
3480 Bethel Rd Se Ste A Port Orchard (98366) *(G-7842)*

Printing Specialties Press — 509 687-9362
4560 Navarre Coulee Rd Chelan (98816) *(G-2562)*

Printing Unlimited — 360 357-8936
2232 63rd Ct Sw Olympia (98512) *(G-7373)*

Printing Washington State Dept — 360 407-6013
300 Desmond Dr Se Lacey (98503) *(G-5578)*

Printonyx Inc — 360 378-2069
470 Reed St Friday Harbor (98250) *(G-4054)*

Printwise Inc — 360 424-5945
2226 Market St Unit Main Mount Vernon (98273) *(G-6826)*

Printworks, Yakima Also called Jones Digital Printing Inc *(G-15602)*

Prism Designs Inc — 206 838-8682
4214 24th Ave W Seattle (98199) *(G-10865)*

Prism Energy, Seattle Also called Prism Motors Inc *(G-10867)*

Prism Graphics Inc — 206 282-1801
7609 5th Ave S Seattle (98108) *(G-10866)*

Prism Kite Technology, Seattle Also called Prism Designs Inc *(G-10865)*

Prism Motors Inc — 425 503-5415
703 Ne Northlake Way Seattle (98105) *(G-10867)*

Prismoid Optical Laboratory — 360 417-1244
216 E 5th St Ste A Port Angeles (98362) *(G-7738)*

Pritchard Woodworks LLC — 206 755-4503
37120 Madrona Blvd Ne Hansville (98340) *(G-4318)*

Privateer Press Inc — 425 643-5900
1705 136th Pl Ne Ste 220 Bellevue (98005) *(G-1084)*

Pro Abrasives Inc — 360 509-4152
1776 3rd Ave W Bremerton (98312) *(G-1990)*

Pro ARC Industries Inc — 916 215-7269
23403 Ne 210th St Battle Ground (98604) *(G-732)*

Pro Clip Products Inc — 509 924-5544
3517 S Fox St Spokane Valley (99206) *(G-12841)*

Pro Controls Inc — 509 457-3386
1312 Gordon Rd Yakima (98901) *(G-15655)*

Pro Fab — 509 879-9293
7505 E Sprague Ave Spokane Valley (99212) *(G-12842)*

Pro Fab Inc — 206 762-5149
211 S Austin St Seattle (98108) *(G-10868)*

Pro Fab Industries Inc — 360 629-4642
8130 311th St Nw Stanwood (98292) *(G-12986)*

Pro Finish Autobody & Auto Sls, Kent Also called Pro Finish Inc *(G-5083)*

Pro Finish Inc — 253 850-9422
1506 Central Ave S Kent (98032) *(G-5083)*

Pro Safety Inc — 360 686-3686
23400 Ne Jehnsen Rd Yacolt (98675) *(G-15492)*

Pro Sales Incorporated (PA) — 253 852-6046
917 Valley Ave Nw Ste C Puyallup (98371) *(G-8226)*

Pro Staff Electric — 360 859-3749
6109 E 18th St Vancouver (98661) *(G-14509)*

Pro Tech Industries Inc (PA) — 360 573-6641
14113 Ne 3rd Ct Vancouver (98685) *(G-14510)*

Pro Tint LLC — 509 468-8468
13409 W Shore Rd Nine Mile Falls (99026) *(G-7082)*

Pro West Mechanical Inc — 509 965-1750
31 Industrial Park Rd Wapato (98951) *(G-14924)*

Pro Wheel Racing Components — 360 691-6459
3729 Menzel Lake Rd Granite Falls (98252) *(G-4283)*

Pro-AM, Bellevue Also called Gekko Corporation *(G-922)*

Pro-Grit Products, Bremerton Also called Pro Abrasives Inc *(G-1990)*

Pro-Litho Inc — 206 547-6462
4411 Wallingford Ave N C Seattle (98103) *(G-10869)*

Pro-TEC Athletics, Redmond Also called Maverick Sports Medicine Inc *(G-8553)*

Probare Industries LLC — 206 334-9840
927 132nd St Sw Apt C4 Everett (98204) *(G-3586)*

Probi Usa Inc (HQ) — 425 883-9518
9609 153rd Ave Ne Redmond (98052) *(G-8632)*

Procedure Products Inc — 360 693-1832
1801 W Fourth Plain Blvd Vancouver (98660) *(G-14511)*

Procedure Products Corp (PA) — 360 693-1832
1801 W Fourth Plain Blvd Vancouver (98660) *(G-14512)*

Process Inc — 425 401-2000
15600 Ne 8th St Bellevue (98008) *(G-1085)*

Process Cntrls Instrumentation — 360 573-4985
21211 Ne 72nd Ave Battle Ground (98604) *(G-733)*

Process Heating Company — 206 682-3414
2732 3rd Ave S Seattle (98134) *(G-10870)*

Process Media Inc — 323 666-3377
1240 W Sims Way Port Townsend (98368) *(G-7919)*

Process Solutions Inc — 360 629-0910
7112 265th St Nw Stanwood (98292) *(G-12987)*

Processing Plant, Chehalis Also called National Frozen Foods Corp *(G-2516)*

Procoat LLC — 425 252-0070
16537 25th Ave Ne Shoreline (98155) *(G-11803)*

Procon Min & Tunnelling US Ltd — 360 685-4253
1313 E Maple St Ste 237 Bellingham (98225) *(G-1506)*

Procter & Gamble Company — 425 313-3511
1180 Nw Maple St Issaquah (98027) *(G-4461)*

Proctor & Associates, Redmond Also called Proctor International LLC *(G-8633)*

Proctor Farm Animal Removal — 360 856-1995
5509 Brookings Rd Sedro Woolley (98284) *(G-11558)*

Proctor International LLC (PA) — 425 881-7000
15305 Ne 95th St Redmond (98052) *(G-8633)*

Proctor Products Co Inc — 425 398-8800
15323 Woodinville Redm Woodinville (98072) *(G-15341)*

Prodeco LLC — 425 827-2573
12832 Ne 70th Pl Kirkland (98033) *(G-5443)*

Production Plating Inc — 425 347-4635
4412 Russell Rd Mukilteo (98275) *(G-6968)*

Professional Business Svc Inc — 360 352-3000
704 Franklin St Se Olympia (98501) *(G-7374)*

Professional Copy 'n' Print, Seattle Also called Quality Copy and Print LLC *(G-10901)*

Professional Crane Inspections, Liberty Lake Also called Mk20 Inc *(G-5847)*

Professional Crane Inspections — 509 226-5302
24810 E Wellesley Ave Otis Orchards (99027) *(G-7516)*

Professional Designed Sewing — 206 234-5955
9051 18th Ave Sw Seattle (98106) *(G-10871)*

Professional Hardwood Floors — 425 741-1017
4205 141st St Se Mill Creek (98012) *(G-6521)*

Professional Mentors & Pro — 832 216-9134
1202 Lincoln St Colton (99113) *(G-2733)*

Professional Mktg Group — 206 322-7303
11416 Rainier Ave S # 18 Seattle (98178) *(G-10872)*

Professional Network Solutions — 509 308-0318
905 S Sharron St Kennewick (99336) *(G-4710)*

Professional Plastics Inc — 425 251-4140
6233 Segale Park Drive D Tukwila (98188) *(G-13795)*

Professional Plastics Inc — 714 446-6500
6412 S 196th St Kent (98032) *(G-5084)*

Professional Plastics Inc — 253 872-7430
6233 Segale Park Drive D Tukwila (98188) *(G-13796)*

Professional Plastics Inc — 253 872-7430
6233 Segale Park Drive D Tukwila (98188) *(G-13797)*

Professional Practice Systems — 253 531-8944
29622 48th Ave S Roy (98580) *(G-9164)*

Professional Sales & Serv — 509 678-4535
250 Thompson Rd Yakima (98908) *(G-15656)*

Professional Sleep Services — 253 759-2700
1818 S Union Ave Ste 2b Tacoma (98405) *(G-13479)*

Professnl Mntrs & Pro Life Skl — 832 216-9134
1202 Lincoln St Colton (99113) *(G-2734)*

Profile Systems Inc — 206 624-7715
5300 4th Ave S Seattle (98108) *(G-10873)*

Profiler Inc — 360 668-3291
17414 Interurban Blvd Snohomish (98296) *(G-11962)*

Proflections Metal Finishing, Auburn Also called Proflections Metal Polishing *(G-539)*

Proflections Metal Polishing — 253 735-6111
131 30th St Ne Ste 20a Auburn (98002) *(G-539)*

Proforma Crtive Prtg Solutions — 360 848-7714
2119 N Trumpeter Dr Mount Vernon (98273) *(G-6827)*

Progenica Therapeutics LLC — 253 347-7018
16016 Se 249th Pl Covington (98042) *(G-2836)*

Progenica Therapeutics LLC — 253 347-7018
16016 Se 249th Pl Covington (98042) *(G-2837)*

Progourmet Foods LLC — 360 769-7420
3643 Beach Dr E Port Orchard (98366) *(G-7843)*

Prographyx — 360 636-1595
735 Commerce Ave Longview (98632) *(G-5945)*

Progressive International Corp (HQ) — 253 850-6111
20435 72nd Ave S Ste 400 Kent (98032) *(G-5085)*

Progressive Machine Inc — 509 547-4062
318 E B Cir Pasco (99301) *(G-7619)*

Progressive Printing Solutions — 425 867-1296
700 Nw Gilman Blvd Ste E Issaquah (98027) *(G-4462)*

Project Machine Inc — 360 446-2858
13424 State Route 507 Rainier (98576) *(G-8320)*

Project Seezit Inc 415 336-4000
4111 E Madison St Seattle (98112) *(G-10874)*
Projul Inc (PA) 844 776-5853
27924 Se 268th St Ravensdale (98051) *(G-8339)*
Prolam Industries Inc 509 926-2001
3808 N Sullivan Rd 29c Spokane Valley (99216) *(G-12843)*
Proliance International 206 764-7028
7951 2nd Ave S Seattle (98108) *(G-10875)*
Proline, Lynnwood *Also called Connelly Skis Inc (G-6098)*
Proline Printer Services 360 697-2336
2049 Ptarmigan Ln Nw Poulsbo (98370) *(G-7992)*
Prologic Engineering Inc 360 734-9625
4041 Bakerview Spur Ste 3 Bellingham (98226) *(G-1507)*
Prologix Instruments, Redmond *Also called Prologix LLC (G-8634)*
Prologix LLC 425 829-8199
16541 Redmond Way 421c Redmond (98052) *(G-8634)*
Promedev LLC 800 500-8384
11335 Ne 122nd Way # 140 Kirkland (98034) *(G-5444)*
Promenade Publishing Inc 800 342-6947
16210 12th Ave Sw Burien (98166) *(G-2122)*
Prometco Inc 425 486-0759
2201 192nd St Se Apt Y102 Bothell (98012) *(G-1891)*
Prometheus Energy Company 425 558-9100
8511 154th Ave Ne Bldg L Redmond (98052) *(G-8635)*
Prometheus Energy Group Inc 425 558-9100
8511 154th Ave Ne Bldg 1 Redmond (98052) *(G-8636)*
Prompt Printery 509 457-5848
313 S 4th Ave Yakima (98902) *(G-15657)*
Propdocket LLC 330 285-6526
3820 219th Pl Se Bothell (98021) *(G-1892)*
Propeller Arprts Pine Feld LLC 425 216-3010
9724 32nd Dr W 2 Everett (98204) *(G-3587)*
Propulsion Controls Engrg 425 257-9065
920 W Marine View Dr Everett (98201) *(G-3588)*
Prorestore Products 412 264-8340
15180 Josh Wilson Rd Burlington (98233) *(G-2182)*
Proshoppers NW 206 852-1127
17604 41st Ave S Seatac (98188) *(G-9300)*
Prospectors Plus LLC 425 750-9290
1311 Skywall Dr Sultan (98294) *(G-13033)*
Prosser Grandview-Publishers 509 786-1711
613 7th St Prosser (99350) *(G-8063)*
Prosser Record Bulletin, Prosser *Also called Prosser Grandview-Publishers (G-8063)*
Prosthetic & Orthotic Services, Walla Walla *Also called Jeffrey A Johnson (G-14828)*
Prosthetic & Orthotic Services, Kennewick *Also called Columbia Basin Prosthetic (G-4646)*
Prosthtic Specialists Wash LLC 425 576-5050
1111417 124th Ave Ne 10 Kirkland (98033) *(G-5445)*
Protac Inc 509 962-5001
110 W 6th Ave Ellensburg (98926) *(G-3221)*
Protech Composites 360 573-7800
11700 Ne 60th Way Ste 3b Vancouver (98682) *(G-14513)*
Protect-A-Board, Tacoma *Also called Caraustar Industries Inc (G-13223)*
Protect-A-Cover Inc 425 408-1072
8112 Ne 145th Pl Kenmore (98028) *(G-4600)*
Protective Coating Consultants 206 762-6119
1501 S 92nd Pl Ste A Seattle (98108) *(G-10876)*
Protek-USA LLC 206 782-8399
3927 1st Ave Ne Apt 31 Seattle (98105) *(G-10877)*
Protium Innovations LLC 206 854-8792
425 Se Dexter St Pullman (99163) *(G-8102)*
Proto Manufacturing Inc 509 535-9683
5959 N Freya St Spokane (99217) *(G-12456)*
Proto Technologies Inc 509 891-4747
22808 E Appleway Ave A Liberty Lake (99019) *(G-5855)*
Proto-Design Inc 425 558-0600
17824 Ne 65th St Redmond (98052) *(G-8637)*
Proto-Rpid McHning Sltions LLC 503 744-0358
3010 Se Menlo Dr Apt 20 Vancouver (98683) *(G-14514)*
Prototek Corp 360 779-1310
19044b Jensen Way Ne Poulsbo (98370) *(G-7993)*
Provail 206 363-7303
21019 66th Ave S Kent (98032) *(G-5086)*
Provident Electric Inc 509 588-3939
64406 N Sr 225 Benton City (99320) *(G-1624)*
Provoke Solutions Inc 206 792-3680
2010 156th Ave Ne Ste 301 Bellevue (98007) *(G-1086)*
Proweld Fabrication LLC 425 835-6477
7609 Mcbeth Ln Ne Moses Lake (98837) *(G-6739)*
Prowse Manufacturing Group 360 403-8910
17617 49th Dr Ne Ste D Arlington (98223) *(G-308)*
Proxygroove LLC 415 264-1906
517 30th Ave E Seattle (98112) *(G-10878)*
Prp Finishing 509 966-0798
401 S 51st Ave Yakima (98908) *(G-15658)*
Prs Group Inc 206 255-7509
3003 Taylor Way Tacoma (98421) *(G-13480)*
Prudent Products Inc 360 445-2556
883 Nw 2nd Ave Oak Harbor (98277) *(G-7162)*
Prune Hill Software LLC 360 834-3067
1013 Nw 36th Ct Camas (98607) *(G-2277)*
Pryde Johnson 1536 LLC 206 352-7000
419 Ne 70th St Seattle (98115) *(G-10879)*
Pryor Giggey Co 360 647-6021
4206 Padden Hills Ct Bellingham (98229) *(G-1508)*
Pryor Giggey, The, Chehalis *Also called Allied Mineral Products Inc (G-2461)*
PS Colors Inc 206 371-1341
7006 42nd Ave S Seattle (98118) *(G-10880)*
Ps2 Group LLC 206 714-3025
18689 Ne 55th St Redmond (98052) *(G-8638)*
Psf Industries Inc (PA) 800 426-1204
65 S Horton St Seattle (98134) *(G-10881)*
PSI Electronics LLC 253 922-7890
5007 Pacific Hwy E Ste 5 Fife (98424) *(G-3984)*
PSI Logistics Intl LLC 855 473-5877
9 S Washington St Ste 301 Spokane (99201) *(G-12457)*
PSI Scientific, Seattle *Also called Peptide Scientific USA Ltd (G-10784)*
PSM Hydraulics 360 282-4998
21307 87th Ave Se Woodinville (98072) *(G-15342)*
PSM LLC 425 486-1232
21307 87th Ave Se Woodinville (98072) *(G-15343)*
PSR, Seattle *Also called Puget Sound Repair Inc (G-10885)*
Pss Rubber Stamp, Kennewick *Also called Print Plus Inc (G-4708)*
Pt Defiance Food Mart 253 761-5084
4601 N Pearl St Tacoma (98407) *(G-13481)*
Pt Shirt 360 385-1911
940 Water St Port Townsend (98368) *(G-7920)*
Ptc Inc 425 455-1930
10900 Ne 8th St Ste 605 Bellevue (98004) *(G-1087)*
Pti, Redmond *Also called Pacific Tool Inc (G-8609)*
Ptsw, Port Townsend *Also called Port Townsend School of Woodwo (G-7915)*
Publications Services, Seattle *Also called University of Washington (G-11382)*
Puddles Barkery LLC 206 495-3072
146 N Canal St Ste 350 Seattle (98103) *(G-10882)*
Puffin Glass 509 328-0661
3904 N Division St Spokane (99207) *(G-12458)*
Puget Bindery Inc 206 621-8898
7820 S 228th St Kent (98032) *(G-5087)*
Puget Bridge Supply (PA) 206 367-3629
2333 N 179th St Shoreline (98133) *(G-11804)*
Puget Lite-Pavers Inc 206 849-7091
309 S Cloverdale St C8 Seattle (98108) *(G-10883)*
Puget Logging & Excavation 360 629-0461
28921 64th Ave Nw Stanwood (98292) *(G-12988)*
Puget Sound Anglers Educ 206 473-1613
18609 182nd Ave Ne Woodinville (98077) *(G-15344)*
Puget Sound Breathalyzers 425 359-9515
3402 65th Dr Ne Marysville (98270) *(G-6372)*
Puget Sound Business Journal, Seattle *Also called Seattle Business Journal Inc (G-11049)*
Puget Sound Canvas Uphols 206 782-5974
17030 418th Ave Se Gold Bar (98251) *(G-4190)*
Puget Sound Commerce Ctr Inc (HQ) 206 623-1635
1801 16th Ave Sw Seattle (98134) *(G-10884)*
Puget Sound Cutting, Kent *Also called Norwood-Wang Inc (G-5037)*
Puget Sound Dumpster Services, Kent *Also called Issak Shamso (G-4962)*
Puget Sound Foods Inc 206 232-2757
8245 Se 59th St Mercer Island (98040) *(G-6481)*
Puget Sound Innovations Inc 206 575-7500
838 Industry Dr Tukwila (98188) *(G-13798)*
Puget Sound Instrument, Fife *Also called PSI Electronics LLC (G-3984)*
Puget Sound Logging 253 310-5923
16516 Littlerock Rd Sw Rochester (98579) *(G-9139)*
Puget Sound Metal Fabrication 253 941-7868
3825 S 312th St Auburn (98001) *(G-540)*
Puget Sound Pattern Inc 206 439-6810
6406 S 143rd St Tukwila (98168) *(G-13799)*
Puget Sound Pattern Works, Tukwila *Also called Puget Sound Pattern Inc (G-13799)*
Puget Sound Pipe and Supply Co 509 783-0474
5950 W Brinkley Rd Kennewick (99338) *(G-4711)*
Puget Sound Pre-Cast, Tacoma *Also called Automatic Wilbert Vault Co Inc (G-13187)*
Puget Sound Precision Inc 360 297-3939
6113 Ne Minder Rd Poulsbo (98370) *(G-7994)*
Puget Sound Qulty Coatings LLC 253 861-8871
6307 7th Street Ct E Fife (98424) *(G-3985)*
Puget Sound Recycling 253 536-2260
222 107th St S Tacoma (98444) *(G-13482)*
Puget Sound Repair Inc 506 556-9722
7410 5th Ave S Seattle (98108) *(G-10885)*
Puget Sound Rope, Anacortes *Also called Cortland Company Inc (G-118)*
Puget Sound Safety 253 770-8888
10720 Woodland Ave E Puyallup (98373) *(G-8227)*
Puget Sound Sand and Grav LLC 360 332-3333
8549 Loomis Trail Ln Blaine (98230) *(G-1698)*
Puget Sound Steel Co Inc 253 854-3600
906 3rd Ave S Kent (98032) *(G-5088)*
Puget Sound Surfacers Inc 360 374-9590
1680 S Forks Ave Forks (98331) *(G-4016)*
Puget Sound Tent & Awning 425 251-9786
18375 Olympic Ave S Tukwila (98188) *(G-13800)*
Puget Sound Welding, Lacey *Also called Integral Fabrications LLC (G-5560)*
Puget Sound Wood Windows LLC 425 828-9736
603 Market St Kirkland (98033) *(G-5446)*

ALPHABETIC

Puget Sound Woodworking LLC — 360 563-0116
112 Long St Snohomish (98290) *(G-11963)*

Puget Sound Workshop LLC — 425 821-7345
14207 100th Ave Ne Kirkland (98034) *(G-5447)*

Puglia Engineering Inc — 360 647-0080
201 Harris Ave Bellingham (98225) *(G-1509)*

Pulley Boys, Lakewood Also called Atkins Machines LLC *(G-5700)*

Pulp Mill, Cosmopolis Also called Weyerhaeuser Company *(G-2802)*

Pulpo Games LLC — 206 371-6924
4412 2nd Ave Ne Seattle (98105) *(G-10886)*

Pulsair Systems Inc — 425 455-1263
13643 Ne 126th Pl Kirkland (98034) *(G-5448)*

Pulse Electronics Inc — 360 944-7551
18110 Se 34th St Bldg 2 Vancouver (98683) *(G-14515)*

Pulse Power Solutions LLC — 206 369-8277
18333 Bothell Way Ne # 510 Bothell (98011) *(G-1785)*

Pulse Publications Inc — 360 671-3933
2423 E Bakerview Rd Bellingham (98226) *(G-1510)*

Pulsed Power Solutions, Bothell Also called Pulse Power Solutions LLC *(G-1785)*

Pumptech, Bellevue Also called Mosesvue LLC *(G-1016)*

Punjab Signs & Printing — 425 501-3336
22307 122nd Ave Se Kent (98031) *(G-5089)*

Puppy Lunch Press — 360 651-9957
10311 110th St Ne Arlington (98223) *(G-309)*

Puppy Stairs — 360 387-4861
355 Melissa St Camano Island (98282) *(G-2222)*

Purcell Systems Inc (HQ) — 509 755-0341
16125 E Euclid Ave Spokane Valley (99216) *(G-12844)*

Pure Blue Tech Inc — 206 724-5707
1200 12th Ave S Ste 1110 Seattle (98144) *(G-10887)*

Pure Drop — 425 351-9007
1515 Sw Roxbury St Seattle (98106) *(G-10888)*

Pure Extracts — 509 679-6556
5526 Industry Ln Ste 1 East Wenatchee (98802) *(G-3030)*

Pure Fire Independent LLC — 206 218-3297
310 1st Ave S Seattle (98104) *(G-10889)*

Pure Health Products LLC — 360 688-7034
8450 30th Ave Ne Lacey (98516) *(G-5579)*

Pure Lite Candle Portland I — 360 909-9499
4115 Nw 118th Cir Vancouver (98685) *(G-14516)*

Pure Safety Group Inc — 253 854-5877
6305 S 231st St Kent (98032) *(G-5090)*

Pure Watercraft — 206 451-0350
2151 N Northlake Way # 210 Seattle (98103) *(G-10890)*

Pureblisnaturals — 253 719-2683
5706 95th Avenue Ct W University Place (98467) *(G-13977)*

Pureheart — 509 535-2323
3704 E 5th Ave Spokane (99202) *(G-12459)*

Purely Tangible — 206 301-9999
2827 14th Ave W Apt 1 Seattle (98119) *(G-10891)*

Purina Animal Nutrition LLC — 425 653-4238
13231 Se 36th St Ste 130 Bellevue (98006) *(G-1088)*

Purina Mills LLC — 509 534-0594
4714 E Trent Ave Spokane (99212) *(G-12460)*

Purple Coyote Inc — 509 754-2488
16 Basin St Sw Ephrata (98823) *(G-3345)*

Purple Star Winery — 509 628-7799
56504 N East Roza Rd Benton City (99320) *(G-1625)*

Purpletrail — 425 292-1811
1495 11th Ave Nw Issaquah (98027) *(G-4463)*

Purposeful Software LLC — 206 855-7927
8150 Hansen Rd Ne Bainbridge Island (98110) *(G-661)*

Purrfect Logos Inc — 509 893-2424
12018 E 1st Ave Spokane Valley (99206) *(G-12845)*

Pursley Logging Co Inc — 360 274-7297
2300 Hazel Dell Rd Castle Rock (98611) *(G-2350)*

Pursuit Distilling Co — 206 406-2263
2321 Cole St Ste 102 Enumclaw (98022) *(G-3312)*

Pushspring Inc — 206 455-6128
712 N 34th St Ste 201 Seattle (98103) *(G-10892)*

Puyallup Casket Company Inc — 253 845-1883
11725 Valley Ave E Puyallup (98372) *(G-8228)*

Puyallup Septic Pumping — 253 785-6553
1214 6th Ave Sw Puyallup (98371) *(G-8229)*

Puzzle Piece Arts — 360 678-3687
3076 Celestial Way Greenbank (98253) *(G-4309)*

Puzzle Pieces Bookkeeping — 360 217-7140
20379 Corbridge Rd Se Monroe (98272) *(G-6609)*

Puzzle Wise, Bellingham Also called Test Best International Inc *(G-1567)*

Pvc Debonding Systems Inc — 866 961-8349
3102 E Trent Ave Ste 208 Spokane (99202) *(G-12461)*

Pw Metal Recovery LLC — 253 537-6301
3522 112th St E Tacoma (98446) *(G-13483)*

Pygmy Boats Inc — 360 385-6143
355 Hudson St Port Townsend (98368) *(G-7921)*

Pygmy Kayak, Port Townsend Also called Pygmy Boats Inc *(G-7921)*

Pyramid Breweries Inc (HQ) — 206 682-8322
91 S Royal Brougham Way Seattle (98134) *(G-10893)*

Pyramid Breweries Inc — 206 682-3377
1201 1st Ave S Seattle (98134) *(G-10894)*

Pyramid Grinding — 425 254-1820
5851 Ne 4th St Renton (98059) *(G-8886)*

Pyramid Materials Kitsap Quar — 360 373-8708
818 Archie Ave W Bremerton (98312) *(G-1991)*

Pyramis Aerospace LLC — 206 407-3406
402 S 333rd St Ste 128 Federal Way (98003) *(G-3774)*

Pyrocom Co, Lynnwood Also called Eustis Co Inc *(G-6115)*

Pyrotek Incorporated (PA) — 509 926-6212
705 W 1st Ave Spokane (99201) *(G-12462)*

Pyrotek Incorporated — 509 926-6211
9601 E Montgomery Ave Spokane Valley (99206) *(G-12846)*

Pyrotek Incorporated — 509 921-8766
3808 N Sullivan Rd 27k Spokane Valley (99216) *(G-12847)*

Pz Wind Down Inc — 206 805-6300
410 W Harrison St Ste 300 Seattle (98119) *(G-10895)*

Q A R Rendering Services Inc — 253 847-7220
23123 Meridian Ave E Graham (98338) *(G-4236)*

Q Otm — 360 802-3700
1713 Garrett St Ste 2 Enumclaw (98022) *(G-3313)*

Q Sea Specialty Services LLC — 360 398-9708
2875 Roeder Ave Ste 8 Bellingham (98225) *(G-1511)*

Qar Redering Service In, Graham Also called Q A R Rendering Services Inc *(G-4236)*

Qi-Infinity, Sammamish Also called Kaenaa Corp *(G-9225)*

Qivu Graphics, Woodinville Also called Nannette Louise Davis *(G-15317)*

QMS 1 Inc (PA) — 360 201-7505
5373 Guide Meridian E2 Bellingham (98226) *(G-1512)*

Qnc Machine Inc — 206 282-5854
3401 17th Ave W Seattle (98119) *(G-10896)*

Qorus Software Inc — 844 516-8000
500 Yale Ave N 100 Seattle (98109) *(G-10897)*

Qr Industries Inc — 360 435-2840
19109 63rd Ave Ne Ste 3 Arlington (98223) *(G-310)*

QSP Packers LLC — 253 770-0315
2316 Inter Ave Ste D Puyallup (98372) *(G-8230)*

Qss, Kennewick Also called Quality Sign Service Inc *(G-4712)*

Quad Group Inc — 509 458-4558
1815 S Lewis St Spokane (99224) *(G-12463)*

Quad Labs, Spokane Also called Quad Group Inc *(G-12463)*

Quadient Data USA Inc — 206 443-0765
1301 5th Ave Ste 1300 Seattle (98101) *(G-10898)*

Quadradyne Technologies LLC — 248 342-5977
14200 Ne 132nd Ave Brush Prairie (98606) *(G-2040)*

Quadrep Northwest Inc — 425 201-0420
19125 North Creek Pkwy Bothell (98011) *(G-1786)*

Quail Meadow Creations — 509 685-1429
615 Rocky Lake Rd Colville (99114) *(G-2770)*

Qual Fab Inc — 206 762-2117
1705 S 93rd St Ste F11 Seattle (98108) *(G-10899)*

Quali Cast Foundry — 360 748-6645
109 Sears Rd Chehalis (98532) *(G-2527)*

Qualident Dental Lab LLC — 360 695-7411
5305 E 18th St Ste 100 Vancouver (98661) *(G-14517)*

Qualitel Corporation — 425 423-8388
11831 Beverly Park Rd A Everett (98204) *(G-3589)*

Qualiteq, Liberty Lake Also called Hundred Horse Panels LLC *(G-5834)*

Quality Backhoe Services Inc — 509 545-0242
26905 Ice Harbor Dr Burbank (99323) *(G-2085)*

Quality Brewing Incorporated — 866 268-5953
159 Hale Barber Rd Kelso (98626) *(G-4543)*

Quality Cabinets Plus Inc — 360 423-1242
2411 Talley Way Kelso (98626) *(G-4544)*

Quality Code Publishing — 206 216-9500
8015 15th Ave Nw Seattle (98117) *(G-10900)*

Quality Concrete Products — 509 758-2655
3050 Wilma Dr Clarkston (99403) *(G-2642)*

Quality Concrete Products Inc — 425 355-5510
4200 78th St Sw Mukilteo (98275) *(G-6969)*

Quality Copy and Print LLC — 206 634-2689
4200 University Way Ne Seattle (98105) *(G-10901)*

Quality Counter — 425 303-9180
1625 E Marine View Dr Everett (98201) *(G-3590)*

Quality Creations — 253 732-4082
7414 202nd Street Ct E Spanaway (98387) *(G-12068)*

Quality Drapery Service — 509 878-1371
120 S Bridge St Palouse (99161) *(G-7547)*

Quality Electronic Assembly, Everett Also called Qualitel Corporation *(G-3589)*

Quality Equipment Supply Inc — 503 544-9779
4400 Ne 77th Ave Ste 275 Vancouver (98662) *(G-14518)*

Quality Fence Builders Inc — 253 939-8533
214 21st St Se Auburn (98002) *(G-541)*

Quality Fuel Trlr & Tank Inc — 425 526-7566
22117 161st Ave Se Monroe (98272) *(G-6610)*

Quality Heating & AC LLC — 360 613-5614
9960 Silverdale Way Nw # 14 Silverdale (98383) *(G-11854)*

Quality Instant Print — 360 274-0337
742 Carnine Rd Castle Rock (98611) *(G-2351)*

Quality Liquid Feeds Inc — 509 854-2311
100 Bailey Ave Granger (98932) *(G-4263)*

Quality Logging LLC — 360 640-1555
1212 Schaffran Rd Castle Rock (98611) *(G-2352)*

Quality Machine — 360 573-8773
13023 Ne Highway 99 Ste 7 Vancouver (98686) *(G-14519)*

Quality Machine & Hydraulic — 206 244-5674
19202 Des Moines Mem Dr S Seatac (98148) *(G-9301)*

Quality Machines, Spokane *Also called Jerry Carter* ***(G-12332)***
Quality Metal Spinning Co 206 242-6751
4031 S 168th St Seatac (98188) ***(G-9302)***
Quality On Time Machining Inc 360 802-3700
1713 Garrett St Ste 2 Enumclaw (98022) ***(G-3314)***
Quality Otbard Boring Sleeving, Mukilteo *Also called Sittauer Industries Inc* ***(G-6977)***
Quality Pallets 360 773-3973
310 Nw 41st St Vancouver (98660) ***(G-14520)***
Quality Polishing and Plating 425 432-5500
21010 196th Ave Se Renton (98058) ***(G-8887)***
Quality Press Inc 206 768-2655
222 S Orcas St Seattle (98108) ***(G-10902)***
Quality Sales Inc 360 694-3165
1304 Ne 154th St Ste 101 Vancouver (98685) ***(G-14521)***
Quality Sign Service Inc 509 586-0585
9312 W 10th Ave Kennewick (99336) ***(G-4712)***
Quality Stairs and Woodworking 425 358-4196
22833 Se 287th Pl Maple Valley (98038) ***(G-6291)***
Quality Used Tires and Wheels 253 446-6002
7602 River Rd E Puyallup (98371) ***(G-8231)***
Qualitylogic Inc 360 882-0201
16700 Ne 12th St Vancouver (98684) ***(G-14522)***
Qualls Stud Welding Pdts Inc (PA) 425 656-9787
7820 S 210th St Ste C103 Kent (98032) ***(G-5091)***
Qualnetics, Bellingham *Also called Road-Iq LLC* ***(G-1518)***
Quanex Building Products Corp 360 345-1241
3003 Sunset Way Se Tumwater (98501) ***(G-13892)***
Quanex Screens LLC 360 748-9201
137 Sears Rd Chehalis (98532) ***(G-2528)***
Quantum 509 751-6407
1524 Lydon Ct Clarkston (99403) ***(G-2643)***
Quantum Corporation 425 201-1400
110 110th Ave Ne Ste 200 Bellevue (98004) ***(G-1089)***
Quantum Development Group, Liberty Lake *Also called Quantum Northwest Inc* ***(G-5856)***
Quantum Northwest Inc 509 624-9290
22910 E Appleway Ave # 4 Liberty Lake (99019) ***(G-5856)***
Quantum Publishing Service 360 734-2906
312 Highland Dr Bellingham (98225) ***(G-1513)***
Quantum Sails 206 634-0636
6319 Seaview Ave Nw Seattle (98107) ***(G-10903)***
Quantum Solutions Inc 360 491-0757
9119 Classic Dr Ne Lacey (98516) ***(G-5580)***
Quantum Technology Corp 604 222-5539
250 H St Pmb 183 Blaine (98230) ***(G-1699)***
Quantum USA, Bellevue *Also called Quantum Corporation* ***(G-1089)***
Quantum Windows and Doors Inc 425 259-6650
2720 34th St Everett (98201) ***(G-3591)***
Quarry S/E Inc 206 525-5270
916 N 143rd St Seattle (98133) ***(G-10904)***
Quarry Tile Company 509 536-2812
6328 E Utah Ave Ste 1 Spokane Valley (99212) ***(G-12848)***
Quarto Pubg Group USA Inc 425 827-7120
11120 Ne 33rd Pl Ste 101 Bellevue (98004) ***(G-1090)***
Queen City Plating Company Inc 425 315-1992
11914 Cyrus Way Mukilteo (98275) ***(G-6970)***
Queen City Shtmtl & Roofg Inc 206 623-6020
22030 84th Ave S Kent (98032) ***(G-5092)***
Queensryche Publishing, Seattle *Also called Tri-Ryche Corporation* ***(G-11332)***
Quest Integrity Group, Kent *Also called Quest Integrity Usa LLC* ***(G-5093)***
Quest Integrity Usa LLC (HQ) 253 893-7070
19823 58th Pl S Ste 100 Kent (98032) ***(G-5093)***
Quest Products LLC 425 451-9876
19017 62nd Ave S Kent (98032) ***(G-5094)***
Quest Software Inc 949 720-1434
1400 Taylor Ave N Apt 302 Seattle (98109) ***(G-10905)***
Questech Unlimited 360 691-2620
509 E Stanley St Granite Falls (98252) ***(G-4284)***
Question Pro.com, Seattle *Also called Survey Analytics LLC* ***(G-11227)***
Quick Collect Inc 360 256-7888
5500 Ne 107th Ave Vancouver (98662) ***(G-14523)***
Quick Cut Inc 360 893-0689
416 Kensington Ave Nw Orting (98360) ***(G-7486)***
Quick Lok, Yakima *Also called Klc Holdings Ltd* ***(G-15608)***
Quick Market Inc 509 653-2268
9951 Us Highway 12 Naches (98937) ***(G-7002)***
Quick Medical Gs, Issaquah *Also called Solcon Inc* ***(G-4480)***
Quick Pressure LLC (PA) 206 219-5567
15600 Redmond Way Ste 101 Redmond (98052) ***(G-8639)***
Quick Print, Tacoma *Also called Quickprint Centers LLC* ***(G-13484)***
Quick Quotes Inc 360 736-3004
210 Northup St Centralia (98531) ***(G-2427)***
Quick Signs and Designs 253 929-4488
12368 Se 221st St Kent (98031) ***(G-5095)***
Quick Tape, Royal City *Also called H A Milton Corp* ***(G-9169)***
Quickprint Centers LLC 253 531-3105
11319 Pacific Ave S Tacoma (98444) ***(G-13484)***
Quicktin Incorporated 253 779-8885
2515 Holgate St Tacoma (98402) ***(G-13485)***
Quiet Giant Brewing Co LLC 253 584-8373
10505 Rainier Ave Sw Lakewood (98499) ***(G-5750)***
Quiet Wing Aerospace LLC 425 451-8565
12324 134th Ct Ne Redmond (98052) ***(G-8640)***
Quikrete Companies LLC 253 396-9996
1420 Port Of Tacoma Rd Tacoma (98421) ***(G-13486)***
Quil Ceda Tanning Co Inc 360 659-1333
3922 88th St Ne Marysville (98270) ***(G-6373)***
Quilceda Creek Vintners Inc 360 568-2389
11306 52nd St Se Snohomish (98290) ***(G-11964)***
Quilcene Marine, Quilcene *Also called Ken Dressler* ***(G-8285)***
Quillisascut Cheese Co 509 738-2011
2409 Pleasant Valley Rd Rice (99167) ***(G-8960)***
Quilters Heaven LLC 800 253-8990
917 Commercial St Leavenworth (98826) ***(G-5814)***
Quilting Fairy LLC 253 845-0462
13507 Meridian E Ste O Puyallup (98373) ***(G-8232)***
Quinault Pride Seafoods 360 276-4431
100 Quinault St Taholah (98587) ***(G-13609)***
Quinault Wood Crafts 360 288-2848
454 N Shore Rd Amanda Park (98526) ***(G-88)***
Quincy Auto Parts, Quincy *Also called Material Inc* ***(G-8303)***
Quincy Foods LLC 509 787-4521
222 Columbia Way Quincy (98848) ***(G-8307)***
Quincy Fresh Fruit LLC 509 787-7100
1015 Industrial Pkwy Quincy (98848) ***(G-8308)***
Quintana Cutting Inc 360 592-5943
6375 Rutsatz Rd Deming (98244) ***(G-2922)***
Quintex, Spokane Valley *Also called Consolidated Container Co LLC* ***(G-12664)***
Quinton Cardiology Systems Inc (HQ) 425 556-9761
3303 Monte Villa Pkwy # 100 Bothell (98021) ***(G-1893)***
Quiring Monuments Inc 206 522-8400
9608 Aurora Ave N Seattle (98103) ***(G-10906)***
Qumulo Inc (PA) 206 260-3588
1501 4th Ave Ste 1600 Seattle (98101) ***(G-10907)***
Quoizel Lighting 360 275-5435
5221 Ne North Shore Rd Belfair (98528) ***(G-771)***
Qwardo Inc 425 753-8865
9440 171st Ave Ne Redmond (98052) ***(G-8641)***
Qwell Pharmaceuticals Inc 206 674-3027
1000 2nd Ave Ste 3700 Seattle (98104) ***(G-10908)***
Qwest, Spokane Valley *Also called Dex Media Holdings Inc* ***(G-12681)***
R & A Manufacturing Inc 425 228-2109
13603 196th Ave Se Renton (98059) ***(G-8888)***
R & B Art Glass 206 323-6430
1813 19th Ave Apt 407 Seattle (98122) ***(G-10909)***
R & D Industries 206 382-1370
2224 1st Ave S Seattle (98134) ***(G-10910)***
R & H Logging & Contract Cutng 360 795-3334
169 Beaver Creek Rd Cathlamet (98612) ***(G-2372)***
R & J Orgnal Kettlekorn Snacks 509 698-5533
10 Fruitspur Dr Selah (98942) ***(G-11595)***
R & K Ventures, Belfair *Also called Richard Meek* ***(G-772)***
R & M Manufacturing LLC 253 503-0956
16909 Park Ave S Spanaway (98387) ***(G-12069)***
R & R Graphics Inc 206 406-3604
203 Airport Way Renton (98057) ***(G-8889)***
R & R Machine 360 568-4844
17918 S Spada Rd Snohomish (98290) ***(G-11965)***
R & R Plastics 360 694-9573
3109 Ne 65th St Ste F Vancouver (98663) ***(G-14524)***
R & R Printing Inc 206 257-9438
2908 Meridian Ave E Edgewood (98371) ***(G-3090)***
R & R Rods 360 423-7935
4543 Columbia Heights Rd Longview (98632) ***(G-5946)***
R & R Woodworking Inc 509 279-9345
23719 W Manila Rd Medical Lake (99022) ***(G-6444)***
R & S Roberts Enterprises Inc 253 333-7567
116 A St Se Auburn (98002) ***(G-542)***
R 2 Manufacturing Inc 360 693-5096
3108 Ne 65th St Ste A Vancouver (98663) ***(G-14525)***
R A Pearson Company (PA) 509 838-6226
8120 W Sunset Hwy Spokane (99224) ***(G-12464)***
R and D Home and Garden Inc 509 826-1730
317 S Main St OMAK (98841) ***(G-7442)***
R and Dee Coatings LLC 509 771-1111
900 N Grape Dr Moses Lake (98837) ***(G-6740)***
R and M Exterminators Inc 509 239-4411
24212 S D St Cheney (99004) ***(G-2591)***
R B Sales 206 870-0741
20714 1st Ave S Des Moines (98198) ***(G-2944)***
R C & L, Black Diamond *Also called Reano Construction & Logging* ***(G-1654)***
R C Systems Inc 425 355-3800
1609 England Ave Everett (98203) ***(G-3592)***
R D F Products 360 253-2181
17706 Ne 72nd St Vancouver (98682) ***(G-14526)***
R D Wing Co Inc 425 821-7222
517 6th St S Kirkland (98033) ***(G-5449)***
R E B Magnetics 360 636-4693
3321 Mount Pleasant Rd Kelso (98626) ***(G-4545)***
R Ellersick Brewing Co 425 374-7248
5030 208th St Sw Lynnwood (98036) ***(G-6185)***
R G Rollin Co 253 274-0882
2702 A St Tacoma (98402) ***(G-13487)***

ALPHABETIC

R Harper Inc 360 985-0806
323 Hadaller Rd Mossyrock (98564) *(G-6765)*
R J M, Auburn *Also called Rjm Corporation (G-548)*
R K I 360 876-0937
9240 Emerald Dr Se Port Orchard (98367) *(G-7844)*
R L Industries (PA) 360 794-1621
14582 172nd Dr Se Monroe (98272) *(G-6611)*
R L Smith Logging Inc 360 943-6540
14612 State Route 8 W Olympia (98502) *(G-7375)*
R L Woodworks 360 607-4471
10012 Ne 142nd Ave Vancouver (98682) *(G-14527)*
R Mathews Optical Works Inc 360 697-6160
26280 Twelve Trees Ln Nw A Poulsbo (98370) *(G-7995)*
R N C Lath & Plaster 360 802-0938
47902 288th Ave Se Enumclaw (98022) *(G-3315)*
R N S Farms Inc 509 545-6775
281 Cottonwood Dr Pasco (99301) *(G-7620)*
R P I, Vancouver *Also called Rubber & Plastics Inc (G-14560)*
R P I, Spokane Valley *Also called Road Products Inc (G-12853)*
R P Signs 425 788-6717
14701 Main St Ne Ste C1 Duvall (98019) *(G-2999)*
R P Signs Screenprinting 425 788-6717
32430 Ne 120th St Duvall (98019) *(G-3000)*
R Plum Corporation (PA) 509 328-2070
1327 N Oak St Spokane (99201) *(G-12465)*
R R Donnelley & Sons Company 206 587-0278
5601 6th Ave S Ste 350 Seattle (98108) *(G-10911)*
R R Donnelly Financial, Seattle *Also called RR Donnelley & Sons Company (G-10989)*
R Ramjet Inc 541 312-1648
11400 Nw Quiet Wtrs Way N Seabeck (98380) *(G-9270)*
R S I, Mount Vernon *Also called Roofing Services Inc (G-6829)*
R S Manufacturing Inc 425 774-1211
5728 204th St Sw Ste 100 Lynnwood (98036) *(G-6186)*
R S Medical, Vancouver *Also called Interntnal Rhbltative Sciences (G-14322)*
R T London Company 360 943-5090
8605 Commerce Place Dr Ne Lacey (98516) *(G-5581)*
R Vision Antq & Restoration 360 280-0328
1911 Farwell Ave Nw Olympia (98502) *(G-7376)*
R Wayne Industries LLC 425 359-0432
20531 129th Ave Se Unit B Snohomish (98296) *(G-11966)*
R&D Enterprises 360 293-4155
1618 22nd St Anacortes (98221) *(G-163)*
R&D Machine LLC 360 694-9573
3109 Ne 65th St Ste B Vancouver (98063) *(G-14528)*
R&J Industries LLC 253 466-3627
402 Valley Ave Nw Ste 105 Puyallup (98371) *(G-8233)*
R&S Forestry and Cnstr LLC 360 436-1771
39115 Sr 530 Ne Arlington (98223) *(G-311)*
R-2 Mfg Inc 360 609-1373
15012 Ne 319th St Battle Ground (98604) *(G-734)*
R.J. Jarvis Enterprise, Spokane *Also called Rj Jarvis Enterprises Inc (G-12477)*
R3bar LLC 647 296-6265
26005 Ne 34th St Redmond (98053) *(G-8642)*
Raad Industries LLC 509 663-8352
2001 N Wenatchee Ave H Wenatchee (98801) *(G-15067)*
RAC Aviation Services LLC 360 256-6698
508 Ne 139th Ave Vancouver (98684) *(G-14529)*
Racal Acoustics Inc 425 297-9700
11910 Beverly Park Rd Everett (98204) *(G-3593)*
Race Horse Studios 206 451-4725
9902 Ne Monsaas Rd Bainbridge Island (98110) *(G-662)*
Racer Mate Inc 206 524-7392
3016 Ne Blakeley St Seattle (98105) *(G-10912)*
Raceway Electric 206 459-5894
8136 Ne 115th Ct Kirkland (98034) *(G-5450)*
Rack & Maintenance Source LLC 509 525-7006
400 W Whitman Dr College Place (99324) *(G-2726)*
Rada & Sons, Pasco *Also called Rada Inc (G-7621)*
Rada Inc 509 547-7232
2707 E Lewis St Pasco (99301) *(G-7621)*
Rader Farms, Lynden *Also called Investure - Wa Inc (G-6023)*
Radiac Abrasives Inc 360 659-6276
13120 Smokey Point Blvd Marysville (98271) *(G-6374)*
Radiac Abrasives Inc 360 659-6201
13120 State Ave Marysville (98271) *(G-6375)*
Radiac Abrasives Inc 360 659-6201
13120 State Ave Marysville (98271) *(G-6376)*
Radial Energy Inc 360 332-0905
225 Marine Dr Ste 210 Blaine (98230) *(G-1700)*
Radian Aerospace Inc 425 235-1936
2210 Ilwaco Ave Ne Renton (98059) *(G-8890)*
Radiant Vision Systems LLC 425 844-0152
18640 Ne 67th Ct Redmond (98052) *(G-8643)*
Radioharness.com, Skykomish *Also called Moore Mfg Co (G-11867)*
Radioracks Aviation Systems 360 651-1200
11616 125th Ave Ne Lake Stevens (98258) *(G-5670)*
Radiorax, Lake Stevens *Also called Radioracks Aviation Systems (G-5670)*
Radix Winery 419 283-7924
4340 Highview Rd Richland (99352) *(G-9037)*
Rads Auto 509 965-5712
1602 S 36th Ave Yakima (98902) *(G-15659)*

Raepop 206 729-3996
6323 Sand Point Way Ne Seattle (98115) *(G-10913)*
Rag Man LLC 206 653-7125
3821 S 250th Pl Kent (98032) *(G-5096)*
Rah Inc 509 482-0943
6510 E Sprague Ave Bldg 1 Spokane Valley (99212) *(G-12849)*
Rahr Malting 509 469-0403
5150 Yakima Valley Hwy Wapato (98951) *(G-14925)*
Raider Boats Inc 509 684-8348
367 Old Dominion Rd Colville (99114) *(G-2771)*
Rail Fx LLC 206 453-1123
1002 E F St Tacoma (98421) *(G-13488)*
Railmakers Northwest 425 259-9236
2944 Cedar St Everett (98201) *(G-3594)*
Railpro of Oregon Inc 360 213-0958
14110 Nw 3rd Ct Vancouver (98685) *(G-14530)*
Railtek Supply, Greenbank *Also called Klas Technologies LLC (G-4308)*
Rain City West Printing LLC 206 767-1151
8133 16th Ave Sw Seattle (98106) *(G-10914)*
Rain City Wood Works LLC 206 378-0494
1611 7th Ave W Seattle (98119) *(G-10915)*
Rain or Shine Kids, Seattle *Also called These Two Girls Llc (G-11289)*
Rain Shadow Cellars LLC 360 320-3115
2291 Roberts Pond Ln Coupeville (98239) *(G-2815)*
Rain Shadow Woodworks Inc 360 385-6789
130 Seton Rd Port Townsend (98368) *(G-7922)*
Rain Song Graphite Guitars, Woodinville *Also called Kuau Technology Ltd (G-15281)*
Rainbow Cloud Kombucha LLC 253 312-3697
2915 29th Ave Sw Ste D Tumwater (98512) *(G-13893)*
Rainbow Metals Inc 360 794-3691
17301 Beaton Rd Se Monroe (98272) *(G-6612)*
Rainbow Racing System Inc 509 326-5470
814 W Rosewood Ave Spokane (99208) *(G-12466)*
Rainestree Timber Marketing 360 462-6197
9100 Se Lynch Rd Shelton (98584) *(G-11723)*
Rainier Building Supply LLC 206 939-2591
12414 Highway 99 Everett (98204) *(G-3595)*
Rainier Clinical Research Ctr 425 251-1720
723 Sw 10th St Ste 100 Renton (98057) *(G-8891)*
Rainier Corp 206 280-4666
4536 University Way Ne Seattle (98105) *(G-10916)*
Rainier Defense LLC 253 218-2999
2504 Auburn Way N Auburn (98002) *(G-543)*
Rainier Distillers Pmb 360 350-9177
14469 Lockwood Ln Se Yelm (98597) *(G-15743)*
Rainier Gravel 206 510-3451
23028 Se 400th St Enumclaw (98022) *(G-3316)*
Rainier Industries 206 622-8219
620 S Industrial Way Seattle (98108) *(G-10917)*
Rainier Industries Ltd 425 251-1800
18375 Olympic Ave S Tukwila (98188) *(G-13801)*
Rainier Orna Ir Fbrication Inc 253 833-0101
19855 Se 342nd St Auburn (98092) *(G-544)*
Rainier Plywood Company 253 383-5533
624 E 15th St Tacoma (98421) *(G-13489)*
Rainier Precision, Seattle *Also called Rp 2000 LLC (G-10988)*
Rainier Ranch Inc 206 243-2044
16644 16th Ave Sw Burien (98166) *(G-2123)*
Rainier Richlite, Tacoma *Also called Rainier Plywood Company (G-13489)*
Rainier Rigging Inc 253 833-4087
16131 Se Green Valley Rd Auburn (98092) *(G-545)*
Rainier Veneer Inc 253 846-0242
8220 Eustis Hunt Rd Spanaway (98387) *(G-12070)*
Rainier Welding Incorporated 425 868-1300
19020 Ne 84th St Redmond (98053) *(G-8644)*
Rainier Wood Recyclers Inc (PA) 425 222-0008
33216 Se Rdmnd Fall Cty Fall City (98024) *(G-3707)*
Rainier Woodworking Co 253 272-5210
3865 Center St Tacoma (98409) *(G-13490)*
Rainier Woodworking Co 253 272-5210
2615 S 80th St Tacoma (98409) *(G-13491)*
Rainmaker Signs Inc 425 861-7446
2020 124th Ave Ne Bellevue (98005) *(G-1091)*
Rainplex Inc 253 576-0157
1512 37th St Nw Gig Harbor (98335) *(G-4150)*
Rainroom Essentials 253 988-5889
11302 205th Ave E Bonney Lake (98391) *(G-1736)*
Rainy Day Artistry 360 484-3681
178 Government Rd Naselle (98638) *(G-7019)*
Rainy Day T-Shirt Gallery, Naselle *Also called Rainy Day Artistry (G-7019)*
Raisbeck Engineering Inc 206 723-2000
4411 S Ryan Way Tukwila (98178) *(G-13802)*
Raisy Kinder Publishing 360 752-0332
1713 Golden Ct Bellingham (98226) *(G-1514)*
Rallito De Luna 509 488-4272
2105 W Bench Rd Othello (99344) *(G-7504)*
Rallito De Luna Tortilla 509 586-8691
213803 E 200 Pr Se Kennewick (99337) *(G-4713)*
Rally Software Development 206 266-8408
16102 Se 46th Way Bellevue (98006) *(G-1092)*
Ralph A Parise 360 387-1794
956 Arrowhead Rd Camano Island (98282) *(G-2223)*

Ralph Doggett 503 998-5935
8515 Ne Hazel Dell Ave Vancouver (98665) **(G-14531)**
Ralph M Eronemo 425 985-1617
11400 Se 66th St Bellevue (98006) **(G-1093)**
Ralston Cunningham Associates 425 455-0316
4050 148th Ave Ne Redmond (98052) **(G-8645)**
Ram Big Horn Brewery-Northgate 206 364-8000
401 Ne Northgate Way Seattle (98125) **(G-10918)**
Ram Bighorn Brewery Kent 253 520-3881
512 Ramsay Way Kent (98032) **(G-5097)**
Ram Cellars LLC 360 909-6714
4554 Rolling Meadows Dr Washougal (98671) **(G-14981)**
Ram Mechanical, Kennewick *Also called Ram Piping Industries Inc* **(G-4714)**
Ram Piping Industries Inc 509 586-0801
109416 E Windward Ln Kennewick (99338) **(G-4714)**
Ram Technologies, Mukilteo *Also called C4 Enterprises Inc* **(G-6902)**
Ram-Bone Industries LLC 360 652-8277
2720 212th St Nw Stanwood (98292) **(G-12989)**
Ramax Printing and Awards 509 928-1222
3209 N Argonne Rd Spokane (99212) **(G-12467)**
Ramco Construction Tools Inc (PA) 253 796-3051
21213 76th Ave S Kent (98032) **(G-5098)**
Ramco Construction Tools Inc 253 796-3051
1217 4th Ave N Kent (98032) **(G-5099)**
Ramco Mechanical Cutting Ltd 360 263-1967
5616 Ne 399th St La Center (98629) **(G-5513)**
Ramgen Power Systems LLC (PA) 425 828-4919
11808 Northup Way W105 Bellevue (98005) **(G-1094)**
Ramlyn Engraving & Sign Co 206 439-8555
14926 Ambaum Blvd Sw Burien (98166) **(G-2124)**
Ramparts, Lake Forest Park *Also called Balance Construction Inc* **(G-5605)**
Rams Custom Cabinets & Wdwkg 253 952-2551
33107 40th Ave S Federal Way (98001) **(G-3775)**
Rams Head Construction Inc 509 997-6962
22 Intercity Airport Rd Winthrop (98862) **(G-15164)**
Ramsay Signs Inc 206 623-3100
727 S 96th St Seattle (98108) **(G-10919)**
Ramsey Bros Logging Inc 253 380-4971
5912 340th St E Eatonville (98328) **(G-3068)**
Ramsey Company Inc 360 748-8918
382 Hamilton Rd Chehalis (98532) **(G-2529)**
Randall Custom Lumber Ltd 360 426-8518
3530 Se Arcadia Rd Shelton (98584) **(G-11724)**
Randl Industries Inc 509 340-0050
3808 N Sullivan Rd 10p Spokane Valley (99216) **(G-12850)**
Randle Steel & Machine Inc 360 497-7477
117 Kehoe Rd Randle (98377) **(G-8327)**
Randles Sand & Gravel Inc (PA) 253 531-6800
5802 192nd St E Puyallup (98375) **(G-8234)**
Random Walk Group LLC 206 724-3621
501 Columbia St Nw Ste H Olympia (98501) **(G-7377)**
Randomalities 253 954-5704
15302 76th Avenue Ct E Puyallup (98375) **(G-8235)**
Randy Wood 360 295-3648
142 Kollock Rd Winlock (98596) **(G-15155)**
Rangemaster Shoulder Therapy, Spokane *Also called Therapeutic Dimension Inc* **(G-12555)**
Ranger Publishing Company Inc 253 584-1212
218 Wilkes St Steilacoom (98388) **(G-13006)**
Ranger Publishing Inc 253 964-2680
1274 Oneil Ct Dupont (98327) **(G-2972)**
Ranger Tugs, Kent *Also called Fluid Motion LLC* **(G-4913)**
Ranger Tugs 360 794-7430
18310 Cascade View Dr Se Monroe (98272) **(G-6613)**
Ranier Welding & Fabrication 360 829-0445
28910 Smner Buckley Hwy E Buckley (98321) **(G-2068)**
Rankin Associates 206 325-9440
2337 13th Ave E Seattle (98102) **(G-10920)**
Raosoft Inc 206 523-9278
6645 Ne Windermere Rd Seattle (98115) **(G-10921)**
Raphoe Press 425 486-5036
6116 Ne 190th St Kenmore (98028) **(G-4601)**
Rapid Machine Inc 360 435-8135
25421 57th Ave Ne Arlington (98223) **(G-312)**
Rapid Print Inc 360 695-6400
3902 Ne 61st Ave Vancouver (98661) **(G-14532)**
Rapid Readymix Co (PA) 509 773-5919
740 W Railroad Ave Goldendale (98620) **(G-4207)**
Rapid Readymix Co 509 493-3153
900 E Steuben St Bingen (98605) **(G-1641)**
Rapp Marine HP LLC 206 286-8162
2260 W Commodore Way Seattle (98199) **(G-10922)**
Raptor Sails Inc 360 775-6039
6319 Seaview Ave Nw Seattle (98107) **(G-10923)**
Raring Corporation 360 892-1659
12007 Ne 95th St Vancouver (98682) **(G-14533)**
Rasa Vineyards LLC 509 252-0900
4122 Power Line Rd Walla Walla (99362) **(G-14858)**
Raston Publishing LLC 206 962-7839
1752 Nw Market St Seattle (98107) **(G-10924)**
Rat Man, Cheney *Also called R and M Exterminators Inc* **(G-2591)**
Rathbun Iron Works Inc 509 865-3717
202 Washington Ave Toppenish (98948) **(G-13671)**
Rattlesnake Mtn Brewing Co 509 783-5747
2696 N Columbia Ctr Blvd Richland (99352) **(G-9038)**
Rauch Industries Inc 800 717-2356
Lakeside Ave Ste 200 Seattle (98122) **(G-10925)**
Rauda Scale Models Inc 206 365-8877
13711 Lake City Way Ne Seattle (98125) **(G-10926)**
Raven Radio Theater 360 943-3206
7605 Boston Harbor Rd Ne Olympia (98506) **(G-7378)**
Raw Advantage Inc 509 738-3344
1156 Highway 25 S Kettle Falls (99141) **(G-5240)**
Raw Chemistry LLC 360 521-2115
1321 Ne 76th St Ste 3d Vancouver (98665) **(G-14534)**
Raw Edge, Seattle *Also called Shah Safari Inc* **(G-11095)**
Rawson Logging 360 829-0474
27312 153rd St E Buckley (98321) **(G-2069)**
Rawson Woodcraft Llc 503 650-4383
109 E 38th St Vancouver (98663) **(G-14535)**
Ray R L Violin Shop LLC 360 570-1085
925 State Ave Ne Olympia (98506) **(G-7379)**
Ray Fanns Whispering Pines 360 384-4750
8746 Delta Line Rd Custer (98240) **(G-2859)**
Ray Summerlin 253 638-0733
29805 148th Ave Se Kent (98042) **(G-5100)**
Raya Publishing LLC 808 635-5908
7718 Swanson Dr Nw Gig Harbor (98335) **(G-4151)**
Rayfield Oneil Timber Cutters 509 925-2061
1307 N Vista Rd Ellensburg (98926) **(G-3222)**
Rayonier Forest Resources LP 360 374-6565
116 Quillayute Rd Forks (98331) **(G-4017)**
Rayonier Inc 425 748-5220
3625 132nd Ave Se 200 Bellevue (98006) **(G-1095)**
Rayonier NW Forest Resources, Forks *Also called Rayonier Forest Resources LP* **(G-4017)**
Rays Custom Cutting 509 684-5544
1043 Miller Rd Colville (99114) **(G-2772)**
Raytheon Company 360 394-3434
610 Dowell St Bldg 894 Keyport (98345) **(G-5244)**
Raytheon Company 360 697-6600
610 Dowell St Bldg 894 Keyport (98345) **(G-5245)**
Raytheon Company 360 394-7559
610 Dowell St Keyport (98345) **(G-5246)**
Raz Arthur John 360 518-2665
20800 Nw Krieger Rd Ridgefield (98642) **(G-9105)**
Razorgirl Press 206 290-7990
130 Sw 112th St Seattle (98146) **(G-10927)**
RB Enterprises, Mukilteo *Also called BM Prgrm & Machining Svc Inc* **(G-6898)**
Rbk Manufacturing Incorporated 253 804-8636
3040 B St Nw Ste 5 Auburn (98001) **(G-546)**
RC & Co 425 774-7511
15603 Main St Ste 101 Mill Creek (98012) **(G-6522)**
Rcc Logging Limited 360 556-8904
1675 View Point Ct Sw Tumwater (98512) **(G-13894)**
Rcd Timber Inc 360 591-9078
16 Hokanson Rd Elma (98541) **(G-3254)**
RCM Enterprise LLC 888 977-6693
614 4th Ave E Olympia (98501) **(G-7380)**
Rdc Enterprises LLC 360 265-0723
3325 Merganser Ln Se Port Orchard (98367) **(G-7845)**
Rdean Enterprises Inc 208 772-8571
6824 N Market St Spokane (99217) **(G-12468)**
Rdgl, Pasco *Also called Vivos Inc* **(G-7650)**
RDL Enterprises Inc 509 529-5480
680 N 13th Ave Walla Walla (99362) **(G-14859)**
Rdl Machine, Walla Walla *Also called RDL Enterprises Inc* **(G-14859)**
RE-Marks Inc 206 548-1008
3610 Albion Pl N Seattle (98103) **(G-10928)**
REA Services Inc 509 394-2305
105 4th St Touchet (99360) **(G-13677)**
Reach For Sky Satellite Servic 509 276-9340
17 N Main Ave Loon Lake (99148) **(G-5977)**
Reach Service LLC 253 370-6229
3800 Bridgeprt Way W A4 University Place (98466) **(G-13978)**
Read E-Z 360 708-8491
11510 Panorama Dr Sedro Woolley (98284) **(G-11559)**
Read Products Inc 206 283-2510
3615 15th Ave W Seattle (98119) **(G-10929)**
Ready Greek Go, Snohomish *Also called Go Manna Inc* **(G-11914)**
Ready Weld 425 391-4211
13620 233rd Way Se Issaquah (98027) **(G-4464)**
Readymix - Pacrock Portabl R/M, Vancouver *Also called Pacific Rock Products LLC* **(G-14473)**
Real Axis Machining Division, Battle Ground *Also called Rivercrest Holdings LLC* **(G-736)**
Real Carriage Door Company 253 853-3815
9803 44th Ave Nw Gig Harbor (98332) **(G-4152)**
Real Estate Book, The, Richland *Also called Custom Publications Wash LLC* **(G-8986)**
Real Estate Sign Service, Brush Prairie *Also called Columbia Sign* **(G-2032)**
Real Fine Publishing 253 318-6553
5123 57th Avenue Ct W University Place (98467) **(G-13979)**
Real Foods, Kent *Also called Taylor Farms Northwest LLC* **(G-5172)**
Real Foods, Kent *Also called Norstar Specialty Foods Inc* **(G-5026)**
Real Love Cupcakes 206 849-9688
16023 19th Avenue Ct E Tacoma (98445) **(G-13492)**

ALPHABETIC

Real Steel Recycling, Kettle Falls *Also called Leake Logging Inc* ***(G-5235)***
Real Time Screen Printinginc...206 818-6346
2051 S 223rd St Des Moines (98198) ***(G-2945)***
Real World Publications, Kingston *Also called Kathleen M Sole* ***(G-5255)***
Reality Plastics Inc...360 653-3949
4700 56th Pl Ne Ste D Marysville (98270) ***(G-6377)***
Realnetworks Inc (PA)...206 674-2700
1501 1st Ave S Ste 600 Seattle (98134) ***(G-10930)***
Realtime Audio, Seattle *Also called Realtime Inc* ***(G-10931)***
Realtime Inc...206 523-8050
336 Ne 89th St Seattle (98115) ***(G-10931)***
Realty Sign Guys...360 909-1540
17912 Ne 37th St Vancouver (98682) ***(G-14536)***
Realty Solutions Inc...206 839-1023
3435 4th Ave S Seattle (98134) ***(G-10932)***
Reano Construction & Logging...360 886-1374
29726 Se 318th St Black Diamond (98010) ***(G-1654)***
Rebec LLC...425 745-4177
3511 132nd St Sw Ste 1 Lynnwood (98087) ***(G-6187)***
Rebell Industries...360 495-4846
310 W Haven Dr Elma (98541) ***(G-3255)***
Rebreathers Usa LLC...425 789-1255
12811 8th Ave W Ste D105 Everett (98204) ***(G-3596)***
Rec Silicon Inc...509 765-2106
3322 Road N Ne Moses Lake (98837) ***(G-6741)***
Rec Silicon Inc...509 793-9015
1800 Road N Ne Moses Lake (98837) ***(G-6742)***
Rec Silicon Inc (HQ)...509 793-9000
1616 S Pioneer Way Moses Lake (98837) ***(G-6743)***
Rec Solar Grade Silicon LLC...509 765-2106
3322 Road N Ne Moses Lake (98837) ***(G-6744)***
Recall...253 272-2813
3995 70th Ave E Ste A Fife (98424) ***(G-3986)***
Recheadz LLC...509 406-2230
285 State Highway 28 W Soap Lake (98851) ***(G-12038)***
Reckless Charm...253 355-1420
1200 Ne Cove Way Pullman (99163) ***(G-8103)***
Reclaimed Wood Products...360 387-1570
724 Halls Hill Rd Stanwood (98282) ***(G-12956)***
Recluse LLC...253 312-2169
10516 36th Street Ct Nw Gig Harbor (98335) ***(G-4153)***
Reco Corporate Sportswear Inc...360 354-2134
210 Nooksack Ave Ste 102 Lynden (98264) ***(G-6048)***
Recognition Unlimited, Seattle *Also called Richard Saunders* ***(G-10962)***
Reconveyance Professionals Inc...425 257-3038
3710 168th St Ne Ste B201 Arlington (98223) ***(G-313)***
Record Printing Inc...509 964-9500
10441 N Thorp Hwy Thorp (98946) ***(G-13629)***
Record Printing Packg & Design, Thorp *Also called Record Printing Inc* ***(G-13629)***
Recordpoint Software USA LLC...425 245-6235
11711 Se 8th St Ste 310 Bellevue (98005) ***(G-1096)***
Recreational Equipment Inc...206 223-1944
222 Yale Ave N Seattle (98109) ***(G-10933)***
Recrochetions...360 450-8757
1203 Nw Drake Way Camas (98607) ***(G-2278)***
Recs, Vancouver *Also called Renewable Enrgy Cmps Sltns LLC* ***(G-14544)***
Recursive Frog LLC...206 745-2561
9222 22nd Ave Sw Seattle (98106) ***(G-10934)***
Red Barn Lavender, Ferndale *Also called Fast Horticultural Services* ***(G-3840)***
Red Creek Apparel and Prom, Olympia *Also called Red Creek Embroidery LLC* ***(G-7381)***
Red Creek Embroidery LLC...360 956-1792
1025 Black Lake Blvd Sw 1f Olympia (98502) ***(G-7381)***
Red Devil Raceway...206 402-6690
10000 Lake City Way Ne Seattle (98125) ***(G-10935)***
Red Dog Fabrication LLC...360 892-3647
1701 W 31st St Bldg C Vancouver (98660) ***(G-14537)***
Red DOT Corporation (PA)...206 151-3840
495 Andover Park E Tukwila (98188) ***(G-13803)***
Red Electric...425 670-7035
4433 Russell Rd Mukilteo (98275) ***(G-6971)***
Red Goat Fabrication Inc...509 240-2896
12339 W Highway 12 Lowden (99360) ***(G-5991)***
Red Hat Lighting LLC...360 624-5773
18508 Ne 73rd St Vancouver (98682) ***(G-14538)***
Red Horse Signs LLC...425 415-0654
8607 219th St Se Ste H Woodinville (98072) ***(G-15345)***
Red Letter Press Corp...206 985-4621
4710 University Way Ne # 100 Seattle (98105) ***(G-10936)***
Red Loon Software...253 353-7963
3800 Bridgeport Way W University Place (98466) ***(G-13980)***
Red Mntain Amrcn Vntners Alnce...509 588-3155
53511 N Sunset Rd Benton City (99320) ***(G-1626)***
Red Mountain Wine Estates, West Richland *Also called Vinmotion Wines LLC* ***(G-15103)***
Red Pearl Systems, Union Gap *Also called Packing House Services Inc* ***(G-13948)***
Red Periscope Technologie...253 851-3968
3467 Edwards Dr Gig Harbor (98335) ***(G-4154)***
Red Propeller LLC...206 452-5664
1605 Boylston Ave Ste 301 Seattle (98122) ***(G-10937)***
Red River Industries...206 992-2446
12990 Phelps Rd Ne Bainbridge Island (98110) ***(G-663)***
Red Rock Creek Inc...509 765-1664
845 Se Greenhill Rd Pullman (99163) ***(G-8104)***
Red Seal Games LLC...425 922-6500
8057 28th Ave Ne Seattle (98115) ***(G-10938)***
Red Sky Winery LLC...425 481-9864
19495 144th Ave Ne B210 Woodinville (98072) ***(G-15346)***
Red Tail Woodworks...360 852-6883
16305 Nw 41st Ave Ridgefield (98642) ***(G-9106)***
Red Wing Brands America Inc...651 388-6233
221 Se Everett Mall Way Everett (98208) ***(G-3597)***
Redbird Sports Inc...206 725-7872
4868 Beacon Ave S Seattle (98108) ***(G-10939)***
Redd Industries LLC...509 572-5752
802 N Keller St Kennewick (99336) ***(G-4715)***
Redden Marine...206 753-0960
12505 Ne Bel Red Rd # 110 Bellevue (98005) ***(G-1097)***
Redemption Press...360 226-3488
1730 Railroad St Enumclaw (98022) ***(G-3317)***
Redi Stair, Asotin *Also called Gc Solutions LLC* ***(G-352)***
Redi-Bag Inc...425 251-9841
17100 W Valley Hwy Tukwila (98188) ***(G-13804)***
Redmond Communications Inc...425 739-4669
1410 Market St Ste 200 Kirkland (98033) ***(G-5451)***
Redmond Town Center...425 702-9158
7525 166th Ave Ne Redmond (98052) ***(G-8646)***
Redmond Wlders Fabricators Inc...425 222-6330
30244 Se High Point Way Issaquah (98027) ***(G-4465)***
Redondo R V Storage, Kent *Also called Redondo Rv Storage & Service* ***(G-5101)***
Redondo Rv Storage & Service...253 941-3662
27641 Pacific Hwy S Kent (98032) ***(G-5101)***
Redpoint International Inc...360 573-5957
9208 Ne Highway 99 107-20 Vancouver (98665) ***(G-14539)***
Redquarry LLC...206 981-5300
708 Broadway Ste 300a Tacoma (98402) ***(G-13493)***
Reds Electric Motors Inc...360 377-3903
2300 6th St Bremerton (98312) ***(G-1992)***
Redside Construction LLC...360 297-9557
600 Winslow Way E Ste 237 Bainbridge Island (98110) ***(G-664)***
Redwood Instrument Co...360 446-2860
17248 Rivendale Ln Se # 5 Rainier (98576) ***(G-8321)***
Redwood Plastics and Rbr Corp...360 225-1491
1901 Schurman Way Woodland (98674) ***(G-15461)***
Redwood Signs By Erl Syverstad, Spanaway *Also called Sign Distributors* ***(G-12073)***
Redwood Subs LLC (PA)...217 493-9499
4316 Leavelle St Nw Olympia (98502) ***(G-7382)***
Reed Composite Solutions LLC...360 637-6867
2210 Port Industrial Rd B Aberdeen (98520) ***(G-31)***
Reed Farms Inc...509 725-4394
41295 State Route 25 N Davenport (99122) ***(G-2876)***
Reed Performance Headers...253 838-7693
33534 18th Ave S Federal Way (98003) ***(G-3776)***
Reel News, The, Lake Stevens *Also called Coordinating Services Inc* ***(G-5640)***
Reelworld Productions Inc (PA)...206 448-1518
2214 Queen Anne Ave N Seattle (98109) ***(G-10940)***
Reese Concrete Products Mfg...509 586-3704
1606 S Ely St Kennewick (99337) ***(G-4716)***
Reese Construction Pdts Mfg, Kennewick *Also called Reese Concrete Products Mfg* ***(G-4716)***
Reesman Co...253 564-7997
606 Regents Blvd Fircrest (98466) ***(G-4004)***
Reeves Cricket Ranch Inc...360 966-3300
3207 Hughes Rd Everson (98247) ***(G-3687)***
Refined Woodworks Inc...206 762-2603
5701 6th Ave S Ste 121 Seattle (98108) ***(G-10941)***
Refiner49er LLC...360 254-0884
24511 Ne Rawson Rd Brush Prairie (98606) ***(G-2041)***
Reflect-A-Life Inc...253 693-8662
20415 Rimrock Rd Monroe (98272) ***(G-6614)***
Reflection Vineyards LLC...360 904-4800
2286 S 31st Ct Ridgefield (98642) ***(G-9107)***
Refocus Laser Engraving-Design...541 998-2047
21420 Locust Way Lynnwood (98036) ***(G-6188)***
Refrelent Software Lab...425 898-9657
4230 194th Pl Ne Sammamish (98074) ***(G-9243)***
Refresco Beverages US Inc...509 582-5200
10 E Bruneau Ave Kennewick (99336) ***(G-4717)***
Refresh Prtg & Promotions LLC...425 391-3223
40 5th Ave Ne Issaquah (98027) ***(G-4466)***
Refrigeration Supplies Distr...503 234-4334
3217 Ne 112th Ave Vancouver (98682) ***(G-14540)***
Refrigeration Supplies Distr...509 452-8689
2 E D St Yakima (98901) ***(G-15660)***
Refuge Music...425 271-4278
16710 133rd Pl Se Renton (98058) ***(G-8892)***
Reg Grays Harbor LLC (HQ)...206 753-0155
1741 1st Ave S Seattle (98134) ***(G-10942)***
Regal Homes Construction LLC...360 606-3486
9901 Ne 26th St Vancouver (98662) ***(G-14541)***
Regal Road Winery...509 838-8024
8224 S Regal Rd Spokane (99223) ***(G-12469)***
Regal Tanks USA Inc...360 707-9948
1733 H St Ste 330 Blaine (98230) ***(G-1701)***
Regency Cleaners LLC...206 650-6933
12825 Des Moines Mem Dr S Burien (98168) ***(G-2125)***

Regenerated Textile Inds LLC 206 427-9343
8715 Dayton Ave N Seattle (98103) *(G-10943)*
Regenx Systems, Lakewood *Also called Renewable Energy Tech Inc (G-5751)*
Reheal LLC 206 440-5948
14333 Interlake Ave N Seattle (98133) *(G-10944)*
Rei, Seattle *Also called Recreational Equipment Inc (G-10933)*
Reichert Shake & Fencing Inc 360 864-6434
207 Kangas Rd Toledo (98591) *(G-13641)*
Reid Signs Inc 206 547-5487
3916 15th Pl W Seattle (98119) *(G-10945)*
Reiff Injection Molding Inc 509 340-1020
131 N Pittsburg St Spokane (99202) *(G-12470)*
Reininger Winery 509 242-3190
824 W Sprague Ave Spokane (99201) *(G-12471)*
Reininger Winery LLC 509 522-1994
5858 Old Highway 12 Walla Walla (99362) *(G-14860)*
Reinkes Fabrication Inc 360 398-2011
5825 Aldrich Rd Bellingham (98226) *(G-1515)*
Reischling Press Inc (PA) 206 905-5999
3325 S 116th St Ste 161 Tukwila (98168) *(G-13805)*
Rejuve - Seattle, Seattle *Also called Rejuvenation Inc (G-10946)*
Rejuvenation Inc 206 382-1901
2910 1st Ave S Seattle (98134) *(G-10946)*
Relentless Publishing LLC 360 929-7530
361 Se Neil St Oak Harbor (98277) *(G-7163)*
Reliable Controls Corp USA 250 475-2036
1465 Slater Rd Ferndale (98248) *(G-3892)*
Reliance Inc 615 218-3929
6416 208th Ave Ne Redmond (98053) *(G-8647)*
Reliance LLC 425 481-3030
14724 173rd Ave Ne Woodinville (98072) *(G-15347)*
Reliance Manufacturing Corp 425 481-3030
8412 219th St Se Woodinville (98072) *(G-15348)*
Reliance Pharmacy, Kennewick *Also called Estm Inc (G-4664)*
Reliance Steel & Aluminum Co 253 395-0614
18325 Olympic Ave S Tukwila (98188) *(G-13806)*
Relief Factor, Kirkland *Also called Promedev LLC (G-5444)*
REM & AES LLC 580 284-3410
15821 136th Avenue Ct E Puyallup (98374) *(G-8236)*
Rembos Hipro 360 492-3100
121 Maple Ln Mineral (98355) *(G-6538)*
Remcon Equipment Inc 509 244-9439
2207 S Lawson St Airway Heights (99001) *(G-61)*
Remember Filtercom 425 359-7905
8418 13th Pl Se Lake Stevens (98258) *(G-5671)*
Remeodiagnostics, Bainbridge Island *Also called Remeopharma Inc (G-665)*
Remeopharma Inc 206 805-9786
9723 Coppertop Park Ste 2 Bainbridge Island (98110) *(G-665)*
Remote Control Technology Inc 425 216-7555
14736 Ne 95th St Redmond (98052) *(G-8648)*
Remote View Daily LLC 360 458-5318
11211 Clark Rd Se Yelm (98597) *(G-15744)*
Rempel Bros Concrete Inc 360 678-4622
27364 State Route 525 Coupeville (98239) *(G-2816)*
Remsberg Trucking, Twisp *Also called Lloyd Remsberg Logging (G-13913)*
Remsing Enterprises 360 521-8049
2111 Ne 49th St Vancouver (98663) *(G-14542)*
Rena Ware International Inc (PA) 425 881-6171
15885 Ne 28th St Bellevue (98008) *(G-1098)*
Renaissance Corporate Services, Vancouver *Also called Renaissance Learning Inc (G-14543)*
Renaissance Fine Woodworking 509 334-7008
525 Se Highland Way Pullman (99163) *(G-8105)*
Renaissance Learning Inc 360 944-8996
4601 Ne 77th Ave Ste 250 Vancouver (98662) *(G-14543)*
Renaissance Marine Group Inc (PA) 509 758-9189
1061 16th Ave Clarkston (99403) *(G-2644)*
Renaissance Rug Corporation 425 698-1073
200 105th Ave Ne Bellevue (98004) *(G-1099)*
Renegade Powder Coating LLC 509 575-4623
916 Rose St Union Gap (98903) *(G-13952)*
Renewable Energy Inc 206 634-3601
3601 Fremont Ave N # 216 Seattle (98103) *(G-10947)*
Renewable Energy Tech Inc 253 267-1965
10321 Lakeview Ave Sw Lakewood (98499) *(G-5751)*
Renewable Enrgy Cmps Sltns LLC 360 695-3238
4400 Se Columbia Way Vancouver (98661) *(G-14544)*
Renewalliance Inc 425 633-3368
1621 114th Ave Se Ste 122 Bellevue (98004) *(G-1100)*
Rental Fleet, Sumner *Also called Cummins Inc (G-13062)*
Rentiel Precision Laser Cutng 253 297-2823
2307 58th Ave Ne Tacoma (98422) *(G-13494)*
Renton Printery Incorporated 425 235-1776
315 S 3rd St Renton (98057) *(G-8893)*
Repair Technology Inc 206 762-6221
400 S 96th St Seattle (98108) *(G-10948)*
Repcon NW Inc 800 325-8707
18307 Ne 221st Ave Brush Prairie (98606) *(G-2042)*
Reprodactyl Inc 206 782-1128
6237 3rd Ave Nw Seattle (98107) *(G-10949)*
Reproduction Services, Seattle *Also called Reprodactyl Inc (G-10949)*
Reprographics Inc 360 423-1237
1444 12th Ave Longview (98632) *(G-5947)*
Republic Locomotive Works 360 577-6479
16 Little Cape Horn Rd Cathlamet (98612) *(G-2373)*
RES Industries LLC 360 225-7955
1555 Down River Dr Woodland (98674) *(G-15462)*
Rescom Railing Systems LLC (PA) 853 243-9841
16910 59th Ave Ne # 215 Arlington (98223) *(G-314)*
Rescue, Spokane Valley *Also called Sterling International Inc (G-12893)*
Research and Development Div, Redmond *Also called Universal Avonics Systems Corp (G-8699)*
Research Nets Incorporated 425 821-7345
8545 152nd Ave Ne Redmond (98052) *(G-8649)*
Research Reactr Sfty/Anylst Sv 509 783-6860
6808 W 15th Ave Kennewick (99338) *(G-4718)*
Resers Fine Foods Inc 509 543-4911
5310 N Industrial Way Pasco (99301) *(G-7622)*
Reserve Industries Corporation 425 432-1241
28131 Rvnsdale Blck Diamn Ravensdale (98051) *(G-8340)*
Reserve Silica, Ravensdale *Also called Reserve Industries Corporation (G-8340)*
Resisters 206 722-3482
3811 S Horton St Seattle (98144) *(G-10950)*
Resolute Medical Inc 800 750-5784
1900 112th Ave Ne Ste 102 Bellevue (98004) *(G-1101)*
Resolve Therapeutics LLC 208 727-7010
454 N 34th St Seattle (98103) *(G-10951)*
Resonant Botanicals LLC 360 969-5065
7459 Maxwelton Rd Clinton (98236) *(G-2694)*
Resonant Solutions LLC 206 619-7672
916 219th Pl Se Bothell (98021) *(G-1894)*
Resonant Systems Inc 206 557-4398
1406 Nw 53rd St Ste 2a Seattle (98107) *(G-10952)*
Resource Accounting Svcs Inc 860 608-0457
8737 Glenwood Rd Sw Port Orchard (98367) *(G-7846)*
Resource Associates Intl 509 466-1894
11721 N Lancelot Dr Spokane (99218) *(G-12472)*
Rest-A-Phone ABC Plastics, Vancouver *Also called Rest-A-Phone Corporation (G-14545)*
Rest-A-Phone Corporation 503 235-6778
2801 Nw Lower River Rd Vancouver (98660) *(G-14545)*
Rest-A-Phone Corporation 360 750-8686
2801 Nw Lower River Rd Vancouver (98660) *(G-14546)*
Restless Prints 772 205-9868
5518 21st Ave S Seattle (98108) *(G-10953)*
Restoration, Seattle *Also called Catherine Tomlinson (G-9646)*
Restore Incorporated 360 909-1161
12110 Nw 41st Ave Vancouver (98685) *(G-14547)*
Restorfx 425 286-5189
1329 56th St Sw Everett (98203) *(G-3598)*
Restorfx International Inc 800 404-4107
2625 Delta Ring Rd Ste 3 Ferndale (98248) *(G-3893)*
Retco Inc 360 341-1487
6694 S Viewmont Dr Clinton (98236) *(G-2695)*
Retip LLC 206 612-5538
5216 Ne 7th Ct Renton (98059) *(G-8894)*
Retired Gorilla Publishing 509 474-9345
1311 S Westcliff Pl # 401 Spokane (99224) *(G-12473)*
Retrodyne Industries LLC 206 906-9762
8560 Greenwood Ave N Seattle (98103) *(G-10954)*
Return My Life LLC 360 584-9799
4400 Fire Willow Way Nw Olympia (98502) *(G-7383)*
Revalesio Corporation 253 922-2600
1202 E D St Ste 101 Tacoma (98421) *(G-13495)*
Revchem Composites Inc 253 305-0303
1132 Thorne Rd Tacoma (98421) *(G-13496)*
Revel Body 206 409-2940
1406 Nw 53rd St Ste 2a Seattle (98107) *(G-10955)*
Revelation Business Servi 360 456-1176
9902 Hampshire Ct Se Olympia (98513) *(G-7384)*
Revelations Yogurt LLC 425 744-6012
527 Main St Edmonds (98020) *(G-3145)*
Reverse Image Technologies LLC 253 219-5345
3310 View Point Cir Ne Tacoma (98422) *(G-13497)*
Revive A Back Inc 360 738-6085
4200 Meridian St Ste 102 Bellingham (98226) *(G-1516)*
Revive Cabinet Closet Pro Llc 425 382-0739
2615 W Casino Rd Ste 6b Everett (98204) *(G-3599)*
Revolution Inc 206 714-3529
3663 1st Ave S Seattle (98134) *(G-10956)*
Revq Inc 360 260-5710
12905 Ne 93rd Ave Vancouver (98662) *(G-14548)*
Rex Plastics Inc 360 892-0366
12515 Ne 95th St Vancouver (98682) *(G-14549)*
Rex, Ron Dairy, Sedro Woolley *Also called Ronald Rex Dairy Farm (G-11561)*
Rexel Capitol Light 425 861-0200
17618 Ne 130th Ct Redmond (98052) *(G-8650)*
Reyes Coca-Cola Bottling LLC 253 503-4341
2115 116th St S Ste 101 Tacoma (98444) *(G-13498)*
Reyes Coca-Cola Bottling LLC 360 475-6528
5001 Auto Center Blvd Bremerton (98312) *(G-1993)*
Reyes Coca-Cola Bottling LLC 509 921-6200
9705 E Montgomery Ave Spokane Valley (99206) *(G-12851)*

ALPHABETIC

Reyes Coca-Cola Bottling LLC 509 762-5480
6819 22nd Ave Ne Moses Lake (98837) ***(G-6745)***
Reyna Moore Advertising 503 230-9440
18514 Ne 23rd St Vancouver (98684) ***(G-14550)***
Reynold Grey & Associates 360 385-1167
321 Otto St Port Townsend (98368) ***(G-7923)***
Reynold Grey McHining Svcs Inc 360 385-1167
321 Otto St Port Townsend (98368) ***(G-7924)***
Reynolds and Reynolds Company 425 985-0194
17121 76th Ave W Edmonds (98026) ***(G-3146)***
Rezabek Vineyards LLC 360 896-0218
5700 Ne 82nd Ave Vancouver (98662) ***(G-14551)***
Rfp LLC 206 523-8996
11712 5th Ave Ne Seattle (98125) ***(G-10957)***
Rfp Manufacturing Inc 253 847-3330
21222 Mountain Hwy E Spanaway (98387) ***(G-12071)***
RG Machining, Port Townsend *Also called Reynold Grey McHining Svcs Inc* ***(G-7924)***
Rgb Soda 206 437-8395
1809 15th Ave Seattle (98122) ***(G-10958)***
Rgb14 LLC 206 818-8207
3629b Courtland Pl S Seattle (98144) ***(G-10959)***
Rgd Enterprises Inc 360 923-9582
8937 27th Ave Se Olympia (98513) ***(G-7385)***
Rgzprints 208 310-0500
1907 W 3rd Ave Spokane (99201) ***(G-12474)***
Rh Airport Commerce 425 454-3030
1800 112th Ave Ne Ste 310 Bellevue (98004) ***(G-1102)***
Rh Appetizing Inc 206 282-0776
1631 15th Ave W Ste 111 Seattle (98119) ***(G-10960)***
Rhinestones Golor, Covington *Also called Dynamic Software* ***(G-2826)***
Rhino Steel Corporation 425 443-2322
4030 Lake Washington Blvd Kirkland (98033) ***(G-5452)***
Rhythm & Brews 360 386-9509
18825 67th Ave Ne Arlington (98223) ***(G-315)***
Rhythmical Steel 360 263-3141
3908 Ne 397th Cir La Center (98629) ***(G-5514)***
Rice Lake Weighing Systems Inc 206 433-0199
19201 62nd Ave S Kent (98032) ***(G-5102)***
Rich Interiors 509 665-8000
2131 N Wenatchee Ave Wenatchee (98801) ***(G-15068)***
Rich Nature Lab, Mukilteo *Also called Rich Nature Nutraceutical Labs* ***(G-6972)***
Rich Nature Nutraceutical Labs 425 493-1885
9700 Harbour Pl Ste 128 Mukilteo (98275) ***(G-6972)***
Rich Nature Organic 425 315-7000
9700 Harbour Pl Ste 128 Mukilteo (98275) ***(G-6973)***
Rich Richmond Logging LLC 509 935-4833
1507 N Pinebrook Dr Chewelah (99109) ***(G-2606)***
Richard & Mike Lynch 360 263-4078
17811 Ne Grinnell Rd Woodland (98674) ***(G-15463)***
Richard Andrews Logging 360 426-1096
170 W Metzler Mill Rd Shelton (98584) ***(G-11725)***
Richard C Busher Jr 206 524-6726
7042 20th Pl Ne Seattle (98115) ***(G-10961)***
Richard Demeules, Redmond *Also called Wood Design* ***(G-8717)***
Richard Evans 509 684-1079
565 Knapp Rd Colville (99114) ***(G-2773)***
Richard Ezetta Stump Grinding 360 687-8054
24000 Ne 101st Ct Battle Ground (98604) ***(G-735)***
Richard Knannlein 360 426-9757
393 Se Dahman Rd Shelton (98584) ***(G-11726)***
Richard Lawson Construction 360 378-4313
1165 W Valley Rd Friday Harbor (98250) ***(G-4055)***
Richard Meek 360 275-4104
210 Ne Belfair Manor Dr Belfair (98528) ***(G-772)***
Richard Saunders 612 861-1061
13716 Lake City Way Ne # 502 Seattle (98125) ***(G-10962)***
Richard Warrington 509 448-8713
3907 W Washington Rd Cheney (99004) ***(G-2592)***
Richards Packaging Inc 253 582-1096
9403 43rd Avenue Ct Sw # 8 Tacoma (98499) ***(G-13499)***
Richards Packaging Inc 253 872-2848
4103 C St Ne Ste 100 Auburn (98002) ***(G-547)***
Richards Packaging Inc 509 545-8690
2105 E Ainsworth St Pasco (99301) ***(G-7623)***
Richardson Bottling Company (PA) 253 535-6447
5410 189th St E Puyallup (98375) ***(G-8237)***
Richardson Coatings LLC 253 861-7611
5930 State Route 508 Morton (98356) ***(G-6672)***
Richardson Log & Land Clearing 360 631-2107
5675 Brookings Rd Sedro Woolley (98284) ***(G-11560)***
Richardson Logging 509 684-4206
2229 Marble Vly Basin Rd Addy (99101) ***(G-47)***
Richardson Precision Machine 509 945-9939
732 N 16th Ave Ste 22 Yakima (98902) ***(G-15661)***
Richart Company Inc 509 935-8857
2714e Quarry Browns Lk Rd Chewelah (99109) ***(G-2607)***
Richert Lina 206 660-3332
1886 Journeys End Ln Camano Island (98282) ***(G-2224)***
Richert Enterprises, Camano Island *Also called Richert Lina* ***(G-2224)***
Richins Printing Inc 425 776-1800
7530 Olympic View Dr # 101 Edmonds (98026) ***(G-3147)***
Richmark Company 206 322-8884
1110 E Pine St Seattle (98122) ***(G-10963)***
Richmark Label, Seattle *Also called Richmark Company* ***(G-10963)***
Richmond Systems Inc 360 455-8284
3721 Griffin Ln Se Olympia (98501) ***(G-7386)***
Rick Carlson 360 691-4421
23212 Scotty Rd Granite Falls (98252) ***(G-4285)***
Rick's Mr Chips, Kennewick *Also called Gold Plating Specialist* ***(G-4668)***
Rickey Canyon Vineyard 206 718-9318
2025 Rickey Canyon Rd Rice (99167) ***(G-8961)***
Rico Instruments, Rainier *Also called Redwood Instrument Co* ***(G-8321)***
Ricter Enterprises 425 482-5942
23128 State Route 9 Se Woodinville (98072) ***(G-15349)***
Ridemind LLC 206 226-0016
4215 Whitman Ave N # 201 Seattle (98103) ***(G-10964)***
Rides Publishing Co LLC 206 789-0827
2442 Nw Market St Ste 43 Seattle (98107) ***(G-10965)***
Ridgeline Graphics Inc 509 662-6858
34 N Chelan Ave Wenatchee (98801) ***(G-15069)***
Ridgerunners Inc 509 248-8531
9007 Scenic Dr Yakima (98908) ***(G-15662)***
Ridgewood Industries Inc 425 774-0170
23110 99th Ave W Edmonds (98020) ***(G-3148)***
Ries Productions LLC 360 627-8795
2600 Burwell St Bremerton (98312) ***(G-1994)***
Ries Tripod, Bremerton *Also called Ries Productions LLC* ***(G-1994)***
Rietdyks Milling Company 360 887-8874
512 Nw Carty Rd Ridgefield (98642) ***(G-9108)***
Rigaku Americas Corporation 206 780-8927
7865 Ne Day Rd W Ste 109 Bainbridge Island (98110) ***(G-666)***
Riggel Productions Limited 509 758-3209
417 Morrison St Clarkston (99403) ***(G-2645)***
Riggsafe Solutions Inc 865 266-9989
15908 E 6th Ln Spokane Valley (99037) ***(G-12852)***
Rikki Usa Inc 425 881-6881
14590 Ne 95th St Redmond (98052) ***(G-8651)***
Riley Hopkins Screen Printing 253 851-9078
196 Fir Dr Nw Gig Harbor (98335) ***(G-4155)***
Riley, Monty Allen, Port Orchard *Also called May Mobile Marine Tech* ***(G-7828)***
Rimini Software LLC 425 785-8819
16650 246th Pl Se Issaquah (98027) ***(G-4467)***
Rios Brick Pavers 206 271-3447
5833 236th Ave Ne Redmond (98053) ***(G-8652)***
Ripley Software 501 773-5519
996 Ne High St Issaquah (98029) ***(G-4468)***
Rippedsheets.com, Benton City *Also called Halldata Inc* ***(G-1615)***
Riptide Charters Inc 360 815-6568
1170 Rene Ct Blaine (98230) ***(G-1702)***
Rise N Grind 360 452-9335
3231 E Highway 101 Port Angeles (98362) ***(G-7739)***
Riser Products, Colton *Also called Professnl Mntrs & Pro Life Skl* ***(G-2734)***
Rising Moon Products 206 439-0338
2017 Sw 146th St Burien (98166) ***(G-2126)***
Risklens Inc 866 936-0191
601 W Main Ave Ste 917 Spokane (99201) ***(G-12475)***
Risley Sons Wldg Fbrcation LLC 509 427-2206
492 Cedar Creek Rd Carson (98610) ***(G-2306)***
Risque Inc 360 738-1280
1122 N State St Bellingham (98225) ***(G-1517)***
Ritzville Adams County Journal, Ritzville *Also called Ruser Publications Inc* ***(G-9122)***
Ritzy Bath Bombs 206 499-7336
2727 E Evergreen Blvd N Vancouver (98661) ***(G-14552)***
Rival Iq Corporation 206 395-8572
500 Union St Ste 500 # 500 Seattle (98101) ***(G-10966)***
River City Brewing LLC 509 413-2388
121 S Cedar St Spokane (99201) ***(G-12476)***
River City Screenprinting 360 428-8985
222 Anderson Rd Ste D Mount Vernon (98273) ***(G-6828)***
River Hollow Creations LLC 509 497-1097
105b Abby Ave Benton City (99320) ***(G-1627)***
River Ridge Hardware, Spokane *Also called Summer Rrh LLC* ***(G-12532)***
River Rock Software Inc 916 797-6746
50 E Blenheim Pl Shelton (98584) ***(G-11727)***
River Town Distillers LLC 425 330-4885
5614 66th Ave Se Snohomish (98290) ***(G-11967)***
River's Edge Winery, Mattawa *Also called J&S Crushing* ***(G-6409)***
Riveraerie Cellars 509 786-2197
548 Cabernet Ct Prosser (99350) ***(G-8064)***
Riverbend Incorporated 509 460-2886
45804 N Whitmore Pr Nw Benton City (99320) ***(G-1628)***
Rivercrest Holdings LLC 360 723-5354
1205 Se Grace Ave Battle Ground (98604) ***(G-736)***
Rivermist Labradoodles 509 427-4810
212 Sprague Landing Rd Stevenson (98648) ***(G-13018)***
Riverport Brewing 509 758-8889
150 9th St Clarkston (99403) ***(G-2646)***
Rivers West Apparel Inc 425 272-2949
1141 Andover Park W Tukwila (98188) ***(G-13807)***
Riversands Distillery 509 492-1015
19 W Canal Dr Kennewick (99336) ***(G-4719)***
Riverside Cabinet Co Inc 360 354-3070
1145 Polinder Rd Lynden (98264) ***(G-6049)***
Riverside Club 509 967-5756
3000 N Riverside Dr Richland (99353) ***(G-9039)***

ALPHABETIC SECTION Rogers Machinery Company Inc

Riverside Scientific Entps 206 842-7513
15708 Point Monroe Dr Ne Bainbridge Island (98110) ***(G-667)***
Rivertrail Roasters, Redmond *Also called Little Bean Coffee LLC* ***(G-8535)***
Rivet & Sway, Seattle *Also called Project Seezit Inc* ***(G-10874)***
Rivet Hammer, Seattle *Also called Blucapp Inc* ***(G-9546)***
Rj Equipment Service, Elma *Also called Ronald Johnson* ***(G-3256)***
RJ Hydraulics Inc 360 693-4399
713 W 11th St Vancouver (98660) ***(G-14553)***
Rj Jarvis Enterprises Inc 509 482-0254
3412 E Bismark Ct Spokane (99217) ***(G-12477)***
Rj Sports Inc 425 227-8777
17622 108th Ave Se Renton (98055) ***(G-8895)***
Rjc Enterprises LLC 425 481-3281
11711 N Creek Pkwy S # 103 Bothell (98011) ***(G-1787)***
Rjh Aerospace NW 425 394-3775
220 Thornton View Rd Cle Elum (98922) ***(G-2677)***
Rjm Corporation 253 887-9100
3220 C St Ne Ste G Auburn (98002) ***(G-548)***
Rjs Marine LLC 509 888-4568
1058 E Woodin Ave Bldg A Chelan (98816) ***(G-2563)***
Rk Burk Meg Murch Artworks 206 954-1297
11810 8th Ave Nw Seattle (98177) ***(G-10967)***
Rk Print Group 206 972-0874
10203 47th Ave Sw Apt C17 Seattle (98146) ***(G-10968)***
Rk Titanium LLC 253 886-1377
27031 114th Ave Se Kent (98030) ***(G-5103)***
Rkba Concealment 360 624-3874
4307 Ne 118th St Vancouver (98686) ***(G-14554)***
Rl Brewer Forestry, Arlington *Also called Ronald Brewer* ***(G-317)***
Rleyh Software LLC 425 837-4643
21293 Se 42nd Pl Issaquah (98029) ***(G-4469)***
Rm Metal Works 253 815-0652
37205 Pacific Hwy S Federal Way (98003) ***(G-3777)***
RMC Incorporated 206 243-4831
7951 2nd Ave S Seattle (98108) ***(G-10969)***
RMC Powder Coating, Seattle *Also called RMC Incorporated* ***(G-10969)***
Rmg Nutrition 253 863-7017
6323 151st Ave E Sumner (98390) ***(G-13096)***
Rmv Industries Inc 253 297-2556
20611 Bothell Everett Hwy Bothell (98012) ***(G-1895)***
Rnd Sign and Design LLC 206 255-1963
34737 27th Ave Sw Federal Way (98023) ***(G-3778)***
Road Products Inc 509 922-1206
12301 E Empire Ave Spokane Valley (99216) ***(G-12853)***
Road Runner Transportation LLC 253 778-3848
4435 S Camano Pl Seattle (98118) ***(G-10970)***
Road-Iq LLC 360 733-4151
2425 E Bakerview Rd # 101 Bellingham (98226) ***(G-1518)***
Roadmaster Inc 360 896-0407
6110 Ne 127th Ave Vancouver (98682) ***(G-14555)***
Roadmaster Inc 360 735-7575
1800 W Fourth Plain Blvd # 115 Vancouver (98660) ***(G-14556)***
Roast House LLC 509 995-6500
423 E Cleveland Ave Ste C Spokane (99207) ***(G-12478)***
Roast Hse From Frm To Cup Mfg, Spokane *Also called Roast House LLC* ***(G-12478)***
Roastmasters LLC 425 284-2327
17725 Ne 65th St 150 Redmond (98052) ***(G-8653)***
Rob Sullivan 425 882-2221
2429 134th Ave Ne Bellevue (98005) ***(G-1103)***
Robbins Company 253 872-0500
5866 S 194th St Kent (98032) ***(G-5104)***
Robbins PBM, Kent *Also called Robbins Company* ***(G-5104)***
Robert Comeau 360 573-2241
5112 Ne 119th St Vancouver (98686) ***(G-14557)***
Robert E Miller 509 485-3032
211 Chesaw Rd Oroville (98844) ***(G-7472)***
Robert Gee Violins 425 776-4002
19330 7th Ave W Lynnwood (98036) ***(G-6189)***
Robert J Parry 509 456-6204
4108 S Scott St Spokane (99203) ***(G-12479)***
Robert Karl Cellars LLC 509 363-1353
115 W Pacific Ave Spokane (99201) ***(G-12480)***
Robert Lloyd Zerck 509 779-4820
17424 N Highway 21 Malo (99150) ***(G-6235)***
Robert Madsen Design Inc 206 588-0090
5448 Shilshole Ave Nw Seattle (98107) ***(G-10971)***
Robert Nickel 239 565-0450
2207 84th St E Tacoma (98445) ***(G-13500)***
Robert Rogers 360 352-9408
3631 113th Ave Sw Olympia (98512) ***(G-7387)***
Robert Rowe 206 632-7997
3809 Interlake Ave N Seattle (98103) ***(G-10972)***
Robert Wickes Od 360 249-3485
118 S Main St Montesano (98563) ***(G-6654)***
Roberta Lowes 253 572-1859
11922 A St S Tacoma (98444) ***(G-13501)***
Roberta Propst 425 681-9760
4957 Lakemont Blvd Se C4 Bellevue (98006) ***(G-1104)***
Roberts Precision Machine Inc 360 805-1000
1166 Village Way Ste B Monroe (98272) ***(G-6615)***
Robertson-Ceco II Corporation 509 244-5611
2714 S Garfield Rd Airway Heights (99001) ***(G-62)***

Robin Ferris Manufacturing 360 757-6804
15254 Flightline Rd Burlington (98233) ***(G-2183)***
Robins Jewelers Ltd 206 622-4337
18604 80th Ave W Edmonds (98026) ***(G-3149)***
Robinson Windword Inc 509 536-1617
2503 S Geiger Blvd Spokane (99224) ***(G-12481)***
Robinsons Inc 360 834-0929
1304 Se 195th Ave Camas (98607) ***(G-2279)***
Robobear LLC 425 453-1391
10505 Main St Apt 654 Bellevue (98004) ***(G-1105)***
Robodub Inc 408 250-5723
4000 Mason Rd Ste 308c Seattle (98195) ***(G-10973)***
Robs Sprnklr Svc Installation 253 581-6491
8103 Steilacoom Blvd Sw Lakewood (98498) ***(G-5752)***
ROC Racing Inc 360 658-4353
14702 Smokey Point Blvd A Marysville (98271) ***(G-6378)***
Rock Bizarre 360 275-9742
2613 Ne Old Belfair Hwy Belfair (98528) ***(G-773)***
Rock Claims Management, Bellevue *Also called Rock Industries LLC* ***(G-1106)***
Rock Industries LLC 206 399-7853
4034 170th Ave Se Bellevue (98008) ***(G-1106)***
Rock Place 425 220-1110
1622 3rd St Marysville (98270) ***(G-6379)***
Rock Services Inc 360 748-8333
258 Hamilton Rd Chehalis (98532) ***(G-2530)***
Rock Services Inc 360 748-8333
258 Hamilton Rd N Chehalis (98532) ***(G-2531)***
Rocket Bakery Inc (PA) 509 462-2345
4124 N Burns Rd Spokane Valley (99216) ***(G-12854)***
Rocket Software 425 502-9684
10900 Ne 8th St Ste 1000 Bellevue (98004) ***(G-1107)***
Rocketcat Games, Bremerton *Also called Rocketcat LLC* ***(G-1995)***
Rocketcat LLC 360 204-4037
7305 Chico Way Nw Bremerton (98312) ***(G-1995)***
Rocking H Woodworking 253 448-7978
3624 232nd St E Spanaway (98387) ***(G-12072)***
Rocking Horse Barns LLC 360 736-5403
2205 Graf Rd Centralia (98531) ***(G-2428)***
Rocking Horse Rita Cstm Hmes 360 600-1000
11077 N Vancouver Way Vancouver (98660) ***(G-14558)***
Rockwall Cellars 509 826-0201
110 Nichols Rd OMAK (98841) ***(G-7443)***
Rockwell Automation Inc 425 519-5109
15375 Se 30th Pl Ste 150 Bellevue (98007) ***(G-1108)***
Rockwell Collins Inc 425 923-2700
11404 Commando Rd W Everett (98204) ***(G-3600)***
Rockwell Collins Inc 425 492-1400
3350 Monte Villa Pkwy # 200 Bothell (98021) ***(G-1896)***
Rocky Mountain Chocolate Fctry 509 927-7623
1330 N Argonne Veradale (99037) ***(G-14750)***
Rocky Mountain Log Holmes, Ellensburg *Also called Slyfield Enterprises* ***(G-3226)***
Rocky Mountain Machining 509 927-8797
1105 S Glenbrook Ct Spokane Valley (99016) ***(G-12855)***
Rocky Pond Winery 206 550-0938
18725 164th Ave Ne Woodinville (98072) ***(G-15350)***
Rocky Pond Winery 206 458-9119
116 Orchard Pl Orondo (98843) ***(G-7460)***
Rocky Prairie Engraving 360 264-2188
840 143rd Ave Se Tenino (98589) ***(G-13622)***
Rod Carr Sailmaker 425 881-2846
3011 177th Ave Ne Redmond (98052) ***(G-8654)***
Rod Thunfield & Custom 253 536-0373
16616 71st Ave E Puyallup (98375) ***(G-8238)***
Rodax Software 206 782-3482
8734 20th Ave Nw Seattle (98117) ***(G-10974)***
Rodda Paint Bellingham Bh51, Bellingham *Also called Rodda Paint Co* ***(G-1519)***
Rodda Paint Co 253 283-6581
920 Nw State Ave Chehalis (98532) ***(G-2532)***
Rodda Paint Co 360 423-4990
541 California Way Longview (98632) ***(G-5948)***
Rodda Paint Co 360 738-6878
747 Ohio St Bellingham (98225) ***(G-1519)***
Rodda Paint Longview Lv55, Longview *Also called Rodda Paint Co* ***(G-5948)***
Rodneys Custom Woodwork 206 542-2517
220 Nw 195th St Shoreline (98177) ***(G-11805)***
Rodocker Woodworks LLC 360 775-1620
1011 W 11th St Port Angeles (98363) ***(G-7740)***
Rods Custom Fiberglass Inc 509 483-2174
2928 N Napa St Spokane (99207) ***(G-12482)***
Roemer Electric Steel Foundry 360 423-1330
523 7th Ave Longview (98632) ***(G-5949)***
Roeracing Slalom Skateboards 206 371-9710
3912 W Bertona St Seattle (98199) ***(G-10975)***
Roger Habon 206 240-0122
17801 Se 146th St Renton (98059) ***(G-8896)***
Rogers & Associates 360 455-1534
7905 Martin Way E Olympia (98516) ***(G-7388)***
Rogers Bob Blldzg & Log Trckg, Olympia *Also called Robert Rogers* ***(G-7387)***
Rogers Custom Woodworking 425 757-1799
19042 Se 161st St Renton (98058) ***(G-8897)***
Rogers Machinery Company Inc 206 763-2530
7800 5th Ave S Seattle (98108) ***(G-10976)***

ALPHABETIC

Rogers Machinery Company Inc ... 360 736-9356
3509 Galvin Rd Centralia (98531) *(G-2429)*
Rogers Machinery Company Inc ... 509 922-0556
16615 E Euclid Ave Spokane Valley (99216) *(G-12856)*
Rogers Rubber Manufacturing ... 253 845-8374
22115 108th Street Ct E Buckley (98321) *(G-2070)*
Rogers Terminal and Shipping ... 253 572-0146
550 Dock St Tacoma (98402) *(G-13502)*
Rogroc LLC ... 360 435-6417
202 E Burke Ave Arlington (98223) *(G-316)*
Rogue Empire Inc ... 253 857-5300
915 26th Ave Nw Gig Harbor (98335) *(G-4156)*
Rojos Famous Inc ... 206 592-6581
19901 1st Ave S Normandy Park (98148) *(G-7097)*
Rolln Dough Ltd (PA) ... 206 763-4300
20620 84th Ave S Kent (98032) *(G-5105)*
Rollo Tomasi Enterprises LLC ... 509 453-9950
101 N 5th Ave Yakima (98902) *(G-15663)*
Romac Foundry Division, Sultan *Also called Romac Industries Inc (G-13034)*
Romac Industries Inc (PA) ... 425 951-6200
21919 20th Ave Se Ste 100 Bothell (98021) *(G-1897)*
Romac Industries Inc ... 425 951-6200
125 S Sultan Basin Rd Sultan (98294) *(G-13034)*
Romanzof Fishing Company LLC ... 206 545-9501
4502 14th Ave Nw Seattle (98107) *(G-10977)*
Romeo and Sylvia LLC ... 425 315-5336
16305 Railroad Way Snohomish (98296) *(G-11968)*
Romine Fuel Inc ... 509 476-3610
105 Frank Rd Riverside (98849) *(G-9126)*
Ron & Leos Welding Svcs Inc ... 360 825-1221
2221 Garrett St Enumclaw (98022) *(G-3318)*
Ron C England ... 509 276-9150
6633 Long Lake Dr Nine Mile Falls (99026) *(G-7083)*
Ron Hall ... 360 468-2294
214 Lopez Rd Lopez Island (98261) *(G-5986)*
Ron Pircey Race Cars, Federal Way *Also called Rm Metal Works (G-3777)*
Ron's Transhop, Seattle *Also called Rons Transmission (G-10979)*
Ronald Brewer ... 360 436-1771
39115 State Route 530 Ne Arlington (98223) *(G-317)*
Ronald F Phillips ... 360 779-5614
22244 Port Gamble Rd Ne Poulsbo (98370) *(G-7996)*
Ronald Finney ... 253 857-7635
3252 Se Nelson Rd Olalla (98359) *(G-7209)*
Ronald G Wahl ... 509 223-3957
300 Chopaka Rd Loomis (98827) *(G-5972)*
Ronald Johnson ... 360 482-4982
861 S Bank Rd Elma (98541) *(G-3256)*
Ronald Rex Dairy Farm ... 360 856-0629
26455 Burmaster Rd Sedro Woolley (98284) *(G-11561)*
Ronald Sand & Gravel Inc ... 509 728-8605
1221 S Thorp Hwy Ellensburg (98926) *(G-3223)*
Ronald Wayne Dagley ... 253 863-4895
14323 16th St E Sumner (98390) *(G-13097)*
Rondys Inc (PA) ... 425 392-6324
5647 229th Ave Se Issaquah (98029) *(G-4470)*
Ronin Green Publishing ... 206 725-2839
6731 29th Ave S Seattle (98108) *(G-10978)*
Rons Transmission ... 206 772-8200
12667 Renton Ave S Seattle (98178) *(G-10979)*
Roof Truss Supply Inc (PA) ... 425 481-0900
5910 234th St Se Woodinville (98072) *(G-15351)*
Rooferpro Software LLC ... 425 503-4298
914 164th St Se Unit 110 Mill Creek (98012) *(G-6523)*
Roofing Services Inc ... 425 347-1146
1005 W Hazel St Mount Vernon (98273) *(G-6829)*
Rooftop Brewing Company ... 206 457-8598
1220 W Nickerson St Seattle (98119) *(G-10980)*
Rook Defense LLC ... 206 518-3593
6821 Udall Pl Se Apt C104 Auburn (98092) *(G-549)*
Room Maker ... 425 432-3324
22218 Se Bain Rd Maple Valley (98038) *(G-6292)*
Roommate Filter LLC ... 863 224-6462
2319 W Smith St Seattle (98199) *(G-10981)*
Rootz ... 509 443-5999
923 E Hoffman Ave Spokane (99207) *(G-12483)*
Rory Thurrott ... 206 941-7297
4710 Ne Eagle Harbor Dr Bainbridge Island (98110) *(G-668)*
Ros Wine Company LLC (PA) ... 509 301-0627
28126 N Hansen Rd Prosser (99350) *(G-8065)*
Rose Brands, Seattle *Also called Tsue Chong Co Inc (G-11346)*
Rose Saviah Winery LLC ... 509 522-2181
1979 J B George Rd Walla Walla (99362) *(G-14861)*
Rose Tucker ... 509 837-8701
70 Ray Rd Sunnyside (98944) *(G-13139)*
Rosebud Ranches ... 509 932-4617
21954 Road I Sw Mattawa (99349) *(G-6412)*
Rosellini Distribution Inc ... 253 867-5648
8637 S 212th St Kent (98031) *(G-5106)*
Rosemount Inc ... 206 329-8600
800 Sw 34th St Ste L Renton (98057) *(G-8898)*
Rosemount Specialty Pdts LLC (HQ) ... 509 881-2100
5545 Nelpar Dr East Wenatchee (98802) *(G-3031)*
Rosemount Specialty Pdts LLC ... 206 329-8600
800 Sw 34th St Ste L Renton (98057) *(G-8899)*
Roslyn Brewing Co Inc ... 509 649-2232
208 W Pennsylvania Ave Roslyn (98941) *(G-9156)*
Ross Andrew Mickel ... 206 267-5252
1910 Frview Ave E Ste 400 Seattle (98102) *(G-10982)*
Ross Andrew Winery, Bellevue *Also called Sussex Clumber LLC (G-1169)*
Ross Creek Logging Inc ... 509 926-0415
18908 E Lincoln Rd Otis Orchards (99027) *(G-7517)*
Ross Group of Companies Inc ... 800 663-8303
210 Duffner Dr Lynden (98264) *(G-6050)*
Ross Metier LLC ... 253 208-8777
6011 256th St E Graham (98338) *(G-4237)*
Ross Packing Co, Selah *Also called Tree Top Inc (G-11602)*
Ross Printing Northwest Inc ... 509 534-0655
1611 E Sprague Ave Spokane (99202) *(G-12484)*
Rotary Offset Press Inc ... 253 813-9900
6600 S 231st St Kent (98032) *(G-5107)*
Rothenbuhler Engineering Co (HQ) ... 360 856-0836
524 Rhodes Rd Sedro Woolley (98284) *(G-11562)*
Rotie Cellars ... 509 529-2011
4 E Main St Walla Walla (99362) *(G-14862)*
Rotovac Corporation ... 425 883-6746
14615 Ne 91st St Ste C Redmond (98052) *(G-8655)*
Rotschy Timber Management ... 360 247-5396
44013 Ne Protzman Rd Amboy (98601) *(G-96)*
Rottler Manufacturing Company ... 253 872-7050
8029 S 200th St Kent (98032) *(G-5108)*
Rousseau Company ... 509 758-3954
1392 Port Dr Clarkston (99403) *(G-2647)*
Routec Industries LLC ... 206 949-2472
9911 198th St Se Snohomish (98296) *(G-11969)*
Rowperfect 3 ... 206 331-5319
3954 Ne 115th St Seattle (98125) *(G-10983)*
Roy Dintelman ... 253 508-9361
5409 S 380th St Auburn (98001) *(G-550)*
Roy McMakin ... 206 323-0111
1128 Poplar Pl S Seattle (98144) *(G-10984)*
Roy Pablo ... 425 750-9941
8825 34th Ave Ne Quil Ceda Village (98271) *(G-8281)*
Royal Aleutian Seafoods Inc ... 206 283-6605
701 Dexter Ave N Ste 403 Seattle (98109) *(G-10985)*
Royal Body Treats, Tacoma *Also called Patricia Avery (G-13460)*
Royal Cabinets ... 253 267-5071
10324 Canyon Rd E Puyallup (98373) *(G-8239)*
Royal Cabinets Inc ... 253 536-6879
5410 96th St E Puyallup (98371) *(G-8240)*
Royal Dental Manufacturing Inc (PA) ... 425 743-0988
12414 Highway 99 Ste 29 Everett (98204) *(G-3601)*
Royal Line Cabinet Co ... 206 767-9125
700 S Orchard St Seattle (98108) *(G-10986)*
Royal Prestige ... 509 544-0330
104 S Oregon Ave Ste D Pasco (99301) *(G-7624)*
Royal Register ... 509 770-8221
813 W 3rd Ave Moses Lake (98837) *(G-6746)*
Royal Ridge Frt Cold Stor LLC (PA) ... 509 346-1520
13215 Road F Sw Royal City (99357) *(G-9174)*
Royal Viking Inc ... 206 783-3818
5303 Shilshole Ave Nw Seattle (98107) *(G-10987)*
Royell Manufacturing Inc ... 425 259-9258
3817 Smith Ave Everett (98201) *(G-3602)*
Roys Salsa LLC ... 253 514-3767
6805 Rosedale St Nw Gig Harbor (98335) *(G-4157)*
Rozema Boat Works, Mount Vernon *Also called Rozema Enterprises Inc (G-6831)*
Rozema Boat Works Inc ... 360 757-6004
11130 Bayview Edison Rd Mount Vernon (98273) *(G-6830)*
Rozema Enterprises Inc ... 360 757-6004
11130 Bayview Edison Rd Mount Vernon (98273) *(G-6831)*
Rp 2000 LLC ... 206 624-8258
13500 Linden Ave N Seattle (98133) *(G-10988)*
RPI, Tukwila *Also called Reischling Press Inc (G-13805)*
RPS Automation, Newman Lake *Also called Hentec Industries Inc (G-7046)*
RR Donnelley & Sons Company ... 206 389-8900
999 3rd Ave Ste 500 Seattle (98104) *(G-10989)*
RR Products ... 509 773-5227
29 Wildcat Rd Goldendale (98620) *(G-4208)*
Rrr Inc ... 206 782-9260
8549 Greenwood Ave N Seattle (98103) *(G-10990)*
Rs Machine Inc ... 360 694-0044
6133 Ne 63rd St Vancouver (98661) *(G-14559)*
Rsa The Security EMC ... 781 515-5000
15500 Se 30th Pl Ste 200 Bellevue (98007) *(G-1109)*
Rsg Forest Products Inc (PA) ... 360 673-2825
985 Nw 2nd St Kalama (98625) *(G-4507)*
Rsg Forest Products Inc ... 360 225-8513
410 N Pekin Rd Woodland (98674) *(G-15464)*
Rss Kennewick ... 206 441-9907
8390 W Gage Blvd Kennewick (99336) *(G-4720)*
Rsvp Seattle ... 425 396-7787
7829 Center Blvd Se 200 Snoqualmie (98065) *(G-12021)*
Rt Industries ... 253 219-8246
12524 127th St E Puyallup (98374) *(G-8241)*

Rt London-Norse, Lacey *Also called R T London Company* ***(G-5581)***
RTC Aerospace - Fife Div Inc.....253 922-3806
7215 45th Street Ct E Fife (98424) ***(G-3987)***
RTC Aerospace LLC (PA).....918 407-0291
7215 45th Street Ct E Fife (98424) ***(G-3988)***
Rti Manufacturing Inc.....360 435-9092
19010 66th Ave Ne Unit 3b Arlington (98223) ***(G-318)***
RTS & BBC Inc.....360 239-1953
911 3rd St Hoquiam (98550) ***(G-4356)***
RTS Lumber, Woodinville *Also called Roof Truss Supply Inc* ***(G-15351)***
RTS Packaging LLC.....206 575-0380
18340 Southcenter Pkwy Tukwila (98188) ***(G-13808)***
Rubber & Plastics Inc.....503 289-7720
7401 Ne 47th Ave Vancouver (98661) ***(G-14560)***
Rubber Granulators Inc.....360 658-7754
3811 152nd St Ne Marysville (98271) ***(G-6380)***
Rubensteins Olympia.....360 753-9156
321 Cleveland Ave Se Tumwater (98501) ***(G-13895)***
Rubythroat Press LLC.....206 634-9173
1325 N Allen Pl Apt 540 Seattle (98103) ***(G-10991)***
Ruckman's, Puyallup *Also called F Ruckman Enterprises* ***(G-8151)***
Ruckus Wireless Inc.....425 896-6000
8815 122nd Ave Ne Kirkland (98033) ***(G-5453)***
Rudd Company Inc.....206 789-1000
1141 Nw 50th St Seattle (98107) ***(G-10992)***
Rudolph Technologies Inc.....425 396-7002
35030 Se Douglas St Snoqualmie (98065) ***(G-12022)***
Rudow Specialty Publishing, Seattle *Also called Northwest Runner* ***(G-10651)***
Ruff Cuts Custom Sawing LLC.....360 249-3926
157 Clemons Rd Montesano (98563) ***(G-6655)***
Rugid Computer.....360 866-0909
6305 Elizan Dr Nw Olympia (98502) ***(G-7389)***
Rulersmith Inc.....360 707-2828
14739 Aurora Ave N Shoreline (98133) ***(G-11806)***
Rum Ruay Inc.....206 660-4647
12711 Evanston Ave N Seattle (98133) ***(G-10993)***
Rumor Games LLC.....585 771-7642
1717 1st Ave N Seattle (98109) ***(G-10994)***
Rumpeltes Enterprises Inc.....509 624-1391
215 W 2nd Ave Spokane (99201) ***(G-12485)***
Runaway Bike Industries LLC.....206 817-1787
4412 Densmore Ave N Seattle (98103) ***(G-10995)***
Rune Inc.....425 766-6134
107 Spring St Seattle (98104) ***(G-10996)***
Running 26 Inc.....425 948-6495
15603 Main St Mill Creek (98012) ***(G-6524)***
Runway Liquidation LLC.....253 474-0610
14050 Janita Dr Ne Ste A Bothell (98011) ***(G-1788)***
Runway Liquidation LLC.....262 253-4000
670 Rising Sun Ln Spokane (99218) ***(G-12486)***
Runway Liquidation LLC.....262 654-0726
7907-09 S Parkside Seattle (98101) ***(G-10997)***
Runway Liquidation LLC.....262 948-7035
12841 Towne Center Dr Seattle (98101) ***(G-10998)***
Runway Liquidation LLC.....304 325-3603
5900 Greenbelt Rd Gig Harbor (98335) ***(G-4158)***
Runway Liquidation LLC.....304 645-2799
3177 Long Beach Rd Kennewick (99336) ***(G-4721)***
Runway Liquidation LLC.....304 825-6364
6003 Big Tree Rd Kennewick (99338) ***(G-4722)***
Runway Liquidation LLC.....304 598-4888
2202 W Artesia Blvd Kirkland (98034) ***(G-5454)***
Runway Liquidation LLC.....304 748-2055
44555 Woodward Ave Lacey (98503) ***(G-5582)***
Runway Liquidation LLC.....304 636-2020
2020 116th Ave Ne Kennewick (99336) ***(G-4723)***
Runway Liquidation LLC.....651 275-3251
480 W Boughton Walla Walla (99362) ***(G-14863)***
Runway Liquidation LLC.....920 387-3180
4 Colebrook Ct Spokane (99205) ***(G-12487)***
Ruser Publications Inc.....509 659-1020
216 W Railroad Ave Ritzville (99169) ***(G-9122)***
Rush Sails Inc.....425 827-9648
16608 Crystal Dr E Enumclaw (98022) ***(G-3319)***
Russell Automation, Battle Ground *Also called Process Cntrls Instrumentation* ***(G-733)***
Russell Lamar Jacquet-Acea.....206 334-2935
4717 Ballard Ave Nw Seattle (98107) ***(G-10999)***
Russell Sign Company.....425 775-7010
21104 70th Ave W Edmonds (98026) ***(G-3150)***
Russells Custom Cabinets Inc.....253 473-7883
5640 S Durango St Ste A Tacoma (98409) ***(G-13503)***
Rust Proved Software.....206 244-0643
11628 30th Ave Sw Burien (98146) ***(G-2127)***
Rustik Kreations.....509 674-7271
486 Sunshine Way Cle Elum (98922) ***(G-2678)***
Rusty Grape Vineyard LLC.....360 513-9338
16712 Ne 219th St Battle Ground (98604) ***(G-737)***
Rusty Rack Guys, The, Pacific *Also called Cedar Recycling Inc* ***(G-7524)***
Rusty's Country Meats, Deer Park *Also called Careks Country Custom Meats* ***(G-2895)***
Ruth Publishing LLC.....253 351-2375
32461 Military Rd S Federal Way (98001) ***(G-3779)***
Rutillo Chaves.....425 775-0651
4202 198th St Sw Ste 3 Lynnwood (98036) ***(G-6190)***
Rv Alpacas.....253 431-6747
10801 133rd Ave Se Rainier (98576) ***(G-8322)***
Rv Comfort Systems LLC.....425 408-3140
24025 Bothell Everett Hwy Bothell (98021) ***(G-1898)***
Rvs Express LLC.....253 249-7043
412 8th St Sw Ste A Auburn (98001) ***(G-551)***
Rw Hot Shot Service.....509 868-6644
202 E Spokane Falls Blvd # 403 Spokane (99202) ***(G-12488)***
Rw Morse Co.....360 943-8600
1515 Lakemoor Loop Sw Olympia (98512) ***(G-7390)***
Rw Precast Inc.....253 770-0100
12216 138th Ave E Puyallup (98374) ***(G-8242)***
Rwc International Ltd.....509 452-5515
1509 S 22nd St Yakima (98901) ***(G-15664)***
Rwoodsii LLC.....206 491-9617
3402 C St Ne Ste 109 Auburn (98002) ***(G-552)***
Rwsd Lumberyard.....503 910-9822
1612 Bishop Rd Chehalis (98532) ***(G-2533)***
RY Investments Inc.....360 701-1261
5238 56th Ave Se Lacey (98503) ***(G-5583)***
Ryan Custom Coatings.....808 652-9731
614 Highland Dr Wenatchee (98801) ***(G-15070)***
Ryan Instruments, Redmond *Also called Sensitech Inc* ***(G-8660)***
Ryan Instruments, Redmond *Also called Sensitech Inc* ***(G-8661)***
Ryan Machine Inc.....253 854-9000
4164 B Pl Nw Auburn (98001) ***(G-553)***
Ryans Machine Shop.....360 427-9490
621 E Leeds Dr Shelton (98584) ***(G-11728)***
Ryco Equipment Inc.....425 744-0444
6810 220th St Sw Mountlake Terrace (98043) ***(G-6867)***
Rygaard Logging Inc (PA).....360 457-4941
401 Monroe Rd Port Angeles (98362) ***(G-7741)***
Ryno Rollers Inc (PA).....253 856-0738
3904 B St Nw Auburn (98001) ***(G-554)***
Ryonet Corporation.....360 576-7188
12303 Ne 56th St Vancouver (98682) ***(G-14561)***
Rypyl, Bellevue *Also called Selah Springs LLC* ***(G-1123)***
S G&C Contractor Services LLC.....360 671-5121
2205 Valencia St Bellingham (98229) ***(G-1520)***
S & B Inc.....425 746-9312
13200 Se 30th St Ste A Bellevue (98005) ***(G-1110)***
S & BS Boutique.....253 631-2718
22721 126th Pl Se Kent (98031) ***(G-5109)***
S & G Engraving.....425 868-4169
22539 Ne 18th St Sammamish (98074) ***(G-9244)***
S & H Auto Parts Inc (PA).....360 354-4468
8123 Guide Meridian Rd Lynden (98264) ***(G-6051)***
S & I Propellers Inc.....425 745-1700
3610 South Rd Ste 100 Mukilteo (98275) ***(G-6974)***
S & J Logging Inc.....360 795-3309
45 Elochoman Valley Rd Cathlamet (98612) ***(G-2374)***
S & R Sheet Metal Inc.....360 425-7020
1300 Walnut St Kelso (98626) ***(G-4546)***
S & R Spiral LLC.....509 747-4723
6747 Kieffer Rd Davenport (99122) ***(G-2877)***
S & S Engine Remanufacturing (PA).....509 325-4558
1023 N Monroe St Spokane (99201) ***(G-12489)***
S & S Metal Fabrication Inc.....253 472-4461
1551 South Tacoma Way Tacoma (98409) ***(G-13504)***
S & S Selden LLC.....253 922-5700
1802 62nd Ave E Fife (98424) ***(G-3989)***
S & S Transportation Services, Ellensburg *Also called S&S Transportation Service* ***(G-3224)***
S & S Welding Inc.....206 793-9943
22131 68th Ave S Kent (98032) ***(G-5110)***
S & S Welding & Repair.....509 657-3340
407 D St Endicott (99125) ***(G-3266)***
S & W Management Co Inc.....425 771-6850
3000 184th St Sw Ste 856 Lynnwood (98037) ***(G-6191)***
S & W Manufacturing Inc.....360 690-8558
7414 Ne 47th Ave Vancouver (98661) ***(G-14562)***
S and R Logging and Cutting.....425 314-7662
18515 75th Ave Nw Stanwood (98292) ***(G-12990)***
S Boone Mechanical Cutting.....360 748-4293
425 N Market Blvd Chehalis (98532) ***(G-2534)***
S C Jr LLC.....253 539-1097
12415 40th Ave E Tacoma (98446) ***(G-13505)***
S D I, Vancouver *Also called Systematic Designs Intl* ***(G-14623)***
S E H America, Vancouver *Also called Shin-Etsu Handotai America Inc* ***(G-14583)***
S E Industries LLC.....503 519-2160
2401 S 17th Way Ridgefield (98642) ***(G-9109)***
S F McKinnon Co Inc (PA).....206 622-4948
1201 Western Ave Ste 100 Seattle (98101) ***(G-11000)***
S J Olsen Publishing Inc.....360 249-3311
109 W Marcy Ave Montesano (98563) ***(G-6656)***
S J W Design, Seattle *Also called S J W Studios Inc* ***(G-11001)***
S J W Studios Inc.....206 323-8020
1424 10th Ave Seattle (98122) ***(G-11001)***
S M Marketing Specialties.....206 230-0710
853 Jericho Pl Ne Renton (98059) ***(G-8900)***

ALPHABETIC

S Mayton Construction Company 360 532-6138
1417 W Huntley St Aberdeen (98520) ***(G-32)***

S S Steiner Inc 509 453-4731
1 W Washington Ave Yakima (98903) ***(G-15665)***

S Scott & Associates LLC 360 576-4830
4719 Ne Salmon Creek St Vancouver (98686) ***(G-14563)***

S Smith 425 529-9244
15205 140th Way Se J101 Renton (98058) ***(G-8901)***

S T A, Bothell *Also called System To Asic Inc* ***(G-1798)***

S T E Electrical Contractors, Fife *Also called Sign-Tech Elc Ltd Lblty Co* ***(G-3993)***

S&J Engines Inc 509 325-4558
817 N Lincoln St Spokane (99201) ***(G-12490)***

S&L Foods LLC 360 627-7809
6349 Juanita Cir Ne Bremerton (98311) ***(G-1996)***

S&L Portable Sawmill LLC 360 417-3085
3578 Monroe Rd Port Angeles (98362) ***(G-7742)***

S&S Industries LLC 360 500-9942
17127 115th Ave E Puyallup (98374) ***(G-8243)***

S&S Industries LLC 360 500-9942
6367 Unit 4 Kimber Rd Cashmere (98815) ***(G-2329)***

S&S NDT LLC 509 688-7996
4711 S South Morrill Ct Spokane (99223) ***(G-12491)***

S&S Repair 360 496-5533
382 Butts Rd Morton (98356) ***(G-6673)***

S&S Transportation Service 509 968-9825
1000 Emerson Rd Ellensburg (98926) ***(G-3224)***

S&T Jewelry, Wenatchee *Also called S&T Trading & More LLC* ***(G-15071)***

S&T Trading & More LLC 509 421-2326
312 N Delaware Ave Wenatchee (98801) ***(G-15071)***

S-K Marine, Cusick *Also called Silver King Mining & Milling* ***(G-2852)***

S.C.I. Door, Yakima *Also called Starline Construction Inc* ***(G-15682)***

S2 Proto Types Inc 425 822-0858
12446 Ne 75th St Kirkland (98033) ***(G-5455)***

S2m Enterprises LLC 509 919-3714
2205 N Woodruff Rd Ste 9 Spokane Valley (99206) ***(G-12857)***

S3j Elctrnics Acquisition Corp 716 206-1309
10323 53rd Ave W Mukilteo (98275) ***(G-6975)***

SA Consumer Products Inc 888 792-4264
4602 20th St E Fife (98424) ***(G-3990)***

Saariswoodworking 360 835-8106
4019 A Loop Washougal (98671) ***(G-14982)***

Sabine F Price 206 780-9211
7555 Madrona Dr Ne Bainbridge Island (98110) ***(G-669)***

Sabre Blasting Industries LLC 360 990-2492
1338 Bertha Ave Nw Bremerton (98312) ***(G-1997)***

Sabre Industries 253 246-7132
26609 79th Ave S Kent (98032) ***(G-5111)***

Sackman Enterprises 509 684-5547
719 Old Arden Hwy Colville (99114) ***(G-2774)***

Saco Sales 253 277-1568
29304 204th Pl Se Kent (98042) ***(G-5112)***

Saco Sales LLC 253 922-6349
4803 Pacific Hwy E Ste 2b Fife (98424) ***(G-3991)***

Sacred Waters Fish Company LLC 503 913-1625
228 Bay Center Rd South Bend (98586) ***(G-12045)***

Safe Bathtub Inc 509 670-2711
3047 Hedding St Entiat (98822) ***(G-3270)***

Safe Boats International LLC 360 674-7161
8800 Sw Barney White Rd Bremerton (98312) ***(G-1998)***

Safe Defense LLC 509 430-5731
8406 W Deschutes Ave Kennewick (99336) ***(G-4724)***

Safe Home Security Products 360 384-1239
1736 Matz Rd Ferndale (98248) ***(G-3894)***

Safe Jack, Pasco *Also called Bogert Manufacturing Inc* ***(G-7556)***

Safe Ride News, Seattle *Also called Willapa Bay Company Inc* ***(G-11476)***

Safe Systems Inc 425 251-8662
18420 68th Ave S Ste 202 Kent (98032) ***(G-5113)***

Safebar, Vancouver *Also called Cascade Specialty Hardware* ***(G-14106)***

Safeco Field 206 346-4000
1250 1st Ave S Seattle (98134) ***(G-11002)***

Safeguard, Pasco *Also called Sbd Inc* ***(G-7625)***

Safeguard Bus Forms & Systems 800 727-9120
617 N Helena St Spokane (99202) ***(G-12492)***

Safetec Compliance Systems Inc 360 567-0280
7700 Ne Parkway Dr # 125 Vancouver (98662) ***(G-14564)***

Safetec Software LLC 888 745-8943
5512 Ne 109th Ct Ste N Vancouver (98662) ***(G-14565)***

Safety Defense Technology 360 718-2078
1900 Fort Vancouver Way Vancouver (98663) ***(G-14566)***

Safety Emergency Systems, Kenmore *Also called SES USA Inc* ***(G-4604)***

Safety Reflection 360 599-1874
6250 Juniper Ln Maple Falls (98266) ***(G-6250)***

Safeworks LLC (HQ) 206 575-6445
365 Upland Dr Tukwila (98188) ***(G-13809)***

Safeworks Holdings Inc 206 575-6445
365 Upland Dr Tukwila (98188) ***(G-13810)***

Safran 425 283-5031
11400 Se 8th St Ste 225 Bellevue (98004) ***(G-1111)***

Safran Cabin Bellingham Inc (HQ) 360 738-2005
3225 Woburn St Bellingham (98226) ***(G-1521)***

Safran Cabin Inc 360 653-2600
12806 State Ave Marysville (98271) ***(G-6381)***

Safran Cabin Inc 360 653-2211
12810 State Ave Marysville (98271) ***(G-6382)***

Safran Cabin Inc 509 447-4122
501 N Newport Ave Newport (99156) ***(G-7065)***

Safran Elec & Pwr USA LLC 425 407-6700
2300 Merrill Creek Pkwy # 100 Everett (98203) ***(G-3603)***

Safran Usa Inc 425 462-8613
11400 Se 8th St Ste 225 Bellevue (98004) ***(G-1112)***

Safran Ventilation System Usa 425 438-1378
7501 Hardeson Rd Everett (98203) ***(G-3604)***

Safs Inc 253 301-0615
629 S Trafton St Apt 2 Tacoma (98405) ***(G-13506)***

Sage Hill Northwest Inc (PA) 509 269-4966
5230 Hollingsworth Rd Mesa (99343) ***(G-6495)***

Sage Manufacturing Corporation 800 952-9827
12715 Miller Rd Ne Bainbridge Island (98110) ***(G-670)***

Sage Manufacturing Corporation 206 842-6608
8500 Ne Day Rd E Bainbridge Island (98110) ***(G-671)***

Sagemax Bioceramics Inc 253 214-0389
34210 9th Ave S Ste 118 Federal Way (98003) ***(G-3780)***

Sagetech Corporation 509 493-2154
1320 Green Tree Ln White Salmon (98672) ***(G-15128)***

Sagetech Corporation 509 493-1364
292 E Jewett Blvd White Salmon (98672) ***(G-15129)***

Sagetech Corporation 509 493-2113
156 Ne Church Ave White Salmon (98672) ***(G-15130)***

Sagra Inc 253 476-1403
5997 Nw Altitude Ln Silverdale (98383) ***(G-11855)***

Sahale Snacks Inc 206 624-7244
3411 S 120th Pl Ste 100 Tukwila (98168) ***(G-13811)***

Saigon Printing 206 722-6788
3311 Rainier Ave S Seattle (98144) ***(G-11003)***

Saint Laurent Winery 509 787-3700
9224 Road S Nw Quincy (98848) ***(G-8309)***

Saint Michelle, Woodinville *Also called Michelle Ste Wine Estates Ltd* ***(G-15310)***

Saint Square Publishing 360 636-2645
191 Inglewood Dr Longview (98632) ***(G-5950)***

Saint-Gobain Prfmce Plas Corp 253 466-5400
507 N Levee Rd Puyallup (98371) ***(G-8244)***

Saitek U S A Inc 425 672-8748
21700 Nootka Rd Woodway (98020) ***(G-15480)***

Sakai Foods America Inc 484 494-4322
5506 6th Ave S Ste 103 Seattle (98108) ***(G-11004)***

Sakco Precision Inc 253 288-9702
3665 C St Ne Auburn (98002) ***(G-555)***

Salem Equipment Inc 503 581-8411
2525 W Firestone Ln Vancouver (98660) ***(G-14567)***

Salesforcecom Inc 206 701-1755
929 108th Ave Ne Bellevue (98004) ***(G-1113)***

Salire Corporation 425 284-0679
16541 Redmond Way Ste 180 Redmond (98052) ***(G-8656)***

Salire Partners, Redmond *Also called Salire Corporation* ***(G-8656)***

Salish Coast Enterprises LLC 360 333-5280
11966 Westar Ln Burlington (98233) ***(G-2184)***

Salish LLC 206 375-7270
1001 Ne Boat St Seattle (98105) ***(G-11005)***

Salish Post Enterprises LLC 360 391-5492
10788 Seaview Ln Mount Vernon (98273) ***(G-6832)***

Salish Screenprinting 360 758-2287
4283 Lummi Shore Dr Ferndale (98248) ***(G-3895)***

Salish Sea Organic Liqueurs 360 890-4927
2641 Willamette Dr Ne Lacey (98516) ***(G-5584)***

Salish Seafoods Company, Shelton *Also called Island Enterprises* ***(G-11702)***

Salish Technology 360 632-4522
7524 Maxwelton Rd Clinton (98236) ***(G-2696)***

Sally and Harry Simmons 206 297-1868
8731 18th Ave Nw Seattle (98117) ***(G-11006)***

Sally Beauty Supply LLC 509 881-2120
300 Simon St Se Ste 3 East Wenatchee (98802) ***(G-3032)***

Sally Beauty Supply LLC 509 783-7292
3180 W Clearwatr Ave C Kennewick (99336) ***(G-4725)***

Salmon Bay Processors, Renton *Also called CFC Fish Company LLC* ***(G-8770)***

Salmon Bay Sand and Gravel Co 206 784-1234
5228 Shilshole Ave Nw Seattle (98107) ***(G-11007)***

Salmon Bay Woodworks 206 612-3993
643 Nw 53rd St Seattle (98107) ***(G-11008)***

Salmon Creek Industries Inc 360 921-5143
34506 Nw 11th Ave La Center (98629) ***(G-5515)***

Salmon Creek Machine 360 573-7958
14503 Nw 56th Ave Vancouver (98685) ***(G-14568)***

Salmon Creek Meats 360 985-7822
139 Koons Rd Mossyrock (98564) ***(G-6766)***

Salmon River Design Inc 425 503-7987
5817 238th St Se Ste 2 Woodinville (98072) ***(G-15352)***

Salsa 7 253 445-6525
506 N Meridian Puyallup (98371) ***(G-8245)***

Salsa Mania LLC 360 432-9240
1290 Se Phillips Rd Shelton (98584) ***(G-11729)***

Salsa With A Kick 253 820-7622
11609 Cloverdale Ct Sw Lakewood (98499) ***(G-5753)***

Salso So Fresh, Shelton *Also called Salsa Mania LLC* ***(G-11729)***

Salt Lake Christmas Tool, Orting *Also called Family Roots Publishing Co LLC* ***(G-7479)***

Salt Studio.......206 784-9652
66 Bell St Apt 1 Seattle (98121) **(G-11009)**
Salted Vinegar Studios.......931 302-0434
9616 Regency Loop Se Olympia (98513) **(G-7391)**
Saltworks Inc.......425 885-7258
16240 Wdinvle Redmnd Ne Woodinville (98072) **(G-15353)**
Sam Bickle Logging Inc.......360 273-5886
201 Jylha Rd Rochester (98579) **(G-9140)**
Sam Knutsons Lumber Co Inc.......509 662-6183
1415 S Wenatchee Ave B Wenatchee (98801) **(G-15072)**
Samish Bay Soaps & Scents.......360 752-9015
1372 Del Bonita Ct Bellingham (98226) **(G-1522)**
Samish Island Winery, Bow *Also called Gary N Lamb* **(G-1929)**
Sammamish.......425 295-7300
22739 Se 29th St Sammamish (98075) **(G-9245)**
Samoa Maritime Company.......206 246-1182
18627 1st Ave S Normandy Park (98148) **(G-7098)**
Sams Press Inc.......425 423-8181
17617 Bagley Pl N Shoreline (98133) **(G-11807)**
Samson Estates Winery.......360 966-4526
1861 Van Dyk Rd Everson (98247) **(G-3688)**
Samson Rope Technologies Inc (HQ).......360 384-4669
2090 Thornton St Ferndale (98248) **(G-3896)**
Samson Sports LLC.......360 833-2507
4327 Nw Lake Rd Camas (98607) **(G-2280)**
Samson's Inland Printing, Bremerton *Also called Tom & Cheryl McCallaum* **(G-2006)**
Samsonite LLC.......253 395-1017
1030 Sw 34th St Ste D Renton (98057) **(G-8902)**
Samuel & Company Inc.......425 883-1220
14690 Ne 95th St Ste 102 Redmond (98052) **(G-8657)**
Samuel Edwards.......253 988-0219
22415 41st Ave S Kent (98032) **(G-5114)**
Samurai Noodle (PA).......206 624-9321
606 5th Ave S Seattle (98104) **(G-11010)**
San Gennaro Foods Inc.......253 872-1900
19255 80th Ave S Kent (98032) **(G-5115)**
San Juan Composites LLC.......360 299-3790
2201 Minnesota Ave Anacortes (98221) **(G-164)**
San Juan Engineering & Mfg Co, Bellingham *Also called Sje Inc* **(G-1540)**
San Juan Islander.......360 378-2798
1010 Guard St Friday Harbor (98250) **(G-4056)**
San Juan Islands Sculpture Pk.......360 370-0035
9083 Roche Harbor Rd Friday Harbor (98250) **(G-4057)**
San Juan Naturals.......360 378-2648
745 Larson St Ste A Friday Harbor (98250) **(G-4058)**
San Juan Publishing.......425 485-2813
18414 57th Ave Ne Kenmore (98028) **(G-4602)**
San Juan Salsa Co.......360 435-2100
5919 195th St Ne Unit 5 Arlington (98223) **(G-319)**
San Mar Corporation.......206 727-3200
30500 Se 79th St Issaquah (98027) **(G-4471)**
San Poil Logging.......509 634-8112
12153 S Highway 21 Keller (99140) **(G-4514)**
Sanchez Pallets LLC.......509 877-4004
6191 Yakima Valley Hwy Wapato (98951) **(G-14926)**
Sanctuary Corporation.......360 477-4384
182 N Ridge View Dr Port Angeles (98362) **(G-7743)**
Sand Blasted Art, Puyallup *Also called Debbie Zachary* **(G-8141)**
Sand Carrier Inc.......206 790-6791
16217 48th Ave S Tukwila (98188) **(G-13812)**
Sand Paper & Ink Inc.......360 705-0918
2918 Ferguson St Sw C1 Tumwater (98512) **(G-13896)**
Sandbox Enterprises LLC.......360 966-6677
3248 Agate Heights Rd Bellingham (98226) **(G-1523)**
Sandcastle Sandblasting.......360 354-5087
861 19th St Lynden (98264) **(G-6052)**
Sandis Signs Inc.......253 862-6885
18317 Veterans Mem Dr E Bonney Lake (98391) **(G-1737)**
Sandland Construction, Lake Forest Park *Also called Clowers Corporation* **(G-5609)**
Sandmaiden Sleepwear.......206 595-4303
2112 Nw 70th St Seattle (98117) **(G-11011)**
Sandpiper Software Inc.......425 788-6175
18448 Ne 199th St Woodinville (98077) **(G-15354)**
Sandra S Berlin.......206 612-4126
914 21st Ave Seattle (98122) **(G-11012)**
Sandra Stroup.......509 754-0822
12199 Dodson Rd Nw Ephrata (98823) **(G-3346)**
Sandstone Distillery.......360 239-7272
842 Wright Rd Se Tenino (98589) **(G-13623)**
Sandvik Special Metals LLC.......509 734-4000
235407 E Sr 397 Kennewick (99337) **(G-4726)**
Sandy Beach Mobile Villa LLC.......509 255-6222
326 S Sandy Beach Ln Liberty Lake (99019) **(G-5857)**
Sandy Jo Franks.......206 367-2669
18212 Ballinger Way Ne Lake Forest Park (98155) **(G-5624)**
Sandy M Serrett, Shelton *Also called Knit Alteration & Design* **(G-11707)**
Sandys Nifty Tees.......360 861-8669
9 Mcconkey Ave McCleary (98557) **(G-6419)**
Sandys Sign & Design.......360 693-9229
4715 Ne 60th St Vancouver (98661) **(G-14569)**
Sanesolution, Bellevue *Also called Yopti LLC* **(G-1231)**
Sanford Art Prints.......509 784-1220
13464 Dunn St Entiat (98822) **(G-3271)**
Sanjuanyachts, Anacortes *Also called San Juan Composites LLC* **(G-164)**
Sansaire, Bellevue *Also called Modernchef Inc* **(G-1013)**
Sansueb Software LLC.......253 630-5208
17019 Se 240th St Kent (98042) **(G-5116)**
Santees Granola Inc.......509 245-3338
2525 E Spangle Waverly Rd Spangle (99031) **(G-12084)**
Santoros Books.......206 784-2113
7405 Greenwood Ave N Seattle (98103) **(G-11013)**
Sapolil Cellars.......509 520-5258
15 E Main St Walla Walla (99362) **(G-14864)**
Sapphire Materials Company.......360 210-5124
750 S 32nd St Washougal (98671) **(G-14983)**
Sapphire Scientific Inc.......928 445-3030
15180 Josh Wilson Rd Burlington (98233) **(G-2185)**
Sara Huey Pblcy Promotions LLC.......206 619-0610
103 Nw 104th St Seattle (98177) **(G-11014)**
Sara June Haskin.......360 873-4257
60623 Beverly Pl Marblemount (98267) **(G-6306)**
Sarangsoft LLC.......425 378-3890
5724 114st Pl Se St Bellevue (98006) **(G-1114)**
Sarco Precision.......360 424-0605
2816 Old Highway 99 S Rd # 4 Mount Vernon (98273) **(G-6833)**
Sars Corporation (PA).......866 276-7277
601 108th Ave Ne Ste 1900 Bellevue (98004) **(G-1115)**
Sarvel Biofuels Lummi Corp.......360 362-0016
4534 Haxton Way Ferndale (98248) **(G-3897)**
Sasquatch Books LLC.......206 467-4300
1904 3rd Ave Ste 710 Seattle (98101) **(G-11015)**
Sasqutch Acqstion Frmerly Name, Seattle *Also called Sasquatch Books LLC* **(G-11015)**
Sassy Dog Wear, Burien *Also called Lk Sewing Co* **(G-2118)**
Sassy Pillows.......425 778-7783
9007 Olympic View Dr Edmonds (98026) **(G-3151)**
Satech, Chehalis *Also called Seamless Attenuating Tech* **(G-2535)**
Satellite Sign Design.......360 986-0067
951 N Stephenson Dr Montesano (98563) **(G-6657)**
Satin Group LLC A.......206 228-1364
1029 Belmont Ave E # 202 Seattle (98102) **(G-11016)**
Saturday Night Inc.......509 928-5816
3520 N Eden Rd Spokane Valley (99216) **(G-12858)**
Satus Networks LLC.......509 575-8382
4901 Scenic Dr Yakima (98908) **(G-15666)**
Sauder Mouldings Inc Ferndale.......360 384-4774
5575 Nordic Pl Ferndale (98248) **(G-3898)**
Sauer Kraut, Sequim *Also called Der Heintzelmann Inc* **(G-11626)**
Sauk Suiattle Indian Tribe Tru.......360 436-0131
5318 Chief Brown Ln B Darrington (98241) **(G-2869)**
Saunders Instruments Inc.......206 842-6651
1416 Elizabeth Pl Nw Bainbridge Island (98110) **(G-672)**
Saunders Solutions Inc.......360 678-4788
701 Ne 4th St Coupeville (98239) **(G-2817)**
Sausage Skateboards.......206 679-3619
2607 Nw 57th St Seattle (98107) **(G-11017)**
Sauther & Assoc Inc.......509 922-7828
2208 N Swing Ln Liberty Lake (99019) **(G-5858)**
Savage Inc.......206 972-8217
6201 15th Ave Nw Seattle (98107) **(G-11018)**
Savage Color LLC.......206 632-2866
3614 2nd Ave Nw Seattle (98107) **(G-11019)**
Savage Gun Coating.......206 485-4125
15405 63rd Ave Ne Kenmore (98028) **(G-4603)**
Savage Screen.......360 321-2040
11247 State Route 525 Clinton (98236) **(G-2697)**
Savang Sine.......206 721-2558
6464 M Luther King Jr Way Seattle (98118) **(G-11020)**
Save Smoke.......425 793-5030
17170 116th Ave Se Renton (98058) **(G-8903)**
Saviah Cellars, Walla Walla *Also called Rose Saviah Winery LLC* **(G-14861)**
Savior Socks Inc.......360 601-8036
307 Sw 20th Ave Battle Ground (98604) **(G-738)**
Savon Caskets and Urns.......206 390-3797
460 Shelton Pl Ne Renton (98056) **(G-8904)**
Savotta Tech LLC.......425 505-9951
1234 244th Pl Se Sammamish (98075) **(G-9246)**
Savoy Candles LLC.......205 281-9031
339 Burnett Ave S Apt 312 Renton (98057) **(G-8905)**
Savoy Truffle.......206 762-7411
5915 Airport Way S Seattle (98108) **(G-11021)**
Saw Industries LLC.......360 306-8988
2009 J St Bellingham (98225) **(G-1524)**
Saw Service Washington Inc.......360 738-6437
1602 Carolina St Ste D9 Bellingham (98229) **(G-1525)**
Sawarne Lumber Co Ltd.......360 380-1290
5530 Nordic Pl Ferndale (98248) **(G-3899)**
Sawbox LLC.......253 277-0506
8623 S 212th St Kent (98031) **(G-5117)**
Sawdust Supply.......206 622-4321
6314 7th Ave S Seattle (98108) **(G-11022)**
Sawtooth Logging.......360 249-6255
81 Winkleman Rd N Montesano (98563) **(G-6658)**

ALPHABETIC

Sawyer & Sawyer Inc 509 486-1304
8d N State Frontage Rd Tonasket (98855) *(G-13658)*
Saxco Pacific Coast LLC 360 892-3451
3812 Ne 112th Ave 100 Vancouver (98682) *(G-14570)*
Saxon Contracting LLC 360 595-2854
322 Rowland Rd Sedro Woolley (98284) *(G-11563)*
Sayitright LLC 401 682-7630
3122 Angela Ln Oak Harbor (98277) *(G-7164)*
Sayitright Media, Oak Harbor *Also called Sayitright LLC (G-7164)*
Sayler Custom Controls Inc 360 816-4193
1708 Midway Ct Centralia (98531) *(G-2430)*
Saywhatclub 425 486-2667
18620 89th Ave Ne Bothell (98011) *(G-1789)*
Sbd Inc 509 545-8845
2521 W Sylvester St Pasco (99301) *(G-7625)*
Sbeusa Medical, Bellingham *Also called Sandbox Enterprises LLC (G-1523)*
Sbf Printing 509 457-2877
313 S 4th Ave Yakima (98902) *(G-15667)*
Sbk Pharma LLC 425 778-7778
7315 212th St Sw Ste 100 Edmonds (98026) *(G-3152)*
Scada Nexus, Spokane *Also called Resource Associates Intl (G-12472)*
Scafco Corporation (PA) 509 343-9000
2800 E Main Ave Spokane (99202) *(G-12493)*
Scafco Corporation 509 343-9012
250 N Altamont St Spokane (99202) *(G-12494)*
Scafco Steel Stud Mfg, Spokane *Also called Scafco Corporation (G-12493)*
Scale Model Boats, Lake Stevens *Also called Isaksen Scale Models (G-5650)*
Scaleout Software Inc 503 643-3422
600 108th Ave Ne Ste 104 Bellevue (98004) *(G-1116)*
Scaler Sales Comp, Mukilteo *Also called Waft Corp (G-6990)*
Scan Marine Equipment, Seattle *Also called Two Mac Inc (G-11354)*
Scanivalve Corp 509 891-9970
1722 N Madson St Liberty Lake (99019) *(G-5859)*
Scared of Genre 206 227-2574
4716 S Orcas St Seattle (98118) *(G-11023)*
Scatter Creek Winery 360 264-9463
3442 180th Ave Sw Tenino (98589) *(G-13624)*
SCC, Bellingham *Also called Skills For Creative Concepts (G-1542)*
SCC Enterprises LLC 425 454-0567
9107 Ne 47th St Yarrow Point (98004) *(G-15723)*
Schaben Logging Inc 360 589-9008
5914 Olympic Hwy Aberdeen (98520) *(G-33)*
Schachere Industries LLC 253 235-5205
33427 Pacific Hwy S E1 Federal Way (98003) *(G-3781)*
Schaeffer Specialized Lubr, Kent *Also called Ray Summerlin (G-5100)*
Schafer Winery LLC 509 522-5444
178 Vineyard Ln Walla Walla (99362) *(G-14865)*
Schafer Winery LLC (PA) 425 985-7000
4402 E Mercer Way Mercer Island (98040) *(G-6482)*
Schattauer Sailmaker Corp 206 783-0173
6010 Seaview Ave Nw Seattle (98107) *(G-11024)*
Schattauer Sails, Seattle *Also called Schattauer Sailmaker Corp (G-11024)*
Schedules Direct 206 701-7800
8613 42nd Ave S Seattle (98118) *(G-11025)*
Scheffler Northwest Inc 360 213-2070
351 Grand Blvd Ste B Vancouver (98661) *(G-14571)*
Scheibler Bros Inc 509 548-7115
15600 Chumstick Hwy Leavenworth (98826) *(G-5815)*
Schell Pump Service 509 922-4756
4312 S Chapman Rd Greenacres (99016) *(G-4302)*
Schenk Packing Co Inc 360 336-2128
1321 S 6th St Mount Vernon (98273) *(G-6834)*
Schermer Construction Inc 360 533-5866
299 Us Highway 101 Hoquiam (98550) *(G-4357)*
Schiferl Woodworking 425 788-3795
19728 Ne 189th St Woodinville (98077) *(G-15355)*
Schilling Cider 208 660-4086
2722 Mayfair Ave N Seattle (98109) *(G-11026)*
Schilling Cider LLC 408 390-8754
4402 D St Nw Ste 101 Auburn (98001) *(G-556)*
Schilling Graphics 253 572-8171
2340 E 11th St Tacoma (98421) *(G-13507)*
Schillinger Enterprises Inc 360 275-2275
4673 E State Route 302 Belfair (98528) *(G-774)*
Schindler Elevator Corporation 509 535-2471
409 N Thierman Rd Ste D Spokane Valley (99212) *(G-12859)*
Schippers & Crew Inc 206 782-2325
5309 Shlshl Ave Nw 100 Seattle (98107) *(G-11027)*
Schmid Family Engraving LLC 360 491-0997
3420 Yorkshire Dr Se Olympia (98513) *(G-7392)*
Schnapsleiche LLC 425 591-2586
19151 144th Ave Ne Ste H Woodinville (98072) *(G-15356)*
Schneider Drainfield Des 360 758-7353
2455 Tuttle Ln Lummi Island (98262) *(G-5993)*
Schneider Elc Buildings LLC 509 892-1121
7222 E Nora Ave Spokane Valley (99212) *(G-12860)*
Schnitzer Steel International (HQ) 253 572-4000
1902 Marine View Dr Tacoma (98422) *(G-13508)*
Schober, Renton *Also called Lumicor Inc (G-8846)*
Schober Woodworks 360 595-7519
3962 Hoff Rd Bellingham (98225) *(G-1526)*
Schoeben & Schoeben Inc 360 794-1945
14792 172nd Dr Se Monroe (98272) *(G-6616)*
Scholastic Inc 509 926-4465
3808 N Sullivan Rd 35d Spokane Valley (99216) *(G-12861)*
School Company, The, Vancouver *Also called Career Development Software (G-14099)*
School of Survival Specialties, Seattle *Also called Survival Inc (G-11229)*
Schoolkit International, Bellevue *Also called Schoolkitcom Inc (G-1117)*
Schoolkitcom Inc 425 454-3373
4505 141st Pl Se Bellevue (98006) *(G-1117)*
Schooner Exact 206 432-9734
3901 1st Ave S Seattle (98134) *(G-11028)*
Schooner Exact Brewing Co., Seattle *Also called Schooner Exact (G-11028)*
Schreiber Foods Inc 425 286-6598
1225 183rd St Se Bothell (98012) *(G-1899)*
Schreiner Construction 509 525-6205
512 Se 6th St College Place (99324) *(G-2727)*
Schroeders Machine Works Inc 360 573-6911
8010 Ne 19th Ct Vancouver (98665) *(G-14572)*
Schumacher Creative Services 206 364-7151
2025 Ne 123rd St Seattle (98125) *(G-11029)*
Schurmans Gas & Glass 360 573-3669
18109 Nw Krieger Rd Ridgefield (98642) *(G-9110)*
Schwager Design & Construction 360 221-8165
3800 E Harbor Rd Langley (98260) *(G-5784)*
Schwaldbe North America 360 384-6468
5501 Hovander Rd Ferndale (98248) *(G-3900)*
Schwartz Brothers Bakery, Renton *Also called Schwartz Brothers Restaurants (G-8906)*
Schwartz Brothers Restaurants 206 623-3134
1010 Sw 34th St Renton (98057) *(G-8906)*
Schwartz Brothers Restaurants 206 623-3134
619 S Nevada St Seattle (98108) *(G-11030)*
Schweitzer Engrg Labs Inc 509 332-1890
2440 Ne Hopkins Ct Pullman (99163) *(G-8106)*
SCI, Redmond *Also called Service Corp International (G-8663)*
Scitus Tech Solutions LLC 360 202-9642
7032 Portal Way R6 Ferndale (98248) *(G-3901)*
Scoggin & Scoggin 509 843-1251
969 Mountain Rd Pomeroy (99347) *(G-7677)*
Scope 5 Inc 206 456-5656
999 N Northlake Way 225 Seattle (98103) *(G-11031)*
Scoring Sports, Fife *Also called Jumbo Dti Corporation (G-3961)*
Scot Industries Inc 360 623-1305
3020 Foron Rd Centralia (98531) *(G-2431)*
Scotsman Guide, Bothell *Also called Scotsman Publishing Inc (G-1901)*
Scotsman Guide Media Inc 425 485-2282
22118 20th Ave Se Ste 129 Bothell (98021) *(G-1900)*
Scotsman Publishing Inc 425 485-2282
22118 20th Ave Se Ste 129 Bothell (98021) *(G-1901)*
Scott Galvanizing, Arlington *Also called Seattle Galvanizing Co Inc (G-322)*
Scott Galvanizing Co Inc 206 783-3100
6010 199th St Ne Arlington (98223) *(G-320)*
Scott Lumber Packaging LLC 425 821-2075
9222 Ne 143rd Pl Bothell (98011) *(G-1790)*
Scott McClure 360 297-7007
27837 Lindvog Rd Kingston (98346) *(G-5262)*
Scott Parrish 360 259-8080
17707 Ne 50th Ave Vancouver (98686) *(G-14573)*
Scott Rl and Associates 253 604-4006
11126 117th Street Ct E Puyallup (98374) *(G-8246)*
Scott Wood Associates LLC 253 509-3742
38 Raft Island Dr Nw Gig Harbor (98335) *(G-4159)*
Scott's Tool & Die, Kingston *Also called Scott McClure (G-5262)*
Scotts Home & Roofing Service 360 297-7524
9750 Ne Kingston Farm Rd Kingston (98346) *(G-5263)*
Scotts Sheet Metal 360 384-3827
6169 Portal Way Ferndale (98248) *(G-3902)*
Scotty's Electric Motor, Vancouver *Also called Scottys Elc Mtr & Pump Repr (G-14574)*
Scottys Elc Mtr & Pump Repr 360 573-9544
7917 Ne St Johns Rd Vancouver (98665) *(G-14574)*
Scougal Rubber Corporation (PA) 206 763-2650
6239 Corson Ave S Seattle (98108) *(G-11032)*
Scout Media Inc 206 313-4932
150 Nickerson St Ste 300 Seattle (98109) *(G-11033)*
Scrappy Punk Brewing LLC 503 810-1655
707 Avenue A Apt A205 Snohomish (98290) *(G-11970)*
Scrappys Bitters LLC 206 632-7257
13749 Midvale Ave N Seattle (98133) *(G-11034)*
Scratch and Peck Feeds, Burlington *Also called Scratch and Peck LLC (G-2186)*
Scratch and Peck LLC 360 318-7585
872 N Hill Blvd Burlington (98233) *(G-2186)*
Scratch Distillery LLC 425 673-5541
20818 44th Ave W Ste 201 Lynnwood (98036) *(G-6192)*
Scratch Distillery LLC 425 442-7306
200 James St Apt 303 Edmonds (98020) *(G-3153)*
Screen Fx 509 966-7515
731 Old Naches Hwy Yakima (98908) *(G-15668)*
Screen Print Northwest Inc 360 577-1534
1141 Commerce Ave Longview (98632) *(G-5951)*
Screen Printing International 678 231-9195
12303 Ne 56th St Vancouver (98682) *(G-14575)*

Screen Printing Northwest Inc 425 303-3381
2526 Colby Ave Everett (98201) *(G-3605)*
Screen Tek Inc 509 928-8322
22902 E Appleway Ave Liberty Lake (99019) *(G-5860)*
Screenlife LLC 206 829-0743
315 5th Ave S Ste 600 Seattle (98104) *(G-11035)*
Screw You LLC 360 400-3648
15826 Lawrence Lake Rd Se Yelm (98597) *(G-15745)*
Scribble Sketch Press 707 364-4072
1525 Nw 57th St Unit 404 Seattle (98107) *(G-11036)*
Scribbly Tees 517 285-3648
3901 Military Rd E Tacoma (98446) *(G-13509)*
Scrub Nogginz LLC 425 931-9251
5919 121st St Se Snohomish (98296) *(G-11971)*
Scrupulous Design 425 788-1812
28326 Ne 146th St Duvall (98019) *(G-3001)*
Sculptures In Glass 509 951-3615
29512 N Elk Chattaroy Rd Chattaroy (99003) *(G-2452)*
Scutters 425 350-7480
14331 148th Pl Se Renton (98059) *(G-8907)*
Scuttlebutt Brewing Co LLC (PA) 425 252-2829
3310 Cedar St Everett (98201) *(G-3606)*
SDaerospace 425 440-9295
19117 63rd Ave Ne Ste B Arlington (98223) *(G-321)*
Sdi, Kirkland *Also called Silicon Designs Inc* *(G-5461)*
Sdp Tech Inc 206 595-3041
227 Bellevue Way Ne Bellevue (98004) *(G-1118)*
SDS Lumber Co 509 493-1444
123 Industrial Rd Bingen (98605) *(G-1642)*
SE Industries LLC 360 256-3775
10212 Ne 219th Ave Vancouver (98682) *(G-14576)*
Sea Alaska Industrial Electric 360 568-7624
415 Maple Ave Snohomish (98290) *(G-11972)*
Sea Com Corporation 425 771-2182
7030 220th St Sw Mountlake Terrace (98043) *(G-6868)*
Sea Cure Technology Inc 360 676-1824
1225 Bowman Rd Acme (98220) *(G-44)*
Sea Island Corp 360 376-4215
340 Gravel Pit Rd Eastsound (98245) *(G-3046)*
Sea Lect Products 253 520-2598
821 3rd Ave S Kent (98032) *(G-5118)*
Sea Pac Transport Services LLC 206 763-0339
3544 W Marginal Way Sw Seattle (98106) *(G-11037)*
Sea Storm Fisheries Inc 206 547-6557
2727 Alaskan Way Pier 69 Seattle (98121) *(G-11038)*
Sea Technology Construction 206 282-9158
309 S Cloverdale St E15 Seattle (98108) *(G-11039)*
Sea To Software LLC 206 617-6893
3626 Fremont Ln N Apt 202 Seattle (98103) *(G-11040)*
Sea West Products Inc 253 854-2942
8801 S 228th St Kent (98031) *(G-5119)*
Sea-Bird Electronics Inc 425 643-9866
13431 Ne 20th St Bellevue (98005) *(G-1119)*
Sea-Dog Corporation (PA) 425 259-0194
3402 Smith Ave Ste C Everett (98201) *(G-3607)*
Sea-Dog Line, Everett *Also called Sea-Dog Corporation* *(G-3607)*
Sea-TAC Lighting & Contrls LLC (PA) 206 575-6865
4439e S 134th Pl Tukwila (98168) *(G-13813)*
Seabear Company (PA) 360 293-4661
605 30th St Anacortes (98221) *(G-165)*
Seaboard Cabinet Company Inc 425 776-2000
5728 204th St Sw Ste 400 Lynnwood (98036) *(G-6193)*
Seacast, Tulalip *Also called Cast 7020 LLC* *(G-13840)*
Seacast Inc (PA) 360 653-9388
6130 31st Ave Ne Tulalip (98271) *(G-13843)*
Seacast Inc 206 767-5759
207 S Bennett St Seattle (98108) *(G-11041)*
Seacast Eagle, Tulalip *Also called Seacast Inc* *(G-13843)*
Seacast Investment Castings, Seattle *Also called Seacast Inc* *(G-11041)*
Seaclear Industries Mfg Inc 360 659-2700
3923 88th St Ne Ste H Marysville (98270) *(G-6383)*
Seafab Metals, Vancouver *Also called Fabricated Products Inc* *(G-14217)*
Seafoam Studios LLC 702 509-4742
6519 Cleopatra Pl Nw Seattle (98117) *(G-11042)*
Seafood Producers Cooperative (PA) 360 733-0120
2417 Meridian St Ste 105 Bellingham (98225) *(G-1527)*
Seafreeze Cold Storage, Seattle *Also called Seafreeze Limited Partnership* *(G-11043)*
Seafreeze Limited Partnership 206 767-7350
206 Sw Michigan St Seattle (98106) *(G-11043)*
Seahurst Lumber Company, Kenmore *Also called Michiels International Inc* *(G-4592)*
Seakamp Engineering Inc 360 734-2788
3985 Hammer Dr Bellingham (98226) *(G-1528)*
Seal Dynamics 503 232-0973
4609 Nw Lincoln Ave Vancouver (98663) *(G-14577)*
Seal Shield, Seattle *Also called D A Graphics Inc* *(G-9777)*
Seal-Guard Corporation 253 833-7080
101 F St Nw Auburn (98001) *(G-557)*
Sealaska Timber Corporation 360 834-3700
532 Ne 3rd Ave Ste 250 Camas (98607) *(G-2281)*
Sealth Aero Marine Co 425 481-0727
16001 Mill Creek Blvd Mill Creek (98012) *(G-6525)*
Sealy Mattress Mfg Co Inc 360 413-6902
2626 Willamette Dr Ne Lacey (98516) *(G-5585)*
Seamax Enterprises Inc 206 323-8886
4227 S Meridian Puyallup (98373) *(G-8247)*
Seamist Marine LLC 253 583-4151
5451 Nw Newberry Hill Rd # 103 Silverdale (98383) *(G-11856)*
Seamless Attenuating Tech 360 748-8711
1769 Bishop Rd Chehalis (98532) *(G-2535)*
Seamobile Inc (PA) 206 838-7700
1200 Westlake Ave N Seattle (98109) *(G-11044)*
Seaplane Landing Area (wa13) 360 647-7839
1622 Euclid Ave Bellingham (98229) *(G-1529)*
Seaport Machine Inc 509 758-2605
1719 13th St Clarkston (99403) *(G-2648)*
Seaport Sound Terminal LLC 253 272-9348
4130 E 11th St Tacoma (98421) *(G-13510)*
Seaport Tile & Marble Inc 425 644-7067
16412 Se 9th St Bellevue (98008) *(G-1120)*
Sears Tents & Awning 509 452-8971
903 S 1st St Yakima (98901) *(G-15669)*
Seasalt Superstore LLC (PA) 425 249-2331
11604 Airport Rd Ste D300 Everett (98204) *(G-3608)*
Seasoft Scuba Inc 253 939-5510
434 Nw Prindle St Chehalis (98532) *(G-2536)*
Seasoningsnet LLC 253 237-0550
8001 S 194th St Kent (98032) *(G-5120)*
Seatac Automotive 253 839-0309
24805 Pacific Hwy S Kent (98032) *(G-5121)*
Seatac Packaging Mfg Corp 253 682-6588
901 N Levee Rd Puyallup (98371) *(G-8248)*
Seatech Publications Inc 360 394-1911
2622 Ne Lillehammer Ln Poulsbo (98370) *(G-7997)*
Seaton Concepts Inc 509 928-0633
18405 E Baldwin Ave Spokane Valley (99016) *(G-12862)*
Seaton Engineering Corporation 509 290-5919
217 W Garden Ct Spokane (99208) *(G-12495)*
Seatons Grove Greenhouse 509 633-0404
Star Rte Coulee Dam (99116) *(G-2808)*
Seatthole Bellingham, Bellingham *Also called Seatthole Inc* *(G-1530)*
Seatthole Inc 360 389-2154
126 W Holly St Bellingham (98225) *(G-1530)*
Seattle 0062, Tacoma *Also called Leggett & Platt Incorporated* *(G-13384)*
Seattle Applied Science Inc 425 773-2673
7015 147th St Sw Edmonds (98026) *(G-3154)*
Seattle Area Tees 425 314-3814
9700 Harbour Pl Ste 130 Mukilteo (98275) *(G-6976)*
Seattle Avionics Inc 425 806-0249
19825 141st Pl Ne Woodinville (98072) *(G-15357)*
Seattle Avionics Software, Woodinville *Also called Seattle Avionics Inc* *(G-15357)*
Seattle Barrel Co 206 622-7218
4716 Airport Way S Seattle (98108) *(G-11045)*
Seattle Bindery 425 656-8210
6540 S Glacier St Ste 120 Tukwila (98188) *(G-13814)*
Seattle Bindery & Finishing, Tukwila *Also called Twelve Thirty-One Incorporated* *(G-13829)*
Seattle Biscuit Company LLC 206 327-2940
6710 35th Ave Nw Seattle (98117) *(G-11046)*
Seattle Boat Works LLC 206 849-4259
2542 Westlake Ave N # 9 Seattle (98109) *(G-11047)*
Seattle Boiler Works Inc 206 762-0737
500 S Myrtle St Seattle (98108) *(G-11048)*
Seattle Business Journal Inc 206 583-0701
801 2nd Ave Ste 210 Seattle (98104) *(G-11049)*
Seattle Cascades 773 387-0502
2610 Western Ave Seattle (98121) *(G-11050)*
Seattle Chinese News, Seattle *Also called USA Printing Corporation* *(G-11395)*
Seattle Chinese Post Inc 206 223-0623
412 Maynard Ave S Seattle (98104) *(G-11051)*
Seattle Chocolate Company LLC 425 264-2800
1180 Andover Park W Tukwila (98188) *(G-13815)*
Seattle Cider Company 206 762-0490
4701 Colorado Ave S Ste C Seattle (98134) *(G-11052)*
Seattle Cotton Works LLC 425 455-8003
405 114th Ave Se Ste 200 Bellevue (98004) *(G-1121)*
Seattle Creative Brands Inc 206 782-6548
3226 26th Ave W Seattle (98199) *(G-11053)*
Seattle Curtain Mfg Co 206 324-0692
104 12th Ave Mill Creek (98012) *(G-6526)*
Seattle Custom Plastics Inc 206 233-0869
309 S Cloverdale St E7 Seattle (98108) *(G-11054)*
Seattle Custom Printing 206 268-0443
18938 13th Pl S Seatac (98148) *(G-9303)*
Seattle Daily Journal Commerce 206 622-8272
83 Columbia St Ste 200 Seattle (98104) *(G-11055)*
Seattle Distilling Company 206 463-0830
19429 Vashon Hwy Sw Vashon (98070) *(G-14741)*
Seattle Drone Sales Llc 206 858-2764
8203 Avalon Dr Mercer Island (98040) *(G-6483)*
Seattle Eco Coatings 253 539-1113
9722 Canyon Rd E Puyallup (98373) *(G-8249)*
Seattle Egg Roll Corp 425 226-6256
106 Lake Ave S Ste B Renton (98057) *(G-8908)*
Seattle Engraving Center LLC 206 420-4604
414 Stewart St Seattle (98101) *(G-11056)*

ALPHABETIC

Seattle Engraving Company, Everett *Also called Seattle Engraving LLC* ***(G-3609)***
Seattle Engraving LLC 425 212-9797
5626 Evergreen Way Ste 1 Everett (98203) ***(G-3609)***
Seattle Espresso Machine Corp 206 284-7171
6133 6th Ave S Seattle (98108) ***(G-11057)***
Seattle Event Printing 253 642-6567
110 42nd St Nw Auburn (98001) ***(G-558)***
Seattle Galvanizing Co Inc 206 783-3100
6010 199th St Ne Arlington (98223) ***(G-322)***
Seattle Gameco 206 767-0922
5932 18th Ave S Seattle (98108) ***(G-11058)***
Seattle Genetics Inc (PA) 425 527-4000
21823 30th Dr Se Bothell (98021) ***(G-1902)***
Seattle Genetics Inc 425 483-1037
22515 29th Dr Se Bothell (98021) ***(G-1903)***
Seattle Glassblowing Studio 206 448-2181
2227 5th Ave Seattle (98121) ***(G-11059)***
Seattle Gold Grills 206 250-0833
901 Occidental Ave S Seattle (98134) ***(G-11060)***
Seattle Gourmet Foods Inc (PA) 425 656-9076
19016 72nd Ave S Seattle (98188) ***(G-11061)***
Seattle Granola Company, Shoreline *Also called 206 Foods LLC* ***(G-11752)***
Seattle Heat Treaters 206 763-2744
521 S Holden St Seattle (98108) ***(G-11062)***
Seattle Kitchen Cabinet Inc 360 437-1344
7446 Oak Bay Rd Port Ludlow (98365) ***(G-7773)***
Seattle Kombucha Company LLC 425 985-2364
1819 Central Ave S C49 Kent (98032) ***(G-5122)***
Seattle Logo Pro, Seattle *Also called Slp Creative LLC* ***(G-11136)***
Seattle Machine Works Inc 206 763-2710
1511 W Thurman St Seattle (98119) ***(G-11063)***
Seattle Manufacturing, Ferndale *Also called Summit Rescue Inc* ***(G-3908)***
Seattle Mariners Baseball Club, Seattle *Also called Baseball Club of Seattle Llp* ***(G-9497)***
Seattle Metropolitan 206 957-2234
509 Olive Way Seattle (98101) ***(G-11064)***
Seattle Music Partners 206 408-8588
1425 Broadway 508 Seattle (98122) ***(G-11065)***
Seattle Northwest Service Corp 206 553-9209
309 S Cloverdale St B11 Seattle (98108) ***(G-11066)***
Seattle Office and Prod Ctr, Seattle *Also called Kemeera Incorporated* ***(G-10335)***
Seattle Oil Solution LLC 206 375-7575
7915 7th Ave Sw Seattle (98106) ***(G-11067)***
Seattle Pacific Industries 253 872-8822
21216 72nd Ave S Kent (98032) ***(G-5123)***
Seattle Plastics, Seattle *Also called Seattle Custom Plastics Inc* ***(G-11054)***
Seattle Pomade Co 206 348-3972
13401 Dumas Rd Apt G304 Mill Creek (98012) ***(G-6527)***
Seattle Popcorn Company Inc 206 937-1292
9320 15th Ave S Ste Cd Seattle (98108) ***(G-11068)***
Seattle Pops 206 714-1354
20111 30th Ave Ne Shoreline (98155) ***(G-11808)***
Seattle Precision Form Inc 253 872-8356
8210 S 222nd St Kent (98032) ***(G-5124)***
Seattle Print House LLC 503 841-7755
26213 116th Ave Se C201 Kent (98030) ***(G-5125)***
Seattle Printing, Seattle *Also called Aastha Inc* ***(G-9331)***
Seattle Printworks, Seattle *Also called Print Works Inc* ***(G-10863)***
Seattle Printworks LLC 206 623-3512
711 9th Ave N Seattle (98109) ***(G-11069)***
Seattle Pure Extracts 206 788-5754
3810 Arprt Way S Ste 110 Seattle (98108) ***(G-11070)***
Seattle Radiator LLC 206 682-5148
5011 Ohio Ave S Seattle (98134) ***(G-11071)***
Seattle Radiator Works, Seattle *Also called Seattle Radiator LLC* ***(G-11071)***
Seattle Rant 206 545-6957
4208 University Way Ne Seattle (98105) ***(G-11072)***
Seattle Safety LLC (PA) 253 395-4321
4502 B St Nw U1 Auburn (98001) ***(G-559)***
Seattle Seams 206 251-8231
13617 165th St E Puyallup (98374) ***(G-8250)***
Seattle Sewing Solutions Inc 253 625-7420
270 S Hanford St Seattle (98134) ***(G-11073)***
Seattle Shipworks LLC 206 763-3133
1801 Fairview Ave E # 100 Seattle (98102) ***(G-11074)***
Seattle Signs & Printing 206 588-5592
1000 2nd Ave Ste 2000 Seattle (98104) ***(G-11075)***
Seattle Software Corp 206 286-7677
6523 California Ave Sw Seattle (98136) ***(G-11076)***
Seattle Software Developers, Bellevue *Also called DOT Com LLC* ***(G-881)***
Seattle Software Works Inc 206 226-9263
7710 190th St Se Snohomish (98296) ***(G-11973)***
Seattle Sound & Vibration 425 497-0660
14810 Ne 95th St Redmond (98052) ***(G-8658)***
Seattle Sport Sciences Inc (PA) 425 939-0015
15320 Ne 92nd St Redmond (98052) ***(G-8659)***
Seattle Sports Company (PA) 206 782-0773
3217 W Smith St Ste 1 Seattle (98199) ***(G-11077)***
Seattle Stair & Design LLC 206 587-5354
3810 4th Ave S Seattle (98134) ***(G-11078)***
Seattle Stump Grinding 206 285-2887
321 Mcgraw St Seattle (98109) ***(G-11079)***
Seattle Synchro 206 856-5239
11410 Ne 124th St Kirkland (98034) ***(G-5456)***
Seattle Systems 360 598-8916
26296 Twelve Trees Ln Nw Poulsbo (98370) ***(G-7998)***
Seattle Tarp Co Inc 206 285-2819
18449 Cascade Ave S Seattle (98188) ***(G-11080)***
Seattle Times - Marysville 360 925-6324
14506 Smokey Point Blvd Marysville (98271) ***(G-6384)***
Seattle Times Company 509 248-1251
114 N 4th St Yakima (98901) ***(G-15670)***
Seattle Times Company (HQ) 206 464-2111
1000 Denny Way Ste 501 Seattle (98109) ***(G-11081)***
Seattle Times Company 425 489-7000
19200 120th Ave Ne Bothell (98011) ***(G-1791)***
Seattle Times Publications, Kent *Also called Rotary Offset Press Inc* ***(G-5107)***
Seattle Times, The, Bothell *Also called Seattle Times Company* ***(G-1791)***
Seattle Turbine Inc 253 770-7567
16706 103rd Avenue Ct E Puyallup (98374) ***(G-8251)***
Seattle Turbine Parts, Puyallup *Also called Seattle Turbine Inc* ***(G-8251)***
Seattle Viet Times Inc 425 678-8872
102 167th St Sw Mill Creek (98012) ***(G-6528)***
Seattle Weekly LLC 206 623-0500
307 3rd Ave S Ste 2002 Seattle (98104) ***(G-11082)***
Seattle Welding Inc 206 763-0980
14622 Prairie Ridge Dr E Bonney Lake (98391) ***(G-1738)***
Seattle Wheelchair Rugby 360 440-2498
18 W Mercer St Ste 400 Seattle (98119) ***(G-11083)***
Seattle Wood Signs 425 422-3750
820 Blanchard St # 1610 Seattle (98121) ***(G-11084)***
Seattle's Child, Bainbridge Island *Also called Northwest Parents Media* ***(G-655)***
Seattlepi.com, Seattle *Also called Hearst Seattle Media LLC* ***(G-10158)***
Seaview Boat Yard Inc (PA) 206 783-6550
6701 Seaview Ave Nw Seattle (98117) ***(G-11085)***
Seaview Boat Yard Inc 206 783-6550
6701 Seaview Ave Nw Seattle (98117) ***(G-11086)***
Seaview Boatyard North Inc 360 676-8282
2652 N Harbor Loop Dr Bellingham (98225) ***(G-1531)***
Seaview Boatyard West Inc 206 783-6550
6701 Seaview Ave Nw Seattle (98117) ***(G-11087)***
Seaview West, Seattle *Also called Seaview Boat Yard Inc* ***(G-11085)***
Seays Lake City Marine LLC 509 483-1461
1617 E Holyoke Ave Spokane (99217) ***(G-12496)***
Second Amendment Foundation (PA) 425 454-7012
12500 Ne 10th Pl Bellevue (98005) ***(G-1122)***
SECOND AMENDMENT REPORTER, Bellevue *Also called Second Amendment Foundation* ***(G-1122)***
Secondhand Hound 253 232-9432
5609 N 51st St Ruston (98407) ***(G-9178)***
Secord Printing Inc 425 883-2182
11332 120th Ave Ne # 119 Kirkland (98033) ***(G-5457)***
Section Magazine LLC 360 694-8571
610 Esther St Ste 200 Vancouver (98660) ***(G-14578)***
Secucred Inc 508 361-0928
413 Adams St Richland (99352) ***(G-9040)***
Secure It LLC 509 992-6190
4022 E Sumac Dr Spokane (99223) ***(G-12497)***
Securitay Inc 425 392-0203
1095 Sunrise Pl Sw Issaquah (98027) ***(G-4472)***
Security Alarms Plus, Wapato *Also called Michael Patrick Matthews* ***(G-14920)***
Security Alarms Plus Inc 509 457-8799
7560 Yakima Valley Hwy Zillah (98953) ***(G-15758)***
Security Door and Window Co, Spokane *Also called Home Builders Service Company* ***(G-12296)***
Seed Factory Northwest Inc 253 395-8813
8439 S 208th St Bldg M Kent (98031) ***(G-5126)***
Seelig Fuel Inc 206 789-6434
8523 18th Ave Nw Seattle (98117) ***(G-11088)***
Sefco LLC 509 921-1121
15215 E Upland Dr Spokane Valley (99216) ***(G-12863)***
SEI Northwest, Seattle *Also called Steel Encounters Inc* ***(G-11186)***
Sekidenko Inc 360 694-7871
2501 Se Columbia Way # 230 Vancouver (98661) ***(G-14579)***
Sel Development LLC 509 332-1890
2440 Ne Hopkins Ct Pullman (99163) ***(G-8107)***
Selah Springs LLC 206 714-6068
16552 Se 28th St Bellevue (98008) ***(G-1123)***
Selco, Everson *Also called South Everson Lumber Co Inc* ***(G-3689)***
Select Fluid Power USA Inc 604 343-1111
17300 W Valley Hwy Tukwila (98188) ***(G-13816)***
Select Selling Inc (HQ) 425 895-8959
550 Kirkland Way Ste 101 Kirkland (98033) ***(G-5458)***
Selectronix Incorporated 425 788-2979
16419 199th Ct Ne Woodinville (98077) ***(G-15358)***
Selfish Apparel and Printing 206 450-2725
7710 197th St Se Snohomish (98296) ***(G-11974)***
Selg and Associates Inc 425 487-6059
15617 212th Ave Ne Woodinville (98077) ***(G-15359)***
Selland Construction Inc 509 662-7119
1285 S Wenatchee Ave Wenatchee (98801) ***(G-15073)***
Sellin Style 360 670-5540
251 W Old Blyn Hwy Sequim (98382) ***(G-11662)***

Semgroup Corp 509 921-7089
16710 E Euclid Ave Spokane Valley (99216) ***(G-12864)***
Semgroup Corporation 509 487-4560
4327 N Thor St Spokane (99217) ***(G-12498)***
Semmaterials LP 509 545-9864
3152 Selph Landing Rd Pasco (99301) ***(G-7626)***
Send4print.com, Kirkland *Also called Worldwide Dgital Solutions Inc* ***(G-5498)***
Seneca Foods Corporation 509 837-3806
1525 S 4th St Sunnyside (98944) ***(G-13140)***
Seneca Foods Corporation 509 382-8323
301 Seneca Way Dayton (99328) ***(G-2884)***
Seneca Foods Corporation 509 457-1089
2418 River Rd Yakima (98902) ***(G-15671)***
Senior Nutrition Department, Shelton *Also called Senior Services For S Sound* ***(G-11730)***
Senior Operations LLC 360 794-4448
14767 172nd Dr Se Monroe (98272) ***(G-6617)***
Senior Operations LLC 360 403-2283
7305 201st St Arlington (98223) ***(G-323)***
Senior Operations LLC 360 435-1116
20350 71st Ave Ne Ste C Arlington (98223) ***(G-324)***
Senior Operations LLC 360 435-1119
20100 71st Ave Ne Arlington (98223) ***(G-325)***
Senior Operations LLC 360 435-1119
7305 201st St Ne Arlington (98223) ***(G-326)***
Senior Operations LLC 360 435-1119
20100 71st Ave Ne Arlington (98223) ***(G-327)***
Senior Services For S Sound 360 426-3697
190 W Sentry Dr Shelton (98584) ***(G-11730)***
Sensi Sweets 206 387-8589
14553 Linden Ave N Unit A Shoreline (98133) ***(G-11809)***
Sensible Horsemanship LLC 509 292-2475
38303 N Chapman Rd Elk (99009) ***(G-3176)***
Sensitech Inc (HQ) 425 883-7926
8801 148th Ave Ne Redmond (98052) ***(G-8660)***
Sensitech Inc 425 883-7926
8801 148th Ave Ne Redmond (98052) ***(G-8661)***
Sensitronics LLC 360 766-8800
16120 Park Pl Bow (98232) ***(G-1932)***
Sensoria Health Inc 425 533-2928
15600 Redmond Way Ste 205 Redmond (98052) ***(G-8662)***
Sensorlink Corporation 360 380-0592
1360 Stonegate Way Ferndale (98248) ***(G-3903)***
Sensormatic Electronics LLC 253 851-6500
5775 Soundview Dr E101 Gig Harbor (98335) ***(G-4160)***
Sentinel Offender Services LLC 206 223-9681
600 5th Ave Fl 8 Seattle (98104) ***(G-11089)***
Sequim Gazette, Sequim *Also called Olympic View Publishing LLC* ***(G-11655)***
Sequoia Scientific Inc 425 641-0944
2700 Richards Rd Ste 107 Bellevue (98005) ***(G-1124)***
Sequoyah Electric 253 520-2064
1319 Central Ave S Kent (98032) ***(G-5127)***
Ser Pro Inc 206 767-3100
11064 1st Ave S Seattle (98168) ***(G-11090)***
Serena Inc 253 939-6509
202 37th St Ne Auburn (98002) ***(G-560)***
Serious Biz LLC 425 454-1906
9628 Hilltop Rd Bellevue (98004) ***(G-1125)***
Serious Cybernetics LLC 646 247-3642
42010 Se 149th Pl North Bend (98045) ***(G-7122)***
Servably Inc 425 216-3333
11410 Ne 124th St Ste 270 Kirkland (98034) ***(G-5459)***
Servatron Inc 509 321-9500
12825 E Mirabeau Pkwy # 104 Spokane Valley (99216) ***(G-12865)***
Service Corp International 425 885-2414
7200 180th Ave Ne Redmond (98052) ***(G-8663)***
Service Hydraulics Inc 253 351-6010
25 37th St Ne Auburn (98002) ***(G-561)***
Service Partners LLC 509 535-4600
125 N Dyer Rd Spokane Valley (99212) ***(G-12866)***
Service Partners of Oregon 360 694-6747
5900 Ne 88th St Ste 100 Vancouver (98665) ***(G-14580)***
Service Printing Co Inc 206 283-6800
3837 13th Ave W Ste 106 Seattle (98119) ***(G-11091)***
Service Surplus & Crafts 360 636-0250
112 Clark Creek Ln Longview (98632) ***(G-5952)***
Service Welding & Machine Co 206 325-1153
1435 S Jackson St Seattle (98144) ***(G-11092)***
Servine Sign Services LLC 509 225-7733
2903 W Yakima Ave Yakima (98902) ***(G-15672)***
SES USA Inc (PA) 425 485-3801
6527 Ne 192nd Pl Kenmore (98028) ***(G-4604)***
Seven Hills Winery LLC 509 529-7198
212 N 3rd Ave Walla Walla (99362) ***(G-14866)***
Seven Twenty Eight CL LLC 206 484-7634
37000 Cypress Dr Ne Hansville (98340) ***(G-4319)***
Seven Up Btlg Co Tri Cities 509 547-1660
2106 W Frontage Rd Pasco (99301) ***(G-7627)***
Seven Up Dr Peper Bottling Co 509 547-1660
2106 W Frontage Rd Pasco (99301) ***(G-7628)***
Seven-K Company 509 863-3429
3120 W Kiernan Ave Spokane (99205) ***(G-12499)***
Seventy Frth St Prductions LLC 206 781-1447
350 N 74th St Seattle (98103) ***(G-11093)***
Sevier Logging LLC 360 791-5527
4570 Avery Ln Se Lacey (98503) ***(G-5586)***
Sevierly Good Gluten Free LLC 253 759-5288
1401 S Sprague Ave Tacoma (98405) ***(G-13511)***
Sevilla LLC 509 280-8447
1203 S Cedar St Spokane (99204) ***(G-12500)***
Sew Athletic Jackets and More 253 446-7115
12110 Meridian E Puyallup (98373) ***(G-8252)***
Seward Fisheries, Seattle *Also called Icicle Seafoods Inc* ***(G-10200)***
Sey Mik Cabinets & Millwork 360 829-0173
23220 Smner Buckley Hwy E Buckley (98321) ***(G-2071)***
Seymour Chnnel Stllite Systems, Colville *Also called Jeffrey Mark Bashe* ***(G-2758)***
Seymour Technology LLC 509 522-3473
504 S Roosevelt St Walla Walla (99362) ***(G-14867)***
SGC World Inc 425 746-6310
13737 Se 26th St Bellevue (98005) ***(G-1126)***
SGC World Inc 425 746-6311
725 172nd Pl Ne Bellevue (98008) ***(G-1127)***
Sgl Atomotive Carbn Fibers LLC 509 762-4600
8781 Randolph Rd Ne Moses Lake (98837) ***(G-6747)***
Sgl Composites LLC 704 593-5177
8781 Randolph Rd Ne Moses Lake (98837) ***(G-6748)***
Sh RTS Off Screen Printing 425 319-1269
403 W Stevens Ave 4/6 Sultan (98294) ***(G-13035)***
Shackelford Vintners 425 350-2719
908 Ash Ct Snohomish (98290) ***(G-11975)***
Shadd Global Industries L 425 374-3946
3616 Colby Ave Ste 774 Everett (98201) ***(G-3610)***
Shade Sunglo & Drapery Co 206 767-4561
5503 Airport Way S Seattle (98108) ***(G-11094)***
Shades of Green 425 387-2335
917 129th Pl Nw Tulalip (98271) ***(G-13844)***
Shadetree Engineering, Silverdale *Also called Michael M Hennessey* ***(G-11850)***
Shadewave 425 557-7788
14532 255th Ave Se Issaquah (98027) ***(G-4473)***
Shadow Master 253 984-0559
11018 Bridgeport Way Sw Lakewood (98499) ***(G-5754)***
Shadow Works LLC 509 251-8306
315 S Dishman Rd Spokane Valley (99206) ***(G-12867)***
Shady Grove Winery LLC 509 767-1400
2297 Dallesport Rd Dallesport (98617) ***(G-2865)***
Shaffer Woodworks LLC 509 697-3023
211 Rainier Ln Selah (98942) ***(G-11596)***
Shah Safari Inc (PA) 206 282-6122
14 W Roy St Seattle (98119) ***(G-11095)***
Shake & Shingle 208, Moclips *Also called Griffiths Inc* ***(G-6539)***
Shaker Craftsman 509 823-4556
2908 Fruitvale Blvd Yakima (98902) ***(G-15673)***
Shaker Innovations LLC 360 886-1873
22411 Se 313th Pl Black Diamond (98010) ***(G-1655)***
Shakertown 1992 Inc 360 785-3501
1200 Nw Kerron St Winlock (98596) ***(G-15156)***
Shaklee Athrzed Dstrs - Resman, Fircrest *Also called Reesman Co* ***(G-4004)***
Shamrock & Spike Maul Pubg Co 360 734-5778
2328 Yew Street Rd Bellingham (98229) ***(G-1532)***
Shamrock Machining Inc 509 534-3031
5704 E 1st Ave Spokane Valley (99212) ***(G-12868)***
Shannock Tapestry Looms 360 573-7264
10402 Nw 11th Ave Vancouver (98685) ***(G-14581)***
Shannon D Agnew 509 926-6209
3808 N Sullivan Rd Spokane Valley (99216) ***(G-12869)***
Shapecut Industries LLC 509 828-3265
3410 E Trent Ave Spokane (99202) ***(G-12501)***
Shared Healthcare Systems Inc 360 299-4000
1601 R Ave Anacortes (98221) ***(G-166)***
Shareway Industries Inc 253 804-0670
2526 E St Ne Auburn (98002) ***(G-562)***
Shark Stainless Systems Inc 866 960-9779
19717 62nd Ave S Ste E102 Kent (98032) ***(G-5128)***
Sharon Mcllhenny 509 493-9259
235 Bates Rd White Salmon (98672) ***(G-15131)***
Sharon Rose 360 341-1898
2838 Sunlight Dr Clinton (98236) ***(G-2698)***
Sharp Synaptics LLC 253 927-2616
700 Sw 368th St Federal Way (98023) ***(G-3782)***
Sharp's Fabricating & Muffler, Moxee *Also called Sharps Welding & Muffler Ctr* ***(G-6885)***
Sharpe Mixers Inc 206 767-5660
1541 S 92nd Pl Ste A Seattle (98108) ***(G-11096)***
Sharps Welding & Muffler Ctr 509 452-2101
212 E Moxee Ave Moxee (98936) ***(G-6885)***
Shasta Beverages Inc 206 575-0525
1227 Andover Park E Tukwila (98188) ***(G-13817)***
Shaw Estate Wines 509 876-2459
26 E Main St Walla Walla (99362) ***(G-14868)***
Shaw Road Development LLC (PA) 253 845-9544
1001 Shaw Rd Puyallup (98372) ***(G-8253)***
Shawnee Construction LLC 425 430-4232
2613 Meadow Ave N Renton (98056) ***(G-8909)***
Shea Edwards Furniture LLP 206 898-1992
32615 Cascade View Dr Sultan (98294) ***(G-13036)***
Shea Your Lips Lip Balm 360 856-4803
190 N Murdock St Apt E107 Sedro Woolley (98284) ***(G-11564)***

ALPHABETIC

(PA)=Parent Co (HQ)=Headquarters (DH)=Div Headquarters
2019 Washington
Manufacturers Register
821

Shear Precision Inc 800 481-4943
10859 1st Ave S Seattle (98168) ***(G-11097)***
Shearer Brothers Chipping LLC 360 426-6466
500 E Millwright Rd Shelton (98584) ***(G-11731)***
Sheets Unlimited, Seattle *Also called Mystic Ltd* ***(G-10583)***
Sheffield Cider Inc 509 269-4610
4665 Sheffield Rd Mesa (99343) ***(G-6496)***
Shelby Super Cars, West Richland *Also called SSC North America LLC* ***(G-15102)***
Sheldon Custom Cabinets Ltd 425 778-0043
20626 50th Ave W Lynnwood (98036) ***(G-6194)***
Shelfbot Co 425 679-1421
1218 3rd Ave Ste 1010 Seattle (98101) ***(G-11098)***
Shelfgenie 206 774-0336
5055 38th Ave Ne Seattle (98105) ***(G-11099)***
Shell Energy North Amer US LP 509 688-6002
601 W 1st Ave Ste 1700 Spokane (99201) ***(G-12502)***
Shellback Ltd 206 463-9054
6702 Sw 240th St Vashon (98070) ***(G-14742)***
Shelly Shay 360 829-2350
29022 State Route 410 E Buckley (98321) ***(G-2072)***
Shelter Peak Publishing LLC 360 460-0751
1654 Cherry St Port Townsend (98368) ***(G-7925)***
Shelterlogic Corp 253 985-0026
9317 47th Ave Sw Bldg 9 Lakewood (98499) ***(G-5755)***
Shelton Publishing Inc 360 426-4412
227 W Cota St Shelton (98584) ***(G-11732)***
Shelton-Mason County Journal, Shelton *Also called Shelton Publishing Inc* ***(G-11732)***
Sheng Mian North America LLC 215 519-5895
76 158th Pl Se Bellevue (98008) ***(G-1128)***
Shepherds Soap Co 360 427-7811
790 E Johns Prairie Rd Shelton (98584) ***(G-11733)***
Shepp Enterprises LLC 206 697-0327
2602 Westridge Ave W E303 Tacoma (98466) ***(G-13512)***
Sheridan Woodworking LLC 509 540-7799
2175 Frog Hollow Rd Walla Walla (99362) ***(G-14869)***
Sherman Technical Inds Inc 509 427-8089
11 Chapman Ave 2226 Carson (98610) ***(G-2307)***
Sherman Technical Inds Inc 509 427-8089
132 Chapman Ave Carson (98610) ***(G-2308)***
Sherpa Adventure Gear LLC 425 251-0760
7857 S 180th St Kent (98032) ***(G-5129)***
Sherpa Foods SPC 425 243-9278
6947 Coal Creek Pkwy Se Newcastle (98059) ***(G-7039)***
Sherri and Brent Wright 360 366-3100
7535 Hickory Ridge Ln Ferndale (98248) ***(G-3904)***
Sherwin-Williams Company 206 417-4502
13318 Lake City Way Ne Seattle (98125) ***(G-11100)***
Sherwin-Williams Company 425 643-8584
3640 Factoria Blvd Se Bellevue (98006) ***(G-1129)***
Sherwood Forest Farms, Seattle *Also called Callisons Inc* ***(G-9608)***
Shield Technologies LLC 425 844-8055
15915 212th Ave Ne Woodinville (98077) ***(G-15360)***
Shields Aerospace Services LLC 425 240-6079
614 6th Ave N Apt 18 Edmonds (98020) ***(G-3155)***
Shiloh Publishing 800 607-6195
16406 Ne 35th St Vancouver (98682) ***(G-14582)***
Shilshole Bioscience Inc 206 459-8341
27213 Se 27th St Sammamish (98075) ***(G-9247)***
Shin-Etsu Handotai America Inc (HQ) 360 883-7000
4111 Ne 112th Ave Vancouver (98682) ***(G-14583)***
Shine Marble Co Inc 425 444-5832
20414 80th Ave Ne Kenmore (98028) ***(G-4605)***
Shine Micro Inc 360 437-2503
9405 Oak Bay Rd Unit A Port Ludlow (98365) ***(G-7774)***
Shine On Signs & Graphics Inc 253 243-7777
259 Sw 41st St Renton (98057) ***(G-8910)***
Shine Quarry Inc 360 437-2415
9861 State Route 104 Port Ludlow (98365) ***(G-7775)***
Shine Specialties & Promotions, Yelm *Also called Lori Shine* ***(G-15738)***
Shining Ocean Inc 253 826-3700
1515 Puyallup St Sumner (98390) ***(G-13098)***
Ship Electronics Inc 206 819-3853
1824 Nw 201st St Shoreline (98177) ***(G-11810)***
Ship N Shore 360 293-8636
4307 Ginnett Rd Anacortes (98221) ***(G-167)***
Ship To Shore Inc 206 284-0406
3456 37th Ave W Seattle (98199) ***(G-11101)***
Shipco Transport Inc 206 444-7447
14900 Interurban Ave S # 215 Tukwila (98168) ***(G-13818)***
Shipp Construction Inc 360 262-0197
262 Larmon Rd Ethel (98542) ***(G-3351)***
Shiprush, Seattle *Also called Descartes Systems (usa) LLC* ***(G-9825)***
Shipyard LLC 360 532-1990
1303 C St Hoquiam (98550) ***(G-4358)***
Shiraul LLC 509 837-6230
410 Factory Rd Sunnyside (98944) ***(G-13141)***
Shire Mountain Log Homes Inc 360 262-9338
812 Rainier Ave Centralia (98531) ***(G-2432)***
Shirley Sunset 360 574-3276
9014 Ne St Johns Rd # 113 Vancouver (98665) ***(G-14584)***
Shirt Image Embroidery 360 870-2837
2200 Simpson Ave Hoquiam (98550) ***(G-4359)***
Shirtbuilders Inc 509 765-3885
206 S Fir St Moses Lake (98837) ***(G-6749)***
Shirthouse , The, Aberdeen *Also called Lorrand Marketing LLC* ***(G-21)***
Shirts Illustrated 425 742-3844
12315 Mukilteo Speedway J Lynnwood (98087) ***(G-6195)***
Shirtworks 509 925-3469
100 W 8th Ave Ellensburg (98926) ***(G-3225)***
Shirtz To Go Inc 206 242-4055
28717 Pacific Hwy S Ste 1 Federal Way (98003) ***(G-3783)***
Shishkaberrys L L C 206 650-3564
1536 Ne 89th St Seattle (98115) ***(G-11102)***
Shocker Metalshop LLC Welding 425 246-5825
5915 322nd Ave Ne Carnation (98014) ***(G-2298)***
Shockwave Medical Inc 425 736-3946
15309 Se 82nd St Newcastle (98059) ***(G-7040)***
Shoemaker Manufacturing Co 509 674-4414
104 N Montgomery Ave Cle Elum (98922) ***(G-2679)***
Shoezandmorecom LLC 216 544-1745
17735 105th Pl Se Renton (98055) ***(G-8911)***
Shonan Usa Inc 509 453-0757
702 Wallace Way Grandview (98930) ***(G-4255)***
Shoot Suit Inc 360 687-3451
1721 Se Grace Ave Ste D Battle Ground (98604) ***(G-739)***
Shope Enterprises Inc 253 848-1551
1618 E Main Puyallup (98372) ***(G-8254)***
Shoppers Weekly, The, Shelton *Also called Tjn Publishing Inc* ***(G-11745)***
Shoreline Cert 206 533-6500
18328 Ashworth Ave N Shoreline (98133) ***(G-11811)***
Shoreline Custom Canvas & Auto 360 874-2702
5056 Sw Lake Helena Rd Port Orchard (98367) ***(G-7847)***
Shoreline Graphics, Lynnwood *Also called K H B Inc* ***(G-6146)***
Shoreline Poleholders LLC 360 659-0826
4019 178th Pl Ne Arlington (98223) ***(G-328)***
Shoreline Sign & Awning, Arlington *Also called Mixign Inc* ***(G-281)***
Show Quality Metal Finish 206 762-6717
18924 13th Pl S Seatac (98148) ***(G-9304)***
Show Quality Metal Finishing 206 762-6717
18924 13th Pl S Seatac (98148) ***(G-9305)***
Showalter Systems Inc 206 236-6276
3047 78th Ave Se Ste 203 Mercer Island (98040) ***(G-6484)***
Showcase Specialties Inc 509 547-3344
702 W Lewis St Pasco (99301) ***(G-7629)***
Shredfast Mobile Data Destruct (PA) 509 244-7076
13026 W Mcfarlane Rd Airway Heights (99001) ***(G-63)***
Shredsupply Inc 509 235-3800
406 1st St Ste D Cheney (99004) ***(G-2593)***
Shrubbery LLC 949 690-9834
1210 E John St Apt 5 Seattle (98102) ***(G-11103)***
Shs, Anacortes *Also called Shared Healthcare Systems Inc* ***(G-166)***
Shunyata Research Corporation 360 598-9935
26273 Twelve Trees Ln Nw D Poulsbo (98370) ***(G-7999)***
Shur - Ooc, Monroe *Also called Jsmd Key Products LLC* ***(G-6583)***
Shur-Loc Fabric System 360 805-4140
14517 Fryelands Blvd Se Monroe (98272) ***(G-6618)***
Shutterpated 360 607-9692
22603 1st Pl W Bothell (98021) ***(G-1904)***
Shutterworks LLC 509 731-4619
3002 W Viola Ave Yakima (98902) ***(G-15674)***
Shuttle Systems, Bellingham *Also called Contemporary Design Co* ***(G-1303)***
Shuttlesystem LLC 425 551-1335
3302 Cedardale Rd E500 Mount Vernon (98274) ***(G-6835)***
Shyft Advanced Mfg LLC 425 398-4009
20004 144th Ave Ne Woodinville (98072) ***(G-15361)***
Shyft AM, Woodinville *Also called Shyft Advanced Mfg LLC* ***(G-15361)***
Sickspeed Inc 509 833-3768
508 Baker St Moxee (98936) ***(G-6886)***
Side Hustle LLC 509 435-6773
1423 N Locust Rd Spokane Valley (99206) ***(G-12870)***
Sideline Sports Inc 206 906-9652
1100 Nw Leary Way Seattle (98107) ***(G-11104)***
Sidetrack Distillery 206 963-5079
27010 78th Ave S Kent (98032) ***(G-5130)***
Siemens 425 507-4380
15900 Se Eastgate Way # 200 Bellevue (98008) ***(G-1130)***
Siemens 425 251-0858
830 Sw 34th St Renton (98057) ***(G-8912)***
Siemens AG 253 922-4297
5013 Pacific Hwy E Fife (98424) ***(G-3992)***
Siemens Gmesa Rnwble Enrgy Inc 509 896-5246
1131 Dot Rd Roosevelt (99356) ***(G-9153)***
Siemens Industry Inc 208 883-8330
6 Odonnell Rd B Pullman (99163) ***(G-8108)***
Siemens Industry Inc 509 891-9070
1225 N Argonne Rd Ste A Spokane Valley (99212) ***(G-12871)***
Siemens Industry Inc 208 883-8330
22010 Se 51st St Issaquah (98029) ***(G-4474)***
Siemens Med Solutions USA Inc 425 392-9180
22010 Se 51st St Issaquah (98029) ***(G-4475)***
Siemens PLM Software, Issaquah *Also called Siemens Product Life Mgmt Sftw* ***(G-4476)***
Siemens Product Life Mgmt Sftw 425 507-1900
22010 Se 51st St Issaquah (98029) ***(G-4476)***
Siemens Solar Industries, Vancouver *Also called Solarworld Industries Amer LP* ***(G-14598)***

Sienna Software Inc ... 206 306-2752
11912 Exeter Ave Ne Seattle (98125) *(G-11105)*
Sienna Technologies Inc ... 425 485-0756
19501 144th Ave Ne F500 Woodinville (98072) *(G-15362)*
Sierra Fishers I N C ... 360 299-1469
14687 Hoxie Ln Anacortes (98221) *(G-168)*
Sierra Industries Inc (PA) ... 425 487-5200
19900 144th Ave Ne Woodinville (98072) *(G-15363)*
Sierra Pacific Industries ... 530 378-8251
204 E Railroad Ave Shelton (98584) *(G-11734)*
Sierra Pacific Industries ... 360 532-2323
301 Hagara St Aberdeen (98520) *(G-34)*
Sierra Pacific Industries ... 360 736-5417
3115 Kuper Rd Centralia (98531) *(G-2433)*
Sifferman & Sifferman ... 360 426-0714
2931 E Mason Lake Dr W Grapeview (98546) *(G-4290)*
Sightman ... 360 934-5886
538 Ostman Rd Raymond (98577) *(G-8358)*
Sigillo Cellars ... 206 919-2326
8353 Meadowbrook Way Se Snoqualmie (98065) *(G-12023)*
Sigma Dg Corporation ... 360 859-3170
5019 Nw 127th St Vancouver (98685) *(G-14585)*
Sign A Rama ... 360 915-9207
2633 Willamette Dr Ne H Lacey (98516) *(G-5587)*
Sign Associates Inc ... 425 885-6100
6825 176th Ave Ne Ste 125 Redmond (98052) *(G-8664)*
Sign Biz ... 360 750-9175
6206 E 18th St Ste A Vancouver (98661) *(G-14586)*
Sign By Tommorrow Kent ... 253 872-7844
22005 68th Ave S Kent (98032) *(G-5131)*
Sign City Gfx ... 253 329-2670
2507 C St Sw Auburn (98001) *(G-563)*
Sign Company ... 253 630-6313
25431 161st Ave Se Covington (98042) *(G-2838)*
Sign Connections, Puyallup *Also called Kts Media Inc (G-8173)*
Sign Corporation ... 509 535-2913
131 N Altamont St Spokane (99202) *(G-12503)*
Sign Crafters Inc ... 509 783-8718
627 N Kellogg St Ste A Kennewick (99336) *(G-4727)*
Sign Department Inc ... 360 708-3823
919 E College Way Ste A Mount Vernon (98273) *(G-6836)*
Sign Distributors ... 253 847-2747
23520 41st Ave E Spanaway (98387) *(G-12073)*
Sign Fracture Care Intl ... 509 371-1107
451 Hills St Ste B Richland (99354) *(G-9041)*
Sign Guys Inc ... 253 942-3688
1714 S 341st Pl Federal Way (98003) *(G-3784)*
Sign Junkies ... 360 273-7553
13906 Vue St Sw Olympia (98512) *(G-7393)*
SIGN LANGUAGE, Tacoma *Also called Tacoma Tent & Awning Co Inc (G-13549)*
Sign Language Interpreter & En ... 509 860-2727
1116 Foothills Ln Wenatchee (98801) *(G-15074)*
Sign Makers Inc ... 425 828-0688
99 10th St S Kirkland (98033) *(G-5460)*
Sign Man ... 509 535-8181
6323 E Mallon Ave Spokane Valley (99212) *(G-12872)*
Sign ME Up Inc ... 360 271-8070
605 Shine Rd Port Ludlow (98365) *(G-7776)*
Sign of Times ... 360 891-9477
5809 Ne 105th Ave Vancouver (98662) *(G-14587)*
Sign Post Inc ... 360 671-1343
2019 E Bakerview Rd Bellingham (98226) *(G-1533)*
Sign Prin6s, Kent *Also called Sign Prints Inc (G-5132)*
Sign Print 360 LLC ... 360 578-2476
305 W Main St Ste B Kelso (98626) *(G-4547)*
Sign Prints Inc ... 253 854-7841
27106 46th Ave S Kent (98032) *(G-5132)*
Sign Pro Inc ... 360 736-6322
321 N Pearl St Centralia (98531) *(G-2434)*
Sign Pro of Lewis County, Centralia *Also called Sign Pro Inc (G-2434)*
Sign Pro of Skagit Valley, Mount Vernon *Also called Skagit City Signs Inc (G-6838)*
Sign Pro of Wenatchee, Wenatchee *Also called Central Wash Media Group LLC (G-15018)*
Sign Pros Inc ... 425 885-3204
17425 Ne 70th St Redmond (98052) *(G-8665)*
Sign Rite ... 253 447-8997
1725 137th Ave E Sumner (98390) *(G-13099)*
Sign Service & Manufacturing, Spokane *Also called Rdean Enterprises Inc (G-12468)*
Sign Shop LLC ... 360 352-5926
1381 Linwood Ave Sw Tumwater (98512) *(G-13897)*
Sign Smart, Kelso *Also called Signsmart USA (G-4548)*
Sign Station ... 360 379-2954
11602 Rhody Dr Port Hadlock (98339) *(G-7762)*
Sign Up Sign Co Inc ... 425 488-9247
18720 Bothell Way Ne Bothell (98011) *(G-1792)*
Sign Wizard ... 206 285-9535
300 Queen Anne Ave N Seattle (98109) *(G-11106)*
Sign Works ... 509 248-8235
915 W Yakima Ave Yakima (98902) *(G-15675)*
Sign Works Custom Concepts, Yakima *Also called Sign Works (G-15675)*
Sign-A-Rama, Lacey *Also called Sign A Rama (G-5587)*
Sign-A-Rama ... 253 474-1991
7610 South Tacoma Way B Tacoma (98409) *(G-13513)*
Sign-O-Lite ... 360 746-8651
477 Peace Portal Dr # 104 Blaine (98230) *(G-1703)*
Sign-Tech Elc Ltd Lblty Co ... 253 922-2146
5113 Pacific Hwy E Ste 7 Fife (98424) *(G-3993)*
Signage ... 206 903-6446
701 Union St Seattle (98101) *(G-11107)*
Signal Hound Inc ... 360 263-5006
1502 Se Commerce Ave # 101 Battle Ground (98604) *(G-740)*
Signal Interface Group ... 425 467-7146
16310 Ne 85th St Redmond (98052) *(G-8666)*
Signature Bakery, Lynnwood *Also called Olsons Baking Company LLC (G-6172)*
Signature Plastics LLC ... 360 366-5044
7837 Custer School Rd Custer (98240) *(G-2860)*
Signature Seafoods Inc ... 206 285-2815
4257 24th Ave W Seattle (98199) *(G-11108)*
Signature Vase ... 253 951-3357
921 Ulery St Se Lacey (98503) *(G-5588)*
Signco, Monroe *Also called Dek Enterprises Inc (G-6564)*
Signdezign LLC ... 360 709-0505
2407 Harrison Ave Nw A Olympia (98502) *(G-7394)*
Signfactory ... 360 833-1515
7711 Ne 317th Pl Camas (98607) *(G-2282)*
Signmaster, Longview *Also called K L Cook Inc (G-5921)*
Signode Industrial Group LLC ... 360 225-9995
701 W Scott Ave Woodland (98674) *(G-15465)*
Signorama ... 425 861-9341
8563 154th Ave Ne Redmond (98052) *(G-8667)*
Signostics Inc ... 425 402-0971
8310 154th Ave Ne Ste 200 Redmond (98052) *(G-8668)*
Signpac Northwest Division, Seattle *Also called National Sign Corporation (G-10590)*
Signs, Seabeck *Also called Magic Mountains Services Inc (G-9268)*
Signs & Designs ... 509 493-8350
1435 Sw Brislawn Loop Rd White Salmon (98672) *(G-15132)*
Signs & More, Vancouver *Also called National Sign Systems Ltd (G-14427)*
Signs 2c ... 206 335-9519
2913 S Court St Seattle (98144) *(G-11109)*
Signs By Tomorrow ... 360 676-7117
420 Ohio St Bellingham (98225) *(G-1534)*
Signs For Success ... 509 489-4200
6824 N Market St Spokane (99217) *(G-12504)*
Signs Now, Kennewick *Also called Sign Crafters Inc (G-4727)*
Signs Now, Spokane *Also called International Trade & Trvl Ltd (G-12324)*
Signs Now In Process Inc (PA) ... 509 928-3467
10502 E Montgomery Dr # 2 Spokane Valley (99206) *(G-12873)*
Signs Now of Moses Lake Inc ... 509 765-8955
1626 W Broadway Ave Ste C Moses Lake (98837) *(G-6750)*
Signs Now Washington, Everett *Also called Bal & Bal 200803466 Inc (G-3382)*
Signs of Grace ... 509 488-5081
430 S 16th Ave Othello (99344) *(G-7505)*
Signs of Seattle Inc ... 206 292-7446
6263 Ellis Ave S Seattle (98108) *(G-11110)*
Signs Plus Inc ... 360 671-7165
766 Marine Dr Bellingham (98225) *(G-1535)*
Signs TEC, Spokane Valley *Also called Bondarchuk Andrey (G-12644)*
Signsmart USA (PA) ... 360 578-2476
305 W Main St Ste B Kelso (98626) *(G-4548)*
Signsouth ... 509 448-4404
4508 S Regal St Spokane (99223) *(G-12505)*
Signworks LLC ... 206 715-1570
14205 Se 36th St Ste 100 Bellevue (98006) *(G-1131)*
Sik Scents LLC ... 206 420-4647
11818 Military Rd S Seattle (98168) *(G-11111)*
Sikorsky, Woodland *Also called Lifeport LLC (G-15447)*
Silent Vineyards Inc ... 360 692-7497
7875 Forest Ridge Dr Ne Bremerton (98311) *(G-1999)*
Silfab Solar WA Inc ... 360 569-4733
800 Cornwall Ave Bellingham (98225) *(G-1536)*
Silgan Containers Mfg Corp ... 509 865-4125
45 E 3rd Ave Toppenish (98948) *(G-13672)*
Silhouette Graphics ... 360 758-4163
2884 Leeward Way Bellingham (98226) *(G-1537)*
Silicle Bay Marina, Seattle *Also called Seaview Boat Yard Inc (G-11086)*
Silicon & Solar Mfg LLC ... 360 703-0701
1401 Industrial Way # 100 Longview (98632) *(G-5953)*
Silicon Chemical Corporation ... 360 210-5124
750 S 32nd St Washougal (98671) *(G-14984)*
Silicon Designs Inc ... 425 391-8329
13905 Ne 128th St Kirkland (98034) *(G-5461)*
Silicon Digital Industries Inc ... 360 332-1349
1127 Se 10th St North Bend (98045) *(G-7123)*
Silicon Forest Electronics Inc ... 360 694-2000
6204 E 18th St Vancouver (98661) *(G-14588)*
Silk From The Hartz, Index *Also called Warren Hartz (G-4372)*
Silk Screen Company The, Seattle *Also called Silkscreen Company (G-11112)*
Silkscreen Company ... 206 763-8108
6336 6th Ave S Seattle (98108) *(G-11112)*
Silvan Craft Inc ... 425 827-7050
11844 Ne 112th St Kirkland (98033) *(G-5462)*
Silver City Brewing Co Inc ... 360 698-5879
2799 Nw Myhre Rd Silverdale (98383) *(G-11857)*

ALPHABETIC

Silver City Lumber Inc (PA) 509 238-6960
3916 E Chattaroy Rd Chattaroy (99003) ***(G-2453)***
Silver City Timber 509 276-5126
518 S Fir Ave Deer Park (99006) ***(G-2914)***
Silver City Timber Company, Chattaroy *Also called Silver City Lumber Inc* ***(G-2453)***
Silver Creek Ice, Silver Creek *Also called Silvercreek Ice* ***(G-11825)***
Silver Horde Fishing Supplies (PA) 425 778-2640
20910 63rd Ave W Lynnwood (98036) ***(G-6196)***
Silver King Mining & Milling 509 445-1406
411352 Highway 20 Cusick (99119) ***(G-2852)***
Silver Lake Publishing 360 532-0308
1119 N Broadway St Aberdeen (98520) ***(G-35)***
Silver Lake Winery, Woodinville *Also called Washington Wine & Beverage Co* ***(G-15402)***
Silver Lining Seafoods, Seattle *Also called Norquest Seafoods Inc* ***(G-10622)***
Silver Moon Woodworks 425 753-4476
1709 S Lander St Seattle (98144) ***(G-11113)***
Silver Star Cabinets, North Bonneville *Also called Silver Star Industies Inc* ***(G-7134)***
Silver Star Industies Inc 509 427-8800
30 Sw Cascade Ave Stevenson (98648) ***(G-13019)***
Silver Star Industies Inc (PA) 509 427-8800
409 Evergreen Dr North Bonneville (98639) ***(G-7133)***
Silver Star Industies Inc 509 427-8800
505 Evergreen Dr North Bonneville (98639) ***(G-7134)***
Silver Star Industies Inc 360 837-3685
412 Silver Star Ln Washougal (98671) ***(G-14985)***
Silver Star Industries, North Bonneville *Also called Silver Star Industies Inc* ***(G-7133)***
Silver Star Industries, Washougal *Also called Silver Star Industies Inc* ***(G-14985)***
Silver Star Street Rods 360 837-1250
3331 Skye Rd Washougal (98671) ***(G-14986)***
Silvercreek Ice 360 985-2385
2879 Us Highway 12 Silver Creek (98585) ***(G-11825)***
Silverdale Orthodontic Lab 360 479-5536
6102 Widgeon Ct Bremerton (98312) ***(G-2000)***
Silverfeather Creations 425 771-9389
18801 Sound View Pl Edmonds (98020) ***(G-3156)***
Silvergen Inc 360 732-5091
170 Embody Rd Port Ludlow (98365) ***(G-7777)***
Simchuk Karene 509 238-2830
16802 N Applewood Ln Mead (99021) ***(G-6436)***
Simerics Inc (PA) 256 489-1480
1750 112th Ave Ne C250 Bellevue (98004) ***(G-1132)***
Simerics Inc 425 502-9978
1750 112th Ave Ne Bellevue (98004) ***(G-1133)***
Simmons Densified Fuels Inc 509 453-6008
8871 State Route 410 Naches (98937) ***(G-7003)***
Simpatico Cellars 408 667-9658
1718 224th Ct Ne Sammamish (98074) ***(G-9248)***
Simple Agile Corporation 425 985-1096
4045 168th Ave Ne Redmond (98052) ***(G-8669)***
Simple Intelligence LLC 425 418-9803
925 Ne Lake St Apt B Pullman (99163) ***(G-8109)***
Simpleline Inc 888 743-7903
2576 Myra Pl Langley (98260) ***(G-5785)***
Simplicity ABC LLC 425 250-1186
7302 Lake Alice Rd Se Fall City (98024) ***(G-3708)***
Simplot Grower Solutions, Moxee *Also called JR Simplot Company* ***(G-6879)***
Simplot Grower Solutions, Othello *Also called JR Simplot Company* ***(G-7498)***
Simply Augmented Inc 206 771-9774
7041 19th Ave Ne Seattle (98115) ***(G-11114)***
Simply Brilliant Press, Kirkland *Also called Dumas Holdings LLC* ***(G-5323)***
Simply Joyful LLC 425 686-5311
215 100th St Sw Everett (98204) ***(G-3611)***
Simply Sinful 206 546-4461
20214 5th Ave Nw Shoreline (98177) ***(G-11812)***
Simply Sweet Cupcakes 360 568-8600
1206 1st St Snohomish (98290) ***(G-11976)***
Simply Wonder LLC 360 866-2482
4719 69th Ave Nw Olympia (98502) ***(G-7395)***
Simplyfun LLC 425 289-0858
11245 Se 6th St Ste 110 Bellevue (98004) ***(G-1134)***
Simpos 360 794-4658
21414 Ricci Rd Monroe (98272) ***(G-6619)***
Simpson Door Company 360 495-3291
400 W Simpson Ave McCleary (98557) ***(G-6420)***
Simpson Gravel Pit 425 879-1024
6610 140th St Nw Stanwood (98292) ***(G-12991)***
Simpson Investment Company (HQ) 253 272-0158
1301 5th Ave Ste 2700 Seattle (98101) ***(G-11115)***
Simpson Tacoma Kraft Co LLC 253 779-6444
801 E Portland Ave Tacoma (98421) ***(G-13514)***
Simrad Fisheries, Lynnwood *Also called Kongsberg Underwater Tech Inc* ***(G-6153)***
Sims Vibration Laboratory Inc 360 427-6031
50 W Rose Nye Way Shelton (98584) ***(G-11735)***
Simulab Corporation 206 297-1260
13001 48th Ave S Tukwila (98168) ***(G-13819)***
Simutech International Inc 360 490-4029
10205 136th Ave Ne Kirkland (98033) ***(G-5463)***
Sinbads Custom Printing 253 232-7367
17501 11th Ave E Spanaway (98387) ***(G-12074)***
Sinbon Technologies West 425 712-8500
6925 216th St Sw Ste D Lynnwood (98036) ***(G-6197)***
Sinclair Apartments The, Port Orchard *Also called Sinclair Companies* ***(G-7848)***
Sinclair Companies 360 874-6772
414 Sw Hayworth Dr Port Orchard (98367) ***(G-7848)***
Singles Going Steady 206 441-7396
2219 2nd Ave Ste C Seattle (98121) ***(G-11116)***
Sinotechusa Inc 360 566-2880
7509 S 5th St Ste 102 Ridgefield (98642) ***(G-9111)***
Sir Speedy, Renton *Also called Graphic Communications Inc* ***(G-8811)***
Sir Speedy, Tacoma *Also called Marshall Marketing Group Inc* ***(G-13400)***
Sir Speedy, Spokane Valley *Also called Print Tech Inc* ***(G-12840)***
Sir Speedy 360 647-7565
810 N State St Bellingham (98225) ***(G-1538)***
Sirascom Inc 425 497-3300
11121 Willows Rd Ne # 200 Redmond (98052) ***(G-8670)***
Sirens Bath Bombs 360 852-4938
3102 Harney St Apt 4 Vancouver (98660) ***(G-14589)***
Sirjmr Inc 509 582-2683
1351 E 3rd Ave Ste C Kennewick (99337) ***(G-4728)***
Sirlin Enterprises 206 883-7988
120 Lakeside Ave Ste 110 Seattle (98122) ***(G-11117)***
Sirt, Ferndale *Also called Nextlevel Training LLC* ***(G-3876)***
SIS Northwest, Sedro Woolley *Also called Skagit Industrial Steel Inc* ***(G-11567)***
SIS Northwest Inc 360 854-0074
500 Metcalf St Sedro Woolley (98284) ***(G-11565)***
Sissys Specialty Foods 360 807-4305
905 Spring Ln Centralia (98531) ***(G-2435)***
Sistahology 206 604-1418
2011 S Nye Pl Seattle (98144) ***(G-11118)***
Sister Souls Gluten Free Bkg 206 909-9054
2809 Ne 110th St Seattle (98125) ***(G-11119)***
Site Welding Services Inc 425 488-2156
19561 144th Ave Ne Woodinville (98072) ***(G-15364)***
Sitec Coatings 360 840-9979
4700 176th St Sw Lynnwood (98037) ***(G-6198)***
Sitelines Pk & Playground Pdts 425 355-5655
4818 Evergreen Way Ste B Everett (98203) ***(G-3612)***
Sitka 2 Publishing LLC 425 522-4231
13326 119th Ave Ne Ste A Kirkland (98034) ***(G-5464)***
Sittauer Industries Inc 425 741-1125
3610 South Rd Ste 101 Mukilteo (98275) ***(G-6977)***
Sittin Pretty Design 206 725-2453
4112 50th Ave S Seattle (98118) ***(G-11120)***
Sitting Room 206 285-2830
108 W Roy St Seattle (98119) ***(G-11121)***
Sivart Software 206 527-2164
3035 Ne 94th St Seattle (98115) ***(G-11122)***
Siverson Design, Redmond *Also called Cory Siverson* ***(G-8427)***
Six LLC 206 466-5186
1319 Dexter Ave N Seattle (98109) ***(G-11123)***
Six Robbles 360 398-7173
150 W Axton Rd Bellingham (98226) ***(G-1539)***
Sjb Enterprises Inc (PA) 509 926-6979
1013 S Mariam St Spokane Valley (99206) ***(G-12874)***
Sje Inc 360 734-1910
4562 Wynn Rd Ste A Bellingham (98226) ***(G-1540)***
Sk Food Group Inc (HQ) 206 935-8100
4600 37th Ave Sw Ste 300 Seattle (98126) ***(G-11124)***
SK&y International LLC 253 833-9525
1221 29th St Nw Ste C Auburn (98001) ***(G-564)***
Skagit Auto Licensing, Burlington *Also called Skagit Vehicle Licensing Inc* ***(G-2190)***
Skagit Cellars LLC 360 708-2801
3200 Shelly Hill Rd Mount Vernon (98274) ***(G-6837)***
Skagit City Signs Inc 360 848-8888
224 Stewart Rd Ste 201 Mount Vernon (98273) ***(G-6838)***
Skagit County Fire Dst 14 360 724-3451
18726 Parkview Ln Burlington (98233) ***(G-2187)***
Skagit Crest Vinyrd Winery LLC 360 630-5176
22230 Cully Rd Sedro Woolley (98284) ***(G-11566)***
Skagit Industrial Steel Inc 360 854-0074
500 Metcalf St Bldg A Sedro Woolley (98284) ***(G-11567)***
Skagit Northwest Holdings Inc (HQ) 360 757-7776
15180 Josh Wilson Rd Burlington (98233) ***(G-2188)***
Skagit Powder Coating 360 428-0413
14805 Jackpot Ln Mount Vernon (98273) ***(G-6839)***
Skagit Publishing 360 424-3251
5763 Honeysuckle Ln Marblemount (98267) ***(G-6307)***
Skagit Ready Mix 360 856-0422
14658 Ovenell Rd Mount Vernon (98273) ***(G-6840)***
Skagit Readymix, Sedro Woolley *Also called Smokey Point Concrete* ***(G-11571)***
Skagit River Reman Company 360 826-4344
8354 S Healy Rd Sedro Woolley (98284) ***(G-11568)***
Skagit Seed Services Inc 360 466-3191
17297 Hulbert Rd Mount Vernon (98273) ***(G-6841)***
Skagit Transmission Inc 360 757-6551
303 Lila Ln Burlington (98233) ***(G-2189)***
Skagit Valley Cheese, Mount Vernon *Also called Joan F Schleh* ***(G-6805)***
Skagit Valley Malting, Burlington *Also called Salish Coast Enterprises LLC* ***(G-2184)***
Skagit Valley Signs 360 755-0356
1289 Bowman Rd Acme (98220) ***(G-45)***
Skagit Vehicle Licensing Inc 360 755-0419
327 S Burlington Blvd Burlington (98233) ***(G-2190)***

Skagit Vly Malting & Brewing, Mount Vernon *Also called Salish Post Enterprises LLC* **(G-6832)**
Skagits Best Salsa....360 610-9022
21146 Falcon Ct Mount Vernon (98274) **(G-6842)**
Skagvale Holsteins, Sedro Woolley *Also called Tenneson Brothers* **(G-11575)**
Skamania County Pioneer, Stevenson *Also called Greenleaf Publishing Inc* **(G-13012)**
Skandia Northwest Mfg....360 599-2681
6807 Mt Baker Hwy Deming (98244) **(G-2923)**
Skate Like A Girl....206 973-8005
305 Harrison St Seattle (98109) **(G-11125)**
Skein Integrated Systems LLC....586 795-2000
6300 Merrill Creek Pkwy Everett (98203) **(G-3613)**
Sketchforschools Pubg Inc....877 397-5655
2716 N University Rd Spokane Valley (99206) **(G-12875)**
Ski Journal....360 752-5559
3620 Irongate Rd Ste 122 Bellingham (98226) **(G-1541)**
Skidmore & Skidmore Inc....360 379-6385
1929 Hill St Port Townsend (98368) **(G-7926)**
Skiers Inc....360 663-7777
30015 Crystal Mountain Bl Enumclaw (98022) **(G-3320)**
Skilfab Industries Inc....425 831-5555
8300 Railroad Ave Se Snoqualmie (98065) **(G-12024)**
Skillcraft, Seattle *Also called Lighthouse For The Blind Inc* **(G-10417)**
Skillet Food Products LLC....206 420-7297
1400 E Union St Seattle (98122) **(G-11126)**
Skilljar, Seattle *Also called Everpath Inc* **(G-9948)**
Skillman Bob Hauling & Logging, Olympia *Also called Skillman Brothers Inc* **(G-7396)**
Skillman Brothers Inc....360 866-7083
5541 Stmboat Island Rd Nw Olympia (98502) **(G-7396)**
Skills Inc....206 782-6000
425 C St Nw Auburn (98001) **(G-565)**
Skills Inc....206 782-6000
825 Nw 47th St Ste 46 Seattle (98107) **(G-11127)**
Skills For Creative Concepts....360 671-1472
3313 Mcalpine Rd Ste C Bellingham (98225) **(G-1542)**
Skilskin....509 326-6760
920 W Riverside Ave Spokane (99201) **(G-12506)**
Skindiver Suits, Kent *Also called Harveys Skin Diving Supplies* **(G-4935)**
Skinmedica Inc....760 448-3600
3645 Sunset Beach Dr Nw Olympia (98502) **(G-7397)**
Skinner Communications....360 980-4906
10214 Ne 65th Ave Vancouver (98686) **(G-14590)**
Skinny Producing....425 443-4552
6617 118th Ave Se Bellevue (98006) **(G-1135)**
Skip Rock Distillers....360 862-0272
104 Avenue C Snohomish (98290) **(G-11977)**
Skip's Dip, Kirkland *Also called Flying Dog Entertainment LLC* **(G-5340)**
Skoflo Industries Inc....425 485-7816
14241 Ne 200th St Woodinville (98072) **(G-15365)**
Skookem Aerospace Mfg....206 365-8027
21019 66th Ave S Kent (98032) **(G-5133)**
Skookum Enterprises LLC....360 475-0756
4525 Auto Center Way Bremerton (98312) **(G-2001)**
Skookum Logging Inc....360 532-2186
819 Shamrock Dr Aberdeen (98520) **(G-36)**
Skookum Sportswear, Centralia *Also called Centralia Knitting Mills Inc* **(G-2390)**
Skooler Inc....425 628-5000
10400 Ne 4th St Bellevue (98004) **(G-1136)**
Skooler US, Bellevue *Also called Skooler Inc* **(G-1136)**
Skt Industries....206 633-4461
802 Nw 97th St Seattle (98117) **(G-11128)**
Skt Publishers Inc....206 789-8116
7342 15th Ave Nw Seattle (98117) **(G-11129)**
Skt2 LLC....775 303-3788
3400 Se 196th Ave Ste 100 Camas (98607) **(G-2283)**
Skunk Brothers Spirits Inc....360 213-3420
2201 Ne 94th Ct Vancouver (98664) **(G-14591)**
Sky Company, Auburn *Also called SK&y International LLC* **(G-564)**
Sky Printing....206 933-5900
4151 Fauntleroy Way Sw Seattle (98126) **(G-11130)**
Sky River Brewing Inc....360 793-6761
14270 Woodinville Redmond Redmond (98052) **(G-8671)**
Sky River Meadery....425 242-3815
14270 Woodinvll Redmd Rd Redmond (98052) **(G-8672)**
Sky Signs Inc....425 417-9063
12428 169th Ave Se Renton (98059) **(G-8913)**
Sky Valley Foods Inc....360 805-1430
17288 Beaton Rd Se Ste C Monroe (98272) **(G-6620)**
Skybreeze Inc....206 764-1872
10021 10th Ave Sw Seattle (98146) **(G-11131)**
Skye Book & Brew....509 382-4677
503 N Willow St Dayton (99328) **(G-2885)**
Skyfish Media LLC....415 779-2132
1425 Broadway 427 Seattle (98122) **(G-11132)**
Skyflight Inc....425 844-9199
18580 142nd Ave Ne Woodinville (98072) **(G-15366)**
Skyflight Mobile, Woodinville *Also called Skyflight Inc* **(G-15366)**
Skyhawk Press LLC....360 598-2211
1230 Nw Finn Hill Rd D Poulsbo (98370) **(G-8000)**
Skyidrones LLC....253 347-7261
18929 Se 292nd Pl Kent (98042) **(G-5134)**
Skykomish Knife Works....509 763-3117
19475 Us Highway 2 Leavenworth (98826) **(G-5816)**
Skyline Fisheries LLC....425 583-7259
4018 226th Pl Ne Arlington (98223) **(G-329)**
Skyline Fluid Power Inc....509 382-4781
109 N Front St Dayton (99328) **(G-2886)**
Skyline International LLC....206 624-1874
4105 Airport Way S Seattle (98108) **(G-11133)**
Skyline Logging LLC....509 935-7200
1670 W Blue Creek Rd Chewelah (99109) **(G-2608)**
Skyline NW Inc A Wash Cor....360 695-6006
7001 Ne 40th Ave Vancouver (98661) **(G-14592)**
Skyline Socks....425 454-1323
10022 Meydenbauer Way Se G3 Bellevue (98004) **(G-1137)**
Skyline Spirits Wine Works Co....509 967-0781
8011 Keene Rd West Richland (99353) **(G-15100)**
Skyline Windows Inc (PA)....206 542-2147
17240 Ronald Pl N Shoreline (98133) **(G-11813)**
Skytech Machine Inc....360 253-6378
10505 Ne Maitland Rd Vancouver (98686) **(G-14593)**
Skyview Fisheries LLC....425 583-7259
4018 226th Pl Ne Arlington (98223) **(G-330)**
Slam Signs....253 927-2616
700 Sw 368th St Federal Way (98023) **(G-3785)**
Slap Stickers LLC....971 238-8329
915 S 96th St Ste A8 Seattle (98108) **(G-11134)**
Slapshot USA Ltd Liability Co....360 560-0245
2637 Maplewood Dr Longview (98632) **(G-5954)**
Slaptastick, Seattle *Also called Slap Stickers LLC* **(G-11134)**
Slave To Lathe....206 937-2129
4132 40th Ave Sw Seattle (98116) **(G-11135)**
Slawek Tiles....253 529-0823
29314 45th Pl S Auburn (98001) **(G-566)**
Slayer Espresso, Seattle *Also called Seattle Espresso Machine Corp* **(G-11057)**
Slays Poulsbo Bakery Inc....360 779-2798
18924 Front St Ne Poulsbo (98370) **(G-8001)**
Sleep Aire Mattress Company (PA)....206 546-4195
19022 Aurora Ave N Shoreline (98133) **(G-11814)**
Sleep Number Corporation....360 671-1266
4210 Meridian St Bellingham (98226) **(G-1543)**
Sleeping Dog Wines, Benton City *Also called Riverbend Incorporated* **(G-1628)**
Sleeping Giant Winery LLC....206 351-0719
19501 144th Ave Ne Woodinville (98072) **(G-15367)**
Sleeping Industries LLC....360 201-4305
9523 232nd St Sw Edmonds (98020) **(G-3157)**
Slingshot Sports LLC....509 427-4950
390 Evergreen Dr Ste Ef North Bonneville (98639) **(G-7135)**
Slope Indicator, Mukilteo *Also called Durham Geo-Enterprises Inc* **(G-6916)**
Slope Indicator Company (inc)....425 806-2200
3450 Monte Villa Pkwy Bothell (98021) **(G-1905)**
Slow Loris Inc....360 588-0321
7238 Square Harbor Ln Anacortes (98221) **(G-169)**
Slowpitch Softball Assoc....206 719-2161
19924 Aurora Ave N Shoreline (98133) **(G-11815)**
Slp Creative LLC....206 935-5646
6521 California Ave Sw Seattle (98136) **(G-11136)**
Sls Development Inc....253 735-0322
3804 B St Nw Auburn (98001) **(G-567)**
Sls Runout LLC (HQ)....360 883-8846
3204 Nw 38th Cir Vancouver (98660) **(G-14594)**
Slumber Ease Mattress Co Inc....360 657-1654
1327 8th St Marysville (98270) **(G-6385)**
Slumber Ease Mattress Factory, Marysville *Also called Slumber Ease Mattress Co Inc* **(G-6385)**
Slyfield Enterprises....509 968-3456
1331 Grindrod Rd Ellensburg (98926) **(G-3226)**
Smad World LLC....253 536-5460
15917 12th Avenue Ct E Tacoma (98445) **(G-13515)**
Smak Plastics Inc....360 882-0410
9116 Ne 130th Ave Vancouver (98682) **(G-14595)**
Small Business Automation....206 324-3820
131 Bellevue Ave E # 403 Seattle (98102) **(G-11137)**
Small Planet Foods Inc (HQ)....800 624-4123
106 Woodworth St Sedro Woolley (98284) **(G-11569)**
Smalldog Net Solutions Inc....360 376-6056
808 Pioneer Hill Rd Olga (98279) **(G-7219)**
Smart Cable Company....253 474-9967
7403 Lakewood Dr W Ste 14 Lakewood (98499) **(G-5756)**
Smart Moves Inc....206 842-6575
12305 Arrow Point Loop Ne Bainbridge Island (98110) **(G-673)**
Smart Office Environments LLC....206 730-8871
4957 Lakemont Blvd Se C4 Bellevue (98006) **(G-1138)**
Smart Start....425 747-4400
13547 Se 27th Pl Ste 4b Bellevue (98005) **(G-1139)**
Smart Start....425 967-5699
18908 Highway 99 Lynnwood (98036) **(G-6199)**
Smart Tech 3d Printing....425 614-6451
4006 Lincoln Ave Ne Renton (98056) **(G-8914)**
Smarte Carte Inc....206 431-0844
17801 International Blvd Seatac (98158) **(G-9306)**
Smartplug Systems LLC....206 285-2990
2500 Westlake Ave N Ste G Seattle (98109) **(G-11138)**

ALPHABETIC

Smartrg Inc (HQ) ALPHABETIC SECTION

Smartrg Inc (HQ).....877 486-6210
501 Se Columbia Shr Vancouver (98661) ***(G-14596)***
Smartstart.....509 317-2050
516 N 20th Ave Ste A Yakima (98902) ***(G-15676)***
Smasne Cellars, Prosser *Also called Ros Wine Company LLC* ***(G-8065)***
SMC Gear.....360 366-5534
6930 Salashan Pkwy Ferndale (98248) ***(G-3905)***
Smelts Sea Mammal Education Le.....360 303-9338
1003 Iowa Heights Rd Sedro Woolley (98284) ***(G-11570)***
Smiley Dog.....206 903-9631
20224 48th Ave Se Bothell (98012) ***(G-1906)***
Smiley Industrial LLC.....509 302-8792
1315 N Oregon Ave Pasco (99301) ***(G-7630)***
Smileys Inc.....360 424-7338
18022 State Route 536 Mount Vernon (98273) ***(G-6843)***
Smith & Nephew Inc.....509 363-0600
12409 E Mirabeau Pkwy # 10 Spokane Valley (99216) ***(G-12876)***
Smith & Reilly Inc.....360 693-9225
3107 Ne 65th St Vancouver (98663) ***(G-14597)***
Smith & Valley Gallery.....360 766-6230
5742 Gilkey Ave Bow (98232) ***(G-1933)***
Smith Auto Electric Inc.....509 453-8275
12 S 3rd Ave Yakima (98902) ***(G-15677)***
Smith Brother Feed Lot, Kent *Also called Smith Brothers Farms Inc* ***(G-5135)***
Smith Brothers Farms Inc (PA).....253 852-1000
32030 4th Ave Sw Kent (98032) ***(G-5135)***
Smith Chrome Plating Inc.....509 525-0993
1012 N 9th Ave Walla Walla (99362) ***(G-14870)***
Smith Custom Woodworking Inc.....509 670-4634
1902 Hideaway Pl Wenatchee (98801) ***(G-15075)***
Smith Fabrication Inc.....253 854-4367
1609 Central Ave S Ste 13 Kent (98032) ***(G-5136)***
Smith Logging & Monkey Bus.....253 857-5900
13698 Fagerud Rd Se Olalla (98359) ***(G-7210)***
Smith Timber, Tonasket *Also called Havillah Lumber* ***(G-13649)***
Smith-Berger Marine Inc.....206 764-4650
7915 10th Ave S Seattle (98108) ***(G-11139)***
Smithco Meats Inc.....253 863-5157
15509 Main St E Sumner (98390) ***(G-13100)***
Smj Industries LLC.....425 442-9785
1831 127th Ave Se Bellevue (98005) ***(G-1140)***
SMK Tri-Cities Inc.....509 547-0412
1125 E Hillsboro St Pasco (99301) ***(G-7631)***
Smma Candelaria Inc.....206 405-2800
701 5th Ave Ste 2150 Seattle (98104) ***(G-11140)***
Smoke Plus.....206 579-3661
23635 104th Ave Se Kent (98031) ***(G-5137)***
Smoke Plus Cigar.....425 673-1390
3333 184th St Sw Lynnwood (98037) ***(G-6200)***
Smokey Point Concrete.....360 856-0422
23315 Gike Rd Sedro Woolley (98284) ***(G-11571)***
Smokey Point Conrete, Mount Vernon *Also called Skagit Ready Mix* ***(G-6840)***
Smokey Point Custom Cabinets.....360 659-6233
14620 Smokey Point Blvd Marysville (98271) ***(G-6386)***
Smokey Point Log Homes Inc.....360 659-7122
15026 Smokey Point Blvd Marysville (98271) ***(G-6387)***
Smokin Legal Anywhere.....509 465-2695
9301 N Division St Ste A Spokane (99218) ***(G-12507)***
Smoothie Essentials.....360 452-8060
213 W 13th St Port Angeles (98362) ***(G-7744)***
Smoothie Ventures LLC.....509 315-4492
14025 E 26th Ave Spokane Valley (99037) ***(G-12877)***
Smuckwell Industries LLC.....206 412-3598
1635 34th Ave Seattle (98122) ***(G-11141)***
Smyth Paulenterprises Inc.....360 598-3262
22922 Indianola Rd Ne Poulsbo (98370) ***(G-8002)***
Smyth Lumber Mills, Poulsbo *Also called Smyth Paulenterprises Inc* ***(G-8002)***
Snackflash LLC.....509 443-0396
6106 E Big Rock Rd Spokane (99223) ***(G-12508)***
Snake River Fence.....509 758-7081
21246 Montgomery Ridge Rd Anatone (99401) ***(G-185)***
Snap Custom Clothing.....206 682-0686
400 Pine St Ste 230 Seattle (98101) ***(G-11142)***
Snapdog Printing.....360 217-8172
815 Avenue D Snohomish (98290) ***(G-11978)***
Snapidle.....509 575-6322
207b W Charron Rd Moxee (98936) ***(G-6887)***
Snappy Ceramics.....206 329-7137
330 29th Ave Seattle (98122) ***(G-11143)***
Snappyduds.....206 243-8478
135 Sw 153rd St Burien (98166) ***(G-2128)***
Sneva Manufacturing.....317 496-8935
1304 W Chelan Ave Spokane (99205) ***(G-12509)***
Snider Burien Draperies.....206 243-3600
247 Sw 153rd St Burien (98166) ***(G-2129)***
Snider Software LLC.....206 790-7570
10444 Ne 16th Pl Bellevue (98004) ***(G-1141)***
Snipahs LLC.....910 922-4693
16808 405th Dr Se Gold Bar (98251) ***(G-4191)***
Snipes Mountain Brewing Inc.....509 837-2739
905 Yakima Valley Hwy Sunnyside (98944) ***(G-13142)***
Sno King Recycling Inc.....425 582-2919
16123 Highway 99 Lynnwood (98087) ***(G-6201)***
Sno King Signs, Edmonds *Also called Sno-King Signs* ***(G-3158)***
Sno King Stamp.....425 771-9373
19832 Highway 99 Lynnwood (98036) ***(G-6202)***
Sno River Manufacturing.....425 338-5200
3105 Silver Crest Dr Mill Creek (98012) ***(G-6529)***
Sno Valley Milk LLC.....360 410-8888
12420 92nd St Se Snohomish (98290) ***(G-11979)***
Sno-King Signs.....425 775-0594
625 Aloha Way Edmonds (98020) ***(G-3158)***
Sno-Mon Stamping Inc.....360 794-6304
20927 Calhoun Rd Monroe (98272) ***(G-6621)***
Sno-Valley Dream Factory LLC.....408 888-8183
101 W North Bend Way # 207 North Bend (98045) ***(G-7124)***
Snogro.....360 863-6935
502 Maple Ave Snohomish (98290) ***(G-11980)***
Snohomish Bakery & CAF.....360 568-1682
920 1st St Snohomish (98290) ***(G-11981)***
Snohomish County Bus Jurnl.....425 339-3000
1213 California St Everett (98201) ***(G-3614)***
Snohomish Iron Works Inc.....360 568-2811
1st St & Ave E Snohomish (98290) ***(G-11982)***
Snohomish Publishing Company.....206 523-7548
605 2nd St Snohomish (98290) ***(G-11983)***
Snoqualmie Gourmet Ice Cream.....360 668-8535
21106 86th Ave Se Snohomish (98296) ***(G-11984)***
Snoqualmie Machine Works.....425 888-1464
8890 Railroad Ave Se Snoqualmie (98065) ***(G-12025)***
Snoqualmie Sand & Gravel, Vancouver *Also called Glacier Northwest Inc* ***(G-14253)***
Snoqualmie Sand & Gravel, Snoqualmie *Also called Glacier Northwest Inc* ***(G-12013)***
Snoqualmie Valley Logging Inc.....360 794-8205
25308 Ben Howard Rd Monroe (98272) ***(G-6622)***
Snoqualmie Valley Record, Snoqualmie *Also called Sound Publishing Inc* ***(G-12026)***
Snoqualmie Vineyards.....509 786-2104
660 Frontier Rd Prosser (99350) ***(G-8066)***
Snotown Embroidery LLC.....425 446-1681
6103 61st Ave Se Snohomish (98290) ***(G-11985)***
Snow & Company Inc.....206 953-7676
5302 26th Ave Nw Seattle (98107) ***(G-11144)***
Snow & Company Inc.....206 396-8997
4606 Whitman Ave N Seattle (98103) ***(G-11145)***
Snow Peak Forest Products Inc (PA).....208 714-4243
3808 N Sullivan Rd N5 Spokane Valley (99216) ***(G-12878)***
Snow Valley Furniture.....509 292-8880
631 Diamond Creek Rd Newport (99156) ***(G-7066)***
Snowbridge Distilling LLC.....206 442-1707
909 5th Ave Unit 1604 Seattle (98164) ***(G-11146)***
Snowden Brothers LLC.....206 624-1752
1100 Bellevue Way Ne # 8 Bellevue (98004) ***(G-1142)***
Snt-Gbain N Vetrotech Amer Inc.....253 333-7592
2108 B St Nw Ste 110 Auburn (98001) ***(G-568)***
So You Want To Write.....760 771-8940
5508 Peninsula Dr Se Olympia (98513) ***(G-7398)***
Soap Aria LLC.....206 229-4351
6529 23rd St Ne Tacoma (98422) ***(G-13516)***
Soaring Heart LLC (PA).....206 282-1717
101 Nickerson St Ste 400 Seattle (98109) ***(G-11147)***
Soaring Heart Natural Bed Co, Seattle *Also called Soaring Heart LLC* ***(G-11147)***
Soaring Heart Natural Bed Co.....206 257-4158
41 Dravus St Seattle (98109) ***(G-11148)***
Soaring Suns Properties LLC.....509 346-9515
4591 Road 13.6 Sw Royal City (99357) ***(G-9175)***
Sobel Guitars.....505 699-4032
716 Nw 179th St Ridgefield (98642) ***(G-9112)***
Socal Lighting & Sign LLC.....425 345-5596
710 Stratford Pl Sultan (98294) ***(G-13037)***
Socco Forest Products, Sumas *Also called Socco Inc* ***(G-13050)***
Socco Inc.....360 988-4900
601 W Front St Ste A Sumas (98295) ***(G-13050)***
Socedo Inc.....206 499-3398
10700 Ne 4th St Unit 1202 Bellevue (98004) ***(G-1143)***
Social Voter Labs LLC.....206 981-9225
936 N 79th St Seattle (98103) ***(G-11149)***
SOCIETY FOR JAPANESE STUDIES, Seattle *Also called Journal of Japanese Studies* ***(G-10308)***
Society For Mining Metallurgy.....509 922-4063
12720 E Nora Ave Ste A Spokane Valley (99216) ***(G-12879)***
Society43 LLC.....206 327-0778
720 N 91st St Seattle (98103) ***(G-11150)***
Sock Doctor Com Inc.....425 223-5173
4 168th Ave Ne Bellevue (98008) ***(G-1144)***
Sock Monster.....206 724-0123
1909 N 45th St Seattle (98103) ***(G-11151)***
Sock Outlet.....435 787-8888
1420 Nw Gilman Blvd Issaquah (98027) ***(G-4477)***
Sock Peddlers.....253 267-0148
6122 Motor Ave Sw Lakewood (98499) ***(G-5757)***
Socks In A Box LLC.....425 533-8316
7938 Ne 181st Pl Kenmore (98028) ***(G-4606)***
Soda Pop Miniatures LLC.....425 260-4638
1895 10th Ave Ne Issaquah (98029) ***(G-4478)***
Sodexo.....425 656-2860
245 Sw 41st St Renton (98057) ***(G-8915)***

Softchoice Corporation.....206 709-9000
1144 Eastlake Ave E # 700 Seattle (98109) ***(G-11152)***
Softec Systems Inc.....425 741-2055
917 134th St Sw Ste A6 Everett (98204) ***(G-3615)***
Softresources LLC.....425 216-4030
11411 Ne 124th St Ste 270 Kirkland (98034) ***(G-5465)***
Softride Inc.....360 647-7420
913 Squalicum Way Ste 201 Bellingham (98225) ***(G-1544)***
Softsource LLC (PA).....360 676-0999
3112 Maple Ridge Ct Bellingham (98229) ***(G-1545)***
Software AG Usa Inc.....425 519-6600
2039 152nd Ave Ne Redmond (98052) ***(G-8673)***
Software In 34th St.....425 557-7953
22014 Se 34th St Issaquah (98075) ***(G-4479)***
Software Ingenuity LLC.....509 924-0093
4923 S Bellaire Ln Veradale (99037) ***(G-14751)***
Software Planning.....509 522-1620
6 E Alder St Ste 224 Walla Walla (99362) ***(G-14871)***
Sog Specialty Knives & Tls LLC (HQ).....425 771-6230
6521 212th St Sw Lynnwood (98036) ***(G-6203)***
Soggy Hawk Software.....425 246-6555
19711 222nd Ave Ne Woodinville (98077) ***(G-15368)***
Soham Inc (PA).....425 445-2125
15375 Se 30th Pl Ste 310 Bellevue (98007) ***(G-1145)***
Soil Science Products LLC.....360 876-3734
2713 Anderson Hill Rd Sw Port Orchard (98367) ***(G-7849)***
Soilcraft Inc (PA).....509 314-9227
2300 E Zillah Dr Zillah (98953) ***(G-15759)***
Soilsoup, Poulsbo *Also called Microbial Magic LLC* ***(G-7983)***
Sojo Foods, Seattle *Also called Tastebud Fusion Inc* ***(G-11272)***
Sol Lighting Inc.....509 789-1092
16124 E Euclid Ave Spokane Valley (99216) ***(G-12880)***
Sol Stone Winery.....425 417-8483
19151 144th Ave Ne Ste G Woodinville (98072) ***(G-15369)***
Sol Sunguard Corporation.....206 283-0409
6525 15th Ave Nw Ste 125 Seattle (98117) ***(G-11153)***
Sola Bothell.....501 487-7652
18333 Bothell Way Ne Bothell (98011) ***(G-1793)***
Sola Bothell Church, Bothell *Also called Sola Bothell* ***(G-1793)***
Solar Graphics Inc.....509 248-1129
2208 Oak Ave Yakima (98903) ***(G-15678)***
Solar Guard Coatings Inc.....425 413-0545
22126 238th Pl Se Maple Valley (98038) ***(G-6293)***
Solar Space Industries Inc.....206 332-9966
701 5th Ave Ste 4620 Seattle (98104) ***(G-11154)***
Solar Spirits Distillery, Richland *Also called Sun Spirits Distillery LLC* ***(G-9043)***
Solaracast, Liberty Lake *Also called Cloudstream Media Inc* ***(G-5828)***
Solarworld Industries Amer LP.....360 944-9251
12016 Ne 95th St Ste 720 Vancouver (98682) ***(G-14598)***
Solcon Inc.....425 222-5963
30200 Se 79th St Unit 120 Issaquah (98027) ***(G-4480)***
Soldano Custom Amplification, Seattle *Also called Gremlin Inc* ***(G-10123)***
Solid Modeling Solutions Inc.....425 246-3943
17708 Se 40th Pl Bellevue (98008) ***(G-1146)***
Solid Solutions Inc.....360 882-9074
2700 Ne Burton Rd Ste B Vancouver (98662) ***(G-14599)***
Solid Surface Solutions, Pacific *Also called Dudley Family Group Inc* ***(G-7525)***
Solid Visions Inc.....206 949-4203
4604 212th St Se Bothell (98021) ***(G-1907)***
Solipsis Publishing, Seattle *Also called Garpike Inc* ***(G-10048)***
Solis Ortus.....206 463-6245
13309 Sw 270th St Vashon (98070) ***(G-14743)***
Solomon Logging LLC.....425 292-0745
14412 447th Ave Se North Bend (98045) ***(G-7125)***
Soloy LLC.....360 754-7000
450 Pat Kennedy Way Sw Tumwater (98501) ***(G-13898)***
Soloy Aviation Solutions, Tumwater *Also called Soloy LLC* ***(G-13898)***
Solta Medical Inc.....425 354-1857
11720 N Creek Pkwy N # 100 Bothell (98011) ***(G-1794)***
Solutec Corp.....509 453-6502
1208 N 1st St Yakima (98901) ***(G-15679)***
Solutions With Innovation.....253 872-0783
6757 S 216th St Kent (98032) ***(G-5138)***
Solvay Chemicals Inc.....360 425-1114
3500 Industrial Way Longview (98632) ***(G-5955)***
Somarakis Inc (PA).....360 574-6722
552 Hendrickson Dr Kalama (98625) ***(G-4508)***
Somatics LLC.....847 234-6761
12911 Nw 25th Ct Vancouver (98685) ***(G-14600)***
Somero Logging.....360 686-3926
36800 Ne 233rd Ave Yacolt (98675) ***(G-15493)***
Somers Automotive Machine, Vancouver *Also called Barbara Somers* ***(G-14057)***
Somerset Software.....425 822-1951
520 6th Ave Apt 4003 Kirkland (98033) ***(G-5466)***
Something For Everybody.....541 805-8495
1212 Se Newgate Dr College Place (99324) ***(G-2728)***
Sonderen Packaging Inc (PA).....509 487-1632
2906 N Crestline St Spokane (99207) ***(G-12510)***
Sonderen Paper Box, Spokane *Also called Sonderen Packaging Inc* ***(G-12510)***
Sondra L Groce.....509 467-8788
9624 N Colfax Rd Spokane (99218) ***(G-12511)***
Songbird Vineyard LLC.....509 318-4044
63704 N 106 Pr Ne Benton City (99320) ***(G-1629)***
Sonic Patch LLC.....425 284-6072
4806 Sw Stevens St Seattle (98116) ***(G-11155)***
Soniccare, Bothell *Also called Philips Oral Healthcare LLC* ***(G-1886)***
Soniq Aerospace LP.....253 750-4592
175 Roy Rd Sw Bldg A Pacific (98047) ***(G-7540)***
Sonoco Products Company.....206 682-0440
1802 Steele Ave Sumner (98390) ***(G-13101)***
Sonoco Products Company.....360 225-1500
1620 Down River Dr Woodland (98674) ***(G-15466)***
Sonodiagnostics.....206 938-7922
5601 32nd Ave Sw Seattle (98126) ***(G-11156)***
Sonofresco LLC.....360 757-2800
1365 Pacific Dr Burlington (98233) ***(G-2191)***
Sonus-USA, Yakima *Also called TAHAc LLC* ***(G-15693)***
Sonus-Usa Inc.....253 272-3090
1901 S Union Ave B2006 Tacoma (98405) ***(G-13517)***
Sony Sewing Co, Seattle *Also called Lammy Industries Inc* ***(G-10374)***
Soos Creek Dental.....253 631-8241
17615 Se 272nd St Ste 108 Covington (98042) ***(G-2839)***
Soos Creek Wine Cellars LLC.....253 631-8775
24012 172nd Ave Se Kent (98042) ***(G-5139)***
Soph-Ware Associates Inc.....509 467-0668
1818 W Francis Ave # 250 Spokane (99205) ***(G-12512)***
Sophies Touch.....253 677-1061
1361 11th Ct Fox Island (98333) ***(G-4025)***
Sorensen Marine Inc.....206 767-4622
9808 17th Ave Sw Seattle (98106) ***(G-11157)***
SOS Finishing Unlimited Inc.....425 746-7385
825 176th Ave Ne Bellevue (98008) ***(G-1147)***
SOS Printing.....360 385-4194
710 Q St Port Townsend (98368) ***(G-7927)***
Soterion Co.....425 259-8181
3201 Rucker Ave Ste 2 Everett (98201) ***(G-3616)***
Souers Custom Plastics, Gig Harbor *Also called Souers Manufacturing Inc* ***(G-4161)***
Souers Manufacturing Inc.....253 735-2488
915 26th Ave Nw Ste C8 Gig Harbor (98335) ***(G-4161)***
Soulier Southbay LLC.....360 459-3015
4003 8th Ave Se Lacey (98503) ***(G-5589)***
Sound Building Supply Inc.....425 264-0264
2701 E Valley Rd Renton (98057) ***(G-8916)***
Sound Glass Sales Inc (PA).....253 473-7477
5501 75th St W Tacoma (98499) ***(G-13518)***
Sound Hydraulics Inc.....206 824-7450
20931 4th Ave S Des Moines (98198) ***(G-2946)***
Sound Machine Products Inc.....253 872-5876
22645 76th Ave S Kent (98032) ***(G-5140)***
Sound Manufacturing Inc.....253 872-8007
5820 S 228th St Kent (98032) ***(G-5141)***
Sound Metal Works Ltd.....360 659-0999
14721 16th Ave Nw Marysville (98271) ***(G-6388)***
Sound Metrics Corp.....425 822-3001
11010 Northup Way Bellevue (98004) ***(G-1148)***
Sound Pharmaceuticals Inc.....206 634-2559
4010 Stone Way N Ste 120 Seattle (98103) ***(G-11158)***
Sound Product Solutions LLC.....360 553-7898
12515 Ne 95th St Vancouver (98682) ***(G-14601)***
Sound Propeller Services Inc.....206 788-4202
7916 8th Ave S Seattle (98108) ***(G-11159)***
Sound Publishing Inc.....253 437-6000
1010 S 336th St Ste 330 Federal Way (98003) ***(G-3786)***
Sound Publishing Inc (HQ).....360 394-5800
11323 Commando Rd W Main Everett (98204) ***(G-3617)***
Sound Publishing Inc.....253 925-5565
1010 S 336th St Ste 330 Federal Way (98003) ***(G-3787)***
Sound Publishing Inc.....360 786-6973
7128 Holmes Island Rd Se Lacey (98503) ***(G-5590)***
Sound Publishing Inc.....360 779-4464
19351 8th Ave Ne Ste 205 Poulsbo (98370) ***(G-8003)***
Sound Publishing Inc.....206 463-9195
17141 Vashon Hwy Sw Ste B Vashon (98070) ***(G-14744)***
Sound Publishing Inc.....360 308-9161
3888 Nw Randall Way # 100 Silverdale (98383) ***(G-11858)***
Sound Publishing Inc.....360 378-5696
640 Mullis St Friday Harbor (98250) ***(G-4059)***
Sound Publishing Inc.....360 376-4500
217 Main St B Eastsound (98245) ***(G-3047)***
Sound Publishing Inc.....360 675-6611
107 S Main St Ste E101 Coupeville (98239) ***(G-2818)***
Sound Publishing Inc.....360 876-4414
2497 Bethel Rd Se Ste 102 Port Orchard (98366) ***(G-7850)***
Sound Publishing Inc.....425 483-3732
11630 Slater Ave Ne Ste 9 Kirkland (98034) ***(G-5467)***
Sound Publishing Inc.....253 872-6600
1010 S 336th St Ste 330 Federal Way (98003) ***(G-3788)***
Sound Publishing Inc.....425 888-2311
8124 Falls Ave Se Snoqualmie (98065) ***(G-12026)***
Sound Publishing Inc.....360 825-2555
1627 Cole St Enumclaw (98022) ***(G-3321)***
Sound Publishing Inc.....360 659-1300
1085 Cedar Ave Marysville (98270) ***(G-6389)***

ALPHABETIC

Sound Publishing Inc — ALPHABETIC SECTION

Sound Publishing Inc 425 355-0717
  11323 Commando Rd W Main Everett (98204) *(G-3618)*
Sound Publishing Holding Inc (HQ) 360 394-5800
  19351 8th Ave Ne Ste 106 Poulsbo (98370) *(G-8004)*
Sound Sails 360 385-3881
  290 10th St Port Townsend (98368) *(G-7928)*
Sound Screen Printing Inc 206 890-2700
  3216 S 136th St Tukwila (98168) *(G-13820)*
Sound Services 360 920-3435
  2531 Eldridge Ave Bellingham (98225) *(G-1546)*
Sound Software 360 375-6375
  1 Marina Dr Blakely Island (98222) *(G-1715)*
Sound Spring Inc 253 859-9499
  830 3rd Ave S Kent (98032) *(G-5142)*
Sound Tanks and Cntrs L L C 425 455-2668
  227 Bellevue Way Ne # 166 Bellevue (98004) *(G-1149)*
Sound Uniform Solutions, Seattle *Also called Seattle Sewing Solutions Inc (G-11073)*
Soundings of The Planet Inc 360 738-9368
  1304 Meador Ave Ste 3 Bellingham (98229) *(G-1547)*
Soundnine Inc 206 245-4463
  10825 Ne 112th St Kirkland (98033) *(G-5468)*
Soundview Graphics LLC 253 851-2007
  3303 Jahn Ave Nw Ste 115 Gig Harbor (98335) *(G-4162)*
Soundworks U S A Inc 425 882-3344
  8300 28th Ct Ne Ste 400 Lacey (98516) *(G-5591)*
Source Dynamics Inc 425 557-3630
  22525 Se 64th Pl Ste 260 Issaquah (98027) *(G-4481)*
Source Engineering LLC (HQ) 360 383-5129
  8858 Guide Meridian Rd Lynden (98264) *(G-6053)*
Source Insight, Issaquah *Also called Source Dynamics Inc (G-4481)*
Source Northwest Inc 360 512-3535
  8329 216th St Se Woodinville (98072) *(G-15370)*
Source TEC Inc 206 972-3172
  13110 Ne 177th Pl 148 Woodinville (98072) *(G-15371)*
Source Window Coverings, Woodinville *Also called Source Northwest Inc (G-15370)*
Souriau, Wenatchee *Also called Pacific Aerospace & Elec Inc (G-15058)*
South Bay Press, Lacey *Also called Soulier Southbay LLC (G-5589)*
South Bend Boat Shop 360 875-5712
  255 W Robert Bush Dr South Bend (98586) *(G-12046)*
South Bend Lathes 360 734-1540
  1821 Valencia St Bellingham (98229) *(G-1548)*
South Bend Products LLC 360 875-6570
  237 W Robert Bush Dr South Bend (98586) *(G-12047)*
South Everson Lumber Co Inc 360 966-2188
  1615 Mission Rd Everson (98247) *(G-3689)*
South Hill Cabinets 253 848-2026
  8418 75th Ave E Puyallup (98371) *(G-8255)*
South Paw Screenprinting 206 762-2926
  309 S Cloverdale St B30 Seattle (98108) *(G-11160)*
South Pierce County Dispatch, Eatonville *Also called Eatonville Dispatch Newspaper (G-3055)*
South Shore Rehabilitation, Kenmore *Also called Southshore Prsthtics Orthotics (G-4607)*
South Sound Aquaponics LLC 206 510-0408
  1847 S 310th St Unit B Federal Way (98003) *(G-3789)*
South Sound Contractors LLC 360 688-5101
  4010 8th Ave Se Lacey (98503) *(G-5592)*
South Sound Metal Inc 253 564-0226
  7406 27th St W Ste 10 University Place (98466) *(G-13981)*
South Sound Screen Printing 360 871-4206
  3370 Arvick Rd Se Port Orchard (98366) *(G-7851)*
South Tacoma Glass Specialists 253 582-2401
  8915 Lakeview Ave Sw Lakewood (98499) *(G-5758)*
Southard Winery 509 697-3003
  670 Tibbling Rd Selah (98942) *(G-11597)*
Southard Winery 509 452-8626
  811 W Yakima Ave Yakima (98902) *(G-15680)*
Southend Machine Inc 253 735-1035
  1802 Pike St Nw Ste C Auburn (98001) *(G-569)*
Southern Explorations 206 641-9241
  2600 2nd Ave Apt 2202 Seattle (98121) *(G-11161)*
Southpark Fuel & Food 206 762-7550
  9525 14th Ave S Seattle (98108) *(G-11162)*
Southshore Prsthtics Orthotics 206 440-1811
  6509 Ne 181st St Kenmore (98028) *(G-4607)*
Southside Enterprises Inc 509 395-2345
  40 Binns Rd Trout Lake (98650) *(G-13683)*
Southwest Concrete Co 360 795-8211
  276 E State Route 4 Cathlamet (98612) *(G-2375)*
Southworth Marine Service 360 871-5610
  11113 Tola Rd Se Southworth (98386) *(G-12051)*
Souz LLC 206 428-8332
  5000 Lake Washington Blvd B102 Renton (98056) *(G-8917)*
Sovereign Manufacturing 253 318-7180
  10506 193rd Street Ct E Graham (98338) *(G-4238)*
Sovrano Di Ricchezza Group 425 449-8011
  13500 Se 24th St Bellevue (98005) *(G-1150)*
Sp Holdings Inc 509 924-7623
  3808 N Sullivan Rd # 21 Spokane Valley (99216) *(G-12881)*
Sp Holdings Inc (PA) 425 291-3500
  1000 Sw 43rd St Renton (98057) *(G-8918)*
Sp Indstrial Lubrication A LLC 360 579-2646
  7190 Terrapin Ln Clinton (98236) *(G-2699)*

Sp Marine Fabrication LLC 360 813-3600
  7510 Bree Dr Bremerton (98312) *(G-2002)*
Space Age Industries LLC 206 992-7731
  1305 E Denny Way Apt 201 Seattle (98122) *(G-11163)*
Space Exploration Tech Corp 425 867-9910
  18390 Ne 6th St Redmond (98052) *(G-8674)*
Space Exploration Tech Corp 425 602-2255
  23020 Ne Alder Crest Dr Redmond (98053) *(G-8675)*
Space Rock It Inc 206 395-8383
  500 Wall St Apt 1502 Seattle (98121) *(G-11164)*
Spacecraft Collective, Seattle *Also called Pow Inc (G-10840)*
Spaceflight Industries Inc (PA) 206 342-9934
  1505 Westlake Ave N # 600 Seattle (98109) *(G-11165)*
Spacelabs Health Care, Snoqualmie *Also called Spacelabs Healthcare Wash (G-12029)*
Spacelabs Healthcare Inc (HQ) 425 396-3300
  35301 Se Center St Snoqualmie (98065) *(G-12027)*
Spacelabs Healthcare LLC 425 396-3300
  35301 Se Center St Snoqualmie (98065) *(G-12028)*
Spacelabs Healthcare Wash (HQ) 425 396-3300
  35301 Se Center St Snoqualmie (98065) *(G-12029)*
Spacelabs Healthcare Wash 425 396-3300
  35301 Se Center St Snoqualmie (98065) *(G-12030)*
Spacewall Northwest, Kent *Also called Spacewall West Inc (G-5143)*
Spacewall West Inc 253 852-0203
  25315 74th Ave S Kent (98032) *(G-5143)*
Spacex, Redmond *Also called Space Exploration Tech Corp (G-8674)*
Spacex Redmond Rr02, Redmond *Also called Space Exploration Tech Corp (G-8675)*
Spanky Burger & Brew 253 720-3344
  601 S Pine St Ste 205 Tacoma (98405) *(G-13519)*
Spanton Business Forms 509 966-7384
  3404 Barge St Yakima (98902) *(G-15681)*
Spargo's Printing, Aberdeen *Also called Clarence H Spargo Jr (G-7)*
Sparkadoodle Baking Co LLC 253 224-0255
  19710 8th Ave E Spanaway (98387) *(G-12075)*
Sparklehorse LLC 253 948-7772
  6820 Kimball Dr Ste C Gig Harbor (98335) *(G-4163)*
Sparkman Cellers 425 398-1045
  19501 144th Ave Ne Woodinville (98072) *(G-15372)*
Sparkon Inc 425 273-3904
  16430 Ne 50th St Redmond (98052) *(G-8676)*
Sparrow Woodworks LLC 206 708-5615
  9829 Ne Coyote Ln Indianola (98342) *(G-4373)*
Spartan Industries L L C 425 822-2071
  13244 Ne 108th St Redmond (98052) *(G-8677)*
Spaz Industries LLC 206 890-7079
  2445 74th Ave Se Mercer Island (98040) *(G-6485)*
Spearman Corp Kent Division 253 236-5980
  7020 Oberto Dr Kent (98032) *(G-5144)*
Spearman Corporation (PA) 360 651-9281
  7020 Oberto Dr Kent (98032) *(G-5145)*
Spec Tech Industries Inc 360 303-9077
  622 Sprague Valley Dr Maple Falls (98266) *(G-6251)*
Specht Coatings 253 732-5662
  27917 129th Ave E Graham (98338) *(G-4239)*
Special Edition Incorporated 253 537-1836
  315 99th St E Tacoma (98445) *(G-13520)*
Special T Signs & Graphics 360 734-7617
  2206 Pacific St Bellingham (98229) *(G-1549)*
Specialists Sealant 509 321-0424
  5610 E Broadway Ave Spokane Valley (99212) *(G-12882)*
Specialized Computing Inc 206 915-9033
  942 N 82nd St Seattle (98103) *(G-11166)*
Specialized Machine Works 206 715-5901
  20021 80th Ave S Kent (98032) *(G-5146)*
Specialized Pharmaceuticals 253 859-3702
  325 W Gowe St Kent (98032) *(G-5147)*
Specialized Safety Pdts LLC 509 707-0068
  6082 22nd Ave Ne Spc 1 Moses Lake (98837) *(G-6751)*
Specialty Chemical Pdts LLC 509 884-4900
  100 S 4th St Rock Island (98850) *(G-9149)*
Specialty Concrete 360 577-4555
  312 Hazel St Kelso (98626) *(G-4549)*
Specialty Embroidery 509 924-1579
  1925 Sorrel Ln Se Lacey (98503) *(G-5593)*
Specialty Graphics, Bellingham *Also called Special T Signs & Graphics (G-1549)*
Specialty Manufacturer, Lynnwood *Also called Arrow International Inc (G-6077)*
Specialty Minerals Inc 509 545-9777
  31829 W Highway 12 Wallula (99363) *(G-14911)*
Specialty Motors Mfg LLC 360 423-9880
  641 California Way Longview (98632) *(G-5956)*
Specialty Pdts Elec Cnstr LLC 425 402-8332
  19495 144th Ave Ne A145 Woodinville (98072) *(G-15373)*
Specialty Products Inc (HQ) 253 588-7101
  2410 104th Street Ct S D Lakewood (98499) *(G-5759)*
Specialty Pump & Well, Snohomish *Also called Specialty Pump and Plbg Inc (G-11986)*
Specialty Pump and Plbg Inc 425 424-8700
  8425 Fobes Rd Snohomish (98290) *(G-11986)*
Specialty Roofing LLC 509 534-8372
  2222 E Mallon Ave Spokane (99202) *(G-12513)*
Specialty Sheet Metal Inc 253 872-5718
  11409 Se 218th Pl Kent (98031) *(G-5148)*
Specialty Steel Fabricators, Olympia *Also called Richmond Systems Inc (G-7386)*

ALPHABETIC SECTION

Springboard Winery LLC

Specialty Stores Inc 206 650-0747
227 Bellevue Way Ne # 59 Bellevue (98004) ***(G-1151)***
Specialty Vetpath 206 453-5691
14810 15th Ave Ne Shoreline (98155) ***(G-11816)***
Specialty Wipers Inc (PA) 425 251-3530
7979 S 180th St Kent (98032) ***(G-5149)***
Specialty Woodworking 360 379-1222
235 Hancock St Port Townsend (98368) ***(G-7929)***
Specialty Woodworks 360 670-6280
124 N Gales St Port Angeles (98362) ***(G-7745)***
Specified Fittings LLC 360 398-7700
164 W Smith Rd Bellingham (98226) ***(G-1550)***
Specified Fittings LLC 360 398-7700
164 W Smith Rd Bellingham (98226) ***(G-1551)***
Spectacle Maker 425 643-5367
1837 156th Ave Ne Ste 202 Bellevue (98007) ***(G-1152)***
Spectech Aerospace LLC 425 286-1101
11805 N Creek Pkwy S Bothell (98011) ***(G-1795)***
Spectracal, Edmonds *Also called Portrait Displays Inc* ***(G-3144)***
Spectralux Avionics, Redmond *Also called Spectralux Corporation* ***(G-8678)***
Spectralux Corporation 425 285-3000
12335 134th Ct Ne Redmond (98052) ***(G-8678)***
Spectroglyph LLC 415 793-1242
101904 Wiser Pkwy Ste 104 Kennewick (99338) ***(G-4729)***
Spectrum Controls Inc 425 462-2087
1705 132nd Ave Ne Bellevue (98005) ***(G-1153)***
Spectrum Embroidery & Printing 206 851-9687
18705 Beardslee Blvd Bothell (98011) ***(G-1796)***
Spectrum Graphics, Edmonds *Also called Ridgewood Industries Inc* ***(G-3148)***
Spectrum Health Systems Inc 253 572-3398
1016 S 28th St Fl 3 Tacoma (98409) ***(G-13521)***
Spectrum Manufacturing 509 982-2257
2194 N Schoonover Rd Odessa (99159) ***(G-7192)***
Spectrum Sign Co Inc 253 939-5500
301 W Main St Auburn (98001) ***(G-570)***
Spectyr Industries Corp 360 863-7720
14327 169th Dr Se Ste 154 Monroe (98272) ***(G-6623)***
Specview Corp (PA) 253 853-3199
3100b Harborview Dr Gig Harbor (98335) ***(G-4164)***
Speechace LLC 425 241-3033
2133 5th Ave Apt 406 Seattle (98121) ***(G-11167)***
Speedfab 360 571-4093
9305 Ne Highway 99 Vancouver (98665) ***(G-14602)***
Speedway Marine Inc 360 658-1288
15008 Smokey Point Blvd F Marysville (98271) ***(G-6390)***
Speedy Litho Inc 360 425-3610
403 Catlin St Kelso (98626) ***(G-4550)***
Speedy Mix Concrete 253 531-3260
8836 E D St Tacoma (98445) ***(G-13522)***
Speedy Signs 425 771-1700
19106 Highway 99 Ste A Lynnwood (98036) ***(G-6204)***
Speedzone By Shadow Master, Lakewood *Also called Shadow Master* ***(G-5754)***
Spencer LLC 360 805-2500
17381 Tye St Se Ste 4 Monroe (98272) ***(G-6624)***
Spencer Cabinetry 360 794-8344
17381 Tye St Se Ste 4 Monroe (98272) ***(G-6625)***
SPI, Aberdeen *Also called Sierra Pacific Industries* ***(G-34)***
SPI, Lakewood *Also called Specialty Products Inc* ***(G-5759)***
Spice Hut Corporation 360 671-2800
131 W Kellogg Rd Bellingham (98226) ***(G-1552)***
Spice Hut, The, Bellingham *Also called Spice Hut Corporation* ***(G-1552)***
Spider, Tukwila *Also called Safeworks LLC* ***(G-13809)***
Spilker Precast LLC 509 487-2261
4231 E Queen Ave Spokane (99217) ***(G-12514)***
Spiller Corporation 206 575-2110
7825 S 180th St Kent (98032) ***(G-5150)***
Spillmasters X LLC 360 461-7910
322 Christmas Tree Ln Port Angeles (98363) ***(G-7746)***
Spin Tees 360 515-0543
2008 Harrison Ave Nw # 101 Olympia (98502) ***(G-7399)***
Spin Tees 253 301-2047
6450 Tacoma Mall Blvd Tacoma (98409) ***(G-13523)***
Spinal Specialties 253 861-7329
2024 Caton Way Sw Ste A Olympia (98502) ***(G-7400)***
Spindrift Rowing LLC 360 344-2233
762 W Park Ave Port Townsend (98368) ***(G-7930)***
Spinner Wood Products LLC 509 653-2222
10533 Old Naches Hwy Naches (98937) ***(G-7004)***
Spinnerrack LLC 425 268-1084
10706 57th Pl W Mukilteo (98275) ***(G-6978)***
Spinning Heads Inc 253 219-5457
420 E 18th St Tacoma (98421) ***(G-13524)***
Spio Inc 253 893-0390
127 Sw 156th St Burien (98166) ***(G-2130)***
Spiral & Railing House, The, Davenport *Also called S & R Spiral LLC* ***(G-2877)***
Spiral Arts 206 768-9765
901 Nw 49th St Seattle (98107) ***(G-11168)***
Spiraltec 360 734-7831
3951 Hammer Dr Bellingham (98226) ***(G-1553)***
Spirit In Wood LLC 509 961-3061
11180 State Route 410 Naches (98937) ***(G-7005)***
Spirit of Winds Incense St 253 293-2743
455 S 305th St Federal Way (98003) ***(G-3790)***
Spirit Trailer, Monroe *Also called Khann Industries Corp* ***(G-6587)***
Splendid Intl USA Corp 253 813-5692
8647 S 212th St Kent (98031) ***(G-5151)***
Splitvane Engineers, Sumas *Also called Mazdak International Inc* ***(G-13047)***
Splunk Inc 206 430-5200
1730 Minor Ave Ste 900 Seattle (98101) ***(G-11169)***
Spnw, Longview *Also called Screen Print Northwest Inc* ***(G-5951)***
Spoiled Dog Winery 360 321-6226
5881 Maxwelton Rd Langley (98260) ***(G-5786)***
Spokanarama Publishing 509 455-8009
627 W 16th Ave Spokane (99203) ***(G-12515)***
Spokane Athors Self-Publishers 509 325-2072
2504 W Walton Ave Spokane (99205) ***(G-12516)***
Spokane County Raceway 509 244-3333
750 N Hayford Rd Airway Heights (99001) ***(G-64)***
Spokane Custom Cabinets Inc 509 487-8416
4515 E Bixel Ct Mead (99021) ***(G-6437)***
Spokane Discount and Brass Co 509 467-8063
6715 N Division St Spokane (99208) ***(G-12517)***
Spokane Forklift Cnstr Eqp Inc 509 868-5962
4907 E Trent Ave Spokane (99212) ***(G-12518)***
Spokane Galvanizing Inc 509 244-4073
2727 S Garfield Rd Airway Heights (99001) ***(G-65)***
Spokane House of Hose Inc 509 535-3638
5520 E Sprague Ave Spokane Valley (99212) ***(G-12883)***
Spokane Hydrogen Hybrids 509 443-5919
13714 E 23rd Ct Spokane Valley (99216) ***(G-12884)***
Spokane Industries Inc (PA) 509 924-0440
3808 N Sullivan Rd Bldg 1 Spokane Valley (99216) ***(G-12885)***
Spokane Industries Inc 509 928-0720
3808 N Sullivan Rd Bldg 4 Spokane Valley (99216) ***(G-12886)***
Spokane Machinery Company (HQ) 509 535-1654
3730 E Trent Ave Spokane (99202) ***(G-12519)***
Spokane Metal Products, Spokane Valley *Also called Spokane Industries Inc* ***(G-12885)***
Spokane Paw Prints LLC 509 475-6885
3929 N Crestline St Spokane (99207) ***(G-12520)***
Spokane Rain Gutter Inc 509 922-4880
8710 E Sprague Ave Spokane Valley (99212) ***(G-12887)***
Spokane Rock Products Inc 509 292-2200
39102 N Newport Hwy Elk (99009) ***(G-3177)***
Spokane Rock Products Inc (PA) 509 244-5421
4418 E 8th Ave Spokane Valley (99212) ***(G-12888)***
Spokane Terminal, Spokane Valley *Also called Ash Grove Cement Company* ***(G-12627)***
Spokane Tin Sheet Ir Works Inc 509 534-0539
3807 E Ferry Ave Spokane (99202) ***(G-12521)***
Spokane Valley Screen Printing 509 921-0207
12005 E Trent Ave Spokane Valley (99206) ***(G-12889)***
Spokane Wilbert Vault Company (PA) 509 325-4573
2215 E Brooklyn Ave Spokane (99217) ***(G-12522)***
Spokaneforklift.com, Spokane *Also called Spokane Forklift Cnstr Eqp Inc* ***(G-12518)***
Spokesinger Prints 206 522-5179
7320 20th Ave Ne Seattle (98115) ***(G-11170)***
Spomac, Spokane *Also called Spokane Machinery Company* ***(G-12519)***
Spoonk Space Inc 360 392-8067
164 Bay Lyn Dr Ste F Lynden (98264) ***(G-6054)***
Spoony Luv 206 240-8584
2336 N 185th St Shoreline (98133) ***(G-11817)***
Spore Incorporated 206 624-9573
2101 9th Ave Ste B1 Seattle (98121) ***(G-11171)***
Sporting Systems Corporation 360 607-0036
7415 Ne Highway 99 # 104 Vancouver (98665) ***(G-14603)***
Sports N Sorts 509 276-6170
7911 W Ridgeway Rd Deer Park (99006) ***(G-2915)***
Sports-Fab Inc 503 408-0920
9505 Ne 84th Ct Vancouver (98662) ***(G-14604)***
Sportsmens Cannery (PA) 360 642-2335
35th & Pacific Hwy Seaview (98644) ***(G-11529)***
Sportsoft Inc 425 822-4613
914 164th St Se Mill Creek (98012) ***(G-6530)***
Spot-On Print & Design Inc 425 558-7768
1803 132nd Ave Ne Ste 1 Bellevue (98005) ***(G-1154)***
Spotter Levels LLC 425 238-5117
6720 Happy Hollow Rd Stanwood (98292) ***(G-12992)***
Spradlin Rock Products Inc 360 532-2994
167 Us Highway 101 Hoquiam (98550) ***(G-4360)***
Spray Center Electronics Inc 509 838-2209
9721 W Flight Dr Spokane (99224) ***(G-12523)***
Spraying Systems Co 425 357-6327
1720 100th Pl Se Ste 102 Everett (98208) ***(G-3619)***
Spring Craft, Spokane *Also called Northwest Bedding Company* ***(G-12411)***
Spring Creek Enterprises 360 876-8884
7997 Van Decar Rd Se Port Orchard (98367) ***(G-7852)***
Spring Creek Industries Inc 509 486-0599
35 Sour Dough Creek Rd Tonasket (98855) ***(G-13659)***
Spring Valley Tasting Room 509 525-1506
18 N 2nd Ave Walla Walla (99362) ***(G-14872)***
Spring Valley Vineyard Winery 509 337-6043
1663 Corkrum Rd Walla Walla (99362) ***(G-14873)***
Springboard Winery LLC 509 929-4247
5090 Naneum Rd Ellensburg (98926) ***(G-3227)***

ALPHABETIC

Springbrook Nurs & Trckg Inc....360 653-6545
9022 84th St Ne Arlington (98223) **(G-331)**
Springcrest Drapery Gallery....509 928-9269
14109 E Sprague Ave Ste 7 Spokane Valley (99216) **(G-12890)**
Springtime Bakery, Burien *Also called Armoire* **(G-2092)**
Sprinkler Fitters Local Un 699, Seattle *Also called United Association of Journeym* **(G-11369)**
Spry Fox LLC....425 835-3320
8730 Ne 124th St Kirkland (98034) **(G-5469)**
Spry Hive Industries....425 503-9790
1113 6th St Kirkland (98033) **(G-5470)**
Spry Product Development LLC....206 556-1246
511 Stadium Pl S Apt 382 Seattle (98104) **(G-11172)**
Sputtertech Inc....360 253-5944
12117 Ne 99th St Ste 1920 Vancouver (98682) **(G-14605)**
Squalicum Marine Inc....360 733-4353
2620 N Harbor Loop Dr # 17 Bellingham (98225) **(G-1554)**
Squalicum Marine Upholstery, Bellingham *Also called Squalicum Marine Inc* **(G-1554)**
Square One Distribution Inc (PA)....425 369-6850
35214 Se Center St Snoqualmie (98065) **(G-12031)**
Squarerigger Inc....360 698-3562
9119 Ridgetop Blvd Nw # 300 Silverdale (98383) **(G-11859)**
Squealock Systems Inc....206 519-4620
126 Sw 148th St Burien (98166) **(G-2131)**
Squires Machine Inc....425 672-7101
19510 21st Ave W Ste B Lynnwood (98036) **(G-6205)**
Squonk Industries....206 250-4355
1015 Ne 72nd St Seattle (98115) **(G-11173)**
SRP Transport Inc....425 770-3031
21005 Brown Rd Monroe (98272) **(G-6626)**
SRS Medical Corp (HQ)....425 882-1101
8672p 154th Ave Ne Redmond (98052) **(G-8679)**
Ss Industrial Inc....509 427-7836
191 S Tucker Rd Stevenson (98648) **(G-13020)**
Ss Trailer Manufacturing....253 750-4724
9409 205th Ave E Bonney Lake (98391) **(G-1739)**
Ssb Manufacturing Company....253 891-3272
13605 52nd St E Ste 200 Sumner (98390) **(G-13102)**
SSC Green Inc....509 967-4753
405 S 54th Ave West Richland (99353) **(G-15101)**
SSC North America LLC....509 967-4753
405 S 54th Ave West Richland (99353) **(G-15102)**
SSP Eyewear, Moses Lake *Also called Specialized Safety Pdts LLC* **(G-6751)**
St Helens Foods, Toppenish *Also called Washington Agricultural Dev* **(G-13673)**
St Helens Press....360 687-1717
25804 Ne Olson Rd Battle Ground (98604) **(G-741)**
St2 Publishing, Longview *Also called Saint Square Publishing* **(G-5950)**
Stabbert & Associates Inc....206 547-6161
2629 Nw 54th St Ste W201 Seattle (98107) **(G-11174)**
Stabbert Mrtime Yacht Ship LLC....206 547-6161
2629 Nw 54th St Ste 201 Seattle (98107) **(G-11175)**
Stabbert Yacht and Ship LLC....206 547-6161
2629 Nw 54th St Ste 201 Seattle (98107) **(G-11176)**
Stach Steel Supply....509 848-2772
3070 Harrah Rd Harrah (98933) **(G-4321)**
Stacya Silverman & Associates....206 270-9465
614 W Mcgraw St Ste 101 Seattle (98119) **(G-11177)**
Stadelman Fruit Frenchman....509 829-5145
111 Meade St Zillah (98953) **(G-15760)**
Stadium Sports, Spokane *Also called Colosseum Ventures LLC* **(G-12188)**
Stafford Press Inc (PA)....425 861-5856
14612 Ne 91st St Redmond (98052) **(G-8680)**
Staffready, Spokane *Also called NW Software Solutions* **(G-12415)**
Stagecraft Industries Inc....206 763-8800
5503 6th Ave S Seattle (98108) **(G-11178)**
Stageplan Inc....360 825-2428
1101 Battersby Ave Enumclaw (98022) **(G-3322)**
Stainless Cable & Railing Inc....360 314-4288
3315 Nw 112th Ave Vancouver (98682) **(G-14606)**
Stair Company The, Lacey *Also called Lawman Industries LLC* **(G-5564)**
Staircrafters Incorporated....360 882-2772
712 Ne 157th Ct Vancouver (98684) **(G-14607)**
Stakana Analytics, Seattle *Also called Stakana LLC* **(G-11179)**
Stakana LLC....206 227-4329
815 1st Ave Ste 287 Seattle (98104) **(G-11179)**
Stambaughs Hungry Harbor Entps....360 777-8289
47 Hungry Harbor Ln Naselle (98638) **(G-7020)**
Stampadoodle Art & Paper, Bellingham *Also called Stampadoodle Inc* **(G-1555)**
Stampadoodle Inc....360 647-9663
1825 Grant St Bellingham (98225) **(G-1555)**
Stampede Forest Products Inc....509 557-3014
1100 E 8th Ave D OMAK (98841) **(G-7444)**
Stanbury Electrical Engrg LLC....206 251-8901
14125 Ne 189th St Woodinville (98072) **(G-15374)**
Standard Digital Print Co Inc....509 624-2985
256 W Riverside Ave Spokane (99201) **(G-12524)**
Standard Environmental Probe, Tumwater *Also called Christopher Ross Dewayne* **(G-13860)**
Standard Nutrition Company....509 839-3500
105 S 11th St Sunnyside (98944) **(G-13143)**
Standard Pallet Co....509 670-0632
5604 Nature Shore Dr Rock Island (98850) **(G-9150)**
Standard Steel Fabg Co Inc....206 767-0499
8155 1st Ave S Seattle (98108) **(G-11180)**
Standard Steel Fabricating Co, Seattle *Also called Duthie Enterprises Inc* **(G-9862)**
Standever Industries Llc....206 687-9610
317 Walbrun Rd Sultan (98294) **(G-13038)**
Stanford Technology Inc....509 638-1191
1010 N Normandie St # 305 Spokane (99201) **(G-12525)**
Stanley Access Tech LLC....425 493-0482
4433 Russell Rd Ste 105 Mukilteo (98275) **(G-6979)**
Stanley Plowing....509 218-2419
32413 N Cedar Rd Deer Park (99006) **(G-2916)**
Stanleys Sanitary Service....360 795-3369
20 Hedlund Rd Cathlamet (98612) **(G-2376)**
Stans Headers Inc....253 854-5310
4715 Auburn Way N Auburn (98002) **(G-571)**
Stanton....360 864-6897
357 Spencer Rd Toledo (98591) **(G-13642)**
Stanwood Cupcakes LLC....360 926-8241
28127 85th Dr Nw Stanwood (98292) **(G-12993)**
Stanwood Redi-Mix Inc....360 652-7777
2431 Larson Rd Stanwood (98292) **(G-12994)**
Stanwood-Camano News Inc....360 629-8066
9005 271st St Nw Stanwood (98292) **(G-12995)**
Star Copy & Reprographics Ctr....360 385-1022
625 Tyler St Port Townsend (98368) **(G-7931)**
Star Forge LLC....206 762-1100
8531 E Marginal Way S Tukwila (98108) **(G-13821)**
Star Industries Corp Inc....360 826-3895
8129 Pipeline Rd Lyman (98263) **(G-5997)**
Star Lumber LLC....316 942-2221
7203 112th St Ne Arlington (98223) **(G-332)**
Star Manufacturing Intl Inc....800 882-6368
6500 Merrill Creek Pkwy Everett (98203) **(G-3620)**
Star Newspaper, The, Grand Coulee *Also called Star Publishing Inc* **(G-4244)**
Star North Woodworks Inc....360 384-0307
6186 Portal Way Ferndale (98248) **(G-3906)**
Star Pipe LLC....253 826-3950
13605 52nd St E Ste 100 Sumner (98390) **(G-13103)**
Star Press Inc....509 525-2425
842 Wallowa Dr Walla Walla (99362) **(G-14874)**
Star Printing, Seattle *Also called Kustom Printing Inc* **(G-10366)**
Star Publishing Inc....509 633-1350
3 Midway Ave Grand Coulee (99133) **(G-4244)**
Star Rentals Inc....509 545-8521
1912 W A St Pasco (99301) **(G-7632)**
Star Steel, Spokane Valley *Also called Kermit Anderson* **(G-12765)**
Star Transport Trailers Inc....509 837-3136
230 State Rt 241 Sunnyside (98944) **(G-13144)**
Star West Satellite....509 545-4996
1320 W A St Pasco (99301) **(G-7633)**
Starbound LLC....206 784-5000
2157 N Northlake Way Seattle (98103) **(G-11181)**
Starcom Computer Corporation....425 486-6464
19515 North Creek Pkwy # 204 Bothell (98011) **(G-1797)**
Stardust Materials LLC....360 260-7399
12518 Ne 95th St Vancouver (98682) **(G-14608)**
Starform Inc....206 446-9657
1501 E Madison St Ste 150 Seattle (98122) **(G-11182)**
Stargate Inc....425 251-0701
19625 62nd Ave S Ste B103 Kent (98032) **(G-5152)**
Stark Raving Foods LLC....425 361-7640
802 134th St Sw Everett (98204) **(G-3621)**
Starkenburg Shavings....360 734-8818
1546 Slater Rd Ferndale (98248) **(G-3907)**
Starlight Desserts Inc....206 284-8770
2001 W Grfield St Bldg 28 Seattle (98119) **(G-11183)**
Starline Construction Inc....509 575-7955
1118 N 6th Ave Ste A Yakima (98902) **(G-15682)**
Starman Metal Fabrications LLC....425 235-1431
17300 Se 132nd St Renton (98059) **(G-8919)**
Starpath Corporation (PA)....206 783-1414
3050 Nw 63rd St Seattle (98107) **(G-11184)**
Starpath School of Navigation, Seattle *Also called Starpath Corporation* **(G-11184)**
Starry Field Services....360 676-7441
4915 Samish Way Unit 19 Bellingham (98229) **(G-1556)**
Starshine Products....425 238-9820
17251 Tye St Se Ste A-7 Monroe (98272) **(G-6627)**
Start 2 Finish Coatings Inc....509 481-8898
24424 E Wellesley Ave Otis Orchards (99027) **(G-7518)**
Starvation Alley Farms, Long Beach *Also called Starvation Alley Socia* **(G-5878)**
Starvation Alley Socia....503 440-0970
15202 Birch St Long Beach (98631) **(G-5878)**
Stason Animal Health Inc....360 200-5300
16821se Mcgllvryblvdst112 # 112 Vancouver (98683) **(G-14609)**
Stat Corporation....425 883-4181
14770 Ne 95th St Redmond (98052) **(G-8681)**
Statcodsi Process Systems....253 249-7539
901 Algona Blvd N Algona (98001) **(G-77)**
Statcorp Medical, Snoqualmie *Also called Spacelabs Healthcare Wash* **(G-12030)**
Stateless Labs LLC....512 387-3115
1425 Broadway 20-1524 Seattle (98122) **(G-11185)**

Stateside Bead Supply......425 644-3448
16830 Se 43rd St Bellevue (98006) ***(G-1155)***
Statesman-Examiner Inc (PA)......509 684-4567
220 S Main St Colville (99114) ***(G-2775)***
Statesman-Examiner Inc......509 276-5043
104 N Main St Deer Park (99006) ***(G-2917)***
Statewide Pubg - Wash Inc......509 734-1186
5009 W Clearwatr Ave K Kennewick (99336) ***(G-4730)***
Stavalaura Vinyards......360 887-1476
29503 Nw 41st Ave Ridgefield (98642) ***(G-9113)***
Stcc, Seattle *Also called Sea Technology Construction* ***(G-11039)***
Stead & Associates, Bellevue *Also called S & B Inc* ***(G-1110)***
Stealth Marine......509 758-8019
1268 Bridge St Clarkston (99403) ***(G-2649)***
Stealth Services & Technology......360 882-7211
3315 Ne 112th Ave Ste 57 Vancouver (98682) ***(G-14610)***
Steam Engine Metal Art......509 302-9941
5412 Koufax Ln Pasco (99301) ***(G-7634)***
Steck Technical Publications......253 630-7279
12613 Se 228th Ct Kent (98031) ***(G-5153)***
Stedman Bee Supplies Inc......360 692-9453
3763 Nw Anderson Hill Rd Silverdale (98383) ***(G-11860)***
Steel Abrasive Finishing Eqp, Kent *Also called Safe Systems Inc* ***(G-5113)***
Steel Encounters Inc......206 281-8500
2300 W Commodore Way # 200 Seattle (98199) ***(G-11186)***
Steel Fab Inc......425 743-9216
6525 188th St Ne Arlington (98223) ***(G-333)***
Steel Fab Nw Inc......360 210-7055
520 S 28th St Washougal (98671) ***(G-14987)***
Steel Magnolia Inc......360 366-5090
7523 Kickerville Rd Blaine (98230) ***(G-1704)***
Steel Painter Division, Kelso *Also called Steel Painters Inc* ***(G-4551)***
Steel Painters Inc......360 425-7720
700 Colorado St Ste A Kelso (98626) ***(G-4551)***
Steel Partners Inc......360 748-9406
154 Devereese Rd Chehalis (98532) ***(G-2537)***
Steel Rule Concepts LLC......905 475-0324
19221 62nd Ave S Kent (98032) ***(G-5154)***
Steel Structures America Inc......509 590-1230
4006 N Division St Spokane (99207) ***(G-12526)***
Steele and Associates Inc......360 297-4555
26112 Iowa Ave Ne Kingston (98346) ***(G-5264)***
Steeler Inc (PA)......206 725-8500
10023 Martin Luther King Seattle (98178) ***(G-11187)***
Steeler Inc......253 572-8200
540 E 15th St Tacoma (98421) ***(G-13525)***
Steeler Inc......509 926-7403
7903 E Harrington Ave Spokane Valley (99212) ***(G-12891)***
Steeler Construction Sup Ltd......206 725-2500
10023 M L King Jr Way S Seattle (98178) ***(G-11188)***
Steeler Construction Supply, Spokane Valley *Also called Steeler Inc* ***(G-12891)***
Steelevest Co, Kingston *Also called Steele and Associates Inc* ***(G-5264)***
Steelhead Communications Inc (PA)......360 829-1330
28120 State Route 410 E A3 Buckley (98321) ***(G-2073)***
Steelhead Specialty Minerals......509 328-5685
1212 N Washington St # 107 Spokane (99201) ***(G-12527)***
Steelscape, Kalama *Also called Imsa Steel Corp* ***(G-4501)***
Steelscape LLC (PA)......360 673-8200
222 W Kalama River Rd Kalama (98625) ***(G-4509)***
Steelscape LLC......360 673-8200
220 W Kalama River Rd Kalama (98625) ***(G-4510)***
Steelscape Washington LLC......360 673-8200
222 W Kalama River Rd Kalama (98625) ***(G-4511)***
Steeltec Supply Inc......253 333-1311
134 37th St Ne Auburn (98002) ***(G-572)***
Steer Straight LLC......360 398-6294
3755 Squalicum Lake Rd Bellingham (98226) ***(G-1557)***
Stelfast Inc......206 574-3078
350 Midland Dr Tukwila (98188) ***(G-13822)***
Stelia Aerospace North America......253 852-4055
8407 S 259th St Ste 303 Kent (98030) ***(G-5155)***
Stella Color Inc......206 223-2303
3131 Elliott Ave Ste 100 Seattle (98121) ***(G-11189)***
Stella-Jones Corporation......360 435-2146
6520 188th St Ne Arlington (98223) ***(G-334)***
Stellar Alpacas......253 208-2107
27810 16th Ave E Spanaway (98387) ***(G-12076)***
Stellar Management Inc......206 724-3973
22608 44th Ave W Mountlake Terrace (98043) ***(G-6869)***
Stellr Inc......425 312-3798
315 5th Ave S Ste 1000 Seattle (98104) ***(G-11190)***
Stemar Media Group LLC......206 877-3560
17438 10th Ave Ne Shoreline (98155) ***(G-11818)***
Stemilt Creek Winery......509 662-3613
110 N Wenatchee Ave Wenatchee (98801) ***(G-15076)***
Stempel Art and Industry LLC......206 718-6562
630 W Nickerson St Seattle (98119) ***(G-11191)***
Stenerson & Sons......360 829-1219
27605 96th St E Buckley (98321) ***(G-2074)***
Stephan J Lesser Woodworking......206 782-9463
940 Nw 49th St Seattle (98107) ***(G-11192)***
Stephen L Nelson Inc......425 885-9499
8434 154th Ave Ne Fl 2 Redmond (98052) ***(G-8682)***
Stephen M Kraft......509 465-1980
1311 W Maxine Ct Spokane (99208) ***(G-12528)***
Stephens Metal Products Inc......509 452-4088
3209 W Washington Ave Yakima (98903) ***(G-15683)***
Stephs Custom Sawyering......425 646-8783
10648 Se 16th St Bellevue (98004) ***(G-1156)***
Steppir Antenna Systems Inc......425 391-1999
14135 233rd Pl Se Issaquah (98027) ***(G-4482)***
Steppir Comm Systems Inc......425 453-1910
13406 Se 32nd St Bellevue (98005) ***(G-1157)***
Stepsavers, Vancouver *Also called Energy Saver Products Inc* ***(G-14202)***
Sterling Breen Crushing Inc......360 736-4240
887 State Route 507 Centralia (98531) ***(G-2436)***
Sterling Business Forms Inc......509 926-8191
13110 E Indiana Ave Spokane Valley (99216) ***(G-12892)***
Sterling Envmtl Resources......360 437-1344
7446 Oak Bay Rd Port Ludlow (98365) ***(G-7778)***
Sterling International Inc......509 926-6766
3808 N Sullivan Rd 16bv Spokane Valley (99216) ***(G-12893)***
Sterlitech Corporation......253 437-0844
22027 70th Ave S Kent (98032) ***(G-5156)***
Stern & Faye......360 770-1967
37607 Cape Horn Rd Sedro Woolley (98284) ***(G-11572)***
Steve Boek Mfg (PA)......503 257-5056
501 8th St Sultan (98294) ***(G-13039)***
Steve Czako Associates......509 624-7018
3025 S Geiger Blvd Spokane (99224) ***(G-12529)***
Steve Hazelwood & Son Trucking......253 863-5721
4703 Ridgewest Dr E Lake Tapps (98391) ***(G-5686)***
Steve Ken Bosman......360 398-7444
539 E Smith Rd Bellingham (98226) ***(G-1558)***
Steve Pool Service Inc......360 533-0421
320 Se Snider Rd Shelton (98584) ***(G-11736)***
Steven Jon Kludt......509 687-4000
200 Quetilquasoon Rd Manson (98831) ***(G-6245)***
Stevens Holding Company Inc......425 446-4928
6920 Seaway Blvd Everett (98203) ***(G-3622)***
Stevens Winery......425 424-9463
11028 Ne 18th Pl Bellevue (98004) ***(G-1158)***
Stevenson Sports Supply, Stevenson *Also called Clifford W Leeson Inc* ***(G-13010)***
Steves Hot Smked Cheese Salmon......360 829-2244
26806 166th St E Buckley (98321) ***(G-2075)***
Steward Publishing......206 283-0077
814 W Emerson St Seattle (98119) ***(G-11193)***
Stewart & Stewart Law Off PS......360 249-4342
101 S 1st St Montesano (98563) ***(G-6659)***
Stewart Industries Inc......206 652-9110
16 S Idaho St Seattle (98134) ***(G-11194)***
Stewart Logging......360 437-2905
300 N Bay Way Port Ludlow (98365) ***(G-7779)***
Stewart Logging Inc......509 684-6746
177 Dubois Rd Colville (99114) ***(G-2776)***
Stewart, James M, Montesano *Also called Stewart & Stewart Law Off PS* ***(G-6659)***
Stewart/Walker Company, Tukwila *Also called Consolidated Container Co LLC* ***(G-13715)***
Stewarts Hanger 21 Inc......509 782-3626
211 Chapel St Cashmere (98815) ***(G-2330)***
Stewarts Markets Inc......360 458-2091
17821 State Route 507 Se Yelm (98597) ***(G-15746)***
Stick & Sand Tutoring......206 721-6261
6515 44th Ave S Seattle (98118) ***(G-11195)***
Stick It Print......360 909-6060
1000 Grand Blvd Vancouver (98661) ***(G-14611)***
Stick It To Violence......360 758-7488
400 Westerly Rd Apt 303 Bellingham (98226) ***(G-1559)***
Stick It Vinyl Sign and Banner, Buckley *Also called Todd Porter Campbell* ***(G-2077)***
Sticker Shock Signs Inc......509 535-0070
4023 E Sprague Ave Spokane (99202) ***(G-12530)***
Stickers Northwest......360 731-0255
2124 N Steele St Tacoma (98406) ***(G-13526)***
Stickers Northwest Inc......253 344-1236
5113 Pacific Hwy E Ste 7 Fife (98424) ***(G-3994)***
Stier Hollister Sales......509 892-1188
10907 E Marietta Ave 1 Spokane Valley (99206) ***(G-12894)***
Stillaquamish Resources LLC......360 474-1999
24913 State Route 9 Ne Arlington (98223) ***(G-335)***
Stilly Venom Baseball Club......360 319-6589
16713 Burn Rd Arlington (98223) ***(G-336)***
Stitch N Wood......360 354-1211
501 Wood Creek Dr Lynden (98264) ***(G-6055)***
Stitch Publications LLC......206 214-5225
1534 45th Ave Sw Seattle (98116) ***(G-11196)***
Stitchblade LLC......206 940-7448
2315 Western Ave Ste 106 Seattle (98121) ***(G-11197)***
Stitchybox......360 450-1089
305 Se Chkalov Dr 111-195 Vancouver (98683) ***(G-14612)***
Stl International Incorporated......253 840-5252
9713 233rd Ave E Buckley (98321) ***(G-2076)***
Stock and Pantry, Seattle *Also called Alex Daisley* ***(G-9373)***
Stockpot Soups, Everett *Also called Garden Fresh Gourmet Foods Inc* ***(G-3491)***

ALPHABETIC

Stockton Cul De Sac 253 854-9358
10955 Se 224th Pl Kent (98031) *(G-5157)*
Stoddard International LLC 360 435-6455
18660 58th Ave Ne Arlington (98223) *(G-337)*
Stoess Manufacturing Inc 509 646-3292
225 North St W Washtucna (99371) *(G-15003)*
Stomani Cellars 425 892-8375
16120 Woodinville Redmond Woodinville (98072) *(G-15375)*
Stone Castle Fabrication LLC 253 205-8435
1501 20th St Nw Auburn (98001) *(G-573)*
Stone Craft LLC 206 762-3920
112 S Mead St Seattle (98108) *(G-11198)*
Stone Drums Inc 425 485-5570
12601 Ne Wdnvlle Dr Ste F Woodinville (98072) *(G-15376)*
Stone Masters Inc 509 667-8833
1604 N Wenatchee Ave Wenatchee (98801) *(G-15077)*
Stonehenge 425 879-9574
32604 149th St Se Sultan (98294) *(G-13040)*
Stones By Marie Inc 206 643-1520
1202 N 10th Pl Apt 1413 Renton (98057) *(G-8920)*
Stoneway Concrete, Seattle *Also called Gary Merlino Cnstr Co Inc (G-10050)*
Stoneway Construction Supply, Seattle *Also called Gary Merlino Cnstr Co Inc (G-10049)*
Stoneway Electric Supply Co 253 859-0224
7011 S 234th St Kent (98032) *(G-5158)*
Stonewood Inc 425 417-5533
9009 Avondale Rd Ne I118 Redmond (98052) *(G-8683)*
Stoney Creek Brewing Co LLC 425 836-0958
19186 Ne 43rd Ct Sammamish (98074) *(G-9249)*
Stong Enterprises LLC 360 326-4752
1720 Ne 64th Ave Ste B Vancouver (98661) *(G-14613)*
Stoothoff Aerospace Inc 360 595-0314
2485 Mosquito Lake Rd Deming (98244) *(G-2924)*
Stop-Sign/Eanthology, Poulsbo *Also called Eacceleration Corp (G-7960)*
Storeanywherecom Inc 425 643-3268
12819 Se 38th St Ste 239 Bellevue (98006) *(G-1159)*
Stork Software LLC 206 669-0644
5216 Ravenna Ave Ne Seattle (98105) *(G-11199)*
Storlie & Graham Cutting Inc 509 962-6494
2700 Willowdale Rd Ellensburg (98926) *(G-3228)*
Stormy Mountain Ranch Inc 509 687-3295
1325 Navarre Coulee Rd Chelan (98816) *(G-2564)*
Stormy Seas Inc 360 779-4439
26287 Twelve Trees Ln Nw Poulsbo (98370) *(G-8005)*
Storopack Inc 253 872-6844
20414 87th Ave S Kent (98031) *(G-5159)*
Storybox Studios LLC 206 310-2626
5608 89th Ave Se Mercer Island (98040) *(G-6486)*
Storytellers Ink Inc 206 365-8265
The Highlands Seattle (98133) *(G-11200)*
Stott Logging Inc 360 533-2971
1102 Simpson Ave Hoquiam (98550) *(G-4361)*
Stottle Winery Tasting Room 360 877-2247
24180 N Us Highway 101 B Hoodsport (98548) *(G-4326)*
Stotts Construction Inc 509 779-4987
17814 N Highway 21 Curlew (99118) *(G-2847)*
Stotts Premix, Curlew *Also called Stotts Construction Inc (G-2847)*
Stourwater Pictures 206 780-6928
11431 Miller Rd Ne Bainbridge Island (98110) *(G-674)*
Stove-Woodward Co, Kelso *Also called Stowe Woodward LLC (G-4552)*
Stover Publishing 206 240-2438
11305 208th Avenue Ct E Bonney Lake (98391) *(G-1740)*
Stowe Woodward LLC 360 636-0330
2209 Talley Way Kelso (98626) *(G-4552)*
Str8 Sheet Fabrications LLC 425 789-1755
4493 Russell Rd Ste D Mukilteo (98275) *(G-6980)*
Straight Edge Asphalt & Maint 206 949-4666
15715 13th Ave Sw Burien (98166) *(G-2132)*
Straight Line Industries Inc 360 366-0223
7634 Zell Rd Custer (98240) *(G-2861)*
Straight Publications Inc 206 324-0618
1007 32nd Ave E Seattle (98112) *(G-11201)*
Straightthrough Inc 425 467-1990
10777 Main St Bellevue (98004) *(G-1160)*
Strain Night Vision & Security 509 926-2025
5709 N Ella St Spokane (99212) *(G-12531)*
Stranger, The, Seattle *Also called Index Publishing (G-10225)*
Strasser Woodenworks Inc 425 402-3080
14237 Ne 200th St Woodinville (98072) *(G-15377)*
Stratagen Systems Inc 425 821-8454
4040 Lake Washington Blvd Kirkland (98033) *(G-5471)*
Strategic News Service LLC 360 378-1023
38 Yew Ln Friday Harbor (98250) *(G-4060)*
Strategic Robotic Systems Inc 425 285-9229
18394 Redmond Way Redmond (98052) *(G-8684)*
Stratford Bottling Company LLC 509 853-3223
2800 S 16th Ave Yakima (98903) *(G-15684)*
Stratodata LLC 425 623-0094
31722 Ne 111th St Carnation (98014) *(G-2299)*
Stratton Woodworks 425 968-2455
420 222nd Ave Ne Sammamish (98074) *(G-9250)*
Strawberry Kids LLC 425 605-8883
16647 Ne 48th St Redmond (98052) *(G-8685)*
Streambox Inc 206 956-0544
1801 130th Ave Ne Ste 200 Bellevue (98005) *(G-1161)*
Streamline International 425 392-2350
200 W Sunset Way Issaquah (98027) *(G-4483)*
Street Corner Caffe, Olympia *Also called Olympic Crest Coffee Roasters (G-7357)*
Streich Bros Inc 253 383-1491
1650 Mar View Dr Ste Main Tacoma (98422) *(G-13527)*
Stresswave Inc 253 259-8796
1130 Andover Park E Tukwila (98188) *(G-13823)*
Stretch 22 Inc 206 375-3358
1913 2nd Ave Seattle (98101) *(G-11202)*
Stretch and Staple 206 607-9277
8005 Greenwood Ave N Seattle (98103) *(G-11203)*
Stretching Charts Inc 253 536-4922
11003 A St S Tacoma (98444) *(G-13528)*
Strictly For Kids, Tacoma *Also called Df Industries Inc (G-13261)*
Strictly Ic 253 941-6611
24920 43rd Ave S Kent (98032) *(G-5160)*
Strike Addiction LLC 206 713-6061
16357 Ahtanum Rd Yakima (98903) *(G-15685)*
Stripes Global Inc 800 690-8219
245 4th St Ste 204 Bremerton (98337) *(G-2003)*
Stromski Repair and Welding 360 452-1661
541 Erving Jacobs Rd Port Angeles (98362) *(G-7747)*
Strong Snax Inc 360 953-3753
6405 Nw 170th Cir Ridgefield (98642) *(G-9114)*
Strongback Metal Boats Inc 206 321-9965
2442 Nw Market St Ste 473 Seattle (98107) *(G-11204)*
Struble Cider LLC 206 766-0009
1817 E Howell St Seattle (98122) *(G-11205)*
Structural Diagnostic Services 360 647-6681
1225 E Sunset Dr Ste 640 Bellingham (98226) *(G-1560)*
Structures Brewing LLC 432 770-1540
1420 N State St Bellingham (98225) *(G-1561)*
Stryve Inc 425 802-3832
1823 Terry Ave Apt 2309 Seattle (98101) *(G-11206)*
STS Trading Co 425 830-6368
6218 167th Ave Se Bellevue (98006) *(G-1162)*
Stuart Orthotics LLC 360 577-3505
1555 3rd Ave Ste B Longview (98632) *(G-5957)*
Students Publication, Pullman *Also called Washington State University (G-8114)*
Studio 3 Signs, Seattle *Also called Goodmar Group LLC (G-10101)*
Studio Equus, Yakima *Also called Nelson Farrier Shop Inc (G-15629)*
Studio Foglio LLC 206 782-8739
2400 Nw 80th St Ste 129 Seattle (98117) *(G-11207)*
Studio Wildcard, Redmond *Also called Wildcard Properties LLC (G-8714)*
Study In The USA Inc 206 622-2075
100 S King St Ste 425 Seattle (98104) *(G-11208)*
Sturtevants Tennis Shop 425 454-6465
1100 Bellevue Way Ne # 7 Bellevue (98004) *(G-1163)*
Stusser Mattson Veneer Inc 425 485-0963
19612 144th Ave Ne Ste 1a Woodinville (98072) *(G-15378)*
Stussers Woodworks, Woodinville *Also called Stusser Mattson Veneer Inc (G-15378)*
Style Plus LLC 206 920-9223
15760 143rd Ave Se Renton (98058) *(G-8921)*
Subaru of America Inc 425 822-0762
4040 Lake Washington Blvd Kirkland (98033) *(G-5472)*
Subaru of America Inc 360 737-7630
3309 Nw Gateway Ave Vancouver (98660) *(G-14614)*
Subdued Brewing LLC 360 656-6611
2529 Grant St Bellingham (98225) *(G-1562)*
Suberizer Inc (PA) 425 747-8900
2625 Northup Way Ste 100 Bellevue (98004) *(G-1164)*
Submeter Solutions Inc 425 228-6831
45 Logan Ave S Renton (98057) *(G-8922)*
Subsea Air Systems LLC 360 563-2400
2610 Bickford Ave Snohomish (98290) *(G-11987)*
Subset Games LLC 206 354-4010
1400 Nw 95th St Seattle (98117) *(G-11209)*
Subsplash Inc 206 965-8090
3257 16th Ave W Ste 200 Seattle (98119) *(G-11210)*
Sudden Printing Inc (PA) 206 243-4444
11009 1st Ave S Seattle (98168) *(G-11211)*
Sue A Priebe 360 398-7647
6759 Lunde Rd Everson (98247) *(G-3690)*
Sue's Stitch In Time, Shelton *Also called Susan Bennett (G-11738)*
Suenos De Salsa 206 334-7496
12524 Lake City Way Ne Seattle (98125) *(G-11212)*
Suez Water Tech & Solution, Bellevue *Also called Suez Wts Systems Usa Inc (G-1165)*
Suez Wts Systems Usa Inc 425 828-2400
3006 Northrup Way Ste 200 Bellevue (98004) *(G-1165)*
Sugar & Stamp 404 944-1354
4846 41st Ave Sw Seattle (98116) *(G-11213)*
Sugar Mountain Livestock LLC 206 322-1644
1725 Westlake Ave N # 200 Seattle (98109) *(G-11214)*
Sugarcrush Hmmade Jams Jellies 253 830-4155
8107 183rd Ave E Bonney Lake (98391) *(G-1741)*
Sugimoto America, Redmond *Also called Sugimoto Seicha Usa Inc (G-8686)*
Sugimoto Seicha Usa Inc 425 558-5552
4070 148th Ave Ne Bldg M Redmond (98052) *(G-8686)*
Sugiyo USA Inc 360 293-0180
3200 T Ave Anacortes (98221) *(G-170)*

Suite Cs Vino 425 949-5006
12601 Ne Woodinville Dr Woodinville (98072) ***(G-15379)***
Sullivan Manufacturing Co, Pasco *Also called Columbia Chain Belt Inc **(G-7562)***
Sullivan Manufacturing Inc 509 545-8000
316 E B Cir Pasco (99301) ***(G-7635)***
Sully N A Saint-Gobain 253 466-5417
507 N Levee Rd Puyallup (98371) ***(G-8256)***
Sumas Mt Log Co 360 966-4781
8373 Westergreen Rd Sumas (98295) ***(G-13051)***
Sumerian Brewing Co LLC 425 486-5330
15510 Woodinvilleredmond Woodinville (98072) ***(G-15380)***
Sumitomo Metal Mining America (HQ) 206 405-2800
701 5th Ave Ste 2150 Seattle (98104) ***(G-11215)***
Sumitomo Metal Mining Ariz Inc 206 405-2800
701 5th Ave Ste 4800 Seattle (98104) ***(G-11216)***
Summer Moon Products 360 826-3157
32069 Lyman Hamilton Hwy Sedro Woolley (98284) ***(G-11573)***
Summer Rrh LLC 509 328-0915
2803 W Garland Ave Spokane (99205) ***(G-12532)***
Summit Biofuels LLC 206 291-6402
20720 111th Ave Sw Vashon (98070) ***(G-14745)***
Summit Carbon Capture LLC 206 780-3551
83 S King St Ste 200 Seattle (98104) ***(G-11217)***
Summit Components LLC 509 750-6629
15509 Road 11 Sw Royal City (99357) ***(G-9176)***
Summit Lake Labs LLC 509 738-4313
8 Enzyme Ln Kettle Falls (99141) ***(G-5241)***
Summit Rescue Inc 360 366-0221
6930 Salashan Pkwy Ferndale (98248) ***(G-3908)***
Summitclimb Inc 360 570-0715
5212 Whiskey Beach Ln Sw Longbranch (98351) ***(G-5880)***
Summitview Tooling Inc 509 966-9859
12105 Klendon Dr Yakima (98908) ***(G-15686)***
Sumner Lawn n Saw LLC 253 435-9284
9318 State Route 162 E Puyallup (98372) ***(G-8257)***
Sumner Stained Glass Company 360 378-2761
91 Cougar Ln Friday Harbor (98250) ***(G-4061)***
Sun Liquor Mfg Inc 206 419-5857
4612 Union Bay Pl Ne Seattle (98105) ***(G-11218)***
Sun News Inc 360 659-1300
6720a 60th Pl Ne Marysville (98270) ***(G-6391)***
Sun Newspaper Daily 360 792-3324
545 5th St Bremerton (98337) ***(G-2004)***
Sun Printing 253 517-5017
33304 Pcf Hwy S Ste 304 Federal Way (98003) ***(G-3791)***
Sun Rise Dental 253 856-3384
10216 Se 256th St Ste 108 Kent (98030) ***(G-5161)***
Sun River Foods Inc 509 249-0820
308 N 22nd Ave Yakima (98902) ***(G-15687)***
Sun River Vintners LLC 509 627-3100
1030 N Center Pkwy Kennewick (99336) ***(G-4731)***
Sun Solutions Inc 509 946-7107
1370 Jadwin Ave Ste 134 Richland (99354) ***(G-9042)***
Sun Spirits Distillery LLC 509 371-1622
2409 Robertson Dr Richland (99354) ***(G-9043)***
Sun Steel Canam, Vancouver *Also called Canam Steel Corporation **(G-14094)***
Sun Valley Collision Center, Yakima *Also called Sun Valley Enterprises **(G-15688)***
Sun Valley Enterprises 509 453-1914
1511 S 1st St Yakima (98901) ***(G-15688)***
Sun-Rype Products (usa) Inc 509 697-7292
1 S Railroad Ave Selah (98942) ***(G-11598)***
Sunbacker Fbrgls Repr Fbrction, Monroe *Also called Sunbacker Fiberglass Inc **(G-6628)***
Sunbacker Fiberglass Inc 360 794-5547
17453 147th St Se Ste 1 Monroe (98272) ***(G-6628)***
Sunbird Aerospace 425 241-8594
13854 Ne 8th St Apt D201 Bellevue (98005) ***(G-1166)***
Suncatchers 360 293-6360
2611 Shannon Point Rd Anacortes (98221) ***(G-171)***
Suncoast Post-Tension Ltd 360 651-2769
13520 45th Ave Ne Marysville (98271) ***(G-6392)***
Sundance Beef Co, Ferndale *Also called Sundance Beef Intl Inc **(G-3909)***
Sundance Beef Intl Inc 360 224-2333
7060 Portal Way Ste 140 Ferndale (98248) ***(G-3909)***
Sundance Equestrian Industries 425 205-3775
18221 236th Ave Ne Woodinville (98077) ***(G-15381)***
Sundog Digitizing & Design, Clarkston *Also called Jodee Maiorana **(G-2637)***
Sundog LLC 206 313-8871
26311 Ne Valley St 219 Duvall (98019) ***(G-3002)***
Sunfreeware, Seattle *Also called Unix Packages LLC **(G-11386)***
Sunfresh Foods Inc 206 764-0940
125 S Kenyon St Seattle (98108) ***(G-11219)***
Sunfresh Freezerves, Seattle *Also called Sunfresh Foods Inc **(G-11219)***
Sunland Bark and Topsoils Co 360 293-7188
12469 Reservation Rd Anacortes (98221) ***(G-172)***
Sunlight Cottage Industries 360 321-8302
2845 Sunlight Dr Clinton (98236) ***(G-2700)***
Sunlight Woodenworks Inc 360 275-5263
876 E Johns Prairie Rd Shelton (98584) ***(G-11737)***
Sunmodo Corporation 360 844-0048
14800 Ne 65th St Vancouver (98682) ***(G-14615)***
Sunn Pharmaceuticals LLC 425 835-0418
23303 56th Ave W Mountlake Terrace (98043) ***(G-6870)***
Sunne Group Ltd Inc 253 839-5240
1302 S 293rd Pl Federal Way (98003) ***(G-3792)***
Sunnyside Daily News Inc 509 837-4500
600 S 6th St Sunnyside (98944) ***(G-13145)***
Sunoco Inc 253 872-8500
8039 S 192nd St Kent (98032) ***(G-5162)***
Sunrice LLC 206 841-2454
3513 Ne Seattle (98105) ***(G-11220)***
Sunrise Bagels & More Inc 360 254-1012
16010 Ne 25th St Vancouver (98684) ***(G-14616)***
Sunrise Identity LLC 425 214-1700
405 114th Ave Se Ste 200 Bellevue (98004) ***(G-1167)***
Sunrise Mattress Company Inc 509 290-5728
328 N Fancher Rd Spokane Valley (99212) ***(G-12895)***
Sunrise W Quarter Horses LLC 509 780-9426
2240 4th Ave Clarkston (99403) ***(G-2650)***
Sunrise Washington Inc 360 574-3512
5900 Ne 88th St Ste 119 Vancouver (98665) ***(G-14617)***
Sunrisebuswerk 360 866-7240
4315 Cooper Point Rd Nw Olympia (98502) ***(G-7401)***
Sunset Collections, Vancouver *Also called Shirley Sunset **(G-14584)***
Sunset Company LLC 425 351-0839
16444 Se 135th St Renton (98059) ***(G-8923)***
Sunset Forge LLC 360 201-0160
3502 Bay Rd Ferndale (98248) ***(G-3910)***
Sunset Manufacturing Corp 425 239-7416
2301 159th Ave Se Snohomish (98290) ***(G-11988)***
Sunset Molding Inc 360 835-3805
37438 Se Sunset View Rd Washougal (98671) ***(G-14988)***
Sunshine Embroidery 360 892-1556
1812 Ne 155th Ave Vancouver (98684) ***(G-14618)***
Sunshine Prtg & Quick Copy Svc 360 671-0191
618 W King Tut Rd Bellingham (98226) ***(G-1563)***
Sunshine Smoothie Inc 425 497-9211
5607 Evergreen Loop Se Auburn (98092) ***(G-574)***
Sunsteel LLC 509 836-3078
312 Se Stnmill Dr Ste 147 Vancouver (98684) ***(G-14619)***
Sunstream Corporation (PA) 253 395-0500
22149 68th Ave S Kent (98032) ***(G-5163)***
Suntower Systems 206 878-0578
21834 12th Ave S Des Moines (98198) ***(G-2947)***
Sunwrist To Go, Lakewood *Also called South Tacoma Glass Specialists **(G-5758)***
Super Anchor Safety, Monroe *Also called American Roof Inc **(G-6548)***
Super Cedar Firestarters, Mukilteo *Also called Northwestern Fuel Ldscpg Sups **(G-6957)***
Super H Corporation 360 687-2824
12403 Ne 60th Way 1d Vancouver (98682) ***(G-14620)***
Super Smoothie 253 671-8883
4502 S Steele St Ste 319 Tacoma (98409) ***(G-13529)***
Super Supplement, Burien *Also called Vitamin Shoppe Industries Inc **(G-2136)***
Super Supplement, Maple Valley *Also called Vitamin Shoppe Industries Inc **(G-6298)***
Super Suris Alpacas 509 475-5110
16219 N Day Mt Spokane Rd Mead (99021) ***(G-6438)***
Super-Keller Industries LLC 360 459-1059
1918 Smmit Lk Shore Rd Nw Olympia (98502) ***(G-7402)***
Supercritical Technologies 518 225-3275
2448 Rocky Point Rd Nw Bremerton (98312) ***(G-2005)***
Superfancy Industries 360 556-9762
1808 5th Ave Se Olympia (98501) ***(G-7403)***
Supergraphics LLC 206 284-2201
2201 15th Ave W Seattle (98119) ***(G-11221)***
Superhero Stuffcom 425 890-3032
34401 Se Cochrane St Snoqualmie (98065) ***(G-12032)***
Superior Asphalt & Paving Co (PA) 509 248-6823
80 Pond Rd Yakima (98901) ***(G-15689)***
Superior Cabinets, Tukwila *Also called Superior Custom Cabinets Inc **(G-13824)***
Superior Coatings 253 405-5424
1325 Bonney Ave Apt 8 Sumner (98390) ***(G-13104)***
Superior Construction, Spokane *Also called Superior Crafted Cabinets **(G-12533)***
Superior Counter Tops, Vancouver *Also called Contour Countertops Inc **(G-14150)***
Superior Crafted Cabinets 509 535-9403
1612 S Campbell St Spokane (99202) ***(G-12533)***
Superior Custom Cabinets Inc (PA) 425 251-1520
7120 S 180th St Tukwila (98188) ***(G-13824)***
Superior Custom Control 206 362-8866
12544 27th Ave Ne Seattle (98125) ***(G-11222)***
Superior Energy Services LLC 360 733-3030
629 Cornwall Ave Bellingham (98225) ***(G-1564)***
Superior Fluid Power Inc (PA) 509 482-7949
9516 E Montgomery Ave # 19 Spokane Valley (99206) ***(G-12896)***
Superior Imprints Inc 206 441-7147
4226 6th Ave S Seattle (98108) ***(G-11223)***
Superior Industrial Services A 360 841-8542
132 Upland Dr Woodland (98674) ***(G-15467)***
Superior Rubber Die Co Inc 206 763-2440
520 S River St Seattle (98108) ***(G-11224)***
Superior Rv Manufacturing 360 693-1398
3801 S Truman Rd Ste 4 Washougal (98671) ***(G-14989)***
Superior Slabjacking Inc 425 970-3986
1603 Glennwood Ave Se Renton (98058) ***(G-8924)***
Superior Sole Wldg Fabrication 360 653-2565
7402 44th Ave Ne Marysville (98270) ***(G-6393)***

ALPHABETIC

Superior Stone Manufacturing 425 931-9303
18619 Ne Wdnvlle Dvall Rd Woodinville (98072) ***(G-15382)***
Superior Stone Manufacturing 425 312-2968
15105 Highway 99 Ste B Lynnwood (98087) ***(G-6206)***
Superior Tramway Co Inc 509 483-6181
2311 E Main Ave Spokane (99202) ***(G-12534)***
Superior Wldg Fabrication LLC 360 430-6766
516 Oak St Kelso (98626) ***(G-4553)***
Superior Wood Treating, Tacoma *Also called Manke Lumber Company Inc* ***(G-13397)***
Superlon Plastics Co Inc 253 383-4000
2116 Taylor Way Tacoma (98421) ***(G-13530)***
Supermedia LLC 425 423-7904
906 Se Everett Mall Way # 210 Everett (98208) ***(G-3623)***
Suplari Inc 425 610-9496
1525 4th Ave Ste 700 Seattle (98101) ***(G-11225)***
Supply Guy 253 531-8600
10735 A St S Ste A Tacoma (98444) ***(G-13531)***
Support The Foot, Kent *Also called Coates Innovations LLC* ***(G-4856)***
Supr Co (HQ) 509 248-6823
2000 E Beech St Yakima (98901) ***(G-15690)***
Surain Industries Inc 253 863-8111
1615 Puyallup St Sumner (98390) ***(G-13105)***
Sure Fit Inc 253 426-1025
13804 50th Ave E Tacoma (98446) ***(G-13532)***
Sure Trax LLC 360 430-8343
5005 Mt Solo Rd Longview (98632) ***(G-5958)***
Sure-Fit Seat Covers 509 326-0122
1730 W Broadway Ave Spokane (99201) ***(G-12535)***
Surewood Custom Cabinets Inc 509 893-9522
3808 N Sullivan Rd 11d Spokane Valley (99216) ***(G-12897)***
Surftech Finishes Co 425 453-9400
500 108th Ave Ne Bellevue (98004) ***(G-1168)***
Surgimark Inc 509 965-1911
1703 Creekside Loop # 110 Yakima (98902) ***(G-15691)***
Surly Industries 206 349-3289
2022 Franklin Ave E B Seattle (98102) ***(G-11226)***
Surphaser, Redmond *Also called Basis Software Inc* ***(G-8397)***
Surprise Al Care Group LLC 775 746-2200
5101 Ne 82nd Ave Ste 200 Vancouver (98662) ***(G-14621)***
Survey Analytics LLC (PA) 800 326-5570
93 S Jackson St 71641 Seattle (98104) ***(G-11227)***
Survey Analytics LLC 800 326-5570
3518 Fremont Ave N 598 Seattle (98103) ***(G-11228)***
Survival Inc 206 726-9363
2633 Eastlake Ave E 103 Seattle (98102) ***(G-11229)***
Survival Gear Systems 866 257-2978
9708 N Nevada St Ste 204 Spokane (99218) ***(G-12536)***
Susan Bennett 360 427-6164
927 W Railroad Ave Shelton (98584) ***(G-11736)***
Susan Eakin 509 966-2014
130 Udell Ln Yakima (98908) ***(G-15692)***
Susan Weinhandl 509 953-4329
3310 W Eagles Nest Ln Spokane (99208) ***(G-12537)***
Susans Custom Embriodery 206 783-3127
2122 Nw 95th St Seattle (98117) ***(G-11230)***
Suse Linux, Seattle *Also called Suse LLC* ***(G-11232)***
Suse LLC (HQ) 206 217-7500
705 5th Ave S Ste 1000 Seattle (98104) ***(G-11231)***
Suse LLC 206 217-7100
705 5th Ave S Ste 1000 Seattle (98104) ***(G-11232)***
Susney Incorporated 253 219-7216
20810 52nd Ave E Spanaway (98387) ***(G-12077)***
Sussex Clumber LLC 206 369-3615
1021 92nd Ave Ne Bellevue (98004) ***(G-1169)***
Sustain Outdoors Inc 949 439-4899
16494 Se 57th Pl Bellevue (98006) ***(G-1170)***
Sustainable Fiber Tech LLC 206 818-4130
234 Sw 43rd St Ste Mb Renton (98057) ***(G-8925)***
Sutliff Candy & Promotions Co (PA) 206 784-5212
7710 Aurora Ave N Seattle (98103) ***(G-11233)***
Sutliff Candy Co, Seattle *Also called Sutliff Candy & Promotions Co* ***(G-11233)***
Sutta Company Incorporated 253 572-2558
2122 Port Of Tacoma Rd Tacoma (98421) ***(G-13533)***
Suzabelle 206 790-5163
5551 Greenwood Ave N Seattle (98103) ***(G-11234)***
Suziperi 425 373-1954
13502 Ne 12th Pl Bellevue (98005) ***(G-1171)***
Svendsen Brothers Fish Inc 206 767-4258
18629 2nd Ave Sw Normandy Park (98166) ***(G-7099)***
Svz Industrial Fruit, Othello *Also called Svz USA Washington Inc* ***(G-7506)***
Svz USA Washington Inc 509 488-6563
1700 N Broadway Ave Othello (99344) ***(G-7506)***
Swaddledesigns LLC 206 971-0426
500 Andover Park E Tukwila (98188) ***(G-13825)***
Swakane Winery 509 881-9688
63 Old Bullard Rd Raymond (98577) ***(G-8359)***
Swanton Hills Press LLC 206 972-1205
524 Ne 80th St Seattle (98115) ***(G-11235)***
Swartz Engineering Company, Snohomish *Also called E T L Corp* ***(G-11903)***
Sweater Stone Inc 425 392-2747
21103 Se 24th St Sammamish (98075) ***(G-9251)***
Sweats Unlimited, Tacoma *Also called Pacific Sportswear Inc* ***(G-13454)***
Sweeny Industries 510 701-0384
13915 120th St E Puyallup (98374) ***(G-8258)***
Sweeny Industries 253 446-7298
17202 110th Ave E Puyallup (98374) ***(G-8259)***
Sweet Creek Creations 509 446-2429
219 E 5th Ave Metaline Falls (99153) ***(G-6498)***
Sweet Dahlia Baking LLC 206 201-3297
9720 Coppertop Loop Ne Bainbridge Island (98110) ***(G-675)***
Sweet Sanity 425 212-7490
9723 Wallingford Ave N Seattle (98103) ***(G-11236)***
Sweet Tees 253 632-9224
28916 218th Ave Se Black Diamond (98010) ***(G-1656)***
Swift Industries 360 966-9697
101 W Madison St Nooksack (98276) ***(G-7087)***
Swift Industries 415 608-8227
1422 20th Ave Seattle (98122) ***(G-11237)***
Swift Machining Inc 360 335-8213
4060 S Grant St Ste 109 Washougal (98671) ***(G-14990)***
Swift Print 360 805-8509
10922 Wagner Rd Snohomish (98290) ***(G-11989)***
Swift Tool Company Inc 206 763-9280
7709 5th Ave S Seattle (98108) ***(G-11238)***
Swiftcarb 800 227-9876
1720 Central Ave S Kent (98032) ***(G-5164)***
Swifty Prtg Dgital Imaging Inc 206 441-0800
2001 3rd Ave Seattle (98121) ***(G-11239)***
Swim Scott 253 968-3389
9933 W Hayes St Tacoma (98431) ***(G-13534)***
Swing Fly Press LLC 616 540-3836
430 Se Dilke St Pullman (99163) ***(G-8110)***
Swinomish Fish Co Inc 360 466-0176
11455 Moorage Way La Conner (98257) ***(G-5526)***
Swire Pacific Holdings Inc 509 921-6200
9705 E Montgomery Ave Spokane Valley (99206) ***(G-12898)***
Swire Pacific Holdings Inc 425 455-2000
1150 124th Ave Ne Bellevue (98005) ***(G-1172)***
Swire Pacific Holdings Inc 509 529-0753
155 Avery St Walla Walla (99362) ***(G-14875)***
Swires 7up, Pasco *Also called Seven Up Dr Peper Bottling Co* ***(G-7628)***
Swirl 425 292-0909
426 Main Ave S North Bend (98045) ***(G-7126)***
Swish 425 644-3545
14603 Ne 20th St Ste 4c Bellevue (98007) ***(G-1173)***
Swiss Ornamental Iron 253 759-6796
3417 6th Ave Tacoma (98406) ***(G-13535)***
Swissa Inc 206 625-9202
1905 Queen Anne Ave N # 101 Seattle (98109) ***(G-11240)***
Swissa Jewelers, Seattle *Also called Swissa Inc* ***(G-11240)***
Swivel Inc 509 557-7000
213 S 4th Ave Walla Walla (99362) ***(G-14876)***
Swivler Inc 360 225-7774
123 Stenerson Rd Woodland (98674) ***(G-15468)***
Sws, Woodinville *Also called Site Welding Services Inc* ***(G-15364)***
Swype Inc 206 547-5250
505 1st Ave S Seattle (98104) ***(G-11241)***
Sycamore Woodworks 360 757-4120
10954 Peter Anderson Rd Burlington (98233) ***(G-2192)***
Sygnet Rail Technologies LLC 360 264-8211
5915 Waldrick Rd Se Tenino (98589) ***(G-13625)***
Sylvia Vanzee 206 284-2977
3050 Magnolia Blvd W Seattle (98199) ***(G-11242)***
Symbol Servers 360 819-5132
416 Washington St Se Olympia (98501) ***(G-7404)***
Symetrix Inc 425 640-3331
6408 216th St Sw Ste A Mountlake Terrace (98043) ***(G-6871)***
Synchronous Aerospace 253 852-9700
821 3rd Ave S Kent (98032) ***(G-5165)***
Syncromsp, Kirkland *Also called Servably Inc* ***(G-5459)***
Syndel USA, Ferndale *Also called Western Chemical Incorporated* ***(G-3923)***
Syndyne Corporation 360 256-8466
12109 Ne 95th St Vancouver (98682) ***(G-14622)***
Synenergy Triad North America, Kingston *Also called Global Enterprise Intl* ***(G-5254)***
Synergistic Technologies Inc (PA) 425 822-7777
11820 Northup Way E200 Bellevue (98005) ***(G-1174)***
Synergy Business Services Inc 206 859-6500
1001 4th Ave Ste 3262 Seattle (98154) ***(G-11243)***
Synergy Welding Inc 360 881-0204
20818 Stephen Ct Ne Kingston (98346) ***(G-5265)***
Synesso Inc 206 764-0600
5610 4th Ave S Seattle (98108) ***(G-11244)***
Syngenta Seeds Inc 509 543-8000
5516 N Industrial Way Pasco (99301) ***(G-7636)***
Synne Cellars 206 851-2048
16110 Woodinville Redmond Woodinville (98072) ***(G-15383)***
Synology America Corp 425 296-3177
3535 Factoria Blvd Se # 200 Bellevue (98006) ***(G-1175)***
Synrad, Mukilteo *Also called Novanta Inc* ***(G-6958)***
Synsor LLC 425 551-1300
1920 Merrill Creek Pkwy Everett (98203) ***(G-3624)***
Syntek, Bellevue *Also called Synergistic Technologies Inc* ***(G-1174)***
Synthesis By Jeffrey Bland PHD 253 238-7898
3414 60th Street Ct E Tacoma (98443) ***(G-13536)***

Synthigen LLC 208 772-7294
717 W Sprague Ave # 1600 Spokane (99201) *(G-12538)*
System & Application Assoc 206 949-4153
6201 15th Ave Nw Seattle (98107) *(G-11245)*
System 1 Software Inc 206 548-1633
501 N 34th St Seattle (98103) *(G-11246)*
System To Asic Inc 425 488-0575
12100 Ne 195th St Ste 180 Bothell (98011) *(G-1798)*
Systematic Designs Intl 360 944-9890
5305 E 187th St Ste 215 Vancouver (98661) *(G-14623)*
Systematic Machinery LLC 509 892-0399
13824 E Francis Ave Spokane (99217) *(G-12539)*
Systems Engineering Inc 206 633-4972
4327 105th Ave Ne Kirkland (98033) *(G-5473)*
Systems Interface Inc 425 481-1225
10802 47th Ave W Mukilteo (98275) *(G-6981)*
Sytech Inc 509 924-7797
3900 E Main Ave Spokane (99202) *(G-12540)*
T & A Supply Company Inc (PA) 206 282-3770
6807 S 216th St Kent (98032) *(G-5166)*
T & A Supply Company Inc 253 872-3682
6821 S 216th St Bldg A Kent (98032) *(G-5167)*
T & D Gruhn Trucking Inc 360 532-1288
6820 Central Park Dr Aberdeen (98520) *(G-37)*
T & D Machine Inc 425 486-8338
8030 Ne Bothell Way Ste A Kenmore (98028) *(G-4608)*
T & G Machinery LLC 425 396-5939
7226 Thompson Ave Se Snoqualmie (98065) *(G-12033)*
T & H Machine Inc 253 735-6521
60 37th St Ne Ste C Auburn (98002) *(G-575)*
T & J Basic Design, Port Orchard *Also called Orpilla Santiago (G-7838)*
T & JS Machine Shop 360 504-2387
92 Sampson Ct Sequim (98382) *(G-11663)*
T & K Cstm Fabrication & Repr 206 242-0197
112 Sw 119th St Seattle (98146) *(G-11247)*
T & K Fab, Seattle *Also called T & K Cstm Fabrication & Repr (G-11247)*
T & K Martin Farms Inc 509 525-4387
2109 S Wilbur Ave Walla Walla (99362) *(G-14877)*
T & R Log Co 509 962-6590
306 S Lookout Mountain Dr Ellensburg (98926) *(G-3229)*
T & R Welding Supplies, Tacoma *Also called Torch & Regulator Repair Co (G-13558)*
T & S Dental Group Corp 714 720-5511
1303 Central Ave S # 202 Kent (98032) *(G-5168)*
T & TS 206 938-0177
7314 28th Ave Sw Seattle (98126) *(G-11248)*
T Bailey Inc 360 293-0682
9628 Marchs Point Rd Anacortes (98221) *(G-173)*
T D Kennedy and Associates Inc 253 922-2558
3404 Pioneer Way E Tacoma (98443) *(G-13537)*
T D Laser Engraving 425 347-6837
10306 19th Pl W Everett (98204) *(G-3625)*
T E C I Inc 509 452-3672
1602 Rudkin Rd Union Gap (98901) *(G-13953)*
T Eight Fincing LLC 360 794-7369
13224 191st Ave Se Monroe (98272) *(G-6629)*
T J Brooks Logging 425 220-2263
1549 Graham Dr Camano Island (98282) *(G-2225)*
T J Pottery 253 946-1974
26620 Pacific Hwy S Kent (98032) *(G-5169)*
T K O Fisheries Inc (PA) 206 285-2815
4257 24th Ave W Seattle (98199) *(G-11249)*
T L C Custom Meats Inc 509 488-9953
93 N Desdemona Dr Othello (99344) *(G-7507)*
T L Fitzer Logging Inc 360 832-4949
11927 Clear Lake S Rd E Eatonville (98328) *(G-3069)*
T M P, Kent *Also called Technical Molded Plastics Inc (G-5174)*
T N T Enterprises 425 742-8210
17121 3rd Ave Se Bothell (98012) *(G-1908)*
T N T Precision Shtmtl Mfg, Bothell *Also called T N T Enterprises (G-1908)*
T N W Inc 206 762-5755
7929 2nd Ave S Seattle (98108) *(G-11250)*
T R Rizzuto Pizza Crust Inc 509 536-9268
3420 E Riverside Ave Spokane (99202) *(G-12541)*
T R S Inc 253 444-1555
7717 Portland Ave E Tacoma (98404) *(G-13538)*
T S I, Oak Harbor *Also called Technical Services Inc (G-7165)*
T S L, Union Gap *Also called Thermoforming Systems LLC (G-13954)*
T Squared Tools LLC 406 260-5232
2139 Humboldt St Bellingham (98225) *(G-1565)*
T T I Acquisition Corp 509 358-2036
1421 N Meadowwood Ln # 40 Liberty Lake (99019) *(G-5861)*
T Town Apparel 253 471-2960
1934 Market St Tacoma (98402) *(G-13539)*
T&B Logging Inc 509 684-4316
563 Finley Gulch Rd Colville (99114) *(G-2777)*
T&C Concepts LLC 253 298-2104
5609 114th Avenue Ct E Puyallup (98372) *(G-8260)*
T-Prints LLC 425 780-9380
6830 Ne 153rd Pl Kenmore (98028) *(G-4609)*
T-Shirt Madness Silk Screen 206 427-8720
945 Nw 51st St Seattle (98107) *(G-11251)*
T-Shirts By Design LLC 360 293-8898
908 31st St Unit Main Anacortes (98221) *(G-174)*
T-Zero Racing Inc 425 222-5800
7700 300th Ave Se Unit A2 Issaquah (98027) *(G-4484)*
T.A.J.J., Everett *Also called Evolving Nutrition (G-3467)*
T14 Creations, Kirkland *Also called T14 Inc (G-5474)*
T14 Inc 425 829-8213
10211 112th Ave Ne Kirkland (98033) *(G-5474)*
T2 Services Inc 509 893-3666
12205 E Empire Ave Spokane Valley (99206) *(G-12899)*
T3 Custom, Woodinville *Also called T3 Publishing LLC (G-15384)*
T3 Publishing LLC (PA) 206 650-0535
14241 Ne Wdnvlle Dvall Rd Woodinville (98072) *(G-15384)*
T3 Technique LLC 425 785-0361
22330 Ne 54th St Redmond (98053) *(G-8687)*
Tabar West, Bellingham *Also called Fownes Brothers & Co Inc (G-1353)*
Table The, Bellingham *Also called Bellingham Pasta Company (G-1267)*
Tableau Ireland LLC (HQ) 206 633-3400
1621 N 34th St Seattle (98103) *(G-11252)*
Tableau Software Inc 206 634-5610
720 4th Ave Ste 120 Kirkland (98033) *(G-5475)*
Tableau Software Inc (PA) 206 633-3400
1621 N 34th St Seattle (98103) *(G-11253)*
Tablesafe Inc 206 516-6100
12220 113th Ave Ne # 220 Kirkland (98034) *(G-5476)*
Tabs To Go Inc 253 854-8227
110 42nd St Nw Auburn (98001) *(G-576)*
TAC Fab LLC 206 755-0519
17024 141st Pl Ne Woodinville (98072) *(G-15385)*
Taco Truck Games LLC 360 218-4967
911 E Pike St Ste 202 Seattle (98122) *(G-11254)*
Tacoma Cabinet & Fixture Co, Tacoma *Also called Tacoma Fixture Co Inc (G-13542)*
Tacoma Community Boat Builders 253 720-8227
1120 E D St Tacoma (98421) *(G-13540)*
Tacoma Fabrication LLC 253 303-1143
1327 N Fir St Tacoma (98406) *(G-13541)*
Tacoma Fixture Co Inc 253 383-5541
1815 E D St Tacoma (98421) *(G-13542)*
Tacoma Glass Blowing Studio 253 383-3499
114 S 23rd St Tacoma (98402) *(G-13543)*
Tacoma Glass Manufacturing Inc 253 581-7679
4424 98th Street Ct Sw B Lakewood (98499) *(G-5760)*
Tacoma Iron Work, Tacoma *Also called Leskajan John (G-13386)*
Tacoma Laser Clinic LLC 253 272-0655
112 S 8th St Ste 200 Tacoma (98402) *(G-13544)*
Tacoma News Inc 253 597-8593
1950 S State St Tacoma (98405) *(G-13545)*
Tacoma Printing 253 470-1454
3711 Center St Tacoma (98409) *(G-13546)*
Tacoma Public Schools 253 571-1170
601 S 8th St Tacoma (98405) *(G-13547)*
Tacoma Range Sheet Metal, Tacoma *Also called T R S Inc (G-13538)*
Tacoma Rubber Stamp Co (PA) 253 383-5433
919 Market St Tacoma (98402) *(G-13548)*
Tacoma Rubber Stamp Co 206 728-8888
5950 6th Ave S Seattle (98108) *(G-11255)*
Tacoma Screw Products Inc 253 395-9770
22123 84th Ave S Kent (98032) *(G-5170)*
Tacoma Screw Products Inc 206 767-3750
1121 S Bailey St Seattle (98108) *(G-11256)*
Tacoma Tent & Awning Co Inc 253 627-4128
121 N G St Tacoma (98403) *(G-13549)*
Tacoma Tofu Inc 253 627-5085
1302 Martin Luther King Tacoma (98405) *(G-13550)*
Tacoma Tofu Inc 253 627-5085
51 Westlake Ave Sw Lakewood (98498) *(G-5761)*
Tacoma Tube Plant, Tacoma *Also called Caraustar Industrial and Con (G-13222)*
Tacoma Woodworks, Seattle *Also called Haun Made LLC (G-10150)*
Tactical Fabs Inc (PA) 360 723-5360
1801 Se Commerce Ave Battle Ground (98604) *(G-742)*
Tactical Tailor Inc 253 984-7854
2916 107th St S Lakewood (98499) *(G-5762)*
Tactile Signs, Kirkland *Also called Sign Makers Inc (G-5460)*
Tactuum LLC 425 941-6958
3822 131st St Ln Se L6 Bellevue (98006) *(G-1176)*
Tag Manufacturing Inc 206 359-8440
1201 3rd Ave Ste 3400 Seattle (98101) *(G-11257)*
Taggart Woodworks LLC 206 729-8028
2311 N 45th St Ste 365 Seattle (98103) *(G-11258)*
Tagline Products LLC 360 927-2719
309 Palm St Bellingham (98225) *(G-1566)*
Tagorbi Publishing LLC 253 466-3214
13802 93rd Ave E Puyallup (98373) *(G-8261)*
TAHAc LLC (PA) 509 248-0933
3810 Kern Way Ste B Yakima (98902) *(G-15693)*
Tahoma Glacier Water, Auburn *Also called Glacier Water Company LLC (G-450)*
Tahoma Technology Inc 206 393-0909
6040 Palatine Ave N Seattle (98103) *(G-11259)*
Tai Incorporated 509 747-6111
501 N Riverpoint Blvd Spokane (99202) *(G-12542)*
Tailored Accents, Tumtum *Also called Tailored Solutions LLC (G-13847)*

ALPHABETIC

(PA)=Parent Co (HQ)=Headquarters (DH)=Div Headquarters
2019 Washington Manufacturers Register
835

Tailored Solutions LLC ALPHABETIC SECTION

Tailored Solutions LLC 509 258-4314
5688 Corkscrew Canyon Rd Tumtum (99034) *(G-13847)*
Taina Hartman Studio 541 806-0053
121 N Main Ave White Salmon (98672) *(G-15133)*
Tainio Biologicals Inc 509 747-5471
4814 S Ben Franklin Ln Spokane (99224) *(G-12543)*
Taiwan Semicdtr Mfg Co Ltd, Camas *Also called Tsmc Development Inc (G-2285)*
Takeda Pharmaceuticals USA Inc 509 747-5551
446 W 18th Ave Spokane (99203) *(G-12544)*
Takovo Led Lights 206 330-6862
8009 7th Ave S Seattle (98108) *(G-11260)*
Tal Holdings LLC 509 682-1617
105 S Bradley St Chelan (98816) *(G-2565)*
Talaera 206 229-0631
1908 8th Ave W Seattle (98119) *(G-11261)*
Talco Services LLC 425 259-0213
34th Ave Ne Bldg B Everett (98201) *(G-3626)*
Talent Shield, Bothell *Also called Talentwise Inc (G-1799)*
Talentwise Inc 425 974-8863
19910 North Creek Pkwy # 200 Bothell (98011) *(G-1799)*
Talgo Inc (HQ) 206 254-7051
1000 2nd Ave Ste 1950 Seattle (98104) *(G-11262)*
Talk To Taracom 206 226-2606
4714 Ballard Ave Nw Seattle (98107) *(G-11263)*
Talkie Tooter 360 856-0836
524 Rhodes Rd Sedro Woolley (98284) *(G-11574)*
Talking Rain Beverage Company 425 222-4900
30520 Se 84th St Preston (98050) *(G-8027)*
Tall Timber Contractoring Inc 509 681-1275
6740 Westside Rd Cle Elum (98922) *(G-2680)*
Tall Timber Contractors, Cle Elum *Also called Tall Timber Contractoring Inc (G-2680)*
Tam Industries Inc 206 763-6868
9420 16th Ave Sw Seattle (98106) *(G-11264)*
Tamarack Software Inc 509 329-0456
1616 W Dean Ave Spokane (99201) *(G-12545)*
Tamer Laboratories Inc 206 364-6761
16825 48th Ave W Ste 310 Lynnwood (98037) *(G-6207)*
Tamu Foods 253 835-1855
1112 S 344th St Federal Way (98003) *(G-3793)*
Tanada Corporation 425 396-1050
1546 Boalch Ave Nw Ste 30 North Bend (98045) *(G-7127)*
Tandar Corp 503 248-0711
13911 Nw 3rd Ct Ste 100 Vancouver (98685) *(G-14624)*
Tangera Technologies Inc 425 652-7969
40 Lake Bellevue Dr # 100 Bellevue (98005) *(G-1177)*
Tangible Ventures LLc 360 818-4000
10710 Ne 10th St Apt 807 Bellevue (98004) *(G-1178)*
Tango Manufacturing Inc 360 693-7228
1222 W Mcloughlin Blvd Vancouver (98660) *(G-14625)*
Tanjuli 509 829-6401
4530 E Zillah Dr Zillah (98953) *(G-15761)*
Tank Wise LLC 206 937-3995
5405 W Marginal Way Sw Seattle (98106) *(G-11265)*
Tap Plastics Inc A Cal Corp 206 389-5900
710 9th Ave N Seattle (98109) *(G-11266)*
Tapenade Inc 509 966-0686
250 Ehler Rd Yakima (98908) *(G-15694)*
Tapenade Inc (PA) 206 325-3051
1103 Grand Ave Seattle (98122) *(G-11267)*
Tapestry Inc 206 729-5908
2680 Ne University Vlg St Seattle (98105) *(G-11268)*
Taphandles LLC (PA) 206 462-6800
1424 4th Ave Ste 201 Seattle (98101) *(G-11269)*
Tarbert Logging Inc 509 738-6567
1505 W Old Kettle Rd Kettle Falls (99141) *(G-5242)*
Target Media Partners 509 765-5681
1428 S Pioneer Way Moses Lake (98837) *(G-6752)*
Target Media Partners 509 662-1405
201 N Mission St Wenatchee (98801) *(G-15078)*
Target Media Partners 509 328-5555
12510 E Sprague Ave Spokane Valley (99216) *(G-12900)*
Target Products, Bellevue *Also called Mutual-Target LLC (G-1021)*
Target System Technology Inc 509 456-4852
14717 E Olympic Ave Spokane Valley (99216) *(G-12901)*
Tarpley Woodworking 360 631-1405
6615 Robe Menzel Rd Granite Falls (98252) *(G-4286)*
Tarpx, Tacoma *Also called Load Control Systems Inc (G-13389)*
Tarr Acquisition LLC 253 859-2979
4510 B St Nw Ste B Auburn (98001) *(G-577)*
Tarra LLC 360 458-4842
34214 102nd Ave S Roy (98580) *(G-9165)*
Tartberry Incorporated 503 295-2700
23516 Ne 120th Ct Battle Ground (98604) *(G-743)*
TAS Group, Kirkland *Also called Select Selling Inc (G-5458)*
Tasc, Seattle *Also called Technical & Assembly Svcs Corp (G-11277)*
Tassels & Wings Publishing 206 725-5075
6208 S Bangor St Seattle (98178) *(G-11270)*
Tasso Inc 608 556-7606
1631 15th Ave W Ste 105 Seattle (98119) *(G-11271)*
Taste of Heaven Baking LLC 509 786-3657
1604 Meade Ave Prosser (99350) *(G-8067)*
Tastebud Fusion Inc 253 826-8700
2025 1st Ave Ste 200 Seattle (98121) *(G-11272)*
Tasting Room Wines Washington 206 770-9463
1924 Post Aly Seattle (98101) *(G-11273)*
Tasting Room, The, Seattle *Also called Tapenade Inc (G-11267)*
Tate Honey Farm 509 924-6669
8900 E Maringo Dr Spokane (99212) *(G-12546)*
Tate Technology Inc 509 534-2500
3102 E Trent Ave Ste 100 Spokane (99202) *(G-12547)*
Tatoosh Distillery LLC (PA) 206 818-0127
309 S Cloverdale St C29 Seattle (98108) *(G-11274)*
Tattoosh Distillery & Spirits, Seattle *Also called Tatoosh Distillery LLC (G-11274)*
Taurman Distributing & Mfg 360 330-5886
2208 Sandra Ave Centralia (98531) *(G-2437)*
Taurus Aerospace Group Inc (PA) 425 423-6200
3121 109th St Sw Everett (98204) *(G-3627)*
Taurus Power and Controls Inc 425 656-4170
8714 S 222nd St Kent (98031) *(G-5171)*
Taylor Communications Inc 509 747-5872
9212 E Montgomry Ave 401-5 Spokane Valley (99206) *(G-12902)*
Taylor Communications Inc 360 699-4013
1498 Se Tech Center Pl # 110 Vancouver (98683) *(G-14626)*
Taylor Dental Studio 360 249-4329
433 E Spruce Ave Montesano (98563) *(G-6660)*
Taylor Drilling Inc 360 262-9274
4304 Jackson Hwy Chehalis (98532) *(G-2538)*
Taylor Farms Northwest LLC 206 764-4499
8030 S 228th St Bldg A Kent (98032) *(G-5172)*
Taylor Mariculture LLC 360 426-6178
130 Se Lynch Rd Shelton (98584) *(G-11739)*
Taylor Metal Inc 425 485-3003
5927 234th St Se Woodinville (98072) *(G-15386)*
Taylor Resources Inc (PA) 360 426-6178
130 Se Lynch Rd Shelton (98584) *(G-11740)*
Taylor Shellfish Company Inc 360 875-5494
378 Bay Center Rd South Bend (98586) *(G-12048)*
Taylor Shellfish Company Inc (HQ) 360 426-6178
130 Se Lynch Rd Shelton (98584) *(G-11741)*
Taylor Technologies, Ridgefield *Also called Tyler Technologies Inc (G-9117)*
Taylor Trucking LLC 360 573-2000
7211 Ne 43rd Ave Ste A Vancouver (98661) *(G-14627)*
Taylor United Inc (PA) 360 426-6178
130 Se Lynch Rd Shelton (98584) *(G-11742)*
Taylor's Custom Exhaust, Electric City *Also called Taylors Marine Center (G-3168)*
Taylor-Made Printing Inc 253 881-1624
217 W Stewart Puyallup (98371) *(G-8262)*
Taylors Marine Center 509 633-2945
236 Coulee Blvd Electric City (99123) *(G-3168)*
Tc Global Inc (PA) 206 233-2070
2003 Western Ave Ste 660 Seattle (98121) *(G-11275)*
Tc Lumber 360 452-2612
3943 Eden Valley Rd Port Angeles (98363) *(G-7748)*
Tc Motorsports 253 887-0500
1302 W Main St Ste 13 Auburn (98001) *(G-578)*
Tc NW Inc 360 683-6655
518 N Sequim Ave Sequim (98382) *(G-11664)*
Tc Span America LLC 425 774-3881
21020 70th Ave W Edmonds (98026) *(G-3159)*
Tcc Printing and Imaging Inc 206 622-4050
616 6th Ave S Seattle (98104) *(G-11276)*
TCI Scales, Snohomish *Also called Curtis Manufacturing Inc (G-11894)*
TCS, Seattle *Also called Telecommunication Systems Inc (G-11280)*
Tdap 509 453-3038
312 S Trail Rd Yakima (98901) *(G-15695)*
Tdb Holdings LLC 360 600-5506
3214 Ne 394th St La Center (98629) *(G-5516)*
Tdm, Centralia *Also called Taurman Distributing & Mfg (G-2437)*
Teaching 2020 LLC 253 232-6822
10631 Orchard Ave Se Olalla (98359) *(G-7211)*
Team Inc 360 848-0353
3302 Cedardale Rd Ste D5 Mount Vernon (98274) *(G-6844)*
Team Chinook Sales 509 949-0929
380 Old River Rd Naches (98937) *(G-7006)*
Team Corporation 360 757-3944
11591 Watertank Rd Burlington (98233) *(G-2193)*
Team Industrial Services 360 757-2589
11837 Watertank Rd Burlington (98233) *(G-2194)*
Team Sport Software LLC 703 971-2005
4415 Holly Ln Nw Gig Harbor (98335) *(G-4165)*
Teammates Sports Products LLC 206 780-2037
410 Robinwood Dr Ne Bainbridge Island (98110) *(G-676)*
Teamster Local 313 ....253 627-0103
220 S 27th St Unit Main Tacoma (98402) *(G-13551)*
Teamsters Union Local 313, Tacoma *Also called Teamster Local 313 (G-13551)*
Teamwest Ltd 425 227-8525
7701 142nd Way Se Newcastle (98059) *(G-7041)*
Teazer 360 387-1737
1256 Country Club Dr Stanwood (98282) *(G-12957)*
Teazer Hats, Stanwood *Also called Teazer (G-12957)*
Tech Heavy Industries Inc 509 557-8492
7 Stansbury Rd Riverside (98849) *(G-9127)*
Tech Industrial Services, Riverside *Also called Tech Heavy Industries Inc (G-9127)*

Tech Machining Usa LLC 425 754-8221
1117 Dale Ln Ste D Mount Vernon (98274) ***(G-6845)***
Tech Marine Enterprises Inc 206 878-7878
5111 4th St E Fife (98424) ***(G-3995)***
Tech-Roll Inc 360 371-4321
5514 Nielsen Ave Ferndale (98248) ***(G-3911)***
Techna NDT LLC 253 872-2415
6707 S 216th St Kent (98032) ***(G-5173)***
Technical & Assembly Svcs Corp (PA) 206 682-2967
2222 N Pacific St Seattle (98103) ***(G-11277)***
Technical Marine and Indus LLC 206 717-4466
24121 56th Ave W Mountlake Terrace (98043) ***(G-6872)***
Technical Molded Plastics Inc 425 251-9710
18506a 80th Pl S Ste A Kent (98032) ***(G-5174)***
Technical Services Inc 360 675-1322
1150 Ne 21st Ct Oak Harbor (98277) ***(G-7165)***
Technical Systems Inc (PA) 425 678-4142
2303 196th St Sw Ste B Lynnwood (98036) ***(G-6208)***
Technical Tooling LLC 253 327-1149
1118 E D St Tacoma (98421) ***(G-13552)***
Technifab Inc 509 534-1022
5714 E 1st Ave Spokane Valley (99212) ***(G-12903)***
Technipfmc US Holdings Inc 509 925-2500
1621 Vantage Hwy Ellensburg (98926) ***(G-3230)***
Technipfmc US Holdings Inc 253 853-5060
13409 53rd Ave Nw Gig Harbor (98332) ***(G-4166)***
Technology Alliance Partners, Friday Harbor *Also called Strategic News Service LLC* ***(G-4060)***
Techpoint Manufacturing Inc 425 387-0305
7823 51st Pl Ne Marysville (98270) ***(G-6394)***
Techtether, Medina *Also called Mary Medina LLC* ***(G-6452)***
Techwood LLC 360 427-9616
121 W Enterprise Rd Shelton (98584) ***(G-11743)***
Teck American Incorporated (HQ) 509 747-6111
501 N Riverpoint Blvd # 300 Spokane (99202) ***(G-12548)***
Teck American Incorporated 509 446-5308
1382 Pend Oreille Mine Rd Metaline Falls (99153) ***(G-6499)***
Teck American Metal Sales Inc 509 747-6111
501 N Riverpoint Blvd Spokane (99202) ***(G-12549)***
Teck Co LLC 509 747-6111
501 N Riverpoint Blvd Spokane (99202) ***(G-12550)***
Tecplot Inc 425 653-1200
3535 Factoria Blvd Se # 550 Bellevue (98006) ***(G-1179)***
Tect Aerospace LLC 253 872-7045
19420 84th Ave S Kent (98032) ***(G-5175)***
Ted Gay 425 742-9566
17709 Highway 99 Lynnwood (98037) ***(G-6209)***
Ted Gruber Software Inc 702 735-1980
212 Beasley Rd Kelso (98626) ***(G-4554)***
Teddy Bear Press 206 402-6947
3703 S Edmunds St Ste 67 Seattle (98118) ***(G-11278)***
Tee-Eight Log, Monroe *Also called T Eight Fincing LLC* ***(G-6629)***
Teeter's Metal Fabricators, Seattle *Also called Kenneth A Edleman* ***(G-10337)***
Teh Industries LLC 425 453-1551
1006 103rd Ave Se Bellevue (98004) ***(G-1180)***
Tek Manufacturing Inc 509 921-5424
6315 E Alki Ave Spokane Valley (99212) ***(G-12904)***
Tekni-Plex Inc 509 663-8541
1121 S Columbia St Wenatchee (98801) ***(G-15079)***
Teknotherm Inc 206 547-5629
3941 Leary Way Nw Seattle (98107) ***(G-11279)***
Tekoa Software Inc 509 340-3580
16201 E Ind Ave Ste 2750 Liberty Lake (99019) ***(G-5862)***
Teladaq LLC 661 373-1168
2040 Lindsay Rd Everson (98247) ***(G-3691)***
Telco Wiring & Repair Inc 509 547-4300
613 N Road 27 Pasco (99301) ***(G-7637)***
Telecom Reseller Inc 360 260-9708
17413 Se 28th St Vancouver (98683) ***(G-14628)***
Telecom Reseller Monthly, Vancouver *Also called Telecom Reseller Inc* ***(G-14628)***
Telecommunication Systems Inc 206 792-2000
2401 Elliott Ave Ste 200 Seattle (98121) ***(G-11280)***
Telect Inc (PA) 509 926-6000
22245 E Appleway Blvd Ste Liberty Lake (99019) ***(G-5863)***
Telegraph Fabrication 360 739-8170
7343 Meadowmist Ln Ferndale (98248) ***(G-3912)***
Telepress Inc (PA) 425 392-1660
19241 62nd Ave S Kent (98032) ***(G-5176)***
Tellwise Inc 425 999-6935
1750 112th Ave Ne D151 Bellevue (98004) ***(G-1181)***
Telmage Consulting, Kirkland *Also called Telspace LLC* ***(G-5478)***
Telos Sales Corporation 425 890-2755
11733 Holmes Point Dr Ne Kirkland (98034) ***(G-5477)***
Telos Wealth Management 509 664-8844
656 N Miller St Wenatchee (98801) ***(G-15080)***
Telos3 LLC 360 900-9274
22277 Stottlemeyer Rd Ne Poulsbo (98370) ***(G-8006)***
Telos3 LLC 360 536-3122
7563 Ne Meadowmeer Ln Bainbridge Island (98110) ***(G-677)***
Telspace LLC 425 953-2801
5400 Carillon Pt Kirkland (98033) ***(G-5478)***
Tempus Cellars 509 368-9267
8 N Post St Ste 8 # 8 Spokane (99201) ***(G-12551)***
Ten Hats 702 375-6504
5411 E Mill Plain Blvd # 7 Vancouver (98661) ***(G-14629)***
Ten Pin Brewing Company 509 750-0396
1165 N Stratford Rd Moses Lake (98837) ***(G-6753)***
Ten Talents 360 256-0205
9005 Ne 162nd St Battle Ground (98604) ***(G-744)***
Ten Talents USA 360 256-2847
2910 Se Blairmont Dr Vancouver (98683) ***(G-14630)***
Tenacious Hgs Jams 360 747-4080
447 23rd Ave Longview (98632) ***(G-5959)***
Teneff Jewelry Mfg Co 509 747-1038
421 W Riverside Ave # 280 Spokane (99201) ***(G-12552)***
Tennant Co 425 788-9711
19915 Ne 175th St Woodinville (98077) ***(G-15387)***
Tenneson Brothers 360 856-6242
10117 Fruitdale Rd Sedro Woolley (98284) ***(G-11575)***
Tennmax America Inc 360 567-0707
7500 Ne St Johns Rd Vancouver (98665) ***(G-14631)***
Tensormake Corporation 206 659-6139
2128 204th Pl Ne Redmond (98074) ***(G-8688)***
Tenth Generation Software 425 226-1939
305 Lynnwood Ave Se Renton (98056) ***(G-8926)***
Teodoro Foundation 253 475-0200
4110 S Washington St Tacoma (98409) ***(G-13553)***
Teras Construction LLC 253 539-2887
4516 176th St E Tacoma (98446) ***(G-13554)***
Terato Products LLC 425 702-6365
2605 151st Pl Ne Redmond (98052) ***(G-8689)***
Terex Corporation 800 536-1800
17275 Ne 67th Ct Redmond (98052) ***(G-8690)***
Terex Utilities Inc 206 764-5025
7829 S 206th St Kent (98032) ***(G-5177)***
Terex Utilities West, Kent *Also called Terex Utilities Inc* ***(G-5177)***
Terra Blanca Vintners, Benton City *Also called Blanca Terra Vineyards Inc* ***(G-1602)***
Terra Vinum LLC 509 628-7799
2514 S Irving St Kennewick (99338) ***(G-4732)***
Terra Vinum LLC 509 551-0854
56204 N East Roza Rd Benton City (99320) ***(G-1630)***
Terramar Instruments LLC 425 306-0174
7930 327th Ave Ne Carnation (98014) ***(G-2300)***
Terrashield Coatings Ltd 206 992-2157
6505 21st Ave Nw Seattle (98117) ***(G-11281)***
Terratrench Usa Inc 360 694-0141
815 Ne 172nd Ave Vancouver (98684) ***(G-14632)***
Terry Albracht 425 252-2997
1035 N Park Dr Everett (98203) ***(G-3628)***
Terry and Kathy Loney 509 375-4005
704 Se Quail Run College Place (99324) ***(G-2729)***
Terry Signs 509 662-6672
527 N Wenatchee Ave Wenatchee (98801) ***(G-15081)***
Terrys Machine & Mfg Inc 425 315-8866
1102 Shuksan Way Ste 200 Everett (98203) ***(G-3629)***
Terrys Precision Products LLC 425 349-2700
1102 Shuksan Way Everett (98203) ***(G-3630)***
Tesla Inc 425 453-5021
233 Bellevue Sq Bellevue (98004) ***(G-1182)***
Tesla Inc 425 519-8070
14408 Ne 20th St Bellevue (98007) ***(G-1183)***
Tesla Motors, Bellevue *Also called Tesla Inc* ***(G-1183)***
Tesla Winery Tours LLC 509 520-5528
422 Diamond Gate Rd Walla Walla (99362) ***(G-14878)***
Teslavision 425 822-6535
401 Parkplace Ctr Ste 319 Kirkland (98033) ***(G-5479)***
Tesoro, Kennewick *Also called Andeavor* ***(G-4617)***
Tesoro, Forks *Also called Andeavor* ***(G-4008)***
Tesoro, Spokane *Also called Andeavor* ***(G-12114)***
Tesoro Companies Inc 253 896-8700
3450 S 344th Way Ste 100 Federal Way (98001) ***(G-3794)***
Tesoro Corporation 360 293-9119
10200 S March Point Rd Anacortes (98221) ***(G-175)***
Tesoro Corporation 509 533-2705
228 S Thor St Spokane (99202) ***(G-12553)***
Tesoro Maritime Company 360 293-3111
10200 S March Point Rd Anacortes (98221) ***(G-176)***
Tesoro Refining & Mktg Co LLC 360 293-9119
10200 W March Point Rd Anacortes (98221) ***(G-177)***
Tesoro Refining and Mktg Co, Anacortes *Also called Tesoro Refining & Mktg Co LLC* ***(G-177)***
Tessenderlo Kerley Inc 509 586-9148
233807 E Straightbank Rd Kennewick (99337) ***(G-4733)***
Test Best International Inc 360 650-0671
3744 Crystal Ct Ste 33 Bellingham (98226) ***(G-1567)***
Tested Field Systems LLC 206 453-4851
4014 47th Ave S Seattle (98118) ***(G-11282)***
Tethers Unlimited Inc 425 486-0100
11711 N Creek Pkwy S Bothell (98011) ***(G-1800)***
Tetra Pak Materials LP 360 693-3664
1616 W 31st St Vancouver (98660) ***(G-14633)***
Tetrachrome Software 425 825-1708
14058 120th Ave Ne Kirkland (98034) ***(G-5480)***

ALPHABETIC

Tevada Publishing Inc ALPHABETIC SECTION

Tevada Publishing Inc 509 783-5455
4812 W Clearwater Ave Kennewick (99336) ***(G-4734)***
Tex Enterprises Inc 253 939-1660
1302 W Main St Ste 13 Auburn (98001) ***(G-579)***
Tex Ware 425 337-3696
13827 51st Dr Se Everett (98208) ***(G-3631)***
Texas Avenue Associates 425 889-9642
10500 Ne 8th St Ste 1900 Bellevue (98004) ***(G-1184)***
Texas Imperial Software, Woodinville *Also called Wftpd Inc* ***(G-15404)***
Texas Instruments Inc 253 927-0754
3455 S 344th Way Federal Way (98001) ***(G-3795)***
Texas Johns 509 659-1402
1455 W 1st Ave Ritzville (99169) ***(G-9123)***
Textured Forest Products Inc 360 835-2164
721 S 28th St Washougal (98671) ***(G-14991)***
Tfi Telemark, Battle Ground *Also called Tactical Fabs Inc* ***(G-742)***
Tfi Telemark 360 723-5360
1801 Se Commerce Ave Battle Ground (98604) ***(G-745)***
That Patchwork Place, Bothell *Also called Martingale & Company Inc* ***(G-1776)***
Thaw Corporation (HQ) 206 505-2100
8300 Military Rd S Seattle (98108) ***(G-11283)***
Thc Partners 347 459-8450
9369 8th Ave S Seattle (98108) ***(G-11284)***
The Creation Station Inc 425 775-7959
2001 71st St Ne Tulalip (98271) ***(G-13845)***
The Euclid Chemical Company 360 848-1202
13527 Farm & Market Rd Mount Vernon (98273) ***(G-6846)***
The Fishermen's News, Seattle *Also called Fishermens News Inc* ***(G-9999)***
The Fuel 206 829-8033
2201 E Aloha St Seattle (98112) ***(G-11285)***
The Habon Company, Renton *Also called Roger Habon* ***(G-8896)***
The Loomis Company, Seattle *Also called Loomis Plastics Corporation* ***(G-10439)***
The Loop, Seattle *Also called Loop Corp* ***(G-10440)***
The McCredy Company 509 773-5340
126 W Main St Goldendale (98620) ***(G-4209)***
The O-Ring Store LLC 208 413-6377
1847 Wilma Dr Clarkston (99403) ***(G-2651)***
The Pacific County Press Inc 360 875-6805
500 W Robert Bush Dr South Bend (98586) ***(G-12049)***
The Riff 509 280-1300
215 W Main Ave Spokane (99201) ***(G-12554)***
The Steel Fabrication Co., Tukwila *Also called Division Five Inc* ***(G-13726)***
The UPS Store Inc 360 400-6245
1201 E Yelm Ave Ste 400 Yelm (98597) ***(G-15747)***
The Windward Cmmncations Group 206 382-1117
504 N 85th St Seattle (98103) ***(G-11286)***
Thee Legacy Woodshop 425 327-0208
2714 179th Pl Ne Arlington (98223) ***(G-338)***
Theelectricaldepot.com, Spokane *Also called C&K Enterprize LLC* ***(G-12165)***
Theo Coram Corporation 425 774-4731
21355 Poplar Way Brier (98036) ***(G-2022)***
Theo Wanne Mouthpieces Instrs 360 392-8416
1221 Fraser St Ste 102 Bellingham (98229) ***(G-1568)***
Theobald Software Inc 425 802-2514
2211 Elliott Ave Ste 200 Seattle (98121) ***(G-11287)***
Therapedic, Auburn *Also called Cascade Manufacturing* ***(G-402)***
Therapeutae Publishing LLC 425 242-1580
414 235th Ave Ne Sammamish (98074) ***(G-9252)***
Therapeutic Dimension Inc 509 323-9275
319 W Hastings Rd Spokane (99218) ***(G-12555)***
Therasigma Inc 800 423-7172
4060 S Grant St Ste 100 Washougal (98671) ***(G-14992)***
Thermal Hydra Plastics LLC 425 483-1877
18800 Wdnvlle Snhomish Rd Woodinville (98072) ***(G-15388)***
Thermal Northwest Inc 253 520-8899
6020 S 226th St Kent (98032) ***(G-5178)***
Thermal Pipe Shields 425 330-3765
29020 40th Ave Nw Stanwood (98292) ***(G-12996)***
Thermal Solar Panels 425 445-0244
1405 N 34th St Renton (98056) ***(G-8927)***
Thermal Solutions Mfg 206 764-7028
14218 Stewart Rd Ste 200b Sumner (98390) ***(G-13106)***
Thermal Solutions Mfg Inc 800 776-4650
400 Industry Dr Ste 160 Tukwila (98188) ***(G-13826)***
Thermal Technologies 425 359-8681
13405 27th St Se Snohomish (98290) ***(G-11990)***
Thermaline Inc 253 833-7168
1531 14th St Nw Auburn (98001) ***(G-580)***
Thermedia Corporation 360 427-1877
301 E W Kneeland Blvd 2 Shelton (98584) ***(G-11744)***
Thermetrics LLC 206 456-9119
4220 24th Ave W Seattle (98199) ***(G-11288)***
Thermion Inc 360 297-5150
5815 Ne Minder Rd Poulsbo (98370) ***(G-8007)***
Thermion Inc 360 692-6469
5813 Ne Minder Rd Poulsbo (98370) ***(G-8008)***
Thermion Inc 360 362-1273
5811 Ne Minder Rd Poulsbo (98370) ***(G-8009)***
Thermion Inc (PA) 360 692-6469
5815 Ne Minder Rd Poulsbo (98370) ***(G-8010)***
Thermoforming Systems LLC 509 454-4578
1601 W Pine St Union Gap (98903) ***(G-13954)***
Thermogenesis Group Inc 425 999-3550
14260 Ne 21st St Bellevue (98007) ***(G-1185)***
These Two Girls Llc 206 200-3620
300 Nw 62nd St Seattle (98107) ***(G-11289)***
Thesoftwareworxcom 425 825-3814
12205 Ne 138th Pl Kirkland (98034) ***(G-5481)***
Thick Film Technologies Inc 425 347-0919
3101 111th St Sw Ste R Everett (98204) ***(G-3632)***
Thin Air Logging LLC 509 670-8139
3000 Ingalls Creek Rd Peshastin (98847) ***(G-7664)***
Thin Dipped Almonds 720 231-9196
115 N 36th St Unit B Seattle (98103) ***(G-11290)***
Thinking Cap Solutions In 360 452-6159
3122 Old Olympic Hwy Port Angeles (98362) ***(G-7749)***
Thinking Industries Inc 206 201-2106
8465 Ne Beck Rd Bainbridge Island (98110) ***(G-678)***
Thinking Man Software Corp 425 313-0607
26518 Se 19th Ct Sammamish (98075) ***(G-9253)***
Third & Wall Art Group LLC 206 443-8425
3455 Thorndyke Ave W # 102 Seattle (98119) ***(G-11291)***
Third Ares Industries LLC 502 592-2463
915 Queen Anne Ave N Seattle (98109) ***(G-11292)***
Third Wave Software Corp 425 825-9082
14033 95th Ave Ne Bothell (98011) ***(G-1801)***
Thirsty Crab Brewery LLC 360 331-3667
4670 Rhodie Ln Freeland (98249) ***(G-4037)***
Thirteen Sheets LLC 888 676-5270
3012 Nw 199th St Ridgefield (98642) ***(G-9115)***
Thirtnspades Metal Fabrication 425 831-6126
43723 Se 149th St North Bend (98045) ***(G-7128)***
Thirty Second Streeet Raccoons 206 526-8169
9518 32nd Ave Ne Seattle (98115) ***(G-11293)***
Thoe John 206 505-6229
2201 Ne 120th St Seattle (98125) ***(G-11294)***
Thomas Dean & Co LLC (PA) 206 355-1009
4957 Lakemont Blvd Se C-145 Bellevue (98006) ***(G-1186)***
Thomas Designs, Anacortes *Also called Ship N Shore* ***(G-167)***
Thomas Grange Holdings Inc 678 921-0499
2716 Elliott Ave Apt 603 Seattle (98121) ***(G-11295)***
Thomas Kemper, Seattle *Also called Pyramid Breweries Inc* ***(G-10893)***
Thomas L Norman Cnstr & Log 253 312-7858
22805 133rd Street Ct E Orting (98360) ***(G-7487)***
Thomas Machine & Foundry Inc 360 651-9100
13100 41st Ave Ne Marysville (98271) ***(G-6395)***
Thomas Mayer 360 945-0354
1886 Washington Dr Point Roberts (98281) ***(G-7670)***
Thomas Products LLC 253 678-8391
4721 Spring Vista Way Bellingham (98226) ***(G-1569)***
Thomas R Keevy 509 245-3457
Rr 1 Spangle (99031) ***(G-12085)***
Thomas Tree Svc & Logging 360 561-9589
4401 37th Ave Se Unit 53 Lacey (98503) ***(G-5594)***
Thomashilfen, Seattle *Also called Exomotion LLC* ***(G-9954)***
Thompson & Cloud LLC 206 218-9991
4842 Rural Rd Sw Apt 301 Tumwater (98512) ***(G-13899)***
Thompson Litho Group Inc 360 892-7888
4018 Ne 112th Ave Ste D9 Vancouver (98682) ***(G-14634)***
Thought Ops LLC 206 427-0165
520 Occidental Ave S # 503 Seattle (98104) ***(G-11296)***
Thrall & Dodge Winery 509 925-4110
111 Dodge Rd Ellensburg (98926) ***(G-3231)***
Three Brothers Vineyard A 503 702-5549
802 Nw 297th Cir Ridgefield (98642) ***(G-9116)***
Three By Three Inc 206 784-5839
3668 Albion Pl N Seattle (98103) ***(G-11297)***
Three By Three Seattle, Seattle *Also called Three By Three Inc* ***(G-11297)***
Three Kees Cider LLC 425 238-3470
22831 Woods Creek Rd Snohomish (98290) ***(G-11991)***
Three of Cups LLC 425 286-6657
18808 142nd Ave Ne Ste 4a Woodinville (98072) ***(G-15389)***
Three Rivers Industrial Mch 360 578-1114
700 Colorado St Ste A Kelso (98626) ***(G-4555)***
Three Rivers Winery, Walla Walla *Also called Walla Walla Wines LLC* ***(G-14897)***
Three Sigma Manufacturing Inc 253 395-1125
22604 58th Pl S Kent (98032) ***(G-5179)***
Three Squared LLC 206 708-5918
9638 Hilltop Rd Bellevue (98004) ***(G-1187)***
Threepenny Software LLC 206 675-1518
4649 Eastern Ave N Seattle (98103) ***(G-11298)***
Thrifty Payless Inc T/A 360 754-8014
305 Cooper Point Rd Nw Olympia (98502) ***(G-7405)***
Thrifty Payless Inc T/A 509 783-1438
101 N Ely St Kennewick (99336) ***(G-4735)***
Thrifty Payless Inc T/A 509 928-9121
1443 N Argonne Rd Spokane Valley (99212) ***(G-12905)***
Thrifty Payless Inc T/A 360 825-2558
232 Roosevelt Ave Enumclaw (98022) ***(G-3323)***
Thrifty Payless Inc T/A 509 925-4232
700 S Main St Ellensburg (98926) ***(G-3232)***
Thrifty Payless Inc T/A 206 324-7111
201 Broadway E Seattle (98102) ***(G-11299)***
Thrifty Payless Inc 206 760-1076
9000 Rainier Ave S Seattle (98118) ***(G-11300)***

Thrifty Payless Inc T/A....206 441-8790
2603 3rd Ave Seattle (98121) *(G-11301)*
Thrifty Payless Inc T/A....360 332-1616
1733 H St Ste 500 Blaine (98230) *(G-1705)*
Thrifty Payless Inc T/A....360 794-0943
18906 State Route 2 Monroe (98272) *(G-6630)*
Thrifty Payless Inc T/A....360 457-3456
1940 E 1st St Ste 110 Port Angeles (98362) *(G-7750)*
Thrifty Payless Inc T/A....206 721-5018
2707 Rainier Ave S Seattle (98144) *(G-11302)*
Thrifty Payless Inc T/A....360 647-2175
3227 Northwest Ave Bellingham (98225) *(G-1570)*
Thryll, Lynnwood *Also called Hbsw Inc (G-6133)*
Thunder Hill Winery LLC....360 681-5209
763 Sporseen Rd Sequim (98382) *(G-11665)*
Thunder Jet, Clarkston *Also called Brunswick Corporation (G-2626)*
Thunder Specialty Printing....253 921-7647
8308 Woodland Ave E Puyallup (98371) *(G-8263)*
Thunderbird Mining Systems, Redmond *Also called Thunderbird Pacific Corp (G-8691)*
Thunderbird Pacific Corp....425 869-2727
2635 151st Pl Ne Redmond (98052) *(G-8691)*
Thurman Enterprises, Shelton *Also called Kennedy Creek Quarry Inc (G-11706)*
Thurston Co Transfer Station....360 459-1901
2420 Hogum Bay Rd Ne Olympia (98516) *(G-7406)*
Thyssenkrupp Elevator Corp....425 828-3110
12530 135th Ave Ne Kirkland (98034) *(G-5482)*
Thyssenkrupp Materials LLC....253 239-6023
5002 D St Nw Ste 104 Auburn (98001) *(G-581)*
Tl Gotham Inc....206 957-8447
413 Pine St Ste 500 Seattle (98101) *(G-11303)*
Tl Northwest Corp....253 445-4104
121 23rd St Se Puyallup (98372) *(G-8264)*
Tiba Medical Inc....503 222-1500
4709 Somerset Pl Se Bellevue (98006) *(G-1188)*
Tibco Software Inc....650 846-1000
2310 N Molter Rd Ste 300 Liberty Lake (99019) *(G-5864)*
Ticket Envelope Company LLC....206 784-7266
4401 E Marginal Way S Seattle (98134) *(G-11304)*
Ticonderoga Enterprises....509 922-2411
5212 N Northwood Dr Spokane (99212) *(G-12556)*
Tidal Vision Products LLC....907 988-8888
5506 Nielsen Ave Ste A Ferndale (98248) *(G-3913)*
Tidewater Holdings Inc (PA)....360 693-1491
6305 Nw Old Lwer River Rd Vancouver (98660) *(G-14635)*
Tidland Hydraulics Inc....360 573-6506
3408 Ne Corbin Rd Vancouver (98686) *(G-14636)*
Tiegrrr Straps Inc....253 520-0303
27005 Cardiff Ave Kent (98032) *(G-5180)*
Tig Aerospace LLC....206 372-6724
1700 Westlake Ave N Seattle (98109) *(G-11305)*
Tiger Oak Media Incorporated....206 284-1750
1417 4th Ave Ste 600 Seattle (98101) *(G-11306)*
Tiger Press....360 468-3737
659 Port Stanley Rd Lopez Island (98261) *(G-5987)*
Tiger Stop, Vancouver *Also called Precision Automation Inc (G-14500)*
Tiger Tail USA, Kent *Also called Polar Fusion LLC (G-5069)*
Tigerstop LLC....360 254-0661
12909 Ne 95th St Vancouver (98682) *(G-14637)*
Tight Group Targets LLC....206 227-0201
15829 Se 167th Pl Renton (98058) *(G-8928)*
Tight Line Industries Inc....360 751-1621
305 Lone Yew Rd Toledo (98591) *(G-13643)*
Tiin-MA Logging....509 874-2040
61 Medicine Valley Rd White Swan (98952) *(G-15139)*
Tik Tik Garment Manufacturing....509 624-0806
160 S Cowley St Spokane (99202) *(G-12557)*
Tilbury Cement, Bellingham *Also called Lehigh Northwest Cement Co (G-1405)*
Tildio Winery LLC....509 687-8463
70 E Wapto Rd Manson (98831) *(G-6246)*
Tilite, Pasco *Also called Tisport LLC (G-7639)*
Tillamook Country Smoker LLC....360 456-2640
7040 Pacific Ave Se Olympia (98503) *(G-7407)*
Tiller LLC....425 770-0855
303 Riverside Ave Winthrop (98862) *(G-15165)*
Tillmans Inc....509 633-2542
3008 Highway 155 Coulee Dam (99116) *(G-2809)*
Tillotson Logging Co, White Salmon *Also called Darrell A Tillotson (G-15114)*
Tiloben Publishing Co Inc....206 323-3070
2600 S Jackson St Seattle (98144) *(G-11307)*
Tilray Inc....206 432-9325
2701 Eastlake Ave E 3 Seattle (98102) *(G-11308)*
Tim Anders....360 944-0806
15816 Ne 36th St Vancouver (98682) *(G-14638)*
Tim Brown Logging Inc....360 274-4422
2970 Tower Rd Castle Rock (98611) *(G-2353)*
Tim Corliss & Son Inc....360 825-2578
29410 Hwy 410 Enumclaw (98022) *(G-3324)*
Tim Eastman Eqp Repr Wldg LLC....360 274-7607
112 Headquarters Rd Castle Rock (98611) *(G-2354)*
Tim Krotzer....509 487-2704
10909 N Iroquois Dr Spokane (99208) *(G-12558)*
Tim's Cascade Snacks, Algona *Also called Kennedy Endeavors Incorporated (G-72)*
Timber Iron Erectors....360 681-8611
1329 Taylor Cutoff Rd Sequim (98382) *(G-11666)*
Timber Savers Inc....208 799-8748
2275 Pitchstone Dr Clarkston (99403) *(G-2652)*
Timberline Controls & Mar Inc....360 335-8598
421 C St Ste 2b Washougal (98671) *(G-14993)*
Timberline Truss and Sup Inc....509 226-0100
25414 E Rowan Ave Newman Lake (99025) *(G-7052)*
Timbers At Towncenter....360 433-9627
608 Ne 86th St Vancouver (98665) *(G-14639)*
Timbersoft Inc....360 750-5575
205 E 11th St Ste 103 Vancouver (98660) *(G-14640)*
Time 4 Fun LLC....425 836-5037
21410 Ne 84th St Redmond (98053) *(G-8692)*
Time Printing Inc....206 633-3320
4411 Wallingford Ave N E Seattle (98103) *(G-11309)*
TIMELESS BOOKS, Spokane *Also called Association For The Developm (G-12123)*
Timeline Press LLC....425 454-7447
6410 129th Pl Se Bellevue (98006) *(G-1189)*
Times....509 337-6631
139 Main St Waitsburg (99361) *(G-14757)*
Times Communications Co, Seattle *Also called Seattle Times Company (G-11081)*
Times Table, Seattle *Also called Origami Inc (G-10714)*
Timextender North America....619 813-7625
411 108th Ave Ne Bellevue (98004) *(G-1190)*
Timezone Raceway Park (PA)....360 687-5100
29718 Ne 132nd Ave Battle Ground (98604) *(G-746)*
Timezone Raceway Park....360 450-3730
6900 Ne 374th St La Center (98629) *(G-5517)*
Timken Motor & Crane Svcs LLC....509 547-1691
4224 E B St Pasco (99301) *(G-7638)*
Timothy Colman....800 631-3086
6521 23rd Ave Ne Seattle (98115) *(G-11310)*
Tims Country Saw Shop....509 486-2798
48 N State Frontage Rd Tonasket (98855) *(G-13660)*
Tims Manufacturing Corp....425 392-2616
11902 124th Ave Ne Kirkland (98034) *(G-5483)*
Timshel Woodworking....206 466-1054
3511 Interlake Ave N Seattle (98103) *(G-11311)*
Tin Can Alley....360 353-0773
160 Huntington Ave N Castle Rock (98611) *(G-2355)*
Tin Can Diva....253 315-5587
42905 260th Ave Se Enumclaw (98022) *(G-3325)*
Tin Can Rocket LLC....206 427-9260
24275 229th Ave Se Maple Valley (98038) *(G-6294)*
Tin Cup LLC....360 866-1580
117 Lilly Rd Ne Olympia (98506) *(G-7408)*
Tin Foil Hat Productions....619 208-5469
3420 Se Navigation Ln Port Orchard (98366) *(G-7853)*
Tin Table....206 320-8458
915 E Pine St Seattle (98122) *(G-11312)*
Tincan Studio LLC....559 906-3521
13308 Wigen Rd Lynnwood (98087) *(G-6210)*
Tinman Software....425 417-2142
22019 Ne 15th St Sammamish (98074) *(G-9254)*
Tinman Systems Inc....425 802-9035
22618 Se 47th Pl Sammamish (98075) *(G-9255)*
Tinplate Toys & Trains....206 715-8118
743 Broadway Tacoma (98402) *(G-13555)*
Tinsley Welding Incorporated....509 786-4000
133401 W Johnson Rd Prosser (99350) *(G-8068)*
Tinypulse....206 455-9424
18 W Mercer St Ste 100 Seattle (98119) *(G-11313)*
Tipke Manufacturing Company....509 534-5336
321 N Helena St Spokane (99202) *(G-12559)*
Tippecanoe Boats Ltd....360 966-7245
4305 Nordum Rd Everson (98247) *(G-3692)*
Tipsy Canyon Winery....425 306-4844
270 Upper Joe Creek Rd Manson (98831) *(G-6247)*
Tiptoes Software LLC....650 267-1907
13330 Se 55th Pl Bellevue (98006) *(G-1191)*
Tiptop Timers LLC....509 448-2819
2225 N Dollar Rd Spokane Valley (99212) *(G-12906)*
Tirtan Publications, Goldendale *Also called Goldendale Sentinel Inc (G-4199)*
Tisport LLC....509 416-4245
2701 W Court St Pasco (99301) *(G-7639)*
Tissue Regeneration Systems....425 576-4032
5400 Carillon Pt Kirkland (98033) *(G-5484)*
Titan Case Inc....206 935-0566
233 S Holden St Seattle (98108) *(G-11314)*
Titan Industries USA LLC....206 466-1300
18473 Ballinger Way Ne Lake Forest Park (98155) *(G-5625)*
Titan Manufacturing, Inc, Monroe *Also called New Star Technology Inc (G-6601)*
Titan Mfg....360 863-1808
17461 147th St Se Monroe (98272) *(G-6631)*
Titanium Industries Inc....425 481-7700
6018 234th St Se Ste C Woodinville (98072) *(G-15390)*
Titanium Sports Tech LLC....509 586-6117
2701 W Court St Pasco (99301) *(G-7640)*
Titus Tool Company Inc (HQ)....206 447-1489
2800 156th Ave Se Ste 135 Bellevue (98007) *(G-1192)*
Titus Tool Company, Inc., Bellevue *Also called Titus Tool Company Inc (G-1192)*

ALPHABETIC

Tj Logging LLC.....509 826-5203
29572 Us Highway 97 OMAK (98841) ***(G-7445)***
Tji II LLC.....360 794-4448
14767 172nd Dr Se Monroe (98272) ***(G-6632)***
Tjn Publishing Inc.....360 426-4677
2505 Olympic Hwy N # 220 Shelton (98584) ***(G-11745)***
Tjs Mechanical Cutting LLC.....360 837-1234
161 Bull Ridge Rd Washougal (98671) ***(G-14994)***
Tk Machine.....509 946-2363
1893 Airport Way Richland (99354) ***(G-9044)***
Tki, Kennewick *Also called Tessenderlo Kerley Inc* ***(G-4733)***
Tl Holdings Inc.....877 743-3509
10424 W Aero Rd Unit G Spokane (99224) ***(G-12560)***
TLC Modular Homes, Goldendale *Also called West Coast Automation Corp* ***(G-4213)***
Tls Printing.....206 522-8289
10331 Aurora Ave N Seattle (98133) ***(G-11315)***
Tmf Inc.....360 598-1750
26273 Twelve Trees Ln Nw B Poulsbo (98370) ***(G-8011)***
TMI, Bellevue *Also called Tri-Mechanical Inc* ***(G-1201)***
Tml Innovative Products LLC.....425 290-3994
12333 Evergreen Dr Mukilteo (98275) ***(G-6982)***
Tmx Aerospace, Auburn *Also called Thyssenkrupp Materials LLC* ***(G-581)***
TNT Crane & Construction.....509 682-7711
4580 Navarre Coulee Rd Chelan (98816) ***(G-2566)***
TNT Horseshoe Art.....253 334-7653
121 3rd Ave N Algona (98001) ***(G-78)***
TNT Industries LLC.....509 279-8011
323 N Flora Rd Spokane Valley (99037) ***(G-12907)***
TNT Machining LLC.....360 988-0274
285 Garfield St Sumas (98295) ***(G-13052)***
TNT Signs & Design Inc.....360 384-3190
6018 Portal Way Ferndale (98248) ***(G-3914)***
TNT Signs Inc.....360 438-3800
4609 Lacey Blvd Se Lacey (98503) ***(G-5595)***
TNT Software Inc.....360 546-0878
2001 Main St Vancouver (98660) ***(G-14641)***
Tntgamble Inc (PA).....425 883-9518
9609 153rd Ave Ne Redmond (98052) ***(G-8693)***
To The T Embroidery.....360 509-0156
6199 Ne Pine St Suquamish (98392) ***(G-13149)***
Toaster Labs Inc.....206 368-3178
2212 Queen Anne Ave N Seattle (98109) ***(G-11316)***
Tobacco City.....425 377-1658
731 State Route 9 Ne # 103 Lake Stevens (98258) ***(G-5672)***
Tobacco Station-WA.....253 517-5618
34815 Pacific Hwy S # 201 Federal Way (98003) ***(G-3796)***
Tobin & Riedesel Logging LLC.....360 482-8127
161 Hokanson Rd Elma (98541) ***(G-3257)***
Tobin and Riedesel Logging LLC.....360 249-8184
100 Brumfield Ave Montesano (98563) ***(G-6661)***
Tobin Cinema Systems Inc.....509 621-0323
19415 E Augusta Ln Spokane Valley (99016) ***(G-12908)***
Tobys Tortillas LLC.....425 344-7653
13709 45th Dr Se Snohomish (98296) ***(G-11992)***
Todays Style.....360 671-4922
1654 Birchwood Ave Bellingham (98225) ***(G-1571)***
Todd Imeson.....509 397-6570
207 E Thorn St Colfax (99111) ***(G-2721)***
Todd M Bearden.....509 624-2875
226 S Washington St Spokane (99201) ***(G-12561)***
Todd Porter Campbell.....253 230-2391
256 S C St Buckley (98321) ***(G-2077)***
Todo Flores Enterprises LLC.....206 450-5123
14019 Se 159th Pl Renton (98058) ***(G-8929)***
Tok, Spokane *Also called Tree of Kindness Inc* ***(G-12567)***
Toka Box.....530 505-1289
13908 Se 42nd Pl Bellevue (98006) ***(G-1193)***
Toke Point Fisheries Inc.....360 753-6917
10415 Stardust Ln Se Olympia (98501) ***(G-7409)***
Tokenyo LLC.....206 851-7046
91 S Jackson St Unit 4581 Seattle (98194) ***(G-11317)***
Toliys Jig Fabrication.....509 534-2261
2530 E 4th Ave Spokane (99202) ***(G-12562)***
Tom & Cheryl McCallaum.....360 377-1606
1222 Park Ave Bremerton (98337) ***(G-2006)***
Tom Bihn Inc.....206 652-4123
4750 Ohio Ave S A Seattle (98134) ***(G-11318)***
Tom Bihn - Portable Culture, Seattle *Also called Tom Bihn Inc* ***(G-11318)***
Tom Bretz.....509 486-2251
2 Tonasket Shop Rd Tonasket (98855) ***(G-13661)***
Tomar Cabinets.....253 538-1183
14606 Pacific Ave S Ste B Tacoma (98444) ***(G-13556)***
Tomar Industries.....509 266-8384
560 Ione Rd Pasco (99301) ***(G-7641)***
Tomatesa Enterprises LLC.....425 778-6708
6333 212th St Sw Lynnwood (98036) ***(G-6211)***
Tommy's Johnson, Tacoma *Also called Nester Brothers LLC* ***(G-13426)***
Toms Prfmce Mch & Repr Inc.....360 256-1722
6707 Ne 117th Ave A Vancouver (98662) ***(G-14642)***
Tonkin Replicas Inc.....206 542-6919
45127 Se 140th St North Bend (98045) ***(G-7129)***
Tony Pecaric.....360 398-9885
236 Pyramid Ln Lynden (98264) ***(G-6056)***
Tonys Custom Cabinets.....425 444-1086
24504 148th Ln Se Kent (98042) ***(G-5181)***
Toolcraft Inc.....360 794-5512
17700 147th St Se Ste E Monroe (98272) ***(G-6633)***
Toolless Plastic Solutions Inc.....425 493-1223
1410 80th St Sw Ste C Everett (98203) ***(G-3633)***
Toolpak, Lakewood *Also called Paktek Inc* ***(G-5745)***
Toonhound Studios LLC.....214 733-9626
20532 2nd Dr Se Bothell (98012) ***(G-1909)***
Top Hat Word & Index.....520 271-2112
1805 134th Ave Se Apt 21 Bellevue (98005) ***(G-1194)***
Top Left Industries.....360 914-1400
8712 57th Dr Ne Marysville (98270) ***(G-6396)***
Top Notch Manufacturing Co.....360 577-9150
1556 3rd Ave Longview (98632) ***(G-5960)***
Top Notch Trailer Mfg.....360 273-0468
19541 Elderberry St Sw Rochester (98579) ***(G-9141)***
Top Notch Trailers, Rochester *Also called Top Notch Trailer Mfg* ***(G-9141)***
Top Quality Woodworks LLC.....509 551-3658
3131 W Hood Ave Apt A105 Kennewick (99336) ***(G-4736)***
Top Shelf Closet Inc.....360 953-1690
21600 Ne 72nd Ave Battle Ground (98604) ***(G-747)***
Top To Bottom.....206 764-7750
9651 15th Ave Sw Seattle (98106) ***(G-11319)***
Top To Bottom Inc.....360 671-7022
2620 N Harbor Loop Dr # 16 Bellingham (98225) ***(G-1572)***
Topcub Aircraft LLC (PA).....401 209-4756
17922 59th Ave Ne Arlington (98223) ***(G-339)***
Topdown Incorporated.....206 920-5566
2691092 Ndavenwste Stanwood (98292) ***(G-12997)***
Topia Press Ltd.....360 754-4449
1508 Bowman Ave Nw Olympia (98502) ***(G-7410)***
Topsoils Northwest Inc.....425 337-0233
9010 Marsh Rd Snohomish (98296) ***(G-11993)***
Toptec Software LLC.....206 331-4420
8524 W Gage Blvd A137 Kennewick (99336) ***(G-4737)***
Toptec Software LLC (PA).....206 331-4420
1766 Fowler St Ste D Richland (99352) ***(G-9045)***
Toray Composite Mtls Amer Inc (HQ).....253 846-1777
19002 50th Ave E Tacoma (98446) ***(G-13557)***
Torc Star Bolting Tools LLC.....334 714-0945
1736 125th Ave Se Bellevue (98005) ***(G-1195)***
Torch & Regulator Repair Co.....253 272-0467
2526 Tacoma Ave S Tacoma (98402) ***(G-13558)***
Torii Mor Winery LLC.....425 408-0086
14525 148th Ave Ne Woodinville (98072) ***(G-15391)***
Tork Lift International Inc (PA).....253 479-0115
322 Railroad Ave N Kent (98032) ***(G-5182)***
Torklift Central Wldg Kent Inc.....253 854-1832
322 Railroad Ave N Kent (98032) ***(G-5183)***
Torklift International, Kent *Also called Tork Lift International Inc* ***(G-5182)***
Tormented Artifacts Ltd.....206 501-8333
9258 9th Ave Nw Seattle (98117) ***(G-11320)***
Torrid Manufacturing Company, Seattle *Also called North Industries Inc* ***(G-10624)***
Torrid Marine LLC.....206 920-9002
8895 Three Tree Ln Ne Bainbridge Island (98110) ***(G-679)***
Tortilla Union.....509 381-5162
808 W Main Ave Spokane (99201) ***(G-12563)***
Tortilleria Jalisco.....253 536-9532
16911 11th Avenue Ct E Spanaway (98387) ***(G-12078)***
Tortilleria Valparaiso.....509 542-1340
1108 W Sylvester St Pasco (99301) ***(G-7642)***
Toss Brion Yacht Rigging Inc.....360 385-1080
313 Jackson St Port Townsend (98368) ***(G-7932)***
Tostrz LLC.....206 595-3044
3114 Sw 172nd St Burien (98166) ***(G-2133)***
Total Battery & Automotive Sup, Olympia *Also called Murphy & Dad Inc* ***(G-7346)***
Total Building Products LLC (PA).....360 380-1100
1810 Scout Pl Ferndale (98248) ***(G-3915)***
Total Cntrl LLC.....425 446-0342
5705 Evergreen Way # 204 Everett (98203) ***(G-3634)***
Total Fabricare Llc.....206 226-3370
417 99th St E Tacoma (98445) ***(G-13559)***
Total Home Control.....509 628-1673
1231 Brentwood Ave Richland (99352) ***(G-9046)***
Total Reclaim Incorporated (PA).....206 343-7443
7021 S 220th St Kent (98032) ***(G-5184)***
Total Sign Service.....253 847-6868
44010 14th Ave E Eatonville (98328) ***(G-3070)***
Totally Blown Glassworks Inc.....206 768-8944
5607 Corson Ave S Seattle (98108) ***(G-11321)***
Totally Chocolate LLC.....360 332-3900
2025 Sweet Rd Blaine (98230) ***(G-1706)***
Totalwave Fitness LLC.....509 361-9089
1300 W Marina Dr Apt 27 Moses Lake (98837) ***(G-6754)***
Totem Electric.....253 327-1500
4310 70th Ave E Fife (98424) ***(G-3996)***
Totem Steel Inc.....425 483-6276
6017 234th St Se Woodinville (98072) ***(G-15392)***
Totten Tileworks.....360 785-3282
200 Se Front St Winlock (98596) ***(G-15157)***

Touch & Go Tees 253 651-7505
4917 63rd Ave Nw Gig Harbor (98335) *(G-4167)*
Touch Color Screen Printing 360 377-5660
2336 8th St Bremerton (98312) *(G-2007)*
Touch Mark Publishing & Print 206 551-0578
1181 Andover Park W Tukwila (98188) *(G-13827)*
Touch of West 509 962-6410
2381 Cooke Canyon Rd Ellensburg (98926) *(G-3233)*
Touch Sky Kites 360 459-2063
7635 11th Ave Se Lacey (98503) *(G-5596)*
Touche Beauty Bar LLC 360 972-2345
1912 State Ave Ne Olympia (98506) *(G-7411)*
Touchet Valley News Inc 509 382-2221
163 E Main St Dayton (99328) *(G-2887)*
Touchet Valley Publishing 509 337-6631
139 Main St Waitsburg (99361) *(G-14758)*
Touchfire Inc 425 466-4177
20206 87th Ave S Kent (98031) *(G-5185)*
Touchmark Printing 206 420-4607
7859 S 180th St Kent (98032) *(G-5186)*
Tough Outdoor Products LLC 509 621-0034
24801 E Wellesley Ave Otis Orchards (99027) *(G-7519)*
Tourmap Company 206 932-2506
1932 1st Ave Ste 625 Seattle (98101) *(G-11322)*
Tournitek Inc 423 620-5475
730 Bellevue Ave E Apt 5 Seattle (98102) *(G-11323)*
Toussint Machine and Mfg LLC 360 840-0705
307 W State St Sedro Woolley (98284) *(G-11576)*
Tova Company 800 729-2886
1832 Scott Rd Ste C5 Freeland (98249) *(G-4038)*
Towaco Screw Machine Pdts Co, Bothell *Also called Towaco Screw Mch Pdts Co LLC* *(G-1910)*
Towaco Screw Mch Pdts Co LLC 425 481-7100
16215 Sunset Rd Bothell (98012) *(G-1910)*
Tower Industries Inc 206 760-3022
5721 34th Ave E Tacoma (98443) *(G-13560)*
Tower Mountain Products 509 448-4000
5721 S Willamette Ln Spokane (99223) *(G-12564)*
Town of Garfield 509 635-1604
405 W California St Garfield (99130) *(G-4069)*
Town Smoke Plus 360 456-8234
3700 Martin Way E Ste 109 Olympia (98506) *(G-7412)*
Townsend Bay Marine LLC 360 385-3981
919 Haines Pl Port Townsend (98368) *(G-7933)*
Townsend Bay Soap Co LLC 360 379-4140
1634 Jackson St Port Townsend (98368) *(G-7934)*
Townsend Ltr For Dctors Ptents 360 385-6021
911 Tyler St Port Townsend (98368) *(G-7935)*
Townshend Cellar 509 481-5465
8022 E Greenbluff Rd Colbert (99005) *(G-2712)*
Townshend Cellar Inc 509 919-3699
1222 N Regal St Spokane (99202) *(G-12565)*
Tph Inc DBA Island Wood Works 360 403-7066
6011 199th St Ne Arlington (98223) *(G-340)*
Tr Wine, Walla Walla *Also called Waters Winery LLC* *(G-14899)*
TRA Industries Inc 509 924-5858
3808 N Sullivan Rd Bldg 2 Spokane Valley (99216) *(G-12909)*
Track Equipment Company LLC 360 201-7881
2630 Jaeger St Bellingham (98225) *(G-1573)*
Tracker Safe LLC 360 213-0363
6317 Ne 63rd St Vancouver (98661) *(G-14643)*
Tracktion Software Corporation 425 273-3376
10820 Ne 108th St Kirkland (98033) *(G-5485)*
Traction Capital Partners Inc 253 922-3090
2516 Holgate St Tacoma (98402) *(G-13561)*
Tractorco.com, Thorp *Also called Bogden Inc* *(G-13627)*
Tracys Print Shop 360 249-5575
210 E Pioneer Ave Montesano (98563) *(G-6662)*
Trade Printery LLC 206 728-1600
317 S Bennett St Seattle (98108) *(G-11324)*
Trade Printery LLC 206 241-3322
16022 Maplewild Ave Sw Burien (98166) *(G-2134)*
Trade-Marx Sign & Display Corp 206 623-7676
818 S Dakota St Seattle (98108) *(G-11325)*
Trader Bay Ltd 253 884-5249
17020 Rouse Rd Sw Lakebay (98351) *(G-5691)*
Traditional Boat Works Inc 360 379-6502
538 Fillmore St Port Townsend (98368) *(G-7936)*
Traditional Concepts 253 884-2818
10626 Wright Bliss Rd Nw Gig Harbor (98329) *(G-4168)*
Traditional Heirlooms 509 722-2620
117 N Columbus Ave Goldendale (98620) *(G-4210)*
Traffic Signs Inc 425 333-6222
2204 Fall City Carnation Carnation (98014) *(G-2301)*
Traffic Tech Inc 206 357-1141
14900 Interurban Ave S # 208 Tukwila (98168) *(G-13828)*
Traight Industries 253 630-1489
14181 Se 255th St Kent (98042) *(G-5187)*
Trail Tech Inc 360 687-4530
1600 Se 18th Ave Battle Ground (98604) *(G-748)*
Trailready Products LLC 425 353-6776
1005 W Hazel St Mount Vernon (98273) *(G-6847)*
Tramco Inc 425 347-3030
3100 112th St Sw Everett (98204) *(G-3635)*
Tramweld LLC 360 425-1240
1605 Burcham St Kelso (98626) *(G-4556)*
Tranche Cellars LLC 509 526-3500
705 Berney Dr Walla Walla (99362) *(G-14879)*
Trane Company 425 455-4148
12031 Ne Northrup 106 Bellevue (98005) *(G-1196)*
Trane US Inc 509 535-9057
10502 E Montgomery Dr # 1 Spokane Valley (99206) *(G-12910)*
Trane US Inc 425 492-2155
19201 120th Ave Ne Bothell (98011) *(G-1802)*
Trane US Inc 206 748-0500
4408 4th Ave S Seattle (98134) *(G-11326)*
Trane US Inc 425 643-4310
2333 158th Ct Ne Bellevue (98008) *(G-1197)*
Trans Pac Enterprises Inc 425 688-0037
9839 Ne 20th St Bellevue (98004) *(G-1198)*
Transact Communications Inc (PA) 425 977-2100
5105 200th St Sw Ste 200 Lynnwood (98036) *(G-6212)*
Transalta Centralia Mining LLC 360 807-8020
913 Big Hanaford Rd Centralia (98531) *(G-2438)*
Transcb-Dot Apprved Desl Tanks, Tukwila *Also called Ironclad Company* *(G-13754)*
Transco Northwest Inc (PA) 425 251-5422
22211 76th Ave S Kent (98032) *(G-5188)*
Transcold Distribution USA Inc 604 519-0600
6858 S 190th St Kent (98032) *(G-5189)*
Transformer Diagnostic Testing 425 486-4110
17529 93rd Ave Ne Bothell (98011) *(G-1803)*
Transgoods America Inc 253 661-0440
33400 9th Ave S Ste 114 Federal Way (98003) *(G-3797)*
Transition Composites Mfg Inc 360 312-1497
2321 E Bakerview Rd Ste E Bellingham (98226) *(G-1574)*
Translation Technologies, Liberty Lake *Also called T T I Acquisition Corp* *(G-5861)*
Transmarine Navigation Corp 206 525-2051
9750 3rd Ave Ne Ste 308 Seattle (98115) *(G-11327)*
Transpac Marinas Inc (PA) 360 293-8888
702 R Ave Anacortes (98221) *(G-178)*
Transparent Classroom, Seattle *Also called Lightsmith Consulting LLC* *(G-10420)*
Transport Logistics Inc 206 824-0667
19600 Intl Blvd Ste 102 Seatac (98188) *(G-9307)*
Transportation Wash State Dept 360 705-7428
310 Maple Park Dr Olympia (98504) *(G-7413)*
Transtech Materials LLC 425 402-3665
24023 26th Dr Se Bothell (98021) *(G-1911)*
Trapp Industries 509 895-4282
491 Buffalo Rd Selah (98942) *(G-11599)*
Travel Wrap, Seattle *Also called R & D Industries* *(G-10910)*
Travelers Tea Bar 206 329-6260
501 E Pine St Seattle (98122) *(G-11328)*
Traveling Designs 360 695-5887
2412 Kingfisher Ln Kelso (98626) *(G-4557)*
Travis Industries Inc (PA) 425 609-2500
12521 Harbour Reach Dr Mukilteo (98275) *(G-6983)*
Travis Pattern & Foundry Inc (PA) 509 466-3545
1413 E Hawthorne Rd Spokane (99218) *(G-12566)*
Travis Pattern & Foundry Inc 509 924-6464
3808 N Sullivan Rd Ste 4b Spokane Valley (99216) *(G-12911)*
Trax At Dupont Station 253 503-0693
1430 Wilmington Dr Dupont (98327) *(G-2973)*
Trax At Dupont Station 253 912-8729
930 Ross Loop Dupont (98327) *(G-2974)*
Treasure Valley Coffee Company, Kennewick *Also called Sirjmr Inc* *(G-4728)*
Tree Flelrs Contract Cutng Log, Belfair *Also called Jeffrey Hembury* *(G-765)*
Tree Island Fastener, Ferndale *Also called Tree Island Industries Ltd* *(G-3916)*
Tree Island Industries Ltd 360 366-0988
6980 Salashan Loop Ferndale (98248) *(G-3916)*
Tree Management Plus Inc 360 978-4305
422 Tucker Rd Toledo (98591) *(G-13644)*
Tree MGT Plus Seeding Sls, Toledo *Also called Tree Management Plus Inc* *(G-13644)*
Tree of Kindness Inc (PA) 509 315-2206
1119 W 1st Ave Spokane (99201) *(G-12567)*
Tree of Life Enterprises Inc 360 894-6038
16100 Lemuria Ln Se Yelm (98597) *(G-15748)*
Tree Top Inc (PA) 509 697-7251
220 E 2nd Ave Selah (98942) *(G-11600)*
Tree Top Inc 509 782-6809
200 Tichenal Rd Cashmere (98815) *(G-2331)*
Tree Top Inc 509 786-2926
2780 Lee Rd Prosser (99350) *(G-8069)*
Tree Top Inc 509 663-8583
3981 Chelan Hwy Wenatchee (98801) *(G-15082)*
Tree Top Inc 509 698-1447
220 E 2nd Ave Selah (98942) *(G-11601)*
Tree Top Inc 509 698-1432
101 S Railroad Ave Selah (98942) *(G-11602)*
Tree-Top Baking 360 720-1937
3650 Orcas Dr Clinton (98236) *(G-2701)*
Treit Equipment Co Inc 253 549-2399
240 Shorewood Ct Fox Island (98333) *(G-4026)*
Trejo Trejo Inc 425 298-3144
409 Ne 70th St Seattle (98115) *(G-11329)*

ALPHABETIC

Trek Global 760 576-5115
4400 Ne 77th Ave Ste 275 Vancouver (98662) *(G-14644)*

Trenzi Inc 206 769-6501
111 S Jackson St Seattle (98104) *(G-11330)*

Tresko Monument Inc (PA) 509 838-3196
1979 W 5th Ave Spokane (99201) *(G-12568)*

Treveri Cellars, Wapato Also called Grieb Optimal Winecrafting LLC *(G-14916)*

Trevors Wood Working LLC 206 940-8000
825 Ne Northgate Way Seattle (98125) *(G-11331)*

Tri City Journal of Business, Kennewick Also called Tricomp Publishing *(G-4741)*

Tri City Pallets 509 543-7500
335 E B Cir Pasco (99301) *(G-7643)*

Tri Coastal Industries 425 353-4384
4204 Russell Rd Mukilteo (98275) *(G-6984)*

Tri County Dead Stock 360 354-3173
714 E Front St Lynden (98264) *(G-6057)*

Tri County Tribune, Colville Also called Statesman-Examiner Inc *(G-2775)*

Tri County Tribune, Deer Park Also called Statesman-Examiner Inc *(G-2917)*

Tri Marine, Bellevue Also called Tri-Marine International Inc *(G-1200)*

Tri Marine Fishing MGT LLC 425 688-1288
10500 Ne 8th St Ste 1888 Bellevue (98004) *(G-1199)*

Tri States Rebar Inc 509 922-5901
7208 E Indiana Ave Spokane Valley (99212) *(G-12912)*

Tri-Cities Wheel Deals, Kennewick Also called Lee Enterprises Incorporated *(G-4688)*

Tri-City Auto Parts, Grand Coulee Also called Material Inc *(G-4243)*

Tri-City Cabinets LLC 509 946-5614
1940 Butler Loop Richland (99354) *(G-9047)*

Tri-City Glass Inc 509 586-0454
304 E Columbia Dr Kennewick (99336) *(G-4738)*

Tri-City Herald, Kennewick Also called McClatchy Newspapers Inc *(G-4693)*

Tri-City Herald, Kennewick Also called Triad Comsural Printing Corp *(G-4740)*

Tri-City Model Railroaders 509 987-7000
101 N Quebec St Kennewick (99336) *(G-4739)*

Tri-City Tees & Screen Prtg 509 420-6993
1834 Marshall Ave Richland (99354) *(G-9048)*

Tri-Cties Orthotics Prostetics, Richland Also called Yakima Orthtics Prosthetics PC *(G-9056)*

Tri-Form Top Company, Spokane Also called Tim Krotzer *(G-12558)*

Tri-Marine International Inc (PA) 425 688-1288
10500 Ne 8th St Ste 1888 Bellevue (98004) *(G-1200)*

Tri-Mechanical Inc 425 391-6016
1824 130th Ave Ne Ste 1 Bellevue (98005) *(G-1201)*

Tri-Point Industries Inc 253 514-8890
10107 74th Ave Nw Gig Harbor (98332) *(G-4169)*

Tri-Ryche Corporation 206 363-8070
10751 Densmore Ave N Seattle (98133) *(G-11332)*

Tri-Shell Cores Shop Inc 360 694-7600
1215 W 19th St Vancouver (98660) *(G-14645)*

Tri-State Machinery Inc 509 786-0400
1531 Stacy Ave Prosser (99350) *(G-8070)*

Tri-TEC Manufacturing LLC 425 251-8777
6915 S 234th St Kent (98032) *(G-5190)*

Tri-Tex Inc 360 274-8511
1140 Dougherty Dr Ne Castle Rock (98611) *(G-2356)*

Tri-Tex Oil Co, Castle Rock Also called Tri-Tex Inc *(G-2356)*

Tri-Way Industries Inc 253 859-4585
506 44th St Nw Auburn (98001) *(G-582)*

Triad Coatings Corp 253 537-4464
14307 7th Ave S Tacoma (98444) *(G-13562)*

Triad Comsural Printing Corp 509 582-1466
333 W Canal Dr Kennewick (99336) *(G-4740)*

Triad Products Corporation 425 514-8363
12414 Highway 99 Ste 40 Everett (98204) *(G-3636)*

Triadd Software Corporation 425 643-3700
13401 Ne Bel Red Rd B10 Bellevue (98005) *(G-1202)*

Triangle C Farms Inc 509 682-2189
175 Turtteman Rd Chelan (98816) *(G-2567)*

Triangle Wellness LLC 727 773-0054
394 Kirner Rd Sequim (98382) *(G-11667)*

Triarii Industries LLC 360 314-6099
15501 Nw 27th Ct Vancouver (98685) *(G-14646)*

Tribal Fishco LLC 509 493-1104
65335 Highway 14 White Salmon (98672) *(G-15134)*

Tribasix Nutrition, Chelan Also called IMS Corporation *(G-2555)*

Tribune Newspapers, Snohomish Also called Market Place Weekly Inc *(G-11943)*

Tribune Office Supply & Prtg 509 674-2511
221 N Pennsylvania Ave Cle Elum (98922) *(G-2681)*

Trick Shot Studios LLC 858 663-7097
122 109th Ave Se Bellevue (98004) *(G-1203)*

Trickinnex Tree Trimming & Fal 509 653-1937
10383 Old Naches Hwy Naches (98937) *(G-7007)*

Tricomp Publishing 509 737-8778
8919 W Grandridge Blvd Kennewick (99336) *(G-4741)*

Trident Carrollton LLC 206 783-3818
5303 Shilshole Ave Nw Seattle (98107) *(G-11333)*

Trident Sea Foods, Seattle Also called Royal Viking Inc *(G-10987)*

Trident Seafoods Asia Inc (HQ) 206 783-3818
5303 Shilshole Ave Nw Seattle (98107) *(G-11334)*

Trident Seafoods Corporation 360 734-8900
2825 Roeder Ave Bellingham (98225) *(G-1575)*

Trident Seafoods Corporation 425 407-4000
1930 Merrill Creek Pkwy B Everett (98203) *(G-3637)*

Trident Seafoods Corporation (PA) 206 783-3818
5303 Shilshole Ave Nw Seattle (98107) *(G-11335)*

Trident Seafoods Corporation 206 783-3818
653 Nw 41st St Seattle (98107) *(G-11336)*

Trident Seafoods Corporation 360 671-0669
400 W Orchard Dr Bellingham (98225) *(G-1576)*

Trident Seafoods Corporation 360 293-7701
1400 4th St Anacortes (98221) *(G-179)*

Trident Seafoods Corporation 360 293-3133
1400 3rd St Anacortes (98221) *(G-180)*

Trident Seafoods Corporation 253 502-5318
401 E Alexander Ave # 592 Tacoma (98421) *(G-13563)*

Trident Seafoods Corporation 360 740-7816
112 Sears Rd Chehalis (98532) *(G-2539)*

Triex Technologies Inc 425 363-2239
8030 Bracken Pl Se Snoqualmie (98065) *(G-12034)*

Trilion Quality Systems LLC 267 565-8062
500 Mercer St Ste C2 Seattle (98109) *(G-11337)*

Trillium Custom Software Inc 425 397-8000
17127 Ok Mill Rd Snohomish (98290) *(G-11994)*

Trim Seal USA Inc (PA) 425 867-1522
17371 Ne 67th Ct Ste A2 Redmond (98052) *(G-8694)*

Trimac Vancouver, Vancouver Also called Northwest Plywood Sales of Ore *(G-14439)*

Trimlite LLC 425 251-8685
901 Sw 39th St Renton (98057) *(G-8930)*

Trimlite Seattle Inc 425 251-8685
901 Sw 39th St Renton (98057) *(G-8931)*

Trinity Farms Inc 509 968-4107
2451 Number 81 Rd Ellensburg (98926) *(G-3234)*

Trinity Glass Intl Inc (PA) 800 803-8182
33615 1st Way S Ste A Federal Way (98003) *(G-3798)*

Trinity Manufacturing Inc 360 474-8639
19009 61st Ave Ne Unit 3 Arlington (98223) *(G-341)*

Trinity Mfg 360 474-8639
19009 61st Ave Ne Unit 3 Arlington (98223) *(G-342)*

Trio Machinery Inc 360 671-6229
1685 H St 876 Blaine (98230) *(G-1707)*

Trio Machinery U S A, Blaine Also called Trio Machinery Inc *(G-1707)*

Trio Native American Entps LLC 206 728-8181
239 Sw 41st St Renton (98057) *(G-8932)*

Triosports Usa LLC 206 953-2394
4040 23rd Ave W Seattle (98199) *(G-11338)*

Triple A Drilling Inc 509 543-3331
785 Tumbleweed Ln Burbank (99323) *(G-2086)*

Triple b Corporation 509 535-7393
3530 E Ferry Ave Spokane (99202) *(G-12569)*

Triple C Fabricators LLC 360 868-4125
3340 E Johns Prairie Rd Shelton (98584) *(G-11746)*

Triple J Farms, Bellingham Also called J J J Farms Inc *(G-1386)*

Triple P Products Inc 509 527-3131
2189 Isaacs Ave Walla Walla (99362) *(G-14880)*

Triple R Enterprises Inc 360 491-1600
1025 Kiwi Ct Nw Olympia (98502) *(G-7414)*

Triple-T Designs Inc 253 284-9200
4037 S Union Ave Tacoma (98409) *(G-13564)*

Triton Aerospace LLC 360 466-4160
813 S 2nd St La Conner (98257) *(G-5527)*

Triton Holdings Inc 360 466-4160
13593 Bayview Edison Rd Mount Vernon (98273) *(G-6848)*

Triton Print and Pour Poor 360 828-8809
8380 Ne Highway 99 Vancouver (98665) *(G-14647)*

Triumph Actuation Systems 509 248-5000
2808 W Washington Ave Yakima (98903) *(G-15696)*

Triumph Aerostructures LLC 310 355-3826
4029 Industrial Way Longview (98632) *(G-5961)*

Triumph Composite Systems Inc 509 623-8536
1514 S Flint Rd Spokane (99224) *(G-12570)*

Triumph Corporation 509 926-7000
1225 N Argonne Rd Ste A Spokane Valley (99212) *(G-12913)*

Triumph Group Inc 425 636-9000
22922 Ne Alder Crest Dr Redmond (98053) *(G-8695)*

Trivan Truck Body LLC 360 380-0773
1385 W Smith Rd Ferndale (98248) *(G-3917)*

Trivan Truck Body Texas LLC 254 799-2360
1385 W Smith Rd Ferndale (98248) *(G-3918)*

Trivitro Corporation 425 251-8340
150 Nickerson St Ste 107 Seattle (98109) *(G-11339)*

Trixie Publishing Inc 360 521-8246
203 Nw 153rd St Vancouver (98685) *(G-14648)*

Trobella Cabinetry Inc 360 947-2114
3201 Nw Lower River Rd Vancouver (98660) *(G-14649)*

Trocar Investments 253 851-9206
9303 N Harborview Dr Gig Harbor (98332) *(G-4170)*

Trogar Awning and Sunscreen Co, Tacoma Also called Troger Enterprises Ltd *(G-13565)*

Troger Enterprises Ltd 253 627-8878
1722 Tacoma Ave S Tacoma (98402) *(G-13565)*

Trojan Lithograph Corporation 425 873-2200
800 Sw 27th St Renton (98057) *(G-8933)*

Trondak Inc 360 794-8250
17631 147th St Se Ste 7 Monroe (98272) *(G-6634)*

Troop Boy Scouts of America 206 284-2164
41 Dravus St Apt 208 Seattle (98109) ***(G-11340)***
Tropic Bird LLC 360 378-5234
618 Harrison St Apt T Friday Harbor (98250) ***(G-4062)***
Tropical Sauna 509 927-7898
5205 N Harvard Rd Otis Orchards (99027) ***(G-7520)***
Trout Lake Farm LLC (PA) 509 395-2025
42 Warner Rd Trout Lake (98650) ***(G-13684)***
Trout-Blue Chelan-Magi Inc 509 689-2511
410 State Way 97 Brewster (98812) ***(G-2017)***
Tru Cut Die Inc 360 571-7158
5906 Ne 41st Ave Vancouver (98661) ***(G-14650)***
Tru Door Inc 509 545-8773
5601 W Clearwater Ave # 101 Kennewick (99336) ***(G-4742)***
Tru Line Laser Alignment Inc 360 371-0552
8231 Blaine Rd Blaine (98230) ***(G-1708)***
Tru Square Metal Products Inc 253 833-2310
640 1st St Sw Auburn (98001) ***(G-583)***
Tru Square Thumler's Tumbler, Auburn *Also called Tru Square Metal Products Inc* ***(G-583)***
Tru-Truss Inc 360 491-8024
2750 Hogum Bay Rd Ne Lacey (98516) ***(G-5597)***
Truck Accessories Group LLC 360 736-9991
2400 Commercial Rd Centralia (98531) ***(G-2439)***
Truckvault Inc (PA) 360 855-0464
315 Twnship St Sdro Wlley Sedro Woolley Sedro Woolley (98284) ***(G-11577)***
True Colors Inc 206 623-2366
1904 3rd Ave Seattle (98101) ***(G-11341)***
True Custom Cabinetry 206 909-4454
22225 76th Ave S Kent (98032) ***(G-5191)***
True Custom Cabinetry Inc 425 919-1966
15255 206th Ave Se Renton (98059) ***(G-8934)***
True Machine 425 610-9669
5410 Barrett Rd Ste B107 Ferndale (98248) ***(G-3919)***
True North Gear LLC 206 723-0735
3723 S Hudson St Seattle (98118) ***(G-11342)***
True North Trading Company, Bremerton *Also called Jett Industries Inc* ***(G-1966)***
True Seals LLC 509 385-0300
1309 N Bradley Rd Spokane Valley (99212) ***(G-12914)***
True Sol Innovations Inc 206 428-7136
8560 Greenwood Ave N Seattle (98103) ***(G-11343)***
Truegem LLC 360 836-0310
4156 Nw 12th Ave Camas (98607) ***(G-2284)***
Truegem Online, Camas *Also called Truegem LLC* ***(G-2284)***
Trueguard LLC 360 835-8547
725 S 32nd St Washougal (98671) ***(G-14995)***
Truepoint Metalworks Wldg Inc 360 273-3412
9616 James Rd Sw Rochester (98579) ***(G-9142)***
Truesonic, Seattle *Also called Resonant Systems Inc* ***(G-10952)***
Trufab LLC 360 229-3028
410 W Enterprise Rd Shelton (98584) ***(G-11747)***
Truhumic Envmtl Solutions LLC 425 232-6903
9617 48th Dr Ne Ste B Marysville (98270) ***(G-6397)***
Trulife Inc 360 714-9000
445 Sequoia Dr Ste 113 Bellingham (98226) ***(G-1577)***
Trulife Inc 360 697-5656
26284 Twelve Trees Ln Nw Poulsbo (98370) ***(G-8012)***
Trumark Industries Inc 509 534-0644
4917 N Penn Ave Spokane (99206) ***(G-12571)***
Trumpeter Public House 360 588-4515
416 Myrtle St Mount Vernon (98273) ***(G-6849)***
Trunek Enterprises Inc 360 734-6860
3883 Irongate Rd Bellingham (98226) ***(G-1578)***
Trunk Show 253 302-4301
7710 29th St W University Place (98466) ***(G-13982)***
Trus-Way Vancouver, Vancouver *Also called Parr Lumber Company* ***(G-14480)***
Truss Co 509 547-2436
355 N Commercial Ave Pasco (99301) ***(G-7644)***
Truss Companies, Tumwater *Also called Truss Components of Washington* ***(G-13901)***
Truss Company and Bldg Sup Inc 509 928-0550
118 S Union Rd Spokane Valley (99206) ***(G-12915)***
Truss Company and Bldg Sup Inc (PA) 253 863-5555
2802 142nd Ave E Sumner (98390) ***(G-13107)***
Truss Components of Washington 360 753-0057
5102 Lambskin St Sw Tumwater (98512) ***(G-13900)***
Truss Components of Washington (PA) 360 753-0057
5232 Joppa St Sw Tumwater (98512) ***(G-13901)***
Truthteller Winery 425 985-3568
7581 Old Redmond Rd Apt 1 Redmond (98052) ***(G-8696)***
Tryb Inc 206 310-9025
3817 Ne 82nd St Seattle (98115) ***(G-11344)***
Trysk Print Solutions LLC 877 605-1164
2201 3rd Ave Apt 2704 Seattle (98121) ***(G-11345)***
Tsmc Development Inc (HQ) 360 817-3000
5509 Nw Parker St Camas (98607) ***(G-2285)***
Tsue Chong Co Inc 206 623-0801
800 S Weller St Seattle (98104) ***(G-11346)***
Tsunami Products Inc 509 868-5731
1711 N Madson St Liberty Lake (99019) ***(G-5865)***
Ttf Aerospace Inc (PA) 253 736-6300
4620 B St Nw Ste 101 Auburn (98001) ***(G-584)***
TTI Inc 509 998-9456
8704 E Red Oak Dr Spokane (99217) ***(G-12572)***
Tts Old Iron Brewery LLC 509 847-4393
8707 E Honorof Ln Spokane (99223) ***(G-12573)***
Tube Art Displays Inc 509 469-8186
2323 W Washington Ave Yakima (98903) ***(G-15697)***
Tube Art Displays Inc (PA) 206 223-1122
11715 Se 5th St Ste 200 Bellevue (98005) ***(G-1204)***
Tube Crazy 206 931-7764
218 Main St Kirkland (98033) ***(G-5486)***
Tubs To Go Inc 425 348-7888
12314 Beverly Park Rd # 119 Lynnwood (98087) ***(G-6213)***
Tucannon Cellars 509 545-9588
40504 N Demoss Rd Benton City (99320) ***(G-1631)***
Tucci & Sons Inc (PA) 253 922-6676
4224 Waller Rd E Tacoma (98443) ***(G-13566)***
Tucker Distillery 360 698-7043
7501 Clover Blossom Ln Ne Bremerton (98311) ***(G-2008)***
Tucker Garner CA 206 236-0856
7256 Holly Hill Dr Mercer Island (98040) ***(G-6487)***
Tucker's Fruit & Produce, Sunnyside *Also called Rose Tucker* ***(G-13139)***
Tuckers Tuffer Coatings Inc 360 707-2168
4667 Humphrey Hill Rd Sedro Woolley (98284) ***(G-11578)***
Tudor Games Inc 800 914-8836
6852 S 224th St Kent (98032) ***(G-5192)***
Tuff Boat, Issaquah *Also called Fields Fabrication Corporation* ***(G-4413)***
Tuff Trailer Inc 360 398-0300
6742 Portal Way Ferndale (98248) ***(G-3920)***
Tuff TS Connection Screen Prtg (PA) 253 588-8897
8012 South Tacoma Way Lakewood (98499) ***(G-5763)***
Tuigis Tek LLC 360 943-9133
3419 Gibraltar Ct Se Olympia (98501) ***(G-7415)***
Tully's Coffee, Seattle *Also called Tc Global Inc* ***(G-11275)***
Tullys Cof Asia PCF Prtners LP 206 233-2070
2003 Western Ave Ste 660 Seattle (98121) ***(G-11347)***
Tumbling Leaf Press 425 885-6315
12230 Ne 32nd St Ste 210 Bellevue (98005) ***(G-1205)***
Tumwater Eye Center Inc 360 352-6060
100 Dennis St Sw Ste F Tumwater (98501) ***(G-13902)***
Tumwater Printing 360 943-2204
7675 New Market St Sw Tumwater (98501) ***(G-13903)***
Tune Inc (PA) 206 508-1318
2200 Western Ave Ste 200 Seattle (98121) ***(G-11348)***
Tungsten Cellars LLC 509 525-3672
704 Beet Rd Walla Walla (99362) ***(G-14881)***
Tunnel Hill Winery 509 682-3243
39 Knapps Coulee Rd Chelan (98816) ***(G-2568)***
Turley Log & Timberland MGT 509 239-4523
24406 S Pine Spring Rd Cheney (99004) ***(G-2594)***
Turn Pro Manufacturing 425 220-8767
938 Warner St Sedro Woolley (98284) ***(G-11579)***
Turn Pt Lghthuse Prsrvtion Soc 360 376-5246
5 Liberty Ln Orcas (98280) ***(G-7456)***
Turner Exhibits Inc 425 776-4930
5631 208th St Sw Ste B Lynnwood (98036) ***(G-6214)***
Turning Point Machining Inc 425 252-7300
710 Ash Ave Marysville (98270) ***(G-6398)***
Turtleback Press 360 376-4625
636 Wildrose Ln Eastsound (98245) ***(G-3048)***
Turtleworks 425 335-0394
6721 60th St Se Everett (98205) ***(G-3638)***
Tuuri Wines LLC 509 525-2299
45 E Main St Walla Walla (99362) ***(G-14882)***
Tuxbits Inc 302 313-6831
722 Crestview Pl Walla Walla (99362) ***(G-14883)***
Tuxedo Park, Lynnwood *Also called Formal Wear Inc* ***(G-6120)***
TV Books, Seattle *Also called Filmateria Studios Inc* ***(G-9992)***
TV Jones Inc 360 930-0418
18916 3rd Ave Ne Poulsbo (98370) ***(G-8013)***
TV Jones Guitars and Pickups, Poulsbo *Also called TV Jones Inc* ***(G-8013)***
Tvan Inc 503 285-2615
3901 Ne 68th St Vancouver (98661) ***(G-14651)***
Twardus Iron & Wire Works Inc 206 723-8234
5269 Rainier Ave S Seattle (98118) ***(G-11349)***
Tweet Promotional Impressions 206 660-6074
6646 Elizabeth Ave Se Auburn (98092) ***(G-585)***
Twelve Thirty-One Incorporated 425 656-8210
6540 S Glacier St Ste 120 Tukwila (98188) ***(G-13829)***
Twice Light Inc 360 573-6101
6137 Ne 63rd St Vancouver Vancouver (98661) ***(G-14652)***
Twilight Bedding Company Inc 509 926-2333
12013 E Trent Ave Ste W2 Spokane Valley (99206) ***(G-12916)***
Twilight Software 206 228-2037
3217 14th Ave S Seattle (98144) ***(G-11350)***
Twin Cities Printing 360 807-1200
540 N Tower Ave Centralia (98531) ***(G-2440)***
Twin City Foods Inc (PA) 206 515-2400
10120 269th Pl Nw Stanwood (98292) ***(G-12998)***
Twin City Foods Inc 509 962-9806
501 W 4th Ave Ellensburg (98926) ***(G-3235)***
Twin City Foods Inc 509 346-1483
12884 Beverly Burke Rd Sw Royal City (99357) ***(G-9177)***
Twin City Foods Inc 509 546-0850
5405 N Industrial Way Pasco (99301) ***(G-7645)***

A L P H A B E T I C

(PA)=Parent Co (HQ)=Headquarters (DH)=Div Headquarters
2019 Washington Manufacturers Register
843

Twin City Foods Inc 509 786-2700
506 6th St Prosser (99350) *(G-8071)*
Twin Country Rv Service, Deming *Also called Skandia Northwest Mfg (G-2923)*
Twin Oaks Cnstr & Metalworks, White Salmon *Also called Krista K Thie (G-15121)*
Twin Ohana Enterprises LLC (PA) 360 882-8022
11011 Ne Burton Rd Vancouver (98682) *(G-14653)*
Twin Ohana Enterprises LLC 360 314-2965
10501 Ne Highway 99 # 27 Vancouver (98686) *(G-14654)*
Twin Peaks 509 427-4759
201 Josheanka Dr Carson (98610) *(G-2309)*
Twin Peaks Cider House & Dist, Wenatchee *Also called Phillippi Fruit Co Inc (G-15062)*
Twintec Inc 253 218-0890
1510 Boundary Blvd # 110 Auburn (98001) *(G-586)*
Twirl Cafe 206 283-4552
2111 Queen Anne Ave N Seattle (98109) *(G-11351)*
Twisted Metal LLC 360 966-5309
1212 Nooksack Ave Everson (98276) *(G-3693)*
Two Blue Mules 206 935-3762
4806 25th Ave Sw Seattle (98106) *(G-11352)*
Two Dog Island Inc 206 325-0609
1118 37th Ave E Seattle (98112) *(G-11353)*
Two Harps 425 432-4128
25360 237th Pl Se Maple Valley (98038) *(G-6295)*
Two Horse Logging Inc 360 592-5244
165 S Garden St Bellingham (98225) *(G-1579)*
Two Mac Inc 206 285-3675
2144 Westlake Ave N Ste D Seattle (98109) *(G-11354)*
Two Mountain Winery 509 829-3900
2151 Cheyne Rd Zillah (98953) *(G-15762)*
Two Rivers Sand and Gravel 509 763-3280
22750 Lake Wenatchee Hwy Leavenworth (98826) *(G-5817)*
Two Sylvias Press 360 447-8735
11264 Hwy 305 Ste 204 Kingston (98346) *(G-5266)*
Two Winey Bitches Winery 509 796-3600
38278 Angels Landing Rd N Ford (99013) *(G-4006)*
Two Zero Six LLC 206 557-4384
920 S Holgate St Ste 103 Seattle (98134) *(G-11355)*
Twobitbear LLC 206 658-5797
1905 E Pine St Seattle (98122) *(G-11356)*
Twopointoh Garmes LLC 360 836-4266
3420 Oakes Ave Anacortes (98221) *(G-181)*
TX Fine Designs Inc 425 271-2866
16550 W Valley Hwy Tukwila (98188) *(G-13830)*
Ty Enterprises 509 826-6597
26 Rosewood Ln Riverside (98849) *(G-9128)*
Tyee Aircraft, Everett *Also called Avtechtyee Inc (G-3378)*
Tyee Aircraft Inc 425 290-3100
6500 Merrill Creek Pkwy Everett (98203) *(G-3639)*
Tyler Technologies Inc 360 852-6696
415 N Allen Creek Dr Ridgefield (98642) *(G-9117)*
Tyler Technologies Inc 360 352-0922
2114 Caton Way Sw Olympia (98502) *(G-7416)*
Tylohelo Inc 425 951-1120
17683 128th Pl Ne Bldg C Woodinville (98072) *(G-15393)*
Tymers Camra Sp Reprographics, Vancouver *Also called Harold Tymer Co Inc (G-14284)*
Tymlez Inc 630 215-7878
600 1st Ave Ste 441 Seattle (98104) *(G-11357)*
Type Cellar, Tukwila *Also called Mary Fleming (G-13768)*
Typebee Lttrpress Prntshop LLC 509 979-6017
914 S Monroe St Spokane (99204) *(G-12574)*
Typesetter Corporation 425 455-3055
9675 Se 36th St Ste 110 Mercer Island (98040) *(G-6488)*
Tyron Global Company 360 734-1789
715 W Orchard Dr Ste 3 Bellingham (98225) *(G-1580)*
Tyson Foods Inc 509 547-7545
13983 Dodd Rd Wallula (99363) *(G-14912)*
Tyson Nutraceuticals Inc 425 869-1192
6531 132nd Ave Ne Kirkland (98033) *(G-5487)*
U Deck It Inc 509 532-9007
5524 E Cataldo Ave Spokane Valley (99212) *(G-12917)*
U Don LLC 206 466-1471
1640 12th Ave Seattle (98122) *(G-11358)*
U E T, Mukilteo *Also called Unienergy Technologies LLC (G-6985)*
U S A Today, Bellevue *Also called Gannett Co Inc (G-918)*
U S Fire Equipment LLC 253 863-1301
4200 150th Avenue Ct E Sumner (98390) *(G-13108)*
U S Practical Shooting Assn 360 855-2245
1639 Lindamood Ln Burlington (98233) *(G-2195)*
U S Scale Incorporated 253 872-4803
8702 S 222nd St Kent (98031) *(G-5193)*
U S Sheet Metal Company Inc 253 272-2444
1325 South Tacoma Way Tacoma (98409) *(G-13567)*
U S Wax & Polymer Inc 509 922-1069
17625 E Euclid Ave Spokane Valley (99216) *(G-12918)*
U-Pull-It Auto Parts Inc 509 895-7655
14 E Washington Ave Yakima (98903) *(G-15698)*
U2 Inc 360 627-8068
5830 W Werner Rd Bremerton (98312) *(G-2009)*
Uav Systems Development Corp 803 767-1351
509 N Bluff West Dr Moses Lake (98837) *(G-6755)*
Ubi Interactive Inc 206 457-2493
1818 Westlake Ave N # 317 Seattle (98109) *(G-11359)*
Ucoinitcom LLC 253 271-0656
18517 111th Ave E Puyallup (98374) *(G-8265)*
Udabomb Bath Bombs 509 331-4100
215 N 14th Ave Othello (99344) *(G-7508)*
Ufp Washington LLC 509 663-1988
4234 Malaga Alcoa Hwy Malaga (98828) *(G-6233)*
Ufp Washington LLC (HQ) 360 568-3185
12027 3 Lakes Rd Snohomish (98290) *(G-11995)*
Ufp Washington LLC 509 966-4610
51 N Mitchell Dr Yakima (98908) *(G-15699)*
Ukush Print and Mail 206 763-0454
2645 S Warsaw St Seattle (98108) *(G-11360)*
Ulis Famous Sausage Inc 206 839-1000
1511 Pike Place Market Seattle (98101) *(G-11361)*
Ulis Famous Sausage LLC 206 839-1000
1511 Pike Pl Seattle (98101) *(G-11362)*
Ulrich Peterson Trucking, Chehalis *Also called Ulrich Trucking Incorporate (G-2540)*
Ulrich Trucking Incorporate 360 748-0026
120 Cabe Rd Chehalis (98532) *(G-2540)*
Ultimate Ears, Camas *Also called Logitech Inc (G-2266)*
Ultimate Intr-Prximal Solution, Vancouver *Also called Contacez LLC (G-14149)*
Ultimate Mtal Fabrications LLC 206 356-9666
330 Sw 43rd St Ste D Renton (98057) *(G-8935)*
Ultimate Product Corp 425 788-7500
20910 Ne 156th St Woodinville (98077) *(G-15394)*
Ultimate Rack Inc 509 393-3526
331 Valley Mall Pkwy # 215 East Wenatchee (98802) *(G-3033)*
Ultimate Seal LLC 866 567-9149
22419 Pacific Hwy S Des Moines (98198) *(G-2948)*
Ultimate Sheepskin 253 677-4384
16014 245th St E Graham (98338) *(G-4240)*
Ultra Carbon 253 922-4266
10203 Lakeview Ave Sw Lakewood (98499) *(G-5764)*
Ultra Paper Co LLC 425 443-5505
15729 142nd Pl Se Renton (98058) *(G-8936)*
Ultra Van Krome Prductions LLC 206 859-3459
13125 Spanaway Loop Rd S Tacoma (98444) *(G-13568)*
Ultra Yield Micronutrients Inc 509 248-4911
213 W Moxee Ave Moxee (98936) *(G-6888)*
Ultrabac Software Inc 425 644-6000
15015 Main St Ste 200 Bellevue (98007) *(G-1206)*
Ultrablock Inc 360 694-0141
815 Ne 172nd Ave Vancouver (98684) *(G-14655)*
Ultrafino Panama Hat, Lynnwood *Also called Tomatesa Enterprises LLC (G-6211)*
Ultrakote, Kent *Also called Litho-Craft Inc (G-4997)*
Ultrashred LLC 509 244-1894
409 N Thierman Rd Ste A Spokane Valley (99212) *(G-12919)*
Ultrashred Sales and Service, Spokane Valley *Also called Ultrashred LLC (G-12919)*
Ultrasonics International Corp 360 676-0056
7044 Portal Way Ferndale (98248) *(G-3921)*
Uluwatu 206 852-7289
4817 44th Ave S Seattle (98118) *(G-11363)*
Umbra Cuscinetti Incorporated 425 405-3500
6707 Hardeson Rd Everett (98203) *(G-3640)*
Umlaut Software Inc 919 321-8324
870 Snoqualm Pl North Bend (98045) *(G-7130)*
Unauthorized Screen Printing 425 224-5602
700 Nw 42nd St Ste 105 Seattle (98107) *(G-11364)*
Unauthorized Screen Printing 425 502-1150
6701 Greenwood Ave N Seattle (98103) *(G-11365)*
Uncaged Creations LLC 509 397-3873
1954 Penawawa Rd Lacrosse (99143) *(G-5604)*
Uncle Woody's Caramel Corn, Seattle *Also called Seattle Popcorn Company Inc (G-11068)*
Uncorked Canvas 253 301-1254
711 St Helens Ave Ste 202 Tacoma (98402) *(G-13569)*
Undead Labs LLC 206 452-0590
308 Occidental Ave S Seattle (98104) *(G-11366)*
Underground1969 Co 747 254-0595
2606 2nd Ave Seattle (98121) *(G-11367)*
Underhorse Entertainment Inc 760 216-0164
6007 150th Ct Ne Redmond (98052) *(G-8697)*
Undershirt Inc 360 740-8048
143 Crest Ln Chehalis (98532) *(G-2541)*
Underwood Fruit & Whse Co LLC (PA) 509 457-6177
401 N 1st Ave Yakima (98902) *(G-15700)*
Unfors Raysafe Inc (HQ) 508 435-5600
6920 Seaway Blvd Everett (98203) *(G-3641)*
Unibest International LLC 509 525-3370
3301 Isaacs Ave Walla Walla (99362) *(G-14884)*
Unicon Inc 425 454-2466
11834 Ne 90th St Kirkland (98033) *(G-5488)*
Unicon International Inc 253 539-7533
7502 135th Street Ct E Puyallup (98373) *(G-8266)*
UNICON INTERNATIONAL INCORPORATED, Puyallup *Also called Unicon International Inc (G-8266)*
Unicorn Booty, Seattle *Also called Skyfish Media LLC (G-11132)*
Unienergy Technologies LLC 425 290-8898
4333 Harbour Pt Blvd Sw Mukilteo (98275) *(G-6985)*
Unified Screening & Crushing 253 872-6595
22020 72nd Ave S Kent (98032) *(G-5194)*
Unified Scrning Crshing-WA LLC 800 562-1971
22020 72nd Ave S Kent (98032) *(G-5195)*

Unifire Inc 509 535-7746
3904 E Trent Ave Spokane (99202) ***(G-12575)***
Uniform Destination, Burlington *Also called Uniform Factory Outl Ariz LLC* ***(G-2196)***
Uniform Factory Outl Ariz LLC 360 707-2608
240 Fashion Way Burlington (98233) ***(G-2196)***
Uniform Trading Company, Bremerton *Also called New Uniformity LLC* ***(G-1980)***
Unify, Normandy Park *Also called Add Corporation* ***(G-7089)***
Unigen Inc 360 486-8200
3005 1st Ave Seattle (98121) ***(G-11368)***
Unilode AVI Solution US Inc (HQ) 206 824-7123
1808 B St Nw Ste 170 Auburn (98001) ***(G-587)***
Uninterruptible Power Systems 509 327-7722
3003 N Crestline St Spokane (99207) ***(G-12576)***
Unionbay Sportswear Juniors, Kent *Also called Seattle Pacific Industries* ***(G-5123)***
Unipar West Inc 360 293-5332
619 30th St Anacortes (98221) ***(G-182)***
Unique Allscapes 425 309-6325
5129 Evergreen Way Everett (98203) ***(G-3642)***
Unique Art Glass LLC 425 467-5599
2619 127th Ave Ne Bellevue (98005) ***(G-1207)***
Unique Beverage Company LLC 425 267-0959
7620 Hardeson Rd Everett (98203) ***(G-3643)***
Unique TS Printing 253 686-3669
1750 Jackson Ave Se # 16 Port Orchard (98366) ***(G-7854)***
Unique Wreaths 206 355-2103
375 Union Ave Se Unit 94 Renton (98059) ***(G-8937)***
Unisource Manufacturing Inc 253 854-0541
1037 4th Ave N Kent (98032) ***(G-5196)***
Unite Seattle Publishing, Seattle *Also called Mike Montgomery* ***(G-10542)***
Unite Stares Arospace, Seatac *Also called Monroe Machined Products Inc* ***(G-9291)***
United American Inc 360 371-7709
8346 Blaine Rd Blaine (98230) ***(G-1709)***
United Association of Journeym 206 441-0737
2800 1st Ave Ste 3 Seattle (98121) ***(G-11369)***
United Contact Lens Inc 360 474-9577
19111 61st Ave Ne Unit 5 Arlington (98223) ***(G-343)***
United Electric Motors Inc 206 624-0044
1510 Nw 46th St Seattle (98107) ***(G-11370)***
United Farms 253 847-4230
23212 86th Ave E Graham (98338) ***(G-4241)***
United Games 360 470-6480
40 Cedar Creek Rd Oakville (98568) ***(G-7176)***
United Home Technologies LLC 360 574-7737
4060 S Grant St Ste 106 Washougal (98671) ***(G-14996)***
United Iron Works Inc 206 767-3630
2215 Davis Ct Ne Tacoma (98422) ***(G-13570)***
United Machine Shops Inc 206 767-0100
9448 17th Ave Sw Seattle (98106) ***(G-11371)***
United Manufacturing Products 425 433-1141
20317 244th Ave Se Maple Valley (98038) ***(G-6296)***
United Print Signs Graphics, Seattle *Also called United Reprographics L L C* ***(G-11372)***
United Reprographics L L C 206 382-1177
1750 4th Ave S Seattle (98134) ***(G-11372)***
United Sales Inc 509 225-0636
1917 S 14th St Union Gap (98903) ***(G-13955)***
United Seating & Mobility LLC 509 484-6720
423 E Cleveland Ave Spokane (99207) ***(G-12577)***
United Sorbents Midwest, Kent *Also called United Sorbents Seattle LLC* ***(G-5197)***
United Sorbents Seattle LLC (HQ) 425 656-4440
18821 90th Ave S Kent (98031) ***(G-5197)***
United Stars Aerospace Inc 253 859-4540
1422 S 192nd St Seatac (98148) ***(G-9308)***
United States Bakery 206 726-7535
2006 S Weller St Seattle (98144) ***(G-11373)***
United States Bakery 509 684-6976
183 Buena Vista Dr Colville (99114) ***(G-2778)***
United States Bakery 509 535-7726
110 N Fancher Rd Spokane Valley (99212) ***(G-12920)***
United States Bakery 206 682-2244
2901 6th Ave S Seattle (98134) ***(G-11374)***
United States Dept of Navy 360 396-2340
610 Dowell St Keyport (98345) ***(G-5247)***
United States Dosimetry Tech 509 946-8738
660 George Washington Way A Richland (99352) ***(G-9049)***
United States Electric Corp 360 427-4218
1101 E Lake Trask Rd Grapeview (98546) ***(G-4291)***
United States Gypsum Company 253 931-6600
401 C St Nw Auburn (98001) ***(G-588)***
United States Sheepskin Inc 253 627-7114
450 Fawcett Ave Tacoma (98402) ***(G-13571)***
United Visual Comms Grp LLC 206 228-5144
1750 4th Ave S Seattle (98134) ***(G-11375)***
United Volleyball Supply LLC 425 576-8835
14615 Ne 91st St Ste B Redmond (98052) ***(G-8698)***
United Western Tech Corp (PA) 509 544-0720
122 S 4th Ave Pasco (99301) ***(G-7646)***
Universal Aerospace Co Inc 360 435-9577
18640 59th Dr Ne Arlington (98223) ***(G-344)***
Universal Alloy Corporation 253 350-4079
5450 Beach Dr Sw Seattle (98136) ***(G-11376)***
Universal Avonics Systems Corp 425 821-2800
11351 Willows Rd Ne Redmond (98052) ***(G-8699)***
Universal Brass Inc 253 939-8282
131 30th St Ne Ste 25 Auburn (98002) ***(G-589)***
Universal Coatings LLC 360 936-2855
215 Turner Ave Apt A103 Shelton (98584) ***(G-11748)***
Universal Engine Heater Co 509 276-5923
6333b Rocky Pines Way Nine Mile Falls (99026) ***(G-7084)***
Universal Forest Products, Snohomish *Also called Ufp Washington LLC* ***(G-11995)***
Universal Paper Box, Seatac *Also called Northwest Paper Box Mfrs Inc* ***(G-9293)***
Universal Plant Services of No 360 757-4646
245 N Hill Blvd Burlington (98233) ***(G-2197)***
Universal Refiner Corporation 360 249-4415
458 Wynooche Valley Rd Montesano (98563) ***(G-6663)***
Universal Repair Shop Inc 206 322-2726
1611 Boylston Ave Seattle (98122) ***(G-11377)***
Universal Sheet Metal Inc 425 483-8384
14400 Ne N Wodinville Way Woodinville (98072) ***(G-15395)***
Universal Sign and Graphics 253 630-0400
14408 Se 256th Pl Kent (98042) ***(G-5198)***
Universal Stl Fabricators LLC 253 891-4224
525 E 15th St Tacoma (98421) ***(G-13572)***
Universal Vault of Washington 360 834-4086
1711 Se 279th Ave Camas (98607) ***(G-2286)***
Universal Wallbeds, Redmond *Also called Wallbeds Northwest Inc* ***(G-8708)***
Universe Builders Inc 206 390-4313
999 3rd Ave Ste 700 Seattle (98104) ***(G-11378)***
University Brass, Monroe *Also called Rainbow Metals Inc* ***(G-6612)***
University News and Info Svc, Seattle *Also called University of Washington* ***(G-11384)***
University of Washington 206 543-5680
3900 7th Ave Ne Seattle (98195) ***(G-11379)***
University of Washington 206 543-2565
4333 Brooklyn Ave Ne Seattle (98195) ***(G-11380)***
University of Washington 206 543-4598
115 Lewis Hall Seattle (98195) ***(G-11381)***
University of Washington 206 543-5680
3900 7th Ave Ne Seattle (98195) ***(G-11382)***
University of Washington 206 543-4050
1326 5th Ave Ste 555 Seattle (98101) ***(G-11383)***
University of Washington 206 543-2580
B54 Gerberding Hall Seattle (98195) ***(G-11384)***
University Publications/Prntng, Pullman *Also called Washington State University* ***(G-8112)***
University Reprographics Inc 206 633-0925
150 Nickerson St Ste 109 Seattle (98109) ***(G-11385)***
University Swaging Corporation (HQ) 425 318-1965
610 Bellevue Way Ne # 200 Bellevue (98004) ***(G-1208)***
University Swaging Corporation 425 318-4500
6525 240th St Se Woodinville (98072) ***(G-15396)***
Uniwest, Pasco *Also called United Western Tech Corp* ***(G-7646)***
Unix Packages LLC 206 310-4610
9257 9th Ave Nw Seattle (98117) ***(G-11386)***
Unlimited Possibilities Now 206 930-9100
20118 107th Ave Ne Bothell (98011) ***(G-1804)***
Unmanned Aerial Systems Dev, Moses Lake *Also called Uav Systems Development Corp* ***(G-6755)***
Up To Grade Concrete Products 253 845-3677
811 7th St Nw Puyallup (98371) ***(G-8267)***
Up4u Inc 206 660-8498
3034 Cloverfield Dr Se Olympia (98501) ***(G-7417)***
Upchurch Scientific, Oak Harbor *Also called Idex Health & Science LLC* ***(G-7153)***
Upland Winery LLC 509 839-2606
3073 Emerald Rd Sunnyside (98944) ***(G-13146)***
Upper Cut Woodworks LLC 425 785-4817
23515 Ne Novelty Hill Rd Redmond (98053) ***(G-8700)***
Upright Posts LLC 253 224-0076
902 Kincaid Ave Sumner (98390) ***(G-13109)***
UPS, Federal Way *Also called Dr Ventures Inc* ***(G-3733)***
UPS Customer Center, Forks *Also called Olympic Graphic Arts Inc* ***(G-4013)***
UPS Store 5427, Redmond *Also called Jack Just Enterprises LLC* ***(G-8518)***
Upstart Industries LLC 206 265-1521
1803 Nw 83rd St Seattle (98117) ***(G-11387)***
Uptake Medical Technology Inc (PA) 206 926-7405
936 N 34th St Ste 200 Seattle (98103) ***(G-11388)***
Uptop Imaging, Tacoma *Also called Shepp Enterprises LLC* ***(G-13512)***
Urban Accessories Inc 253 572-1112
465 E 15th St Tacoma (98421) ***(G-13573)***
Urban Buggy Farm, The, Seattle *Also called Urban Buggy LLC* ***(G-11389)***
Urban Buggy LLC 206 743-5727
308 22nd Ave S Ste 101 Seattle (98144) ***(G-11389)***
Urban Cabinets 425 286-2977
19300 144th Ave Ne Woodinville (98072) ***(G-15397)***
Urban Diamond Tools 206 824-6819
23260 25th Ave S Des Moines (98198) ***(G-2949)***
Urban Family Brewing Co 206 861-6769
4441 26th Ave W Seattle (98199) ***(G-11390)***
Urban Press Inc 206 325-4060
317 S Bennett St Seattle (98108) ***(G-11391)***
Urban Stoneworks LLC 808 333-6675
252 N Green Gables Loop Ridgefield (98642) ***(G-9118)***
Urethane Cast Parts Inc 253 539-4282
5612 163rd St E Puyallup (98375) ***(G-8268)***
Urethane Technologies, Monroe *Also called Northwest Inc* ***(G-6602)***

ALPHABETIC

(PA)=Parent Co (HQ)=Headquarters (DH)=Div Headquarters
2019 Washington Manufacturers Register
845

Urns Throgh Time, McCleary *Also called Dugger and Associates Inc* ***(G-6415)***
US Attachments Inc......360 501-4484
211 Hazel St Kelso (98626) ***(G-4558)***
US Biopharma Inc......425 242-0208
4710 140th Ave Ne Bellevue (98005) ***(G-1209)***
US Builders Team LLC......425 466-2611
7438 159th Pl Ne Redmond (98052) ***(G-8701)***
US Castings LLC......509 784-1001
14351 Shamel St Entiat (98822) ***(G-3272)***
US Cryogenics Inc......360 835-2475
1422 E St Washougal (98671) ***(G-14997)***
US Dies Inc......509 248-0404
315 S 4th Ave Yakima (98902) ***(G-15701)***
US Fab......206 623-1635
1801 16th Ave Sw Seattle (98134) ***(G-11392)***
US Federal Shredding, Cheney *Also called Shredsupply Inc* ***(G-2593)***
US Filter Vancouver......360 892-6977
11606 Ne 66th Cir Vancouver (98662) ***(G-14656)***
US Hospitality Publishers Inc......615 956-0080
1406 Se 164th Ave Ste 200 Vancouver (98683) ***(G-14657)***
US Marine Chemists & Engrg......206 200-6912
4986 Dover Ct Mukilteo (98275) ***(G-6986)***
US Mat Systems LLC......509 763-4000
17400 Winton Rd Leavenworth (98826) ***(G-5818)***
US Micro, Bellevue *Also called US Micro Pc Inc* ***(G-1210)***
US Micro Pc Inc......425 462-7300
13600 Ne 20th St Ste C Bellevue (98005) ***(G-1210)***
US Mill Works LLC......206 355-5143
2203 N 59th St Seattle (98103) ***(G-11393)***
US Mower Inc......360 757-7555
11949 Westar Ln Burlington (98233) ***(G-2198)***
US Natural Resources Inc......360 841-6346
1981 Schurman Way Woodland (98674) ***(G-15469)***
US Oil & Refining Co (HQ)......253 383-1651
3001 Marshall Ave Tacoma (98421) ***(G-13574)***
US Polyco Inc......509 413-1006
8914 N Torrey Ln Spokane (99208) ***(G-12578)***
US Printing, Seattle *Also called Jet City Imaging LLC* ***(G-10293)***
US Sign Girl......801 644-1108
772 Big Tree Dr Nw Issaquah (98027) ***(G-4485)***
US Sign One LLC......253 236-8074
7808 River Rd E Puyallup (98371) ***(G-8269)***
US Starcraft Corporation......206 762-0607
703 30th Ave Apt B Seattle (98122) ***(G-11394)***
US Syntec, Yakima *Also called US Syntec Corporation* ***(G-15702)***
US Syntec Corporation......509 452-4476
2809 Fruitvale Blvd Yakima (98902) ***(G-15702)***
US Water Services Inc......360 695-1270
2700 W Firestone Ln Vancouver (98660) ***(G-14658)***
US Workboats Inc (PA)......360 808-2292
60 Airpark Rd Sequim (98382) ***(G-11668)***
USA Milk Processing LLC......202 657-5399
120 State Ave Ne Ste 1014 Olympia (98501) ***(G-7418)***
USA Oil LLC......425 226-5555
3002 Ne Sunset Blvd Renton (98056) ***(G-8938)***
USA Printing Corporation......206 682-2423
2010 Ne 137th St Seattle (98125) ***(G-11395)***
Usbdrive, Kent *Also called Jmtek LLC* ***(G-4969)***
USI Commerical, Arlington *Also called Rescom Railing Systems LLC* ***(G-314)***
Usjade LLC......509 535-3411
3606 N Garry Rd Otis Orchards (99027) ***(G-7521)***
Usl Technologies LLC......360 379-0684
260 Kala Heights Dr Port Townsend (98368) ***(G-7937)***
Usnr LLC (PA)......360 225-8267
1981 Schurman Way Woodland (98674) ***(G-15470)***
Usnr LLC......360 225-8267
1981 Schurman Way Woodland (98674) ***(G-15471)***
Uswp Manufacuring, Spokane Valley *Also called U S Wax & Polymer Inc* ***(G-12918)***
UTC Aerospace Systems, Spokane *Also called Collins Aerospace* ***(G-12187)***
UTC Aerospace Systems, Kirkland *Also called Goodrich Corporation* ***(G-5351)***
Ute Ltd......206 510-8621
12622 4th Ave Sw Burien (98146) ***(G-2135)***
Utec Metals Inc......509 891-7833
17305 E Euclid Ave Spokane Valley (99216) ***(G-12921)***
Utilikilts Co LLC......206 282-4226
620 1st Ave Seattle (98104) ***(G-11396)***
Utilities Service Company Inc......206 246-5674
12608 E Marginal Way S Tukwila (98168) ***(G-13831)***
Utility Supply Group......360 626-1086
24355 Nordvie Pl Nw Poulsbo (98370) ***(G-8014)***
Utr Manufacturing Inc......360 901-1435
8010 Ne 19th Ct Vancouver (98665) ***(G-14659)***
Utrip Inc......509 954-9393
2101 4th Ave Ste 1020 Seattle (98121) ***(G-11397)***
Uv Systems Inc......425 228-9988
16605 127th Ave Se Renton (98058) ***(G-8939)***
V 4 Software LLC......813 870-6666
4271 E Lake Sammamish Sammamish (98075) ***(G-9256)***
V F Services Inc Jansport......425 407-4040
1202 Shuksan Way Everett (98203) ***(G-3644)***
V O Printers Inc......360 577-0038
1213 14th Ave Longview (98632) ***(G-5962)***
V S P Jewelry Design Gallery......206 367-7310
17171 Bothell Way Ne A137 Lake Forest Park (98155) ***(G-5626)***
V&C LLC......509 773-1976
9774 Highway 14 Goldendale (98620) ***(G-4211)***
V-Care Health Systems Inc......509 670-9068
2601 N Alder St Ellensburg (98926) ***(G-3236)***
Vaagen Bros Lumber Inc (PA)......509 684-5071
565 W 5th Ave Colville (99114) ***(G-2779)***
Vaagen Timbers LLC......509 684-5071
1245 North Highway Colville (99114) ***(G-2780)***
Vaccines 2 U......509 475-1347
17110 E Daybreak Ln Spokane Valley (99016) ***(G-12922)***
Vacupractor, Redmond *Also called Cornerstone Attache Group Inc* ***(G-8426)***
Valberg Mfg Inc......206 920-1296
316 181st Pl Sw Bothell (98012) ***(G-1912)***
Valco Instruments Company LP......360 697-9199
26295 Twelve Trees Ln Nw Poulsbo (98370) ***(G-8015)***
Valcom Inc......509 865-5511
1111 Buena Rd Buena (98921) ***(G-2081)***
Valcon Games LLC......425 223-4672
16701 Ne 80th St Ste 204 Redmond (98052) ***(G-8702)***
Valence Surface Tech LLC......206 762-5855
8135 1st Ave S Seattle (98108) ***(G-11398)***
Valhalla Brewing and Bev Co LL......206 243-6346
402 Baker Blvd Tukwila (98188) ***(G-13832)***
Validigm Biotechnology Inc......415 205-3377
3417 Evanston Ave N # 327 Seattle (98103) ***(G-11399)***
Valin Corporation......509 924-4914
3808 N Sullivan Rd 18p Spokane Valley (99216) ***(G-12923)***
Valley Aero Mfg......206 841-9652
314 Williams Ave S # 4141 Renton (98057) ***(G-8940)***
Valley Automotive Machine......360 336-9722
331 E Blackburn Rd Mount Vernon (98273) ***(G-6850)***
Valley Bugler LLC......360 414-1246
15554 207th Pl Se Renton (98059) ***(G-8941)***
Valley Cabinet Shop Inc......509 786-2717
22502 S Ward Gap Rd Prosser (99350) ***(G-8072)***
Valley Cabinets & More Inc......360 428-0916
18362 Burkland Rd Mount Vernon (98274) ***(G-6851)***
Valley Fuel LLC......509 937-2230
3080 Highway 231 Valley (99181) ***(G-13995)***
Valley Graphics Inc......509 937-4055
3091 5th Ave Valley (99181) ***(G-13996)***
Valley Instant Printing Inc......509 924-8040
1014 N Pines Rd Ste 118 Spokane Valley (99206) ***(G-12924)***
Valley Machine & Manufacturing, Puyallup *Also called B G Bender Inc* ***(G-8125)***
Valley Machine and Fabrication, Winthrop *Also called Rams Head Construction Inc* ***(G-15164)***
Valley Machine Shop Inc......425 226-5040
1166 6th Ave N Kent (98032) ***(G-5199)***
Valley Manufactured Hsing Inc......509 839-9409
1717 S 4th St Sunnyside (98944) ***(G-13147)***
Valley Orthopedics Inc......509 922-5040
509 N Homestead Dr Liberty Lake (99019) ***(G-5866)***
Valley Printing Inc......253 845-0960
4601 6th Street Pl Se A Puyallup (98374) ***(G-8270)***
Valley Processing, Sunnyside *Also called Mountain Valley Products Inc* ***(G-13134)***
Valley Processing Inc (PA)......509 837-8084
108 Blaine Ave Sunnyside (98944) ***(G-13148)***
Valley Publishing Company Inc......509 882-3712
308 Division St Grandview (98930) ***(G-4256)***
Valley Publishing Company Inc (PA)......509 786-1711
613 7th St Prosser (99350) ***(G-8073)***
Valley Rubber & Gasket, Kent *Also called Lewis-Goetz and Company Inc* ***(G-4994)***
Valley Steel & Stone......360 378-5758
2435 San Juan Valley Rd Friday Harbor (98250) ***(G-4063)***
Valley Supply Company (PA)......360 217-4400
8310 Maltby Rd Woodinville (98072) ***(G-15398)***
Valleyford Metal Crafters LLC......509 448-5583
6313 E Rutter Ave Spokane (99212) ***(G-12579)***
Valmet Inc......253 927-2200
34320 Pacific Hwy S Federal Way (98003) ***(G-3799)***
Valmet Inc......360 753-8831
9730 Lathrop Indus Dr Olympia (98512) ***(G-7419)***
Valmont Industries Inc......509 921-0290
12720 E Nora Ave Ste A Spokane Valley (99216) ***(G-12925)***
Valmont Northwest Inc (HQ)......509 547-1623
4225 N Capitol Ave Pasco (99301) ***(G-7647)***
Valon Kone North America......509 434-6436
3808 N Sullivan Rd Spokane Valley (99216) ***(G-12926)***
Valtech......360 779-6748
610 Nw Gurley Ct Poulsbo (98370) ***(G-8016)***
Value Plus......509 468-0393
9623 N Indian Trail Rd Spokane (99208) ***(G-12580)***
Valve Adjusters Co Intl......425 322-4241
10711 Washington Way Everett (98204) ***(G-3645)***
Vamco Ltd Inc......509 877-2138
5250 Yakima Valley Hwy Wapato (98951) ***(G-14927)***
Vampt America Inc (PA)......800 508-6149
2212 Queen Anne Ave N Seattle (98109) ***(G-11400)***
Vampt Beverage USA Corp......800 508-6149
2212 Queen Anne Ave N Seattle (98109) ***(G-11401)***

Van Brynns Wheelchair......360 687-8546
8319 Ne 316th St La Center (98629) ***(G-5518)***
Van Dam Welding Inc......360 761-7297
28421 112th St E Buckley (98321) ***(G-2078)***
Van Doren Sales Inc (PA)......509 886-1837
10 Ne Cascade Ave East Wenatchee (98802) ***(G-3034)***
Van Dyk & Son Logging Inc......360 592-5951
5240 Mosquito Lake Rd Deming (98244) ***(G-2925)***
Van Dyke Logging Incorporated......509 442-3852
221 Mckay St Ione (99139) ***(G-4376)***
Van Essen Instruments Division......520 203-3445
12123 Harbour Reach Dr Mukilteo (98275) ***(G-6987)***
Van Harten......360 868-2011
318 Mill St Shelton (98584) ***(G-11749)***
Van Horn Mfd Homes......253 370-7263
15216 91st Avenue Ct E Puyallup (98375) ***(G-8271)***
Van Orman Guitars LLC......253 269-8660
179 S Union Rd Elma (98541) ***(G-3258)***
Van Quill Larry R......360 736-1776
712 W Main St Centralia (98531) ***(G-2441)***
Van's Cabinet Shop, Lynden *Also called Vans Cabinets LLC* ***(G-6059)***
Vana Life Foods LP......347 446-6504
98 S Jackson St Seattle (98104) ***(G-11402)***
Vanarnam Vineyards......360 904-4800
1305 Gilbert Rd Zillah (98953) ***(G-15763)***
Vanatoo LLC......206 486-1002
28838 52nd Pl S Auburn (98001) ***(G-590)***
Vancouver Business Journal, Vancouver *Also called Warrior Brown Publishing LLC* ***(G-14677)***
Vancouver Business Journal......360 695-2442
1251 Officers Row Vancouver (98661) ***(G-14660)***
Vancouver Button Makers, Vancouver *Also called Yvette J Cooke* ***(G-14707)***
Vancouver Door Company Inc......253 845-9581
203 5th St Nw Puyallup (98371) ***(G-8272)***
Vancouver Foundry Company......360 695-3914
1200 W 13th St Vancouver (98660) ***(G-14661)***
Vancouver Iron & Steel Inc......360 695-3914
1200 W 13th St Vancouver (98660) ***(G-14662)***
Vancouver Iron and Steel, Vancouver *Also called Varicast Inc* ***(G-14666)***
Vancouver Sign Co Inc......360 693-4773
2600 Ne Andresen Rd # 50 Vancouver (98661) ***(G-14663)***
Vancouver Woodworks Inc......360 696-8590
3000 Ne Andresen Rd A101 Vancouver (98661) ***(G-14664)***
Vandalez Industries Inc......509 228-9000
3020 N Sullivan Rd Ste E Spokane Valley (99216) ***(G-12927)***
Vandermeer Forest Products Inc......360 657-2518
1364 State Ave Bldg B Marysville (98270) ***(G-6399)***
Vanderpol Building Components......360 354-5883
841 E Badger Rd Lynden (98264) ***(G-6058)***
Vanetten Fine Art......509 928-2385
626 N Best Rd Spokane Valley (99216) ***(G-12928)***
Vanex Industries LLC......206 860-0455
186 35th Ave E Seattle (98112) ***(G-11403)***
Vanguard Foods......206 355-5938
3416 B St Nw Ste C Auburn (98001) ***(G-591)***
Vanguard Press......206 782-1448
8300 Greenwood Ave N Seattle (98103) ***(G-11404)***
Vanities......425 453-5353
1405 132nd Ave Ne Bellevue (98005) ***(G-1211)***
Vans Inc......360 254-3075
8700 Ne Vncvr Mll Dr 25 Vancouver (98662) ***(G-14665)***
Vans Cabinets LLC......360 354-5845
426 E Wiser Lake Rd Lynden (98264) ***(G-6059)***
Vansh Foods LLC......425 743-1043
13414 11th Pl W Everett (98204) ***(G-3646)***
Vanwerven Inc......360 435-2600
17928 59th Ave Ne Arlington (98223) ***(G-345)***
Vaporpath Inc......306 208-2747
9300 North Town Dr Ne Bainbridge Island (98110) ***(G-680)***
Vaportech Solutions LLC......888 746-8955
10011 3rd Ave Se Ste J Everett (98208) ***(G-3647)***
Varicast, Vancouver *Also called Vancouver Iron & Steel Inc* ***(G-14662)***
Varicast Inc (PA)......360 816-7350
1200 W 13th St Vancouver (98660) ***(G-14666)***
Variety Show Studios LLC......571 242-1724
1545 Nw Market St Apt 205 Seattle (98107) ***(G-11405)***
Varsity Communications Inc......425 412-7070
4114 198th St Sw Ste 5 Lynnwood (98036) ***(G-6215)***
Varsity Screen Prtg & Awards......509 829-3700
905 Vintage Valley Pkwy Zillah (98953) ***(G-15764)***
Vartan Product Support LLC......425 374-8914
Mukilteo Speedway Ste 204 Mukilteo (98275) ***(G-6988)***
Vashon Island Technology, Vashon *Also called M M Enterprises* ***(G-14731)***
Vashon Trading Co LLC......206 463-2278
25826 75th Ave Sw Vashon (98070) ***(G-14746)***
Vashon-Mury Island Beachcomber, Vashon *Also called Sound Publishing Inc* ***(G-14744)***
Vaughan Co Inc (PA)......360 249-4042
364 Monte Elma Rd Montesano (98563) ***(G-6664)***
Vaupell Industrial Plas Inc (HQ)......206 784-9050
1144 Nw 53rd St Seattle (98107) ***(G-11406)***
Vaupell Molding & Tooling Inc (HQ)......206 784-9050
1144 Nw 53rd St Seattle (98107) ***(G-11407)***
Vaupell NW Molding & Tooling, Everett *Also called Vaupell Rapid Solutions* ***(G-3648)***
Vaupell Rapid Solutions......206 784-9050
11323 Commando Rd W Everett (98204) ***(G-3648)***
Vavako Fine Chocolates......425 453-4553
10149 Main St Bellevue (98004) ***(G-1212)***
Vbs Reachout Adventures......206 365-0860
14830 Wallingford Ave N Shoreline (98133) ***(G-11819)***
Veatch Custom Cabinetry LLC......425 418-3693
22620 29th Pl Ne Granite Falls (98252) ***(G-4287)***
Vector Blue Services LLC......425 219-2528
10900 Ne 4th St Ste 2300 Bellevue (98004) ***(G-1213)***
Vector R&D Inc (PA)......877 883-7455
2810 69th Ave W University Place (98466) ***(G-13983)***
Vector Research & Development, University Place *Also called Vector R&D Inc* ***(G-13983)***
Vectored Solutions Inc......425 355-8038
9800 29th Ave W Unit E101 Everett (98204) ***(G-3649)***
Vectra Fitness Inc......425 291-9550
18840 Se 42nd St Issaquah (98027) ***(G-4486)***
Vehicle Licensing......360 336-9348
700 S 2nd St Ste 201 Mount Vernon (98273) ***(G-6852)***
Vehicle Monitor Corporation......425 881-5560
6825 176th Ave Ne Ste 100 Redmond (98052) ***(G-8703)***
Velendo Inc (PA)......360 828-7174
6501 Ne 47th Ave Vancouver (98661) ***(G-14667)***
Velotron Heavy Industries......206 799-5089
3515 Meridian Ave N Seattle (98103) ***(G-11408)***
Vendorhawk Inc......360 903-3744
12038 70th Pl S Seattle (98178) ***(G-11409)***
Venetian Interiors, Woodinville *Also called Venetian Stone Works LLC* ***(G-15399)***
Venetian Stone Works LLC......425 486-1234
16110 Woodinville Redmond Woodinville (98072) ***(G-15399)***
Vennco Rubber Inc......360 249-6924
285 Geissler Rd Montesano (98563) ***(G-6665)***
Venspark Inc......206 588-2756
2700 4th Ave S Seattle (98134) ***(G-11410)***
Ventec Life Systems Inc......425 686-1728
22002 26th Ave Se Ste 104 Bothell (98021) ***(G-1913)***
Venture Pacific Marine, Seattle *Also called Stabbert Mrtime Yacht Ship LLC* ***(G-11175)***
Venturi Holdings LLC......206 305-0642
719 S Monroe St Seattle (98108) ***(G-11411)***
Venus Gusmer, Kent *Also called Pmc Inc* ***(G-5068)***
Venus Laboratories Inc......360 455-8933
8735 Commerce Place Dr Ne Lacey (98516) ***(G-5598)***
Veracious Printing LLC......360 823-7395
11301 Ne 7th St Apt H5 Vancouver (98684) ***(G-14668)***
Verallia......206 762-0660
5801 E Marginal Way S Seattle (98134) ***(G-11412)***
Verathon Inc (HQ)......425 867-1348
20001 North Creek Pkwy Bothell (98011) ***(G-1805)***
Verax Chemical Co......360 668-2431
20102 Broadway Ave Snohomish (98296) ***(G-11996)***
Verdesian Life Science US LLC......919 825-1901
821 S Chestnut Ave Pasco (99301) ***(G-7648)***
Vergent Software......425 880-4158
27915 Ne 26th St Redmond (98053) ***(G-8704)***
Vergon Medical Products, Mount Vernon *Also called National Wirecraft Company Inc* ***(G-6816)***
Vericlouds......844 532-5332
555 8th Ave Seattle (98125) ***(G-11413)***
Veritas Custom Woodworks......425 346-5576
17725 17th Ave W Lynnwood (98037) ***(G-6216)***
Verizon Communications Inc......425 641-5900
14510 Ne 20th St Bellevue (98007) ***(G-1214)***
Verlindas......253 437-5217
22510 43rd Ave S Kent (98032) ***(G-5200)***
Vernon Publications LLC......425 488-3211
12437 Ne 173rd Pl Woodinville (98072) ***(G-15400)***
Verns Moses Lake Meats Inc......509 765-5671
3954 Mae Valley Rd Ne Moses Lake (98837) ***(G-6756)***
Verns Rent It......360 458-3302
19302 Elderberry St Sw Rochester (98579) ***(G-9143)***
Verone Sausage Company......253 759-7532
1456 S Ferdinand Dr Tacoma (98405) ***(G-13575)***
Veronica Dlndba Gold Star Pubg......360 398-2446
4764 Corona Ct Bellingham (98226) ***(G-1581)***
Versaly Games Inc......425 577-0208
1065 1st Pl Se Issaquah (98027) ***(G-4487)***
Versatile Machining Inc......206 855-8296
7873 Ne Day Rd W Bainbridge Island (98110) ***(G-681)***
Vertek Ois Inc......425 455-9921
3910 S Union Ct Spokane Valley (99206) ***(G-12929)***
Verti Technology Group Inc......425 279-1200
3600 136th Pl Se Ste 400 Bellevue (98006) ***(G-1215)***
Vertical Dimensions LLC......206 767-8022
1115 Andover Park W Tukwila (98188) ***(G-13833)***
Vertical Gardens Northwest LLC......425 891-7183
2808 16th St Everett (98201) ***(G-3650)***
Vertical Lift Solutions......360 928-1126
763 Oxenford Rd Port Angeles (98363) ***(G-7751)***
Vertical Limits LLC......509 294-9878
4116 W Indian Trail Rd Spokane (99208) ***(G-12581)***

ALPHABETIC

Vertical Technologies 509 382-2119
609 S 5th St Dayton (99328) ***(G-2888)***
Vertical Visual Solutions 425 361-1562
7036 220th St Sw Mountlake Terrace (98043) ***(G-6873)***
Vertical Welder 360 265-5457
4851 Geiger Rd Se Port Orchard (98367) ***(G-7855)***
Vertical Works LLC 509 251-0513
13120 W Meadow Lake Rd Cheney (99004) ***(G-2595)***
Vertiv, Kirkland *Also called Avocent Redmond Corp* ***(G-5287)***
Vertx Industries LLC 206 619-1479
32319 Se 42nd Ln Fall City (98024) ***(G-3709)***
Verzitelle LLC 360 829-1628
13119 Fettig Rd E Buckley (98321) ***(G-2079)***
Ves Company Inc 206 940-5742
20416 Richmond Bch Dr Nw Shoreline (98177) ***(G-11820)***
Vesi, Spokane Valley *Also called Virtual Education Software Inc* ***(G-12931)***
Vessel Printing Studio 360 441-4622
107 Grand Ave Bellingham (98225) ***(G-1582)***
Vessels Archtctral Woodturning 509 927-0721
6801 E 3rd Ave Spokane Valley (99212) ***(G-12930)***
Vesta, Bellevue *Also called Precision Appliance Technology* ***(G-1079)***
Vestas-American Wind Tech Inc 509 382-1800
517 Cameron St Dayton (99328) ***(G-2889)***
Vestcom Retail Solutions, Auburn *Also called Electronic Imaging Svcs Inc* ***(G-432)***
Vestdavit Inc 425 355-4652
170 W Dayton St Ste 101 Edmonds (98020) ***(G-3160)***
Vetch Construction LLC 425 387-3244
159 Chelsea Ln Camano Island (98282) ***(G-2226)***
Veteran Awards Inc 360 925-6019
3416 97th Dr Se Lake Stevens (98258) ***(G-5673)***
Veterans Express 253 517-3798
1300 Sw Campus Dr 14-7 Federal Way (98023) ***(G-3800)***
Veterans Memorial Pro Shop, Walla Walla *Also called We-Man Vets Golf Inc* ***(G-14900)***
Veva Company LLC 360 687-8550
20117 Ne 279th St Battle Ground (98604) ***(G-749)***
Vevaco, Battle Ground *Also called Veva Company LLC* ***(G-749)***
Vf Outdoor LLC 425 455-7349
1001 Bellevue Sq Bellevue (98004) ***(G-1216)***
Via Airlift Inc 206 258-6844
815 Industry Dr Tukwila (98188) ***(G-13834)***
Viar Visual Communications 425 391-8443
20867 Se 20th St Sammamish (98075) ***(G-9257)***
Viavi Solutions Inc 425 398-1298
22215 26th Ave Se Bothell (98021) ***(G-1914)***
Vibratrim LLC 253 238-0675
5114 Point Fosdick Dr Nw Gig Harbor (98335) ***(G-4171)***
Vici Metronics Inc 360 697-9199
26295 Twelve Trees Ln Nw Poulsbo (98370) ***(G-8017)***
Vicis Inc 206 456-6680
570 Mercer St Seattle (98109) ***(G-11414)***
Victor Gutierrez 509 301-4915
2316 Garrison St Walla Walla (99362) ***(G-14885)***
Victorian Hearts 509 926-1425
20419 E 1st Ave Greenacres (99016) ***(G-4303)***
Victories Organic Gardens, Kettle Falls *Also called China Bend Vineyards* ***(G-5228)***
Victory Circle Signs 509 489-3083
2212 E Decatur Ave Spokane (99208) ***(G-12582)***
Victory Enterprises LLC 360 420-1161
1510 Windsor Dr Mount Vernon (98273) ***(G-6853)***
Victory Millwork LLC 360 592-6090
2077 Main St Lynden (98264) ***(G-6060)***
Vidor 425 827-9967
13002 Ne 101st Pl Kirkland (98033) ***(G-5489)***
Vietnam Filter Project 425 772-5401
14831 19th Ave W Lynnwood (98087) ***(G-6217)***
Vietnamese Baptist Church Tin 360 953-8311
7814 Ne 20th St Vancouver (98664) ***(G-14669)***
Vietnamese NW Newsppr & Annual 206 722-6984
6951 M L King Jr Way S Seattle (98118) ***(G-11415)***
Vietnamese NW Newsppr & Yellow, Seattle *Also called Vietnamese NW Newsppr & Annual* ***(G-11415)***
View Point Global Inc 206 714-4884
1700 7th St Ave Ste 110 Seattle (98101) ***(G-11416)***
Vigor Alaska, Port Angeles *Also called Vigor Industrial LLC* ***(G-7752)***
Vigor Fab LLC 206 623-1635
1801 16th Ave Sw Seattle (98134) ***(G-11417)***
Vigor Industrial LLC 360 457-8470
202 N Cedar St Ste 1 Port Angeles (98363) ***(G-7752)***
Vigor Industrial LLC 253 627-9136
313 E F St Tacoma (98421) ***(G-13576)***
Vigor Marine LLC 253 627-9136
313 E F St Tacoma (98421) ***(G-13577)***
Vigor Marine LLC 206 623-1635
1801 16th Ave Sw Seattle (98134) ***(G-11418)***
Vigor Marine Tacoma, Tacoma *Also called Vigor Marine LLC* ***(G-13577)***
Vigor Shipyards Inc 206 623-1635
1801 16th Ave Sw Seattle (98134) ***(G-11419)***
Vigor Works LLC 360 699-1547
3515 Se Columbia Way 48 Vancouver (98661) ***(G-14670)***
Vigor Works LLC 360 694-7636
3515 Se Columbia Way Vancouver (98661) ***(G-14671)***
Viking Cabinets Inc 253 875-1555
24215 Mountain Hwy E Spanaway (98387) ***(G-12079)***
Viking Fire 206 715-8052
4710 Ballard Ave Nw Seattle (98107) ***(G-11420)***
Viking Industrial Group Inc 360 666-1110
2118 Se 12th Ave Ste 104 Battle Ground (98604) ***(G-750)***
Viking Packaging Machinery (PA) 509 452-7143
3800 W Washington Ave Yakima (98903) ***(G-15703)***
Village Frame & Gallery 206 824-3068
22507 Marine View Dr S Des Moines (98198) ***(G-2950)***
Villas Josey 360 405-1944
3451 Partridge Holw Ne Bremerton (98310) ***(G-2010)***
Vilma Signs, Federal Way *Also called Vilmas Family Corporation* ***(G-3801)***
Vilmas Family Corporation 253 941-9008
30432 Military Rd S Federal Way (98003) ***(G-3801)***
Vimly Benefit Solutions Inc 425 771-7359
12121 Harbour Reach Dr Mukilteo (98275) ***(G-6989)***
Vin Du Lac Winery 509 682-2882
105 Highway 150 Chelan (98816) ***(G-2569)***
Vinal Letter Specialist, Carnation *Also called Traffic Signs Inc* ***(G-2301)***
Vincent R Taylor 509 397-3305
100 E Upton St Colfax (99111) ***(G-2722)***
Vindico Printing and Design 425 329-4739
2100 196th St Sw Ste 117 Lynnwood (98036) ***(G-6218)***
Vinegar & Oil 425 454-8497
2086 Bellevue Sq Bellevue (98004) ***(G-1217)***
Vinmotion Wines LLC 509 967-7477
8111 Keene Rd West Richland (99353) ***(G-15103)***
Vino Aquino Tacoma Inc 253 272-5511
4417 6th Ave Tacoma (98406) ***(G-13578)***
Vino Verite 206 324-0324
4908 Rainier Ave S Ste C Seattle (98118) ***(G-11421)***
Vintage ADS 253 278-3297
2207 144th St E Tacoma (98445) ***(G-13579)***
Vintage Embroidery 360 668-1923
15723 Broadway Ave Snohomish (98296) ***(G-11997)***
Vintage Idaho Prints 509 217-8453
19711 W Mcfarlane Rd Medical Lake (99022) ***(G-6445)***
Vintage Investments Inc 360 293-2596
3014 Commercial Ave Ste D Anacortes (98221) ***(G-183)***
Vintage Quilting 253 852-6596
20004 106th Ave Se Kent (98031) ***(G-5201)***
Vinyl Lab NW LLC 425 870-8702
16401 43rd Pl W Lynnwood (98087) ***(G-6219)***
Vinyl Status 206 601-3598
10710 Ne 10th St Apt 504 Bellevue (98004) ***(G-1218)***
Vioguard Inc 425 280-7735
19201 120th Ave Ne # 200 Bothell (98011) ***(G-1806)***
Vioguard LLC 425 406-8009
12220 113th Ave Ne # 100 Kirkland (98034) ***(G-5490)***
Viper Protective Coatings, Vancouver *Also called Polyurethane Sales & Svc LLC* ***(G-14494)***
Viper R/C Solutions Inc 425 968-5389
2731 152nd Ave Ne Redmond (98052) ***(G-8705)***
Viper RC Solutions, Redmond *Also called Viper R/C Solutions Inc* ***(G-8705)***
Viper Tactical LLC 425 341-0529
107 Jordan Rd Salkum (98582) ***(G-9181)***
Virgil L L C Fax Company, Onalaska *Also called Birchfield Winery Inc* ***(G-7446)***
Viridian Sciences Inc 360 719-4451
2114 Main St Ste 101 Vancouver (98660) ***(G-14672)***
Virtual Education Software Inc 509 891-7219
16201 E Ind Ave Ste 1450 Spokane Valley (99216) ***(G-12931)***
Virtual Imprints LLC 425 998-9994
330 102nd Ave Se Bellevue (98004) ***(G-1219)***
Virtual Professional Audio, Vashon *Also called Nickolay Philip and Wendy LLC* ***(G-14736)***
Virtual Stream 206 938-3886
9751 43rd Pl Sw Seattle (98136) ***(G-11422)***
Virtual Timbers Inc 509 935-4680
2126 Old Hwy Nw Chewelah (99109) ***(G-2609)***
Vishay Precision Group Inc 253 872-1910
5920 S 194th St Kent (98032) ***(G-5202)***
Vision Leadership Inc 206 418-0808
14306 22nd Ave Ne Seattle (98125) ***(G-11423)***
Vision Press Inc 206 782-8476
4018 2nd Ave Nw Seattle (98107) ***(G-11424)***
Vision Woodworks 425 432-6772
21639 290th Ave Se Maple Valley (98038) ***(G-6297)***
Vision X Offroad LLC 888 489-9820
1601 Boundary Blvd Auburn (98001) ***(G-592)***
Vision X Offroad Lighting, Auburn *Also called Vision X Offroad LLC* ***(G-592)***
Visions In Print, Vancouver *Also called Thompson Litho Group Inc* ***(G-14634)***
Visiprinting 253 565-4713
2014 112th St E Tacoma (98445) ***(G-13580)***
Visitors Guide Publications, Bellingham *Also called Visual Communications Dev* ***(G-1583)***
Vista Copy and Print 206 715-2011
12354 15th Ave Ne Ste E Seattle (98125) ***(G-11425)***
Vista Precision Solutions Inc 908 829-3471
2350 Lindberg Loop Richland (99354) ***(G-9050)***
Vistaprint 617 838-2434
11287 Borgen Loop Gig Harbor (98332) ***(G-4172)***
Vistaprint 703 868-1794
12545 Phinney Ave N Seattle (98133) ***(G-11426)***

Vistaprint 206 973-0324
3406 18th Ave S Seattle (98144) ***(G-11427)***
Visual Communications Dev 360 676-8625
215 W Holly St Ste H24 Bellingham (98225) ***(G-1583)***
Visual Health Information, Tacoma *Also called Stretching Charts Inc* ***(G-13528)***
Visual Options Inc 253 472-1440
4302 S Washington St C Tacoma (98409) ***(G-13581)***
Visual Print Solutions, Black Diamond *Also called Abcd Ventures LLC* ***(G-1644)***
Visual Verve Design Print LLC 509 773-4596
2308 Centerville Hwy Centerville (98613) ***(G-2378)***
Vital Choice Seafood Spc 360 325-0104
615 17th St Bellingham (98225) ***(G-1584)***
Vital Force Publishing LLC 253 350-6359
5922 16th Street Ct Ne Tacoma (98422) ***(G-13582)***
Vital Juice Co Inc 206 258-4203
1424 4th Ave Ste 800 Seattle (98101) ***(G-11428)***
Vital Signs Ministries 360 659-2726
6118 Mission Beach Rd Tulalip (98271) ***(G-13846)***
Vital Signs Notary 206 387-6622
14641 Se 276th Pl Kent (98042) ***(G-5203)***
Vitamin Shoppe Industries Inc 855 715-8530
15870 1st Ave S Burien (98148) ***(G-2136)***
Vitamin Shoppe Industries Inc 855 235-9431
26710 Maple Vlly Blck Dia Maple Valley (98038) ***(G-6298)***
Viterra USA LLC 509 349-8464
1875 W 1st St Warden (98857) ***(G-14936)***
Viva Publishing 360 394-3756
1995 Miss Ellis Loop Ne Poulsbo (98370) ***(G-8018)***
Vivasource Inc 253 627-3853
3131 S Lawrence St Tacoma (98409) ***(G-13583)***
Vivid Learning Systems Inc 509 545-1800
5728 Bedford St Pasco (99301) ***(G-7649)***
Vivonet Halo Pos, Bellingham *Also called Vivonet Incorporated* ***(G-1585)***
Vivonet Incorporated (PA) 866 512-2033
1225 E Sunset Dr Ste 14 Bellingham (98226) ***(G-1585)***
Vivos Inc 509 736-4000
11316 W Court St Pasco (99301) ***(G-7650)***
Vixon Corporation 360 607-5817
3315 Ne 112th Ave Ste 51 Vancouver (98682) ***(G-14673)***
Vixon Custom Cabinets, Vancouver *Also called Vixon Corporation* ***(G-14673)***
Vleds 360 543-5700
130 W Axton Rd Bellingham (98226) ***(G-1586)***
Vm Products, Puyallup *Also called Vm Solutions Inc* ***(G-8273)***
Vm Solutions Inc 253 841-2939
11208 62nd Ave E Puyallup (98373) ***(G-8273)***
VMS, Kent *Also called Valley Machine Shop Inc* ***(G-5199)***
Vn Graphics, Redmond *Also called Hazelwood Farm LLC* ***(G-8489)***
Vodka Is Vegan LLC 206 278-4257
1425 Broadway Ste 474 Seattle (98122) ***(G-11429)***
Voice of The Valley, Covington *Also called Hipple Family Ltd Liability Co* ***(G-2829)***
Voicelever Inc 425 864-7676
7349 148th Ave Ne Redmond (98052) ***(G-8706)***
Voise Susage By Schumacher Inc 509 982-2956
7 S Ist St Odessa (99159) ***(G-7193)***
Voiss Wood Products Inc 360 794-1062
14582 172nd Dr Se Ste 5 Monroe (98272) ***(G-6635)***
Volant Aerospace Holdings LLC 360 757-2376
11817 Westar Ln Burlington (98233) ***(G-2199)***
Volcanic Bikes, North Bonneville *Also called Volcanic Manufacturing LLC* ***(G-7136)***
Volcanic Manufacturing LLC 509 427-8623
28 Cbd Mall St North Bonneville (98639) ***(G-7136)***
Volometrix Inc 425 706-7507
1 Microsoft Way Redmond (98052) ***(G-8707)***
Voltaire Inc 425 274-7000
40 Lake Bellevue Dr # 100 Bellevue (98005) ***(G-1220)***
Von Grey Custom Cabinets Inc 360 679-8641
920 Silver Lake Rd Oak Harbor (98277) ***(G-7166)***
Vose Technical Systems Inc (PA) 253 272-7273
711 Commerce St Ste 12 Tacoma (98402) ***(G-13584)***
Voyager Rcordings Publications 206 323-1112
424 35th Ave Seattle (98122) ***(G-11430)***
VPI, Spokane *Also called Jeld-Wen Holding Inc* ***(G-12331)***
Vpt Inc 425 353-3010
19909 120th Ave Ne # 102 Bothell (98011) ***(G-1807)***
Vrieze & Olson Custom Wdwkg 253 445-9733
2313 E Pioneer Puyallup (98372) ***(G-8274)***
Vs Foods LLC 425 279-8089
728 177th Ln Ne Bellevue (98008) ***(G-1221)***
Vsp, Lacey *Also called Capitol Optical Corp* ***(G-5538)***
Vts, Tacoma *Also called Vose Technical Systems Inc* ***(G-13584)***
Vts Aviation LLC 253 272-7273
711 Commerce St Ste 12 Tacoma (98402) ***(G-13585)***
Vue Internationalk Ltd 206 878-1061
3237 S 202nd St Seatac (98198) ***(G-9309)***
Vulcan Global LLC 509 528-2000
2014 W 6th Ave Kennewick (99336) ***(G-4743)***
Vulcan Global Solutions, Kennewick *Also called Vulcan Global LLC* ***(G-4743)***
Vulcan Oracle 360 609-9272
815 E 20th St Vancouver (98663) ***(G-14674)***
Vulcan Performance 360 450-4237
2112 Ne 236th St Ridgefield (98642) ***(G-9119)***
Vulcan Products Company Inc 425 806-6000
6210 234th St Se Woodinville (98072) ***(G-15401)***
Vulcan Software LLC 206 407-3057
14416 18th Ave W Lynnwood (98087) ***(G-6220)***
Vulcan Technologies LLC 206 342-2000
505 5th Ave S Ste 900 Seattle (98104) ***(G-11431)***
W & S Enterprises 253 848-9189
12602 106th Avenue Ct E Puyallup (98374) ***(G-8275)***
W B & L Machine Inc 360 225-5020
1665 Schurman Way Woodland (98674) ***(G-15472)***
W B Mason Co Inc 888 926-2766
18351 Cascade Ave S Tukwila (98188) ***(G-13835)***
W C I, Shoreline *Also called West Coast Industries Inc* ***(G-11821)***
W H Autopilots Inc 206 780-2175
12685 Miller Rd Ne # 1400 Bainbridge Island (98110) ***(G-682)***
W K O, Carson *Also called Wilkins Kaiser & Olsen Inc* ***(G-2310)***
W R Meadows Inc 707 745-6666
826 3rd Ave S Kent (98032) ***(G-5204)***
W Systems 425 616-2512
906 14th Ave E Seattle (98112) ***(G-11432)***
W W Wells, Everett *Also called Wells Ww Millwork LLC* ***(G-3654)***
W-4 Construction Inc 509 529-1603
1646 University Dr Walla Walla (99362) ***(G-14886)***
WA Cutting and Logging 360 520-0464
1648 Us Highway 12 Ethel (98542) ***(G-3352)***
Wabo, Lacey *Also called Washington Assn Bldg Officials* ***(G-5599)***
Wachtler Inc 253 225-1904
6659 Kimball Dr Ste D404 Gig Harbor (98335) ***(G-4173)***
Waddell Woodworking LLC 503 752-1940
12323 Ne 39th St Vancouver (98682) ***(G-14675)***
Wade Sumpter Industries Inc 425 486-9541
17321 31st Dr Se Bothell (98012) ***(G-1915)***
Wafer Reclaim Services LLC 360 254-0221
12117 Ne 99th St Ste 1900 Vancouver (98682) ***(G-14676)***
Wafertech LLC 360 817-3000
5509 Nw Parker St Camas (98607) ***(G-2287)***
Waft Corp 425 743-4601
9806 Marine View Dr Mukilteo (98275) ***(G-6990)***
Wagging Tails Vineyard 509 847-5287
9419 E Big Meadows Rd Chattaroy (99003) ***(G-2454)***
Wagstaff Inc (PA) 509 922-1404
3910 N Flora Rd Spokane Valley (99216) ***(G-12932)***
Wahkiakum County Eagle, Cathlamet *Also called Bob Nelson* ***(G-2360)***
Wahluke Wine Company Inc 509 932-0030
23934 Road T.1 Sw Mattawa (99349) ***(G-6413)***
Wahoo Fabrication 360 353-3478
1171 3rd Ave Longview (98632) ***(G-5963)***
Waite Speciality Mch Work Inc 360 577-0777
1356 Tennant Way Longview (98632) ***(G-5964)***
Waiv Aerospace LLC 206 276-2306
11747 Ne 1st St Ste 201 Bellevue (98005) ***(G-1222)***
Wakefield Art 425 260-0257
11203 100th Ave Ne Kirkland (98033) ***(G-5491)***
Wal Med Inc 253 845-6633
11302 164th St E Puyallup (98374) ***(G-8276)***
Wala Wala Winery, Walla Walla *Also called Ww Village Winery* ***(G-14905)***
Waldon Abel Guide Pins LLC 509 684-2009
1467 Onion Creek Rd Colville (99114) ***(G-2781)***
Walflor Industries 425 766-4161
4820 Whitney St Bellingham (98229) ***(G-1587)***
Waliser Winery LLC 509 522-4206
1956 J B George Rd Walla Walla (99362) ***(G-14887)***
Walker Blocker, Seattle *Also called Allied Body Works Inc* ***(G-9381)***
Walker Custom Cabinets, Kirkland *Also called Silvan Craft Inc* ***(G-5462)***
Walker Engine & Machine, Chehalis *Also called Kenneth Walker* ***(G-2508)***
Walker Goldsmiths 360 758-2601
2603 Finkbonner Rd Bellingham (98226) ***(G-1588)***
Walla Walla Environmental Inc 509 522-0490
4 E Rees Ave Walla Walla (99362) ***(G-14888)***
Walla Walla Farmers Co Op 509 529-5750
928 W Main St Walla Walla (99362) ***(G-14889)***
Walla Walla Foundry Inc (PA) 509 522-2114
405 Woodland Ave Walla Walla (99362) ***(G-14890)***
Walla Walla Foundry Inc 509 525-5690
944 N 9th Ave Walla Walla (99362) ***(G-14891)***
Walla Walla Gravel & Rock Llc 509 301-1050
1133 Smith Rd Walla Walla (99362) ***(G-14892)***
Walla Walla Motor Supply Inc 509 525-2940
1830 Isaacs Ave Walla Walla (99362) ***(G-14893)***
Walla Walla Sprinkler Comp, Walla Walla *Also called Nelson Irrigation Corporation* ***(G-14850)***
Walla Walla Sweets 509 522-2255
109 E Main St Ste C Walla Walla (99362) ***(G-14894)***
Walla Walla Union Bulletin 509 525-3300
112 S 1st Ave Walla Walla (99362) ***(G-14895)***
Walla Walla Valley Mobile LLC 509 386-8549
349 Ne Myra Rd College Place (99324) ***(G-2730)***
Walla Walla Vintners LLC 509 525-4724
225 Vineyard Ln Walla Walla (99362) ***(G-14896)***
Walla Walla Wines LLC 509 526-9463
5641 Old Highway 12 Walla Walla (99362) ***(G-14897)***
Wallbeds Northwest Inc 206 256-1700
2801 1st Ave Ste D Seattle (98121) ***(G-11433)***

ALPHABETIC

Wallbeds Northwest Inc (PA) 425 284-6692
17646 Ne 65th St Redmond (98052) ***(G-8708)***

Wallfam Inc 509 786-2163
1520 Sheridan Ave Prosser (99350) ***(G-8074)***

Walls Vineyards 509 876-0200
1015 W Pine St Walla Walla (99362) ***(G-14898)***

Walman Optical 425 462-2576
1247 120th Ave Ne Bellevue (98005) ***(G-1223)***

Walman Optical Company 253 872-7137
20417 80th Ave S Kent (98032) ***(G-5205)***

Walt Racing LLP 253 847-8221
5110 184th St E Tacoma (98446) ***(G-13586)***

Walter Dacon Wines, Shelton *Also called Anderson Resources Inc* ***(G-11678)***

Walton Beverage Co 360 380-1660
1350 Pacific Pl Ferndale (98248) ***(G-3922)***

Walts Organic Fert Co Inc 206 297-9092
2209 W Elmore St Seattle (98199) ***(G-11434)***

Wanderback Distillery LLC 206 390-7530
333 W Kinnear Pl Seattle (98119) ***(G-11435)***

Wane Flitch 253 414-2783
701 E 72nd St Tacoma (98404) ***(G-13587)***

Wapato Independent, Toppenish *Also called Flint Publishing Inc* ***(G-13669)***

Wapato Pawn & Trade 509 877-6405
201 S Wapato Ave Wapato (98951) ***(G-14928)***

Wapenish Sand & Gravel, Toppenish *Also called D & S Rock LLC* ***(G-13665)***

Wapiti Woolies Inc 360 663-2268
58414 State Route 410 E Enumclaw (98022) ***(G-3326)***

Warden Fluid Dynamics, Spokane Valley *Also called George W Warden Co Inc* ***(G-12716)***

Warden Welding Inc 509 349-2478
116 N Ash Ave Warden (98857) ***(G-14937)***

Wargaming Seattle Inc 425 250-0209
500 108th Ave Ne Ste 300 Bellevue (98004) ***(G-1224)***

Warm Company, The, Lynnwood *Also called Warm Products Inc* ***(G-6221)***

Warm Products Inc (PA) 425 248-2424
5529 186th Pl Sw Lynnwood (98037) ***(G-6221)***

Warmington & North Co Inc 206 324-5043
3408 Densmore Ave N Seattle (98103) ***(G-11436)***

Warners Cabinets 425 222-7386
33516 Se 114th St Issaquah (98027) ***(G-4488)***

Warren Hartz 360 793-0691
51211 Avenue A Index (98256) ***(G-4372)***

Warren Welding 425 761-1777
8824 60th St Ne Marysville (98270) ***(G-6400)***

Warriners Originals Inc 509 973-2705
15702 N Rothrock Rd Prosser (99350) ***(G-8075)***

Warrington Publications 425 793-9629
11100 Se Petrovitsky Rd A104 Renton (98055) ***(G-8942)***

Warrington Studios, Cheney *Also called Richard Warrington* ***(G-2592)***

Warrior Brown Publishing LLC 360 695-2442
1251 Officers Row Vancouver (98661) ***(G-14677)***

Washigton Field Services Inc 253 813-6681
11325 Se 264th Pl Kent (98030) ***(G-5206)***

Washington Agricultural Dev 509 865-2121
201 Elmwood Rd Toppenish (98948) ***(G-13673)***

Washington Alder LLC 360 542-1900
13421 Farm To Market Rd Mount Vernon (98273) ***(G-6854)***

Washington Assn Bldg Officials 360 628-8321
4405 7th Ave Se Ste 205 Lacey (98503) ***(G-5599)***

Washington Assn of Sheriffs 360 438-6618
3060 Willamette Dr Ne # 200 Lacey (98516) ***(G-5600)***

Washington Auto Carriage, Spokane Valley *Also called Fabrication & Truck Eqp Inc* ***(G-12698)***

Washington Beef LLC 509 865-2121
201 Elmwood Rd Toppenish (98948) ***(G-13674)***

Washington Bio-Oils Inc 509 713-3299
2720 Crimson Way Richland (99354) ***(G-9051)***

Washington Biodiesel LLC 206 297-6107
1730 Nw Greenbrier Way Seattle (98177) ***(G-11437)***

Washington Chain & Supply Inc (HQ) 206 623-8500
2901 Utah Ave S Seattle (98134) ***(G-11438)***

Washington Cncil Plice Sheriff 360 352-8224
200 Union Ave Se Olympia (98501) ***(G-7420)***

Washington Crab Producers Inc (HQ) 360 268-9161
1980 N Nyhus St Westport (98595) ***(G-15107)***

Washington Crane Hoist Co Inc 360 694-9844
4707 Ne Minnehaha St # 503 Vancouver (98661) ***(G-14678)***

Washington Design Center, Lynnwood *Also called Cypress Semiconductor Corp* ***(G-6104)***

Washington Dily Dcsion Svc LLC 206 250-1138
7018 19th Ave Nw Seattle (98117) ***(G-11439)***

Washington Dupont WA 253 964-3403
1575 Wilmington Dr # 120 Dupont (98327) ***(G-2975)***

Washington Eqp Mfg Co Inc (PA) 509 244-4773
5510 W Thorpe Rd Spokane (99224) ***(G-12583)***

Washington Fire Safety, Woodinville *Also called Source TEC Inc* ***(G-15371)***

Washington Fruit & Produce Co 509 932-7981
19253 Road 5 Sw Quincy (98848) ***(G-8310)***

Washington Graphics LLC 425 376-0877
15340 Ne 92nd St Ste B Redmond (98052) ***(G-8709)***

Washington Hardwoods and 206 283-7574
1200 Nw Kerron St Ste 200 Winlock (98596) ***(G-15158)***

Washington Hardwoods Co LLC 206 283-7574
3257 17th Ave W Seattle (98119) ***(G-11440)***

Washington Haykingdom Inc 509 925-7000
7931 Reecer Creek Rd Ellensburg (98926) ***(G-3237)***

Washington Healthcare News, Kirkland *Also called Peel David and Associates* ***(G-5432)***

Washington Ignition Interlock 206 824-6849
23452 30th Ave S Ste 102 Kent (98032) ***(G-5207)***

Washington Iron Works Inc 360 679-4868
3144 Ne Halyard Ln Oak Harbor (98277) ***(G-7167)***

Washington Jones Tasting Room 509 787-8108
2101 F St Sw Quincy (98848) ***(G-8311)***

Washington Machine Works, Seattle *Also called Blue Heron Group Inc* ***(G-9548)***

Washington Marine Repair LLC 360 457-8470
202 N Cedar St Ste 1 Port Angeles (98363) ***(G-7753)***

Washington Media Services Inc 360 754-4543
407 West Bay Dr Nw Olympia (98502) ***(G-7421)***

Washington Mso Inc 253 984-7247
4901 108th St Sw Tacoma (98499) ***(G-13588)***

Washington Newspaper Publisher 360 515-0974
1204 4th Ave E Ste 4 Olympia (98506) ***(G-7422)***

Washington Poster Company, Centralia *Also called Blanc Industries Inc* ***(G-2385)***

Washington Potato, Warden *Also called Oregon Potato Company* ***(G-14935)***

Washington Potato Company, Pasco *Also called Oregon Potato Company* ***(G-7609)***

Washington Potato Company Inc 509 349-8803
1900 1st Ave W Warden (98857) ***(G-14938)***

Washington Pottery Co 425 656-7277
18815 72nd Ave S Kent (98032) ***(G-5208)***

Washington Powerscreen Inc 253 236-4153
7915 S 261st St Kent (98032) ***(G-5209)***

Washington Precast Products 360 598-1631
20519 Chief Sealth Dr Ne Indianola (98342) ***(G-4374)***

Washington Publishing Company (PA) 425 562-2245
2107 Elliott Ave Ste 305 Seattle (98121) ***(G-11441)***

Washington Publishing Hse LLC 425 406-9891
16035 Ne 117th Way Redmond (98052) ***(G-8710)***

Washington Rock Quarries Inc 360 893-7701
29104 Camp 1 Rd E Orting (98360) ***(G-7488)***

Washington Schl Info Proc Coop 425 349-6600
2121 W Casino Rd Everett (98204) ***(G-3651)***

Washington Screnprint Graphics, Redmond *Also called Washington Graphics LLC* ***(G-8709)***

Washington State Apple Comm 509 663-9600
2900 Euclid Ave Wenatchee (98801) ***(G-15083)***

Washington State Gifts, Edmonds *Also called Fascinaturals LLC* ***(G-3111)***

Washington State Horseshoe Pit 253 735-0213
16010 Se 322nd St Auburn (98092) ***(G-593)***

Washington State University 509 335-2947
2 Cooper Bldg Pullman (99164) ***(G-8111)***

Washington State University 509 335-3518
Cooper Publications Bldg Pullman (99164) ***(G-8112)***

Washington State University 509 335-4014
Food Quality Bldg Rm 101 Pullman (99164) ***(G-8113)***

Washington State University 509 372-7400
2710 Crimson Way Ste 101 Richland (99354) ***(G-9052)***

Washington State University 509 335-4573
113 Murrow Comm Ctr Pullman (99164) ***(G-8114)***

Washington Stone, Spokane *Also called Tresko Monument Inc* ***(G-12568)***

Washington Teck Incorporated 509 446-4516
1382 Pend Oreille Mine Rd Metaline Falls (99153) ***(G-6500)***

Washington Tent & Awning Inc 253 581-7177
3419 Chapel St S Lakewood (98499) ***(G-5765)***

Washington Tractor Inc 509 452-2880
3110 Fruitvale Blvd Yakima (98902) ***(G-15704)***

Washington Tractor Inc (PA) 253 863-4436
2700 136th Avenue Ct E Sumner (98390) ***(G-13110)***

Washington Tractor Inc 360 533-6393
5015 Olympic Hwy Aberdeen (98520) ***(G-38)***

Washington Tractor Inc 509 422-3030
1 Patrol St Okanogan (98840) ***(G-7204)***

Washington Vg Inc 425 823-4518
13600 Ne 126th Pl Ste A Kirkland (98034) ***(G-5492)***

Washington Web Company Inc 206 441-1844
600 S Spokane St Seattle (98134) ***(G-11442)***

Washington Wind Sports Inc 360 676-1146
104 E Maple St Bellingham (98225) ***(G-1589)***

Washington Wine & Beverage Co (PA) 425 485-2437
14701 148th Ave Ne Woodinville (98072) ***(G-15402)***

Washingtonian Print, Hoquiam *Also called Harbor Graphics Inc* ***(G-4339)***

Washougal Baselt Rock Qua 360 335-0111
404 Ne 367th Ave Washougal (98671) ***(G-14998)***

Washougal Manufacturing Co 360 261-2199
952 W T St Washougal (98671) ***(G-14999)***

Wasser Corp 360 870-3513
4118 B Pl Nw Ste B Auburn (98001) ***(G-594)***

Wasser High-Tech Coatings, Auburn *Also called Wasser Corp* ***(G-594)***

Watchguard Technologies Inc (PA) 206 613-6600
505 5th Ave S Ste 500 Seattle (98104) ***(G-11443)***

Water Beetle USA (PA) 702 899-2266
13511 36th Ave Ne Seattle (98125) ***(G-11444)***

Water Empire Press, East Wenatchee *Also called Empire Press Co* ***(G-3011)***

Water Well Drilling, Benton City *Also called Carpenter Drilling LLC* ***(G-1603)***

Waterax Corporation 360 574-1818
3801 Ne 109th Ave Ste A Vancouver (98682) ***(G-14679)***

ALPHABETIC SECTION
West Coast Fiber Inc

Waterfront Solutions Inc............360 348-1874
820 12th Ave N Edmonds (98020) **(G-3161)**
Waterline Envirotech Ltd............360 676-9635
4301 Squalicum Lake Rd Bellingham (98226) **(G-1590)**
Watermark Art & Framing............360 871-2906
3857 E Nautical Cove Way Port Orchard (98366) **(G-7856)**
Watermark Binderies............360 379-0186
1510 Hastings Ave Port Townsend (98368) **(G-7938)**
Watermark Scuba, Chehalis *Also called Seasoft Scuba Inc* **(G-2536)**
Waterra USA Inc............360 738-3366
5108 Mountain Hm Rnch Rd Peshastin (98847) **(G-7665)**
Waters Edge Gallery & Framery............253 858-7449
7808 Pioneer Way Gig Harbor (98335) **(G-4174)**
Waters Winery LLC............541 203-0020
6 W Rose St Ste 103 Walla Walla (99362) **(G-14899)**
Waterstation Technology LLC (PA)............877 475-7717
2732 Grand Ave Ste 122 Everett (98201) **(G-3652)**
Waterstone Brands Inc............800 579-3644
1211 E Denny Way Ste 22b Seattle (98122) **(G-11445)**
Watford Tanikka............360 499-6327
8535 Commerce Place Dr Ne Lacey (98516) **(G-5601)**
Watson Desking, Poulsbo *Also called Watson Furniture Group Inc* **(G-8019)**
Watson Dispatch, Poulsbo *Also called Watson Furniture Group Inc* **(G-8020)**
Watson Furniture Group Inc (PA)............360 394-1300
26246 Twelve Trees Ln Nw Poulsbo (98370) **(G-8019)**
Watson Furniture Group Inc............360 394-1300
26246 Twelve Trees Ln Nw Poulsbo (98370) **(G-8020)**
Watsons Wooden Words LLC............253 348-7995
6809 183rd Ave E Bonney Lake (98391) **(G-1742)**
Watts Brothers Frozen Foods, Paterson *Also called Lamb Weston Inc* **(G-7658)**
Watts Specialties LLC............253 848-9288
2323 E Pioneer Ste A Puyallup (98372) **(G-8277)**
Waugh Enterprises LLC............360 468-4372
1008 Dill Rd Ste C Lopez Island (98261) **(G-5988)**
Waupaca Materials, Parker *Also called Waupaca Northwoods LLC* **(G-7550)**
Waupaca Northwoods LLC............509 877-2830
81 N Track Rd Parker (98939) **(G-7550)**
Wautoma Wines LLC............509 378-1163
1022 Meadow Hills Dr Richland (99352) **(G-9053)**
Wave Engine Solutions Inc............317 554-7201
3101 Se 197th Ct Camas (98607) **(G-2288)**
Wave Holdco Corporation............425 576-8200
401 Kirkland Parkpl Kirkland (98033) **(G-5493)**
Waving Tree Vineyard & Winery............509 773-6552
2 Maryhill Hwy Goldendale (98620) **(G-4212)**
Wawawai Canyon Winery............509 338-4916
5602 State Route 270 Pullman (99163) **(G-8115)**
Wax Barn Inc............425 228-8537
13009 172nd Ave Se Renton (98059) **(G-8943)**
Wax Orchards Inc............800 634-6132
3041 Ne 166th St Lake Forest Park (98155) **(G-5627)**
Waya Group Inc............877 277-6999
1205 Craftsman Way # 111 Everett (98201) **(G-3653)**
Wayne - Dalton of Yakima, Kennewick *Also called Hrh Door Corp* **(G-4672)**
Wayne Davidson............425 333-4242
32405 Ne 12th Pl Carnation (98014) **(G-2302)**
Wayne Pond Logging Inc............509 684-8732
1264 Slide Creek Rd Colville (99114) **(G-2782)**
Waypoint Sign Company, Seattle *Also called Blue Water Projects Inc* **(G-9554)**
Wazzbizz Inc............360 332-5276
1100 Yew Ave Blaine (98230) **(G-1710)**
Wb Mobile Modular Service............253 952-4630
11005 20th St E Edgewood (98372) **(G-3091)**
Wbsb, Bellevue *Also called Great Artisan Beverage LLC* **(G-933)**
Wc Manufacturing LLC............425 890-9709
3217 S 374th St Auburn (98001) **(G-595)**
Wcp Solutions, Kent *Also called West Coast Paper Company* **(G-5212)**
WD&I Machine Co (PA)............360 225-5020
1665 Schurman Way Woodland (98674) **(G-15473)**
Wdk Signs............509 758-0483
1249 7th St Clarkston (99403) **(G-2653)**
We Are Wild, Vancouver *Also called Favorite Discovery LLC* **(G-14225)**
We Industries LLC............206 853-4505
1519 10th Ave W Seattle (98119) **(G-11446)**
We-Man Vets Golf Inc............509 527-4507
201 E Rees Ave Walla Walla (99362) **(G-14900)**
Wear-Tek Inc............509 747-4139
8021 W Highway 2 Spokane (99224) **(G-12584)**
Weaver Family Winery............509 386-8018
5223 Detour Rd Touchet (99360) **(G-13678)**
Web Press LLC............253 620-4747
701 E D St Tacoma (98421) **(G-13589)**
Web Printing & Bindery, Woodinville *Also called Good News Printing & Graphics* **(G-15253)**
Webers Radiator Service Inc............509 452-3747
310 S 3rd Ave Yakima (98902) **(G-15705)**
Webgirl............253 473-6895
6406 Fawcett Ave Tacoma (98408) **(G-13590)**
Webley Lumber Inc............509 684-3980
578d Webley Mill Rd Colville (99114) **(G-2783)**
Weddings Sochic............360 438-6540
441 Cougar St Se Olympia (98503) **(G-7423)**
Wedge Mountain Winery............509 548-7068
9534 Saunders Rd Peshastin (98847) **(G-7666)**
Weeks Waterjet & Mfg............206 261-1954
104 49th St Nw Auburn (98001) **(G-596)**
Wegners Wire Inc............253 535-0945
7308 139th Street Ct E Puyallup (98373) **(G-8278)**
Weigh Tronix Company Store, Tukwila *Also called Avery Weigh-Tronix LLC* **(G-13694)**
Weissert Tool & Design Inc............360 835-7256
540 Washougal River Rd Washougal (98671) **(G-15000)**
Welch Foods Inc A Cooperative............509 582-1010
10 E Bruneau Ave Kennewick (99336) **(G-4744)**
Welch Foods Inc A Cooperative............509 882-1711
504 Birch Ave Grandview (98930) **(G-4257)**
Welch Foods Inc A Cooperative............509 882-3112
401 Grandridge Rd Grandview (98930) **(G-4258)**
Welch's, Kennewick *Also called Welch Foods Inc A Cooperative* **(G-4744)**
Welco Sales LLC............425 771-9043
18401 76th Ave W Edmonds (98026) **(G-3162)**
Welcome Ramp Systems Inc............425 754-0489
3902 B St Nw Ste B Auburn (98001) **(G-597)**
Welcome Road Winery............206 778-3028
4415 Sw Stevens St Seattle (98116) **(G-11447)**
Weld-Rite Mfg LLC............509 927-9353
3519 N Eden Rd Spokane Valley (99216) **(G-12933)**
Weld-Tech Fabrication Inc............425 591-5912
10320 James Rd Sw Rochester (98579) **(G-9144)**
Weldco-Beales Mfg Corp............253 383-0180
11106 25th Ave E Ste B Tacoma (98445) **(G-13591)**
Weldcraft Marine Industries............509 758-9831
908 4th St Clarkston (99403) **(G-2654)**
Welding & Machine Shop, Snohomish *Also called Snohomish Iron Works Inc* **(G-11982)**
Welding &MAchine Shop, Langley *Also called Williamson Brock Wldg Mch Sp* **(G-5788)**
Welding By Craig............253 307-3936
4225 114th Ave E Edgewood (98372) **(G-3092)**
Welding Shop Inc............425 888-0911
939 Nw 14th St North Bend (98045) **(G-7131)**
Wellons Inc (PA)............360 750-3500
2525 W Firestone Ln Vancouver (98660) **(G-14680)**
Wellons Inc............360 750-3500
2600 W Firestone Ln Vancouver (98660) **(G-14681)**
Wellons Group Inc............360 750-3500
2525 W Firestone Ln Vancouver (98660) **(G-14682)**
Wellpepper Inc............206 455-7377
3502 Fremont Ave N Seattle (98103) **(G-11448)**
Wells Signs Mfg & Distrg............360 225-0520
109 Brothers Rd Woodland (98674) **(G-15474)**
Wells Ww Millwork LLC............425 405-3252
3202 Mcdougall Ave Everett (98201) **(G-3654)**
Welwater............360 909-7970
2924 Ne 116th Ave Vancouver (98682) **(G-14683)**
Wemco, Spokane *Also called Washington Eqp Mfg Co Inc* **(G-12583)**
Wenatchee Business Journal............509 663-6730
201 Cottage Ave Ste 4 Cashmere (98815) **(G-2332)**
Wenatchee Petroleum Co (PA)............509 662-4423
601e N Wenatchee Ave Wenatchee (98801) **(G-15084)**
Wenatchee Qlty Wldg Fbrication............509 782-0807
5830 Sunset Hwy Cashmere (98815) **(G-2333)**
Wenatchee Red Apple Flyers............509 881-7884
1123 2nd St Se East Wenatchee (98802) **(G-3035)**
Wenatchee Valley Brewery, Wenatchee *Also called Wenatchee Vly Brewing Co LLC* **(G-15085)**
Wenatchee Vly Brewing Co LLC............509 888-8088
7 N Worthen St Wenatchee (98801) **(G-15085)**
Wenatchee World, Wenatchee *Also called World Publishing Company* **(G-15087)**
Wendy Rawley............253 531-6785
9918 Portland Ave E Tacoma (98445) **(G-13592)**
Wesco Sales Group Inc............206 227-5980
24210 23rd Ave Se Bothell (98021) **(G-1916)**
Wescold Inc............206 284-5710
4816 15th Ave Nw Seattle (98107) **(G-11449)**
Wescold Systems, Seattle *Also called Integrated Marine Systems Inc* **(G-10246)**
Wesley Todd............509 926-0344
1605 S Clinton Rd Spokane Valley (99216) **(G-12934)**
Wesmar Company Inc............206 783-5344
5720 204th St Sw Lynnwood (98036) **(G-6222)**
Wesnip............360 306-0345
424 W Bakerview Rd # 105 Bellingham (98226) **(G-1591)**
West Bay Boat & Manufacturing............360 683-4066
1451 W Sequim Bay Rd Sequim (98382) **(G-11669)**
West Coast Athletic LLC............425 413-9200
23220 Maple Valley B Maple Valley (98038) **(G-6299)**
West Coast Automation Corp............509 773-5055
1600 S Roosevelt St Goldendale (98620) **(G-4213)**
West Coast Custom Metal Design............360 738-2884
3950 Hammer Dr Ste 104 Bellingham (98226) **(G-1592)**
West Coast Elevator LLC............206 878-9378
111 S 197th St Des Moines (98148) **(G-2951)**
West Coast Fabrication Inc............206 790-1496
3202 C St Ne B Auburn (98002) **(G-598)**
West Coast Fiber Inc............253 850-5606
832 3rd Ave S Kent (98032) **(G-5210)**

ALPHABETIC

West Coast Fire & Rescue Inc......253 826-9852
18322 9th St E Lake Tapps (98391) *(G-5687)*
West Coast Gemstones Inc......509 522-4851
360 Sw 12th St College Place (99324) *(G-2731)*
West Coast Goalkeeping, Maple Valley *Also called West Coast Athletic LLC (G-6299)*
West Coast Industries Inc......206 365-7513
14900 Whitman Ave N Shoreline (98133) *(G-11821)*
West Coast Insulation Inc......206 459-2233
2426 W Commodore Way Seattle (98199) *(G-11450)*
West Coast Laminating LLC......253 395-5225
8939 S 190th St Ste 104 Kent (98031) *(G-5211)*
West Coast Manufacturing Inc......208 667-5121
1515 75th St Sw Ste 600 Everett (98203) *(G-3655)*
West Coast Mining, College Place *Also called West Coast Gemstones Inc (G-2731)*
West Coast Paper Company (PA)......253 850-1900
6703 S 234th St Ste 120 Kent (98032) *(G-5212)*
West Coast Plastics Inc......509 575-0727
1110 N 20th Ave Yakima (98902) *(G-15706)*
West Coast Screen Printing......360 581-6466
323 W Market St Aberdeen (98520) *(G-39)*
West Coast Stair Company......206 406-4927
16908 Se May Valley Rd Renton (98059) *(G-8944)*
West Coast Waterjet, Seattle *Also called West Coast Insulation Inc (G-11450)*
West Columbia Carriers LLC......509 488-5000
435 N Desdemona Ave Othello (99344) *(G-7509)*
West Fork Timber Co LLC......253 383-5871
3819 100th St Sw Ste 5b Lakewood (98499) *(G-5766)*
West Isle Air Inc......425 235-1996
1328 W Woodin Ave Chelan (98816) *(G-2570)*
West Pacific Resources Inc......425 210-6427
17204 Mcrae Rd Nw Arlington (98223) *(G-346)*
West Quarter Horses LLC......360 969-0791
1593 Baker Ranch Ln Oak Harbor (98277) *(G-7168)*
West Road Candles......360 682-5822
1504 Sw 2nd Ct Oak Harbor (98277) *(G-7169)*
West Seattle Brewing Company......206 708-6627
2613 58th Ave Sw Seattle (98116) *(G-11451)*
West Seattle Brewing Company L, Seattle *Also called West Seattle Brewing Company (G-11451)*
West Side Record Journal, Ferndale *Also called Ferndale Record Inc (G-3844)*
West Ward Fishing Co, Seattle *Also called Westward Seafoods Inc (G-11458)*
West Worldwide Services Inc......509 764-2177
151 S Hamilton Rd Moses Lake (98837) *(G-6757)*
Westar Medical Products Inc......425 290-3945
18930 59th Ave Ne Arlington (98223) *(G-347)*
Westbay Auto Parts Inc......360 373-1424
1550 Navy Yard Hwy Bremerton (98312) *(G-2011)*
Westbay Industrial Sales, Bremerton *Also called Westbay Auto Parts Inc (G-2011)*
Westco Engineering......425 481-7271
17011 174th Ave Ne Woodinville (98072) *(G-15403)*
Westco Lifts, Woodinville *Also called Westco Engineering (G-15403)*
Westcoast Telemetry Specialist......253 536-1351
1909 159th Street Ct S Spanaway (98387) *(G-12080)*
Westec Tool & Productions Inc......253 476-3404
6229 S Adams St Ste A Tacoma (98409) *(G-13593)*
Westech Aerosol Corporation......206 930-9291
26268 Twlve Trees Ln Nw Suquamish (98392) *(G-13150)*
Westech Industries LLC......509 751-0401
1487 15th St Clarkston (99403) *(G-2655)*
Westek Marketing LLC......425 888-1988
7415 W Ridgecrest Ave Nine Mile Falls (99026) *(G-7085)*
Westerberg & Associates Inc......509 951-4399
1421 N Meadowwood Ln # 20 Liberty Lake (99019) *(G-5867)*
Westerlund Log Handlers LLC......503 325-9877
496 Parpala Rd Naselle (98638) *(G-7021)*
Westerly Wood Working......360 480-4840
6920 Zangle Rd Ne Olympia (98506) *(G-7424)*
Western Adhesive Solutions......360 904-5005
15601 Ne 194th Ct Brush Prairie (98606) *(G-2043)*
Western Aerospace & Engrg LLC......360 253-8282
12401 Ne 60th Way Unit A1 Vancouver (98682) *(G-14684)*
Western Animal Nutrition, Woodland *Also called Northwest Pet Products Inc (G-15452)*
Western Avionics Inc......509 534-7371
6095 E Rutter Ave Ste 1 Spokane (99212) *(G-12585)*
Western Business Forms & Sups......503 285-8738
14917 Ne 269th St Battle Ground (98604) *(G-751)*
Western Cabinets......253 269-2742
3411 C St Ne Ste 16 Auburn (98002) *(G-599)*
Western Chemical Incorporated......360 384-5898
1441 W Smith Rd Ferndale (98248) *(G-3923)*
Western Clear View Railing......253 395-3113
7818 S 194th St Kent (98032) *(G-5213)*
Western Continental, Spokane Valley *Also called Helena Silver Mines Inc (G-12729)*
Western Energy Group Inc......253 306-4748
9817 132nd Street Ct E D Puyallup (98373) *(G-8279)*
Western Engineers, Seattle *Also called Wescold Inc (G-11449)*
Western Equipment Repr & Wldg......253 922-8351
115 54th Ave E Fife (98424) *(G-3997)*
Western Fabrication Center LLC......360 575-1500
700 Colorado St Ste A Kelso (98626) *(G-4559)*
Western Foil Corporation......206 624-3645
2900 1st Ave S Seattle (98134) *(G-11452)*
Western Forest Products US LLC......360 403-1400
19406 68th Dr Ne A Arlington (98223) *(G-348)*
Western Forest Products US LLC......360 735-9700
4303 Nw Fruit Valley Rd Vancouver (98660) *(G-14685)*
Western Glove Co, Tacoma *Also called Oregon Glove Company (G-13446)*
Western Graphics Inc......206 241-2526
5009 Pacific Hwy E Ste 12 Fife (98424) *(G-3998)*
Western Group Pacific......253 964-6201
3250 International Pl Dupont (98327) *(G-2976)*
Western Hydro LLC......509 546-9999
1116 N Oregon Ave Pasco (99301) *(G-7651)*
Western Hydro LLC......360 428-4704
902 S Spruce St Burlington (98233) *(G-2200)*
Western Industrial Products, Redmond *Also called Western Industrial Tooling Inc (G-8711)*
Western Industrial Tooling Inc......425 883-6644
14511 Ne 87th St Redmond (98052) *(G-8711)*
Western Land Timber......360 987-2170
66 Badger Rd Hoquiam (98550) *(G-4362)*
Western Lime Corp......604 249-1997
800 5th Ave Seattle (98104) *(G-11453)*
Western Machine Works Inc......253 627-6538
652 E 11th St Tacoma (98421) *(G-13594)*
Western Materials Inc......509 547-3301
317 S 5th Ave Pasco (99301) *(G-7652)*
Western Metal Products LLC......509 962-4895
2613 Hwy 97 Ellensburg (98926) *(G-3238)*
Western Neon Inc......206 682-7738
2902 4th Ave S Seattle (98134) *(G-11454)*
Western Optical Corporation......206 622-7627
1200 Mercer St Seattle (98109) *(G-11455)*
Western Pacific Log Exports, Snohomish *Also called Global Pacific Forest Products (G-11913)*
Western Pneumatic Tube Co LLC (HQ)......425 822-8271
835 6th St S Kirkland (98033) *(G-5494)*
Western Print Systems Inc......206 794-0045
1313 Bonneville Ave # 103 Snohomish (98290) *(G-11998)*
Western Products......509 994-1288
406 N G St Sprague (99032) *(G-12949)*
Western Security Systems, Deer Park *Also called Darren Mode (G-2897)*
Western Skylights, Kent *Also called KDL Enterprises Inc (G-4973)*
Western Specialties Co......425 353-9282
7924 40th Ave W Mukilteo (98275) *(G-6991)*
Western States Asphalt LLC (HQ)......509 487-4560
4327 N Thor St Spokane (99217) *(G-12586)*
Western States Asphalt LLC......509 545-9864
3152 Selph Landing Rd Pasco (99301) *(G-7653)*
Western States Fire Equipment......360 723-0032
1604 Nw 1st Ave Battle Ground (98604) *(G-752)*
Western States Group LLC (PA)......509 487-4560
4327 N Thor St Spokane (99217) *(G-12587)*
Western Sttes Stl Fbrction Inc......509 489-8046
1515 E Holyoke Ave Spokane (99217) *(G-12588)*
Western Superior Structurals......360 943-0339
7380 New Market St Sw Tumwater (98501) *(G-13904)*
Western Systems Inc......425 438-1133
1122 Industry St Ste B Everett (98203) *(G-3656)*
Western Systems & Fabrication, Spokane Valley *Also called Wsf LLC (G-12944)*
Western Tag and Label, Redmond *Also called Stafford Press Inc (G-8680)*
Western Technology Inc......360 917-0080
3517 W Arsenal Way Bremerton (98312) *(G-2012)*
Western Timber Inc......360 769-0639
6845 Se King Rd Port Orchard (98367) *(G-7857)*
Western Towboat Company......206 789-9000
617 Nw 40th St Seattle (98107) *(G-11456)*
Western Typographers Inc......425 967-4700
6327 204th St Sw 201 Lynnwood (98036) *(G-6223)*
Western Wash Safety Conslt......253 815-7920
34213 31st Ave Sw Federal Way (98023) *(G-3802)*
Western Wire Works Inc......253 964-6201
3250 International Pl Dupont (98327) *(G-2977)*
Western Wood Preserving Co......253 863-8191
1310 Zehnder St Sumner (98390) *(G-13111)*
Western Yacht Systems Inc......360 384-3648
1720 Kaas Rd Ferndale (98248) *(G-3924)*
Westfall Gooden Sfo Co......253 344-1025
500 S 336th St Federal Way (98003) *(G-3803)*
Westland Distillery......206 763-5381
2931 1st Ave S Seattle (98134) *(G-11457)*
Westlands Resources Corp Inc (PA)......360 740-1970
2451 Ne Kresky Ave Unit J Chehalis (98532) *(G-2542)*
Westman Marine Inc......360 332-5051
218 Mcmillan Ave Blaine (98230) *(G-1711)*
Westmark Industries Inc......425 251-8444
19115 68th Ave S Ste H101 Kent (98032) *(G-5214)*
Westom Tools......360 355-6741
520 Haussler Rd Kelso (98626) *(G-4560)*
Westover Scientific Inc......425 368-0444
22025 20th Ave Se Ste 100 Bothell (98021) *(G-1917)*
Westport LLC......360 268-1800
1807 N Nyhus St Westport (98595) *(G-15108)*

ALPHABETIC SECTION

Westport LLC 360 452-5095
  3500 E Highway 101 Port Angeles (98362) *(G-7754)*
Westport LLC 360 452-5095
  2140 W 18th St 1050 Port Angeles (98363) *(G-7755)*
Westport Winery Inc 360 648-2224
  1 S Arbor Rd Aberdeen (98520) *(G-40)*
Westrock Company 360 575-5256
  300 Fibre Way Longview (98632) *(G-5965)*
Westrock Rkt Company 425 885-5851
  8720 148th Ave Ne Redmond (98052) *(G-8712)*
Westside Concrete ACC Inc 360 892-0203
  11412 Ne 76th St Vancouver (98662) *(G-14686)*
Westward Seafoods Inc (HQ) 206 682-5949
  3015 112th Ave Ne Ste 100 Bellevue (98004) *(G-1225)*
Westward Seafoods Inc 206 341-9996
  413 3rd Ave W Seattle (98119) *(G-11458)*
Westweld Inc 253 862-1107
  9117 207th Ave E Bonney Lake (98391) *(G-1743)*
Westwood Logging 509 548-7681
  9264 Foster Rd Cashmere (98815) *(G-2334)*
Westwood Precision Inc 425 742-7011
  7509 Hardeson Rd Everett (98203) *(G-3657)*
Westwynd Publishing LLC 253 588-3066
  9709 73rd St Sw Lakewood (98498) *(G-5767)*
Wet Fly, Snohomish Also called Carlson & Fitzwater LLC *(G-11885)*
Wet Noses Natural Dog Treat Co 360 794-7950
  14439 167th Ave Se Monroe (98272) *(G-6636)*
Weyerhaeuser Co 425 455-1111
  1899 120th Ave Ne Bellevue (98005) *(G-1226)*
Weyerhaeuser Company (PA) 206 539-3000
  220 Occidental Ave S Seattle (98104) *(G-11459)*
Weyerhaeuser Company 360 942-6302
  51 Ellis St Raymond (98577) *(G-8360)*
Weyerhaeuser Company 360 532-7110
  1701 E 1st St Cosmopolis (98537) *(G-2802)*
Weyerhaeuser Company 360 491-1200
  7727 Union Mill Rd Se Olympia (98503) *(G-7425)*
Weyerhaeuser Company 509 453-4741
  600 W Ahtanum Rd Union Gap (98903) *(G-13956)*
Weyerhaeuser Company 360 736-2811
  3000 Galvin Rd Centralia (98531) *(G-2442)*
Weyerhaeuser Company 360 425-2150
  3401 Industrial Way Longview (98632) *(G-5966)*
Weyerhaeuser Company 206 467-3600
  601 Union St Ste 3100 Seattle (98101) *(G-11460)*
Weyerhaeuser Company 360 577-6678
  120 Industrial Way Longview (98632) *(G-5967)*
Weyerhaeuser Company 631 863-1117
  6210 207th Ave E Sumner (98391) *(G-13112)*
Weyerhaeuser Company 360 446-2420
  16506 Vail Loop Se Rainier (98576) *(G-8323)*
Weyerhaeuser Company 360 291-3229
  1098 Muller Rd Pe Ell (98572) *(G-7661)*
Weyerhaeuser Company 253 924-6373
  220 Occidental Ave S Seattle (98104) *(G-11461)*
Weyerhaeuser Company 360 274-3058
  500 Burma Rd Castle Rock (98611) *(G-2357)*
Weyerhaeuser Company 425 210-5880
  220 Occidental Ave S Seattle (98104) *(G-11462)*
Weyerhaeuser Company 360 245-3245
  246 Boistfort Rd Curtis (98538) *(G-2849)*
Weyerhaeuser Company 253 924-3030
  33663 Weyerhaeuser Way S Tacoma (98477) *(G-13595)*
Weyerhaeuser Company 253 924-2345
  220 Occidental Ave S Seattle (98104) *(G-11463)*
Weyerhaeuser Company 360 482-2521
  505 Elma Mccleary Rd Elma (98541) *(G-3259)*
Weyerhaeuser Hardwoods, Centralia Also called Weyerhaeuser Company *(G-2442)*
Weyerhaeuser Tech Ctr Div, Seattle Also called Weyerhaeuser Company *(G-11461)*
Weyhaeuser Co, Longview Also called Weyerhaeuser Company *(G-5966)*
Wfc Lynden Convenience Store, Lynden Also called CHS-Sub Whatcom Inc *(G-6008)*
Wfc Nooksack Convenience Store, Everson Also called CHS-Sub Whatcom Inc *(G-3671)*
Wfc Nooksack Country Store, Nooksack Also called CHS-Sub Whatcom Inc *(G-7086)*
Wfi Vancouver, Vancouver Also called Whipple Falls Industries *(G-14688)*
Wfm Select Fish Inc 512 542-0676
  15 Lake Bellevue Dr # 100 Bellevue (98005) *(G-1227)*
Wfs Networks, Edmonds Also called Waterfront Solutions Inc *(G-3161)*
Wftpd Inc 206 428-1991
  23921 57th Ave Se Woodinville (98072) *(G-15404)*
Wh International Casting LLC 425 498-7531
  6605 Hardeson Rd Ste 101 Everett (98203) *(G-3658)*
Wh International Casting LLC 562 521-0727
  5075 Randolph Rd Ne Moses Lake (98837) *(G-6758)*
Whab Technologies LLC 800 506-2770
  13716 Manor Way Lynnwood (98087) *(G-6224)*
Whaer Inc 919 946-5720
  16405 Se 145th St Renton (98059) *(G-8945)*
Whalen Furniture Manufacturing 425 427-0115
  1605 Nw Sammamish Rd # 111 Issaquah (98027) *(G-4489)*
Whalestooth Publishing 360 376-2784
  131 Bond Mill Rd Olga (98279) *(G-7220)*

What S Next 425 235-1696
  4403 Se 4th St Renton (98059) *(G-8946)*
Whatcom Farmers Coop, Lynden Also called CHS-Sub Whatcom Inc *(G-6007)*
Whatcom Watch Newspaper 360 734-6007
  3008 Tulip Rd Bellingham (98225) *(G-1593)*
Whatcounts Inc 206 709-8250
  101 Yesler Way Ste 500 Seattle (98104) *(G-11464)*
Whats On Tap, Bellingham Also called Innovative Manufacturing Inc *(G-1379)*
Whats Your Sign Inc 253 475-7446
  3838 S Warner St Tacoma (98409) *(G-13596)*
Whatzit Machining Inc 360 378-6874
  474a Dexter Ln Friday Harbor (98250) *(G-4064)*
Wheatland Alpacas 509 526-4847
  2010 Stovall Rd Walla Walla (99362) *(G-14901)*
Wheel 206 956-0334
  1902 2nd Ave Seattle (98101) *(G-11465)*
Wheel Deals, Spokane Valley Also called Target Media Partners *(G-12900)*
Wheel Haus Mfg Inc 360 719-1030
  1417 Ne 76th St Ste F Vancouver (98665) *(G-14687)*
Wheelchair Adl Solutions 509 228-8293
  23614 E Sprague Ave Liberty Lake (99019) *(G-5868)*
Wheelchairs and More LLC 509 926-9337
  9904 E 50th Ave Spokane Valley (99206) *(G-12935)*
Wheelchairs For Nigeria 206 932-6129
  1542 Palm Ave Sw Seattle (98116) *(G-11466)*
Wheeler Industries Inc 509 534-4556
  1118 N Howe Rd Spokane Valley (99212) *(G-12936)*
Wheeler, Delbert L Logging Co, White Swan Also called Delbert L Wheeler *(G-15137)*
Wheels Northwest Inc 206 909-6735
  18930 State Route 9 Se Snohomish (98296) *(G-11999)*
Wheels Up LLC 206 588-1573
  1735 Westlake Ave N # 110 Seattle (98109) *(G-11467)*
Whidbey Auto Parts Inc 360 675-5946
  1370 Sw Barlow St Oak Harbor (98277) *(G-7170)*
Whidbey Cruzers 253 299-6442
  953 Se 4th Ave Oak Harbor (98277) *(G-7171)*
Whidbey Design Works 360 321-8221
  2715 Evening Glory Ct Clinton (98236) *(G-2702)*
Whidbey Examiner LLC 360 678-8060
  107 S Main St Ste 101 Coupeville (98239) *(G-2819)*
Whidbey Island Ice Cream LLC 425 359-6372
  1715 Main St Freeland (98249) *(G-4039)*
Whidbey Island Ntural Pdts Inc 360 929-2461
  2133 Lancaster Rd Freeland (98249) *(G-4040)*
Whidbey Island Prtg & Off Sup, Clinton Also called Sharon Rose *(G-2698)*
Whidbey Island Sign Sltons LLC 360 299-0430
  789 Chrysler Dr Burlington (98233) *(G-2201)*
Whidbey Island Soap Company, Freeland Also called Whidbey Island Ntural Pdts Inc *(G-4040)*
Whidbey Island Vintners 360 331-3544
  4591 Honeymoon Bay Rd Greenbank (98253) *(G-4310)*
Whidbey Island Vinyard Winery 360 221-2040
  5237 Langley Rd Langley (98260) *(G-5787)*
Whidbey Marketplace & News LLC 360 682-2341
  390 Ne Midway Blvd B203 Oak Harbor (98277) *(G-7172)*
Whidbey News Times, Coupeville Also called Sound Publishing Inc *(G-2818)*
Whidbey Printers, Oak Harbor Also called Bte Printing Inc *(G-7143)*
Whidbey Publishing, Clinton Also called D Powers Consulting *(G-2688)*
Whidbey Sign Co 360 720-2015
  751 Ne Midway Blvd Oak Harbor (98277) *(G-7173)*
Whidbeyfresh, Greenbank Also called Wildeberry LLC *(G-4311)*
Whipple Falls Industries 360 573-0863
  15612 Ne 57th Ave Vancouver (98686) *(G-14688)*
Whipsaw Brewing LLC 360 463-0436
  704 N Wenas St Ellensburg (98926) *(G-3239)*
Whirlpool Corporation 253 875-7100
  19700 38th Ave E Spanaway (98387) *(G-12081)*
Whisd Craft 253 850-7126
  10825 Se 233rd Pl Kent (98031) *(G-5215)*
Whiskey Ridge Mfg Inc 360 426-6100
  21 Adonai Ct Shelton (98584) *(G-11750)*
Whisler Communications, Tumwater Also called Whislers Inc *(G-13905)*
Whislers Inc (PA) 360 352-8777
  2875 R W Johnson Blvd Sw Tumwater (98512) *(G-13905)*
Whistle Pig LLC 509 949-1584
  1042 Mahoney Rd Yakima (98908) *(G-15707)*
Whistle Stop Studios LLC 360 652-9728
  5919 Happy Hollow Rd Stanwood (98292) *(G-12999)*
Whistle Workwear Shoreline LLC 206 364-2253
  15240 Aurora Ave N Shoreline (98133) *(G-11822)*
Whitbys Whimsies 206 937-1312
  6717 Holly Pl Sw Seattle (98136) *(G-11468)*
White & Zumstein Inc 360 263-6114
  35006 Nw Seibler Dr La Center (98629) *(G-5519)*
White Block Co Inc 509 534-0651
  6219 E Trent Ave Spokane Valley (99212) *(G-12937)*
White Cellars 425 246-1419
  1307 240th Way Se Sammamish (98075) *(G-9258)*
White Center Glass & Uphl 206 762-8088
  9443 Delridge Way Sw Seattle (98106) *(G-11469)*

White Cloud Alpacas 253 853-6984
8535 Se Willock Rd Olalla (98359) **(G-7212)**
White Creek Project LLC 360 737-9692
9611 Ne 117th Ave Vancouver (98662) **(G-14689)**
White Dog Press 800 257-2226
321 High School Rd Ne Bainbridge Island (98110) **(G-683)**
White Heron 206 246-5080
15217 8th Ave S Burien (98148) **(G-2137)**
White Light Publications LLC 206 575-4236
1201 Monster Rd Sw # 430 Renton (98057) **(G-8947)**
White Logging LLC 509 997-0279
110 Lookout Mnt Rd Twisp (98856) **(G-13917)**
White Matter LLC 510 409-0144
4431 Ferncroft Rd Mercer Island (98040) **(G-6489)**
White Mountainhouse 360 835-5442
4211 L Cir Washougal (98671) **(G-15001)**
White Rabbit Ventures Inc 360 474-5828
6000 Ne 88th St Ste D102 Vancouver (98665) **(G-14690)**
White River Distillers LLC 253 219-5100
25714 Se 400th St Enumclaw (98022) **(G-3327)**
White River Fabrication LLC 253 261-8718
2321 Cole St Ste 101 Enumclaw (98022) **(G-3328)**
White River Logging 360 829-1630
27115 Smner Buckley Hwy E Buckley (98321) **(G-2080)**
White Signs 425 745-0760
15107 Highway 99 Lynnwood (98087) **(G-6225)**
White Stone Calcium Corp 509 935-0838
2432 Highway 395 S Chewelah (99109) **(G-2610)**
White Stone Calcium Corp (PA) 509 738-6571
Rittinger Rd Kettle Falls (99141) **(G-5243)**
White Stone Co, Chewelah *Also called White Stone Calcium Corp* **(G-2610)**
White Stone Co, Kettle Falls *Also called White Stone Calcium Corp* **(G-5243)**
Whitefab 253 277-4047
22803 86th Ave S Kent (98031) **(G-5216)**
Whitehouse Antique & Candy 425 486-8453
23712 Bothell Everett Hwy Bothell (98021) **(G-1918)**
Whitelatch-Hoch LLC 509 586-7337
175 E Aeronca Ave # 202 Walla Walla (99362) **(G-14902)**
Whitelatch-Hoch LLC 509 956-9311
313 W Kennewick Ave Kennewick (99336) **(G-4745)**
Whitepages Inc (PA) 206 973-5100
1301 5th Ave Ste 1600 Seattle (98101) **(G-11470)**
Whites Boots Inc 509 535-1875
4002 E Ferry Ave Spokane (99202) **(G-12589)**
Whites Custom Woodworking LLC 509 582-9474
510 E 31st Ct Kennewick (99337) **(G-4746)**
Whitestone Winery Inc 509 636-2001
42399 Jump Canyon Rd N Creston (99117) **(G-2843)**
Whitewall Brewing LLC 360 454-0464
14524 Smokey Point Blvd # 1 Marysville (98271) **(G-6401)**
Whitley Evergreen Inc 360 653-5790
14219 Smokey Point Blvd Marysville (98271) **(G-6402)**
Whitman Cabinets and Wdwkg 360 825-6466
1732 Harding St Enumclaw (98022) **(G-3329)**
Whitmus Enterprises Inc 509 398-0144
16051 Railroad St Nw Ephrata (98823) **(G-3347)**
Whitstran Brewing Company Inc 509 786-4922
1427 Wine Country Rd Prosser (99350) **(G-8076)**
Whitten Group International 360 560-3319
2622 Lilac St Longview (98632) **(G-5968)**
Whittier Machine & Tool Co 509 276-7855
4632 Oregon Way Clayton (99110) **(G-2660)**
Whodat Towers 360 786-1984
1708 Midway Ct Centralia (98531) **(G-2443)**
Whole Energy Fuels Corporation 888 600-8611
20 Alder Ln Mount Vernon (98273) **(G-6855)**
Whole Shebang 360 941-5125
401 Bennett St Sedro Woolley (98284) **(G-11580)**
Wholesale Forms Inc 800 826-7095
17449 Jordan St Sw Rochester (98579) **(G-9145)**
Wholesale Neon A Division 253 939-0716
1450 32nd St Se Auburn (98002) **(G-600)**
Wholesale Printers Inc 360 687-5500
10816 Ne 189th St Battle Ground (98604) **(G-753)**
Whooshh Innovations Inc 206 801-3565
2001 W Grfeld St Bldg 156 Seattle (98119) **(G-11471)**
Whyte & Sons Incorporated 425 885-3571
11609 172nd Ave Ne Redmond (98052) **(G-8713)**
Wiard H Groeneveld 360 793-1638
29126 Fern Bluff Rd Monroe (98272) **(G-6637)**
Wibotic Inc 503 484-3930
4545 Roosevelt Way Ne # 400 Seattle (98105) **(G-11472)**
Wicked Lures LLC 360 460-6078
23 Valley Center Pl Sequim (98382) **(G-11670)**
Wickman Electric, Lake Forest Park *Also called L & B Service LLC* **(G-5619)**
Wide Format Geeks 509 868-2319
2929 168th St Se Ofc Bothell (98012) **(G-1919)**
Wiebold & Sons Logging Inc 360 573-2149
10715 Ne 72nd Ave Vancouver (98686) **(G-14691)**
Wiegardt Bros Inc 360 665-4111
3215 273rd St Ocean Park (98640) **(G-7183)**
Wiese and Son Inc 509 455-8610
4125 W Thorpe Rd Spokane (99224) **(G-12590)**
Wiest Logging 360 423-3560
1616 Abernathy Creek Rd Longview (98632) **(G-5969)**
Wieweck LLC 360 576-0509
14314 Nw 8th Ct Vancouver (98685) **(G-14692)**
Wigfur Productions 206 545-4306
3658 Dayton Ave N Apt 104 Seattle (98103) **(G-11473)**
Wilbert Precast, Spokane *Also called Spokane Wilbert Vault Company* **(G-12522)**
Wilbert Precast, Yakima *Also called Wilbert Spokane Vault Company* **(G-15708)**
Wilbert Spokane Vault Company 509 248-1984
2309 S 38th Ave Yakima (98903) **(G-15708)**
Wilbur Register Inc 509 647-5551
110 Se Main Ave Wilbur (99185) **(G-15142)**
Wilcor Grounding Systems, Seattle *Also called Wilson and Associates NW* **(G-11479)**
Wilcox & Flegel, Spokane *Also called Wilson Oil Inc* **(G-12594)**
Wilcox Farms Inc 360 458-6903
40400 Harts Lake Vly Rd Roy (98580) **(G-9166)**
Wild Birds Unlimited, Gig Harbor *Also called Bear Inc* **(G-4078)**
Wild Flavors Inc 509 773-4008
1501 S Columbus Ave Goldendale (98620) **(G-4214)**
Wild Horse Graphics 425 413-5080
21036 Se 232nd St Maple Valley (98038) **(G-6300)**
Wild Noodle 206 935-1100
1615 Sunset Ave Sw Seattle (98116) **(G-11474)**
Wild River Press, Bothell *Also called Wild River Publishing Inc* **(G-1920)**
Wild River Publishing Inc 425 486-3638
2315 210th St Se Bothell (98021) **(G-1920)**
Wild Rose Graphics, Spokane *Also called Wildrose Ltd* **(G-12591)**
Wild Tree Woodworks LLC 206 650-2565
1405 E John St Apt 9 Seattle (98112) **(G-11475)**
Wild Wood Splitting 206 909-8342
25124 215th Pl Se Maple Valley (98038) **(G-6301)**
Wildcard Properties LLC 425 296-0896
8383 158th Ave Ne Ste 200 Redmond (98052) **(G-8714)**
Wildeberry LLC 360 222-3626
23923 Sr 525 Greenbank (98253) **(G-4311)**
Wilder Technologies LLC 360 859-3041
6101 A 18th St Vancouver (98661) **(G-14693)**
Wildfire Safe LLC 509 670-3816
5930 Sunburst Ln Cashmere (98815) **(G-2335)**
Wildrose Ltd 509 535-8555
134 N Madelia St Spokane (99202) **(G-12591)**
Wildtangent Inc 425 497-4500
18578 Ne 67th Ct Bldg 5 Redmond (98052) **(G-8715)**
Wilford Noorda Foundation 509 487-6832
1318 E Nebraska Ave Spokane (99208) **(G-12592)**
Wilkerson Weld & Fbrcn Inc 509 545-3181
1100 E Columbia St B-7 Pasco (99301) **(G-7654)**
Wilkeson Sandstone Quarry LLC 360 829-0999
29115 Quinnon Rd E Wilkeson (98396) **(G-15144)**
Wilkins Kaiser & Olsen Inc 509 427-5967
2022 Wind River Hwy Carson (98610) **(G-2310)**
Wilkins Precision Inc 253 851-9736
927 34th Ave Nw Gig Harbor (98335) **(G-4175)**
Wilkinson Baking Company, Walla Walla *Also called Wilkinson Group LLC* **(G-14903)**
Wilkinson Group LLC 509 529-5800
2465 Old Milton Hwy Walla Walla (99362) **(G-14903)**
Will Logging & Construction 509 223-3560
2049 Sinlahekin Rd Loomis (98827) **(G-5973)**
Willamette Valley Lumber LLC (PA) 509 331-0442
1885 W Herman Rd Othello (99344) **(G-7510)**
Willapa Bay Company Inc 206 465-5616
220 Allaha 303 Seattle (98109) **(G-11476)**
Willapa Hills Cheese LLC 360 291-3937
4680 State Route 6 Chehalis (98532) **(G-2543)**
Willapa Logging Company Inc 360 875-5670
2770 Ocean Ave Raymond (98577) **(G-8361)**
Willapa Marine Products Inc 360 942-2151
2 Green Creek Rd Raymond (98577) **(G-8362)**
Willapa Printing 360 942-5580
422 Franklin St Raymond (98577) **(G-8363)**
Willard Newman 509 442-3265
25282 Le Clerc Rd N Ione (99139) **(G-4377)**
Willard Newman Logging, Ione *Also called Willard Newman* **(G-4377)**
William Blockley Contracting 360 592-5843
5725 Mt Baker Hwy Deming (98244) **(G-2926)**
William Bounds Custom Frames 360 404-2002
1034 S Anacortes St Burlington (98233) **(G-2202)**
William E Munson Company 360 707-2752
15806 Preston Pl Burlington (98233) **(G-2203)**
William Grssie Wine Esttes LLC 913 461-4601
35922 Se 46th St Fall City (98024) **(G-3710)**
William H Olson Inc (PA) 360 249-3691
2203 Pacific Ave Se Olympia (98501) **(G-7426)**
William H Olson Inc 360 754-2858
2203 Pacific Ave Se Olympia (98501) **(G-7427)**
William Louis Becker 509 624-3466
3617 S Abbott Rd Spokane (99224) **(G-12593)**
William Minniear 360 254-6764
9503 Ne 82nd Ave Vancouver (98662) **(G-14694)**
William Ob Co Woodwork, Seattle *Also called O B Williams Company* **(G-10677)**
William Reed & Associates 509 534-4727
5702 E Alki Ave Ste C Spokane Valley (99212) **(G-12938)**

William Walker Woodworking....206 780-5301
10115 Ne Kitsap St Bainbridge Island (98110) ***(G-684)***
William Willis....360 885-2045
7212 Ne 58th St Vancouver (98662) ***(G-14695)***
Williams Elite Machining & Mfg....253 228-2288
9200 Applegate Loop Sw Rochester (98579) ***(G-9146)***
Williamson Brock Wldg Mch Sp....360 321-3227
5017 Bayview Rd Langley (98260) ***(G-5788)***
Williamson Illustration....360 734-5497
5989 Longdin Rd Ferndale (98248) ***(G-3925)***
Willingham Inc....425 432-9867
20008 244th Ave Se Maple Valley (98038) ***(G-6302)***
Willis Enterprises, Cle Elum *Also called Longview Fibre Ppr & Packg Inc* ***(G-2671)***
Willis Enterprises Inc (PA)....360 273-9266
208 Park St Oakville (98568) ***(G-7177)***
Willow Crest Winery (PA)....509 786-7999
590 Willow Dr Prosser (99350) ***(G-8077)***
Willow Crest Winery Estates, Prosser *Also called Willow Crest Winery* ***(G-8077)***
Willow Wind Organic Farms Inc....509 796-4006
38278 Angels Landing Rd N Ford (99013) ***(G-4007)***
Willys Canvas Works....425 923-7810
12315 4th Pl W Everett (98204) ***(G-3659)***
Wilo Inc....425 793-4862
16958 Woodside Dr Se Renton (98058) ***(G-8948)***
Wilridge Winery....206 770-9463
1924 Post Aly Seattle (98101) ***(G-11477)***
Wilridge Winery and Vineyard, Yakima *Also called Tapenade Inc* ***(G-15694)***
Wilson & Hayes Inc....206 323-6758
1601 Eastlake Ave E Seattle (98102) ***(G-11478)***
Wilson Air Technologies Inc....253 474-9928
5045 Yakima Ave Tacoma (98408) ***(G-13597)***
Wilson and Associates NW....206 292-9756
4045 7th Ave S Seattle (98108) ***(G-11479)***
Wilson Art, Algona *Also called Wilsonart LLC* ***(G-79)***
Wilson Dairy....360 736-6001
2560 Lincoln Creek Rd Rochester (98579) ***(G-9147)***
Wilson Machine Works Inc....206 282-7560
1038 Elliott Ave W Seattle (98119) ***(G-11480)***
Wilson Oil Inc....509 536-3550
220 N Haven St Spokane (99202) ***(G-12594)***
Wilson Operations....360 496-6565
324 Davis Lake Rd Morton (98356) ***(G-6674)***
Wilson Tool & Manufacturing Co....509 928-9441
2622 N Dartmouth Ln Spokane Valley (99206) ***(G-12939)***
Wilson Tools & Gages, Cashmere *Also called L E Wilson Inc* ***(G-2324)***
Wilsonart LLC....253 833-0551
400 Boundary Blvd Algona (98001) ***(G-79)***
Wilsons Custom Cabinets Inc....425 334-3522
13008 27th Pl Ne Lake Stevens (98258) ***(G-5674)***
Wiman Corporation....360 757-8880
527 N Hill Blvd Burlington (98233) ***(G-2204)***
Wimetrics Corp....253 593-1220
711 E 11th St Tacoma (98421) ***(G-13598)***
Winchell's Donut House, Longview *Also called Yum Yum Donut Shops Inc* ***(G-5970)***
Wincraft Incorporated....507 454-5510
16750 Woodinville Redmond Woodinville (98072) ***(G-15405)***
Wind Machine Sales, Wapato *Also called Vamco Ltd Inc* ***(G-14927)***
Wind Play Inc....206 784-0414
8326 24th Ave Nw Seattle (98117) ***(G-11481)***
Wind River Cellar....509 493-2324
196 Spring Creek Rd Husum (98623) ***(G-4367)***
Wind Talker Innovations Inc....253 883-3615
5007 Pacific Hwy E Ste 4 Fife (98424) ***(G-3999)***
Windbreak Inc....817 306-9587
2515 Ne 163rd St Ridgefield (98642) ***(G-9120)***
Windemere Camino Island Realty....360 387-3411
1283 Elger Bay Rd Ste A Stanwood (98282) ***(G-12958)***
Windfall Lumber Inc....360 352-2250
711 Tumwater Blvd Sw D Tumwater (98501) ***(G-13906)***
Windorco Supply Inc....206 784-9440
1201 Nw 92nd St Seattle (98117) ***(G-11482)***
Windowscape Designs....360 468-3510
948 Cross Rd Lopez Island (98261) ***(G-5989)***
Windtogreen LLC....509 382-4034
610 Patit Rd Dayton (99328) ***(G-2890)***
Windtones LLC....360 349-9083
2203 Wilkins Pl Se Olympia (98501) ***(G-7428)***
Windwalker Vineyard....541 490-4011
133 Wnuk Rd White Salmon (98672) ***(G-15135)***
Windward Press, Seattle *Also called Livingston Printing Inc* ***(G-10431)***
Windward Ways II LLC....206 364-5236
12236 10th Ave Nw Seattle (98177) ***(G-11483)***
Windy Acres....360 491-2177
9546 Glory Dr Se Olympia (98513) ***(G-7429)***
Wine & Labels By Vino Aquino, Tacoma *Also called Vino Aquino Tacoma Inc* ***(G-13578)***
Wine Erna A I D Inc....360 332-4888
399 H St Ste 6 Blaine (98230) ***(G-1712)***
Wineblock LLC....877 919-4921
4412 31st Ave W Seattle (98199) ***(G-11484)***
Winegar's, Ellensburg *Also called Gariko LLC* ***(G-3201)***
Winery Compliance Northwe....509 528-0905
2257 Morris Ave Richland (99352) ***(G-9054)***
Winery Fulfillment Svcs LLC....509 529-2497
1491 W Rose St Walla Walla (99362) ***(G-14904)***
Winerybound LLC....206 458-2831
80 Vine St Apt 703 Seattle (98121) ***(G-11485)***
Wines Company....509 292-8820
36103 N Conklin Rd Elk (99009) ***(G-3178)***
Wines of Substance....206 745-7456
1136 S Albro Pl Seattle (98108) ***(G-11486)***
Winescape, Spokane *Also called Butterfield Cellars LLC* ***(G-12163)***
Wingardner Sand and Gravel....509 480-3847
1300 Roza Dr Zillah (98953) ***(G-15765)***
Winigent, Woodinville *Also called MNC Services Inc* ***(G-15312)***
Winigent, Bellevue *Also called MNC Services Inc* ***(G-1011)***
Winn Enterprises LLC....425 482-6000
20702 Bothell Everett Hwy Bothell (98012) ***(G-1921)***
Winn/Devon Art Group Ltd (PA)....604 276-4551
6015 6th Ave S Seattle (98108) ***(G-11487)***
Winning Times, Steilacoom *Also called Ranger Publishing Company Inc* ***(G-13006)***
Winshuttle LLC (PA)....425 368-2708
19820 North Creek Pkwy # 200 Bothell (98011) ***(G-1808)***
Winshuttle Software Canada Inc....425 368-2708
20021 120th Ave Ne Bothell (98011) ***(G-1809)***
Winsol Laboratories Inc....206 782-5500
1417 Nw 51st St Seattle (98107) ***(G-11488)***
Winsor Fireform LLC....360 786-8200
3401 Mottman Rd Sw Tumwater (98512) ***(G-13907)***
Winston Quarry Inc....360 985-0487
269 Winston Creek Rd Mossyrock (98564) ***(G-6767)***
Winter Mattias....206 579-5275
500c E Main St Monroe (98272) ***(G-6638)***
Winterhalter Inc....360 652-6337
5219 220th St Nw Stanwood (98292) ***(G-13000)***
Winthrop Wood Works....509 996-2037
810 E Side Rd Winthrop (98862) ***(G-15166)***
Wintran Trading....425 501-7818
3601 97th Pl Se Everett (98208) ***(G-3660)***
Wipro Givon Usa Inc....425 355-3330
2300 Merrill Creek Pkwy # 300 Everett (98203) ***(G-3661)***
Wirefab Company, Mount Vernon *Also called National Wirecraft Company Inc* ***(G-6817)***
Wirekat Enterprises....425 413-6946
18531 Se 224th St Kent (98042) ***(G-5217)***
Wirtanen Logging Inc....360 686-3042
30606 Ne 247th Ave Yacolt (98675) ***(G-15494)***
Wisdom Elite LLC....806 201-3953
10614 Westwood Dr Sw Lakewood (98499) ***(G-5768)***
Wisdoms Marionettes....206 243-6172
4509 S 139th St Tukwila (98168) ***(G-13836)***
Wise Choice Custom Coatings....360 326-3809
6100 Ne 79th Ave Vancouver (98662) ***(G-14696)***
Wise Owl Productions, Blaine *Also called Wine Erna A I D Inc* ***(G-1712)***
Wise Publishing Group, Seattle *Also called My City Wise LLC* ***(G-10578)***
Wiseworth Canada, Ferndale *Also called Nuovo Parts Inc* ***(G-3879)***
Wishkah River Distillery LLC....360 612-4756
2210 Port Industrial Rd Aberdeen (98520) ***(G-41)***
Within Power Publishing....425 241-4214
9231 118th Pl Se Newcastle (98056) ***(G-7042)***
Wits Cellars....509 786-1311
2880 Lee Rd Prosser (99350) ***(G-8078)***
Wittco Separation Systems Inc....360 495-3100
260 Mccleary Rd McCleary (98557) ***(G-6421)***
Wizard International Inc....425 551-4300
4600 116th St Sw Mukilteo (98275) ***(G-6992)***
Wizard Shipping & Receiving, Mukilteo *Also called Wizard International Inc* ***(G-6992)***
Wizard Works....509 486-2654
32156 Highway 97 Tonasket (98855) ***(G-13662)***
Wizards of Coast LLC (HQ)....425 226-6500
1600 Lind Ave Sw Ste 400 Renton (98057) ***(G-8949)***
Wizz Signs....360 779-3103
20373 Viking Ave Nw D Poulsbo (98370) ***(G-8021)***
Wldg Wilkerson & Fabrication....509 438-9667
1100 E Columbia St D7 Pasco (99301) ***(G-7655)***
Wli Recycling, Lakewood *Also called E Power Systems & Battery Inc* ***(G-5716)***
Wli Recycling Inc....253 267-1965
10321 Lakeview Ave Sw Lakewood (98499) ***(G-5769)***
Wm Bolthouse Farms Inc....509 894-4460
10 Sonova Rd Prosser (99350) ***(G-8079)***
Wn Inc....509 966-9409
3271 Mapleway Rd Yakima (98908) ***(G-15709)***
Wntr Ski Academy LLC....425 829-1384
614 10th Ave W Kirkland (98033) ***(G-5495)***
Wof Pnw Pog 1 LLC....206 624-2144
601 Union St Ste 630 Seattle (98101) ***(G-11489)***
Woitchek Printing LLC....425 869-8212
7126 180th Ave Ne C104 Redmond (98052) ***(G-8716)***
Wojtanowicz Wood Works....253 225-2252
5902 Reid Dr Nw Gig Harbor (98335) ***(G-4176)***
Wolf Pack, Gold Bar *Also called G Wolf Enterprises Inc* ***(G-4188)***
Wolfetone Pickups Co....206 417-3548
18944 40th Pl Ne Lake Forest Park (98155) ***(G-5628)***
Wolff Defense....425 284-2000
4040 Lake Wash Blvd Ne Kirkland (98033) ***(G-5496)***

ALPHABETIC

Wolfkill Feed & Fert Corp (PA)....360 794-7065
217 E Stretch St Monroe (98272) ***(G-6639)***
Wollin Woodworking Inc....360 929-5895
725 N 1st St Mount Vernon (98273) ***(G-6856)***
Wompmobile Inc....888 625-8144
1117 Ellis St Bellingham (98225) ***(G-1594)***
Womsley Enterprises, Langley *Also called Womsley Logging Company* ***(G-5789)***
Womsley Logging Company....360 321-5321
4869 Lakeside Dr Langley (98260) ***(G-5789)***
Won-Door Corporation....206 726-9449
2141 E Hamlin St Seattle (98112) ***(G-11490)***
Wonderball, Seattle *Also called Play Impossible Corporation* ***(G-10821)***
Wonderware Pacwest, Bothell *Also called Industrial Software Solutns* ***(G-1767)***
Woobox LLC....360 450-5200
101 E 6th St Ste 220 Vancouver (98660) ***(G-14697)***
Wood & Son Earthwork & Utility....360 352-1022
2840 Black Lake Blvd Sw Tumwater (98512) ***(G-13908)***
Wood Box Factory, Mattawa *Also called Mattawa Wood Products Corp* ***(G-6410)***
Wood Care Systems....425 827-6000
719 Kirkland Ave Kirkland (98033) ***(G-5497)***
Wood Crafts By Pear Company....360 532-6246
617 Kuhn Ave Hoquiam (98550) ***(G-4363)***
Wood Creations....360 491-1616
4303 68th Ave Ne Olympia (98516) ***(G-7430)***
Wood Design....425 883-8842
11421 206th Ave Ne Redmond (98053) ***(G-8717)***
Wood House Custom Cabinets....360 293-2890
3111 T Ave Anacortes (98221) ***(G-184)***
Wood Resources LLC (PA)....360 432-5048
204 E Railroad Ave Shelton (98584) ***(G-11751)***
Wood Shed Inc....253 405-8890
373 Pacific Ave N Pacific (98047) ***(G-7541)***
Wood Stone Corporation....360 650-1111
1801 W Bakerview Rd Bellingham (98226) ***(G-1595)***
Wood Way Mfg Inc....360 366-4854
2183 Burk Rd Blaine (98230) ***(G-1713)***
Wood Works By Rob....206 497-6345
2812 H St Se Auburn (98002) ***(G-601)***
Wood-Works Cabinetry & Design....206 257-3335
401 S Brandon St Seattle (98108) ***(G-11491)***
Woodcraft Inc....800 225-1153
5015 208th St Sw Ste 3 Lynnwood (98036) ***(G-6226)***
Woodcraft Studio....404 426-1229
301 13th St Bremerton (98337) ***(G-2013)***
Woodcraft Supply LLC....206 767-6394
5963 Corson Ave S Ste 120 Seattle (98108) ***(G-11492)***
Wooden Pallets Recycled....360 624-3935
6905 Ne 119th St Vancouver (98686) ***(G-14698)***
Woodford Phoenix Aerospace Mfg....360 736-9689
112 E 1st St Centralia (98531) ***(G-2444)***
Woodhouse Family Cellars....425 527-0608
15500 Wdnville Rdmnd Woodinville (98072) ***(G-15406)***
Woodinville Printing Company, Woodinville *Also called Nta Inc* ***(G-15325)***
Woodinville Signs Inc....425 483-0296
13317 Ne 175th St Ste Z Woodinville (98072) ***(G-15407)***
Woodinville Weekly, Woodinville *Also called Ed Print Inc* ***(G-15233)***
Woodinville Whiskey Co LLC....425 486-1199
14509 Wdnvl Red Rd Ne Woodinville (98072) ***(G-15408)***
Woodinville Wine Co....425 481-8860
17721 132nd Ave Ne Woodinville (98072) ***(G-15409)***
Woodinvl Fclty McHne Shp/Wrhs, Woodinville *Also called Young Corporation* ***(G-15413)***
Woodland Pallet Repair LLC....360 624-3935
104 Whalen Rd Woodland (98674) ***(G-15475)***
Woodland Pattern Inc....253 475-3131
5408 S Proctor St Tacoma (98409) ***(G-13599)***
Woodland Paving....360 225-8317
3730 Old Lewis River Rd Woodland (98674) ***(G-15476)***
Woodland Services Inc....360 652-0412
17215 3rd Ave Ne Arlington (98223) ***(G-349)***
Woodland Windows & Doors....360 260-5466
11405 Ne 65th Ave Vancouver (98686) ***(G-14699)***
Woodmark Design, Sequim *Also called Dwight Hostvedt* ***(G-11631)***
Woodone-US Corp....206 850-0230
23209 Se 27th St Sammamish (98075) ***(G-9259)***
Woodpecker Graphics....509 481-8406
1119 N Bowdish Rd Spokane Valley (99206) ***(G-12940)***
Woodrock Inc....253 565-6090
1515 Dock St Ste 1 Tacoma (98402) ***(G-13600)***
Woodruff Aviation Co, Trout Lake *Also called Mount Adams Lumber Co Inc* ***(G-13681)***
Woods Bee Co....360 623-3359
919 W Reynolds Ave Centralia (98531) ***(G-2445)***
Woodstock International Inc (PA)....360 734-3482
1821 Valencia St Bellingham (98229) ***(G-1596)***
Woodward & White Manufacturing....253 839-7581
27051 10th Ave S Des Moines (98198) ***(G-2952)***
Woodward Canyon Winery Inc....509 525-4129
11920 W Highway 12 Lowden (99360) ***(G-5992)***
Woodward White Mch Manufacturi, Des Moines *Also called Woodward & White Manufacturing* ***(G-2952)***
Woodwise, Redmond *Also called Design Hardwood Products Inc* ***(G-8439)***
Woodwork Specialties LLC....360 687-5880
12501 Ne 308th St Battle Ground (98604) ***(G-754)***
Woodwork Tattoo and Gallery....360 626-1965
19494 7th Ave Ne Ste 144 Poulsbo (98370) ***(G-8022)***
Woodwork Unlimited Inc....425 334-5702
2608 Hartford Dr Lake Stevens (98258) ***(G-5675)***
Woodworkers Outpost....253 653-8607
25914 193rd Pl Se Covington (98042) ***(G-2840)***
Woodworking Services....253 678-7951
6614 Vickery Ave E Tacoma (98443) ***(G-13601)***
Woodworking Unlimited....425 481-7451
21819 1st Ave W Bothell (98021) ***(G-1922)***
Woodworks Cnstr & Cabinets....253 846-1918
17019 33rd Ave S Seatac (98188) ***(G-9310)***
Woody's Accessories, Kelso *Also called Kaper II Inc* ***(G-4533)***
Woodys Relics....360 849-4257
223 N Welcome Slough Rd Cathlamet (98612) ***(G-2377)***
Wooldridge Boats Inc....206 722-8998
1303 S 96th St Seattle (98108) ***(G-11493)***
Woolman Coatings LLC....206 402-2960
16227 Railroad Way Snohomish (98296) ***(G-12000)***
Woolys Tree Service Inc....360 944-7786
5321 Ne 72nd Ave Vancouver (98661) ***(G-14700)***
Word & Raby LLC....206 795-5267
260 Ne 43rd St Seattle (98105) ***(G-11494)***
Word & Raby Publishing, Seattle *Also called Word & Raby LLC* ***(G-11494)***
Word Up Publishing....253 859-7002
1600 Central Ave S Kent (98032) ***(G-5218)***
Worden's Lures, Granger *Also called Yakima Bait Co* ***(G-4264)***
Workbench Productions LLC....206 853-3742
1715 36th Ave S Seattle (98144) ***(G-11495)***
Workhorse Incorporated....360 835-9417
711 Ne 332nd Ct Washougal (98671) ***(G-15002)***
Workhorse Ind....206 257-5374
129 N 85th St Seattle (98103) ***(G-11496)***
Workskiff Inc....360 707-5622
500 Metcalf St Ste F1 Sedro Woolley (98284) ***(G-11581)***
Worktank Creative Media, Seattle *Also called Worktank Enterprises LLC* ***(G-11497)***
Worktank Enterprises LLC....206 254-0950
400 E Pine St Ste 301 Seattle (98122) ***(G-11497)***
World Diamonds....425 765-7119
1429 Bellevue Way Ne F Bellevue (98004) ***(G-1228)***
World Knives Ltd....866 862-5233
2103 Harrison Ave Nw 2-646 Olympia (98502) ***(G-7431)***
World Publishing Co....509 884-7575
110 N Wenatchee Ave Wenatchee (98801) ***(G-15086)***
World Publishing Company....509 663-5161
14 N Mission St Wenatchee (98801) ***(G-15087)***
World Trends Holdings LLC....559 474-2361
4170 Norris St Richland (99352) ***(G-9055)***
World Tube Company....253 756-6489
2608 N 15th St Tacoma (98406) ***(G-13602)***
World Wide Gourmet Foods Inc....360 668-9404
21616 87th Ave Se Woodinville (98072) ***(G-15410)***
World Wide Packets Inc (HQ)....509 242-9000
115 N Sullivan Rd Spokane Valley (99037) ***(G-12941)***
World Wide Store.com, Vancouver *Also called Far Star Products* ***(G-14222)***
Worldwide Botanicals Inc....206 518-1878
4463 S 175th St Seatac (98188) ***(G-9311)***
Worldwide Dgital Solutions Inc....425 605-0923
11251 120th Ave Ne # 142 Kirkland (98033) ***(G-5498)***
Worley Logging, Elk *Also called Michael D Worley* ***(G-3174)***
Wound Wood Technologies LLC....206 762-0400
9131 10th Ave S Seattle (98108) ***(G-11498)***
Wow Mom Corporation....206 240-4068
14200 69th Dr Se Unit B3 Snohomish (98296) ***(G-12001)***
Wozeniak Gordon Trucking, Buckley *Also called White River Logging* ***(G-2080)***
Wrap Pack Inc....509 453-2830
1728 Presson Pl Yakima (98903) ***(G-15710)***
Wrapper Press....425 443-4389
23010 Se 222nd St Maple Valley (98038) ***(G-6303)***
Wrbq Inc....509 927-7181
111 N Vista Rd Ste 1d Spokane Valley (99212) ***(G-12942)***
Wreathe Havoc....206 979-6838
17629 76th Ave W Edmonds (98026) ***(G-3163)***
Wright Business Forms Inc....253 872-0200
7015 S 212th St Kent (98032) ***(G-5219)***
Wright Designs....800 866-1245
17701 108th Ave Se Renton (98055) ***(G-8950)***
Wright Enterprises....360 985-7060
103 Shanklin Rd Onalaska (98570) ***(G-7454)***
Wright Machine, Seattle *Also called Venturi Holdings LLC* ***(G-11411)***
Wright Machine Inc....206 305-0642
719 S Monroe St Seattle (98108) ***(G-11499)***
Wright Surgical Arts LLC....509 792-1404
5908 Bedford St Pasco (99301) ***(G-7656)***
Wright T Company, The, Renton *Also called Wright Designs* ***(G-8950)***
Wrigley Jr Co....408 528-4376
1522 217th Pl Se Bothell (98021) ***(G-1923)***
Write Spark, Sammamish *Also called Marketech* ***(G-9230)***
Writing Hands....360 893-1606
1206 Williams St Nw Orting (98360) ***(G-7489)***

Wrs Materials, Vancouver *Also called Wafer Reclaim Services LLC* ***(G-14676)***
Wry Ink Publishing LLC 206 714-3178
2400 Nw 80th St Seattle (98117) ***(G-11500)***
Wsa-Hl Inc 509 921-7089
16710 E Euclid Ave Spokane Valley (99216) ***(G-12943)***
Wsb Sheetmetal Company 425 844-2061
14701 Main St Ne Ste C3 Duvall (98019) ***(G-3003)***
Wsf LLC (PA) 509 922-1300
911 N Thierman Rd Spokane Valley (99212) ***(G-12944)***
Wsu Bulletin Office 509 335-2857
2580 Nw Grimes Way Pullman (99164) ***(G-8116)***
Wt Vintners LLC 425 610-9463
14818 Ne 195th St Woodinville (98072) ***(G-15411)***
Wti, Fife *Also called Wind Talker Innovations Inc* ***(G-3999)***
Ww Village Winery 509 529-5300
107 S 3rd Ave Walla Walla (99362) ***(G-14905)***
Wws, Bellingham *Also called Washington Wind Sports Inc* ***(G-1589)***
Wwvwa 509 526-3117
13 1/2 E Main St Ste 214 Walla Walla (99362) ***(G-14906)***
Www Qualitylacecom 425 996-0523
2031 248th Pl Se Sammamish (98075) ***(G-9260)***
Www.bestbuyhorsetack.com, Port Orchard *Also called Imc-Innvtive Mktg Cnnction LLC* ***(G-7816)***
Www.hotfoilgraphics.com, Vancouver *Also called Foil Graphics* ***(G-14236)***
Www.multiplication.com, Prosser *Also called Krimsten Publishing LLC* ***(G-8047)***
Wychwood Inc 209 667-8188
161 Bunge Rd Elk (99009) ***(G-3179)***
Wyckoff Farms Incorporated (PA) 509 882-3934
160602 Evans Rd Grandview (98930) ***(G-4259)***
Wynakos Machine Inc 360 794-9057
17461 147th St Se Ste 7 Monroe (98272) ***(G-6640)***
Wyndsor Cabinet Group LLC 425 775-9828
200 2nd Ave N Apt 202 Edmonds (98020) ***(G-3164)***
Wynoochee River Winery 360 580-4452
79 Wheeler Rd Montesano (98563) ***(G-6666)***
Wyss Logging Inc 509 452-5893
7601 Wyss Ln Yakima (98901) ***(G-15711)***
X Bolt Signs LLC 509 945-6780
111 Blue Spruce Ln Naches (98937) ***(G-7008)***
X L F Aerospace LLC 206 592-2249
19550 Intl Blvd Ste 205 Seatac (98188) ***(G-9312)***
X Media Communications 206 789-6758
113 Nw 56th St Seattle (98107) ***(G-11501)***
X Press Ink Co 253 588-1818
4001 100th St Sw Lakewood (98499) ***(G-5770)***
X Products LLC 971 302-6127
1110 W 17th St Vancouver (98660) ***(G-14701)***
X Tracted 206 294-3308
3423 4th Ave S Seattle (98134) ***(G-11502)***
X'Tex, Issaquah *Also called Xextex Corporation USA* ***(G-4490)***
X-Cap, Olympia *Also called Extreme Capacitor Inc* ***(G-7281)***
X-Cel Feeds Inc 253 472-5140
5436 S Washington St Tacoma (98409) ***(G-13603)***
Xafax Corporation 360 389-5630
2045 Aldergrove Rd Ferndale (98248) ***(G-3926)***
Xanfab Inc 206 717-2185
19108 Des Moines Mem Dr Seatac (98148) ***(G-9313)***
Xd Vintners 425 210-1554
19501 144th Ave Ne C300 Woodinville (98072) ***(G-15412)***
Xenex Group, Seattle *Also called Xenex Seattle* ***(G-11503)***
Xenex Seattle 206 281-9370
3600 15th Ave W Ste 201 Seattle (98119) ***(G-11503)***
Xenon Arc Inc (PA) 425 646-1063
777 108th Ave Ne Ste 1750 Bellevue (98004) ***(G-1229)***
Xenophile Books, Seattle *Also called Studio Foglio LLC* ***(G-11207)***
Xensource Inc 425 881-9479
8461 154th Ave Ne Redmond (98052) ***(G-8718)***
Xeriton Corporation 425 369-2279
336 228th Ave Ne Ste 301 Sammamish (98074) ***(G-9261)***
Xerium Technologies Inc 360 636-0330
2209 Talley Way Kelso (98626) ***(G-4561)***
Xerox 360 923-8640
8535 Commerce Place Dr Ne A Lacey (98516) ***(G-5602)***
Xerox 253 437-4000
435 Minkler Blvd Tukwila (98188) ***(G-13837)***
Xerox Corp Xerox Corporat 425 947-7046
18005 Ne 68th St Ste A120 Redmond (98052) ***(G-8719)***
Xeta Technologies Inc 425 653-4500
10303 Meridian Ave N # 101 Seattle (98133) ***(G-11504)***
Xeta Technologies Inc 425 316-0721
3425 S 116th St Ste 101 Tukwila (98168) ***(G-13838)***
Xextex Corporation USA 425 392-3848
70 E Sunset Way Ste 188 Issaquah (98027) ***(G-4490)***
Xkl LLC 425 869-9050
12020 113th Ave Ne 100 Redmond (98052) ***(G-8720)***
Xmedius America Inc (HQ) 425 951-1600
20000 North Creek Pkwy # 200 Bothell (98011) ***(G-1810)***
Xmedius Buyer LLC (PA) 866 368-0400
20000 North Creek Pkwy Bothell (98011) ***(G-1811)***
Xn Technologies Inc 509 235-2672
2416 Cheney Spokane Rd Cheney (99004) ***(G-2596)***
Xnrgi Inc 425 272-2703
22722 29th Dr Se Ste 100 Bothell (98021) ***(G-1924)***
Xoceco USA 509 808-2480
225 N Holiday Hills Dr Liberty Lake (99019) ***(G-5869)***
Xoceco USA 425 670-3968
4100 194th St Sw Lynnwood (98036) ***(G-6227)***
Xtaeros Inc 206 883-4034
113 Cherry St Ste 58189 Seattle (98104) ***(G-11505)***
Xtr Off-Road Products 208 717-1515
2014 Andreasen Dr Clarkston (99403) ***(G-2656)***
Xtreme Pet Products LLC 206 772-2000
200 S Tobin St Ste D Renton (98057) ***(G-8951)***
Xtrudx Technologies Inc 206 568-3100
3410 A St Se Bldg B Auburn (98002) ***(G-602)***
XYZ Manufacturing 206 402-1936
1611 Sw 325th Pl Federal Way (98023) ***(G-3804)***
Y-Verge Llc 360 975-9277
3100 Se 168th Ave Apt 258 Vancouver (98683) ***(G-14702)***
Ya We Can Do That 360 253-5555
8905 Ne 136th Ave Vancouver (98682) ***(G-14703)***
Yacht Masters Northwest LLC 206 285-3460
1341 N Northlake Way # 100 Seattle (98103) ***(G-11506)***
Yacht Specialties 360 423-9995
111 Speer Dr Kelso (98626) ***(G-4562)***
Yachtfish Marine Inc (PA) 206 623-3233
1141 Fairview Ave N Seattle (98109) ***(G-11507)***
Yaculta Companies Inc (PA) 360 887-7493
805 Broadway St Ste 700 Vancouver (98660) ***(G-14704)***
Yager Company Inc 509 922-2772
9209 E Mission Ave Spokane Valley (99206) ***(G-12945)***
Yager Sails & Canvas, Spokane Valley *Also called Yager Company Inc* ***(G-12945)***
Yainax Medical LLC 503 516-7173
1915 E 5th St Ste C Vancouver (98661) ***(G-14705)***
Yakama Forest Products, White Swan *Also called Yakama Nation* ***(G-15140)***
Yakama Nation 509 874-2901
3191 Wesley Rd White Swan (98952) ***(G-15140)***
Yakama Yogert Shack LLC 509 965-5569
110 S 72nd Ave Yakima (98908) ***(G-15712)***
Yakima Bait Co 509 854-1311
1000 Bailey Ave Granger (98932) ***(G-4264)***
Yakima Chief-Hopunion LLC (PA) 509 453-4792
203 Division St Yakima (98902) ***(G-15713)***
Yakima Forklift LLC 509 985-3568
890 Rocky Ford Rd Toppenish (98948) ***(G-13675)***
Yakima Freightliner, Union Gap *Also called Freedom Truck Centers Inc* ***(G-13931)***
Yakima Grinding Co 509 575-1977
515 S 2nd St Yakima (98901) ***(G-15714)***
Yakima Herald Republic, Yakima *Also called Seattle Times Company* ***(G-15670)***
Yakima Herald Republic-309 ....509 367-6376
309 S Front St Yakima (98901) ***(G-15715)***
Yakima Herald-Republic Inc 509 452-7355
114 N 4th St Yakima (98901) ***(G-15716)***
Yakima Orthtics Prosthetics PC 509 943-8561
317 Wellsian Way Richland (99352) ***(G-9056)***
Yakima Press Company LLC 509 480-0642
361 Charlie Ln Naches (98937) ***(G-7009)***
Yakima Tent & Awning Co Ltd 509 457-6169
1015 E Lincoln Ave Yakima (98901) ***(G-15717)***
Yakima Valley Cabinets Inc 509 248-0472
701 Madison Ave Yakima (98902) ***(G-15718)***
Yakima Valley Pepsi Pak 509 952-0318
201 Merinda Dr Selah (98942) ***(G-11603)***
Yakima Valley Publishing, Yakima *Also called Yakima Valley Senior Times* ***(G-15719)***
Yakima Valley Senior Times 509 457-4886
416 S 3rd St Yakima (98901) ***(G-15719)***
Yakima Valley Teen Magazine 509 865-4055
16 W 1st Ave Toppenish (98948) ***(G-13676)***
Yakima Water Solutions LLC 509 941-9607
5808 Summitview Ave 71 Yakima (98908) ***(G-15720)***
Yamato Engine Specialists 1990, Bellingham *Also called North American Atk Corporation* ***(G-1463)***
Yancey Pallet Inc 509 331-0442
1885 W Herman Rd Othello (99344) ***(G-7511)***
Yangarra Alpacas 253 630-5422
25915 160th Ave Se Covington (98042) ***(G-2841)***
Yardarm Knot Inc 206 216-0220
2440 W Commodore Way # 200 Seattle (98199) ***(G-11508)***
Yazdi Corporation (PA) 425 787-6328
1815 N 45th St Ste 208 Seattle (98103) ***(G-11509)***
Yazdi Imports, Seattle *Also called Yazdi Corporation* ***(G-11509)***
Yehun LLC 425 533-9641
2729 S Elmwood Pl Seattle (98144) ***(G-11510)***
Yes Cabinet & Graent 253 572-1188
3702 Center St Tacoma (98409) ***(G-13604)***
YES MAGAZINE, Bainbridge Island *Also called Positive Futures Network* ***(G-660)***
Yesco, Tacoma *Also called Young Electric Sign Company* ***(G-13605)***
Yippie-Pie-Yay 206 227-9665
2625 13th Ave W Apt 405 Seattle (98119) ***(G-11511)***
Yk Products LLC 425 244-5000
12428 Highway 99 Ste 53 Everett (98204) ***(G-3662)***
YKK (usa) Inc 425 277-2503
1300 Sw 7th St Ste 109 Renton (98057) ***(G-8952)***

ALPHABETIC

Yms 206 354-2048
3635 S Findlay St Seattle (98118) ***(G-11512)***
Yo Gs Gh 253 858-9647
4784 Borgen Blvd Ste E Gig Harbor (98332) ***(G-4177)***
Yo Yakima 509 426-2925
2401 S 1st St Yakima (98903) ***(G-15721)***
Yon LLC 360 947-5895
1312 Nw 148th St Vancouver (98685) ***(G-14706)***
Yong Feng America Inc 425 271-8057
11220 Se 64th St Bellevue (98006) ***(G-1230)***
Yopti LLC 347 979-1735
227 Bellevue Way Ne # 257 Bellevue (98004) ***(G-1231)***
Yorkston Card Lock Fuels, Bellingham *Also called Yorkston Oil Co* ***(G-1597)***
Yorkston Oil Co (PA) 360 734-2201
2801 Roeder Ave Bellingham (98225) ***(G-1597)***
You Are Better Publishing 425 776-8640
716 Maple St Edmonds (98020) ***(G-3165)***
Youlookfab LLC 206 709-9541
1600 29th Ave Seattle (98122) ***(G-11513)***
Young Corporation 206 623-3274
3444 13th Ave Sw Seattle (98134) ***(G-11514)***
Young Corporation 206 623-3274
3444 13th Ave Sw Seattle (98134) ***(G-11515)***
Young Corporation 425 488-2427
16219 Woodinvlle Redmnd Woodinville (98072) ***(G-15413)***
Young Electric Sign Company 253 722-5753
7515 Portland Ave E Ste A Tacoma (98404) ***(G-13605)***
Young Gun NW 360 996-4275
2249 Jackson Hwy Chehalis (98532) ***(G-2544)***
Youngquist Boat Repair 206 283-9555
2476 Westlake Ave N Ste D Seattle (98109) ***(G-11516)***
Youngs Market of Washington 206 808-6124
3215 Lind Ave Sw Renton (98057) ***(G-8953)***
Youngs Neon Sign Co 253 946-1286
30318 13th Ave S Federal Way (98003) ***(G-3805)***
Youngwol Noodle 253 941-2002
31260 Pacific Hwy S Federal Way (98003) ***(G-3806)***
Younique 509 842-6908
17417 E Apollo Rd Spokane Valley (99016) ***(G-12946)***
Your Daily Dose LLC 360 749-7414
477 Agren Rd Castle Rock (98611) ***(G-2358)***
Yourceba LLC 509 747-5027
5123 N Post St Spokane (99205) ***(G-12595)***
Youth With A Mission 425 771-1153
7825 230th St Sw Edmonds (98026) ***(G-3166)***
Yue Fon USA Inc 206 303-0148
6840 Montevista Dr Se Auburn (98092) ***(G-603)***
Yum Yum Donut Shops Inc 360 423-0150
1560 15th Ave Longview (98632) ***(G-5970)***
Yummy Designs LLC 509 525-2072
636 Washington St Walla Walla (99362) ***(G-14907)***
Yurt, Vineyard & Winery, Creston *Also called Whitestone Winery Inc* ***(G-2843)***
Yvette J Cooke 360 718-0306
2403 Nw 148th St Vancouver (98685) ***(G-14707)***
Yvonne Roberts 253 531-3105
11319 Pacific Ave S Tacoma (98444) ***(G-13606)***
Ywam Publishing, Edmonds *Also called Youth With A Mission* ***(G-3166)***
Z & Z Art LLC 206 669-3323
2440 Western Ave Apt 212 Seattle (98121) ***(G-11517)***
Z Recyclers Inc 360 398-2161
6129 Guide Meridian Rd Lynden (98264) ***(G-6061)***
Z-Axis Prints 509 842-6680
6213 E Valleyview Dr Spokane Valley (99212) ***(G-12947)***
Z-Machine LLC 509 991-8628
35611 N Dunn Rd Chattaroy (99003) ***(G-2455)***
Z2live Inc (HQ) 206 890-4996
1420 5th Ave Ste 1900 Seattle (98101) ***(G-11518)***
Zacklift International Inc 509 674-4426
1102 E 1st St Cle Elum (98922) ***(G-2682)***
Zango Inc (PA) 425 279-1200
3600 136th Pl Se Ste 200 Bellevue (98006) ***(G-1232)***
Zebra Computers, Centralia *Also called Expert Computer Tech Inc* ***(G-2401)***
Zebra Print and Copy, Seattle *Also called Hilltop Management Inc* ***(G-10174)***
Zebra Print and Copy 206 223-1800
701 5th Ave Seattle (98104) ***(G-11519)***
Zebra Printing 425 656-3700
18439 E Valley Hwy # 103 Kent (98032) ***(G-5220)***
Zebra Printing Inc 425 462-9775
2021 130th Ave Ne Ste I Bellevue (98005) ***(G-1233)***
Zebra Technical Services LLC 425 485-8700
17270 Woodinville Redmond Woodinville (98072) ***(G-15414)***
Zebra Trans LLC 360 993-0451
4500 Nicholson Rd Apt E23 Vancouver (98661) ***(G-14708)***
Zeigler's Welding & Hitch Shop, Olympia *Also called Ziglers Welding Shop Inc* ***(G-7432)***
Zemax LLC (PA) 425 305-2800
10230 Ne Pints Dr Ste 540 Kirkland (98033) ***(G-5499)***
Zen Bakery, MA, Seattle *Also called Pin Hsiao & Associates LLC* ***(G-10808)***
Zen Dog Software LLC 425 861-8777
3741 122nd Ave Ne Bellevue (98005) ***(G-1234)***
Zender Bros & Wilburn Logging 360 599-2859
6269 Mt Baker Hwy Deming (98244) ***(G-2927)***
Zender Joe & Sons Logging Shop, Deming *Also called Joe Zender & Sons Inc* ***(G-2920)***
Zender Logging Co Inc 360 966-5693
2181 Central Rd Everson (98247) ***(G-3694)***
Zepher, Bingen *Also called Carbon Consultants LLC* ***(G-1634)***
Zepher Inc 509 637-2520
310 S Larch St Bingen (98605) ***(G-1643)***
Zephyrwerks 360 385-2720
521 Snagstead Way Port Townsend (98368) ***(G-7939)***
Zepp Resources 360 470-4622
225 Dunlap Rd Elma (98541) ***(G-3260)***
Zercks Logging LLC 509 779-4820
17424 N Highway 21 Malo (99150) ***(G-6236)***
Zero Gravity Bldrs Studio LLC 509 942-8439
1865 Bronco Ln Richland (99354) ***(G-9057)***
Zero One Vintners 206 601-2407
7050 S 216th St Kent (98032) ***(G-5221)***
Zero One Vintners 425 242-0735
131 Lake St S Kirkland (98033) ***(G-5500)***
Zeta Software Inc 503 371-4340
15606 Ne 40th St Apt I136 Redmond (98052) ***(G-8721)***
Zetec Inc (HQ) 425 974-2700
8226 Bracken Pl Se # 100 Snoqualmie (98065) ***(G-12035)***
Zhongtao 425 344-9373
11228 Ne 143rd Ct Kirkland (98034) ***(G-5501)***
Zhuro Software LLC 206 607-9073
2639 Sw Nevada St Seattle (98126) ***(G-11520)***
Ziglers Welding Shop Inc 360 357-6077
322 Capitol Way N Olympia (98501) ***(G-7432)***
Zila Works LLC 425 777-6813
4308 Ne 19th St Renton (98059) ***(G-8954)***
Zillow Group Inc (PA) 206 470-7000
1301 2nd Ave Fl 31 Seattle (98101) ***(G-11521)***
Zilyn LLC 360 509-2436
1323 Boren Ave Apt 603 Seattle (98101) ***(G-11522)***
Zimmel Unruh Cellars LLC 503 313-2235
17011 Se 5th St Vancouver (98684) ***(G-14709)***
Zions River 253 473-1838
4602 S 56th St Tacoma (98409) ***(G-13607)***
Zip-Vac, Auburn *Also called Danner Corporation* ***(G-422)***
Zipfizz Corporation 425 398-4240
14400 Ne 145th St Ste 201 Woodinville (98072) ***(G-15415)***
Zippro Press, Redmond *Also called Bryan Zippro* ***(G-8411)***
Zippy Pop Inc (PA) 855 404-3300
225 Marine Dr Blaine (98230) ***(G-1714)***
Zipwire Incorporated 425 591-4924
8201 164th Ave Ne Ste 200 Redmond (98052) ***(G-8722)***
Zirconia Inc 206 219-9236
4611 S 134th Pl Ste 240 Tukwila (98168) ***(G-13839)***
Zirkus Inc 360 385-5478
910 Calhoun St Port Townsend (98368) ***(G-7940)***
Zkl Printing Company LLC 206 369-6156
1445 R St Nw Auburn (98001) ***(G-604)***
Zoal & Associates LLC 425 355-9590
4609 Marble Ln Everett (98203) ***(G-3663)***
Zoal Precission Machining, Everett *Also called Zoal & Associates LLC* ***(G-3663)***
Zodiac Aerospace 425 791-3302
6300 Merrill Creek Pkwy B100 Everett (98203) ***(G-3664)***
Zodiac Aerospace 360 653-2600
18825 67th Ave Ne Arlington (98223) ***(G-350)***
Zodiac Aerospace 425 257-2044
2204 Hewitt Ave Everett (98201) ***(G-3665)***
Zodiac Arospc Engineered Mtls 360 653-2600
12806 State Ave Marysville (98271) ***(G-6403)***
Zodiac Lighting Solutions, Redmond *Also called Idd Aerospace Corp* ***(G-8505)***
Zojo Coffee, Longview *Also called NW Coffee Rosters LLC* ***(G-5939)***
Zombie Inc 206 623-9655
8477 Ne New Brooklyn Rd Bainbridge Island (98110) ***(G-685)***
Zombie Studios, Bainbridge Island *Also called Zombie Inc* ***(G-685)***
Zombie Tinder 360 548-3132
20611 67th Ave Ne Arlington (98223) ***(G-351)***
Zometek LLC 888 505-7953
616 S Lucile St Seattle (98108) ***(G-11523)***
Zometek Decking, Seattle *Also called Zometek LLC* ***(G-11523)***
Zonar Systems Inc (PA) 206 878-2459
18200 Cascade Ave S # 200 Seattle (98188) ***(G-11524)***
Zonecro Llc 760 702-9290
1810 Ne Rustic Ln Bremerton (98310) ***(G-2014)***
Zooka 425 363-3922
44027 Se Tanner Rd Ste A North Bend (98045) ***(G-7132)***
Zooka Sports Corporation 425 861-0111
8447 154th Ave Ne Redmond (98052) ***(G-8723)***
Zoomnet Postal + ...360 719-0973
7617 Nw 16th Ave Vancouver (98665) ***(G-14710)***
Zorn Manufacturing Co 360 456-4747
6714 Shincke Rd Ne Lacey (98506) ***(G-5603)***
Zorzi Corporation 425 334-0160
17103 14th St Ne Snohomish (98290) ***(G-12002)***
Zsolutionz LLC 425 502-6970
415 210th Pl Se Sammamish (98074) ***(G-9262)***
Ztron Labs Inc 425 289-8794
6405 158th St Se Snohomish (98296) ***(G-12003)***
Zuber Polymers LLC 360 929-7888
3005 Nw Market St A214 Seattle (98107) ***(G-11525)***

ALPHABETIC SECTION — Zzaphoria Spirits

Zultimate Self Defense Studios......425 688-7888
330 Bellevue Way Ne Bellevue (98004) *(G-1235)*

Zumar Industries Inc (PA)......253 536-7740
12015 Steele St S Tacoma (98444) *(G-13608)*

Zumedix LP......206 618-2848
3410 47th Ave Ne Seattle (98105) *(G-11526)*

Zumstein Logging Co (PA)......360 225-7505
1801 Ne Hayes Rd Woodland (98674) *(G-15477)*

Zumstein Logging Co......253 225-7521
302 E Scott Ave Woodland (98674) *(G-15478)*

Zuribella......253 227-2988
20621 74th Ave E Spanaway (98387) *(G-12082)*

Zymogenetics Inc (HQ)......206 442-6600
1201 Eastlake Ave E Seattle (98102) *(G-11527)*

Zymogenetics Inc......425 398-9637
3450 Monte Villa Pkwy Bothell (98021) *(G-1925)*

Zz Inc......360 734-2290
407 S Clarkwood Dr Bellingham (98225) *(G-1598)*

Zzaphoria Spirits......206 450-1353
20614 4th Ave Sw Normandy Park (98166) *(G-7100)*

(PA)=Parent Co (HQ)=Headquarters (DH)=Div Headquarters

PRODUCT INDEX

• Product categories are listed in alphabetical order.

A

ABRASIVES
ABRASIVES: Diamond Powder
ACCELERATION INDICATORS & SYSTEM COMPONENTS: Aerospace
ACCELERATORS: Particle, High Voltage
ACCOMMODATION LOCATING SVCS
ACCOUNTING MACHINES & CASH REGISTERS
ACCOUNTING SVCS, NEC
ACCOUNTING SVCS: Certified Public
ACIDS: Sulfuric, Oleum
ACTUATORS: Indl, NEC
ADDITIVE BASED PLASTIC MATERIALS: Plasticizers
ADHESIVES
ADHESIVES & SEALANTS
ADVERTISING AGENCIES
ADVERTISING AGENCIES: Consultants
ADVERTISING CURTAINS
ADVERTISING DISPLAY PRDTS
ADVERTISING MATERIAL DISTRIBUTION
ADVERTISING REPRESENTATIVES: Electronic Media
ADVERTISING REPRESENTATIVES: Magazine
ADVERTISING REPRESENTATIVES: Media
ADVERTISING REPRESENTATIVES: Newspaper
ADVERTISING REPRESENTATIVES: Printed Media
ADVERTISING SPECIALTIES, WHOLESALE
ADVERTISING SVCS, NEC
ADVERTISING SVCS: Coupon Distribution
ADVERTISING SVCS: Direct Mail
ADVERTISING SVCS: Display
ADVERTISING SVCS: Outdoor
ADVERTISING SVCS: Transit
ADVERTISING: Aerial
AERIAL WORK PLATFORMS
AEROSOLS
AGENTS & MANAGERS: Entertainers
AGENTS, BROKERS & BUREAUS: Personal Service
AGRICULTURAL CHEMICALS: Trace Elements
AGRICULTURAL DISINFECTANTS
AGRICULTURAL EQPT: BARN, SILO, POULTRY, DAIRY/LIVESTOCK MACH
AGRICULTURAL EQPT: Dusters, Mechanical
AGRICULTURAL EQPT: Elevators, Farm
AGRICULTURAL EQPT: Fertilizng, Sprayng, Dustng/Irrigatn Mach
AGRICULTURAL EQPT: Grade, Clean & Sort Machines, Fruit/Veg
AGRICULTURAL EQPT: Harvesters, Fruit, Vegetable, Tobacco
AGRICULTURAL EQPT: Haying Mach, Mowers, Rakes, Stackers, Etc
AGRICULTURAL EQPT: Irrigation Eqpt, Self-Propelled
AGRICULTURAL EQPT: Loaders, Manure & General Utility
AGRICULTURAL EQPT: Tractors, Farm
AGRICULTURAL EQPT: Trailers & Wagons, Farm
AGRICULTURAL EQPT: Troughs, Water
AGRICULTURAL EQPT: Turf & Grounds Eqpt
AGRICULTURAL MACHINERY & EQPT REPAIR
AGRICULTURAL MACHINERY & EQPT: Wholesalers
AGRICULTURAL PROGRAM REGULATION OFFICES, GOVERNMENT: State
AIR CLEANING SYSTEMS
AIR CONDITIONERS: Motor Vehicle
AIR CONDITIONING & VENTILATION EQPT & SPLYS: Wholesales
AIR CONDITIONING EQPT
AIR CONDITIONING EQPT, WHOLE HOUSE: Wholesalers
AIR CONDITIONING UNITS: Complete, Domestic Or Indl
AIR MATTRESSES: Plastic
AIR POLLUTION CONTROL EQPT & SPLYS WHOLESALERS
AIR PURIFICATION EQPT
AIR TRAFFIC CONTROL SYSTEMS & EQPT
AIRCRAFT & AEROSPACE FLIGHT INSTRUMENTS & GUIDANCE SYSTEMS
AIRCRAFT & HEAVY EQPT REPAIR SVCS
AIRCRAFT ASSEMBLY PLANTS
AIRCRAFT CLEANING & JANITORIAL SVCS
AIRCRAFT CONTROL SYSTEMS:
AIRCRAFT CONTROL SYSTEMS: Electronic Totalizing Counters
AIRCRAFT DEALERS
AIRCRAFT ENGINES & ENGINE PARTS: Air Scoops
AIRCRAFT ENGINES & ENGINE PARTS: Cooling Systems
AIRCRAFT ENGINES & ENGINE PARTS: Engine Heaters
AIRCRAFT ENGINES & ENGINE PARTS: Exhaust Systems
AIRCRAFT ENGINES & ENGINE PARTS: Mount Parts
AIRCRAFT ENGINES & ENGINE PARTS: Research & Development, Mfr
AIRCRAFT ENGINES & PARTS
AIRCRAFT EQPT & SPLYS WHOLESALERS
AIRCRAFT FLIGHT INSTRUMENT REPAIR SVCS
AIRCRAFT FLIGHT INSTRUMENTS
AIRCRAFT FUELING SVCS
AIRCRAFT LIGHTING
AIRCRAFT MAINTENANCE & REPAIR SVCS
AIRCRAFT PARTS & AUX EQPT: Panel Assy/Hydro Prop Test Stands
AIRCRAFT PARTS & AUXILIARY EQPT: Aircraft Training Eqpt
AIRCRAFT PARTS & AUXILIARY EQPT: Assys, Subassemblies/Parts
AIRCRAFT PARTS & AUXILIARY EQPT: Body & Wing Assys & Parts
AIRCRAFT PARTS & AUXILIARY EQPT: Body Assemblies & Parts
AIRCRAFT PARTS & AUXILIARY EQPT: Elevators
AIRCRAFT PARTS & AUXILIARY EQPT: Fins
AIRCRAFT PARTS & AUXILIARY EQPT: Flaps, Wing
AIRCRAFT PARTS & AUXILIARY EQPT: Landing Assemblies & Brakes
AIRCRAFT PARTS & AUXILIARY EQPT: Lighting/Landing Gear Assy
AIRCRAFT PARTS & AUXILIARY EQPT: Military Eqpt & Armament
AIRCRAFT PARTS & AUXILIARY EQPT: Oxygen Systems
AIRCRAFT PARTS & AUXILIARY EQPT: Refueling Eqpt, In Flight
AIRCRAFT PARTS & AUXILIARY EQPT: Research & Development, Mfr
AIRCRAFT PARTS & AUXILIARY EQPT: Rotor Blades, Helicopter
AIRCRAFT PARTS & AUXILIARY EQPT: Rudders
AIRCRAFT PARTS & AUXILIARY EQPT: Tanks, Fuel
AIRCRAFT PARTS & AUXILIARY EQPT: Wing Assemblies & Parts
AIRCRAFT PARTS & EQPT, NEC
AIRCRAFT PARTS WHOLESALERS
AIRCRAFT PARTS/AUX EQPT: Airframe Assy, Exc Guided Missiles
AIRCRAFT PROPELLERS & PARTS
AIRCRAFT RADIO EQPT REPAIR SVCS
AIRCRAFT SEATS
AIRCRAFT SERVICING & REPAIRING
AIRCRAFT TIRES
AIRCRAFT TURBINES
AIRCRAFT: Airplanes, Fixed Or Rotary Wing
AIRCRAFT: Airships
AIRCRAFT: Autogiros
AIRCRAFT: Motorized
AIRCRAFT: Research & Development, Manufacturer
AIRLOCKS
AIRPORT
AIRPORTS, FLYING FIELDS & SVCS
ALARMS: Burglar
ALARMS: Fire
ALCOHOL TREATMENT CLINIC, OUTPATIENT
ALCOHOL, GRAIN: For Beverage Purposes
ALCOHOL: Methyl & Methanol, Synthetic
ALKALIES & CHLORINE
ALLOYS: Additive, Exc Copper Or Made In Blast Furnaces
ALTERNATORS: Automotive
ALUMINUM
ALUMINUM & BERYLLIUM ORES MINING
ALUMINUM PRDTS
ALUMINUM: Ingots & Slabs
ALUMINUM: Ingots, Primary
ALUMINUM: Slabs, Primary
AMMONIA & LIQUOR: Chemical Recovery Coke Oven
AMMUNITION
AMMUNITION: Cartridges, 30 mm & Below
AMMUNITION: Mines & Parts, Ordnance
AMPLIFIERS
AMPLIFIERS: Pulse Amplifiers
AMPLIFIERS: RF & IF Power
AMUSEMENT & RECREATION SVCS: Art Gallery, Commercial
AMUSEMENT & RECREATION SVCS: Bridge Club, Non-Membership
AMUSEMENT & RECREATION SVCS: Diving Instruction, Underwater
AMUSEMENT & RECREATION SVCS: Fishing Boat Operations, Party
AMUSEMENT & RECREATION SVCS: Golf Club, Membership
AMUSEMENT & RECREATION SVCS: Golf Professionals
AMUSEMENT & RECREATION SVCS: Gun Club, Membership
AMUSEMENT & RECREATION SVCS: Lottery Tickets, Sales
AMUSEMENT & RECREATION SVCS: Physical Fitness Instruction
AMUSEMENT & RECREATION SVCS: Picnic Ground Operation
AMUSEMENT & RECREATION SVCS: Rafting Tours
AMUSEMENT & RECREATION SVCS: Recreation SVCS
AMUSEMENT & RECREATION SVCS: Riding & Rodeo Svcs
AMUSEMENT & RECREATION SVCS: Tennis Club, Membership
AMUSEMENT & RECREATION SVCS: Yoga Instruction
AMUSEMENT PARK DEVICES & RIDES
AMUSEMENT PARK DEVICES & RIDES Carousels Or Merry-Go-Rounds
AMUSEMENT PARK DEVICES & RIDES: Carnival Mach & Eqpt, NEC
ANALGESICS
ANALYZERS: Moisture
ANALYZERS: Network
ANESTHESIA EQPT
ANIMAL BASED MEDICINAL CHEMICAL PRDTS
ANIMAL FEED & SUPPLEMENTS: Livestock & Poultry
ANIMAL FEED: Wholesalers
ANIMAL FOOD & SUPPLEMENTS: Alfalfa Or Alfalfa Meal
ANIMAL FOOD & SUPPLEMENTS: Bird Food, Prepared
ANIMAL FOOD & SUPPLEMENTS: Cat
ANIMAL FOOD & SUPPLEMENTS: Dog
ANIMAL FOOD & SUPPLEMENTS: Dog & Cat
ANIMAL FOOD & SUPPLEMENTS: Feed Concentrates
ANIMAL FOOD & SUPPLEMENTS: Feed Premixes
ANIMAL FOOD & SUPPLEMENTS: Feed Supplements
ANIMAL FOOD & SUPPLEMENTS: Hay, Cubed
ANIMAL FOOD & SUPPLEMENTS: Livestock
ANIMAL FOOD & SUPPLEMENTS: Meat Meal & Tankage
ANIMAL FOOD & SUPPLEMENTS: Mineral feed supplements
ANIMAL FOOD & SUPPLEMENTS: Pet, Exc Dog & Cat, Dry
ANIMAL FOOD & SUPPLEMENTS: Poultry
ANIMAL FOOD & SUPPLEMENTS: Stock Feeds, Dry
ANNEALING: Metal
ANODIZING SVC
ANTENNAS: Radar Or Communications
ANTENNAS: Receiving
ANTIMONY ORE MINING
ANTIQUE FURNITURE RESTORATION & REPAIR
ANTIQUES, WHOLESALE
APPAREL DESIGNERS: Commercial
APPLIANCES, HOUSEHOLD: Kitchen, Major, Exc Refrigs & Stoves
APPLIANCES, HOUSEHOLD: Laundry Machines, Incl Coin-Operated
APPLIANCES, HOUSEHOLD: Refrigs, Mechanical & Absorption
APPLIANCES, HOUSEHOLD: Shampooers, Carpet
APPLIANCES: Household, NEC
APPLIANCES: Household, Refrigerators & Freezers
APPLIANCES: Small, Electric
APPLICATIONS SOFTWARE PROGRAMMING

PRODUCT INDEX

APPRAISAL SVCS, EXC REAL ESTATE
AQUARIUMS & ACCESS: Plastic
ARCHITECT'S SUPPLIES WHOLESALERS
ARCHITECTURAL SVCS
ARCHITECTURAL SVCS: House Designer
ARMATURE REPAIRING & REWINDING SVC
ARMOR PLATES
AROMATIC CHEMICAL PRDTS
ART & ORNAMENTAL WARE: Pottery
ART DEALERS & GALLERIES
ART DESIGN SVCS
ART GALLERIES
ART GOODS & SPLYS WHOLESALERS
ART GOODS, WHOLESALE
ART RELATED SVCS
ART SCHOOL, EXC COMMERCIAL
ART SPLY STORES
ARTIFICIAL FLOWER SHOPS
ARTIFICIAL FLOWERS & TREES
ARTISTS' MATERIALS, WHOLESALE
ARTISTS' MATERIALS: Boards, Drawing
ARTISTS' MATERIALS: Canvas, Prepared On Frames
ARTISTS' MATERIALS: Colors, Water & Oxide Ceramic Glass
ARTISTS' MATERIALS: Frames, Artists' Canvases
ARTISTS' MATERIALS: Paints, China Painting
ARTISTS' MATERIALS: Paints, Exc Gold & Bronze
ARTISTS' MATERIALS: Paints, Gold Or Bronze
ARTS & CRAFTS SCHOOL
ARTWORK: Framed
ASBESTOS PRODUCTS
ASBESTOS REMOVAL EQPT
ASHLAR: Cast Stone
ASPHALT & ASPHALT PRDTS
ASPHALT COATINGS & SEALERS
ASPHALT PLANTS INCLUDING GRAVEL MIX TYPE
ASSEMBLING SVC: Plumbing Fixture Fittings, Plastic
ASSOCIATIONS: Business
ASSOCIATIONS: Fraternal
ASSOCIATIONS: Real Estate Management
ATHLETIC CLUB & GYMNASIUMS, MEMBERSHIP
ATOMIZERS
AUDIO & VIDEO EQPT, EXC COMMERCIAL
AUDIO COMPONENTS
AUDIO ELECTRONIC SYSTEMS
AUDIOLOGICAL EQPT: Electronic
AUTO & HOME SUPPLY STORES: Auto & Truck Eqpt & Parts
AUTO & HOME SUPPLY STORES: Auto Air Cond Eqpt, Sell/Install
AUTO & HOME SUPPLY STORES: Automotive Access
AUTO & HOME SUPPLY STORES: Automotive parts
AUTO & HOME SUPPLY STORES: Trailer Hitches, Automotive
AUTO & HOME SUPPLY STORES: Truck Eqpt & Parts
AUTO SPLYS & PARTS, NEW, WHSLE: Exhaust Sys, Mufflers, Etc
AUTOCLAVES: Indl
AUTOMATED TELLER MACHINE NETWORK
AUTOMATIC REGULATING CNTRLS: Liq Lvl, Residential/Comm Heat
AUTOMATIC REGULATING CONTROL: Building Svcs Monitoring, Auto
AUTOMATIC REGULATING CONTROLS: AC & Refrigeration
AUTOMATIC REGULATING CONTROLS: Elect Air Cleaner, Automatic
AUTOMATIC REGULATING CONTROLS: Hardware, Environmental Reg
AUTOMATIC REGULATING CONTROLS: Humidity, Air-Conditioning
AUTOMATIC REGULATING CONTROLS: Pneumatic Relays, Air-Cond
AUTOMATIC REGULATING CTRLS: Damper, Pneumatic Or Electric
AUTOMATIC REGULATING CTRLS: Elec Heat Proportion, Modultg
AUTOMATIC TELLER MACHINES
AUTOMOBILE DRIVING SCHOOLS
AUTOMOBILES & OTHER MOTOR VEHICLES WHOLESALERS
AUTOMOTIVE & TRUCK GENERAL REPAIR SVC
AUTOMOTIVE AIR CONDITIONING REPAIR SHOPS
AUTOMOTIVE BATTERIES WHOLESALERS
AUTOMOTIVE BODY SHOP
AUTOMOTIVE BODY, PAINT & INTERIOR REPAIR & MAINTENANCE SVC
AUTOMOTIVE CUSTOMIZING SVCS, NONFACTORY BASIS
AUTOMOTIVE GLASS REPLACEMENT SHOPS
AUTOMOTIVE LETTERING SVCS
AUTOMOTIVE PAINT SHOP
AUTOMOTIVE PARTS, ACCESS & SPLYS
AUTOMOTIVE PARTS: Plastic
AUTOMOTIVE PRDTS: Rubber
AUTOMOTIVE RADIATOR REPAIR SHOPS
AUTOMOTIVE REPAIR SHOPS: Brake Repair
AUTOMOTIVE REPAIR SHOPS: Carburetor Repair
AUTOMOTIVE REPAIR SHOPS: Diesel Engine Repair
AUTOMOTIVE REPAIR SHOPS: Electrical Svcs
AUTOMOTIVE REPAIR SHOPS: Engine Rebuilding
AUTOMOTIVE REPAIR SHOPS: Engine Repair
AUTOMOTIVE REPAIR SHOPS: Engine Repair, Exc Diesel
AUTOMOTIVE REPAIR SHOPS: Frame & Front End Repair Svcs
AUTOMOTIVE REPAIR SHOPS: Fuel System Repair
AUTOMOTIVE REPAIR SHOPS: Machine Shop
AUTOMOTIVE REPAIR SHOPS: Muffler Shop, Sale/Rpr/Installation
AUTOMOTIVE REPAIR SHOPS: Powertrain Components Repair Svcs
AUTOMOTIVE REPAIR SHOPS: Sound System Svc & Installation
AUTOMOTIVE REPAIR SHOPS: Trailer Repair
AUTOMOTIVE REPAIR SHOPS: Truck Engine Repair, Exc Indl
AUTOMOTIVE REPAIR SVC
AUTOMOTIVE SPLYS & PARTS, NEW, WHOL: Auto Servicing Eqpt
AUTOMOTIVE SPLYS & PARTS, NEW, WHOLESALE: Brakes
AUTOMOTIVE SPLYS & PARTS, NEW, WHOLESALE: Engines/Eng Parts
AUTOMOTIVE SPLYS & PARTS, NEW, WHOLESALE: Filters, Air & Oil
AUTOMOTIVE SPLYS & PARTS, NEW, WHOLESALE: Radiators
AUTOMOTIVE SPLYS & PARTS, NEW, WHOLESALE: Seat Covers
AUTOMOTIVE SPLYS & PARTS, NEW, WHOLESALE: Splys
AUTOMOTIVE SPLYS & PARTS, NEW, WHOLESALE: Trailer Parts
AUTOMOTIVE SPLYS & PARTS, USED, WHOLESALE: Dry Cell Batt
AUTOMOTIVE SPLYS & PARTS, WHOLESALE, NEC
AUTOMOTIVE SPLYS, USED, WHOLESALE & RETAIL
AUTOMOTIVE SPLYS/PARTS, NEW, WHOL: Body Rpr/Paint Shop Splys
AUTOMOTIVE SVCS
AUTOMOTIVE SVCS, EXC REPAIR & CARWASHES: Glass Tinting
AUTOMOTIVE SVCS, EXC REPAIR & CARWASHES: Insp & Diagnostic
AUTOMOTIVE SVCS, EXC REPAIR & CARWASHES: Maintenance
AUTOMOTIVE TOWING & WRECKING SVC
AUTOMOTIVE TOWING SVCS
AUTOMOTIVE UPHOLSTERY SHOPS
AUTOMOTIVE WELDING SVCS
AUTOMOTIVE: Bodies
AUTOMOTIVE: Seating
AWNINGS & CANOPIES
AWNINGS & CANOPIES: Awnings, Fabric, From Purchased Matls
AWNINGS & CANOPIES: Canopies, Fabric, From Purchased Matls
AWNINGS & CANOPIES: Fabric
AWNINGS: Fiberglass
AWNINGS: Metal
AWNINGS: Wood
AXES & HATCHETS
AXLES

B

BACKHOES
BADGES, WHOLESALE
BADGES: Identification & Insignia
BAGS & CONTAINERS: Textile, Exc Sleeping
BAGS: Canvas
BAGS: Duffle, Canvas, Made From Purchased Materials
BAGS: Garment, Plastic Film, Made From Purchased Materials
BAGS: Paper
BAGS: Paper, Made From Purchased Materials
BAGS: Plastic
BAGS: Plastic, Made From Purchased Materials
BAGS: Tea, Fabric, Made From Purchased Materials
BAGS: Textile
BAGS: Vacuum cleaner, Made From Purchased Materials
BAGS: Wardrobe, Closet Access, Made From Purchased Materials
BAIT, FISHING, WHOLESALE
BAKERIES, COMMERCIAL: On Premises Baking Only
BAKERIES: On Premises Baking & Consumption
BAKERY FOR HOME SVC DELIVERY
BAKERY MACHINERY
BAKERY PRDTS: Bagels, Fresh Or Frozen
BAKERY PRDTS: Bakery Prdts, Partially Cooked, Exc frozen
BAKERY PRDTS: Bread, All Types, Fresh Or Frozen
BAKERY PRDTS: Buns, Bread Type, Fresh Or Frozen
BAKERY PRDTS: Cakes, Bakery, Exc Frozen
BAKERY PRDTS: Cakes, Bakery, Frozen
BAKERY PRDTS: Cones, Ice Cream
BAKERY PRDTS: Cookies
BAKERY PRDTS: Cookies & crackers
BAKERY PRDTS: Cracker Meal & Crumbs
BAKERY PRDTS: Doughnuts, Exc Frozen
BAKERY PRDTS: Dry
BAKERY PRDTS: Frozen
BAKERY PRDTS: Pies, Exc Frozen
BAKERY PRDTS: Pretzels
BAKERY PRDTS: Rolls, Bread Type, Fresh Or Frozen
BAKERY PRDTS: Wholesalers
BAKERY PRDTS: Zwieback
BAKERY: Wholesale Or Wholesale & Retail Combined
BALLASTS: Lighting
BALLOONS: Hot Air
BALLOONS: Novelty & Toy
BANKING SCHOOLS, TRAINING
BANKS: Mortgage & Loan
BANKS: National Commercial
BANNERS: Fabric
BANQUET HALL FACILITIES
BAR
BARBECUE EQPT
BARGES BUILDING & REPAIR
BARRICADES: Metal
BARS, COLD FINISHED: Steel, From Purchased Hot-Rolled
BARS, PIPES, PLATES & SHAPES: Lead/Lead Alloy Bars, Pipe
BARS: Concrete Reinforcing, Fabricated Steel
BASALT: Crushed & Broken
BASALT: Dimension
BASES, BEVERAGE
BATH SALTS
BATH SHOPS
BATHMATS: Rubber
BATHROOM ACCESS & FITTINGS: Vitreous China & Earthenware
BATHTUBS: Concrete
BATTERIES: Lead Acid, Storage
BATTERIES: Nickel-Cadmium
BATTERIES: Rechargeable
BATTERIES: Storage
BATTERIES: Wet
BATTERY CASES: Plastic Or Plastics Combination
BATTERY CHARGERS
BATTERY CHARGERS: Storage, Motor & Engine Generator Type
BATTERY CHARGING GENERATORS
BEARINGS & PARTS Ball
BEARINGS: Plastic
BEARINGS: Roller & Parts
BEARINGS: Wooden
BEAUTY & BARBER SHOP EQPT
BEAUTY SALONS
BED & BREAKFAST INNS
BED SHEETING, COTTON
BEDDING & BEDSPRINGS STORES
BEDDING, BEDSPREADS, BLANKETS & SHEETS
BEDDING, BEDSPREADS, BLANKETS & SHEETS: Comforters & Quilts
BEDS & ACCESS STORES
BEDS: Hospital
BEDS: Institutional
BEEKEEPERS' SPLYS
BEEKEEPERS' SPLYS: Honeycomb Foundations
BEER & ALE WHOLESALERS

PRODUCT INDEX

BEER & ALE, WHOLESALE: Beer & Other Fermented Malt Liquors
BEER, WINE & LIQUOR STORES
BEER, WINE & LIQUOR STORES: Hard Liquor
BEER, WINE & LIQUOR STORES: Wine
BEER, WINE & LIQUOR STORES: Wine & Beer
BEESWAX PROCESSING
BELLOWS
BELTING: Fabric
BELTING: Rubber
BELTS & BELT PRDTS
BELTS: Chain
BELTS: Conveyor, Made From Purchased Wire
BELTS: Seat, Automotive & Aircraft
BELTS: V
BEVERAGE BASES & SYRUPS
BEVERAGE POWDERS
BEVERAGE PRDTS: Brewers' Grain
BEVERAGE STORES
BEVERAGE, NONALCOHOLIC: Iced Tea/Fruit Drink, Bottled/Canned
BEVERAGES, ALCOHOLIC: Ale
BEVERAGES, ALCOHOLIC: Beer
BEVERAGES, ALCOHOLIC: Beer & Ale
BEVERAGES, ALCOHOLIC: Bourbon Whiskey
BEVERAGES, ALCOHOLIC: Brandy & Brandy Spirits
BEVERAGES, ALCOHOLIC: Brandy Spirits
BEVERAGES, ALCOHOLIC: Cocktails
BEVERAGES, ALCOHOLIC: Distilled Liquors
BEVERAGES, ALCOHOLIC: Liquors, Malt
BEVERAGES, ALCOHOLIC: Near Beer
BEVERAGES, ALCOHOLIC: Neutral Spirits, Exc Fruit
BEVERAGES, ALCOHOLIC: Vodka
BEVERAGES, ALCOHOLIC: Wines
BEVERAGES, MALT
BEVERAGES, NONALCOHOLIC: Bottled & canned soft drinks
BEVERAGES, NONALCOHOLIC: Carbonated
BEVERAGES, NONALCOHOLIC: Carbonated, Canned & Bottled, Etc
BEVERAGES, NONALCOHOLIC: Cider
BEVERAGES, NONALCOHOLIC: Flavoring extracts & syrups, nec
BEVERAGES, NONALCOHOLIC: Fruit Drnks, Under 100% Juice, Can
BEVERAGES, NONALCOHOLIC: Fruits, Crushed, For Fountain Use
BEVERAGES, NONALCOHOLIC: Soft Drinks, Canned & Bottled, Etc
BEVERAGES, NONALCOHOLIC: Tea, Iced, Bottled & Canned, Etc
BEVERAGES, WINE & DISTILLED ALCOHOLIC, WHOLESALE: Liquor
BEVERAGES, WINE & DISTILLED ALCOHOLIC, WHOLESALE: Wine
BEVERAGES, WINE/DISTILLED ALCOH, WHOL: Brandy/Brandy Spirits
BICYCLE SHOPS
BICYCLES, PARTS & ACCESS
BINDING SVC: Books & Manuals
BINDING SVC: Trade
BIOLOGICAL PRDTS: Exc Diagnostic
BIOLOGICAL PRDTS: Extracts
BIOLOGICAL PRDTS: Vaccines
BIOLOGICAL PRDTS: Vaccines & Immunizing
BIOLOGICAL PRDTS: Venoms
BIOLOGICAL PRDTS: Veterinary
BITUMINOUS & LIGNITE COAL LOADING & PREPARATION
BLADES: Knife
BLADES: Saw, Hand Or Power
BLANKBOOKS & LOOSELEAF BINDERS
BLANKBOOKS: Albums, Record
BLANKBOOKS: Checkbooks & Passbooks, Bank
BLANKBOOKS: Scrapbooks
BLANKETS, INSULATING: Aircraft, Asbestos
BLANKETS: Horse
BLASTING SVC: Sand, Metal Parts
BLINDS & SHADES: Mini
BLINDS & SHADES: Vertical
BLINDS : Window
BLOCKS & BLANKS: Bobbin, Wood
BLOCKS & BRICKS: Concrete
BLOCKS: Landscape Or Retaining Wall, Concrete
BLOCKS: Paving, Composition
BLOCKS: Sewer & Manhole, Concrete

BLOCKS: Standard, Concrete Or Cinder
BLOWER FILTER UNITS: Furnace Blowers
BLOWERS & FANS
BLOWERS & FANS
BLUEPRINTING SVCS
BOAT & BARGE COMPONENTS: Metal, Prefabricated
BOAT BUILDING & REPAIR
BOAT BUILDING & REPAIRING: Fiberglass
BOAT BUILDING & REPAIRING: Kayaks
BOAT BUILDING & REPAIRING: Lifeboats
BOAT BUILDING & REPAIRING: Motorboats, Inboard Or Outboard
BOAT BUILDING & REPAIRING: Motorized
BOAT BUILDING & REPAIRING: Non-Motorized
BOAT BUILDING & REPAIRING: Pontoons, Exc Aircraft & Inflat
BOAT BUILDING & REPAIRING: Rowboats
BOAT BUILDING & REPAIRING: Tenders, Small Motor Craft
BOAT BUILDING & REPAIRING: Yachts
BOAT BUILDING & RPRG: Fishing, Small, Lobster, Crab, Oyster
BOAT DEALERS
BOAT DEALERS: Canoes
BOAT DEALERS: Inboard
BOAT DEALERS: Kayaks
BOAT DEALERS: Marine Splys & Eqpt
BOAT DEALERS: Motor
BOAT DEALERS: Sailboats & Eqpt
BOAT DEALERS: Sails & Eqpt
BOAT LIFTS
BOAT REPAIR SVCS
BOAT YARD: Boat yards, storage & incidental repair
BOATS & OTHER MARINE EQPT: Plastic
BOATS: Plastic, Nonrigid
BODIES: Truck & Bus
BODY PARTS: Automobile, Stamped Metal
BOILER & HEATING REPAIR SVCS
BOILER REPAIR SHOP
BONDS, RAIL: Electric, Propulsion & Signal Circuit Uses
BOOK STORES
BOOK STORES: College
BOOKS, WHOLESALE
BOOTS: Men's
BOOTS: Women's
BOTTLED GAS DEALERS: Propane
BOTTLES: Plastic
BOULDER: Crushed & Broken
BOX & CARTON MANUFACTURING EQPT
BOXES & CRATES: Rectangular, Wood
BOXES & SHOOK: Nailed Wood
BOXES, METER: Concrete
BOXES: Corrugated
BOXES: Mail Or Post Office, Collection/Storage, Sheet Metal
BOXES: Packing & Shipping, Metal
BOXES: Paperboard, Folding
BOXES: Paperboard, Set-Up
BOXES: Plastic
BOXES: Stamped Metal
BOXES: Wooden
BRAKES & BRAKE PARTS
BRAKES: Metal Forming
BRASS GOODS, WHOLESALE
BRAZING SVCS
BRICK, STONE & RELATED PRDTS WHOLESALERS
BRICKS & BLOCKS: Structural
BRICKS : Ceramic Glazed, Clay
BRIDAL SHOPS
BROADCASTING & COMMS EQPT: Antennas, Transmitting/Comms
BROADCASTING & COMMS EQPT: Rcvr-Transmitter Unt, Transceiver
BROADCASTING & COMMUNICATIONS EQPT: Cellular Radio Telephone
BROADCASTING & COMMUNICATIONS EQPT: Studio Eqpt, Radio & TV
BROADCASTING STATIONS, RADIO: Educational
BROKERS: Fish
BROKERS: Food
BROKERS: Log & Lumber
BROKERS: Mortgage, Arranging For Loans
BROKERS: Printing
BRONZE FOUNDRY, NEC
BROOMS & BRUSHES
BROOMS & BRUSHES: Street Sweeping, Hand Or Machine

BROOMS & BRUSHES: Vacuum Cleaners & Carpet Sweepers
BRUSH BLOCKS: Carbon Or Molded Graphite
BUCKLES & PARTS
BUILDING & STRUCTURAL WOOD MBRS: Timbers, Struct, Lam Lumber
BUILDING & STRUCTURAL WOOD MEMBERS
BUILDING CLEANING & MAINTENANCE SVCS
BUILDING COMPONENT CLEANING SVCS
BUILDING COMPONENTS: Structural Steel
BUILDING INSPECTION SVCS
BUILDING PRDTS & MATERIALS DEALERS
BUILDING PRDTS: Concrete
BUILDING PRDTS: Stone
BUILDING STONE, ARTIFICIAL: Concrete
BUILDINGS & COMPONENTS: Prefabricated Metal
BUILDINGS, PREFABRICATED: Wholesalers
BUILDINGS: Farm & Utility
BUILDINGS: Farm, Prefabricated Or Portable, Wood
BUILDINGS: Geodesic Domes, Prefabricated, Wood
BUILDINGS: Mobile, For Commercial Use
BUILDINGS: Portable
BUILDINGS: Prefabricated, Metal
BUILDINGS: Prefabricated, Wood
BUILDINGS: Prefabricated, Wood
BULLETIN BOARDS: Cork
BULLETPROOF VESTS
BUOYS: Plastic
BURGLAR ALARM MAINTENANCE & MONITORING SVCS
BURIAL VAULTS: Concrete Or Precast Terrazzo
BURIAL VAULTS: Stone
BUS BARS: Electrical
BUS CHARTER SVC: Local
BUS CHARTER SVC: Long-Distance
BUSINESS ACTIVITIES: Non-Commercial Site
BUSINESS FORMS WHOLESALERS
BUSINESS FORMS: Printed, Manifold
BUSINESS FORMS: Unit Sets, Manifold
BUSINESS MACHINE REPAIR, ELECTRIC
BUSINESS SUPPORT SVCS
BUTTONS

C

CABINETS & CASES: Show, Display & Storage, Exc Wood
CABINETS, HOUSING: For Radium, Metal Plate
CABINETS: Bathroom Vanities, Wood
CABINETS: Entertainment
CABINETS: Entertainment Units, Household, Wood
CABINETS: Factory
CABINETS: Filing, Wood
CABINETS: Kitchen, Wood
CABINETS: Office, Wood
CABINETS: Radio & Television, Metal
CABINETS: Show, Display, Etc, Wood, Exc Refrigerated
CABINETS: Stereo, Wood
CABLE & OTHER PAY TELEVISION DISTRIBUTION
CABLE WIRING SETS: Battery, Internal Combustion Engines
CABLE: Fiber Optic
CABLE: Noninsulated
CABLE: Steel, Insulated Or Armored
CAFES
CAFETERIAS
CAGES: Wire
CAMERA & PHOTOGRAPHIC SPLYS STORES
CAMERA CARRYING BAGS
CAMERAS & RELATED EQPT: Photographic
CAMPERS: Truck Mounted
CAMPERS: Truck, Slide-In
CAMSHAFTS
CANDLES
CANDLES: Wholesalers
CANDY & CONFECTIONS: Candy Bars, Including Chocolate Covered
CANDY & CONFECTIONS: Chocolate Candy, Exc Solid Chocolate
CANDY & CONFECTIONS: Fruit & Fruit Peel
CANDY & CONFECTIONS: Fruit, Chocolate Covered, Exc Dates
CANDY & CONFECTIONS: Popcorn Balls/Other Trtd Popcorn Prdts
CANDY, NUT & CONFECTIONERY STORE: Popcorn, Incl Caramel Corn
CANDY, NUT & CONFECTIONERY STORES: Candy
CANDY, NUT & CONFECTIONERY STORES: Confectionery

PRODUCT INDEX

CANDY, NUT & CONFECTIONERY STORES: Produced For Direct Sale
CANDY: Chocolate From Cacao Beans
CANDY: Hard
CANNED SPECIALTIES
CANOE BUILDING & REPAIR
CANOPIES: Sheet Metal
CANS: Beer, Metal
CANS: Composite Foil-Fiber, Made From Purchased Materials
CANS: Garbage, Stamped Or Pressed Metal
CANS: Metal
CANS: Tin
CANVAS PRDTS
CANVAS PRDTS, WHOLESALE
CANVAS PRDTS: Boat Seats
CANVAS PRDTS: Convertible Tops, Car/Boat, Fm Purchased Mtrl
CAPACITORS: NEC
CAPS: Plastic
CAPS: Rubber, Vulcanized Or Rubberized Fabric
CAR WASH EQPT
CARBIDES
CARBON & GRAPHITE PRDTS, NEC
CARDIOVASCULAR SYSTEM DRUGS, EXC DIAGNOSTIC
CARDS: Color
CARDS: Greeting
CARDS: Identification
CARPETS & RUGS: Tufted
CARPETS, RUGS & FLOOR COVERING
CARPETS: Textile Fiber
CARRIAGES: Horse Drawn
CARRIERS: Infant, Textile
CARS: Electric
CASEMENTS: Aluminum
CASES, WOOD
CASES: Carrying
CASES: Carrying, Clothing & Apparel
CASES: Nonrefrigerated, Exc Wood
CASES: Plastic
CASES: Shipping, Nailed Or Lock Corner, Wood
CASES: Shipping, Wood, Wirebound
CASH REGISTER REPAIR SVCS
CASH REGISTERS & PARTS
CASH REGISTERS WHOLESALERS
CASKETS & ACCESS
CASKETS WHOLESALERS
CASKS: Atomic Waste
CAST STONE: Concrete
CASTERS
CASTINGS GRINDING: For The Trade
CASTINGS: Aerospace Investment, Ferrous
CASTINGS: Aerospace, Aluminum
CASTINGS: Aerospace, Nonferrous, Exc Aluminum
CASTINGS: Aluminum
CASTINGS: Brass, NEC, Exc Die
CASTINGS: Bronze, NEC, Exc Die
CASTINGS: Die, Aluminum
CASTINGS: Die, Lead
CASTINGS: Die, Nonferrous
CASTINGS: Ductile
CASTINGS: Gray Iron
CASTINGS: Precision
CASTINGS: Rubber
CASTINGS: Steel
CATALOG & MAIL-ORDER HOUSES
CATALOG SHOWROOMS
CATAPULTS
CATCH BASIN CLEANING SVC
CATCH BASIN COVERS: Concrete
CATERERS
CATTLE WHOLESALERS
CEILING SYSTEMS: Luminous, Commercial
CEMENT ROCK: Crushed & Broken
CEMENT: Hydraulic
CEMENT: Masonry
CEMENT: Portland
CEMETERIES: Real Estate Operation
CEMETERY MEMORIAL DEALERS
CERAMIC FIBER
CHAMBERS OF COMMERCE
CHAMBERS: Fumigating, Metal Plate
CHANGE MAKING MACHINES
CHARCOAL
CHARCOAL: Activated
CHART & GRAPH DESIGN SVCS

CHASSIS: Automobile House Trailer
CHASSIS: Motor Vehicle
CHEMICAL CLEANING SVCS
CHEMICAL ELEMENTS
CHEMICAL PROCESSING MACHINERY & EQPT
CHEMICAL SPLYS FOR FOUNDRIES
CHEMICALS & ALLIED PRDTS WHOLESALERS, NEC
CHEMICALS & ALLIED PRDTS, WHOLESALE: Adhesives
CHEMICALS & ALLIED PRDTS, WHOLESALE: Chemicals, Indl
CHEMICALS & ALLIED PRDTS, WHOLESALE: Compressed Gas
CHEMICALS & ALLIED PRDTS, WHOLESALE: Detergent/Soap
CHEMICALS & ALLIED PRDTS, WHOLESALE: Plastics Film
CHEMICALS & ALLIED PRDTS, WHOLESALE: Plastics Prdts, NEC
CHEMICALS & ALLIED PRDTS, WHOLESALE: Plastics Sheets & Rods
CHEMICALS & ALLIED PRDTS, WHOLESALE: Resins
CHEMICALS, AGRICULTURE: Wholesalers
CHEMICALS: Agricultural
CHEMICALS: Aluminum Compounds
CHEMICALS: Aluminum Sulfate
CHEMICALS: Calcium & Calcium Compounds
CHEMICALS: Cyanides
CHEMICALS: Fire Retardant
CHEMICALS: High Purity, Refined From Technical Grade
CHEMICALS: Hydrogen Peroxide
CHEMICALS: Inorganic, NEC
CHEMICALS: Isotopes, Radioactive
CHEMICALS: Medicinal
CHEMICALS: Medicinal, Organic, Uncompounded, Bulk
CHEMICALS: NEC
CHEMICALS: Nonmetallic Compounds
CHEMICALS: Organic, NEC
CHEMICALS: Phenol
CHEMICALS: Reagent Grade, Refined From Technical Grade
CHEMICALS: Sodium Bicarbonate
CHEMICALS: Water Treatment
CHEWING GUM
CHICKEN SLAUGHTERING & PROCESSING
CHILD & YOUTH SVCS, NEC
CHILDREN'S & INFANTS' CLOTHING STORES
CHILDREN'S WEAR STORES
CHINAWARE WHOLESALERS
CHIPPER MILL
CHLORINE
CHOCOLATE, EXC CANDY FROM BEANS: Chips, Powder, Block, Syrup
CHOCOLATE, EXC CANDY FROM PURCH CHOC: Chips, Powder, Block
CHUTES: Coal, Sheet Metal, Prefabricated
CIGARETTE & CIGAR PRDTS & ACCESS
CINCHONA & DERIVATIVES
CIRCUIT BOARDS, PRINTED: Television & Radio
CIRCUIT BREAKERS
CIRCUITS: Electronic
CIVIL SVCS TRAINING SCHOOL
CLAMPS: Ground, Electric-Wiring Devices
CLAMPS: Metal
CLAY MINING, COMMON
CLEANING & DYEING PLANTS, EXC RUGS
CLEANING EQPT: Blast, Dustless
CLEANING EQPT: Commercial
CLEANING EQPT: High Pressure
CLEANING OR POLISHING PREPARATIONS, NEC
CLEANING PRDTS: Automobile Polish
CLEANING PRDTS: Bleaches, Household, Dry Or Liquid
CLEANING PRDTS: Degreasing Solvent
CLEANING PRDTS: Disinfectants, Household Or Indl Plant
CLEANING PRDTS: Laundry Preparations
CLEANING PRDTS: Leather Dressings & Finishes
CLEANING PRDTS: Sanitation Preparations
CLEANING PRDTS: Sanitation Preps, Disinfectants/Deodorants
CLEANING PRDTS: Specialty
CLEANING PRDTS: Window Cleaning Preparations
CLEATS: Porcelain
CLIPS & FASTENERS, MADE FROM PURCHASED WIRE
CLOTHING & ACCESS STORES
CLOTHING & ACCESS, WOMEN, CHILD & INFANT, WHSLE: Sportswear
CLOTHING & ACCESS, WOMEN, CHILDREN & INFANT, WHOL: Gloves

CLOTHING & ACCESS, WOMEN, CHILDREN & INFANT, WHOL: Sweaters
CLOTHING & ACCESS, WOMEN, CHILDREN/INFANT, WHOL: Baby Goods
CLOTHING & ACCESS, WOMEN, CHILDREN/INFANT, WHOL: Outerwear
CLOTHING & ACCESS, WOMENS, CHILDREN & INFANTS, WHOL: Hats
CLOTHING & ACCESS: Costumes, Theatrical
CLOTHING & ACCESS: Handicapped
CLOTHING & ACCESS: Hospital Gowns
CLOTHING & ACCESS: Men's Miscellaneous Access
CLOTHING & APPAREL STORES: Custom
CLOTHING & FURNISHINGS, MEN'S & BOYS', WHOLESALE: Caps
CLOTHING & FURNISHINGS, MEN'S & BOYS', WHOLESALE: Gloves
CLOTHING & FURNISHINGS, MEN'S & BOYS', WHOLESALE: Hats
CLOTHING & FURNISHINGS, MEN'S & BOYS', WHOLESALE: Outerwear
CLOTHING & FURNISHINGS, MEN'S & BOYS', WHOLESALE: Shirts
CLOTHING & FURNISHINGS, MEN'S & BOYS', WHOLESALE: Uniforms
CLOTHING & FURNISHINGS, MEN/BOY, WHOL: Hats, Scarves/Gloves
CLOTHING & FURNISHINGS, MENS & BOYS, WHOLESALE: Apprl Belts
CLOTHING STORES, NEC
CLOTHING STORES: Designer Apparel
CLOTHING STORES: Leather
CLOTHING STORES: Shirts, Custom Made
CLOTHING STORES: T-Shirts, Printed, Custom
CLOTHING STORES: Uniforms & Work
CLOTHING STORES: Unisex
CLOTHING STORES: Work
CLOTHING, WOMEN & CHILD, WHLSE: Dress, Suit, Skirt & Blouse
CLOTHING: Access
CLOTHING: Access, Women's & Misses'
CLOTHING: Aprons, Exc Rubber/Plastic, Women, Misses, Junior
CLOTHING: Aprons, Harness
CLOTHING: Aprons, Waterproof, From Purchased Materials
CLOTHING: Aprons, Work, Exc Rubberized & Plastic, Men's
CLOTHING: Athletic & Sportswear, Men's & Boys'
CLOTHING: Athletic & Sportswear, Women's & Girls'
CLOTHING: Band Uniforms
CLOTHING: Bathing Suits & Swimwear, Knit
CLOTHING: Blouses & Shirts, Girls' & Children's
CLOTHING: Blouses, Women's & Girls'
CLOTHING: Blouses, Womens & Juniors, From Purchased Mtrls
CLOTHING: Bridal Gowns
CLOTHING: Buntings, Infants'
CLOTHING: Capes & Jackets, Women's & Misses'
CLOTHING: Caps, Baseball
CLOTHING: Children & Infants'
CLOTHING: Children's, Girls'
CLOTHING: Coats & Jackets, Leather & Sheep-Lined
CLOTHING: Coats & Suits, Men's & Boys'
CLOTHING: Coats, Hunting & Vests, Men's
CLOTHING: Collar & Cuff Sets, Knit
CLOTHING: Costumes
CLOTHING: Disposable
CLOTHING: Dresses
CLOTHING: Foundation Garments, Women's
CLOTHING: Furs
CLOTHING: Gowns & Dresses, Wedding
CLOTHING: Hats & Caps, NEC
CLOTHING: Hats & Caps, Uniform
CLOTHING: Hats & Headwear, Knit
CLOTHING: Hats, Panama
CLOTHING: Hosiery, Men's & Boys'
CLOTHING: Jackets, Field, Military
CLOTHING: Jackets, Knit
CLOTHING: Jeans, Men's & Boys'
CLOTHING: Leather & sheep-lined clothing
CLOTHING: Lounge, Bed & Leisurewear
CLOTHING: Men's & boy's clothing, nec
CLOTHING: Men's & boy's underwear & nightwear
CLOTHING: Mens & Boys Jackets, Sport, Suede, Leatherette
CLOTHING: Neckwear

PRODUCT INDEX

CLOTHING: Outerwear, Lthr, Wool/Down-Filled, Men, Youth/Boy
CLOTHING: Outerwear, Women's & Misses' NEC
CLOTHING: Overalls & Coveralls
CLOTHING: Raincoats, Exc Vulcanized Rubber, Purchased Matls
CLOTHING: Service Apparel, Women's
CLOTHING: Sheep-Lined
CLOTHING: Shirts
CLOTHING: Shirts & T-Shirts, Knit
CLOTHING: Shirts, Dress, Men's & Boys'
CLOTHING: Shirts, Sports & Polo, Men's & Boys'
CLOTHING: Socks
CLOTHING: Sportswear, Women's
CLOTHING: Suits & Skirts, Women's & Misses'
CLOTHING: Sweaters & Sweater Coats, Knit
CLOTHING: T-Shirts & Tops, Knit
CLOTHING: T-Shirts & Tops, Women's & Girls'
CLOTHING: Tailored Suits & Formal Jackets
CLOTHING: Trousers & Slacks, Men's & Boys'
CLOTHING: Tuxedos, From Purchased Materials
CLOTHING: Underwear, Knit
CLOTHING: Underwear, Women's & Children's
CLOTHING: Uniforms & Vestments
CLOTHING: Uniforms, Ex Athletic, Women's, Misses' & Juniors'
CLOTHING: Uniforms, Men's & Boys'
CLOTHING: Uniforms, Military, Men/Youth, Purchased Materials
CLOTHING: Uniforms, Team Athletic
CLOTHING: Uniforms, Work
CLOTHING: Vests
CLOTHING: Waterproof Outerwear
CLOTHING: Work, Men's
CLOTHING: Work, Waterproof, Exc Raincoats
CLOTHS: Polishing, Plain
COAL MINING SERVICES
COAL MINING: Bituminous Coal & Lignite-Surface Mining
COAL MINING: Bituminous, Strip
COAL MINING: Bituminous, Surface, NEC
COAL MINING: Underground, Subbituminous
COAL, MINERALS & ORES, WHOLESALE: Coal & Coke
COATED OR PLATED PRDTS
COATING COMPOUNDS: Tar
COATING SVC
COATING SVC: Aluminum, Metal Prdts
COATING SVC: Hot Dip, Metals Or Formed Prdts
COATING SVC: Metals & Formed Prdts
COATING SVC: Rust Preventative
COATINGS: Polyurethane
COCKTAIL LOUNGE
COFFEE MAKERS: Electric
COFFEE SVCS
COILS & TRANSFORMERS
COIN COUNTERS
COIN OPERATED LAUNDRIES & DRYCLEANERS
COINS & TOKENS: Non-Currency
COLLECTION AGENCIES
COLLEGES, UNIVERSITIES & PROFESSIONAL SCHOOLS
COLORS: Pigments, Inorganic
COMBINATION UTILITIES, NEC
COMFORTERS & QUILTS, FROM MANMADE FIBER OR SILK
COMMERCIAL & OFFICE BUILDINGS RENOVATION & REPAIR
COMMERCIAL ART & GRAPHIC DESIGN SVCS
COMMERCIAL ART & ILLUSTRATION SVCS
COMMERCIAL CONTAINERS WHOLESALERS
COMMERCIAL EQPT WHOLESALERS, NEC
COMMERCIAL EQPT, WHOL: Soda Fountain Fixtures, Exc Refrig
COMMERCIAL EQPT, WHOLESALE: Bakery Eqpt & Splys
COMMERCIAL EQPT, WHOLESALE: Coin counters
COMMERCIAL EQPT, WHOLESALE: Display Eqpt, Exc Refrigerated
COMMERCIAL EQPT, WHOLESALE: Neon Signs
COMMERCIAL EQPT, WHOLESALE: Restaurant, NEC
COMMERCIAL EQPT, WHOLESALE: Scales, Exc Laboratory
COMMERCIAL PRINTING & NEWSPAPER PUBLISHING COMBINED
COMMERCIAL REFRIGERATORS WHOLESALERS
COMMODITY CONTRACT TRADING COMPANIES
COMMON SAND MINING
COMMUNICATIONS EQPT & SYSTEMS, NEC
COMMUNICATIONS EQPT WHOLESALERS

COMMUNICATIONS EQPT: Microwave
COMMUNICATIONS EQPT: Radio, Marine
COMMUNICATIONS SVCS: Cellular
COMMUNICATIONS SVCS: Data
COMMUNICATIONS SVCS: Electronic Mail
COMMUNICATIONS SVCS: Facsimile Transmission
COMMUNICATIONS SVCS: Internet Host Svcs
COMMUNICATIONS SVCS: Online Svc Providers
COMMUNICATIONS SVCS: Telephone, Local
COMMUNICATIONS SVCS: Telephone, Voice
COMMUNITY CENTERS: Adult
COMMUNITY CENTERS: Youth
COMMUNITY COLLEGE
COMMUTATORS: Electric Motors
COMMUTATORS: Electronic
COMPACT LASER DISCS: Prerecorded
COMPOST
COMPRESSORS: Air & Gas
COMPRESSORS: Air & Gas, Including Vacuum Pumps
COMPRESSORS: Refrigeration & Air Conditioning Eqpt
COMPRESSORS: Repairing
COMPUTER & COMPUTER SOFTWARE STORES
COMPUTER & COMPUTER SOFTWARE STORES: Peripheral Eqpt
COMPUTER & COMPUTER SOFTWARE STORES: Personal Computers
COMPUTER & COMPUTER SOFTWARE STORES: Software & Access
COMPUTER & COMPUTER SOFTWARE STORES: Software, Bus/Non-Game
COMPUTER & COMPUTER SOFTWARE STORES: Software, Computer Game
COMPUTER & DATA PROCESSING EQPT REPAIR & MAINTENANCE
COMPUTER & OFFICE MACHINE MAINTENANCE & REPAIR
COMPUTER FACILITIES MANAGEMENT SVCS
COMPUTER FORMS
COMPUTER GRAPHICS SVCS
COMPUTER HARDWARE REQUIREMENTS ANALYSIS
COMPUTER INTERFACE EQPT: Indl Process
COMPUTER PERIPHERAL EQPT REPAIR & MAINTENANCE
COMPUTER PERIPHERAL EQPT, NEC
COMPUTER PERIPHERAL EQPT, WHOLESALE
COMPUTER PERIPHERAL EQPT: Decoders
COMPUTER PERIPHERAL EQPT: Encoders
COMPUTER PERIPHERAL EQPT: Graphic Displays, Exc Terminals
COMPUTER PERIPHERAL EQPT: Input Or Output
COMPUTER PERIPHERAL EQPT: Output To Microfilm Units
COMPUTER PROCESSING SVCS
COMPUTER PROGRAMMING SVCS
COMPUTER PROGRAMMING SVCS: Custom
COMPUTER RELATED MAINTENANCE SVCS
COMPUTER RELATED SVCS, NEC
COMPUTER SOFTWARE DEVELOPMENT
COMPUTER SOFTWARE DEVELOPMENT & APPLICATIONS
COMPUTER SOFTWARE SYSTEMS ANALYSIS & DESIGN: Custom
COMPUTER SOFTWARE WRITERS
COMPUTER STORAGE DEVICES, NEC
COMPUTER STORAGE UNITS: Auxiliary
COMPUTER SYSTEMS ANALYSIS & DESIGN
COMPUTER TERMINALS
COMPUTER TIME-SHARING
COMPUTER TRAINING SCHOOLS
COMPUTER-AIDED DESIGN SYSTEMS SVCS
COMPUTER-AIDED ENGINEERING SYSTEMS SVCS
COMPUTER-AIDED SYSTEM SVCS
COMPUTERS, NEC
COMPUTERS, NEC, WHOLESALE
COMPUTERS, PERIPH & SOFTWARE, WHLSE: Personal & Home Entrtn
COMPUTERS, PERIPHERALS & SOFTWARE, WHOLESALE: Printers
COMPUTERS, PERIPHERALS & SOFTWARE, WHOLESALE: Software
COMPUTERS: Mini
COMPUTERS: Personal
CONCRETE BUILDING PRDTS WHOLESALERS
CONCRETE CURING & HARDENING COMPOUNDS
CONCRETE PLANTS
CONCRETE PRDTS

CONCRETE PRDTS, PRECAST, NEC
CONCRETE: Dry Mixture
CONCRETE: Ready-Mixed
CONDENSERS: Heat Transfer Eqpt, Evaporative
CONDUITS & FITTINGS: Electric
CONFECTIONERY PRDTS WHOLESALERS
CONFECTIONS & CANDY
CONFINEMENT SURVEILLANCE SYS MAINTENANCE & MONITORING SVCS
CONNECTORS & TERMINALS: Electrical Device Uses
CONNECTORS: Electrical
CONNECTORS: Electronic
CONNECTORS: Power, Electric
CONSTRUCTION & MINING MACHINERY WHOLESALERS
CONSTRUCTION EQPT REPAIR SVCS
CONSTRUCTION EQPT: Attachments
CONSTRUCTION EQPT: Backhoes, Tractors, Cranes & Similar Eqpt
CONSTRUCTION EQPT: Blade, Grader, Scraper, Dozer/Snow Plow
CONSTRUCTION EQPT: Buckets, Excavating, Clamshell, Etc
CONSTRUCTION EQPT: Crane Carriers
CONSTRUCTION EQPT: Cranes
CONSTRUCTION EQPT: Dozers, Tractor Mounted, Material Moving
CONSTRUCTION EQPT: Entrenching Machines
CONSTRUCTION EQPT: Finishers & Spreaders
CONSTRUCTION EQPT: Mud Jacks
CONSTRUCTION EQPT: Rock Crushing Machinery, Portable
CONSTRUCTION EQPT: Roofing Eqpt
CONSTRUCTION EQPT: Tractors
CONSTRUCTION EQPT: Tunneling
CONSTRUCTION EQPT: Wrecker Hoists, Automobile
CONSTRUCTION MATERIALS, WHOL: Concrete/Cinder Bldg Prdts
CONSTRUCTION MATERIALS, WHOLESALE: Aggregate
CONSTRUCTION MATERIALS, WHOLESALE: Architectural Metalwork
CONSTRUCTION MATERIALS, WHOLESALE: Awnings
CONSTRUCTION MATERIALS, WHOLESALE: Block, Concrete & Cinder
CONSTRUCTION MATERIALS, WHOLESALE: Blocks, Building, NEC
CONSTRUCTION MATERIALS, WHOLESALE: Building Stone
CONSTRUCTION MATERIALS, WHOLESALE: Building Stone, Granite
CONSTRUCTION MATERIALS, WHOLESALE: Building, Exterior
CONSTRUCTION MATERIALS, WHOLESALE: Building, Interior
CONSTRUCTION MATERIALS, WHOLESALE: Cement
CONSTRUCTION MATERIALS, WHOLESALE: Concrete Mixtures
CONSTRUCTION MATERIALS, WHOLESALE: Door Frames
CONSTRUCTION MATERIALS, WHOLESALE: Doors, Sliding
CONSTRUCTION MATERIALS, WHOLESALE: Drywall Materials
CONSTRUCTION MATERIALS, WHOLESALE: Fiberglass Building Mat
CONSTRUCTION MATERIALS, WHOLESALE: Glass
CONSTRUCTION MATERIALS, WHOLESALE: Gravel
CONSTRUCTION MATERIALS, WHOLESALE: Guardrails, Metal
CONSTRUCTION MATERIALS, WHOLESALE: Hardboard
CONSTRUCTION MATERIALS, WHOLESALE: Insulation, Thermal
CONSTRUCTION MATERIALS, WHOLESALE: Limestone
CONSTRUCTION MATERIALS, WHOLESALE: Masons' Materials
CONSTRUCTION MATERIALS, WHOLESALE: Millwork
CONSTRUCTION MATERIALS, WHOLESALE: Pallets, Wood
CONSTRUCTION MATERIALS, WHOLESALE: Paving Materials
CONSTRUCTION MATERIALS, WHOLESALE: Plywood
CONSTRUCTION MATERIALS, WHOLESALE: Prefabricated Structures
CONSTRUCTION MATERIALS, WHOLESALE: Roof, Asphalt/Sheet Metal
CONSTRUCTION MATERIALS, WHOLESALE: Roofing & Siding Material
CONSTRUCTION MATERIALS, WHOLESALE: Sand
CONSTRUCTION MATERIALS, WHOLESALE: Septic Tanks
CONSTRUCTION MATERIALS, WHOLESALE: Stone, Crushed Or Broken

PRODUCT INDEX

CONSTRUCTION MATERIALS, WHOLESALE: Stucco
CONSTRUCTION MATERIALS, WHOLESALE: Windows
CONSTRUCTION MATLS, WHOL: Composite Board Prdts, Woodboard
CONSTRUCTION MATLS, WHOL: Lumber, Rough, Dressed/Finished
CONSTRUCTION SAND MINING
CONSTRUCTION SITE PREPARATION SVCS
CONSTRUCTION: Apartment Building
CONSTRUCTION: Athletic & Recreation Facilities
CONSTRUCTION: Bridge
CONSTRUCTION: Commercial & Institutional Building
CONSTRUCTION: Commercial & Office Building, New
CONSTRUCTION: Dams, Waterways, Docks & Other Marine
CONSTRUCTION: Dock
CONSTRUCTION: Drainage System
CONSTRUCTION: Electric Power Line
CONSTRUCTION: Factory
CONSTRUCTION: Farm Building
CONSTRUCTION: Food Prdts Manufacturing or Packing Plant
CONSTRUCTION: Greenhouse
CONSTRUCTION: Heavy
CONSTRUCTION: Heavy Highway & Street
CONSTRUCTION: Indl Building & Warehouse
CONSTRUCTION: Indl Building, Prefabricated
CONSTRUCTION: Indl Buildings, New, NEC
CONSTRUCTION: Indl Plant
CONSTRUCTION: Land Preparation
CONSTRUCTION: Marine
CONSTRUCTION: Mausoleum
CONSTRUCTION: Multi-family Dwellings, New
CONSTRUCTION: Nonresidential Buildings, Custom
CONSTRUCTION: Pipeline, NEC
CONSTRUCTION: Power Plant
CONSTRUCTION: Residential, Nec
CONSTRUCTION: Retaining Wall
CONSTRUCTION: Roads, Gravel or Dirt
CONSTRUCTION: Sewer Line
CONSTRUCTION: Single-Family Housing
CONSTRUCTION: Single-family Housing, New
CONSTRUCTION: Single-family Housing, Prefabricated
CONSTRUCTION: Steel Buildings
CONSTRUCTION: Street Surfacing & Paving
CONSTRUCTION: Svc Station
CONSTRUCTION: Swimming Pools
CONSTRUCTION: Tunnel
CONSTRUCTION: Utility Line
CONSTRUCTION: Warehouse
CONSTRUCTION: Waste Water & Sewage Treatment Plant
CONSTRUCTION: Water & Sewer Line
CONSTRUCTION: Water Main
CONSULTING SVC: Business, NEC
CONSULTING SVC: Chemical
CONSULTING SVC: Computer
CONSULTING SVC: Educational
CONSULTING SVC: Engineering
CONSULTING SVC: Management
CONSULTING SVC: Marketing Management
CONSULTING SVC: Online Technology
CONSULTING SVC: Personnel Management
CONSULTING SVC: Sales Management
CONSULTING SVC: Telecommunications
CONSULTING SVCS, BUSINESS: Agricultural
CONSULTING SVCS, BUSINESS: Economic
CONSULTING SVCS, BUSINESS: Employee Programs Administration
CONSULTING SVCS, BUSINESS: Environmental
CONSULTING SVCS, BUSINESS: Fishery
CONSULTING SVCS, BUSINESS: Publishing
CONSULTING SVCS, BUSINESS: Sys Engnrg, Exc Computer/Prof
CONSULTING SVCS, BUSINESS: Systems Analysis & Engineering
CONSULTING SVCS, BUSINESS: Systems Analysis Or Design
CONSULTING SVCS, BUSINESS: Urban Planning & Consulting
CONSULTING SVCS: Oil
CONSULTING SVCS: Scientific
CONTACT LENSES
CONTAINERS, GLASS: Food
CONTAINERS: Air Cargo, Metal
CONTAINERS: Cargo, Wood & Wood With Metal
CONTAINERS: Corrugated
CONTAINERS: Food & Beverage
CONTAINERS: Frozen Food & Ice Cream
CONTAINERS: Glass
CONTAINERS: Laminated Phenolic & Vulcanized Fiber
CONTAINERS: Liquid Tight Fiber, From Purchased Materials
CONTAINERS: Metal
CONTAINERS: Plastic
CONTAINERS: Plywood & Veneer, Wood
CONTAINERS: Sanitary, Food
CONTAINERS: Shipping & Mailing, Fiber
CONTAINERS: Shipping, Metal, Milk, Fluid
CONTAINERS: Wood
CONTAINMENT VESSELS: Reactor, Metal Plate
CONTRACT DIVING SVC
CONTRACTOR: Rigging & Scaffolding
CONTRACTORS: Access Flooring System Installation
CONTRACTORS: Acoustical & Ceiling Work
CONTRACTORS: Acoustical & Insulation Work
CONTRACTORS: Asbestos Removal & Encapsulation
CONTRACTORS: Asphalt
CONTRACTORS: Blasting, Exc Building Demolition
CONTRACTORS: Boring, Building Construction
CONTRACTORS: Building Eqpt & Machinery Installation
CONTRACTORS: Building Sign Installation & Mntnce
CONTRACTORS: Building Site Preparation
CONTRACTORS: Caisson Drilling
CONTRACTORS: Carpentry Work
CONTRACTORS: Carpentry, Cabinet & Finish Work
CONTRACTORS: Carpentry, Cabinet Building & Installation
CONTRACTORS: Commercial & Office Building
CONTRACTORS: Computer Installation
CONTRACTORS: Computerized Controls Installation
CONTRACTORS: Concrete
CONTRACTORS: Concrete Reinforcement Placing
CONTRACTORS: Construction Site Cleanup
CONTRACTORS: Core Drilling & Cutting
CONTRACTORS: Countertop Installation
CONTRACTORS: Demolition, Building & Other Structures
CONTRACTORS: Demountable Partition Installation
CONTRACTORS: Dewatering
CONTRACTORS: Directional Oil & Gas Well Drilling Svc
CONTRACTORS: Driveway
CONTRACTORS: Drywall
CONTRACTORS: Earthmoving
CONTRACTORS: Electric Power Systems
CONTRACTORS: Electrical
CONTRACTORS: Excavating
CONTRACTORS: Excavating Slush Pits & Cellars Svcs
CONTRACTORS: Fence Construction
CONTRACTORS: Fiber Optic Cable Installation
CONTRACTORS: Fiberglass Work
CONTRACTORS: Fire Detection & Burglar Alarm Systems
CONTRACTORS: Fire Sprinkler System Installation Svcs
CONTRACTORS: Floor Laying & Other Floor Work
CONTRACTORS: Flooring
CONTRACTORS: Foundation Building
CONTRACTORS: Garage Doors
CONTRACTORS: Gas Detection & Analysis Svcs
CONTRACTORS: Gas Field Svcs, NEC
CONTRACTORS: General Electric
CONTRACTORS: Geothermal Drilling
CONTRACTORS: Glass Tinting, Architectural & Automotive
CONTRACTORS: Glass, Glazing & Tinting
CONTRACTORS: Grave Excavation
CONTRACTORS: Grouting Work
CONTRACTORS: Gutters & Downspouts
CONTRACTORS: Heating & Air Conditioning
CONTRACTORS: Heating Systems Repair & Maintenance Svc
CONTRACTORS: Highway & Street Construction, General
CONTRACTORS: Highway & Street Paving
CONTRACTORS: Hot Shot Svcs
CONTRACTORS: Hydraulic Eqpt Installation & Svcs
CONTRACTORS: Indl Building Renovation, Remodeling & Repair
CONTRACTORS: Insulation Installation, Building
CONTRACTORS: Kitchen & Bathroom Remodeling
CONTRACTORS: Kitchen Cabinet Installation
CONTRACTORS: Land Reclamation
CONTRACTORS: Lighting Syst
CONTRACTORS: Maintenance, Parking Facility Eqpt
CONTRACTORS: Marble Installation, Interior
CONTRACTORS: Masonry & Stonework
CONTRACTORS: Mechanical
CONTRACTORS: Multi-Family Home Remodeling
CONTRACTORS: Office Furniture Installation
CONTRACTORS: Oil & Gas Well Casing Cement Svcs
CONTRACTORS: Oil & Gas Well Drilling Svc
CONTRACTORS: Oil Field Haulage Svcs
CONTRACTORS: Oil Field Lease Tanks: Erectg, Clng/Rprg Svcs
CONTRACTORS: Oil Field Pipe Testing Svcs
CONTRACTORS: Oil/Gas Field Casing,Tube/Rod Running,Cut/Pull
CONTRACTORS: Oil/Gas Well Construction, Rpr/Dismantling Svcs
CONTRACTORS: On-Site Welding
CONTRACTORS: Ornamental Metal Work
CONTRACTORS: Painting & Wall Covering
CONTRACTORS: Painting, Commercial, Interior
CONTRACTORS: Painting, Residential
CONTRACTORS: Patio & Deck Construction & Repair
CONTRACTORS: Petroleum Storage Tanks, Pumping & Draining
CONTRACTORS: Playground Construction & Eqpt Installation
CONTRACTORS: Plumbing
CONTRACTORS: Pole Cutting
CONTRACTORS: Post Disaster Renovations
CONTRACTORS: Posthole Digging
CONTRACTORS: Prefabricated Window & Door Installation
CONTRACTORS: Process Piping
CONTRACTORS: Refractory or Acid Brick Masonry
CONTRACTORS: Refrigeration
CONTRACTORS: Rock Removal
CONTRACTORS: Roofing
CONTRACTORS: Roustabout Svcs
CONTRACTORS: Safety & Security Eqpt
CONTRACTORS: Sandblasting Svc, Building Exteriors
CONTRACTORS: Seismograph Survey Svcs
CONTRACTORS: Septic System
CONTRACTORS: Sheet Metal Work, NEC
CONTRACTORS: Sheet metal Work, Architectural
CONTRACTORS: Shoring & Underpinning
CONTRACTORS: Siding
CONTRACTORS: Single-family Home General Remodeling
CONTRACTORS: Solar Energy Eqpt
CONTRACTORS: Solar Reflecting Insulation Film Installation
CONTRACTORS: Sound Eqpt Installation
CONTRACTORS: Special Trades, NEC
CONTRACTORS: Spraying, Nonagricultural
CONTRACTORS: Steam Cleaning, Building Exterior
CONTRACTORS: Storage Tank Erection, Metal
CONTRACTORS: Store Fixture Installation
CONTRACTORS: Structural Iron Work, Structural
CONTRACTORS: Structural Steel Erection
CONTRACTORS: Svc Station Eqpt Installation, Maint & Repair
CONTRACTORS: Svc Well Drilling Svcs
CONTRACTORS: Tile Installation, Ceramic
CONTRACTORS: Timber Removal
CONTRACTORS: Underground Utilities
CONTRACTORS: Ventilation & Duct Work
CONTRACTORS: Vinyl Flooring Installation, Tile & Sheet
CONTRACTORS: Warm Air Heating & Air Conditioning
CONTRACTORS: Water Intake Well Drilling Svc
CONTRACTORS: Water Well Drilling
CONTRACTORS: Water Well Servicing
CONTRACTORS: Waterproofing
CONTRACTORS: Well Bailing, Cleaning, Swabbing & Treating Svc
CONTRACTORS: Well Surveying Svcs
CONTRACTORS: Windows & Doors
CONTRACTORS: Wood Floor Installation & Refinishing
CONTRACTORS: Wrecking & Demolition
CONTROL EQPT: Electric
CONTROL PANELS: Electrical
CONTROLS & ACCESS: Indl, Electric
CONTROLS & ACCESS: Motor
CONTROLS: Access, Motor
CONTROLS: Adjustable Speed Drive
CONTROLS: Air Flow, Refrigeration
CONTROLS: Automatic Temperature
CONTROLS: Crane & Hoist, Including Metal Mill
CONTROLS: Electric Motor
CONTROLS: Environmental
CONTROLS: Hydronic
CONTROLS: Marine & Navy, Auxiliary
CONTROLS: Numerical
CONTROLS: Relay & Ind
CONTROLS: Thermostats
CONTROLS: Water Heater

PRODUCT INDEX

CONVENIENCE STORES
CONVERTERS: Data
CONVERTERS: Torque, Exc Auto
CONVEYOR SYSTEMS
CONVEYOR SYSTEMS: Belt, General Indl Use
CONVEYOR SYSTEMS: Bucket Type
CONVEYOR SYSTEMS: Bulk Handling
CONVEYOR SYSTEMS: Robotic
CONVEYORS & CONVEYING EQPT
COOKING & FOOD WARMING EQPT: Commercial
COOKING & FOODWARMING EQPT: Coffee Brewing
COOKING & FOODWARMING EQPT: Commercial
COOKING & FOODWARMING EQPT: Popcorn Machines, Commercial
COOKING EQPT, HOUSEHOLD: Indoor
COOKING EQPT, HOUSEHOLD: Ranges, Gas
COOKWARE, STONEWARE: Coarse Earthenware & Pottery
COOLING TOWERS: Metal
COPING MATERIALS
COPPER ORES
COPPER: Cakes, Primary
COPPER: Rolling & Drawing
COPY MACHINES WHOLESALERS
CORD & TWINE
CORES: Magnetic
CORK & CORK PRDTS: Tiles
CORRECTIONAL INSTITUTIONS
CORRECTIONAL INSTITUTIONS, GOVERNMENT: Jail
CORRUGATED PRDTS: Boxes, Partition, Display Items, Sheet/Pad
CORRUGATING MACHINES
COSMETIC PREPARATIONS
COSMETICS & TOILETRIES
COSMETICS WHOLESALERS
COSTUME JEWELRY & NOVELTIES: Apparel, Exc Precious Metals
COSTUME JEWELRY & NOVELTIES: Bracelets, Exc Precious Metals
COSTUME JEWELRY & NOVELTIES: Costume Novelties
COSTUME JEWELRY & NOVELTIES: Exc Semi & Precious
COSTUME JEWELRY & NOVELTIES: Keychains, Exc Precious Metal
COSTUME JEWELRY & NOVELTIES: Pins, Exc Precious Metals
COUNTER & SINK TOPS
COUNTERS & COUNTING DEVICES
COUNTERS OR COUNTER DISPLAY CASES, EXC WOOD
COUPLINGS: Hose & Tube, Hydraulic Or Pneumatic
COUPLINGS: Shaft
COURIER SVCS, AIR: Parcel Delivery, Private
COURIER SVCS: Package By Vehicle
COVERS & PADS Chair, Made From Purchased Materials
COVERS: Automobile Seat
COVERS: Book, Fabric
COVERS: Hot Tub & Spa
CRANE & AERIAL LIFT SVCS
CRANES: Indl Plant
CRANES: Indl Truck
CRANES: Overhead
CRANKSHAFTS & CAMSHAFTS: Machining
CRAYONS
CREATIVE SVCS: Advertisers, Exc Writers
CREDIT & OTHER FINANCIAL RESPONSIBILITY INSURANCE
CREDIT AGENCIES: Federal & Federally Sponsored
CREDIT CARD SVCS
CREDIT INST, SHORT-TERM BUSINESS: Financing Dealers
CRUDE PETROLEUM & NATURAL GAS PRODUCTION
CRUDE PETROLEUM & NATURAL GAS PRODUCTION
CRUDE PETROLEUM PRODUCTION
CRYSTALS
CULTURE MEDIA
CULVERTS: Sheet Metal
CUPS & PLATES: Foamed Plastics
CUPS: Plastic Exc Polystyrene Foam
CURBING: Granite Or Stone
CURTAIN & DRAPERY FIXTURES: Poles, Rods & Rollers
CURTAINS: Shower
CUSHIONS & PILLOWS
CUSHIONS & PILLOWS: Bed, From Purchased Materials
CUSHIONS & PILLOWS: Boat
CUSHIONS: Carpet & Rug, Foamed Plastics
CUSTOMIZING SVCS
CUT STONE & STONE PRODUCTS
CUTLERY
CUTLERY WHOLESALERS
CUTOUTS: Paper or Paperboard, Made From Purchased Materials
CYCLIC CRUDES & INTERMEDIATES
CYLINDER & ACTUATORS: Fluid Power

D

DAIRY EQPT
DAIRY PRDTS STORE: Cheese
DAIRY PRDTS STORE: Ice Cream, Packaged
DAIRY PRDTS STORES
DAIRY PRDTS WHOLESALERS: Fresh
DAIRY PRDTS: Butter
DAIRY PRDTS: Cheese
DAIRY PRDTS: Cheese, Cottage
DAIRY PRDTS: Cream, Aerated
DAIRY PRDTS: Dietary Supplements, Dairy & Non-Dairy Based
DAIRY PRDTS: Dips & Spreads, Cheese Based
DAIRY PRDTS: Evaporated Milk
DAIRY PRDTS: Frozen Desserts & Novelties
DAIRY PRDTS: Ice Cream & Ice Milk
DAIRY PRDTS: Ice Cream, Bulk
DAIRY PRDTS: Milk, Condensed & Evaporated
DAIRY PRDTS: Milk, Fluid
DAIRY PRDTS: Milk, Processed, Pasteurized, Homogenized/Btld
DAIRY PRDTS: Natural Cheese
DAIRY PRDTS: Pastes, Cheese
DAIRY PRDTS: Powdered Milk
DAIRY PRDTS: Processed Cheese
DAIRY PRDTS: Yogurt, Exc Frozen
DAIRY PRDTS: Yogurt, Frozen
DANCE INSTRUCTOR & SCHOOL
DATA PROCESSING & PREPARATION SVCS
DATA PROCESSING SVCS
DAVITS
DECALS, WHOLESALE
DECORATIVE WOOD & WOODWORK
DEFENSE SYSTEMS & EQPT
DEGREASING MACHINES
DEHUMIDIFIERS: Electric
DEHYDRATION EQPT
DENTAL EQPT
DENTAL EQPT & SPLYS
DENTAL EQPT & SPLYS WHOLESALERS
DENTAL EQPT & SPLYS: Dental Hand Instruments, NEC
DENTAL EQPT & SPLYS: Dental Materials
DENTAL EQPT & SPLYS: Denture Materials
DENTAL EQPT & SPLYS: Enamels
DENTAL EQPT & SPLYS: Orthodontic Appliances
DENTAL EQPT & SPLYS: Teeth, Artificial, Exc In Dental Labs
DENTAL EQPT & SPLYS: Tools, NEC
DENTISTS' OFFICES & CLINICS
DEODORANTS: Personal
DEPARTMENT STORES
DEPARTMENT STORES: Country General
DERMATOLOGICALS
DESIGN SVCS, NEC
DESIGN SVCS: Commercial & Indl
DESIGN SVCS: Computer Integrated Systems
DETECTION APPARATUS: Electronic/Magnetic Field, Light/Heat
DETECTION EQPT: Aeronautical Electronic Field
DETECTION EQPT: Magnetic Field
DETECTORS: Water Leak
DIAGNOSTIC SUBSTANCES
DIAGNOSTIC SUBSTANCES OR AGENTS: Enzyme & Isoenzyme
DIAGNOSTIC SUBSTANCES OR AGENTS: Hematology
DIAGNOSTIC SUBSTANCES OR AGENTS: In Vitro
DIAGNOSTIC SUBSTANCES OR AGENTS: Microbiology & Virology
DIAGNOSTIC SUBSTANCES OR AGENTS: Radioactive
DIAGNOSTIC SUBSTANCES OR AGENTS: Veterinary
DIAMONDS, GEMS, WHOLESALE
DIAMONDS: Cutting & Polishing
DIAPERS: Disposable
DIATOMACEOUS EARTH MINING SVCS
DIE SETS: Presses, Metal Stamping
DIES & TOOLS: Special
DIES: Cutting, Exc Metal
DIES: Paper Cutting
DIES: Plastic Forming
DIES: Steel Rule
DIODES: Light Emitting
DIRECT SELLING ESTABLISHMENTS, NEC
DIRECT SELLING ESTABLISHMENTS: Bakery Goods, House-To-House
DIRECT SELLING ESTABLISHMENTS: Beverage Svcs
DIRECT SELLING ESTABLISHMENTS: Food Svc, Coffee-Cart
DIRECT SELLING ESTABLISHMENTS: Food Svcs
DIRECT SELLING ESTABLISHMENTS: Housewares, House-To-House
DIRECT SELLING ESTABLISHMENTS: Snacks
DIRECT SELLING ESTABLISHMENTS: Telemarketing
DISHWASHING EQPT: Household
DISK & DISKETTE CONVERSION SVCS
DISK DRIVES: Computer
DISKETTE DUPLICATING SVCS
DISPENSERS: Soap
DISPENSING EQPT & PARTS, BEVERAGE: Beer
DISPENSING EQPT & PARTS, BEVERAGE: Fountain/Other Beverage
DISPLAY CASES: Refrigerated
DISPLAY FIXTURES: Showcases, Wood, Exc Refrigerated
DISPLAY FIXTURES: Wood
DISPLAY LETTERING SVCS
DISTILLERS DRIED GRAIN & SOLUBLES
DOCKS: Floating, Wood
DOCKS: Prefabricated Metal
DOCUMENT DESTRUCTION SVC
DOLLIES: Industrial
DOLOMITIC MARBLE: Crushed & Broken
DOOR & WINDOW REPAIR SVCS
DOOR FRAMES: Wood
DOOR OPERATING SYSTEMS: Electric
DOORS & WINDOWS WHOLESALERS: All Materials
DOORS & WINDOWS: Screen & Storm
DOORS & WINDOWS: Storm, Metal
DOORS: Fiberglass
DOORS: Fire, Metal
DOORS: Garage, Overhead, Metal
DOORS: Garage, Overhead, Wood
DOORS: Glass
DOORS: Wooden
DOWN FEATHERS
DRAFTING SVCS
DRAPERIES & CURTAINS
DRAPERIES: Plastic & Textile, From Purchased Materials
DRAPERY & UPHOLSTERY STORES: Draperies
DRILLING MACHINERY & EQPT: Oil & Gas
DRILLING MACHINERY & EQPT: Water Well
DRILLS: Hand
DRINK MIXES, NONALCOHOLIC: Cocktail
DRINKING PLACES: Alcoholic Beverages
DRINKING PLACES: Bars & Lounges
DRINKING PLACES: Beer Garden
DRINKING PLACES: Tavern
DRIVE SHAFTS
DRIVES: High Speed Indl, Exc Hydrostatic
DRUG STORES
DRUG TESTING KITS: Blood & Urine
DRUGS & DRUG PROPRIETARIES, WHOLESALE: Medicinals/Botanicals
DRUGS & DRUG PROPRIETARIES, WHOLESALE: Pharmaceuticals
DRUGS & DRUG PROPRIETARIES, WHOLESALE: Vitamins & Minerals
DRUGS ACTING ON THE CENTRAL NERVOUS SYSTEM & SENSE ORGANS
DRYCLEANING & LAUNDRY SVCS: Commercial & Family
DRYCLEANING EQPT & SPLYS: Commercial
DRYCLEANING SVC: Drapery & Curtain
DUCTS: Sheet Metal
DUMPSTERS: Garbage
DURABLE GOODS WHOLESALERS, NEC
DUST OR FUME COLLECTING EQPT: Indl
DYES: Synthetic Organic
DYNAMOMETERS

E

EATING PLACES
EDUCATIONAL SVCS
EDUCATIONAL SVCS, NONDEGREE GRANTING: Continuing Education
EGG WHOLESALERS
ELECTRIC & OTHER SERVICES COMBINED
ELECTRIC MOTOR REPAIR SVCS

PRODUCT INDEX

ELECTRIC POWER DISTRIBUTION TO CONSUMERS
ELECTRIC POWER, COGENERATED
ELECTRIC SERVICES
ELECTRIC SVCS, NEC Power Marketers
ELECTRIC SVCS, NEC: Power Generation
ELECTRIC WATER HEATERS WHOLESALERS
ELECTRICAL APPARATUS & EQPT WHOLESALERS
ELECTRICAL APPLIANCES, TELEVISIONS & RADIOS WHOLESALERS
ELECTRICAL CURRENT CARRYING WIRING DEVICES
ELECTRICAL DISCHARGE MACHINING, EDM
ELECTRICAL EQPT & SPLYS
ELECTRICAL EQPT FOR ENGINES
ELECTRICAL EQPT REPAIR & MAINTENANCE
ELECTRICAL EQPT REPAIR SVCS
ELECTRICAL EQPT: Household
ELECTRICAL GOODS, WHOL: Antennas, Receiving/Satellite Dishes
ELECTRICAL GOODS, WHOL: Vid Camera-Aud Recorders/Camcorders
ELECTRICAL GOODS, WHOLESALE: Batteries, Dry Cell
ELECTRICAL GOODS, WHOLESALE: Batteries, Storage, Indl
ELECTRICAL GOODS, WHOLESALE: Circuit Breakers
ELECTRICAL GOODS, WHOLESALE: Electrical Entertainment Eqpt
ELECTRICAL GOODS, WHOLESALE: Electronic Parts
ELECTRICAL GOODS, WHOLESALE: Fittings & Construction Mat
ELECTRICAL GOODS, WHOLESALE: Generators
ELECTRICAL GOODS, WHOLESALE: Lighting Fixtures, Comm & Indl
ELECTRICAL GOODS, WHOLESALE: Lighting Fixtures, Residential
ELECTRICAL GOODS, WHOLESALE: Motors
ELECTRICAL GOODS, WHOLESALE: Security Control Eqpt & Systems
ELECTRICAL GOODS, WHOLESALE: Semiconductor Devices
ELECTRICAL GOODS, WHOLESALE: Signaling, Eqpt
ELECTRICAL GOODS, WHOLESALE: Sound Eqpt
ELECTRICAL GOODS, WHOLESALE: Telephone Eqpt
ELECTRICAL GOODS, WHOLESALE: VCR & Access
ELECTRICAL GOODS, WHOLESALE: Wire & Cable
ELECTRICAL GOODS, WHOLESALE: Wire & Cable, Electronic
ELECTRICAL MEASURING INSTRUMENT REPAIR & CALIBRATION SVCS
ELECTRICAL SPLYS
ELECTRICAL SUPPLIES: Porcelain
ELECTROMEDICAL EQPT
ELECTROMETALLURGICAL PRDTS
ELECTRON BEAM: Cutting, Forming, Welding
ELECTRON TUBES: Cathode Ray
ELECTRONIC COMPONENTS
ELECTRONIC DETECTION SYSTEMS: Aeronautical
ELECTRONIC DEVICES: Solid State, NEC
ELECTRONIC EQPT REPAIR SVCS
ELECTRONIC LOADS & POWER SPLYS
ELECTRONIC PARTS & EQPT WHOLESALERS
ELECTRONIC SHOPPING
ELECTRONIC TRAINING DEVICES
ELECTROPLATING & PLATING SVC
ELEMENTARY & SECONDARY SCHOOLS, SPECIAL EDUCATION
ELEVATORS & EQPT
ELEVATORS WHOLESALERS
ELEVATORS: Installation & Conversion
ELEVATORS: Stair, Motor Powered
EMBLEMS: Embroidered
EMBOSSING SVC: Paper
EMBROIDERING & ART NEEDLEWORK FOR THE TRADE
EMBROIDERING SVC
EMBROIDERING SVC: Schiffli Machine
EMBROIDERY ADVERTISING SVCS
EMERGENCY ALARMS
EMERGENCY SHELTERS
EMPLOYMENT AGENCY SVCS
ENCODERS: Digital
ENERGY MEASUREMENT EQPT
ENGINE REBUILDING: Diesel
ENGINEERING HELP SVCS
ENGINEERING SVCS
ENGINEERING SVCS: Acoustical
ENGINEERING SVCS: Aviation Or Aeronautical
ENGINEERING SVCS: Building Construction

ENGINEERING SVCS: Chemical
ENGINEERING SVCS: Construction & Civil
ENGINEERING SVCS: Electrical Or Electronic
ENGINEERING SVCS: Energy conservation
ENGINEERING SVCS: Fire Protection
ENGINEERING SVCS: Industrial
ENGINEERING SVCS: Machine Tool Design
ENGINEERING SVCS: Marine
ENGINEERING SVCS: Mechanical
ENGINEERING SVCS: Mining
ENGINEERING SVCS: Pollution Control
ENGINEERING SVCS: Professional
ENGINEERING SVCS: Sanitary
ENGINEERING SVCS: Structural
ENGINES & ENGINE PARTS: Guided Missile, Research & Develpt
ENGINES: Diesel & Semi-Diesel Or Duel Fuel
ENGINES: Gasoline, NEC
ENGINES: Internal Combustion, NEC
ENGINES: Jet Propulsion
ENGINES: Marine
ENGINES: Steam
ENGRAVING SVC, NEC
ENGRAVING SVC: Jewelry & Personal Goods
ENGRAVING SVCS
ENGRAVING: Currency
ENGRAVING: Steel line, For The Printing Trade
ENGRAVINGS: Plastic
ENTERTAINMENT SVCS
ENVELOPES
ENVELOPES WHOLESALERS
ENVIRON QUALITY PROGS ADMIN, GOVT: Water Control & Quality
EPOXY RESINS
EQUIPMENT: Pedestrian Traffic Control
EQUIPMENT: Rental & Leasing, NEC
ETCHING & ENGRAVING SVC
ETHYLENE-PROPYLENE RUBBERS: EPDM Polymers
EXCAVATING EQPT
EXCURSION BOATS
EXERCISE EQPT STORES
EXHAUST SYSTEMS: Eqpt & Parts
EXPLORATION, METAL MINING
EXPLOSIVES
EXPLOSIVES: Gunpowder
EXTRACTS, FLAVORING
EYEGLASSES
EYES & HOOKS Screw
EYES: Artificial

F

FABRIC STORES
FABRICATED METAL PRODUCTS, NEC
FABRICS & CLOTH: Quilted
FABRICS: Alpacas, Cotton
FABRICS: Alpacas, Mohair, Woven
FABRICS: Animal Fiber, Woven, Exc Wool
FABRICS: Apparel & Outerwear, Cotton
FABRICS: Bags & Bagging, Cotton
FABRICS: Broadwoven, Cotton
FABRICS: Broadwoven, Synthetic Manmade Fiber & Silk
FABRICS: Broadwoven, Wool
FABRICS: Canvas
FABRICS: Coated Or Treated
FABRICS: Denims
FABRICS: Fiberglass, Broadwoven
FABRICS: Filter Cloth, Cotton
FABRICS: Glass & Fiberglass, Broadwoven
FABRICS: Metallized
FABRICS: Nonwoven
FABRICS: Nylon, Broadwoven
FABRICS: Pin Stripes, Cotton
FABRICS: Polyester, Broadwoven
FABRICS: Print, Cotton
FABRICS: Resin Or Plastic Coated
FABRICS: Rubberized
FABRICS: Satin
FABRICS: Surgical Fabrics, Cotton
FABRICS: Table Cover, Cotton
FABRICS: Trimmings
FABRICS: Warp Knit, Lace & Netting
FABRICS: Woven Wire, Made From Purchased Wire
FABRICS: Woven, Narrow Cotton, Wool, Silk
FACIAL SALONS
FACILITIES SUPPORT SVCS

FACSIMILE COMMUNICATION EQPT
FAMILY CLOTHING STORES
FANS, VENTILATING: Indl Or Commercial
FARM & GARDEN MACHINERY WHOLESALERS
FARM MACHINERY REPAIR SVCS
FARM PRDTS, RAW MATERIALS, WHOLESALE: Hides
FARM PRDTS, RAW MATERIALS, WHOLESALE: Hops
FARM SPLY STORES
FARM SPLYS WHOLESALERS
FARM SPLYS, WHOLESALE: Beekeeping Splys, Nondurable
FARM SPLYS, WHOLESALE: Feed
FARM SPLYS, WHOLESALE: Fertilizers & Agricultural Chemicals
FARM SPLYS, WHOLESALE: Garden Splys
FASTENERS: Metal
FASTENERS: Notions, NEC
FASTENERS: Notions, Zippers
FATTY ACID ESTERS & AMINOS
FAUCETS & SPIGOTS: Metal & Plastic
FEDERAL SAVINGS BANKS
FENCE POSTS: Iron & Steel
FENCES & FENCING MATERIALS
FENCES OR POSTS: Ornamental Iron Or Steel
FENCING DEALERS
FENCING MATERIALS: Docks & Other Outdoor Prdts, Wood
FENCING MATERIALS: Plastic
FENCING MATERIALS: Snow Fence, Wood
FENCING MATERIALS: Wood
FENCING: Chain Link
FENDERS: Automobile, Stamped Or Pressed Metal
FERRIES: Operating Across Rivers Or Within Harbors
FERTILIZER MINERAL MINING
FERTILIZER, AGRICULTURAL: Wholesalers
FERTILIZERS: NEC
FERTILIZERS: Nitrogenous
FERTILIZERS: Phosphatic
FIBER & FIBER PRDTS: Acrylic
FIBER & FIBER PRDTS: Fluorocarbon
FIBER & FIBER PRDTS: Organic, Noncellulose
FIBER & FIBER PRDTS: Synthetic Cellulosic
FIBER OPTICS
FIBERS: Carbon & Graphite
FILLERS & SEALERS: Putty, Wood
FILLING SVCS: Pressure Containers
FILM & SHEET: Unsuppported Plastic
FILM BASE: Cellulose Acetate Or Nitrocellulose Plastics
FILM: Motion Picture
FILTER CLEANING SVCS
FILTER ELEMENTS: Fluid & Hydraulic Line
FILTERS
FILTERS & SOFTENERS: Water, Household
FILTERS & STRAINERS: Pipeline
FILTERS: Air
FILTERS: Air Intake, Internal Combustion Engine, Exc Auto
FILTERS: General Line, Indl
FILTERS: Oil, Internal Combustion Engine, Exc Auto
FILTRATION DEVICES: Electronic
FINANCIAL INVESTMENT ADVICE
FINGERNAILS, ARTIFICIAL
FINISHING SVCS
FIRE ALARM MAINTENANCE & MONITORING SVCS
FIRE ARMS, SMALL: Guns Or Gun Parts, 30 mm & Below
FIRE ARMS, SMALL: Machine Guns/Machine Gun Parts, 30mm/below
FIRE ARMS, SMALL: Pistols Or Pistol Parts, 30 mm & below
FIRE ARMS, SMALL: Shotguns Or Shotgun Parts, 30 mm & Below
FIRE DETECTION SYSTEMS
FIRE EXTINGUISHER CHARGES
FIRE EXTINGUISHER SVC
FIRE EXTINGUISHERS, WHOLESALE
FIRE EXTINGUISHERS: Portable
FIRE OR BURGLARY RESISTIVE PRDTS
FIRE PROTECTION EQPT
FIREARMS & AMMUNITION, EXC SPORTING, WHOLESALE
FIREARMS: Large, Greater Than 30mm
FIREARMS: Small, 30mm or Less
FIREBRICK: Clay
FIREPLACE & CHIMNEY MATERIAL: Concrete
FIREPLACE EQPT & ACCESS
FIRING OVEN & ACCESS: Clay
FIRST AID SPLYS, WHOLESALE
FISH & SEAFOOD PROCESSORS: Canned Or Cured
FISH & SEAFOOD PROCESSORS: Fresh Or Frozen
FISH & SEAFOOD WHOLESALERS

PRODUCT INDEX

FISH EGGS: Packaged For Use As Bait
FISH FOOD
FISHING EQPT: Lures
FISHING EQPT: Nets & Seines
FITTINGS & ASSEMBLIES: Hose & Tube, Hydraulic Or Pneumatic
FITTINGS: Pipe
FIXTURES & EQPT: Kitchen, Metal, Exc Cast Aluminum
FIXTURES: Cut Stone
FLAGS: Fabric
FLAGSTONES
FLARES
FLAT GLASS: Construction
FLAT GLASS: Ophthalmic
FLAT GLASS: Skylight
FLAT GLASS: Tempered
FLAT GLASS: Window, Clear & Colored
FLIGHT TRAINING SCHOOLS
FLOOR CLEANING & MAINTENANCE EQPT: Household
FLOOR COVERING STORES
FLOOR COVERING STORES: Carpets
FLOOR COVERING: Plastic
FLOOR COVERINGS WHOLESALERS
FLOOR COVERINGS: Textile Fiber
FLOOR COVERINGS: Tile, Support Plastic
FLOORING & GRATINGS: Open, Construction Applications
FLOORING: Hard Surface
FLOORING: Hardwood
FLOORING: Tile
FLORISTS
FLORISTS' SPLYS, WHOLESALE
FLOWER ARRANGEMENTS: Artificial
FLOWER POTS Plastic
FLOWER POTS: Red Earthenware
FLOWERS & FLORISTS' SPLYS WHOLESALERS
FLOWERS: Artificial & Preserved
FLUES & PIPES: Stove Or Furnace
FLUID METERS & COUNTING DEVICES
FLUID POWER PUMPS & MOTORS
FLUID POWER VALVES & HOSE FITTINGS
FLUMES: Metal Plate
FLY TRAPS: Electrical
FLYING FIELDS, EXC MAINTAINED BY CLUBS
FOIL: Aluminum
FOIL: Laminated To Paper Or Other Materials
FOIL: Magnesium & Magnesium-Base Alloy
FOIL: Tin
FOOD COLORINGS
FOOD CONTAMINATION TESTING OR SCREENING KITS
FOOD PRDTS & SEAFOOD: Shellfish, Fresh, Shucked
FOOD PRDTS, CANNED OR FRESH PACK: Fruit Juices
FOOD PRDTS, CANNED OR FRESH PACK: Vegetable Juices
FOOD PRDTS, CANNED: Applesauce
FOOD PRDTS, CANNED: Barbecue Sauce
FOOD PRDTS, CANNED: Ethnic
FOOD PRDTS, CANNED: Fruit Juices, Fresh
FOOD PRDTS, CANNED: Fruit Pie Mixes & Fillings
FOOD PRDTS, CANNED: Fruit Purees
FOOD PRDTS, CANNED: Fruits
FOOD PRDTS, CANNED: Fruits
FOOD PRDTS, CANNED: Fruits & Fruit Prdts
FOOD PRDTS, CANNED: Jams, Including Imitation
FOOD PRDTS, CANNED: Jams, Jellies & Preserves
FOOD PRDTS, CANNED: Jellies, Edible, Including Imitation
FOOD PRDTS, CANNED: Mexican, NEC
FOOD PRDTS, CANNED: Spaghetti
FOOD PRDTS, CANNED: Vegetables
FOOD PRDTS, CANNED: Vegetables
FOOD PRDTS, CONFECTIONERY, WHOLESALE: Candy
FOOD PRDTS, CONFECTIONERY, WHOLESALE: Snack Foods
FOOD PRDTS, DAIRY, WHOLESALE: Frozen Dairy Desserts
FOOD PRDTS, FISH & SEAFOOD, WHOLESALE: Fresh
FOOD PRDTS, FISH & SEAFOOD, WHOLESALE: Frozen, Unpackaged
FOOD PRDTS, FISH & SEAFOOD, WHOLESALE: Seafood
FOOD PRDTS, FISH & SEAFOOD: Broth, Canned, Jarred, Etc
FOOD PRDTS, FISH & SEAFOOD: Canned & Jarred, Etc
FOOD PRDTS, FISH & SEAFOOD: Crabmeat, Fresh, Pkgd Nonsealed
FOOD PRDTS, FISH & SEAFOOD: Fish, Canned & Cured
FOOD PRDTS, FISH & SEAFOOD: Fish, Cured, NEC
FOOD PRDTS, FISH & SEAFOOD: Fish, Fresh, Prepared
FOOD PRDTS, FISH & SEAFOOD: Fish, Frozen, Prepared
FOOD PRDTS, FISH & SEAFOOD: Fish, Smoked
FOOD PRDTS, FISH & SEAFOOD: Fresh, Prepared
FOOD PRDTS, FISH & SEAFOOD: Fresh/Frozen Chowder, Soup/Stew
FOOD PRDTS, FISH & SEAFOOD: Oysters, Canned, Jarred, Etc
FOOD PRDTS, FISH & SEAFOOD: Oysters, Preserved & Cured
FOOD PRDTS, FISH & SEAFOOD: Prepared Cakes & Sticks
FOOD PRDTS, FISH & SEAFOOD: Salmon, Canned, Jarred, Etc
FOOD PRDTS, FISH & SEAFOOD: Salmon, Cured, NEC
FOOD PRDTS, FISH & SEAFOOD: Salmon, Smoked
FOOD PRDTS, FISH & SEAFOOD: Seafood, Frozen, Prepared
FOOD PRDTS, FISH & SEAFOOD: Shellfish, Canned & Cured
FOOD PRDTS, FISH & SEAFOOD: Shellfish, Canned, Jarred, Etc
FOOD PRDTS, FISH & SEAFOOD: Shellfish, Frozen, Prepared
FOOD PRDTS, FISH & SEAFOOD: Tuna Fish, Canned, Jarred, Etc
FOOD PRDTS, FISH & SEAFOOD: Tuna Fish, Preserved & Cured
FOOD PRDTS, FROZEN: Breakfasts, Packaged
FOOD PRDTS, FROZEN: Ethnic Foods, NEC
FOOD PRDTS, FROZEN: Fruit Juice, Concentrates
FOOD PRDTS, FROZEN: Fruits
FOOD PRDTS, FROZEN: Fruits & Vegetables
FOOD PRDTS, FROZEN: Fruits, Juices & Vegetables
FOOD PRDTS, FROZEN: NEC
FOOD PRDTS, FROZEN: Pizza
FOOD PRDTS, FROZEN: Potato Prdts
FOOD PRDTS, FROZEN: Soups
FOOD PRDTS, FROZEN: Vegetables, Exc Potato Prdts
FOOD PRDTS, FROZEN: Waffles
FOOD PRDTS, FRUITS & VEGETABLES, FRESH, WHOLESALE
FOOD PRDTS, FRUITS & VEGETABLES, FRESH, WHOLESALE: Potatoes
FOOD PRDTS, FRUITS & VEGETABLES, FRESH, WHOLESALE: Vegetable
FOOD PRDTS, MEAT & MEAT PRDTS, WHOLESALE: Cured Or Smoked
FOOD PRDTS, MEAT & MEAT PRDTS, WHOLESALE: Fresh
FOOD PRDTS, WHOL: Canned Goods, Fruit, Veg, Seafood/Meats
FOOD PRDTS, WHOLESALE: Beverages, Exc Coffee & Tea
FOOD PRDTS, WHOLESALE: Chocolate
FOOD PRDTS, WHOLESALE: Coffee & Tea
FOOD PRDTS, WHOLESALE: Coffee, Green Or Roasted
FOOD PRDTS, WHOLESALE: Condiments
FOOD PRDTS, WHOLESALE: Crackers
FOOD PRDTS, WHOLESALE: Dried or Canned Foods
FOOD PRDTS, WHOLESALE: Flavorings & Fragrances
FOOD PRDTS, WHOLESALE: Grains
FOOD PRDTS, WHOLESALE: Health
FOOD PRDTS, WHOLESALE: Natural & Organic
FOOD PRDTS, WHOLESALE: Organic & Diet
FOOD PRDTS, WHOLESALE: Pasta & Rice
FOOD PRDTS, WHOLESALE: Salad Dressing
FOOD PRDTS, WHOLESALE: Sandwiches
FOOD PRDTS, WHOLESALE: Sauces
FOOD PRDTS, WHOLESALE: Sausage Casings
FOOD PRDTS, WHOLESALE: Specialty
FOOD PRDTS, WHOLESALE: Spices & Seasonings
FOOD PRDTS, WHOLESALE: Water, Mineral Or Spring, Bottled
FOOD PRDTS, WHOLESALE: Wine Makers' Eqpt & Splys
FOOD PRDTS: Almond Pastes
FOOD PRDTS: Animal & marine fats & oils
FOOD PRDTS: Breakfast Bars
FOOD PRDTS: Cereals
FOOD PRDTS: Chicken, Processed, Cooked
FOOD PRDTS: Chicken, Processed, NEC
FOOD PRDTS: Chocolate Coatings & Syrup
FOOD PRDTS: Cocoa & Cocoa Prdts
FOOD PRDTS: Cocoa, Powdered
FOOD PRDTS: Coffee
FOOD PRDTS: Coffee Extracts
FOOD PRDTS: Coffee Roasting, Exc Wholesale Grocers
FOOD PRDTS: Coffee, Ground, Mixed With Grain Or Chicory
FOOD PRDTS: Corn Meal
FOOD PRDTS: Cottonseed Oil, Cake & Meal
FOOD PRDTS: Dessert Mixes & Fillings
FOOD PRDTS: Dips, Exc Cheese & Sour Cream Based
FOOD PRDTS: Dough, Biscuit
FOOD PRDTS: Dressings, Salad, Raw & Cooked Exc Dry Mixes
FOOD PRDTS: Dried & Dehydrated Fruits, Vegetables & Soup Mix
FOOD PRDTS: Edible Oil Prdts, Exc Corn Oil
FOOD PRDTS: Edible fats & oils
FOOD PRDTS: Eggs, Processed
FOOD PRDTS: Fish Meal
FOOD PRDTS: Fish Oil
FOOD PRDTS: Flour
FOOD PRDTS: Flour & Other Grain Mill Products
FOOD PRDTS: Flour Mixes & Doughs
FOOD PRDTS: Flours & Flour Mixes, From Purchased Flour
FOOD PRDTS: Freeze-Dried Coffee
FOOD PRDTS: Fresh Vegetables, Peeled Or Processed
FOOD PRDTS: Fruit Juices
FOOD PRDTS: Fruits & Vegetables, Pickled
FOOD PRDTS: Fruits, Dehydrated Or Dried
FOOD PRDTS: Fruits, Dried Or Dehydrated, Exc Freeze-Dried
FOOD PRDTS: Granola & Energy Bars, Nonchocolate
FOOD PRDTS: Honey
FOOD PRDTS: Ice, Blocks
FOOD PRDTS: Macaroni, Noodles, Spaghetti, Pasta, Etc
FOOD PRDTS: Malt
FOOD PRDTS: Milled Corn By-Prdts
FOOD PRDTS: Mixes, Doughnut From Purchased Flour
FOOD PRDTS: Mixes, Gingerbread From Purchased Flour
FOOD PRDTS: Mixes, Pizza
FOOD PRDTS: Mixes, Sauces, Dry
FOOD PRDTS: Mixes, Seasonings, Dry
FOOD PRDTS: Nuts & Seeds
FOOD PRDTS: Olive Oil
FOOD PRDTS: Pasta, Rice/Potatoes, Uncooked, Pkgd
FOOD PRDTS: Pasta, Uncooked, Packaged With Other Ingredients
FOOD PRDTS: Pickles, Vinegar
FOOD PRDTS: Pizza Doughs From Purchased Flour
FOOD PRDTS: Pork Rinds
FOOD PRDTS: Potato & Corn Chips & Similar Prdts
FOOD PRDTS: Potato Chips & Other Potato-Based Snacks
FOOD PRDTS: Potatoes, Dried
FOOD PRDTS: Preparations
FOOD PRDTS: Prepared Sauces, Exc Tomato Based
FOOD PRDTS: Prepared Seafood Sauces Exc Tomato & Dry
FOOD PRDTS: Raw cane sugar
FOOD PRDTS: Salads
FOOD PRDTS: Sandwiches
FOOD PRDTS: Seasonings & Spices
FOOD PRDTS: Soup Mixes
FOOD PRDTS: Soup Powders
FOOD PRDTS: Soy Sauce
FOOD PRDTS: Spices, Including Ground
FOOD PRDTS: Starch, Edible Root
FOOD PRDTS: Starch, Potato
FOOD PRDTS: Sugar
FOOD PRDTS: Tea
FOOD PRDTS: Tofu, Exc Frozen Desserts
FOOD PRDTS: Tortilla Chips
FOOD PRDTS: Tortillas
FOOD PRDTS: Vegetable Oil Mills, NEC
FOOD PRDTS: Vegetable Oil, Refined, Exc Corn
FOOD PRDTS: Vegetables, Dehydrated Or Dried
FOOD PRDTS: Vegetables, Pickled
FOOD PRDTS: Vinegar
FOOD PRODUCTS MACHINERY
FOOD STORES: Convenience, Chain
FOOD STORES: Convenience, Independent
FOOD STORES: Delicatessen
FOOD STORES: Grocery, Chain
FOOD STORES: Grocery, Independent
FOOTWEAR: Cut Stock
FOOTWEAR: Except Rubber, NEC
FORESTRY RELATED EQPT
FORGINGS
FORGINGS: Aluminum
FORGINGS: Anchors
FORGINGS: Armor Plate, Iron Or Steel
FORGINGS: Automotive & Internal Combustion Engine
FORGINGS: Gear & Chain
FORGINGS: Machinery, Ferrous

PRODUCT INDEX

FORGINGS: Nuclear Power Plant, Ferrous
FORGINGS: Plumbing Fixture, Nonferrous
FORMS HANDLING EQPT
FORMS: Concrete, Sheet Metal
FOUNDRIES: Aluminum
FOUNDRIES: Brass, Bronze & Copper
FOUNDRIES: Gray & Ductile Iron
FOUNDRIES: Iron
FOUNDRIES: Nonferrous
FOUNDRIES: Steel
FOUNDRIES: Steel Investment
FRACTIONATION PRDTS OF CRUDE PETROLEUM, HYDROCARBONS, NEC
FRAMES & FRAMING WHOLESALE
FRANCHISES, SELLING OR LICENSING
FREIGHT CAR LOADING & UNLOADING SVCS
FREIGHT TRANSPORTATION ARRANGEMENTS
FRICTION MATERIAL, MADE FROM POWDERED METAL
FRUIT & VEGETABLE MARKETS
FRUIT STANDS OR MARKETS
FRUITS & VEGETABLES WHOLESALERS: Fresh
FUEL ADDITIVES
FUEL CELL FORMS: Cardboard, Made From Purchased Materials
FUEL CELLS: Solid State
FUEL DEALERS: Coal
FUEL DEALERS: Wood
FUEL OIL DEALERS
FUEL TREATING
FUEL: Rocket Engine, Organic
FUELS: Diesel
FUELS: Ethanol
FUELS: Nuclear
FUNERAL HOME
FUNERAL HOMES & SVCS
FUNGICIDES OR HERBICIDES
FUR APPAREL STORES
FUR APPAREL STORES: Made To Custom Order
FUR: Hats
FURNACES & OVENS: Indl
FURNITURE & CABINET STORES: Cabinets, Custom Work
FURNITURE & CABINET STORES: Custom
FURNITURE & FIXTURES Factory
FURNITURE PARTS: Metal
FURNITURE REFINISHING SVCS
FURNITURE REPAIR & MAINTENANCE SVCS
FURNITURE STOCK & PARTS: Carvings, Wood
FURNITURE STOCK & PARTS: Dimension Stock, Hardwood
FURNITURE STOCK & PARTS: Hardwood
FURNITURE STOCK & PARTS: Squares, Hardwood
FURNITURE STORES
FURNITURE STORES: Cabinets, Kitchen, Exc Custom Made
FURNITURE STORES: Custom Made, Exc Cabinets
FURNITURE STORES: Office
FURNITURE STORES: Outdoor & Garden
FURNITURE WHOLESALERS
FURNITURE, HOUSEHOLD: Wholesalers
FURNITURE, MATTRESSES: Wholesalers
FURNITURE, OFFICE: Wholesalers
FURNITURE, WHOLESALE: Bedsprings
FURNITURE, WHOLESALE: Racks
FURNITURE: Bed Frames & Headboards, Wood
FURNITURE: Bedroom, Wood
FURNITURE: Box Springs, Assembled
FURNITURE: Camp, Metal
FURNITURE: Chairs, Dental
FURNITURE: Chests, Cedar
FURNITURE: China Closets
FURNITURE: Church
FURNITURE: Desks & Tables, Office, Exc Wood
FURNITURE: Dining Room, Wood
FURNITURE: Dressers, Household, Wood
FURNITURE: Fiberglass & Plastic
FURNITURE: Foundations & Platforms
FURNITURE: Garden, Exc Wood, Metal, Stone Or Concrete
FURNITURE: Household, Metal
FURNITURE: Household, NEC
FURNITURE: Household, Upholstered On Metal Frames
FURNITURE: Household, Upholstered, Exc Wood Or Metal
FURNITURE: Household, Wood
FURNITURE: Institutional, Exc Wood
FURNITURE: Juvenile, Wood
FURNITURE: Kitchen & Dining Room
FURNITURE: Lawn & Garden, Except Wood & Metal
FURNITURE: Living Room, Upholstered On Wood Frames
FURNITURE: Mattresses & Foundations
FURNITURE: Mattresses, Box & Bedsprings
FURNITURE: Mattresses, Innerspring Or Box Spring
FURNITURE: NEC
FURNITURE: Office Panel Systems, Exc Wood
FURNITURE: Office Panel Systems, Wood
FURNITURE: Office, Exc Wood
FURNITURE: Office, Wood
FURNITURE: Outdoor, Wood
FURNITURE: Picnic Tables Or Benches, Park
FURNITURE: Rockers, Wood, Exc Upholstered
FURNITURE: School
FURNITURE: Ship
FURNITURE: Sleep
FURNITURE: Storage Chests, Household, Wood
FURNITURE: Studio Couches
FURNITURE: Table Tops, Marble
FURNITURE: Tables & Table Tops, Wood
FURNITURE: Unfinished, Wood
FURNITURE: Upholstered
FURNITURE: Vehicle
FURS, DRESSED, WHOLESALE
Furs

G

GAITERS: Rubber Or Rubber Soled Fabric
GAMES & TOYS: Bells
GAMES & TOYS: Blocks
GAMES & TOYS: Board Games, Children's & Adults'
GAMES & TOYS: Carriages, Baby
GAMES & TOYS: Craft & Hobby Kits & Sets
GAMES & TOYS: Dolls, Exc Stuffed Toy Animals
GAMES & TOYS: Electronic
GAMES & TOYS: Game Machines, Exc Coin-Operated
GAMES & TOYS: Kits, Science, Incl Microscopes/Chemistry Sets
GAMES & TOYS: Models, Airplane, Toy & Hobby
GAMES & TOYS: Models, Railroad, Toy & Hobby
GAMES & TOYS: Puzzles
GAMES & TOYS: Rocking Horses
GAMES & TOYS: Scooters, Children's
GAMES & TOYS: Sleds, Children's
GAMES & TOYS: Trains & Eqpt, Electric & Mechanical
GARAGE DOOR REPAIR SVCS
GARBAGE DISPOSERS & COMPACTORS: Commercial
GAS & OIL FIELD EXPLORATION SVCS
GAS & OIL FIELD SVCS, NEC
GAS APPLIANCE REPAIR SVCS
GAS STATIONS
GAS: Refinery
GASES: Acetylene
GASES: Carbon Dioxide
GASES: Helium
GASES: Hydrogen
GASES: Indl
GASES: Neon
GASES: Nitrogen
GASES: Oxygen
GASKETS
GASKETS & SEALING DEVICES
GASOLINE FILLING STATIONS
GASOLINE WHOLESALERS
GATES: Ornamental Metal
GEARS: Power Transmission, Exc Auto
GEM STONES MINING, NEC: Natural
GENERAL & INDUSTRIAL LOAN INSTITUTIONS
GENERAL MERCHANDISE, NONDURABLE, WHOLESALE
GENERATING APPARATUS & PARTS: Electrical
GENERATION EQPT: Electronic
GENERATOR SETS: Motor
GENERATORS: Electric
GENERATORS: Electrochemical, Fuel Cell
GENERATORS: Storage Battery Chargers
GENERATORS: Vehicles, Gas-Electric Or Oil-Electric
GIFT SHOP
GIFT WRAPPING SVCS
GIFT, NOVELTY & SOUVENIR STORES: Artcraft & carvings
GIFT, NOVELTY & SOUVENIR STORES: Gift Baskets
GIFT, NOVELTY & SOUVENIR STORES: Gifts & Novelties
GIFT, NOVELTY & SOUVENIR STORES: Party Favors
GIFTS & NOVELTIES: Wholesalers
GIFTWARE: Brass
GLASS & GLASS CERAMIC PRDTS, PRESSED OR BLOWN: Tableware
GLASS FABRICATORS
GLASS PRDTS, FROM PURCHASED GLASS: Art
GLASS PRDTS, FROM PURCHASED GLASS: Glassware
GLASS PRDTS, FROM PURCHASED GLASS: Insulating
GLASS PRDTS, PRESSED OR BLOWN: Bulbs, Electric Lights
GLASS PRDTS, PRESSED OR BLOWN: Glass Fibers, Textile
GLASS PRDTS, PRESSED OR BLOWN: Glassware, Art Or Decorative
GLASS PRDTS, PRESSED OR BLOWN: Glassware, Novelty
GLASS PRDTS, PRESSED OR BLOWN: Optical
GLASS PRDTS, PRESSED OR BLOWN: Ornaments, Christmas Tree
GLASS PRDTS, PRESSED OR BLOWN: Vases
GLASS PRDTS, PRESSED/BLOWN: Glassware, Art, Decor/Novelty
GLASS PRDTS, PRESSED/BLOWN: Lenses, Lantern, Flshlght, Etc
GLASS PRDTS, PURCHSD GLASS: Ornamental, Cut, Engraved/Décor
GLASS STORE: Leaded Or Stained
GLASS STORES
GLASS: Fiber
GLASS: Flat
GLASS: Insulating
GLASS: Leaded
GLASS: Plate
GLASS: Pressed & Blown, NEC
GLASS: Stained
GLASS: Tempered
GLASSWARE STORES
GLASSWARE WHOLESALERS
GLASSWARE, NOVELTY, WHOLESALE
GLASSWARE: Cut & Engraved
GLASSWARE: Laboratory
GLOBAL POSITIONING SYSTEMS & EQPT
GLOBES, GEOGRAPHICAL
GLOVES: Fabric
GLOVES: Leather
GLOVES: Leather, Work
GLOVES: Safety
GLOVES: Work
GLYCERIN
GOLD ORE MINING
GOLD ORES
GOLD ORES PROCESSING
GOLD STAMPING, EXC BOOKS
GOLF CARTS: Powered
GOLF CLUB & EQPT REPAIR SVCS
GOLF COURSES: Public
GOLF EQPT
GOLF GOODS & EQPT
GOURMET FOOD STORES
GOVERNMENT, EXECUTIVE OFFICES: City & Town Managers' Offices
GOVERNMENT, GENERAL: Administration
GRAIN & FIELD BEANS WHOLESALERS
GRANITE: Crushed & Broken
GRANITE: Cut & Shaped
GRANITE: Dimension
GRAPHIC ARTS & RELATED DESIGN SVCS
GRAPHIC LAYOUT SVCS: Printed Circuitry
GRATINGS: Open Steel Flooring
GRATINGS: Tread, Fabricated Metal
GRAVE MARKERS: Concrete
GRAVEL & PEBBLE MINING
GRAVEL MINING
GREASES & INEDIBLE FATS, RENDERED
GREENHOUSES: Prefabricated Metal
GREETING CARD SHOPS
GRENADES: Grenades, Hand
GRILLES & REGISTERS: Ornamental Metal Work
GRINDING BALLS: Ceramic
GRINDING SVC: Precision, Commercial Or Indl
GRINDING SVCS: Ophthalmic Lens, Exc Prescription
GRIPS OR HANDLES: Rubber
GRITS: Crushed & Broken
GROCERIES WHOLESALERS, NEC
GROCERIES, GENERAL LINE WHOLESALERS
GUARD SVCS
GUIDED MISSILES & SPACE VEHICLES
GUIDED MISSILES & SPACE VEHICLES: Research & Development
GUM & WOOD CHEMICALS
GUN STOCKS: Wood
GUN SVCS

PRODUCT INDEX

GUNSMITHS
GUTTERS
GUTTERS: Sheet Metal
GYPSUM PRDTS

H

HAIR & HAIR BASED PRDTS
HAIR ACCESS WHOLESALERS
HAIR ACCESS: Rubber
HAIR CARE PRDTS
HAIR DRESSING, FOR THE TRADE
HAIR REPLACEMENT & WEAVING SVCS
HAIRBRUSHES, WHOLESALE
HAIRDRESSERS
HAND TOOLS, NEC: Wholesalers
HANDBAGS
HANDBAGS: Women's
HANDLES: Brush Or Tool, Plastic
HANDLES: Wood
HANG GLIDERS
HANGERS: Garment, Home & Store, Wooden
HARDWARE
HARDWARE & BUILDING PRDTS: Plastic
HARDWARE & EQPT: Stage, Exc Lighting
HARDWARE STORES
HARDWARE STORES: Builders'
HARDWARE STORES: Chainsaws
HARDWARE STORES: Pumps & Pumping Eqpt
HARDWARE STORES: Tools
HARDWARE STORES: Tools, Hand
HARDWARE STORES: Tools, Power
HARDWARE WHOLESALERS
HARDWARE, WHOLESALE: Builders', NEC
HARDWARE, WHOLESALE: Chains
HARDWARE, WHOLESALE: Power Tools & Access
HARDWARE, WHOLESALE: Saw Blades
HARDWARE: Aircraft
HARDWARE: Aircraft & Marine, Incl Pulleys & Similar Items
HARDWARE: Builders'
HARDWARE: Cabinet
HARDWARE: Door Opening & Closing Devices, Exc Electrical
HARDWARE: Furniture
HARDWARE: Harness
HARNESS ASSEMBLIES: Cable & Wire
HARNESSES, HALTERS, SADDLERY & STRAPS
HEADPHONES: Radio
HEALTH AIDS: Exercise Eqpt
HEALTH AIDS: Vaporizers
HEALTH CLUBS
HEALTH PRACTITIONERS' OFFICES, NEC
HEALTH SCREENING SVCS
HEARING AIDS
HEAT EMISSION OPERATING APPARATUS
HEAT EXCHANGERS
HEAT TREATING: Metal
HEATERS: Swimming Pool, Electric
HEATING & AIR CONDITIONING EQPT & SPLYS WHOLESALERS
HEATING & AIR CONDITIONING UNITS, COMBINATION
HEATING EQPT & SPLYS
HEATING EQPT: Complete
HEATING SYSTEMS: Radiant, Indl Process
HEATING UNITS & DEVICES: Indl, Electric
HEATING UNITS: Gas, Infrared
HELICOPTERS
HELMETS: Leather
HELP SUPPLY SERVICES
HIGH ENERGY PARTICLE PHYSICS EQPT
HIGHWAY & STREET MAINTENANCE SVCS
HITCHES: Trailer
HOBBY, TOY & GAME STORES: Arts & Crafts & Splys
HOBBY, TOY & GAME STORES: Ceramics Splys
HOBBY, TOY & GAME STORES: Chess, Backgammon/Other Drbl Games
HOBBY, TOY & GAME STORES: Children's Toys & Games, Exc Dolls
HOBBY, TOY & GAME STORES: Dolls & Access
HOBBY, TOY & GAME STORES: Hobbies, NEC
HOBBY, TOY & GAME STORES: Kites
HOBBY, TOY & GAME STORES: Toys & Games
HOISTING SLINGS
HOISTS
HOISTS: Aircraft Loading
HOISTS: Hand
HOISTS: Mine

HOLDERS, PAPER TOWEL, GROCERY BAG, ETC: Plastic
HOLDING COMPANIES, NEC
HOLDING COMPANIES: Investment, Exc Banks
HOLDING COMPANIES: Personal, Exc Banks
HOME DELIVERY NEWSPAPER ROUTES
HOME ENTERTAINMENT EQPT: Electronic, NEC
HOME FURNISHINGS WHOLESALERS
HOME HEALTH CARE SVCS
HOMEBUILDERS & OTHER OPERATIVE BUILDERS
HOMEFURNISHING STORES: Lighting Fixtures
HOMEFURNISHING STORES: Mirrors
HOMEFURNISHING STORES: Pictures, Wall
HOMEFURNISHING STORES: Pottery
HOMEFURNISHING STORES: Venetian Blinds
HOMEFURNISHING STORES: Vertical Blinds
HOMEFURNISHING STORES: Window Furnishings
HOMEFURNISHINGS & SPLYS, WHOLESALE: Decorative
HOMEFURNISHINGS, WHOLESALE: Carpets
HOMEFURNISHINGS, WHOLESALE: Grills, Barbecue
HOMEFURNISHINGS, WHOLESALE: Kitchenware
HOMEFURNISHINGS, WHOLESALE: Pottery
HOMEFURNISHINGS, WHOLESALE: Window Covering Parts & Access
HOMEFURNISHINGS, WHOLESALE: Wood Flooring
HOMES, MODULAR: Wooden
HOMES: Log Cabins
HONES
HOPPERS: Sheet Metal
HORMONE PREPARATIONS
HORNS: Marine, Compressed Air Or Steam
HORSE & PET ACCESSORIES: Textile
HORSE ACCESS: Harnesses & Riding Crops, Etc, Exc Leather
HORSE ACCESS: Saddle Cloth
HORSESHOEING SVCS
HORSESHOES
HOSE: Air Line Or Air Brake, Rubber Or Rubberized Fabric
HOSE: Flexible Metal
HOSE: Vacuum Cleaner, Rubber
HOSES & BELTING: Rubber & Plastic
HOSPITAL EQPT REPAIR SVCS
HOSPITAL HOUSEKEEPING SVCS
HOSPITALS: Orthopedic
HOT TUBS
HOT TUBS: Plastic & Fiberglass
HOUSEHOLD APPLIANCE STORES
HOUSEHOLD ARTICLES, EXC KITCHEN: Pottery
HOUSEHOLD ARTICLES: Metal
HOUSEHOLD FURNISHINGS, NEC
HOUSEKEEPING & MAID SVCS
HOUSEWARE STORES
HOUSEWARES, ELECTRIC, EXC COOKING APPLIANCES & UTENSILS
HOUSEWARES, ELECTRIC: Cooking Appliances
HOUSEWARES, ELECTRIC: Extractors, Juice
HOUSEWARES, ELECTRIC: Heaters, Sauna
HOUSEWARES, ELECTRIC: Heating, Bsbrd/Wall, Radiant Heat
HOUSEWARES, ELECTRIC: Irons, Curling
HOUSEWARES, ELECTRIC: Massage Machines, Exc Beauty/Barber
HOUSEWARES, ELECTRIC: Popcorn Poppers
HOUSEWARES, ELECTRIC: Roasters
HOUSEWARES: Dishes, Plastic
HOUSEWARES: Kettles & Skillets, Cast Iron
HUMIDIFIERS & DEHUMIDIFIERS
HYDRAULIC EQPT REPAIR SVC
HYDRAULIC FLUIDS: Synthetic Based
HYDROPHONES
HYDROPONIC EQPT
Hard Rubber & Molded Rubber Prdts

I

ICE
ICE CREAM & ICES WHOLESALERS
ICE WHOLESALERS
ICE: Dry
IDENTIFICATION TAGS, EXC PAPER
IGNEOUS ROCK: Crushed & Broken
IGNITION APPARATUS & DISTRIBUTORS
INCENSE
INCINERATORS
INDL & PERSONAL SVC PAPER WHOLESALERS
INDL & PERSONAL SVC PAPER, WHOL: Boxes, Corrugtd/Solid Fiber

INDL & PERSONAL SVC PAPER, WHOL: Boxes, Paperbrd/Plastic
INDL & PERSONAL SVC PAPER, WHOL: Container, Paper/Plastic
INDL & PERSONAL SVC PAPER, WHOL: Cups, Disp, Plastic/Paper
INDL & PERSONAL SVC PAPER, WHOL: Paper, Wrap/Coarse/Prdts
INDL & PERSONAL SVC PAPER, WHOLESALE: Boxes & Containers
INDL & PERSONAL SVC PAPER, WHOLESALE: Boxes, Fldng Pprboard
INDL & PERSONAL SVC PAPER, WHOLESALE: Paper Tubes & Cores
INDL & PERSONAL SVC PAPER, WHOLESALE: Shipping Splys
INDL CONTRACTORS: Exhibit Construction
INDL EQPT SVCS
INDL GASES WHOLESALERS
INDL MACHINERY & EQPT WHOLESALERS
INDL MACHINERY REPAIR & MAINTENANCE
INDL PATTERNS: Foundry Cores
INDL PATTERNS: Foundry Patternmaking
INDL PROCESS INSTR: Transmit, Process Variables
INDL PROCESS INSTRUMENTS: Absorp Analyzers, Infrared, X-Ray
INDL PROCESS INSTRUMENTS: Control
INDL PROCESS INSTRUMENTS: Controllers, Process Variables
INDL PROCESS INSTRUMENTS: Digital Display, Process Variables
INDL PROCESS INSTRUMENTS: Fluidic Devices, Circuit & Systems
INDL PROCESS INSTRUMENTS: On-Stream Gas Or Liquid Analysis
INDL PROCESS INSTRUMENTS: Water Quality Monitoring/Cntrl Sys
INDL SPLYS WHOLESALERS
INDL SPLYS, WHOL: Fasteners, Incl Nuts, Bolts, Screws, Etc
INDL SPLYS, WHOLESALE: Barrels, New Or Reconditioned
INDL SPLYS, WHOLESALE: Bearings
INDL SPLYS, WHOLESALE: Chains, Power Transmission
INDL SPLYS, WHOLESALE: Electric Tools
INDL SPLYS, WHOLESALE: Fasteners & Fastening Eqpt
INDL SPLYS, WHOLESALE: Fittings
INDL SPLYS, WHOLESALE: Gaskets
INDL SPLYS, WHOLESALE: Gaskets & Seals
INDL SPLYS, WHOLESALE: Lapidary Eqpt
INDL SPLYS, WHOLESALE: Rubber Goods, Mechanical
INDL SPLYS, WHOLESALE: Seals
INDL SPLYS, WHOLESALE: Staplers & Tackers
INDL SPLYS, WHOLESALE: Tools
INDL SPLYS, WHOLESALE: Tools, NEC
INDL SPLYS, WHOLESALE: Valves & Fittings
INDUCTORS
INDUSTRIAL & COMMERCIAL EQPT INSPECTION SVCS
INFORMATION RETRIEVAL SERVICES
INFRARED OBJECT DETECTION EQPT
INK OR WRITING FLUIDS
INK: Printing
INNER TUBES: Truck Or Bus
INSECTICIDES
INSECTICIDES & PESTICIDES
INSPECTION & TESTING SVCS
INSTRUMENTS, LAB: Spectroscopic/Optical Properties Measuring
INSTRUMENTS, LABORATORY: Analyzers, Automatic Chemical
INSTRUMENTS, LABORATORY: Analyzers, Thermal
INSTRUMENTS, LABORATORY: Blood Testing
INSTRUMENTS, LABORATORY: Dust Sampling & Analysis
INSTRUMENTS, LABORATORY: Infrared Analytical
INSTRUMENTS, LABORATORY: Magnetic/Elec Properties Measuring
INSTRUMENTS, MEASURING & CNTRG: Plotting, Drafting/Map Rdg
INSTRUMENTS, MEASURING & CNTRL: Gauges, Auto, Computer
INSTRUMENTS, MEASURING & CNTRL: Geophysical & Meteorological
INSTRUMENTS, MEASURING & CNTRL: Radiation & Testing, Nuclear
INSTRUMENTS, MEASURING & CNTRLG: Aircraft & Motor Vehicle

PRODUCT INDEX

INSTRUMENTS, MEASURING & CNTRLG: Electrogamma Ray Loggers
INSTRUMENTS, MEASURING & CNTRLG: Thermometers/Temp Sensors
INSTRUMENTS, MEASURING & CNTRLNG: Press & Vac Ind, Acft Eng
INSTRUMENTS, MEASURING & CONTROLLING: Anamometers
INSTRUMENTS, MEASURING & CONTROLLING: Breathalyzers
INSTRUMENTS, MEASURING & CONTROLLING: Dosimetry, Personnel
INSTRUMENTS, MEASURING & CONTROLLING: Polygraph
INSTRUMENTS, MEASURING & CONTROLLING: Reactor Controls, Aux
INSTRUMENTS, MEASURING & CONTROLLING: Seismoscopes
INSTRUMENTS, MEASURING/CNTRL: Gauging, Ultrasonic Thickness
INSTRUMENTS, MEASURING/CNTRL: Testing/Measuring, Kinematic
INSTRUMENTS, MEASURING/CNTRLNG: Med Diagnostic Sys, Nuclear
INSTRUMENTS, OPTICAL: Light Sources, Standard
INSTRUMENTS, OPTICAL: Polarizers
INSTRUMENTS, OPTICAL: Prisms
INSTRUMENTS, OPTICAL: Test & Inspection
INSTRUMENTS, SURGICAL & MEDICAL: Biopsy
INSTRUMENTS, SURGICAL & MEDICAL: Blood & Bone Work
INSTRUMENTS, SURGICAL & MEDICAL: Catheters
INSTRUMENTS, SURGICAL & MEDICAL: Lasers, Surgical
INSTRUMENTS, SURGICAL & MEDICAL: Operating Tables
INSTRUMENTS, SURGICAL & MEDICAL: Optometers
INSTRUMENTS, SURGICAL & MEDICAL: Retractors
INSTRUMENTS, SURGICAL & MEDICAL: Saws, Surgical
INSTRUMENTS, SURGICAL & MEDICAL: Skin Grafting
INSTRUMENTS, SURGICAL & MEDICAL: Stapling Devices, Surgical
INSTRUMENTS, SURGICAL & MEDICAL: Suction Therapy
INSTRUMENTS, SURGICAL & MEDICAL: Trocars
INSTRUMENTS: Analytical
INSTRUMENTS: Analyzers, Spectrum
INSTRUMENTS: Drafting
INSTRUMENTS: Electrocardiographs
INSTRUMENTS: Electroencephalographs
INSTRUMENTS: Endoscopic Eqpt, Electromedical
INSTRUMENTS: Flow, Indl Process
INSTRUMENTS: Frequency Meters, Electrical, Mech & Electronic
INSTRUMENTS: Frequency Synthesizers
INSTRUMENTS: Generators, Pulse, Signal
INSTRUMENTS: Indl Process Control
INSTRUMENTS: Laser, Scientific & Engineering
INSTRUMENTS: Measurement, Indl Process
INSTRUMENTS: Measuring & Controlling
INSTRUMENTS: Measuring Electricity
INSTRUMENTS: Measuring, Current, NEC
INSTRUMENTS: Measuring, Electrical Energy
INSTRUMENTS: Measuring, Electrical, Field Strgth & Intensity
INSTRUMENTS: Medical & Surgical
INSTRUMENTS: Nautical
INSTRUMENTS: Optical, Analytical
INSTRUMENTS: Pressure Measurement, Indl
INSTRUMENTS: Radar Testing, Electric
INSTRUMENTS: Temperature Measurement, Indl
INSTRUMENTS: Test, Digital, Electronic & Electrical Circuits
INSTRUMENTS: Test, Electrical, Engine
INSTRUMENTS: Test, Electronic & Electric Measurement
INSTRUMENTS: Test, Electronic & Electrical Circuits
INSTRUMENTS: Testing, Semiconductor
INSTRUMENTS: Vibration
INSULATING COMPOUNDS
INSULATION & CUSHIONING FOAM: Polystyrene
INSULATION & ROOFING MATERIALS: Wood, Reconstituted
INSULATION MATERIALS WHOLESALERS
INSULATION: Fiberglass
INSULATORS & INSULATION MATERIALS: Electrical
INSURANCE AGENTS, NEC
INSURANCE CARRIERS: Automobile
INSURANCE CARRIERS: Direct Accident & Health
INSURANCE CARRIERS: Life
INSURANCE INSPECTION & INVESTIGATIONS SVCS
INSURANCE: Agents, Brokers & Service

INTEGRATED CIRCUITS, SEMICONDUCTOR NETWORKS, ETC
INTERCOMMUNICATIONS SYSTEMS: Electric
INTERIOR DESIGN SVCS, NEC
INTERIOR DESIGNING SVCS
INVERTERS: Nonrotating Electrical
INVESTMENT ADVISORY SVCS
INVESTMENT FUNDS, NEC
INVESTMENT RESEARCH SVCS
INVESTORS, NEC
IRON & STEEL PRDTS: Hot-Rolled
IRON & STEEL: Corrugating, Cold-Rolled
IRON ORES
IRRIGATION EQPT WHOLESALERS

J

JACKS: Hydraulic
JANITORIAL & CUSTODIAL SVCS
JANITORIAL EQPT & SPLYS WHOLESALERS
JAZZ MUSIC GROUP OR ARTISTS
JEWELERS' FINDINGS & MATERIALS
JEWELERS' FINDINGS & MATERIALS: Castings
JEWELERS' FINDINGS & MTLS: Jewel Prep, Instr, Tools, Watches
JEWELRY & PRECIOUS STONES WHOLESALERS
JEWELRY APPAREL
JEWELRY FINDINGS & LAPIDARY WORK
JEWELRY FINDINGS WHOLESALERS
JEWELRY REPAIR SVCS
JEWELRY STORES
JEWELRY STORES: Precious Stones & Precious Metals
JEWELRY, PREC METAL: Mountings, Pens, Lthr, Etc, Gold/Silver
JEWELRY, PRECIOUS METAL: Bracelets
JEWELRY, PRECIOUS METAL: Cigar & Cigarette Access
JEWELRY, PRECIOUS METAL: Medals, Precious Or Semiprecious
JEWELRY, PRECIOUS METAL: Necklaces
JEWELRY, PRECIOUS METAL: Pins
JEWELRY, PRECIOUS METAL: Rings, Finger
JEWELRY, PRECIOUS METAL: Settings & Mountings
JEWELRY, WHOLESALE
JEWELRY: Decorative, Fashion & Costume
JEWELRY: Precious Metal
JIGS & FIXTURES
JOB PRINTING & NEWSPAPER PUBLISHING COMBINED
JOB TRAINING & VOCATIONAL REHABILITATION SVCS
JOB TRAINING SVCS
JOINTS: Swivel & Universal, Exc Aircraft & Auto

K

KAOLIN MINING
KEYBOARDS: Computer Or Office Machine
KILNS & FURNACES: Ceramic
KITCHEN & COOKING ARTICLES: Pottery
KITCHEN & TABLE ARTICLES: Coarse Earthenware
KITCHEN CABINET STORES, EXC CUSTOM
KITCHEN CABINETS WHOLESALERS
KITCHEN TOOLS & UTENSILS WHOLESALERS
KITCHEN UTENSILS: Bakers' Eqpt, Wood
KITCHEN UTENSILS: Food Handling & Processing Prdts, Wood
KITCHENWARE STORES
KITCHENWARE: Plastic

L

LABELS: Paper, Made From Purchased Materials
LABOR UNION
LABORATORIES, TESTING: Forensic
LABORATORIES, TESTING: Metallurgical
LABORATORIES, TESTING: Prdt Certification, Sfty/Performance
LABORATORIES, TESTING: Product Testing
LABORATORIES, TESTING: Product Testing, Safety/Performance
LABORATORIES: Biological Research
LABORATORIES: Biotechnology
LABORATORIES: Dental
LABORATORIES: Dental Orthodontic Appliance Production
LABORATORIES: Electronic Research
LABORATORIES: Environmental Research
LABORATORIES: Medical
LABORATORIES: Noncommercial Research
LABORATORIES: Physical Research, Commercial

LABORATORIES: Testing
LABORATORIES: Testing
LABORATORY APPARATUS & FURNITURE
LABORATORY APPARATUS: Laser Beam Alignment Device
LABORATORY APPARATUS: Physics, NEC
LABORATORY APPARATUS: Sample Preparation Apparatus
LABORATORY APPARATUS: Shakers & Stirrers
LABORATORY CHEMICALS: Organic
LABORATORY EQPT, EXC MEDICAL: Wholesalers
LABORATORY EQPT: Centrifuges
LABORATORY EQPT: Clinical Instruments Exc Medical
LABORATORY EQPT: Distilling
LABORATORY EQPT: Sterilizers
LADDER & WORKSTAND COMBINATION ASSEMBLIES: Metal
LADDERS: Metal
LADDERS: Permanent Installation, Metal
LAMINATED PLASTICS: Plate, Sheet, Rod & Tubes
LAMINATING SVCS
LAMP BASES: Pottery
LAMP BULBS & TUBES, ELECTRIC: Electric Light
LAMP BULBS & TUBES, ELECTRIC: For Specialized Applications
LAMP BULBS & TUBES, ELECTRIC: Light, Complete
LAMPS: Ultraviolet
LAND SUBDIVIDERS & DEVELOPERS: Commercial
LAND SUBDIVIDERS & DEVELOPERS: Residential
LAND SUBDIVISION & DEVELOPMENT
LANDING MATS: Aircraft, Metal
LASER SYSTEMS & EQPT
LASERS: Welding, Drilling & Cutting Eqpt
LATH: Wood
LATHES
LAUNDRY & GARMENT SVCS: Tailor Shop, Exc Custom/Merchant
LAUNDRY EQPT: Commercial
LAUNDRY SVC: Flame & Heat Resistant Clothing Sply
LAWN & GARDEN EQPT
LAWN & GARDEN EQPT STORES
LAWN & GARDEN EQPT: Rototillers
LAWN & GARDEN EQPT: Tractors & Eqpt
LAWN MOWER REPAIR SHOP
LEAD & ZINC ORES
LEAD PENCILS & ART GOODS
LEASING & RENTAL SVCS: Cranes & Aerial Lift Eqpt
LEASING & RENTAL SVCS: Earth Moving Eqpt
LEASING & RENTAL: Computers & Eqpt
LEASING & RENTAL: Construction & Mining Eqpt
LEASING & RENTAL: Medical Machinery & Eqpt
LEASING & RENTAL: Other Real Estate Property
LEASING: Passenger Car
LEATHER GOODS: Aprons, Welders', Blacksmiths', Etc
LEATHER GOODS: Card Cases
LEATHER GOODS: Holsters
LEATHER GOODS: NEC
LEATHER GOODS: Personal
LEATHER GOODS: Saddles Or Parts
LEATHER GOODS: Spats
LEATHER GOODS: Wallets
LEATHER GOODS: Whips
LEATHER TANNING & FINISHING
LEATHER: Accessory Prdts
LEATHER: Shoe
LEATHER: Specialty, NEC
LEATHER: Upholstery
LECTURING SVCS
LEGAL OFFICES & SVCS
LEGAL SVCS: General Practice Attorney or Lawyer
LEGAL SVCS: Malpractice & Negligence Law
LESSORS: Farm Land
LICENSE TAGS: Automobile, Stamped Metal
LIE DETECTION SVCS
LIFE RAFTS: Rubber
LIGHT SENSITIVE DEVICES
LIGHTING EQPT: Flashlights
LIGHTING EQPT: Floodlights
LIGHTING EQPT: Locomotive & Railroad Car Lights
LIGHTING EQPT: Miners' Lamps
LIGHTING EQPT: Motor Vehicle, NEC
LIGHTING EQPT: Outdoor
LIGHTING EQPT: Spotlights
LIGHTING EQPT: Strobe Lighting Systems
LIGHTING FIXTURES WHOLESALERS
LIGHTING FIXTURES, NEC
LIGHTING FIXTURES: Arc

PRODUCT INDEX

LIGHTING FIXTURES: Indl & Commercial
LIGHTING FIXTURES: Motor Vehicle
LIGHTING FIXTURES: Ornamental, Commercial
LIGHTING FIXTURES: Residential
LIGHTING FIXTURES: Street
LIME
LIMESTONE & MARBLE: Dimension
LIMESTONE: Crushed & Broken
LIMESTONE: Ground
LINEN SPLY SVC: Clothing
LINERS & COVERS: Fabric
LINERS & LINING
LININGS: Apparel, Made From Purchased Materials
LININGS: Fabric, Apparel & Other, Exc Millinery
LIP BALMS
LIPSTICK
LOCKS
LOCKS & LOCK SETS, WHOLESALE
LOCKS: Safe & Vault, Metal
LOG LOADING & UNLOADING SVCS
LOGGING
LOGGING CAMPS & CONTRACTORS
LOGGING: Peeler Logs
LOGGING: Saw Logs
LOGGING: Stump Harvesting
LOGGING: Timber, Cut At Logging Camp
LOGGING: Wood Chips, Produced In The Field
LOGGING: Wooden Logs
LOGS: Gas, Fireplace
LOOMS
LOOSELEAF BINDERS
LOTIONS OR CREAMS: Face
LOUDSPEAKERS
LUBRICANTS: Corrosion Preventive
LUBRICATING EQPT: Indl
LUBRICATING OIL & GREASE WHOLESALERS
LUGGAGE & BRIEFCASES
LUGGAGE & LEATHER GOODS STORES
LUGGAGE: Traveling Bags
LUMBER & BLDG MATLS DEALER, RET: Electric Constructn Matls
LUMBER & BLDG MATLS DEALER, RET: Garage Doors, Sell/Install
LUMBER & BLDG MATRLS DEALERS, RET: Bath Fixtures, Eqpt/Sply
LUMBER & BLDG MATRLS DEALERS, RETAIL: Doors, Wood/Metal
LUMBER & BLDG MTRLS DEALERS, RET: Doors, Storm, Wood/Metal
LUMBER & BLDG MTRLS DEALERS, RET: Planing Mill Prdts/Lumber
LUMBER & BLDG MTRLS DEALERS, RET: Windows, Storm, Wood/Metal
LUMBER & BUILDING MATERIAL DEALERS, RETAIL: Roofing Material
LUMBER & BUILDING MATERIALS DEALER, RET: Door & Window Prdts
LUMBER & BUILDING MATERIALS DEALER, RET: Masonry Matls/Splys
LUMBER & BUILDING MATERIALS DEALERS, RET: Solar Heating Eqpt
LUMBER & BUILDING MATERIALS DEALERS, RETAIL: Brick
LUMBER & BUILDING MATERIALS DEALERS, RETAIL: Cement
LUMBER & BUILDING MATERIALS DEALERS, RETAIL: Countertops
LUMBER & BUILDING MATERIALS DEALERS, RETAIL: Flooring, Wood
LUMBER & BUILDING MATERIALS DEALERS, RETAIL: Modular Homes
LUMBER & BUILDING MATERIALS DEALERS, RETAIL: Sand & Gravel
LUMBER & BUILDING MATERIALS RET DEALERS: Millwork & Lumber
LUMBER & BUILDING MATLS DEALERS, RET: Concrete/Cinder Block
LUMBER: Cut Stock, Softwood
LUMBER: Dimension, Hardwood
LUMBER: Fiberboard
LUMBER: Flooring, Dressed, Softwood
LUMBER: Fuelwood, From Mill Waste
LUMBER: Furniture Dimension Stock, Softwood
LUMBER: Hardwood Dimension
LUMBER: Hardwood Dimension & Flooring Mills
LUMBER: Kiln Dried
LUMBER: Panels, Plywood, Softwood
LUMBER: Piles, Foundation & Marine Construction, Treated
LUMBER: Plywood, Hardwood
LUMBER: Plywood, Hardwood or Hardwood Faced
LUMBER: Plywood, Prefinished, Hardwood
LUMBER: Plywood, Softwood
LUMBER: Plywood, Softwood
LUMBER: Poles & Pole Crossarms, Treated
LUMBER: Rails, Fence, Round Or Split
LUMBER: Resawn, Small Dimension
LUMBER: Siding, Dressed
LUMBER: Stacking Or Sticking
LUMBER: Treated
LUMBER: Veneer, Hardwood
LUMBER: Veneer, Softwood

M

MACHINE PARTS: Stamped Or Pressed Metal
MACHINE SHOPS
MACHINE TOOL ACCESS: Boring Attachments
MACHINE TOOL ACCESS: Cutting
MACHINE TOOL ACCESS: Diamond Cutting, For Turning, Etc
MACHINE TOOL ACCESS: Machine Attachments & Access, Drilling
MACHINE TOOL ACCESS: Milling Machine Attachments
MACHINE TOOL ACCESS: Pushers
MACHINE TOOL ACCESS: Shaping Tools
MACHINE TOOL ACCESS: Sockets
MACHINE TOOL ACCESS: Tools & Access
MACHINE TOOL ATTACHMENTS & ACCESS
MACHINE TOOLS & ACCESS
MACHINE TOOLS, METAL CUTTING: Drilling
MACHINE TOOLS, METAL CUTTING: Drilling & Boring
MACHINE TOOLS, METAL CUTTING: Electrolytic
MACHINE TOOLS, METAL CUTTING: Exotic, Including Explosive
MACHINE TOOLS, METAL CUTTING: Grind, Polish, Buff, Lapp
MACHINE TOOLS, METAL CUTTING: Home Workshop
MACHINE TOOLS, METAL CUTTING: Lathes
MACHINE TOOLS, METAL CUTTING: Tool Replacement & Rpr Parts
MACHINE TOOLS, METAL FORMING: Bending
MACHINE TOOLS, METAL FORMING: Headers
MACHINE TOOLS, METAL FORMING: High Energy Rate
MACHINE TOOLS, METAL FORMING: Magnetic Forming
MACHINE TOOLS, METAL FORMING: Rebuilt
MACHINE TOOLS: Metal Cutting
MACHINE TOOLS: Metal Forming
MACHINERY & EQPT FINANCE LEASING
MACHINERY & EQPT, AGRICULTURAL, WHOL: Farm Eqpt Parts/Splys
MACHINERY & EQPT, AGRICULTURAL, WHOLESALE: Agricultural, NEC
MACHINERY & EQPT, AGRICULTURAL, WHOLESALE: Farm Implements
MACHINERY & EQPT, AGRICULTURAL, WHOLESALE: Landscaping Eqpt
MACHINERY & EQPT, AGRICULTURAL, WHOLESALE: Lawn & Garden
MACHINERY & EQPT, INDL, WHOL: Controlling Instruments/Access
MACHINERY & EQPT, INDL, WHOL: Environ Pollution Cntrl, Air
MACHINERY & EQPT, INDL, WHOL: Meters, Consumption Registerng
MACHINERY & EQPT, INDL, WHOLESALE: Alcoholic Beverage Mfrg
MACHINERY & EQPT, INDL, WHOLESALE: Cement Making
MACHINERY & EQPT, INDL, WHOLESALE: Chainsaws
MACHINERY & EQPT, INDL, WHOLESALE: Conveyor Systems
MACHINERY & EQPT, INDL, WHOLESALE: Cranes
MACHINERY & EQPT, INDL, WHOLESALE: Crushing
MACHINERY & EQPT, INDL, WHOLESALE: Drilling Bits
MACHINERY & EQPT, INDL, WHOLESALE: Drilling, Exc Bits
MACHINERY & EQPT, INDL, WHOLESALE: Engines & Parts, Diesel
MACHINERY & EQPT, INDL, WHOLESALE: Engs/Transportation Eqpt
MACHINERY & EQPT, INDL, WHOLESALE: Food Manufacturing
MACHINERY & EQPT, INDL, WHOLESALE: Food Product Manufacturng
MACHINERY & EQPT, INDL, WHOLESALE: Hydraulic Systems
MACHINERY & EQPT, INDL, WHOLESALE: Indl Machine Parts
MACHINERY & EQPT, INDL, WHOLESALE: Instruments & Cntrl Eqpt
MACHINERY & EQPT, INDL, WHOLESALE: Lift Trucks & Parts
MACHINERY & EQPT, INDL, WHOLESALE: Machine Tools & Access
MACHINERY & EQPT, INDL, WHOLESALE: Machine Tools & Metalwork
MACHINERY & EQPT, INDL, WHOLESALE: Measure/Test, Electric
MACHINERY & EQPT, INDL, WHOLESALE: Packaging
MACHINERY & EQPT, INDL, WHOLESALE: Paper Manufacturing
MACHINERY & EQPT, INDL, WHOLESALE: Petroleum Industry
MACHINERY & EQPT, INDL, WHOLESALE: Pneumatic Tools
MACHINERY & EQPT, INDL, WHOLESALE: Processing & Packaging
MACHINERY & EQPT, INDL, WHOLESALE: Pulp Manufacturing, Wood
MACHINERY & EQPT, INDL, WHOLESALE: Recycling
MACHINERY & EQPT, INDL, WHOLESALE: Safety Eqpt
MACHINERY & EQPT, INDL, WHOLESALE: Sawmill
MACHINERY & EQPT, INDL, WHOLESALE: Stackers
MACHINERY & EQPT, INDL, WHOLESALE: Tanks, Storage
MACHINERY & EQPT, INDL, WHOLESALE: Trailers, Indl
MACHINERY & EQPT, INDL, WHOLESALE: Winches
MACHINERY & EQPT, INDL, WHOLESALE: Woodworking
MACHINERY & EQPT, WHOLESALE: Construction, Cranes
MACHINERY & EQPT, WHOLESALE: Construction, General
MACHINERY & EQPT, WHOLESALE: Contractors Materials
MACHINERY & EQPT, WHOLESALE: Crushing, Pulverizng & Screeng
MACHINERY & EQPT, WHOLESALE: Drilling, Wellpoints
MACHINERY & EQPT, WHOLESALE: Logging
MACHINERY & EQPT, WHOLESALE: Logging & Forestry
MACHINERY & EQPT, WHOLESALE: Masonry
MACHINERY & EQPT: Farm
MACHINERY & EQPT: Gas Producers, Generators/Other RItd Eqpt
MACHINERY & EQPT: Liquid Automation
MACHINERY & EQPT: Petroleum Refinery
MACHINERY & EQPT: Smelting & Refining
MACHINERY & EQPT: Vibratory Parts Handling Eqpt
MACHINERY BASES
MACHINERY, COMM LAUNDRY: Rug Cleaning, Drying Or Napping
MACHINERY, COMMERCIAL LAUNDRY & Drycleaning: Ironers
MACHINERY, COMMERCIAL LAUNDRY & Drycleaning: Pressing
MACHINERY, COMMERCIAL LAUNDRY: Dryers, Incl Coin-Operated
MACHINERY, EQPT & SUPPLIES: Parking Facility
MACHINERY, FLOOR SANDING: Commercial
MACHINERY, FOOD PRDTS: Beverage
MACHINERY, FOOD PRDTS: Cutting, Chopping, Grinding, Mixing
MACHINERY, FOOD PRDTS: Distillery
MACHINERY, FOOD PRDTS: Flour Mill
MACHINERY, FOOD PRDTS: Food Processing, Smokers
MACHINERY, FOOD PRDTS: Homogenizing, Dairy, Fruit/Vegetable
MACHINERY, FOOD PRDTS: Malt Mills
MACHINERY, FOOD PRDTS: Milk Processing, Dry
MACHINERY, FOOD PRDTS: Ovens, Bakery
MACHINERY, FOOD PRDTS: Pasta
MACHINERY, FOOD PRDTS: Presses, Cheese, Beet, Cider & Sugar
MACHINERY, FOOD PRDTS: Processing, Fish & Shellfish
MACHINERY, FOOD PRDTS: Roasting, Coffee, Peanut, Etc.
MACHINERY, LUBRICATION: Automatic
MACHINERY, MAILING: Mail Tying Or Bundling
MACHINERY, MAILING: Mailing
MACHINERY, MAILING: Postage Meters
MACHINERY, METALWORKING: Assembly, Including Robotic
MACHINERY, METALWORKING: Coilers, Metalworking
MACHINERY, OFFICE: Paper Handling
MACHINERY, OFFICE: Typing & Word Processing
MACHINERY, PACKAGING: Canning, Food
MACHINERY, PACKAGING: Carton Packing

PRODUCT INDEX

MACHINERY, PACKAGING: Packing & Wrapping
MACHINERY, PAPER INDUSTRY: Coating & Finishing
MACHINERY, PAPER INDUSTRY: Paper Mill, Plating, Etc
MACHINERY, PAPER INDUSTRY: Pulp Mill
MACHINERY, PRINTING TRADES: Copy Holders
MACHINERY, PRINTING TRADES: Plates
MACHINERY, PRINTING TRADES: Printing Trade Parts & Attchts
MACHINERY, PRINTING TRADES: Type & Type Making
MACHINERY, SERVICING: Coin-Operated, Exc Dry Clean & Laundry
MACHINERY, SEWING: Bag Seaming & Closing
MACHINERY, SEWING: Sewing & Hat & Zipper Making
MACHINERY, TEXTILE: Cloth Spreading
MACHINERY, TEXTILE: Embroidery
MACHINERY, TEXTILE: Fiber & Yarn Preparation
MACHINERY, TEXTILE: Picker
MACHINERY, TEXTILE: Spinning
MACHINERY, TEXTILE: Wool Processing, Carbonizing
MACHINERY, WOODWORKING: Bandsaws
MACHINERY, WOODWORKING: Cabinet Makers'
MACHINERY, WOODWORKING: Planers
MACHINERY, WOODWORKING: Sanding, Exc Portable Floor Sanders
MACHINERY/EQPT, INDL, WHOL: Cleaning, High Press, Sand/Steam
MACHINERY/EQPT, INDL, WHOL: Machinist Precision Measrng Tool
MACHINERY: Ammunition & Explosives Loading
MACHINERY: Assembly, Exc Metalworking
MACHINERY: Automotive Maintenance
MACHINERY: Automotive Related
MACHINERY: Banking
MACHINERY: Bottle Washing & Sterilzing
MACHINERY: Brewery & Malting
MACHINERY: Cement Making
MACHINERY: Centrifugal
MACHINERY: Concrete Prdts
MACHINERY: Construction
MACHINERY: Cryogenic, Industrial
MACHINERY: Custom
MACHINERY: Deburring
MACHINERY: Die Casting
MACHINERY: Electronic Component Making
MACHINERY: Engraving
MACHINERY: General, Industrial, NEC
MACHINERY: Glassmaking
MACHINERY: Industrial, NEC
MACHINERY: Kilns
MACHINERY: Kilns, Lumber
MACHINERY: Logging Eqpt
MACHINERY: Marking, Metalworking
MACHINERY: Metalworking
MACHINERY: Milling
MACHINERY: Mining
MACHINERY: Packaging
MACHINERY: Paper Industry Miscellaneous
MACHINERY: Pharmaciutical
MACHINERY: Plastic Working
MACHINERY: Polishing & Buffing
MACHINERY: Pottery Making
MACHINERY: Printing Presses
MACHINERY: Recycling
MACHINERY: Riveting
MACHINERY: Road Construction & Maintenance
MACHINERY: Saw & Sawing
MACHINERY: Screening Eqpt, Electric
MACHINERY: Semiconductor Manufacturing
MACHINERY: Separators, Mineral
MACHINERY: Service Industry, NEC
MACHINERY: Sheet Metal Working
MACHINERY: Sifting & Screening
MACHINERY: Specialty
MACHINERY: Stone Working
MACHINERY: Tapping
MACHINERY: Textile
MACHINERY: Voting
MACHINERY: Wire Drawing
MACHINERY: Woodworking
MACHINES: Forming, Sheet Metal
MACHINISTS' TOOLS: Measuring, Precision
MACHINISTS' TOOLS: Precision
MACHINISTS' TOOLS: Scales, Measuring, Precision
MAGAZINES, WHOLESALE
MAGNESIUM

MAGNETIC TAPE, AUDIO: Prerecorded
MAGNETS: Ceramic
MAGNETS: Permanent
MAIL-ORDER HOUSE, NEC
MAIL-ORDER HOUSES: Arts & Crafts Eqpt & Splys
MAIL-ORDER HOUSES: Books, Exc Book Clubs
MAIL-ORDER HOUSES: Computer Eqpt & Electronics
MAIL-ORDER HOUSES: Food
MAIL-ORDER HOUSES: Fruit
MAIL-ORDER HOUSES: General Merchandise
MAIL-ORDER HOUSES: Jewelry
MAIL-ORDER HOUSES: Stamps
MAIL-ORDER HOUSES: Women's Apparel
MAILBOX RENTAL & RELATED SVCS
MAILING & MESSENGER SVCS
MAILING LIST: Compilers
MAILING SVCS, NEC
MANAGEMENT CONSULTING SVCS: Business
MANAGEMENT CONSULTING SVCS: Business Planning & Organizing
MANAGEMENT CONSULTING SVCS: Construction Project
MANAGEMENT CONSULTING SVCS: Food & Beverage
MANAGEMENT CONSULTING SVCS: General
MANAGEMENT CONSULTING SVCS: Hospital & Health
MANAGEMENT CONSULTING SVCS: Incentive Or Award Program
MANAGEMENT CONSULTING SVCS: Industrial
MANAGEMENT CONSULTING SVCS: Industrial & Labor
MANAGEMENT CONSULTING SVCS: Industry Specialist
MANAGEMENT CONSULTING SVCS: Information Systems
MANAGEMENT CONSULTING SVCS: Manufacturing
MANAGEMENT CONSULTING SVCS: Public Utilities
MANAGEMENT CONSULTING SVCS: Training & Development
MANAGEMENT CONSULTING SVCS: Transportation
MANAGEMENT SERVICES
MANAGEMENT SVCS, FACILITIES SUPPORT: Environ Remediation
MANAGEMENT SVCS: Administrative
MANAGEMENT SVCS: Business
MANAGEMENT SVCS: Construction
MANAGEMENT SVCS: Restaurant
MANHOLES & COVERS: Metal
MANICURE PREPARATIONS
MANPOWER POOLS
MANUFACTURING INDUSTRIES, NEC
MAPS
MARBLE, BUILDING: Cut & Shaped
MARBLE: Crushed & Broken
MARINAS
MARINE CARGO HANDLING SVCS: Loading & Unloading
MARINE CARGO HANDLING SVCS: Waterfront Terminal Operations
MARINE ENGINE REPAIR SVCS
MARINE HARDWARE
MARINE PROPELLER REPAIR SVCS
MARINE RELATED EQPT
MARINE SPLY DEALERS
MARINE SPLYS WHOLESALERS
MARKETS: Meat & fish
MARKING DEVICES
MARKING DEVICES: Canceling Stamps, Hand, Rubber Or Metal
MARKING DEVICES: Date Stamps, Hand, Rubber Or Metal
MARKING DEVICES: Embossing Seals & Hand Stamps
MARKING DEVICES: Printing Dies, Marking Mach, Rubber/Plastic
MARKING DEVICES: Screens, Textile Printing
MASKS: Gas
MASSAGE MACHINES, ELECTRIC: Barber & Beauty Shops
MATERIAL GRINDING & PULVERIZING SVCS NEC
MATERIALS HANDLING EQPT WHOLESALERS
MATS OR MATTING, NEC: Rubber
MATS, MATTING & PADS: Nonwoven
MATTRESS STORES
MEAT & FISH MARKETS: Fish
MEAT & FISH MARKETS: Seafood
MEAT & MEAT PRDTS WHOLESALERS
MEAT CUTTING & PACKING
MEAT MARKETS
MEAT PRDTS: Bacon, Slab & Sliced, From Slaughtered Meat
MEAT PRDTS: Boxed Beef, From Slaughtered Meat
MEAT PRDTS: Canned
MEAT PRDTS: Frozen
MEAT PRDTS: Lamb, From Slaughtered Meat

MEAT PRDTS: Pork, From Slaughtered Meat
MEAT PRDTS: Prepared Beef Prdts From Purchased Beef
MEAT PRDTS: Roast Beef, From Purchased Meat
MEAT PRDTS: Sausage Casings, Natural
MEAT PRDTS: Sausages, From Purchased Meat
MEAT PRDTS: Sausages, From Slaughtered Meat
MEAT PRDTS: Smoked
MEAT PRDTS: Snack Sticks, Incl Jerky, From Purchased Meat
MEAT PROCESSED FROM PURCHASED CARCASSES
MEAT PROCESSING MACHINERY
MEATS, PACKAGED FROZEN: Wholesalers
MECHANICAL INSTRUMENT REPAIR SVCS
MEDIA: Magnetic & Optical Recording
MEDICAL & HOSPITAL EQPT WHOLESALERS
MEDICAL & SURGICAL SPLYS: Applicators, Cotton Tipped
MEDICAL & SURGICAL SPLYS: Autoclaves
MEDICAL & SURGICAL SPLYS: Braces, Orthopedic
MEDICAL & SURGICAL SPLYS: Clothing, Fire Resistant & Protect
MEDICAL & SURGICAL SPLYS: Drapes, Surgical, Cotton
MEDICAL & SURGICAL SPLYS: Foot Appliances, Orthopedic
MEDICAL & SURGICAL SPLYS: Hydrotherapy
MEDICAL & SURGICAL SPLYS: Limbs, Artificial
MEDICAL & SURGICAL SPLYS: Models, Anatomical
MEDICAL & SURGICAL SPLYS: Orthopedic Appliances
MEDICAL & SURGICAL SPLYS: Personal Safety Eqpt
MEDICAL & SURGICAL SPLYS: Prosthetic Appliances
MEDICAL & SURGICAL SPLYS: Stretchers
MEDICAL & SURGICAL SPLYS: Supports, Abdominal, Ankle, Etc
MEDICAL & SURGICAL SPLYS: Technical Aids, Handicapped
MEDICAL & SURGICAL SPLYS: Traction Apparatus
MEDICAL & SURGICAL SPLYS: Welders' Hoods
MEDICAL CENTERS
MEDICAL EQPT: CAT Scanner Or Computerized Axial Tomography
MEDICAL EQPT: Defibrillators
MEDICAL EQPT: Diagnostic
MEDICAL EQPT: Electromedical Apparatus
MEDICAL EQPT: Electrotherapeutic Apparatus
MEDICAL EQPT: Heart-Lung Machines, Exc Iron Lungs
MEDICAL EQPT: Laser Systems
MEDICAL EQPT: PET Or Position Emission Tomography Scanners
MEDICAL EQPT: Patient Monitoring
MEDICAL EQPT: Ultrasonic, Exc Cleaning
MEDICAL EQPT: X-Ray Apparatus & Tubes, Radiographic
MEDICAL SVCS ORGANIZATION
MEDICAL, DENTAL & HOSP EQPT, WHOLESALE: X-ray Film & Splys
MEDICAL, DENTAL & HOSPITAL EQPT, WHOL: Hosptl Eqpt/Furniture
MEDICAL, DENTAL & HOSPITAL EQPT, WHOLESALE: Med Eqpt & Splys
MEMBERSHIP ORGANIZATIONS, CIVIC, SOCIAL/FRAT: Youth Orgs
MEMBERSHIP ORGANIZATIONS, NEC: Charitable
MEMBERSHIP ORGANIZATIONS, NEC: Personal Interest
MEMBERSHIP ORGANIZATIONS, PROF: Education/Teacher Assoc
MEMBERSHIP ORGANIZATIONS, REL: Churches, Temples & Shrines
MEMBERSHIP ORGANIZATIONS, REL: Covenant & Evangelical Church
MEMBERSHIP ORGANIZATIONS, RELIGIOUS: Assembly Of God Church
MEMBERSHIP ORGANIZATIONS, RELIGIOUS: Lutheran Church
MEMBERSHIP ORGANIZATIONS, RELIGIOUS: Nonchurch
MEMBERSHIP ORGS, CIVIC, SOCIAL & FRATERNAL: Civic Assoc
MEMBERSHIP ORGS, RELIGIOUS: Non-Denominational Church
MEMBERSHIP SPORTS & RECREATION CLUBS
MEMORIALS, MONUMENTS & MARKERS
MEN'S & BOYS' CLOTHING STORES
MEN'S & BOYS' CLOTHING WHOLESALERS, NEC
MEN'S & BOYS' HATS STORES
MEN'S & BOYS' SPORTSWEAR CLOTHING STORES
MEN'S & BOYS' SPORTSWEAR WHOLESALERS
MEN'S & BOYS' WORK CLOTHING WHOLESALERS
MENTAL HEALTH CLINIC, OUTPATIENT
MENTAL HEALTH PRACTITIONERS' OFFICES
MERCHANDISING MACHINE OPERATORS: Vending

PRODUCT INDEX

METAL CUTTING SVCS
METAL DETECTORS
METAL FABRICATORS: Architechtural
METAL FABRICATORS: Plate
METAL FABRICATORS: Sheet
METAL FABRICATORS: Structural, Ship
METAL FABRICATORS: Structural, Ship
METAL FINISHING SVCS
METAL MINING SVCS
METAL OXIDE SILICONE OR MOS DEVICES
METAL SERVICE CENTERS & OFFICES
METAL SPINNING FOR THE TRADE
METAL STAMPING, FOR THE TRADE
METAL STAMPINGS: Ornamental
METAL TREATING: Cryogenic
METALS SVC CENTERS & WHOLESALERS: Bale Ties, Wire
METALS SVC CENTERS & WHOLESALERS: Bars, Metal
METALS SVC CENTERS & WHOLESALERS: Cable, Wire
METALS SVC CENTERS & WHOLESALERS: Concrete Reinforcing Bars
METALS SVC CENTERS & WHOLESALERS: Copper Prdts
METALS SVC CENTERS & WHOLESALERS: Iron & Steel Prdt, Ferrous
METALS SVC CENTERS & WHOLESALERS: Piling, Iron & Steel
METALS SVC CENTERS & WHOLESALERS: Pipe & Tubing, Steel
METALS SVC CENTERS & WHOLESALERS: Rope, Wire, Exc Insulated
METALS SVC CENTERS & WHOLESALERS: Sheets, Metal
METALS SVC CENTERS & WHOLESALERS: Steel
METALS SVC CENTERS & WHOLESALERS: Tubing, Metal
METALS: Precious NEC
METALWORK: Miscellaneous
METALWORK: Ornamental
METER READERS: Remote
METERS: Power Factor & Phase Angle
MGMT CONSULTING SVCS: Matls, Incl Purch, Handle & Invntry
MICROCIRCUITS, INTEGRATED: Semiconductor
MICROFILM SVCS
MICROPROCESSORS
MICROSCOPES
MICROSCOPES: Electron & Proton
MILITARY GOODS & REGALIA STORES
MILITARY INSIGNIA, TEXTILE
MILL PRDTS: Structural & Rail
MILLING: Corn Grits & Flakes, For Brewers' Use
MILLING: Grains, Exc Rice
MILLWORK
MINE & QUARRY SVCS: Nonmetallic Minerals
MINE EXPLORATION SVCS: Nonmetallic Minerals
MINE PREPARATION SVCS
MINERAL ABRASIVES MINING SVCS
MINERAL MINING: Nonmetallic
MINERAL WOOL
MINERAL WOOL INSULATION PRDTS
MINERALS: Ground or Treated
MINIATURES
MINING EXPLORATION & DEVELOPMENT SVCS
MINING MACHINES & EQPT: Amalgamators, Metallurgical/Mining
MINING MACHINES & EQPT: Augers
MINING MACHINES & EQPT: Crushers, Stationary
MINING MACHINES & EQPT: Mineral Beneficiation
MINING MACHINES & EQPT: Rock Crushing, Stationary
MINING MACHINES & EQPT: Trucks, Dollies
MINING SVCS, NEC: Bituminous
MINING: Oil Sand
MISCELLANEOUS FINANCIAL INVEST ACT: Oil/Gas Lease Brokers
MISSILES: Guided
MITTENS: Woven Or Knit, From Purchased Materials
MIXTURES & BLOCKS: Asphalt Paving
MOBILE COMMUNICATIONS EQPT
MOBILE HOME REPAIR SVCS
MOBILE HOMES
MOBILE HOMES: Indl Or Commercial Use
MOBILE HOMES: Personal Or Private Use
MODELS
MODELS: Airplane, Exc Toy
MODELS: Boat, Exc Toy
MODELS: General, Exc Toy
MODULES: Computer Logic
MOLDED RUBBER PRDTS

MOLDING COMPOUNDS
MOLDINGS & TRIM: Wood
MOLDINGS: Picture Frame
MOLDS: Indl
MOLDS: Plastic Working & Foundry
MONOFILAMENTS: Nontextile
MONUMENTS & GRAVE MARKERS, EXC TERRAZZO
MONUMENTS & GRAVE MARKERS, WHOLESALE
MONUMENTS: Cut Stone, Exc Finishing Or Lettering Only
MOTEL
MOTION PICTURE & VIDEO DISTRIBUTION
MOTION PICTURE & VIDEO PRODUCTION SVCS
MOTION PICTURE & VIDEO PRODUCTION SVCS: Educational
MOTION PICTURE & VIDEO PRODUCTION SVCS: Training
MOTION PICTURE EQPT
MOTOR HOME DEALERS
MOTOR HOMES
MOTOR REBUILDING SVCS, EXC AUTOMOTIVE
MOTOR REPAIR SVCS
MOTOR SCOOTERS & PARTS
MOTOR VEHICLE ASSEMBLY, COMPLETE: Ambulances
MOTOR VEHICLE ASSEMBLY, COMPLETE: Autos, Incl Specialty
MOTOR VEHICLE ASSEMBLY, COMPLETE: Fire Department Vehicles
MOTOR VEHICLE ASSEMBLY, COMPLETE: Military Motor Vehicle
MOTOR VEHICLE ASSEMBLY, COMPLETE: Truck & Tractor Trucks
MOTOR VEHICLE ASSEMBLY, COMPLETE: Truck Tractors, Highway
MOTOR VEHICLE ASSEMBLY, COMPLETE: Universal Carriers, Mil
MOTOR VEHICLE ASSEMBLY, COMPLETE: Wreckers, Tow Truck
MOTOR VEHICLE DEALERS: Automobiles, New & Used
MOTOR VEHICLE DEALERS: Cars, Used Only
MOTOR VEHICLE DEALERS: Pickups, New & Used
MOTOR VEHICLE PARTS & ACCESS: Air Conditioner Parts
MOTOR VEHICLE PARTS & ACCESS: Booster Cables, Jump-Start
MOTOR VEHICLE PARTS & ACCESS: Cylinder Heads
MOTOR VEHICLE PARTS & ACCESS: Electrical Eqpt
MOTOR VEHICLE PARTS & ACCESS: Engines & Parts
MOTOR VEHICLE PARTS & ACCESS: Fuel Systems & Parts
MOTOR VEHICLE PARTS & ACCESS: Heaters
MOTOR VEHICLE PARTS & ACCESS: Instrument Board Assemblies
MOTOR VEHICLE PARTS & ACCESS: Lifting Mechanisms, Dump Truck
MOTOR VEHICLE PARTS & ACCESS: Mufflers, Exhaust
MOTOR VEHICLE PARTS & ACCESS: Pickup Truck Bed Liners
MOTOR VEHICLE PARTS & ACCESS: Propane Conversion Eqpt
MOTOR VEHICLE PARTS & ACCESS: Pumps, Hydraulic Fluid Power
MOTOR VEHICLE PARTS & ACCESS: Sanders, Safety
MOTOR VEHICLE PARTS & ACCESS: Trailer Hitches
MOTOR VEHICLE PARTS & ACCESS: Transmission Housings Or Parts
MOTOR VEHICLE PARTS & ACCESS: Transmissions
MOTOR VEHICLE PARTS & ACCESS: Windshield Frames
MOTOR VEHICLE PARTS & ACCESS: Wipers, Windshield
MOTOR VEHICLE SPLYS & PARTS WHOLESALERS: New
MOTOR VEHICLE SPLYS & PARTS WHOLESALERS: Used
MOTOR VEHICLE: Radiators
MOTOR VEHICLES & CAR BODIES
MOTOR VEHICLES, WHOLESALE: Ambulances
MOTOR VEHICLES, WHOLESALE: Trailers, Truck, New & Used
MOTORCYCLE & BICYCLE PARTS: Frames
MOTORCYCLE ACCESS
MOTORCYCLE DEALERS
MOTORCYCLE PARTS & ACCESS DEALERS
MOTORCYCLE REPAIR SHOPS
MOTORCYCLES & RELATED PARTS
MOTORS: Electric
MOTORS: Generators
MUSEUMS & ART GALLERIES
MUSIC BOXES
MUSIC LICENSING & ROYALTIES
MUSIC RECORDING PRODUCER
MUSIC SCHOOLS

MUSICAL INSTRUMENT PARTS & ACCESS, WHOLESALE
MUSICAL INSTRUMENT REPAIR
MUSICAL INSTRUMENTS & ACCESS: Carrying Cases
MUSICAL INSTRUMENTS & ACCESS: NEC
MUSICAL INSTRUMENTS & ACCESS: Pipe Organs
MUSICAL INSTRUMENTS & ACCESS: Stands
MUSICAL INSTRUMENTS & PARTS: Percussion
MUSICAL INSTRUMENTS & PARTS: String
MUSICAL INSTRUMENTS & SPLYS STORES
MUSICAL INSTRUMENTS & SPLYS STORES: Organs
MUSICAL INSTRUMENTS & SPLYS STORES: String instruments
MUSICAL INSTRUMENTS WHOLESALERS
MUSICAL INSTRUMENTS: Accordions & Parts
MUSICAL INSTRUMENTS: Chimes & Parts
MUSICAL INSTRUMENTS: Electric & Electronic
MUSICAL INSTRUMENTS: Flutes & Parts
MUSICAL INSTRUMENTS: Guitars & Parts, Electric & Acoustic
MUSICAL INSTRUMENTS: Ocarinas
MUSICAL INSTRUMENTS: Organ Parts & Materials
MUSICAL INSTRUMENTS: Organs
MUSICAL INSTRUMENTS: Reeds, Organ
MUSICAL INSTRUMENTS: Violins & Parts
MUSICIAN

N

NAIL SALONS
NAME PLATES: Engraved Or Etched
NAMEPLATES
NAPALM
NATIONAL SECURITY FORCES
NATIONAL SECURITY, GOVERNMENT: Navy
NATURAL GAS DISTRIBUTION TO CONSUMERS
NATURAL GAS LIQUIDS PRODUCTION
NATURAL GAS PRODUCTION
NATURAL GASOLINE PRODUCTION
NATURAL PROPANE PRODUCTION
NAUTICAL & NAVIGATIONAL INSTRUMENT REPAIR SVCS
NAUTICAL REPAIR SVCS
NAVIGATIONAL SYSTEMS & INSTRUMENTS
NET & NETTING PRDTS
NETTING: Plastic
NEWSPAPERS, WHOLESALE
NEWSSTAND
NICKEL ALLOY
NONCLASSIFIABLE ESTABLISHMENTS
NONDAIRY BASED FROZEN DESSERTS
NONDURABLE GOODS WHOLESALERS, NEC
NONFERROUS: Rolling & Drawing, NEC
NONMETALLIC MINERALS DEVELOPMENT & TEST BORING SVC
NONMETALLIC MINERALS: Support Activities, Exc Fuels
NOVELTIES
NOVELTIES & SPECIALTIES: Metal
NOVELTIES, DURABLE, WHOLESALE
NOVELTIES: Leather
NOVELTIES: Plastic
NOVELTY SHOPS
NOZZLES & SPRINKLERS Lawn Hose
NOZZLES: Spray, Aerosol, Paint Or Insecticide
NURSERIES & LAWN & GARDEN SPLY STORE, RET: Lawn/Garden Splys
NURSERIES & LAWN & GARDEN SPLY STORES, RETAIL
NURSERIES & LAWN & GARDEN SPLY STORES, RETAIL: Fertilizer
NURSERIES & LAWN & GARDEN SPLY STORES, RETAIL: Sod
NURSERIES & LAWN & GARDEN SPLY STORES, RETAIL: Top Soil
NURSERIES & LAWN/GARDEN SPLY STORE, RET: Lawnmowers/Tractors
NURSERIES & LAWN/GARDEN SPLY STORES, RET: Garden Splys/Tools
NURSERIES/LAWN/GRDN SPLY STORE, RET: Nursery Stck, Seed/Bulb
NURSERY & GARDEN CENTERS
NURSERY STOCK, WHOLESALE
NURSING HOME, EXC SKILLED & INTERMEDIATE CARE FACILITY
NUTRITION SVCS
NUTS: Metal
NYLON RESINS

PRODUCT INDEX

O

OFFENDER SELF-HELP AGENCY
OFFICE EQPT WHOLESALERS
OFFICE FIXTURES: Exc Wood
OFFICE FIXTURES: Wood
OFFICE MACHINES, NEC
OFFICE SPLY & STATIONERY STORES
OFFICE SPLY & STATIONERY STORES: Office Forms & Splys
OFFICE SPLY & STATIONERY STORES: School Splys
OFFICE SPLY & STATIONERY STORES: Writing Splys
OFFICE SPLYS, NEC, WHOLESALE
OFFICES & CLINICS DOCTORS OF MED: Intrnl Med Practitioners
OFFICES & CLINICS OF DENTISTS: Dentists' Office
OFFICES & CLINICS OF DOCTORS OF MEDICINE: Radiologist
OFFICES & CLINICS OF HEALTH PRACTITIONERS: Naturopath
OFFICES & CLINICS OF HEALTH PRACTITIONERS: Nutritionist
OFFICES & CLINICS OF OPTOMETRISTS: Specialist, Optometrists
OIL & GAS FIELD MACHINERY
OIL ABSORPTION Eqpt
OIL FIELD MACHINERY & EQPT
OIL FIELD SVCS, NEC
OIL TREATING COMPOUNDS
OILS & ESSENTIAL OILS
OILS & GREASES: Blended & Compounded
OILS & GREASES: Lubricating
OILS: Anise
OILS: Essential
OILS: Lubricating
OILS: Lubricating
OILS: Magnetic Inspection Or Powder
ON-LINE DATABASE INFORMATION RETRIEVAL SVCS
OPEN PIT GOLD MINING
OPERATOR: Apartment Buildings
OPERATOR: Nonresidential Buildings
OPHTHALMIC GOODS
OPHTHALMIC GOODS WHOLESALERS
OPHTHALMIC GOODS: Eyewear, Protective
OPHTHALMIC GOODS: Frames & Parts, Eyeglass & Spectacle
OPHTHALMIC GOODS: Frames, Lenses & Parts, Eyeglasses
OPHTHALMIC GOODS: Lenses, Ophthalmic
OPHTHALMIC GOODS: Spectacles
OPTICAL GOODS STORES
OPTICAL GOODS STORES: Eyeglasses, Prescription
OPTICAL GOODS STORES: Opticians
OPTICAL INSTRUMENTS & APPARATUS
OPTICAL INSTRUMENTS & LENSES
OPTOMETRIC EQPT & SPLYS WHOLESALERS
OPTOMETRISTS' OFFICES
ORAL PREPARATIONS
ORDNANCE
ORGANIZATIONS: Biotechnical Research, Noncommercial
ORGANIZATIONS: Civic & Social
ORGANIZATIONS: Medical Research
ORGANIZATIONS: Physical Research, Noncommercial
ORGANIZATIONS: Professional
ORGANIZATIONS: Religious
ORGANIZATIONS: Research Institute
ORGANIZATIONS: Safety Research, Noncommercial
ORNAMENTS: Christmas Tree, Exc Electrical & Glass
OSCILLATORS
OUTBOARD MOTOR DEALERS
OVENS: Infrared

P

PACKAGE DESIGN SVCS
PACKAGED FROZEN FOODS WHOLESALERS, NEC
PACKAGING & LABELING SVCS
PACKAGING MATERIALS, INDL: Wholesalers
PACKAGING MATERIALS, WHOLESALE
PACKAGING MATERIALS: Paper
PACKAGING MATERIALS: Paper, Coated Or Laminated
PACKAGING MATERIALS: Paperboard Backs For Blister/Skin Pkgs
PACKAGING MATERIALS: Plastic Film, Coated Or Laminated
PACKAGING MATERIALS: Polystyrene Foam
PACKING & CRATING SVC
PACKING & CRATING SVCS: Containerized Goods For Shipping
PACKING MATERIALS: Mechanical
PACKING SVCS: Shipping
PADS: Solid Fiber, Made From Purchased Materials
PAGING SVCS
PAINT & PAINTING SPLYS STORE
PAINT STORE
PAINTING SVC: Metal Prdts
PAINTS & ADDITIVES
PAINTS & ALLIED PRODUCTS
PAINTS, VARNISHES & SPLYS WHOLESALERS
PAINTS, VARNISHES & SPLYS, WHOLESALE: Paints
PAINTS: Lead-In-Oil
PAINTS: Marine
PAINTS: Oil Or Alkyd Vehicle Or Water Thinned
PALLET REPAIR SVCS
PALLETIZERS & DEPALLETIZERS
PALLETS
PALLETS & SKIDS: Wood
PALLETS: Corrugated
PALLETS: Plastic
PALLETS: Wooden
PANEL & DISTRIBUTION BOARDS & OTHER RELATED APPARATUS
PANEL & DISTRIBUTION BOARDS: Electric
PANELS: Building, Metal
PANELS: Building, Plastic, NEC
PANELS: Building, Wood
PANELS: Control & Metering, Generator
PANELS: Wood
PAPER & BOARD: Die-cut
PAPER CONVERTING
PAPER MANUFACTURERS: Exc Newsprint
PAPER PRDTS
PAPER PRDTS: Feminine Hygiene Prdts
PAPER PRDTS: Infant & Baby Prdts
PAPER PRDTS: Pressed & Molded Pulp & Fiber Prdts
PAPER PRDTS: Sanitary
PAPER PRDTS: Sanitary Tissue Paper
PAPER PRDTS: Towels, Napkins/Tissue Paper, From Purchd Mtrls
PAPER, WHOLESALE: Printing
PAPER: Adhesive
PAPER: Building Laminated, Made From Purchased Materials
PAPER: Building, Insulating & Packaging
PAPER: Business Form
PAPER: Cardboard
PAPER: Coated & Laminated, NEC
PAPER: Corrugated
PAPER: Fine
PAPER: Greaseproof Wrapping
PAPER: Newsprint
PAPER: Printer
PAPER: Specialty
PAPER: Specialty Or Chemically Treated
PAPER: Tissue
PAPER: Wallpaper
PAPER: Wrapping & Packaging
PAPER: Wrapping, Waterproof Or Coated
PAPERBOARD
PAPERBOARD CONVERTING
PAPERBOARD PRDTS: Automobile Board
PAPERBOARD PRDTS: Building Insulating & Packaging
PAPERBOARD PRDTS: Container Board
PAPERBOARD PRDTS: Folding Boxboard
PAPERBOARD PRDTS: Packaging Board
PAPERBOARD: Coated
PARTICLEBOARD
PARTITIONS & FIXTURES: Except Wood
PARTITIONS: Solid Fiber, Made From Purchased Materials
PARTITIONS: Wood & Fixtures
PARTITIONS: Wood, Floor Attached
PARTS: Metal
PATCHING PLASTER: Household
PATENT OWNERS & LESSORS
PATTERNS: Indl
PAVERS
PAWN SHOPS
PENS & PARTS: Ball Point
PERFUME: Concentrated
PERFUMES
PERISCOPES
PERSONAL CREDIT INSTITUTIONS: Financing, Autos, Furniture
PERSONAL DOCUMENT & INFORMATION SVCS
PEST CONTROL IN STRUCTURES SVCS
PESTICIDES
PESTICIDES WHOLESALERS
PET ACCESS: Collars, Leashes, Etc, Exc Leather
PET COLLARS, LEASHES, MUZZLES & HARNESSES: Leather
PET FOOD WHOLESALERS
PET SPLYS
PET SPLYS WHOLESALERS
PETROLEUM & PETROLEUM PRDTS, WHOL Svc Station Splys, Petro
PETROLEUM & PETROLEUM PRDTS, WHOLESALE Diesel Fuel
PETROLEUM & PETROLEUM PRDTS, WHOLESALE Engine Fuels & Oils
PETROLEUM & PETROLEUM PRDTS, WHOLESALE Fuel Oil
PETROLEUM & PETROLEUM PRDTS, WHOLESALE Petroleum Brokers
PETROLEUM & PETROLEUM PRDTS, WHOLESALE Petroleum Terminals
PETROLEUM & PETROLEUM PRDTS, WHOLESALE: Bulk Stations
PETROLEUM BULK STATIONS & TERMINALS
PETROLEUM PRDTS WHOLESALERS
PETS & PET SPLYS, WHOLESALE
PHARMACEUTICAL PREPARATIONS: Druggists' Preparations
PHARMACEUTICAL PREPARATIONS: Medicines, Capsule Or Ampule
PHARMACEUTICAL PREPARATIONS: Proprietary Drug PRDTS
PHARMACEUTICAL PREPARATIONS: Solutions
PHARMACEUTICAL PREPARATIONS: Tablets
PHARMACEUTICALS
PHARMACEUTICALS: Medicinal & Botanical Prdts
PHOSPHATE ROCK MINING
PHOTOCOPYING & DUPLICATING SVCS
PHOTOELECTRIC CELLS: Electronic Eye, Solid State
PHOTOENGRAVING SVC
PHOTOFINISHING LABORATORIES
PHOTOGRAPH DEVELOPING & RETOUCHING SVCS
PHOTOGRAPHIC EQPT & CAMERAS, WHOLESALE
PHOTOGRAPHIC EQPT & SPLY: Sound Recordg/Reprod Eqpt, Motion
PHOTOGRAPHIC EQPT & SPLYS
PHOTOGRAPHIC EQPT & SPLYS: Developers, Not Chemical Plants
PHOTOGRAPHIC EQPT & SPLYS: Graphic Arts Plates, Sensitized
PHOTOGRAPHIC EQPT & SPLYS: Printing Eqpt
PHOTOGRAPHIC EQPT & SPLYS: Printing Frames
PHOTOGRAPHIC EQPT & SPLYS: Toners, Prprd, Not Chem Plnts
PHOTOGRAPHY SVCS: Commercial
PHOTOGRAPHY SVCS: Portrait Studios
PHOTOGRAPHY SVCS: Still Or Video
PHYSICAL FITNESS CENTERS
PHYSICIANS' OFFICES & CLINICS: Medical doctors
PICTURE FRAMES: Metal
PICTURE FRAMES: Wood
PICTURE FRAMING SVCS, CUSTOM
PIECE GOODS, NOTIONS & DRY GOODS, WHOL: Fabrics, Fiberglass
PIECE GOODS, NOTIONS & DRY GOODS, WHOL: Textiles, Woven
PIECE GOODS, NOTIONS & DRY GOODS, WHOLESALE: Belt/Bckl Kits
PIECE GOODS, NOTIONS & OTHER DRY GOODS, WHOL: Flags/Banners
PIECE GOODS, NOTIONS & OTHER DRY GOODS, WHOLESALE: Fabrics
PIECE GOODS, NOTIONS/DRY GOODS, WHOL: Drapery Mtrl, Woven
PIGMENTS, INORGANIC: Chrome Green, Chrome Yellow, Zinc Yellw
PILLOW FILLING MTRLS: Curled Hair, Cotton Waste, Moss
PILLOWCASES
PINS
PIPE & FITTING: Fabrication
PIPE & FITTINGS: Cast Iron
PIPE & TUBES: Seamless
PIPE CLEANERS
PIPE SECTIONS, FABRICATED FROM PURCHASED PIPE

PRODUCT INDEX

PIPE: Concrete
PIPE: Plastic
PIPE: Plate Fabricated, Large Diameter
PIPE: Water, Cast Iron
PIPELINE & POWER LINE INSPECTION SVCS
PIPELINES: Crude Petroleum
PIPELINES: Refined Petroleum
PIPES & FITTINGS: Fiber, Made From Purchased Materials
PIPES & TUBES
PIPES & TUBES: Steel
PIPES & TUBES: Welded
PIPES: Tobacco
PLANING MILL, NEC
PLANING MILLS: Independent, Exc Millwork
PLANING MILLS: Millwork
PLANT HORMONES
PLANTERS & FLOWER POTS, WHOLESALE
PLANTERS: Plastic
PLAQUES: Picture, Laminated
PLASMAS
PLASTIC PRDTS
PLASTIC WOOD
PLASTICS FILM & SHEET
PLASTICS FILM & SHEET: Polyethylene
PLASTICS FILM & SHEET: Polyvinyl
PLASTICS FILM & SHEET: Vinyl
PLASTICS FINISHED PRDTS: Laminated
PLASTICS MATERIAL & RESINS
PLASTICS MATERIALS, BASIC FORMS & SHAPES WHOLESALERS
PLASTICS PROCESSING
PLASTICS SHEET: Packing Materials
PLASTICS: Cast
PLASTICS: Extruded
PLASTICS: Finished Injection Molded
PLASTICS: Injection Molded
PLASTICS: Molded
PLASTICS: Polystyrene Foam
PLASTICS: Thermoformed
PLATED WARE, ALL METALS
PLATEMAKING SVC: Color Separations, For The Printing Trade
PLATES
PLATING & POLISHING SVC
PLATING SVC: Chromium, Metals Or Formed Prdts
PLATING SVC: Electro
PLATING SVC: Gold
PLATING SVC: NEC
PLAYGROUND EQPT
PLEATING & STITCHING SVC
PLUMBING & HEATING EQPT & SPLY, WHOL: Htg Eqpt/Panels, Solar
PLUMBING & HEATING EQPT & SPLY, WHOLESALE: Hydronic Htg Eqpt
PLUMBING & HEATING EQPT & SPLYS WHOLESALERS
PLUMBING & HEATING EQPT & SPLYS, WHOL: Pipe/Fitting, Plastic
PLUMBING & HEATING EQPT & SPLYS, WHOL: Plumbing Fitting/Sply
PLUMBING & HEATING EQPT & SPLYS, WHOL: Water Purif Eqpt
PLUMBING & HEATING EQPT, WHOLESALE: Water Heaters/Purif
PLUMBING FIXTURES
PLUMBING FIXTURES: Brass, Incl Drain Cocks, Faucets/Spigots
PLUMBING FIXTURES: Plastic
PLUMBING FIXTURES: Vitreous
POINT OF SALE DEVICES
POKER CHIPS
POLES & POSTS: Concrete
POLISHING SVC: Metals Or Formed Prdts
PONTOONS: Rubber
POPCORN & SUPPLIES WHOLESALERS
POPULAR MUSIC GROUPS OR ARTISTS
PORCELAIN ENAMELED PRDTS & UTENSILS
POSTERS & DECALS, WHOLESALE
POTTERY
POTTERY: Laboratory & Indl
POULTRY & SMALL GAME SLAUGHTERING & PROCESSING
POWDER: Metal
POWDER: Silver
POWER DISTRIBUTION BOARDS: Electric
POWER GENERATORS

POWER SPLY CONVERTERS: Static, Electronic Applications
POWER SUPPLIES: All Types, Static
POWER SWITCHING EQPT
POWER TOOL REPAIR SVCS
POWER TOOLS, HAND: Chain Saws, Portable
POWER TRANSMISSION EQPT WHOLESALERS
POWER TRANSMISSION EQPT: Aircraft
POWER TRANSMISSION EQPT: Mechanical
PRECAST TERRAZZO OR CONCRETE PRDTS
PRECIOUS METALS WHOLESALERS
PRECIOUS STONE MINING SVCS, NEC
PRECIOUS STONES & METALS, WHOLESALE
PRECIOUS STONES WHOLESALERS
PRECISION INSTRUMENT REPAIR SVCS
PREFABRICATED BUILDING DEALERS
PREPARING SHAFTS OR TUNNELS, METAL MINING
PRERECORDED TAPE, COMPACT DISC & RECORD STORES: Records
PRERECORDED TAPES & CASSETTES WHOLESALERS
PRESSED & MOLDED PULP PRDTS, NEC: From Purchased Materials
PRESSED FIBER & MOLDED PULP PRDTS, EXC FOOD PRDTS
PRESTRESSED CONCRETE PRDTS
PRIMARY METAL PRODUCTS
PRINT CARTRIDGES: Laser & Other Computer Printers
PRINTED CIRCUIT BOARDS
PRINTERS & PLOTTERS
PRINTERS' SVCS: Folding, Collating, Etc
PRINTERS: Computer
PRINTERS: Magnetic Ink, Bar Code
PRINTING & BINDING: Books
PRINTING & BINDING: Pamphlets
PRINTING & ENGRAVING: Invitation & Stationery
PRINTING & ENGRAVING: Poster & Decal
PRINTING & STAMPING: Fabric Articles
PRINTING & STAMPING: Tip, On Fabric
PRINTING & WRITING PAPER WHOLESALERS
PRINTING MACHINERY
PRINTING MACHINERY, EQPT & SPLYS: Wholesalers
PRINTING TRADES MACHINERY & EQPT REPAIR SVCS
PRINTING, COMMERCIAL Newspapers, NEC
PRINTING, COMMERCIAL: Business Forms, NEC
PRINTING, COMMERCIAL: Cards, Visiting, Incl Business, NEC
PRINTING, COMMERCIAL: Circulars, NEC
PRINTING, COMMERCIAL: Coupons, NEC
PRINTING, COMMERCIAL: Decals, NEC
PRINTING, COMMERCIAL: Directories, Exc Telephone, NEC
PRINTING, COMMERCIAL: Directories, Telephone, NEC
PRINTING, COMMERCIAL: Envelopes, NEC
PRINTING, COMMERCIAL: Imprinting
PRINTING, COMMERCIAL: Invitations, NEC
PRINTING, COMMERCIAL: Labels & Seals, NEC
PRINTING, COMMERCIAL: Letterpress & Screen
PRINTING, COMMERCIAL: Literature, Advertising, NEC
PRINTING, COMMERCIAL: Maps, NEC
PRINTING, COMMERCIAL: Post Cards, Picture, NEC
PRINTING, COMMERCIAL: Promotional
PRINTING, COMMERCIAL: Publications
PRINTING, COMMERCIAL: Ready
PRINTING, COMMERCIAL: Screen
PRINTING, LITHOGRAPHIC: Advertising Posters
PRINTING, LITHOGRAPHIC: Catalogs
PRINTING, LITHOGRAPHIC: Color
PRINTING, LITHOGRAPHIC: Decals
PRINTING, LITHOGRAPHIC: Forms & Cards, Business
PRINTING, LITHOGRAPHIC: Forms, Business
PRINTING, LITHOGRAPHIC: Letters, Circular Or Form
PRINTING, LITHOGRAPHIC: Offset & photolithographic printing
PRINTING, LITHOGRAPHIC: On Metal
PRINTING, LITHOGRAPHIC: Promotional
PRINTING, LITHOGRAPHIC: Publications
PRINTING: Books
PRINTING: Books
PRINTING: Broadwoven Fabrics. Cotton
PRINTING: Checkbooks
PRINTING: Commercial, NEC
PRINTING: Engraving & Plate
PRINTING: Fabric, Narrow
PRINTING: Flexographic
PRINTING: Gravure, Business Form & Card
PRINTING: Gravure, Color
PRINTING: Gravure, Forms, Business

PRINTING: Gravure, Job
PRINTING: Gravure, Labels
PRINTING: Gravure, Rotogravure
PRINTING: Gravure, Seals
PRINTING: Gravure, Stationery & Invitation
PRINTING: Laser
PRINTING: Letterpress
PRINTING: Lithographic
PRINTING: Offset
PRINTING: Photo-Offset
PRINTING: Roller, Manmade Fiber & Silk, Broadwoven Fabric
PRINTING: Screen, Broadwoven Fabrics, Cotton
PRINTING: Screen, Fabric
PRINTING: Screen, Manmade Fiber & Silk, Broadwoven Fabric
PRINTING: Thermography
PRIVATE INVESTIGATOR SVCS
PROFESSIONAL EQPT & SPLYS, WHOL: Metal Locating Eqpt/Access
PROFESSIONAL EQPT & SPLYS, WHOLESALE: Analytical Instruments
PROFESSIONAL EQPT & SPLYS, WHOLESALE: Optical Goods
PROFESSIONAL EQPT & SPLYS, WHOLESALE: Precision Tools
PROFESSIONAL EQPT & SPLYS, WHOLESALE: Scientific & Engineerg
PROFESSIONAL EQPT & SPLYS, WHOLESALE: Scientific Recording
PROFESSIONAL INSTRUMENT REPAIR SVCS
PROFILE SHAPES: Unsupported Plastics
PROGRAMMERS: Indl Process
PROMOTION SVCS
PROPELLERS: Boat & Ship, Cast
PROPELLERS: Boat & Ship, Machined
PROPELLERS: Ship, Nec
PROPULSION UNITS: Guided Missiles & Space Vehicles
PROTECTIVE FOOTWEAR: Rubber Or Plastic
PUBLIC RELATIONS SVCS
PUBLISHERS: Art Copy
PUBLISHERS: Art Copy & Poster
PUBLISHERS: Book
PUBLISHERS: Books, No Printing
PUBLISHERS: Catalogs
PUBLISHERS: Comic Books, No Printing
PUBLISHERS: Directories, NEC
PUBLISHERS: Directories, Telephone
PUBLISHERS: Magazines, No Printing
PUBLISHERS: Miscellaneous
PUBLISHERS: Music Book & Sheet Music
PUBLISHERS: Music, Sheet
PUBLISHERS: Newsletter
PUBLISHERS: Newspaper
PUBLISHERS: Newspapers, No Printing
PUBLISHERS: Pamphlets, No Printing
PUBLISHERS: Periodical, With Printing
PUBLISHERS: Periodicals, Magazines
PUBLISHERS: Periodicals, No Printing
PUBLISHERS: Sheet Music
PUBLISHERS: Shopping News
PUBLISHERS: Technical Manuals
PUBLISHERS: Technical Manuals & Papers
PUBLISHERS: Telephone & Other Directory
PUBLISHERS: Textbooks, No Printing
PUBLISHERS: Trade journals, No Printing
PUBLISHING & BROADCASTING: Internet Only
PUBLISHING & PRINTING: Art Copy
PUBLISHING & PRINTING: Book Clubs
PUBLISHING & PRINTING: Books
PUBLISHING & PRINTING: Catalogs
PUBLISHING & PRINTING: Directories, NEC
PUBLISHING & PRINTING: Directories, Telephone
PUBLISHING & PRINTING: Magazines: publishing & printing
PUBLISHING & PRINTING: Music, Book
PUBLISHING & PRINTING: Newsletters, Business Svc
PUBLISHING & PRINTING: Newspapers
PUBLISHING & PRINTING: Pamphlets
PUBLISHING & PRINTING: Periodical Statistical Reports
PUBLISHING & PRINTING: Posters
PUBLISHING & PRINTING: Textbooks
PUBLISHING & PRINTING: Trade Journals
PULLEYS: Power Transmission
PULP MILLS
PULP MILLS: Chemical & Semichemical Processing
PULP MILLS: Dissolving Pulp Processing

PRODUCT INDEX

PULP MILLS: Mech Pulp, Incl Groundwood & Thermomechanical
PULP MILLS: Mechanical & Recycling Processing
PULP MILLS: Wood Based Pulp, NEC
PUMPS
PUMPS & PARTS: Indl
PUMPS & PUMPING EQPT REPAIR SVCS
PUMPS & PUMPING EQPT WHOLESALERS
PUMPS, HEAT: Electric
PUMPS: Aircraft, Hydraulic
PUMPS: Domestic, Water Or Sump
PUMPS: Fluid Power
PUMPS: Hydraulic Power Transfer
PUMPS: Measuring & Dispensing
PUMPS: Vacuum, Exc Laboratory
PUPPETS & MARIONETTES
PURIFICATION & DUST COLLECTION EQPT

Q

QUARTZ CRYSTAL MINING SVCS
QUARTZ CRYSTALS: Electronic
QUILTING SVC
QUILTING SVC & SPLYS, FOR THE TRADE

R

RACETRACKS
RACEWAYS
RACKS: Bicycle, Automotive
RACKS: Display
RACKS: Pallet, Exc Wood
RACKS: Railroad Car, Vehicle Transportation, Steel
RACKS: Trash, Metal Rack
RADAR SYSTEMS & EQPT
RADIO & TELEVISION COMMUNICATIONS EQUIPMENT
RADIO & TELEVISION REPAIR
RADIO BROADCASTING & COMMUNICATIONS EQPT
RADIO BROADCASTING STATIONS
RADIO COMMUNICATIONS: Airborne Eqpt
RADIO RECEIVER NETWORKS
RADIO, TELEVISION & CONSUMER ELECTRONICS STORES: Eqpt, NEC
RADIO, TELEVISION & CONSUMER ELECTRONICS STORES: TV Sets
RADIO, TV & CONSUMER ELEC STORES: Automotive Sound Eqpt
RADIO, TV & CONSUMER ELEC STORES: Radios, Receiver Type
RADIO, TV/CONSUMER ELEC STORES: Antennas, Satellite Dish
RAIL & STRUCTURAL SHAPES: Aluminum rail & structural shapes
RAILINGS: Prefabricated, Metal
RAILINGS: Wood
RAILROAD CAR RENTING & LEASING SVCS
RAILROAD CARGO LOADING & UNLOADING SVCS
RAILROAD EQPT
RAILROAD EQPT & SPLYS WHOLESALERS
RAILROAD EQPT: Cars & Eqpt, Train, Freight Or Passenger
RAILROAD RELATED EQPT: Railway Track
RAILROAD TIES: Concrete
RAILS: Steel Or Iron
RAMPS: Prefabricated Metal
RAZORS, RAZOR BLADES
REACTORS: Current Limiting
REAL ESTATE AGENCIES & BROKERS
REAL ESTATE AGENTS & MANAGERS
REAL ESTATE FIDUCIARIES' OFFICES
REAL ESTATE INVESTMENT TRUSTS
REAL ESTATE OPERATORS, EXC DEVELOPERS: Commercial/Indl Bldg
RECEIVERS: Radio Communications
RECLAIMED RUBBER: Reworked By Manufacturing Process
RECORDING HEADS: Speech & Musical Eqpt
RECORDS & TAPES: Prerecorded
RECOVERY SVCS: Metal
RECREATIONAL & SPORTING CAMPS
RECREATIONAL SPORTING EQPT REPAIR SVCS
RECREATIONAL VEHICLE DEALERS
RECREATIONAL VEHICLE PARKS & CAMPGROUNDS
RECREATIONAL VEHICLE PARTS & ACCESS STORES
RECREATIONAL VEHICLE: Wholesalers
RECYCLABLE SCRAP & WASTE MATERIALS WHOLESALERS
RECYCLING: Paper
REFINERS & SMELTERS: Copper

REFINERS & SMELTERS: Gold
REFINERS & SMELTERS: Nonferrous Metal
REFINING: Petroleum
REFLECTIVE ROAD MARKERS, WHOLESALE
REFRACTORIES: Brick
REFRACTORIES: Clay
REFRACTORIES: Graphite, Carbon Or Ceramic Bond
REFRACTORIES: Nonclay
REFRACTORY MATERIALS WHOLESALERS
REFRIGERATION & HEATING EQUIPMENT
REFRIGERATION EQPT & SPLYS WHOLESALERS
REFRIGERATION EQPT & SPLYS, WHOLESALE: Beverage Dispensers
REFRIGERATION EQPT & SPLYS, WHOLESALE: Commercial Eqpt
REFRIGERATION EQPT: Complete
REFRIGERATION REPAIR SVCS
REFRIGERATION SVC & REPAIR
REFRIGERATOR REPAIR SVCS
REFUSE SYSTEMS
REHABILITATION CENTER, OUTPATIENT TREATMENT
RELIGIOUS SCHOOL
REMOTE DATABASE INFORMATION RETRIEVAL SVCS
REMOVERS & CLEANERS
REMOVERS: Paint
RENDERING PLANT
RENTAL CENTERS: Party & Banquet Eqpt & Splys
RENTAL CENTERS: Tools
RENTAL SVCS: Aircraft & Indl Truck
RENTAL SVCS: Business Machine & Electronic Eqpt
RENTAL SVCS: Clothing
RENTAL SVCS: Costume
RENTAL SVCS: Garage Facility & Tool
RENTAL SVCS: Mobile Communication Eqpt
RENTAL SVCS: Recreational Vehicle
RENTAL SVCS: Sign
RENTAL SVCS: Sporting Goods, NEC
RENTAL SVCS: Trailer
RENTAL SVCS: Vending Machine
RENTAL SVCS: Video Cassette Recorder & Access
RENTAL: Portable Toilet
RENTAL: Video Tape & Disc
REPAIR SERVICES, NEC
REPLATING SHOP, EXC SILVERWARE
REPRODUCTION SVCS: Video Tape Or Disk
RESEARCH, DEVELOPMENT & TEST SVCS, COMM: Business Analysis
RESEARCH, DEVELOPMENT & TEST SVCS, COMM: Cmptr Hardware Dev
RESEARCH, DEVELOPMENT & TEST SVCS, COMM: Research, Exc Lab
RESEARCH, DEVELOPMENT & TESTING SVCS, COMM: Agricultural
RESEARCH, DEVELOPMENT & TESTING SVCS, COMM: Research Lab
RESEARCH, DEVELOPMENT & TESTING SVCS, COMMERCIAL: Business
RESEARCH, DEVELOPMENT & TESTING SVCS, COMMERCIAL: Energy
RESEARCH, DEVELOPMENT & TESTING SVCS, COMMERCIAL: Physical
RESEARCH, DVLPT & TESTING SVCS, COMM: Mkt, Bus & Economic
RESIDENTIAL REMODELERS
RESINS: Custom Compound Purchased
RESISTORS
RESPIRATORS
RESPIRATORY SYSTEM DRUGS
RESTAURANT EQPT REPAIR SVCS
RESTAURANT EQPT: Food Wagons
RESTAURANTS:Full Svc, American
RESTAURANTS:Full Svc, Barbecue
RESTAURANTS:Full Svc, Family
RESTAURANTS:Full Svc, Indian-Pakistan
RESTAURANTS:Full Svc, Italian
RESTAURANTS:Full Svc, Seafood
RESTAURANTS:Limited Svc, Chicken
RESTAURANTS:Limited Svc, Coffee Shop
RESTAURANTS:Limited Svc, Grill
RESTAURANTS:Limited Svc, Ice Cream Stands Or Dairy Bars
RESTAURANTS:Ltd Svc, Ice Cream, Soft Drink/Fountain Stands
RETAIL BAKERY: Bagels
RETAIL BAKERY: Bread

RETAIL BAKERY: Cakes
RETAIL BAKERY: Doughnuts
RETAIL BAKERY: Pastries
RETAIL BAKERY: Pretzels
RETAIL FIREPLACE STORES
RETAIL LUMBER YARDS
RETAIL STORES, NEC
RETAIL STORES: Air Purification Eqpt
RETAIL STORES: Alarm Signal Systems
RETAIL STORES: Alcoholic Beverage Making Eqpt & Splys
RETAIL STORES: Awnings
RETAIL STORES: Banners
RETAIL STORES: Business Machines & Eqpt
RETAIL STORES: Canvas Prdts
RETAIL STORES: Cleaning Eqpt & Splys
RETAIL STORES: Coins
RETAIL STORES: Concrete Prdts, Precast
RETAIL STORES: Cosmetics
RETAIL STORES: Decals
RETAIL STORES: Educational Aids & Electronic Training Mat
RETAIL STORES: Electronic Parts & Eqpt
RETAIL STORES: Engine & Motor Eqpt & Splys
RETAIL STORES: Farm Eqpt & Splys
RETAIL STORES: Fire Extinguishers
RETAIL STORES: Flags
RETAIL STORES: Foam & Foam Prdts
RETAIL STORES: Hair Care Prdts
RETAIL STORES: Hearing Aids
RETAIL STORES: Ice
RETAIL STORES: Maps & Charts
RETAIL STORES: Medical Apparatus & Splys
RETAIL STORES: Mobile Telephones & Eqpt
RETAIL STORES: Monuments, Finished To Custom Order
RETAIL STORES: Motors, Electric
RETAIL STORES: Orthopedic & Prosthesis Applications
RETAIL STORES: Perfumes & Colognes
RETAIL STORES: Pet Food
RETAIL STORES: Pet Splys
RETAIL STORES: Pets
RETAIL STORES: Photocopy Machines
RETAIL STORES: Picture Frames, Ready Made
RETAIL STORES: Plumbing & Heating Splys
RETAIL STORES: Police Splys
RETAIL STORES: Religious Goods
RETAIL STORES: Rock & Stone Specimens
RETAIL STORES: Rubber Stamps
RETAIL STORES: Safety Splys & Eqpt
RETAIL STORES: Spas & Hot Tubs
RETAIL STORES: Telephone & Communication Eqpt
RETAIL STORES: Tents
RETAIL STORES: Theatrical Eqpt & Splys
RETAIL STORES: Toilet Preparations
RETAIL STORES: Vaults & Safes
RETAIL STORES: Water Purification Eqpt
RETAIL STORES: Welding Splys
RETAIL STORES: Wheelchair Lifts
REUPHOLSTERY & FURNITURE REPAIR
REUPHOLSTERY SVCS
REWINDING SVCS
RHEOSTATS: Electronic
RIFLES: Recoilless
RIPRAP QUARRYING
ROAD MATERIALS: Bituminous
ROAD MATERIALS: Bituminous, Not From Refineries
ROBOTS: Assembly Line
ROCKETS: Space & Military
ROD & BAR: Aluminum
RODS: Steel & Iron, Made In Steel Mills
ROLL COVERINGS: Rubber
ROLLERS & FITTINGS: Window Shade
ROLLING MILL MACHINERY
ROOF DECKS
ROOFING MATERIALS: Asphalt
ROOFING MATERIALS: Sheet Metal
ROOFING PRDTS: Wood Fiber
ROPE
RUBBER
RUBBER PRDTS
RUBBER PRDTS: Mechanical
RUBBER PRDTS: Medical & Surgical Tubing, Extrudd & Lathe-Cut
RUBBER PRDTS: Sponge
RUBBER PRDTS: Wet Suits
RUBBER STRUCTURES: Air-Supported
RUGS : Hand & Machine Made

PRODUCT INDEX

S

SADDLERY STORES
SAFES & VAULTS: Metal
SAFETY EQPT & SPLYS WHOLESALERS
SAILBOAT BUILDING & REPAIR
SAILS
SALT
SAND & GRAVEL
SAND MINING
SAND: Hygrade
SAND: Silica
SANDBLASTING EQPT
SANDBLASTING SVC: Building Exterior
SANDSTONE: Crushed & Broken
SANDSTONE: Dimension
SANITARY SVC, NEC
SANITARY SVCS: Dead Animal Disposal
SANITARY SVCS: Environmental Cleanup
SANITARY SVCS: Oil Spill Cleanup
SANITARY SVCS: Refuse Collection & Disposal Svcs
SANITARY SVCS: Waste Materials, Recycling
SANITARY WARE: Metal
SANITATION CHEMICALS & CLEANING AGENTS
SASHES: Door Or Window, Metal
SATCHELS
SATELLITE COMMUNICATIONS EQPT
SATELLITES: Communications
SAUNA ROOMS: Prefabricated
SAW BLADES
SAWDUST & SHAVINGS
SAWING & PLANING MILLS
SAWING & PLANING MILLS: Custom
SAWMILL MACHINES
SAWS & SAWING EQPT
SAWS: Hand, Metalworking Or Woodworking
SCALE REPAIR SVCS
SCALES & BALANCES, EXC LABORATORY
SCALES: Counting
SCALES: Indl
SCALES: Truck
SCANNING DEVICES: Optical
SCHOOL SPLYS, EXC BOOKS: Wholesalers
SCHOOLS: Elementary & Secondary
SCISSORS: Hand
SCRAP & WASTE MATERIALS, WHOLESALE: Bottles
SCRAP & WASTE MATERIALS, WHOLESALE: Ferrous Metal
SCRAP & WASTE MATERIALS, WHOLESALE: Metal
SCRAP & WASTE MATERIALS, WHOLESALE: Nonferrous Metals Scrap
SCRAP & WASTE MATERIALS, WHOLESALE: Plastics Scrap
SCRAP STEEL CUTTING
SCREENS: Door, Wood Frame
SCREENS: Window, Metal
SCREW MACHINE PRDTS
SCREWS: Metal
SEALANTS
SEALS: Hermetic
SEARCH & DETECTION SYSTEMS, EXC RADAR
SEARCH & NAVIGATION SYSTEMS
SEAT BELTS: Automobile & Aircraft
SEATING: Stadium
SECRETARIAL SVCS
SECURE STORAGE SVC: Document
SECURITY CONTROL EQPT & SYSTEMS
SECURITY DEVICES
SECURITY EQPT STORES
SECURITY SYSTEMS SERVICES
SEEDS: Coated Or Treated, From Purchased Seeds
SEMICONDUCTOR & RELATED DEVICES: Read-Only Memory Or ROM
SEMICONDUCTOR CIRCUIT NETWORKS
SEMICONDUCTOR DEVICES: Wafers
SEMICONDUCTORS & RELATED DEVICES
SENSORS: Infrared, Solid State
SENSORS: Radiation
SEPTIC TANK CLEANING SVCS
SEPTIC TANKS: Concrete
SEPTIC TANKS: Plastic
SETTLEMENT HOUSE
SEWAGE & WATER TREATMENT EQPT
SEWING CONTRACTORS
SEWING KITS: Novelty
SEWING MACHINES & PARTS: Household
SEWING, NEEDLEWORK & PIECE GOODS STORES: Knitting Splys
SEXTANTS
SHADES: Lamp & Light, Residential
SHADES: Window
SHAPES & PILINGS, STRUCTURAL: Steel
SHAVING PREPARATIONS
SHAVINGS, WOOD, WHOLESALE
SHEARLING, PREPARED SHEEPSKIN
SHEET METAL SPECIALTIES, EXC STAMPED
SHEET MUSIC STORES
SHEET MUSIC, WHOLESALE
SHEETING: Laminated Plastic
SHEETING: Window, Plastic
SHEETS & STRIPS: Aluminum
SHEETS: Fabric, From Purchased Materials
SHELLAC
SHELTERED WORKSHOPS
SHIP BUILDING & REPAIRING: Boats, Crew
SHIP BUILDING & REPAIRING: Cargo Vessels
SHIP BUILDING & REPAIRING: Cargo, Commercial
SHIP BUILDING & REPAIRING: Combat Vessels
SHIP BUILDING & REPAIRING: Ferryboats
SHIP BUILDING & REPAIRING: Fishing Vessels, Large
SHIP BUILDING & REPAIRING: Lighters, Marine
SHIP BUILDING & REPAIRING: Lighthouse Tenders
SHIP BUILDING & REPAIRING: Military
SHIP BUILDING & REPAIRING: Offshore Sply Boats
SHIP BUILDING & REPAIRING: Rigging, Marine
SHIP BUILDING & REPAIRING: Sailing Vessels, Commercial
SHIP BUILDING & REPAIRING: Trawlers
SHIPBUILDING & REPAIR
SHIPPING AGENTS
SHIPPING DOCUMENTS PREPARATION SVCS
SHIPS WHOLESALERS
SHOCK ABSORBERS: Indl
SHOE & BOOT ACCESS
SHOE MATERIALS: Counters
SHOE MATERIALS: Quarters
SHOE STORES
SHOE STORES: Athletic
SHOE STORES: Boots, Men's
SHOE STORES: Custom & Orthopedic
SHOE STORES: Men's
SHOES & BOOTS WHOLESALERS
SHOES: Infants' & Children's
SHOES: Men's
SHOES: Plastic Or Rubber
SHOES: Sandals, Rubber
SHOES: Women's
SHOES: Women's, Dress
SHOWCASES & DISPLAY FIXTURES: Office & Store
SHOWER STALLS: Plastic & Fiberglass
SHREDDERS: Indl & Commercial
SHUTTERS, DOOR & WINDOW: Metal
SHUTTERS: Window, Wood
SIDING & STRUCTURAL MATERIALS: Wood
SIDING MATERIALS
SIGN LETTERING & PAINTING SVCS
SIGN PAINTING & LETTERING SHOP
SIGNALING APPARATUS: Electric
SIGNALING DEVICES: Sound, Electrical
SIGNALS: Traffic Control, Electric
SIGNALS: Transportation
SIGNS & ADVERTISING SPECIALTIES
SIGNS & ADVERTISING SPECIALTIES: Artwork, Advertising
SIGNS & ADVERTISING SPECIALTIES: Displays, Paint Process
SIGNS & ADVERTISING SPECIALTIES: Letters For Signs, Metal
SIGNS & ADVERTISING SPECIALTIES: Novelties
SIGNS & ADVERTISING SPECIALTIES: Signs
SIGNS & ADVERTSG SPECIALTIES: Displays/Cutouts Window/Lobby
SIGNS, ELECTRICAL: Wholesalers
SIGNS, EXC ELECTRIC, WHOLESALE
SIGNS: Electrical
SIGNS: Neon
SILICA MINING
SILICON & CHROMIUM
SILICON WAFERS: Chemically Doped
SILICON: Pure
SILK SCREEN DESIGN SVCS
SILVER ORES
SILVERSMITHS
SIMULATORS: Electronic Countermeasure
SIRENS: Vehicle, Marine, Indl & Warning
SIZES
SKIN CARE PRDTS: Suntan Lotions & Oils
SKYLIGHTS
SLAB & TILE, ROOFING: Concrete
SLAB & TILE: Precast Concrete, Floor
SLABS: Steel
SLATE PRDTS
SLAUGHTERING & MEAT PACKING
SLIDES & EXHIBITS: Prepared
SLINGS: Lifting, Made From Purchased Wire
SLINGS: Rope
SLOT MACHINES
SMOKE DETECTORS
SMOKERS' ARTICLES: Pottery
SNOWMOBILES
SOAPS & DETERGENTS
SOAPS & DETERGENTS: Textile
SOCIAL SVCS, HANDICAPPED
SOFT DRINKS WHOLESALERS
SOFTWARE PUBLISHERS: Application
SOFTWARE PUBLISHERS: Business & Professional
SOFTWARE PUBLISHERS: Computer Utilities
SOFTWARE PUBLISHERS: Education
SOFTWARE PUBLISHERS: Home Entertainment
SOFTWARE PUBLISHERS: NEC
SOFTWARE PUBLISHERS: Operating Systems
SOFTWARE PUBLISHERS: Publisher's
SOFTWARE PUBLISHERS: Word Processing
SOFTWARE TRAINING, COMPUTER
SOIL CONDITIONERS
SOLAR CELLS
SOLAR HEATING EQPT
SOLDERING EQPT: Electrical, Exc Handheld
SOLDERING SVC: Jewelry
SOLVENTS
SOLVENTS: Organic
SONAR SYSTEMS & EQPT
SONG WRITING SVCS
SOUND EFFECTS & MUSIC PRODUCTION: Motion Picture
SOUND EQPT: Underwater
SOUVENIR SHOPS
SOYBEAN PRDTS
SPACE PROPULSION UNITS & PARTS
SPACE RESEARCH & TECHNOLOGY, GOVT: Space Research/Developt
SPACE VEHICLE EQPT
SPACE VEHICLES
SPAS
SPEAKER MONITORS
SPEAKER SYSTEMS
SPECIAL PRODUCT SAWMILLS, NEC
SPECIALTY FOOD STORES, NEC
SPECIALTY FOOD STORES: Coffee
SPECIALTY FOOD STORES: Dietetic Foods
SPECIALTY FOOD STORES: Dried Fruit
SPECIALTY FOOD STORES: Food Gift Baskets
SPECIALTY FOOD STORES: Health & Dietetic Food
SPECIALTY FOOD STORES: Juices, Fruit Or Vegetable
SPECIALTY FOOD STORES: Vitamin
SPECIALTY SAWMILL PRDTS
SPECULATIVE BUILDERS: Single-Family Housing
SPICE & HERB STORES
SPORTING & ATHLETIC GOODS: Balls, Baseball, Football, Etc
SPORTING & ATHLETIC GOODS: Boomerangs
SPORTING & ATHLETIC GOODS: Bowling Alleys & Access
SPORTING & ATHLETIC GOODS: Camping Eqpt & Splys
SPORTING & ATHLETIC GOODS: Darts & Table Sports Eqpt & Splys
SPORTING & ATHLETIC GOODS: Decoys, Duck & Other Game Birds
SPORTING & ATHLETIC GOODS: Dumbbells & Other Weight Eqpt
SPORTING & ATHLETIC GOODS: Exercising Cycles
SPORTING & ATHLETIC GOODS: Fencing Eqpt
SPORTING & ATHLETIC GOODS: Fishing Bait, Artificial
SPORTING & ATHLETIC GOODS: Fishing Eqpt
SPORTING & ATHLETIC GOODS: Fishing Tackle, General
SPORTING & ATHLETIC GOODS: Flies, Fishing, Artificial
SPORTING & ATHLETIC GOODS: Football Eqpt & Splys, NEC
SPORTING & ATHLETIC GOODS: Gymnasium Eqpt
SPORTING & ATHLETIC GOODS: Hooks, Fishing

PRODUCT INDEX

SPORTING & ATHLETIC GOODS: Hunting Eqpt
SPORTING & ATHLETIC GOODS: Masks, Hockey, Baseball, Etc
SPORTING & ATHLETIC GOODS: Polo Eqpt & Splys, NEC
SPORTING & ATHLETIC GOODS: Pools, Swimming, Exc Plastic
SPORTING & ATHLETIC GOODS: Protective Sporting Eqpt
SPORTING & ATHLETIC GOODS: Reels, Fishing
SPORTING & ATHLETIC GOODS: Rods & Rod Parts, Fishing
SPORTING & ATHLETIC GOODS: Shafts, Golf Club
SPORTING & ATHLETIC GOODS: Shooting Eqpt & Splys, General
SPORTING & ATHLETIC GOODS: Skateboards
SPORTING & ATHLETIC GOODS: Snow Skiing Eqpt & Sply, Exc Skis
SPORTING & ATHLETIC GOODS: Snow Skis
SPORTING & ATHLETIC GOODS: Soccer Eqpt & Splys
SPORTING & ATHLETIC GOODS: Strings, Tennis Racket
SPORTING & ATHLETIC GOODS: Target Shooting Eqpt
SPORTING & ATHLETIC GOODS: Targets, Archery & Rifle Shooting
SPORTING & ATHLETIC GOODS: Team Sports Eqpt
SPORTING & ATHLETIC GOODS: Track & Field Athletic Eqpt
SPORTING & ATHLETIC GOODS: Trampolines & Eqpt
SPORTING & ATHLETIC GOODS: Water Skiing Eqpt & Splys
SPORTING & ATHLETIC GOODS: Water Skis
SPORTING & ATHLETIC GOODS: Water Sports Eqpt
SPORTING & ATHLETIC GOODS: Winter Sports
SPORTING & RECREATIONAL GOODS & SPLYS WHOLESALERS
SPORTING & RECREATIONAL GOODS, WHOL: Sharpeners, Sporting
SPORTING & RECREATIONAL GOODS, WHOLESALE: Bicycle
SPORTING & RECREATIONAL GOODS, WHOLESALE: Boat Access & Part
SPORTING & RECREATIONAL GOODS, WHOLESALE: Exercise
SPORTING & RECREATIONAL GOODS, WHOLESALE: Fishing
SPORTING & RECREATIONAL GOODS, WHOLESALE: Fishing Tackle
SPORTING & RECREATIONAL GOODS, WHOLESALE: Fitness
SPORTING & RECREATIONAL GOODS, WHOLESALE: Motorboats
SPORTING & RECREATIONAL GOODS, WHOLESALE: Sailboats
SPORTING & RECREATIONAL GOODS, WHOLESALE: Skiing
SPORTING & RECREATIONAL GOODS, WHOLESALE: Spa
SPORTING & RECREATIONAL GOODS, WHOLESALE: Surfing
SPORTING FIREARMS WHOLESALERS
SPORTING GOODS
SPORTING GOODS STORES, NEC
SPORTING GOODS STORES: Ammunition
SPORTING GOODS STORES: Bait & Tackle
SPORTING GOODS STORES: Firearms
SPORTING GOODS STORES: Fishing Eqpt
SPORTING GOODS STORES: Gymnasium Eqpt, NEC
SPORTING GOODS STORES: Playground Eqpt
SPORTING GOODS STORES: Soccer Splys
SPORTING GOODS STORES: Team sports Eqpt
SPORTING GOODS STORES: Water Sport Eqpt
SPORTING GOODS: Archery
SPORTING GOODS: Fishing Nets
SPORTING GOODS: Sailboards
SPORTING GOODS: Skin Diving Eqpt
SPORTING GOODS: Sleeping Bags
SPORTING GOODS: Surfboards
SPORTING/ATHLETIC GOODS: Gloves, Boxing, Handball, Etc
SPORTS APPAREL STORES
SPRAYING EQPT: Agricultural
SPRINGS: Clock, Precision
SPRINGS: Coiled Flat
SPRINGS: Steel
SPRINGS: Wire
SPRINKLER SYSTEMS: Field
SPRINKLING SYSTEMS: Fire Control
STACKS: Smoke
STAGE LIGHTING SYSTEMS
STAINED GLASS ART SVCS
STAINLESS STEEL

STAINLESS STEEL WARE
STAINS: Wood
STAIRCASES & STAIRS, WOOD
STAMPED ART GOODS FOR EMBROIDERING
STAMPINGS: Automotive
STAMPINGS: Metal
STATIONARY & OFFICE SPLYS, WHOL: Computer/Photocopying Splys
STATIONARY & OFFICE SPLYS, WHOLESALE: Blank Books
STATIONARY & OFFICE SPLYS, WHOLESALE: Laser Printer Splys
STATIONARY & OFFICE SPLYS, WHOLESALE: Manifold Business Form
STATIONARY & OFFICE SPLYS, WHOLESALE: Office Filing Splys
STATIONER'S SUNDRIES: Rubber
STATIONERY & OFFICE SPLYS WHOLESALERS
STATIONERY PRDTS
STATORS REWINDING SVCS
STATUARY GOODS, EXC RELIGIOUS: Wholesalers
STEEL & ALLOYS: Tool & Die
STEEL FABRICATORS
STEEL MILLS
STEEL: Cold-Rolled
STENCILS & LETTERING MATERIALS: Die-Cut
STILLS: Pressure, Metal Plate
STITCHING SVCS
STONE: Crushed & Broken, NEC
STONE: Dimension, NEC
STONE: Quarrying & Processing, Own Stone Prdts
STONES, SYNTHETIC: Gem Stone & Indl Use
STONEWARE PRDTS: Pottery
STORE FIXTURES, EXC REFRIGERATED: Wholesalers
STORE FIXTURES: Wood
STORES: Auto & Home Supply
STORES: Drapery & Upholstery
STOVES: Wood & Coal Burning
STRADDLE CARRIERS: Mobile
STRAPS: Cotton Webbing
STRAW GOODS
STRAWS: Drinking, Made From Purchased Materials
STRINGING BEADS
STRUCTURAL SUPPORT & BUILDING MATERIAL: Concrete
STUCCO
STUDIOS: Artist
STUDIOS: Artist's
STUDS & JOISTS: Sheet Metal
SUBMARINE BUILDING & REPAIR
SUBSCRIPTION FULFILLMENT SVCS: Magazine, Newspaper, Etc
SUBSTANCE ABUSE COUNSELING
SUGAR SUBSTITUTES: Organic
SUNDRIES & RELATED PRDTS: Medical & Laboratory, Rubber
SUNROOMS: Prefabricated Metal
SUPERMARKETS & OTHER GROCERY STORES
SURFACERS: Concrete Grinding
SURGICAL APPLIANCES & SPLYS
SURGICAL APPLIANCES & SPLYS
SURGICAL EQPT: See Also Instruments
SURGICAL IMPLANTS
SURGICAL INSTRUMENT REPAIR SVCS
SURVEYING & MAPPING: Land Parcels
SUSPENSION SYSTEMS: Acoustical, Metal
SVC ESTABLISHMENT EQPT & SPLYS WHOLESALERS
SVC ESTABLISHMENT EQPT, WHOL: Cleaning & Maint Eqpt & Splys
SVC ESTABLISHMENT EQPT, WHOLESALE: Beauty Parlor Eqpt & Sply
SVC ESTABLISHMENT EQPT, WHOLESALE: Firefighting Eqpt
SVC ESTABLISHMENT EQPT, WHOLESALE: Laundry Eqpt & Splys
SVC ESTABLISHMENT EQPT, WHOLESALE: Vacuum Cleaning Systems
SVC ESTABLISHMENT EQPT, WHOLESALE: Voting Machines
SWEEPING COMPOUNDS
SWIMMING POOL & HOT TUB CLEANING & MAINTENANCE SVCS
SWIMMING POOL EQPT: Filters & Water Conditioning Systems
SWITCHES: Electronic
SWITCHES: Electronic Applications
SWITCHES: Thermostatic

SWITCHES: Time, Electrical Switchgear Apparatus
SWITCHGEAR & SWITCHBOARD APPARATUS
SWITCHGEAR & SWITCHGEAR ACCESS, NEC
SYNCHROS
SYNTHETIC RESIN FINISHED PRDTS, NEC
SYRUPS, DRINK
SYRUPS, FLAVORING, EXC DRINK
SYSTEMS ENGINEERING: Computer Related
SYSTEMS INTEGRATION SVCS
SYSTEMS INTEGRATION SVCS: Local Area Network
SYSTEMS SOFTWARE DEVELOPMENT SVCS

T

TABLE OR COUNTERTOPS, PLASTIC LAMINATED
TABLECLOTHS & SETTINGS
TABLES: Lift, Hydraulic
TABLETS & PADS
TABLETS: Bronze Or Other Metal
TABLEWARE OR KITCHEN ARTICLES: Commercial, Fine Earthenware
TABLEWARE: Household & Commercial, Semivitreous
TAGS: Paper, Blank, Made From Purchased Paper
TALLOW: Animal
TALLOW: Vegetable
TANK COMPONENTS: Military, Specialized
TANK REPAIR & CLEANING SVCS
TANKS & OTHER TRACKED VEHICLE CMPNTS
TANKS: Concrete
TANKS: Fuel, Including Oil & Gas, Metal Plate
TANKS: Plastic & Fiberglass
TANKS: Standard Or Custom Fabricated, Metal Plate
TANKS: Storage, Farm, Metal Plate
TANKS: Water, Metal Plate
TANNERIES: Leather
TAPE DRIVES
TAPE MEASURES
TAPES: Fabric
TAPES: Slide Fastener
TARGET DRONES
TARPAULINS
TELECOMMUNICATION EQPT REPAIR SVCS, EXC TELEPHONES
TELECOMMUNICATION SYSTEMS & EQPT
TELECOMMUNICATIONS CARRIERS & SVCS: Wired
TELEGRAPH STATION EQPT & PARTS: Wire
TELEMETERING EQPT
TELEPHONE EQPT INSTALLATION
TELEPHONE EQPT: Modems
TELEPHONE EQPT: NEC
TELEPHONE SET REPAIR SVCS
TELEPHONE STATION EQPT & PARTS: Wire
TELEPHONE SVCS
TELEPHONE: Automatic Dialers
TELEPHONE: Fiber Optic Systems
TELEPHONE: Headsets
TELEVISION BROADCASTING & COMMUNICATIONS EQPT
TELEVISION BROADCASTING STATIONS
TELEVISION SETS WHOLESALERS
TELEVISION: Cameras
TELEVISION: Monitors
TENT REPAIR SHOP
TENTS: All Materials
TEST KITS: Pregnancy
TESTERS: Environmental
TESTERS: Physical Property
TESTERS: Water, Exc Indl Process
TESTING SVCS
TEXTILE & APPAREL SVCS
TEXTILE BAGS WHOLESALERS
TEXTILE FABRICATORS
TEXTILE FINISHING: Sponging, Cotton, Broadwoven, Trade
TEXTILE MACHINERY ACCESS, HARDWOOD
TEXTILE PRDTS: Hand Woven & Crocheted
TEXTILE: Goods, NEC
TEXTILES: Carbonized Rags
TEXTILES: Crash, Linen
TEXTILES: Fibers, Textile, Rcvrd From Mill Waste/Rags
TEXTILES: Jute & Flax Prdts
THERMOCOUPLES
THERMOPLASTIC MATERIALS
THERMOPLASTICS
THIN FILM CIRCUITS
THREAD: All Fibers
THREAD: Embroidery
THREAD: Natural Fiber

PRODUCT INDEX

THREAD: Sewing
TIES, FORM: Metal
TILE: Brick & Structural, Clay
TILE: Mosaic, Ceramic
TILE: Precast Terrazzo, Floor
TILE: Wall & Floor, Ceramic
TILE: Wall, Ceramic
TIN
TIN-BASE ALLOYS, PRIMARY
TINPLATE
TIRE CORD & FABRIC
TIRE DEALERS
TIRE RECAPPING & RETREADING
TIRES & INNER TUBES
TIRES & TUBES, WHOLESALE: Automotive
TIRES: Auto
TITANIUM MILL PRDTS
TOBACCO & PRDTS, WHOLESALE: Smoking
TOBACCO & TOBACCO PRDTS WHOLESALERS
TOBACCO STORES & STANDS
TOBACCO: Cigarettes
TOBACCO: Cigars
TOBACCO: Smoking
TOILET SEATS: Wood
TOILETRIES, COSMETICS & PERFUME STORES
TOILETRIES, WHOLESALE: Razor Blades
TOILETRIES, WHOLESALE: Toilet Soap
TOOL & DIE STEEL
TOOLS & EQPT: Used With Sporting Arms
TOOLS: Carpenters', Including Levels & Chisels, Exc Saws
TOOLS: Hand
TOOLS: Hand, Hammers
TOOLS: Hand, Jewelers'
TOOLS: Hand, Mechanics
TOOLS: Hand, Plumbers'
TOOLS: Hand, Power
TOOTHPASTES, GELS & TOOTHPOWDERS
TOPS: Automobile, Stamped Metal
TOWELETTES: Premoistened
TOWELS: Paper
TOWERS, SECTIONS: Transmission, Radio & Television
TOWERS: Cooling, Sheet Metal
TOWING & TUGBOAT SVC
TOWING BARS & SYSTEMS
TOWING SVCS: Marine
TOYS
TOYS & HOBBY GOODS & SPLYS, WHOL: Toy Novelties & Amusements
TOYS & HOBBY GOODS & SPLYS, WHOLESALE: Arts/Crafts Eqpt/Sply
TOYS & HOBBY GOODS & SPLYS, WHOLESALE: Balloons, Novelty
TOYS & HOBBY GOODS & SPLYS, WHOLESALE: Toys & Games
TOYS & HOBBY GOODS & SPLYS, WHOLESALE: Toys, NEC
TOYS, HOBBY GOODS & SPLYS WHOLESALERS
TOYS: Dolls, Stuffed Animals & Parts
TOYS: Kites
TOYS: Video Game Machines
TRAFFIC CONTROL FLAGGING SVCS
TRAILERS & CHASSIS: Camping
TRAILERS & PARTS: Boat
TRAILERS & PARTS: Truck & Semi's
TRAILERS & TRAILER EQPT
TRAILERS OR VANS: Horse Transportation, Fifth-Wheel Type
TRAILERS: Bodies
TRAILERS: Bus, Tractor Type
TRAILERS: Demountable Cargo Containers
TRAILERS: House, Exc Permanent Dwellings
TRAILERS: Semitrailers, Truck Tractors
TRAILERS: Truck, Chassis
TRANSFORMERS: Distribution
TRANSFORMERS: Doorbell, Electric
TRANSFORMERS: Electric
TRANSFORMERS: Meters, Electronic
TRANSFORMERS: Power Related
TRANSFORMERS: Specialty
TRANSMISSIONS: Motor Vehicle
TRANSPORTATION EQPT & SPLYS, WHOLESALE: Acft/Space Vehicle
TRANSPORTATION EQPT & SPLYS, WHOLESALE: Marine Crafts/Splys
TRANSPORTATION EQPT & SPLYS, WHOLESALE: Pulleys
TRANSPORTATION EPQT & SPLYS, WHOLESALE: Tanks & Tank Compnts
TRANSPORTATION EPQT/SPLYS, WHOL: Marine Propulsn Mach/Eqpt
TRANSPORTATION EQPT & SPLYS WHOLESALERS, NEC
TRANSPORTATION EQUIPMENT, NEC
TRANSPORTATION SVCS, AIR, NONSCHEDULED: Air Cargo Carriers
TRANSPORTATION SVCS, WATER: Boat Cleaning
TRANSPORTATION SVCS, WATER: Log Rafting & Towing
TRANSPORTATION SVCS, WATER: River, Exc St Lawrence Seaway
TRANSPORTATION SVCS, WATER: Surveyors, Marine
TRANSPORTATION SVCS: Airport
TRANSPORTATION SVCS: Rental, Local
TRANSPORTATION: Air, Scheduled Passenger
TRANSPORTATION: Deep Sea Domestic Freight
TRANSPORTATION: Deep Sea Foreign Freight
TRANSPORTATION: Great Lakes Domestic Freight
TRANSPORTATION: Local Passenger, NEC
TRAPS: Animal & Fish, Wire
TRAPS: Crab, Steel
TRAPS: Stem
TRAVEL TRAILERS & CAMPERS
TRAVELER ACCOMMODATIONS, NEC
TROPHIES, PLATED, ALL METALS
TROPHIES, WHOLESALE
TROPHIES: Metal, Exc Silver
TROPHY & PLAQUE STORES
TRUCK & BUS BODIES: Automobile Wrecker Truck
TRUCK & BUS BODIES: Car Carrier
TRUCK & BUS BODIES: Dump Truck
TRUCK & BUS BODIES: Truck Beds
TRUCK & BUS BODIES: Truck, Motor Vehicle
TRUCK & BUS BODIES: Utility Truck
TRUCK & FREIGHT TERMINALS & SUPPORT ACTIVITIES
TRUCK BODIES: Body Parts
TRUCK BODY SHOP
TRUCK GENERAL REPAIR SVC
TRUCK PAINTING & LETTERING SVCS
TRUCK PARTS & ACCESSORIES: Wholesalers
TRUCKING & HAULING SVCS: Animal & Farm Prdt
TRUCKING & HAULING SVCS: Contract Basis
TRUCKING & HAULING SVCS: Garbage, Collect/Transport Only
TRUCKING & HAULING SVCS: Heavy, NEC
TRUCKING & HAULING SVCS: Lumber & Log, Local
TRUCKING & HAULING SVCS: Lumber & Timber
TRUCKING & HAULING SVCS: Machinery, Heavy
TRUCKING & HAULING SVCS: Steel, Local
TRUCKING, DUMP
TRUCKING: Except Local
TRUCKING: Local, With Storage
TRUCKING: Local, Without Storage
TRUCKS & TRACTORS: Industrial
TRUCKS: Forklift
TRUCKS: Indl
TRUNKS
TRUSSES & FRAMING: Prefabricated Metal
TRUSSES: Wood, Floor
TRUSSES: Wood, Roof
TRUST MANAGEMENT SVCS: Charitable
TUBE & TUBING FABRICATORS
TUBES: Generator, Electron Beam, Beta Ray
TUBES: Paper
TUBES: Steel & Iron
TUBES: Vacuum
TUBES: Wrought, Welded Or Lock Joint
TUBING: Flexible, Metallic
TUBING: Glass
TUBING: Plastic
TUGBOAT SVCS
TURBINES & TURBINE GENERATOR SET UNITS, COMPLETE
TURBINES & TURBINE GENERATOR SETS
TURBINES & TURBINE GENERATOR SETS & PARTS
TURBINES: Hydraulic, Complete
TWINE
TYPESETTING SVC
TYPESETTING SVC: Computer
TYPESETTING SVC: Linotype Composition, For Printing Trade
TYPOGRAPHY

U

ULTRASONIC EQPT: Cleaning, Exc Med & Dental
UMBRELLAS & CANES
UNDERCOATINGS: Paint
UNIFORM STORES
UNISEX HAIR SALONS
UNIVERSITY
UPHOLSTERY MATERIALS, BROADWOVEN
UPHOLSTERY WORK SVCS
URANIUM ORE MINING, NEC
UREA
URNS: Cut Stone
USED BOOK STORES
USED CAR DEALERS
USED MERCHANDISE STORES
USED MERCHANDISE STORES: Computers & Access
UTENSILS: Cast Aluminum, Cooking Or Kitchen
UTILITY TRAILER DEALERS

V

VACUUM CLEANERS: Household
VACUUM CLEANERS: Indl Type
VALUE-ADDED RESELLERS: Computer Systems
VALVES
VALVES & PIPE FITTINGS
VALVES: Aerosol, Metal
VALVES: Aircraft
VALVES: Aircraft, Control, Hydraulic & Pneumatic
VALVES: Aircraft, Hydraulic
VALVES: Control, Automatic
VALVES: Fire Hydrant
VALVES: Fluid Power, Control, Hydraulic & pneumatic
VALVES: Gas Cylinder, Compressed
VALVES: Indl
VALVES: Plumbing & Heating
VALVES: Regulating & Control, Automatic
VALVES: Water Works
VARIETY STORE MERCHANDISE, WHOLESALE
VARIETY STORES
VASES & URNS: Gypsum & Papier-Mache
VASES: Pottery
VAULTS & SAFES WHOLESALERS
VEHICLES: All Terrain
VEHICLES: Recreational
VENDING MACHINES & PARTS
VENETIAN BLINDS & SHADES
VENTILATING EQPT: Metal
VENTURE CAPITAL COMPANIES
VETERANS AFFAIRS ADMINISTRATION SVCS
VETERINARY PHARMACEUTICAL PREPARATIONS
VIBRATORS, ELECTRIC: Beauty & Barber Shop
VIDEO & AUDIO EQPT, WHOLESALE
VIDEO EQPT
VIDEO PRODUCTION SVCS
VIDEO TAPE WHOLESALERS, RECORDED
VIDEO TRIGGERS EXC REMOTE CONTROL TV DEVICES
VINYL RESINS, NEC
VISUAL COMMUNICATIONS SYSTEMS
VISUAL EFFECTS PRODUCTION SVCS
VITAMINS: Natural Or Synthetic, Uncompounded, Bulk
VITAMINS: Pharmaceutical Preparations
VOCATIONAL COUNSELING
VOCATIONAL REHABILITATION AGENCY
VOCATIONAL TRAINING AGENCY
VOLCANIC ROCK: Crushed & Broken

W

WALLBOARD: Gypsum
WALLPAPER & WALL COVERINGS
WALLPAPER STORE
WAREHOUSING & STORAGE FACILITIES, NEC
WAREHOUSING & STORAGE, REFRIGERATED: Cold Storage Or Refrig
WAREHOUSING & STORAGE, REFRIGERATED: Frozen Or Refrig Goods
WAREHOUSING & STORAGE: General
WAREHOUSING & STORAGE: General
WAREHOUSING & STORAGE: Miniwarehouse
WAREHOUSING & STORAGE: Refrigerated
WARM AIR HEAT & AC EQPT & SPLYS, WHOLESALE Fan, Heat & Vent
WARM AIR HEATING & AC EQPT & SPLYS, WHOL: Dust Collecting

PRODUCT INDEX

WARM AIR HEATING & AC EQPT & SPLYS, WHOL: Elec Heating Eqpt
WARM AIR HEATING & AC EQPT & SPLYS, WHOLESALE Air Filters
WARM AIR HEATING & AC EQPT & SPLYS, WHOLESALE Condensing
WARM AIR HEATING/AC EQPT/SPLYS, WHOL Warm Air Htg Eqpt/Splys
WASHERS
WASHERS: Plastic
WASTE CLEANING SVCS
WATCH REPAIR SVCS
WATCHCASES
WATCHES & PARTS, WHOLESALE
WATER HEATERS WHOLESALERS EXCEPT ELECTRIC
WATER PURIFICATION EQPT: Household
WATER PURIFICATION PRDTS: Chlorination Tablets & Kits
WATER SOFTENER SVCS
WATER SUPPLY
WATER TREATMENT EQPT: Indl
WATER: Distilled
WATER: Mineral, Carbonated, Canned & Bottled, Etc
WATER: Pasteurized & Mineral, Bottled & Canned
WATER: Pasteurized, Canned & Bottled, Etc
WATERPROOFING COMPOUNDS
WAX REMOVERS
WEATHER RELATED SVCS
WEATHER VANES
WEB SEARCH PORTALS: Internet
WEIGHING MACHINERY & APPARATUS
WELDING & CUTTING APPARATUS & ACCESS, NEC
WELDING EQPT
WELDING EQPT & SPLYS WHOLESALERS
WELDING EQPT & SPLYS: Arc Welders, Transformer-Rectifier
WELDING EQPT & SPLYS: Electrodes
WELDING EQPT & SPLYS: Generators, Arc Welding, AC & DC
WELDING EQPT & SPLYS: Resistance, Electric
WELDING EQPT REPAIR SVCS
WELDING REPAIR SVC
WELDING TIPS: Heat Resistant, Metal
WESTERN APPAREL STORES
WET CORN MILLING
WHEEL BALANCING EQPT: Automotive
WHEELCHAIR LIFTS
WHEELCHAIRS
WHEELS
WHEELS & PARTS
WHEELS, GRINDING: Artificial
WHEELS: Abrasive
WHEELS: Disc, Wheelbarrow, Stroller, Etc, Stamped Metal

WHISTLES
WIND TUNNELS
WINDMILLS: Electric Power Generation
WINDOW & DOOR FRAMES
WINDOW FRAMES & SASHES: Plastic
WINDOW FRAMES, MOLDING & TRIM: Vinyl
WINDOW FURNISHINGS WHOLESALERS
WINDOW SASHES, WOOD
WINDOWS, LOUVER: Metal
WINDOWS: Frames, Wood
WINDOWS: Wood
WINDSHIELD WIPER SYSTEMS
WINE & DISTILLED ALCOHOLIC BEVERAGES WHOLESALERS
WINE CELLARS, BONDED: Wine, Blended
WIRE
WIRE & CABLE: Aluminum
WIRE & CABLE: Nonferrous, Aircraft
WIRE & CABLE: Nonferrous, Automotive, Exc Ignition Sets
WIRE & CABLE: Nonferrous, Building
WIRE & WIRE PRDTS
WIRE FABRIC: Welded Steel
WIRE MATERIALS: Copper
WIRE MATERIALS: Steel
WIRE PRDTS: Steel & Iron
WIRE: Communication
WIRE: Mesh
WIRE: Nonferrous
WIRE: Steel, Insulated Or Armored
WIRE: Wire, Ferrous Or Iron
WOMEN'S & CHILDREN'S CLOTHING WHOLESALERS, NEC
WOMEN'S & GIRLS' SPORTSWEAR WHOLESALERS
WOMEN'S CLOTHING STORES
WOMEN'S CLOTHING STORES: Ready-To-Wear
WOMEN'S SPECIALTY CLOTHING STORES
WOMEN'S SPORTSWEAR STORES
WOOD & WOOD BY-PRDTS, WHOLESALE
WOOD CHIPS, PRODUCED AT THE MILL
WOOD EXTRACT PRDTS
WOOD PRDTS
WOOD PRDTS: Applicators
WOOD PRDTS: Barrels & Barrel Parts
WOOD PRDTS: Beekeeping Splys
WOOD PRDTS: Box Shook
WOOD PRDTS: Door Trim
WOOD PRDTS: Engraved
WOOD PRDTS: Furniture Inlays, Veneers
WOOD PRDTS: Jalousies, Glass, Wood Framed
WOOD PRDTS: Ladders & Stepladders
WOOD PRDTS: Laundry
WOOD PRDTS: Logs Of Sawdust & Wood Particles, Pressed

WOOD PRDTS: Mantels
WOOD PRDTS: Moldings, Unfinished & Prefinished
WOOD PRDTS: Mulch Or Sawdust
WOOD PRDTS: Mulch, Wood & Bark
WOOD PRDTS: Novelties, Fiber
WOOD PRDTS: Oars & Paddles
WOOD PRDTS: Outdoor, Structural
WOOD PRDTS: Panel Work
WOOD PRDTS: Poles
WOOD PRDTS: Policemen's Clubs
WOOD PRDTS: Reed, Rattan, Wicker & Willow ware, Exc Furnitr
WOOD PRDTS: Sawdust
WOOD PRDTS: Shoe & Boot Prdts
WOOD PRDTS: Signboards
WOOD PRDTS: Stoppers & Plugs
WOOD PRDTS: Survey Stakes
WOOD PRDTS: Trophy Bases
WOOD PRDTS: Window Backs, Store Or Lunchroom, Prefabricated
WOOD PRODUCTS: Reconstituted
WOOD TREATING: Bridges
WOOD TREATING: Creosoting
WOOD TREATING: Flooring, Block
WOOD TREATING: Structural Lumber & Timber
WOOD TREATING: Wood Prdts, Creosoted
WOODWORK & TRIM: Exterior & Ornamental
WOODWORK & TRIM: Interior & Ornamental
WOODWORK: Carved & Turned
WOODWORK: Interior & Ornamental, NEC
WOODWORK: Ornamental, Cornices, Mantels, Etc.
WOOL PULLING SVC
WORD PROCESSING SVCS
WOVEN WIRE PRDTS, NEC
WREATHS: Artificial
WRITING FOR PUBLICATION SVCS

X

X-RAY EQPT & TUBES

Y

YARN: Knitting, Spun
YARN: Manmade & Synthetic Fiber, Twisting Or Winding
YARN: Plastic Coated, Made From Purchased Yarn
YARNS & ROVING: Coir
YOGURT WHOLESALERS

Z

ZINC ORE MINING

PRODUCT SECTION

Product category → **BOXES: Folding**
Edgar & Son Paperboard ....G...... 999 999-9999
  Yourtown *(G-11480)*
Ready Box Co.............................E...... 999 999-9999
  Anytown *(G-7097)*
City

Indicates approximate employment figure
A = Over 500 employees, B = 251-500
C = 101-250, D = 51-100, E = 20-50
F = 10-19, G = 2-9
Business phone
Geographic Section entry number where full company information appears.

See footnotes for symbols and codes identification.
• Refer to the Industrial Product Index preceding this section to locate product headings.

ABRASIVES

Lapo Inc ....G....... 360 314-4546
  Vancouver *(G-14359)*
Pro Abrasives Inc.............................G....... 360 509-4152
  Bremerton *(G-1990)*
Radiac Abrasives Inc......................D....... 360 659-6201
  Marysville *(G-6375)*

ABRASIVES: Diamond Powder

Mt Baker Powder Coating ....G....... 360 366-3233
  Bellingham *(G-1449)*

ACCELERATION INDICATORS & SYSTEM COMPONENTS: Aerospace

Aero-Space Port Intl Group Inc ....G....... 425 264-1000
  Renton *(G-8729)*
Electrijet Research Foundation ....G....... 509 990-9474
  Greenacres *(G-4297)*
Kgr Corporation ....G....... 360 403-7330
  Arlington *(G-266)*
Roberts Precision Machine Inc..........F....... 360 805-1000
  Monroe *(G-6615)*
RTC Aerospace - Fife Div Inc ....D....... 253 922-3806
  Fife *(G-3987)*
Sakco Precision Inc..........................G....... 253 288-9702
  Auburn *(G-555)*

ACCELERATORS: Particle, High Voltage

Interworld Elec Cmpt Inds Inc ....G....... 425 223-4311
  Point Roberts *(G-7668)*

ACCOMMODATION LOCATING SVCS

Deming Log Show Inc ....G....... 360 592-3051
  Bellingham *(G-1322)*

ACCOUNTING MACHINES & CASH REGISTERS

D S Thermal ....G....... 206 789-2271
  Seattle *(G-9782)*

ACCOUNTING SVCS, NEC

Nora Haugan....................................G....... 360 877-0602
  Lilliwaup *(G-5872)*

ACCOUNTING SVCS: Certified Public

John H Wolf CPA PC ....G....... 509 465-9165
  Spokane *(G-12338)*

ACIDS: Sulfuric, Oleum

Chemtrade Chemicals US LLC ....E....... 360 299-1560
  Anacortes *(G-111)*

ACTUATORS: Indl, NEC

J Bozeat & Associates LLC................G....... 206 937-5719
  Seattle *(G-10267)*

ADDITIVE BASED PLASTIC MATERIALS: Plasticizers

Mapletex Inc ....G....... 253 572-3608
  Tacoma *(G-13399)*

ADHESIVES

Adhesive Products Inc ....F....... 206 762-7459
  Seattle *(G-9352)*
Advanced Adhesive..........................G....... 360 373-1156
  Bremerton *(G-1934)*
Atwood Adhesives Inc......................G....... 206 762-7455
  Seattle *(G-9460)*
Evans Adhesives Corporation............G....... 614 410-6027
  Camas *(G-2250)*
HB Fuller Company..........................E....... 360 574-8828
  Vancouver *(G-14288)*
Westech Aerosol Corporation............E....... 206 930-9291
  Suquamish *(G-13150)*
Western Adhesive Solutions.............G....... 360 904-5005
  Brush Prairie *(G-2043)*

ADHESIVES & SEALANTS

Atacs Products Inc ....F....... 206 433-9000
  Seattle *(G-9449)*
Atlas Supply Inc...............................G....... 509 924-2417
  Spokane Valley *(G-12628)*
Blue Seal Inc...................................G....... 360 568-2098
  Lynnwood *(G-6084)*
Building Envlope Innvtions LLC.........G....... 206 985-3788
  Seattle *(G-9597)*

ADVERTISING AGENCIES

B & D Advertising Prtg & Svc ....G....... 206 542-3262
  Shoreline *(G-11758)*
Bensussen Deutsch & Assoc LLC ......B....... 425 492-6111
  Woodinville *(G-15188)*
Brecht-Pacific Publishing Inc ....E....... 360 425-4671
  Longview *(G-5890)*
Devaul Publishing Inc.......................E....... 360 748-3335
  Chehalis *(G-2489)*
Prime West of Washington Inc ....E....... 360 424-5783
  Kent *(G-5081)*
Richard Saunders ....G....... 612 861-1061
  Seattle *(G-10962)*
Shepp Enterprises LLC ....G....... 206 697-0327
  Tacoma *(G-13512)*
Target Media Partners ....F....... 509 662-1405
  Wenatchee *(G-15078)*
Washington Media Services Inc ....G....... 360 754-4543
  Olympia *(G-7421)*
Zango Inc ....C....... 425 279-1200
  Bellevue *(G-1232)*

ADVERTISING AGENCIES: Consultants

Pacific Printing Inc...........................G....... 360 377-0844
  Bremerton *(G-1984)*

ADVERTISING CURTAINS

Grigg Farms LLC..............................E....... 509 787-3225
  Quincy *(G-8299)*
Jensen Seed Farm Inc ....G....... 509 896-2312
  Bickleton *(G-1632)*
Mollys Salads LLC ....G....... 206 512-3075
  Seattle *(G-10558)*
Northwest Wholesale Inc ....D....... 509 662-3563
  Wenatchee *(G-15092)*

ADVERTISING DISPLAY PRDTS

Bayside EMB & Screenprint..............G....... 253 565-1521
  Tacoma *(G-13191)*
Skyline International LLC..................E....... 206 624-1874
  Seattle *(G-11133)*

ADVERTISING MATERIAL DISTRIBUTION

Northwest Pioneer Inc......................D....... 253 872-9693
  Kent *(G-5034)*
Noteadscom Inc ....G....... 360 705-4548
  Lacey *(G-5569)*

ADVERTISING REPRESENTATIVES: Electronic Media

Avalonphilly LLC..............................G....... 800 405-7024
  Bellevue *(G-800)*
Hollywood Triangle Productions ....G....... 323 301-3003
  Seattle *(G-10179)*

ADVERTISING REPRESENTATIVES: Magazine

Crave Magazine...............................G....... 360 991-9332
  Vancouver *(G-14152)*
Family Values Mag Clark Cnty ....G....... 360 909-5945
  Vancouver *(G-14221)*

ADVERTISING REPRESENTATIVES: Media

Ron Hall ....G....... 360 468-2294
  Lopez Island *(G-5986)*

ADVERTISING REPRESENTATIVES: Newspaper

El Mundo Communications Inc ....G....... 509 663-5737
  Wenatchee *(G-15029)*
Seattle Times Company ....C....... 509 248-1251
  Yakima *(G-15670)*
Target Media Partners ....C....... 509 328-5555
  Spokane Valley *(G-12900)*
Yakima Herald-Republic Inc.............C....... 509 452-7355
  Yakima *(G-15716)*

ADVERTISING REPRESENTATIVES: Printed Media

Sauther & Assoc Inc........................E....... 509 922-7828
  Liberty Lake *(G-5858)*

ADVERTISING SPECIALTIES, WHOLESALE

American Image Displays ....F....... 425 556-9511
  Port Orchard *(G-7786)*
Arctic Circle Holdings LLC ....G....... 206 625-9226
  Seattle *(G-9422)*
Athletic Awards Company Inc ....G....... 206 624-3995
  Seattle *(G-9452)*
Bensussen Deutsch & Assoc LLC ......B....... 425 492-6111
  Woodinville *(G-15188)*
Bergen Screen Print ....G....... 509 965-2511
  Yakima *(G-15519)*
Envision Custom EMB & Designs .....G....... 360 693-2588
  Vancouver *(G-14204)*
Go Usa Inc ....E....... 509 662-3387
  Wenatchee *(G-15034)*
Jackyes Enterprises Inc...................G....... 425 355-5997
  Everett *(G-3521)*
Jmh Enterprises..............................G....... 509 628-2191
  Richland *(G-9015)*
Lasting Impressions Inc...................G....... 360 659-1255
  Marysville *(G-6353)*
Mattress Makers Incorporated..........F....... 253 984-1730
  Tacoma *(G-13401)*
Northstar Investment Co ....G....... 360 297-2260
  Kingston *(G-5258)*

ADVERTISING SPECIALTIES, WHOLESALE

Printcom Inc ....F 206 763-7600
  Burien *(G-2121)*
Signs Now of Moses Lake Inc..................G...... 509 765-8955
  Moses Lake *(G-6750)*
Tru Line Laser Alignment Inc..................G...... 360 371-0552
  Blaine *(G-1708)*

ADVERTISING SVCS, NEC

Wild Horse Graphics..................................G...... 425 413-5080
  Maple Valley *(G-6300)*

ADVERTISING SVCS: Coupon Distribution

Dualos LLC ....G...... 253 750-5125
  Tacoma *(G-13266)*
Karlas Hand Bindery Inc ....E 206 405-3350
  Seattle *(G-10328)*
Seatac Automotive ....G...... 253 839-0309
  Kent *(G-5121)*

ADVERTISING SVCS: Direct Mail

Alphaprint Inc ....G...... 425 771-1140
  Lynnwood *(G-6073)*
Copy-Rite Inc ....G...... 509 624-8503
  Spokane *(G-12200)*
Direct Connect Group (dcg) LLC............B...... 206 784-6892
  Seattle *(G-9833)*
EE Printing LLC ....G...... 425 656-1250
  Kent *(G-4885)*
Graphics Place Inc ....F 425 486-3323
  Woodinville *(G-15255)*
Kp LLC ....C 425 204-6355
  Renton *(G-8838)*
Mediamax ....G...... 509 627-2358
  Richland *(G-9026)*
Snohomish Publishing Company............E 206 523-7548
  Snohomish *(G-11983)*
Sudden Printing Inc ....E 206 243-4444
  Seattle *(G-11211)*

ADVERTISING SVCS: Display

American Image Displays ....F 425 556-9511
  Port Orchard *(G-7786)*
Fastsigns International Inc ....G...... 253 835-9450
  Federal Way *(G-3737)*
Meyer Sign & Advertising Co..................F 360 424-1325
  Mount Vernon *(G-6813)*
Prime West of Washington Inc ....E 360 424-5783
  Kent *(G-5081)*
Sunbacker Fiberglass Inc ....G...... 360 794-5547
  Monroe *(G-6628)*

ADVERTISING SVCS: Outdoor

Mustang Signs LLC ....F 509 735-4607
  Kennewick *(G-4698)*
OMega Graphics and Signs LLC............G...... 206 789-5480
  Seattle *(G-10697)*
X Products LLC ....E 971 302-6127
  Vancouver *(G-14701)*

ADVERTISING SVCS: Transit

Showcase Specialties Inc ....G...... 509 547-3344
  Pasco *(G-7629)*

ADVERTISING: Aerial

Sky Signs Inc..G...... 425 417-9063
  Renton *(G-8913)*

AERIAL WORK PLATFORMS

Genie Manufacturing Inc ....A 425 881-1800
  Redmond *(G-8475)*
Genie Manufacturing Inc ....C 509 762-3200
  Moses Lake *(G-6712)*
Washington Eqp Mfg Co Inc ....E 509 244-4773
  Spokane *(G-12583)*

AEROSOLS

Homax Group Inc ....E 360 733-9029
  Bellingham *(G-1371)*

AGENTS & MANAGERS: Entertainers

Ultra Van Krome Prductions LLC..........G...... 206 859-3459
  Tacoma *(G-13568)*

AGENTS, BROKERS & BUREAUS: Personal Service

Island Blueback Inc ....G...... 360 385-0871
  Port Townsend *(G-7892)*
Machstem Inc ....G...... 801 259-3305
  Nine Mile Falls *(G-7078)*
Nu Element Inc ....G...... 206 356-4525
  Tacoma *(G-13437)*
Shoezandmorecom LLC ....F 216 544-1745
  Renton *(G-8911)*

AGRICULTURAL CHEMICALS: Trace Elements

Truhumic Envmtl Solutions LLC ....G...... 425 232-6903
  Marysville *(G-6397)*

AGRICULTURAL DISINFECTANTS

Agrasyst Inc ....F 509 467-2167
  Spokane *(G-12103)*
Custom Chemicals Co Inc ....F 509 349-7000
  Warden *(G-14930)*

AGRICULTURAL EQPT: BARN, SILO, POULTRY, DAIRY/LIVESTOCK MACH

Suberizer Inc ....G...... 425 747-8900
  Bellevue *(G-1164)*

AGRICULTURAL EQPT: Dusters, Mechanical

Hahn Manufacturing Inc ....G...... 509 930-1621
  Yakima *(G-15580)*

AGRICULTURAL EQPT: Elevators, Farm

Anderson Machinery Inc ....G...... 509 964-2225
  Thorp *(G-13626)*

AGRICULTURAL EQPT: Fertilizng, Sprayng, Dustng/Irrigatn Mach

Agri-Trac Inc ....G...... 509 265-4327
  Mesa *(G-6490)*

AGRICULTURAL EQPT: Grade, Clean & Sort Machines, Fruit/Veg

CCS Equipment Inc ....E 509 248-4001
  Union Gap *(G-13925)*
GP Graders LLC ....F 253 239-3727
  East Wenatchee *(G-3016)*
Nolan & Sons Northwest Inc..................G...... 509 658-2604
  Naches *(G-7000)*
Packing House Services Inc ....G...... 509 452-5002
  Union Gap *(G-13948)*

AGRICULTURAL EQPT: Harvesters, Fruit, Vegetable, Tobacco

De Kleine Machine Company LLC........G...... 509 832-1108
  Prosser *(G-8038)*
Furford Picker Co ....G...... 360 267-3303
  Grayland *(G-4294)*
Korvan Industries Inc ....D...... 360 354-1500
  Lynden *(G-6029)*
Northwest Wildfoods Co Inc ....G...... 360 757-7940
  Burlington *(G-2176)*
Perrault Manufacturing Inc ....G...... 509 248-9905
  Moxee *(G-6884)*

AGRICULTURAL EQPT: Haying Mach, Mowers, Rakes, Stackers, Etc

Mikes Rental Machinery Inc ....E 509 925-6126
  Ellensburg *(G-3215)*

AGRICULTURAL EQPT: Irrigation Eqpt, Self-Propelled

Custom Technology Co Inc......................F 509 965-3333
  Yakima *(G-15546)*
Irrigation Accessories Co ....F 360 896-9440
  Vancouver *(G-14324)*
Isaacs & Associates Inc ....G...... 509 529-2286
  Walla Walla *(G-14825)*
Travis Pattern & Foundry Inc ....B...... 509 466-3545
  Spokane *(G-12566)*

AGRICULTURAL EQPT: Loaders, Manure & General Utility

All Pole Corporation ....F 360 933-1806
  Blaine *(G-1658)*
Town of Garfield..G...... 509 635-1604
  Garfield *(G-4069)*

AGRICULTURAL EQPT: Tractors, Farm

EFC Equipment LLC ....G...... 509 713-7230
  Richland *(G-8992)*
Eldred Bros Farms LLC ....G...... 360 398-9757
  Bellingham *(G-1332)*
Frog Creek Co ....G...... 509 276-6467
  Deer Park *(G-2903)*

AGRICULTURAL EQPT: Trailers & Wagons, Farm

REA Services Inc ....F 509 394-2305
  Touchet *(G-13677)*

AGRICULTURAL EQPT: Troughs, Water

Backwoods ....G...... 509 826-0758
  OMAK *(G-7434)*

AGRICULTURAL EQPT: Turf & Grounds Eqpt

US Mower Inc ....F 360 757-7555
  Burlington *(G-2198)*

AGRICULTURAL MACHINERY & EQPT REPAIR

AG Enterprise Supply Inc ....F 509 235-2006
  Cheney *(G-2575)*
Cannon Engineering Solutions ....G...... 360 840-6731
  Port Townsend *(G-7871)*
Hahn Manufacturing Inc ....G...... 509 930-1621
  Yakima *(G-15580)*
Prathers Welding & Fabrication ....G...... 509 632-5321
  Coulee City *(G-2805)*

AGRICULTURAL MACHINERY & EQPT: Wholesalers

Kemps Machine Co ....F 509 784-1326
  Yakima *(G-15606)*
Mikes Rental Machinery Inc ....E 509 925-6126
  Ellensburg *(G-3215)*
Rathbun Iron Works Inc ....G...... 509 865-3717
  Toppenish *(G-13671)*
Spray Center Electronics Inc ....G...... 509 838-2209
  Spokane *(G-12523)*

AGRICULTURAL PROGRAM REGULATION OFFICES, GOVERNMENT: State

Fruit Commission Wash State ....E 509 453-4837
  Yakima *(G-15574)*

AIR CLEANING SYSTEMS

All-Pro Services Ran LLC ....G...... 425 746-4829
  Redmond *(G-8379)*
Lawrence Enterprises...............................G...... 360 750-8551
  Vancouver *(G-14366)*
Omnitec Design Inc ....F 425 290-3922
  Mukilteo *(G-6960)*

AIR CONDITIONERS: Motor Vehicle

Red DOT Corporation ....B...... 206 151-3840
  Tukwila *(G-13803)*

AIR CONDITIONING & VENTILATION EQPT & SPLYS: Wholesales

Wescold Inc ....E 206 284-5710
  Seattle *(G-11449)*

AIR CONDITIONING EQPT

Trane US Inc ....F 509 535-9057
  Spokane Valley *(G-12910)*

PRODUCT SECTION

AIRCRAFT CONTROL SYSTEMS: Electronic Totalizing Counters

AIR CONDITIONING EQPT, WHOLE HOUSE: Wholesalers

Refrigeration Supplies Distr ....G...... 503 234-4334
 Vancouver *(G-14540)*

AIR CONDITIONING UNITS: Complete, Domestic Or Indl

Usnr LLC..G...... 360 225-8267
 Woodland *(G-15470)*
Whirlpool Corporation.............................E...... 253 875-7100
 Spanaway *(G-12081)*

AIR MATTRESSES: Plastic

Cascade Designs Inc ....B...... 206 505-9500
 Seattle *(G-9640)*

AIR POLLUTION CONTROL EQPT & SPLYS WHOLESALERS

Direct Contact LLC ....E...... 425 235-1723
 Tukwila *(G-13725)*
Dust Control Technologies Inc ....G...... 360 256-2479
 Brush Prairie *(G-2033)*

AIR PURIFICATION EQPT

Computer Systems Sales & Svcs...........G...... 206 979-1731
 Kent *(G-4859)*
Mpm Technologies Inc ....G...... 973 599-4416
 Spokane Valley *(G-12795)*
Raring Corporation..................................G...... 360 892-1659
 Vancouver *(G-14533)*

AIR TRAFFIC CONTROL SYSTEMS & EQPT

Innov8 Cabin Solutions LLC ....G...... 425 241-8378
 Sammamish *(G-9220)*

AIRCRAFT & AEROSPACE FLIGHT INSTRUMENTS & GUIDANCE SYSTEMS

Aaco Incorporated ....G...... 206 722-1571
 Seattle *(G-9329)*
Aeries Enterprises LLC ....G...... 425 739-9997
 Kirkland *(G-5273)*
Aircraft Solutions LLC.............................G...... 509 838-8883
 Spokane *(G-12105)*
Applewhite Aero LLC ....G...... 206 762-5285
 Seattle *(G-9412)*
Applied Navigation LLC ....G...... 503 329-3126
 Bothell *(G-1821)*
Bae Systems Controls Inc......................E...... 607 770-2000
 Redmond *(G-8396)*
Cascade Family Flyers ....G...... 425 750-4249
 Snohomish *(G-11886)*
Eaton Corporation ....G...... 425 451-4954
 Bellevue *(G-890)*
Eldec Corporation....................................A...... 425 743-1313
 Lynnwood *(G-6114)*
Epi Inc ....G...... 360 247-5858
 Amboy *(G-92)*
Esterline Europe Company LLC ....G...... 425 453-9400
 Bellevue *(G-900)*
King Aerospace Inc ....G...... 360 257-6610
 Oak Harbor *(G-7155)*
Maren-Go Solutions Corporation ....G...... 217 506-2749
 Vancouver *(G-14393)*
Pacific Aircraft Modifications ....G...... 360 403-7282
 Arlington *(G-297)*
Pacific NW Arospc Aliance ....G...... 425 885-0290
 Redmond *(G-8607)*
Random Walk Group LLC ....G...... 206 724-3621
 Olympia *(G-7377)*
Soniq Aerospace LP ....G...... 253 750-4592
 Pacific *(G-7540)*
Spectralux Corporation............................D...... 425 285-3000
 Redmond *(G-8678)*
Stratodata LLC ....G...... 425 623-0094
 Carnation *(G-2299)*
Stresswave Inc ....G...... 253 259-8796
 Tukwila *(G-13823)*
Volant Aerospace Holdings LLC............G...... 360 757-2376
 Burlington *(G-2199)*
Zodiac Aerospace ....G...... 360 653-2600
 Arlington *(G-350)*

AIRCRAFT & HEAVY EQPT REPAIR SVCS

Aero Controls Inc ....C...... 253 269-3000
 Auburn *(G-364)*
Flying Wrench Svc ....F...... 360 638-0044
 Kingston *(G-5251)*
Pape Machinery Inc ....F...... 360 575-9959
 Kelso *(G-4541)*
Spokane Forklift Cnstr Eqp Inc ....G...... 509 868-5962
 Spokane *(G-12518)*

AIRCRAFT ASSEMBLY PLANTS

Air Technics..G...... 425 316-0587
 Everett *(G-3364)*
AR Northwest..G...... 425 485-9000
 Bothell *(G-1748)*
Barefoote Concrete Inc ....G...... 509 879-3736
 Spokane Valley *(G-12636)*
Bcb Enterprises LLC ....G...... 360 435-1047
 Arlington *(G-210)*
Boeing Arospc Operations Inc ....G...... 253 773-9906
 Puyallup *(G-8132)*
Boeing China Inc.....................................G...... 206 655-2121
 Tukwila *(G-13699)*
Boeing Co ....G...... 206 351-8601
 Des Moines *(G-2931)*
Boeing Commercial Airplane...................E...... 425 237-2019
 Everett *(G-3394)*
Boeing Commercial Airplanes ....G...... 206 662-9615
 Seatac *(G-9275)*
Boeing Company ....E...... 312 544-2000
 Kent *(G-4818)*
Boeing Company ....E...... 206 655-9974
 Tukwila *(G-13700)*
Boeing Company ....G...... 425 266-0616
 Mukilteo *(G-6900)*
Boeing Company ....F...... 312 544-2000
 Bellevue *(G-821)*
Boeing Company ....G...... 206 544-2374
 Renton *(G-8758)*
Boeing Company ....G...... 253 657-0675
 Seatac *(G-9277)*
Boeing Company ....A...... 253 872-5545
 Kent *(G-4819)*
Boeing Company ....G...... 206 544-4524
 Tukwila *(G-13702)*
Boeing Company ....A...... 206 655-1131
 Tukwila *(G-13703)*
Boeing Company ....E...... 206 655-2121
 Tukwila *(G-13704)*
Boeing Company ....G...... 206 544-9246
 Tukwila *(G-13705)*
Boeing Company Incorporated ....E...... 425 965-4300
 Tukwila *(G-13706)*
Boeing Domestic Sales Corp..................G...... 206 655-2121
 Tukwila *(G-13707)*
Boeing Employees Flying Assn ....G...... 425 271-2332
 Renton *(G-8763)*
Cadence Aerospace LLC........................G...... 425 353-0405
 Everett *(G-3407)*
Carbon Aerospace ....G...... 206 697-3832
 Seattle *(G-9627)*
Commet Precision Products ....G...... 360 403-7600
 Arlington *(G-220)*
Composite Aircraft Tech LLC..................G...... 360 864-6271
 Toledo *(G-13636)*
Conachen Aviation...................................G...... 360 516-7740
 Sequim *(G-11618)*
Cub Crafters Services LLC ....F...... 509 248-1025
 Yakima *(G-15543)*
Eaton Corporation ....G...... 425 451-4954
 Bellevue *(G-890)*
Forged Chaos LLC..................................G...... 360 630-1947
 Arlington *(G-237)*
General Aerospace Inc ....G...... 425 422-5462
 Lynnwood *(G-6127)*
Glasair Aviation LLC ....G...... 360 435-8533
 Arlington *(G-240)*
Glasair Aviation Usa LLC ....E...... 360 435-8533
 Arlington *(G-241)*
Grace AVI & Logistics Support ....G...... 425 269-9424
 Sammamish *(G-9210)*
Helipower Helicopter Inc ....G...... 425 232-0972
 Lynnwood *(G-6134)*
Independent Aero Space Svcs ....G...... 702 237-9953
 Kent *(G-4949)*
Kenmore Air Harbor Inc ....D...... 425 486-3224
 Kenmore *(G-4587)*
Kit Planes Northwest ....G...... 360 403-0679
 Arlington *(G-267)*

Kono Fixed Income Fund 1511 LP.........F...... 360 686-7688
 Bellevue *(G-972)*
Left Full Rudder Aerospace LLC ....G...... 516 330-0633
 Woodinville *(G-15287)*
Lehenengo Aerospace Inc ....G...... 425 256-1376
 Kirkland *(G-5386)*
Lfr Aerospace ....G...... 516 330-0633
 Kirkland *(G-5388)*
Lockheed Martin Corporation..................G...... 360 779-4682
 Poulsbo *(G-7976)*
Lockheed Martin Corporation..................G...... 360 779-4682
 Poulsbo *(G-7977)*
Loki Aerospace Incorporated ....G...... 425 361-2353
 Brier *(G-2021)*
Merlyn Products Inc................................F...... 509 838-7500
 Spokane *(G-12390)*
Monroe Machined Products Inc ....E...... 206 242-4898
 Seatac *(G-9291)*
Morgan Aerospace LLC...........................F...... 360 435-9755
 Arlington *(G-284)*
Nexus Aerospace.....................................G...... 253 797-0700
 Federal Way *(G-3762)*
Northwing Uninsured Ultralight................F...... 509 682-4359
 Chelan *(G-2561)*
Page Aerospace Inc ....G...... 425 650-1459
 Kirkland *(G-5426)*
Pyramis Aerospace LLC ....G...... 206 407-3406
 Federal Way *(G-3774)*
RAC Aviation Services LLC ....G...... 360 256-6698
 Vancouver *(G-14529)*
Rjh Aerospace NW ....G...... 425 394-3775
 Cle Elum *(G-2677)*
Sandy Jo Franks ....G...... 206 367-2669
 Lake Forest Park *(G-5624)*
Seaplane Landing Area (wa13)...............G...... 360 647-7839
 Bellingham *(G-1529)*
Senior Operations LLC ....G...... 360 403-2283
 Arlington *(G-323)*
Shields Aerospace Services LLC ....G...... 425 240-6079
 Edmonds *(G-3155)*
Simple Intelligence LLC ....G...... 425 418-9803
 Pullman *(G-8109)*
Soloy LLC ....E...... 360 754-7000
 Tumwater *(G-13898)*
Spectech Aerospace LLC........................G...... 425 286-1101
 Bothell *(G-1795)*
Stewarts Hanger 21 Inc ....G...... 509 782-3626
 Cashmere *(G-2330)*
Sunbird Aerospace ....G...... 425 241-8594
 Bellevue *(G-1166)*
Thyssenkrupp Materials LLC..................G...... 253 239-6023
 Auburn *(G-581)*
Topcub Aircraft LLC.................................G...... 401 209-4756
 Arlington *(G-339)*
Triumph Aerostructures LLC ....G...... 310 355-3826
 Longview *(G-5961)*
Up4u Inc ....G...... 206 660-8498
 Olympia *(G-7417)*
Vectored Solutions Inc ....G...... 425 355-8038
 Everett *(G-3649)*
Western Avionics Inc ....G...... 509 534-7371
 Spokane *(G-12585)*
X L F Aerospace LLC ....G...... 206 592-2249
 Seatac *(G-9312)*
Zero Gravity Bldrs Studio LLC ....G...... 509 942-8439
 Richland *(G-9057)*
Ztron Labs Inc ....G...... 425 289-8794
 Snohomish *(G-12003)*

AIRCRAFT CLEANING & JANITORIAL SVCS

Cascade Flying Service LLC..................G...... 509 635-1212
 Garfield *(G-4067)*
REM & AES LLC ....G...... 580 284-3410
 Puyallup *(G-8236)*

AIRCRAFT CONTROL SYSTEMS:

Eldec Corporation....................................G...... 425 882-3100
 Redmond *(G-8447)*
Esterline Technologies Corp ....E...... 425 453-9400
 Bellevue *(G-902)*
Triumph Actuation Systems ....B...... 509 248-5000
 Yakima *(G-15696)*

AIRCRAFT CONTROL SYSTEMS: Electronic Totalizing Counters

Nat Seattle Inc ....E...... 425 424-3370
 Bothell *(G-1878)*

AIRCRAFT DEALERS   PRODUCT SECTION

AIRCRAFT DEALERS

Kenmore Air Harbor Inc .... D 425 486-3224
   Kenmore *(G-4587)*
Pyramis Aerospace LLC .... G 206 407-3406
   Federal Way *(G-3774)*

AIRCRAFT ENGINES & ENGINE PARTS: Air Scoops

Omohundro Co Kitsap Composites ...... D 360 519-3047
   Port Orchard *(G-7837)*
Precision Engines LLC .... D 425 347-2800
   Everett *(G-3584)*

AIRCRAFT ENGINES & ENGINE PARTS: Cooling Systems

Coolpc Incorporated .... G 425 821-6400
   Kirkland *(G-5313)*

AIRCRAFT ENGINES & ENGINE PARTS: Engine Heaters

Universal Engine Heater Co .... G 509 276-5923
   Nine Mile Falls *(G-7084)*

AIRCRAFT ENGINES & ENGINE PARTS: Exhaust Systems

Belair Composites Inc .... F 509 482-0442
   Spokane *(G-12144)*

AIRCRAFT ENGINES & ENGINE PARTS: Mount Parts

Double D Mfg LLC .... G 206 954-8099
   Marysville *(G-6331)*
Gms Procurement LLC .... G 253 852-6552
   Auburn *(G-453)*

AIRCRAFT ENGINES & ENGINE PARTS: Research & Development, Mfr

ADI Solar Corporation .... G 206 484-2879
   Monroe *(G-6542)*
Falcon Rennissance Systems Inc .... G 360 378-3900
   Friday Harbor *(G-4044)*
Mr Rpm LLC .... G 360 387-2272
   Camano Island *(G-2218)*
Tethers Unlimited Inc .... G 425 486-0100
   Bothell *(G-1800)*

AIRCRAFT ENGINES & PARTS

Aeroform Inc .... E 360 403-1919
   Arlington *(G-195)*
Associated Aircraft & Mar Svcs .... G 253 631-3082
   Kent *(G-4794)*
Bspace Corporation .... G 208 559-7806
   Seattle *(G-9591)*
Cascade Arcft Conversions LLC .... G 509 635-1212
   Garfield *(G-4066)*
Cascade Flying Service LLC .... G 509 635-1212
   Garfield *(G-4067)*
CFI Blue Sky II LLC .... E 253 627-1903
   Sumner *(G-13058)*
David Olson Honeywell Arspc .... G 509 321-7368
   Spokane *(G-12220)*
Doyon Technical Services LLC .... G 253 344-5300
   Federal Way *(G-3732)*
Elmo Fokker Inc .... E 253 395-2652
   Sumner *(G-13068)*
Exotic Metals Forming Co LLC .... B 253 220-5900
   Kent *(G-4900)*
General Electric Company 253 351-2200
   Auburn *(G-448)*
Honeywell International Inc .... B 425 885-3711
   Redmond *(G-8496)*
Honeywell International Inc .... A 509 534-5226
   Spokane Valley *(G-12732)*
Honeywell International Inc .... A 760 339-5592
   Renton *(G-8819)*
Honeywell International Inc .... E 425 921-4598
   Lynnwood *(G-6135)*
Honeywell International Inc .... G 425 413-2453
   Maple Valley *(G-6273)*
Honeywell International Inc .... G 360 253-8100
   Mercer Island *(G-6466)*
Honeywell International Inc .... G 253 966-0203
   Lewis Mcchord *(G-5820)*
Honeywell International Inc .... G 425 885-8944
   Redmond *(G-8497)*
Honeywell International Inc .... G 425 885-3711
   Redmond *(G-8498)*
Honeywell International Inc .... A 425 885-3711
   Redmond *(G-8499)*
Honeywell International Inc .... A 425 885-3711
   Redmond *(G-8500)*
Kurtisfactor LLC .... G 208 863-6180
   Tacoma *(G-13379)*
Luma Technologies LLC .... F 425 643-4000
   Bellevue *(G-990)*
Merlyn Products Inc .... F 509 838-7500
   Spokane *(G-12390)*
Norfil LLC .... E 253 863-5888
   Pacific *(G-7534)*
Pmw Capital Inc .... G 253 272-5119
   Tacoma *(G-13468)*
Precision Airmotive LLC .... E 360 659-7348
   Marysville *(G-6371)*
Precision Machine Works Inc .... C 253 272-5119
   Tacoma *(G-13474)*
Rentiel Precision Laser Cutng .... G 253 297-2823
   Tacoma *(G-13494)*
Safran Usa Inc .... E 425 462-8613
   Bellevue *(G-1112)*
Skein Integrated Systems LLC .... D 586 795-2000
   Everett *(G-3613)*
Triumph Actuation Systems .... B 509 248-5000
   Yakima *(G-15696)*
Triumph Composite Systems Inc .... B 509 623-8536
   Spokane *(G-12570)*

AIRCRAFT EQPT & SPLYS WHOLESALERS

Aero Controls Inc .... C 253 269-3000
   Auburn *(G-364)*
Aviation Spares & Svcs Intl Co .... F 425 869-7799
   Redmond *(G-8393)*
Composite Solutions Corp .... D 253 833-1878
   Sumner *(G-13060)*
Marketing Masters Inc .... F 425 454-5610
   Issaquah *(G-4445)*
Safran Usa Inc .... E 425 462-8613
   Bellevue *(G-1112)*
Seaton Engineering Corporation .... G 509 290-5919
   Spokane *(G-12495)*
Toussint Machine and Mfg LLC .... G 360 840-0705
   Sedro Woolley *(G-11576)*

AIRCRAFT FLIGHT INSTRUMENT REPAIR SVCS

Aircraft Solutions LLC .... G 509 838-8883
   Spokane *(G-12105)*
Honeywell International Inc .... C 425 251-9511
   Renton *(G-8820)*

AIRCRAFT FLIGHT INSTRUMENTS

Redwood Instrument Co .... G 360 446-2860
   Rainier *(G-8321)*

AIRCRAFT FUELING SVCS

Advanced Fuel Systems .... G 425 526-7566
   Fall City *(G-3698)*

AIRCRAFT LIGHTING

B/E Aerospace Inc .... B 425 923-2700
   Everett *(G-3381)*
Idd Aerospace Corp .... C 425 885-0617
   Redmond *(G-8505)*

AIRCRAFT MAINTENANCE & REPAIR SVCS

Heatcon Inc .... D 206 575-0815
   Tukwila *(G-13745)*
Interntnal Arospc Coatings Inc .... D 509 321-0342
   Spokane *(G-12325)*
Parkwater Aviation Inc .... F 509 536-1969
   Spokane *(G-12430)*
Petrichor Industries LLC 425 454-8281
   Bellevue *(G-1073)*
Soloy LLC .... E 360 754-7000
   Tumwater *(G-13898)*

AIRCRAFT PARTS & AUX EQPT: Panel Assy/Hydro Prop Test Stands

Idd Aerospace Corp .... C 425 885-0617
   Redmond *(G-8505)*

AIRCRAFT PARTS & AUXILIARY EQPT: Aircraft Training Eqpt

Parkwater Aviation Inc .... F 509 536-1969
   Spokane *(G-12430)*

AIRCRAFT PARTS & AUXILIARY EQPT: Assys, Subassemblies/Parts

A & M Prcsion Msuring Svcs Inc .... F 425 432-7554
   Kent *(G-4750)*
Aim Aerospace Inc .... C 425 235-2750
   Renton *(G-8732)*
Aim Aerospace Auburn Inc .... C 253 804-3355
   Auburn *(G-365)*
Aim Aerospace Sumner Inc .... C 253 804-3355
   Auburn *(G-366)*
Aim Aerospace Sumner Inc .... C 253 863-7868
   Sumner *(G-13054)*
Airworthness Drctive Solutions .... G 425 876-9742
   Mukilteo *(G-6891)*
Bogert Aviation Inc .... G 509 736-1513
   Pasco *(G-7554)*
Composite Solutions Corp .... D 253 833-1878
   Sumner *(G-13060)*
Esterline International Co .... G 425 453-9400
   Bellevue *(G-901)*
Esterline Technologies Corp .... G 253 796-4527
   Kent *(G-4897)*
Esterline Technologies Corp .... E 425 453-9400
   Bellevue *(G-902)*
Exotic Metals Forming Co LLC .... B 253 220-5900
   Kent *(G-4900)*
G B C Enterprises Inc .... G 360 275-3522
   Tahuya *(G-13610)*
Gcm North American Arospc LLC ...... D 253 872-7488
   Algona *(G-69)*
GE Aviation Systems LLC .... C 206 662-2934
   Tukwila *(G-13737)*
Hirschler Mfg Inc .... E 425 827-9384
   Kirkland *(G-5358)*
Icarus Aero Components LLC .... G 386 299-0529
   Kirkland *(G-5366)*
Janicki Industries Inc .... E 360 856-5143
   Sedro Woolley *(G-11545)*
Linear Controls Inc 425 876-9742
   Mukilteo *(G-6949)*
Mechanical Specialties LLC .... G 360 273-7604
   Olympia *(G-7335)*
Nabtesco Aerospace Inc .... E 425 602-8400
   Kirkland *(G-5407)*
Palomar Products Inc .... G 425 453-9400
   Bellevue *(G-1061)*
Safran Cabin Inc .... C 509 447-4122
   Newport *(G-7065)*
Spartan Industries L L C .... G 425 822-2071
   Redmond *(G-8677)*
Surftech Finishes Co .... G 425 453-9400
   Bellevue *(G-1168)*
Umbra Cuscinetti Incorporated .... D 425 405-3500
   Everett *(G-3640)*
Wipro Givon Usa Inc .... E 425 355-3330
   Everett *(G-3661)*

AIRCRAFT PARTS & AUXILIARY EQPT: Body & Wing Assys & Parts

Aim Group USA Inc 425 235-2750
   Renton *(G-8733)*
Dabs M&A LLC .... E 253 872-2200
   Kent *(G-4869)*
Primus International Inc .... G 425 688-0444
   Auburn *(G-537)*
Primus International Inc .... C 253 854-2995
   Algona *(G-75)*
Primus International Inc .... B 425 318-4500
   Woodinville *(G-15340)*
Primus International Inc .... C 253 876-1500
   Algona *(G-76)*
Tect Aerospace LLC .... D 253 872-7045
   Kent *(G-5175)*

PRODUCT SECTION

AIRCRAFT PARTS & EQPT, NEC

AIRCRAFT PARTS & AUXILIARY EQPT: Body Assemblies & Parts

Aeroacoustics Inc .... G 425 438-0215
  Everett *(G-3363)*
After Market Products Inc .... F 360 825-6500
  Enumclaw *(G-3275)*
Cobalt Enterprises LLC .... D 360 691-2298
  Granite Falls *(G-4267)*
Danner Corporation .... C 253 833-5333
  Auburn *(G-422)*
Intergrated Aerospace LLC .... G 360 691-2298
  Lake Stevens *(G-5649)*
Petrichor Industries LLC .... G 425 454-8281
  Bellevue *(G-1073)*
Pnw Aerospace LLC .... G 360 292-0909
  Lacey *(G-5577)*
Routec Industries LLC .... G 206 949-2472
  Snohomish *(G-11969)*

AIRCRAFT PARTS & AUXILIARY EQPT: Elevators

Lift Solutions Inc .... G 360 862-8328
  Lake Stevens *(G-5657)*

AIRCRAFT PARTS & AUXILIARY EQPT: Fins

Omohundro Co Kitsap Composites .... D 360 519-3047
  Port Orchard *(G-7837)*

AIRCRAFT PARTS & AUXILIARY EQPT: Flaps, Wing

Double D Mfg LLC .... G 206 954-8099
  Marysville *(G-6331)*

AIRCRAFT PARTS & AUXILIARY EQPT: Landing Assemblies & Brakes

Northwest Dynamics Inc .... G 360 253-3656
  Vancouver *(G-14434)*
Triumph Composite Systems Inc .... B 509 623-8536
  Spokane *(G-12570)*

AIRCRAFT PARTS & AUXILIARY EQPT: Lighting/Landing Gear Assy

Goodrich Corporation .... E 425 261-8700
  Everett *(G-3503)*
Landing Gear Work LLC .... G 509 884-9546
  Renton *(G-8840)*

AIRCRAFT PARTS & AUXILIARY EQPT: Military Eqpt & Armament

Boeing Commercial Airplane .... E 425 237-2019
  Everett *(G-3394)*

AIRCRAFT PARTS & AUXILIARY EQPT: Oxygen Systems

Humbay Health LLC .... G 425 922-0200
  Kirkland *(G-5363)*

AIRCRAFT PARTS & AUXILIARY EQPT: Refueling Eqpt, In Flight

Spearman Corp Kent Division .... F 253 236-5980
  Kent *(G-5144)*

AIRCRAFT PARTS & AUXILIARY EQPT: Research & Development, Mfr

Plexsys Interface Products Inc .... E 360 838-2500
  Camas *(G-2275)*
Raisbeck Engineering Inc .... F 206 723-2000
  Tukwila *(G-13802)*
West Coast Fabrication Inc .... G 206 790-1496
  Auburn *(G-598)*

AIRCRAFT PARTS & AUXILIARY EQPT: Rotor Blades, Helicopter

Vts Aviation LLC .... G 253 272-7273
  Tacoma *(G-13585)*

AIRCRAFT PARTS & AUXILIARY EQPT: Rudders

Bayview Engineering Inds LLC .... G 360 421-2126
  Oak Harbor *(G-7141)*

AIRCRAFT PARTS & AUXILIARY EQPT: Tanks, Fuel

Protium Innovations LLC .... G 206 854-8792
  Pullman *(G-8102)*

AIRCRAFT PARTS & AUXILIARY EQPT: Wing Assemblies & Parts

Aviation Partners Inc .... F 206 762-1171
  Seattle *(G-9471)*

AIRCRAFT PARTS & EQPT, NEC

AAA Precise Machine Inc .... G 509 375-3268
  Benton City *(G-1599)*
Absolute Aviation Services LLC .... E 509 747-2904
  Spokane *(G-12094)*
Accra Manufacturing Inc .... D 425 424-1000
  Bothell *(G-1814)*
Accurus Aerospace Kent LLC .... D 253 872-8541
  Kent *(G-4757)*
Aero Controls Inc .... C 253 269-3000
  Auburn *(G-364)*
Aerocell Corporation .... C 360 653-2211
  Marysville *(G-6311)*
Aeroforge Manufacturing Inc .... E 253 286-2525
  Puyallup *(G-8118)*
Aeroform Inc .... E 360 403-1919
  Arlington *(G-195)*
Aerojet Rocketdyne Inc .... E 425 885-5000
  Redmond *(G-8373)*
Aeronautical Testing Service .... G 360 363-4276
  Arlington *(G-196)*
Aerospace Defense Inc .... E 360 548-8017
  Arlington *(G-197)*
Aerospace International LLC .... G 206 334-7426
  Kent *(G-4763)*
Air Metal Fabricators Inc .... G 509 923-2274
  Pateros *(G-7657)*
Airborne Ecs LLC .... F 319 538-1051
  Port Angeles *(G-7679)*
Aj Aerospace .... G 253 335-7775
  Algona *(G-66)*
American Edge LLC .... F 509 937-4404
  Valley *(G-13987)*
Asko Industrial Repair .... F 206 284-2659
  Mukilteo *(G-6894)*
Astronics Advncd Electrnc Sys .... A 425 881-1700
  Kirkland *(G-5283)*
Astronics Cstm Ctrl Cncpts Inc .... D 206 575-0933
  Kent *(G-4795)*
Atacs Products Inc .... F 206 433-9000
  Seattle *(G-9449)*
Aviation Covers Inc .... G 360 435-0342
  Arlington *(G-205)*
Aviation Innovations LLC .... G 360 907-0888
  Yacolt *(G-15481)*
Aviation Spares & Svcs Intl Co .... F 425 869-7799
  Redmond *(G-8393)*
Avistar Aerospace LLC .... G 206 838-6869
  Seattle *(G-9472)*
Avtechtyee Inc .... C 425 290-3100
  Everett *(G-3378)*
B/E Aerospace Inc .... B 360 657-5197
  Everett *(G-3380)*
B/E Aerospace Inc .... B 425 923-2700
  Everett *(G-3381)*
Ballard Technology Inc .... D 425 339-0281
  Everett *(G-3383)*
Blr Aerospace Llc .... E 425 353-6591
  Everett *(G-3389)*
Boeing Company .... C 253 931-2121
  Auburn *(G-395)*
Boeing Company .... A 425 865-3311
  Bellevue *(G-824)*
Brooks Tactical Systems .... F 253 549-2703
  Fox Island *(G-4019)*
Bucher Aerospace Corporation .... E 425 355-2202
  Everett *(G-3402)*
C&D Zodiac Inc .... D 360 653-2211
  Marysville *(G-6318)*
Cadence Aerospace LLC .... F 425 353-0405
  Everett *(G-3408)*
Carbon Consultants LLC .... E 509 637-2520
  Bingen *(G-1634)*
Cascade Aviation Services Inc .... E 425 493-1707
  Marysville *(G-6322)*
Cashmere Manufacturing LLC .... E 509 888-2141
  East Wenatchee *(G-3009)*
Center Trade Corporation .... G 206 992-2374
  Kirkland *(G-5302)*
Collins Aerospace .... E 509 744-6000
  Spokane *(G-12187)*
Compass Aerospace Northwest, I ...... D 253 852-9700
  Kent *(G-4858)*
Component Products Corporation .... F 425 355-6800
  Mukilteo *(G-6904)*
Core Tech LLC .... E 253 457-3239
  Tacoma *(G-13243)*
Crane Aerospace Inc .... E 425 743-1313
  Lynnwood *(G-6100)*
Cub Crafters Inc .... E 509 248-9491
  Yakima *(G-15541)*
Dakota Cub .... G 509 453-3412
  Yakima *(G-15549)*
Dance Air Inc .... E 425 222-6789
  Snoqualmie *(G-12009)*
Defense Sales Intl LLC .... G 206 999-8684
  Renton *(G-8782)*
Diamond Machine Works Inc .... E 206 633-3960
  Seattle *(G-9827)*
Dowty Aerospace .... G 509 248-5000
  Yakima *(G-15558)*
Dynamic Safety LLC .... G 425 290-9399
  Mukilteo *(G-6917)*
Eldec Corporation .... A 425 743-1313
  Lynnwood *(G-6114)*
Ellison Fluid Systems Inc .... G 425 271-3220
  Renton *(G-8793)*
EM Global Manufacturing Inc .... G 253 655-5206
  Tacoma *(G-13276)*
Esterline Corporation .... G 425 453-9400
  Bellevue *(G-899)*
Esterline Technologies Corp .... E 425 297-9624
  Everett *(G-3462)*
Exotic Metals Forming Co LLC .... G 253 395-3710
  Kent *(G-4901)*
Fabrication Technologies LLC .... G 360 293-3707
  Anacortes *(G-127)*
Fatigue Technology Inc .... C 206 246-2010
  Tukwila *(G-13732)*
Fiberdyne Aerospace .... G 206 326-8581
  Seattle *(G-9987)*
Flight Structures Inc .... C 360 651-8537
  Everett *(G-3475)*
Fly Girls Aero Covers .... G 509 466-7794
  Spokane *(G-12260)*
Frisbie Company .... G 253 939-0363
  Auburn *(G-444)*
Gemini Management Ltd .... G 425 739-6800
  Kirkland *(G-5347)*
Giddens Aerospace Inc .... G 425 353-0405
  Everett *(G-3497)*
Giddens Holdings Inc .... G 425 353-0405
  Everett *(G-3498)*
Giddens Industries Inc .... G 425 353-0405
  Everett *(G-3499)*
Giddens Industries Inc .... G 425 353-0405
  Everett *(G-3500)*
Goodrich Aerostructures Integr .... G 425 318-9276
  Everett *(G-3502)*
Goodrich Corporation .... F 425 822-9851
  Kirkland *(G-5351)*
Goodrich Corporation .... E 509 744-6000
  Spokane *(G-12278)*
Harper Engineering Company .... D 425 255-0414
  Renton *(G-8817)*
Hexcel Corporation .... C 360 757-7212
  Burlington *(G-2163)*
Hexcel Corporation .... C 253 872-7500
  Kent *(G-4941)*
Hydro Systems USA Inc .... C 253 876-2100
  Kent *(G-4946)*
J C Manufacturing Inc .... F 206 824-7650
  Des Moines *(G-2938)*
J D Ott Co Inc .... C 206 749-0777
  Seattle *(G-10269)*
Jamco America Inc .... C 425 347-4735
  Everett *(G-3522)*
Jamco America Inc .... G 425 347-4735
  Everett *(G-3523)*
Jet Parts Engineering LLC .... E 206 281-0963
  Seattle *(G-10295)*

Employee Codes: A=Over 500 employees, B=251-500
C=101-250, D=51-100, E=20-50, F=10-19, G=2-9

2019 Washington Manufacturers Register

887

AIRCRAFT PARTS & EQPT, NEC

Kira Aviation Services LLC ....G...... 425 361-1060
  Lynnwood *(G-6151)*
Klune Industries Inc ....C...... 253 872-7488
  Kent *(G-4979)*
Krismark Group Inc ....G...... 425 396-0829
  Snoqualmie *(G-12015)*
L & R Industries LLC ....G...... 425 226-2780
  Renton *(G-8839)*
Lamar Technologies LLC ....F...... 360 651-8869
  Marysville *(G-6352)*
Lifeport Inc ....G...... 360 225-3200
  Woodland *(G-15445)*
Lifeport Inc ....E...... 360 225-6690
  Woodland *(G-15446)*
Lifeport LLC ....D...... 360 225-1212
  Woodland *(G-15447)*
Lkd Aerospace LLC ....F...... 425 396-0829
  Snoqualmie *(G-12017)*
LMI Aerospace Inc ....G...... 425 293-0340
  Everett *(G-3538)*
LMI Aerospace Inc ....C...... 253 288-9379
  Auburn *(G-489)*
Longwell Company ....D...... 425 289-0160
  Bellevue *(G-989)*
Lrt Inc ....G...... 425 742-0333
  Mill Creek *(G-6516)*
Lumicor Inc ....G...... 425 255-4000
  Renton *(G-8846)*
Majestic Aerotech Inc ....F...... 360 528-4142
  Tacoma *(G-13396)*
Manufacturing Technology Inc ....G...... 206 763-3161
  Seattle *(G-10473)*
Marketing Masters Inc ....F...... 425 454-5610
  Issaquah *(G-4445)*
Mercer Products & Mfg Co ....G...... 425 742-0333
  Mill Creek *(G-6517)*
Merlyn Products Inc ....F...... 509 838-7500
  Spokane *(G-12390)*
Micro Aerodynamics Inc ....F...... 360 293-8082
  Anacortes *(G-146)*
Morgan Aero Products Inc ....G...... 425 438-9600
  Everett *(G-3551)*
Northstone Industries LLC ....G...... 509 844-7775
  Spokane *(G-12410)*
Northwest Aerospace Tech Inc ....G...... 425 212-5001
  Everett *(G-3556)*
Northwest Aerospace Tech Inc ....D...... 425 257-2044
  Everett *(G-3555)*
Olympic Aerospace Inc ....G...... 253 835-4984
  Federal Way *(G-3767)*
Olympic Areospace Inc ....G...... 253 835-4984
  Federal Way *(G-3768)*
Onboard Systems Intl LLC ....E...... 360 546-3072
  Vancouver *(G-14451)*
Pacific Aerospace & Elec LLC ....C...... 855 885-5200
  Wenatchee *(G-15059)*
Pmw Capital Inc ....G...... 253 272-5119
  Tacoma *(G-13468)*
Precision Machine Works Inc ....C...... 253 272-5119
  Tacoma *(G-13474)*
Primus Bumstead Manufacturing ....G...... 425 688-0444
  Algona *(G-74)*
Primus International ....G...... 425 424-1085
  Bothell *(G-1889)*
Quality On Time Machining Inc ....G...... 360 802-3700
  Enumclaw *(G-3314)*
Quiet Wing Aerospace LLC ....G...... 425 451-8565
  Redmond *(G-8640)*
Radioracks Aviation Systems ....G...... 360 651-1200
  Lake Stevens *(G-5670)*
RMC Incorporated ....E...... 206 243-4831
  Seattle *(G-10969)*
Roberts Precision Machine Inc ....F...... 360 805-1000
  Monroe *(G-6615)*
Royell Manufacturing Inc ....D...... 425 259-9258
  Everett *(G-3602)*
RTC Aerospace LLC ....F...... 918 407-0291
  Fife *(G-3988)*
Rti Manufacturing Inc ....G...... 360 435-9092
  Arlington *(G-318)*
Safran Cabin Bellingham Inc ....C...... 360 738-2005
  Bellingham *(G-1521)*
Safran Cabin Inc ....C...... 360 653-2600
  Marysville *(G-6381)*
Safran Cabin Inc ....D...... 360 653-2211
  Marysville *(G-6382)*
Safran Ventilation System Usa ....E...... 425 438-1378
  Everett *(G-3604)*
Sakco Precision Inc ....G...... 253 288-9702
  Auburn *(G-555)*
Samuel Edwards ....G...... 253 988-0219
  Kent *(G-5114)*
Sea West Products Inc ....F...... 253 854-2942
  Kent *(G-5119)*
Seaton Engineering Corporation ....G...... 509 290-5919
  Spokane *(G-12495)*
Seattle Turbine Inc ....G...... 253 770-7567
  Puyallup *(G-8251)*
Senior Operations LLC ....B...... 360 435-1119
  Arlington *(G-325)*
Senior Operations LLC ....G...... 360 435-1119
  Arlington *(G-326)*
Skills Inc ....E...... 206 782-6000
  Seattle *(G-11127)*
Soloy LLC ....E...... 360 754-7000
  Tumwater *(G-13898)*
Spearman Corporation ....E...... 360 651-9281
  Kent *(G-5145)*
Spokane Industries Inc ....E...... 509 928-0720
  Spokane Valley *(G-12886)*
Stoddard International LLC ....E...... 360 435-6455
  Arlington *(G-337)*
Subaru of America Inc ....G...... 425 822-0762
  Kirkland *(G-5472)*
Synchronous Aerospace ....G...... 253 852-9700
  Kent *(G-5165)*
Terrys Precision Products LLC ....G...... 425 349-2700
  Everett *(G-3630)*
Toolcraft Inc ....F...... 360 794-5512
  Monroe *(G-6633)*
Triton Aerospace LLC ....F...... 360 466-4160
  La Conner *(G-5527)*
Triumph Actuation Systems ....B...... 509 248-5000
  Yakima *(G-15696)*
Triumph Group Inc ....F...... 425 636-9000
  Redmond *(G-8695)*
Ttf Aerospace Inc ....C...... 253 736-6300
  Auburn *(G-584)*
Tyee Aircraft Inc ....G...... 425 290-3100
  Everett *(G-3639)*
Universal Aerospace Co Inc ....C...... 360 435-9577
  Arlington *(G-344)*
University Swaging Corporation ....C...... 425 318-1965
  Bellevue *(G-1208)*
University Swaging Corporation ....G...... 425 318-4500
  Woodinville *(G-15396)*
Valley Machine Shop Inc ....E...... 425 226-5040
  Kent *(G-5199)*
Waiv Aerospace LLC ....G...... 206 276-2306
  Bellevue *(G-1222)*
West Isle Air Inc ....F...... 425 235-1996
  Chelan *(G-2570)*
Western Aerospace & Engrg LLC ....G...... 360 253-8282
  Vancouver *(G-14684)*
Woodford Phoenix Aerospace Mfg ....G...... 360 736-9689
  Centralia *(G-2444)*
Zepher Inc ....F...... 509 637-2520
  Bingen *(G-1643)*
Zodiac Aerospace ....G...... 425 791-3302
  Everett *(G-3664)*
Zodiac Aerospace ....G...... 425 257-2044
  Everett *(G-3665)*
Zodiac Arospc Engineered Mtls ....G...... 360 653-2600
  Marysville *(G-6403)*

AIRCRAFT PARTS WHOLESALERS

Aeroforge Inc ....E...... 253 286-2525
  Puyallup *(G-8117)*
Avio Corporation ....A...... 425 739-6800
  Kirkland *(G-5286)*
Cub Crafters Inc ....E...... 509 248-9491
  Yakima *(G-15541)*
Longwell Company ....D...... 425 289-0160
  Bellevue *(G-989)*
Subsea Air Systems LLC ....G...... 360 563-2400
  Snohomish *(G-11987)*

AIRCRAFT PARTS/AUX EQPT: Airframe Assy, Exc Guided Missiles

Horizon Flight ....G...... 509 521-4244
  Pasco *(G-7590)*
Vaupell Rapid Solutions ....G...... 206 784-9050
  Everett *(G-3648)*

AIRCRAFT PROPELLERS & PARTS

Aircraft Propulsion Systems ....G...... 425 413-4127
  Maple Valley *(G-6254)*

AIRCRAFT RADIO EQPT REPAIR SVCS

Western Avionics Inc ....G...... 509 534-7371
  Spokane *(G-12585)*

AIRCRAFT SEATS

B/E Aerospace Inc ....B...... 425 923-2700
  Everett *(G-3381)*

AIRCRAFT SERVICING & REPAIRING

Aeronautical Testing Service ....G...... 360 363-4276
  Arlington *(G-196)*
Air Metal Fabricators Inc ....G...... 509 923-2274
  Pateros *(G-7657)*
Bogert Aviation Inc ....G...... 509 736-1513
  Pasco *(G-7554)*

AIRCRAFT TIRES

Michelin Mounting Center ....G...... 253 872-0868
  Kent *(G-5010)*

AIRCRAFT TURBINES

Subsea Air Systems LLC ....G...... 360 563-2400
  Snohomish *(G-11987)*

AIRCRAFT: Airplanes, Fixed Or Rotary Wing

A & B Plastics Inc ....G...... 509 248-9166
  Union Gap *(G-13919)*
Adrenaline Products LLC ....G...... 503 805-4525
  Ridgefield *(G-9059)*
Boeing ....G...... 360 348-0394
  Snohomish *(G-11879)*
Boeing Classic ....G...... 206 381-7804
  Seattle *(G-9562)*
Boeing Commercial Airplane ....G...... 206 662-9615
  Kent *(G-4817)*
Boeing Company ....B...... 425 413-3400
  Maple Valley *(G-6261)*
Boeing Company ....A...... 425 417-5612
  Kirkland *(G-5295)*
Boeing Company ....A...... 425 359-3777
  Bothell *(G-1831)*
Boeing Company ....A...... 425 493-8267
  Mukilteo *(G-6899)*
Boeing Company ....A...... 206 662-6863
  Renton *(G-8756)*
Boeing Company ....A...... 206 655-1131
  Tukwila *(G-13701)*
Boeing Company ....A...... 206 766-2770
  Renton *(G-8757)*
Boeing Company ....A...... 206 662-9615
  Seatac *(G-9276)*
Boeing Company ....E...... 425 865-6915
  Bellevue *(G-822)*
Boeing Company ....G...... 425 407-1400
  Everett *(G-3395)*
Boeing Company ....A...... 206 655-1131
  Seattle *(G-9563)*
Boeing Company ....G...... 425 342-2121
  Everett *(G-3396)*
Boeing Company ....G...... 425 306-8112
  Renton *(G-8759)*
Boeing Company ....A...... 312 544-2000
  Seatac *(G-9278)*
Boeing Company ....A...... 425 865-3308
  Bellevue *(G-823)*
Boeing Company ....A...... 425 865-3311
  Bellevue *(G-824)*
Boeing Company ....A...... 253 657-5616
  Renton *(G-8761)*
Boeing Company ....A...... 206 655-1131
  Renton *(G-8762)*
Boeing Company ....A...... 312 544-2000
  Everett *(G-3397)*
Boeing Operations Intl Inc ....G...... 206 655-2121
  Tukwila *(G-13708)*
Client Service Center ....G...... 206 237-0821
  Seattle *(G-9696)*
Flightways Corporation ....G...... 425 747-6903
  Bellevue *(G-912)*
Roy Dintelman ....G...... 253 508-9361
  Auburn *(G-550)*
Sodexo ....G...... 425 656-2860
  Renton *(G-8915)*
Uav Systems Development Corp ....B...... 803 767-1351
  Moses Lake *(G-6755)*

PRODUCT SECTION　　　　　　　　　　　　　　　　　　　　　　　　　　　AMUSEMENT & RECREATION SVCS: Picnic Ground Operation

AIRCRAFT: Airships
Plimp Inc .... G 206 795-3292
  Seattle *(G-10823)*

AIRCRAFT: Autogiros
Vose Technical Systems Inc .... G 253 272-7273
  Tacoma *(G-13584)*

AIRCRAFT: Motorized
Cub Crafters Group LLC .... G 509 248-9491
  Yakima *(G-15542)*
Droneworks LLC .... G 253 261-3888
  Auburn *(G-429)*
Druid Mountain Drones .... G 206 321-4771
  Puyallup *(G-8146)*
Interntnal Arospc Coatings Inc .... D 509 321-0342
  Spokane *(G-12325)*
Pacific Northwest Drone Svcs .... G 509 679-0863
  Lacey *(G-5573)*
Robodub Inc .... G 408 250-5723
  Seattle *(G-10973)*
Seattle Drone Sales Llc .... G 206 858-2764
  Mercer Island *(G-6483)*
Skyidrones LLC .... G 253 347-7261
  Kent *(G-5134)*

AIRCRAFT: Research & Development, Manufacturer
4r Aviation LLC .... G 206 336-9415
  Seattle *(G-9323)*
Jetoptera Inc .... G 516 456-7609
  Edmonds *(G-3123)*
Jetprop LLC .... G 509 535-4401
  Spokane *(G-12333)*
Radian Aerospace Inc .... G 425 235-1936
  Renton *(G-8890)*

AIRLOCKS
Airlock LLC .... G 206 992-3996
  Seattle *(G-9362)*

AIRPORT
Kenmore Air Harbor Inc .... D 425 486-3224
  Kenmore *(G-4587)*

AIRPORTS, FLYING FIELDS & SVCS
Aeroacoustics Inc .... G 425 438-0215
  Everett *(G-3363)*
Center Trade Corporation .... G 206 992-2374
  Kirkland *(G-5302)*
Honeywell International Inc .... C 425 251-9511
  Renton *(G-8821)*
Kono Fixed Income Fund 1511 LP .... F 360 686-7688
  Bellevue *(G-972)*

ALARMS: Burglar
Foundation International .... G 425 391-1281
  Bellevue *(G-916)*

ALARMS: Fire
General Fire Prtection Systems .... F 509 535-4255
  Spokane *(G-12268)*
Inland Alarm LLC .... G 509 457-6065
  Yakima *(G-15589)*

ALCOHOL TREATMENT CLINIC, OUTPATIENT
Innovation Resource Center .... G 509 836-2400
  Sunnyside *(G-13127)*

ALCOHOL, GRAIN: For Beverage Purposes
Skyline Spirits Wine Works Co .... G 509 967-0781
  West Richland *(G-15100)*

ALCOHOL: Methyl & Methanol, Synthetic
Northwest Innovation Works Ka .... F 360 673-7800
  Kalama *(G-4505)*
Pan-Pacific Energy Corp .... F 360 673-7800
  Kalama *(G-4506)*

ALKALIES & CHLORINE
Buckeye International Inc .... G 206 575-1185
  Seatac *(G-9279)*

ALLOYS: Additive, Exc Copper Or Made In Blast Furnaces
Travis Pattern & Foundry Inc .... B 509 466-3545
  Spokane *(G-12566)*

ALTERNATORS: Automotive
Life Safer .... G 800 328-9890
  Bremerton *(G-1973)*

ALUMINUM
Alacan Solatens .... G 509 462-2310
  Spokane Valley *(G-12603)*
AMG Aluminum North America LLC .... D 509 663-2165
  Malaga *(G-6231)*
Gnr Aerospace Inc .... G 360 652-4040
  Arlington *(G-244)*
Kaiser Aluminum Fab Pdts LLC .... D 509 375-0900
  Richland *(G-9016)*
Mavin Mfg Inc .... G 360 663-0354
  Enumclaw *(G-3304)*

ALUMINUM & BERYLLIUM ORES MINING
Kaiser Aluminum Washington LLC .... G 949 614-1740
  Spokane Valley *(G-12761)*

ALUMINUM PRDTS
A & B Fabricators Inc .... G 253 887-0442
  Auburn *(G-355)*
Alaskan Copper Companies Inc .... G 206 623-5800
  Seattle *(G-9368)*
How-Mac Manufacturing Inc .... E 360 855-2649
  Sedro Woolley *(G-11540)*
Hydro Extrusion North Amer LLC .... G 503 802-3000
  Vancouver *(G-14307)*
Industrial Revolution Inc .... E 425 285-1111
  Tukwila *(G-13752)*
Isla Carmen LLC .... G 360 836-5955
  Vancouver *(G-14325)*
Kaiser Aluminum Fab Pdts LLC .... A 509 927-6508
  Spokane Valley *(G-12760)*
Kaiser Aluminum Fab Pdts LLC .... F 509 375-0900
  Richland *(G-9017)*
Kaiser Alutek Inc .... G 509 924-2689
  Spokane Valley *(G-12762)*
Pyrotek Incorporated .... D 509 926-6211
  Spokane Valley *(G-12846)*
Universal Alloy Corporation .... C 253 350-4079
  Seattle *(G-11376)*

ALUMINUM: Ingots & Slabs
Nupro Products Inc .... G 509 698-6983
  Selah *(G-11593)*

ALUMINUM: Ingots, Primary
Intalco Aluminum LLC .... A 360 384-7061
  Ferndale *(G-3859)*

ALUMINUM: Slabs, Primary
Custom Bilt Holdings LLC .... G 509 533-1703
  Spokane *(G-12212)*

AMMONIA & LIQUOR: Chemical Recovery Coke Oven
Ace Galvanizing .... G 206 687-7688
  Burien *(G-2090)*
Inland Empire Resteel .... G 509 863-9870
  Spokane *(G-12308)*

AMMUNITION
Slapshot USA Ltd Liability Co .... G 360 560-0245
  Longview *(G-5954)*

AMMUNITION: Cartridges, 30 mm & Below
Eco Cartridge Store .... G 425 820-3570
  Kirkland *(G-5329)*

AMMUNITION: Mines & Parts, Ordnance
Chiwawa Mines Inc .... G 509 455-8080
  Spokane *(G-12180)*

AMPLIFIERS
Dehavilland Elc Amplifier Co .... G 360 891-6570
  Vancouver *(G-14174)*
Gremlin Inc .... G 206 781-4636
  Seattle *(G-10123)*

AMPLIFIERS: Pulse Amplifiers
Clear Rf LLC .... F 855 321-9527
  Spokane Valley *(G-12658)*

AMPLIFIERS: RF & IF Power
Aci Communications Inc .... E 253 854-9802
  Kent *(G-4758)*
AR Kalmus Corp .... E 425 485-9000
  Bothell *(G-1822)*

AMUSEMENT & RECREATION SVCS: Art Gallery, Commercial
Fremont Fine Arts Foundry Inc .... G 206 588-6981
  Seattle *(G-10024)*
Third & Wall Art Group LLC .... F 206 443-8425
  Seattle *(G-11291)*
Vanetten Fine Art .... G 509 928-2385
  Spokane Valley *(G-12928)*

AMUSEMENT & RECREATION SVCS: Bridge Club, Non-Membership
Sears Tents & Awning .... G 509 452-8971
  Yakima *(G-15669)*

AMUSEMENT & RECREATION SVCS: Diving Instruction, Underwater
Top To Bottom Inc .... G 360 671-7022
  Bellingham *(G-1572)*

AMUSEMENT & RECREATION SVCS: Fishing Boat Operations, Party
Sierra Fishers I N C .... G 360 299-1469
  Anacortes *(G-168)*

AMUSEMENT & RECREATION SVCS: Golf Club, Membership
Members Club At Aldarra .... G 206 232-8580
  Mercer Island *(G-6473)*

AMUSEMENT & RECREATION SVCS: Golf Professionals
We-Man Vets Golf Inc .... E 509 527-4507
  Walla Walla *(G-14900)*

AMUSEMENT & RECREATION SVCS: Gun Club, Membership
U S Practical Shooting Assn .... F 360 855-2245
  Burlington *(G-2195)*

AMUSEMENT & RECREATION SVCS: Lottery Tickets, Sales
Chevron Kalama .... F 360 673-2972
  Kalama *(G-4495)*

AMUSEMENT & RECREATION SVCS: Physical Fitness Instruction
Momentum Gear .... G 360 524-2098
  Vancouver *(G-14424)*

AMUSEMENT & RECREATION SVCS: Picnic Ground Operation
Oakwood Cellars .... G 509 588-1900
  Benton City *(G-1622)*

Employee Codes: A=Over 500 employees, B=251-500
C=101-250, D=51-100, E=20-50, F=10-19, G=2-9

AMUSEMENT & RECREATION SVCS: Rafting Tours

Olympic Outdoor Center .... E 360 297-4659
  Port Gamble *(G-7757)*

AMUSEMENT & RECREATION SVCS: Recreation SVCS

Bremerton Trap & Skeet Club .... G 360 674-2438
  Port Orchard *(G-7796)*
County of Lewis .... C 360 748-9121
  Chehalis *(G-2485)*

AMUSEMENT & RECREATION SVCS: Riding & Rodeo Svcs

Kitc Radio Inc .... G 360 876-1400
  Port Orchard *(G-7823)*

AMUSEMENT & RECREATION SVCS: Tennis Club, Membership

Sturtevants Tennis Shop .... G 425 454-6465
  Bellevue *(G-1163)*

AMUSEMENT & RECREATION SVCS: Yoga Instruction

Six LLC .... G 206 466-5186
  Seattle *(G-11123)*

AMUSEMENT PARK DEVICES & RIDES

Allegis Corporation .... G 425 242-6680
  Kent *(G-4772)*
Bentriver Tech Inc .... G 360 335-1345
  Washougal *(G-14945)*
Bombora Global LLC .... G 206 617-6996
  Sammamish *(G-9191)*
Dabs Manufacturing & Assembly .... F 253 872-2200
  Kent *(G-4870)*
Fluid Process Engineering LLC .... G 425 868-0899
  Sammamish *(G-9207)*
Fred J Kimball Machine Shop .... G 509 529-5339
  Walla Walla *(G-14810)*

AMUSEMENT PARK DEVICES & RIDES: Carousels Or Merry-Go-Rounds

Dentzel Carousel Co .... G 360 385-1068
  Port Townsend *(G-7879)*

AMUSEMENT PARK DEVICES & RIDES: Carnival Mach & Eqpt, NEC

Freeman Companies .... G 425 656-1255
  Renton *(G-8804)*
Jim s Machining Service Inc .... G 509 926-1868
  Spokane Valley *(G-12753)*
Pape Machinery Inc .... F 360 575-9959
  Kelso *(G-4541)*

ANALGESICS

Neobiotech Global Corporation .... G 253 732-3573
  Auburn *(G-506)*

ANALYZERS: Moisture

Abode Specialist Inspection SE .... G 253 209-0878
  Tacoma *(G-13193)*

ANALYZERS: Network

Brightwire Networks LLC .... G 360 528-6017
  Olympia *(G-7242)*
Professional Network Solutions .... G 509 308-0318
  Kennewick *(G-4710)*

ANESTHESIA EQPT

G Dundas Co Inc .... G 253 631-8008
  Black Diamond *(G-1648)*
M2 Anesthesia PLLC .... G 206 605-5933
  Lake Tapps *(G-5682)*
Patcen Healthcare Inc .... G 425 495-5143
  Bellevue *(G-1064)*

ANIMAL BASED MEDICINAL CHEMICAL PRDTS

Ian Enterprises LLC .... G 425 413-0371
  Maple Valley *(G-6275)*

ANIMAL FEED & SUPPLEMENTS: Livestock & Poultry

Baker Commodities Inc .... D 206 243-4781
  Seattle *(G-9478)*
Bear Inc .... G 253 851-2575
  Gig Harbor *(G-4078)*
Cargill Incorporated .... F 360 757-4012
  Burlington *(G-2140)*
Cargill Incorporated .... G 509 854-1035
  Granger *(G-4260)*
Cargill Incorporated .... E 360 656-5784
  Ferndale *(G-3823)*
Country Store .... G 509 534-1412
  Spokane Valley *(G-12667)*
Epl Feed LLC .... G 360 988-5811
  Everson *(G-3674)*
Feed Commodities LLC .... F 626 799-1196
  Tacoma *(G-13293)*
Grain Craft Inc .... D 206 898-3079
  Seattle *(G-10104)*
Iron Horse Hay & Feed .... G 425 432-0636
  Maple Valley *(G-6277)*
Land OLakes Inc .... F 509 488-5208
  Othello *(G-7501)*
Land OLakes Inc .... G 360 592-5115
  Everson *(G-3681)*
Lenroc Co .... F 509 754-5266
  Ephrata *(G-3341)*
Mid-Valley Milling Inc .... G 509 786-1300
  Prosser *(G-8056)*
National Food Corporation .... G 360 435-9207
  Arlington *(G-286)*
Pautzke Bait Co Inc .... G 509 925-6154
  Ellensburg *(G-3218)*
Purina Animal Nutrition LLC .... G 425 653-4238
  Bellevue *(G-1088)*
Quality Liquid Feeds Inc .... G 509 854-2311
  Granger *(G-4263)*
Raw Advantage Inc .... G 509 738-3344
  Kettle Falls *(G-5240)*
Thomas Products LLC .... G 253 678-8391
  Bellingham *(G-1569)*
Valcom Inc .... G 509 865-5511
  Buena *(G-2081)*
Washington Haykingdom Inc .... G 509 925-7000
  Ellensburg *(G-3237)*
Wet Noses Natural Dog Treat Co .... E 360 794-7950
  Monroe *(G-6636)*
X-Cel Feeds Inc .... E 253 472-5140
  Tacoma *(G-13603)*

ANIMAL FEED: Wholesalers

Archer-Daniels-Midland Company ...... G 509 534-2636
  Spokane Valley *(G-12624)*
Dairy Export Co Inc .... G 206 284-7220
  Seattle *(G-9786)*
Iron Horse Hay & Feed .... G 425 432-0636
  Maple Valley *(G-6277)*
Land OLakes Inc .... G 360 592-5115
  Everson *(G-3681)*

ANIMAL FOOD & SUPPLEMENTS: Alfalfa Or Alfalfa Meal

Scratch and Peck LLC .... E 360 318-7585
  Burlington *(G-2186)*

ANIMAL FOOD & SUPPLEMENTS: Bird Food, Prepared

Global Harvest Foods Ltd .... G 509 466-0539
  Mead *(G-6428)*
Global Harvest Foods Ltd .... G 206 957-1350
  Tukwila *(G-13741)*
Global Harvest Foods Ltd .... G 206 957-1350
  Tukwila *(G-13742)*
Seed Factory Northwest Inc .... G 253 395-8813
  Kent *(G-5126)*

ANIMAL FOOD & SUPPLEMENTS: Cat

Good Pet Food Inc .... G 310 430-3833
  Seattle *(G-10099)*

ANIMAL FOOD & SUPPLEMENTS: Dog

Blue Dog Bakery Group Inc .... F 206 323-6958
  Seattle *(G-9547)*
Himalayan Corporation .... D 425 322-4295
  Mukilteo *(G-6934)*
Miss Mags LLC .... G 208 301-0549
  Palouse *(G-7545)*
Nancy Baer .... G 360 668-0350
  Snohomish *(G-11949)*
Northwest Pet Products Inc .... E 360 225-8855
  Woodland *(G-15452)*
Petforia LLC .... G 425 945-2300
  Bellevue *(G-1072)*
Puddles Barkery LLC .... G 206 495-3072
  Seattle *(G-10882)*
Wet Noses Natural Dog Treat Co .... E 360 794-7950
  Monroe *(G-6636)*

ANIMAL FOOD & SUPPLEMENTS: Dog & Cat

Arrow Reliance Inc .... F 206 324-7387
  Tukwila *(G-13692)*
Natural Pet Pantry .... G 206 762-5575
  Seattle *(G-10593)*
Northwest Farm Food Coop .... E 360 757-4225
  Burlington *(G-2175)*

ANIMAL FOOD & SUPPLEMENTS: Feed Concentrates

Eh Enterprises Management Inc .... F 206 596-8600
  Seattle *(G-9889)*
Elenbaas Company Inc .... E 360 354-3577
  Lynden *(G-6014)*
Epl Feed LLC .... E 360 988-5811
  Sumas *(G-13044)*
La Belle Associates Inc .... F 360 671-5122
  Bellingham *(G-1400)*
Standard Nutrition Company .... G 509 839-3500
  Sunnyside *(G-13143)*

ANIMAL FOOD & SUPPLEMENTS: Feed Premixes

Deyoungs Farm and Garden .... E 425 483-9600
  Woodinville *(G-15225)*
Rietdyks Milling Company .... G 360 887-8874
  Ridgefield *(G-9108)*

ANIMAL FOOD & SUPPLEMENTS: Feed Supplements

Luna Lactation .... G 360 693-7616
  Vancouver *(G-14387)*
Mmusa Inc .... G 360 306-5383
  Lynnwood *(G-6165)*

ANIMAL FOOD & SUPPLEMENTS: Hay, Cubed

Sage Hill Northwest Inc .... F 509 269-4966
  Mesa *(G-6495)*

ANIMAL FOOD & SUPPLEMENTS: Livestock

Agriaccess Inc .... G 425 806-9356
  Bothell *(G-1817)*
Cooperative AG Producers Inc .... E 509 523-3032
  Rosalia *(G-9154)*
Wolfkill Feed & Fert Corp .... F 360 794-7065
  Monroe *(G-6639)*

ANIMAL FOOD & SUPPLEMENTS: Meat Meal & Tankage

Arrow Reliance Inc .... F 206 324-7387
  Tukwila *(G-13692)*

ANIMAL FOOD & SUPPLEMENTS: Mineral feed supplements

Coenzyme-A Technologies Inc .... F 425 438-8586
  Lynnwood *(G-6094)*

ANIMAL FOOD & SUPPLEMENTS: Pet, Exc Dog & Cat, Dry

Kritter Kookies Ltd .... G 509 233-8414
  Loon Lake *(G-5975)*

PRODUCT SECTION

ARTISTS' MATERIALS: Boards, Drawing

ANIMAL FOOD & SUPPLEMENTS: Poultry
Baker Commodities Inc ....F...... 509 837-8686
  Grandview (G-4245)

ANIMAL FOOD & SUPPLEMENTS: Stock Feeds, Dry
Land OLakes Inc ....F...... 425 653-4200
  Bellevue (G-976)
Purina Mills LLC ....E...... 509 534-0594
  Spokane (G-12460)

ANNEALING: Metal
Utec Metals Inc ....G...... 509 891-7833
  Spokane Valley (G-12921)

ANODIZING SVC
Novation Inc ....E...... 509 922-1912
  Spokane Valley (G-12812)

ANTENNAS: Radar Or Communications
Steppir Antenna Systems Inc ....G...... 425 391-1999
  Issaquah (G-4482)
Whislers Inc ....G...... 360 352-8777
  Tumwater (G-13905)

ANTENNAS: Receiving
Jag Technologies ....G...... 360 910-2933
  Vancouver (G-14332)
Lhc2 Inc ....G...... 509 723-4517
  Liberty Lake (G-5843)
Omohundro Co Kitsap Composites ......D...... 360 519-3047
  Port Orchard (G-7837)

ANTIMONY ORE MINING
Precision Metal Works LLC ....G...... 509 945-8433
  Union Gap (G-13951)

ANTIQUE FURNITURE RESTORATION & REPAIR
Omega Silversmithing Inc ....G...... 360 863-6771
  Snohomish (G-11956)

ANTIQUES, WHOLESALE
Whitehouse Antique & Candy ....G...... 425 486-8453
  Bothell (G-1918)

APPAREL DESIGNERS: Commercial
Enlighting Struck Design LLC ....G...... 206 229-9438
  Kent (G-4893)
Florian Design ....G...... 425 742-7212
  Mill Creek (G-6511)

APPLIANCES, HOUSEHOLD: Kitchen, Major, Exc Refrigs & Stoves
Daves TV & Appliance Inc ....G...... 360 293-5129
  Mount Vernon (G-6787)
Judd & Black Electric Inc ....F...... 425 258-4557
  Everett (G-3526)
Natural Machines Inc ....F...... 206 747-9483
  Seattle (G-10591)

APPLIANCES, HOUSEHOLD: Laundry Machines, Incl Coin-Operated
Whirlpool Corporation ....E...... 253 875-7100
  Spanaway (G-12081)

APPLIANCES, HOUSEHOLD: Refrigs, Mechanical & Absorption
Andersons Rebuilding ....G...... 360 779-5287
  Poulsbo (G-7944)
Whirlpool Corporation ....E...... 253 875-7100
  Spanaway (G-12081)

APPLIANCES, HOUSEHOLD: Shampooers, Carpet
Hydramaster LLC ....D...... 425 775-7272
  Mukilteo (G-6938)
Rotovac Corporation ....E...... 425 883-6746
  Redmond (G-8655)

APPLIANCES: Household, NEC
Cypress Houseworks LLC ....G...... 360 676-9778
  Bellingham (G-1315)

APPLIANCES: Household, Refrigerators & Freezers
General Electric Company ....G...... 253 351-2200
  Auburn (G-448)
I-90 Express LLC ....G...... 509 855-6280
  Ephrata (G-3337)
Judd & Black Electric Inc ....F...... 425 258-4557
  Everett (G-3526)

APPLIANCES: Small, Electric
Amhi Inc ....G...... 425 883-4040
  Kirkland (G-5278)
Esterbrook Inc ....G...... 509 783-6826
  Kennewick (G-4663)
Farmer Bros Co ....E...... 425 881-7030
  Redmond (G-8459)

APPLICATIONS SOFTWARE PROGRAMMING
Cyrus Biotechnology Inc ....G...... 503 489-8460
  Seattle (G-9775)
Realnetworks Inc ....C...... 206 674-2700
  Seattle (G-10930)
Swype Inc ....D...... 206 547-5250
  Seattle (G-11241)
Unix Packages LLC ....G...... 206 310-4610
  Seattle (G-11386)
Vendorhawk Inc ....G...... 360 903-3744
  Seattle (G-11409)

APPRAISAL SVCS, EXC REAL ESTATE
Coin Market LLC ....G...... 425 745-1659
  Lynnwood (G-6095)

AQUARIUMS & ACCESS: Plastic
J R Setina Manufacturing Co ....D...... 360 491-6197
  Olympia (G-7310)

ARCHITECT'S SUPPLIES WHOLESALERS
University Reprographics Inc ....G...... 206 633-0925
  Seattle (G-11385)

ARCHITECTURAL SVCS
Architect David Vandervort ....G...... 206 784-1614
  Seattle (G-9420)
George G Sharp Inc ....D...... 360 476-8896
  Bremerton (G-1957)
Guido Perla & Associates Inc ....E...... 206 463-2217
  Seattle (G-10132)
Robert Madsen Design Inc ....G...... 206 588-0090
  Seattle (G-10971)

ARCHITECTURAL SVCS: House Designer
Custom Building Services Inc ....G...... 509 422-5746
  Okanogan (G-7195)
Northwest Home Designing Inc .....G...... 253 584-6309
  Tacoma (G-13433)
Pan Abode Cedar Homes Inc ....E...... 425 255-8260
  Renton (G-8874)
Pan Abode Homes Inc ....E...... 425 255-8260
  Renton (G-8875)

ARMATURE REPAIRING & REWINDING SVC
Atlas Electric Inc ....E...... 509 534-8389
  Spokane (G-12124)
Bills Marine Service ....G...... 509 826-5564
  OMAK (G-7435)
Smith Auto Electric Inc ....G...... 509 453-8275
  Yakima (G-15677)
Superior Industrial Services A ....E...... 360 841-8542
  Woodland (G-15467)

ARMOR PLATES
Sienna Technologies Inc ....F...... 425 485-0756
  Woodinville (G-15362)

AROMATIC CHEMICAL PRDTS
Specialty Chemical Pdts LLC ....G...... 509 884-4900
  Rock Island (G-9149)

ART & ORNAMENTAL WARE: Pottery
Catherine Tomlinson ....G...... 206 789-4405
  Seattle (G-9646)
Handyworks Inc ....G...... 509 299-4918
  Medical Lake (G-6441)
Jans Ceramics ....G...... 360 425-3540
  Longview (G-5920)
Nelson Farrier Shop Inc ....G...... 509 966-9598
  Yakima (G-15629)
Orcas Island Pottery ....G...... 360 376-2813
  Eastsound (G-3042)

ART DEALERS & GALLERIES
Flying Arts Ranch Inc ....G...... 509 659-1819
  Ritzville (G-9121)
Kirsten Gallery Inc ....G...... 206 522-2011
  Gig Harbor (G-4126)
S J W Studios Inc ....F...... 206 323-8020
  Seattle (G-11001)
Third & Wall Art Group LLC ....F...... 206 443-8425
  Seattle (G-11291)
Waters Edge Gallery & Framery .....G...... 253 858-7449
  Gig Harbor (G-4174)

ART DESIGN SVCS
Arctic Circle Holdings LLC ....G...... 206 625-9226
  Seattle (G-9422)
Designer Decal Inc ....F...... 509 535-0267
  Spokane (G-12226)
Ideal Commercial Uniforms ....G...... 360 876-1767
  Port Orchard (G-7814)
Printcom Inc ....F...... 206 763-7600
  Burien (G-2121)
Western Graphics Inc ....G...... 206 241-2526
  Fife (G-3998)

ART GALLERIES
Smith & Valley Gallery ....G...... 360 766-6230
  Bow (G-1933)

ART GOODS & SPLYS WHOLESALERS
Printers Shopper LLC ....G...... 425 822-7766
  Kirkland (G-5442)

ART GOODS, WHOLESALE
For Art Sake Inc ....G...... 253 858-8087
  Gig Harbor (G-4101)
Kirsten Gallery Inc ....G...... 206 522-2011
  Gig Harbor (G-4126)

ART RELATED SVCS
Marked Departure Pottery ....G...... 360 991-5910
  Vancouver (G-14394)

ART SCHOOL, EXC COMMERCIAL
Puffin Glass ....G...... 509 328-0661
  Spokane (G-12458)

ART SPLY STORES
Book N Brush ....G...... 360 748-6221
  Chehalis (G-2472)
Stampadoodle Inc ....G...... 360 647-9663
  Bellingham (G-1555)

ARTIFICIAL FLOWER SHOPS
Hope Chest Crafts ....G...... 509 865-5666
  Toppenish (G-13670)

ARTIFICIAL FLOWERS & TREES
Lavender Heart Ltd ....G...... 206 568-4441
  Seattle (G-10384)

ARTISTS' MATERIALS, WHOLESALE
Tcc Printing and Imaging Inc ....E...... 206 622-4050
  Seattle (G-11276)

ARTISTS' MATERIALS: Boards, Drawing
PBS Supply Co Inc ....F...... 253 395-5550
  Kent (G-5063)

ARTISTS' MATERIALS: Canvas, Prepared On Frames

Cubby B & Friends .... G 253 537-6266
Tacoma *(G-13250)*

ARTISTS' MATERIALS: Colors, Water & Oxide Ceramic Glass

Geo Lastomirsky Ceramic A .... G 206 782-4695
Seattle *(G-10062)*
Grey Gull Ceramics .... G 360 321-1582
Langley *(G-5779)*

ARTISTS' MATERIALS: Frames, Artists' Canvases

Alb Framing Gallery & Gift .... G 425 432-5505
Maple Valley *(G-6255)*
Museum Quality Discount Frmng ...... F 206 624-1057
Seattle *(G-10574)*

ARTISTS' MATERIALS: Paints, China Painting

Kilian & Kilian Artists .... G 360 654-1799
Stanwood *(G-12977)*

ARTISTS' MATERIALS: Paints, Exc Gold & Bronze

Ginny Hardings Equine Classics .... G 509 582-7924
Kennewick *(G-4667)*

ARTISTS' MATERIALS: Paints, Gold Or Bronze

Biscomb Fleudeliza S (artist) .... G 206 842-6417
Bainbridge Island *(G-618)*
Robinsons Inc .... G 360 834-0929
Camas *(G-2279)*

ARTS & CRAFTS SCHOOL

Covenant Art Glass Inc .... G 425 252-4232
Everett *(G-3429)*

ARTWORK: Framed

Charles Friedman .... G 206 781-0608
Seattle *(G-9667)*
Dejay Products LLC .... G 206 784-8200
Lakewood *(G-5711)*
Hopp Industries .... G 253 732-7348
Tacoma *(G-13343)*
Liz Tran .... G 206 720-7165
Seattle *(G-10432)*
Precision Art Works .... G 206 714-7074
Seattle *(G-10848)*
Sirlin Enterprises .... G 206 883-7988
Seattle *(G-11117)*
Watermark Art & Framing .... G 360 871-2906
Port Orchard *(G-7856)*
Waters Edge Gallery & Framery ...... G 253 858-7449
Gig Harbor *(G-4174)*

ASBESTOS PRODUCTS

A1 Asbestos LLC .... G 509 881-0074
Cashmere *(G-2311)*
Asbestos Northwest .... G 253 941-4343
Federal Way *(G-3717)*

ASBESTOS REMOVAL EQPT

Air Tech Abatement Tech Inc .... E 509 315-4550
Spokane *(G-12104)*

ASHLAR: Cast Stone

Cams-Usa Inc .... F 253 639-3890
Kent *(G-4835)*
J & R Commercial Inc .... G 253 639-3890
Kent *(G-4963)*

ASPHALT & ASPHALT PRDTS

Bainter Bainter & Bainter LLC .... G 360 267-5521
Grayland *(G-4292)*
Lakeside Industries Inc .... D 425 313-2600
Issaquah *(G-4437)*
Lakeside Industries Inc .... E 360 491-5460
Olympia *(G-7318)*
Lakeside Industries Inc .... E 360 423-6882
Longview *(G-5925)*
Lakeside Industries Inc .... E 360 794-7779
Monroe *(G-6590)*
Lakeside Industries Inc .... E 360 604-1869
Vancouver *(G-14356)*
Looker & Associates Inc .... E 253 210-5200
Puyallup *(G-8179)*
Miles Resources LLC .... C 253 383-3585
Puyallup *(G-8192)*
Mitchell Trucking and Paving .... G 509 884-5928
East Wenatchee *(G-3026)*
Naselle Rock & Asphalt Company ... F 360 484-3443
Naselle *(G-7017)*
Superior Asphalt & Paving Co .... F 509 248-6823
Yakima *(G-15689)*
Yk Products LLC .... G 425 244-5000
Everett *(G-3662)*

ASPHALT COATINGS & SEALERS

Custom Bilt Holdings LLC .... E 253 872-7330
Lakewood *(G-5709)*
Gardner-Fields Inc .... G 253 627-4098
Tacoma *(G-13304)*
Hco Holding I Corporation .... G 503 255-3767
Vancouver *(G-14289)*
Iko Pacific Inc .... E 360 988-9103
Sumas *(G-13046)*
Johns Manville Corporation .... D 800 654-3103
Kent *(G-4970)*
Mates Seal Smart .... G 509 489-6346
Spokane *(G-12386)*
Metal Sales Manufacturing Corp ...... F 253 872-5750
Kent *(G-5007)*
Pabco Building Products LLC .... C 253 284-1200
Tacoma *(G-13449)*
Perfection Coatings .... G 509 599-2538
Spokane Valley *(G-12828)*
Richard Lawson Construction .... E 360 378-4313
Friday Harbor *(G-4055)*
Road Products Inc .... G 509 922-1206
Spokane Valley *(G-12853)*

ASPHALT PLANTS INCLUDING GRAVEL MIX TYPE

Albina Holdings Inc .... D 360 696-3408
Vancouver *(G-14017)*
Asphalt Equipment & Service Co ..... E 253 939-4150
Auburn *(G-379)*
US Oil & Refining Co .... C 253 383-1651
Tacoma *(G-13574)*
Western States Asphalt LLC .... F 509 487-4560
Spokane *(G-12586)*
Western States Asphalt LLC .... G 509 545-9864
Pasco *(G-7653)*
Western States Group LLC .... G 509 487-4560
Spokane *(G-12587)*

ASSEMBLING SVC: Plumbing Fixture Fittings, Plastic

Tubs To Go Inc .... G 425 348-7888
Lynnwood *(G-6213)*

ASSOCIATIONS: Business

Kalispel Tribe of Indians .... E 509 242-7000
Airway Heights *(G-54)*
Point Roberts Press Inc .... G 360 945-0413
Blaine *(G-1696)*
Prime West of Washington Inc .... E 360 424-5783
Kent *(G-5081)*
Tarr Acquisition LLC .... G 253 859-2979
Auburn *(G-577)*

ASSOCIATIONS: Fraternal

Veterans Express .... G 253 517-3798
Federal Way *(G-3800)*

ASSOCIATIONS: Real Estate Management

Impact Property Mgnt .... G 425 334-6361
Lake Stevens *(G-5647)*
McFarland Cascade Holdings Inc .... G 360 273-5541
Rochester *(G-9136)*
McFarland Cascade Holdings Inc .... D 253 572-3033
Tacoma *(G-13404)*

ATHLETIC CLUB & GYMNASIUMS, MEMBERSHIP

Elite Athletics Training LLC .... G 509 221-1898
Richland *(G-8993)*

ATOMIZERS

195 Industries Inc .... F 509 245-3735
Spangle *(G-12083)*
Abraham Industries LLC .... F 509 329-8260
Tacoma *(G-13155)*
Allco Manufacturing Inc .... G 702 616-2081
Federal Way *(G-3714)*
ATF Mfg LLC .... G 509 762-2421
Moses Lake *(G-6681)*
Haytools Inc .... G 509 933-1102
Ellensburg *(G-3207)*
Insitu Inc .... F 509 493-8600
Bingen *(G-1637)*
Interstate Industries Inc .... G 206 387-2364
Kent *(G-4959)*
Kenwood Manufacturing Inc .... G 602 625-4012
Tukwila *(G-13764)*
Northwest Marine Inds LLC .... G 360 389-5351
Bellingham *(G-1468)*
Shah Safari Inc .... E 206 282-6122
Seattle *(G-11095)*
Thomas Grange Holdings Inc .... F 678 921-0499
Seattle *(G-11295)*

AUDIO & VIDEO EQPT, EXC COMMERCIAL

Audiocontrol Inc .... F 425 775-8461
Spokane *(G-12126)*
Bayview Pro Audio Inc .... G 360 867-1798
Olympia *(G-7235)*
Cco Holdings LLC .... G 509 293-4177
Wenatchee *(G-15016)*
Cco Holdings LLC .... G 509 643-3364
Sunnyside *(G-13116)*
Electric AMP Innvtions USA LLC ..... G 509 455-7469
Spokane *(G-12239)*
Fusion9 Design LLC .... G 360 831-0899
Camano Island *(G-2214)*
High Definition Audio Video .... G 360 398-8265
Lynden *(G-6021)*
Impulse Audio Inc .... G 206 650-0075
Seattle *(G-10217)*
Lavry Engineering .... G 360 598-9757
Poulsbo *(G-7974)*
Mackie Designs Inc .... G 425 868-0555
Redmond *(G-8544)*
Nepoware Corporation .... G 425 802-8821
Medina *(G-6453)*
Pb Inc .... G 206 747-0347
Bellevue *(G-1066)*
Savang Sine .... G 206 721-2558
Seattle *(G-11020)*
Shunyata Research Corporation ...... F 360 598-9935
Poulsbo *(G-7999)*
The Riff .... G 509 280-1300
Spokane *(G-12554)*

AUDIO COMPONENTS

Allied Forces Inc .... G 360 387-5713
Camano Island *(G-2206)*
Condor Technical Services .... G 206 633-5190
Seattle *(G-9726)*
Modwright Instruments Inc .... G 360 247-6688
Amboy *(G-95)*

AUDIO ELECTRONIC SYSTEMS

Acoustic Info Proc Lab LLC .... G 509 427-5374
Stevenson *(G-13008)*
Advanced Autosound .... G 509 453-5363
Yakima *(G-15500)*
Audiocontrol Inc .... E 425 775-8461
Mountlake Terrace *(G-6859)*
Cloudstream Media Inc .... G 858 245-0034
Liberty Lake *(G-5828)*
Jo Bee Inc .... G 509 483-1118
Spokane *(G-12336)*
Live Sound & Recording Co LLC ..... G 425 308-2868
Everett *(G-3537)*
Loud Audio LLC .... G 425 892-6500
Woodinville *(G-15294)*

PRODUCT SECTION

AUTOMOTIVE BODY, PAINT & INTERIOR REPAIR & MAINTENANCE SVC

McCauley International Inc ....G....... 253 229-8900
  Puyallup *(G-8187)*
Nickolay Philip and Wendy LLC ....G....... 206 463-7997
  Vashon *(G-14736)*
Playnetwork Inc ....C....... 425 497-8100
  Redmond *(G-8626)*
Shadow Master ....G....... 253 984-0559
  Lakewood *(G-5754)*
Vanatoo LLC ....G....... 206 486-1002
  Auburn *(G-590)*
Westek Marketing LLC ....G....... 425 888-1988
  Nine Mile Falls *(G-7085)*

AUDIOLOGICAL EQPT: Electronic

Mind Modulations ....G....... 626 863-7379
  Marysville *(G-6360)*

AUTO & HOME SUPPLY STORES: Auto & Truck Eqpt & Parts

Maren-Go Solutions Corporation ....G....... 217 506-2749
  Vancouver *(G-14393)*
Whidbey Auto Parts Inc ....G....... 360 675-5946
  Oak Harbor *(G-7170)*

AUTO & HOME SUPPLY STORES: Auto Air Cond Eqpt, Sell/Install

U-Pull-It Auto Parts Inc ....G....... 509 895-7655
  Yakima *(G-15698)*

AUTO & HOME SUPPLY STORES: Automotive Access

Heininger Holdings LLC ....G....... 360 756-2411
  Bellingham *(G-1368)*
Linex of Olympia ....G....... 360 709-0363
  Tumwater *(G-13884)*

AUTO & HOME SUPPLY STORES: Automotive parts

Afco Performance Group LLC ....G....... 360 453-2030
  Monroe *(G-6543)*
D & G Auto Parts ....G....... 360 696-3631
  Vancouver *(G-14161)*
Diebels Welding & Machine ....G....... 509 422-0457
  Okanogan *(G-7196)*
Dynamic Automotive Distrs ....G....... 206 725-4474
  Seattle *(G-9864)*
Genuine Parts Company ....F....... 509 484-4400
  Spokane *(G-12269)*
Jones Automotive Engine Inc ....E....... 509 838-3625
  Spokane *(G-12341)*
Kroll Machine & Supply Inc ....G....... 509 397-4666
  Colfax *(G-2715)*
Material Inc ....F....... 509 754-4695
  Ephrata *(G-3342)*
Material Inc ....G....... 509 633-1740
  Grand Coulee *(G-4243)*
Material Inc ....G....... 509 787-4585
  Quincy *(G-8303)*
Oceanwest Rvm LLC ....G....... 503 569-6969
  Lynden *(G-6041)*
Olsons Gaskets ....G....... 360 871-1207
  Port Orchard *(G-7836)*
S & H Auto Parts Inc ....G....... 360 354-4468
  Lynden *(G-6051)*
Smith Auto Electric Inc ....G....... 509 453-8275
  Yakima *(G-15677)*
Trail Tech Inc ....G....... 360 687-4530
  Battle Ground *(G-748)*
Walla Walla Motor Supply Inc ....F....... 509 525-2940
  Walla Walla *(G-14893)*
Westbay Auto Parts Inc ....F....... 360 373-1424
  Bremerton *(G-2011)*

AUTO & HOME SUPPLY STORES: Trailer Hitches, Automotive

Fab-Tech Inc ....G....... 360 755-0215
  Burlington *(G-2156)*
Macklin Welding ....G....... 509 926-3597
  Spokane Valley *(G-12781)*

AUTO & HOME SUPPLY STORES: Truck Eqpt & Parts

4k Lift Services Inc ....G....... 509 679-9997
  East Wenatchee *(G-3004)*

BTS Exchange LLC ....G....... 253 859-5450
  Kent *(G-4825)*
Canopy World Inc ....G....... 253 531-5192
  Tacoma *(G-13219)*
Fab Shop LLC ....E....... 253 568-9124
  Edgewood *(G-3077)*
Kenneth Walker ....G....... 360 748-7519
  Chehalis *(G-2508)*
Nelson Truck Equipment Co Inc ....F....... 206 622-3825
  Seattle *(G-10598)*
Nelson Truck Equipment Co Inc ....E....... 253 395-3825
  Kent *(G-5018)*

AUTO SPLYS & PARTS, NEW, WHSLE: Exhaust Sys, Mufflers, Etc

Marine Engine Repair Co Inc ....E....... 206 286-1817
  Seattle *(G-10480)*

AUTOCLAVES: Indl

Sunsteel LLC ....E....... 509 836-3078
  Vancouver *(G-14619)*

AUTOMATED TELLER MACHINE NETWORK

Core Corporation ....G....... 425 485-0574
  Bothell *(G-1757)*

AUTOMATIC REGULATING CNTRLS: Liq Lvl, Residential/Comm Heat

P G K Inc ....G....... 425 432-0945
  Maple Valley *(G-6285)*

AUTOMATIC REGULATING CONTROL: Building Svcs Monitoring, Auto

Branom Operating Company LLC ....E....... 206 762-6050
  Seattle *(G-9578)*
Enertec Bas ....G....... 360 786-1257
  Olympia *(G-7277)*
Schneider Elc Buildings LLC ....F....... 509 892-1121
  Spokane Valley *(G-12860)*
Sentinel Offender Services LLC ....E....... 206 223-9681
  Seattle *(G-11089)*
West Coast Stair Company ....G....... 206 406-4927
  Renton *(G-8944)*

AUTOMATIC REGULATING CONTROLS: AC & Refrigeration

Siemens Industry Inc ....D....... 208 883-8330
  Pullman *(G-8108)*

AUTOMATIC REGULATING CONTROLS: Elect Air Cleaner, Automatic

P & RS Mobile Services Inc ....G....... 425 652-1394
  Maple Valley *(G-6284)*

AUTOMATIC REGULATING CONTROLS: Hardware, Environmental Reg

Million Tree Prj For Somalia ....G....... 206 731-9164
  Renton *(G-8855)*

AUTOMATIC REGULATING CONTROLS: Humidity, Air-Conditioning

Sporting Systems Corporation ....G....... 360 607-0036
  Vancouver *(G-14603)*

AUTOMATIC REGULATING CONTROLS: Pneumatic Relays, Air-Cond

Twintec Inc ....G....... 253 218-0890
  Auburn *(G-586)*

AUTOMATIC REGULATING CTRLS: Damper, Pneumatic Or Electric

Smart Moves Inc ....G....... 206 842-6575
  Bainbridge Island *(G-673)*

AUTOMATIC REGULATING CTRLS: Elec Heat Proportion, Modultg

Waft Corp ....F....... 425 743-4601
  Mukilteo *(G-6990)*

AUTOMATIC TELLER MACHINES

American Bancard LLC ....E....... 360 713-0690
  Vancouver *(G-14026)*
Burlington Shell ....G....... 360 755-0400
  Burlington *(G-2138)*
Chevron Kalama ....F....... 360 673-2972
  Kalama *(G-4495)*
Core Corporation ....G....... 425 485-0574
  Bothell *(G-1757)*

AUTOMOBILE DRIVING SCHOOLS

Defensive Driving School Inc ....G....... 425 643-0116
  Kirkland *(G-5320)*

AUTOMOBILES & OTHER MOTOR VEHICLES WHOLESALERS

Freedom Truck Centers Inc ....E....... 509 248-9478
  Union Gap *(G-13931)*
Harris-Ford Inc ....C....... 425 678-0391
  Lynnwood *(G-6132)*

AUTOMOTIVE & TRUCK GENERAL REPAIR SVC

Bobs Welding & Auto Repair ....G....... 509 427-5094
  Carson *(G-2303)*
Custom Chemicals Co Inc ....F....... 509 349-7000
  Warden *(G-14930)*
Eagle Systems Inc ....E....... 509 535-8654
  Spokane Valley *(G-12685)*
Eds Automotive and Machine Sp ....G....... 425 355-7268
  Mukilteo *(G-6919)*
EDS Garage & Welding ....G....... 253 845-8741
  Puyallup *(G-8149)*
Freedom Truck Centers Inc ....E....... 509 248-9478
  Union Gap *(G-13931)*
Haldex Brake Products Corp ....G....... 360 944-3070
  Vancouver *(G-14279)*
Heiser George Body Co Inc ....E....... 206 622-7985
  Tukwila *(G-13748)*
K & M Unibody Works Inc ....F....... 509 922-2083
  Spokane Valley *(G-12758)*
Methow Valley Industrial LLC ....E....... 509 997-7777
  Twisp *(G-13914)*
North Bend Automotives ....G....... 425 888-4522
  North Bend *(G-7119)*
Northwest Truck & Auto AC ....F....... 206 242-6034
  Federal Way *(G-3765)*
Perfect Reflections Auto Body ....G....... 360 426-0805
  Shelton *(G-11721)*
Pioneer Metal Works Inc ....G....... 509 787-4425
  Quincy *(G-8306)*
Sjb Enterprises Inc ....G....... 509 926-6979
  Spokane Valley *(G-12874)*

AUTOMOTIVE AIR CONDITIONING REPAIR SHOPS

Northwest Truck & Auto AC ....F....... 206 242-6034
  Federal Way *(G-3765)*

AUTOMOTIVE BATTERIES WHOLESALERS

Wli Recycling Inc ....G....... 253 267-1965
  Lakewood *(G-5769)*

AUTOMOTIVE BODY SHOP

Andersons Rebuilding ....G....... 360 779-5287
  Poulsbo *(G-7944)*
Auto Body Specialties ....G....... 360 424-1313
  Mount Vernon *(G-6772)*
Pro Finish Inc ....G....... 253 850-9422
  Kent *(G-5083)*

AUTOMOTIVE BODY, PAINT & INTERIOR REPAIR & MAINTENANCE SVC

Csr Marine Inc ....E....... 206 632-2001
  Seattle *(G-9761)*
Harris-Ford Inc ....C....... 425 678-0391
  Lynnwood *(G-6132)*
K & M Unibody Works Inc ....F....... 509 922-2083
  Spokane Valley *(G-12758)*
Luann Ayling ....G....... 509 633-2839
  Electric City *(G-3167)*
Perfect Reflections Auto Body ....G....... 360 426-0805
  Shelton *(G-11721)*

Employee Codes: A=Over 500 employees, B=251-500
C=101-250, D=51-100, E=20-50, F=10-19, G=2-9

AUTOMOTIVE CUSTOMIZING SVCS, NONFACTORY BASIS

Custom Welding .... G 206 242-5047
  Burien *(G-2100)*

AUTOMOTIVE GLASS REPLACEMENT SHOPS

Clear View Auto & Window Glass .... G 360 539-5909
  Lacey *(G-5542)*
Gaynors Glass & Restoration .... G 253 538-2501
  Tacoma *(G-13305)*

AUTOMOTIVE LETTERING SVCS

Comeau Lettering .... G 360 573-2216
  Vancouver *(G-14141)*

AUTOMOTIVE PAINT SHOP

Heiser George Body Co Inc .... E 206 622-7985
  Tukwila *(G-13748)*
Sun Valley Enterprises .... G 509 453-1914
  Yakima *(G-15688)*

AUTOMOTIVE PARTS, ACCESS & SPLYS

Afco Performance Group LLC .... G 360 453-2030
  Monroe *(G-6543)*
ARB USA .... G 866 293-9078
  Auburn *(G-376)*
Art Morrison Enterprises Inc .... E 253 344-0161
  Fife *(G-3933)*
Billet Connection Llc .... G 509 467-7584
  Spokane *(G-12148)*
Bnb International LLC .... G 425 712-1687
  Edmonds *(G-3097)*
Brooks Tactical Systems .... F 253 549-2703
  Fox Island *(G-4019)*
Corner Stone R V Center LLC .... G 360 704-4441
  Tumwater *(G-13865)*
Cummins Inc .... E 509 455-4411
  Spokane *(G-12211)*
Cummins Inc .... E 360 748-8841
  Tumwater *(G-13867)*
Current Drives LLC .... G 206 697-6073
  Seattle *(G-9765)*
Delphis Creative Bus Solutions .... G 360 689-4063
  Gig Harbor *(G-4094)*
Dogfence of North America .... G 509 991-0385
  Clayton *(G-2657)*
Drive Line Svc of Bellingham .... G 360 734-7828
  Bellingham *(G-1326)*
Ford Motor Credit Company LLC .... D 425 643-0454
  Bellevue *(G-914)*
Harris-Ford Inc .... C 425 678-0391
  Lynnwood *(G-6132)*
Heininger Holdings LLC .... G 360 756-2411
  Bellingham *(G-1368)*
Instrument Sales and Svc Inc .... E 253 796-5400
  Kent *(G-4954)*
Jones Automotive Engine Inc .... E 509 838-3625
  Spokane *(G-12341)*
Joyson Safety Systems .... C 509 762-5549
  Moses Lake *(G-6718)*
Kic-N Corp .... G 360 696-9595
  Vancouver *(G-14349)*
Lifeport Inc .... E 360 225-6690
  Woodland *(G-15446)*
Lithia Motors Inc .... G 509 321-7300
  Spokane *(G-12373)*
Meritor Inc .... C 360 737-0175
  Vancouver *(G-14411)*
Model A Wheel Colors .... G 206 264-4944
  Seatac *(G-9290)*
N C Power Systems Co .... C 425 251-5877
  Tukwila *(G-13774)*
North American Atk Corporation .... E 360 733-1916
  Bellingham *(G-1463)*
Offroad Outpost .... G 360 910-0021
  Vancouver *(G-14448)*
Paccar Inc .... C 425 828-5000
  Kirkland *(G-5424)*
Paccar Inc .... B 425 468-7400
  Bellevue *(G-1058)*
Potter-Webster Co .... G 360 577-9632
  Longview *(G-5944)*
Prism Motors Inc .... G 425 503-5415
  Seattle *(G-10867)*
Pro Tech Industries Inc .... C 360 573-6641
  Vancouver *(G-14510)*

Rebreathers Usa LLC .... G 425 789-1255
  Everett *(G-3596)*
Roadmaster Inc .... G 360 896-0407
  Vancouver *(G-14555)*
Roadmaster Inc .... G 360 735-7575
  Vancouver *(G-14556)*
S & S Engine Remanufacturing .... E 509 325-4558
  Spokane *(G-12489)*
Seattle Radiator LLC .... G 206 682-5148
  Seattle *(G-11071)*
South Sound Metal Inc .... G 253 564-0226
  University Place *(G-13981)*
Subaru of America Inc .... G 360 737-7630
  Vancouver *(G-14614)*
T3 Technique LLC .... G 425 785-0361
  Redmond *(G-8687)*
Tesla Inc .... C 425 453-5021
  Bellevue *(G-1182)*
Thermal Solutions Mfg .... G 206 764-7028
  Sumner *(G-13106)*
Thermal Solutions Mfg Inc .... G 800 776-4650
  Tukwila *(G-13826)*
TNT Machining LLC .... G 360 988-0274
  Sumas *(G-13052)*
Toolcraft Inc .... F 360 794-5512
  Monroe *(G-6633)*
Topdown Incorporated .... G 206 920-5566
  Stanwood *(G-12997)*
Tork Lift International Inc .... F 253 479-0115
  Kent *(G-5182)*
Triad Products Corporation .... G 425 514-8363
  Everett *(G-3636)*
Truckvault Inc .... G 360 855-0464
  Sedro Woolley *(G-11577)*
Ultra Carbon .... G 253 922-4266
  Lakewood *(G-5764)*
Viper Tactical LLC .... G 425 341-0529
  Salkum *(G-9181)*
Vulcan Performance .... G 360 450-4237
  Ridgefield *(G-9119)*
Xtr Off-Road Products .... G 208 717-1515
  Clarkston *(G-2656)*
Ya We Can Do That .... G 360 253-5555
  Vancouver *(G-14703)*
Yakima Grinding Co .... F 509 575-1977
  Yakima *(G-15714)*

AUTOMOTIVE PARTS: Plastic

FA Green Company .... E 425 888-0007
  Snoqualmie *(G-12012)*
Ktn Thermo Dynamics .... G 509 823-0560
  Yakima *(G-15610)*
Max-Five Importing Company .... G 253 887-8665
  Auburn *(G-492)*
Nova Verta USA Inc .... G 509 444-7910
  Spokane Valley *(G-12811)*
Rod Thunfield & Custom .... G 253 536-0373
  Puyallup *(G-8238)*

AUTOMOTIVE PRDTS: Rubber

EZ Lip LLC .... G 425 753-6814
  Renton *(G-8798)*

AUTOMOTIVE RADIATOR REPAIR SHOPS

Harrys Radiator Shop Inc .... G 509 765-8581
  Moses Lake *(G-6713)*
Seattle Radiator LLC .... G 206 682-5148
  Seattle *(G-11071)*
Webers Radiator Service Inc .... G 509 452-3747
  Yakima *(G-15705)*

AUTOMOTIVE REPAIR SHOPS: Brake Repair

Stans Headers Inc .... F 253 854-5310
  Auburn *(G-571)*

AUTOMOTIVE REPAIR SHOPS: Carburetor Repair

Carburetors Unlimited Inc .... G 253 833-4106
  Auburn *(G-401)*

AUTOMOTIVE REPAIR SHOPS: Diesel Engine Repair

Cummins Inc .... F 509 248-9033
  Yakima *(G-15545)*
Western Equipment Repr & Wldg .... G 253 922-8351
  Fife *(G-3997)*

AUTOMOTIVE REPAIR SHOPS: Electrical Svcs

Electrical Services & SEC Inc .... G 206 276-6629
  Kent *(G-4887)*
Smith Auto Electric Inc .... G 509 453-8275
  Yakima *(G-15677)*

AUTOMOTIVE REPAIR SHOPS: Engine Rebuilding

Jones Automotive Engine Inc .... E 509 838-3625
  Spokane *(G-12341)*
S & S Engine Remanufacturing .... E 509 325-4558
  Spokane *(G-12489)*
Tims Country Saw Shop .... G 509 486-2798
  Tonasket *(G-13660)*
Toms Prfmce Mch & Repr Inc .... G 360 256-1722
  Vancouver *(G-14642)*

AUTOMOTIVE REPAIR SHOPS: Engine Repair

Seatac Automotive .... G 253 839-0309
  Kent *(G-5121)*

AUTOMOTIVE REPAIR SHOPS: Engine Repair, Exc Diesel

Easterday Diesel Manufacturing .... G 509 269-4577
  Mesa *(G-6492)*

AUTOMOTIVE REPAIR SHOPS: Frame & Front End Repair Svcs

Norms Truck & Equipment Inc .... F 253 833-8339
  Pacific *(G-7535)*
R & A Manufacturing Inc .... G 425 228-2109
  Renton *(G-8888)*

AUTOMOTIVE REPAIR SHOPS: Fuel System Repair

Defbooty LLC .... G 800 311-5887
  Chehalis *(G-2488)*

AUTOMOTIVE REPAIR SHOPS: Machine Shop

Auto Spring Service Inc .... G 253 839-3780
  Kent *(G-4799)*
Automotive Machine Specialties .... G 425 355-0802
  Everett *(G-3376)*
Dg Machine .... G 253 735-1373
  Auburn *(G-426)*
Heads Up Inc .... G 253 833-4546
  Auburn *(G-461)*
Johnsons Machine and Prfmce Sp .... G 360 352-4465
  Olympia *(G-7313)*
Valley Automotive Machine .... G 360 336-9722
  Mount Vernon *(G-6850)*
Yakima Grinding Co .... F 509 575-1977
  Yakima *(G-15714)*

AUTOMOTIVE REPAIR SHOPS: Muffler Shop, Sale/Rpr/Installation

Airport Welding & Muffler Inc .... G 360 568-7135
  Snohomish *(G-11872)*
Barnes Welding Inc .... G 509 745-8588
  Waterville *(G-15005)*
Sharps Welding & Muffler Ctr .... G 509 452-2101
  Moxee *(G-6885)*
Stans Headers Inc .... F 253 854-5310
  Auburn *(G-571)*
Taylors Marine Center .... G 509 633-2945
  Electric City *(G-3168)*

AUTOMOTIVE REPAIR SHOPS: Powertrain Components Repair Svcs

Precision Driveshaft Inc .... G 253 236-5640
  Kent *(G-5077)*

AUTOMOTIVE REPAIR SHOPS: Sound System Svc & Installation

Instrument Sales and Svc Inc .... E 253 796-5400
  Kent *(G-4954)*

PRODUCT SECTION

BADGES, WHOLESALE

AUTOMOTIVE REPAIR SHOPS: Trailer Repair
Carrier Transports Inc .... G 509 452-0136
  Yakima *(G-15528)*
Gibbs Trailer Mfg & Repr .... G 509 547-8241
  Pasco *(G-7586)*
Marquez Mfg Ltd .... E 509 837-6230
  Sunnyside *(G-13133)*

AUTOMOTIVE REPAIR SHOPS: Truck Engine Repair, Exc Indl
Cummins Inc .... E 360 748-8841
  Tumwater *(G-13867)*
Endicott Truck & Tractor .... G 509 657-3436
  Endicott *(G-3264)*

AUTOMOTIVE REPAIR SVC
Braun Northwest Inc .... C 800 245-6303
  Chehalis *(G-2474)*
Dr Dans Alternative Fuel Werks .... G 206 783-5728
  Seattle *(G-9851)*
Drive Line Svc of Bellingham .... G 360 734-7828
  Bellingham *(G-1326)*
Jjs Automotive & Auto Elc LLC .... G 509 248-2622
  Union Gap *(G-13935)*
Maverick Metalworks LLC .... G 253 345-1590
  Spanaway *(G-12063)*
Performance Radiator PCF LLC .... E 253 472-0586
  Tacoma *(G-13464)*
Rads Auto .... G 509 965-5712
  Yakima *(G-15659)*

AUTOMOTIVE SPLYS & PARTS, NEW, WHOL: Auto Servicing Eqpt
D&J Custom Metal Fabrication .... G 206 242-3238
  Burien *(G-2101)*

AUTOMOTIVE SPLYS & PARTS, NEW, WHOLESALE: Brakes
Global Direct Components LLC .... F 253 661-1100
  Federal Way *(G-3741)*

AUTOMOTIVE SPLYS & PARTS, NEW, WHOLESALE: Engines/Eng Parts
Kroll Machine & Supply Inc .... G 509 397-4666
  Colfax *(G-2715)*
Lkq Corporation .... G 800 733-1916
  Bellingham *(G-1412)*

AUTOMOTIVE SPLYS & PARTS, NEW, WHOLESALE: Filters, Air & Oil
Precision Airmotive LLC .... G 360 403-4803
  Arlington *(G-305)*

AUTOMOTIVE SPLYS & PARTS, NEW, WHOLESALE: Radiators
Performance Radiator PCF LLC .... E 253 472-0586
  Tacoma *(G-13464)*
Performance Radiator PCF LLC .... G 206 624-2440
  Seattle *(G-10787)*

AUTOMOTIVE SPLYS & PARTS, NEW, WHOLESALE: Seat Covers
United States Sheepskin Inc .... F 253 627-7114
  Tacoma *(G-13571)*
Willingham Inc .... F 425 432-9867
  Maple Valley *(G-6302)*

AUTOMOTIVE SPLYS & PARTS, NEW, WHOLESALE: Splys
Sp Indstrial Lubrication A LLC .... G 360 579-2646
  Clinton *(G-2699)*

AUTOMOTIVE SPLYS & PARTS, NEW, WHOLESALE: Trailer Parts
Top Notch Trailer Mfg .... F 360 273-0468
  Rochester *(G-9141)*

AUTOMOTIVE SPLYS & PARTS, USED, WHOLESALE: Dry Cell Batt
E Power Systems & Battery Inc .... G 253 267-1965
  Lakewood *(G-5716)*

AUTOMOTIVE SPLYS & PARTS, WHOLESALE, NEC
Cummins Inc .... E 360 748-8841
  Tumwater *(G-13867)*
D & G Auto Parts .... G 360 696-3631
  Vancouver *(G-14161)*
Dynamic Automotive Distrs .... G 206 725-4474
  Seattle *(G-9864)*
Genuine Parts Company .... E 206 575-8100
  Renton *(G-8806)*
Material Inc .... F 509 754-4695
  Ephrata *(G-3342)*
S & H Auto Parts Inc .... G 360 354-4468
  Lynden *(G-6051)*
Safran Usa Inc .... E 425 462-8613
  Bellevue *(G-1112)*
Smith Auto Electric Inc .... G 509 453-8275
  Yakima *(G-15677)*
Valley Automotive Machine .... G 360 336-9722
  Mount Vernon *(G-6850)*
Walla Walla Motor Supply Inc .... F 509 525-2940
  Walla Walla *(G-14893)*
Westbay Auto Parts Inc .... F 360 373-1424
  Bremerton *(G-2011)*
Yakima Grinding Co .... F 509 575-1977
  Yakima *(G-15714)*

AUTOMOTIVE SPLYS, USED, WHOLESALE & RETAIL
Giant Metals Inc .... G 206 592-0963
  Seatac *(G-9285)*
Gundies Inc .... E 360 733-5036
  Bellingham *(G-1364)*
Power Equipment Supply Llc .... G 206 817-5627
  Everett *(G-3580)*

AUTOMOTIVE SPLYS/PARTS, NEW, WHOL: Body Rpr/Paint Shop Splys
K & L Unlimited .... G 509 965-6451
  Yakima *(G-15604)*

AUTOMOTIVE SVCS
Camas Auto License .... G 360 835-2977
  Camas *(G-2236)*

AUTOMOTIVE SVCS, EXC REPAIR & CARWASHES: Glass Tinting
Custom Win Tnting Graphics Inc .... G 509 453-4293
  Yakima *(G-15547)*

AUTOMOTIVE SVCS, EXC REPAIR & CARWASHES: Insp & Diagnostic
A & M Prcsion Msuring Svcs Inc .... F 425 432-7554
  Kent *(G-4750)*

AUTOMOTIVE SVCS, EXC REPAIR & CARWASHES: Maintenance
A A Auto Towing .... G 360 892-2924
  Vancouver *(G-14002)*

AUTOMOTIVE TOWING & WRECKING SVC
Patriot Towing Recovery .... G 360 890-9288
  Lacey *(G-5575)*

AUTOMOTIVE TOWING SVCS
Bobs Welding & Auto Repair .... G 509 427-5094
  Carson *(G-2303)*
SRP Transport Inc .... G 425 770-3031
  Monroe *(G-6626)*

AUTOMOTIVE UPHOLSTERY SHOPS
Willingham Inc .... F 425 432-9867
  Maple Valley *(G-6302)*

AUTOMOTIVE WELDING SVCS
Gt Machining .... G 509 922-8395
  Spokane Valley *(G-12726)*

AUTOMOTIVE: Bodies
Sickspeed Inc .... G 509 833-3768
  Moxee *(G-6886)*

AUTOMOTIVE: Seating
Exomotion LLC .... G 206 763-0754
  Seattle *(G-9954)*
Johnson Controls Inc .... G 509 747-8053
  Spokane *(G-12339)*

AWNINGS & CANOPIES
CDI Custom Design Inc .... E 360 650-1150
  Bellingham *(G-1294)*
FO Berg Company .... F 509 624-8921
  Spokane Valley *(G-12706)*
Outdoor Leisure Centers .... G 509 599-2150
  Spokane *(G-12423)*
T&C Concepts LLC .... G 253 298-2104
  Puyallup *(G-8260)*

AWNINGS & CANOPIES: Awnings, Fabric, From Purchased Matls
Everett Tent & Awning Inc .... G 425 252-8213
  Everett *(G-3464)*
Troger Enterprises Ltd .... G 253 627-8878
  Tacoma *(G-13565)*
Washington Tent & Awning Inc .... G 253 581-7177
  Lakewood *(G-5765)*

AWNINGS & CANOPIES: Canopies, Fabric, From Purchased Matls
Barrett Enclosures Inc .... G 206 285-8100
  Seattle *(G-9494)*

AWNINGS & CANOPIES: Fabric
Bumperchute Co .... G 206 232-8189
  Mercer Island *(G-6457)*

AWNINGS: Fiberglass
Pic Sentry Rail Inc .... G 425 349-3606
  Mukilteo *(G-6965)*

AWNINGS: Metal
Metals USA Building Pdts LP .... F 425 251-0589
  Kent *(G-5008)*

AWNINGS: Wood
Sign Post Inc .... F 360 671-1343
  Bellingham *(G-1533)*

AXES & HATCHETS
American Tomahawk Company LLC .... G 253 884-1940
  Anderson Island *(G-186)*

AXLES
Hendrickson International Corp .... G 360 906-0222
  Vancouver *(G-14293)*
Jantz Engineering .... G 360 598-2773
  Poulsbo *(G-7968)*

BACKHOES
ABC Water Specialty Inc .... G 425 355-9826
  Lake Stevens *(G-5629)*
Affordble Trctr Bckhoe Svc LLC .... G 360 306-1533
  Maple Valley *(G-6253)*
Agate Backhoe Tractor .... G 360 426-7085
  Shelton *(G-11673)*
Les Ware Backhoe .... G 425 508-2252
  Monroe *(G-6591)*
Quality Backhoe Services Inc .... G 509 545-0242
  Burbank *(G-2085)*

BADGES, WHOLESALE
Badge Boys Awards & Engraving .... G 360 876-8414
  Port Orchard *(G-7792)*
United States Dosimetry Tech .... G 509 946-8738
  Richland *(G-9049)*

Employee Codes: A=Over 500 employees, B=251-500
C=101-250, D=51-100, E=20-50, F=10-19, G=2-9

BADGES: Identification & Insignia

BADGES: Identification & Insignia
Brady Worldwide Inc ....E 800 854-6832
  Seattle *(G-9576)*
Brady Worldwide Inc ....E 206 323-8100
  Seattle *(G-9577)*
Pacific Knight Emblem & Insig ....G 206 354-2060
  Kent *(G-5052)*

BAGS & CONTAINERS: Textile, Exc Sleeping
American Edge LLC ....F 509 937-4404
  Valley *(G-13987)*
AMICK Tactical LLC ....G 253 301-7619
  Yelm *(G-15726)*
Last US Bag Co ....G 360 993-2247
  Vancouver *(G-14361)*
Lk Sewing Co ....G 206 240-9973
  Burien *(G-2118)*
Outdoor Research LLC ....C 206 467-8197
  Seattle *(G-10717)*
Seattle Northwest Service Corp ....F 206 553-9209
  Seattle *(G-11066)*

BAGS: Canvas
International Athletic ....G 360 384-6868
  Ferndale *(G-3860)*
Misty Mountain Manufacturing ....E 206 763-4055
  Seattle *(G-10548)*

BAGS: Duffle, Canvas, Made From Purchased Materials
Amjay Inc ....G 360 676-1165
  Bellingham *(G-1247)*
Bad Bags Inc ....G 206 722-0916
  Seattle *(G-9476)*

BAGS: Garment, Plastic Film, Made From Purchased Materials
STS Trading Co ....G 425 830-6368
  Bellevue *(G-1162)*

BAGS: Paper
AAA Sandbags ....G 509 979-4029
  Spokane *(G-12093)*
Hood Packaging Corporation ....C 360 695-1251
  Vancouver *(G-14302)*

BAGS: Paper, Made From Purchased Materials
Portco Corporation ....F 360 696-1641
  Woodland *(G-15460)*
Seatac Packaging Mfg Corp ....D 253 682-6588
  Puyallup *(G-8248)*

BAGS: Plastic
A Well Balanced Home LLC ....G 206 280-5532
  Seattle *(G-9327)*
Portland Plastics ....B 360 887-2230
  Ridgefield *(G-9103)*

BAGS: Plastic, Made From Purchased Materials
American Plastic Mfg Inc ....F 206 763-1055
  Seattle *(G-9394)*
Ampac Packaging LLC ....C 253 939-8206
  Auburn *(G-374)*
Chunder Bag ....G 253 987-6224
  Renton *(G-8772)*
Elkay Plastics Co Inc ....F 425 251-1488
  Kent *(G-4890)*
Envision Inc ....G 509 247-5732
  Fairchild Afb *(G-3695)*

BAGS: Tea, Fabric, Made From Purchased Materials
Motovotano LLC ....G 206 363-0338
  Anacortes *(G-148)*

BAGS: Textile
Carry Gear Solutions LLC ....E 206 957-6800
  Seattle *(G-9636)*

Lammy Industries Inc ....E 206 654-0010
  Seattle *(G-10374)*
Outdoor Research-Canada Inc ....G 206 467-8197
  Seattle *(G-10718)*
Paktek Inc ....E 253 584-4914
  Lakewood *(G-5745)*
Seattle Seams ....G 206 251-8231
  Puyallup *(G-8250)*
Sundog LLC ....G 206 313-8871
  Duvall *(G-3002)*
Swaddledesigns LLC ....E 206 971-0426
  Tukwila *(G-13825)*
Swift Industries ....G 415 608-8227
  Seattle *(G-11237)*
Tom Bihn Inc ....D 206 652-4123
  Seattle *(G-11318)*
Yakima Tent & Awning Co Ltd ....F 509 457-6169
  Yakima *(G-15717)*

BAGS: Vacuum cleaner, Made From Purchased Materials
Green Label Manufacturing Inc ....G 954 445-0001
  Vancouver *(G-14270)*

BAGS: Wardrobe, Closet Access, Made From Purchased Materials
Top Shelf Closet Inc ....G 360 953-1690
  Battle Ground *(G-747)*

BAIT, FISHING, WHOLESALE
George Gehrkes Gink ....G 509 243-4100
  Asotin *(G-353)*

BAKERIES, COMMERCIAL: On Premises Baking Only
Anjou Bakery and Catering ....G 509 782-4360
  Cashmere *(G-2314)*
Anne & Mollys Inc ....D 253 872-8390
  Kent *(G-4785)*
Artisan Baking Company ....G 206 240-4713
  Seattle *(G-9440)*
Baked LLC ....G 206 307-4847
  Seattle *(G-9477)*
Barn Owl Bakery Inc ....G 360 468-3492
  Lopez Island *(G-5979)*
Bimbo Bakeries Usa Inc ....F 509 452-6293
  Yakima *(G-15521)*
Bimbo Bakeries Usa Inc ....F 509 662-4731
  Wenatchee *(G-15013)*
Bimbo Bakeries Usa Inc ....E 425 415-6745
  Woodinville *(G-15191)*
Bimbo Bakery USA ....F 425 347-3900
  Everett *(G-3388)*
Bread Garden Ltd ....D 253 838-1639
  Auburn *(G-396)*
Campbell Soup Company ....B 425 415-2000
  Woodinville *(G-15204)*
CCS Baking Co ....G 206 200-5195
  Lake Stevens *(G-5637)*
Celebrity Bakery & Cafe ....D 253 627-4773
  Tacoma *(G-13229)*
Companion Baking LLC ....G 206 856-4080
  Seattle *(G-9722)*
Cookie Fairy ....G 360 568-0868
  Snohomish *(G-11891)*
Cupcakes of Auburn ....G 253 733-5547
  Auburn *(G-419)*
Ener-G Foods Inc ....E 206 767-3928
  Seattle *(G-9922)*
Fairlight Bakery Inc ....F 360 576-8587
  Vancouver *(G-14220)*
Gais Bakery ....G 425 743-2460
  Lynnwood *(G-6123)*
House of Rising Buns ....G 360 718-8330
  Vancouver *(G-14304)*
Itty Bitty Baking Company LLC ....G 206 715-6134
  Bothell *(G-1868)*
Just American Desserts ....G 509 927-2253
  Spokane Valley *(G-12757)*
L M Cupcakes LLC ....G 425 427-9558
  Issaquah *(G-4436)*
Les Boulangers Associes Inc ....E 206 241-9343
  Seatac *(G-9288)*
Lupitas ....G 253 838-6132
  Federal Way *(G-3754)*
Mc Gavins Bakery ....G 360 373-2414
  Bremerton *(G-1977)*

Miss Mfftts Mystcal Cpckes LLC ....G 360 890-4403
  Olympia *(G-7341)*
Pasteleria Del Castillo ....G 206 242-6247
  Seattle *(G-10762)*
Petite Chat LLC ....G 509 468-2720
  Spokane *(G-12438)*
Piper 2600 Investments LLC ....G 971 409-7596
  Ridgefield *(G-9102)*
Real Love Cupcakes ....G 206 849-9688
  Tacoma *(G-13492)*
Rocket Bakery Inc ....G 509 462-2345
  Spokane Valley *(G-12854)*
S & W Management Co Inc ....E 425 771-6850
  Lynnwood *(G-6191)*
San Juan Salsa Co ....G 360 435-2100
  Arlington *(G-319)*
Savoy Truffle ....G 206 762-7411
  Seattle *(G-11021)*
Schwartz Brothers Restaurants ....C 206 623-3134
  Renton *(G-8906)*
Schwartz Brothers Restaurants ....C 206 623-3134
  Seattle *(G-11030)*
Sister Souls Gluten Free Bkg ....G 206 909-9054
  Seattle *(G-11119)*
Slays Poulsbo Bakery Inc ....E 360 779-2798
  Poulsbo *(G-8001)*
Sweet Dahlia Baking LLC ....G 206 201-3297
  Bainbridge Island *(G-675)*
Sweet Sanity ....G 425 212-7490
  Seattle *(G-11236)*
Tree-Top Baking ....G 360 720-1937
  Clinton *(G-2701)*
Watford Tanikka ....G 360 499-6327
  Lacey *(G-5601)*
Wilkinson Group LLC ....F 509 529-5800
  Walla Walla *(G-14903)*
World Wide Gourmet Foods Inc ....F 360 668-9404
  Woodinville *(G-15410)*
Yum Yum Donut Shops Inc ....G 360 423-0150
  Longview *(G-5970)*

BAKERIES: On Premises Baking & Consumption
Armoire ....G 206 397-4703
  Burien *(G-2092)*
Barn Owl Bakery Inc ....G 360 468-3492
  Lopez Island *(G-5979)*
D Floured LLC ....F 206 395-4623
  Seattle *(G-9781)*
Gingerbread Factory ....G 509 548-6592
  Leavenworth *(G-5803)*
Grand Central Bakery Inc ....D 206 768-0320
  Seattle *(G-10106)*
Mc Gavins Bakery ....G 360 373-2414
  Bremerton *(G-1977)*
Savoy Truffle ....G 206 762-7411
  Seattle *(G-11021)*
Sunrise Bagels & More Inc ....F 360 254-1012
  Vancouver *(G-14616)*

BAKERY FOR HOME SVC DELIVERY
Fresh Flours ....G 206 297-3300
  Seattle *(G-10026)*
Pacific Wholesale Banner & Sup ....G 509 487-4189
  Spokane *(G-12427)*

BAKERY MACHINERY
Belshaw Bros Inc ....C 206 322-5474
  Auburn *(G-391)*
Food Equipment International ....G 509 924-0181
  Spokane Valley *(G-12707)*
Hobart Corporation ....C 360 893-5554
  Orting *(G-7480)*
ITW Food Equipment Group LLC ....E 360 893-5554
  Orting *(G-7482)*

BAKERY PRDTS: Bagels, Fresh Or Frozen
Pike Place Bagel Bakery Inc ....F 206 382-4297
  Seattle *(G-10806)*
Sunrise Bagels & More Inc ....F 360 254-1012
  Vancouver *(G-14616)*

BAKERY PRDTS: Bakery Prdts, Partially Cooked, Exc frozen
Flax 4 Life ....G 360 715-1944
  Bellingham *(G-1349)*

PRODUCT SECTION

BAKERY PRDTS: Bread, All Types, Fresh Or Frozen

Baker Boys Northwest LLC ....G...... 253 383-3113
 Tacoma *(G-13188)*
D & N Farms Partnership ....G...... 509 771-1714
 Moses Lake *(G-6702)*
M and J Distribution ....G...... 360 455-4675
 Olympia *(G-7327)*

BAKERY PRDTS: Buns, Bread Type, Fresh Or Frozen

Northwest Baking Ltd Partnr ....D...... 253 863-0373
 Sumner *(G-13089)*

BAKERY PRDTS: Cakes, Bakery, Exc Frozen

D Floured LLC ....F...... 206 395-4623
 Seattle *(G-9781)*
Oroweat ....G...... 253 872-8237
 Kent *(G-5049)*
Simply Sweet Cupcakes ....G...... 360 568-8600
 Snohomish *(G-11976)*

BAKERY PRDTS: Cakes, Bakery, Frozen

Bella Bella Cupcakes LLC ....F...... 253 509-3158
 Gig Harbor *(G-4079)*
Kellis Creations ....G...... 206 371-7130
 Lynnwood *(G-6147)*
Zuribella ....G...... 253 227-2988
 Spanaway *(G-12082)*

BAKERY PRDTS: Cones, Ice Cream

Elkins Distribution Inc ....G...... 206 241-0333
 Seattle *(G-9898)*
Gelatello Inc ....G...... 425 214-1267
 Federal Way *(G-3740)*

BAKERY PRDTS: Cookies

Brown Sugar Baking Company LLC .....G...... 202 558-8422
 Seattle *(G-9590)*
Sunne Group Ltd Inc ....G...... 253 839-5240
 Federal Way *(G-3792)*
Tsue Chong Co Inc ....E...... 206 623-0801
 Seattle *(G-11346)*

BAKERY PRDTS: Cookies & crackers

Ana Oven ....G...... 661 878-4277
 Tacoma *(G-13170)*
Biscottea Baking Company LLC ....G...... 206 695-2614
 Seattle *(G-9533)*
Campbell Soup Company ....B...... 425 415-2000
 Woodinville *(G-15204)*
Ener-G Foods Inc ....E...... 206 767-3928
 Seattle *(G-9922)*
Fairlight Bakery Inc ....F...... 360 576-8587
 Vancouver *(G-14220)*
Schwartz Brothers Restaurants ....C...... 206 623-3134
 Renton *(G-8906)*
Slays Poulsbo Bakery Inc ....E...... 360 779-2798
 Poulsbo *(G-8001)*
Sugar & Stamp ....G...... 404 944-1354
 Seattle *(G-11213)*
Sunrise Bagels & More Inc ....F...... 360 254-1012
 Vancouver *(G-14616)*

BAKERY PRDTS: Cracker Meal & Crumbs

Madrona Specialty Foods LLC ....E...... 206 903-0500
 Seattle *(G-10465)*

BAKERY PRDTS: Doughnuts, Exc Frozen

Choukette ....G...... 206 466-6906
 Seattle *(G-9680)*
Donut Star Inc ....G...... 253 833-2980
 Auburn *(G-428)*
Ever Green Donuts ....G...... 425 673-5331
 Lynnwood *(G-6117)*
Happy Donut ....G...... 253 852-3286
 Kent *(G-4932)*
Henrys Donuts ....G...... 360 653-4044
 Marysville *(G-6344)*
Henrys Donuts ....F...... 425 258-6887
 Everett *(G-3509)*
Krispy Kreme Doughnuts ....G...... 206 316-7090
 Seattle *(G-10358)*

Pigs & Angels Inc ....F...... 360 293-4053
 Anacortes *(G-161)*

BAKERY PRDTS: Dry

Bake Works Inc ....E...... 360 213-2001
 Vancouver *(G-14054)*
Bite ME Inc ....E...... 253 244-7194
 Lakewood *(G-5703)*
Entenmanns Oroweat Foods ....F...... 360 475-8283
 Bremerton *(G-1952)*
Indulge LLC ....G...... 360 589-7226
 Richland *(G-9008)*
Kusher LLC ....G...... 800 445-0655
 Fife *(G-3963)*
Kusina Fillipina ....G...... 206 322-9433
 Seattle *(G-10365)*
Pacific NW Cookie Co LLC ....G...... 360 280-4179
 Chehalis *(G-2519)*
Snohomish Bakery & CAF ....G...... 360 568-1682
 Snohomish *(G-11981)*

BAKERY PRDTS: Frozen

Brown Sugar Baking Company LLC .....G...... 202 558-8422
 Seattle *(G-9590)*
Conagra Brands Inc ....C...... 425 251-0761
 Kent *(G-4861)*
Ericka J Thielke ....G...... 206 214-7530
 Seattle *(G-9937)*
Les Boulangers Associes Inc ....E...... 206 241-9343
 Seatac *(G-9288)*
Mondelez Global LLC ....G...... 253 395-4237
 Kent *(G-5015)*
Norstar Specialty Foods Inc ....E...... 206 764-4499
 Kent *(G-5026)*
Olsons Baking Company LLC ....C...... 425 774-9164
 Lynnwood *(G-6172)*
Paris Gourmet Dessert ....F...... 206 767-9097
 Seattle *(G-10756)*
Starlight Desserts Inc ....G...... 206 284-8770
 Seattle *(G-11183)*

BAKERY PRDTS: Pies, Exc Frozen

Brown Sugar Baking Company LLC .....G...... 202 558-8422
 Seattle *(G-9590)*
La Waffletz LLC ....G...... 206 432-7548
 Federal Way *(G-3750)*

BAKERY PRDTS: Pretzels

Evas Crackers LLC ....G...... 206 353-5691
 Seattle *(G-9944)*

BAKERY PRDTS: Rolls, Bread Type, Fresh Or Frozen

Jenny Maes Gluten-Free Goodies ....G...... 509 833-5096
 Yakima *(G-15600)*

BAKERY PRDTS: Wholesalers

Cake Time Unque Tste Sweet LLC ......G...... 253 886-9366
 Dupont *(G-2956)*
Ethos Bakery LLC ....G...... 509 942-8799
 Richland *(G-8994)*
Grain Craft Inc ....D...... 206 898-3079
 Seattle *(G-10104)*
Grand Central Bakery Inc ....D...... 206 768-0320
 Seattle *(G-10106)*
United States Bakery ....A...... 206 726-7535
 Seattle *(G-11373)*
United States Bakery ....B...... 509 535-7726
 Spokane Valley *(G-12920)*
United States Bakery ....C...... 206 682-2244
 Seattle *(G-11374)*

BAKERY PRDTS: Zwieback

Nancy Zwieback ....G...... 206 306-0411
 Seattle *(G-10584)*

BAKERY: Wholesale Or Wholesale & Retail Combined

An-Xuyen Bakery Co ....G...... 253 887-7823
 Auburn *(G-375)*
Au Gavroche Inc ....G...... 206 284-8770
 Seattle *(G-9461)*
Berry Haven LLC ....G...... 509 521-4902
 Pasco *(G-7553)*

Bimbo Bakeries Usa Inc ....F...... 509 469-3707
 Union Gap *(G-13923)*
Bimbo Bakeries Usa Inc ....F...... 509 688-3966
 Spokane Valley *(G-12639)*
Flowers Bkg Co Thomasville Inc ....G...... 253 433-4455
 Kent *(G-4912)*
Frosty Bay Seafoods LLC ....G...... 360 387-7685
 Camano Island *(G-2213)*
Grand Central Bakery Inc ....D...... 206 768-0320
 Seattle *(G-10106)*
Great Harvest Bread Co Inc ....E...... 509 535-1146
 Spokane *(G-12281)*
Hancocks Bakery ....G...... 425 885-3780
 Redmond *(G-8487)*
Kotelnikov Zinaida ....G...... 206 728-6195
 Seattle *(G-10357)*
Kylie BS Pastry Case LLC ....G...... 206 935-6335
 Kent *(G-4985)*
Lattins Country Cider ....E...... 360 491-7328
 Olympia *(G-7319)*
Laval ....G...... 360 491-8118
 Olympia *(G-7320)*
Masons Cheesecake Co LLC ....G...... 206 602-4563
 Federal Way *(G-3756)*
Mount Bakery ....G...... 360 715-2195
 Bellingham *(G-1445)*
New Sage Bakery LLC ....G...... 208 596-5331
 Uniontown *(G-13957)*
Olsons Baking Company LLC ....C...... 425 774-9164
 Lynnwood *(G-6172)*
Ono Cakes and Delights ....G...... 206 257-9046
 Seattle *(G-10703)*
Pin Hsiao & Associates LLC ....E...... 253 863-0337
 Sumner *(G-13094)*
Pin Hsiao & Associates LLC ....F...... 206 818-0155
 Seattle *(G-10808)*
Pin Hsiao & Associates LLC ....G...... 425 637-3357
 Redmond *(G-8622)*
Rolln Dough Ltd ....E...... 206 763-4300
 Kent *(G-5105)*
Stanwood Cupcakes LLC ....G...... 360 926-8241
 Stanwood *(G-12993)*
Taste of Heaven Baking LLC ....G...... 509 786-3657
 Prosser *(G-8067)*
Tower Mountain Products ....G...... 509 448-4000
 Spokane *(G-12564)*
United States Bakery ....A...... 206 726-7535
 Seattle *(G-11373)*
United States Bakery ....G...... 509 684-6976
 Colville *(G-2778)*
United States Bakery ....B...... 509 535-7726
 Spokane Valley *(G-12920)*
United States Bakery ....C...... 206 682-2244
 Seattle *(G-11374)*

BALLASTS: Lighting

Envirolux Energy Systems LLC ....G...... 800 914-8779
 Vancouver *(G-14203)*

BALLOONS: Hot Air

Avian Balloon Company ....G...... 509 928-6847
 Spokane Valley *(G-12631)*
Balloon Masters ....G...... 253 566-0201
 University Place *(G-13960)*

BALLOONS: Novelty & Toy

Paul Parish Limited ....G...... 509 735-9820
 Kennewick *(G-4705)*

BANKING SCHOOLS, TRAINING

First Millennium Bank ....G...... 360 797-5108
 Sequim *(G-11634)*

BANKS: Mortgage & Loan

Bookmark Publishing Co ....G...... 425 562-0909
 Bellevue *(G-826)*

BANKS: National Commercial

First Millennium Bank ....G...... 360 797-5108
 Sequim *(G-11634)*

BANNERS: Fabric

Countryman Signs Screen Prtrs ....G...... 425 355-1037
 Everett *(G-3428)*
Robinson Windword Inc ....F...... 509 536-1617
 Spokane *(G-12481)*

Employee Codes: A=Over 500 employees, B=251-500
C=101-250, D=51-100, E=20-50, F=10-19, G=2-9

BANNERS: Fabric

Wincraft Incorporated ....E 507 454-5510
  Woodinville (G-15405)

BANQUET HALL FACILITIES

Boundary Bay Brewing Company ....E 360 647-5593
  Bellingham (G-1281)

BAR

Fishtail Pub ....E 360 943-3650
  Olympia (G-7287)
Silver City Brewing Co Inc ....D 360 698-5879
  Silverdale (G-11857)

BARBECUE EQPT

P&M Products Inc ....G 425 939-8349
  Kirkland (G-5423)
Sno-Valley Dream Factory LLC ....G 408 888-8183
  North Bend (G-7124)

BARGES BUILDING & REPAIR

Bennett Lumber Products Inc ....C 509 758-5558
  Clarkston (G-2623)
Campbell Maritime Inc ....G 206 794-0232
  Seattle (G-9614)
Deep Ocean Expeditions LLC ....G 801 390-7025
  Seattle (G-9814)

BARRICADES: Metal

Highlands Welding Repair Inc ....G 206 283-0080
  Seattle (G-10172)
J Freitag Enterprises Inc ....G 509 453-4461
  Yakima (G-15595)

BARS, COLD FINISHED: Steel, From Purchased Hot-Rolled

DCB Industries Inc ....G 360 750-0009
  Vancouver (G-14169)

BARS, PIPES, PLATES & SHAPES: Lead/Lead Alloy Bars, Pipe

Flashco Manufacturing Inc ....G 360 225-4662
  Woodland (G-15432)

BARS: Concrete Reinforcing, Fabricated Steel

ABG ....G 253 896-1372
  Fife (G-3927)
Alliance Steel Fabrication ....E 253 538-7935
  Tacoma (G-13166)
Big C Industries LLC ....G 844 406-2442
  Longview (G-5888)
CMC Steel Fabricators Inc ....G 253 833-9060
  Auburn (G-409)
Daines Corporation ....G 425 212-3169
  Everett (G-3438)
DCB Industries Inc ....G 360 750-0009
  Vancouver (G-14170)
Jodal Manufacturing ....G 206 763-8848
  Seattle (G-10300)
Katana Industries Inc ....D 509 754-5600
  Ephrata (G-3340)
Kiln Cart Construction ....G 360 319-0414
  Bellingham (G-1394)
McVays Mobile Welding LLC ....G 360 657-0360
  Marysville (G-6358)
ONeill Steel Fabrication Inc ....F 509 467-5309
  Spokane (G-12421)
Western Fabrication Center LLC ....F 360 575-1500
  Kelso (G-4559)

BASALT: Crushed & Broken

Lodestone Quarry Incorporated ....G 360 942-0400
  South Bend (G-12044)
Sterling Breen Crushing Inc ....E 360 736-4240
  Centralia (G-2436)

BASALT: Dimension

Naselle Rock & Asphalt Company ....F 360 484-3443
  Naselle (G-7017)

BASES, BEVERAGE

Diamond Knot Brewing Co Inc ....D 425 355-4488
  Mukilteo (G-6912)

BATH SALTS

Aveda Environmental Lifestyles ....G 509 624-5028
  Spokane (G-12132)
Beyoutiful Bath Bombs More ....G 509 315-9608
  Spokane (G-12146)
Ritzy Bath Bombs ....G 206 499-7336
  Vancouver (G-14552)
Sirens Bath Bombs ....G 360 852-4938
  Vancouver (G-14589)
Udabomb Bath Bombs ....G 509 331-4100
  Othello (G-7508)

BATH SHOPS

Aveda Environmental Lifestyles ....G 509 624-5028
  Spokane (G-12132)

BATHMATS: Rubber

Innocor Foam Technologies LLC ....F 360 575-8844
  Longview (G-5918)

BATHROOM ACCESS & FITTINGS: Vitreous China & Earthenware

Pacarc LLC ....G 206 547-4591
  Seattle (G-10726)

BATHTUBS: Concrete

Chip Away Bathtub Repair ....G 425 246-1306
  North Bend (G-7107)
Melcher Manufacturing Co Inc ....G 509 534-9119
  Spokane Valley (G-12787)

BATTERIES: Lead Acid, Storage

E Power Systems & Battery Inc ....G 253 267-1965
  Lakewood (G-5716)
Energy Battery Systems Inc ....G 253 267-1965
  Lakewood (G-5719)
Enersys ....F 253 299-0005
  Sumner (G-13069)
Wli Recycling Inc ....G 253 267-1965
  Lakewood (G-5769)

BATTERIES: Nickel-Cadmium

Brightvolt Inc ....D 863 603-7640
  Redmond (G-8409)

BATTERIES: Rechargeable

Green-On-Green Energy Inc ....G 206 701-7321
  Auburn (G-457)
Maxx Distribution LLC ....G 888 507-6790
  Tacoma (G-13402)

BATTERIES: Storage

56 Thunder Batteries ....G 253 267-0059
  Tacoma (G-13152)
East Penn Manufacturing Co ....G 253 983-9622
  Lakewood (G-5718)
Egis Group LLC ....G 360 768-1211
  Bellingham (G-1331)
Energy Sales ....F 425 883-2343
  Woodinville (G-15236)
Exide Technologies ....G 509 922-3135
  Spokane Valley (G-12697)
Exide Technologies ....G 253 863-5134
  Sumner (G-13071)
Kibbey Battery Service Inc ....G 253 845-9155
  Puyallup (G-8172)
Megabess Us Inc ....G 425 890-9175
  Bellevue (G-1002)
Ralph M Eronemo ....G 425 985-1617
  Bellevue (G-1093)
Unienergy Technologies LLC ....D 425 290-8898
  Mukilteo (G-6985)
Uninterruptible Power Systems ....G 509 327-7722
  Spokane (G-12576)

BATTERIES: Wet

Austin Else LLC ....F 888 654-4450
  Spokane (G-12128)

Khancell Corporation ....G 646 385-7243
  Blaine (G-1678)
Kibbey Battery Service Inc ....G 253 845-9155
  Puyallup (G-8172)

BATTERY CASES: Plastic Or Plastics Combination

Kaenaa Corp ....G 425 283-3072
  Sammamish (G-9225)
Porex Technologies Corporation ....C 253 284-8000
  Fife (G-3982)

BATTERY CHARGERS

Ample Power Company LLC ....G 206 789-0827
  Seattle (G-9400)
Charge Solutions LLC ....G 425 381-7922
  Sammamish (G-9196)
Exide Technologies ....G 509 922-3135
  Spokane Valley (G-12697)
Exide Technologies ....G 253 863-5134
  Sumner (G-13071)

BATTERY CHARGERS: Storage, Motor & Engine Generator Type

Electrijet Flight Systems Inc ....G 509 990-9474
  Liberty Lake (G-5831)
Global Emergent Tech LLC ....G 425 999-9021
  Seattle (G-10083)
Renewable Energy Tech Inc ....G 253 267-1965
  Lakewood (G-5751)

BATTERY CHARGING GENERATORS

Murphy & Dad Inc ....G 360 438-2747
  Olympia (G-7346)

BEARINGS & PARTS Ball

Richert Lina ....G 206 660-3332
  Camano Island (G-2224)

BEARINGS: Plastic

Edt Corp ....F 360 574-7294
  Ferndale (G-3837)

BEARINGS: Roller & Parts

Modern Siding LLC ....G 813 484-9498
  Everett (G-3550)

BEARINGS: Wooden

D-Way Tools Inc ....G 360 432-9509
  Shelton (G-11694)
Pacific Woodtech Corporation ....C 360 707-2200
  Burlington (G-2177)

BEAUTY & BARBER SHOP EQPT

Advanced Lean Mfg LLC ....E 425 402-8300
  Woodinville (G-15172)
American Innovative Mfg LLC ....G 509 244-2730
  Spokane Valley (G-12611)
Archer-Daniels-Midland Company ....F 509 754-5266
  Ephrata (G-3331)
Avitech International Corp ....F 425 885-3863
  Redmond (G-8395)
B Line Mfg ....G 360 718-2158
  Vancouver (G-14052)
Black Dog Industries ....G 509 946-6400
  Richland (G-8973)
Calib Designs LLC ....G 206 548-9217
  Seattle (G-9606)
Croix Industries Ltd ....G 206 528-5555
  Seattle (G-9754)
Denmar Industries Inc ....G 206 579-9316
  Anacortes (G-121)
Diversified Mfg Techologies ....G 360 424-9300
  Mount Vernon (G-6790)
Ellipse Mfg Inc ....G 253 653-5554
  Tacoma (G-13275)
Evil Industries ....G 206 612-3293
  Duvall (G-2987)
Foxbat Heavy Industries Inc ....G 425 890-0410
  Port Townsend (G-7885)
Frame It Ltd ....G 206 364-7477
  Seattle (G-10019)
Hardwood Industries Inc ....F 425 420-1050
  Snohomish (G-11919)

PRODUCT SECTION

Harris Manufacturing Irri .... G 509 539-1725
 Burbank *(G-2084)*
J & G Industries Inc .... G 206 246-3782
 Normandy Park *(G-7095)*
J D Precision Mfg Inc .... G 509 496-2607
 Colbert *(G-2709)*
Kresek Brothers Manufacturing .... G 509 322-0808
 Tonasket *(G-13652)*
Ledford Industries LLC .... G 253 446-6508
 Puyallup *(G-8177)*
Looker Industries Inc .... G 360 691-1596
 Granite Falls *(G-4279)*
Mid Mountain Materials Inc .... E 360 435-9622
 Arlington *(G-278)*
Mutual Materials .... D 425 452-2300
 Bellevue *(G-1020)*
Neptune Global LLC .... G 310 752-9992
 Seattle *(G-10601)*
Northwest Territorial Mint LLC .... F 253 833-7780
 Kent *(G-5036)*
Nth Degree Inc .... G 253 926-6705
 Milton *(G-6537)*
Olympic Manufacturing Inc .... G 425 679-6303
 Bellevue *(G-1048)*
Polar Fusion LLC .... G 206 779-5238
 Kent *(G-5070)*
Powell Industries Inc .... G 509 922-0463
 Spokane Valley *(G-12835)*
Prowse Manufacturing Group .... E 360 403-8910
 Arlington *(G-308)*
Skilskin .... G 509 326-6760
 Spokane *(G-12506)*
Star Industries Corp Inc .... G 360 826-3895
 Lyman *(G-5997)*
Sweeny Industries .... G 510 701-0384
 Puyallup *(G-8258)*
Todays Style .... G 360 671-4922
 Bellingham *(G-1571)*
TRA Industries Inc .... F 509 924-5858
 Spokane Valley *(G-12909)*
Wheels Up LLC .... G 206 588-1573
 Seattle *(G-11467)*
Xextex Corporation USA .... G 425 392-3848
 Issaquah *(G-4490)*

BEAUTY SALONS

Paulas Choice LLC .... C 425 988-6068
 Seattle *(G-10772)*
Touche Beauty Bar LLC .... G 360 972-2345
 Olympia *(G-7411)*

BED & BREAKFAST INNS

La Toscana Bed Brakfast Winery .... G 509 548-5448
 Cashmere *(G-2325)*

BED SHEETING, COTTON

Fabrications Inc .... G 888 808-9878
 Mercer Island *(G-6462)*

BEDDING & BEDSPRINGS STORES

Slumber Ease Mattress Co Inc .... G 360 657-1654
 Marysville *(G-6385)*

BEDDING, BEDSPREADS, BLANKETS & SHEETS

Bucky Inc .... E 206 545-8790
 Seattle *(G-9592)*

BEDDING, BEDSPREADS, BLANKETS & SHEETS: Comforters & Quilts

Laura Townsend-Faber .... G 206 517-5739
 Seattle *(G-10381)*

BEDS & ACCESS STORES

Dream On Futon Co .... G 360 739-2103
 Bellingham *(G-1325)*
Professional Sleep Services .... G 253 759-2700
 Tacoma *(G-13479)*

BEDS: Hospital

Evolution Technologies USA .... G 360 392-8600
 Ferndale *(G-3839)*
Kci Commercial Inc .... G 253 475-4363
 Tacoma *(G-13373)*

BEDS: Institutional

Exomotion LLC .... G 206 763-0754
 Seattle *(G-9954)*
Welco Sales LLC .... G 425 771-9043
 Edmonds *(G-3162)*

BEEKEEPERS' SPLYS

Bee Keeper Gordons Gold .... G 360 202-9523
 Mount Vernon *(G-6779)*
Knox Cellars .... G 425 392-7536
 Sammamish *(G-9226)*
Tate Honey Farm .... F 509 924-6669
 Spokane *(G-12546)*
Tree of Life Enterprises Inc .... G 360 894-6038
 Yelm *(G-15748)*

BEEKEEPERS' SPLYS: Honeycomb Foundations

Stedman Bee Supplies Inc .... G 360 692-9453
 Silverdale *(G-11860)*
University of Washington .... B 206 543-2565
 Seattle *(G-11380)*

BEER & ALE WHOLESALERS

Blend Wine Shop .... G 253 884-9688
 Lakebay *(G-5688)*

BEER & ALE, WHOLESALE: Beer & Other Fermented Malt Liquors

Farmstrong LLC .... G 360 873-8852
 Mount Vernon *(G-6795)*
Laht Neppur Ventures Inc .... G 509 337-6261
 Waitsburg *(G-14755)*
Lynch Distributing Co .... F 509 248-0880
 Yakima *(G-15613)*

BEER, WINE & LIQUOR STORES

Island Enterprises .... G 360 426-4933
 Shelton *(G-11701)*
Island Enterprises .... F 360 426-3442
 Shelton *(G-11703)*

BEER, WINE & LIQUOR STORES: Hard Liquor

Lynden Liquor Agency 570 .... G 360 354-4744
 Lynden *(G-6033)*

BEER, WINE & LIQUOR STORES: Wine

Alexandria Nicole Cellars LLC .... F 509 786-3497
 Prosser *(G-8029)*
Anderson Resources Inc .... G 360 426-5913
 Shelton *(G-11678)*
Balboa Winery .... G 509 529-0461
 Walla Walla *(G-14767)*
Bartholomew Winery Inc .... G 206 755-5296
 Kennewick *(G-4625)*
Bonair Winery Inc .... F 509 829-6027
 Zillah *(G-15750)*
Chinook Wines .... G 509 786-2725
 Prosser *(G-8033)*
Cinq Cellars LLC .... G 206 954-4626
 Redmond *(G-8420)*
Craftsman Cellars LLC .... G 509 328-3960
 Spokane *(G-12206)*
DRM Holdings Inc .... G 509 338-4699
 Pullman *(G-8089)*
Esther Brcques Wnery Vnyrd LLC .... G 509 476-2861
 Oroville *(G-7465)*
Gilbert Cellars LLC .... G 509 249-9049
 Yakima *(G-15576)*
Ginkgo Forest Winery LLC .... G 509 932-0082
 Mattawa *(G-6406)*
Hoodsport Winery Inc .... G 360 877-9894
 Hoodsport *(G-4325)*
Kiona Vineyards LLC .... F 509 588-6716
 Benton City *(G-1618)*
Knipprath Cellars Inc .... G 208 699-3393
 Spokane *(G-12353)*
Latah Creek Wine Cellars Ltd .... G 509 926-0164
 Spokane Valley *(G-12773)*
Laurelhurst Cellars LLC .... G 206 992-2875
 Seattle *(G-10383)*
Naches Heights Vineyard LLC .... G 509 966-4355
 Yakima *(G-15627)*
Pepper Bridge Winery LLC .... G 425 483-7026
 Woodinville *(G-15334)*
Plain Cellars LLC .... F 509 548-5412
 Leavenworth *(G-5813)*
Rose Saviah Winery LLC .... G 509 522-2181
 Walla Walla *(G-14861)*
Samson Estates Winery .... G 360 966-4526
 Everson *(G-3688)*
Vin Du Lac Winery .... G 509 682-2882
 Chelan *(G-2569)*
Waving Tree Vineyard & Winery .... G 509 773-6552
 Goldendale *(G-4212)*

BEER, WINE & LIQUOR STORES: Wine & Beer

Boundary Bay Brewing Company .... E 360 647-5593
 Bellingham *(G-1281)*
Eaton Hill Winery .... G 509 854-2220
 Granger *(G-4261)*
Washington Wine & Beverage Co .... F 425 485-2437
 Woodinville *(G-15402)*

BEESWAX PROCESSING

Bainbridge Beeswax Works .... G 206 618-2569
 Bainbridge Island *(G-613)*

BELLOWS

Whipple Falls Industries .... G 360 573-0863
 Vancouver *(G-14688)*

BELTING: Fabric

Osp Sling Inc .... E 360 683-4109
 Sequim *(G-11657)*

BELTING: Rubber

Rubber & Plastics Inc .... E 503 289-7720
 Vancouver *(G-14560)*

BELTS & BELT PRDTS

K&W Enterprises Inc .... G 425 255-4316
 Renton *(G-8835)*

BELTS: Chain

Mac Chain Company Limited .... E 800 663-0072
 Woodland *(G-15448)*

BELTS: Conveyor, Made From Purchased Wire

Ammeraal Beltech Inc .... F 510 352-3770
 Kent *(G-4781)*
Donamo Co .... G 360 835-5634
 Washougal *(G-14952)*
Northwest Belt & Equipment Co .... G 360 533-7051
 Aberdeen *(G-24)*

BELTS: Seat, Automotive & Aircraft

Bridport-Air Carrier Inc .... E 253 872-7205
 Kent *(G-4823)*
Pioneer Aerofab Company Inc .... F 360 757-4780
 Burlington *(G-2181)*

BELTS: V

Aahed Logistics LLC .... G 757 395-7063
 Port Orchard *(G-7782)*

BEVERAGE BASES & SYRUPS

Milne Aseptics LLC .... F 509 786-2240
 Prosser *(G-8058)*
Side Hustle LLC .... G 509 435-6773
 Spokane Valley *(G-12870)*

BEVERAGE POWDERS

Zipfizz Corporation .... B 425 398-4240
 Woodinville *(G-15415)*

BEVERAGE PRDTS: Brewers' Grain

Yakima Chief-Hopunion LLC .... G 509 453-4792
 Yakima *(G-15713)*

BEVERAGE STORES

BEVERAGE STORES

Coca-Cola Btlg Co of NY Inc .... E 509 886-1136
  Wenatchee *(G-15089)*
Gbjc Inc .... G 360 321-5262
  Mukilteo *(G-6927)*
Henrys Donuts .... F 425 258-6887
  Everett *(G-3509)*

BEVERAGE, NONALCOHOLIC: Iced Tea/Fruit Drink, Bottled/Canned

Side Hustle LLC .... G 509 435-6773
  Spokane Valley *(G-12870)*

BEVERAGES, ALCOHOLIC: Ale

Diamond Knot Brewing Co Inc .... F 425 315-0703
  Mukilteo *(G-6913)*
Diamond Knot Brewing Co Inc .... E 425 355-4488
  Mukilteo *(G-6914)*
Elysian Brewing Company Inc .... E 206 860-3977
  Seattle *(G-9908)*
Mac & Jacks Brewery Inc .... F 425 558-9697
  Redmond *(G-8543)*
Mule and Elk Brewing Co LLC .... G 206 909-9622
  Cle Elum *(G-2672)*
Pyramid Breweries Inc .... D 206 682-8322
  Seattle *(G-10893)*

BEVERAGES, ALCOHOLIC: Beer

Big House Brewing Inc .... E 509 522-2440
  Walla Walla *(G-14771)*
Big Time Brewery Company Inc .... E 206 545-4509
  Seattle *(G-9526)*
Bighorn Brewery Warehouse .... G 253 474-7465
  Tacoma *(G-13200)*
Boundary Bay Brewing Company ...... E 360 647-5593
  Bellingham *(G-1281)*
Cascade Ales Company .... G 360 520-6040
  Longview *(G-5895)*
Cascadia Homebrew .... G 360 943-2337
  Olympia *(G-7247)*
Chief Springs Fire & Irons Brw .... G 509 382-4677
  Dayton *(G-2879)*
Crucible Brewing Company .... G 425 374-7293
  Everett *(G-3431)*
Diamond Knot Brewery Inc .... E 425 355-4488
  Mukilteo *(G-6911)*
Dirty Couch LLC .... G 203 303-8661
  Seattle *(G-9835)*
Dwinell LLC .... G 312 343-8607
  Goldendale *(G-4195)*
Elliott Bay Brewing Company .... E 206 246-4211
  Seattle *(G-9900)*
Farmstrong LLC .... G 360 873-8852
  Mount Vernon *(G-6795)*
Fish Brewing Co .... F 360 943-3650
  Olympia *(G-7286)*
Fishtail Pub .... E 360 943-3650
  Olympia *(G-7287)*
Genus Brewing Company LLC .... G 509 808-2395
  Spokane Valley *(G-12715)*
Ghost Runners Brewery .... G 360 989-3912
  Vancouver *(G-14251)*
Great Artisan Beverage LLC .... G 425 467-7952
  Bellevue *(G-933)*
Heavy Metal Brewing Co LLC .... G 503 710-6296
  Vancouver *(G-14292)*
Hilliards Beer LLC .... F 206 257-4486
  Seattle *(G-10173)*
Hopunion Craft Brewing Sls LLC .... G 509 457-3200
  Yakima *(G-15584)*
Ice Harbor Brewing Company .... E 509 586-3181
  Kennewick *(G-4673)*
Ice Harbor Brewing Company .... E 509 545-0927
  Kennewick *(G-4674)*
Iron Hop Brewing Co LLC .... G 360 421-8138
  Monroe *(G-6581)*
Joe Nestor .... G 509 264-0800
  Cashmere *(G-2323)*
Kulshan Brewing Company .... G 360 389-5348
  Bellingham *(G-1399)*
Laht Neppur Ventures Inc .... G 509 337-6261
  Waitsburg *(G-14755)*
Ls Brewing Inc .... G 425 423-7700
  Everett *(G-3541)*
Maritime Pacific Brewing Co .... F 206 782-6181
  Seattle *(G-10485)*
Narrows Brewing LLP .... G 253 327-1400
  Tacoma *(G-13424)*

New World Market LP .... G 206 653-7754
  Federal Way *(G-3761)*
Northern Ales Inc .... G 509 738-6913
  Kettle Falls *(G-5238)*
Northwest Peaks Brewery LLC .... G 206 853-0525
  Seattle *(G-10649)*
Orlison Brewing Co .... G 503 894-2917
  Airway Heights *(G-59)*
Pike Brewing Company .... E 206 622-6044
  Seattle *(G-10805)*
Port Townsend Brewing Co .... G 360 385-9967
  Port Townsend *(G-7908)*
Pyramid Breweries Inc .... D 206 682-3377
  Seattle *(G-10894)*
R Ellersick Brewing Co .... G 425 374-7248
  Lynnwood *(G-6185)*
Ram Big Horn Brewery-Northgate ..... G 206 364-8000
  Seattle *(G-10918)*
Ram Bighorn Brewery Kent .... G 253 520-3881
  Kent *(G-5097)*
River City Brewing LLC .... G 509 413-2388
  Spokane *(G-12476)*
Riverport Brewing .... G 509 758-8889
  Clarkston *(G-2646)*
Rooftop Brewing Company .... G 206 457-8598
  Seattle *(G-10980)*
Roslyn Brewing Co Inc .... G 509 649-2232
  Roslyn *(G-9156)*
Schooner Exact .... G 206 432-9734
  Seattle *(G-11028)*
Scuttlebutt Brewing Co LLC .... F 425 252-2829
  Everett *(G-3606)*
Skye Book & Brew .... G 509 382-4677
  Dayton *(G-2885)*
Smith & Reilly Inc .... G 360 693-9225
  Vancouver *(G-14597)*
Structures Brewing LLC .... G 432 770-1540
  Bellingham *(G-1561)*
Subdued Brewing LLC .... G 360 656-6611
  Bellingham *(G-1562)*
Sumerian Brewing Co LLC .... G 425 486-5330
  Woodinville *(G-15380)*
Tapenade Inc .... G 509 966-0686
  Yakima *(G-15694)*
Wenatchee Vly Brewing Co LLC .... G 509 888-8088
  Wenatchee *(G-15085)*
Whitstran Brewing Company Inc .... G 509 786-4922
  Prosser *(G-8076)*
Youngs Market of Washington .... E 206 808-6124
  Renton *(G-8953)*

BEVERAGES, ALCOHOLIC: Beer & Ale

20 Corners Brewing LLC .... F 800 840-3346
  Woodinville *(G-15169)*
Alpine Brewing Co .... G 509 476-9662
  Oroville *(G-7461)*
Ambrew LLC .... G 425 774-1717
  Edmonds *(G-3094)*
Aslan Brewing Company LLC .... G 360 393-4106
  Bellingham *(G-1254)*
Bad Dog Distillery LLC .... G 360 435-3981
  Arlington *(G-207)*
Bastion Brewing Company LLC .... G 360 420-8223
  Oak Harbor *(G-7139)*
Bellevue Brewing Company LLC .... F 425 497-8686
  Bellevue *(G-809)*
Black Fleet Brewing .... G 425 432-6868
  Tacoma *(G-13203)*
Brews Customs .... G 253 334-1694
  Auburn *(G-397)*
Brier Brewing LLC .... G 206 258-4987
  Brier *(G-2018)*
Brotherhood Brewing Co LLC .... G 509 585-6765
  Kennewick *(G-4634)*
Chehalis Brewing Group LLC .... G 360 701-7873
  Chehalis *(G-2483)*
Chuckanut Bay Distillery Inc .... G 360 739-0361
  Bellingham *(G-1297)*
Come On Get Hoppy .... G 509 276-6288
  Nine Mile Falls *(G-7069)*
Cross Current Brewing .... G 253 952-2105
  Tacoma *(G-13249)*
Dungeness Brewing Co .... G 360 775-1877
  Port Angeles *(G-7700)*
Elysian Brewing Company Inc .... F 206 767-0210
  Seattle *(G-9907)*
Figurehead Brewing Company LLC .. G 206 492-7981
  Seattle *(G-9991)*
Foggy Noggin Brewing .... G 425 486-1070
  Bothell *(G-1855)*

Four Generals Brewing .... G 425 282-4360
  Renton *(G-8803)*
Gb Acquisition Inc .... G 206 405-4205
  Seattle *(G-10054)*
Gig Harbor Brewing Co .... G 253 474-0672
  Tacoma *(G-13308)*
Grains of Wrath Brewery .... G 847 727-5100
  Camas *(G-2255)*
Green Lake Brewing Company LLC ..D 206 300-9337
  Seattle *(G-10117)*
Half Lion Brewing Company LLC ...... G 253 561-1115
  Auburn *(G-459)*
Harmon Brewing Company L L C .... F 253 853-1585
  Gig Harbor *(G-4113)*
Holm Brewing Enterpises LLC .... G 425 827-9307
  Kirkland *(G-5359)*
Hopunion CBS LLC .... G 509 574-5124
  Yakima *(G-15583)*
Hoquiam Brewing Co .... G 360 637-8252
  Hoquiam *(G-4342)*
Independent Brewers Untd Corp .... F 206 682-8322
  Seattle *(G-10222)*
Jellyfish Brewing Company .... G 206 517-4497
  Seattle *(G-10291)*
Lagunitas .... G 206 784-2230
  Seattle *(G-10373)*
Lantern Brewing LLC .... G 206 729-5350
  Seattle *(G-10377)*
McMenamins Inc .... F 206 285-4722
  Seattle *(G-10510)*
Meconi Pub & Eatery .... G 253 383-3388
  Tacoma *(G-13405)*
Methow House Watch Inc .... G 509 996-3332
  Winthrop *(G-15163)*
Naan & Brew .... G 425 330-3891
  Bellingham *(G-1456)*
Northern Lights Brewing Co .... G 509 242-2739
  Spokane *(G-12408)*
O-Town Brewing LLC .... G 360 701-4706
  Lacey *(G-5571)*
Optimism Brewing LLC .... F 206 651-5429
  Seattle *(G-10709)*
Quiet Giant Brewing Co LLC .... G 253 584-8373
  Lakewood *(G-5750)*
Rattlesnake Mtn Brewing Co .... E 509 783-5747
  Richland *(G-9038)*
Rhythm & Brews .... G 360 386-9509
  Arlington *(G-315)*
Scrappy Punk Brewing LLC .... G 503 810-1655
  Snohomish *(G-11970)*
Seattle Cider Company .... F 206 762-0490
  Seattle *(G-11052)*
Silver City Brewing Co Inc .... D 360 698-5879
  Silverdale *(G-11857)*
Snipes Mountain Brewing Inc .... E 509 837-2739
  Sunnyside *(G-13142)*
Spanky Burger & Brew .... G 253 720-3344
  Tacoma *(G-13519)*
Stoney Creek Brewing Co LLC .... G 425 836-0958
  Sammamish *(G-9249)*
Thirsty Crab Brewery LLC .... G 360 331-3667
  Freeland *(G-4037)*
Tts Old Iron Brewery LLC .... G 509 847-4393
  Spokane *(G-12573)*
Urban Family Brewing Co .... G 206 861-6769
  Seattle *(G-11390)*
Valhalla Brewing and Bev Co LL .... G 206 243-6361
  Tukwila *(G-13832)*
Vampt Beverage USA Corp .... F 800 508-6149
  Seattle *(G-11401)*
West Seattle Brewing Company .... G 206 708-6677
  Seattle *(G-11451)*
Westland Distillery .... F 206 763-5381
  Seattle *(G-11457)*
Whipsaw Brewing LLC .... F 360 463-0436
  Ellensburg *(G-3239)*

BEVERAGES, ALCOHOLIC: Bourbon Whiskey

Cadee Distillery LLC .... G 360 969-6041
  Clinton *(G-2685)*

BEVERAGES, ALCOHOLIC: Brandy & Brandy Spirits

Devorah Creek Vinyards .... G 206 579-8906
  Auburn *(G-425)*
Efeste .... G 206 535-6997
  Seattle *(G-9886)*

Marketplace Cellars ....G.... 509 795-8500
Spokane *(G-12382)*
Southard Winery ....G.... 509 452-8626
Yakima *(G-15680)*
Stomani Cellars ....G.... 425 892-8375
Woodinville *(G-15375)*
Tatoosh Distillery LLC ....G.... 206 818-0127
Seattle *(G-11274)*
White Heron ....G.... 206 246-5080
Burien *(G-2137)*

BEVERAGES, ALCOHOLIC: Brandy Spirits

New World Market LP ....G.... 206 653-7754
Federal Way *(G-3761)*

BEVERAGES, ALCOHOLIC: Cocktails

Black Magic Beverages LLC ....G.... 206 632-7257
Seattle *(G-9537)*
Seattle Kombucha Company LLC ....G.... 425 985-2364
Kent *(G-5122)*

BEVERAGES, ALCOHOLIC: Distilled Liquors

3 Howls ....G.... 206 747-8400
Seattle *(G-9321)*
Alaska Distributors Co ....G.... 206 682-1517
Seattle *(G-9365)*
Batch 206 Distillery LLC ....G.... 206 216-2803
Seattle *(G-9500)*
Big Derby Distilling Co ....G.... 206 504-7604
Seattle *(G-9522)*
Blend Wine Shop ....G.... 253 884-9688
Lakebay *(G-5688)*
Brovo Spirits LLC ....G.... 206 354-3919
Woodinville *(G-15198)*
Cadee Distillery LLC ....G.... 360 969-5565
Langley *(G-5772)*
Caudill Bros Distillery ....G.... 360 460-6172
Port Angeles *(G-7692)*
Caudill Distillery ....G.... 360 457-0947
Port Angeles *(G-7693)*
Chambers Bay Distillery ....G.... 503 819-0542
University Place *(G-13964)*
Chehalis Brewing Group LLC ....G.... 360 628-8259
Olympia *(G-7248)*
Dawson-Alley LLC ....G.... 360 217-8244
Snohomish *(G-11895)*
Dead Oak Distilling LLC ....G.... 509 882-2794
Prosser *(G-8040)*
Deception Distilling LLC ....G.... 360 588-1000
Anacortes *(G-120)*
Delich Distillery ....G.... 360 552-2282
Belfair *(G-760)*
Distiller LLC ....G.... 206 659-4759
Kirkland *(G-5321)*
Distillers Way LLC ....G.... 360 927-8781
Ferndale *(G-3836)*
Distillery A Creative LLC ....G.... 206 696-0597
Seattle *(G-9836)*
Distillery Loft Events ....G.... 206 262-1022
Seattle *(G-9837)*
Distillery Provisions LLC ....G.... 206 861-5350
Seattle *(G-9838)*
Distillery Seaspirits ....G.... 360 820-0770
Woodinville *(G-15227)*
Evil Roys Elixirs ....G.... 360 463-6105
Sequim *(G-11633)*
Gabrielli Distillers ....G.... 503 421-2797
Vancouver *(G-14246)*
Grapeworks Distilling LLC ....G.... 425 478-7181
Woodinville *(G-15254)*
Highside Distilling LLC ....G.... 425 417-9000
Bremerton *(G-1960)*
Its 5 LLC ....G.... 509 679-9771
Cashmere *(G-2322)*
James Bay Distillers Ltd ....G.... 703 930-8453
Edmonds *(G-3121)*
JP Trodden Distilling LLC ....G.... 206 399-6291
Bothell *(G-1871)*
JP Trodden Distilling LLC ....G.... 425 286-2756
Woodinville *(G-15275)*
Latitude 47 Distillers ....G.... 206 794-0852
Seattle *(G-10379)*
Liquid Brands Distillery LLC ....G.... 509 413-1885
Spokane *(G-12370)*
Mark Anthony Brands Inc ....D.... 206 267-4444
Seattle *(G-10486)*
Mastrogiannis Distillery LLC ....G.... 206 383-2463
Renton *(G-8850)*
Nightside Distillery LLC ....G.... 253 906-4265
Edgewood *(G-3087)*
Novo Fogo ....G.... 425 256-2527
Issaquah *(G-4455)*
Old Soldier Distillery ....G.... 253 223-4306
Tacoma *(G-13441)*
Pursuit Distilling Co ....G.... 206 406-2263
Enumclaw *(G-3312)*
Rainier Distillers Pmb ....G.... 360 350-9177
Yelm *(G-15743)*
River Town Distillers LLC ....G.... 425 330-4885
Snohomish *(G-11967)*
Riversands Distillery ....G.... 509 492-1015
Kennewick *(G-4719)*
Sandstone Distillery ....G.... 360 239-7272
Tenino *(G-13623)*
Schnapsleiche LLC ....G.... 425 591-2586
Woodinville *(G-15356)*
Scratch Distillery LLC ....G.... 425 673-5541
Lynnwood *(G-6192)*
Scratch Distillery LLC ....G.... 425 442-7306
Edmonds *(G-3153)*
Seattle Distilling Company ....G.... 206 463-0830
Vashon *(G-14741)*
Sidetrack Distillery ....G.... 206 963-5079
Kent *(G-5130)*
Skip Rock Distillers ....G.... 360 862-0272
Snohomish *(G-11977)*
Snowbridge Distilling LLC ....G.... 206 442-1707
Seattle *(G-11146)*
Sun Spirits Distillery LLC ....G.... 509 371-1622
Richland *(G-9043)*
Tucker Distillery ....G.... 360 698-7043
Bremerton *(G-2008)*
Wanderback Distillery LLC ....G.... 206 390-7530
Seattle *(G-11435)*
White River Distillers LLC ....G.... 253 219-5100
Enumclaw *(G-3327)*
Wishkah River Distillery LLC ....G.... 360 612-4756
Aberdeen *(G-41)*
Woodinville Whiskey Co LLC ....F.... 425 486-1199
Woodinville *(G-15408)*

BEVERAGES, ALCOHOLIC: Liquors, Malt

English Setter Brewing ....G.... 509 413-3663
Spokane Valley *(G-12692)*

BEVERAGES, ALCOHOLIC: Near Beer

Sparklehorse LLC ....G.... 253 948-7772
Gig Harbor *(G-4163)*

BEVERAGES, ALCOHOLIC: Neutral Spirits, Exc Fruit

Skunk Brothers Spirits Inc ....G.... 360 213-3420
Vancouver *(G-14591)*

BEVERAGES, ALCOHOLIC: Vodka

Dry Fly Distilling Inc ....F.... 509 489-2112
Spokane *(G-12232)*
Lynden Liquor Agency 570 ....G.... 360 354-4744
Lynden *(G-6033)*
Vodka Is Vegan LLC ....G.... 206 278-4257
Seattle *(G-11429)*

BEVERAGES, ALCOHOLIC: Wines

21cellars ....G.... 253 353-2317
Tacoma *(G-13151)*
37 Cellars ....G.... 509 679-0668
Leavenworth *(G-5793)*
50st Seattle Winery LLC ....G.... 206 409-0994
Chelan *(G-2545)*
Adamant Cellars ....G.... 509 529-4161
Walla Walla *(G-14760)*
Agate Creek Farm ....G.... 360 740-1692
Chehalis *(G-2459)*
Agate Field Vineyard ....G.... 509 829-6097
Zillah *(G-15749)*
Airport Ranch Estates LLC ....F.... 509 786-7401
Prosser *(G-8028)*
Airport Ranch Estates LLC ....G.... 425 877-1006
Woodinville *(G-15174)*
Alexander Grape ....G.... 509 942-9850
West Richland *(G-15093)*
Alexandria Nicole Cellars LLC ....F.... 509 786-3497
Prosser *(G-8029)*
Alia Wines LLC ....G.... 360 794-0421
Snohomish *(G-11873)*
Alpine Wines ....G.... 208 354-9463
Anacortes *(G-98)*
Alta Cellars ....G.... 425 424-9218
Woodinville *(G-15175)*
Amavi Cellars ....G.... 509 525-3541
Walla Walla *(G-14761)*
American Wine Trade Inc ....E.... 206 357-0607
Seattle *(G-9396)*
American Wine Trade Inc ....F.... 509 588-3155
Benton City *(G-1601)*
Amos Rome Vineyards ....G.... 206 890-4482
Manson *(G-6238)*
Ancient Lake Wine Company LLC ....F.... 509 787-2022
Quincy *(G-8288)*
Anderson Resources Inc ....G.... 360 426-5913
Shelton *(G-11678)*
Andrew Ross Winery ....G.... 425 487-9463
Woodinville *(G-15178)*
Antoine Creek Vineyards LLC ....G.... 509 682-4448
Chelan *(G-2547)*
Antolin Cellars ....G.... 509 833-5765
Yakima *(G-15510)*
Ardor Cellars ....G.... 509 876-8086
Walla Walla *(G-14765)*
Arlington Road Cellars ....G.... 425 482-1801
Woodinville *(G-15180)*
Ash Hollow Winery LLC ....G.... 509 529-7565
Olympia *(G-7232)*
Aspenwood Cellars ....G.... 425 844-2233
Woodinville *(G-15182)*
Atam Company LLC ....G.... 509 687-4421
Manson *(G-6239)*
Avennia Winery ....G.... 425 392-3191
Woodinville *(G-15183)*
Badger Mountain Inc ....F.... 509 627-4986
Kennewick *(G-4623)*
Badger Mountain Vineyards LLC ....G.... 509 627-4986
Kennewick *(G-4624)*
Baer Winery LLC ....G.... 425 483-7060
Woodinville *(G-15184)*
Bainbridge Vineyards LLC ....G.... 206 842-9463
Bainbridge Island *(G-615)*
Balboa Winery ....G.... 509 529-0461
Walla Walla *(G-14767)*
Barnard-Griffin Inc ....F.... 509 627-0266
Richland *(G-8971)*
Barrage Cellars LLC ....G.... 425 381-9675
Woodinville *(G-15185)*
Barrister Winery ....G.... 509 465-3591
Spokane *(G-12139)*
Bartholomew Winery ....G.... 206 395-8460
Seattle *(G-9496)*
Bartholomew Winery Inc ....F.... 206 755-5296
Kennewick *(G-4626)*
Bartholomew Winery Inc ....G.... 206 755-5296
Kennewick *(G-4625)*
Basalt Cellars ....G.... 509 758-6442
Clarkston *(G-2622)*
Basel Cellars Estate Winery ....G.... 509 522-0200
Walla Walla *(G-14768)*
Bear Wildfire ....G.... 360 379-8915
Port Townsend *(G-7868)*
Benson Vineyards ....G.... 509 687-0313
Manson *(G-6240)*
Bergdorf Cellars ....G.... 509 548-7638
Leavenworth *(G-5796)*
Berghan Vineyeards ....G.... 509 301-9229
Walla Walla *(G-14769)*
Bertelsen Winery & Tasting Rm ....G.... 360 445-2300
Mount Vernon *(G-6780)*
Bethany Vineyard & Winery ....G.... 360 887-3525
Ridgefield *(G-9067)*
Betz Cellars LLC ....G.... 425 861-9823
Redmond *(G-8402)*
Bieler and Smith LLC ....G.... 509 526-5230
Walla Walla *(G-14770)*
Birchfield Winery ....G.... 360 978-6176
Chehalis *(G-2471)*
Birchfield Winery Inc ....G.... 360 280-8998
Onalaska *(G-7446)*
Bonair Winery Inc ....F.... 509 829-6027
Zillah *(G-15750)*
Bontzu Cellars ....G.... 425 205-3482
Walla Walla *(G-14773)*
Bookwalter LLC ....G.... 425 488-1983
Woodinville *(G-15196)*
Bookwalter Winery LLC ....F.... 509 627-5000
Richland *(G-8976)*
Bouchard Lake Winery LLC ....G.... 425 803-5076
Kirkland *(G-5296)*

PRODUCT

Employee Codes: A=Over 500 employees, B=251-500
C=101-250, D=51-100, E=20-50, F=10-19, G=2-9
2019 Washington
Manufacturers Register
901

BEVERAGES, ALCOHOLIC: Wines PRODUCT SECTION

Boulder Estates Winery G 509 628-1209
Richland ***(G-8977)***
Boutique Imports LLC G 206 650-5555
Seattle ***(G-9571)***
Buckmaster Cellars G 509 627-1321
Richland ***(G-8979)***
Bunnell Family Cellular G 425 286-2964
Woodinville ***(G-15200)***
Butterfield Cellars LLC G 509 994-0382
Spokane ***(G-12163)***
Buty Winery G 509 527-0901
Walla Walla ***(G-14776)***
Cadaretta G 509 525-1352
Walla Walla ***(G-14777)***
Callahan Cellars G 425 877-1842
Woodinville ***(G-15203)***
Camarda Corporation G 206 463-9227
Vashon ***(G-14715)***
Canoe Ridge Vineyard G 206 267-5252
Seattle ***(G-9619)***
Canoe Ridge Vineyard LLC F 509 527-0885
Walla Walla ***(G-14778)***
Castillo De Feliciana G 541 558-3656
Walla Walla ***(G-14779)***
Castle Bridge Winery G 425 251-0983
Renton ***(G-8768)***
Cave B Estate Winery G 509 785-3500
Quincy ***(G-8292)***
Cavu Cellars G 509 540-6352
Walla Walla ***(G-14780)***
Cayuse Vineyards G 509 526-0686
Walla Walla ***(G-14781)***
Cedar River Cellars G 206 229-2104
Renton ***(G-8769)***
Cellars Nodland G 509 927-7770
Spokane Valley ***(G-12653)***
Champoux Vineyards LLC G 360 563-1330
Snohomish ***(G-11889)***
Chandler Reach Vineyard Estate G 509 588-8800
Benton City ***(G-1605)***
Charles Lybecker G 509 687-0555
Manson ***(G-6241)***
Charles Smith Vineyards LLC G 509 526-5230
Walla Walla ***(G-14783)***
Chateau Faire Le Pont LLC G 509 667-9463
Wenatchee ***(G-15020)***
Chateau Plateau Winery Inc G 360 825-2466
Enumclaw ***(G-3281)***
Chateau Rollat Winery LLC G 509 529-4511
Walla Walla ***(G-14784)***
Chelan Estate Winery LLC G 509 682-5454
Chelan ***(G-2550)***
China Bend Vineyards G 509 732-6123
Kettle Falls ***(G-5228)***
Chinook Wines G 509 786-2725
Prosser ***(G-8033)***
Cinq Cellars LLC G 206 954-4626
Redmond ***(G-8420)***
Cloudlift Cellars G 206 622-2004
Seattle ***(G-9701)***
Col Solare LLP G 509 588-6806
Benton City ***(G-1607)***
Columbia Cascade Winery Assn G 509 782-3845
Cashmere ***(G-2318)***
Columbia Gorge Winery Inc G 509 365-2900
Lyle ***(G-5995)***
Columbia Winery F 425 488-2776
Woodinville ***(G-15208)***
Confluence Vineyards G 360 887-2343
Ridgefield ***(G-9075)***
Connerlee Vineyards Inc G 509 932-4267
Sammamish ***(G-9199)***
Copper Mountain Vineyards G 509 476-2762
Oroville ***(G-7463)***
Corkycellars LLC G 425 226-5479
Renton ***(G-8775)***
Corliss Estates G 509 526-4400
Walla Walla ***(G-14790)***
Corus Estates & Vineyards LLC G 206 728-9063
Seattle ***(G-9744)***
Corus Estates & Vineyards LLC E 503 538-7724
Yakima ***(G-15538)***
Cote Bonneville G 509 840-4596
Sunnyside ***(G-13117)***
Cougar Hills LLC G 425 398-9999
Redmond ***(G-8428)***
Cougar Hills LLC G 509 241-3850
Spokane ***(G-12201)***
Cougar Hills LLC F 509 529-5980
Walla Walla ***(G-14791)***
Coventry Vale Winery Inc E 509 882-4100
Grandview ***(G-4246)***
Covington Cellars G 425 806-8636
Woodinville ***(G-15214)***
Covington Cellars LLC G 253 347-9463
Bothell ***(G-1844)***
Cox Canyon Vineyards G 206 940-5086
Ellensburg ***(G-3191)***
Coyote Canyon Winery LLC G 509 786-7686
Prosser ***(G-8036)***
Craftsman Cellars LLC G 509 328-3960
Spokane ***(G-12206)***
Cranberry Road Winery G 425 254-8400
Bonney Lake ***(G-1719)***
Crowder Family Winery G 509 834-3270
Manson ***(G-6243)***
Crucible Wines LLC G 206 605-2953
Seattle ***(G-9759)***
Cuillin Hills Winery G 425 402-1907
Woodinville ***(G-15217)***
Damsel Cellars G 206 465-2433
Woodinville ***(G-15218)***
Dancing Alder Winery G 425 402-6300
Woodinville ***(G-15219)***
Darby Winery G 206 954-4700
Seattle ***(G-9792)***
Darby Winery Inc G 206 954-4700
Woodinville ***(G-15220)***
Davis Degrass Enterprises Inc G 360 332-2097
Blaine ***(G-1667)***
Dead Canyon Vineyard LLC G 509 786-2665
Prosser ***(G-8039)***
Delille Cellars Inc G 425 489-0544
Redmond ***(G-8437)***
Des Voigne Melissa G 206 478-2021
Woodinville ***(G-15221)***
Desert Wind Vineyard E 509 786-7277
Prosser ***(G-8041)***
Devona LLC G 509 520-2524
Walla Walla ***(G-14796)***
Dineen Family Wine Company LLC G 509 829-6897
Zillah ***(G-15753)***
Distefano Winery Ltd G 425 487-1648
Woodinville ***(G-15226)***
Dodger and Powers Wines G 509 627-4986
Kennewick ***(G-4655)***
Domanico Cellars LLC G 206 465-9406
Seattle ***(G-9845)***
Doubleback G 509 525-3334
Walla Walla ***(G-14798)***
Dubrul Vineyard LLC G 509 837-7746
Sunnyside ***(G-13122)***
Dunham Cellars LLC G 509 529-4685
Walla Walla ***(G-14799)***
Dusted Valley G 509 525-1337
Walla Walla ***(G-14800)***
Dusty Cellars Winery G 360 387-2171
Camano Island ***(G-2211)***
DVinery G 509 548-7059
Leavenworth ***(G-5798)***
Eagle Creek Winery G 509 548-7059
Leavenworth ***(G-5799)***
Eaton Hill Winery G 509 854-2220
Granger ***(G-4261)***
Eight Bells Winery G 206 294-4131
Seattle ***(G-9890)***
Eleven Winery Inc F 206 780-0905
Bainbridge Island ***(G-628)***
Ellensburg Canyon Winery LLC G 509 933-3523
Ellensburg ***(G-3194)***
Elsom Cellars LLC G 425 298-3082
Seattle ***(G-9905)***
Elsom Cllars Winery 3pp Pnw Hq G 775 848-1771
Seattle ***(G-9906)***
Entiat Valley Vineyards LLC G 509 884-1152
East Wenatchee ***(G-3012)***
Errant Cellars G 509 289-9660
Quincy ***(G-8298)***
Esther Brcques Wnery Vnyrd LLC G 509 476-2861
Oroville ***(G-7465)***
Evalesco Inc G 425 486-5959
Woodinville ***(G-15238)***
Eye of Needle Winery G 425 210-7463
Woodinville ***(G-15240)***
Fall Line Winery LLC G 206 406-4249
Seattle ***(G-9965)***
Farmhand Winery G 509 308-7203
Kennewick ***(G-4665)***
Felamere Vineyard LLC G 360 652-7414
Stanwood ***(G-12970)***
Fidelitas G 509 521-1553
Richland ***(G-8996)***
Fidelitas Wines LLC G 509 588-3469
Benton City ***(G-1611)***
Figgins Family Wine Estates G 509 525-1428
Walla Walla ***(G-14804)***
Firesteed Corporation G 503 623-8683
Issaquah ***(G-4415)***
Five Star Cellars Inc G 509 527-8400
Walla Walla ***(G-14805)***
Fletcher Bay Winery G 206 780-9463
Bainbridge Island ***(G-634)***
Flying Trout Wines LLC G 509 520-7701
Walla Walla ***(G-14806)***
Fools Prairie Vineyards LLC G 509 319-0752
Spokane ***(G-12261)***
Force Majeure Winery G 425 892-9848
Woodinville ***(G-15247)***
Forgeron Cellars G 425 908-7683
Redmond ***(G-8463)***
Forgeron Cellars LLC G 509 522-9463
Walla Walla ***(G-14807)***
Fort Walla Walla Cellars LLC G 509 520-1095
Walla Walla ***(G-14808)***
Foundry Vineyards LLC G 509 529-0736
Walla Walla ***(G-14809)***
Fountaine Estates Winery G 509 972-8123
Naches ***(G-6996)***
Francisco Gomez Vineyard Svcs G 559 567-7013
Pasco ***(G-7583)***
Frichette Winery G 509 426-3227
Benton City ***(G-1612)***
Furion Cellars LLC G 425 314-8922
Everett ***(G-3489)***
Gallo Winery G 509 947-4520
Sunnyside ***(G-13126)***
Garlic Crush G 425 968-2539
Redmond ***(G-8469)***
Gary N Lamb G 360 766-6086
Bow ***(G-1929)***
Generations Winery LLC G 206 351-0933
Everett ***(G-3493)***
Genoa Cellars G 425 296-9660
Woodinville ***(G-15251)***
Gifford Hirlinger Winery G 509 301-9229
Walla Walla ***(G-14811)***
Gilbert Cellars LLC G 509 249-9049
Yakima ***(G-15576)***
Ginkgo Forest Winery G 253 301-4372
Tacoma ***(G-13309)***
Ginkgo Forest Winery LLC G 509 932-0082
Mattawa ***(G-6406)***
Gino Cuneo Cellars LLC G 509 876-4738
Walla Walla ***(G-14812)***
Glacier Peak Winery G 360 419-9107
Mount Vernon ***(G-6799)***
Glacier View Winery G 206 719-1331
Woodinville ***(G-15252)***
Glencorrie G 509 525-2585
Walla Walla ***(G-14813)***
Goose Ridge LLC F 509 837-4427
Benton City ***(G-1613)***
Goose Ridge Vineyards LLC F 509 627-1618
Benton City ***(G-1614)***
Gordon Brothers Cellars Inc E 509 547-6331
Pasco ***(G-7588)***
Gouger Cellars G 360 693-2700
Ridgefield ***(G-9086)***
Gramercy Cellars F 509 876-2427
Walla Walla ***(G-14815)***
Grand Reve Vintners G 425 892-9848
Carnation ***(G-2294)***
Grape Visions LLC E 509 525-1337
Walla Walla ***(G-14816)***
Greenwood Cider Co LLC G 360 961-2902
Seattle ***(G-10122)***
Greg Michael Cellars LLC G 509 465-3591
Spokane ***(G-12283)***
Grieb Optimal Winecrafting LLC G 509 877-0925
Wapato ***(G-14916)***
Hamilton Cellars LLC G 509 628-8227
Benton City ***(G-1616)***
Hanatoro Winery G 404 312-5891
Walla Walla ***(G-14818)***
Hard Row To Hoe Vineyards G 509 687-3000
Manson ***(G-6244)***
Heathen Estate Vineyards G 360 768-5199
Vancouver ***(G-14291)***
Hestia Cellars G 425 333-4270
Redmond ***(G-8492)***

PRODUCT SECTION BEVERAGES, ALCOHOLIC: Wines

Heymann Whinery Etc ......G 360 623-1106
Chehalis (G-2502)
Hezel Vineyard and Cellars LLC ......G 360 321-4898
Clinton (G-2689)
Hierophant Meadery LLC ......G 509 294-0134
Mead (G-6429)
Hightower Cellars ......G 509 588-2867
Benton City (G-1617)
Hogue Cellars Ltd ......D 509 786-4557
Prosser (G-8042)
Hollywood Hill Vineyards LLC ......G 425 753-0093
Woodinville (G-15260)
Holmes Family Winery LLC ......G 253 906-6317
Federal Way (G-3743)
Holmes Harbor Cellars LLC ......G 360 331-3544
Greenbank (G-4306)
Hoodsport Winery Inc ......G 360 877-9894
Hoodsport (G-4325)
Horan Estates Winery ......G 509 679-8705
East Wenatchee (G-3020)
Icicle Ridge Winery ......G 509 548-7019
Peshastin (G-7663)
Icicle Ridge Winery ......G 509 548-7019
Leavenworth (G-5807)
Icon Cellars LLC ......G 425 223-7300
Sammamish (G-9219)
Isenhower Cellars ......G 425 488-2299
Woodinville (G-15269)
Isenhower Cellars ......G 509 526-7896
Walla Walla (G-14826)
Island Vintners ......G 206 451-4344
Bainbridge Island (G-643)
J As Winery ......G 206 409-4841
Sammamish (G-9221)
J M Cellars Company ......G 425 485-6508
Woodinville (G-15270)
J M Cellars Company ......G 206 321-0052
Seattle (G-10272)
J&S Crushing ......G 509 787-3537
Mattawa (G-6409)
J-NH Wine Group LLC ......F 425 481-5502
Woodinville (G-15271)
Januik Winery ......G 425 481-5502
Woodinville (G-15272)
JB Neufeld LLC ......G 509 945-1887
Yakima (G-15596)
JB Neufeld LLC ......G 509 895-9979
Yakima (G-15597)
Jester Cellars ......G 425 785-9217
Redmond (G-8519)
Johnson Ward Winery ......G 206 284-2635
Seattle (G-10303)
K Vintners LLC ......G 509 526-5230
Walla Walla (G-14830)
K-W Cellars ......G 509 525-6222
Walla Walla (G-14831)
Kana Winery ......G 509 453-6611
Yakima (G-15605)
Karma Kanyon LLC ......G 509 669-5753
Chelan (G-2556)
Kestrel Vintners ......F 509 786-2675
Prosser (G-8046)
Kestrel Vintners ......G 425 398-1199
Woodinville (G-15278)
Kestrel Vintners ......G 509 548-7348
Leavenworth (G-5808)
Kevin W Lantz ......G 425 770-2599
Lake Stevens (G-5653)
Kevin White Winery ......G 206 992-5746
Woodinville (G-15279)
Kiona Vineyards LLC ......F 509 588-6716
Benton City (G-1618)
Klickitat Canyon Winery ......G 509 365-2900
Lyle (G-5996)
Knipprath Cellars Inc ......G 208 699-3393
Spokane (G-12353)
Knox Cellars Mason Bees ......G 360 286-2025
Bremerton (G-1971)
Koi Pond Cellars ......G 360 281-2716
Ridgefield (G-9093)
Lachini Winery ......G 503 864-4553
Medina (G-6450)
Lake Chelan Trading Company ......F 509 687-9463
Chelan (G-2557)
Lane Gibbons Vineyard Inc ......G 360 264-8466
Tenino (G-13620)
Latah Creek Wine Cellars Ltd ......G 509 926-0164
Spokane Valley (G-12773)
Laurelhurst Cellars LLC ......G 206 992-2875
Seattle (G-10383)
Lauren Ashton Cellars LLC ......G 206 504-8546
Woodinville (G-15285)
Lawrence Cellars ......G 425 286-2198
Woodinville (G-15286)
Lawrence Cellars LLC ......G 509 346-2585
Royal City (G-9171)
Lawrence Fruit Inc ......G 509 925-1095
Ellensburg (G-3212)
Locati Cellars LLC ......G 509 529-5871
Walla Walla (G-14838)
Long Road Winery ......G 206 859-7697
Belfair (G-767)
Long Shadows Vintners LLC ......F 509 526-0905
Seattle (G-10436)
Lost River Winery LLC ......G 509 996-2888
Mazama (G-6414)
Lowden Schoolhouse Corporation ......G 509 525-0940
Walla Walla (G-14839)
Lowden Schoolhouse Corporation ......F 509 525-0940
Lowden (G-5990)
Lupine Vineyards LLC ......G 206 915-5862
Lynnwood (G-6160)
Lynch Distributing Co ......F 509 248-0880
Yakima (G-15613)
Madsen Family Cellars ......G 360 357-3015
Olympia (G-7329)
Maison Bleue Winery ......G 509 525-9084
Walla Walla (G-14840)
Mark Ryan Winery LLC ......F 425 481-7070
Kirkland (G-5397)
Market Vineyards ......G 509 396-4798
Richland (G-9024)
Market Vineyards ......G 425 486-1171
Woodinville (G-15302)
Marshals Winery Inc ......G 509 767-4633
Dallesport (G-2864)
Martedi Winery ......G 425 444-2840
Woodinville (G-15303)
Martinez and Martinez Winery ......G 509 786-2424
Prosser (G-8050)
Maryhill Winery ......G 509 443-3832
Spokane (G-12384)
Masset Winery ......G 509 877-6675
Wapato (G-14918)
Matthews Cellars ......G 425 487-9810
Woodinville (G-15305)
Matthews Estate LLC ......G 425 488-3883
Woodinville (G-15306)
McKinley Springs LLC ......G 509 894-4528
Prosser (G-8052)
Meade Winery ......G 509 972-4443
Yakima (G-15617)
Mercer Wine Estates LLC ......F 509 786-2097
Prosser (G-8054)
Mercer Wine Estates LLC ......F 509 832-2810
Prosser (G-8055)
Michelle Chateau Ste ......G 425 488-1133
Woodinville (G-15308)
Michelle Ste Wine Estates Ltd ......F 509 875-4227
Paterson (G-7659)
Michelle Ste Wine Estates Ltd ......G 425 488-1133
Woodinville (G-15309)
Michelle Ste Wine Estates Ltd ......F 509 875-2061
Paterson (G-7660)
Michelle Ste Wine Estates Ltd ......F 509 882-3928
Grandview (G-4253)
Michelle Ste Wine Estates Ltd ......F 425 488-1133
Woodinville (G-15310)
Mike Scott Orchards & Winery ......G 509 787-3538
Wenatchee (G-15091)
Milbrandt Vineyards Inc ......F 509 788-0030
Prosser (G-8057)
Mill Lane Winery Yakima LLC ......G 206 817-5767
Yakima (G-15622)
Minnick Hills Vineyard LL ......G 509 525-5076
Walla Walla (G-14845)
Miracles Vintners LLC ......G 253 606-6202
Walla Walla (G-14846)
Monson Ranches ......G 425 488-0200
Woodinville (G-15314)
Monson Ranches ......E 509 628-3880
Richland (G-9029)
Monte Scarlatto Estate Winery ......G 509 531-3081
Benton City (G-1620)
Moose Canyon Winery ......G 253 225-1985
Edgewood (G-3086)
Mosquito Fleet Winery LLC ......G 360 710-8788
Belfair (G-768)
Naches Heights Vineyard LLC ......G 509 966-4355
Yakima (G-15627)
Napeequa Vintners ......G 509 763-1600
Leavenworth (G-5810)
Nefarious Cellers ......G 509 682-9505
Chelan (G-2560)
No Grass Winery ......G 509 784-5101
Entiat (G-3269)
Northstar Winery ......G 509 525-6100
Walla Walla (G-14851)
Nota Bene Cellars Ltd ......G 206 762-5581
Seattle (G-10657)
Novelty Hill Winery LLC ......F 425 481-5502
Woodinville (G-15324)
Novelty Hill Winery LLC ......G 206 664-2522
Seattle (G-10660)
Noviello Vineyards LLC ......G 509 784-0544
Orondo (G-7458)
O S Winery LLC ......G 206 243-3427
Mercer Island (G-6475)
Oldfield Cellars LLC ......G 425 398-7200
Woodinville (G-15326)
Olsen Estates LLC ......E 509 973-2203
Prosser (G-8061)
Olympic Cellars LLC ......G 360 452-0160
Port Angeles (G-7728)
One Tree Hard Cider ......G 509 315-9856
Spokane Valley (G-12820)
Owen Kotler Selections LLC ......G 917 912-0678
Seattle (G-10724)
Page Cellars ......G 253 232-9463
Woodinville (G-15331)
Palouse Winery ......G 206 567-4994
Vashon (G-14740)
Paradisos Del Sol Winery Inc ......G 509 829-9000
Zillah (G-15757)
Pasek Cellars Winery Inc ......G 888 350-9463
Mount Vernon (G-6822)
Passing Time Winery ......G 425 892-8684
Woodinville (G-15333)
Patit Creek Cellars ......G 509 868-4045
Spokane (G-12431)
Pepper Bridge Winery LLC ......G 425 483-7026
Woodinville (G-15334)
Pepper Bridge Winery LLC ......F 509 525-6502
Walla Walla (G-14855)
Piety Flats Winery ......G 509 877-3115
Yakima (G-15647)
Plain Cellars LLC ......F 509 548-5412
Leavenworth (G-5813)
Pleasant Hill Winery LLC ......G 425 333-6770
Bonney Lake (G-1734)
Plumb Cellars ......G 509 540-5632
Walla Walla (G-14856)
Pondera Winery LLC ......G 425 486-8500
Woodinville (G-15337)
Pontin Del Roza Winery ......G 509 786-4449
Prosser (G-8062)
Port Townsend Vineyards Winery ......G 360 385-0694
Port Townsend (G-7917)
Precept Brands LLC ......D 206 267-5252
Seattle (G-10845)
Purple Star Winery ......G 509 628-7799
Benton City (G-1625)
Quilceda Creek Vintners Inc ......G 360 568-2389
Snohomish (G-11964)
Radix Winery ......G 419 283-7924
Richland (G-9037)
Red Mntain Amrcn Vntners Alnce ......G 509 588-3155
Benton City (G-1626)
Red Sky Winery LLC ......G 425 481-9864
Woodinville (G-15346)
Reflection Vineyards LLC ......G 360 904-4800
Ridgefield (G-9107)
Regal Road Winery ......G 509 838-8024
Spokane (G-12469)
Reininger Winery ......G 509 242-3190
Spokane (G-12471)
Reininger Winery LLC ......G 509 522-1994
Walla Walla (G-14860)
Rezabek Vineyards LLC ......G 360 896-0218
Vancouver (G-14551)
Riveraerie Cellars ......G 509 786-2197
Prosser (G-8064)
Riverbend Incorporated ......G 509 460-2886
Benton City (G-1628)
Robert Karl Cellars LLC ......G 509 363-1353
Spokane (G-12480)
Rockwall Cellars ......G 509 826-0201
OMAK (G-7443)
Rocky Pond Winery ......G 206 550-0938
Woodinville (G-15350)

Employee Codes: A=Over 500 employees, B=251-500
C=101-250, D=51-100, E=20-50, F=10-19, G=2-9

Rocky Pond Winery ......G...... 206 458-9119
Orondo *(G-7460)*
Ros Wine Company LLC ......G...... 509 301-0627
Prosser *(G-8065)*
Rose Saviah Winery LLC ......G...... 509 522-2181
Walla Walla *(G-14861)*
Rose Tucker ......G...... 509 837-8701
Sunnyside *(G-13139)*
Rosebud Ranches ......E...... 509 932-4617
Mattawa *(G-6412)*
Ross Andrew Mickel ......G...... 206 267-5252
Seattle *(G-10982)*
Rotie Cellars ......G...... 509 529-2011
Walla Walla *(G-14862)*
Rusty Grape Vineyard LLC ......G...... 360 513-9338
Battle Ground *(G-737)*
S&S Industries LLC ......G...... 360 500-9942
Cashmere *(G-2329)*
Saint Laurent Winery ......G...... 509 787-3700
Quincy *(G-8309)*
Samson Estates Winery ......G...... 360 966-4526
Everson *(G-3688)*
Sapolil Cellars ......G...... 509 520-5258
Walla Walla *(G-14864)*
Scatter Creek Winery ......G...... 360 264-9463
Tenino *(G-13624)*
Schafer Winery LLC ......G...... 509 522-5444
Walla Walla *(G-14865)*
Seven Hills Winery LLC ......G...... 509 529-7198
Walla Walla *(G-14866)*
Shady Grove Winery LLC ......G...... 509 767-1400
Dallesport *(G-2865)*
Shaw Estate Wines ......G...... 509 876-2459
Walla Walla *(G-14868)*
Sigillo Cellars ......G...... 206 919-2326
Snoqualmie *(G-12023)*
Skagit Cellars LLC ......G...... 360 708-2801
Mount Vernon *(G-6837)*
Skagit Crest Vinyrd Winery LLC ......G...... 360 630-5176
Sedro Woolley *(G-11566)*
Sky River Brewing Inc ......G...... 360 793-6761
Redmond *(G-8671)*
Sky River Meadery ......F...... 425 242-3815
Redmond *(G-8672)*
Sleeping Giant Winery LLC ......F...... 206 351-0719
Woodinville *(G-15367)*
Snoqualmie Vineyards ......E...... 509 786-2104
Prosser *(G-8066)*
Sol Stone Winery ......G...... 425 417-8483
Woodinville *(G-15369)*
Songbird Vineyard LLC ......G...... 509 318-4044
Benton City *(G-1629)*
Soos Creek Wine Cellars LLC ......G...... 253 631-8775
Kent *(G-5139)*
Southard Winery ......G...... 509 697-3003
Selah *(G-11597)*
Sparkman Cellers ......G...... 425 398-1045
Woodinville *(G-15372)*
Spoiled Dog Winery ......G...... 360 321-6226
Langley *(G-5786)*
Spring Valley Tasting Room ......G...... 509 525-1506
Walla Walla *(G-14872)*
Spring Valley Vineyard Winery ......G...... 509 337-6043
Walla Walla *(G-14873)*
Stavalaura Vinyards ......G...... 360 887-1476
Ridgefield *(G-9113)*
Stemilt Creek Winery ......G...... 509 662-3613
Wenatchee *(G-15076)*
Stevens Winery ......G...... 425 424-9463
Bellevue *(G-1158)*
Stoney Creek Brewing Co LLC ......G...... 425 836-0958
Sammamish *(G-9249)*
Stottle Winery Tasting Room ......G...... 360 877-2247
Hoodsport *(G-4326)*
Sun River Vintners LLC ......G...... 509 627-3100
Kennewick *(G-4731)*
Sussex Clumber LLC ......G...... 206 369-3615
Bellevue *(G-1169)*
Swakane Winery ......G...... 509 881-9688
Raymond *(G-8359)*
Synne Cellars ......G...... 206 851-2048
Woodinville *(G-15383)*
Tanjuli ......G...... 509 829-6401
Zillah *(G-15761)*
Tapenade Inc ......G...... 206 325-3051
Seattle *(G-11267)*
Tasting Room Wines Washington ......G...... 206 770-9463
Seattle *(G-11273)*
Tempus Cellars ......G...... 509 368-9267
Spokane *(G-12551)*
Terra Vinum LLC ......G...... 509 628-7799
Kennewick *(G-4732)*
Terra Vinum LLC ......G...... 509 551-0854
Benton City *(G-1630)*
Tesla Winery Tours LLC ......G...... 509 520-5528
Walla Walla *(G-14878)*
Thrall & Dodge Winery ......G...... 509 925-4110
Ellensburg *(G-3231)*
Three Brothers Vineyard A ......G...... 503 702-5549
Ridgefield *(G-9116)*
Tildio Winery LLC ......G...... 509 687-8463
Manson *(G-6246)*
Tipsy Canyon Winery ......G...... 425 306-4844
Manson *(G-6247)*
Torii Mor Winery LLC ......G...... 425 408-0086
Woodinville *(G-15391)*
Townshend Cellar Inc ......G...... 509 919-3699
Spokane *(G-12565)*
Truthteller Winery ......G...... 425 985-3568
Redmond *(G-8696)*
Tucannon Cellars ......G...... 509 545-9588
Benton City *(G-1631)*
Tunnel Hill Winery ......G...... 509 682-3243
Chelan *(G-2568)*
Tuuri Wines LLC ......G...... 509 525-2299
Walla Walla *(G-14882)*
Two Mountain Winery ......G...... 509 829-3900
Zillah *(G-15762)*
Two Winey Bitches Winery ......G...... 509 796-3600
Ford *(G-4006)*
Upland Winery LLC ......G...... 509 839-2606
Sunnyside *(G-13146)*
V&C LLC ......F...... 509 773-1976
Goldendale *(G-4211)*
Vanarnam Vineyards ......G...... 360 904-4800
Zillah *(G-15763)*
Victor Gutierrez ......G...... 509 301-4915
Walla Walla *(G-14885)*
Vin Du Lac Winery ......G...... 509 682-2882
Chelan *(G-2569)*
Vinmotion Wines LLC ......G...... 509 967-7477
West Richland *(G-15103)*
Vino Aquino Tacoma Inc ......G...... 253 272-5511
Tacoma *(G-13578)*
Vino Verite ......G...... 206 324-0324
Seattle *(G-11421)*
Wahluke Wine Company Inc ......E...... 509 932-0030
Mattawa *(G-6413)*
Waliser Winery LLC ......G...... 509 522-4206
Walla Walla *(G-14887)*
Walla Walla Vintners LLC ......G...... 509 525-4724
Walla Walla *(G-14896)*
Walla Walla Wines LLC ......F...... 509 526-9463
Walla Walla *(G-14897)*
Wallfam Inc ......G...... 509 786-2163
Prosser *(G-8074)*
Walls Vineyards ......G...... 509 876-0200
Walla Walla *(G-14898)*
Washington Jones Tasting Room ......G...... 509 787-8108
Quincy *(G-8311)*
Washington Wine & Beverage Co ......F...... 425 485-2437
Woodinville *(G-15402)*
Waters Winery LLC ......G...... 541 203-0020
Walla Walla *(G-14899)*
Wautoma Wines LLC ......G...... 509 378-1163
Richland *(G-9053)*
Waving Tree Vineyard & Winery ......G...... 509 773-6552
Goldendale *(G-4212)*
Wawawai Canyon Winery ......G...... 509 338-4916
Pullman *(G-8115)*
Weaver Family Winery ......G...... 509 386-8018
Touchet *(G-13678)*
Wedge Mountain Winery ......G...... 509 548-7068
Peshastin *(G-7666)*
Welcome Road Winery ......G...... 206 778-3028
Seattle *(G-11447)*
Westport Winery Inc ......F...... 360 648-2224
Aberdeen *(G-40)*
Whidbey Island Vintners ......G...... 360 331-3544
Greenbank *(G-4310)*
Whidbey Island Vinyard Winery ......G...... 360 221-2040
Langley *(G-5787)*
White Cellars ......G...... 425 246-1419
Sammamish *(G-9258)*
Whitelatch-Hoch LLC ......G...... 509 956-9311
Kennewick *(G-4745)*
Whitestone Winery Inc ......G...... 509 636-2001
Creston *(G-2843)*
Whitewall Brewing LLC ......G...... 360 454-0464
Marysville *(G-6401)*
William Grssie Wine Esttes LLC ......G...... 913 461-4601
Fall City *(G-3710)*
Willow Crest Winery ......G...... 509 786-7999
Prosser *(G-8077)*
Wilridge Winery ......G...... 206 770-9463
Seattle *(G-11477)*
Wind River Cellar ......G...... 509 493-2324
Husum *(G-4367)*
Windwalker Vineyard ......G...... 541 490-4011
White Salmon *(G-15135)*
Winery Compliance Northwe ......G...... 509 528-0905
Richland *(G-9054)*
Winery Fulfillment Svcs LLC ......G...... 509 529-2497
Walla Walla *(G-14904)*
Winerybound LLC ......G...... 206 458-2831
Seattle *(G-11485)*
Wines of Substance ......F...... 206 745-7456
Seattle *(G-11486)*
Woodhouse Family Cellars ......G...... 425 527-0608
Woodinville *(G-15406)*
Woodinville Wine Co ......G...... 425 481-8860
Woodinville *(G-15409)*
Woodward Canyon Winery Inc ......F...... 509 525-4129
Lowden *(G-5992)*
Wt Vintners LLC ......G...... 425 610-9463
Woodinville *(G-15411)*
Ww Village Winery ......G...... 509 529-5300
Walla Walla *(G-14905)*
Wwvwa ......G...... 509 526-3117
Walla Walla *(G-14906)*
Wyckoff Farms Incorporated ......E...... 509 882-3934
Grandview *(G-4259)*
Wynoochee River Winery ......G...... 360 580-4452
Montesano *(G-6666)*
Zimmel Unruh Cellars LLC ......G...... 503 313-2235
Vancouver *(G-14709)*

BEVERAGES, MALT

Harmon Brewing Company L L C ......E...... 253 383-2739
Tacoma *(G-13331)*
LDB Beverage Company ......F...... 509 651-0381
Stevenson *(G-13015)*
Vampt America Inc ......G...... 800 508-6149
Seattle *(G-11400)*

BEVERAGES, NONALCOHOLIC: Bottled & canned soft drinks

A & W Bottling Company Inc ......E...... 425 355-0100
Everett *(G-3353)*
Bottling Group LLC ......C...... 509 535-0605
Spokane *(G-12158)*
Cliffstar LLC ......D...... 509 522-8608
Walla Walla *(G-14786)*
Coca Cola Bottling Co ......E...... 509 529-0753
Walla Walla *(G-14787)*
Coca-Cola Bottling Co ......E...... 509 248-1855
Yakima *(G-15535)*
Coca-Cola Bottling Co ......D...... 509 547-6712
Pasco *(G-7561)*
Coca-Cola Company ......F...... 404 676-0887
Bellevue *(G-857)*
Coca-Cola Refreshments ......G...... 425 226-6004
Renton *(G-8774)*
Concordia Coffee Company Inc ......E...... 425 453-2800
Redmond *(G-8422)*
Custom Bottling Company ......G...... 509 528-3196
Benton City *(G-1608)*
Greenland Inc ......F...... 206 623-2577
Seattle *(G-10119)*
Pacific Coca Cola Bottling ......G...... 509 762-6987
Moses Lake *(G-6734)*
Pepsi Cola Bottling Co Pasco ......E...... 509 545-8585
Pasco *(G-7615)*
Reyes Coca-Cola Bottling LLC ......C...... 253 503-4341
Tacoma *(G-13498)*
Reyes Coca-Cola Bottling LLC ......D...... 360 475-6528
Bremerton *(G-1993)*
Reyes Coca-Cola Bottling LLC ......D...... 509 921-6200
Spokane Valley *(G-12851)*
Reyes Coca-Cola Bottling LLC ......F...... 509 762-5480
Moses Lake *(G-6745)*
Richards Packaging Inc ......G...... 509 545-8690
Pasco *(G-7623)*
Salish Sea Organic Liqueurs ......G...... 360 890-4927
Lacey *(G-5584)*
Scuttlebutt Brewing Co LLC ......F...... 425 252-2829
Everett *(G-3606)*
Seven Up Btlg Co Tri Cities ......F...... 509 547-1660
Pasco *(G-7627)*

Stratford Bottling Company LLC ....G...... 509 853-3223
  Yakima *(G-15684)*
Swire Pacific Holdings Inc ....G...... 509 921-6200
  Spokane Valley *(G-12898)*
Swire Pacific Holdings Inc ....G...... 425 455-2000
  Bellevue *(G-1172)*

BEVERAGES, NONALCOHOLIC: Carbonated

Corwin Beverage Co ....D...... 360 696-0766
  Ridgefield *(G-9076)*
Corwin Beverage Co ....E...... 360 696-0766
  Ridgefield *(G-9077)*
Pepsico ....G...... 253 778-7107
  Tacoma *(G-13463)*
Struble Cider LLC ....G...... 206 766-0009
  Seattle *(G-11205)*
Unique Beverage Company LLC ....G...... 425 267-0959
  Everett *(G-3643)*

BEVERAGES, NONALCOHOLIC: Carbonated, Canned & Bottled, Etc

Custom Smoothie ....G...... 206 462-6264
  Seattle *(G-9772)*
Hyperfizzics ....G...... 904 253-5137
  Seattle *(G-10198)*
Johanna Beverage Company LLC ......D...... 509 455-8059
  Spokane *(G-12337)*
LDB Beverage Company ....F...... 509 651-0381
  Stevenson *(G-13015)*
Rainbow Cloud Kombucha LLC ....G...... 253 312-3697
  Tumwater *(G-13893)*
Refresco Beverages US Inc ....E...... 509 582-5200
  Kennewick *(G-4717)*
Rgb Soda ....G...... 206 437-8395
  Seattle *(G-10958)*

BEVERAGES, NONALCOHOLIC: Cider

Incline Cider Company ....G...... 503 830-4414
  Auburn *(G-475)*
Jester and Judge Cider Company ......E...... 509 651-0381
  Stevenson *(G-13013)*
Lattins Country Cider ....E...... 360 491-7328
  Olympia *(G-7319)*
Schilling Cider LLC ....F...... 408 390-8754
  Auburn *(G-556)*
Sheffield Cider Inc ....G...... 509 269-4610
  Mesa *(G-6496)*

BEVERAGES, NONALCOHOLIC: Flavoring extracts & syrups, nec

Callisons Inc ....E...... 360 748-3316
  Chehalis *(G-2477)*
Coca-Cola Btlg Co of NY Inc ....E...... 509 886-1136
  Wenatchee *(G-15089)*
Dawn Food Products Inc ....E...... 206 623-7740
  Seattle *(G-9803)*
Gavriel Jecan ....G...... 206 332-0993
  Seattle *(G-10053)*
J M Smucker Company ....E...... 509 882-1530
  Grandview *(G-4248)*
Jet Farms Inc ....F...... 509 346-2588
  Royal City *(G-9170)*
McStevens Inc ....E...... 360 944-5788
  Vancouver *(G-14407)*
S S Steiner Inc ....E...... 509 453-4731
  Yakima *(G-15665)*
Scrappys Bitters LLC ....G...... 206 632-7257
  Seattle *(G-11034)*
Shrubbery LLC ....G...... 949 690-9834
  Seattle *(G-11103)*
Simchuk Karene ....G...... 509 238-2830
  Mead *(G-6436)*
Tree Top Inc ....D...... 509 782-6809
  Cashmere *(G-2331)*
Wild Flavors Inc ....G...... 509 773-4008
  Goldendale *(G-4214)*

BEVERAGES, NONALCOHOLIC: Fruit Drnks, Under 100% Juice, Can

Shonan Usa Inc ....E...... 509 453-0757
  Grandview *(G-4255)*

BEVERAGES, NONALCOHOLIC: Fruits, Crushed, For Fountain Use

Allan Bros Inc ....D...... 509 653-2625
  Naches *(G-6993)*
International Glace Inc ....G...... 503 267-7917
  Spokane *(G-12323)*

BEVERAGES, NONALCOHOLIC: Soft Drinks, Canned & Bottled, Etc

American Bottling Company ....D...... 509 328-6984
  Spokane Valley *(G-12608)*
Coca-Cola Btlg Co of NY Inc ....E...... 509 886-1136
  Wenatchee *(G-15089)*
Cola Cola Enterprises ....G...... 509 921-6229
  Spokane Valley *(G-12660)*
Harbor Pacific Bottling Inc ....E...... 360 482-4820
  Elma *(G-3248)*
Jones Soda Co ....E...... 206 624-3357
  Seattle *(G-10307)*
L & E Bottling Co Inc ....D...... 360 357-3812
  Tumwater *(G-13882)*
Noel Corporation ....C...... 509 248-4545
  Yakima *(G-15630)*
Orca Beverage Inc ....F...... 425 349-5655
  Mukilteo *(G-6961)*
Pepsi ....G...... 509 536-5585
  Spokane Valley *(G-12827)*
Pepsi Cola 7 Up Bottling Co ....G...... 360 757-0044
  Burlington *(G-2180)*
Pepsi Northwest Beverages LLC ....C...... 206 326-7487
  Seattle *(G-10782)*
Pepsi Northwest Beverages LLC ....C...... 360 357-9090
  Tumwater *(G-13891)*
Pepsi-Cola Metro Btlg Co Inc ....D...... 206 326-7431
  Seattle *(G-10783)*
Seven Up Dr Peper Bottling Co ....F...... 509 547-1660
  Pasco *(G-7628)*
Shasta Beverages Inc ....E...... 206 575-0525
  Tukwila *(G-13817)*
Swire Pacific Holdings Inc ....E...... 509 529-0753
  Walla Walla *(G-14875)*
Walton Beverage Co ....C...... 360 380-1660
  Ferndale *(G-3922)*
Yakima Valley Pepsi Pak ....G...... 509 952-0318
  Selah *(G-11603)*

BEVERAGES, NONALCOHOLIC: Tea, Iced, Bottled & Canned, Etc

Kombucha Town ....G...... 360 224-2974
  Bellingham *(G-1398)*

BEVERAGES, WINE & DISTILLED ALCOHOLIC, WHOLESALE: Liquor

Alaska Distributors Co ....G...... 206 682-1517
  Seattle *(G-9365)*
Schooner Exact ....G...... 206 432-9734
  Seattle *(G-11028)*

BEVERAGES, WINE & DISTILLED ALCOHOLIC, WHOLESALE: Wine

Ancient Lake Wine Company LLC .....F...... 509 787-2022
  Quincy *(G-8288)*
Anderson Resources Inc ....G...... 360 426-5913
  Shelton *(G-11678)*
Badger Mountain Inc ....F...... 509 627-4986
  Kennewick *(G-4623)*
Bartholomew Winery Inc ....G...... 206 755-5296
  Kennewick *(G-4625)*
Bonair Winery Inc ....F...... 509 829-6027
  Zillah *(G-15750)*
Canoe Ridge Vineyard ....G...... 206 267-5252
  Seattle *(G-9619)*
Canoe Ridge Vineyard LLC ....F...... 509 527-0885
  Walla Walla *(G-14778)*
Coyote Canyon Winery LLC ....G...... 509 786-7686
  Prosser *(G-8036)*
Gilbert Cellars LLC ....G...... 509 249-9049
  Yakima *(G-15576)*
Knipprath Cellars Inc ....G...... 208 699-3393
  Spokane *(G-12353)*
Locati Cellars LLC ....G...... 509 529-5871
  Walla Walla *(G-14838)*
Lynch Distributing Co ....F...... 509 248-0880
  Yakima *(G-15613)*
Mpm Vintners LLC ....E...... 509 525-2469
  Walla Walla *(G-14847)*
Naches Heights Vineyard LLC ....G...... 509 966-4355
  Yakima *(G-15627)*
Plain Cellars LLC ....F...... 509 548-5412
  Leavenworth *(G-5813)*
Rose Saviah Winery LLC ....G...... 509 522-2181
  Walla Walla *(G-14861)*
Tapenade Inc ....G...... 509 966-0686
  Yakima *(G-15694)*
Whitelatch-Hoch LLC ....G...... 509 956-9311
  Kennewick *(G-4745)*

BEVERAGES, WINE/DISTILLED ALCOH, WHOL: Brandy/Brandy Spirits

Tatoosh Distillery LLC ....G...... 206 818-0127
  Seattle *(G-11274)*

BICYCLE SHOPS

Elliott Bay Bicycles Inc ....F...... 206 441-9998
  Seattle *(G-9899)*

BICYCLES, PARTS & ACCESS

Cee Gees & Co ....G...... 509 465-8231
  Spokane *(G-12174)*
Classic Cycle ....F...... 206 842-9191
  Bainbridge Island *(G-622)*
Elliott Bay Bicycles Inc ....F...... 206 441-9998
  Seattle *(G-9899)*
J & B Importers Inc ....G...... 253 395-0441
  Sumner *(G-13075)*
Ridemind LLC ....G...... 206 226-0016
  Seattle *(G-10964)*

BINDING SVC: Books & Manuals

Armadillo Press Inc ....G...... 425 355-5588
  Everett *(G-3373)*
B & R Bindery and Collating ....G...... 360 944-0326
  Vancouver *(G-14050)*
Budget Printing Center ....G...... 509 736-7511
  Kennewick *(G-4636)*
Cascade Printing Company ....F...... 253 472-5500
  Tacoma *(G-13227)*
Catholic Printery Inc ....G...... 206 767-0660
  Seattle *(G-9648)*
Consolidated Press LLC ....E...... 206 447-9659
  Seattle *(G-9730)*
ESP Printing Inc ....E...... 425 251-6240
  Seattle *(G-9940)*
Fedex Office & Print Svcs Inc ....F...... 360 694-8584
  Vancouver *(G-14226)*
Fedex Office & Print Svcs Inc ....E...... 206 467-1767
  Seattle *(G-9981)*
Fedex Office & Print Svcs Inc ....E...... 206 244-8884
  Tukwila *(G-13733)*
Fedex Office & Print Svcs Inc ....E...... 360 647-1114
  Bellingham *(G-1344)*
Good News Printing & Graphics ....G...... 425 483-2510
  Woodinville *(G-15253)*
Marshall Marketing Group Inc ....E...... 253 473-0765
  Tacoma *(G-13400)*
North West Book Oper Co Inc ....G...... 877 591-8608
  Bellingham *(G-1465)*
NRG Resources Inc ....D...... 509 588-4786
  Benton City *(G-1621)*
Plese Printing & Marketing ....F...... 509 534-2355
  Spokane *(G-12448)*
Prestige Copy and Print ....G...... 206 365-5770
  Seattle *(G-10857)*
Printgraphics Inc ....E...... 503 641-8811
  Vancouver *(G-14508)*
Quality Press Inc ....E...... 206 768-2655
  Seattle *(G-10902)*
Sketchforschools Pubg Inc ....G...... 877 397-5655
  Spokane Valley *(G-12875)*
Snohomish Publishing Company ....E...... 206 523-7548
  Snohomish *(G-11983)*
SOS Finishing Unlimited Inc ....F...... 425 746-7385
  Bellevue *(G-1147)*
Sudden Printing Inc ....E...... 206 243-4444
  Seattle *(G-11211)*
University Reprographics Inc ....G...... 206 633-0925
  Seattle *(G-11385)*
Van Quill Larry R ....G...... 360 736-1776
  Centralia *(G-2441)*

Employee Codes: A=Over 500 employees, B=251-500
C=101-250, D=51-100, E=20-50, F=10-19, G=2-9

BINDING SVC: Trade

PRODUCT SECTION

BINDING SVC: Trade

Cullen Bindery LLC .... F 206 799-6295
   Covington *(G-2824)*

BIOLOGICAL PRDTS: Exc Diagnostic

Absci LLC .... E 360 949-1041
   Vancouver *(G-14005)*
Alder Biopharmaceuticals Inc .... D 425 205-2900
   Bothell *(G-1745)*
Alpha Biopartners LLC .... G 405 603-1917
   Seattle *(G-9386)*
Amplex Bioresources LLC .... G 425 285-0628
   Bellevue *(G-787)*
Aquabiotics Corporation .... G 206 842-1708
   Bainbridge Island *(G-609)*
Chondrex Inc .... G 425 702-6365
   Redmond *(G-8419)*
Glycocept Inc .... G 425 647-7446
   Sammamish *(G-9209)*
Healionics Corporation .... G 206 432-9060
   Seattle *(G-10155)*
Immunex Corporation .... A 206 551-5169
   Seattle *(G-10210)*
Immunobioscience Corp .... G 425 367-4601
   Mukilteo *(G-6942)*
Juno Therapeutics Inc .... E 206 582-1600
   Seattle *(G-10317)*
Just Biotherapeutics Inc .... D 206 651-5094
   Seattle *(G-10318)*
Kamiya Biomedical Company LLC .... F 206 575-8068
   Tukwila *(G-13760)*
Prorestore Products .... E 412 264-8340
   Burlington *(G-2182)*
Qwell Pharmaceuticals Inc .... G 206 674-3027
   Seattle *(G-10908)*
Seattle Genetics Inc .... B 425 527-4000
   Bothell *(G-1902)*
Seattle Genetics Inc .... G 425 483-1037
   Bothell *(G-1903)*

BIOLOGICAL PRDTS: Extracts

Advanced Extracts .... G 360 949-5325
   Brush Prairie *(G-2027)*
Ballard Extracts .... G 206 499-4476
   Seattle *(G-9480)*
Chemill Inc .... F 425 286-5229
   Bothell *(G-1755)*
Hops Extract Corp America .... F 509 575-6440
   Yakima *(G-15582)*
Optimum Extracts .... G 206 491-9617
   Auburn *(G-519)*
Pure Extracts .... G 509 679-6556
   East Wenatchee *(G-3030)*
Seattle Pure Extracts .... G 206 788-5754
   Seattle *(G-11070)*

BIOLOGICAL PRDTS: Vaccines

Inventprise LLC .... F 206 858-8472
   Redmond *(G-8514)*
Path Vaccine Solutions .... G 206 285-3500
   Seattle *(G-10766)*
Vaccines 2 U .... G 509 475-1347
   Spokane Valley *(G-12922)*

BIOLOGICAL PRDTS: Vaccines & Immunizing

Thrifty Payless Inc T/A .... G 360 754-8014
   Olympia *(G-7405)*
Thrifty Payless Inc T/A .... G 509 783-1438
   Kennewick *(G-4735)*
Thrifty Payless Inc T/A .... G 509 928-9121
   Spokane Valley *(G-12905)*
Thrifty Payless Inc T/A .... G 360 825-2558
   Enumclaw *(G-3323)*
Thrifty Payless Inc T/A .... G 509 925-4232
   Ellensburg *(G-3232)*
Thrifty Payless Inc T/A .... G 206 324-7111
   Seattle *(G-11299)*
Thrifty Payless Inc .... G 206 760-1076
   Seattle *(G-11300)*
Thrifty Payless Inc T/A .... G 206 441-8790
   Seattle *(G-11301)*
Thrifty Payless Inc T/A .... G 360 332-1616
   Blaine *(G-1705)*
Thrifty Payless Inc T/A .... G 360 794-0943
   Monroe *(G-6630)*
Thrifty Payless Inc T/A .... G 360 457-3456
   Port Angeles *(G-7750)*
Thrifty Payless Inc T/A .... G 206 721-5018
   Seattle *(G-11302)*
Thrifty Payless Inc T/A .... G 360 647-2175
   Bellingham *(G-1570)*

BIOLOGICAL PRDTS: Venoms

Cascadia Venom Collection .... G 360 556-3177
   Rochester *(G-9129)*
East Vancouver Venom .... G 360 518-1658
   Vancouver *(G-14192)*
Natural Venom All Star .... G 253 370-7986
   Tacoma *(G-13425)*
Stilly Venom Baseball Club .... G 360 319-6589
   Arlington *(G-336)*

BIOLOGICAL PRDTS: Veterinary

Pellets Inc .... G 360 733-3012
   Bellingham *(G-1495)*
Specialty Vetpath .... G 206 453-5691
   Shoreline *(G-11816)*

BITUMINOUS & LIGNITE COAL LOADING & PREPARATION

Coalview Ltd LLC .... E 360 623-7525
   Centralia *(G-2394)*

BLADES: Knife

Skykomish Knife Works .... G 509 763-3117
   Leavenworth *(G-5816)*

BLADES: Saw, Hand Or Power

Carbide Online Sales LLC .... G 253 476-1338
   University Place *(G-13962)*

BLANKBOOKS & LOOSELEAF BINDERS

Automatic Funds Transfer Svcs .... E 206 254-0975
   Seattle *(G-9467)*
Gentzen LLC .... G 206 768-1297
   Tukwila *(G-13738)*

BLANKBOOKS: Albums, Record

Voyager Rcordings Publications .... G 206 323-1112
   Seattle *(G-11430)*

BLANKBOOKS: Checkbooks & Passbooks, Bank

Micrprint Inc .... G 253 539-1103
   Tacoma *(G-13412)*

BLANKBOOKS: Scrapbooks

All Scrapped Up Inc .... G 206 824-3762
   Des Moines *(G-2928)*
Doodlebugs .... G 360 683-3154
   Sequim *(G-11628)*
Finely Finished LLC .... G 360 709-0602
   Olympia *(G-7284)*
Lizzy and Alex Enterprises LLC .... G 425 698-1439
   Bellevue *(G-987)*
Papercraft Cottage .... G 360 426-1038
   Shelton *(G-11720)*
Quick Quotes Inc .... F 360 736-3004
   Centralia *(G-2427)*
Triple-T Designs Inc .... G 253 284-9200
   Tacoma *(G-13564)*

BLANKETS, INSULATING: Aircraft, Asbestos

Thermal Northwest Inc .... F 253 520-8899
   Kent *(G-5178)*

BLANKETS: Horse

Kims Horse Blankets .... G 360 623-9567
   Silver Creek *(G-11824)*

BLASTING SVC: Sand, Metal Parts

Powder Coating Inc .... G 425 743-4393
   Mukilteo *(G-6967)*
Powder Vision Inc .... G 425 222-6363
   Preston *(G-8026)*

BLINDS & SHADES: Mini

A & I Manufacturing Inc .... E 360 805-0858
   Monroe *(G-6540)*
American Drpery Blind Crpt Inc .... C 360 676-1121
   Renton *(G-8743)*

BLINDS & SHADES: Vertical

Go Vertical Corporation .... G 360 830-5447
   Seabeck *(G-9264)*
Otis Elevator Company .... G 206 285-2285
   Tukwila *(G-13784)*
Vertical Gardens Northwest LLC .... G 425 891-7183
   Everett *(G-3650)*
Vertical Lift Solutions .... G 360 928-1126
   Port Angeles *(G-7751)*
Vertical Limits LLC .... G 509 294-9878
   Spokane *(G-12581)*
Vertical Technologies .... G 509 382-2119
   Dayton *(G-2888)*
Vertical Welder .... G 360 265-5457
   Port Orchard *(G-7855)*
Vertical Works LLC .... G 509 251-0513
   Cheney *(G-2595)*

BLINDS : Window

HK Window Fashions .... G 509 466-4202
   Nine Mile Falls *(G-7076)*
Home Sweet Home Indoor .... G 509 327-9637
   Spokane *(G-12297)*

BLOCKS & BLANKS: Bobbin, Wood

Wound Wood Technologies LLC .... F 206 762-0400
   Seattle *(G-11498)*

BLOCKS & BRICKS: Concrete

Basalite Building Products LLC .... E 253 964-5000
   Dupont *(G-2955)*
Cascade Concrete Industries .... F 360 757-2900
   Burlington *(G-2141)*
Cemex Cnstr Mtls PCF LLC .... E 360 486-3557
   Snohomish *(G-11888)*
Quality Concrete Products .... G 509 758-2655
   Clarkston *(G-2642)*

BLOCKS: Landscape Or Retaining Wall, Concrete

Greenland Industries LLC .... G 503 841-1835
   Port Orchard *(G-7811)*
Kp2 LLC .... G 509 663-4983
   Wenatchee *(G-15041)*
Landsol LLC .... F 425 242-5198
   Kirkland *(G-5382)*

BLOCKS: Paving, Composition

Bayview Composites LLC .... D 360 466-4160
   Mount Vernon *(G-6775)*

BLOCKS: Sewer & Manhole, Concrete

Columbia Precast Products LLC .... F 360 335-8400
   Woodland *(G-15424)*

BLOCKS: Standard, Concrete Or Cinder

Cemex Cnstr Mtls PCF LLC .... E 425 355-2111
   Lynnwood *(G-6091)*
Cemex Cnstr Mtls PCF LLC .... G 360 474-0173
   Arlington *(G-218)*
Eastside Masonry Products Inc .... E 425 868-0303
   Redmond *(G-8445)*
Holroyd Block Company Inc .... F 253 474-8481
   Tacoma *(G-13339)*
Kelley Blocks LLC .... G 253 922-9848
   Lake Tapps *(G-5680)*
White Block Co Inc .... E 509 534-0651
   Spokane Valley *(G-12937)*

BLOWER FILTER UNITS: Furnace Blowers

Argo Blower & Mfg Co .... F 206 762-9336
   Seattle *(G-9428)*

BLOWERS & FANS

Corrosion Companies Inc .... E 360 835-2171
   Washougal *(G-14949)*

Dust Control Technologies Inc ....G.... 360 256-2479
Brush Prairie *(G-2033)*
Higher Power Supplies Inc ....G.... 425 438-0990
Mukilteo *(G-6933)*
Mechatronics Inc ....C.... 425 222-5900
Issaquah *(G-4447)*
Mobile Air Applied Science ....G.... 206 953-3786
Bellevue *(G-1012)*
Orchard-Rite Limited Inc ....E.... 509 834-2029
Union Gap *(G-13947)*
Pyrotek Incorporated ....D.... 509 926-6211
Spokane Valley *(G-12846)*

BLOWERS & FANS

Nidec America Corporation ....G.... 360 666-2445
Battle Ground *(G-724)*
Rogers Machinery Company Inc ....E.... 206 763-2530
Seattle *(G-10976)*
Rogers Machinery Company Inc ....E.... 360 736-9356
Centralia *(G-2429)*
Rogers Machinery Company Inc ....F.... 509 922-0556
Spokane Valley *(G-12856)*

BLUEPRINTING SVCS

Applied Digital Imaging Inc ....E.... 360 671-9465
Bellingham *(G-1250)*
Panther Printing ....G.... 509 344-4600
Spokane Valley *(G-12825)*
Printonyx Inc ....G.... 360 378-2069
Friday Harbor *(G-4054)*
Risque Inc ....F.... 360 738-1280
Bellingham *(G-1517)*
Standard Digital Print Co Inc ....F.... 509 624-2985
Spokane *(G-12524)*
University Reprographics Inc ....G.... 206 633-0925
Seattle *(G-11385)*

BOAT & BARGE COMPONENTS: Metal, Prefabricated

Vigor Works LLC ....D.... 360 694-7636
Vancouver *(G-14671)*

BOAT BUILDING & REPAIR

All American Marine Inc ....E.... 360 647-7602
Bellingham *(G-1243)*
All Ocean Services LLC ....G.... 206 632-7692
Everett *(G-3367)*
American Flex & Exhaust Pdts ....G.... 206 789-1353
Seattle *(G-9392)*
Amphibious Marine Inc ....G.... 360 426-3170
Shelton *(G-11677)*
Armstrong Consolidated LLC ....G.... 360 477-7558
Port Townsend *(G-7864)*
Armstrong Marine USA Inc ....D.... 360 457-5752
Port Angeles *(G-7686)*
Arrants Boat Works ....G.... 425 293-4660
Camano Island *(G-2207)*
Baycraft Marine Sales Inc ....G.... 253 863-8522
Chehalis *(G-2470)*
Bear Creek Boatworks Inc ....G.... 425 558-4086
Woodinville *(G-15186)*
Bitter End Boatworks ....G.... 360 920-3862
Bellingham *(G-1274)*
Blue Oval Co ....G.... 509 448-2894
Spokane *(G-12155)*
Boat-Tech ....G.... 206 281-9828
Seattle *(G-9559)*
Boatworks Gallery LLC ....G.... 360 626-1284
Poulsbo *(G-7950)*
Boatworks Long Lake ....G.... 509 979-0936
Nine Mile Falls *(G-7068)*
Brunswick Corporation ....D.... 509 769-2142
Clarkston *(G-2626)*
Bushwacker Boats ....G.... 360 969-1648
Burlington *(G-2139)*
C D Boat Works ....G.... 360 942-3669
Raymond *(G-8344)*
Celebration Boatworks ....G.... 206 321-0794
Bothell *(G-1838)*
Chinook Marine Repair Inc ....G.... 360 777-8361
Chinook *(G-2615)*
Christensen Shipyards LLC ....F.... 360 831-9800
Vancouver *(G-14119)*
Commercial Plastics Corp ....F.... 206 682-4832
Seattle *(G-9717)*
Csr Marine Inc ....E.... 206 632-2001
Seattle *(G-9761)*
Dakota Creek Industries Inc ....A.... 360 293-9575
Anacortes *(G-119)*
Dale A West Specialty Wdwkg ....G.... 360 683-9419
Sequim *(G-11623)*
Defiance Boats LLC ....G.... 360 674-7098
Bremerton *(G-1945)*
Defiance Boats LLC ....E.... 360 329-6865
Bremerton *(G-1946)*
Devlin Designing Boatbuilders ....G.... 360 866-0164
Seattle *(G-9826)*
Down Island Trading Co ....G.... 360 376-4056
Deer Harbor *(G-2891)*
Eagle Rock Boat Repair ....G.... 360 391-3219
Anacortes *(G-125)*
Edwing Boat Inc ....G.... 360 777-8771
Chinook *(G-2616)*
Fields Fabrication Corporation ....G.... 425 222-5905
Issaquah *(G-4413)*
First Boat Company ....G.... 425 931-9433
Everett *(G-3473)*
Fishing Vessel Owners Mar Way ....F.... 206 282-6421
Seattle *(G-10000)*
Fitz Custom Marine ....G.... 253 732-5669
Gig Harbor *(G-4100)*
Gig Harbor Boat Works Inc ....G.... 253 851-2126
Gig Harbor *(G-4107)*
Global Marine Specialties Inc ....G.... 206 414-0819
Kent *(G-4923)*
Granite Boatworks Inc ....G.... 360 466-1280
Mount Vernon *(G-6801)*
Grapeview Point ....G.... 360 277-9015
Allyn *(G-83)*
Group 2 Inc ....G.... 206 378-0900
Seattle *(G-10126)*
H F S-Vitek ....G.... 360 293-8054
Anacortes *(G-133)*
Hansen Fabrication ....G.... 206 283-9181
Seattle *(G-10139)*
Hard Drive Marine ....G.... 360 306-8685
Bellingham *(G-1365)*
Haven Boatworks LLC ....G.... 360 385-5727
Port Townsend *(G-7889)*
Haven Boatworks LLC ....F.... 360 385-5727
Port Townsend *(G-7890)*
Helicat LLC ....G.... 253 376-8273
Spanaway *(G-12059)*
Ice Floe LLC ....C.... 360 331-5500
Freeland *(G-4030)*
Ivie Boat Building ....G.... 360 892-2883
Vancouver *(G-14328)*
Jonathan Quinn Barnett Ltd ....G.... 206 322-2152
Seattle *(G-10305)*
Kalhovde Boat Works ....G.... 360 398-1262
Bellingham *(G-1389)*
Kettle River Boat Works LLC ....G.... 509 738-2872
Kettle Falls *(G-5234)*
Kevin Philbin Yacht Detail ....G.... 206 949-0162
Seattle *(G-10339)*
Leclercq Marine Construction ....E.... 206 283-8555
Seattle *(G-10396)*
Lee Shore Boats Inc ....G.... 360 385-1491
Port Townsend *(G-7895)*
Left Coast Composites ....G.... 305 923-4590
Port Angeles *(G-7723)*
Level Sky Boatworks ....G.... 206 789-5655
Seattle *(G-10410)*
Lovrics Sea Craft Inc ....G.... 360 293-2042
Anacortes *(G-144)*
Marine Servicenter Inc ....G.... 206 323-2405
Seattle *(G-10484)*
Martian Boat Works ....G.... 360 427-8629
Shelton *(G-11711)*
Maven Watersports Designs LLC ....G.... 360 481-2521
Puyallup *(G-8185)*
Mercer Marine Inc ....F.... 425 641-2090
Fall City *(G-3703)*
Miller & Miller Boatyard Co ....G.... 206 285-5958
Seattle *(G-10543)*
Nichols Diversified Inds LLC ....F.... 360 331-7230
Freeland *(G-4035)*
North Hbr Diesl Yacht Svc Inc ....E.... 360 293-5551
Anacortes *(G-153)*
North Industries Inc ....G.... 206 940-0842
Seattle *(G-10624)*
Northwest Dock Systems LLC ....G.... 360 832-2295
Eatonville *(G-3064)*
Northwest Yachts Inc ....G.... 360 299-0777
Anacortes *(G-156)*
Oceanus Plastics Inc ....G.... 360 366-7474
Custer *(G-2858)*
Olympic Outdoor Center ....E.... 360 297-4659
Port Gamble *(G-7757)*
Outdoor Synergy ....G.... 360 435-3330
Arlington *(G-296)*
Pacific Ship Repr Fbrction Inc ....C.... 360 674-2480
Bremerton *(G-1985)*
Pacific Skiffs Nw Inc ....G.... 360 658-7111
Marysville *(G-6367)*
Papenhause Composites Inc ....G.... 206 669-3260
Seattle *(G-10747)*
Performance Marine Inc ....F.... 425 258-9292
Everett *(G-3571)*
Peter Kaupat Easy ....F.... 425 228-3633
Tukwila *(G-13791)*
Pierres Dock Inc ....G.... 425 488-8600
Kenmore *(G-4598)*
Port Townsend Sails Inc ....F.... 360 385-1640
Port Townsend *(G-7914)*
Port Townsend Shipwrights Coop ....E.... 360 385-6138
Port Townsend *(G-7916)*
Puget Sound Repair Inc ....G.... 506 556-9722
Seattle *(G-10885)*
Raider Boats Inc ....F.... 509 684-8348
Colville *(G-2771)*
Railmakers Northwest ....F.... 425 259-9236
Everett *(G-3594)*
Rozema Enterprises Inc ....G.... 360 757-6004
Mount Vernon *(G-6831)*
Safe Boats International LLC ....B.... 360 674-7161
Bremerton *(G-1998)*
Seamist Marine LLC ....G.... 253 583-4151
Silverdale *(G-11856)*
Seattle Boat Works LLC ....G.... 206 849-4259
Seattle *(G-11047)*
Seaview Boat Yard Inc ....E.... 206 783-6550
Seattle *(G-11085)*
Seaview Boat Yard Inc ....F.... 206 783-6550
Seattle *(G-11086)*
Seaview Boatyard North Inc ....E.... 360 676-8282
Bellingham *(G-1531)*
Seaview Boatyard West Inc ....G.... 206 783-6550
Seattle *(G-11087)*
Sifferman & Sifferman ....G.... 360 426-0714
Grapeview *(G-4290)*
Snow & Company Inc ....E.... 206 953-7676
Seattle *(G-11144)*
South Bend Boat Shop ....G.... 360 875-5712
South Bend *(G-12046)*
Southworth Marine Service ....G.... 360 871-5610
Southworth *(G-12051)*
Spring Creek Industries Inc ....G.... 509 486-0599
Tonasket *(G-13659)*
Stabbert Yacht and Ship LLC ....E.... 206 547-6161
Seattle *(G-11176)*
Sunbacker Fiberglass Inc ....G.... 360 794-5547
Monroe *(G-6628)*
Top To Bottom ....G.... 206 764-7750
Seattle *(G-11319)*
Top To Bottom Inc ....G.... 360 671-7022
Bellingham *(G-1572)*
Toss Brion Yacht Rigging Inc ....G.... 360 385-1080
Port Townsend *(G-7932)*
Townsend Bay Marine LLC ....F.... 360 385-3981
Port Townsend *(G-7933)*
Traditional Boat Works Inc ....G.... 360 379-6502
Port Townsend *(G-7936)*
University Swaging Corporation ....C.... 425 318-1965
Bellevue *(G-1208)*
US Workboats Inc ....G.... 360 808-2292
Sequim *(G-11668)*
West Bay Boat & Manufacturing ....G.... 360 683-4066
Sequim *(G-11669)*
Western Towboat Company ....C.... 206 789-9000
Seattle *(G-11456)*
Wooldridge Boats Inc ....F.... 206 722-8998
Seattle *(G-11493)*
Yacht Masters Northwest LLC ....E.... 206 285-3460
Seattle *(G-11506)*
Youngquist Boat Repair ....G.... 206 283-9555
Seattle *(G-11516)*

BOAT BUILDING & REPAIRING: Fiberglass

B & J Fiberglass LLC ....G.... 360 398-9342
Bellingham *(G-1256)*
Custom Fiberglass Mfr ....G.... 360 457-5092
Port Angeles *(G-7696)*
Fluid Motion LLC ....E.... 253 839-5213
Kent *(G-4913)*
Jenneth Technologies Inc ....G.... 509 547-8977
Kennewick *(G-4680)*

BOAT BUILDING & REPAIRING: Fiberglass

Martin Boats Inc .... G 360 380-7331
  Bellingham *(G-1425)*
Modutech Marine Inc .... E 253 272-9319
  Tacoma *(G-13418)*
Moe Howard Enterprises Inc .... E 360 538-1622
  Hoquiam *(G-4349)*
Nordic Tugs Incorporated .... E 360 757-8847
  Burlington *(G-2172)*
Norstar Boats Inc .... G 360 671-3669
  Bellingham *(G-1462)*
Ranger Tugs .... G 360 794-7430
  Monroe *(G-6613)*
Renaissance Marine Group Inc .... D 509 758-9189
  Clarkston *(G-2644)*
Richard Knannlein .... G 360 426-9757
  Shelton *(G-11726)*
Sorensen Marine Inc .... G 206 767-4622
  Seattle *(G-11157)*
Stambaughs Hungry Harbor Entps ...... G 360 777-8289
  Naselle *(G-7020)*
William E Munson Company .... D 360 707-2752
  Burlington *(G-2203)*
Workskiff Inc .... G 360 707-5622
  Sedro Woolley *(G-11581)*

BOAT BUILDING & REPAIRING: Kayaks

Auburn Marine .... G 253 941-3046
  Auburn *(G-382)*
Pygmy Boats Inc .... G 360 385-6143
  Port Townsend *(G-7921)*

BOAT BUILDING & REPAIRING: Lifeboats

Cap Sante International Inc .... E 360 293-3145
  Anacortes *(G-109)*
Palfinger Marine USA Inc .... G 360 299-4585
  Anacortes *(G-160)*

BOAT BUILDING & REPAIRING: Motorboats, Inboard Or Outboard

Duckworth Boat Works Inc .... E 509 758-9831
  Clarkston *(G-2633)*
Fletcher Boats Inc .... G 360 452-8430
  Port Angeles *(G-7707)*
Hewes Marine Co Inc .... D 509 684-5235
  Colville *(G-2756)*
Nexus Marine Corporation .... G 425 252-8330
  Everett *(G-3552)*
Speedway Marine Inc .... G 360 658-1288
  Marysville *(G-6390)*
Waya Group Inc .... G 877 277-6999
  Everett *(G-3653)*
Weldcraft Marine Industries .... C 509 758-9831
  Clarkston *(G-2654)*

BOAT BUILDING & REPAIRING: Motorized

Alexander S Service Repair .... G 509 773-7010
  Goldendale *(G-4192)*
Concorde Marine Inc .... G 360 755-3471
  Anacortes *(G-115)*
Rjs Marine LLC .... G 509 888-4568
  Chelan *(G-2563)*

BOAT BUILDING & REPAIRING: Non-Motorized

Howard Fabrication .... G 360 380-1721
  Ferndale *(G-3854)*
Jr Grennay Co .... G 509 484-5056
  Valleyford *(G-13997)*
Redden Marine .... G 206 753-0960
  Bellevue *(G-1097)*
Spindrift Rowing LLC .... G 360 344-2233
  Port Townsend *(G-7930)*

BOAT BUILDING & REPAIRING: Pontoons, Exc Aircraft & Inflat

Silver King Mining & Milling .... G 509 445-1406
  Cusick *(G-2852)*

BOAT BUILDING & REPAIRING: Rowboats

Pocock Racing Shells Inc .... F 425 438-9048
  Everett *(G-3577)*

BOAT BUILDING & REPAIRING: Tenders, Small Motor Craft

M & M Craftworks .... G 360 675-9138
  Oak Harbor *(G-7157)*

BOAT BUILDING & REPAIRING: Yachts

Cap Sante Marine Ltd .... E 360 293-3145
  Anacortes *(G-110)*
Delta Marine Industries Inc .... B 206 763-0760
  Seattle *(G-9818)*
First Cabin Yachts Inc .... G 206 595-6657
  Seattle *(G-9995)*
Joseph Artese Design .... G 206 365-4326
  Lake Forest Park *(G-5617)*
Legendary Yacht Inc .... F 360 835-0342
  Washougal *(G-14963)*
North Island Boat Company Inc .... F 360 293-2565
  Anacortes *(G-154)*
Northcoast Yachts Inc .... E 253 383-3803
  Seattle *(G-10630)*
Pacific Asian Enterprises Inc .... G 206 223-3624
  Seattle *(G-10727)*
Passage Inc .... G 425 743-5600
  Everett *(G-3570)*
San Juan Composites LLC .... E 360 299-3790
  Anacortes *(G-164)*
Time 4 Fun LLC .... G 425 836-5037
  Redmond *(G-8692)*
Western Yacht Systems Inc .... G 360 384-3648
  Ferndale *(G-3924)*
Westport LLC .... C 360 268-1800
  Westport *(G-15108)*
Westport LLC .... C 360 452-5095
  Port Angeles *(G-7754)*
Westport LLC .... F 360 452-5095
  Port Angeles *(G-7755)*
Yacht Specialties .... G 360 423-9995
  Kelso *(G-4562)*
Yachtfish Marine Inc .... F 206 623-3233
  Seattle *(G-11507)*

BOAT BUILDING & RPRG: Fishing, Small, Lobster, Crab, Oyster

D&L Summers Inc .... G 360 268-0769
  Westport *(G-15104)*
F/V Native Star .... G 360 267-6348
  Grayland *(G-4293)*
Fv Fast Break .... G 360 642-3753
  Ilwaco *(G-4370)*
Lorelei II Inc .... G 206 783-6045
  Seattle *(G-10443)*
Mezich Allegiance Inc .... G 206 782-1767
  Seattle *(G-10526)*
Novus Composites Incorporated .... G 253 476-8582
  Tacoma *(G-13436)*
Petrzelka Bros Inc .... G 360 424-8095
  Mount Vernon *(G-6824)*
S Mayton Construction Company .... G 360 532-6138
  Aberdeen *(G-32)*
Sierra Fishers I N C .... G 360 299-1469
  Anacortes *(G-168)*
Skyline Fisheries LLC .... G 425 583-7259
  Arlington *(G-329)*
Skyview Fisheries LLC .... G 425 583-7259
  Arlington *(G-330)*
Sp Marine Fabrication LLC .... F 360 813-3600
  Bremerton *(G-2002)*
Tony Pecaric .... G 360 398-9885
  Lynden *(G-6056)*
Westward Seafoods Inc .... G 206 341-9996
  Seattle *(G-11458)*

BOAT DEALERS

Ade Holding Inc .... D 206 789-3600
  Seattle *(G-9350)*
Fletcher Boats Inc .... G 360 452-8430
  Port Angeles *(G-7707)*
Gig Harbor Boat Works Inc .... G 253 851-2126
  Gig Harbor *(G-4107)*
Jh Marine LLC .... G 425 241-6801
  Kirkland *(G-5373)*
Legendary Yacht Inc .... F 360 835-0342
  Washougal *(G-14963)*
Marine Servicenter Inc .... G 206 323-2405
  Seattle *(G-10484)*
Nexus Marine Corporation .... G 425 252-8330
  Everett *(G-3552)*
North Island Boat Company Inc .... F 360 293-2565
  Anacortes *(G-154)*
Northern Lights Inc .... D 206 789-3600
  Seattle *(G-10632)*
Pygmy Boats Inc .... G 360 385-6143
  Port Townsend *(G-7921)*
Rod Carr Sailmaker .... G 425 881-2846
  Redmond *(G-8654)*
Rozema Enterprises Inc .... G 360 757-6004
  Mount Vernon *(G-6831)*
Ship To Shore Inc .... G 206 284-0406
  Seattle *(G-11101)*
Spindrift Rowing LLC .... G 360 344-2233
  Port Townsend *(G-7930)*
US Workboats Inc .... G 360 808-2292
  Sequim *(G-11668)*
Yachtfish Marine Inc .... F 206 623-3233
  Seattle *(G-11507)*

BOAT DEALERS: Canoes

Easy Rider Canoe & Kayak Co .... G 425 228-3633
  Tukwila *(G-13727)*

BOAT DEALERS: Inboard

Waya Group Inc .... G 877 277-6999
  Everett *(G-3653)*

BOAT DEALERS: Kayaks

Auburn Marine .... G 253 941-3046
  Auburn *(G-382)*
Olympic Outdoor Center .... E 360 297-4659
  Port Gamble *(G-7757)*

BOAT DEALERS: Marine Splys & Eqpt

M & I Systems Inc .... G 206 547-7899
  Everett *(G-3542)*
North Hbr Diesl Yacht Svc Inc .... E 360 293-5551
  Anacortes *(G-153)*
Redden Marine .... G 206 753-0960
  Bellevue *(G-1097)*
Safe Boats International LLC .... B 360 674-7161
  Bremerton *(G-1998)*

BOAT DEALERS: Motor

Jened Inc .... G 509 926-6894
  Spokane Valley *(G-12751)*
Performance Marine Inc .... F 425 258-9292
  Everett *(G-3571)*
Petrzelka Bros Inc .... G 360 424-8095
  Mount Vernon *(G-6824)*
Sorensen Marine Inc .... G 206 767-4622
  Seattle *(G-11157)*
Taylors Marine Center .... G 509 633-2945
  Electric City *(G-3168)*
West Bay Boat & Manufacturing .... G 360 683-4066
  Sequim *(G-11669)*

BOAT DEALERS: Sailboats & Eqpt

Pacific Radar Inc .... G 425 775-0400
  Everett *(G-3566)*
Quantum Sails .... G 206 634-0636
  Seattle *(G-10903)*

BOAT DEALERS: Sails & Eqpt

Port Townsend Sails Inc .... F 360 385-1640
  Port Townsend *(G-7914)*
Schattauer Sailmaker Corp .... G 206 783-0173
  Seattle *(G-11024)*

BOAT LIFTS

Accumar Corporation .... G 360 779-7795
  Poulsbo *(G-7942)*
Aqua-Lift Inc .... G 253 845-4010
  Puyallup *(G-8124)*
Basta Inc .... E 425 641-8911
  Bellevue *(G-807)*
Boat Tote .... G 360 600-1364
  Vancouver *(G-14073)*
Marine Restoration & Cnstr LLC .... G 425 576-8661
  Kirkland *(G-5396)*
Sierra Industries Inc .... C 425 487-5200
  Woodinville *(G-15363)*
Specialty Motors Mfg LLC .... G 360 423-9880
  Longview *(G-5956)*
Sunstream Corporation .... E 253 395-0500
  Kent *(G-5163)*

PRODUCT SECTION

BOAT REPAIR SVCS

Company	Code	Phone
Blue Oval Co	G	509 448-2894
Spokane *(G-12155)*		
Leclercq Marine Construction	E	206 283-8555
Seattle *(G-10396)*		
Marine Servicenter Inc	G	206 323-2405
Seattle *(G-10484)*		
Maritime Fabrications Inc	E	360 466-3629
La Conner *(G-5524)*		
Mercer Marine Inc	F	425 641-2090
Fall City *(G-3703)*		
Miller & Miller Boatyard Co	G	206 285-5958
Seattle *(G-10543)*		
North Island Boat Company Inc	F	360 293-2565
Anacortes *(G-154)*		
R&D Enterprises	G	360 293-4155
Anacortes *(G-163)*		
Snow & Company Inc	E	206 953-7676
Seattle *(G-11144)*		
Top To Bottom Inc	G	360 671-7022
Bellingham *(G-1572)*		
Townsend Bay Marine LLC	F	360 385-3981
Port Townsend *(G-7933)*		
Western Yacht Systems Inc	G	360 384-3648
Ferndale *(G-3924)*		

BOAT YARD: Boat yards, storage & incidental repair

Company	Code	Phone
H F S-Vitek	G	360 293-8054
Anacortes *(G-133)*		

BOATS & OTHER MARINE EQPT: Plastic

Company	Code	Phone
Oceanus Plastics Inc	G	360 366-7474
Custer *(G-2858)*		
Pure Watercraft Inc	G	206 451-0350
Seattle *(G-10890)*		
Tdap	G	509 453-3038
Yakima *(G-15695)*		

BOATS: Plastic, Nonrigid

Company	Code	Phone
Rods Custom Fiberglass Inc	G	509 483-2174
Spokane *(G-12482)*		

BODIES: Truck & Bus

Company	Code	Phone
Allied Body Works Inc	F	206 763-7811
Seattle *(G-9381)*		
Amrep Inc	G	253 939-6265
Pacific *(G-7523)*		
Freedom Truck Centers Inc	E	509 248-9478
Union Gap *(G-13931)*		
Geo Heiser Body Co LLC	E	206 622-7985
Tukwila *(G-13739)*		
Imperial Group Mfg Inc	C	360 748-4201
Chehalis *(G-2504)*		
Nelson Truck Equipment Co Inc	E	253 395-3825
Kent *(G-5018)*		
Paccar Inc	B	425 468-7400
Bellevue *(G-1058)*		
Pacifica Marine Inc	F	206 764-1646
Seattle *(G-10742)*		
Road Runner Transportation LLC	G	253 778-3848
Seattle *(G-10970)*		
Truck Accessories Group LLC	D	360 736-9991
Centralia *(G-2439)*		
U S Fire Equipment LLC	F	253 863-1301
Sumner *(G-13108)*		

BODY PARTS: Automobile, Stamped Metal

Company	Code	Phone
A-Star Distributing Inc	F	509 467-6809
Spokane *(G-12091)*		
Billy Bob Customs	G	360 637-9147
Elma *(G-3242)*		
Carburetors Unlimited Inc	G	253 833-4106
Auburn *(G-401)*		
Genuine Parts Company	F	509 484-4400
Spokane *(G-12269)*		
J R Setina Manufacturing Co	D	360 491-6197
Olympia *(G-7310)*		
Joe Constance	F	425 347-8920
Everett *(G-3524)*		
Kryki Sports	G	206 660-7359
Seattle *(G-10360)*		
Shoot Suit Inc	G	360 687-3451
Battle Ground *(G-739)*		
Zhongtao	G	425 344-9373
Kirkland *(G-5501)*		

BOILER & HEATING REPAIR SVCS

Company	Code	Phone
Specialty Pump and Plbg Inc	G	425 424-8700
Snohomish *(G-11986)*		

BOILER REPAIR SHOP

Company	Code	Phone
CH Murphy/Clark-Ullman Inc	D	253 475-6566
Tacoma *(G-13232)*		

BONDS, RAIL: Electric, Propulsion & Signal Circuit Uses

Company	Code	Phone
Bluefin Marine LLC	G	206 276-4087
Kirkland *(G-5293)*		
Magnix Usa Inc	G	206 304-8129
Redmond *(G-8545)*		

BOOK STORES

Company	Code	Phone
Fantagraphics Books Inc	E	206 524-1967
Seattle *(G-9968)*		
Globe	G	206 527-2480
Seattle *(G-10086)*		
Indaba Management Company LLC	F	360 546-5528
Vancouver *(G-14312)*		
Mindcastle Books Incorporated	G	206 801-7338
Shoreline *(G-11789)*		
Oxalis Group	G	509 838-3295
Spokane *(G-12424)*		
Skye Book & Brew	G	509 382-4677
Dayton *(G-2885)*		
Starpath Corporation	G	206 783-1414
Seattle *(G-11184)*		
Studio Foglio LLC	G	206 782-8739
Seattle *(G-11207)*		

BOOK STORES: College

Company	Code	Phone
Book N Brush	G	360 748-6221
Chehalis *(G-2472)*		

BOOKS, WHOLESALE

Company	Code	Phone
Alex Daisley	G	206 623-5555
Seattle *(G-9373)*		
Cascade Publishing Inc	G	206 430-6021
Seattle *(G-9643)*		
Homestead Book Co	G	206 782-4532
Seattle *(G-10180)*		
Illumination Arts Inc	G	360 984-5173
Vancouver *(G-14308)*		
Indaba Management Company LLC	F	360 546-5528
Vancouver *(G-14312)*		
Test Best International Inc	F	360 650-0671
Bellingham *(G-1567)*		

BOOTS: Men's

Company	Code	Phone
Amgb Inc	G	509 309-2903
Spokane *(G-12112)*		
Whites Boots Inc	C	509 535-1875
Spokane *(G-12589)*		

BOOTS: Women's

Company	Code	Phone
Amgb Inc	G	509 309-2903
Spokane *(G-12112)*		

BOTTLED GAS DEALERS: Propane

Company	Code	Phone
Blue Water Inc	G	509 682-5544
Chelan *(G-2548)*		

BOTTLES: Plastic

Company	Code	Phone
Amcor Rigid Packaging Usa LLC	D	509 525-0230
Walla Walla *(G-14762)*		
Consolidated Container Co LLC	E	425 251-0303
Tukwila *(G-13715)*		
Evergreen Plastic Container	F	360 828-7174
Vancouver *(G-14209)*		
Graham Packaging Company LP	E	509 698-4545
Selah *(G-11589)*		
Green Willow Trucking Inc	F	360 687-7171
Battle Ground *(G-705)*		
Green Willow Trucking Inc	E	360 687-7171
Battle Ground *(G-706)*		
Okanogan Label & Print Ltd	F	250 328-8660
Walla Walla *(G-14853)*		
Richards Packaging Inc	E	253 582-1096
Tacoma *(G-13499)*		
Richards Packaging Inc	E	253 872-2848
Auburn *(G-547)*		
Velendo Inc	F	360 828-7174
Vancouver *(G-14667)*		

BOULDER: Crushed & Broken

Company	Code	Phone
Dulin Construction Inc	F	360 736-9225
Centralia *(G-2399)*		
Good Crushing Inc	F	360 864-2974
Toledo *(G-13639)*		
H B Q Inc	G	509 653-1939
Naches *(G-6997)*		
Jones Quarry Inc	G	360 352-1022
Tumwater *(G-13879)*		
Rock Services Inc	G	360 748-8333
Chehalis *(G-2531)*		

BOX & CARTON MANUFACTURING EQPT

Company	Code	Phone
ASC Machine Tools Inc	C	509 534-6600
Spokane Valley *(G-12626)*		
H R Spinner Corporation	E	509 453-9111
Yakima *(G-15579)*		

BOXES & CRATES: Rectangular, Wood

Company	Code	Phone
Armour Mfg & Cnstr Inc	G	253 984-1213
Tacoma *(G-13180)*		
Atomic Crate & Case Inc	G	425 264-0336
Seatac *(G-9273)*		
Commercial Crting Box Pckg Inc	F	253 804-8616
Auburn *(G-410)*		
G M Pallet Inc	G	253 435-1040
Tacoma *(G-13303)*		

BOXES & SHOOK: Nailed Wood

Company	Code	Phone
Macro Plastics Inc	E	509 452-1200
Union Gap *(G-13940)*		
Northwest Cstm Crating Box Inc	G	253 232-3244
Puyallup *(G-8203)*		
Ufp Washington LLC	F	509 663-1988
Malaga *(G-6233)*		
Ufp Washington LLC	D	360 568-3185
Snohomish *(G-11995)*		
Ufp Washington LLC	E	509 966-4610
Yakima *(G-15699)*		
World Wide Gourmet Foods Inc	F	360 668-9404
Woodinville *(G-15410)*		

BOXES, METER: Concrete

Company	Code	Phone
Fog Tite Meter Seal Inc	E	206 935-8000
Seattle *(G-10010)*		

BOXES: Corrugated

Company	Code	Phone
Alliance Packaging LLC	D	509 924-7623
Spokane Valley *(G-12605)*		
Alliance Packaging LLC	C	425 291-3500
Renton *(G-8738)*		
Allpak Container LLC	D	425 227-0400
Renton *(G-8739)*		
Allpak Container LLC	E	509 535-4112
Renton *(G-8740)*		
Box Maker Inc	G	425 291-1291
Kent *(G-4820)*		
Georgia-Pacific LLC	C	360 491-1310
Olympia *(G-7295)*		
Great Little Box Co Inc	G	425 349-4522
Everett *(G-3506)*		
International Paper Company	C	509 765-0262
Moses Lake *(G-6716)*		
Longview Fibre Ppr & Packg Inc	D	206 762-7170
Seattle *(G-10437)*		
Orora Packaging Solutions	F	253 796-6200
Kent *(G-5048)*		
Pacific Container Corp	D	206 682-1778
Tacoma *(G-13450)*		
Packaging Corporation America	C	509 575-3689
Yakima *(G-15641)*		
Packaging Corporation America	F	800 223-2307
Algona *(G-73)*		
Packaging Corporation America	G	360 891-8796
Vancouver *(G-14475)*		
Packaging Corporation America	C	509 545-3202
Wallula *(G-14910)*		
Sp Holdings Inc	E	509 924-7623
Spokane Valley *(G-12881)*		
Sp Holdings Inc	C	425 291-3500
Renton *(G-8918)*		
Weyerhaeuser Company	C	360 491-1200
Olympia *(G-7425)*		

Employee Codes: A=Over 500 employees, B=251-500 C=101-250, D=51-100, E=20-50, F=10-19, G=2-9

BOXES: Mail Or Post Office, Collection/Storage, Sheet Metal

BOXES: Mail Or Post Office, Collection/Storage, Sheet Metal

Kingston Mail Center Inc ....G...... 360 297-2173
  Kingston *(G-5256)*
Mailboxes Depot ....G...... 360 651-2651
  Arlington *(G-272)*
Post All Expressions ....G...... 509 684-3723
  Colville *(G-2769)*

BOXES: Packing & Shipping, Metal

Avista Corporation ....A...... 509 489-0500
  Spokane *(G-12134)*
Steel Fab Inc ....E...... 425 743-9216
  Arlington *(G-333)*

BOXES: Paperboard, Folding

Charles Hanson ....G...... 360 871-2173
  Port Orchard *(G-7797)*
Decomp ....G...... 360 306-8516
  Bellingham *(G-1321)*
Graphic Packaging Intl Inc ....C...... 425 235-3300
  Renton *(G-8812)*
Michelsen Packaging Company ....C...... 509 248-6270
  Yakima *(G-15619)*
Sonderen Packaging Inc ....C...... 509 487-1632
  Spokane *(G-12510)*
Trojan Lithograph Corporation ....C...... 425 873-2200
  Renton *(G-8933)*
X Tracted ....G...... 206 294-3308
  Seattle *(G-11502)*

BOXES: Paperboard, Set-Up

Northwest Paper Box Mfrs Inc ....E...... 206 782-7105
  Seatac *(G-9293)*

BOXES: Plastic

Northwest Paper Box Mfrs Inc ....E...... 206 782-7105
  Seatac *(G-9293)*

BOXES: Stamped Metal

N2 Storage Systems Inc ....G...... 509 981-8097
  Mead *(G-6434)*

BOXES: Wooden

Duncans Woods ....G...... 360 604-7140
  Vancouver *(G-14190)*
Encased Specialty Mfg LLC ....G...... 509 396-0755
  Kennewick *(G-4660)*
Harbor Action Inc ....F...... 360 417-1316
  Port Angeles *(G-7708)*
Industrial Crating & Packing ....F...... 425 226-9200
  Mercer Island *(G-6467)*
Mattawa Wood Products Corp ....G...... 509 932-6420
  Mattawa *(G-6410)*
Northwest Dovetail Inc ....G...... 509 248-2056
  Yakima *(G-15634)*
Quinault Wood Crafts ....G...... 360 288-2848
  Amanda Park *(G-88)*
Wood Design ....G...... 425 883-8842
  Redmond *(G-8717)*

BRAKES & BRAKE PARTS

Genuine Parts Company ....E...... 206 575-8100
  Renton *(G-8806)*
Haldex Brake Products Corp ....G...... 360 944-3070
  Vancouver *(G-14279)*
Metal Frictions Company Inc ....G...... 425 776-0336
  Edmonds *(G-3133)*

BRAKES: Metal Forming

Metal Frictions Company Inc ....G...... 425 776-0336
  Edmonds *(G-3133)*

BRASS GOODS, WHOLESALE

J & H Printing Inc ....G...... 509 332-0782
  Pullman *(G-8094)*

BRAZING SVCS

Bennett Industries Inc ....E...... 253 627-7775
  Tacoma *(G-13194)*

BRICK, STONE & RELATED PRDTS WHOLESALERS

Eastside Masonry Products Inc ....E...... 425 868-0303
  Redmond *(G-8445)*
Fred Hill Materials ....F...... 360 779-4431
  Sequim *(G-11635)*
Gary Merlino Cnstr Co Inc ....F...... 206 763-2134
  Seattle *(G-10050)*
Glacier Northwest Inc ....D...... 253 912-8500
  Dupont *(G-2964)*
Glacier Northwest Inc ....E...... 425 888-9795
  Snoqualmie *(G-12013)*
Graymont Western US Inc ....E...... 253 572-7600
  Tacoma *(G-13319)*
James Hardie Building Pdts Inc ....D...... 253 847-8700
  Tacoma *(G-13355)*
Mario & Son Inc ....E...... 509 536-6079
  Liberty Lake *(G-5845)*
Milestone Products Co ....F...... 425 882-1987
  Redmond *(G-8589)*
North Hill Resources Inc ....F...... 360 757-1866
  Burlington *(G-2173)*
Samoa Maritime Company ....G...... 206 246-1182
  Normandy Park *(G-7098)*
Spilker Precast LLC ....G...... 509 487-2261
  Spokane *(G-12514)*

BRICKS & BLOCKS: Structural

Mutual Materials Company ....E...... 509 924-2120
  Mica *(G-6501)*

BRICKS : Ceramic Glazed, Clay

Ty Enterprises ....G...... 509 826-6597
  Riverside *(G-9128)*

BRIDAL SHOPS

Fashion Corner ....G...... 509 837-7345
  Sunnyside *(G-13125)*

BROADCASTING & COMMS EQPT: Antennas, Transmitting/Comms

Morad Electronics Corporation ....G...... 206 789-2525
  Bellingham *(G-1442)*
Omohundro Co Kitsap Composites ....D...... 360 519-3047
  Port Orchard *(G-7837)*
Steppir Comm Systems Inc ....G...... 425 453-1910
  Bellevue *(G-1157)*

BROADCASTING & COMMS EQPT: Rcvr-Transmitter Unt, Transceiver

SGC World Inc ....F...... 425 746-6310
  Bellevue *(G-1126)*
Unlimited Possibilities Now ....G...... 206 930-9100
  Bothell *(G-1804)*

BROADCASTING & COMMUNICATIONS EQPT: Cellular Radio Telephone

Huawei Device USA Inc ....F...... 425 247-2700
  Bellevue *(G-951)*

BROADCASTING & COMMUNICATIONS EQPT: Studio Eqpt, Radio & TV

Race Horse Studios ....G...... 206 451-4725
  Bainbridge Island *(G-662)*
Roberta Lowes ....G...... 253 572-1859
  Tacoma *(G-13501)*
Washington State University ....G...... 509 372-7400
  Richland *(G-9052)*

BROADCASTING STATIONS, RADIO: Educational

Shoezandmorecom LLC ....F...... 216 544-1745
  Renton *(G-8911)*

BROKERS: Fish

Trident Seafoods Corporation ....C...... 360 293-7701
  Anacortes *(G-179)*

BROKERS: Food

Del Rio Food Processing Corp ....F...... 206 767-9102
  Seattle *(G-9816)*

Vs Foods LLC ....G...... 425 279-8089
  Bellevue *(G-1221)*

BROKERS: Log & Lumber

Barry Rankin Logging Inc ....G...... 360 436-1947
  Darrington *(G-2866)*
Miller Shingle Company LLC ....G...... 360 691-7727
  Granite Falls *(G-4281)*
Phillip L Remsberg ....G...... 509 997-3231
  Twisp *(G-13916)*

BROKERS: Mortgage, Arranging For Loans

Eakin Enterprises Inc ....F...... 509 698-3200
  Selah *(G-11587)*

BROKERS: Printing

William Reed & Associates ....G...... 509 534-4727
  Spokane Valley *(G-12938)*

BRONZE FOUNDRY, NEC

Frasers Bronze Foundry Inc ....G...... 877 264-1064
  Marysville *(G-6336)*
Fremont Fine Arts Foundry Inc ....G...... 206 588-6981
  Seattle *(G-10024)*

BROOMS & BRUSHES

Cascade Brush Company ....G...... 509 965-6603
  Yakima *(G-15529)*
Sherwin-Williams Company ....G...... 425 643-8584
  Bellevue *(G-1129)*

BROOMS & BRUSHES: Street Sweeping, Hand Or Machine

Tennant Co ....G...... 425 788-9711
  Woodinville *(G-15387)*

BROOMS & BRUSHES: Vacuum Cleaners & Carpet Sweepers

3tac Distribution Inc ....G...... 206 257-1552
  Tukwila *(G-13685)*

BRUSH BLOCKS: Carbon Or Molded Graphite

Transition Composites Mfg Inc ....G...... 360 312-1497
  Bellingham *(G-1574)*

BUCKLES & PARTS

Ralston Cunningham Associates ....G...... 425 455-0316
  Redmond *(G-8645)*

BUILDING & STRUCTURAL WOOD MBRS: Timbers, Struct, Lam Lumber

Murphy Company ....C...... 360 482-2521
  Elma *(G-3250)*
Weyerhaeuser Company ....D...... 360 482-2521
  Elma *(G-3259)*

BUILDING & STRUCTURAL WOOD MEMBERS

AAA Truss ....G...... 509 365-2690
  Appleton *(G-187)*
Bamboo Hardwoods Inc ....G...... 800 607-2414
  Seattle *(G-9488)*
BMC West LLC ....E...... 360 943-8050
  Lakewood *(G-5704)*
Builders Firstsource Inc ....D...... 509 783-8148
  Kennewick *(G-4637)*
Canfor USA Corporation ....G...... 360 647-2434
  Bellingham *(G-1290)*
Dis-Tran Wood Products LLC ....G...... 360 735-9356
  Vancouver *(G-14181)*
G R Plume Co ....F...... 360 384-2800
  Ferndale *(G-3846)*
Matthaeis Camco Inc ....E...... 360 426-7900
  Shelton *(G-11712)*
Precision Beam & Timber Inc ....G...... 509 525-1381
  Walla Walla *(G-14857)*
Professional Hardwood Floors ....G...... 425 741-1017
  Mill Creek *(G-6521)*
Sign Post Inc ....F...... 360 671-1343
  Bellingham *(G-1533)*

PRODUCT SECTION

Stusser Mattson Veneer Inc ....F...... 425 485-0963
  Woodinville *(G-15378)*
Summit Components LLC ....G...... 509 750-6629
  Royal City *(G-9176)*
Vanderpol Building Components ....F...... 360 354-5883
  Lynden *(G-6058)*

BUILDING CLEANING & MAINTENANCE SVCS

Endresen Pressure Washing ....G...... 253 858-7743
  Gig Harbor *(G-4098)*
Pringles Power-Vac Inc ....G...... 509 375-0500
  Richland *(G-9036)*

BUILDING COMPONENT CLEANING SVCS

Coyote Cleaning Systems Inc ....G...... 425 776-8002
  Mukilteo *(G-6907)*

BUILDING COMPONENTS: Structural Steel

Big C Industries LLC ....G...... 844 406-2442
  Longview *(G-5888)*
Burlingame Steel Inc ....F...... 509 535-3735
  Spokane *(G-12161)*
C & S Welding Inc ....G...... 253 520-2095
  Kent *(G-4828)*
Canam Steel Corporation ....G...... 360 329-7048
  Sunnyside *(G-13115)*
Division Five Inc ....F...... 206 988-5004
  Tukwila *(G-13726)*
Industrial Welding Service ....G...... 425 334-2686
  Everett *(G-3515)*
Inline Steel Fabricators Inc ....E...... 509 248-4554
  Yakima *(G-15591)*
Metals Fabrication Company Inc ....D...... 509 244-2909
  Airway Heights *(G-56)*
Mt Norway Fabrication LLC ....G...... 360 836-0322
  Washougal *(G-14970)*
Nelson Construction Inc ....F...... 253 931-6696
  Auburn *(G-505)*
One Build Inc ....G...... 206 801-1675
  Seattle *(G-10701)*
Oszman Service Inc ....G...... 360 532-4552
  Hoquiam *(G-4351)*
Pacific A Crgo Transf Systems ....E...... 253 735-5277
  Auburn *(G-522)*
Rj Jarvis Enterprises Inc ....E...... 509 482-0254
  Spokane *(G-12477)*
Steel Fab Nw Inc ....G...... 360 210-7055
  Washougal *(G-14987)*
Totem Steel Inc ....F...... 425 483-6276
  Woodinville *(G-15392)*
Western Superior Structurals ....F...... 360 943-0439
  Tumwater *(G-13904)*

BUILDING INSPECTION SVCS

Washington Assn Bldg Officials ....F...... 360 628-8321
  Lacey *(G-5599)*

BUILDING PRDTS & MATERIALS DEALERS

Fixture Engineering Inc ....G...... 360 671-9052
  Bellingham *(G-1347)*
Glacier Northwest Inc ....E...... 425 888-9795
  Snoqualmie *(G-12013)*
Ode Products LLC ....G...... 253 859-7902
  Sumner *(G-13090)*
Parker Lumber Co Inc ....E...... 253 806-7253
  Bremerton *(G-1986)*
Pls Pacific Laser Systems LLC ....D...... 415 453-5780
  Everett *(G-3576)*
Speedy Mix Concrete ....G...... 253 531-3260
  Tacoma *(G-13522)*
Staircrafters Incorporated ....G...... 360 882-2772
  Vancouver *(G-14607)*
Superior Custom Cabinets Inc ....E...... 425 251-1520
  Tukwila *(G-13824)*
Tim Krotzer ....G...... 509 487-2704
  Spokane *(G-12558)*
Wintran Trading ....G...... 425 501-7818
  Everett *(G-3660)*

BUILDING PRDTS: Concrete

Burke Meadow LLC ....G...... 253 439-6092
  Auburn *(G-399)*
Mikron Industries Inc ....F...... 815 335-2372
  Yakima *(G-15621)*
Quanex Building Products Corp ....G...... 360 345-1241
  Tumwater *(G-13892)*

BUILDING PRDTS: Stone

Designers Holding Company Inc ....G...... 425 487-9887
  Woodinville *(G-15222)*

BUILDING STONE, ARTIFICIAL: Concrete

Splendid Intl USA Corp ....G...... 253 813-5692
  Kent *(G-5151)*

BUILDINGS & COMPONENTS: Prefabricated Metal

American Container Homes Inc ....G...... 509 531-3286
  Mead *(G-6424)*
ASC Profiles LLC ....E...... 509 535-0600
  Spokane *(G-12120)*
ASC Profiles LLC ....E...... 253 383-4955
  Tacoma *(G-13184)*
D S Fabrication & Design Inc ....G...... 360 600-9706
  Vancouver *(G-14163)*
Gimpy Ninja LLC ....G...... 253 282-9943
  Gig Harbor *(G-4108)*
Grenlar Holdings Inc ....G...... 425 419-4430
  Kenmore *(G-4578)*
Integrated Systems Design ....G...... 360 746-0812
  Bellingham *(G-1380)*
Joom 3d ....G...... 413 566-6330
  Olympia *(G-7314)*
K&M Storage ....G...... 253 862-3515
  Sumner *(G-13076)*
Latium USA Trading Inc ....G...... 253 850-4530
  Kent *(G-4990)*
Metal Structures LLC ....G...... 703 628-7808
  Battle Ground *(G-721)*
Northside Metal Carports LLC ....G...... 360 262-9354
  Chehalis *(G-2518)*
Pacific N W Sheds Buildings ....G...... 360 573-7433
  Vancouver *(G-14466)*
Peninsula Iron ....G...... 253 857-8844
  Gig Harbor *(G-4143)*
Port A Cover & More Inc ....G...... 509 928-9264
  Spokane Valley *(G-12832)*
Shelterlogic Corp ....G...... 253 985-0026
  Lakewood *(G-5755)*
Steel Structures America Inc ....G...... 509 590-1230
  Spokane *(G-12526)*
Verns Rent It ....G...... 360 458-3302
  Rochester *(G-9143)*

BUILDINGS, PREFABRICATED: Wholesalers

Pan Abode Cedar Homes Inc ....E...... 425 255-8260
  Renton *(G-8874)*
Pan Abode Homes Inc ....E...... 425 255-8260
  Renton *(G-8875)*

BUILDINGS: Farm & Utility

Mac Arthur Co ....E...... 253 863-8830
  Sumner *(G-13080)*

BUILDINGS: Farm, Prefabricated Or Portable, Wood

Mobile Storage Units Inc ....G...... 509 276-8220
  Deer Park *(G-2909)*
Protect-A-Cover Inc ....G...... 425 408-1072
  Kenmore *(G-4600)*

BUILDINGS: Geodesic Domes, Prefabricated, Wood

Geodesic Structures Inc ....G...... 509 535-0220
  Spokane *(G-12270)*

BUILDINGS: Mobile, For Commercial Use

Aladdin Valley Modular Mfg ....G...... 509 732-6159
  Colville *(G-2735)*
F W Enterprises LLC ....G...... 253 439-8090
  Buckley *(G-2058)*
US Builders Team LLC ....G...... 425 466-2611
  Redmond *(G-8701)*

BUILDINGS: Portable

Garco Building Systems Inc ....C...... 509 244-5611
  Airway Heights *(G-52)*
Pacific Contractors & Supply ....G...... 509 534-4304
  Spokane Valley *(G-12822)*

BUILDINGS: Prefabricated, Metal

Atomic Fabrications LLC ....G...... 206 767-8036
  Seattle *(G-9456)*
Canam Steel Corporation ....C...... 509 837-7008
  Vancouver *(G-14094)*
Robertson-Ceco II Corporation ....D...... 509 244-5611
  Airway Heights *(G-62)*

BUILDINGS: Prefabricated, Wood

Aspen Creek Log Homes ....G...... 509 590-5541
  Spokane *(G-12122)*
Cascade Joinery Inc ....F...... 360 527-0119
  Ferndale *(G-3826)*
Choice Construction Inc ....F...... 360 340-2206
  Olalla *(G-7205)*
Cynthia Rochlitzer ....G...... 509 796-4199
  Spokane *(G-12213)*
Green Flush Technologies LLC ....G...... 360 718-7595
  Washougal *(G-14957)*
K&M Storage ....G...... 253 862-3515
  Sumner *(G-13076)*
Pacific Bay Inc ....G...... 253 848-5541
  Sumner *(G-13092)*
Star Lumber LLC ....G...... 316 942-2221
  Arlington *(G-332)*
Whitley Evergreen Inc ....E...... 360 653-5790
  Marysville *(G-6402)*

BUILDINGS: Prefabricated, Wood

International Homes Cedar Inc ....F...... 360 668-8511
  Woodinville *(G-15266)*
Joom 3d ....G...... 413 566-6330
  Olympia *(G-7314)*
Lindal Cedar Homes Inc ....D...... 206 725-0900
  Seattle *(G-10423)*
Modern Building Systems Inc ....F...... 800 682-1422
  Pacific *(G-7532)*
Pan Abode Cedar Homes Inc ....E...... 425 255-8260
  Renton *(G-8874)*
Pan Abode Homes Inc ....E...... 425 255-8260
  Renton *(G-8875)*

BULLETIN BOARDS: Cork

PBS Supply Co Inc ....F...... 253 395-5550
  Kent *(G-5063)*

BULLETPROOF VESTS

Elite Group Management Corp ....G...... 253 631-1175
  Kent *(G-4889)*

BUOYS: Plastic

Polyform US Ltd ....D...... 253 872-0300
  Kent *(G-5072)*

BURGLAR ALARM MAINTENANCE & MONITORING SVCS

Michael Patrick Matthews ....G...... 509 457-8799
  Wapato *(G-14920)*

BURIAL VAULTS: Concrete Or Precast Terrazzo

All About Safes and Vaults ....G...... 570 839-1980
  Auburn *(G-368)*
Automatic Wilbert Vault Co Inc ....E...... 253 531-2656
  Tacoma *(G-13187)*
Capsule Urn LLC ....G...... 360 695-2618
  Vancouver *(G-14097)*
Centralia Box & Vault Co ....G...... 360 736-4757
  Centralia *(G-2389)*
Coffee Vault LLC ....G...... 253 227-5798
  Buckley *(G-2052)*
Fantasy Sports Vault ....G...... 206 219-9833
  Seattle *(G-9969)*
Green Vault Systems LLC ....G...... 206 900-2036
  Snohomish *(G-11916)*
Gregory Diede ....G...... 509 662-1009
  Wenatchee *(G-15038)*
NW Pole Vault Camps ....G...... 206 526-0436
  Seattle *(G-10674)*
Phone Vault ....G...... 360 867-8535
  Ocean Park *(G-7182)*
Spokane Wilbert Vault Company ....G...... 509 325-4573
  Spokane *(G-12522)*
Universal Vault of Washington ....G...... 360 834-4086
  Camas *(G-2286)*

Employee Codes: A=Over 500 employees, B=251-500
C=101-250, D=51-100, E=20-50, F=10-19, G=2-9

BURIAL VAULTS: Stone

East WA Burial Vaults Inc ..... G 509 662-5684
Wenatchee *(G-15027)*
Service Corp International ..... G 425 885-2414
Redmond *(G-8663)*

BUS BARS: Electrical

Blue Sea Systems Inc ..... E 360 738-8230
Bellingham *(G-1278)*

BUS CHARTER SVC: Local

Northwest Smoking & Curing ..... G 360 733-3666
Bellingham *(G-1470)*

BUS CHARTER SVC: Long-Distance

Northwest Smoking & Curing ..... G 360 733-3666
Bellingham *(G-1470)*

BUSINESS ACTIVITIES: Non-Commercial Site

8stem Inc ..... G 360 317-7448
Eastsound *(G-3036)*
Aav Group ..... F 972 834-2750
Bellevue *(G-779)*
Ada Signage and Spc Inc ..... G 253 651-1748
Eatonville *(G-3049)*
Adaptelligence LLC ..... G 509 432-1812
Pullman *(G-8082)*
Addison Construction Sup Inc ..... D 253 474-0711
Tacoma *(G-13157)*
Advanced Cargo Control LLC ..... G 206 498-5824
Snohomish *(G-11870)*
Aerospace International LLC ..... G 206 334-7426
Kent *(G-4763)*
Alairx LLC ..... G 425 281-3180
Carnation *(G-2289)*
Alphawave Systems ..... G 719 888-9283
Vancouver *(G-14024)*
Angstrom Innovations Inc ..... G 425 750-6329
Mountlake Terrace *(G-6857)*
Arabella Software LLC ..... G 206 963-6460
Seattle *(G-9418)*
Ario Inc ..... G 206 852-4877
Seattle *(G-9429)*
Battery Recycler ..... G 562 434-4502
Bellingham *(G-1259)*
Bella Cupcake Couture LLC ..... G 425 260-3224
Newcastle *(G-7026)*
Benjamin D Schreiner ..... G 206 417-4663
Lake Forest Park *(G-5606)*
Benthic Fishing LLC ..... E 253 219-1500
Bremerton *(G-1938)*
Bit Elixir LLC ..... G 509 842-4121
Spokane Valley *(G-12641)*
Brown Lumber Co ..... G 509 779-4738
Curlew *(G-2844)*
Browsereport ..... G 206 948-2640
Federal Way *(G-3718)*
Budwiz Inc ..... G 360 508-2771
Olympia *(G-7246)*
Butterfield Cellars LLC ..... G 509 994-0382
Spokane *(G-12163)*
Cake Time Unque Tste Sweet LLC ..... G 253 886-9366
Dupont *(G-2956)*
Cannon Engineering Solutions ..... G 360 840-6731
Port Townsend *(G-7871)*
Charge Solutions LLC ..... G 425 381-7922
Sammamish *(G-9196)*
Chasco LLC ..... G 503 803-4675
Battle Ground *(G-695)*
Chekin MD LLC ..... G 425 894-9896
Sammamish *(G-9197)*
Chiminera LLC ..... G 401 326-2820
Seattle *(G-9677)*
Coach Cheetah Inc ..... G 206 914-8313
Seattle *(G-9703)*
Coates Innovations LLC ..... G 907 617-5801
Kent *(G-4856)*
Color ME House Inc ..... G 360 742-8646
Olympia *(G-7252)*
Commerce Retail Sales Inc ..... G 509 926-1724
Spokane *(G-12191)*
Counting Stick Software LLC ..... G 425 750-1028
Lynnwood *(G-6099)*
Craft Labor & Support Svcs LLC ..... G 206 304-4543
Edmonds *(G-3103)*
Craig Fleener ..... G 509 872-3016
Palouse *(G-7544)*
Curnutt Inc ..... G 208 520-2598
Pasco *(G-7574)*
Da Vincis Garage LLC ..... G 206 579-1333
Seattle *(G-9783)*
Daniel Oneill ..... G 509 939-7916
Newman Lake *(G-7043)*
David T Mitchell ..... G 425 227-7111
Renton *(G-8781)*
DC Engineering Consulting Inc ..... G 360 932-2367
Rainier *(G-8313)*
Descartes Biometrics Inc ..... G 650 743-4435
Blaine *(G-1668)*
Diamond Knot Brewery Inc ..... G 425 355-4488
Mukilteo *(G-6911)*
Dna Growers LLC ..... G 509 793-6606
Moses Lake *(G-6706)*
DOT Com LLC ..... G 425 256-2815
Bellevue *(G-881)*
Ekko Bioscience LLC ..... G 844 822-9300
Vancouver *(G-14196)*
Emerald Energy Nw LLC ..... G 425 830-2757
Bothell *(G-1851)*
Emmrod Fishing Gear Inc ..... G 509 979-2222
Spokane Valley *(G-12691)*
Energy Consulting Services LLC ..... G 701 580-9732
Long Beach *(G-5874)*
Entraq Medical ..... G 425 495-5143
Redmond *(G-8450)*
Ericka J Thielke ..... G 206 214-7530
Seattle *(G-9937)*
Fantasy Index Magazines LLC ..... G 206 527-4444
Redmond *(G-8457)*
Farm Breeze International LLC ..... G 253 365-0542
Tacoma *(G-13291)*
Farm Built Fab LLC ..... G 360 213-8458
La Center *(G-5504)*
Fifth Star Labs LLC ..... G 206 369-3956
Seattle *(G-9990)*
Finishing Touch ..... G 360 391-2108
Camano Island *(G-2212)*
Fizikl Inc ..... G 360 393-0714
Bellingham *(G-1348)*
Flying Sofa LLC ..... G 206 275-3935
Mercer Island *(G-6463)*
Formula Web LLC ..... G 425 835-3259
Bellevue *(G-915)*
Freakn Genius Inc ..... G 425 301-4258
Kirkland *(G-5343)*
Garjen Corp ..... G 253 862-6140
Bonney Lake *(G-1724)*
Gdp Group Ltd Spc ..... G 253 459-3447
Gig Harbor *(G-4106)*
General Computers Inc ..... G 425 405-0588
Bellevue *(G-923)*
Ghost Runners Brewery ..... G 360 989-3912
Vancouver *(G-14251)*
Go Planit LLC ..... G 206 227-0660
Mattawa *(G-6407)*
Grace Harvest & Assoc LLC ..... F 206 973-2363
Mercer Island *(G-6464)*
Great Graphics & Signs Inc ..... F 206 948-9480
Orondo *(G-7457)*
Greenland Industries LLC ..... G 503 841-1835
Port Orchard *(G-7811)*
H Brothers Inc ..... G 206 999-9837
Seattle *(G-10134)*
Harbor Vascular Inc ..... G 425 420-6009
Sammamish *(G-9215)*
Harmonious Development LLC ..... G 425 248-5794
Seattle *(G-10142)*
Hbsw Inc ..... G 217 377-9043
Lynnwood *(G-6133)*
Hexen Glass Studio LLC ..... G 360 807-4217
Centralia *(G-2406)*
High Liftt LLC ..... G 425 216-3050
Mattawa *(G-6408)*
Hirelytics LLC ..... G 843 900-4473
Seattle *(G-10175)*
Hobi Instrument Services LLC ..... G 425 223-3438
Bellevue *(G-946)*
Howard & Son Excavating LLC ..... G 360 983-3922
Silver Creek *(G-11823)*
Hulett and Company ..... G 425 922-5224
Snohomish *(G-11925)*
Hurkin LLC ..... G 425 437-0100
Maple Valley *(G-6274)*
Icarus Aero Components LLC ..... G 386 299-0529
Kirkland *(G-5366)*
IMS Corporation ..... G 509 687-8116
Chelan *(G-2555)*
Innovative Outdoor Pdts LLC ..... G 509 826-0219
Tonasket *(G-13651)*
Irish Foundry & Mfg Inc ..... G 206 623-7147
Seattle *(G-10259)*
Isonetic Inc ..... G 800 670-8871
Vashon *(G-14726)*
J M Cellars Company ..... G 206 321-0052
Seattle *(G-10272)*
JC Fabworks LLC ..... G 253 389-5842
Graham *(G-4228)*
Jim Johnson & Son Trucking LLC ..... F 360 770-5073
Sedro Woolley *(G-11548)*
Joan F Schleh ..... G 360 424-4112
Mount Vernon *(G-6805)*
Jointmetrix Medical LLC ..... G 425 246-7799
Seattle *(G-10304)*
Jolly Hatchet Games LLC ..... G 360 624-2758
Vancouver *(G-14341)*
Juntlabs LLC ..... G 253 987-1750
Federal Way *(G-3747)*
Kashoo Cloud Accunting USA Inc ..... E 888 520-5274
Bellingham *(G-1391)*
King Northern Inc ..... F 520 604-6379
Auburn *(G-484)*
Kp2 LLC ..... G 509 663-4983
Wenatchee *(G-15041)*
Krn Services ..... G 509 366-3431
Richland *(G-9019)*
Kurtisfactor LLC ..... G 208 863-6180
Tacoma *(G-13379)*
LA Excav & Select Log Inc ..... G 360 856-4111
Mount Vernon *(G-6806)*
Leaftail Labs LLC ..... G 206 399-4233
Seattle *(G-10394)*
Leake Logging Inc ..... G 509 738-3033
Kettle Falls *(G-5235)*
Leisure Loyalty Inc ..... G 425 223-5102
Bellevue *(G-981)*
Lemmino Inc ..... G 571 229-3854
Seattle *(G-10401)*
Light It Bright Products LLC ..... G 253 666-2278
Tacoma *(G-13388)*
Lodestone Quarry Incorparated ..... G 360 942-0400
South Bend *(G-12044)*
Lost City Digital LLC ..... G 206 327-4537
Des Moines *(G-2940)*
Maelstrom Interactive ..... G 206 841-6071
Kirkland *(G-5393)*
Magnapro Business Systems Inc ..... G 206 280-6222
Edmonds *(G-3131)*
Manta Network Technologies LLC ..... G 202 713-0508
Mukilteo *(G-6952)*
Maren-Go Solutions Corporation ..... G 217 506-2749
Vancouver *(G-14393)*
Master Vac LLC ..... G 253 875-0074
Graham *(G-4231)*
Metal Structures LLC ..... G 703 628-7808
Battle Ground *(G-721)*
Mint Valley Paper Company Inc ..... G 360 931-9055
Battle Ground *(G-723)*
Molson Runner Sleds ..... G 425 445-2975
Covington *(G-2834)*
Mora LLC ..... E 206 855-1112
Poulsbo *(G-7985)*
Mustang Signs LLC ..... F 509 735-4607
Kennewick *(G-4698)*
Nepoware Corporation ..... G 425 802-8821
Medina *(G-6453)*
Nestor Enterprises LLC ..... G 206 794-4989
Edmonds *(G-3136)*
Nion Beauty Inc ..... G 206 228-5988
Bothell *(G-1880)*
Nlpcore LLC ..... G 206 883-7616
Seattle *(G-10613)*
Noahs Ark Foods LLC ..... G 509 595-8642
Palouse *(G-7546)*
Norman Lancaster Brown ..... G 509 678-5980
Tieton *(G-13631)*
Northwest Metal Craft ..... G 509 999-5280
Spokane Valley *(G-12807)*
Nutesla Corporation ..... G 910 688-3752
Washougal *(G-14974)*
Omega Silversmithing Inc ..... G 360 863-6771
Snohomish *(G-11956)*
Ong Innovations LLC ..... G 253 777-0186
Renton *(G-8864)*
Outbouts LLC ..... G 253 921-0155
Bonney Lake *(G-1731)*

PRODUCT SECTION CABINETS: Factory

Pacific Knight Emblem & Insig .... G 206 354-2060
  Kent *(G-5052)*
Pacific Northwest Iron LLC .... G 509 499-0668
  Nine Mile Falls *(G-7081)*
Palouse Gutters and Cnstr LLC .... G 509 397-0404
  Colfax *(G-2719)*
Parentasoft LLC .... G 425 877-8574
  Redmond *(G-8615)*
Patricia Avery .... G 206 602-0017
  Tacoma *(G-13460)*
Pb Inc .... G 206 747-0347
  Bellevue *(G-1066)*
Pc2 LLC .... G 360 921-8066
  Battle Ground *(G-730)*
Phone Flare Inc .... G 425 346-9230
  Duvall *(G-2998)*
Plimp Inc .... G 206 795-3292
  Seattle *(G-10823)*
Portland Stirling Incorporated .... G 206 855-0819
  Bainbridge Island *(G-659)*
Powerhuse Brnds Consulting LLC .... G 503 317-4925
  Ridgefield *(G-9104)*
Prism Motors Inc .... G 425 503-5415
  Seattle *(G-10867)*
Pushspring Inc .... G 206 455-6128
  Seattle *(G-10892)*
R3bar LLC .... G 647 296-6265
  Redmond *(G-8642)*
Rain Shadow Cellars LLC .... G 360 320-3115
  Coupeville *(G-2815)*
Red Seal Games LLC .... G 425 922-6500
  Seattle *(G-10938)*
REM & AES LLC .... G 580 284-3410
  Puyallup *(G-8236)*
Resonant Solutions LLC .... G 206 619-7672
  Bothell *(G-1894)*
Rgb14 LLC .... G 206 818-8207
  Seattle *(G-10959)*
Richard Warrington .... G 509 448-8713
  Cheney *(G-2592)*
Roommate Filter LLC .... G 863 224-6462
  Seattle *(G-10981)*
Roy Pablo .... G 425 750-9941
  Quil Ceda Village *(G-8281)*
S & S Welding & Repair .... G 509 657-3340
  Endicott *(G-3266)*
S&T Trading & More LLC .... G 509 421-2326
  Wenatchee *(G-15071)*
Safe Bathtub Inc .... G 509 670-2711
  Entiat *(G-3270)*
Sandmaiden Sleepwear .... G 206 595-4303
  Seattle *(G-11011)*
Sandra S Berlin .... G 206 612-4126
  Seattle *(G-11012)*
Sara June Haskin .... G 360 873-4257
  Marblemount *(G-6306)*
Savotta Tech LLC .... G 425 505-9951
  Sammamish *(G-9246)*
Seafoam Studios LLC .... G 702 509-4742
  Seattle *(G-11042)*
Seattle Viet Times Inc .... G 425 678-8872
  Mill Creek *(G-6528)*
Seymour Technology LLC .... G 509 522-3473
  Walla Walla *(G-14867)*
Sheffield Cider Inc .... G 509 269-4610
  Mesa *(G-6496)*
Sheng Mian North America LLC .... G 215 519-5895
  Bellevue *(G-1128)*
Signature Vase .... G 253 951-3357
  Lacey *(G-5588)*
Simple Agile Corporation .... G 425 985-1096
  Redmond *(G-8669)*
Skunk Brothers Spirits Inc .... G 360 213-3420
  Vancouver *(G-14591)*
Slapshot USA Ltd Liability Co .... G 360 560-0245
  Longview *(G-5954)*
Smad World LLC .... G 253 536-5460
  Tacoma *(G-13515)*
Snipahs LLC .... G 910 922-4693
  Gold Bar *(G-4191)*
Soap Aria LLC .... G 206 229-4351
  Tacoma *(G-13516)*
Southside Enterprises Inc .... F 509 395-2345
  Trout Lake *(G-13683)*
Space Rock It Inc .... G 206 395-8383
  Seattle *(G-11164)*
Star Press Inc .... E 509 525-2425
  Walla Walla *(G-14874)*
Stones By Marie Inc .... G 206 643-1520
  Renton *(G-8920)*

Strawberry Kids LLC .... G 425 605-8883
  Redmond *(G-8685)*
Stryve Inc .... G 425 802-3832
  Seattle *(G-11206)*
Sumner Lawn n Saw LLC .... F 253 435-9284
  Puyallup *(G-8257)*
Supercritical Technologies .... G 518 225-3275
  Bremerton *(G-2005)*
Tactuum LLC .... G 425 941-6958
  Bellevue *(G-1176)*
Tailored Solutions LLC .... G 509 258-4314
  Tumtum *(G-13847)*
Thirteen Sheets LLC .... G 888 676-5270
  Ridgefield *(G-9115)*
Three Kees Cider LLC .... G 425 238-3470
  Snohomish *(G-11991)*
TNT Machining LLC .... G 360 988-0274
  Sumas *(G-13052)*
Toonhound Studios LLC .... G 214 733-9626
  Bothell *(G-1909)*
Tracktion Software Corporation .... G 425 273-3376
  Kirkland *(G-5485)*
Truegem LLC .... G 360 836-0310
  Camas *(G-2284)*
Truhumic Envmtl Solutions LLC .... G 425 232-6903
  Marysville *(G-6397)*
TV Jones Inc .... G 360 930-0418
  Poulsbo *(G-8013)*
Uv Systems Inc .... G 425 228-9988
  Renton *(G-8939)*
Variety Show Studios LLC .... G 571 242-1724
  Seattle *(G-11405)*
Weld-Tech Fabrication Inc .... G 425 591-5912
  Rochester *(G-9144)*
Whaer Inc .... G 919 946-5720
  Renton *(G-8945)*
White Cloud Alpacas .... G 253 853-6984
  Olalla *(G-7212)*
Wildeberry LLC .... G 360 222-3626
  Greenbank *(G-4311)*
Windward Ways II LLC .... G 206 364-5236
  Seattle *(G-11483)*
Word & Raby LLC .... G 206 795-5267
  Seattle *(G-11494)*
Y-Verge Llc .... G 360 975-9277
  Vancouver *(G-14702)*
Yehun LLC .... G 425 533-9641
  Seattle *(G-11510)*
Yvette J Cooke .... G 360 718-0306
  Vancouver *(G-14707)*
Zimmel Unruh Cellars LLC .... G 503 313-2235
  Vancouver *(G-14709)*

BUSINESS FORMS WHOLESALERS

A-Z Business Forms .... G 206 363-8170
  Shoreline *(G-11753)*
Control Seneca Corporation .... E 425 602-4700
  Woodinville *(G-15212)*
Norwest Business Forms & Sups .... G 206 938-4387
  Seattle *(G-10655)*
Printcom Inc .... F 206 763-7600
  Burien *(G-2121)*
Sterling Business Forms Inc .... E 509 926-8191
  Spokane Valley *(G-12892)*

BUSINESS FORMS: Printed, Manifold

Garland Printing Co Inc .... G 509 327-5556
  Spokane *(G-12267)*
Horizon Printing Company LLC .... G 509 663-8414
  Wenatchee *(G-15040)*
Inland Empire Bus Solutions .... G 509 922-7492
  Spokane Valley *(G-12742)*
Kaye-Smith Enterprises Inc .... C 425 455-0923
  Bellevue *(G-967)*
Merrill Corporation .... C 360 794-3157
  Monroe *(G-6596)*
Potter & Associates Inc .... G 206 623-8844
  Edmonds *(G-10839)*
Reynolds and Reynolds Company .... E 425 985-0194
  Edmonds *(G-3146)*
Sand Paper & Ink Inc .... G 360 705-0918
  Tumwater *(G-13896)*
Sterling Business Forms Inc .... E 509 926-8191
  Spokane Valley *(G-12892)*
Stretching Charts Inc .... E 253 536-4922
  Tacoma *(G-13528)*
Taylor Communications Inc .... G 509 747-5872
  Spokane Valley *(G-12902)*
Wright Business Forms Inc .... E 253 872-0200
  Kent *(G-5219)*

BUSINESS FORMS: Unit Sets, Manifold

Evergreen Forms Services .... G 425 740-2927
  Mukilteo *(G-6925)*

BUSINESS MACHINE REPAIR, ELECTRIC

Bellingham Business Machines .... G 360 734-3630
  Bellingham *(G-1264)*

BUSINESS SUPPORT SVCS

Western Group Pacific .... G 253 964-6201
  Dupont *(G-2976)*
Western States Fire Equipment .... G 360 723-0032
  Battle Ground *(G-752)*

BUTTONS

Buttonsmith Inc .... G 800 789-4364
  Carnation *(G-2290)*

CABINETS & CASES: Show, Display & Storage, Exc Wood

All In Wood .... G 360 457-8337
  Port Angeles *(G-7682)*
Aristocratic Cabinets Inc .... D 360 740-0609
  Chehalis *(G-2467)*
Butler Did It .... G 360 662-0629
  Bremerton *(G-1941)*
Dru Wood .... G 360 213-7444
  Vancouver *(G-14188)*
Higher Plane Cabinetworks .... F 360 733-4322
  Bellingham *(G-1370)*
Museum Resource LLC .... G 206 547-4047
  Seatac *(G-9292)*

CABINETS, HOUSING: For Radium, Metal Plate

Dep Homes Corporation .... G 206 322-1241
  Seattle *(G-9824)*

CABINETS: Bathroom Vanities, Wood

AE Downs Enterprises Inc .... E 206 295-9831
  Kent *(G-4761)*
Benandre LLC .... F 425 298-8635
  Arlington *(G-211)*
Bilt-Rite Custom Cabinets .... G 360 829-0663
  Buckley *(G-2049)*
Colbasia Cabinets Inc .... G 509 765-0718
  Moses Lake *(G-6694)*
Dewils Industries Inc .... C 360 892-0300
  Vancouver *(G-14177)*
Strasser Woodenworks Inc .... D 425 402-3080
  Woodinville *(G-15377)*

CABINETS: Entertainment

Acorn Custom Cabinetry Inc .... E 425 235-8366
  Renton *(G-8727)*
AE Downs Enterprises Inc .... E 206 295-9831
  Kent *(G-4761)*
Markay Cabinets Inc .... F 360 779-3443
  Poulsbo *(G-7982)*
Michael B Knutson .... G 509 398-7312
  Wenatchee *(G-15050)*
Seaboard Cabinet Company Inc .... F 425 776-2000
  Lynnwood *(G-6193)*
Wood Way Mfg Inc .... G 360 366-4854
  Blaine *(G-1713)*

CABINETS: Entertainment Units, Household, Wood

Pacific Crest Industries Inc .... C 253 321-3011
  Sumner *(G-13093)*
Valley Cabinets & More Inc .... G 360 428-0916
  Mount Vernon *(G-6851)*

CABINETS: Factory

Cabinet Masters Inc .... G 360 695-6615
  Vancouver *(G-14089)*
F H Sullivan Co Inc .... E 360 442-4222
  Kelso *(G-4525)*
Frankenstein Incorporated .... G 206 915-1011
  Seattle *(G-10021)*
Haun Made LLC .... G 253 242-6105
  Seattle *(G-10150)*

CABINETS: Factory

CABINETS: Filing, Wood

Company		Phone
Markay Cabinets Inc	F	360 779-3443
Poulsbo (G-7982)		
Nygards Custom Cabinetry	G	360 425-1777
Kelso (G-4540)		

CABINETS: Filing, Wood

Company		Phone
AAA Cabinets & Millwork Inc	F	509 484-7152
Airway Heights (G-48)		
Liberty Casework LLC	G	253 651-7891
Graham (G-4230)		
Michael B Knutson	G	509 398-7312
Wenatchee (G-15050)		
Tacoma Fixture Co Inc	D	253 383-5541
Tacoma (G-13542)		
Valley Cabinets & More Inc	G	360 428-0916
Mount Vernon (G-6851)		

CABINETS: Kitchen, Wood

Company		Phone
A & J Custom Cabinets Inc	D	360 694-4833
Vancouver (G-14001)		
Acorn Custom Cabinetry Inc	E	425 235-8366
Renton (G-8727)		
Alpine Cabinet	G	509 679-6380
Leavenworth (G-5794)		
Alpine Woodworking	G	253 565-4560
University Place (G-13958)		
American Cabinet Doors Inc	F	509 574-3176
Yakima (G-15506)		
Andrews Fixture Company Inc	F	253 627-7481
Tacoma (G-13172)		
Arcomm Inc	G	253 581-9800
Lakewood (G-5699)		
Aristocratic Cabinets Inc	D	360 740-0609
Chehalis (G-2467)		
Aurora Quality Buildings Inc	G	360 658-9967
Marysville (G-6314)		
Authentic Woodcraft Inc	G	253 939-8119
Auburn (G-383)		
Avella LLC	G	509 217-0347
Liberty Lake (G-5827)		
Bagdons Inc	E	509 662-1411
Wenatchee (G-15011)		
Belina Interiors Inc	D	253 474-0276
Tacoma (G-13193)		
Beltecno Inc	G	360 512-4000
Monroe (G-6552)		
Best Cabinet & Granite Sup Inc	G	503 285-1838
Vancouver (G-14062)		
Blase S Gorny Design Inc	G	360 426-5613
Shelton (G-11685)		
Blue Horizon Cabinet Co LLC	G	509 254-1430
Clarkston (G-2625)		
Cabinet Aesthetics	G	808 268-1822
North Bend (G-7103)		
Cabinet Fx	G	425 879-6690
Marysville (G-6319)		
Cabinet Guys	G	425 344-5882
Everett (G-3406)		
Cabinet Masters Inc	G	360 695-6615
Vancouver (G-14089)		
Cabinet Refacing of Seattle	G	425 405-7961
Woodinville (G-15202)		
Cabinet Tech LLC	G	509 575-0180
Yakima (G-15526)		
Cabinets & Countertops LLC	G	206 933-9385
Seattle (G-9603)		
Cabinets Inc	G	360 778-1780
Bellingham (G-1286)		
Caledonia Bay Cabinets Inc	G	253 905-7368
Federal Way (G-3720)		
Canyon Creek Cabinet Company	G	509 921-7807
Spokane Valley (G-12650)		
Cascade Cabinetry LLC	G	253 395-6670
Kent (G-4840)		
CBS Cabinet Center	G	253 582-8088
Lakewood (G-5706)		
Cherry Grove Cabinets	G	360 687-8820
Ridgefield (G-9071)		
Chets Cabinets	G	360 659-7500
Marysville (G-6325)		
Clearwater Cabinet Co	G	253 853-3644
Gig Harbor (G-4090)		
CM Cabinets L L C	G	360 921-3493
Vancouver (G-14125)		
Columbia Cabinets LLC	G	509 325-8995
Spokane (G-12189)		
Columbia Cultured Marble Inc	G	509 582-5660
Kennewick (G-4647)		
Copperwood LLC	G	360 674-3122
Bremerton (G-1944)		
Covenant Cabinets	G	425 481-4799
Bothell (G-1843)		
Creative Cabinet Design	G	509 452-2777
Yakima (G-15540)		
Creekside Cabinet & Design	G	360 692-7070
Silverdale (G-11830)		
Curry Custom Cabinets Corp	G	425 315-9355
Mukilteo (G-6909)		
Custom Cabinet Design	G	360 679-8729
Oak Harbor (G-7144)		
Custom Source Woodworking Inc	E	360 491-9365
Tumwater (G-13868)		
D and D Trim and Cabinets Inc	G	360 736-4279
Centralia (G-2398)		
D-Mac Carpentry	G	509 326-6601
Spokane (G-12214)		
Daniel Cabinets LLC	G	509 949-0855
Selah (G-11586)		
Days Gone By Cabinetry	G	425 868-5132
Redmond (G-8436)		
Dean Powell & Magda Velarde	G	253 535-4195
Kent (G-4872)		
Dean Thoemke	G	253 640-2232
Yakima (G-15551)		
Designcraft Cabinets Inc	G	509 758-2160
Clarkston (G-2631)		
Dewils Industries Inc	D	360 892-0300
Vancouver (G-14178)		
Dmm Incorporated	E	360 435-5252
Arlington (G-229)		
Dogstar Cabinets Inc	G	509 674-4229
Cle Elum (G-2665)		
Dream Line Cabinets LLC	G	503 841-8575
Vancouver (G-14187)		
DWhittle Shop Inc	G	509 627-3050
Richland (G-8990)		
Dwight Hostvedt	G	360 683-2315
Sequim (G-11631)		
E & S Custom Cabinets Inc	E	253 405-2732
Puyallup (G-8147)		
Eagle Harbor Cabinets LLC	G	206 317-6942
Bainbridge Island (G-625)		
Econo Quality Signs Inc	G	253 531-3943
Tacoma (G-13270)		
Elander Persson Fine Wdwrk LLC	G	206 818-2882
Snohomish (G-11904)		
Elkwood Custom Cabinetry LLC	G	360 886-1989
Ravensdale (G-8335)		
Emerald City Cabinet Co LLC	G	425 429-7887
Mukilteo (G-6923)		
Encore Cabinets Inc	F	425 259-0100
Everett (G-3461)		
Ernest R Howald Inc	G	360 491-1758
Olympia (G-7279)		
Evergreen Granite & Cab Sup	G	425 423-9681
Everett (G-3465)		
EZ Line Cabinets	G	206 775-2226
Kent (G-4902)		
F H Sullivan Co Inc	E	360 442-4222
Kelso (G-4525)		
F Ruckman Enterprises	E	253 531-9132
Puyallup (G-8151)		
Ferguson Woodworking Inc	G	360 398-1543
Bellingham (G-1345)		
Ferrier Cabinets	G	425 788-0230
Duvall (G-2988)		
Firehouse Custom Cabinets	G	253 864-4894
Puyallup (G-8153)		
Freeze Furniture and Mfg Co	F	509 924-3545
Spokane Valley (G-12710)		
Frontier Door & Cabinet LLC	D	206 768-2524
Tacoma (G-13302)		
Gary R Howe	G	253 857-5835
Gig Harbor (G-4105)		
Goodnight Wood Designs	G	360 652-7765
Tulalip (G-13841)		
Gordon Becker Construction	G	425 883-8545
Redmond (G-8481)		
Great Northwest Industries	F	425 861-9768
Redmond (G-8483)		
Green Ndle Cbnets Moldings LLC	G	206 235-3061
Auburn (G-456)		
H & E Building Enterprises	G	253 848-3534
Edgewood (G-3081)		
Heirloom Custom Cabinetry	G	509 370-9012
Spokane Valley (G-12727)		
Heirloom Custom Cabinets Inc	G	360 354-7851
Lynden (G-6020)		
Henderson Cabinet Refinishing	G	206 963-0874
Kenmore (G-4579)		
Hertco Kitchens LLC	D	360 380-1100
Ferndale (G-3851)		
Hewitt Cabinets & Interiors	F	253 272-0404
Tacoma (G-13336)		
J M C Cabinets & Interiors	E	425 258-1204
Everett (G-3520)		
James Hellar Cabinetry	G	360 376-5727
Eastsound (G-3037)		
Jesse Bay Cabinetry	G	360 417-8122
Port Angeles (G-7717)		
JI Cabinet Refacing LLC	G	253 514-5975
Gig Harbor (G-4124)		
John Duane King	G	360 736-6707
Centralia (G-2412)		
K & M Wdwrkers Port Angles Inc	G	360 457-9773
Port Angeles (G-7722)		
Kc Fine Cabinetry	G	425 359-8491
Monroe (G-6584)		
Kenco Manufacturing Inc	G	425 743-1080
Lynnwood (G-6148)		
King Brothers Woodworking Inc	E	509 453-4683
Union Gap (G-13936)		
Kings Kitchen LLC	G	253 212-3623
Tacoma (G-13376)		
Kitchen Cabinet and Granite	G	509 783-9500
Kennewick (G-4683)		
Kitchens Etc	G	360 430-4272
Longview (G-5923)		
Kristines	G	360 437-0136
Port Ludlow (G-7769)		
Lb Steele Cabinet Co	G	360 446-4114
Rainier (G-8316)		
Legacy Mill and Cabinet LLC	G	509 440-4884
Kennewick (G-4689)		
Leon Green Co Fine Woodworking	G	425 822-8210
Kirkland (G-5387)		
Lj Backdoor Inc	E	206 767-2434
Seattle (G-10433)		
M and M Cabinets	G	253 503-0756
Spanaway (G-12061)		
Markay Cabinets Inc	F	360 779-3443
Poulsbo (G-7982)		
Master Millwork Inc	E	253 770-2023
Puyallup (G-8182)		
Masterbrand Cabinets Inc	F	812 482-2527
Bellevue (G-998)		
Michael B Knutson	G	509 398-7312
Wenatchee (G-15050)		
Millers Quality Cabinets	G	360 275-4349
Grapeview (G-4289)		
Millwork Cabinet Specialist	G	253 377-4334
Tacoma (G-13415)		
Morgan Electric & Plumbing Inc	F	206 547-1617
Seattle (G-10562)		
Mountainside Cabinets	G	253 278-8400
Spanaway (G-12066)		
Murdocks	G	253 858-9697
Gig Harbor (G-4135)		
Murphy Runa Inc	G	206 782-2664
Seattle (G-10572)		
My Cabinetry	G	509 879-0086
Spokane Valley (G-12797)		
Neil Levinson Enterprises	G	425 828-3833
Kirkland (G-5409)		
Nelson S Cabinet Installa	G	253 770-3975
Puyallup (G-8198)		
North West Cab & Refacing LLC	G	360 415-9999
Bremerton (G-1981)		
Northwest Cab & Countertop LLC	G	253 446-7193
Puyallup (G-8201)		
Northwest Cabinet & Refacing	G	970 497-8230
Poulsbo (G-7987)		
Northwest Cabinetry & Design	G	360 434-0740
Poulsbo (G-7988)		
Northwest Custom Cabinets Inc	F	360 757-8788
Burlington (G-2174)		
Northwood Cabinets Inc	E	360 314-2446
Vancouver (G-14443)		
Northwood Cabinets Inc	E	360 225-1001
Woodland (G-15453)		
On The Level Custom Cabinets	G	360 666-9058
La Center (G-5510)		
Optima Cabinets	G	509 868-5691
Bremerton (G-1983)		
Ovenell Custom Cabinets	G	509 782-3400
Cashmere (G-2328)		
Pacific Crest Building Supply	E	360 857-3120
Ridgefield (G-9098)		
Pacific Crest Industries Inc	C	253 321-3011
Sumner (G-13093)		

PRODUCT SECTION

CAMERAS & RELATED EQPT: Photographic

Pacific Door & Window Inc ....F 360 577-9121
  Longview *(G-5940)*
Paneltech International LLC ....E 360 538-1480
  Hoquiam *(G-4353)*
Park Avenue Construction Inc ....F 206 783-3693
  Seattle *(G-10758)*
Parr Cabinet Outlet ....G 253 926-0505
  Fife *(G-3978)*
Pauls Cabinetry ....G 425 343-7930
  Sultan *(G-13032)*
Pauls Custom Cabinets ....G 253 536-6330
  Tacoma *(G-13461)*
Peterson Manufacturing Co ....F 360 425-4170
  Longview *(G-5943)*
Pine Ridge Cabinets ....G 509 486-0789
  Tonasket *(G-13657)*
Precision Custom Cabinets LLC ....F 253 397-4240
  Auburn *(G-534)*
R S Manufacturing Inc ....E 425 774-1211
  Lynnwood *(G-6186)*
Refined Woodworks Inc ....G 206 762-2603
  Seattle *(G-10941)*
Revive Cabinet Closet Pro Llc ....G 425 382-0739
  Everett *(G-3599)*
Rich Interiors ....G 509 665-8000
  Wenatchee *(G-15068)*
Riverside Cabinet Co Inc ....G 360 354-3070
  Lynden *(G-6049)*
Rogers & Associates ....G 360 455-1534
  Olympia *(G-7388)*
Ronald G Wahl ....G 509 223-3957
  Loomis *(G-5972)*
Room Maker ....G 425 432-3324
  Maple Valley *(G-6292)*
Royal Cabinets ....G 253 267-5071
  Puyallup *(G-8239)*
Royal Cabinets Inc ....G 253 536-6879
  Puyallup *(G-8240)*
Russells Custom Cabinets Inc ....G 253 473-7883
  Tacoma *(G-13503)*
Sam Knutsons Lumber Co Inc ....G 509 662-6183
  Wenatchee *(G-15072)*
Schwager Design & Construction ....G 360 221-8165
  Langley *(G-5784)*
Seaboard Cabinet Company Inc ....F 425 776-2000
  Lynnwood *(G-6193)*
Seattle Kitchen Cabinet Inc ....G 360 437-1344
  Port Ludlow *(G-7773)*
Sey Mik Cabinets & Millwork ....G 360 829-0173
  Buckley *(G-2071)*
Shark Stainless Systems Inc ....G 866 960-9779
  Kent *(G-5128)*
Sheldon Custom Cabinets Ltd ....G 425 778-0043
  Lynnwood *(G-6194)*
Silvan Craft Inc ....G 425 827-7050
  Kirkland *(G-5462)*
Smokey Point Custom Cabinets ....F 360 659-6233
  Marysville *(G-6386)*
South Hill Cabinets ....G 253 848-2026
  Puyallup *(G-8255)*
Spencer LLC ....G 360 805-2500
  Monroe *(G-6624)*
Spencer Cabinetry ....G 360 794-8344
  Monroe *(G-6625)*
Spokane Custom Cabinets Inc ....G 509 487-8416
  Mead *(G-6437)*
Stonewood Inc ....G 425 417-5533
  Redmond *(G-8683)*
Superior Crafted Cabinets ....G 509 535-9403
  Spokane *(G-12533)*
Superior Custom Cabinets Inc ....E 425 251-1520
  Tukwila *(G-13824)*
T R S Inc ....F 253 444-1555
  Tacoma *(G-13538)*
Tacoma Fixture Co Inc ....D 253 383-5541
  Tacoma *(G-13542)*
Tomar Cabinets ....G 253 538-1183
  Tacoma *(G-13556)*
Tonys Custom Cabinets ....G 425 444-1086
  Kent *(G-5181)*
Total Building Products LLC ....F 360 380-1100
  Ferndale *(G-3915)*
Tri-City Cabinets LLC ....G 509 946-5614
  Richland *(G-9047)*
True Custom Cabinetry ....G 206 909-4454
  Kent *(G-5191)*
True Custom Cabinetry Inc ....G 425 919-1966
  Renton *(G-8934)*
Urban Cabinets ....G 425 286-2977
  Woodinville *(G-15397)*

Valley Cabinet Shop Inc ....F 509 786-2717
  Prosser *(G-8072)*
Valley Cabinets & More Inc ....G 360 428-0916
  Mount Vernon *(G-6851)*
Vanities ....G 425 453-5353
  Bellevue *(G-1211)*
Vans Cabinets LLC ....G 360 354-5845
  Lynden *(G-6059)*
Veatch Custom Cabinetry LLC ....G 425 418-3693
  Granite Falls *(G-4287)*
Viking Cabinets Inc ....F 253 875-1555
  Spanaway *(G-12079)*
Vision Woodworks ....G 425 432-6772
  Maple Valley *(G-6297)*
Vixon Corporation ....G 360 607-5817
  Vancouver *(G-14673)*
Von Grey Custom Cabinets Inc ....G 360 679-8641
  Oak Harbor *(G-7166)*
W & S Enterprises ....G 253 848-9189
  Puyallup *(G-8275)*
Warners Cabinets ....G 425 222-7386
  Issaquah *(G-4488)*
Wells Ww Millwork LLC ....F 425 405-3252
  Everett *(G-3654)*
West Coast Laminating LLC ....F 253 395-5225
  Kent *(G-5211)*
Western Cabinets ....G 253 269-2742
  Auburn *(G-599)*
William H Olson Inc ....G 360 249-3691
  Olympia *(G-7426)*
William H Olson Inc ....G 360 754-2858
  Olympia *(G-7427)*
Wilsons Custom Cabinets Inc ....G 425 334-3522
  Lake Stevens *(G-5674)*
Wood House Custom Cabinets ....G 360 293-2890
  Anacortes *(G-184)*
Wood Way Mfg Inc ....G 360 366-4854
  Blaine *(G-1713)*
Wood-Works Cabinetry & Design ....G 206 257-3335
  Seattle *(G-11491)*
Woodwork Unlimited Inc ....G 425 334-5702
  Lake Stevens *(G-5675)*
Woodworks Cnstr & Cabinets ....G 253 846-1918
  Seatac *(G-9310)*
Wyndsor Cabinet Group LLC ....G 425 775-9828
  Edmonds *(G-3164)*
Yakima Valley Cabinets Inc ....G 509 248-0472
  Yakima *(G-15718)*
Yes Cabinet & Graent ....G 253 572-1188
  Tacoma *(G-13604)*

CABINETS: Office, Wood

Burgeners Woodworking Inc ....E 360 694-9408
  Vancouver *(G-14086)*
Cedar Mountain Woodwrights ....G 509 933-2602
  Ellensburg *(G-3188)*
Columbia Cabinets LLC ....G 509 325-8995
  Spokane *(G-12189)*
Filliols Custom Cab Doors Inc ....F 509 453-8098
  Yakima *(G-15570)*
Flory Cabinets LLC ....G 360 894-2504
  Yelm *(G-15733)*
Fred Misner ....G 425 398-7184
  Bothell *(G-1856)*
Inland Fixtures Co Inc ....G 509 487-2759
  Spokane *(G-12309)*
Kristines ....G 360 437-0136
  Port Ludlow *(G-7769)*
Northwest Woodworks Inc ....E 425 482-9663
  Woodinville *(G-15322)*
Prp Finishing ....G 509 966-0798
  Yakima *(G-15658)*
Quality Cabinets Plus Inc ....G 360 423-1242
  Kelso *(G-4544)*
R S Manufacturing Inc ....E 425 774-1211
  Lynnwood *(G-6186)*
Sawbox LLC ....G 253 277-0506
  Kent *(G-5117)*
Sunlight Woodenworks Inc ....G 360 275-5263
  Shelton *(G-11737)*

CABINETS: Radio & Television, Metal

Purcell Systems Inc ....D 509 755-0341
  Spokane Valley *(G-12844)*

CABINETS: Show, Display, Etc, Wood, Exc Refrigerated

Andrew M Baldwin ....G 425 481-6245
  Woodinville *(G-15177)*

Bagdons Inc ....E 509 662-1411
  Wenatchee *(G-15011)*
Commercial Cabinet Works ....G 360 857-3130
  Ridgefield *(G-9074)*
Journeyman Cabinets Inc ....G 509 483-6864
  Spokane *(G-12343)*
Kermits Wood Products ....G 425 316-6823
  Everett *(G-3530)*
Room Maker ....G 425 432-3324
  Maple Valley *(G-6292)*
Royal Line Cabinet Co ....G 206 767-9125
  Seattle *(G-10986)*
Silver Star Industies Inc ....E 509 427-8800
  North Bonneville *(G-7134)*
Silver Star Industies Inc ....F 360 837-3685
  Washougal *(G-14985)*
Vrieze & Olson Custom Wdwkg ....F 253 445-9733
  Puyallup *(G-8274)*

CABINETS: Stereo, Wood

Lou Hinkley ....G 360 312-3604
  Ferndale *(G-3866)*

CABLE & OTHER PAY TELEVISION DISTRIBUTION

Cco Holdings LLC ....G 509 293-4177
  Wenatchee *(G-15016)*
Cco Holdings LLC ....G 509 643-3364
  Sunnyside *(G-13116)*

CABLE WIRING SETS: Battery, Internal Combustion Engines

Hydra Group LLC ....G 503 957-0975
  Washougal *(G-14959)*

CABLE: Fiber Optic

Manta Network Technologies LLC ....G 202 713-0508
  Mukilteo *(G-6952)*
Ruckus Wireless Inc ....E 425 896-6000
  Kirkland *(G-5453)*

CABLE: Noninsulated

Mantec Services Inc ....E 206 285-5656
  Seattle *(G-10472)*
Smart Cable Company ....G 253 474-9967
  Lakewood *(G-5756)*

CABLE: Steel, Insulated Or Armored

Suncoast Post-Tension Ltd ....G 360 651-2769
  Marysville *(G-6392)*

CAFES

Freeland Cafe ....F 360 331-9945
  Freeland *(G-4028)*
Twirl Cafe ....G 206 283-4552
  Seattle *(G-11351)*

CAFETERIAS

Grand Central Bakery Inc ....D 206 768-0320
  Seattle *(G-10106)*

CAGES: Wire

David L Flink ....G 253 735-5417
  Auburn *(G-423)*

CAMERA & PHOTOGRAPHIC SPLYS STORES

Harold Tymer Co Inc ....F 360 573-6053
  Vancouver *(G-14284)*

CAMERA CARRYING BAGS

Padded Spaces LLC ....G 872 222-7767
  Lake Stevens *(G-5668)*

CAMERAS & RELATED EQPT: Photographic

Contour Inc ....F 206 792-5226
  Seattle *(G-9734)*
Immersive Media Company ....E 360 609-3419
  Washougal *(G-14960)*
Triosports Usa LLC ....G 206 953-2394
  Seattle *(G-11338)*

Employee Codes: A=Over 500 employees, B=251-500
C=101-250, D=51-100, E=20-50, F=10-19, G=2-9

CAMPERS: Truck Mounted

CAMPERS: Truck Mounted
Alaskan Campers Inc .... G 360 748-6494
  Chehalis *(G-2460)*

CAMPERS: Truck, Slide-In
D & R Rv LLC .... F 360 755-3218
  Burlington *(G-2150)*

CAMSHAFTS
Oregon CAM Grinding Inc .... G 503 252-5505
  Vancouver *(G-14456)*

CANDLES
A 2 Z Mfg LLC .... G 360 398-2126
  Lynden *(G-5998)*
A Path To Avalon .... G 360 403-8884
  Arlington *(G-189)*
Bee Hive Candles Inc .... G 360 599-9725
  Maple Falls *(G-6248)*
Big Dipper Wax Works .... G 206 767-7322
  Seattle *(G-9523)*
Candeo Candle Factory LLC .... G 360 524-2310
  Vancouver *(G-14095)*
Claro Candles .... G 253 678-1173
  Tacoma *(G-13235)*
Common Industries LLC .... G 206 963-6649
  Seattle *(G-9719)*
Country Flicker Candle Co .... G 509 286-3031
  Latah *(G-5790)*
Creative Outlook .... G 360 607-4013
  Battle Ground *(G-696)*
Dark Star Candle Company .... G 206 280-5902
  Seattle *(G-9795)*
Dragonfire Candles LLC .... G 206 851-4235
  Everett *(G-3446)*
Glassy Baby LLC .... E 206 568-7368
  Seattle *(G-10081)*
Greenfire Candles LLC .... G 206 240-9225
  Seattle *(G-10118)*
Hood River Candle Works .... G 503 213-4487
  Port Angeles *(G-7711)*
Julias Glows .... G 206 722-0411
  Seattle *(G-10315)*
Lighthouse Candles .... G 360 671-2598
  Bellingham *(G-1410)*
Long Life Candles .... G 360 866-1127
  Olympia *(G-7325)*
Madretierra Candle Company LLC .... G 786 374-5913
  Kennewick *(G-4690)*
McLaren Destiny .... G 971 217-5877
  La Center *(G-5509)*
Melt Candle Company LLC .... G 360 200-0993
  Oak Harbor *(G-7158)*
Morning Dew Candles .... G 206 772-5611
  Seattle *(G-10563)*
Old Soul Candle Company LLC .... G 206 915-0224
  Renton *(G-8863)*
Posh Digs .... G 425 286-6245
  Bothell *(G-1888)*
Pure Lite Candle Portland I .... G 360 909-9499
  Vancouver *(G-14516)*
Savoy Candles LLC .... G 205 281-9031
  Renton *(G-8905)*
Thompson & Cloud LLC .... G 206 218-9991
  Tumwater *(G-13899)*
Wax Barn Inc .... F 425 228-8537
  Renton *(G-8943)*
Webgirl .... G 253 473-6895
  Tacoma *(G-13590)*
West Road Candles .... G 360 682-5822
  Oak Harbor *(G-7169)*
Wieweck LLC .... G 360 576-0509
  Vancouver *(G-14692)*

CANDLES: Wholesalers
Lighthouse Candles .... G 360 671-2598
  Bellingham *(G-1410)*
Olympic Mountain Products Inc .... E 253 850-2343
  Kent *(G-5044)*

CANDY & CONFECTIONS: Candy Bars, Including Chocolate Covered
Hershey Company .... G 800 468-1714
  Bellevue *(G-942)*
Sensi Sweets .... G 206 387-8589
  Shoreline *(G-11809)*

CANDY & CONFECTIONS: Chocolate Candy, Exc Solid Chocolate
Boehms Candies Inc .... E 425 392-6652
  Issaquah *(G-4387)*
Cobbs LLC .... G 360 302-2692
  Olympia *(G-7250)*
Emerald City Promotions LLC .... G 206 271-2880
  Mercer Island *(G-6461)*

CANDY & CONFECTIONS: Fruit & Fruit Peel
Liberty Orchards Company Inc .... D 509 782-4088
  Cashmere *(G-2326)*

CANDY & CONFECTIONS: Fruit, Chocolate Covered, Exc Dates
Shishkaberrys L L C .... G 206 650-3564
  Seattle *(G-11102)*

CANDY & CONFECTIONS: Popcorn Balls/Other Trtd Popcorn Prdts
Killian Korn Inc .... G 800 528-7861
  Othello *(G-7500)*
Moosoo Corporation .... G 866 966-6766
  Kent *(G-5016)*
R & J Orgnal Kettlekorn Snacks .... G 509 698-5533
  Selah *(G-11595)*
Seattle Popcorn Company Inc .... G 206 937-1292
  Seattle *(G-11068)*
Simply Sinful .... G 206 546-4461
  Shoreline *(G-11812)*

CANDY, NUT & CONFECTIONERY STORE: Popcorn, Incl Caramel Corn
Killian Korn Inc .... G 800 528-7861
  Othello *(G-7500)*

CANDY, NUT & CONFECTIONERY STORES: Candy
Baums Candy .... G 509 967-9340
  Kennewick *(G-4628)*
Boehms Candies Inc .... E 425 392-6652
  Issaquah *(G-4387)*
Bright Candies .... G 509 525-5533
  Walla Walla *(G-14774)*
Chocolate Necessity Inc .... G 360 676-0589
  Bellingham *(G-1296)*
Frans Chocolates Ltd .... E 206 322-0233
  Seattle *(G-10022)*
Rocky Mountain Chocolate Fctry .... G 509 927-7623
  Veradale *(G-14750)*

CANDY, NUT & CONFECTIONERY STORES: Confectionery
Clarks Country Kitchen .... G 509 586-6909
  Richland *(G-8981)*

CANDY, NUT & CONFECTIONERY STORES: Produced For Direct Sale
Hallett Confections .... F 509 484-6454
  Spokane *(G-12286)*
Simchuk Karene .... G 509 238-2830
  Mead *(G-6436)*

CANDY: Chocolate From Cacao Beans
Adams Place Country Gourmet .... G 509 582-8564
  Kennewick *(G-4611)*
Chocolate Necessity Inc .... G 360 676-0589
  Bellingham *(G-1296)*
Rocky Mountain Chocolate Fctry .... G 509 927-7623
  Veradale *(G-14750)*

CANDY: Hard
Apricots & Lollipops .... G 509 216-0325
  Liberty Lake *(G-5826)*
Lollipoppassions .... G 206 617-4217
  Woodinville *(G-15293)*

CANNED SPECIALTIES
Effortless Atms LLC .... G 206 456-4130
  Seattle *(G-9888)*

Kastoria Inc .... G 206 633-4170
  Seattle *(G-10329)*
Kraft Heinz Foods Company .... C 800 255-5750
  Kent *(G-4984)*

CANOE BUILDING & REPAIR
Easy Rider Canoe & Kayak Co .... G 425 228-3633
  Tukwila *(G-13727)*
Nucanoe Inc .... F 360 543-9019
  Bellingham *(G-1474)*

CANOPIES: Sheet Metal
Bestworth - Rommel Inc .... E 360 435-2927
  Arlington *(G-213)*

CANS: Beer, Metal
Xafax Corporation .... G 360 389-5630
  Ferndale *(G-3926)*

CANS: Composite Foil-Fiber, Made From Purchased Materials
LP Composites Inc .... F 509 493-4447
  Bingen *(G-1639)*
Technical Tooling LLC .... G 253 327-1149
  Tacoma *(G-13552)*

CANS: Garbage, Stamped Or Pressed Metal
Capital Industries Inc .... D 206 762-8585
  Seattle *(G-9624)*

CANS: Metal
Ball .... G 253 854-9950
  Kent *(G-4806)*
Crown Cork & Seal Usa Inc .... C 360 491-4900
  Olympia *(G-7261)*
Crown Cork & Seal Usa Inc .... C 206 575-4260
  Tukwila *(G-13719)*
Crown Cork & Seal Usa Inc .... C 206 575-4260
  Tukwila *(G-13720)*
Crown Cork & Seal Usa Inc .... E 206 575-4260
  Tukwila *(G-13718)*
Silgan Containers Mfg Corp .... D 509 865-4125
  Toppenish *(G-13672)*

CANS: Tin
Tin Can Alley .... G 360 353-0773
  Castle Rock *(G-2355)*
Tin Can Diva .... G 253 315-5587
  Enumclaw *(G-3325)*
Tin Can Rocket LLC .... G 206 427-9260
  Maple Valley *(G-6294)*

CANVAS PRDTS
AGM Fabric Products Inc .... G 253 946-3200
  Federal Way *(G-3713)*
Bridport-Air Carrier Inc .... E 253 872-7205
  Kent *(G-4823)*
Canvas Creations .... G 425 210-5993
  Tonasket *(G-13647)*
Canvas Man .... G 360 293-2812
  Anacortes *(G-108)*
Canvas Shoppe .... G 360 457-2773
  Port Angeles *(G-7691)*
Canvas Supply Co Inc .... E 206 784-0711
  Seattle *(G-9621)*
Coulter Canvas .... G 509 246-2188
  Soap Lake *(G-12037)*
Duane Ruud .... F 206 682-1082
  Seattle *(G-9856)*
Eastside Tent & Awning Co .... G 425 454-7766
  Bellevue *(G-888)*
Evolution Covers .... G 425 478-2043
  Mill Creek *(G-6509)*
In Canvas .... G 425 355-4102
  Everett *(G-3513)*
Inland Tarp & Cover Inc .... G 509 766-7024
  Moses Lake *(G-6715)*
Integrated Systems Design .... G 360 746-0812
  Bellingham *(G-1380)*
Kvamme Ltd .... G 425 787-1669
  Lynnwood *(G-6154)*
Puget Sound Tent & Awning .... G 425 251-9786
  Tukwila *(G-13800)*
Raptor Sails Inc .... G 360 775-6039
  Seattle *(G-10923)*

PRODUCT SECTION

Walla Walla Farmers Co Op ....G....... 509 529-5750
 Walla Walla *(G-14889)*
Willys Canvas Works ....G....... 425 923-7810
 Everett *(G-3659)*

CANVAS PRDTS, WHOLESALE

Walla Walla Farmers Co Op ....G....... 509 529-5750
 Walla Walla *(G-14889)*
Yager Company Inc..............................G....... 509 922-2772
 Spokane Valley *(G-12945)*

CANVAS PRDTS: Boat Seats

Power Equipment Supply Llc ....G....... 206 817-5627
 Everett *(G-3580)*

CANVAS PRDTS: Convertible Tops, Car/Boat, Fm Purchased Mtrl

Churchill Brothers ....G....... 360 293-2700
 Everett *(G-3417)*
Squalicum Marine Inc...........................G....... 360 733-4353
 Bellingham *(G-1554)*

CAPACITORS: NEC

Extreme Capacitor Inc ....G....... 360 878-9749
 Olympia *(G-7281)*
Hexa Materials LLC............................G....... 541 337-3669
 Seattle *(G-10168)*

CAPS: Plastic

Intelligent Lids LLC..............................G....... 206 920-6484
 Seattle *(G-10247)*
Vaporpath Inc ....G....... 306 208-2747
 Bainbridge Island *(G-680)*

CAPS: Rubber, Vulcanized Or Rubberized Fabric

Sally Beauty Supply LLC ....G....... 509 881-2120
 East Wenatchee *(G-3032)*
Sally Beauty Supply LLC......................G....... 509 783-7292
 Kennewick *(G-4725)*

CAR WASH EQPT

Cloth Creations Inc.............................G....... 360 573-7348
 Vancouver *(G-14124)*
Francis & Wall Shell............................G....... 509 467-5493
 Spokane *(G-12262)*

CARBIDES

Carbide Web Sales LLC ....G....... 253 353-2595
 University Place *(G-13963)*
K2 Carbide ....G....... 425 761-2335
 Bellevue *(G-966)*

CARBON & GRAPHITE PRDTS, NEC

Hexa Materials LLC............................G....... 541 337-3669
 Seattle *(G-10168)*
Pyrotek Incorporated...........................D....... 509 926-6211
 Spokane Valley *(G-12846)*
Sgl Composites LLC ....G....... 704 593-5177
 Moses Lake *(G-6748)*
Toray Composite Mtls Amer Inc ....A....... 253 846-1777
 Tacoma *(G-13557)*
Young Corporation ....E....... 206 623-3274
 Seattle *(G-11514)*

CARDIOVASCULAR SYSTEM DRUGS, EXC DIAGNOSTIC

Choice Cardiovascular Pllc..................G....... 253 229-7003
 Gig Harbor *(G-4087)*

CARDS: Color

Northwest Executive Corp ....G....... 425 883-9010
 Redmond *(G-8598)*
Puget Bridge Supply ....G....... 206 367-3629
 Shoreline *(G-11804)*

CARDS: Greeting

Alder Grove Distributors ....G....... 360 423-3138
 Longview *(G-5885)*
Blue Lantern Publishing Inc ....G....... 206 447-9229
 Seattle *(G-9551)*

Bookmark Publishing Co ....G....... 425 562-0909
 Bellevue *(G-826)*
Compendium Incorporated...................E....... 206 812-1640
 Seattle *(G-9724)*
Emery Burton Inc................................G....... 206 323-7351
 Seattle *(G-9917)*
Ganapati Studios ....G....... 206 547-2239
 Coupeville *(G-2813)*
Gentle Dragon Cards Inc ....G....... 206 546-3593
 Edmonds *(G-3114)*
Goodall Productions Inc ....G....... 206 722-0544
 Seattle *(G-10100)*
Original Hearts ....G....... 253 857-0700
 Gig Harbor *(G-4140)*
Paper Delights....................................G....... 206 547-1002
 Seattle *(G-10748)*
Uncaged Creations LLC ....G....... 509 397-3873
 Lacrosse *(G-5604)*

CARDS: Identification

Delestine Designs................................G....... 206 524-6980
 Seattle *(G-9817)*

CARPETS & RUGS: Tufted

Mohawk Industries Inc ....G....... 253 395-3277
 Kent *(G-5014)*

CARPETS, RUGS & FLOOR COVERING

A Touch of Class Creations ....G....... 425 489-3472
 Woodinville *(G-15170)*
Bentley Mills Inc..................................G....... 206 622-8228
 Seattle *(G-9514)*
Breezy Upholstery & Canvas ....G....... 206 545-8538
 Seattle *(G-9582)*
G&S Trading International...................G....... 253 859-1097
 Kent *(G-4920)*
Howatt Company Inc ....F....... 425 743-4682
 Mukilteo *(G-6937)*
Le Beau Tapis ....G....... 360 734-9786
 Bellingham *(G-1404)*
Level 5 Inc..G....... 425 260-3440
 Monroe *(G-6592)*
Mohawk Esv Inc ....G....... 253 395-3277
 Kent *(G-5013)*
Noel Corporation ....F....... 509 248-3412
 Yakima *(G-15631)*
Rubensteins Olympia ....G....... 360 753-9156
 Tumwater *(G-13895)*
Specialty Wipers Inc ....G....... 425 251-3530
 Kent *(G-5149)*
Z & Z Art LLC ....G....... 206 669-3323
 Seattle *(G-11517)*

CARPETS: Textile Fiber

Aladdin Manufacturing Corp................E....... 253 395-3277
 Kent *(G-4767)*
Carpet Plus LLC ....G....... 253 874-0525
 Federal Way *(G-3721)*

CARRIAGES: Horse Drawn

SRP Transport Inc ....G....... 425 770-3031
 Monroe *(G-6626)*

CARRIERS: Infant, Textile

Seattle Cotton Works LLC..................F....... 425 455-8003
 Bellevue *(G-1121)*

CARS: Electric

Tesla Inc..C....... 425 453-5021
 Bellevue *(G-1182)*

CASEMENTS: Aluminum

Alpine Industries Inc............................B....... 425 481-7101
 Bothell *(G-1818)*

CASES, WOOD

Baye Enterprises Inc ....E....... 253 536-2277
 Tacoma *(G-13190)*
J R Reding Company Inc....................G....... 253 474-9938
 Tacoma *(G-13354)*
Museum Resource LLC ....G....... 206 547-4047
 Seatac *(G-9292)*
Shawnee Construction LLC ....G....... 425 430-4232
 Renton *(G-8909)*

CASES: Carrying

Darbonnier Tactical Supply LLC..........G....... 360 672-0216
 Oak Harbor *(G-7146)*
True North Gear LLC ....G....... 206 723-0735
 Seattle *(G-11342)*

CASES: Carrying, Clothing & Apparel

Imperial Motion LLC ....G....... 253 779-4400
 Tacoma *(G-13347)*
Lady 12 LLC.......................................G....... 425 218-3080
 Redmond *(G-8528)*
Presidential...G....... 509 669-1230
 Wenatchee *(G-15066)*

CASES: Nonrefrigerated, Exc Wood

Ennco Display Systems Inc ....F....... 425 883-1650
 Redmond *(G-8449)*

CASES: Plastic

Burke Gibson LLC ....E....... 253 735-4444
 Auburn *(G-398)*

CASES: Shipping, Nailed Or Lock Corner, Wood

Shipco Transport Inc ....G....... 206 444-7447
 Tukwila *(G-13818)*

CASES: Shipping, Wood, Wirebound

Northwest Container Svcs Inc.............E....... 360 864-2571
 Toledo *(G-13640)*

CASH REGISTER REPAIR SVCS

Joseph Gillum ....G....... 800 624-4578
 Centralia *(G-2413)*

CASH REGISTERS & PARTS

Edge Technologies Inc ....G....... 253 383-9181
 University Place *(G-13966)*
Posera USA Inc ....C....... 206 364-8686
 Lynnwood *(G-6183)*

CASH REGISTERS WHOLESALERS

Posera USA Inc ....C....... 206 364-8686
 Lynnwood *(G-6183)*

CASKETS & ACCESS

Puyallup Casket Company Inc.............G....... 253 845-1883
 Puyallup *(G-8228)*

CASKETS WHOLESALERS

Savon Caskets and Urns ....G....... 206 390-3797
 Renton *(G-8904)*

CASKS: Atomic Waste

Atomic Fabrications LLC ....G....... 206 767-8036
 Seattle *(G-9456)*

CAST STONE: Concrete

Concrete Works Statuary Inc..............G....... 509 922-6168
 Spokane *(G-12197)*
Novustone LLC ....G....... 206 457-4443
 Seattle *(G-10661)*

CASTERS

Advanced Caster Corporati ....G....... 425 821-6574
 Kirkland *(G-5269)*
Durable Superior Casters....................G....... 253 750-0379
 Sumner *(G-13067)*
Reproductyl Inc ....G....... 206 782-1128
 Seattle *(G-10949)*

CASTINGS GRINDING: For The Trade

All Seasons Stump Grinding ....G....... 425 775-7977
 Lynnwood *(G-6071)*
Blackies Grinding Service Inc ....G....... 253 735-1835
 Auburn *(G-394)*
Browns Daily Grind.............................G....... 360 556-3525
 Shelton *(G-11687)*
City Grind Works.................................G....... 206 769-0006
 Shoreline *(G-11765)*

CASTINGS GRINDING: For The Trade

Company		Phone
Daily Grind	G	253 632-7992
Buckley (G-2056)		
Daily Grind Uptown	G	509 448-1281
Spokane (G-12215)		
Delta Grind LLC	G	360 459-8205
Olympia (G-7267)		
Foss Stump Grinding	G	360 799-2100
Gold Bar (G-4187)		
Frontside Grind LLC	G	206 246-5697
Seattle (G-10030)		
Fuse Weld Grind	G	360 261-2722
Vancouver (G-14244)		
Grit City Grind House LLC	G	203 898-5627
Tacoma (G-13326)		
Highway Grind Inc	G	509 466-5061
Mead (G-6430)		
Hwy Grind Inc	G	509 710-7704
Spokane (G-12300)		
Johnsons Stump Grinding S	G	360 334-4832
Snohomish (G-11928)		
Pyramid Grinding	G	425 254-1820
Renton (G-8886)		
Richard Ezetta Stump Grinding	G	360 687-8054
Battle Ground (G-735)		
Rise N Grind	G	360 452-9335
Port Angeles (G-7739)		
Seattle Stump Grinding	G	206 285-2887
Seattle (G-11079)		

CASTINGS: Aerospace Investment, Ferrous

Company		Phone
Ecs Machining Inc	F	509 317-2557
Yakima (G-15563)		
Elite Aircraft Deburring	G	360 435-2652
Arlington (G-234)		
Hard Metal Solutions Inc	F	360 548-8017
Arlington (G-249)		
Precision Castparts Corp	B	425 957-6938
Bellevue (G-1080)		

CASTINGS: Aerospace, Aluminum

Company		Phone
Aerofab Industries Inc	E	360 403-8994
Arlington (G-194)		
HB Aerospace LLC	E	425 432-3440
Hobart (G-4323)		
Omada International LLC	C	425 242-5400
Sumner (G-13091)		
Pacific Aerospace & Elec Inc	F	360 683-4167
Sequim (G-11658)		
Senior Operations LLC	C	360 794-4448
Monroe (G-6617)		

CASTINGS: Aerospace, Nonferrous, Exc Aluminum

Company		Phone
Aerofab NDT LLC	G	253 395-8706
Kent (G-4762)		
Precision Technology Corp	E	360 403-0254
Arlington (G-306)		
Senior Operations LLC	C	360 794-4448
Monroe (G-6617)		
Transition Composites Mfg Inc	G	360 312-1497
Bellingham (G-1574)		

CASTINGS: Aluminum

Company		Phone
Consolidated Metco Inc	D	360 828-2599
Vancouver (G-14147)		
Consolidated Metco Inc	F	360 828-2689
Vancouver (G-14148)		
Creative Casting Company	G	253 475-2643
Tacoma (G-13248)		
Gray Mold Company Inc	F	360 671-5711
Bellingham (G-1361)		
Irish Foundry & Mfg Inc	G	206 623-7147
Seattle (G-10259)		
Morel Industries Inc	E	360 691-9722
Arlington (G-283)		
Pentz Design Pattern Fndry Inc	E	425 788-6490
Duvall (G-2997)		
Pyrotek Incorporated	D	509 926-6212
Spokane (G-12462)		
Thomas Machine & Foundry Inc	G	360 651-9100
Marysville (G-6395)		
US Castings LLC	D	509 784-1001
Entiat (G-3272)		

CASTINGS: Brass, NEC, Exc Die

Company		Phone
Morel Industries Inc	E	360 691-9722
Arlington (G-283)		

CASTINGS: Bronze, NEC, Exc Die

Company		Phone
Irish Foundry & Mfg Inc	G	206 623-7147
Seattle (G-10259)		
Rainbow Metals Inc	G	360 794-3691
Monroe (G-6612)		
Walla Walla Foundry Inc	C	509 522-2114
Walla Walla (G-14890)		

CASTINGS: Die, Aluminum

Company		Phone
Consolidated Metco Inc	D	360 828-2599
Vancouver (G-14147)		
Consolidated Metco Inc	F	360 828-2689
Vancouver (G-14148)		
Gils Aluminum & Shell Core Sp	G	206 762-1726
Seattle (G-10071)		
HNG Group LLC	G	206 723-6848
Tukwila (G-13749)		

CASTINGS: Die, Lead

Company		Phone
Walla Walla Foundry Inc	G	509 525-5690
Walla Walla (G-14891)		

CASTINGS: Die, Nonferrous

Company		Phone
Jerry H Hyman	G	360 479-1724
Bremerton (G-1965)		
Tru Cut Die Inc	G	360 571-7158
Vancouver (G-14650)		
Wagstaff Inc	B	509 922-1404
Spokane Valley (G-12932)		
Wear-Tek Inc	G	509 747-4139
Spokane (G-12584)		

CASTINGS: Ductile

Company		Phone
Varicast Inc	D	360 816-7350
Vancouver (G-14666)		

CASTINGS: Gray Iron

Company		Phone
D & L Foundry Inc	C	509 765-7952
Moses Lake (G-6701)		
Dallesport Foundry Inc	E	509 767-1183
Dallesport (G-2862)		
Mackenzie Spcalty Castings Inc	E	360 435-5539
Arlington (G-271)		
N E W Castings	E	509 924-6464
Spokane Valley (G-12799)		
Travis Pattern & Foundry Inc	B	509 924-6464
Spokane Valley (G-12911)		

CASTINGS: Precision

Company		Phone
Spokane Industries Inc	C	509 924-0440
Spokane Valley (G-12885)		
Travis Pattern & Foundry Inc	B	509 466-3545
Spokane (G-12566)		

CASTINGS: Rubber

Company		Phone
Proto Technologies Inc	D	509 891-4747
Liberty Lake (G-5855)		

CASTINGS: Steel

Company		Phone
Bradken Inc	B	253 475-4600
Tacoma (G-13207)		
North Star Casteel Pdts Inc	E	206 622-0068
Seattle (G-10627)		
Roemer Electric Steel Foundry	E	360 423-1330
Longview (G-5949)		
Spokane Industries Inc	C	509 924-0440
Spokane Valley (G-12885)		
Varicast Inc	D	360 816-7350
Vancouver (G-14666)		

CATALOG & MAIL-ORDER HOUSES

Company		Phone
Barker Creek Publishing Inc	F	360 881-0292
Poulsbo (G-7946)		
CC Filson Co	C	206 624-4437
Seattle (G-9649)		
Christmas Forest	E	360 245-3202
Curtis (G-2848)		
Filson Manufacturing Inc	G	206 242-9579
Seattle (G-9993)		
Micks Peppourri Inc	G	509 966-2328
Yakima (G-15620)		
Northstone Industries LLC	G	509 844-7775
Spokane (G-12410)		
Price Jensen Surveys Inc	E	425 747-4143
Bellevue (G-1081)		
Rena Ware International Inc	E	425 881-6171
Bellevue (G-1098)		
Seasalt Superstore LLC	E	425 249-2331
Everett (G-3608)		

CATALOG SHOWROOMS

Company		Phone
Direct Connect Group (dcg) LLC	B	206 784-6892
Seattle (G-9833)		

CATAPULTS

Company		Phone
Catapult Solutions	G	509 849-2660
Prescott (G-8023)		

CATCH BASIN CLEANING SVC

Company		Phone
Precisionhx LLC	G	509 951-1266
Chattaroy (G-2451)		

CATCH BASIN COVERS: Concrete

Company		Phone
Columbia Precast Products LLC	F	360 335-8400
Woodland (G-15424)		

CATERERS

Company		Phone
Anjou Bakery and Catering	G	509 782-4360
Cashmere (G-2314)		
Ethos Bakery LLC	G	509 942-8799
Richland (G-8994)		

CATTLE WHOLESALERS

Company		Phone
Kurt Timmermeister	G	206 696-0989
Vashon (G-14729)		

CEILING SYSTEMS: Luminous, Commercial

Company		Phone
Envirolux Energy Systems LLC	G	800 914-8779
Vancouver (G-14203)		

CEMENT ROCK: Crushed & Broken

Company		Phone
Penny Creek Quarry	G	360 765-3413
Quilcene (G-8287)		

CEMENT: Hydraulic

Company		Phone
Calportland Company	G	206 764-3000
Port Ludlow (G-7764)		
Glacier Northwest Inc	E	253 572-7412
Tacoma (G-13310)		
Lafarge North America Inc	G	360 695-9208
Vancouver (G-14355)		
Lafarge North America Inc	D	206 937-8025
Seattle (G-10371)		
Lafarge North America Inc	G	509 893-0034
Spokane Valley (G-12770)		
Mutual-Target LLC	E	425 452-2300
Bellevue (G-1021)		

CEMENT: Masonry

Company		Phone
Ash Grove Cement Company	D	206 623-5596
Seattle (G-9443)		

CEMENT: Portland

Company		Phone
Ash Grove Cement Company	G	509 928-4343
Spokane Valley (G-12627)		
Calportland Company	D	425 486-3281
Kenmore (G-4568)		
Holcim (us) Inc	G	360 695-9208
Vancouver (G-14300)		
Lehigh Northwest Cement Co	F	360 733-6720
Bellingham (G-1405)		
Lehigh Northwest Cement Co	F	800 752-6794
Tacoma (G-13385)		

CEMETERIES: Real Estate Operation

Company		Phone
Fir Lane Memorial Pk & Fnrl HM	F	253 531-6600
Spanaway (G-12058)		

CEMETERY MEMORIAL DEALERS

Company		Phone
High Cascade Incorporated	G	509 763-2195
Leavenworth (G-5806)		
M&E Memorial Markers Inc	G	509 662-6469
Wenatchee (G-15048)		

PRODUCT SECTION

CHEMICALS: Fire Retardant

CERAMIC FIBER
Ceradyne Inc .... G 206 763-2170
 Seattle *(G-9656)*
Lapel Solutions LLC .... F 360 597-4958
 Vancouver *(G-14358)*
Sienna Technologies Inc .... F 425 485-0756
 Woodinville *(G-15362)*

CHAMBERS OF COMMERCE
Kent Chamber of Commerce Inc .... G 253 854-1770
 Kent *(G-4975)*

CHAMBERS: Fumigating, Metal Plate
Fort Vancouver Bee LLC .... G 360 274-3396
 Silverlake *(G-11864)*

CHANGE MAKING MACHINES
Coinstar Automated Ret Canada ...... G 425 943-8000
 Bellevue *(G-858)*

CHARCOAL
Kingsford Smith Charles .... G 360 738-6959
 Bellingham *(G-1396)*

CHARCOAL: Activated
Charcoir Corporation .... G 213 379-4040
 Seattle *(G-9666)*

CHART & GRAPH DESIGN SVCS
Flying Arts Ranch Inc .... G 509 659-1819
 Ritzville *(G-9121)*
Jackson Signs & Graphics .... G 360 457-3703
 Port Angeles *(G-7716)*
Stretching Charts Inc .... E 253 536-4922
 Tacoma *(G-13528)*

CHASSIS: Automobile House Trailer
Adventurer LP .... C 509 895-7064
 Yakima *(G-15501)*
Tuff Trailer Inc .... G 360 398-0300
 Ferndale *(G-3920)*

CHASSIS: Motor Vehicle
Eight Star Group of America .... G 206 243-8888
 Lynnwood *(G-6113)*

CHEMICAL CLEANING SVCS
Mechpro Inc .... G 206 445-5230
 Auburn *(G-496)*

CHEMICAL ELEMENTS
Cultured Elements LLC .... G 425 442-4595
 Cheney *(G-2583)*
Element .... G 425 941-5373
 Othello *(G-7494)*
Element 8 .... G 208 870-8471
 Seattle *(G-9896)*
Element Electric LLC .... G 360 304-9918
 Olympia *(G-7274)*
Elemental Cremation & Burial .... G 206 357-1141
 Bellevue *(G-893)*
Elements of Iron & Wood LLC .... G 360 789-0840
 Olympia *(G-7275)*
Hot Yoga Elements .... G 360 676-9642
 Bellingham *(G-1373)*
NW Elements .... G 206 440-9135
 Shoreline *(G-11795)*

CHEMICAL PROCESSING MACHINERY & EQPT
Lundberg LLC .... E 425 283-5070
 Redmond *(G-8541)*

CHEMICAL SPLYS FOR FOUNDRIES
Northwest Solutions Inc .... G 360 380-3807
 Bellingham *(G-1471)*
Theo Coram Corporation .... G 425 774-4731
 Brier *(G-2022)*
Washington Biodiesel LLC .... G 206 297-6107
 Seattle *(G-11437)*

CHEMICALS & ALLIED PRDTS WHOLESALERS, NEC
Articland Ice .... G 509 582-5808
 Kennewick *(G-4620)*
Haldex Brake Products Corp .... G 360 944-3070
 Vancouver *(G-14279)*
Kepler Absorbents LLC .... G 844 453-7537
 Fife *(G-3962)*
L & L Nursery Supply Inc .... E 909 591-0461
 Fife *(G-3964)*
Oil Spills Services Inc .... G 425 823-6500
 Kirkland *(G-5416)*
Vaportech Solutions LLC .... F 888 746-8955
 Everett *(G-3647)*
Washington Biodiesel LLC .... G 206 297-6107
 Seattle *(G-11437)*
West Coast Paper Company .... E 253 850-1900
 Kent *(G-5212)*

CHEMICALS & ALLIED PRDTS, WHOLESALE: Adhesives
Atacs Products Inc .... F 206 433-9000
 Seattle *(G-9449)*

CHEMICALS & ALLIED PRDTS, WHOLESALE: Chemicals, Indl
BBC Biochemical Corporation .... C 360 542-8400
 Mount Vernon *(G-6777)*
Jci Jones Chemicals Inc .... E 253 274-0104
 Tacoma *(G-13356)*
Kemira Chemicals Inc .... F 360 835-8725
 Washougal *(G-14962)*
Pacific NW Reps LLC .... G 509 823-7008
 Yakima *(G-15640)*
Winsol Laboratories Inc .... G 206 782-5500
 Seattle *(G-11488)*

CHEMICALS & ALLIED PRDTS, WHOLESALE: Compressed Gas
Airgas Usa LLC .... E 253 872-7000
 Kent *(G-4766)*
Vulcan Global LLC .... G 509 528-2000
 Kennewick *(G-4743)*

CHEMICALS & ALLIED PRDTS, WHOLESALE: Detergent/Soap
Formula Corp .... E 253 880-0170
 Auburn *(G-442)*

CHEMICALS & ALLIED PRDTS, WHOLESALE: Plastics Film
Layfield Plastics Incorporated .... G 425 254-1075
 Renton *(G-8841)*

CHEMICALS & ALLIED PRDTS, WHOLESALE: Plastics Prdts, NEC
Dongalen Enterprises Inc .... G 253 395-4885
 Kent *(G-4877)*

CHEMICALS & ALLIED PRDTS, WHOLESALE: Plastics Sheets & Rods
Northwest Laminating Co Inc .... F 206 789-5536
 Seattle *(G-10648)*

CHEMICALS & ALLIED PRDTS, WHOLESALE: Resins
Hydro Consulting LLC .... G 509 302-1034
 Pasco *(G-7591)*
Tam Industries Inc .... F 206 763-6868
 Seattle *(G-11264)*

CHEMICALS, AGRICULTURE: Wholesalers
Crockers Fish Oil Inc .... G 509 787-4983
 Quincy *(G-8295)*
Helena Chemical Company .... G 901 761-0050
 Spokane *(G-12292)*
JR Simplot Company .... F 509 248-5756
 Moxee *(G-6879)*
L & L Nursery Supply Inc .... E 909 591-0461
 Fife *(G-3964)*

Northwest Wholesale Inc .... D 509 662-3563
 Wenatchee *(G-15092)*

CHEMICALS: Agricultural
Agrium US Inc .... C 509 586-5500
 Kennewick *(G-4613)*
Bw Liberty Inn Dupont .... G 253 912-8777
 Bothell *(G-1832)*
Dow Agroscience .... G 509 332-3650
 Pullman *(G-8088)*
Dupont Co .... G 425 260-0257
 Kirkland *(G-5325)*
Dupont De Nemours Inc .... G 253 212-2278
 Dupont *(G-2958)*
Dupont Delivery LLC .... G 253 884-2824
 Dupont *(G-2959)*
Dupont Library .... G 253 548-3326
 Dupont *(G-2960)*
Dupont Pet Sitting & Services .... G 816 517-7045
 Dupont *(G-2961)*
Dupont Veterinary Center .... G 253 267-5431
 Dupont *(G-2962)*
Helena Chemical Company .... G 509 539-5761
 Moses Lake *(G-6714)*
Home Team Dupont .... G 253 576-1907
 Dupont *(G-2966)*
Home2 Suites By Hilton Dupont ...... G 253 912-1000
 Dupont *(G-2967)*
JR Simplot Company .... F 509 248-5756
 Moxee *(G-6879)*
Life Church Dupont .... G 253 279-1507
 Dupont *(G-2969)*
Moms Club of Dupont .... G 206 209-9048
 Dupont *(G-2970)*
Monsanto .... G 509 760-0707
 Moses Lake *(G-6726)*
Monsanto Company .... E 509 349-2327
 Warden *(G-14933)*
Monsanto Company .... G 509 488-0821
 Hatton *(G-4322)*
Nutrien AG Solutions Inc .... G 509 547-9771
 Pasco *(G-7606)*
Pace International LLC .... F 509 877-2830
 Parker *(G-7549)*
R and M Exterminators Inc .... E 509 239-4411
 Cheney *(G-2591)*
Solutec Corp .... G 509 453-6502
 Yakima *(G-15679)*
Syngenta Seeds Inc .... C 509 543-8000
 Pasco *(G-7636)*
Tidal Vision Products LLC .... F 907 988-8888
 Ferndale *(G-3913)*
Trax At Dupont Station .... G 253 503-0693
 Dupont *(G-2973)*
Trax At Dupont Station .... G 253 912-8729
 Dupont *(G-2974)*
Washington Dupont WA .... G 253 964-3403
 Dupont *(G-2975)*
Waupaca Northwoods LLC .... D 509 877-2830
 Parker *(G-7550)*

CHEMICALS: Aluminum Compounds
Sienna Technologies Inc .... F 425 485-0756
 Woodinville *(G-15362)*

CHEMICALS: Aluminum Sulfate
Chemtrade Chemicals US LLC .... G 360 693-1379
 Vancouver *(G-14114)*

CHEMICALS: Calcium & Calcium Compounds
Columbia River Carbonates .... D 360 225-6505
 Woodland *(G-15425)*
Graymont Western US Inc .... G 253 572-7600
 Tacoma *(G-13320)*
Northwest Carbonate Inc .... E 360 225-6505
 Woodland *(G-15451)*

CHEMICALS: Cyanides
Ceylon & Cyanide .... G 509 638-7772
 Spokane *(G-12177)*

CHEMICALS: Fire Retardant
Fsi Inc .... G 360 452-9194
 Seattle *(G-10033)*
United American Inc .... E 360 371-7709
 Blaine *(G-1709)*

Employee Codes: A=Over 500 employees, B=251-500
C=101-250, D=51-100, E=20-50, F=10-19, G=2-9

CHEMICALS: Fire Retardant

Viking Fire .... G 206 715-8052
  Seattle *(G-11420)*

CHEMICALS: High Purity, Refined From Technical Grade

Helena Chemical Company .... G 901 761-0050
  Spokane *(G-12292)*
Reg Grays Harbor LLC .... E 206 753-0155
  Seattle *(G-10942)*
Structural Diagnostic Services .... G 360 647-6681
  Bellingham *(G-1560)*

CHEMICALS: Hydrogen Peroxide

Solvay Chemicals Inc .... E 360 425-1114
  Longview *(G-5955)*

CHEMICALS: Inorganic, NEC

Agrium US Inc .... C 509 586-5500
  Kennewick *(G-4613)*
Ascensus Specialties LLC .... D 360 482-8819
  Elma *(G-3240)*
Bhs Marketing LLC .... G 208 740-9369
  Tacoma *(G-13199)*
Carbon Northwest .... G 425 820-0873
  Kirkland *(G-5297)*
Commercial Chemtech Inc .... G 206 932-0841
  Seattle *(G-9716)*
Element .... E 360 682-5649
  Oak Harbor *(G-7149)*
Element .... G 253 335-8342
  Bonney Lake *(G-1722)*
Element 6 .... G 206 282-0877
  Seattle *(G-9895)*
Element Group Inc .... G 206 784-3355
  Seattle *(G-9897)*
Energ2 Inc .... F 206 465-7243
  Seattle *(G-9923)*
Energ2 Technologies Inc .... G 206 547-0445
  Seattle *(G-9924)*
Excelsior Nanotech Corporation .... G 206 898-9477
  Bellevue *(G-905)*
Graymont Western US Inc .... E 253 572-7600
  Tacoma *(G-13319)*
Jci Jones Chemicals Inc .... E 253 274-0104
  Tacoma *(G-13356)*
Lenroc Co .... F 509 754-5266
  Ephrata *(G-3341)*
Moravek Biochemicals Inc .... G 509 375-5124
  Richland *(G-9030)*
Nouryon Pulp & Prfmce Chem LLC .... C 509 765-6400
  Moses Lake *(G-6733)*
Tessenderlo Kerley Inc .... G 509 586-9148
  Kennewick *(G-4733)*
Traffic Tech Inc .... G 206 357-1141
  Tukwila *(G-13828)*
Tyron Global Company .... G 360 734-1789
  Bellingham *(G-1580)*
US Syntec Corporation .... G 509 452-4476
  Yakima *(G-15702)*

CHEMICALS: Isotopes, Radioactive

Vivos Inc .... G 509 736-4000
  Pasco *(G-7650)*

CHEMICALS: Medicinal

Botanical Blu L L C .... G 360 866-8251
  Olympia *(G-7240)*
Modulien Inc .... G 208 874-2219
  Pullman *(G-8099)*
Peptide Scientific USA Ltd .... F 718 618-5025
  Seattle *(G-10784)*

CHEMICALS: Medicinal, Organic, Uncompounded, Bulk

Worldwide Botanicals Inc .... G 206 518-1878
  Seatac *(G-9311)*

CHEMICALS: NEC

Adiprene Direct Inc .... E 425 999-3805
  Bellevue *(G-781)*
Arch Wood Protection Inc .... G 360 673-5099
  Kalama *(G-4492)*
Argent Chemical Labs Inc .... G 425 885-3777
  Redmond *(G-8385)*
Bearded Fellows Elixir LLC .... G 253 750-3060
  Bonney Lake *(G-1717)*
Beryllium LLC .... G 206 780-8900
  Bainbridge Island *(G-617)*
Buckeye International Inc .... G 206 575-1185
  Seatac *(G-9279)*
Central Washington Wtr Ctr Inc .... F 509 663-1177
  Wenatchee *(G-15019)*
Chemtrade Solutions LLC .... E 360 293-2171
  Anacortes *(G-112)*
Cr Callen LLC .... G 206 363-7648
  Edmonds *(G-3102)*
Cytec Industries Materials .... G 425 274-0485
  Bellevue *(G-871)*
Eakin Enterprises Inc .... F 509 698-3200
  Selah *(G-11587)*
Eco Tec Inc .... G 253 884-6804
  Gig Harbor *(G-4097)*
Gelene Legault .... G 425 481-5560
  Bothell *(G-1860)*
Integrity Industries Inc .... G 425 264-9401
  Renton *(G-8828)*
Jetwest .... G 801 223-9149
  Sequim *(G-11643)*
Kamiya Biomedical Company LLC .... F 206 575-8068
  Tukwila *(G-13760)*
Kemira Chemicals Inc .... F 360 835-8725
  Washougal *(G-14962)*
Larry Lisk .... G 425 252-5475
  Everett *(G-3534)*
Lonza Inc .... G 360 673-5099
  Kalama *(G-4504)*
Lumisands Inc .... G 206 403-7887
  Seattle *(G-10452)*
Magaway Fire LLC .... G 253 394-3255
  Tacoma *(G-13394)*
Mercurius Biofuels LLC .... G 360 941-7207
  Ferndale *(G-3869)*
Nalco Company LLC .... G 509 928-7713
  Spokane *(G-12401)*
Network Collaborative 4 LLC .... F 206 898-5869
  Seattle *(G-10602)*
Talk To Taracom .... G 206 226-2606
  Seattle *(G-11263)*
The Euclid Chemical Company .... G 360 848-1202
  Mount Vernon *(G-6846)*
Vaportech Solutions LLC .... F 888 746-8955
  Everett *(G-3647)*
Walla Walla Environmental Inc .... F 509 522-0490
  Walla Walla *(G-14888)*
Xtrudx Technologies Inc .... G 206 568-3100
  Auburn *(G-602)*

CHEMICALS: Nonmetallic Compounds

Finishing Touch .... G 360 391-2108
  Camano Island *(G-2212)*

CHEMICALS: Organic, NEC

Agrium US Inc .... C 509 586-5500
  Kennewick *(G-4613)*
Ascensus Specialties LLC .... D 425 448-1679
  Bellevue *(G-796)*
Clean-Vantage .... G 509 392-2793
  Richland *(G-8982)*
Dynamic Food Ingredients Corp .... G 303 459-5908
  Spokane *(G-12234)*
Envirosorb Co .... G 425 778-7485
  Edmonds *(G-3109)*
Gaynors Glass & Restoration .... G 253 538-2501
  Tacoma *(G-13305)*
Gen-X Energy Group Inc .... G 509 547-2447
  Pasco *(G-7585)*
GR Silicate Nano- .... F 253 267-8781
  Tacoma *(G-13318)*
Hudson Technologies Inc .... G 253 887-7707
  Auburn *(G-468)*
International Chem Systems Inc .... F 253 263-8038
  Gig Harbor *(G-4122)*
Inventure Chemical Inc .... G 253 576-1577
  Tacoma *(G-13350)*
Janicki Energy .... G 360 856-2068
  Sedro Woolley *(G-11544)*
Kopius Energy Solutions LLC .... G 425 322-2853
  Seattle *(G-10355)*
Moses Lake Industries Inc .... D 509 762-5336
  Moses Lake *(G-6727)*
Renewable Energy Inc .... G 206 634-3601
  Seattle *(G-10947)*
Sunoco Inc .... G 253 872-8500
  Kent *(G-5162)*

Tidal Vision Products LLC .... F 907 988-8888
  Ferndale *(G-3913)*
Ultimate Seal LLC .... G 866 567-9149
  Des Moines *(G-2948)*
Washington Bio-Oils Inc .... G 509 713-3299
  Richland *(G-9051)*

CHEMICALS: Phenol

Sunoco Inc .... G 253 872-8500
  Kent *(G-5162)*

CHEMICALS: Reagent Grade, Refined From Technical Grade

BBC Biochemical Corporation .... C 360 542-8400
  Mount Vernon *(G-6777)*
Delozier Recovery Services .... G 360 385-1258
  Port Townsend *(G-7878)*

CHEMICALS: Sodium Bicarbonate

Church & Dwight Co Inc .... G 253 838-3385
  Federal Way *(G-3723)*
Solvay Chemicals Inc .... E 360 425-1114
  Longview *(G-5955)*

CHEMICALS: Water Treatment

Kemira Water Solutions Inc .... F 509 922-2244
  Spokane Valley *(G-12764)*
Pace International LLC .... G 800 936-6750
  Wapato *(G-14922)*
Tidal Vision Products LLC .... F 907 988-8888
  Ferndale *(G-3913)*
Truhumic Envmtl Solutions LLC .... G 425 232-6903
  Marysville *(G-6397)*
US Water Services Inc .... G 360 695-1270
  Vancouver *(G-14658)*

CHEWING GUM

Wrigley Jr Co .... G 408 528-4376
  Bothell *(G-1923)*

CHICKEN SLAUGHTERING & PROCESSING

Foster Poultry Farms .... A 360 425-8957
  Kelso *(G-4526)*
Lues Debeaking .... G 360 438-9207
  Olympia *(G-7326)*

CHILD & YOUTH SVCS, NEC

Northwest Center .... C 206 285-9140
  Seattle *(G-10639)*
Northwest Center .... E 425 355-1855
  Everett *(G-3557)*

CHILDREN'S & INFANTS' CLOTHING STORES

Country Clothiers .... G 206 632-3319
  Seattle *(G-9747)*

CHILDREN'S WEAR STORES

Beanpop LLC .... G 509 499-5322
  Spokane *(G-12142)*

CHINAWARE WHOLESALERS

Rena Ware International Inc .... E 425 881-6171
  Bellevue *(G-1098)*

CHIPPER MILL

Columbia Cascade Company .... D 360 693-8558
  Vancouver *(G-14129)*
Granger Company .... E 509 758-9458
  Vancouver *(G-14261)*
Local Manufacturing Inc .... F 360 533-0190
  Aberdeen *(G-20)*
Longview Fibre Ppr & Packg Inc .... G 509 674-1791
  Cle Elum *(G-2671)*
Pacific Fibre Products Inc .... D 360 577-7112
  Longview *(G-5941)*
Willis Enterprises Inc .... G 360 273-9266
  Oakville *(G-7177)*

CHLORINE

Hasa Inc .... E 360 578-9300
  Longview *(G-5916)*

PRODUCT SECTION

CLEANING PRDTS: Sanitation Preps, Disinfectants/Deodorants

CHOCOLATE, EXC CANDY FROM BEANS: Chips, Powder, Block, Syrup

Ames International Inc	D	253 946-4779	
Fife (G-3932)			
Ardezan Chocolate LLC	G	206 244-4440	
Seattle (G-9426)			
Armoire	G	206 397-4703	
Burien (G-2092)			
Bright Candies	G	509 525-5533	
Walla Walla (G-14774)			
Brown & Haley	C	253 620-3077	
Tacoma (G-13211)			
Hershey Company	G	800 468-1714	
Bellevue (G-942)			
Progourmet Foods LLC	G	360 769-7420	
Port Orchard (G-7843)			
R & S Roberts Enterprises Inc	F	253 333-7567	
Auburn (G-542)			

CHOCOLATE, EXC CANDY FROM PURCH CHOC: Chips, Powder, Block

- Cocoa Future Spc .... G 206 877-3347
  Seattle (G-9709)
- Frans Chocolates Ltd .... E 206 322-0233
  Seattle (G-10022)
- Intrigue Chocolates Co .... G 206 829-8810
  Seattle (G-10253)
- Kristine Aumspach .... G 360 681-4277
  Sequim (G-11645)
- Rh Appetizing Inc .... G 206 282-0776
  Seattle (G-10960)
- Seattle Chocolate Company LLC .... E 425 264-2800
  Tukwila (G-13815)
- Vavako Fine Chocolates .... G 425 453-4553
  Bellevue (G-1212)

CHUTES: Coal, Sheet Metal, Prefabricated

- Independent Chute Company .... G 206 321-8911
  Puyallup (G-8166)

CIGARETTE & CIGAR PRDTS & ACCESS

- 99 Smokers Paradise .... G 425 775-8081
  Lynnwood (G-6063)
- Aura Accessories Inc .... G 208 850-1603
  Seattle (G-9463)
- Cigarland Gig Harbor .... G 253 851-5515
  Gig Harbor (G-4089)
- Fuze Create LLC .... G 425 212-8807
  Seattle (G-10043)
- Orillia Smoke .... G 425 656-1219
  Kent (G-5046)

CINCHONA & DERIVATIVES

- Heather & Company For Ibs LLC .... F 206 264-8069
  Kent (G-4938)

CIRCUIT BOARDS, PRINTED: Television & Radio

- Infinetix Corp .... F 509 922-5629
  Spokane Valley (G-12739)
- M-Tronic Inc .... G 509 484-3572
  Spokane (G-12377)
- Printed Circuits Assembly .... C 425 641-7455
  Bellevue (G-1082)
- Printed Circuits Assembly .... C 425 644-7754
  Bellevue (G-1083)
- Schippers & Crew Inc .... D 206 782-2325
  Seattle (G-11027)

CIRCUIT BREAKERS

- Eaton Corporation .... E 425 644-5800
  Bellevue (G-889)

CIRCUITS: Electronic

- Acacia Controls Inc .... G 253 277-1206
  Kent (G-4755)
- Checksum LLC .... E 360 435-5510
  Arlington (G-219)
- Crystalfontz America Inc .... F 509 892-1200
  Spokane Valley (G-12671)
- D & D Controls Inc .... G 360 695-8931
  Vancouver (G-14160)
- Data I/O Corporation .... C 425 881-6444
  Redmond (G-8433)
- David T Mitchell .... G 425 227-7111
  Renton (G-8781)
- Eagle Harbor Technologies Inc .... F 206 402-5241
  Seattle (G-9868)
- Electronic Prgrm & Design .... G 206 767-7262
  Seattle (G-9894)
- Ernit LLC .... G 425 922-3867
  Bellevue (G-898)
- Holmes and Associates .... G 360 793-9723
  Monroe (G-6578)
- Honeywell Electronic Mtls Inc .... A 509 252-2200
  Spokane Valley (G-12731)
- Imat Inc .... E 360 256-5600
  Vancouver (G-14310)
- Krn Services .... G 509 366-3431
  Richland (G-9019)
- Lumber Line Laser Repair .... G 360 686-3340
  Yacolt (G-15486)
- Mantec Services Inc .... E 206 285-5656
  Seattle (G-10472)
- Micro Current Technology Inc .... E 206 938-5288
  Seattle (G-10531)
- Microtemp Electronics .... G 360 256-6789
  Vancouver (G-14420)
- Pacific Aerospace & Elec LLC .... C 855 885-5200
  Wenatchee (G-15059)
- Paradise Technolgy Inc .... G 253 370-3682
  Lakebay (G-5690)
- Pulse Power Solutions LLC .... G 206 369-8277
  Bothell (G-1785)
- Scrupulous Design .... G 425 788-1812
  Duvall (G-3001)
- Seymour Technology LLC .... G 509 522-3473
  Walla Walla (G-14867)
- Signature Plastics LLC .... F 360 366-5044
  Custer (G-2860)
- Stargate Inc .... G 425 251-0701
  Kent (G-5152)
- Tate Technology Inc .... E 509 534-2500
  Spokane (G-12547)
- Technical Services Inc .... C 360 675-1322
  Oak Harbor (G-7165)
- Thick Film Technologies Inc .... G 425 347-0919
  Everett (G-3632)
- White Mountainhouse .... G 360 835-5442
  Washougal (G-15001)
- World Wide Packets Inc .... E 509 242-9000
  Spokane Valley (G-12941)

CIVIL SVCS TRAINING SCHOOL

- Machstem Inc .... G 801 259-3305
  Nine Mile Falls (G-7078)

CLAMPS: Ground, Electric-Wiring Devices

- Wilson and Associates NW .... F 206 292-9756
  Seattle (G-11479)

CLAMPS: Metal

- Industrial Revolution Inc .... E 425 285-1111
  Tukwila (G-13752)
- Matchlock Clamp Co .... G 360 262-9942
  Chehalis (G-2512)

CLAY MINING, COMMON

- Imerys Minerals California Inc .... D 509 787-4575
  Quincy (G-8300)

CLEANING & DYEING PLANTS, EXC RUGS

- Downtown Cleaners & Tailoring .... G 206 363-5455
  Shoreline (G-11769)

CLEANING EQPT: Blast, Dustless

- Go Ventures Inc .... G 253 313-4070
  Tacoma (G-13315)

CLEANING EQPT: Commercial

- Dri-Eaz Products Inc .... C 360 757-7776
  Burlington (G-2152)
- Northwest Envmtl & Eqp Inc .... G 253 435-5115
  Puyallup (G-8204)
- Sapphire Scientific Inc .... E 928 445-3030
  Burlington (G-2185)
- Skagit Northwest Holdings Inc .... C 360 757-7776
  Burlington (G-2188)

CLEANING EQPT: High Pressure

- Afirm Construction Inc .... G 509 928-4361
  Spokane Valley (G-12601)
- Fsx Equipment Inc .... F 360 691-2999
  Granite Falls (G-4272)
- Karcher North America Inc .... D 360 833-1600
  Camas (G-2261)
- Pauls Mobile Washing .... G 509 954-1910
  Spokane (G-12432)
- Randy Wood .... G 360 295-3648
  Winlock (G-15155)

CLEANING OR POLISHING PREPARATIONS, NEC

- Formula Corp .... E 253 880-0170
  Auburn (G-442)
- Maid Naturally LLC .... E 509 994-3685
  Spokane (G-12379)
- Paramount Chemical Spc Inc .... E 425 882-2673
  Redmond (G-8614)
- Roadmaster Inc .... G 360 735-7575
  Vancouver (G-14556)

CLEANING PRDTS: Automobile Polish

- Ant Fx International LLC .... G 253 302-7414
  Ferndale (G-3814)
- Clear-Fx LLC .... F 800 408-3701
  Ferndale (G-3832)
- Fir Line Trans & Brake .... G 509 684-5484
  Colville (G-2752)
- Northwest Euro LLC .... G 206 981-8002
  Seattle (G-10642)
- Restorfx .... G 425 286-5189
  Everett (G-3598)
- Restorfx International Inc .... G 800 404-4107
  Ferndale (G-3893)
- Sellin Style .... G 360 670-5540
  Sequim (G-11662)

CLEANING PRDTS: Bleaches, Household, Dry Or Liquid

- Bhs Marketing LLC .... G 208 740-9369
  Tacoma (G-13199)
- Country Save Products Corp .... G 360 435-9868
  Arlington (G-223)

CLEANING PRDTS: Degreasing Solvent

- Olympic Jantr Sup & Svc LLC .... G 360 692-0832
  Bremerton (G-1982)

CLEANING PRDTS: Disinfectants, Household Or Indl Plant

- Alcide Corporation .... E 425 882-2555
  Redmond (G-8377)
- Medetech Development Corp .... G 425 891-9151
  Bellevue (G-1000)
- Verax Chemical Co .... G 360 668-2431
  Snohomish (G-11996)

CLEANING PRDTS: Laundry Preparations

- NW Laundry Service .... G 206 242-5500
  Tukwila (G-13781)
- Western Products .... G 509 994-1288
  Sprague (G-12949)

CLEANING PRDTS: Leather Dressings & Finishes

- Bee Natural Leathercare LLC .... G 360 891-7178
  Vancouver (G-14059)

CLEANING PRDTS: Sanitation Preparations

- Hassler & Associates Inc .... G 253 851-3248
  Gig Harbor (G-4115)

CLEANING PRDTS: Sanitation Preps, Disinfectants/Deodorants

- Ekko Bioscience LLC .... G 844 822-9300
  Vancouver (G-14196)
- Oxiscience LLC .... G 425 777-5488
  Redmond (G-8605)
- Walla Walla Environmental Inc .... F 509 522-0490
  Walla Walla (G-14888)

Employee Codes: A=Over 500 employees, B=251-500
C=101-250, D=51-100, E=20-50, F=10-19, G=2-9

CLEANING PRDTS: Specialty

A and V Inc ....G 425 968-5881
  Sammamish *(G-9182)*
Buckeye International Inc ....G 206 575-1185
  Seatac *(G-9279)*
Cardinal Clean ....G 360 629-4399
  Stanwood *(G-12964)*
Discovery Products Corporation ......G 877 530-2999
  Lynnwood *(G-6109)*
Pace International LLC ....E 800 936-6750
  East Wenatchee *(G-3028)*
Procter & Gamble Company ....C 425 313-3511
  Issaquah *(G-4461)*
Tower Industries Inc ....F 206 760-3022
  Tacoma *(G-13560)*
Winsol Laboratories Inc ....G 206 782-5500
  Seattle *(G-11488)*

CLEANING PRDTS: Window Cleaning Preparations

Regency Cleaners LLC ....G 206 650-6933
  Burien *(G-2125)*

CLEATS: Porcelain

Bestfitt Gasket Company Inc ....G 253 863-9521
  Sumner *(G-13056)*

CLIPS & FASTENERS, MADE FROM PURCHASED WIRE

Lulabop Inc ....G 206 225-0049
  Seattle *(G-10448)*
Pacific Wire Group Inc ....F 253 249-0249
  Auburn *(G-525)*

CLOTHING & ACCESS STORES

About Printing and Apparel ....G 360 584-9159
  Lacey *(G-5529)*
Bergen Screen Print ....G 509 965-2511
  Yakima *(G-15519)*
Flying Arts Ranch Inc ....G 509 659-1819
  Ritzville *(G-9121)*
North Star Embroidery ....G 360 588-0530
  Anacortes *(G-155)*
West Coast Screen Printing ....G 360 581-6466
  Aberdeen *(G-39)*

CLOTHING & ACCESS, WOMEN, CHILD & INFANT, WHSLE: Sportswear

Embroidery Plus LLC ....G 253 630-2616
  Kent *(G-4891)*
Newtown Inc ....F 253 395-9028
  Kent *(G-5022)*

CLOTHING & ACCESS, WOMEN, CHILDREN & INFANT, WHOL: Gloves

Fownes Brothers & Co Inc ....G 360 738-3126
  Bellingham *(G-1353)*

CLOTHING & ACCESS, WOMEN, CHILDREN & INFANT, WHOL: Sweaters

San Mar Corporation ....C 206 727-3200
  Issaquah *(G-4471)*

CLOTHING & ACCESS, WOMEN, CHILDREN/INFANT, WHOL: Baby Goods

Specialty Stores Inc ....G 206 650-0747
  Bellevue *(G-1151)*

CLOTHING & ACCESS, WOMEN, CHILDREN/INFANT, WHOL: Outerwear

Dawn Workman Lularoe ....G 360 955-1324
  Yelm *(G-15731)*
Kakadu Traders Australia Inc ....F 360 836-5820
  Ridgefield *(G-9091)*

CLOTHING & ACCESS, WOMENS, CHILDREN & INFANTS, WHOL: Hats

Teazer ....G 360 387-1737
  Stanwood *(G-12957)*

CLOTHING & ACCESS: Costumes, Theatrical

Costume Atlier Msque Pettycote ....G 360 819-4296
  Olympia *(G-7257)*

CLOTHING & ACCESS: Handicapped

Itc USA LLC ....F 206 669-3442
  Seattle *(G-10262)*
Maurices Incorporated ....G 253 845-5577
  Puyallup *(G-8184)*
Momentum Gear ....G 360 524-2098
  Vancouver *(G-14424)*
Newtown Inc ....F 253 395-9028
  Kent *(G-5022)*

CLOTHING & ACCESS: Hospital Gowns

Malone Manufacturing LLC ....G 360 366-9964
  Custer *(G-2857)*

CLOTHING & ACCESS: Men's Miscellaneous Access

Coal Headwear LLC ....F 206 632-1601
  Seattle *(G-9704)*
Esquel Apparel Inc ....G 206 223-7338
  Seattle *(G-9941)*
Inspired ....G 360 504-2590
  Port Angeles *(G-7713)*
Kakadu Traders Australia Inc ....G 360 836-5820
  Ridgefield *(G-9091)*
Offerup Inc ....G 844 633-3787
  Bellevue *(G-1043)*

CLOTHING & APPAREL STORES: Custom

Casual Fridays ....G 360 425-8841
  Longview *(G-5897)*
Creating Memories Together ....G 360 944-8393
  Vancouver *(G-14153)*
D A Graphics Inc ....G 206 760-5886
  Seattle *(G-9777)*
Fourplay Awd ....G 971 706-7646
  Vancouver *(G-14237)*
Kushco ....G 206 772-9333
  Seattle *(G-10363)*
Secure It LLC ....G 509 992-6190
  Spokane *(G-12497)*
Sew Athletic Jackets and More ....G 253 446-7115
  Puyallup *(G-8252)*
Steele and Associates Inc ....G 360 297-4555
  Kingston *(G-5264)*

CLOTHING & FURNISHINGS, MEN'S & BOYS', WHOLESALE: Caps

Ajaxx Design Inc ....G 206 522-4545
  Seattle *(G-9363)*

CLOTHING & FURNISHINGS, MEN'S & BOYS', WHOLESALE: Gloves

North Star Glove Company ....E 253 627-7107
  Tacoma *(G-13429)*

CLOTHING & FURNISHINGS, MEN'S & BOYS', WHOLESALE: Hats

Teazer ....G 360 387-1737
  Stanwood *(G-12957)*

CLOTHING & FURNISHINGS, MEN'S & BOYS', WHOLESALE: Outerwear

Embroidery Plus LLC ....G 253 630-2616
  Kent *(G-4891)*
Kakadu Traders Australia Inc ....F 360 836-5820
  Ridgefield *(G-9091)*

CLOTHING & FURNISHINGS, MEN'S & BOYS', WHOLESALE: Shirts

Logo Unltd ....F 425 896-8412
  Woodinville *(G-15292)*
Phazr LLC ....G 509 329-8306
  Spokane *(G-12440)*
Thomas Dean & Co LLC ....G 206 355-1009
  Bellevue *(G-1186)*
Tuff TS Connection Screen Prtg ......G 253 588-8897
  Lakewood *(G-5763)*

CLOTHING & FURNISHINGS, MEN'S & BOYS', WHOLESALE: Uniforms

10-20 Services Inc ....G 253 503-6000
  Lakewood *(G-5692)*

CLOTHING & FURNISHINGS, MEN/BOY, WHOL: Hats, Scarves/Gloves

Seattle Northwest Service Corp ....F 206 553-9209
  Seattle *(G-11066)*

CLOTHING & FURNISHINGS, MENS & BOYS, WHOLESALE: Apprl Belts

Guess Inc ....E 206 682-7005
  Seattle *(G-10131)*

CLOTHING STORES, NEC

Pacific Northwest Jewelers ....G 509 927-8923
  Greenacres *(G-4300)*

CLOTHING STORES: Designer Apparel

Wntr Ski Academy LLC ....G 425 829-1384
  Kirkland *(G-5495)*

CLOTHING STORES: Leather

Emu Emprium Hlthy Alternatives .....G 360 269-3459
  Chehalis *(G-2492)*
North Star Trading Co LLP ....G 360 341-2953
  Clinton *(G-2692)*

CLOTHING STORES: Shirts, Custom Made

Ajaxx Design Inc ....G 206 522-4545
  Seattle *(G-9363)*
Logo Unltd ....F 425 896-8412
  Woodinville *(G-15292)*

CLOTHING STORES: T-Shirts, Printed, Custom

Amjay Inc ....G 360 676-1165
  Bellingham *(G-1247)*
Cachanilla Design ....G 425 207-6396
  Kent *(G-4832)*
Rainy Day Artistry ....G 360 484-3681
  Naselle *(G-7019)*
Saturday Night Inc ....F 509 928-5816
  Spokane Valley *(G-12858)*
Shirtz To Go Inc ....G 206 242-4055
  Federal Way *(G-3783)*
Showcase Specialties Inc ....G 509 547-3344
  Pasco *(G-7629)*
Symbol Servers ....G 360 819-5132
  Olympia *(G-7404)*
Tuff TS Connection Screen Prtg ......G 253 588-8897
  Lakewood *(G-5763)*

CLOTHING STORES: Uniforms & Work

Crystal Blue Screen Printing ....G 509 337-8201
  Waitsburg *(G-14753)*
Darbonnier Tactical Supply LLC ......G 360 672-0216
  Oak Harbor *(G-7146)*
Highway Specialties LLC ....G 360 823-0511
  Vancouver *(G-14298)*
Pacific Knight Emblem & Insig ....G 206 354-2060
  Kent *(G-5052)*
Rag Man LLC ....G 206 653-7125
  Kent *(G-5096)*

CLOTHING STORES: Unisex

Vf Outdoor LLC ....E 425 455-7349
  Bellevue *(G-1216)*

CLOTHING STORES: Work

Helly Hansen (us) Inc ....E 800 435-5901
  Sumner *(G-13073)*
Tims Country Saw Shop ....G 509 486-2798
  Tonasket *(G-13660)*

CLOTHING, WOMEN & CHILD, WHLSE: Dress, Suit, Skirt & Blouse

Helly Hansen (us) Inc ....E 800 435-5901
  Sumner *(G-13073)*

PRODUCT SECTION

CLOTHING: Access

Better Off Threads .... G 425 408-1304
  Woodinville (G-15189)
Filson Manufacturing Inc .... G 206 805-3730
  Seatac (G-9284)
Knit Alteration & Design .... G 360 426-5078
  Shelton (G-11707)
Morningstar Business Group Inc .... G 509 476-2944
  Oroville (G-7469)
Per Gioia .... G 206 240-4216
  Seattle (G-10785)
Seven Twenty Eight CL LLC .... G 206 484-7634
  Hansville (G-4319)
South Sound Screen Printing .... G 360 871-4206
  Port Orchard (G-7851)
Susans Custom Embroidery .... G 206 783-3127
  Seattle (G-11230)

CLOTHING: Access, Women's & Misses'

Coal Headwear LLC .... F 206 632-1601
  Seattle (G-9704)
Pkfashions Inc .... G 425 359-6510
  Mill Creek (G-6520)

CLOTHING: Aprons, Exc Rubber/Plastic, Women, Misses, Junior

Domestique .... G 206 545-3769
  Seattle (G-9846)

CLOTHING: Aprons, Harness

Ballenger International LLC .... G 970 641-9494
  Arlington (G-209)
Misty Mountain Manufacturing .... E 206 763-4055
  Seattle (G-10548)

CLOTHING: Aprons, Waterproof, From Purchased Materials

Locknane Inc .... E 425 493-8300
  Mukilteo (G-6950)

CLOTHING: Aprons, Work, Exc Rubberized & Plastic, Men's

Fabrications Inc .... G 888 808-9878
  Mercer Island (G-6462)

CLOTHING: Athletic & Sportswear, Men's & Boys'

Certified Branching Habit .... G 206 286-9685
  Seattle (G-9659)
Chicago Title Insurance Co .... G 509 765-8820
  Moses Lake (G-6693)
Dawn Workman Lularoe .... G 360 955-1324
  Yelm (G-15731)
DUO Wear Inc .... G 425 251-0760
  Kent (G-4879)
Ers Group Inc .... G 360 895-1318
  Port Orchard (G-7808)
Ex Officio LLC .... G 206 283-1471
  Seattle (G-9951)
Global Sportswear Corporation .... G 253 813-9788
  Kent (G-4924)
Great King of Americas LLC .... G 206 957-0987
  Seattle (G-10113)
Guides Chice AP Spcialists LLC .... G 206 931-3838
  Kent (G-4931)
K-L Mfg Co Inc .... E 509 232-8655
  Spokane (G-12347)
McCoy International Ltd .... G 206 284-7734
  Seattle (G-10505)
Pacific Sportswear LLC .... E 253 582-4444
  Tacoma (G-13455)
Seattle Cotton Works LLC .... F 425 455-8003
  Bellevue (G-1121)
Sherpa Adventure Gear LLC .... F 425 251-0760
  Kent (G-5129)
Sunrise Identity LLC .... G 425 214-1700
  Bellevue (G-1167)

CLOTHING: Athletic & Sportswear, Women's & Girls'

Crystalli Inc .... G 253 905-6784
  Federal Way (G-3727)

Nuu-Muu LLC .... G 360 223-7151
  Bellingham (G-1475)
Pacific Sportswear LLC .... E 253 582-4444
  Tacoma (G-13455)
Sherpa Adventure Gear LLC .... F 425 251-0760
  Kent (G-5129)
Sunrise Identity LLC .... G 425 214-1700
  Bellevue (G-1167)

CLOTHING: Band Uniforms

Islanders .... G 253 588-9246
  Tacoma (G-13351)

CLOTHING: Bathing Suits & Swimwear, Knit

Blueseventy LLC .... G 206 547-5273
  Seattle (G-9557)
Mix Creations .... G 425 392-1123
  Issaquah (G-4450)

CLOTHING: Blouses & Shirts, Girls' & Children's

Beanpop LLC .... G 509 499-5322
  Spokane (G-12142)
Chrysanthemum .... G 206 722-1031
  Seattle (G-9683)

CLOTHING: Blouses, Women's & Girls'

Fashion Sales Inc .... G 206 441-3282
  Seattle (G-9973)
Yazdi Corporation .... G 425 787-6328
  Seattle (G-11509)

CLOTHING: Blouses, Womens & Juniors, From Purchased Mtrls

Sweet Creek Creations .... G 509 446-2429
  Metaline Falls (G-6498)

CLOTHING: Bridal Gowns

Happily Ever After .... G 206 226-8814
  Mountlake Terrace (G-6863)
Happy Thoughts .... G 360 468-2880
  Lopez Island (G-5983)
La Belle Reve LLC .... G 425 454-7772
  Bellevue (G-974)
Pacific Coast Bride LLC .... G 360 303-5047
  Bellingham (G-1484)

CLOTHING: Buntings, Infants'

Swaddledesigns LLC .... E 206 971-0426
  Tukwila (G-13825)

CLOTHING: Capes & Jackets, Women's & Misses'

Illusion Wear Capes .... G 360 674-2357
  Port Orchard (G-7815)

CLOTHING: Caps, Baseball

Walla Walla Sweets .... G 509 522-2255
  Walla Walla (G-14894)

CLOTHING: Children & Infants'

Country Clothiers .... G 206 632-3319
  Seattle (G-9747)
Lil Squirtz .... G 360 521-9598
  Vancouver (G-14376)
Long Construction LLC .... G 360 202-2664
  Anacortes (G-143)
Pacific Northwest Wovens LLC .... G 714 392-0634
  Lewis McChord (G-5821)

CLOTHING: Children's, Girls'

Country Clothiers .... G 206 632-3319
  Seattle (G-9747)
Lil Squirtz .... G 360 521-9598
  Vancouver (G-14376)
McC Enterprises Inc .... G 509 928-9676
  Spokane Valley (G-12785)
These Two Girls Llc .... G 206 200-3620
  Seattle (G-11289)

CLOTHING: Coats & Jackets, Leather & Sheep-Lined

Bigfoot Trading Inc .... G 360 340-7332
  Allyn (G-81)

CLOTHING: Coats & Suits, Men's & Boys'

J & Ree Fashions .... G 360 281-8610
  Vancouver (G-14330)
Leo Roux LLC .... G 512 565-3406
  Seattle (G-10403)
Locknane Inc .... E 425 493-8300
  Mukilteo (G-6950)
Mustang Survival Holdings Inc .... D 360 676-1782
  Bellingham (G-1453)
Susan Bennett .... G 360 427-6164
  Shelton (G-11738)

CLOTHING: Coats, Hunting & Vests, Men's

CC Filson Co .... C 206 624-4437
  Seattle (G-9649)
Insect Shield LLC .... G 206 624-9307
  Seattle (G-10241)

CLOTHING: Collar & Cuff Sets, Knit

Bella Tutto Inc .... G 425 898-8680
  Sammamish (G-9189)

CLOTHING: Costumes

Embroidery For Soul .... G 425 319-1269
  Monroe (G-6568)
Janice Arnold .... G 360 273-8548
  Centralia (G-2410)
Superhero Stuffcom .... G 425 890-3032
  Snoqualmie (G-12032)
Tormented Artifacts Ltd .... G 206 501-8333
  Seattle (G-11320)

CLOTHING: Disposable

Sandmaiden Sleepwear .... G 206 595-4303
  Seattle (G-11011)

CLOTHING: Dresses

Charlies Coat LLC .... G 206 323-2191
  Seattle (G-9669)
Runway Liquidation LLC .... G 253 474-0610
  Bothell (G-1788)
Runway Liquidation LLC .... G 262 253-4000
  Spokane (G-12486)
Runway Liquidation LLC .... G 262 654-0726
  Seattle (G-10997)
Runway Liquidation LLC .... G 262 948-7035
  Seattle (G-10998)
Runway Liquidation LLC .... G 304 325-3603
  Gig Harbor (G-4158)
Runway Liquidation LLC .... G 304 645-2799
  Kennewick (G-4721)
Runway Liquidation LLC .... G 304 825-6364
  Kennewick (G-4722)
Runway Liquidation LLC .... G 304 598-4888
  Kirkland (G-5454)
Runway Liquidation LLC .... G 304 748-2055
  Lacey (G-5582)
Runway Liquidation LLC .... G 304 636-2020
  Kennewick (G-4723)
Runway Liquidation LLC .... G 651 275-3251
  Walla Walla (G-14863)
Runway Liquidation LLC .... G 920 387-3180
  Spokane (G-12487)
Yazdi Corporation .... G 425 787-6328
  Seattle (G-11509)

CLOTHING: Foundation Garments, Women's

Michelle Schwartzman .... G 360 629-5255
  Stanwood (G-12979)

CLOTHING: Furs

Harts Lake Trading Post .... G 360 458-3477
  Roy (G-9160)
Noel Inc .... G 206 784-1894
  Seattle (G-10618)

CLOTHING: Gowns & Dresses, Wedding

Asabooks Inc .... G 425 885-1889
  Sammamish (G-9186)

Employee Codes: A=Over 500 employees, B=251-500
C=101-250, D=51-100, E=20-50, F=10-19, G=2-9

CLOTHING: Gowns & Dresses, Wedding

Central Party & Costume .... G 509 962-3934
  Ellensburg *(G-3189)*
Fashion Corner .... G 509 837-7345
  Sunnyside *(G-13125)*
Fern Hollow LLC .... G 360 504-2323
  Poulsbo *(G-7963)*
Specialty Stores Inc .... G 206 650-0747
  Bellevue *(G-1151)*
Weddings Sochic .... G 360 438-6540
  Olympia *(G-7423)*

CLOTHING: Hats & Caps, NEC

Century 21 Promotions Inc .... E 206 282-8827
  Seattle *(G-9655)*
Hatterdashery .... G 206 322-6149
  Seattle *(G-10147)*
Irrational Hats N Stuff .... G 253 460-5565
  University Place *(G-13974)*
Kavu Inc .... F 206 456-9305
  Seattle *(G-10332)*
Kushco Clothing LLC .... G 206 772-9333
  Seattle *(G-10364)*
Suziperi .... G 425 373-1954
  Bellevue *(G-1171)*

CLOTHING: Hats & Caps, Uniform

Seattle Northwest Service Corp ...... F 206 553-9209
  Seattle *(G-11066)*

CLOTHING: Hats & Headwear, Knit

Teazer .... G 360 387-1737
  Stanwood *(G-12957)*
Wapiti Woolies Inc .... G 360 663-2268
  Enumclaw *(G-3326)*

CLOTHING: Hats, Panama

Tomatesa Enterprises LLC .... G 425 778-6708
  Lynnwood *(G-6211)*

CLOTHING: Hosiery, Men's & Boys'

Ellsworth & Company LLC .... G 253 301-2800
  Steilacoom *(G-13004)*

CLOTHING: Jackets, Field, Military

Survival Gear Systems .... G 866 257-2978
  Spokane *(G-12536)*

CLOTHING: Jackets, Knit

10-20 Services Inc .... G 253 503-6000
  Lakewood *(G-5692)*
Centralia Knitting Mills Inc .... E 360 736-3994
  Centralia *(G-2390)*

CLOTHING: Jeans, Men's & Boys'

Guess Inc .... E 206 682-7005
  Seattle *(G-10131)*

CLOTHING: Leather & sheep-lined clothing

Harts Lake Trading Post .... G 360 458-3477
  Roy *(G-9160)*

CLOTHING: Lounge, Bed & Leisurewear

Choraks Sportsmans Inn .... G 206 463-0940
  Vashon *(G-14719)*
Freeland Cafe .... F 360 331-9945
  Freeland *(G-4028)*

CLOTHING: Men's & boy's clothing, nec

Cenveo Inc .... G 503 224-7777
  Kent *(G-4848)*
R B Sales .... G 206 870-0741
  Des Moines *(G-2944)*

CLOTHING: Men's & boy's underwear & nightwear

Decent Exposures Inc .... F 206 364-4540
  Seattle *(G-9810)*

CLOTHING: Mens & Boys Jackets, Sport, Suede, Leatherette

Locknane Inc .... E 425 493-8300
  Mukilteo *(G-6950)*

Tostrz LLC .... G 206 595-3044
  Burien *(G-2133)*

CLOTHING: Neckwear

Formal Wear Inc .... G 425 776-1088
  Lynnwood *(G-6120)*

CLOTHING: Outerwear, Lthr, Wool/Down-Filled, Men, Youth/Boy

Vf Outdoor LLC .... E 425 455-7349
  Bellevue *(G-1216)*

CLOTHING: Outerwear, Women's & Misses' NEC

Baxis Inc .... G 360 797-0084
  Sequim *(G-11614)*
Certified Branching Habit .... G 206 286-9685
  Seattle *(G-9659)*
Custom Veils & Accessories .... G 509 258-7810
  Valley *(G-13989)*
Derek Andrew Inc .... F 425 453-9888
  Bellevue *(G-877)*
Dogfish Bay Studios LLC .... G 772 335-8711
  Poulsbo *(G-7959)*
DUO Wear Inc .... G 425 251-0760
  Kent *(G-4879)*
Ers Group Inc .... G 360 895-1318
  Port Orchard *(G-7808)*
Ex Officio LLC .... G 206 283-1471
  Seattle *(G-9951)*
Item House Inc .... E 253 627-7168
  Tacoma *(G-13352)*
Jumbo Dti Corporation .... F 253 272-9764
  Fife *(G-3961)*
K-L Mfg Co Inc .... E 509 232-8655
  Spokane *(G-12347)*
Mustang Survival Holdings Inc ...... D 360 676-1782
  Bellingham *(G-1453)*
Seattle Pacific Industries .... D 253 872-8822
  Kent *(G-5123)*
Shah Safari Inc .... E 206 282-6122
  Seattle *(G-11095)*
Thaw Corporation .... C 206 505-2100
  Seattle *(G-11283)*
Tik Tik Garment Manufacturing ..... F 509 624-0806
  Spokane *(G-12557)*

CLOTHING: Overalls & Coveralls

Buffalo Industries Inc .... G 206 682-9900
  Seattle *(G-9595)*
Maulcor Inc .... G 773 696-2783
  Seattle *(G-10502)*

CLOTHING: Raincoats, Exc Vulcanized Rubber, Purchased Matls

Darbonnier Tactical Supply LLC .... G 360 672-0216
  Oak Harbor *(G-7146)*
Fibrearts Inc .... G 425 432-1454
  Maple Valley *(G-6269)*
McKenzie & Adams Inc .... G 425 672-8668
  Woodinville *(G-15307)*
Sweet Creek Creations .... G 509 446-2429
  Metaline Falls *(G-6498)*

CLOTHING: Service Apparel, Women's

Margaret OLeary Inc .... G 206 729-5934
  Seattle *(G-10476)*

CLOTHING: Sheep-Lined

United States Sheepskin Inc .... F 253 627-7114
  Tacoma *(G-13571)*

CLOTHING: Shirts

Arctic Circle Enterprises LLC .... D 253 872-8525
  Kent *(G-4789)*

CLOTHING: Shirts & T-Shirts, Knit

Cheers To Life .... G 425 697-2966
  Lynnwood *(G-6092)*
Nwd Ink International Inc .... G 425 454-0707
  Bellevue *(G-1040)*
Pt Shirt .... G 360 385-1911
  Port Townsend *(G-7920)*

CLOTHING: Shirts, Dress, Men's & Boys'

Nidekken Ltd .... F 425 885-1587
  Redmond *(G-8595)*

CLOTHING: Shirts, Sports & Polo, Men's & Boys'

Waterstone Brands Inc .... G 800 579-3644
  Seattle *(G-11445)*

CLOTHING: Socks

16 Cents Corp .... F 509 329-1600
  Spokane *(G-12086)*
Ballard Sock Critters .... G 206 218-9215
  Seattle *(G-9485)*
Danalco Inc .... E 626 303-4019
  Seattle *(G-9790)*
Laylas Fun Socks .... G 509 279-8343
  Spokane *(G-12359)*
OK Sock LLC .... G 509 209-6598
  Mead *(G-6435)*
Savior Socks Inc .... G 360 601-8036
  Battle Ground *(G-738)*
Skyline Socks .... G 425 454-1323
  Bellevue *(G-1137)*
Sock Doctor Com Inc .... G 425 223-5173
  Bellevue *(G-1144)*
Sock Monster .... G 206 724-0123
  Seattle *(G-11151)*
Sock Outlet .... E 435 787-8888
  Issaquah *(G-4477)*
Sock Peddlers .... G 253 267-0148
  Lakewood *(G-5757)*
Socks In A Box LLC .... G 425 533-8316
  Kenmore *(G-4606)*

CLOTHING: Sportswear, Women's

Two Dog Island Inc .... G 206 325-0609
  Seattle *(G-11353)*
Younique .... G 509 842-6908
  Spokane Valley *(G-12946)*

CLOTHING: Suits & Skirts, Women's & Misses'

Yazdi Corporation .... G 425 787-6328
  Seattle *(G-11509)*

CLOTHING: Sweaters & Sweater Coats, Knit

Knitwear Network Inc .... G 206 353-1337
  Seattle *(G-10347)*

CLOTHING: T-Shirts & Tops, Knit

Ajaxx Design Inc .... G 206 522-4545
  Seattle *(G-9363)*
Archivalry .... G 206 420-3899
  Seattle *(G-9421)*
Blackwood Fiber Co .... G 206 387-3854
  Tacoma *(G-13205)*
My T-Shirt Source .... G 425 746-7447
  Bellevue *(G-1022)*
Seatthole Inc .... G 360 389-2154
  Bellingham *(G-1530)*

CLOTHING: T-Shirts & Tops, Women's & Girls'

Arctic Circle Enterprises LLC .... D 253 872-8525
  Kent *(G-4789)*

CLOTHING: Tailored Suits & Formal Jackets

Bellevue Tailors and Formal Wr ..... G 425 643-0741
  Bellevue *(G-815)*
Downtown Cleaners & Tailoring ..... G 206 363-5455
  Shoreline *(G-11769)*

CLOTHING: Trousers & Slacks, Men's & Boys'

Nidekken Ltd .... F 425 885-1587
  Redmond *(G-8595)*
Utilikilts Co LLC .... F 206 282-4226
  Seattle *(G-11396)*
V F Services Inc Jansport .... G 425 407-4040
  Everett *(G-3644)*

PRODUCT SECTION

COATING SVC: Aluminum, Metal Prdts

CLOTHING: Tuxedos, From Purchased Materials

Formal Wear Inc .... G 425 776-1088
Lynnwood *(G-6120)*

CLOTHING: Underwear, Knit

Decent Exposures Inc .... F 206 364-4540
Seattle *(G-9810)*

CLOTHING: Underwear, Women's & Children's

Country Clothiers .... G 206 632-3319
Seattle *(G-9747)*
Decent Exposures Inc .... F 206 364-4540
Seattle *(G-9810)*

CLOTHING: Uniforms & Vestments

Seattle Sewing Solutions Inc .... E 253 625-7420
Seattle *(G-11073)*

CLOTHING: Uniforms, Ex Athletic, Women's, Misses' & Juniors'

Tik Tik Garment Manufacturing .... F 509 624-0806
Spokane *(G-12557)*

CLOTHING: Uniforms, Men's & Boys'

Maulcor Inc .... G 773 696-2783
Seattle *(G-10502)*

CLOTHING: Uniforms, Military, Men/Youth, Purchased Materials

New Uniformity LLC .... G 360 373-2785
Bremerton *(G-1980)*
Seattle Northwest Service Corp .... F 206 553-9209
Seattle *(G-11066)*
Survival Gear Systems .... G 866 257-2978
Spokane *(G-12536)*

CLOTHING: Uniforms, Team Athletic

Seattle Northwest Service Corp .... F 206 553-9209
Seattle *(G-11066)*

CLOTHING: Uniforms, Work

Moor Innovative Tech LLC .... G 253 343-2216
Tacoma *(G-13419)*
Uniform Factory Outl Ariz LLC .... G 360 707-2608
Burlington *(G-2196)*

CLOTHING: Vests

Steele and Associates Inc .... G 360 297-4555
Kingston *(G-5264)*

CLOTHING: Waterproof Outerwear

Advadri LLC .... G 425 228-7558
Renton *(G-8728)*
Florian Design .... G 425 742-7212
Mill Creek *(G-6511)*
Rivers West Apparel Inc .... E 425 272-2949
Tukwila *(G-13807)*
Stormy Seas Inc .... F 360 779-4439
Poulsbo *(G-8005)*

CLOTHING: Work, Men's

CC Filson Co .... C 206 624-4437
Seattle *(G-9649)*
Department Crrctons Wash State .... B 509 526-6375
Walla Walla *(G-14795)*
Evolution Revolution LLC .... G 623 703-5042
Leavenworth *(G-5802)*
Filson Manufacturing Inc .... G 206 242-9579
Seattle *(G-9993)*
Kushco .... G 206 772-9333
Seattle *(G-10363)*
Locknane Inc .... E 425 493-8300
Mukilteo *(G-6950)*
Misty Mountain Manufacturing .... E 360 763-4055
Seattle *(G-10548)*
R B Sales .... G 206 870-0741
Des Moines *(G-2944)*
San Mar Corporation .... C 206 727-3200
Issaquah *(G-4471)*

Zonecro Llc .... G 760 702-9290
Bremerton *(G-2014)*

CLOTHING: Work, Waterproof, Exc Raincoats

Shoot Suit Inc .... G 360 687-3451
Battle Ground *(G-739)*

CLOTHS: Polishing, Plain

Buffalo Industries Inc .... G 206 682-9900
Seattle *(G-9595)*

COAL MINING SERVICES

Clowers Corporation .... G 206 420-1202
Lake Forest Park *(G-5609)*
Groundhog Mines LLC .... G 425 609-6901
Lake Stevens *(G-5645)*
Hart Crowser Inc .... D 206 324-9530
Seattle *(G-10145)*
Nika Mines LLC .... G 425 609-6901
Lake Stevens *(G-5664)*
Triumph Corporation .... G 509 926-7000
Spokane Valley *(G-12913)*

COAL MINING: Bituminous Coal & Lignite-Surface Mining

Morning Sun Inc .... G 253 922-6589
Lakewood *(G-5739)*

COAL MINING: Bituminous, Strip

Usnr LLC .... G 360 225-8267
Woodland *(G-15470)*

COAL MINING: Bituminous, Surface, NEC

Green Mtn Mine Oper Co LLC .... G 206 451-7105
Granite Falls *(G-4276)*
Pacific Coast Coal Company .... G 360 886-1060
Black Diamond *(G-1652)*

COAL MINING: Underground, Subbituminous

Transalta Centralia Mining LLC .... A 360 807-8020
Centralia *(G-2438)*

COAL, MINERALS & ORES, WHOLESALE: Coal & Coke

Giant Metals Inc .... G 206 592-0963
Seatac *(G-9285)*

COATED OR PLATED PRDTS

Renegade Powder Coating LLC .... G 509 575-4623
Union Gap *(G-13952)*

COATING COMPOUNDS: Tar

Pacific Coatings Inc .... F 206 722-1413
Seattle *(G-10730)*
Seattle Eco Coatings 253 539-1113
Puyallup *(G-8249)*

COATING SVC

2h Protective Coatings Inc .... G 425 346-3306
Lynnwood *(G-6062)*
A & S Powder Coating .... G 360 880-2487
Chehalis *(G-2456)*
Advanced Prtctive Coatings LLC .... G 425 818-2820
Kirkland *(G-5271)*
Air Specialty Coatings LLC .... G 206 713-2070
Monroe *(G-6546)*
Bear Creek Coatings LLC .... G 253 722-4220
Gig Harbor *(G-4077)*
Black River Seal Coating Wesle .... G 509 836-0125
Sunnyside *(G-13114)*
Bullhide Liner Corp .... G 509 532-9007
Spokane Valley *(G-12647)*
C and R Coatings LLC .... G 509 949-8515
Moxee *(G-6876)*
California Coating .... G 609 405-2683
Battle Ground *(G-694)*
Can AM Coatings .... G 360 386-9692
Marysville *(G-6320)*
Carls Powder Coating 425 864-7950
North Bend *(G-7104)*

Cobalt Investments LLC .... G 360 691-2298
Granite Falls *(G-4268)*
Contour Coatings LLC .... G 253 830-4994
Tacoma *(G-13241)*
Craftwork Coatings .... G 253 508-9358
Puyallup *(G-8138)*
Critchlow Custom Coatings LLC .... G 253 651-9675
University Place *(G-13965)*
D & R Quality Coatings Inc .... G 253 209-5441
Orting *(G-7478)*
Deans Mean Prfmce Coatings .... G 509 406-4713
Yakima *(G-15552)*
Diversified Coatings LLC .... G 360 264-2099
Tenino *(G-13617)*
Dm Coating LLC .... G 509 420-0961
Pasco *(G-7578)*
Dynamic Coatings LLC .... G 360 755-3649
Anacortes *(G-124)*
Endurance Coatings LLC .... G 206 234-8793
Snohomish *(G-11905)*
Feller Custom Coatings .... G 360 551-2045
Lakewood *(G-5722)*
Fox Coatings .... G 360 574-7471
Vancouver *(G-14238)*
Franks Custom Coatings LLC .... G 253 973-4361
Puyallup *(G-8154)*
Integrity First Coatings LLC .... G 509 619-9983
Pasco *(G-7592)*
J and T Prtective Coatings LLC .... G 206 498-6147
Seattle *(G-10266)*
J T Coatings Inc .... G 509 944-1669
Pasco *(G-7594)*
Kings of Coatings Inc .... G 360 721-0636
Vancouver *(G-14350)*
Kitsap Coatings .... G 360 550-3777
Bremerton *(G-1968)*
Kitsap Custom Coatings LLC .... G 360 471-3095
Silverdale *(G-11842)*
Kitsap Custom Coatings LLC .... G 360 471-3095
Bremerton *(G-1969)*
M & M Coatings Inc .... G 360 480-6425
Yelm *(G-15739)*
Mad Custom Coating .... G 360 621-6525
Poulsbo *(G-7980)*
Meticulous Coating Applicators 206 251-3684
Everett *(G-3547)*
Multi App Coatings LLC .... G 253 841-1256
Puyallup *(G-8196)*
North West Coating & Svcs LLC .... G 360 649-1548
Port Orchard *(G-7834)*
Pesani Genuine Coatings LLC .... G 509 860-3426
Wenatchee *(G-15061)*
R and Dee Coatings LLC .... G 509 771-1111
Moses Lake *(G-6740)*
Richardson Coatings LLC .... G 253 861-7611
Morton *(G-6672)*
Rocky Prairie Engraving .... G 360 264-2188
Tenino *(G-13622)*
Ryan Custom Coatings .... G 808 652-9731
Wenatchee *(G-15070)*
Savage Gun Coating .... G 206 485-4125
Kenmore *(G-4603)*
Shannon D Agnew .... G 509 926-6209
Spokane Valley *(G-12869)*
Sitec Coatings .... G 360 840-9979
Lynnwood *(G-6198)*
Solar Guard Coatings Inc .... G 425 413-0545
Maple Valley *(G-6293)*
Specht Coatings .... G 253 732-5662
Graham *(G-4239)*
Start 2 Finish Coatings Inc .... G 509 481-8898
Otis Orchards *(G-7518)*
Superior Coatings .... G 253 405-5424
Sumner *(G-13104)*
Terrashield Coatings Ltd .... G 206 992-2157
Seattle *(G-11281)*
Triad Coatings Corp .... G 253 537-4464
Tacoma *(G-13562)*
Universal Coatings LLC .... G 360 936-2855
Shelton *(G-11748)*
Wise Choice Custom Coatings .... G 360 326-3809
Vancouver *(G-14696)*
Woolman Coatings LLC .... G 206 402-2960
Snohomish *(G-12000)*

COATING SVC: Aluminum, Metal Prdts

North PCF Indus Coatings LLC .... G 907 865-8400
Renton *(G-8859)*
Steelscape LLC .... C 360 673-8200
Kalama *(G-4509)*

COATING SVC: Aluminum, Metal Prdts

Steelscape LLC .... C 360 673-8200
  Kalama *(G-4510)*
Steelscape Washington LLC .... C 360 673-8200
  Kalama *(G-4511)*

COATING SVC: Hot Dip, Metals Or Formed Prdts

Abel Flamespray .... G 360 925-6125
  Arlington *(G-190)*
Kens Powder Coating .... G 253 539-5845
  Tacoma *(G-13375)*
Powdertech Mr Shannon .... F 509 927-5804
  Spokane Valley *(G-12834)*

COATING SVC: Metals & Formed Prdts

Advanced Powder Coating NW .... G 360 398-1460
  Bellingham *(G-1240)*
Applied Finishing Inc .... E 425 513-2505
  Mukilteo *(G-6893)*
Artisan Finishing Systems Inc .... G 360 658-0686
  Marysville *(G-6313)*
Asko Processing Inc .... F 206 634-2080
  Seattle *(G-9444)*
Biec International Inc .... G 360 750-5791
  Vancouver *(G-14065)*
Bowmans Electro Painting .... G 360 668-1389
  Snohomish *(G-11880)*
Cascade Powder Coating LLC .... G 509 663-9080
  Wenatchee *(G-15015)*
Doug House Powder Coating .... G 360 681-5412
  Sequim *(G-11629)*
Ecolite Manufacturing Co .... D 509 922-8888
  Spokane Valley *(G-12687)*
Electronic Coating Tech Inc .... G 425 265-2212
  Everett *(G-3457)*
Farwest Operating LLC .... G 509 453-1663
  Moxee *(G-6878)*
Finishing Specialist LLC .... G 509 248-5510
  Union Gap *(G-13930)*
Flamespray Northwest Inc .... F 206 508-6779
  Seattle *(G-10004)*
Forever Powder Coating LLC .... G 360 786-6345
  Tumwater *(G-13872)*
I-90 Express Finishing Inc .... E 509 922-2297
  Spokane Valley *(G-12736)*
Imsa Steel Corp .... B 360 673-8200
  Kalama *(G-4501)*
Kitsap Powder Coating LLC .... G 360 297-0015
  Poulsbo *(G-7971)*
Metal Finishing Inc .... F 360 659-1971
  Arlington *(G-274)*
Metron Powdercoating Inc .... G 509 766-1278
  Moses Lake *(G-6725)*
Olympia Powder Coat .... G 360 570-9100
  Olympia *(G-7353)*
Pacific NW Powdr Coating .... F 509 535-9950
  Spokane *(G-12426)*
Pacific Performance Coatings .... G 425 339-5528
  Everett *(G-3565)*
Pacific Powder Coating Inc .... G 360 383-9100
  Ferndale *(G-3882)*
Perfection Powder Coating & FA .... G 253 875-0010
  Puyallup *(G-8221)*
Performance Coatings Inc .... G 253 735-1919
  Auburn *(G-531)*
Powder Vision Inc .... G 425 222-6363
  Preston *(G-8026)*
Powder-Fab Inc .... E 360 435-0793
  Arlington *(G-303)*
Powdertech Inc .... G 509 927-0189
  Spokane Valley *(G-12833)*
Production Plating Inc .... D 425 347-4635
  Mukilteo *(G-6968)*
Protective Coating Consultants .... G 206 762-6119
  Seattle *(G-10876)*
RMC Incorporated .... G 206 243-4831
  Seattle *(G-10969)*
Skagit Powder Coating .... G 360 428-0413
  Mount Vernon *(G-6839)*
Skills Inc .... D 206 782-6000
  Auburn *(G-565)*
U Deck It Inc .... G 509 532-9007
  Spokane Valley *(G-12917)*
Vivasource Inc .... E 253 627-3853
  Tacoma *(G-13583)*

COATING SVC: Rust Preventative

Ameron International Corp .... C 509 547-3689
  Pasco *(G-7552)*

No Graf Network Inc .... G 509 531-1334
  Kennewick *(G-4703)*
Powder Coating Inc .... G 425 743-4393
  Mukilteo *(G-6967)*

COATINGS: Polyurethane

CDI Coding .... G 360 653-6437
  Woodinville *(G-15207)*
Curnutt Inc .... G 208 520-2598
  Pasco *(G-7574)*
Polyurethane Sales & Svc LLC .... G 360 334-5364
  Vancouver *(G-14494)*
Specialty Products Inc .... E 253 588-7101
  Lakewood *(G-5759)*

COCKTAIL LOUNGE

Freeland Cafe .... F 360 331-9945
  Freeland *(G-4028)*

COFFEE MAKERS: Electric

Mavam LLC .... G 360 789-0639
  Seattle *(G-10503)*
Tml Innovative Products LLC .... F 425 290-3994
  Mukilteo *(G-6982)*

COFFEE SVCS

Cascade Coffee Inc .... F 425 347-3995
  Everett *(G-3410)*
Sirjmr Inc .... E 509 582-2683
  Kennewick *(G-4728)*

COILS & TRANSFORMERS

AMG Aluminum North America LLC ..... D 509 663-2165
  Malaga *(G-6231)*
Kemcor Inc .... E 425 488-7400
  Woodinville *(G-15276)*
Polytech Coil Winding .... G 253 324-3044
  Tacoma *(G-13470)*

COIN COUNTERS

Gene L Henry Inc .... G 425 392-1485
  Issaquah *(G-4418)*
Lone Ranger LLC .... G 425 355-7474
  Everett *(G-3539)*

COIN OPERATED LAUNDRIES & DRYCLEANERS

Samish Bay Soaps & Scents .... G 360 752-9015
  Bellingham *(G-1522)*

COINS & TOKENS: Non-Currency

Coinforcecom LLC .... G 253 682-2825
  Olympia *(G-7251)*

COLLECTION AGENCIES

Quick Collect Inc .... E 360 256-7888
  Vancouver *(G-14523)*

COLLEGES, UNIVERSITIES & PROFESSIONAL SCHOOLS

Center For East Asian Studies .... E 360 650-3836
  Bellingham *(G-1295)*
University of Washington .... C 206 543-5680
  Seattle *(G-11382)*

COLORS: Pigments, Inorganic

Stardust Materials LLC .... G 360 260-7399
  Vancouver *(G-14608)*

COMBINATION UTILITIES, NEC

Direct Contact LLC .... E 425 235-1723
  Tukwila *(G-13725)*
Global Emergent Tech LLC .... G 425 999-9021
  Seattle *(G-10083)*

COMFORTERS & QUILTS, FROM MANMADE FIBER OR SILK

Dan Coats .... G 360 892-2730
  Vancouver *(G-14166)*
Yong Feng America Inc .... G 425 271-8057
  Bellevue *(G-1230)*

COMMERCIAL & OFFICE BUILDINGS RENOVATION & REPAIR

Grenlar Holdings Inc .... G 425 419-4430
  Kenmore *(G-4578)*
Noel Corporation .... F 509 248-3412
  Yakima *(G-15631)*
Patriot Jabez Construction JV .... G 253 293-7100
  Auburn *(G-527)*
Warmington & North Co Inc .... F 206 324-5043
  Seattle *(G-11436)*

COMMERCIAL ART & GRAPHIC DESIGN SVCS

4 Over LLC .... G 818 246-1170
  Milton *(G-6531)*
AAA Printing & Graphics Inc .... F 425 454-0156
  Bellevue *(G-778)*
Bayshore Office Products Inc .... F 360 293-4669
  Anacortes *(G-102)*
Benjamin Moore Inc .... G 206 329-8607
  Seattle *(G-9513)*
Brecht-Pacific Publishing Inc .... E 360 425-4671
  Longview *(G-5890)*
Community Networkers LLC .... G 509 826-5154
  OMAK *(G-7437)*
Electronic Charts Co Inc .... G 206 282-4990
  Seattle *(G-9893)*
Fedex Office & Print Svcs Inc .... G 206 546-7600
  Shoreline *(G-11771)*
Holm Bing .... F 509 454-2277
  Yakima *(G-15581)*
Imagesmart Sign Company LLC .... G 509 525-4343
  Walla Walla *(G-14821)*
Magna Vis Graphic Impressions .... G 509 684-5659
  Colville *(G-2764)*
Nannette Louise Davis .... G 425 485-5570
  Woodinville *(G-15317)*
National Color .... F 206 281-9400
  Seattle *(G-10587)*
Olympic Graphic Arts Inc .... G 360 374-6020
  Forks *(G-4013)*
Potter & Associates Inc .... G 206 623-8844
  Seattle *(G-10839)*
Prime West of Washington Inc .... E 360 424-5783
  Kent *(G-5081)*
Print Services Northwest Inc .... G 206 763-9230
  Seattle *(G-10860)*
Quarto Pubg Group USA Inc .... E 425 827-7120
  Bellevue *(G-1090)*
Rainbow Racing System Inc .... F 509 326-5470
  Spokane *(G-12466)*
Sand Paper & Ink Inc .... G 360 705-0918
  Tumwater *(G-13896)*
Saturday Night Inc .... F 509 928-5816
  Spokane Valley *(G-12858)*
Stemar Media Group LLC .... G 206 877-3560
  Shoreline *(G-11818)*
Winsor Fireform LLC .... E 360 786-8200
  Tumwater *(G-13907)*
Yehun LLC .... G 425 533-9641
  Seattle *(G-11510)*

COMMERCIAL ART & ILLUSTRATION SVCS

Absolute Graphix Inc .... G 425 771-6087
  Lynnwood *(G-6067)*
Schumacher Creative Services .... G 206 364-7151
  Seattle *(G-11029)*
Tourmap Company .... G 206 932-2506
  Seattle *(G-11322)*

COMMERCIAL CONTAINERS WHOLESALERS

Adaptive Cargo Solutions LLC .... F 240 475-6521
  Everett *(G-3360)*
Graham Packaging Company LP .... E 509 698-4545
  Selah *(G-11589)*

COMMERCIAL EQPT WHOLESALERS, NEC

Econo Quality Signs Inc .... G 253 531-3943
  Tacoma *(G-13270)*
Farmer Bros Co .... E 425 881-7030
  Redmond *(G-8459)*
Norma Industries .... G 253 208-1728
  Puyallup *(G-8200)*
Safs Inc .... G 253 301-0615
  Tacoma *(G-13506)*

COMMERCIAL EQPT, WHOL: Soda Fountain Fixtures, Exc Refrig

Coca-Cola Company.................................F...... 404 676-0887
  Bellevue *(G-857)*

COMMERCIAL EQPT, WHOLESALE: Bakery Eqpt & Splys

Hobart Corporation..................................C...... 360 893-5554
  Orting *(G-7480)*

COMMERCIAL EQPT, WHOLESALE: Coin counters

Cummins - Allison Corp...........................G...... 206 763-3900
  Tukwila *(G-13721)*

COMMERCIAL EQPT, WHOLESALE: Display Eqpt, Exc Refrigerated

Imagicorps Inc...E...... 425 869-0599
  Redmond *(G-8506)*

COMMERCIAL EQPT, WHOLESALE: Neon Signs

Reid Signs Inc..G...... 206 547-5487
  Seattle *(G-10945)*
Sno-King Signs.......................................G...... 425 775-0594
  Edmonds *(G-3158)*

COMMERCIAL EQPT, WHOLESALE: Restaurant, NEC

Bargreen-Ellingson Inc..........................D...... 253 475-9201
  Tacoma *(G-13189)*
Bargreen-Ellingson Inc..........................E...... 253 722-2573
  Fife *(G-3937)*
Beverage Specialist Inc.........................E...... 206 763-0255
  Tukwila *(G-13697)*
Food Equipment International..............G...... 509 924-0181
  Spokane Valley *(G-12707)*

COMMERCIAL EQPT, WHOLESALE: Scales, Exc Laboratory

Avery Weigh-Tronix LLC......................G...... 206 575-1992
  Tukwila *(G-13694)*
Pacific Northwest Scale Co..................G...... 425 259-4720
  Snohomish *(G-11960)*
Tandar Corp...F...... 503 248-0711
  Vancouver *(G-14624)*
U S Scale Incorporated.........................G...... 253 872-4803
  Kent *(G-5193)*

COMMERCIAL PRINTING & NEWSPAPER PUBLISHING COMBINED

Columbia Basin Publishing Co.............D...... 509 765-4561
  Moses Lake *(G-6696)*
Courier-Herald...F...... 360 825-2555
  Enumclaw *(G-3283)*
Daily Herald Company...........................D...... 425 339-3000
  Everett *(G-3437)*
Ed Print Inc...F...... 425 483-0606
  Woodinville *(G-15233)*
Grand Image Ltd....................................F...... 206 624-0444
  Seattle *(G-10107)*
Issaquah Sammamish Reporter..........G...... 425 391-0363
  Bellevue *(G-963)*
Journal-News Publishing Co.................F...... 509 754-4636
  Ephrata *(G-3339)*
Journal-News Publishing Co................G...... 509 725-0101
  Davenport *(G-2872)*
Journal-News Publishing Co................E...... 509 235-6184
  Cheney *(G-2588)*
Ken Robinson Publications Inc...........G...... 360 794-7116
  Monroe *(G-6585)*
Key Peninsula News..............................G...... 253 884-4699
  Vaughn *(G-14747)*
Kingston Community News...................E...... 360 779-4464
  Poulsbo *(G-7970)*
Kitsap Sun..D...... 360 792-3350
  Bremerton *(G-1970)*
Lafromboise Newspapers......................D...... 360 736-3311
  Centralia *(G-2415)*
Lafromboise Newspapers......................F...... 360 807-8716
  Centralia *(G-2416)*
McClatchy Newspapers Inc..................C...... 360 676-2600
  Bellingham *(G-1428)*
North American Post Publishing..........G...... 206 726-6460
  Seattle *(G-10623)*
Northwest Media Washington LP.........E...... 360 681-2390
  Sequim *(G-11653)*
Northwest Publications Inc...................G...... 360 379-4080
  Port Townsend *(G-7901)*
Nw Asian Weekly....................................G...... 206 223-5559
  Seattle *(G-10672)*
Oroville Gazette Inc...............................G...... 509 476-3602
  Oroville *(G-7470)*
Pareto-Curve Marketing Inc.................G...... 360 357-1000
  Tumwater *(G-13889)*
R R Donnelley & Sons Company.........G...... 206 587-0278
  Seattle *(G-10911)*
Seattle Times Company........................B...... 425 489-7000
  Bothell *(G-1791)*
Tricomp Publishing.................................G...... 509 737-8778
  Kennewick *(G-4741)*
Valley Publishing Company Inc...........F...... 509 786-1711
  Prosser *(G-8073)*
Whidbey Examiner LLC..........................G...... 360 678-8060
  Coupeville *(G-2819)*
World Publishing Company...................D...... 509 663-5161
  Wenatchee *(G-15087)*
Yakima Herald-Republic Inc.................G...... 509 452-7355
  Yakima *(G-15716)*

COMMERCIAL REFRIGERATORS WHOLESALERS

Refrigeration Supplies Distr..................G...... 503 234-4334
  Vancouver *(G-14540)*

COMMODITY CONTRACT TRADING COMPANIES

Lagunamoon Beauty Intl Ltd LLC........F...... 480 925-7577
  Seattle *(G-10372)*

COMMON SAND MINING

Davis Sand & Gravel Inc.......................G...... 360 683-5680
  Sequim *(G-11625)*

COMMUNICATIONS EQPT & SYSTEMS, NEC

American Digital......................................G...... 800 765-2580
  Kirkland *(G-5277)*
Fathem LLC...G...... 360 403-7418
  Arlington *(G-236)*
James Wile..G...... 360 606-0706
  Camas *(G-2259)*
Jay Pathy...G...... 425 890-9526
  Medina *(G-6449)*
Junefalsetta..G...... 253 536-3576
  Tacoma *(G-13370)*
Tim Anders...G...... 360 944-0806
  Vancouver *(G-14638)*

COMMUNICATIONS EQPT WHOLESALERS

Diversified Marketing Intl LLC..............G...... 509 585-9377
  Kennewick *(G-4654)*
Pacific Tchnical Solutions Inc.............F...... 425 489-5700
  Redmond *(G-8608)*

COMMUNICATIONS EQPT: Microwave

Diversified Marketing Intl LLC..............G...... 509 585-9377
  Kennewick *(G-4654)*
Loop Devices Inc...................................G...... 206 965-9828
  Seattle *(G-10441)*
PSI Electronics LLC...............................F...... 253 922-7890
  Fife *(G-3984)*

COMMUNICATIONS EQPT: Radio, Marine

Mahler & Assoc Inc.................................G...... 206 365-3800
  Lake Forest Park *(G-5620)*
Rothenbuhler Engineering Co..............F...... 360 856-0836
  Sedro Woolley *(G-11562)*
Xoceco USA..G...... 509 808-2480
  Liberty Lake *(G-5869)*

COMMUNICATIONS SVCS: Cellular

Bluecosmo Inc..G...... 877 258-3496
  Seattle *(G-9555)*
Dannys Electronics Inc.........................G...... 253 314-5056
  Tacoma *(G-13253)*
New Cingular Wireless Svcs Inc..........F...... 425 288-3132
  Bothell *(G-1779)*
Verizon Communications Inc................F...... 425 641-5900
  Bellevue *(G-1214)*

COMMUNICATIONS SVCS: Data

Action Communications Inc.................G...... 206 625-1234
  Seattle *(G-9344)*
Viar Visual Communications................G...... 425 391-8443
  Sammamish *(G-9257)*
Wind Talker Innovations Inc................G...... 253 883-3615
  Fife *(G-3999)*

COMMUNICATIONS SVCS: Electronic Mail

Telecommunication Systems Inc.........C...... 206 792-2000
  Seattle *(G-11280)*

COMMUNICATIONS SVCS: Facsimile Transmission

King Enterprises....................................G...... 360 568-1644
  Snohomish *(G-11933)*

COMMUNICATIONS SVCS: Internet Host Svcs

Washington Media Services Inc..........G...... 360 754-4543
  Olympia *(G-7421)*

COMMUNICATIONS SVCS: Online Svc Providers

Local Church Publishing.......................G...... 360 710-8751
  Bremerton *(G-1974)*
Mind Modulations..................................G...... 626 863-7379
  Marysville *(G-6360)*
Zango Inc..C...... 425 279-1200
  Bellevue *(G-1232)*
Zillow Group Inc....................................C...... 206 470-7000
  Seattle *(G-11521)*

COMMUNICATIONS SVCS: Telephone, Local

Verizon Communications Inc................F...... 425 641-5900
  Bellevue *(G-1214)*

COMMUNICATIONS SVCS: Telephone, Voice

Bluecosmo Inc..G...... 877 258-3496
  Seattle *(G-9555)*

COMMUNITY CENTERS: Adult

County of Lewis.....................................C...... 360 748-9121
  Chehalis *(G-2485)*
Senior Services For S Sound...............G...... 360 426-3697
  Shelton *(G-11730)*

COMMUNITY CENTERS: Youth

Marysville Awards Inc...........................G...... 360 653-4811
  Marysville *(G-6356)*

COMMUNITY COLLEGE

Green River College..............................E...... 253 856-9595
  Kent *(G-4928)*

COMMUTATORS: Electric Motors

Cutsforth Inc..E...... 800 290-6458
  Ferndale *(G-3835)*

COMMUTATORS: Electronic

Misiu Systems LLC................................G...... 425 402-8700
  Bothell *(G-1877)*

COMPACT LASER DISCS: Prerecorded

Alpha Audio Group Inc..........................G...... 253 846-1536
  Tacoma *(G-13167)*
Arrowdisc LLC.......................................D...... 253 518-3900
  Kent *(G-4792)*
Media Holdings LLC..............................G...... 503 313-0676
  Olympia *(G-7338)*

COMPOST

Brm Marketing LLC................................G...... 509 350-5844
  Moses Lake *(G-6688)*

Employee Codes: A=Over 500 employees, B=251-500
C=101-250, D=51-100, E=20-50, F=10-19, G=2-9

COMPOST

Cedar Grove Composting Inc ....C...... 425 212-2515
  Everett *(G-3412)*
Columbia Valley Compost LLC.........G...... 509 551-7202
  Prosser *(G-8035)*
Compost Manufacturing Alliance ....G...... 206 755-8309
  Port Orchard *(G-7798)*
Compost Tea By Seaneen ....G...... 360 678-3288
  Coupeville *(G-2811)*
H & H Wood Recyclers Inc ....E...... 360 892-2805
  Vancouver *(G-14278)*
Hawaiian Earth Products ....G...... 808 682-5895
  Seattle *(G-10152)*
Microbial Magic LLC ....G...... 360 297-2224
  Poulsbo *(G-7983)*
Neilson Organic Compost ....G...... 360 983-8125
  Mossyrock *(G-6763)*
Northwest Compost LLC ....G...... 509 932-0215
  Mattawa *(G-6411)*
O2compost ....G...... 360 563-6709
  Snohomish *(G-11955)*
Olysunrise Compost Concierge ....G...... 360 551-0674
  Olympia *(G-7360)*
Sawdust Supply ....G...... 206 622-4321
  Seattle *(G-11022)*
Sunland Bark and Topsoils Co ....G...... 360 293-7188
  Anacortes *(G-172)*
Trinity Farms Inc ....G...... 509 968-4107
  Ellensburg *(G-3234)*

COMPRESSORS: Air & Gas

Atlas Copco Compressors LLC.........F...... 425 251-1040
  Kent *(G-4797)*
Atlas Copco Compressors LLC ....G...... 360 530-2130
  Arlington *(G-204)*
Compressed Air Systems LLC ....G...... 425 328-0755
  Arlington *(G-222)*
Dresser-Rand Company ....G...... 425 828-4919
  Bellevue *(G-884)*
I 90 Enterprises Inc ....G...... 509 988-0380
  Odessa *(G-7190)*
Ingersoll-Rand Company ....E...... 253 931-8600
  Kent *(G-4952)*
Magnum Venus Products Inc ....D...... 253 854-2660
  Kent *(G-5000)*
Ron C England ....G...... 509 276-9150
  Nine Mile Falls *(G-7083)*
Somarakis Inc ....F...... 360 574-6722
  Kalama *(G-4508)*
Thermion Inc ....G...... 360 362-1273
  Poulsbo *(G-8009)*

COMPRESSORS: Air & Gas, Including Vacuum Pumps

Northwest Truck & Auto AC ....F...... 206 242-6034
  Federal Way *(G-3765)*

COMPRESSORS: Refrigeration & Air Conditioning Eqpt

Frascold USA Corporation ....G...... 855 547-5600
  Everett *(G-3485)*
Pacific NW Reps LLC ....G...... 509 823-7008
  Yakima *(G-15640)*

COMPRESSORS: Repairing

Integrity Dental LLC ....G...... 253 691-7292
  Orting *(G-7481)*
Rogers Machinery Company Inc ....E...... 206 763-2530
  Seattle *(G-10976)*
Rogers Machinery Company Inc ....E...... 360 736-9356
  Centralia *(G-2429)*
Rogers Machinery Company Inc ....F...... 509 922-0556
  Spokane Valley *(G-12856)*

COMPUTER & COMPUTER SOFTWARE STORES

Airwavz Inc ....G...... 206 696-6649
  Renton *(G-8734)*
Custom Computer Creat CCC LLC.........G...... 800 295-3381
  Seattle *(G-9766)*
Glenn Waldren ....G...... 360 570-8400
  Olympia *(G-7297)*
Riverside Scientific Entps ....G...... 206 842-7513
  Bainbridge Island *(G-667)*
T T I Acquisition Corp ....F...... 509 358-2036
  Liberty Lake *(G-5861)*

COMPUTER & COMPUTER SOFTWARE STORES: Peripheral Eqpt

Cartridge World ....G...... 509 469-9711
  Kennewick *(G-4643)*
Computer Clinic Northwest Inc ....G...... 360 658-1234
  Marysville *(G-6327)*
Engineering Solutions Inc ....F...... 206 241-9395
  Renton *(G-8795)*
Northwest Technologies ....G...... 206 528-5353
  Seattle *(G-10652)*

COMPUTER & COMPUTER SOFTWARE STORES: Personal Computers

US Micro Pc Inc ....G...... 425 462-7300
  Bellevue *(G-1210)*

COMPUTER & COMPUTER SOFTWARE STORES: Software & Access

Defsec Solutions LLC ....G...... 855 933-3732
  Mill Creek *(G-6506)*
JC Global Supply LLC ....G...... 253 275-6093
  Kent *(G-4966)*
Magnapro Business Systems Inc ....G...... 206 280-6222
  Edmonds *(G-3131)*
Proforma Crtive Prtg Solutions ....G...... 360 848-7714
  Mount Vernon *(G-6827)*

COMPUTER & COMPUTER SOFTWARE STORES: Software, Bus/Non-Game

Democracy Live Inc ....F...... 855 655-8683
  Seattle *(G-9819)*

COMPUTER & COMPUTER SOFTWARE STORES: Software, Computer Game

Cetrestec Inc ....G...... 206 650-8676
  Seattle *(G-9662)*

COMPUTER & DATA PROCESSING EQPT REPAIR & MAINTENANCE

Opticon Inc ....E...... 425 651-2120
  Renton *(G-8865)*
Profile Systems Inc ....F...... 206 624-7715
  Seattle *(G-10873)*
Unix Packages LLC ....G...... 206 310-4610
  Seattle *(G-11386)*

COMPUTER & OFFICE MACHINE MAINTENANCE & REPAIR

Grays Harbor Electronics ....G...... 360 532-3474
  Hoquiam *(G-4338)*
M M Enterprises ....G...... 206 463-1927
  Vashon *(G-14731)*
Mikes Help Key LLC ....G...... 360 897-2880
  Buckley *(G-2064)*
Northwest Technologies ....G...... 206 528-5353
  Seattle *(G-10652)*
Washington Schl Info Proc Coop ....C...... 425 349-6600
  Everett *(G-3651)*
Wendy Rawley ....G...... 253 531-6785
  Tacoma *(G-13592)*

COMPUTER FACILITIES MANAGEMENT SVCS

Desema Company ....G...... 425 202-7572
  Redmond *(G-8438)*
Horizon Professional Cmpt Svcs ....F...... 425 883-6588
  Redmond *(G-8501)*
Manta Network Technologies LLC ....G...... 202 713-0508
  Mukilteo *(G-6952)*
Space Rock It Inc ....G...... 206 395-8383
  Seattle *(G-11164)*

COMPUTER FORMS

Apperson Inc ....E...... 206 336-1015
  Renton *(G-8746)*
Now Impressions Inc ....G...... 425 881-5911
  Redmond *(G-8601)*

COMPUTER GRAPHICS SVCS

American Bancard LLC ....E...... 360 713-0690
  Vancouver *(G-14026)*
Denny Mountain Media LLC ....D...... 425 831-7130
  Seattle *(G-9822)*
Dimensional Products Inc ....F...... 206 352-9065
  Seattle *(G-9831)*
Dumas Holdings LLC ....G...... 425 576-4227
  Kirkland *(G-5323)*
Filmateria Studios Inc ....G...... 206 938-6791
  Seattle *(G-9992)*
Graphic Communications Inc ....G...... 425 251-8680
  Renton *(G-8811)*
L G Artworks Inc ....G...... 425 355-9143
  Everett *(G-3533)*
Vertical Visual Solutions ....G...... 425 361-1562
  Mountlake Terrace *(G-6873)*
Whab Technologies LLC ....G...... 800 506-2770
  Lynnwood *(G-6224)*

COMPUTER HARDWARE REQUIREMENTS ANALYSIS

Secure It LLC ....G...... 509 992-6190
  Spokane *(G-12497)*

COMPUTER INTERFACE EQPT: Indl Process

Empire Controls LLC ....G...... 509 795-5615
  Chelan *(G-2553)*
Expert Computer Tech Inc ....G...... 360 736-7000
  Centralia *(G-2401)*
Fermium It LLC ....G...... 541 213-9291
  Vancouver *(G-14227)*
R C Systems Inc ....G...... 425 355-3800
  Everett *(G-3592)*
Remote Control Technology Inc ....G...... 425 216-7555
  Redmond *(G-8648)*

COMPUTER PERIPHERAL EQPT REPAIR & MAINTENANCE

CCS Computer Systems Inc ....F...... 425 672-4806
  Lynnwood *(G-6089)*
Spacelabs Healthcare Inc ....A...... 425 396-3300
  Snoqualmie *(G-12027)*
Spacelabs Healthcare LLC ....B...... 425 396-3300
  Snoqualmie *(G-12028)*
Spacelabs Healthcare Wash ....C...... 425 396-3300
  Snoqualmie *(G-12029)*

COMPUTER PERIPHERAL EQPT, NEC

4m Sigma Corporation ....G...... 206 285-9181
  Seattle *(G-9322)*
Antipodes Inc ....G...... 253 444-5555
  Tacoma *(G-13173)*
Antipodes Inc ....F...... 253 444-5555
  Tacoma *(G-13174)*
Astronics Cstm Ctrl Cncpts Inc ....D...... 206 575-0933
  Kent *(G-4795)*
Avocent ....G...... 425 398-0294
  Bothell *(G-1749)*
Avocent Redmond Corp ....D...... 425 861-5858
  Kirkland *(G-5287)*
Black Box Corporation ....G...... 800 733-0274
  Kent *(G-4814)*
Black Box Corporation ....G...... 406 522-3944
  Spokane *(G-12151)*
Black Box Corporation ....G...... 406 652-1956
  Spokane *(G-12152)*
Black Box Corporation ....G...... 406 652-1956
  Spokane *(G-12153)*
Blue Heron Lake Farms Inc ....G...... 360 966-5241
  Bellingham *(G-1277)*
Byte Brothers ....E...... 425 917-8380
  Medina *(G-6447)*
Cisco Systems Inc ....A...... 206 256-3229
  Seattle *(G-9686)*
Computer Technology Link Corp ....G...... 253 872-3608
  Kent *(G-4860)*
Copytonix ....G...... 503 968-0364
  Bellevue *(G-865)*
David G McAlees ....G...... 425 641-0318
  Bellevue *(G-875)*
Engineering Solutions Inc ....F...... 206 241-9395
  Renton *(G-8795)*
Enravel Inc ....G...... 206 414-8884
  Seattle *(G-9928)*
Exorvision Inc ....G...... 206 254-0220
  Seattle *(G-9955)*
Fantasy Content ....G...... 425 653-2207
  Bellevue *(G-907)*

Fox Bay Industries Inc ... G ... 253 941-9155
Auburn *(G-443)*

Francis Scientific Inc ... G ... 360 687-7019
Battle Ground *(G-702)*

Gsl Solutions Inc ... E ... 360 896-5354
Vancouver *(G-14275)*

Intel Corporation ... F ... 253 371-1052
Bellevue *(G-959)*

Intermec Technologies Corp ... A ... 425 348-2600
Lynnwood *(G-6140)*

Ioline Corporation ... E ... 425 398-8282
Woodinville *(G-15267)*

Jaspreet Singh ... G ... 253 239-3250
Kent *(G-4965)*

Key Tronic Corporation ... E ... 509 928-8000
Spokane Valley *(G-12766)*

Key Tronic Corporation ... G ... 509 927-5225
Spokane Valley *(G-12768)*

Koolance Inc ... G ... 253 249-7669
Auburn *(G-485)*

Microsoft Corporation ... A ... 425 882-8080
Redmond *(G-8580)*

Microstar Laboratories Inc ... E ... 425 453-2345
Redmond *(G-8585)*

Motek Inc ... G ... 206 632-7795
Seattle *(G-10565)*

Next Biometrics Inc ... F ... 617 510-4086
Bellevue *(G-1029)*

Next Biometrics Inc ... E ... 425 406-7055
Bellevue *(G-1030)*

Oroville Reman & Reload Inc ... E ... 509 476-2935
Oroville *(G-7471)*

PC Networks Inc ... G ... 360 362-9684
Silverdale *(G-11853)*

Professional Sales & Serv ... G ... 509 678-4535
Yakima *(G-15656)*

Prologic Engineering Inc ... D ... 360 734-9625
Bellingham *(G-1507)*

Prologix LLC ... G ... 425 829-8199
Redmond *(G-8634)*

R C Systems Inc ... G ... 425 355-3800
Everett *(G-3592)*

Ralph Doggett ... G ... 503 998-5935
Vancouver *(G-14531)*

Signal Interface Group ... G ... 425 467-7146
Redmond *(G-8666)*

Smart Cable Company ... G ... 253 474-9967
Lakewood *(G-5756)*

Softec Systems Inc ... G ... 425 741-2055
Everett *(G-3615)*

Stick It To Violence ... G ... 360 758-7488
Bellingham *(G-1559)*

Transport Logistics Inc ... G ... 206 824-0667
Seatac *(G-9307)*

Troop Boy Scouts of America ... G ... 206 284-2164
Seattle *(G-11340)*

US Micro Pc Inc ... G ... 425 462-7300
Bellevue *(G-1210)*

Wendy Rawley ... G ... 253 531-6785
Tacoma *(G-13592)*

Xerox ... G ... 360 923-8640
Lacey *(G-5602)*

Xerox ... G ... 253 437-4000
Tukwila *(G-13837)*

Zebra Trans LLC ... G ... 360 993-0451
Vancouver *(G-14708)*

COMPUTER PERIPHERAL EQPT, WHOLESALE

Computer Technology Link Corp ... G ... 253 872-3608
Kent *(G-4860)*

Northwest Technologies ... G ... 206 528-5353
Seattle *(G-10652)*

Pacific Custom Cable Inc ... F ... 253 373-0800
Auburn *(G-523)*

COMPUTER PERIPHERAL EQPT: Decoders

Netacquire Corporation ... E ... 425 821-3100
Kirkland *(G-5410)*

COMPUTER PERIPHERAL EQPT: Encoders

Lone Ranger LLC ... E ... 425 355-7474
Everett *(G-3539)*

COMPUTER PERIPHERAL EQPT: Graphic Displays, Exc Terminals

Graphic Control System Inc ... G ... 360 833-9522
Vancouver *(G-14262)*

COMPUTER PERIPHERAL EQPT: Input Or Output

Leancode Inc ... F ... 425 533-5219
Redmond *(G-8532)*

Logitech Inc ... F ... 360 817-1200
Camas *(G-2266)*

Tahoma Technology Inc ... G ... 206 393-0909
Seattle *(G-11259)*

COMPUTER PERIPHERAL EQPT: Output To Microfilm Units

Allied Telesis Inc ... C ... 408 519-8700
Bothell *(G-1746)*

COMPUTER PROCESSING SVCS

Automatic Funds Transfer Svcs ... E ... 206 254-0975
Seattle *(G-9467)*

Mediapro Holdings LLC ... E ... 425 483-4700
Bothell *(G-1777)*

COMPUTER PROGRAMMING SVCS

Amdocs Qpass Inc ... F ... 206 447-6000
Seattle *(G-9391)*

AMP Engineering Services LLC ... G ... 480 512-1186
Ellensburg *(G-3183)*

Applied Navigation LLC ... G ... 503 329-3126
Bothell *(G-1821)*

August Systems Inc ... E ... 509 468-2988
Spokane *(G-12127)*

Avaya Inc ... C ... 425 881-7544
Bellevue *(G-802)*

Biblesoft Inc ... F ... 206 824-0547
Des Moines *(G-2929)*

Career Development Software ... F ... 360 696-3529
Vancouver *(G-14099)*

CCS Computer Systems Inc ... F ... 425 672-4806
Lynnwood *(G-6089)*

Coastal Software & Consulting ... G ... 360 891-6174
Vancouver *(G-14127)*

Computer Human Interaction LLC ... E ... 425 282-6900
Tukwila *(G-13714)*

Congruent Software (usa) Inc ... D ... 425 460-0172
Bellevue *(G-861)*

Constructivision Inc ... G ... 425 741-4413
Mill Creek *(G-6504)*

Crema Development LLC ... G ... 360 918-6978
Olympia *(G-7260)*

Descartes Systems (usa) LLC ... F ... 206 812-7874
Seattle *(G-9825)*

Desema Company ... G ... 425 202-7572
Redmond *(G-8438)*

Digital Product Studio LLC ... G ... 206 484-8439
Seattle *(G-9829)*

Eduongo Inc ... F ... 206 451-7325
Bellevue *(G-892)*

Enhanced Software Products Inc ... E ... 509 534-1514
Spokane Valley *(G-12693)*

Far Star Products ... G ... 360 604-0080
Vancouver *(G-14222)*

Flying Lab Software LLC ... F ... 206 272-9815
Seattle *(G-10009)*

Global Software LLC ... F ... 425 822-3140
Bothell *(G-1861)*

Hidden Path Entertainment Inc ... E ... 425 452-7284
Bellevue *(G-945)*

Hunt Hosted Solutions ... G ... 425 222-0098
Fall City *(G-3702)*

Infinetix Corp ... F ... 509 922-5629
Spokane Valley *(G-12739)*

Infoharvest Inc ... G ... 206 686-2729
Seattle *(G-10233)*

Infometrix Inc ... F ... 425 402-1450
Bothell *(G-1768)*

Krimsten Publishing LLC ... G ... 509 786-7978
Prosser *(G-8047)*

Lenco Mobile Inc ... D ... 800 557-4148
Seattle *(G-10402)*

M I S Construction Software ... G ... 425 882-3027
Kirkland *(G-5389)*

Microquill Software Publishing ... G ... 425 827-7200
Kirkland *(G-5401)*

Microstar Laboratories Inc ... E ... 425 453-2345
Redmond *(G-8585)*

Moxie Software Cim Corp ... D ... 425 467-5000
Bellevue *(G-1018)*

Nbk Associates Inc ... G ... 216 408-8685
Kirkland *(G-5408)*

Oak Bay Technologies Inc ... G ... 360 437-0718
Port Ludlow *(G-7771)*

Pixel Planet Inc ... G ... 206 669-7371
Seattle *(G-10816)*

Ptc Inc ... E ... 425 455-1930
Bellevue *(G-1087)*

R K I ... G ... 360 876-0937
Port Orchard *(G-7844)*

Racer Mate Inc ... E ... 206 524-7392
Seattle *(G-10912)*

Rleyh Software LLC ... G ... 425 837-4643
Issaquah *(G-4469)*

RY Investments Inc ... G ... 360 701-1261
Lacey *(G-5583)*

Siemens Med Solutions USA Inc ... C ... 425 392-9180
Issaquah *(G-4475)*

Software Planning ... G ... 509 522-1620
Walla Walla *(G-14871)*

Source Dynamics Inc ... G ... 425 557-3630
Issaquah *(G-4481)*

Suntower Systems ... F ... 206 878-0578
Des Moines *(G-2947)*

Tahoma Technology Inc ... G ... 206 393-0909
Seattle *(G-11259)*

Talentwise Inc ... B ... 425 974-8863
Bothell *(G-1799)*

Threepenny Software LLC ... G ... 206 675-1518
Seattle *(G-11298)*

TNT Software Inc ... F ... 360 546-0878
Vancouver *(G-14641)*

Triadd Software Corporation ... G ... 425 643-3700
Bellevue *(G-1202)*

Trulife Inc ... C ... 360 697-5656
Poulsbo *(G-8012)*

Vertek Ois Inc ... G ... 425 455-9921
Spokane Valley *(G-12929)*

Washington Schl Info Proc Coop ... C ... 425 349-6600
Everett *(G-3651)*

Wftpd Inc ... G ... 206 428-1991
Woodinville *(G-15404)*

Wildtangent Inc ... D ... 425 497-4500
Redmond *(G-8715)*

COMPUTER PROGRAMMING SVCS: Custom

Concur Technologies Inc ... A ... 425 590-5000
Bellevue *(G-860)*

Foof LLC ... G ... 425 260-8897
Cle Elum *(G-2666)*

COMPUTER RELATED MAINTENANCE SVCS

Cray Inc ... A ... 206 701-2000
Seattle *(G-9751)*

Magnolia Desktop Computing LLC ... G ... 206 282-7161
Seattle *(G-10467)*

Portrait Displays Inc ... F ... 206 420-7514
Edmonds *(G-3144)*

COMPUTER RELATED SVCS, NEC

Avocent ... G ... 425 398-0294
Bothell *(G-1749)*

COMPUTER SOFTWARE DEVELOPMENT

Alitheon Inc ... F ... 888 606-7445
Bellevue *(G-784)*

All Wave Innovations Inc ... G ... 509 308-7230
Benton City *(G-1600)*

ARS Nova Software ... G ... 425 869-0625
Redmond *(G-8386)*

Attachmate Corporation ... B ... 206 217-7100
Seattle *(G-9458)*

Attachmate Intl Sls Corp ... G ... 206 217-7500
Seattle *(G-9459)*

Author-It Software Corporation ... F ... 888 999-1021
Seattle *(G-9466)*

Bob Bracht Llc ... G ... 206 678-5168
Lake Forest Park *(G-5608)*

Byteware LLC ... G ... 503 914-8020
Woodinville *(G-15201)*

Candela Technologies Inc ... G ... 360 380-1618
Ferndale *(G-3822)*

Circle Systems Inc ... G ... 206 682-3783
Seattle *(G-9685)*

PRODUCT

Employee Codes: A=Over 500 employees, B=251-500
C=101-250, D=51-100, E=20-50, F=10-19, G=2-9

2019 Washington
Manufacturers Register

929

Comtronic Systems LLC ....F 509 573-4300
Cle Elum *(G-2662)*
Dealer Info Systems Corp ....D 360 733-7610
Bellingham *(G-1320)*
Dwight Company LLC ....G 360 262-9844
Chehalis *(G-2490)*
E L F Software Distributors ....G 360 577-6163
Longview *(G-5908)*
Energy Efficiency Systems Corp ....E 360 835-7838
Washougal *(G-14953)*
Expert Computer Tech Inc ....G 360 736-7000
Centralia *(G-2401)*
Express Imaging Systems LLC ....F 206 720-1798
Renton *(G-8796)*
Faithlife Corporation ....C 360 685-2300
Bellingham *(G-1342)*
Global Studios Consulting LLC ....E 425 223-5291
Bellevue *(G-929)*
Graphicode Inc ....E 360 282-4888
Snohomish *(G-11915)*
Hash Inc ....F 360 750-0042
Vancouver *(G-14287)*
Incontrol Systems Corp ....G 425 424-9707
Everett *(G-3514)*
Infosoft Solutions Inc ....G 360 738-3060
Bellingham *(G-1377)*
Intuitive Mfg Systems Inc ....D 425 821-0740
Kirkland *(G-5370)*
Jj 206 LLC ....G 206 453-0186
Seattle *(G-10297)*
Kennewick Computer Company ....G 509 371-0600
Richland *(G-9018)*
Leidos Inc ....E 425 267-5600
Lynnwood *(G-6157)*
Leidos Inc ....G 360 394-8870
Poulsbo *(G-7975)*
Lumedx Corporation ....D 425 450-9774
Bellevue *(G-991)*
Magnapro Business Systems Inc ....G 206 280-6222
Edmonds *(G-3131)*
Microsoft Corporation ....A 425 882-8080
Redmond *(G-8580)*
Multico Rating Systems ....F 206 357-3928
Seattle *(G-10569)*
National Management Software ....E 509 327-0192
Spokane *(G-12403)*
Northwest Technologies ....G 206 528-5353
Seattle *(G-10652)*
Peach Fuzzer LLC ....F 206 453-0339
Seattle *(G-10775)*
Portrait Displays Inc ....F 206 420-7514
Edmonds *(G-3144)*
Precision Shapes Nw LLC ....G 206 605-4396
Seattle *(G-10852)*
Quadient Data USA Inc ....D 206 443-0765
Seattle *(G-10898)*
Raosoft Inc ....G 206 523-9278
Seattle *(G-10921)*
Renaissance Learning Inc ....D 360 944-8996
Vancouver *(G-14543)*
Shared Healthcare Systems Inc ....E 360 299-4000
Anacortes *(G-166)*
Soph-Ware Associates Inc ....F 509 467-0668
Spokane *(G-12512)*
Splunk Inc ....G 206 430-5200
Seattle *(G-11169)*
Starcom Computer Corporation ....F 425 486-6464
Bothell *(G-1797)*
Systematic Designs Intl ....F 360 944-9890
Vancouver *(G-14623)*
Thomas Grange Holdings Inc ....F 678 921-0499
Seattle *(G-11295)*
Timbersoft Inc ....F 360 750-5575
Vancouver *(G-14640)*
Tincan Studio LLC ....G 559 906-3521
Lynnwood *(G-6210)*
Transact Communications Inc ....F 425 977-2100
Lynnwood *(G-6212)*
Virtual Education Software Inc ....F 509 891-7219
Spokane Valley *(G-12931)*
Woobox LLC ....G 360 450-5200
Vancouver *(G-14697)*
Zombie Inc ....E 206 623-9655
Bainbridge Island *(G-685)*

COMPUTER SOFTWARE DEVELOPMENT & APPLICATIONS

Alphawave Systems ....G 719 888-9283
Vancouver *(G-14024)*
APM Games LLC ....G 512 961-6515
Vancouver *(G-14038)*
Astronics Cstm Ctrl Cncpts Inc ....D 206 575-0933
Kent *(G-4795)*
Blucapp Inc ....F 206 629-8887
Seattle *(G-9546)*
Bluepenguin Software Inc ....G 561 459-5393
Sequim *(G-11615)*
Builder Box LLC ....E 206 778-4753
Seattle *(G-9596)*
Certifly LLC ....G 888 415-9119
Seattle *(G-9660)*
Coach Cheetah Inc ....G 206 914-8313
Seattle *(G-9703)*
Crescent Moon Studios Inc ....G 509 322-7730
Riverside *(G-9124)*
Crimpd LLC ....G 847 436-0433
Seattle *(G-9753)*
Custom Computer Creat CCC LLC ....G 800 295-3381
Seattle *(G-9766)*
Dinesync Inc ....G 206 620-2550
Seattle *(G-9832)*
Eclipse Technology LLC ....G 406 270-6366
Seattle *(G-9875)*
Energy Arrow ....G 267 932-7769
Stanwood *(G-12969)*
Energysavvy Inc ....E 206 462-2206
Seattle *(G-9926)*
Garjen Corp ....G 253 862-6140
Bonney Lake *(G-1724)*
Harbor Vascular Inc ....G 425 420-6009
Sammamish *(G-9215)*
I2nnovations LLC ....G 425 298-3143
Sammamish *(G-9218)*
Itraq Inc ....G 844 694-8727
Redmond *(G-8516)*
Itron Inc ....B 509 924-9900
Liberty Lake *(G-5838)*
Juntlabs LLC ....G 253 987-1750
Federal Way *(G-3747)*
Librofm Inc ....G 206 730-2463
Seattle *(G-10413)*
Mainstem Inc ....F 844 623-4084
Seattle *(G-10469)*
Momentum Interactive LLC ....G 915 203-5349
Bellingham *(G-1440)*
Nexus Life Cycle MGT LLC ....G 541 400-0765
Stevenson *(G-13016)*
Nintendo Software Technology ....E 425 497-7500
Redmond *(G-8596)*
Random Walk Group LLC ....G 206 724-3621
Olympia *(G-7377)*
Reliance Inc ....F 615 218-3929
Redmond *(G-8647)*
Road-Iq LLC ....F 360 733-4151
Bellingham *(G-1518)*
Sarangsoft LLC ....G 425 378-3890
Bellevue *(G-1114)*
Selah Springs LLC ....G 206 714-6068
Bellevue *(G-1123)*
Simply Augmented Inc ....G 206 771-9774
Seattle *(G-11114)*
Starform Inc ....G 206 446-9657
Seattle *(G-11182)*
Starpath Corporation ....G 206 783-1414
Seattle *(G-11184)*
Tova Company ....F 800 729-2886
Freeland *(G-4038)*
Universe Builders Inc ....G 206 390-4313
Seattle *(G-11378)*
Wizards of Coast LLC ....B 425 226-6500
Renton *(G-8949)*
Zsolutionz LLC ....G 425 502-6970
Sammamish *(G-9262)*

COMPUTER SOFTWARE SYSTEMS ANALYSIS & DESIGN: Custom

A & E Systems ....G 509 886-1092
East Wenatchee *(G-3005)*
Aynano Technology LLC ....G 208 596-9865
Pullman *(G-8084)*
Cellar Door Media LLC ....G 253 732-9560
Tacoma *(G-13230)*
Coherent Knowledge Systems LLC ....G 206 519-6410
Mercer Island *(G-6458)*
Datapark LLC ....E 360 224-2157
Sumas *(G-13043)*
Fluentpro Software Corporation ....G 855 358-3688
Redmond *(G-8462)*
GE Healthcare Inc ....B 206 622-9558
Seattle *(G-10055)*
Gekko Corporation ....G 425 679-9188
Bellevue *(G-922)*
General Computers Inc ....G 425 405-0588
Bellevue *(G-923)*
Ieg7 Inc ....G 206 501-6193
Auburn *(G-470)*
Onsite Computer Services ....G 360 650-1079
Bellingham *(G-1480)*
Pat-Co Inc ....G 206 937-8927
Seattle *(G-10765)*
Professional Practice Systems ....F 253 531-8944
Roy *(G-9164)*
Speechace LLC ....G 425 241-3033
Seattle *(G-11167)*
Stanford Technology Inc ....G 509 638-1191
Spokane *(G-12525)*
Trillium Custom Software Inc ....G 425 397-8000
Snohomish *(G-11994)*
Vector Blue Services LLC ....F 425 219-2528
Bellevue *(G-1213)*

COMPUTER SOFTWARE WRITERS

Global Software Systems Inc ....G 425 427-8215
Issaquah *(G-4421)*
Griptonite Inc ....C 425 825-6800
Kirkland *(G-5355)*
Tested Field Systems LLC ....G 206 453-4851
Seattle *(G-11282)*

COMPUTER STORAGE DEVICES, NEC

Advanced Digital Info Corp ....B 425 881-8004
Redmond *(G-8370)*
Allsop Inc ....D 360 734-9090
Bellingham *(G-1244)*
Avere Systems Inc ....D 425 706-7507
Redmond *(G-8392)*
Benjamin Anderson ....G 206 228-8174
Seattle *(G-9512)*
E McS2 ....G 971 295-4641
Port Ludlow *(G-7765)*
EMC Corporation ....D 206 623-1227
Seattle *(G-9909)*
EMC Corporation ....F 425 378-9209
Bellevue *(G-895)*
EMC Nursing Services ....G 425 346-5982
Everett *(G-3459)*
Ergo Design Inc ....G 360 427-5779
Olympia *(G-7278)*
Expert Computer Tech Inc ....G 360 736-7000
Centralia *(G-2401)*
Fmj Storage Inc ....G 206 605-1394
Woodinville *(G-15244)*
Grubstake EMC ....G 509 775-2041
Republic *(G-8957)*
Hewlett-Packard Company ....C 800 325-5372
Vancouver *(G-14294)*
James Clay ....G 360 891-8147
Vancouver *(G-14333)*
Jmtek LLC ....E 425 251-9400
Kent *(G-4969)*
Optistor Technologies Inc ....F 425 283-5227
Bellevue *(G-1052)*
Pohlman Knowles ....G 206 933-7450
Seattle *(G-10827)*
Quantum Corporation ....D 425 201-1400
Bellevue *(G-1089)*
Quantum Solutions Inc ....G 360 491-0757
Lacey *(G-5580)*
Qumulo Inc ....D 206 260-3588
Seattle *(G-10907)*
Rsa The Security EMC ....G 781 515-5000
Bellevue *(G-1109)*
Valtech ....G 360 779-6748
Poulsbo *(G-8016)*

COMPUTER STORAGE UNITS: Auxiliary

Isilon Systems LLC ....B 206 315-7500
Seattle *(G-10260)*
Leancode Inc ....F 425 533-5219
Redmond *(G-8532)*

COMPUTER SYSTEMS ANALYSIS & DESIGN

Add Corporation ....D 206 452-7498
Normandy Park *(G-7089)*
Alphawave Systems ....G 719 888-9283
Vancouver *(G-14024)*

PRODUCT SECTION

CONCRETE PRDTS

Space Rock It Inc .... G 206 395-8383
  Seattle *(G-11164)*

COMPUTER TERMINALS

Hasco Inc .... G 425 643-2525
  Bellevue *(G-937)*
Igt Global Solutions Corp .... E 360 412-2140
  Lacey *(G-5559)*
Leyda Computers .... G 425 335-1273
  Lake Stevens *(G-5655)*

COMPUTER TIME-SHARING

Digital Impressions Inc .... G 206 443-1234
  Seattle *(G-9828)*
Pamar Systems Inc .... G 360 992-4120
  Vancouver *(G-14477)*

COMPUTER TRAINING SCHOOLS

Media Matrix Digital Center .... G 360 693-6455
  Vancouver *(G-14408)*
Nbk Associates Inc .... G 216 408-8685
  Kirkland *(G-5408)*

COMPUTER-AIDED DESIGN SYSTEMS SVCS

De Kleine Machine Company LLC .... G 509 832-1108
  Prosser *(G-8038)*
Softsource LLC .... G 360 676-0999
  Bellingham *(G-1545)*

COMPUTER-AIDED ENGINEERING SYSTEMS SVCS

Tuigis Tek LLC .... G 360 943-9133
  Olympia *(G-7415)*

COMPUTER-AIDED SYSTEM SVCS

Apana Inc .... F 360 746-2276
  Bellingham *(G-1249)*
Barn2door Inc .... G 206 459-4338
  Seattle *(G-9493)*

COMPUTERS, NEC

Allview Services Inc .... G 425 483-6103
  Lynnwood *(G-6072)*
Amy Stevens .... G 206 706-2528
  Seattle *(G-9401)*
Armstrong & Associates LLC .... G 253 548-6148
  Kennewick *(G-4619)*
Assurware Inc .... G 509 531-8336
  Richland *(G-8968)*
Atomrock Llc .... G 425 281-2371
  Issaquah *(G-4384)*
Bang & Jack Montgomery .... G 360 403-9444
  Lynnwood *(G-6081)*
Christian Hamilton .... G 360 442-4900
  Longview *(G-5899)*
Constant Computer .... G 253 227-0532
  Tacoma *(G-13239)*
Corban Tech LLC .... G 253 353-0849
  Tacoma *(G-13242)*
County of Asotin .... F 509 758-1668
  Clarkston *(G-2628)*
Cray Inc .... A 206 701-2000
  Seattle *(G-9751)*
Electronic Systems Tech Inc .... F 509 735-9092
  Kennewick *(G-4657)*
Engineering Solutions Inc .... F 206 241-9395
  Renton *(G-8795)*
Expert Computer Tech Inc .... G 360 736-7000
  Centralia *(G-2401)*
General Computers Inc .... G 425 405-0588
  Bellevue *(G-923)*
Grays Harbor Electronics .... G 360 532-3474
  Hoquiam *(G-4338)*
Honeywell International Inc .... C 425 251-9511
  Renton *(G-8821)*
Itron Inc .... E 509 924-9900
  Spokane Valley *(G-12748)*
Itron Manufacturing Inc .... E 509 924-9900
  Spokane Valley *(G-12749)*
James Moore .... G 206 799-0399
  Seattle *(G-10283)*
Key Tronic Corporation .... C 509 928-8000
  Spokane Valley *(G-12767)*
Kingtime LLC .... G 206 375-7422
  Renton *(G-8837)*

M K Hansen Company .... G 509 884-1396
  East Wenatchee *(G-3023)*
M M Enterprises .... G 206 463-1927
  Vashon *(G-14731)*
Meet Your Price Inc .... G 360 260-2066
  Battle Ground *(G-720)*
Michael Blackwell .... G 253 759-2906
  Tacoma *(G-13410)*
Micro Standard .... G 425 882-1722
  Redmond *(G-8557)*
Patrick Clarke .... G 206 365-8804
  Seattle *(G-10770)*
Phytec America LLC .... F 206 780-9047
  Bainbridge Island *(G-658)*
Rugid Computer .... G 360 866-0909
  Olympia *(G-7389)*
Sensitronics LLC .... G 360 766-8800
  Bow *(G-1932)*
Skinner Communications .... G 360 980-4906
  Vancouver *(G-14590)*
Sound Services .... G 360 920-3435
  Bellingham *(G-1546)*
Stadelman Fruit Frenchman .... G 509 829-5145
  Zillah *(G-15760)*
Storeanywherecom Inc .... G 425 643-3268
  Bellevue *(G-1159)*
Voicelever Inc .... D 425 864-7676
  Redmond *(G-8706)*

COMPUTERS, NEC, WHOLESALE

Hewlett-Packard Company .... C 800 325-5372
  Vancouver *(G-14294)*
Opticon Inc .... E 425 651-2120
  Renton *(G-8865)*
Reynolds and Reynolds Company .... E 425 985-0194
  Edmonds *(G-3146)*
US Micro Pc Inc .... G 425 462-7300
  Bellevue *(G-1210)*

COMPUTERS, PERIPH & SOFTWARE, WHLSE: Personal & Home Entrtn

Allsop Inc .... D 360 734-9090
  Bellingham *(G-1244)*

COMPUTERS, PERIPHERALS & SOFTWARE, WHOLESALE: Printers

Kemeera Incorporated .... E 206 582-1062
  Seattle *(G-10335)*

COMPUTERS, PERIPHERALS & SOFTWARE, WHOLESALE: Software

Career Development Software .... F 360 696-3529
  Vancouver *(G-14099)*
Gekko Corporation .... G 425 679-9188
  Bellevue *(G-922)*
Krantz News Service Inc .... G 253 857-6590
  Gig Harbor *(G-4128)*
Magnavon Business Systems Inc .... G 206 280-6222
  Edmonds *(G-3131)*
Ontario Systems LLC .... C 360 256-7358
  Vancouver *(G-14452)*
Pamar Systems Inc .... G 360 992-4120
  Vancouver *(G-14477)*
Securitay Inc .... G 425 392-0203
  Issaquah *(G-4472)*
Stretching Charts Inc .... E 253 536-4922
  Tacoma *(G-13528)*
T T I Acquisition Corp .... F 509 358-2036
  Liberty Lake *(G-5861)*
Tova Company .... F 800 729-2886
  Freeland *(G-4038)*
Virtual Stream .... G 206 938-3886
  Seattle *(G-11422)*

COMPUTERS: Mini

Elarm Inc .... G 206 395-9604
  Seattle *(G-9892)*
Maren-Go Solutions Corporation .... G 217 506-2749
  Vancouver *(G-14393)*

COMPUTERS: Personal

Adams Apple Cider LLC .... G 509 933-1025
  Ellensburg *(G-3180)*
Apple Brooke LLC .... G 509 922-0696
  Spokane Valley *(G-12623)*

Apple City Electric LLC .... G 509 782-2334
  Cashmere *(G-2315)*
Apple Earthworks LLC .... G 253 847-3755
  Graham *(G-4216)*
Apple For Hire .... G 206 722-3205
  Seattle *(G-9411)*
Apple of My Pie LLC .... G 509 860-8881
  East Wenatchee *(G-3007)*
Apple Street L L C .... G 253 988-4120
  Tacoma *(G-13177)*
Bad Apple .... G 360 899-5183
  Mount Vernon *(G-6773)*
Carburetors Unlimited Inc .... G 253 833-4106
  Auburn *(G-401)*
Chris Barber Apple .... G 360 875-8112
  Raymond *(G-8345)*
Golden Apple Inc .... G 253 473-7880
  Tacoma *(G-13316)*
HP Inc .... F 650 857-1501
  Seattle *(G-10190)*
Lisa Appel .... G 360 521-5472
  Vancouver *(G-14378)*
Michael P Appleby .... G 360 652-1178
  Stanwood *(G-12978)*
Moms Carmel Apples & More LLC .... G 509 515-8153
  Kennewick *(G-4696)*
Monument Apples LLC .... G 509 787-5700
  Quincy *(G-8305)*
P Apple LLC .... G 206 290-9898
  Everett *(G-3561)*
Poison Apple Tacoma .... G 253 304-1874
  Tacoma *(G-13469)*
Sammamish .... G 425 295-7300
  Sammamish *(G-9245)*
Washington State Apple Comm .... G 509 663-9600
  Wenatchee *(G-15083)*
Wenatchee Red Apple Flyers .... G 509 881-7884
  East Wenatchee *(G-3035)*

CONCRETE BUILDING PRDTS WHOLESALERS

Atlas Construction Spc Co Inc .... E 206 283-2000
  Seattle *(G-9455)*
Barefoote Concrete Inc .... G 509 879-3736
  Spokane Valley *(G-12636)*
Cascade Concrete Industries .... F 360 757-2900
  Burlington *(G-2141)*
Central Pre-Mix Concrete Co .... A 509 534-6221
  Spokane Valley *(G-12654)*
Concrete Shop Inc .... F 360 573-5775
  Vancouver *(G-14145)*
D & S Rock LLC .... F 509 877-7400
  Toppenish *(G-13665)*
East West General Inc .... G 360 673-6404
  Kalama *(G-4497)*

CONCRETE CURING & HARDENING COMPOUNDS

Mad Concrete Cutting & Coring .... G 206 367-0263
  Lynnwood *(G-6161)*

CONCRETE PLANTS

Miles Sand & Gravel Company .... F 360 427-0946
  Shelton *(G-11714)*

CONCRETE PRDTS

Advanced Cement Tech LLC .... G 360 332-7060
  Blaine *(G-1657)*
Ameron International Corp .... E 909 944-4100
  Vancouver *(G-14031)*
Atlas Construction Spc Co Inc .... E 206 283-2000
  Seattle *(G-9455)*
Barefoote Concrete Inc .... G 509 879-3736
  Spokane Valley *(G-12636)*
Bernard Manufacturing .... F 206 242-4017
  Burien *(G-2093)*
Bethlehem Construction Inc .... E 509 782-1001
  Cashmere *(G-2317)*
C T Sales Inc .... G 253 874-8737
  Federal Way *(G-3719)*
Chelan Concrete Inc .... F 509 682-2915
  Chelan *(G-2549)*
Concrete Creations .... G 509 826-5409
  OMAK *(G-7438)*
Concrete Products Co Ore LLC .... E 360 834-3459
  Camas *(G-2242)*

Employee Codes: A=Over 500 employees, B=251-500
C=101-250, D=51-100, E=20-50, F=10-19, G=2-9

Concrete Products Inc.....G..... 253 864-2774
Puyallup *(G-8136)*
CPM Development Corporation.....B..... 509 534-6221
Spokane Valley *(G-12668)*
Creative Concrete Concepts.....G..... 425 466-4479
Carnation *(G-2292)*
Curtiss R Grenz.....E..... 509 893-0317
Greenacres *(G-4296)*
Eucon Corporation.....F..... 509 529-6400
Walla Walla *(G-14803)*
Forterra Inc.....G..... 360 943-1600
Olympia *(G-7291)*
Gary Merlino Cnstr Co Inc.....F..... 206 763-2134
Seattle *(G-10050)*
Glacier Northwest Inc.....E..... 425 486-3281
Seattle *(G-10076)*
Glacier Northwest Inc.....G..... 360 896-8922
Vancouver *(G-14255)*
Hanson Aggregates LLC.....F..... 360 795-3221
Cathlamet *(G-2368)*
In Cascade Concrete Industries.....G..... 425 747-0956
Bellevue *(G-955)*
James Hardie Building Pdts Inc.....D..... 253 847-8700
Tacoma *(G-13355)*
Mikron Industries Inc.....C..... 253 854-8020
Kent *(G-5011)*
Milestone Products Co.....F..... 425 882-1987
Redmond *(G-8589)*
Oldcastle Apg.....G..... 509 926-8235
Spokane Valley *(G-12816)*
Oldcastle Precast Inc.....D..... 253 839-3500
Auburn *(G-517)*
Pacific Precast Inc.....F..... 360 750-0099
Vancouver *(G-14470)*
Pacific Rock Products LLC.....E..... 360 254-7770
Vancouver *(G-14474)*
Panelsuppliers.....G..... 253 217-1668
Pacific *(G-7537)*
Peninsula Tanks Inc.....G..... 360 683-4714
Sequim *(G-11659)*
Quanex Screens LLC.....F..... 360 748-9201
Chehalis *(G-2528)*
Schneider Drainfield Des.....G..... 360 758-7353
Lummi Island *(G-5993)*
Stonehenge.....G..... 425 879-9574
Sultan *(G-13040)*
Ultrablock Inc.....E..... 360 694-0141
Vancouver *(G-14655)*
Up To Grade Concrete Products.....F..... 253 845-3677
Puyallup *(G-8267)*
W R Meadows Inc.....G..... 707 745-6666
Kent *(G-5204)*
Wilbert Spokane Vault Company.....E..... 509 248-1984
Yakima *(G-15708)*

CONCRETE PRDTS, PRECAST, NEC

Absolute Concreteworks LLC.....G..... 360 297-5055
Port Townsend *(G-7859)*
Ameron International Corp.....E..... 909 944-4100
Vancouver *(G-14028)*
Basalite Building Products LLC.....E..... 253 964-5000
Dupont *(G-2955)*
Bodes Precast Inc.....F..... 360 354-3912
Everson *(G-3668)*
Cascade Concrete.....G..... 360 354-8901
Lynden *(G-6005)*
Concrete Shop Inc.....F..... 360 573-5775
Vancouver *(G-14145)*
Custom Concrete Casting Corp.....F..... 425 333-4737
Carnation *(G-2293)*
Diamond Concrete Products.....G..... 360 659-6277
Arlington *(G-228)*
East West General Inc.....G..... 360 673-6404
Kalama *(G-4497)*
Eldorado Stone LLC.....E..... 425 349-4107
Everett *(G-3453)*
Encon United Company.....F..... 360 834-3459
Camas *(G-2248)*
H2 Pre- Cast Inc.....D..... 509 884-6644
East Wenatchee *(G-3018)*
Master Precaster Inc.....G..... 253 770-9119
Puyallup *(G-8183)*
Mutual Materials Company.....G..... 425 353-9686
Marysville *(G-6362)*
Mutual Materials Company.....F..... 360 573-5683
Vancouver *(G-14426)*
Mutual Materials Company.....G..... 253 838-0803
Auburn *(G-502)*
Northwest Precast Llc.....E..... 253 770-9119
Puyallup *(G-8207)*
Pc2 LLC.....G..... 360 921-8066
Battle Ground *(G-730)*
Precast By Design Inc.....G..... 509 292-2988
Elk *(G-3175)*
Quality Concrete Products Inc.....E..... 425 355-5510
Mukilteo *(G-6969)*
Shope Enterprises Inc.....E..... 253 848-1551
Puyallup *(G-8254)*
Spilker Precast LLC.....G..... 509 487-2261
Spokane *(G-12514)*
Washington Precast Products.....G..... 360 598-1631
Indianola *(G-4374)*
Western Materials Inc.....D..... 509 547-3301
Pasco *(G-7652)*
White Block Co Inc.....E..... 509 534-0651
Spokane Valley *(G-12937)*

CONCRETE: Dry Mixture

Jet Set Northwest Inc.....G..... 206 762-0434
Tukwila *(G-13756)*
Quikrete Companies LLC.....E..... 253 396-9996
Tacoma *(G-13486)*

CONCRETE: Ready-Mixed

A A A Redi Mix II Inc.....F..... 509 765-1923
Moses Lake *(G-6677)*
Angeles Concrete Products Inc.....G..... 360 681-5429
Sequim *(G-11611)*
Apex Mobile Mix LLC.....G..... 360 304-8797
Chehalis *(G-2466)*
Atlas Concrete Products Inc.....F..... 360 736-7642
Centralia *(G-2384)*
Bayside Redi-Mix.....G..... 360 426-4987
Shelton *(G-11682)*
Bayview Redi Mix Inc.....G..... 360 875-9993
Raymond *(G-8342)*
Bayview Redi Mix Inc.....G..... 360 482-3444
Elma *(G-3241)*
Bayview Redi Mix Inc.....E..... 360 533-7372
Aberdeen *(G-5)*
Best Way Concrete.....G..... 360 825-5494
Enumclaw *(G-3279)*
Cadman Inc.....B..... 425 867-1234
Redmond *(G-8413)*
Cadman (seattle) Inc.....C..... 425 316-9100
Mill Creek *(G-6502)*
Cadman Holding Company Inc.....G..... 425 868-1234
Redmond *(G-8415)*
Calportland.....G..... 206 764-3000
Seattle *(G-9609)*
Calportland Company.....G..... 360 423-8112
Longview *(G-5893)*
Calportland Company.....D..... 206 764-3075
Seattle *(G-9610)*
Calportland Company.....D..... 360 892-5100
Woodland *(G-15422)*
Calportland Company.....E..... 360 892-5100
Vancouver *(G-14091)*
Calportland Company.....G..... 253 912-8500
Dupont *(G-2957)*
Cascade Mobile Mix.....G..... 253 833-1956
Graham *(G-4220)*
Case Mix Analysis Inc.....G..... 206 285-2576
Seattle *(G-9644)*
Cemex Cnstr Mtls Fla LLC.....G..... 425 513-6651
Everett *(G-3413)*
Cemex Cnstr Mtls PCF LLC.....G..... 425 252-8600
Everett *(G-3414)*
Cemex Materials LLC.....E..... 360 254-7770
Vancouver *(G-14111)*
Central Pre-Mix Concrete Co.....A..... 509 534-6221
Spokane Valley *(G-12654)*
Chelan Concrete Inc.....F..... 509 682-2915
Chelan *(G-2549)*
Clark Site Mix Con Spokane LLC.....G..... 509 991-7730
Spokane *(G-12182)*
Cm2931 LLC.....E..... 253 447-7537
Fife *(G-3944)*
Columbia Asphalt & Gravel Inc.....G..... 509 457-3654
Wapato *(G-14913)*
Columbia Ready Mix Inc.....D..... 509 453-2063
Parker *(G-7548)*
Colville Valley Concrete Corp.....E..... 509 684-2534
Colville *(G-2747)*
Concrete & Aggregate Supply Co.....G..... 253 853-2887
Nine Mile Falls *(G-7070)*
Connell Sand & Gravel Inc.....F..... 509 545-4066
Pasco *(G-7567)*
Cowden Inc.....D..... 360 592-4200
Bellingham *(G-1309)*
CPM Development Corporation.....D..... 509 248-2041
Yakima *(G-15539)*
CPM Development Corporation.....F..... 509 865-2975
Toppenish *(G-13664)*
CPM Development Corporation.....B..... 509 534-6221
Spokane Valley *(G-12668)*
CPM Development Corporation.....E..... 509 536-3355
Spokane Valley *(G-12669)*
CPM Development Corporation.....G..... 509 932-4525
Mattawa *(G-6405)*
CPM Development Corporation.....D..... 509 837-5171
Sunnyside *(G-13118)*
CPM Development Corporation.....G..... 509 762-5366
Moses Lake *(G-6699)*
CPM Development Corporation.....G..... 509 754-5287
Ephrata *(G-3332)*
CPM Development Corporation.....G..... 509 663-5141
Wenatchee *(G-15024)*
CPM Development Corporation.....G..... 509 886-4853
Wenatchee *(G-15090)*
CPM Development Corporation.....G..... 509 488-2614
Othello *(G-7493)*
Dinners Ready.....G..... 425 337-7955
Mill Creek *(G-6507)*
DTI Ready Mix Company.....G..... 509 937-4683
Valley *(G-13991)*
Ferndale Ready-Mix.....F..... 360 354-1400
Lynden *(G-6017)*
Ferndale Ready-Mix.....F..... 360 384-8087
Ferndale *(G-3843)*
Fred Hill Materials.....F..... 360 779-4431
Sequim *(G-11635)*
Gary Merlino Cnstr Co Inc.....F..... 206 763-2134
Seattle *(G-10050)*
Gary Merlino Cnstr Co Inc.....B..... 206 763-9552
Seattle *(G-10049)*
Glacier Northwest Inc.....G..... 425 486-3281
Bothell *(G-1766)*
Glacier Northwest Inc.....F..... 360 694-9420
Vancouver *(G-14253)*
Glacier Northwest Inc.....G..... 360 694-1627
Vancouver *(G-14254)*
Glacier Northwest Inc.....G..... 360 896-8922
Vancouver *(G-14255)*
Glacier Northwest Inc.....F..... 360 736-1131
Centralia *(G-2403)*
Glacier Northwest Inc.....E..... 360 892-5100
Vancouver *(G-14256)*
Glacier Northwest Inc.....F..... 206 764-3075
Seattle *(G-10077)*
Glacier Northwest Inc.....D..... 253 912-8500
Dupont *(G-2964)*
Glacier Northwest Inc.....E..... 425 486-3281
Seattle *(G-10076)*
Glacier Northwest Inc.....E..... 425 888-9795
Snoqualmie *(G-12013)*
Godbey Red-E-Mix Concrete Inc.....G..... 509 689-2415
Brewster *(G-2016)*
Hanson Lehigh Inc.....G..... 425 867-1234
Issaquah *(G-4425)*
Hardrock Incorporated.....E..... 360 779-3700
Poulsbo *(G-7965)*
Holroyd Company Inc.....D..... 253 474-0725
Tacoma *(G-13340)*
Holroyd Company Inc.....D..... 253 627-0571
Tacoma *(G-13341)*
Holroyd Company Inc.....E..... 253 474-0725
Olympia *(G-7308)*
Interstate Concrete and Asp Co.....G..... 509 375-1021
Richland *(G-9012)*
Interstate Concrete and Asp Co.....G..... 509 529-6400
Walla Walla *(G-14824)*
Interstate Concrete and Asp Co.....G..... 509 547-2380
Prosser *(G-8043)*
Interstate Concrete and Asp Co.....E..... 509 547-2380
Pasco *(G-7593)*
Jason Thompson.....G..... 757 867-6494
Spokane *(G-12329)*
Jerry Nybo Construction Inc.....G..... 253 691-1797
Eatonville *(G-3060)*
Krieg Concrete Products Inc.....F..... 360 675-2727
Oak Harbor *(G-7156)*
Kubeshs Site Mixed Con Inc.....G..... 509 684-1381
Colville *(G-2763)*
Lafarge North America Inc.....G..... 509 893-0034
Spokane Valley *(G-12770)*
Lopez Redi Mix Inc.....G..... 360 468-2485
Lopez Island *(G-5985)*
Miles Sand & Gravel Company.....B..... 253 833-3705
Puyallup *(G-8193)*

PRODUCT SECTION

CONSTRUCTION EQPT: Finishers & Spreaders

Miles Sand & Gravel Company ....C....... 360 757-3121
  Burlington *(G-2171)*
Miles Sand & Gravel Company ....F....... 360 435-5511
  Lake Stevens *(G-5661)*
Miles Sand & Gravel Company ....E....... 253 922-9116
  Tacoma *(G-13414)*
Miles Sand & Gravel Company ....F....... 360 675-2626
  Oak Harbor *(G-7159)*
Miles Sand & Gravel Company ....E....... 360 734-1956
  Everson *(G-3682)*
Miles Sand & Gravel Company ....F....... 360 427-0946
  Shelton *(G-11714)*
Mix It Up LLC ....G....... 425 396-7345
  Snoqualmie *(G-12019)*
Okanogan Valley Concrete Inc ....G....... 509 422-3211
  Okanogan *(G-7203)*
Oldcastle Materials Inc ....E....... 253 872-9466
  Kent *(G-5042)*
Oldcastle Materials Inc ....D....... 509 926-8235
  Spokane Valley *(G-12817)*
Oldcastle Materials Inc ....F....... 509 534-6221
  Spokane Valley *(G-12818)*
Rapid Readymix Co ....G....... 509 773-5919
  Goldendale *(G-4207)*
Rapid Readymix Co ....G....... 509 493-3153
  Bingen *(G-1641)*
Rempel Bros Concrete Inc ....F....... 360 678-4622
  Coupeville *(G-2816)*
Richard Lawson Construction ....E....... 360 378-4313
  Friday Harbor *(G-4055)*
Salmon Bay Sand and Gravel Co ....D....... 206 784-1234
  Seattle *(G-11007)*
Samoa Maritime Company ....G....... 206 246-1182
  Normandy Park *(G-7098)*
Skagit Ready Mix ....G....... 360 856-0422
  Mount Vernon *(G-6840)*
Smokey Point Concrete ....F....... 360 856-0422
  Sedro Woolley *(G-11571)*
Southwest Concrete Co ....G....... 360 795-8211
  Cathlamet *(G-2375)*
Specialty Concrete ....G....... 360 577-4555
  Kelso *(G-4549)*
Speedy Mix Concrete ....G....... 253 531-3260
  Tacoma *(G-13522)*
Spokane Rock Products Inc ....F....... 509 292-2200
  Elk *(G-3177)*
Stanwood Redi-Mix Inc ....E....... 360 652-7777
  Stanwood *(G-12994)*
Stotts Construction Inc ....F....... 509 779-4987
  Curlew *(G-2847)*
Tillmans Inc ....G....... 509 633-2542
  Coulee Dam *(G-2809)*
Tim Corliss & Son Inc ....G....... 360 825-2578
  Enumclaw *(G-3324)*
Two Rivers Sand and Gravel ....G....... 509 763-3280
  Leavenworth *(G-5817)*
Whyte & Sons Incorporated ....G....... 425 885-3571
  Redmond *(G-8713)*

CONDENSERS: Heat Transfer Eqpt, Evaporative

Direct Contact LLC ....E....... 425 235-1723
  Tukwila *(G-13725)*

CONDUITS & FITTINGS: Electric

Wilson and Associates NW ....F....... 206 292-9756
  Seattle *(G-11479)*

CONFECTIONERY PRDTS WHOLESALERS

Johnson Candy Co Inc ....G....... 253 272-8504
  Tacoma *(G-13363)*

CONFECTIONS & CANDY

Ames International Inc ....D....... 253 946-4779
  Fife *(G-3932)*
Baums Candy ....G....... 509 967-9340
  Kennewick *(G-4628)*
Bright Candies ....G....... 509 525-5533
  Walla Walla *(G-14774)*
Brown & Haley ....C....... 253 620-3067
  Tacoma *(G-13210)*
Brown & Haley ....C....... 253 620-3077
  Tacoma *(G-13211)*
Brown & Haley ....C....... 253 620-3000
  Fife *(G-3940)*
Candy Fix ....G....... 253 770-8242
  Orting *(G-7475)*
Chehalis Mints Co Corp ....G....... 360 736-9899
  Centralia *(G-2392)*
Clarks Country Kitchen ....G....... 509 586-6909
  Richland *(G-8981)*
Hallett Confections ....F....... 509 484-6454
  Spokane *(G-12286)*
Jackson Yukon ....G....... 206 349-8566
  Seattle *(G-10278)*
Johnson Candy Co Inc ....G....... 253 272-8504
  Tacoma *(G-13363)*
Jonboy Caramels LLC ....G....... 206 850-4225
  Seattle *(G-10306)*
Katies Candies Inc ....F....... 360 748-8967
  Chehalis *(G-2507)*
Lucks Company ....C....... 253 383-4815
  Tacoma *(G-13391)*
Motovotano LLC ....G....... 206 363-0338
  Anacortes *(G-148)*
Mt Baker Candy Co ....G....... 360 756-0661
  Bellingham *(G-1446)*
Murphy Nathanial ....G....... 509 386-0727
  Waitsburg *(G-14756)*
Nutradried Creations LLP ....G....... 360 332-2101
  Blaine *(G-1690)*
OH Cholocolate LLC ....E....... 206 232-4974
  Mercer Island *(G-6477)*
Powers Candy and Nut Company ....F....... 509 489-1955
  Spokane *(G-12452)*
R & S Roberts Enterprises Inc ....F....... 253 333-7567
  Auburn *(G-542)*
Rh Appetizing Inc ....G....... 206 282-0776
  Seattle *(G-10960)*
Seattle Gourmet Foods Inc ....D....... 425 656-9076
  Seattle *(G-11061)*
Skiers Inc ....G....... 360 663-7777
  Enumclaw *(G-3320)*
Sutliff Candy & Promotions Co ....G....... 206 784-5212
  Seattle *(G-11233)*
Thin Dipped Almonds ....G....... 720 231-9196
  Seattle *(G-11290)*
Totally Chocolate LLC ....E....... 360 332-3900
  Blaine *(G-1706)*
Trejo Trejo Inc ....G....... 425 298-3144
  Seattle *(G-11329)*
Whitehouse Antique & Candy ....G....... 425 486-8453
  Bothell *(G-1918)*

CONFINEMENT SURVEILLANCE SYS MAINTENANCE & MONITORING SVCS

Keyking Inc ....G....... 360 977-7870
  Camas *(G-2262)*

CONNECTORS & TERMINALS: Electrical Device Uses

ABB Installation Products Inc ....E....... 206 548-1595
  Seattle *(G-9332)*
Safran Usa Inc ....E....... 425 462-8613
  Bellevue *(G-1112)*

CONNECTORS: Electrical

Best Connection LLC ....G....... 360 241-8244
  Vancouver *(G-14063)*
Wilder Technologies LLC ....G....... 360 859-3041
  Vancouver *(G-14693)*

CONNECTORS: Electronic

C&J Offshore Systems LLC ....G....... 360 293-4200
  Anacortes *(G-106)*
Cory Siverson ....G....... 425 869-8303
  Redmond *(G-8427)*
Dash Connector Technology Inc ....G....... 509 465-1903
  Spokane *(G-12218)*
Gravity Square Inc ....G....... 206 524-0063
  Seattle *(G-10111)*
Smartplug Systems LLC ....G....... 206 285-2990
  Seattle *(G-11138)*

CONNECTORS: Power, Electric

Omni Technology ....G....... 425 823-9295
  Kirkland *(G-5419)*

CONSTRUCTION & MINING MACHINERY WHOLESALERS

Advanced Traffic Products Inc ....F....... 425 347-6208
  Everett *(G-3361)*
Birch Equipment Company Inc ....E....... 360 734-5744
  Bellingham *(G-1272)*
Haven Boatworks LLC ....F....... 360 385-5727
  Port Townsend *(G-7890)*
Impact Service Corporation ....E....... 509 468-7900
  Spokane *(G-12305)*
Kono Fixed Income Fund 1511 LP ....F....... 360 686-7688
  Bellevue *(G-972)*
Pape Machinery Inc ....F....... 360 575-9959
  Kelso *(G-4541)*
Steeler Inc ....D....... 206 725-8500
  Seattle *(G-11187)*

CONSTRUCTION EQPT REPAIR SVCS

Centric Corporation ....F....... 253 833-4342
  Auburn *(G-403)*
Tim Eastman Eqp Repr Wldg LLC ....F....... 360 274-7607
  Castle Rock *(G-2354)*

CONSTRUCTION EQPT: Attachments

Elliot Attachments Inc ....G....... 360 636-2203
  Kelso *(G-4524)*
Tim Eastman Eqp Repr Wldg LLC ....F....... 360 274-7607
  Castle Rock *(G-2354)*

CONSTRUCTION EQPT: Backhoes, Tractors, Cranes & Similar Eqpt

D W Pape Inc ....G....... 509 586-0522
  Kennewick *(G-4652)*
Ed Ka Manufacturing Inc ....G....... 509 635-1521
  Garfield *(G-4068)*
Neil F Lampson Inc ....C....... 509 586-0411
  Kennewick *(G-4700)*

CONSTRUCTION EQPT: Blade, Grader, Scraper, Dozer/Snow Plow

All Seasons Sweeping Service ....G....... 509 782-8015
  Cashmere *(G-2312)*
Weldco-Beales Mfg Corp ....E....... 253 383-0180
  Tacoma *(G-13591)*

CONSTRUCTION EQPT: Buckets, Excavating, Clamshell, Etc

Iron Horse Vac LLC ....G....... 509 586-2446
  Kennewick *(G-4677)*

CONSTRUCTION EQPT: Crane Carriers

A Millican Crane Service Inc ....G....... 360 779-6723
  Poulsbo *(G-7941)*
Professional Crane Inspections ....G....... 509 226-5302
  Otis Orchards *(G-7516)*
Rapp Marine HP LLC ....E....... 206 286-8162
  Seattle *(G-10922)*
Ulrich Trucking Incorporate ....G....... 360 748-0026
  Chehalis *(G-2540)*

CONSTRUCTION EQPT: Cranes

PSM Hydraulics ....E....... 360 282-4998
  Woodinville *(G-15342)*
Terex Corporation ....F....... 800 536-1800
  Redmond *(G-8690)*
TNT Crane & Construction ....G....... 509 682-7711
  Chelan *(G-2566)*

CONSTRUCTION EQPT: Dozers, Tractor Mounted, Material Moving

J&L Enterprises Inc ....G....... 360 262-3735
  Onalaska *(G-7449)*

CONSTRUCTION EQPT: Entrenching Machines

Precisionhx LLC ....G....... 509 951-1266
  Chattaroy *(G-2451)*
Terratrench Usa Inc ....G....... 360 694-0141
  Vancouver *(G-14632)*

CONSTRUCTION EQPT: Finishers & Spreaders

Natural Stone Restorers ....G....... 360 825-3199
  Enumclaw *(G-3307)*

Employee Codes: A=Over 500 employees, B=251-500
C=101-250, D=51-100, E=20-50, F=10-19, G=2-9

CONSTRUCTION EQPT: Mud Jacks

Superior Slabjacking Inc .... G 425 970-3986
Renton *(G-8924)*

CONSTRUCTION EQPT: Rock Crushing Machinery, Portable

North Hill Resources Inc .... F 360 757-1866
Burlington *(G-2173)*

CONSTRUCTION EQPT: Roofing Eqpt

Miramac Metals Inc .... F 509 483-5331
Mead *(G-6433)*

CONSTRUCTION EQPT: Tractors

J TS Tractor Work .... G 360 263-3016
La Center *(G-5508)*

CONSTRUCTION EQPT: Tunneling

Robbins Company .... E 253 872-0500
Kent *(G-5104)*

CONSTRUCTION EQPT: Wrecker Hoists, Automobile

A A Auto Towing .... G 360 892-2924
Vancouver *(G-14002)*
Dude Wheres My Car .... G 509 249-5440
Yakima *(G-15559)*
Horseshoe Lake Auto Wreck .... G 253 857-3866
Gig Harbor *(G-4119)*
Junk Car Removal 1 .... G 206 369-7832
Seattle *(G-10316)*

CONSTRUCTION MATERIALS, WHOL: Concrete/Cinder Bldg Prdts

Angeles Concrete Products Inc .... G 360 681-5429
Sequim *(G-11611)*
Bair Construction Inc .... G 360 491-2285
Lacey *(G-5535)*
Calportland Company .... G 253 912-8500
Dupont *(G-2957)*

CONSTRUCTION MATERIALS, WHOLESALE: Aggregate

James A Wright Cnstr LLC .... G 509 996-3249
Winthrop *(G-15162)*

CONSTRUCTION MATERIALS, WHOLESALE: Architectural Metalwork

Knights Welding .... G 509 412-1103
Pasco *(G-7596)*

CONSTRUCTION MATERIALS, WHOLESALE: Awnings

Canvas Supply Co Inc .... E 206 784-0711
Seattle *(G-9621)*

CONSTRUCTION MATERIALS, WHOLESALE: Block, Concrete & Cinder

Glacier Northwest Inc .... E 253 572-7412
Tacoma *(G-13310)*
Miles Sand & Gravel Company .... F 360 427-0946
Shelton *(G-11714)*
Mutual Materials Company .... F 360 573-5683
Vancouver *(G-14426)*

CONSTRUCTION MATERIALS, WHOLESALE: Blocks, Building, NEC

Rock Place .... G 425 220-1110
Marysville *(G-6379)*

CONSTRUCTION MATERIALS, WHOLESALE: Building Stone

Building Specialty Systems .... G 425 483-6875
Ellensburg *(G-3185)*
White Stone Calcium Corp .... G 509 935-0838
Chewelah *(G-2610)*

CONSTRUCTION MATERIALS, WHOLESALE: Building Stone, Granite

Cascade Marble & Granite .... G 509 533-0476
Spokane *(G-12171)*

CONSTRUCTION MATERIALS, WHOLESALE: Building, Exterior

Valley Supply Company .... E 360 217-4400
Woodinville *(G-15398)*

CONSTRUCTION MATERIALS, WHOLESALE: Building, Interior

Edensaw Woods Ltd .... G 253 216-1150
Tacoma *(G-13271)*
Read Products Inc .... F 206 283-2510
Seattle *(G-10929)*

CONSTRUCTION MATERIALS, WHOLESALE: Cement

Glacier Northwest Inc .... G 360 896-8922
Vancouver *(G-14255)*
Lehigh Northwest Cement Co .... F 800 752-6794
Tacoma *(G-13385)*
Lehigh Northwest Cement Co .... G 360 733-6720
Bellingham *(G-1405)*

CONSTRUCTION MATERIALS, WHOLESALE: Concrete Mixtures

Oldcastle Materials Inc .... D 509 926-8235
Spokane Valley *(G-12817)*

CONSTRUCTION MATERIALS, WHOLESALE: Door Frames

Oregon PCF Bldg Pdts Exch Inc .... D 509 892-5555
Spokane Valley *(G-12821)*

CONSTRUCTION MATERIALS, WHOLESALE: Doors, Sliding

Automatic Door Solutions LLC .... G 253 802-0888
Orting *(G-7473)*

CONSTRUCTION MATERIALS, WHOLESALE: Drywall Materials

Steeltec Supply Inc .... G 253 333-1311
Auburn *(G-572)*
Western Materials Inc .... D 509 547-3301
Pasco *(G-7652)*

CONSTRUCTION MATERIALS, WHOLESALE: Fiberglass Building Mat

All American Metal Products .... G 360 380-6202
Ferndale *(G-3811)*
Revchem Composites Inc .... G 253 305-0303
Tacoma *(G-13496)*

CONSTRUCTION MATERIALS, WHOLESALE: Glass

Gaffer Glass USA Limited .... G 253 395-3361
Kent *(G-4921)*
Hy-Grade Glass Inc .... F 509 248-9919
Union Gap *(G-13932)*

CONSTRUCTION MATERIALS, WHOLESALE: Gravel

Beans & Rocks LLC .... F 360 942-5414
Raymond *(G-8343)*
Highland Quarry LLC .... G 509 624-4136
Spokane *(G-12294)*
J L Shrman Excvtg Rock Crshing .... F 509 447-4214
Newport *(G-7059)*
Lakeside Industries Inc .... D 425 313-2600
Issaquah *(G-4437)*
Lakeside Industries Inc .... E 360 491-5460
Olympia *(G-7318)*
Lakeside Industries Inc .... E 360 423-6882
Longview *(G-5925)*
Lakeside Industries Inc .... G 360 794-7779
Monroe *(G-6590)*

Lakeside Industries Inc .... E 360 604-1869
Vancouver *(G-14356)*
Topsoils Northwest Inc .... F 425 337-0233
Snohomish *(G-11993)*

CONSTRUCTION MATERIALS, WHOLESALE: Guardrails, Metal

Twisted Metal LLC .... G 360 966-5309
Everson *(G-3693)*

CONSTRUCTION MATERIALS, WHOLESALE: Hardboard

Neil Levinson Enterprises .... G 425 828-3833
Kirkland *(G-5409)*

CONSTRUCTION MATERIALS, WHOLESALE: Insulation, Thermal

Service Partners LLC .... D 509 535-4600
Spokane Valley *(G-12866)*

CONSTRUCTION MATERIALS, WHOLESALE: Limestone

Hemphill Brothers Inc .... G 206 842-0748
Bainbridge Island *(G-639)*

CONSTRUCTION MATERIALS, WHOLESALE: Masons' Materials

Mutual Materials Company .... G 253 838-0803
Auburn *(G-502)*

CONSTRUCTION MATERIALS, WHOLESALE: Millwork

Armstrong Lumber Co Inc .... E 253 833-6666
Auburn *(G-377)*
Washington Hardwoods and .... F 206 283-7574
Winlock *(G-15158)*

CONSTRUCTION MATERIALS, WHOLESALE: Pallets, Wood

G M Pallet Inc .... G 253 435-1040
Tacoma *(G-13303)*

CONSTRUCTION MATERIALS, WHOLESALE: Paving Materials

Degerstrom Corporation .... E 509 928-3333
Spokane Valley *(G-12680)*

CONSTRUCTION MATERIALS, WHOLESALE: Plywood

Precision Countertops Inc .... E 253 867-5317
Kent *(G-5076)*

CONSTRUCTION MATERIALS, WHOLESALE: Prefabricated Structures

Steeltec Supply Inc .... G 253 333-1311
Auburn *(G-572)*

CONSTRUCTION MATERIALS, WHOLESALE: Roof, Asphalt/Sheet Metal

Custom Bilt Holdings LLC .... G 509 533-1703
Spokane *(G-12212)*
Metal Mill Corporation .... G 360 262-9080
Chehalis *(G-2514)*
Sinotechusa Inc .... G 360 566-2880
Ridgefield *(G-9111)*

CONSTRUCTION MATERIALS, WHOLESALE: Roofing & Siding Material

Sound Building Supply Inc .... E 425 264-0264
Renton *(G-8916)*
Western Materials Inc .... D 509 547-3301
Pasco *(G-7652)*

CONSTRUCTION MATERIALS, WHOLESALE: Sand

Cadman Holding Company Inc .... G 425 868-1234
Redmond *(G-8415)*

PRODUCT SECTION

CONSTRUCTION: Indl Building & Warehouse

Colville Valley Concrete Corp .... E 509 684-2534
  Colville *(G-2747)*
Connell Sand & Gravel Inc .... F 509 234-3221
  Connell *(G-2793)*
Ferndale Ready-Mix .... F 360 354-1400
  Lynden *(G-6017)*
Holroyd Company Inc .... D 253 474-0725
  Tacoma *(G-13340)*
Miles Sand & Gravel Company .... B 253 833-3705
  Puyallup *(G-8193)*
Miles Sand & Gravel Company .... E 360 734-1956
  Everson *(G-3682)*
Miles Sand & Gravel Company .... C 360 757-3121
  Burlington *(G-2171)*
Pacific Topsoils Inc .... E 425 337-2700
  Everett *(G-3568)*
Salmon Bay Sand and Gravel Co .... D 206 784-1234
  Seattle *(G-11007)*
Tim Corliss & Son Inc .... G 360 825-2578
  Enumclaw *(G-3324)*
Two Rivers Sand and Gravel .... G 509 763-3280
  Leavenworth *(G-5817)*

CONSTRUCTION MATERIALS, WHOLESALE: Septic Tanks

Bodes Precast Inc .... F 360 354-3912
  Everson *(G-3668)*

CONSTRUCTION MATERIALS, WHOLESALE: Stone, Crushed Or Broken

Lynch Creek Quarry LLC .... G 360 832-4269
  Eatonville *(G-3062)*
Okanogan Valley Concrete Inc .... G 509 422-3211
  Okanogan *(G-7203)*
Richard Lawson Construction .... E 360 378-4313
  Friday Harbor *(G-4055)*
Washington Rock Quarries Inc .... F 360 893-7701
  Orting *(G-7488)*

CONSTRUCTION MATERIALS, WHOLESALE: Stucco

Service Partners of Oregon .... E 360 694-6747
  Vancouver *(G-14580)*

CONSTRUCTION MATERIALS, WHOLESALE: Windows

Sylvia Vanzee .... G 206 284-2977
  Seattle *(G-11242)*

CONSTRUCTION MATLS, WHOL: Composite Board Prdts, Woodboard

San Juan Composites LLC .... E 360 299-3790
  Anacortes *(G-164)*

CONSTRUCTION MATLS, WHOL: Lumber, Rough, Dressed/Finished

Brazier Lumber Company Inc .... G 206 441-8184
  Mercer Island *(G-6456)*
Camco Inc .... G 866 856-4826
  Tacoma *(G-13218)*
Canfor USA Corporation .... G 360 647-2434
  Bellingham *(G-1290)*
Cedar Farms LLC .... G 360 779-3575
  Poulsbo *(G-7954)*
Evergreen Timber Corp .... F 206 579-2925
  Seattle *(G-9946)*
Green Diamond Resource Company .... G 360 426-0737
  Grapeview *(G-4288)*
Manke Lumber Company Inc .... D 253 863-4495
  Sumner *(G-13084)*
Marine Lumber Service Inc .... F 206 767-4730
  Seattle *(G-10482)*
Matthaeis Camco Inc .... E 360 426-7900
  Shelton *(G-11712)*
Michiels International Inc .... G 206 365-4060
  Kenmore *(G-4592)*
Nielsen Brothers Inc .... D 360 671-9078
  Sedro Woolley *(G-11552)*
Snow Peak Forest Products Inc .... G 208 714-4243
  Spokane Valley *(G-12878)*
Trumark Industries Inc .... E 509 534-0644
  Spokane *(G-12571)*
Wayne Davidson .... G 425 333-4242
  Carnation *(G-2302)*

Weyerhaeuser Company .... E 425 210-5880
  Seattle *(G-11462)*
Willapa Logging Company Inc .... E 360 875-5670
  Raymond *(G-8361)*

CONSTRUCTION SAND MINING

Builders Sand and Gravel Inc .... F 425 743-3333
  Snohomish *(G-11884)*
Northwest Rock Inc .... G 360 533-3050
  Aberdeen *(G-25)*
Northwest Rock Inc .... G 360 249-2245
  Montesano *(G-6651)*
Rainier Gravel .... G 206 510-3451
  Enumclaw *(G-3316)*

CONSTRUCTION SITE PREPARATION SVCS

Bradley Heavy Construction .... G 360 341-5967
  Clinton *(G-2684)*
Jack H Hill .... G 360 864-4939
  Winlock *(G-15152)*
Karvonen Sand & Gravel Inc .... G 360 687-2549
  Battle Ground *(G-712)*
Parker Pacific Inc .... E 253 862-9133
  Buckley *(G-2066)*
Puget Logging & Excavation .... G 360 629-0461
  Stanwood *(G-12988)*

CONSTRUCTION: Apartment Building

Grenlar Holdings Inc .... G 425 419-4430
  Kenmore *(G-4578)*

CONSTRUCTION: Athletic & Recreation Facilities

Professional Crane Inspections .... G 509 226-5302
  Otis Orchards *(G-7516)*

CONSTRUCTION: Bridge

Dulin Construction Inc .... F 360 736-9225
  Centralia *(G-2399)*
Krista K Thie .... G 509 493-2626
  White Salmon *(G-15121)*
McCain Timber & Bridge Inc .... G 360 520-6595
  Napavine *(G-7011)*

CONSTRUCTION: Commercial & Institutional Building

Design Construction Heritg Inc .... G 206 634-1989
  Everett *(G-3442)*
Harbor Action Inc .... F 360 417-1316
  Port Angeles *(G-7708)*
K&M Storage .... G 253 862-3515
  Sumner *(G-13076)*
Newcore Aviation LLC .... G 509 276-8200
  Deer Park *(G-2910)*
Newcore Enterprises LLC .... G 509 276-8200
  Deer Park *(G-2911)*
Skagit Industrial Steel Inc .... E 360 854-0074
  Sedro Woolley *(G-11567)*
Skookum Enterprises LLC .... D 360 475-0756
  Bremerton *(G-2001)*
Valley Steel & Stone .... G 360 378-5758
  Friday Harbor *(G-4063)*
Will Logging & Construction .... F 509 223-3560
  Loomis *(G-5973)*

CONSTRUCTION: Commercial & Office Building, New

Bethlehem Construction Inc .... E 509 782-1001
  Cashmere *(G-2317)*
Custom Building Services Inc .... G 509 422-5746
  Okanogan *(G-7195)*
Dan McMullen Well Drilling .... G 707 998-9252
  Ethel *(G-3350)*
Electric Concept Labs Inc .... G 503 244-3000
  Castle Rock *(G-2342)*
Greenland Industries LLC .... G 503 841-1835
  Port Orchard *(G-7811)*
Larry Guthrie Co .... G 509 922-6121
  Spokane Valley *(G-12772)*
Sun Valley Enterprises .... G 509 453-1914
  Yakima *(G-15688)*

CONSTRUCTION: Dams, Waterways, Docks & Other Marine

Blue Marine LLC .... G 253 225-8228
  Gig Harbor *(G-4082)*

CONSTRUCTION: Dock

Mantle Industries LLC .... F 360 332-5276
  Blaine *(G-1683)*
Wazzbizz Inc .... G 360 332-5276
  Blaine *(G-1710)*

CONSTRUCTION: Drainage System

Frank J Martin Company .... E 206 523-7665
  Lynnwood *(G-6122)*

CONSTRUCTION: Electric Power Line

Crux Subsurface Inc .... D 509 892-9409
  Spokane Valley *(G-12670)*

CONSTRUCTION: Factory

Farm Built Fab LLC .... G 360 213-8458
  La Center *(G-5504)*

CONSTRUCTION: Farm Building

Milman Engineering Inc .... G 360 273-5080
  Rochester *(G-9137)*

CONSTRUCTION: Food Prdts Manufacturing or Packing Plant

Wax Orchards Inc .... G 800 634-6132
  Lake Forest Park *(G-5627)*

CONSTRUCTION: Greenhouse

Global Emergent Tech LLC .... G 425 999-9021
  Seattle *(G-10083)*

CONSTRUCTION: Heavy

Ronald Brewer .... G 360 436-1771
  Arlington *(G-317)*

CONSTRUCTION: Heavy Highway & Street

Arris Kollman Trucking Inc .... E 360 532-0351
  Aberdeen *(G-2)*
B & B Logging Inc .... G 360 247-5237
  Amboy *(G-89)*
Burns Construction Inc .... G 360 957-4183
  Cathlamet *(G-2361)*
East Valley Sand and Gravel .... E 360 403-7520
  Arlington *(G-232)*
Garkse Logging & Road Bldg LLC .... G 360 520-2707
  Chehalis *(G-2498)*
Granite Construction Company .... G 360 676-2450
  Everson *(G-3676)*
Kenneth Maupin Logging Cnstr .... G 509 442-3484
  Ione *(G-4375)*
Miles Resources LLC .... C 253 383-3585
  Puyallup *(G-8192)*
North Fork Timber Company Corp .... F 360 748-8333
  Centralia *(G-2420)*
Richard & Mike Lynch .... G 360 263-4078
  Woodland *(G-15463)*
Selland Construction Inc .... C 509 662-7119
  Wenatchee *(G-15073)*
Shipp Construction Inc .... E 360 262-0197
  Ethel *(G-3351)*
Willapa Logging Company Inc .... E 360 875-5670
  Raymond *(G-8361)*

CONSTRUCTION: Indl Building & Warehouse

Chemithon Enterprises Inc .... C 206 937-9954
  Seattle *(G-9672)*
Geodesic Structures Inc .... G 509 535-0220
  Spokane *(G-12270)*
Gibraltar Maint & Cnstr Inc .... G 206 365-4440
  Redmond *(G-8477)*
Greenberry Industrial LLC .... G 360 366-3767
  Ferndale *(G-3849)*
High Caliber Mill .... E 360 984-6669
  Vancouver *(G-14295)*
Layfield Plastics Incorporated .... G 425 254-1075
  Renton *(G-8841)*
Skagit Industrial Steel Inc .... E 360 854-0074
  Sedro Woolley *(G-11567)*

Employee Codes: A=Over 500 employees, B=251-500
C=101-250, D=51-100, E=20-50, F=10-19, G=2-9

CONSTRUCTION: Indl Building & Warehouse

W-4 Construction Inc .... F 509 529-1603
   Walla Walla *(G-14886)*

CONSTRUCTION: Indl Building, Prefabricated

Puglia Engineering Inc .... C 360 647-0080
   Bellingham *(G-1509)*

CONSTRUCTION: Indl Buildings, New, NEC

Grenlar Holdings Inc .... G 425 419-4430
   Kenmore *(G-4578)*
McDowall Bros Insulation .... G 509 762-9530
   Moses Lake *(G-6724)*
Patriot Jabez Construction JV .... G 253 293-7100
   Auburn *(G-527)*
Sierra Industries Inc .... C 425 487-5200
   Woodinville *(G-15363)*

CONSTRUCTION: Indl Plant

Halme Construction Inc .... E 509 725-4200
   Spokane *(G-12287)*

CONSTRUCTION: Land Preparation

Dahlquist Logging Inc .... G 253 804-9112
   Auburn *(G-421)*
Kaplan Homes Unlimited LLC .... G 360 855-1675
   Sedro Woolley *(G-11549)*
Kemp West Inc .... D 425 334-5572
   Snohomish *(G-11932)*
Pilot Knob Construction Inc .... G 509 493-4196
   White Salmon *(G-15127)*
Sunland Bark and Topsoils Co .... G 360 293-7188
   Anacortes *(G-172)*

CONSTRUCTION: Marine

Bellingham Marine Industries .... D 360 676-2800
   Bellingham *(G-1266)*
Columbia Navigation Inc .... G 509 684-4335
   Kettle Falls *(G-5222)*
Craftsmen United Inc .... F 360 379-2500
   Port Townsend *(G-7874)*
Redside Construction LLC .... G 360 297-9557
   Bainbridge Island *(G-664)*

CONSTRUCTION: Mausoleum

Spokane Wilbert Vault Company .... G 509 325-4573
   Spokane *(G-12522)*

CONSTRUCTION: Multi-family Dwellings, New

Buddy Shelters LLC .... G 425 239-8104
   Arlington *(G-216)*

CONSTRUCTION: Nonresidential Buildings, Custom

I-5 Design Build Inc .... D 360 459-3200
   Lacey *(G-5558)*
Kaes Enterprises LLC .... E 800 252-5237
   Puyallup *(G-8171)*

CONSTRUCTION: Pipeline, NEC

McKinstry Co LLC .... B 206 762-3311
   Seattle *(G-10509)*

CONSTRUCTION: Power Plant

Psf Industries Inc .... E 800 426-1204
   Seattle *(G-10881)*

CONSTRUCTION: Residential, Nec

Dyers Construction & Excav .... G 903 486-1881
   Ocean Park *(G-7181)*
Modern Siding LLC .... G 813 484-9498
   Everett *(G-3550)*
Vintage Investments Inc .... G 360 293-2596
   Anacortes *(G-183)*

CONSTRUCTION: Retaining Wall

Mutual Materials Company .... G 425 353-9686
   Marysville *(G-6362)*
Mutual Materials Company .... G 360 573-5683
   Vancouver *(G-14426)*

Mutual Materials Company .... G 253 838-0803
   Auburn *(G-502)*
Mutual Materials Company Inc .... G 253 589-6434
   Tacoma *(G-13423)*

CONSTRUCTION: Roads, Gravel or Dirt

Rock Services Inc .... G 360 748-8333
   Chehalis *(G-2531)*

CONSTRUCTION: Sewer Line

Dickson Company .... D 253 472-4489
   Tacoma *(G-13263)*

CONSTRUCTION: Single-Family Housing

Archibald Log Homes Inc .... G 509 782-3703
   Cashmere *(G-2316)*
Cascade Country Cabins .... G 509 427-8515
   Stevenson *(G-13009)*
Cowlitz Electric Construction .... G 253 355-7163
   Tacoma *(G-13247)*
Dagner Construction .... G 509 349-8944
   Warden *(G-14931)*
Ewing Construction .... G 509 624-2246
   Spokane *(G-12252)*
Hill Woodworking .... G 425 488-7943
   Kenmore *(G-4581)*
Jerry Nybo Construction Inc .... G 253 691-1797
   Eatonville *(G-3060)*
Kaplan Homes Unlimited LLC .... G 360 855-1675
   Sedro Woolley *(G-11549)*
McCain Timber & Bridge Inc .... G 360 520-6595
   Napavine *(G-7011)*
Milman Engineering Inc .... G 360 273-5080
   Rochester *(G-9137)*
Murphy JP Construction .... G 425 222-7299
   Seattle *(G-10571)*
Pacific Contractors & Supply .... G 509 534-4304
   Spokane Valley *(G-12822)*
Pacific Mobile Structures Inc .... G 509 244-8335
   Airway Heights *(G-60)*
Vanderpol Building Components .... F 360 354-5883
   Lynden *(G-6058)*
Vintage Investments Inc .... G 360 293-2596
   Anacortes *(G-183)*
Wizard Works .... G 509 486-2654
   Tonasket *(G-13662)*

CONSTRUCTION: Single-family Housing, New

Boettcher & Sons Inc .... G 360 832-3943
   Eatonville *(G-3051)*
Cascade Joinery Inc .... F 360 527-0119
   Ferndale *(G-3826)*
Custom Building Services Inc .... G 509 422-5746
   Okanogan *(G-7195)*
Gary R Howe .... G 253 857-5835
   Gig Harbor *(G-4105)*
Regal Homes Construction LLC .... G 360 606-3486
   Vancouver *(G-14541)*
Tacoma Community Boat Builders .... G 253 720-8227
   Tacoma *(G-13540)*

CONSTRUCTION: Single-family Housing, Prefabricated

Cedar Homes of Washington Inc .... G 360 668-8242
   Snohomish *(G-11887)*

CONSTRUCTION: Steel Buildings

Hci Steel Buildings LLC .... F 360 403-4900
   Arlington *(G-250)*

CONSTRUCTION: Street Surfacing & Paving

CPM Development Corporation .... G 509 754-5287
   Ephrata *(G-3332)*
CPM Development Corporation .... G 509 663-5141
   Wenatchee *(G-15024)*
Degerstrom Corporation .... E 509 928-3333
   Spokane Valley *(G-12680)*
Jones Logging and Cnstr LLC .... F 509 422-3147
   Okanogan *(G-7198)*
Superior Asphalt & Paving Co .... F 509 248-6823
   Yakima *(G-15689)*
Woodland Paving .... G 360 225-8317
   Woodland *(G-15476)*

CONSTRUCTION: Svc Station

Bestworth - Rommel Inc .... E 360 435-2927
   Arlington *(G-213)*

CONSTRUCTION: Swimming Pools

JW Custom Construction .... G 509 679-2959
   Stehekin *(G-13003)*
Melcher Manufacturing Co Inc .... G 509 534-9119
   Spokane Valley *(G-12787)*

CONSTRUCTION: Tunnel

North Hill Resources Inc .... F 360 757-1866
   Burlington *(G-2173)*

CONSTRUCTION: Utility Line

Halme Construction Inc .... E 509 725-4200
   Spokane *(G-12287)*
Lloyd Logging Inc .... F 509 997-2441
   Twisp *(G-13912)*
M A C I Inc .... E 360 424-7013
   Mount Vernon *(G-6808)*

CONSTRUCTION: Warehouse

Bethlehem Construction Inc .... E 509 782-1001
   Cashmere *(G-2317)*

CONSTRUCTION: Waste Water & Sewage Treatment Plant

Bamboo Hardwoods Inc .... E 206 264-2414
   Seattle *(G-9489)*

CONSTRUCTION: Water & Sewer Line

James A Wright Cnstr LLC .... G 509 996-3249
   Winthrop *(G-15162)*

CONSTRUCTION: Water Main

Gary Merlino Cnstr Co Inc .... B 206 763-9552
   Seattle *(G-10049)*

CONSULTING SVC: Business, NEC

Almeda Cottage Inc .... E 206 285-1674
   Seattle *(G-9384)*
Apex Curb & Turf LLC .... F 509 758-1543
   Clarkston *(G-2620)*
Avalonphilly LLC .... G 800 405-7024
   Bellevue *(G-800)*
Blend Wine Shop .... G 253 884-9688
   Lakebay *(G-5688)*
Bobek Enterprises .... G 360 683-8785
   Sequim *(G-11616)*
Camoflage .... G 425 744-0764
   Edmonds *(G-3099)*
Case Mix Analysis Inc .... G 206 285-2576
   Seattle *(G-9644)*
Casey Communications Inc .... G 206 448-5902
   Seattle *(G-9645)*
Coastal Software & Consulting .... G 360 891-6174
   Vancouver *(G-14127)*
E B Associates Inc .... G 253 709-1433
   Enumclaw *(G-3288)*
Edwin Laird .... G 206 587-6537
   Seattle *(G-9885)*
Electronic Prgrm & Design .... G 206 767-7262
   Seattle *(G-9894)*
Evans - Hamilton Inc .... G 206 526-5622
   Seattle *(G-9943)*
Filmateria Studios Inc .... G 206 938-6791
   Seattle *(G-9992)*
Fox Architectural Signs Inc .... G 503 512-8757
   Woodland *(G-15433)*
International Bar Coding .... F 800 661-5570
   Oroville *(G-7467)*
J A Ratto Company .... G 206 240-5601
   Bellevue *(G-964)*
Manta Network Technologies LLC .... G 202 713-0508
   Mukilteo *(G-6952)*
Medical Equipment Dev Co LLC .... G 206 364-3894
   Shoreline *(G-11788)*
Paul Parish Limited .... G 509 735-9820
   Kennewick *(G-4705)*
Precision Fldpower Systems LLC .... G 206 938-2894
   Seattle *(G-10851)*
Ron C England 509 276-9150
   Nine Mile Falls *(G-7083)*

Shine Micro Inc ....F 360 437-2503
Port Ludlow (G-7774)
Tomatesa Enterprises LLC ....G 425 778-6708
Lynnwood (G-6211)

CONSULTING SVC: Chemical

Beryllium LLC ....G 206 780-8900
Bainbridge Island (G-617)

CONSULTING SVC: Computer

2 C Media LLC ....E 206 522-7211
Seattle (G-9318)
Applied Navigation LLC ....G 503 329-3126
Bothell (G-1821)
Author-It Software Corporation ....F 888 999-1021
Seattle (G-9466)
Cetrestec Inc ....G 206 650-8676
Seattle (G-9662)
Chase Scientific Co ....G 360 221-8455
Langley (G-5774)
Cronus Ventures LLC ....G 425 641-4497
Bellevue (G-869)
Custom Computer Creat CCC LLC ....G 800 295-3381
Seattle (G-9766)
Discovery Tools ....G 253 288-1720
Enumclaw (G-3285)
Dugger and Associates Inc ....G 425 785-6940
McCleary (G-6415)
Glarus Group Inc ....G 425 572-5907
Newcastle (G-7030)
Gsl Solutions Inc ....E 360 896-5354
Vancouver (G-14275)
Leyda Computers ....G 425 335-1273
Lake Stevens (G-5655)
Manta Network Technologies LLC ....G 202 713-0508
Mukilteo (G-6952)
Mediapro Holdings LLC ....E 425 483-4700
Bothell (G-1777)
MNC Services Inc ....G 425 527-9031
Woodinville (G-15312)
MNC Services Inc ....G 425 527-9031
Bellevue (G-1011)
Pat-Co Inc ....G 206 937-8927
Seattle (G-10765)
Peach Fuzzer LLC ....F 206 453-0339
Seattle (G-10775)
Pra Inc ....F 408 743-5300
Arlington (G-304)
Risklens Inc ....F 866 936-0191
Spokane (G-12475)
Simerics Inc ....F 256 489-1480
Bellevue (G-1132)
Simerics Inc ....F 425 502-9978
Bellevue (G-1133)
Skookum Enterprises LLC ....D 360 475-0756
Bremerton (G-2001)
Space Rock It Inc ....G 206 395-8383
Seattle (G-11164)
Vector Blue Services LLC ....F 425 219-2528
Bellevue (G-1213)
Zsolutionz LLC ....G 425 502-6970
Sammamish (G-9262)

CONSULTING SVC: Educational

Campbell & Associates Inc ....G 360 652-9502
Stanwood (G-12963)
Leading Beyond Tradition LLC ....G 425 275-7665
Snohomish (G-11938)
Machstem Inc ....G 801 259-3305
Nine Mile Falls (G-7078)
Math Perspectives ....G 360 715-2782
Bellingham (G-1426)

CONSULTING SVC: Engineering

4m Sigma Corporation ....G 206 285-9181
Seattle (G-9322)
A H Lundberg Inc ....G 425 258-4617
Everett (G-3354)
Aeronautical Testing Service ....G 360 363-4276
Arlington (G-196)
AG Energy Solutions Inc ....F 509 343-3156
Spokane Valley (G-12602)
B/E Aerospace Inc ....B 360 657-5197
Everett (G-3380)
Brockett Ocean Services Inc ....F 425 869-1834
Redmond (G-8410)
Flight Structures Inc ....C 360 651-8537
Everett (G-3475)
Guido Perla & Associates Inc ....E 206 463-2217
Seattle (G-10132)
Laser Techniques Company LLC ....F 425 885-0607
Redmond (G-8530)
Lhc2 Inc ....G 509 723-4517
Liberty Lake (G-5843)
Linda J Mohr ....G 509 946-0941
Richland (G-9022)
Mazdak International Inc ....G 360 988-6058
Sumas (G-13047)
Pulsair Systems Inc ....G 425 455-1263
Kirkland (G-5448)
Resource Associates Intl ....G 509 466-1894
Spokane (G-12472)
Team Corporation ....E 360 757-3944
Burlington (G-2193)
Tidland Hydraulics Inc ....G 360 573-6506
Vancouver (G-14636)

CONSULTING SVC: Management

Framatome Inc ....F 425 250-2775
Redmond (G-8465)
Girandola ....G 206 289-0523
Seattle (G-10073)
Glarus Group Inc ....G 425 572-5907
Newcastle (G-7030)
Green River College ....E 253 856-9595
Kent (G-4928)
Intelligent Technologies Inc ....G 360 254-4211
Vancouver (G-14321)
Lilibete LLC ....G 206 407-6890
Kent (G-4996)
Manta Network Technologies LLC ....G 202 713-0508
Mukilteo (G-6952)
Pacific Ally LLC ....G 360 760-4266
La Center (G-5511)
Reynolds and Reynolds Company ....E 425 985-0194
Edmonds (G-3146)
Sand Paper & Ink Inc ....G 360 705-0918
Tumwater (G-13896)
Stretching Charts Inc ....E 253 536-4922
Tacoma (G-13528)
Unlimited Possibilities Now ....G 206 930-9100
Bothell (G-1804)
Vimly Benefit Solutions Inc ....D 425 771-7359
Mukilteo (G-6989)
Volometrix Inc ....G 425 706-7507
Redmond (G-8707)

CONSULTING SVC: Marketing Management

Cascadia Dynamix LLC ....G 360 584-3044
Tenino (G-13613)
Cronus Ventures LLC ....G 425 641-4497
Bellevue (G-869)
Deluxe ....G 360 794-3157
Monroe (G-6565)
Denny Mountain Media LLC ....D 425 831-7130
Seattle (G-9822)
Direct Connect Group (dcg) LLC ....B 206 784-6892
Seattle (G-9833)
Ds-Iq Inc ....D 425 974-1400
Bellevue (G-885)
Electronic Imaging Svcs Inc ....E 253 887-1237
Auburn (G-432)
I2nnovations LLC ....G 425 298-3143
Sammamish (G-9218)
Imagicorps Inc ....E 425 869-0599
Redmond (G-8506)
Lift Solutions Inc ....G 360 862-8328
Lake Stevens (G-5657)
NRG Resources Inc ....D 509 588-4786
Benton City (G-1621)
Pacific NW Print Flfllment Inc ....F 509 242-7857
Spokane Valley (G-12823)
Pareto-Curve Marketing Inc ....G 360 357-1000
Tumwater (G-13889)
Powerhuse Brnds Consulting LLC ....G 503 317-4925
Ridgefield (G-9104)
Stemar Media Group LLC ....G 206 877-3560
Shoreline (G-11818)
Taphandles LLC ....E 206 462-6800
Seattle (G-11269)

CONSULTING SVC: Online Technology

Differential Networks LLC ....G 360 366-8123
Bellingham (G-1323)
Far Star Products ....G 360 604-0080
Vancouver (G-14222)
Fluentpro Software Corporation ....G 855 358-3688
Redmond (G-8462)
Intentionet Inc ....G 206 579-6567
Redmond (G-8512)
RY Investments Inc ....G 360 701-1261
Lacey (G-5583)

CONSULTING SVC: Personnel Management

Grief Inc ....G 253 929-0649
Puyallup (G-8160)

CONSULTING SVC: Sales Management

AVI Marie Hair Collection LLC ....G 425 409-9924
Renton (G-8749)
Great Artisan Beverage LLC ....G 425 467-7952
Bellevue (G-933)

CONSULTING SVC: Telecommunications

Telspace LLC ....E 425 953-2801
Kirkland (G-5478)

CONSULTING SVCS, BUSINESS: Agricultural

Terra Vinum LLC ....G 509 551-0854
Benton City (G-1630)

CONSULTING SVCS, BUSINESS: Economic

Girandola ....G 206 289-0523
Seattle (G-10073)

CONSULTING SVCS, BUSINESS: Employee Programs Administration

Vimly Benefit Solutions Inc ....D 425 771-7359
Mukilteo (G-6989)

CONSULTING SVCS, BUSINESS: Environmental

American Petro Envmtl Svcs LLC ....G 253 538-5252
Puyallup (G-8122)
Battery Recycler ....G 562 434-4502
Bellingham (G-1259)
Directed Technologies Drlg Inc ....G 800 239-5950
Bremerton (G-1948)
Eco Tec Inc ....G 253 884-6804
Gig Harbor (G-4097)
Ecotech Recycling LLC ....E 360 673-3860
Kalama (G-4498)
Emerald Services Inc ....C 206 430-7795
Seattle (G-9913)
Hart Crowser Inc ....D 206 324-9530
Seattle (G-10145)
Parametrix Inc ....D 206 394-3700
Puyallup (G-8219)

CONSULTING SVCS, BUSINESS: Fishery

Aquabiotics Corporation ....G 206 842-1708
Bainbridge Island (G-609)
Biosonics Inc ....F 206 782-2211
Seattle (G-9530)
Hydroacoustic Technology Inc ....F 206 633-3383
Seattle (G-10196)

CONSULTING SVCS, BUSINESS: Publishing

Hoffmann Petra ....G 360 321-4733
Langley (G-5780)
Pizzicato Publishing Co ....G 206 361-0444
Seattle (G-10819)
Printcom Inc ....F 206 763-7600
Burien (G-2121)
Study In The USA Inc ....G 206 622-2075
Seattle (G-11208)
Vernon Publications LLC ....F 425 488-3211
Woodinville (G-15400)
Whalestooth Publishing ....G 360 376-2784
Olga (G-7220)

CONSULTING SVCS, BUSINESS: Sys Engnrg, Exc Computer/Prof

Christian Hamilton ....G 360 442-4900
Longview (G-5899)
Helldyne Inc ....G 206 855-1227
Bainbridge Island (G-638)
Isonetic Inc ....G 800 670-8871
Vashon (G-14726)

Employee Codes: A=Over 500 employees, B=251-500
C=101-250, D=51-100, E=20-50, F=10-19, G=2-9
2019 Washington
Manufacturers Register
937

CONSULTING SVCS, BUSINESS: Sys Engnrg, Exc Computer/Prof

Manceps Inc .... G 503 922-1164
 Camas (G-2267)
R D F Products .... G 360 253-2181
 Vancouver (G-14526)
Tuxbits Inc .... G 302 313-6831
 Walla Walla (G-14883)

CONSULTING SVCS, BUSINESS: Systems Analysis & Engineering

ADS LLC .... G 206 762-5070
 Tukwila (G-13687)
Armstrong & Associates LLC .... G 253 548-6148
 Kennewick (G-4619)
Custom Computer Creat CCC LLC .... G 800 295-3381
 Seattle (G-9766)
Glarus Group Inc .... G 425 572-5907
 Newcastle (G-7030)
Monster Concepts Inc .... G 206 706-6730
 Seattle (G-10560)

CONSULTING SVCS, BUSINESS: Systems Analysis Or Design

Conveyor Dynamics Inc .... F 360 671-2200
 Bellingham (G-1305)
Industrial Control Group .... G 509 965-5967
 Yakima (G-15587)

CONSULTING SVCS, BUSINESS: Urban Planning & Consulting

Vanetten Fine Art .... G 509 928-2385
 Spokane Valley (G-12928)

CONSULTING SVCS: Oil

Amiraq Cnsltnts Inc .... G 936 448-1480
 Woodland (G-15418)
QMS 1 Inc .... G 360 201-7505
 Bellingham (G-1512)

CONSULTING SVCS: Scientific

Infometrix Inc .... F 425 402-1450
 Bothell (G-1768)
Jan Scientific Inc .... G 206 632-1814
 Seattle (G-10285)

CONTACT LENSES

United Contact Lens Inc .... G 360 474-9577
 Arlington (G-343)

CONTAINERS, GLASS: Food

Vashon Trading Co LLC .... G 206 463-2278
 Vashon (G-14746)

CONTAINERS: Air Cargo, Metal

Container Stuffers LLC .... G 206 255-3187
 Auburn (G-414)
Gimpy Ninja LLC .... G 253 282-9943
 Gig Harbor (G-4108)

CONTAINERS: Cargo, Wood & Wood With Metal

Moberg & Company .... G 360 380-5257
 Ferndale (G-3873)
Unicon International Inc .... D 253 539-7533
 Puyallup (G-8266)

CONTAINERS: Corrugated

Commercial Crting Box Pckg Inc .... F 253 804-8616
 Auburn (G-410)
Gbc International Bank .... G 425 214-8435
 Bellevue (G-921)
Heritage Gbc .... G 360 392-8541
 Bellingham (G-1369)
Industrial Crating & Packing .... F 425 226-9200
 Mercer Island (G-6467)
Kapstone Seattle .... G 206 762-7170
 Seattle (G-10327)
Longview Fibre Ppr & Packg Inc .... A 360 425-1550
 Longview (G-5930)
Menasha Packaging Company LLC ..... C 425 677-7788
 Issaquah (G-4448)
Port Townsend Holdings Co Inc .... B 360 385-3170
 Port Townsend (G-7911)
RTS Packaging LLC .... G 206 575-0380
 Tukwila (G-13808)
Sonoco Products Company .... D 360 225-1500
 Woodland (G-15466)
Weyerhaeuser Co .... G 425 455-1111
 Bellevue (G-1226)
Weyerhaeuser Company .... C 509 453-4741
 Union Gap (G-13956)

CONTAINERS: Food & Beverage

Pacific Market Intl LLC .... C 206 441-1400
 Seattle (G-10735)

CONTAINERS: Frozen Food & Ice Cream

Stark Raving Foods LLC .... G 425 361-7640
 Everett (G-3621)

CONTAINERS: Glass

Adaptive Cargo Solutions LLC .... F 240 475-6521
 Everett (G-3360)
Ardagh Glass Inc .... A 765 741-7985
 Seattle (G-9425)
Verallia .... G 206 762-0660
 Seattle (G-11412)

CONTAINERS: Laminated Phenolic & Vulcanized Fiber

Paneltech Intl Holdings Inc .... F 360 538-1480
 Hoquiam (G-4354)

CONTAINERS: Liquid Tight Fiber, From Purchased Materials

Tetra Pak Materials LP .... C 360 693-3664
 Vancouver (G-14633)

CONTAINERS: Metal

Armour Mfg & Cnstr Inc .... G 253 984-1213
 Tacoma (G-13180)
Blefa Kegs Inc .... G 615 267-1385
 Vancouver (G-14068)
Industrial Container Svcs LLC .... E 206 763-2345
 Seattle (G-10231)
Jet City Partners LLC .... G 206 999-0047
 Auburn (G-479)
Omnifab Inc .... E 253 931-5151
 Auburn (G-518)
Scot Industries Inc .... D 360 623-1305
 Centralia (G-2431)
Seattle Barrel Co .... G 206 622-7218
 Seattle (G-11045)

CONTAINERS: Plastic

Adaptive Cargo Solutions LLC .... F 240 475-6521
 Everett (G-3360)
Amcor Rigid Packaging Usa LLC .... B 360 753-4162
 Tumwater (G-13851)
Battery Recycler 562 434-4502
 Bellingham (G-1259)
Berry Global Inc .... C 253 627-2151
 Tacoma (G-13198)
Big Blok LLC .... G 360 442-0655
 Vancouver (G-14066)
Captive Plastics LLC .... D 253 627-2151
 Tacoma (G-13220)
Clear Cut Plastics Inc .... G 206 545-9131
 Seattle (G-9694)
Consolidated Container Co LLC .... E 509 891-2483
 Spokane Valley (G-12664)
Elkhart Plastics .... D 360 887-2230
 Ridgefield (G-9080)
Fastcap LLC .... E 888 443-3748
 Ferndale (G-3841)
Fuze Create LLC 425 212-8807
 Seattle (G-10043)
Graham Packaging Company LP .... E 509 698-4545
 Selah (G-11589)
Joseph S Heagney 360 631-2982
 Arlington (G-10263)
Mixie Manufacturing LLC .... G 360 696-4943
 Vancouver (G-14422)
Peninsula Packaging LLC .... D 509 575-5341
 Yakima (G-15644)
Portland Plastics 360 887-2230
 Ridgefield (G-9103)
Signature Plastics LLC .... F 360 366-5044
 Custer (G-2860)
Tap Plastics Inc A Cal Corp 206 389-5900
 Seattle (G-11266)

CONTAINERS: Plywood & Veneer, Wood

Weyerhaeuser Company .... C 509 453-4741
 Union Gap (G-13956)

CONTAINERS: Sanitary, Food

Dart Container Corp Georgia .... E 360 352-7045
 Tumwater (G-13870)
Sheng Mian North America LLC .... G 215 519-5895
 Bellevue (G-1128)
Tetra Pak Materials LP .... C 360 693-3664
 Vancouver (G-14633)

CONTAINERS: Shipping & Mailing, Fiber

JC Global Supply LLC .... G 253 275-6093
 Kent (G-4966)

CONTAINERS: Shipping, Metal, Milk, Fluid

Ocean Cargo Container Inc .... G 253 381-9098
 Gig Harbor (G-4138)

CONTAINERS: Wood

Cedar Grove Wood Specialty .... G 360 494-5295
 Randle (G-8324)
Contrary Design .... G 253 653-0275
 Auburn (G-415)
Fastcap LLC .... E 888 443-3748
 Ferndale (G-3841)
Havillah Shake Co .... G 509 486-1467
 Tonasket (G-13650)
Howatt Company Inc .... F 425 743-4682
 Mukilteo (G-6937)
Spinner Wood Products LLC .... G 509 653-2222
 Naches (G-7004)

CONTAINMENT VESSELS: Reactor, Metal Plate

Centerline Fabricators LLC .... G 253 922-3226
 Fife (G-3941)

CONTRACT DIVING SVC

Top To Bottom Inc .... G 360 671-7022
 Bellingham (G-1572)

CONTRACTOR: Rigging & Scaffolding

Neil F Lampson Inc .... C 509 586-0411
 Kennewick (G-4700)
Toss Brion Yacht Rigging Inc .... G 360 385-1080
 Port Townsend (G-7932)

CONTRACTORS: Access Flooring System Installation

Dep Homes Corporation .... G 206 322-1241
 Seattle (G-9824)

CONTRACTORS: Acoustical & Ceiling Work

Dlm Inc .... F 425 348-3204
 Mukilteo (G-6915)
Forrest Sound Products LLC .... G 425 881-1111
 Redmond (G-8464)

CONTRACTORS: Acoustical & Insulation Work

Distribution International Inc .... B 425 228-4111
 Renton (G-8785)

CONTRACTORS: Asbestos Removal & Encapsulation

Dickson Company .... D 253 472-4489
 Tacoma (G-13263)

CONTRACTORS: Asphalt

Bainter Bainter & Bainter LLC .... G 360 267-5521
 Grayland (G-4292)
CPM Development Corporation .... B 509 534-6221
 Spokane Valley (G-12668)

PRODUCT SECTION

Granite Construction Company............G....... 360 676-2450
  Everson *(G-3676)*
Jimini Construction LLC ....G....... 360 426-9918
  Shelton *(G-11705)*
Looker & Associates Inc ....E....... 253 210-5200
  Puyallup *(G-8179)*
Miles Resources LLC ....C....... 253 383-3585
  Puyallup *(G-8192)*

CONTRACTORS: Blasting, Exc Building Demolition

Gibbons Drilling Inc..............................G....... 360 671-3040
  Stanwood *(G-12974)*

CONTRACTORS: Boring, Building Construction

Christopher Ross Dewayne ....G....... 360 918-4586
  Tumwater *(G-13860)*

CONTRACTORS: Building Eqpt & Machinery Installation

Schindler Elevator Corporation............E....... 509 535-2471
  Spokane Valley *(G-12859)*

CONTRACTORS: Building Sign Installation & Mntnce

Sign Crafters Inc ....G....... 509 783-8718
  Kennewick *(G-4727)*
Sign-A-Rama ....G....... 253 474-1991
  Tacoma *(G-13513)*
Vancouver Sign Co Inc ....E....... 360 693-4773
  Vancouver *(G-14663)*

CONTRACTORS: Building Site Preparation

M A C I Inc..E....... 360 424-7013
  Mount Vernon *(G-6808)*

CONTRACTORS: Caisson Drilling

Pacific Foundation Inc..........................F....... 360 200-6608
  Vancouver *(G-14464)*

CONTRACTORS: Carpentry Work

Anderson Fine Woods...........................G....... 425 422-2753
  Lake Stevens *(G-5631)*
Kaplan Homes Unlimited LLC..............G....... 360 855-1675
  Sedro Woolley *(G-11549)*
Ornamental Iron Works Inc ....G....... 509 662-8294
  Wenatchee *(G-15054)*
T R S Inc..F....... 253 444-1555
  Tacoma *(G-13538)*
Tacoma Fixture Co Inc..........................D....... 253 383-5541
  Tacoma *(G-13542)*

CONTRACTORS: Carpentry, Cabinet & Finish Work

AE Downs Enterprises Inc ....E....... 206 295-9831
  Kent *(G-4761)*
Authentic Woodcraft Inc ....G....... 253 939-8119
  Auburn *(G-383)*
Conestoga Wood Spc Corp ....G....... 253 437-1320
  Kent *(G-4863)*
Curry Custom Cabinets Corp ....G....... 425 315-9355
  Mukilteo *(G-6909)*
Dream Line Cabinets LLC ....G....... 503 841-8575
  Vancouver *(G-14187)*
DWhittle Shop Inc ....G....... 509 627-3050
  Richland *(G-8990)*
Heirloom Custom Cabinets Inc............G....... 360 354-7851
  Lynden *(G-6020)*
Higher Plane Cabinetworks ....F....... 360 733-4322
  Bellingham *(G-1370)*
John Duane King ....G....... 360 736-6707
  Centralia *(G-2412)*
Michael B Knutson................................G....... 509 398-7312
  Wenatchee *(G-15050)*
Northwest Woodworks Inc ....E....... 425 482-9663
  Woodinville *(G-15322)*
Olympic Mountain Millwork LLC ....G....... 360 432-2992
  Shelton *(G-11717)*
Rainier Woodworking Co ....F....... 253 272-5210
  Tacoma *(G-13491)*
Wood Way Mfg Inc ....G....... 360 366-4854
  Blaine *(G-1713)*

CONTRACTORS: Carpentry, Cabinet Building & Installation

A & J Custom Cabinets Inc ....D....... 360 694-4833
  Vancouver *(G-14001)*
A & V Investments Inc ....E....... 509 276-5088
  Deer Park *(G-2892)*
Artistic Cabinets & Millwork ....G....... 509 575-4788
  Yakima *(G-15514)*
B Plus Inc..G....... 360 426-5038
  Shelton *(G-11681)*
Dogstar Cabinets Inc ....G....... 509 674-4229
  Cle Elum *(G-2665)*
Ernest R Howald Inc ....G....... 360 491-1758
  Olympia *(G-7279)*
F H Sullivan Co Inc ....E....... 360 442-4222
  Kelso *(G-4525)*
Fredricksons Furn & Cabinets.............G....... 206 782-5310
  Seattle *(G-10023)*
H & E Building Enterprises ....G....... 253 848-3534
  Edgewood *(G-3081)*
Warmington & North Co Inc ....F....... 206 324-5043
  Seattle *(G-11436)*

CONTRACTORS: Commercial & Office Building

McDowall Bros Insulation ....G....... 509 762-9530
  Moses Lake *(G-6724)*
Roy Pablo ....G....... 425 750-9941
  Quil Ceda Village *(G-8281)*
Vulcan Global LLC ....G....... 509 528-2000
  Kennewick *(G-4743)*

CONTRACTORS: Computer Installation

CCS Computer Systems Inc ....F....... 425 672-4806
  Lynnwood *(G-6089)*
Christian Hamilton................................G....... 360 442-4900
  Longview *(G-5899)*
Expert Computer Tech Inc ....G....... 360 736-7000
  Centralia *(G-2401)*
Pacific Custom Cable Inc ....F....... 253 373-0800
  Auburn *(G-523)*
Space Rock It Inc ....G....... 206 395-8383
  Seattle *(G-11164)*

CONTRACTORS: Computerized Controls Installation

Ikonika Corp ....G....... 253 344-1523
  Fife *(G-3960)*
Resource Associates Intl ....G....... 509 466-1894
  Spokane *(G-12472)*
True Machine ....G....... 425 610-9669
  Ferndale *(G-3919)*

CONTRACTORS: Concrete

Best Way Concrete ....G....... 360 825-5494
  Enumclaw *(G-3279)*
CPM Development Corporation............G....... 509 762-5366
  Moses Lake *(G-6699)*
CPM Development Corporation............G....... 509 886-4853
  Wenatchee *(G-15090)*
CPM Development Corporation............G....... 509 488-2614
  Othello *(G-7493)*
M A C I Inc..E....... 360 424-7013
  Mount Vernon *(G-6808)*
Mitchell Trucking and Paving ....G....... 509 884-5928
  East Wenatchee *(G-3026)*
Patriot Jabez Construction JV ....G....... 253 293-7100
  Auburn *(G-527)*
Speedy Mix Concrete............................G....... 253 531-3260
  Tacoma *(G-13522)*

CONTRACTORS: Concrete Reinforcement Placing

CMC Steel Fabricators Inc ....G....... 253 833-9060
  Auburn *(G-409)*
Tri States Rebar Inc ....E....... 509 922-5901
  Spokane Valley *(G-12912)*

CONTRACTORS: Construction Site Cleanup

Jesse W Palmer.....................................F....... 509 634-1494
  Keller *(G-4513)*

CONTRACTORS: Electrical

CONTRACTORS: Core Drilling & Cutting

American Drilling Corp LLC.................E....... 509 921-7836
  Spokane Valley *(G-12610)*
Carpenter Drilling LLC.........................F....... 509 627-6642
  Benton City *(G-1603)*

CONTRACTORS: Countertop Installation

Absolute GM LLC..................................E....... 425 814-1011
  Kirkland *(G-5267)*
Arcomm Inc ....G....... 253 581-9800
  Lakewood *(G-5699)*
Lakewood Counter Tops Inc ....F....... 253 588-8550
  Lakewood *(G-5733)*
Room Maker ....G....... 425 432-3324
  Maple Valley *(G-6292)*

CONTRACTORS: Demolition, Building & Other Structures

Dickson Company..................................D....... 253 472-4489
  Tacoma *(G-13263)*

CONTRACTORS: Demountable Partition Installation

L Clasen Corp.......................................G....... 360 658-1823
  Snohomish *(G-11935)*

CONTRACTORS: Dewatering

Clear Water Compliance LLC...............E....... 425 412-5700
  Everett *(G-3419)*

CONTRACTORS: Directional Oil & Gas Well Drilling Svc

Directed Technologies Drlg Inc ....G....... 800 239-5950
  Bremerton *(G-1948)*
Division Piedmont Directional ....G....... 425 482-9022
  Woodinville *(G-15228)*
Taylor Drilling Inc.................................F....... 360 262-9274
  Chehalis *(G-2538)*

CONTRACTORS: Driveway

Hillcar & Fletcher Inc ....G....... 360 327-3844
  Beaver *(G-757)*

CONTRACTORS: Drywall

Jon Lonning Drywall.............................G....... 253 851-4866
  Gig Harbor *(G-4125)*

CONTRACTORS: Earthmoving

Emerson Logging Corporation ....G....... 509 647-5658
  Wilbur *(G-15141)*
Robert Rogers ....G....... 360 352-9408
  Olympia *(G-7387)*

CONTRACTORS: Electric Power Systems

Kaes Enterprises LLC...........................E....... 800 252-5237
  Puyallup *(G-8171)*
Liberty Casework LLC ....G....... 253 651-7891
  Graham *(G-4230)*

CONTRACTORS: Electrical

Battery X-Change & Repair Inc............G....... 206 682-2981
  Tukwila *(G-13695)*
Berry Neon Co Inc................................E....... 425 776-8835
  Everett *(G-3385)*
Enertec Bas ....G....... 360 786-1257
  Olympia *(G-7277)*
Grays Electric Inc.................................G....... 509 662-6834
  Wenatchee *(G-15037)*
Industrial Electric Co Inc.....................G....... 360 424-3239
  Mount Vernon *(G-6804)*
Industrial Support Service LLC ....G....... 509 276-5131
  Deer Park *(G-2906)*
Island Electric.......................................G....... 360 293-9275
  Anacortes *(G-136)*
K J M Electric Co Inc ....G....... 206 624-5294
  Seattle *(G-10320)*
NW Utility Services LLC ....E....... 253 891-7802
  Pacific *(G-7536)*
Olympic SEC Comm Sys Inc................G....... 360 652-1088
  Arlington *(G-294)*
Picatti Brothers Inc ....D....... 509 248-2540
  Yakima *(G-15646)*

Employee Codes: A=Over 500 employees, B=251-500
C=101-250, D=51-100, E=20-50, F=10-19, G=2-9

CONTRACTORS: Electrical

Company		Phone
Plumb Signs Inc ....E		253 474-6702
Tacoma *(G-13466)*		
Prairie Electric Inc.............................D		509 545-1752
Pasco *(G-7618)*		
Provident Electric Inc ....F		509 588-3939
Benton City *(G-1624)*		
Red Electric ....G		425 670-7035
Mukilteo *(G-6971)*		
Totem Electric ....G		253 327-1500
Fife *(G-3996)*		
Twice Light Inc ....F		360 573-6101
Vancouver *(G-14652)*		
United States Electric Corp...............G		360 427-4218
Grapeview *(G-4291)*		
Utilities Service Company Inc...........G		206 246-5674
Tukwila *(G-13831)*		

CONTRACTORS: Excavating

- Alan Loghry Excavation Inc ....G 360 461-0660
  Port Angeles *(G-7681)*
- Bradley Heavy Construction ....G 360 341-5967
  Clinton *(G-2684)*
- Bruce & Walter Webster ....G 360 697-3975
  Poulsbo *(G-7953)*
- Cherry Valley Logging Company ....F 206 396-0002
  Duvall *(G-2981)*
- Dyers Construction & Excav ....G 903 486-1881
  Ocean Park *(G-7181)*
- Fred Nanamkin ....G 509 634-8110
  Keller *(G-4512)*
- Howard & Son Excavating LLC ....G 360 983-3922
  Silver Creek *(G-11823)*
- James A Wright Cnstr LLC ....G 509 996-3249
  Winthrop *(G-15162)*
- John Dalrymple ....G 509 837-2117
  Sunnyside *(G-13129)*
- Jones Logging and Cnstr LLC............F 509 422-3147
  Okanogan *(G-7198)*
- Kemp West Inc ....D 425 334-5572
  Snohomish *(G-11932)*
- LA Excav & Select Log Inc ....G 360 856-4111
  Mount Vernon *(G-6806)*
- Leon Wickizer Excavating ....G 253 261-2978
  Buckley *(G-2061)*
- Lloyd Logging Inc ....F 509 997-2441
  Twisp *(G-13912)*
- Lodestone Construction Inc ....G 360 875-6960
  South Bend *(G-12043)*
- Mt Adams Lumber Company Inc ....G 509 395-2131
  Trout Lake *(G-13682)*
- Pierson & Son Construction ....G 360 642-2796
  Long Beach *(G-5877)*
- Plano Bros Paving Inc ....G 425 226-8210
  Newcastle *(G-7038)*
- Puget Logging & Excavation ....G 360 629-0461
  Stanwood *(G-12988)*
- Reano Construction & Logging..........G 360 886-1374
  Black Diamond *(G-1654)*
- Richard Lawson Construction ....E 360 378-4313
  Friday Harbor *(G-4055)*
- Robert Rogers ....G 360 352-9408
  Olympia *(G-7387)*
- Stotts Construction Inc ....F 509 779-4987
  Curlew *(G-2847)*
- Whyte & Sons Incorporated ....G 425 885-3571
  Redmond *(G-8713)*

CONTRACTORS: Excavating Slush Pits & Cellars Svcs

- Fox Island Excavation LLC ....G 253 677-7291
  Fox Island *(G-4020)*
- Precisionhx LLC.................................G 509 951-1266
  Chattaroy *(G-2451)*

CONTRACTORS: Fence Construction

- All In Cnstr & Ldscpg LLC ....G 360 840-7990
  Mount Vernon *(G-6770)*
- Basic Homes LLC ....G 253 579-2724
  Eatonville *(G-3050)*
- Bradley Robling ....G 360 832-6778
  Spanaway *(G-12054)*
- Cowlitz Fence Co ....G 360 577-6110
  Kelso *(G-4522)*
- Ellensburg Fence Co ....G 509 929-4090
  Ellensburg *(G-3196)*
- Northwest Fence Co ....G 360 683-4673
  Sequim *(G-11652)*
- Quality Fence Builders Inc ....E 253 939-8533
  Auburn *(G-541)*

CONTRACTORS: Fiber Optic Cable Installation

- Dial One Telecommunications............G 360 629-2085
  Stanwood *(G-12966)*
- Fat Daddys Fabrication LLC ....G 253 677-8005
  Roy *(G-9159)*
- Mira Technology................................G 425 678-0183
  Lynnwood *(G-6164)*

CONTRACTORS: Fiberglass Work

- B & J Fiberglass LLC.........................G 360 398-9342
  Bellingham *(G-1256)*
- Environmental Insul Contg LLC ....E 360 647-2532
  Bellingham *(G-1336)*

CONTRACTORS: Fire Detection & Burglar Alarm Systems

- General Fire Prtection Systems..........F 509 535-4255
  Spokane *(G-12268)*
- Johnson Controls ....C 206 291-1400
  Seattle *(G-10302)*
- Michael Patrick Matthews ....G 509 457-8799
  Wapato *(G-14920)*
- Security Alarms Plus Inc ....G 509 457-8799
  Zillah *(G-15758)*

CONTRACTORS: Fire Sprinkler System Installation Svcs

- Johnson Controls ....C 206 291-1400
  Seattle *(G-10302)*

CONTRACTORS: Floor Laying & Other Floor Work

- D Ds Hardwood Floors ....G 206 726-8808
  Seattle *(G-9780)*

CONTRACTORS: Flooring

- D Ds Hardwood Floors ....G 206 726-8808
  Seattle *(G-9780)*
- Extreme Hardwood Floors ....G 425 985-6735
  Renton *(G-8797)*
- Nfi Enterprises LLC ....E 253 245-5500
  Auburn *(G-507)*
- T & A Supply Company Inc ....D 206 282-3770
  Kent *(G-5166)*
- T & A Supply Company Inc ....G 253 872-3682
  Kent *(G-5167)*

CONTRACTORS: Foundation Building

- Pacific Foundation Inc.......................F 360 200-6608
  Vancouver *(G-14464)*

CONTRACTORS: Garage Doors

- S G&C Contractor Services LLC ....G 360 671-5121
  Bellingham *(G-1520)*

CONTRACTORS: Gas Detection & Analysis Svcs

- Vista Precision Solutions Inc.............G 908 829-3471
  Richland *(G-9050)*

CONTRACTORS: Gas Field Svcs, NEC

- First Choice Market Inc ....E 360 253-9149
  Brush Prairie *(G-2035)*
- M A C I Inc..E 360 424-7013
  Mount Vernon *(G-6808)*
- Washigton Field Services Inc ....G 253 813-6681
  Kent *(G-5206)*

CONTRACTORS: General Electric

- Control Dynamics Inc ....E 800 738-5004
  Everett *(G-3425)*
- Custom Controls Corporation ....F 253 922-5874
  Fife *(G-3947)*
- M R K Electric ....G 360 253-8310
  Brush Prairie *(G-2037)*
- Mountain Sttes Elec Contrs Inc ....F 509 532-0110
  Spokane *(G-12399)*
- Poppleton Electric & Mchy Co...........F 206 762-9160
  Kent *(G-5073)*
- Sign-Tech Elc Ltd Lblty Co ....E 253 922-2146
  Fife *(G-3993)*
- Timken Motor & Crane Svcs LLC ......E 509 547-1691
  Pasco *(G-7638)*

CONTRACTORS: Geothermal Drilling

- Carpenter Drilling LLC ....F 509 627-6642
  Benton City *(G-1603)*
- Crux Subsurface Inc ....D 509 892-9409
  Spokane Valley *(G-12670)*

CONTRACTORS: Glass Tinting, Architectural & Automotive

- Epic Wheel and Tire Inc....................E 253 691-1785
  Tacoma *(G-13280)*
- Shadow Master..................................G 253 984-0559
  Lakewood *(G-5754)*

CONTRACTORS: Glass, Glazing & Tinting

- Annapurna Glass & Wood Inc ....G 206 525-0777
  Seattle *(G-9404)*
- Bancheros Glass and Etching ....G 253 854-4877
  Kent *(G-4807)*
- Gaynors Glass & Restoration ....G 253 538-2501
  Tacoma *(G-13305)*
- Glass Doctor of Wenatchee ....G 509 415-3400
  East Wenatchee *(G-3014)*
- Sound Glass Sales Inc ....D 253 473-7477
  Tacoma *(G-13518)*
- Steel Encounters Inc ....F 206 281-8500
  Seattle *(G-11186)*

CONTRACTORS: Grave Excavation

- Precisionhx LLC.................................G 509 951-1266
  Chattaroy *(G-2451)*

CONTRACTORS: Grouting Work

- Hydro Consulting LLC ....G 509 302-1034
  Pasco *(G-7591)*

CONTRACTORS: Gutters & Downspouts

- Custom Bilt Holdings LLC ....G 509 533-1703
  Spokane *(G-12212)*
- Custom Bilt Holdings LLC ....E 253 872-7330
  Lakewood *(G-5709)*
- J & E Jensen Inc ....G 253 851-2282
  Bremerton *(G-1963)*
- Spokane Rain Gutter Inc ....F 509 922-4880
  Spokane Valley *(G-12887)*

CONTRACTORS: Heating & Air Conditioning

- Enertec Bas ....G 360 786-1257
  Olympia *(G-7277)*
- Filter Clean Recycling LLC ....G 360 798-1012
  Vancouver *(G-14230)*
- Scotts Sheet Metal ....G 360 384-3827
  Ferndale *(G-3902)*

CONTRACTORS: Heating Systems Repair & Maintenance Svc

- Air Pro Heating & Cooling LLC ....F 360 423-9165
  Longview *(G-5884)*
- Harolds Power Vac Inc ....G 509 529-2088
  Walla Walla *(G-14820)*
- Specialty Pump and Plbg Inc.............G 425 424-8700
  Snohomish *(G-11986)*

CONTRACTORS: Highway & Street Construction, General

- ALRT Corporation ....D 360 592-5300
  Everson *(G-3666)*
- Basic Homes LLC ....G 253 579-2724
  Eatonville *(G-3050)*
- Crux Subsurface Inc ....D 509 892-9409
  Spokane Valley *(G-12670)*
- Dickson Company ....G 253 472-4489
  Tacoma *(G-13263)*
- Dyers Construction & Excav ....G 903 486-1881
  Ocean Park *(G-7181)*
- Ecco Contractors Incorporated ....G 425 957-1735
  Bellevue *(G-891)*

PRODUCT SECTION

CONTRACTORS: On-Site Welding

Gary C Horsley ....G...... 360 274-4502
  Winlock *(G-15150)*
Gary Merlino Cnstr Co Inc ....B...... 206 763-9552
  Seattle *(G-10049)*
Gibson & Son Road Building Inc ....F...... 509 925-2017
  Ellensburg *(G-3202)*
Halme Construction Inc ....E...... 509 725-4200
  Spokane *(G-12287)*
James Smith Trucking ....G...... 360 423-1027
  Kelso *(G-4531)*
Jensen Barton W Inc ....F...... 360 825-3750
  Enumclaw *(G-3297)*
Lloyd Logging Inc ....F...... 509 997-2441
  Twisp *(G-13912)*
Northwest Rock Inc ....G...... 360 533-3050
  Aberdeen *(G-25)*
Northwest Rock Inc ....G...... 360 249-2245
  Montesano *(G-6651)*
Pilot Knob Construction Inc ....G...... 509 493-4196
  White Salmon *(G-15127)*
Samoa Maritime Company ....G...... 206 246-1182
  Normandy Park *(G-7098)*
Southside Enterprises Inc ....F...... 509 395-2345
  Trout Lake *(G-13683)*
Tucci & Sons Inc ....D...... 253 922-6676
  Tacoma *(G-13566)*

CONTRACTORS: Highway & Street Paving

Lakeside Industries Inc ....D...... 425 313-2600
  Issaquah *(G-4437)*
Lakeside Industries Inc ....E...... 360 491-5460
  Olympia *(G-7318)*
Lakeside Industries Inc ....E...... 360 423-6882
  Longview *(G-5925)*
Lakeside Industries Inc ....E...... 360 794-7779
  Monroe *(G-6590)*
Lakeside Industries Inc ....E...... 360 604-1869
  Vancouver *(G-14356)*
Poe Asphalt Paving Inc ....E...... 509 334-6400
  Pullman *(G-8101)*
Supr Co ....E...... 509 248-6823
  Yakima *(G-15690)*

CONTRACTORS: Hot Shot Svcs

Hot Shot Express Inc ....G...... 206 241-5516
  Burien *(G-2112)*
Hot Shot Site Dots ....G...... 206 604-8980
  Seattle *(G-10185)*
McLeod Pilot Car & Hot Sht Svc ....G...... 360 701-5827
  Olympia *(G-7334)*
Rw Hot Shot Service ....G...... 509 868-6644
  Spokane *(G-12488)*

CONTRACTORS: Hydraulic Eqpt Installation & Svcs

American Min & Tunneling LLC ....G...... 509 921-7836
  Spokane Valley *(G-12612)*
Clarus Technologies LLC ....G...... 360 671-1514
  Bellingham *(G-1299)*
Dessert Industries Inc ....G...... 425 487-3244
  Snohomish *(G-11898)*

CONTRACTORS: Indl Building Renovation, Remodeling & Repair

Clowers Corporation ....G...... 206 420-1202
  Lake Forest Park *(G-5609)*
Madrona Log HM Repr & Care LLC ....G...... 360 202-2842
  Marysville *(G-6354)*

CONTRACTORS: Insulation Installation, Building

Curnutt Inc ....G...... 208 520-2598
  Pasco *(G-7574)*
IW International Inc ....E...... 509 735-8411
  Kennewick *(G-4679)*
Petrochem Insulation Inc ....E...... 360 254-8953
  Vancouver *(G-14487)*
Service Partners LLC ....D...... 509 535-4600
  Spokane Valley *(G-12866)*
West Coast Insulation Inc ....G...... 206 459-2233
  Seattle *(G-11450)*

CONTRACTORS: Kitchen & Bathroom Remodeling

Above and Beyond Cnstr LLC ....G...... 509 521-8081
  Kennewick *(G-4610)*
Custom Building Services Inc ....G...... 509 422-5746
  Okanogan *(G-7195)*
Designers Marble Inc ....G...... 425 487-9887
  Woodinville *(G-15223)*
Stephan J Lesser Woodworking ....G...... 206 782-9463
  Seattle *(G-11192)*

CONTRACTORS: Kitchen Cabinet Installation

Food Service Eqp Repr Inc ....G...... 206 730-2662
  Shoreline *(G-11773)*
Kern Construction Inc ....G...... 360 805-5598
  Monroe *(G-6586)*

CONTRACTORS: Land Reclamation

American Min & Tunneling LLC ....G...... 509 921-7836
  Spokane Valley *(G-12612)*

CONTRACTORS: Lighting Syst

Netzero Energy LLC ....G...... 360 636-5337
  Longview *(G-5934)*

CONTRACTORS: Maintenance, Parking Facility Eqpt

All Seasons Sweeping Service ....G...... 509 782-8015
  Cashmere *(G-2312)*

CONTRACTORS: Marble Installation, Interior

Pacific Stone & Tile LLC ....F...... 360 352-3960
  Olympia *(G-7365)*

CONTRACTORS: Masonry & Stonework

Custom Masonry & Stove Inc ....G...... 206 524-4714
  Lake Forest Park *(G-5610)*
Mutual Materials ....D...... 425 452-2300
  Bellevue *(G-1020)*

CONTRACTORS: Mechanical

Apollo Sheet Metal Inc ....A...... 509 586-1104
  Kennewick *(G-4618)*
Greenberry Industrial LLC ....G...... 360 366-3767
  Ferndale *(G-3849)*
Ram Piping Industries Inc ....F...... 509 586-0801
  Kennewick *(G-4714)*
Ronald Johnson ....G...... 360 482-4982
  Elma *(G-3256)*
Schneider Elc Buildings LLC ....F...... 509 892-1121
  Spokane Valley *(G-12860)*

CONTRACTORS: Multi-Family Home Remodeling

Above and Beyond Cnstr LLC ....G...... 509 521-8081
  Kennewick *(G-4610)*
Designers Holding Company Inc ....G...... 425 487-9887
  Woodinville *(G-15222)*

CONTRACTORS: Office Furniture Installation

Outsmart Office Solutions Inc ....G...... 888 688-8154
  Mercer Island *(G-6478)*

CONTRACTORS: Oil & Gas Well Casing Cement Svcs

Firepak Oil and Gas Inds LLC ....G...... 360 679-1747
  Oak Harbor *(G-7152)*
On-Site Safety Inc ....G...... 701 774-2022
  Kirkland *(G-5421)*

CONTRACTORS: Oil & Gas Well Drilling Svc

C J Warren & Sons Well Drlg ....G...... 509 924-3872
  Veradale *(G-14749)*
Holman Drilling Corporation ....G...... 509 534-1013
  Spokane Valley *(G-12730)*
Scheffler Northwest Inc ....G...... 360 213-2070
  Vancouver *(G-14571)*

CONTRACTORS: Oil Field Haulage Svcs

Emerald Phoenix Oil Co Llc ....G...... 509 466-0555
  Spokane *(G-12242)*

CONTRACTORS: Oil Field Lease Tanks: Erectg, Clng/Rprg Svcs

NRC Environmental Services Inc ....D...... 206 607-3000
  Seattle *(G-10663)*

CONTRACTORS: Oil Field Pipe Testing Svcs

Ricter Enterprises ....G...... 425 482-5942
  Woodinville *(G-15349)*

CONTRACTORS: Oil/Gas Field Casing,Tube/Rod Running,Cut/Pull

Tube Crazy ....G...... 206 931-7764
  Kirkland *(G-5486)*

CONTRACTORS: Oil/Gas Well Construction, Rpr/Dismantling Svcs

Burnstead Construction Co ....F...... 425 635-1090
  Bellevue *(G-831)*
Dagner Construction ....G...... 509 349-8944
  Warden *(G-14931)*
Dyers Construction & Excav ....G...... 903 486-1881
  Ocean Park *(G-7181)*
Gibraltar Maint & Cnstr Inc ....G...... 206 365-4440
  Redmond *(G-8477)*
Hammer & Tongs LLC ....G...... 206 526-0549
  Seattle *(G-10137)*
Katerra Inc ....A...... 650 422-3572
  Seattle *(G-10330)*
Lorache Cad/lt Services LLC ....F...... 206 328-4227
  Seattle *(G-10442)*
Lyle W Pulling ....G...... 360 825-6129
  Enumclaw *(G-3302)*
M&S Custom Remodeling ....G...... 425 739-0262
  Kirkland *(G-5391)*
Madrona Log HM Repr & Care LLC ....G...... 360 202-2842
  Marysville *(G-6354)*
Master Vac LLC ....G...... 253 875-0074
  Graham *(G-4231)*
McLeod Masonry USA Inc ....F...... 360 734-4427
  Bellingham *(G-1429)*
Murphy JP Construction ....G...... 425 222-7299
  Seattle *(G-10571)*
Northwest REO Preservation LLC ....G...... 360 521-6761
  Vancouver *(G-14440)*
Parametrix Inc ....D...... 206 394-3700
  Puyallup *(G-8219)*
Paynestaking Detail ....G...... 509 599-2207
  Spokane *(G-12433)*
South Sound Contractors LLC ....F...... 360 688-5101
  Lacey *(G-5592)*

CONTRACTORS: On-Site Welding

Associated Mch Fabrication Inc ....F...... 253 395-1155
  Auburn *(G-380)*
B & B Parrotts Welding Inc ....G...... 360 825-0565
  Enumclaw *(G-3277)*
B K Welding and Fabrication ....G...... 360 871-0490
  Port Orchard *(G-7791)*
Centralia Supply & Fabrication ....G...... 360 736-7277
  Centralia *(G-2391)*
Custom Welding ....G...... 206 242-5047
  Burien *(G-2100)*
D&J Custom Metal Fabrication ....G...... 206 242-3238
  Burien *(G-2101)*
Fab-Tech Inc ....G...... 360 755-0215
  Burlington *(G-2156)*
Ferrotek Corporation ....F...... 360 366-7444
  Ferndale *(G-3845)*
Jason Dunton ....G...... 360 293-7256
  Anacortes *(G-137)*
Lorenz Welding ....G...... 360 384-5258
  Ferndale *(G-3865)*
Maintenance Welding Service ....G...... 360 533-4318
  Hoquiam *(G-4348)*
Precision Machine & Mfg ....G...... 360 734-1081
  Bellingham *(G-1502)*
Precision Machine & Tool Inc ....G...... 425 745-6229
  Lynnwood *(G-6184)*
Site Welding Services Inc ....E...... 425 488-2156
  Woodinville *(G-15364)*
Synergy Welding Inc ....G...... 360 881-0204
  Kingston *(G-5265)*
Wenatchee Qlty Wldg Fbrication ....F...... 509 782-0807
  Cashmere *(G-2333)*

CONTRACTORS: Ornamental Metal Work

CONTRACTORS: Ornamental Metal Work

A & B Fabricators Inc ....G....... 253 887-0442
  Auburn (G-355)
Decorative Metal Arts ....G....... 206 782-4009
  Seattle (G-9812)
European Wrought Iron 509 548-4879
  Leavenworth (G-5801)
Homers Ornamental Iron ....G....... 509 327-8673
  Spokane (G-12298)
Little Mexico Ornamental Iron ....G....... 425 334-1082
  Lake Stevens (G-5658)
Northwest Metal Craft ....G....... 509 999-5280
  Spokane Valley (G-12807)
Risley Sons Wldg Fbrcation LLC 509 427-2206
  Carson (G-2306)
Steel Magnolia Inc ....G....... 360 366-5090
  Blaine (G-1704)

CONTRACTORS: Painting & Wall Covering

Bowmans Electro Painting ....G....... 360 668-1389
  Snohomish (G-11880)
Clean Lines LLC ....G....... 509 939-2957
  Deer Park (G-2896)
Kaplan Homes Unlimited LLC ....G....... 360 855-1675
  Sedro Woolley (G-11549)
Rdean Enterprises Inc ....F....... 208 772-8571
  Spokane (G-12468)

CONTRACTORS: Painting, Commercial, Interior

Colosseum Ventures LLC ....F....... 509 533-0366
  Spokane (G-12188)

CONTRACTORS: Painting, Residential

Bennett Painting ....G....... 360 426-6489
  Shelton (G-11683)
Hauge & Hassain Incorporated ....E....... 206 789-8842
  Seattle (G-10149)
Sherwin-Williams Company ....G....... 206 417-4502
  Seattle (G-11100)

CONTRACTORS: Patio & Deck Construction & Repair

Basta Inc ....E....... 425 641-8911
  Bellevue (G-807)
Kitsap Vinyl Deck & Rail LLC ....G....... 360 830-5959
  Seabeck (G-9266)

CONTRACTORS: Petroleum Storage Tanks, Pumping & Draining

Quality Fuel Trlr & Tank Inc ....G....... 425 526-7566
  Monroe (G-6610)

CONTRACTORS: Playground Construction & Eqpt Installation

Child Inc ....G....... 425 775-9076
  Edmonds (G-3100)
Northstar Attachments LLC ....G....... 509 453-8271
  Union Gap (G-13946)

CONTRACTORS: Plumbing

Harris Acquisition IV LLC ....G....... 360 734-3600
  Bellingham (G-1366)
Harris Acquisition IV LLC ....G....... 360 734-3600
  Bellingham (G-1367)
McKinstry Co LLC ....B....... 206 762-3311
  Seattle (G-10509)

CONTRACTORS: Pole Cutting

Weyerhaeuser Company ....G....... 360 245-3245
  Curtis (G-2849)

CONTRACTORS: Post Disaster Renovations

Belfor USA Group Inc ....E....... 206 632-0800
  Tukwila (G-13696)
Belfor USA Group Inc ....G....... 509 453-8551
  Yakima (G-15518)

CONTRACTORS: Posthole Digging

J TS Tractor Work ....G....... 360 263-3016
  La Center (G-5508)

CONTRACTORS: Prefabricated Window & Door Installation

Great Gates NW Inc ....G....... 360 879-5554
  Eatonville (G-3058)
Island Sash & Door Inc ....F....... 360 331-7752
  Freeland (G-4031)
Lindal Cedar Homes Inc ....D....... 206 725-0900
  Seattle (G-10423)
Mitchell Door and Trim Inc ....F....... 360 874-8901
  Port Orchard (G-7830)

CONTRACTORS: Process Piping

Centurion Process LLC ....G....... 509 759-3001
  Selah (G-11584)

CONTRACTORS: Refractory or Acid Brick Masonry

CH Murphy/Clark-Ullman Inc ....D....... 253 475-6566
  Tacoma (G-13232)

CONTRACTORS: Refrigeration

Alaska Marine Refrigeration ....F....... 360 871-4414
  Port Orchard (G-7785)
Metal Smith ....F....... 509 884-4851
  East Wenatchee (G-3025)

CONTRACTORS: Rock Removal

Alan Good ....F....... 360 864-2974
  Toledo (G-13635)

CONTRACTORS: Roofing

Ark Commercial Roofing Inc ....F....... 509 443-9300
  Spokane Valley (G-12625)
Custom Building Services Inc ....G....... 509 422-5746
  Okanogan (G-7195)
Gutters Inc ....G....... 425 482-2679
  Bothell (G-1863)
Krueger Sheet Metal Co ....D....... 509 489-0221
  Spokane (G-12355)
Pacific Sheet Metal Inc ....E....... 206 682-5354
  Seattle (G-10740)
Queen City Shtmtl & Roofg Inc ....E....... 206 623-6020
  Kent (G-5092)
Scotts Home & Roofing Service ....G....... 360 297-7524
  Kingston (G-5263)
White Rabbit Ventures Inc ....G....... 360 474-5828
  Vancouver (G-14690)

CONTRACTORS: Roustabout Svcs

Loreen Home Servicing ....G....... 509 325-4290
  Spokane (G-12375)

CONTRACTORS: Safety & Security Eqpt

Keyking Inc ....G....... 360 977-7870
  Camas (G-2262)

CONTRACTORS: Sandblasting Svc, Building Exteriors

Barnes Welding Inc ....G....... 509 745-8588
  Waterville (G-15005)
Machinists Inc ....C....... 206 763-0990
  Seattle (G-10460)
North PCF Indus Coatings LLC ....G....... 907 865-8400
  Renton (G-8859)

CONTRACTORS: Seismograph Survey Svcs

Cascadia Seismic Inc ....G....... 206 801-5999
  Bothell (G-1837)

CONTRACTORS: Septic System

James A Wright Cnstr LLC ....G....... 509 996-3249
  Winthrop (G-15162)
Long Septic Services ....E....... 253 852-0550
  Lake Stevens (G-5659)
Northwest Cascade Inc ....C....... 253 848-2371
  Puyallup (G-8202)
Okanogan Valley Concrete Inc ....G....... 509 422-3211
  Okanogan (G-7203)
Peninsula Tanks Inc 360 683-4714
  Sequim (G-11659)
Puyallup Septic Pumping ....G....... 253 785-6553
  Puyallup (G-8229)

Rada Inc ....G....... 509 547-7232
  Pasco (G-7621)

CONTRACTORS: Sheet Metal Work, NEC

Capital Heating & Cooling Inc ....E....... 360 491-7450
  Lacey (G-5537)
Mutual Industries Inc ....G....... 206 767-6647
  Seattle (G-10577)
N A I Inc ....G....... 509 453-4778
  Union Gap (G-13945)
North Park Heating Company Inc ....F....... 206 365-1414
  Lake Forest Park (G-5622)
S & R Sheet Metal Inc ....D....... 360 425-7020
  Kelso (G-4546)
Sound Metal Works Ltd ....F....... 360 659-0999
  Marysville (G-6388)
Steel Encounters Inc ....F....... 206 281-8500
  Seattle (G-11186)
T R S Inc 253 444-1555
  Tacoma (G-13538)
U S Sheet Metal Company Inc ....F....... 253 272-2444
  Tacoma (G-13567)

CONTRACTORS: Sheet metal Work, Architectural

Air Pro Heating & Cooling LLC ....F....... 360 423-9165
  Longview (G-5884)
Bestworth - Rommel Inc ....E....... 360 435-2927
  Arlington (G-213)
Risley Sons Wldg Fbrcation LLC ....G....... 509 427-2206
  Carson (G-2306)

CONTRACTORS: Shoring & Underpinning

Pacific Foundation Inc ....F....... 360 200-6608
  Vancouver (G-14464)

CONTRACTORS: Siding

American Vinyl Industries Inc ....G....... 253 473-4731
  Fife (G-3931)

CONTRACTORS: Single-family Home General Remodeling

Dan McMullen Well Drilling ....G....... 707 998-9252
  Ethel (G-3350)
Fred Nanamkin 509 634-8110
  Keller (G-4512)
G R Plume Co ....F....... 360 384-2800
  Ferndale (G-3846)
Hewitt Cabinets & Interiors ....F....... 253 272-0404
  Tacoma (G-13336)
Maizefield Company ....G....... 360 385-6789
  Port Townsend (G-7896)
Warmington & North Co Inc ....F....... 206 324-5043
  Seattle (G-11436)

CONTRACTORS: Solar Energy Eqpt

Global Emergent Tech LLC ....G....... 425 999-9021
  Seattle (G-10083)

CONTRACTORS: Solar Reflecting Insulation Film Installation

Custom Win Tnting Graphics Inc ....G....... 509 453-4293
  Yakima (G-15547)

CONTRACTORS: Sound Eqpt Installation

Fusion9 Design LLC ....G....... 360 831-0899
  Camano Island (G-2214)

CONTRACTORS: Special Trades, NEC

Hensleys Mobile Welding ....G....... 360 532-1633
  Aberdeen (G-16)
Inland Woodworks ....G....... 509 701-0985
  Spokane (G-12314)
Slyfield Enterprises ....G....... 509 968-3456
  Ellensburg (G-3226)
Staircrafters Incorporated ....G....... 360 882-2772
  Vancouver (G-14607)

CONTRACTORS: Spraying, Nonagricultural

Tailored Solutions LLC ....G....... 509 258-4314
  Tumtum (G-13847)

PRODUCT SECTION

CONTROLS: Air Flow, Refrigeration

CONTRACTORS: Steam Cleaning, Building Exterior

Go Ventures Inc .... G 253 313-4070
  Tacoma *(G-13315)*

CONTRACTORS: Storage Tank Erection, Metal

Down Island Trading Co .... G 360 376-4056
  Deer Harbor *(G-2891)*
Risley Sons Wldg Fbrcation LLC .... G 509 427-2206
  Carson *(G-2306)*

CONTRACTORS: Store Fixture Installation

Turner Exhibits Inc .... E 425 776-4930
  Lynnwood *(G-6214)*

CONTRACTORS: Structural Iron Work, Structural

Hci Steel Buildings LLC .... F 360 403-4900
  Arlington *(G-250)*
Oneils Foundry Forging Metal & .... G 360 941-7557
  Sedro Woolley *(G-11553)*
Pacific Northwest Iron LLC .... G 509 499-0668
  Nine Mile Falls *(G-7081)*

CONTRACTORS: Structural Steel Erection

Acufab Inc .... G 509 525-3833
  Walla Walla *(G-14759)*
CBI Services LLC .... E 425 258-2350
  Everett *(G-3411)*
Harris Rebar Seattle Inc .... E 253 847-5001
  Tacoma *(G-13332)*
Morgan Steel & Metal Works .... G 360 301-6611
  Poulsbo *(G-7986)*
Psf Industries Inc .... E 800 426-1204
  Seattle *(G-10881)*
Steel Encounters Inc .... F 206 281-8500
  Seattle *(G-11186)*
Steel Fab Nw Inc .... G 360 210-7055
  Washougal *(G-14987)*
Streich Bros Inc .... E 253 383-1491
  Tacoma *(G-13527)*
Sunset Company LLC .... G 425 351-0839
  Renton *(G-8923)*
Swiss Ornamental Iron .... G 253 759-6796
  Tacoma *(G-13535)*

CONTRACTORS: Svc Station Eqpt Installation, Maint & Repair

OK Tool & Machine Works .... G 360 736-8350
  Centralia *(G-2422)*

CONTRACTORS: Svc Well Drilling Svcs

Barker Drilling .... G 425 252-4686
  Mount Vernon *(G-6774)*
Carpenter Drilling LLC .... F 509 627-6642
  Benton City *(G-1603)*
Malcom Drilling .... G 206 623-0776
  Seattle *(G-10470)*
Pacific NW Probe & Drlg Inc .... G 253 651-2477
  Puyallup *(G-8218)*

CONTRACTORS: Tile Installation, Ceramic

Designers Marble Inc .... G 425 487-9887
  Woodinville *(G-15223)*
Seaport Tile & Marble Inc .... E 425 644-7067
  Bellevue *(G-1120)*

CONTRACTORS: Timber Removal

D & H Enterprises .... G 360 374-9500
  Forks *(G-4009)*
Forsyth Enterprises .... G 360 297-2684
  Kingston *(G-5252)*

CONTRACTORS: Underground Utilities

Diversified Northwest Inc .... F 425 710-0753
  Everett *(G-3444)*
Lloyd Enterprises Inc .... D 253 874-6692
  Federal Way *(G-3753)*
McCain Timber & Bridge Inc .... G 360 520-6595
  Napavine *(G-7011)*

Northwest Cascade Inc .... C 253 848-2371
  Puyallup *(G-8202)*
NW Utility Services LLC .... E 253 891-7802
  Pacific *(G-7536)*

CONTRACTORS: Ventilation & Duct Work

Capital Heating & Cooling Inc .... E 360 491-7450
  Lacey *(G-5537)*

CONTRACTORS: Vinyl Flooring Installation, Tile & Sheet

Dean Thoemke .... G 253 640-2232
  Yakima *(G-15551)*

CONTRACTORS: Warm Air Heating & Air Conditioning

Louis Stoffer & Son .... G 360 736-3820
  Centralia *(G-2418)*
North Park Heating Company Inc ..... F 206 365-1414
  Lake Forest Park *(G-5622)*
Wilson Air Technologies Inc .... G 253 474-9928
  Tacoma *(G-13597)*

CONTRACTORS: Water Intake Well Drilling Svc

Dan McMullen Well Drilling .... G 707 998-9252
  Ethel *(G-3350)*
Daughtrey Machine .... G 509 834-9786
  Yakima *(G-15550)*
Triple A Drilling Inc .... G 509 543-3331
  Burbank *(G-2086)*

CONTRACTORS: Water Well Drilling

Barker Drilling .... G 425 252-4686
  Mount Vernon *(G-6774)*
Blue Star Enterprises NW Inc .... F 509 946-9388
  Richland *(G-8975)*
C J Warren & Sons Well Drlg .... G 509 924-3872
  Veradale *(G-14749)*

CONTRACTORS: Water Well Servicing

Holman Drilling Corporation .... G 509 534-1013
  Spokane Valley *(G-12730)*
Specialty Pump and Plbg Inc .... G 425 424-8700
  Snohomish *(G-11986)*

CONTRACTORS: Waterproofing

Kitsap Vinyl Deck & Rail LLC .... G 360 830-5959
  Seabeck *(G-9266)*
Queen City Shtmtl & Roofg Inc .... E 206 623-6020
  Kent *(G-5092)*

CONTRACTORS: Well Bailing, Cleaning, Swabbing & Treating Svc

Praxair Services Inc .... G 360 676-8215
  Bellingham *(G-1501)*

CONTRACTORS: Well Surveying Svcs

Foster Surveying Inc .... G 503 997-1100
  Camas *(G-2253)*

CONTRACTORS: Windows & Doors

Automatic Door Solutions LLC .... G 253 802-0888
  Orting *(G-7473)*
Tri-City Glass Inc .... G 509 586-0454
  Kennewick *(G-4738)*

CONTRACTORS: Wood Floor Installation & Refinishing

T & A Supply Company Inc .... D 206 282-3770
  Kent *(G-5166)*
T & A Supply Company Inc .... G 253 872-3682
  Kent *(G-5167)*

CONTRACTORS: Wrecking & Demolition

Bobby Wolford Trucking & Salv .... E 425 481-1800
  Woodinville *(G-15195)*
East Valley Sand and Gravel .... E 360 403-7520
  Arlington *(G-232)*
McCain Timber & Bridge Inc .... G 360 520-6595
  Napavine *(G-7011)*

Mulvaney Trucking and Excav .... G 509 784-4502
  Entiat *(G-3268)*
R&S Forestry and Cnstr LLC .... G 360 436-1771
  Arlington *(G-311)*

CONTROL EQPT: Electric

Controls Group The Inc .... G 425 828-4149
  Kirkland *(G-5312)*
Digitron Electronics LLC .... F 509 427-4005
  Stevenson *(G-13011)*
Heatcon Inc .... D 206 575-0815
  Tukwila *(G-13745)*
Heatcon Composite Systems Inc ...... G 206 575-1333
  Tukwila *(G-13746)*
Heatcon Composite Systems Inc ...... D 206 575-1333
  Tukwila *(G-13747)*
Maple Systems Inc .... E 425 745-3229
  Everett *(G-3545)*
Process Solutions Inc .... E 360 629-0910
  Stanwood *(G-12987)*
Usnr LLC .... G 360 225-8267
  Woodland *(G-15470)*

CONTROL PANELS: Electrical

Applied Power & Control Inc .... G 425 710-9911
  Everett *(G-3370)*
Cets LLC .... G 206 992-6993
  Seattle *(G-9663)*
Controlled Power Incorporated .... E 425 485-1778
  Bothell *(G-1842)*
Electrical Packaging Co Inc .... F 425 745-5466
  Everett *(G-3455)*
Equipment Technology & Design ..... G 509 747-5550
  Spokane *(G-12248)*
Evergreen Controls LLC .... G 253 405-3770
  Tacoma *(G-13283)*
Evs Manufacturing Inc .... G 360 863-6413
  Monroe *(G-6570)*
Hundred Horse Panels LLC .... G 509 227-5686
  Liberty Lake *(G-5834)*
Imco Inc .... F 360 694-7121
  Ridgefield *(G-9089)*
Lilibete LLC .... G 206 407-6890
  Kent *(G-4996)*
Ornelas LLC .... G 206 388-2267
  Wenatchee *(G-15055)*

CONTROLS & ACCESS: Indl, Electric

Asphalt Equipment & Service Co ...... E 253 939-4150
  Auburn *(G-379)*
Electric Concept Labs Inc .... G 503 244-3000
  Castle Rock *(G-2342)*
Industrial Systems Inc .... G 503 262-0367
  Vancouver *(G-14314)*
Mekltek Engineering & Mfg .... G 360 384-1607
  Ferndale *(G-3868)*
Precision Data Technology Inc .... G 425 259-9237
  Everett *(G-3583)*
Taurus Power and Controls Inc .... G 425 656-4170
  Kent *(G-5171)*

CONTROLS & ACCESS: Motor

Ces Enterprises .... G 206 443-1742
  Seattle *(G-9661)*
Eaton Agency Inc .... G 509 448-6556
  Spokane *(G-12238)*
Eaton Corp .... G 253 375-6013
  Graham *(G-4224)*
Ink For You Tattoo .... G 360 649-6972
  Port Orchard *(G-7817)*
United Games .... G 360 470-6480
  Oakville *(G-7176)*

CONTROLS: Access, Motor

Stoneway Electric Supply Co .... F 253 859-0224
  Kent *(G-5158)*

CONTROLS: Adjustable Speed Drive

Rogers Terminal and Shipping .... F 253 572-0146
  Tacoma *(G-13502)*

CONTROLS: Air Flow, Refrigeration

Aso Inc .... G 360 883-3962
  Vancouver *(G-14044)*

CONTROLS: Automatic Temperature

CONTROLS: Automatic Temperature

AMP Engineering Services LLC .... G 480 512-1186
  Ellensburg *(G-3183)*
Ample Power Company LLC .... G 206 789-0827
  Seattle *(G-9400)*
Ats Inland Nw LLC .... G 509 892-1000
  Spokane Valley *(G-12630)*

CONTROLS: Crane & Hoist, Including Metal Mill

Checkmate Industries Inc .... G 360 691-1753
  Granite Falls *(G-4266)*
Liftex .... G 253 395-4458
  Kent *(G-4995)*

CONTROLS: Electric Motor

North Coast Electric Company .... F 360 671-1100
  Bellingham *(G-1464)*

CONTROLS: Environmental

Ademco Inc .... G 253 872-7128
  Kent *(G-4759)*
Ademco Inc .... G 509 534-7300
  Spokane *(G-12098)*
Ademco Inc .... G 425 485-3938
  Bothell *(G-1815)*
Controls Group The Inc .... G 425 828-4149
  Kirkland *(G-5312)*
Engineered Bldg Contrls LLC .... G 206 229-7475
  Burien *(G-2105)*
Essential Building Tech LLC .... G 360 573-3200
  Vancouver *(G-14206)*
M K Hansen Company .... G 509 884-1396
  East Wenatchee *(G-3023)*
Nugent Gis & Environmental Svc ...... G 206 324-0059
  Seattle *(G-10668)*
P N D Corporation .... G 425 562-7252
  Bellevue *(G-1057)*
Pacific Environmental Inc .... G 760 877-9796
  Fall City *(G-3705)*
Primeone Products LLC .... G 509 448-8818
  Spokane *(G-12455)*
Reliable Controls Corp USA .... G 250 475-2036
  Ferndale *(G-3892)*
Synergistic Technologies Inc .... G 425 822-7777
  Bellevue *(G-1174)*
Zebra Technical Services LLC .... G 425 485-8700
  Woodinville *(G-15414)*

CONTROLS: Hydronic

A Thousand Hills Inc .... G 360 437-9805
  Port Ludlow *(G-7763)*
Golden Harvest Inc .... D 360 757-4334
  Burlington *(G-2159)*

CONTROLS: Marine & Navy, Auxiliary

Astrake Inc .... G 503 470-4470
  Seattle *(G-9446)*
R G Rollin Co .... G 253 274-0882
  Tacoma *(G-13487)*
Systems Engineering Inc .... G 206 633-4972
  Kirkland *(G-5473)*
W H Autopilots Inc .... F 206 780-2175
  Bainbridge Island *(G-682)*

CONTROLS: Numerical

Camtronics Inc .... G 425 487-0013
  Bothell *(G-1753)*

CONTROLS: Relay & Ind

Anderson Electric Controls .... E 206 575-4444
  Kent *(G-4783)*
Bunker Hill Diagnostics .... G 206 579-1440
  Renton *(G-8765)*
Charter Controls Inc .... F 360 695-2161
  Vancouver *(G-14113)*
Controlfreek Inc .... G 509 979-5677
  Spokane Valley *(G-12666)*
Custom Controls Corporation .... F 253 922-5874
  Fife *(G-3947)*
DC Engineering Consulting Inc .... G 360 932-2367
  Rainier *(G-8313)*
Duren Controls .... G 206 745-4987
  Edmonds *(G-3108)*

Fisher-Rosemount Systems Inc .... G 425 488-4111
  Bothell *(G-1853)*
Norgren Gt Development Corp .... C 206 244-1305
  Auburn *(G-509)*
P G K Inc .... G 425 432-0945
  Maple Valley *(G-6285)*
Rockwell Automation Inc .... F 425 519-5109
  Bellevue *(G-1108)*
S & B Inc .... G 425 746-9312
  Bellevue *(G-1110)*
Seattle Sound & Vibration .... G 425 497-0660
  Redmond *(G-8658)*
Talkie Tooter .... E 360 856-0836
  Sedro Woolley *(G-11574)*
Tiptop Timers LLC .... G 509 448-2819
  Spokane Valley *(G-12906)*

CONTROLS: Thermostats

Automated Tech Solutions LLC .... G 425 999-1297
  Maple Valley *(G-6259)*
Aynano Technology LLC .... G 208 596-9865
  Pullman *(G-8084)*

CONTROLS: Water Heater

Torrid Marine LLC .... G 206 920-9002
  Bainbridge Island *(G-679)*

CONVENIENCE STORES

Chevron Corporation .... G 509 534-4077
  Spokane *(G-12179)*
Chevron Kalama .... F 360 673-2972
  Kalama *(G-4495)*
Pacific Fuel and Convenience .... G 253 631-8512
  Kent *(G-5051)*
Quick Market Inc .... G 509 653-2268
  Naches *(G-7002)*

CONVERTERS: Data

Cisco Systems Inc .... G 360 352-3657
  Lacey *(G-5541)*
Cisco Systems Inc .... C 425 468-0800
  Bellevue *(G-854)*
Evans - Hamilton Inc .... G 206 526-5622
  Seattle *(G-9943)*

CONVERTERS: Torque, Exc Auto

Premier Torque Converter .... G 253 288-2233
  Auburn *(G-535)*

CONVEYOR SYSTEMS

A-1 Welding Inc .... F 360 671-9414
  Bellingham *(G-1237)*

CONVEYOR SYSTEMS: Belt, General Indl Use

Agjet LLC .... F 509 654-9449
  Yakima *(G-15502)*
Columbia Chain Belt Inc .... G 509 546-2000
  Pasco *(G-7562)*
Conveyor Works Inc .... G 360 829-5378
  Buckley *(G-2053)*

CONVEYOR SYSTEMS: Bucket Type

Washington Eqp Mfg Co Inc .... E 509 244-4773
  Spokane *(G-12583)*

CONVEYOR SYSTEMS: Bulk Handling

Atlas Systems LLC .... G 509 535-7775
  Spokane Valley *(G-12629)*

CONVEYOR SYSTEMS: Robotic

Byron Automation LLC .... F 509 653-2100
  Naches *(G-6994)*

CONVEYORS & CONVEYING EQPT

Accucon Inc .... G 509 534-4460
  Spokane Valley *(G-12599)*
Aerogo Inc .... D 206 575-3344
  Tukwila *(G-13689)*
Austin-Mac Inc .... F 206 624-7066
  Seattle *(G-9465)*
Carsoe US Inc .... G 206 408-5869
  Seattle *(G-9637)*

Custom Technology Co Inc .... F 509 965-3333
  Yakima *(G-15546)*
Dematic Corp .... A 206 674-4578
  Tukwila *(G-13723)*
Easterday Diesel Manufacturing .... G 509 269-4577
  Mesa *(G-6492)*
Edco Inc .... E 360 424-6600
  Mount Vernon *(G-6792)*
Empire Rubber & Supply Co .... F 509 547-0026
  Pasco *(G-7579)*
Fish Transport Systems LLC .... G 206 801-3565
  Seattle *(G-9997)*
Harrah Farm Shop .... G 509 848-2941
  Harrah *(G-4320)*
Intermountain Fabricators Inc .... F 509 534-1676
  Spokane Valley *(G-12746)*
Pomona Service & Supply Co .... G 509 452-7121
  Yakima *(G-15649)*
Pro West Mechanical Inc .... F 509 965-1750
  Wapato *(G-14924)*
Reconveyance Professionals Inc .... G 425 257-3038
  Arlington *(G-313)*
Remcon Equipment Inc .... F 509 244-9439
  Airway Heights *(G-61)*
Source Engineering LLC .... E 360 383-5129
  Lynden *(G-6053)*
T & K Cstm Fabrication & Repr .... G 206 242-0197
  Seattle *(G-11247)*
Tramco Inc .... G 425 347-3030
  Everett *(G-3635)*
Transco Northwest Inc .... E 425 251-5422
  Kent *(G-5188)*
Whooshh Innovations Inc .... F 206 801-3565
  Seattle *(G-11471)*

COOKING & FOOD WARMING EQPT: Commercial

Almeda Cottage Inc .... E 206 285-1674
  Seattle *(G-9384)*
Beverage Specialist Inc .... E 206 763-0255
  Tukwila *(G-13697)*
Davis Development & Mfg .... G 360 892-7802
  Vancouver *(G-14168)*
Legend Brands .... G 360 757-7776
  Burlington *(G-2168)*

COOKING & FOODWARMING EQPT: Coffee Brewing

Coffee Catcher LLC .... G 202 704-2868
  Seattle *(G-9711)*
Creative Concepts .... G 425 743-4671
  Edmonds *(G-3104)*
Inland Coffee and Beverage .... G 509 228-9239
  Spokane Valley *(G-12741)*
La Marzocco International LLC .... G 206 706-9104
  Seattle *(G-10367)*
Original Expresso Machine .... G 360 686-3643
  Yacolt *(G-15490)*
Quality Brewing Incorporated .... G 866 268-5953
  Kelso *(G-4543)*
Synesso Inc .... F 206 764-0600
  Seattle *(G-11244)*

COOKING & FOODWARMING EQPT: Commercial

Capstan Fund .... G 206 626-0800
  Seattle *(G-9626)*
Star Manufacturing Intl Inc .... C 800 882-6368
  Everett *(G-3620)*

COOKING & FOODWARMING EQPT: Popcorn Machines, Commercial

Cellular To Go Inc .... G 253 255-1955
  Gig Harbor *(G-4085)*
Jts Kettlecorn .... G 509 962-2524
  Ellensburg *(G-3209)*

COOKING EQPT, HOUSEHOLD: Indoor

Modernchef Inc .... G 425 202-6252
  Bellevue *(G-1013)*

COOKING EQPT, HOUSEHOLD: Ranges, Gas

Whirlpool Corporation .... E 253 875-7100
  Spanaway *(G-12081)*

PRODUCT SECTION

COOKWARE, STONEWARE: Coarse Earthenware & Pottery

Cook On Clay .... G 360 678-1818
  Coupeville *(G-2812)*
Gurglepot Inc .... G 253 670-6240
  Pacific *(G-7528)*

COOLING TOWERS: Metal

Evergreen Cooling Tech Inc .... G 360 983-3691
  Mossyrock *(G-6761)*

COPING MATERIALS

Hamilton Materials Wash LLC .... D 360 225-6888
  Woodland *(G-15439)*

COPPER ORES

Silver King Mining & Milling .... G 509 445-1406
  Cusick *(G-2852)*

COPPER: Cakes, Primary

Peekaboo Cupcakery .... G 206 458-6986
  Seattle *(G-10778)*

COPPER: Rolling & Drawing

Kenneth A Edleman .... G 206 524-2814
  Seattle *(G-10337)*

COPY MACHINES WHOLESALERS

Business Equipment Center Inc .... F 509 747-2964
  Spokane *(G-12162)*
Overnight Prtg & Graphics Inc .... G 206 621-9412
  Seattle *(G-10721)*
Preferred Business Solutions .... G 425 251-1202
  Kent *(G-5079)*

CORD & TWINE

Bridport-Air Carrier Inc .... E 253 872-7205
  Kent *(G-4823)*
Coppertop Enterprises Inc .... E 360 966-9622
  Everson *(G-3672)*
Craft International of Wash .... G 360 785-3606
  Winlock *(G-15148)*
Mid Mountain Materials Inc .... E 206 762-7600
  Seattle *(G-10539)*
Noreastern Trawl Systems Inc .... E 206 842-5623
  Bainbridge Island *(G-652)*
Pnw Select Marketing Group LLC ..... G 360 746-8270
  Ferndale *(G-3888)*
Romanzof Fishing Company LLC ..... F 206 545-9501
  Seattle *(G-10977)*
Samson Rope Technologies Inc .... C 360 384-4669
  Ferndale *(G-3896)*
Seattle Tarp Co Inc .... E 206 285-2819
  Seattle *(G-11080)*

CORES: Magnetic

Allstar Magnetics LLC .... E 360 693-0213
  Vancouver *(G-14022)*

CORK & CORK PRDTS: Tiles

Slawek Tiles .... G 253 529-0823
  Auburn *(G-566)*

CORRECTIONAL INSTITUTIONS

Department Crrctons Wash State ..... B 509 526-6375
  Walla Walla *(G-14795)*

CORRECTIONAL INSTITUTIONS, GOVERNMENT: Jail

County of Asotin .... F 509 758-1668
  Clarkston *(G-2628)*

CORRUGATED PRDTS: Boxes, Partition, Display Items, Sheet/Pad

Easy Fold Fixtures .... F 425 209-0167
  Kent *(G-4883)*
Medical Equipment Dev Co LLC .... G 206 364-3894
  Shoreline *(G-11788)*

CORRUGATING MACHINES

Alliance Mch Systems Intl LLC .... B 509 842-5104
  Spokane Valley *(G-12604)*

COSMETIC PREPARATIONS

Antica Farmacista LLC .... G 206 329-3966
  Seattle *(G-9406)*
Arbordoun .... G 360 468-2508
  Lopez Island *(G-5978)*
Chimeras LLC .... G 360 754-9217
  Olympia *(G-7249)*
Econet Inc .... E 360 486-8300
  Seattle *(G-9880)*
Grace Harvest & Assoc LLC .... F 206 973-2363
  Mercer Island *(G-6464)*
Honey House Naturals Inc .... F 253 926-8193
  Fife *(G-3958)*
Jeffrey James LLC .... G 562 541-6976
  Seattle *(G-10290)*
Koh Gen Do Americas LLC .... G 253 267-1769
  Dupont *(G-2968)*
Nion Beauty Inc .... G 206 228-5988
  Bothell *(G-1880)*
Paulas Choice LLC .... C 425 988-6068
  Seattle *(G-10772)*
Paulas Choice Holdings Inc .... G 425 988-6068
  Seattle *(G-10773)*
Renewalliance Inc .... G 425 633-3368
  Bellevue *(G-1100)*

COSMETICS & TOILETRIES

12 Scents .... G 206 588-0314
  Seattle *(G-9316)*
Art of Shaving - Fl LLC .... G 206 737-8370
  Seattle *(G-9437)*
Art of Shaving - Fl LLC .... G 253 777-0993
  Tacoma *(G-13181)*
Basic Topicals LLC .... G 206 397-3309
  Seattle *(G-9498)*
Biozn LLC .... G 206 388-7865
  Bellevue *(G-818)*
Butter London LLC .... G 206 624-1085
  Seattle *(G-9602)*
Camille .... G 206 284-0407
  Seattle *(G-9613)*
Crystalwolfe Blends .... G 509 217-2132
  Cheney *(G-2582)*
Enervana LLC .... G 253 220-8413
  Tukwila *(G-13729)*
Everlasting Scents LLC .... G 509 534-4790
  Spokane Valley *(G-12695)*
Favorite Discovery LLC .... G 646 337-3574
  Vancouver *(G-14225)*
Fiddle and Fern .... G 206 898-4165
  Sammamish *(G-9206)*
Franklin and Franklin Company .... G 360 254-4767
  Vancouver *(G-14239)*
Herbivore Botanicals LLC .... G 206 226-5008
  Seattle *(G-10167)*
House of Matriarch Inc .... G 425 466-7783
  Bellevue *(G-950)*
K&G Scents .... G 206 380-1831
  Seattle *(G-10321)*
Kona Gold Corp .... G 425 836-0389
  Kirkland *(G-5377)*
Maysbeautproductscom .... G 253 318-8772
  Auburn *(G-493)*
National Hsptlity Rsources LLC .... G 360 413-1654
  Olympia *(G-7348)*
Natural Essences .... G 509 820-3242
  Kennewick *(G-4699)*
Nester Brothers LLC .... G 253 320-9405
  Tacoma *(G-13426)*
Olympic Mountain Products Inc .... E 253 850-2343
  Kent *(G-5044)*
Organic Creations .... G 503 891-0479
  Vancouver *(G-14457)*
Pureblisnaturals .... G 253 719-2683
  University Place *(G-13977)*
Rainborn Essentials .... G 253 988-5889
  Bonney Lake *(G-1736)*
Resonant Botanicals LLC .... G 360 969-5065
  Clinton *(G-2694)*
Scrub Nogginz LLC .... G 425 931-9251
  Snohomish *(G-11971)*
Seattle Pomade Co .... G 206 348-3972
  Mill Creek *(G-6527)*
Shadow Works LLC .... G 509 251-8306
  Spokane Valley *(G-12867)*

COUNTER & SINK TOPS

Sik Scents LLC .... G 206 420-4647
  Seattle *(G-11111)*
Simply Joyful LLC .... G 425 686-5311
  Everett *(G-3611)*
Underground1969 Co .... G 747 254-0595
  Seattle *(G-11367)*
Whidbey Island Ntural Pdts Inc .... G 360 929-2461
  Freeland *(G-4040)*
Yon LLC .... G 360 947-5895
  Vancouver *(G-14706)*

COSMETICS WHOLESALERS

Nion Beauty Inc .... G 206 228-5988
  Bothell *(G-1880)*
Shadow Works LLC .... G 509 251-8306
  Spokane Valley *(G-12867)*
Something For Everybody .... G 541 805-8495
  College Place *(G-2728)*

COSTUME JEWELRY & NOVELTIES: Apparel, Exc Precious Metals

Flatter Heights .... G 509 238-6192
  Chattaroy *(G-2446)*
Nora Haugan .... G 360 877-0602
  Lilliwaup *(G-5872)*

COSTUME JEWELRY & NOVELTIES: Bracelets, Exc Precious Metals

Build-A-Bracelet .... G 919 757-1219
  Covington *(G-2821)*
Fallen Hero Bracelets .... G 253 537-1212
  Tacoma *(G-13288)*

COSTUME JEWELRY & NOVELTIES: Costume Novelties

Flytes of Fancy .... G 206 306-9233
  Shoreline *(G-11772)*

COSTUME JEWELRY & NOVELTIES: Exc Semi & Precious

Jane Martin .... G 206 842-4569
  Bainbridge Island *(G-644)*
Plateau Jewelers Inc .... G 425 313-0657
  Sammamish *(G-9242)*
Stones By Marie Inc .... G 206 643-1520
  Renton *(G-8920)*
Turtleworks .... G 425 335-0394
  Everett *(G-3638)*

COSTUME JEWELRY & NOVELTIES: Keychains, Exc Precious Metal

Minnysonoda Corporation .... F 360 863-8141
  Monroe *(G-6597)*

COSTUME JEWELRY & NOVELTIES: Pins, Exc Precious Metals

Yvette J Cooke .... G 360 718-0306
  Vancouver *(G-14707)*

COUNTER & SINK TOPS

Carlson Custom .... G 360 756-0351
  Bellingham *(G-1291)*
Contour Countertops Inc .... F 503 654-2245
  Vancouver *(G-14150)*
Counter Intuitive .... G 360 264-5150
  Tenino *(G-13614)*
Countertops For Less .... G 360 306-3921
  Bellingham *(G-1308)*
Edgebanding Services Inc .... F 866 395-7002
  Kent *(G-4884)*
Gds Direct Countertops Ltd .... G 360 312-9688
  Ferndale *(G-3848)*
Lakewood Counter Tops Inc .... F 253 588-8550
  Lakewood *(G-5733)*
Lg Hausys America Inc .... G 425 251-3698
  Tukwila *(G-13765)*
Madrona Stone LLC .... G 253 750-5064
  Sumner *(G-13083)*
Quality Counter .... G 425 303-9180
  Everett *(G-3590)*
Valley Cabinets & More Inc .... G 360 428-0916
  Mount Vernon *(G-6851)*

Employee Codes: A=Over 500 employees, B=251-500
C=101-250, D=51-100, E=20-50, F=10-19, G=2-9

COUNTERS & COUNTING DEVICES

COUNTERS & COUNTING DEVICES
Kichi Systems LLC ....G....... 509 924-7672
  Spokane *(G-12350)*
Triex Technologies Inc ....G....... 425 363-2239
  Snoqualmie *(G-12034)*
Wesco Sales Group Inc ....G....... 206 227-5980
  Bothell *(G-1916)*

COUNTERS OR COUNTER DISPLAY CASES, EXC WOOD
Tim Krotzer ....G....... 509 487-2704
  Spokane *(G-12558)*
Venetian Stone Works LLC ....F....... 425 486-1234
  Woodinville *(G-15399)*

COUPLINGS: Hose & Tube, Hydraulic Or Pneumatic
RJ Hydraulics Inc ....F....... 360 693-4399
  Vancouver *(G-14553)*

COUPLINGS: Shaft
Magnadrive Corporation ....E....... 425 487-2881
  Woodinville *(G-15299)*

COURIER SVCS, AIR: Parcel Delivery, Private
Critical Delivery Service LLC ....G....... 206 724-3653
  Bellevue *(G-868)*

COURIER SVCS: Package By Vehicle
Federal Express Corporation ....G....... 800 463-3339
  Spokane *(G-12253)*
Jack Just Enterprises LLC ....G....... 425 836-7755
  Redmond *(G-8518)*
Urban Buggy LLC ....G....... 206 743-5727
  Seattle *(G-11389)*

COVERS & PADS Chair, Made From Purchased Materials
Malone Manufacturing LLC ....G....... 360 366-9964
  Custer *(G-2857)*

COVERS: Automobile Seat
United States Sheepskin Inc ....F....... 253 627-7114
  Tacoma *(G-13571)*
Willingham Inc ....F....... 425 432-9867
  Maple Valley *(G-6302)*

COVERS: Book, Fabric
Betty OGuin ....G....... 360 876-0803
  Port Orchard *(G-7794)*

COVERS: Hot Tub & Spa
Leisure Home & Spa ....G....... 360 647-5529
  Bellingham *(G-1406)*

CRANE & AERIAL LIFT SVCS
Mikes Custom Welding ....G....... 360 754-3719
  Tumwater *(G-13887)*
Washington Crane Hoist Co Inc ....G....... 360 694-9844
  Vancouver *(G-14678)*

CRANES: Indl Plant
Ederer LLC ....F....... 800 464-1320
  Seattle *(G-9883)*
High Caliber Mill ....E....... 360 984-6669
  Vancouver *(G-14295)*
Timken Motor & Crane Svcs LLC ....E....... 509 547-1691
  Pasco *(G-7638)*
Washington Crane Hoist Co Inc ....G....... 360 694-9844
  Vancouver *(G-14678)*

CRANES: Indl Truck
Hawthorne Hill ....G....... 253 572-3744
  Tacoma *(G-13333)*

CRANES: Overhead
Washington Eqp Mfg Co Inc ....E....... 509 244-4773
  Spokane *(G-12583)*

CRANKSHAFTS & CAMSHAFTS: Machining
J & L Machining and More LLC ....G....... 503 317-8284
  La Center *(G-5507)*
Omega Architectural Pdts Inc ....G....... 425 821-7222
  Kirkland *(G-5417)*
Proto-Rpid McHning Sltions LLC ....G....... 503 744-0358
  Vancouver *(G-14514)*
Toliys Jig Fabrication ....G....... 509 534-2261
  Spokane *(G-12562)*

CRAYONS
Color ME House Inc ....G....... 360 742-8646
  Olympia *(G-7252)*

CREATIVE SVCS: Advertisers, Exc Writers
Advangelists LLC ....G....... 734 546-4989
  Seattle *(G-9355)*

CREDIT & OTHER FINANCIAL RESPONSIBILITY INSURANCE
Ford Motor Credit Company LLC ....D....... 425 643-0454
  Bellevue *(G-914)*

CREDIT AGENCIES: Federal & Federally Sponsored
Trans Pac Enterprises Inc ....F....... 425 688-0037
  Bellevue *(G-1198)*

CREDIT CARD SVCS
American Bancard LLC ....E....... 360 713-0690
  Vancouver *(G-14026)*

CREDIT INST, SHORT-TERM BUSINESS: Financing Dealers
Ford Motor Credit Company LLC ....D....... 425 643-0454
  Bellevue *(G-914)*
Paccar Inc ....B....... 425 468-7400
  Bellevue *(G-1058)*

CRUDE PETROLEUM & NATURAL GAS PRODUCTION
Energy Consulting Services LLC ....G....... 701 580-9732
  Long Beach *(G-5874)*
Summit Carbon Capture LLC ....G....... 206 780-3551
  Seattle *(G-11217)*

CRUDE PETROLEUM & NATURAL GAS PRODUCTION
Annointed Oil Inc ....G....... 206 242-6925
  Seattle *(G-9405)*
Camwest Inc ....G....... 425 776-7900
  Lynnwood *(G-6086)*
Coinstar LLC ....G....... 866 733-2693
  Vancouver *(G-14128)*
Cool Racing Oil ....G....... 971 235-7611
  Sequim *(G-11619)*
Daybreak Oil and Gas Inc ....G....... 509 232-7674
  Spokane Valley *(G-12679)*
Dose Oil LLC ....G....... 954 494-7976
  Mill Creek *(G-6508)*
Ephrata Oil Change Express ....G....... 509 398-8740
  Ephrata *(G-3334)*
Grease Heads Lube and Oil LLC ....G....... 509 930-3786
  East Wenatchee *(G-3017)*
Green Star Energies Inc ....G....... 360 989-5549
  Vancouver *(G-14271)*
Jackson Oil Anthony Schnell ....G....... 253 847-2566
  Graham *(G-4227)*
K & S Oil Field Services Inc ....G....... 509 998-5738
  Elk *(G-3171)*
Khans Oil LLC ....G....... 360 668-6415
  Vancouver *(G-14347)*
Myinterzone ....G....... 206 679-4566
  Seattle *(G-10581)*
One Oil Lovin Mama ....G....... 360 572-4511
  Stanwood *(G-12984)*
Seattle Oil Solution LLC ....G....... 206 375-7575
  Seattle *(G-11067)*
Shell Energy North Amer US LP ....G....... 509 688-6002
  Spokane *(G-12502)*
Skinny Producing ....G....... 425 443-4552
  Bellevue *(G-1135)*

(continued)
Starry Field Services ....G....... 360 676-7441
  Bellingham *(G-1556)*
Tesoro Companies Inc ....D....... 253 896-8700
  Federal Way *(G-3794)*
Tesoro Maritime Company ....G....... 360 293-3111
  Anacortes *(G-176)*
USA Oil LLC ....G....... 425 226-5555
  Renton *(G-8938)*
Weyerhaeuser Company ....A....... 206 467-3600
  Seattle *(G-11460)*

CRUDE PETROLEUM PRODUCTION
Andeavor ....G....... 509 586-2117
  Kennewick *(G-4617)*
Andeavor ....G....... 509 928-5632
  Spokane Valley *(G-12617)*
Andeavor ....G....... 360 374-2038
  Forks *(G-4008)*
Andeavor ....G....... 509 487-9235
  Spokane *(G-12114)*
BP West Coast Products LLC ....B....... 360 856-5022
  Sedro Woolley *(G-11533)*
BP West Coast Products LLC ....A....... 360 371-1500
  Blaine *(G-1665)*
Tesoro Corporation ....G....... 509 533-2705
  Spokane *(G-12553)*

CRYSTALS
Epson Toyocom Seattle Inc ....F....... 360 200-5537
  Longview *(G-5909)*

CULTURE MEDIA
Carol Braden Inc ....G....... 206 715-9397
  Seattle *(G-9635)*
Greyslade ....G....... 253 332-5985
  Tacoma *(G-13325)*
Kc Wheelwright ....G....... 206 799-9822
  Seattle *(G-10333)*
New Culture Media ....G....... 206 406-1934
  Bothell *(G-1780)*

CULVERTS: Sheet Metal
Cascade Pipe & Feed Supply ....G....... 509 997-0720
  Twisp *(G-13910)*

CUPS & PLATES: Foamed Plastics
Dart Container Corp Georgia ....E....... 360 352-7045
  Tumwater *(G-13870)*

CUPS: Plastic Exc Polystyrene Foam
Northwest Plastic Tech LLC ....E....... 206 499-6292
  Edmonds *(G-3138)*

CURBING: Granite Or Stone
Antony Architectural Stone ....G....... 425 424-0051
  Woodinville *(G-15179)*
Lee R Mason Inc ....G....... 253 863-8666
  Sumner *(G-13079)*
Stone Castle Fabrication LLC ....G....... 253 205-8435
  Auburn *(G-573)*
Zorzi Corporation ....G....... 425 334-0160
  Snohomish *(G-12002)*

CURTAIN & DRAPERY FIXTURES: Poles, Rods & Rollers
American Drpery Blind Crpt Inc ....E....... 425 793-4477
  Renton *(G-8742)*
Creative Window Concepts ....G....... 425 351-2246
  Issaquah *(G-4400)*
Johnson Enterprises ....G....... 253 537-8056
  Tacoma *(G-13365)*
Seattle Curtain Mfg Co ....E....... 206 324-0692
  Mill Creek *(G-6526)*
Source Northwest Inc ....D....... 360 512-3535
  Woodinville *(G-15370)*
Traditional Concepts ....G....... 253 884-2818
  Gig Harbor *(G-4168)*

CURTAINS: Shower
Agalite Seattle ....G....... 425 656-2626
  Tukwila *(G-13690)*

PRODUCT SECTION

CUSHIONS & PILLOWS

Alex Daisley..G....... 206 623-5555
  Seattle *(G-9373)*
Corona Decor Company.......................F....... 206 763-1600
  Seattle *(G-9741)*
Pacific Coast Feather LLC ....C....... 206 624-1057
  Seattle *(G-10729)*

CUSHIONS & PILLOWS: Bed, From Purchased Materials

West Coast Fiber Inc...............................F....... 253 850-5606
  Kent *(G-5210)*

CUSHIONS & PILLOWS: Boat

Jh Marine LLC..G....... 425 241-6801
  Kirkland *(G-5373)*

CUSHIONS: Carpet & Rug, Foamed Plastics

American Excelsior Company ....E....... 509 575-5794
  Yakima *(G-15507)*

CUSTOMIZING SVCS

Armour Mfg & Cnstr Inc ....G....... 253 984-1213
  Tacoma *(G-13180)*
Pra Inc ....F....... 408 743-5300
  Arlington *(G-304)*

CUT STONE & STONE PRODUCTS

Bedrock Industries Inc ....F....... 206 283-7625
  Seattle *(G-9508)*
Cascade Marble & Granite ....G....... 509 533-0476
  Spokane *(G-12171)*
Columbia Cultured MBL II LLC ....G....... 509 582-5660
  Kennewick *(G-4648)*
Gabrielle England Inc ....G....... 360 956-1017
  Olympia *(G-7292)*
Gary Merlino Cnstr Co Inc.....................F....... 206 763-2134
  Seattle *(G-10050)*
Kings Kitchen LLC ....G....... 253 212-3623
  Tacoma *(G-13376)*
Lapel Solutions LLC ....F....... 360 597-4958
  Vancouver *(G-14358)*
Manufacturers Mineral Company ....F....... 425 228-2120
  Renton *(G-8847)*
Mario & Son Inc......................................E....... 509 536-6079
  Liberty Lake *(G-5845)*
Nichols Bros Stoneworks Ltd ....E....... 360 668-5434
  Snohomish *(G-11951)*
Premier Memorial LLC ....E....... 253 472-0369
  Tacoma *(G-13477)*
Quiring Monuments Inc..........................E....... 206 522-8400
  Seattle *(G-10906)*
Rock Place...G....... 425 220-1110
  Marysville *(G-6379)*

CUTLERY

Bladegallery Inc ....G....... 425 889-5980
  Kirkland *(G-5292)*
Pacific Hide & Fur Depot ....E....... 509 545-0688
  Pasco *(G-7611)*

CUTLERY WHOLESALERS

Rena Ware International Inc..................E....... 425 881-6171
  Bellevue *(G-1098)*

CUTOUTS: Paper or Paperboard, Made From Purchased Materials

Nippon Dynawave Packaging Co ....G....... 360 414-3379
  Federal Way *(G-3763)*

CYCLIC CRUDES & INTERMEDIATES

Emerald Kalama Chemical LLC ....C....... 360 673-2550
  Kalama *(G-4499)*

CYLINDER & ACTUATORS: Fluid Power

American West Industries Inc................F....... 509 535-5040
  Spokane *(G-12111)*
Custom Hydraulic & Machine Inc ....F....... 253 854-4666
  Kent *(G-4868)*
GE Aviation Systems LLC ....C....... 206 662-2934
  Tukwila *(G-13737)*
Nabtesco Aerospace Inc ....E....... 425 602-8400
  Kirkland *(G-5407)*

Service Hydraulics Inc............................F....... 253 351-6010
  Auburn *(G-561)*
Superior Fluid Power Inc........................G....... 509 482-7949
  Spokane Valley *(G-12896)*

DAIRY EQPT

Diamond Blue Manufacturing Co ....E....... 360 428-1744
  Mount Vernon *(G-6789)*
Excel Dairy Service Inc..........................E....... 360 848-9494
  Mount Vernon *(G-6794)*
Wilson Dairy ....G....... 360 736-6001
  Rochester *(G-9147)*

DAIRY PRDTS STORE: Cheese

Bay City Sausage Co Inc ....G....... 360 648-2344
  Aberdeen *(G-4)*
Steves Hot Smked Cheese Salmon.......G....... 360 829-2244
  Buckley *(G-2075)*

DAIRY PRDTS STORE: Ice Cream, Packaged

Baskin-Robbins..G....... 425 793-3544
  Bellevue *(G-806)*
Jesus Romero ....G....... 509 545-9551
  Pasco *(G-7595)*
Snoqualmie Gourmet Ice Cream ....G....... 360 668-8535
  Snohomish *(G-11984)*

DAIRY PRDTS STORES

Evolving Nutrition ....F....... 425 355-5682
  Everett *(G-3467)*
Farm Breeze International LLC..............G....... 253 365-0542
  Tacoma *(G-13291)*

DAIRY PRDTS WHOLESALERS: Fresh

Andersen Dairy Inc ....D....... 360 687-7171
  Battle Ground *(G-687)*
Dairyland Orthopedics Pubg ....G....... 509 868-0096
  Spokane *(G-12216)*
Inland Northwest Dairies LLC ....D....... 509 489-8600
  Spokane *(G-12310)*
Northwest Dairy Association ....C....... 206 284-7220
  Seattle *(G-10641)*

DAIRY PRDTS: Butter

Balleywood Creamery ....G....... 206 920-5173
  Seattle *(G-9486)*
Cokedale Creamery LLC ....G....... 360 856-1695
  Sedro Woolley *(G-11535)*
Cosmic Creamery LLC ....G....... 425 633-7742
  Kirkland *(G-5314)*
Darigold Inc ....D....... 425 392-6463
  Issaquah *(G-4402)*
Darigold Inc ....D....... 509 489-8600
  Spokane *(G-12217)*
Dungeness Valley Creamery ....G....... 360 683-0716
  Sequim *(G-11630)*
Ethos Bakery LLC ....G....... 509 942-8799
  Richland *(G-8994)*
Ferndale Creamery Co LLC...................G....... 360 255-7062
  Ferndale *(G-3842)*

DAIRY PRDTS: Cheese

Appel Farms LLC ....F....... 360 384-4996
  Ferndale *(G-3815)*
Black Sheep Creamery ....M....... 360 520-3397
  Seattle *(G-9538)*
Joan F Schleh ....G....... 360 424-4112
  Mount Vernon *(G-6805)*
Northwest Dairy Association ....C....... 206 284-7220
  Seattle *(G-10641)*
Washington State University ....D....... 509 335-4014
  Pullman *(G-8113)*

DAIRY PRDTS: Cheese, Cottage

Darigold Inc ....D....... 425 392-6463
  Issaquah *(G-4402)*

DAIRY PRDTS: Cream, Aerated

Northwest Dairy Association ....C....... 206 284-7220
  Seattle *(G-10641)*

DAIRY PRDTS: Dietary Supplements, Dairy & Non-Dairy Based

25 Bits Inc ....G....... 206 861-3836
  Kent *(G-4747)*
Aloe 2000 ....G....... 206 420-8785
  Seattle *(G-9385)*
Astamed..G....... 206 812-0270
  Seattle *(G-9445)*
Astareal Inc...E....... 509 855-4370
  Moses Lake *(G-6680)*
Bharat Ratan LLC ....G....... 206 458-3322
  Renton *(G-8755)*
BHP Holdings Inc ....F....... 425 462-8414
  Woodinville *(G-15190)*
Cascade Intgrtive Medicine LLC ....G....... 425 391-5270
  Issaquah *(G-4390)*
Columbia Nutritional LLC......................C....... 360 737-9966
  Vancouver *(G-14135)*
Emerald City Smoothie...........................G....... 253 826-6664
  Bonney Lake *(G-1723)*
Evolving Nutrition ....F....... 425 355-5682
  Everett *(G-3467)*
IMS Corporation ....G....... 509 687-8116
  Chelan *(G-2555)*
Pharma Terra Inc ....G....... 800 215-3957
  Mercer Island *(G-6479)*
Probi Usa Inc ....G....... 425 883-9518
  Redmond *(G-8632)*
Pure Health Products LLC ....G....... 360 688-7034
  Lacey *(G-5579)*
Reesman Co ....G....... 253 564-7997
  Fircrest *(G-4004)*
Summit Lake Labs LLC ....F....... 509 738-4313
  Kettle Falls *(G-5241)*
Terato Products LLC..............................G....... 425 702-6365
  Redmond *(G-8689)*
Tntgamble Inc...E....... 425 883-9518
  Redmond *(G-8693)*

DAIRY PRDTS: Dips & Spreads, Cheese Based

Bfy Food Group LLC ....G....... 425 298-5523
  Bellevue *(G-816)*

DAIRY PRDTS: Evaporated Milk

Nestle Usa Inc ....C....... 425 844-3201
  Carnation *(G-2296)*

DAIRY PRDTS: Frozen Desserts & Novelties

A J R Enterprises Inc ....G....... 253 946-1708
  Federal Way *(G-3711)*
Baskin Robbins 1361..............................G....... 425 226-3113
  Renton *(G-8751)*
Baskin-Robbins..G....... 425 793-3544
  Bellevue *(G-806)*
Cowboyz ....G....... 206 793-6831
  Tacoma *(G-13246)*
Dina Helmts ....G....... 509 521-9866
  Pasco *(G-7577)*
Emerald City Smoothie...........................G....... 253 564-1966
  Tacoma *(G-13277)*
Faith Dairy Inc ....E....... 253 531-3398
  Tacoma *(G-13287)*
Gariko LLC ....G....... 509 933-1821
  Ellensburg *(G-3201)*
Heavenly Gelato Inc...............................F....... 360 426-0696
  Shelton *(G-11699)*
Jesus Romero ....G....... 509 545-9551
  Pasco *(G-7595)*
M-K-D Distributors Inc ....C....... 425 251-0809
  Kent *(G-4999)*
Megan Nieforth ....G....... 509 380-6543
  Pasco *(G-7602)*
Molly Moons Homemade Ice Cream......G....... 206 547-5105
  Seattle *(G-10557)*
Mora LLC ....E....... 206 855-1112
  Poulsbo *(G-7985)*
Nestle Dreyers Ice Cream Co ....D....... 425 251-0809
  Kent *(G-5019)*
Paleteria Lanorpeana..............................G....... 509 839-5802
  Sunnyside *(G-13136)*
Seattle Pops ....G....... 206 714-1354
  Shoreline *(G-11808)*
Snoqualmie Gourmet Ice Cream ....G....... 360 668-8535
  Snohomish *(G-11984)*
Transcold Distribution USA Inc ....G....... 604 519-0600
  Kent *(G-5189)*

Employee Codes: A=Over 500 employees, B=251-500
C=101-250, D=51-100, E=20-50, F=10-19, G=2-9

DAIRY PRDTS: Frozen Desserts & Novelties

Washington State University .... D 509 335-4014
 Pullman *(G-8113)*
Whidbey Island Ice Cream LLC .... G 425 359-6372
 Freeland *(G-4039)*

DAIRY PRDTS: Ice Cream & Ice Milk

Hain Refrigerated Foods Inc .... F 425 485-2476
 Mountlake Terrace *(G-6862)*

DAIRY PRDTS: Ice Cream, Bulk

Cherry De Pon .... G 253 277-1907
 Covington *(G-2823)*
Cherry De Pon .... G 425 226-5246
 Renton *(G-8771)*
Marias Hawaiian Snow .... G 509 217-1612
 Colbert *(G-2711)*
Yo Gs Gh .... G 253 858-9647
 Gig Harbor *(G-4177)*
Yo Yakima .... G 509 426-2925
 Yakima *(G-15721)*

DAIRY PRDTS: Milk, Condensed & Evaporated

Dairy Queens Vancouver .... E 360 256-7302
 Vancouver *(G-14164)*
Deboer Dairy LLC .... E 360 757-2660
 Burlington *(G-2151)*
Northwest Dairy Association .... C 206 284-7220
 Seattle *(G-10641)*
USA Milk Processing LLC .... G 202 657-5399
 Olympia *(G-7418)*
Washington State University .... D 509 335-4014
 Pullman *(G-8113)*

DAIRY PRDTS: Milk, Fluid

Castle Rock Goat Farm LLC .... G 509 961-5613
 Zillah *(G-15751)*
Country Morning Farms Inc .... E 509 349-2958
 Warden *(G-14929)*
Darigold Inc .... B 206 722-2655
 Seattle *(G-9793)*
Faith Dairy Inc .... E 253 531-3398
 Tacoma *(G-13287)*
Harvest House .... G 509 238-6970
 Colbert *(G-2707)*
Inland Northwest Dairies LLC .... D 509 489-8600
 Spokane *(G-12310)*
Smith Brothers Farms Inc .... E 253 852-1000
 Kent *(G-5135)*
Sno Valley Milk LLC .... F 360 410-8888
 Snohomish *(G-11979)*
Wilcox Farms Inc .... F 360 458-6903
 Roy *(G-9166)*

DAIRY PRDTS: Milk, Processed, Pasteurized, Homogenized/Btld

Andersen Dairy Inc .... D 360 687-7171
 Battle Ground *(G-687)*
Auburn Dairy Products Inc .... E 253 833-3400
 Auburn *(G-381)*
Darigold Inc .... D 509 489-8600
 Spokane *(G-12217)*
Lukens Farms Inc .... G 360 366-4151
 Custer *(G-2856)*

DAIRY PRDTS: Natural Cheese

Good Planet Foods LLC .... G 425 449-8134
 Bellevue *(G-931)*
Kurt Timmermeister .... G 206 696-0989
 Vashon *(G-14728)*
Laurels Crown LLC .... G 509 860-2510
 Wenatchee *(G-15042)*
Omicron Investment Corporation .... G 360 413-7569
 Olympia *(G-7361)*
Port Townsend Lcl Mktplc LLC .... G 360 732-0696
 Chimacum *(G-2613)*
Quillisascut Cheese Co .... G 509 738-2011
 Rice *(G-8960)*
Willapa Hills Cheese LLC .... G 360 291-3937
 Chehalis *(G-2543)*

DAIRY PRDTS: Pastes, Cheese

Nutradried Food Company LLC .... D 360 366-4567
 Ferndale *(G-3880)*

DAIRY PRDTS: Powdered Milk

Commercial Creamery Co .... D 509 747-4131
 Spokane *(G-12192)*
Commercial Creamery Co Ida Inc .... D 509 747-4131
 Spokane *(G-12193)*

DAIRY PRDTS: Processed Cheese

Annette Kraft .... G 501 319-5073
 Bellingham *(G-1248)*
Kraft .... G 509 375-2992
 Pasco *(G-7597)*
Kraft Foods .... G 253 395-4237
 Kent *(G-4983)*
Kurt Timmermeister .... G 206 696-0989
 Vashon *(G-14729)*
Schreiber Foods Inc .... C 425 286-6598
 Bothell *(G-1899)*
Stephen M Kraft .... G 509 465-1980
 Spokane *(G-12528)*

DAIRY PRDTS: Yogurt, Exc Frozen

Berry Nutty .... G 425 265-1680
 Everett *(G-3386)*
Finnegan Frost .... G 509 572-2477
 Richland *(G-8997)*
Flying Cow Creamery LLC .... G 360 273-1045
 Rochester *(G-9132)*
Froyo Earth .... G 509 888-7201
 Chelan *(G-2554)*
Froyo Fresh .... G 206 447-4599
 Seattle *(G-10031)*
Go Manna Inc .... G 360 794-7480
 Snohomish *(G-11914)*
Houghton Plaza .... G 425 298-4857
 Kirkland *(G-5360)*
Isaacs Incrdbl Frz Yogurt LLC .... G 509 928-9497
 Spokane Valley *(G-12747)*
Joe Froyo LLC .... G 909 204-1301
 Tacoma *(G-13361)*
Yakama Yogert Shack LLC .... G 509 965-5569
 Yakima *(G-15712)*

DAIRY PRDTS: Yogurt, Frozen

Revelations Yogurt LLC .... F 425 744-6012
 Edmonds *(G-3145)*
Swirl .... G 425 292-0909
 North Bend *(G-7126)*
Tartberry Incorporated .... G 503 295-2700
 Battle Ground *(G-743)*

DANCE INSTRUCTOR & SCHOOL

Ascendance Pole & Aerial Arts .... G 425 256-2246
 Renton *(G-8748)*

DATA PROCESSING & PREPARATION SVCS

Arcblock Inc .... F 425 442-5101
 Bellevue *(G-793)*
Financial Management Systems .... G 425 881-8687
 Issaquah *(G-4414)*
Omage Labs Inc .... G 844 662-4326
 Seattle *(G-10696)*
Rleyh Software LLC .... G 425 837-4643
 Issaquah *(G-4469)*

DATA PROCESSING SVCS

Enhanced Software Products Inc .... E 509 534-1514
 Spokane Valley *(G-12693)*
Omega Labs Inc .... G 425 296-0886
 Kirkland *(G-5418)*
Pacific Ally LLC .... G 360 760-4266
 La Center *(G-5511)*

DAVITS

Nick Jackson Co Inc .... F 425 481-1381
 Redmond *(G-8594)*
Vestdavit Inc .... G 425 355-4692
 Edmonds *(G-3160)*

DECALS, WHOLESALE

Decal Factory .... G 509 465-8931
 Spokane *(G-12222)*

DECORATIVE WOOD & WOODWORK

Aayers .... G 253 872-5108
 Kent *(G-4753)*
AGC Cww .... G 360 608-4642
 Vancouver *(G-14011)*
Barbanc .... G 206 552-0852
 Seattle *(G-9491)*
Cascade Woodwrights .... G 360 771-3908
 Vancouver *(G-14108)*
CDI Custom Design Inc .... E 360 650-1150
 Bellingham *(G-1294)*
DOE Run Studios .... G 360 765-0935
 Quilcene *(G-8282)*
Erics Woodwork .... G 206 860-6174
 Seattle *(G-9938)*
Kadi Manufacturing .... G 360 668-5633
 Snohomish *(G-11929)*
Kern Construction Inc .... G 360 805-5598
 Monroe *(G-6586)*
Louisiana-Pacific Corporation .... F 503 821-5001
 Vancouver *(G-14383)*
Michael Dresdner .... G 253 770-1664
 Puyallup *(G-8191)*
Orpilla Santiago .... G 360 876-1976
 Port Orchard *(G-7838)*
Pacific Coast Evergreen Inc .... E 360 876-2061
 Port Orchard *(G-7840)*
Peter Blue Woodworks .... G 206 542-4281
 Shoreline *(G-11800)*
Planned Solutions LLC .... G 425 827-4277
 Kirkland *(G-5435)*
Rising Moon Products .... G 206 439-0338
 Burien *(G-2126)*
Rustik Kreations .... G 509 674-7271
 Cle Elum *(G-2678)*
Salmon River Design Inc .... G 425 503-7987
 Woodinville *(G-15352)*
Solis Ortus .... G 206 463-6245
 Vashon *(G-14743)*
Stitch N Wood .... G 360 354-1211
 Lynden *(G-6055)*
Sunrisebuswerk .... G 360 866-7240
 Olympia *(G-7401)*
Ten Talents .... G 360 256-0205
 Battle Ground *(G-744)*
Westerly Wood Working .... G 360 480-4840
 Olympia *(G-7424)*
Whisd Craft .... G 253 850-7126
 Kent *(G-5215)*

DEFENSE SYSTEMS & EQPT

Argus Defense LLC .... G 206 707-6373
 Kent *(G-4790)*
Boeing Company .... C 206 689-4059
 Renton *(G-8760)*
Burg Criminal & Dui Defense .... G 206 467-3190
 Seattle *(G-9599)*
Ckreed Defense LLC .... G 206 297-2116
 Burien *(G-2096)*
Defensestorm Inc .... G 858 228-1903
 Seattle *(G-9815)*
Diversified Defense .... G 253 327-0862
 Edgewood *(G-3075)*
Do or Dye Self Defense .... G 253 653-5696
 Des Moines *(G-2934)*
Kidd Defense .... G 509 290-6171
 Spokane *(G-12351)*
Lc Logic Defense and Space LLC .... G 425 270-5169
 Everett *(G-3535)*
Rainier Defense LLC .... G 253 218-2999
 Auburn *(G-543)*
Raytheon Company .... C 360 394-7559
 Keyport *(G-5246)*
Rook Defense LLC .... G 206 518-3593
 Auburn *(G-549)*
Safe Defense LLC .... G 509 430-5731
 Kennewick *(G-4724)*
Safety Defense Technology .... G 360 718-2078
 Vancouver *(G-14566)*
Swim Scott .... G 253 968-3389
 Tacoma *(G-13534)*
Wolff Defense .... G 425 284-2000
 Kirkland *(G-5496)*
Zultimate Self Defense Studios .... G 425 688-7888
 Bellevue *(G-1235)*

DEGREASING MACHINES

Franklin Machinery .... G 360 581-5079
 Aberdeen *(G-11)*

PRODUCT SECTION

Oliver Machinery Company ....G........ 253 867-0334
   Kent *(G-5043)*

DEHUMIDIFIERS: Electric

Wilson Air Technologies Inc ....G........ 253 474-9928
   Tacoma *(G-13597)*

DEHYDRATION EQPT

Marel Seattle Inc..D........ 206 781-1827
   Seattle *(G-10475)*

DENTAL EQPT

Aseptico Inc...D........ 425 487-3157
   Woodinville *(G-15181)*
Gator Dental Equip ....G........ 360 770-3502
   Concrete *(G-2786)*
Integrity Dental LLC ....G........ 253 691-7292
   Orting *(G-7481)*
Pascal Company Inc ....E........ 425 827-4694
   Bellevue *(G-1063)*
Reach Service LLC ....G........ 253 370-6229
   University Place *(G-13978)*

DENTAL EQPT & SPLYS

Airway Metrics LLC ....G........ 206 949-8839
   Tacoma *(G-13159)*
Alvelogro Inc ....G........ 425 831-1110
   Snoqualmie *(G-12004)*
Central Dental Technicians ....G........ 509 663-4113
   Wenatchee *(G-15017)*
Clay In Motion Inc ....F........ 509 529-6146
   Walla Walla *(G-14785)*
Contacez LLC ....F........ 360 694-1000
   Vancouver *(G-14149)*
Dental X Ray Support Systems ....F........ 509 279-2061
   Spokane *(G-12224)*
Fairy Floss ....G........ 206 364-3218
   Seattle *(G-9963)*
Hf Acquisition Co LLC ....E........ 800 331-1984
   Mukilteo *(G-6932)*
Im3 Inc..F........ 360 254-2981
   Vancouver *(G-14309)*
Innovative Dental Tech Inc ....G........ 971 303-5659
   Camas *(G-2257)*
Parts Warehouse Inc ....G........ 360 354-4722
   Lynden *(G-6045)*
Phazr LLC ....G........ 509 329-8306
   Spokane *(G-12440)*
Philips Oral Healthcare LLC ....A........ 425 487-7000
   Bothell *(G-1886)*
Qualident Dental Lab LLC ....E........ 360 695-7411
   Vancouver *(G-14517)*
Sagemax Bioceramics Inc...........................E........ 253 214-0389
   Federal Way *(G-3780)*
Shadewave ....G........ 425 557-7788
   Issaquah *(G-4473)*

DENTAL EQPT & SPLYS WHOLESALERS

Parts Warehouse Inc ....G........ 360 354-4722
   Lynden *(G-6045)*

DENTAL EQPT & SPLYS: Dental Hand Instruments, NEC

Ems Dental Designs Inc ....G........ 425 584-7206
   Covington *(G-2827)*
Vector R&D Inc ....G........ 877 883-7455
   University Place *(G-13983)*

DENTAL EQPT & SPLYS: Dental Materials

Comfort Acrylics Inc ....G........ 360 834-9218
   Camas *(G-2241)*

DENTAL EQPT & SPLYS: Denture Materials

Taylor Dental Studio ....G........ 360 249-4329
   Montesano *(G-6660)*

DENTAL EQPT & SPLYS: Enamels

Award Dental II LLC ....G........ 253 520-0100
   Kent *(G-4804)*
Bellevue Dental Excellence ....G........ 425 378-1600
   Bellevue *(G-810)*
Carssow John ....G........ 425 820-7995
   Woodinville *(G-15206)*
Center For Dental Implants ....G........ 509 765-5141
   Moses Lake *(G-6690)*

Fouad Farhat ....G........ 206 628-0404
   Seattle *(G-10016)*
Generations Dental ....G........ 360 379-1591
   Port Townsend *(G-7886)*
Jerry Brown ....G........ 509 684-3736
   Colville *(G-2759)*
Olympic Peninsula Implants ....G........ 360 385-5121
   Port Townsend *(G-7904)*
Osbourne Square Dental ....G........ 425 225-5757
   Mill Creek *(G-6519)*
Peaceful Sole ....G........ 425 652-7043
   Issaquah *(G-4458)*
Rutillo Chaves ....G........ 425 775-0651
   Lynnwood *(G-6190)*
Soos Creek Dental ....F........ 253 631-8241
   Covington *(G-2839)*
Sun Rise Dental ....G........ 253 856-3384
   Kent *(G-5161)*

DENTAL EQPT & SPLYS: Orthodontic Appliances

Hager Worldwide Inc ....G........ 360 210-5084
   Washougal *(G-14958)*
Pacific Coast Manufacturing..........................F........ 425 485-8866
   Woodinville *(G-15328)*
Pacific Orthodontic Laboratory ....G........ 425 224-4193
   Everett *(G-3564)*
Silverdale Orthodontic Lab ....G........ 360 479-5536
   Bremerton *(G-2000)*

DENTAL EQPT & SPLYS: Teeth, Artificial, Exc In Dental Labs

Seattle Gold Grills ....G........ 206 250-0833
   Seattle *(G-11060)*
T & S Dental Group Corp.............................G........ 714 720-5511
   Kent *(G-5168)*

DENTAL EQPT & SPLYS: Tools, NEC

Myotronics-Noromed Inc...............................F........ 206 243-4214
   Kent *(G-5017)*

DENTISTS' OFFICES & CLINICS

Soos Creek Dental ....F........ 253 631-8241
   Covington *(G-2839)*
T & S Dental Group Corp.............................G........ 714 720-5511
   Kent *(G-5168)*

DEODORANTS: Personal

Miracle Studios ....G........ 833 728-3233
   Bonney Lake *(G-1729)*
Procter & Gamble Company ....C........ 425 313-3511
   Issaquah *(G-4461)*

DEPARTMENT STORES

Vertical Visual Solutions ....G........ 425 361-1562
   Mountlake Terrace *(G-6873)*

DEPARTMENT STORES: Country General

Endicott Truck & Tractor ....G........ 509 657-3436
   Endicott *(G-3264)*

DERMATOLOGICALS

Adapt Labs Inc ....G........ 206 842-2040
   Bainbridge Island *(G-606)*
Grove and Kane Inc ....G........ 425 407-3454
   Everett *(G-3507)*
Sol Sunguard Corporation ....E........ 206 283-0409
   Seattle *(G-11153)*

DESIGN SVCS, NEC

American Bnchmark Mch Wrks LLC ....G........ 360 584-9303
   Olympia *(G-7224)*
Centurion Process LLC ....G........ 509 759-3001
   Selah *(G-11584)*
Dwight Company LLC....................................G........ 360 262-9844
   Chehalis *(G-2490)*
Holmes and Associates ....G........ 360 793-9723
   Monroe *(G-6578)*
L G Artworks Inc ....G........ 425 355-9143
   Everett *(G-3533)*
Mango and Lime Design LLC.......................G........ 425 985-8994
   Redmond *(G-8547)*
Mr Rpm LLC...G........ 360 387-2272
   Camano Island *(G-2218)*

DIAGNOSTIC SUBSTANCES

Simplicity ABC LLC ....G........ 425 250-1186
   Fall City *(G-3708)*
TX Fine Designs Inc ....G........ 425 271-2866
   Tukwila *(G-13830)*

DESIGN SVCS: Commercial & Indl

Go2origins LLC ....G........ 425 413-4134
   Ravensdale *(G-8336)*
L Clasen Corp..G........ 360 658-1823
   Snohomish *(G-11935)*
Nozzleworks Inc ....G........ 360 668-2548
   Bothell *(G-1881)*
Precision Fldpower Systems LLC ....G........ 206 938-2894
   Seattle *(G-10851)*
Waiv Aerospace LLC ....G........ 206 276-2306
   Bellevue *(G-1222)*

DESIGN SVCS: Computer Integrated Systems

Amdocs Qpass Inc..F........ 206 447-6000
   Seattle *(G-9391)*
Astrake Inc..G........ 503 470-4470
   Seattle *(G-9446)*
Aynano Technology LLC ....G........ 208 596-9865
   Pullman *(G-8084)*
Cronus Ventures LLC ....G........ 425 641-4497
   Bellevue *(G-869)*
Desema Company ....G........ 425 202-7572
   Redmond *(G-8438)*
F5 Networks Inc ....C........ 206 272-5555
   Seattle *(G-9959)*
Graphicode Inc ....E........ 360 282-4888
   Snohomish *(G-11915)*
Helldyne Inc..G........ 206 855-1227
   Bainbridge Island *(G-638)*
Hewlett-Packard Company............................C........ 800 325-5372
   Vancouver *(G-14294)*
Hildebrand Consulting ....G........ 206 465-1729
   Lake Forest Park *(G-5614)*
ID Integration Inc ....F........ 425 438-2533
   Mukilteo *(G-6940)*
Incremental Systems Corp............................G........ 425 732-2377
   Bellevue *(G-956)*
Lorache Cad/It Services LLC ....F........ 206 328-4227
   Seattle *(G-10442)*
M I S Construction Software ....G........ 425 882-3027
   Kirkland *(G-5389)*
Monaco Enterprises Inc................................D........ 509 926-6277
   Spokane Valley *(G-12793)*
Oatridge-Evergreen 8a2 JV LLC ....G........ 253 627-3794
   Tacoma *(G-13439)*
Squarerigger Inc ....F........ 360 698-3562
   Silverdale *(G-11859)*
Verizon Communications Inc ....F........ 425 641-5900
   Bellevue *(G-1214)*

DETECTION APPARATUS: Electronic/Magnetic Field, Light/Heat

Gallivan Gallivan & Omelia ....F........ 206 652-1441
   Seattle *(G-10046)*
Northwest Marine Tech Inc ....E........ 360 468-3375
   Shaw Island *(G-11671)*
Sensormatic Electronics LLC ....D........ 253 851-6500
   Gig Harbor *(G-4160)*

DETECTION EQPT: Aeronautical Electronic Field

Skookem Aerospace Mfg ....G........ 206 365-8027
   Kent *(G-5133)*

DETECTION EQPT: Magnetic Field

Auroraview LLC ....F........ 206 724-5953
   Redmond *(G-8388)*

DETECTORS: Water Leak

Detec Systems LLC ....G........ 253 272-3252
   Tacoma *(G-13260)*

DIAGNOSTIC SUBSTANCES

Abr Inc...G........ 509 334-2968
   Pullman *(G-8080)*
Cell Systems Corporation ....G........ 425 823-1010
   Kirkland *(G-5301)*
Kamiya Biomedical Company LLC...............F........ 206 575-8068
   Tukwila *(G-13760)*

DIAGNOSTIC SUBSTANCES

Kent Laboratories Inc .... F 360 398-8641
  Bellingham *(G-1392)*

DIAGNOSTIC SUBSTANCES OR AGENTS: Enzyme & Isoenzyme

Genzyme Corporation .... D 425 245-1221
  Lynnwood *(G-6129)*

DIAGNOSTIC SUBSTANCES OR AGENTS: Hematology

Photon Biosciences LLC .... G 509 595-0159
  Pullman *(G-8100)*

DIAGNOSTIC SUBSTANCES OR AGENTS: In Vitro

Bio-RAD Laboratories Inc .... C 425 881-8300
  Redmond *(G-8403)*
Biotangent Diagnostics LLC .... G 503 713-3339
  Issaquah *(G-4385)*
Mep Labs LLC .... G 206 229-2525
  Renton *(G-8852)*
Prevencio Inc .... G 425 576-1200
  Kirkland *(G-5441)*
S2m Enterprises LLC .... G 509 919-3714
  Spokane Valley *(G-12857)*

DIAGNOSTIC SUBSTANCES OR AGENTS: Microbiology & Virology

Eurofins Microbiology Labs Inc .... G 425 686-1996
  Bothell *(G-1762)*

DIAGNOSTIC SUBSTANCES OR AGENTS: Radioactive

Cardinal Health 414 LLC .... G 206 763-4411
  Seattle *(G-9630)*
Petnet Solutions Inc .... G 425 656-1640
  Kent *(G-5065)*
Petnet Solutions Inc .... G 509 455-4178
  Spokane *(G-12439)*

DIAGNOSTIC SUBSTANCES OR AGENTS: Veterinary

J J J Farms Inc .... G 360 398-8641
  Bellingham *(G-1386)*

DIAMONDS, GEMS, WHOLESALE

Pacific Gem Inc .... G 206 448-7700
  Seattle *(G-10733)*
Urban Diamond Tools .... G 206 824-6819
  Des Moines *(G-2949)*

DIAMONDS: Cutting & Polishing

Diamond Tech Innovations Inc .... E 360 866-1337
  Olympia *(G-7270)*
Pacific Jewelers .... G 360 693-3410
  Vancouver *(G-14465)*

DIAPERS: Disposable

Malone Manufacturing LLC .... G 360 366-9964
  Custer *(G-2857)*

DIATOMACEOUS EARTH MINING SVCS

Distribution Northwest Inc .... G 206 963-6126
  Bothell *(G-1846)*

DIE SETS: Presses, Metal Stamping

U S Wax & Polymer Inc .... E 509 922-1069
  Spokane Valley *(G-12918)*

DIES & TOOLS: Special

Alliance Mfg Group LLC .... G 253 922-3090
  Tacoma *(G-13165)*
Danielson Tool & Die .... E 509 924-5734
  Spokane Valley *(G-12678)*
Dry Fly or Die .... G 509 252-5022
  Spokane *(G-12233)*
Global Product Development .... G 509 487-1155
  Spokane Valley *(G-12720)*
Gurian Instruments Inc .... G 206 467-7990
  Seattle *(G-10133)*

Hubbard Jointers Incorporated .... G 509 235-2148
  Cheney *(G-2587)*
J C Ross Co Inc .... G 206 241-0715
  Seattle *(G-10268)*
Mikes Machine .... G 360 652-4046
  Stanwood *(G-12980)*
Pacific Die Cast Inc .... E 360 571-9681
  Vancouver *(G-14463)*
Pacific Tool Inc .... D 425 882-1970
  Redmond *(G-8609)*
Precision Tooling and Die .... G 253 872-8217
  Renton *(G-8883)*
Stewart Industries Inc .... E 206 652-9110
  Seattle *(G-11194)*
Traction Capital Partners Inc .... G 253 922-3090
  Tacoma *(G-13561)*
West Coast Automation Corp .... E 509 773-5055
  Goldendale *(G-4213)*

DIES: Cutting, Exc Metal

Precision Steel Rule Die Co .... G 206 397-3982
  Seattle *(G-10853)*
US Dies Inc .... G 509 248-0404
  Yakima *(G-15701)*

DIES: Paper Cutting

Graphic Impressions Inc .... E 253 872-0555
  Kent *(G-4925)*

DIES: Plastic Forming

Altek Inc .... C 509 921-0597
  Liberty Lake *(G-5825)*
Weissert Tool & Design Inc .... G 360 835-7256
  Washougal *(G-15000)*

DIES: Steel Rule

US Dies Inc .... G 509 248-0404
  Yakima *(G-15701)*

DIODES: Light Emitting

Dennis Nelson .... G 360 320-4237
  Oak Harbor *(G-7148)*
Global Display North Amer Ltd .... G 425 698-1938
  Bellevue *(G-927)*
Growlife Inc .... F 866 781-5559
  Kirkland *(G-5356)*
Optic Led Grow Lights LLC .... G 971 704-2912
  Tacoma *(G-13444)*
Wirekat Enterprises .... G 425 413-6946
  Kent *(G-5217)*

DIRECT SELLING ESTABLISHMENTS, NEC

S & W Management Co Inc .... E 425 771-6850
  Lynnwood *(G-6191)*
Urban Buggy LLC .... G 206 743-5727
  Seattle *(G-11389)*

DIRECT SELLING ESTABLISHMENTS: Bakery Goods, House-To-House

Cake Time Unque Tste Sweet LLC .... G 253 886-9366
  Dupont *(G-2956)*

DIRECT SELLING ESTABLISHMENTS: Beverage Svcs

Connelly Company Inc .... G 509 935-6755
  Chewelah *(G-2601)*
I-90 Express LLC .... G 509 855-6280
  Ephrata *(G-3337)*

DIRECT SELLING ESTABLISHMENTS: Food Svc, Coffee-Cart

Fstopcafe LLC .... G 206 842-0335
  Bainbridge Island *(G-635)*
Little Bean Coffee LLC .... G 425 829-8289
  Redmond *(G-8535)*

DIRECT SELLING ESTABLISHMENTS: Food Svcs

Sodexo .... G 425 656-2860
  Renton *(G-8915)*

DIRECT SELLING ESTABLISHMENTS: Housewares, House-To-House

Rena Ware International Inc .... E 425 881-6171
  Bellevue *(G-1098)*

DIRECT SELLING ESTABLISHMENTS: Snacks

Freedom Snacks LLC .... G 253 886-1838
  Normandy Park *(G-7094)*

DIRECT SELLING ESTABLISHMENTS: Telemarketing

Bad Bags Inc .... G 206 722-0916
  Seattle *(G-9476)*

DISHWASHING EQPT: Household

Whirlpool Corporation .... E 253 875-7100
  Spanaway *(G-12081)*

DISK & DISKETTE CONVERSION SVCS

Diversified Systems Group Inc .... E 425 947-1500
  Redmond *(G-8442)*

DISK DRIVES: Computer

Diversified Systems Group Inc .... E 425 947-1500
  Kent *(G-4875)*
Mikes Help Key LLC .... G 360 897-2880
  Buckley *(G-2064)*

DISKETTE DUPLICATING SVCS

McG Health Llc .... E 206 389-5300
  Seattle *(G-10507)*

DISPENSERS: Soap

Mill Race Farm .... G 509 964-2473
  Thorp *(G-13628)*

DISPENSING EQPT & PARTS, BEVERAGE: Beer

Innovative Manufacturing Inc .... G 360 966-7250
  Bellingham *(G-1379)*
Ten Pin Brewing Company .... G 509 750-0396
  Moses Lake *(G-6753)*

DISPENSING EQPT & PARTS, BEVERAGE: Fountain/Other Beverage

Pepsi Cola Bottling Co Pasco .... E 509 248-1313
  Pasco *(G-7616)*

DISPLAY CASES: Refrigerated

Synsor LLC .... C 425 551-1300
  Everett *(G-3624)*

DISPLAY FIXTURES: Showcases, Wood, Exc Refrigerated

Ennco Display Systems Inc .... F 425 883-1650
  Redmond *(G-8449)*

DISPLAY FIXTURES: Wood

Burke Gibson LLC .... E 253 735-4444
  Auburn *(G-398)*
Imagicorps Inc .... E 425 869-0599
  Redmond *(G-8506)*
Northwest Building Tech Inc .... E 206 767-4012
  Seattle *(G-10638)*
Spacewall West Inc .... G 253 852-0203
  Kent *(G-5143)*
Synsor LLC .... C 425 551-1300
  Everett *(G-3624)*

DISPLAY LETTERING SVCS

Terry Signs .... G 509 662-6672
  Wenatchee *(G-15081)*

DISTILLERS DRIED GRAIN & SOLUBLES

Bainbridge Organic Distillers .... G 206 842-3184
  Bainbridge Island *(G-614)*

PRODUCT SECTION

DRINKING PLACES: Bars & Lounges

Double V Distillery ....G....... 360 666-0716
  Battle Ground *(G-699)*
Heritage Distilling Co Inc ....G....... 253 509-0008
  Gig Harbor *(G-4118)*

DOCKS: Floating, Wood

Northwest Dock Systems LLC ....G....... 360 832-2295
  Eatonville *(G-3064)*
Transpac Marinas Inc ....G....... 360 293-8888
  Anacortes *(G-178)*

DOCKS: Prefabricated Metal

Bellingham Marine Industries ....D....... 360 676-2800
  Bellingham *(G-1266)*

DOCUMENT DESTRUCTION SVC

Entrust Community Services ....D....... 509 839-8066
  Sunnyside *(G-13124)*

DOLLIES: Industrial

T E C I Inc..F....... 509 452-3672
  Union Gap *(G-13953)*

DOLOMITIC MARBLE: Crushed & Broken

White Stone Calcium Corp......................G....... 509 935-0838
  Chewelah *(G-2610)*
White Stone Calcium Corp......................G....... 509 738-6571
  Kettle Falls *(G-5243)*

DOOR & WINDOW REPAIR SVCS

Automatic Door Solutions LLC.................G....... 253 802-0888
  Orting *(G-7473)*

DOOR FRAMES: Wood

A 1 Doors Inc..G....... 604 591-1044
  Kent *(G-4751)*
Custom Choice Door LLC ....G....... 253 472-0963
  Lakewood *(G-5710)*

DOOR OPERATING SYSTEMS: Electric

Automatic Door Solutions LLC.................G....... 253 802-0888
  Orting *(G-7473)*
Hrh Door Corp..F....... 509 575-0832
  Kennewick *(G-4672)*
Hy-Security Gate Inc ....E....... 253 867-3700
  Kent *(G-4945)*
Stanley Access Tech LLC........................G....... 425 493-0482
  Mukilteo *(G-6979)*

DOORS & WINDOWS WHOLESALERS: All Materials

Hrh Door Corp..D....... 360 736-7651
  Centralia *(G-2409)*
J M C Cabinets & Interiors ....E....... 425 258-1204
  Everett *(G-3520)*
Tri-City Glass Inc...................................G....... 509 586-0454
  Kennewick *(G-4738)*
Trimlite Seattle Inc ....E....... 425 251-8685
  Renton *(G-8931)*
White Rabbit Ventures Inc.......................F....... 360 474-5828
  Vancouver *(G-14690)*

DOORS & WINDOWS: Screen & Storm

A Thrifty Custom Screens ....G....... 425 337-2211
  Bothell *(G-1813)*
Ceco Door Products ....G....... 253 872-8174
  Kent *(G-4843)*
Lundgren Enterprises..............................G....... 206 789-1122
  Seattle *(G-10453)*

DOORS & WINDOWS: Storm, Metal

Home Builders Service Company ....F....... 509 747-1206
  Spokane *(G-12296)*
Windorco Supply Inc ....G....... 206 784-9440
  Seattle *(G-11482)*

DOORS: Fiberglass

Fabtek Industries Llc...............................F....... 360 322-7367
  Arlington *(G-235)*
Tri-City Glass Inc...................................G....... 509 586-0454
  Kennewick *(G-4738)*

DOORS: Fire, Metal

Building Specialty Systems ....G....... 425 483-6875
  Ellensburg *(G-3185)*

DOORS: Garage, Overhead, Metal

Overhead Door Corporation ....G....... 253 520-8008
  Fife *(G-3977)*
S G&C Contractor Services LLC ....G....... 360 671-5121
  Bellingham *(G-1520)*
Starline Construction Inc ....G....... 509 575-7955
  Yakima *(G-15682)*

DOORS: Garage, Overhead, Wood

Building Specialty Systems ....G....... 425 483-6875
  Ellensburg *(G-3185)*
Jim Lemons Doors & Cabinets.................G....... 360 871-4001
  Port Orchard *(G-7820)*
S G&C Contractor Services LLC ....G....... 360 671-5121
  Bellingham *(G-1520)*
Starline Construction Inc ....G....... 509 575-7955
  Yakima *(G-15682)*

DOORS: Glass

AAA Kartak Co ....G....... 425 844-8555
  Everett *(G-3355)*
Atrium Windows and Door Wash ....B....... 509 248-4462
  Union Gap *(G-13921)*
ESP Supply Company LLC ....F....... 503 256-2933
  Vancouver *(G-14205)*
Hartung Glass Industries ....D....... 206 772-7800
  Tukwila *(G-13743)*
Hartung Glass Industries ....G....... 206 772-7800
  Tukwila *(G-13744)*
Real Carriage Door Company ....G....... 253 853-3815
  Gig Harbor *(G-4152)*

DOORS: Wooden

Bagdons Inc...E....... 509 662-1411
  Wenatchee *(G-15011)*
Bellevue Door & Millwork Co ....G....... 425 885-3009
  Kirkland *(G-5290)*
Buffelen Woodworking Co ....D....... 253 627-1191
  Tacoma *(G-13212)*
Crafted Northwest Doors Inc ....F....... 509 484-3722
  Spokane *(G-12205)*
Elochoman Millwork Inc..........................G....... 360 795-3637
  Cathlamet *(G-2365)*
Fircrest Pre-Fit Door Co Inc ....G....... 253 564-6921
  Tacoma *(G-13296)*
Hrh Door Corp..D....... 360 736-7651
  Centralia *(G-2409)*
Kamilche Company.................................G....... 206 224-5800
  Seattle *(G-10326)*
Lynden Door Inc.....................................E....... 360 354-5676
  Lynden *(G-6032)*
McKenna Door and Millwork ....G....... 360 458-5467
  Roy *(G-9162)*
Overhead Door Corporation ....G....... 253 520-8008
  Fife *(G-3977)*
Pacific Crest Building Pdts ....F....... 253 447-7686
  Puyallup *(G-8217)*
Pacific Door & Window Inc ....F....... 360 577-9121
  Longview *(G-5940)*
Price & Visser Millwork Inc.....................F....... 360 734-7700
  Bellingham *(G-1504)*
Simpson Investment Company ....D....... 253 272-0158
  Seattle *(G-11115)*
Star North Woodworks Inc......................E....... 360 384-0307
  Ferndale *(G-3906)*
Trinity Glass Intl Inc ....D....... 800 803-8182
  Federal Way *(G-3798)*
Vancouver Door Company Inc.................E....... 253 845-9581
  Puyallup *(G-8272)*

DOWN FEATHERS

Pangaea Ltd...G....... 206 292-9911
  Seattle *(G-10746)*

DRAFTING SVCS

JV Designs Inc ....G....... 509 786-2588
  Prosser *(G-8045)*

DRAPERIES & CURTAINS

Evergreen Textiles ....G....... 253 852-6565
  Auburn *(G-434)*

DRAPERIES: Plastic & Textile, From Purchased Materials

American Drpery Blind Crpt Inc ....E....... 425 793-4477
  Renton *(G-8742)*
American Drpery Blind Crpt Inc ....C....... 360 676-1121
  Renton *(G-8743)*
Chinook Acoustics Inc ....G....... 425 307-1976
  Redmond *(G-8418)*
Custom Made Draperies Etc ....G....... 425 485-2724
  Kenmore *(G-4570)*
Hoss A W & Sons Furn & Mfg ....F....... 206 522-1229
  Seattle *(G-10182)*
Penthouse Drapery Clrs & Mfrs ....E....... 206 292-8336
  Seattle *(G-10781)*
Seattle Curtain Mfg Co ....E....... 206 324-0692
  Mill Creek *(G-6526)*
Shade Sunglo & Drapery Co ....G....... 206 767-4561
  Seattle *(G-11094)*
Snider Burien Draperies ....G....... 206 243-3600
  Burien *(G-2129)*
Springcrest Drapery Gallery ....G....... 509 928-9269
  Spokane Valley *(G-12890)*

DRAPERY & UPHOLSTERY STORES: Draperies

Custom Made Draperies Etc ....G....... 425 485-2724
  Kenmore *(G-4570)*
Gaes Draperies......................................G....... 360 293-9732
  Anacortes *(G-132)*
Snider Burien Draperies ....G....... 206 243-3600
  Burien *(G-2129)*

DRILLING MACHINERY & EQPT: Oil & Gas

Airgas Usa LLC ....G....... 360 293-6171
  Anacortes *(G-97)*
Nuovo Parts Inc......................................G....... 360 738-1888
  Ferndale *(G-3879)*
US Mat Systems LLC ....F....... 509 763-4000
  Leavenworth *(G-5818)*

DRILLING MACHINERY & EQPT: Water Well

Bayview Pumps......................................G....... 360 301-3600
  Nordland *(G-7088)*
Blue Star Enterprises NW Inc ....F....... 509 946-9388
  Richland *(G-8975)*
QSP Packers LLC..................................G....... 253 770-0315
  Puyallup *(G-8230)*
R 2 Manufacturing Inc ....G....... 360 693-5096
  Vancouver *(G-14525)*
Schell Pump Service ....G....... 509 922-4756
  Greenacres *(G-4302)*

DRILLS: Hand

Jmd Property Preservation ....G....... 267 713-2277
  Lakewood *(G-5730)*

DRINK MIXES, NONALCOHOLIC: Cocktail

Gourmet Mixes Inc.................................G....... 206 764-6006
  Seattle *(G-10103)*
Sharon McIlhenny ....G....... 509 493-9259
  White Salmon *(G-15131)*

DRINKING PLACES: Alcoholic Beverages

Arbor Crest Wineries & Nursery ....F....... 509 927-9463
  Spokane *(G-12115)*
Big Time Brewery Company Inc ....E....... 206 545-4509
  Seattle *(G-9526)*
Boundary Bay Brewing Company ....E....... 360 647-5593
  Bellingham *(G-1281)*
Eco Inc ....F....... 206 784-6611
  Seattle *(G-9878)*
Elliott Bay Brewing Company ....E....... 206 246-4211
  Seattle *(G-9900)*
Fish Brewing Co.....................................F....... 360 943-3650
  Olympia *(G-7286)*
Pyramid Breweries Inc ....D....... 206 682-8322
  Seattle *(G-10893)*

DRINKING PLACES: Bars & Lounges

Diamond Knot Brewing Co Inc ....D....... 425 355-4488
  Mukilteo *(G-6912)*
Odo ....G....... 303 915-9652
  Spokane *(G-12418)*
Rattlesnake Mtn Brewing Co ....E....... 509 783-5747
  Richland *(G-9038)*

DRINKING PLACES: Beer Garden

Farmstrong LLC ....G....... 360 873-8852
  Mount Vernon (G-6795)
River City Brewing LLC ....G....... 509 413-2388
  Spokane (G-12476)

DRINKING PLACES: Tavern

Cascade Ales Company ....G....... 360 520-6040
  Longview (G-5895)
Meconi Pub & Eatery ....G....... 253 383-3388
  Tacoma (G-13405)
Mule and Elk Brewing Co LLC ....G....... 206 909-9622
  Cle Elum (G-2672)
Pike Brewing Company ....E....... 206 622-6044
  Seattle (G-10805)

DRIVE SHAFTS

Precision Driveshaft Inc ....G....... 253 236-5640
  Kent (G-5077)

DRIVES: High Speed Indl, Exc Hydrostatic

Peregrine Manufacturing Inc ....G....... 425 673-5600
  Lynnwood (G-6179)

DRUG STORES

Genoa Healthcare Mass LLC ....G....... 425 789-3050
  Everett (G-3495)
Halls Drug Center Inc ....E....... 360 736-5000
  Centralia (G-2405)

DRUG TESTING KITS: Blood & Urine

American Mobile Drug Testing ....G....... 509 921-2730
  Spokane Valley (G-12613)
Data Quest LLC ....G....... 360 568-8708
  Everett (G-3439)
Drug Interv Service Amer ....G....... 360 299-2700
  Anacortes (G-123)
Innovation Resource Center ....G....... 509 836-2400
  Sunnyside (G-13127)
Walla Walla Valley Mobile LLC ....G....... 509 386-8549
  College Place (G-2730)

DRUGS & DRUG PROPRIETARIES, WHOLESALE: Medicinals/Botanicals

Agro Technic LLC ....F....... 206 669-2446
  Bellevue (G-782)
Tilray Inc ....G....... 206 432-9325
  Seattle (G-11308)

DRUGS & DRUG PROPRIETARIES, WHOLESALE: Pharmaceuticals

Central Admxture Phrm Svcs Inc ....E....... 253 395-8700
  Kent (G-4846)
Normed Inc ....E....... 800 288-8200
  Tukwila (G-13779)

DRUGS & DRUG PROPRIETARIES, WHOLESALE: Vitamins & Minerals

Avid Health Inc ....G....... 360 737-6800
  Vancouver (G-14048)
Betsy Bells Natyural Solutions ....G....... 206 933-1889
  Seattle (G-9518)
Northwest Natural Products Inc ....C....... 360 737-6800
  Ridgefield (G-9096)
Pacific Nutritional Inc ....G....... 360 253-3197
  Vancouver (G-14467)
Terato Products LLC ....G....... 425 702-6365
  Redmond (G-8689)
Zipfizz Corporation ....B....... 425 398-4240
  Woodinville (G-15215)

DRUGS ACTING ON THE CENTRAL NERVOUS SYSTEM & SENSE ORGANS

Sound Pharmaceuticals Inc ....F....... 206 634-2559
  Seattle (G-11158)

DRYCLEANING & LAUNDRY SVCS: Commercial & Family

Northwest Center ....C....... 206 285-9140
  Seattle (G-10639)

DRYCLEANING EQPT & SPLYS: Commercial

Northwest Laundry Supply Inc ....G....... 509 487-4800
  Spokane Valley (G-12806)

DRYCLEANING SVC: Drapery & Curtain

Penthouse Drapery Clrs & Mfrs ....E....... 206 292-8336
  Seattle (G-10781)

DUCTS: Sheet Metal

ECB Corp ....E....... 425 514-8334
  Everett (G-3451)
Ershigs Inc ....F....... 360 733-2620
  Bellingham (G-1338)

DUMPSTERS: Garbage

Issak Shamso ....G....... 253 457-2964
  Kent (G-4962)
Lucky Dumpster ....G....... 360 766-4049
  Bow (G-1930)
Thurston Co Transfer Station ....G....... 360 459-1901
  Olympia (G-7406)

DURABLE GOODS WHOLESALERS, NEC

Cenex Supply & Marketing Inc ....G....... 509 488-5261
  Othello (G-7491)

DUST OR FUME COLLECTING EQPT: Indl

3 Phase Energy Systems Inc ....F....... 253 736-2248
  Auburn (G-354)
Viking Packaging Machinery ....G....... 509 452-7143
  Yakima (G-15703)
Woodstock International Inc ....E....... 360 734-3482
  Bellingham (G-1596)

DYES: Synthetic Organic

Botanical Colors LLC ....G....... 206 518-7073
  Seattle (G-9566)
Botanical Colors LLC ....G....... 206 518-7073
  Seattle (G-9567)

DYNAMOMETERS

Dyno Resource Corp ....G....... 425 391-6084
  Issaquah (G-4407)
Dynolab ....G....... 206 243-8877
  Normandy Park (G-7091)

EATING PLACES

Bean Collection Coffee Inc ....G....... 206 382-1966
  Seattle (G-9505)
Big House Brewing Inc ....E....... 509 522-2440
  Walla Walla (G-14771)
Boundary Bay Brewing Company ....E....... 360 647-5593
  Bellingham (G-1281)
Eco Inc ....F....... 206 784-6611
  Seattle (G-9878)
Elliott Bay Brewing Company ....E....... 206 246-4211
  Seattle (G-9900)
Elysian Brewing Company Inc ....E....... 206 860-3977
  Seattle (G-9908)
Fish Brewing Co ....F....... 360 943-3650
  Olympia (G-7286)
Framatome Inc ....F....... 425 250-2775
  Redmond (G-8465)
Garden Fresh Foods Inc ....D....... 425 483-5467
  Woodinville (G-15250)
Gb Acquisition Inc ....G....... 206 405-4205
  Seattle (G-10054)
Great Harvest Bread Co Inc ....E....... 509 535-1146
  Spokane (G-12281)
Harmon Brewing Company L L C ....F....... 253 853-1585
  Gig Harbor (G-4113)
Henrys Donuts ....F....... 425 258-6887
  Everett (G-3509)
Ice Harbor Brewing Company ....E....... 509 586-3181
  Kennewick (G-4673)
ISC Inc ....E....... 253 395-5465
  Kent (G-4961)
Kings Kitchen LLC ....G....... 253 212-3623
  Tacoma (G-13376)
Kusina Fillipina ....G....... 206 322-9433
  Seattle (G-10365)
Lilly Tin ....F....... 509 888-8101
  Chelan (G-2559)
McMenamins Inc ....F....... 206 285-4722
  Seattle (G-10510)

Meconi Pub & Eatery ....G....... 253 383-3388
  Tacoma (G-13405)
Noodle Express ....F....... 509 927-4117
  Spokane (G-12405)
Odyssey Enterprises Inc ....C....... 206 285-7445
  Seattle (G-10685)
Pelican Packers Inc ....F....... 360 398-8825
  Bellingham (G-1494)
Pike Brewing Company ....E....... 206 622-6044
  Seattle (G-10805)
Pioneer Coffee Roasting Co LLC ....G....... 509 674-4100
  Cle Elum (G-2676)
Quillisascut Cheese Co ....G....... 509 738-2011
  Rice (G-8960)
Rattlesnake Mtn Brewing Co ....G....... 509 783-5747
  Richland (G-9038)
Scuttlebutt Brewing Co LLC ....F....... 425 252-2829
  Everett (G-3606)
Silver City Brewing Co Inc ....D....... 360 698-5879
  Silverdale (G-11857)
Snipes Mountain Brewing Inc ....E....... 509 837-2739
  Sunnyside (G-13142)
We-Man Vets Golf Inc ....G....... 509 527-4507
  Walla Walla (G-14900)
Whidbey Island Vinyard Winery ....G....... 360 221-2040
  Langley (G-5787)

EDUCATIONAL SVCS

Heatcon Composite Systems Inc ....D....... 206 575-1333
  Tukwila (G-13747)
Instructional Technologies Inc ....F....... 360 576-5976
  Vancouver (G-14320)
Leading Beyond Tradition LLC ....G....... 425 275-7665
  Snohomish (G-11938)
Mediapro Holdings LLC ....G....... 425 483-4700
  Bothell (G-1777)
Second Amendment Foundation ....F....... 425 454-7012
  Bellevue (G-1122)
Skooler Inc ....G....... 425 628-5000
  Bellevue (G-1136)
Smelts Sea Mammal Education Le ......G....... 360 303-9338
  Sedro Woolley (G-11570)
Starpath Corporation ....G....... 206 783-1414
  Seattle (G-11184)

EDUCATIONAL SVCS, NONDEGREE GRANTING: Continuing Education

Goodmans Ski and Sports Inc ....G....... 360 733-8937
  Bellingham (G-1358)

EGG WHOLESALERS

Dynes Farms Inc ....E....... 360 757-4025
  Burlington (G-2154)
National Food Corporation ....D....... 360 653-2904
  Arlington (G-285)

ELECTRIC & OTHER SERVICES COMBINED

Airgas Usa LLC ....G....... 360 293-6171
  Anacortes (G-97)

ELECTRIC MOTOR REPAIR SVCS

A1 Electric Motor Inc ....G....... 360 568-3409
  Snohomish (G-11869)
All Electric Motor Service ....G....... 253 845-1938
  Puyallup (G-8120)
B & B Electric Motors Inc ....G....... 206 763-3538
  Kent (G-4805)
Ballard Electric ....G....... 800 873-3526
  Seattle (G-9479)
Bl Best Inc ....G....... 509 534-0237
  Spokane (G-12150)
C & R Electric Motor Service ....G....... 360 736-2521
  Centralia (G-2387)
Center Electric Inc ....F....... 253 383-4416
  Tacoma (G-13231)
Cooper Electric Motor Svc Co ....F....... 509 452-9550
  Yakima (G-15536)
Cubbys Elc Mtr & Pump Repr ....G....... 509 544-9317
  Pasco (G-7572)
D and D Electric Motor Svc Inc ....G....... 509 762-6136
  Moses Lake (G-6703)
Dipietro Enterprises Inc ....F....... 206 423-7633
  Tukwila (G-13724)
F W B Enterprises Inc ....G....... 425 377-2628
  Snohomish (G-11908)
Grays Electric Inc ....G....... 509 662-6834
  Wenatchee (G-15037)

Industrial Electric Co Inc ..... G 360 424-3239
Mount Vernon *(G-6804)*
Industrial Electric Service Co ..... F 360 533-2792
Aberdeen *(G-19)*
JS Uniform ..... G 509 467-8416
Spokane *(G-12344)*
K & N Electric Motors Inc ..... D 509 838-8000
Spokane Valley *(G-12759)*
K J M Electric Co Inc ..... G 206 624-5294
Seattle *(G-10320)*
M R K Electric ..... G 360 253-8310
Brush Prairie *(G-2037)*
Mac & Mac Electric Company ..... G 360 734-6530
Bellingham *(G-1418)*
Panasonic Corp North America ..... G 425 883-9290
Redmond *(G-8613)*
Poppleton Electric & Mchy Co ..... F 206 762-9160
Kent *(G-5073)*
Reds Electric Motors Inc ..... G 360 377-3903
Bremerton *(G-1992)*
Scottys Elc Mtr & Pump Repr ..... G 360 573-9544
Vancouver *(G-14574)*
Sea Alaska Industrial Electric ..... G 360 568-7624
Snohomish *(G-11972)*
Timken Motor & Crane Svcs LLC ..... E 509 547-1691
Pasco *(G-7638)*
United Electric Motors Inc ..... G 206 624-0044
Seattle *(G-11370)*

ELECTRIC POWER DISTRIBUTION TO CONSUMERS

Avista Corporation ..... A 509 489-0500
Spokane *(G-12134)*
Energy Efficiency Systems Corp ..... E 360 835-7838
Washougal *(G-14953)*

ELECTRIC POWER, COGENERATED

Wellons Group Inc ..... F 360 750-3500
Vancouver *(G-14682)*

ELECTRIC SERVICES

Avista Capital Inc ..... G 509 489-0500
Spokane *(G-12133)*
City of Sattle-City Light Dept ..... E 509 446-3083
Metaline Falls *(G-6497)*
Total Home Control ..... G 509 628-1673
Richland *(G-9046)*

ELECTRIC SVCS, NEC Power Marketers

Glarus Group Inc ..... G 425 572-5907
Newcastle *(G-7030)*

ELECTRIC SVCS, NEC: Power Generation

Kaes Enterprises LLC ..... E 800 252-5237
Puyallup *(G-8171)*

ELECTRIC WATER HEATERS WHOLESALERS

Kauffmann Industries Inc ..... G 425 770-5781
Bothell *(G-1872)*
Torrid Marine LLC ..... G 206 920-9002
Bainbridge Island *(G-679)*

ELECTRICAL APPARATUS & EQPT WHOLESALERS

Ademco Inc ..... G 253 872-7128
Kent *(G-4759)*
Ademco Inc ..... G 509 534-7300
Spokane *(G-12098)*
Ademco Inc ..... G 425 485-3938
Bothell *(G-1815)*
Board Shark LLC ..... E 503 351-5424
Vancouver *(G-14072)*
Controlled Products of Wash ..... G 206 575-2249
Tukwila *(G-13717)*
Eaton Corporation ..... F 253 833-5021
Auburn *(G-431)*
Picatti Brothers Inc ..... D 509 248-2540
Yakima *(G-15646)*
Sea-TAC Lighting & Contrls LLC ..... F 206 575-6865
Tukwila *(G-13813)*
Siemens ..... G 425 507-4380
Bellevue *(G-1130)*
Siemens ..... G 425 251-0858
Renton *(G-8912)*
Utility Supply Group ..... G 360 626-1086
Poulsbo *(G-8014)*

ELECTRICAL APPLIANCES, TELEVISIONS & RADIOS WHOLESALERS

Almeda Cottage Inc ..... E 206 285-1674
Seattle *(G-9384)*
Cco Holdings LLC ..... G 509 293-4177
Wenatchee *(G-15016)*
Cco Holdings LLC ..... G 509 643-3364
Sunnyside *(G-13116)*

ELECTRICAL CURRENT CARRYING WIRING DEVICES

Acacia Controls Inc ..... G 253 277-1206
Kent *(G-4755)*
Alset Corporation ..... G 206 335-3700
Sequim *(G-11610)*
Carlisle Inc ..... A 425 251-0700
Kent *(G-4836)*
Carlyle Holdings Inc ..... C 425 251-0700
Kent *(G-4839)*
Fastcap LLC ..... E 888 443-3748
Ferndale *(G-3841)*
Gcm North American Arospc LLC ..... D 253 872-7488
Algona *(G-69)*
Honeywell Electronic Mtls Inc ..... A 509 252-2200
Spokane Valley *(G-12731)*
Jjp Electric ..... G 509 325-5266
Spokane *(G-12335)*
Leviton Manufacturing Co Inc ..... C 425 486-2222
Bothell *(G-1874)*
Mountain Sttes Elec Contrs Inc ..... E 509 532-0110
Spokane *(G-12399)*
PA&e International Inc ..... C 509 667-9600
Wenatchee *(G-15056)*
Pacific Aerospace & Elec Inc ..... G 855 285-5200
Wenatchee *(G-15058)*
Pacific Aerospace & Elec LLC ..... C 855 885-5200
Wenatchee *(G-15059)*
Valberg Mfg Inc ..... G 206 920-1296
Bothell *(G-1912)*

ELECTRICAL DISCHARGE MACHINING, EDM

Seattle Precision Form Inc ..... G 253 872-8356
Kent *(G-5124)*

ELECTRICAL EQPT & SPLYS

All Wave Innovations Inc ..... G 509 308-7230
Benton City *(G-1600)*
Atlas Electric Inc ..... E 509 534-8389
Spokane *(G-12124)*
Battery X-Change & Repair Inc ..... G 360 373-2921
Bremerton *(G-1937)*
Bridgeways ..... D 425 513-2989
Everett *(G-3401)*
Burke Electric ..... G 509 633-8046
Coulee Dam *(G-2806)*
Columbia Electric Supply ..... G 509 473-9156
Spokane Valley *(G-12661)*
Cooper Power Systems Inc ..... G 206 499-9473
Maple Valley *(G-6265)*
Cowlitz Electric Construction ..... G 253 355-7163
Tacoma *(G-13247)*
Ditco Inc ..... F 253 854-1002
Kent *(G-4874)*
Eaton Hydraulics LLC ..... G 360 834-0653
Camas *(G-2245)*
Elmor Inc ..... G 206 213-0111
Seattle *(G-9903)*
ESP Seattle ..... G 206 388-4800
Tukwila *(G-13730)*
Graybar Electric Company Inc ..... E 425 203-1500
Renton *(G-8813)*
Gsl Solutions Inc ..... E 360 896-5354
Vancouver *(G-14275)*
Herrington Marine Tech Inc ..... G 360 222-3106
Greenbank *(G-4305)*
Hiline Engrg & Fabrication Inc ..... E 509 943-9043
Richland *(G-9006)*
Hyak Electroworks ..... E 360 737-0157
Vancouver *(G-14306)*
Island Electric ..... G 360 293-9275
Anacortes *(G-136)*
Itraq Inc ..... G 844 694-8727
Redmond *(G-8516)*
Jjs Automotive & Auto Elc LLC ..... G 509 248-2622
Union Gap *(G-13935)*
Kanon Electric ..... G 253 447-7831
Edgewood *(G-3083)*
L3 Systems Inc ..... G 425 836-5438
Sammamish *(G-9228)*
Laughlin Industries Inc ..... G 360 514-9218
Vancouver *(G-14364)*
Lavry Engineering Inc ..... F 206 842-3552
Bainbridge Island *(G-648)*
Malone Electronics ..... G 360 687-1034
Battle Ground *(G-719)*
McCoy Electric ..... G 360 829-5273
Buckley *(G-2063)*
Mitsubishi Electric & Elec USA ..... G 425 202-7671
Kirkland *(G-5404)*
Morpac Industries Inc ..... E 253 735-8922
Pacific *(G-7533)*
Nextlevel Training LLC ..... G 360 933-4640
Ferndale *(G-3876)*
Nova Services ..... E 509 928-1588
Spokane Valley *(G-12810)*
Polarity Elec ..... G 206 546-3539
Shoreline *(G-11802)*
Power Breaker LLC Seattle ..... G 425 286-4276
Monroe *(G-6607)*
Prairie Electric Inc ..... D 509 545-1752
Pasco *(G-7618)*
Pro Staff Electric ..... G 360 859-3749
Vancouver *(G-14509)*
Provident Electric Inc ..... F 509 588-3939
Benton City *(G-1624)*
Red Electric ..... G 425 670-7035
Mukilteo *(G-6971)*
Sea-TAC Lighting & Contrls LLC ..... F 206 575-6865
Tukwila *(G-13813)*
Sequoyah Electric ..... G 253 520-2064
Kent *(G-5127)*
Siemens ..... G 425 507-4380
Bellevue *(G-1130)*
Siemens ..... G 425 251-0858
Renton *(G-8912)*
Specialty Pdts Elec Cnstr LLC ..... G 425 402-8332
Woodinville *(G-15373)*
Terex Utilities Inc ..... E 206 764-5025
Kent *(G-5177)*
Totem Electric ..... G 253 327-1500
Fife *(G-3996)*
United States Electric Corp ..... G 360 427-4218
Grapeview *(G-4291)*
Utility Supply Group ..... G 360 626-1086
Poulsbo *(G-8014)*

ELECTRICAL EQPT FOR ENGINES

Baton Labs Inc ..... G 509 467-4203
Spokane *(G-12140)*
Jantz Engineering ..... G 360 598-2773
Poulsbo *(G-7968)*
North PCF Ign Interlock Svc ..... G 360 480-4919
Lacey *(G-5567)*
S&J Engines Inc ..... F 509 325-4558
Spokane *(G-12490)*
Schumacher Creative Services ..... G 206 364-7151
Seattle *(G-11029)*
Smart Start ..... G 425 747-4400
Bellevue *(G-1139)*

ELECTRICAL EQPT REPAIR & MAINTENANCE

Berry Neon Co Inc ..... E 425 776-8835
Everett *(G-3385)*
Custom Bilt Holdings LLC ..... E 253 872-7330
Lakewood *(G-5709)*
Honeywell International Inc ..... C 425 251-9511
Renton *(G-8820)*
Lower Valley Machine Shop ..... F 509 882-3881
Grandview *(G-4251)*
National Sign Corporation ..... E 206 282-0700
Seattle *(G-10590)*
Servatron Inc ..... C 509 321-9500
Spokane Valley *(G-12865)*
Shamrock Machining Inc ..... E 509 534-3031
Spokane Valley *(G-12868)*
Sondra L Groce ..... G 509 467-8788
Spokane *(G-12511)*
Three Rivers Industrial Mch ..... G 360 578-1114
Kelso *(G-4555)*
Valmet Inc ..... E 253 927-2200
Federal Way *(G-3799)*

PRODUCT

Employee Codes: A=Over 500 employees, B=251-500
C=101-250, D=51-100, E=20-50, F=10-19, G=2-9

2019 Washington
Manufacturers Register

953

ELECTRICAL EQPT REPAIR SVCS

ELECTRICAL EQPT REPAIR SVCS
Christian Hamilton .... G 360 442-4900
  Longview *(G-5899)*
Practec LLC .... F 425 881-8202
  Redmond *(G-8630)*

ELECTRICAL EQPT: Household
Toaster Labs Inc .... G 206 368-3178
  Seattle *(G-11316)*

ELECTRICAL GOODS, WHOL: Antennas, Receiving/Satellite Dishes
Bluecosmo Inc .... G 877 258-3496
  Seattle *(G-9555)*

ELECTRICAL GOODS, WHOL: Vid Camera-Aud Recorders/Camcorders
Northwest Video Wall .... G 360 403-7773
  Arlington *(G-291)*

ELECTRICAL GOODS, WHOLESALE: Batteries, Dry Cell
Energy Sales .... F 425 883-2343
  Woodinville *(G-15236)*

ELECTRICAL GOODS, WHOLESALE: Batteries, Storage, Indl
Austin Else LLC .... F 888 654-4450
  Spokane *(G-12128)*

ELECTRICAL GOODS, WHOLESALE: Circuit Breakers
Eaton Corporation .... E 425 644-5800
  Bellevue *(G-889)*

ELECTRICAL GOODS, WHOLESALE: Electrical Entertainment Eqpt
Lavry Engineering .... G 360 598-9757
  Poulsbo *(G-7974)*
Mackie Designs Inc .... G 425 868-0555
  Redmond *(G-8544)*

ELECTRICAL GOODS, WHOLESALE: Electronic Parts
Allstar Magnetics LLC .... E 360 693-0213
  Vancouver *(G-14022)*
Ecotech Recycling LLC .... E 360 673-3860
  Kalama *(G-4498)*
Huntron Inc .... F 425 743-3171
  Mill Creek *(G-6513)*
Interworld Elec Cmpt Inds Inc 425 223-4311
  Point Roberts *(G-7668)*
Jauch Quartz America Inc .... G 360 633-7200
  Seabeck *(G-9265)*
Lauterbach Inc 360 567-2666
  Vancouver *(G-14365)*
Seymour Technology LLC .... G 509 522-3473
  Walla Walla *(G-14867)*

ELECTRICAL GOODS, WHOLESALE: Fittings & Construction Mat
Industrial Electric Service Co .... F 360 533-2792
  Aberdeen *(G-19)*

ELECTRICAL GOODS, WHOLESALE: Generators
Pacific Power Group LLC .... E 360 887-5980
  Ridgefield *(G-9099)*
Pacific Power Group LLC .... E 253 395-9077
  Auburn *(G-524)*
Pacific Power Group LLC .... D 360 887-7400
  Vancouver *(G-14469)*

ELECTRICAL GOODS, WHOLESALE: Lighting Fixtures, Comm & Indl
Light It Bright Products LLC .... G 253 666-2278
  Tacoma *(G-13388)*
Rexel Capitol Light .... G 425 861-0200
  Redmond *(G-8650)*

ELECTRICAL GOODS, WHOLESALE: Lighting Fixtures, Residential
C & H Lighting Associates Inc .... G 253 531-1270
  Tacoma *(G-13213)*

ELECTRICAL GOODS, WHOLESALE: Motors
C & R Electric Motor Service .... G 360 736-2521
  Centralia *(G-2387)*
Center Electric Inc .... F 253 383-4416
  Tacoma *(G-13231)*
D and D Electric Motor Svc Inc .... G 509 762-6136
  Moses Lake *(G-6703)*
F W B Enterprises Inc 425 377-2628
  Snohomish *(G-11908)*
K & N Electric Motors Inc .... D 509 838-8000
  Spokane Valley *(G-12759)*
Mac & Mac Electric Company .... G 360 734-6530
  Bellingham *(G-1418)*
Nidec America Corporation .... G 360 666-2445
  Battle Ground *(G-724)*
Sea Alaska Industrial Electric .... G 360 568-7624
  Snohomish *(G-11972)*
Timken Motor & Crane Svcs LLC .... E 509 547-1691
  Pasco *(G-7638)*
United Electric Motors Inc .... G 206 624-0044
  Seattle *(G-11370)*

ELECTRICAL GOODS, WHOLESALE: Security Control Eqpt & Systems
Controlled Products of Wash .... G 206 575-2249
  Tukwila *(G-13717)*
Darren Mode .... G 509 292-2438
  Deer Park *(G-2897)*
Keyking Inc .... G 360 977-7870
  Camas *(G-2262)*

ELECTRICAL GOODS, WHOLESALE: Semiconductor Devices
Eaton Corporation .... E 425 644-5800
  Bellevue *(G-889)*
Shin-Etsu Handotai America Inc .... A 360 883-7000
  Vancouver *(G-14583)*

ELECTRICAL GOODS, WHOLESALE: Signaling, Eqpt
Timberline Controls & Mar Inc .... F 360 335-8598
  Washougal *(G-14993)*

ELECTRICAL GOODS, WHOLESALE: Sound Eqpt
Mitsubishi Electric & Elec USA .... G 425 202-7671
  Kirkland *(G-5404)*

ELECTRICAL GOODS, WHOLESALE: Telephone Eqpt
Telco Wiring & Repair Inc .... G 509 547-4300
  Pasco *(G-7637)*

ELECTRICAL GOODS, WHOLESALE: VCR & Access
Elite Enterprise Co .... G 360 756-0205
  Bellingham *(G-1333)*

ELECTRICAL GOODS, WHOLESALE: Wire & Cable
Carlisle Inc .... A 425 251-0700
  Kent *(G-4836)*
Carlyle Holdings Inc .... C 425 251-0700
  Kent *(G-4839)*

ELECTRICAL GOODS, WHOLESALE: Wire & Cable, Electronic
Connectzonecom LLC .... E 425 212-4400
  Lynnwood *(G-6097)*
Mechatronics Inc .... C 425 222-5900
  Issaquah *(G-4447)*

ELECTRICAL MEASURING INSTRUMENT REPAIR & CALIBRATION SVCS
Aldergrove LLC .... G 360 253-7378
  Vancouver *(G-14018)*

ELECTRICAL SPLYS
BI Best Inc .... G 509 534-0237
  Spokane *(G-12150)*
Columbia Electric Supply .... G 509 473-9156
  Spokane Valley *(G-12661)*
Graybar Electric Company Inc .... E 425 203-1500
  Renton *(G-8813)*
North Coast Electric Company .... F 360 671-1100
  Bellingham *(G-1464)*
Stoneway Electric Supply Co .... F 253 859-0224
  Kent *(G-5158)*

ELECTRICAL SUPPLIES: Porcelain
Colorific Porcelain .... G 425 743-1591
  Lynnwood *(G-6096)*
Pyrotek Incorporated .... D 509 926-6211
  Spokane Valley *(G-12846)*

ELECTROMEDICAL EQPT
A-M Systems LLC .... E 360 683-8300
  Sequim *(G-11604)*
Aqueduct Neurosciences Inc .... G 206 661-1538
  Seattle *(G-9417)*
Biolife Solutions Inc .... G 425 402-1400
  Bothell *(G-1827)*
Biolife Solutions Inc .... E 425 402-1400
  Bothell *(G-1828)*
Blaze Metrics LLC .... G 206 972-3890
  Quil Ceda Village *(G-8280)*
Breast Care Center .... F 360 424-6161
  Sedro Woolley *(G-11534)*
Cadwell Laboratories Inc .... D 509 735-6481
  Kennewick *(G-4638)*
Cardiodynamics Intl Corp 208 332-2502
  Bothell *(G-1834)*
Echo-Sense Inc .... G 360 833-9032
  Camas *(G-2246)*
Emergent Detection Inc .... G 206 391-4876
  Seattle *(G-9915)*
General Electric Company .... G 253 351-2200
  Auburn *(G-448)*
Innerscan Inc .... G 425 419-7718
  Bothell *(G-1769)*
Innovaura Corporation 425 272-2702
  Edmonds *(G-3120)*
Iopi Medical LLC .... G 425 549-0139
  Woodinville *(G-15268)*
Medtronic Inc 425 867-4000
  Redmond *(G-8554)*
Medtronic Usa Inc .... E 425 803-0708
  Bellevue *(G-1001)*
Mindray Medical USA Corp 425 881-0361
  Redmond *(G-8590)*
Myotronics-Noromed Inc .... F 206 243-4214
  Kent *(G-5017)*
Natus Medical Incorporated .... F 206 767-3500
  Seattle *(G-10594)*
Olympic Medical Corp .... D 206 767-3500
  Seattle *(G-10692)*
Palo Alto Health Sciences Inc .... F 925 594-8404
  Kirkland *(G-5427)*
Philips North America LLC .... C 206 664-5000
  Seattle *(G-10794)*
Seattle Espresso Machine Corp .... G 206 284-7171
  Seattle *(G-11057)*
Siemens Med Solutions USA Inc .... C 425 392-9180
  Issaquah *(G-4475)*
Solta Medical Inc .... F 425 354-1857
  Bothell *(G-1794)*
Somatics LLC 847 234-6761
  Vancouver *(G-14600)*
Spacelabs Healthcare LLC .... B 425 396-3300
  Snoqualmie *(G-12028)*
Tiba Medical Inc 503 222-1500
  Bellevue *(G-1188)*
Tournitek Inc .... G 423 620-5475
  Seattle *(G-11323)*

ELECTROMETALLURGICAL PRDTS
Teck American Metal Sales Inc .... G 509 747-6111
  Spokane *(G-12549)*

PRODUCT SECTION

EMBROIDERING SVC

Young Corporation .... E 206 623-3274
  Seattle *(G-11514)*

ELECTRON BEAM: Cutting, Forming, Welding

Kent Enterprises .... G 360 403-0242
  Arlington *(G-264)*

ELECTRON TUBES: Cathode Ray

Ceradyne Inc .... G 206 763-2170
  Seattle *(G-9656)*

ELECTRONIC COMPONENTS

Creepcocom .... G 206 547-7020
  Seattle *(G-9752)*
Emerald City Electronics .... G 425 649-1006
  Bellevue *(G-896)*
Lauterbach Inc .... G 360 567-2666
  Vancouver *(G-14365)*
Mackie Designs Inc .... G 425 868-0555
  Redmond *(G-8544)*

ELECTRONIC DETECTION SYSTEMS: Aeronautical

Pacific Radar Inc .... G 425 775-0400
  Everett *(G-3566)*
Sensitronics LLC .... G 360 766-8800
  Bow *(G-1932)*

ELECTRONIC DEVICES: Solid State, NEC

Blink Device Company LLC .... F 206 708-6043
  Seattle *(G-9542)*
Jj 206 LLC .... G 206 453-0186
  Seattle *(G-10297)*
Resonant Systems Inc .... G 206 557-4398
  Seattle *(G-10952)*

ELECTRONIC EQPT REPAIR SVCS

Condor Technical Services .... G 206 633-5190
  Seattle *(G-9726)*

ELECTRONIC LOADS & POWER SPLYS

Aees Inc .... G 425 803-2170
  Kirkland *(G-5272)*
Altair Advanced Industries .... E 360 756-4900
  Bellingham *(G-1245)*
Austin Else LLC .... F 888 654-4450
  Spokane *(G-12128)*
Cabi .... G 425 413-8772
  Renton *(G-8766)*
Crane Electronics Inc .... B 425 882-3100
  Redmond *(G-8429)*
Crane Electronics Inc .... G 425 882-3100
  Redmond *(G-8430)*
Microvision Inc .... C 425 936-6847
  Redmond *(G-8587)*
Powerguard Corporation .... G 206 764-8882
  Kent *(G-5074)*

ELECTRONIC PARTS & EQPT WHOLESALERS

Carlisle Inc .... A 425 251-0700
  Kent *(G-4836)*
Carlyle Holdings Inc .... C 425 251-0700
  Kent *(G-4839)*
Crystalfontz America Inc .... F 509 892-1200
  Spokane Valley *(G-12671)*
Mackie Designs Inc .... G 425 868-0555
  Redmond *(G-8544)*
Mekltek Engineering & Mfg .... G 360 384-1607
  Ferndale *(G-3868)*
North Coast Electric Company .... F 360 671-1100
  Bellingham *(G-1464)*
Scafco Corporation .... C 509 343-9000
  Spokane *(G-12493)*
Scafco Corporation .... F 509 343-9012
  Spokane *(G-12494)*
Waft Corp .... F 425 743-4601
  Mukilteo *(G-6990)*

ELECTRONIC SHOPPING

Austin Else LLC .... F 888 654-4450
  Spokane *(G-12128)*

Carbide Online Sales LLC .... G 253 476-1338
  University Place *(G-13962)*
Imc-Innvtive Mktg Cnnction LLC .... G 360 895-0178
  Port Orchard *(G-7816)*
Mainstem Inc .... F 844 623-4084
  Seattle *(G-10469)*
Tight Group Targets LLC .... G 206 227-0201
  Renton *(G-8928)*

ELECTRONIC TRAINING DEVICES

Disman Bakner Northwest Inc .... G 425 837-3913
  Issaquah *(G-4406)*

ELECTROPLATING & PLATING SVC

Friedman Slversmiths Repr Pltg .... G 360 752-3119
  Bellingham *(G-1354)*

ELEMENTARY & SECONDARY SCHOOLS, SPECIAL EDUCATION

Machstem Inc .... G 801 259-3305
  Nine Mile Falls *(G-7078)*

ELEVATORS & EQPT

Chinook Elevator Solutions .... G 425 213-0784
  Kent *(G-4851)*
J Fillips LLC .... G 425 277-1011
  Renton *(G-8830)*
Schindler Elevator Corporation .... E 509 535-2471
  Spokane Valley *(G-12859)*
Vertical Dimensions LLC .... G 206 767-8022
  Tukwila *(G-13833)*

ELEVATORS WHOLESALERS

Otis Elevator Intl Inc .... F 509 483-7328
  Spokane *(G-12422)*

ELEVATORS: Installation & Conversion

Chinook Elevator Solutions .... G 425 213-0784
  Kent *(G-4851)*

ELEVATORS: Stair, Motor Powered

Olympic Home Modification LLC .... G 253 858-9941
  Gig Harbor *(G-4139)*

EMBLEMS: Embroidered

Arctic Circle Holdings LLC .... G 206 625-9226
  Seattle *(G-9422)*
Casual Fridays .... G 360 425-8841
  Longview *(G-5897)*
Color Grphics Scrnprinting Inc .... F 360 352-3970
  Tumwater *(G-13862)*
Emblems & More X3 .... G 253 248-2400
  Fife *(G-3950)*
Fashion Embroidery Inc .... G 425 820-7125
  Kirkland *(G-5337)*
Ink Inc .... F 253 565-4000
  University Place *(G-13973)*
Lannoye Emblems Inc .... G 425 844-8411
  Woodinville *(G-15283)*
Two Harps .... G 425 432-4128
  Maple Valley *(G-6295)*

EMBOSSING SVC: Paper

Badge Boys Awards & Engraving .... G 360 876-8414
  Port Orchard *(G-7792)*
Go Usa Inc .... E 509 662-3387
  Wenatchee *(G-15034)*
Graphic Impressions Inc .... E 253 872-0555
  Kent *(G-4925)*

EMBROIDERING & ART NEEDLEWORK FOR THE TRADE

Allstar Specialty Designs .... G 425 820-0285
  Kirkland *(G-5275)*
AZ Arts Inc .... F 253 584-8155
  Lakewood *(G-5701)*
Bellevue Embroidery .... G 425 646-9191
  Bellevue *(G-811)*
Bergen & Company .... F 360 676-7503
  Bellingham *(G-1271)*
Beth Donalley .... G 206 366-8445
  Lake Forest Park *(G-5607)*
Casual Fridays Custom E M B .... G 360 425-8841
  Longview *(G-5898)*

Contract Sew & Repair Inc .... F 253 395-7910
  Kent *(G-4865)*
Creative Garment Design & EMB .... G 509 457-3482
  Union Gap *(G-13927)*
Durado Enterprise .... G 509 882-3247
  Grandview *(G-4247)*
Embroidery By Design .... G 509 582-2858
  Kennewick *(G-4658)*
Embroidery Plus LLC .... G 253 630-2616
  Kent *(G-4891)*
GPA Embroidery .... G 509 662-1929
  Wenatchee *(G-15035)*
Graphic Apparel .... G 509 525-7630
  College Place *(G-2724)*
H W Image Works Inc .... G 760 343-3869
  Bellevue *(G-935)*
Hawkins Lettering .... F 425 481-1938
  Bothell *(G-1864)*
Hellroaring Company .... G 509 364-3522
  Glenwood *(G-4184)*
Huntington Pier International .... G 310 640-8358
  Tukwila *(G-13750)*
J & R Mercantile .... G 425 486-6402
  Kenmore *(G-4583)*
Jodee Maiorana .... G 509 758-1035
  Clarkston *(G-2637)*
Johnnie Montice .... G 360 452-6549
  Port Angeles *(G-7719)*
Much More Embroidery .... F 360 289-0955
  Ocean Shores *(G-7186)*
N-Vee Embroidery .... G 425 246-3125
  Kirkland *(G-5406)*
Purrfect Logos Inc .... G 509 893-2424
  Spokane Valley *(G-12845)*
Sandra Stroup .... G 509 754-0822
  Ephrata *(G-3346)*
Sew Athletic Jackets and More .... G 253 446-7115
  Puyallup *(G-8252)*
Sherri and Brent Wright .... G 360 366-3100
  Ferndale *(G-3904)*
Snappyduds .... G 206 243-8478
  Burien *(G-2128)*
Snotown Embroidery LLC .... G 425 446-1681
  Snohomish *(G-11985)*
Stitchybox .... G 360 450-1089
  Vancouver *(G-14612)*
Sunshine Embroidery .... G 360 892-1556
  Vancouver *(G-14618)*
To The T Embroidery .... G 360 509-0156
  Suquamish *(G-13149)*
Vintage Embroidery .... G 360 668-1923
  Snohomish *(G-11997)*

EMBROIDERING SVC

AJS Custom Embroidery .... G 360 993-1987
  Vancouver *(G-14015)*
Art N Stitches Inc .... G 253 248-1900
  Fife *(G-3934)*
Bayside EMB & Screenprint .... G 253 565-1521
  Tacoma *(G-13917)*
Bellingham Promotional Pdts .... G 360 676-5416
  Bellingham *(G-1268)*
Bent Needle Designs .... G 253 531-9440
  Tacoma *(G-13196)*
Bergen Screen Print .... G 509 965-2511
  Yakima *(G-15519)*
Cachanilla Design .... G 425 207-6396
  Kent *(G-4832)*
Cascade Apparel & Embroidery .... G 360 253-3022
  Vancouver *(G-14102)*
EMB Create Inc .... G 360 384-8072
  Ferndale *(G-3838)*
Embroidered Effects LLC .... G 360 380-1928
  Bellingham *(G-1334)*
Embroidery Northwest .... G 509 248-1186
  Yakima *(G-15564)*
Emerald City Embroidery .... G 253 922-8838
  Milton *(G-6534)*
Envision Custom EMB & Designs .... G 360 693-2588
  Vancouver *(G-14204)*
Excel Designs Inc .... G 360 892-1412
  Vancouver *(G-14213)*
Go Usa Inc .... E 509 662-3387
  Wenatchee *(G-15034)*
Hull Marigail .... G 425 643-3737
  Bellevue *(G-952)*
Jmh Enterprises .... G 509 628-2191
  Richland *(G-9015)*
Little Indian Embroidery .... G 360 414-4165
  Longview *(G-5927)*

Employee Codes: A=Over 500 employees, B=251-500
C=101-250, D=51-100, E=20-50, F=10-19, G=2-9

EMBROIDERING SVC

Logo Unltd ....F 425 896-8412
  Woodinville *(G-15292)*
Mr TS Trophies ....G 360 424-9339
  Mount Vernon *(G-6815)*
North Star Embroidery ....G 360 588-0530
  Anacortes *(G-155)*
Olympic Embroidery ....E 425 413-2848
  Ravensdale *(G-8338)*
Prographyx ....G 360 636-1595
  Longview *(G-5945)*
Reco Corporate Sportswear Inc ....G 360 354-2134
  Lynden *(G-6048)*
Showcase Specialties Inc ....G 509 547-3344
  Pasco *(G-7629)*

EMBROIDERING SVC: Schiffli Machine

Accent By Design ....G 360 256-6607
  Vancouver *(G-14006)*
Chings Embroidery ....G 360 613-9861
  Bremerton *(G-1942)*
Cruiser Creations ....G 360 832-7078
  Graham *(G-4222)*

EMBROIDERY ADVERTISING SVCS

Art N Stitches Inc ....G 253 248-1900
  Fife *(G-3934)*
Fashion Embroidery Inc ....G 425 820-7125
  Kirkland *(G-5337)*
Northstar Investment Co ....G 360 297-2260
  Kingston *(G-5258)*
Shirts Illustrated ....G 425 742-3844
  Lynnwood *(G-6195)*

EMERGENCY ALARMS

Ademco Inc ....G 253 872-7128
  Kent *(G-4759)*
Ademco Inc ....G 509 534-7300
  Spokane *(G-12098)*
Ademco Inc ....G 425 485-3938
  Bothell *(G-1815)*
Advanced Aero Safety Inc ....G 360 387-8472
  Stanwood *(G-12952)*
Electrical Services & SEC Inc ....G 206 276-6629
  Kent *(G-4887)*
Johnson Controls ....C 206 291-1400
  Seattle *(G-10302)*
Johnson Controls ....E 509 534-6055
  Spokane Valley *(G-12754)*
Michael Patrick Matthews ....G 509 457-8799
  Wapato *(G-14920)*
Monaco Enterprises Inc ....D 509 926-6277
  Spokane Valley *(G-12793)*
Motek Inc ....G 206 632-7795
  Seattle *(G-10565)*
Oatridge-Evergreen 8a2 JV LLC ....G 253 627-3794
  Tacoma *(G-13439)*
Surprise AI Care Group LLC ....G 775 746-2200
  Vancouver *(G-14621)*

EMERGENCY SHELTERS

Hydra Group LLC ....G 503 957-0975
  Washougal *(G-14959)*

EMPLOYMENT AGENCY SVCS

C E Publications Inc ....F 425 806-5200
  Bothell *(G-1833)*
Gildeane Group ....G 206 362-0336
  Kenmore *(G-4575)*
Nova Services ....E 509 928-1588
  Spokane Valley *(G-12810)*
Wafertech LLC ....A 360 817-3000
  Camas *(G-2287)*

ENCODERS: Digital

Differential Networks LLC ....G 360 366-8123
  Bellingham *(G-1323)*
Eln Communications Inc ....G 206 256-0420
  Seattle *(G-9904)*

ENERGY MEASUREMENT EQPT

Randl Industries Inc ....G 509 340-0050
  Spokane Valley *(G-12850)*

ENGINE REBUILDING: Diesel

Energy Conversions Inc ....G 253 922-6670
  Fife *(G-3951)*

Eriksen Diesel Repair Inc ....G 425 778-8237
  Edmonds *(G-3110)*
J & M Diesel Inc ....F 425 353-3050
  Lynnwood *(G-6142)*
Pacific Power Group LLC ....D 360 887-5980
  Ridgefield *(G-9100)*
Pacific Power Group LLC ....D 360 887-7400
  Vancouver *(G-14469)*
Yaculta Companies Inc ....B 360 887-7493
  Vancouver *(G-14704)*

ENGINEERING HELP SVCS

American Min & Tunneling LLC ....G 509 921-7836
  Spokane Valley *(G-12612)*

ENGINEERING SVCS

Adobe Systems Incorporated ....B 206 675-7000
  Seattle *(G-9353)*
Ahtna Engineering Services LLC ....D 425 864-1695
  Seatac *(G-9272)*
Airtran Wireless Technologies ....G 360 430-3179
  Vancouver *(G-14014)*
All Ocean Services LLC ....G 206 632-7692
  Everett *(G-3367)*
Astronics Cstm Ctrl Cncpts Inc ....D 206 575-0933
  Kent *(G-4795)*
Cascade Joinery Inc ....F 360 527-0119
  Ferndale *(G-3826)*
Conveyor Dynamics Inc ....G 360 671-2200
  Bellingham *(G-1305)*
DC Engineering Consulting Inc ....G 360 932-2367
  Rainier *(G-8313)*
Electric Boat Corporation ....E 360 598-5115
  Silverdale *(G-11833)*
Elkhart Plastics ....D 360 887-2230
  Ridgefield *(G-9080)*
Grow Plastics LLC ....G 206 954-4564
  Seattle *(G-10128)*
Holmes and Associates ....G 360 793-9723
  Monroe *(G-6578)*
ID Integration Inc ....F 425 438-2533
  Mukilteo *(G-6940)*
Immersive Media Company ....E 360 609-3419
  Washougal *(G-14960)*
Insitu Inc ....F 509 493-8600
  Bingen *(G-1637)*
Moco Engineering & Fabrication ....F 509 226-0199
  Spokane Valley *(G-12792)*
Modelwerks Inc ....F 206 340-6007
  Seattle *(G-10553)*
Mohr Test and Measurement LLC ....G 888 852-0408
  Richland *(G-9028)*
Mohr Test and Measurement LLC ....F 509 946-0941
  Richland *(G-9027)*
Monolithic Power Systems Inc ....C 425 296-9956
  Kirkland *(G-5405)*
Nbk Associates Inc ....G 216 408-8685
  Kirkland *(G-5408)*
Neumeier Engineering Inc ....E 253 854-3635
  Kent *(G-5020)*
Novex LLC ....G 360 296-3467
  Bellingham *(G-1473)*
Oiltrap Environmental Pdts Inc ....F 360 943-6495
  Olympia *(G-7350)*
Omni Technology ....G 425 823-9295
  Kirkland *(G-5419)*
Opticon Inc ....G 425 651-2120
  Renton *(G-8865)*
Phoenix Power Control Inc ....F 360 794-8550
  Monroe *(G-6606)*
Power Conversion Inc ....E 425 487-1337
  Woodinville *(G-15338)*
Raisbeck Engineering Inc ....F 206 723-2000
  Tukwila *(G-13802)*
Siemens Industry Inc ....F 509 891-9070
  Spokane Valley *(G-12871)*
Soloy LLC ....E 360 754-7000
  Tumwater *(G-13898)*
Somarakis Inc ....F 360 574-6722
  Kalama *(G-4508)*
Tecplot Inc ....F 425 653-1200
  Bellevue *(G-1179)*
Trilion Quality Systems LLC ....E 267 565-8062
  Seattle *(G-11337)*
United Home Technologies LLC ....F 360 574-7737
  Washougal *(G-14996)*
Wescold Inc ....E 206 284-5710
  Seattle *(G-11449)*
Westco Engineering ....G 425 481-7271
  Woodinville *(G-15403)*

ENGINEERING SVCS: Acoustical

Bucher Aerospace Corporation ....E 425 355-2202
  Everett *(G-3402)*

ENGINEERING SVCS: Aviation Or Aeronautical

Aim Aerospace Sumner Inc ....C 253 863-7868
  Sumner *(G-13054)*
Electrijet Flight Systems Inc ....G 509 990-9474
  Liberty Lake *(G-5831)*
Insitu Inc ....A 509 493-8600
  Bingen *(G-1638)*
Northwest Aerospace Tech Inc ....D 425 257-2044
  Everett *(G-3555)*
Northwest Aerospace Tech Inc ....G 425 212-5001
  Everett *(G-3556)*
Tethers Unlimited Inc ....G 425 486-0100
  Bothell *(G-1800)*
Ttf Aerospace Inc ....C 253 736-6300
  Auburn *(G-584)*

ENGINEERING SVCS: Building Construction

Greence Inc ....G 360 727-3528
  Ridgefield *(G-9087)*
Hope Moffat ....G 401 527-4234
  Bainbridge Island *(G-640)*

ENGINEERING SVCS: Chemical

Direct Contact LLC ....E 425 235-1723
  Tukwila *(G-13725)*

ENGINEERING SVCS: Construction & Civil

North Hill Resources Inc ....F 360 757-1866
  Burlington *(G-2173)*

ENGINEERING SVCS: Electrical Or Electronic

D & E Enterprises ....G 509 684-6618
  Colville *(G-2749)*
Dynolab ....G 206 243-8877
  Normandy Park *(G-7091)*
Engineering Solutions Inc ....F 206 241-9395
  Renton *(G-8795)*
Frencken America Inc ....E 509 924-9777
  Liberty Lake *(G-5832)*
Helldyne Inc ....G 206 855-1227
  Bainbridge Island *(G-638)*
Infinetix Corp ....F 509 922-5629
  Spokane Valley *(G-12739)*
Monsoon Solutions Inc ....E 425 378-8081
  Bellevue *(G-1014)*
Picatti Brothers Inc ....D 509 248-2540
  Yakima *(G-15646)*
Selectronix Incorporated ....G 425 788-2979
  Woodinville *(G-15358)*
Silicon Designs Inc ....E 425 391-8329
  Kirkland *(G-5461)*

ENGINEERING SVCS: Energy conservation

3 Phase Energy Systems Inc ....F 253 736-2248
  Auburn *(G-354)*
Lundberg LLC ....E 425 283-5070
  Redmond *(G-8541)*

ENGINEERING SVCS: Fire Protection

Jesse W Palmer ....F 509 634-1494
  Keller *(G-4513)*

ENGINEERING SVCS: Industrial

D & D Controls Inc ....G 360 695-8931
  Vancouver *(G-14160)*
Richmond Systems Inc ....E 360 455-8284
  Olympia *(G-7386)*
Workhorse Incorporated ....G 360 835-9417
  Washougal *(G-15002)*

ENGINEERING SVCS: Machine Tool Design

Monster Concepts Inc ....G 206 706-6730
  Seattle *(G-10560)*

ENGINEERING SVCS: Marine

Dli Engineering Corporation ....F 206 842-7656
  Poulsbo *(G-7958)*

PRODUCT SECTION — ETCHING & ENGRAVING SVC

Engineered Products Entps ....F 253 826-6185
  Edgewood *(G-3076)*

ENGINEERING SVCS: Mechanical

Byron Automation LLC ....F 509 653-2100
  Naches *(G-6994)*
Centurion Process LLC ....G 509 759-3001
  Selah *(G-11584)*
Hardy Engineering & Mfg Inc ....E 253 735-6488
  Auburn *(G-460)*
Hiline Engrg & Fabrication Inc ....E 509 943-9043
  Richland *(G-9006)*
Opi Wind Technologies Inc ....G 206 999-5373
  Seattle *(G-10706)*
Protium Innovations LLC ....G 206 854-8792
  Pullman *(G-8102)*
Source Engineering LLC ....E 360 383-5129
  Lynden *(G-6053)*

ENGINEERING SVCS: Mining

Infomine Usa Inc ....G 509 328-8023
  Spokane Valley *(G-12740)*

ENGINEERING SVCS: Pollution Control

Mpm Technologies Inc ....G 973 599-4416
  Spokane Valley *(G-12795)*

ENGINEERING SVCS: Professional

Transpac Marinas Inc ....G 360 293-8888
  Anacortes *(G-178)*

ENGINEERING SVCS: Sanitary

Parametrix Inc ....D 206 394-3700
  Puyallup *(G-8219)*

ENGINEERING SVCS: Structural

Earthbound Corporation ....F 360 863-0722
  Monroe *(G-6567)*

ENGINES & ENGINE PARTS: Guided Missile, Research & Develpt

Spaceflight Industries Inc ....E 206 342-9934
  Seattle *(G-11165)*

ENGINES: Diesel & Semi-Diesel Or Duel Fuel

Cummins Inc ....G 425 277-5342
  Sumner *(G-13062)*
Wave Engine Solutions Inc ....G 317 554-7201
  Camas *(G-2288)*

ENGINES: Gasoline, NEC

Walt Racing LLP ....G 253 847-8221
  Tacoma *(G-13586)*

ENGINES: Internal Combustion, NEC

ADI Thermal Power Corp ....G 206 484-2879
  Woodinville *(G-15171)*
Austin Resources LLC ....E 253 472-1703
  Tacoma *(G-13185)*
Cummins - Allison Corp ....G 206 763-3900
  Tukwila *(G-13721)*
Cummins Inc ....G 541 276-2561
  Pasco *(G-7573)*
Cummins Inc ....E 509 455-4411
  Spokane *(G-12211)*
Cummins Inc ....F 509 248-9033
  Yakima *(G-15545)*
Cummins Inc ....G 360 748-8841
  Tumwater *(G-13867)*
Eds Automotive and Machine Sp ...G 425 355-7268
  Mukilteo *(G-6919)*
Johnson Marine ....G 360 437-0467
  Port Ludlow *(G-7768)*
May Mobile Marine Tech ....G 360 552-2561
  Port Orchard *(G-7828)*
Mobile Marine Maintenance ....G 360 777-0001
  Chinook *(G-2617)*
N C Power Systems Co ....C 425 251-5877
  Tukwila *(G-13774)*
Sje Inc ....E 360 734-1910
  Bellingham *(G-1540)*

ENGINES: Jet Propulsion

Electrijet Flight Systems Inc ....G 509 990-9474
  Liberty Lake *(G-5831)*

ENGINES: Marine

Hatch & Kirk Inc ....F 206 783-2766
  Seattle *(G-10146)*
Hydra-Com Inc ....G 253 862-9140
  Pacific *(G-7529)*
Man Diesel North America Inc ....G 253 479-6800
  Kent *(G-5002)*
US Marine Chemists & Engrg ....G 206 200-6912
  Mukilteo *(G-6986)*

ENGINES: Steam

Steam Engine Metal Art ....G 509 302-9941
  Pasco *(G-7634)*

ENGRAVING SVC, NEC

Awards Etc ....G 509 758-3537
  Clarkston *(G-2621)*
Bellevue Fine Art Reproductn ....G 425 749-7396
  Bellevue *(G-812)*
Care Engraving Company ....G 360 456-0831
  Lacey *(G-5539)*
Delta C Dynamics LLC ....G 888 704-3626
  Kennewick *(G-4653)*
Geometric ....G 206 244-2222
  Tukwila *(G-13740)*
KB Hanks Enterprises ....G 425 221-1040
  Renton *(G-8836)*
Kens Engraving Emporium Inc ....G 360 578-0844
  Longview *(G-5922)*
Spring Creek Enterprises ....G 360 876-8884
  Port Orchard *(G-7852)*

ENGRAVING SVC: Jewelry & Personal Goods

Awards N More Usa Inc ....G 360 577-3646
  Longview *(G-5886)*
Bay Trophies & Engraving Inc ....G 360 676-0868
  Bellingham *(G-1261)*
DOE Run Studios ....G 360 765-0935
  Quilcene *(G-8282)*
Harrington Trophies ....G 509 943-2593
  Richland *(G-9005)*
Krysaliis LLC ....G 888 579-7254
  Blaine *(G-1679)*
Marysville Awards Inc ....G 360 653-4811
  Marysville *(G-6356)*
Mr TS Trophies ....G 360 424-9339
  Mount Vernon *(G-6815)*
Pats Blue Ribbons & Trophies ....F 360 676-8292
  Ferndale *(G-3884)*
Richard Saunders ....G 612 861-1061
  Seattle *(G-10962)*
Schmid Family Engraving LLC ......G 360 491-0997
  Olympia *(G-7392)*
Universal Brass Inc ....F 253 939-8282
  Auburn *(G-589)*

ENGRAVING SVCS

Image Masters Inc ....G 253 939-5868
  Auburn *(G-471)*
Jackyes Enterprises Inc ....G 425 355-5997
  Everett *(G-3521)*
Pcs Laser and Memorial ....G 208 746-1033
  Clarkston *(G-2640)*
Seattle Engraving LLC ....G 425 212-9797
  Everett *(G-3609)*
Sno King Stamp ....G 425 771-9373
  Lynnwood *(G-6202)*

ENGRAVING: Currency

Seattle Engraving Center LLC ....G 206 420-4604
  Seattle *(G-11056)*

ENGRAVING: Steel line, For The Printing Trade

Sanctuary Corporation ....G 360 477-4384
  Port Angeles *(G-7743)*

ENGRAVINGS: Plastic

Veva Company LLC ....G 360 687-8550
  Battle Ground *(G-749)*

ENTERTAINMENT SVCS

Avalonphilly LLC ....G 800 405-7024
  Bellevue *(G-800)*

ENVELOPES

Cenveo Worldwide Limited ....B 206 576-4300
  Kent *(G-4849)*
Direct Connect Group (dcg) LLC ..B 206 784-6892
  Seattle *(G-9833)*
Envelope Converting Service ....G 206 767-3653
  Seattle *(G-9932)*
Value Plus ....G 509 468-0393
  Spokane *(G-12580)*
West Coast Paper Company ....E 253 850-1900
  Kent *(G-5212)*

ENVELOPES WHOLESALERS

Cenveo Worldwide Limited ....B 206 576-4300
  Kent *(G-4849)*

ENVIRON QUALITY PROGS ADMIN, GOVT: Water Control & Quality

County of Pierce ....F 360 893-2844
  Orting *(G-7477)*

EPOXY RESINS

Leggari Products LLC ....G 509 727-2979
  Pasco *(G-7600)*

EQUIPMENT: Pedestrian Traffic Control

Nestor Inc ....D 253 395-0285
  Tukwila *(G-13776)*

EQUIPMENT: Rental & Leasing, NEC

Bair Construction Inc ....G 360 491-2285
  Lacey *(G-5535)*
Beverage Specialist Inc ....E 206 763-0255
  Tukwila *(G-13697)*
Blue Water Inc ....G 509 682-5544
  Chelan *(G-2548)*
Factory Trawler Supply Inc ....G 206 285-6732
  Seattle *(G-9961)*
Fedex Office & Print Svcs Inc ....E 360 647-1114
  Bellingham *(G-1344)*
Landa Inc ....D 360 833-9100
  Camas *(G-2263)*
Mikes Rental Machinery Inc ....E 509 925-6126
  Ellensburg *(G-3215)*
Olympic Outdoor Center ....E 360 297-4659
  Port Gamble *(G-7757)*
Rozema Enterprises Inc ....G 360 757-6004
  Mount Vernon *(G-6831)*
Summer Rrh LLC ....F 509 328-0915
  Spokane *(G-12532)*

ETCHING & ENGRAVING SVC

Acu-Line Corporation ....G 206 634-1618
  Seattle *(G-9347)*
Armor Performance Coating LLC ..G 509 551-1294
  Richland *(G-8967)*
Cutting Edge Engraving Inc ....G 360 863-2184
  Monroe *(G-6563)*
Dimensional Imaging Inc ....G 206 285-0450
  Seattle *(G-9830)*
Enlighting Struck Design LLC ....G 206 229-9438
  Kent *(G-4893)*
Extreme Indus Coatings LLC ....G 509 991-1773
  Airway Heights *(G-51)*
Jet City Partners LLC ....G 206 999-0047
  Auburn *(G-479)*
Lazer Trends LLC ....G 253 886-5600
  Auburn *(G-487)*
M S I Engineering Corporation ......F 425 827-6797
  Kirkland *(G-5390)*
Omnifab Inc ....E 253 931-5151
  Auburn *(G-518)*
Ries Productions LLC ....G 360 627-8795
  Bremerton *(G-1994)*
Sanctuary Corporation ....G 360 477-4384
  Port Angeles *(G-7743)*

Employee Codes: A=Over 500 employees, B=251-500
C=101-250, D=51-100, E=20-50, F=10-19, G=2-9

ETHYLENE-PROPYLENE RUBBERS: EPDM Polymers

ETHYLENE-PROPYLENE RUBBERS: EPDM Polymers
Zuber Polymers LLC ....G....... 360 929-7888
  Seattle *(G-11525)*

EXCAVATING EQPT
Cline Rentals LLC ....G....... 206 375-0705
  Bothell *(G-1839)*
D & M Machine Division Inc ....F....... 360 249-3366
  Montesano *(G-6643)*

EXCURSION BOATS
Northwest Yachts Inc ....G....... 360 299-0777
  Anacortes *(G-156)*

EXERCISE EQPT STORES
Vectra Fitness Inc ....C....... 425 291-9550
  Issaquah *(G-4486)*

EXHAUST SYSTEMS: Eqpt & Parts
Makk Motoring LLC ....G....... 509 855-2638
  Moses Lake *(G-6723)*
Pacbrake Company ....G....... 360 332-4717
  Blaine *(G-1692)*

EXPLORATION, METAL MINING
Goldrich Mining Company ....F....... 509 535-7367
  Spokane *(G-12277)*
Hunt Family Ltd Partnership ....G....... 509 892-5287
  Greenacres *(G-4299)*
Hunt Mining Corp ....G....... 509 290-5659
  Liberty Lake *(G-5835)*
Teck American Incorporated ....E....... 509 747-6111
  Spokane *(G-12548)*
Teck Co LLC ....G....... 509 747-6111
  Spokane *(G-12550)*
Washington Teck Incorporated ....B....... 509 446-4516
  Metaline Falls *(G-6500)*

EXPLOSIVES
Dyno Nobel Inc ....G....... 360 740-0128
  Chehalis *(G-2491)*
Natures Provision ....G....... 360 307-0113
  Silverdale *(G-11851)*

EXPLOSIVES: Gunpowder
Desparado Cowboy Bullets LLC ....G....... 509 382-8926
  Dayton *(G-2881)*
Gunpowder Creek LLC ....G....... 860 502-9202
  Walla Walla *(G-14817)*

EXTRACTS, FLAVORING
Deekay Essentials LLC ....G....... 732 809-7284
  Vancouver *(G-14173)*
Northwest Naturals LLC ....E....... 425 885-5252
  Bothell *(G-1781)*

EYEGLASSES
Tumwater Eye Center Inc ....G....... 360 352-6060
  Tumwater *(G-13902)*
Western Optical Corporation ....D....... 206 622-7627
  Seattle *(G-11455)*

EYES & HOOKS Screw
Suncatchers ....G....... 360 293-6360
  Anacortes *(G-171)*

EYES: Artificial
Erickson Inc ....G....... 509 747-6148
  Spokane *(G-12250)*
House of Lashes ....G....... 206 522-5277
  Seattle *(G-10186)*

FABRIC STORES
Chemical Cloth Co ....G....... 360 582-9684
  Sequim *(G-11617)*
Pendleton Woolen Mills Inc ....C....... 360 835-2131
  Washougal *(G-14977)*
Starman Metal Fabrications LLC ....G....... 425 235-1431
  Renton *(G-8919)*
Sweet Creek Creations ....G....... 509 446-2429
  Metaline Falls *(G-6498)*

FABRICATED METAL PRODUCTS, NEC
Creon LLC ....G....... 360 318-1559
  Lynden *(G-6010)*
Heavy Metal Fabrication ....G....... 509 493-2979
  White Salmon *(G-15116)*
Iron Rangers LLC ....G....... 509 891-9355
  Newman Lake *(G-7047)*
Mark S Vorobik ....G....... 360 766-6252
  Bow *(G-1931)*
Metalistics Inc ....G....... 425 348-9377
  Everett *(G-3546)*
Nipr LLC ....G....... 253 261-6840
  Enumclaw *(G-3310)*
Pivot Custom Metal Fabrication ....G....... 206 762-3755
  Seattle *(G-10815)*
Ralph A Parise ....G....... 360 387-1794
  Camano Island *(G-2223)*
Rory Thurrott ....G....... 206 941-7297
  Bainbridge Island *(G-668)*
Tacoma Fabrication LLC ....G....... 253 303-1143
  Tacoma *(G-13541)*
Thirtnspades Metal Fabrication ....G....... 425 831-6126
  North Bend *(G-7128)*
Tough Outdoor Products LLC ....F....... 509 621-0034
  Otis Orchards *(G-7519)*
Valley Steel & Stone ....G....... 360 378-5758
  Friday Harbor *(G-4063)*
Winter Mattias ....G....... 206 579-5275
  Monroe *(G-6638)*

FABRICS & CLOTH: Quilted
Dream Works Machine Quilting ....G....... 360 668-0864
  Snohomish *(G-11901)*

FABRICS: Alpacas, Cotton
Glenbar Alpacas Inc ....G....... 360 574-5428
  Ridgefield *(G-9085)*
White Cloud Alpacas ....G....... 253 853-6984
  Olalla *(G-7212)*

FABRICS: Alpacas, Mohair, Woven
Alpaca Mentors ....G....... 253 880-6469
  Enumclaw *(G-3276)*
Alpaca This LLC ....G....... 425 432-7227
  Maple Valley *(G-6256)*
Alpacas Northwest Inc ....G....... 503 519-7587
  Vancouver *(G-14023)*
Alpacas of Wintercreek ....G....... 253 332-4026
  Auburn *(G-372)*
Alpacas Paradise Pt ....G....... 360 263-2092
  Ridgefield *(G-9060)*
Brush Prairie Alpacas ....G....... 360 892-1011
  Brush Prairie *(G-2031)*
Cascade Rose Alpacas ....G....... 206 715-6910
  Carnation *(G-2291)*
Cusichaca Alpacas ....G....... 360 936-3259
  La Center *(G-5503)*
Fiber Meadows Alpacas LLC ....G....... 360 856-5740
  Sedro Woolley *(G-11537)*
Meadowrock Alpacas ....G....... 509 395-2266
  Trout Lake *(G-13680)*
Merrimac Alpacas ....G....... 425 387-7586
  Snohomish *(G-11946)*
Mt Peak Alpacas LLC ....G....... 253 297-4083
  Enumclaw *(G-3306)*
Rv Alpacas ....G....... 253 431-6747
  Rainier *(G-8322)*
Stellar Alpacas ....G....... 253 208-2107
  Spanaway *(G-12076)*
Super Suris Alpacas ....G....... 509 475-5110
  Mead *(G-6438)*
Wheatland Alpacas ....G....... 509 526-4847
  Walla Walla *(G-14901)*
Yangarra Alpacas ....G....... 253 630-5422
  Covington *(G-2841)*

FABRICS: Animal Fiber, Woven, Exc Wool
Peoh Point Alpaca Farm ....G....... 509 674-9120
  Cle Elum *(G-2675)*

FABRICS: Apparel & Outerwear, Cotton
Billdon LLC ....G....... 425 736-4316
  Sammamish *(G-9190)*
Fourplay Awd ....G....... 971 706-7646
  Vancouver *(G-14237)*
Lady 12 LLC ....G....... 425 218-3080
  Redmond *(G-8528)*

Wntr Ski Academy LLC ....G....... 425 829-1384
  Kirkland *(G-5495)*

FABRICS: Bags & Bagging, Cotton
Justus Bag Company Inc ....G....... 509 765-6981
  Moses Lake *(G-6720)*

FABRICS: Broadwoven, Cotton
Circa 15 Fabric Studio LLC ....G....... 425 309-9553
  Anacortes *(G-113)*
Clothworks Textiles Inc ....E....... 206 762-7886
  Seattle *(G-9698)*
Gaes Draperies ....G....... 360 293-9732
  Anacortes *(G-132)*

FABRICS: Broadwoven, Synthetic Manmade Fiber & Silk
Campbell Pet Company ....F....... 360 892-9786
  Vancouver *(G-14093)*
Danalco Inc ....E....... 626 303-4019
  Seattle *(G-9790)*
Paul Sessions ....G....... 360 265-1658
  Bremerton *(G-1987)*
Redwood Plastics and Rbr Corp ....E....... 360 225-1491
  Woodland *(G-15461)*
Xerium Technologies Inc ....G....... 360 636-0330
  Kelso *(G-4561)*

FABRICS: Broadwoven, Wool
Pendleton Woolen Mills Inc ....C....... 360 835-2131
  Washougal *(G-14977)*

FABRICS: Canvas
Canvas ....G....... 206 829-9858
  Seattle *(G-9620)*
Canvas Traditions ....G....... 206 313-0223
  Seattle *(G-9622)*
Coffee On Canvas ....G....... 419 605-2529
  Fircrest *(G-4001)*
Cookes Canvas & Sewing ....G....... 360 384-1636
  Ferndale *(G-3833)*
Crimson Canvas Arts ....G....... 610 235-7605
  Sammamish *(G-9200)*
Hanging Canvas ....G....... 206 937-3525
  Seattle *(G-10138)*
Life On Canvas ....G....... 503 470-9474
  Auburn *(G-488)*
Northwest Sails & Canvas Inc ....G....... 360 301-3204
  Port Townsend *(G-7902)*
Northwest Tarp & Canvas ....G....... 360 296-2321
  Bellingham *(G-1472)*
Port Townsend Community ....G....... 360 385-0120
  Port Townsend *(G-7909)*
Puget Sound Canvas Uphols ....G....... 206 782-5974
  Gold Bar *(G-4190)*
Shoreline Custom Canvas & Auto ....G....... 360 874-2702
  Port Orchard *(G-7847)*
Stretch and Staple ....G....... 206 607-9277
  Seattle *(G-11203)*
Uncorked Canvas ....G....... 253 301-1254
  Tacoma *(G-13569)*

FABRICS: Coated Or Treated
California Industrial Faciliti ....F....... 360 863-9333
  Monroe *(G-6562)*
Detro Manufacturing Inc ....G....... 360 687-9960
  Battle Ground *(G-697)*
Mid Mountain Materials Inc ....E....... 206 762-7600
  Seattle *(G-10539)*

FABRICS: Denims
Denim Dreamz ....G....... 425 712-1001
  Edmonds *(G-3106)*
Denim Duds ....G....... 360 432-1183
  Shelton *(G-11696)*
Denim Frills ....G....... 360 844-5163
  Vancouver *(G-14175)*

FABRICS: Fiberglass, Broadwoven
Comptex Inc ....F....... 360 466-5453
  La Conner *(G-5522)*
R&D Enterprises ....G....... 360 293-4155
  Anacortes *(G-163)*
Revchem Composites Inc ....G....... 253 305-0303
  Tacoma *(G-13496)*

PRODUCT SECTION

FARM SPLYS, WHOLESALE: Feed

Sunbacker Fiberglass Inc .... G 360 794-5547
  Monroe *(G-6628)*

FABRICS: Filter Cloth, Cotton

Thermedia Corporation .... G 360 427-1877
  Shelton *(G-11744)*

FABRICS: Glass & Fiberglass, Broadwoven

B & C Fiberglass Inc .... G 907 842-4767
  Bellingham *(G-1255)*
Bedrock Industries Inc .... F 206 283-7625
  Seattle *(G-9508)*

FABRICS: Metallized

C&J Industries Inc .... E 253 852-0634
  Kent *(G-4831)*
Precision Metal Works LLC .... G 509 945-8433
  Union Gap *(G-13951)*

FABRICS: Nonwoven

Warm Products Inc .... E 425 248-2424
  Lynnwood *(G-6221)*

FABRICS: Nylon, Broadwoven

Load Control Systems Inc .... G 253 284-0351
  Tacoma *(G-13389)*
Tactical Tailor Inc .... D 253 984-7854
  Lakewood *(G-5762)*

FABRICS: Pin Stripes, Cotton

Comeau Lettering .... G 360 573-2216
  Vancouver *(G-14141)*

FABRICS: Polyester, Broadwoven

Tiegrrr Straps Inc .... G 253 520-0303
  Kent *(G-5180)*

FABRICS: Print, Cotton

Wright Designs 800 866-1245
  Renton *(G-8950)*

FABRICS: Resin Or Plastic Coated

Crown Films LLC .... G 360 757-8880
  Burlington *(G-2149)*
Paneltech Intl Holdings Inc .... F 360 538-1480
  Hoquiam *(G-4354)*

FABRICS: Rubberized

Bowhead Manufacturing Co LLC .... G 206 957-5321
  Seattle *(G-9572)*

FABRICS: Satin

Satin Group LLC A .... G 206 228-1364
  Seattle *(G-11016)*

FABRICS: Surgical Fabrics, Cotton

Jovipak Corporation .... F 206 575-1656
  Kent *(G-4971)*

FABRICS: Table Cover, Cotton

Quilting Fairy LLC .... G 253 845-0462
  Puyallup *(G-8232)*

FABRICS: Trimmings

Advantage Precision Graphics .... F 425 285-9787
  Redmond *(G-8371)*
Alki Sports LLC .... F 206 898-1305
  Redmond *(G-8378)*
Arctic Circle Enterprises LLC .... D 253 872-8525
  Kent *(G-4789)*
Arctic Circle Holdings LLC .... G 206 625-9226
  Seattle *(G-9422)*
Blanc Industries Inc .... E 360 736-8988
  Centralia *(G-2385)*
Budd Bay Embroidery Inc .... F 360 709-0483
  Olympia *(G-7244)*
Classic Impressions .... E 206 766-9121
  Seattle *(G-9340)*
Colosseum Ventures LLC .... F 509 533-0366
  Spokane *(G-12188)*
Gompf Brackets Inc .... F 425 348-5002
  Mukilteo *(G-6929)*

Ink Inc .... F 253 565-4000
  University Place *(G-13973)*
Marysville Printing Inc .... G 360 658-9195
  Marysville *(G-6357)*
Merrill Corporation .... C 360 794-3157
  Monroe *(G-6596)*
Moss Green Inc .... F 206 285-4020
  Seattle *(G-10564)*
Northwest Designs Ink Inc .... F 425 454-0707
  Bellevue *(G-1035)*
NW Solar Protection LLC .... G 509 294-9878
  Spokane *(G-12416)*
Pacific Sportswear Inc .... E 253 582-4444
  Tacoma *(G-13454)*
Plastic Sales & Service Inc .... F 206 524-8312
  Lynnwood *(G-6181)*
Post Indus Stress & Design .... C 253 572-9782
  Tacoma *(G-13472)*
Ramax Printing and Awards .... G 509 928-1222
  Spokane *(G-12467)*
Screen Tek Inc .... E 509 928-8322
  Liberty Lake *(G-5860)*
Shirley Sunset .... G 360 574-3276
  Vancouver *(G-14584)*
Silkscreen Company .... E 206 763-8108
  Seattle *(G-11112)*
Trailready Products LLC .... F 425 353-6776
  Mount Vernon *(G-6847)*
Western Foil Corporation 206 624-3645
  Seattle *(G-11452)*
Western Graphics Inc .... G 206 241-2526
  Fife *(G-3998)*
Wildrose Ltd .... F 509 535-8555
  Spokane *(G-12591)*

FABRICS: Warp Knit, Lace & Netting

Pacific Netting Products Inc .... F 360 697-5540
  Kingston *(G-5260)*

FABRICS: Woven Wire, Made From Purchased Wire

Western Group Pacific .... G 253 964-6201
  Dupont *(G-2976)*

FABRICS: Woven, Narrow Cotton, Wool, Silk

Mid Mountain Materials Inc .... E 206 762-7600
  Seattle *(G-10539)*

FACIAL SALONS

Wright Surgical Arts LLC .... G 509 792-1404
  Pasco *(G-7656)*

FACILITIES SUPPORT SVCS

All Ocean Services LLC .... G 206 632-7692
  Everett *(G-3367)*
All Pole Corporation .... F 360 933-1806
  Blaine *(G-1658)*

FACSIMILE COMMUNICATION EQPT

Bellingham Business Machines .... G 360 734-3630
  Bellingham *(G-1264)*

FAMILY CLOTHING STORES

Bergen & Company .... F 360 676-7503
  Bellingham *(G-1271)*
Garage .... G 425 640-6021
  Lynnwood *(G-6126)*
Johnnie Montice .... G 360 452-6549
  Port Angeles *(G-7719)*
Northwest Sports 206 463-5906
  Vashon *(G-14738)*

FANS, VENTILATING: Indl Or Commercial

Efficient Dryer Vent Services .... G 360 687-7643
  Battle Ground *(G-700)*
Injectidry Systems Inc 425 822-3851
  Lynnwood *(G-6138)*
Unifire Inc .... F 509 535-7746
  Spokane *(G-12575)*

FARM & GARDEN MACHINERY WHOLESALERS

Blueline Equipment Co LLC .... G 509 525-4550
  Walla Walla *(G-14772)*

Furford Picker Co .... G 360 267-3303
  Grayland *(G-4294)*
L & L Nursery Supply Inc .... E 909 591-0461
  Fife *(G-3964)*
Newcore Aviation LLC .... G 509 276-8200
  Deer Park *(G-2910)*
Newcore Enterprises LLC .... G 509 276-8200
  Deer Park *(G-2911)*
Northstar Attachments LLC .... G 509 452-1651
  Yakima *(G-15632)*
Nutrien AG Solutions Inc .... G 509 547-9771
  Pasco *(G-7606)*
Oxbo International Corporation .... G 509 544-0362
  Pasco *(G-7610)*
US Mower Inc .... F 360 757-7555
  Burlington *(G-2198)*
Washington Tractor Inc .... C 253 863-4436
  Sumner *(G-13110)*
Washington Tractor Inc .... G 360 533-6393
  Aberdeen *(G-38)*
Washington Tractor Inc .... F 509 422-3030
  Okanogan *(G-7204)*

FARM MACHINERY REPAIR SVCS

Kile Machine & Manufacturing .... G 509 569-3814
  Rosalia *(G-9155)*
Lower Valley Machine Shop .... F 509 882-3881
  Grandview *(G-4251)*
REA Services Inc .... F 509 394-2305
  Touchet *(G-13677)*
Smileys Inc 360 424-7338
  Mount Vernon *(G-6843)*
Washington Tractor Inc .... C 253 863-4436
  Sumner *(G-13110)*
Washington Tractor Inc .... G 360 533-6393
  Aberdeen *(G-38)*
Washington Tractor Inc .... F 509 422-3030
  Okanogan *(G-7204)*

FARM PRDTS, RAW MATERIALS, WHOLESALE: Hides

Mason Meat Packing Co .... G 509 447-3788
  Newport *(G-7060)*

FARM PRDTS, RAW MATERIALS, WHOLESALE: Hops

S S Steiner Inc .... E 509 453-4731
  Yakima *(G-15665)*

FARM SPLY STORES

CHS-Sub Whatcom Inc .... E 360 354-2108
  Lynden *(G-6007)*
Elenbaas Company Inc .... E 360 354-3577
  Lynden *(G-6014)*
Epl Feed LLC .... E 360 988-5811
  Sumas *(G-13044)*
Rietdyks Milling Company .... G 360 887-8874
  Ridgefield *(G-9108)*

FARM SPLYS WHOLESALERS

Agrium US Inc .... C 509 586-5355
  Kennewick *(G-4614)*
Cascade Flying Service LLC .... G 509 635-1212
  Garfield *(G-4067)*
CHS-Sub Whatcom Inc .... E 360 354-2108
  Lynden *(G-6007)*
CHS-Sub Whatcom Inc .... G 360 966-4193
  Nooksack *(G-7086)*
CHS-Sub Whatcom Inc .... G 360 354-1198
  Lynden *(G-6008)*
CHS-Sub Whatcom Inc .... E 360 966-4782
  Everson *(G-3671)*
Graymont Western US Inc .... E 253 572-7600
  Tacoma *(G-13319)*
Skagit Seed Services Inc .... G 360 466-3191
  Mount Vernon *(G-6841)*

FARM SPLYS, WHOLESALE: Beekeeping Splys, Nondurable

Langes Honey Skep Inc .... G 360 757-1073
  Burlington *(G-2167)*

FARM SPLYS, WHOLESALE: Feed

Cargill Incorporated .... E 360 656-5784
  Ferndale *(G-3823)*

Employee Codes: A=Over 500 employees, B=251-500
C=101-250, D=51-100, E=20-50, F=10-19, G=2-9

FARM SPLYS, WHOLESALE: Feed

Northwest Farm Food Coop .... E 360 757-4225
  Burlington *(G-2175)*
Rietdyks Milling Company .... G 360 887-8874
  Ridgefield *(G-9108)*
Scratch and Peck LLC .... E 360 318-7585
  Burlington *(G-2186)*
X-Cel Feeds Inc .... E 253 472-5140
  Tacoma *(G-13603)*

FARM SPLYS, WHOLESALE: Fertilizers & Agricultural Chemicals

Truhumic Envmtl Solutions LLC .... G 425 232-6903
  Marysville *(G-6397)*

FARM SPLYS, WHOLESALE: Garden Splys

De Jong Sawdust & Shavings .... F 425 252-1566
  Lake Stevens *(G-5643)*
Micro Ag Inc .... G 509 397-4278
  Steptoe *(G-13007)*
Sls Runout LLC .... D 360 883-8846
  Vancouver *(G-14594)*

FASTENERS: Metal

Complex Aerospace LLC .... G 253 886-1323
  Auburn *(G-412)*
Earthbound Corporation .... F 360 863-0722
  Monroe *(G-6567)*
Jerry Carter .... G 509 487-8294
  Spokane *(G-12332)*
Twisted Metal LLC .... G 360 966-5309
  Everson *(G-3693)*

FASTENERS: Notions, NEC

A & P Fasteners Inc .... G 425 486-9562
  Kenmore *(G-4563)*
Allspec Fasteners Inc .... G 512 263-2593
  Everett *(G-3368)*
Centrix Inc .... D 253 872-4773
  Kent *(G-4847)*
Fastener Training 562 400-3009
  Olympia *(G-7282)*
Icg Corp 425 315-0200
  Mukilteo *(G-6939)*
Leads Manufacturing Company .... G 541 259-1128
  Vancouver *(G-14367)*
Northwest Lcknut Specialty Inc .... G 253 604-4860
  Puyallup *(G-8206)*

FASTENERS: Notions, Zippers

YKK (usa) Inc .... G 425 277-2503
  Renton *(G-8952)*

FATTY ACID ESTERS & AMINOS

Manuflaxsterit Llc .... D 360 384-0485
  Ferndale *(G-3867)*

FAUCETS & SPIGOTS: Metal & Plastic

Masons Supply Company .... G 206 883-5550
  Seattle *(G-10496)*
Part Works Inc .... E 206 632-8900
  Seattle *(G-10760)*

FEDERAL SAVINGS BANKS

First Millennium Bank .... G 360 797-5108
  Sequim *(G-11634)*

FENCE POSTS: Iron & Steel

Cowlitz Fence Co .... G 360 577-6110
  Kelso *(G-4522)*
Innotech Metal Designs LLC .... F 360 393-4108
  Bellingham *(G-1378)*

FENCES & FENCING MATERIALS

Merchants Metals LLC .... E 253 531-5454
  Tacoma *(G-13408)*

FENCES OR POSTS: Ornamental Iron Or Steel

Ballard Ornamental Ironworks .... G 206 782-3343
  Seattle *(G-9481)*
Big C Industries LLC .... G 844 406-2442
  Longview *(G-5888)*
Dag Industries Inc .... G 425 228-4962
  Renton *(G-8779)*
Fence Store By Eagle Vinyl LLC .... G 509 860-3603
  Wenatchee *(G-15032)*
Leskajan John .... G 253 539-8018
  Tacoma *(G-13386)*
Northwest Fence Co .... G 360 683-4673
  Sequim *(G-11652)*
Rainier Orna Ir Fbrication Inc .... G 253 833-0101
  Auburn *(G-544)*

FENCING DEALERS

Cowlitz Fence Co .... G 360 577-6110
  Kelso *(G-4522)*
Oneils Foundry Forging Metal & .... G 360 941-7557
  Sedro Woolley *(G-11553)*
T Eight Fincing LLC .... G 360 794-7369
  Monroe *(G-6629)*

FENCING MATERIALS: Docks & Other Outdoor Prdts, Wood

Greenhill Lumber Co Inc .... F 509 767-0010
  Dallesport *(G-2863)*
White Rabbit Ventures Inc .... F 360 474-5828
  Vancouver *(G-14690)*

FENCING MATERIALS: Plastic

Bradley Robling .... G 360 832-6778
  Spanaway *(G-12054)*
Michellaine Lee Larry Bergsma .... G 360 873-4005
  Marblemount *(G-6305)*

FENCING MATERIALS: Snow Fence, Wood

Michellaine Lee Larry Bergsma .... G 360 873-4005
  Marblemount *(G-6305)*

FENCING MATERIALS: Wood

Alta Forest Products LLC .... G 360 426-9721
  Chehalis *(G-2464)*
Alta Forest Products LLC .... G 800 599-5596
  Chehalis *(G-2465)*
Cedartone Specialties Inc .... C 253 852-6628
  Kent *(G-4845)*
Reichert Shake & Fencing Inc .... E 360 864-6434
  Toledo *(G-13641)*
Rsg Forest Products Inc .... C 360 673-2825
  Kalama *(G-4507)*
T Eight Fincing LLC .... G 360 794-7369
  Monroe *(G-6629)*

FENCING: Chain Link

Michellaine Lee Larry Bergsma .... G 360 873-4005
  Marblemount *(G-6305)*

FENDERS: Automobile, Stamped Or Pressed Metal

Capital Industries Inc .... D 206 762-8585
  Seattle *(G-9624)*

FERRIES: Operating Across Rivers Or Within Harbors

Foss Marine Holdings Inc .... G 206 381-5800
  Seattle *(G-10014)*

FERTILIZER MINERAL MINING

Verdesian Life Science US LLC .... F 919 825-1901
  Pasco *(G-7648)*

FERTILIZER, AGRICULTURAL: Wholesalers

Agrium US Inc .... C 509 586-5500
  Kennewick *(G-4613)*
Perfect Blend LLC .... E 509 488-5570
  Bellevue *(G-1069)*
Perfect Blend LLC .... E 509 488-5570
  Othello *(G-7503)*
Tessenderlo Kerley Inc .... E 509 586-9148
  Kennewick *(G-4733)*

FERTILIZERS: NEC

CHS-Sub Whatcom Inc .... E 360 354-2108
  Lynden *(G-6007)*
CHS-Sub Whatcom Inc .... G 360 966-4193
  Nooksack *(G-7086)*
CHS-Sub Whatcom Inc .... G 360 354-1198
  Lynden *(G-6008)*
CHS-Sub Whatcom Inc .... E 360 966-4782
  Everson *(G-3671)*
De Jong Sawdust & Shavings .... F 425 252-1566
  Lake Stevens *(G-5643)*
Helena Agri-Enterprises LLC .... F 509 549-3566
  Pomeroy *(G-7674)*
JR Simplot Company .... E 509 488-2132
  Othello *(G-7498)*
JR Simplot Company .... E 509 248-5756
  Moxee *(G-6879)*
Kronos Micronutrients LP .... E 509 248-4911
  Moxee *(G-6880)*
L & L Nursery Supply Inc .... G 909 591-0461
  Fife *(G-3964)*
Natural Selection Farms Inc .... F 509 837-3501
  Sunnyside *(G-13135)*
Northwest AG Pdts LLC .... E 509 547-8234
  Pasco *(G-7604)*
Nutrien AG Solutions Inc .... G 509 547-9771
  Pasco *(G-7606)*
Pacific Topsoils Inc .... F 425 337-2700
  Everett *(G-3568)*
Ronald F Phillips .... G 360 779-5614
  Poulsbo *(G-7996)*
Sarvel Biofuels Lummi Corp .... G 360 362-0016
  Ferndale *(G-3897)*
Wolfkill Feed & Fert Corp .... G 360 794-7065
  Monroe *(G-6639)*

FERTILIZERS: Nitrogenous

Agrium US Inc .... C 509 586-5500
  Kennewick *(G-4613)*
Agrium US Inc .... C 509 586-5355
  Kennewick *(G-4614)*
McGregor Company .... G 509 549-3635
  Pomeroy *(G-7675)*
Nhthree LLC .... C 509 396-2082
  Richland *(G-9031)*
Ultra Yield Micronutrients Inc .... E 509 248-4911
  Moxee *(G-6888)*
Waupaca Northwoods LLC .... D 509 877-2830
  Parker *(G-7550)*
Windtogreen LLC .... G 509 382-4034
  Dayton *(G-2890)*

FERTILIZERS: Phosphatic

JR Simplot Company .... E 509 488-2132
  Othello *(G-7498)*
McGregor Company .... F 509 397-4360
  Colfax *(G-2716)*
Northwest AG Pdts LLC .... E 509 547-8234
  Pasco *(G-7604)*
Soil Science Products LLC .... G 360 876-3734
  Port Orchard *(G-7849)*
Tessenderlo Kerley Inc .... E 509 586-9148
  Kennewick *(G-4733)*

FIBER & FIBER PRDTS: Acrylic

Plastic Sales & Service Inc .... F 206 524-8312
  Lynnwood *(G-6181)*

FIBER & FIBER PRDTS: Fluorocarbon

Carbitex Inc .... G 509 591-9775
  Kennewick *(G-4642)*

FIBER & FIBER PRDTS: Organic, Noncellulose

Day Creek Organic Farms Inc .... G 360 856-4770
  Sedro Woolley *(G-11536)*
Rich Nature Nutraceutical Labs .... F 425 493-1885
  Mukilteo *(G-6972)*
Tidal Vision Products LLC .... F 907 988-8888
  Ferndale *(G-3913)*

FIBER & FIBER PRDTS: Synthetic Cellulosic

Aidapak Services LLC .... F 360 448-2090
  Vancouver *(G-14013)*
Spillmasters X LLC .... G 360 461-7910
  Port Angeles *(G-7746)*

PRODUCT SECTION — FIRE PROTECTION EQPT

FIBER OPTICS
Agile Data Technology Inc ....G...... 206 280-9512
  Seattle *(G-9359)*
Dennis Nelson ....G...... 360 320-4237
  Oak Harbor *(G-7148)*

FIBERS: Carbon & Graphite
A To Z Composites Inc ....F...... 435 680-3762
  Bellingham *(G-1236)*
Innovative Composite Engrg Inc ....D...... 509 493-4484
  White Salmon *(G-15119)*
Sgl Atomotive Carbn Fibers LLC ....D...... 509 762-4600
  Moses Lake *(G-6747)*

FILLERS & SEALERS: Putty, Wood
Wade Sumpter Industries Inc ....G...... 425 486-9541
  Bothell *(G-1915)*

FILLING SVCS: Pressure Containers
Norco Inc ....G...... 509 754-3518
  Ephrata *(G-3343)*

FILM & SHEET: Unsuppported Plastic
Bemis Company Inc ....G...... 206 632-2246
  Seattle *(G-9511)*
Flexible Containment Pdts Inc........E...... 509 624-8921
  Spokane Valley *(G-12705)*
ISO Poly Films Inc ....F...... 864 684-8198
  Vancouver *(G-14326)*
Layfield Plastics Incorporated .....G...... 425 254-1075
  Renton *(G-8841)*
Orbis Rpm LLC ....F...... 253 333-0606
  Auburn *(G-520)*

FILM BASE: Cellulose Acetate Or Nitrocellulose Plastics
Nobelus LLC ....G...... 800 895-2747
  Seattle *(G-10614)*

FILM: Motion Picture
Indie Flix Inc ....F...... 206 829-9112
  Seattle *(G-10226)*
Northwest Video Wall ....G...... 360 403-7773
  Arlington *(G-291)*
Oppenheimer Camera Pdts Inc.....G...... 206 467-8666
  Seattle *(G-10707)*
Outdoor Specialties LLC ....G...... 425 432-0507
  Renton *(G-8869)*
Stourwater Pictures ....G...... 206 780-6928
  Bainbridge Island *(G-674)*
Tarra LLC ....G...... 360 458-4842
  Roy *(G-9165)*

FILTER CLEANING SVCS
Aaire Particle Control Co Inc .....G...... 206 767-6692
  Seattle *(G-9330)*
Filter Clean Recycling LLC ....G...... 360 798-1012
  Vancouver *(G-14230)*

FILTER ELEMENTS: Fluid & Hydraulic Line
RJ Hydraulics Inc ....F...... 360 693-4399
  Vancouver *(G-14553)*

FILTERS
Advance Pattern & Tooling Inc ...G...... 253 638-0300
  Kent *(G-4760)*
Armadillo Equipment & Parts .....G...... 360 829-4107
  Buckley *(G-2046)*
Clarus Technologies LLC ....G...... 360 671-1514
  Bellingham *(G-1299)*
Ervin H Tennyson ....G...... 360 445-2434
  Mount Vernon *(G-6793)*
Filter Clean Recycling LLC ....G...... 360 798-1012
  Vancouver *(G-14230)*
Fourth Corner Wtr Filters LLC ....G...... 360 296-1647
  Blaine *(G-1670)*
Fsx Incorporated ....G...... 360 691-2999
  Granite Falls *(G-4274)*
Hdc Filters LLC ....G...... 253 964-0707
  Dupont *(G-2965)*
Highwater Filters ....G...... 509 685-0933
  Colville *(G-2757)*
Inskiwrx Tool & Machine LLC ....G...... 425 238-2738
  Arlington *(G-255)*

Mal Inc ....D...... 360 491-2900
  Olympia *(G-7331)*
NW Filters ....G...... 253 859-4099
  Kent *(G-5039)*
Oberg Filters LLC ....G...... 360 403-3222
  Arlington *(G-292)*
Pine Filter LLC ....G...... 360 262-9132
  Chehalis *(G-2525)*
Remember Filtercom ....G...... 425 359-7905
  Lake Stevens *(G-5671)*
True Machine ....G...... 425 610-9669
  Ferndale *(G-3919)*
US Filter Vancouver ....G...... 360 892-6977
  Vancouver *(G-14656)*
Vietnam Filter Project ....G...... 425 772-5401
  Lynnwood *(G-6217)*

FILTERS & SOFTENERS: Water, Household
Emerald City Water LLC ....G...... 425 821-0800
  Kirkland *(G-5332)*
Health Guard Industries Inc ......G...... 360 474-9298
  Arlington *(G-251)*
N R G Enterprises Inc ....D...... 425 556-3993
  Redmond *(G-8592)*
Northwest Water Treatment LLC ....G...... 360 354-2044
  Lynden *(G-6040)*
Rena Ware International Inc ......E...... 425 881-6171
  Bellevue *(G-1098)*
Treit Equipment Co Inc ....G...... 253 549-2399
  Fox Island *(G-4026)*

FILTERS & STRAINERS: Pipeline
Deer Path Industrial Tech ....G...... 425 391-9223
  Issaquah *(G-4404)*

FILTERS: Air
Aaire Particle Control Co Inc ....G...... 206 767-6692
  Seattle *(G-9330)*
Allred Heating Cooling Elc LLC......F...... 206 359-2164
  Federal Way *(G-3715)*
American Air Filter Co Inc ....G...... 253 395-8860
  Kent *(G-4776)*

FILTERS: Air Intake, Internal Combustion Engine, Exc Auto
Claudes Accurate Machining .....G...... 360 546-5840
  Vancouver *(G-14120)*

FILTERS: General Line, Indl
Evoqua Water Technologies LLC ......G...... 360 699-7392
  Brush Prairie *(G-2034)*
Water Beetle USA ....G...... 702 899-2266
  Seattle *(G-11444)*

FILTERS: Oil, Internal Combustion Engine, Exc Auto
Clarification Techology Inc ....G...... 425 820-4850
  Kirkland *(G-5307)*
Oberg Manufacturing Inc ....G...... 360 435-8161
  Arlington *(G-293)*

FILTRATION DEVICES: Electronic
Source TEC Inc ....G...... 206 972-3172
  Woodinville *(G-15371)*

FINANCIAL INVESTMENT ADVICE
Global Incorporated ....F...... 206 763-4424
  Seattle *(G-10084)*

FINGERNAILS, ARTIFICIAL
Nitwit Lice Removal ....G...... 206 327-5782
  Seattle *(G-10611)*

FINISHING SVCS
Elite Aircraft Deburring ....G...... 360 435-2652
  Arlington *(G-234)*

FIRE ALARM MAINTENANCE & MONITORING SVCS
Direct Fire Suppression System ......G...... 509 215-0852
  Medical Lake *(G-6440)*

Fire Solutions NW LLC ....G...... 855 876-3473
  Bremerton *(G-1954)*
General Fire Prtection Systems ....F...... 509 535-4255
  Spokane *(G-12268)*

FIRE ARMS, SMALL: Guns Or Gun Parts, 30 mm & Below
Blood Eagle Weaponry LLC ....G...... 360 929-9567
  Oak Harbor *(G-7142)*
Bullet Hole LLC ....G...... 509 868-8884
  Spokane Valley *(G-12646)*
Crt Less Lethal ....G...... 425 337-6875
  Snohomish *(G-11893)*
Dayton Traister Co Inc ....G...... 360 675-3421
  Oak Harbor *(G-7147)*
Defense Sales Intl LLC ....G...... 206 999-8684
  Renton *(G-8782)*
Hamilton Equipment ....G...... 509 775-3445
  Republic *(G-8958)*
Modular Driven Tech Inc ....F...... 604 393-0800
  Sumas *(G-13049)*
Olympic Arms Inc ....D...... 360 456-3471
  Olympia *(G-7356)*
Sims Vibration Laboratory Inc ....D...... 360 427-6031
  Shelton *(G-11735)*

FIRE ARMS, SMALL: Machine Guns/Machine Gun Parts, 30mm/below
Okanogan Arms Co LLC ....G...... 509 422-4123
  Okanogan *(G-7202)*

FIRE ARMS, SMALL: Pistols Or Pistol Parts, 30 mm & below
L E Wilson Inc ....G...... 509 782-1328
  Cashmere *(G-2324)*

FIRE ARMS, SMALL: Shotguns Or Shotgun Parts, 30 mm & Below
Aero Precision LLC ....E...... 253 272-8188
  Tacoma *(G-13158)*

FIRE DETECTION SYSTEMS
Fire Protection Inc ....G...... 206 440-5763
  Seattle *(G-9994)*
Performnce Fire Protection Inc ...G...... 253 778-8039
  Kent *(G-5064)*

FIRE EXTINGUISHER CHARGES
Nu Element Inc ....G...... 206 356-4525
  Tacoma *(G-13437)*

FIRE EXTINGUISHER SVC
Austin Speciaties Inc ....G...... 360 629-6662
  Stanwood *(G-12959)*
U S Fire Equipment LLC ....F...... 253 863-1301
  Sumner *(G-13108)*

FIRE EXTINGUISHERS, WHOLESALE
Austin Speciaties Inc ....G...... 360 629-6662
  Stanwood *(G-12959)*
Direct Fire Suppression System ......G...... 509 215-0852
  Medical Lake *(G-6440)*

FIRE EXTINGUISHERS: Portable
Austin Speciaties Inc ....G...... 360 629-6662
  Stanwood *(G-12959)*
Direct Fire Suppression System ......G...... 509 215-0852
  Medical Lake *(G-6440)*
Hawk International Inc ....G...... 253 851-3444
  Gig Harbor *(G-4116)*
Kolibaba and Associates ....G...... 253 752-0368
  Tacoma *(G-13378)*

FIRE OR BURGLARY RESISTIVE PRDTS
Dylan Manufacturing Inc ....F...... 253 333-8260
  Auburn *(G-430)*

FIRE PROTECTION EQPT
American Roof Inc ....F...... 360 668-3206
  Monroe *(G-6548)*
Fire Def Tech Safety Pdts Inc .....G...... 509 619-0261
  Richland *(G-8998)*

Employee Codes: A=Over 500 employees, B=251-500 C=101-250, D=51-100, E=20-50, F=10-19, G=2-9

FIRE PROTECTION EQPT

U S Fire Equipment LLC ....F 253 863-1301
  Sumner *(G-13108)*
Western States Fire Equipment ....G 360 723-0032
  Battle Ground *(G-752)*

FIREARMS & AMMUNITION, EXC SPORTING, WHOLESALE

Aero Precision LLC ....E 253 272-8188
  Tacoma *(G-13158)*
Blood Eagle Weaponry LLC ....G 360 929-9567
  Oak Harbor *(G-7142)*
Bullet Hole LLC ....G 509 868-8884
  Spokane Valley *(G-12646)*
Lionheart Industries LLC ....G 888 552-4743
  Renton *(G-8845)*
Pacific Northwest Jewelers ....G 509 927-8923
  Greenacres *(G-4300)*

FIREARMS: Large, Greater Than 30mm

Spec Tech Industries Inc ....G 360 303-9077
  Maple Falls *(G-6251)*
X Products LLC ....E 971 302-6127
  Vancouver *(G-14701)*

FIREARMS: Small, 30mm or Less

Go Planit LLC ....G 206 227-0660
  Mattawa *(G-6407)*
Hardened Arms LLC ....E 425 530-0837
  Friday Harbor *(G-4050)*
Lionheart Industries LLC ....G 888 552-4743
  Renton *(G-8845)*
Ortwein International ....G 503 313-0514
  Vancouver *(G-14458)*
Tech Heavy Industries Inc ....G 509 557-8492
  Riverside *(G-9127)*
Wynakos Machine Inc ....G 360 794-9057
  Monroe *(G-6640)*

FIREBRICK: Clay

Allied Mineral Products Inc ....G 360 748-9295
  Chehalis *(G-2461)*

FIREPLACE & CHIMNEY MATERIAL: Concrete

Fireside Hearth & Home Inc ....F 425 251-9447
  Kent *(G-4907)*

FIREPLACE EQPT & ACCESS

Aqua Rec Inc ....G 253 826-2561
  Bonney Lake *(G-1716)*
Aqua Rec Inc ....G 253 770-9447
  Puyallup *(G-8123)*

FIRING OVEN & ACCESS: Clay

Burn Manufacturing Co ....G 331 444-2876
  Vashon *(G-14714)*

FIRST AID SPLYS, WHOLESALE

Normed Inc ....E 800 288-8200
  Tukwila *(G-13779)*

FISH & SEAFOOD PROCESSORS: Canned Or Cured

Americn-Canadian Fisheries Inc ....E 360 398-1117
  Bellingham *(G-1246)*
Bell Buoy Crab Co Inc ....G 360 777-8272
  Chinook *(G-2614)*
Benthic Fishing LLC ....E 253 219-1500
  Bremerton *(G-1938)*
Cape Greig LLC ....G 206 545-9501
  Renton *(G-8767)*
Dockside Cannery ....G 360 642-8870
  Ilwaco *(G-4369)*
Dungeness Development Assoc ....F 360 875-5507
  Seattle *(G-9860)*
Glacier Bay Fisheries LLC ....F 206 298-1200
  Seattle *(G-10075)*
North Pacific Seafoods Inc ....E 206 726-9900
  Seattle *(G-10626)*
Norton Sound Fish Company LLC ....E 206 298-1200
  Seattle *(G-10654)*
Ocean Beauty Seafoods LLC ....C 206 285-6800
  Seattle *(G-10682)*
Pelican Packers Inc ....F 360 398-8825
  Bellingham *(G-1494)*
Wfm Select Fish Inc ....F 512 542-0676
  Bellevue *(G-1227)*

FISH & SEAFOOD PROCESSORS: Fresh Or Frozen

Alaska Seafood Holdings Inc ....G 360 734-8175
  Bellingham *(G-1242)*
Aleutian Spray Reverse LLC ....G 206 784-5000
  Seattle *(G-9372)*
Alyeska Ocean Inc ....G 360 293-4677
  Anacortes *(G-99)*
American Seafoods Company LLC ....D 206 448-0300
  Seattle *(G-9395)*
Arctic Fjord Inc ....G 206 547-6557
  Seattle *(G-9423)*
Arctic Storm Inc ....G 206 547-6557
  Seattle *(G-9424)*
Bay Center Mariculture Co ....G 360 875-6172
  Bay Center *(G-755)*
Bear & Wolf LLC ....F 206 281-7777
  Seattle *(G-9506)*
Big Creek Fisheries LLC ....C 425 742-8609
  Everett *(G-3387)*
Blau Oyster Company Inc ....G 360 766-6171
  Bow *(G-1927)*
Blue Sea Fisheries ....G 360 299-0936
  Anacortes *(G-103)*
CFC Fish Company LLC ....C 253 478-5160
  Renton *(G-8770)*
Clipper Seafoods Ltd ....C 206 284-1162
  Seattle *(G-9697)*
Coast Seafoods Company ....E 360 875-5557
  South Bend *(G-12040)*
Coastal Star Inc ....D 206 282-0988
  Seattle *(G-9706)*
Cold Locker Processing LLC ....F 253 321-3233
  Sumner *(G-13059)*
Cooke Seafood Usa Inc ....G 206 282-0988
  Seattle *(G-9737)*
Copper River Smoking Co ....G 253 446-0634
  Puyallup *(G-8137)*
Custom Seafood Services Inc ....E 360 267-2666
  Seattle *(G-9771)*
Deep Sea Fisheries ....G 206 743-3381
  Lynnwood *(G-6106)*
Dignon Co Inc ....G 206 448-6677
  Lake Forest Park *(G-5612)*
Dungeness Development Assoc ....F 360 875-5507
  Seattle *(G-9860)*
Julie Cake Fisheries Inc ....G 360 636-3621
  Kelso *(G-4532)*
Kanaway Seafoods Inc ....D 425 485-7755
  Kenmore *(G-4586)*
King & Prince Seafood Corp ....E 360 733-9090
  Bellingham *(G-1395)*
Kiska Sea Northern LLC ....G 206 784-5000
  Seattle *(G-10346)*
Norquest Seafoods Inc ....D 425 349-2563
  Everett *(G-3553)*
Norquest Seafoods Inc ....E 206 281-7022
  Seattle *(G-10622)*
North Star Cold Storage Inc ....E 360 629-9591
  Stanwood *(G-12983)*
Northern Fish Products Inc ....G 253 475-3858
  Tacoma *(G-13430)*
Northern Wave LLC ....F 206 217-4518
  Seattle *(G-10633)*
Ocean Beauty Seafoods LLC ....C 206 285-6800
  Seattle *(G-10682)*
Ocean Peace Inc ....D 206 282-6100
  Seattle *(G-10683)*
Orient Food Production ....G 253 926-1389
  Fife *(G-3976)*
Paragon Seafood Company ....G 425 788-6077
  Woodinville *(G-15332)*
Portlock Smked Sfds-Bllard Ret ....G 206 466-1931
  Seattle *(G-10836)*
Q Sea Specialty Services LLC ....E 360 398-9708
  Bellingham *(G-1511)*
Quinault Pride Seafoods ....E 360 276-4431
  Taholah *(G-13609)*
Royal Aleutian Seafoods Inc ....G 206 283-6605
  Seattle *(G-10985)*
Royal Viking Inc ....G 206 783-3818
  Seattle *(G-10987)*
Sea Storm Fisheries Inc ....G 206 547-6557
  Seattle *(G-11038)*
South Bend Products LLC ....D 360 875-6570
  South Bend *(G-12047)*
Starbound LLC ....C 206 784-5000
  Seattle *(G-11181)*
Sugiyo USA Inc ....D 360 293-0180
  Anacortes *(G-170)*
Taylor Mariculture LLC ....G 360 426-6178
  Shelton *(G-11739)*
Taylor Resources Inc ....C 360 426-6178
  Shelton *(G-11740)*
Toke Point Fisheries Inc ....G 360 753-6917
  Olympia *(G-7409)*
Trader Bay Ltd ....D 253 884-5691
  Lakebay *(G-5691)*
Tribal Fishco LLC ....F 509 493-1104
  White Salmon *(G-15134)*
Trident Carrollton LLC ....G 206 783-3818
  Seattle *(G-11333)*
Trident Seafoods Corporation ....C 425 407-4000
  Everett *(G-3637)*
Trident Seafoods Corporation ....B 360 293-3133
  Anacortes *(G-180)*
Trident Seafoods Corporation ....B 253 502-5318
  Tacoma *(G-13563)*
Trident Seafoods Corporation ....B 360 740-7816
  Chehalis *(G-2539)*
Trident Seafoods Corporation ....C 360 293-7701
  Anacortes *(G-179)*
Trio Machinery Inc ....G 360 671-6229
  Blaine *(G-1707)*
Wiegardt Bros Inc ....E 360 665-4111
  Ocean Park *(G-7183)*

FISH & SEAFOOD WHOLESALERS

Barleans Fishery Inc ....G 360 384-0325
  Ferndale *(G-3817)*
D P Clarke ....G 360 647-8185
  Bellingham *(G-1317)*
E & E Foods Inc ....E 206 768-8979
  Renton *(G-8789)*
Kono Fixed Income Fund 1511 LP ....F 360 686-7688
  Bellevue *(G-972)*
Northwest Smoking & Curing ....G 360 733-3666
  Bellingham *(G-1470)*
Quinault Pride Seafoods ....E 360 276-4431
  Taholah *(G-13609)*
Taylor Shellfish Company Inc ....E 360 875-5494
  South Bend *(G-12048)*
World Wide Gourmet Foods Inc ....F 360 668-9404
  Woodinville *(G-15410)*

FISH EGGS: Packaged For Use As Bait

Pautzke Bait Co Inc ....G 509 925-6154
  Ellensburg *(G-3218)*

FISH FOOD

Bio-Tope Research Inc ....G 509 684-1512
  Colville *(G-2739)*
Bio-Tope Research Inc ....G 509 684-1154
  Colville *(G-2740)*
Dr Dons Fishfood LLC ....G 360 533-6620
  Aberdeen *(G-8)*
Fat-Cat Fish LLC ....E 360 715-1994
  Bellingham *(G-1343)*
Tastebud Fusion Inc ....E 253 826-8700
  Seattle *(G-11272)*

FISHING EQPT: Lures

George Gehrkes Gink ....G 509 243-4100
  Asotin *(G-353)*
Noors Lures LLC ....G 360 896-4032
  Vancouver *(G-14433)*
Wicked Lures LLC ....G 360 460-6078
  Sequim *(G-11670)*

FISHING EQPT: Nets & Seines

Everson Cordage Works LLC ....E 360 966-4613
  Everson *(G-3675)*

FITTINGS & ASSEMBLIES: Hose & Tube, Hydraulic Or Pneumatic

Central Hose and Fittings Inc ....F 509 547-6460
  Pasco *(G-7558)*
Hose Pro ....G 253 448-1304
  Puyallup *(G-8162)*
Hose Shop Inc ....G 360 757-3776
  Burlington *(G-2165)*

PRODUCT SECTION

Kaman Fluid Power LLC .... G 253 922-5710
  Tacoma *(G-13372)*
Kaman Fluid Power LLC .... G 360 738-1264
  Bellingham *(G-1390)*
Spokane House of Hose Inc .... E 509 535-3638
  Spokane Valley *(G-12883)*

FITTINGS: Pipe

Romac Industries Inc .... C 425 951-6200
  Bothell *(G-1897)*

FIXTURES & EQPT: Kitchen, Metal, Exc Cast Aluminum

Arlenes Kitchen .... G 208 254-0591
  Sequim *(G-11612)*
Lumpinee Inc .... F 425 497-8383
  Redmond *(G-8540)*
Premier Stainless Installers .... G 253 370-0521
  Puyallup *(G-8224)*

FIXTURES: Cut Stone

Columbia Cultured Marble Inc .... G 509 582-5660
  Kennewick *(G-4647)*

FLAGS: Fabric

Direct Hit Golf Flags LLC .... G 253 946-6263
  Federal Way *(G-3729)*
Snow & Company Inc .... G 206 396-8997
  Seattle *(G-11145)*

FLAGSTONES

Flagstone .... G 425 892-9134
  Bothell *(G-1854)*
Flagstone Wildlife Artisrty .... G 360 967-2005
  Silverlake *(G-11863)*

FLARES

Hacienda Las Flares .... G 208 819-8879
  Spokane *(G-12285)*

FLAT GLASS: Construction

Impulse Construction & Glass .... G 425 530-7728
  Snohomish *(G-11927)*
Valley Supply Company .... E 360 217-4400
  Woodinville *(G-15398)*

FLAT GLASS: Ophthalmic

Lapel Solutions LLC .... F 360 597-4958
  Vancouver *(G-14358)*

FLAT GLASS: Skylight

KDL Enterprises Inc .... E 253 395-3113
  Kent *(G-4973)*
Tam Industries Inc .... F 206 763-6868
  Seattle *(G-11264)*

FLAT GLASS: Tempered

Snt-Gbain N Vetrotech Amer Inc .... G 253 333-7592
  Auburn *(G-568)*

FLAT GLASS: Window, Clear & Colored

Clear View Auto & Window Glass .... G 360 539-5909
  Lacey *(G-5542)*
Endurance Window Co .... G 425 883-1345
  Bellevue *(G-897)*
Gabrielles Glassworks .... G 509 585-9394
  Kennewick *(G-4666)*
Marlin Windows Inc .... E 509 535-3015
  Spokane Valley *(G-12784)*
Northwestern Industries Inc .... E 206 285-3140
  Seattle *(G-10653)*
Pro Tint LLC .... G 509 468-8468
  Nine Mile Falls *(G-7082)*
South Tacoma Glass Specialists .... E 253 582-2401
  Lakewood *(G-5758)*
White Center Glass & Uphl .... G 206 762-8088
  Seattle *(G-11469)*

FLIGHT TRAINING SCHOOLS

Kenmore Air Harbor Inc .... D 425 486-3224
  Kenmore *(G-4587)*

FLOOR CLEANING & MAINTENANCE EQPT: Household

Applicator Technology Inc .... G 253 859-9501
  Kent *(G-4786)*
Fredericks Appliance Centers .... E 425 885-0000
  Redmond *(G-8466)*

FLOOR COVERING STORES

Arcomm Inc .... G 253 581-9800
  Lakewood *(G-5699)*
Nfi Enterprises LLC .... E 253 245-5500
  Auburn *(G-507)*
Read Products Inc .... F 206 283-2510
  Seattle *(G-10929)*

FLOOR COVERING STORES: Carpets

American Drpery Blind Crpt Inc .... C 360 676-1121
  Renton *(G-8743)*
Carpet Plus LLC .... G 253 874-0525
  Federal Way *(G-3721)*
Gilyard Co .... G 509 782-1817
  Cashmere *(G-2321)*

FLOOR COVERING: Plastic

Alaska Wholesale Hardwoods .... G 360 704-4444
  Tumwater *(G-13850)*

FLOOR COVERINGS WHOLESALERS

Alaska Wholesale Hardwoods .... G 360 704-4444
  Tumwater *(G-13850)*
Out Peak Services Inc .... F 360 255-7282
  Blaine *(G-1691)*
T & A Supply Company Inc .... G 253 872-3682
  Kent *(G-5167)*
T & A Supply Company Inc .... D 206 282-3770
  Kent *(G-5166)*

FLOOR COVERINGS: Textile Fiber

Nielsen Bros & Sons Inc .... G 425 776-9191
  Edmonds *(G-3137)*

FLOOR COVERINGS: Tile, Support Plastic

Zometek LLC .... G 888 505-7953
  Seattle *(G-11523)*

FLOORING & GRATINGS: Open, Construction Applications

Alabama Metal Industries Corp .... C 253 926-1600
  Fife *(G-3928)*
McNichols Company .... F 253 922-4296
  Fife *(G-3970)*

FLOORING: Hard Surface

Nce Inc .... G 253 884-6255
  Longbranch *(G-5879)*
Seamless Attenuating Tech .... E 360 748-8711
  Chehalis *(G-2535)*

FLOORING: Hardwood

Alaska Wholesale Hardwoods .... G 360 704-4444
  Tumwater *(G-13850)*
All Things New LLC .... G 253 255-4954
  Lakewood *(G-5697)*
Aurora Hardwood Seattle LLC .... G 253 236-8985
  Kent *(G-4798)*
D Ds Hardwood Floors .... G 206 726-8808
  Seattle *(G-9780)*
Eurocraft Hardwood Floors Llc .... G 425 670-6769
  Woodinville *(G-15237)*
Extreme Hardwood Floors .... G 425 985-6735
  Renton *(G-8797)*
Ifloorcom .... G 206 438-3022
  Tukwila *(G-13751)*
JM Ventures Inc .... G 206 718-3355
  Bothell *(G-1771)*
Nfi Enterprises LLC .... E 253 245-5500
  Auburn *(G-507)*
Professional Hardwood Floors .... G 425 741-1017
  Mill Creek *(G-6521)*

FLOORING: Tile

Quarry Tile Company .... D 509 536-2812
  Spokane Valley *(G-12848)*

FLORISTS

Heritage Professional Ldscpg .... G 509 737-8580
  Kennewick *(G-4669)*

FLORISTS' SPLYS, WHOLESALE

Callisons Inc .... E 360 412-3340
  Lacey *(G-5536)*
Pacific Coast Evergreen Inc .... E 360 876-2061
  Port Orchard *(G-7840)*

FLOWER ARRANGEMENTS: Artificial

Klein Joanne Klein Kevin .... G 360 435-8615
  Arlington *(G-268)*

FLOWER POTS Plastic

Surain Industries Inc .... G 253 863-8111
  Sumner *(G-13105)*

FLOWER POTS: Red Earthenware

Washington Pottery Co .... G 425 656-7277
  Kent *(G-5208)*

FLOWERS & FLORISTS' SPLYS WHOLESALERS

L & L Nursery Supply Inc .... E 909 591-0461
  Fife *(G-3964)*
Ljs Plants & Crafts .... G 253 854-9407
  Kent *(G-4998)*

FLOWERS: Artificial & Preserved

Sweet Creek Creations .... G 509 446-2429
  Metaline Falls *(G-6498)*

FLUES & PIPES: Stove Or Furnace

Air Pro Heating & Cooling LLC .... F 360 423-9165
  Longview *(G-5884)*

FLUID METERS & COUNTING DEVICES

Cobalt Utility Products .... G 425 823-0708
  Kirkland *(G-5310)*
Eldec Corporation .... A 425 743-1313
  Lynnwood *(G-6114)*
S Scott & Associates LLC .... G 360 576-4830
  Vancouver *(G-14563)*

FLUID POWER PUMPS & MOTORS

Airborne Ecs LLC .... F 319 538-1051
  Port Angeles *(G-7679)*
Bogert Manufacturing Inc .... F 509 735-2106
  Pasco *(G-7556)*
Ditco Inc .... F 253 854-1002
  Kent *(G-4874)*
Eagle Pump & Equipment Inc .... G 509 534-1111
  Spokane *(G-12237)*
Parker-Hannifin Corporation .... G 509 764-5430
  Moses Lake *(G-6737)*
Parker-Hannifin Corporation .... G 509 764-5430
  Moses Lake *(G-6738)*
Parker-Hannifin Corporation .... G 425 284-2925
  Redmond *(G-8616)*

FLUID POWER VALVES & HOSE FITTINGS

Bridgestone Hosepower LLC .... E 206 767-4670
  Seattle *(G-9585)*
Custom Hydraulic & Machine Inc .... F 253 854-4666
  Kent *(G-4868)*

FLUMES: Metal Plate

Nu Way Flume & Equipment Co .... G 360 942-3581
  Raymond *(G-8356)*

FLY TRAPS: Electrical

Hunter Fish Enterprises .... G 253 852-8357
  Renton *(G-8822)*

FLYING FIELDS, EXC MAINTAINED BY CLUBS

Mt Adams Lumber Company Inc .... G 509 395-2131
  Trout Lake *(G-13682)*

FOIL: Aluminum

Chemi-Con Materials Corp ....D....... 509 762-8788
  Moses Lake *(G-6692)*
Novelis Corporation ....E....... 509 462-2310
  Spokane Valley *(G-12813)*

FOIL: Laminated To Paper Or Other Materials

Western Foil Corporation ....G....... 206 624-3645
  Seattle *(G-11452)*

FOIL: Magnesium & Magnesium-Base Alloy

Proto Technologies Inc ....D....... 509 891-4747
  Liberty Lake *(G-5855)*

FOIL: Tin

Tin Foil Hat Productions ....G....... 619 208-5469
  Port Orchard *(G-7853)*

FOOD COLORINGS

Lucks Company ....C....... 253 383-4815
  Tacoma *(G-13390)*

FOOD CONTAMINATION TESTING OR SCREENING KITS

Biocontrol Systems Inc ....F....... 425 603-1123
  Bellevue *(G-817)*

FOOD PRDTS & SEAFOOD: Shellfish, Fresh, Shucked

Heckes Clams Inc ....G....... 360 665-4371
  Nahcotta *(G-7010)*
Taylor Shellfish Company Inc ....E....... 360 875-5494
  South Bend *(G-12048)*
Taylor Shellfish Company Inc ....C....... 360 426-6178
  Shelton *(G-11741)*
Taylor United Inc ....E....... 360 426-6178
  Shelton *(G-11742)*

FOOD PRDTS, CANNED OR FRESH PACK: Fruit Juices

Dairy Export Co Inc ....G....... 206 284-7220
  Seattle *(G-9786)*
Ocean Spray Cranberries Inc ....D....... 360 648-2515
  Aberdeen *(G-26)*
Odwalla Inc ....E....... 206 242-8519
  Tukwila *(G-13782)*
Starvation Alley Socia ....G....... 503 440-0970
  Long Beach *(G-5878)*
Tree Top Inc ....A....... 509 697-7251
  Selah *(G-11600)*
Tree Top Inc ....D....... 509 782-6809
  Cashmere *(G-2331)*
Welch Foods Inc A Cooperative ....C....... 509 582-1010
  Kennewick *(G-4744)*

FOOD PRDTS, CANNED OR FRESH PACK: Vegetable Juices

Vital Juice Co Inc ....E....... 206 258-4203
  Seattle *(G-11428)*

FOOD PRDTS, CANNED: Applesauce

Tree Top Inc ....C....... 509 786-2926
  Prosser *(G-8069)*

FOOD PRDTS, CANNED: Barbecue Sauce

Longhorn Barbecue Inc ....C....... 509 922-0702
  Spokane Valley *(G-12777)*
McNerney Enterprises LLC ....G....... 206 850-5023
  Sammamish *(G-9232)*
Pheasant Brothers LLC ....G....... 509 539-5899
  Benton City *(G-1623)*

FOOD PRDTS, CANNED: Ethnic

Salsa Mania LLC ....G....... 360 432-9240
  Shelton *(G-11729)*
Sheng Mian North America LLC ....G....... 215 519-5895
  Bellevue *(G-1128)*
Texas Johns ....E....... 509 659-1402
  Ritzville *(G-9123)*

FOOD PRDTS, CANNED: Fruit Juices, Fresh

Backyard Bounty Co-Op ....G....... 360 574-6937
  Ridgefield *(G-9065)*
Tree Top Inc ....D....... 509 698-1432
  Selah *(G-11602)*

FOOD PRDTS, CANNED: Fruit Pie Mixes & Fillings

Canter-Berry Farms ....G....... 253 939-2706
  Auburn *(G-400)*

FOOD PRDTS, CANNED: Fruit Purees

Svz USA Washington Inc ....E....... 509 488-6563
  Othello *(G-7506)*

FOOD PRDTS, CANNED: Fruits

Allan Bros Inc ....D....... 509 653-2625
  Naches *(G-6993)*
Fruit Packers Supply ....G....... 509 888-3059
  Wenatchee *(G-15033)*
Quincy Fresh Fruit LLC ....F....... 509 787-7100
  Quincy *(G-8308)*
Welch Foods Inc A Cooperative ....E....... 509 882-1711
  Grandview *(G-4257)*

FOOD PRDTS, CANNED: Fruits

Campbell Soup Company ....B....... 425 415-2000
  Woodinville *(G-15204)*
Coventry Vale Winery Inc ....E....... 509 882-4100
  Grandview *(G-4246)*
J M Smucker Company ....E....... 509 882-1530
  Grandview *(G-4248)*
Johnson Concentrates Inc ....E....... 509 837-4600
  Sunnyside *(G-13130)*
Oly Kraut LLC ....G....... 360 561-4532
  Olympia *(G-7352)*
Rose Tucker ....E....... 509 837-8701
  Sunnyside *(G-13139)*
Tree Top Inc ....D....... 509 698-1447
  Selah *(G-11601)*
Tree Top Inc ....E....... 509 663-8583
  Wenatchee *(G-15082)*

FOOD PRDTS, CANNED: Fruits & Fruit Prdts

Farm Breeze International LLC ....G....... 253 365-0542
  Tacoma *(G-13291)*
Underwood Fruit & Whse Co LLC ....G....... 509 457-6177
  Yakima *(G-15700)*

FOOD PRDTS, CANNED: Jams, Including Imitation

Blue Cottage Jams ....G....... 425 836-9580
  Redmond *(G-8406)*
General Mills Inc ....E....... 763 764-7600
  Sedro Woolley *(G-11539)*
Simchuk Karene ....G....... 509 238-2830
  Mead *(G-6436)*

FOOD PRDTS, CANNED: Jams, Jellies & Preserves

Artisanal Goods Northwest LLC ....G....... 503 803-7228
  Washougal *(G-14944)*
Cindy Lous Artisan Jams ....G....... 360 873-4178
  Marblemount *(G-6304)*
Sugarcrush Hmmade Jams Jellies ....G....... 253 830-4155
  Bonney Lake *(G-1741)*
Tenacious Hgs Jams ....G....... 360 747-4080
  Longview *(G-5959)*
Welch Foods Inc A Cooperative ....G....... 509 882-3112
  Grandview *(G-4258)*

FOOD PRDTS, CANNED: Jellies, Edible, Including Imitation

Micks Peppourri Inc ....G....... 509 966-2328
  Yakima *(G-15620)*

FOOD PRDTS, CANNED: Mexican, NEC

Ljro Inc ....F....... 360 693-2443
  Vancouver *(G-14380)*

FOOD PRDTS, CANNED: Spaghetti

Campbell Soup Company ....B....... 425 415-2000
  Woodinville *(G-15204)*

FOOD PRDTS, CANNED: Vegetables

G Wolf Enterprises Inc ....G....... 360 793-2988
  Gold Bar *(G-4188)*
Johnson Foods Inc ....E....... 509 837-4188
  Sunnyside *(G-13131)*
Maika Foods LLC ....G....... 310 893-7050
  Spokane *(G-12380)*
Seneca Foods Corporation ....C....... 509 382-8323
  Dayton *(G-2884)*

FOOD PRDTS, CANNED: Vegetables

Pacific Prepac Inc ....E....... 360 653-1661
  Marysville *(G-6366)*
Snipahs LLC ....G....... 910 922-4693
  Gold Bar *(G-4191)*

FOOD PRDTS, CONFECTIONERY, WHOLESALE: Candy

Brown & Haley ....C....... 253 620-3067
  Tacoma *(G-13210)*
Hallett Confections ....F....... 509 484-6454
  Spokane *(G-12286)*

FOOD PRDTS, CONFECTIONERY, WHOLESALE: Snack Foods

Jumbo Foods Inc ....C....... 425 355-1103
  Mukilteo *(G-6946)*
Sahale Snacks Inc ....D....... 206 624-7244
  Tukwila *(G-13811)*

FOOD PRDTS, DAIRY, WHOLESALE: Frozen Dairy Desserts

Baskin-Robbins ....G....... 425 793-3544
  Bellevue *(G-806)*

FOOD PRDTS, FISH & SEAFOOD, WHOLESALE: Fresh

Northern Fish Products Inc ....E....... 253 475-3858
  Tacoma *(G-13430)*

FOOD PRDTS, FISH & SEAFOOD, WHOLESALE: Frozen, Unpackaged

CFC Fish Company LLC ....F....... 253 478-5160
  Renton *(G-8770)*

FOOD PRDTS, FISH & SEAFOOD, WHOLESALE: Seafood

Blau Oyster Company Inc ....F....... 360 766-6171
  Bow *(G-1927)*
Odyssey Enterprises Inc ....C....... 206 285-7445
  Seattle *(G-10685)*
Seafood Producers Cooperative ....E....... 360 733-0120
  Bellingham *(G-1527)*
Trident Seafoods Asia Inc ....F....... 206 783-3818
  Seattle *(G-11334)*
Trident Seafoods Corporation ....G....... 360 671-0669
  Bellingham *(G-1576)*
Trident Seafoods Corporation ....B....... 206 783-3818
  Seattle *(G-11335)*

FOOD PRDTS, FISH & SEAFOOD: Broth, Canned, Jarred, Etc

Cauldron Investment Group LLC ....G....... 360 671-1098
  Bellingham *(G-1293)*

FOOD PRDTS, FISH & SEAFOOD: Canned & Jarred, Etc

Dungeness Development Assoc ....E....... 425 481-0600
  Kirkland *(G-5324)*
Maruha Capital Investment Inc ....F....... 206 382-0640
  Bellevue *(G-996)*
Peter Pan Seafoods Inc ....C....... 206 728-6000
  Bellevue *(G-1071)*

PRODUCT SECTION

FOOD PRDTS, FISH & SEAFOOD: Crabmeat, Fresh, Pkgd Nonsealed

Alaska Fresh Seafoods Inc ....G....... 206 285-2412
  Shoreline *(G-11755)*
Golden Shamrock Inc ....G....... 206 282-5825
  Seattle *(G-10095)*
Nelson Crab Inc......................................E....... 360 267-2911
  Tokeland *(G-13633)*
Shining Ocean Inc ....C....... 253 826-3700
  Sumner *(G-13098)*
Washington Crab Producers Inc ....G....... 360 268-9161
  Westport *(G-15107)*

FOOD PRDTS, FISH & SEAFOOD: Fish, Canned & Cured

Quinault Pride Seafoods ....E....... 360 276-4431
  Taholah *(G-13609)*

FOOD PRDTS, FISH & SEAFOOD: Fish, Cured, NEC

Sacred Waters Fish Company LLC ....G....... 503 913-1625
  South Bend *(G-12045)*

FOOD PRDTS, FISH & SEAFOOD: Fish, Fresh, Prepared

Bornstein Seafoods Inc..........................D....... 360 734-7990
  Bellingham *(G-1280)*
Phoenix Processor Ltd Partnr ....C....... 206 286-8584
  Seattle *(G-10796)*

FOOD PRDTS, FISH & SEAFOOD: Fish, Frozen, Prepared

High Tide Seafoods Inc ....E....... 360 452-8488
  Port Angeles *(G-7710)*
Mike Breckon ....G....... 360 380-0622
  Ferndale *(G-3871)*
Nova Fisheries Inc ....G....... 206 781-2000
  Seattle *(G-10658)*
Orca Bay Foods LLC ....B....... 206 762-7364
  Seattle *(G-10711)*
Pacific Sea Food Co Inc ....E....... 360 225-8553
  Woodland *(G-15456)*
Yardarm Knot Inc ....E....... 206 216-0220
  Seattle *(G-11508)*

FOOD PRDTS, FISH & SEAFOOD: Fish, Smoked

Barleans Fishery Inc...............................G....... 360 384-0325
  Ferndale *(G-3817)*

FOOD PRDTS, FISH & SEAFOOD: Fresh, Prepared

Alaska Star Inc ....D....... 206 282-0988
  Seattle *(G-9366)*
Alaska Wathervane Seafoods LLC ....G....... 253 582-2580
  Lakewood *(G-5696)*
Alber Seafoods Inc ....G....... 360 642-3773
  Seattle *(G-9369)*
Alyeska Seafoods Inc............................D....... 206 682-5949
  Bellevue *(G-785)*
Bell Buoy Crab Co Inc ....E....... 360 777-8272
  Chinook *(G-2614)*
Boundary Fish Company ....E....... 360 332-6715
  Blaine *(G-1662)*
Briney Sea Delicacies Inc......................G....... 360 956-1797
  Tumwater *(G-13853)*
Dutch Harbor Seafoods Ltd...................E....... 425 881-8181
  Redmond *(G-8444)*
E & E Foods Inc......................................E....... 206 768-8979
  Renton *(G-8789)*
Gasllc Ltd Liability Company..................C....... 206 441-1990
  Seattle *(G-10051)*
Home Port Seafood Inc ....D....... 360 676-4707
  Bellingham *(G-1372)*
Independent Packers Corp ....E....... 206 285-6000
  Seattle *(G-10223)*
Interntional Seafoods Alsk Inc ....G....... 206 284-4830
  Lynnwood *(G-6141)*
Peter Pan Seafoods Inc ....C....... 206 728-6000
  Bellevue *(G-1071)*
Seafreeze Limited Partnership ....D....... 206 767-7350
  Seattle *(G-11043)*

Trident Seafoods Corporation ....C....... 360 734-8900
  Bellingham *(G-1575)*
Westward Seafoods Inc.........................C....... 206 682-5949
  Bellevue *(G-1225)*

FOOD PRDTS, FISH & SEAFOOD: Fresh/Frozen Chowder, Soup/Stew

D P Clarke ....G....... 360 647-8185
  Bellingham *(G-1317)*
Jgc Food Co LLC ....F....... 206 622-0420
  Seattle *(G-10296)*
Ocean Gold Seafoods Inc ....C....... 360 268-2510
  Westport *(G-15106)*

FOOD PRDTS, FISH & SEAFOOD: Oysters, Canned, Jarred, Etc

Coast Seafoods Company ....D....... 360 875-5577
  Bellevue *(G-856)*
Island Enterprises..................................G....... 360 426-4933
  Shelton *(G-11701)*
Island Enterprises..................................E....... 360 426-4933
  Shelton *(G-11702)*
Island Enterprises..................................F....... 360 426-3442
  Shelton *(G-11703)*
Wiegardt Bros Inc ....E....... 360 665-4111
  Ocean Park *(G-7183)*

FOOD PRDTS, FISH & SEAFOOD: Oysters, Preserved & Cured

Taylor Shellfish Company Inc................E....... 360 875-5494
  South Bend *(G-12048)*

FOOD PRDTS, FISH & SEAFOOD: Prepared Cakes & Sticks

Signature Seafoods Inc ....G....... 206 285-2815
  Seattle *(G-11108)*
T K O Fisheries Inc ....G....... 206 285-2815
  Seattle *(G-11249)*

FOOD PRDTS, FISH & SEAFOOD: Salmon, Canned, Jarred, Etc

Icicle Seafoods Inc.................................D....... 206 282-0988
  Seattle *(G-10200)*
Sportsmens Cannery ....F....... 360 642-2335
  Seaview *(G-11529)*
Vital Choice Seafood Spc......................E....... 360 325-0104
  Bellingham *(G-1584)*

FOOD PRDTS, FISH & SEAFOOD: Salmon, Cured, NEC

Fishers Choice Wild Salmon..................G....... 360 671-6478
  Bellingham *(G-1346)*
Svendsen Brothers Fish Inc ....F....... 206 767-4258
  Normandy Park *(G-7099)*

FOOD PRDTS, FISH & SEAFOOD: Salmon, Smoked

Kasilof Fish Company ....E....... 360 658-7552
  Everett *(G-3529)*
Northwest Smoking & Curing ....G....... 360 733-3666
  Bellingham *(G-1470)*
Seabear Company ....E....... 360 293-4661
  Anacortes *(G-165)*
Steves Hot Smked Cheese Salmon.......G....... 360 829-2244
  Buckley *(G-2075)*
World Wide Gourmet Foods Inc ....F....... 360 668-9404
  Woodinville *(G-15410)*

FOOD PRDTS, FISH & SEAFOOD: Seafood, Frozen, Prepared

Gallatin International LLC ....G....... 425 557-4356
  Issaquah *(G-4416)*
New Continent Food USA Inc ....G....... 425 644-6448
  Bellevue *(G-1026)*
Odyssey Enterprises Inc ....C....... 206 285-7445
  Seattle *(G-10685)*
Seafood Producers Cooperative ....E....... 360 733-0120
  Bellingham *(G-1527)*
Swinomish Fish Co Inc..........................G....... 360 466-0176
  La Conner *(G-5526)*
Trident Seafoods Asia Inc ....F....... 360 783-3818
  Seattle *(G-11334)*

Trident Seafoods Corporation ....B....... 206 783-3818
  Seattle *(G-11335)*
Trident Seafoods Corporation ....G....... 206 783-3818
  Seattle *(G-11336)*
Trident Seafoods Corporation ....G....... 360 671-0669
  Bellingham *(G-1576)*

FOOD PRDTS, FISH & SEAFOOD: Shellfish, Canned & Cured

Washington Crab Producers Inc ....G....... 360 268-9161
  Westport *(G-15107)*

FOOD PRDTS, FISH & SEAFOOD: Shellfish, Canned, Jarred, Etc

Taylor Shellfish Company Inc................C....... 360 426-6178
  Shelton *(G-11741)*
Taylor United Inc ....E....... 360 426-6178
  Shelton *(G-11742)*

FOOD PRDTS, FISH & SEAFOOD: Shellfish, Frozen, Prepared

Cooke Aquaculture Pacific LLC ....F....... 206 282-0988
  Seattle *(G-9736)*
Cooke Aquaculture Pacific LLC ....G....... 360 293-9448
  Anacortes *(G-117)*
Icicle Seafoods Inc.................................D....... 206 282-0988
  Seattle *(G-10200)*

FOOD PRDTS, FISH & SEAFOOD: Tuna Fish, Canned, Jarred, Etc

Tri Marine Fishing MGT LLC ....F....... 425 688-1288
  Bellevue *(G-1199)*
Tri-Marine International Inc ....G....... 425 688-1288
  Bellevue *(G-1200)*

FOOD PRDTS, FISH & SEAFOOD: Tuna Fish, Preserved & Cured

Fishing Vessel St Jude LLC ....G....... 425 378-0680
  Bellevue *(G-911)*

FOOD PRDTS, FROZEN: Breakfasts, Packaged

Continental Mills Inc ....C....... 206 816-7000
  Tukwila *(G-13716)*

FOOD PRDTS, FROZEN: Ethnic Foods, NEC

Sakai Foods America Inc ....G....... 484 494-4322
  Seattle *(G-11004)*

FOOD PRDTS, FROZEN: Fruit Juice, Concentrates

Johnson Concentrates Inc.....................E....... 509 837-4600
  Sunnyside *(G-13130)*
Milne Fruit Products Inc ....D....... 509 786-0019
  Prosser *(G-8059)*
Sun-Rype Products (usa) Inc.................D....... 509 697-7292
  Selah *(G-11598)*
Tree Top Inc ....C....... 509 786-2926
  Prosser *(G-8069)*
Valley Processing Inc ....D....... 509 837-8084
  Sunnyside *(G-13148)*

FOOD PRDTS, FROZEN: Fruits

Clarks Berry Farm Inc............................E....... 360 354-1294
  Lynden *(G-6009)*
General Mills Inc ....E....... 763 764-7600
  Sedro Woolley *(G-11539)*
National Frozen Foods Corp..................C....... 360 748-9963
  Chehalis *(G-2516)*
Sunfresh Foods Inc ....G....... 206 764-0940
  Seattle *(G-11219)*
Twin City Foods Inc ....B....... 509 786-2700
  Prosser *(G-8071)*

FOOD PRDTS, FROZEN: Fruits & Vegetables

Noon International LLC..........................F....... 206 283-8400
  Seattle *(G-10619)*

FOOD PRDTS, FROZEN: Fruits, Juices & Vegetables

FOOD PRDTS, FROZEN: Fruits, Juices & Vegetables

Birds Eye Foods Inc .... G 253 833-0255
  Auburn *(G-393)*
David Lynn Smoothies LLC .... G 907 242-4564
  Redmond *(G-8435)*
Drr Fruit Products Co Inc .... E 509 836-2051
  Sunnyside *(G-13121)*
Firestone Pacific Foods Inc .... D 360 695-9484
  Vancouver *(G-14232)*
Graces Kitchen Inc .... G 425 635-4609
  Bellevue *(G-932)*
Investure - Wa Inc .... D 360 354-6574
  Lynden *(G-6023)*
Jake Maberry Packing Inc .... G 206 366-5411
  Custer *(G-2855)*
JR Simplot Company .... E 509 765-5663
  Othello *(G-7499)*
JR Simplot Company .... G 509 765-3443
  Moses Lake *(G-6719)*
Lamb Weston Inc .... G 509 375-4181
  Richland *(G-9020)*
Lamb Weston Inc .... G 509 713-7200
  Richland *(G-9021)*
Lamb Weston Inc .... A 509 547-8851
  Pasco *(G-7598)*
National Frozen Foods Corp .... A 206 322-8900
  Seattle *(G-10588)*
National Frozen Foods Corp .... E 509 766-0793
  Moses Lake *(G-6730)*
Ocean Spray Cranberries Inc .... D 360 648-2515
  Aberdeen *(G-26)*
Pacific Northwest Packers Inc .... E 360 354-0776
  Lynden *(G-6044)*
Quincy Foods LLC .... G 509 787-4521
  Quincy *(G-8307)*
Royal Ridge Frt Cold Stor LLC .... D 509 346-1520
  Royal City *(G-9174)*
Six LLC .... G 206 466-5186
  Seattle *(G-11123)*
Smoothie Essentials .... G 360 452-8060
  Port Angeles *(G-7744)*
Smoothie Ventures LLC .... G 509 315-4492
  Spokane Valley *(G-12877)*
Solutions With Innovation .... G 253 872-0783
  Kent *(G-5138)*
Sunshine Smoothie Inc .... G 425 497-9211
  Auburn *(G-574)*
Super Smoothie .... G 253 671-8883
  Tacoma *(G-13529)*
Tree Top Inc .... G 509 663-8583
  Wenatchee *(G-15082)*
Tree Top Inc .... A 509 697-7251
  Selah *(G-11600)*
Twin City Foods Inc .... G 509 346-1483
  Royal City *(G-9177)*
Twin City Foods Inc .... B 509 546-0850
  Pasco *(G-7645)*
Washington Fruit & Produce Co .... E 509 932-7981
  Quincy *(G-8310)*
Wyckoff Farms Incorporated .... E 509 882-3934
  Grandview *(G-4259)*

FOOD PRDTS, FROZEN: NEC

Campbell Soup Company .... B 425 415-2000
  Woodinville *(G-15204)*
Ed Bohl .... G 360 264-5822
  Tenino *(G-13618)*
January Company .... E 253 872-9919
  Kent *(G-4964)*
Lamb Weston Inc .... A 509 547-8851
  Pasco *(G-7598)*
Luvo Usa Llc .... G 604 730-0387
  Blaine *(G-1681)*
Man Pies .... G 360 201-4294
  Bellingham *(G-1421)*
McCain Foods Usa Inc .... A 509 488-9611
  Othello *(G-7502)*
Michael Eckles .... G 253 568-2934
  Tacoma *(G-13411)*
National Frozen Foods Corp .... C 360 748-9963
  Chehalis *(G-2516)*
Northwest Frozen LLC .... E 206 388-3551
  Seattle *(G-10645)*

FOOD PRDTS, FROZEN: Pizza

AC Larocco Pizza Co .... G 509 924-9113
  Spokane Valley *(G-12597)*

FOOD PRDTS, FROZEN: Potato Prdts

Lamb Weston Inc .... B 509 735-4651
  Kennewick *(G-4685)*
Lamb Weston Holdings Inc .... C 509 786-2700
  Prosser *(G-8048)*
Lamb Weston Sales Inc .... C 509 735-4651
  Kennewick *(G-4686)*
McCain Foods Usa Inc .... A 509 488-9611
  Othello *(G-7502)*
Ochoa AG Unlimited Foods Inc .... C 509 349-2210
  Warden *(G-14934)*

FOOD PRDTS, FROZEN: Soups

Ivars Inc .... E 425 493-1402
  Mukilteo *(G-6945)*

FOOD PRDTS, FROZEN: Vegetables, Exc Potato Prdts

Crf Frozen Foods LLC .... E 509 542-0018
  Pasco *(G-7570)*
Seneca Foods Corporation .... C 509 382-8323
  Dayton *(G-2884)*
Twin City Foods Inc .... D 206 515-2400
  Stanwood *(G-12998)*
Twin City Foods Inc .... C 509 962-9806
  Ellensburg *(G-3235)*
Willow Wind Organic Farms Inc .... G 509 796-4006
  Ford *(G-4007)*

FOOD PRDTS, FROZEN: Waffles

P&Js Waffle Delight .... G 510 335-5393
  Tacoma *(G-13448)*

FOOD PRDTS, FRUITS & VEGETABLES, FRESH, WHOLESALE

Triple b Corporation .... D 509 535-7393
  Spokane *(G-12569)*

FOOD PRDTS, FRUITS & VEGETABLES, FRESH, WHOLESALE: Potatoes

Lamb Weston Inc .... A 509 547-8851
  Pasco *(G-7598)*

FOOD PRDTS, FRUITS & VEGETABLES, FRESH, WHOLESALE: Vegetable

Mollys Salads LLC .... G 206 512-3075
  Seattle *(G-10558)*

FOOD PRDTS, MEAT & MEAT PRDTS, WHOLESALE: Cured Or Smoked

Verns Moses Lake Meats Inc .... F 509 765-5671
  Moses Lake *(G-6756)*

FOOD PRDTS, MEAT & MEAT PRDTS, WHOLESALE: Fresh

Ameristar Meats Inc .... C 509 535-2049
  Spokane Valley *(G-12616)*
Smithco Meats Inc .... E 253 863-5157
  Sumner *(G-13100)*

FOOD PRDTS, WHOL: Canned Goods, Fruit, Veg, Seafood/Meats

Coast Seafoods Company .... D 360 875-5577
  Bellevue *(G-856)*
Underwood Fruit & Whse Co LLC .... G 509 457-6177
  Yakima *(G-15700)*

FOOD PRDTS, WHOLESALE: Beverages, Exc Coffee & Tea

Coca-Cola Refreshments .... G 425 226-6004
  Renton *(G-8774)*
Lynch Distributing Co .... F 509 248-0880
  Yakima *(G-15613)*

FOOD PRDTS, WHOLESALE: Chocolate

Intrigue Chocolates Co .... G 206 829-8810
  Seattle *(G-10253)*

FOOD PRDTS, WHOLESALE: Coffee & Tea

Farmer Bros Co .... G 509 457-6031
  Union Gap *(G-13929)*
Gariko LLC .... G 509 933-1821
  Ellensburg *(G-3201)*
Gbjc Inc .... G 360 321-5262
  Mukilteo *(G-6927)*
Java Java Coffee Company Inc .... G 425 432-5261
  Maple Valley *(G-6278)*
Joes Garage LLC .... F 206 466-5579
  Tukwila *(G-13758)*
Sirjmr Inc .... G 509 582-2683
  Kennewick *(G-4728)*

FOOD PRDTS, WHOLESALE: Coffee, Green Or Roasted

Bean Collection Coffee Inc .... G 206 382-1966
  Seattle *(G-9505)*
Cascade Coffee Inc .... F 425 347-3995
  Everett *(G-3410)*
Dillanos Coffee Roasters Inc .... E 253 826-1807
  Sumner *(G-13066)*
Field Roast Grain Meat Co Spc .... C 800 311-9797
  Seattle *(G-9989)*
Haley & Bros .... G 253 851-4977
  Gig Harbor *(G-4109)*
Java Trading Co LLC .... G 425 917-2920
  Renton *(G-8832)*
Jumbo Foods Inc .... C 425 355-1103
  Mukilteo *(G-6946)*
Lighthouse Roasters Inc .... G 206 633-4775
  Seattle *(G-10418)*
Sonofresco LLC .... G 360 757-2800
  Burlington *(G-2191)*
Tc Global Inc .... D 206 233-2070
  Seattle *(G-11275)*

FOOD PRDTS, WHOLESALE: Condiments

Zz Inc .... G 360 734-2290
  Bellingham *(G-1598)*

FOOD PRDTS, WHOLESALE: Crackers

Madrona Specialty Foods LLC .... E 206 903-0500
  Seattle *(G-10465)*

FOOD PRDTS, WHOLESALE: Dried or Canned Foods

Cherry Chukar Company .... E 509 786-2055
  Prosser *(G-8032)*
Sheng Mian North America LLC .... G 215 519-5895
  Bellevue *(G-1128)*

FOOD PRDTS, WHOLESALE: Flavorings & Fragrances

Wisdom Elite LLC .... G 806 201-3953
  Lakewood *(G-5768)*

FOOD PRDTS, WHOLESALE: Grains

CHS Inc .... F 509 488-9681
  Othello *(G-7492)*
Cooperative AG Producers Inc .... E 509 523-3032
  Rosalia *(G-9154)*
Northwest Pea & Bean Company .... F 509 534-3821
  Spokane Valley *(G-12808)*
Pacific NW Frmrs Coop Inc .... F 509 283-2124
  Fairfield *(G-3697)*

FOOD PRDTS, WHOLESALE: Health

Bioplex Nutrition Inc .... F 360 332-2101
  Blaine *(G-1661)*

FOOD PRDTS, WHOLESALE: Natural & Organic

Small Planet Foods Inc .... E 800 624-4123
  Sedro Woolley *(G-11569)*
Urban Buggy LLC .... G 206 743-5727
  Seattle *(G-11389)*
Watford Tanikka .... G 360 499-6327
  Lacey *(G-5601)*

PRODUCT SECTION

FOOD PRDTS: Dried & Dehydrated Fruits, Vegetables & Soup Mix

FOOD PRDTS, WHOLESALE: Organic & Diet
- Matrix Health .... G 360 816-1200
  Vancouver *(G-14402)*
- Trout Lake Farm LLC .... E 509 395-2025
  Trout Lake *(G-13684)*

FOOD PRDTS, WHOLESALE: Pasta & Rice
- Carsos Pasta Company Inc .... E 206 283-8227
  Lynnwood *(G-6087)*

FOOD PRDTS, WHOLESALE: Salad Dressing
- Johnnys Fine Foods Inc .... E 253 383-4597
  Tacoma *(G-13362)*

FOOD PRDTS, WHOLESALE: Sandwiches
- Mollys Salads LLC .... G 206 512-3075
  Seattle *(G-10558)*

FOOD PRDTS, WHOLESALE: Sauces
- Fortun Foods Inc .... F 425 827-1977
  Kirkland *(G-5342)*

FOOD PRDTS, WHOLESALE: Sausage Casings
- Oversea Casing Company LLC .... E 206 682-6845
  Seattle *(G-10722)*

FOOD PRDTS, WHOLESALE: Specialty
- Friday Harbor House of Jerky .... G 360 207-9652
  Friday Harbor *(G-4046)*
- Grand Temple .... G 509 715-7876
  Liberty Lake *(G-5833)*
- Innovasian Cuisine Entps Inc .... E 800 324-5140
  Tukwila *(G-13753)*
- Reesman Co .... G 253 564-7997
  Fircrest *(G-4004)*

FOOD PRDTS, WHOLESALE: Spices & Seasonings
- Broussards Creole Foods Inc .... G 253 638-2098
  Kent *(G-4824)*
- Spice Hut Corporation .... F 360 671-2800
  Bellingham *(G-1552)*

FOOD PRDTS, WHOLESALE: Water, Mineral Or Spring, Bottled
- Firesteed Corporation .... G 503 623-8683
  Issaquah *(G-4415)*

FOOD PRDTS, WHOLESALE: Wine Makers' Eqpt & Splys
- Ice Harbor Brewing Company .... E 509 545-0927
  Kennewick *(G-4674)*
- Johnson Ward Winery .... G 206 284-2635
  Seattle *(G-10303)*

FOOD PRDTS: Almond Pastes
- Golden Boy Foods (usa) Inc .... G 360 332-1990
  Blaine *(G-1671)*

FOOD PRDTS: Animal & marine fats & oils
- Baker Commodities Inc .... D 206 243-4781
  Seattle *(G-9478)*
- J & S Manufacturing Inc .... G 360 384-5553
  Ferndale *(G-3861)*

FOOD PRDTS: Breakfast Bars
- B3 Breakfast & Burger Bar .... G 425 672-3666
  Lynnwood *(G-6079)*

FOOD PRDTS: Cereals
- 206 Foods LLC .... G 206 387-5881
  Shoreline *(G-11752)*
- Grain Craft Inc .... D 206 898-3079
  Seattle *(G-10104)*
- Kellogg Company .... E 253 872-3826
  Kent *(G-4974)*
- Mountain Muesli LLC .... G 253 426-8092
  Tacoma *(G-13421)*

- Natures Path Foods USA Inc .... E 360 332-1111
  Blaine *(G-1686)*
- Natures Path Foods USA Inc .... D 360 603-7200
  Blaine *(G-1687)*
- Sherpa Foods SPC .... F 425 243-9278
  Newcastle *(G-7039)*
- Tree Top Inc .... D 509 698-1432
  Selah *(G-11602)*
- Watford Tanikka .... G 360 499-6327
  Lacey *(G-5601)*

FOOD PRDTS: Chicken, Processed, Cooked
- Salmon Creek Meats .... G 360 985-7822
  Mossyrock *(G-6766)*

FOOD PRDTS: Chicken, Processed, NEC
- Perdue Foods LLC .... B 360 424-7947
  Mount Vernon *(G-6823)*

FOOD PRDTS: Chocolate Coatings & Syrup
- Wax Orchards Inc .... G 800 634-6132
  Lake Forest Park *(G-5627)*

FOOD PRDTS: Cocoa & Cocoa Prdts
- McStevens Inc .... E 360 944-5788
  Vancouver *(G-14407)*

FOOD PRDTS: Cocoa, Powdered
- Costellinis LLC .... G 877 889-8266
  Bellevue *(G-866)*

FOOD PRDTS: Coffee
- Austin Chase Coffee Inc .... G 206 281-8040
  Seattle *(G-9464)*
- Boyd Coffee Company .... G 425 744-1394
  Lynnwood *(G-6085)*
- Caffe Appassionato Inc .... G 206 281-8040
  Seattle *(G-9605)*
- Chadao Tea Co Inc .... G 206 335-6585
  Seattle *(G-9664)*
- Dillanos Coffee Roasters Inc .... E 253 826-1807
  Sumner *(G-13066)*
- Distant Lands Trading Co .... G 800 758-4437
  Renton *(G-8784)*
- Fstopcafe LLC .... G 206 842-0335
  Bainbridge Island *(G-635)*
- Gbjc Inc .... G 360 321-5262
  Mukilteo *(G-6927)*
- Haley & Bros .... G 253 851-4977
  Gig Harbor *(G-4109)*
- Hook Line and Espresso .... G 360 691-7095
  Granite Falls *(G-4277)*
- Java Trading Co LLC .... C 425 917-2920
  Renton *(G-8832)*
- Keurig Green Mountain Inc .... C 253 447-9100
  Sumner *(G-13078)*
- L Lazy Corp .... G 509 448-3426
  Spokane *(G-12357)*
- Little Bean Coffee LLC .... G 425 829-8289
  Redmond *(G-8535)*
- Mark Sholtys .... G 509 930-1725
  Moxee *(G-6881)*
- Millars Organic WD Roasted Cof .... G 360 686-3643
  Yacolt *(G-15487)*
- NW Coffee Roasters LLC .... F 360 442-4111
  Longview *(G-5939)*
- Pioneer Coffee Roasting Co LLC .... G 509 674-4100
  Cle Elum *(G-2676)*
- Roast House LLC .... G 509 995-6500
  Spokane *(G-12478)*
- Sirjmr Inc .... E 509 582-2683
  Kennewick *(G-4728)*
- South Sound Aquaponics LLC .... G 206 510-0408
  Federal Way *(G-3789)*
- Tullys Cof Asia PCF Prtners LP .... G 206 233-2070
  Seattle *(G-11347)*

FOOD PRDTS: Coffee Extracts
- Emerald Hills Coffee Inc .... G 800 562-6015
  Mukilteo *(G-6924)*

FOOD PRDTS: Coffee Roasting, Exc Wholesale Grocers
- Bean Collection Coffee Inc .... G 206 382-1966
  Seattle *(G-9505)*

- Cascade Coffee Inc .... F 425 347-3995
  Everett *(G-3410)*
- Commencement Bay Coffee Co .... G 253 851-8259
  Gig Harbor *(G-4092)*
- Farmer Bros Co .... G 509 457-6031
  Union Gap *(G-13929)*
- Farmer Bros Co .... E 425 881-7030
  Redmond *(G-8459)*
- Fidalgo Bay Coffee Inc .... G 360 757-8818
  Burlington *(G-2158)*
- Java Java Coffee Company Inc .... G 425 432-5261
  Maple Valley *(G-6278)*
- Joes Garage LLC .... F 206 466-5579
  Tukwila *(G-13758)*
- Lighthouse Roasters Inc .... F 206 633-4775
  Seattle *(G-10418)*
- Olympic Crest Coffee Roasters .... G 360 459-5756
  Olympia *(G-7357)*
- Tc Global Inc .... D 206 233-2070
  Seattle *(G-11275)*

FOOD PRDTS: Coffee, Ground, Mixed With Grain Or Chicory
- Cafe Las Americas .... G 253 272-0644
  Tacoma *(G-13216)*
- Grounds For Change Inc .... G 360 779-0401
  Poulsbo *(G-7964)*

FOOD PRDTS: Corn Meal
- San Gennaro Foods Inc .... F 253 872-1900
  Kent *(G-5115)*

FOOD PRDTS: Cottonseed Oil, Cake & Meal
- Syngenta Seeds Inc .... C 509 543-8000
  Pasco *(G-7636)*

FOOD PRDTS: Dessert Mixes & Fillings
- Dawn Food Products Inc .... E 206 623-7740
  Seattle *(G-9803)*

FOOD PRDTS: Dips, Exc Cheese & Sour Cream Based
- Bad Breath Garlic Co .... G 253 223-1835
  Puyallup *(G-8127)*
- D A M Salsa LLC .... G 206 527-0300
  Seattle *(G-9778)*
- Finas Salsa .... G 360 951-5218
  Olympia *(G-7283)*
- Just Salsa .... G 253 455-4618
  Puyallup *(G-8170)*
- Roys Salsa LLC .... G 253 514-3767
  Gig Harbor *(G-4157)*
- Salsa 7 .... G 253 445-6525
  Puyallup *(G-8245)*
- Salsa With A Kick .... G 253 820-7622
  Lakewood *(G-5753)*
- Skagits Best Salsa .... G 360 610-9022
  Mount Vernon *(G-6842)*
- Suenos De Salsa .... G 206 334-7496
  Seattle *(G-11212)*

FOOD PRDTS: Dough, Biscuit
- Seattle Biscuit Company LLC .... G 206 327-2940
  Seattle *(G-11046)*

FOOD PRDTS: Dressings, Salad, Raw & Cooked Exc Dry Mixes
- Rikki Usa Inc .... F 425 881-6881
  Redmond *(G-8651)*
- Wm Bolthouse Farms Inc .... G 509 894-4460
  Prosser *(G-8079)*

FOOD PRDTS: Dried & Dehydrated Fruits, Vegetables & Soup Mix
- Ames International Inc .... D 253 946-4779
  Fife *(G-3932)*
- Basic American Inc .... C 509 765-7807
  Moses Lake *(G-6685)*
- Blue Bird Inc .... F 509 486-2160
  Tonasket *(G-13646)*
- Dodson Rd Orchard LLC .... D 509 787-3537
  Quincy *(G-8296)*
- Lamb Weston Inc .... A 509 547-8851
  Pasco *(G-7598)*

Employee Codes: A=Over 500 employees, B=251-500
C=101-250, D=51-100, E=20-50, F=10-19, G=2-9

FOOD PRDTS: Dried & Dehydrated Fruits, Vegetables & Soup Mix

McCain Foods Usa Inc................................A....... 509 488-9611
  Othello (G-7502)
Mountain Valley Products Inc..................E....... 509 837-8084
  Sunnyside (G-13134)
Newly Weds Foods Inc..............................D....... 253 584-9270
  Lakewood (G-5741)
Northwest Pea & Bean Company ....F....... 509 534-3821
  Spokane Valley (G-12808)
Royal Ridge Frt Cold Stor LLC ....D....... 509 346-1520
  Royal City (G-9174)
Seneca Foods Corporation ....E....... 509 457-1089
  Yakima (G-15671)
Washington Potato Company Inc.............D....... 509 349-8803
  Warden (G-14938)
Wyckoff Farms Incorporated ....E....... 509 882-3934
  Grandview (G-4259)

FOOD PRDTS: Edible Oil Prdts, Exc Corn Oil

Evergreen Production LLC ....G....... 206 818-5054
  Raymond (G-8347)
Hot Oil Company LLC ....G....... 509 338-5678
  Seattle (G-10184)

FOOD PRDTS: Edible fats & oils

Apresvin Enterprises Ave Inc ....G....... 509 967-3045
  West Richland (G-15094)

FOOD PRDTS: Eggs, Processed

National Food Corporation ....D....... 360 653-2904
  Arlington (G-285)
National Food Corporation ....F....... 509 457-4031
  Moxee (G-6883)

FOOD PRDTS: Fish Meal

Ocean Protein LLC ....E....... 360 538-7400
  Hoquiam (G-4350)

FOOD PRDTS: Fish Oil

Crockers Fish Oil Inc ....G....... 509 787-4983
  Quincy (G-8295)

FOOD PRDTS: Flour

Ener-G Foods Inc ....E....... 206 767-3928
  Seattle (G-9922)
Gateway Milling LLC ....G....... 509 639-2431
  Almira (G-85)
Grain Craft Inc ....D....... 206 898-3079
  Seattle (G-10104)

FOOD PRDTS: Flour & Other Grain Mill Products

ADM Milling Co..E....... 509 535-2995
  Spokane (G-12099)
Archer-Daniels-Midland Company ....G....... 509 533-9632
  Spokane (G-12117)
Archer-Daniels-Midland Company ....F....... 509 754-5266
  Ephrata (G-3331)
Archer-Daniels-Midland Company ....G....... 509 534-2636
  Spokane Valley (G-12624)
Cascade Organic Flour LLC ....F....... 509 855-7450
  Royal City (G-9168)
Farnworth Group.......................................G....... 425 894-8643
  Kirkland (G-5336)
Field Roast Grain Meat Co Spc ....C....... 800 311-9797
  Seattle (G-9989)
GF Blends Inc...G....... 509 375-0909
  Richland (G-9001)
Highland Milling LLC ....G....... 360 901-8332
  Vancouver (G-14297)
J&R Hennings Inc ....G....... 509 659-0102
  Sprague (G-12948)
Kaniksu Feeds Inc ....G....... 509 406-1995
  Deer Park (G-2907)
Kemason Inc...G....... 360 757-9947
  Burlington (G-2166)
Newly Weds Foods Inc ....D....... 253 584-9270
  Lakewood (G-5741)
Todd Imeson ....G....... 509 397-6570
  Colfax (G-2721)

FOOD PRDTS: Flour Mixes & Doughs

Dawn Food Products Inc ....D....... 206 763-1711
  Seattle (G-9804)
Dawn Food Products Inc ....E....... 206 623-7740
  Seattle (G-9803)

FOOD PRDTS: Flours & Flour Mixes, From Purchased Flour

Continental Mills Inc ....C....... 206 816-7000
  Tukwila (G-13716)
Continental Mills Inc ....C....... 206 816-7799
  Kent (G-4864)

FOOD PRDTS: Freeze-Dried Coffee

Eko Brands LLC ....E....... 800 833-0622
  Woodinville (G-15234)

FOOD PRDTS: Fresh Vegetables, Peeled Or Processed

Farm To Market Foods LLC......................G....... 360 708-6103
  Burlington (G-2157)
Garden Fresh Foods Inc..........................D....... 425 483-5467
  Woodinville (G-15250)
Mercer Ranches Inc.................................D....... 509 894-4773
  Prosser (G-8053)
National Frozen Foods Corp.....................E....... 509 766-0793
  Moses Lake (G-6730)

FOOD PRDTS: Fruit Juices

Cliffstar LLC..D....... 509 522-8608
  Walla Walla (G-14786)
Fresh Fruit Juice LLC ....G....... 206 329-5979
  Seattle (G-10027)
Naumes Concentrates Inc.......................E....... 509 877-8882
  Wapato (G-14921)
Phillippi Fruit Co Inc ....E....... 509 662-8522
  Wenatchee (G-15062)
Welch Foods Inc A Cooperative ....E....... 509 882-3112
  Grandview (G-4258)

FOOD PRDTS: Fruits & Vegetables, Pickled

How Pickle Got Out of A Jam...................G....... 206 940-6532
  Seattle (G-10187)
Leonhards Pickles LLC ....G....... 509 280-4267
  Spokane (G-12361)

FOOD PRDTS: Fruits, Dehydrated Or Dried

Mutiny Bay Blues LLC ....G....... 360 678-4315
  Freeland (G-4033)
Sun River Foods Inc ....F....... 509 249-0820
  Yakima (G-15687)

FOOD PRDTS: Fruits, Dried Or Dehydrated, Exc Freeze-Dried

Cherry Chukar Company..........................E....... 509 786-2055
  Prosser (G-8032)
Tree Top Inc ....C....... 509 663-8583
  Wenatchee (G-15082)
Tree Top Inc ....A....... 509 697-7251
  Selah (G-11600)
Tree Top Inc ....D....... 509 698-1432
  Selah (G-11602)

FOOD PRDTS: Granola & Energy Bars, Nonchocolate

Lifestyle Granolas Inc..............................G....... 509 768-5126
  Spokane (G-12364)

FOOD PRDTS: Honey

Hoffman Honey Co...................................G....... 360 568-5210
  Snohomish (G-11921)
Langes Honey Skep Inc...........................G....... 360 757-1073
  Burlington (G-2167)
Miracle Studios..G....... 833 728-3233
  Bonney Lake (G-1729)
My Local Co..F....... 360 989-6903
  Seattle (G-10579)

FOOD PRDTS: Ice, Blocks

Inland Ice & Fuel Inc ....G....... 509 457-6151
  Yakima (G-15590)

R Plum Corporation ....F....... 509 328-2070
  Spokane (G-12465)
Silvercreek Ice..G....... 360 985-2385
  Silver Creek (G-11825)

FOOD PRDTS: Macaroni, Noodles, Spaghetti, Pasta, Etc

Cucina Fresca Inc ....E....... 206 903-0825
  Seattle (G-9763)
Maninis LLC ....F....... 206 686-4600
  Kent (G-5003)

FOOD PRDTS: Malt

Great Western Malting Co ....G....... 360 859-0940
  Vancouver (G-14266)
Great Western Malting Co ....G....... 360 991-0888
  Vancouver (G-14267)
Great Western Malting Co ....G....... 360 693-3661
  Vancouver (G-14268)
Great Western Malting Co ....F....... 360 695-3484
  Vancouver (G-14269)
Rahr Malting ....G....... 509 469-0403
  Wapato (G-14925)
Salish Coast Enterprises LLC ....G....... 360 333-5280
  Burlington (G-2184)
Salish Post Enterprises LLC ....G....... 360 391-5492
  Mount Vernon (G-6832)

FOOD PRDTS: Milled Corn By-Prdts

Central Wash Corn Prcssors Inc ....G....... 509 623-1144
  Spokane (G-12176)

FOOD PRDTS: Mixes, Doughnut From Purchased Flour

Yum Yum Donut Shops Inc ....G....... 360 423-0150
  Longview (G-5970)

FOOD PRDTS: Mixes, Gingerbread From Purchased Flour

Gingerbread Factory................................G....... 509 548-6592
  Leavenworth (G-5803)

FOOD PRDTS: Mixes, Pizza

AC Larocco Pizza Co ....G....... 509 924-9113
  Spokane Valley (G-12597)

FOOD PRDTS: Mixes, Sauces, Dry

Fortun Foods Inc......................................F....... 425 827-1977
  Kirkland (G-5342)
Jot Products Co ....G....... 206 331-6677
  Renton (G-8833)

FOOD PRDTS: Mixes, Seasonings, Dry

Cascade Mountain Blends NW LLC ....G....... 425 275-3344
  Lynnwood (G-6088)
J&Ds Down Home Entps Inc....................G....... 206 388-3395
  Seattle (G-10275)
Johnnys Fine Foods Inc ....E....... 253 383-4597
  Tacoma (G-13362)
Pride of The West Inc ....G....... 360 694-4976
  Vancouver (G-14504)

FOOD PRDTS: Nuts & Seeds

Ames International Inc ....D....... 253 946-4779
  Fife (G-3932)
Brian Gannon ....G....... 206 782-2276
  Seattle (G-9583)
Jud Calvary Inc ....G....... 708 323-8758
  Redmond (G-8524)
Nut Factory Inc...E....... 509 926-6666
  Spokane Valley (G-12815)

FOOD PRDTS: Olive Oil

Olive Omg Oils ....G....... 206 340-4114
  Seattle (G-10690)
Olive Seattle Oil Co ....G....... 425 740-6055
  Mukilteo (G-6959)
View Point Global Inc ....F....... 206 714-4884
  Seattle (G-11416)

FOOD PRDTS: Pizza Blends LLC (listed at top)

Kof Enterprises LLC.................................F....... 206 328-2972
  Seattle (G-10351)
Newly Weds Foods Inc.............................D....... 253 584-9270
  Lakewood (G-5741)
Pizza Blends LLC ....F....... 800 826-1200
  Bellevue (G-1076)

PRODUCT SECTION

FOOD PRDTS: Pasta, Rice/Potatoes, Uncooked, Pkgd

Kof Enterprises LLC .... F 206 328-2972
   Seattle *(G-10351)*
Passport Food Group LLC .... E 253 520-9299
   Kent *(G-5060)*

FOOD PRDTS: Pasta, Uncooked, Packaged With Other Ingredients

Bellingham Pasta Company .... F 360 594-6000
   Bellingham *(G-1267)*
Cucina Fresca Inc .... F 206 903-0825
   Seattle *(G-9763)*

FOOD PRDTS: Pickles, Vinegar

General Mills Inc .... E 763 764-7600
   Sedro Woolley *(G-11539)*

FOOD PRDTS: Pizza Doughs From Purchased Flour

T R Rizzuto Pizza Crust Inc .... D 509 536-9268
   Spokane *(G-12541)*

FOOD PRDTS: Pork Rinds

Old Timers Pork Rinds .... G 509 438-8999
   Prosser *(G-8060)*

FOOD PRDTS: Potato & Corn Chips & Similar Prdts

Bright Candies .... G 509 525-5533
   Walla Walla *(G-14774)*
Campbell Soup Company .... B 425 415-2000
   Woodinville *(G-15204)*
Daisy Maiz LLC..................................... G 360 718-8288
   Vancouver *(G-14165)*
Noahs Ark Foods LLC .... G 509 595-8642
   Palouse *(G-7546)*
Pop Gourmet LLC .... D 425 277-5225
   Tukwila *(G-13792)*
S & W Management Co Inc .... E 425 771-6850
   Lynnwood *(G-6191)*
T D Kennedy and Associates Inc .... G 253 922-2558
   Tacoma *(G-13537)*
Watford Tanikka .... G 360 499-6327
   Lacey *(G-5601)*

FOOD PRDTS: Potato Chips & Other Potato-Based Snacks

Frito-Lay North America Inc .... A 360 737-3000
   Vancouver *(G-14241)*
Kennedy Endeavors Incorporated .... D 253 833-0255
   Algona *(G-72)*
Lamb Weston Bsw LLC .... E 509 349-2210
   Warden *(G-14932)*

FOOD PRDTS: Potatoes, Dried

Basic American Inc .... C 509 765-8601
   Moses Lake *(G-6684)*
Oregon Potato Company .... E 509 547-8772
   Pasco *(G-7608)*
Oregon Potato Company .... D 509 349-8803
   Warden *(G-14935)*
Oregon Potato Company .... G 509 545-4545
   Pasco *(G-7609)*

FOOD PRDTS: Preparations

Ayurveg Inc .... G 360 863-2457
   Gold Bar *(G-4186)*
B & B Foods Inc .... G 906 493-6962
   Walla Walla *(G-14766)*
Basic American Inc .... C 509 765-8601
   Moses Lake *(G-6684)*
Bumblebar Inc .... F 509 924-2080
   Spokane Valley *(G-12648)*
Butler Did It .... G 360 737-2672
   Vancouver *(G-14087)*
Central Market Incorporated .... G 509 787-5100
   Quincy *(G-8293)*
Cherrys Jubilee .... G 253 862-6751
   Lake Tapps *(G-5677)*
Conifer Specialties Inc .... D 425 486-3334
   Woodinville *(G-15210)*

Consolidated Food Management .... G 253 589-5654
   Lakewood *(G-5708)*
Daddy Daughter Diner LLC .... G 425 442-8307
   Bothell *(G-1845)*
Damn Good Pepper .... G 206 675-0540
   Seattle *(G-9789)*
Del Rio Food Processing Corp .... F 206 767-9102
   Seattle *(G-9816)*
Dodson Rd Orchard LLC .... D 509 787-3537
   Quincy *(G-8296)*
Don Pancho Authenti .... E 509 575-4489
   Yakima *(G-15557)*
Dynamic Food Ingredients Corp .... G 303 459-5908
   Spokane *(G-12234)*
Eclaire Farm LLC .... G 360 524-9775
   Vancouver *(G-14193)*
Fantazimo Food .... G 206 484-8232
   Mountlake Terrace *(G-6860)*
Farmer Bros Co .... E 425 881-7030
   Redmond *(G-8459)*
Ferris Fun Foods .... G 253 964-2828
   Dupont *(G-2963)*
Flora Inc .... D 360 354-2110
   Lynden *(G-6019)*
Food Master (pnw) Corp .... E 253 846-2600
   Tacoma *(G-13300)*
Four Seasons Gourmet Food Proc .... G 847 636-9879
   Seattle *(G-10017)*
Freedom Snacks LLC .... G 253 886-1838
   Normandy Park *(G-7094)*
Friday Harbor Exports Inc .... G 360 378-6086
   Friday Harbor *(G-4045)*
Garvey C Maury .... G 425 641-0232
   Bellevue *(G-919)*
General Mills Inc .... E 763 764-7600
   Sedro Woolley *(G-11539)*
Golden Nut Company (usa) Inc .... E 360 332-1990
   Blaine *(G-1673)*
Golden State Foods Corp .... G 509 928-9055
   Spokane Valley *(G-12722)*
Grand Temple .... G 509 715-7876
   Liberty Lake *(G-5833)*
Grandma Ednas .... G 425 200-5435
   Marysville *(G-6340)*
Gruma Corporation .... G 253 896-4483
   Fife *(G-3957)*
Guadalupe Foods Inc .... G 360 736-0298
   Rochester *(G-9133)*
Hearthside Usa LLC .... G 206 745-0850
   Seatac *(G-9286)*
Humming Hemp LLC .... G 503 559-6476
   Richland *(G-9007)*
Imagine Food .... G 917 428-4173
   Covington *(G-2830)*
Innovative Freeze Dried Fd LLC .... E 855 836-3233
   Ferndale *(G-3857)*
Innovative Solutions Intl .... F 206 365-7200
   Mercer Island *(G-6468)*
Island Bankra Caribbean Foods .... G 360 698-8345
   Silverdale *(G-11839)*
January Company .... E 253 872-9919
   Kent *(G-4964)*
Jgc Food Co LLC .... F 206 622-0420
   Seattle *(G-10296)*
JR Simplot Company .... E 509 765-3443
   Moses Lake *(G-6719)*
JR Simplot Company .... G 509 765-5663
   Othello *(G-7499)*
Lamb Weston Holdings Inc .... B 509 234-5511
   Connell *(G-2795)*
Lamb Weston Holdings Inc .... E 509 882-1417
   Prosser *(G-8049)*
Lamb Weston Inc .... A 509 787-3567
   Quincy *(G-8301)*
Lamb Weston Inc .... C 509 875-2423
   Paterson *(G-7658)*
Lolo Foods Inc .... G 509 860-8021
   Wenatchee *(G-15045)*
Lopez Island Chamber Commerce ...... G 360 468-4664
   Olga *(G-7215)*
Lostacos Locos .... G 360 573-1327
   Vancouver *(G-14382)*
Loving Superfoods LLC .... G 214 717-3321
   Vancouver *(G-14384)*
Matrix Health .... G 360 816-1200
   Vancouver *(G-14402)*
McCain Foods Usa Inc .... A 509 488-9611
   Othello *(G-7502)*
Medallion Foods Inc .... D 253 846-2600
   Tacoma *(G-13406)*

FOOD PRDTS: Prepared Sauces, Exc Tomato Based

Metabolic Global .... G 206 660-7243
   Seattle *(G-10519)*
Mountain Valley Products Inc .... E 509 837-8084
   Sunnyside *(G-13134)*
Mustard and Co LLC .... G 734 904-9877
   Seattle *(G-10576)*
Natural Matters Inc .... G 206 387-7054
   Seattle *(G-10592)*
Newgem Foods LLC .... F 209 948-1508
   Fife *(G-3973)*
Newly Weds Foods Inc .... D 253 584-9270
   Lakewood *(G-5741)*
Northwest Brewery Works Inc .... G 425 255-0698
   Newcastle *(G-7037)*
Nut Factory Inc .... E 509 926-6666
   Spokane Valley *(G-12815)*
Pacific Nutritional Inc .... C 360 253-3197
   Vancouver *(G-14467)*
Pacific NW Frmrs Coop Inc .... F 509 283-2124
   Fairfield *(G-3697)*
Pacwest Dental Lab .... G 360 635-3976
   Vancouver *(G-14476)*
Premium World Food Corporation .... G 206 267-8914
   Renton *(G-8885)*
Resers Fine Foods Inc .... D 509 543-4911
   Pasco *(G-7622)*
Rich Nature Organic .... G 425 315-7000
   Mukilteo *(G-6973)*
Rojos Famous Inc .... G 206 592-6581
   Normandy Park *(G-7097)*
S&L Foods LLC .... G 360 627-7809
   Bremerton *(G-1996)*
Saltworks Inc .... D 425 885-7258
   Woodinville *(G-15353)*
Santees Granola Inc .... G 509 245-3338
   Spangle *(G-12084)*
Schilling Cider .... G 208 660-4086
   Seattle *(G-11026)*
Seattle Egg Roll Corp .... G 425 226-6256
   Renton *(G-8908)*
Seneca Foods Corporation .... C 509 837-3806
   Sunnyside *(G-13140)*
Seneca Foods Corporation .... E 509 457-1089
   Yakima *(G-15671)*
Senior Services For S Sound .... G 360 426-3697
   Shelton *(G-11730)*
Sevierly Good Gluten Free LLC .... G 253 759-5288
   Tacoma *(G-13511)*
Sharon McIlhenny .... G 509 493-9259
   White Salmon *(G-15131)*
Sissys Specialty Foods .... G 360 807-4305
   Centralia *(G-2435)*
Sk Food Group Inc .... F 206 935-8100
   Seattle *(G-11124)*
Skillet Food Products LLC .... G 206 420-7297
   Seattle *(G-11126)*
Sky Valley Foods Inc .... G 360 805-1430
   Monroe *(G-6620)*
Small Planet Foods Inc .... E 800 624-4123
   Sedro Woolley *(G-11569)*
Snackflash LLC .... G 509 443-0396
   Spokane *(G-12508)*
Sunrice LLC .... G 206 841-2454
   Seattle *(G-11220)*
Tacoma Tofu Inc .... G 253 627-5085
   Tacoma *(G-13550)*
Tamu Foods .... G 253 835-1855
   Federal Way *(G-3793)*
Tsue Chong Co Inc .... E 206 623-0801
   Seattle *(G-11346)*
Twin City Foods Inc .... C 509 962-9806
   Ellensburg *(G-3235)*
Twin City Foods Inc .... B 509 786-2700
   Prosser *(G-8071)*
Vana Life Foods LP .... G 347 446-6504
   Seattle *(G-11402)*
Vansh Foods LLC .... G 425 743-1043
   Everett *(G-3646)*
Washington Potato Company Inc .... D 509 349-8803
   Warden *(G-14938)*

FOOD PRDTS: Prepared Sauces, Exc Tomato Based

De Marss LLC .... G 425 218-3454
   Bellevue *(G-876)*
Garden Fresh Gourmet Foods Inc .... C 425 407-6400
   Everett *(G-3491)*

FOOD PRDTS: Prepared Seafood Sauces Exc Tomato & Dry

Onefarstar LLC .... G 425 999-4894
 Bellevue (G-1049)
Sheng Mian North America LLC .... G 215 519-5895
 Bellevue (G-1128)

FOOD PRDTS: Raw cane sugar

Scutters .... G 425 350-7480
 Renton (G-8907)

FOOD PRDTS: Salads

Evergreens Salad .... G 206 973-4400
 Seattle (G-9947)
Triple b Corporation .... D 509 535-7393
 Spokane (G-12569)

FOOD PRDTS: Sandwiches

Jumbo Foods Inc .... C 425 355-1103
 Mukilteo (G-6946)

FOOD PRDTS: Seasonings & Spices

Broussards Creole Foods Inc .... G 253 638-2098
 Kent (G-4824)
For The Love of Spice .... G 253 858-0272
 Gig Harbor (G-4102)
Grampas Garlic Salt LLC .... G 425 513-0446
 Everett (G-3504)
Pizza Blends LLC .... F 800 826-1200
 Bellevue (G-1076)
Seasalt Superstore LLC .... E 425 249-2331
 Everett (G-3608)
Seasoningsnet LLC .... G 253 237-0550
 Kent (G-5120)
Spice Hut Corporation .... F 360 671-2800
 Bellingham (G-1552)
Travelers Tea Bar .... E 206 329-6260
 Seattle (G-11328)

FOOD PRDTS: Soup Mixes

Country Harvest Soup .... G 509 535-8357
 Spokane (G-12202)

FOOD PRDTS: Soup Powders

Fortun Foods Inc .... F 425 827-1977
 Kirkland (G-5342)

FOOD PRDTS: Soy Sauce

Kof Enterprises LLC .... F 206 328-2972
 Seattle (G-10351)

FOOD PRDTS: Spices, Including Ground

Puget Sound Foods Inc .... F 206 232-2757
 Mercer Island (G-6481)

FOOD PRDTS: Starch, Edible Root

David P Rush .... G 509 865-5338
 Zillah (G-15752)

FOOD PRDTS: Starch, Potato

Penford Products Co .... E 509 375-1261
 Richland (G-9034)

FOOD PRDTS: Sugar

Larry S Ayre .... G 509 582-8925
 Kennewick (G-4687)

FOOD PRDTS: Tea

Ethen Foods Inc .... G 206 778-0931
 Newcastle (G-7029)
Greenland Inc .... F 206 623-2577
 Seattle (G-10119)
Guy Chai Inc .... G 360 710-5962
 Bremerton (G-1959)
Samuel & Company Inc .... G 425 883-1220
 Bremerton (G-8657)
Sugimoto Seicha Usa Inc .... G 425 558-5552
 Redmond (G-8686)

FOOD PRDTS: Tofu, Exc Frozen Desserts

Tacoma Tofu Inc .... G 253 627-5085
 Lakewood (G-5761)

FOOD PRDTS: Tortilla Chips

Gruma Corporation .... C 253 896-4483
 Fife (G-3957)
Jalisco LLC .... F 360 432-9397
 Shelton (G-11704)
La Michoacana .... G 360 658-1635
 Marysville (G-6349)
Tortilleria Jalisco .... G 253 536-9532
 Spanaway (G-12078)

FOOD PRDTS: Tortillas

Bimbo Bakeries Usa Inc .... G 253 759-2146
 Tacoma (G-13201)
El Dorado Tortillas LLC .... G 719 459-2576
 Kirkland (G-5330)
Ernestinas Tortillas LLC .... G 360 669-0319
 Centralia (G-2400)
Kracker Tortilla Distribution .... G 253 380-2690
 Edgewood (G-3084)
La Mexicana Inc .... E 206 763-1488
 Seattle (G-10368)
Rallito De Luna .... G 509 488-4272
 Othello (G-7504)
Rallito De Luna Tortilla .... G 509 586-8691
 Kennewick (G-4713)
Tobys Tortillas LLC .... G 425 344-7653
 Snohomish (G-11992)
Tortilla Union .... G 509 381-5162
 Spokane (G-12563)
Tortilleria Valparaiso .... G 509 542-1340
 Pasco (G-7642)

FOOD PRDTS: Vegetable Oil Mills, NEC

Syngenta Seeds Inc .... C 509 543-8000
 Pasco (G-7636)

FOOD PRDTS: Vegetable Oil, Refined, Exc Corn

Barleans Organic Oils LLC .... C 360 384-0485
 Ferndale (G-3818)
Viterra USA LLC .... F 509 349-8464
 Warden (G-14936)

FOOD PRDTS: Vegetables, Dehydrated Or Dried

Double Dutch LLC .... G 509 837-6539
 Sunnyside (G-13120)

FOOD PRDTS: Vegetables, Pickled

Foster Family Farm .... D 509 543-9330
 Pasco (G-7582)

FOOD PRDTS: Vinegar

Anacortes Oil Vinegar Bar LLC .... G 360 293-6410
 Anacortes (G-100)
Desimone Oil and Vinegar Mkt .... G 253 709-5576
 Renton (G-8783)
Oil & Vinegar Retail .... G 509 838-7115
 Spokane (G-12420)
Oil Vinegar .... G 206 285-0517
 Seattle (G-10688)
Olive Navidis Oil & Vinegars .... G 360 600-9836
 Washougal (G-14975)
Salted Vinegar Studios .... G 931 302-0434
 Olympia (G-7391)
Vinegar & Oil .... G 425 454-8497
 Bellevue (G-1217)

FOOD PRODUCTS MACHINERY

Arr Tech Manufacturing .... E 509 966-4300
 Yakima (G-15512)
B & B Equipment Co Inc .... F 509 786-3838
 Prosser (G-8030)
Baader North America .... G 253 333-0422
 Auburn (G-388)
Bioplex Nutrition Inc .... F 360 332-2101
 Blaine (G-1661)
Carnitech US Inc .... G 206 781-1827
 Seattle (G-9634)
Cascadia Dynamix LLC .... G 360 584-3044
 Tenino (G-13613)
JV Designs Inc .... G 509 786-2588
 Prosser (G-8045)
Key Technology Inc .... B 509 529-2161
 Walla Walla (G-14833)
Key Technology Inc .... G 509 529-2161
 Walla Walla (G-14834)
Klc Holdings Ltd .... F 509 248-4770
 Yakima (G-15608)
MCD Technologies Inc .... F 253 564-2420
 Tacoma (G-13403)
McKinnon International .... G 206 633-1616
 Seattle (G-10508)
Mohr Test and Measurement LLC .... G 888 852-0408
 Richland (G-9028)
Mohr Test and Measurement LLC .... E 509 946-0941
 Richland (G-9027)
Nether Industries Inc .... E 360 825-7940
 Enumclaw (G-3309)
North Connection Corp .... G 425 637-7787
 Bellevue (G-1034)
Northwest Bagger Company Inc .... G 509 575-1950
 Yakima (G-15633)
Nutrifaster Inc .... G 206 767-5054
 Seattle (G-10670)
Pacific Vision Enterprises .... G 509 895-4199
 Wapato (G-14923)
Pomona Service & Supply Co .... G 509 452-7121
 Yakima (G-15649)
Prater Enterprises Inc .... G 360 893-3620
 Graham (G-4235)
Pro Sales Incorporated .... E 253 852-6046
 Puyallup (G-8226)
Professional Mktg Group .... G 206 322-7303
 Seattle (G-10872)
Sagra Inc .... G 253 476-1403
 Silverdale (G-11855)
Star Manufacturing Intl Inc .... C 800 882-6368
 Everett (G-3620)
Technipfmc US Holdings Inc .... F 253 853-5060
 Gig Harbor (G-4166)
Tramco Inc .... G 425 347-3030
 Everett (G-3635)
Tri-State Machinery Inc .... G 509 786-0400
 Prosser (G-8070)

FOOD STORES: Convenience, Chain

Conocophillips Company .... F 253 584-0583
 Lakewood (G-5707)
Yorkston Oil Co .... F 360 734-2201
 Bellingham (G-1597)

FOOD STORES: Convenience, Independent

Wenatchee Petroleum Co .... E 509 662-4423
 Wenatchee (G-15084)

FOOD STORES: Delicatessen

Island Enterprises .... E 360 426-4933
 Shelton (G-11702)
Island Enterprises .... F 360 426-3442
 Shelton (G-11703)
Northwest Sausage & Deli .... F 360 736-7760
 Centralia (G-2421)
Rolln Dough Ltd .... G 206 763-4300
 Kent (G-5105)

FOOD STORES: Grocery, Chain

Sno-Valley Dream Factory LLC .... G 408 888-8183
 North Bend (G-7124)

FOOD STORES: Grocery, Independent

Dynamic Automotive Distrs .... G 206 725-4474
 Seattle (G-9864)
Green Willow Trucking Inc .... E 360 687-7171
 Battle Ground (G-706)
Green Willow Trucking Inc .... F 360 687-7171
 Battle Ground (G-705)

FOOTWEAR: Cut Stock

Northwest Sports .... G 206 463-5906
 Vashon (G-14738)
Rah Inc .... E 509 482-0943
 Spokane Valley (G-12849)
Windbreak Inc .... G 817 306-9587
 Ridgefield (G-9120)

PRODUCT SECTION

FOOTWEAR: Except Rubber, NEC

Fleet Feet Sports .... G....... 509 309-2174
  Spokane Valley (G-12704)

FORESTRY RELATED EQPT

Armadillo Equipment & Parts .... G....... 360 829-4107
  Buckley (G-2046)
Danzco Inc .... G....... 360 264-2141
  Tenino (G-13616)
Ramsey Company Inc .... G....... 360 748-8918
  Chehalis (G-2529)

FORGINGS

12th Avenue Iron Inc .... G....... 206 325-0792
  Seattle (G-9317)
Custom Gear Inc .... F....... 206 767-9448
  Tukwila (G-13722)
Fss Holdings LLC .... G....... 425 820-5455
  Kirkland (G-5345)
Interntonal Hearth Melting LLC .... D....... 509 371-2500
  Richland (G-9011)
Jfc Holding Corporation .... E....... 206 762-1100
  Tukwila (G-13757)
Peregrine Manufacturing Inc .... G....... 425 673-5600
  Lynnwood (G-6179)
Snohomish Iron Works Inc .... G....... 360 568-2811
  Snohomish (G-11982)
Timber Iron Erectors .... G....... 360 681-8611
  Sequim (G-11666)

FORGINGS: Aluminum

Star Forge LLC .... C....... 206 762-1100
  Tukwila (G-13821)

FORGINGS: Anchors

All American Corporation .... F....... 509 315-9951
  Mead (G-6423)
Contech Systems Inc .... G....... 360 332-1718
  Tacoma (G-13240)
Forfjord Supply Co .... G....... 206 784-8171
  Seattle (G-10012)
Lister Chain and Forge Inc .... E....... 360 332-4323
  Blaine (G-1680)

FORGINGS: Armor Plate, Iron Or Steel

Hesco Armor Inc .... E....... 360 580-1146
  Aberdeen (G-17)

FORGINGS: Automotive & Internal Combustion Engine

American Engine & Machine Inc .... G....... 509 487-3332
  Spokane (G-12110)

FORGINGS: Gear & Chain

Jorgensen Forge Corporation .... C....... 206 762-1100
  Tukwila (G-13759)
Star Forge LLC .... C....... 206 762-1100
  Tukwila (G-13821)

FORGINGS: Machinery, Ferrous

Innotech Metal Designs LLC .... F....... 360 393-4108
  Bellingham (G-1378)

FORGINGS: Nuclear Power Plant, Ferrous

Electrino Group Inc .... G....... 360 491-9373
  Lacey (G-5548)

FORGINGS: Plumbing Fixture, Nonferrous

Fix Brothers Inc .... G....... 206 246-5127
  Seattle (G-10002)

FORMS HANDLING EQPT

Process Inc .... G....... 425 401-2000
  Bellevue (G-1085)

FORMS: Concrete, Sheet Metal

Bair Construction Inc .... G....... 360 491-2285
  Lacey (G-5535)
Efco Corp .... G....... 360 566-0300
  Vancouver (G-14194)
Efco Corp .... F....... 253 852-3800
  Kent (G-4886)

Naps Forming Systems .... G....... 800 922-2082
  Sumner (G-13087)
Peri Formwork Systems Inc .... E....... 360 225-3583
  Woodland (G-15458)
Star Rentals Inc .... F....... 509 545-8521
  Pasco (G-7632)
Westside Concrete ACC Inc .... G....... 360 892-0203
  Vancouver (G-14686)

FOUNDRIES: Aluminum

Bergstrom Foundry Inc .... F....... 360 532-6981
  Aberdeen (G-6)
Frasers Bronze Foundry Inc .... G....... 877 264-1064
  Marysville (G-6336)
Jerry H Hyman .... G....... 360 479-1724
  Bremerton (G-1965)
Olympic Foundry Inc .... E....... 206 764-6200
  Seattle (G-10691)
Puget Sound Repair Inc .... G....... 506 556-9722
  Seattle (G-10885)
Pyrotek Incorporated .... F....... 509 921-8766
  Spokane Valley (G-12847)
Seacast Inc .... C....... 360 653-9388
  Tulalip (G-13843)

FOUNDRIES: Brass, Bronze & Copper

Bergstrom Foundry Inc .... F....... 360 532-6981
  Aberdeen (G-6)
Creative Casting Company .... G....... 253 475-2643
  Tacoma (G-13248)
Garden Expressions .... G....... 360 403-9532
  Arlington (G-239)
Jerry H Hyman .... G....... 360 479-1724
  Bremerton (G-1965)
Mission Africa .... F....... 206 850-9155
  Auburn (G-499)
Olympic Foundry Inc .... E....... 206 764-6200
  Seattle (G-10691)

FOUNDRIES: Gray & Ductile Iron

Ej Usa Inc .... G....... 360 651-6144
  Marysville (G-6332)
Indepndent Distr Rexall Showca .... G....... 253 565-6595
  University Place (G-13972)
Jerry H Hyman .... G....... 360 479-1724
  Bremerton (G-1965)
Mazdak International Inc .... G....... 360 988-6058
  Sumas (G-13047)
Travis Pattern & Foundry Inc .... B....... 509 466-3545
  Spokane (G-12566)
Wear-Tek Inc .... D....... 509 747-4139
  Spokane (G-12584)
Wh International Casting LLC .... G....... 425 498-7531
  Everett (G-3658)
Wh International Casting LLC .... G....... 562 521-0727
  Moses Lake (G-6758)

FOUNDRIES: Iron

Olympic Foundry Inc .... E....... 206 764-6200
  Seattle (G-10691)
Spokane Industries Inc .... C....... 509 924-0440
  Spokane Valley (G-12885)

FOUNDRIES: Nonferrous

Bergstrom Foundry Inc .... F....... 360 532-6981
  Aberdeen (G-6)
Cashmere Manufacturing LLC .... E....... 509 888-2141
  East Wenatchee (G-3009)
Jerry H Hyman .... G....... 360 479-1724
  Bremerton (G-1965)
Mackenzie Spcalty Castings Inc .... E....... 360 435-5539
  Arlington (G-271)
Pentz Design Pattern Fndry Inc .... E....... 425 788-6490
  Duvall (G-2997)
Port Townsend Foundry LLC .... F....... 360 385-6425
  Port Townsend (G-7910)
Precision Castparts Corp .... B....... 425 957-6938
  Bellevue (G-1080)
Roemer Electric Steel Foundry .... E....... 360 423-1330
  Longview (G-5949)
Salish Technology .... G....... 360 632-4522
  Clinton (G-2696)
Seacast Inc .... E....... 206 767-5759
  Seattle (G-11041)
Thomas Machine & Foundry Inc .... D....... 360 651-9100
  Marysville (G-6395)
Wear-Tek Inc .... D....... 509 747-4139
  Spokane (G-12584)

FOUNDRIES: Steel

Anderson Foundry Forge .... G....... 360 270-2008
  Silverlake (G-11862)
Bradken - Atlas LLC .... D....... 360 748-6645
  Chehalis (G-2473)
Decker Foundry .... G....... 206 225-9000
  Seattle (G-9811)
Jerry H Hyman .... G....... 360 479-1724
  Bremerton (G-1965)
Machstem Inc .... G....... 801 259-3305
  Nine Mile Falls (G-7078)
Mackenzie Spcalty Castings Inc .... E....... 360 435-5539
  Arlington (G-271)
Mt Baker Mining and Mtls LLC .... F....... 360 595-4445
  Bellingham (G-1447)
Mt Baker Mining and Mtls LLC .... F....... 360 739-7264
  Bellingham (G-1448)
Nucor Corporation .... C....... 206 933-2222
  Seattle (G-10666)
Olympic Foundry Inc .... E....... 206 764-6200
  Seattle (G-10691)
Puget Sound Repair Inc .... G....... 506 556-9722
  Seattle (G-10885)
Romac Industries Inc .... D....... 425 951-6200
  Sultan (G-13034)
Vancouver Foundry Company .... G....... 360 695-3914
  Vancouver (G-14661)
Vancouver Iron & Steel Inc .... D....... 360 695-3914
  Vancouver (G-14662)
Wear-Tek Inc .... D....... 509 747-4139
  Spokane (G-12584)
Young Corporation .... G....... 206 623-3274
  Seattle (G-11515)
Young Corporation .... E....... 206 623-3274
  Seattle (G-11514)

FOUNDRIES: Steel Investment

Cast 7020 LLC .... D....... 401 885-9555
  Tulalip (G-13840)
Gray Mold Company Inc .... F....... 360 671-5711
  Bellingham (G-1361)
Seacast Inc .... C....... 360 653-9388
  Tulalip (G-13843)
Seacast Inc .... E....... 206 767-5759
  Seattle (G-11041)

FRACTIONATION PRDTS OF CRUDE PETROLEUM, HYDROCARBONS, NEC

Paramount Petroleum Corp .... E....... 503 273-4700
  Seattle (G-10752)

FRAMES & FRAMING WHOLESALE

Museum Quality Discount Frmng .... F....... 206 624-1057
  Seattle (G-10574)

FRANCHISES, SELLING OR LICENSING

Artistic Iron Furniture Mfrs .... F....... 360 398-9351
  Lynden (G-6002)
Mips Tech Inc .... G....... 408 610-5900
  Bellevue (G-1008)
Normed Inc .... E....... 800 288-8200
  Tukwila (G-13779)

FREIGHT CAR LOADING & UNLOADING SVCS

North Mason Fiber Company .... G....... 360 275-0228
  Belfair (G-769)
Oroville Reman & Reload Inc .... E....... 509 476-2935
  Oroville (G-7471)

FREIGHT TRANSPORTATION ARRANGEMENTS

Adaptive Cargo Solutions LLC .... F....... 240 475-6521
  Everett (G-3360)
Berg Manufacturing Inc .... C....... 509 624-8921
  Spokane Valley (G-12638)
Frank Harkness Trckg & Log LLC .... F....... 360 826-6087
  Acme (G-42)
Frank Harkness Trckg & Log LLC .... G....... 360 595-2496
  Concrete (G-2785)
I-90 Express LLC .... G....... 509 855-6280
  Ephrata (G-3337)
Shipco Transport Inc .... G....... 206 444-7447
  Tukwila (G-13818)

Employee Codes: A=Over 500 employees, B=251-500
C=101-250, D=51-100, E=20-50, F=10-19, G=2-9

FRICTION MATERIAL, MADE FROM POWDERED METAL

Quadradyne Technologies LLC.............G....... 248 342-5977
Brush Prairie *(G-2040)*

FRUIT & VEGETABLE MARKETS

Garlic Crush...G....... 425 968-2539
Redmond *(G-8469)*

FRUIT STANDS OR MARKETS

Rose Tucker..G....... 509 837-8701
Sunnyside *(G-13139)*

FRUITS & VEGETABLES WHOLESALERS: Fresh

Grow Northwest.......................................G....... 360 398-1155
Everson *(G-3678)*
Maury Hill Farm Enterprises.................G....... 206 463-6193
Vashon *(G-14733)*

FUEL ADDITIVES

Pacrim Technologies LLC.....................G....... 425 284-7300
Kirkland *(G-5425)*

FUEL CELL FORMS: Cardboard, Made From Purchased Materials

Plug Power Inc..F....... 509 228-6694
Spokane Valley *(G-12829)*

FUEL CELLS: Solid State

Avista Capital Inc..................................G....... 509 489-0500
Spokane *(G-12133)*

FUEL DEALERS: Coal

Articland Ice..G....... 509 582-5808
Kennewick *(G-4620)*
Inland Ice & Fuel Inc............................G....... 509 457-6151
Yakima *(G-15590)*

FUEL DEALERS: Wood

Grizzly Firestarters North.....................G....... 360 659-3948
Marysville *(G-6341)*
Grizzly Firestarters North.....................G....... 360 652-2100
Mount Vernon *(G-6802)*

FUEL OIL DEALERS

Allied Grinders Inc................................F....... 425 493-1313
Mukilteo *(G-6892)*
Deyoungs Farm and Garden...............E....... 425 483-9600
Woodinville *(G-15225)*
Inland Ice & Fuel Inc............................G....... 509 457-6151
Yakima *(G-15590)*

FUEL TREATING

Lightning Nuggets Inc..........................F....... 509 725-6211
Davenport *(G-2873)*

FUEL: Rocket Engine, Organic

Sovrano Di Ricchezza Group...............G....... 425 449-8011
Bellevue *(G-1150)*

FUELS: Diesel

Diesel Prfmce Unlimited LLC...............G....... 509 546-9997
Pasco *(G-7576)*
Dr Dans Alternative Fuel Werks..........G....... 206 783-5728
Seattle *(G-9851)*
Flotbunker LLC......................................G....... 206 354-5205
Bellevue *(G-913)*
S&S Transportation Service................G....... 509 968-9825
Ellensburg *(G-3224)*

FUELS: Ethanol

Arneson Fuels LLC...............................G....... 425 823-1096
Kirkland *(G-5280)*
Blue Star Gas - Seattle Co...................G....... 206 762-2583
Tukwila *(G-13698)*
Coulee View Food and Fuel................G....... 509 633-2951
Coulee Dam *(G-2807)*
Escape Fuel Game One LLC...............G....... 425 883-8054
Redmond *(G-8453)*

Flex Fuel...G....... 360 520-9773
Chehalis *(G-2497)*
Fuel Coffee...G....... 206 634-2700
Seattle *(G-10035)*
Fuel100 LLC...G....... 206 898-4904
Seattle *(G-10036)*
Garrison Fuel Tech................................G....... 360 739-2634
Ferndale *(G-3847)*
Global Enterprise Intl............................F....... 303 928-3208
Kingston *(G-5254)*
Imperium Renewables Inc....................G....... 360 532-2387
Longview *(G-5917)*
K and M Fuel LLC................................G....... 509 675-3005
Colville *(G-2761)*
Mileage Maxer LLC..............................G....... 360 550-5809
Poulsbo *(G-7984)*
Northwest Biofuels...............................G....... 509 927-4548
Spokane Valley *(G-12805)*
Northwestern Fuel Ldscpg Sups.........G....... 425 743-1550
Mukilteo *(G-6957)*
Pacific Fuel and Convenience.............G....... 253 631-8512
Kent *(G-5051)*
Patroit Fuels LLC..................................G....... 253 507-6256
Auburn *(G-528)*
Pickens Fuel Corp................................G....... 206 824-8181
Seatac *(G-9299)*
Romine Fuel Inc....................................G....... 509 476-3610
Riverside *(G-9126)*
Seelig Fuel Inc......................................G....... 206 789-6434
Seattle *(G-11088)*
Southpark Fuel & Food........................G....... 206 762-7550
Seattle *(G-11162)*
Summit Biofuels LLC............................G....... 206 291-6402
Vashon *(G-14745)*
The Fuel..G....... 206 829-8033
Seattle *(G-11285)*
Valley Fuel LLC.....................................G....... 509 937-2230
Valley *(G-13995)*
Wof Pnw Pog 1 LLC.............................G....... 206 624-2144
Seattle *(G-11489)*

FUELS: Nuclear

Sandvik Special Metals LLC................C....... 509 734-4000
Kennewick *(G-4726)*

FUNERAL HOME

Fir Lane Memorial Pk & Fnrl HM.........F....... 253 531-6600
Spanaway *(G-12058)*

FUNERAL HOMES & SVCS

Funeral Directors Research..................G....... 360 736-7105
Centralia *(G-2402)*

FUNGICIDES OR HERBICIDES

Pace International LLC........................G....... 800 936-6750
Wapato *(G-14922)*

FUR APPAREL STORES

United States Sheepskin Inc...............F....... 253 627-7114
Tacoma *(G-13571)*

FUR APPAREL STORES: Made To Custom Order

Olympic Print and Apparel...................G....... 206 402-3642
Seattle *(G-10693)*

FUR: Hats

Etc Tacoma..G....... 253 223-5459
Tacoma *(G-13282)*

FURNACES & OVENS: Indl

Advanced Combustn Systems Inc.......E....... 360 676-6005
Bellingham *(G-1239)*
King Electrical Mfg Co.........................D....... 206 762-0400
Seattle *(G-10345)*

FURNITURE & CABINET STORES: Cabinets, Custom Work

Acorn Custom Cabinetry Inc................E....... 425 235-8366
Renton *(G-8727)*
F H Sullivan Co Inc..............................E....... 360 442-4222
Kelso *(G-4525)*
Haun Made LLC....................................G....... 253 242-6105
Seattle *(G-10150)*

John Duane King..................................G....... 360 736-6707
Centralia *(G-2412)*
New Whatcom Interiors........................F....... 360 671-3389
Bellingham *(G-1459)*
Prp Finishing...G....... 509 966-0798
Yakima *(G-15658)*
R&J Industries LLC..............................G....... 253 466-3627
Puyallup *(G-8233)*
Rainier Woodworking Co......................F....... 253 272-5210
Tacoma *(G-13491)*
Smokey Point Custom Cabinets..........F....... 360 659-6233
Marysville *(G-6386)*
Windfall Lumber Inc.............................E....... 360 352-2250
Tumwater *(G-13906)*

FURNITURE & CABINET STORES: Custom

IB Wood Inc...G....... 253 395-8886
Kent *(G-4948)*
Kelseys Collection Inc..........................G....... 206 355-4333
Lake Forest Park *(G-5618)*
Modern Classics Inc.............................G....... 360 733-6400
Bellingham *(G-1438)*

FURNITURE & FIXTURES Factory

International Wood Processors............D....... 360 299-9996
Anacortes *(G-135)*

FURNITURE PARTS: Metal

Fuze Create LLC..................................G....... 425 212-8807
Seattle *(G-10043)*
Origami Inc..G....... 206 784-9133
Seattle *(G-10714)*
West Coast Fabrication Inc..................G....... 206 790-1496
Auburn *(G-598)*

FURNITURE REFINISHING SVCS

J R Reding Company Inc.....................G....... 253 474-9938
Tacoma *(G-13354)*

FURNITURE REPAIR & MAINTENANCE SVCS

Prp Finishing...G....... 509 966-0798
Yakima *(G-15658)*

FURNITURE STOCK & PARTS: Carvings, Wood

Eagles Nest..G....... 360 876-9522
Port Orchard *(G-7806)*
Grassroots Woodworks LLC.................G....... 360 836-1313
Bellingham *(G-1360)*
Kelseys Collection Inc..........................G....... 206 355-4333
Lake Forest Park *(G-5618)*
Norman Lancaster Brown....................G....... 509 678-5980
Tieton *(G-13631)*

FURNITURE STOCK & PARTS: Dimension Stock, Hardwood

Fredricksons Furn & Cabinets.............G....... 206 782-5310
Seattle *(G-10023)*

FURNITURE STOCK & PARTS: Hardwood

Custom Office Design Inc....................F....... 253 735-8777
Auburn *(G-420)*
Dwight Hostvedt....................................G....... 360 683-2315
Sequim *(G-11631)*
North Country Forest Resources........G....... 509 486-2882
Tonasket *(G-13655)*
S & S Selden LLC................................G....... 253 922-5700
Fife *(G-3989)*

FURNITURE STOCK & PARTS: Squares, Hardwood

Crafted Northwest Doors Inc................F....... 509 484-3722
Spokane *(G-12205)*

FURNITURE STORES

Briarwood Furniture Ltd Inc.................G....... 425 868-7707
Kingston *(G-5249)*
Columbia Furniture Mfg Inc.................F....... 509 534-7147
Spokane *(G-12190)*
Hoss A W & Sons Furn & Mfg............F....... 206 522-1229
Seattle *(G-10182)*
S F McKinnon Co Inc..........................G....... 206 622-4948
Seattle *(G-11000)*

PRODUCT SECTION

FURNITURE: Household, Wood

Twilight Bedding Company Inc..............G...... 509 926-2333
  Spokane Valley *(G-12916)*
Vancouver Woodworks Inc ....G...... 360 696-8590
  Vancouver *(G-14664)*
Wallbeds Northwest Inc ....G...... 206 256-1700
  Seattle *(G-11433)*
Warners Cabinets ....G...... 425 222-7386
  Issaquah *(G-4488)*

FURNITURE STORES: Cabinets, Kitchen, Exc Custom Made

Dean Thoemke ....G...... 253 640-2232
  Yakima *(G-15551)*
Valley Cabinet Shop Inc ....F...... 509 786-2717
  Prosser *(G-8072)*
William H Olson Inc ....G...... 360 249-3691
  Olympia *(G-7426)*
William H Olson Inc ....G...... 360 754-2858
  Olympia *(G-7427)*

FURNITURE STORES: Custom Made, Exc Cabinets

Pioneer Woodworks Company Inc.........G...... 206 362-5637
  Seattle *(G-10812)*

FURNITURE STORES: Office

Bayshore Office Products Inc...............F...... 360 293-4669
  Anacortes *(G-102)*
Thermogenesis Group Inc ....F...... 425 999-3550
  Bellevue *(G-1185)*
W B Mason Co Inc................................E...... 888 926-2766
  Tukwila *(G-13835)*

FURNITURE STORES: Outdoor & Garden

Central Washington Wtr Ctr Inc.............F...... 509 663-1177
  Wenatchee *(G-15019)*

FURNITURE WHOLESALERS

Company K LLC ....G...... 206 632-0509
  Seattle *(G-9723)*
Global Industries Inc ....G...... 425 291-9282
  Renton *(G-8807)*
Kings Kitchen LLC................................G...... 253 212-3623
  Tacoma *(G-13376)*
Kristines ....G...... 360 437-0136
  Port Ludlow *(G-7769)*
Prp Finishing ....G...... 509 966-0798
  Yakima *(G-15658)*
Whalen Furniture Manufacturing..........G...... 425 427-0115
  Issaquah *(G-4489)*

FURNITURE, HOUSEHOLD: Wholesalers

Emerald Home Furnishings LLC ....B...... 253 922-1400
  Tacoma *(G-13278)*
IB Wood Inc ....G...... 253 395-8886
  Kent *(G-4948)*

FURNITURE, MATTRESSES: Wholesalers

Sleep Number Corporation ....G...... 360 671-1266
  Bellingham *(G-1543)*
Ssb Manufacturing Company ....C...... 253 891-3272
  Sumner *(G-13102)*

FURNITURE, OFFICE: Wholesalers

Custom Office Design Inc ....F...... 253 735-8777
  Auburn *(G-420)*
Professional Business Svc Inc..............F...... 360 352-3000
  Olympia *(G-7374)*

FURNITURE, WHOLESALE: Bedsprings

Slumber Ease Mattress Co Inc ....G...... 360 657-1654
  Marysville *(G-6385)*

FURNITURE, WHOLESALE: Racks

Rack & Maintenance Source LLC.........G...... 509 525-7006
  College Place *(G-2726)*
Ultimate Rack Inc ....G...... 509 393-3526
  East Wenatchee *(G-3033)*

FURNITURE: Bed Frames & Headboards, Wood

A & J Brokerage Co Inc ....E...... 509 483-3003
  Spokane *(G-12088)*

FURNITURE: Bedroom, Wood

All Wood Concepts Inc..........................G...... 253 255-6518
  Tacoma *(G-13164)*
Grassroots Woodworks LLC ....G...... 360 836-1313
  Bellingham *(G-1360)*
Kessler Wood Products ....G...... 509 937-2500
  Valley *(G-13992)*

FURNITURE: Box Springs, Assembled

Cascade Manufacturing ....G...... 206 762-3750
  Auburn *(G-402)*

FURNITURE: Camp, Metal

Camp Time Inc ....F...... 509 928-3051
  Spokane Valley *(G-12649)*

FURNITURE: Chairs, Dental

Royal Dental Manufacturing Inc ....D...... 425 743-0988
  Everett *(G-3601)*
Westar Medical Products Inc ....F...... 425 290-3945
  Arlington *(G-347)*

FURNITURE: Chests, Cedar

Deer Creek Cedar Products Inc ....G...... 360 435-4707
  Arlington *(G-227)*

FURNITURE: China Closets

Glassique...G...... 206 963-4400
  Seattle *(G-10080)*

FURNITURE: Church

Douglas L Perry ....G...... 253 303-0537
  Gig Harbor *(G-4095)*

FURNITURE: Desks & Tables, Office, Exc Wood

Thermogenesis Group Inc ....F...... 425 999-3550
  Bellevue *(G-1185)*

FURNITURE: Dining Room, Wood

Two Zero Six LLC ....G...... 206 557-4384
  Seattle *(G-11355)*

FURNITURE: Dressers, Household, Wood

Freeze Furniture and Mfg Co ....F...... 509 924-3545
  Spokane Valley *(G-12710)*

FURNITURE: Fiberglass & Plastic

Douglas L Perry ....G...... 253 303-0537
  Gig Harbor *(G-4095)*

FURNITURE: Foundations & Platforms

NW Closets ....F...... 253 246-7596
  Kent *(G-5038)*
Summitclimb Inc ....G...... 360 570-0715
  Longbranch *(G-5880)*

FURNITURE: Garden, Exc Wood, Metal, Stone Or Concrete

Green Store Inc ....G...... 253 939-5757
  Algona *(G-70)*
Potrisers Inc..G...... 206 240-5579
  Snohomish *(G-11961)*

FURNITURE: Household, Metal

Alairx LLC ....G...... 425 281-3180
  Carnation *(G-2289)*
Artistic Iron Furniture Mfrs ....F...... 360 398-9351
  Lynden *(G-6002)*
Jpl Habitability Inc ....F...... 360 377-7660
  Bremerton *(G-1967)*
Northwest Metal Craft ....G...... 509 999-5280
  Spokane Valley *(G-12807)*

FURNITURE: Household, NEC

Kitty Cribs LLC.....................................G...... 360 312-8102
  Ferndale *(G-3864)*
Patricia Kinsella ....G...... 206 285-5885
  Seattle *(G-10769)*

FURNITURE: Household, Upholstered On Metal Frames

David Gulassa & Co Inc........................E...... 206 283-1810
  Seattle *(G-9800)*
Schreiner Construction ....G...... 509 525-6205
  College Place *(G-2727)*

FURNITURE: Household, Upholstered, Exc Wood Or Metal

Wallbeds Northwest Inc ....E...... 425 284-6692
  Redmond *(G-8708)*

FURNITURE: Household, Wood

All Points East......................................G...... 360 863-8971
  Monroe *(G-6545)*
Barnes Wood Inc..................................G...... 360 658-0145
  Marysville *(G-6315)*
Beltecno Inc..G...... 360 512-4000
  Monroe *(G-6552)*
Bernard Manufacturing ....F...... 206 242-4017
  Burien *(G-2093)*
Bilt-Rite Custom Cabinets....................G...... 360 829-0663
  Buckley *(G-2049)*
Briarwood Furniture Ltd Inc..................G...... 425 868-7707
  Kingston *(G-5249)*
Brooks Properties.................................G...... 360 733-5170
  Bellingham *(G-1284)*
Canyon Creek Cabinet Company ....G...... 509 921-7807
  Spokane Valley *(G-12650)*
Charles Hanson ....G...... 360 871-2173
  Port Orchard *(G-7797)*
D-Mac Carpentry ....G...... 509 326-6601
  Spokane *(G-12214)*
Dale A West Specialty Wdwkg ....G...... 360 683-9419
  Sequim *(G-11623)*
Dale M Shafman LLC ....G...... 206 499-4408
  Seattle *(G-9787)*
David Gray Furnituremaker Inc ....G...... 360 321-4514
  Langley *(G-5776)*
David Gulassa & Co Inc........................E...... 206 283-1810
  Seattle *(G-9800)*
Diy Table Legs LLC ....G...... 206 659-8669
  Lynnwood *(G-6110)*
Dmm Incorporated ....E...... 360 435-5252
  Arlington *(G-229)*
Douglas L Perry ....G...... 253 303-0537
  Gig Harbor *(G-4095)*
Emerald Home Furnishings LLC ....B...... 253 922-1400
  Tacoma *(G-13278)*
Erb Woodcraft LLC ....G...... 509 467-1134
  Spokane *(G-12249)*
Ferguson Woodworking Inc..................G...... 360 398-1543
  Bellingham *(G-1345)*
Furniture By Foss ....G...... 206 783-3626
  Seattle *(G-10040)*
Heirloom Custom Cabinets Inc.............G...... 360 354-7851
  Lynden *(G-6020)*
Jpl Habitability Inc ....F...... 360 377-7660
  Bremerton *(G-1967)*
Kristines..G...... 360 437-0136
  Port Ludlow *(G-7769)*
Leader Manufacturing Inc ....E...... 360 895-1184
  Port Orchard *(G-7825)*
Lewis Cnty Work Opportunities ....E...... 360 748-9921
  Chehalis *(G-2509)*
Maine Cottage Inc ....G...... 866 366-3505
  Poulsbo *(G-7981)*
Maywood Shops Inc ....F...... 360 748-9244
  Chehalis *(G-2513)*
Modern Classics Inc ....G...... 360 733-6400
  Bellingham *(G-1438)*
Nordal Denver ....G...... 509 456-8969
  Spokane *(G-12406)*
Petit and Olson.....................................G...... 206 201-3262
  Bainbridge Island *(G-657)*
Pioneer Woodworks Company Inc........G...... 206 362-5637
  Seattle *(G-10812)*
Precision Woodcraft ....G...... 509 276-1362
  Deer Park *(G-2913)*
Preston Woodcraft LLC.........................G...... 425 749-8074
  Issaquah *(G-4460)*

Employee Codes: A=Over 500 employees, B=251-500
C=101-250, D=51-100, E=20-50, F=10-19, G=2-9

FURNITURE: Household, Wood

Quality Cabinets Plus Inc .... G 360 423-1242
  Kelso *(G-4544)*
Quality Creations .... G 253 732-4082
  Spanaway *(G-12068)*
Reclaimed Wood Products .... G 360 387-1570
  Stanwood *(G-12956)*
Roy McMakin .... G 206 323-0111
  Seattle *(G-10984)*
S F McKinnon Co Inc .... G 206 622-4948
  Seattle *(G-11000)*
Shaker Craftsman .... G 509 823-4556
  Yakima *(G-15673)*
Shea Edwards Furniture LLP .... F 206 898-1992
  Sultan *(G-13036)*
Shelfgenie .... G 206 774-0336
  Seattle *(G-11099)*
Ship N Shore .... G 360 293-8636
  Anacortes *(G-167)*
Shuttlesystem LLC .... F 425 551-1335
  Mount Vernon *(G-6835)*
Snow Valley Furniture .... F 509 292-8880
  Newport *(G-7066)*
Style Plus LLC .... E 206 920-9223
  Renton *(G-8921)*
Surewood Custom Cabinets Inc .... G 509 893-9522
  Spokane Valley *(G-12897)*
Thoe John .... G 206 505-6229
  Seattle *(G-11294)*
Traditional Heirlooms .... G 509 722-2620
  Goldendale *(G-4210)*
Wallbeds Northwest Inc .... E 425 284-6692
  Redmond *(G-8708)*
Whidbey Design Works .... G 360 321-8221
  Clinton *(G-2702)*
William Walker Woodworking .... G 206 780-5301
  Bainbridge Island *(G-684)*
Winthrop Wood Works .... G 509 996-2037
  Winthrop *(G-15166)*
Wood-Works Cabinetry & Design .... G 206 257-3335
  Seattle *(G-11491)*
Woodcraft Inc .... G 800 225-1153
  Lynnwood *(G-6226)*
Woodcraft Studio 404 426-1229
  Bremerton *(G-2013)*
Woodworking Unlimited .... G 425 481-7451
  Bothell *(G-1922)*

FURNITURE: Institutional, Exc Wood

Dream Line Cabinets LLC .... G 503 841-8575
  Vancouver *(G-14187)*
Genothen Holdings LLC .... D 360 352-3636
  Tumwater *(G-13873)*
Trevors Wood Working LLC .... G 206 940-8000
  Seattle *(G-11331)*
Watson Furniture Group Inc .... G 360 394-1300
  Poulsbo *(G-8020)*
Watson Furniture Group Inc .... G 360 394-1300
  Poulsbo *(G-8019)*

FURNITURE: Juvenile, Wood

Simplicity ABC LLC .... G 425 250-1186
  Fall City *(G-3708)*

FURNITURE: Kitchen & Dining Room

Henry Products Incorporated .... D 206 624-5656
  Seattle *(G-10166)*

FURNITURE: Lawn & Garden, Except Wood & Metal

Vancouver Woodworks Inc .... G 360 696-8590
  Vancouver *(G-14664)*

FURNITURE: Living Room, Upholstered On Wood Frames

Kaasco Inc .... C 425 412-2460
  Mukilteo *(G-6947)*
William Bounds Custom Frames .... G 360 404-2002
  Burlington *(G-2202)*

FURNITURE: Mattresses & Foundations

Bayshore Office Products Inc .... F 360 293-4669
  Anacortes *(G-102)*
Emerald Home Furnishings LLC .... B 253 922-1400
  Tacoma *(G-13278)*
Sleep Aire Mattress Company .... E 206 546-4195
  Shoreline *(G-11814)*
Slumber Ease Mattress Co Inc .... G 360 657-1654
  Marysville *(G-6385)*
Soaring Heart Natural Bed Co .... G 206 257-4158
  Seattle *(G-11148)*
Twilight Bedding Company Inc .... G 509 926-2333
  Spokane Valley *(G-12916)*

FURNITURE: Mattresses, Box & Bedsprings

Canvas Supply Co Inc .... E 206 784-0711
  Seattle *(G-9621)*
Cascade Designs Inc .... B 206 505-9500
  Seattle *(G-9640)*
Leggett & Platt Incorporated .... G 801 825-9739
  Tacoma *(G-13384)*
Sleep Number Corporation .... G 360 671-1266
  Bellingham *(G-1543)*
Soaring Heart LLC .... F 206 282-1717
  Seattle *(G-11147)*

FURNITURE: Mattresses, Innerspring Or Box Spring

Mattress Makers Incorporated .... F 253 984-1730
  Tacoma *(G-13401)*
Northwest Bedding Company .... E 509 244-3000
  Spokane *(G-12411)*
Sealy Mattress Mfg Co Inc .... C 360 413-6902
  Lacey *(G-5585)*
Ssb Manufacturing Company .... G 253 891-3272
  Sumner *(G-13102)*

FURNITURE: NEC

Judith Ames Furniture .... G 206 324-8538
  Seattle *(G-10313)*
Leigh Interiors .... G 206 351-5158
  Bellevue *(G-980)*
Two Blue Mules .... G 206 935-3762
  Seattle *(G-11352)*

FURNITURE: Office Panel Systems, Exc Wood

Kenco Construction Inc .... E 206 783-3300
  Seattle *(G-10336)*

FURNITURE: Office Panel Systems, Wood

Watson Furniture Group Inc .... C 360 394-1300
  Poulsbo *(G-8019)*

FURNITURE: Office, Exc Wood

Artiks Inc .... G 206 849-4335
  Redmond *(G-8387)*
Global Industries Inc .... G 425 291-9282
  Renton *(G-8807)*
Jpl Habitability Inc .... F 360 377-7660
  Bremerton *(G-1967)*
Loop Corp .... G 206 499-0679
  Seattle *(G-10440)*
Meyer Wells Inc .... E 206 282-0076
  Seattle *(G-10525)*
Warmington & North Co Inc .... F 206 324-5043
  Seattle *(G-11436)*

FURNITURE: Office, Wood

Acorn Custom Cabinetry Inc .... E 425 235-8366
  Renton *(G-8727)*
Andrews Fixture Company Inc .... F 253 627-7481
  Tacoma *(G-13172)*
Belina Interiors Inc .... D 253 474-0276
  Tacoma *(G-13193)*
Canyon Creek Cabinet Company .... G 509 921-7807
  Spokane Valley *(G-12650)*
Contempo Inc 509 758-1694
  Clarkston *(G-2627)*
Custom Office Design Inc .... F 253 735-8777
  Auburn *(G-420)*
Dogstar Cabinets Inc .... G 509 674-4229
  Cle Elum *(G-2665)*
Douglas L Perry .... G 253 303-0537
  Gig Harbor *(G-4095)*
Elpis Works Inc .... G 206 317-4647
  Everett *(G-3458)*
Family Endurance Corporation .... F 253 872-3900
  Kent *(G-4903)*
Freeze Furniture and Mfg Co .... F 509 924-3545
  Spokane Valley *(G-12710)*
Furniture By Foss .... G 206 783-3626
  Seattle *(G-10040)*
Genothen Holdings LLC .... D 360 352-3636
  Tumwater *(G-13873)*
Interior Environments Inc .... E 206 432-8800
  Seattle *(G-10248)*
Johnnystand .... G 206 412-2982
  Redmond *(G-8520)*
Jpl Habitability Inc .... F 360 377-7660
  Bremerton *(G-1967)*
Ken Boudreau Inc .... D 425 402-8001
  Woodinville *(G-15277)*
Kings Kitchen LLC .... G 253 212-3623
  Tacoma *(G-13376)*
Knoll Inc .... F 206 624-0174
  Seattle *(G-10348)*
Loop Corp .... G 206 499-0679
  Seattle *(G-10440)*
Markay Cabinets Inc .... F 360 779-3443
  Poulsbo *(G-7982)*
Maywood Shops Inc .... F 360 748-9244
  Chehalis *(G-2513)*
Pacific Crest Industries Inc .... C 253 321-3011
  Sumner *(G-13093)*
R T London Company .... G 360 943-5090
  Lacey *(G-5581)*
Seaboard Cabinet Company Inc .... F 425 776-2000
  Lynnwood *(G-6193)*
Smart Office Environments LLC .... G 206 730-8871
  Bellevue *(G-1138)*
Solid Visions Inc .... E 206 949-4203
  Bothell *(G-1907)*
Trevors Wood Working LLC .... G 206 940-8000
  Seattle *(G-11331)*
Wells Ww Millwork LLC .... F 425 405-3252
  Everett *(G-3654)*
Windfall Lumber Inc .... E 360 352-2250
  Tumwater *(G-13906)*

FURNITURE: Outdoor, Wood

Wintran Trading .... G 425 501-7818
  Everett *(G-3660)*

FURNITURE: Picnic Tables Or Benches, Park

Cape Dissapointment State Park .... F 360 642-3078
  Ilwaco *(G-4368)*

FURNITURE: Rockers, Wood, Exc Upholstered

Greg Aanes Furniture Inc .... G 360 733-9101
  Bellingham *(G-1362)*

FURNITURE: School

Bradley Saxton .... G 800 643-3512
  Kent *(G-4821)*
Df Industries Inc .... F 253 472-0422
  Tacoma *(G-13261)*
S2 Proto Types Inc .... G 425 822-0858
  Kirkland *(G-5455)*
Smarte Carte Inc .... G 206 431-0844
  Seatac *(G-9306)*

FURNITURE: Ship

Belina Interiors Inc .... D 253 474-0276
  Tacoma *(G-13193)*
Tri-Way Industries Inc .... D 253 859-4585
  Auburn *(G-582)*
Wilson & Hayes Inc .... G 206 323-6758
  Seattle *(G-11478)*

FURNITURE: Sleep

Americas Sleep Comfort Center .... G 253 548-8890
  Tacoma *(G-13169)*
Wallbeds Northwest Inc .... G 206 256-1700
  Seattle *(G-11433)*

FURNITURE: Storage Chests, Household, Wood

Arrowood Mini Storage .... G 360 769-7400
  Port Orchard *(G-7789)*
Larry Guthrie Co .... G 509 922-6121
  Spokane Valley *(G-12772)*

PRODUCT SECTION

FURNITURE: Studio Couches

Heavenly Mountain Studios .... G 360 437-2298
  Port Hadlock (G-7759)
Laser Reflections .... G 206 818-2940
  Poulsbo (G-7973)
Paradise Studios .... G 360 789-5744
  Kirkland (G-5428)

FURNITURE: Table Tops, Marble

Northwest Granite and MBL LLC .... F 206 228-6881
  Redmond (G-8599)
Seaport Tile & Marble Inc .... E 425 644-7067
  Bellevue (G-1120)

FURNITURE: Tables & Table Tops, Wood

Collectible Creations .... G 360 613-1799
  Bremerton (G-1943)

FURNITURE: Unfinished, Wood

Company K LLC .... G 206 632-0509
  Seattle (G-9723)

FURNITURE: Upholstered

Barbara Bogart .... G 360 385-0815
  Port Townsend (G-7867)
Columbia Furniture Mfg Inc .... F 509 534-7147
  Spokane (G-12190)
Design Craft Upholstery Inc .... G 425 775-7620
  Lynnwood (G-6107)
Ecobalanza LLC .... G 888 220-6020
  Seattle (G-9879)
Empire Upholstery .... G 509 467-5263
  Spokane (G-12247)
Epoch Design LLC .... F 425 284-0880
  Redmond (G-8452)
Freeze Furniture and Mfg Co .... F 509 924-3545
  Spokane Valley (G-12710)
Maywood Shops Inc .... F 360 748-9244
  Chehalis (G-2513)
Style Plus LLC .... E 206 920-9223
  Renton (G-8921)
Wn Inc .... G 509 966-9409
  Yakima (G-15709)

FURNITURE: Vehicle

Tri-Way Industries Inc .... D 253 859-4585
  Auburn (G-582)

FURS, DRESSED, WHOLESALE

Pacific Northwest Jewelers .... G 509 927-8923
  Greenacres (G-4300)

Furs

All Fur One .... G 206 281-8412
  Seattle (G-9379)
Lunas Custom Puppets .... G 360 721-9672
  Battle Ground (G-717)

GAITERS: Rubber Or Rubber Soled Fabric

Outdoor Research LLC .... C 206 467-8197
  Seattle (G-10717)

GAMES & TOYS: Bells

Metal Art Bells .... G 360 546-2018
  Vancouver (G-14414)

GAMES & TOYS: Blocks

OShell Delmont .... G 360 427-9600
  Shelton (G-11719)

GAMES & TOYS: Board Games, Children's & Adults'

Break From Reality Games LLC .... G 513 884-4940
  Seattle (G-9581)
Storybox Studios LLC .... G 206 310-2626
  Mercer Island (G-6486)
T14 Inc .... G 425 829-8213
  Kirkland (G-5474)
Wizards of Coast LLC .... B 425 226-6500
  Renton (G-8949)

GAMES & TOYS: Carriages, Baby

Mamma-Kin LLC .... G 425 922-9505
  Kirkland (G-5395)

GAMES & TOYS: Craft & Hobby Kits & Sets

C & M Country Creations .... G 253 535-3327
  Tacoma (G-13214)
Craft International of Wash .... G 360 785-3606
  Winlock (G-15148)
Family Treasures .... G 206 282-1194
  Seattle (G-9967)
Koehler Enterprise Inc .... G 360 261-0390
  Longview (G-5924)
Ljs Plants & Crafts .... G 253 854-9407
  Kent (G-4998)
Log Cabin Crafts .... G 425 885-9049
  Redmond (G-8537)
Milestone Products Co .... F 425 882-1987
  Redmond (G-8589)
The Creation Station Inc .... G 425 775-7959
  Tulalip (G-13845)
Whitbys Whimsies .... G 206 937-1312
  Seattle (G-11468)

GAMES & TOYS: Dolls, Exc Stuffed Toy Animals

Dolls By Arlene .... G 360 687-4321
  Battle Ground (G-698)
Warriners Originals Inc .... G 509 973-2705
  Prosser (G-8075)

GAMES & TOYS: Electronic

Bungie Inc .... G 425 440-6800
  Bellevue (G-830)
Flowplay Inc .... F 206 903-0457
  Seattle (G-10007)
Griptonite Inc .... C 425 825-6800
  Kirkland (G-5355)
Olive Games Corporation .... G 425 649-1136
  Bellevue (G-1046)
Red Seal Games LLC .... G 425 922-6500
  Seattle (G-10938)
Simplyfun LLC .... E 425 289-0858
  Bellevue (G-1134)
Smad World LLC .... G 253 536-5460
  Tacoma (G-13515)
Universe Builders Inc .... G 206 390-4313
  Seattle (G-11378)

GAMES & TOYS: Game Machines, Exc Coin-Operated

GAEMS Inc .... F 855 754-2367
  Redmond (G-8468)

GAMES & TOYS: Kits, Science, Incl Microscopes/Chemistry Sets

Creative Dimensions .... G 360 733-5024
  Bellingham (G-1310)
Washington Vg Inc .... F 425 823-4518
  Kirkland (G-5492)

GAMES & TOYS: Models, Airplane, Toy & Hobby

Eagle Tree Systems LLC .... G 425 614-0450
  Bellevue (G-886)

GAMES & TOYS: Models, Railroad, Toy & Hobby

Oso Railworks Inc .... G 406 375-7555
  Arlington (G-295)

GAMES & TOYS: Puzzles

Artifactory .... G 360 260-2660
  Brush Prairie (G-2029)
Doug Puzzle .... G 425 647-0464
  Bellevue (G-883)
Exit Puzzles .... G 360 930-9686
  Olympia (G-7280)
Kick Ass Puzzles .... G 425 275-2381
  Lynnwood (G-6150)
Pavel S Puzzles .... G 425 643-0204
  Bellevue (G-1065)
Puzzle Piece Arts .... G 360 678-3687
  Greenbank (G-4309)
Puzzle Pieces Bookkeeping .... G 360 217-7140
  Monroe (G-6609)

GAMES & TOYS: Rocking Horses

Crisman Rocking Horses LLC .... G 206 408-7465
  Vashon (G-14720)
Rocking Horse Barns LLC .... G 360 736-5403
  Centralia (G-2428)
Rocking Horse Rita Cstm Hmes .... G 360 600-1000
  Vancouver (G-14558)

GAMES & TOYS: Scooters, Children's

Jaxjox Inc .... G 425 324-3017
  Vancouver (G-14335)

GAMES & TOYS: Sleds, Children's

Molson Runner Sleds .... G 425 445-2975
  Covington (G-2834)

GAMES & TOYS: Trains & Eqpt, Electric & Mechanical

Republic Locomotive Works .... G 360 577-6479
  Cathlamet (G-2373)

GARAGE DOOR REPAIR SVCS

Jim Lemons Doors & Cabinets .... G 360 871-4001
  Port Orchard (G-7820)

GARBAGE DISPOSERS & COMPACTORS: Commercial

Jerrys Iron Works Inc .... G 425 788-1467
  Duvall (G-2993)
Stanleys Sanitary Service .... G 360 795-3369
  Cathlamet (G-2376)

GAS & OIL FIELD EXPLORATION SVCS

Access US Oil & Gas Inc .... G 206 792-7575
  Lacey (G-5530)
American Petro Envmtl Svcs LLC .... G 253 538-5252
  Puyallup (G-8122)
Blackhawk Synergies Inc .... G 509 627-9726
  Kennewick (G-4632)
Bud Clary Properties LLC .... G 800 899-1926
  Longview (G-5891)
Carbon Cycle Crush LLC .... G 509 476-3667
  Oroville (G-7462)
Empire Creek Exploration Co .... G 509 747-0996
  Spokane (G-12244)
Ground Source Energy Nw .... G 253 852-5926
  Kent (G-4930)
Longshot Oil LLC .... G 509 455-5924
  Spokane (G-12374)
Radial Energy Inc .... G 360 332-0905
  Blaine (G-1700)
Rk Burk Meg Murch Artworks .... G 206 954-1297
  Seattle (G-10967)
Shepp Enterprises LLC .... G 206 697-0327
  Tacoma (G-13512)
Tucker Garner CA .... G 206 236-0856
  Mercer Island (G-6487)
Weyerhaeuser Company .... A 206 539-3000
  Seattle (G-11459)
Xextex Corporation USA .... G 425 392-3848
  Issaquah (G-4490)

GAS & OIL FIELD SVCS, NEC

Diligence Group Oil & Gas Biof .... G 360 892-0745
  Vancouver (G-14180)
Genesis Wellness .... G 425 337-3944
  Everett (G-3494)
Northwest Envmtl Solutions Inc .... G 253 241-6213
  Puyallup (G-8205)
Western Energy Group Inc .... G 253 306-4748
  Puyallup (G-8279)

GAS APPLIANCE REPAIR SVCS

Air Pro Heating & Cooling LLC .... F 360 423-9165
  Longview (G-5884)

GAS STATIONS

Richard Andrews Logging .... G 360 426-1096
  Shelton (G-11725)

Employee Codes: A=Over 500 employees, B=251-500
C=101-250, D=51-100, E=20-50, F=10-19, G=2-9

GAS STATIONS

Sauk Suiattle Indian Tribe Tru.................F....... 360 436-0131
  Darrington (G-2869)

GAS: Refinery

US Oil & Refining Co ....C....... 253 383-1651
  Tacoma (G-13574)

GASES: Acetylene

Norco Inc ....G....... 509 754-3518
  Ephrata (G-3343)

GASES: Carbon Dioxide

Praxair Distribution Inc ....E....... 253 620-1620
  Tacoma (G-13473)
We-Man Vets Golf Inc ....E....... 509 527-4507
  Walla Walla (G-14900)

GASES: Helium

Helium ....G....... 206 650-4822
  Sammamish (G-9216)
Helium Advisors.....................................G....... 425 214-1533
  Bellevue (G-939)
Helium Development LLC ....G....... 360 550-3322
  Port Orchard (G-7813)

GASES: Hydrogen

Air Liquide America LP ....G....... 360 673-1400
  Kalama (G-4491)
Hydrogen 2o2 LLC ....G....... 704 906-3770
  Lake Stevens (G-5646)
Hydrogen Fueled Vehicles ....G....... 425 502-7170
  Bellevue (G-953)
Spokane Hydrogen Hybrids..................G....... 509 443-5919
  Spokane Valley (G-12884)

GASES: Indl

Air Liquide ....G....... 509 793-9590
  Eltopia (G-3261)
Airgas Usa LLC ....G....... 360 293-6171
  Anacortes (G-97)
Airgas Usa LLC ....E....... 253 872-7000
  Kent (G-4766)
Eco Inc ....F....... 206 784-6611
  Seattle (G-9878)
Linde North America Inc ....G....... 360 834-9519
  Camas (G-2264)
Messer LLC ....F....... 509 738-6611
  Vancouver (G-14413)
Norco Inc ....G....... 509 764-5032
  Moses Lake (G-6731)
Praxair Inc ....G....... 425 821-2423
  Kirkland (G-5440)
Praxair Inc ....G....... 360 734-3955
  Bellingham (G-1499)
Praxair Inc ....G....... 206 632-7138
  Seattle (G-10843)
Praxair Inc ....G....... 360 733-0971
  Bellingham (G-1500)
Praxair Inc ....G....... 425 259-0188
  Everett (G-3582)
Praxair Inc ....F....... 360 371-2900
  Ferndale (G-3890)
Praxair Inc ....G....... 206 264-2881
  Seattle (G-10844)
Praxair Distribution Inc ....E....... 360 694-1338
  Vancouver (G-14497)
Praxair Distribution Inc ....G....... 360 504-2086
  Sequim (G-11661)
Rec Silicon Inc ....D....... 509 765-2106
  Moses Lake (G-6741)
Vulcan Global LLC ....G....... 509 528-2000
  Kennewick (G-4743)

GASES: Neon

Neon Labs Inc ....G....... 415 854-8795
  Seattle (G-10599)
Neon Pig LLC ....G....... 509 244-5319
  Airway Heights (G-57)
Neon Taco ....G....... 323 577-3045
  Seattle (G-10600)
Noble Gas Neon Company ....G....... 206 708-6290
  Seattle (G-10615)
Ross Metier LLC...................................G....... 253 208-8777
  Graham (G-4237)
Western Neon Inc.................................G....... 206 682-7738
  Seattle (G-11454)

GASES: Nitrogen

Matheson Tri-Gas Inc ....G....... 253 284-9295
  Fife (G-3969)
Messer LLC ....D....... 360 695-1255
  Vancouver (G-14412)

GASES: Oxygen

Med-Core Services Inc ....G....... 360 455-5425
  Olympia (G-7337)

GASKETS

Bestfitt Gasket Company Inc ....G....... 253 863-9521
  Sumner (G-13056)
Cascade Gasket & Mfg Co Inc ....C....... 253 854-1800
  Kent (G-4841)
True Seals LLC ....G....... 509 385-0300
  Spokane Valley (G-12914)

GASKETS & SEALING DEVICES

Engineered Piping Systems..................G....... 360 225-5302
  Woodland (G-15429)
Jetseal Inc ....E....... 509 467-9133
  Spokane Valley (G-12752)
Seal-Guard Corporation ....G....... 253 833-7080
  Auburn (G-557)

GASOLINE FILLING STATIONS

Chevron Kalama ....F....... 360 673-2972
  Kalama (G-4495)
Conocophillips Company.......................F....... 509 536-8417
  Spokane Valley (G-12663)
Conocophillips Company.......................F....... 253 584-0583
  Lakewood (G-5707)
Wenatchee Petroleum Co......................E....... 509 662-4423
  Wenatchee (G-15084)

GASOLINE WHOLESALERS

Wenatchee Petroleum Co......................E....... 509 662-4423
  Wenatchee (G-15084)

GATES: Ornamental Metal

Automated Equipment Company ....E....... 206 767-9080
  Tukwila (G-13693)

GEARS: Power Transmission, Exc Auto

Aahed Logistics LLC ....G....... 757 395-7063
  Port Orchard (G-7782)
Cascade Indus & Hydraulic LLC...........G....... 509 452-1752
  Union Gap (G-13924)

GEM STONES MINING, NEC: Natural

West Coast Gemstones Inc...................G....... 509 522-4851
  College Place (G-2731)

GENERAL & INDUSTRIAL LOAN INSTITUTIONS

General Electric Company ....G....... 253 351-2200
  Auburn (G-448)

GENERAL MERCHANDISE, NONDURABLE, WHOLESALE

Global Product Mfg Corp ....F....... 425 512-9129
  Everett (G-3501)

GENERATING APPARATUS & PARTS: Electrical

Energy Efficiency Systems Corp...........E....... 360 835-7838
  Washougal (G-14953)

GENERATION EQPT: Electronic

All Systems Integrated Inc ....F....... 253 770-5570
  Puyallup (G-8121)
Alpha Mfg ....G....... 360 794-8573
  Snohomish (G-11874)
Industrial Support Service LLC ....G....... 509 276-5131
  Deer Park (G-2906)
Lift Av LLC ....G....... 425 242-7339
  Renton (G-8843)
Quadrep Northwest Inc ....G....... 425 201-0420
  Bothell (G-1786)

PRODUCT SECTION

Shine Micro Inc ....F....... 360 437-2503
  Port Ludlow (G-7774)
Sinbon Technologies West ....G....... 425 712-8500
  Lynnwood (G-6197)
Specialty Pdts Elec Cnstr LLC ....G....... 425 402-8332
  Woodinville (G-15373)
Stanbury Electrical Engrg LLC ....F....... 206 251-8901
  Woodinville (G-15374)
Wibotic Inc ....G....... 503 484-3930
  Seattle (G-11472)

GENERATOR SETS: Motor

Pacific Power Group LLC ....E....... 360 887-5980
  Ridgefield (G-9099)
Pacific Power Group LLC ....E....... 253 395-9077
  Auburn (G-524)
Pacific Power Group LLC ....D....... 360 887-7400
  Vancouver (G-14469)

GENERATORS: Electric

Nine Mile Power Station ....G....... 509 466-5322
  Nine Mile Falls (G-7080)
Portland Stirling Incorporated ....G....... 206 855-0819
  Bainbridge Island (G-659)

GENERATORS: Electrochemical, Fuel Cell

Kontak LLC ....G....... 425 442-5929
  Redmond (G-8525)
Midnite Solar Inc ....E....... 360 403-7207
  Arlington (G-279)
Plug Power Inc ....G....... 509 228-6638
  Spokane Valley (G-12830)

GENERATORS: Storage Battery Chargers

Kaenaa Corp ....G....... 425 283-3072
  Sammamish (G-9225)

GENERATORS: Vehicles, Gas-Electric Or Oil-Electric

Ecotech Services LLC ....G....... 509 995-5809
  Spokane Valley (G-12689)

GIFT SHOP

Community Networkers LLC................G....... 509 826-5154
  OMAK (G-7437)
Diamond Store Inc ....G....... 253 272-3377
  Tacoma (G-13262)
Gingerbread Factory ....G....... 509 548-6592
  Leavenworth (G-5803)
Highway Shoppers.................................G....... 360 494-7641
  Packwood (G-7543)
Hogue Cellars Ltd ....D....... 509 786-4557
  Prosser (G-8042)
Inspired ....G....... 360 504-2590
  Port Angeles (G-7713)
Jans Ceramics ....G....... 360 425-3540
  Longview (G-5920)
Klein Joanne Klein Kevin ....G....... 360 435-8615
  Arlington (G-268)
Kusina Fillipina ....G....... 206 322-9433
  Seattle (G-10365)
Lavender Heart Ltd ....G....... 206 568-4441
  Seattle (G-10384)
Lighthouse Envmtl Programs................G....... 360 579-4489
  Coupeville (G-2814)
Paper Delights ....G....... 206 547-1002
  Seattle (G-10748)
Seabear Company.................................E....... 360 293-4661
  Anacortes (G-165)
Ship To Shore Inc ....G....... 206 284-0406
  Seattle (G-11101)
Spokane Discount and Brass Co ....G....... 509 467-8063
  Spokane (G-12517)
Vavako Fine Chocolates.......................G....... 425 453-4553
  Bellevue (G-1212)
Village Frame & Gallery ....G....... 206 824-3068
  Des Moines (G-2950)

GIFT WRAPPING SVCS

Pickle Papers..G....... 509 665-8661
  Wenatchee (G-15064)

PRODUCT SECTION

GLASS: Flat

GIFT, NOVELTY & SOUVENIR STORES: Artcraft & carvings
- Artists Edge Inc .... G 360 779-2337
  Poulsbo *(G-7945)*
- Artists Edge Inc .... G 360 698-3113
  Silverdale *(G-11826)*

GIFT, NOVELTY & SOUVENIR STORES: Gift Baskets
- Canter-Berry Farms .... G 253 939-2706
  Auburn *(G-400)*
- Christmas Forest .... E 360 245-3202
  Curtis *(G-2848)*

GIFT, NOVELTY & SOUVENIR STORES: Gifts & Novelties
- Olde English Crackers Inc .... G 360 715-2972
  Bellingham *(G-1478)*

GIFT, NOVELTY & SOUVENIR STORES: Party Favors
- Party City Corporation .... F 206 575-0502
  Tukwila *(G-13790)*

GIFTS & NOVELTIES: Wholesalers
- Alex Daisley .... G 206 623-5555
  Seattle *(G-9373)*
- Debbie Mumm Inc .... G 509 939-1479
  Spokane *(G-12221)*
- Kolibaba and Associates .... G 253 752-0368
  Tacoma *(G-13378)*
- Play Visions Inc .... E 425 482-2836
  Woodinville *(G-15335)*
- Skyflight Inc .... G 425 844-9199
  Woodinville *(G-15366)*

GIFTWARE: Brass
- Universal Brass Inc .... F 253 939-8282
  Auburn *(G-589)*

GLASS & GLASS CERAMIC PRDTS, PRESSED OR BLOWN: Tableware
- Karen Nichols .... G 360 497-2778
  Randle *(G-8326)*

GLASS FABRICATORS
- Bedrock Industries Inc .... F 206 283-7625
  Seattle *(G-9508)*
- Cardinal Corp .... G 360 242-4400
  Chehalis *(G-2478)*
- Cardinal Glass Industries Inc .... D 360 956-9002
  Tumwater *(G-13858)*
- Cardinal Tg .... F 360 242-4352
  Chehalis *(G-2480)*
- Central Glass Works .... G 360 623-1099
  Centralia *(G-2388)*
- Denny Park Glass Studio LLC .... F 206 388-5725
  Seattle *(G-9823)*
- Evergreen House Inc .... G 425 821-1005
  Kirkland *(G-5334)*
- Fibres International Inc .... E 425 455-9811
  Everett *(G-3472)*
- Fibres International Inc .... D 425 455-9811
  Everett *(G-3471)*
- Gary L Jordanger .... G 425 271-2617
  Renton *(G-8805)*
- Guy Sunglass .... G 509 489-2963
  Deer Park *(G-2904)*
- M7m Investments .... G 253 922-2030
  Fife *(G-3967)*
- Milestone Products Co .... F 425 882-1987
  Redmond *(G-8589)*
- National Glass Industries Inc .... E 425 488-8126
  Woodinville *(G-15319)*
- Northwestern Industries Inc .... E 206 285-3140
  Seattle *(G-10653)*
- Opal Art Glass .... G 360 532-9268
  Cosmopolis *(G-2801)*
- Rogue Empire Inc .... F 253 857-5300
  Gig Harbor *(G-4156)*
- Steel Encounters Inc .... F 206 281-8500
  Seattle *(G-11186)*
- Trivitro Corporation .... F 425 251-8340
  Seattle *(G-11339)*
- Unique Art Glass LLC .... G 425 467-5599
  Bellevue *(G-1207)*

GLASS PRDTS, FROM PURCHASED GLASS: Art
- Batho Studios .... G 503 282-1460
  Vashon *(G-14712)*
- David Wight Glass Art Inc .... G 360 389-2844
  Bellingham *(G-1319)*
- Maslach Art Glass A Corp .... G 206 842-9212
  Seattle *(G-11528)*
- Morrison Art Glass Inc .... G 360 714-8732
  Bellingham *(G-1443)*

GLASS PRDTS, FROM PURCHASED GLASS: Glassware
- Debbie Zachary .... G 253 848-5011
  Puyallup *(G-8141)*
- Sandcastle Sandblasting .... G 360 354-5087
  Lynden *(G-6052)*

GLASS PRDTS, FROM PURCHASED GLASS: Insulating
- Cardinal Glass Industries Inc .... C 360 242-4336
  Winlock *(G-15147)*
- Sound Glass Sales Inc .... D 253 473-7477
  Tacoma *(G-13518)*

GLASS PRDTS, PRESSED OR BLOWN: Bulbs, Electric Lights
- Issaquah Lanscaping Inc .... G 425 392-6123
  Issaquah *(G-4430)*

GLASS PRDTS, PRESSED OR BLOWN: Glass Fibers, Textile
- Comptex Inc .... F 360 466-5453
  La Conner *(G-5522)*
- Mid Mountain Materials Inc .... E 206 762-7600
  Seattle *(G-10539)*

GLASS PRDTS, PRESSED OR BLOWN: Glassware, Art Or Decorative
- Chihuly Inc .... C 206 781-8707
  Seattle *(G-9675)*
- Fantasy Glass Works Inc .... G 425 557-6642
  Issaquah *(G-4412)*
- Glasshouse Studio .... G 206 682-9939
  Seattle *(G-10079)*
- Gribskov Glassblowing .... G 360 795-8419
  Skamokawa *(G-11865)*
- Hot Glass Color & Supply .... G 206 448-1199
  Seattle *(G-10183)*
- Idea Company .... G 253 891-8140
  Pacific *(G-7530)*
- Trimlite LLC .... E 425 251-8685
  Renton *(G-8930)*
- Trimlite Seattle Inc .... E 425 251-8685
  Renton *(G-8931)*

GLASS PRDTS, PRESSED OR BLOWN: Glassware, Novelty
- Seattle Glassblowing Studio .... E 206 448-2181
  Seattle *(G-11059)*

GLASS PRDTS, PRESSED OR BLOWN: Optical
- Veteran Awards Inc .... G 360 925-6019
  Lake Stevens *(G-5673)*

GLASS PRDTS, PRESSED OR BLOWN: Ornaments, Christmas Tree
- Far Star Products .... G 360 604-0080
  Vancouver *(G-14222)*
- Rauch Industries Inc .... F 800 717-2356
  Seattle *(G-10925)*

GLASS PRDTS, PRESSED OR BLOWN: Vases
- Often On Glass .... G 206 725-5306
  Seattle *(G-10687)*
- Signature Vase .... G 253 951-3357
  Lacey *(G-5588)*

GLASS PRDTS, PRESSED/BLOWN: Glassware, Art, Decor/Novelty
- Maslach Art Glass A Corp .... G 206 842-9212
  Seattle *(G-11528)*
- R & B Art Glass .... G 206 323-6430
  Seattle *(G-10909)*
- Totally Blown Glassworks Inc .... G 206 768-8944
  Seattle *(G-11321)*

GLASS PRDTS, PRESSED/BLOWN: Lenses, Lantern, Flshlght, Etc
- Momentum Interactive LLC .... G 915 203-5349
  Bellingham *(G-1440)*

GLASS PRDTS, PURCHSD GLASS: Ornamental, Cut, Engraved/Décor
- Bancheros Glass and Etching .... G 253 854-4877
  Kent *(G-4807)*
- Blackwaters Metal .... G 425 213-0154
  Port Orchard *(G-7795)*
- Veteran Awards Inc .... G 360 925-6019
  Lake Stevens *(G-5673)*

GLASS STORE: Leaded Or Stained
- Covenant Art Glass Inc .... G 425 252-4232
  Everett *(G-3429)*
- Expressions Glass II .... G 206 242-2860
  Burien *(G-2106)*

GLASS STORES
- Fantasy Glass Works Inc .... G 425 557-6642
  Issaquah *(G-4412)*
- Oldcastle Buildingenvelope Inc .... D 360 816-7777
  Battle Ground *(G-725)*
- Sound Glass Sales Inc .... D 253 473-7477
  Tacoma *(G-13518)*
- Sumner Stained Glass Company .... G 360 378-2761
  Friday Harbor *(G-4061)*
- Tri-City Glass Inc .... G 509 586-0454
  Kennewick *(G-4738)*

GLASS: Fiber
- Absolute Concreteworks LLC .... G 360 297-5055
  Port Townsend *(G-7859)*
- Composite Aquatic Innovations .... F 360 403-7707
  Arlington *(G-221)*
- Composites Consolidation Compa .... G 509 877-2228
  Wapato *(G-14914)*
- Composites Consolidation LLC .... G 509 877-2228
  Wapato *(G-14915)*
- McClarin Plastics LLC .... B 509 877-5950
  Wapato *(G-14919)*
- Pacific Interconnection LLC .... G 425 277-9527
  Renton *(G-8872)*
- Pyrotek Incorporated .... D 509 926-6211
  Spokane Valley *(G-12846)*

GLASS: Flat
- Cardinal Glass Industries Inc .... C 360 242-4300
  Winlock *(G-15146)*
- Cardinal Glass Industries Inc .... D 360 242-4400
  Chehalis *(G-2479)*
- Cardinal Glass Industries Inc .... C 360 242-4336
  Winlock *(G-15147)*
- Gaffer Glass USA Limited .... E 253 395-3361
  Kent *(G-4921)*
- Pilkington North America Inc .... C 509 534-4899
  Spokane *(G-12442)*
- Pilkington North America Inc .... F 425 438-8442
  Everett *(G-3573)*
- Sumner Stained Glass Company .... G 360 378-2761
  Friday Harbor *(G-4061)*
- Tacoma Glass Manufacturing Inc .... E 253 581-7679
  Lakewood *(G-5760)*

Employee Codes: A=Over 500 employees, B=251-500
C=101-250, D=51-100, E=20-50, F=10-19, G=2-9

GLASS: Insulating

Hy-Grade Glass Inc.................................F 509 248-9919
  Union Gap *(G-13932)*
IW International Inc.............................E 509 735-8411
  Kennewick *(G-4679)*

GLASS: Leaded

Annapurna Glass & Wood Inc..............G 206 525-0777
  Seattle *(G-9404)*

GLASS: Plate

Glasshape North America LP..............G 206 538-5416
  Friday Harbor *(G-4048)*

GLASS: Pressed & Blown, NEC

Benjamin Moore Inc..............................G 206 329-8607
  Seattle *(G-9513)*
Blowing Sands.......................................G 206 783-5314
  Seattle *(G-9545)*
Connectzonecom LLC............................E 425 212-4400
  Lynnwood *(G-6097)*
Cq2 Enterprises.....................................G 253 941-4488
  Federal Way *(G-3726)*
Cultus Bay Tiles Inc..............................G 360 579-3079
  Clinton *(G-2687)*
Frantz Glass Gallery.............................F 360 426-6712
  Shelton *(G-11697)*
M-Space Inc..G 253 779-0101
  Seattle *(G-10457)*
Martin Blank Studios...........................F 206 621-9733
  Seattle *(G-10493)*
Oak Bros Curved Glass........................G 253 752-4055
  Olympia *(G-7349)*
Richards Packaging Inc......................G 509 545-8690
  Pasco *(G-7623)*
Sculptures In Glass............................G 509 951-3615
  Chattaroy *(G-2452)*
Seattle Creative Brands Inc...............G 206 782-6548
  Seattle *(G-11053)*
Stempel Art and Industry LLC..........G 206 718-6562
  Seattle *(G-11191)*
Tacoma Glass Blowing Studio...........G 253 383-3499
  Tacoma *(G-13543)*
Walman Optical Company...................E 253 872-7137
  Kent *(G-5205)*

GLASS: Stained

Charles Parriott...................................G 206 725-1765
  Seattle *(G-9668)*
Covenant Art Glass Inc......................G 425 252-4232
  Everett *(G-3429)*
Eidos Stained Glass............................G 360 468-3577
  Lopez Island *(G-5982)*
Expressions Glass II............................G 206 242-2860
  Burien *(G-2106)*
Hexen Glass Studio LLC.....................G 360 807-4217
  Centralia *(G-2406)*
Perry Stained Glass Studio................G 425 392-1600
  Issaquah *(G-4459)*
Windowscape Designs.........................G 360 468-3510
  Lopez Island *(G-5989)*

GLASS: Tempered

Oldcastle Buildingenvelope Inc...........D 360 816-7777
  Battle Ground *(G-725)*

GLASSWARE STORES

D A Graphics Inc..................................G 206 760-5886
  Seattle *(G-9777)*
Glasshouse Studio................................G 206 682-9939
  Seattle *(G-10079)*

GLASSWARE WHOLESALERS

Richards Packaging Inc......................G 509 545-8690
  Pasco *(G-7623)*

GLASSWARE, NOVELTY, WHOLESALE

Totally Blown Glassworks Inc.............G 206 768-8944
  Seattle *(G-11321)*

GLASSWARE: Cut & Engraved

Crystal Barone......................................G 206 621-7810
  Seattle *(G-9760)*

GLASSWARE: Laboratory

Matsunami Glass USA Inc....................G 360 302-5575
  Bellingham *(G-1427)*

GLOBAL POSITIONING SYSTEMS & EQPT

Stoothoff Aerospace Inc........................G 360 595-0314
  Deming *(G-2924)*

GLOBES, GEOGRAPHICAL

Orbis Company LLC................................G 360 376-4320
  Eastsound *(G-3041)*

GLOVES: Fabric

Blackbirds Nest.....................................G 509 946-1978
  Richland *(G-8974)*
Churchill N Mfg Co Inc........................F 360 736-9923
  Centralia *(G-2393)*
Danalco Inc...E 626 303-4019
  Seattle *(G-9790)*
Neetas Creations.................................G 585 233-1896
  Bellevue *(G-1024)*

GLOVES: Leather

Oregon Glove Company........................G 253 475-6733
  Tacoma *(G-13446)*

GLOVES: Leather, Work

Churchill N Mfg Co Inc........................F 360 736-9923
  Centralia *(G-2393)*
Darbonnier Tactical Supply LLC........G 360 672-0216
  Oak Harbor *(G-7146)*
North Star Glove Company..................E 253 627-7107
  Tacoma *(G-13429)*

GLOVES: Safety

Amerisafe Inc..G 360 943-5634
  Tumwater *(G-13852)*

GLOVES: Work

Brooks Tactical Systems......................F 253 549-2703
  Fox Island *(G-4019)*
Maulcor Inc...G 773 696-2783
  Seattle *(G-10502)*
North Star Glove Company..................E 253 627-7107
  Tacoma *(G-13429)*
Outdoor Research LLC.........................C 206 467-8197
  Seattle *(G-10717)*

GLYCERIN

Whole Energy Fuels Corporation..........G 888 600-8611
  Mount Vernon *(G-6855)*

GOLD ORE MINING

American Cordillera Min Corp............G 509 671-9401
  Spokane *(G-12109)*
Bazooka Gold Mining Co LLC.............G 360 202-5953
  Mount Vernon *(G-6776)*
Boulder Gold LLC.................................G 425 308-4316
  Everett *(G-3399)*
Diversified Development Co................G 360 734-1480
  Bellingham *(G-1324)*
Gold Reserve Inc..................................G 509 623-1500
  Spokane *(G-12276)*
Josephine Mining Corp........................G 509 343-3193
  Spokane *(G-12342)*
Kinross Gold Usa Inc..........................C 509 775-3157
  Republic *(G-8959)*
Lka Gold Incorporated........................G 253 514-6661
  Gig Harbor *(G-4133)*
Lovitt Resources Inc............................G 509 668-8170
  Wenatchee *(G-15047)*

GOLD ORES

3dx Industries Inc................................G 360 244-4339
  Ferndale *(G-3808)*
Alto Group Holdings Inc.....................G 801 816-2520
  Wenatchee *(G-15088)*
Goldrich Mining Company...................F 509 535-7367
  Spokane *(G-12277)*
Great Basin Energies Inc....................G 509 623-1500
  Spokane *(G-12280)*
Rondys Inc..G 425 392-6324
  Issaquah *(G-4470)*

Timbers At Towncenter........................G 360 433-9627
  Vancouver *(G-14639)*

GOLD ORES PROCESSING

Walker Goldsmiths...............................G 360 758-2601
  Bellingham *(G-1588)*

GOLD STAMPING, EXC BOOKS

Ramax Printing and Awards...............G 509 928-1222
  Spokane *(G-12467)*

GOLF CARTS: Powered

Pacer Design & Manufacturing..........F 425 481-5300
  Bothell *(G-1883)*

GOLF CLUB & EQPT REPAIR SVCS

Par 4 Golf Services...............................G 360 376-4462
  Eastsound *(G-3045)*

GOLF COURSES: Public

Caitac USA Corp...................................B 360 671-1700
  Bellingham *(G-1287)*
We-Man Vets Golf Inc...........................E 509 527-4507
  Walla Walla *(G-14900)*

GOLF EQPT

Direct Hit Golf Flags LLC....................G 253 946-6263
  Federal Way *(G-3729)*
Etsoutdoors...G 509 481-3938
  Nine Mile Falls *(G-7073)*
Golfco International Inc......................G 425 861-7755
  Redmond *(G-8480)*
Omega Pacific Inc................................D 509 456-0170
  Airway Heights *(G-58)*
Redbird Sports Inc..............................F 206 725-7872
  Seattle *(G-10939)*

GOLF GOODS & EQPT

We-Man Vets Golf Inc...........................E 509 527-4507
  Walla Walla *(G-14900)*

GOURMET FOOD STORES

Ayurveg Inc...G 360 863-2457
  Gold Bar *(G-4186)*
La Mexicana Inc...................................E 206 763-1488
  Seattle *(G-10368)*

GOVERNMENT, EXECUTIVE OFFICES: City & Town Managers' Offices

City of Yakima.......................................G 509 575-6177
  Yakima *(G-15532)*

GOVERNMENT, GENERAL: Administration

County of King......................................E 206 263-3113
  Seattle *(G-9748)*
Printing Washington State Dept.........G 360 407-6013
  Lacey *(G-5578)*

GRAIN & FIELD BEANS WHOLESALERS

Cascade Organic Flour LLC................F 509 855-7450
  Royal City *(G-9168)*

GRANITE: Crushed & Broken

Alan Good..F 360 864-2974
  Toledo *(G-13635)*

GRANITE: Cut & Shaped

Absolute GM LLC..................................E 425 814-1011
  Kirkland *(G-5267)*
Ddbd Construction..............................G 253 576-6769
  Bonney Lake *(G-1721)*
Debroeck Solid Surface Inc................G 509 525-1349
  Walla Walla *(G-14794)*
Dudley Family Group Inc....................G 253 863-9282
  Pacific *(G-7525)*
Homchick Michael Stone Work...........E 425 481-2783
  Kenmore *(G-4582)*
J R Stone Services................................G 425 227-8513
  Renton *(G-8831)*
Kaes Enterprises LLC...........................E 800 252-5237
  Puyallup *(G-8171)*

PRODUCT SECTION

GUTTERS

Marmo E Granito Inc ....G...... 206 368-0990
  Shoreline *(G-11785)*
Norhtwest Stone Pros ....G...... 206 824-2458
  Kent *(G-5025)*
Precision Waterjet Inc ....G...... 509 888-7954
  Wenatchee *(G-15065)*
Stone Craft LLC ....G...... 206 762-3920
  Seattle *(G-11198)*

GRANITE: Dimension

Cadman Holding Company Inc ....G...... 425 868-1234
  Redmond *(G-8415)*
Columbia Granite LLC ....G...... 360 943-4072
  Olympia *(G-7253)*

GRAPHIC ARTS & RELATED DESIGN SVCS

Advertising Services Intl LLC ....G...... 206 623-6963
  Seattle *(G-9356)*
Copy Cat Graphics ....G...... 360 452-3635
  Port Angeles *(G-7695)*
Designs Unlimited ....G...... 360 792-1372
  Port Orchard *(G-7802)*
Digital Impressions Inc ....G...... 206 443-1234
  Seattle *(G-9828)*
Eagle Printing Inc ....G...... 509 943-2611
  Richland *(G-8991)*
Garjen Corp ....G...... 253 862-6140
  Bonney Lake *(G-1724)*
Graphic Advertising Svcs Inc ....F...... 425 688-9980
  Richland *(G-9003)*
Graphics Place Inc ....F...... 425 486-3323
  Woodinville *(G-15255)*
I-5 Design Build Inc ....D...... 360 459-3200
  Lacey *(G-5558)*
In Graphic Detail LLC ....G...... 360 582-0002
  Sequim *(G-11641)*
Industrial Screenprint Inc ....G...... 253 735-5111
  Kent *(G-4951)*
Inland Saxum Printing LLC ....G...... 509 525-0467
  Walla Walla *(G-14823)*
J N W Inc ....E...... 509 489-9191
  Spokane *(G-12327)*
Marshall Marketing Group Inc ....E...... 253 473-0765
  Tacoma *(G-13400)*
Mary Fleming ....G...... 206 246-4871
  Tukwila *(G-13768)*
Mustang Signs LLC ....F...... 509 735-4607
  Kennewick *(G-4698)*
Pacific Printing Inc ....G...... 360 377-0844
  Bremerton *(G-1984)*
Primal Screens LLC ....G...... 206 784-5266
  Seattle *(G-10859)*
Record Printing Inc ....F...... 509 964-9500
  Thorp *(G-13629)*
Reyna Moore Advertising ....G...... 503 230-9440
  Vancouver *(G-14550)*
Ridgeline Graphics Inc ....G...... 509 662-6858
  Wenatchee *(G-15069)*
Ron Hall ....G...... 360 468-2294
  Lopez Island *(G-5986)*
Stat Corporation ....F...... 425 883-4181
  Redmond *(G-8681)*
Whidbey Island Sign Sltons LLC ....G...... 360 299-0430
  Burlington *(G-2201)*
Wild Horse Graphics ....G...... 425 413-5080
  Maple Valley *(G-6300)*

GRAPHIC LAYOUT SVCS: Printed Circuitry

Helldyne Inc ....G...... 206 855-1227
  Bainbridge Island *(G-638)*

GRATINGS: Open Steel Flooring

Grating Pacific LLC ....G...... 253 872-7733
  Kent *(G-4926)*

GRATINGS: Tread, Fabricated Metal

Grating Fabricators Inc ....F...... 360 696-0886
  Vancouver *(G-14164)*

GRAVE MARKERS: Concrete

Murdock Roach Inc ....G...... 509 302-1054
  Kennewick *(G-4697)*
Pioneer Rock & Monument LLC ....G...... 509 773-4702
  Goldendale *(G-4206)*

GRAVEL & PEBBLE MINING

Bishop-Red Rock Inc ....G...... 509 773-5335
  Goldendale *(G-4193)*
James A Wright Cnstr LLC ....G...... 509 996-3249
  Winthrop *(G-15162)*
Konen Rock Crushing Inc ....G...... 509 382-2768
  Dayton *(G-2883)*

GRAVEL MINING

Beans & Rocks LLC ....F...... 360 942-5414
  Raymond *(G-8343)*
Burns Construction Inc ....G...... 360 957-4183
  Cathlamet *(G-2361)*
Cadman Holding Company Inc ....G...... 425 868-1234
  Redmond *(G-8415)*
Cowden Inc ....D...... 360 592-4200
  Bellingham *(G-1309)*
Doris J Johnson ....G...... 509 586-3646
  Kennewick *(G-4656)*
Jensen Barton W Inc ....F...... 360 825-3750
  Enumclaw *(G-3297)*
Krieg Concrete Products Inc ....F...... 360 675-2727
  Oak Harbor *(G-7156)*
O L Luther Co ....G...... 509 837-2527
  Granger *(G-4262)*

GREASES & INEDIBLE FATS, RENDERED

Darling Ingredients Inc ....E...... 253 572-3922
  Tacoma *(G-13254)*
Rainier Ranch Inc ....G...... 206 243-2044
  Burien *(G-2123)*

GREENHOUSES: Prefabricated Metal

Evergreen House Inc ....F...... 425 821-1005
  Kirkland *(G-5334)*

GREETING CARD SHOPS

Potluck Press LLC ....G...... 206 328-1300
  Seattle *(G-10838)*
Purpletrail ....G...... 425 292-1811
  Issaquah *(G-4463)*

GRENADES: Grenades, Hand

Fire Solutions NW LLC ....G...... 855 876-3473
  Bremerton *(G-1954)*

GRILLES & REGISTERS: Ornamental Metal Work

Home Builders Service Company ....F...... 509 747-1206
  Spokane *(G-12296)*
Ornamental Iron Specialists ....G...... 253 630-0328
  Kent *(G-5047)*
Shoemaker Manufacturing Co ....D...... 509 674-4414
  Cle Elum *(G-2679)*

GRINDING BALLS: Ceramic

Lapel Solutions LLC ....F...... 360 597-4958
  Vancouver *(G-14358)*

GRINDING SVC: Precision, Commercial Or Indl

Blackies Grinding Service Inc ....G...... 253 735-1835
  Auburn *(G-394)*
Marketech International Inc ....F...... 360 379-6707
  Sequim *(G-11647)*

GRINDING SVCS: Ophthalmic Lens, Exc Prescription

Capitol Optical Corp ....E...... 360 352-7502
  Lacey *(G-5538)*

GRIPS OR HANDLES: Rubber

Grab On Grips LLC ....F...... 509 529-9800
  Walla Walla *(G-14814)*

GRITS: Crushed & Broken

Amery Rock & Construction Inc ....G...... 509 365-4122
  Lyle *(G-5994)*

GROCERIES WHOLESALERS, NEC

A & W Bottling Company Inc ....E...... 425 355-0100
  Everett *(G-3353)*
Au Gavroche Inc ....G...... 206 284-8770
  Seattle *(G-9461)*
Diamond Knot Brewery Inc ....G...... 425 355-4488
  Mukilteo *(G-6911)*
Go Manna Inc ....G...... 360 794-7480
  Snohomish *(G-11914)*
Golden State Foods Corp ....G...... 509 928-9055
  Spokane Valley *(G-12722)*
Mutiny Bay Blues LLC ....G...... 360 678-4315
  Freeland *(G-4033)*
Natures Path Foods USA Inc ....D...... 360 603-7200
  Blaine *(G-1687)*
Norstar Specialty Foods Inc ....E...... 206 764-4499
  Kent *(G-5026)*
Phoenix Processor Ltd Partnr ....C...... 206 286-8584
  Seattle *(G-10796)*
Port Townsend Brewing Co ....G...... 360 385-9967
  Port Townsend *(G-7908)*
Schwartz Brothers Restaurants ....C...... 206 623-3134
  Renton *(G-8906)*
Scuttlebutt Brewing Co LLC ....F...... 425 252-2829
  Everett *(G-3606)*
Swire Pacific Holdings Inc ....E...... 509 529-0753
  Walla Walla *(G-14875)*
Walton Beverage Co ....C...... 360 380-1660
  Ferndale *(G-3922)*
Washington Potato Company Inc ....D...... 509 349-8803
  Warden *(G-14938)*

GROCERIES, GENERAL LINE WHOLESALERS

Boyd Coffee Company ....G...... 425 744-1394
  Lynnwood *(G-6085)*
Farmer Bros Co ....E...... 425 881-7030
  Redmond *(G-8459)*
Global Harvest Foods Ltd ....G...... 206 957-1350
  Tukwila *(G-13741)*
Golden State Foods Corp ....G...... 509 928-9055
  Spokane Valley *(G-12722)*

GUARD SVCS

Oatridge-Evergreen 8a2 JV LLC ....G...... 253 627-3794
  Tacoma *(G-13439)*

GUIDED MISSILES & SPACE VEHICLES

Boeing Company ....A...... 425 865-3311
  Bellevue *(G-824)*
Bspace Corporation ....G...... 208 559-7806
  Seattle *(G-9591)*
Kurtisfactor LLC ....G...... 208 863-6180
  Tacoma *(G-13379)*

GUIDED MISSILES & SPACE VEHICLES: Research & Development

Northrop Grumman Systems Corp ....E...... 360 315-3976
  Silverdale *(G-11852)*
Spaceflight Industries Inc ....E...... 206 342-9934
  Seattle *(G-11165)*

GUM & WOOD CHEMICALS

Arch Wood Protection Inc ....G...... 360 673-5099
  Kalama *(G-4492)*
Chemco Acquisition Corporation ....E...... 360 366-3500
  Ferndale *(G-3830)*

GUN STOCKS: Wood

Dem-Bart Checkering Tools Inc ....G...... 360 568-7356
  Snohomish *(G-11897)*

GUN SVCS

Bowlbys Sporting Goods ....G...... 509 248-8281
  Yakima *(G-15524)*

GUNSMITHS

Aro-Tek Ltd ....G...... 360 754-2770
  Olympia *(G-7230)*

GUTTERS

Gutters Inc ....G...... 425 482-2679
  Bothell *(G-1863)*

Employee Codes: A=Over 500 employees, B=251-500
C=101-250, D=51-100, E=20-50, F=10-19, G=2-9

GUTTERS: Sheet Metal

GUTTERS: Sheet Metal
5-Star Enterprises Inc .... G 360 577-0829
   Kelso *(G-4515)*
J & E Jensen Inc .... G 253 851-2282
   Bremerton *(G-1963)*
Ode Products LLC .... G 253 859-7902
   Sumner *(G-13090)*
Palouse Gutters and Cnstr LLC .... G 509 397-0404
   Colfax *(G-2719)*
Precision Fabricators LLC .... G 206 362-1195
   Seattle *(G-10850)*

GYPSUM PRDTS
Certainteed Gypsum Inc .... D 425 291-9099
   Kent *(G-4850)*
New West Gypsum Inc .... F 253 380-1079
   Kent *(G-5021)*
United States Gypsum Company .... E 253 931-6600
   Auburn *(G-588)*

HAIR & HAIR BASED PRDTS
AVI Marie Hair Collection LLC .... G 425 409-9924
   Renton *(G-8749)*
Qr Industries Inc .... G 360 435-2840
   Arlington *(G-310)*

HAIR ACCESS WHOLESALERS
Creative Collections Co Inc .... E 360 866-8840
   Olympia *(G-7259)*

HAIR ACCESS: Rubber
Creative Collections Co Inc .... E 360 866-8840
   Olympia *(G-7259)*

HAIR CARE PRDTS
Beyond Zone Inc .... G 206 363-2147
   Shoreline *(G-11761)*
Innovative Salon Products Inc .... G 360 805-0794
   Monroe *(G-6580)*
J King Formulas Inc .... G 360 683-6908
   Sequim *(G-11642)*

HAIR DRESSING, FOR THE TRADE
Beigeblond Inc .... G 360 693-3283
   Vancouver *(G-14060)*

HAIR REPLACEMENT & WEAVING SVCS
AVI Marie Hair Collection LLC .... G 425 409-9924
   Renton *(G-8749)*

HAIRBRUSHES, WHOLESALE
Creative Collections Co Inc .... E 360 866-8840
   Olympia *(G-7259)*

HAIRDRESSERS
Artistic Talents Styling Salon .... G 360 456-0100
   Lacey *(G-5533)*

HAND TOOLS, NEC: Wholesalers
Center Electric Inc .... F 253 383-4416
   Tacoma *(G-13231)*
Kestrel Tool .... G 360 468-2103
   Lopez Island *(G-5984)*
Pacific Coatings Inc .... F 206 722-1413
   Seattle *(G-10730)*
Power Equipment Supply Llc .... G 206 817-5627
   Everett *(G-3580)*

HANDBAGS
Domino Fashion LLC .... G 425 646-0500
   Bellevue *(G-879)*

HANDBAGS: Women's
Alchemy Goods LLC .... G 206 484-9469
   Seattle *(G-9370)*
Colour Coach .... G 206 478-6159
   Everett *(G-3423)*
Proshoppers NW .... G 206 852-1127
   Seatac *(G-9300)*
Tapestry Inc .... G 206 729-5908
   Seattle *(G-11268)*

HANDLES: Brush Or Tool, Plastic
Taphandles LLC .... E 206 462-6800
   Seattle *(G-11269)*

HANDLES: Wood
Taphandles LLC .... E 206 462-6800
   Seattle *(G-11269)*

HANG GLIDERS
Hang Gliding Adventures .... G 360 357-1460
   Tumwater *(G-13875)*

HANGERS: Garment, Home & Store, Wooden
Garden Expressions .... G 360 403-9532
   Arlington *(G-239)*

HARDWARE
Bainbridge Manufacturing Inc .... E 800 255-4702
   Waterville *(G-15004)*
Bridgestone Hosepower LLC .... E 206 767-4670
   Seattle *(G-9585)*
Broomflds Wldg Met Fabrication .... G 206 784-9267
   Seattle *(G-9589)*
Conestoga Wood Spc Corp .... G 253 437-1320
   Kent *(G-4863)*
Department Crrctons Wash State .... B 509 526-6375
   Walla Walla *(G-14795)*
Dooley Enterprises LLC .... G 303 619-7101
   Bothell *(G-1847)*
Doug & June Holt .... G 425 228-6067
   Newcastle *(G-7028)*
Electroimpact Inc .... D 425 348-8090
   Mukilteo *(G-6920)*
Empire Rubber & Supply Co .... F 509 547-0026
   Pasco *(G-7579)*
Kaisers Welding & Mfg .... G 509 738-6855
   Kettle Falls *(G-5233)*
Markey Machinery Co Inc .... F 206 763-0383
   Seattle *(G-10490)*
Mitchell Hardware W Linn Inc .... G 253 752-2000
   Tacoma *(G-13416)*
Monroe Machined Products Inc .... E 206 242-4898
   Seatac *(G-9291)*
North Industries Inc .... G 206 940-0842
   Seattle *(G-10624)*
Pacific Coast Marine Inds Inc .... D 425 743-9550
   Lynnwood *(G-6177)*
Paxton Sales Corporation .... F 509 453-0397
   Yakima *(G-15642)*
Pcs Mill Work Inc .... G 425 820-5688
   Kirkland *(G-5431)*
Proctor International LLC .... G 425 881-7000
   Redmond *(G-8633)*
R G Rollin Co .... G 253 274-0882
   Tacoma *(G-13487)*
Rads Auto .... G 509 965-5712
   Yakima *(G-15659)*
Stone Masters Inc .... G 509 667-8833
   Wenatchee *(G-15077)*
Tethers Unlimited Inc .... G 425 486-0100
   Bothell *(G-1800)*
Titus Tool Company Inc .... F 206 447-1489
   Bellevue *(G-1192)*
Tri-Way Industries Inc .... D 253 859-4585
   Auburn *(G-582)*
Triad Products Corporation .... G 425 514-8363
   Everett *(G-3636)*
Washington Chain & Supply Inc .... E 206 623-8500
   Seattle *(G-11438)*
Zephyrwerks .... G 360 385-2720
   Port Townsend *(G-7939)*

HARDWARE & BUILDING PRDTS: Plastic
Fabriform LLC .... E 206 587-5303
   Seattle *(G-9960)*
P & M Fiberglass Company Inc .... G 206 784-1940
   Seattle *(G-10725)*
Reflect-A-Life Inc .... G 253 693-8662
   Monroe *(G-6614)*
Toolless Plastic Solutions Inc .... E 425 493-1223
   Everett *(G-3633)*

HARDWARE & EQPT: Stage, Exc Lighting
J & R Commercial Inc .... G 253 639-3890
   Kent *(G-4963)*
Lightbank Studio .... G 206 409-0939
   Seattle *(G-10416)*
Stagecraft Industries Inc .... G 206 763-8800
   Seattle *(G-11178)*

HARDWARE STORES
Central Hose and Fittings Inc .... F 509 547-6460
   Pasco *(G-7558)*
Morgan Electric & Plumbing Inc .... F 206 547-1617
   Seattle *(G-10562)*
Steeler Inc .... G 509 926-7403
   Spokane Valley *(G-12891)*

HARDWARE STORES: Builders'
Old & Elegant Distributing .... F 425 455-4660
   Bellevue *(G-1045)*
Summer Rrh LLC .... F 509 328-0915
   Spokane *(G-12532)*

HARDWARE STORES: Chainsaws
Sumner Lawn n Saw LLC .... F 253 435-9284
   Puyallup *(G-8257)*
Tims Country Saw Shop .... G 509 486-2798
   Tonasket *(G-13660)*

HARDWARE STORES: Pumps & Pumping Eqpt
Cascade Indus & Hydraulic LLC .... G 509 452-1752
   Union Gap *(G-13924)*
Pacific Pipe & Pump LLC .... F 425 640-0376
   Mountlake Terrace *(G-6865)*
Reds Electric Motors Inc .... G 360 377-3903
   Bremerton *(G-1992)*
Valley Supply Company .... E 360 217-4400
   Woodinville *(G-15398)*

HARDWARE STORES: Tools
Birch Equipment Company Inc .... E 360 734-5744
   Bellingham *(G-1272)*
Cowlitz River Rigging Inc .... F 360 425-6720
   Longview *(G-5903)*

HARDWARE STORES: Tools, Hand
Kestrel Tool .... G 360 468-2103
   Lopez Island *(G-5984)*
Woodcraft Supply LLC .... F 206 767-6394
   Seattle *(G-11492)*

HARDWARE STORES: Tools, Power
Eastside Saw & Sales Inc .... E 425 454-7627
   Bellevue *(G-887)*

HARDWARE WHOLESALERS
Blaser Die Casting Co .... D 206 767-7800
   Seattle *(G-9540)*
Frank J Martin Company .... E 206 523-7665
   Lynnwood *(G-6122)*
Washington Chain & Supply Inc .... E 206 623-8500
   Seattle *(G-11438)*
YKK (usa) Inc .... G 425 277-2503
   Renton *(G-8952)*

HARDWARE, WHOLESALE: Builders', NEC
Builders Firstsource Inc .... D 509 783-8148
   Kennewick *(G-4637)*
Evergreen Construction Spc Inc .... F 253 288-8455
   Auburn *(G-433)*
Old & Elegant Distributing .... F 425 455-4660
   Bellevue *(G-1045)*
Steeler Inc .... D 206 725-8500
   Seattle *(G-11187)*
Steeler Inc .... G 253 572-8200
   Tacoma *(G-13525)*

HARDWARE, WHOLESALE: Chains
North Star Casteel Pdts Inc .... E 206 622-0068
   Seattle *(G-10627)*

HARDWARE, WHOLESALE: Power Tools & Access
Hope Moffat .... G 401 527-4234
   Bainbridge Island *(G-640)*

PRODUCT SECTION

Shelly Shay ....G....... 360 829-2350
  Buckley (G-2072)

HARDWARE, WHOLESALE: Saw Blades

Emerald Tool Inc ....G....... 206 767-5670
  Seattle (G-9914)

HARDWARE: Aircraft

A & G Machine Inc ....D....... 253 887-8433
  Auburn (G-357)
A & G Machine Inc ....G....... 253 887-8433
  Auburn (G-358)
Aeroforge Inc..E....... 253 286-2525
  Puyallup (G-8117)
Art Brass Aerospace Finshg Inc ....G....... 206 209-3010
  Seattle (G-9435)
Avia Marine Company ....G....... 253 373-1644
  Kent (G-4803)
Esterline Technologies Corp ....E....... 425 453-9400
  Bellevue (G-902)
Fabrication Technologies LLC ....G....... 360 293-3707
  Anacortes (G-127)
Northstone Industries LLC ....G....... 509 844-7775
  Spokane (G-12410)
Toussint Machine and Mfg LLC ....G....... 360 840-0705
  Sedro Woolley (G-11576)

HARDWARE: Aircraft & Marine, Incl Pulleys & Similar Items

Power Equipment Supply Llc ....G....... 206 817-5627
  Everett (G-3580)

HARDWARE: Builders'

Dodge Systems LLC ....G....... 253 405-3967
  Lakewood (G-5712)
Dormakaba USA Inc....................................F....... 253 864-4484
  Puyallup (G-8145)
Karcher Design ....D....... 253 220-8244
  Tukwila (G-13761)
Precision Builders ....G....... 509 882-2232
  Grandview (G-4254)

HARDWARE: Cabinet

Northwest Cabinet Hardware ....G....... 360 281-5869
  Yacolt (G-15489)
R&J Industries LLC.....................................G....... 253 466-3627
  Puyallup (G-8233)

HARDWARE: Door Opening & Closing Devices, Exc Electrical

Automatic Door Solutions LLC...................G....... 253 802-0888
  Orting (G-7473)
Tri-City Glass Inc..G....... 509 586-0454
  Kennewick (G-4738)

HARDWARE: Furniture

Blaser Die Casting Co ....D....... 206 767-7800
  Seattle (G-9540)

HARDWARE: Harness

Pure Safety Group Inc ....G....... 253 854-5877
  Kent (G-5090)

HARNESS ASSEMBLIES: Cable & Wire

AFL Ig LLC ....E....... 425 291-4200
  Kent (G-4765)
Bic Inc ....G....... 360 691-1452
  Granite Falls (G-4265)
Carlisle Interconnect Tech Inc ....G....... 425 656-5235
  Kent (G-4837)
Carlisle Interconnect Tech Inc ....B....... 425 291-3991
  Kent (G-4838)
Custom Interface Inc ....E....... 509 493-8756
  Bingen (G-1636)
Hydra Group LLC ....G....... 503 957-0975
  Washougal (G-14959)
Logan Industries Inc ....D....... 509 462-7400
  Spokane Valley (G-12776)
Northwest Applied Marine LLC ....G....... 509 936-4316
  Chewelah (G-2605)
Pacific Custom Cable Inc ....F....... 253 373-0800
  Auburn (G-523)
Paragon Manufacturing Corp ....E....... 425 438-0800
  Everett (G-3569)

Wegners Wire Inc ....G....... 253 535-0945
  Puyallup (G-8278)

HARNESSES, HALTERS, SADDLERY & STRAPS

Ch Leather & Supply..................................G....... 360 966-0183
  Everson (G-3670)

HEADPHONES: Radio

Multisonus Audio Inc..................................G....... 425 241-1112
  Bellingham (G-1451)

HEALTH AIDS: Exercise Eqpt

Contemporary Design Co...........................F....... 360 599-2833
  Bellingham (G-1303)
D & P Products Inc....................................G....... 425 551-1380
  Everett (G-3435)
Dyaco Coml & Med N Amer LLC ....G....... 408 966-4239
  Bothell (G-1850)
Lemond Fitness Inc ....F....... 425 615-0116
  Woodinville (G-15288)
Level 10 Fitness Products LLC ....G....... 503 572-5530
  Vancouver (G-14372)
Maverick Sports Medicine Inc....................E....... 425 497-0887
  Redmond (G-8553)
Precor Incorporated ....B....... 425 486-9292
  Woodinville (G-15339)
Revive A Back Inc ....G....... 360 738-6085
  Bellingham (G-1516)
Sports-Fab Inc ....G....... 503 408-0920
  Vancouver (G-14604)
Totalwave Fitness LLC ....G....... 509 361-9089
  Moses Lake (G-6754)
Vectra Fitness Inc ....C....... 425 291-9550
  Issaquah (G-4486)

HEALTH AIDS: Vaporizers

Spry Product Development LLC.................G....... 206 556-1246
  Seattle (G-11172)
Twin Ohana Enterprises LLC ....G....... 360 882-8022
  Vancouver (G-14653)
Twin Ohana Enterprises LLC ....G....... 360 314-2965
  Vancouver (G-14654)

HEALTH CLUBS

Giorgios Fitness Center ....G....... 509 922-8833
  Spokane Valley (G-12718)

HEALTH PRACTITIONERS' OFFICES, NEC

Peryl Professional Touch ....G....... 253 537-8181
  Tacoma (G-13465)

HEALTH SCREENING SVCS

Cardinal Health Inc ....E....... 206 763-8500
  Seattle (G-9629)
Feminina Group Inc ....G....... 310 237-5733
  Seattle (G-9983)

HEARING AIDS

Saywhatclub ....G....... 425 486-2667
  Bothell (G-1789)
Sonus-Usa Inc ....G....... 253 272-3090
  Tacoma (G-13517)
TAHAc LLC..G....... 509 248-0933
  Yakima (G-15693)

HEAT EMISSION OPERATING APPARATUS

Kisslers Machine & Fabrication..................G....... 509 877-1177
  Wapato (G-14917)

HEAT EXCHANGERS

Trunek Enterprises Inc ....F....... 360 734-6860
  Bellingham (G-1578)

HEAT TREATING: Metal

Almet Incorporated ....F....... 253 852-1690
  Kent (G-4773)
Bodycote Imt Inc ....E....... 360 833-1120
  Camas (G-2234)
Cascade Metallurgical Inc ....E....... 253 838-0477
  Kent (G-4842)
Copperheat ....G....... 360 757-2589
  Burlington (G-2146)

HEATING UNITS: Gas, Infrared

Frontier Mtal Fabrications Inc....................F....... 360 514-0961
  Vancouver (G-14242)
Inland NW Metallurgical Svcs ....F....... 509 922-7663
  Spokane Valley (G-12745)
Pacific Metallurgical Inc ....E....... 206 292-9205
  Kent (G-5055)
Seattle Heat Treaters ....G....... 206 763-2744
  Seattle (G-11062)
Team Inc...E....... 360 848-0353
  Mount Vernon (G-6844)
Team Industrial Services ....G....... 360 757-2589
  Burlington (G-2194)
Thermal Technologies ....G....... 425 359-8681
  Snohomish (G-11990)

HEATERS: Swimming Pool, Electric

Coates Heater Company Inc ....G....... 253 872-7256
  Kent (G-4855)

HEATING & AIR CONDITIONING EQPT & SPLYS WHOLESALERS

A-Star Distributing Inc................................F....... 509 467-6809
  Spokane (G-12091)
Siemens Industry Inc ....F....... 509 891-9070
  Spokane Valley (G-12871)

HEATING & AIR CONDITIONING UNITS, COMBINATION

Wsb Sheetmetal Company ....G....... 425 844-2061
  Duvall (G-3003)

HEATING EQPT & SPLYS

Custom Masonry & Stove Inc ....G....... 206 524-4714
  Lake Forest Park (G-5610)
Eclipse Inc ....G....... 754 581-1513
  Seattle (G-9874)
Fives N Amercn Combustn Inc ....E....... 360 659-7432
  Marysville (G-6334)
Greenwood Clean Energy Inc ....G....... 888 788-3090
  Redmond (G-8485)
Hearth & Home Technologies LLC ....B....... 509 684-3745
  Colville (G-2755)
Lighthouse International Ltd ....E....... 509 466-2502
  Spokane (G-12365)
Marine Hardware Inc ....E....... 425 883-0651
  Redmond (G-8549)
North Industries Inc ....G....... 206 940-0842
  Seattle (G-10624)
Pacific Hide & Fur Depot ....E....... 509 545-0688
  Pasco (G-7611)
Paragon Energy Solutions ....G....... 425 445-6471
  Kirkland (G-5429)
Two Mac Inc ....G....... 206 285-3675
  Seattle (G-11354)

HEATING EQPT: Complete

Biosmart Technologies LLC ....G....... 360 888-8638
  Yelm (G-15729)
Dry Air Technology Inc ....F....... 360 755-9176
  Burlington (G-2153)
Ducoterra LLC...G....... 360 788-4200
  Bellingham (G-1327)
Innovative Thermal Solutions.....................G....... 253 830-4550
  Edgewood (G-3082)
King Electrical Mfg Co................................D....... 206 762-0400
  Seattle (G-10345)
Rv Comfort Systems LLC...........................G....... 425 408-3140
  Bothell (G-1898)

HEATING SYSTEMS: Radiant, Indl Process

Prestyl USA LLC ....G....... 509 703-7661
  Spokane Valley (G-12838)

HEATING UNITS & DEVICES: Indl, Electric

Ducoterra LLC...G....... 360 788-4200
  Bellingham (G-1327)
Tank Wise LLC ....G....... 206 937-3995
  Seattle (G-11265)
Team Inc...E....... 360 848-0353
  Mount Vernon (G-6844)

HEATING UNITS: Gas, Infrared

J S OWill Inc ....G....... 360 226-3637
  Enumclaw (G-3296)

Employee Codes: A=Over 500 employees, B=251-500
C=101-250, D=51-100, E=20-50, F=10-19, G=2-9

2019 Washington
Manufacturers Register

HELICOPTERS | PRODUCT SECTION

HELICOPTERS
Fairlane Helicopters Inc ....G 360 398-1015
  Lynden *(G-6016)*
Glacier Aviation Inc ....F 360 705-3214
  Olympia *(G-7296)*
Helitrak Inc ....G 253 857-0890
  Gig Harbor *(G-4117)*
Mechanical Specilities ....G 360 273-7604
  Olympia *(G-7336)*

HELMETS: Leather
TI Holdings Inc ....F 877 743-3509
  Spokane *(G-12560)*

HELP SUPPLY SERVICES
Avantech Inc ....D 509 943-6706
  Richland *(G-8969)*

HIGH ENERGY PARTICLE PHYSICS EQPT
Helion Energy Inc ....E 425 332-7463
  Redmond *(G-8490)*
Validigm Biotechnology Inc ....G 415 205-3377
  Seattle *(G-11399)*

HIGHWAY & STREET MAINTENANCE SVCS
Hansen Logging LLC ....E 509 935-4515
  Chewelah *(G-2602)*
Michael H Wold Company Inc ....G 360 435-6953
  Arlington *(G-275)*
Road Products Inc ....G 509 922-1206
  Spokane Valley *(G-12853)*

HITCHES: Trailer
Chase Race 425 269-5636
  Duvall *(G-2980)*
Itec Inc ....G 509 452-3672
  Union Gap *(G-13934)*
Pacific Rim International LLC ....G 503 781-2394
  Vancouver *(G-14472)*

HOBBY, TOY & GAME STORES: Arts & Crafts & Splys
Expressions Glass II ....G 206 242-2860
  Burien *(G-2106)*
Ferguson Merchandising LLC ....D 425 883-2050
  Redmond *(G-8460)*
Hope Chest Crafts ....G 509 865-5666
  Toppenish *(G-13670)*
Stampadoodle Inc ....G 360 647-9663
  Bellingham *(G-1555)*

HOBBY, TOY & GAME STORES: Ceramics Splys
Colorific Porcelain ....G 425 743-1591
  Lynnwood *(G-6096)*

HOBBY, TOY & GAME STORES: Chess, Backgammon/Other Drbl Games
Puget Bridge Supply ....G 206 367-3629
  Shoreline *(G-11804)*

HOBBY, TOY & GAME STORES: Children's Toys & Games, Exc Dolls
LB Games Inc ....G 360 794-7803
  Snohomish *(G-11937)*

HOBBY, TOY & GAME STORES: Dolls & Access
One Atta Time Doll Co ....G 360 956-1091
  Olympia *(G-7362)*

HOBBY, TOY & GAME STORES: Hobbies, NEC
Michaels Stores Inc ....E 360 892-4494
  Vancouver *(G-14417)*

HOBBY, TOY & GAME STORES: Kites
Wind Play Inc ....G 206 784-0414
  Seattle *(G-11481)*

HOBBY, TOY & GAME STORES: Toys & Games
Novel Inc ....E 425 956-3096
  Kirkland *(G-5414)*
OShell Delmont ....G 360 427-9600
  Shelton *(G-11719)*

HOISTING SLINGS
Columbia Rigging Corporation ....G 509 545-4657
  Pasco *(G-7564)*

HOISTS
Callahan Manufacturing Inc ....E 509 346-2208
  Royal City *(G-9167)*
Safeworks LLC ....D 206 575-6445
  Tukwila *(G-13809)*

HOISTS: Aircraft Loading
Pf Fishpole Hoists Inc ....G 206 767-3887
  Renton *(G-8878)*

HOISTS: Hand
A Terex Genie Company ....G 800 536-1800
  Redmond *(G-8365)*
Genie Holdings Inc ....G 425 881-1800
  Redmond *(G-8471)*
Genie Industries Inc ....A 425 881-1800
  Redmond *(G-8472)*
Genie Industries Inc ....E 425 881-1800
  Redmond *(G-8473)*
Genie Industries Inc ....E 425 881-1800
  Moses Lake *(G-6711)*
Genie Industries Inc 425 888-4600
  North Bend *(G-7112)*

HOISTS: Mine
Access Equipment LLC ....G 360 376-2679
  Orcas *(G-7455)*

HOLDERS, PAPER TOWEL, GROCERY BAG, ETC: Plastic
Corbitz Ltd ....G 206 241-9877
  Burien *(G-2099)*
Pro Clip Products Inc ....G 509 924-5544
  Spokane Valley *(G-12841)*

HOLDING COMPANIES, NEC
Continental Holdings III ....G 425 502-7055
  Seattle *(G-9732)*

HOLDING COMPANIES: Investment, Exc Banks
Batp Inc ....G 253 677-4706
  Edgewood *(G-3072)*
Nathan Capital LLC ....G 360 835-1211
  Washougal *(G-14971)*

HOLDING COMPANIES: Personal, Exc Banks
Western States Group LLC ....G 509 487-4560
  Spokane *(G-12587)*

HOME DELIVERY NEWSPAPER ROUTES
Korea Times Los Angeles Inc ....E 206 622-2229
  Seattle *(G-10356)*

HOME ENTERTAINMENT EQPT: Electronic, NEC
Innovative Advantage Inc ....G 206 910-7528
  Redmond *(G-8508)*
U2 Inc ....F 360 627-8068
  Bremerton *(G-2009)*

HOME FURNISHINGS WHOLESALERS
Aladdin Manufacturing Corp ....E 253 395-3277
  Kent *(G-4767)*
American Drpery Blind Crpt Inc .....C 360 676-1121
  Renton *(G-8743)*
Penthouse Drapery Clrs & Mfrs .....E 206 292-8336
  Seattle *(G-10781)*

HOME HEALTH CARE SVCS
Cascade Intgrtive Medicine LLC ....G 425 391-5270
  Issaquah *(G-4390)*
Omage Labs Inc ....G 844 662-4326
  Seattle *(G-10696)*

HOMEBUILDERS & OTHER OPERATIVE BUILDERS
M A C I Inc ....E 360 424-7013
  Mount Vernon *(G-6808)*
US Builders Team LLC ....G 425 466-2611
  Redmond *(G-8701)*

HOMEFURNISHING STORES: Lighting Fixtures
Rich Interiors ....G 509 665-8000
  Wenatchee *(G-15068)*

HOMEFURNISHING STORES: Mirrors
Tri-City Glass Inc ....G 509 586-0454
  Kennewick *(G-4738)*

HOMEFURNISHING STORES: Pictures, Wall
Carson/Corbett LLC ....G 206 524-9782
  Seattle *(G-9639)*

HOMEFURNISHING STORES: Pottery
Jans Ceramics ....G 360 425-3540
  Longview *(G-5920)*
Kennedy Creek Pottery ....G 360 866-3937
  Olympia *(G-7316)*
Marked Departure Pottery ....G 360 991-5910
  Vancouver *(G-14394)*
Orcas Island Pottery ....G 360 376-2813
  Eastsound *(G-3042)*

HOMEFURNISHING STORES: Venetian Blinds
Penthouse Drapery Clrs & Mfrs .....E 206 292-8336
  Seattle *(G-10781)*
Shade Sunglo & Drapery Co ....G 206 767-4561
  Seattle *(G-11094)*

HOMEFURNISHING STORES: Vertical Blinds
Gaes Draperies ....G 360 293-9732
  Anacortes *(G-132)*

HOMEFURNISHING STORES: Window Furnishings
Rodda Paint Co ....G 360 423-4990
  Longview *(G-5948)*
Rodda Paint Co ....G 360 738-6878
  Bellingham *(G-1519)*

HOMEFURNISHINGS & SPLYS, WHOLESALE: Decorative
Alex Daisley ....G 206 623-5555
  Seattle *(G-9373)*
Married To Metal ....G 206 244-2238
  Pacific *(G-7531)*
S J W Studios Inc ....F 206 323-8020
  Seattle *(G-11001)*

HOMEFURNISHINGS, WHOLESALE: Carpets
Pacific Mat & Coml Flrg LLC ....E 800 345-6287
  Kent *(G-5053)*

HOMEFURNISHINGS, WHOLESALE: Grills, Barbecue
P&M Products Inc ....G 425 939-8349
  Kirkland *(G-5423)*

HOMEFURNISHINGS, WHOLESALE: Kitchenware
Lectent LLC ....D 360 574-7737
  Vancouver *(G-14369)*
Progressive International Corp ......D 253 850-6111
  Kent *(G-5085)*

HOMEFURNISHINGS, WHOLESALE: Pottery
Clayport Pottery .... G 425 335-0678
 Lake Stevens *(G-5638)*

HOMEFURNISHINGS, WHOLESALE: Window Covering Parts & Access
Johnson Enterprises .... G 253 537-8056
 Tacoma *(G-13365)*

HOMEFURNISHINGS, WHOLESALE: Wood Flooring
NW Wood Holding LLC .... G 360 326-8794
 Vancouver *(G-14445)*

HOMES, MODULAR: Wooden
Blokable Inc .... G 800 928-6778
 Seattle *(G-9544)*
Blokable Inc .... F 800 928-6778
 Vancouver *(G-14069)*
Northwest Modular Service .... G 253 631-2802
 Covington *(G-2835)*
West Coast Automation Corp .... E 509 773-5055
 Goldendale *(G-4213)*

HOMES: Log Cabins
Amish Log Homes .... G 360 491-4132
 Lacey *(G-5532)*
Archibald Log Homes Inc .... G 509 782-3703
 Cashmere *(G-2316)*
Cascade Country Cabins .... G 509 427-8515
 Stevenson *(G-13009)*
Cedar Homes of Washington Inc .... G 360 668-8242
 Snohomish *(G-11887)*
Custom Building Services Inc .... G 509 422-5746
 Okanogan *(G-7195)*
Forest View Inc .... G 360 909-9890
 Ridgefield *(G-9083)*
JW Custom Construction .... G 509 679-2959
 Stehekin *(G-13003)*
Mountain Log Homes Inc .... F 360 799-0533
 Startup *(G-13002)*
Regal Homes Construction LLC .... G 360 606-3486
 Vancouver *(G-14541)*
Shire Mountain Log Homes Inc .... G 360 262-9338
 Centralia *(G-2432)*
Slyfield Enterprises .... G 509 968-3456
 Ellensburg *(G-3226)*
Smokey Point Log Homes Inc .... G 360 659-7122
 Marysville *(G-6387)*

HONES
Fresh Impressions By Honey D .... G 253 503-7887
 Lakewood *(G-5723)*

HOPPERS: Sheet Metal
Marks Design & Metalworks LLC .... D 360 859-3535
 Vancouver *(G-14396)*

HORMONE PREPARATIONS
Nobu Integrative Medicine LLC .... G 425 363-2970
 North Bend *(G-7118)*
Vitamin Shoppe Industries Inc .... G 855 715-8530
 Burien *(G-2136)*
Vitamin Shoppe Industries Inc .... G 855 235-9431
 Maple Valley *(G-6298)*

HORNS: Marine, Compressed Air Or Steam
Olympic Instruments Inc .... F 206 463-3604
 Vashon *(G-14739)*

HORSE & PET ACCESSORIES: Textile
Imc-Innvtive Mktg Cnnction LLC .... G 360 895-0178
 Port Orchard *(G-7816)*
Lk Sewing Co .... G 206 240-9973
 Burien *(G-2118)*

HORSE ACCESS: Harnesses & Riding Crops, Etc, Exc Leather
Colburn Enterprise .... G 509 292-2310
 Elk *(G-3169)*

HORSE ACCESS: Saddle Cloth
Puget Sound Workshop LLC .... G 425 821-7345
 Kirkland *(G-5447)*

HORSESHOEING SVCS
Nelson Farrier Shop Inc .... G 509 966-9598
 Yakima *(G-15629)*

HORSESHOES
Horseshoe Cove Cabin Owne .... G 509 966-4087
 Yakima *(G-15585)*
Horseshoe Falls LLC .... G 360 256-0668
 Vancouver *(G-14303)*
Horseshoe Grange 965 .... G 360 668-3939
 Snohomish *(G-11922)*
Horseshoe Lake Estates Assn .... G 253 851-3514
 Gig Harbor *(G-4120)*
TNT Horseshoe Art .... G 253 334-7653
 Algona *(G-78)*
Washington State Horseshoe Pit .... G 253 735-0213
 Auburn *(G-593)*

HOSE: Air Line Or Air Brake, Rubber Or Rubberized Fabric
Belair Composites Inc .... F 509 482-0442
 Spokane *(G-12144)*

HOSE: Flexible Metal
Proto Technologies Inc .... D 509 891-4747
 Liberty Lake *(G-5855)*
Senior Operations LLC .... B 360 435-1119
 Arlington *(G-327)*

HOSE: Vacuum Cleaner, Rubber
Hide-A-Hose Inc .... G 425 750-7636
 Monroe *(G-6577)*

HOSES & BELTING: Rubber & Plastic
Custom Hydraulic & Machine Inc .... F 253 854-4666
 Kent *(G-4868)*
Lewis-Goetz and Company Inc .... F 206 623-5650
 Kent *(G-4994)*
Nxedge Inc .... G 425 990-0091
 Bellevue *(G-1041)*
Ves Company Inc .... G 206 940-5742
 Shoreline *(G-11820)*

HOSPITAL EQPT REPAIR SVCS
Spacelabs Healthcare Inc .... A 425 396-3300
 Snoqualmie *(G-12027)*
Spacelabs Healthcare LLC .... B 425 396-3300
 Snoqualmie *(G-12028)*
Spacelabs Healthcare Wash .... C 425 396-3300
 Snoqualmie *(G-12029)*

HOSPITAL HOUSEKEEPING SVCS
REM & AES LLC .... G 580 284-3410
 Puyallup *(G-8236)*

HOSPITALS: Orthopedic
Valley Orthopedics Inc .... G 509 922-5040
 Liberty Lake *(G-5866)*

HOT TUBS
Apollo Antenna & Sales Inc .... G 509 534-6972
 Spokane Valley *(G-12622)*
Griese Enterprises .... G 509 868-7963
 Spokane *(G-12284)*
Hollibaugh Manufacturing .... G 360 653-8612
 Marysville *(G-6345)*

HOT TUBS: Plastic & Fiberglass
Composites Consolidation Compa ...... G 509 877-2228
 Wapato *(G-14914)*
Hydra Plastics Inc .... E 425 483-1877
 Woodinville *(G-15262)*
Maax Hydro Swirl Mfg Co .... D 360 734-0616
 Bellingham *(G-1417)*
McClarin Plastics LLC .... B 509 877-5950
 Wapato *(G-14919)*
Thermal Hydra Plastics LLC .... D 425 483-1877
 Woodinville *(G-15388)*

HOUSEHOLD APPLIANCE STORES
McLaren Destiny .... G 971 217-5877
 La Center *(G-5509)*
Read Products Inc .... F 206 283-2510
 Seattle *(G-10929)*
Refrigeration Supplies Distr .... G 509 452-8689
 Yakima *(G-15660)*

HOUSEHOLD ARTICLES, EXC KITCHEN: Pottery
Clayport Pottery .... G 425 335-0678
 Lake Stevens *(G-5638)*

HOUSEHOLD ARTICLES: Metal
Cut Above Enterprise Inc .... F 509 928-5091
 Spokane Valley *(G-12674)*
D&J Custom Metal Fabrication .... G 206 242-3238
 Burien *(G-2101)*
Fabrictn Melton & Precision .... G 509 284-2620
 Tekoa *(G-13611)*
Married To Metal .... G 206 244-2238
 Pacific *(G-7531)*

HOUSEHOLD FURNISHINGS, NEC
Alderwood Park .... G 425 774-5266
 Lynnwood *(G-6069)*
Dream On Futon Co .... G 360 739-2103
 Bellingham *(G-1325)*
Dutena Blankets .... G 253 581-0312
 Lakewood *(G-5715)*
Edgewalker Woodworks Ltd .... G 360 468-2839
 Lopez Island *(G-5981)*
Globalmax Associates Inc .... F 425 392-4848
 Issaquah *(G-4422)*
Heritage Professional Ldscpg .... G 509 737-8580
 Kennewick *(G-4669)*
Holy Lamb Organics Inc .... G 360 402-5781
 Olympia *(G-7309)*
Khann Industries Corp .... G 360 794-1033
 Monroe *(G-6587)*
Northwest Native Designs .... G 206 679-5847
 Snohomish *(G-11953)*
Seattle Curtain Mfg Co .... E 206 324-0692
 Mill Creek *(G-6526)*

HOUSEKEEPING & MAID SVCS
Maid Naturally LLC .... E 509 994-3685
 Spokane *(G-12379)*

HOUSEWARE STORES
The McCredy Company .... G 509 773-5340
 Goldendale *(G-4209)*

HOUSEWARES, ELECTRIC, EXC COOKING APPLIANCES & UTENSILS
Magellan Group Ltd .... G 360 332-6868
 Blaine *(G-1682)*

HOUSEWARES, ELECTRIC: Cooking Appliances
Precision Appliance Technology .... F 206 960-2467
 Bellevue *(G-1079)*

HOUSEWARES, ELECTRIC: Extractors, Juice
Nutrifaster Inc .... G 206 767-5054
 Seattle *(G-10670)*

HOUSEWARES, ELECTRIC: Heaters, Sauna
Tylohelo Inc .... E 425 951-1120
 Woodinville *(G-15393)*

HOUSEWARES, ELECTRIC: Heating, Bsbrd/Wall, Radiant Heat
Ducoterra LLC .... G 360 788-4200
 Bellingham *(G-1327)*
Glen Dimplex Americas Company ..... C 360 693-2505
 Vancouver *(G-14257)*
King Electrical Mfg Co .... D 206 762-0400
 Seattle *(G-10345)*

HOUSEWARES, ELECTRIC: Irons, Curling
Curly Clutch LLC .... G 253 732-3647
  Puyallup *(G-8139)*

HOUSEWARES, ELECTRIC: Massage Machines, Exc Beauty/Barber
Artistic Talents Styling Salon .... G 360 456-0100
  Lacey *(G-5533)*
Polar Fusion LLC .... G 206 395-7811
  Kent *(G-5069)*
Revel Body .... G 206 409-2940
  Seattle *(G-10955)*

HOUSEWARES, ELECTRIC: Popcorn Poppers
Zippy Pop Inc .... G 855 404-3300
  Blaine *(G-1714)*

HOUSEWARES, ELECTRIC: Roasters
Mokajoe Inc .... G 360 714-1953
  Bellingham *(G-1439)*

HOUSEWARES: Dishes, Plastic
New Top Dog LLC .... G 206 817-3395
  Bellevue *(G-1028)*
Plastics Dynamics Inc .... E 206 762-2164
  Kent *(G-5067)*
United Home Technologies LLC .... F 360 574-7737
  Washougal *(G-14996)*

HOUSEWARES: Kettles & Skillets, Cast Iron
Royal Prestige .... G 509 544-0330
  Pasco *(G-7624)*

HUMIDIFIERS & DEHUMIDIFIERS
Munters Moisture Control Svcs .... G 707 863-4189
  Auburn *(G-501)*
Sporting Systems Corporation .... G 360 607-0036
  Vancouver *(G-14603)*

HYDRAULIC EQPT REPAIR SVC
American West Industries Inc .... F 509 535-5040
  Spokane *(G-12111)*
Asko Industrial Repair .... F 206 284-2659
  Mukilteo *(G-6894)*
Asko Processing Inc .... F 206 284-2659
  Mukilteo *(G-6895)*
Dessert Industries Inc .... G 425 487-3244
  Snohomish *(G-11898)*
Fluid Power Service Inc .... G 360 496-6888
  Morton *(G-6669)*
Hydro-Tech Genertr Repair Plus .... F 509 276-2063
  Chattaroy *(G-2447)*
Hydro-Tech Genertr Repair Plus .... F 509 536-9464
  Spokane Valley *(G-12734)*
PSM Hydraulics .... E 360 282-4998
  Woodinville *(G-15342)*
RJ Hydraulics Inc .... G 360 693-4399
  Vancouver *(G-14553)*
Service Hydraulics Inc .... F 253 351-6010
  Auburn *(G-561)*
Skyline Fluid Power Inc .... G 509 382-4781
  Dayton *(G-2886)*
Sound Hydraulics Inc .... G 206 824-7450
  Des Moines *(G-2946)*
Universal Repair Shop Inc .... F 206 322-2726
  Seattle *(G-11377)*
Valin Corporation .... G 509 924-4914
  Spokane Valley *(G-12923)*
Webers Radiator Service Inc .... G 509 452-3747
  Yakima *(G-15705)*

HYDRAULIC FLUIDS: Synthetic Based
Dyna Flow .... G 253 381-9736
  Gig Harbor *(G-4096)*

HYDROPHONES
Life-Gro Inc .... G 253 682-1669
  Tacoma *(G-13387)*

HYDROPONIC EQPT
NW Hydroponics .... G 360 778-3254
  Bellingham *(G-1476)*

Hard Rubber & Molded Rubber Prdts
Bestfitt Gasket Company Inc .... G 253 863-9521
  Sumner *(G-13056)*
Image Masters Inc .... G 253 939-5868
  Auburn *(G-471)*
Perception Plastics Inc .... G 509 624-5408
  Spokane *(G-12437)*
Stampadoodle Inc .... G 360 647-9663
  Bellingham *(G-1555)*

ICE
Airgas Usa LLC .... E 253 872-7000
  Kent *(G-4766)*
Allied Grinders Inc .... F 425 493-1313
  Mukilteo *(G-6892)*
Articland Ice .... G 509 582-5808
  Kennewick *(G-4620)*
Columbia Basin Ice LLC .... E 509 736-9583
  Kennewick *(G-4645)*
Crystal Clear Ice Co .... G 509 525-1042
  Walla Walla *(G-14792)*
Lynden Meat Company LLC .... F 360 354-5227
  Lynden *(G-6034)*
Nanoice .... G 206 257-3380
  Tukwila *(G-13775)*
Nanoice Inc .... G 206 257-3380
  Woodinville *(G-15318)*

ICE CREAM & ICES WHOLESALERS
M-K-D Distributors Inc .... C 425 251-0809
  Kent *(G-4999)*
Nestle Dreyers Ice Cream Co .... D 425 251-0809
  Kent *(G-5019)*
Whidbey Island Ice Cream LLC .... G 425 359-6372
  Freeland *(G-4039)*

ICE WHOLESALERS
Lynden Meat Company LLC .... F 360 354-5227
  Lynden *(G-6034)*
Rays Custom Cutting .... G 509 684-5544
  Colville *(G-2772)*

ICE: Dry
Rosellini Distribution Inc .... G 253 867-5648
  Kent *(G-5106)*

IDENTIFICATION TAGS, EXC PAPER
Jrotc Dog Tags Inc .... G 509 292-0410
  Elk *(G-3170)*

IGNEOUS ROCK: Crushed & Broken
De Rosier Trucking Inc .... E 360 577-1636
  Kelso *(G-4523)*
J L Shrman Excvtg Rock Crshing .... F 509 447-4214
  Newport *(G-7059)*
Olivine Corp .... G 360 733-3332
  Bellingham *(G-1479)*
Rock Services Inc .... G 360 748-8333
  Chehalis *(G-2530)*
Sawyer & Sawyer Inc .... E 509 486-1304
  Tonasket *(G-13658)*
Shine Quarry Inc .... F 360 437-2415
  Port Ludlow *(G-7775)*

IGNITION APPARATUS & DISTRIBUTORS
Smart Start .... G 425 967-5699
  Lynnwood *(G-6199)*
Smartstart .... G 509 317-2050
  Yakima *(G-15676)*
Washington Ignition Interlock .... G 206 824-6849
  Kent *(G-5207)*

INCENSE
Higher Mind Incense .... G 541 702-1560
  Port Ludlow *(G-7767)*
Spirit of Winds Incense St .... G 253 293-2743
  Federal Way *(G-3790)*

INCINERATORS
Olivine Corp .... G 360 733-3332
  Bellingham *(G-1479)*

INDL & PERSONAL SVC PAPER WHOLESALERS
Gerris Dry Bunk .... G 509 782-2653
  Cashmere *(G-2320)*

INDL & PERSONAL SVC PAPER, WHOL: Boxes, Corrugtd/Solid Fiber
Alliance Packaging LLC .... D 509 924-7623
  Spokane Valley *(G-12605)*
Allpak Container LLC .... D 425 227-0400
  Renton *(G-8739)*
Northwest Pioneer Inc .... D 253 872-9693
  Kent *(G-5034)*
Sp Holdings Inc .... C 425 291-3500
  Renton *(G-8918)*

INDL & PERSONAL SVC PAPER, WHOL: Boxes, Paperbrd/Plastic
H R Spinner Corporation .... E 509 453-9111
  Yakima *(G-15579)*

INDL & PERSONAL SVC PAPER, WHOL: Container, Paper/Plastic
Michelsen Packaging Co Cal .... D 509 248-6270
  Yakima *(G-15618)*

INDL & PERSONAL SVC PAPER, WHOL: Cups, Disp, Plastic/Paper
Nippon Dynawave Packaging Co .... G 360 414-3379
  Federal Way *(G-3763)*
Nippon Dynawave Packg Co LLC .... A 360 425-2150
  Longview *(G-5935)*

INDL & PERSONAL SVC PAPER, WHOL: Paper, Wrap/Coarse/Prdts
Orora Packaging Solutions .... F 253 796-6200
  Kent *(G-5048)*

INDL & PERSONAL SVC PAPER, WHOLESALE: Boxes & Containers
Ocean Cargo Container Inc .... G 253 381-9098
  Gig Harbor *(G-4138)*

INDL & PERSONAL SVC PAPER, WHOLESALE: Boxes, Fldng Pprboard
Michelsen Packaging Company .... C 509 248-6270
  Yakima *(G-15619)*

INDL & PERSONAL SVC PAPER, WHOLESALE: Paper Tubes & Cores
Pac Rite Inc .... G 253 833-7071
  Puyallup *(G-8215)*

INDL & PERSONAL SVC PAPER, WHOLESALE: Shipping Splys
Park Postal LLC .... G 206 860-7678
  Seattle *(G-10759)*
PSI Logistics Intl LLC .... G 855 473-5877
  Spokane *(G-12457)*

INDL CONTRACTORS: Exhibit Construction
Turner Exhibits Inc .... E 425 776-4930
  Lynnwood *(G-6214)*

INDL EQPT SVCS
Centralia Supply & Fabrication .... G 360 736-7277
  Centralia *(G-2391)*
Industrial Support Service LLC .... G 509 276-5131
  Deer Park *(G-2906)*
Precision Industrial Equi .... G 509 571-1725
  Yakima *(G-15650)*
Superior Fluid Power Inc .... G 509 482-7949
  Spokane Valley *(G-12896)*

INDL GASES WHOLESALERS
Air Products and Chemicals Inc .... G 253 845-4000
  Puyallup *(G-8119)*

PRODUCT SECTION

INDL SPLYS, WHOLESALE: Bearings

Norco Inc .... G 509 764-5032
  Moses Lake *(G-6731)*

INDL MACHINERY & EQPT WHOLESALERS

Aerogo Inc .... D 206 575-3344
  Tukwila *(G-13689)*
Chemithon Enterprises Inc .... C 206 937-9954
  Seattle *(G-9672)*
Custom Bilt Holdings LLC .... E 253 872-7330
  Lakewood *(G-5709)*
Drive Line Svc of Bellingham .... G 360 734-7828
  Bellingham *(G-1326)*
Enterprises International Inc .... G 360 533-6222
  Hoquiam *(G-4336)*
Franklin Machinery .... G 360 581-5079
  Aberdeen *(G-11)*
Go Ventures Inc .... G 253 313-4070
  Tacoma *(G-13315)*
H D Fowler Co Inc .... D 425 746-8400
  Bellevue *(G-934)*
Hydra-Com Inc .... G 253 862-9140
  Pacific *(G-7529)*
J Calman Industries .... G 360 398-1932
  Lynden *(G-6024)*
Leading Edge Labeling Inc .... E 425 821-4137
  Redmond *(G-8531)*
Mainland Machinery LLC .... G 360 354-2348
  Lynden *(G-6036)*
McGregor Company .... F 509 397-4360
  Colfax *(G-2716)*
Nicholson Manufacturing Co .... D 206 682-2752
  Seattle *(G-10607)*
Norma Industries .... G 253 208-1728
  Puyallup *(G-8200)*
Northwest Envmtl & Eqp Inc .... G 253 435-5115
  Puyallup *(G-8204)*
Pollution Control Systems Corp .... G 206 523-7220
  Seattle *(G-10828)*
Praxair Distribution Inc .... E 360 694-1338
  Vancouver *(G-14497)*
Pro Controls Inc .... G 509 457-3386
  Yakima *(G-15655)*
Process Heating Company .... G 206 682-3414
  Seattle *(G-10870)*
Rogers Machinery Company Inc .... E 206 763-2530
  Seattle *(G-10976)*
Rogers Machinery Company Inc .... E 360 736-9356
  Centralia *(G-2429)*
Rogers Machinery Company Inc .... G 509 922-0556
  Spokane Valley *(G-12856)*
Simutech International Inc .... G 360 490-4029
  Kirkland *(G-5463)*
Sound Tanks and Cntrs L L C .... G 425 455-2668
  Bellevue *(G-1149)*
Spokane Machinery Company .... F 509 535-1654
  Spokane *(G-12519)*
Ss Industrial Inc .... G 509 427-7836
  Stevenson *(G-13020)*
Utilities Service Company Inc .... G 206 246-5674
  Tukwila *(G-13831)*
Van Doren Sales Inc .... D 509 886-1837
  East Wenatchee *(G-3034)*
Workhorse Incorporated .... G 360 835-9417
  Washougal *(G-15002)*

INDL MACHINERY REPAIR & MAINTENANCE

Argo Blower & Mfg Co .... F 206 762-9336
  Seattle *(G-9428)*
C H W Enterprises Inc .... F 360 425-8700
  Longview *(G-5892)*
DK Machining LLC .... G 509 991-6110
  Nine Mile Falls *(G-7072)*
Extreme Indus Coatings LLC .... G 509 991-1773
  Airway Heights *(G-51)*
Flamespray Northwest Inc .... F 206 508-6779
  Seattle *(G-10004)*
Hard Rock Machine Works Inc .... G 509 529-9833
  Walla Walla *(G-14819)*
Impact Service Corporation .... E 509 468-7900
  Spokane *(G-12305)*
Intech Enterprises Inc .... E 360 835-8785
  Washougal *(G-14961)*
Machine Repair & Design Inc .... F 253 826-6329
  Sumner *(G-13081)*
Maintenance Welding Service .... G 360 533-4318
  Hoquiam *(G-4348)*
N C Power Systems Co .... C 425 251-5877
  Tukwila *(G-13774)*
New Tec LLC .... F 509 738-6621
  Kettle Falls *(G-5237)*

Repair Technology Inc .... F 206 762-6221
  Seattle *(G-10948)*
Steve Pool Service Inc .... G 360 533-0421
  Shelton *(G-11736)*
Superior Industrial Services A .... E 360 841-8542
  Woodland *(G-15467)*
Toussint Machine and Mfg LLC .... G 360 840-0705
  Sedro Woolley *(G-11576)*
Unilode AVI Solution US Inc .... G 206 824-7123
  Auburn *(G-587)*
Utilities Service Company Inc .... G 206 246-5674
  Tukwila *(G-13831)*

INDL PATTERNS: Foundry Cores

Continuous Casting Co .... F 206 623-7688
  Seattle *(G-9733)*
Gils Aluminum & Shell Core Sp .... G 206 762-1726
  Seattle *(G-10071)*

INDL PATTERNS: Foundry Patternmaking

Roemer Electric Steel Foundry .... E 360 423-1330
  Longview *(G-5949)*

INDL PROCESS INSTR: Transmit, Process Variables

Airtran Wireless Technologies .... G 360 430-3179
  Vancouver *(G-14014)*
Soundnine Inc .... G 206 245-4463
  Kirkland *(G-5468)*

INDL PROCESS INSTRUMENTS: Absorp Analyzers, Infrared, X-Ray

Academy Infrared Training Inc .... G 360 676-1915
  Bellingham *(G-1238)*

INDL PROCESS INSTRUMENTS: Control

Cambria Corporation .... G 206 782-8380
  Seattle *(G-9612)*
Centurion Process LLC .... G 509 759-3001
  Selah *(G-11584)*
Clearsign Combustion Corp .... F 206 673-4848
  Tukwila *(G-13712)*
Geartrology Corporation .... G 425 347-1300
  Everett *(G-3492)*
Mk Optimization and Ctrl LLC .... G 509 656-3321
  Seattle *(G-10550)*
Mount Fury Co Inc .... G 425 391-0747
  Issaquah *(G-4451)*
Selectronix Incorporated .... G 425 788-2979
  Woodinville *(G-15358)*
Spectrum Controls Inc .... D 425 462-2087
  Bellevue *(G-1153)*
Systems Interface Inc .... E 425 481-1225
  Mukilteo *(G-6981)*

INDL PROCESS INSTRUMENTS: Controllers, Process Variables

Pantrol Inc .... F 509 535-9061
  Spokane *(G-12428)*

INDL PROCESS INSTRUMENTS: Digital Display, Process Variables

Digatron LLC .... E 509 467-3128
  Spokane *(G-12227)*
Digi Resources LLC .... F 888 775-3444
  Sammamish *(G-9201)*
Worktank Enterprises LLC .... E 206 254-0950
  Seattle *(G-11497)*

INDL PROCESS INSTRUMENTS: Fluidic Devices, Circuit & Systems

Astrake Inc .... G 503 470-4470
  Seattle *(G-9446)*
Lee Company .... G 425 488-5842
  Bothell *(G-1773)*
Novex LLC .... G 360 296-3467
  Bellingham *(G-1473)*

INDL PROCESS INSTRUMENTS: On-Stream Gas Or Liquid Analysis

Valco Instruments Company LP .... G 360 697-9199
  Poulsbo *(G-8015)*

Vici Metronics Inc .... E 360 697-9199
  Poulsbo *(G-8017)*

INDL PROCESS INSTRUMENTS: Water Quality Monitoring/Cntrl Sys

Branom Operating Company LLC .... E 206 762-6050
  Seattle *(G-9578)*
Cape Horn Maintenance Co .... G 360 826-9105
  Concrete *(G-2784)*
Dungeness Envmtl Solutions Inc .... G 888 481-0326
  Everett *(G-3447)*
Evoqua Water Technologies LLC .... G 360 699-7392
  Brush Prairie *(G-2034)*
Northwest Envmtl & Eqp Inc .... G 253 435-5115
  Puyallup *(G-8204)*
Northwest Water Systems Inc .... G 360 876-0958
  Port Orchard *(G-7835)*
Ovivo USA LLC .... C 360 253-3440
  Vancouver *(G-14460)*
Resource Associates Intl .... G 509 466-1894
  Spokane *(G-12472)*
Unibest International LLC .... G 509 525-3370
  Walla Walla *(G-14884)*
Waterline Envirotech Ltd .... G 360 676-9635
  Bellingham *(G-1590)*

INDL SPLYS WHOLESALERS

Arbon Equipment Corporation .... F 253 395-7099
  Kent *(G-4787)*
Blue Oval Co .... G 509 448-2894
  Spokane *(G-12155)*
Capital Industrial Supply Inc .... E 360 786-1890
  Tumwater *(G-13856)*
Center Electric Inc .... F 253 383-4416
  Tacoma *(G-13231)*
Centralia Supply & Fabrication .... G 360 736-7277
  Centralia *(G-2391)*
Chemical Cloth Co .... G 360 582-9684
  Sequim *(G-11617)*
Chemithon Enterprises Inc .... C 206 937-9954
  Seattle *(G-9672)*
Gran Quartz Trading Inc .... G 206 973-7640
  Seattle *(G-10105)*
Grating Pacific LLC .... G 253 872-7733
  Kent *(G-4926)*
Great Little Box Co Inc .... G 425 349-4522
  Everett *(G-3506)*
H D Fowler Co Inc .... D 425 746-8400
  Bellevue *(G-934)*
Industrial Ceramics Inc .... G 905 878-2848
  Seattle *(G-10230)*
Leading Edge Labeling Inc .... E 425 821-4137
  Redmond *(G-8531)*
Monarch Machine and TI Co Inc .... E 509 547-7753
  Pasco *(G-7603)*
P F M Industries Inc .... G 425 776-3112
  Edmonds *(G-3142)*
Spokane Machinery Company .... F 509 535-1654
  Spokane *(G-12519)*
Transco Northwest Inc .... E 425 251-5422
  Kent *(G-5188)*
Valmont Northwest Inc .... F 509 547-1623
  Pasco *(G-7647)*
West Coast Paper Company .... E 253 850-1900
  Kent *(G-5212)*

INDL SPLYS, WHOL: Fasteners, Incl Nuts, Bolts, Screws, Etc

A & P Fasteners Inc .... G 425 486-9562
  Kenmore *(G-4563)*
Multifab Inc .... C 509 924-6631
  Spokane Valley *(G-12796)*
Tacoma Screw Products Inc .... G 253 395-9770
  Kent *(G-5170)*

INDL SPLYS, WHOLESALE: Barrels, New Or Reconditioned

Seattle Barrel Co .... G 206 622-7218
  Seattle *(G-11045)*

INDL SPLYS, WHOLESALE: Bearings

Mechatronics Inc .... C 425 222-5900
  Issaquah *(G-4447)*

Employee Codes: A=Over 500 employees, B=251-500
C=101-250, D=51-100, E=20-50, F=10-19, G=2-9

INDL SPLYS, WHOLESALE: Chains, Power Transmission

Caskey Industrial Supply Co ....G....... 360 533-6366
  Cosmopolis *(G-2798)*

INDL SPLYS, WHOLESALE: Electric Tools

Ferguson ....G....... 206 767-7700
  Auburn *(G-440)*

INDL SPLYS, WHOLESALE: Fasteners & Fastening Eqpt

Titus Tool Company Inc ....F....... 206 447-1489
  Bellevue *(G-1192)*

INDL SPLYS, WHOLESALE: Fittings

Bridgestone Hosepower LLC ....E....... 206 767-4670
  Seattle *(G-9585)*

INDL SPLYS, WHOLESALE: Gaskets

Paramount Supply Co ....G....... 360 647-8328
  Bellingham *(G-1489)*

INDL SPLYS, WHOLESALE: Gaskets & Seals

Beckwith & Kuffel ....E....... 509 922-5222
  Spokane Valley *(G-12637)*

INDL SPLYS, WHOLESALE: Lapidary Eqpt

Lortone Inc ....F....... 425 493-1600
  Mukilteo *(G-6951)*

INDL SPLYS, WHOLESALE: Rubber Goods, Mechanical

Empire Rubber & Supply Co ....F....... 509 547-0026
  Pasco *(G-7579)*

INDL SPLYS, WHOLESALE: Seals

4 M Company Inc ....D....... 425 227-4100
  Tukwila *(G-13686)*

INDL SPLYS, WHOLESALE: Staplers & Tackers

Strong Snax Inc ....G....... 360 953-3753
  Ridgefield *(G-9114)*

INDL SPLYS, WHOLESALE: Tools

Hd International Corp ....G....... 503 997-9325
  Vancouver *(G-14290)*

INDL SPLYS, WHOLESALE: Tools, NEC

Emerald Tool Inc ....G....... 206 767-5670
  Seattle *(G-9914)*
Kestrel Tool ....G....... 360 468-2103
  Lopez Island *(G-5984)*
Woodstock International Inc ....E....... 360 734-3482
  Bellingham *(G-1596)*

INDL SPLYS, WHOLESALE: Valves & Fittings

Kaman Fluid Power LLC ....G....... 360 738-1264
  Bellingham *(G-1390)*
Valin Corporation ....G....... 509 924-4914
  Spokane Valley *(G-12923)*

INDUCTORS

Power Conversion Inc ....E....... 425 487-1337
  Woodinville *(G-15338)*

INDUSTRIAL & COMMERCIAL EQPT INSPECTION SVCS

S&S NDT LLC ....G....... 509 688-7996
  Spokane *(G-12491)*

INFORMATION RETRIEVAL SERVICES

Elarm Inc ....G....... 206 395-9604
  Seattle *(G-9892)*
Enhanced Software Products Inc ....E....... 509 534-1514
  Spokane Valley *(G-12693)*
Iocurrents Inc ....G....... 206 494-0099
  Seattle *(G-10258)*

Microsoft Corporation ....A....... 425 882-8080
  Redmond *(G-8580)*
Salesforcecom Inc ....G....... 206 701-1755
  Bellevue *(G-1113)*
Stanwood-Camano News Inc ....E....... 360 629-8066
  Stanwood *(G-12995)*
Washington Media Services Inc ....G....... 360 754-4543
  Olympia *(G-7421)*
Zombie Inc ....E....... 206 623-9655
  Bainbridge Island *(G-685)*

INFRARED OBJECT DETECTION EQPT

PSI Electronics LLC ....F....... 253 922-7890
  Fife *(G-3984)*

INK OR WRITING FLUIDS

Cartridge World ....G....... 509 469-9711
  Kennewick *(G-4643)*

INK: Printing

American Printing and Pubg ....G....... 253 395-3349
  Kent *(G-4779)*
Outsmart Office Solutions Inc ....G....... 888 688-8154
  Mercer Island *(G-6478)*
Pencils and Inks Inc ....G....... 206 683-4441
  Seattle *(G-10780)*
Sunoco Inc ....G....... 253 872-8500
  Kent *(G-5162)*

INNER TUBES: Truck Or Bus

West Worldwide Services Inc ....G....... 509 764-2177
  Moses Lake *(G-6757)*

INSECTICIDES

Walla Walla Environmental Inc ....F....... 509 522-0490
  Walla Walla *(G-14888)*

INSECTICIDES & PESTICIDES

Homax Group Inc ....E....... 360 733-9029
  Bellingham *(G-1371)*
Plunk LLC ....G....... 425 770-1287
  Kirkland *(G-5436)*

INSPECTION & TESTING SVCS

A & M Prcsion Msuring Svcs Inc ....F....... 425 432-7554
  Kent *(G-4750)*
Magnetic Penetrant Svcs Co Inc ....D....... 206 762-5855
  Seattle *(G-10466)*
Quest Integrity Usa LLC ....D....... 253 893-7070
  Kent *(G-5093)*
Sensitech Inc ....E....... 425 883-7926
  Redmond *(G-8660)*
Sensitech Inc ....C....... 425 883-7926
  Redmond *(G-8661)*
Structural Diagnostic Services ....G....... 360 647-6681
  Bellingham *(G-1560)*
Valence Surface Tech LLC ....C....... 206 762-5855
  Seattle *(G-11398)*
Zetec Inc ....C....... 425 974-2700
  Snoqualmie *(G-12035)*

INSTRUMENTS, LAB: Spectroscopic/Optical Properties Measuring

Sekidenko Inc ....E....... 360 694-7871
  Vancouver *(G-14579)*

INSTRUMENTS, LABORATORY: Analyzers, Automatic Chemical

Compound Photonics US Corp ....E....... 360 597-3654
  Vancouver *(G-14143)*

INSTRUMENTS, LABORATORY: Analyzers, Thermal

GE Totten & Associates LLC ....G....... 206 788-0188
  Seattle *(G-10056)*

INSTRUMENTS, LABORATORY: Blood Testing

Bio-RAD Laboratories Inc ....C....... 425 881-8300
  Redmond *(G-8403)*
Pacific Biomarkers Inc ....E....... 206 298-0068
  Seattle *(G-10728)*

INSTRUMENTS, LABORATORY: Dust Sampling & Analysis

Protac Inc ....G....... 509 962-5001
  Ellensburg *(G-3221)*

INSTRUMENTS, LABORATORY: Infrared Analytical

Georadar Imaging ....G....... 425 392-7688
  Sammamish *(G-9208)*

INSTRUMENTS, LABORATORY: Magnetic/Elec Properties Measuring

Riverside Scientific Entps ....G....... 206 842-7513
  Bainbridge Island *(G-667)*

INSTRUMENTS, MEASURING & CNTRG: Plotting, Drafting/Map Rdg

Axama Corporation ....G....... 509 922-8400
  Spokane Valley *(G-12632)*

INSTRUMENTS, MEASURING & CNTRL: Gauges, Auto, Computer

Cartech Industries Inc ....G....... 360 693-3616
  Vancouver *(G-14100)*

INSTRUMENTS, MEASURING & CNTRL: Geophysical & Meteorological

Hobi Instrument Services LLC ....G....... 425 223-3438
  Bellevue *(G-946)*
Sea-Bird Electronics Inc ....C....... 425 643-9866
  Bellevue *(G-1119)*

INSTRUMENTS, MEASURING & CNTRL: Radiation & Testing, Nuclear

Linda J Mohr ....G....... 509 946-0941
  Richland *(G-9022)*

INSTRUMENTS, MEASURING & CNTRLG: Aircraft & Motor Vehicle

Heatcon Composite Systems Inc ....D....... 206 575-1333
  Tukwila *(G-13747)*

INSTRUMENTS, MEASURING & CNTRLG: Electrogamma Ray Loggers

Log Max Inc ....F....... 360 699-7300
  Vancouver *(G-14381)*

INSTRUMENTS, MEASURING & CNTRLG: Thermometers/Temp Sensors

Mindplace Company ....G....... 360 376-6494
  Eastsound *(G-3040)*

INSTRUMENTS, MEASURING & CNTRLNG: Press & Vac Ind, Acft Eng

Electrijet Flight Systems Inc ....G....... 509 990-9474
  Liberty Lake *(G-5831)*

INSTRUMENTS, MEASURING & CONTROLLING: Anamometers

Pra Inc ....F....... 408 743-5300
  Arlington *(G-304)*

INSTRUMENTS, MEASURING & CONTROLLING: Breathalyzers

Guardian Interlock Systems ....G....... 360 423-4766
  Longview *(G-5913)*
Puget Sound Breathalyzers ....G....... 425 359-9515
  Marysville *(G-6372)*

INSTRUMENTS, MEASURING & CONTROLLING: Dosimetry, Personnel

United States Dosimetry Tech ....G....... 509 946-8738
  Richland *(G-9049)*

PRODUCT SECTION

INSTRUMENTS: Indl Process Control

INSTRUMENTS, MEASURING & CONTROLLING: Polygraph

Gillespie Polygraph .... G 425 775-9015
　Lynnwood *(G-6130)*
Richard Evans .... G 509 684-1079
　Colville *(G-2773)*

INSTRUMENTS, MEASURING & CONTROLLING: Reactor Controls, Aux

Durham Geo-Enterprises Inc .... E 770 465-7557
　Mukilteo *(G-6916)*

INSTRUMENTS, MEASURING & CONTROLLING: Seismoscopes

Michael Shaw .... G 206 669-7597
　Federal Way *(G-3758)*

INSTRUMENTS, MEASURING/CNTRL: Gauging, Ultrasonic Thickness

Echo Ultrasonics LLC .... G 360 671-9121
　Bellingham *(G-1328)*

INSTRUMENTS, MEASURING/CNTRL: Testing/Measuring, Kinematic

Chemchek Instruments Inc .... G 509 943-5000
　Richland *(G-8980)*

INSTRUMENTS, MEASURING/CNTRLNG: Med Diagnostic Sys, Nuclear

Cardinal Health Inc .... E 206 763-8500
　Seattle *(G-9629)*
Physicians Sleep Scoring .... G 360 403-7685
　Arlington *(G-301)*

INSTRUMENTS, OPTICAL: Light Sources, Standard

Usl Technologies LLC .... G 360 379-0684
　Port Townsend *(G-7937)*

INSTRUMENTS, OPTICAL: Polarizers

Lightspeed Design Inc .... G 425 637-2818
　Bellevue *(G-983)*

INSTRUMENTS, OPTICAL: Prisms

Fractal Filters LLC .... G 206 854-0968
　Normandy Park *(G-7093)*

INSTRUMENTS, OPTICAL: Test & Inspection

Eyeon LLC .... G 425 652-9556
　Issaquah *(G-4410)*
Refiner49er LLC .... G 360 254-0884
　Brush Prairie *(G-2041)*

INSTRUMENTS, SURGICAL & MEDICAL: Biopsy

Perfint Healthcare Corp USA .... G 425 629-9207
　Redmond *(G-8618)*

INSTRUMENTS, SURGICAL & MEDICAL: Blood & Bone Work

American Bnchmark Mch Wrks LLC ..... G 360 584-9303
　Olympia *(G-7224)*
Harbor Vascular Inc .... G 425 420-6009
　Sammamish *(G-9215)*
Hyprotek Inc .... G 509 343-3121
　Spokane *(G-12301)*
Magnolia Medical Tech Inc .... E 206 673-2500
　Seattle *(G-10468)*
Medworks Instruments .... G 360 597-3754
　Vancouver *(G-14409)*
SRS Medical Corp .... F 425 882-1101
　Redmond *(G-8679)*
V-Care Health Systems Inc .... G 509 670-9068
　Ellensburg *(G-3236)*

INSTRUMENTS, SURGICAL & MEDICAL: Catheters

Atossa Genetics Inc .... G 206 325-6086
　Seattle *(G-9457)*
Innovation Associates .... G 206 455-2332
　Bellevue *(G-958)*

INSTRUMENTS, SURGICAL & MEDICAL: Lasers, Surgical

Claus Paws Animal Hospital LLC .... F 360 896-7449
　Vancouver *(G-14121)*
Laser Support Services Inc .... G 253 531-9008
　Tacoma *(G-13382)*
Tacoma Laser Clinic LLC .... F 253 272-0655
　Tacoma *(G-13544)*

INSTRUMENTS, SURGICAL & MEDICAL: Operating Tables

or Specific Inc .... G 800 937-7949
　Vancouver *(G-14453)*

INSTRUMENTS, SURGICAL & MEDICAL: Optometers

Robert Wickes Od .... G 360 249-3485
　Montesano *(G-6654)*

INSTRUMENTS, SURGICAL & MEDICAL: Retractors

Dawling Spay Retractor LLC .... G 360 482-4970
　Elma *(G-3244)*

INSTRUMENTS, SURGICAL & MEDICAL: Saws, Surgical

Wright Surgical Arts LLC .... G 509 792-1404
　Pasco *(G-7656)*

INSTRUMENTS, SURGICAL & MEDICAL: Skin Grafting

Kean Center .... G 206 465-4879
　Seattle *(G-10334)*

INSTRUMENTS, SURGICAL & MEDICAL: Stapling Devices, Surgical

Sara June Haskin .... G 360 873-4257
　Marblemount *(G-6306)*

INSTRUMENTS, SURGICAL & MEDICAL: Suction Therapy

Reheal LLC .... G 206 440-5948
　Seattle *(G-10944)*

INSTRUMENTS, SURGICAL & MEDICAL: Trocars

Trocar Investments .... G 253 851-9206
　Gig Harbor *(G-4170)*

INSTRUMENTS: Analytical

Amnis LLC .... E 206 374-7000
　Seattle *(G-9399)*
Analytical Reaserch Consulting .... G 360 573-5700
　Vancouver *(G-14033)*
Bio-RAD Laboratories Inc .... B 425 498-1933
　Woodinville *(G-15192)*
Biotangent Diagnostics LLC .... G 503 713-3339
　Issaquah *(G-4385)*
Brooks Rand Inc .... G 206 632-6206
　Seattle *(G-9588)*
Bruker Axs Handheld Inc .... E 509 783-9850
　Kennewick *(G-4635)*
Customarray Inc .... G 425 609-0923
　Bothell *(G-1758)*
Easyxafs LLC .... G 208 697-4076
　Renton *(G-8790)*
Fialab Instruments Inc .... G 206 258-2290
　Seattle *(G-9986)*
Full Spectrum Analytics Inc .... G 206 729-0775
　Seattle *(G-10037)*
Global Scientific Systems .... G 360 504-5100
　Sequim *(G-11636)*
Idex Health & Science LLC .... C 360 679-2528
　Oak Harbor *(G-7153)*
Metricstory Incorporated .... G 206 755-4511
　Seattle *(G-10523)*
Microbiologique Inc .... F 206 714-5275
　Seattle *(G-10533)*
Plexera LLC .... G 425 368-7410
　Woodinville *(G-15336)*
Reheal LLC .... G 206 440-5948
　Seattle *(G-10944)*
Rigaku Americas Corporation .... G 206 780-8927
　Bainbridge Island *(G-666)*
Spectroglyph LLC .... G 415 793-1242
　Kennewick *(G-4729)*
Viavi Solutions Inc .... F 425 398-1298
　Bothell *(G-1914)*

INSTRUMENTS: Analyzers, Spectrum

Pacific Wireless Systems LLC .... G 509 375-3533
　Richland *(G-9033)*

INSTRUMENTS: Drafting

Pro Fab .... G 509 879-9293
　Spokane Valley *(G-12842)*

INSTRUMENTS: Electrocardiographs

Mindplace Company .... G 360 376-6494
　Eastsound *(G-3040)*
Resolute Medical Inc .... G 800 750-5784
　Bellevue *(G-1101)*

INSTRUMENTS: Electroencephalographs

Cadence Neuroscience Inc .... G 425 681-6863
　Sammamish *(G-9194)*

INSTRUMENTS: Endoscopic Eqpt, Electromedical

Simulab Corporation .... E 206 297-1260
　Tukwila *(G-13819)*

INSTRUMENTS: Flow, Indl Process

ADS LLC .... G 206 762-5070
　Tukwila *(G-13687)*

INSTRUMENTS: Frequency Meters, Electrical, Mech & Electronic

R D F Products .... G 360 253-2181
　Vancouver *(G-14526)*

INSTRUMENTS: Frequency Synthesizers

Synthesis By Jeffrey Bland PHD .... G 253 238-7898
　Tacoma *(G-13536)*

INSTRUMENTS: Generators, Pulse, Signal

Nutesla Corporation .... G 910 688-3752
　Washougal *(G-14974)*

INSTRUMENTS: Indl Process Control

Airmagnet Inc .... G 800 283-5853
　Everett *(G-3365)*
Cognex .... G 206 448-2343
　Seattle *(G-9712)*
Combustion Technology LLC .... G 360 253-9600
　Vancouver *(G-14140)*
Control Systems America Inc .... G 360 210-7475
　Camas *(G-2243)*
Control Technology Inc .... G 425 823-3878
　Kirkland *(G-15311)*
Emerson Electric Co .... G 360 805-0590
　Monroe *(G-6569)*
Emerson Process Management .... G 425 391-8565
　Sammamish *(G-9204)*
Fisher-Rosemount Systems Inc .... G 425 488-4111
　Bothell *(G-1853)*
Fortive Corporation .... C 425 446-5000
　Everett *(G-3483)*
Francis Scientific Inc .... G 360 687-7019
　Battle Ground *(G-702)*
General Dynmics Ots Arospc Inc .... A 425 420-9311
　Bothell *(G-1765)*
Global Fia Inc .... G 253 549-2223
　Fox Island *(G-4022)*
Heckman Inc .... G 360 724-4580
　Burlington *(G-2162)*

Employee Codes: A=Over 500 employees, B=251-500
C=101-250, D=51-100, E=20-50, F=10-19, G=2-9

INSTRUMENTS: Indl Process Control

Hexagon Metrology Inc ....G....... 253 872-2443
 Kent *(G-4940)*
Idex Health & Science LLC.................C....... 360 679-2528
 Oak Harbor *(G-7153)*
Instrumentation Northwest Inc ....E....... 425 822-4434
 Kent *(G-4955)*
Micro Motion Inc ....G....... 360 896-0522
 Vancouver *(G-14418)*
Pacific Biomarkers Inc ....E....... 206 298-0068
 Seattle *(G-10728)*
Pollution Control Systems Corp.................G....... 206 523-7220
 Seattle *(G-10828)*
Precision Automation Inc ....G....... 360 254-0661
 Vancouver *(G-14500)*
Process Cntrls Instrumentation ....G....... 360 573-4985
 Battle Ground *(G-733)*
Process Solutions Inc ....E....... 360 629-0910
 Stanwood *(G-12987)*
Rosemount Specialty Pdts LLC.................E....... 509 881-2100
 East Wenatchee *(G-3031)*
Rosemount Specialty Pdts LLC.................E....... 206 329-8600
 Renton *(G-8899)*
Sekidenko Inc.................E....... 360 694-7871
 Vancouver *(G-14579)*
Silicon Designs Inc ....E....... 425 391-8329
 Kirkland *(G-5461)*
Slope Indicator Company (inc).................E....... 425 806-2200
 Bothell *(G-1905)*
Tigerstop LLC.................E....... 360 254-0661
 Vancouver *(G-14637)*

INSTRUMENTS: Laser, Scientific & Engineering

Empire Lab Automtn Systems LLC ....G....... 509 808-6050
 Spokane *(G-12245)*
Hc Laserlign Inc ....G....... 253 852-2001
 Kent *(G-4936)*
Klar Scientific LLC ....G....... 509 330-2103
 Pullman *(G-8096)*
Sightman.................G....... 360 934-5886
 Raymond *(G-8358)*

INSTRUMENTS: Measurement, Indl Process

Creative Microsystems Inc.................F....... 425 235-4335
 Renton *(G-8776)*
Fluke Corporation.................F....... 425 446-5600
 Everett *(G-3476)*
Fluke Corporation.................E....... 888 993-5853
 Everett *(G-3477)*
Fluke Electronics Corporation.................A....... 425 347-6100
 Everett *(G-3478)*
Fluke Electronics Corporation.................B....... 425 446-5610
 Everett *(G-3479)*
Fluke Electronics Corporation.................E....... 888 993-5853
 Everett *(G-3481)*
Krill Systems Inc ....G....... 206 780-2901
 Bainbridge Island *(G-647)*
Mach Transonic Inc ....G....... 206 853-6909
 Seattle *(G-10459)*
Marqmetrix Inc ....F....... 206 971-3625
 Seattle *(G-10492)*
Showalter Systems Inc.................G....... 206 236-6276
 Mercer Island *(G-6484)*

INSTRUMENTS: Measuring & Controlling

Automated Mechanical Controls.................G....... 425 881-8226
 Redmond *(G-8389)*
Avac Inc ....G....... 425 869-2822
 Redmond *(G-8391)*
Avocent Redmond Corp.................D....... 425 861-5858
 Kirkland *(G-5287)*
Basis Software Inc ....G....... 425 861-9390
 Redmond *(G-8397)*
Beco Inc ....G....... 425 885-2603
 Redmond *(G-8399)*
Custom Sensor Design Inc ....G....... 425 778-4980
 Lynnwood *(G-6102)*
Ec/Ndt LLC.................G....... 253 815-0797
 Federal Way *(G-3734)*
Hart Scientific ....G....... 425 446-5400
 Everett *(G-3508)*
Itron Inc.................B....... 509 924-9900
 Liberty Lake *(G-5838)*
Itron Brazil II LLC.................G....... 509 924-9900
 Liberty Lake *(G-5839)*
Itron International Inc ....G....... 866 374-8766
 Liberty Lake *(G-5840)*
Joescan Inc ....G....... 360 993-0069
 Vancouver *(G-14338)*

Know Labs Inc.................F....... 206 903-1351
 Seattle *(G-10349)*
Lawrenson Electronics Co Inc.................G....... 206 243-7310
 Burien *(G-2117)*
Measurement Technology NW Inc.................E....... 206 634-1308
 Seattle *(G-10512)*
Northwest Metrology LLC.................F....... 253 853-3183
 Gig Harbor *(G-4136)*
Northwest Technical Services ....G....... 425 419-4321
 Snohomish *(G-11954)*
Olympic Instruments Inc ....F....... 206 463-3604
 Vashon *(G-14739)*
Precision Data Technology Inc.................G....... 425 259-9237
 Everett *(G-3583)*
Rjc Enterprises LLC.................F....... 425 481-3281
 Bothell *(G-1787)*
Rudolph Technologies Inc ....G....... 425 396-7002
 Snoqualmie *(G-12022)*
Siemens Industry Inc.................F....... 509 891-9070
 Spokane Valley *(G-12871)*
Synergistic Technologies Inc.................G....... 425 822-7777
 Bellevue *(G-1174)*
Techna NDT LLC.................F....... 253 872-2415
 Kent *(G-5173)*
Terramar Instruments LLC.................G....... 425 306-0174
 Carnation *(G-2300)*
Unicon Inc.................G....... 425 454-2466
 Kirkland *(G-5488)*
United Western Tech Corp ....E....... 509 544-0720
 Pasco *(G-7646)*
Universal Avionics Systems Corp ....G....... 425 821-2800
 Redmond *(G-8699)*
Van Essen Instruments Division ....G....... 520 203-3445
 Mukilteo *(G-6987)*
Zetec Inc ....C....... 425 974-2700
 Snoqualmie *(G-12035)*

INSTRUMENTS: Measuring Electricity

Agilent Technologies Inc.................G....... 425 255-6320
 Renton *(G-8731)*
Agilent Technologies Inc.................D....... 509 921-3525
 Liberty Lake *(G-5824)*
Ahtna Engineering Services LLC ....D....... 425 864-1695
 Seatac *(G-9272)*
Alpha Test Corporation.................E....... 360 462-0201
 Shelton *(G-11675)*
Anewin LLC.................G....... 360 606-5591
 Vancouver *(G-14036)*
Astronics Advances Electronic ....G....... 425 895-4622
 Kirkland *(G-5282)*
Astronics Corporation.................B....... 425 881-1700
 Kirkland *(G-5284)*
Dualos LLC ....G....... 253 750-5125
 Tacoma *(G-13266)*
Ets-Lindgren Inc.................G....... 425 868-2558
 Sammamish *(G-9205)*
Itron US Gas LLC ....G....... 509 924-9900
 Liberty Lake *(G-5841)*
KLA Fuels Reductions.................G....... 509 680-0110
 Chewelah *(G-2603)*
Landis Gyr ....G....... 425 458-9363
 Kirkland *(G-5381)*
Lite-Check LLC.................F....... 509 535-7512
 Spokane *(G-12371)*
Metriguard Technologies Inc ....E....... 509 332-7526
 Pullman *(G-8098)*
Novatech Instruments Inc ....G....... 206 284-0704
 Lynnwood *(G-6171)*
Pacific Engineering & Mfg Co ....G....... 360 274-8323
 Castle Rock *(G-2349)*
Schweitzer Engrg Labs Inc ....E....... 509 332-1890
 Pullman *(G-8106)*
Siemens Industry Inc.................G....... 208 883-8330
 Issaquah *(G-4474)*
Zetec Inc ....C....... 425 974-2700
 Snoqualmie *(G-12035)*

INSTRUMENTS: Measuring, Current, NEC

Vm Solutions Inc.................F....... 253 841-2939
 Puyallup *(G-8273)*

INSTRUMENTS: Measuring, Electrical Energy

Sensorlink Corporation ....E....... 360 380-0592
 Ferndale *(G-3903)*

INSTRUMENTS: Measuring, Electrical, Field Strgth & Intensity

Quad Group Inc.................F....... 509 458-4558
 Spokane *(G-12463)*

INSTRUMENTS: Medical & Surgical

A-M Systems LLC ....E....... 360 683-8300
 Sequim *(G-11604)*
American Medical Concepts ....G....... 425 844-2840
 Duvall *(G-2979)*
Aortica Corporation ....G....... 425 209-0272
 Mercer Island *(G-6454)*
Aqueduct Critical Care Inc ....F....... 425 984-6090
 Seattle *(G-9416)*
Arrhythmia Solutions Inc ....G....... 509 389-7366
 Spokane *(G-12118)*
Ats ....G....... 509 534-2822
 Spokane *(G-12125)*
Bens Precision Instrs Inc.................D....... 253 883-5040
 Fife *(G-3938)*
Bining Health Inc.................G....... 604 540-8288
 Seattle *(G-9529)*
Bodypoint Inc.................E....... 206 405-4555
 Seattle *(G-9560)*
Boston Sceintifics ....G....... 608 323-3377
 Redmond *(G-8407)*
Btpsurgical LLC ....G....... 425 657-0805
 Issaquah *(G-4389)*
Cadwell Laboratories Inc ....D....... 509 735-6481
 Kennewick *(G-4638)*
Cardiac Insight Inc.................F....... 206 596-2060
 Bellevue *(G-839)*
Cellcyte Genetics Corporation ....G....... 425 519-3755
 Bellevue *(G-843)*
Cinterion Wireless Modu ....G....... 630 517-0198
 Issaquah *(G-4394)*
Convergent Technology ....G....... 206 352-5357
 Seattle *(G-9735)*
Cortex Manufacturing Inc.................G....... 425 334-2277
 Lake Stevens *(G-5641)*
Crh Medical Corporation ....F....... 425 284-7890
 Kirkland *(G-5318)*
Draxis Health Inc.................G....... 509 489-5656
 Spokane *(G-12231)*
Echonous Inc ....E....... 425 482-6213
 Redmond *(G-8446)*
Ekos Corporation ....C....... 425 415-3100
 Bothell *(G-1760)*
Ent Solutions Inc ....G....... 206 769-1735
 Seattle *(G-9929)*
Evergreen Orthpd RES Lab LLC ....G....... 425 284-7262
 Kirkland *(G-5335)*
FA Green Company ....E....... 425 888-0007
 Snoqualmie *(G-12012)*
Fresenius Med Care Hldings Inc ....D....... 509 276-7338
 Deer Park *(G-2902)*
Fukuda Denshi Usa Inc ....F....... 425 881-7737
 Redmond *(G-8467)*
Funeral Directors Research ....G....... 360 736-7105
 Centralia *(G-2402)*
Gestsure Technologies Ltd.................G....... 800 510-2485
 Seattle *(G-10067)*
Ginacor Inc ....F....... 206 860-1595
 Seattle *(G-10072)*
Howellcorp ....F....... 206 954-8011
 Seattle *(G-10189)*
Impulse Medical Tech Inc ....G....... 360 829-0400
 Buckley *(G-2059)*
Interntnal Rhbltative Sciences.................D....... 360 892-0339
 Vancouver *(G-14322)*
Joylux Inc ....F....... 206 219-6444
 Seattle *(G-10309)*
Karl-Sons LLC ....G....... 509 627-0152
 Kennewick *(G-4681)*
Kestra Medical Tech Inc ....G....... 425 279-8002
 Kirkland *(G-5375)*
Lifeport Inc ....G....... 360 944-9606
 Vancouver *(G-14374)*
Medtronic Inc.................G....... 509 991-0159
 Spokane *(G-12388)*
Mobile Air Applied Science ....G....... 206 953-3786
 Bellevue *(G-1012)*
Myotronics-Noromed Inc ....F....... 206 243-4214
 Kent *(G-5017)*
Nexus Surgical Innovations ....G....... 509 499-0937
 Spokane *(G-12404)*
Novo Contour Inc ....G....... 425 773-2673
 Edmonds *(G-3139)*

PRODUCT SECTION

INSURANCE: Agents, Brokers & Service

Novuson Surgical Inc .... G 425 481-7165
  Bothell *(G-1783)*
Olympic Medical Corp .... D 206 767-3500
  Seattle *(G-10692)*
Opticyte Inc .... G 206 696-3957
  Seattle *(G-10708)*
Pacific Bioscience Labs Inc .... C 888 525-2747
  Redmond *(G-8606)*
Personal Medical Corp .... G 425 497-1044
  Redmond *(G-8620)*
Precision Biometrics Inc .... G 206 448-3464
  Seattle *(G-10849)*
Procedure Products Corp .... G 360 693-1832
  Vancouver *(G-14512)*
Quinton Cardiology Systems Inc .... G 425 556-9761
  Bothell *(G-1893)*
Redpoint International Inc .... F 360 573-5957
  Vancouver *(G-14539)*
Redwood Instrument Co .... G 360 446-2860
  Rainier *(G-8321)*
Seattle Applied Science Inc .... G 425 773-2673
  Edmonds *(G-3154)*
Sensoria Health Inc .... G 425 533-2928
  Redmond *(G-8662)*
Ship N Shore .... G 360 293-8636
  Anacortes *(G-167)*
Sign Fracture Care Intl .... E 509 371-1107
  Richland *(G-9041)*
Signostics Inc .... F 425 402-0971
  Redmond *(G-8668)*
Smith & Nephew Inc .... E 509 363-0600
  Spokane Valley *(G-12876)*
South Sound Metal Inc .... G 253 564-0226
  University Place *(G-13981)*
Spacelabs Healthcare Inc .... A 425 396-3300
  Snoqualmie *(G-12027)*
Spacelabs Healthcare LLC .... B 425 396-3300
  Snoqualmie *(G-12028)*
Spacelabs Healthcare Wash .... E 425 396-3300
  Snoqualmie *(G-12030)*
Spio Inc .... G 253 893-0390
  Burien *(G-2130)*
Stripes Global Inc .... G 800 690-8219
  Bremerton *(G-2003)*
Surgimark Inc .... G 509 965-1911
  Yakima *(G-15691)*
Therapeutic Dimension Inc .... G 509 323-9275
  Spokane *(G-12555)*
Tissue Regeneration Systems .... G 425 576-4032
  Kirkland *(G-5484)*
Todo Flores Enterprises LLC .... G 206 450-5123
  Renton *(G-8929)*
Triad Products Corporation .... G 425 514-8363
  Everett *(G-3636)*
Unfors Raysafe Inc .... E 508 435-5600
  Everett *(G-3641)*
Uptake Medical Technology Inc .... G 206 926-7405
  Seattle *(G-11388)*
Vioguard Inc .... G 425 280-7735
  Bothell *(G-1806)*
Vioguard LLC .... F 425 406-8009
  Kirkland *(G-5490)*
Yourceba LLC .... G 509 747-5027
  Spokane *(G-12595)*

INSTRUMENTS: Nautical

Brockett Ocean Services Inc .... F 425 869-1834
  Redmond *(G-8410)*
Mintaka Instruments LLC .... G 206 783-1414
  Seattle *(G-10546)*
Sequoia Scientific Inc .... G 425 641-0944
  Bellevue *(G-1124)*

INSTRUMENTS: Optical, Analytical

Fenologica Biosciences Inc .... G 206 726-1200
  Seattle *(G-9985)*

INSTRUMENTS: Pressure Measurement, Indl

Celestial Monitoring Corp .... G 800 477-2506
  Lynnwood *(G-6090)*
Dynavest Inc .... E 206 728-0777
  Seattle *(G-9865)*
Hart Systems Inc .... G 253 858-8481
  Gig Harbor *(G-4114)*
Quick Pressure LLC .... G 206 219-5567
  Redmond *(G-8639)*
Rosemount Inc .... G 206 329-8600
  Renton *(G-8898)*

S & B Inc .... F 425 746-9312
  Bellevue *(G-1110)*
Scanivalve Corp .... E 509 891-9970
  Liberty Lake *(G-5859)*

INSTRUMENTS: Radar Testing, Electric

Thermetrics LLC .... G 206 456-9119
  Seattle *(G-11288)*

INSTRUMENTS: Temperature Measurement, Indl

Pra Inc .... F 408 743-5300
  Arlington *(G-304)*
Sensitech Inc .... E 425 883-7926
  Redmond *(G-8660)*
Sensitech Inc .... C 425 883-7926
  Redmond *(G-8661)*
Voltaire Inc .... E 425 274-7000
  Bellevue *(G-1220)*

INSTRUMENTS: Test, Digital, Electronic & Electrical Circuits

Chase Scientific Co .... G 360 221-8455
  Langley *(G-5774)*
Daniel Oneill .... G 509 939-7916
  Newman Lake *(G-7043)*
Dynon Instruments Inc .... G 425 402-0433
  Woodinville *(G-15231)*
Helldyne Inc .... E 206 855-1227
  Bainbridge Island *(G-638)*
Lite-Check Fleet Solutions Inc .... E 509 535-7512
  Spokane *(G-12372)*
Novatech Instruments Inc .... G 206 301-8986
  Redmond *(G-8600)*

INSTRUMENTS: Test, Electrical, Engine

Mohr Test and Measurement LLC .... E 509 946-0941
  Richland *(G-9027)*

INSTRUMENTS: Test, Electronic & Electric Measurement

Applied Precision LLC .... C 425 557-1000
  Issaquah *(G-4380)*
Colby Instruments LLC .... G 425 452-8889
  Bellevue *(G-859)*
Emeasure Inc .... G 844 382-7326
  Winthrop *(G-15159)*
Esterline Technologies Corp .... F 206 281-1312
  Seattle *(G-9942)*
Fluke Electronics Corporation .... A 425 347-6100
  Everett *(G-3478)*
Fluke Electronics Corporation .... B 425 446-5610
  Everett *(G-3479)*
Fluke Electronics Corporation .... B 425 446-5858
  Everett *(G-3480)*
Fluke Electronics Corporation .... E 888 993-5853
  Everett *(G-3481)*
Huntron Inc .... F 425 743-3171
  Mill Creek *(G-6513)*
ID Integration Inc .... F 425 438-2533
  Mukilteo *(G-6940)*
Innovaura Corporation .... G 425 272-2702
  Edmonds *(G-3120)*
Interstate Electronics Corp .... G 360 779-3723
  Silverdale *(G-11838)*
Nanoport Technologies LLC .... G 206 403-1714
  Friday Harbor *(G-4052)*
North Star High Voltage Corp .... G 520 780-9030
  Bainbridge Island *(G-653)*
Practec LLC .... F 425 881-8202
  Redmond *(G-8630)*
Signal Hound Inc .... G 360 263-5006
  Battle Ground *(G-740)*
Silicon Designs Inc .... E 425 391-8329
  Kirkland *(G-5461)*

INSTRUMENTS: Test, Electronic & Electrical Circuits

General Dynmics Ots Arospc Inc .... A 425 420-9311
  Bothell *(G-1765)*
Seattle Safety LLC .... E 253 395-4321
  Auburn *(G-559)*

INSTRUMENTS: Testing, Semiconductor

Applied Precision Holdings LLC .... C 425 557-1000
  Issaquah *(G-4381)*

INSTRUMENTS: Vibration

Dli Engineering Corporation .... F 206 842-7656
  Poulsbo *(G-7958)*
G G Consultants .... F 541 223-9519
  Ridgefield *(G-9084)*
Team Corporation .... E 360 757-3944
  Burlington *(G-2193)*

INSULATING COMPOUNDS

Angstrom Innovations Inc .... G 425 750-6329
  Mountlake Terrace *(G-6857)*

INSULATION & CUSHIONING FOAM: Polystyrene

Distribution International Inc .... B 425 228-4111
  Renton *(G-8785)*
Fxi Inc .... D 253 872-0170
  Kent *(G-4919)*
Johns Manville Corporation .... D 800 654-3103
  Kent *(G-4970)*

INSULATION & ROOFING MATERIALS: Wood, Reconstituted

Northwest Heli Structures .... G 360 734-1073
  Bellingham *(G-1467)*

INSULATION MATERIALS WHOLESALERS

Distribution International Inc .... B 425 228-4111
  Renton *(G-8785)*
Mac Arthur Co .... E 253 863-8830
  Sumner *(G-13080)*
Paragon Industries Inc .... E 253 872-0800
  Tukwila *(G-13789)*
Service Partners of Oregon .... E 360 694-6747
  Vancouver *(G-14580)*

INSULATION: Fiberglass

Environmental Insul Contg LLC .... E 360 647-2532
  Bellingham *(G-1336)*
Pmc Inc .... D 206 854-2660
  Kent *(G-5068)*
West Coast Insulation Inc .... G 206 459-2233
  Seattle *(G-11450)*

INSULATORS & INSULATION MATERIALS: Electrical

Jpmorgan Chase Bank Nat Assn .... G 206 505-1501
  Seattle *(G-10310)*

INSURANCE AGENTS, NEC

Gary G Guzzie Insurance .... G 509 674-4433
  Cle Elum *(G-2668)*

INSURANCE CARRIERS: Automobile

Ford Motor Credit Company LLC .... D 425 643-0454
  Bellevue *(G-914)*

INSURANCE CARRIERS: Direct Accident & Health

Washington Mso Inc .... F 253 984-7247
  Tacoma *(G-13588)*

INSURANCE CARRIERS: Life

Washington Mso Inc .... F 253 984-7247
  Tacoma *(G-13588)*

INSURANCE INSPECTION & INVESTIGATIONS SVCS

Ecm Maritime Services LLC .... G 206 780-9980
  Seattle *(G-9876)*

INSURANCE: Agents, Brokers & Service

Automotive Machine Specialties .... G 425 355-0802
  Everett *(G-3376)*

Employee Codes: A=Over 500 employees, B=251-500
C=101-250, D=51-100, E=20-50, F=10-19, G=2-9

INSURANCE: Agents, Brokers & Service

Stellar Management Inc .... G 206 724-3973
  Mountlake Terrace *(G-6869)*
Vimly Benefit Solutions Inc .... D 425 771-7359
  Mukilteo *(G-6989)*

INTEGRATED CIRCUITS, SEMICONDUCTOR NETWORKS, ETC

Arm Inc .... C 425 602-0915
  Bellevue *(G-794)*
Arm Inc .... C 408 576-1500
  Olympia *(G-7229)*
Conation Technologies LLC .... C 253 864-8234
  Puyallup *(G-8135)*
Galaxy Cmpund Smconductors Inc ...... F 509 892-1114
  Spokane Valley *(G-12712)*
Leidos Inc .... E 425 267-5600
  Lynnwood *(G-6157)*
Leidos Inc .... E 360 394-8870
  Poulsbo *(G-7975)*
Matrix Visions LLC .... G 206 368-3824
  Lake Forest Park *(G-5621)*
System To Asic Inc .... F 425 488-0575
  Bothell *(G-1798)*
Xnrgi Inc .... G 425 272-2703
  Bothell *(G-1924)*

INTERCOMMUNICATIONS SYSTEMS: Electric

J Fillips LLC .... G 425 277-1011
  Renton *(G-8830)*
Linc Technology Corporation .... E 425 882-2206
  Issaquah *(G-4439)*
Waterfront Solutions Inc .... G 360 348-1874
  Edmonds *(G-3161)*
Zonar Systems Inc .... C 206 878-2459
  Seattle *(G-11524)*

INTERIOR DESIGN SVCS, NEC

Eleganza Designs Inc .... G 360 499-2710
  Lacey *(G-5549)*
I-5 Design Build Inc .... D 360 459-3200
  Lacey *(G-5558)*
Nfi Enterprises LLC .... E 253 245-5500
  Auburn *(G-507)*

INTERIOR DESIGNING SVCS

Bagdons Inc .... E 509 662-1411
  Wenatchee *(G-15011)*
Noel Corporation .... C 509 248-4545
  Yakima *(G-15630)*

INVERTERS: Nonrotating Electrical

Blue Frog Solar LLC .... G 206 855-5149
  Poulsbo *(G-7948)*

INVESTMENT ADVISORY SVCS

Capstan Fund .... G 206 626-0800
  Seattle *(G-9626)*

INVESTMENT FUNDS, NEC

Traction Capital Partners Inc .... G 253 922-3090
  Tacoma *(G-13561)*

INVESTMENT RESEARCH SVCS

Random Walk Group LLC .... G 206 724-3621
  Olympia *(G-7377)*

INVESTORS, NEC

Maruha Capital Investment Inc .... F 206 382-0640
  Bellevue *(G-996)*

IRON & STEEL PRDTS: Hot-Rolled

Consolidated Metco Inc .... D 360 828-2599
  Vancouver *(G-14147)*

IRON & STEEL: Corrugating, Cold-Rolled

Master Roll Manufacturing .... E 425 641-1566
  Bellevue *(G-997)*

IRON ORES

Giant Metals Inc .... G 206 592-0963
  Seatac *(G-9285)*

IRRIGATION EQPT WHOLESALERS

Isaacs & Associates Inc .... G 509 529-2286
  Walla Walla *(G-14825)*
Omak Machine Shop Inc .... G 509 826-1030
  OMAK *(G-7440)*

JACKS: Hydraulic

Specialty Motors Mfg LLC .... G 360 423-9880
  Longview *(G-5956)*

JANITORIAL & CUSTODIAL SVCS

C&T Northwest Services .... G 509 680-4890
  Colville *(G-2742)*
Entrust Community Services .... D 509 839-8066
  Sunnyside *(G-13124)*

JANITORIAL EQPT & SPLYS WHOLESALERS

Coyote Cleaning Systems Inc .... G 425 776-8002
  Mukilteo *(G-6907)*
Northwest Solutions Inc .... G 360 380-3807
  Bellingham *(G-1471)*

JAZZ MUSIC GROUP OR ARTISTS

Juice & Jam Inc .... G 206 734-5136
  Seattle *(G-10314)*

JEWELERS' FINDINGS & MATERIALS

Gem Cut Company .... G 206 780-0113
  Bainbridge Island *(G-636)*

JEWELERS' FINDINGS & MATERIALS: Castings

Le Bijou Corporation .... G 206 622-9453
  Seattle *(G-10389)*

JEWELERS' FINDINGS & MTLS: Jewel Prep, Instr, Tools, Watches

Stateside Bead Supply .... G 425 644-3448
  Bellevue *(G-1155)*

JEWELRY & PRECIOUS STONES WHOLESALERS

Bailey and Bailey Inc .... F 253 649-0568
  Gig Harbor *(G-4075)*
European Creations Inc .... G 425 898-0685
  Redmond *(G-8454)*
Frank Lau Jewelry Inc .... G 206 323-6343
  Seattle *(G-10020)*

JEWELRY APPAREL

A1 Services .... G 509 946-6269
  Richland *(G-8962)*
Dream It Inc .... G 360 379-1070
  Port Townsend *(G-7881)*
Elegantly Yours .... G 425 478-2873
  Duvall *(G-2985)*
Faris LLC .... G 206 992-6453
  Seattle *(G-9972)*
G L Kluh & Sons Jewelers Inc ...... F 360 491-3530
  Lacey *(G-5552)*
Goldenrod Inc .... G 253 840-8114
  Edgewood *(G-3080)*
Kit A Jeweler Designed For You ... G 253 851-5546
  Gig Harbor *(G-4127)*

JEWELRY FINDINGS & LAPIDARY WORK

Cosmic Resources .... G 360 730-8574
  Langley *(G-5775)*
Handmaiden Bead & Jwly Shoppe ...... G 509 680-5785
  Colville *(G-2754)*
John Knutson Lapidary .... G 509 653-2111
  Naches *(G-6998)*
Juicy Gems .... G 425 232-3567
  Spokane *(G-12346)*
M B Lapidary .... G 253 271-7515
  Spanaway *(G-12062)*
Mend .... G 949 355-9925
  Seattle *(G-10516)*
Nutshell .... G 360 438-1054
  Lacey *(G-5570)*
Stockton Cul De Sac .... G 253 854-9358
  Kent *(G-5157)*

PRODUCT SECTION

Teneff Jewelry Mfg Co .... E 509 747-1038
  Spokane *(G-12552)*
True Colors Inc .... G 206 623-2366
  Seattle *(G-11341)*
Usjade LLC .... G 509 535-3411
  Otis Orchards *(G-7521)*

JEWELRY FINDINGS WHOLESALERS

Cosmic Resources .... G 360 730-8574
  Langley *(G-5775)*

JEWELRY REPAIR SVCS

A U Cornerstone Inc .... G 360 336-5234
  Mount Vernon *(G-6768)*
Brothers Jewelers Inc .... G 509 946-7989
  Richland *(G-8978)*
Carlson Brothers Inc .... F 253 472-9232
  Tacoma *(G-13224)*
Handmaiden Bead & Jwly Shoppe ...... G 509 680-5785
  Colville *(G-2754)*
Hartley Jewelers .... G 360 754-6161
  Olympia *(G-7304)*
Jay Lauris & Company Inc .... G 206 243-9890
  Burien *(G-2114)*
Larkin Jewelers .... G 253 756-0712
  Tacoma *(G-13381)*
Originals By Chad Jwly Design .... G 360 318-0210
  Lynden *(G-6042)*
Pacific Northwest Jewelers .... G 509 927-8923
  Greenacres *(G-4300)*
RC & Co .... G 425 774-7511
  Mill Creek *(G-6522)*
Teneff Jewelry Mfg Co .... E 509 747-1038
  Spokane *(G-12552)*

JEWELRY STORES

Cline Manufacturing Jewelers .... G 425 673-7979
  Edmonds *(G-3101)*
Columbia Gem House Inc .... E 360 514-0569
  Vancouver *(G-14130)*
Diamondcraft Jewels .... G 509 758-1449
  Clarkston *(G-2632)*
Handmaiden Bead & Jwly Shoppe ...... G 509 680-5785
  Colville *(G-2754)*
Larkin Jewelers .... G 253 756-0712
  Tacoma *(G-13381)*
Neetas Creations .... G 585 233-1896
  Bellevue *(G-1024)*
Pacific Jewelers .... G 360 693-3410
  Vancouver *(G-14465)*
S&T Trading & More LLC .... G 509 421-2326
  Wenatchee *(G-15071)*
West Coast Gemstones Inc .... G 509 522-4851
  College Place *(G-2731)*
Zirkus Inc .... G 360 385-5478
  Port Townsend *(G-7940)*

JEWELRY STORES: Precious Stones & Precious Metals

ADI Corporation .... G 425 455-4561
  Bellevue *(G-780)*
Bailey and Bailey Inc .... F 253 649-0568
  Gig Harbor *(G-4075)*
Carlson Brothers Inc .... F 253 472-9232
  Tacoma *(G-13224)*
Diamond Store Inc .... G 253 272-3377
  Tacoma *(G-13262)*
DOriginal Jewelers .... G 425 454-5559
  Bellevue *(G-880)*
Dynamic Designs Jewelry Inc .... G 425 827-7722
  Kirkland *(G-5326)*
Eldorado AG .... G 360 491-0394
  Lacey *(G-5547)*
European Creations Inc .... G 425 898-0685
  Redmond *(G-8454)*
Fairhaven Gold Inc .... G 360 733-4667
  Bellingham *(G-1341)*
G L Kluh & Sons Jewelers Inc ...... F 360 491-3530
  Lacey *(G-5552)*
Gold Mine of Jewelry Inc .... G 206 622-3333
  Seattle *(G-10093)*
Goldenrod Inc .... G 253 840-8114
  Edgewood *(G-3080)*
Hartley Jewelers .... G 360 754-6161
  Olympia *(G-7304)*
J Lanning Jewelers .... G 360 693-9940
  Vancouver *(G-14331)*

PRODUCT SECTION

Jane Martin ....G...... 206 842-4569
  Bainbridge Island *(G-644)*
Jay Lauris & Company Inc ....G...... 206 243-9890
  Burien *(G-2114)*
Jewelry Design Center Inc ....E...... 509 487-5905
  Spokane *(G-12334)*
Kogita Custom Mfg & Repair ....G...... 425 453-9547
  Bellevue *(G-970)*
Ofner and Company ....G...... 425 485-0437
  Kenmore *(G-4595)*
Plateau Jewelers Inc ....G...... 425 313-0657
  Sammamish *(G-9242)*
Prestige Fine Jewelry ....G...... 206 623-0085
  Mount Vernon *(G-6825)*
Robins Jewelers Ltd ....G...... 206 622-4337
  Edmonds *(G-3149)*
V S P Jewelry Design Gallery ....G...... 206 367-7310
  Lake Forest Park *(G-5626)*

JEWELRY, PREC METAL: Mountings, Pens, Lthr, Etc, Gold/Silver

Coin Market LLC ....G...... 425 745-1659
  Lynnwood *(G-6095)*

JEWELRY, PRECIOUS METAL: Bracelets

Daughters of Mary ....G...... 360 943-2186
  Olympia *(G-7264)*
S&T Trading & More LLC ....G...... 509 421-2326
  Wenatchee *(G-15071)*

JEWELRY, PRECIOUS METAL: Cigar & Cigarette Access

Sauk Suiattle Indian Tribe Tru ....F...... 360 436-0131
  Darrington *(G-2869)*

JEWELRY, PRECIOUS METAL: Medals, Precious Or Semiprecious

Marathon N More ....G...... 360 380-5242
  Bellingham *(G-1423)*

JEWELRY, PRECIOUS METAL: Necklaces

DOriginal Jewelers ....G...... 425 454-5559
  Bellevue *(G-880)*

JEWELRY, PRECIOUS METAL: Pins

Zirkus Inc ....G...... 360 385-5478
  Port Townsend *(G-7940)*

JEWELRY, PRECIOUS METAL: Rings, Finger

Carlson Brothers Inc ....F...... 253 472-9232
  Tacoma *(G-13224)*

JEWELRY, PRECIOUS METAL: Settings & Mountings

Pacific Northwest Jewelers ....G...... 509 927-8923
  Greenacres *(G-4300)*
Robins Jewelers Ltd ....G...... 206 622-4337
  Edmonds *(G-3149)*

JEWELRY, WHOLESALE

A U Cornerstone Inc ....G...... 360 336-5234
  Mount Vernon *(G-6768)*
ADI Corporation ....G...... 425 455-4561
  Bellevue *(G-780)*
Jane Martin ....G...... 206 842-4569
  Bainbridge Island *(G-644)*
Jewelry Boutique LLC ....G...... 360 866-2278
  Olympia *(G-7311)*
Le Bijou Corporation ....G...... 206 622-9453
  Seattle *(G-10389)*
Pacific Jewelers ....G...... 360 693-3410
  Vancouver *(G-14465)*
Swissa Inc ....G...... 206 625-9202
  Seattle *(G-11240)*

JEWELRY: Decorative, Fashion & Costume

Baubles ....G...... 360 647-3857
  Bellingham *(G-1260)*
Creative Collections Co Inc ....E...... 360 866-8840
  Olympia *(G-7259)*
Daughters of Mary ....G...... 360 943-2186
  Olympia *(G-7264)*
Deborah Funches Jewelry Design ....G...... 503 381-4017
  Camas *(G-2244)*
Degroot Designs ....G...... 253 472-7279
  Tacoma *(G-13256)*
Gold Impressions ....G...... 509 886-0866
  East Wenatchee *(G-3015)*
Infinite Caste ....G...... 206 335-4058
  Renton *(G-8825)*
Kjs Handcrafted Jewelry ....G...... 425 582-8488
  Brier *(G-2020)*
Mike Frantz Inc ....G...... 800 839-6712
  Shelton *(G-11713)*
Millianna LLC ....G...... 415 505-8507
  Spokane *(G-12394)*
Nexappeal ....G...... 360 293-5054
  Anacortes *(G-151)*
Northwest Family Strands ....F...... 206 779-8997
  Seattle *(G-10643)*
Seattle Gold Grills ....G...... 206 250-0833
  Seattle *(G-11060)*
The McCredy Company ....G...... 509 773-5340
  Goldendale *(G-4209)*
Yue Fon USA Inc ....G...... 206 303-0148
  Auburn *(G-603)*

JEWELRY: Precious Metal

A U Cornerstone Inc ....G...... 360 336-5234
  Mount Vernon *(G-6768)*
ADI Corporation ....G...... 425 455-4561
  Bellevue *(G-780)*
Angelwear ....G...... 206 230-9594
  Seattle *(G-9403)*
Astral Holdings Inc ....G...... 206 762-4800
  Seattle *(G-9447)*
Brothers Jewelers Inc ....G...... 509 946-7989
  Richland *(G-8978)*
Cascade Custom Jewelers ....G...... 253 535-2121
  Tacoma *(G-13226)*
Cline Manufacturing Jewelers ....G...... 425 673-7979
  Edmonds *(G-3101)*
Columbia Gem House Inc ....E...... 360 514-0569
  Vancouver *(G-14130)*
Deborah Designs ....G...... 253 848-3274
  Puyallup *(G-8142)*
Diamond Store Inc ....G...... 253 272-3377
  Tacoma *(G-13262)*
Diamondcraft Jewels ....G...... 509 758-1449
  Clarkston *(G-2632)*
Dynamic Designs Jewelry Inc ....G...... 425 827-7722
  Kirkland *(G-5326)*
Eastern Merchandise Co Inc ....G...... 206 448-4466
  Seattle *(G-9871)*
Eldorado AG ....G...... 360 491-0394
  Lacey *(G-5547)*
European Creations Inc ....G...... 425 898-0685
  Redmond *(G-8454)*
Fairhaven Gold Inc ....G...... 360 733-4667
  Bellingham *(G-1341)*
Feather and Skull ....G...... 206 227-7951
  Seattle *(G-9979)*
Frank Lau Jewelry Inc ....G...... 206 323-6343
  Seattle *(G-10020)*
Gem East Corporation ....E...... 206 441-1700
  Lake Forest Park *(G-5613)*
Gems n Gold ....G...... 360 574-5085
  Vancouver *(G-14249)*
Glo Tech Inc ....G...... 360 403-8928
  Arlington *(G-242)*
Goedecke & Goedecke ....G...... 425 481-1153
  Bothell *(G-1862)*
Gold Mine of Jewelry Inc ....G...... 206 622-3333
  Seattle *(G-10093)*
Hartley Jewelers ....G...... 360 754-6161
  Olympia *(G-7304)*
Idea Company ....G...... 253 891-8140
  Pacific *(G-7530)*
J Lanning Jewelers ....G...... 360 693-9940
  Vancouver *(G-14331)*
Jay Lauris & Company Inc ....G...... 206 243-9890
  Burien *(G-2114)*
Jewelry Boutique LLC ....G...... 360 866-2278
  Olympia *(G-7311)*
Jewelry Design Center Inc ....E...... 509 487-5905
  Spokane *(G-12334)*
John M Smith ....G...... 360 484-7738
  Naselle *(G-7013)*
Kogita Custom Mfg & Repair ....G...... 425 453-9547
  Bellevue *(G-970)*
Larkin Jewelers ....G...... 253 756-0712
  Tacoma *(G-13381)*
Marcin Jewelry Inc ....F...... 425 883-7884
  Woodinville *(G-15301)*
Norris Techniques ....G...... 360 871-1458
  Port Orchard *(G-7833)*
Ofner and Company ....G...... 425 485-0437
  Kenmore *(G-4595)*
Originals By Chad Jwly Design ....G...... 360 318-0210
  Lynden *(G-6042)*
Pacific Gem Inc ....G...... 206 448-7700
  Seattle *(G-10733)*
Prestige Fine Jewelry ....G...... 206 623-0085
  Mount Vernon *(G-6825)*
RC & Co ....G...... 425 774-7511
  Mill Creek *(G-6522)*
Swissa Inc ....G...... 206 625-9202
  Seattle *(G-11240)*
Taina Hartman Studio ....G...... 541 806-0053
  White Salmon *(G-15133)*
Teneff Jewelry Mfg Co ....E...... 509 747-1038
  Spokane *(G-12552)*
V S P Jewelry Design Gallery ....G...... 206 367-7310
  Lake Forest Park *(G-5626)*
Wapato Pawn & Trade ....G...... 509 877-6405
  Wapato *(G-14928)*

JIGS & FIXTURES

Triad Products Corporation ....G...... 425 514-8363
  Everett *(G-3636)*

JOB PRINTING & NEWSPAPER PUBLISHING COMBINED

Flint Publishing Inc ....G...... 509 314-6400
  Toppenish *(G-13669)*
Odessa Record ....G...... 509 982-2632
  Odessa *(G-7191)*
OfficeMax North America Inc ....E...... 360 455-4068
  Lacey *(G-5572)*
Ruser Publications Inc ....G...... 509 659-1020
  Ritzville *(G-9122)*
Shelton Publishing Inc ....E...... 360 426-4412
  Shelton *(G-11732)*
Stanwood-Camano News Inc ....E...... 360 629-8066
  Stanwood *(G-12995)*
Sun News Inc ....E...... 360 659-1300
  Marysville *(G-6391)*
Zebra Print and Copy ....G...... 206 223-1800
  Seattle *(G-11519)*

JOB TRAINING & VOCATIONAL REHABILITATION SVCS

Glacier Aviation Inc ....F...... 360 705-3214
  Olympia *(G-7296)*
Math Perspectives ....G...... 360 715-2782
  Bellingham *(G-1426)*
Pioneer Human Services ....D...... 206 768-1990
  Seattle *(G-10809)*
Westerberg & Associates Inc ....G...... 509 951-4399
  Liberty Lake *(G-5867)*

JOB TRAINING SVCS

Cartech Industries Inc ....G...... 360 693-3616
  Vancouver *(G-14100)*
Vivid Learning Systems Inc ....D...... 509 545-1800
  Pasco *(G-7649)*

JOINTS: Swivel & Universal, Exc Aircraft & Auto

Carson NC Inc ....G...... 509 427-8616
  Carson *(G-2304)*

KAOLIN MINING

J M Huber Corporation ....G...... 206 762-4263
  Seattle *(G-10273)*

KEYBOARDS: Computer Or Office Machine

Circuit Imaging LLC ....G...... 509 315-3400
  Spokane Valley *(G-12657)*
Touchfire Inc ....G...... 425 466-4177
  Kent *(G-5185)*

KILNS & FURNACES: Ceramic

Bricor Ceramic Industries ....G...... 360 377-9197
  Bremerton *(G-1940)*

Employee Codes: A=Over 500 employees, B=251-500
C=101-250, D=51-100, E=20-50, F=10-19, G=2-9

KITCHEN & COOKING ARTICLES: Pottery

Clay In Motion Inc .... F 509 529-6146
  Walla Walla *(G-14785)*
Creative Interaction LLC .... G 509 466-4612
  Spokane *(G-12207)*

KITCHEN & TABLE ARTICLES: Coarse Earthenware

Read Products Inc .... F 206 283-2510
  Seattle *(G-10929)*

KITCHEN CABINET STORES, EXC CUSTOM

American Cabinet Doors Inc .... F 509 574-3176
  Yakima *(G-15506)*
Cedar Mountain Woodwrights .... G 509 933-2602
  Ellensburg *(G-3188)*
Morgan Electric & Plumbing Inc .... F 206 547-1617
  Seattle *(G-10562)*
Von Grey Custom Cabinets Inc .... G 360 679-8641
  Oak Harbor *(G-7166)*
Yakima Valley Cabinets Inc .... G 509 248-0472
  Yakima *(G-15718)*

KITCHEN CABINETS WHOLESALERS

American Cabinet Doors Inc .... F 509 574-3176
  Yakima *(G-15506)*
Haun Made LLC .... G 253 242-6105
  Seattle *(G-10150)*
John Duane King .... G 360 736-6707
  Centralia *(G-2412)*
R&J Industries LLC .... G 253 466-3627
  Puyallup *(G-8233)*

KITCHEN TOOLS & UTENSILS WHOLESALERS

Arcomm Inc .... G 253 581-9800
  Lakewood *(G-5699)*

KITCHEN UTENSILS: Bakers' Eqpt, Wood

Pacific NW Fine WD Pdts LLC .... G 360 275-5397
  Belfair *(G-770)*

KITCHEN UTENSILS: Food Handling & Processing Prdts, Wood

Conagra Foods Specialty Potato .... G 509 547-8851
  Pasco *(G-7566)*
Northwest Sushi LLC .... G 360 878-3464
  Vancouver *(G-14441)*

KITCHENWARE STORES

Food Equipment International .... G 509 924-0181
  Spokane Valley *(G-12707)*
Sunrise Bagels & More Inc .... F 360 254-1012
  Vancouver *(G-14616)*

KITCHENWARE: Plastic

Lectent LLC .... D 360 574-7737
  Vancouver *(G-14369)*

LABELS: Paper, Made From Purchased Materials

Desi Telephone Labels Inc .... F 360 571-0713
  Vancouver *(G-14176)*
Go Usa Inc .... E 509 662-3387
  Wenatchee *(G-15034)*
Label Company Inc .... G 206 568-6000
  Seattle *(G-10369)*
Merchant Investments Inc .... E 425 235-8675
  Kent *(G-5006)*
Wholesale Forms Inc .... G 800 826-7095
  Rochester *(G-9145)*

LABOR UNION

Teamster Local 313 .... G 253 627-0103
  Tacoma *(G-13551)*

LABORATORIES, TESTING: Forensic

Secure It LLC .... G 509 992-6190
  Spokane *(G-12497)*

LABORATORIES, TESTING: Metallurgical

Dwight Company LLC .... G 360 262-9844
  Chehalis *(G-2490)*
PM Testing Laboratory Inc .... D 253 922-1321
  Fife *(G-3981)*

LABORATORIES, TESTING: Prdt Certification, Sfty/Performance

Appesteem Corporation .... F 240 461-5689
  Bellevue *(G-789)*

LABORATORIES, TESTING: Product Testing

Integrated Technologies Inc .... D 425 349-2084
  Everett *(G-3518)*

LABORATORIES, TESTING: Product Testing, Safety/Performance

Lawrenson Electronics Co Inc .... G 206 243-7310
  Burien *(G-2117)*

LABORATORIES: Biological Research

Athira Pharma Inc .... F 206 221-8112
  Seattle *(G-9451)*
Biolife Solutions Inc .... E 425 402-1400
  Bothell *(G-1828)*
Novuson Surgical Inc .... G 425 481-7165
  Bothell *(G-1783)*

LABORATORIES: Biotechnology

Biocontrol Systems Inc .... F 425 603-1123
  Bellevue *(G-817)*
Cell Systems Corporation .... G 425 823-1010
  Kirkland *(G-5301)*
Gilead Sciences Inc .... D 206 728-5090
  Seattle *(G-10070)*
Immunex Corporation .... A 206 551-5169
  Seattle *(G-10210)*
Juno Therapeutics Inc .... E 206 582-1600
  Seattle *(G-10317)*
Just Biotherapeutics Inc .... D 206 651-5094
  Seattle *(G-10318)*
Seattle Genetics Inc .... B 425 527-4000
  Bothell *(G-1902)*
Sequoia Scientific Inc .... G 425 641-0944
  Bellevue *(G-1124)*

LABORATORIES: Dental

Central Dental Technicians .... G 509 663-4113
  Wenatchee *(G-15017)*
Qualident Dental Lab LLC .... E 360 695-7411
  Vancouver *(G-14517)*
Sagemax Bioceramics Inc .... E 253 214-0389
  Federal Way *(G-3780)*

LABORATORIES: Dental Orthodontic Appliance Production

Pacific Orthodontic Laboratory .... G 425 224-4193
  Everett *(G-3564)*
Silverdale Orthodontic Lab .... G 360 479-5536
  Bremerton *(G-2000)*

LABORATORIES: Electronic Research

Dynon Avionics Inc .... D 425 402-0433
  Woodinville *(G-15230)*
Falcon Rcnnissance Systems Inc .... G 360 378-3900
  Friday Harbor *(G-4044)*
Prologic Engineering Inc .... D 360 734-9625
  Bellingham *(G-1507)*

LABORATORIES: Environmental Research

Clipper Seafoods Ltd .... C 206 284-1162
  Seattle *(G-9697)*

LABORATORIES: Medical

Breast Care Center .... F 360 424-6161
  Sedro Woolley *(G-11534)*

LABORATORIES: Noncommercial Research

Esther Brcques Wnery Vnyrd LLC ...... G 509 476-2861
  Oroville *(G-7465)*
Infinetix Corp .... F 509 922-5629
  Spokane Valley *(G-12739)*

LABORATORIES: Physical Research, Commercial

A-M Systems LLC .... E 360 683-8300
  Sequim *(G-11604)*
Bio-Tope Research Inc .... G 509 684-1512
  Colville *(G-2739)*
Columbia Mfg & Tech Ctr LLC .... G 360 835-0922
  Washougal *(G-14948)*
Immune Design Corp .... D 206 682-0645
  Seattle *(G-10209)*
Microconnex Corporation .... G 425 396-5707
  Snoqualmie *(G-12018)*
Nbk Associates Inc .... G 216 408-8685
  Kirkland *(G-5408)*
Nu Element Inc .... G 206 356-4525
  Tacoma *(G-13437)*
Pacific Biomarkers Inc .... E 206 298-0068
  Seattle *(G-10728)*
Random Walk Group LLC .... G 206 724-3621
  Olympia *(G-7377)*
Spaceflight Industries Inc .... E 206 342-9934
  Seattle *(G-11165)*
Stardust Materials LLC .... G 360 260-7399
  Vancouver *(G-14608)*
Universal Avonics Systems Corp .... C 425 821-2800
  Redmond *(G-8699)*
Zymogenetics Inc .... C 206 442-6600
  Seattle *(G-11527)*

LABORATORIES: Testing

Pacific Biomarkers Inc .... E 206 298-0068
  Seattle *(G-10728)*

LABORATORIES: Testing

Magnetic Penetrant Svcs Co Inc .... D 206 762-5855
  Seattle *(G-10466)*
Meridian Valley Laboratories .... G 206 209-4200
  Tukwila *(G-13771)*
Pacific Biomarkers Inc .... E 206 298-0068
  Seattle *(G-10728)*
Pacific Northwest Scale Co .... G 425 259-4720
  Snohomish *(G-11960)*
Quad Group Inc .... F 509 458-4558
  Spokane *(G-12463)*
Seacast Inc .... E 206 767-5759
  Seattle *(G-11041)*
United States Dosimetry Tech .... G 509 946-8738
  Richland *(G-9049)*
Valence Surface Tech LLC .... C 206 762-5855
  Seattle *(G-11398)*
Vpt Inc .... G 425 353-3010
  Bothell *(G-1807)*
Zetec Inc .... C 425 974-2700
  Snoqualmie *(G-12035)*

LABORATORY APPARATUS & FURNITURE

Atlas Bimetal Labs Inc .... E 360 385-3123
  Port Townsend *(G-7865)*
BBC .... G 360 629-4477
  Stanwood *(G-12960)*
Loder Instrument Company Inc .... G 425 869-3861
  Redmond *(G-8536)*
Mobile Air Applied Science .... G 206 953-3786
  Bellevue *(G-1012)*
Quantum Technology Corp .... G 604 222-5539
  Blaine *(G-1699)*

LABORATORY APPARATUS: Laser Beam Alignment Device

Basis Software Inc .... G 425 861-9390
  Redmond *(G-8397)*
Pls Pacific Laser Systems LLC .... D 415 453-5780
  Everett *(G-3576)*
Tru Line Laser Alignment Inc .... G 360 371-0552
  Blaine *(G-1708)*

LABORATORY APPARATUS: Physics, NEC

Tested Field Systems LLC .... G 206 453-4851
  Seattle *(G-11282)*

LABORATORY APPARATUS: Sample Preparation Apparatus

Diamond Machine Works Inc .... E 206 633-3960
  Seattle *(G-9827)*

PRODUCT SECTION

LABORATORY APPARATUS: Shakers & Stirrers
Shaker Innovations LLC ....G....... 360 886-1873
  Black Diamond *(G-1655)*

LABORATORY CHEMICALS: Organic
BBC Biochemical Corporation ....C....... 360 542-8400
  Mount Vernon *(G-6777)*

LABORATORY EQPT, EXC MEDICAL: Wholesalers
Washington Vg Inc................................F....... 425 823-4518
  Kirkland *(G-5492)*

LABORATORY EQPT: Centrifuges
Numeric Control LLC ....G....... 360 269-1497
  Morton *(G-6670)*

LABORATORY EQPT: Clinical Instruments Exc Medical
Mill Creek Spine Injury Inc PS ....G....... 425 344-6835
  Lake Stevens *(G-5662)*
Modus Health LLC ....G....... 703 835-0055
  Edmonds *(G-3135)*

LABORATORY EQPT: Distilling
Eden Labs LLC ....F....... 888 626-3271
  Seattle *(G-9882)*

LABORATORY EQPT: Sterilizers
Bmt - Usa LLC ....E....... 360 863-2252
  Monroe *(G-6557)*

LADDER & WORKSTAND COMBINATION ASSEMBLIES: Metal
Metal Werks Inc ....F....... 360 651-0300
  Marysville *(G-6359)*

LADDERS: Metal
American Lifting Products Inc ....G....... 253 572-8981
  Tacoma *(G-13168)*
Marchant Ladders Inc ....G....... 509 882-1912
  Grandview *(G-4252)*

LADDERS: Permanent Installation, Metal
Integrated Stair Systems Inc................E....... 360 829-4220
  Buckley *(G-2060)*
Louisville Ladder ....G....... 206 762-4888
  Seattle *(G-10444)*

LAMINATED PLASTICS: Plate, Sheet, Rod & Tubes
Bridgestone Hosepower LLC ....E....... 206 767-4670
  Seattle *(G-9585)*
Hesco Armor LLC ....E....... 360 637-6867
  Aberdeen *(G-18)*
Innovative Composite Engrg Inc ....D....... 509 493-4484
  White Salmon *(G-15119)*
Interior Form Tops Inc ....E....... 253 927-8171
  Milton *(G-6535)*
Prolam Industries Inc ....E....... 509 926-2001
  Spokane Valley *(G-12843)*
Sound Manufacturing Inc ....E....... 253 872-8007
  Kent *(G-5141)*

LAMINATING SVCS
Plastic Sales & Service Inc ....F....... 206 524-8312
  Lynnwood *(G-6181)*

LAMP BASES: Pottery
Scott Parrish...G....... 360 259-8080
  Vancouver *(G-14573)*

LAMP BULBS & TUBES, ELECTRIC: Electric Light
Envirolux Energy Systems LLC...........G....... 800 914-8779
  Vancouver *(G-14203)*

LAMP BULBS & TUBES, ELECTRIC: For Specialized Applications
Differential Energy Global Ltd ....G....... 360 895-1184
  Port Orchard *(G-7803)*

LAMP BULBS & TUBES, ELECTRIC: Light, Complete
Netzero Energy LLC...........................G....... 360 636-5337
  Longview *(G-5934)*

LAMPS: Ultraviolet
Uv Systems Inc ....G....... 425 228-9988
  Renton *(G-8939)*

LAND SUBDIVIDERS & DEVELOPERS: Commercial
Land Co LLC..G....... 360 484-7712
  Naselle *(G-7016)*
Lloyd Enterprises Inc ....D....... 253 874-6692
  Federal Way *(G-3753)*
McFarland Cascade Holdings Inc.........G....... 360 273-5541
  Rochester *(G-9136)*
McFarland Cascade Holdings Inc.........D....... 253 572-3033
  Tacoma *(G-13404)*
Northwest Executive Corp ....E....... 425 883-9010
  Redmond *(G-8598)*

LAND SUBDIVIDERS & DEVELOPERS: Residential
Lovitt Mining Company Inc ....G....... 509 668-8170
  Wenatchee *(G-15046)*

LAND SUBDIVISION & DEVELOPMENT
All American Corporation ....F....... 509 315-9951
  Mead *(G-6423)*
Bullfrog Land Co Inc............................G....... 509 223-3055
  Loomis *(G-5971)*
Mac Arthur Land & Timber ....G....... 509 442-3805
  Cusick *(G-2851)*
Merrill & Ring Inc ....E....... 360 452-2367
  Port Angeles *(G-7725)*
Vintage Investments Inc ....G....... 360 293-2596
  Anacortes *(G-183)*

LANDING MATS: Aircraft, Metal
Vartan Product Support LLC.................E....... 425 374-8914
  Mukilteo *(G-6988)*

LASER SYSTEMS & EQPT
Auroma Technologies Co LLC..............F....... 425 582-8674
  Everett *(G-3375)*
Cartridge Care Inc ....G....... 360 459-8845
  Lacey *(G-5540)*
JP Innovations LLC ....G....... 360 805-3124
  Monroe *(G-6582)*
Kings Wok ....G....... 360 337-2512
  Silverdale *(G-11841)*
Laser Techniques Company LLC ....F....... 425 885-0607
  Redmond *(G-8530)*
Lumberline Laser Inc ....G....... 360 686-3077
  Vancouver *(G-14386)*
Nlight Inc...B....... 360 566-4460
  Vancouver *(G-14432)*
Novanta Inc...C....... 425 349-1359
  Mukilteo *(G-6958)*
Pls Pacific Laser Systems LLC.............D....... 415 453-5780
  Everett *(G-3576)*
T D Laser Engraving ....G....... 425 347-6837
  Everett *(G-3625)*

LASERS: Welding, Drilling & Cutting Eqpt
Fablab LLC ....G....... 253 426-1267
  Tacoma *(G-13286)*
Laserfab Inc..F....... 509 762-0400
  Puyallup *(G-8176)*
Naimor Inc ....E....... 360 756-9700
  Bellingham *(G-1457)*
Northwest Laser Systems Inc..............G....... 877 623-1342
  Kent *(G-5032)*
Rentiel Precision Laser Cutng.............G....... 253 297-2823
  Tacoma *(G-13494)*

LATH: Wood
Don Larson Logging Inc......................G....... 509 722-6612
  Fruitland *(G-4065)*

LATHES
First Impressions Co Inc.....................G....... 206 372-0361
  Kent *(G-4908)*
R N C Lath & Plaster............................G....... 360 802-0938
  Enumclaw *(G-3315)*
Slave To Lathe ....G....... 206 937-2129
  Seattle *(G-11135)*
South Bend Lathes ....G....... 360 734-1540
  Bellingham *(G-1548)*

LAUNDRY & GARMENT SVCS: Tailor Shop, Exc Custom/Merchant
Bellevue Tailors and Formal Wr ....G....... 425 643-0741
  Bellevue *(G-815)*

LAUNDRY EQPT: Commercial
Hoofsbeat Blankets ....G....... 206 390-0016
  Monroe *(G-6579)*
SK&y International LLC ....G....... 253 833-9525
  Auburn *(G-564)*
Ultrasonics International Corp ....G....... 360 676-0056
  Ferndale *(G-3921)*

LAUNDRY SVC: Flame & Heat Resistant Clothing Sply
Darbonnier Tactical Supply LLC...........G....... 360 672-0216
  Oak Harbor *(G-7146)*

LAWN & GARDEN EQPT
D & M Machine Division Inc ....F....... 360 249-3366
  Montesano *(G-6643)*
Garden Guys LLC ....G....... 206 257-4024
  Burien *(G-2110)*
Pacific Topsoils Inc..............................E....... 425 337-2700
  Everett *(G-3568)*
Sls Runout LLC ....D....... 360 883-8846
  Vancouver *(G-14594)*
Snogro ....G....... 360 863-6935
  Snohomish *(G-11980)*
US Mower Inc ....F....... 360 757-7555
  Burlington *(G-2198)*

LAWN & GARDEN EQPT STORES
EFC Equipment LLC ....G....... 509 713-7230
  Richland *(G-8992)*

LAWN & GARDEN EQPT: Rototillers
Northwest Tillers Inc............................G....... 509 575-1950
  Yakima *(G-15635)*

LAWN & GARDEN EQPT: Tractors & Eqpt
Rootz ....G....... 509 443-5999
  Spokane *(G-12483)*

LAWN MOWER REPAIR SHOP
Alexander S Service Repair ....G....... 509 773-7010
  Goldendale *(G-4192)*
Sondra L Groce ....G....... 509 467-8788
  Spokane *(G-12511)*
Sumner Lawn n Saw LLC ....F....... 253 435-9284
  Puyallup *(G-8257)*

LEAD & ZINC ORES
Lka Gold Incorporated.........................G....... 253 514-6661
  Gig Harbor *(G-4133)*

LEAD PENCILS & ART GOODS
Chabre Bros ....G....... 509 629-0342
  Walla Walla *(G-14782)*
Milestone Products Co ....F....... 425 882-1987
  Redmond *(G-8589)*

LEASING & RENTAL SVCS: Cranes & Aerial Lift Eqpt
Neil F Lampson Inc ....C....... 509 586-0411
  Kennewick *(G-4700)*

Employee Codes: A=Over 500 employees, B=251-500
C=101-250, D=51-100, E=20-50, F=10-19, G=2-9

LEASING & RENTAL SVCS: Earth Moving Eqpt

Birch Equipment Company Inc .... E 360 734-5744
Bellingham *(G-1272)*
International Cnstr Eqp Inc .... G 206 764-4787
Seattle *(G-10249)*

LEASING & RENTAL: Computers & Eqpt

Fedex Office & Print Svcs Inc .... E 360 647-1114
Bellingham *(G-1344)*

LEASING & RENTAL: Construction & Mining Eqpt

Best Way Concrete .... G 360 825-5494
Enumclaw *(G-3279)*
Efco Corp .... F 253 852-3800
Kent *(G-4886)*
Mikes Custom Welding .... G 360 754-3719
Tumwater *(G-13887)*
Mikes Rental Machinery Inc .... E 509 925-6126
Ellensburg *(G-3215)*
Spokane Forklift Cnstr Eqp Inc .... G 509 868-5962
Spokane *(G-12518)*
Springbrook Nurs & Trckg Inc .... D 360 653-6545
Arlington *(G-331)*
Star Rentals Inc .... F 509 545-8521
Pasco *(G-7632)*
Washington Tractor Inc .... C 253 863-4436
Sumner *(G-13110)*
Washington Tractor Inc .... E 360 533-6393
Aberdeen *(G-38)*
Washington Tractor Inc .... F 509 422-3030
Okanogan *(G-7204)*

LEASING & RENTAL: Medical Machinery & Eqpt

Norco Inc .... G 509 764-5032
Moses Lake *(G-6731)*

LEASING & RENTAL: Other Real Estate Property

Longwell Company .... D 425 289-0160
Bellevue *(G-989)*

LEASING: Passenger Car

Harris-Ford Inc .... C 425 678-0391
Lynnwood *(G-6132)*

LEATHER GOODS: Aprons, Welders', Blacksmiths', Etc

Oregon Glove Company .... G 253 475-6733
Tacoma *(G-13446)*

LEATHER GOODS: Card Cases

Pioneer Square Brands Inc .... G 360 733-5608
Seattle *(G-10811)*

LEATHER GOODS: Holsters

Crew Custom Holsters .... G 360 270-3588
Longview *(G-5904)*
Kramer Handgun Leather Inc .... F 253 564-6652
University Place *(G-13975)*

LEATHER GOODS: NEC

5 Shot Leather .... G 509 844-3969
Colbert *(G-2705)*
Ape Artisan Leather .... G 206 399-0967
Seattle *(G-9408)*
Burnish Leather Co .... G 360 723-8533
Washougal *(G-14946)*
Desert Leathercraft LLC .... G 509 392-2589
Richland *(G-8987)*
Dog House Leathers .... G 206 257-0231
Seattle *(G-9841)*
Good Wear Leather Coat Company .... G 206 724-6325
Mountlake Terrace *(G-6861)*
Hi-Lineleather .... G 360 263-7898
La Center *(G-5505)*
L Leather LLC .... G 253 733-9196
Tacoma *(G-13380)*
Luans Leathers .... G 360 546-5050
Vancouver *(G-14385)*

Patriot Leather Company .... G 360 393-1392
Sedro Woolley *(G-11555)*
Reckless Charm .... G 253 355-1420
Pullman *(G-8103)*
Rkba Concealment .... G 360 624-3874
Vancouver *(G-14554)*

LEATHER GOODS: Personal

Christopher Pallis Inc .... G 206 619-4146
Tacoma *(G-13234)*
College Portfolios 425 427-0126
Sammamish *(G-9198)*

LEATHER GOODS: Saddles Or Parts

Indiana Harness Co .... G 509 535-3400
Spokane Valley *(G-12738)*

LEATHER GOODS: Spats

Touche Beauty Bar LLC .... G 360 972-2345
Olympia *(G-7411)*

LEATHER GOODS: Wallets

Foldz Wallet LLC 206 730-6381
Edmonds *(G-3112)*
Subsplash Inc .... E 206 965-8090
Seattle *(G-11210)*

LEATHER GOODS: Whips

Nelson Estate .... G 206 241-9463
Burien *(G-2119)*

LEATHER TANNING & FINISHING

High Mountain Tannery .... G 509 435-3478
Clayton *(G-2658)*
Obenaufs Online .... G 509 254-3542
Clarkston *(G-2639)*
Outlaw Leather LLC .... G 206 679-7483
Seattle *(G-10719)*

LEATHER: Accessory Prdts

Bochans Custom Leather Work .... G 425 337-6128
Snohomish *(G-11878)*

LEATHER: Shoe

McKenzie & Adams Inc .... G 425 672-8668
Woodinville *(G-15307)*

LEATHER: Specialty, NEC

Tidal Vision Products LLC .... F 907 988-8888
Ferndale *(G-3913)*

LEATHER: Upholstery

Sure-Fit Seat Covers .... G 509 326-0122
Spokane *(G-12535)*

LECTURING SVCS

Leading Beyond Tradition LLC .... G 425 275-7665
Snohomish *(G-11938)*

LEGAL OFFICES & SVCS

Custom Office Design Inc .... F 253 735-8777
Auburn *(G-420)*
Jury Verdicts Northwest .... G 425 487-9848
Burien *(G-2115)*
S J Olsen Publishing Inc .... F 360 249-3311
Montesano *(G-6656)*

LEGAL SVCS: General Practice Attorney or Lawyer

Faubion William J Atty At Law .... G 360 795-3367
Cathlamet *(G-2366)*
Montgomery Law Firm .... G 509 684-2519
Colville *(G-2766)*
Stewart & Stewart Law Off PS .... G 360 249-4342
Montesano *(G-6659)*

LEGAL SVCS: Malpractice & Negligence Law

Morgan Electric & Plumbing Inc .... F 206 547-1617
Seattle *(G-10562)*

LESSORS: Farm Land

Sage Hill Northwest Inc .... F 509 269-4966
Mesa *(G-6495)*

LICENSE TAGS: Automobile, Stamped Metal

Battle Ground Auto License .... G 360 687-5115
Battle Ground *(G-691)*
Camano Island Licensing .... F 360 387-4700
Stanwood *(G-12954)*
Camas Auto License .... G 360 835-2977
Camas *(G-2236)*
Defensive Driving School Inc .... G 425 643-0116
Kirkland *(G-5320)*
Drivers License Examining .... G 253 872-2782
Kent *(G-4878)*
Fifes Vehicle Vessel .... G 253 926-8227
Fife *(G-3952)*
Gundersons Auto License .... G 360 695-2122
Vancouver *(G-14276)*
Hawkbird Auto An Boat Listing .... G 360 491-3015
Lacey *(G-5554)*
Hwy 99 Auto License .... G 360 573-6226
Vancouver *(G-14305)*
Skagit Vehicle Licensing Inc .... G 360 755-0419
Burlington *(G-2190)*
Vehicle Licensing .... G 360 336-9348
Mount Vernon *(G-6852)*

LIE DETECTION SVCS

Gillespie Polygraph .... G 425 775-9015
Lynnwood *(G-6130)*

LIFE RAFTS: Rubber

Tacoma Community Boat Builders .... G 253 720-8227
Tacoma *(G-13540)*

LIGHT SENSITIVE DEVICES

Applied Precision LLC .... C 425 557-1000
Issaquah *(G-4380)*
Applied Precision Holdings LLC .... C 425 557-1000
Issaquah *(G-4381)*

LIGHTING EQPT: Flashlights

Mag Lite Warranty .... G 360 398-9798
Bellingham *(G-1420)*
Zonecro Llc 760 702-9290
Bremerton *(G-2014)*

LIGHTING EQPT: Floodlights

Netzero Energy LLC .... G 360 636-5337
Longview *(G-5934)*

LIGHTING EQPT: Locomotive & Railroad Car Lights

Klas Technologies LLC .... G 360 678-8705
Greenbank *(G-4308)*

LIGHTING EQPT: Miners' Lamps

Global Mining .... G 509 863-9724
Spokane Valley *(G-12719)*
Nevada Lithium Corp .... G 360 318-8352
Lynden *(G-6039)*

LIGHTING EQPT: Motor Vehicle, NEC

Kent D Bruce .... G 360 886-9410
Black Diamond *(G-1649)*

LIGHTING EQPT: Outdoor

Event Power & Lighting Inc .... G 360 225-3830
Woodland *(G-15431)*
Laser Guidance Inc .... G 206 679-3909
Redmond *(G-8529)*
Mfg Universe Corp .... G 800 883-8779
Tukwila *(G-13772)*
Ncs Power Inc .... F 360 896-4063
Vancouver *(G-14429)*

LIGHTING EQPT: Spotlights

Deaf Spotlight .... G 206 466-4693
Seattle *(G-9808)*

PRODUCT SECTION

LIGHTING EQPT: Strobe Lighting Systems

Nortn Coast Lighting Cash ....G..... 425 454-2122
  Bellevue *(G-1038)*

LIGHTING FIXTURES WHOLESALERS

NW Lighting Solutions LLC ....G..... 253 246-2959
  Kent *(G-5040)*
Sol Lighting Inc..................................G..... 509 789-1092
  Spokane Valley *(G-12880)*
Uv Systems Inc ....G..... 425 228-9988
  Renton *(G-8939)*

LIGHTING FIXTURES, NEC

Avio Corporation...............................G..... 425 739-6800
  Kirkland *(G-5286)*
Avtechtyee Inc..................................C..... 425 290-3100
  Everett *(G-3378)*
Belfair Garden & Lighting ....G..... 360 275-2130
  Belfair *(G-759)*
C & H Lighting Associates Inc ....G..... 253 531-1270
  Tacoma *(G-13213)*
Christie Lites Seattle LLC ....F..... 206 223-7200
  Kent *(G-4852)*
Eco Safe Technologies LLC..............G..... 360 567-1923
  Camas *(G-2247)*
Electric Mirror LLC ....B..... 425 776-4946
  Everett *(G-3454)*
Emerald City Lighting........................G..... 206 234-8554
  Kirkland *(G-5331)*
Escent Lighting.................................G..... 509 838-9028
  Spokane *(G-12251)*
Fishtrap Creek Lighting LLC.............G..... 360 354-7900
  Lynden *(G-6018)*
Grakon LLC.......................................C..... 206 824-6000
  Des Moines *(G-2936)*
Industrial Revolution Inc ....E..... 425 285-1111
  Tukwila *(G-13752)*
Leader Manufacturing Inc ....E..... 360 895-1184
  Port Orchard *(G-7825)*
Lightloom..G..... 206 228-5001
  Shoreline *(G-11782)*
Lumenomics Inc................................E..... 206 327-9037
  Seattle *(G-10451)*
Northwest Outdoor Lighting..............G..... 425 633-6074
  Duvall *(G-2996)*
NW Lighting Solutions LLC ....G..... 253 929-4657
  Auburn *(G-514)*
Plc-Multipoint Inc ....G..... 425 353-7552
  Everett *(G-3575)*
Quoizel Lighting ....G..... 360 275-5435
  Belfair *(G-771)*
Red Hat Lighting LLC ....G..... 360 624-5773
  Vancouver *(G-14538)*
Rejuvenation Inc...............................F..... 206 382-1901
  Seattle *(G-10946)*
Steel Partners Inc.............................F..... 360 748-9406
  Chehalis *(G-2537)*
Takovo Led Lights ....G..... 206 330-6862
  Seattle *(G-11260)*
Vleds ....G..... 360 543-5700
  Bellingham *(G-1586)*

LIGHTING FIXTURES: Arc

NW Lighting Solutions LLC ....G..... 253 246-2959
  Kent *(G-5040)*

LIGHTING FIXTURES: Indl & Commercial

Aleddra Inc ....G..... 425 430-4555
  Renton *(G-8735)*
Aleddra Inc ....G..... 425 430-4555
  Renton *(G-8736)*
Charles Loomis Inc..........................F..... 425 823-4560
  Kirkland *(G-5303)*
Dynesco Corporation Inc ....G..... 360 256-0116
  Mukilteo *(G-6918)*
Every Watt Matters LLC ....E..... 425 985-2171
  Vancouver *(G-14211)*
Every Watt Matters LLC ....D..... 503 221-2113
  Vancouver *(G-14212)*
Form Lighting and Controls LLC......G..... 206 854-8689
  Seattle *(G-10013)*
Iunu Inc...G..... 253 307-1858
  Seattle *(G-10263)*
Lagoon Conservation LLC ....G..... 253 202-6479
  Des Moines *(G-2939)*
Leader Manufacturing Inc ....E..... 360 895-1184
  Port Orchard *(G-7825)*

Legitiment Light Co ....G..... 206 542-3268
  Shoreline *(G-11781)*
Light Edge Inc ....E..... 360 567-1680
  Vancouver *(G-14375)*
Light It Bright Products LLC.............G..... 253 666-2278
  Tacoma *(G-13388)*
Lightel Technologies Inc ....E..... 425 277-8000
  Renton *(G-8844)*
Lighting Group Northwest Inc ....G..... 206 298-9000
  Seattle *(G-10419)*
Lumenex LLC ....G..... 206 909-3474
  Seattle *(G-10450)*
Netzero Energy LLC.........................G..... 360 636-5337
  Longview *(G-5934)*
ORyan Industries Inc ....E..... 360 892-0447
  Vancouver *(G-14459)*
Rexel Capitol Light ....G..... 425 861-0200
  Redmond *(G-8650)*
Roy Pablo ....G..... 425 750-9941
  Quil Ceda Village *(G-8281)*
S3j Elctrnics Acquisition Corp ....G..... 716 206-1309
  Mukilteo *(G-6975)*
Vision X Offroad LLC ....E..... 888 489-9820
  Auburn *(G-592)*
Western Technology Inc...................G..... 360 917-0080
  Bremerton *(G-2012)*

LIGHTING FIXTURES: Motor Vehicle

Altus Industries Inc..........................G..... 360 255-7699
  Blaine *(G-1659)*
Xenon Arc Inc...................................E..... 425 646-1063
  Bellevue *(G-1229)*

LIGHTING FIXTURES: Ornamental, Commercial

Graypants Inc ....G..... 206 420-3912
  Seattle *(G-10112)*
I-5 Design Build Inc..........................D..... 360 459-3200
  Lacey *(G-5558)*

LIGHTING FIXTURES: Residential

Howard Lamp Company....................G..... 425 776-7914
  Seattle *(G-10188)*
Michael Ashford Design ....G..... 360 352-0694
  Olympia *(G-7339)*
Rexel Capitol Light ....G..... 425 861-0200
  Redmond *(G-8650)*
Sevilla LLC ....G..... 509 280-8447
  Spokane *(G-12500)*
Steel Partners Inc.............................F..... 360 748-9406
  Chehalis *(G-2537)*

LIGHTING FIXTURES: Street

Patriot Sales Inc ....F..... 360 855-0737
  Sedro Woolley *(G-11556)*

LIME

Graymont Western US Inc................E..... 253 572-7600
  Tacoma *(G-13319)*
Lime Solutions..................................G..... 425 502-7651
  Bellevue *(G-984)*
Mango and Lime Design LLC...........G..... 425 985-8994
  Redmond *(G-8547)*
Western Lime Corp ....G..... 604 249-1997
  Seattle *(G-11453)*

LIMESTONE & MARBLE: Dimension

Highland Quarry LLC........................G..... 509 624-4136
  Spokane *(G-12294)*
Northwest Lime Co LLC ....G..... 360 815-0304
  Ferndale *(G-3877)*
Urban Stoneworks LLC ....G..... 808 333-6675
  Ridgefield *(G-9118)*

LIMESTONE: Crushed & Broken

Clauson Quarry LLC.........................G..... 360 599-2731
  Maple Falls *(G-6249)*
Hemphill Brothers Inc......................G..... 206 842-0748
  Bainbridge Island *(G-639)*
Hemphill Brothers Inc......................G..... 509 732-4481
  Northport *(G-7138)*
Legacy Vulcan LLC ....E..... 206 284-7717
  Seattle *(G-10400)*
Martin Marietta Materials Inc...........F..... 360 424-3441
  Mount Vernon *(G-6810)*

Martin Marietta Materials Inc...........G..... 360 856-5870
  Mount Vernon *(G-6811)*
Pyramid Materials Kitsap Quar........G..... 360 373-8708
  Bremerton *(G-1991)*
Rondys Inc..G..... 425 392-6324
  Issaquah *(G-4470)*
Sawyer & Sawyer Inc ....E..... 509 486-1304
  Tonasket *(G-13658)*

LIMESTONE: Ground

J A Jack & Sons Inc ....F..... 206 762-7622
  Seattle *(G-10265)*
Pacific Calcium Incorporated ....E..... 509 486-1201
  Tonasket *(G-13656)*

LINEN SPLY SVC: Clothing

Itc USA LLC ....F..... 206 669-3442
  Seattle *(G-10262)*

LINERS & COVERS: Fabric

Cedar Mountain Spa Covers ....F..... 253 872-8993
  Kent *(G-4844)*

LINERS & LINING

Foss Marine Holdings Inc ....G..... 206 381-5800
  Seattle *(G-10014)*

LININGS: Apparel, Made From Purchased Materials

Strawberry Kids LLC ....G..... 425 605-8883
  Redmond *(G-8685)*

LININGS: Fabric, Apparel & Other, Exc Millinery

Embroidery For Soul ....G..... 425 319-1269
  Monroe *(G-6568)*
Sh RTS Off Screen Printing ....G..... 425 319-1269
  Sultan *(G-13035)*

LIP BALMS

Dr Bieseckers LLC............................G..... 360 386-1530
  Stanwood *(G-12967)*
Miracle Studios ....G..... 833 728-3233
  Bonney Lake *(G-1729)*
Shea Your Lips Lip Balm ....G..... 360 856-4803
  Sedro Woolley *(G-11564)*
Wineblock LLC ....G..... 877 919-4921
  Seattle *(G-11484)*

LIPSTICK

I Hart Lipstick ....G..... 253 720-7126
  Tacoma *(G-13345)*
Lipstick Mission ....G..... 360 455-3212
  Lacey *(G-5565)*

LOCKS

Clark Security Products Inc ....G..... 206 467-3000
  Seattle *(G-9689)*
Cobra Key Systems LLC ....G..... 509 466-1918
  Colbert *(G-2706)*
S C Jr LLC...G..... 253 539-1097
  Tacoma *(G-13505)*

LOCKS & LOCK SETS, WHOLESALE

Clark Security Products Inc ....G..... 206 467-3000
  Seattle *(G-9689)*

LOCKS: Safe & Vault, Metal

SA Consumer Products Inc ....G..... 888 792-4264
  Fife *(G-3990)*

LOG LOADING & UNLOADING SVCS

Feller Logging Inc ....G..... 509 364-3435
  Glenwood *(G-4181)*
H & D Logging Company Inc ....F..... 509 548-7358
  Leavenworth *(G-5805)*

LOGGING

3 X Bar Inc ....G..... 360 274-4502
  Castle Rock *(G-2336)*
7 Arrows Logging LLC ....G..... 509 930-8059
  White Swan *(G-15136)*

Employee Codes: A=Over 500 employees, B=251-500
C=101-250, D=51-100, E=20-50, F=10-19, G=2-9

LOGGING

PRODUCT SECTION

AAA Tree Service & Logging LLC ....G 360 463-7553
  Shelton *(G-11672)*
Acorn Tree and Stump Services ....G 360 509-0145
  Port Gamble *(G-7756)*
Adams Timber Service LLC ....G 360 636-7766
  Silverlake *(G-11861)*
Aeneas Valley Cnstr & Log ....G 206 391-8408
  Ravensdale *(G-8328)*
AG Tree Service LLC 425 830-8820
  Kirkland *(G-5274)*
Alan Loghry Excavation Inc ....G 360 461-0660
  Port Angeles *(G-7681)*
Allen Bros Diving Logging ....G 360 866-3643
  Olympia *(G-7222)*
Allways Logging LLC ....G 360 893-2724
  Graham *(G-4215)*
Altels Logging Inc ....G 509 782-5808
  Cashmere *(G-2313)*
Amanda Park Services Inc ....G 360 288-2230
  Amanda Park *(G-87)*
American Forest Lands Wash ....G 425 358-5235
  Maple Valley *(G-6258)*
American Timber Resources LLC ....G 360 796-4236
  Brinnon *(G-2023)*
Andrew A Kroiss ....G 509 684-4929
  Colville *(G-2736)*
Andrew Russell Pond ....G 509 690-8509
  Colville *(G-2737)*
Arg Logging LLC ....G 253 606-5047
  Yelm *(G-15728)*
B L Logging ....G 360 748-8248
  Chehalis *(G-2469)*
Baldwin Logging Incorporated ....G 360 520-4484
  Salkum *(G-9179)*
Bdn Logging Inc ....G 360 785-4119
  Winlock *(G-15145)*
Bear Mountin Cutters Inc ....G 360 875-0035
  South Bend *(G-12039)*
Bearly Loggin ....G 509 493-1706
  White Salmon *(G-15111)*
Bell Creek Contracting Inc ....G 360 592-3300
  Bellingham *(G-1262)*
Bennett Painting ....G 360 426-6489
  Shelton *(G-11683)*
Bethel Lutheran Church ....G 360 892-4231
  Brush Prairie *(G-2030)*
Bill Anderson ....G 509 281-0055
  White Salmon *(G-15112)*
Black Lk Bb Camp Cnference Ctr ....F 360 539-5337
  Olympia *(G-7236)*
Bme Logging LLC ....G 360 931-6797
  La Center *(G-5502)*
Boettcher & Sons Inc ....G 360 832-3943
  Eatonville *(G-3051)*
Bradley Heavy Construction ....G 360 341-5967
  Clinton *(G-2684)*
Bremerton Trap & Skeet Club ....G 360 674-2438
  Port Orchard *(G-7796)*
Brian D Ames ....G 360 561-5119
  Olympia *(G-7241)*
Brian Martell ....G 509 738-3041
  Kettle Falls *(G-5227)*
Brindle Technical Logging Inc ....G 360 985-7459
  Mossyrock *(G-6759)*
Brintech Inc ....G 360 985-7459
  Mossyrock *(G-6760)*
Brown Lumber Co ....G 509 779-4738
  Curlew *(G-2844)*
Bueler Farms Inc ....G 360 668-5289
  Snohomish *(G-11883)*
Bullfrog Land Co Inc ....G 509 223-3055
  Loomis *(G-5971)*
Butchs Bulldozing & Backhoe ....G 360 652-0473
  Stanwood *(G-12962)*
Carl Emil Seastrom ....F 509 722-5414
  Inchelium *(G-4371)*
Carlson and Sons Logging Inc ....G 360 795-3068
  Cathlamet *(G-2362)*
Chandler W Jeppsen ....G 541 466-0908
  Tacoma *(G-13233)*
Charles Washington ....G 509 466-9098
  Mead *(G-6427)*
Charlo Timberlands Inc ....G 509 447-3671
  Newport *(G-7055)*
Chavez Nolberto ....G 360 426-9550
  Shelton *(G-11691)*
Claquato Farms Inc ....G 360 748-6220
  Chehalis *(G-2484)*
Clark Contract Cutting Inc ....G 360 705-0355
  Tumwater *(G-13861)*

Clear and Level Logging LLC ....G 360 247-5989
  Amboy *(G-90)*
Colburn Timber Inc ....F 360 208-4501
  Raymond *(G-8346)*
Colburn Timber Inc ....G 360 875-6565
  Rainier *(G-8312)*
Columbia Navigation Inc ....G 509 684-4335
  Kettle Falls *(G-5222)*
Copper Creek Logging LLC ....G 253 203-5915
  Wilkeson *(G-15143)*
Corporation of the President ....G 509 656-2344
  Cle Elum *(G-2663)*
Crawford Enterprises ....G 360 866-4972
  Olympia *(G-7258)*
Crw Timber ....G 360 425-4858
  Longview *(G-5905)*
Curtins Heritage Logging Inc ....G 360 518-5735
  Washougal *(G-14950)*
D E Metlow Logging LLC ....G 509 937-2233
  Valley *(G-13990)*
Dahlquist Logging Inc ....G 253 804-9112
  Auburn *(G-421)*
Dave Bekkevar Logging & Trckg ....F 360 683-3655
  Sequim *(G-11624)*
Deming Log Show Inc ....G 360 592-3051
  Bellingham *(G-1322)*
Derek Mefford ....G 360 580-9166
  Hoquiam *(G-4333)*
Diamond Timber Company ....F 360 274-7914
  Castle Rock *(G-2339)*
Don Glaser Logging ....G 206 462-9638
  Eatonville *(G-3053)*
Don Larson Logging Inc ....G 509 722-6612
  Fruitland *(G-4065)*
Double a Logging Inc ....F 509 476-2907
  Oroville *(G-7464)*
Dozing & Ditching ....G 425 308-2063
  Lake Stevens *(G-5644)*
Dw Cornwall Farms Inc ....G 509 291-5011
  Fairfield *(G-3696)*
Edward Laurence Pelanconi ....G 360 435-2725
  Arlington *(G-233)*
Elder Logging Co ....G 360 886-2779
  Black Diamond *(G-1647)*
ENB Logging & Construction ....F 360 673-2696
  Kalama *(G-4500)*
Endicott Truck & Tractor ....G 509 657-3436
  Endicott *(G-3264)*
Evergreen Fibre Inc ....E 360 452-2670
  Port Angeles *(G-7704)*
Ewing Construction ....G 509 624-2246
  Spokane *(G-12252)*
F and F Excavating and Logging ....G 509 637-2551
  Glenwood *(G-4180)*
Far West Inc ....G 360 942-3270
  Raymond *(G-8348)*
Faubion William J Atty At Law ....G 360 795-3367
  Cathlamet *(G-2366)*
Filla Company LLC ....G 360 864-2531
  Toledo *(G-13638)*
Fir Lane Memorial Pk & Fnrl HM ....F 253 531-6600
  Spanaway *(G-12058)*
Flory Cabinets LLC ....G 360 894-2504
  Yelm *(G-15733)*
Forsyth Enterprises ....G 360 297-2684
  Kingston *(G-5252)*
Frank Harkness Trckg & Log LLC ....F 360 826-6087
  Acme *(G-42)*
Frank Harkness Trckg & Log LLC ....G 360 595-2496
  Concrete *(G-2785)*
Fred B Moe Logging Co ....G 360 273-6049
  Oakville *(G-7174)*
Fur Tree Forestry ....G 360 426-6252
  Elma *(G-3246)*
Garkse Logging & Road Bldg LLC ....G 360 520-2707
  Chehalis *(G-2498)*
Gary C Horsley ....G 360 274-4502
  Winlock *(G-15150)*
Gary G Guzzie Insurance ....G 509 674-4433
  Cle Elum *(G-2668)*
Gary L Ostenson DDS PS ....G 360 896-9595
  Vancouver *(G-14248)*
Gibbons Drilling Inc ....G 360 671-3040
  Stanwood *(G-12974)*
Haulin Somethin Inc ....G 509 738-4144
  Kettle Falls *(G-5232)*
Havillah Lumber ....G 509 486-4650
  Tonasket *(G-13649)*
Herbrand Company ....F 253 848-7700
  Puyallup *(G-8161)*

Hicks Logging Christmas T ....G 253 208-8914
  Olympia *(G-7306)*
Ho Stafford Logging ....G 360 853-8816
  Rockport *(G-9152)*
Horsley Timber & Construction ....G 360 274-7272
  Castle Rock *(G-2345)*
Howard & Son Excavating LLC ....G 360 983-3922
  Silver Creek *(G-11823)*
Islas Cedar LLC ....G 360 590-2176
  Hoquiam *(G-4345)*
J L & O Enterprises Inc ....G 360 636-5427
  Kelso *(G-4530)*
J&M Heavy Cnstr & Log Co LLC ....G 360 747-2735
  Port Orchard *(G-7818)*
J&N Land Trucking ....G 360 677-2274
  Skykomish *(G-11866)*
Jack H Hill ....G 360 864-4939
  Winlock *(G-15152)*
James & Eileen Kaski ....G 360 687-4214
  Battle Ground *(G-711)*
James Smith Trucking ....G 360 423-1027
  Kelso *(G-4531)*
JB Timberline Logging ....G 360 871-0956
  Olalla *(G-7207)*
Jeff Hauenstein Logging ....G 360 826-3490
  Concrete *(G-2788)*
Jeffrey Gould ....F 360 274-7914
  Castle Rock *(G-2346)*
Jim Davis ....G 360 374-5659
  Forks *(G-4010)*
Jimini Construction LLC ....G 360 426-9918
  Shelton *(G-11705)*
Jon Lonning Drywall ....G 253 851-4866
  Gig Harbor *(G-4125)*
Jones Logging and Cnstr LLC ....F 509 422-3147
  Okanogan *(G-7198)*
Jones Logging LLC ....G 509 732-4511
  Colville *(G-2760)*
JP Logging LLC ....G 208 596-7069
  Spokane Valley *(G-12755)*
Jrj Inc ....F 360 691-2528
  Seattle *(G-10311)*
JSB Logging ....G 360 301-9675
  Brinnon *(G-2024)*
Judd Timber Cutting LLC ....G 360 928-9011
  Port Angeles *(G-7720)*
Justin Maine Logging Inc ....G 360 262-4105
  Winlock *(G-15153)*
Kaski Tom Logging & Cat Work ....G 360 247-5707
  Yacolt *(G-15484)*
Kayser Farms ....G 360 274-6277
  Castle Rock *(G-2347)*
Kcpk Trucking Inc ....G 360 592-2260
  Everson *(G-3680)*
Keith Austin Logging ....G 509 684-8869
  Colville *(G-2762)*
Keith Cooper Logging Inc ....G 360 459-3553
  Olympia *(G-7315)*
Ken Olson Cutting ....G 360 374-5052
  Forks *(G-4011)*
Kenneth Maupin Logging Cnstr ....G 509 442-3484
  Ione *(G-4375)*
Knot Hole Inc ....G 541 806-0950
  White Salmon *(G-15120)*
Krueger Logging Inc ....G 360 687-5558
  Battle Ground *(G-714)*
Kurt Muonio Contract Cutting ....G 360 686-1809
  Yacolt *(G-15485)*
LA Excav & Select Log Inc ....G 360 856-4111
  Mount Vernon *(G-6806)*
Land Co LLC ....G 360 484-7712
  Naselle *(G-7016)*
Leon Wickizer Excavating ....G 253 261-2978
  Buckley *(G-2061)*
Levanen Lee John ....G 360 687-7478
  Battle Ground *(G-716)*
Lewis Cnty Work Opportunities ....E 360 748-9921
  Chehalis *(G-2509)*
Liberty Logging Inc ....G 360 423-5454
  Kelso *(G-4535)*
Living Waters Logging LLC ....G 360 749-6333
  Longview *(G-5928)*
Lloyd Remsberg Logging ....G 509 997-7362
  Twisp *(G-13913)*
Lodestone Construction Inc ....G 360 875-6960
  South Bend *(G-12043)*
Lorz & Lorz Inc ....G 509 486-2202
  Tonasket *(G-13653)*
Loudin Logging LLC ....G 253 691-8679
  Eatonville *(G-3061)*

Lynch Creek Quarry LLC G 360 832-4269
Eatonville *(G-3062)*

M & M Logging G 360 280-5973
McCleary *(G-6418)*

Mac Arthur Land & Timber G 509 442-3805
Cusick *(G-2851)*

Macarthur Logging G 509 675-8045
Elk *(G-3172)*

Manastash Logging Inc G 206 937-8311
Seattle *(G-10471)*

Manke Lumber Company Inc G 360 426-5536
Shelton *(G-11710)*

McClure Ranch G 509 634-4685
Nespelem *(G-7022)*

Mechanical Fuels Treatment LLC G 509 486-1438
Tonasket *(G-13654)*

Mesa Resources Inc G 360 683-1912
Sequim *(G-11648)*

Michael D Worley G 509 290-0927
Elk *(G-3174)*

Mike Nilles G 509 299-3653
Medical Lake *(G-6442)*

Mnr Logging LLC G 360 532-3631
Aberdeen *(G-23)*

Mnr Logging LLC G 360 249-2213
Montesano *(G-6648)*

Moerke Family 3 LLC G 360 748-8952
Chehalis *(G-2515)*

Montgomery Law Firm G 509 684-2519
Colville *(G-2766)*

Moose Creek Logging Inc G 360 631-3728
Arlington *(G-282)*

Mor-Log Inc G 360 426-7872
Shelton *(G-11715)*

Mount Adams Lumber Co Inc G 509 395-2122
Trout Lake *(G-13681)*

Mountain Tree Farm Company E 253 924-2345
Federal Way *(G-3760)*

Mulvaney Trucking and Excav G 509 784-4502
Entiat *(G-3268)*

Newport Equipment Entps Inc E 509 447-4688
Newport *(G-7062)*

Nielsen Brothers Inc D 360 671-9078
Sedro Woolley *(G-11552)*

NW Logging Company G 360 226-2691
Tacoma *(G-13438)*

Pacific Marine Contractors G 360 532-2765
Aberdeen *(G-27)*

Pacific Marine Investments G 360 532-2765
Aberdeen *(G-28)*

Pacific Rim Portfolios Ltd E 360 595-2854
Sedro Woolley *(G-11554)*

Paul E Sevier G 360 491-1334
Olympia *(G-7367)*

Petes Logging LLC G 509 684-6231
Colville *(G-2768)*

Phillip L Remsberg G 509 997-3231
Twisp *(G-13916)*

Phillips & Reichert Shake Mill G 360 978-4392
Chehalis *(G-2524)*

Plaas Timber LLC F 360 832-2440
Eatonville *(G-3066)*

Puget Logging & Excavation G 360 629-0461
Stanwood *(G-12988)*

Puget Sound Logging G 253 310-5923
Rochester *(G-9139)*

Quality Logging LLC G 360 640-1555
Castle Rock *(G-2352)*

R & H Logging & Contract Cutng G 360 795-3334
Cathlamet *(G-2372)*

R Harper Inc G 360 985-0806
Mossyrock *(G-6765)*

R&S Forestry and Cnstr LLC G 360 436-1771
Arlington *(G-311)*

Rayonier Inc E 425 748-5220
Bellevue *(G-1095)*

Rcc Logging Limited G 360 556-8904
Tumwater *(G-13894)*

Richard & Mike Lynch G 360 263-4078
Woodland *(G-15463)*

Richard Meek G 360 275-4104
Belfair *(G-772)*

Richardson Log & Land Clearing G 360 631-2107
Sedro Woolley *(G-11560)*

Robert E Miller G 509 485-3032
Oroville *(G-7472)*

Robert Lloyd Zerck G 509 779-4820
Malo *(G-6235)*

Robert Rogers G 360 352-9408
Olympia *(G-7387)*

Ronald Brewer G 360 436-1771
Arlington *(G-317)*

Ronald Rex Dairy Farm G 360 856-0629
Sedro Woolley *(G-11561)*

Rotschy Timber Management G 360 247-5396
Amboy *(G-96)*

RTS & BBC Inc G 360 239-1953
Hoquiam *(G-4356)*

S and R Logging and Cutting G 425 314-7662
Stanwood *(G-12990)*

Schaben Logging Inc G 360 589-9008
Aberdeen *(G-33)*

Scotts Home & Roofing Service G 360 297-7524
Kingston *(G-5263)*

Sevier Logging LLC G 360 791-5527
Lacey *(G-5586)*

Shipp Construction Inc E 360 262-0197
Ethel *(G-3351)*

Smith Logging & Monkey Bus G 253 857-5900
Olalla *(G-7210)*

Solomon Logging LLC G 425 292-0745
North Bend *(G-7125)*

Southside Enterprises Inc F 509 395-2345
Trout Lake *(G-13683)*

Steve Hazelwood & Son Trucking G 253 863-5721
Lake Tapps *(G-5686)*

Stewart & Stewart Law Off PS G 360 249-4342
Montesano *(G-6659)*

Storlie & Graham Cutting Inc G 509 962-6494
Ellensburg *(G-3228)*

Stormy Mountain Ranch Inc G 509 687-3295
Chelan *(G-2564)*

Sumas Mt Log Co G 360 966-4781
Sumas *(G-13051)*

T & D Gruhn Trucking Inc G 360 532-1288
Aberdeen *(G-37)*

T & R Log Co G 509 962-6590
Ellensburg *(G-3229)*

T J Brooks Logging G 425 220-2263
Camano Island *(G-2225)*

Tall Timber Contractoring Inc G 509 681-1275
Cle Elum *(G-2680)*

Tdb Holdings LLC G 360 600-5506
La Center *(G-5516)*

Teamster Local 313 G 253 627-0103
Tacoma *(G-13551)*

Tenneson Brothers G 360 856-6242
Sedro Woolley *(G-11575)*

Thin Air Logging LLC G 509 670-8139
Peshastin *(G-7664)*

Thomas L Norman Cnstr & Log G 253 312-7858
Orting *(G-7487)*

Thomas Tree Svc & Logging G 360 561-9589
Lacey *(G-5594)*

Tight Line Industries Inc F 360 751-1621
Toledo *(G-13643)*

Tiin-MA Logging E 509 874-2040
White Swan *(G-15139)*

Tj Logging LLC G 509 826-5203
OMAK *(G-7445)*

Tjs Mechanical Cutting LLC G 360 837-1234
Washougal *(G-14994)*

Tobin & Riedesel Logging LLC E 360 482-8127
Elma *(G-3257)*

Tri-Tex Inc E 360 274-8511
Castle Rock *(G-2356)*

Triangle C Farms Inc G 509 682-2189
Chelan *(G-2567)*

Trickinnex Tree Trimming & Fal G 509 653-1937
Naches *(G-7007)*

Two Horse Logging Inc G 360 592-5244
Bellingham *(G-1579)*

W-4 Construction Inc F 509 529-1603
Walla Walla *(G-14886)*

Wayne Pond Logging Inc G 509 684-8732
Colville *(G-2782)*

Westerlund Log Handlers LLC E 503 325-9877
Naselle *(G-7021)*

Westlands Resources Corp Inc G 360 740-1970
Chehalis *(G-2542)*

Weyerhaeuser Company C 360 274-3058
Castle Rock *(G-2357)*

Weyerhaeuser Company B 253 924-3030
Tacoma *(G-13595)*

Weyerhaeuser Company B 360 425-2150
Longview *(G-5966)*

Weyerhaeuser Company C 360 291-3229
Pe Ell *(G-7661)*

White & Zumstein Inc F 360 263-6114
La Center *(G-5519)*

White Logging LLC G 509 997-0279
Twisp *(G-13917)*

Wiard H Groeneveld G 360 793-1638
Monroe *(G-6637)*

Wilkins Kaiser & Olsen Inc C 509 427-5967
Carson *(G-2310)*

William Blockley Contracting G 360 592-5843
Deming *(G-2926)*

Wilson Operations G 360 496-6565
Morton *(G-6674)*

Windemere Camino Island Realty E 360 387-3411
Stanwood *(G-12958)*

Wood Shed Inc G 253 405-8890
Pacific *(G-7541)*

Woodland Services Inc G 360 652-0412
Arlington *(G-349)*

Woolys Tree Service Inc G 360 944-7786
Vancouver *(G-14700)*

Zender Logging Co Inc E 360 966-5693
Everson *(G-3694)*

Zercks Logging LLC G 509 779-4820
Malo *(G-6236)*

Zumstein Logging Co G 253 225-7521
Woodland *(G-15478)*

LOGGING CAMPS & CONTRACTORS

A & RS Logging Inc F 360 249-4017
Montesano *(G-6641)*

A&C Logging LLC G 509 493-3160
White Salmon *(G-15109)*

Ace Logging Inc F 360 537-6843
Hoquiam *(G-4327)*

Ah Logging G 509 935-4565
Chewelah *(G-2598)*

Ahola Timber Inc G 360 892-2243
Brush Prairie *(G-2028)*

AK Logging Lumber & Millwork G 360 461-3764
Port Angeles *(G-7680)*

ALRT Corporation D 360 592-5300
Everson *(G-3666)*

American Forest Lands G 425 432-5004
Maple Valley *(G-6257)*

Arthur D Fulford Jr G 509 826-2225
OMAK *(G-7433)*

Ash Logging Company Inc G 360 264-4367
Tenino *(G-13612)*

B & B Logging Inc G 360 247-5237
Amboy *(G-89)*

B & M Logging Inc E 360 748-6904
Chehalis *(G-2468)*

B & W Excavating & Cnstr G 509 937-2028
Valley *(G-13988)*

B&M Logging Inc G 360 985-0150
Ethel *(G-3348)*

Barry Rankin Logging Inc G 360 436-1947
Darrington *(G-2866)*

Beardslee Logging G 509 675-2400
Kettle Falls *(G-5224)*

Breithaupt Logging Inc G 360 732-4225
Chimacum *(G-2612)*

Bremmeyer Logging E 425 432-9310
Ravensdale *(G-8332)*

Bresch Logging G 509 258-9620
Springdale *(G-12950)*

Bruce & Walter Webster G 360 697-3975
Poulsbo *(G-7953)*

Bucks Logging Inc G 360 985-0758
Ethel *(G-3349)*

Burgess Logging Inc F 509 763-3119
Leavenworth *(G-5797)*

Burya Logging and Trucking Inc F 509 935-6816
Chewelah *(G-2599)*

C & C Logging LLC D 360 636-0300
Kelso *(G-4519)*

C & H Logging Inc E 509 364-3420
Glenwood *(G-4178)*

C Swanson Logging G 360 886-0237
Black Diamond *(G-1646)*

Caribou Creek Logging Inc G 509 962-6700
Ellensburg *(G-3186)*

Carlson Login Inc G 360 795-3068
Cathlamet *(G-2363)*

Castle & Coleman Logging Co G 360 426-0840
Shelton *(G-11688)*

Cherry Valley Logging Company F 206 396-0002
Duvall *(G-2981)*

Chilton Logging Inc E 360 225-0427
Woodland *(G-15423)*

D & D Logging G 425 308-2063
Lake Stevens *(G-5642)*

PRODUCT

Employee Codes: A=Over 500 employees, B=251-500
C=101-250, D=51-100, E=20-50, F=10-19, G=2-9
2019 Washington
Manufacturers Register
997

D Creek Timber Inc.....G..... 360 262-3786
Winlock *(G-15149)*
Dale Bradeen Logging.....G..... 509 738-6132
Kettle Falls *(G-5230)*
Darrell A Tillotson.....G..... 509 493-2376
White Salmon *(G-15114)*
David Littlejohn Logging.....G..... 360 352-5858
Olympia *(G-7265)*
Deep Creek Logging Inc.....G..... 360 533-2390
Hoquiam *(G-4332)*
Delbert L Wheeler.....E..... 509 874-2471
White Swan *(G-15137)*
Denise Haase.....G..... 360 264-4680
Tumwater *(G-13871)*
Dennis Davis Logging Co Inc.....F..... 360 864-2548
Toledo *(G-13637)*
Dills Creek Inc.....G..... 360 826-3841
Hamilton *(G-4312)*
Don Boehme & Sons Logging.....G..... 360 871-1571
Port Orchard *(G-7804)*
Don Painter Logging Inc.....F..... 360 832-3683
Eatonville *(G-3054)*
Donald R Jacobson.....G..... 360 425-4346
Longview *(G-5907)*
Donner Logging LLC.....G..... 509 675-2717
Colville *(G-2751)*
Double D Logging Co Inc.....G..... 360 533-7168
Hoquiam *(G-4334)*
Drolz Log and Rock Inc.....G..... 360 987-2343
Hoquiam *(G-4335)*
Duane Bruner Logging Inc.....E..... 360 274-7103
Castle Rock *(G-2340)*
Eagle Logging Inc.....G..... 509 226-1329
Spokane Valley *(G-12684)*
Eddie ODell.....G..... 360 797-7549
Sequim *(G-11632)*
Edwards Logging Co.....F..... 360 457-7330
Port Angeles *(G-7702)*
Eiger Skyline Inc.....G..... 509 548-6808
Leavenworth *(G-5800)*
Elder Logging Inc.....G..... 360 825-7158
Enumclaw *(G-3289)*
Elk Creek Contractors Inc.....F..... 509 364-3692
Glenwood *(G-4179)*
Emerson Logging Corporation.....G..... 509 647-5658
Wilbur *(G-15141)*
Emery Enterprises.....G..... 360 532-0102
Aberdeen *(G-10)*
Engeseth Logging.....F..... 360 327-3391
Beaver *(G-756)*
Erickson Busheling Inc.....G..... 360 928-3232
Port Angeles *(G-7703)*
Erickson Logging.....G..... 253 846-2646
Graham *(G-4225)*
Erickson Logging Inc.....F..... 360 832-8627
Eatonville *(G-3056)*
F A Koenig & Sons Inc.....G..... 360 793-1711
Sultan *(G-13024)*
Fagernes Cutting Inc.....G..... 360 245-3249
Chehalis *(G-2496)*
Farrer Logging Co.....G..... 509 773-5069
Goldendale *(G-4197)*
Feller Logging Inc.....G..... 509 364-3435
Glenwood *(G-4181)*
Florek Logging Ltd Inc.....G..... 360 795-8058
Cathlamet *(G-2367)*
Forest Land Services Inc.....F..... 360 652-9044
Stanwood *(G-12971)*
Fred Nanamkin.....G..... 509 634-8110
Keller *(G-4512)*
G&L Horse Logging.....G..... 360 247-5156
Amboy *(G-94)*
Galivan Logging Inc.....G..... 360 866-1431
Olympia *(G-7293)*
Gamble Bay Timber.....G..... 360 297-0555
Kingston *(G-5253)*
Gamble Logging.....G..... 253 857-3294
Gig Harbor *(G-4104)*
George Anderson Company.....G..... 425 333-0707
Redmond *(G-8476)*
Gibson & Son Road Building Inc.....F..... 509 925-2017
Ellensburg *(G-3202)*
Global Pacific Forest Products.....F..... 360 568-1111
Snohomish *(G-11913)*
Gould & Sons Logging Inc.....E..... 360 274-9425
Castle Rock *(G-2343)*
Gould-Sunrise Logging Inc.....F..... 360 274-8000
Castle Rock *(G-2344)*
Greg Robertson Logging Inc.....G..... 208 660-3616
Newport *(G-7058)*

Griffiths Inc.....G..... 360 276-4122
Moclips *(G-6539)*
Gronlund Logging Inc.....G..... 509 548-5039
Leavenworth *(G-5804)*
Hadaller Logging Inc.....F..... 360 425-0602
Kelso *(G-4527)*
Handly & Phillips Logging Inc.....G..... 360 765-3578
Quilcene *(G-8284)*
Hansen & Spies Logging Inc.....F..... 509 364-3385
Glenwood *(G-4183)*
Hansen Logging LLC.....E..... 509 935-4515
Chewelah *(G-2602)*
Harry Wiebold Logging.....G..... 360 687-2129
Battle Ground *(G-708)*
Hofstrand Logging Inc.....E..... 509 968-3197
Ellensburg *(G-3208)*
Holbrook Inc.....E..... 360 754-9390
Olympia *(G-7307)*
Hood Canal Logging Co Inc.....G..... 360 275-4676
Belfair *(G-763)*
Howard Denson Logging.....G..... 360 988-4910
Sumas *(G-13045)*
Hubster Logging Inc.....G..... 253 200-7183
Eatonville *(G-3059)*
Hurworth Logging.....G..... 360 457-4776
Port Angeles *(G-7712)*
J H Holm.....G..... 360 825-4276
Enumclaw *(G-3295)*
Jerry Debriae Logging Co Inc.....D..... 360 795-3309
Cathlamet *(G-2369)*
Jerry Hart & Son Logging.....G..... 360 871-7037
Port Orchard *(G-7819)*
Jim Hamilton.....G..... 360 875-6170
South Bend *(G-12041)*
Joe Gordon Logging Inc.....G..... 360 470-1631
McCleary *(G-6417)*
Joe Zender & Sons Inc.....G..... 360 599-2064
Deming *(G-2920)*
John Harkness Logging.....F..... 360 595-2260
Acme *(G-43)*
John Meadows Logging.....G..... 509 427-4330
Stevenson *(G-13014)*
John Meek Logging.....G..... 360 491-6976
Olympia *(G-7312)*
Johnson Forestry Contracting.....G..... 360 484-3311
Naselle *(G-7014)*
K & L Logging.....G..... 360 273-9916
Rochester *(G-9134)*
Kennedy Creek Quarry Inc.....F..... 360 426-4743
Shelton *(G-11706)*
Knoll Tree Care & Logging.....G..... 253 630-1520
Kent *(G-4981)*
Knutz Logging & Farming.....G..... 509 779-4713
Malo *(G-6234)*
Kovash Logging Ltd.....E..... 360 825-4263
Enumclaw *(G-3299)*
Krume Logging Excavation.....F..... 360 274-8667
Castle Rock *(G-2348)*
Leake Logging Inc.....G..... 509 738-3033
Kettle Falls *(G-5235)*
Levanen Inc.....F..... 360 687-4314
Battle Ground *(G-715)*
Log Processors Inc.....F..... 509 773-3043
Goldendale *(G-4202)*
Lost Creek Logging.....G..... 509 442-3218
Cusick *(G-2850)*
Lv Logging.....G..... 360 837-3144
Washougal *(G-14964)*
Macmillan & Company.....F..... 360 249-1148
Montesano *(G-6645)*
Mark 3 Logging.....G..... 360 577-8833
Longview *(G-5931)*
Martin Frank.....G..... 509 292-2685
Deer Park *(G-2908)*
McFadden & Mcfadden Logging.....G..... 253 847-7695
Graham *(G-4232)*
McKay & Son.....G..... 360 532-2285
Aberdeen *(G-22)*
McNamee & Sons Logging.....G..... 509 292-8656
Elk *(G-3173)*
Mike Brandeberry.....F..... 206 524-9656
North Bend *(G-7116)*
Mikes Logging.....G..... 360 893-5336
Tacoma *(G-13413)*
Miller Shingle Company LLC.....G..... 360 691-7727
Granite Falls *(G-4281)*
Mischel Bros Logging Inc.....G..... 360 649-7101
Port Orchard *(G-7829)*
Mitzner Logging.....G..... 509 422-6834
Okanogan *(G-7200)*

Monk Logging Inc.....G..... 509 447-4526
Newport *(G-7061)*
Montes Logging & Firewood.....G..... 360 943-3181
Olympia *(G-7342)*
Mountain Logging Inc.....E..... 509 493-3511
White Salmon *(G-15123)*
Mountain Logging Inc.....E..... 509 493-3511
Bingen *(G-1640)*
Mulrony Logging LLC.....G..... 509 261-1549
Goldendale *(G-4204)*
NDC Timber Inc.....E..... 360 482-4645
Elma *(G-3251)*
Norm Stoken Logging Inc.....G..... 360 683-0908
Sequim *(G-11651)*
North Fork Timber Company Corp.....G..... 360 273-5541
Rochester *(G-9138)*
North Fork Timber Company Corp.....F..... 360 748-8333
Centralia *(G-2420)*
North Fork Timber Company Corp.....G..... 360 748-8333
Chehalis *(G-2517)*
Northman Logging.....G..... 425 870-4727
Granite Falls *(G-4282)*
Oster Logging Inc.....G..... 425 397-0585
Lake Stevens *(G-5665)*
Pacific Force MGT & Harvest.....G..... 360 484-3854
Naselle *(G-7018)*
Pacific Logging Inc.....E..... 425 334-3600
Marysville *(G-6365)*
Pacific Logging LLC.....G..... 425 508-9150
Lake Stevens *(G-5667)*
Pacific Reign Enterprises.....G..... 360 580-4447
Humptulips *(G-4364)*
Parker Pacific Inc.....E..... 253 862-9133
Buckley *(G-2066)*
Perkins Timber LLC.....G..... 360 754-2892
Olympia *(G-7368)*
Pierson & Son Construction.....G..... 360 642-2796
Long Beach *(G-5877)*
Pleines Logging Inc.....G..... 360 374-6373
Forks *(G-4015)*
Pries Logging.....G..... 360 985-0044
Onalaska *(G-7453)*
Pursley Logging Co Inc.....G..... 360 274-7297
Castle Rock *(G-2350)*
R L Smith Logging Inc.....F..... 360 943-6540
Olympia *(G-7375)*
Rainestree Timber Marketing.....G..... 360 462-6197
Shelton *(G-11723)*
Ramco Mechanical Cutting Ltd.....E..... 360 263-1967
La Center *(G-5513)*
Ramsey Bros Logging Inc.....G..... 253 380-4971
Eatonville *(G-3068)*
Rawson Logging.....G..... 360 829-0474
Buckley *(G-2069)*
Rayonier Forest Resources LP.....F..... 360 374-6565
Forks *(G-4017)*
Reano Construction & Logging.....G..... 360 886-1374
Black Diamond *(G-1654)*
Rich Richmond Logging LLC.....E..... 509 935-4833
Chewelah *(G-2606)*
Richard Andrews Logging.....G..... 360 426-1096
Shelton *(G-11725)*
Richardson Logging.....G..... 509 684-4206
Addy *(G-47)*
Rick Carlson.....G..... 360 691-4421
Granite Falls *(G-4285)*
Ross Creek Logging Inc.....G..... 509 926-0415
Otis Orchards *(G-7517)*
Rygaard Logging Inc.....F..... 360 457-4941
Port Angeles *(G-7741)*
S & J Logging Inc.....G..... 360 795-3309
Cathlamet *(G-2374)*
Sam Bickle Logging Inc.....G..... 360 273-5886
Rochester *(G-9140)*
San Poil Logging.....G..... 509 634-8112
Keller *(G-4514)*
Sawtooth Logging.....G..... 360 249-6255
Montesano *(G-6658)*
Saxon Contracting LLC.....E..... 360 595-2854
Sedro Woolley *(G-11563)*
Skillman Brothers Inc.....G..... 360 866-7083
Olympia *(G-7396)*
Skookum Logging Inc.....F..... 360 532-2186
Aberdeen *(G-36)*
Skyline Logging LLC.....G..... 509 935-7200
Chewelah *(G-2608)*
Snoqualmie Valley Logging Inc.....G..... 360 794-8205
Monroe *(G-6622)*
Somero Logging.....G..... 360 686-3926
Yacolt *(G-15493)*

PRODUCT SECTION

LUMBER & BLDG MATRLS DEALERS, RET: Bath Fixtures, Eqpt/Sply

Spradlin Rock Products Inc .... G 360 532-2994
  Hoquiam *(G-4360)*
Stewart Logging .... G 360 437-2905
  Port Ludlow *(G-7779)*
Stewart Logging Inc .... G 509 684-6746
  Colville *(G-2776)*
Stott Logging Inc .... F 360 533-2971
  Hoquiam *(G-4361)*
T L Fitzer Logging Inc .... E 360 832-4949
  Eatonville *(G-3069)*
T&B Logging Inc .... G 509 684-4316
  Colville *(G-2777)*
Tarbert Logging Inc .... F 509 738-6567
  Kettle Falls *(G-5242)*
Tc Lumber .... G 360 452-2612
  Port Angeles *(G-7748)*
Tim Brown Logging Inc .... E 360 274-4422
  Castle Rock *(G-2353)*
Tree Management Plus Inc .... F 360 978-4305
  Toledo *(G-13644)*
Turley Log & Timberland MGT .... G 509 239-4523
  Cheney *(G-2594)*
Van Dyk & Son Logging Inc .... G 360 592-5951
  Deming *(G-2925)*
Van Dyke Logging Incorporated .... G 509 442-3852
  Ione *(G-4376)*
WA Cutting and Logging .... G 360 520-0464
  Ethel *(G-3352)*
West Pacific Resources Inc .... F 425 210-6427
  Arlington *(G-346)*
Western Land Timber .... E 360 987-2170
  Hoquiam *(G-4362)*
Western Timber Inc .... G 360 769-0639
  Port Orchard *(G-7857)*
Westwood Logging .... G 509 548-7681
  Cashmere *(G-2334)*
Weyerhaeuser Company .... C 360 446-2420
  Rainier *(G-8323)*
White River Logging .... F 360 829-1630
  Buckley *(G-2080)*
Wiebold & Sons Logging Inc .... G 360 573-2149
  Vancouver *(G-14691)*
Wiest Logging .... G 360 423-3560
  Longview *(G-5969)*
Will Logging & Construction .... F 509 223-3560
  Loomis *(G-5973)*
Willapa Logging Company Inc .... E 360 875-5670
  Raymond *(G-8361)*
Willard Newman .... G 509 442-3265
  Ione *(G-4377)*
Wines Company .... G 509 292-8820
  Elk *(G-3178)*
Wirtanen Logging Inc .... G 360 686-3042
  Yacolt *(G-15494)*
Womsley Logging Company .... G 360 321-5321
  Langley *(G-5789)*
Wyss Logging Inc .... E 509 452-5893
  Yakima *(G-15711)*
Zender Bros & Wilburn Logging .... G 360 599-2859
  Deming *(G-2927)*
Zepp Resources .... F 360 470-4622
  Elma *(G-3260)*
Zumstein Logging Co .... G 360 225-7505
  Woodland *(G-15477)*

LOGGING: Peeler Logs

Silver City Timber .... G 509 276-5126
  Deer Park *(G-2914)*

LOGGING: Saw Logs

SDS Lumber Co .... C 509 493-1444
  Bingen *(G-1642)*

LOGGING: Stump Harvesting

Kriegers Stump Removal Inc .... G 360 225-1703
  Woodland *(G-15443)*

LOGGING: Timber, Cut At Logging Camp

Anderson & Middleton Company .... F 360 533-2410
  Olympia *(G-7225)*
Basic Homes LLC .... G 253 579-2724
  Eatonville *(G-3050)*
Cascade Tree Service LLC .... G 425 241-9326
  North Bend *(G-7106)*
Frank Swiger Trucking Inc .... G 509 258-7226
  Ford *(G-4005)*
Glenwood Timber Inc .... G 509 364-4158
  Glenwood *(G-4182)*
Green Diamond Resource Company ..... G 360 426-0737
  Grapeview *(G-4288)*
H & D Logging Company Inc .... F 509 548-7358
  Leavenworth *(G-5805)*
Hitchcock Cutting .... G 360 748-7480
  Chehalis *(G-2503)*
Hunter Creek Property Ltd .... G 509 675-4949
  Hunters *(G-4365)*
J & O Timber Falling Inc .... G 360 978-4590
  Onalaska *(G-7448)*
Jeffrey Hembury .... G 360 535-3737
  Belfair *(G-765)*
Jim Johnson & Son Trucking LLC .... F 360 770-5073
  Sedro Woolley *(G-11548)*
Kiona Creek Timber Inc .... G 360 983-3786
  Mossyrock *(G-6762)*
Macmillan and Company .... E 360 470-1535
  Montesano *(G-6646)*
Mvr Timber Cutting Inc .... F 360 459-7409
  Olympia *(G-7347)*
Pope Resources .... G 253 851-7009
  Gig Harbor *(G-4147)*
Quintana Cutting Inc .... G 360 592-5943
  Deming *(G-2922)*
Rayfield Oneil Timber Cutters .... G 509 925-2061
  Ellensburg *(G-3222)*
Richart Company Inc .... G 509 935-8857
  Chewelah *(G-2607)*
S Boone Mechanical Cutting .... G 360 748-4293
  Chehalis *(G-2534)*
Sealaska Timber Corporation .... G 360 834-3700
  Camas *(G-2281)*
Stanton .... G 360 864-6897
  Toledo *(G-13642)*
West Fork Timber Co LLC .... F 253 383-5871
  Lakewood *(G-5766)*
Weyerhaeuser Company .... A 206 539-3000
  Seattle *(G-11459)*

LOGGING: Wood Chips, Produced In The Field

Evergreen Fibre Inc .... F 360 452-3341
  Port Angeles *(G-7705)*
Schillinger Enterprises Inc .... G 360 275-2275
  Belfair *(G-774)*

LOGGING: Wooden Logs

C & J Logging Co Inc .... E 360 484-7256
  Naselle *(G-7012)*
Evergreen Timber Corp .... F 206 579-2925
  Seattle *(G-9946)*
Interfor US Inc .... D 360 575-3600
  Longview *(G-5919)*
Kilponen Bros Logging Inc .... G 360 484-7758
  Naselle *(G-7015)*
Longview Fibre Ppr & Packg Inc .... D 206 762-7170
  Seattle *(G-10437)*
Tobin and Riedesel Logging LLC .... G 360 249-8184
  Montesano *(G-6661)*

LOGS: Gas, Fireplace

Home Fire Prest Logs Ltd .... F 360 366-2200
  Ferndale *(G-3852)*

LOOMS

Shannock Tapestry Looms .... G 360 573-7264
  Vancouver *(G-14581)*

LOOSELEAF BINDERS

Trim Seal USA Inc .... G 425 867-1522
  Redmond *(G-8694)*

LOTIONS OR CREAMS: Face

All Natural Botanicals Inc .... G 253 939-2600
  Kent *(G-4771)*
Bon Logic Corporation .... G 509 991-9643
  Spokane *(G-12157)*
Emu Emprium Hlthy Alternatives .... G 360 269-3459
  Chehalis *(G-2492)*
Fascinaturals LLC .... G 425 954-7151
  Edmonds *(G-3111)*
Fast Horticultural Services .... G 360 393-7057
  Ferndale *(G-3840)*
Lch Enterprises .... G 253 313-5665
  Gig Harbor *(G-4129)*
Little Bay Inc .... G 646 300-3694
  Seattle *(G-10429)*
Micro Current Technology Inc .... E 206 938-5800
  Seattle *(G-10530)*
Moon Valley Natural Pdts LLC .... G 360 595-0500
  Deming *(G-2921)*
Paula S Choice .... G 425 988-2931
  Kent *(G-5062)*
Wisdom Elite LLC .... G 806 201-3953
  Lakewood *(G-5768)*

LOUDSPEAKERS

Genesis Advanced Technologies .... F 206 762-8383
  Seattle *(G-10060)*
Leeds Look Listen Inc .... G 208 252-6075
  Seattle *(G-10398)*
Sound Product Solutions LLC .... G 360 553-7898
  Vancouver *(G-14601)*

LUBRICANTS: Corrosion Preventive

Sandbox Enterprises LLC .... G 360 966-6677
  Bellingham *(G-1523)*

LUBRICATING EQPT: Indl

Altix North America Inc .... G 425 285-4477
  Redmond *(G-8381)*
Quantum .... G 509 751-6407
  Clarkston *(G-2643)*
Sp Indstrial Lubrication A LLC .... G 360 579-2646
  Clinton *(G-2699)*

LUBRICATING OIL & GREASE WHOLESALERS

Power Punch Distributors LLC .... G 360 479-0673
  Bremerton *(G-1989)*
Pulsair Systems Inc .... G 425 455-1263
  Kirkland *(G-5448)*

LUGGAGE & BRIEFCASES

CC Filson Co .... C 206 624-4437
  Seattle *(G-9649)*
Filson Manufacturing Inc .... G 206 242-9579
  Seattle *(G-9993)*
Lammy Industries Inc .... E 206 654-0010
  Seattle *(G-10374)*
Northwest Design & Mfg .... G 360 714-8513
  Bellingham *(G-1466)*
Poros .... F 773 504-2908
  Seattle *(G-10833)*
Resource Accounting Svcs Inc .... G 860 608-0457
  Port Orchard *(G-7846)*
Samsonite LLC .... A 253 395-1017
  Renton *(G-8902)*
Titan Case Inc .... G 206 935-0566
  Seattle *(G-11314)*

LUGGAGE & LEATHER GOODS STORES

Tom Bihn Inc .... D 206 652-4123
  Seattle *(G-11318)*

LUGGAGE: Traveling Bags

Jeri -Ohs .... G 206 722-5918
  Seattle *(G-10292)*
Outdoor Research LLC .... C 206 467-8197
  Seattle *(G-10717)*
R & D Industries .... G 206 382-1370
  Seattle *(G-10910)*
Vf Outdoor LLC .... E 425 455-7349
  Bellevue *(G-1216)*

LUMBER & BLDG MATLS DEALER, RET: Electric Constructn Matls

Builders Firstsource Inc .... D 509 783-8148
  Kennewick *(G-4637)*

LUMBER & BLDG MATLS DEALER, RET: Garage Doors, Sell/Install

Hrh Door Corp .... F 509 575-0832
  Kennewick *(G-4672)*

LUMBER & BLDG MATRLS DEALERS, RET: Bath Fixtures, Eqpt/Sply

Arcomm Inc .... G 253 581-9800
  Lakewood *(G-5699)*

Employee Codes: A=Over 500 employees, B=251-500
C=101-250, D=51-100, E=20-50, F=10-19, G=2-9

LUMBER & BLDG MATRLS DEALERS, RETAIL: Doors, Wood/Metal

LUMBER & BLDG MATRLS DEALERS, RETAIL: Doors, Wood/Metal

Building Specialty Systems .... G 425 483-6875
  Ellensburg *(G-3185)*

LUMBER & BLDG MTRLS DEALERS, RET: Doors, Storm, Wood/Metal

Tru Door Inc .... F 509 545-8773
  Kennewick *(G-4742)*

LUMBER & BLDG MTRLS DEALERS, RET: Planing Mill Prdts/Lumber

Brown Lumber Co .... G 509 779-4738
  Curlew *(G-2844)*
Manke Lumber Company Inc .... G 360 426-5536
  Shelton *(G-11710)*
McClanahan Lumber Inc .... G 360 374-5887
  Forks *(G-4012)*

LUMBER & BLDG MTRLS DEALERS, RET: Windows, Storm, Wood/Metal

Pacific Door & Window Inc .... F 360 577-9121
  Longview *(G-5940)*
Puget Sound Wood Windows LLC ..... G 425 828-9736
  Kirkland *(G-5446)*

LUMBER & BUILDING MATERIAL DEALERS, RETAIL: Roofing Material

Metal Mill Corporation .... G 360 262-9080
  Chehalis *(G-2514)*
Western Materials Inc .... D 509 547-3301
  Pasco *(G-7652)*

LUMBER & BUILDING MATERIALS DEALER, RET: Door & Window Prdts

BMC West LLC .... E 360 943-8050
  Lakewood *(G-5704)*
Northwest Door and Millwork .... G 509 782-4525
  Wenatchee *(G-15053)*

LUMBER & BUILDING MATERIALS DEALER, RET: Masonry Matls/Splys

Bair Construction Inc .... G 360 491-2285
  Lacey *(G-5535)*
Concrete Creations .... G 509 826-5409
  OMAK *(G-7438)*
Mutual Materials Company .... G 425 353-9686
  Marysville *(G-6362)*
Okanogan Valley Concrete Inc .... G 509 422-3211
  Okanogan *(G-7203)*
Oldcastle Materials Inc .... E 253 872-9466
  Kent *(G-5042)*

LUMBER & BUILDING MATERIALS DEALERS, RET: Solar Heating Eqpt

Blue Frog Solar LLC .... G 206 855-5149
  Poulsbo *(G-7948)*
Offset Solar LLC .... E 866 376-9559
  Liberty Lake *(G-5849)*

LUMBER & BUILDING MATERIALS DEALERS, RETAIL: Brick

Mutual Materials Company .... G 253 838-0803
  Auburn *(G-502)*

LUMBER & BUILDING MATERIALS DEALERS, RETAIL: Cement

Angeles Concrete Products Inc .... G 360 681-5429
  Sequim *(G-11611)*
Best Way Concrete .... G 360 825-5494
  Enumclaw *(G-3279)*
Glacier Northwest Inc .... F 360 736-1131
  Centralia *(G-2403)*

LUMBER & BUILDING MATERIALS DEALERS, RETAIL: Countertops

Venetian Stone Works LLC .... F 425 486-1234
  Woodinville *(G-15399)*

LUMBER & BUILDING MATERIALS DEALERS, RETAIL: Flooring, Wood

NW Wood Holding LLC .... G 360 326-8794
  Vancouver *(G-14445)*

LUMBER & BUILDING MATERIALS DEALERS, RETAIL: Modular Homes

Pan Abode Homes Inc .... E 425 255-8260
  Renton *(G-8875)*

LUMBER & BUILDING MATERIALS DEALERS, RETAIL: Sand & Gravel

Action Materials Inc .... E 509 448-9386
  Cheney *(G-2573)*
Bayview Redi Mix Inc .... G 360 533-7372
  Aberdeen *(G-5)*
Cadman Holding Company Inc .... G 425 868-1234
  Redmond *(G-8415)*
Chelan Concrete Inc .... F 509 682-2915
  Chelan *(G-2549)*
East Valley Sand and Gravel .... E 360 403-7520
  Arlington *(G-232)*
Lopez Redi Mix Inc .... G 360 468-2485
  Lopez Island *(G-5985)*
Miles Sand & Gravel Company .... C 360 757-3121
  Burlington *(G-2171)*
Salmon Bay Sand and Gravel Co ...... D 206 784-1234
  Seattle *(G-11007)*
Stanwood Redi-Mix Inc .... G 360 652-7777
  Stanwood *(G-12994)*

LUMBER & BUILDING MATERIALS RET DEALERS: Millwork & Lumber

Armstrong Lumber Co Inc .... E 253 833-6666
  Auburn *(G-377)*
R L Industries .... F 360 794-1621
  Monroe *(G-6611)*

LUMBER & BLDG MATLS DEALERS, RET: Concrete/Cinder Block

Calportland Company .... G 253 912-8500
  Dupont *(G-2957)*
Glacier Northwest Inc .... E 253 572-7412
  Tacoma *(G-13310)*
Miles Sand & Gravel Company .... F 360 427-0946
  Shelton *(G-11714)*
Mutual Materials Company .... F 360 573-5683
  Vancouver *(G-14426)*

LUMBER: Cut Stock, Softwood

Trumark Industries Inc .... E 509 534-0644
  Spokane *(G-12571)*

LUMBER: Dimension, Hardwood

Bamboo Hardwoods Inc .... G 800 607-2414
  Seattle *(G-9488)*
Bamboo Hardwoods Inc .... E 206 264-2414
  Seattle *(G-9489)*

LUMBER: Fiberboard

Plum Creek Timberlands LP .... F 206 467-3600
  Seattle *(G-10825)*

LUMBER: Flooring, Dressed, Softwood

C Johnson Lumber Company Inc .... G 425 353-4222
  Mukilteo *(G-6901)*
Mercer Timber Products LLC .... G 206 674-4639
  Tukwila *(G-13770)*
Windfall Lumber Inc .... G 360 352-2250
  Tumwater *(G-13906)*

LUMBER: Fuelwood, From Mill Waste

H & H Wood Recyclers Inc .... E 360 892-2805
  Vancouver *(G-14278)*

LUMBER: Furniture Dimension Stock, Softwood

Heirloom Quality Modern LLC .... G 206 291-7331
  Seattle *(G-10160)*

LUMBER: Hardwood Dimension

Allweather Wood LLC .... D 360 835-8547
  Washougal *(G-14941)*
Bennett Lumber Products Inc .... C 208 875-1321
  Clarkston *(G-2624)*
Cascade Hardwoods LLC .... C 360 748-3317
  Chehalis *(G-2482)*
D S Hardwood Corporation .... G 509 369-3442
  Graham *(G-4223)*
Northwest Hardwoods Inc .... A 253 568-6800
  Tacoma *(G-13432)*
Snow Peak Forest Products Inc .... G 208 714-4243
  Spokane Valley *(G-12878)*

LUMBER: Hardwood Dimension & Flooring Mills

Carpet Plus LLC .... G 253 874-0525
  Federal Way *(G-3721)*
Dahlstrom Lumber Co Inc .... E 360 533-0448
  Hoquiam *(G-4331)*
Great Western Lumber Company ...... D 360 966-3061
  Everson *(G-3677)*
Macmillan & Company .... F 360 249-1148
  Montesano *(G-6645)*
NW Wood Holding LLC .... G 360 326-8794
  Vancouver *(G-14445)*
Planeta Works LLC .... G 206 250-4311
  Shoreline *(G-11801)*
Robert Madsen Design Inc .... G 206 588-0090
  Seattle *(G-10971)*
Weyerhaeuser Company .... C 360 736-2811
  Centralia *(G-2442)*
Weyerhaeuser Company .... C 360 577-6678
  Longview *(G-5967)*
Weyerhaeuser Company .... E 425 210-5880
  Seattle *(G-11462)*

LUMBER: Kiln Dried

Cedar Farms LLC .... G 360 779-3575
  Poulsbo *(G-7954)*
Empire Lumber Co .... G 509 534-0266
  Spokane *(G-12246)*
F A Koenig & Sons Inc .... G 360 793-1711
  Sultan *(G-13024)*
Havillah Shake Co .... G 509 486-1467
  Tonasket *(G-13650)*
Ld Forest Inc .... G 360 733-1606
  Bellingham *(G-1403)*
Rainier Veneer Inc .... D 253 846-0242
  Spanaway *(G-12070)*
Socco Inc .... F 360 988-4900
  Sumas *(G-13050)*
Western Forest Products US LLC ...... E 360 735-9700
  Vancouver *(G-14685)*

LUMBER: Panels, Plywood, Softwood

Pacific Trim Panels Inc .... E 360 841-8438
  Woodland *(G-15457)*

LUMBER: Piles, Foundation & Marine Construction, Treated

Blue Marine LLC .... G 253 225-8228
  Gig Harbor *(G-4082)*
Pacific Foundation Inc .... F 360 200-6608
  Vancouver *(G-14464)*
Pile Protectors .... G 360 683-3926
  Sequim *(G-11660)*

LUMBER: Plywood, Hardwood

Alsea Veneer Inc .... G 360 891-2020
  Vancouver *(G-14025)*
Belina Interiors Inc .... D 253 474-0276
  Tacoma *(G-13193)*
Boise Cascade Company .... D 509 738-3200
  Kettle Falls *(G-5226)*
Danzer Veneer Americas Inc .... G 253 770-4664
  Sumner *(G-13065)*
Drc Specialty Veneering LLC .... G 253 301-0443
  Tacoma *(G-13265)*
Edensaw Woods Ltd .... G 253 216-1150
  Tacoma *(G-13271)*
Edwin Enterprises Inc .... G 253 272-7090
  Tacoma *(G-13274)*
Hardel Mutual Plywood Corp .... C 360 740-0232
  Chehalis *(G-2501)*

| Northwest Plywood Sales of Ore........F...... 360 750-1561
Vancouver *(G-14439)*
NW Hardwoods LLC......................G...... 206 784-9369
Mill Creek *(G-6518)*
Olympic Panel Products LLC..........G...... 360 432-5033
Shelton *(G-11718)*
Plum Creek Northwest Plywd Inc....G...... 206 467-3600
Seattle *(G-10824)*
Potlatchdeltic Mfg L L C..................G...... 509 835-1500
Spokane *(G-12449)*
Techwood LLC.................................D...... 360 427-9616
Shelton *(G-11743)*
Weyerhaeuser Company..................A...... 206 539-3000
Seattle *(G-11459)*
Weyerhaeuser Company..................B...... 253 924-3030
Tacoma *(G-13595)*

LUMBER: Plywood, Hardwood or Hardwood Faced

Kamilche Company.........................G...... 206 224-5800
Seattle *(G-10326)*
Mt Baker Products Inc....................C...... 360 733-3960
Bellingham *(G-1450)*

LUMBER: Plywood, Prefinished, Hardwood

Delta Pntg & Prefinishing Co..........G...... 253 588-8278
Tacoma *(G-13258)*
Prolam Industries Inc......................G...... 509 926-2001
Spokane Valley *(G-12843)*

LUMBER: Plywood, Softwood

Boise Cascade Company.................D...... 509 738-3200
Kettle Falls *(G-5226)*
Hoquiam Plywood Products Inc......C...... 360 533-3060
Hoquiam *(G-4343)*
Plum Creek Timberlands LP............F...... 206 467-3600
Seattle *(G-10825)*
Plywood Components Inc................E...... 253 863-6323
Sumner *(G-13095)*
SDS Lumber Co................................C...... 509 493-1444
Bingen *(G-1642)*
Yakama Nation.................................F...... 509 874-2901
White Swan *(G-15140)*

LUMBER: Plywood, Softwood

Decorado Fabrication.......................G...... 360 694-6832
Vancouver *(G-14171)*
Edwin Enterprises Inc.....................G...... 253 272-7090
Tacoma *(G-13274)*
Erosion Ctrl Innovations LLC...........G...... 206 962-9580
Enumclaw *(G-3290)*
Infinity Building Mtls LLC................G...... 804 921-0810
Ferndale *(G-3856)*
Murphy Company............................C...... 360 482-2521
Elma *(G-3250)*
Plum Creek Northwest Plywd Inc....G...... 206 467-3600
Seattle *(G-10824)*
Stusser Mattson Veneer Inc............F...... 425 485-0963
Woodinville *(G-15378)*
Textured Forest Products Inc..........G...... 360 835-2164
Washougal *(G-14991)*
Weyerhaeuser Company..................D...... 360 482-2521
Elma *(G-3259)*

LUMBER: Poles & Pole Crossarms, Treated

Flannery Comerford Inc...................G...... 509 242-5000
Spokane *(G-12258)*
Hamilton Spray................................G...... 360 748-9615
Chehalis *(G-2500)*
McFarland Cascade Holdings Inc....G...... 360 273-5541
Rochester *(G-9136)*
McFarland Cascade Holdings Inc....D...... 253 572-3033
Tacoma *(G-13404)*

LUMBER: Rails, Fence, Round Or Split

All In Cnstr & Ldscpg LLC................G...... 360 840-7990
Mount Vernon *(G-6770)*
Ellensburg Fence Co........................G...... 509 929-4090
Ellensburg *(G-3196)*
Michellaine Lee Larry Bergsma........G...... 360 873-4045
Marblemount *(G-6305)*

LUMBER: Resawn, Small Dimension

Canfor USA Corporation..................E...... 360 647-2434
Bellingham *(G-1289)*

Rfp Manufacturing Inc.....................E...... 253 847-3330
Spanaway *(G-12071)*
Skagit River Reman Company........E...... 360 826-4344
Sedro Woolley *(G-11568)*

LUMBER: Siding, Dressed

Sylvia Vanzee..................................G...... 206 284-2977
Seattle *(G-11242)*

LUMBER: Stacking Or Sticking

Holbrook Inc....................................E...... 360 754-9390
Olympia *(G-7307)*
Mapel Mill LLC.................................G...... 360 508-1313
Winlock *(G-15154)*
Willamette Valley Lumber LLC........F...... 509 331-0442
Othello *(G-7510)*

LUMBER: Treated

Exterior Wood Inc...........................C...... 360 835-8561
Washougal *(G-14955)*
Great Northern Holdings Inc...........E...... 253 572-3033
Tacoma *(G-13321)*
Kaplan Homes Unlimited LLC.........G...... 360 855-1675
Sedro Woolley *(G-11549)*
Manke Lumber Company Inc..........B...... 253 572-6252
Tacoma *(G-13397)*
McFarland Cascade Holdings Inc....D...... 800 426-8430
Spokane *(G-12387)*
Stella-Jones Corporation.................D...... 360 435-2146
Arlington *(G-334)*
Transpac Marinas Inc.....................G...... 360 293-8888
Anacortes *(G-178)*
Western Wood Preserving Co........E...... 253 863-8191
Sumner *(G-13111)*
Wood Care Systems.......................G...... 425 827-6000
Kirkland *(G-5497)*

LUMBER: Veneer, Hardwood

Dmm Incorporated..........................E...... 360 435-5252
Arlington *(G-229)*
Rainier Veneer Inc...........................D...... 253 846-0242
Spanaway *(G-12070)*

LUMBER: Veneer, Softwood

Alsea Veneer Inc.............................G...... 360 891-2020
Vancouver *(G-14025)*

MACHINE PARTS: Stamped Or Pressed Metal

B & S Enterprises...........................G...... 253 859-3605
Auburn *(G-387)*
D S Fabrication & Design Inc.........G...... 360 210-7526
Washougal *(G-14951)*
Dylan Manufacturing Inc................F...... 253 333-8260
Auburn *(G-430)*
H C U Inc..G...... 425 885-0564
Redmond *(G-8486)*
High-Tech Mfg Svcs Inc..................F...... 360 696-1611
Vancouver *(G-14296)*
Liedtke Tool and Gage Inc.............G...... 360 694-9573
Vancouver *(G-14373)*
Marine Diesel Inc............................G...... 206 767-9594
Seattle *(G-10479)*
Middco Tool & Equipment Inc........F...... 509 535-1701
Spokane Valley *(G-12789)*
New Star Technology Inc...............G...... 425 350-7611
Monroe *(G-6601)*
Quality On Time Machining Inc.....G...... 360 802-3700
Enumclaw *(G-3314)*
Raad Industries LLC.......................E...... 509 663-8352
Wenatchee *(G-15067)*
Swift Machining Inc........................G...... 360 335-8213
Washougal *(G-14990)*

MACHINE SHOPS

Bluewater Industries Inc.................F...... 509 765-4623
Moses Lake *(G-6687)*
Brockman Machine Works LLC......F...... 509 735-1354
Kennewick *(G-4633)*
Bullock Machining Co.....................G...... 425 432-8261
Ravensdale *(G-8333)*
C T Specialties...............................G...... 360 786-0274
Tumwater *(G-13854)*
Delta Camshaft Inc.........................G...... 253 383-4152
Tacoma *(G-13257)*
Diesel America West Inc................G...... 360 378-4182
Friday Harbor *(G-4042)*

Edco Inc..E...... 360 424-6600
Mount Vernon *(G-6792)*
Elkay Ssp LLC..................................E...... 509 533-0808
Spokane *(G-12241)*
Fab Shop LLC..................................E...... 253 568-9124
Edgewood *(G-3077)*
Fabrication Enterprises Inc............F...... 503 240-0878
Vancouver *(G-14218)*
Farwest Operating LLC...................D...... 509 453-1663
Moxee *(G-6878)*
Gem Welding & Fabrication...........G...... 360 378-5818
Friday Harbor *(G-4047)*
Gilmour Machinery..........................G...... 360 263-5515
Battle Ground *(G-704)*
Go Planit LLC..................................G...... 206 227-0660
Mattawa *(G-6407)*
Hamiltonjet Inc................................E...... 206 784-8400
Woodinville *(G-15259)*
High Liftt LLC..................................G...... 425 216-3050
Mattawa *(G-6408)*
Intek Manufacturing Inc.................G...... 253 857-5073
Olalla *(G-7206)*
John M Smith..................................G...... 360 484-7738
Naselle *(G-7013)*
Krista K Thie...................................G...... 509 493-2626
White Salmon *(G-15121)*
L & M Prcision Fabrication Inc.......E...... 509 244-5446
Airway Heights *(G-55)*
Milman Engineering Inc..................G...... 360 273-5080
Rochester *(G-9137)*
New Tech Industries Inc.................E...... 425 374-3814
Mukilteo *(G-6955)*
Northstone Industries LLC.............E...... 509 844-7775
Spokane *(G-12410)*
Northwest Center............................E...... 360 403-7330
Arlington *(G-289)*
Northwest Center............................C...... 206 285-9140
Seattle *(G-10639)*
Northwest Center............................E...... 425 355-1855
Everett *(G-3557)*
Olympic Machine & Welding Inc....G...... 253 627-8571
Tacoma *(G-13443)*
Pasco Processing LLC.....................D...... 509 544-6700
Pasco *(G-7614)*
Richmond Systems Inc...................E...... 360 455-8284
Olympia *(G-7386)*
Roberts Precision Machine Inc......F...... 360 805-1000
Monroe *(G-6615)*
Sno-Mon Stamping Inc...................G...... 360 794-6304
Monroe *(G-6621)*
U S Wax & Polymer Inc..................E...... 509 922-1069
Spokane Valley *(G-12918)*
Venturi Holdings LLC......................G...... 206 305-0642
Seattle *(G-11411)*
Waite Speciality Mch Work Inc......D...... 360 577-0777
Longview *(G-5964)*

MACHINE TOOL ACCESS: Boring Attachments

Digital Control Incorporated...........D...... 425 251-0701
Kent *(G-4873)*

MACHINE TOOL ACCESS: Cutting

Cutting Tool Control Inc..................F...... 206 789-7277
Seattle *(G-9773)*
International Carbide Corp.............F...... 800 422-8665
Roy *(G-9161)*
Omax Corporation..........................C...... 253 872-2300
Kent *(G-5045)*
Swiftcarb..G...... 800 227-9876
Kent *(G-5164)*

MACHINE TOOL ACCESS: Diamond Cutting, For Turning, Etc

Concut Inc......................................E...... 253 872-3507
Kent *(G-4862)*
Urban Diamond Tools.....................G...... 206 824-6819
Des Moines *(G-2949)*

MACHINE TOOL ACCESS: Machine Attachments & Access, Drilling

Fostco Inc......................................G...... 509 725-3765
Davenport *(G-2870)*

MACHINE TOOL ACCESS: Milling Machine Attachments

PRODUCT SECTION

MACHINE TOOL ACCESS: Milling Machine Attachments

Precision Spring Stamping Corp............E...... 253 852-6911
   Kent *(G-5078)*
Swift Machining Inc...........................G...... 360 335-8213
   Washougal *(G-14990)*

MACHINE TOOL ACCESS: Pushers

Bit Pusher LLC.................................G...... 206 457-5242
   Seattle *(G-9534)*
Marnis Petal Pushers........................G...... 360 249-8382
   Montesano *(G-6647)*
Paleo Pushers LLC...........................G...... 253 539-3848
   Tacoma *(G-13457)*
Pedal Pushers Bike Rntl & RPR..........G...... 208 689-3436
   Spokane *(G-12435)*

MACHINE TOOL ACCESS: Shaping Tools

East County Machine LLC..................G...... 360 249-4114
   Montesano *(G-6644)*

MACHINE TOOL ACCESS: Sockets

NW Evergreen Products....................G...... 509 276-7825
   Deer Park *(G-2912)*

MACHINE TOOL ACCESS: Tools & Access

Cannon Lauree................................G...... 509 627-0505
   Kennewick *(G-4640)*
Lonnie Hansen................................G...... 253 847-4632
   Spanaway *(G-12060)*
Woodstock International Inc................E...... 360 734-3482
   Bellingham *(G-1596)*

MACHINE TOOL ATTACHMENTS & ACCESS

Bogert Aviation Inc............................G...... 509 736-1513
   Pasco *(G-7554)*
Ceba Systems LLC...........................G...... 360 891-1823
   Vancouver *(G-14109)*
Imaginetics Holdings LLC...................G...... 253 735-0156
   Auburn *(G-472)*
Imaginetics LLC................................D...... 253 735-0156
   Auburn *(G-473)*
Janicki Industries Inc.........................B...... 360 856-5143
   Hamilton *(G-4313)*

MACHINE TOOLS & ACCESS

Almar Tls & Cutter Grinders Co...........F...... 503 255-2763
   Camas *(G-2227)*
Bridge City Arbors Inc........................G...... 360 600-3803
   Ridgefield *(G-9069)*
Chasco LLC.....................................G...... 503 803-4675
   Battle Ground *(G-695)*
Cnc Tooling Solutions Inc...................G...... 425 250-6295
   Kirkland *(G-5309)*
Danielson Tool & Die.........................E...... 509 924-5734
   Spokane Valley *(G-12678)*
Dem-Bart Checkering Tools Inc...........G...... 360 568-7356
   Snohomish *(G-11897)*
Emerald Tool Inc...............................G...... 206 767-5670
   Seattle *(G-9914)*
Fam Waterjet Inc..............................G...... 425 353-6111
   Everett *(G-3469)*
Global Product Development...............G...... 509 487-1155
   Spokane Valley *(G-12720)*
Harris Machine LLC...........................G...... 253 347-6230
   Kent *(G-4934)*
J & J Precision Machine LLC...............G...... 509 315-9319
   Spokane Valley *(G-12750)*
Manufacturing Technology Inc.............G...... 206 763-3161
   Seattle *(G-10473)*
Northwest Carbide Tool & Svc............G...... 253 872-7848
   Kent *(G-5029)*
Peregrine Manufacturing Inc...............G...... 425 673-5600
   Lynnwood *(G-6179)*
Proto-Design Inc...............................F...... 425 558-0600
   Redmond *(G-8237)*
Radiac Abrasives Inc.........................D...... 360 659-6201
   Marysville *(G-6376)*
Spotter Levels LLC............................G...... 425 238-5117
   Stanwood *(G-12992)*

MACHINE TOOLS, METAL CUTTING: Drilling

Crux Subsurface Inc..........................D...... 509 892-9409
   Spokane Valley *(G-12670)*

MACHINE TOOLS, METAL CUTTING: Drilling & Boring

Geologic Drill Explorations..................G...... 509 466-5241
   Spokane *(G-12271)*
Ground Piercing Inc..........................G...... 509 961-8241
   Yakima *(G-15577)*
Rottler Manufacturing Company..........E...... 253 872-7050
   Kent *(G-5108)*

MACHINE TOOLS, METAL CUTTING: Electrolytic

Davincis Workshop LLC.....................G...... 206 244-7000
   Seatac *(G-9280)*

MACHINE TOOLS, METAL CUTTING: Exotic, Including Explosive

Q Otm..F...... 360 802-3700
   Enumclaw *(G-3313)*
Swift Tool Company Inc.....................G...... 206 763-9280
   Seattle *(G-11238)*

MACHINE TOOLS, METAL CUTTING: Grind, Polish, Buff, Lapp

Lortone Inc.......................................F...... 425 493-1600
   Mukilteo *(G-6951)*

MACHINE TOOLS, METAL CUTTING: Home Workshop

Automated AG Systems LLC...............G...... 813 786-7282
   Moses Lake *(G-6682)*

MACHINE TOOLS, METAL CUTTING: Lathes

Aem-Network LLC.............................G...... 509 946-0813
   Richland *(G-8966)*
Cutting Edge Machine & Mfg...............G...... 253 926-8514
   Tacoma *(G-13252)*
Cw Machine LLC...............................G...... 360 829-4171
   Buckley *(G-2055)*
Larsen Equipment Design Inc.............G...... 206 789-5121
   Seattle *(G-10378)*
Mc Ilvanie Machine Works Inc.............F...... 509 452-3131
   Yakima *(G-15616)*

MACHINE TOOLS, METAL CUTTING: Tool Replacement & Rpr Parts

C N C Repair & Sales Inc...................G...... 408 331-1970
   Lynden *(G-6004)*
J & J Precision Machine LLC...............G...... 509 315-9319
   Spokane Valley *(G-12750)*
Rams Head Construction Inc..............G...... 509 997-6962
   Winthrop *(G-15164)*

MACHINE TOOLS, METAL FORMING: Bending

Jesse Engineering Company...............E...... 253 552-1500
   Tacoma *(G-13358)*

MACHINE TOOLS, METAL FORMING: Headers

Reed Performance Headers................G...... 253 838-7693
   Federal Way *(G-3776)*
Rhino Steel Corporation.....................G...... 425 443-2322
   Kirkland *(G-5452)*

MACHINE TOOLS, METAL FORMING: High Energy Rate

Ektos LLC..G...... 800 783-0383
   Woodinville *(G-15235)*
High Energy Metals Inc......................F...... 360 683-6390
   Sequim *(G-11638)*

MACHINE TOOLS, METAL FORMING: Magnetic Forming

Flux Drive Inc...................................F...... 253 826-9002
   Kent *(G-4914)*

MACHINE TOOLS, METAL FORMING: Rebuilt

U-Pull-It Auto Parts Inc......................G...... 509 895-7655
   Yakima *(G-15698)*

MACHINE TOOLS: Metal Cutting

3dx Industries Inc.............................G...... 360 244-4339
   Ferndale *(G-3807)*
A H Lundberg Inc..............................G...... 425 258-4617
   Everett *(G-3354)*
Almar Tls & Cutter Grinders Co...........F...... 503 255-2763
   Camas *(G-2227)*
Cut Technologies Metal LLC...............F...... 360 733-0460
   Bellingham *(G-1312)*
Dilbeck Tools Inc...............................G...... 509 452-3405
   Yakima *(G-15555)*
Norwood-Wang Inc...........................G...... 206 304-8769
   Kent *(G-5037)*
Noxon Inc..G...... 509 926-0557
   Spokane Valley *(G-12814)*
Pacific Hide & Fur Depot....................E...... 509 545-0688
   Pasco *(G-7611)*
Romac Industries Inc.........................C...... 425 951-6200
   Bothell *(G-1897)*
S&S Repair.......................................G...... 360 496-5533
   Morton *(G-6673)*
Serena Inc.......................................G...... 253 939-6509
   Auburn *(G-560)*
Tru Square Metal Products Inc...........G...... 253 833-2310
   Auburn *(G-583)*
Universal Refiner Corporation.............G...... 360 249-4415
   Montesano *(G-6663)*
W B & L Machine Inc.........................E...... 360 225-5020
   Woodland *(G-15472)*

MACHINE TOOLS: Metal Forming

Cincinnati Incorporated......................E...... 425 263-9216
   Everett *(G-3418)*
Covlet Machine & Design Inc..............F...... 360 658-1977
   Marysville *(G-6328)*
EDJ Precision Machine Inc.................E...... 425 745-3937
   Everett *(G-3452)*
Electroimpact Inc..............................D...... 425 348-8090
   Mukilteo *(G-6920)*
Electroimpact Inc..............................F...... 425 348-8090
   Mukilteo *(G-6921)*
Flower Racing..................................G...... 360 793-2196
   Sultan *(G-13025)*
Gemmells Wldg Fabrication LLC.........G...... 509 547-5200
   Pasco *(G-7584)*
J&M Rifle Works................................G...... 360 985-0445
   Onalaska *(G-7450)*
Wagstaff Inc.....................................B...... 509 922-1404
   Spokane Valley *(G-12932)*

MACHINERY & EQPT FINANCE LEASING

Reynolds and Reynolds Company........E...... 425 985-0194
   Edmonds *(G-3146)*

MACHINERY & EQPT, AGRICULTURAL, WHOL: Farm Eqpt Parts/Splys

AG Enterprise Supply Inc....................F...... 509 235-2006
   Cheney *(G-2575)*

MACHINERY & EQPT, AGRICULTURAL, WHOLESALE: Agricultural, NEC

Vamco Ltd Inc..................................G...... 509 877-2138
   Wapato *(G-14927)*

MACHINERY & EQPT, AGRICULTURAL, WHOLESALE: Farm Implements

Dairy Export Co Inc...........................G...... 206 284-7220
   Seattle *(G-9786)*

MACHINERY & EQPT, AGRICULTURAL, WHOLESALE: Landscaping Eqpt

Concrete Creations............................G...... 509 826-5409
   OMAK *(G-7438)*
Ervin H Tennyson..............................G...... 360 445-2434
   Mount Vernon *(G-6793)*
Everett Bark Supply Inc......................G...... 425 353-9024
   Everett *(G-3463)*
H D Fowler Co Inc.............................D...... 425 746-8400
   Bellevue *(G-934)*

MACHINERY & EQPT, AGRICULTURAL, WHOLESALE: Lawn & Garden

Cascade Pipe & Feed Supply .... G 509 997-0720
Twisp *(G-13910)*

MACHINERY & EQPT, INDL, WHOL: Controlling Instruments/Access

Eustis Co Inc .... E 425 423-9996
Lynnwood *(G-6115)*

MACHINERY & EQPT, INDL, WHOL: Environ Pollution Cntrl, Air

Hallmark Refining Corporation .... D 360 428-5880
Mount Vernon *(G-6803)*

MACHINERY & EQPT, INDL, WHOL: Meters, Consumption Registerng

Pacific Meter & Equipment Inc .... G 253 872-3374
Kent *(G-5056)*

MACHINERY & EQPT, INDL, WHOLESALE: Alcoholic Beverage Mfrg

Golden Hills Brewing Co .... G 509 389-6253
Airway Heights *(G-53)*

MACHINERY & EQPT, INDL, WHOLESALE: Cement Making

Nobelus LLC .... G 800 895-2747
Seattle *(G-10614)*

MACHINERY & EQPT, INDL, WHOLESALE: Chainsaws

Tims Country Saw Shop .... G 509 486-2798
Tonasket *(G-13660)*

MACHINERY & EQPT, INDL, WHOLESALE: Conveyor Systems

Agjet LLC .... F 509 654-9449
Yakima *(G-15502)*
Empire Rubber & Supply Co .... F 509 547-0026
Pasco *(G-7579)*
Flsmidth Inc .... G 509 434-8605
Spokane *(G-12259)*
North Coast Electric Company .... F 360 671-1100
Bellingham *(G-1464)*
Northwest Belt & Equipment Co .... G 360 533-7051
Aberdeen *(G-24)*
Smartstart .... G 509 317-2050
Yakima *(G-15676)*
T & K Cstm Fabrication & Repr .... G 206 242-0197
Seattle *(G-11247)*
Transco Northwest Inc .... E 425 251-5422
Kent *(G-5188)*

MACHINERY & EQPT, INDL, WHOLESALE: Cranes

Halme Construction Inc .... E 509 725-4200
Spokane *(G-12287)*

MACHINERY & EQPT, INDL, WHOLESALE: Crushing

Impact Service Corporation .... E 509 468-7900
Spokane *(G-12305)*

MACHINERY & EQPT, INDL, WHOLESALE: Drilling Bits

Carbide Online Sales LLC .... G 253 476-1338
University Place *(G-13962)*

MACHINERY & EQPT, INDL, WHOLESALE: Drilling, Exc Bits

Fostco Inc .... G 509 725-3765
Davenport *(G-2870)*

MACHINERY & EQPT, INDL, WHOLESALE: Engines & Parts, Diesel

Cummins Inc .... G 541 276-2561
Pasco *(G-7573)*
Cummins Inc .... E 509 455-4411
Spokane *(G-12211)*
Cummins Inc .... F 509 248-9033
Yakima *(G-15545)*
Cummins Inc .... E 360 748-8841
Tumwater *(G-13867)*
Defbooty LLC .... G 800 311-5887
Chehalis *(G-2488)*
Hatch & Kirk Inc .... F 206 783-2766
Seattle *(G-10146)*
North Hbr Diesl Yacht Svc Inc .... G 360 293-5551
Anacortes *(G-153)*
North Island Boat Company Inc .... F 360 293-2565
Anacortes *(G-154)*
Pacific Power Group LLC .... D 360 887-5980
Ridgefield *(G-9100)*
Pacific Power Group LLC .... D 360 887-7400
Vancouver *(G-14469)*
Parkers Truck & Equipment Repr .... G 253 833-3696
Pacific *(G-7538)*
Rwc International Ltd .... G 509 452-5515
Yakima *(G-15664)*
Valley Automotive Machine .... G 360 336-9722
Mount Vernon *(G-6850)*

MACHINERY & EQPT, INDL, WHOLESALE: Engs/Transportation Eqpt

B & G Machine Inc .... E 206 767-6071
Seattle *(G-9473)*

MACHINERY & EQPT, INDL, WHOLESALE: Food Manufacturing

Nolan & Sons Northwest Inc .... G 509 658-2604
Naches *(G-7000)*

MACHINERY & EQPT, INDL, WHOLESALE: Food Product Manufacturng

Lectro Tek Services Inc .... E 509 663-2891
Wenatchee *(G-15043)*

MACHINERY & EQPT, INDL, WHOLESALE: Hydraulic Systems

Central Hose and Fittings Inc .... F 509 547-6460
Pasco *(G-7558)*
George W Warden Co Inc .... G 509 534-2880
Spokane Valley *(G-12716)*
Kaman Fluid Power LLC .... G 253 922-5710
Tacoma *(G-13372)*
Kaman Fluid Power LLC .... G 360 738-1264
Bellingham *(G-1390)*
Kinematics Marine Eqp Inc .... G 360 659-5415
Marysville *(G-6348)*
RJ Hydraulics Inc .... F 360 693-4399
Vancouver *(G-14553)*
Skyline Fluid Power Inc .... G 509 382-4781
Dayton *(G-2886)*
Superior Fluid Power Inc .... G 509 482-7949
Spokane Valley *(G-12896)*
Unisource Manufacturing Inc .... G 253 854-0541
Kent *(G-5196)*
Valin Corporation .... G 509 924-4914
Spokane Valley *(G-12923)*

MACHINERY & EQPT, INDL, WHOLESALE: Indl Machine Parts

Trinity Mfg .... G 360 474-8639
Arlington *(G-342)*

MACHINERY & EQPT, INDL, WHOLESALE: Instruments & Cntrl Eqpt

Paramount Supply Co .... G 360 647-8328
Bellingham *(G-1489)*
United States Dosimetry Tech .... G 509 946-8738
Richland *(G-9049)*

MACHINERY & EQPT, INDL, WHOLESALE: Lift Trucks & Parts

BTS Exchange LLC .... G 253 859-5450
Kent *(G-4825)*

MACHINERY & EQPT, INDL, WHOLESALE: Machine Tools & Access

Alliance Mfg Group LLC .... G 253 922-3090
Tacoma *(G-13165)*
Bjorklund Machine and Tool Co .... G 425 949-5761
Bothell *(G-1830)*
Precision Spring Stamping Corp .... E 253 852-6911
Kent *(G-5078)*
Traction Capital Partners Inc .... G 253 922-3090
Tacoma *(G-13561)*

MACHINERY & EQPT, INDL, WHOLESALE: Machine Tools & Metalwork

Cnc Tooling Solutions Inc .... G 425 250-6295
Kirkland *(G-5309)*

MACHINERY & EQPT, INDL, WHOLESALE: Measure/Test, Electric

Synergistic Technologies Inc .... G 425 822-7777
Bellevue *(G-1174)*

MACHINERY & EQPT, INDL, WHOLESALE: Packaging

Intech Enterprises Inc .... E 360 835-8785
Washougal *(G-14961)*
Phillips Industrial Supply Inc .... F 206 523-0477
Everett *(G-3572)*
West Coast Paper Company .... E 253 850-1900
Kent *(G-5212)*

MACHINERY & EQPT, INDL, WHOLESALE: Paper Manufacturing

North Pacific Paper Co LLC .... B 360 636-6400
Longview *(G-5937)*

MACHINERY & EQPT, INDL, WHOLESALE: Petroleum Industry

Clarus Technologies LLC .... G 360 671-1514
Bellingham *(G-1299)*

MACHINERY & EQPT, INDL, WHOLESALE: Pneumatic Tools

Twintec Inc .... G 253 218-0890
Auburn *(G-586)*

MACHINERY & EQPT, INDL, WHOLESALE: Processing & Packaging

Ron C England .... G 509 276-9150
Nine Mile Falls *(G-7083)*

MACHINERY & EQPT, INDL, WHOLESALE: Pulp Manufacturing, Wood

A H Lundberg Inc .... G 425 258-4617
Everett *(G-3354)*
Somarakis Inc .... F 360 574-6722
Kalama *(G-4508)*

MACHINERY & EQPT, INDL, WHOLESALE: Recycling

Deer Path Industrial Tech .... G 425 391-9223
Issaquah *(G-4404)*
Total Reclaim Incorporated .... C 206 343-7443
Kent *(G-5184)*

MACHINERY & EQPT, INDL, WHOLESALE: Safety Eqpt

Almx-Security Inc .... G 425 485-3801
Kenmore *(G-4564)*
Lilibete LLC .... G 206 407-6890
Kent *(G-4996)*
SES USA Inc .... G 425 485-3801
Kenmore *(G-4604)*

Employee Codes: A=Over 500 employees, B=251-500
C=101-250, D=51-100, E=20-50, F=10-19, G=2-9

MACHINERY & EQPT, INDL, WHOLESALE: Safety Eqpt

Western Optical Corporation..........D...... 206 622-7627
 Seattle *(G-11455)*

MACHINERY & EQPT, INDL, WHOLESALE: Sawmill

Salem Equipment Inc..........F...... 503 581-8411
 Vancouver *(G-14567)*
Usnr LLC..........G...... 360 225-8267
 Woodland *(G-15470)*

MACHINERY & EQPT, INDL, WHOLESALE: Stackers

Arr Tech Manufacturing..........E...... 509 966-4300
 Yakima *(G-15512)*

MACHINERY & EQPT, INDL, WHOLESALE: Tanks, Storage

Down Island Trading Co..........G...... 360 376-4056
 Deer Harbor *(G-2891)*

MACHINERY & EQPT, INDL, WHOLESALE: Trailers, Indl

Top Notch Trailer Mfg..........F...... 360 273-0468
 Rochester *(G-9141)*

MACHINERY & EQPT, INDL, WHOLESALE: Winches

Nelson Truck Equipment Co Inc..........F...... 206 622-3825
 Seattle *(G-10598)*

MACHINERY & EQPT, INDL, WHOLESALE: Woodworking

Oliver Machinery Company..........G...... 253 867-0334
 Kent *(G-5043)*

MACHINERY & EQPT, WHOLESALE: Construction, Cranes

Safeworks LLC..........D...... 206 575-6445
 Tukwila *(G-13809)*

MACHINERY & EQPT, WHOLESALE: Construction, General

D W Pape Inc..........G...... 509 586-0522
 Kennewick *(G-4652)*
Mikes Rental Machinery Inc..........E...... 509 925-6126
 Ellensburg *(G-3215)*
Monarch Machine and TI Co Inc..........E...... 509 547-7753
 Pasco *(G-7603)*
N C Power Systems Co..........C...... 425 251-5877
 Tukwila *(G-13774)*
Pacific Coatings Inc..........F...... 206 722-1413
 Seattle *(G-10730)*
Spokane Machinery Company..........F...... 509 535-1654
 Spokane *(G-12519)*

MACHINERY & EQPT, WHOLESALE: Contractors Materials

Blue Water Inc..........G...... 509 682-5544
 Chelan *(G-2548)*
Central Machinery Sales Inc..........F...... 509 547-9003
 Pasco *(G-7559)*
Pape Machinery Inc..........E...... 509 838-5252
 Spokane *(G-12429)*
Star Rentals Inc..........F...... 509 545-8521
 Pasco *(G-7632)*
Westside Concrete ACC Inc..........G...... 360 892-0203
 Vancouver *(G-14686)*

MACHINERY & EQPT, WHOLESALE: Crushing, Pulverizng & Screeng

Omh Innovations Usa Inc..........G...... 509 264-1129
 Chattaroy *(G-2450)*

MACHINERY & EQPT, WHOLESALE: Drilling, Wellpoints

Pacific Foundation Inc..........F...... 360 200-6608
 Vancouver *(G-14464)*

MACHINERY & EQPT, WHOLESALE: Logging

Emery Enterprises..........G...... 360 532-0102
 Aberdeen *(G-10)*

MACHINERY & EQPT, WHOLESALE: Logging & Forestry

Joseph Gillum..........G...... 800 624-4578
 Centralia *(G-2413)*

MACHINERY & EQPT, WHOLESALE: Masonry

Mutual Materials Company..........G...... 253 838-0803
 Auburn *(G-502)*

MACHINERY & EQPT: Farm

AG Engineering & Development..........F...... 509 582-8900
 Kennewick *(G-4612)*
AG Enterprise Supply Inc..........F...... 509 235-2006
 Cheney *(G-2575)*
AGCO..........G...... 253 964-2313
 Dupont *(G-2954)*
Asnw Inc..........F...... 509 297-4272
 Eltopia *(G-3262)*
Athletic Cases..........G...... 206 569-8677
 Seattle *(G-9453)*
Bills Welding & Machine Shop..........G...... 509 334-2222
 Pullman *(G-8085)*
Blueline Equipment Co LLC..........G...... 509 785-2595
 Quincy *(G-8290)*
Blueline Equipment Co LLC..........G...... 509 525-4550
 Walla Walla *(G-14772)*
Blueline Equipment Co LLC..........E...... 509 248-8411
 Moxee *(G-6875)*
Blueline Equipment Co LLC..........E...... 509 248-8411
 Seattle *(G-9556)*
Blueline Equipment Co LLC..........E...... 509 248-8411
 Yakima *(G-15522)*
Blueline Mfg Co..........E...... 509 248-8411
 Yakima *(G-15523)*
C & V Machinery..........G...... 509 657-3392
 Endicott *(G-3263)*
Callahan Manufacturing Inc..........E...... 509 346-2208
 Royal City *(G-9167)*
Case42..........G...... 509 270-3500
 Otis Orchards *(G-7513)*
Central Machinery Sales Inc..........F...... 509 547-9003
 Pasco *(G-7559)*
Dari-Tech Inc..........E...... 360 354-6900
 Lynden *(G-6013)*
Dauenhauer Manufacturing Inc..........G...... 509 865-3300
 Toppenish *(G-13666)*
Delaval Inc..........F...... 360 428-1744
 Mount Vernon *(G-6788)*
Edwards Equipment Co Inc..........F...... 509 248-1770
 Union Gap *(G-13928)*
Jason C Bailes Pllc..........G...... 360 975-4687
 Vancouver *(G-14334)*
Jerrys Iron Works Inc..........G...... 425 788-1467
 Duvall *(G-2993)*
K & D Machine LLC..........F...... 509 882-2239
 Grandview *(G-4249)*
Kile Machine & Manufacturing..........G...... 509 569-3814
 Rosalia *(G-9155)*
Lower Valley Machine Shop..........F...... 509 882-3881
 Grandview *(G-4251)*
McGregor Company..........F...... 509 397-4360
 Colfax *(G-2716)*
Microbial Magic LLC..........G...... 360 297-2224
 Poulsbo *(G-7983)*
Nelson Irrigation Corporation..........C...... 509 525-7660
 Walla Walla *(G-14850)*
Nicholson Manufacturing Co..........D...... 206 682-2752
 Seattle *(G-10607)*
Norma Industries..........G...... 253 208-1728
 Puyallup *(G-8200)*
Northstar Attachments LLC..........E...... 509 452-1651
 Yakima *(G-15632)*
Northwest Tillers Inc..........G...... 509 575-1950
 Yakima *(G-15635)*
Orchard-Rite Limited Inc..........E...... 509 834-2029
 Yakima *(G-15639)*
Orchard-Rite Limited Inc..........E...... 509 834-2029
 Union Gap *(G-13947)*
Oxbo International Corporation..........G...... 509 544-0362
 Pasco *(G-7610)*
Parsons Equipment Inc..........G...... 509 632-5205
 Coulee City *(G-2804)*
Prathers Welding & Fabrication..........G...... 509 632-5321
 Coulee City *(G-2805)*

Scafco Corporation..........C...... 509 343-9000
 Spokane *(G-12493)*
Scafco Corporation..........F...... 509 343-9012
 Spokane *(G-12494)*
Spray Center Electronics Inc..........G...... 509 838-2209
 Spokane *(G-12523)*
Stoess Manufacturing Inc..........G...... 509 646-3292
 Washtucna *(G-15003)*
Valmont Northwest Inc..........F...... 509 547-1623
 Pasco *(G-7647)*
Van Doren Sales Inc..........D...... 509 886-1837
 East Wenatchee *(G-3034)*
Washington Eqp Mfg Co Inc..........E...... 509 244-4773
 Spokane *(G-12583)*
Washington Tractor Inc..........F...... 509 452-2880
 Yakima *(G-15704)*
Washington Tractor Inc..........C...... 253 863-4436
 Sumner *(G-13110)*
Washington Tractor Inc..........E...... 360 533-6393
 Aberdeen *(G-38)*
Washington Tractor Inc..........F...... 509 422-3030
 Okanogan *(G-7204)*

MACHINERY & EQPT: Gas Producers, Generators/Other Rltd Eqpt

Algas-Sdi International LLC..........D...... 206 789-5410
 Seattle *(G-9374)*
Vulcan Global LLC..........G...... 509 528-2000
 Kennewick *(G-4743)*

MACHINERY & EQPT: Liquid Automation

Deines Automation LLC..........G...... 509 230-2369
 Spokane *(G-12223)*
Pulsair Systems Inc..........G...... 425 455-1263
 Kirkland *(G-5448)*

MACHINERY & EQPT: Petroleum Refinery

Whitten Group International..........F...... 360 560-3319
 Longview *(G-5968)*

MACHINERY & EQPT: Smelting & Refining

Aquamira Technologies Inc..........G...... 360 392-2730
 Bellingham *(G-1251)*

MACHINERY & EQPT: Vibratory Parts Handling Eqpt

Armadillo Equipment & Parts..........G...... 360 829-4107
 Buckley *(G-2046)*
Process Inc..........G...... 425 401-2000
 Bellevue *(G-1085)*

MACHINERY BASES

N E S Enterprises..........G...... 509 928-9151
 Spokane Valley *(G-12798)*

MACHINERY, COMM LAUNDRY: Rug Cleaning, Drying Or Napping

Hydramaster LLC..........F...... 425 775-7272
 Mukilteo *(G-6938)*

MACHINERY, COMMERCIAL LAUNDRY & Drycleaning: Ironers

REM & AES LLC..........G...... 580 284-3410
 Puyallup *(G-8236)*

MACHINERY, COMMERCIAL LAUNDRY & Drycleaning: Pressing

Total Fabricare Llc..........G...... 206 226-3370
 Tacoma *(G-13559)*

MACHINERY, COMMERCIAL LAUNDRY: Dryers, Incl Coin-Operated

Chauncey and Shirah Bell Inc..........G...... 206 437-7556
 Seattle *(G-9670)*

MACHINERY, EQPT & SUPPLIES: Parking Facility

Dog On It Parks Inc..........G...... 425 512-8489
 Everett *(G-3445)*
Nite-Hawk Sweepers LLC..........F...... 253 872-2077
 Kent *(G-5024)*

PRODUCT SECTION

MACHINERY, FLOOR SANDING: Commercial
Quick Cut Inc .... G 360 893-0689
  Orting *(G-7486)*

MACHINERY, FOOD PRDTS: Beverage
Perlage Systems Inc .... G 253 632-0891
  Federal Way *(G-3770)*
Perlage Systems Inc .... G 206 973-7500
  Seattle *(G-10789)*

MACHINERY, FOOD PRDTS: Cutting, Chopping, Grinding, Mixing
Hydro Consulting LLC .... G 509 302-1034
  Pasco *(G-7591)*

MACHINERY, FOOD PRDTS: Distillery
Olympic Distillers LLC .... G 360 920-9645
  Port Angeles *(G-7729)*

MACHINERY, FOOD PRDTS: Flour Mill
US Natural Resources Inc .... E 360 841-6346
  Woodland *(G-15469)*

MACHINERY, FOOD PRDTS: Food Processing, Smokers
Flodin Inc .... E 509 766-2996
  Moses Lake *(G-6709)*
Innotech Metal Designs LLC .... F 360 393-4108
  Bellingham *(G-1378)*
Ryco Equipment Inc .... E 425 744-0444
  Mountlake Terrace *(G-6867)*

MACHINERY, FOOD PRDTS: Homogenizing, Dairy, Fruit/Vegetable
Plantsplus .... G 360 628-8368
  Olympia *(G-7371)*

MACHINERY, FOOD PRDTS: Malt Mills
Jimboneys Malt Mills & More .... G 541 571-1144
  Chehalis *(G-2506)*

MACHINERY, FOOD PRDTS: Milk Processing, Dry
Morice Engineering .... G 360 754-9217
  Olympia *(G-7343)*

MACHINERY, FOOD PRDTS: Ovens, Bakery
Wood Stone Corporation .... C 360 650-1111
  Bellingham *(G-1595)*

MACHINERY, FOOD PRDTS: Pasta
Pasteria Lucchese .... G 206 420-4939
  Seattle *(G-10763)*

MACHINERY, FOOD PRDTS: Presses, Cheese, Beet, Cider & Sugar
Columbia Cove LLC .... G 360 739-7373
  Rock Island *(G-9148)*

MACHINERY, FOOD PRDTS: Processing, Fish & Shellfish
Coastline Equipment Inc .... E 360 734-8509
  Bellingham *(G-1301)*
Environmental Tech Group .... F 253 804-2507
  Pacific *(G-7526)*
Kami Steel US Inc .... F 206 283-9655
  Seattle *(G-10325)*
Smith-Berger Marine Inc .... E 206 764-4650
  Seattle *(G-11139)*
Steve Pool Service Inc .... G 360 533-0421
  Shelton *(G-11736)*

MACHINERY, FOOD PRDTS: Roasting, Coffee, Peanut, Etc.
Roastmasters LLC .... G 425 284-2327
  Redmond *(G-8653)*
Sonofresco LLC .... G 360 757-2800
  Burlington *(G-2191)*

MACHINERY, LUBRICATION: Automatic
King Machine LLC .... F 425 743-5464
  Mukilteo *(G-6948)*

MACHINERY, MAILING: Mail Tying Or Bundling
LSI Logistic Svc Solutions LLC .... F 253 872-8970
  Puyallup *(G-8180)*

MACHINERY, MAILING: Mailing
Pinpoint LLC .... G 425 442-4764
  Redmond *(G-8623)*

MACHINERY, MAILING: Postage Meters
American Postage Scale Corp .... G 509 299-6144
  Medical Lake *(G-6439)*
Pitney Bowes Inc .... E 509 363-3694
  Spokane *(G-12444)*
Pitney Bowes Inc .... E 509 835-1272
  Spokane *(G-12445)*
Pitney Bowes Inc .... D 253 395-8717
  Kent *(G-5066)*
Pitney Bowes Inc .... E 509 838-0115
  Spokane *(G-12446)*

MACHINERY, METALWORKING: Assembly, Including Robotic
Bionic Builders LLC .... G 509 435-1114
  Spokane Valley *(G-12640)*

MACHINERY, METALWORKING: Coilers, Metalworking
ASC Machine Tools Inc .... C 509 534-6600
  Spokane Valley *(G-12626)*

MACHINERY, OFFICE: Paper Handling
Preferred Business Solutions .... G 425 251-1202
  Kent *(G-5079)*
Wizard International Inc .... D 425 551-4300
  Mukilteo *(G-6992)*

MACHINERY, OFFICE: Typing & Word Processing
Peace Arch Business Center .... G 360 366-8500
  Blaine *(G-1693)*

MACHINERY, PACKAGING: Canning, Food
Cascade Caning .... G 360 258-1738
  Vancouver *(G-14103)*

MACHINERY, PACKAGING: Carton Packing
R A Pearson Company .... C 509 838-6226
  Spokane *(G-12464)*

MACHINERY, PACKAGING: Packing & Wrapping
Emerald Automation LLC .... E 509 783-1369
  Kennewick *(G-4659)*
Kemps Machine Co .... F 509 784-1326
  Yakima *(G-15606)*
Maf Industries Inc .... F 509 574-8775
  Union Gap *(G-13941)*

MACHINERY, PAPER INDUSTRY: Coating & Finishing
Leather Guard Div Int Renovatn .... G 425 827-4895
  Kirkland *(G-5384)*
Simutech International Inc .... G 360 490-4029
  Kirkland *(G-5463)*

MACHINERY, PAPER INDUSTRY: Paper Mill, Plating, Etc
North Pacific Paper Co LLC .... B 360 636-6400
  Longview *(G-3937)*
Northwest Paper Converters Inc ...... F 800 681-9748
  Ferndale *(G-3878)*

MACHINERY, PAPER INDUSTRY: Pulp Mill
Legacy Automation Inc .... F 360 538-2550
  Hoquiam *(G-4346)*

MACHINERY, PRINTING TRADES: Copy Holders
Green Office Supplies .... G 408 871-8887
  Redmond *(G-8484)*

MACHINERY, PRINTING TRADES: Plates
Anderson & Vreeland Inc .... G 419 636-5002
  Kent *(G-4782)*
Hazelwood Farm LLC .... F 425 454-5165
  Redmond *(G-8489)*
Preflex Digital Prepress Svcs .... F 253 583-9100
  Lakewood *(G-5747)*

MACHINERY, PRINTING TRADES: Printing Trade Parts & Attchts
Heath Graphics LLC .... G 253 856-1422
  Auburn *(G-462)*

MACHINERY, PRINTING TRADES: Type & Type Making
Machine Works Inc .... G 253 750-0238
  Sumner *(G-13082)*

MACHINERY, SERVICING: Coin-Operated, Exc Dry Clean & Laundry
Clarus Technologies LLC .... G 360 671-1514
  Bellingham *(G-1299)*

MACHINERY, SEWING: Bag Seaming & Closing
Integrated Systems Design .... G 360 746-0812
  Bellingham *(G-1380)*

MACHINERY, SEWING: Sewing & Hat & Zipper Making
Morley Machine Tool Algnmt Inc ...... E 253 926-1515
  Milton *(G-6536)*

MACHINERY, TEXTILE: Cloth Spreading
Vintage Quilting .... G 253 852-6596
  Kent *(G-5201)*

MACHINERY, TEXTILE: Embroidery
National Specialties LLC .... G 253 581-4908
  Lakewood *(G-5740)*
R K I .... G 360 876-0937
  Port Orchard *(G-7844)*

MACHINERY, TEXTILE: Fiber & Yarn Preparation
Cosmopolis Specialty Fiber .... G 360 533-7531
  Cosmopolis *(G-2800)*
Hansencrafts LLC .... G 360 747-7746
  Port Townsend *(G-7888)*

MACHINERY, TEXTILE: Picker
Furford Picker .... G 360 267-3303
  Aberdeen *(G-12)*

MACHINERY, TEXTILE: Spinning
Windy Acres .... G 360 491-2177
  Olympia *(G-7429)*

MACHINERY, TEXTILE: Wool Processing, Carbonizing
Protech Composites .... E 360 573-7800
  Vancouver *(G-14513)*

MACHINERY, WOODWORKING: Bandsaws
Cut Technologies Usa Inc .... E 360 733-0460
  Bellingham *(G-1313)*
Holiday Engineering & Mfg Co .... G 253 238-0671
  Tacoma *(G-13338)*

MACHINERY, WOODWORKING: Cabinet Makers'

MACHINERY, WOODWORKING: Cabinet Makers'

Mt Pickett Woodworking ....G....... 360 376-2449
  Olga *(G-7216)*
Skidmore & Skidmore Inc ....G....... 360 379-6385
  Port Townsend *(G-7926)*
Trobella Cabinetry Inc ....E....... 360 947-2114
  Vancouver *(G-14649)*

MACHINERY, WOODWORKING: Planers

Woodcraft Supply LLC ....F....... 206 767-6394
  Seattle *(G-11492)*

MACHINERY, WOODWORKING: Sanding, Exc Portable Floor Sanders

D D M Corporation ....G....... 206 282-3422
  Seattle *(G-9779)*

MACHINERY/EQPT, INDL, WHOL: Cleaning, High Press, Sand/Steam

Northwest Solutions Inc ....G....... 360 380-3807
  Bellingham *(G-1471)*

MACHINERY/EQPT, INDL, WHOL: Machinist Precision Measrng Tool

Automatic Products Mfg Co LLC ....G....... 253 395-7173
  Kent *(G-4801)*

MACHINERY: Ammunition & Explosives Loading

Wellons Inc ....G....... 360 750-3500
  Vancouver *(G-14681)*

MACHINERY: Assembly, Exc Metalworking

Frencken America Inc ....E....... 509 924-9777
  Liberty Lake *(G-5832)*
Robert J Parry ....G....... 509 456-6204
  Spokane *(G-12479)*
Skytech Machine Inc ....G....... 360 253-6378
  Vancouver *(G-14593)*

MACHINERY: Automotive Maintenance

McCulley Inc ....G....... 509 891-4134
  Spokane Valley *(G-12786)*
R 2 Manufacturing Inc ....G....... 360 693-5096
  Vancouver *(G-14525)*
Skookum Enterprises LLC ....D....... 360 475-0756
  Bremerton *(G-2001)*

MACHINERY: Automotive Related

Aritex USA Inc ....G....... 425 922-3819
  Seattle *(G-9430)*
Automotive Repair Corporation ....F....... 509 244-2730
  Spokane *(G-12131)*
GTC Innovations LLC ....G....... 866 241-3149
  Renton *(G-8815)*

MACHINERY: Banking

First Millennium Bank ....G....... 360 797-5108
  Sequim *(G-11634)*

MACHINERY: Bottle Washing & Sterilzing

Saxco Pacific Coast LLC ....F....... 360 892-3451
  Vancouver *(G-14570)*

MACHINERY: Brewery & Malting

Green Air Supply Inc ....G....... 877 427-4361
  Tacoma *(G-13323)*
Picobrew Inc ....G....... 425 503-0132
  Seattle *(G-10802)*

MACHINERY: Cement Making

Joom 3d ....G....... 413 566-6330
  Olympia *(G-7314)*

MACHINERY: Centrifugal

Numeric Control LLC ....G....... 360 269-1497
  Morton *(G-6670)*

MACHINERY: Concrete Prdts

Columbia Machine Inc ....B....... 360 694-1501
  Vancouver *(G-14131)*
Columbia Machine Inc ....G....... 360 905-1611
  Vancouver *(G-14132)*
Columbia Machine Inc ....C....... 360 694-1501
  Vancouver *(G-14133)*

MACHINERY: Construction

Action Materials Inc ....E....... 509 448-9386
  Cheney *(G-2573)*
Aerofab Inc ....G....... 253 863-8402
  Ravensdale *(G-8329)*
Anbo Mfg Inc ....F....... 509 684-6559
  Veradale *(G-14748)*
Anthony Rousseau ....G....... 509 758-8379
  Clarkston *(G-2619)*
Austin Jordan Inc ....G....... 253 265-1903
  Gig Harbor *(G-4074)*
Bizzybee LLC ....G....... 206 707-9417
  Seattle *(G-9535)*
Caterpillar Inc ....E....... 509 623-4640
  Spokane *(G-12173)*
Caterpillar Inc ....G....... 425 562-2060
  Bellevue *(G-842)*
Central Machinery Sales Inc ....F....... 509 547-9003
  Pasco *(G-7559)*
Centric Corporation ....E....... 253 833-4342
  Auburn *(G-403)*
Concut Inc ....E....... 253 872-3507
  Kent *(G-4862)*
Construction Parts ....G....... 253 271-6133
  Spanaway *(G-12055)*
Construction Parts LLC ....G....... 253 255-1775
  Graham *(G-4221)*
Dandy Digger and Supply Inc ....F....... 360 795-3617
  Cathlamet *(G-2364)*
Dyers Construction & Excav ....G....... 903 486-1881
  Ocean Park *(G-7181)*
Fabrication Products Inc ....E....... 503 283-3218
  Vancouver *(G-14219)*
Fluid Power Service Inc ....G....... 360 496-6888
  Morton *(G-6669)*
Global Marine Logistics LLC ....E....... 206 854-0201
  Kirkland *(G-5350)*
Hansen Fabrication ....G....... 206 283-9181
  Seattle *(G-10139)*
Hanson Worldwide LLC ....G....... 509 252-9290
  Spokane *(G-12289)*
Industrial Welding Co Inc ....F....... 509 598-2356
  Spokane *(G-12306)*
International Cnstr Eqp Inc ....G....... 206 764-4787
  Seattle *(G-10249)*
Kemp West Inc ....D....... 425 334-5572
  Snohomish *(G-11932)*
Konecranes Inc ....G....... 503 548-4078
  Vancouver *(G-14353)*
Machine Development Company ....G....... 360 479-4484
  Bremerton *(G-1975)*
Morgan Creek Envmtl Rsrces Inc ....G....... 360 202-6536
  Sedro Woolley *(G-11551)*
Morpac Industries Inc ....E....... 253 735-8922
  Pacific *(G-7533)*
Northstar Attachments LLC ....G....... 509 453-8271
  Union Gap *(G-13946)*
Northwest Equipment Sales Inc ....G....... 253 835-1802
  Federal Way *(G-3764)*
Pape Machinery Inc ....E....... 509 838-5252
  Spokane *(G-12429)*
Performance Cnstr Eqp Inc ....G....... 360 794-6220
  Monroe *(G-6605)*
PSM LLC ....E....... 425 486-1232
  Woodinville *(G-15343)*
Safeworks LLC ....D....... 206 575-6445
  Tukwila *(G-13809)*
Steer Straight LLC ....G....... 360 398-6294
  Bellingham *(G-1557)*
Stella-Jones Corporation ....D....... 360 435-2146
  Arlington *(G-334)*
Track Equipment Company LLC ....G....... 360 201-7881
  Bellingham *(G-1573)*
Twin Peaks ....G....... 509 427-4759
  Carson *(G-2309)*
Young Corporation ....E....... 206 623-3274
  Seattle *(G-11514)*
Young Corporation ....E....... 425 488-2427
  Woodinville *(G-15413)*

MACHINERY: Cryogenic, Industrial

Universal Refiner Corporation ....G....... 360 249-4415
  Montesano *(G-6663)*

MACHINERY: Custom

All American Spacer Co LLC ....G....... 509 633-3440
  Grand Coulee *(G-4242)*
Automated Systems Tacoma LLC ....E....... 253 475-0200
  Tacoma *(G-13186)*
Bair Metal ....G....... 425 231-1944
  Arlington *(G-208)*
Camano Mold Inc ....E....... 360 387-0961
  Camano Island *(G-2209)*
Coherent Resources Inc ....F....... 509 747-3541
  Cheney *(G-2581)*
Corvus and Columba LLC ....G....... 206 673-7860
  Seattle *(G-9745)*
Custom Craft LLC ....E....... 253 826-5450
  Sumner *(G-13064)*
Elliott Bay Holding Co LLC ....G....... 206 762-6560
  Seattle *(G-9901)*
Jemco Cmpnents Fabrication Inc ....D....... 425 827-7611
  Kirkland *(G-5372)*
Kinematics Marine Eqp Inc ....G....... 360 659-5415
  Marysville *(G-6348)*
Korvan Industries Inc ....D....... 360 354-1500
  Lynden *(G-6029)*
Larock Enterprises Inc ....F....... 509 966-4542
  Union Gap *(G-13938)*
Lasermach Inc ....G....... 425 485-3169
  Woodinville *(G-15284)*
Moco Engineering & Fabrication ....F....... 509 226-0199
  Spokane Valley *(G-12792)*
Overseas Security ....G....... 206 364-6784
  Seattle *(G-10723)*
Paul Schurman Machine Inc ....F....... 360 887-3193
  Ridgefield *(G-9101)*
Rjm Corporation ....F....... 253 887-9100
  Auburn *(G-548)*
Tango Manufacturing Inc ....G....... 360 693-7228
  Vancouver *(G-14625)*
Tidland Hydraulics Inc ....G....... 360 573-6506
  Vancouver *(G-14636)*
Universal Plant Services of No ....E....... 360 757-4646
  Burlington *(G-2197)*

MACHINERY: Deburring

Complete Deburr Inc ....F....... 253 887-0997
  Auburn *(G-411)*

MACHINERY: Die Casting

Tonkin Replicas Inc ....E....... 206 542-6919
  North Bend *(G-7129)*

MACHINERY: Electronic Component Making

Alpha Test Corporation ....E....... 360 462-0201
  Shelton *(G-11675)*
Brandon Company Inc ....G....... 425 290-5427
  Everett *(G-3400)*
Electro Erosion Specialties ....G....... 425 251-9440
  Renton *(G-8792)*
Powell Industries Inc ....F....... 206 402-3591
  Tukwila *(G-13793)*

MACHINERY: Engraving

Evergreen Engravers ....G....... 253 852-6766
  Kent *(G-4899)*

MACHINERY: General, Industrial, NEC

Atkins Machines LLC ....G....... 253 588-2350
  Lakewood *(G-5700)*
Clark Machinery Inc ....G....... 360 825-1840
  Enumclaw *(G-3282)*
Cnc Diversified Manufacturing ....G....... 253 852-6869
  Kent *(G-4854)*
Industrial Systems LLC ....E....... 503 262-0367
  Vancouver *(G-14315)*
Kinetic Solutions Intl ....G....... 503 490-8642
  Ridgefield *(G-9092)*
Membane Solutions Corp ....G....... 253 487-5134
  Kent *(G-5005)*
Osmonics Inc ....G....... 425 204-5508
  Renton *(G-8867)*
Precision Industrial Equi ....G....... 509 571-1725
  Yakima *(G-15650)*

PRODUCT SECTION

Rrr Inc ....G..... 206 782-9260
Seattle *(G-10990)*
Stevens Holding Company Inc ....G..... 425 446-4928
Everett *(G-3622)*
Unisource Manufacturing Inc ....G..... 253 854-0541
Kent *(G-5196)*

MACHINERY: Glassmaking

Spiral Arts ....G..... 206 768-9765
Seattle *(G-11168)*

MACHINERY: Industrial, NEC

Airnexion Inc ....G..... 425 771-5924
Woodinville *(G-15173)*
Amazon Tool Shed ....G..... 206 429-2185
Normandy Park *(G-7090)*
Anchor Cnc LLC ....G..... 360 516-3501
Poulsbo *(G-7943)*
B Triplex Inc ....G..... 360 904-5981
Battle Ground *(G-689)*
Basic Machining & Electronics ....G..... 509 308-6341
Kennewick *(G-4627)*
Buried Hatchet Tool Co LLC ....G..... 253 677-9730
Seattle *(G-9600)*
Cascade Cnc LLC ....G..... 360 366-2580
Custer *(G-2853)*
Config-Systems ....G..... 360 871-8091
Port Orchard *(G-7799)*
Crossrads Precision Rifles LLC ....G..... 360 931-4505
Vancouver *(G-14154)*
Dans Tool Truck ....G..... 509 520-4531
Dayton *(G-2880)*
Element 13 Precision LLC ....G..... 360 597-3195
Vancouver *(G-14198)*
Finco Corp ....G..... 360 854-0772
Sedro Woolley *(G-11538)*
Five Tool Food Service LLC ....G..... 253 761-5621
Tacoma *(G-13298)*
Foust Fabrication Co ....G..... 509 684-3754
Colville *(G-2753)*
Glamazon Salon LLC ....G..... 509 703-7145
Spokane *(G-12275)*
Island Custom Machining ....G..... 360 341-5687
Clinton *(G-2690)*
Jadron Tools ....G..... 253 862-3908
Lakewood *(G-5729)*
Kjar Industrial ....G..... 206 992-7151
Lynnwood *(G-6152)*
Merlins Workshop LLC ....G..... 206 817-9677
Port Hadlock *(G-7760)*
Nelscorp Inc ....G..... 206 660-6313
Stanwood *(G-12982)*
Otogear ....G..... 360 852-0250
Seattle *(G-10716)*
Oyate Research & Training Cons ....G..... 360 239-2281
Yelm *(G-15742)*
Peter K Grossman ....G..... 206 824-6626
Renton *(G-8877)*
Peterson Tools ....G..... 425 870-0137
Marysville *(G-6368)*
Precision Alias ....G..... 425 222-0744
Fall City *(G-3706)*
Precision Machine Supply ....G..... 509 922-1666
Spokane Valley *(G-12837)*
Robobear LLC ....G..... 425 453-1391
Bellevue *(G-1105)*
Sapphire Materials Company ....G..... 360 210-5124
Washougal *(G-14983)*
Screw You LLC ....G..... 360 400-3648
Yelm *(G-15745)*
Snoqualmie Machine Works ....G..... 425 888-1464
Snoqualmie *(G-12025)*
Synthigen LLC ....G..... 208 772-7294
Spokane *(G-12538)*
T Squared Tools LLC ....G..... 406 260-5232
Bellingham *(G-1565)*
Torc Star Bolting Tools LLC ....G..... 334 714-0945
Bellevue *(G-1195)*
Valleyford Metal Crafters LLC ....E..... 509 448-5583
Spokane *(G-12579)*
Wenatchee Qlty Wldg Fbrication ....F..... 509 782-0807
Cashmere *(G-2333)*
Westom Tools ....G..... 360 355-6741
Kelso *(G-4560)*
Z-Machine LLC ....G..... 509 991-8628
Chattaroy *(G-2455)*
Zombie Tinder ....G..... 360 548-3132
Arlington *(G-351)*

MACHINERY: Kilns

Arlington Dry Kilns LLC ....F..... 360 403-3566
Arlington *(G-200)*
Kiln Core Holdings LLC ....G..... 206 859-1114
Seattle *(G-10343)*

MACHINERY: Kilns, Lumber

Wellons Inc ....C..... 360 750-3500
Vancouver *(G-14680)*

MACHINERY: Logging Eqpt

Briggs Mch & Fabrication LLC ....F..... 509 535-0125
Spokane Valley *(G-12645)*
Joseph Gillum ....G..... 800 624-4578
Centralia *(G-2413)*

MACHINERY: Marking, Metalworking

Trinity Mfg ....G..... 360 474-8639
Arlington *(G-342)*

MACHINERY: Metalworking

A & M Prcsion Msuring Svcs Inc ....F..... 425 432-7554
Kent *(G-4750)*
Industrial Tech Intl LLC ....G..... 509 248-0959
Yakima *(G-15588)*
Micro Machining LLC ....G..... 360 835-3200
Washougal *(G-14967)*
Provail ....E..... 206 363-7303
Kent *(G-5086)*
Pyrotek Incorporated ....D..... 509 926-6211
Spokane Valley *(G-12846)*
Rottler Manufacturing Company ....E..... 253 872-7050
Kent *(G-5108)*
Summitview Tooling Inc ....G..... 509 966-9859
Yakima *(G-15686)*
Westec Tool & Productions Inc ....G..... 253 476-3404
Tacoma *(G-13593)*
Western Machine Works Inc ....F..... 253 627-6538
Tacoma *(G-13594)*

MACHINERY: Milling

Grizzly Machining Solutions ....G..... 406 396-4087
Sultan *(G-13026)*

MACHINERY: Mining

Hanson Worldwide LLC ....D..... 509 252-9290
Spokane *(G-12289)*
Impact Service Corporation ....E..... 509 468-7900
Spokane *(G-12305)*
New Tec LLC ....F..... 509 738-6621
Kettle Falls *(G-5237)*
QSP Packers LLC ....G..... 253 770-0315
Puyallup *(G-8230)*
Rainier Rigging Inc ....F..... 253 833-4087
Auburn *(G-545)*
Thunderbird Pacific Corp ....G..... 425 869-2727
Redmond *(G-8691)*
Williams Elite Machining & Mfg ....G..... 253 228-2288
Rochester *(G-9146)*

MACHINERY: Packaging

Buren Sheet Metal Inc ....E..... 509 575-1950
Yakima *(G-15525)*
C & C Packaging Services Inc ....E..... 425 673-6347
Camano Island *(G-2208)*
Crown Cork & Seal Usa Inc ....E..... 206 575-4260
Tukwila *(G-13718)*
Design Service Corporation ....F..... 509 248-8531
Yakima *(G-15553)*
Intech Enterprises Inc ....E..... 360 835-8785
Washougal *(G-14961)*
Jerry Carter ....G..... 509 487-8294
Spokane *(G-12332)*
Klc Holdings Ltd ....F..... 509 248-4770
Yakima *(G-15608)*
Kwik Loc Corp ....G..... 253 564-3574
University Place *(G-13976)*
Kwik Lok Corporation ....C..... 509 248-4770
Union Gap *(G-13937)*
Marq Packaging Systems Inc ....E..... 509 966-4300
Yakima *(G-15615)*
Pomona Service & Supply Co ....G..... 509 452-7121
Yakima *(G-15649)*
Ridgerunners Inc ....G..... 509 248-8531
Yakima *(G-15662)*

MACHINERY: Screening Eqpt, Electric

Thermoforming Systems LLC ....E..... 509 454-4578
Union Gap *(G-13954)*
United Sales Inc ....F..... 509 225-0636
Union Gap *(G-13955)*
Viking Packaging Machinery ....G..... 509 452-7143
Yakima *(G-15703)*

MACHINERY: Paper Industry Miscellaneous

A H Lundberg Inc ....G..... 425 258-4617
Everett *(G-3354)*
Diane M Young ....G..... 310 284-8704
Burien *(G-2102)*
Enterprises International Inc ....G..... 360 533-6222
Hoquiam *(G-4336)*
Valmet Inc ....G..... 360 753-8831
Olympia *(G-7419)*

MACHINERY: Pharmaciutical

Nextrx Corporation ....F..... 425 402-3485
Bothell *(G-1879)*

MACHINERY: Plastic Working

Diy Tech Shop LLC ....G..... 360 258-1519
Vancouver *(G-14184)*
General Plastics Machines ....G..... 360 694-8836
Vancouver *(G-14250)*

MACHINERY: Polishing & Buffing

Coyote Cleaning Systems Inc ....G..... 425 776-8002
Mukilteo *(G-6907)*
Levetec Surface Prep Mchy LLC ....G..... 425 629-8200
Redmond *(G-8533)*

MACHINERY: Pottery Making

Birdseed ....G..... 360 574-7516
Vancouver *(G-14067)*
Northstar Equipment Inc ....F..... 509 235-9200
Cheney *(G-2589)*
S & BS Boutique ....G..... 253 631-2718
Kent *(G-5109)*

MACHINERY: Printing Presses

Jones Digital Printing Inc ....G..... 509 452-8238
Yakima *(G-15602)*
Pad Printing Services Inc ....G..... 206 362-4544
Seattle *(G-10744)*
Scheibler Bros Inc ....G..... 509 548-7115
Leavenworth *(G-5815)*
Web Press LLC ....E..... 253 620-4747
Tacoma *(G-13589)*

MACHINERY: Recycling

Cedar Recycling Inc ....F..... 253 863-5353
Pacific *(G-7524)*
Composite Recycling Tech Ctr ....G..... 360 819-1204
Port Angeles *(G-7694)*
Puget Sound Recycling ....G..... 253 536-2260
Tacoma *(G-13482)*
Total Reclaim Incorporated ....C..... 206 343-7443
Kent *(G-5184)*

MACHINERY: Riveting

Electroimpact Inc ....B..... 425 348-8090
Mukilteo *(G-6922)*

MACHINERY: Road Construction & Maintenance

County Public Works ....G..... 509 674-2502
Cle Elum *(G-2664)*
Kc McCoy Inc ....G..... 360 376-5619
Eastsound *(G-3038)*
McCafferty NW Land Dev LLC ....G..... 509 483-1222
White Salmon *(G-15122)*
Vetch Construction LLC ....G..... 425 387-3244
Camano Island *(G-2226)*

MACHINERY: Saw & Sawing

Maulcor Inc ....G..... 773 696-2783
Seattle *(G-10502)*

MACHINERY: Screening Eqpt, Electric

Schilling Graphics ....E..... 253 572-8171
Tacoma *(G-13507)*

MACHINERY: Screening Eqpt, Electric

Unified Scrning Crshing-WA LLC ....G....... 800 562-1971
Kent *(G-5195)*

MACHINERY: Semiconductor Manufacturing

Advanced Technology Resources ....G....... 253 229-3415
Yelm *(G-15725)*
Ochoa Brothers Inc ....G....... 509 544-6553
Pasco *(G-7607)*
Perco Inc ....G....... 425 373-1252
Bellevue *(G-1068)*
QSP Packers LLC ....G....... 253 770-0315
Puyallup *(G-8230)*
Tactical Fabs Inc ....E....... 360 723-5360
Battle Ground *(G-742)*
Zepher Inc ....E....... 509 637-2520
Bingen *(G-1643)*

MACHINERY: Separators, Mineral

Wittco Separation Systems Inc ....G....... 360 495-3100
McCleary *(G-6421)*

MACHINERY: Service Industry, NEC

Compactors Nw ....G....... 206 747-7316
Seattle *(G-9721)*
Endresen Pressure Washing ....G....... 253 858-7743
Gig Harbor *(G-4098)*
Geogenius LLC ....G....... 206 838-8125
Seattle *(G-10063)*
MA & Kt Inc ....G....... 360 321-4019
Freeland *(G-4032)*
Machine Technology ....G....... 425 334-1951
Snohomish *(G-11942)*

MACHINERY: Sheet Metal Working

ASC Machine Tools Inc ....C....... 509 534-6600
Spokane Valley *(G-12626)*

MACHINERY: Sifting & Screening

Aerospace Mltxis Machining Inc ....F....... 253 856-1068
Kent *(G-4764)*

MACHINERY: Specialty

Fobes District Water & Assn ....G....... 425 334-3311
Snohomish *(G-11910)*
Innovatech Pdts & Eqp Co Inc ....G....... 425 402-1881
Woodinville *(G-15265)*
Peri-USA ....G....... 410 712-7225
Woodland *(G-15459)*
Pishwacom ....G....... 509 991-8972
Spokane *(G-12443)*
Renewable Enrgy Cmps Sltns LLC ...G....... 360 695-3238
Vancouver *(G-14544)*
Wilford Noorda Foundation ....G....... 509 487-6832
Spokane *(G-12592)*
World Diamonds ....G....... 425 765-7119
Bellevue *(G-1228)*

MACHINERY: Stone Working

Gran Quartz Trading Inc ....G....... 206 973-7640
Seattle *(G-10105)*
Tru Square Metal Products Inc ....G....... 253 833-2310
Auburn *(G-583)*

MACHINERY: Tapping

Milman Engineering Inc ....G....... 360 273-5080
Rochester *(G-9137)*

MACHINERY: Textile

Ioline Corporation ....E....... 425 398-8282
Woodinville *(G-15267)*
Mountain Loom Co ....G....... 360 295-3856
Vader *(G-13986)*

MACHINERY: Voting

Democracy Live Inc ....F....... 855 655-8683
Seattle *(G-9819)*

MACHINERY: Wire Drawing

4evergreen Fabricators LLC ....G....... 253 691-6752
Sumner *(G-13053)*
Stelia Aerospace North America ......G....... 253 852-4055
Kent *(G-5155)*

MACHINERY: Woodworking

American Machine Works ....G....... 509 968-4415
Ellensburg *(G-3182)*
Andritz Iggesund Tools Inc ....G....... 360 574-1440
Vancouver *(G-14035)*
Globe Machine Manufacturing Co ....C....... 253 383-2584
Tacoma *(G-13314)*
Hill Woodworking ....G....... 425 488-7943
Kenmore *(G-4581)*
Multi Score Inc ....G....... 206 524-7591
Seattle *(G-10568)*
New Tec LLC ....F....... 509 738-6621
Kettle Falls *(G-5237)*
Nicholson Manufacturing Co ....G....... 206 682-2752
Seattle *(G-10607)*
Nicholson Manufacturing Co ....G....... 206 291-8849
Kent *(G-5023)*
Seaport Machine Inc ....F....... 509 758-2605
Clarkston *(G-2648)*
T & G Machinery LLC ....G....... 425 396-5939
Snoqualmie *(G-12033)*
Woodward & White Manufacturing ...G....... 253 839-7581
Des Moines *(G-2952)*

MACHINES: Forming, Sheet Metal

L & M Prcision Fabrication Inc ....E....... 509 244-5446
Airway Heights *(G-55)*
North Park Heating Company Inc .....F....... 206 365-1414
Lake Forest Park *(G-5622)*

MACHINISTS' TOOLS: Measuring, Precision

Hexagon Metrology Inc ....G....... 253 872-2443
Kent *(G-4940)*
Trilion Quality Systems LLC ....E....... 267 565-8062
Seattle *(G-11337)*
Wilkins Precision Inc ....G....... 253 851-9736
Gig Harbor *(G-4175)*

MACHINISTS' TOOLS: Precision

Innova Mfg LLC ....G....... 509 946-7461
Richland *(G-9010)*
Mecadaq Aerospace LLC ....F....... 714 442-9703
Kirkland *(G-5399)*
Polaris Manufacturing Inc ....E....... 360 653-7676
Marysville *(G-6370)*
Tmf Inc ....F....... 360 598-1750
Poulsbo *(G-8011)*
Vanwerven Inc ....G....... 360 435-2600
Arlington *(G-345)*

MACHINISTS' TOOLS: Scales, Measuring, Precision

Acf Idea Works Inc ....G....... 425 335-0958
Lake Stevens *(G-5630)*
Bibbi Co LLC ....G....... 206 453-4152
Seattle *(G-9520)*
Cheyenne Scale Co Inc ....G....... 206 933-7904
Seattle *(G-9673)*

MAGAZINES, WHOLESALE

Clam Digger ....G....... 360 299-3444
Anacortes *(G-114)*

MAGNESIUM

Northwest Alloys Inc ....G....... 509 935-3300
Addy *(G-46)*

MAGNETIC TAPE, AUDIO: Prerecorded

Soundings of The Planet Inc ....G....... 360 738-9368
Bellingham *(G-1547)*

MAGNETS: Ceramic

Baker Enterprises ....G....... 360 452-1349
Port Angeles *(G-7688)*

MAGNETS: Permanent

Armstrong Magnetics Inc ....G....... 360 647-8438
Bellingham *(G-1252)*

MAIL-ORDER HOUSE, NEC

Art On File Inc ....G....... 206 329-9607
Seattle *(G-9438)*

Computergear Inc ....G....... 425 487-3600
Woodinville *(G-15209)*
International Athletic ....G....... 360 384-6868
Ferndale *(G-3860)*
Liberty Orchards Company Inc ....D....... 509 782-4088
Cashmere *(G-2326)*
Pacific Rim Tonewoods Inc ....F....... 360 826-6101
Concrete *(G-2790)*
Pacific Rim Tonewoods Inc ....F....... 360 826-6101
Bellingham *(G-1488)*
Rainbow Racing System Inc ....F....... 509 326-5470
Spokane *(G-12466)*
Skyflight Inc ....G....... 425 844-9199
Woodinville *(G-15366)*

MAIL-ORDER HOUSES: Arts & Crafts Eqpt & Splys

Village Frame & Gallery ....G....... 206 824-3068
Des Moines *(G-2950)*

MAIL-ORDER HOUSES: Books, Exc Book Clubs

Gildeane Group ....G....... 206 362-0336
Kenmore *(G-4575)*
Pathfinder Press ....G....... 360 687-4319
Battle Ground *(G-729)*

MAIL-ORDER HOUSES: Computer Eqpt & Electronics

Christian Hamilton ....G....... 360 442-4900
Longview *(G-5899)*

MAIL-ORDER HOUSES: Food

Ener-G Foods Inc ....E....... 206 767-3928
Seattle *(G-9922)*
Frans Chocolates Ltd ....E....... 206 322-0233
Seattle *(G-10022)*
Seabear Company ....E....... 360 293-4661
Anacortes *(G-165)*
Taylor Shellfish Company Inc ....E....... 360 875-5494
South Bend *(G-12048)*

MAIL-ORDER HOUSES: Fruit

Cherry Chukar Company ....E....... 509 786-2055
Prosser *(G-8032)*
Coyote Canyon Winery LLC ....G....... 509 786-7686
Prosser *(G-8036)*

MAIL-ORDER HOUSES: General Merchandise

Far Star Products ....G....... 360 604-0080
Vancouver *(G-14222)*
Magellan Group Ltd ....G....... 360 332-6868
Blaine *(G-1682)*
Sandbox Enterprises LLC ....G....... 360 966-6677
Bellingham *(G-1523)*

MAIL-ORDER HOUSES: Jewelry

Jewelry Boutique LLC ....G....... 360 866-2278
Olympia *(G-7311)*

MAIL-ORDER HOUSES: Stamps

American Postage Scale Corp ....G....... 509 299-6144
Medical Lake *(G-6439)*

MAIL-ORDER HOUSES: Women's Apparel

Decent Exposures Inc ....F....... 206 364-4540
Seattle *(G-9810)*
Lady 12 LLC ....G....... 425 218-3080
Redmond *(G-8528)*

MAILBOX RENTAL & RELATED SVCS

Andrews Nation Inc ....G....... 360 989-1700
Vancouver *(G-14034)*
Dr Ventures Inc ....G....... 253 874-6583
Federal Way *(G-3733)*
Post All Expressions ....G....... 509 684-3723
Colville *(G-2769)*
The UPS Store Inc ....G....... 360 400-6245
Yelm *(G-15747)*

PRODUCT SECTION

MANUFACTURING INDUSTRIES, NEC

MAILING & MESSENGER SVCS
Computer Assisted Message Inc ....F 425 392-2496
 Issaquah *(G-4399)*
McG Health Llc ....E 206 389-5300
 Seattle *(G-10507)*

MAILING LIST: Compilers
Labels & Lists Inc ....F 425 822-1984
 Bothell *(G-1772)*
Vancouver Business Journal ....F 360 695-2442
 Vancouver *(G-14660)*

MAILING SVCS, NEC
Direct Mailing Solutions ....G 425 739-4568
 Lynnwood *(G-6108)*
Merril Mail Marketing Inc ....G 425 454-7009
 Bellevue *(G-1003)*
Rotary Offset Press Inc ....C 253 813-9900
 Kent *(G-5107)*

MANAGEMENT CONSULTING SVCS: Business
Allied Forces Inc ....G 360 387-5713
 Camano Island *(G-2206)*
Allstar Magnetics LLC ....E 360 693-0213
 Vancouver *(G-14022)*
Chauncey and Shirah Bell Inc ....G 206 437-7556
 Seattle *(G-9670)*
Leading Beyond Tradition LLC ....G 425 275-7665
 Snohomish *(G-11938)*
M B G Management Services ....G 360 493-0522
 Olympia *(G-7328)*
Parametrix Inc ....D 206 394-3700
 Puyallup *(G-8219)*

MANAGEMENT CONSULTING SVCS: Business Planning & Organizing
Reliance Inc ....F 615 218-3929
 Redmond *(G-8647)*
Stillaquamish Resources LLC ....G 360 474-1999
 Arlington *(G-335)*

MANAGEMENT CONSULTING SVCS: Construction Project
Northstar Attachments LLC ....G 509 453-8271
 Union Gap *(G-13946)*

MANAGEMENT CONSULTING SVCS: Food & Beverage
LDB Beverage Company ....F 509 651-0381
 Stevenson *(G-13015)*

MANAGEMENT CONSULTING SVCS: General
Cleaning Consultants Services ....G 206 682-9748
 Seattle *(G-9692)*

MANAGEMENT CONSULTING SVCS: Hospital & Health
Callidus Software Inc ....F 503 579-4484
 Vancouver *(G-14090)*

MANAGEMENT CONSULTING SVCS: Incentive Or Award Program
Jmh Enterprises ....G 509 628-2191
 Richland *(G-9015)*

MANAGEMENT CONSULTING SVCS: Industrial
Intech Enterprises Inc ....E 360 835-8785
 Washougal *(G-14961)*

MANAGEMENT CONSULTING SVCS: Industrial & Labor
Unisource Manufacturing Inc ....G 253 854-0541
 Kent *(G-5196)*

MANAGEMENT CONSULTING SVCS: Industry Specialist
Electronic Prgrm & Design ....G 206 767-7262
 Seattle *(G-9894)*
Wallfam Inc ....G 509 786-2163
 Prosser *(G-8074)*

MANAGEMENT CONSULTING SVCS: Information Systems
Nexus Life Cycle MGT LLC ....G 541 400-0765
 Stevenson *(G-13016)*

MANAGEMENT CONSULTING SVCS: Manufacturing
Mfg Universe Corp ....G 800 883-8779
 Tukwila *(G-13772)*

MANAGEMENT CONSULTING SVCS: Public Utilities
Avista Capital Inc ....G 509 489-0500
 Spokane *(G-12133)*

MANAGEMENT CONSULTING SVCS: Training & Development
Eduongo Inc ....F 206 451-7325
 Bellevue *(G-892)*
Gildeane Group ....G 206 362-0336
 Kenmore *(G-4575)*
Leidos Inc ....E 425 267-5600
 Lynnwood *(G-6157)*
Leidos Inc ....G 360 394-8870
 Poulsbo *(G-7975)*
Vision Leadership Inc ....G 206 418-0808
 Seattle *(G-11423)*

MANAGEMENT CONSULTING SVCS: Transportation
Adaptive Cargo Solutions LLC ....F 240 475-6521
 Everett *(G-3360)*

MANAGEMENT SERVICES
Glacier Water Services Inc ....G 360 413-7272
 Lacey *(G-5553)*
Green Valley Management LLC ....G 509 830-5240
 Mabton *(G-6228)*
Marq Packaging Systems Inc ....E 509 966-4300
 Yakima *(G-15615)*
Oatridge-Evergreen 8a2 JV LLC ....G 253 627-3794
 Tacoma *(G-13439)*
Talkie Tooter ....E 360 856-0836
 Sedro Woolley *(G-11574)*
Waft Corp ....F 425 743-4601
 Mukilteo *(G-6990)*

MANAGEMENT SVCS, FACILITIES SUPPORT: Environ Remediation
Anderson Rock Dem Pits II LLC ....G 509 965-3621
 Yakima *(G-15509)*
Ecotech Recycling LLC ....E 360 673-3860
 Kalama *(G-4498)*

MANAGEMENT SVCS: Administrative
Alyeska Ocean Inc ....E 360 293-4677
 Anacortes *(G-99)*

MANAGEMENT SVCS: Business
Constellation Homebuilder Syst ....G 888 723-2222
 Redmond *(G-8424)*
Itc USA LLC ....F 206 669-3442
 Seattle *(G-10262)*
Reliance Inc ....F 615 218-3929
 Redmond *(G-8647)*

MANAGEMENT SVCS: Construction
Lorache Cad/It Services LLC ....F 206 328-4227
 Seattle *(G-10442)*

MANAGEMENT SVCS: Restaurant
Ektos LLC ....G 800 783-0383
 Woodinville *(G-15235)*

Sitting Room ....G 206 285-2830
 Seattle *(G-11121)*

MANHOLES & COVERS: Metal
Pfc Inc ....G 360 398-8889
 Bellingham *(G-1497)*

MANICURE PREPARATIONS
Amera Sales Inc ....G 509 735-1531
 Kennewick *(G-4615)*
Mani Pedi ....G 509 522-6264
 Walla Walla *(G-14841)*
Polish Nail Spa ....G 425 771-1458
 Lynnwood *(G-6182)*

MANPOWER POOLS
K & D Services Inc ....G 425 252-0906
 Everett *(G-3527)*

MANUFACTURING INDUSTRIES, NEC
206 Industries LLC ....G 206 390-8449
 Seattle *(G-9319)*
2x4 Industries ....G 253 205-0359
 Seattle *(G-9320)*
613 Industries Inc ....G 612 823-3606
 Seattle *(G-9325)*
A & S Manufacturing Entps ....G 425 334-6606
 Marysville *(G-6309)*
Abbott Industries Inc ....G 360 894-6230
 Yelm *(G-15724)*
Ace Anthony Equity MGT LLC ....F 425 333-6024
 Duvall *(G-2978)*
Act Manufacturing Inc ....G 509 893-4100
 Spokane Valley *(G-12600)*
AGM Industries Inc ....G 716 256-9470
 Redmond *(G-8375)*
Alexander Industries LLC ....G 253 686-6066
 Renton *(G-8737)*
Alpine Industries LLC ....G 253 261-1500
 Lake Tapps *(G-5676)*
Alpine Shed LLC ....G 509 322-0808
 Tonasket *(G-13645)*
Aseptic Manufacturing Svcs LLC ....G 509 869-4867
 Spokane *(G-12121)*
Axis Mfg ....G 509 368-9895
 Spokane Valley *(G-12634)*
B & B Manufacturing LLC ....G 360 988-5020
 Sumas *(G-13041)*
Back To Basics Lean Mfg ....G 253 353-4281
 Puyallup *(G-8126)*
Balros Industries ....G 206 963-6114
 Seattle *(G-9487)*
Bear Industries LLC ....G 509 981-8618
 Spokane *(G-12143)*
Belshire Industries ....G 360 910-9209
 Ridgefield *(G-9066)*
Bestway Industries LLC ....G 360 513-2000
 Vancouver *(G-14064)*
Big C Industries LLC ....G 360 773-5873
 Ridgefield *(G-9068)*
Big Rock Industries ....G 360 659-3308
 Lake Stevens *(G-5634)*
Big Rock Industries LLC ....G 425 314-8710
 Monroe *(G-6553)*
Big Smooth Industries LLC ....G 206 356-5888
 Gig Harbor *(G-4081)*
Bigoni Stiner & Assoc ....G 253 826-5824
 Edgewood *(G-3073)*
Black Mouse Inc ....G 253 677-3491
 Tacoma *(G-13204)*
Bloomfield Light Industries ....G 360 877-5718
 Lilliwaup *(G-5870)*
Bmt Industries Inc ....G 509 838-4400
 Spokane *(G-12156)*
Board Systems ....G 253 307-0166
 Roy *(G-9157)*
Boulder Creek Industriescom ....G 425 879-2322
 Arlington *(G-214)*
Bre & Car Industries LLC ....G 206 268-0204
 Seattle *(G-9580)*
Bridgetown Industries L L ....G 503 953-3580
 Vancouver *(G-14083)*
Brushwood Industries Ltd ....G 509 447-2266
 Newport *(G-7054)*
Buck Snort Industries ....G 509 939-7777
 Deer Park *(G-2894)*
Buckley Industries ....G 425 286-6443
 Kenmore *(G-4567)*

Employee Codes: A=Over 500 employees, B=251-500
C=101-250, D=51-100, E=20-50, F=10-19, G=2-9

2019 Washington Manufacturers Register

1009

Budo Industries LLC G 206 349-8085
Seattle *(G-9593)*
C M F Industries Inc G 425 282-5065
Kent *(G-4830)*
Cannon Ball Industries G 206 781-1833
Seattle *(G-9618)*
Cascade Ridge Industries G 509 237-1534
Quincy *(G-8291)*
Center For Advanced G 253 298-7490
Tukwila *(G-13711)*
Chambong Industries LLC G 608 335-1882
Seattle *(G-9665)*
Chrome Industries G 206 682-1343
Seattle *(G-9682)*
CJ Manufacturing I Inc G 360 543-5297
Ferndale *(G-3831)*
Cns Industries Inc G 360 424-1624
Mount Vernon *(G-6785)*
Cobblestone Industries LLC G 509 447-4518
Newport *(G-7056)*
Colubia AG & Mfg G 509 382-4849
Waitsburg *(G-14752)*
Columbia Manufacturing G 360 210-5124
Camas *(G-2240)*
Columbia Mfg & Tech Ctr LLC G 360 835-0922
Washougal *(G-14948)*
Columbia River Mfg Inc G 509 493-3460
White Salmon *(G-15113)*
Columbia River Mfg Svcs LLC G 801 652-3008
Kennewick *(G-4649)*
Conner Industries G 360 261-0265
Kelso *(G-4520)*
Cooper T Kirsch Glass LLC G 206 718-8183
Seattle *(G-9738)*
Cor-Tread LLC G 425 268-6377
Mukilteo *(G-6905)*
Corallie Industries G 253 576-5240
Spanaway *(G-12056)*
Core Training Industries Inc G 206 250-2050
Federal Way *(G-3725)*
Correctional Industries G 360 963-3332
Clallam Bay *(G-2618)*
Correctional Industries G 360 427-4613
Shelton *(G-11692)*
Cowin In-Situ Science LLC G 509 392-1329
Richland *(G-8985)*
Curvetec Mfg G 425 760-2844
Mukilteo *(G-6910)*
Custom Mfg Ambassador LLC G 206 963-9853
Seattle *(G-9769)*
Cuzd Industries G 360 742-3126
Lacey *(G-5544)*
CWC Industries LLC A Washingto G 206 528-8090
Seattle *(G-9774)*
Db Industries LLC G 360 432-8239
Shelton *(G-11695)*
Decatur Industries Inc G 206 368-3178
Lake Forest Park *(G-5611)*
Deep Cell Industries G 206 909-3858
Seattle *(G-9813)*
Desert View Manufactured Home G 509 967-3456
West Richland *(G-15095)*
Df Industries Inc G 253 445-7940
Puyallup *(G-8143)*
Dogwood Industries G 425 949-7379
Bothell *(G-1759)*
Drake Industries LLC G 425 672-8266
Edmonds *(G-3107)*
Duncan Stone LLC G 360 820-0823
Seattle *(G-9859)*
Dunmire Manufacturing G 360 241-9099
Bremerton *(G-1949)*
E and S Industries LLC G 253 678-1539
Tacoma *(G-13268)*
Eagle Rock Manufacturing Inc G 360 989-0863
Granite Falls *(G-4271)*
Edinger Mfg Inc G 425 413-4008
Ravensdale *(G-8334)*
Envision Manufacturing Co G 206 963-7352
Kent *(G-4895)*
Epik Industries G 360 303-6488
Bellingham *(G-1337)*
Erik Doane Manufacturing G 360 799-0997
Sultan *(G-13023)*
Etz Industries LLC G 253 630-2915
Kent *(G-4898)*
Evergreen Sales Group Inc G 425 368-2000
Woodinville *(G-15239)*
Evo Industries LLC G 717 665-0406
Ellensburg *(G-3199)*
Excel Industries Incorporated G 360 790-3577
Lynden *(G-6015)*
F&S Industries LLC G 206 501-5347
Seattle *(G-9957)*
Fab5ventures LLC G 425 310-2543
University Place *(G-13967)*
Farstad Industries LLC G 360 316-9485
Oak Harbor *(G-7150)*
Fasola Tools G 360 293-9231
Anacortes *(G-128)*
Fenix Industries Inc G 206 695-2582
Seattle *(G-9984)*
Ferguson - Gagnon Industries G 509 337-6207
Waitsburg *(G-14754)*
Ferryboat Music LLC G 509 996-3528
Winthrop *(G-15160)*
First Strike LLC G 360 285-4000
Olympia *(G-7285)*
Five Star Industries LLC G 206 706-2754
Seattle *(G-10001)*
Fortynine Industries G 253 632-3081
Maple Valley *(G-6270)*
Fps West Inc G 206 242-4888
Normandy Park *(G-7092)*
Frontier Manufacturing Inc G 360 652-4046
Stanwood *(G-12972)*
Function Works G 206 219-5636
Oroville *(G-7466)*
Fusion Industries G 425 703-2867
Bellevue *(G-917)*
Gale Industries G 360 659-7674
Marysville *(G-6338)*
Gale Industries Inc G 360 479-6271
Bremerton *(G-1955)*
Garvie Industries LLC G 360 691-1233
Granite Falls *(G-4275)*
Giesbrecht & Sons LLC G 509 269-4087
Mesa *(G-6493)*
Globodyne Industries Inc G 425 321-9471
Mukilteo *(G-6928)*
Gman Industries Ltd G 425 228-2518
Renton *(G-8809)*
Gms Industries Inc G 425 454-9500
Bellevue *(G-930)*
Gorman Industries G 509 899-3933
Ellensburg *(G-3204)*
Graymark Industries Inc G 360 437-5121
Port Hadlock *(G-7758)*
Greenlife Industries G 360 566-3984
Vancouver *(G-14272)*
Greenlite Heavy Industries LLC G 206 226-3523
Mercer Island *(G-6465)*
Ham Industries G 360 201-8439
Seattle *(G-10136)*
Haolifts Industries G 425 836-3968
Sammamish *(G-9214)*
Harbor Steel Fabrication G 253 858-8804
Gig Harbor *(G-4112)*
Hard Industries HI G 360 913-2063
Arlington *(G-248)*
Harlane Co LLC G 404 771-9300
Vancouver *(G-14283)*
Harvest Helper G 360 515-5491
Olympia *(G-7305)*
Helm Industries LLC G 206 419-3973
Seattle *(G-10163)*
Hjalmar Industries Inc G 360 957-4302
Seattle *(G-10177)*
Hodge Industries G 253 266-6921
Bonney Lake *(G-1726)*
Hoober Industries Inc G 253 370-9553
Tacoma *(G-13342)*
Hot Sox LLC G 509 947-5193
West Richland *(G-15096)*
Hpf Manufacturing G 425 486-8031
Snohomish *(G-11923)*
Ht Industries LLC G 360 863-2029
Snohomish *(G-11924)*
Huney Jun LLC G 805 903-2011
Peshastin *(G-7662)*
Ideal Industries Intl Inc G 360 761-9958
Puyallup *(G-8164)*
Infinity Industries LLC G 425 418-1151
Bothell *(G-1866)*
Inland Northwest Mfg LLC G 509 218-7424
Spokane *(G-12311)*
Innovate For All Spc G 425 681-2191
Seattle *(G-10240)*
Intelligent Industries LLC G 206 372-7273
Federal Way *(G-3746)*
Interstate Industries Inc G 425 226-2135
Kent *(G-4960)*
Irondog Industries LLC G 509 586-0479
Kennewick *(G-4678)*
J D Mfg G 360 864-8271
Winlock *(G-15151)*
J L Innovations Inc G 425 823-8540
Kenmore *(G-4584)*
Jamar Industries LLC G 206 725-3409
Seattle *(G-10281)*
JD Bargen Industries LLC G 360 354-5676
Lynden *(G-6026)*
JD Fabrication G 360 691-4550
Granite Falls *(G-4278)*
Jett Industries Inc G 360 649-3840
Bremerton *(G-1966)*
Jharc Industries LLC G 571 205-5422
Tacoma *(G-13360)*
Jph Industries LLC G 425 269-8966
Redmond *(G-8522)*
JWB Manufacturing LLC G 253 222-1671
South Prairie *(G-12050)*
K and K Industries LLC G 425 951-0502
Edmonds *(G-3128)*
K Line Industries LLC G 425 870-4228
Camano Island *(G-2215)*
K Sports Manufacturing Inc G 206 251-5211
Renton *(G-8834)*
K Stauffer Manufacturing LLC G 360 626-1462
Poulsbo *(G-7969)*
K&J Mfg Inc G 425 503-2174
North Bend *(G-7114)*
Kam Manufacturing G 360 625-8321
Enumclaw *(G-3298)*
Katana Industries Inc G 360 293-0682
Anacortes *(G-139)*
Kelly Industries LLC G 206 676-2338
Snohomish *(G-11931)*
Kentucky Chrome Industries G 816 522-1783
Seattle *(G-10338)*
Kf Industries LLC G 360 628-8473
Lacey *(G-5563)*
Kfj Industries LLC G 425 922-2889
Kirkland *(G-5376)*
Kobelt Manufacturing G 360 676-2774
Bellingham *(G-1397)*
Koehler Industries Inc G 360 793-9101
Bellevue *(G-969)*
Kova Industries LLC G 360 567-5371
Battle Ground *(G-713)*
Kramerica Industries LLC G 360 931-9690
Vancouver *(G-14354)*
L Rock Industries Inc G 360 575-8868
Cathlamet *(G-2370)*
Labore Industries G 206 533-8709
Shoreline *(G-11780)*
Lancs Industries Holdings LLC D 425 823-6634
Kirkland *(G-5379)*
Lawman Industries LLC G 360 915-7807
Lacey *(G-5564)*
Lazerwood Industries G 206 650-2367
Seattle *(G-10388)*
Leeward Industries Inc G 360 830-0765
Seabeck *(G-9267)*
Lg Industries LLC G 425 557-7993
Issaquah *(G-4438)*
Lgk Industries Inc G 360 299-3140
Anacortes *(G-141)*
Living Stone Industries Inc G 425 679-6278
Edmonds *(G-3130)*
Lohr Industries G 360 802-4351
Enumclaw *(G-3301)*
Lomax Industries LLC G 206 687-7499
Seattle *(G-10435)*
Longhorn Industries G 509 899-5475
Ellensburg *(G-3213)*
Loth Industries Inc G 425 418-5897
Snohomish *(G-11940)*
Luckyhorse Industries G 206 227-3383
Issaquah *(G-4441)*
M Squared Manufacturing LLC G 206 380-0233
Vashon *(G-14732)*
M&L Industries Inc G 425 894-7147
Redmond *(G-8542)*
M24 Industries LLC G 360 348-3578
Monroe *(G-6594)*
Macaw Rescue and Santuary G 425 788-4721
Carnation *(G-2295)*
Macro Mfg LLC G 360 750-3544
Vancouver *(G-14391)*

Madboy Industries.....G....... 206 707-9394
Seattle *(G-10464)*
Malone Industries LLC.....G....... 360 636-1383
Kelso *(G-4536)*
Match Grade Industries LLC.....G....... 425 949-8110
Woodinville *(G-15304)*
Mattress Manufacturing Prize.....G....... 509 946-1194
Richland *(G-9025)*
McMullen Mfg Services.....G....... 360 891-3662
Vancouver *(G-14406)*
McNeeley Mfg.....G....... 206 255-7818
Covington *(G-2832)*
McNeeley Mfg.....G....... 253 236-4969
Auburn *(G-495)*
Meadowbrook Manufacturing LLC.....G....... 206 297-1029
Seattle *(G-10511)*
Meier Manufacturing.....G....... 253 545-9798
Tacoma *(G-13407)*
Menace Industries LLC.....G....... 360 595-4095
Bellingham *(G-1432)*
Meyle Industries LLC.....G....... 360 250-6114
Vancouver *(G-14416)*
Michaels Manufacturing.....G....... 253 459-4384
Bonney Lake *(G-1728)*
Microscan Mfg LLC.....G....... 425 226-5700
Renton *(G-8854)*
Miller Manufacturing.....G....... 360 844-5403
Washougal *(G-14968)*
Millman Industries LLC.....G....... 425 471-0854
Langley *(G-5783)*
MJM Manufacturing.....G....... 305 620-2020
Orting *(G-7485)*
Mjv Mfg.....G....... 509 735-1662
Kennewick *(G-4695)*
Mk Industries LLC.....G....... 425 922-0139
Bellevue *(G-1010)*
Mkg Mfg.....G....... 360 398-7518
Bellingham *(G-1437)*
Mm Industries LLC.....G....... 360 629-4595
Stanwood *(G-12981)*
Monkey Wrench Fabrication LLC.....G....... 206 992-8509
Bainbridge Island *(G-650)*
Moonstuff Inc.....G....... 509 947-2981
West Richland *(G-15099)*
Moore Manufacturing LLC.....G....... 360 400-3277
Roy *(G-9163)*
Morwenstow.....G....... 425 483-0320
Woodinville *(G-15315)*
Mount Evergreen Industries.....G....... 360 584-9620
Olympia *(G-7344)*
Mountain View Industries Inc.....G....... 360 894-0499
Yelm *(G-15741)*
Mt Baker Manufacturing.....G....... 360 778-1238
Lynden *(G-6038)*
Mudslayer Manufacturing LLC.....G....... 360 477-0251
Sequim *(G-11649)*
Mybock Manufacturing LLC.....G....... 716 913-4157
Seattle *(G-10580)*
Natural Nutrition Mfg LLC.....G....... 509 966-8849
Yakima *(G-15628)*
Nightmare Industries.....G....... 425 330-1084
Snohomish *(G-11952)*
Nordick Mfg Co.....G....... 425 488-2427
Woodinville *(G-15321)*
Northwest Labor Industries.....G....... 206 388-6135
Seattle *(G-10647)*
Northwind Industries.....G....... 360 424-6689
Mount Vernon *(G-6818)*
NW Center Industries 5307.....A....... 206 285-9140
Seattle *(G-10673)*
O Neil Industries LLC.....G....... 509 828-0213
Spokane *(G-12417)*
Oe Two Industries LLC.....G....... 425 657-0958
Sammamish *(G-9238)*
Omen Board Industries LLC.....G....... 425 967-3434
Lynnwood *(G-6174)*
Orion Mfg LLC.....G....... 206 979-5511
Kirkland *(G-5422)*
Ortech Controls.....G....... 206 633-7914
Shoreline *(G-11798)*
Orvella Industries Corp.....G....... 206 778-2743
Renton *(G-8866)*
Otter Creek Industries L L C.....G....... 509 954-3998
Loon Lake *(G-5976)*
Ozette Industries LLC.....G....... 360 460-4272
Port Angeles *(G-7734)*
Pacific Northwest Industries.....G....... 206 841-3144
Seatac *(G-9298)*
Pacific Spring Mfg Co.....G....... 360 832-3633
Eatonville *(G-3065)*
Palmer Industries LLC.....G....... 509 989-1069
Moses Lake *(G-6736)*
Park Place Industries.....G....... 360 584-9762
Tumwater *(G-13890)*
Paulty Mfg LLC.....G....... 509 470-1791
Leavenworth *(G-5812)*
Pcs Industries LLC.....G....... 509 406-5852
Naches *(G-7001)*
Peak Industries.....G....... 509 448-5793
Spokane *(G-12434)*
Pei Manufacturing LLC.....D....... 360 210-4165
Camas *(G-2274)*
Pelling Industries Inc.....G....... 206 243-1941
Burien *(G-2120)*
Pentech Industries LLC.....G....... 360 989-7903
La Center *(G-5512)*
Peone Industries.....G....... 509 443-4710
Spokane *(G-12436)*
Peters Industries.....G....... 360 254-9889
Vancouver *(G-14486)*
Phunnybaggscom.....G....... 253 709-9481
Lake Tapps *(G-5685)*
PM Industries.....G....... 253 666-8977
Tacoma *(G-13467)*
Polaris Manufacturing Inc.....G....... 206 230-9235
Mercer Island *(G-6480)*
Porter Etuv Manufacturing Inc.....G....... 360 796-3172
Brinnon *(G-2026)*
Precision Industries LLC.....G....... 253 255-3814
Eatonville *(G-3067)*
Premier Industries.....G....... 253 514-0977
Gig Harbor *(G-4148)*
Prime Biodiesel.....G....... 360 969-3966
Arlington *(G-307)*
Pro ARC Industries Inc.....G....... 916 215-7269
Battle Ground *(G-732)*
Probare Industries LLC.....G....... 206 334-9840
Everett *(G-3586)*
Prudent Products Inc.....G....... 360 445-2556
Oak Harbor *(G-7162)*
R & M Manufacturing LLC.....G....... 253 503-0956
Spanaway *(G-12069)*
R-2 Mfg Inc.....G....... 360 609-1373
Battle Ground *(G-734)*
Rainier Industries.....G....... 206 622-8219
Seattle *(G-10917)*
Ram-Bone Industries LLC.....G....... 360 652-8277
Stanwood *(G-12989)*
Rebell Industries.....G....... 360 495-4846
Elma *(G-3255)*
Red River Industries.....G....... 206 992-2446
Bainbridge Island *(G-663)*
Redd Industries LLC.....G....... 509 572-5752
Kennewick *(G-4715)*
RES Industries LLC.....G....... 360 225-7955
Woodland *(G-15462)*
Retrodyne Industries LLC.....G....... 206 906-9762
Seattle *(G-10954)*
Rmv Industries Inc.....G....... 253 297-2556
Bothell *(G-1895)*
Rock Industries LLC.....G....... 206 399-7853
Bellevue *(G-1106)*
Rt Industries.....G....... 253 219-8246
Puyallup *(G-8241)*
Runaway Bike Industries LLC.....G....... 206 817-1787
Seattle *(G-10995)*
S E Industries LLC.....G....... 503 519-2160
Ridgefield *(G-9109)*
S&S Industries LLC.....G....... 360 500-9942
Puyallup *(G-8243)*
Sabre Blasting Industries LLC.....G....... 360 990-2492
Bremerton *(G-1997)*
Sabre Industries.....G....... 253 246-7132
Kent *(G-5111)*
Saunders Solutions Inc.....G....... 360 678-4788
Coupeville *(G-2817)*
Saw Industries LLC.....G....... 360 306-8988
Bellingham *(G-1524)*
Schachere Industries LLC.....G....... 253 235-5205
Federal Way *(G-3781)*
SE Industries LLC.....G....... 360 256-3775
Vancouver *(G-14576)*
Seven-K Company.....G....... 509 863-3429
Spokane *(G-12499)*
Shadd Global Industries L.....G....... 425 374-3946
Everett *(G-3610)*
Shapecut Industries LLC.....G....... 509 828-3265
Spokane *(G-12501)*
Sigma Dg Corporation.....G....... 360 859-3170
Vancouver *(G-14585)*
Silicon Digital Industries Inc.....G....... 360 332-1349
North Bend *(G-7123)*
Skt Industries.....G....... 206 633-4461
Seattle *(G-11128)*
Sleeping Industries LLC.....G....... 360 201-4305
Edmonds *(G-3157)*
Smj Industries LLC.....G....... 425 442-9785
Bellevue *(G-1140)*
Smuckwell Industries LLC.....G....... 206 412-3598
Seattle *(G-11141)*
Sneva Manufacturing.....G....... 317 496-8935
Spokane *(G-12509)*
Sno River Manufacturing.....G....... 425 338-5200
Mill Creek *(G-6529)*
Solar Space Industries Inc.....G....... 206 332-9966
Seattle *(G-11154)*
Sovereign Manufacturing.....G....... 253 318-7180
Graham *(G-4238)*
Space Age Industries LLC.....G....... 206 992-7731
Seattle *(G-11163)*
Spaz Industries LLC.....G....... 206 890-7079
Mercer Island *(G-6485)*
Spectrum Manufacturing.....G....... 509 982-2257
Odessa *(G-7192)*
Spectyr Industries Corp.....G....... 360 863-7720
Monroe *(G-6623)*
Spinnerrack LLC.....G....... 425 268-1084
Mukilteo *(G-6978)*
Spry Hive Industries.....G....... 425 503-9790
Kirkland *(G-5470)*
Squonk Industries.....G....... 206 250-4355
Seattle *(G-11173)*
Ss Trailer Manufacturing.....G....... 253 750-4724
Bonney Lake *(G-1739)*
Standever Industries Llc.....G....... 206 687-9610
Sultan *(G-13038)*
Sun Liquor Mfg Inc.....G....... 206 419-5857
Seattle *(G-11218)*
Sundance Equestrian Industries.....G....... 425 205-3775
Woodinville *(G-15381)*
Sunlight Cottage Industries.....G....... 360 321-8302
Clinton *(G-2700)*
Sunset Manufacturing Corp.....G....... 425 239-7416
Snohomish *(G-11988)*
Super-Keller Industries LLC.....G....... 360 459-1059
Olympia *(G-7402)*
Superfancy Industries.....G....... 360 556-9762
Olympia *(G-7403)*
Superior Stone Manufacturing.....G....... 425 931-9303
Woodinville *(G-15382)*
Superior Stone Manufacturing.....G....... 425 312-2968
Lynnwood *(G-6206)*
Surly Industries.....G....... 206 349-3289
Seattle *(G-11226)*
Sweeny Industries.....G....... 253 446-7298
Puyallup *(G-8259)*
Swift Industries.....G....... 360 966-9697
Nooksack *(G-7087)*
Tag Manufacturing Inc.....G....... 206 359-8440
Seattle *(G-11257)*
Taurman Distributing & Mfg.....G....... 360 330-5886
Centralia *(G-2437)*
Techpoint Manufacturing Inc.....G....... 425 387-0305
Marysville *(G-6394)*
Teh Industries LLC.....G....... 425 453-1551
Bellevue *(G-1180)*
Thinking Industries Inc.....G....... 206 201-2106
Bainbridge Island *(G-678)*
Third Ares Industries LLC.....G....... 502 592-2463
Seattle *(G-11292)*
Tims Manufacturing Corp.....G....... 425 392-2616
Kirkland *(G-5483)*
Titan Industries USA LLC.....G....... 206 466-1300
Lake Forest Park *(G-5625)*
Titan Mfg.....G....... 360 863-1808
Monroe *(G-6631)*
TNT Industries LLC.....G....... 509 279-8011
Spokane Valley *(G-12907)*
Tomar Industries.....G....... 509 266-8384
Pasco *(G-7641)*
Top Left Industries.....G....... 360 914-1400
Marysville *(G-6396)*
Traight Industries.....G....... 253 630-1489
Kent *(G-5187)*
Transtech Materials LLC.....G....... 425 402-3665
Bothell *(G-1911)*
Trapp Industries.....G....... 509 895-4282
Selah *(G-11599)*
Tri Coastal Industries.....G....... 425 353-4384
Mukilteo *(G-6984)*

Employee Codes: A=Over 500 employees, B=251-500
C=101-250, D=51-100, E=20-50, F=10-19, G=2-9
2019 Washington
Manufacturers Register
1011

MANUFACTURING INDUSTRIES, NEC

PRODUCT SECTION

Tri-Point Industries Inc .... G 253 514-8890
  Gig Harbor *(G-4169)*
Triarii Industries LLC .... G 360 314-6099
  Vancouver *(G-14646)*
Turn Pro Manufacturing .... G 425 220-8767
  Sedro Woolley *(G-11579)*
Ucoinitcom LLC .... G 253 271-0656
  Puyallup *(G-8265)*
Unisource Manufacturing Inc .... G 253 854-0541
  Kent *(G-5196)*
Upstart Industries LLC .... G 206 265-1521
  Seattle *(G-11387)*
Valley Aero Mfg .... G 206 841-9652
  Renton *(G-8940)*
Vandalez Industries Inc .... G 509 228-9000
  Spokane Valley *(G-12927)*
Velotron Heavy Industries .... G 206 799-5089
  Seattle *(G-11408)*
Vertx Industries LLC .... G 206 619-1479
  Fall City *(G-3709)*
Walflor Industries .... G 425 766-4161
  Bellingham *(G-1587)*
Washougal Manufacturing Co .... G 360 261-2199
  Washougal *(G-14999)*
Wc Manufacturing LLC .... G 425 890-9709
  Auburn *(G-595)*
We Industries LLC .... G 206 853-4505
  Seattle *(G-11446)*
Weeks Waterjet & Mfg .... G 206 261-1954
  Auburn *(G-596)*
West Coast Fire & Rescue Inc .... G 253 826-9852
  Lake Tapps *(G-5687)*
Westech Industries LLC .... G 509 751-0401
  Clarkston *(G-2655)*
Whalen Furniture Manufacturing .... G 425 427-0115
  Issaquah *(G-4489)*
Wheel Haus Mfg Inc .... G 360 719-1030
  Vancouver *(G-14687)*
Whitmus Enterprises Inc .... G 509 398-0144
  Ephrata *(G-3347)*
Woods Bee Co .... G 360 623-3359
  Centralia *(G-2445)*
XYZ Manufacturing .... G 206 402-1936
  Federal Way *(G-3804)*
Zorn Manufacturing Co .... G 360 456-4747
  Lacey *(G-5603)*

MAPS

Green Trails Inc .... G 206 546-6277
  Shoreline *(G-11775)*

MARBLE, BUILDING: Cut & Shaped

Bailey and Bailey Inc .... F 253 649-0568
  Gig Harbor *(G-4075)*
Designers Marble Inc .... G 425 487-9887
  Woodinville *(G-15223)*
Pacific Stone & Tile LLC .... F 360 352-3960
  Olympia *(G-7365)*
Rock Bizarre .... G 360 275-9742
  Belfair *(G-773)*
Shine Marble Co Inc .... F 425 444-5832
  Kenmore *(G-4605)*

MARBLE: Crushed & Broken

Manufacturers Mineral Company .... F 425 228-2120
  Renton *(G-8847)*

MARINAS

Richard Knannlein .... G 360 426-9757
  Shelton *(G-11726)*

MARINE CARGO HANDLING SVCS: Loading & Unloading

Tesoro Refining & Mktg Co LLC .... G 360 293-9119
  Anacortes *(G-177)*

MARINE CARGO HANDLING SVCS: Waterfront Terminal Operations

Foss Maritime Company Llc .... D 206 281-3800
  Seattle *(G-10015)*

MARINE ENGINE REPAIR SVCS

Bills Marine Service .... G 509 826-5564
  OMAK *(G-7435)*
Chinook Marine Repair Inc .... G 360 777-8361
  Chinook *(G-2615)*
North Hbr Diesl Yacht Svc Inc .... E 360 293-5551
  Anacortes *(G-153)*
Performance Marine Inc .... F 425 258-9292
  Everett *(G-3571)*
Pierres Dock Inc .... G 425 488-8600
  Kenmore *(G-4598)*
Propulsion Controls Engrg .... F 425 257-9065
  Everett *(G-3588)*
Systems Engineering Inc .... G 206 633-4972
  Kirkland *(G-5473)*

MARINE HARDWARE

Battery X-Change & Repair Inc .... G 206 682-2981
  Tukwila *(G-13695)*
Complete Controls .... G 360 904-7525
  Vancouver *(G-14142)*
Datrex Inc .... G 206 762-9070
  Seattle *(G-9797)*
Engineered Products Entps .... F 253 826-6185
  Edgewood *(G-3076)*
Harbor Island Supply Corp .... F 206 762-1900
  Seattle *(G-10141)*
Marine Hardware Inc .... E 425 883-0651
  Redmond *(G-8549)*
National Products Inc .... C 206 763-8361
  Seattle *(G-10589)*
New Found Metals Incorporated .... G 360 385-3315
  Port Townsend *(G-7899)*
Oceanwest Rvm LLC .... G 503 569-6969
  Lynden *(G-6041)*
Sea Cure Technology Inc .... G 360 676-1824
  Acme *(G-44)*
Sea-Dog Corporation .... D 425 259-0194
  Everett *(G-3607)*
Sealth Aero Marine Co .... E 425 481-0727
  Mill Creek *(G-6525)*
Sje Inc .... G 360 734-1910
  Bellingham *(G-1540)*
Smith-Berger Marine Inc .... E 206 764-4650
  Seattle *(G-11139)*

MARINE PROPELLER REPAIR SVCS

Sound Propeller Services Inc .... E 206 788-4202
  Seattle *(G-11159)*

MARINE RELATED EQPT

Fessco Fleet and Marine Inc .... E 509 534-5880
  Spokane *(G-12255)*
Kinematics Marine Eqp Inc .... G 360 659-5415
  Marysville *(G-6348)*
Man Diesel North America Inc .... G 253 479-6800
  Kent *(G-5002)*
Markey Machinery Co Inc .... G 206 622-4697
  Seattle *(G-10489)*
Markey Machinery Co Inc .... F 206 763-0383
  Seattle *(G-10490)*
Naust Marine Usa Inc .... F 206 484-5710
  Seattle *(G-10595)*
RMC Incorporated .... E 206 243-4831
  Seattle *(G-10969)*
Willapa Marine Products Inc .... G 360 942-2151
  Raymond *(G-8362)*

MARINE SPLY DEALERS

B & J Fiberglass LLC .... G 360 398-9342
  Bellingham *(G-1256)*
Harbor Island Supply Corp .... F 206 762-1900
  Seattle *(G-10141)*
Speedway Marine Inc .... G 360 658-1288
  Marysville *(G-6390)*

MARINE SPLYS WHOLESALERS

Datrex Inc .... G 206 762-9070
  Seattle *(G-9797)*
Harbor Island Supply Corp .... F 206 762-1900
  Seattle *(G-10141)*
Sea Cure Technology Inc .... G 360 676-1824
  Acme *(G-44)*
Sea-Dog Corporation .... D 425 259-0194
  Everett *(G-3607)*
Washington Chain & Supply Inc .... E 206 623-8500
  Seattle *(G-11438)*

MARKETS: Meat & fish

Quinault Pride Seafoods .... E 360 276-4431
  Taholah *(G-13609)*

MARKING DEVICES

Ace Stamp & Engraving .... G 253 582-3322
  Lakewood *(G-5695)*
Budget Printing Center .... G 509 736-7511
  Kennewick *(G-4636)*
Grays Harbor Stamp Works .... G 360 533-3830
  Aberdeen *(G-14)*
Great Impressions Rbr Stamps .... F 360 807-8462
  Centralia *(G-2404)*
Martronics Corporation .... E 360 985-2999
  Salkum *(G-9180)*
Northwest Business Stamp Inc .... G 509 483-0308
  Spokane *(G-12412)*
Peterson Manufacturing Co .... F 360 425-4170
  Longview *(G-5943)*
Sabine F Price .... G 206 780-9211
  Bainbridge Island *(G-669)*
Stampadoodle Inc .... G 360 647-9663
  Bellingham *(G-1555)*
Tacoma Rubber Stamp Co .... F 206 728-8888
  Seattle *(G-11255)*
Tacoma Rubber Stamp Co .... E 253 383-5433
  Tacoma *(G-13548)*

MARKING DEVICES: Canceling Stamps, Hand, Rubber Or Metal

S M Marketing Specialties .... G 206 230-0710
  Renton *(G-8900)*

MARKING DEVICES: Date Stamps, Hand, Rubber Or Metal

Rumpeltes Enterprises Inc .... E 509 624-1391
  Spokane *(G-12485)*

MARKING DEVICES: Embossing Seals & Hand Stamps

Print Plus Inc .... G 509 735-6303
  Kennewick *(G-4708)*
Sno King Stamp .... G 425 771-9373
  Lynnwood *(G-6202)*

MARKING DEVICES: Printing Dies, Marking Mach, Rubber/Plastic

Superior Rubber Die Co Inc .... G 206 763-2440
  Seattle *(G-11224)*

MARKING DEVICES: Screens, Textile Printing

Dimensional Products Inc .... F 206 352-9065
  Seattle *(G-9831)*
Jackyes Enterprises Inc .... G 425 355-5997
  Everett *(G-3521)*
Swivler Inc .... E 360 225-7774
  Woodland *(G-15468)*
Symbol Servers .... G 360 819-5132
  Olympia *(G-7404)*

MASKS: Gas

Koolmask Inc .... F 206 886-5248
  Bellevue *(G-973)*

MASSAGE MACHINES, ELECTRIC: Barber & Beauty Shops

Peryl Professional Touch .... G 253 537-8181
  Tacoma *(G-13465)*

MATERIAL GRINDING & PULVERIZING SVCS NEC

Hn Goods & Services LLc .... G 360 841-8414
  Woodland *(G-15441)*
Northwest Carbide Tool & Svc .... G 253 872-7848
  Kent *(G-5029)*
Northwest Grinding Co LLC .... G 509 727-5774
  Pasco *(G-7605)*
Pacific Grinding .... G 208 412-5945
  Liberty Lake *(G-5850)*

PRODUCT SECTION

MEAT PROCESSING MACHINERY

MATERIALS HANDLING EQPT WHOLESALERS

Arbon Equipment Corporation ....F 253 395-7099
  Kent *(G-4787)*
Globe International Inc ....G 253 383-2584
  Tacoma *(G-13313)*
Pacific Integrated Hdlg Inc ....E 253 535-5888
  Tacoma *(G-13451)*
Washington Crane Hoist Co Inc ....G 360 694-9844
  Vancouver *(G-14678)*

MATS OR MATTING, NEC: Rubber

Howatt Company Inc ....F 425 743-4682
  Mukilteo *(G-6937)*

MATS, MATTING & PADS: Nonwoven

Ezion Global Inc ....G 206 446-9476
  Bellevue *(G-906)*
Mat Salleh Satay LLC ....G 206 547-0597
  Seattle *(G-10500)*
Out Peak Services Inc ....F 360 255-7282
  Blaine *(G-1691)*
Spoonk Space Inc ....G 360 392-8067
  Lynden *(G-6054)*

MATTRESS STORES

Mattress Manufacturing Prize ....G 509 946-1194
  Richland *(G-9025)*
Northwest Bedding Company ....E 509 244-3000
  Spokane *(G-12411)*
Sleep Aire Mattress Company ....E 206 546-4195
  Shoreline *(G-11814)*
Sleep Number Corporation ....G 360 671-1266
  Bellingham *(G-1543)*
Soaring Heart LLC ....F 206 282-1717
  Seattle *(G-11147)*
Soaring Heart Natural Bed Co ....G 206 257-4158
  Seattle *(G-11148)*

MEAT & FISH MARKETS: Fish

World Wide Gourmet Foods Inc ....F 360 668-9404
  Woodinville *(G-15410)*

MEAT & FISH MARKETS: Seafood

Bay City Sausage Co Inc ....G 360 648-2344
  Aberdeen *(G-4)*
Dockside Cannery ....G 360 642-8870
  Ilwaco *(G-4369)*

MEAT & MEAT PRDTS WHOLESALERS

Bavarian Meat Products Inc ....F 206 448-3540
  Seattle *(G-9501)*

MEAT CUTTING & PACKING

Ahtanum Custom Meats ....G 509 966-3642
  Yakima *(G-15503)*
BJ & Bobs Farm Butchering ....G 360 274-4202
  Castle Rock *(G-2338)*
Careks Country Custom Meats ....G 509 276-2237
  Deer Park *(G-2895)*
Cullens Custom Meats ....G 509 837-0079
  Sunnyside *(G-13119)*
Del Fox Custom Meats Inc ....G 360 629-3723
  Stanwood *(G-12965)*
Empire Packing ....D 360 459-3745
  Olympia *(G-7276)*
Erickson Custom Meats ....G 509 962-6099
  Ellensburg *(G-3198)*
Field Roast Grain Meat Co Spc ....C 800 311-9797
  Seattle *(G-9989)*
Hormel Foods Corporation ....G 425 635-0109
  Bellevue *(G-948)*
Longhorn Barbecue Prod Ctr ....E 509 922-0702
  Spokane Valley *(G-12778)*
Mason Meat Packing Co ....G 509 447-3788
  Newport *(G-7060)*
Matts Custom Meats ....G 360 414-1073
  Kelso *(G-4537)*
Meat & Bread US Inc ....G 604 819-1728
  Seattle *(G-10513)*
Oberto ....G 425 251-4563
  Renton *(G-8862)*
Patriotic Packing ....G 360 942-3054
  Raymond *(G-8357)*

Quick Market Inc ....G 509 653-2268
  Naches *(G-7002)*
Rays Custom Cutting ....G 509 684-5544
  Colville *(G-2772)*
Smithco Meats Inc ....E 253 863-5157
  Sumner *(G-13100)*
Stewarts Markets Inc ....E 360 458-2091
  Yelm *(G-15746)*
T L C Custom Meats Inc ....G 509 488-9953
  Othello *(G-7507)*
Tyson Foods Inc ....A 509 547-7545
  Wallula *(G-14912)*
Verns Moses Lake Meats Inc ....F 509 765-5671
  Moses Lake *(G-6756)*
Vincent R Taylor ....G 509 397-3305
  Colfax *(G-2722)*

MEAT MARKETS

Bavarian Meat Products Inc ....F 206 448-3540
  Seattle *(G-9501)*
Careks Country Custom Meats ....G 509 276-2237
  Deer Park *(G-2895)*
Cascioppo Bros Meats Inc ....F 206 784-6121
  Kirkland *(G-5298)*
Cullens Custom Meats ....G 509 837-0079
  Sunnyside *(G-13119)*
Emu Emprium Hlthy Alternatives ....G 360 269-3459
  Chehalis *(G-2492)*
Friday Harbor House of Jerky ....G 360 207-9652
  Friday Harbor *(G-4046)*
Mason Meat Packing Co ....G 509 447-3788
  Newport *(G-7060)*
Mayers Custom Meats Inc ....G 360 574-2828
  Vancouver *(G-14404)*
Owens Meats Inc ....G 509 674-2530
  Cle Elum *(G-2674)*
Stewarts Markets Inc ....E 360 458-2091
  Yelm *(G-15746)*
Sundance Beef Intl Inc ....G 360 224-2333
  Ferndale *(G-3909)*
Verns Moses Lake Meats Inc ....F 509 765-5671
  Moses Lake *(G-6756)*

MEAT PRDTS: Bacon, Slab & Sliced, From Slaughtered Meat

Beck Pack Systems Inc ....E 425 222-9515
  Preston *(G-8024)*

MEAT PRDTS: Boxed Beef, From Slaughtered Meat

Prime West Beef Co Inc ....G 360 306-1831
  Ferndale *(G-3891)*
Sugar Mountain Livestock LLC ....F 206 322-1644
  Seattle *(G-11214)*
Sundance Beef Intl Inc ....G 360 224-2333
  Ferndale *(G-3909)*

MEAT PRDTS: Canned

Sakai Foods America Inc ....G 484 494-4322
  Seattle *(G-11004)*

MEAT PRDTS: Frozen

Innovasian Cuisine Entps Inc ....E 800 324-5140
  Tukwila *(G-13753)*

MEAT PRDTS: Lamb, From Slaughtered Meat

Conagra Fods Clmbia Base Blnds ....D 509 544-2110
  Pasco *(G-7565)*

MEAT PRDTS: Pork, From Slaughtered Meat

Kapowsin Meats Inc ....F 253 847-1777
  Graham *(G-4229)*

MEAT PRDTS: Prepared Beef Prdts From Purchased Beef

BP Marketing ....G 509 475-7125
  Renton *(G-8764)*

MEAT PRDTS: Roast Beef, From Purchased Meat

Field Roast Grain Meat Co Spc ....C 800 311-9797
  Seattle *(G-9989)*

Greenleaf Foods Spc ....E 206 762-5961
  Seattle *(G-10120)*
Greenleaf Foods Spc ....G 206 762-5961
  Seattle *(G-10121)*

MEAT PRDTS: Sausage Casings, Natural

Oversea Casing Company LLC ....E 206 682-6845
  Seattle *(G-10722)*

MEAT PRDTS: Sausages, From Purchased Meat

Bavarian Meat Products Inc ....F 206 448-3540
  Seattle *(G-9501)*
Bay City Sausage Co Inc ....G 360 648-2344
  Aberdeen *(G-4)*
ISC Inc ....E 253 395-5465
  Kent *(G-4961)*
January Company ....E 253 872-9919
  Kent *(G-4964)*
Northwest Sausage & Deli ....F 360 736-7760
  Centralia *(G-2421)*
Oberto Snacks Inc ....C 253 437-6100
  Kent *(G-5041)*
Ulis Famous Sausage LLC ....G 206 839-1000
  Seattle *(G-11362)*
Voise Susage By Schumacher Inc ......G 509 982-2956
  Odessa *(G-7193)*

MEAT PRDTS: Sausages, From Slaughtered Meat

Adalbert & Nagy Sausage Co LLC ....G 206 356-3305
  Issaquah *(G-4378)*
Jahrs European Sausage & Cstm ....G 509 697-8904
  Selah *(G-11591)*

MEAT PRDTS: Smoked

Black Diamond Smoked Meats ....G 541 228-2758
  Black Diamond *(G-1645)*
Longhorn Barbecue Prod Ctr ....E 509 922-0702
  Spokane Valley *(G-12778)*

MEAT PRDTS: Snack Sticks, Incl Jerky, From Purchased Meat

Friday Harbor House of Jerky ....G 360 207-9652
  Friday Harbor *(G-4046)*
Tillamook Country Smoker LLC ....G 360 456-2640
  Olympia *(G-7407)*

MEAT PROCESSED FROM PURCHASED CARCASSES

Bels International Corporation ....F 206 722-3365
  Seattle *(G-9510)*
Cascioppo Bros Meats Inc ....F 206 784-6121
  Kirkland *(G-5298)*
Crimson Cove LLC ....G 360 598-2683
  Poulsbo *(G-7956)*
Eldons Sausage Inc ....G 509 309-3140
  Spokane Valley *(G-12690)*
Hillshire Brands Company ....D 253 437-3700
  Kent *(G-4942)*
Hillshire Brands Company ....F 253 395-3444
  Kent *(G-4943)*
Kings Command Foods LLC ....C 425 251-6788
  Kent *(G-4977)*
Longhorn Barbecue Inc ....C 509 922-0702
  Spokane Valley *(G-12777)*
Mayers Custom Meats Inc ....G 360 574-2828
  Vancouver *(G-14404)*
Smithco Meats Inc ....E 253 863-5157
  Sumner *(G-13100)*
Smoke Plus Cigar ....G 425 673-1390
  Lynnwood *(G-6200)*
Tyson Foods Inc ....A 509 547-7545
  Wallula *(G-14912)*
Ulis Famous Sausage Inc ....G 206 839-1000
  Seattle *(G-11361)*
Verone Sausage Company ....G 253 759-7532
  Tacoma *(G-13575)*

MEAT PROCESSING MACHINERY

Ameristar Meats Inc ....C 509 535-2049
  Spokane Valley *(G-12616)*

MEATS, PACKAGED FROZEN: Wholesalers

Smithco Meats Inc .... E 253 863-5157
Sumner *(G-13100)*

MECHANICAL INSTRUMENT REPAIR SVCS

Morley Machine Tool Algnmt Inc .... E 253 926-1515
Milton *(G-6536)*

MEDIA: Magnetic & Optical Recording

Intermedianet Inc .... F 425 451-3393
Bellevue *(G-960)*
Master Peace Productions .... G 360 600-2736
Vancouver *(G-14398)*
Realtime Inc .... G 206 523-8050
Seattle *(G-10931)*

MEDICAL & HOSPITAL EQPT WHOLESALERS

Alliance Mfg Group LLC .... G 253 922-3090
Tacoma *(G-13165)*
Amfit Inc .... E 360 573-9100
Vancouver *(G-14032)*
Bodypoint Inc .... E 206 405-4555
Seattle *(G-9560)*
Fukuda Denshi Usa Inc .... E 425 881-7737
Redmond *(G-8467)*
G Dundas Co Inc .... G 253 631-8008
Black Diamond *(G-1648)*
Ginacor Inc .... F 206 860-1595
Seattle *(G-10072)*
Gsl Solutions Inc .... G 360 896-5354
Vancouver *(G-14275)*
Impulse Medical Tech Inc .... F 360 829-0400
Buckley *(G-2059)*
Medtronic Usa Inc .... E 425 803-0708
Bellevue *(G-1001)*
Solcon Inc .... E 425 222-5963
Issaquah *(G-4480)*
Stl International Incorporated .... E 253 840-5252
Buckley *(G-2076)*
Traction Capital Partners Inc .... G 253 922-3090
Tacoma *(G-13561)*

MEDICAL & SURGICAL SPLYS: Applicators, Cotton Tipped

Buffalo Industries Inc .... G 206 682-9900
Seattle *(G-9595)*

MEDICAL & SURGICAL SPLYS: Autoclaves

Wright Surgical Arts LLC .... G 509 792-1404
Pasco *(G-7656)*

MEDICAL & SURGICAL SPLYS: Braces, Orthopedic

Valley Orthopedics Inc .... G 509 922-5040
Liberty Lake *(G-5866)*

MEDICAL & SURGICAL SPLYS: Clothing, Fire Resistant & Protect

Davidson Prosthetics LLC .... G 253 770-6578
Puyallup *(G-8140)*
Lancs Industries Inc .... E 425 823-6634
Kirkland *(G-5380)*
Safety Reflection .... G 360 599-1874
Maple Falls *(G-6250)*
Survival Inc .... E 206 726-9363
Seattle *(G-11229)*

MEDICAL & SURGICAL SPLYS: Drapes, Surgical, Cotton

or Specific Inc .... G 800 937-7949
Vancouver *(G-14453)*

MEDICAL & SURGICAL SPLYS: Foot Appliances, Orthopedic

Cox Orthotics Inc .... G 425 493-8015
Mukilteo *(G-6906)*
Northwest Podiatric Laboratory .... D 360 332-8411
Blaine *(G-1689)*
Pacific Orthotic LLC .... G 425 486-4292
Woodinville *(G-15330)*

Stuart Orthotics LLC .... G 360 577-3505
Longview *(G-5957)*

MEDICAL & SURGICAL SPLYS: Hydrotherapy

Meridian Valley Laboratories .... G 206 209-4200
Tukwila *(G-13771)*

MEDICAL & SURGICAL SPLYS: Limbs, Artificial

Cascade Dafo Inc .... B 360 543-9306
Ferndale *(G-3825)*
Center For Prosthetic .... F 206 328-4276
Seattle *(G-9652)*
Columbia Basin Prosthetic .... G 509 737-8322
Kennewick *(G-4646)*
Cornerstone Prsthtics Orthtics .... F 425 339-2559
Everett *(G-3427)*
Cornerstone Prsthtics Orthtics .... G 360 734-0298
Bellingham *(G-1306)*
Dolans Dog Doodads LLC .... G 206 257-4518
Seattle *(G-9844)*
Fabtech Systems LLC .... G 425 349-9557
Everett *(G-3468)*
Hanger Prsthetcs & Ortho Inc .... G 253 372-7478
Gig Harbor *(G-4110)*
Hanger Prsthetcs & Ortho Inc .... G 509 624-3314
Spokane *(G-12288)*
Independent Tech Service LLC .... G 253 891-1976
Puyallup *(G-8167)*
Jeffrey A Johnson .... G 509 525-8322
Walla Walla *(G-14828)*
Maughan Prosthetic Orthotic S .... G 360 338-0284
Olympia *(G-7332)*
Maughan Prsthetic Orthotic Inc .... G 360 447-0770
Silverdale *(G-11849)*
Out On A Limb .... G 360 607-3429
Stevenson *(G-13017)*
Out On A Limb Enterprises .... G 360 457-8479
Port Angeles *(G-7733)*
Out On A Limb Tree Co .... G 206 938-3779
Lake Forest Park *(G-5623)*
Preferred Orthotic & Prosthetc .... G 253 572-1282
Tacoma *(G-13476)*
Prosthtic Specialists Wash LLC .... G 425 576-5050
Kirkland *(G-5445)*
Yakima Orthtics Prosthetics PC .... G 509 943-8561
Richland *(G-9056)*

MEDICAL & SURGICAL SPLYS: Models, Anatomical

Andersen Models International .... G 253 952-2135
Milton *(G-6532)*

MEDICAL & SURGICAL SPLYS: Orthopedic Appliances

A1a Inc .... G 509 455-5000
Spokane *(G-12092)*
Cresap Orthotics & Prosthetics .... G 509 764-8500
Moses Lake *(G-6700)*
Flood & Associates Inc .... G 253 531-7305
Tacoma *(G-13299)*
Hanger Prsthetcs & Ortho Inc .... F 360 423-6049
Longview *(G-5915)*
Hanger Prsthetcs & Ortho Inc .... G 509 946-2520
Richland *(G-9004)*
Integrity Orthotic Laboratory .... E 360 435-0703
Arlington *(G-256)*
Pacific Orthotic LLC .... G 425 417-3742
Issaquah *(G-4457)*
Pedologic Orthotics .... G 360 318-3452
Arlington *(G-299)*
Reheal LLC .... G 206 440-5948
Seattle *(G-10944)*

MEDICAL & SURGICAL SPLYS: Personal Safety Eqpt

Control Dynamics Inc .... E 800 738-5004
Everett *(G-3425)*
Future Machine & Mfg Inc .... F 509 891-5600
Spokane Valley *(G-12711)*
I1 Sensortech Inc .... F 425 372-7811
Kirkland *(G-5365)*
Western Wash Safety Conslt .... G 253 815-7920
Federal Way *(G-3802)*

MEDICAL & SURGICAL SPLYS: Prosthetic Appliances

Cascade Prsthtics Orthtics Inc .... F 360 384-1858
Ferndale *(G-3828)*
Cascade Prsthtics Orthtics Inc .... G 360 428-4003
Mount Vernon *(G-6783)*
Center For Prosthetic .... G 425 454-4276
Bellevue *(G-845)*
Custom Ocular Prosthetics .... G 206 522-4222
Seattle *(G-9770)*
Douglass Certified Prosthetics .... G 206 363-7790
Seattle *(G-9850)*
Evergreen Prosthetcs & Orthotc .... F 360 213-2088
Vancouver *(G-14210)*
Hanger Orthopedic Group Inc .... F 253 383-4447
Tacoma *(G-13330)*
Hattingh Holdings Inc .... E 206 323-4040
Seattle *(G-10148)*
Island Prosthetics & Orthotics .... G 360 331-7070
Clinton *(G-2691)*
Missoula Orthotics & Prosthet .... G 406 549-0921
Spokane *(G-12396)*
RCM Enterprise LLC .... G 888 977-6693
Olympia *(G-7380)*
Southshore Prsthtics Orthotics .... G 206 440-1811
Kenmore *(G-4607)*
Trulife Inc .... C 360 697-5656
Poulsbo *(G-8012)*

MEDICAL & SURGICAL SPLYS: Stretchers

Dollar Stretcher .... G 509 895-7744
Yakima *(G-15556)*
Lifeport LLC .... D 360 225-1212
Woodland *(G-15447)*

MEDICAL & SURGICAL SPLYS: Supports, Abdominal, Ankle, Etc

Fox Bay Industries Inc .... G 253 941-9155
Auburn *(G-443)*

MEDICAL & SURGICAL SPLYS: Technical Aids, Handicapped

Jan A Thompson Lcpo .... G 509 241-3820
Spokane *(G-12328)*

MEDICAL & SURGICAL SPLYS: Traction Apparatus

Sure Trax LLC .... G 360 430-8343
Longview *(G-5958)*

MEDICAL & SURGICAL SPLYS: Welders' Hoods

All Metal Arts Seattle .... G 206 200-9496
Seattle *(G-9380)*
Kurt A Flechel .... G 509 953-8358
Spokane *(G-12356)*
Perkins Performance .... G 253 389-9669
Puyallup *(G-8222)*

MEDICAL CENTERS

Derma Medical Spa .... G 360 350-5321
Olympia *(G-7268)*

MEDICAL EQPT: CAT Scanner Or Computerized Axial Tomography

Myovision .... G 800 969-6961
Seattle *(G-10582)*

MEDICAL EQPT: Defibrillators

Physio-Control Intl Inc .... A 425 867-4000
Redmond *(G-8621)*

MEDICAL EQPT: Diagnostic

CM Innovations Inc .... G 425 641-0460
Issaquah *(G-4395)*
D E Hokanson Inc .... F 425 882-1689
Bellevue *(G-872)*
Isoray Inc .... E 509 375-1202
Richland *(G-9013)*
Isoray Medical Inc .... E 509 375-1202
Richland *(G-9014)*

PRODUCT SECTION

Jointmetrix Medical LLC .... G 425 246-7799
  Seattle *(G-10304)*
Kent Laboratories Inc .... F 360 398-8641
  Bellingham *(G-1392)*
Pet/X LLC .... G 206 715-5743
  Seattle *(G-10791)*
Shockwave Medical Inc .... G 425 736-3946
  Newcastle *(G-7040)*
Siemens Med Solutions USA Inc .... C 425 392-9180
  Issaquah *(G-4475)*
Sonodiagnostics .... G 206 938-7922
  Seattle *(G-11156)*
Spacelabs Healthcare Wash 425 396-3300
  Snoqualmie *(G-12029)*
Tasso Inc .... G 608 556-7606
  Seattle *(G-11271)*

MEDICAL EQPT: Electromedical Apparatus

ATL International LLC 425 487-7000
  Bothell *(G-1825)*
Biodynamics Corporation .... G 206 526-0205
  Shoreline *(G-11762)*
Ftv Business Services LLC .... F 425 347-6100
  Everett *(G-3486)*
Philips Ultrasound Inc .... C 800 982-2011
  Bothell *(G-1887)*
Ventec Life Systems Inc .... E 425 686-1728
  Bothell *(G-1913)*
Verathon Inc .... C 425 867-1348
  Bothell *(G-1805)*

MEDICAL EQPT: Electrotherapeutic Apparatus

Emulate Therapeutics Inc .... G 206 708-2288
  Seattle *(G-9918)*
Impulse Medical Tech Inc .... F 360 829-0400
  Buckley *(G-2059)*

MEDICAL EQPT: Heart-Lung Machines, Exc Iron Lungs

Courageous Heart Healing LLC .... G 541 517-6222
  Seattle *(G-9749)*

MEDICAL EQPT: Laser Systems

Columbia Laser Centers Inc .... G 509 529-7711
  College Place *(G-2723)*
Derma Medical Spa .... G 360 350-5321
  Olympia *(G-7268)*
Flourish Skin & Laser LLC .... F 360 636-1411
  Longview *(G-5911)*
Lockheed Martin Aculight Corp .... D 425 482-1100
  Bothell *(G-1875)*

MEDICAL EQPT: PET Or Position Emission Tomography Scanners

Pet/CT Imaging At Swdish Cncer .... F 206 215-6433
  Seattle *(G-10790)*

MEDICAL EQPT: Patient Monitoring

J & J Engineering Inc .... F 360 779-3853
  Poulsbo *(G-7967)*
Spacelabs Healthcare Wash .... C 425 396-3300
  Snoqualmie *(G-12029)*

MEDICAL EQPT: Ultrasonic, Exc Cleaning

Carrot Medical LLC .... F 425 318-8089
  Bothell *(G-1836)*
Cerevast Medical Inc .... G 425 748-7529
  Bothell *(G-1754)*
Fujifilm Sonosite Inc .... B 425 951-1200
  Bothell *(G-1858)*
Fujifilm Sonosite Inc .... C 425 951-1200
  Bothell *(G-1859)*
Spacelabs Healthcare Inc .... A 425 396-3300
  Snoqualmie *(G-12027)*

MEDICAL EQPT: X-Ray Apparatus & Tubes, Radiographic

P S Northwest Radiography .... G 253 627-3988
  Tacoma *(G-13447)*

MEDICAL SVCS ORGANIZATION

Med-Core Services Inc .... G 360 455-5425
  Olympia *(G-7337)*

MEDICAL, DENTAL & HOSP EQPT, WHOLESALE: X-ray Film & Splys

CMX Corporation .... E 425 656-1269
  Tukwila *(G-13713)*

MEDICAL, DENTAL & HOSPITAL EQPT, WHOL: Hosptl Eqpt/Furniture

Capital Instruments Ltd .... G 425 271-3756
  Bellevue *(G-838)*
United States Dosimetry Tech .... G 509 946-8738
  Richland *(G-9049)*

MEDICAL, DENTAL & HOSPITAL EQPT, WHOLESALE: Med Eqpt & Splys

A Well Balanced Home LLC .... G 206 280-5532
  Seattle *(G-9327)*
Halls Drug Center Inc .... E 360 736-5000
  Centralia *(G-2405)*
Medical Equipment Dev Co LLC .... G 206 364-3894
  Shoreline *(G-11788)*
Therapeutic Dimension Inc 509 323-9275
  Spokane *(G-12555)*

MEMBERSHIP ORGANIZATIONS, CIVIC, SOCIAL/FRAT: Youth Orgs

Dot4kids .... G 503 884-8838
  Olympia *(G-7273)*

MEMBERSHIP ORGANIZATIONS, NEC: Charitable

Aav Group .... F 972 834-2750
  Bellevue *(G-779)*
Association For The Developm .... G 509 838-3575
  Spokane *(G-12123)*
Dot4kids .... G 503 884-8838
  Olympia *(G-7273)*
Million Tree Prj For Somalia .... G 206 731-9164
  Renton *(G-8855)*
Partners In Emrgncy Prpredness .... G 509 335-3530
  Tacoma *(G-13459)*

MEMBERSHIP ORGANIZATIONS, NEC: Personal Interest

Bowet & Poet Inc .... G 360 385-9005
  Port Townsend *(G-7870)*

MEMBERSHIP ORGANIZATIONS, PROF: Education/Teacher Assoc

Virtual Education Software Inc .... F 509 891-7219
  Spokane Valley *(G-12931)*

MEMBERSHIP ORGANIZATIONS, REL: Churches, Temples & Shrines

Corporation of The President .... G 509 656-2344
  Cle Elum *(G-2663)*
Flourish Church Rainier Valley .... G 206 769-7950
  Seattle *(G-10006)*
Good News Church 509 544-0938
  Pasco *(G-7587)*
Hearts In Motion Ministries .... G 360 798-0275
  Ridgefield *(G-9088)*

MEMBERSHIP ORGANIZATIONS, REL: Covenant & Evangelical Church

Black Lk Bb Camp Cnference Ctr .... F 360 539-5337
  Olympia *(G-7236)*

MEMBERSHIP ORGANIZATIONS, RELIGIOUS: Assembly Of God Church

Grove Church .... G 360 386-5760
  Marysville *(G-6342)*

MEMBERSHIP ORGANIZATIONS, RELIGIOUS: Lutheran Church

Bethel Lutheran Church .... G 360 892-4231
  Brush Prairie *(G-2030)*

MEMBERSHIP ORGANIZATIONS, RELIGIOUS: Nonchurch

Tubs To Go Inc .... G 425 348-7888
  Lynnwood *(G-6213)*

MEMBERSHIP ORGS, CIVIC, SOCIAL & FRATERNAL: Civic Assoc

Copper Creek Fabrications LLC .... G 360 582-9676
  Sequim *(G-11620)*

MEMBERSHIP ORGS, RELIGIOUS: Non-Denominational Church

Zions River .... G 253 473-1838
  Tacoma *(G-13607)*

MEMBERSHIP SPORTS & RECREATION CLUBS

Recreational Equipment Inc .... B 206 223-1944
  Seattle *(G-10933)*

MEMORIALS, MONUMENTS & MARKERS

Koppenberg Enterprises Inc .... F 360 793-1600
  Monroe *(G-6589)*
M&E Memorial Markers Inc .... G 509 662-6469
  Wenatchee *(G-15048)*
Sandcastle Sandblasting .... G 360 354-5087
  Lynden *(G-6052)*

MEN'S & BOYS' CLOTHING STORES

CC Filson Co .... C 206 624-4437
  Seattle *(G-9649)*
Filson Manufacturing Inc .... G 206 242-9579
  Seattle *(G-9993)*
Shirtz To Go Inc .... G 206 242-4055
  Federal Way *(G-3783)*

MEN'S & BOYS' CLOTHING WHOLESALERS, NEC

Certified Branching Habit .... G 206 286-9685
  Seattle *(G-9659)*
Contract Sew & Repair Inc .... F 253 395-7910
  Kent *(G-4865)*
Etc Tacoma .... G 253 223-5459
  Tacoma *(G-13282)*
Hope Moffat .... G 401 527-4234
  Bainbridge Island *(G-640)*

MEN'S & BOYS' HATS STORES

Hatterdashery 206 322-6149
  Seattle *(G-10147)*

MEN'S & BOYS' SPORTSWEAR CLOTHING STORES

Northwest Designs Ink Inc .... F 425 454-0707
  Bellevue *(G-1035)*
Swivler Inc .... E 360 225-7774
  Woodland *(G-15468)*

MEN'S & BOYS' SPORTSWEAR WHOLESALERS

Bensussen Deutsch & Assoc LLC .... B 425 492-6111
  Woodinville *(G-15188)*
Northwest Designs Ink Inc .... F 425 454-0707
  Bellevue *(G-1035)*
Seattle Pacific Industries .... D 253 872-8822
  Kent *(G-5123)*
Shah Safari Inc .... E 206 282-6122
  Seattle *(G-11095)*

MEN'S & BOYS' WORK CLOTHING WHOLESALERS

R B Sales .... G 206 870-0741
  Des Moines *(G-2944)*

Employee Codes: A=Over 500 employees, B=251-500
C=101-250, D=51-100, E=20-50, F=10-19, G=2-9

MENTAL HEALTH CLINIC, OUTPATIENT
Bridgeways..................................D....... 425 513-2989
  Everett *(G-3401)*

MENTAL HEALTH PRACTITIONERS' OFFICES
Herald Cheraine PHD.....................G....... 253 564-1193
  Tacoma *(G-13335)*

MERCHANDISING MACHINE OPERATORS: Vending
Cardlock Vending Inc......................G....... 888 487-5040
  Bothell *(G-1835)*
Noel Corporation..............................C....... 509 248-4545
  Yakima *(G-15630)*

METAL CUTTING SVCS
Farwest Operating LLC....................D....... 509 453-1663
  Moxee *(G-6878)*
Five Star Industries LLC..................G....... 206 706-2754
  Seattle *(G-10001)*
H2o Jet Inc...E....... 360 866-7161
  Tumwater *(G-13874)*
Precision Steel Rule Die Co.............G....... 206 397-3982
  Seattle *(G-10853)*
White River Fabrication LLC...........G....... 253 261-8718
  Enumclaw *(G-3328)*

METAL DETECTORS
Prospectors Plus LLC.......................G....... 425 750-9290
  Sultan *(G-13033)*
Prototek Corp...................................F....... 360 779-1310
  Poulsbo *(G-7993)*

METAL FABRICATORS: Architechtural
A & B Fabricators Inc......................G....... 253 887-0442
  Auburn *(G-355)*
A One Ornamental Iron Works.......G....... 206 622-4033
  Seatac *(G-9271)*
Acufab Inc..G....... 509 525-3833
  Walla Walla *(G-14759)*
AGS Stainless Inc............................F....... 206 842-9492
  Bainbridge Island *(G-607)*
All Metal Fab Inc.............................F....... 253 737-5154
  Auburn *(G-370)*
Allied Steel Fabricators Inc.............E....... 425 861-9558
  Redmond *(G-8380)*
American Metal Specialties.............G....... 253 272-9344
  University Place *(G-13959)*
American Railworks.........................G....... 425 582-8990
  Lynnwood *(G-6075)*
Argent Fabrication LLC...................F....... 206 438-0068
  Seattle *(G-9427)*
Artistic Iron Furniture Mfrs.............F....... 360 398-9351
  Lynden *(G-6002)*
Benjamin D Schreiner.....................G....... 206 417-4663
  Lake Forest Park *(G-5606)*
Blazen Metal Works........................G....... 360 897-2053
  Orting *(G-7474)*
Brassfinders Inc...............................G....... 509 747-7412
  Spokane *(G-12160)*
Buyken Metal Products Inc............E....... 253 852-0634
  Kent *(G-4827)*
Callison Architecture LLC...............G....... 206 623-4646
  Seattle *(G-9607)*
Click It Picket LLC...........................G....... 253 750-0182
  Auburn *(G-408)*
Decorative Metal Services Inc........G....... 360 695-7052
  Vancouver *(G-14172)*
Earthen Alchemy..............................G....... 360 926-8467
  Stanwood *(G-12968)*
Ecolite Manufacturing Co...............D....... 509 922-8888
  Spokane Valley *(G-12687)*
Ecolite Manufacturing Co...............D....... 509 922-8888
  Spokane Valley *(G-12688)*
Evergreen Fabrication Inc...............G....... 509 534-9096
  Spokane Valley *(G-12694)*
Fast Flashings LLC..........................G....... 425 827-8367
  Seattle *(G-9974)*
Fast Flashings LLC..........................G....... 206 364-3612
  Seattle *(G-9975)*
Gerald McCallum.............................G....... 509 467-8456
  Spokane *(G-12273)*
Holland Ornamental Iron Inc..........G....... 253 564-5671
  University Place *(G-13971)*
Honolds Ornamental Ironwork........G....... 206 779-0668
  Langley *(G-5781)*
Intermountain Fabricators Inc.........F....... 509 534-1676
  Spokane Valley *(G-12746)*
Ironhouse Ornamental......................G....... 509 993-7601
  Spokane *(G-12326)*
J and S Ironworks LLC....................G....... 509 276-5887
  Nine Mile Falls *(G-7077)*
Leader Manufacturing Inc...............E....... 360 895-1184
  Port Orchard *(G-7825)*
Lous Welding & Fabricating...........F....... 425 483-0300
  Woodinville *(G-15295)*
McKinstry Co LLC............................B....... 206 762-3311
  Seattle *(G-10509)*
Michael Enterprises Co...................G....... 253 630-4259
  Covington *(G-2833)*
Modern Metals LLC........................E....... 425 405-6994
  Everett *(G-3549)*
Ornamental Iron Works Inc............G....... 509 662-8294
  Wenatchee *(G-15054)*
Perfect Reflections Auto Body........G....... 360 426-0805
  Shelton *(G-11721)*
Pfc Inc..G....... 360 398-8889
  Bellingham *(G-1497)*
Proweld Fabrication LLC.................G....... 425 835-6477
  Moses Lake *(G-6739)*
Railmakers Northwest......................F....... 425 259-9236
  Everett *(G-3594)*
Reliance Manufacturing Corp.........E....... 425 481-3030
  Woodinville *(G-15348)*
Rj Jarvis Enterprises Inc.................G....... 509 482-0254
  Spokane *(G-12477)*
S & S Welding Inc...........................E....... 206 793-9943
  Kent *(G-5110)*
Safeworks LLC.................................D....... 206 575-6445
  Tukwila *(G-13809)*
Snake River Fence..........................G....... 509 758-7081
  Anatone *(G-185)*
Swiss Ornamental Iron....................G....... 253 759-6796
  Tacoma *(G-13535)*
TAC Fab LLC....................................G....... 206 755-0519
  Woodinville *(G-15385)*
US Starcraft Corporation.................G....... 206 762-0607
  Seattle *(G-11394)*
West Coast Custom Metal Design..G....... 360 738-2884
  Bellingham *(G-1592)*

METAL FABRICATORS: Plate
Acufab Inc..G....... 509 525-3833
  Walla Walla *(G-14759)*
Alaskan Copper Companies Inc.....B....... 206 623-5800
  Kent *(G-4768)*
Alaskan Copper Companies Inc.....G....... 206 623-5800
  Seattle *(G-9367)*
Alaskan Copper Companies Inc.....E....... 206 623-5800
  Kent *(G-4769)*
Alco Investment Company..............C....... 206 623-5800
  Kent *(G-4770)*
Calhoun Tanks and Services..........G....... 253 517-7356
  Milton *(G-6533)*
Calhoun Tnks & Servces Inc..........G....... 206 870-0802
  Tacoma *(G-13217)*
CBI Services LLC.............................E....... 425 258-2350
  Everett *(G-3411)*
CH Murphy/Clark-Ullman Inc........G....... 253 475-6566
  Tacoma *(G-13232)*
Consolidated Metco Inc..................D....... 360 828-2599
  Vancouver *(G-14147)*
Contech Engnered Solutions LLC...F....... 509 244-3694
  Airway Heights *(G-50)*
Contech Engnered Solutions LLC...F....... 360 357-9735
  Olympia *(G-7255)*
Edco Inc...E....... 360 424-6600
  Mount Vernon *(G-6792)*
Efco Corp..F....... 253 852-3800
  Kent *(G-4886)*
Erickson Tank & Pump LLC............F....... 509 785-2955
  Quincy *(G-8297)*
Fat Daddys Fabrication LLC...........G....... 253 677-8005
  Roy *(G-9159)*
Gemmells Wldg Fabrication LLC....G....... 509 547-5200
  Pasco *(G-7584)*
Global Incorporated.........................F....... 206 763-4424
  Seattle *(G-10621)*
Greenberry Industrial LLC...............G....... 360 366-3767
  Ferndale *(G-3849)*
Hallmark Refining Corporation........D....... 360 428-5880
  Mount Vernon *(G-6803)*
Industrial Container Svcs LLC........E....... 206 763-2345
  Seattle *(G-10231)*
Jet City Partners LLC......................G....... 206 999-0047
  Auburn *(G-479)*
Macro Plastics Inc...........................E....... 509 452-1200
  Union Gap *(G-13940)*
Omnifab Inc.....................................E....... 253 931-5151
  Auburn *(G-518)*
Piece of Mind LLC..........................G....... 509 868-0850
  Spokane *(G-12441)*
Rainier Welding Incorporated.........E....... 425 868-1300
  Redmond *(G-8644)*
Safran Cabin Inc..............................C....... 360 653-2600
  Marysville *(G-6381)*
Spokane Industries Inc....................C....... 509 924-0440
  Spokane Valley *(G-12885)*
Statcodsi Process Systems.............G....... 253 249-7539
  Algona *(G-77)*
Wellons Group Inc...........................F....... 360 750-3500
  Vancouver *(G-14682)*

METAL FABRICATORS: Sheet
A & B Fabricators Inc......................G....... 253 887-0442
  Auburn *(G-355)*
ABC Sheet Metal Inc.......................G....... 360 574-4884
  Ridgefield *(G-9058)*
Accra-Fab Inc...................................D....... 509 922-3300
  Liberty Lake *(G-5822)*
Accra-Fab Inc...................................G....... 509 922-3300
  Liberty Lake *(G-5823)*
Accurate Sheet Metal Inc................E....... 425 745-6786
  Mukilteo *(G-6889)*
Acufab Inc..G....... 509 525-3833
  Walla Walla *(G-14759)*
Advanced Metal Fabrication............G....... 509 534-0671
  Spokane *(G-12102)*
Apex Industries Inc..........................D....... 509 928-8450
  Spokane Valley *(G-12621)*
Apollo Sheet Metal Inc....................A....... 509 586-1104
  Kennewick *(G-4618)*
Ark Commercial Roofing Inc...........F....... 509 443-9300
  Spokane Valley *(G-12625)*
ASap Metal Fabricators Inc............G....... 509 469-3572
  Yakima *(G-15515)*
ASap Metal Fabricators Inc............G....... 509 453-9143
  Yakima *(G-15516)*
Automated Metal Tech Inc..............F....... 425 895-9733
  Redmond *(G-8390)*
B & J Metal Fab..............................G....... 360 887-8548
  Ridgefield *(G-9063)*
Barrys Steve Pool Service LLC......G....... 360 533-0421
  Aberdeen *(G-3)*
BBH Sheet Metal LLC.....................G....... 425 637-0360
  Bellevue *(G-808)*
Bending Solutions Incorporated......E....... 360 651-2443
  Marysville *(G-6316)*
Brewster Manufacturing Inc............F....... 509 923-2264
  Brewster *(G-2015)*
Brownfield Manufacturing Inc.........E....... 360 568-0572
  Monroe *(G-6559)*
Buyken Metal Products Inc............G....... 253 852-0634
  Kent *(G-4827)*
Canopy World Inc............................G....... 206 824-3877
  Des Moines *(G-2932)*
Capital Heating & Cooling Inc........E....... 360 491-7450
  Lacey *(G-5537)*
Carlson Sheet Metal Works Inc......F....... 509 535-4228
  Spokane *(G-12170)*
Ccw LLC..G....... 206 363-4916
  Shoreline *(G-11764)*
Central Fabricators Inc....................F....... 206 633-4762
  Seattle *(G-9654)*
City Sheet Metal Heating & Air......G....... 253 852-2174
  Auburn *(G-407)*
Cleveland Enterprises Inc...............G....... 360 694-0435
  Vancouver *(G-14123)*
Colored Metal Roofing....................G....... 360 887-4524
  Ridgefield *(G-9073)*
Columbia Stainless Metal-Fab........G....... 509 662-9078
  Wenatchee *(G-15022)*
Competitive Development & Mfg....G....... 360 691-7816
  Granite Falls *(G-4270)*
Copper Creek Fabrications LLC.....G....... 360 582-9676
  Sequim *(G-11620)*
Copper Ridge Fabrication LLC.......G....... 360 582-3898
  Sequim *(G-11621)*
Crystal Distribution Inc...................F....... 253 736-0016
  Fife *(G-3946)*
Custom Bilt Holdings LLC...............E....... 253 872-7330
  Lakewood *(G-5709)*
Custom Sheet Metal Inc.................G....... 360 754-5220
  Olympia *(G-7262)*

PRODUCT SECTION — METAL MINING SVCS

Custom Technology Co Inc ....F 509 965-3333
  Yakima *(G-15546)*
David Gulassa & Co Inc ....E 206 283-1810
  Seattle *(G-9800)*
Decorative Metal Arts ....G 206 782-4009
  Seattle *(G-9812)*
DK Machining LLC ....G 509 991-6110
  Nine Mile Falls *(G-7072)*
Elkay Ssp LLC ....E 509 533-0808
  Spokane *(G-12241)*
Evergreen Fabrication Inc ....G 509 534-9096
  Spokane Valley *(G-12694)*
Exact Aerospace Inc ....E 253 854-1017
  Auburn *(G-436)*
Fabrication Products Inc ....E 503 283-3218
  Vancouver *(G-14219)*
Farwest Operating LLC ....D 509 453-1663
  Moxee *(G-6878)*
First Metals Inc ....G 303 915-2426
  Renton *(G-8800)*
Gaudet Sheetmetal Inc ....G 360 892-5772
  Battle Ground *(G-703)*
Gcm North American Arospc LLC ....D 253 872-7488
  Algona *(G-69)*
Gensco Inc ....C 253 620-8203
  Fife *(G-3954)*
Gibraltar Industries Inc ....C 253 926-1600
  Fife *(G-3955)*
Glenns Welding and Mfg Inc ....E 425 743-2226
  Lynnwood *(G-6131)*
Global Incorporated ....F 206 763-4424
  Seattle *(G-10084)*
Gompf Brackets Inc ....F 425 348-5002
  Mukilteo *(G-6929)*
Home Builders Service Company ....F 509 747-1206
  Spokane *(G-12296)*
Hulett and Company ....G 425 922-5224
  Snohomish *(G-11925)*
Ifh Group West LLC ....G 844 434-9378
  Arlington *(G-253)*
Imaginetics Holdings LLC ....G 253 735-0156
  Auburn *(G-472)*
Imaginetics LLC ....D 253 735-0156
  Auburn *(G-473)*
J S Vail ....G 509 886-8708
  East Wenatchee *(G-3022)*
Jemco Cmpnents Fabrication Inc ....D 425 827-7611
  Kirkland *(G-5372)*
Jet City Partners LLC ....G 206 999-0047
  Auburn *(G-479)*
Jpl Habitability Inc ....F 360 377-7660
  Bremerton *(G-1967)*
Kauffmann Industries Inc ....G 425 770-5781
  Bothell *(G-1872)*
KDL Enterprises Inc ....E 253 395-3113
  Kent *(G-4973)*
Klw Manufacturing & Design Inc .....F 360 435-6288
  Arlington *(G-270)*
Kollmar Incorporated ....E 509 882-3148
  Grandview *(G-4250)*
Krueger Sheet Metal Co ....D 509 489-0221
  Spokane *(G-12355)*
L & E Tubing LLC ....E 425 778-4123
  Lynnwood *(G-6155)*
Laz Tool and Manufacturing ....E 360 568-5749
  Snohomish *(G-11936)*
Lee Fabricators Inc ....F 360 698-1190
  Silverdale *(G-11843)*
Lighthouse For The Blind Inc ....B 206 322-4200
  Seattle *(G-10417)*
Lloyd Industries LLC ....E 509 468-8691
  Spokane Valley *(G-12775)*
Louis Stoffer & Son ....G 360 736-3820
  Centralia *(G-2648)*
Lous Welding & Fabricating ....F 425 483-0300
  Woodinville *(G-15295)*
M & M Fabricators Inc ....G 509 248-8890
  Union Gap *(G-13939)*
Magic Metals Inc ....C 509 453-1690
  Union Gap *(G-13942)*
McKinstry Co LLC ....B 206 762-3311
  Seattle *(G-10509)*
Metal Rollforming Systems Inc ....E 509 315-8737
  Spokane *(G-12392)*
Metal Sales Manufacturing Corp .....F 253 872-5750
  Kent *(G-5007)*
Metals Fabrication Company Inc .....D 509 244-2909
  Airway Heights *(G-56)*
Metals McHning Fabricators Inc ......F 509 248-8890
  Union Gap *(G-13944)*

Moses Lake Sheet Metal Inc ....E 509 765-1614
  Moses Lake *(G-6728)*
Mutual Industries Inc ....G 206 767-6647
  Seattle *(G-10577)*
Noll/Norwesco LLC ....C 253 926-1600
  Fife *(G-3974)*
Northern Mountain Metals LLC ....G 509 226-1957
  Newman Lake *(G-7049)*
Ogle Equipment Co ....G 509 489-6306
  Spokane *(G-12419)*
Olympia Sheet Metal Inc ....E 360 491-1123
  Olympia *(G-7354)*
Omnifab Inc ....E 253 931-5151
  Auburn *(G-518)*
Omnimax International Inc ....F 509 535-0344
  Spokane Valley *(G-12819)*
Orion Industries ....C 253 661-7805
  Auburn *(G-521)*
Orion Industries ....C 425 355-1253
  Mukilteo *(G-6962)*
P&A Metal Fab Inc ....G 253 435-8947
  Puyallup *(G-8213)*
Pacer Design By Sharp Pdts Inc .....F 360 217-8120
  Monroe *(G-6603)*
Pacific Coast Marine Inds Inc ....D 425 743-9550
  Lynnwood *(G-6177)*
Pacific Metal Fabrication Inc ....G 253 833-3362
  Kent *(G-5054)*
Pacific Northwest ....G 206 453-3182
  Seattle *(G-10736)*
Pacific Sheet Metal Inc ....E 206 682-5354
  Seattle *(G-10740)*
Peninsula Sheet Metal Inc ....G 360 642-2102
  Long Beach *(G-5876)*
Pioneer Human Services ....D 206 768-1990
  Seattle *(G-10809)*
Pioneer Human Services ....C 206 762-7737
  Seattle *(G-10810)*
Polaris Manufacturing Inc ....E 360 653-7676
  Marysville *(G-6370)*
Power Plus Incorporated ....F 509 489-8308
  Spokane *(G-12451)*
Precision Sheet Metal LLC ....G 509 969-0055
  Yakima *(G-15652)*
Precision Sheet Metal & Heatin ....G 503 939-8600
  Vancouver *(G-14502)*
Premier Manufacturing Inc ....D 509 927-9860
  Liberty Lake *(G-5854)*
Proctor Products Co Inc ....F 425 398-8800
  Woodinville *(G-15341)*
Proto Manufacturing Inc ....D 509 535-9683
  Spokane *(G-12456)*
Queen City Shtmtl & Roofg Inc ....E 206 623-6020
  Kent *(G-5092)*
Quicktin Incorporated ....D 253 779-8885
  Tacoma *(G-13485)*
Reliance Steel & Aluminum Co ....E 253 395-0614
  Tukwila *(G-13806)*
Rogroc LLC ....G 360 435-6417
  Arlington *(G-316)*
Roofing Services Inc ....F 425 347-1146
  Mount Vernon *(G-6829)*
Rozema Boat Works Inc ....F 360 757-6004
  Mount Vernon *(G-6830)*
S & R Sheet Metal Inc ....D 360 425-7020
  Kelso *(G-4546)*
S & S Metal Fabrication Inc ....F 253 472-4461
  Tacoma *(G-13504)*
Scafco Corporation ....C 509 343-9000
  Spokane *(G-12493)*
Sea Lect Products ....G 253 520-2598
  Kent *(G-5118)*
Seaport Machine Inc ....F 509 758-2605
  Clarkston *(G-2648)*
Sharps Welding & Muffler Ctr ....G 509 452-2101
  Moxee *(G-6885)*
Shoemaker Manufacturing Co ....D 509 674-4414
  Cle Elum *(G-2679)*
Skilfab Industries Inc ....G 425 831-5555
  Snoqualmie *(G-12024)*
SMK Tri-Cities Inc ....E 509 547-0412
  Pasco *(G-7631)*
Sound Building Supply Inc ....E 425 264-0264
  Renton *(G-8916)*
Sound Metal Works Ltd ....F 360 659-0999
  Marysville *(G-6388)*
Specialty Sheet Metal Inc ....F 253 872-5718
  Kent *(G-5148)*
Spiraltec ....G 360 734-7831
  Bellingham *(G-1553)*

Spokane Tin Sheet Ir Works Inc ......F 509 534-0539
  Spokane *(G-12521)*
Steel Fab Inc ....E 425 743-9216
  Arlington *(G-333)*
Steeler Construction Sup Ltd ....E 206 725-2500
  Seattle *(G-11188)*
Steeltec Supply Inc ....G 253 333-1311
  Auburn *(G-572)*
Str8 Sheet Fabrications LLC ....E 425 789-1755
  Mukilteo *(G-6980)*
T N T Enterprises ....E 425 742-8210
  Bothell *(G-1908)*
T2 Services Inc ....F 509 893-3666
  Spokane Valley *(G-12899)*
TI Northwest Corp ....F 253 445-4104
  Puyallup *(G-8264)*
Top Notch Manufacturing Co ....G 360 577-9150
  Longview *(G-5960)*
Tri-Mechanical Inc ....F 425 391-6016
  Bellevue *(G-1201)*
Tri-Way Industries Inc ....D 253 859-4585
  Auburn *(G-582)*
Truepoint Metalworks Wldg Inc ....E 360 273-3412
  Rochester *(G-9142)*
U S Sheet Metal Company Inc ....F 253 272-2444
  Tacoma *(G-13567)*
Viking Packaging Machinery ....G 509 452-7143
  Yakima *(G-15703)*
West Coast Custom Metal Design ...G 360 738-2884
  Bellingham *(G-1592)*
West Coast Manufacturing Inc ....G 208 667-5121
  Everett *(G-3655)*
Wldg Wilkerson & Fabrication ....G 509 438-9667
  Pasco *(G-7655)*
Wsf LLC ....E 509 922-1300
  Spokane Valley *(G-12944)*

METAL FABRICATORS: Structural, Ship

Bennett Industries Inc ....E 253 627-7775
  Tacoma *(G-13194)*
Sea Technology Construction ....F 206 282-9158
  Seattle *(G-11039)*

METAL FABRICATORS: Structural, Ship

Alpha Iron LLC ....E 360 823-1777
  Ridgefield *(G-9061)*
Twisted Metal LLC ....G 360 966-5309
  Everson *(G-3693)*

METAL FINISHING SVCS

Almet Metal Refinishing ....G 206 234-8555
  Fall City *(G-3699)*
Applied Finishing Inc ....E 425 513-2505
  Mukilteo *(G-6893)*
Artisan Finishing Systems Inc ....G 360 658-0686
  Marysville *(G-6313)*
Blue Streak Finishers LLC ....D 425 347-1944
  Everett *(G-3392)*
Hytek Finishes Co ....C 253 872-7160
  Kent *(G-4947)*
Metal Finishing Inc ....F 360 659-1971
  Arlington *(G-274)*
Pacmet ....G 253 854-4241
  Kent *(G-5058)*
PM Testing Laboratory Inc ....D 253 922-1321
  Fife *(G-3981)*
Pro Finish Inc ....G 253 850-9422
  Kent *(G-5083)*
Schoeben & Schoeben Inc ....E 360 794-1945
  Monroe *(G-6616)*
Show Quality Metal Finishing ....G 206 762-6717
  Seatac *(G-9305)*

METAL MINING SVCS

Adamera Minerals LLC ....F 509 237-7731
  Republic *(G-8955)*
Alaska Standard Mining Inc ....G 360 432-8797
  Shelton *(G-11674)*
Boart Longyear ....G 509 926-9575
  Otis Orchards *(G-7512)*
Cannabis Leaf Incorporated ....G 206 430-6250
  Seattle *(G-9617)*
Fam USA Inc ....G 509 468-2677
  Nine Mile Falls *(G-7074)*
Global Metal Technologies LLC ....G 425 956-3506
  Bellevue *(G-928)*
Golden Claw Ventures Inc ....G 360 927-8276
  Blaine *(G-1672)*

Employee Codes: A=Over 500 employees, B=251-500
C=101-250, D=51-100, E=20-50, F=10-19, G=2-9

METAL MINING SVCS

Hart Crowser Inc .... D 206 324-9530
 Seattle *(G-10145)*
Hiett Logging Inc .... G 360 724-5505
 Burlington *(G-2164)*
High Cascade Incorporated .... G 509 763-2195
 Leavenworth *(G-5806)*
Iron Mountain Quarry LLC .... G 425 338-0607
 Bothell *(G-1867)*
Mascota Resources Corp .... G 206 818-4799
 Black Diamond *(G-1650)*
Raz Arthur John .... F 360 518-2665
 Ridgefield *(G-9105)*
Selland Construction Inc .... C 509 662-7119
 Wenatchee *(G-15073)*
Smma Candelaria Inc .... G 206 405-2800
 Seattle *(G-11140)*
Sumitomo Metal Mining America .... G 206 405-2800
 Seattle *(G-11215)*
Tai Incorporated .... G 509 747-6111
 Spokane *(G-12542)*
Teck American Incorporated .... D 509 446-5308
 Metaline Falls *(G-6499)*

METAL OXIDE SILICONE OR MOS DEVICES

Rec Silicon Inc .... D 509 765-2106
 Moses Lake *(G-6741)*

METAL SERVICE CENTERS & OFFICES

American Lifting Products Inc .... G 253 572-8981
 Tacoma *(G-13168)*
Bergstrom Foundry Inc .... F 360 532-6981
 Aberdeen *(G-6)*
Fixture Engineering Inc .... G 360 671-9052
 Bellingham *(G-1347)*
HB Jaeger Company LLc .... G 360 707-5958
 Burlington *(G-2161)*
Metal Sales Manufacturing Corp .... F 253 872-5750
 Kent *(G-5007)*
Reliance Steel & Aluminum Co .... E 253 395-0614
 Tukwila *(G-13806)*

METAL SPINNING FOR THE TRADE

Custom Metal Spinning LLC .... G 206 762-2707
 Seattle *(G-9768)*
Northwest Metal Spinning .... G 253 351-8489
 Auburn *(G-512)*
Quality Metal Spinning Co .... G 206 242-6751
 Seatac *(G-9302)*

METAL STAMPING, FOR THE TRADE

Gillaspie Manufacturing Inc .... F 360 260-1975
 Vancouver *(G-14252)*
Hill Aerosystems Inc .... D 360 802-8300
 Enumclaw *(G-3293)*

METAL STAMPINGS: Ornamental

Sound Spring Inc .... F 253 859-9499
 Kent *(G-5142)*

METAL TREATING: Cryogenic

US Cryogenics Inc .... G 360 835-2475
 Washougal *(G-14997)*

METALS SVC CENTERS & WHOLESALERS: Bale Ties, Wire

Pacific Wire Group Inc .... F 253 249-0249
 Auburn *(G-525)*

METALS SVC CENTERS & WHOLESALERS: Bars, Metal

Scot Industries Inc .... D 360 623-1305
 Centralia *(G-2431)*

METALS SVC CENTERS & WHOLESALERS: Cable, Wire

Connectzonecom LLC .... E 425 212-4400
 Lynnwood *(G-6097)*

METALS SVC CENTERS & WHOLESALERS: Concrete Reinforcing Bars

CMC Steel Fabricators Inc .... G 253 833-9060
 Auburn *(G-409)*

METALS SVC CENTERS & WHOLESALERS: Copper Prdts

Alaskan Copper Companies Inc .... G 206 623-5800
 Seattle *(G-9368)*

METALS SVC CENTERS & WHOLESALERS: Iron & Steel Prdt, Ferrous

Waite Speciality Mch Work Inc .... D 360 577-0777
 Longview *(G-5964)*

METALS SVC CENTERS & WHOLESALERS: Piling, Iron & Steel

Bigfoot Pipe & Piling LLC .... G 425 882-1000
 Puyallup *(G-8130)*

METALS SVC CENTERS & WHOLESALERS: Pipe & Tubing, Steel

Ameron International Corp .... D 909 944-4100
 Vancouver *(G-14029)*
Cascade Pipe & Feed Supply .... G 509 997-0720
 Twisp *(G-13910)*
Northwest Pipe Company .... B 303 289-4080
 Vancouver *(G-14438)*
Paramount Supply Co .... G 360 647-8328
 Bellingham *(G-1489)*

METALS SVC CENTERS & WHOLESALERS: Rope, Wire, Exc Insulated

Washington Chain & Supply Inc .... E 206 623-8500
 Seattle *(G-11438)*

METALS SVC CENTERS & WHOLESALERS: Sheets, Metal

Central Fabricators Inc .... F 206 633-4762
 Seattle *(G-9654)*

METALS SVC CENTERS & WHOLESALERS: Steel

Bills Welding & Machine Shop .... G 509 334-2222
 Pullman *(G-8085)*
Centralia Supply & Fabrication .... G 360 736-7277
 Centralia *(G-2391)*
Efco Corp .... F 253 852-3800
 Kent *(G-4886)*
Greer Steel Inc .... E 253 581-4100
 Lakewood *(G-5727)*
McNichols Company .... F 253 922-4296
 Fife *(G-3970)*
Olympic Foundry Inc .... G 206 764-6200
 Seattle *(G-10691)*
Stach Steel Supply .... G 509 848-2772
 Harrah *(G-4321)*
Western Sttes Stl Fbrction Inc .... E 509 489-8046
 Spokane *(G-12588)*

METALS SVC CENTERS & WHOLESALERS: Tubing, Metal

Pacific Hide & Fur Depot .... E 509 545-0688
 Pasco *(G-7611)*

METALS: Precious NEC

Fusion Silver .... G 253 740-8117
 Auburn *(G-446)*
Precious Metals Min & Ref Co .... G 509 927-2685
 Spokane Valley *(G-12836)*
Sure Fit Inc .... G 253 426-1025
 Tacoma *(G-13532)*

METALWORK: Miscellaneous

Arbon Equipment Corporation .... F 253 395-7099
 Kent *(G-4787)*
Arbon Equipment Corporation .... E 253 796-0004
 Kent *(G-4788)*
Berg Manufacturing Inc .... C 509 624-8921
 Spokane Valley *(G-12638)*
Bite-A-Lite LLC .... G 360 687-2995
 Battle Ground *(G-693)*
Canam Steel Corporation .... C 509 837-7008
 Vancouver *(G-14094)*
Cutting Edge Manufacturing .... G 425 348-0626
 Everett *(G-3434)*
D&E Kustoms LLC .... G 360 681-0511
 Sequim *(G-11622)*
Harris Rebar Seattle Inc .... E 253 847-5001
 Tacoma *(G-13332)*
Homecare Products Inc .... C 253 249-1108
 Algona *(G-71)*
Joy Specialty Metals LLC .... G 206 542-5161
 Shoreline *(G-11778)*
Knights Welding .... G 509 412-1103
 Pasco *(G-7596)*
Morgan Steel & Metal Works .... G 360 301-6611
 Poulsbo *(G-7986)*
National Wirecraft Company Inc .... F 360 424-1129
 Mount Vernon *(G-6816)*
Nucor Corporation .... C 206 933-2222
 Seattle *(G-10666)*
Pfc Inc .... G 360 398-8889
 Bellingham *(G-1497)*
Pickett Spring .... G 360 376-6982
 Olga *(G-7218)*
Ries Productions LLC .... G 360 627-8795
 Bremerton *(G-1994)*
Titanium Sports Tech LLC .... D 509 586-6117
 Pasco *(G-7640)*
Tri States Rebar Inc .... E 509 922-5901
 Spokane Valley *(G-12912)*
Ultimate Mtal Fabrications LLC .... F 206 356-9666
 Renton *(G-8935)*
West Coast Custom Metal Design .... G 360 738-2884
 Bellingham *(G-1592)*

METALWORK: Ornamental

Bfc Architectural Metals Inc .... F 206 763-0530
 Seatac *(G-9274)*
Corona Steel Inc .... G 253 874-4766
 Tacoma *(G-13244)*
Garys Garden Gate .... G 360 357-5607
 Olympia *(G-7294)*
Quali Cast Foundry .... G 360 748-6645
 Chehalis *(G-2527)*
Urban Accessories Inc .... E 253 572-1112
 Tacoma *(G-13573)*

METER READERS: Remote

Resource Associates Intl .... G 509 466-1894
 Spokane *(G-12472)*

METERS: Power Factor & Phase Angle

Submeter Solutions Inc .... G 425 228-6831
 Renton *(G-8922)*

MGMT CONSULTING SVCS: Matls, Incl Purch, Handle & Invntry

Fascinaturals LLC .... G 425 954-7151
 Edmonds *(G-3111)*

MICROCIRCUITS, INTEGRATED: Semiconductor

Ecorsys Inc .... G 347 282-6888
 Seattle *(G-9881)*

MICROFILM SVCS

Business Equipment Center Inc .... F 509 747-2964
 Spokane *(G-12162)*

MICROPROCESSORS

Mips Tech Inc .... G 408 610-5900
 Bellevue *(G-1008)*
New Age Processors LLC .... G 425 656-0174
 Renton *(G-8857)*
Texas Instruments Inc .... G 253 927-0754
 Federal Way *(G-3795)*

MICROSCOPES

Toussint Machine and Mfg LLC .... G 360 840-0705
 Sedro Woolley *(G-11576)*
Westover Scientific Inc .... D 425 368-0444
 Bothell *(G-1917)*

MICROSCOPES: Electron & Proton

Hummingbird Precision Mch Co .... F 360 252-2737
 Lacey *(G-5556)*
Hummingbird Scientific LLC .... F 360 252-2737
 Lacey *(G-5557)*

PRODUCT SECTION

MILLWORK

MILITARY GOODS & REGALIA STORES
Sandbox Enterprises LLC ....G...... 360 966-6677
  Bellingham *(G-1523)*

MILITARY INSIGNIA, TEXTILE
AMICK Tactical LLC ....G...... 253 301-7619
  Yelm *(G-15726)*

MILL PRDTS: Structural & Rail
Steel Painters Inc ....E...... 360 425-7720
  Kelso *(G-4551)*

MILLING: Corn Grits & Flakes, For Brewers' Use
Golden Hills Brewing Co ....G...... 509 389-6253
  Airway Heights *(G-53)*

MILLING: Grains, Exc Rice
ADM Milling Co ....E...... 509 534-2636
  Spokane *(G-12100)*
ADM Milling Co ....F...... 509 235-6216
  Cheney *(G-2574)*
ADM Milling Co ....G...... 509 534-2636
  Spokane *(G-12101)*

MILLWORK
A and R Cabinets & Wdwkg L L C .....G...... 360 863-8417
  Monroe *(G-6541)*
Acadie Woodworks ....G...... 509 924-1256
  Spokane *(G-12095)*
Acadie Woodworks Incorporated ....G...... 509 230-6874
  Spokane Valley *(G-12598)*
Alexandria Moulding Inc ....C...... 509 248-2120
  Moxee *(G-6874)*
Als Custom Woodworking ....G...... 360 354-2407
  Lynden *(G-6000)*
American Woodworking Supply ....G...... 509 424-3800
  Yakima *(G-15508)*
Anderson Woodworks ....G...... 360 923-2203
  Olympia *(G-7226)*
Archetype Woodworking LLC ....G...... 360 977-0565
  Vancouver *(G-14039)*
Argusea Mar Wdwkg & Finshg LLC ....G...... 360 708-9702
  Bow *(G-1926)*
Artisan Stone Wood Works Inc ....G...... 253 740-7102
  Tacoma *(G-13182)*
Artistic Cabinets & Millwork ....G...... 509 575-4788
  Yakima *(G-15514)*
Avn Floor & Mill Work LLC ....G...... 425 345-6071
  Everett *(G-3377)*
B Plus Inc ....G...... 360 426-5038
  Shelton *(G-11681)*
Bahmiller Woodworks ....G...... 509 929-6300
  Ellensburg *(G-3184)*
Baraa Woodworking ....G...... 360 752-0608
  Bellingham *(G-1257)*
Bayne Junction Woodworks ....G...... 360 886-8908
  Ravensdale *(G-8331)*
Beaver Lake Woodworks ....G...... 425 391-0661
  Sammamish *(G-9188)*
Bernstein Woodworks ....G...... 206 605-1796
  Seattle *(G-9516)*
Blue Heron Woodworks ....G...... 360 766-4475
  Bow *(G-1928)*
Blue Streak Woodworks ....G...... 360 379-0414
  Port Townsend *(G-7869)*
Bob Johnson Woodworking ....G...... 360 668-9456
  Snohomish *(G-11877)*
Bolt Woodworks Corp ....G...... 206 734-5845
  Everett *(G-3398)*
Brad O Connor Woodworking ....G...... 206 302-8424
  Seattle *(G-9575)*
Bush Woodcraft ....G...... 206 323-2020
  Seattle *(G-9601)*
C & M Woodworks ....G...... 253 503-9440
  Graham *(G-4219)*
Cabin Mill LLC ....G...... 509 235-1808
  Cheney *(G-2579)*
Centerpiece Customs ....G...... 360 490-8636
  Shelton *(G-11690)*
Chetties Woodworking LLC ....G...... 360 500-9099
  Rochester *(G-9130)*
Chuckanut Woodworks ....G...... 360 724-3129
  Burlington *(G-2143)*
Coastline Woodworking ....G...... 360 678-7572
  Coupeville *(G-2810)*

Colville Wdwkg & Stained GL ....G...... 509 684-7670
  Colville *(G-2748)*
Complete Mllwk Solutions Inc ....G...... 253 875-6769
  Federal Way *(G-3724)*
Conestoga Wood Spc Corp ....G...... 253 437-1320
  Kent *(G-4863)*
Contemporary Woodworks LLC ....G...... 360 897-2162
  Orting *(G-7476)*
Contour Countertops Inc ....F...... 503 654-2245
  Vancouver *(G-14150)*
Conwood Construction Inc ....G...... 360 694-5195
  Vancouver *(G-14151)*
Cornerstone Real Property ....G...... 360 455-0862
  Olympia *(G-7256)*
Costom Woodwork 425 828-2579
  Kirkland *(G-5315)*
Crafty Woodworking 425 822-9618
  Kirkland *(G-5316)*
Craig Yamamoto Woodworker LLC ....G...... 206 571-5821
  Clinton *(G-2686)*
Creative Millwork & Moulding ....G...... 425 343-4799
  Snohomish *(G-11892)*
Crucible NW Woodworks LLC ....G...... 206 661-3545
  Seattle *(G-9758)*
Csw Inc ....G...... 360 491-9365
  Tumwater *(G-13866)*
Curry Custom Cabinets Corp ....G...... 425 315-9355
  Mukilteo *(G-6909)*
Custom Wood Finishes ....G...... 360 468-4383
  Lopez Island *(G-5980)*
Custom Woodworking ....G...... 360 739-3961
  Lynden *(G-6011)*
Cutting Edge Woodworks LLC ....G...... 360 929-5386
  Oak Harbor *(G-7145)*
D & D Millwork Inc ....F...... 800 627-8437
  Lynnwood *(G-6105)*
D Haitre Woodworks LLC ....G...... 360 752-0405
  Bellingham *(G-1316)*
Daniels Woodworks ....G...... 360 264-7311
  Tenino *(G-13615)*
Dave Yocoms Wood Creations ....G...... 425 220-5628
  Everett *(G-3440)*
Delta Pntg & Prefinishing Co ....G...... 253 588-8278
  Tacoma *(G-13258)*
Discount Doors & Millwork LLC ....G...... 360 687-1942
  Vancouver *(G-14182)*
Dkr Wood Working ....G...... 509 943-2273
  Richland *(G-8989)*
Doors & Millwork Inc ....G...... 509 921-7663
  Spokane Valley *(G-12682)*
Dreamers Woods ....G...... 360 477-5888
  Port Angeles *(G-7698)*
Duncan J Woodworking ....G...... 360 765-0745
  Quilcene *(G-8283)*
Edwin Enterprises Inc ....G...... 253 272-7090
  Tacoma *(G-13274)*
Emma Danforth ....G...... 360 931-5060
  Vancouver *(G-14201)*
Epping-Jordan Fine Wdwkg LLC ....G...... 206 588-2700
  Seattle *(G-9935)*
F Ruckman Enterprises ....E...... 253 531-9132
  Puyallup *(G-8151)*
Flanagan Woodworks Inc ....G...... 360 221-3352
  Langley *(G-5777)*
Fox Island Woodworks ....G...... 253 549-7019
  Fox Island *(G-4021)*
G R Plume Co ....F...... 360 384-2800
  Ferndale *(G-3846)*
Garage Sports Woodworking ....G...... 206 433-1645
  Burien *(G-2109)*
Ghl Architectural Millwork LLC ....G...... 206 467-5004
  Seattle *(G-10068)*
Glacier Mouldings Ltd ....F...... 360 629-5313
  Stanwood *(G-12975)*
Gnw Corporation ....G...... 425 869-6218
  Redmond *(G-8479)*
Goddard Woodworking Llcpetr Go ....G...... 206 920-8675
  Seattle *(G-10092)*
Great Northwest Industries ....F...... 425 861-9768
  Redmond *(G-8483)*
Haase Woodworks ....G...... 360 681-2600
  Sequim *(G-11637)*
Hacienda Custom Woodwork LLC .....G...... 206 922-9330
  Renton *(G-8816)*
Hacienda Custom Woodwork LLC .....G...... 206 922-9330
  Maple Valley *(G-6272)*
Havens Woodworks & Refinishing ......G...... 360 833-9446
  Camas *(G-2256)*
Heirloom Woodworks ....G...... 509 315-9275
  Spokane Valley *(G-12728)*

Hicks Leathermaking and Wdwkg ......G...... 253 833-8873
  Auburn *(G-465)*
High Country Woodworks ....G...... 360 942-2996
  Raymond *(G-8353)*
Howat Fine Woodworking Inc ....G...... 360 681-3451
  Sequim *(G-11640)*
Hugh Montgomery ....G...... 206 369-9356
  Bainbridge Island *(G-641)*
Independent Woodworks ....G...... 206 239-8577
  Seattle *(G-10224)*
Inland Fixtures Co Inc ....G...... 509 487-2759
  Spokane *(G-12309)*
Inland Millwork ....G...... 509 481-7765
  Spokane Valley *(G-12744)*
Interior Construction Spc ....F...... 425 745-8343
  Mukilteo *(G-6944)*
Interior Wdwkg Specialists Inc ....E...... 425 881-1328
  Redmond *(G-8513)*
Island Wood Works ....G...... 360 403-7066
  Arlington *(G-258)*
J & K Woodworks ....G...... 425 392-3758
  Issaquah *(G-4433)*
J & R Wood Products Inc ....G...... 360 687-1662
  Battle Ground *(G-710)*
J Wanamaker Cabinetry & Wdwrk .....G...... 206 762-3494
  Seattle *(G-10274)*
Jaks Custom Woodwork ....G...... 425 443-6210
  Duvall *(G-2992)*
Jays Custom Woodworks ....G...... 360 807-0976
  Centralia *(G-2411)*
Jaywick Woodworks LLC ....G...... 206 793-7208
  Seattle *(G-10286)*
JB Woodworking ....G...... 509 949-3683
  Yakima *(G-15598)*
Jbs Millwork Inc ....G...... 509 248-3412
  Yakima *(G-15599)*
Jet Door LLC ....E...... 253 531-2261
  Tacoma *(G-13359)*
Ji Woodwork ....G...... 360 790-4083
  Gig Harbor *(G-4123)*
Jsg Fine Cstm Cbntry Wdwrk LLC ....G...... 253 906-9043
  Tacoma *(G-13369)*
Jubilee Woodworks LLC ....G...... 206 734-0344
  Seattle *(G-10312)*
JW Woodworks ....G...... 206 719-4229
  Federal Way *(G-3748)*
Jwoodworking ....G...... 253 229-9581
  Tacoma *(G-13371)*
K & S Woodworks LLC ....G...... 360 354-1043
  Lynden *(G-6027)*
Kaci Woodworks LLC ....G...... 206 601-0395
  Seattle *(G-10324)*
Kieu Danh ....G...... 360 548-9649
  Marysville *(G-6347)*
Kincaid Woodworking ....G...... 518 810-1374
  Tumwater *(G-13880)*
Klm Custom Sash LLC ....G...... 360 403-7400
  Arlington *(G-269)*
Korben Mathis Woodworking Inc ....G...... 360 598-6797
  Poulsbo *(G-7972)*
Kyle O Meara ....G...... 206 874-2626
  Federal Way *(G-3749)*
Lak Woodworks ....G...... 253 495-0611
  Lakewood *(G-5732)*
Leaves In Wind Woodworks LLC ....G...... 360 574-6750
  Vancouver *(G-14368)*
Left Coast Woodworks LLC ....G...... 360 790-3188
  Centralia *(G-2417)*
Loan Goat Woodworks ....G...... 360 395-8996
  Sedro Woolley *(G-11550)*
Lr Woodworking ....G...... 281 813-1169
  Poulsbo *(G-7978)*
Lucky Dog Woodworking ....G...... 507 218-6767
  Okanogan *(G-7199)*
M L Woodworks ....G...... 360 264-4859
  Tenino *(G-13621)*
Mark Thomas Woodworks ....G...... 505 220-7560
  Walla Walla *(G-14842)*
Marke Woodworking ....G...... 360 945-4023
  Point Roberts *(G-7669)*
Master Millwork Inc ....E...... 253 770-2023
  Puyallup *(G-8182)*
McKeons Fine Wdwkg LLC Gc ....G...... 206 920-6724
  Shoreline *(G-11787)*
Metrie Inc ....E...... 360 863-1730
  Ferndale *(G-3870)*
Miles Woodworking ....G...... 360 306-3048
  Bellingham *(G-1435)*
Mill City Brew Werks ....G...... 360 210-4761
  Camas *(G-2270)*

Employee Codes: A=Over 500 employees, B=251-500
C=101-250, D=51-100, E=20-50, F=10-19, G=2-9

MILLWORK

PRODUCT SECTION

Mill Creek Woodworking Inc .... G 509 526-5660
  Walla Walla *(G-14844)*
Modern Art Woodwork LLC .... G 360 303-6054
  Ferndale *(G-3874)*
Modern Yacht Joinery .... G 360 928-0214
  Port Angeles *(G-7726)*
Monroe Door & Millwork Inc .... F 360 863-9882
  Monroe *(G-6598)*
Mountain Springs Building Co .... G 206 550-4380
  Bellevue *(G-1017)*
Mystic Woodworking .... G 425 736-1416
  Newcastle *(G-7036)*
Neucor Inc .... G 866 638-2671
  Vancouver *(G-14430)*
New Touch Woodworking .... G 360 930-1118
  Hansville *(G-4316)*
New Whatcom Interiors .... F 360 671-3389
  Bellingham *(G-1459)*
Nicos Woodworking .... G 206 755-8110
  Shoreline *(G-11793)*
Nissen Woodworks .... G 425 216-3575
  North Bend *(G-7117)*
Nk Woodworking LLC .... G 206 257-4395
  Seattle *(G-10612)*
Noel Corporation .... F 509 248-3412
  Yakima *(G-15631)*
Northwest Custom Podiums Inc .... G 360 830-5858
  Seabeck *(G-9269)*
Northwest Millwork Door Co .... G 360 297-0802
  Bainbridge Island *(G-654)*
Northwest Woodworking LLC .... G 425 488-9597
  Kenmore *(G-4594)*
NW Woodworks LLC .... G 206 780-6753
  Bainbridge Island *(G-656)*
O B Williams Company .... E 206 623-2494
  Seattle *(G-10677)*
Oceanus Plastics Inc .... G 360 366-7474
  Custer *(G-2858)*
Oka Woodworks Inc .... G 425 221-2573
  Sammamish *(G-9239)*
Old Dominion Woodworks .... G 509 684-7931
  Colville *(G-2767)*
Old Plank Woodworks .... G 360 455-7366
  Olympia *(G-7351)*
Old Woodworking Inc .... G 253 770-3650
  Puyallup *(G-8209)*
Olsen Cabinet & Millwork .... G 206 242-1188
  Seatac *(G-9295)*
Olympic Millwork .... G 360 480-6650
  Olympia *(G-7359)*
Olympic Mountain Millwork LLC .... G 360 432-2992
  Shelton *(G-11717)*
Once Again Woodworking .... G 425 327-9733
  Snohomish *(G-11957)*
Orcas Island Tonewoods .... G 360 376-2747
  Olga *(G-7217)*
Oropeza Woodworks .... G 360 668-0438
  Snohomish *(G-11958)*
Osborne Woodworks .... G 360 428-0245
  Mount Vernon *(G-6819)*
Outside In Woodworks LLC .... G 208 403-9067
  Port Orchard *(G-7839)*
Pacific Crest Industries Inc .... C 253 321-3011
  Sumner *(G-13093)*
Pan Abode Cedar Homes Inc .... E 425 255-8260
  Renton *(G-8874)*
Pearson Millwork Inc .... F 360 435-9516
  Arlington *(G-298)*
Pedersons Custom Woodworking .... G 509 981-0720
  Spokane Valley *(G-12826)*
Port Townsend School of Woodwo .... G 303 910-0016
  Port Townsend *(G-7915)*
Possession Point Woodworking .... G 360 579-2183
  Clinton *(G-2693)*
Precision Customer Woodworking .... G 360 983-3297
  Mossyrock *(G-6764)*
Pritchard Woodworks LLC .... G 206 755-4503
  Hansville *(G-4318)*
Procoat LLC .... G 425 252-0070
  Shoreline *(G-11803)*
Puget Sound Woodworking LLC .... G 360 563-0116
  Snohomish *(G-11963)*
Quality Stairs and Woodworking .... G 425 358-4196
  Maple Valley *(G-6291)*
R & R Woodworking Inc .... G 509 279-9345
  Medical Lake *(G-6444)*
R L Woodworks .... G 360 607-4471
  Vancouver *(G-14527)*
R Vision Antq & Restoration .... G 360 280-0328
  Olympia *(G-7376)*

Rain City Wood Works LLC .... G 206 378-0494
  Seattle *(G-10915)*
Rain Shadow Woodworks Inc .... G 360 385-6789
  Port Townsend *(G-7922)*
Rainier Woodworking Co .... E 253 272-5210
  Tacoma *(G-13490)*
Rams Custom Cabinets & Wdwkg .... G 253 952-2551
  Federal Way *(G-3775)*
River Hollow Creations LLC .... G 509 497-1097
  Benton City *(G-1627)*
Rocking H Woodworking .... G 253 448-7978
  Spanaway *(G-12072)*
Rodocker Woodworks LLC .... G 360 775-1620
  Port Angeles *(G-7740)*
Rogers Custom Woodworking .... G 425 757-1799
  Renton *(G-8897)*
Romeo and Sylvia LLC .... G 425 315-5336
  Snohomish *(G-11968)*
Rwsd Lumberyard .... G 503 910-9822
  Chehalis *(G-2533)*
Saariswoodworking .... G 360 835-8106
  Washougal *(G-14982)*
Salmon Bay Woodworks .... G 206 612-3993
  Seattle *(G-11008)*
Schiferl Woodworking .... G 425 788-3795
  Woodinville *(G-15355)*
Schober Woodworks .... G 360 595-7519
  Bellingham *(G-1526)*
Shaffer Woodworks LLC .... G 509 697-3023
  Selah *(G-11596)*
Sheridan Woodworking LLC .... G 509 540-7799
  Walla Walla *(G-14869)*
Silver Moon Woodworks .... G 425 753-4476
  Seattle *(G-11113)*
Simpson Door Company .... B 360 495-3291
  McCleary *(G-6420)*
Smith Custom Woodworking Inc .... G 509 670-4634
  Wenatchee *(G-15075)*
Sparrow Woodworks LLC .... G 206 708-5615
  Indianola *(G-4373)*
Specialty Woodworking .... G 360 379-1222
  Port Townsend *(G-7929)*
Specialty Woodworks .... G 360 670-6280
  Port Angeles *(G-7745)*
Spirit In Wood LLC .... G 509 961-3061
  Naches *(G-7005)*
Stephan J Lesser Woodworking .... G 206 782-9463
  Seattle *(G-11192)*
Stratton Woodworks .... G 425 968-2455
  Sammamish *(G-9250)*
Sycamore Woodworks .... G 360 757-4120
  Burlington *(G-2192)*
T & A Supply Company Inc .... G 253 872-3682
  Kent *(G-5167)*
T R S Inc .... F 253 444-1555
  Tacoma *(G-13538)*
Taggart Woodworks LLC .... G 206 729-8028
  Seattle *(G-11258)*
Tarpley Woodworking .... G 360 631-1405
  Granite Falls *(G-4286)*
Techwood LLC .... D 360 427-9616
  Shelton *(G-11743)*
Timshel Woodworking .... G 206 466-1054
  Seattle *(G-11311)*
Top Quality Woodworks LLC .... G 509 551-3658
  Kennewick *(G-4736)*
Tph Inc DBA Island Wood Works .... G 360 403-7066
  Arlington *(G-340)*
Tru Door Inc .... F 509 545-8773
  Kennewick *(G-4742)*
Trumark Industries Inc .... E 509 534-0644
  Spokane *(G-12571)*
Upper Cut Woodworks LLC .... G 425 785-4817
  Redmond *(G-8700)*
US Mill Works LLC .... G 206 355-5143
  Seattle *(G-11393)*
Veritas Custom Woodworks .... G 425 346-5576
  Lynnwood *(G-6216)*
Victory Millwork LLC .... E 360 592-6090
  Lynden *(G-6060)*
Voiss Wood Products Inc .... G 360 794-1062
  Monroe *(G-6635)*
Vrieze & Olson Custom Wdwkg .... F 253 445-9733
  Puyallup *(G-8274)*
Waddell Woodworking LLC .... G 503 752-1940
  Vancouver *(G-14675)*
Washington Hardwoods and .... F 206 283-7574
  Winlock *(G-15158)*
Washington Hardwoods Co LLC .... G 206 283-7574
  Seattle *(G-11440)*

Wells Ww Millwork LLC .... F 425 405-3252
  Everett *(G-3654)*
Weyerhaeuser Company .... B 253 924-2345
  Seattle *(G-11463)*
Whites Custom Woodworking LLC .... G 509 582-9474
  Kennewick *(G-4746)*
Whitman Cabinets and Wdwkg .... G 360 825-6466
  Enumclaw *(G-3329)*
Wild Tree Woodworks LLC .... G 206 650-2565
  Seattle *(G-11475)*
Wild Wood Splitting .... G 206 909-8342
  Maple Valley *(G-6301)*
Wojtanowicz Wood Works .... G 253 225-2252
  Gig Harbor *(G-4176)*
Wollin Woodworking Inc .... G 360 929-5895
  Mount Vernon *(G-6856)*
Wood Creations .... G 360 491-1616
  Olympia *(G-7430)*
Wood Works By Rob .... G 206 497-6345
  Auburn *(G-601)*
Woodwork Tattoo and Gallery .... G 360 626-1965
  Poulsbo *(G-8022)*
Woodworkers Outpost .... G 253 653-8607
  Covington *(G-2840)*
Woodworking Services .... G 253 678-7951
  Tacoma *(G-13601)*

MINE & QUARRY SVCS: Nonmetallic Minerals

Crossroads Group Inc .... G 206 855-3146
  Everett *(G-3430)*
French Man Hills Quarry .... G 509 346-2111
  Othello *(G-7496)*
Hart Crowser Inc .... D 206 324-9530
  Seattle *(G-10145)*
Kennedy Creek Quarry Inc .... F 360 426-4743
  Shelton *(G-11706)*
Pacific NW Aggregates Inc .... G 509 748-9188
  Wishram *(G-15167)*

MINE EXPLORATION SVCS: Nonmetallic Minerals

American Drilling Corp LLC .... E 509 921-7836
  Spokane Valley *(G-12610)*
Gold Reserve Inc .... G 509 623-1500
  Spokane *(G-12276)*
Goldmountain Exploration Corp .... G 360 332-0905
  Blaine *(G-1674)*
Lka Gold Incorporated .... G 253 514-6661
  Gig Harbor *(G-4133)*
Lovitt Mining Company Inc .... G 509 668-8170
  Wenatchee *(G-15046)*

MINE PREPARATION SVCS

American Min & Tunneling LLC .... G 509 921-7836
  Spokane Valley *(G-12612)*
Procon Min & Tunnelling US Ltd .... F 360 685-4253
  Bellingham *(G-1506)*

MINERAL ABRASIVES MINING SVCS

Axiom Drilling Corp .... F 509 921-7836
  Spokane Valley *(G-12633)*

MINERAL MINING: Nonmetallic

Olympic Manganese Mining Co .... G 360 426-9273
  Shelton *(G-11716)*
Society For Mining Metallurgy .... G 509 922-4063
  Spokane Valley *(G-12879)*

MINERAL WOOL

Johns Manville Corporation .... D 800 654-3103
  Kent *(G-4970)*

MINERAL WOOL INSULATION PRDTS

Service Partners LLC .... D 509 535-4600
  Spokane Valley *(G-12866)*
Service Partners of Oregon .... E 360 694-6747
  Vancouver *(G-14580)*

MINERALS: Ground or Treated

Columbia Rock & Aggregates Inc .... F 360 892-0510
  Vancouver *(G-14137)*
Imerys Minerals California Inc .... D 509 787-4575
  Quincy *(G-8300)*

PRODUCT SECTION

MOLDS: Indl

Konen Rock Crushing Inc .... G 509 382-2768
 Dayton *(G-2883)*
Lane Mt Silica Co .... E 206 762-7622
 Valley *(G-13993)*
Magic Earth .... G 509 738-2801
 Kettle Falls *(G-5236)*
Manufacturers Mineral Company ...... F 425 228-2120
 Renton *(G-8847)*
Puget Sound Surfacers Inc .... G 360 374-9590
 Forks *(G-4016)*
Rec Silicon Inc .... D 509 765-2106
 Moses Lake *(G-6741)*
Specialty Minerals Inc .... G 509 545-9777
 Wallula *(G-14911)*
Steelhead Specialty Minerals .... G 509 328-5685
 Spokane *(G-12527)*

MINIATURES

Soda Pop Miniatures LLC .... G 425 260-4638
 Issaquah *(G-4478)*

MINING EXPLORATION & DEVELOPMENT SVCS

Andritz Hydro Corp .... G 704 943-4343
 Spokane Valley *(G-12618)*
Ce Metal Fabrication .... F 360 673-9663
 Kalama *(G-4494)*
Christopher Ross Dewayne .... G 360 918-4586
 Tumwater *(G-13860)*
LI3 LLC .... G 509 332-2109
 Pullman *(G-8097)*
Master Vac LLC .... G 253 875-0074
 Graham *(G-4231)*
North Star Mining Co Inc .... G 360 793-0848
 Sultan *(G-13030)*
Pilot Knob Construction Inc .... G 509 493-4196
 White Salmon *(G-15127)*

MINING MACHINES & EQPT: Amalgamators, Metallurgical/Mining

Rebec LLC .... G 425 745-4177
 Lynnwood *(G-6187)*

MINING MACHINES & EQPT: Augers

Courtright Enterprises Inc .... E 509 764-9600
 Moses Lake *(G-6698)*

MINING MACHINES & EQPT: Crushers, Stationary

Bedford Industries Inc .... G 360 805-9099
 Monroe *(G-6551)*
Flsmidth Inc .... G 509 434-8605
 Spokane *(G-12259)*

MINING MACHINES & EQPT: Mineral Beneficiation

Novex LLC .... G 360 296-3467
 Bellingham *(G-1473)*

MINING MACHINES & EQPT: Rock Crushing, Stationary

LLP Enterprises LLC .... G 509 423-7580
 Wenatchee *(G-15044)*

MINING MACHINES & EQPT: Trucks, Dollies

Joy Glbal Lngview Oprtions LLC .... G 253 588-1726
 Lakewood *(G-5731)*

MINING SVCS, NEC: Bituminous

Sumitomo Metal Mining Ariz Inc .... G 206 405-2800
 Seattle *(G-11216)*

MINING: Oil Sand

Green Section 30 LLC .... G 253 433-4130
 Enumclaw *(G-3292)*

MISCELLANEOUS FINANCIAL INVEST ACT: Oil/Gas Lease Brokers

Procon Min & Tunnelling US Ltd .... F 360 685-4253
 Bellingham *(G-1506)*

MISSILES: Guided

Boeing Company .... A 206 655-1131
 Seattle *(G-9563)*

MITTENS: Woven Or Knit, From Purchased Materials

Mittens By Ann .... G 253 862-1050
 Edgewood *(G-3085)*

MIXTURES & BLOCKS: Asphalt Paving

Clean Lines LLC .... G 509 939-2957
 Deer Park *(G-2896)*
CPM Development Corporation .... G 509 663-5141
 Wenatchee *(G-15024)*
Degerstrom Corporation .... E 509 928-3333
 Spokane Valley *(G-12680)*
Granite Construction Company .... G 360 676-2450
 Everson *(G-3676)*
Interstate Asphalt Paving Inc .... G 425 318-5008
 Arlington *(G-257)*
Karvonen Sand & Gravel Inc .... G 360 687-2549
 Battle Ground *(G-712)*
Koch Industries Inc .... G 509 487-4560
 Spokane *(G-12354)*
MA Assoc .... G 206 719-1363
 Bothell *(G-1775)*
Michael H Wold Company Inc .... G 360 435-6953
 Arlington *(G-275)*
Poe Asphalt Paving Inc .... E 509 334-6400
 Pullman *(G-8101)*
Semgroup Corp .... G 509 921-7089
 Spokane Valley *(G-12864)*
Semgroup Corporation .... G 509 487-4560
 Spokane *(G-12498)*
Semmaterials LP .... G 509 545-9864
 Pasco *(G-7626)*
Straight Edge Asphalt & Maint .... G 206 949-4666
 Burien *(G-2132)*
Supr Co .... E 509 248-6823
 Yakima *(G-15690)*
Tucci & Sons Inc .... D 253 922-6676
 Tacoma *(G-13566)*
Unique Allscapes .... G 425 309-6325
 Everett *(G-3642)*
US Polyco Inc .... G 509 413-1006
 Spokane *(G-12578)*
Woodland Paving .... G 360 225-8317
 Woodland *(G-15476)*

MOBILE COMMUNICATIONS EQPT

Admiralty Crane LLC .... G 360 461-2092
 Sequim *(G-11606)*
Bluecosmo Inc .... G 877 258-3496
 Seattle *(G-9555)*
Complete Music .... G 509 927-3535
 Spokane *(G-12195)*
Konnectone LLC .... F 425 502-7371
 Bellevue *(G-971)*
Mary Medina LLC .... G 206 719-1730
 Medina *(G-6452)*
Pacific Tchnical Solutions Inc .... F 425 489-5700
 Redmond *(G-8608)*
Swype Inc .... D 206 547-5250
 Seattle *(G-11241)*

MOBILE HOME REPAIR SVCS

Rwc International Ltd .... G 509 452-5515
 Yakima *(G-15664)*

MOBILE HOMES

A & S Contractors .... G 509 930-7994
 Yakima *(G-15496)*
Basic Homes LLC .... G 253 579-2724
 Eatonville *(G-3050)*
Clayton Homes Inc .... G 509 452-9228
 Union Gap *(G-13926)*
Glen Hidden Mhc LLC .... G 253 537-9383
 Puyallup *(G-8159)*
Lake Samish Terrace Park .... G 360 671-2741
 Bellingham *(G-1401)*
Mantheys Country Mobile Park .... G 360 384-5623
 Bellingham *(G-1422)*
Pacific Mat & Coml Flrg LLC .... E 800 345-6287
 Kent *(G-5053)*
Sandy Beach Mobile Villa LLC .... G 509 255-6222
 Liberty Lake *(G-5857)*
Valley Manufactured Hsing Inc .... C 509 839-9409
 Sunnyside *(G-13147)*
Van Horn Mfd Homes .... G 253 370-7263
 Puyallup *(G-8271)*

MOBILE HOMES: Indl Or Commercial Use

Pacific Mobile Structures Inc .... G 509 244-8335
 Airway Heights *(G-60)*

MOBILE HOMES: Personal Or Private Use

J&K Enterprise .... G 360 854-0020
 Sedro Woolley *(G-11542)*

MODELS

Concept Reality Inc .... F 360 695-3860
 Vancouver *(G-14144)*
Rauda Scale Models Inc .... F 206 365-8877
 Seattle *(G-10926)*

MODELS: Airplane, Exc Toy

Dynon Avionics Inc .... D 425 402-0433
 Woodinville *(G-15230)*
Insitu Inc .... A 509 493-8600
 Bingen *(G-1638)*

MODELS: Boat, Exc Toy

Isaksen Scale Models .... G 425 334-2807
 Lake Stevens *(G-5650)*

MODELS: General, Exc Toy

Galaxy Hobby Inc .... G 425 670-0454
 Lynnwood *(G-6124)*
Northwest Park Models LLC .... G 509 235-2522
 Cheney *(G-2590)*
Rh Airport Commerce .... E 425 454-3030
 Bellevue *(G-1102)*

MODULES: Computer Logic

Critical Delivery Service LLC .... G 206 724-3653
 Bellevue *(G-868)*

MOLDED RUBBER PRDTS

4 M Company Inc .... D 425 227-4100
 Tukwila *(G-13686)*
Cascade Gasket & Mfg Co Inc .... C 253 854-1800
 Kent *(G-4841)*
Scougal Rubber Corporation .... D 206 763-2650
 Seattle *(G-11032)*

MOLDING COMPOUNDS

A To Z Composites Inc .... F 435 680-3762
 Bellingham *(G-1236)*
Cypress Designs LLC .... G 360 384-6572
 Bellingham *(G-1314)*
Signature Plastics LLC .... F 360 366-5044
 Custer *(G-2860)*

MOLDINGS & TRIM: Wood

Artistic Home & Garden LLC .... G 360 834-7021
 Camas *(G-2229)*
R L Industries .... F 360 794-1621
 Monroe *(G-6611)*

MOLDINGS: Picture Frame

Groove Incorporated .... G 360 786-9605
 Olympia *(G-7300)*
Larson-Juhl US LLC .... E 206 433-6002
 Kent *(G-4989)*

MOLDS: Indl

American Mold Inspection .... G 425 770-4375
 Bainbridge Island *(G-608)*
Bay City Mold Inspection Svcs .... G 415 925-0801
 Olga *(G-7213)*
Mold Dmage Rmval Pros Lakewood . G 253 343-0497
 Lakewood *(G-5738)*
Northwest Center .... E 360 403-7330
 Arlington *(G-289)*
NW Mold Removal .... G 360 433-7353
 Vancouver *(G-14444)*
Tri-Shell Cores Shop Inc .... F 360 694-7600
 Vancouver *(G-14645)*

Employee Codes: A=Over 500 employees, B=251-500
C=101-250, D=51-100, E=20-50, F=10-19, G=2-9

MOLDS: Plastic Working & Foundry

Inject Tool & Die Inc..................G........ 360 679-6160
  Oak Harbor (G-7154)
Modelwerks Inc..........................F........ 206 340-6007
  Seattle (G-10553)

MONOFILAMENTS: Nontextile

Advanced Cargo Control LLC.........G........ 206 498-5824
  Snohomish (G-11870)
Avante Technology LLC.................G........ 425 273-4740
  Bellevue (G-801)

MONUMENTS & GRAVE MARKERS, EXC TERRAZZO

Edgewood Monuments..................G........ 253 561-2498
  Puyallup (G-8148)
Inspired Monumental...................G........ 253 468-4835
  Gig Harbor (G-4121)
Majestic Monument & Stone............G........ 509 699-8937
  Ellensburg (G-3214)
Monument Wheelworks LLC............G........ 206 856-9509
  Seattle (G-10561)
Monumental Chewelah..................G........ 509 935-6962
  Chewelah (G-2604)
Monumental Task........................G........ 509 449-8286
  Okanogan (G-7201)
Premier Memorial LLC..................E........ 253 472-0369
  Tacoma (G-13477)

MONUMENTS & GRAVE MARKERS, WHOLESALE

Quiring Monuments Inc.................E........ 206 522-8400
  Seattle (G-10906)

MONUMENTS: Cut Stone, Exc Finishing Or Lettering Only

Tresko Monument Inc...................F........ 509 838-3196
  Spokane (G-12568)

MOTEL

Morgan Electric & Plumbing Inc........F........ 206 547-1617
  Seattle (G-10562)

MOTION PICTURE & VIDEO DISTRIBUTION

Greenfire Productions...................G........ 360 572-0554
  Arlington (G-245)
Jjs Productions LLC......................G........ 360 630-5294
  Anacortes (G-138)

MOTION PICTURE & VIDEO PRODUCTION SVCS

Career Development Software..........F........ 360 696-3529
  Vancouver (G-14099)
Cascade Chalet...........................E........ 206 463-4628
  Vashon (G-14716)
Cinematix LLC.............................G........ 425 533-1024
  Kirkland (G-5305)
Lavry Engineering.........................G........ 360 598-9757
  Poulsbo (G-7974)

MOTION PICTURE & VIDEO PRODUCTION SVCS: Educational

Committee For Children.................D........ 206 343-1223
  Seattle (G-9718)

MOTION PICTURE & VIDEO PRODUCTION SVCS: Training

Mediapro Holdings LLC..................E........ 425 483-4700
  Bothell (G-1777)

MOTION PICTURE EQPT

Lightspeed Design Inc...................G........ 425 637-2818
  Bellevue (G-983)

MOTOR HOME DEALERS

D & R Rv LLC..............................F........ 360 755-3218
  Burlington (G-2150)

MOTOR HOMES

Redondo Rv Storage & Service.........G........ 253 941-3662
  Kent (G-5101)

MOTOR REBUILDING SVCS, EXC AUTOMOTIVE

Barbara Somers..........................G........ 360 699-5205
  Vancouver (G-14057)
Seatac Automotive.......................G........ 253 839-0309
  Kent (G-5121)

MOTOR REPAIR SVCS

Picatti Brothers Inc......................D........ 509 248-2540
  Yakima (G-15646)
Rwc International Ltd...................G........ 509 452-5515
  Yakima (G-15664)
Seays Lake City Marine LLC............G........ 509 483-1461
  Spokane (G-12496)

MOTOR SCOOTERS & PARTS

Lets Ride LLC.............................G........ 253 225-3630
  Gig Harbor (G-4131)
Lucky Scooter Parts LLC................G........ 425 558-0715
  Redmond (G-8539)

MOTOR VEHICLE ASSEMBLY, COMPLETE: Ambulances

Braun Northwest Inc....................C........ 800 245-6303
  Chehalis (G-2474)

MOTOR VEHICLE ASSEMBLY, COMPLETE: Autos, Incl Specialty

Ford Motor Credit Company LLC.......D........ 425 643-0454
  Bellevue (G-914)
Jensen Race Cars.........................G........ 425 745-8000
  Lynnwood (G-6144)
Rm Metal Works...........................G........ 253 815-0652
  Federal Way (G-3777)
Silver Star Street Rods..................G........ 360 837-1250
  Washougal (G-14986)

MOTOR VEHICLE ASSEMBLY, COMPLETE: Fire Department Vehicles

Central Kitsap Fire Rescu...............G........ 360 447-3575
  Silverdale (G-11828)
County of Lewis..........................G........ 360 494-4123
  Packwood (G-7542)
Patrick Corp...............................G........ 509 925-1300
  Ellensburg (G-3217)
Shoreline Cert............................G........ 206 533-6500
  Shoreline (G-11811)
Wildfire Safe LLC.........................G........ 509 670-3816
  Cashmere (G-2335)

MOTOR VEHICLE ASSEMBLY, COMPLETE: Military Motor Vehicle

Kurtisfactor LLC..........................G........ 208 863-6180
  Tacoma (G-13379)

MOTOR VEHICLE ASSEMBLY, COMPLETE: Truck & Tractor Trucks

Paccar Inc..................................C........ 425 828-5000
  Kirkland (G-5424)
Paccar Inc..................................C........ 360 757-5357
  Mount Vernon (G-6820)
Paccar Inc..................................B........ 425 468-7400
  Bellevue (G-1058)
Paccar Inc..................................C........ 425 254-4400
  Renton (G-8870)
Paccar Inc..................................B........ 425 227-5800
  Renton (G-8871)
Paccar Inc..................................B........ 206 764-5400
  Tukwila (G-13786)

MOTOR VEHICLE ASSEMBLY, COMPLETE: Truck Tractors, Highway

Herrera Isael Gomez....................G........ 509 270-7022
  Spokane (G-12293)

MOTOR VEHICLE ASSEMBLY, COMPLETE: Universal Carriers, Mil

Defense Sales Intl LLC..................G........ 206 999-8684
  Renton (G-8782)

MOTOR VEHICLE ASSEMBLY, COMPLETE: Wreckers, Tow Truck

Ncw Towing................................G........ 509 630-7155
  Wenatchee (G-15051)

MOTOR VEHICLE DEALERS: Automobiles, New & Used

Harris-Ford Inc............................C........ 425 678-0391
  Lynnwood (G-6132)
Subaru of America Inc..................G........ 360 737-7630
  Vancouver (G-14614)
U-Pull-It Auto Parts Inc.................G........ 509 895-7655
  Yakima (G-15698)

MOTOR VEHICLE DEALERS: Cars, Used Only

Emery Enterprises.......................G........ 360 532-0102
  Aberdeen (G-10)
Pro Finish Inc..............................G........ 253 850-9422
  Kent (G-5083)
Showcase Specialties Inc..............G........ 509 547-3344
  Pasco (G-7629)

MOTOR VEHICLE DEALERS: Pickups, New & Used

Showcase Specialties Inc..............G........ 509 547-3344
  Pasco (G-7629)

MOTOR VEHICLE PARTS & ACCESS: Air Conditioner Parts

Energy Efficiency Systems Corp........E........ 360 835-7838
  Washougal (G-14953)
Five Food Inc..............................G........ 509 855-6914
  Moses Lake (G-6708)

MOTOR VEHICLE PARTS & ACCESS: Booster Cables, Jump-Start

Hydra Group LLC..........................G........ 503 957-0975
  Washougal (G-14959)

MOTOR VEHICLE PARTS & ACCESS: Cylinder Heads

Heads Up Inc..............................G........ 253 833-4546
  Auburn (G-461)

MOTOR VEHICLE PARTS & ACCESS: Electrical Eqpt

Evs Manufacturing Inc..................G........ 360 863-6413
  Monroe (G-6570)
Vehicle Monitor Corporation...........F........ 425 881-5560
  Redmond (G-8703)

MOTOR VEHICLE PARTS & ACCESS: Engines & Parts

Hytech Power Inc.........................F........ 425 890-1180
  Redmond (G-8504)
Motor Works Inc..........................D........ 509 535-9240
  Spokane (G-12398)
Olsons Gaskets...........................G........ 360 871-1207
  Port Orchard (G-7836)
Sje Inc.......................................E........ 360 734-1910
  Bellingham (G-1540)
Universal Engine Heater Co............G........ 509 276-5923
  Nine Mile Falls (G-7084)

MOTOR VEHICLE PARTS & ACCESS: Fuel Systems & Parts

Consolidated Metco Inc................D........ 360 828-2599
  Vancouver (G-14147)
Precision Airmotive LLC................G........ 360 403-4803
  Arlington (G-305)

PRODUCT SECTION — MUSIC BOXES

MOTOR VEHICLE PARTS & ACCESS: Heaters
Red DOT Corporation .... B 206 151-3840
 Tukwila *(G-13803)*

MOTOR VEHICLE PARTS & ACCESS: Instrument Board Assemblies
Bic Inc .... G 360 691-1452
 Granite Falls *(G-4265)*

MOTOR VEHICLE PARTS & ACCESS: Lifting Mechanisms, Dump Truck
Workhorse Incorporated .... G 360 835-9417
 Washougal *(G-15002)*

MOTOR VEHICLE PARTS & ACCESS: Mufflers, Exhaust
Taylors Marine Center .... G 509 633-2945
 Electric City *(G-3168)*

MOTOR VEHICLE PARTS & ACCESS: Pickup Truck Bed Liners
Ted Gay .... G 425 742-9566
 Lynnwood *(G-6209)*
Tuckers Tuffer Coatings Inc .... G 360 707-2168
 Sedro Woolley *(G-11578)*

MOTOR VEHICLE PARTS & ACCESS: Propane Conversion Eqpt
Pacific Meter & Equipment Inc .... G 253 872-3374
 Kent *(G-5056)*

MOTOR VEHICLE PARTS & ACCESS: Pumps, Hydraulic Fluid Power
Bogert International Inc .... G 509 736-1512
 Pasco *(G-7555)*
Et Hydraulics LLC .... G 206 718-7372
 Snohomish *(G-11906)*
Skyline Fluid Power Inc .... G 509 382-4781
 Dayton *(G-2886)*

MOTOR VEHICLE PARTS & ACCESS: Sanders, Safety
Fact Motorcycle Training Inc .... G 509 248-2373
 Yakima *(G-15567)*

MOTOR VEHICLE PARTS & ACCESS: Trailer Hitches
C & V Machinery .... G 509 657-3392
 Endicott *(G-3263)*

MOTOR VEHICLE PARTS & ACCESS: Transmission Housings Or Parts
Whidbey Cruzers .... G 253 299-6442
 Oak Harbor *(G-7171)*

MOTOR VEHICLE PARTS & ACCESS: Transmissions
Skagit Transmission Inc .... G 360 757-6551
 Burlington *(G-2189)*

MOTOR VEHICLE PARTS & ACCESS: Windshield Frames
Luann Ayling .... G 509 633-2839
 Electric City *(G-3167)*
Navan Enterprises LLC .... G 206 214-6227
 Seattle *(G-10596)*
Ppr Industries Corporation .... E 360 863-9500
 Monroe *(G-6608)*

MOTOR VEHICLE PARTS & ACCESS: Wipers, Windshield
South Tacoma Glass Specialists .... E 253 582-2401
 Lakewood *(G-5758)*

MOTOR VEHICLE SPLYS & PARTS WHOLESALERS: New
A-Star Distributing Inc .... F 509 467-6809
 Spokane *(G-12091)*
Advanced Fuel Systems .... G 425 526-7566
 Fall City *(G-3698)*
Ellison Fluid Systems Inc .... G 425 271-3220
 Renton *(G-8793)*
Haldex Brake Products Corp .... G 360 944-3070
 Vancouver *(G-14279)*
Material Inc .... G 509 787-4585
 Quincy *(G-8303)*
Paccar Inc .... B 425 468-7400
 Bellevue *(G-1058)*
Phazr LLC .... G 509 329-8306
 Spokane *(G-12440)*

MOTOR VEHICLE SPLYS & PARTS WHOLESALERS: Used
Haldex Brake Products Corp .... G 360 944-3070
 Vancouver *(G-14279)*
Olsons Gaskets .... G 360 871-1207
 Port Orchard *(G-7836)*

MOTOR VEHICLE: Radiators
Performance Radiator PCF LLC .... G 206 624-2440
 Seattle *(G-10787)*
Performance Radiator PCF LLC .... E 253 472-0586
 Tacoma *(G-13464)*

MOTOR VEHICLES & CAR BODIES
Andrew McDonald .... G 253 964-5020
 Lewis McChord *(G-5819)*
Andyman Online .... G 425 761-5921
 Renton *(G-8744)*
Art Morrison Enterprises Inc .... E 253 344-0161
 Fife *(G-3933)*
Ferrotek Corporation .... F 360 366-7444
 Ferndale *(G-3845)*
Jamie Kinney .... G 206 953-9302
 Seattle *(G-10284)*
Lifeport Inc .... E 360 225-6690
 Woodland *(G-15446)*
Nite-Hawk Sweepers LLC .... F 253 872-2077
 Kent *(G-5024)*
Paccar Inc .... G 206 214-0418
 Seatac *(G-9297)*
Paccar Inc .... E 425 468-7400
 Bellevue *(G-1059)*
Paul Parish Limited .... G 509 735-9820
 Kennewick *(G-4705)*
Skagit County Fire Dst 14 .... E 360 724-3451
 Burlington *(G-2187)*
SSC Green Inc .... G 509 967-4753
 West Richland *(G-15101)*
SSC North America LLC .... G 509 967-4753
 West Richland *(G-15102)*
Subaru of America Inc .... G 360 737-7630
 Vancouver *(G-14614)*
Susan Eakin .... G 509 966-2014
 Yakima *(G-15692)*
Tesla Inc .... G 425 519-8070
 Bellevue *(G-1183)*

MOTOR VEHICLES, WHOLESALE: Ambulances
Braun Northwest Inc .... C 800 245-6303
 Chehalis *(G-2474)*

MOTOR VEHICLES, WHOLESALE: Trailers, Truck, New & Used
Allied Body Works Inc .... F 206 763-7811
 Seattle *(G-9381)*

MOTORCYCLE & BICYCLE PARTS: Frames
Volcanic Manufacturing LLC .... G 509 427-8623
 North Bonneville *(G-7136)*

MOTORCYCLE ACCESS
Ace of Spades Inc .... G 360 807-6442
 Centralia *(G-2381)*
DMC Sidecars LLC .... F 360 825-4610
 Buckley *(G-2057)*

Lt Racing .... G 360 871-2259
 Port Orchard *(G-7826)*

MOTORCYCLE DEALERS
Liberty Lake Powersports LLC .... G 509 926-5044
 Liberty Lake *(G-5844)*
Shamrock Machining Inc .... E 509 534-3031
 Spokane Valley *(G-12868)*

MOTORCYCLE PARTS & ACCESS DEALERS
Kens Powder Coating .... G 253 539-5845
 Tacoma *(G-13375)*

MOTORCYCLE REPAIR SHOPS
Flower Racing .... G 360 793-2196
 Sultan *(G-13025)*

MOTORCYCLES & RELATED PARTS
Ace Race Parts Inc .... G 844 223-7223
 Tumwater *(G-13848)*
Bgs Cycle Parts .... G 808 368-8122
 Battle Ground *(G-692)*
Choppers By Kriss .... G 509 570-2737
 Spokane *(G-12181)*
Hardtail Choppers Inc .... G 360 750-6780
 Vancouver *(G-14282)*
Liberty Lake Powersports LLC .... G 509 926-5044
 Liberty Lake *(G-5844)*
Metal Frictions Company Inc .... G 425 776-0336
 Edmonds *(G-3133)*
Motherwell Products Usa Inc .... G 360 366-2600
 Ferndale *(G-3875)*
Pro Wheel Racing Components .... F 360 691-6459
 Granite Falls *(G-4283)*
Puget Sound Safety .... G 253 770-8888
 Puyallup *(G-8227)*

MOTORS: Electric
Ev Drives .... F 360 302-5226
 Port Townsend *(G-7882)*
Nidec America Corporation .... G 360 666-2445
 Battle Ground *(G-724)*
Safran .... G 425 283-5031
 Bellevue *(G-1111)*
Viper R/C Solutions Inc .... G 425 968-5389
 Redmond *(G-8705)*

MOTORS: Generators
Airborne Ecs LLC .... F 319 538-1051
 Port Angeles *(G-7679)*
Automated Controls Inc .... G 206 246-6499
 Auburn *(G-384)*
C H W Enterprises Inc .... F 360 425-8700
 Longview *(G-5892)*
City of Sattle-City Light Dept .... E 509 446-3083
 Metaline Falls *(G-6497)*
D Square Energy LLC .... F 425 888-2882
 North Bend *(G-7110)*
Gen-Set Co .... G 509 891-8452
 Spokane Valley *(G-12714)*
Gen-Tech LLC .... G 206 634-3399
 Seattle *(G-10059)*
K & N Electric Motors Inc .... D 509 838-8000
 Spokane Valley *(G-12759)*
Oscilla Power Inc .... G 206 557-7032
 Seattle *(G-10715)*
Power Conversion Inc .... E 425 487-1337
 Woodinville *(G-15338)*
Safran Usa Inc .... E 425 462-8613
 Bellevue *(G-1112)*
Tsunami Products Inc .... G 509 868-5731
 Liberty Lake *(G-5865)*

MUSEUMS & ART GALLERIES
Mach 2 Arts Inc .... G 206 953-0575
 Seattle *(G-10458)*
Maslach Art Glass A Corp .... G 206 842-9212
 Seattle *(G-11528)*

MUSIC BOXES
Skybreeze Inc .... G 206 764-1872
 Seattle *(G-11131)*

MUSIC LICENSING & ROYALTIES

Leopona Inc .... F 206 701-7931
Seattle *(G-10404)*

MUSIC RECORDING PRODUCER

Ultra Van Krome Prductions LLC .... G 206 859-3459
Tacoma *(G-13568)*

MUSIC SCHOOLS

Magical Strings .... G 253 857-3716
Olalla *(G-7208)*

MUSICAL INSTRUMENT PARTS & ACCESS, WHOLESALE

Dusty Strings Co .... E 206 634-1656
Seattle *(G-9861)*

MUSICAL INSTRUMENT REPAIR

Fluteworks .... G 206 729-1903
Seattle *(G-10008)*

MUSICAL INSTRUMENTS & ACCESS: Carrying Cases

Music Express LLC .... G 206 842-6317
Bainbridge Island *(G-651)*

MUSICAL INSTRUMENTS & ACCESS: NEC

A I S .... G 509 972-2064
Yakima *(G-15497)*
Alan R & Sara Balmforth .... G 206 363-7349
Shoreline *(G-11754)*
Casey Burns Flutes .... G 360 297-4020
Kingston *(G-5250)*
Graphite Guitar Systems .... G 360 273-7744
Oakville *(G-7175)*
Howling Wolf Drums .... G 425 391-2540
Issaquah *(G-4426)*
Magical Strings .... G 253 857-3716
Olalla *(G-7208)*
Olympic Musical Instrumen .... G 360 779-4620
Poulsbo *(G-7989)*
Pacific Rim Tonewoods Inc .... F 360 826-6101
Concrete *(G-2790)*
Pacific Rim Tonewoods Inc .... F 360 826-6101
Bellingham *(G-1488)*
Seattle Music Partners .... G 206 408-8588
Seattle *(G-11065)*
Sobel Guitars .... G 505 699-4032
Ridgefield *(G-9112)*
Summer Moon Products .... G 360 826-3157
Sedro Woolley *(G-11573)*
Theo Wanne Mouthpieces Instrs .... G 360 392-8416
Bellingham *(G-1568)*
Wolfetone Pickups Co .... G 206 417-3548
Lake Forest Park *(G-5628)*

MUSICAL INSTRUMENTS & ACCESS: Pipe Organs

Northwest Pipe Organ .... G 425 432-5039
Maple Valley *(G-6283)*

MUSICAL INSTRUMENTS & ACCESS: Stands

Manhasset Specialty Co Inc .... E 509 248-3810
Yakima *(G-15614)*

MUSICAL INSTRUMENTS & PARTS: Percussion

Other Worlds .... G 360 459-2323
Olympia *(G-7363)*

MUSICAL INSTRUMENTS & PARTS: String

Dusty Strings Co .... E 206 634-1656
Seattle *(G-9861)*
Gurian Instruments Inc .... G 206 467-7990
Seattle *(G-10133)*
Ray R L Violin Shop LLC .... G 360 570-1085
Olympia *(G-7379)*

MUSICAL INSTRUMENTS & SPLYS STORES

Gremlin Inc .... G 206 781-4636
Seattle *(G-10123)*
Petosa Accordions Inc .... G 206 632-2700
Lynnwood *(G-6180)*
Ray R L Violin Shop LLC .... G 360 570-1085
Olympia *(G-7379)*
Sensitronics LLC .... G 360 766-8800
Bow *(G-1932)*

MUSICAL INSTRUMENTS & SPLYS STORES: Organs

Northwest Pipe Organ .... G 425 432-5039
Maple Valley *(G-6283)*

MUSICAL INSTRUMENTS & SPLYS STORES: String instruments

Dusty Strings Co .... E 206 634-1656
Seattle *(G-9861)*

MUSICAL INSTRUMENTS WHOLESALERS

Ray R L Violin Shop LLC .... G 360 570-1085
Olympia *(G-7379)*

MUSICAL INSTRUMENTS: Accordions & Parts

Petosa Accordions Inc .... G 206 632-2700
Lynnwood *(G-6180)*

MUSICAL INSTRUMENTS: Chimes & Parts

Windtones LLC .... G 360 349-9083
Olympia *(G-7428)*

MUSICAL INSTRUMENTS: Electric & Electronic

Intellitouch Communicatons .... G 858 457-3300
Liberty Lake *(G-5837)*

MUSICAL INSTRUMENTS: Flutes & Parts

Fluteworks .... G 206 729-1903
Seattle *(G-10008)*

MUSICAL INSTRUMENTS: Guitars & Parts, Electric & Acoustic

Arnquist Musical Designs .... G 206 420-1639
Seattle *(G-9431)*
Big Lloyde .... G 509 233-2293
Loon Lake *(G-5974)*
Kuau Technology Ltd .... F 425 485-7551
Woodinville *(G-15281)*
Mad Ape .... G 206 201-3275
Bainbridge Island *(G-649)*
T & K Martin Farms Inc .... G 509 525-4387
Walla Walla *(G-14877)*
TV Jones Inc .... G 360 930-0418
Poulsbo *(G-8013)*
Van Orman Guitars LLC .... G 253 269-8660
Elma *(G-3258)*

MUSICAL INSTRUMENTS: Ocarinas

Ocarina Arena .... G 206 446-5354
Seattle *(G-10680)*

MUSICAL INSTRUMENTS: Organ Parts & Materials

Syndyne Corporation .... G 360 256-8466
Vancouver *(G-14622)*

MUSICAL INSTRUMENTS: Organs

Artisan Instruments Inc .... F 425 486-6555
Kenmore *(G-4566)*

MUSICAL INSTRUMENTS: Reeds, Organ

L & B Service LLC .... G 206 650-4607
Lake Forest Park *(G-5619)*

MUSICAL INSTRUMENTS: Violins & Parts

Bowet & Poet Inc .... G 360 385-9005
Port Townsend *(G-7870)*
David T Vanzandt Co .... G 206 789-7294
Seattle *(G-9801)*
Duncan Macdonald Violins LLC .... G 206 352-7219
Seattle *(G-9858)*
Flyingviolin Inc .... G 209 595-9709
Olympia *(G-7288)*
Kenmore Violins .... G 425 481-5638
Kenmore *(G-4588)*
Robert Gee Violins .... G 425 776-4002
Lynnwood *(G-6189)*

MUSICIAN

Islanders .... G 253 588-9246
Tacoma *(G-13351)*

NAIL SALONS

Lexys Nails & Spa .... G 360 352-5044
Tumwater *(G-13883)*

NAME PLATES: Engraved Or Etched

GM Nameplate Inc .... C 206 284-2201
Seattle *(G-10090)*

NAMEPLATES

Adhesa-Plate Manufacturing Co .... E 206 682-0141
Seattle *(G-9351)*
Interntonal Graphics Nameplate .... F 360 699-4808
Vancouver *(G-14323)*

NAPALM

Napalm Racing .... G 509 991-9759
Chattaroy *(G-2448)*

NATIONAL SECURITY FORCES

Dla Document Services .... G 509 527-7231
Walla Walla *(G-14797)*
Dla Document Services .... E 360 315-4014
Silverdale *(G-11832)*

NATIONAL SECURITY, GOVERNMENT: Navy

United States Dept of Navy .... C 360 396-2340
Keyport *(G-5247)*

NATURAL GAS DISTRIBUTION TO CONSUMERS

Avista Corporation .... A 509 489-0500
Spokane *(G-12134)*

NATURAL GAS LIQUIDS PRODUCTION

Emerald Energy Nw LLC .... G 425 830-2757
Bothell *(G-1851)*
Prometheus Energy Company .... F 425 558-9100
Redmond *(G-8635)*
Prometheus Energy Group Inc .... G 425 558-9100
Redmond *(G-8636)*

NATURAL GAS PRODUCTION

Pacificorp .... G 360 827-6467
Chehalis *(G-2520)*

NATURAL GASOLINE PRODUCTION

Pt Defiance Food Mart .... F 253 761-5084
Tacoma *(G-13481)*

NATURAL PROPANE PRODUCTION

Wenatchee Petroleum Co .... E 509 662-4423
Wenatchee *(G-15084)*

NAUTICAL & NAVIGATIONAL INSTRUMENT REPAIR SVCS

W H Autopilots Inc .... F 206 780-2175
Bainbridge Island *(G-682)*

NAUTICAL REPAIR SVCS

Basta Inc .... E 425 641-8911
Bellevue *(G-807)*
Conglobal Industries LLC .... D 206 624-8180
Seattle *(G-9728)*
Npm LLC .... G 206 782-8999
Seattle *(G-10662)*
Puget Sound Repair Inc .... G 506 556-9722
Seattle *(G-10885)*

PRODUCT SECTION

NAVIGATIONAL SYSTEMS & INSTRUMENTS
Electronic Charts Co Inc .... G 206 282-4990
 Seattle *(G-9893)*
Guided Reality Corporation .... G 206 856-8819
 Bainbridge Island *(G-637)*
Novus Composites Incorporated ...... G 253 476-8582
 Tacoma *(G-13436)*

NET & NETTING PRDTS
Cascade Nets Inc .... G 866 738-8071
 Ferndale *(G-3827)*
Coppertop Enterprises Inc .... E 360 966-9622
 Everson *(G-3672)*
Net Services LLC .... F 360 651-1955
 Tulalip *(G-13842)*
Pacific Netting Products Inc .... G 360 697-5540
 Poulsbo *(G-7990)*

NETTING: Plastic
American Nettings & Fabric Inc .... F 360 366-2630
 Ferndale *(G-3813)*
Norplex Inc .... F 360 736-0727
 Centralia *(G-2419)*
Norplex Inc .... E 253 735-3431
 Auburn *(G-510)*

NEWSPAPERS, WHOLESALE
Target Media Partners .... G 509 765-5681
 Moses Lake *(G-6752)*

NEWSSTAND
Endex Newspaper LLC .... G 206 322-4194
 Seattle *(G-9921)*

NICKEL ALLOY
Nichol Prfmce & Ctrl Automatio .... G 360 961-2833
 Everson *(G-3684)*
Robert Nickel .... G 239 565-0450
 Tacoma *(G-13500)*

NONCLASSIFIABLE ESTABLISHMENTS
Pettibon Bio-Mechanics Inst .... G 360 748-4207
 Gig Harbor *(G-4144)*

NONDAIRY BASED FROZEN DESSERTS
Paris Gourmet Dessert .... F 206 767-9097
 Seattle *(G-10756)*

NONDURABLE GOODS WHOLESALERS, NEC
De Jong Sawdust & Shavings .... F 425 252-1566
 Lake Stevens *(G-5643)*
Network Collaborative 4 LLC .... F 206 898-5869
 Seattle *(G-10602)*

NONFERROUS: Rolling & Drawing, NEC
Interntnal Hearth Melting LLC .... D 509 371-2500
 Richland *(G-9011)*
Tungsten Cellars LLC .... G 509 525-3672
 Walla Walla *(G-14881)*
West Coast Plastics Inc .... G 509 575-0727
 Yakima *(G-15706)*

NONMETALLIC MINERALS DEVELOPMENT & TEST BORING SVC
Geocom Resources Inc .... G 360 392-2898
 Bellingham *(G-1357)*

NONMETALLIC MINERALS: Support Activities, Exc Fuels
Dickson Company .... D 253 472-4489
 Tacoma *(G-13263)*
Procon Min & Tunnelling US Ltd ...... F 360 685-4253
 Bellingham *(G-1506)*

NOVELTIES
Ship To Shore Inc .... G 206 284-0406
 Seattle *(G-11101)*
Sweater Stone Inc .... G 425 392-2747
 Sammamish *(G-9251)*

NOVELTIES & SPECIALTIES: Metal
Custom Fab .... G 360 466-1199
 La Conner *(G-5523)*
Safs Inc .... G 253 301-0615
 Tacoma *(G-13506)*

NOVELTIES, DURABLE, WHOLESALE
Screen Print Northwest Inc .... G 360 577-1534
 Longview *(G-5951)*

NOVELTIES: Leather
Pioneer Aerofab Company Inc .... F 360 757-4780
 Burlington *(G-2181)*

NOVELTIES: Plastic
Bite Buddy LLC .... G 360 749-4781
 Kelso *(G-4518)*
Finest Accessories Inc .... G 425 831-7001
 Preston *(G-8025)*
Globalmax Associates Inc .... F 425 392-4848
 Issaquah *(G-4422)*
Lucky Break Wishbone Corp .... G 206 933-8700
 Seattle *(G-10446)*

NOVELTY SHOPS
Grays Harbor Stamp Works .... G 360 533-3830
 Aberdeen *(G-14)*

NOZZLES & SPRINKLERS Lawn Hose
Desert Rain .... G 509 545-1900
 Burbank *(G-2083)*
Forever Green Sprinklers .... G 509 796-2676
 Nine Mile Falls *(G-7075)*
Robs Sprnklr Svc Installation .... G 253 581-6491
 Lakewood *(G-5752)*

NOZZLES: Spray, Aerosol, Paint Or Insecticide
Spraying Systems Co .... G 425 357-6327
 Everett *(G-3619)*

NURSERIES & LAWN & GARDEN SPLY STORE, RET: Lawn/Garden Splys
Angeles Concrete Products Inc .... G 360 681-5429
 Sequim *(G-11611)*
Calportland Company .... G 253 912-8500
 Dupont *(G-2957)*
Glacier Northwest Inc .... F 360 736-1131
 Centralia *(G-2403)*
Lynch Creek Quarry LLC .... G 360 832-4269
 Eatonville *(G-3062)*

NURSERIES & LAWN & GARDEN SPLY STORES, RETAIL
Topsoils Northwest Inc .... F 425 337-0233
 Snohomish *(G-11993)*

NURSERIES & LAWN & GARDEN SPLY STORES, RETAIL: Fertilizer
Crockers Fish Oil Inc .... G 509 787-4983
 Quincy *(G-8295)*
Deyoungs Farm and Garden .... E 425 483-9600
 Woodinville *(G-15225)*
McGregor Company .... F 509 397-4360
 Colfax *(G-2716)*
Nutrien AG Solutions Inc .... G 509 547-9771
 Pasco *(G-7606)*
Perfect Blend LLC .... F 509 968-3316
 Ellensburg *(G-3219)*

NURSERIES & LAWN & GARDEN SPLY STORES, RETAIL: Sod
Pacific Topsoils Inc .... E 425 337-2700
 Everett *(G-3568)*

NURSERIES & LAWN & GARDEN SPLY STORES, RETAIL: Top Soil
De Jong Sawdust & Shavings .... F 425 252-1566
 Lake Stevens *(G-5643)*

Sunland Bark and Topsoils Co .... G 360 293-7188
 Anacortes *(G-172)*

NURSERIES & LAWN/GARDEN SPLY STORE, RET: Lawnmowers/Tractors
Carls Mower and Saw .... G 360 384-0799
 Ferndale *(G-3824)*
Fab-Tech Inc .... G 360 755-0215
 Burlington *(G-2156)*
Sumner Lawn n Saw LLC .... F 253 435-9284
 Puyallup *(G-8257)*
Tims Country Saw Shop .... G 509 486-2798
 Tonasket *(G-13660)*
Washington Tractor Inc .... C 253 863-4436
 Sumner *(G-13110)*
Washington Tractor Inc .... E 360 533-6393
 Aberdeen *(G-38)*
Washington Tractor Inc .... F 509 422-3030
 Okanogan *(G-7204)*

NURSERIES & LAWN/GARDEN SPLY STORES, RET: Garden Splys/Tools
Micro Ag Inc .... G 509 397-4278
 Steptoe *(G-13007)*

NURSERIES/LAWN/GRDN SPLY STORE, RET: Nursery Stck, Seed/Bulb
John McLean Seed Co .... G 509 632-8709
 Coulee City *(G-2803)*
Springbrook Nurs & Trckg Inc .... D 360 653-6545
 Arlington *(G-331)*

NURSERY & GARDEN CENTERS
Ervin H Tennyson .... G 360 445-2434
 Mount Vernon *(G-6793)*

NURSERY STOCK, WHOLESALE
Brothers United Inc .... F 360 426-3959
 Shelton *(G-11686)*
South Sound Aquaponics LLC .... G 206 510-0408
 Federal Way *(G-3789)*
Springbrook Nurs & Trckg Inc .... D 360 653-6545
 Arlington *(G-331)*

NURSING HOME, EXC SKILLED & INTERMEDIATE CARE FACILITY
Omage Labs Inc .... G 844 662-4326
 Seattle *(G-10696)*

NUTRITION SVCS
BHP Holdings Inc .... F 425 462-8414
 Woodinville *(G-15190)*
Evolving Nutrition .... F 425 355-5682
 Everett *(G-3467)*
Strong Snax Inc .... G 360 953-3753
 Ridgefield *(G-9114)*
Yummy Designs LLC .... G 509 525-2072
 Walla Walla *(G-14907)*

NUTS: Metal
Lyn-Tron Inc .... D 509 456-4545
 Spokane *(G-12376)*

NYLON RESINS
Nylatech Incorporated .... F 360 966-2838
 Everson *(G-3685)*

OFFENDER SELF-HELP AGENCY
Department Crrctons Wash State ...... B 509 526-6375
 Walla Walla *(G-14795)*

OFFICE EQPT WHOLESALERS
Simpleline Inc .... G 888 743-7903
 Langley *(G-5785)*

OFFICE FIXTURES: Exc Wood
Pacific Enviroments Corp .... E 408 836-7581
 Kent *(G-5050)*

OFFICE FIXTURES: Wood — PRODUCT SECTION

OFFICE FIXTURES: Wood

Inland Fixtures Co Inc .... G 509 487-2759
  Spokane *(G-12309)*
Stageplan Inc .... E 360 825-2428
  Enumclaw *(G-3322)*

OFFICE MACHINES, NEC

Abadan Repo Graphics .... E 509 946-7697
  Richland *(G-8963)*

OFFICE SPLY & STATIONERY STORES

Andrews Nation Inc .... G 360 989-1700
  Vancouver *(G-14034)*
Fedex Office & Print Svcs Inc ...... E 253 565-4882
  Tacoma *(G-13292)*
OfficeMax North America Inc ...... G 360 455-4068
  Lacey *(G-5572)*
Pickle Papers .... G 509 665-8661
  Wenatchee *(G-15064)*

OFFICE SPLY & STATIONERY STORES: Office Forms & Splys

Beach Bee Inc .... G 360 289-2244
  Ocean Shores *(G-7184)*
Cummins - Allison Corp .... G 206 763-3900
  Tukwila *(G-13721)*
JC Global Supply LLC .... G 253 275-6093
  Kent *(G-4966)*
Martin Business Systems .... G 509 582-3159
  Kennewick *(G-4692)*
Olympic Graphic Arts Inc .... G 360 374-6020
  Forks *(G-4013)*
Oroville Gazette Inc .... G 509 476-3602
  Oroville *(G-7470)*
Pioneer Printing and Forms .... G 509 248-7393
  Yakima *(G-15648)*
Rapid Print Inc .... G 360 695-6400
  Vancouver *(G-14532)*
Sharon Rose .... G 360 341-1898
  Clinton *(G-2698)*
SOS Printing .... G 360 385-4194
  Port Townsend *(G-7927)*
Valley Publishing Company Inc ... F 509 786-1711
  Prosser *(G-8073)*
W B Mason Co Inc .... G 888 926-2766
  Tukwila *(G-13835)*
Wright Business Forms Inc .... E 253 872-0200
  Kent *(G-5219)*

OFFICE SPLY & STATIONERY STORES: School Splys

The Creation Station Inc .... G 425 775-7959
  Tulalip *(G-13845)*

OFFICE SPLY & STATIONERY STORES: Writing Splys

Go Usa Inc .... E 509 662-3387
  Wenatchee *(G-15034)*

OFFICE SPLYS, NEC, WHOLESALE

Bayshore Office Products Inc ..... F 360 293-4669
  Anacortes *(G-102)*
Clark Office Products Inc .... G 360 657-2018
  Marysville *(G-6326)*
Professional Business Svc Inc .... F 360 352-3000
  Olympia *(G-7374)*
Stanwood-Camano News Inc ..... E 360 629-8066
  Stanwood *(G-12995)*

OFFICES & CLINICS DOCTORS OF MED: Intrnl Med Practitioners

Washington Mso Inc .... F 253 984-7247
  Tacoma *(G-13588)*

OFFICES & CLINICS OF DENTISTS: Dentists' Office

Gary L Ostenson DDS PS .... G 360 896-9595
  Vancouver *(G-14248)*

OFFICES & CLINICS OF DOCTORS OF MEDICINE: Radiologist

Breast Care Center .... F 360 424-6161
  Sedro Woolley *(G-11534)*

OFFICES & CLINICS OF HEALTH PRACTITIONERS: Naturopath

Nobu Integrative Medicine LLC ... G 425 363-2970
  North Bend *(G-7118)*

OFFICES & CLINICS OF HEALTH PRACTITIONERS: Nutritionist

Cascade Intgrtive Medicine LLC . G 425 391-5270
  Issaquah *(G-4390)*

OFFICES & CLINICS OF OPTOMETRISTS: Specialist, Optometrists

East Hill Optometry .... G 253 859-0942
  Kent *(G-4882)*

OIL & GAS FIELD MACHINERY

AG Energy Solutions Inc .... F 509 343-3156
  Spokane Valley *(G-12602)*
Cameron International Corp .... E 425 438-8726
  Everett *(G-3409)*
Technipfmc US Holdings Inc ...... G 509 925-2500
  Ellensburg *(G-3230)*

OIL ABSORPTION Eqpt

Healthy Pet LP .... C 360 734-7415
  Ferndale *(G-3850)*

OIL FIELD MACHINERY & EQPT

Highwood Global LP .... E 509 655-7711
  Spokane *(G-12295)*
Oil Spills Services Inc .... G 425 823-6500
  Kirkland *(G-5416)*

OIL FIELD SVCS, NEC

Dai Environmental Services .... E 360 354-1134
  Lynden *(G-6012)*
Global Fire Response & Safety ... G 701 774-2022
  Kirkland *(G-5349)*
Impact Property Mgnt .... G 425 334-6361
  Lake Stevens *(G-5647)*
On Site Safety Inc .... G 970 876-1908
  Kirkland *(G-5420)*
Petrogas Lift Tech LLC .... G 425 891-7403
  Sammamish *(G-9240)*
S Smith .... G 425 529-9244
  Renton *(G-8901)*
Superior Energy Services LLC ... E 360 733-3030
  Bellingham *(G-1564)*
Woodrock Inc .... F 253 565-6090
  Tacoma *(G-13600)*

OIL TREATING COMPOUNDS

Gimpy Ninja LLC .... G 253 282-9943
  Gig Harbor *(G-4108)*
Power Punch Distributors LLC ... G 360 479-0673
  Bremerton *(G-1989)*

OILS & ESSENTIAL OILS

Callisons Inc .... E 360 412-3340
  Lacey *(G-5536)*
Callisons Inc .... F 206 545-3900
  Seattle *(G-9608)*
Natures Inventory LLC .... F 425 775-2000
  Enumclaw *(G-3308)*
Tree of Kindness Inc .... G 509 315-2206
  Spokane *(G-12567)*

OILS & GREASES: Blended & Compounded

Peninsula Lubricants .... G 360 452-8376
  Port Angeles *(G-7736)*

OILS & GREASES: Lubricating

Bardahl Manufacturing Corp .... E 206 783-4851
  Seattle *(G-9492)*
G and T Renewables .... G 206 412-2352
  Seattle *(G-10044)*

Gimpy Ninja LLC .... G 253 282-9943
  Gig Harbor *(G-4108)*
Gobers Fuel Oil Inc .... F 509 924-5372
  Spokane Valley *(G-12721)*
Interlube International Inc .... G 360 332-2132
  Blaine *(G-1675)*
Interlube International Inc .... E 360 734-3832
  Bellingham *(G-1381)*
Mpl Innovations Inc .... G 425 398-1310
  Seattle *(G-10566)*
Prs Group Inc .... F 206 255-7509
  Tacoma *(G-13480)*
Ray Summerlin .... G 253 638-0733
  Kent *(G-5100)*
Restore Incorporated .... G 360 909-1161
  Vancouver *(G-14547)*
Wal Med Inc .... G 253 845-6633
  Puyallup *(G-8276)*
Wilson Oil Inc .... F 509 536-3550
  Spokane *(G-12594)*

OILS: Anise

Inland Synthetics .... G 509 466-6101
  Spokane *(G-12313)*

OILS: Essential

Essex Laboratories LLC .... G 360 740-1770
  Chehalis *(G-2494)*

OILS: Lubricating

AAA Superlubes Inc .... G 425 353-4901
  Port Orchard *(G-7781)*

OILS: Lubricating

Mobile One Lube Ex Everett .... G 425 374-8862
  Everett *(G-3548)*
Winn Enterprises LLC .... G 425 482-6000
  Bothell *(G-1921)*

OILS: Magnetic Inspection Or Powder

S&S NDT LLC .... G 509 688-7996
  Spokane *(G-12491)*

ON-LINE DATABASE INFORMATION RETRIEVAL SVCS

Hunt Hosted Solutions .... G 425 222-0098
  Fall City *(G-3702)*
Meet Your Price Inc .... G 360 260-2066
  Battle Ground *(G-720)*

OPEN PIT GOLD MINING

NA Degerstrom Inc .... E 509 928-3333
  Spokane Valley *(G-12800)*

OPERATOR: Apartment Buildings

Brooks Properties .... G 360 733-5170
  Bellingham *(G-1284)*
Nordal Denver .... G 509 456-8969
  Spokane *(G-12406)*
Parberry Inc .... E 360 734-2340
  Bellingham *(G-1491)*

OPERATOR: Nonresidential Buildings

Noel Corporation .... C 509 248-4545
  Yakima *(G-15630)*

OPHTHALMIC GOODS

Commercial Plastics Corp .... F 206 682-4832
  Seattle *(G-9717)*
East Hill Optometry .... G 253 859-0942
  Kent *(G-4882)*
Northwest Eye Design LLC .... G 425 823-1861
  Kirkland *(G-5413)*
Project Seezit Inc .... G 415 336-4000
  Seattle *(G-10874)*
Society43 LLC .... G 206 327-0778
  Seattle *(G-11150)*
Specialized Safety Pdts LLC ...... G 509 707-0068
  Moses Lake *(G-6751)*
Walman Optical Company .... E 253 872-7137
  Kent *(G-5205)*

PRODUCT SECTION

PACKAGING MATERIALS: Paper

OPHTHALMIC GOODS WHOLESALERS
Impulse Medical Tech Inc .... F ... 360 829-0400
  Buckley *(G-2059)*
Prismoid Optical Laboratory .... G ... 360 417-1244
  Port Angeles *(G-7738)*
Western Optical Corporation .... D ... 206 622-7627
  Seattle *(G-11455)*

OPHTHALMIC GOODS: Eyewear, Protective
Ellensburg Eye & Cntact Lens C 509 925-1000
  Ellensburg *(G-3195)*

OPHTHALMIC GOODS: Frames & Parts, Eyeglass & Spectacle
Island Construction .... G ... 360 426-3442
  Shelton *(G-11700)*

OPHTHALMIC GOODS: Frames, Lenses & Parts, Eyeglasses
Peninsula Optical Lab Inc .... E ... 800 540-4640
  Tacoma *(G-13462)*

OPHTHALMIC GOODS: Lenses, Ophthalmic
Hoya Optical Laboratories .... E ... 253 475-7809
  Tacoma *(G-13344)*
Market Optical .... G ... 206 448-7739
  Seattle *(G-10488)*
Prismoid Optical Laboratory .... G ... 360 417-1244
  Port Angeles *(G-7738)*

OPHTHALMIC GOODS: Spectacles
Council For Edctl Trvl US Amer .... E ... 949 940-1140
  Bellingham *(G-1307)*
Elles Island Spectacle .... G ... 206 715-9475
  Bainbridge Island *(G-629)*
Spectacle Maker .... G ... 425 643-5367
  Bellevue *(G-1152)*

OPTICAL GOODS STORES
Capitol Optical Corp .... E ... 360 352-7502
  Lacey *(G-5538)*
Prismoid Optical Laboratory .... G ... 360 417-1244
  Port Angeles *(G-7738)*
Schwaldbe North America .... G ... 360 384-6468
  Ferndale *(G-3900)*
Walman Optical Company .... E ... 253 872-7137
  Kent *(G-5205)*

OPTICAL GOODS STORES: Eyeglasses, Prescription
Market Optical .... G ... 206 448-7739
  Seattle *(G-10488)*

OPTICAL GOODS STORES: Opticians
East Hill Optometry .... G ... 253 859-0942
  Kent *(G-4882)*
Robert Wickes Od .... G ... 360 249-3485
  Montesano *(G-6654)*
Western Optical Corporation .... D ... 206 622-7627
  Seattle *(G-11455)*

OPTICAL INSTRUMENTS & APPARATUS
Key Technology .... G ... 509 529-2161
  Walla Walla *(G-14832)*
Ocular Instruments Inc .... D ... 425 455-5200
  Bellevue *(G-1042)*
Saunders Instruments Inc .... G ... 206 842-6651
  Bainbridge Island *(G-672)*

OPTICAL INSTRUMENTS & LENSES
BE Meyers & Co Inc .... C ... 425 881-6648
  Redmond *(G-8398)*
Jan Scientific Inc .... G ... 206 632-1814
  Seattle *(G-10285)*
Luxel Corporation .... F ... 360 378-0064
  Friday Harbor *(G-4051)*
Nimbus Technologies LLC .... G ... 206 724-5507
  Seattle *(G-10610)*
Paradigm Optics Incorporated .... G ... 360 573-6500
  Vancouver *(G-14479)*
Quantum Northwest Inc .... G ... 509 624-9290
  Liberty Lake *(G-5856)*

R Mathews Optical Works Inc .... G ... 360 697-6160
  Poulsbo *(G-7995)*
Radiant Vision Systems LLC .... C ... 425 844-0152
  Redmond *(G-8643)*
Walman Optical .... G ... 425 462-2576
  Bellevue *(G-1223)*

OPTOMETRIC EQPT & SPLYS WHOLESALERS
Walman Optical .... G ... 425 462-2576
  Bellevue *(G-1223)*

OPTOMETRISTS' OFFICES
Tumwater Eye Center Inc .... G ... 360 352-6060
  Tumwater *(G-13902)*

ORAL PREPARATIONS
Beaming White LLC .... E ... 360 635-5600
  Vancouver *(G-14058)*
Quest Products LLC .... F ... 425 451-9876
  Kent *(G-5094)*

ORDNANCE
Jr Moore .... G ... 360 607-6128
  Vancouver *(G-14342)*

ORGANIZATIONS: Biotechnical Research, Noncommercial
Cerevast Medical Inc .... G ... 425 748-7529
  Bothell *(G-1754)*
CTI Biopharma Corp .... D ... 206 282-7100
  Seattle *(G-9762)*
Grow Plastics LLC .... G ... 206 954-4564
  Seattle *(G-10128)*

ORGANIZATIONS: Civic & Social
Pariyatti .... G ... 360 978-4998
  Onalaska *(G-7452)*

ORGANIZATIONS: Medical Research
Impel Neuropharma Inc .... G ... 206 568-1466
  Seattle *(G-10211)*
Orthocare Innovations LLC .... F ... 425 771-0797
  Edmonds *(G-3141)*

ORGANIZATIONS: Physical Research, Noncommercial
Eagle Harbor Technologies Inc .... F ... 206 402-5241
  Seattle *(G-9868)*

ORGANIZATIONS: Professional
Washington Cncil Plice Sheriff .... G ... 360 352-8224
  Olympia *(G-7420)*

ORGANIZATIONS: Religious
Cross and Crown Church .... G ... 206 498-3551
  Seattle *(G-9755)*
Markarts Inc .... G ... 425 895-0651
  Redmond *(G-8551)*

ORGANIZATIONS: Research Institute
Cascade Designs Inc .... B ... 206 505-9500
  Seattle *(G-9640)*

ORGANIZATIONS: Safety Research, Noncommercial
Lilibete LLC .... G ... 206 407-6890
  Kent *(G-4996)*

ORNAMENTS: Christmas Tree, Exc Electrical & Glass
Brothers United Inc .... F ... 360 426-3959
  Shelton *(G-11686)*

OSCILLATORS
Orbiter Inc .... G ... 253 627-5588
  Tacoma *(G-13445)*

OUTBOARD MOTOR DEALERS
Bills Marine Service .... G ... 509 826-5564
  OMAK *(G-7435)*
Mercer Marine Inc .... F ... 425 641-2090
  Fall City *(G-3703)*
Northwest Yachts Inc .... G ... 360 299-0777
  Anacortes *(G-156)*

OVENS: Infrared
Ets Inc .... F ... 509 276-2015
  Deer Park *(G-2901)*

PACKAGE DESIGN SVCS
Medical Equipment Dev Co LLC .... G ... 206 364-3894
  Shoreline *(G-11788)*

PACKAGED FROZEN FOODS WHOLESALERS, NEC
Del Rio Food Processing Corp .... F ... 206 767-9102
  Seattle *(G-9816)*
Kastoria Inc .... G ... 206 633-4170
  Seattle *(G-10329)*
Odyssey Enterprises Inc .... C ... 206 285-7445
  Seattle *(G-10685)*
Schenk Packing Co Inc .... E ... 360 336-2128
  Mount Vernon *(G-6834)*
Swinomish Fish Co Inc .... G ... 360 466-0176
  La Conner *(G-5526)*

PACKAGING & LABELING SVCS
Atlas Pacific Engineering Co .... G ... 509 665-6911
  Wenatchee *(G-15010)*
Craft International of Wash .... G ... 360 785-3606
  Winlock *(G-15148)*
Decal Factory .... G ... 509 465-8931
  Spokane *(G-12222)*
Fedex Office & Print Svcs Inc .... F ... 253 872-5539
  Kent *(G-4906)*
Fedexoffice .... G ... 206 467-5885
  Seattle *(G-9982)*
Northwest Center .... C ... 206 285-9140
  Seattle *(G-10639)*
Northwest Flexo Spc LLC .... G ... 425 776-4315
  Lynnwood *(G-6170)*
Pride of The West Inc .... G ... 360 694-4976
  Vancouver *(G-14504)*

PACKAGING MATERIALS, INDL: Wholesalers
H R Spinner Corporation .... E ... 509 453-9111
  Yakima *(G-15579)*
Industrial Crating & Packing .... F ... 425 226-9200
  Mercer Island *(G-6467)*

PACKAGING MATERIALS, WHOLESALE
Alliance Packaging LLC .... D ... 509 924-7623
  Spokane Valley *(G-12605)*
Craft International of Wash .... G ... 360 785-3606
  Winlock *(G-15148)*
Matrix Applications Company .... G ... 509 547-7609
  Vancouver *(G-14400)*
Medical Equipment Dev Co LLC .... G ... 206 364-3894
  Shoreline *(G-11788)*
Tekni-Plex Inc .... C ... 509 663-8541
  Wenatchee *(G-15079)*

PACKAGING MATERIALS: Paper
Adhesive Products Inc .... F ... 206 762-7459
  Seattle *(G-9352)*
Alliance Packaging LLC .... D ... 509 924-7623
  Spokane Valley *(G-12605)*
Allpak Container LLC .... D ... 425 227-0400
  Renton *(G-8739)*
Atlas Pacific Engineering Co .... G ... 509 665-6911
  Wenatchee *(G-15010)*
Caraustar Industrial and Con .... E ... 253 272-1648
  Tacoma *(G-13222)*
Emerald City Label Inc .... F ... 425 347-3479
  Everett *(G-3460)*
Glacier Packaging Inc .... F ... 253 272-4682
  Lakewood *(G-5726)*
Leading Edge Labeling Inc .... E ... 425 821-4137
  Redmond *(G-8531)*
Merrill Corporation .... C ... 360 794-3157
  Monroe *(G-6596)*

Employee Codes: A=Over 500 employees, B=251-500
C=101-250, D=51-100, E=20-50, F=10-19, G=2-9

PACKAGING MATERIALS: Paper

Packaging Corporation America .... D 509 545-3260
   Wallula (G-14909)
Pactiv LLC .... D 847 482-2000
   Auburn (G-526)
Portland Plastics .... B 360 887-2230
   Ridgefield (G-9103)
Sonoco Products Company .... D 360 225-1500
   Woodland (G-15466)
Sp Holdings Inc .... E 509 924-7623
   Spokane Valley (G-12881)
Stafford Press Inc .... F 425 861-5856
   Redmond (G-8680)
Sutta Company Incorporated .... G 253 572-2558
   Tacoma (G-13533)
Tacoma Rubber Stamp Co .... E 253 383-5433
   Tacoma (G-13548)
Trojan Lithograph Corporation .... C 425 873-2200
   Renton (G-8933)
Western Foil Corporation .... G 206 624-3645
   Seattle (G-11452)

PACKAGING MATERIALS: Paper, Coated Or Laminated

Cascades Sonoco Inc. .... E 253 584-4295
   Tacoma (G-13228)
Hexacomb Corporation .... F 253 288-2820
   Auburn (G-464)

PACKAGING MATERIALS: Paperboard Backs For Blister/Skin Pkgs

Nippon Dynawave Packg Co LLC .... A 360 425-2150
   Longview (G-5935)

PACKAGING MATERIALS: Plastic Film, Coated Or Laminated

Cassel Inc .... C 206 909-9584
   Bellevue (G-841)
CP Films Custom Printed Films .... G 253 261-9404
   Kent (G-4867)
Csi Group LLC .... G 360 334-5455
   Vancouver (G-14157)
Sterling International Inc .... C 509 926-6766
   Spokane Valley (G-12893)

PACKAGING MATERIALS: Polystyrene Foam

Adalis Corporation .... E 360 574-8828
   Vancouver (G-14008)
Alliance Packaging LLC .... C 425 291-3500
   Renton (G-8738)
C4 Enterprises Inc .... E 425 347-9200
   Mukilteo (G-6902)
Cryovac Inc. .... C 509 539-2923
   Prosser (G-8037)
Entrust Community Services .... D 509 839-8066
   Sunnyside (G-13124)
Fps Manufacturing LLC .... G 509 248-0423
   Yakima (G-15573)
JC Global Supply LLC .... G 253 275-6093
   Kent (G-4966)
Matrix Applications Company .... G 509 547-7609
   Vancouver (G-14400)
Matrix Applications Company .... G 360 256-2534
   Vancouver (G-14401)
Pac Rite Inc. .... G 253 833-7071
   Puyallup (G-8215)
Pactiv LLC .... D 847 482-2000
   Auburn (G-526)
Storopack Inc .... F 253 872-6844
   Kent (G-5159)
Tekni-Plex Inc .... C 509 663-8541
   Wenatchee (G-15079)
Zoomnet Postal + ... G 360 719-0973
   Vancouver (G-14710)

PACKING & CRATING SVC

Global Harvest Foods Ltd .... G 206 957-1350
   Tukwila (G-13741)
Global Harvest Foods Ltd .... G 206 957-1350
   Tukwila (G-13742)
Industrial Crating & Packing .... F 425 226-9200
   Mercer Island (G-6467)

PACKING & CRATING SVCS: Containerized Goods For Shipping

JC Global Supply LLC .... G 253 275-6093
   Kent (G-4966)

PACKING MATERIALS: Mechanical

Concept Fabrication Inc .... F 509 534-9235
   Spokane (G-12196)
Scott RI and Associates .... G 253 604-4006
   Puyallup (G-8246)

PACKING SVCS: Shipping

Sea Pac Transport Services LLC .... E 206 763-0339
   Seattle (G-11037)

PADS: Solid Fiber, Made From Purchased Materials

Michelsen Packaging Co Cal .... D 509 248-6270
   Yakima (G-15618)

PAGING SVCS

Pacific Radar Inc .... G 425 775-0400
   Everett (G-3566)

PAINT & PAINTING SPLYS STORE

Farwest Paint Manufacturing Co .... F 206 244-8844
   Tukwila (G-13731)

PAINT STORE

Dalys Inc .... E 425 454-3093
   Seattle (G-9788)
Rodda Paint Co .... G 360 423-4990
   Longview (G-5948)
Rodda Paint Co .... G 360 738-6878
   Bellingham (G-1519)
The McCredy Company .... G 509 773-5340
   Goldendale (G-4209)
Vanetten Fine Art .... G 509 928-2385
   Spokane Valley (G-12928)

PAINTING SVC: Metal Prdts

Blue Streak Finishers LLC .... D 425 347-1944
   Everett (G-3392)
Steel Painters Inc .... E 360 425-7720
   Kelso (G-4551)

PAINTS & ADDITIVES

Behr Process Corporation .... F 253 887-8410
   Algona (G-67)
Farwest Paint Manufacturing Co .... F 206 244-8844
   Tukwila (G-13731)
Forrest Paint Co .... G 509 924-3785
   Spokane Valley (G-12708)
Rodda Paint Co .... G 360 423-4990
   Longview (G-5948)
Rodda Paint Co .... G 360 738-6878
   Bellingham (G-1519)

PAINTS & ALLIED PRODUCTS

A Quality Painting .... G 509 362-2398
   Spokane (G-12090)
Asahipen America Inc .... F 206 371-7931
   Seattle (G-9441)
Behr Paint & Stain .... G 253 887-9337
   Auburn (G-390)
Cardinal Industrial Finishes .... F 425 483-5665
   Woodinville (G-15205)
Columbia Indus Coatings LLC .... G 509 531-7310
   Richland (G-8983)
Dalys Inc .... G 425 454-3093
   Seattle (G-9788)
Design Hardwood Products Inc .... F 425 869-0859
   Redmond (G-8439)
Dux Technologies Inc .... G 206 248-0808
   Burien (G-2103)
Forrest Paint Co .... F 253 854-6372
   Kent (G-4917)
Hauge & Hassain Incorporated .... E 206 789-8842
   Seattle (G-10149)
Industrial Control Dev Inc .... E 360 546-2286
   Ridgefield (G-9090)
International Paint LLC .... F 206 763-5884
   Seattle (G-10251)
Jim Suzuki .... G 253 804-6070
   Auburn (G-482)
Mad Label Industries Inc .... G 844 623-4897
   Bremerton (G-1976)
Metal Finishing Inc .... F 360 659-1971
   Arlington (G-274)
PPG Industries .... G 253 804-4350
   Auburn (G-533)
PPG Industries Inc .... G 425 885-3848
   Redmond (G-8629)
Precision Paint .... G 425 235-0340
   Renton (G-8882)
Primer Specialties Inc .... G 360 518-3716
   Vancouver (G-14505)
Rodda Paint Co .... G 253 283-6581
   Chehalis (G-2532)
Sherwin-Williams Company .... G 206 417-4502
   Seattle (G-11100)
T N W Inc. .... G 206 762-5755
   Seattle (G-11250)
Walla Walla Environmental Inc .... F 509 522-0490
   Walla Walla (G-14888)

PAINTS, VARNISHES & SPLYS WHOLESALERS

Forrest Paint Co .... G 509 924-3785
   Spokane Valley (G-12708)
Homax Group Inc .... E 360 733-9029
   Bellingham (G-1371)
Phazr LLC .... G 509 329-8306
   Spokane (G-12440)
Sherwin-Williams Company .... G 425 643-8584
   Bellevue (G-1129)

PAINTS, VARNISHES & SPLYS, WHOLESALE: Paints

Alpine Products Inc .... G 253 351-9828
   Auburn (G-373)
Buffalo Industries LLC .... E 206 682-9900
   Kent (G-4826)
Rodda Paint Co .... G 360 423-4990
   Longview (G-5948)
Rodda Paint Co .... G 360 738-6878
   Bellingham (G-1519)

PAINTS: Lead-In-Oil

Wakefield Art .... G 425 260-0257
   Kirkland (G-5491)

PAINTS: Marine

G C P LLC .... G 206 781-1162
   Seattle (G-10045)
Wasser Corp .... G 360 870-3513
   Auburn (G-594)

PAINTS: Oil Or Alkyd Vehicle Or Water Thinned

Eco Chemical Inc .... F 206 448-7930
   Seattle (G-9877)

PALLET REPAIR SVCS

Standard Pallet Co .... G 509 670-0632
   Rock Island (G-9150)

PALLETIZERS & DEPALLETIZERS

Columbia Machine Inc .... B 360 694-1501
   Vancouver (G-14131)
Columbia Machine Inc .... C 360 694-1501
   Vancouver (G-14133)
Columbia/Okura LLC .... E 360 735-1952
   Vancouver (G-14139)

PALLETS

A & C Pallet Sales .... G 509 669-0653
   Wenatchee (G-15006)
Angels Pallets .... G 253 426-1770
   Lakewood (G-5698)
Ellensburg Pallet .... G 509 962-1373
   Ellensburg (G-3197)
Pallet Place Inc. .... G 509 484-4889
   Spokane Valley (G-12824)
Pallets Unlimited .... G 360 354-1395
   Everson (G-3686)

PRODUCT SECTION

PAPER: Adhesive

Prime Pallets and Recycling .... G 360 410-0238
  Blaine *(G-1697)*
Sanchez Pallets LLC .... G 509 877-4004
  Wapato *(G-14926)*
Standard Pallet Co .... G 509 670-0632
  Rock Island *(G-9150)*
Tri City Pallets .... G 509 543-7500
  Pasco *(G-7643)*
Wooden Pallets Recycled .... G 360 624-3935
  Vancouver *(G-14698)*

PALLETS & SKIDS: Wood

Alta Forest Products LLC .... D 360 426-9721
  Shelton *(G-11676)*
Armour Mfg & Cnstr Inc .... G 253 984-1213
  Tacoma *(G-13180)*
Ballenger International LLC .... G 970 641-9494
  Arlington *(G-209)*
Bison Fiber Pallet .... G 206 291-0778
  Des Moines *(G-2930)*
Emmanuel Pallets LLC .... G 509 439-0924
  Sunnyside *(G-13123)*
Lewis Cnty Work Opportunities .... E 360 748-9921
  Chehalis *(G-2509)*
Pallet Services Inc .... G 509 543-3541
  Pasco *(G-7612)*
Rcd Timber Inc .... G 360 591-9078
  Elma *(G-3254)*
Robertson-Ceco II Corporation .... D 509 244-5611
  Airway Heights *(G-62)*

PALLETS: Corrugated

Unilode AVI Solution US Inc .... F 206 824-7123
  Auburn *(G-587)*

PALLETS: Plastic

Consolidated Container Co LLC .... E 425 251-0303
  Tukwila *(G-13715)*
Prime Pallets and Recycling .... G 360 410-0238
  Blaine *(G-1697)*

PALLETS: Wooden

A & J Brokerage Co Inc .... E 509 483-3003
  Spokane *(G-12088)*
A 1 Pallets Inc .... E 253 395-3119
  Kent *(G-4752)*
Basin Pallett Inc .... F 509 765-8083
  Moses Lake *(G-6686)*
Columbia Pallet LLC .... G 509 430-9647
  Pasco *(G-7563)*
F PS Pallet Recycling Inc .... G 253 312-7122
  Eatonville *(G-3057)*
G M Pallet Inc .... G 253 435-1040
  Tacoma *(G-13303)*
Girard Management Group LLC .... D 253 845-0505
  Puyallup *(G-8156)*
Girard Wood Products Inc .... E 253 845-0505
  Puyallup *(G-8157)*
Girard Wood Products Inc .... D 360 482-5151
  Elma *(G-3247)*
Illinois Tool Works Inc .... G 360 225-9995
  Woodland *(G-15442)*
Lane Pierce Partners Inc .... F 509 926-1033
  Spokane Valley *(G-12771)*
Once Upon A Pallet .... G 360 798-6294
  Battle Ground *(G-726)*
Pallet Services Inc .... G 360 424-8171
  Burlington *(G-2178)*
Pallet Services Inc .... G 360 424-8171
  Burlington *(G-2179)*
Perry Enterprises .... E 360 366-5239
  Ferndale *(G-3885)*
Pilchuck Pallets Inc .... G 425 530-1857
  Arlington *(G-302)*
Quality Pallets .... G 360 773-3973
  Vancouver *(G-14520)*
S & W Manufacturing Inc .... G 360 690-8558
  Vancouver *(G-14562)*
Spinner Wood Products LLC .... G 509 653-2222
  Naches *(G-7004)*
Ufp Washington LLC .... F 509 663-1988
  Malaga *(G-6233)*
Ufp Washington LLC .... D 360 568-3185
  Snohomish *(G-11995)*
Ufp Washington LLC .... E 509 966-4610
  Yakima *(G-15699)*
Woodland Pallet Repair LLC .... G 360 624-3935
  Woodland *(G-15475)*

Yancey Pallet Inc .... D 509 331-0442
  Othello *(G-7511)*

PANEL & DISTRIBUTION BOARDS & OTHER RELATED APPARATUS

Heritage Electrical Group Inc .... G 425 774-7595
  Everett *(G-3511)*
Korry Electronics Co .... A 425 297-9700
  Everett *(G-3532)*
Polaris Glove & Safety In .... G 206 789-5887
  Redmond *(G-8627)*

PANEL & DISTRIBUTION BOARDS: Electric

M & I Systems Inc .... G 206 547-7899
  Everett *(G-3542)*

PANELS: Building, Metal

Front Panel Express LLC .... F 206 768-0602
  Seattle *(G-10029)*

PANELS: Building, Plastic, NEC

Fiberglass Technology Inds Inc .... E 509 928-8880
  Spokane Valley *(G-12701)*
Modular Arts Inc .... G 206 788-4210
  Kent *(G-5012)*

PANELS: Building, Wood

Armstrong Lumber Co Inc .... E 253 833-6666
  Auburn *(G-377)*
Shaw Road Development LLC .... G 253 845-9544
  Puyallup *(G-8253)*
Vaagen Timbers LLC .... G 509 684-5071
  Colville *(G-2780)*
West Coast Laminating LLC .... F 253 395-5225
  Kent *(G-5211)*

PANELS: Control & Metering, Generator

Green-On-Green Energy Inc .... G 206 701-7321
  Auburn *(G-457)*

PANELS: Wood

Alpac Components Co .... E 360 466-2024
  La Conner *(G-5520)*
Infinity Building Mtls LLC .... G 804 921-0810
  Ferndale *(G-3856)*
Stusser Mattson Veneer Inc .... F 425 485-0963
  Woodinville *(G-15378)*
Wachtler Inc .... G 253 225-1904
  Gig Harbor *(G-4173)*
Wood Resources LLC .... G 360 432-5048
  Shelton *(G-11751)*

PAPER & BOARD: Die-cut

Arrow International Inc .... D 425 407-1475
  Lynnwood *(G-6077)*
Cascades Sonoco Inc .... E 253 584-4295
  Tacoma *(G-13228)*
Cowlitz Cont & Diecutting Inc .... F 360 577-8748
  Kelso *(G-4521)*
Graphic Impressions Inc .... E 253 872-0555
  Kent *(G-4925)*
Tabs To Go Inc .... G 253 854-8227
  Auburn *(G-576)*

PAPER CONVERTING

American Paper Converting Inc .... D 360 225-0488
  Woodland *(G-15417)*
Caraustar Industrial and Con .... E 253 272-1648
  Tacoma *(G-13222)*
Caraustar Industries Inc .... E 360 423-3420
  Longview *(G-5894)*
Cascade Paper Converting Inc .... G 360 735-1602
  Vancouver *(G-14105)*
Intellipaper LLC .... F 509 343-9410
  Spokane *(G-12321)*
Nelson-Ball Paper Products .... C 360 423-3420
  Longview *(G-5933)*
Northwest Pioneer Inc .... D 253 872-9693
  Kent *(G-5034)*
Pabco Building Products LLC .... C 253 284-1200
  Tacoma *(G-13449)*
Pacific Paper Products Inc .... D 253 272-9195
  Tacoma *(G-13453)*
Paneltech Intl Holdings Inc .... F 360 538-1480
  Hoquiam *(G-4354)*

Paper Stuffcom .... G 206 462-6079
  Seattle *(G-10750)*
Seattle Rant .... G 206 545-6957
  Seattle *(G-11072)*
Signode Industrial Group LLC .... E 360 225-9995
  Woodland *(G-15465)*
Ultra Paper Co LLC .... G 425 443-5505
  Renton *(G-8936)*

PAPER MANUFACTURERS: Exc Newsprint

Bob Nagel Inc .... F 503 869-6933
  Vancouver *(G-14074)*
Boise Cascade Company .... D 360 690-7028
  Vancouver *(G-14076)*
Boise Cascade Company .... D 360 891-8787
  Vancouver *(G-14077)*
Boise White Paper LLC .... E 509 545-3293
  Wallula *(G-14908)*
Caraustar Industrial and Con .... D 253 627-1197
  Tacoma *(G-13221)*
Clearwater Paper Corporation .... C 509 344-5900
  Spokane *(G-12183)*
Crown Paper Group Inc .... F 360 385-3170
  Port Townsend *(G-7875)*
Domtar Paper Company LLC .... B 253 924-2345
  Federal Way *(G-3730)*
International Paper Company .... E 509 576-3158
  Union Gap *(G-13933)*
International Paper Company .... D 253 372-1360
  Kent *(G-4957)*
Kamilche Company .... G 206 224-5800
  Seattle *(G-10326)*
McKinley Paper Company .... E 360 457-4474
  Port Angeles *(G-7724)*
Nippon Paper Inds USA Co Ltd .... G 360 457-4474
  Longview *(G-5936)*
Packaging Corporation America .... D 509 545-3260
  Wallula *(G-14909)*
Simpson Investment Company .... D 253 272-0158
  Seattle *(G-11115)*

PAPER PRDTS

Northwest Flexo Spc LLC .... G 425 776-4315
  Lynnwood *(G-6170)*

PAPER PRDTS: Feminine Hygiene Prdts

Feminina Group Inc .... G 310 237-5733
  Seattle *(G-9983)*

PAPER PRDTS: Infant & Baby Prdts

J K Properties Inc .... G 360 354-6719
  Lynden *(G-6025)*
Kimberly-Clark Corporation .... F 425 373-5900
  Bellevue *(G-968)*

PAPER PRDTS: Pressed & Molded Pulp & Fiber Prdts

Fibro Corporation .... G 253 503-3568
  Tacoma *(G-13294)*

PAPER PRDTS: Sanitary

Georgia-Pacific LLC .... C 404 652-4000
  Camas *(G-2254)*
Gerris Dry Bunk .... G 509 782-2653
  Cashmere *(G-2320)*

PAPER PRDTS: Sanitary Tissue Paper

Kimberly-Clark Corporation .... F 425 373-5900
  Bellevue *(G-968)*

PAPER PRDTS: Towels, Napkins/Tissue Paper, From Purchd Mtrls

Five Food Inc .... G 509 855-6914
  Moses Lake *(G-6708)*
Procter & Gamble Company .... C 425 313-3511
  Issaquah *(G-4461)*

PAPER, WHOLESALE: Printing

Now Impressions Inc .... G 425 881-5911
  Redmond *(G-8601)*

PAPER: Adhesive

Decal Factory .... G 509 465-8931
  Spokane *(G-12222)*

Employee Codes: A=Over 500 employees, B=251-500
C=101-250, D=51-100, E=20-50, F=10-19, G=2-9

2019 Washington Manufacturers Register

PAPER: Building Laminated, Made From Purchased Materials

Harpo Investment Inc ....F...... 360 532-5516
  Aberdeen *(G-15)*

PAPER: Building, Insulating & Packaging

Pinatas Tradedia ....G....... 509 836-2442
  Sunnyside *(G-13138)*
Sunrise Washington Inc ....G....... 360 574-3512
  Vancouver *(G-14617)*

PAPER: Business Form

Glenn Waldren ....G....... 360 570-8400
  Olympia *(G-7297)*

PAPER: Cardboard

Expensive Cardboard ....G....... 214 564-2670
  Seattle *(G-9956)*
Forged From Cardboard ....G....... 425 399-0715
  Everett *(G-3482)*
Kaddy ....G....... 360 438-3636
  Lacey *(G-5562)*

PAPER: Coated & Laminated, NEC

Adhesa-Plate Manufacturing Co ....E....... 206 682-0141
  Seattle *(G-9351)*
Adhesive Products Inc ....F....... 206 762-7459
  Seattle *(G-9352)*
Avery Dennison Corporation ....F....... 253 872-6993
  Kent *(G-4802)*
Caraustar Industries Inc ....E....... 360 423-3420
  Longview *(G-5894)*
Fedex Office & Print Svcs Inc ....F....... 360 694-8584
  Vancouver *(G-14226)*
Halldata Inc ....E....... 509 588-5080
  Benton City *(G-1615)*
Litho-Craft Inc ....G....... 253 872-9161
  Kent *(G-4997)*
Northwest Label/Design Inc ....E....... 206 282-5568
  Seattle *(G-10646)*
NRG Resources Inc ....D....... 509 588-4786
  Benton City *(G-1621)*
Paneltech International LLC ....E....... 360 538-1480
  Hoquiam *(G-4353)*
Paneltech Products Inc ....E....... 360 538-1480
  Hoquiam *(G-4355)*
Rainier Plywood Company ....E....... 253 383-5533
  Tacoma *(G-13489)*

PAPER: Corrugated

Sno King Recycling Inc ....G....... 425 582-2919
  Lynnwood *(G-6201)*

PAPER: Fine

Georgia-Pacific LLC ....G....... 253 631-3250
  Covington *(G-2828)*
Grays Harbor Paper LLC ....F....... 877 548-3424
  Renton *(G-8814)*

PAPER: Greaseproof Wrapping

Bella Cupcake Couture LLC ....G....... 425 260-3224
  Newcastle *(G-7026)*

PAPER: Newsprint

Cowles Publishing Company ....B....... 509 459-5000
  Spokane *(G-12204)*
Inland Empire Paper Company ....C....... 509 924-1911
  Spokane *(G-12307)*
North Pacific Paper Co LLC ....B....... 360 636-6400
  Longview *(G-5937)*
NP Paper Company LLC ....G....... 360 636-6400
  Longview *(G-5938)*
Ponderay Newsprint Company ....C....... 509 445-2133
  Usk *(G-13985)*
Tevada Publishing Inc ....F....... 509 783-5455
  Kennewick *(G-4734)*

PAPER: Printer

Alexander Printing Co Inc ....G....... 425 252-4212
  Everett *(G-3366)*
J & H Printing Inc ....G....... 509 332-0782
  Pullman *(G-8094)*

PAPER: Specialty

Pac-Paper Inc ....C....... 800 223-4981
  Vancouver *(G-14461)*

PAPER: Specialty Or Chemically Treated

Westrock Company ....G....... 360 575-5256
  Longview *(G-5965)*

PAPER: Tissue

Clearwater Paper Oklahoma ....G....... 405 717-5104
  Spokane *(G-12184)*
Wrap Pack Inc ....F....... 509 453-2830
  Yakima *(G-15710)*

PAPER: Wallpaper

Butler Design Inc ....G....... 360 380-1651
  Ferndale *(G-3819)*

PAPER: Wrapping & Packaging

Cassel Inc ....C....... 206 909-9584
  Bellevue *(G-841)*
Dolco Packaging Corp ....E....... 509 662-8415
  Wenatchee *(G-15026)*
LSI Logistic Svc Solutions LLC ....F....... 253 872-8970
  Puyallup *(G-8180)*
Nippon Dynawave Packg Co LLC ....A....... 360 425-2150
  Longview *(G-5935)*

PAPER: Wrapping, Waterproof Or Coated

Korblu Mfg Solutions LLC ....G....... 509 930-2010
  Yakima *(G-15609)*

PAPERBOARD

Boise Inc ....G....... 509 685-9825
  Colville *(G-2741)*
Caraustar Industrial and Con ....D....... 253 627-1197
  Tacoma *(G-13221)*
Clearwater Paper Corporation ....C....... 509 344-5900
  Spokane *(G-12183)*
Core Pack LLC ....G....... 509 426-2511
  Yakima *(G-15537)*
Packaging Corporation America ....D....... 509 545-3260
  Wallula *(G-14909)*
Port Townsend Paper Corp ....B....... 360 385-3170
  Port Townsend *(G-7912)*
Simpson Tacoma Kraft Co LLC ....G....... 253 779-6444
  Tacoma *(G-13514)*
Sonoco Products Company ....D....... 206 682-0440
  Sumner *(G-13101)*
Sonoco Products Company ....D....... 360 225-1500
  Woodland *(G-15466)*
Weyerhaeuser Company ....C....... 509 453-4741
  Union Gap *(G-13956)*

PAPERBOARD CONVERTING

Pacific Mount Inc ....F....... 253 473-2580
  Tacoma *(G-13452)*

PAPERBOARD PRDTS: Automobile Board

Action Equipment Inc ....G....... 360 897-0890
  Buckley *(G-2045)*

PAPERBOARD PRDTS: Building Insulating & Packaging

Paragon Industries Inc ....E....... 253 872-0800
  Tukwila *(G-13789)*

PAPERBOARD PRDTS: Container Board

Longview Fibre Ppr & Packg Inc ....D....... 206 762-7170
  Seattle *(G-10437)*

PAPERBOARD PRDTS: Folding Boxboard

Graphic Packaging Intl Inc ....C....... 425 235-3300
  Renton *(G-8812)*

PAPERBOARD PRDTS: Packaging Board

Nippon Dynawave Packaging Co ....G....... 360 414-3379
  Federal Way *(G-3763)*
Nippon Dynawave Packg Co LLC ....A....... 360 425-2150
  Longview *(G-5935)*

PAPERBOARD: Coated

Caraustar Industries Inc ....E....... 360 423-3420
  Longview *(G-5894)*

PARTICLEBOARD

Plywood Components Inc ....E....... 253 863-6323
  Sumner *(G-13095)*

PARTITIONS & FIXTURES: Except Wood

Belina Interiors Inc ....D....... 253 474-0276
  Tacoma *(G-13193)*
Bfc Architectural Metals Inc ....F....... 206 763-0530
  Seatac *(G-9274)*
Jpl Habitability Inc ....F....... 360 377-7660
  Bremerton *(G-1967)*
Multifab Inc ....C....... 509 924-6631
  Spokane Valley *(G-12796)*
Northwest Building Tech Inc ....E....... 206 767-4012
  Seattle *(G-10638)*
Obcon Inc ....G....... 253 931-0455
  Auburn *(G-516)*
Souers Manufacturing Inc ....G....... 253 735-2488
  Gig Harbor *(G-4161)*
T R S Inc ....F....... 253 444-1555
  Tacoma *(G-13538)*
Won-Door Corporation ....G....... 206 726-9449
  Seattle *(G-11490)*

PARTITIONS: Solid Fiber, Made From Purchased Materials

Westrock Rkt Company ....E....... 425 885-5851
  Redmond *(G-8712)*

PARTITIONS: Wood & Fixtures

Conestoga Wood Spc Corp ....G....... 253 437-1320
  Kent *(G-4863)*
Custom Craft LLC ....E....... 253 826-5450
  Sumner *(G-13064)*
King Brothers Woodworking Inc ....E....... 509 453-4683
  Union Gap *(G-13936)*
Lake Sunset LLC ....G....... 718 683-2269
  Olympia *(G-7317)*
Northwest Woodworks Inc ....E....... 425 482-9663
  Woodinville *(G-15322)*
R S Manufacturing Inc ....E....... 425 774-1211
  Lynnwood *(G-6186)*
Silver Star Industies Inc ....G....... 509 427-8800
  Stevenson *(G-13019)*
T R S Inc ....F....... 253 444-1555
  Tacoma *(G-13538)*
Tacoma Fixture Co Inc ....D....... 253 383-5541
  Tacoma *(G-13542)*
Tim Krotzer ....G....... 509 487-2704
  Spokane *(G-12558)*
Turner Exhibits Inc ....E....... 425 776-4930
  Lynnwood *(G-6214)*

PARTITIONS: Wood, Floor Attached

L Clasen Corp ....G....... 360 658-1823
  Snohomish *(G-11935)*

PARTS: Metal

All Metal Solutions ....G....... 509 426-2400
  Yakima *(G-15504)*
Gepford Welding Inc ....G....... 509 624-6610
  Spokane *(G-12272)*
Ries Productions LLC ....G....... 360 627-8795
  Bremerton *(G-1994)*
South Sound Metal Inc ....G....... 253 564-0226
  University Place *(G-13981)*

PATCHING PLASTER: Household

Energy Saver Products Inc ....G....... 888 778-4537
  Vancouver *(G-14202)*

PATENT OWNERS & LESSORS

Battle Ground Auto License ....G....... 360 687-5115
  Battle Ground *(G-691)*
Microtemp Electronics ....G....... 360 256-6789
  Vancouver *(G-14420)*

PATTERNS: Indl

Aim Aerospace Sumner Inc ....F....... 253 804-3355
  Auburn *(G-366)*

PRODUCT SECTION

PETROLEUM PRDTS WHOLESALERS

Functional Patterns Llc ....G...... 619 565-3955
Seattle *(G-10038)*
Model One ....G...... 206 383-0380
Seattle *(G-10552)*
Modern Pattern Works Inc ....G...... 206 762-2227
Seattle *(G-10554)*
Pattern Integrity LLC ....G...... 503 752-6018
Camas *(G-2273)*
Patterns In Nature LLC ....G...... 360 918-2629
Olympia *(G-7366)*
Precision Pattern ....G...... 253 572-4333
Tacoma *(G-13475)*
Puget Sound Pattern Inc ....G...... 206 439-6810
Tukwila *(G-13799)*
Woodland Pattern Inc ....F...... 253 475-3131
Tacoma *(G-13599)*

PAVERS

Bc Pavers Inc ....G...... 425 413-2110
Renton *(G-8753)*
Plano Bros Paving Inc ....G...... 425 226-8210
Newcastle *(G-7038)*
Puget Lite-Pavers Inc ....G...... 206 849-7091
Seattle *(G-10883)*
Rios Brick Pavers ....G...... 206 271-3447
Redmond *(G-8652)*

PAWN SHOPS

Bowlbys Sporting Goods ....G...... 509 248-8281
Yakima *(G-15524)*
Wapato Pawn & Trade ....G...... 509 877-6405
Wapato *(G-14928)*

PENS & PARTS: Ball Point

Djs Pens ....G...... 360 565-0145
Port Angeles *(G-7697)*

PERFUME: Concentrated

Marie-Luce Enterprises ....G...... 360 876-7925
Port Orchard *(G-7827)*

PERFUMES

Altera Inc ....F...... 509 901-9292
Yakima *(G-15505)*
Green Global Solution Inc ....G...... 253 202-2304
Tacoma *(G-13324)*
Le Labo ....G...... 206 420-2835
Seattle *(G-10390)*
Patricia Avery ....G...... 206 602-0017
Tacoma *(G-13460)*
Raw Chemistry LLC ....G...... 360 521-2115
Vancouver *(G-14534)*

PERISCOPES

Periscope Sls & Analytics LLC ....G...... 503 707-1907
Vancouver *(G-14485)*
Red Periscope Technologie ....G...... 253 851-3968
Gig Harbor *(G-4154)*

PERSONAL CREDIT INSTITUTIONS: Financing, Autos, Furniture

Ford Motor Credit Company LLC ....D...... 425 643-0454
Bellevue *(G-914)*

PERSONAL DOCUMENT & INFORMATION SVCS

5th Wave Mobile Tech Inc ....G...... 425 898-8161
Gig Harbor *(G-4070)*

PEST CONTROL IN STRUCTURES SVCS

R and M Exterminators Inc ....E...... 509 239-4411
Cheney *(G-2591)*

PESTICIDES

Freedomweeder Company LLC ....G...... 509 673-0014
Tieton *(G-13630)*
Matson LLC ....E...... 425 888-6212
North Bend *(G-7115)*
Tanada Corporation ....G...... 425 396-1050
North Bend *(G-7127)*

PESTICIDES WHOLESALERS

J L Innovations Inc ....G...... 425 823-8540
Kenmore *(G-4584)*

PET ACCESS: Collars, Leashes, Etc, Exc Leather

Browbandsbydesigncom ....G...... 360 779-9339
Poulsbo *(G-7952)*
Sandbox Enterprises LLC ....G...... 360 966-6677
Bellingham *(G-1523)*

PET COLLARS, LEASHES, MUZZLES & HARNESSES: Leather

Campbell Pet Company ....F...... 360 892-9786
Vancouver *(G-14093)*
Dolans Dog Doodads LLC ....G...... 206 257-4518
Seattle *(G-9844)*

PET FOOD WHOLESALERS

Bio-Tope Research Inc ....G...... 509 684-1512
Colville *(G-2739)*
Cobbs LLC ....G...... 360 302-2692
Olympia *(G-7250)*
Good Pet Food Inc ....G...... 310 430-3833
Seattle *(G-10099)*
Landy Corporation ....G...... 253 835-1427
Federal Way *(G-3751)*
Natural Pet Pantry ....G...... 206 762-5575
Seattle *(G-10593)*
Pet Media Plus LLC ....G...... 360 425-0188
Longview *(G-5942)*

PET SPLYS

3 CS ....G...... 509 246-1451
Soap Lake *(G-12036)*
Ballboy LLC ....G...... 425 281-9152
North Bend *(G-7101)*
D&S Innovative Enterprises ....G...... 509 467-2032
Nine Mile Falls *(G-7071)*
Dk9 Dog Walking ....G...... 425 922-4685
Covington *(G-2825)*
Dogsdream Corporation ....G...... 425 737-2810
Seattle *(G-9843)*
Drama Nine LLP ....G...... 206 949-2953
Seattle *(G-9854)*
Fido N-Scratch ....G...... 206 588-2111
Seattle *(G-9988)*
Grizzly Pet Products LLC ....G...... 425 481-1110
Woodinville *(G-15257)*
Healthy Pet LP ....C...... 360 734-7415
Ferndale *(G-3850)*
Kason Pet Supply ....G...... 360 886-2306
Maple Valley *(G-6279)*
Landy Corporation ....E...... 253 835-1427
Federal Way *(G-3751)*
Lucky Dog Eqp Inc DBA Pet Pros ....E...... 425 402-8833
Woodinville *(G-15297)*
Moore-Clark USA Inc ....E...... 360 425-6715
Longview *(G-5932)*
Nordkyn Outfitters ....G...... 253 847-4128
Eatonville *(G-3063)*
Northwest Seed & Pet Inc ....F...... 509 484-7387
Spokane *(G-12414)*
Ocean In A Box ....G...... 360 573-2250
Vancouver *(G-14446)*
Pacific Sales & Service ....G...... 425 271-9000
Renton *(G-8873)*
Pam S Bubble Mobile ....G...... 360 630-5511
Mount Vernon *(G-6821)*
Pawpular Companions Bouti ....G...... 509 850-6070
Liberty Lake *(G-5851)*
Pet Media Plus LLC ....G...... 360 425-0188
Longview *(G-5942)*
Platinum Pets LLC ....F...... 360 859-4027
Vancouver *(G-14489)*
Poopless In Seattle ....G...... 425 444-6930
North Bend *(G-7121)*
Puppy Stairs ....G...... 360 387-4861
Camano Island *(G-2222)*
Recall ....G...... 253 272-2813
Fife *(G-3986)*
Rivermist Labradoodles ....G...... 509 427-4810
Stevenson *(G-13018)*
Sally and Harry Simmons ....G...... 206 297-1868
Seattle *(G-11006)*
Secondhand Hound ....G...... 253 232-9432
Ruston *(G-9178)*
Smiley Dog ....G...... 206 903-9631
Bothell *(G-1906)*
Sophies Touch ....G...... 253 677-1061
Fox Island *(G-4025)*
United Farms ....F...... 253 847-4230
Graham *(G-4241)*
Vanex Industries LLC ....G...... 206 860-0455
Seattle *(G-11403)*
Wesnip ....G...... 360 306-0345
Bellingham *(G-1591)*
Wychwood Inc ....G...... 209 667-8188
Elk *(G-3179)*
Xtreme Pet Products LLC ....G...... 206 772-2000
Renton *(G-8951)*

PET SPLYS WHOLESALERS

Fido N-Scratch ....G...... 206 588-2111
Seattle *(G-9988)*
Pet Media Plus LLC ....G...... 360 425-0188
Longview *(G-5942)*
Raw Advantage Inc ....G...... 509 738-3344
Kettle Falls *(G-5240)*

PETROLEUM & PETROLEUM PRDTS, WHOL Svc Station Splys, Petro

Ironclad Company ....G...... 206 588-2272
Tukwila *(G-13754)*
Whitten Group International ....F...... 360 560-3319
Longview *(G-5968)*

PETROLEUM & PETROLEUM PRDTS, WHOLESALE Diesel Fuel

Cenex Supply & Marketing Inc ....G...... 509 488-5261
Othello *(G-7491)*

PETROLEUM & PETROLEUM PRDTS, WHOLESALE Engine Fuels & Oils

Defbooty LLC ....G...... 800 311-5887
Chehalis *(G-2488)*
Filter Clean Recycling LLC ....G...... 360 798-1012
Vancouver *(G-14230)*
Tesoro Refining & Mktg Co LLC ....G...... 360 293-9119
Anacortes *(G-177)*

PETROLEUM & PETROLEUM PRDTS, WHOLESALE Fuel Oil

Sovrano Di Ricchezza Group ....G...... 425 449-8011
Bellevue *(G-1150)*

PETROLEUM & PETROLEUM PRDTS, WHOLESALE Petroleum Brokers

Yorkston Oil Co ....F...... 360 734-2201
Bellingham *(G-1597)*

PETROLEUM & PETROLEUM PRDTS, WHOLESALE Petroleum Terminals

Sunoco Inc ....G...... 253 872-8500
Kent *(G-5162)*

PETROLEUM & PETROLEUM PRDTS, WHOLESALE: Bulk Stations

Tri-Tex Inc ....E...... 360 274-8511
Castle Rock *(G-2356)*

PETROLEUM BULK STATIONS & TERMINALS

Conocophillips Company ....F...... 509 536-8417
Spokane Valley *(G-12663)*
Semgroup Corp ....G...... 509 921-7089
Spokane Valley *(G-12864)*
Semgroup Corporation ....G...... 509 487-4560
Spokane *(G-12498)*

PETROLEUM PRDTS WHOLESALERS

Interlube International Inc ....E...... 360 734-3832
Bellingham *(G-1381)*
Tri-Tex Inc ....E...... 360 274-8511
Castle Rock *(G-2356)*

Employee Codes: A=Over 500 employees, B=251-500
C=101-250, D=51-100, E=20-50, F=10-19, G=2-9

PETS & PET SPLYS, WHOLESALE

PETS & PET SPLYS, WHOLESALE

Stason Animal Health Inc .... G 360 200-5300
  Vancouver (G-14609)

PHARMACEUTICAL PREPARATIONS: Druggists' Preparations

David Bol .... G 425 802-0804
  Spokane (G-12219)
Implicit Bioscience Inc .... G 650 851-3133
  Seattle (G-10215)

PHARMACEUTICAL PREPARATIONS: Medicines, Capsule Or Ampule

Promedev LLC .... G 800 500-8384
  Kirkland (G-5444)

PHARMACEUTICAL PREPARATIONS: Proprietary Drug PRDTS

Altan Inc .... G 360 331-1595
  Greenbank (G-4304)

PHARMACEUTICAL PREPARATIONS: Solutions

CMC Biologics SARI Corp .... E 425 485-1900
  Bothell (G-1840)
Olympic Protein Sciences LLC .... G 206 849-9811
  Seattle (G-10694)

PHARMACEUTICAL PREPARATIONS: Tablets

Nuun & Company Inc .... D 206 219-9237
  Seattle (G-10671)

PHARMACEUTICALS

ABT 360 LLC .... G 509 592-8144
  Pullman (G-8081)
Achieve Life Science Inc .... G 425 686-1500
  Bothell (G-1744)
Achieve Life Sciences Inc .... G 425 686-1500
  Seattle (G-9342)
AGC Biologics Inc .... C 425 485-0280
  Bothell (G-1816)
Alder Biopharmaceuticals Inc .... D 425 205-2900
  Bothell (G-1745)
Aletheia Therapeutics LLC .... G 206 473-2435
  Seattle (G-9371)
Alphapharma Inc .... G 206 413-5122
  Renton (G-8741)
Alpine Immune Sciences Inc .... E 206 788-4545
  Seattle (G-9388)
Amgen Inc .... A 206 265-7504
  Seattle (G-9397)
Aptevo Therapeutics Inc .... D 206 838-0500
  Seattle (G-9414)
Aq Usa Inc .... G 800 663-8303
  Lynden (G-6001)
Artemisia Biomedical Inc .... G 425 444-5619
  Newcastle (G-7024)
Athira Pharma Inc .... F 206 221-8112
  Seattle (G-9451)
Atossa Genetics Inc .... G 206 325-6086
  Seattle (G-9457)
Avantbio Corporation .... G 360 521-8904
  Seattle (G-9470)
Avantbio Corporation .... G 360 521-8904
  Vancouver (G-14046)
Bausch Health Americas Inc .... G 425 346-2472
  Bothell (G-1751)
Bayer Healthcare LLC .... C 425 245-1392
  Lynnwood (G-6082)
Bayer Healthcare LLC .... G 360 886-8182
  Ravensdale (G-8330)
Bergstrom Nutrition .... G 360 693-0601
  Vancouver (G-14061)
Briotech Inc .... G 425 488-4300
  Woodinville (G-15197)
Cardeas Pharma Corporation .... F 206 973-1026
  Seattle (G-9628)
Cardinal Health 414 LLC .... G 206 763-4411
  Seattle (G-9630)
Celgene Corporation .... D 415 839-7058
  Seattle (G-9650)
Central Admxture Phrm Svcs Inc ...... E 253 395-8700
  Kent (G-4846)
Cocrystal Pharma Inc .... F 786 459-1831
  Bothell (G-1756)
Coronado Biosciences .... G 206 826-7168
  Seattle (G-9742)
CTI Biopharma Corp .... D 206 282-7100
  Seattle (G-9762)
Cytodyn Operations Inc .... G 360 980-8524
  Vancouver (G-14159)
Dendreon Corporation .... B 877 256-4545
  Seattle (G-9820)
Dendreon Corporation .... C 206 256-4545
  Seattle (G-9821)
Endpoint LLC .... G 206 780-2905
  Bainbridge Island (G-630)
Estm Inc .... G 509 545-0596
  Kennewick (G-4664)
Faraday Pharmaceuticals Inc .... G 206 946-1989
  Seattle (G-9971)
Furtim Therapeutics LLC .... G 425 273-1035
  Seattle (G-10041)
Genoa Healthcare LLC .... G 206 971-9707
  Seattle (G-10061)
Gilead Sciences Inc .... G 206 728-5090
  Seattle (G-10070)
Glaxosmithkline LLC .... E 206 755-5725
  Bellevue (G-926)
Glaxosmithkline LLC .... E 206 856-5663
  Kenmore (G-4576)
Hebert Sam-E LLC .... G 206 650-4489
  Seattle (G-10159)
Helix Biomedix Inc .... G 425 402-8400
  Bothell (G-1865)
Immune Design Corp .... D 206 682-0645
  Seattle (G-10209)
Immunex Corporation .... A 206 551-5169
  Seattle (G-10210)
Impel Neuropharma Inc .... G 206 568-1466
  Seattle (G-10211)
Integrity Biopharma Services .... G 509 474-1481
  Spokane (G-12320)
Jubilant Hollisterstier LLC .... B 509 482-4945
  Spokane (G-12345)
Jubilant Hollisterstier LLC .... G 509 482-3287
  Spokane Valley (G-12756)
Key Technology Inc .... B 509 529-2161
  Walla Walla (G-14833)
Kiadis Pharma US Corporation .... G 585 397-1074
  Seattle (G-10342)
Lyell Immunopharma Inc .... G 206 909-3809
  Seattle (G-10455)
Medicines Co .... G 425 829-2540
  Snohomish (G-11945)
Medicis Technologies Corp .... D 425 420-2100
  Bothell (G-1778)
Mk Perrigo Realtor .... G 425 478-6694
  Seattle (G-10551)
Morton A Kimball .... G 360 458-5251
  Yelm (G-15740)
Novartis Vccnes Dagnostics Inc .... C 862 778-2100
  Seattle (G-10659)
Oberon Pharma .... G 206 713-5467
  Mercer Island (G-6476)
Omeros Corporation .... C 206 676-5000
  Seattle (G-10698)
Pd Pharmatech LLC .... G 800 452-4682
  Seattle (G-10774)
Permesys Inc .... G 860 961-5367
  Bothell (G-1885)
Pfizer Inc .... C 360 701-0799
  Lacey (G-5576)
Poa Pharma North America LLC ...... G 855 416-6826
  Vancouver (G-14491)
Pz Wind Down Inc .... G 206 805-6300
  Seattle (G-10895)
Rainier Clinical Research Ctr .... E 425 251-1720
  Renton (G-8891)
Remeopharma Inc .... F 206 805-9786
  Bainbridge Island (G-665)
Resolve Therapeutics LLC .... G 208 727-7010
  Seattle (G-10951)
Ross Group of Companies Inc .... G 800 663-8303
  Lynden (G-6050)
Sbk Pharma LLC .... G 425 778-7778
  Edmonds (G-3152)
Skinmedica Inc .... G 760 448-3600
  Olympia (G-7397)
Specialized Pharmaceuticals .... G 253 859-3702
  Kent (G-5147)
Stier Hollister Sales .... G 509 892-1188
  Spokane Valley (G-12894)
Sunn Pharmaceuticals LLC .... G 425 835-0418
  Mountlake Terrace (G-6870)
Takeda Pharmaceuticals USA Inc .... G 509 747-5551
  Spokane (G-12544)
Tyson Nutraceuticals Inc .... G 425 869-1192
  Kirkland (G-5487)
Unigen Inc .... F 360 486-8200
  Seattle (G-11368)
US Biopharma Inc .... G 425 242-0208
  Bellevue (G-1209)
Zumedix LP .... G 206 618-2848
  Seattle (G-11526)
Zymogenetics Inc .... C 206 442-6600
  Seattle (G-11527)
Zymogenetics Inc .... G 425 398-9637
  Bothell (G-1925)

PHARMACEUTICALS: Medicinal & Botanical Prdts

Awakened Heart .... G 360 556-6168
  Olympia (G-7233)
Blue Moon Marine LLC .... G 360 378-2498
  Friday Harbor (G-4041)
Econet Inc .... E 360 486-8300
  Seattle (G-9880)
Farwell Products Inc .... G 509 663-6212
  Wenatchee (G-15030)
Glykon Technologies Group LLC ...... G 510 289-4331
  Seattle (G-10089)
Human Science LLC .... G 253 321-6800
  Sumner (G-13074)
Integrity Supplements LLC .... G 800 210-4863
  Bremerton (G-1962)
Nbty Inc .... G 425 369-1771
  Issaquah (G-4452)
Pacific Coast Cascara Bark Co .... G 360 249-3503
  Montesano (G-6652)
Tilray Inc .... G 206 432-9325
  Seattle (G-11308)
Trout Lake Farm LLC .... E 509 395-2025
  Trout Lake (G-13684)
Urban Buggy LLC .... G 206 743-5727
  Seattle (G-11389)

PHOSPHATE ROCK MINING

NA Degerstrom Inc .... E 509 928-3333
  Spokane Valley (G-12800)

PHOTOCOPYING & DUPLICATING SVCS

A & H Printers Inc .... G 509 765-0283
  Moses Lake (G-6676)
Abadan Repo Graphics .... E 509 946-7697
  Richland (G-8963)
B & B Express Printing .... G 509 783-7383
  Kennewick (G-4622)
Bellevue Printing LLC .... G 425 558-1862
  Bellevue (G-814)
Business Equipment Center Inc .... F 509 747-2964
  Spokane (G-12162)
Copy Break .... G 206 782-7506
  Seattle (G-9739)
Copy Shop .... G 509 962-2679
  Ellensburg (G-3190)
Copy-Rite Inc .... G 509 624-8503
  Spokane (G-12200)
Digital Impressions Inc .... G 206 443-1234
  Seattle (G-9828)
Fedex Office & Print Svcs Inc .... F 509 922-4929
  Spokane Valley (G-12700)
Fedex Office & Print Svcs Inc .... E 360 647-1114
  Bellingham (G-1344)
Fedex Office & Print Svcs Inc .... E 509 484-0601
  Spokane (G-12254)
Fedex Office & Print Svcs Inc .... F 360 694-8584
  Vancouver (G-14226)
Fedex Office & Print Svcs Inc .... E 206 467-1767
  Seattle (G-9981)
Fedex Office & Print Svcs Inc .... E 206 244-8884
  Tukwila (G-13733)
Fedex Office & Print Svcs Inc .... E 253 841-3557
  Puyallup (G-8152)
Fedex Office & Print Svcs Inc .... E 206 546-7600
  Shoreline (G-11771)
Fedex Office & Print Svcs Inc .... E 253 565-4882
  Tacoma (G-13292)
Fedexoffice .... G 206 467-5885
  Seattle (G-9982)
Graphic Communications Inc .... G 425 251-8680
  Renton (G-8811)

PRODUCT SECTION

Harold Tymer Co Inc .... F 360 573-6053
  Vancouver *(G-14284)*
In Graphic Detail LLC .... G 360 582-0002
  Sequim *(G-11641)*
Inland Saxum Printing LLC ....G 509 525-0467
  Walla Walla *(G-14823)*
Jet City Printing Inc .... G 425 485-8611
  Kenmore *(G-4585)*
King Enterprises .... G 360 568-1644
  Snohomish *(G-11933)*
Kitsap Business Services Inc .... G 360 297-2173
  Kingston *(G-5257)*
Marshall Marketing Group Inc .... E 253 473-0765
  Tacoma *(G-13400)*
Master Printing Inc .... G 509 684-5869
  Colville *(G-2765)*
Mountain Top Inc .... G 360 416-3433
  Mount Vernon *(G-6814)*
Nannette Louise Davis .... G 425 485-5570
  Woodinville *(G-15317)*
Northwest Executive Corp .... G 425 883-9010
  Redmond *(G-8598)*
P I P Printing Inc .... F 360 456-4742
  Olympia *(G-7364)*
Prestige Copy and Print .... G 206 365-5770
  Seattle *(G-10857)*
Print NW LLC .... D 253 284-2300
  Tacoma *(G-13478)*
Sams Press Inc .... G 425 423-8181
  Shoreline *(G-11807)*
SOS Printing .... G 360 385-4194
  Port Townsend *(G-7927)*
Stat Corporation .... F 425 883-4181
  Redmond *(G-8681)*
Sudden Printing Inc .... E 206 243-4444
  Seattle *(G-11211)*
Tcc Printing and Imaging Inc .... G 206 622-4050
  Seattle *(G-11276)*
Tom & Cheryl McCallaum .... G 360 377-1606
  Bremerton *(G-2006)*
Van Quill Larry R .... G 360 736-1776
  Centralia *(G-2441)*
Yvonne Roberts .... G 253 531-3105
  Tacoma *(G-13606)*
Zebra Printing Inc .... F 425 462-9775
  Bellevue *(G-1233)*

PHOTOELECTRIC CELLS: Electronic Eye, Solid State

Nec Corp of America .... G 425 373-4400
  Bellevue *(G-1023)*

PHOTOENGRAVING SVC

William Louis Becker .... G 509 624-3466
  Spokane *(G-12593)*

PHOTOFINISHING LABORATORIES

Signs For Success .... G 509 489-4200
  Spokane *(G-12504)*

PHOTOGRAPH DEVELOPING & RETOUCHING SVCS

Media Matrix Digital Center .... G 360 693-6455
  Vancouver *(G-14408)*

PHOTOGRAPHIC EQPT & CAMERAS, WHOLESALE

Ries Productions LLC .... G 360 627-8795
  Bremerton *(G-1994)*

PHOTOGRAPHIC EQPT & SPLY: Sound Recordg/Reprod Eqpt, Motion

Beats4legends .... G 253 218-5075
  Seattle *(G-9507)*
Component Engineering Inc .... F 206 284-9171
  Shoreline *(G-11767)*

PHOTOGRAPHIC EQPT & SPLYS

Business Computing Solutions .... G 425 644-6174
  Bellevue *(G-832)*
Comp U Charge Inc .... F 509 484-1918
  Spokane *(G-12194)*
Express Imaging Systems LLC .... F 206 720-1798
  Renton *(G-8796)*
Freefly Systems Inc .... E 425 485-5500
  Woodinville *(G-15249)*
Tobin Cinema Systems Inc .... G 509 621-0323
  Spokane Valley *(G-12908)*
Xerox Corp Xerox Corporat .... G 425 947-7046
  Redmond *(G-8719)*

PHOTOGRAPHIC EQPT & SPLYS: Developers, Not Chemical Plants

CMX Corporation .... E 425 656-1269
  Tukwila *(G-13713)*
Pryde Johnson 1536 LLC .... G 206 352-7000
  Seattle *(G-10879)*

PHOTOGRAPHIC EQPT & SPLYS: Graphic Arts Plates, Sensitized

Printers Shopper LLC .... G 425 822-7766
  Kirkland *(G-5442)*

PHOTOGRAPHIC EQPT & SPLYS: Printing Eqpt

Brooke Engrg Photographic Eqp .... F 360 638-2591
  Hansville *(G-4314)*

PHOTOGRAPHIC EQPT & SPLYS: Printing Frames

Silhouette Graphics .... G 360 758-4163
  Bellingham *(G-1537)*

PHOTOGRAPHIC EQPT & SPLYS: Toners, Prprd, Not Chem Plnts

Profile Systems Inc .... F 206 624-7715
  Seattle *(G-10873)*
Rgd Enterprises Inc .... G 360 923-9582
  Olympia *(G-7385)*

PHOTOGRAPHY SVCS: Commercial

Goodall Productions Inc .... G 206 722-0544
  Seattle *(G-10100)*
Mitchell Osborne .... G 360 379-2427
  Port Townsend *(G-7898)*
Richard C Busher Jr .... G 206 524-6726
  Seattle *(G-10961)*
University Reprographics Inc .... G 206 633-0925
  Seattle *(G-11385)*

PHOTOGRAPHY SVCS: Portrait Studios

Bizzybee LLC .... G 206 707-9417
  Seattle *(G-9535)*
Media Matrix Digital Center .... G 360 693-6455
  Vancouver *(G-14408)*
Washington Media Services Inc .... G 360 754-4543
  Olympia *(G-7421)*

PHOTOGRAPHY SVCS: Still Or Video

Creating Memories Together .... G 360 944-8393
  Vancouver *(G-14153)*
Kith D Lazelles Nture Phtgrphy .... G 360 765-3697
  Quilcene *(G-8286)*

PHYSICAL FITNESS CENTERS

Stretch 22 Inc .... G 206 375-3358
  Seattle *(G-11202)*

PHYSICIANS' OFFICES & CLINICS: Medical doctors

Biodynamics Corporation .... G 206 526-0205
  Shoreline *(G-11762)*
Coenzyme-A Technologies Inc .... F 425 438-8586
  Lynnwood *(G-6094)*
Custom Ocular Prosthetics .... G 206 522-4222
  Seattle *(G-9770)*
Ellensburg Eye & Cntact Lens C .... G 509 925-1000
  Ellensburg *(G-3195)*
Howard F Harrison M D .... G 509 575-8307
  Yakima *(G-15586)*
Hoya Optical Laboratories .... E 253 475-7809
  Tacoma *(G-13344)*
Northwest Runner .... G 206 527-5301
  Seattle *(G-10651)*
P S Northwest Radiography .... G 253 627-3988
  Tacoma *(G-13447)*
United Contact Lens Inc .... G 360 474-9577
  Arlington *(G-343)*

PICTURE FRAMES: Metal

Elite Frames Inc .... G 360 247-7300
  Amboy *(G-91)*

PICTURE FRAMES: Wood

Artists Edge Inc .... G 360 779-2337
  Poulsbo *(G-7945)*
Artists Edge Inc .... G 360 698-3113
  Silverdale *(G-11826)*
Book N Brush .... G 360 748-6221
  Chehalis *(G-2472)*
Elite Frames Inc .... G 360 247-7300
  Amboy *(G-91)*
Ferguson Merchandising LLC .... D 425 883-2050
  Redmond *(G-8460)*
Frame It Ltd .... G 206 364-7477
  Seattle *(G-10019)*
Julias Lumber .... G 509 966-0925
  Yakima *(G-15603)*
Pacific Frame Source LLC .... G 800 292-3202
  Woodinville *(G-15329)*
Summer Rrh LLC .... F 509 328-0915
  Spokane *(G-12532)*
Village Frame & Gallery .... G 206 824-3068
  Des Moines *(G-2950)*
Williamson Illustration .... G 360 734-5497
  Ferndale *(G-3925)*

PICTURE FRAMING SVCS, CUSTOM

Ferguson Merchandising LLC .... D 425 883-2050
  Redmond *(G-8460)*
Its A Wrap Washington Inc .... G 425 827-2000
  Kirkland *(G-5371)*

PIECE GOODS, NOTIONS & DRY GOODS, WHOL: Fabrics, Fiberglass

George Broom Sons Inc .... G 206 282-0800
  Seattle *(G-10064)*

PIECE GOODS, NOTIONS & DRY GOODS, WHOL: Textiles, Woven

Northwest Linings & Geo .... E 253 872-0244
  Kent *(G-5033)*

PIECE GOODS, NOTIONS & DRY GOODS, WHOLESALE: Belt/Bckl Kits

Ralston Cunningham Associates .... G 425 455-0316
  Redmond *(G-8645)*

PIECE GOODS, NOTIONS & OTHER DRY GOODS, WHOL: Flags/Banners

American Edge LLC .... F 509 937-4404
  Valley *(G-13987)*
Decal Factory .... G 509 465-8931
  Spokane *(G-12222)*
Sandbox Enterprises LLC .... G 360 966-6677
  Bellingham *(G-1523)*

PIECE GOODS, NOTIONS & OTHER DRY GOODS, WHOLESALE: Fabrics

Tiegrrr Straps Inc .... G 253 520-0303
  Kent *(G-5180)*

PIECE GOODS, NOTIONS/DRY GOODS, WHOL: Drapery Mtrl, Woven

Evergreen Textiles .... G 253 852-6565
  Auburn *(G-434)*

PIGMENTS, INORGANIC: Chrome Green, Chrome Yellow, Zinc Yellw

Glass Restoration Specialists .... E 253 473-7779
  Tacoma *(G-13311)*

PILLOW FILLING MTRLS: Curled Hair, Cotton Waste, Moss

Sassy Pillows .... G 425 778-7783
  Edmonds *(G-3151)*

Employee Codes: A=Over 500 employees, B=251-500
C=101-250, D=51-100, E=20-50, F=10-19, G=2-9

PILLOWCASES

Milo & Gabby LLC ....G...... 206 257-1957
  Seattle *(G-10544)*
Nestor Enterprises LLC ....G...... 206 794-4989
  Edmonds *(G-3136)*

PINS

Closest To The Pin Inc ....G...... 425 820-2297
  Kirkland *(G-5308)*
J & R Mercantile ....G...... 425 486-6402
  Kenmore *(G-4583)*
Pin City Wrestling Club ....G...... 425 327-8518
  Lake Stevens *(G-5669)*
Waldon Abel Guide Pins LLC ....G...... 509 684-2009
  Colville *(G-2781)*

PIPE & FITTING: Fabrication

Alaskan Copper Companies Inc ....B...... 206 623-5800
  Kent *(G-4768)*
Alaskan Copper Companies Inc ....G...... 206 623-5800
  Seattle *(G-9367)*
Alaskan Copper Companies Inc ....E...... 206 623-5800
  Kent *(G-4769)*
Alco Investment Company ....C...... 206 623-5800
  Kent *(G-4770)*
Centerline Fabricators LLC ....G...... 253 922-3226
  Fife *(G-3941)*
Chinook Mechanical LLC ....G...... 360 947-9035
  Vancouver *(G-14118)*
Fluid Controls and Components ....F...... 253 922-3226
  Fife *(G-3953)*
Metal Meister Inc ....G...... 480 845-6717
  Valleyford *(G-13998)*
Northwest Pipe Company ....F...... 801 326-6044
  Vancouver *(G-14437)*
Offshore Products Inc ....G...... 206 567-5404
  Edmonds *(G-3140)*
Star Pipe LLC ....G...... 253 826-3950
  Sumner *(G-13103)*
University Swaging Corporation ....C...... 425 318-1965
  Bellevue *(G-1208)*

PIPE & FITTINGS: Cast Iron

Specified Fittings LLC ....C...... 360 398-7700
  Bellingham *(G-1551)*

PIPE & TUBES: Seamless

Scot Industries Inc ....D...... 360 623-1305
  Centralia *(G-2431)*

PIPE CLEANERS

Pringles Power-Vac Inc ....G...... 509 375-0500
  Richland *(G-9036)*

PIPE SECTIONS, FABRICATED FROM PURCHASED PIPE

Harris Acquisition IV LLC ....G...... 360 734-3600
  Bellingham *(G-1366)*
Harris Acquisition IV LLC ....G...... 360 734-3600
  Bellingham *(G-1367)*

PIPE: Concrete

Ameron International Corp ....D...... 909 944-4100
  Vancouver *(G-14029)*
Reese Concrete Products Mfg ....F...... 509 586-3704
  Kennewick *(G-4716)*

PIPE: Plastic

Advanced Drainage Systems Inc ....E...... 360 943-3313
  Olympia *(G-7221)*
Advanced Drainage Systems Inc ....E...... 360 835-8523
  Washougal *(G-14939)*
Cresline-Northwest LLC ....E...... 360 740-0700
  Chehalis *(G-2487)*
Ershigs Inc ....F...... 360 733-2620
  Bellingham *(G-1338)*
Hancor Inc ....E...... 360 943-3313
  Olympia *(G-7302)*
J-M Manufacturing Company Inc ....E...... 509 837-7800
  Sunnyside *(G-13128)*
Norma Industries ....G...... 253 208-1728
  Puyallup *(G-8200)*
Plactic Services and Products ....E...... 360 736-5616
  Centralia *(G-2424)*

Simpson Investment Company ....D...... 253 272-0158
  Seattle *(G-11115)*
Superlon Plastics Co Inc ....F...... 253 383-4000
  Tacoma *(G-13530)*

PIPE: Plate Fabricated, Large Diameter

Ram Piping Industries Inc ....F...... 509 586-0801
  Kennewick *(G-4714)*

PIPE: Water, Cast Iron

H D Fowler Co Inc ....D...... 425 746-8400
  Bellevue *(G-934)*

PIPELINE & POWER LINE INSPECTION SVCS

Shepp Enterprises LLC ....G...... 206 697-0327
  Tacoma *(G-13512)*

PIPELINES: Crude Petroleum

Conocophillips Company ....F...... 509 536-8417
  Spokane Valley *(G-12663)*
Semgroup Corp ....G...... 509 921-7089
  Spokane Valley *(G-12864)*
Semgroup Corporation ....G...... 509 487-4560
  Spokane *(G-12498)*

PIPELINES: Refined Petroleum

Conocophillips Company ....F...... 509 536-8417
  Spokane Valley *(G-12663)*

PIPES & FITTINGS: Fiber, Made From Purchased Materials

Pipe Vlves Fttngs Wrldwide Inc ....G...... 509 991-7191
  Newman Lake *(G-7051)*

PIPES & TUBES

Thermal Pipe Shields ....G...... 425 330-3765
  Stanwood *(G-12996)*

PIPES & TUBES: Steel

Ameron International Corp ....C...... 909 944-4100
  Vancouver *(G-14030)*
Ameron International Corp ....E...... 909 944-4100
  Vancouver *(G-14031)*
Bigfoot Pipe & Piling LLC ....G...... 425 882-1000
  Puyallup *(G-8130)*
Garmire Iron Works Inc ....G...... 360 651-1001
  Marysville *(G-6339)*
Metal One America Inc ....G...... 206 223-2273
  Seattle *(G-10520)*
Mill Man Steel Inc ....F...... 909 854-7020
  Spokane Valley *(G-12790)*
Puget Sound Pipe and Supply Co ....F...... 509 783-0474
  Kennewick *(G-4711)*

PIPES & TUBES: Welded

Northwest Pipe Company ....D...... 360 397-6250
  Vancouver *(G-14436)*

PIPES: Tobacco

King Mountain Tobacco Co Inc ....D...... 509 874-9935
  White Swan *(G-15138)*

PLANING MILL, NEC

Bennett Lumber Products Inc ....C...... 208 875-1321
  Clarkston *(G-2624)*
Hampton Dist Companies LLC ....D...... 360 496-5115
  Randle *(G-8325)*

PLANING MILLS: Independent, Exc Millwork

Peterson Manufacturing Co ....F...... 360 425-4170
  Longview *(G-5943)*

PLANING MILLS: Millwork

King Brothers Woodworking Inc ....E...... 509 453-4683
  Union Gap *(G-13936)*

PLANT HORMONES

Plant Hormones LLC ....G...... 253 332-6131
  Auburn *(G-532)*

PLANTERS & FLOWER POTS, WHOLESALE

Washington Pottery Co ....G...... 425 656-7277
  Kent *(G-5208)*

PLANTERS: Plastic

Camoflage ....G...... 425 744-0764
  Edmonds *(G-3099)*
Dp West ....G...... 360 825-7660
  Enumclaw *(G-3287)*
Garden Bucket LLC ....G...... 425 828-6500
  Kirkland *(G-5346)*

PLAQUES: Picture, Laminated

Don Macintosh ....G...... 425 821-1499
  Kirkland *(G-5322)*

PLASMAS

Csl Plasma Inc ....G...... 253 275-2243
  Federal Way *(G-3728)*
Guys Plasma NW LLC ....G...... 360 878-9826
  Olympia *(G-7301)*
Octapharma Plasma ....G...... 360 450-3135
  Vancouver *(G-14447)*
Octapharma Plasma ....G...... 253 922-7753
  Fife *(G-3975)*
Plasma Biolife Services L P ....G...... 509 545-3008
  Pasco *(G-7617)*
Plasma Steel LLC ....G...... 360 801-0444
  Bremerton *(G-1988)*

PLASTIC PRDTS

Advanced Plastic & Metal Wldng ....G...... 509 466-1986
  Nine Mile Falls *(G-7067)*
AP Interprices ....G...... 360 837-2548
  Washougal *(G-14943)*
Desco Plastics LLC ....G...... 360 413-7787
  Olympia *(G-7269)*
Graves Spray Supply Inc ....G...... 253 854-2660
  Kent *(G-4927)*
Mercury Plastics LLC ....G...... 360 693-0627
  Vancouver *(G-14410)*
Michael W Sherer ....G...... 206 230-8541
  Mercer Island *(G-6474)*
R Wayne Industries LLC ....G...... 425 359-0432
  Snohomish *(G-11966)*
Reed Composite Solutions LLC ....G...... 360 637-6867
  Aberdeen *(G-31)*
S Scott & Associates LLC ....G...... 360 576-4830
  Vancouver *(G-14563)*

PLASTIC WOOD

Aqua-Lift Inc ....G...... 253 845-4010
  Puyallup *(G-8124)*

PLASTICS FILM & SHEET

Novolex Shields LLC ....B...... 800 541-8630
  Yakima *(G-15636)*

PLASTICS FILM & SHEET: Polyethylene

Ampac Packaging LLC ....C...... 253 939-8206
  Auburn *(G-374)*
Paragon Films Inc ....E...... 509 424-3700
  Union Gap *(G-13949)*

PLASTICS FILM & SHEET: Polyvinyl

Achilles Usa Inc ....C...... 425 353-7000
  Everett *(G-3357)*
Redi-Bag Inc ....E...... 425 251-9841
  Tukwila *(G-13804)*
Wiman Corporation ....G...... 360 757-8880
  Burlington *(G-2204)*

PLASTICS FILM & SHEET: Vinyl

Custom Win Tnting Graphics Inc ....G...... 509 453-4293
  Yakima *(G-15547)*

PLASTICS FINISHED PRDTS: Laminated

Acrylic Concepts Inc ....G...... 425 881-3603
  Redmond *(G-8369)*
Dmm Incorporated ....E...... 360 435-5252
  Arlington *(G-229)*
Pexco Aerospace Inc ....C...... 509 248-9166
  Union Gap *(G-13950)*

Rulersmith Inc .... E 360 707-2828
Shoreline (G-11806)

PLASTICS MATERIAL & RESINS

3s Plastics LLC .... G 425 747-2827
Bellevue (G-775)
All Composite Inc .... G 253 847-5106
Spanaway (G-12053)
American Excelsior Company .... E 509 575-5794
Yakima (G-15507)
Arclin Surfaces LLC .... E 253 572-5600
Tacoma (G-13178)
Axiall Corporation .... D 360 577-3232
Longview (G-5887)
Columbia Cultured Marble Inc .... G 509 582-5660
Kennewick (G-4647)
Concept Fabrication Inc .... F 509 534-9235
Spokane (G-12196)
Corrosion Companies Inc .... E 360 835-2171
Washougal (G-14949)
Epic Polymer Systems Corp .... F 360 225-1496
Woodland (G-15430)
General Plastics Mfg Co .... C 253 473-5000
Tacoma (G-13306)
Honeywell International Inc .... A 425 885-3711
Redmond (G-8500)
Interplastic Corporation .... E 253 872-8067
Kent (G-4958)
James Koehnline .... G 206 783-6846
Seattle (G-10282)
K Rounds LLC .... G 206 452-0466
Kent (G-4972)
Microgreen Polymers Inc .... E 360 435-7400
Arlington (G-276)
Microgreen Polymers Inc .... G 360 435-7400
Arlington (G-277)
North American Composites Co .... G 253 351-9994
Kent (G-5027)
Orca Composites .... G 206 782-0660
Seattle (G-10712)
Pexco LLC .... C 253 284-8000
Fife (G-3980)
Plasticreations Inc .... G 425 558-1075
Redmond (G-8624)
Polythermics LLC .... G 425 823-5568
Kirkland (G-5438)
Professional Plastics Inc .... F 425 251-4140
Tukwila (G-13795)
Professional Plastics Inc .... G 714 446-6500
Kent (G-5084)
Professional Plastics Inc .... F 253 872-7430
Tukwila (G-13797)
R & R Plastics .... G 360 694-9573
Vancouver (G-14524)
Redwood Plastics and Rbr Corp .... E 360 225-1491
Woodland (G-15461)
Tex Enterprises Inc .... G 253 939-1660
Auburn (G-579)
Visual Options Inc .... E 253 472-1440
Tacoma (G-13581)
Wilsonart LLC .... E 253 833-0551
Algona (G-79)

PLASTICS MATERIALS, BASIC FORMS & SHAPES WHOLESALERS

Professional Plastics Inc .... F 253 872-7430
Tukwila (G-13796)

PLASTICS PROCESSING

Acrylic Arts & Fabrication .... G 360 802-0808
Enumclaw (G-3274)
American Cnc Fabricating Inc .... G 509 315-4095
Spokane Valley (G-12609)
Applied Finishing Inc .... E 425 513-2505
Mukilteo (G-6893)
Belair Composites Inc .... F 509 482-0442
Spokane (G-12144)
Composites Consolidation Compa .... G 509 877-2228
Wapato (G-14914)
Dongalen Enterprises Inc .... G 253 395-4885
Kent (G-4877)
Ershigs Inc .... E 360 887-3580
Ridgefield (G-9081)
Georges Custom Plastic Inc .... G 253 939-1575
Bonney Lake (G-1725)
Gigglydoo LLC .... G 425 344-5594
Ellensburg (G-3203)
Northwest Composites Inc .... E 360 653-2211
Marysville (G-6364)
Obcon Inc .... G 253 931-0455
Auburn (G-516)
Polymer Foundry Inc .... G 360 574-1617
Vancouver (G-14493)
Professional Plastics Inc .... F 253 872-7430
Tukwila (G-13796)
Redwood Plastics and Rbr Corp .... E 360 225-1491
Woodland (G-15461)
Sunbacker Fiberglass Inc .... G 360 794-5547
Monroe (G-6628)
U S Wax & Polymer Inc .... E 509 922-1069
Spokane Valley (G-12918)

PLASTICS SHEET: Packing Materials

Cordstrap USA Inc .... G 253 886-5000
Auburn (G-417)
Portco Corporation .... F 360 696-1641
Woodland (G-15460)
Tekni-Plex Inc .... C 509 663-8541
Wenatchee (G-15079)

PLASTICS: Cast

Go2origins LLC .... G 425 413-4134
Ravensdale (G-8336)

PLASTICS: Extruded

West Coast Plastics Inc .... G 509 575-0727
Yakima (G-15706)

PLASTICS: Finished Injection Molded

Artisan Industries Inc .... F 360 474-1282
Arlington (G-203)
CFM Consolidated Inc .... F 253 922-2700
Fife (G-3942)
CFM Consolidated Inc .... E 253 922-2700
Fife (G-3943)
Consolidated Metco Inc .... D 360 828-2599
Vancouver (G-14147)
Mapp Tool LLC .... G 509 228-9449
Spokane Valley (G-12783)
Rex Plastics Inc .... E 360 892-0366
Vancouver (G-14549)
Rp 2000 LLC .... G 206 624-8258
Seattle (G-10988)
Skills For Creative Concepts .... G 360 671-1472
Bellingham (G-1542)
Stewart Industries Inc .... E 206 652-9110
Seattle (G-11194)
Technical Molded Plastics Inc .... E 425 251-9710
Kent (G-5174)

PLASTICS: Injection Molded

All Craft Plastics .... G 253 887-1768
Auburn (G-369)
Alpine Precision Tooling Inc .... G 360 474-0547
Arlington (G-199)
Altek Inc .... C 509 921-0597
Liberty Lake (G-5825)
Artech Sinrud Industries Inc .... G 360 435-3520
Arlington (G-202)
Avid Products LLC .... G 888 271-3616
Redmond (G-8394)
Benchmark Injection Molding .... G 425 263-9171
Lynnwood (G-6083)
Blaser Casting Corporation .... E 206 767-7800
Seattle (G-9539)
Commercial Plastics Corp .... F 206 682-4832
Seattle (G-9717)
Davis Tool Inc .... G 509 891-5568
Newman Lake (G-7044)
Diversified Plastics West Inc .... F 360 825-7660
Enumclaw (G-3286)
Exotec .... G 425 488-0691
Kenmore (G-4574)
Jatal Inc .... E 253 854-0034
Auburn (G-478)
Kaso Plastics Inc .... D 360 254-3980
Vancouver (G-14344)
Legacy Plastics L L C .... G 360 413-7787
Olympia (G-7321)
Lnp LLC .... G 206 467-4556
Tukwila (G-13767)
Loomis Plastics Corporation .... E 206 292-0111
Seattle (G-10439)
Macro Plastics Inc .... E 509 452-1200
Union Gap (G-13940)
Minds-I Inc .... G 509 252-5725
Liberty Lake (G-5846)
Myco Molding Inc .... F 360 676-9656
Bellingham (G-1454)
Pacific Injection Molding .... G 360 733-7466
Bellingham (G-1485)
Piller Aimmco Inc .... D 360 835-2103
Washougal (G-14979)
Plastic Forming Services LLC .... F 360 335-9755
Washougal (G-14980)
Plastic Injection Molding Inc .... G 509 375-4260
Richland (G-9035)
Plastics Northwest Inc .... F 360 823-0505
Vancouver (G-14488)
Plexus Manufacturing Inc .... G 425 355-2997
Mukilteo (G-6966)
Reality Plastics Inc .... G 360 653-3949
Marysville (G-6377)
Seattle Custom Plastics Inc .... F 206 233-0869
Seattle (G-11054)
Sensitech Inc .... E 425 883-7926
Redmond (G-8660)
Sensitech Inc .... C 425 883-7926
Redmond (G-8661)
Shyft Advanced Mfg LLC .... F 425 398-4009
Woodinville (G-15361)
Sinotechusa Inc .... G 360 566-2880
Ridgefield (G-9111)
Stl International Incorporated .... E 253 840-5252
Buckley (G-2076)
Vaupell Industrial Plas Inc .... B 206 784-9050
Seattle (G-11406)
Vaupell Molding & Tooling Inc .... D 206 784-9050
Seattle (G-11407)
WD&I Machine Co .... E 360 225-5020
Woodland (G-15473)

PLASTICS: Molded

Aska Company .... G 360 753-4233
Lacey (G-5534)
Cascade Quality Molding Inc .... F 509 248-9642
Yakima (G-15530)
Dana-Saad Company .... E 509 924-6711
Spokane Valley (G-12677)
Dans Striping and Molding Inc .... G 206 533-1495
Woodway (G-15479)
Focal Point Plastics Inc .... F 206 282-0433
Washougal (G-14956)
Globaltech Plastics LLC .... D 253 327-1333
Fife (G-3956)
Goodwinds LLC .... G 206 362-6151
Mount Vernon (G-6800)
Jim Suzuki .... G 253 804-6070
Auburn (G-482)
McClarin Plastics LLC .... B 509 877-5950
Wapato (G-14919)
Northwest Inc .... G 360 794-7473
Monroe (G-6602)
Proto Technologies Inc .... D 509 891-4747
Liberty Lake (G-5855)
Reiff Injection Molding Inc .... G 509 340-1020
Spokane (G-12470)
Smak Plastics Inc .... E 360 882-0410
Vancouver (G-14595)
Sound Manufacturing Inc .... E 253 872-8007
Kent (G-5141)
Sunset Molding Inc .... G 360 835-3805
Washougal (G-14988)
Tailored Solutions LLC .... G 509 258-4314
Tumtum (G-13847)
Urethane Cast Parts Inc .... G 253 539-4282
Puyallup (G-8268)

PLASTICS: Polystyrene Foam

Cams-Usa Inc .... F 253 639-3890
Kent (G-4835)
Concept Fabrication Inc .... F 509 534-9235
Spokane (G-12196)
Five Food Inc .... G 509 855-6914
Moses Lake (G-6708)
General Plastics Mfg Co .... C 253 473-5000
Tacoma (G-13306)
Grab On Grips LLC .... F 509 529-9800
Walla Walla (G-14814)
How-Mac Manufacturing Inc .... E 360 855-2649
Sedro Woolley (G-11540)
Innocor Inc .... G 844 824-9348
Issaquah (G-4429)
J & R Commercial Inc .... G 253 639-3890
Kent (G-4963)
Mantec Services Inc .... E 206 285-5656
Seattle (G-10472)

PLASTICS: Polystyrene Foam

Mr Ed Floats .... G 360 834-3986
  Camas *(G-2272)*

PLASTICS: Thermoformed

Conrad Manufacturing Co Inc .... F 253 852-3420
  Auburn *(G-413)*
Grow Plastics LLC .... G 206 954-4564
  Seattle *(G-10128)*
Kel-Tech Plastics Inc .... E 253 472-9654
  Tacoma *(G-13374)*
Lemac Manufacturing Co Inc .... G 360 756-1720
  Bellingham *(G-1407)*
Saint-Gobain Prfmce Plas Corp .... C 253 466-5400
  Puyallup *(G-8244)*
Sully N A Saint-Gobain .... G 253 466-5417
  Puyallup *(G-8256)*
Thermoforming Systems LLC .... E 509 454-4578
  Union Gap *(G-13954)*

PLATED WARE, ALL METALS

Carl Zapffe Inc .... G 206 364-1919
  Seattle *(G-9633)*

PLATEMAKING SVC: Color Separations, For The Printing Trade

Imagine Color Service LLC .... E 206 281-5703
  Seattle *(G-10207)*

PLATES

Graphic Advertising Svcs Inc .... F 425 688-9980
  Richland *(G-9003)*
Graphic Impressions Inc .... E 253 872-0555
  Kent *(G-4925)*
Hazelwood Farm LLC .... F 425 454-5165
  Redmond *(G-8489)*
Preflex Digital Prepress Svcs .... F 253 583-9100
  Lakewood *(G-5747)*
Refocus Laser Engraving-Design .... G 541 998-2047
  Lynnwood *(G-6188)*
Tacoma Rubber Stamp Co .... E 253 383-5433
  Tacoma *(G-13548)*

PLATING & POLISHING SVC

American Powder Works .... G 360 220-3104
  Lynnwood *(G-6074)*
Ameristar 124 .... G 509 783-7518
  Kennewick *(G-4616)*
Bluerose Processing .... G 360 281-7371
  Vancouver *(G-14070)*
Carl Zapffe Inc .... G 206 364-1919
  Seattle *(G-9633)*
Complete Deburr Inc .... F 253 887-0997
  Auburn *(G-411)*
D G Hard Surface LLC .... G 206 718-4700
  Bellevue *(G-873)*
Denise Mayward .... G 253 927-0219
  Tacoma *(G-13259)*
Magnetic Penetrant Svcs Co Inc .... D 206 762-5855
  Seattle *(G-10466)*
Pacific NW Powdr Coating .... F 509 535-9950
  Spokane *(G-12426)*
Pioneer Human Services .... C 206 762-7737
  Seattle *(G-10810)*
Repair Technology Inc .... F 206 762-6221
  Seattle *(G-10948)*
Show Quality Metal Finish .... G 206 762-6717
  Seatac *(G-9304)*
Skyline NW Inc A Wash Cor .... G 360 695-6006
  Vancouver *(G-14592)*
Spokane Galvanizing Inc .... E 509 244-4073
  Airway Heights *(G-65)*
Triangle Wellness LLC .... G 727 773-0054
  Sequim *(G-11667)*
Valence Surface Tech LLC .... C 206 762-5855
  Seattle *(G-11398)*

PLATING SVC: Chromium, Metals Or Formed Prdts

Crown Plating Inc .... G 360 693-3040
  Vancouver *(G-14155)*
Finishing Unlimited Inc .... G 425 881-7300
  Redmond *(G-8461)*
Harrys Radiator Shop Inc .... G 509 765-8581
  Moses Lake *(G-6713)*
Smith Chrome Plating Inc .... G 509 525-0993
  Walla Walla *(G-14870)*

PLATING SVC: Electro

Asko Processing Inc .... F 206 634-2080
  Seattle *(G-9444)*
Asko Processing Inc .... G 206 298-9730
  Mukilteo *(G-6896)*
Dlm Inc .... F 425 348-3204
  Mukilteo *(G-6915)*
Electrofinishing Inc .... G 253 850-0540
  Kent *(G-4888)*
Production Plating Inc .... D 425 347-4635
  Mukilteo *(G-6968)*
Queen City Plating Company Inc .... G 425 315-1992
  Mukilteo *(G-6970)*

PLATING SVC: Gold

Omega Silversmithing Inc .... G 360 863-6771
  Snohomish *(G-11956)*

PLATING SVC: NEC

American Plating .... G 360 736-0052
  Centralia *(G-2383)*
Art Brass Plating Inc .... D 206 767-4443
  Seattle *(G-9436)*
Fc Plating Inc .... G 360 679-4665
  Oak Harbor *(G-7151)*
Gamblin Enterprises Inc .... G 206 795-3817
  Lynnwood *(G-6125)*
Gold Plating Specialist .... G 509 582-3430
  Kennewick *(G-4668)*
Inland Empire Plating Inc .... F 509 535-1704
  Spokane Valley *(G-12743)*
Mastercraft Metal Finishing .... G 206 622-6380
  Seattle *(G-10498)*
Pacific NW Plating Inc .... F 360 735-9000
  Vancouver *(G-14468)*
Proflections Metal Polishing .... G 253 735-6111
  Auburn *(G-539)*
Quality Polishing and Plating .... F 425 432-5500
  Renton *(G-8887)*
Universal Brass Inc .... F 253 939-8282
  Auburn *(G-589)*

PLAYGROUND EQPT

Allplay Systems LLC .... G 360 808-5925
  Sequim *(G-11609)*
Jesternick Systems LLC .... G 509 338-4837
  Pullman *(G-8095)*
Pacific Outdoor Products Inc .... F 425 432-6000
  Maple Valley *(G-6287)*
Perch and Play .... G 360 393-4925
  Bellingham *(G-1496)*
Sitelines Pk & Playground Pdts .... G 425 355-5655
  Everett *(G-3612)*

PLEATING & STITCHING SVC

Arctic Circle Enterprises LLC .... D 253 872-8525
  Kent *(G-4789)*
Availble Creat Screen Prtg EMB .... G 360 576-8542
  Vancouver *(G-14045)*
Chings Embroidery .... G 360 613-9861
  Bremerton *(G-1942)*
Classic Impressions .... E 206 766-9121
  Seattle *(G-9690)*
Colosseum Ventures LLC .... F 509 533-0366
  Spokane *(G-12188)*
Fast Lane Auto Sports .... G 253 584-3676
  Lakewood *(G-5721)*
Jackyes Enterprises Inc .... G 425 355-5997
  Everett *(G-3521)*
Larsen Sign Company .... G 253 581-4313
  Lakewood *(G-5736)*
Post Indus Stress & Design .... F 253 572-9782
  Tacoma *(G-13472)*
Wildrose Ltd .... F 509 535-8555
  Spokane *(G-12591)*

PLUMBING & HEATING EQPT & SPLY, WHOL: Htg Eqpt/Panels, Solar

Jx Crystals Inc .... G 425 392-5237
  Issaquah *(G-4435)*

PLUMBING & HEATING EQPT & SPLY, WHOLESALE: Hydronic Htg Eqpt

Gensco Inc .... C 253 620-8203
  Fife *(G-3954)*

PLUMBING & HEATING EQPT & SPLYS WHOLESALERS

Pat Files .... G 206 405-4370
  Seattle *(G-10764)*
Siemens Industry Inc .... F 509 891-9070
  Spokane Valley *(G-12871)*

PLUMBING & HEATING EQPT & SPLYS, WHOL: Pipe/Fitting, Plastic

Fluid Controls and Components .... F 253 922-3226
  Fife *(G-3953)*
Paramount Supply Co .... G 360 647-8328
  Bellingham *(G-1489)*
Superlon Plastics Co Inc .... F 253 383-4000
  Tacoma *(G-13530)*

PLUMBING & HEATING EQPT & SPLYS, WHOL: Plumbing Fitting/Sply

Keller Supply Co .... F 509 925-2400
  Ellensburg *(G-3210)*
Keller Supply Co .... G 253 863-9271
  Sumner *(G-13077)*
Pac West Sales Inc .... F 425 493-9680
  Mukilteo *(G-6963)*
Pacific Plumbing Supply Co LLC .... F 425 251-0604
  Seattle *(G-10738)*
Part Works Inc .... E 206 632-8900
  Seattle *(G-10760)*

PLUMBING & HEATING EQPT & SPLYS, WHOL: Water Purif Eqpt

Aquatech .... G 360 957-5203
  Castle Rock *(G-2337)*

PLUMBING & HEATING EQPT, WHOLESALE: Water Heaters/Purif

Dep Homes Corporation .... G 206 322-1241
  Seattle *(G-9824)*

PLUMBING FIXTURES

Accor Technology Inc .... E 509 662-0608
  East Wenatchee *(G-3006)*
Ferguson .... G 206 767-7700
  Auburn *(G-440)*
Gordon Exports LLC .... G 503 313-6544
  Redmond *(G-8482)*
K & M Unibody Works Inc .... F 509 922-2083
  Spokane Valley *(G-12758)*
Keller Supply Co .... G 509 922-6388
  Spokane Valley *(G-12763)*
Keller Supply Co .... G 253 863-9271
  Sumner *(G-13077)*
Keller Supply Co .... F 509 925-2400
  Ellensburg *(G-3210)*
Pac West Sales Inc .... F 425 493-9680
  Mukilteo *(G-6963)*
Pipemasters Inc .... G 253 377-0717
  Gig Harbor *(G-4146)*
Quality Sales Inc .... F 360 694-3165
  Vancouver *(G-14521)*

PLUMBING FIXTURES: Brass, Incl Drain Cocks, Faucets/Spigots

JI Distribution Ltd .... G 206 743-1148
  Arlington *(G-262)*
Old & Elegant Distributing .... F 425 455-4660
  Bellevue *(G-1045)*

PLUMBING FIXTURES: Plastic

Columbia Cultured Marble Inc .... G 509 582-5660
  Kennewick *(G-4647)*
Pat Files .... G 206 405-4370
  Seattle *(G-10764)*
Pvc Debonding Systems Inc .... G 866 961-8349
  Spokane *(G-12461)*

PLUMBING FIXTURES: Vitreous

Cascade Specialty Hardware .... G 360 823-3995
  Vancouver *(G-14106)*

PRODUCT SECTION — PRESSED FIBER & MOLDED PULP PRDTS, EXC FOOD PRDTS

POINT OF SALE DEVICES
Softec Systems Inc ....G...... 425 741-2055
  Everett *(G-3615)*

POKER CHIPS
Freelocalpoker Co ....G...... 360 794-5173
  Monroe *(G-6574)*

POLES & POSTS: Concrete
Altus Industries Inc ....G...... 360 255-7699
  Blaine *(G-1659)*

POLISHING SVC: Metals Or Formed Prdts
Alloy Polishing Co ....G...... 360 736-2716
  Centralia *(G-2382)*
Diamond Polishing Systems ....G...... 253 770-0508
  Puyallup *(G-8144)*
Ketchum Metal Polishing ....G...... 360 403-8726
  Arlington *(G-265)*
Marble Plsg Stone Rstrtion LLC ....G...... 425 564-8284
  Federal Way *(G-3755)*

PONTOONS: Rubber
Blackbear Pontoons Fabrication ....G...... 206 372-9998
  Montesano *(G-6642)*

POPCORN & SUPPLIES WHOLESALERS
Moosoo Corporation ....G...... 866 966-6766
  Kent *(G-5016)*
Seattle Popcorn Company Inc ....G...... 206 937-1292
  Seattle *(G-11068)*

POPULAR MUSIC GROUPS OR ARTISTS
Foxfacerabbitfish LLC ....G...... 206 856-7222
  Seattle *(G-10018)*
Magical Strings ....G...... 253 857-3716
  Olalla *(G-7208)*

PORCELAIN ENAMELED PRDTS & UTENSILS
Lasting Memories ....G...... 509 548-6393
  Leavenworth *(G-5809)*

POSTERS & DECALS, WHOLESALE
Washington Graphics LLC ....F....... 425 376-0877
  Redmond *(G-8709)*

POTTERY
Atlas Ceramic ....G...... 206 280-0041
  Seattle *(G-9454)*
Audrey Josias Ceramics ....G...... 253 862-2365
  Buckley *(G-2047)*
Canterburys Dental Ceramics ....G...... 509 966-3622
  Yakima *(G-15527)*
Geo Lastomirsky Ceramic A ....G...... 206 782-4695
  Seattle *(G-10062)*
Glazy Daze Ceramics ....G...... 253 770-2979
  Puyallup *(G-8158)*
Jadeflower Ceramics ....G...... 253 720-6036
  Seattle *(G-10279)*
Kennedy Creek Pottery ....G...... 360 866-3937
  Olympia *(G-7316)*
Mardie Rees Artist LLC ....G...... 253 279-3244
  Gig Harbor *(G-4134)*
Sandra S Berlin ....G...... 206 612-4126
  Seattle *(G-11012)*

POTTERY: Laboratory & Indl
Bodycote Imt Inc ....E....... 360 833-1120
  Camas *(G-2234)*

POULTRY & SMALL GAME SLAUGHTERING & PROCESSING
Dynes Farms Inc ....E....... 360 757-4025
  Burlington *(G-2154)*
Jeff Potter ....G...... 206 819-4224
  Seattle *(G-10289)*
Perdue Foods LLC ....G...... 360 748-9466
  Chehalis *(G-2523)*
Perdue Foods LLC ....F....... 360 398-2911
  Lynden *(G-6046)*

POWDER: Metal
Iasco ....E....... 253 474-0497
  Tacoma *(G-13346)*
J L Powder Ctg ....G...... 360 380-3898
  Ferndale *(G-3863)*
N A I Inc ....G...... 509 453-4778
  Union Gap *(G-13945)*
Northwest Powder Soultions ....G...... 253 395-6282
  Kent *(G-5035)*

POWDER: Silver
Custom Coat ....G...... 509 542-9431
  Pasco *(G-7575)*

POWER DISTRIBUTION BOARDS: Electric
C&K Enterprize LLC ....G...... 509 448-2866
  Spokane *(G-12165)*

POWER GENERATORS
Innovatek Inc ....G...... 509 375-1093
  Kennewick *(G-4676)*
Koma Kulshan Associates ....G...... 360 853-8530
  Concrete *(G-2789)*
Silvergen Inc ....G...... 360 732-5091
  Port Ludlow *(G-7777)*

POWER SPLY CONVERTERS: Static, Electronic Applications
E T L Corp ....F....... 360 568-1473
  Snohomish *(G-11903)*
Vpt Inc ....G...... 425 353-3010
  Bothell *(G-1807)*

POWER SUPPLIES: All Types, Static
Ant Lamp Corp ....G...... 360 600-1031
  Vancouver *(G-14037)*
Microconnex Corporation ....G...... 425 396-5707
  Snoqualmie *(G-12018)*
Nidec America Corporation ....G...... 360 666-2445
  Battle Ground *(G-724)*

POWER SWITCHING EQPT
Leach International Corp ....G...... 425 519-1826
  Bellevue *(G-979)*

POWER TOOL REPAIR SVCS
Carls Mower and Saw ....G...... 360 384-0799
  Ferndale *(G-3824)*

POWER TOOLS, HAND: Chain Saws, Portable
Specialty Motors Mfg LLC ....G...... 360 423-9880
  Longview *(G-5956)*

POWER TRANSMISSION EQPT WHOLESALERS
Tramco Inc ....G...... 425 347-3030
  Everett *(G-3635)*

POWER TRANSMISSION EQPT: Aircraft
Matsushita Avionics Co ....G...... 206 246-6200
  Seatac *(G-9289)*

POWER TRANSMISSION EQPT: Mechanical
Aahed Logistics LLC ....G...... 757 395-7063
  Port Orchard *(G-7782)*
Cablecraft Motion Controls LLC ....D...... 253 475-1080
  Tacoma *(G-13215)*
Gms Procurement LLC ....G...... 253 852-6552
  Auburn *(G-453)*
Jerry Fry ....G...... 509 765-4367
  Moses Lake *(G-6717)*
Joint Way International Inc ....G...... 503 286-7781
  Vancouver *(G-14340)*
Moxee Innovations Corporation ....G...... 509 575-6322
  Yakima *(G-15625)*
Moxee Innovations Corporation ....G...... 509 575-6322
  Moxee *(G-6882)*
Powerlink Transmission Co LLC ....G...... 360 314-6840
  Vancouver *(G-14496)*
Snapidle ....G...... 509 575-6322
  Moxee *(G-6887)*

Valin Corporation ....G...... 509 924-4914
  Spokane Valley *(G-12923)*

PRECAST TERRAZZO OR CONCRETE PRDTS
Bayview Redi Mix Inc ....E....... 360 533-7372
  Aberdeen *(G-5)*
Creative Concrete Products LLC ....G...... 360 419-9909
  Mount Vernon *(G-6786)*
Cuz Concrete Products Inc ....G...... 360 435-0769
  Arlington *(G-225)*
Krieg Concrete Products Inc ....F....... 360 675-2727
  Oak Harbor *(G-7156)*
Lynden Precast LLC ....G...... 360 354-8901
  Lynden *(G-6035)*
Ornamental Stone Inc ....G...... 360 275-4241
  Allyn *(G-84)*
Precast Oldcastle ....G...... 800 509-6150
  Vancouver *(G-14498)*
Quality Concrete Products ....G...... 509 758-2655
  Clarkston *(G-2642)*
Rw Precast Inc ....F....... 253 770-0100
  Puyallup *(G-8242)*

PRECIOUS METALS WHOLESALERS
Ecotech Recycling LLC ....E....... 360 673-3860
  Kalama *(G-4498)*

PRECIOUS STONE MINING SVCS, NEC
Goldrich Mining Company ....F....... 509 535-7367
  Spokane *(G-12277)*
Huntmountain Resources Ltd ....G...... 509 290-5659
  Liberty Lake *(G-5836)*

PRECIOUS STONES & METALS, WHOLESALE
Eastern Merchandise Co Inc ....G...... 206 448-4466
  Seattle *(G-9871)*

PRECIOUS STONES WHOLESALERS
Columbia Gem House Inc ....E....... 360 514-0569
  Vancouver *(G-14130)*

PRECISION INSTRUMENT REPAIR SVCS
Signal Hound Inc ....G...... 360 263-5006
  Battle Ground *(G-740)*

PREFABRICATED BUILDING DEALERS
Cedar Homes of Washington Inc ....G...... 360 668-8242
  Snohomish *(G-11887)*
Mobile Storage Units Inc ....G...... 509 276-8220
  Deer Park *(G-2909)*

PREPARING SHAFTS OR TUNNELS, METAL MINING
Chooch Enterprises Inc ....G...... 425 273-4794
  Maple Valley *(G-6264)*

PRERECORDED TAPE, COMPACT DISC & RECORD STORES: Records
Globe ....G...... 206 527-2480
  Seattle *(G-10086)*

PRERECORDED TAPES & CASSETTES WHOLESALERS
Soundworks U S A Inc ....G...... 425 882-3344
  Lacey *(G-5591)*

PRESSED & MOLDED PULP PRDTS, NEC: From Purchased Materials
Tabs To Go Inc ....G...... 253 854-8227
  Auburn *(G-576)*

PRESSED FIBER & MOLDED PULP PRDTS, EXC FOOD PRDTS
Maxcess International Corp ....D...... 360 834-2345
  Camas *(G-2268)*

PRESTRESSED CONCRETE PRDTS

PRESTRESSED CONCRETE PRDTS
Ameron International Corp .... E 425 258-2616
  Everett *(G-3369)*

PRIMARY METAL PRODUCTS
Chevy Metal .... G 360 694-7295
  Vancouver *(G-14115)*
D & D Dividers LLC .... G 360 951-4852
  Centralia *(G-2397)*
Meyer Engineered Materials LLC .... G 253 854-6117
  Kent *(G-5009)*
Smiley Industrial LLC .... G 509 302-8792
  Pasco *(G-7630)*
Sunset Forge LLC .... G 360 201-0160
  Ferndale *(G-3910)*

PRINT CARTRIDGES: Laser & Other Computer Printers
Aplus Inkworks .... G 206 910-9082
  Bothell *(G-1747)*
Blender LLC .... G 509 210-3373
  Spokane *(G-12154)*
Lazer Cartridges Plus LLC .... G 509 529-0200
  Walla Walla *(G-14835)*
Olympic Printer Resources Inc .... F 360 297-8384
  Kingston *(G-5259)*
Rgd Enterprises Inc .... G 360 923-9582
  Olympia *(G-7385)*

PRINTED CIRCUIT BOARDS
Acacia Controls Inc 253 277-1206
  Kent *(G-4755)*
Almax Manufacturing Co .... G 425 889-8708
  Kirkland *(G-5276)*
Applied Technical Svcs Corp 425 249-5555
  Everett *(G-3371)*
Board Shark LLC .... E 503 351-5424
  Vancouver *(G-14072)*
Circuit Services Worldwide .... E 425 454-7181
  Bellevue *(G-852)*
Circuit Services Worldwide LLC .... F 425 454-7181
  Bellevue *(G-853)*
Constant Computer 253 227-0532
  Tacoma *(G-13239)*
Four Barr Industries 360 659-8182
  Marysville *(G-6335)*
I2nnovations LLC 425 298-3143
  Sammamish *(G-9218)*
Industrial Control Group 509 965-5967
  Yakima *(G-15587)*
Jabil Def & Arospc Svcs LLC .... G 206 257-0243
  Seattle *(G-10276)*
Jabil Inc .... G 206 257-0243
  Seattle *(G-10277)*
Monsoon Solutions Inc .... E 425 378-8081
  Bellevue *(G-1014)*
Out of Box Manufacturing LLC .... E 253 214-7448
  Renton *(G-8868)*
Pantrol Inc .... F 509 535-9061
  Spokane *(G-12428)*
Pcb Universe Inc 360 256-7228
  Vancouver *(G-14481)*
Plc-Multipoint Inc 425 353-7552
  Everett *(G-3575)*
Servatron Inc .... C 509 321-9500
  Spokane Valley *(G-12865)*
Sherman Technical Inds Inc 509 427-8089
  Carson *(G-2307)*
Sherman Technical Inds Inc .... G 509 427-8089
  Carson *(G-2308)*
Silicon Forest Electronics Inc .... C 360 694-2000
  Vancouver *(G-14588)*
Technical & Assembly Svcs Corp .... E 206 682-2967
  Seattle *(G-11287)*
White Matter LLC .... G 510 409-0144
  Mercer Island *(G-6489)*
Xanfab Inc .... G 206 717-2185
  Seatac *(G-9313)*

PRINTERS & PLOTTERS
AZ Imprint .... G 360 578-2476
  Kelso *(G-4517)*
Northwest Hydroprint .... G 360 249-2220
  Montesano *(G-6650)*
Trio Native American Entps LLC .... G 206 728-8181
  Renton *(G-8932)*

PRINTERS' SVCS: Folding, Collating, Etc
Dumas Holdings LLC .... G 425 576-4227
  Kirkland *(G-5323)*
United Reprographics L L C .... E 206 382-1177
  Seattle *(G-11372)*

PRINTERS: Computer
B G Instruments Inc .... G 509 893-9881
  Spokane Valley *(G-12635)*
Kemeera Incorporated .... E 206 582-1062
  Seattle *(G-10335)*

PRINTERS: Magnetic Ink, Bar Code
5th Wave Mobile Tech Inc .... G 425 898-8161
  Gig Harbor *(G-4070)*
Barcode Equipment Recyling Co .... G 360 393-4232
  Bellingham *(G-1258)*
Intermec Inc .... F 425 348-2600
  Lynnwood *(G-6139)*
International Bar Coding .... F 800 661-5570
  Oroville *(G-7467)*
Scitus Tech Solutions LLC .... G 360 202-9642
  Ferndale *(G-3901)*
Sportsoft Inc .... G 425 822-4613
  Mill Creek *(G-6530)*

PRINTING & BINDING: Books
Johnson Cox Co Inc .... E 253 272-2238
  Tacoma *(G-13364)*
Quarto Pubg Group USA Inc .... E 425 827-7120
  Bellevue *(G-1090)*

PRINTING & BINDING: Pamphlets
AAA Printing Inc .... E 425 454-0156
  Bellevue *(G-777)*

PRINTING & ENGRAVING: Invitation & Stationery
King Enterprises .... G 360 568-1644
  Snohomish *(G-11933)*
Party City Corporation .... F 206 575-0502
  Tukwila *(G-13790)*
Pickle Papers .... G 509 665-8661
  Wenatchee *(G-15064)*

PRINTING & ENGRAVING: Poster & Decal
Decal Factory .... G 509 465-8931
  Spokane *(G-12222)*

PRINTING & STAMPING: Fabric Articles
Ammonite Ink .... G 907 227-2719
  Spokane *(G-12113)*
Computergear Inc .... G 425 487-3600
  Woodinville *(G-15209)*

PRINTING & STAMPING: Tip, On Fabric
Blackstar .... G 360 426-7470
  Shelton *(G-11684)*

PRINTING & WRITING PAPER WHOLESALERS
Wholesale Forms Inc .... G 800 826-7095
  Rochester *(G-9145)*

PRINTING MACHINERY
Applied Mfg & Engrg Tech Inc .... F 253 852-5378
  Edmonds *(G-3095)*
E H P & Associates Inc .... F 206 764-3344
  Burien *(G-2104)*
Embodi3d LLC .... G 425 429-6193
  Bellevue *(G-894)*
Enterprises International Inc .... G 360 533-6222
  Hoquiam *(G-4336)*
Exone Company .... G 253 394-0357
  Auburn *(G-439)*
Ioline Corporation .... E 425 398-8282
  Woodinville *(G-15267)*
Ovalstrapping Incorporated .... G 360 532-9101
  Hoquiam *(G-4352)*
Prodeco LLC .... G 425 827-2573
  Kirkland *(G-5443)*
Sdp Tech Inc .... G 206 595-3041
  Bellevue *(G-1118)*

PRINTING MACHINERY, EQPT & SPLYS: Wholesalers
Anderson & Vreeland Inc .... G 419 636-5002
  Kent *(G-4782)*
Dimensional Products Inc .... F 206 352-9065
  Seattle *(G-9831)*

PRINTING TRADES MACHINERY & EQPT REPAIR SVCS
E H P & Associates Inc .... F 206 764-3344
  Burien *(G-2104)*

PRINTING, COMMERCIAL Newspapers, NEC
Triad Comsural Printing Corp .... F 509 582-1466
  Kennewick *(G-4740)*

PRINTING, COMMERCIAL: Business Forms, NEC
Liberty Business Forms Inc .... D 509 536-0515
  Spokane *(G-12362)*
Pacific Dealer Services .... G 509 299-7269
  Medical Lake *(G-6443)*
Pioneer Printing and Forms .... G 509 248-7393
  Yakima *(G-15648)*
Sand Paper & Ink Inc .... G 360 705-0918
  Tumwater *(G-13896)*
Wholesale Forms Inc .... G 800 826-7095
  Rochester *(G-9145)*

PRINTING, COMMERCIAL: Cards, Visiting, Incl Business, NEC
NW Wood Box .... G 360 939-2434
  Camano Island *(G-2220)*

PRINTING, COMMERCIAL: Circulars, NEC
Catholic Printery Inc .... E 206 767-0660
  Seattle *(G-9648)*

PRINTING, COMMERCIAL: Coupons, NEC
Tacoma Public Schools .... G 253 571-1170
  Tacoma *(G-13547)*

PRINTING, COMMERCIAL: Decals, NEC
Atlas Pacific Engineering Co .... G 509 665-6911
  Wenatchee *(G-15010)*
Designer Decal Inc .... F 509 535-0267
  Spokane *(G-12226)*
Mountain Top Inc .... G 360 416-3333
  Mount Vernon *(G-6814)*

PRINTING, COMMERCIAL: Directories, Exc Telephone, NEC
Snohomish Publishing Company .... E 206 523-7548
  Snohomish *(G-11983)*

PRINTING, COMMERCIAL: Directories, Telephone, NEC
City Books Yellow Pages Inc .... F 805 473-1686
  Burlington *(G-2144)*

PRINTING, COMMERCIAL: Envelopes, NEC
Coprintco Business Forms Inc .... E 360 425-1810
  Longview *(G-5902)*
Envelopes Unlimited Inc .... G 425 451-9622
  Redmond *(G-8451)*
Herzog Envelope Inc .... G 206 618-6765
  Redmond *(G-8491)*

PRINTING, COMMERCIAL: Imprinting
Getting Personal Imprinting .... G 253 302-5566
  Lakewood *(G-5725)*
Information Management Tech .... G 425 322-5078
  Maple Valley *(G-6276)*

PRINTING, COMMERCIAL: Invitations, NEC
Chic Ink .... G 425 392-3943
  Issaquah *(G-4393)*
Mango Ink .... G 509 990-9085
  Mead *(G-6431)*

PRINTING, COMMERCIAL: Labels & Seals, NEC

Bar Code Labels & Equipment .... G 206 567-5577
　Vashon *(G-14711)*
Creative Label Incorporated .... G 425 821-8810
　Kirkland *(G-5317)*
Emerald City Label Inc .... F 425 347-3479
　Everett *(G-3460)*
Global Product Mfg Corp .... F 425 512-9129
　Everett *(G-3501)*
Intermec Technologies Corp .... A 425 348-2600
　Lynnwood *(G-6140)*
Label Masters Inc .... G 425 869-2422
　Kent *(G-4987)*
Labels & Lists Inc .... F 425 822-1984
　Bothell *(G-1772)*
Masterpress Inc .... E 206 524-1444
　Seattle *(G-10499)*
Merchant Investments Inc .... E 425 235-8675
　Kent *(G-5006)*
Northwest Label/Design Inc .... E 206 282-5568
　Seattle *(G-10646)*
Okanogan Label & Print Ltd .... F 250 328-8660
　Walla Walla *(G-14853)*
Pacific Labels .... G 360 671-6507
　Bellingham *(G-1486)*
Richmark Company .... D 206 322-8884
　Seattle *(G-10963)*
Stafford Press Inc .... F 425 861-5856
　Redmond *(G-8680)*

PRINTING, COMMERCIAL: Letterpress & Screen

Ideal Commercial Uniforms .... G 360 876-1767
　Port Orchard *(G-7814)*
Skyhawk Press LLC .... G 360 598-2211
　Poulsbo *(G-8000)*

PRINTING, COMMERCIAL: Literature, Advertising, NEC

Duvall Graphics LLC .... G 425 788-7578
　Duvall *(G-2984)*
Sauther & Assoc Inc .... E 509 922-7828
　Liberty Lake *(G-5858)*
Writing Hands .... G 360 893-1606
　Orting *(G-7489)*

PRINTING, COMMERCIAL: Maps, NEC

Phoenix Maps .... G 509 697-5059
　Selah *(G-11594)*

PRINTING, COMMERCIAL: Post Cards, Picture, NEC

Printing Services Inc .... G 253 858-5350
　Port Orchard *(G-7842)*

PRINTING, COMMERCIAL: Promotional

Arrow International Inc .... B 425 745-3700
　Lynnwood *(G-6076)*
D & J Marketing Inc .... G 360 413-9173
　Lacey *(G-5545)*
Enlighting Struck Design LLC .... G 206 229-9438
　Kent *(G-4893)*
Ever-Mark LLc .... G 425 486-7200
　Kenmore *(G-4573)*
Expressive Promotions .... G 253 863-4211
　Lake Tapps *(G-5678)*
Logo Loft Inc .... G 360 394-5638
　Silverdale *(G-11848)*
Pad Printing Services Inc .... G 206 362-4544
　Seattle *(G-10744)*
Proforma Crtive Prtg Solutions .... G 360 848-7714
　Mount Vernon *(G-6827)*
Purpletrail .... G 425 292-1811
　Issaquah *(G-4463)*
Sbd Inc .... G 509 545-8845
　Pasco *(G-7625)*

PRINTING, COMMERCIAL: Publications

Apex Marketing Strategy .... G 360 402-6487
　Olympia *(G-7228)*
Cedar Creek Printing Co .... G 360 757-7588
　Burlington *(G-2142)*

Commerce Retail Sales Inc .... G 509 926-1724
　Spokane *(G-12191)*
Environmental Fincl Info Svcs .... G 206 283-4210
　Seattle *(G-9933)*
Griffin Publishing Inc .... E 509 534-3625
　Spokane Valley *(G-12724)*
Jen Gar Corp .... G 253 862-6140
　Bonney Lake *(G-1727)*
Lawton Printing Inc .... E 509 534-1044
　Spokane *(G-12358)*
Mediamax .... G 509 627-2358
　Richland *(G-9026)*
Metrix Software .... G 425 361-2415
　Edmonds *(G-3134)*
Northern Kittitas Cnty Tribune .... G 509 674-2511
　Cle Elum *(G-2673)*
P G I Publications Inc .... G 425 743-0110
　Everett *(G-3562)*
Pariyatti .... G 360 978-4998
　Onalaska *(G-7452)*
Pgi Publications .... G 206 588-2968
　Seattle *(G-10792)*
Section Magazine LLC .... G 360 694-8571
　Vancouver *(G-14578)*
Washington State University .... F 509 335-2947
　Pullman *(G-8111)*
Welco Sales LLC .... G 425 771-9043
　Edmonds *(G-3162)*

PRINTING, COMMERCIAL: Ready

Vanetten Fine Art .... G 509 928-2385
　Spokane Valley *(G-12928)*

PRINTING, COMMERCIAL: Screen

253 Custom Tees .... G 253 244-7117
　Lakewood *(G-5693)*
A & J Graphics & Design .... G 206 439-1766
　Burien *(G-2087)*
Absolute Graphix Inc .... G 425 771-6087
　Lynnwood *(G-6067)*
Action Sports & Locks Inc .... G 360 435-9505
　Arlington *(G-193)*
Action Sportswear & Printables .... F 509 328-5861
　Spokane *(G-12097)*
All Pro Screen Prtg & EMB LLC .... G 360 438-0304
　Lacey *(G-5531)*
American Graphic Arts .... G 425 378-8065
　Bellevue *(G-786)*
Angel Screen Printing .... G 253 872-3040
　Kent *(G-4784)*
Arctic Circle Enterprises LLC .... D 253 872-8525
　Kent *(G-4789)*
ASAP Sign & Design .... G 360 757-1570
　Mount Vernon *(G-6771)*
Atomic Screen Printing & EMB .... E 509 585-2866
　Kennewick *(G-4621)*
Bellingham Promotional Pdts .... G 360 676-5416
　Bellingham *(G-1268)*
Bergen & Company .... F 360 676-7503
　Bellingham *(G-1271)*
Blackstar .... G 360 426-7470
　Shelton *(G-11684)*
Brainless Tees Inc .... G 360 608-8417
　Vancouver *(G-14080)*
Buy More Caps Co .... G 509 599-2944
　Spokane *(G-12164)*
C S Adventurecorp LLC .... G 425 679-1172
　Ferndale *(G-3821)*
Choke Shirt Company .... G 206 624-4444
　Seattle *(G-9679)*
Classic Impressions .... E 206 766-9121
　Seattle *(G-9690)*
Co C Graphics .... G 360 571-8488
　Vancouver *(G-14126)*
Cole Graphic Solutions Inc .... E 253 564-4600
　Tacoma *(G-13238)*
Color Grphics Scrnprinting Inc .... F 360 352-3970
　Tumwater *(G-13862)*
Colosseum Ventures LLC .... F 509 533-0366
　Spokane *(G-12188)*
Corey Sign & Display Inc .... G 360 297-5490
　Poulsbo *(G-7955)*
Cory A Stemp .... G 509 491-3847
　Kennewick *(G-4650)*
Creative Edge Graphics .... G 253 735-5115
　Auburn *(G-418)*
Custom Pressed Tees LLC .... G 425 264-5909
　Renton *(G-8777)*
Denrick Tees .... G 509 429-6675
　Riverside *(G-9125)*

Desert Graphics Inc .... G 509 765-8082
　Moses Lake *(G-6704)*
Designs Unlimited .... G 360 792-1372
　Port Orchard *(G-7802)*
Diversified Systems Group Inc .... E 425 947-1500
　Redmond *(G-8442)*
E Teez .... G 425 645-9514
　Everett *(G-3450)*
Eclipse Technical Graphics LLC .... F 509 922-7700
　Spokane Valley *(G-12686)*
Edmonds Athletic Supply Co .... G 425 778-7322
　Lynnwood *(G-6111)*
Excel Designs Inc .... G 360 892-1412
　Vancouver *(G-14213)*
Fine Arts Litho .... G 360 876-5649
　Port Orchard *(G-7809)*
Fkc Co Ltd .... G 360 452-9472
　Port Angeles *(G-7706)*
Flexabili-Tees .... G 360 260-3163
　Vancouver *(G-14234)*
Funky Screenprint .... G 509 674-5121
　Cle Elum *(G-2667)*
Gnarly Tees .... G 360 326-3770
　Vancouver *(G-14260)*
Gorilla Screen Printing .... G 206 621-1728
　Seattle *(G-10102)*
Green Karma Inc .... G 206 786-1988
　Kirkland *(G-5354)*
Greenes Tees LLC .... G 206 801-7725
　Shoreline *(G-11776)*
Hamilton Priniting .... G 425 778-1975
　Edmonds *(G-3116)*
Hs Print Works Difficult .... G 253 251-0045
　Puyallup *(G-8163)*
Hull Marigail .... G 425 643-3737
　Bellevue *(G-952)*
Idk Wear .... G 425 346-1904
　Des Moines *(G-2937)*
Industrial Screenprint Inc .... G 253 735-5111
　Kent *(G-4951)*
Ink It Your Way .... G 425 789-1669
　Lake Stevens *(G-5648)*
Inkwell Screenprinting .... G 206 551-1713
　Seattle *(G-10236)*
Jaytees Management Group LLC .... G 360 352-0038
　Tumwater *(G-13877)*
Jet City Vtg Tees .... G 310 500-0577
　Seattle *(G-10294)*
Jmh Enterprises .... G 509 628-2191
　Richland *(G-9015)*
Johnnie Montice .... G 360 452-6549
　Port Angeles *(G-7719)*
L & P Screen Printing .... G 253 859-8787
　Kent *(G-4986)*
L&P Screen Printing Inc .... G 253 951-2482
　Auburn *(G-486)*
Larrys Screen Printing .... G 425 885-3644
　Bellevue *(G-978)*
Lasting Impressions Inc .... G 360 659-1255
　Marysville *(G-6353)*
Laurel Graphics Fabrication Co .... E 253 872-7617
　Kent *(G-4991)*
Logo House .... G 206 890-3051
　Seattle *(G-10434)*
Lorrand Marketing LLC .... G 360 532-7510
　Aberdeen *(G-21)*
Miller Purr Fect Prints .... G 360 687-1186
　Yacolt *(G-15488)*
Moss Green Inc .... F 206 285-4020
　Seattle *(G-10564)*
Mvp Athletic Inc .... G 360 915-8715
　Tumwater *(G-13888)*
Plastic Sales & Service Inc .... F 206 524-8312
　Lynnwood *(G-6181)*
Post Indus Stress & Design .... F 253 572-9782
　Tacoma *(G-13472)*
Powder-Fab Inc .... E 360 435-0793
　Arlington *(G-303)*
Print Solutions .... G 253 435-1928
　Puyallup *(G-8225)*
PS Colors Inc .... G 206 371-1341
　Seattle *(G-10880)*
Purple Coyote Inc .... G 509 754-2488
　Ephrata *(G-3345)*
R P Signs .... G 425 788-6717
　Duvall *(G-2999)*
Reco Corporate Sportswear Inc .... G 360 354-2134
　Lynden *(G-6048)*
River City Screenprinting .... G 360 428-8985
　Mount Vernon *(G-6828)*

PRINTING, COMMERCIAL: Screen

Rulersmith Inc .... E 360 707-2828
  Shoreline *(G-11806)*
Salish Screenprinting .... G 360 758-2287
  Ferndale *(G-3895)*
Sandys Nifty Tees .... G 360 861-8669
  McCleary *(G-6419)*
Savage Screen .... G 360 321-2040
  Clinton *(G-2697)*
Screen Fx .... G 509 966-7515
  Yakima *(G-15668)*
Screen Printing Northwest Inc .... G 425 303-3381
  Everett *(G-3605)*
Screen Tek Inc .... E 509 928-8322
  Liberty Lake *(G-5860)*
Scribbly Tees .... G 517 285-3648
  Tacoma *(G-13509)*
Seattle Area Tees .... G 425 314-3814
  Mukilteo *(G-6976)*
Shirley Sunset .... G 360 574-3276
  Vancouver *(G-14584)*
Shirt Image Embroidery .... G 360 870-2837
  Hoquiam *(G-4359)*
Shirts Illustrated .... G 425 742-3844
  Lynnwood *(G-6195)*
Shirtworks .... G 509 925-3469
  Ellensburg *(G-3225)*
Shirtz To Go Inc .... G 206 242-4055
  Federal Way *(G-3783)*
Showcase Specialties Inc .... G 509 547-3344
  Pasco *(G-7629)*
Shur-Loc Fabric System .... G 360 805-4140
  Monroe *(G-6618)*
Silkscreen Company .... E 206 763-8108
  Seattle *(G-11112)*
Slow Loris Inc .... G 360 588-0321
  Anacortes *(G-169)*
Slp Creative LLC .... G 206 935-5646
  Seattle *(G-11136)*
Snap Custom Clothing .... G 206 682-0686
  Seattle *(G-11142)*
Solar Graphics Inc .... G 509 248-1129
  Yakima *(G-15678)*
Soundview Graphics LLC .... G 253 851-2007
  Gig Harbor *(G-4162)*
South Paw Screenprinting .... G 206 762-2926
  Seattle *(G-11160)*
Spectrum Sign Co Inc .... F 253 939-5500
  Auburn *(G-570)*
Spin Tees .... G 360 515-0543
  Olympia *(G-7399)*
Spin Tees .... G 253 301-2047
  Tacoma *(G-13523)*
Spokane Valley Screen Printing .... G 509 921-0207
  Spokane Valley *(G-12889)*
Starshine Products .... G 425 238-9820
  Monroe *(G-6627)*
Stickers Northwest .... G 360 731-0255
  Tacoma *(G-13526)*
Stickers Northwest Inc .... G 253 344-1236
  Fife *(G-3994)*
Stitchblade LLC .... G 206 940-7448
  Seattle *(G-11197)*
Sweet Tees .... G 253 632-9224
  Black Diamond *(G-1656)*
T & TS .... G 206 938-0177
  Seattle *(G-11248)*
T Town Apparel .... G 253 471-2960
  Tacoma *(G-13539)*
Tc Span America LLC .... F 425 774-3881
  Edmonds *(G-3159)*
Theo Coram Corporation .... G 425 774-4731
  Brier *(G-2022)*
Touch & Go Tees .... G 253 651-7505
  Gig Harbor *(G-4167)*
Touch Color Screen Printing .... G 360 377-5660
  Bremerton *(G-2007)*
TX Fine Designs Inc .... G 425 271-2866
  Tukwila *(G-13830)*
Undershirt Inc .... G 360 740-8048
  Chehalis *(G-2541)*
Van Quill Larry R .... G 360 736-1776
  Centralia *(G-2441)*
Vindico Printing and Design .... G 425 329-4739
  Lynnwood *(G-6218)*
Vinyl Status .... G 206 601-3598
  Bellevue *(G-1218)*
Washington Graphics LLC .... F 425 376-0877
  Redmond *(G-8709)*
West Coast Screen Printing .... G 360 581-6466
  Aberdeen *(G-39)*
Western Graphics Inc .... G 206 241-2526
  Fife *(G-3998)*
Wild Horse Graphics .... G 425 413-5080
  Maple Valley *(G-6300)*
Workhorse Ind .... G 206 257-5374
  Seattle *(G-11496)*
Wright Enterprises .... G 360 985-7060
  Onalaska *(G-7454)*
Yehun LLC .... G 425 533-9641
  Seattle *(G-11510)*

PRINTING, LITHOGRAPHIC: Advertising Posters

Forger3d LLC .... G 425 440-0662
  Renton *(G-8802)*
Sharon Rose .... G 360 341-1898
  Clinton *(G-2698)*

PRINTING, LITHOGRAPHIC: Catalogs

Amaze Graphics Inc .... G 425 481-8877
  Woodinville *(G-15176)*

PRINTING, LITHOGRAPHIC: Color

Hilltop Management Inc .... G 206 933-5900
  Seattle *(G-10174)*
National Color Graphics Inc .... F 509 326-6464
  Spokane *(G-12402)*

PRINTING, LITHOGRAPHIC: Decals

Duramark Technologies Inc .... G 206 473-9212
  Woodinville *(G-15229)*

PRINTING, LITHOGRAPHIC: Forms & Cards, Business

Clark Office Products Inc .... G 360 657-2018
  Marysville *(G-6326)*
Purple Coyote Inc .... G 509 754-2488
  Ephrata *(G-3345)*
Saturday Night Inc .... F 509 928-5816
  Spokane Valley *(G-12858)*

PRINTING, LITHOGRAPHIC: Forms, Business

Coprintco Business Forms Inc .... E 360 425-1810
  Longview *(G-5902)*

PRINTING, LITHOGRAPHIC: Letters, Circular Or Form

Impression Printing Co Inc .... G 206 762-6211
  Seattle *(G-10216)*

PRINTING, LITHOGRAPHIC: Offset & photolithographic printing

505 Printing .... G 360 864-6510
  Toledo *(G-13634)*
Lewis Publishing Company Inc .... E 360 354-4444
  Lynden *(G-6031)*
Tom & Cheryl McCallaum .... G 360 377-1606
  Bremerton *(G-2006)*

PRINTING, LITHOGRAPHIC: On Metal

A & A Printing Inc .... E 206 285-1700
  Seattle *(G-9326)*
Kalastar Holdings Inc .... E 509 534-0655
  Spokane *(G-12348)*
Kp LLC .... C 425 204-6355
  Renton *(G-8838)*
Lincoln Advertiser .... G 509 725-8007
  Davenport *(G-2874)*
Prompt Printery .... G 509 457-5848
  Yakima *(G-15657)*
Sams Press Inc .... G 425 423-8181
  Shoreline *(G-11807)*

PRINTING, LITHOGRAPHIC: Promotional Images

.... G 509 736-9508
  Kennewick *(G-4675)*

PRINTING, LITHOGRAPHIC: Publications

Consolidated Press LLC .... E 206 447-9659
  Seattle *(G-9730)*
Consolidated Press LLC .... D 253 922-3195
  Fife *(G-3945)*
Jomar Holdings Inc .... G 425 881-7125
  Redmond *(G-8521)*

PRINTING: Books

Literaryroad Com .... G 206 909-1672
  Seattle *(G-10426)*
United Reprographics L L C .... E 206 382-1177
  Seattle *(G-11372)*

PRINTING: Books

American Printing and Pubg .... G 253 395-3349
  Kent *(G-4779)*
Potter & Associates Inc .... G 206 623-8844
  Seattle *(G-10839)*
Ps2 Group LLC .... G 206 714-3025
  Redmond *(G-8638)*

PRINTING: Broadwoven Fabrics. Cotton

Jag Enterprizes Inc .... G 509 832-2836
  Prosser *(G-8044)*

PRINTING: Checkbooks

Deluxe .... G 360 794-3157
  Monroe *(G-6565)*

PRINTING: Commercial, NEC

360 Apparel LLC .... G 509 924-5219
  Spokane *(G-12087)*
4 Colour Inc .... G 509 249-0955
  Yakima *(G-15495)*
4 Over LLC .... G 818 246-1170
  Milton *(G-6531)*
A & R Enterprise .... G 425 453-0010
  Lynnwood *(G-6064)*
A and M Impressions LLC .... G 206 595-1111
  Burien *(G-2088)*
A B Graphics .... G 360 566-3666
  Vancouver *(G-14003)*
A-K Printing LLC .... G 253 249-7133
  Spanaway *(G-12052)*
AAA Printing & Graphics Inc .... F 425 454-0156
  Bellevue *(G-778)*
Aastha Inc .... G 206 382-4118
  Seattle *(G-9331)*
Abadan Repo Graphics .... E 509 946-7697
  Richland *(G-8963)*
About Printing and Apparel .... G 360 584-9159
  Lacey *(G-5529)*
Abracadabra Printing Inc .... G 206 343-9087
  Seattle *(G-9334)*
Absolute Sportswear .... G 206 890-1531
  Seattle *(G-9335)*
Adhesa-Plate Manufacturing Co .... E 206 682-0141
  Seattle *(G-9351)*
Advocate Printing .... G 360 748-3335
  Chehalis *(G-2458)*
Aero Safety Graphics Inc .... G 425 957-0712
  Redmond *(G-8372)*
Alexander Printing Co Inc .... G 425 252-4212
  Everett *(G-3366)*
All Print .... G 509 328-9344
  Spokane *(G-12106)*
Allied Envelope Company- Boise .... G 509 328-9800
  Spokane *(G-12107)*
American Printing and Pubg .... G 253 395-3349
  Kent *(G-4779)*
Apperson Print Management .... G 425 251-1850
  Renton *(G-8747)*
B & B Express Printing .... G 509 783-7383
  Kennewick *(G-4622)*
Ballard Outdoor .... F 206 552-0760
  Seattle *(G-9482)*
Barking Dog Inc .... G 425 822-6542
  Kirkland *(G-5288)*
Belgate Printing & Copy Inc .... F 425 451-9048
  Redmond *(G-8400)*
Bellevue Printing LLC .... G 425 558-1862
  Bellevue *(G-814)*
Bentson Printing LLC .... G 253 272-6563
  Tacoma *(G-13197)*
Biaflex Printing Solutions LLC .... G 509 895-7076
  Yakima *(G-15520)*
Blue Ink .... G 206 588-0739
  Seattle *(G-9549)*
Bob Bracht Llc .... G 206 678-5168
  Lake Forest Park *(G-5608)*

PRODUCT SECTION PRINTING: Fabric, Narrow

Brian E Styke .... G 360 331-0527
Freeland *(G-4027)*
Brightwork Specialty Printing .... G 360 930-0218
Poulsbo *(G-7951)*
Bte Printing Inc .... G 360 675-8837
Oak Harbor *(G-7143)*
Budget Printing Center .... G 509 736-7511
Kennewick *(G-4636)*
Business Equipment Center Inc .... F 509 747-2964
Spokane *(G-12162)*
Captivating Covers .... G 800 975-8198
Tukwila *(G-13710)*
Cascade Printing Direct .... G 253 661-6213
Federal Way *(G-3722)*
Chelan Printing .... G 509 682-5157
Chelan *(G-2551)*
Clam Digger .... G 360 299-3444
Anacortes *(G-114)*
Columbia Office and Bus .... G 360 695-6245
Vancouver *(G-14136)*
Colville Printing LLC .... G 509 684-5869
Colville *(G-2745)*
Community Networkers LLC .... G 509 826-5154
OMAK *(G-7437)*
Continuum .... G 509 534-0655
Spokane *(G-12199)*
Copy Break .... G 206 782-7506
Seattle *(G-9739)*
Copy-Rite Inc .... G 509 624-8503
Spokane *(G-12200)*
Countryman Signs Screen Prtrs .... G 425 355-1037
Everett *(G-3428)*
County of Lewis .... C 360 748-9121
Chehalis *(G-2485)*
D & H Printing .... G 360 427-7423
Shelton *(G-11693)*
D & L Screen Printing .... G 206 781-1977
Seattle *(G-9776)*
D A Graphics Inc .... G 206 760-5886
Seattle *(G-9777)*
Digital Documents Inc .... G 509 775-2425
Republic *(G-8956)*
Digital Image .... G 509 375-6001
Richland *(G-8988)*
Direct Mailing Solutions .... G 425 739-4568
Lynnwood *(G-6108)*
Dnlvi Business Solutions .... G 360 827-5210
Rochester *(G-9131)*
Dreamworks Printing Inc .... G 425 970-4625
Renton *(G-8788)*
Dynea Overlays Inc .... F 253 572-5600
Tacoma *(G-13267)*
East Washingtonian .... G 509 843-1313
Pomeroy *(G-7672)*
Editorial Consultants Inc .... G 206 329-6499
Seattle *(G-9884)*
Eiki Digital Systems Inc .... G 206 957-2626
Seattle *(G-9891)*
Electronic Imaging Svcs Inc .... E 253 887-1237
Auburn *(G-432)*
Fedex Office & Print Svcs Inc .... F 509 922-4929
Spokane Valley *(G-12700)*
Fedex Office & Print Svcs Inc .... E 206 467-1767
Seattle *(G-9981)*
Fine Design Inc .... E 425 271-2866
Tukwila *(G-13735)*
Foster Press .... G 425 334-9317
Everett *(G-3484)*
Garjen Corp .... G 253 862-6140
Bonney Lake *(G-1724)*
Garland Printing Co Inc .... G 509 327-5556
Spokane *(G-12267)*
Gdansk Inc .... E 509 279-2034
Spokane Valley *(G-12713)*
Gordon Gruel .... G 509 226-1309
Newman Lake *(G-7045)*
Graphic Communications .... F 360 786-5110
Olympia *(G-7299)*
Greendisk Inc .... G 425 392-8700
Sammamish *(G-9211)*
Gt Recording .... G 206 783-6911
Seattle *(G-10130)*
Harold Tymer Co Inc .... F 360 573-6053
Vancouver *(G-14284)*
Hemlock Printers USA Inc .... G 206 241-8311
Seattle *(G-10165)*
ID Integration Inc .... F 425 438-2533
Mukilteo *(G-6940)*
ID Label Inc .... F 206 323-8100
Seattle *(G-10202)*
Impact Studio .... G 425 890-3914
Sedro Woolley *(G-11541)*
In Graphic Detail LLC .... G 360 582-0002
Sequim *(G-11641)*
Ink Inc .... F 253 565-4000
University Place *(G-13973)*
Ink Ability .... G 360 342-8174
Battle Ground *(G-709)*
Integrity Printing LLC .... G 253 841-3161
Puyallup *(G-8169)*
Invitationinabottlecom .... G 800 489-8048
Everett *(G-3519)*
Ito Enterprises Inc .... G 425 556-0819
Redmond *(G-8515)*
James Lund .... G 425 742-9135
Lynnwood *(G-6143)*
Jeremy Nichols .... G 509 930-6352
Yakima *(G-15601)*
Journal-News Publishing Co .... F 509 754-4636
Ephrata *(G-3339)*
Journal-News Publishing Co .... G 509 725-0101
Davenport *(G-2872)*
K Smith Enterprises .... G 425 455-0923
Bellevue *(G-965)*
Kool Change Printing Inc .... G 360 794-9019
Monroe *(G-6588)*
Kp LLC .... C 425 204-6355
Renton *(G-8838)*
Kwang Nam Hwang .... F 206 433-8811
Burien *(G-2116)*
Lakeside Gardens .... G 360 483-8889
Lynden *(G-6030)*
Legend Data Systems Inc .... F 425 251-1670
Kent *(G-4992)*
Marked Departure Pottery .... G 360 991-5910
Vancouver *(G-14394)*
Markon Inc .... G 503 222-3966
Vancouver *(G-14395)*
Martin Business Systems .... G 509 582-3159
Kennewick *(G-4692)*
Marysville Printing Inc .... G 360 658-9195
Marysville *(G-6357)*
McClatchy Newspapers Inc .... C 509 582-1500
Kennewick *(G-4693)*
McMann & Tate Inc .... G 360 676-4396
Bellingham *(G-1430)*
Merrill Corp Resource MGT .... G 509 326-7892
Spokane *(G-12391)*
Merrill Corporation .... C 360 794-3157
Monroe *(G-6596)*
Myseps .... G 858 231-2774
Port Orchard *(G-7831)*
National Color .... F 206 281-9400
Seattle *(G-10587)*
Newmata Screen Printing .... G 360 631-7860
Arlington *(G-288)*
Nova Graphics .... G 206 248-3489
Seatac *(G-9294)*
NRG Resources Inc .... D 509 588-4786
Benton City *(G-1621)*
Nta Inc .... G 425 487-2679
Woodinville *(G-15325)*
Omega Printing .... G 425 339-8538
Everett *(G-3559)*
Oroville Reman & Reload Inc .... E 509 476-2935
Oroville *(G-7471)*
P I P Printing Inc .... F 360 456-4742
Olympia *(G-7364)*
Panther Printing .... G 509 344-4600
Spokane Valley *(G-12825)*
Paper Muses .... G 425 241-3710
Maple Valley *(G-6288)*
Park Postal LLC .... G 206 860-7678
Seattle *(G-10759)*
Peetz Enterprises .... G 509 276-2608
Clayton *(G-2659)*
Pen Print Inc .... G 360 457-3404
Port Angeles *(G-7735)*
Penway Limited Inc .... G 360 435-6445
Arlington *(G-300)*
Perfect Copy & Print Inc .... G 206 325-4733
Seattle *(G-10786)*
Perfect Printing & Signs .... G 509 786-3811
Yakima *(G-15645)*
Potter & Associates Inc .... G 206 623-8844
Seattle *(G-10839)*
Print NW LLC .... D 253 284-2300
Tacoma *(G-13478)*
Print24com USA LP .... G 206 607-0639
Seattle *(G-10864)*
Printing Washington State Dept .... G 360 407-6013
Lacey *(G-5578)*
Progressive Printing Solutions .... G 425 867-1296
Issaquah *(G-4462)*
Proline Printer Services .... G 360 697-2336
Poulsbo *(G-7992)*
Quality Press Inc .... E 206 768-2655
Seattle *(G-10902)*
Rainbow Racing System Inc .... F 509 326-5470
Spokane *(G-12466)*
Rainier Corp .... G 206 280-4666
Seattle *(G-10916)*
Real Time Screen Printinginc .... G 206 818-6346
Des Moines *(G-2945)*
Revolution Inc .... F 206 714-3529
Seattle *(G-10956)*
Roberta Propst .... G 425 681-9760
Bellevue *(G-1104)*
Ronald Finney .... G 253 857-7635
Olalla *(G-7209)*
RR Donnelley & Sons Company .... F 206 389-8900
Seattle *(G-10989)*
Saco Sales LLC .... G 253 922-6349
Fife *(G-3991)*
Savage Inc .... G 206 972-8217
Seattle *(G-11018)*
Sbf Printing .... G 509 457-2877
Yakima *(G-15667)*
Sideline Sports Inc .... G 206 906-9652
Seattle *(G-11104)*
Sno-King Signs .... G 425 775-0594
Edmonds *(G-3158)*
Sound Publishing Inc .... D 425 355-0717
Everett *(G-3618)*
Specialty Embroidery .... G 509 924-1579
Lacey *(G-5593)*
Star Copy & Reprographics Ctr .... E 360 385-1022
Port Townsend *(G-7931)*
Stat Corporation .... F 425 883-4181
Redmond *(G-8681)*
Stephen L Nelson Inc .... G 425 885-9499
Redmond *(G-8682)*
Steve Czako Associates .... G 509 624-7018
Spokane *(G-12529)*
Stone Drums Inc .... G 425 485-5570
Woodinville *(G-15376)*
Streamline International .... G 425 392-2350
Issaquah *(G-4483)*
Sun Printing .... G 253 517-5017
Federal Way *(G-3791)*
Super H Corporation .... G 360 687-2824
Vancouver *(G-14620)*
Swift Print .... G 360 805-8509
Snohomish *(G-11989)*
Tacoma Printing .... G 253 470-1454
Tacoma *(G-13546)*
Taylor Communications Inc .... G 360 699-4013
Vancouver *(G-14626)*
Tcc Printing and Imaging Inc .... E 206 622-4050
Seattle *(G-11276)*
Thomas Mayer .... G 360 945-0354
Point Roberts *(G-7670)*
Ticket Envelope Company LLC .... G 206 784-7266
Seattle *(G-11304)*
Tiger Press .... G 360 468-3737
Lopez Island *(G-5987)*
Time Printing Inc .... G 206 633-3320
Seattle *(G-11309)*
Touchmark Printing .... G 206 420-4607
Kent *(G-5186)*
Twin Cities Printing .... G 360 807-1200
Centralia *(G-2440)*
Typesetter Corporation .... F 425 455-3055
Mercer Island *(G-6488)*
Vanguard Press .... G 206 782-1448
Seattle *(G-11404)*
Vietnamese NW Newsppr & Annual .... F 206 722-6984
Seattle *(G-11415)*
Western Typographers Inc .... G 425 967-4700
Lynnwood *(G-6223)*
Wide Format Geeks .... G 509 868-2319
Bothell *(G-1919)*

PRINTING: Engraving & Plate

S & G Engraving .... G 425 868-4169
Sammamish *(G-9244)*

PRINTING: Fabric, Narrow

Traveling Designs .... G 360 695-5887
Kelso *(G-4557)*

PRODUCT

PRINTING: Flexographic

Tacoma Rubber Stamp Co .... E 253 383-5433
  Tacoma *(G-13548)*

PRINTING: Gravure, Business Form & Card

American Solutions For Bus .... G 509 276-8700
  Deer Park *(G-2893)*

PRINTING: Gravure, Color

United Reprographics L L C .... E 206 382-1177
  Seattle *(G-11372)*

PRINTING: Gravure, Forms, Business

Pioneer Printing and Forms .... G 509 248-7393
  Yakima *(G-15648)*

PRINTING: Gravure, Job

Exone Company .... G 360 286-0556
  Bremerton *(G-1953)*

PRINTING: Gravure, Labels

Bcwest LLC .... E 206 323-8100
  Seattle *(G-9504)*

PRINTING: Gravure, Rotogravure

Color Press Publishing Inc .... E 509 525-6030
  Walla Walla *(G-14789)*
Integrity Press Inc .... G 425 868-3120
  Redmond *(G-8511)*
RR Donnelley & Sons Company .... F 206 389-8900
  Seattle *(G-10989)*
Sbd Inc .... G 509 545-8845
  Pasco *(G-7625)*

PRINTING: Gravure, Seals

Aesseal Inc .... G 360 414-0118
  Longview *(G-5883)*

PRINTING: Gravure, Stationery & Invitation

Citlali Creativo .... G 206 779-5664
  Burien *(G-2095)*

PRINTING: Laser

Metrix Create Space .... G 206 357-9406
  Seattle *(G-10524)*
Pcs Laser and Memorial .... G 208 746-1033
  Clarkston *(G-2640)*

PRINTING: Letterpress

Arts & Crafts Press Inc .... G 360 871-7707
  Tacoma *(G-13183)*
Bison Bkbinding Letterpress LP .... G 360 734-0481
  Bellingham *(G-1273)*
Bremerton Letterpress Co LLC .... G 360 620-8967
  Bremerton *(G-1939)*
Clarence H Spargo Jr .... G 360 532-1505
  Aberdeen *(G-7)*
Commercial Printing Inc .... F 509 663-4772
  Wenatchee *(G-15023)*
Control Seneca Corporation .... E 425 602-4700
  Woodinville *(G-15212)*
Dunsire Printers Inc .... G 360 532-8791
  Aberdeen *(G-9)*
F D Company .... G 253 531-7087
  Tacoma *(G-13285)*
Girlie Press Inc .... G 206 720-1237
  Seattle *(G-10074)*
Harbor Graphics Inc .... G 360 532-1234
  Hoquiam *(G-4339)*
Horizon Printing Company LLC .... G 509 663-8414
  Wenatchee *(G-15040)*
Impression Printing Co Inc .... G 206 762-6211
  Seattle *(G-10216)*
L & L Printing Inc .... G 253 848-5546
  Puyallup *(G-8174)*
Letterpress Distilling LLC .... G 206 227-4522
  Seattle *(G-10408)*
Luckiest Letterpress .... G 425 241-8229
  Bothell *(G-1774)*
Prompt Printery .... G 509 457-5848
  Yakima *(G-15657)*
Ramax Printing and Awards .... G 509 928-1222
  Spokane *(G-12467)*

Record Printing Inc .... F 509 964-9500
  Thorp *(G-13629)*
Seattle Chinese Post Inc .... E 206 223-0623
  Seattle *(G-11051)*
Swifty Prtg Dgital Imaging Inc .... E 206 441-0800
  Seattle *(G-11239)*

PRINTING: Lithographic

1 Wild Print .... G 360 550-1916
  Vancouver *(G-14000)*
3d Mail Results .... G 253 859-7310
  Kent *(G-4748)*
A & R Enterprise .... G 425 453-0010
  Lynnwood *(G-6064)*
A & R Print Services Inc .... G 206 321-5263
  Buckley *(G-2044)*
A D G Data Systems Inc .... G 425 771-7603
  Lynnwood *(G-6065)*
A Plus Printing .... G 509 714-5514
  Spokane *(G-12089)*
A Printing .... G 509 235-5160
  Cheney *(G-2572)*
A-K Printing .... G 253 391-1784
  Maple Valley *(G-6252)*
A-Z Business Forms .... G 206 363-8170
  Shoreline *(G-11753)*
AAA Printing & Graphics Inc .... F 425 454-0156
  Bellevue *(G-778)*
Aceface Printing .... G 206 427-2272
  Seattle *(G-9341)*
Adam Welch .... G 206 329-8697
  Seattle *(G-9348)*
Adhesa-Plate Manufacturing Co .... E 206 682-0141
  Seattle *(G-9351)*
Advanced Laser Printer Service .... G 360 835-1824
  Washougal *(G-14940)*
Airport Prints .... G 425 760-2235
  Arlington *(G-198)*
All City Print .... G 360 718-2448
  Vancouver *(G-14019)*
American Printing and Pubg .... G 253 395-3349
  Kent *(G-4779)*
Andrews Nation Inc .... G 360 989-1700
  Vancouver *(G-14034)*
Apparel Dude Printing .... G 425 283-3051
  Redmond *(G-8382)*
Apple Valley Printers .... G 509 679-9592
  Wenatchee *(G-15009)*
Applied Digital Imaging Inc .... E 360 671-9465
  Bellingham *(G-1250)*
ARC Document Solutions Inc .... G 425 883-1110
  Bellevue *(G-792)*
Arch Parent Inc .... A 206 664-0217
  Burien *(G-2091)*
Ardor Printing LLC .... G 425 786-4361
  Snohomish *(G-11875)*
Arrow International Inc .... D 425 407-1475
  Lynnwood *(G-6077)*
Artillery Graphic Design & SCR .... G 360 709-3351
  Olympia *(G-7231)*
Ats .... G 360 260-2627
  Camas *(G-2230)*
B & J Printing Inc .... G 360 692-3470
  Bremerton *(G-1936)*
Bas Inc .... G 509 943-2611
  Richland *(G-8972)*
Bastet Screen Printing .... G 360 880-2717
  Seattle *(G-9499)*
Bay Printing Inc .... G 360 679-3816
  Oak Harbor *(G-7140)*
Beach Bee Inc .... G 360 289-2244
  Ocean Shores *(G-7184)*
Belgate Printing & Copy Inc .... F 425 451-9048
  Redmond *(G-8400)*
Bellingham Screen Printing .... G 360 920-0114
  Bellingham *(G-1269)*
Belltown Prtg & Graphics Inc .... G 206 448-8919
  Seattle *(G-9509)*
Bentson Printing LLC .... G 253 272-6563
  Tacoma *(G-13197)*
Best Practices Wiki .... G 206 708-1572
  Seattle *(G-9517)*
Bigwoods Screen Printing .... G 253 208-3990
  Puyallup *(G-8131)*
Blanksi LLC .... G 425 453-1224
  Bellevue *(G-820)*
Blue Print .... G 425 870-5599
  Everett *(G-3390)*
Blue Prints Plus .... G 425 888-8815
  North Bend *(G-7102)*

Blue Ribbon Printing .... G 425 478-7628
  Everett *(G-3391)*
Bob Nelson .... G 360 795-3391
  Cathlamet *(G-2360)*
Boruck Prtg & Silk Screening .... G 206 522-8500
  Shoreline *(G-11763)*
Brands Reco .... G 360 428-8985
  Lynden *(G-6003)*
Bright Signs Screen Printing .... G 360 695-6444
  Vancouver *(G-14084)*
Bryan Zippro .... G 425 881-9780
  Redmond *(G-8411)*
Bulldog Printing LLC .... G 360 217-7317
  Monroe *(G-6560)*
Cadena Printing .... G 253 951-7545
  Kent *(G-4833)*
Carlyle Printing .... G 360 537-0266
  Hoquiam *(G-4330)*
Cascadia Screen Printing .... G 509 362-8900
  Spokane Valley *(G-12651)*
Cascadia Screen Printing .... G 541 490-7012
  Spokane *(G-12172)*
Cassandra Watterson .... G 509 306-0205
  Ellensburg *(G-3187)*
Catholic Printery Inc .... E 206 767-0660
  Seattle *(G-9648)*
Chameleon Prints .... G 425 493-3071
  Marysville *(G-6323)*
Child Evngelism Fellowship Inc .... E 509 662-2320
  Wenatchee *(G-15021)*
Child Evngelism Fellowship Inc .... E 360 424-1014
  Mount Vernon *(G-6784)*
Child Evngelism Fellowship Inc .... E 509 928-2820
  Spokane Valley *(G-12655)*
Child Evngelism Fellowship Inc .... E 425 252-6314
  Everett *(G-3416)*
Color Press Publishing Inc .... E 509 525-6030
  Walla Walla *(G-14789)*
Colorgraphics .... G 206 576-4300
  Kent *(G-4857)*
County of King .... E 206 263-3113
  Seattle *(G-9748)*
Cross Roads Printing .... G 509 328-1627
  Spokane *(G-12209)*
Curt Arneson Enterprises Inc .... F 253 383-4377
  Tacoma *(G-13251)*
Curts Printing .... G 360 456-3041
  Lacey *(G-5543)*
Custom Prints NW LLC .... G 253 225-7725
  Gig Harbor *(G-4093)*
Deer Park Printing .... G 509 276-9712
  Deer Park *(G-2899)*
Devaul Publishing Inc .... E 360 748-3335
  Chehalis *(G-2489)*
Digital Imaging Services Inc .... G 360 567-1260
  Vancouver *(G-14179)*
Direct Connect Group (dcg) LLC .... B 206 784-6892
  Seattle *(G-9833)*
DI Logos .... G 360 385-3101
  Port Townsend *(G-7880)*
Dla Document Services .... G 509 527-7231
  Walla Walla *(G-14797)*
Dla Document Services .... E 360 315-4014
  Silverdale *(G-11832)*
Dolphin Press Inc .... G 253 735-1856
  Auburn *(G-427)*
Dotink LLC .... G 509 655-0828
  Spokane Valley *(G-12683)*
Dr Ventures Inc .... G 253 874-6583
  Federal Way *(G-3733)*
Eagle Harbor Print Co LLC .... G 970 441-0000
  Port Orchard *(G-7805)*
Ecographics Inc .... G 425 825-1888
  Bainbridge Island *(G-627)*
Empress Print LLC .... G 509 826-5154
  Tonasket *(G-13648)*
ESP Printing Inc .... G 425 251-6240
  Seattle *(G-9940)*
Eternal Color Prints .... G 360 771-9408
  Vancouver *(G-14207)*
Everything Prints .... G 360 447-8217
  Puyallup *(G-8150)*
Evolution Press Inc .... G 206 783-5522
  Seattle *(G-9949)*
Fedex Office & Print Svcs Inc .... E 509 484-0601
  Spokane *(G-12254)*
Fedex Office & Print Svcs Inc .... E 253 841-3557
  Puyallup *(G-8152)*
Fedex Office & Print Svcs Inc .... E 206 546-7600
  Shoreline *(G-11771)*

Fedex Office & Print Svcs Inc F 253 872-5539
Kent (G-4906)
Fedex Office & Print Svcs Inc F 360 694-8584
Vancouver (G-14226)
Fedex Office & Print Svcs Inc E 206 467-1767
Seattle (G-9981)
Fedex Office & Print Svcs Inc E 206 244-8884
Tukwila (G-13733)
Fedex Office & Print Svcs Inc E 253 565-4882
Tacoma (G-13292)
Fedex Office Print & Ship Ctr G 425 641-1174
Bellevue (G-909)
Fedexoffice G 206 467-5885
Seattle (G-9982)
Felony Prints G 509 443-6702
Cheney (G-2585)
Fifty Fifty Print G 360 936-9516
Vancouver (G-14228)
Fifty Fifty Print Co G 360 718-2448
Vancouver (G-14229)
Fine Arts Litho G 360 876-5649
Port Orchard (G-7809)
Fine Print WA LLC G 206 859-8469
Spanaway (G-12057)
Finger Prints of His Grace G 253 514-6150
Gig Harbor (G-4099)
Flake Printing G 425 210-6371
Everett (G-3474)
Footeprints Incorporated G 360 754-8779
Olympia (G-7289)
Footeprints Inc G 360 491-8195
Olympia (G-7290)
Foremost Printing G 206 861-6576
Kent (G-4916)
Fox Printing G 206 595-7055
Edmonds (G-3113)
Freda Britt Prints G 206 409-4701
Vashon (G-14722)
Freedomprint LLC G 860 333-2448
Silverdale (G-11835)
Fremont Printing Co G 206 632-3759
Seattle (G-10025)
Full Color Printing NW G 360 721-2110
Vancouver (G-14243)
Gill Print G 509 535-2521
Spokane (G-12274)
Girlie Press Inc G 206 720-1237
Seattle (G-10074)
Good Impressions Inc G 360 225-9080
Woodland (G-15434)
Grandview Screen USA Inc G 360 481-3490
Olympia (G-7298)
Great White Smile Instant G 253 255-0456
Tacoma (G-13322)
Ground Print LLC G 206 852-2622
Maple Valley (G-6271)
Hamilton Printing Systems G 425 778-1936
Edmonds (G-3117)
Harbor Graphics Inc G 253 858-7909
Gig Harbor (G-4111)
Heaton Printing G 360 353-3720
Kelso (G-4528)
Heir Wear LLC G 425 760-0990
Snohomish (G-11920)
Herff Jones LLC G 425 488-7213
Kenmore (G-4580)
Herzog Envelope Inc G 206 618-6765
Redmond (G-8491)
Highroad Products Inc G 253 474-9900
Tacoma (G-13337)
Historic Photos Prints Cds LLC G 360 695-6151
Vancouver (G-14299)
Hitech Publications Group G 520 378-1155
Lacey (G-5555)
Hoof Prints Kitsap G 360 932-3992
Bremerton (G-1961)
Huskey Printing & Envelop G 206 901-1792
Seattle (G-10194)
Im Printing G 206 300-7511
Seattle (G-10206)
Imagine Visual Service LLC G 206 281-5703
Seattle (G-10208)
Impressive Printing G 253 538-2948
Tacoma (G-13348)
Imprints Northwest G 360 254-8700
Vancouver (G-14311)
In An Instant G 206 465-0644
Seattle (G-10218)
In An Instant Art LLC G 206 294-3570
Seattle (G-10219)

Ink Doctor Printing G 509 237-1644
Ephrata (G-3338)
Ink Smiths Screen Printing LLC G 253 446-7126
Puyallup (G-8168)
Ink Well Printers Inc G 206 623-1701
Federal Way (G-3745)
Inker Prints LLC G 206 499-7379
Seattle (G-10235)
Inkwell LLC G 425 277-3655
Renton (G-8826)
Instant Access Videocom G 425 273-3496
Newcastle (G-7031)
Instant Auction Co G 509 448-0279
Spokane (G-12315)
Instant Cheer Illstrations LLC G 206 999-5515
Seattle (G-10245)
Instant Gratification LLP G 206 361-2966
Lake Forest Park (G-5615)
Instant Option G 509 290-6481
Spokane (G-12316)
Insty-Prints G 509 334-4275
Pullman (G-8092)
Integrated Print Solutions Inc G 888 716-5666
Everett (G-3517)
Iron Street Printing LLC G 360 734-5809
Bellingham (G-1383)
J Salgado LLC G 425 367-3188
Marysville (G-6346)
Jasper Know Print G 425 486-7147
Bothell (G-1869)
Jeanne Jolivette G 360 750-4447
Vancouver (G-14336)
Jma Printing G 509 395-2145
Trout Lake (G-13679)
Johnson Cox Co Inc E 253 272-2238
Tacoma (G-13364)
Johnston Printing Inc E 509 892-2055
Spokane (G-12340)
Journal-News Publishing Co F 509 754-4636
Ephrata (G-3339)
K H B Inc G 425 771-0881
Lynnwood (G-6146)
Kennewick Press LLC G 509 491-3801
Kennewick (G-4682)
Kewanna Screen Printing Inc G 574 817-0682
Bellingham (G-1393)
Kolorkraze LLC G 360 609-2771
Vancouver (G-14352)
L & L Printing Inc G 253 848-5546
Puyallup (G-8174)
Lane Chestnut Prints G 206 397-3108
Seattle (G-10375)
Laser Printers Plus Inc G 206 786-0107
Bothell (G-1873)
Liberty Print Solutions G 509 536-0515
Spokane (G-12363)
Litho Inc G 206 632-0211
Seattle (G-10428)
Lithos Craftsmen Inc G 206 949-9787
Woodinville (G-15290)
Lj Print Group LLC G 360 852-0914
Vancouver (G-14379)
Local Church Publishing G 360 710-8751
Bremerton (G-1974)
Logos Church G 425 378-0276
Bellevue (G-988)
Lonjina Design and Print G 206 852-6197
Seattle (G-10438)
Lori Shine G 360 400-6006
Yelm (G-15738)
Lx Packaging & Printing Svc G 206 714-5479
Seattle (G-10454)
M C Printing G 360 573-7499
Vancouver (G-14390)
Madsam Printing LLC G 425 445-1949
Kirkland (G-5392)
Mail Well Envelope G 206 576-4300
Kent (G-5001)
Marshall Dt Company F 425 869-2525
Kirkland (G-5398)
Mass Media Outlet Corporation G 206 274-8475
Shoreline (G-11786)
McClatchy Newspapers Inc C 360 754-5400
Olympia (G-7333)
Merrill Corporation C 360 794-3157
Monroe (G-6596)
Metrix Software G 425 361-2415
Edmonds (G-3134)
Minute Man Press G 360 738-3539
Bellingham (G-1436)

Minuteman Press G 360 258-2411
Vancouver (G-14421)
Minuteman Press G 206 577-9199
Seattle (G-10547)
Minuteman Press G 509 435-0863
Spokane Valley (G-12791)
Minuteman Press G 360 577-3257
Kelso (G-4538)
Minuteman Press Intl Inc G 360 692-3470
Bremerton (G-1979)
Minuteman Press Renton G 425 251-0781
Renton (G-8856)
Morris Printer Solutions G 360 891-3812
Vancouver (G-14425)
Mountainview Screen Print G 509 773-6290
Goldendale (G-4203)
Mr Print One G 253 693-2802
Tacoma (G-13422)
MSC Print House G 206 708-1423
Seattle (G-10567)
Newman Burrows LLC E 206 324-5644
Tukwila (G-13777)
Nielsens Graphic Service Inc F 206 463-2430
Vashon (G-14737)
Northwest Fine Art Printing G 425 947-1501
Kent (G-5031)
Norwest Business Forms & Sups G 206 938-4387
Seattle (G-10655)
Noteadscom Inc G 360 705-4548
Lacey (G-5569)
Now Impressions Inc G 425 881-5911
Redmond (G-8601)
OH Snap Prints G 509 901-7719
Yakima (G-15638)
Olympic Print and Apparel G 206 402-3642
Seattle (G-10693)
Ooak Prints LLC G 253 886-1539
Buckley (G-2065)
Orange Homes LLC G 360 450-4640
Vancouver (G-14454)
Out of Woods Printing LLC G 509 447-2590
Newport (G-7063)
P & Ds IMG-N-That Spcalty Prtg G 509 346-1170
Royal City (G-9173)
P and S Print Company LLC G 509 398-6504
Ephrata (G-3344)
P I P Printing Inc F 360 456-4742
Olympia (G-7364)
Pacific NW Print Flfllment Inc F 509 242-7857
Spokane Valley (G-12823)
Pacific Printing Inc G 360 377-0844
Bremerton (G-1984)
Pacific Screen Printers G 360 225-7771
Woodland (G-15455)
Park & Moazez Enterprises Inc G 206 464-0100
Seattle (G-10757)
Pen Print Inc G 360 457-3404
Port Angeles (G-7735)
Peril Prints G 323 599-1447
Seattle (G-10788)
Pink Power Printing G 425 295-4324
Maple Valley (G-6290)
Pinnacle Printing Foundation G 425 271-7089
Renton (G-8879)
Pressed In Time Prtg Prmtons L G 253 833-1351
Auburn (G-536)
Prins Robert P G 360 293-3101
Anacortes (G-162)
Prins Williams Analytics LLC G 253 549-0740
Fox Island (G-4024)
Print & Play Productions G 503 750-5316
Vancouver (G-14506)
Print Concierge G 206 801-9996
Redmond (G-8631)
Print Easy G 800 562-0888
Friday Harbor (G-4053)
Print Guys G 509 453-6369
Yakima (G-15653)
Print It Northwest G 360 840-0807
Sedro Woolley (G-11557)
Print N Surf G 360 693-1710
Vancouver (G-14507)
Print Pro G 360 807-8716
Centralia (G-2426)
Print Rogue LLC G 360 791-0914
Olympia (G-7372)
Print Tech Inc G 509 535-1460
Spokane Valley (G-12840)
Print Works Inc G 206 623-3512
Seattle (G-10863)

Employee Codes: A=Over 500 employees, B=251-500
C=101-250, D=51-100, E=20-50, F=10-19, G=2-9
2019 Washington
Manufacturers Register
1043

PRINTING: Lithographic

Printing Hope .... G 253 358-3348
  Gig Harbor *(G-4149)*
Printing Perfection .... G 509 843-7455
  Pomeroy *(G-7676)*
Printing Unlimited .... G 360 357-8936
  Olympia *(G-7373)*
Printonyx Inc .... G 360 378-2069
  Friday Harbor *(G-4054)*
Printwise Inc .... F 360 424-5945
  Mount Vernon *(G-6826)*
Pro-Litho Inc .... G 206 547-6462
  Seattle *(G-10869)*
Punjab Signs & Printing .... G 425 501-3336
  Kent *(G-5089)*
R & R Printing Inc .... G 206 257-9438
  Edgewood *(G-3090)*
Refresh Prtg & Promotions LLC ..... G 425 391-3223
  Issaquah *(G-4466)*
Restless Prints .... G 772 205-9868
  Seattle *(G-10953)*
Revelation Business Servi .... G 360 456-1176
  Olympia *(G-7384)*
Rgzprints .... G 208 310-0500
  Spokane *(G-12474)*
Ridgeline Graphics Inc .... G 509 662-6858
  Wenatchee *(G-15069)*
Ridgewood Industries Inc .... F 425 774-0170
  Edmonds *(G-3148)*
Riley Hopkins Screen Printing .... G 253 851-9078
  Gig Harbor *(G-4155)*
Risque Inc .... F 360 738-1280
  Bellingham *(G-1517)*
Rk Print Group .... G 206 972-0874
  Seattle *(G-10968)*
Rss Kennewick .... G 206 441-9907
  Kennewick *(G-4720)*
Ruser Publications Inc .... G 509 659-1020
  Ritzville *(G-9122)*
Ryonet Corporation .... D 360 576-7188
  Vancouver *(G-14561)*
Safeguard Bus Forms & Systems .. G 800 727-9120
  Spokane *(G-12492)*
Sanford Art Prints .... G 509 784-1220
  Entiat *(G-3271)*
Screen Printing International .... G 678 231-9195
  Vancouver *(G-14575)*
Screen Tek Inc .... E 509 928-8322
  Liberty Lake *(G-5860)*
Seattle Custom Printing .... G 206 268-0443
  Seatac *(G-9303)*
Seattle Daily Journal Commerce ... E 206 622-8272
  Seattle *(G-11055)*
Seattle Event Printing .... G 253 642-6567
  Auburn *(G-558)*
Seattle Print House LLC .... G 503 841-7755
  Kent *(G-5125)*
Seattle Printworks LLC .... G 206 623-3512
  Seattle *(G-11069)*
Seattle Signs & Printing .... G 206 588-5592
  Seattle *(G-11075)*
Selfish Apparel and Printing .... G 206 450-2725
  Snohomish *(G-11974)*
Sensible Horsemanship LLC .... G 509 292-2475
  Elk *(G-3176)*
Shelton Publishing Inc .... E 360 426-4412
  Shelton *(G-11732)*
Sign Print 360 LLC .... G 360 578-2476
  Kelso *(G-4547)*
Sinbads Custom Printing .... G 253 232-7367
  Spanaway *(G-12074)*
Sir Speedy .... G 360 647-7565
  Bellingham *(G-1538)*
Sky Printing .... G 206 933-5900
  Seattle *(G-11130)*
Sls Development Inc .... G 253 735-0322
  Auburn *(G-567)*
Smart Tech 3d Printing .... G 425 614-6451
  Renton *(G-8914)*
Snapdog Printing .... G 360 217-8172
  Snohomish *(G-11978)*
Snohomish Publishing Company .. E 206 523-7548
  Snohomish *(G-11983)*
Soterion Co .... G 425 259-8181
  Everett *(G-3616)*
Soulier Southbay LLC .... G 360 459-3015
  Lacey *(G-5589)*
Sound Screen Printing Inc .... G 206 890-2700
  Tukwila *(G-13820)*
Spectrum Embroidery & Printing ... G 206 851-9687
  Bothell *(G-1796)*
Spectrum Health Systems Inc .... A 253 572-3398
  Tacoma *(G-13521)*
Spokane Paw Prints LLC .... G 509 475-6885
  Spokane *(G-12520)*
Spokesinger Prints .... G 206 522-5179
  Seattle *(G-11170)*
Stafford Press Inc .... F 425 861-5856
  Redmond *(G-8680)*
Standard Digital Print Co Inc .... F 509 624-2985
  Spokane *(G-12524)*
Stanwood-Camano News Inc .... E 360 629-8066
  Stanwood *(G-12995)*
Statesman-Examiner Inc .... E 509 684-4567
  Colville *(G-2775)*
Stella Color Inc .... F 206 223-2303
  Seattle *(G-11189)*
Stick It Print .... G 360 909-6060
  Vancouver *(G-14611)*
Sun News Inc .... E 360 659-1300
  Marysville *(G-6391)*
Sun Printing .... G 253 517-5017
  Federal Way *(G-3791)*
Superior Imprints Inc .... F 206 441-7147
  Seattle *(G-11223)*
T-Prints LLC .... G 425 780-9380
  Kenmore *(G-4609)*
T-Shirt Madness Silk Screen .... G 206 427-8720
  Seattle *(G-11251)*
Telepress Inc .... E 425 392-1660
  Kent *(G-5176)*
Thought Ops LLC .... G 206 427-0165
  Seattle *(G-11296)*
Thunder Specialty Printing .... G 253 921-7647
  Puyallup *(G-8263)*
Tiger Press .... G 360 468-3737
  Lopez Island *(G-5987)*
Time Printing Inc .... G 206 633-3320
  Seattle *(G-11309)*
Tls Printing .... G 206 522-8289
  Seattle *(G-11315)*
Touch Mark Publishing & Print ...... G 206 551-0578
  Tukwila *(G-13827)*
Tri-City Tees & Screen Prtg .... G 509 420-6993
  Richland *(G-9048)*
Triad Comsural Printing Corp .... F 509 582-1466
  Kennewick *(G-4740)*
Triton Print and Pour Poor .... G 360 828-8809
  Vancouver *(G-14647)*
Trojan Lithograph Corporation ...... C 425 873-2200
  Renton *(G-8933)*
Typebee Lttrpress Prntshop LLC .. G 509 979-6017
  Spokane *(G-12574)*
Ukush Print and Mail .... G 206 763-0454
  Seattle *(G-11360)*
Unauthorized Screen Printing .... G 425 224-5602
  Seattle *(G-11364)*
Unauthorized Screen Printing .... G 425 502-1150
  Seattle *(G-11365)*
Unique TS Printing .... G 253 686-3669
  Port Orchard *(G-7854)*
University of Washington .... C 206 543-5680
  Seattle *(G-11379)*
University of Washington .... C 206 543-5680
  Seattle *(G-11382)*
Van Quill Larry R .... G 360 736-1776
  Centralia *(G-2441)*
Varsity Screen Prtg & Awards .... G 509 829-3700
  Zillah *(G-15764)*
Veracious Printing LLC .... G 360 823-7395
  Vancouver *(G-14668)*
Vessel Printing Studio .... G 360 441-4622
  Bellingham *(G-1582)*
Villas Josey .... G 360 405-1944
  Bremerton *(G-2010)*
Vintage ADS .... G 253 278-3297
  Tacoma *(G-13579)*
Vintage Idaho Prints .... G 509 217-8453
  Medical Lake *(G-6445)*
Virtual Imprints LLC .... G 425 998-9994
  Bellevue *(G-1219)*
Vistaprint 617 838-2434
  Gig Harbor *(G-4172)*
Vistaprint .... G 703 868-1794
  Seattle *(G-11426)*
Vistaprint .... G 206 973-0324
  Seattle *(G-11427)*
Visual Verve Design Print LLC ...... G 509 773-4596
  Centerville *(G-2378)*
W B Mason Co Inc .... E 888 926-2766
  Tukwila *(G-13835)*
Washington State University .... D 509 335-3518
  Pullman *(G-8112)*
Wenatchee Business Journal .... G 509 663-6730
  Cashmere *(G-2332)*
Wilbur Register Inc .... G 509 647-5551
  Wilbur *(G-15142)*
William Willis .... G 360 885-2045
  Vancouver *(G-14695)*
Woodpecker Graphics .... G 509 481-8406
  Spokane Valley *(G-12940)*
Worldwide Dgital Solutions Inc ..... G 425 605-0923
  Kirkland *(G-5498)*
Z-Axis Prints .... G 509 842-6680
  Spokane Valley *(G-12947)*
Zebra Printing .... G 425 656-3700
  Kent *(G-5220)*
Zkl Printing Company LLC .... G 206 369-6156
  Auburn *(G-604)*

PRINTING: Offset

A & H Printers Inc .... G 509 765-0283
  Moses Lake *(G-6676)*
A D G Printing .... G 425 771-7603
  Lynnwood *(G-6066)*
Abbotts Printing Inc .... G 509 452-8202
  Yakima *(G-15498)*
Abbotts Printing Inc .... F 509 452-8202
  Yakima *(G-15499)*
ABC Printers Inc .... G 360 423-6991
  Longview *(G-5881)*
ABC Printing Inc .... E 360 456-4545
  Lacey *(G-5528)*
Abcd Ventures LLC .... G 206 686-6089
  Black Diamond *(G-1644)*
Abracadabra Printing Inc .... G 206 343-9087
  Seattle *(G-9334)*
Access Printing Inc .... G 425 656-0563
  Kent *(G-4756)*
Advantage Screen Printing .... G 360 425-7343
  Longview *(G-5882)*
All Pro Printer Service LLC .... G 360 818-4592
  Vancouver *(G-14020)*
AlphaGraphics .... G 206 343-5037
  Seattle *(G-9387)*
Alphaprint Inc .... G 425 771-1140
  Lynnwood *(G-6073)*
Amica Inc .... G 253 872-9600
  Kent *(G-4780)*
Anacortes Printing .... G 360 293-2131
  Anacortes *(G-101)*
Arctic Printing & Graphics Inc .... F 425 967-0700
  Mountlake Terrace *(G-6858)*
Artcraft Printing Co .... G 509 323-5266
  Spokane *(G-12119)*
Asher Graphics .... G 206 546-6500
  Shoreline *(G-11756)*
B & B Express Printing .... G 509 783-7383
  Kennewick *(G-4622)*
B & D Advertising Prtg & Svc .... G 206 542-3262
  Shoreline *(G-11758)*
B C T Inc .... E 206 343-9355
  Seattle *(G-9474)*
Ballard Printing .... G 206 782-7892
  Seattle *(G-9483)*
Bellevue Printing LLC .... G 425 558-1862
  Bellevue *(G-814)*
Bettendorfs Printing & Design ...... G 509 586-7473
  Kennewick *(G-4630)*
Blue Sky Printing LLC .... G 360 779-2681
  Poulsbo *(G-7949)*
BNC Printing .... G 503 318-5916
  Vancouver *(G-14071)*
Bte Printing Inc .... G 360 675-8837
  Oak Harbor *(G-7143)*
Budget Printing & Mailing .... F 253 872-9969
  Woodinville *(G-15199)*
Budget Printing Center .... G 509 736-7511
  Kennewick *(G-4636)*
Capitol City Press Inc .... E 360 943-3556
  Tumwater *(G-13857)*
Carrolls Printing Inc .... G 360 345-1399
  Chehalis *(G-2481)*
Cascade Printing Company .... F 253 472-5500
  Tacoma *(G-13227)*
Chelan Printing .... G 509 682-5157
  Chelan *(G-2551)*
Clarence H Spargo Jr .... G 360 532-1505
  Aberdeen *(G-7)*
Classic Printing Inc .... G 509 452-1231
  Yakima *(G-15533)*

Cleland Investment LC ....F 509 326-5898
Spokane Valley (G-12659)
Color Art Printing Inc........G 206 762-0784
Seattle (G-9715)
Color Printing Systems Inc........F 206 763-7704
Burien (G-2097)
Columbia Litho Inc........G 360 834-4662
Camas (G-2239)
Commercial Printing Inc........F 509 663-4772
Wenatchee (G-15023)
Copy Break........G 206 782-7506
Seattle (G-9739)
Copy Co........G 206 622-4050
Seattle (G-9740)
Copy Shop........G 509 962-2679
Ellensburg (G-3190)
Copy-Rite Inc........G 509 624-8503
Spokane (G-12200)
Cover ME Screen Printing........G 509 552-1940
Clarkston (G-2629)
Crown Media & Printing Inc........G 509 315-8114
Liberty Lake (G-5829)
Custom Printing Company........G 206 842-1606
Bainbridge Island (G-624)
Daruma Graphics........G 206 365-5644
Seattle (G-9796)
Digital Impressions Inc........G 206 443-1234
Seattle (G-9828)
Dittos Print & Copy Center Inc........F 509 533-0025
Spokane (G-12229)
Domenics Printing Inc........G 425 251-4925
Kent (G-4876)
Donnelley Financial LLC........F 206 853-5460
Seattle (G-9847)
Dont Stop Printing........G 360 292-8610
Olympia (G-7272)
Dove Printing Inc........G 509 483-6164
Spokane (G-12230)
Dtg Inc........G 206 622-4387
Brier (G-2019)
Dumas Holdings LLC........G 425 576-4227
Kirkland (G-5323)
Dunsire Printers Inc........G 360 532-8791
Aberdeen (G-9)
Eagle Printing Inc........G 509 943-2611
Richland (G-8991)
East County Journal........G 360 496-5993
Morton (G-6668)
Eastlake Minuteman Press........G 425 402-7900
Woodinville (G-15232)
Edmonds Printing Co Inc........G 425 775-7907
Lynnwood (G-6112)
EE Printing LLC........G 425 656-1250
Kent (G-4885)
Emerald City Graphics Inc........D 253 520-2600
Kent (G-4892)
Encompass Print Solutions LLC........G 425 922-6170
Seattle (G-9919)
Esprit Grphic Cmmnications Inc........F 509 586-7858
Kennewick (G-4662)
Evergreen Printing & Graphics........G 425 338-2900
Everett (G-3466)
F D Company........G 253 531-7087
Tacoma (G-13285)
First Imprssions Creative Prtg........G 509 483-6822
Spokane (G-12257)
Four U Printers Inc........G 360 671-2032
Bellingham (G-1352)
Garcia Ink Corp........G 425 391-4950
Issaquah (G-4417)
Garland Printing Co Inc........G 509 327-5556
Spokane (G-12267)
Garrett Press........G 206 362-1466
Shoreline (G-11774)
Gateway Printing Inc........G 425 453-3272
Bellevue (G-920)
Good News Printing & Graphics........G 425 483-2510
Woodinville (G-15253)
GOS Printing Corporation........G 253 939-3131
Auburn (G-454)
Graphic Advertising Svcs Inc........F 425 688-9980
Richland (G-9003)
Graphic Communications........G 360 426-8628
Shelton (G-11698)
Graphic Communications Inc........G 425 251-8680
Renton (G-8811)
Graphics Place Inc........F 425 486-3323
Woodinville (G-15255)
Hamilton Jan Printing Systems........G 425 778-1975
Edmonds (G-3115)
Harbor Graphics Inc........G 360 532-1234
Hoquiam (G-4339)
Hearn Brothers Printing Inc........G 509 324-2882
Spokane (G-12291)
Hill Print Inc........G 425 255-7700
Auburn (G-467)
Holly Press Inc........G 206 623-2444
Seattle (G-10178)
Hook & Ladder Printing Co LLC........G 206 568-0588
Seattle (G-10181)
Horizon Printing Company LLC........G 509 663-8414
Wenatchee (G-15040)
Inland Saxum Printing LLC........G 509 525-0467
Walla Walla (G-14823)
Inprint Printing Inc........G 509 884-1454
East Wenatchee (G-3021)
Instant Imprints........G 360 694-9711
Vancouver (G-14318)
Instant Press Inc........F 509 457-6195
Yakima (G-15592)
Jdkk Investment Group Inc........G 253 565-4713
Tacoma (G-13357)
Jet City Imaging LLC........G 206 447-0600
Seattle (G-10293)
Jet City Printing Inc........G 425 485-8611
Kenmore (G-4585)
K & H Prntrs-Lithographers Inc........D 425 446-3300
Everett (G-3528)
Kool Change Printing Inc........G 360 794-9019
Monroe (G-6588)
Kustom Printing Inc........F 206 282-8400
Seattle (G-10366)
Kwang Nam Hwang........F 206 433-8811
Burien (G-2116)
Lakewood Printing Inc........F 253 582-6670
Lakewood (G-5735)
Lawton Printing Inc........E 509 534-1044
Spokane (G-12358)
Leatherback Publishing Inc........E 425 822-1202
Kirkland (G-5385)
Litho Design Inc........F 206 574-3000
Tukwila (G-13766)
Litho-Craft Inc........G 253 872-9161
Kent (G-4997)
Lithograph Reproduction Inc........G 509 926-9526
Spokane Valley (G-12774)
Lithtex Northwest LLC........G 360 424-5945
Mount Vernon (G-6807)
Lithtex Northwest LLC........F 360 676-1977
Bellingham (G-1411)
Livingston Printing Inc........F 206 382-1117
Seattle (G-10431)
Marshall Marketing Group Inc........E 253 473-0765
Tacoma (G-13400)
Martin William Owens........G 253 564-5950
Fircrest (G-4002)
Marymoor Press Inc........G 425 867-9073
Seattle (G-10495)
Master Printing Inc........G 509 684-5869
Colville (G-2765)
Maxart Inc........G 425 778-1108
Mountlake Terrace (G-6864)
Mc BAC Inc........F 360 699-4466
Vancouver (G-14405)
Minuteman Fund of Washington........G 253 584-5411
Olympia (G-7340)
Minuteman Press Intl Inc........G 253 841-3161
Puyallup (G-8195)
Minuteman Press Intl Inc........G 509 452-6144
Yakima (G-15623)
Nannette Louise Davis........G 425 485-5570
Woodinville (G-15317)
Norberg Press Inc........G 206 938-3905
Seattle (G-10620)
Northwest Impressions........G 253 474-1119
Tacoma (G-13434)
Nta Inc........G 425 487-2679
Woodinville (G-15325)
NW Fine Art Printing........G 425 947-1539
Redmond (G-8602)
Olympic Graphic Arts Inc........G 360 374-6020
Forks (G-4013)
Olympus Press Inc........E 206 242-2700
Tukwila (G-13783)
Overnight Prtg & Graphics Inc........G 206 621-9412
Seattle (G-10721)
Pacific Art Press Inc........G 425 778-8095
Lake Stevens (G-5666)
Paradyce Industries Inc........G 360 736-4474
Centralia (G-2423)
Perfect Press Printing Inc........G 425 562-0507
Bellevue (G-1070)
Perfect Printing & Signs........G 509 786-3811
Yakima (G-15645)
Pickles Printing........G 360 456-3230
Olympia (G-7370)
PIP Building LLC........G 360 961-1702
Ferndale (G-3887)
PIP McKay Unlimited LLC........G 206 390-0988
Seattle (G-10813)
PJ Finney Corporation........F 206 282-8400
Seattle (G-10820)
Pk Graphics Inc........G 425 251-8083
Renton (G-8881)
Plese Printing & Marketing........G 509 534-2355
Spokane (G-12447)
Plese Printing & Marketing........F 509 534-2355
Spokane (G-12448)
Potter & Associates Inc........G 206 623-8844
Seattle (G-10839)
Ppcs Inc........G 425 883-7464
Redmond (G-8628)
Precise Printing Inc........F 206 343-0942
Seattle (G-10846)
Precision Printing Inc........G 360 736-7232
Centralia (G-2425)
Pressworks........F 509 462-7627
Spokane (G-12454)
Prestige Copy and Print........G 206 365-5770
Seattle (G-10857)
Print & Copy Factory LLC........G 360 738-4931
Bellingham (G-1505)
Print Center LLC........G 509 979-8272
Spokane Valley (G-12839)
Print House Inc........G 425 742-1434
Everett (G-3585)
Print NW LLC........D 253 284-2300
Tacoma (G-13478)
Print Place........G 206 878-1380
Des Moines (G-2943)
Print Plus Inc........G 509 735-6303
Kennewick (G-4708)
Print Plus Inc........G 509 735-6303
Kennewick (G-4709)
Print Services Northwest Inc........G 206 763-9230
Seattle (G-10860)
Print Services Northwest Inc........G 253 236-8224
Auburn (G-538)
Print Solutions and Consulting........G 206 726-8053
Seattle (G-10861)
Print Stop Inc........G 360 354-5100
Lynden (G-6047)
Print Time Inc........F 206 682-1000
Seattle (G-10862)
Printcom Inc........F 206 763-7600
Burien (G-2121)
Printers Bloc........G 253 576-6043
Lakewood (G-5749)
Printgraphics Inc........E 503 641-8811
Vancouver (G-14508)
Printing Conexions........G 206 383-4516
Bonney Lake (G-1735)
Printing Control Services Inc........D 206 575-4114
Kent (G-5082)
Printing Ngo LLC........G 206 569-8388
Bothell (G-1890)
Printing Services Inc........G 253 858-5350
Port Orchard (G-7842)
Printing Specialties Press........G 509 687-9362
Chelan (G-2562)
Professional Business Svc Inc........F 360 352-3000
Olympia (G-7374)
Purely Tangible........G 206 301-9999
Seattle (G-10891)
Quality Copy and Print LLC........G 206 634-2689
Seattle (G-10901)
Quality Instant Print........G 360 274-0337
Castle Rock (G-2351)
Quality Press Inc........E 206 768-2655
Seattle (G-10902)
Quickprint Centers LLC........G 253 531-3105
Tacoma (G-13484)
Rain City West Printing LLC........G 206 767-1151
Seattle (G-10914)
Ramax Printing and Awards........G 509 928-1222
Spokane (G-12467)
Rapid Print Inc........G 360 695-6400
Vancouver (G-14532)
Record Printing Inc........F 509 964-9500
Thorp (G-13629)

PRINTING: Offset

Reischling Press Inc .... E ... 206 905-5999
  Tukwila (G-13805)
Renton Printery Incorporated .... G ... 425 235-1776
  Renton (G-8893)
Reprographics Inc .... G ... 360 423-1237
  Longview (G-5947)
Richins Printing Inc .... G ... 425 776-1800
  Edmonds (G-3147)
Ross Printing Northwest Inc .... E ... 509 534-0655
  Spokane (G-12484)
Rotary Offset Press Inc .... C ... 253 813-9900
  Kent (G-5107)
Saigon Printing .... G ... 206 722-6788
  Seattle (G-11003)
Savage Color LLC .... G ... 206 632-2866
  Seattle (G-11019)
Secord Printing Inc .... G ... 425 883-2182
  Kirkland (G-5457)
Service Printing Co Inc .... G ... 206 283-6800
  Seattle (G-11091)
SOS Printing .... G ... 360 385-4194
  Port Townsend (G-7927)
Special Edition Incorporated .... G ... 253 537-1836
  Tacoma (G-13520)
Speedy Litho Inc .... G ... 360 425-3610
  Kelso (G-4550)
Spot-On Print & Design Inc .... G ... 425 558-7768
  Bellevue (G-1154)
Stat Corporation .... F ... 425 883-4181
  Redmond (G-8681)
Stern & Faye .... G ... 360 770-1967
  Sedro Woolley (G-11572)
Sudden Printing Inc .... E ... 206 243-4444
  Seattle (G-11211)
Sunshine Prtg & Quick Copy Svc .... G ... 360 671-0191
  Bellingham (G-1563)
Swifty Prtg Dgital Imaging Inc .... E ... 206 441-0800
  Seattle (G-11239)
Taylor-Made Printing Inc .... G ... 253 881-1624
  Puyallup (G-8262)
The Windward Cmmncations Group G ... 206 382-1117
  Seattle (G-11286)
Thompson Litho Group Inc .... G ... 360 892-7888
  Vancouver (G-14634)
Times .... G ... 509 337-6631
  Waitsburg (G-14757)
Touchet Valley News Inc .... G ... 509 382-2221
  Dayton (G-2887)
Tracys Print Shop .... G ... 360 249-5575
  Montesano (G-6662)
Trade Printery LLC .... G ... 206 728-1600
  Seattle (G-11324)
Trade Printery LLC .... G ... 206 241-3322
  Burien (G-2134)
Tribune Office Supply & Prtg .... G ... 509 674-2511
  Cle Elum (G-2681)
Triple P Products Inc .... G ... 509 527-3131
  Walla Walla (G-14880)
Trysk Print Solutions LLC .... G ... 877 605-1464
  Seattle (G-11345)
Tumwater Printing .... F ... 360 943-2204
  Tumwater (G-13903)
United Reprographics L L C .... E ... 206 382-1177
  Seattle (G-11372)
University Reprographics Inc .... G ... 206 633-0925
  Seattle (G-11385)
Urban Press Inc .... G ... 206 325-4060
  Seattle (G-11391)
V O Printers Inc .... G ... 360 577-0038
  Longview (G-5962)
Valley Instant Printing Inc .... G ... 509 924-8040
  Spokane Valley (G-12924)
Valley Printing Inc .... G ... 253 845-0960
  Puyallup (G-8270)
Valley Publishing Company Inc .... F ... 509 786-1711
  Prosser (G-8073)
Vision Press Inc .... G ... 206 782-8476
  Seattle (G-11424)
Visiprinting .... G ... 253 565-4713
  Tacoma (G-13580)
Vista Copy and Print .... G ... 206 715-2011
  Seattle (G-11425)
Western Business Forms & Sups .... G ... 503 285-8738
  Battle Ground (G-751)
Western Print Systems Inc .... G ... 206 794-0045
  Snohomish (G-11998)
Wholesale Printers Inc .... E ... 360 687-5500
  Battle Ground (G-753)
Willapa Printing .... G ... 360 942-5580
  Raymond (G-8363)
Wilo Inc .... G ... 425 793-4862
  Renton (G-8948)
Woitchek Printing LLC .... G ... 425 869-8212
  Redmond (G-8716)
Yvonne Roberts .... G ... 253 531-3105
  Tacoma (G-13606)
Zebra Print and Copy .... G ... 206 223-1800
  Seattle (G-11519)
Zebra Printing Inc .... F ... 425 462-9775
  Bellevue (G-1233)

PRINTING: Photo-Offset

Its A Wrap Washington Inc .... G ... 425 827-2000
  Kirkland (G-5371)

PRINTING: Roller, Manmade Fiber & Silk, Broadwoven Fabric

Ryno Rollers Inc .... G ... 253 856-0738
  Auburn (G-554)

PRINTING: Screen, Broadwoven Fabrics, Cotton

Bayside EMB & Screenprint .... G ... 253 565-1521
  Tacoma (G-13191)
Go Designs .... G ... 206 719-0936
  Seattle (G-10091)
Ink Inc .... F ... 253 565-4000
  University Place (G-13973)
Jacknut Apparel .... G ... 360 742-3523
  Tumwater (G-13876)
Jsmd Key Products LLC .... G ... 360 805-4140
  Monroe (G-6583)
T-Shirts By Design LLC .... G ... 360 293-8898
  Anacortes (G-174)

PRINTING: Screen, Fabric

Action Apparel Washington Inc .... G ... 509 328-5861
  Spokane (G-12096)
All Color Screen Printing .... G ... 253 536-2822
  Tacoma (G-13162)
American Edge LLC .... F ... 509 937-4404
  Valley (G-13987)
Ariel Screenprinting & Design .... G ... 425 337-1918
  Everett (G-3372)
Availble Creat Screen Prtg EMB ...... G ... 360 576-8542
  Vancouver (G-14045)
Bad Habit Ltd .... G ... 360 385-3101
  Port Townsend (G-7866)
Brooks Products & Services .... G ... 425 742-4214
  Edmonds (G-3098)
Centurion Enterprises .... G ... 509 787-2345
  Quincy (G-8294)
Competitive Edge Athletics .... G ... 206 246-7211
  Burien (G-2098)
Countryman Signs Screen Prtrs .... G ... 425 355-1037
  Everett (G-3428)
Crystal Blue Screen Printing .... G ... 509 337-8201
  Waitsburg (G-14753)
D A Graphics Inc .... G ... 206 760-5886
  Seattle (G-9777)
H W Image Works Inc .... G ... 760 343-3869
  Bellevue (G-935)
Hope Moffat .... G ... 401 527-4234
  Bainbridge Island (G-640)
International Athletic .... G ... 360 384-6868
  Ferndale (G-3860)
Kitsap Screen Printing LLC .... G ... 360 876-5101
  Port Orchard (G-7824)
Magna Vis Graphic Impressions ...... G ... 509 684-5659
  Colville (G-2764)
Primal Screens LLC .... G ... 206 784-5266
  Seattle (G-10859)
Rainy Day Artistry .... G ... 360 484-3681
  Naselle (G-7019)
Rollo Tomasi Enterprises LLC .... G ... 509 453-9950
  Yakima (G-15663)
Saturday Night Inc .... F ... 509 928-5816
  Spokane Valley (G-12858)
Screen Print Northwest Inc .... G ... 360 577-1534
  Longview (G-5951)
Shirtbuilders Inc .... G ... 509 765-3885
  Moses Lake (G-6749)
Sports N Sorts .... G ... 509 276-6170
  Deer Park (G-2915)
Sunrise Identity LLC .... G ... 425 214-1700
  Bellevue (G-1167)
Tuff TS Connection Screen Prtg ...... G ... 253 588-8897
  Lakewood (G-5763)
Valley Graphics Inc .... G ... 509 937-4055
  Valley (G-13996)
Vilmas Family Corporation .... G ... 253 941-9008
  Federal Way (G-3801)
Western Specialties Co .... G ... 425 353-9282
  Mukilteo (G-6991)

PRINTING: Screen, Manmade Fiber & Silk, Broadwoven Fabric

Pacific Sportswear Inc .... E ... 253 582-4444
  Tacoma (G-13454)

PRINTING: Thermography

Bras Thermography .... G ... 425 677-8430
  Issaquah (G-4388)
Nicole Lewis/Northwest Breast .... G ... 360 989-0312
  Vancouver (G-14431)
Scott Wood Associates LLC .... G ... 253 509-3742
  Gig Harbor (G-4159)

PRIVATE INVESTIGATOR SVCS

Biscomb Fleudeliza S (artist) .... G ... 206 842-6417
  Bainbridge Island (G-618)

PROFESSIONAL EQPT & SPLYS, WHOL: Metal Locating Eqpt/Access

Pauley Rodine Inc .... G ... 509 773-3200
  Goldendale (G-4205)

PROFESSIONAL EQPT & SPLYS, WHOLESALE: Analytical Instruments

Rigaku Americas Corporation .... G ... 206 780-8927
  Bainbridge Island (G-666)

PROFESSIONAL EQPT & SPLYS, WHOLESALE: Optical Goods

United Contact Lens Inc .... G ... 360 474-9577
  Arlington (G-343)
Walman Optical Company .... E ... 253 872-7137
  Kent (G-5205)

PROFESSIONAL EQPT & SPLYS, WHOLESALE: Precision Tools

Morley Machine Tool Algnmt Inc ..... E ... 253 926-1515
  Milton (G-6536)

PROFESSIONAL EQPT & SPLYS, WHOLESALE: Scientific & Engineerg

Ries Productions LLC .... G ... 360 627-8795
  Bremerton (G-1994)

PROFESSIONAL EQPT & SPLYS, WHOLESALE: Scientific Recording

Eustis Co Inc .... E ... 425 423-9996
  Lynnwood (G-6115)

PROFESSIONAL INSTRUMENT REPAIR SVCS

Pacific Ship Repr Fbrction Inc .... E ... 425 409-5060
  Everett (G-3567)

PROFILE SHAPES: Unsupported Plastics

Envision Manufacturing & Servi .... G ... 253 941-1739
  Kent (G-4894)
Extrusion Technology Group Inc ..... G ... 253 583-8283
  Lakewood (G-5720)
Middy Marine Products Inc .... G ... 425 883-4600
  Redmond (G-8588)
Porex Technologies Corporation ...... C ... 253 284-8000
  Fife (G-3982)

PROGRAMMERS: Indl Process

Data I/O Corporation .... C ... 425 881-6444
  Redmond (G-8433)
Lilibete LLC .... G ... 206 407-6890
  Kent (G-4996)

PRODUCT SECTION

PROMOTION SVCS

Images .... G 509 736-9508
  Kennewick *(G-4675)*
Woobox LLC .... G 360 450-5200
  Vancouver *(G-14697)*

PROPELLERS: Boat & Ship, Cast

North Harbor Propeller .... G 360 299-8266
  Anacortes *(G-152)*
Olympic Propeller Company .... G 360 299-8266
  Anacortes *(G-157)*
Pacific Propeller Inter LLC .... G 206 575-5107
  Tukwila *(G-13787)*
Propeller Arprts Pine Feld LLC .... G 425 216-3010
  Everett *(G-3587)*
Red Propeller LLC .... G 206 452-5664
  Seattle *(G-10937)*
S & I Propellers Inc .... G 425 745-1700
  Mukilteo *(G-6974)*
Sound Propeller Services Inc .... E 206 788-4202
  Seattle *(G-11159)*

PROPELLERS: Boat & Ship, Machined

Nor Prop Inc .... E 253 939-1200
  Auburn *(G-508)*
Power Equipment Supply Llc .... G 206 817-5627
  Everett *(G-3580)*

PROPELLERS: Ship, Nec

NW Propeller Operations Inc .... G 253 858-5061
  Lakewood *(G-5743)*

PROPULSION UNITS: Guided Missiles & Space Vehicles

Atk Manufacturing Inc .... G 951 660-1218
  Ridgefield *(G-9062)*

PROTECTIVE FOOTWEAR: Rubber Or Plastic

Vans Inc .... F 360 254-3075
  Vancouver *(G-14665)*

PUBLIC RELATIONS SVCS

Krantz News Service Inc .... G 253 857-6590
  Gig Harbor *(G-4128)*
University of Washington .... F 206 543-2580
  Seattle *(G-11384)*

PUBLISHERS: Art Copy

Slap Stickers LLC .... G 971 238-8329
  Seattle *(G-11134)*

PUBLISHERS: Art Copy & Poster

Kith D Lazelles Nture Phtgrphy .... G 360 765-3697
  Quilcene *(G-8286)*
Third & Wall Art Group LLC .... F 206 443-8425
  Seattle *(G-11291)*
Timothy Colman .... G 800 631-3086
  Seattle *(G-11310)*
Winn/Devon Art Group Ltd .... G 604 276-4551
  Seattle *(G-11487)*

PUBLISHERS: Book

A H Tom Publishing .... G 360 385-2059
  Port Townsend *(G-7858)*
Ampersan Press Inc .... G 360 379-5187
  Port Townsend *(G-7861)*
Ananse Press .... G 206 325-8205
  Seattle *(G-9402)*
Association For The Developm .... G 509 838-3575
  Spokane *(G-12123)*
B Karnes Books Inc .... G 360 828-7132
  Vancouver *(G-14051)*
Bergman LLC .... G 206 910-0138
  Seattle *(G-9515)*
Blue Lantern Publishing Inc .... G 206 447-9229
  Seattle *(G-9551)*
Bonfire Productions Inc .... F 425 748-5041
  Bellevue *(G-825)*
Boundless Immigration Inc .... G 855 268-6353
  Seattle *(G-9569)*
Bridge City Publishing .... G 360 600-0558
  Vancouver *(G-14082)*
Campbell & Associates Inc .... G 360 652-9502
  Stanwood *(G-12963)*
Cascade Publishing Inc .... G 206 430-6021
  Seattle *(G-9643)*
Cedarbrook .... G 360 354-5770
  Lynden *(G-6006)*
Celesticomp Inc .... G 206 463-9626
  Vashon *(G-14717)*
Center For East Asian Studies .... E 360 650-3836
  Bellingham *(G-1295)*
Center For The Def Free Entp .... G 425 455-5038
  Bellevue *(G-846)*
Contracts Company .... G 360 299-9900
  Anacortes *(G-116)*
Debbie Mumm Inc .... G 509 939-1479
  Spokane *(G-12221)*
Delta Production .... G 206 567-4373
  Vashon *(G-14721)*
Djangobookscom .... G 206 528-9873
  Seattle *(G-9839)*
Ex Ophidia Press LLC .... G 360 385-9966
  Bainbridge Island *(G-632)*
Farber News Service .... G 253 565-1131
  Tacoma *(G-13290)*
Feral House Inc .... G 323 666-3311
  Port Townsend *(G-7884)*
Forest Publications Inc .... G 360 609-4400
  Camas *(G-2252)*
Hoffmann Petra .... G 360 321-4753
  Langley *(G-5780)*
Hundman Publishing Inc .... G 425 742-1214
  Edmonds *(G-3119)*
Illumination Arts Inc .... G 360 984-5173
  Vancouver *(G-14308)*
Intelligent Technologies Inc .... G 360 254-4211
  Vancouver *(G-14321)*
Jerry P Osborne .... G 360 385-1200
  Port Townsend *(G-7893)*
Kathleen M Sole .... G 360 297-4650
  Kingston *(G-5255)*
King Northern Inc .... F 520 604-6379
  Auburn *(G-484)*
Kiowna Publishing Inc .... G 509 947-0675
  Moses Lake *(G-6721)*
Kurt Blume .... G 206 371-9337
  Seattle *(G-10362)*
La Mesa Fiction .... G 206 459-2664
  Kirkland *(G-5378)*
Mabo Publishers .... G 425 746-9934
  Bellevue *(G-994)*
Many Rivers Company .... G 360 221-1324
  Langley *(G-5782)*
Mary Ellen McCaffree .... G 253 820-0731
  Snohomish *(G-11944)*
Members Club At Aldarra .... G 206 232-8580
  Mercer Island *(G-6473)*
Northlight Communications .... F 425 493-1903
  Seattle *(G-10635)*
Northstar Investment Co .... G 360 297-2260
  Kingston *(G-5258)*
Northwest Press LLC .... G 646 926-6427
  Seattle *(G-10650)*
Pe Ell Pub .... G 360 291-2707
  Chehalis *(G-2522)*
Pizzicato Publishing Co .... G 206 361-0444
  Seattle *(G-10819)*
Portland Press Inc .... F 253 274-8883
  Tacoma *(G-13471)*
Process Media Inc .... G 323 666-3377
  Port Townsend *(G-7919)*
Quantum Publishing Service .... G 360 734-2906
  Bellingham *(G-1513)*
Refuge Music .... G 425 271-4278
  Renton *(G-8892)*
Rides Publishing Co LLC .... G 206 789-0827
  Seattle *(G-10965)*
Riggsafe Solutions Inc .... G 865 266-9989
  Spokane Valley *(G-12852)*
Rw Morse Co .... G 360 943-8600
  Olympia *(G-7390)*
Saint Square Publishing .... G 360 636-2645
  Longview *(G-5950)*
Santoros Books .... G 206 784-2113
  Seattle *(G-11013)*
Silver Lake Publishing .... G 360 532-0308
  Aberdeen *(G-35)*
Simply Wonder LLC .... G 360 866-2482
  Olympia *(G-7395)*
Sound Publishing Inc .... F 360 779-4464
  Poulsbo *(G-8003)*

PUBLISHERS: Books, No Printing

Sound Publishing Inc .... F 206 463-9195
  Vashon *(G-14744)*
Sound Publishing Inc .... G 360 376-4500
  Eastsound *(G-3047)*
Sound Publishing Inc .... E 360 675-6611
  Coupeville *(G-2818)*
St Helens Press .... G 360 687-1717
  Battle Ground *(G-741)*
Statesman-Examiner Inc .... E 509 684-4567
  Colville *(G-2775)*
Susney Incorporated .... G 253 219-7216
  Spanaway *(G-12077)*
Test Best International Inc .... F 360 650-0671
  Bellingham *(G-1567)*
Thinking Cap Solutions In .... G 360 452-6159
  Port Angeles *(G-7749)*
Trillium Custom Software Inc .... G 425 397-8000
  Snohomish *(G-11994)*
Turtleback Press .... G 360 376-4625
  Eastsound *(G-3048)*
Washington State University .... D 509 335-3518
  Pullman *(G-8112)*
Westerberg & Associates Inc .... G 509 951-4399
  Liberty Lake *(G-5867)*
Willapa Bay Company Inc .... G 206 465-5616
  Seattle *(G-11476)*
Youth With A Mission .... F 425 771-1153
  Edmonds *(G-3166)*

PUBLISHERS: Books, No Printing

American Printing and Pubg .... G 253 395-3349
  Kent *(G-4779)*
Barker Creek Publishing Inc .... F 360 881-0292
  Poulsbo *(G-7946)*
Bilingual Books Inc .... G 206 284-4211
  Seattle *(G-9527)*
Blind Eye Books .... G 360 715-9117
  Bellingham *(G-1276)*
Blue Lantern Publishing Inc .... G 206 632-7075
  Seattle *(G-9550)*
Calico Press LLC .... G 206 855-1903
  Bainbridge Island *(G-619)*
Center For Touch Drawing .... G 360 221-5745
  Langley *(G-5773)*
Cherbo Publishing Group Inc .... F 818 783-0040
  Lynnwood *(G-6093)*
Clyde Curley .... G 360 738-6862
  Bellingham *(G-1300)*
Coffey Communications Inc .... C 509 525-0101
  Walla Walla *(G-14788)*
Columbia Games Inc .... G 360 366-2228
  Custer *(G-2854)*
Crescent Moon Studios Inc .... G 509 322-7730
  Riverside *(G-9124)*
D & E Enterprises .... G 509 684-6618
  Colville *(G-2749)*
D Powers Consulting .... G 360 341-1533
  Clinton *(G-2688)*
Documentary Media LLC .... G 206 935-9292
  Seattle *(G-9840)*
Douglass Hemingway & Co LLC .... G 360 299-0420
  Anacortes *(G-122)*
Epicenter Press Inc .... G 425 485-6822
  Kenmore *(G-4571)*
Filmateria Studios Inc .... G 206 938-6791
  Seattle *(G-9992)*
H&H Publications LLP .... G 360 730-1206
  Freeland *(G-4029)*
Health Research .... F 509 843-2385
  Pomeroy *(G-7673)*
Homestead Book Co .... G 206 782-4532
  Seattle *(G-10180)*
Houstory Publishing LLC .... G 877 962-6500
  Ferndale *(G-3853)*
Infomine Usa Inc .... G 509 328-8023
  Spokane Valley *(G-12740)*
Justice Systems Press .... G 360 417-8845
  Port Angeles *(G-7721)*
Krimsten Publishing LLC .... G 509 786-7978
  Prosser *(G-8047)*
Latitude Blue Press LLC .... G 360 421-1934
  Kirkland *(G-5383)*
Librofm Inc .... G 206 730-2463
  Seattle *(G-10413)*
Living Free .... G 360 446-3032
  Rainier *(G-8317)*
Lundquist Joegil .... G 425 454-5830
  Medina *(G-6451)*
Martingale & Company Inc .... E 425 483-3313
  Bothell *(G-1776)*

Employee Codes: A=Over 500 employees, B=251-500
C=101-250, D=51-100, E=20-50, F=10-19, G=2-9

PUBLISHERS: Books, No Printing

Merril Mail Marketing Inc ....G....... 425 454-7009
  Bellevue *(G-1003)*
Mindcastle Books Incorporated ....G....... 206 801-7338
  Shoreline *(G-11789)*
Northwest Home Designing Inc ....G....... 253 584-6309
  Tacoma *(G-13433)*
Old Growth Northwest ....G....... 206 856-6293
  Seattle *(G-10689)*
Our House Publishing ....G....... 360 676-0428
  Bellingham *(G-1482)*
Overdue Media LLC ....G....... 206 860-2199
  Seattle *(G-10720)*
P F M Industries Inc ....G....... 425 776-3112
  Edmonds *(G-3142)*
Paizo Inc ....E....... 425 289-0060
  Redmond *(G-8611)*
Paper Jam Publishing Co LLP ....G....... 360 376-3200
  Eastsound *(G-3044)*
Pathfinder Press ....G....... 360 687-4319
  Battle Ground *(G-729)*
Portland Press Incorporated ....G....... 206 297-1304
  Seattle *(G-10835)*
Red Letter Press Corp ....G....... 206 985-4621
  Seattle *(G-10936)*
Reelworld Productions Inc ....G....... 206 448-1518
  Seattle *(G-10940)*
Ruth Publishing LLC ....G....... 253 351-2375
  Federal Way *(G-3779)*
San Juan Naturals ....G....... 360 378-2648
  Friday Harbor *(G-4058)*
Sasquatch Books LLC ....F....... 206 467-4300
  Seattle *(G-11015)*
Scholastic Inc ....G....... 509 926-4465
  Spokane Valley *(G-12861)*
Seventy Frth St Prductions LLC ....G....... 206 781-1447
  Seattle *(G-11093)*
Shiloh Publishing ....G....... 800 607-6195
  Vancouver *(G-14582)*
Snohomish Publishing Company ....E....... 206 523-7548
  Snohomish *(G-11983)*
Storytellers Ink Inc ....G....... 206 365-8265
  Seattle *(G-11200)*
Tassels & Wings Publishing ....G....... 206 725-5075
  Seattle *(G-11270)*
Two Sylvias Press ....G....... 360 447-8735
  Kingston *(G-5266)*
University of Washington ....E....... 206 543-4050
  Seattle *(G-11383)*
Vidor ....G....... 425 827-9967
  Kirkland *(G-5489)*
Wild River Publishing Inc ....G....... 425 486-3638
  Bothell *(G-1920)*
Wine Erna A I D Inc ....G....... 360 332-4888
  Blaine *(G-1712)*
Word & Raby LLC ....G....... 206 795-5267
  Seattle *(G-11494)*

PUBLISHERS: Catalogs

Coffey Communications Inc ....C....... 509 525-0101
  Walla Walla *(G-14788)*
Richard C Busher Jr ....G....... 206 524-6726
  Seattle *(G-10961)*
Visual Communications Dev ....G....... 360 676-8625
  Bellingham *(G-1583)*

PUBLISHERS: Comic Books, No Printing

Grow Northwest ....G....... 360 398-1155
  Everson *(G-3678)*
Phillips Publishing Group ....G....... 206 429-2429
  Normandy Park *(G-7096)*
Studio Foglio LLC ....G....... 206 782-8739
  Seattle *(G-11207)*
Toonhound Studios LLC ....G....... 214 733-9626
  Bothell *(G-1909)*

PUBLISHERS: Directories, NEC

Bravo Publications Inc ....G....... 206 937-3264
  Seattle *(G-9579)*
Macgregor Publishing Co ....E....... 800 581-5040
  Mount Vernon *(G-6809)*
Northwest Multiple Listing Svc ....G....... 253 566-2331
  Graham *(G-4234)*
Slowpitch Softball Assoc ....G....... 206 719-2161
  Shoreline *(G-11815)*
Tiger Oak Media Incorporated ....E....... 206 284-1750
  Seattle *(G-11306)*

PUBLISHERS: Directories, Telephone

Verizon Communications Inc ....F....... 425 641-5900
  Bellevue *(G-1214)*

PUBLISHERS: Magazines, No Printing

Arrow Point Media Inc ....G....... 425 885-3922
  Bellevue *(G-795)*
Boundless Enterprises Inc ....G....... 206 789-7350
  Seattle *(G-9568)*
C E Publications Inc ....F....... 425 806-5200
  Bothell *(G-1833)*
Community Values Magazine ....G....... 360 459-8292
  Olympia *(G-7254)*
Eastside Parent ....G....... 206 441-0191
  Seattle *(G-9873)*
Focus Group Inc ....G....... 206 281-1977
  Burien *(G-2108)*
Fruit Commission Wash State ....E....... 509 453-4837
  Yakima *(G-15574)*
Grist Magazine Inc ....E....... 206 876-2020
  Seattle *(G-10125)*
Hundman Publishing Inc ....G....... 425 742-1214
  Edmonds *(G-3119)*
Kiowna Publishing Inc ....G....... 509 947-0675
  Moses Lake *(G-6721)*
Loggers World Publications ....G....... 360 262-3376
  Chehalis *(G-2510)*
My City Wise LLC ....G....... 206 409-0818
  Seattle *(G-10578)*
Northwest Fly Fishing LLC ....G....... 206 667-9359
  Seattle *(G-10644)*
Northwest Horse Source LLC ....G....... 360 332-5579
  Blaine *(G-1688)*
Omega Ministries Inc ....G....... 360 477-4180
  Sequim *(G-11656)*
Pgri Incorporated ....G....... 425 449-3000
  Kirkland *(G-5433)*
Pricemedia Inc ....G....... 206 418-0747
  Seattle *(G-10858)*
Rfp LLC ....G....... 206 523-8996
  Seattle *(G-10957)*
Scotsman Guide Media Inc ....G....... 425 485-2282
  Bothell *(G-1900)*
Scotsman Publishing Inc ....E....... 425 485-2282
  Bothell *(G-1901)*
Seattle Metropolitan ....F....... 206 957-2234
  Seattle *(G-11064)*
Second Amendment Foundation ....F....... 425 454-7012
  Bellevue *(G-1122)*
TI Gotham Inc ....A....... 206 957-8447
  Seattle *(G-11303)*
Tiger Oak Media Incorporated ....E....... 206 284-1750
  Seattle *(G-11306)*
Varsity Communications Inc ....F....... 425 412-7070
  Lynnwood *(G-6215)*
Vernon Publications LLC ....F....... 425 488-3211
  Woodinville *(G-15400)*
Washington Cncil Plice Sheriff ....G....... 360 352-8224
  Olympia *(G-7420)*
White Light Publications LLC ....E....... 206 575-4236
  Renton *(G-8947)*

PUBLISHERS: Miscellaneous

7 Ocean Express Inc ....G....... 206 250-9239
  Kent *(G-4749)*
Aapkispace LLC ....G....... 425 614-6465
  Redmond *(G-8366)*
AG Creative Publishing ....G....... 206 375-0934
  Seattle *(G-9358)*
Alki Press LLC ....G....... 206 854-1148
  Seattle *(G-9378)*
Alry Publications LLC ....G....... 206 274-8204
  Seattle *(G-9389)*
Amaral Music ....G....... 206 853-9847
  Kent *(G-4775)*
Anagram Press LLC ....G....... 253 310-8770
  Tacoma *(G-13171)*
Anaphora Press ....G....... 360 379-4004
  Port Townsend *(G-7862)*
Ann Silvers ....G....... 253 853-7049
  Gig Harbor *(G-4072)*
Anniversary Year Press ....G....... 360 348-7945
  Monroe *(G-6550)*
Apollonian Publications LLC ....G....... 206 922-7910
  Tacoma *(G-13176)*
Arbuckle Press ....G....... 206 409-2091
  Bainbridge Island *(G-610)*
ARS Nova Press Inc DBA ARS Nov ......G....... 206 783-9671
  Seattle *(G-9433)*
Art On File Inc ....G....... 206 329-9607
  Seattle *(G-9438)*
Atlantis Publications Inc ....G....... 206 497-0894
  Lynnwood *(G-6078)*
Avoa Publishing LLC ....G....... 509 594-9778
  Yakima *(G-15517)*
Azure Fire Publishing ....G....... 206 380-2036
  Shoreline *(G-11757)*
Banana Blossom Press ....G....... 206 719-3887
  Seattle *(G-9490)*
Barefoot Btnik Pblications LLC ....G....... 360 275-0798
  Allyn *(G-80)*
Barnard Press ....G....... 253 851-2208
  Gig Harbor *(G-4076)*
Bayview Publishing LLC ....G....... 425 282-4640
  Renton *(G-8752)*
Bellingham Business Journal ....G....... 360 647-8805
  Bellingham *(G-1263)*
Bent Whisker Press ....G....... 206 914-3556
  Shoreline *(G-11760)*
Bewitching Moon Press ....G....... 206 380-3807
  Auburn *(G-392)*
Bicycle Quarterly ....G....... 206 789-0424
  Seattle *(G-9521)*
Big Door Music Publishing ....G....... 206 890-1269
  Edmonds *(G-3096)*
Billabong Publishing & ME ....G....... 206 391-8300
  Maple Valley *(G-6260)*
Blue Lantern Publishing Inc ....G....... 206 447-9229
  Seattle *(G-9551)*
Bluer Skies Publishing LLC ....G....... 813 675-7588
  Gig Harbor *(G-4083)*
Bonnie Press ....G....... 360 807-4442
  Longview *(G-5889)*
Brecht-Pacific Publishing Inc ....E....... 360 425-4671
  Longview *(G-5890)*
Brindle Press LLC ....G....... 360 434-3302
  Seattle *(G-9586)*
Bunny Bear Press ....G....... 425 894-0944
  Redmond *(G-8412)*
Bunnybud Books ....G....... 360 293-4675
  Anacortes *(G-105)*
C & C Associates Technologies ....G....... 509 710-4464
  Cheney *(G-2578)*
Calkins Publishing Company LLC ......G....... 425 836-3548
  Sammamish *(G-9195)*
Cape Point Press LLC ....G....... 206 324-2126
  Seattle *(G-9623)*
Capital A Publications LL ....G....... 509 279-0832
  Spokane *(G-12168)*
Cargo Express Inc ....G....... 253 630-7294
  Covington *(G-2822)*
Case Enterprises ....G....... 425 827-2056
  Kirkland *(G-5299)*
Cedar Coast Press ....G....... 206 451-4568
  Bainbridge Island *(G-620)*
Center For Religious Humanism ....F....... 206 281-2988
  Seattle *(G-9653)*
Centricity Publishing LLC ....G....... 360 692-6162
  Bellevue *(G-847)*
Chin Music Press Inc ....G....... 206 457-8752
  Seattle *(G-9678)*
Choix Publishing ....G....... 425 821-2752
  Kirkland *(G-5304)*
Claudja Inc ....G....... 206 842-6303
  Bainbridge Island *(G-623)*
Clever Fox Editing ....G....... 805 910-6938
  Snohomish *(G-11890)*
Climate Publishing LLC ....G....... 206 515-1795
  Bellevue *(G-855)*
Conlan Press Incorporated ....G....... 650 267-9651
  Bellingham *(G-1302)*
Constancy Press LLC ....G....... 206 522-7513
  Seattle *(G-9731)*
Copbong428 LLC ....G....... 206 778-1436
  Auburn *(G-416)*
Copper Canyon Press ....G....... 360 385-4925
  Port Townsend *(G-7872)*
Corvidae Press ....G....... 360 379-1934
  Port Townsend *(G-7873)*
Counterbalance Poetry ....G....... 206 282-2677
  Seattle *(G-9746)*
Coyote Hill Press ....G....... 951 295-9552
  Camano Island *(G-2210)*
Crystal Triangle Publishing ....G....... 360 546-2497
  Vancouver *(G-14156)*
Cuddletunes Com ....G....... 206 284-4991
  Seattle *(G-9764)*
Custom Publications Wash LLC ....G....... 509 628-3500
  Richland *(G-8986)*

D B Express LLC … G … 509 265-4511
Mesa *(G-6491)*

Dahlia Press … G … 206 229-0817
Seattle *(G-9784)*

Dairyland Orthopedics Pubg … G … 509 868-0096
Spokane *(G-12216)*

Dark Coast Press Co … G … 206 902-0906
Seattle *(G-9794)*

Debbie Mumm Inc … G … 509 939-1479
Spokane *(G-12221)*

Different Drummers … G … 509 216-2098
Liberty Lake *(G-5830)*

Digital Color Press … G … 509 362-1152
Spokane *(G-12228)*

Dmfrank Publication … G … 360 446-6113
Rainier *(G-8314)*

Doremus & Fahey Publishing … G … 253 507-8848
Lakewood *(G-5713)*

Douglas Green … G … 360 260-9708
Vancouver *(G-14186)*

Dow Publishing LLC … G … 425 572-6540
Renton *(G-8787)*

Dragondyne Publishing … G … 206 619-1577
Seatac *(G-9281)*

Eagle Harbor Editing … G … 206 293-4264
Bainbridge Island *(G-626)*

Ed Stephan … G … 360 733-4781
Bellingham *(G-1330)*

Edgetown Pubg & Productions … G … 360 626-1242
Poulsbo *(G-7961)*

Edwin Laird … G … 206 587-6537
Seattle *(G-9885)*

El Mundo Communications Inc … G … 509 663-5737
Wenatchee *(G-15029)*

Encore Publishing Inc … G … 206 443-0445
Seattle *(G-9920)*

Evergreen Eye Center Inc Ps … F … 206 212-2163
Federal Way *(G-3735)*

Evergreen Pacific Publishing … G … 425 493-1451
Mukilteo *(G-6926)*

Evergreen Publications … G … 360 734-4158
Bellingham *(G-1339)*

Everlasting Publishing … G … 509 225-9829
Yakima *(G-15566)*

Evil Genius Publishing LLC … G … 253 929-6710
Auburn *(G-435)*

Express Messenger … G … 360 992-9999
Vancouver *(G-14214)*

Family Roots Publishing Co LLC … G … 801 949-7259
Orting *(G-7479)*

Federal Express Corporation … G … 800 463-3339
Spokane *(G-12253)*

Fenwick Publishing Group Inc … G … 206 842-3981
Bainbridge Island *(G-633)*

Final State Press LLC … G … 253 237-2474
Des Moines *(G-2935)*

Fisher Publications Inc … G … 206 923-2000
Seattle *(G-9998)*

Flagship Custom Publishing LLC … G … 310 245-9550
Seattle *(G-10003)*

Flannery Publications LLC … G … 360 942-0060
Raymond *(G-8349)*

Fly By Night Express Frei … G … 360 420-0844
Mount Vernon *(G-6797)*

Flying Trout Press … G … 360 647-5740
Bellingham *(G-1351)*

Frog Hollow Press L L C … G … 509 943-3331
Richland *(G-8999)*

Frogchart Press … G … 206 284-7156
Seattle *(G-10028)*

From Field … G … 360 446-7689
Rainier *(G-8315)*

Fruhla LLC … G … 206 633-4652
Seattle *(G-10032)*

Fundamentals Publishing … G … 509 334-8787
Pullman *(G-8090)*

G B E Publishers Inc … G … 360 438-5779
Lacey *(G-5551)*

Gagne International LLC … G … 360 733-9500
Bellingham *(G-1356)*

Gambia Press Union GPU-USA … G … 425 357-6483
Everett *(G-3490)*

Gannett Co Inc … E … 425 391-2530
Bellevue *(G-918)*

Garpike Inc … F … 206 719-7820
Seattle *(G-10048)*

Gemelli Press LLC … G … 360 420-7721
Seattle *(G-10058)*

Gfg Publishing … F … 509 853-3520
Yakima *(G-15575)*

Giraffe Family Press … G … 360 437-8018
Port Ludlow *(G-7766)*

Glen Cove Press LLC … G … 509 318-5934
Richland *(G-9002)*

Global Press … G … 425 254-9323
Renton *(G-8808)*

Glori Publishing LLC … G … 425 202-7714
Redmond *(G-8478)*

Goldfinch Press … G … 206 696-2933
Seattle *(G-10096)*

Goldfish Press … G … 206 380-4181
Seattle *(G-10097)*

Gorman Publicity … G … 360 676-9393
Bellingham *(G-1359)*

Grand Image Ltd … F … 206 624-0444
Seattle *(G-10107)*

Grapecity Inc … G … 425 828-4440
Kirkland *(G-5352)*

Greybeard Publishing … G … 360 495-4107
McCleary *(G-6416)*

Grief Inc … G … 253 929-0649
Puyallup *(G-8160)*

Gsf Publications … G … 206 789-7548
Seattle *(G-10129)*

H Brothers Inc … G … 206 999-9837
Seattle *(G-10134)*

Hal Burton Publishing & Dist … G … 360 877-0613
Lilliwaup *(G-5871)*

Halfmoon Publishing LLC … G … 360 934-5387
Raymond *(G-8352)*

Harrison Gray Publishing LLC … G … 206 783-5682
Seattle *(G-10144)*

Haskill Creek Publishing … G … 509 467-9439
Spokane *(G-12290)*

Healing Mountain Pubg Inc … G … 509 433-4719
East Wenatchee *(G-3019)*

Hearthland Publishing LLC … G … 253 588-2149
Steilacoom *(G-13005)*

Heiret Publications … G … 253 852-1254
Kent *(G-4939)*

Hexagon Blue … G … 425 890-5351
Sammamish *(G-9217)*

Higher Age Press … G … 425 891-9129
Seattle *(G-10171)*

Holmes Publishing Group LLC … G … 360 681-2900
Sequim *(G-11639)*

Hot Off Press … G … 253 255-2829
Graham *(G-4226)*

How 2 Publishing LLC … G … 360 878-9274
Centralia *(G-2408)*

Hoyem Publications Inc … G … 360 676-0864
Bellingham *(G-1374)*

Hrh Press … G … 206 781-1279
Seattle *(G-10191)*

Huckleberry Press … G … 844 344-8344
Davenport *(G-2871)*

Hummingbird Press … G … 617 921-6502
Seattle *(G-10193)*

Impact Health Publishing … G … 509 624-2599
Spokane *(G-12304)*

Imperial Publishing … G … 800 210-5033
Kirkland *(G-5367)*

Impressions Express Inc … G … 253 874-2923
Auburn *(G-474)*

Informatica Pubg Group LLC … G … 480 361-6300
Burien *(G-2113)*

Intention Publishing Co … G … 206 463-9777
Vashon *(G-14724)*

International Comanche Society … G … 360 332-2743
Blaine *(G-1676)*

Itty Bits Publications … G … 360 894-3288
Yelm *(G-15736)*

Joyful Noise Publications … G … 425 774-7078
Edmonds *(G-3127)*

JP Publications … G … 425 835-0021
Mill Creek *(G-6514)*

Jury Verdicts Northwest … G … 425 487-9848
Burien *(G-2115)*

Jvs Publications LLC … G … 360 412-0516
Lacey *(G-5561)*

Key Publishing Group LLC … F … 360 882-3488
Vancouver *(G-14345)*

Kingdom Life Publishing … G … 509 465-0672
Colbert *(G-2710)*

Kirsten Gallery Inc … G … 206 522-2011
Gig Harbor *(G-4126)*

Lab Door Press … G … 425 408-0672
Woodinville *(G-15282)*

Lafromboise Newspapers … F … 360 458-2681
Yelm *(G-15737)*

Larson Rv Publishing … G … 360 733-8576
Bellingham *(G-1402)*

Lawyer Avenue … G … 425 243-7958
Seattle *(G-10387)*

Lead Cat Press LLC … G … 206 349-3226
Seattle *(G-10391)*

Lee Enterprises Incorporated … G … 509 783-5555
Kennewick *(G-4688)*

Leonsdeli Express … G … 360 863-1998
Buckley *(G-2062)*

Lewis and Clark Publishing … G … 253 631-8712
Kent *(G-4993)*

Lexington Publishing Co LLC … G … 425 344-0909
Snohomish *(G-11939)*

Lexington Publishing Company … G … 800 774-1170
Lake Stevens *(G-5654)*

Life Chronicles … G … 253 508-8876
Federal Way *(G-3752)*

Life Spring Press … G … 360 872-8452
Orting *(G-7484)*

Lifecodex Publishing … G … 206 453-0235
Mercer Island *(G-6471)*

Lifesmart Publication … G … 253 851-3169
Gig Harbor *(G-4132)*

Lightmark Press … G … 206 463-0831
Vashon *(G-14730)*

Liquid Industry LLC … G … 206 718-3360
Enumclaw *(G-3300)*

Literary Fatale … G … 425 239-2126
Lynnwood *(G-6158)*

Litfuse Publicity Group … G … 206 947-3743
Seattle *(G-10427)*

Little Picture Press … G … 206 542-7808
Shoreline *(G-11783)*

Live Music Project … G … 206 329-8125
Seattle *(G-10430)*

Lone Pine Publishing Inc … G … 253 394-0400
Auburn *(G-490)*

Low Orbit Publications … G … 425 398-0598
Kenmore *(G-4590)*

Lynnsville Press Patterns … G … 360 573-1396
Vancouver *(G-14388)*

Maas Publications LLC … G … 425 445-7845
Maple Valley *(G-6281)*

Mach Publishing Company Inc … F … 425 258-9396
Snohomish *(G-11941)*

Mammoth Media Inc … G … 206 275-3183
Mercer Island *(G-6472)*

Markarts Inc … G … 425 895-0651
Redmond *(G-8551)*

Marketech … G … 425 391-1886
Sammamish *(G-9230)*

Martian Publishing LLC … G … 425 572-0743
Renton *(G-8848)*

Math Perspectives … G … 360 715-2782
Bellingham *(G-1426)*

Mathemechanix … G … 360 944-2029
Vancouver *(G-14399)*

Max Monitor & Publications LLC … G … 206 280-6489
Seattle *(G-10504)*

MC Publishing LLC … G … 253 678-3105
Puyallup *(G-8186)*

Mdr Publishing … G … 360 691-5908
Granite Falls *(G-4280)*

Media Directed Inc … G … 509 886-5759
East Wenatchee *(G-3024)*

Mediterranean Express … G … 206 860-3989
Seattle *(G-10514)*

Melange Publishing … G … 360 387-2395
Camano Island *(G-2217)*

Mfml Publishing … G … 360 603-6148
Bellingham *(G-1434)*

Mike Montgomery … G … 206 306-4599
Seattle *(G-10542)*

Mindware Inc … G … 425 415-3921
Kenmore *(G-4593)*

Mitchell Osborne … G … 360 379-2427
Port Townsend *(G-7898)*

Mobile Game Partners LLC … G … 310 926-3932
Woodinville *(G-15313)*

Mogul Express … G … 206 386-8070
Seattle *(G-10556)*

Momma DOT Publishing LLC … G … 425 322-3486
Lake Stevens *(G-5663)*

Mondello Publishing … G … 425 775-9695
Lynnwood *(G-6166)*

Moon Donkey Press LLC … G … 425 990-8149
Clyde Hill *(G-2704)*

Mtd Publishing … G … 509 525-7289
Walla Walla *(G-14848)*

PRODUCT

PUBLISHERS: Miscellaneous

Multiple Streams Marketin .... G 206 650-6769
  Shoreline (G-11791)
Nabat Publishing .... G 509 869-8707
  Spokane (G-12400)
Natural Wonder Publishing .... G 253 905-1583
  Puyallup (G-8197)
Naturally NW Publications .... G 360 332-1777
  Blaine (G-1685)
Netherfield Publishing LLC .... G 360 903-8512
  Montesano (G-6649)
New Foundation Press .... G 509 783-5237
  Kennewick (G-4701)
Newtonia Publishing LLC .... G 206 790-6628
  Seattle (G-10604)
Nickel One Ad Newspaper .... G 360 423-3141
  Kennewick (G-4702)
Non Sequitur Music .... G 360 733-7145
  Bellingham (G-1460)
Noonday Design .... G 253 517-8293
  Bonney Lake (G-1730)
Noreah/Brownfield Press LLC .... G 360 849-4857
  Cathlamet (G-2371)
Normandy Press LLC .... G 206 285-2881
  Seattle (G-10621)
Northwest Company Intl .... G 253 365-6316
  Tacoma (G-13431)
Northwest Publishing Ctr LLC .... G 206 324-5644
  Tukwila (G-13780)
Norwegian American .... G 206 784-4617
  Shoreline (G-11794)
Nubble Road Music & Pubg LLC .... G 206 283-0696
  Seattle (G-10665)
NW Publishing Center .... G 206 242-1822
  Seattle (G-10675)
Oakbridge University .... G 360 681-5233
  Sequim (G-11654)
Object Publishing Software .... G 206 414-9440
  Seattle (G-10678)
Occasional Publishing Inc .... G 877 373-8273
  Seattle (G-10681)
October Mist Publishing .... G 206 933-1414
  Seattle (G-10684)
On Purpose Publishing .... G 206 789-9677
  Seattle (G-10700)
One Earth Press .... G 206 784-1641
  Seattle (G-10702)
Pacific Publishing Studio LLC .... G 206 371-5628
  Seattle (G-10739)
Page Last Publishing .... G 360 289-4165
  Ocean Shores (G-7189)
Panesko Publishing .... G 360 748-0505
  Chehalis (G-2521)
Paradigm Publishing NW LLC .... G 206 257-0214
  Seattle (G-10751)
Paraversal Publishing LLC .... G 206 366-1981
  Seattle (G-10755)
Peel and Press LLC .... G 206 937-1457
  Seattle (G-10779)
Penchant Press International .... G 206 687-2401
  Blaine (G-1694)
Peridot Publishing LLC .... G 509 242-7752
  Liberty Lake (G-5853)
Philos Press .... G 360 456-5106
  Olympia (G-7369)
Piecemeal Publishing LLC .... G 425 432-3043
  Maple Valley (G-6289)
Pike Street Press .... G 206 971-0120
  Seattle (G-10807)
Pink Slug Press .... G 206 430-2637
  Hansville (G-4317)
Platinum Rail Publications LLC .... G 360 658-2485
  Marysville (G-6369)
Pleasure Boat Studio .... G 206 962-0460
  Seattle (G-10822)
Plus Six Publishing .... G 360 553-2316
  Vancouver (G-14490)
PM Weizenbaum .... G 206 427-4127
  Seattle (G-10826)
Point Roberts Press Inc .... G 360 945-0413
  Blaine (G-1696)
Polyventure International .... G 360 898-7013
  Union (G-13918)
Ponder Press .... G 206 861-0448
  Seattle (G-10830)
Post Alley Press .... G 206 522-5963
  Seattle (G-10837)
Potluck Press LLC .... G 206 328-1300
  Seattle (G-10838)
Powerhuse Brnds Consulting LLC .... G 503 317-4925
  Ridgefield (G-9104)

Press .... G 509 869-2242
  Spokane (G-12453)
Press .... G 206 290-7392
  Seattle (G-10856)
Price Jensen Surveys Inc .... E 425 747-4143
  Bellevue (G-1081)
Print Guys Inc .... G 509 453-6369
  Yakima (G-15654)
Privateer Press Inc .... E 425 643-5900
  Bellevue (G-1084)
Promenade Publishing Inc .... G 800 342-6947
  Burien (G-2122)
Puppy Lunch Press .... G 360 651-9957
  Arlington (G-309)
Quality Code Publishing .... G 206 216-9500
  Seattle (G-10900)
Raepop .... G 206 729-3996
  Seattle (G-10913)
Raisy Kinder Publishing .... G 360 752-0332
  Bellingham (G-1514)
Raphoe Press .... G 425 486-5036
  Kenmore (G-4601)
Raston Publishing LLC .... G 206 962-7839
  Seattle (G-10924)
Rauda Scale Models Inc .... F 206 365-8877
  Seattle (G-10926)
Raven Radio Theater .... G 360 943-3206
  Olympia (G-7378)
Raya Publishing LLC .... G 808 635-5908
  Gig Harbor (G-4151)
Razorgirl Press .... G 206 290-7990
  Seattle (G-10927)
Read E-Z .... G 360 708-8491
  Sedro Woolley (G-11559)
Redemption Press .... G 360 226-3488
  Enumclaw (G-3317)
Retired Gorilla Publishing .... G 509 474-9345
  Spokane (G-12473)
Ronin Green Publishing .... G 206 725-2839
  Seattle (G-10978)
Rubythroat Press LLC .... G 206 634-9173
  Seattle (G-10991)
Russell Lamar Jacquet-Acea .... G 206 334-2935
  Seattle (G-10999)
San Juan Publishing .... G 425 485-2813
  Kenmore (G-4602)
Sara Huey Pblcy Promotions LLC .... G 206 619-0610
  Seattle (G-11014)
Schedules Direct .... G 206 701-7800
  Seattle (G-11025)
Scribble Sketch Press .... G 707 364-4072
  Seattle (G-11036)
Seatech Publications Inc .... G 360 394-1911
  Poulsbo (G-7997)
Serious Biz LLC .... G 425 454-1906
  Bellevue (G-1125)
Service Surplus & Crafts .... G 360 636-0250
  Longview (G-5952)
Shamrock & Spike Maul Pubg Co .... G 360 734-5778
  Bellingham (G-1532)
Sistahology .... G 206 604-1418
  Seattle (G-11118)
Sitka 2 Publishing LLC .... G 425 522-4231
  Kirkland (G-5464)
Skagit Publishing .... F 360 424-3251
  Marblemount (G-6307)
So You Want To Write .... G 760 771-8940
  Olympia (G-7398)
Soph-Ware Associates Inc .... F 509 467-0668
  Spokane (G-12512)
Spinning Heads Inc .... G 253 219-5457
  Tacoma (G-13524)
Spokane Athors Self-Publishers .... G 509 325-2072
  Spokane (G-12516)
Star Press Inc .... E 509 525-2425
  Walla Walla (G-14874)
Steck Technical Publications .... G 253 630-7279
  Kent (G-5153)
Stitch Publications LLC .... G 206 214-5225
  Seattle (G-11196)
Stover Publishing .... G 206 240-2438
  Bonney Lake (G-1740)
Straight Publications Inc .... G 206 324-0618
  Seattle (G-11201)
Strategic News Service LLC .... F 360 378-1023
  Friday Harbor (G-4060)
Strictly Ic .... G 253 941-6611
  Kent (G-5160)
Study In The USA Inc .... G 206 622-2075
  Seattle (G-11208)

Supermedia LLC .... B 425 423-7904
  Everett (G-3623)
Swanton Hills Press LLC .... G 206 972-1205
  Seattle (G-11235)
T3 Publishing LLC .... G 206 650-0535
  Woodinville (G-15384)
Tagorbi Publishing LLC .... G 253 466-3214
  Puyallup (G-8261)
Target Media Partners .... G 509 765-5681
  Moses Lake (G-6752)
Target Media Partners .... C 509 328-5555
  Spokane Valley (G-12900)
Target Media Partners .... F 509 662-1405
  Wenatchee (G-15078)
Teddy Bear Press .... G 206 402-6947
  Seattle (G-11278)
Tevada Publishing Inc .... F 509 783-5455
  Kennewick (G-4734)
Therapeutae Publishing LLC .... G 425 242-1580
  Sammamish (G-9252)
Thirty Second Streeet Raccoons .... G 206 526-8169
  Seattle (G-11293)
Tiloben Publishing Co Inc .... G 206 323-3070
  Seattle (G-11307)
Timeline Press LLC .... G 425 454-7447
  Bellevue (G-1189)
Toka Box .... G 530 505-1289
  Bellevue (G-1193)
Top Hat Word & Index .... G 520 271-2112
  Bellevue (G-1194)
Topia Press Ltd .... G 360 754-4449
  Olympia (G-7410)
Touchet Valley Publishing .... G 509 337-6631
  Waitsburg (G-14758)
Tourmap Company .... G 206 932-2506
  Seattle (G-11322)
Transportation Wash State Dept .... G 360 705-7428
  Olympia (G-7413)
Trixie Publishing Inc .... G 360 521-8246
  Vancouver (G-14648)
Tropic Bird LLC .... G 360 378-5234
  Friday Harbor (G-4062)
Trumpeter Public House .... G 360 588-4515
  Mount Vernon (G-6849)
Tumbling Leaf Press .... G 425 885-6315
  Bellevue (G-1205)
University of Washington .... G 206 543-4598
  Seattle (G-11381)
USA Printing Corporation .... G 206 682-2423
  Seattle (G-11395)
Valcon Games LLC .... G 425 223-4672
  Redmond (G-8702)
Vanguard Foods .... G 206 355-5938
  Auburn (G-591)
Vbs Reachout Adventures .... G 206 365-0860
  Shoreline (G-11819)
Veronica Dlndba Gold Star Pubg .... G 360 398-2446
  Bellingham (G-1581)
Veterans Express .... G 253 517-3798
  Federal Way (G-3800)
Vital Force Publishing LLC .... G 253 350-6359
  Tacoma (G-13582)
Viva Publishing .... G 360 394-3756
  Poulsbo (G-8018)
Warrington Publications .... G 425 793-9629
  Renton (G-8942)
Washington Publishing Company .... G 425 562-2245
  Seattle (G-11441)
Washington Publishing Hse LLC .... F 425 406-9891
  Redmond (G-8710)
Westwynd Publishing LLC .... G 253 588-3066
  Lakewood (G-5767)
Whalestooth Publishing .... G 360 376-2784
  Olga (G-7220)
Whidbey Marketplace & News LLC .... G 360 682-2341
  Oak Harbor (G-7172)
White Dog Press .... G 800 257-2226
  Bainbridge Island (G-683)
Within Power Publishing .... G 425 241-4214
  Newcastle (G-7042)
Word Up Publishing .... G 253 859-7002
  Kent (G-5218)
World Trends Holdings LLC .... G 559 474-2361
  Richland (G-9055)
Wow Mom Corporation .... G 206 240-4068
  Snohomish (G-12001)
Wrapper Press .... G 425 443-4389
  Maple Valley (G-6303)
Wry Ink Publishing LLC .... G 206 714-3178
  Seattle (G-11500)

PRODUCT SECTION

X Media Communications ....G...... 206 789-6758
Seattle *(G-11501)*
X Press Ink Co ....G...... 253 588-1818
Lakewood *(G-5770)*
Yakima Press Company LLC ....G...... 509 480-0642
Naches *(G-7009)*
Yakima Valley Senior Times ....G...... 509 457-4886
Yakima *(G-15719)*
Yopti LLC ....G...... 347 979-1735
Bellevue *(G-1231)*
You Are Better Publishing ....G...... 425 776-8640
Edmonds *(G-3165)*

PUBLISHERS: Music Book & Sheet Music

Hometown Band ....G...... 206 842-2084
Silverdale *(G-11837)*
Juice & Jam Inc ....G...... 206 734-5136
Seattle *(G-10314)*
Leopona Inc ....F...... 206 701-7931
Seattle *(G-10404)*
Relentless Publishing LLC ....G...... 360 929-7530
Oak Harbor *(G-7163)*
Tri-Ryche Corporation ....G...... 206 363-8070
Seattle *(G-11332)*

PUBLISHERS: Music, Sheet

Equity Publishing ....G...... 509 994-0505
Deer Park *(G-2900)*

PUBLISHERS: Newsletter

Newsdata LLC ....F...... 206 285-4848
Seattle *(G-10603)*
Redmond Communications Inc ....F...... 425 739-4669
Kirkland *(G-5451)*
University of Washington ....F...... 206 543-2580
Seattle *(G-11384)*

PUBLISHERS: Newspaper

11 Times Creative LLC ....G...... 206 523-2985
Seattle *(G-9315)*
Advocate Printing ....G...... 360 748-3335
Chehalis *(G-2458)*
Animal People Inc ....G...... 360 579-2505
Clinton *(G-2683)*
Avaric Letter Press ....G...... 360 836-5993
Vancouver *(G-14047)*
Brian Murphy ....G...... 206 323-8001
Seattle *(G-9584)*
Budo LLC ....G...... 206 854-1161
Seattle *(G-9594)*
Business To Business ....G...... 360 748-6848
Chehalis *(G-2475)*
Buy Monthly Deals ....G...... 360 321-6748
Langley *(G-5771)*
Catholic Northwest Progress ....F...... 206 382-4850
Seattle *(G-9647)*
Clyde Hill Publishing LLC ....G...... 425 454-8220
Clyde Hill *(G-2703)*
Columbia River Reader ....G...... 360 636-6097
Longview *(G-5900)*
Devaul Publishing Inc ....E...... 360 748-3335
Chehalis *(G-2489)*
Double Up LLC ....G...... 908 398-9088
Sammamish *(G-9202)*
Echo Springs Publishing ....G...... 360 417-1346
Port Angeles *(G-7701)*
Edmund Lucy ....G...... 425 703-4155
Issaquah *(G-4409)*
Executive Media Corp ....G...... 509 933-2993
Ellensburg *(G-3200)*
Fanipin Korea Corp ....G...... 425 218-6555
Mill Creek *(G-6510)*
Golden Child Inc ....G...... 206 901-9502
Seattle *(G-10094)*
Gutsy Services LLC ....G...... 503 750-9024
Vancouver *(G-14277)*
Herald Classified Want ADS ....G...... 425 339-3100
Everett *(G-3510)*
Hispanic Yellow Pages ....G...... 206 297-8532
Seattle *(G-10176)*
Horizon of Change ....G...... 425 355-1712
Everett *(G-3512)*
Horvitz Newspapers Inc ....G...... 425 274-4782
Bellevue *(G-949)*
Inside Real Estate ....G...... 360 379-0139
Port Townsend *(G-7891)*
Investigatewest ....G...... 206 441-4288
Seattle *(G-10255)*

Jason K Miller ....G...... 360 853-8213
Concrete *(G-2787)*
Jasper Publishing LLC ....G...... 360 875-8383
Raymond *(G-8355)*
Katherine Ottaway Dr ....G...... 360 385-3826
Port Townsend *(G-7894)*
Kaye Mag LLC ....G...... 360 668-8989
Snohomish *(G-11930)*
Korea Times Los Angeles Inc ....E...... 206 622-2229
Seattle *(G-10356)*
Letter & Sphere LLC ....G...... 206 473-7534
Seattle *(G-10407)*
Little Nickel-Bremerton ....G...... 360 308-0279
Silverdale *(G-11845)*
Living Snoqualmie LLC ....G...... 425 396-7304
Snoqualmie *(G-12016)*
Mach Publishing Company Inc ....F...... 425 258-9396
Snohomish *(G-11941)*
Methow Valley Publishing LLC ....F...... 509 997-7011
Twisp *(G-13915)*
Mid-Columbia Newspaper Pubhs ....G...... 509 845-5253
Kennewick *(G-4694)*
Ncw Media Inc ....G...... 509 782-3781
Cashmere *(G-2327)*
Nguoi Viet Ngay Nay ....G...... 206 725-8384
Seattle *(G-10606)*
Night Shift LLC ....G...... 206 334-2548
Tukwila *(G-13778)*
North Cascades Broadcasting ....G...... 509 826-0100
OMAK *(G-7439)*
Northern Kittitas Cnty Tribune ....G...... 509 674-2511
Cle Elum *(G-2673)*
Northsound Shopping ....G...... 425 258-3455
Everett *(G-3554)*
Northwest Flyer Inc ....G...... 253 471-9888
Lakewood *(G-5742)*
Northwest Parents Media ....F...... 206 842-8500
Bainbridge Island *(G-655)*
Northwest Satellite Network ....G...... 425 885-5986
Bellevue *(G-1037)*
Orcas Memories LLC ....G...... 650 325-9400
Eastsound *(G-3043)*
Page Editorial ....G...... 253 597-8634
Tacoma *(G-13456)*
Paper Panduh ....G...... 206 538-0202
Seattle *(G-10749)*
Paul Middlewood ....G...... 425 778-4771
Mountlake Terrace *(G-6866)*
Paul Razore ....G...... 360 734-4845
Bellingham *(G-1492)*
Periodico Laraza ....G...... 253 961-5008
Fife *(G-3979)*
Prentis Literary LLC ....G...... 425 260-7753
Kent *(G-5080)*
Prosser Grandview-Publishers ....F...... 509 786-1711
Prosser *(G-8063)*
Randomalities ....G...... 253 954-5704
Puyallup *(G-8235)*
Real Fine Publishing ....G...... 253 318-6553
University Place *(G-13979)*
Return My Life LLC ....G...... 360 584-9799
Olympia *(G-7383)*
Royal Register ....G...... 509 770-8221
Moses Lake *(G-6746)*
Seattle Chinese Post Inc ....E...... 206 223-0623
Seattle *(G-11051)*
Shelter Peak Publishing LLC ....G...... 360 460-0751
Port Townsend *(G-7925)*
Snohomish Publishing Company .....E...... 206 523-7548
Snohomish *(G-11983)*
Spokanarama Publishing ....G...... 509 455-8009
Spokane *(G-12515)*
Statesman-Examiner Inc ....G...... 509 276-5043
Deer Park *(G-2917)*
Swing Fly Press LLC ....G...... 616 540-3836
Pullman *(G-8110)*
Target Media Partners ....F...... 509 662-1405
Wenatchee *(G-15078)*
Telecom Reseller Inc ....G...... 360 260-9708
Vancouver *(G-14628)*
Touchet Valley News Inc ....G...... 509 382-2221
Dayton *(G-2887)*
University of Washington ....F...... 206 543-2580
Seattle *(G-11384)*
US Hospitality Publishers Inc ....G...... 615 956-0080
Vancouver *(G-14657)*
USA Printing Corporation ....G...... 206 682-2423
Seattle *(G-11395)*
Walla Walla Union Bulletin ....D...... 509 525-3300
Walla Walla *(G-14895)*

PUBLISHERS: Newspapers, No Printing

Washington State University ....C...... 509 335-4573
Pullman *(G-8114)*
Whole Shebang ....G...... 360 941-5125
Sedro Woolley *(G-11580)*
Wilbur Register Inc ....G...... 509 647-5551
Wilbur *(G-15142)*
Woodys Relics ....G...... 360 849-4257
Cathlamet *(G-2377)*
World Publishing Co ....G...... 509 884-7575
Wenatchee *(G-15086)*
Your Daily Dose LLC ....G...... 360 749-7414
Castle Rock *(G-2358)*

PUBLISHERS: Newspapers, No Printing

Beacon Publishing Inc ....F...... 425 347-1711
Mukilteo *(G-6897)*
Bilingual Press Publishing Co ....G...... 509 483-2523
Spokane *(G-12147)*
Bob Nelson ....G...... 360 795-3391
Cathlamet *(G-2360)*
Camas-Washougal Post-Record .....F...... 360 834-2141
Camas *(G-2237)*
Chewelah Independent Inc ....G...... 509 935-8422
Chewelah *(G-2600)*
Chronicle ....E...... 509 826-1110
OMAK *(G-7436)*
Coordinating Services Inc ....G...... 425 334-8966
Lake Stevens *(G-5640)*
Daily Ellensburg Record Inc ....E...... 509 925-1414
Ellensburg *(G-3192)*
Der Heintzelmann Inc ....G...... 360 683-4740
Sequim *(G-11626)*
East County Journal ....G...... 360 496-5993
Morton *(G-6668)*
Eatonville Dispatch Newspaper ....F...... 360 832-4411
Eatonville *(G-3055)*
El Mundo Communications Inc ....G...... 509 663-5737
Wenatchee *(G-15029)*
Empire Press Co ....G...... 509 886-8668
East Wenatchee *(G-3011)*
Facts Newspaper ....G...... 206 324-0552
Seattle *(G-9962)*
Ferndale Record Inc ....G...... 360 384-1411
Ferndale *(G-3844)*
Fishermens News Inc ....G...... 206 282-7545
Seattle *(G-9999)*
Franklin County Graphic ....G...... 509 234-3181
Connell *(G-2794)*
Giraffe Project ....G...... 360 221-7989
Langley *(G-5778)*
Goldendale Grapplers ....G...... 509 314-9975
Goldendale *(G-4198)*
Goldendale Sentinel Inc ....G...... 509 773-3777
Goldendale *(G-4199)*
Greenleaf Publishing Inc ....G...... 509 427-8444
Stevenson *(G-13012)*
Havre Daily News ....G...... 206 284-4424
Seattle *(G-10151)*
Index Publishing ....D...... 206 323-7101
Seattle *(G-10225)*
Inland Publications Inc ....E...... 509 325-0634
Spokane *(G-12312)*
Lafromboise Newspapers ....F...... 360 458-2681
Yelm *(G-15737)*
Lee Enterprises Incorporated ....G...... 509 783-5555
Kennewick *(G-4688)*
McClatchy Newspapers Inc ....C...... 360 754-5400
Olympia *(G-7333)*
Ncw Media Inc ....G...... 509 548-5286
Leavenworth *(G-5811)*
Northwest Media Washington LP ....G...... 425 274-4782
Bellevue *(G-1036)*
Northwest Prime Time ....G...... 206 824-8600
Des Moines *(G-2941)*
Olympian Newspaper ....G...... 360 754-5402
Olympia *(G-7355)*
Olympic View Publishing LLC ....G...... 360 374-3311
Forks *(G-4014)*
Olympic View Publishing LLC ....E...... 360 683-3311
Sequim *(G-11655)*
Orcas Island Growlers ....G...... 360 927-9265
Bellingham *(G-1481)*
Ranger Publishing Company Inc .....F...... 253 584-1212
Steilacoom *(G-13006)*
Ranger Publishing Inc ....F...... 253 964-2680
Dupont *(G-2972)*
S J Olsen Publishing Inc ....F...... 360 249-3311
Montesano *(G-6656)*
San Juan Islander ....G...... 360 378-2798
Friday Harbor *(G-4056)*

Employee Codes: A=Over 500 employees, B=251-500
C=101-250, D=51-100, E=20-50, F=10-19, G=2-9

PUBLISHERS: Newspapers, No Printing

Seattle Business Journal Inc...................D.......206 583-0701
  Seattle *(G-11049)*
Seattle Daily Journal Commerce..........E.......206 622-8272
  Seattle *(G-11055)*
Seattle Times Company.........................C.......509 248-1251
  Yakima *(G-15670)*
Seattle Weekly LLC................................E.......206 623-0500
  Seattle *(G-11082)*
Shoezandmorecom LLC..........................F.......216 544-1745
  Renton *(G-8911)*
Sound Publishing Inc..............................G.......253 437-6000
  Federal Way *(G-3786)*
Sound Publishing Inc..............................D.......360 394-5800
  Everett *(G-3617)*
Sound Publishing Inc..............................G.......253 925-5565
  Federal Way *(G-3787)*
Sound Publishing Inc..............................G.......360 786-6973
  Lacey *(G-5590)*
Sound Publishing Inc..............................F.......360 779-4464
  Poulsbo *(G-8003)*
Sound Publishing Inc..............................F.......206 463-9195
  Vashon *(G-14744)*
Sound Publishing Inc..............................g.......360 376-4500
  Eastsound *(G-3047)*
Sound Publishing Inc..............................E.......360 675-6611
  Coupeville *(G-2818)*
Sound Publishing Inc..............................g.......360 876-4414
  Port Orchard *(G-7850)*
Sound Publishing Inc..............................g.......425 483-3732
  Kirkland *(G-5467)*
Sound Publishing Inc..............................E.......253 872-6600
  Federal Way *(G-3788)*
Sound Publishing Inc..............................g.......360 825-2555
  Enumclaw *(G-3321)*
Sound Publishing Inc..............................F.......360 659-1300
  Marysville *(G-6389)*
Souz LLC...g.......206 428-8332
  Renton *(G-8917)*
Star Publishing Inc.................................G.......509 633-1350
  Grand Coulee *(G-4244)*
Statesman-Examiner Inc.........................E.......509 684-4567
  Colville *(G-2775)*
Tacoma News Inc....................................B.......253 597-8593
  Tacoma *(G-13545)*
Times...G.......509 337-6631
  Waitsburg *(G-14757)*
Tjn Publishing Inc...................................G.......360 426-4677
  Shelton *(G-11745)*
Valley Bugler LLC...................................G.......360 414-1246
  Renton *(G-8941)*
Valley Publishing Company Inc.............G.......509 882-3712
  Grandview *(G-4256)*
Washington Newspaper Publisher.........G.......360 515-0974
  Olympia *(G-7422)*
Yakima Valley Senior Times..................G.......509 457-4886
  Yakima *(G-15719)*

PUBLISHERS: Pamphlets, No Printing

Intellicard Inc..G.......509 965-9266
  Yakima *(G-15593)*
M B G Management Services..................G.......360 493-0522
  Olympia *(G-7328)*
Macgregor Publishing Co.......................E.......800 581-5040
  Mount Vernon *(G-6809)*

PUBLISHERS: Periodical, With Printing

Elliott Bay Publishing Inc......................G.......206 283-8144
  Tukwila *(G-13728)*
Laser Writing...G.......253 686-6909
  Tacoma *(G-13383)*
Northwest Architectural League............G.......206 971-5596
  Seattle *(G-10637)*
Saco Sales LLC.......................................G.......253 922-6349
  Fife *(G-3991)*
Washington Media Services Inc.............G.......360 754-4543
  Olympia *(G-7421)*

PUBLISHERS: Periodicals, Magazines

Al Jadid Magazine..................................G.......360 936-1765
  Vancouver *(G-14016)*
Alice E Marwick.....................................G.......206 329-9565
  Seattle *(G-9376)*
Andrew Hoover......................................G.......425 869-1123
  Bellevue *(G-788)*
Bellingham Business Journal.................G.......360 647-8805
  Bellingham *(G-1263)*
Coffey Communications Inc..................C.......509 525-0101
  Walla Walla *(G-14788)*
Edwin Laird..G.......206 587-6537
  Seattle *(G-9885)*
Everything Quarterly LLC.....................G.......425 478-2173
  Lynnwood *(G-6118)*
Farm Aquisition RES & MGT LLC........G.......425 869-0624
  Redmond *(G-8458)*
Feral House Inc......................................G.......323 666-3311
  Port Townsend *(G-7883)*
Funny Feeling...G.......360 671-7386
  Bellingham *(G-1355)*
G A News..G.......253 471-9888
  Lakewood *(G-5724)*
Kent Chamber of Commerce Inc..........G.......253 854-1770
  Kent *(G-4975)*
Magazine For Gigging Musicans...........G.......425 503-0421
  Sammamish *(G-9229)*
Magnet Magazine....................................G.......206 977-7696
  Kirkland *(G-5394)*
Master Printing Inc.................................G.......509 684-5869
  Colville *(G-2765)*
Naval Magazine Code 4214...................G.......360 396-2187
  Port Hadlock *(G-7761)*
Nickel One Ad Newspaper.....................g.......360 423-3141
  Kennewick *(G-4702)*
Nova Graphics..G.......509 251-2575
  Newman Lake *(G-7050)*
Paizo Publishing LLC............................G.......425 289-0060
  Redmond *(G-8612)*
Pamela McAllister..................................G.......206 783-9534
  Seattle *(G-10745)*
Peel David and Associates.....................G.......425 577-8980
  Kirkland *(G-5432)*
Pope John...G.......206 320-0686
  Seattle *(G-10832)*
Portland Press Inc..................................F.......253 274-8883
  Tacoma *(G-13471)*
Powell Publishing Inc............................G.......360 886-6650
  Black Diamond *(G-1653)*
Redmond Communications Inc.............F.......425 739-4669
  Kirkland *(G-5451)*
Rsvp Seattle..G.......425 396-7787
  Snoqualmie *(G-12021)*
Seattle Business Journal Inc..................D.......206 583-0701
  Seattle *(G-11049)*
Steward Publishing.................................G.......206 283-0077
  Seattle *(G-11193)*
Terry and Kathy Loney..........................G.......509 375-4005
  College Place *(G-2729)*
Ticonderoga Enterprises........................G.......509 922-2411
  Spokane *(G-12556)*
University of Washington......................G.......206 543-4598
  Seattle *(G-11381)*
Washington Assn Bldg Officials.............F.......360 628-8321
  Lacey *(G-5599)*
Washington State University..................D.......509 335-3518
  Pullman *(G-8112)*
Yakima Valley Teen Magazine...............G.......509 865-4055
  Toppenish *(G-13676)*

PUBLISHERS: Periodicals, No Printing

Charles Cerar...G.......425 392-1821
  Issaquah *(G-4392)*
J & M Reports LLC................................G.......360 260-8620
  Vancouver *(G-14329)*
Seattle Viet Times Inc............................G.......425 678-8872
  Mill Creek *(G-6528)*
Sound Publishing Inc..............................G.......253 437-6000
  Federal Way *(G-3786)*
Sound Publishing Inc..............................G.......360 786-6973
  Lacey *(G-5590)*
Wenatchee Business Journal..................G.......509 663-6730
  Cashmere *(G-2332)*

PUBLISHERS: Sheet Music

Ascap...G.......206 324-0561
  Seattle *(G-9442)*

PUBLISHERS: Shopping News

Ferndale Record Inc...............................G.......360 384-1411
  Ferndale *(G-3844)*
Geekwire LLC...F.......206 913-7926
  Seattle *(G-10057)*
Highway Shoppers..................................G.......360 494-7641
  Packwood *(G-7543)*
Sound Publishing Inc..............................G.......253 437-6000
  Federal Way *(G-3786)*
Sound Publishing Inc..............................G.......360 786-6973
  Lacey *(G-5590)*

PUBLISHERS: Technical Manuals

Girandola..G.......206 289-0523
  Seattle *(G-10073)*

PUBLISHERS: Technical Manuals & Papers

Jessy Wilkinson LLC..............................G.......509 578-1650
  West Richland *(G-15097)*
L & L Ink..G.......206 605-4561
  Snohomish *(G-11934)*

PUBLISHERS: Telephone & Other Directory

Coastal Cruise Guides............................G.......206 448-4488
  Seattle *(G-9705)*
Dex Media Holdings Inc........................E.......509 922-1026
  Spokane Valley *(G-12681)*
First Index Inc..E.......888 535-8583
  Spokane Valley *(G-12703)*
Hibu Inc..D.......425 454-1762
  Bellevue *(G-944)*
Statewide Pubg - Wash Inc....................F.......509 734-1186
  Kennewick *(G-4730)*

PUBLISHERS: Textbooks, No Printing

Bamonte A Trnado Crk Pblction...........G.......509 838-7114
  Spokane *(G-12138)*
Leading Beyond Tradition LLC.............G.......425 275-7665
  Snohomish *(G-11938)*

PUBLISHERS: Trade journals, No Printing

Builders Exchange Wash Inc..................F.......425 743-3244
  Everett *(G-3403)*
Fantagraphics Books Inc.......................E.......206 524-1967
  Seattle *(G-9968)*

PUBLISHING & BROADCASTING: Internet Only

Afar Interactive Inc................................G.......425 442-5101
  Seattle *(G-9357)*
Callidus Software Inc.............................F.......503 579-4484
  Vancouver *(G-14090)*
Cellartracker LLC...................................G.......206 601-7226
  Seattle *(G-9651)*
Denny Mountain Media LLC.................D.......425 831-7130
  Seattle *(G-9822)*
Digital Product Studio LLC...................G.......206 484-8439
  Seattle *(G-9829)*
Equipment Inc..G.......206 826-9577
  Kirkland *(G-5333)*
Formula Web LLC..................................G.......425 835-3259
  Bellevue *(G-915)*
Hollywood Triangle Productions...........G.......323 301-3003
  Seattle *(G-10179)*
Hunt Hosted Solutions..........................G.......425 222-0098
  Fall City *(G-3702)*
Keychain Social LLC..............................G.......425 876-3261
  Snoqualmie *(G-12014)*
M&L Research Inc..................................G.......877 321-8766
  Seattle *(G-10456)*
Myyearlook...G.......303 523-2468
  Port Orchard *(G-7832)*
Scout Media Inc.....................................E.......206 313-4932
  Seattle *(G-11033)*
Skyfish Media LLC.................................G.......415 779-2132
  Seattle *(G-11132)*
Stemar Media Group LLC......................G.......206 877-3560
  Shoreline *(G-11818)*
Transact Communications Inc...............F.......425 977-2100
  Lynnwood *(G-6212)*
Ultra Van Krome Prductions LLC.........G.......206 859-3459
  Tacoma *(G-13568)*
Whitepages Inc.......................................D.......206 973-5100
  Seattle *(G-11470)*

PUBLISHING & PRINTING: Art Copy

Chromaworks Corporation....................G.......206 622-7107
  Seattle *(G-9681)*
Dunsire Printers Inc..............................G.......360 532-8791
  Aberdeen *(G-9)*
For Art Sake Inc.....................................G.......253 858-8087
  Gig Harbor *(G-4101)*

PUBLISHING & PRINTING: Book Clubs

Barbara Karnes Books Inc....................G.......360 828-7132
  Vancouver *(G-14056)*

Cascade Publications ....G.... 360 638-0404
Hansville (G-4315)
Deca Stories LLC ....G.... 302 219-0373
Seattle (G-9809)

PUBLISHING & PRINTING: Books

Cadwallader and Stern LLC ....G.... 206 931-8018
Seattle (G-9604)
Cepher Publishing Group LLC ....G.... 406 889-7583
Everett (G-3415)
Cleaning Consultants Services ....G.... 206 682-9748
Seattle (G-9692)
Double Vision Partners Inc ....G.... 360 378-4331
Friday Harbor (G-4043)
Fine Edge ....G.... 360 299-8500
Anacortes (G-130)
Oxalis Group ....G.... 509 838-3295
Spokane (G-12424)
Peel Productions Inc ....G.... 360 256-2450
Vancouver (G-14482)
Pgi Publications ....G.... 206 588-2968
Seattle (G-10792)
Premier Agendas Inc ....D.... 360 734-1153
Bellingham (G-1503)
Saco Sales LLC ....G.... 253 922-6349
Fife (G-3991)
Wesley Todd ....G.... 509 926-0344
Spokane Valley (G-12934)

PUBLISHING & PRINTING: Catalogs

North Cross Aluminum LLC ....G.... 360 821-1481
Freeland (G-4036)
Scared of Genre ....G.... 206 227-2574
Seattle (G-11023)

PUBLISHING & PRINTING: Directories, NEC

Dex Media Holdings Inc ....F.... 360 830-0807
Silverdale (G-11831)
Kannberg Media Corp ....G.... 509 468-4226
Spokane (G-12349)
Wrbq Inc ....G.... 509 927-7181
Spokane Valley (G-12942)

PUBLISHING & PRINTING: Directories, Telephone

Action Pages Consolidated Inc ....E.... 360 848-0870
Mount Vernon (G-6769)
Cellular Directory Corp ....G.... 425 646-4917
Bellevue (G-844)
City of Naches ....G.... 509 653-1400
Naches (G-6995)

PUBLISHING & PRINTING: Magazines: publishing & printing

American News Company LLC ....G.... 866 466-7231
Fife (G-3930)
Artful Dragon Press LLC ....G.... 800 630-1117
Sammamish (G-9185)
Blue Water Publishers LLC ....G.... 360 805-6474
Monroe (G-6555)
Cleaning Consultants Services ....G.... 206 682-9748
Seattle (G-9692)
Clintron Publishing Inc ....G.... 509 448-9878
Spokane (G-12185)
Crave Magazine ....G.... 360 991-9332
Vancouver (G-14152)
Family Values Mag Clark Cnty ....G.... 360 909-5945
Vancouver (G-14221)
Fantasy Index Magazines LLC ....G.... 206 527-4444
Redmond (G-8457)
Guild of American Luthiers ....G.... 253 472-7853
Tacoma (G-13329)
Iocolor LLP ....G.... 206 223-1845
Seattle (G-10257)
Lenswork Publishing ....G.... 360 588-1343
Anacortes (G-140)
Mj Directions LLC ....G.... 425 656-3621
Seattle (G-10549)
Northwest Runner ....G.... 206 527-5301
Seattle (G-10651)
Poetry Northwest ....G.... 425 388-9395
Everett (G-3578)
Positive Futures Network ....E.... 206 842-0216
Bainbridge Island (G-660)
Pulse Publications Inc ....F.... 360 671-3933
Bellingham (G-1510)
Skt Publishers Inc ....G.... 206 789-8116
Seattle (G-11129)
Starpath Corporation ....G.... 206 783-1414
Seattle (G-11184)
Townsend Ltr For Dctors Ptents ....F.... 360 385-6021
Port Townsend (G-7935)
U S Practical Shooting Assn ....F.... 360 855-2245
Burlington (G-2195)

PUBLISHING & PRINTING: Music, Book

Lets Play Stella LLC ....G.... 206 365-6249
Seattle (G-10406)

PUBLISHING & PRINTING: Newsletters, Business Svc

AAA Printing Inc ....E.... 425 454-0156
Bellevue (G-777)
Dumas Holdings LLC ....G.... 425 576-4227
Kirkland (G-5323)
Genoa Healthcare Mass LLC ....G.... 425 789-3050
Everett (G-3495)
Marlene Marshall ....G.... 360 733-6479
Bellingham (G-1424)

PUBLISHING & PRINTING: Newspapers

Allied Daily Newspapers Wash ....G.... 360 943-9960
Olympia (G-7223)
Bellingham Business Journal ....G.... 360 647-8805
Bellingham (G-1263)
Bellingham Escape ....G.... 360 519-9213
Bellingham (G-1265)
Big Sky Publishing Co ....F.... 406 587-4491
Seattle (G-9525)
Blethen Corporation ....C.... 206 464-2471
Seattle (G-9541)
British Footpaths ....G.... 206 525-2466
Seattle (G-9587)
Cabin Fever Media ....G.... 509 544-2155
Pasco (G-7557)
Cascadia Newspaper Company LLC ....G.... 360 647-8200
Bellingham (G-1292)
Casey Communications Inc ....G.... 206 448-5902
Seattle (G-9645)
Cowles Publishing Company ....B.... 509 459-5000
Spokane (G-12204)
Daily Bulletin ....G.... 509 397-3332
Colfax (G-2713)
Daily Conner ....G.... 360 643-0056
Port Townsend (G-7876)
Daily Dessert LLC ....G.... 757 746-7744
Seattle (G-9785)
Daily Plant-It ....G.... 425 677-4948
Issaquah (G-4401)
Daily Toils & Troubles ....G.... 360 337-9028
Poulsbo (G-7957)
Deer Park Gazette LLC ....G.... 509 276-7737
Deer Park (G-2898)
Douglas Green ....G.... 360 260-9708
Vancouver (G-14186)
Dow Jones & Company Inc ....E.... 253 661-8850
Federal Way (G-3731)
East Oregonian Publishing Co ....G.... 360 642-8181
Long Beach (G-5873)
East Washingtonian ....G.... 509 843-1313
Pomeroy (G-7672)
Eastern News Inc ....G.... 206 760-9168
Seattle (G-9872)
Endex Newspaper LLC ....G.... 206 322-4194
Seattle (G-9921)
Examinercom ....G.... 206 459-0562
Auburn (G-437)
Focusbloom LLC ....G.... 360 894-2362
Yelm (G-15734)
Frontier Publication Inc ....G.... 206 463-5656
Vashon (G-14723)
Gannett Co Inc ....E.... 425 391-2530
Bellevue (G-918)
Gatehouse Media LLC ....F.... 360 532-4000
Aberdeen (G-13)
Good News Church ....G.... 509 544-0938
Pasco (G-7587)
Hearst Corporation ....C.... 206 448-8000
Seattle (G-10157)
Hearst Seattle Media LLC ....G.... 206 448-8000
Seattle (G-10158)
Herald Cheraine PHD ....G.... 253 564-1193
Tacoma (G-13335)
Hipple Family Ltd Liability Co ....G.... 425 432-9696
Covington (G-2829)
Horizon Publications Inc ....F.... 509 276-5043
Deer Park (G-2905)
House Reporter LLC ....G.... 360 678-4931
Greenbank (G-4307)
International Examiner ....G.... 206 624-3925
Seattle (G-10250)
Joongang USA ....B.... 206 365-4000
Edmonds (G-3126)
Korean Sunday News of Seattle ....G.... 425 778-6747
Edmonds (G-3129)
Lee Publications Inc ....F.... 360 577-2500
Longview (G-5926)
Lewis Publishing Company Inc ....E.... 360 354-4444
Lynden (G-6031)
Maine Marketing Inc ....G.... 425 487-9111
Woodinville (G-15300)
Market Place Weekly Inc ....F.... 360 568-4121
Snohomish (G-11943)
McClatchy Newspapers Inc ....C.... 509 582-1500
Kennewick (G-4693)
Morning News Tribune ....G.... 253 597-8511
Tacoma (G-13420)
Motorsports ....G.... 360 799-0865
Sultan (G-13029)
Mukilteo Beacon ....G.... 425 347-5634
Mukilteo (G-6954)
News Trbune Schlrship Fndation ....G.... 253 597-8593
Tacoma (G-13427)
News Tribune The 1950 S ....G.... 253 841-2481
Puyallup (G-8199)
Nickel One Ad Newspaper ....G.... 360 423-3141
Kennewick (G-4702)
North Beach Media Inc ....G.... 360 289-2441
Ocean Shores (G-7188)
Obituaries and Legals ....G.... 253 597-8605
Tacoma (G-13440)
Olympic Cascade Publishing ....E.... 253 274-7344
Tacoma (G-13442)
Pacific Northwest Newspaper ....G.... 206 448-8125
Seattle (G-10737)
Pacific Pilot Services LLC ....G.... 509 899-0858
Ellensburg (G-3216)
Penny Savers ....G.... 360 723-0740
Battle Ground (G-731)
Phuong Dng Times ....G.... 206 760-9168
Seattle (G-10798)
Point Roberts Press Inc ....G.... 360 945-0413
Blaine (G-1696)
Port Townsend Publishing Co ....E.... 360 385-2900
Port Townsend (G-7913)
Remote View Daily LLC ....G.... 360 458-5318
Yelm (G-15744)
Resisters ....G.... 206 722-3482
Seattle (G-10950)
Seattle Times - Marysville ....G.... 360 925-6324
Marysville (G-6384)
Seattle Times Company ....C.... 206 464-2111
Seattle (G-11081)
Ski Journal ....G.... 360 752-5559
Bellingham (G-1541)
Snohomish County Bus Jurnl ....G.... 425 339-3000
Everett (G-3614)
Sound Publishing Inc ....G.... 360 308-9161
Silverdale (G-11858)
Sound Publishing Inc ....G.... 360 378-5696
Friday Harbor (G-4059)
Sound Publishing Inc ....G.... 425 888-2311
Snoqualmie (G-12026)
Sound Publishing Inc ....D.... 425 355-0717
Everett (G-3618)
Sound Publishing Holding Inc ....E.... 360 394-5800
Poulsbo (G-8004)
Sun Newspaper Daily ....G.... 360 792-3324
Bremerton (G-2004)
Sunnyside Daily News Inc ....F.... 509 837-4500
Sunnyside (G-13145)
Tex Ware ....G.... 425 337-3696
Everett (G-3631)
The Pacific County Press Inc ....G.... 360 875-6805
South Bend (G-12049)
Tri-City Model Railroaders ....G.... 509 987-7000
Kennewick (G-4739)
University of Washington ....G.... 206 543-4598
Seattle (G-11381)
Vancouver Business Journal ....F.... 360 695-2442
Vancouver (G-14660)
Warrior Brown Publishing LLC ....F.... 360 695-2442
Vancouver (G-14677)
Washington Dily Dcsion Svc LLC ....G.... 206 250-1138
Seattle (G-11439)

Employee Codes: A=Over 500 employees, B=251-500
C=101-250, D=51-100, E=20-50, F=10-19, G=2-9
2019 Washington
Manufacturers Register
1053

PUBLISHING & PRINTING: Newspapers

Washington Web Company Inc .... C 206 441-1844
  Seattle *(G-11442)*
Whatcom Watch Newspaper .... G 360 734-6007
  Bellingham *(G-1593)*
Wsu Bulletin Office .... F 509 335-2857
  Pullman *(G-8116)*
Yakima Herald Republic-309 .... G 509 367-6376
  Yakima *(G-15715)*

PUBLISHING & PRINTING: Pamphlets

AAA Printing Inc .... E 425 454-0156
  Bellevue *(G-777)*
Code Publishing Company Inc .... F 206 527-6831
  Seattle *(G-9710)*
Purple Coyote Inc .... G 509 754-2488
  Ephrata *(G-3345)*

PUBLISHING & PRINTING: Periodical Statistical Reports

Data Shaping Solutions LLC .... G 425 837-4767
  Issaquah *(G-4403)*
Stakana LLC .... G 206 227-4329
  Seattle *(G-11179)*

PUBLISHING & PRINTING: Posters

1 World Globes & Maps LLC .... G 206 781-1400
  Seattle *(G-9314)*
Carrolls Printing Inc .... G 360 345-1399
  Chehalis *(G-2481)*
Poetry Posters .... G 425 831-5809
  North Bend *(G-7120)*
Purple Coyote Inc .... G 509 754-2488
  Ephrata *(G-3345)*
Red Horse Signs LLC .... G 425 415-0654
  Woodinville *(G-15345)*
Viar Visual Communications .... G 425 391-8443
  Sammamish *(G-9257)*

PUBLISHING & PRINTING: Textbooks

Committee For Children .... D 206 343-1223
  Seattle *(G-9718)*

PUBLISHING & PRINTING: Trade Journals

Avalonphilly LLC .... G 800 405-7024
  Bellevue *(G-800)*
Gildeane Group .... G 206 362-0336
  Kenmore *(G-4575)*
Journal of Japanese Studies .... G 206 543-9302
  Seattle *(G-10308)*
Susney Incorporated .... G 253 219-7216
  Spanaway *(G-12077)*

PULLEYS: Power Transmission

Tech-Roll Inc .... G 360 371-4321
  Ferndale *(G-3911)*

PULP MILLS

Bagcraft .... G 360 695-7771
  Vancouver *(G-14053)*
Columbia Pulp I LLC .... E 509 288-4892
  Starbuck *(G-13001)*
Core Pack LLC .... G 509 426-2511
  Yakima *(G-15537)*
Fibres International Inc .... D 425 455-9811
  Everett *(G-3471)*
Kamilche Company .... G 206 224-5800
  Seattle *(G-10326)*
Longview Fibre Ppr & Packg Inc .... G 509 674-1791
  Cle Elum *(G-2671)*
Nippon Dynawave Packg Co LLC .... A 360 425-2150
  Longview *(G-5935)*
Nippon Paper Inds USA Co Ltd .... F 360 457-4474
  Port Angeles *(G-7727)*
Parberry Inc .... E 360 734-2340
  Bellingham *(G-1491)*
Port Townsend Holdings Co Inc .... B 360 385-3170
  Port Townsend *(G-7911)*
Simpson Investment Company .... D 253 272-0158
  Seattle *(G-11115)*
Weyerhaeuser Company .... B 360 532-7110
  Cosmopolis *(G-2802)*
Weyerhaeuser Company .... F 253 924-6373
  Seattle *(G-11461)*
Weyerhaeuser Company .... A 206 539-3000
  Seattle *(G-11459)*

PULP MILLS: Chemical & Semichemical Processing

Mint Valley Paper Company Inc .... G 360 931-9055
  Battle Ground *(G-723)*

PULP MILLS: Dissolving Pulp Processing

Cosmo Specialty Fibers Inc .... C 360 500-4600
  Cosmopolis *(G-2799)*

PULP MILLS: Mech Pulp, Incl Groundwood & Thermomechanical

Braven Metals LLC .... G 206 963-2234
  Lake Stevens *(G-5635)*
Sustainable Fiber Tech LLC .... G 206 818-4130
  Renton *(G-8925)*

PULP MILLS: Mechanical & Recycling Processing

Eh Metal Recycling .... G 360 334-6005
  Vancouver *(G-14195)*
Faithful Enterprises Inc .... E 509 865-7300
  Toppenish *(G-13667)*
Yms .... G 206 354-2048
  Seattle *(G-11512)*

PULP MILLS: Wood Based Pulp, NEC

Buddy Shelters LLC .... G 425 239-8104
  Arlington *(G-216)*
Cowles Publishing Company .... B 509 459-5000
  Spokane *(G-12204)*
Northwest Cpitl Apprcation Inc .... A 206 689-5615
  Seattle *(G-10640)*

PUMPS

2 M Company Inc .... G 509 765-0867
  Moses Lake *(G-6675)*
Aquatech .... G 360 957-5203
  Castle Rock *(G-2337)*
Beckwith & Kuffel .... E 509 922-5222
  Spokane Valley *(G-12637)*
Consolidated Pump & Supply .... G 509 891-1313
  Spokane Valley *(G-12665)*
Consolidated Pump & Supply .... G 509 543-7241
  Pasco *(G-7568)*
Flow International Corporation .... B 253 850-3500
  Kent *(G-4909)*
H2o Jet Inc .... E 360 866-7161
  Tumwater *(G-13874)*
Hallmark Refining Corporation .... D 360 428-5880
  Mount Vernon *(G-6803)*
HB Jaeger Company LLc .... G 360 707-5958
  Burlington *(G-2161)*
Ingersoll-Rand Company .... C 253 398-3900
  Kent *(G-4953)*
Lufkin Industries LLC .... B 425 295-7676
  Issaquah *(G-4442)*
Mal Inc .... D 360 491-2900
  Olympia *(G-7331)*
Mitchell Lewis & Staver .... G 253 589-2141
  Lakewood *(G-5737)*
Mosesvue LLC .... F 425 644-8501
  Bellevue *(G-1016)*
Omax Corporation .... C 253 872-2300
  Kent *(G-5045)*
Pacific Rim Con Pmpg Eqp Co .... G 425 453-8140
  Bellevue *(G-1060)*
Precision Castparts Corp .... G 206 433-2600
  Tukwila *(G-13794)*
Puyallup Septic Pumping .... G 253 785-6553
  Puyallup *(G-8229)*
Qualitylogic Inc .... G 360 882-0201
  Vancouver *(G-14522)*
Robert Comeau .... G 360 573-2241
  Vancouver *(G-14557)*
Sharpe Mixers Inc .... E 206 767-5660
  Seattle *(G-11096)*
Somarakis Inc .... F 360 574-6722
  Kalama *(G-4508)*
Stealth Services & Technology .... G 360 882-7211
  Vancouver *(G-14610)*
Thesoftwareworxcom .... G 425 825-3814
  Kirkland *(G-5481)*
Waterax Corporation .... G 360 574-1818
  Vancouver *(G-14679)*
Waterra USA Inc .... G 360 738-3366
  Peshastin *(G-7665)*
Western Hydro LLC .... G 509 546-9999
  Pasco *(G-7651)*
Western Hydro LLC .... G 360 428-4704
  Burlington *(G-2200)*

PUMPS & PARTS: Indl

Bradleys Metal Works Inc .... G 509 448-2307
  Spokane *(G-12159)*
Centurion Process LLC .... G 509 759-3001
  Selah *(G-11584)*
Flowserve Corporation .... F 360 573-5211
  Ridgefield *(G-9082)*
Flowserve Corporation .... G 360 676-0702
  Bellingham *(G-1350)*
Grundfos CBS Inc .... F 206 433-2600
  Tacoma *(G-13328)*
Revalesio Corporation .... E 253 922-2600
  Tacoma *(G-13495)*
Rogers Machinery Company Inc .... E 206 763-2530
  Seattle *(G-10976)*
Rogers Machinery Company Inc .... E 360 736-9356
  Centralia *(G-2429)*
Rogers Machinery Company Inc .... F 509 922-0556
  Spokane Valley *(G-12856)*
Vaughan Co Inc .... C 360 249-4042
  Montesano *(G-6664)*

PUMPS & PUMPING EQPT REPAIR SVCS

Grays Electric Inc .... G 509 662-6834
  Wenatchee *(G-15037)*
Grundfos CBS Inc .... F 206 433-2600
  Tacoma *(G-13328)*
Industrial Electric Co Inc .... G 360 424-3239
  Mount Vernon *(G-6804)*
Mal Inc .... D 360 491-2900
  Olympia *(G-7331)*
North Ridge Machine LLC .... G 509 765-8928
  Moses Lake *(G-6732)*

PUMPS & PUMPING EQPT WHOLESALERS

Beckwith & Kuffel .... E 509 922-5222
  Spokane Valley *(G-12637)*
Consolidated Pump & Supply .... G 509 543-7241
  Pasco *(G-7568)*
Grundfos CBS Inc .... F 206 433-2600
  Tacoma *(G-13328)*
HB Jaeger Company LLc .... G 360 707-5958
  Burlington *(G-2161)*
Mitchell Lewis & Staver .... G 253 589-2141
  Lakewood *(G-5737)*
Pacer Design & Manufacturing .... F 425 481-5300
  Bothell *(G-1883)*
Pacific Rim Con Pmpg Eqp Co .... G 425 453-8140
  Bellevue *(G-1060)*
Part Works Inc .... E 206 632-8900
  Seattle *(G-10760)*
Reds Electric Motors Inc .... G 360 377-3903
  Bremerton *(G-1992)*

PUMPS, HEAT: Electric

Economy Hearth & Home Inc .... G 360 692-8709
  Bremerton *(G-1950)*

PUMPS: Aircraft, Hydraulic

Eriks .... G 253 395-4770
  Kent *(G-4896)*

PUMPS: Domestic, Water Or Sump

Erickson Tank & Pump LLC .... F 509 785-2955
  Quincy *(G-8297)*
Flow International Corporation .... G 812 590-4922
  Kent *(G-4910)*
Specialty Pump and Plbg Inc .... F 425 424-8700
  Snohomish *(G-11986)*

PUMPS: Fluid Power

Dessert Industries Inc .... G 425 487-3244
  Snohomish *(G-11898)*
Environmental Technologies Inc .... F 253 804-2507
  Pacific *(G-7527)*

PUMPS: Hydraulic Power Transfer

Precision Fldpower Systems LLC .... G 206 938-2894
  Seattle *(G-10851)*

PRODUCT SECTION

RAILINGS: Prefabricated, Metal

PUMPS: Measuring & Dispensing
Adamatic Corporation ....G....... 206 322-5474
  Auburn *(G-362)*
Belshaw Bros Inc ....C....... 206 322-5474
  Auburn *(G-391)*
Fire Lion Global LLC.................................G....... 360 901-9828
  Vancouver *(G-14231)*
Petroleum Svc & Solutions LLC ....G....... 253 987-5143
  Lake Tapps *(G-5684)*

PUMPS: Vacuum, Exc Laboratory
Stealth Services & Technology..............G....... 360 882-7211
  Vancouver *(G-14610)*

PUPPETS & MARIONETTES
Fussy Cloud Puppet Slam......................G....... 206 235-9109
  Seattle *(G-10042)*
Wisdoms Marionettes..............................G....... 206 243-6172
  Tukwila *(G-13836)*
Yummy Designs LLC ....G....... 509 525-2072
  Walla Walla *(G-14907)*

PURIFICATION & DUST COLLECTION EQPT
Fsx Equipment Inc ....F....... 360 691-2999
  Granite Falls *(G-4272)*
Fsx Equipment Inc ....G....... 360 691-2999
  Granite Falls *(G-4273)*

QUARTZ CRYSTAL MINING SVCS
Caesarstone Usa Inc..............................F....... 425 251-8668
  Kent *(G-4834)*

QUARTZ CRYSTALS: Electronic
C Quartz Inc..G....... 360 393-1254
  Ferndale *(G-3820)*
Jauch Quartz America Inc......................G....... 360 633-7200
  Seabeck *(G-9265)*
Laser Materials Corporation ....G....... 360 254-4180
  Vancouver *(G-14360)*

QUILTING SVC
Material Girls Quilting..............................G....... 360 354-2930
  Lynden *(G-6037)*

QUILTING SVC & SPLYS, FOR THE TRADE
Autocraft Incorporated ....G....... 509 926-7002
  Greenacres *(G-4295)*
Palouse River Quilts ....G....... 509 397-2278
  Colfax *(G-2720)*
Susan Bennett..G....... 360 427-6164
  Shelton *(G-11738)*

RACETRACKS
Ephrata Raceway Park LLC ....E....... 509 398-7110
  Ephrata *(G-3333)*

RACEWAYS
Ephrata Raceway Park LLC ....E....... 509 398-7110
  Ephrata *(G-3333)*
Grays Harbor Raceway..........................G....... 360 482-4374
  Vancouver *(G-14265)*
Pacific Slot Car Raceways LLC ....G....... 253 446-5039
  Edgewood *(G-3089)*
Raceway Electric.....................................G....... 206 459-5894
  Kirkland *(G-5450)*
Red Devil Raceway.................................G....... 206 402-6690
  Seattle *(G-10935)*
Spokane County Raceway ....G....... 509 244-3333
  Airway Heights *(G-64)*
Timezone Raceway Park ....G....... 360 687-5100
  Battle Ground *(G-746)*
Timezone Raceway Park ....G....... 360 450-3730
  La Center *(G-5517)*

RACKS: Bicycle, Automotive
Cyns Insanitys..G....... 360 694-2459
  Vancouver *(G-14158)*
Heininger Holdings LLC ....G....... 360 756-2411
  Bellingham *(G-1368)*
ROC Racing Inc.......................................G....... 360 658-4353
  Marysville *(G-6378)*
Ultimate Rack Inc ....G....... 509 393-3526
  East Wenatchee *(G-3033)*

RACKS: Display
Metal Werks Inc......................................F....... 360 651-0300
  Marysville *(G-6359)*

RACKS: Pallet, Exc Wood
Frazier Industrial Company....................G....... 509 698-4100
  Selah *(G-11588)*

RACKS: Railroad Car, Vehicle Transportation, Steel
C J & M Transport Inc ....F....... 206 510-8296
  Kent *(G-4829)*

RACKS: Trash, Metal Rack
S Scott & Associates LLC ....G....... 360 576-4830
  Vancouver *(G-14563)*

RADAR SYSTEMS & EQPT
Fidelitad Inc..G....... 509 637-3938
  White Salmon *(G-15115)*
Omohundro Co Kitsap Composites ......D....... 360 519-3047
  Port Orchard *(G-7837)*

RADIO & TELEVISION COMMUNICATIONS EQUIPMENT
AR Worldwide..G....... 425 485-9000
  Bothell *(G-1823)*
Astronics Cstm Ctrl Cncpts Inc.............D....... 206 575-0933
  Kent *(G-4795)*
Bbtline LLC...G....... 425 273-3712
  Kirkland *(G-5289)*
Behringer Usa Inc ....D....... 425 672-0816
  Bothell *(G-1752)*
Boeing Company ....B....... 425 413-3400
  Maple Valley *(G-6261)*
Boeing Company ....A....... 206 662-9615
  Seatac *(G-9276)*
Cco Holdings LLC ....G....... 509 293-4177
  Wenatchee *(G-15016)*
Cco Holdings LLC ....G....... 509 643-3364
  Sunnyside *(G-13116)*
Ciena Corporation...................................G....... 509 242-9000
  Spokane Valley *(G-12656)*
Commscope Technologies LLC ....F....... 425 888-2370
  North Bend *(G-7109)*
Integrated Design Group Inc.................G....... 509 328-4244
  Spokane *(G-12319)*
Itron Inc..E....... 509 924-9900
  Spokane Valley *(G-12748)*
Itron Manufacturing Inc..........................E....... 509 924-9900
  Spokane Valley *(G-12749)*
Kitc Radio Inc...G....... 360 876-1400
  Port Orchard *(G-7823)*
Ludlow Mortgage Inc..............................G....... 360 437-1344
  Port Ludlow *(G-7770)*
Neocific Inc..G....... 425 451-8278
  Bellevue *(G-1025)*
Pathfinder Wireless Corp.......................G....... 206 409-5767
  Seattle *(G-10767)*
Pulse Electronics Inc..............................D....... 360 944-7551
  Vancouver *(G-14515)*
Ruckus Wireless Inc..............................E....... 425 896-6000
  Kirkland *(G-5453)*
Sea Com Corporation............................F....... 425 771-2182
  Mountlake Terrace *(G-6868)*
SGC World Inc ....G....... 425 746-6311
  Bellevue *(G-1127)*
Streambox Inc ....E....... 206 956-0544
  Bellevue *(G-1161)*
Symetrix Inc..E....... 425 640-3331
  Mountlake Terrace *(G-6871)*
Wave Holdco Corporation.....................G....... 425 576-8200
  Kirkland *(G-5493)*
Xoceco USA...G....... 425 670-3968
  Lynnwood *(G-6227)*

RADIO & TELEVISION REPAIR
Powercom Inc..D....... 425 489-8549
  Bothell *(G-1784)*
Puget Sound Repair Inc ....G....... 506 556-9722
  Seattle *(G-10885)*

RADIO BROADCASTING & COMMUNICATIONS EQPT
Airwavz Inc...G....... 206 696-6649
  Renton *(G-8734)*
Influx LLC...G....... 360 200-4323
  Vancouver *(G-14316)*
Kzbg Big Country 977.............................G....... 509 751-0977
  Clarkston *(G-2638)*
Lhc2 Inc ....G....... 509 723-4517
  Liberty Lake *(G-5843)*
Meteorcomm LLC....................................C....... 253 872-2521
  Renton *(G-8853)*
Oak Bay Technologies Inc ....G....... 360 437-0718
  Port Ludlow *(G-7771)*
Oneradio Corporation.............................G....... 206 393-2900
  Redmond *(G-8603)*
Skt2 LLC ....G....... 775 303-3788
  Camas *(G-2283)*

RADIO BROADCASTING STATIONS
Complete Music ....G....... 509 927-3535
  Spokane *(G-12195)*
North Cascades Broadcasting..............G....... 509 826-0100
  OMAK *(G-7439)*

RADIO COMMUNICATIONS: Airborne Eqpt
Action Communications Inc ....G....... 206 625-1234
  Seattle *(G-9344)*
Boeing Company ....A....... 206 655-1131
  Seattle *(G-9563)*
Boeing Company ....A....... 312 544-2000
  Everett *(G-3397)*
Zonar Systems Inc ....C....... 206 878-2459
  Seattle *(G-11524)*

RADIO RECEIVER NETWORKS
Katz Media Group Inc.............................G....... 206 777-1800
  Seattle *(G-10331)*
Wind Talker Innovations Inc ....G....... 253 883-3615
  Fife *(G-3999)*

RADIO, TELEVISION & CONSUMER ELECTRONICS STORES: Eqpt, NEC
Industrial Generosity Inc.......................G....... 206 336-2268
  Seattle *(G-10232)*
Shepp Enterprises LLC..........................G....... 206 697-0327
  Tacoma *(G-13512)*

RADIO, TELEVISION & CONSUMER ELECTRONICS STORES: TV Sets
Grays Harbor Electronics.......................G....... 360 532-3474
  Hoquiam *(G-4338)*

RADIO, TV & CONSUMER ELEC STORES: Automotive Sound Eqpt
Instrument Sales and Svc Inc...............E....... 253 796-5400
  Kent *(G-4954)*

RADIO, TV & CONSUMER ELEC STORES: Radios, Receiver Type
Whislers Inc..G....... 360 352-8777
  Tumwater *(G-13905)*

RADIO, TV/CONSUMER ELEC STORES: Antennas, Satellite Dish
Bluecosmo Inc ....G....... 877 258-3496
  Seattle *(G-9555)*
Reach For Sky Satellite Servic ....G....... 509 276-9340
  Loon Lake *(G-5977)*

RAIL & STRUCTURAL SHAPES: Aluminum rail & structural shapes
Buddy Shelters LLC................................G....... 425 239-8104
  Arlington *(G-216)*

RAILINGS: Prefabricated, Metal
Inline Design LLC....................................F....... 425 405-5505
  Seattle *(G-10238)*
Rail Fx LLC ....G....... 206 453-1123
  Tacoma *(G-13488)*

RAILINGS: Wood

Rail Fx LLC ....G....... 206 453-1123
 Tacoma (G-13488)

RAILROAD CAR RENTING & LEASING SVCS

Paneltech Intl Holdings Inc ....F....... 360 538-1480
 Hoquiam (G-4354)

RAILROAD CARGO LOADING & UNLOADING SVCS

Parametrix Inc ....D....... 206 394-3700
 Puyallup (G-8219)
PSI Logistics Intl LLC ....G....... 855 473-5877
 Spokane (G-12457)

RAILROAD EQPT

Marine Recuriting ....G....... 206 763-5050
 Seattle (G-10483)
Pacifica Resources LLC ....F....... 206 764-1646
 Seattle (G-10743)
Railpro of Oregon Inc ....G....... 360 213-0958
 Vancouver (G-14530)
Transgoods America Inc ....G....... 253 661-0440
 Federal Way (G-3797)

RAILROAD EQPT & SPLYS WHOLESALERS

Transgoods America Inc ....G....... 253 661-0440
 Federal Way (G-3797)

RAILROAD EQPT: Cars & Eqpt, Train, Freight Or Passenger

Edward Fisher ....G....... 253 566-4335
 Tacoma (G-13273)
Pacifica Marine Inc ....F....... 206 764-1646
 Seattle (G-10742)
Talgo Inc ....E....... 206 254-7051
 Seattle (G-11262)

RAILROAD RELATED EQPT: Railway Track

Trail Tech Inc ....G....... 360 687-4530
 Battle Ground (G-748)

RAILROAD TIES: Concrete

Cxt Incorporated ....D....... 509 924-6300
 Spokane Valley (G-12675)
Cxt Incorporated ....E....... 509 921-7878
 Spokane Valley (G-12676)

RAILS: Steel Or Iron

Fat Daddys Fabrication LLC ....G....... 253 677-8005
 Roy (G-9159)
Steel Magnolia Inc ....G....... 360 366-5090
 Blaine (G-1704)

RAMPS: Prefabricated Metal

Homecare Products Inc ....C....... 253 249-1108
 Algona (G-71)
Mantle Industries LLC ....F....... 360 332-5276
 Blaine (G-1683)
Wazzbizz Inc ....G....... 360 332-5276
 Blaine (G-1710)
Welcome Ramp Systems Inc ....G....... 425 754-0489
 Auburn (G-597)

RAZORS, RAZOR BLADES

Art of Shaving - Fl LLC ....G....... 206 737-8370
 Seattle (G-9437)
Art of Shaving - Fl LLC ....G....... 253 777-0993
 Tacoma (G-13181)
Procter & Gamble Company ....C....... 425 313-3511
 Issaquah (G-4461)

REACTORS: Current Limiting

Research Reactr Sfty/Anylst Sv ....G....... 509 783-6860
 Kennewick (G-4718)
Sel Development LLC ....F....... 509 332-1890
 Pullman (G-8107)

REAL ESTATE AGENCIES & BROKERS

Port Blakely Company ....G....... 206 624-5810
 Seattle (G-10834)

Windemere Camino Island Realty ....E....... 360 387-3411
 Stanwood (G-12958)
Zillow Group Inc ....C....... 206 470-7000
 Seattle (G-11521)

REAL ESTATE AGENTS & MANAGERS

Green Leaf Family Estates ....G....... 360 894-4945
 Yelm (G-15735)
Northwest Multiple Listing Svc ....G....... 253 566-2331
 Graham (G-4234)
Pinnacle NW ....G....... 360 264-5484
 Shelton (G-11722)
Scafco Corporation ....F....... 509 343-9012
 Spokane (G-12494)
Tjn Publishing Inc ....G....... 360 426-4677
 Shelton (G-11745)
Vintage Investments Inc ....G....... 360 293-2596
 Anacortes (G-183)

REAL ESTATE FIDUCIARIES' OFFICES

First Millennium Bank ....G....... 360 797-5108
 Sequim (G-11634)

REAL ESTATE INVESTMENT TRUSTS

Weyerhaeuser Company ....A....... 206 467-3600
 Seattle (G-11460)
Weyerhaeuser Company ....A....... 206 539-3000
 Seattle (G-11459)

REAL ESTATE OPERATORS, EXC DEVELOPERS: Commercial/Indl Bldg

M7m Investments ....G....... 253 922-2030
 Fife (G-3967)
Parberry Inc ....E....... 360 734-2340
 Bellingham (G-1491)
Tramco Inc ....G....... 425 347-3030
 Everett (G-3635)

RECEIVERS: Radio Communications

Piccell LLC ....G....... 206 780-0478
 Seattle (G-10799)

RECLAIMED RUBBER: Reworked By Manufacturing Process

Rubber Granulators Inc ....G....... 360 658-7754
 Marysville (G-6380)

RECORDING HEADS: Speech & Musical Eqpt

Behringer Usa Inc ....D....... 425 672-0816
 Bothell (G-1752)

RECORDS & TAPES: Prerecorded

Career Development Software ....F....... 360 696-3529
 Vancouver (G-14099)
Gt Recording ....G....... 206 783-6911
 Seattle (G-10130)
Pure Fire Independent LLC ....G....... 206 218-3297
 Seattle (G-10889)
Singles Going Steady ....G....... 206 441-7396
 Seattle (G-11116)
Soundworks U S A Inc ....G....... 425 882-3344
 Lacey (G-5591)

RECOVERY SVCS: Metal

Pw Metal Recovery LLC ....G....... 253 537-6301
 Tacoma (G-13483)

RECREATIONAL & SPORTING CAMPS

Compass Outdoor Adventures LLC ....G....... 425 281-0267
 Snoqualmie (G-12007)

RECREATIONAL SPORTING EQPT REPAIR SVCS

Body Builders Gym Equipment ....G....... 253 631-8274
 Kent (G-4816)

RECREATIONAL VEHICLE DEALERS

Meili Manufacturing ....G....... 509 489-9180
 Spokane (G-12389)
Nelson Truck Equipment Co Inc ....F....... 206 622-3825
 Seattle (G-10598)

Recreational Equipment Inc ....B....... 206 223-1944
 Seattle (G-10933)

RECREATIONAL VEHICLE PARKS & CAMPGROUNDS

Cape Dissapointment State Park ....F....... 360 642-3078
 Ilwaco (G-4368)

RECREATIONAL VEHICLE PARTS & ACCESS STORES

Manns Welding & Trailer Hitch ....G....... 206 542-7434
 Shoreline (G-11784)

RECREATIONAL VEHICLE: Wholesalers

Quality Fuel Trlr & Tank Inc ....G....... 425 526-7566
 Monroe (G-6610)

RECYCLABLE SCRAP & WASTE MATERIALS WHOLESALERS

Buffalo Industries LLC ....E....... 206 682-9900
 Kent (G-4826)
Longview Auto Wrecking ....G....... 360 423-9327
 Longview (G-5929)

RECYCLING: Paper

Green Brothers of Seattle LLC ....G....... 303 295-7669
 Seattle (G-10115)
Marilyns Recycle Inc ....G....... 425 788-1716
 Duvall (G-2995)
Paneltech Intl Holdings Inc ....F....... 360 538-1480
 Hoquiam (G-4354)

REFINERS & SMELTERS: Copper

Freeprt-Mcmran Expiration Corp ....G....... 509 928-0704
 Spokane Valley (G-12709)

REFINERS & SMELTERS: Gold

Hallmark Refining Corporation ....D....... 360 428-5880
 Mount Vernon (G-6803)

REFINERS & SMELTERS: Nonferrous Metal

Alaska Metal Recycling Co ....E....... 907 349-4833
 Tacoma (G-13160)
American Recycling Corp ....E....... 509 535-4271
 Spokane Valley (G-12614)
Ecotech Recycling LLC ....E....... 360 673-3860
 Kalama (G-4498)
Fibres International Inc ....D....... 425 455-9811
 Everett (G-3471)
Fran Hunter ....G....... 253 876-0434
 Port Orchard (G-7810)
Hallmark Refining Corporation ....D....... 360 428-5880
 Mount Vernon (G-6803)
Parberry Inc ....E....... 360 734-2340
 Bellingham (G-1491)
Schnitzer Steel International ....G....... 253 572-4000
 Tacoma (G-13508)
Z Recyclers Inc ....F....... 360 398-2161
 Lynden (G-6061)

REFINING: Petroleum

BP America Inc ....A....... 360 371-0373
 Blaine (G-1663)
BP Arco Seattle Terminal ....G....... 206 623-4637
 Seattle (G-9574)
BP Corporation North Amer Inc ....B....... 360 371-1500
 Blaine (G-1664)
Chevron Corporation ....G....... 360 887-8101
 Camas (G-2238)
Chevron Corporation ....G....... 509 534-4077
 Spokane (G-12179)
Chevron Corporation ....G....... 425 413-8881
 Maple Valley (G-6263)
Christine Jamison ....G....... 253 887-1095
 Auburn (G-406)
Conocophillips Company ....F....... 509 536-8417
 Spokane Valley (G-12663)
Conocophillips Company ....F....... 253 584-0583
 Lakewood (G-5707)
Doug Skrivan ....G....... 253 584-7323
 Lakewood (G-5714)
Emerald Services Inc ....C....... 206 430-7795
 Seattle (G-9913)

Equilon Enterprises LLC .... B 360 293-0800
  Anacortes *(G-126)*
L Stop-N-Go .... G 509 896-6089
  Mabton *(G-6229)*
Par Tacoma LLC .... G 253 383-1651
  Tacoma *(G-13458)*
Paramount Petroleum Corp .... F 503 273-4705
  Seattle *(G-10753)*
Paramount Petroleum Corp .... F 206 542-3121
  Seattle *(G-10754)*
Phillips 66 Company .... G 509 534-5040
  Wenatchee *(G-15063)*
Phillips 66 Company .... D 360 384-1011
  Ferndale *(G-3886)*
Sinclair Companies .... C 360 874-6772
  Port Orchard *(G-7848)*
Sunoco Inc .... G 253 872-8500
  Kent *(G-5162)*
Tesoro Companies Inc .... D 253 896-8700
  Federal Way *(G-3794)*
Tesoro Corporation .... E 360 293-9119
  Anacortes *(G-175)*
Westfall Gooden Sfo Co .... G 253 344-1025
  Federal Way *(G-3803)*

REFLECTIVE ROAD MARKERS, WHOLESALE

Alpine Products Inc .... G 253 351-9828
  Auburn *(G-373)*

REFRACTORIES: Brick

Bricking Solutions .... G 360 794-1277
  Monroe *(G-6558)*

REFRACTORIES: Clay

Harbisonwalker Intl Inc .... E 253 872-2552
  Kent *(G-4933)*
Mutual Materials Company .... E 509 924-2120
  Mica *(G-6501)*

REFRACTORIES: Graphite, Carbon Or Ceramic Bond

Industrial Ceramics Inc .... G 905 878-2848
  Seattle *(G-10230)*
Seal Dynamics .... G 503 232-0973
  Vancouver *(G-14577)*

REFRACTORIES: Nonclay

Allied Mineral Products Inc .... G 360 748-9295
  Chehalis *(G-2461)*
Aluminum Technologies Inc .... G 206 323-6900
  Seattle *(G-9390)*
CH Murphy/Clark-Ullman Inc .... D 253 475-6566
  Tacoma *(G-13232)*
Pryor Giggey Co .... G 360 647-6021
  Bellingham *(G-1508)*

REFRACTORY MATERIALS WHOLESALERS

Allied Mineral Products Inc .... G 360 748-9295
  Chehalis *(G-2461)*
Aluminum Technologies Inc .... G 206 323-6900
  Seattle *(G-9390)*
CH Murphy/Clark-Ullman Inc .... D 253 475-6566
  Tacoma *(G-13232)*

REFRIGERATION & HEATING EQUIPMENT

Anatoliy Semenko .... G 509 525-4486
  Walla Walla *(G-14763)*
Custom Mech Solutions Inc .... F 206 973-3900
  Seattle *(G-9767)*
Hoshizaki Western Dist Ctr Inc .... G 253 922-8589
  Fife *(G-3959)*
Joshua M Lennox MA .... G 253 590-8952
  Tacoma *(G-13368)*
Lennox Inc .... G 360 970-8954
  Olympia *(G-7322)*
Lennox Industries Commeri .... G 206 607-1585
  Fife *(G-3965)*
Lennox Stores (partsplus) .... G 206 607-1818
  Fife *(G-3966)*
Lenox Clothing LLC .... G 360 213-9634
  Vancouver *(G-14371)*
Lenox Independent Dealer .... G 509 837-6400
  Sunnyside *(G-13132)*

Msr Marine & Vhcl Htg Systems .... G 206 546-5670
  Shoreline *(G-11790)*
Quality Heating & AC LLC .... F 360 613-5614
  Silverdale *(G-11854)*
Rob Sullivan .... G 425 882-2221
  Bellevue *(G-1103)*
Siemens Industry Inc .... G 208 883-8330
  Issaquah *(G-4474)*
Trane Company .... E 425 455-4148
  Bellevue *(G-1196)*
Trane US Inc .... G 425 492-2155
  Bothell *(G-1802)*
Trane US Inc .... G 206 748-0500
  Seattle *(G-11326)*
Trane US Inc .... D 425 643-4310
  Bellevue *(G-1197)*

REFRIGERATION EQPT & SPLYS WHOLESALERS

Refrigeration Supplies Distr .... G 509 452-8689
  Yakima *(G-15660)*
Teknotherm Inc .... D 206 547-5629
  Seattle *(G-11279)*
Wescold Inc .... E 206 284-5710
  Seattle *(G-11449)*

REFRIGERATION EQPT & SPLYS, WHOLESALE: Beverage Dispensers

Coca-Cola Refreshments .... G 425 226-6004
  Renton *(G-8774)*

REFRIGERATION EQPT & SPLYS, WHOLESALE: Commercial Eqpt

Cold Sea Refrigeration Inc .... G 360 466-5850
  La Conner *(G-5521)*
Pacific NW Reps LLC .... G 509 823-7008
  Yakima *(G-15640)*

REFRIGERATION EQPT: Complete

Alaska Marine Refrigeration .... F 360 871-4414
  Port Orchard *(G-7785)*
Cold Sea Refrigeration Inc .... G 360 466-5850
  La Conner *(G-5521)*
Integrated Marine Systems Inc .... E 360 385-0077
  Seattle *(G-10246)*
ISO-Quip Corp .... F 360 695-4243
  Vancouver *(G-14327)*
Johnson Controls Inc .... G 360 448-7771
  Vancouver *(G-14339)*
Refrigeration Supplies Distr .... G 503 234-4334
  Vancouver *(G-14540)*
Refrigeration Supplies Distr .... G 509 452-8689
  Yakima *(G-15660)*
Teknotherm Inc .... D 206 547-5629
  Seattle *(G-11279)*
Wescold Inc .... E 206 284-5710
  Seattle *(G-11449)*

REFRIGERATION REPAIR SVCS

Alaska Marine Refrigeration .... F 360 871-4414
  Port Orchard *(G-7785)*
Teknotherm Inc .... D 206 547-5629
  Seattle *(G-11279)*
Wescold Inc .... E 206 284-5710
  Seattle *(G-11449)*

REFRIGERATION SVC & REPAIR

M A C I Inc .... E 360 424-7013
  Mount Vernon *(G-6808)*
Tri-Mechanical Inc .... F 425 391-6016
  Bellevue *(G-1201)*

REFRIGERATOR REPAIR SVCS

HNG Group LLC .... G 206 723-6848
  Tukwila *(G-13749)*

REFUSE SYSTEMS

American Recycling Corp .... E 509 535-4271
  Spokane Valley *(G-12614)*
Ecotech Recycling LLC .... E 360 673-3860
  Kalama *(G-4498)*
Girard Wood Products Inc .... E 253 845-0505
  Puyallup *(G-8157)*

H & H Wood Recyclers Inc .... E 360 892-2805
  Vancouver *(G-14278)*
New West Gypsum Inc .... F 253 380-1079
  Kent *(G-5021)*

REHABILITATION CENTER, OUTPATIENT TREATMENT

Revive A Back Inc .... G 360 738-6085
  Bellingham *(G-1516)*

RELIGIOUS SCHOOL

Sola Bothell .... G 501 487-7652
  Bothell *(G-1793)*

REMOTE DATABASE INFORMATION RETRIEVAL SVCS

Maren-Go Solutions Corporation .... G 217 506-2749
  Vancouver *(G-14393)*
Medworks Instruments .... G 360 597-3754
  Vancouver *(G-14409)*

REMOVERS & CLEANERS

Stanley Plowing .... G 509 218-2419
  Deer Park *(G-2916)*

REMOVERS: Paint

Homax Group Inc .... E 360 733-9029
  Bellingham *(G-1371)*
I M A C .... G 509 747-3607
  Spokane *(G-12302)*

RENDERING PLANT

Baker Commodities Inc .... E 509 535-5435
  Spokane *(G-12136)*
Proctor Farm Animal Removal .... G 360 856-1995
  Sedro Woolley *(G-11558)*
Q A R Rendering Services Inc .... G 253 847-7220
  Graham *(G-4236)*
Tri County Dead Stock .... G 360 354-3173
  Lynden *(G-6057)*

RENTAL CENTERS: Party & Banquet Eqpt & Splys

Bella Cupcake Couture LLC .... G 425 260-3224
  Newcastle *(G-7026)*
Doodlebugs .... G 360 683-3154
  Sequim *(G-11628)*

RENTAL CENTERS: Tools

Star Rentals Inc .... F 509 545-8521
  Pasco *(G-7632)*

RENTAL SVCS: Aircraft & Indl Truck

Helitrak Inc .... G 253 857-0890
  Gig Harbor *(G-4117)*

RENTAL SVCS: Business Machine & Electronic Eqpt

Dana-Saad Company .... E 509 924-6711
  Spokane Valley *(G-12677)*
Pitney Bowes Inc .... E 509 363-3694
  Spokane *(G-12444)*
Pitney Bowes Inc .... E 509 835-1272
  Spokane *(G-12445)*
Pitney Bowes Inc .... D 253 395-8717
  Kent *(G-5066)*
Pitney Bowes Inc .... E 509 838-0115
  Spokane *(G-12446)*
Wizard International Inc .... D 425 551-4300
  Mukilteo *(G-6992)*

RENTAL SVCS: Clothing

Costume Atlier Msque Pettycote .... G 360 819-4296
  Olympia *(G-7257)*

RENTAL SVCS: Costume

Party City Corporation .... F 206 575-0502
  Tukwila *(G-13790)*

Employee Codes: A=Over 500 employees, B=251-500
C=101-250, D=51-100, E=20-50, F=10-19, G=2-9

RENTAL SVCS: Garage Facility & Tool

Mobile Storage Units Inc .... G 509 276-8220
Deer Park *(G-2909)*

RENTAL SVCS: Mobile Communication Eqpt

Bluecosmo Inc .... G 877 258-3496
Seattle *(G-9555)*

RENTAL SVCS: Recreational Vehicle

Lithia Motors Inc .... G 509 321-7300
Spokane *(G-12373)*
Quality Fuel Trlr & Tank Inc .... G 425 526-7566
Monroe *(G-6610)*

RENTAL SVCS: Sign

J Freitag Enterprises Inc .... G 509 453-4461
Yakima *(G-15595)*
National Sign Corporation .... E 206 282-0700
Seattle *(G-10590)*
Ramsay Signs Inc .... G 206 623-3100
Seattle *(G-10919)*
Vancouver Sign Co Inc .... E 360 693-4773
Vancouver *(G-14663)*

RENTAL SVCS: Sporting Goods, NEC

Mvp Athletic Inc .... G 360 915-8715
Tumwater *(G-13888)*

RENTAL SVCS: Trailer

Cline Rentals LLC .... G 206 375-0705
Bothell *(G-1839)*

RENTAL SVCS: Vending Machine

Cinevend Inc .... G 206 388-3784
Seattle *(G-9684)*

RENTAL SVCS: Video Cassette Recorder & Access

Westek Marketing LLC .... G 425 888-1988
Nine Mile Falls *(G-7085)*

RENTAL: Portable Toilet

Emerald Services Inc .... C 206 430-7795
Seattle *(G-9913)*
Northwest Cascade Inc .... C 253 848-2371
Puyallup *(G-8202)*

RENTAL: Video Tape & Disc

Kusina Fillipina .... G 206 322-9433
Seattle *(G-10365)*

REPAIR SERVICES, NEC

Jr Grennay Co .... G 509 484-5056
Valleyford *(G-13997)*
Navan Enterprises LLC .... G 206 214-6227
Seattle *(G-10596)*
Scitus Tech Solutions LLC .... G 360 202-9642
Ferndale *(G-3901)*

REPLATING SHOP, EXC SILVERWARE

Carl Zapffe Inc .... G 206 364-1919
Seattle *(G-9633)*

REPRODUCTION SVCS: Video Tape Or Disk

2 C Media LLC .... E 206 522-7211
Seattle *(G-9318)*

RESEARCH, DEVELOPMENT & TEST SVCS, COMM: Business Analysis

Reliance Inc .... F 615 218-3929
Redmond *(G-8647)*

RESEARCH, DEVELOPMENT & TEST SVCS, COMM: Cmptr Hardware Dev

Datapark LLC .... E 360 224-2157
Sumas *(G-13043)*

RESEARCH, DEVELOPMENT & TEST SVCS, COMM: Research, Exc Lab

Modumetal Inc .... E 877 632-4242
Seattle *(G-10555)*
Research Reactr Sfty/Anylst Sv .... G 509 783-6860
Kennewick *(G-4718)*

RESEARCH, DEVELOPMENT & TESTING SVCS, COMM: Agricultural

De Kleine Machine Company LLC .... G 509 832-1108
Prosser *(G-8038)*

RESEARCH, DEVELOPMENT & TESTING SVCS, COMM: Research Lab

Eden Labs LLC .... F 888 626-3271
Seattle *(G-9882)*
Esther Brcques Wnery Vnyrd LLC .... G 509 476-2861
Oroville *(G-7465)*
Landrace Labs .... G 360 273-9277
Rochester *(G-9135)*
Microgreen Polymers Inc .... E 360 435-7400
Arlington *(G-276)*

RESEARCH, DEVELOPMENT & TESTING SVCS, COMMERCIAL: Business

Lockheed Martin Aculight Corp .... D 425 482-1100
Bothell *(G-1875)*

RESEARCH, DEVELOPMENT & TESTING SVCS, COMMERCIAL: Energy

Avista Capital Inc .... G 509 489-0500
Spokane *(G-12133)*
Aynano Technology LLC .... G 208 596-9865
Pullman *(G-8084)*
Electrijet Research Foundation .... G 509 990-9474
Greenacres *(G-4297)*
Innovatek Inc .... G 509 375-1093
Kennewick *(G-4676)*
Xnrgi Inc .... G 425 272-2703
Bothell *(G-1924)*

RESEARCH, DEVELOPMENT & TESTING SVCS, COMMERCIAL: Physical

Energy Efficiency Systems Corp .... E 360 835-7838
Washougal *(G-14953)*
Leidos Inc .... E 425 267-5600
Lynnwood *(G-6157)*
Leidos Inc .... G 360 394-8870
Poulsbo *(G-7975)*
Protium Innovations LLC .... G 206 854-8792
Pullman *(G-8102)*

RESEARCH, DVLPT & TESTING SVCS, COMM: Mkt, Bus & Economic

Girandola .... G 206 289-0523
Seattle *(G-10073)*

RESIDENTIAL REMODELERS

Madrona Log HM Repr & Care LLC .... G 360 202-2842
Marysville *(G-6354)*
Olympic Home Modification LLC .... G 253 858-9941
Gig Harbor *(G-4139)*
White Rabbit Ventures Inc .... F 360 474-5828
Vancouver *(G-14690)*

RESINS: Custom Compound Purchased

Bellwether Gate C LLC .... G 360 738-1940
Bellingham *(G-1270)*
Innovative Technologies Inc .... G 425 258-4773
Everett *(G-3516)*
Polydrop LLC .... G 206 601-2191
Kent *(G-5071)*

RESISTORS

First Choice Marketing Inc .... G 206 306-1100
Seattle *(G-9996)*
Vishay Precision Group Inc .... G 253 872-1910
Kent *(G-5202)*

RESPIRATORS

A-M Systems LLC .... E 360 683-8300
Sequim *(G-11604)*

RESPIRATORY SYSTEM DRUGS

Avalyn Pharma Inc .... F 206 707-0340
Seattle *(G-9469)*

RESTAURANT EQPT REPAIR SVCS

Crescent Machine Works Inc .... G 509 328-2820
Spokane *(G-12208)*

RESTAURANT EQPT: Food Wagons

Dingeys LLC .... G 360 789-0853
Olympia *(G-7271)*

RESTAURANTS: Full Svc, American

Big Time Brewery Company Inc .... E 206 545-4509
Seattle *(G-9526)*
Diamond Knot Brewing Co Inc .... E 425 355-4488
Mukilteo *(G-6914)*
Little Bean Coffee LLC .... G 425 829-8289
Redmond *(G-8535)*
Texas Johns .... E 509 659-1402
Ritzville *(G-9123)*

RESTAURANTS: Full Svc, Barbecue

Longhorn Barbecue Inc .... C 509 922-0702
Spokane Valley *(G-12777)*

RESTAURANTS: Full Svc, Family

Wenatchee Vly Brewing Co LLC .... G 509 888-8088
Wenatchee *(G-15085)*

RESTAURANTS: Full Svc, Indian-Pakistan

Travelers Tea Bar .... E 206 329-6260
Seattle *(G-11328)*

RESTAURANTS: Full Svc, Italian

Bellingham Pasta Company .... F 360 594-6000
Bellingham *(G-1267)*

RESTAURANTS: Full Svc, Seafood

Coast Seafoods Company .... E 360 875-5557
South Bend *(G-12040)*
Taylor United Inc .... E 360 426-6178
Shelton *(G-11742)*

RESTAURANTS: Limited Svc, Chicken

Harmon Brewing Company L L C .... E 253 383-2739
Tacoma *(G-13331)*

RESTAURANTS: Limited Svc, Coffee Shop

Armoire .... G 206 397-4703
Burien *(G-2092)*
Austin Chase Coffee Inc .... E 206 281-8040
Seattle *(G-9464)*
Caffe Appassionato Inc .... E 206 281-8040
Seattle *(G-9605)*
Emerald Hills Coffee Inc .... G 800 562-6015
Mukilteo *(G-6924)*
Farmer Bros Co .... E 425 881-7030
Redmond *(G-8459)*
Java Java Coffee Company Inc .... G 425 432-5261
Maple Valley *(G-6278)*
Lighthouse Roasters Inc .... F 206 633-4775
Seattle *(G-10418)*
New Sage Bakery LLC .... G 208 596-5331
Uniontown *(G-13957)*
Olympic Crest Coffee Roasters .... G 360 459-5756
Olympia *(G-7357)*
Sunrise Bagels & More Inc .... F 360 254-1012
Vancouver *(G-14616)*
Wapiti Woolies Inc .... G 360 663-2268
Enumclaw *(G-3326)*

RESTAURANTS: Limited Svc, Grill

Diamond Knot Brewing Co Inc .... D 425 355-4488
Mukilteo *(G-6912)*

PRODUCT SECTION

RESTAURANTS: Limited Svc, Ice Cream Stands Or Dairy Bars

Baskin Robbins 1361 .... G 425 226-3113
  Renton *(G-8751)*
Baskin-Robbins .... G 425 793-3544
  Bellevue *(G-806)*
Dairy Queens Vancouver .... E 360 256-7302
  Vancouver *(G-14164)*

RESTAURANTS: Ltd Svc, Ice Cream, Soft Drink/Fountain Stands

Gariko LLC .... G 509 933-1821
  Ellensburg *(G-3201)*

RETAIL BAKERY: Bagels

Pike Place Bagel Bakery Inc .... F 206 382-4297
  Seattle *(G-10806)*

RETAIL BAKERY: Bread

Great Harvest Bread Co Inc .... E 509 535-1146
  Spokane *(G-12281)*
Rocket Bakery Inc .... G 509 462-2345
  Spokane Valley *(G-12854)*
Slays Poulsbo Bakery Inc .... E 360 779-2798
  Poulsbo *(G-8001)*

RETAIL BAKERY: Cakes

Cake Time Unque Tste Sweet LLC G ... 253 886-9366
  Dupont *(G-2956)*
Cakes Be We .... G 509 460-1399
  Kennewick *(G-4639)*
Just American Desserts .... G 509 927-2253
  Spokane Valley *(G-12757)*

RETAIL BAKERY: Doughnuts

Donut Star Inc .... G 253 833-2980
  Auburn *(G-428)*
Ever Green Donuts .... G 425 673-5331
  Lynnwood *(G-6117)*
Happy Donut .... G 253 852-3286
  Kent *(G-4932)*
Henrys Donuts .... G 360 653-4044
  Marysville *(G-6344)*
Krispy Kreme Doughnuts .... G 206 316-7090
  Seattle *(G-10358)*
Yum Yum Donut Shops Inc .... G 360 423-0150
  Longview *(G-5970)*

RETAIL BAKERY: Pastries

Snohomish Bakery & CAF .... G 360 568-1682
  Snohomish *(G-11981)*

RETAIL BAKERY: Pretzels

S & W Management Co Inc .... E 425 771-6850
  Lynnwood *(G-6191)*

RETAIL FIREPLACE STORES

Mount Baker Fireplace Shop .... G 360 384-3507
  Bellingham *(G-1444)*

RETAIL LUMBER YARDS

Adams Timber Service LLC .... G 360 636-7766
  Silverlake *(G-11861)*
BMC West LLC .... D 425 303-0661
  Everett *(G-3393)*
Cedar Farms LLC .... G 360 779-3575
  Poulsbo *(G-7954)*
D Ds Hardwood Floors .... G 206 726-8808
  Seattle *(G-9780)*
Edensaw Woods Ltd .... G 253 216-1150
  Tacoma *(G-13271)*
Havillah Shake Co .... G 509 486-1467
  Tonasket *(G-13650)*
Tal Holdings LLC .... G 509 682-1617
  Chelan *(G-2565)*

RETAIL STORES, NEC

Community Thrift Shop LLC .... G 509 438-1302
  Richland *(G-8984)*
Sawdust Supply .... G 206 622-4321
  Seattle *(G-11022)*

RETAIL STORES: Air Purification Eqpt

Dust Control Technologies Inc .... G 360 256-2479
  Brush Prairie *(G-2033)*
Fireside Hearth & Home Inc .... F 425 251-9447
  Kent *(G-4907)*

RETAIL STORES: Alarm Signal Systems

Shadow Master .... G 253 984-0559
  Lakewood *(G-5754)*

RETAIL STORES: Alcoholic Beverage Making Eqpt & Splys

J & H Printing Inc .... G 509 332-0782
  Pullman *(G-8094)*
Joseph Gillum .... G 800 624-4578
  Centralia *(G-2413)*
Pacific Meter & Equipment Inc ... G 253 872-3374
  Kent *(G-5056)*
Tru Line Laser Alignment Inc ..... G 360 371-0552
  Blaine *(G-1708)*

RETAIL STORES: Awnings

Canvas Supply Co Inc .... E 206 784-0711
  Seattle *(G-9621)*
Eastside Tent & Awning Co .... G 425 454-7766
  Bellevue *(G-888)*
Sears Tents & Awning .... G 509 452-8971
  Yakima *(G-15669)*

RETAIL STORES: Banners

Bellingham Promotional Pdts ..... G 360 676-5416
  Bellingham *(G-1268)*
Creating Memories Together ...... G 360 944-8393
  Vancouver *(G-14153)*
Fastsigns International Inc .... G 253 835-9450
  Federal Way *(G-3737)*
Flexabili-Tees .... G 360 260-3163
  Vancouver *(G-14234)*
HI Tech Signs & Banners .... G 360 736-6322
  Centralia *(G-2407)*
Pacific Wholesale Banner & Sup . G 509 487-4189
  Spokane *(G-12427)*
Sign Crafters Inc .... G 509 783-8718
  Kennewick *(G-4727)*

RETAIL STORES: Business Machines & Eqpt

Cummins - Allison Corp .... G 206 763-3900
  Tukwila *(G-13721)*
Legend Data Systems Inc .... F 425 251-1670
  Kent *(G-4992)*

RETAIL STORES: Canvas Prdts

Canvas Man .... G 360 293-2812
  Anacortes *(G-108)*
Yager Company Inc .... G 509 922-2772
  Spokane Valley *(G-12945)*

RETAIL STORES: Cleaning Eqpt & Splys

Coyote Cleaning Systems Inc ..... G 425 776-8002
  Mukilteo *(G-6907)*
Higher Power Supplies Inc .... G 425 438-0990
  Mukilteo *(G-6933)*
Western Products .... G 509 994-1288
  Sprague *(G-12949)*

RETAIL STORES: Coins

Coin Market LLC .... G 425 745-1659
  Lynnwood *(G-6095)*

RETAIL STORES: Concrete Prdts, Precast

Reese Concrete Products Mfg .... F 509 586-3704
  Kennewick *(G-4716)*

RETAIL STORES: Cosmetics

Nion Beauty Inc .... G 206 228-5988
  Bothell *(G-1880)*

RETAIL STORES: Decals

Industry Sign & Graphics Inc ..... F 253 854-2333
  Auburn *(G-476)*

RETAIL STORES: Educational Aids & Electronic Training Mat

Cleaning Consultants Services ... G 206 682-9748
  Seattle *(G-9692)*
Test Best International Inc .... F 360 650-0671
  Bellingham *(G-1567)*

RETAIL STORES: Electronic Parts & Eqpt

Dannys Electronics Inc .... G 253 314-5056
  Tacoma *(G-13253)*
Seymour Technology LLC .... G 509 522-3473
  Walla Walla *(G-14867)*

RETAIL STORES: Engine & Motor Eqpt & Splys

All Electric Motor Service .... G 253 845-1938
  Puyallup *(G-8120)*
Atlas Electric Inc .... E 509 534-8389
  Spokane *(G-12124)*
Ballard Electric .... G 800 873-3526
  Seattle *(G-9479)*
Beckwith & Kuffel .... E 509 922-5222
  Spokane Valley *(G-12637)*

RETAIL STORES: Farm Eqpt & Splys

Barnes Welding Inc .... G 509 745-8588
  Waterville *(G-15005)*
Dari-Tech Inc .... E 360 354-6900
  Lynden *(G-6013)*
Dolco Packaging Corp .... E 509 662-8415
  Wenatchee *(G-15026)*
Prathers Welding & Fabrication . G 509 632-5321
  Coulee City *(G-2805)*
Spray Center Electronics Inc ..... G 509 838-2209
  Spokane *(G-12523)*
Vamco Ltd Inc .... G 509 877-2138
  Wapato *(G-14927)*

RETAIL STORES: Fire Extinguishers

On-Site Safety Inc .... G 701 774-2022
  Kirkland *(G-5421)*

RETAIL STORES: Flags

Its A Wrap Washington Inc .... G 425 827-2000
  Kirkland *(G-5371)*

RETAIL STORES: Foam & Foam Prdts

Cams-Usa Inc .... F 253 639-3890
  Kent *(G-4835)*

RETAIL STORES: Hair Care Prdts

Art of Shaving - FI LLC .... G 206 737-8370
  Seattle *(G-9437)*
Art of Shaving - FI LLC .... G 253 777-0993
  Tacoma *(G-13181)*
Beyond Zone Inc .... G 206 363-2147
  Shoreline *(G-11761)*
Grace Harvest & Assoc LLC .... F 206 973-2363
  Mercer Island *(G-6464)*

RETAIL STORES: Hearing Aids

Sonus-Usa Inc .... G 253 272-3090
  Tacoma *(G-13517)*

RETAIL STORES: Ice

Allied Grinders Inc .... F 425 493-1313
  Mukilteo *(G-6892)*
Articland Ice .... G 509 582-5808
  Kennewick *(G-4620)*
Crystal Clear Ice Co .... G 509 525-1042
  Walla Walla *(G-14792)*

RETAIL STORES: Maps & Charts

1 World Globes & Maps LLC ...... G 206 781-1400
  Seattle *(G-9314)*

RETAIL STORES: Medical Apparatus & Splys

Btpsurgical LLC .... G 425 657-0805
  Issaquah *(G-4389)*
Cornerstone Prsthtics Orthtics .. F 425 339-2559
  Everett *(G-3427)*

Employee Codes: A=Over 500 employees, B=251-500
C=101-250, D=51-100, E=20-50, F=10-19, G=2-9

RETAIL STORES: Medical Apparatus & Splys

Ginacor Inc .... F 206 860-1595
 Seattle *(G-10072)*
Solcon Inc .... E 425 222-5963
 Issaquah *(G-4480)*
Traction Capital Partners Inc .... G 253 922-3090
 Tacoma *(G-13561)*

RETAIL STORES: Mobile Telephones & Eqpt

Scitus Tech Solutions LLC .... G 360 202-9642
 Ferndale *(G-3901)*

RETAIL STORES: Monuments, Finished To Custom Order

Pioneer Rock & Monument LLC .... G 509 773-4702
 Goldendale *(G-4206)*
Quiring Monuments Inc .... E 206 522-8400
 Seattle *(G-10906)*
Service Corp International .... G 425 885-2414
 Redmond *(G-8663)*

RETAIL STORES: Motors, Electric

C & R Electric Motor Service .... G 360 736-2521
 Centralia *(G-2387)*
Industrial Electric Co Inc .... G 360 424-3239
 Mount Vernon *(G-6804)*
K & N Electric Motors Inc .... D 509 838-8000
 Spokane Valley *(G-12759)*
Mac & Mac Electric Company .... G 360 734-6530
 Bellingham *(G-1418)*
United Electric Motors Inc .... G 206 624-0044
 Seattle *(G-11370)*

RETAIL STORES: Orthopedic & Prosthesis Applications

Cascade Prsthtics Orthtics Inc .... G 360 428-4003
 Mount Vernon *(G-6783)*
Center For Prosthetic .... G 425 454-4276
 Bellevue *(G-845)*
Cornerstone Prsthtics Orthtics .... G 360 734-0298
 Bellingham *(G-1306)*
Custom Ocular Prosthetics .... G 206 522-4222
 Seattle *(G-9770)*
Maughan Prosthetic Orthotic S .... G 360 338-0284
 Olympia *(G-7332)*
Preferred Orthotic & Prosthetc .... G 253 838-6726
 Federal Way *(G-3772)*
Spinal Specialties .... G 253 861-7329
 Olympia *(G-7400)*
Yakima Orthtics Prosthetics PC .... G 509 943-8561
 Richland *(G-9056)*

RETAIL STORES: Perfumes & Colognes

Aveda Environmental Lifestyles .... G 509 624-5028
 Spokane *(G-12132)*

RETAIL STORES: Pet Food

EFC Equipment LLC .... G 509 713-7230
 Richland *(G-8992)*

RETAIL STORES: Pet Splys

Emu Emprium Hlthy Alternatives .... G 360 269-3459
 Chehalis *(G-2492)*
Lucky Dog Eqp Inc DBA Pet Pros .... E 425 402-8833
 Woodinville *(G-15297)*

RETAIL STORES: Pets

Xtreme Pet Products LLC .... G 206 772-2000
 Renton *(G-8951)*

RETAIL STORES: Photocopy Machines

Bellingham Business Machines .... G 360 734-3630
 Bellingham *(G-1264)*

RETAIL STORES: Picture Frames, Ready Made

Alb Framing Gallery & Gift .... G 425 432-5505
 Maple Valley *(G-6255)*
Ferguson Merchandising LLC .... D 425 883-2050
 Redmond *(G-8460)*
Frame It Ltd .... G 206 364-7477
 Seattle *(G-10019)*
Lee Frame Shoppe Inc .... G 509 624-2715
 Spokane *(G-12360)*

Village Frame & Gallery .... G 206 824-3068
 Des Moines *(G-2950)*

RETAIL STORES: Plumbing & Heating Splys

Cascade Pipe & Feed Supply .... G 509 997-0720
 Twisp *(G-13910)*
Morgan Electric & Plumbing Inc .... F 206 547-1617
 Seattle *(G-10562)*

RETAIL STORES: Police Splys

Pacific Knight Emblem & Insig .... G 206 354-2060
 Kent *(G-5052)*
Survival Gear Systems 866 257-2978
 Spokane *(G-12536)*

RETAIL STORES: Religious Goods

Daughters of Mary .... G 360 943-2186
 Olympia *(G-7264)*

RETAIL STORES: Rock & Stone Specimens

Exquisitecrystals Com LLC .... G 360 573-6787
 Vancouver *(G-14215)*
Jones Quarry Inc .... G 360 352-1022
 Tumwater *(G-13879)*

RETAIL STORES: Rubber Stamps

Budget Printing Center .... G 509 736-7511
 Kennewick *(G-4636)*
Grays Harbor Stamp Works .... G 360 533-3830
 Aberdeen *(G-14)*
Sno King Stamp .... G 425 771-9373
 Lynnwood *(G-6202)*

RETAIL STORES: Safety Splys & Eqpt

On Site Safety Inc .... G 970 876-1908
 Kirkland *(G-5420)*

RETAIL STORES: Spas & Hot Tubs

Apollo Antenna & Sales Inc .... G 509 534-6972
 Spokane Valley *(G-12622)*
Central Washington Wtr Ctr Inc .... F 509 663-1177
 Wenatchee *(G-15019)*
Hollibaugh Manufacturing .... G 360 653-8612
 Marysville *(G-6345)*

RETAIL STORES: Telephone & Communication Eqpt

Halls Drug Center Inc .... E 360 736-5000
 Centralia *(G-2405)*

RETAIL STORES: Tents

Hilleberg Inc 425 883-0101
 Redmond *(G-8493)*
Home Sweet Home Indoor .... G 509 327-9637
 Spokane *(G-12297)*

RETAIL STORES: Theatrical Eqpt & Splys

BB Citc LLC .... F 425 776-4950
 Everett *(G-3384)*

RETAIL STORES: Toilet Preparations

Butter London LLC .... G 206 624-1085
 Seattle *(G-9602)*

RETAIL STORES: Vaults & Safes

Tracker Safe LLC .... G 360 213-0363
 Vancouver *(G-14643)*

RETAIL STORES: Water Purification Eqpt

Down Island Trading Co .... G 360 376-4056
 Deer Harbor *(G-2891)*

RETAIL STORES: Welding Splys

Praxair Distribution Inc .... E 253 620-1620
 Tacoma *(G-13473)*

RETAIL STORES: Wheelchair Lifts

Olympic Home Modification LLC .... G 253 858-9941
 Gig Harbor *(G-4139)*

REUPHOLSTERY & FURNITURE REPAIR

Douglas L Perry .... G 253 303-0537
 Gig Harbor *(G-4095)*

REUPHOLSTERY SVCS

Hoss A W & Sons Furn & Mfg .... F 206 522-1229
 Seattle *(G-10182)*

REWINDING SVCS

Northwest Paper Converters Inc .... F 800 681-9748
 Ferndale *(G-3878)*

RHEOSTATS: Electronic

Manufacturing Services Inc .... E 509 735-8444
 Kennewick *(G-4691)*

RIFLES: Recoilless

N C I Inc .... G 360 225-9701
 Woodland *(G-15449)*

RIPRAP QUARRYING

County of Pierce .... F 360 893-2844
 Orting *(G-7477)*

ROAD MATERIALS: Bituminous

Wsa-Hl Inc .... G 509 921-7089
 Spokane Valley *(G-12943)*

ROAD MATERIALS: Bituminous, Not From Refineries

Jesse W Palmer .... F 509 634-1494
 Keller *(G-4513)*

ROBOTS: Assembly Line

Advanced Robotic Vehicles Inc .... G 206 310-1122
 Tukwila *(G-13688)*
Flow International Corporation .... B 253 850-3501
 Kent *(G-4911)*

ROCKETS: Space & Military

Space Exploration Tech Corp .... A 425 867-9910
 Redmond *(G-8674)*
Space Exploration Tech Corp .... C 425 602-2255
 Redmond *(G-8675)*

ROD & BAR: Aluminum

AMG Aluminum North America LLC .... D 509 663-2165
 Malaga *(G-6231)*

RODS: Steel & Iron, Made In Steel Mills

Puget Sound Steel Co Inc .... E 253 854-3600
 Kent *(G-5088)*

ROLL COVERINGS: Rubber

Stowe Woodward LLC .... E 360 636-0330
 Kelso *(G-4552)*
Valmet Inc .... E 253 927-2200
 Federal Way *(G-3799)*

ROLLERS & FITTINGS: Window Shade

Fusion9 Design LLC .... G 360 831-0899
 Camano Island *(G-2214)*

ROLLING MILL MACHINERY

Metal Roofing & Siding Sup Inc .... F 509 466-6854
 Mead *(G-6432)*
Precision Shapes Nw LLC .... G 206 605-4396
 Seattle *(G-10852)*

ROOF DECKS

All American Metal Products .... G 360 380-6202
 Ferndale *(G-3811)*
Interlock Industries Inc .... G 253 872-5750
 Kent *(G-4956)*
Interlock Industries Inc .... G 360 713-3036
 Stanwood *(G-12976)*
Metal Mill Corporation .... G 360 262-9080
 Chehalis *(G-2514)*
Taylor Metal Inc .... F 425 485-3003
 Woodinville *(G-15386)*

PRODUCT SECTION

ROOFING MATERIALS: Asphalt
Fields Company LLC .... D 253 627-4098
  Tacoma *(G-13295)*

ROOFING MATERIALS: Sheet Metal
Metal Sales Manufacturing Corp .... E 509 536-6000
  Spokane *(G-12393)*
Metal Smith .... F 509 884-4851
  East Wenatchee *(G-3025)*
Nu-Ray Metal Products Inc .... F 253 833-8637
  Auburn *(G-513)*
Specialty Roofing LLC .... G 509 534-8372
  Spokane *(G-12513)*
Spokane Rain Gutter Inc .... F 509 922-4880
  Spokane Valley *(G-12887)*

ROOFING PRDTS: Wood Fiber
Little Nut Inc .... G 360 327-3394
  Beaver *(G-758)*

ROPE
Cortland Company Inc .... E 360 293-8488
  Anacortes *(G-118)*

RUBBER
Cascades Sonoco Inc .... E 253 584-4295
  Tacoma *(G-13228)*
Farley Desighn and Inc .... G 425 259-5946
  Everett *(G-3470)*
Innovative Technologies Inc .... G 425 258-4773
  Everett *(G-3516)*
Jeremy Rieken .... G 360 428-7736
  Sedro Woolley *(G-11546)*
Tex Enterprises Inc .... G 253 939-1660
  Auburn *(G-579)*
Vennco Rubber Inc .... G 360 249-6924
  Montesano *(G-6665)*

RUBBER PRDTS
Docufeed Technologies .... G 360 793-2001
  Sultan *(G-13022)*

RUBBER PRDTS: Mechanical
Rogers Rubber Manufacturing .... G 253 845-8374
  Buckley *(G-2070)*
U S Wax & Polymer Inc .... E 509 922-1069
  Spokane Valley *(G-12918)*

RUBBER PRDTS: Medical & Surgical Tubing, Extrudd & Lathe-Cut
Kasaganaan Enterprise .... G 206 361-2645
  Shoreline *(G-11779)*

RUBBER PRDTS: Sponge
Calendars Northwest LLC .... F 425 454-1145
  Hunts Point *(G-4366)*

RUBBER PRDTS: Wet Suits
Harveys Skin Diving Supplies .... E 206 824-1114
  Kent *(G-4935)*

RUBBER STRUCTURES: Air-Supported
Canflex (usa) Inc .... F 206 282-8233
  Anacortes *(G-107)*

RUGS : Hand & Machine Made
Renaissance Rug Corporation .... G 425 698-1073
  Bellevue *(G-1099)*

SADDLERY STORES
Indiana Harness Co .... G 509 535-3400
  Spokane Valley *(G-12738)*

SAFES & VAULTS: Metal
Tracker Safe LLC .... G 360 213-0363
  Vancouver *(G-14643)*

SAFETY EQPT & SPLYS WHOLESALERS
On Site Safety Inc .... G 970 876-1908
  Kirkland *(G-5420)*
Pure Safety Group Inc .... G 253 854-5877
  Kent *(G-5090)*
Road-Iq LLC .... F 360 733-4151
  Bellingham *(G-1518)*

SAILBOAT BUILDING & REPAIR
Better Boats Inc .... F 360 797-1244
  Port Angeles *(G-7690)*
Quantum Sails .... G 206 634-0636
  Seattle *(G-10903)*

SAILS
Port Townsend Sails Inc .... F 360 385-1640
  Port Townsend *(G-7914)*
Rod Carr Sailmaker .... G 425 881-2846
  Redmond *(G-8654)*
Rush Sails Inc .... G 425 827-9648
  Enumclaw *(G-3319)*
Schattauer Sailmaker Corp .... G 206 783-0173
  Seattle *(G-11024)*
Sound Sails .... G 360 385-3881
  Port Townsend *(G-7928)*
Yager Company Inc .... G 509 922-2772
  Spokane Valley *(G-12945)*

SALT
Lake City Naturopathic Care In .... G 509 590-1343
  Liberty Lake *(G-5842)*
Old Salt Merchants LLC .... G 888 995-7258
  Port Townsend *(G-7903)*
Salt Studio .... G 206 784-9652
  Seattle *(G-11009)*

SAND & GRAVEL
Anderson Rock Dem Pits II LLC .... G 509 965-3621
  Yakima *(G-15509)*
Associated Sand Gravel .... G 425 348-6309
  Gold Bar *(G-4185)*
Bayside Redi-Mix .... G 360 426-4987
  Shelton *(G-11682)*
Burien Sand and Gravel LLC .... G 206 244-1023
  Burien *(G-2094)*
Chelan Concrete Inc .... F 509 682-2915
  Chelan *(G-2549)*
Chelan Sand & Gravel LLC .... G 509 682-2569
  Chelan *(G-2552)*
Conex Sand & Gravel .... G 503 437-0536
  Vancouver *(G-14146)*
Connell Sand & Gravel Inc .... E 509 234-3221
  Connell *(G-2792)*
Connell Sand & Gravel Inc .... F 509 234-3221
  Connell *(G-2793)*
D & S Rock LLC .... F 509 877-7400
  Toppenish *(G-13665)*
Diamondback Construction LLC .... G 206 730-1239
  Shoreline *(G-11768)*
Dickson Company .... D 253 472-4489
  Tacoma *(G-13263)*
East Valley Sand & Gravel Inc .... G 360 403-7520
  Arlington *(G-231)*
East Valley Sand and Gravel .... E 360 403-7520
  Arlington *(G-232)*
Eucon Corporation .... D 509 547-4402
  Pasco *(G-7580)*
Gary Merlino Cnstr Co Inc .... F 206 763-2134
  Seattle *(G-10050)*
Gillingham Sand & Gravel Co .... G 509 456-5527
  Cheney *(G-2586)*
Glacier Northwest Inc .... D 253 912-8500
  Dupont *(G-2964)*
Glacier Northwest Inc .... E 425 486-3281
  Seattle *(G-10076)*
Glacier Northwest Inc .... E 253 572-7412
  Tacoma *(G-13310)*
Glacier Northwest Inc .... G 360 896-8922
  Vancouver *(G-14255)*
Glacier Northwest Inc .... E 425 888-9795
  Snoqualmie *(G-12013)*
Gravel .... G 360 930-5777
  Silverdale *(G-11836)*
Gravel Doctor of Washington .... G 509 899-1608
  Ellensburg *(G-3205)*
Gravel Flat Crop Dusting LLC .... G 509 398-8617
  Ephrata *(G-3336)*
Gravel Tones Productions Inc .... G 248 202-5757
  Seattle *(G-10109)*
Gravelroad LLC .... G 760 840-7174
  Seattle *(G-10110)*
Hermann Intermountain Corp .... G 509 445-0966
  Usk *(G-13984)*
Hood River Sand Gravel .... G 509 773-0314
  Goldendale *(G-4200)*
J A Jack & Sons Inc .... F 360 479-4659
  Bremerton *(G-1964)*
Jones Company Inc .... G 360 352-1022
  Tumwater *(G-13878)*
Lincoln Sand & Gravel .... G 509 725-4531
  Davenport *(G-2875)*
Lloyd Enterprises Inc .... D 253 874-6692
  Federal Way *(G-3753)*
Lloyd Logging Inc .... F 509 997-2441
  Twisp *(G-13912)*
Lynch Creek Quarry LLC .... G 360 832-4269
  Puyallup *(G-8181)*
Manufacturers Mineral Company .... F 425 228-2120
  Renton *(G-8847)*
Miles Sand & Gravel Company .... C 360 757-3121
  Burlington *(G-2171)*
Mountain Side Sand & Grav LLC .... G 360 701-1241
  Rainier *(G-8318)*
Mt Baker Stump Grinding & Grav .... G 360 684-1695
  Everson *(G-3683)*
Neshkaw Sand and Gravel LLC .... G 360 482-0274
  Elma *(G-3252)*
Northside Sand & Gravel .... G 509 551-5830
  Chattaroy *(G-2449)*
Northwest Rock Inc .... G 360 482-3550
  Elma *(G-3253)*
P & R Rock Sand & Gravel .... G 503 278-3512
  Battle Ground *(G-727)*
Pacific Rock Products LLC .... G 360 896-8721
  Vancouver *(G-14473)*
Pipkin-Goodfellow Venture LLC .... G 509 884-2400
  East Wenatchee *(G-3029)*
Port Orchard Sand & Gravel .... E 360 681-2526
  Port Ludlow *(G-7772)*
Puget Sound Sand and Grav LLC .... G 360 332-3333
  Blaine *(G-1698)*
Randles Sand & Gravel Inc .... D 253 531-6800
  Puyallup *(G-8234)*
Redside Construction LLC .... G 360 297-9557
  Bainbridge Island *(G-664)*
Ronald Sand & Gravel Inc .... G 509 728-8605
  Ellensburg *(G-3223)*
Sand Carrier Inc .... G 206 790-6791
  Tukwila *(G-13812)*
Sea Island Corp .... F 360 376-4215
  Eastsound *(G-3046)*
Simpson Gravel Pit .... G 425 879-1024
  Stanwood *(G-12991)*
Spokane Rock Products Inc .... G 509 244-5421
  Spokane Valley *(G-12888)*
Stick & Sand Tutoring .... G 206 721-6261
  Seattle *(G-11195)*
Stillaquamish Resources LLC .... G 360 474-1999
  Arlington *(G-335)*
Supply Guy .... G 253 531-8600
  Tacoma *(G-13531)*
Tim Corliss & Son Inc .... G 360 825-2578
  Enumclaw *(G-3324)*
Timber Savers Inc .... G 208 799-8748
  Clarkston *(G-2652)*
Walla Walla Gravel & Rock Llc .... G 509 301-1050
  Walla Walla *(G-14892)*
Washington Rock Quarries Inc .... F 360 893-7701
  Orting *(G-7488)*
Wingardner Sand and Gravel .... G 509 480-3847
  Zillah *(G-15765)*
Winston Quarry Inc .... G 360 985-0487
  Mossyrock *(G-6767)*

SAND MINING
Cadman (rock) Inc .... D 425 867-1234
  Redmond *(G-8414)*
Taylor Trucking LLC .... F 360 573-2000
  Vancouver *(G-14627)*

SAND: Hygrade
Lane Mt Silica Co .... E 206 762-7622
  Valley *(G-13993)*

SAND: Silica
Reserve Industries Corporation .... G 425 432-1241
  Ravensdale *(G-8340)*

Employee Codes: A=Over 500 employees, B=251-500
C=101-250, D=51-100, E=20-50, F=10-19, G=2-9

SANDBLASTING EQPT

SANDBLASTING EQPT
- North Pacific Industrial .... G 425 251-0335
  Issaquah *(G-4454)*
- Safe Systems Inc .... F 425 251-8662
  Kent *(G-5113)*

SANDBLASTING SVC: Building Exterior
- Mikes Custom Welding .... G 360 754-3719
  Tumwater *(G-13887)*

SANDSTONE: Crushed & Broken
- Hillcar & Fletcher Inc .... G 360 327-3844
  Beaver *(G-757)*

SANDSTONE: Dimension
- Quarry S/E Inc .... G 206 525-5270
  Seattle *(G-10904)*
- Wilkeson Sandstone Quarry LLC ... G 360 829-0999
  Wilkeson *(G-15144)*

SANITARY SVC, NEC
- B & B Logging Inc .... G 360 247-5237
  Amboy *(G-89)*

SANITARY SVCS: Dead Animal Disposal
- Q A R Rendering Services Inc .... G 253 847-7220
  Graham *(G-4236)*

SANITARY SVCS: Environmental Cleanup
- Foss Maritime Company Llc .... D 206 281-3800
  Seattle *(G-10015)*

SANITARY SVCS: Oil Spill Cleanup
- Oil Spills Services Inc .... G 425 823-6500
  Kirkland *(G-5416)*

SANITARY SVCS: Refuse Collection & Disposal Svcs
- Emerald Services Inc .... C 206 430-7795
  Seattle *(G-9913)*
- Fibres International Inc .... D 425 455-9811
  Everett *(G-3471)*

SANITARY SVCS: Waste Materials, Recycling
- Fibres International Inc .... E 425 455-9811
  Everett *(G-3472)*
- J A Jack & Sons Inc .... F 360 479-4659
  Bremerton *(G-1964)*
- Parberry Inc .... E 360 734-2340
  Bellingham *(G-1491)*
- Rebec LLC .... G 425 745-4177
  Lynnwood *(G-6187)*
- Sno King Recycling Inc .... G 425 582-2919
  Lynnwood *(G-6201)*
- Sunland Bark and Topsoils Co ...... G 360 293-7188
  Anacortes *(G-172)*

SANITARY WARE: Metal
- Elkay Ssp LLC .... G 509 533-0808
  Spokane *(G-12240)*
- Elkay Ssp LLC .... E 509 533-0808
  Spokane *(G-12241)*
- Familian Northwest Seattle 07 ...... G 206 767-7700
  Seattle *(G-9966)*

SANITATION CHEMICALS & CLEANING AGENTS
- Alpine Products Inc .... G 253 351-9828
  Auburn *(G-373)*
- Cgt Inc .... G 253 833-8849
  Auburn *(G-405)*
- Chimcare Vancouver .... G 360 696-8309
  Vancouver *(G-14117)*
- Chimcare West Seattle .... G 206 673-2203
  Seattle *(G-9676)*
- Design Hardwood Products Inc .... G 425 869-0859
  Redmond *(G-8440)*
- Ecolab Inc .... E 253 733-3000
  Tacoma *(G-13269)*
- Gerris Dry Bunk .... G 509 782-2653
  Cashmere *(G-2320)*

- Glass Restoration Specialists .... E 253 473-7779
  Tacoma *(G-13311)*
- Jay One Ball .... G 360 275-2834
  Belfair *(G-764)*
- Kepler Absorbents LLC .... G 844 453-7537
  Fife *(G-3962)*
- Waupaca Northwoods LLC .... D 509 877-2830
  Parker *(G-7550)*
- Wesmar Company Inc .... D 206 783-5344
  Lynnwood *(G-6222)*

SASHES: Door Or Window, Metal
- Milgard Manufacturing Inc .... C 253 922-6030
  Fife *(G-3971)*

SATCHELS
- Magic Satchel .... G 509 342-8914
  Spokane Valley *(G-12782)*

SATELLITE COMMUNICATIONS EQPT
- Channel Korea .... G 425 557-5970
  Issaquah *(G-4391)*
- Star West Satellite .... G 509 545-4996
  Pasco *(G-7633)*

SATELLITES: Communications
- DMC Satellite Systems Inc .... G 360 681-4204
  Sequim *(G-11627)*
- Emerging Mkts Cmmnications LLC .. G 206 454-8300
  Seattle *(G-9916)*
- Integrated Technologies Inc .... D 425 349-2084
  Everett *(G-3518)*
- Jeffrey Mark Bashe .... G 509 684-6925
  Colville *(G-2758)*
- Kymeta Corporation .... D 425 896-3700
  Redmond *(G-8526)*
- Kymeta Corporation .... D 425 896-3700
  Redmond *(G-8527)*
- Reach For Sky Satellite Servic ...... G 509 276-9340
  Loon Lake *(G-5977)*
- Seamobile Inc .... G 206 838-7700
  Seattle *(G-11044)*
- Ship Electronics Inc .... G 206 819-3853
  Shoreline *(G-11810)*

SAUNA ROOMS: Prefabricated
- Seamax Enterprises Inc .... F 206 323-8886
  Puyallup *(G-8247)*
- Tropical Sauna .... G 509 927-7898
  Otis Orchards *(G-7520)*

SAW BLADES
- Concut Inc .... E 253 872-3507
  Kent *(G-4862)*
- Cut Technologies Usa Inc .... E 360 733-0460
  Bellingham *(G-1313)*
- Eastside Saw & Sales Inc .... G 425 454-7627
  Bellevue *(G-887)*
- Saw Service Washington Inc .... G 360 738-6437
  Bellingham *(G-1525)*

SAWDUST & SHAVINGS
- Ace International Inc .... G 360 736-9999
  Centralia *(G-2380)*
- Bobby Wolford Trucking & Salv ... E 425 481-1800
  Woodinville *(G-15195)*
- De Jong Sawdust & Shavings ...... F 425 252-1566
  Lake Stevens *(G-5643)*
- Full Circle Natural Products .... G 425 337-8844
  Everett *(G-3487)*
- Pacific Topsoils Inc .... E 425 337-2700
  Everett *(G-3568)*
- Starkenburg Shavings .... G 360 734-8818
  Ferndale *(G-3907)*
- Topsoils Northwest Inc .... F 425 337-0233
  Snohomish *(G-11993)*

SAWING & PLANING MILLS
- A JS Custom Portable Sawmilli .... G 425 775-7999
  Bothell *(G-1812)*
- Ace International Inc .... E 360 736-3937
  Centralia *(G-2379)*
- Alsea Veneer Inc .... G 360 891-2020
  Vancouver *(G-14025)*
- Alta Forest Products LLC .... B 360 219-0008
  Morton *(G-6667)*

PRODUCT SECTION

- Alta Forest Products LLC .... D 360 426-9721
  Shelton *(G-11676)*
- Alta Forest Products LLC .... G 360 288-2234
  Amanda Park *(G-86)*
- Beam Machine .... G 425 222-5587
  Fall City *(G-3700)*
- Blue North Forest Products LLC ... F 208 935-2547
  Seattle *(G-9552)*
- Burgess Logging Inc .... F 509 763-3119
  Leavenworth *(G-5797)*
- Butteville Lumber Co .... E 360 978-6098
  Onalaska *(G-7447)*
- Carpinito Brothers Inc .... G 253 627-3121
  Tacoma *(G-13225)*
- Columbia Cedar Inc .... G 509 738-4711
  Colville *(G-2744)*
- Edwin Enterprises Inc .... G 253 272-7090
  Tacoma *(G-13274)*
- Erosion Ctrl Innovations LLC .... G 206 962-9582
  Enumclaw *(G-3290)*
- Faye Gear Rhonda .... G 509 380-0950
  Pasco *(G-7581)*
- Hampton Affiliates .... G 360 403-8213
  Arlington *(G-246)*
- Interfor US Inc .... C 360 457-6266
  Port Angeles *(G-7714)*
- James Hardie Building Pdts Inc ... D 253 847-8700
  Tacoma *(G-13355)*
- James Richard Simpson .... G 509 679-9720
  Tenino *(G-13619)*
- Jarvis Saw Mill LLC .... G 360 733-7591
  Bellingham *(G-1387)*
- Little River Inc .... G 360 532-7490
  Hoquiam *(G-4347)*
- Manke Lumber Company Inc .... G 360 426-5536
  Shelton *(G-11710)*
- Manke Timber Company Inc .... G 253 572-9029
  Tacoma *(G-13398)*
- Matthaeis Camco Inc .... E 360 426-7900
  Shelton *(G-11712)*
- Meyer Wells Inc .... E 206 282-0076
  Seattle *(G-10525)*
- Mhj Wood Works .... G 360 901-8889
  Battle Ground *(G-722)*
- Michiels International Inc .... G 206 365-4060
  Kenmore *(G-4592)*
- Miller Shingle Company LLC .... G 360 691-7727
  Granite Falls *(G-4281)*
- Milmor Lumber Manufacturing ..... G 253 474-1001
  Fircrest *(G-4003)*
- Mount Adams Lumber Co Inc .... G 509 395-2122
  Trout Lake *(G-13681)*
- Mt Adams Lumber Company Inc .. G 509 395-2131
  Trout Lake *(G-13682)*
- North Fork Timber Company Corp .. G 360 273-5541
  Rochester *(G-9138)*
- Northern Industrial Inc .... E 206 682-2752
  Seattle *(G-10631)*
- Oroville Reman & Reload Inc .... E 509 476-2935
  Oroville *(G-7471)*
- Pacific Northwest Timbers LLC ..... G 360 379-2792
  Port Townsend *(G-7906)*
- Pat Lydon Saw Mill LLC .... G 360 666-0900
  Battle Ground *(G-728)*
- Pleasant Hill Sawmill .... G 360 274-7888
  Kelso *(G-4542)*
- Port Angeles Hardwood LLC .... G 360 452-6041
  Port Angeles *(G-7737)*
- Robert Madsen Design Inc .... G 206 588-0090
  Seattle *(G-10971)*
- Rsg Forest Products Inc .... E 360 225-8513
  Woodland *(G-15464)*
- Ruff Cuts Custom Sawing LLC ...... G 360 249-3926
  Montesano *(G-6655)*
- S&L Portable Sawmill LLC .... G 360 417-3085
  Port Angeles *(G-7742)*
- Sawarne Lumber Co Ltd .... E 360 380-1290
  Ferndale *(G-3899)*
- Shakertown 1992 Inc .... G 360 785-3501
  Winlock *(G-15156)*
- Silver City Lumber Inc .... E 509 238-6960
  Chattaroy *(G-2453)*
- Stella-Jones Corporation .... D 360 435-2146
  Arlington *(G-334)*
- Thee Legacy Woodshop .... G 425 327-0208
  Arlington *(G-338)*
- W-4 Construction Inc .... F 509 529-1603
  Walla Walla *(G-14886)*
- Wayne Davidson .... G 425 333-4242
  Carnation *(G-2302)*

PRODUCT SECTION

SEARCH & NAVIGATION SYSTEMS

Webley Lumber Inc ....G....... 509 684-3980
  Colville *(G-2783)*
Western Forest Products US LLC ....G....... 360 403-1400
  Arlington *(G-348)*
Weyerhaeuser Company ....C....... 360 736-2811
  Centralia *(G-2442)*
Weyerhaeuser Company ....C....... 360 577-6678
  Longview *(G-5967)*

SAWING & PLANING MILLS: Custom

Artic Timber..G....... 360 533-6490
  Cosmopolis *(G-2797)*
Randall Custom Lumber Ltd.....................G....... 360 426-8518
  Shelton *(G-11724)*
South Everson Lumber Co Inc ....C....... 360 966-2188
  Everson *(G-3689)*
Weyerhaeuser Company ....C....... 631 863-1117
  Sumner *(G-13112)*

SAWMILL MACHINES

Miller Manufacturing Inc..........................F....... 360 335-1236
  Washougal *(G-14969)*
Northern Industrial Inc ....E....... 206 682-2752
  Seattle *(G-10631)*
Salem Equipment Inc................................F....... 503 581-8411
  Vancouver *(G-14567)*
Usnr LLC..C....... 360 225-8267
  Woodland *(G-15471)*
Usnr LLC..G....... 360 225-8267
  Woodland *(G-15470)*
Wellons Group Inc ....F....... 360 750-3500
  Vancouver *(G-14682)*

SAWS & SAWING EQPT

Blue Water Inc ....G....... 509 682-5544
  Chelan *(G-2548)*
Carls Mower and Saw ....G....... 360 384-0799
  Ferndale *(G-3824)*
Cascade Pipe & Feed Supply....................G....... 509 997-0720
  Twisp *(G-13910)*
Shelly Shay ....G....... 360 829-2350
  Buckley *(G-2072)*
Sondra L Groce...G....... 509 467-8788
  Spokane *(G-12511)*
Sumner Lawn n Saw LLC ....F....... 253 435-9284
  Puyallup *(G-8257)*
Tims Country Saw Shop ....G....... 509 486-2798
  Tonasket *(G-13660)*
Unifire Inc ....F....... 509 535-7746
  Spokane *(G-12575)*

SAWS: Hand, Metalworking Or Woodworking

Two Blue Mules...G....... 206 935-3762
  Seattle *(G-11352)*
Www Qualitylacecom ....G....... 425 996-0523
  Sammamish *(G-9260)*

SCALE REPAIR SVCS

Avery Weigh-Tronix LLC.........................G....... 206 575-1992
  Tukwila *(G-13694)*
Christian Hamilton ....G....... 360 442-4900
  Longview *(G-5899)*
Tandar Corp ....F....... 503 248-0711
  Vancouver *(G-14624)*

SCALES & BALANCES, EXC LABORATORY

Solcon Inc ....E....... 425 222-5963
  Issaquah *(G-4480)*
Tandar Corp ....F....... 503 248-0711
  Vancouver *(G-14624)*

SCALES: Counting

U S Scale Incorporated..............................G....... 253 872-4803
  Kent *(G-5193)*

SCALES: Indl

Avery Weigh-Tronix LLC.........................G....... 206 575-1992
  Tukwila *(G-13694)*
Curtis Manufacturing Inc...........................F....... 425 353-4384
  Snohomish *(G-11894)*

SCALES: Truck

Bee Jay Scales Inc ....G....... 509 837-8280
  Sunnyside *(G-13113)*

Creative Microsystems Inc.....................F....... 425 235-4335
  Renton *(G-8776)*
Pacific Northwest Technology................G....... 360 493-8344
  Lacey *(G-5574)*

SCANNING DEVICES: Optical

Microvision Inc.......................................C....... 425 936-6847
  Redmond *(G-8587)*
Opticon Inc ....E....... 425 651-2120
  Renton *(G-8865)*

SCHOOL SPLYS, EXC BOOKS: Wholesalers

Grief Inc ....G....... 253 929-0649
  Puyallup *(G-8160)*

SCHOOLS: Elementary & Secondary

Physware Inc...G....... 562 491-1600
  Bellevue *(G-1074)*

SCISSORS: Hand

Shear Precision Inc................................G....... 800 481-4943
  Seattle *(G-11097)*

SCRAP & WASTE MATERIALS, WHOLESALE: Bottles

Sno King Recycling Inc..........................G....... 425 582-2919
  Lynnwood *(G-6201)*

SCRAP & WASTE MATERIALS, WHOLESALE: Ferrous Metal

Alaska Metal Recycling Co ....E....... 907 349-4833
  Tacoma *(G-13160)*
E Power Systems & Battery Inc..............G....... 253 267-1965
  Lakewood *(G-5716)*
Gundies Inc ....E....... 360 733-5036
  Bellingham *(G-1364)*
Schnitzer Steel International...................G....... 253 572-4000
  Tacoma *(G-13508)*

SCRAP & WASTE MATERIALS, WHOLESALE: Metal

Giant Metals Inc ....G....... 206 592-0963
  Seatac *(G-9285)*

SCRAP & WASTE MATERIALS, WHOLESALE: Nonferrous Metals Scrap

American Recycling Corp ....E....... 509 535-4271
  Spokane Valley *(G-12614)*
Z Recyclers Inc.......................................F....... 360 398-2161
  Lynden *(G-6061)*

SCRAP & WASTE MATERIALS, WHOLESALE: Plastics Scrap

Yms ....G....... 206 354-2048
  Seattle *(G-11512)*

SCRAP STEEL CUTTING

American Recycling Corp ....E....... 509 535-4271
  Spokane Valley *(G-12614)*

SCREENS: Door, Wood Frame

Mill Frame LLC ....G....... 425 599-5992
  Sumas *(G-13048)*

SCREENS: Window, Metal

Skyline Windows Inc..............................G....... 206 542-2147
  Shoreline *(G-11813)*
Sun Solutions Inc....................................G....... 509 946-7107
  Richland *(G-9042)*

SCREW MACHINE PRDTS

Automatic Products Co Inc....................D....... 253 872-0203
  Kent *(G-4800)*
Ems & Sales LLC ....G....... 253 208-9062
  Renton *(G-8794)*
Fkc Co Ltd ....F....... 360 452-9472
  Port Angeles *(G-7706)*
Go Planit LLC ....G....... 206 227-0660
  Mattawa *(G-6407)*

Grizzly Machining Solutions ....G....... 406 396-4087
  Sultan *(G-13026)*
Jet City Partners LLC ....G....... 206 999-0047
  Auburn *(G-479)*
Jevco International Inc ....F....... 253 858-2605
  Auburn *(G-480)*
Mico Welding & Machining Inc ....G....... 509 467-5082
  Nine Mile Falls *(G-7079)*
Northstone Industries LLC....................G....... 509 844-7775
  Spokane *(G-12410)*
Omnifab Inc ....E....... 253 931-5151
  Auburn *(G-518)*
Roberts Precision Machine Inc..............F....... 360 805-1000
  Monroe *(G-6615)*
Saco Sales ....G....... 253 277-1568
  Kent *(G-5112)*
Tacoma Screw Products Inc ....G....... 253 395-9770
  Kent *(G-5170)*
Tacoma Screw Products Inc ....G....... 206 767-3750
  Seattle *(G-11256)*
Towaco Screw Mch Pdts Co LLC ....G....... 425 481-7100
  Bothell *(G-1910)*

SCREWS: Metal

Steeler Inc ....G....... 509 926-7403
  Spokane Valley *(G-12891)*

SEALANTS

Northwest Adhesives Inc ....F....... 360 260-1227
  Washougal *(G-14972)*
Specialists Sealant ....G....... 509 321-0424
  Spokane Valley *(G-12882)*

SEALS: Hermetic

Biocom Systems Inc...............................G....... 509 241-0505
  Wenatchee *(G-15014)*
Pacific Aerospace & Elec Inc ....C....... 509 667-9600
  Wenatchee *(G-15057)*

SEARCH & DETECTION SYSTEMS, EXC RADAR

Strategic Robotic Systems Inc ....G....... 425 285-9229
  Redmond *(G-8684)*

SEARCH & NAVIGATION SYSTEMS

Advanced Aero Safety Inc......................G....... 360 387-8472
  Stanwood *(G-12952)*
Aerocell Corporation ....C....... 360 653-2211
  Marysville *(G-6311)*
Aeroforge Manufacturing Inc..................E....... 253 286-2525
  Puyallup *(G-8118)*
Airborne Ecs LLC..................................F....... 319 538-1051
  Port Angeles *(G-7679)*
Avtechtyee Inc..C....... 425 290-3100
  Everett *(G-3378)*
B/E Aerospace Inc ....B....... 360 657-5197
  Everett *(G-3380)*
Bae Systems Tech Sol Srvc Inc ....G....... 360 598-8800
  Silverdale *(G-11827)*
Ballard Technology Inc...........................D....... 425 339-0281
  Everett *(G-3383)*
Biosonics Inc..F....... 206 782-2211
  Seattle *(G-9530)*
Biosonics Telemetry LP ....G....... 206 783-9356
  Seattle *(G-9531)*
Boeing Company ....C....... 253 931-2121
  Auburn *(G-395)*
Boeing Company ....B....... 425 413-3400
  Maple Valley *(G-6261)*
Bridgeways...D....... 425 513-2989
  Everett *(G-3401)*
Brooks Tactical Systems........................F....... 253 549-2703
  Fox Island *(G-4019)*
Dabs Manufacturing & Assembly ....F....... 253 872-2200
  Kent *(G-4870)*
Digital Control Incorporated ....D....... 425 251-0701
  Kent *(G-4873)*
Echodyne Corp ....C....... 206 713-1216
  Kirkland *(G-5328)*
Engine & Aircraft Strategies ....G....... 425 432-2800
  Maple Valley *(G-6268)*
Gcm North American Arospc LLC ....D....... 253 872-7488
  Algona *(G-69)*
General Dynamics Corporation ....E....... 425 885-5010
  Duvall *(G-2989)*
Honeywell International Inc ....C....... 425 251-9511
  Renton *(G-8820)*

Employee Codes: A=Over 500 employees, B=251-500
C=101-250, D=51-100, E=20-50, F=10-19, G=2-9

Idd Aerospace Corp.......C....... 425 885-0617
Redmond *(G-8505)*
Iocurrents Inc.......G....... 206 494-0099
Seattle *(G-10258)*
Jtc Aerospace LLC.......G....... 425 869-6812
Redmond *(G-8523)*
Krismark Group Inc.......G....... 425 396-0829
Snoqualmie *(G-12015)*
LMI Aerospace Inc.......C....... 253 288-9379
Auburn *(G-489)*
Lockheed Martin Corporation.......F....... 425 482-1100
Bothell *(G-1876)*
Lockheed Martin Corporation.......B....... 360 396-8591
Silverdale *(G-11846)*
Lockheed Martin Corporation.......C....... 360 697-6844
Silverdale *(G-11847)*
Nabtesco Aerospace Inc.......E....... 425 602-8400
Kirkland *(G-5407)*
Neumeier Engineering Inc.......E....... 253 854-3635
Kent *(G-5020)*
Newcore Aviation LLC.......G....... 509 276-8200
Deer Park *(G-2910)*
Newcore Enterprises LLC.......G....... 509 276-8200
Deer Park *(G-2911)*
Nova-Tech Engineering LP.......G....... 425 245-7000
Bothell *(G-1782)*
Papec.......G....... 253 862-6148
Lake Tapps *(G-5683)*
Prototek Corp.......F....... 360 779-1310
Poulsbo *(G-7993)*
R Ramjet Inc.......G....... 541 312-1648
Seabeck *(G-9270)*
Raisbeck Engineering Inc.......F....... 206 723-2000
Tukwila *(G-13802)*
Rockwell Collins Inc.......G....... 425 923-2700
Everett *(G-3600)*
Rockwell Collins Inc.......E....... 425 492-1400
Bothell *(G-1896)*
Sagetech Corporation.......D....... 509 493-2154
White Salmon *(G-15128)*
Sagetech Corporation.......D....... 509 493-1364
White Salmon *(G-15129)*
Sagetech Corporation.......D....... 509 493-2113
White Salmon *(G-15130)*
Sealth Aero Marine Co.......E....... 425 481-0727
Mill Creek *(G-6525)*
Ship Electronics Inc.......G....... 206 819-3853
Shoreline *(G-11810)*
Stargate Inc.......G....... 425 251-0701
Kent *(G-5152)*
Tig Aerospace LLC.......G....... 206 372-6724
Seattle *(G-11305)*
Tji II LLC.......C....... 360 794-4448
Monroe *(G-6632)*
Toolcraft Inc.......F....... 360 794-5512
Monroe *(G-6633)*
Universal Avonics Systems Corp.......C....... 425 821-2800
Redmond *(G-8699)*
Valley Machine Shop Inc.......E....... 425 226-5040
Kent *(G-5199)*

SEAT BELTS: Automobile & Aircraft

Bridport-Air Carrier Inc.......E....... 253 872-7205
Kent *(G-4823)*
Pioneer Aerofab Company Inc.......F....... 360 757-4780
Burlington *(G-2181)*

SEATING: Stadium

Federal Way Memorial Field.......G....... 253 945-5575
Federal Way *(G-3738)*
Safeco Field.......G....... 206 346-4000
Seattle *(G-11002)*
United Seating & Mobility LLC.......G....... 509 484-6720
Spokane *(G-12577)*

SECRETARIAL SVCS

D & E Enterprises.......G....... 509 684-6618
Colville *(G-2749)*

SECURE STORAGE SVC: Document

Pacific Ally LLC.......G....... 360 760-4266
La Center *(G-5511)*

SECURITY CONTROL EQPT & SYSTEMS

Affordable Electronics Inc.......G....... 425 484-0964
Monroe *(G-6544)*
Apollo Video Technology LLC.......C....... 425 483-7100
Bothell *(G-1820)*
Cascadia Video Pdts Cvp LLC.......G....... 509 202-4230
Cheney *(G-2580)*
Darren Mode.......G....... 509 292-2438
Deer Park *(G-2897)*
Jan-R Corporation.......E....... 360 856-0836
Sedro Woolley *(G-11543)*
Keyking Inc.......G....... 360 977-7870
Camas *(G-2262)*
Nationwide SEC Solutions Inc.......G....... 800 908-8992
Vancouver *(G-14428)*
Newton Security Inc.......E....... 425 251-9494
Renton *(G-8858)*
Northwest Monitoring Services.......G....... 509 326-6270
Spokane *(G-12413)*
PC Open Incorporated.......C....... 509 777-6736
Liberty Lake *(G-5852)*
Stardust Materials LLC.......G....... 360 260-7399
Vancouver *(G-14608)*
T & K Cstm Fabrication & Repr.......G....... 206 242-0197
Seattle *(G-11247)*

SECURITY DEVICES

Controlled Products of Wash.......G....... 206 575-2249
Tukwila *(G-13717)*
E2 Systems LLC.......G....... 253 284-3707
Lakewood *(G-5717)*
Frank J Martin Company.......E....... 206 523-7665
Lynnwood *(G-6122)*
N W Sound & Security Tech LLC.......F....... 360 213-1619
Ridgefield *(G-9095)*
Next Biometrics Inc.......E....... 425 406-7055
Bellevue *(G-1030)*
Nuid Inc.......G....... 360 927-4682
Seattle *(G-10669)*
Olympic SEC Comm Sys Inc.......G....... 360 652-1088
Arlington *(G-294)*
Patroltag Inc.......G....... 650 678-3790
Seattle *(G-10771)*
Pb Inc.......G....... 206 747-0347
Bellevue *(G-1066)*
Quality Fence Builders Inc.......E....... 253 939-8533
Auburn *(G-541)*
Safe Home Security Products.......G....... 360 384-1239
Ferndale *(G-3894)*
Strain Night Vision & Security.......G....... 509 926-2025
Spokane *(G-12531)*

SECURITY EQPT STORES

Richards Packaging Inc.......G....... 509 545-8690
Pasco *(G-7623)*
Spokane House of Hose Inc.......E....... 509 535-3638
Spokane Valley *(G-12883)*

SECURITY SYSTEMS SERVICES

Aaab Consulting LLC.......G....... 206 612-7041
Seattle *(G-9328)*
Bluewave Technologies LLC.......G....... 800 636-1428
Seattle *(G-9558)*
Cleaning Consultants Services.......G....... 206 682-9748
Seattle *(G-9692)*
Electrical Services & SEC Inc.......G....... 206 276-6629
Kent *(G-4887)*
Monaco Enterprises Inc.......D....... 509 926-6277
Spokane Valley *(G-12793)*
Oatridge-Evergreen 8a2 JV LLC.......G....... 253 627-3794
Tacoma *(G-13439)*

SEEDS: Coated Or Treated, From Purchased Seeds

Skagit Seed Services Inc.......G....... 360 466-3191
Mount Vernon *(G-6841)*

SEMICONDUCTOR & RELATED DEVICES: Read-Only Memory Or ROM

Monolithic Power Systems Inc.......G....... 408 826-0600
Seattle *(G-10559)*

SEMICONDUCTOR CIRCUIT NETWORKS

Impinj Inc.......C....... 206 517-5300
Seattle *(G-10212)*
Impinj Inc.......F....... 206 315-4449
Seattle *(G-10214)*
Tsmc Development Inc.......C....... 360 817-3000
Camas *(G-2285)*
Wafertech LLC.......A....... 360 817-3000
Camas *(G-2287)*

SEMICONDUCTOR DEVICES: Wafers

Jx Crystals Inc.......G....... 425 392-5237
Issaquah *(G-4435)*
Linear Technology Corporation.......C....... 360 834-1900
Camas *(G-2265)*
Shin-Etsu Handotai America Inc.......A....... 360 883-7000
Vancouver *(G-14583)*
Tactical Fabs Inc.......E....... 360 723-5360
Battle Ground *(G-742)*

SEMICONDUCTORS & RELATED DEVICES

Aard Technology LLC.......G....... 425 785-0682
Sammamish *(G-9183)*
Advanced Energy Industries Inc.......G....... 360 759-2713
Vancouver *(G-14010)*
Analog Devices Inc.......G....... 360 834-1900
Camas *(G-2228)*
Bobek Enterprises.......G....... 360 683-8785
Sequim *(G-11616)*
Broadcom Corporation.......G....... 425 748-5076
Bellevue *(G-829)*
Canelle Citron.......G....... 206 241-4657
Seattle *(G-9616)*
Constant Computer.......G....... 253 227-0532
Tacoma *(G-13239)*
Convergent Earned Value Assoc.......G....... 206 293-6931
Bellevue *(G-864)*
Cypress Microsystems Inc.......F....... 425 787-4400
Lynnwood *(G-6103)*
Cypress Semiconductor Corp.......F....... 425 787-4400
Lynnwood *(G-6104)*
Data I/O Corporation.......C....... 425 881-6444
Redmond *(G-8433)*
Eaton Corporation.......E....... 425 644-5800
Bellevue *(G-889)*
Ejimcom.......G....... 360 459-4785
Lacey *(G-5546)*
Eldec Corporation.......A....... 425 743-1313
Lynnwood *(G-6114)*
First Silicon Designs LLC.......G....... 303 883-6891
Vancouver *(G-14233)*
Greence Inc.......G....... 360 727-3528
Ridgefield *(G-9087)*
Hd Pacific Inc.......F....... 425 481-3031
Mukilteo *(G-6931)*
Honeywell Electronic Mtls Inc.......A....... 509 252-2200
Spokane Valley *(G-12731)*
Impinj Inc.......G....... 206 834-1098
Seattle *(G-10213)*
Isilon Systems LLC.......B....... 206 315-7500
Seattle *(G-10260)*
Jet City Electronics Inc.......G....... 206 529-0351
Lake Forest Park *(G-5616)*
Lam Research Corporation.......D....... 360 260-0352
Vancouver *(G-14357)*
Lauda-Noah LP.......F....... 360 993-1395
Vancouver *(G-14362)*
Lauda-Noah LP.......G....... 360 993-1395
Vancouver *(G-14363)*
Leader Manufacturing Inc.......E....... 360 895-1184
Port Orchard *(G-7825)*
Lightel Technologies Inc.......E....... 425 277-8000
Renton *(G-8844)*
Lumotive LLC.......G....... 907 306-6267
Bellevue *(G-992)*
Marketech International Inc.......G....... 360 379-6707
Port Townsend *(G-7897)*
Marvell Semiconductor Inc.......G....... 408 222-2500
Redmond *(G-8552)*
Mellanox Technologies Inc.......G....... 512 239-8282
Redmond *(G-8555)*
Micrametal Inc.......G....... 206 508-1405
Seattle *(G-10529)*
Micron Technology Inc.......G....... 206 294-7015
Seattle *(G-10535)*
Monolithic Power Systems Inc.......C....... 425 296-9956
Kirkland *(G-5405)*
Muscleclub 4 Men.......G....... 206 624-9785
Seattle *(G-10573)*
Nlight Inc.......B....... 360 566-4460
Vancouver *(G-14432)*
Nxedge Inc.......G....... 425 990-0091
Bellevue *(G-1041)*
Professional Mentors & Pro.......G....... 832 216-9134
Colton *(G-2733)*
Professnl Mntrs & Pro Life Skl.......G....... 832 216-9134
Colton *(G-2734)*
Rec Silicon Inc.......G....... 509 793-9015
Moses Lake *(G-6742)*

PRODUCT SECTION

SHIP BUILDING & REPAIRING: Combat Vessels

Sputtertech Inc ....G....... 360 253-5944
  Vancouver *(G-14605)*
Tfi Telemark ....D....... 360 723-5360
  Battle Ground *(G-745)*
Wafer Reclaim Services LLC ....G....... 360 254-0221
  Vancouver *(G-14676)*
Xkl LLC ....E....... 425 869-9050
  Redmond *(G-8720)*

SENSORS: Infrared, Solid State

Automated Tech Solutions LLC...........G....... 425 999-1297
  Maple Valley *(G-6259)*

SENSORS: Radiation

Momentum Interactive LLC...................G....... 915 203-5349
  Bellingham *(G-1440)*

SEPTIC TANK CLEANING SVCS

Gobers Fuel Oil Inc ....F....... 509 924-5372
  Spokane Valley *(G-12721)*
Iron Horse Vac LLC ....G....... 509 586-2446
  Kennewick *(G-4677)*
Northwest Cascade Inc ....C....... 253 848-2371
  Puyallup *(G-8202)*

SEPTIC TANKS: Concrete

Atlas Concrete Products Inc..............F....... 360 736-7642
  Centralia *(G-2384)*
Cuz Concrete Products Inc ....E....... 360 435-5531
  Arlington *(G-224)*
D & K Concrete Products Inc............F....... 360 573-4020
  Vancouver *(G-14162)*
John Dalrymple ....G....... 509 837-2117
  Sunnyside *(G-13129)*
Long Septic Services..........................E....... 253 852-0550
  Lake Stevens *(G-5659)*
Lopez Redi Mix Inc.............................G....... 360 468-2485
  Lopez Island *(G-5985)*
M 1 Tanks Inc ....G....... 509 766-2914
  Moses Lake *(G-6722)*
Northwest Cascade Inc ....C....... 253 848-2371
  Puyallup *(G-8202)*
Rada Inc ....G....... 509 547-7232
  Pasco *(G-7621)*
Rapid Readymix Co ....G....... 509 493-3153
  Bingen *(G-1641)*

SEPTIC TANKS: Plastic

Lowridge On Site Tech LLC ....G....... 877 476-8823
  Lake Stevens *(G-5660)*
Norwesco Inc......................................F....... 360 835-3021
  Washougal *(G-14973)*

SETTLEMENT HOUSE

Pioneer Human Services ....D....... 206 768-1990
  Seattle *(G-10809)*

SEWAGE & WATER TREATMENT EQPT

Advance Septic Trtmnt Systems ....G....... 360 856-0550
  Sedro Woolley *(G-11531)*
Clear Water Compliance LLC............E....... 425 412-5700
  Everett *(G-3419)*
Evoqua Water Technologies LLC.......G....... 360 699-7392
  Brush Prairie *(G-2034)*
Fobes District Water & Assn..............F....... 425 334-3311
  Snohomish *(G-11910)*
King County Wastewater Trtmnt ....G....... 206 463-0102
  Vashon *(G-14727)*
Landa Inc ....D....... 360 833-9100
  Camas *(G-2263)*
Microhaops Inc....................................G....... 206 595-6426
  Seattle *(G-10534)*
Pure Blue Tech Inc.............................G....... 206 724-5707
  Seattle *(G-10887)*
Selg and Associates Inc.....................G....... 425 487-6059
  Woodinville *(G-15359)*

SEWING CONTRACTORS

Contract Sew & Repair Inc ....F....... 253 395-7910
  Kent *(G-4865)*
Duane Ruud ....F....... 206 682-1082
  Seattle *(G-9856)*
Lammy Industries Inc ....E....... 206 654-0010
  Seattle *(G-10374)*
Pacific Coast Manufacturing ....F....... 425 485-8866
  Woodinville *(G-15328)*

Robinson Windword Inc......................F....... 509 536-1617
  Spokane *(G-12481)*
Washington Tent & Awning Inc...........G....... 253 581-7177
  Lakewood *(G-5765)*

SEWING KITS: Novelty

Heartwarmer Designs ....G....... 253 630-7408
  Kent *(G-4937)*

SEWING MACHINES & PARTS: Household

Conterra Inc..F....... 360 734-2311
  Bellingham *(G-1304)*
Professional Designed Sewing............G....... 206 234-5955
  Seattle *(G-10871)*

SEWING, NEEDLEWORK & PIECE GOODS STORES: Knitting Splys

Emma Knits Inc..................................G....... 509 999-8583
  Spokane *(G-12243)*

SEXTANTS

NW Sextant LLC ....G....... 425 746-6475
  Bellevue *(G-1039)*

SHADES: Lamp & Light, Residential

Shades of Green ....G....... 425 387-2335
  Tulalip *(G-13844)*
Twice Light Inc ....F....... 360 573-6101
  Vancouver *(G-14652)*

SHADES: Window

Shade Sunglo & Drapery Co ....G....... 206 767-4561
  Seattle *(G-11094)*

SHAPES & PILINGS, STRUCTURAL: Steel

Accurate Sheet Metal Inc ....E....... 425 745-6786
  Mukilteo *(G-6889)*
Fabrication Products Inc.....................E....... 503 283-3218
  Vancouver *(G-14219)*
Hci Steel Buildings LLC ....F....... 360 403-4900
  Arlington *(G-250)*

SHAVING PREPARATIONS

Stacya Silverman & Associates..........G....... 206 270-9465
  Seattle *(G-11177)*

SHAVINGS, WOOD, WHOLESALE

Starkenburg Shavings.........................G....... 360 734-8818
  Ferndale *(G-3907)*

SHEARLING, PREPARED SHEEPSKIN

Aircraft Sheepskin Company...............G....... 800 874-5747
  Ocean Park *(G-7178)*

SHEET METAL SPECIALTIES, EXC STAMPED

Applied Mfg & Engrg Tech Inc ....F....... 253 852-5378
  Edmonds *(G-3095)*
B & D Sheet Metal LLC ....G....... 206 533-0350
  Shoreline *(G-11759)*
Ballard Sheet Metal Works Inc...........E....... 206 784-0545
  Seattle *(G-9484)*
Coastal Manufacturing Inc..................E....... 425 407-0624
  Everett *(G-3421)*
Competitive Development & Mfg.........F....... 360 691-7816
  Granite Falls *(G-4269)*
Fabtech Precision Mfg Inc ....E....... 509 534-7660
  Spokane Valley *(G-12699)*
Gnr Aerospace Inc ....G....... 360 652-4040
  Arlington *(G-244)*
J & R Mtlcraft Fabricators Inc ....E....... 425 254-0392
  Renton *(G-8829)*
James Homola ....G....... 360 686-3549
  Yacolt *(G-15483)*
Jit Manufacturing Inc ....E....... 425 487-0672
  Woodinville *(G-15274)*
Kenneth A Edleman ....G....... 206 524-2814
  Seattle *(G-10337)*
Kollmar Sheet Metal Works Inc..........G....... 206 283-2330
  Seattle *(G-10353)*
Metaltech Inc ....E....... 253 863-7532
  Sumner *(G-13086)*
National Indus Concepts Inc...............C....... 425 489-4300
  Woodinville *(G-15320)*

Optimum Precision Inc........................G....... 425 778-1455
  Lynnwood *(G-6175)*
Qual Fab Inc.......................................E....... 206 762-2117
  Seattle *(G-10899)*
Smith Fabrication Inc..........................G....... 253 854-4367
  Kent *(G-5136)*
Sol Lighting Inc ....G....... 509 789-1092
  Spokane Valley *(G-12880)*
Stephens Metal Products Inc..............G....... 509 452-4088
  Yakima *(G-15683)*
Sytech Inc ....E....... 509 924-7797
  Spokane *(G-12540)*
Universal Sheet Metal Inc...................E....... 425 483-8384
  Woodinville *(G-15395)*

SHEET MUSIC STORES

Reelworld Productions Inc..................G....... 206 448-1518
  Seattle *(G-10940)*

SHEET MUSIC, WHOLESALE

Non Sequitur Music.............................G....... 360 733-7145
  Bellingham *(G-1460)*

SHEETING: Laminated Plastic

Northwest Laminating Co Inc ....F....... 206 789-5536
  Seattle *(G-10648)*

SHEETING: Window, Plastic

Middy Marine Products Inc ....G....... 425 883-4600
  Redmond *(G-8588)*

SHEETS & STRIPS: Aluminum

Alcoa Inc...C....... 253 272-8413
  Tacoma *(G-13161)*
American Alloy LLC ....D....... 509 921-5794
  Spokane Valley *(G-12607)*

SHEETS: Fabric, From Purchased Materials

Glorious Comfort ....G....... 253 884-1465
  Lakebay *(G-5689)*

SHELLAC

Linex of Olympia ....G....... 360 709-0363
  Tumwater *(G-13884)*

SHELTERED WORKSHOPS

Entrust Community Services...............D....... 509 839-8066
  Sunnyside *(G-13124)*
Lewis Cnty Work Opportunities ....E....... 360 748-9921
  Chehalis *(G-2509)*

SHIP BUILDING & REPAIRING: Boats, Crew

Snow & Company Inc ....G....... 206 396-8997
  Seattle *(G-11145)*
Strongback Metal Boats Inc................G....... 206 321-9965
  Seattle *(G-11204)*

SHIP BUILDING & REPAIRING: Cargo Vessels

Aircraft Cargo Pods ....G....... 509 238-1165
  Mead *(G-6422)*
General Steamship Intl Ltd ....G....... 425 329-1040
  Lynnwood *(G-6128)*
Stabbert Mrtime Yacht Ship LLC ....F....... 206 547-6161
  Seattle *(G-11175)*

SHIP BUILDING & REPAIRING: Cargo, Commercial

Abcd Marine ....G....... 206 527-3428
  Seattle *(G-9333)*
George G Sharp Inc...........................D....... 360 476-8896
  Bremerton *(G-1957)*
Lovrics Sea Craft Inc ....G....... 360 293-2042
  Anacortes *(G-144)*

SHIP BUILDING & REPAIRING: Combat Vessels

Metro Machine Corp ....D....... 360 782-5600
  Bremerton *(G-1978)*
Pacific Ship Repr Fbrction Inc.............C....... 360 674-2480
  Bremerton *(G-1985)*

Employee Codes: A=Over 500 employees, B=251-500
C=101-250, D=51-100, E=20-50, F=10-19, G=2-9

SHIP BUILDING & REPAIRING: Combat Vessels

Puget Sound Commerce Ctr Inc ....D...... 206 623-1635
  Seattle *(G-10884)*

SHIP BUILDING & REPAIRING: Ferryboats

Dakota Creek Industries Inc ....A...... 360 293-9575
  Anacortes *(G-119)*

SHIP BUILDING & REPAIRING: Fishing Vessels, Large

Cape San Lucas Fishing LP ....E...... 425 688-1288
  Bellevue *(G-836)*
F/V Neahkahnie LLC ....G...... 206 547-6557
  Seattle *(G-9958)*
Fishing Vessel Owners Mar Way ....F...... 206 282-6421
  Seattle *(G-10000)*
Gardner Boat Repair Inc ....G...... 206 784-0854
  Seattle *(G-10047)*
Pacific Fishermen Inc ....D...... 206 784-2562
  Seattle *(G-10731)*
Pequod Inc ....G...... 425 742-7456
  Edmonds *(G-3143)*
Westman Marine Inc ....G...... 360 332-5051
  Blaine *(G-1711)*
Winterhalter Inc ....G...... 360 652-6337
  Stanwood *(G-13000)*

SHIP BUILDING & REPAIRING: Lighters, Marine

Ken Dressler ....G...... 360 765-3131
  Quilcene *(G-8285)*

SHIP BUILDING & REPAIRING: Lighthouse Tenders

Lighthouse Envmtl Programs ....G...... 360 579-4489
  Coupeville *(G-2814)*
Quilters Heaven LLC ....G...... 800 253-8990
  Leavenworth *(G-5814)*
Turn Pt Lghthuse Prsrvtion Soc ....G...... 360 376-5246
  Orcas *(G-7456)*

SHIP BUILDING & REPAIRING: Military

Fabtek Industries Llc ....F...... 360 322-7367
  Arlington *(G-235)*
Terry Albracht 425 252-2997
  Everett *(G-3628)*
US Fab ....G...... 206 623-1635
  Seattle *(G-11392)*

SHIP BUILDING & REPAIRING: Offshore Sply Boats

J Calman Industries ....G...... 360 398-1932
  Lynden *(G-6024)*
Palmer Hayes Offshore ....G...... 253 310-7162
  Gig Harbor *(G-4142)*
Xtaeros Inc. ....G...... 206 883-4034
  Seattle *(G-11505)*

SHIP BUILDING & REPAIRING: Rigging, Marine

Hansen Marine Repair & Rigging ....G...... 360 705-1252
  Olympia *(G-7303)*
Toss Brion Yacht Rigging Inc ....G...... 360 385-1080
  Port Townsend *(G-7932)*
University Swaging Corporation ....C...... 425 318-1965
  Bellevue *(G-1208)*

SHIP BUILDING & REPAIRING: Sailing Vessels, Commercial

Highlands Welding Repair Inc ....G...... 206 283-0080
  Seattle *(G-10172)*

SHIP BUILDING & REPAIRING: Trawlers

Lfs Inc ....E...... 360 734-6825
  Bellingham *(G-1408)*
Lfs Inc ....E...... 360 734-3336
  Bellingham *(G-1409)*

SHIPBUILDING & REPAIR

Al Fletcher ....G...... 360 963-2241
  Sekiu *(G-11582)*
All Ocean Services LLC ....G...... 206 632-7692
  Everett *(G-3367)*
American Flex & Exhaust Pdts ....G...... 206 789-1353
  Seattle *(G-9392)*
Argo West Inc ....G...... 360 213-1503
  Vancouver *(G-14040)*
Clarus Fluid Intelligence LLC ....E...... 360 671-1514
  Bellingham *(G-1298)*
Clarus Technologies LLC ....G...... 360 671-1514
  Bellingham *(G-1299)*
Conglobal Industries LLC ....E...... 206 624-8180
  Seattle *(G-9727)*
Craft Labor & Support Svcs LLC ....G...... 206 304-4543
  Edmonds *(G-3103)*
Daves Mobile Welding LLC ....G...... 360 302-0069
  Port Townsend *(G-7877)*
Duwamish Marine Services LLC ....G...... 206 870-3027
  Seattle *(G-9863)*
Ecm Maritime Services LLC ....G...... 206 780-9980
  Seattle *(G-9876)*
Federal Marine & Def Svcs LLC ....E...... 206 322-5529
  Seattle *(G-9980)*
Foss Maritime Company Llc ....D...... 206 281-3800
  Seattle *(G-10015)*
General Dynamics Nascco ....G...... 360 373-2845
  Bremerton *(G-1956)*
Guido Perla & Associates Inc ....E...... 206 463-2217
  Seattle *(G-10132)*
J M Mrtnac Shipbuilding Corp ....C...... 253 572-4005
  Tacoma *(G-13353)*
Jt Marine Inc ....E...... 360 750-1300
  Vancouver *(G-14343)*
Kurtisfactor LLC ....G...... 208 863-6180
  Tacoma *(G-13379)*
Marine Fluid Systems Inc ....F...... 206 706-0858
  Seattle *(G-10481)*
Mavrik Marine Inc ....D...... 360 296-4051
  La Conner *(G-5525)*
Northlake Shipyard Inc ....F...... 206 632-1441
  Seattle *(G-10634)*
Npm LLC ....G...... 206 782-8999
  Seattle *(G-10662)*
Pac Ship 425 622-9030
  Everett *(G-3563)*
Pacific Fshrmen Shpyrd Elc LLC ....D...... 206 784-2562
  Seattle *(G-10732)*
Pacific Pipe & Pump LLC ....F...... 425 640-0376
  Mountlake Terrace *(G-6865)*
Pacific Ship Repr Fbrction Inc ....E...... 425 409-5060
  Everett *(G-3567)*
Propulsion Controls Engrg ....E...... 425 257-9065
  Everett *(G-3588)*
Puglia Engineering Inc ....C...... 360 647-0080
  Bellingham *(G-1509)*
Rozema Boat Works Inc ....F...... 360 757-6004
  Mount Vernon *(G-6830)*
Rozema Enterprises Inc ....G...... 360 757-6004
  Mount Vernon *(G-6831)*
Seattle Shipworks LLC ....D...... 206 763-3133
  Seattle *(G-11074)*
Seaview Boat Yard Inc ....F...... 206 783-6550
  Seattle *(G-11086)*
Shipyard LLC ....G...... 360 532-1990
  Hoquiam *(G-4358)*
Snow & Company Inc ....E...... 206 953-7676
  Seattle *(G-11144)*
Stabberr & Associates Inc ....C...... 206 547-6161
  Seattle *(G-11174)*
Stabberr Yacht and Ship LLC ....E...... 206 547-6161
  Seattle *(G-11176)*
Stealth Marine ....G...... 509 758-8019
  Clarkston *(G-2649)*
Sterling Envmtl Resources ....D...... 360 437-1344
  Port Ludlow *(G-7778)*
Technical Marine and Indus LLC ....G...... 206 717-4466
  Mountlake Terrace *(G-6872)*
Tidewater Holdings Inc ....G...... 360 693-1491
  Vancouver *(G-14635)*
Vigor Fab LLC ....G...... 206 623-1635
  Seattle *(G-11417)*
Vigor Industrial LLC ....E...... 360 457-8470
  Port Angeles *(G-7752)*
Vigor Industrial LLC ....F...... 253 627-9136
  Tacoma *(G-13576)*
Vigor Marine LLC ....D...... 253 627-9136
  Tacoma *(G-13577)*
Vigor Marine LLC ....B...... 206 623-1635
  Seattle *(G-11418)*
Vigor Shipyards Inc ....A...... 206 623-1635
  Seattle *(G-11419)*
Washington Marine Repair LLC ....E...... 360 457-8470
  Port Angeles *(G-7753)*

SHIPPING AGENTS

General Steamship Intl Ltd ....G...... 425 329-1040
  Lynnwood *(G-6128)*
Kitsap Business Services Inc ....G...... 360 297-2173
  Kingston *(G-5257)*

SHIPPING DOCUMENTS PREPARATION SVCS

Kingston Mail Center Inc ....G...... 360 297-2173
  Kingston *(G-5256)*

SHIPS WHOLESALERS

Northwest Yachts Inc ....G...... 360 299-0777
  Anacortes *(G-156)*

SHOCK ABSORBERS: Indl

Innofresh LLC ....G...... 206 438-3541
  Seattle *(G-10239)*

SHOE & BOOT ACCESS

DBa Euroimport Company Inc ....G...... 206 763-7303
  Seattle *(G-9805)*

SHOE MATERIALS: Counters

Counterpane Inc ....G...... 253 535-0145
  Tacoma *(G-13245)*
Precision Counter Tech Inc ....G...... 425 486-8629
  Kent *(G-5075)*
Solid Solutions Inc ....G...... 360 882-9074
  Vancouver *(G-14599)*

SHOE MATERIALS: Quarters

Eagles Eductl Consulting LLC ....G...... 360 482-6093
  Elma *(G-3245)*
Fence Quarter LLC ....G...... 800 205-0128
  Lynnwood *(G-6119)*
French Quarter ....G...... 509 624-5350
  Spokane *(G-12265)*
Irish Acres Foundation Quarter ....G...... 360 966-4677
  Everson *(G-3679)*
Monte Whtzel Con Qarter Cir Ha ....G...... 509 220-8449
  Springdale *(G-12951)*
No Quarter LLC ....G...... 206 412-4311
  Kirkland *(G-5411)*
Sunrise W Quarter Horses LLC ....G...... 509 780-9426
  Clarkston *(G-2650)*
West Quarter Horses LLC ....G...... 360 969-0791
  Oak Harbor *(G-7168)*

SHOE STORES

Fleet Feet Sports ....G...... 509 309-2174
  Spokane Valley *(G-12704)*
Indiana Harness Co ....G...... 509 535-3400
  Spokane Valley *(G-12738)*

SHOE STORES: Athletic

Action Sports & Locks Inc ....G...... 360 435-9505
  Arlington *(G-193)*
Alki Sports LLC ....F...... 206 898-1305
  Redmond *(G-8378)*

SHOE STORES: Boots, Men's

Whites Boots Inc ....C...... 509 535-1875
  Spokane *(G-12589)*

SHOE STORES: Custom & Orthopedic

Stuart Orthotics LLC ....G...... 360 577-3505
  Longview *(G-5957)*

SHOE STORES: Men's

Rah Inc ....E...... 509 482-0943
  Spokane Valley *(G-12849)*

SHOES & BOOTS WHOLESALERS

Fleet Feet Sports ....G...... 509 309-2174
  Spokane Valley *(G-12704)*

SHOES: Infants' & Children's

No Name Boot Company ....G...... 509 226-1980
  Otis Orchards *(G-7515)*

PRODUCT SECTION

SIGNS & ADVERTISING SPECIALTIES

Red Wing Brands America Inc ....G....... 651 388-6233
  Everett *(G-3597)*

SHOES: Men's

Billdon LLC ....G....... 425 736-4316
  Sammamish *(G-9190)*
Kulien Shoe Factory ....G....... 360 736-6943
  Centralia *(G-2414)*
North Star Trading Co LLP ....G....... 360 341-2953
  Clinton *(G-2692)*
Rah Inc ....E....... 509 482-0943
  Spokane Valley *(G-12849)*
Snowden Brothers LLC ....G....... 206 624-1752
  Bellevue *(G-1142)*

SHOES: Plastic Or Rubber

AAA Victory Vending Inc ....G....... 425 235-0378
  Renton *(G-8725)*
Nike Inc ....G....... 206 527-3554
  Seattle *(G-10609)*
Nike Inc ....G....... 425 747-2848
  Bellevue *(G-1031)*

SHOES: Sandals, Rubber

Combat Flip Flops LLC ....G....... 206 913-9971
  Issaquah *(G-4396)*
Combat Flip Flops LLC ....G....... 206 913-9971
  Issaquah *(G-4397)*

SHOES: Women's

Billdon LLC ....G....... 425 736-4316
  Sammamish *(G-9190)*
Kulien Shoe Factory ....G....... 360 736-6943
  Centralia *(G-2414)*
North Star Trading Co LLP ....G....... 360 341-2953
  Clinton *(G-2692)*
Rah Inc ....E....... 509 482-0943
  Spokane Valley *(G-12849)*
Snowden Brothers LLC ....G....... 206 624-1752
  Bellevue *(G-1142)*
Whites Boots Inc ....C....... 509 535-1875
  Spokane *(G-12589)*

SHOES: Women's, Dress

Domino Fashion LLC ....G....... 425 646-0500
  Bellevue *(G-879)*

SHOWCASES & DISPLAY FIXTURES: Office & Store

Idx Corporation ....C....... 253 445-9000
  Puyallup *(G-8165)*
Out For A Walk ....G....... 360 793-4419
  Sultan *(G-13031)*
Pacific Integrated Hdlg Inc ....E....... 253 535-5888
  Tacoma *(G-13451)*
Spokane Discount and Brass Co ....G....... 509 467-8063
  Spokane *(G-12517)*

SHOWER STALLS: Plastic & Fiberglass

Aquatic Co ....C....... 360 458-3900
  Yelm *(G-15727)*

SHREDDERS: Indl & Commercial

Ci Support LLC ....G....... 509 586-6090
  Kennewick *(G-4644)*
Document MGT Archives LLC ....G....... 360 501-5047
  Longview *(G-5906)*
McLane Foodservice Dist Inc ....G....... 253 891-6943
  Sumner *(G-13085)*
Shredfast Mobile Data Destruct .....E....... 509 244-7076
  Airway Heights *(G-63)*
Shredsupply Inc ....G....... 509 235-3800
  Cheney *(G-2593)*
Ultrashred LLC ....G....... 509 244-1894
  Spokane Valley *(G-12919)*

SHUTTERS, DOOR & WINDOW: Metal

Fabtek Industries Llc ....F....... 360 322-7367
  Arlington *(G-235)*
Shutterpated ....G....... 360 607-9692
  Bothell *(G-1904)*
Shutterworks LLC ....G....... 509 731-4619
  Yakima *(G-15674)*

SHUTTERS: Window, Wood

Alan and Linda Murray LLC ....G....... 206 527-0841
  Seattle *(G-9364)*

SIDING & STRUCTURAL MATERIALS: Wood

Acme Forge ....G....... 253 217-3801
  Auburn *(G-360)*
Builders Firstsource Inc ....E....... 253 847-2900
  Graham *(G-4217)*
E-Green Building Systems ....G....... 206 219-9236
  Seattle *(G-9867)*
Mutual Materials Company Inc ......G....... 253 589-6434
  Tacoma *(G-13423)*
Valley Supply Company ....E....... 360 217-4400
  Woodinville *(G-15398)*

SIDING MATERIALS

Remsing Enterprises ....G....... 360 521-8049
  Vancouver *(G-14542)*

SIGN LETTERING & PAINTING SVCS

Athletic Awards Company Inc ....G....... 206 624-3995
  Seattle *(G-9452)*
King Graphics ....G....... 360 423-9781
  Kelso *(G-4534)*
Spectrum Sign Co Inc ....F....... 253 939-5500
  Auburn *(G-570)*

SIGN PAINTING & LETTERING SHOP

Bellandi Signs Inc ....G....... 253 841-1144
  Puyallup *(G-8129)*
Budget Signs Inc ....G....... 253 473-1760
  Fircrest *(G-4000)*
Flexabili-Tees ....G....... 360 260-3163
  Vancouver *(G-14234)*
Foley Sign Company Inc ....F....... 206 324-3040
  Seattle *(G-10011)*
Larsen Sign Company ....G....... 253 581-4313
  Lakewood *(G-5736)*
Markon Inc ....G....... 503 222-3966
  Vancouver *(G-14395)*
Messenger Corporation ....E....... 206 623-4525
  Seattle *(G-10518)*
Meyer Sign & Advertising Co ....F....... 360 424-1325
  Mount Vernon *(G-6813)*
Morup Signs Inc ....G....... 425 883-6337
  Bellevue *(G-1015)*
OMega Graphics and Signs LLC ....G....... 206 789-5480
  Seattle *(G-10697)*
Rumpeltes Enterprises Inc ....E....... 509 624-1391
  Spokane *(G-12485)*
Solar Graphics Inc ....G....... 509 248-1129
  Yakima *(G-15678)*

SIGNALING APPARATUS: Electric

Almx-Security Inc ....G....... 425 485-3801
  Kenmore *(G-4564)*
Highway Specialties LLC ....G....... 360 823-0511
  Vancouver *(G-14298)*
SES USA Inc ....G....... 425 485-3801
  Kenmore *(G-4604)*

SIGNALING DEVICES: Sound, Electrical

NW Utility Services LLC ....E....... 253 891-7802
  Pacific *(G-7536)*

SIGNALS: Traffic Control, Electric

McCain Inc ....G....... 760 734-5086
  Issaquah *(G-4446)*
Northwest Traffic Control Inc ....G....... 360 604-5655
  Brush Prairie *(G-2038)*
Western Systems Inc ....E....... 425 438-1133
  Everett *(G-3656)*

SIGNALS: Transportation

Advanced Traffic Products Inc ....F....... 425 347-6208
  Everett *(G-3361)*
B C Traffic ....G....... 360 895-1000
  Port Orchard *(G-7790)*
K & D Services Inc ....G....... 425 252-0906
  Everett *(G-3527)*
National Barricade & Sign Co ....G....... 509 534-2619
  Spokane Valley *(G-12801)*
Road-Iq LLC ....F....... 360 733-4151
  Bellingham *(G-1518)*

Top Notch Manufacturing Co ....G....... 360 577-9150
  Longview *(G-5960)*

SIGNS & ADVERTISING SPECIALTIES

A-1 Illuminated Sign Company ......F....... 509 534-6134
  Spokane Valley *(G-12596)*
A-1 Pro Sign ....G....... 425 765-8836
  Renton *(G-8724)*
Accent Signs Inc ....G....... 509 967-7446
  Richland *(G-8965)*
Ad Sign Design ....G....... 425 259-3000
  Everett *(G-3359)*
Ada Signage and Spc Inc ....G....... 253 651-1748
  Eatonville *(G-3049)*
Advanced Signs LLC ....G....... 253 987-5909
  Auburn *(G-363)*
Advertising Signs & More ....G....... 360 452-7785
  Port Angeles *(G-7678)*
Alderwood Signs ....G....... 425 744-6555
  Lynnwood *(G-6070)*
Allpak Container LLC ....D....... 425 227-0400
  Renton *(G-8739)*
American Architectural Signage ....G....... 509 624-5842
  Spokane *(G-12108)*
American Laser Works ....G....... 360 871-3738
  Port Orchard *(G-7787)*
American Sign & Indicator ....G....... 509 926-6979
  Spokane Valley *(G-12615)*
Amigo Arts LLC ....G....... 425 443-5744
  Monroe *(G-6549)*
Arrows Sign Servicing LLC ....G....... 206 412-4922
  Federal Way *(G-3716)*
Artco Sign Co Inc ....G....... 206 622-5262
  Seattle *(G-9439)*
ASAP Sign & Design ....G....... 360 757-1570
  Mount Vernon *(G-6771)*
Asi Signage Innovations ....G....... 360 668-1636
  Snohomish *(G-11876)*
Baby Signs By Laurie Hals ....G....... 425 557-6537
  Sammamish *(G-9187)*
Bal & Bal 200803466 Inc ....G....... 425 481-4900
  Everett *(G-3382)*
Balcony Signs & Laminating ....G....... 425 454-5500
  Bellevue *(G-805)*
Barking Dog Inc ....G....... 425 822-6542
  Kirkland *(G-5288)*
Bc Signs Inc ....G....... 360 835-3570
  Camas *(G-2231)*
Bellandi Signs Inc ....G....... 253 841-1144
  Puyallup *(G-8129)*
Birklor LLC ....G....... 206 368-7331
  Seattle *(G-9532)*
Blazing Banners ....G....... 360 756-9990
  Bellingham *(G-1275)*
Blue Water Projects Inc ....F....... 206 452-1332
  Seattle *(G-9554)*
Bolander Sign Co ....G....... 360 943-2447
  Olympia *(G-7239)*
Bondarchuk Andrey ....G....... 509 290-2525
  Spokane Valley *(G-12644)*
Brighten Sign ....G....... 360 608-5863
  Vancouver *(G-14085)*
Budget Signs Inc ....G....... 253 473-1760
  Fircrest *(G-4000)*
Bullene Sign ....G....... 425 260-3311
  Seattle *(G-9598)*
CBS Outdoor ....G....... 509 892-4720
  Spokane Valley *(G-12652)*
Central Wash Media Group LLC ....G....... 509 667-8112
  Wenatchee *(G-15018)*
Central Washington Sign Co ....G....... 509 765-1818
  Moses Lake *(G-6691)*
Christine Woodcock ....G....... 509 773-4747
  Goldendale *(G-4194)*
Classic Sign and Graphics ....G....... 253 862-8035
  Buckley *(G-2051)*
Classic Vinyl LLC ....G....... 509 656-3011
  Cle Elum *(G-2661)*
Clearway Signs ....G....... 253 324-1706
  Tacoma *(G-13236)*
Cogent Holdings-1 LLC ....G....... 425 776-8835
  Everett *(G-3422)*
Cogent Holdings-1 LLC ....E....... 425 776-8835
  Tacoma *(G-13237)*
Color Grphics Scrnprinting Inc ......F....... 360 352-3970
  Tumwater *(G-13862)*
Columbia Basin Sign and Ltg ....G....... 509 764-8121
  Moses Lake *(G-6697)*
Commercial Displayers ....G....... 206 622-8039
  Everett *(G-3424)*

Employee Codes: A=Over 500 employees, B=251-500
C=101-250, D=51-100, E=20-50, F=10-19, G=2-9

Commercial Plastics Corp F 206 682-4832
Seattle *(G-9717)*

Copy Cat Graphics G 360 452-3635
Port Angeles *(G-7695)*

Corwin Scott Thomas Imag G 253 350-6984
Edgewood *(G-3074)*

Cottage Sign Co G 360 312-1565
Ferndale *(G-3834)*

Countryman Signs Screen Prtrs G 425 355-1037
Everett *(G-3428)*

Creating Memories Together G 360 944-8393
Vancouver *(G-14153)*

Creative ADS G 360 981-1106
Silverdale *(G-11829)*

Creative Enterprises Inc G 425 775-7010
Edmonds *(G-3105)*

Creative Imagery G 360 871-6529
Port Orchard *(G-7801)*

Custom Win Tnting Graphics Inc G 509 453-4293
Yakima *(G-15547)*

D A Graphics Inc G 206 760-5886
Seattle *(G-9777)*

Decal Factory G 509 465-8931
Spokane *(G-12222)*

Dek Enterprises Inc G 360 794-8614
Monroe *(G-6564)*

Department Crrctons Wash State B 509 526-6375
Walla Walla *(G-14795)*

Design Centre G 509 534-6461
Spokane *(G-12225)*

Dick and Janes Spot G 509 925-3224
Ellensburg *(G-3193)*

Eagle Scoreboard Systems G 509 751-7228
Clarkston *(G-2634)*

Eagles Nest Holding Inc G 206 368-7331
Seattle *(G-9869)*

Econo Quality Signs Inc G 253 531-3943
Tacoma *(G-13270)*

Econo Sign of America G 360 739-8480
Bellingham *(G-1329)*

Eden Sign G 360 377-3040
Bremerton *(G-1951)*

Effective Design Studio LLC G 206 328-8989
Seattle *(G-9887)*

Electric Avenue Sign Co G 360 903-5447
Vancouver *(G-14197)*

Expressions Signs Inc G 425 844-6415
Monroe *(G-6571)*

Fast Sign Man LLC G 360 592-4599
Deming *(G-2919)*

Fast Signs G 253 942-9444
Federal Way *(G-3736)*

Fastsigns G 206 682-2129
Seattle *(G-9977)*

Fastsigns G 425 746-4151
Bellevue *(G-908)*

Fastsigns G 360 567-3313
Vancouver *(G-14224)*

Fastsigns G 206 886-3860
Seattle *(G-9978)*

Fastsigns G 360 692-1660
Silverdale *(G-11834)*

Fastsigns G 206 575-2110
Kent *(G-4904)*

Fastsigns 632 G 206 577-4077
Burien *(G-2107)*

Fastsigns International Inc G 253 835-9450
Federal Way *(G-3737)*

Fastsigns of Auburn G 360 480-1097
Kent *(G-4905)*

Felts Signs G 360 299-0430
Anacortes *(G-129)*

Flip Signs G 509 965-2822
Yakima *(G-15572)*

Flying Arts Ranch Inc G 509 659-1819
Ritzville *(G-9121)*

Foley Sign Company Inc F 206 324-3040
Seattle *(G-10011)*

Footprint Promotions Inc G 425 408-0966
Woodinville *(G-15245)*

Gerrard Inc G 253 804-8001
Auburn *(G-449)*

Global Professional Svcs LLC G 808 682-0404
University Place *(G-13970)*

Gotagscom LLC G 509 754-2760
Ephrata *(G-3335)*

Grand D Signs G 253 929-9963
Federal Way *(G-3742)*

Graphic Art Productions Inc G 509 536-3278
Spokane Valley *(G-12723)*

Great Graphics & Signs Inc F 206 948-9480
Orondo *(G-7457)*

Greensleeves LLC G 360 606-1934
Vancouver *(G-14273)*

Hafa Adai Signs & Graphics LLC G 253 394-0600
Auburn *(G-458)*

Holm Bing F 509 454-2277
Yakima *(G-15581)*

Home Design Expo G 425 864-6313
Redmond *(G-8495)*

I Concept Signs LLC G 206 658-1158
Seattle *(G-10199)*

Image Signs and Design LLC G 360 533-0133
Hoquiam *(G-4344)*

Imagesmart Sign Company LLC G 509 525-4343
Walla Walla *(G-14821)*

Imagicorps Inc E 425 869-0599
Redmond *(G-8506)*

In The Zone Promotions G 425 246-6313
Issaquah *(G-4428)*

Incentives By Design Inc G 206 623-4310
Seattle *(G-10220)*

Indigo Vinylworks LLC G 425 463-7460
Renton *(G-8823)*

Indigo Vinylworks Llc G 425 278-4411
Seattle *(G-10227)*

Infinity Sign & Marketing Inc G 253 539-6771
Lakewood *(G-5728)*

Insignia Sign Inc F 425 917-2109
Renton *(G-8827)*

International Trade & Trvl Ltd G 509 981-2307
Spokane *(G-12324)*

Island Dog Sign Company F 206 381-0661
Duvall *(G-2991)*

Issaquah Signs Inc G 425 391-3010
Issaquah *(G-4431)*

J Freitag Enterprises Inc G 509 453-4461
Yakima *(G-15595)*

Jakes Electrical Sign Service G 509 901-1012
Selah *(G-11592)*

James I Manning G 425 774-4275
Edmonds *(G-3122)*

Johnson Signs of Federal Way G 253 678-4304
Tacoma *(G-13366)*

Jolly Family Corp G 425 438-9350
Everett *(G-3525)*

Jrotc Dog Tags Inc G 509 292-0410
Elk *(G-3170)*

King Graphics G 360 423-9781
Kelso *(G-4534)*

Kjj Enterprises Inc G 253 474-6607
Tacoma *(G-13377)*

Kolorkraze G 360 609-2771
Vancouver *(G-14351)*

Kts Media Inc G 253 845-0771
Puyallup *(G-8173)*

Landd Ventures Inc G 425 775-9709
Lynnwood *(G-6156)*

Larsen Sign Company G 253 581-4313
Lakewood *(G-5736)*

Leader Manufacturing Inc E 360 895-1184
Port Orchard *(G-7825)*

Lee Signs G 360 750-0689
Vancouver *(G-14370)*

Lennox Ergonomics & Co G 253 268-0830
Gig Harbor *(G-4130)*

Lettering Arts G 206 310-6599
Bellevue *(G-982)*

Lid Signs LLC G 206 290-7536
Seattle *(G-10414)*

Lifesigns Plus G 425 330-3710
Lake Stevens *(G-5656)*

Linden Vic B & Sons Sign Advg G 509 624-0663
Spokane *(G-12368)*

LLC Putnam Brothers G 509 679-4981
Quincy *(G-8302)*

Loewen Group LLC G 425 775-9709
Lynnwood *(G-6159)*

Lonnies Sign Service G 509 543-7446
Pasco *(G-7601)*

Loomis Plastics Corporation E 206 292-0111
Seattle *(G-10439)*

Magic Mountains Services Inc G 360 830-0634
Seabeck *(G-9268)*

Magnolia Signs G 253 592-5121
Tacoma *(G-13395)*

Mail It Sign It LLC G 360 515-5198
Tumwater *(G-13886)*

Maple Valley Signs Inc G 425 413-1430
Maple Valley *(G-6282)*

Mark Lasting Technology G 425 836-4317
Redmond *(G-8550)*

Medford Technologies Inc G 206 963-0589
Tukwila *(G-13769)*

Media Incorporated G 425 251-5145
Renton *(G-8851)*

Merrill Corporation C 360 794-3157
Monroe *(G-6596)*

Meyer Sign & Advertising Co F 360 424-1325
Mount Vernon *(G-6813)*

Michael L White G 509 526-6923
Walla Walla *(G-14843)*

Morup Signs Inc G 425 883-6337
Bellevue *(G-1015)*

Mustang Signs LLC F 509 735-4607
Kennewick *(G-4698)*

Neon Moon Longhorned Cattle G 360 293-2721
Anacortes *(G-150)*

Nwsignwerxs G 253 217-0053
Auburn *(G-515)*

Olympic Print and Apparel G 206 402-3642
Seattle *(G-10693)*

OMega Graphics and Signs LLC G 206 789-5480
Seattle *(G-10697)*

Pad Printing Services Inc G 206 362-4544
Seattle *(G-10744)*

Patrick E & Patricia M Lydon G 425 226-3216
Renton *(G-8876)*

Patriot Towing Recovery G 360 890-9288
Lacey *(G-5575)*

Patriot Wood LLC G 360 393-7082
Ferndale *(G-3883)*

PDQ Signs G 253 531-8010
Puyallup *(G-8220)*

Peekay Inc F 818 754-1201
Auburn *(G-529)*

Pens By Bill G 509 628-3288
Kennewick *(G-4706)*

Perfect Printing & Signs G 509 786-3811
Yakima *(G-15645)*

Petroglyph Printing & Signs G 509 447-2590
Newport *(G-7064)*

Phoenix Sign Company F 360 612-3267
Aberdeen *(G-29)*

Pixelan Works G 425 379-0339
Everett *(G-3574)*

Premium Sign Inc G 253 267-0547
Lakewood *(G-5748)*

Quick Signs and Designs G 253 929-4488
Kent *(G-5095)*

R & R Graphics Inc G 206 406-3604
Renton *(G-8889)*

R E B Magnetics G 360 636-4693
Kelso *(G-4545)*

R P Signs Screenprinting G 425 788-6717
Duvall *(G-3000)*

Rainier Industries Ltd C 425 251-1800
Tukwila *(G-13801)*

Ramlyn Engraving & Sign Co G 206 439-8555
Burien *(G-2124)*

Ramsay Signs Inc G 206 623-3100
Seattle *(G-10919)*

Realty Sign Guys G 360 909-1540
Vancouver *(G-14536)*

Realty Solutions Inc F 206 839-1023
Seattle *(G-10932)*

Rnd Sign and Design LLC G 206 255-1963
Federal Way *(G-3778)*

Russell Sign Company G 425 775-7010
Edmonds *(G-3150)*

Sandys Sign & Design G 360 693-9229
Vancouver *(G-14569)*

Satellite Sign Design G 360 986-0067
Montesano *(G-6657)*

Schurmans Gas & Glass G 360 573-3669
Ridgefield *(G-9110)*

Screen Print Northwest Inc G 360 577-1534
Longview *(G-5951)*

Screen Tek Inc E 509 928-8322
Liberty Lake *(G-5860)*

Seaton Concepts Inc G 509 928-0633
Spokane Valley *(G-12862)*

Seattle Engraving LLC G 425 212-9797
Everett *(G-3609)*

Seattle Wood Signs G 425 422-3750
Seattle *(G-11084)*

Servine Sign Services LLC G 509 225-7733
Yakima *(G-15672)*

Sign A Rama G 360 915-9207
Lacey *(G-5587)*

Sign Biz.....G..... 360 750-9175
Vancouver *(G-14586)*
Sign By Tommorrow Kent.....G..... 253 872-7844
Kent *(G-5131)*
Sign City Gfx.....G..... 253 329-2670
Auburn *(G-563)*
Sign Company.....G..... 253 630-6313
Covington *(G-2838)*
Sign Crafters Inc.....G..... 509 783-8718
Kennewick *(G-4727)*
Sign Department Inc.....G..... 360 708-3823
Mount Vernon *(G-6836)*
Sign Distributors.....G..... 253 847-2747
Spanaway *(G-12073)*
Sign Guys Inc.....G..... 253 942-3688
Federal Way *(G-3784)*
Sign Junkies.....G..... 360 273-7553
Olympia *(G-7393)*
Sign Language Interpreter & En.....G..... 509 860-2727
Wenatchee *(G-15074)*
Sign Makers Inc.....G..... 425 828-0688
Kirkland *(G-5460)*
Sign ME Up Inc.....G..... 360 271-8070
Port Ludlow *(G-7776)*
Sign of Times.....G..... 360 891-9477
Vancouver *(G-14587)*
Sign Prints Inc.....G..... 253 854-7841
Kent *(G-5132)*
Sign Rite.....G..... 253 447-8997
Sumner *(G-13099)*
Sign Wizard.....G..... 206 285-9535
Seattle *(G-11106)*
Sign-A-Rama.....G..... 253 474-1991
Tacoma *(G-13513)*
Sign-O-Lite.....G..... 360 746-8651
Blaine *(G-1703)*
Signage.....G..... 206 903-6446
Seattle *(G-11107)*
Signdezign LLC.....G..... 360 709-0505
Olympia *(G-7394)*
Signorama.....G..... 425 861-9341
Redmond *(G-8667)*
Signs & Designs.....G..... 509 493-8350
White Salmon *(G-15132)*
Signs 2c.....G..... 206 335-9519
Seattle *(G-11109)*
Signs By Tomorrow.....G..... 360 676-7117
Bellingham *(G-1534)*
Signs For Success.....G..... 509 489-4200
Spokane *(G-12504)*
Signs Now In Process Inc.....G..... 509 928-3467
Spokane Valley *(G-12873)*
Signs Now of Moses Lake Inc.....G..... 509 765-8955
Moses Lake *(G-6750)*
Signs of Grace.....G..... 509 488-5081
Othello *(G-7505)*
Signs of Seattle Inc.....G..... 206 292-7446
Seattle *(G-11110)*
Signs Plus Inc.....F..... 360 671-7165
Bellingham *(G-1535)*
Signsmart USA.....G..... 360 578-2476
Kelso *(G-4548)*
Signworks LLC.....G..... 206 715-1570
Bellevue *(G-1131)*
Sjb Enterprises Inc.....G..... 509 926-6979
Spokane Valley *(G-12874)*
Skagit City Signs Inc.....G..... 360 848-8888
Mount Vernon *(G-6838)*
Sky Signs Inc.....G..... 425 417-9063
Renton *(G-8913)*
Slam Signs.....G..... 253 927-2616
Federal Way *(G-3785)*
Socal Lighting & Sign LLC.....G..... 425 345-5596
Sultan *(G-13037)*
Spanton Business Forms.....G..... 509 966-7384
Yakima *(G-15681)*
Special T Signs & Graphics.....F..... 360 734-7617
Bellingham *(G-1549)*
Spectrum Sign Co Inc.....F..... 253 939-5500
Auburn *(G-570)*
Spiller Corporation.....G..... 206 575-2110
Kent *(G-5150)*
Spring Creek Enterprises.....G..... 360 876-8884
Port Orchard *(G-7852)*
Steve Boek Mfg.....G..... 503 257-5056
Sultan *(G-13039)*
Sticker Shock Signs Inc.....G..... 509 535-0070
Spokane *(G-12530)*
Stong Enterprises LLC.....G..... 360 326-4752
Vancouver *(G-14613)*
Sudden Printing Inc.....E..... 206 243-4444
Seattle *(G-11211)*
Supergraphics LLC.....E..... 206 284-2201
Seattle *(G-11221)*
Tacoma Tent & Awning Co Inc.....E..... 253 627-4128
Tacoma *(G-13549)*
Terry Signs.....G..... 509 662-6672
Wenatchee *(G-15081)*
TNT Signs Inc.....G..... 360 438-3800
Lacey *(G-5595)*
Todd Porter Campbell.....G..... 253 230-2391
Buckley *(G-2077)*
Top Notch Manufacturing Co.....G..... 360 577-9150
Longview *(G-5960)*
Total Sign Service.....G..... 253 847-6868
Eatonville *(G-3070)*
Traffic Signs Inc.....G..... 425 333-6222
Carnation *(G-2301)*
Tube Art Displays Inc.....G..... 509 469-8186
Yakima *(G-15697)*
United Visual Comms Grp LLC.....G..... 206 228-5144
Seattle *(G-11375)*
Universal Sign and Graphics.....G..... 253 630-0400
Kent *(G-5198)*
US Sign Girl.....G..... 801 644-1108
Issaquah *(G-4485)*
US Sign One LLC.....G..... 253 236-8074
Puyallup *(G-8269)*
Viar Visual Communications.....G..... 425 391-8443
Sammamish *(G-9257)*
Victory Circle Signs.....G..... 509 489-3083
Spokane *(G-12582)*
Vilmas Family Corporation.....G..... 253 941-9008
Federal Way *(G-3801)*
Vinyl Lab NW LLC.....G..... 425 870-8702
Lynnwood *(G-6219)*
Vital Signs Ministries.....G..... 360 659-2726
Tulalip *(G-13846)*
Vital Signs Notary.....G..... 206 387-6622
Kent *(G-5203)*
Watsons Wooden Words LLC.....G..... 253 348-7995
Bonney Lake *(G-1742)*
Wdk Signs.....G..... 509 758-0483
Clarkston *(G-2653)*
Western Graphics Inc.....G..... 206 241-2526
Fife *(G-3998)*
Whats Your Sign Inc.....G..... 253 475-7446
Tacoma *(G-13596)*
Whidbey Island Sign Sltons LLC.....G..... 360 299-0430
Burlington *(G-2201)*
Whidbey Sign Co.....G..... 360 720-2015
Oak Harbor *(G-7173)*
Wildrose Ltd.....F..... 509 535-8555
Spokane *(G-12591)*
Winsor Fireform LLC.....E..... 360 786-8200
Tumwater *(G-13907)*
Wizz Signs.....G..... 360 779-3103
Poulsbo *(G-8021)*
X Bolt Signs LLC.....G..... 509 945-6780
Naches *(G-7008)*
Young Gun NW.....G..... 360 996-4275
Chehalis *(G-2544)*
Zumar Industries Inc.....D..... 253 536-7740
Tacoma *(G-13608)*

SIGNS & ADVERTISING SPECIALTIES: Artwork, Advertising

Ad One Corp.....G..... 253 942-3688
Federal Way *(G-3712)*
Dancing Clouds LLC.....G..... 360 289-0790
Ocean Shores *(G-7185)*
Prism Graphics Inc.....G..... 206 282-1801
Seattle *(G-10866)*
Reyna Moore Advertising.....G..... 503 230-9440
Vancouver *(G-14550)*
Upright Posts LLC.....G..... 253 224-0076
Sumner *(G-13109)*

SIGNS & ADVERTISING SPECIALTIES: Displays, Paint Process

Elevation Exhibits LLC.....E..... 774 696-2549
Redmond *(G-8448)*

SIGNS & ADVERTISING SPECIALTIES: Letters For Signs, Metal

Dynamic Specialties.....G..... 509 447-2755
Newport *(G-7057)*
Shine On Signs & Graphics Inc.....G..... 253 243-7777
Renton *(G-8910)*
Wells Signs Mfg & Distrg.....G..... 360 225-0520
Woodland *(G-15474)*

SIGNS & ADVERTISING SPECIALTIES: Novelties

Abracadabra Printing Inc.....G..... 206 343-9087
Seattle *(G-9334)*

SIGNS & ADVERTISING SPECIALTIES: Signs

Accent Signs & Engraving Inc.....G..... 509 946-8998
Richland *(G-8964)*
Advance Sign Design Inc.....G..... 206 789-6051
Seattle *(G-9354)*
Advanced Metal Creations.....G..... 509 662-0335
Wenatchee *(G-15008)*
Apco Northwest.....F..... 800 815-8028
Tukwila *(G-13691)*
Bear Signs.....G..... 509 888-4477
Wenatchee *(G-15012)*
Bellevue Instant Sign.....G..... 425 451-8218
Redmond *(G-8401)*
Blanc Industries Inc.....E..... 360 736-8988
Centralia *(G-2385)*
Brown & Balsley Sign Co.....G..... 360 705-3099
Olympia *(G-7243)*
Colville Sign Co.....G..... 509 685-2185
Colville *(G-2746)*
Creo Industrial Arts LLC.....D..... 425 775-7444
Woodinville *(G-15216)*
Crossroads Sign & Graphic.....G..... 425 481-9411
Lynnwood *(G-6101)*
Davis Sign Company Inc.....G..... 206 287-9800
Seattle *(G-9802)*
Eastside Signs.....G..... 425 888-6764
Snoqualmie *(G-12011)*
Goodmar Group LLC.....G..... 206 622-8204
Seattle *(G-10101)*
HI Tech Signs & Banners.....G..... 360 736-6322
Centralia *(G-2407)*
Industry Sign & Graphics Inc.....F..... 253 854-2333
Auburn *(G-476)*
Instant Sign Factory.....G..... 509 456-3333
Spokane *(G-12317)*
J N W Inc.....E..... 509 489-9191
Spokane *(G-12327)*
Jackson Signs & Graphics.....G..... 360 457-3703
Port Angeles *(G-7716)*
Jamison Signs Inc.....G..... 509 226-2000
Newman Lake *(G-7048)*
K L Cook Inc.....G..... 360 423-0195
Longview *(G-5921)*
Kitsap Business Services Inc.....G..... 360 297-2173
Kingston *(G-5257)*
Liberty Sign Shoppe LLC.....G..... 425 482-2811
Woodinville *(G-15289)*
Lumin Art Signs Inc.....G..... 253 833-2800
Tacoma *(G-13392)*
Messenger Corporation.....E..... 206 623-4525
Seattle *(G-10518)*
Mike Lavalle Inc.....G..... 360 563-0501
Snohomish *(G-11947)*
National Sign Systems Ltd.....G..... 360 699-3055
Vancouver *(G-14427)*
North West Barricades & Signs.....E..... 206 243-8004
Seattle *(G-10629)*
Olysigns.....G..... 360 417-5254
Port Angeles *(G-7730)*
OReilly Signs.....G..... 206 623-5135
Seattle *(G-10713)*
Rainmaker Signs Inc.....G..... 425 861-7446
Bellevue *(G-1091)*
Reid Signs Inc.....G..... 206 547-5487
Seattle *(G-10945)*
Sandis Signs Inc.....G..... 253 862-6885
Bonney Lake *(G-1737)*
Sign Associates Inc.....G..... 425 885-6100
Redmond *(G-8664)*
Sign Man.....G..... 509 535-8181
Spokane Valley *(G-12872)*
Sign Post Inc.....F..... 360 671-1343
Bellingham *(G-1533)*
Sign Pros Inc.....F..... 425 885-3204
Redmond *(G-8665)*
Sign Up Sign Co Inc.....G..... 425 488-9247
Bothell *(G-1792)*
Skagit Valley Signs.....G..... 360 755-0356
Acme *(G-45)*

PRODUCT

SIGNS & ADVERTISING SPECIALTIES: Signs

Steve Ken Bosman .... G 360 398-7444
  Bellingham *(G-1558)*
Tacoma Rubber Stamp Co .... E 253 383-5433
  Tacoma *(G-13548)*
TNT Signs & Design Inc .... G 360 384-3190
  Ferndale *(G-3914)*
Woodinville Signs Inc .... G 425 483-0296
  Woodinville *(G-15407)*

SIGNS & ADVERTSG SPECIALTIES: Displays/Cutouts Window/Lobby

American Image Displays .... F 425 556-9511
  Port Orchard *(G-7786)*
Seatons Grove Greenhouse .... G 509 633-0404
  Coulee Dam *(G-2808)*
Veva Company LLC .... G 360 687-8550
  Battle Ground *(G-749)*

SIGNS, ELECTRICAL: Wholesalers

Ramsay Signs Inc .... G 206 623-3100
  Seattle *(G-10919)*
Viar Visual Communications .... G 425 391-8443
  Sammamish *(G-9257)*

SIGNS, EXC ELECTRIC, WHOLESALE

Badge Boys Awards & Engraving .... G 360 876-8414
  Port Orchard *(G-7792)*
Cogent Holdings-1 LLC .... G 425 776-8835
  Everett *(G-3422)*
Fedex Office & Print Svcs Inc .... F 253 872-5539
  Kent *(G-4906)*
Fedexoffice .... G 206 467-5885
  Seattle *(G-9982)*
Grays Harbor Stamp Works .... G 360 533-3830
  Aberdeen *(G-14)*
How-Mac Manufacturing Inc .... E 360 855-2649
  Sedro Woolley *(G-11540)*
Signage .... G 206 903-6446
  Seattle *(G-11107)*
Traffic Signs Inc .... G 425 333-6222
  Carnation *(G-2301)*
Viar Visual Communications .... G 425 391-8443
  Sammamish *(G-9257)*
Youngs Neon Sign Co .... G 253 946-1286
  Federal Way *(G-3805)*

SIGNS: Electrical

Acclaim Sign & Display Partner .... G 206 706-3900
  Seattle *(G-9336)*
Advanced Electric Signs Inc .... G 360 225-6826
  Woodland *(G-15416)*
Berry Neon Co Inc .... E 425 776-8835
  Everett *(G-3385)*
Biz Design & Sign .... G 253 472-3070
  Tacoma *(G-13202)*
Cascade Sign .... G 509 945-1578
  Yakima *(G-15531)*
CDI Custom Design Inc .... E 360 650-1150
  Bellingham *(G-1294)*
Columbia Sign .... G 360 696-1919
  Brush Prairie *(G-2032)*
Columbia Sign Inc .... G 360 696-1919
  Vancouver *(G-14138)*
Eagle Signs LLC .... G 509 453-8159
  Yakima *(G-15561)*
Eagle Signs LLC .... F 509 453-5511
  Yakima *(G-15562)*
Federal Way Sign .... G 253 529-2011
  Federal Way *(G-3739)*
Graybeal Signs .... F 509 662-6926
  Wenatchee *(G-15036)*
I-5 Design Build Inc .... D 360 459-3200
  Lacey *(G-5558)*
JJ&d Signs Inc .... G 206 623-3100
  Seattle *(G-10298)*
Magnificent Signs Inc .... G 509 468-2794
  Spokane *(G-12378)*
Mark Grid Signs Inc .... G 509 323-0328
  Spokane *(G-12381)*
Martin Signs & Fabrication .... G 206 768-5183
  Seattle *(G-10494)*
Misapplied Sciences Inc .... G 425 999-9582
  Redmond *(G-8591)*
Mixign Inc .... G 206 542-8737
  Arlington *(G-281)*
Mountain Dog Sign Company Inc .... G 509 891-9999
  Spokane Valley *(G-12794)*

National Sign Corporation .... E 206 282-0700
  Seattle *(G-10590)*
Neon Electric Sign Co .... G 206 405-4001
  Issaquah *(G-4453)*
Phoenix Sign Company .... G 360 532-1111
  Montesano *(G-6653)*
Plumb Signs Inc .... E 253 474-6702
  Tacoma *(G-13466)*
Quality Sign Service Inc .... F 509 586-0585
  Kennewick *(G-4712)*
Rdean Enterprises Inc .... F 208 772-8571
  Spokane *(G-12468)*
Roy Pablo .... G 425 750-9941
  Quil Ceda Village *(G-8281)*
Sign Corporation .... F 509 535-2913
  Spokane *(G-12503)*
Sign Pro Inc .... G 360 736-6322
  Centralia *(G-2434)*
Sign Shop LLC .... G 360 352-5926
  Tumwater *(G-13897)*
Sign Works .... G 509 248-8235
  Yakima *(G-15675)*
Sign-Tech Elc Ltd Lblty Co .... E 253 922-2146
  Fife *(G-3993)*
Signfactory .... G 360 833-1515
  Camas *(G-2282)*
Signsouth .... G 509 448-4404
  Spokane *(G-12505)*
Sno-King Signs .... G 425 775-0594
  Edmonds *(G-3158)*
Speedy Signs .... G 425 771-1700
  Lynnwood *(G-6204)*
Tube Art Displays Inc .... E 206 223-1122
  Bellevue *(G-1204)*
Vancouver Sign Co Inc .... E 360 693-4773
  Vancouver *(G-14663)*
White Signs .... G 425 745-0760
  Lynnwood *(G-6225)*
Young Electric Sign Company .... F 253 722-5753
  Tacoma *(G-13605)*

SIGNS: Neon

American Neon Inc .... F 253 627-7446
  Gig Harbor *(G-4071)*
City Lites Neon Inc .... G 206 789-4747
  Seattle *(G-9687)*
Esco Pacific Signs Inc .... G 360 748-6461
  Chehalis *(G-2493)*
Fox Architectural Signs Inc .... G 503 512-7757
  Woodland *(G-15433)*
Garrett Sign Co Inc .... F 360 693-9081
  Vancouver *(G-14247)*
Jim Manning .... G 425 774-1964
  Edmonds *(G-3124)*
Neon Connection .... G 360 224-3061
  Sumner *(G-13088)*
Neon Systems Inc .... G 425 501-6447
  Lynnwood *(G-6168)*
Noble Neon .... G 206 708-6290
  Seattle *(G-10616)*
Ross Metier LLC .... G 253 208-8777
  Graham *(G-4237)*
Teslavision .... G 425 822-6535
  Kirkland *(G-5479)*
Trade-Marx Sign & Display Corp .... E 206 623-7676
  Seattle *(G-11325)*
Wholesale Neon A Division .... G 253 939-0716
  Auburn *(G-600)*
Youngs Neon Sign Co .... G 253 946-1286
  Federal Way *(G-3805)*

SILICA MINING

Hemphill Brothers Inc .... G 206 842-0748
  Bainbridge Island *(G-639)*
Lane Mt Silica Co .... G 206 762-7622
  Seattle *(G-10376)*

SILICON & CHROMIUM

Rec Silicon Inc .... F 509 793-9000
  Moses Lake *(G-6743)*
Rec Solar Grade Silicon LLC .... C 509 765-2106
  Moses Lake *(G-6744)*

SILICON WAFERS: Chemically Doped

Asimi .... G 509 766-9641
  Moses Lake *(G-6679)*

SILICON: Pure

Silicon Chemical Corporation .... E 360 210-5124
  Washougal *(G-14984)*

SILK SCREEN DESIGN SVCS

Computergear Inc .... G 425 487-3600
  Woodinville *(G-15209)*
Countryman Signs Screen Prtrs .... G 425 355-1037
  Everett *(G-3428)*
Markon Inc .... G 503 222-3966
  Vancouver *(G-14395)*
Purrfect Logos Inc .... G 509 893-2424
  Spokane Valley *(G-12845)*
R E B Magnetics .... G 360 636-4693
  Kelso *(G-4545)*

SILVER ORES

3dx Industries Inc .... G 360 244-4339
  Ferndale *(G-3808)*
Alto Group Holdings Inc .... G 801 816-2520
  Wenatchee *(G-15088)*
Gold Reserve Inc .... G 509 623-1500
  Spokane *(G-12276)*
Helena Silver Mines Inc .... G 509 922-3035
  Spokane Valley *(G-12729)*
Lka Gold Incorporated .... G 253 514-6661
  Gig Harbor *(G-4133)*
Silver King Mining & Milling .... G 509 445-1406
  Cusick *(G-2852)*

SILVERSMITHS

Friedman Slversmiths Repr Pltg .... G 360 752-3119
  Bellingham *(G-1354)*
John Marshall Metalsmith Inc .... G 206 546-5643
  Edmonds *(G-3125)*
Omega Silversmithing Inc .... G 360 863-6771
  Snohomish *(G-11956)*

SIMULATORS: Electronic Countermeasure

Rowperfect 3 .... G 206 331-5319
  Seattle *(G-10983)*

SIRENS: Vehicle, Marine, Indl & Warning

Smelts Sea Mammal Education Le .... G 360 303-9338
  Sedro Woolley *(G-11570)*

SIZES

Life Size 3 D Animal Targ .... G 206 432-9147
  Maple Valley *(G-6280)*
P S Plus Sizes Tukwila .... G 206 575-3690
  Tukwila *(G-13785)*

SKIN CARE PRDTS: Suntan Lotions & Oils

Brown Toes LLC .... G 360 873-8407
  Anacortes *(G-104)*

SKYLIGHTS

Crystalite Inc .... E 425 259-6000
  Everett *(G-3432)*
Crystalite Inc .... G 509 921-9585
  Spokane Valley *(G-12672)*
Crystalite Inc .... E 425 259-6000
  Everett *(G-3433)*
Evergreen House Inc .... F 425 821-1005
  Kirkland *(G-5334)*
Lumenomics Inc .... E 206 327-9037
  Seattle *(G-10451)*

SLAB & TILE, ROOFING: Concrete

Boral Roofing LLC .... E 253 581-3666
  Lakewood *(G-5705)*

SLAB & TILE: Precast Concrete, Floor

Armstrong NW .... G 425 251-0353
  Kent *(G-4791)*
Gc Solutions LLC .... G 509 243-6030
  Asotin *(G-352)*

SLABS: Steel

Kindle Eithan .... G 509 558-7023
  Spokane *(G-12352)*

PRODUCT SECTION

SLATE PRDTS
Southern Explorations ....G..... 206 641-9241
  Seattle *(G-11161)*

SLAUGHTERING & MEAT PACKING
Crowd Cow Inc ....G..... 717 333-0740
  Seattle *(G-9756)*
Owens Meats Inc ....G..... 509 674-2530
  Cle Elum *(G-2674)*
Schenk Packing Co Inc ....E..... 360 336-2128
  Mount Vernon *(G-6834)*
Washington Agricultural Dev ......G..... 509 865-2121
  Toppenish *(G-13673)*
Washington Beef LLC ....A..... 509 865-2121
  Toppenish *(G-13674)*

SLIDES & EXHIBITS: Prepared
Bering Street Studio LLC ....G..... 253 677-4870
  Gig Harbor *(G-4080)*
Mach 2 Arts Inc ....G..... 206 953-0575
  Seattle *(G-10458)*
Pacific Studio Inc ....D..... 206 783-5226
  Seattle *(G-10741)*

SLINGS: Lifting, Made From Purchased Wire
Munks Livestock Sling Mfg ....G..... 360 293-6581
  Anacortes *(G-149)*

SLINGS: Rope
Open Water Splicing ....G..... 360 510-8059
  Ferndale *(G-3881)*

SLOT MACHINES
Agt Inc ....G..... 509 935-6140
  Chewelah *(G-2597)*

SMOKE DETECTORS
Save Smoke ....G..... 425 793-5030
  Renton *(G-8903)*

SMOKERS' ARTICLES: Pottery
Puffin Glass ....G..... 509 328-0661
  Spokane *(G-12458)*

SNOWMOBILES
Holz Enterprises Inc ....G..... 360 398-7006
  Lynden *(G-6022)*
Mountainview Polaris Inc ....G..... 509 765-9340
  Moses Lake *(G-6729)*
Powder Keg LLC ....G..... 509 758-7300
  Clarkston *(G-2641)*
Team Chinook Sales ....G..... 509 949-0929
  Naches *(G-7006)*

SOAPS & DETERGENTS
Agbanga Karite LLC ....G..... 360 515-9013
  Tumwater *(G-13849)*
Azure Mountain Botanicals ....G..... 425 478-3902
  Dayton *(G-2878)*
Bon Logic Corporation ....G..... 509 991-9643
  Spokane *(G-12157)*
Bubbles Bakery ....G..... 360 945-1816
  Point Roberts *(G-7667)*
Curlew Country Herbs ....G..... 509 779-4941
  Curlew *(G-2845)*
Dandelion & Tea LLC ....G..... 206 353-2048
  Seattle *(G-9791)*
Diana Thompson ....G..... 360 665-0102
  Ocean Park *(G-7179)*
Dr Bieseckers LLC ....G..... 360 386-1530
  Stanwood *(G-12967)*
Earth Soap Company ....G..... 425 677-8540
  Issaquah *(G-4408)*
Eliza K Trowbridge ....G..... 360 376-5152
  Olga *(G-7214)*
Heavenly Soap ....G..... 206 349-7982
  Monroe *(G-6575)*
Marvin Batcheller ....G..... 509 784-7018
  Entiat *(G-3267)*
Pureheart ....G..... 509 535-2323
  Spokane *(G-12459)*
Quail Meadow Creations ....G..... 509 685-1429
  Colville *(G-2770)*

Secure It LLC ....G..... 509 992-6190
  Spokane *(G-12497)*
Shepherds Soap Co ....G..... 360 427-7811
  Shelton *(G-11733)*
Something For Everybody ....G..... 541 805-8495
  College Place *(G-2728)*
Venus Laboratories Inc ....E..... 360 455-8933
  Lacey *(G-5598)*

SOAPS & DETERGENTS: Textile
Dave Ledgerwood ....G..... 509 843-3677
  Pomeroy *(G-7671)*
Whidbey Island Ntural Pdts Inc ....G..... 360 929-2461
  Freeland *(G-4040)*

SOCIAL SVCS, HANDICAPPED
Skilskin ....G..... 509 326-6760
  Spokane *(G-12506)*

SOFT DRINKS WHOLESALERS
Bottling Group LLC ....C..... 509 535-0605
  Spokane *(G-12158)*
Coca-Cola Btlg Co of NY Inc ....E..... 509 886-1136
  Wenatchee *(G-15089)*
Pepsi Cola Bottling Co Pasco ......E..... 509 248-1313
  Pasco *(G-7616)*
Shasta Beverages Inc ....E..... 206 575-0525
  Tukwila *(G-13817)*

SOFTWARE PUBLISHERS: Application
8stem Inc ....G..... 360 317-7448
  Eastsound *(G-3036)*
Aav Group ....F..... 972 834-2750
  Bellevue *(G-779)*
Accordent Technologies Inc ....F..... 310 374-7491
  Seattle *(G-9337)*
Adaptelligence LLC ....G..... 509 432-1812
  Pullman *(G-8082)*
Afar Interactive Inc ....G..... 425 442-5101
  Seattle *(G-9357)*
Antenna Dexterra Inc ....G..... 425 939-3100
  Bothell *(G-1819)*
APM Games LLC ....G..... 512 961-6515
  Vancouver *(G-14038)*
App Grinder LLC ....G..... 206 293-9632
  Seattle *(G-9410)*
Appattach Inc ....G..... 425 202-5676
  Kirkland *(G-5279)*
Appesteem Corporation ....F..... 240 461-5689
  Bellevue *(G-789)*
Arcblock Inc ....F..... 425 442-5101
  Bellevue *(G-793)*
Arigato LLC ....G..... 713 492-3858
  Issaquah *(G-4382)*
Ascendance Pole & Aerial Arts ....G..... 425 256-2246
  Renton *(G-8748)*
Barn2door Inc ....G..... 206 459-4338
  Seattle *(G-9493)*
Bcard Inc ....G..... 206 963-5211
  Spokane *(G-12141)*
Bluewave Technologies LLC ....G..... 800 636-1428
  Seattle *(G-9558)*
Bravura Software LLC ....G..... 425 881-7305
  Redmond *(G-8408)*
Budwiz Inc ....G..... 360 508-2771
  Olympia *(G-7246)*
Byteware LLC ....G..... 503 914-8020
  Woodinville *(G-15201)*
Ca Inc ....D..... 509 252-5080
  Spokane *(G-12166)*
Ca Inc ....D..... 425 201-3500
  Bellevue *(G-834)*
Cadence Design Systems Inc ......G..... 425 451-2360
  Bellevue *(G-835)*
Cakes Be We ....G..... 509 460-1399
  Kennewick *(G-4639)*
Campusce Corporation ....G..... 206 686-8003
  Seattle *(G-9615)*
Cardswapper LLC ....G..... 253 549-8600
  Gig Harbor *(G-4084)*
Care Zone Inc ....E..... 206 707-9127
  Seattle *(G-9632)*
Casaba Security LLC ....G..... 888 869-6708
  Redmond *(G-8416)*
Cellar Door Media LLC ....G..... 253 732-9560
  Tacoma *(G-13230)*
Certifly LLC ....G..... 888 415-9119
  Seattle *(G-9660)*

SOFTWARE PUBLISHERS: Application

Champlin Technologies LLC ....G..... 425 736-8935
  Bellevue *(G-849)*
Chekin MD LLC ....G..... 425 894-9896
  Sammamish *(G-9197)*
Cirrato Technologies Inc ....G..... 425 999-4500
  Kirkland *(G-5306)*
Cloudcoreo Inc ....G..... 206 851-0130
  Seattle *(G-9700)*
Community Thrift Shop LLC ....G..... 509 438-1302
  Richland *(G-8984)*
Computer Clinic Northwest Inc ....G..... 360 658-1234
  Marysville *(G-6327)*
Continuum Creative LLC ....G..... 404 985-6648
  Mercer Island *(G-6459)*
Conveyor Dynamics Inc ....F..... 360 671-2200
  Bellingham *(G-1305)*
Crema Development LLC ....G..... 360 918-6978
  Olympia *(G-7260)*
Crimpd LLC ....G..... 847 436-0433
  Seattle *(G-9753)*
Cross and Crown Church ....G..... 206 498-3551
  Seattle *(G-9755)*
Custom Computer Creat CCC LLC ...G..... 800 295-3381
  Seattle *(G-9766)*
Cyrus Biotechnology Inc ....G..... 503 489-8460
  Seattle *(G-9775)*
Da Vincis Garage LLC ....G..... 206 579-1333
  Seattle *(G-9783)*
Darklight Inc ....G..... 509 940-1818
  Redmond *(G-8432)*
Datapark LLC ....E..... 360 224-2157
  Sumas *(G-13043)*
Deal Perch Inc ....G..... 425 372-8514
  Snohomish *(G-11896)*
Destiny Software Inc ....G..... 425 415-1777
  Woodinville *(G-15224)*
Dining Solutions LLC ....G..... 425 268-6190
  Bellevue *(G-878)*
Dogfish Software Corporation .....G..... 206 395-9050
  Seattle *(G-9842)*
Dot4kids ....G..... 503 884-8838
  Olympia *(G-7273)*
Dragon Head Studios LLC ....G..... 925 813-2881
  Shoreline *(G-11770)*
Dreamtones Inc ....G..... 650 265-0576
  Bothell *(G-1849)*
Dumb Luck LLC ....G..... 206 406-1011
  Mercer Island *(G-6460)*
Dwight Company LLC ....G..... 360 262-9844
  Chehalis *(G-2490)*
Eclipse Technology LLC ....G..... 406 270-6366
  Seattle *(G-9875)*
Elguji Software LLC ....G..... 360 450-5022
  Vancouver *(G-14199)*
Elite Athletics Training LLC ....G..... 509 221-1898
  Richland *(G-8993)*
Encore Analytics LLC ....G..... 866 890-4331
  Tacoma *(G-13279)*
Etios Health LLC ....G..... 585 217-1716
  Bellevue *(G-903)*
Exceptionally Smart ....G..... 206 321-0721
  Seattle *(G-9952)*
Exquisitecrystals Com LLC ....G..... 360 573-6787
  Vancouver *(G-14215)*
Ezr Communications Inc ....G..... 360 936-0070
  Vancouver *(G-14216)*
Falx Games ....G..... 253 439-9121
  Tacoma *(G-13289)*
Fanapptic LLC ....G..... 253 548-7443
  University Place *(G-13968)*
Fastdataio Inc ....F..... 888 707-3346
  Seattle *(G-9976)*
Float Technologies LLC ....G..... 916 947-6646
  Kirkland *(G-5339)*
Flourish Church Rainier Valley ....G..... 206 769-7950
  Seattle *(G-10006)*
Flying Sofa LLC ....G..... 206 275-3935
  Mercer Island *(G-6463)*
Foof LLC ....G..... 425 260-8897
  Cle Elum *(G-2666)*
Freakn Genius Inc ....G..... 425 301-4258
  Kirkland *(G-5343)*
Free Birthday Fun LLC ....G..... 509 999-7517
  Spokane *(G-12264)*
Gatheredtable Inc ....F..... 206 735-4886
  Seattle *(G-10052)*
Gengler Veterinary Svcs Pllc ......F..... 425 788-2620
  Duvall *(G-2990)*
Global Software LLC ....F..... 425 822-3140
  Bothell *(G-1861)*

Employee Codes: A=Over 500 employees, B=251-500
C=101-250, D=51-100, E=20-50, F=10-19, G=2-9

Gomotive Inc G 206 462-6379 Seattle ***(G-10098)***
Gooseworks Media LLC G 425 487-8766 Kenmore ***(G-4577)***
Gravity Labs Inc G 509 220-0817 Spokane ***(G-12279)***
Grcc Student Chapter Saf F 253 288-3331 Auburn ***(G-455)***
Greater Intelligence Inc G 703 989-2281 Kirkland ***(G-5353)***
Green Hills Software LLC G 206 447-1373 Seattle ***(G-10116)***
Grove Church G 360 386-5760 Marysville ***(G-6342)***
Hado Labs LLC G 425 891-7124 Seattle ***(G-10135)***
Happy Tab LLC G 773 231-8223 Kirkland ***(G-5357)***
Hbsw Inc G 217 377-9043 Lynnwood ***(G-6133)***
Hearform Software LLC G 888 453-8806 Northport ***(G-7137)***
Hearts In Motion Ministries G 360 798-0275 Ridgefield ***(G-9088)***
Her Interactive Inc E 425 460-8787 Bellevue ***(G-940)***
Hirelytics LLC G 843 900-4473 Seattle ***(G-10175)***
Hussey Software LLC G 206 409-0959 Seattle ***(G-10195)***
Indulo Inc G 206 383-0373 Seattle ***(G-10228)***
Industrial Generosity Inc G 206 336-2268 Seattle ***(G-10232)***
Industrial Systems Laboratory G 425 226-7585 Renton ***(G-8824)***
Infometrix Inc F 425 402-1450 Bothell ***(G-1768)***
Inner Fence Holdings Inc G 888 922-8277 Redmond ***(G-8507)***
Inside Out Medicine Inc G 206 920-8959 Seattle ***(G-10243)***
Insightful Corporation D 206 283-8802 Seattle ***(G-10244)***
Instructional Technologies Inc F 360 576-5976 Vancouver ***(G-14320)***
Konnekti Incorporated G 925 878-5083 Seattle ***(G-10354)***
Koowalla Inc G 206 948-1803 Woodinville ***(G-15280)***
Kragworks Llc G 208 871-6413 Naches ***(G-6999)***
Krantz News Service Inc G 253 857-6590 Gig Harbor ***(G-4128)***
Krill Systems Inc G 206 780-2901 Bainbridge Island ***(G-647)***
Lagunamoon Beauty Intl Ltd LLC F 480 925-7577 Seattle ***(G-10372)***
Laud Social Inc G 213 797-0744 Seattle ***(G-10380)***
Lawsuite Technologies LLC G 206 349-2227 Seattle ***(G-10386)***
Leadscorz Inc G 206 899-4665 Seattle ***(G-10392)***
Life Recovery Solutions Inc G 208 771-2161 Olympia ***(G-7323)***
Limelyte Technology Group Inc G 509 241-0138 Spokane ***(G-12366)***
Loqu8 Inc G 650 892-8901 Bellingham ***(G-1414)***
Lost City Digital LLC G 206 327-4537 Des Moines ***(G-2940)***
Lost Signal LLC G 360 601-2227 Tumwater ***(G-13885)***
Lpr Park LLC G 888 884-9507 Seattle ***(G-10445)***
Magnolia Desktop Computing LLC G 206 282-7161 Seattle ***(G-10467)***
Mangoapps Inc D 425 274-9950 Issaquah ***(G-4443)***
Materiant Inc E 425 209-1943 Bellevue ***(G-999)***
Microquill Software Publishing G 425 827-7200 Kirkland ***(G-5401)***
Microsoft Corporation D 509 787-6900 Quincy ***(G-8304)***
Microsoft Corporation D 425 705-1900 Bellevue ***(G-1004)***
Microsoft Corporation D 425 705-6218 Redmond ***(G-8558)***
Microsoft Corporation D 425 705-1900 Bellevue ***(G-1006)***
Microsoft Corporation A 425 882-8080 Redmond ***(G-8566)***
Microsoft Corporation A 425 882-8080 Redmond ***(G-8567)***
Microsoft Corporation A 425 882-8080 Redmond ***(G-8568)***
Microsoft Corporation A 425 882-8080 Redmond ***(G-8569)***
Microsoft Corporation A 425 828-8080 Redmond ***(G-8570)***
Microsoft Corporation A 425 882-8080 Redmond ***(G-8571)***
Microsoft Corporation A 425 882-8080 Redmond ***(G-8572)***
Microsoft Corporation A 425 882-8080 Redmond ***(G-8573)***
Microsoft Corporation A 425 882-8080 Redmond ***(G-8574)***
Microsoft Corporation A 425 882-8080 Redmond ***(G-8575)***
Microsoft Corporation A 425 882-8080 Redmond ***(G-8576)***
Microsoft Corporation A 425 882-8080 Redmond ***(G-8577)***
Microsoft Corporation A 425 882-8080 Redmond ***(G-8578)***
Microsoft Corporation G 425 882-8080 Redmond ***(G-8579)***
Microsoft Corporation E 425 435-8457 Bellevue ***(G-1007)***
Mobimaging LLC G 859 559-5138 Camas ***(G-2271)***
Mordi Software G 425 301-4897 Snohomish ***(G-11948)***
Navit LLC G 425 647-3580 Seattle ***(G-10597)***
Nlpcore LLC G 206 883-7616 Seattle ***(G-10613)***
Noonum Llc G 425 894-1202 Redmond ***(G-8597)***
Nostopsign LLC G 213 422-1750 Seattle ***(G-10656)***
Nuance Communications Inc C 781 565-5000 Seattle ***(G-10664)***
Omage Labs Inc G 844 662-4326 Seattle ***(G-10696)***
Ong Innovations LLC G 253 777-0186 Renton ***(G-8864)***
Open Mobile Solutions Inc G 206 290-2314 Kenmore ***(G-4596)***
Outbouts LLC G 253 921-0155 Bonney Lake ***(G-1731)***
Parentasoft LLC G 425 877-8574 Redmond ***(G-8615)***
Partners In Emrgncy Prpredness G 509 335-3530 Tacoma ***(G-13459)***
Picmonkey Inc F 206 486-2106 Seattle ***(G-10801)***
Pipelinedeals Inc F 866 702-7303 Seattle ***(G-10814)***
Pixelan Software G 831 222-0339 Bellingham ***(G-1498)***
Platalytics Inc E 916 835-9584 Redmond ***(G-8625)***
Pop Pop LLC G 206 384-8121 Seattle ***(G-10831)***
Propdocket LLC G 330 285-6526 Bothell ***(G-1892)***
Realnetworks Inc C 206 674-2700 Seattle ***(G-10930)***
Recursive Frog LLC G 206 745-2561 Seattle ***(G-10934)***
Reliance Inc F 615 218-3929 Redmond ***(G-8647)***
Retip LLC G 206 612-5538 Renton ***(G-8894)***
Reverse Image Technologies LLC G 253 219-5345 Tacoma ***(G-13497)***
Reynolds and Reynolds Company E 425 985-0194 Edmonds ***(G-3146)***
Risklens Inc F 866 936-0191 Spokane ***(G-12475)***
Robert Rowe G 206 632-7997 Seattle ***(G-10972)***
Rodax Software G 206 782-3482 Seattle ***(G-10974)***
Roommate Filter LLC G 863 224-6462 Seattle ***(G-10981)***
Rune Inc G 425 766-6134 Seattle ***(G-10996)***
RY Investments Inc G 360 701-1261 Lacey ***(G-5583)***
Satus Networks LLC G 509 575-8382 Yakima ***(G-15666)***
Savotta Tech LLC G 425 505-9951 Sammamish ***(G-9246)***
Sayitright LLC G 401 682-7630 Oak Harbor ***(G-7164)***
Scaleout Software Inc G 503 643-3422 Bellevue ***(G-1116)***
Scope 5 Inc G 206 456-5656 Seattle ***(G-11031)***
Secucred Inc G 508 361-0928 Richland ***(G-9040)***
Securitay Inc G 425 392-0203 Issaquah ***(G-4472)***
Serious Cybernetics LLC G 646 247-3642 North Bend ***(G-7122)***
Sharp Synaptics LLC G 253 927-2616 Federal Way ***(G-3782)***
Shelfbot Co G 425 679-1421 Seattle ***(G-11098)***
Shield Technologies LLC G 425 844-8055 Woodinville ***(G-15360)***
Simple Agile Corporation G 425 985-1096 Redmond ***(G-8669)***
Sivart Software G 206 527-2164 Seattle ***(G-11122)***
Six LLC G 206 466-5186 Seattle ***(G-11123)***
Smalldog Net Solutions Inc G 360 376-6056 Olga ***(G-7219)***
Soham Inc D 425 445-2125 Bellevue ***(G-1145)***
Sola Bothell G 501 487-7652 Bothell ***(G-1793)***
Space Rock It Inc G 206 395-8383 Seattle ***(G-11164)***
Specview Corp G 253 853-3199 Gig Harbor ***(G-4164)***
Squealock Systems Inc G 206 519-4620 Burien ***(G-2131)***
Starform Inc G 206 446-9657 Seattle ***(G-11182)***
Stateless Labs LLC G 512 387-3115 Seattle ***(G-11185)***
Stellar Management Inc G 206 724-3973 Mountlake Terrace ***(G-6869)***
Stellr Inc F 425 312-3798 Seattle ***(G-11190)***
Stretch 22 Inc G 206 375-3358 Seattle ***(G-11202)***
Stryve Inc G 425 802-3832 Seattle ***(G-11206)***
Subset Games LLC G 206 354-4010 Seattle ***(G-11209)***
Swivel Inc G 509 557-7000 Walla Walla ***(G-14876)***
System & Application Assoc G 206 949-4153 Seattle ***(G-11245)***
Tangible Ventures LLc G 360 818-4000 Bellevue ***(G-1178)***
Tecplot Inc E 425 653-1200 Bellevue ***(G-1179)***
Tiller LLC G 425 770-0855 Winthrop ***(G-15165)***
Timbersoft Inc F 360 750-5575 Vancouver ***(G-14640)***
Tokenyo LLC G 206 851-7046 Seattle ***(G-11317)***
Trenzi Inc G 206 769-6501 Seattle ***(G-11330)***
Trick Shot Studios LLC G 858 663-7097 Bellevue ***(G-1203)***
Truegem LLC G 360 836-0310 Camas ***(G-2284)***
Tryb Inc G 206 310-9025 Seattle ***(G-11344)***
Tuxbits Inc G 302 313-6831 Walla Walla ***(G-14883)***
Ubi Interactive Inc G 206 457-2493 Seattle ***(G-11359)***
Umlaut Software Inc G 919 321-8324 North Bend ***(G-7130)***
Undead Labs LLC G 206 452-0590 Seattle ***(G-11366)***
Variety Show Studios LLC G 571 242-1724 Seattle ***(G-11405)***

PRODUCT SECTION

SOFTWARE PUBLISHERS: Business & Professional

Vector Blue Services LLC .... F 425 219-2528
 Bellevue *(G-1213)*
Via Airlift Inc .... G 206 258-6844
 Tukwila *(G-13834)*
Victory Enterprises LLC .... G 360 420-1161
 Mount Vernon *(G-6853)*
Viridian Sciences Inc .... G 360 719-4451
 Vancouver *(G-14672)*
Vivonet Incorporated .... G 866 512-2033
 Bellingham *(G-1585)*
Vulcan Software LLC .... G 206 407-3057
 Lynnwood *(G-6220)*
Vulcan Technologies LLC .... G 206 342-2000
 Seattle *(G-11431)*
Whab Technologies LLC .... G 800 506-2770
 Lynnwood *(G-6224)*
Wompmobile Inc .... G 888 625-8144
 Bellingham *(G-1594)*
Woobox LLC .... G 360 450-5200
 Vancouver *(G-14697)*
Zango Inc .... C 425 279-1200
 Bellevue *(G-1232)*
Zilyn LLC .... G 360 509-2436
 Seattle *(G-11522)*
Zions River .... G 253 473-1838
 Tacoma *(G-13607)*
Zipwire Incorporated .... G 425 591-4924
 Redmond *(G-8722)*
Zsolutionz LLC .... G 425 502-6970
 Sammamish *(G-9262)*

SOFTWARE PUBLISHERS: Business & Professional

Aaab Consulting LLC .... G 206 612-7041
 Seattle *(G-9328)*
Add Corporation .... D 206 452-7498
 Normandy Park *(G-7089)*
All Software Tools Inc .... G 360 883-2981
 Vancouver *(G-14021)*
Apana Inc .... F 360 746-2276
 Bellingham *(G-1249)*
Automated Options Inc .... G 509 467-9860
 Spokane *(G-12130)*
Avado Inc .... G 415 662-8236
 Newcastle *(G-7025)*
B-Side Software LLC .... G 206 708-6973
 Seattle *(G-9475)*
Barking Ant Software LLC .... G 360 281-1118
 Battle Ground *(G-690)*
Biblesoft Inc .... F 206 824-0547
 Des Moines *(G-2929)*
Bittitan Inc .... F 206 428-6030
 Kirkland *(G-5291)*
Bittium Usa Inc .... G 425 780-4480
 Bothell *(G-1829)*
Bizlogr Inc .... G 800 366-4484
 Redmond *(G-8405)*
Blucapp Inc .... F 206 629-8887
 Seattle *(G-9546)*
Bocada LLC .... E 425 818-4400
 Kirkland *(G-5294)*
Byndl AMC LLC .... E 855 462-9635
 Bellevue *(G-833)*
Candela Technologies Inc .... G 360 380-1618
 Ferndale *(G-3822)*
Certain Software Inc .... G 415 353-5330
 Bellevue *(G-848)*
Coastal Software & Consulting .... G 360 891-6174
 Vancouver *(G-14127)*
Cobalt Group Inc .... B 206 269-6363
 Seattle *(G-9708)*
Coherent Knowledge Systems LLC ... G 206 519-6410
 Mercer Island *(G-6458)*
Comscore Inc .... E 206 447-1860
 Seattle *(G-9725)*
Concur Technologies Inc .... A 425 590-5000
 Bellevue *(G-860)*
Congruent Software .... G 206 301-0553
 Seattle *(G-9729)*
Connx Solutions Inc .... E 206 519-6600
 Redmond *(G-8423)*
Constellation Homebuilder Syst ...... G 888 723-2222
 Redmond *(G-8424)*
Context Reality Inc .... G 425 241-5860
 Redmond *(G-8425)*
Cronus Ventures LLC .... G 425 641-4497
 Bellevue *(G-869)*
Crystal Point Inc .... F 425 487-3656
 Mill Creek *(G-6505)*

Data Enterprises of The NW .... G 425 688-8805
 Bellevue *(G-874)*
Dauntless Inc .... E 206 494-3338
 Redmond *(G-8434)*
Dealer Info Systems Corp .... D 360 733-7610
 Bellingham *(G-1320)*
Descartes Biometrics Inc .... G 650 743-4435
 Blaine *(G-1668)*
Descartes Systems (usa) LLC .... F 206 812-7874
 Seattle *(G-9825)*
Dinesync Inc .... G 206 620-2550
 Seattle *(G-9832)*
E/Step Software Inc .... G 509 853-5000
 Yakima *(G-15560)*
Eacceleration Corp .... E 360 697-9260
 Poulsbo *(G-7960)*
Enprecis Inc .... E 206 274-0122
 Seattle *(G-9927)*
Entirely Inc .... G 206 979-9092
 Seattle *(G-9930)*
Event 1 Software Inc .... F 360 567-3752
 Vancouver *(G-14208)*
Everpath Inc .... G 206 682-7259
 Seattle *(G-9948)*
Exacttarget Inc .... G 866 362-4538
 Bellevue *(G-904)*
Fileonq Inc .... F 206 575-3488
 Tukwila *(G-13734)*
Fizikl Inc .... G 360 393-0714
 Bellingham *(G-1348)*
Flexe Inc .... G 855 733-7788
 Seattle *(G-10005)*
Followone Inc .... G 206 518-8844
 Kirkland *(G-5341)*
Gekko Corporation .... G 425 679-9188
 Bellevue *(G-922)*
Ghost Inspector Inc .... G 206 395-3635
 Seattle *(G-10069)*
Global Studios Consulting LLC .... E 425 223-5291
 Bellevue *(G-929)*
Groupware Incorporated .... E 360 397-1000
 Vancouver *(G-14274)*
Harbinger Knowledge Pdts Inc .... G 425 861-8400
 Redmond *(G-8488)*
Headlight Software Inc .... G 206 985-4431
 Seattle *(G-10154)*
Health Guardian Inc .... G 206 999-8153
 Seattle *(G-10156)*
Horizon Professional Cmpt Svcs ..... F 425 883-6588
 Redmond *(G-8501)*
Hyperfish Inc .... G 425 332-6567
 Kirkland *(G-5364)*
Icopyright Inc .... G 206 484-8561
 Seattle *(G-10201)*
Ieg7 Inc .... G 206 501-6193
 Auburn *(G-470)*
Ifooddecisionsciences Inc .... E 206 219-3703
 Seattle *(G-10204)*
Imprev Inc .... G 800 809-3356
 Bellevue *(G-954)*
Integrated Computer Systems .... F 425 820-6120
 Redmond *(G-8510)*
Invio Inc .... G 206 915-3563
 Seattle *(G-10256)*
Iunu Inc .... G 253 307-1858
 Seattle *(G-10263)*
Kashoo Cloud Accunting USA Inc .... E 888 520-5274
 Bellingham *(G-1391)*
Kentico Software LLC .... G 206 674-4507
 Tukwila *(G-13763)*
Klicktrack Inc .... F 206 557-3223
 Bainbridge Island *(G-646)*
Krell Software Inc .... G 425 298-9519
 Mill Creek *(G-6515)*
Kronos Incorporated .... E 206 696-1505
 Seattle *(G-10359)*
Legal+plus Software Group Inc ...... G 206 286-3600
 Newcastle *(G-7034)*
Leisure Loyalty Inc .... G 425 223-5102
 Bellevue *(G-981)*
Lemmino Inc .... G 571 229-3854
 Seattle *(G-10401)*
Lincoln Data Inc .... G 509 466-1744
 Spokane *(G-12367)*
Linedata Services .... G 206 545-9522
 Seattle *(G-10425)*
Links Business Group LLC .... G 425 961-0565
 Issaquah *(G-4440)*
Loki Systems Inc .... G 800 961-5654
 Bellingham *(G-1413)*

Lumatax Inc .... G 206 450-2004
 Seattle *(G-10449)*
Mainstem Inc .... F 844 623-4084
 Seattle *(G-10469)*
Majesco Software Inc .... G 425 242-0327
 Bellevue *(G-995)*
Medida Health LLC .... G 425 985-5214
 Kirkland *(G-5400)*
Microsoft Payments Inc .... F 425 722-0528
 Redmond *(G-8583)*
MNC Services Inc .... G 425 527-9031
 Woodinville *(G-15312)*
Mobetize Corp .... G 778 588-5563
 Blaine *(G-1684)*
Moxie Software Cim Corp .... D 425 467-5000
 Bellevue *(G-1018)*
Mscsoftware Corporation .... G 855 672-7638
 Bellevue *(G-1019)*
Nexus Life Cycle MGT LLC .... G 541 400-0765
 Stevenson *(G-13016)*
NW Software Solutions .... G 509 252-3550
 Spokane *(G-12415)*
Observa Inc .... F 206 499-4444
 Seattle *(G-10679)*
Olympic Sytems Inc .... G 206 547-5777
 Seattle *(G-10695)*
Omnim2m LLC .... F 425 278-4090
 Issaquah *(G-4456)*
Ontario Systems LLC .... G 360 256-7358
 Vancouver *(G-14452)*
Opportunity Interactive Inc .... F 206 870-1880
 Seatac *(G-9296)*
Oracle Corporation .... B 425 945-8200
 Bellevue *(G-1053)*
Pacific Ally LLC .... G 360 760-4266
 La Center *(G-5511)*
Pearson Business Mgt Svcs .... G 206 382-1457
 Seattle *(G-10777)*
Phone Flare Inc .... G 425 346-9230
 Duvall *(G-2998)*
Point Inside Inc .... D 425 590-9522
 Bellevue *(G-1077)*
Projul Inc .... G 844 776-5853
 Ravensdale *(G-8339)*
Pushspring Inc .... G 206 455-6128
 Seattle *(G-10892)*
Qorus Software Inc .... G 844 516-8000
 Seattle *(G-10897)*
Redquarry LLC .... F 206 981-5300
 Tacoma *(G-13493)*
Resonant Solutions LLC .... G 206 619-7672
 Bothell *(G-1894)*
Rival Iq Corporation .... F 206 395-8572
 Seattle *(G-10966)*
Rooferpro Software LLC .... G 425 503-4298
 Mill Creek *(G-6523)*
Safetec Compliance Systems Inc .... D 360 567-0280
 Vancouver *(G-14564)*
Safetec Software LLC .... G 888 745-8943
 Vancouver *(G-14565)*
Salesforcecom Inc .... G 206 701-1755
 Bellevue *(G-1113)*
Salire Corporation .... E 425 284-0679
 Redmond *(G-8656)*
Seattle Avionics Inc .... G 425 806-0249
 Woodinville *(G-15357)*
Selah Springs LLC .... G 206 714-6068
 Bellevue *(G-1123)*
Select Selling Inc .... E 425 895-8959
 Kirkland *(G-5458)*
Servably Inc .... G 425 216-3333
 Kirkland *(G-5459)*
Siemens Product Life Mgmt Sftw ... E 425 507-1900
 Issaquah *(G-4476)*
Simply Augmented Inc .... G 206 771-9774
 Seattle *(G-11114)*
Socedo Inc .... G 206 499-3398
 Bellevue *(G-1143)*
Softresources LLC .... G 425 216-4030
 Kirkland *(G-5465)*
Software AG Usa Inc .... G 425 519-6600
 Redmond *(G-8673)*
Software Ingenuity LLC .... G 509 924-0093
 Veradale *(G-14751)*
Software Planning .... G 509 522-1620
 Walla Walla *(G-14871)*
Squarerigger Inc .... F 360 698-3562
 Silverdale *(G-11859)*
Stratagen Systems Inc .... E 425 821-8454
 Kirkland *(G-5471)*

Employee Codes: A=Over 500 employees, B=251-500
C=101-250, D=51-100, E=20-50, F=10-19, G=2-9

2019 Washington Manufacturers Register

1073

Suplari Inc ... G ... 425 610-9496
Seattle *(G-11225)*
Survey Analytics LLC ... F ... 800 326-5570
Seattle *(G-11227)*
Survey Analytics LLC ... E ... 800 326-5570
Seattle *(G-11228)*
Tableau Ireland LLC ... G ... 206 633-3400
Seattle *(G-11252)*
Tableau Software Inc ... C ... 206 633-3400
Seattle *(G-11253)*
Tactuum LLC ... G ... 425 941-6958
Bellevue *(G-1176)*
Talaera ... G ... 206 229-0631
Seattle *(G-11261)*
Talentwise Inc ... B ... 425 974-8863
Bothell *(G-1799)*
Tamarack Software Inc ... G ... 509 329-0456
Spokane *(G-12545)*
Tellwise Inc ... G ... 425 999-6935
Bellevue *(G-1181)*
Tensormake Corporation ... G ... 206 659-6139
Redmond *(G-8688)*
Theobald Software Inc ... G ... 425 802-2514
Seattle *(G-11287)*
Timextender North America ... G ... 619 813-7625
Bellevue *(G-1190)*
Tinypulse ... E ... 206 455-9424
Seattle *(G-11313)*
Toptec Software LLC ... G ... 206 331-4420
Richland *(G-9045)*
Tune Inc ... C ... 206 508-1318
Seattle *(G-11348)*
Utrip Inc ... F ... 509 954-9393
Seattle *(G-11397)*
Vimly Benefit Solutions Inc ... D ... 425 771-7359
Mukilteo *(G-6989)*
Volometrix Inc ... G ... 425 706-7507
Redmond *(G-8707)*
Watchguard Technologies Inc ... C ... 206 613-6600
Seattle *(G-11443)*
Wellpepper Inc ... G ... 206 455-7377
Seattle *(G-11448)*
Whatcounts Inc ... E ... 206 709-8250
Seattle *(G-11464)*
Wimetrics Corp ... F ... 253 593-1220
Tacoma *(G-13598)*
Winshuttle LLC ... C ... 425 368-2708
Bothell *(G-1808)*
Zillow Group Inc ... C ... 206 470-7000
Seattle *(G-11521)*

SOFTWARE PUBLISHERS: Computer Utilities

Advangelists LLC ... G ... 734 546-4989
Seattle *(G-9355)*
Algorithmia Inc ... G ... 415 741-1491
Seattle *(G-9375)*
Battery Informatics Inc ... G ... 443 534-7671
Poulsbo *(G-7947)*
Bourgeois Bits LLC ... G ... 434 535-2487
Seattle *(G-9570)*
Chiminera LLC ... G ... 401 326-2820
Seattle *(G-9677)*
Glarus Group Inc ... G ... 425 572-5907
Newcastle *(G-7030)*
Incremental Systems Corp ... G ... 425 732-2377
Bellevue *(G-956)*
Intentionet Inc ... G ... 206 579-6567
Redmond *(G-8512)*
Qwardo Inc ... G ... 425 753-8865
Redmond *(G-8641)*
Smartrg Inc ... E ... 877 486-6210
Vancouver *(G-14596)*
Ultrabac Software Inc ... E ... 425 644-6000
Bellevue *(G-1206)*

SOFTWARE PUBLISHERS: Education

Actively Learn Inc ... G ... 857 540-6670
Seattle *(G-9346)*
Ann H McCormick PHD ... G ... 650 451-8020
Leavenworth *(G-5795)*
Arrhythmia Solutions Inc ... G ... 509 389-7366
Spokane *(G-12118)*
Blackboard Cyphr Educ Consltng ... G ... 360 870-8429
Olympia *(G-7237)*
Browsereport ... G ... 206 948-2640
Federal Way *(G-3718)*
Career Development Software ... F ... 360 696-3529
Vancouver *(G-14099)*
Competentum-Usa Ltd ... F ... 425 996-4201
Issaquah *(G-4398)*
Digitlis Educatn Solutions Inc ... F ... 360 616-8915
Bremerton *(G-1947)*
Discovery Tools ... G ... 253 288-1720
Enumclaw *(G-3285)*
Earshot LLC ... G ... 917 822-6074
Seattle *(G-9870)*
Eduongo Inc ... F ... 206 451-7325
Bellevue *(G-892)*
Fifth Star Labs LLC ... G ... 206 369-3956
Seattle *(G-9990)*
Infosoft Solutions Inc ... G ... 360 738-3060
Bellingham *(G-1377)*
Intradata Inc ... G ... 425 836-8654
Newcastle *(G-7032)*
Jam Developers Inc ... E ... 206 448-5225
Seattle *(G-10280)*
Lightsmith Consulting LLC ... G ... 312 953-1193
Seattle *(G-10420)*
Maelstrom Interactive ... G ... 206 841-6071
Kirkland *(G-5393)*
Mediapro Holdings LLC ... E ... 425 483-4700
Bothell *(G-1777)*
Omega Labs Inc ... G ... 425 296-0886
Kirkland *(G-5418)*
Pulpo Games LLC ... G ... 206 371-6924
Seattle *(G-10886)*
Renaissance Learning Inc ... D ... 360 944-8996
Vancouver *(G-14543)*
Schoolkitcom Inc ... F ... 425 454-3373
Bellevue *(G-1117)*
Social Voter Labs LLC ... G ... 206 981-9225
Seattle *(G-11149)*
Speechace LLC ... G ... 425 241-3033
Seattle *(G-11167)*
Teaching 2020 LLC ... G ... 253 232-6822
Olalla *(G-7211)*
Virtual Education Software Inc ... F ... 509 891-7219
Spokane Valley *(G-12931)*
Washington Schl Info Proc Coop ... C ... 425 349-6600
Everett *(G-3651)*
Wild Noodle ... G ... 206 935-1100
Seattle *(G-11474)*

SOFTWARE PUBLISHERS: Home Entertainment

Blockpartygg LLC ... G ... 206 409-6562
Seattle *(G-9543)*
Builder Box LLC ... E ... 206 778-4753
Seattle *(G-9596)*
Cannonbot Games LLC ... G ... 510 473-6871
Spokane *(G-12167)*
Cinematix LLC ... G ... 425 533-1024
Kirkland *(G-5305)*
DOT Com LLC ... G ... 425 256-2815
Bellevue *(G-881)*
Foxfacerabbitfish LLC ... G ... 206 856-7222
Seattle *(G-10018)*
Harmonious Development LLC ... G ... 425 248-5794
Seattle *(G-10142)*
Hidden Path Entertainment Inc ... E ... 425 452-7284
Bellevue *(G-945)*
Jolly Hatchet Games LLC ... G ... 360 624-2758
Vancouver *(G-14341)*
Leaftail Labs LLC ... G ... 206 399-4233
Seattle *(G-10394)*
Leviathan Games Inc ... G ... 206 432-9949
Seattle *(G-10411)*
Lill Creates ... G ... 206 355-4409
Seattle *(G-10422)*
North Sky Games Inc ... G ... 425 283-9634
Sammamish *(G-9237)*
Oliver Henry Games LLC ... G ... 971 231-9141
Woodinville *(G-15327)*
Panthercorn Studios ... G ... 425 501-9717
Mukilteo *(G-6964)*
Pixvana Inc ... F ... 206 910-5747
Seattle *(G-10818)*
Proxygroove LLC ... G ... 415 264-1906
Seattle *(G-10878)*
Rleyh Software LLC ... G ... 425 837-4643
Issaquah *(G-4469)*
Rocketcat LLC ... G ... 360 204-4037
Bremerton *(G-1995)*
Rumor Games LLC ... G ... 585 771-7642
Seattle *(G-10994)*
Seafoam Studios LLC ... G ... 702 509-4742
Seattle *(G-11042)*
Spry Fox LLC ... G ... 425 835-3320
Kirkland *(G-5469)*
Taco Truck Games LLC ... G ... 360 218-4967
Seattle *(G-11254)*
Twobitbear LLC ... G ... 206 658-5797
Seattle *(G-11356)*
Underhorse Entertainment Inc ... G ... 760 216-0164
Redmond *(G-8697)*
Wildcard Properties LLC ... E ... 425 296-0896
Redmond *(G-8714)*
Z2live Inc ... E ... 206 890-4996
Seattle *(G-11518)*

SOFTWARE PUBLISHERS: NEC

1strategy LLC ... G ... 801 824-5660
Bainbridge Island *(G-605)*
2 C Media LLC ... E ... 206 522-7211
Seattle *(G-9318)*
5 By 5 Software Ventures Ltd ... G ... 206 779-6234
Seattle *(G-9324)*
7 Grapes Software ... G ... 425 653-2308
Bellevue *(G-776)*
8th Shore Inc ... G ... 425 681-1157
Redmond *(G-8364)*
A & E Systems ... G ... 509 886-1092
East Wenatchee *(G-3005)*
Accounting Software Inc ... G ... 253 952-6040
Tacoma *(G-13156)*
Acg Software ... G ... 425 828-1456
Redmond *(G-8368)*
ACS Technologies Group Inc ... D ... 843 413-8032
Seattle *(G-9343)*
Activated Content ... G ... 206 448-3260
Seattle *(G-9345)*
Adobe Systems Incorporated ... B ... 206 675-7000
Seattle *(G-9353)*
Agile Advantage Inc ... E ... 425 629-6361
Redmond *(G-8374)*
Agilecore Software LLC ... G ... 360 910-3140
Vancouver *(G-14012)*
Aircon Soft ... G ... 206 851-8476
Seattle *(G-9361)*
Akamai Technologies Inc ... G ... 206 674-5900
Bellevue *(G-783)*
Alcatel-Lucent USA Inc ... E ... 425 497-2400
Redmond *(G-8376)*
Alitheon Inc ... F ... 888 606-7445
Bellevue *(G-784)*
Alphawave Systems ... G ... 719 888-9283
Vancouver *(G-14024)*
Amdocs Qpass Inc ... F ... 206 447-6000
Seattle *(G-9391)*
Appagare Software Inc ... G ... 253 857-4675
Port Orchard *(G-7788)*
Appgen Business Software ... G ... 253 857-9400
Gig Harbor *(G-4073)*
Apptio Inc ... C ... 866 470-0320
Bellevue *(G-790)*
Arabella Software LLC ... G ... 206 963-6460
Seattle *(G-9418)*
Arbitrary Software LLC ... G ... 425 644-7428
Bellevue *(G-791)*
Archer USA Inc ... E ... 206 567-5343
Seattle *(G-9419)*
Archive Solution Providers ... G ... 425 440-0228
Redmond *(G-8384)*
Arrays Software LLC ... G ... 206 414-8250
Seattle *(G-9432)*
ARS Nova Software ... G ... 425 869-0625
Redmond *(G-8386)*
Ascentis Corporation ... E ... 425 519-0241
Bellevue *(G-797)*
Assetic Inc ... G ... 425 658-6603
Kirkland *(G-5281)*
At Once Sales Software Inc ... G ... 509 845-2453
Seattle *(G-9448)*
Attachmate Corporation ... B ... 206 217-7100
Seattle *(G-9458)*
Attachmate Intl Sls Corp ... G ... 206 217-7500
Seattle *(G-9459)*
Auction Edge Inc ... E ... 206 858-4808
Seattle *(G-9462)*
August Systems Inc ... E ... 509 468-2988
Spokane *(G-12127)*
Author-It Software Corporation ... F ... 888 999-1021
Seattle *(G-9466)*
Automic Software Inc ... D ... 425 644-2121
Bellevue *(G-799)*
Avalara Inc ... D ... 206 826-4900
Seattle *(G-9468)*

SOFTWARE PUBLISHERS: NEC

Avidian Technologies Inc .... E 800 399-8980
  Bellevue *(G-804)*
Avst Parent LLC .... D 425 951-1600
  Bothell *(G-1750)*
Aware Software Inc .... G 206 232-5709
  Mercer Island *(G-6455)*
Barn Door Productions .... G 206 780-3535
  Bainbridge Island *(G-616)*
Barshay Software Inc .... G 206 370-2393
  Seattle *(G-9495)*
Bc Software .... G 425 831-0550
  Snoqualmie *(G-12005)*
Bellevue Parent LLC .... G 866 470-0320
  Bellevue *(G-813)*
Best Guess Software .... G 360 876-3272
  Port Orchard *(G-7793)*
Big Fish Premium LLC .... F 206 269-3573
  Seattle *(G-9524)*
Bill Dibenedetto .... G 206 963-0499
  Seattle *(G-9528)*
Bit Elixir LLC .... G 509 842-4121
  Spokane Valley *(G-12641)*
Bitpeg Software Inc .... G 509 290-5216
  Mead *(G-6425)*
Bittitan Inc .... D 206 428-6030
  Bellevue *(G-819)*
Bkd Software .... G 425 487-1475
  Woodinville *(G-15194)*
Blue Martini Software .... G 360 754-2207
  Olympia *(G-7238)*
Blueberry Meringue Software .... G 425 830-5414
  Monroe *(G-6556)*
Bluepenguin Software Inc .... G 561 459-5393
  Sequim *(G-11615)*
Bobolink Software .... G 509 684-2800
  Kettle Falls *(G-5225)*
Brad Pendleton Software LLC .... G 425 898-0309
  Sammamish *(G-9193)*
Brak Software Inc .... G 206 280-7157
  Bellevue *(G-828)*
Bubbie Bit N Bundle .... G 360 733-8315
  Bellingham *(G-1285)*
C Davis Software Con .... G 847 436-6225
  Lake Stevens *(G-5636)*
Caminova Inc .... G 206 919-2110
  Mill Creek *(G-6503)*
Care Zone Inc .... G 888 407-7785
  Seattle *(G-9631)*
Cartogram Inc .... E 425 628-0395
  Bellevue *(G-840)*
Cascade Medical Technologies .... G 360 896-6944
  Vancouver *(G-14104)*
Cascade Software Corp .... G 425 558-9017
  Redmond *(G-8417)*
CCS Computer Systems Inc .... F 425 672-4806
  Lynnwood *(G-6089)*
CHI-Square Labs LLC .... G 206 282-8246
  Seattle *(G-9674)*
Chronus Corporation .... F 425 629-6327
  Bellevue *(G-851)*
Circle Systems Inc .... G 206 682-3783
  Seattle *(G-9685)*
Citrix Systems Inc .... G 425 895-4700
  Redmond *(G-8421)*
Clario Medical .... G 206 315-5410
  Seattle *(G-9688)*
Cnc Software Inc .... G 253 858-6677
  Gig Harbor *(G-4091)*
Coach Cheetah Inc .... G 206 914-8313
  Seattle *(G-9703)*
Coinstax LLC .... G 206 629-8831
  Seattle *(G-9713)*
Columbus Systems Inc .... G 360 943-4165
  Tumwater *(G-13863)*
Columbus Systems Inc .... G 360 943-4165
  Tumwater *(G-13864)*
Company 43 LLC .... G 425 269-0430
  Bothell *(G-1841)*
Compass Northwest .... G 206 546-1178
  Shoreline *(G-11766)*
Computer Assisted Message Inc .... F 425 392-2496
  Issaquah *(G-4399)*
Computer Connections .... G 360 736-2177
  Centralia *(G-2185)*
Computer Human Interaction LLC .... E 425 282-6900
  Tukwila *(G-13714)*
Comtronic Systems LLC .... F 509 573-4300
  Cle Elum *(G-2662)*
Congruent Software (usa) Inc .... D 425 460-0172
  Bellevue *(G-861)*

Constructivision Inc .... G 425 741-4413
  Mill Creek *(G-6504)*
Content Master .... G 425 274-1970
  Bellevue *(G-862)*
Continental Data Graphics .... G 425 562-4050
  Bellevue *(G-863)*
Coptracker Inc .... G 214 542-2351
  Mattawa *(G-6404)*
Cornerstone Software Systems .... G 425 788-9681
  Woodinville *(G-15213)*
Corporate Vat Management Inc .... G 206 292-0300
  Seattle *(G-9743)*
Coverity .... G 206 467-5967
  Seattle *(G-9750)*
Cowlitz River Software Inc .... G 253 856-3111
  Kent *(G-4866)*
Dauntless Software Inc .... G 206 489-4942
  Renton *(G-8780)*
Dave Peck Software Development .... G 206 931-7572
  Seattle *(G-9798)*
Defsec Solutions LLC .... G 855 933-3732
  Mill Creek *(G-6506)*
Desema Company .... G 425 202-7572
  Redmond *(G-8438)*
Desi Telephone Labels Inc .... F 360 571-0713
  Vancouver *(G-14176)*
Detonator Games LLC .... F 206 355-6682
  Duvall *(G-2982)*
Directeq LLC .... G 425 818-9510
  Darrington *(G-2867)*
Diversified Systems Group Inc .... E 425 947-1500
  Redmond *(G-8442)*
Dm2 Software Inc .... E 360 574-6984
  Vancouver *(G-14185)*
Dojo LLC .... G 203 903-0079
  Renton *(G-8786)*
Dose Safety Co .... G 206 282-7086
  Seattle *(G-9848)*
Doublebit Software .... G 425 503-0692
  Bellevue *(G-882)*
Dowling Software Consulta .... G 425 489-3026
  Bothell *(G-1848)*
Dr Software LLC .... G 206 526-1371
  Seattle *(G-9852)*
Duck Software LLC .... G 206 935-9722
  Seattle *(G-9857)*
Dwaynes Software .... G 425 379-7741
  Everett *(G-3448)*
Dynamic Software .... G 253 630-7026
  Covington *(G-2826)*
Dynamic Software Innovations .... G 425 432-5313
  Maple Valley *(G-6267)*
E B Associates Inc .... G 253 709-1433
  Enumclaw *(G-3288)*
E L F Software Distributors .... G 360 577-6163
  Longview *(G-5908)*
E W Bachtal Inc .... G 425 241-2505
  Snoqualmie *(G-12010)*
Electromagnetic Software .... G 425 557-4716
  Sammamish *(G-9203)*
Emerald City Software LLC .... G 206 321-5252
  Seattle *(G-9911)*
Energsoft Inc .... G 425 246-1675
  Seattle *(G-9925)*
Energysavvy Inc .... E 206 462-2206
  Seattle *(G-9926)*
Engineering .... G 360 275-7384
  Belfair *(G-761)*
Enhanced Software Products Inc .... E 509 534-1514
  Spokane Valley *(G-12693)*
Entropy Killer Software .... G 206 526-2488
  Seattle *(G-9931)*
Epicore .... G 360 659-1986
  Marysville *(G-6333)*
Eric Gibbs Software .... G 206 784-0741
  Seattle *(G-9936)*
Esi Distribution Ltd .... G 206 780-9623
  Bainbridge Island *(G-631)*
Esoteric Software LLC .... G 206 618-3331
  Seattle *(G-9939)*
Eternity Software .... G 425 486-1622
  Bothell *(G-1852)*
Excelerate Systems LLC .... F 425 605-8515
  Redmond *(G-8455)*
Exo Labs Inc .... G 206 659-1249
  Seattle *(G-9953)*
Expert Ig .... G 360 335-0555
  Washougal *(G-14954)*
F5 LLC .... G 425 882-8080
  Redmond *(G-8456)*

F5 Networks Inc .... C 206 272-5555
  Seattle *(G-9959)*
Falconstor Software Inc .... G 206 652-3312
  Seattle *(G-9964)*
Fast Yeti Inc .... G 253 573-1877
  University Place *(G-13969)*
Firecracker Software LLC .... G 509 443-5308
  Spokane Valley *(G-12702)*
Florence L Ellis .... G 360 213-2475
  Vancouver *(G-14235)*
Fluentpro Software Corporation .... G 855 358-3688
  Redmond *(G-8462)*
Flying Lab Software LLC .... F 206 272-9815
  Seattle *(G-10009)*
Forword Input Inc .... F 206 227-0191
  Lynnwood *(G-6121)*
Francis Scientific Inc .... G 360 687-7019
  Battle Ground *(G-702)*
Fti Consulting Tech Sftwr .... D 206 373-6500
  Seattle *(G-10034)*
Fund RR LLC .... G 425 530-7120
  Marysville *(G-6337)*
Future Software Systems Inc .... G 360 629-9973
  Stanwood *(G-12973)*
GE Healthcare Inc .... B 206 622-9558
  Seattle *(G-10055)*
Ghost Ridge Software Inc .... G 425 646-4822
  Kirkland *(G-5348)*
Girt John .... G 206 399-4977
  Issaquah *(G-4420)*
Global Software Systems Inc .... G 425 427-8215
  Issaquah *(G-4421)*
Global Vision .... G 425 985-9325
  Mill Creek *(G-6512)*
Globalwxdatacom .... G 425 644-4010
  Seattle *(G-10085)*
Globys Inc .... D 206 352-3055
  Seattle *(G-10088)*
Graphicode Inc .... E 360 282-4888
  Snohomish *(G-11915)*
Gratrack .... G 571 357-4728
  Seattle *(G-10108)*
Grigsby Software Developm .... G 360 942-5240
  Raymond *(G-8351)*
Groupfabric Inc .... G 425 681-2927
  Seattle *(G-10127)*
Growfast Software .... G 360 224-5484
  Bellingham *(G-1363)*
Hahn Software LLC .... G 206 724-4735
  Burien *(G-2111)*
Harvest Food Solutions .... G 503 926-6499
  Vancouver *(G-14286)*
Hash Inc .... F 360 750-0042
  Vancouver *(G-14287)*
Helcorp Interactive LLC .... G 917 446-8506
  Seattle *(G-10162)*
Hella Shaggy Software LLC .... G 206 533-1468
  Edmonds *(G-3118)*
HI Baby Software .... G 206 372-8936
  Bellevue *(G-943)*
High Rise Software Group Inc .... G 206 290-6087
  Seattle *(G-10170)*
Hildebrand Consulting .... G 206 465-1729
  Lake Forest Park *(G-5614)*
Holder Software .... G 509 338-0692
  Pullman *(G-8091)*
Holdiman Software .... G 509 582-5085
  Kennewick *(G-4671)*
Hough Software Consulting .... G 425 881-2339
  Redmond *(G-8502)*
Howard F Harrison M D .... G 509 575-8307
  Yakima *(G-15586)*
Hoylu Inc .... G 425 269-3299
  Kirkland *(G-5361)*
Hoylu Inc .... G 425 829-2316
  Kirkland *(G-5362)*
Hurkin LLC .... G 425 437-0100
  Maple Valley *(G-6274)*
Ilinklive Inc .... G 509 464-0062
  Spokane *(G-12303)*
Immersive Media Company .... E 360 609-3419
  Washougal *(G-14960)*
Impinj Inc .... C 206 517-5300
  Seattle *(G-10212)*
Incycle Software Corp .... G 425 880-9200
  Bellevue *(G-957)*
Indaba Management Company LLC .... F 360 546-5528
  Vancouver *(G-14312)*
Industrial Software Solutns .... E 425 368-7310
  Bothell *(G-1767)*

Employee Codes: A=Over 500 employees, B=251-500
C=101-250, D=51-100, E=20-50, F=10-19, G=2-9

SOFTWARE PUBLISHERS: NEC

Company	Code	Phone
Infinity Digital LLC — Kelso *(G-4529)*	G	715 298-3530
Infoharvest Inc — Seattle *(G-10233)*	G	206 686-2729
Information Builders Inc — Seattle *(G-10234)*	F	206 624-9055
Ingio/Vinbalance LLC — Walla Walla *(G-14822)*	G	509 522-1621
Insights Works Inc — Kirkland *(G-5368)*	G	425 577-2206
Insomania Software — Redmond *(G-8509)*	G	425 837-1525
Instantiations Inc — Vancouver *(G-14319)*	F	503 770-0861
Intelligenteffects LLC — Kirkland *(G-5369)*	G	323 206-0499
Interlocking Software Corp — Poulsbo *(G-7966)*	G	360 394-5900
Internet Motors Company — Bellevue *(G-961)*	G	425 654-1154
Interworks US LLC — Seattle *(G-10252)*	G	206 934-1074
Intuitive Mfg Systems Inc — Kirkland *(G-5370)*	D	425 821-0740
Intuitive Software Solution — Stanwood *(G-12955)*	G	360 387-2271
Ipr-Now Inc — North Bend *(G-7113)*	G	425 888-6190
Iron Software Development LLC — Bothell *(G-1770)*	G	425 892-2287
Iship Inc — Bellevue *(G-962)*	E	425 602-4848
Isonetic Inc — Vashon *(G-14726)*	G	800 670-8871
J A Ratto Company — Bellevue *(G-964)*	G	206 240-5601
Jayam Software — Sammamish *(G-9222)*	G	425 208-6467
Jazzie Software — Seattle *(G-10287)*	G	206 905-7411
Jima Software Incorporated — Bothell *(G-1870)*	G	206 354-7309
JM Software — Seattle *(G-10299)*	G	206 453-3544
John H Wolf CPA PC — Spokane *(G-12338)*	G	509 465-9165
Justin-Grace Inc — Seattle *(G-10319)*	G	206 992-4292
Kennewick Computer Company — Richland *(G-9018)*	G	509 371-0600
Keypict — Seattle *(G-10340)*	G	206 522-5201
Knights Edge Software — Kenmore *(G-4589)*	G	425 488-3552
Kokako Software — Seattle *(G-10352)*	G	425 922-1115
Kuo Software LLC — Sammamish *(G-9227)*	G	425 961-0197
Lambda Software LLC — Bellevue *(G-975)*	G	425 882-3464
Laplink Software Inc — Bellevue *(G-977)*	E	425 952-6000
Ldl- Software Inc — Renton *(G-8842)*	G	425 652-1473
Leavelogic Inc — Seattle *(G-10395)*	G	757 655-3283
Led Software — Mercer Island *(G-6470)*	G	206 232-2812
Legal + Plus Software Group — Newcastle *(G-7033)*	G	206 286-3600
Lenco Mobile Inc — Seattle *(G-10402)*	D	800 557-4148
Lifter Apps LLC — Seattle *(G-10415)*	G	206 289-0407
Lightshine Software LLC — Monroe *(G-6593)*	G	425 231-9320
Likebright Inc — Seattle *(G-10421)*	G	206 669-2536
Lionfort Software Inc — Redmond *(G-8534)*	G	425 698-7403
Little Sun Software LLC — Woodinville *(G-15291)*	G	425 442-4911
Loudscoop Inc — Redmond *(G-8538)*	G	425 391-7159
Lumedx Corporation — Bellevue *(G-991)*	D	425 450-9774
M I S Construction Software — Kirkland *(G-5389)*	G	425 882-3027
Mackichan Software Inc — Poulsbo *(G-7979)*	F	360 394-6033
Magnapro Business Systems Inc — Edmonds *(G-3131)*	G	206 280-6222
Magnum Opus Software & Co — Newcastle *(G-7035)*	G	425 227-7712
Manceps Inc — Camas *(G-2267)*	G	503 922-1164
Marcia Hardy — Redmond *(G-8548)*	G	425 880-4460
Margate Software LLC — Seattle *(G-10477)*	G	206 381-9120
Mark Muzi — Seattle *(G-10487)*	G	206 523-6954
Matersmost Software LLC — Sammamish *(G-9231)*	G	425 392-6165
Mathsoft Inc — Seattle *(G-10501)*	G	206 283-8802
Matthews Cellars — Woodinville *(G-15305)*	G	425 487-9810
McG Health Llc — Seattle *(G-10507)*	E	206 389-5300
McObject LLC — Federal Way *(G-3757)*	F	425 888-8505
Media Matrix Digital Center — Vancouver *(G-14408)*	G	360 693-6455
Mettler Toledo NW — Lynnwood *(G-6163)*	G	425 774-3510
Mgs Software LLC — Puyallup *(G-8190)*	G	253 841-1573
Micro Focus Software Inc — Seattle *(G-10532)*	A	206 217-7100
Microchips Software — Vancouver *(G-14419)*	G	360 921-8562
Microsoft Corporation — Redmond *(G-8559)*	E	425 706-0040
Microsoft Corporation — Sammamish *(G-9233)*	G	425 281-6768
Microsoft Corporation — Seattle *(G-10536)*	G	206 290-9669
Microsoft Corporation — Seattle *(G-10537)*	G	425 533-6624
Microsoft Corporation — Bellevue *(G-1005)*	G	770 235-8794
Microsoft Corporation — Kirkland *(G-5402)*	E	206 724-8130
Microsoft Corporation — Issaquah *(G-4449)*	E	425 882-8080
Microsoft Corporation — Redmond *(G-8560)*	E	425 706-6640
Microsoft Corporation — Redmond *(G-8561)*	E	425 861-0581
Microsoft Corporation — Redmond *(G-8562)*	E	425 706-0033
Microsoft Corporation — Redmond *(G-8563)*	E	425 882-8080
Microsoft Corporation — Redmond *(G-8564)*	G	360 863-0642
Microsoft Corporation — Redmond *(G-8565)*	E	425 867-6537
Microsoft Corporation — Seattle *(G-10538)*	E	206 883-5474
Microsoft Corporation — Redmond *(G-8580)*	A	425 882-8080
Microsoft Corporation — Sammamish *(G-9234)*	G	425 633-4929
Microsoft Corporation — Redmond *(G-8581)*	G	206 816-0190
Microsoft Corporation — Redmond *(G-8582)*	E	425 556-9348
Microsoft Corporation — Woodinville *(G-15311)*	G	425 703-6921
Mighty Ai LLC — Seattle *(G-10540)*	E	425 753-3167
Mike Houston — Kirkland *(G-5403)*	G	425 889-0682
Minapsys Software Corp — Spokane *(G-12395)*	G	425 891-1460
Mindcast Software — Federal Way *(G-3759)*	G	425 341-0450
Minima Software LLC — Seattle *(G-10545)*	G	206 659-9646
MNC Services Inc — Bellevue *(G-1011)*	G	425 527-9031
Modeling Dynamics Inc — Sammamish *(G-9235)*	G	425 392-2262
Modular Software Systems Inc — Enumclaw *(G-3305)*	G	360 886-8882
Moneymindersoftware — Bellingham *(G-1441)*		360 255-4300
Morcant Software — Yakima *(G-15624)*	G	509 225-6807
Multico Rating Systems — Seattle *(G-10569)*	F	206 357-3928
Multimodal Health Inc — Seattle *(G-10570)*	G	651 245-2326
Mutiny Bay Software LLC — Freeland *(G-4034)*	G	360 331-5170
National Management Software — Spokane *(G-12403)*	E	509 327-0192
Nbk Associates Inc — Kirkland *(G-5408)*	G	216 408-8685
Neil Butler — Snohomish *(G-11950)*		360 668-9555
Newline Software Inc — Redmond *(G-8593)*	G	425 442-1126
Nextgen Apps Co — Seattle *(G-10605)*	G	206 395-6770
Niftybrick Software — Seattle *(G-10608)*	G	206 588-5696
Nintendo Software Technology — Redmond *(G-8596)*	E	425 497-7500
Nintex Usa Inc — Bellevue *(G-1032)*	D	425 324-2400
Noda Software — Seattle *(G-10617)*	G	206 726-1125
Norcom Inc — Sammamish *(G-9236)*	G	425 868-9973
Norman Langseth — Bellevue *(G-1033)*	G	425 643-7751
Northwest Internet — East Wenatchee *(G-3027)*		509 888-2020
Northwest Sftwr Professionals — Bellingham *(G-1469)*	G	360 734-5747
Northwest Synergistic Software — Renton *(G-8860)*	G	425 271-1491
Northwest Technologies — Seattle *(G-10652)*	G	206 528-5353
Novaleaf Software LLC — Woodinville *(G-15323)*	G	425 486-1242
Nrs Software LLC — Yakima *(G-15637)*	G	509 969-4769
O2d Software Inc — Shoreline *(G-11796)*	G	206 364-0055
Office Timeline LLC — Bellevue *(G-1044)*	E	425 296-9002
Oltis Software LLC — Bellevue *(G-1047)*	F	800 557-1780
Omni Development Inc — Seattle *(G-10699)*	E	206 523-4152
Onsite Computer Services — Bellingham *(G-1480)*	G	360 650-1079
Open Text Inc — Bellevue *(G-1051)*	E	425 455-6000
Oracle Corporation — Seattle *(G-10710)*	G	206 695-9000
Oracle Fisheries LLC — Port Angeles *(G-7732)*	G	360 477-9829
Oracle Hypnosis — Dupont *(G-2971)*	G	859 893-8147
Oracles of God Ministries — Bellevue *(G-1054)*	G	425 449-8663
Orderport LLC — Bellevue *(G-1055)*	F	425 746-2926
Os Nexus Inc — Bellevue *(G-1056)*	F	425 279-0172
Pacific Applied Technology — Vancouver *(G-14462)*	G	360 693-4292
Pagemark Technology Inc — Redmond *(G-8610)*	F	425 444-3735
Paladin Data Systems Corp — Poulsbo *(G-7991)*	D	360 779-2400
Pamar Systems Inc — Vancouver *(G-14477)*	G	360 992-4120
Panda Dental Software Inc — Bellevue *(G-1062)*	G	800 517-7716
Panther Systems Northwest Inc — Vancouver *(G-14478)*	E	360 750-9783
Pat-Co Inc — Seattle *(G-10765)*	G	206 937-8927
Pateric Software — Kirkland *(G-5430)*	G	425 814-4949
PC Consulting & Development — Redmond *(G-8617)*	G	425 836-0645
Peach Fuzzer LLC — Seattle *(G-10775)*	F	206 453-0339
Peach Fuzzer LLC — Seattle *(G-10776)*		844 557-3224
Pendown Software LLC — Yakima *(G-15643)*	G	509 480-8232
Performance Software Corp — Bothell *(G-1884)*	G	425 481-4956

Physware Inc ... G ... 562 491-1600
Bellevue *(G-1074)*
PI Technologies ... G ... 206 877-3720
Bellevue *(G-1075)*
Pixelsaurus Games LLC ... G ... 617 893-7755
Seattle *(G-10817)*
Pixotec LLC ... G ... 425 255-0789
Renton *(G-8880)*
Portlock Software ... G ... 425 247-0545
Kenmore *(G-4599)*
Portrait Displays Inc ... F ... 206 420-7514
Edmonds *(G-3144)*
Posabit Inc ... F ... 903 641-7604
Kirkland *(G-5439)*
Powder Monkey Games LLC ... G ... 206 501-2340
Seattle *(G-10842)*
Powell Software Inc ... E ... 425 974-9692
Yarrow Point *(G-15722)*
Powersoft ... G ... 425 637-8088
Bellevue *(G-1078)*
Premiere Software ... G ... 206 399-7495
Seattle *(G-10855)*
Proctor International LLC ... G ... 425 881-7000
Redmond *(G-8633)*
Professional Practice Systems ... F ... 253 531-8944
Roy *(G-9164)*
Prune Hill Software LLC ... G ... 360 834-3067
Camas *(G-2277)*
Ptc Inc ... E ... 425 455-1930
Bellevue *(G-1087)*
Purposeful Software LLC ... G ... 206 855-7927
Bainbridge Island *(G-661)*
Quadient Data USA Inc ... D ... 206 443-0765
Seattle *(G-10898)*
Quest Integrity Usa LLC ... D ... 253 893-7070
Kent *(G-5093)*
Quest Software Inc ... E ... 949 720-1434
Seattle *(G-10905)*
Quick Collect Inc ... E ... 360 256-7888
Vancouver *(G-14523)*
Racer Mate Inc ... E ... 206 524-7392
Seattle *(G-10912)*
Rainplex Inc ... G ... 253 576-0157
Gig Harbor *(G-4150)*
Rally Software Development ... G ... 206 266-8408
Bellevue *(G-1092)*
Rankin Associates ... G ... 206 325-9440
Seattle *(G-10920)*
Raosoft Inc ... G ... 206 523-9278
Seattle *(G-10921)*
Recheadz LLC ... G ... 509 406-2230
Soap Lake *(G-12038)*
Recordpoint Software USA LLC ... G ... 425 245-6235
Bellevue *(G-1096)*
Red Loon Software ... G ... 253 353-7963
University Place *(G-13980)*
Refrelent Software Lab ... G ... 425 898-9657
Sammamish *(G-9243)*
Revq Inc ... G ... 360 260-5710
Vancouver *(G-14548)*
Rgb14 LLC ... G ... 206 818-8207
Seattle *(G-10959)*
Riggel Productions Limited ... G ... 509 758-3209
Clarkston *(G-2645)*
Rimini Software LLC ... G ... 425 785-8819
Issaquah *(G-4467)*
Ripley Software ... G ... 501 773-5519
Issaquah *(G-4468)*
River Rock Software Inc ... G ... 916 797-6746
Shelton *(G-11727)*
Rocket Software ... G ... 425 502-9684
Bellevue *(G-1107)*
Rust Proved Software ... G ... 206 244-0643
Burien *(G-2127)*
Sandpiper Software Inc ... G ... 425 788-6175
Woodinville *(G-15354)*
Sansueb Software LLC ... G ... 253 630-5208
Kent *(G-5116)*
Sarangsoft LLC ... G ... 425 378-3890
Bellevue *(G-1114)*
Sars Corporation ... F ... 866 276-7277
Bellevue *(G-1115)*
SCC Enterprises LLC ... G ... 425 454-0567
Yarrow Point *(G-15723)*
Sea To Software LLC ... G ... 206 617-6893
Seattle *(G-11040)*
Seattle Software Corp ... G ... 206 286-7677
Seattle *(G-11076)*
Seattle Software Works Inc ... G ... 206 226-9263
Snohomish *(G-11973)*

Shared Healthcare Systems Inc ... E ... 360 299-4000
Anacortes *(G-166)*
Sienna Software Inc ... G ... 206 306-2752
Seattle *(G-11105)*
Simerics Inc ... F ... 256 489-1480
Bellevue *(G-1132)*
Simerics Inc ... F ... 425 502-9978
Bellevue *(G-1133)*
Simpos ... G ... 360 794-4658
Monroe *(G-6619)*
Sirascom Inc ... G ... 425 497-3300
Redmond *(G-8670)*
Sitting Room ... G ... 206 285-2830
Seattle *(G-11121)*
Small Business Automation ... G ... 206 324-3820
Seattle *(G-11137)*
Snider Software LLC ... G ... 206 790-7570
Bellevue *(G-1141)*
Softchoice Corporation ... G ... 206 709-9000
Seattle *(G-11152)*
Softsource LLC ... G ... 360 676-0999
Bellingham *(G-1545)*
Software In 34th St ... G ... 425 557-7953
Issaquah *(G-4479)*
Soggy Hawk Software ... G ... 425 246-6555
Woodinville *(G-15368)*
Somerset Software ... G ... 425 822-1951
Kirkland *(G-5466)*
Sound Software ... G ... 360 375-6375
Blakely Island *(G-1715)*
Source Dynamics Inc ... G ... 425 557-3630
Issaquah *(G-4481)*
Sparkon Inc ... G ... 425 273-3904
Redmond *(G-8676)*
Specialized Computing Inc ... G ... 206 915-9033
Seattle *(G-11166)*
Splunk Inc ... G ... 206 430-5200
Seattle *(G-11169)*
Stanford Technology Inc ... G ... 509 638-1191
Spokane *(G-12525)*
Starcom Computer Corporation ... F ... 425 486-6464
Bothell *(G-1797)*
Stork Software LLC ... G ... 206 669-0644
Seattle *(G-11199)*
Straightthrough Inc ... G ... 425 467-1990
Bellevue *(G-1160)*
Suntower Systems ... F ... 206 878-0578
Des Moines *(G-2947)*
Suse LLC ... E ... 206 217-7500
Seattle *(G-11231)*
Suse LLC ... G ... 206 217-7100
Seattle *(G-11232)*
Synergy Business Services Inc ... E ... 206 859-6500
Seattle *(G-11243)*
System 1 Software Inc ... G ... 206 548-1633
Seattle *(G-11246)*
Systematic Designs Intl ... F ... 360 944-9890
Vancouver *(G-14623)*
T T I Acquisition Corp ... F ... 509 358-2036
Liberty Lake *(G-5861)*
Tableau Software Inc ... F ... 206 634-5610
Kirkland *(G-5475)*
Tangera Technologies Inc ... G ... 425 652-7969
Bellevue *(G-1177)*
Target System Technology Inc ... G ... 509 456-4852
Spokane Valley *(G-12901)*
Team Sport Software LLC ... G ... 703 971-2005
Gig Harbor *(G-4165)*
Ted Gruber Software Inc ... G ... 702 735-1980
Kelso *(G-4554)*
Tekoa Software Inc ... G ... 509 340-3580
Liberty Lake *(G-5862)*
Telos Sales Corporation ... G ... 425 890-2755
Kirkland *(G-5477)*
Telos Wealth Management ... G ... 509 664-8844
Wenatchee *(G-15080)*
Telos3 LLC ... G ... 360 900-9274
Poulsbo *(G-8006)*
Telos3 LLC ... G ... 360 536-3122
Bainbridge Island *(G-677)*
Telspace LLC ... E ... 425 953-2801
Kirkland *(G-5478)*
Tenth Generation Software ... G ... 425 226-1939
Renton *(G-8926)*
Tetrachrome Software ... G ... 425 825-1708
Kirkland *(G-5480)*
Thinking Man Software Corp ... G ... 425 313-0607
Sammamish *(G-9253)*
Third Wave Software Corp ... G ... 425 825-9082
Bothell *(G-1801)*

Threepenny Software LLC ... G ... 206 675-1518
Seattle *(G-11298)*
Tibco Software Inc ... F ... 650 846-1000
Liberty Lake *(G-5864)*
Tinman Software ... G ... 425 417-2142
Sammamish *(G-9254)*
Tinman Systems Inc ... G ... 425 802-9035
Sammamish *(G-9255)*
Tiptoes Software LLC ... G ... 650 267-1907
Bellevue *(G-1191)*
TNT Software Inc ... F ... 360 546-0878
Vancouver *(G-14641)*
Toptec Software LLC ... G ... 206 331-4420
Kennewick *(G-4737)*
Total Cntrl LLC ... F ... 425 446-0342
Everett *(G-3634)*
Tova Company ... F ... 800 729-2886
Freeland *(G-4038)*
Tracktion Software Corporation ... G ... 425 273-3376
Kirkland *(G-5485)*
Trek Global ... G ... 760 576-5115
Vancouver *(G-14644)*
Triadd Software Corporation ... G ... 425 643-3700
Bellevue *(G-1202)*
Twilight Software ... G ... 206 228-2037
Seattle *(G-11350)*
Tyler Technologies Inc ... E ... 360 852-6696
Ridgefield *(G-9117)*
Tyler Technologies Inc ... E ... 360 352-0922
Olympia *(G-7416)*
Tymlez Inc ... G ... 630 215-7878
Seattle *(G-11357)*
Unix Packages LLC ... G ... 206 310-4610
Seattle *(G-11386)*
V 4 Software LLC ... G ... 813 870-6666
Sammamish *(G-9256)*
Vendorhawk Inc ... G ... 360 903-3744
Seattle *(G-11409)*
Vergent Software ... G ... 425 880-4158
Redmond *(G-8704)*
Vericlouds ... E ... 844 532-5332
Seattle *(G-11413)*
Versaly Games Inc ... G ... 425 577-0208
Issaquah *(G-4487)*
Vertek Ois Inc ... G ... 425 455-9921
Spokane Valley *(G-12929)*
Verti Technology Group Inc ... G ... 425 279-1200
Bellevue *(G-1215)*
Vivid Learning Systems Inc ... D ... 509 545-1800
Pasco *(G-7649)*
Vulcan Oracle ... G ... 360 609-9272
Vancouver *(G-14674)*
Washington Mso Inc ... F ... 253 984-7247
Tacoma *(G-13588)*
Wftpd Inc ... G ... 206 428-1991
Woodinville *(G-15404)*
Whaer Inc ... G ... 919 946-5720
Renton *(G-8945)*
Wildtangent Inc ... D ... 425 497-4500
Redmond *(G-8715)*
William Minniear ... G ... 360 254-6764
Vancouver *(G-14694)*
Winshuttle Software Canada Inc ... G ... 425 368-2708
Bothell *(G-1809)*
Xenex Seattle ... G ... 206 281-9370
Seattle *(G-11503)*
Xensource Inc ... G ... 425 881-9479
Redmond *(G-8718)*
Xeriton Corporation ... E ... 425 369-2279
Sammamish *(G-9261)*
Xmedius America Inc ... E ... 425 951-1600
Bothell *(G-1810)*
Xmedius Buyer LLC ... G ... 866 368-0400
Bothell *(G-1811)*
Y-Verge Llc ... G ... 360 975-9277
Vancouver *(G-14702)*
Zemax LLC ... D ... 425 305-2800
Kirkland *(G-5499)*
Zen Dog Software LLC ... G ... 425 861-8777
Bellevue *(G-1234)*
Zeta Software Inc ... G ... 503 371-4340
Redmond *(G-8721)*
Zhuro Software LLC ... G ... 206 607-9073
Seattle *(G-11520)*
Zombie Inc ... E ... 206 623-9655
Bainbridge Island *(G-685)*

SOFTWARE PUBLISHERS: Operating Systems

SOFTWARE PUBLISHERS: Operating Systems
- Add Three Inc .... E 206 568-3772
  Seattle *(G-9349)*
- Dose Safety Inc .... G 206 276-3385
  Redmond *(G-8443)*
- Financial Management Systems .... G 425 881-8687
  Issaquah *(G-4414)*
- Gate Technologies LLC .... G 206 229-9947
  North Bend *(G-7111)*
- Microsoft Tech Licensing LLC .... G 425 882-8080
  Redmond *(G-8584)*

SOFTWARE PUBLISHERS: Publisher's
- American Labelmark Company .... E 206 256-0889
  Seattle *(G-9393)*
- Counting Stick Software LLC .... G 425 750-1028
  Lynnwood *(G-6099)*
- Ds-Iq Inc .... G 425 974-1400
  Bellevue *(G-885)*
- Energy Arrow .... G 267 932-7769
  Stanwood *(G-12969)*
- Freemo Inc .... G 425 280-9661
  Kirkland *(G-5344)*
- Horizon Imaging LLC .... G 509 525-2860
  College Place *(G-2725)*
- Pinnion Inc .... F 206 577-3070
  Kirkland *(G-5434)*
- Pixel Planet Inc .... G 206 669-7371
  Seattle *(G-10816)*
- Solid Modeling Solutions Inc .... G 425 246-3943
  Bellevue *(G-1146)*

SOFTWARE PUBLISHERS: Word Processing
- Provoke Solutions Inc .... G 206 792-3680
  Bellevue *(G-1086)*

SOFTWARE TRAINING, COMPUTER
- Defsec Solutions LLC .... G 855 933-3732
  Mill Creek *(G-6506)*
- Eduongo Inc .... F 206 451-7325
  Bellevue *(G-892)*
- R D F Products .... G 360 253-2181
  Vancouver *(G-14526)*
- Risklens Inc .... F 866 936-0191
  Spokane *(G-12475)*

SOIL CONDITIONERS
- Northwest AG Pdts LLC .... E 509 547-8234
  Pasco *(G-7604)*

SOLAR CELLS
- Itekenergy LLC .... D 360 647-9531
  Bellingham *(G-1385)*
- Northlight Power LLC .... G 206 780-3551
  Seattle *(G-10636)*
- Silfab Solar WA Inc .... F 360 569-4733
  Bellingham *(G-1536)*
- Solarworld Industries Amer LP .... D 360 944-9251
  Vancouver *(G-14598)*

SOLAR HEATING EQPT
- Cleanpwr .... G 425 334-6100
  Lake Stevens *(G-5639)*
- Offset Solar LLC .... E 866 376-9559
  Liberty Lake *(G-5849)*

SOLDERING EQPT: Electrical, Exc Handheld
- Component Tinning Services Inc ...... F 509 315-5840
  Spokane Valley *(G-12662)*
- Hentec Industries Inc .... E 509 891-1680
  Newman Lake *(G-7046)*

SOLDERING SVC: Jewelry
- Bodle Diamond Industries .... G 360 939-0242
  Stanwood *(G-12953)*

SOLVENTS
- Inlet Petroleum Solvents .... G 907 274-3835
  Seattle *(G-10237)*

SOLVENTS: Organic
- Tarr Acquisition LLC .... G 253 859-2979
  Auburn *(G-577)*

SONAR SYSTEMS & EQPT
- Hydroacoustic Technology Inc .... F 206 633-3383
  Seattle *(G-10196)*
- Kongsberg Underwater Tech Inc ..... E 425 712-1107
  Lynnwood *(G-6153)*
- Ocean Instruments Wash LLC .... G 425 281-1471
  Fall City *(G-3704)*
- Raytheon Company .... C 360 394-3434
  Keyport *(G-5244)*
- Raytheon Company .... B 360 697-6600
  Keyport *(G-5245)*
- Sound Metrics Corp .... G 425 822-3001
  Bellevue *(G-1148)*

SONG WRITING SVCS
- Ultra Van Krome Prductions LLC ..... G 206 859-3459
  Tacoma *(G-13568)*

SOUND EFFECTS & MUSIC PRODUCTION: Motion Picture
- Foxfacerabbitfish LLC .... G 206 856-7222
  Seattle *(G-10018)*
- Juice & Jam Inc .... G 206 734-5136
  Seattle *(G-10314)*

SOUND EQPT: Underwater
- Cetrestec Inc .... G 206 650-8676
  Seattle *(G-9662)*

SOUVENIR SHOPS
- Martin Business Systems .... G 509 582-3159
  Kennewick *(G-4692)*

SOYBEAN PRDTS
- Syngenta Seeds Inc .... C 509 543-8000
  Pasco *(G-7636)*

SPACE PROPULSION UNITS & PARTS
- Boeing Company .... B 425 413-3400
  Maple Valley *(G-6261)*
- Bspace Corporation .... G 208 559-7806
  Seattle *(G-9591)*
- Electrijet Research Foundation .... G 509 990-9474
  Greenacres *(G-4297)*
- General Dynamics Ordna .... D 509 762-5381
  Moses Lake *(G-6710)*
- General Dynmics Ots Arospc Inc ..... A 425 420-9311
  Bothell *(G-1765)*
- Northrop Grumman Systems Corp ... E 360 315-3976
  Silverdale *(G-11852)*

SPACE RESEARCH & TECHNOLOGY, GOVT: Space Research/Developt
- Electrijet Research Foundation .... G 509 990-9474
  Greenacres *(G-4297)*

SPACE VEHICLE EQPT
- Accra Manufacturing Inc .... D 425 424-1000
  Bothell *(G-1814)*
- Boeing Domestic Sales Corp .... G 206 655-2121
  Tukwila *(G-13707)*
- Eldec Corporation .... A 425 743-1313
  Lynnwood *(G-6114)*
- Electroimpact Inc .... D 425 348-8090
  Mukilteo *(G-6920)*
- Fabrication Technologies LLC .... G 360 293-3707
  Anacortes *(G-127)*
- General Dynamics Ordna .... D 509 762-5381
  Moses Lake *(G-6710)*
- Infinity Fabrication Inc .... G 360 435-7460
  Arlington *(G-254)*
- Jim Suzuki .... G 253 804-6070
  Auburn *(G-482)*
- Neumeier Engineering Inc .... E 253 854-3635
  Kent *(G-5020)*
- Omohundro Co Kitsap Composites ... D 360 519-3047
  Port Orchard *(G-7837)*
- Primus International Inc .... C 253 876-1500
  Algona *(G-76)*

Tethers Unlimited Inc
Tethers Unlimited Inc .... G 425 486-0100
  Bothell *(G-1800)*

SPACE VEHICLES
- Blue Origin LLC .... D 253 872-0411
  Kent *(G-4815)*

SPAS
- Derma Medical Spa .... G 360 350-5321
  Olympia *(G-7268)*

SPEAKER MONITORS
- Couple Power .... G 425 641-0278
  Bellevue *(G-867)*

SPEAKER SYSTEMS
- Chapman Audio Systems .... G 206 463-3008
  Vashon *(G-14718)*
- Half Families Enterprises LLC .... G 425 629-3232
  Sammamish *(G-9213)*
- Matamp Distribution USA .... G 509 455-7469
  Spokane *(G-12385)*
- McCauley Sound Inc .... E 253 848-0363
  Puyallup *(G-8188)*

SPECIAL PRODUCT SAWMILLS, NEC
- Acuna Cedar Products .... G 425 359-3224
  Sedro Woolley *(G-11530)*
- N J L Inc .... G 360 590-8100
  Ocean Shores *(G-7187)*

SPECIALTY FOOD STORES, NEC
- Grand Temple .... G 509 715-7876
  Liberty Lake *(G-5833)*

SPECIALTY FOOD STORES: Coffee
- Biscottea Baking Company LLC ...... G 206 695-2614
  Seattle *(G-9533)*
- Cascade Coffee Inc .... F 425 347-3995
  Everett *(G-3410)*
- Fidalgo Bay Coffee Inc .... E 360 757-8818
  Burlington *(G-2158)*
- Grounds For Change Inc .... G 360 779-0401
  Poulsbo *(G-7964)*
- Joes Garage LLC .... F 206 466-5579
  Tukwila *(G-13758)*
- Keurig Green Mountain Inc .... C 253 447-9100
  Sumner *(G-13078)*
- Lighthouse Roasters Inc .... G 206 633-4775
  Seattle *(G-10418)*
- NW Coffee Rosters LLC .... F 360 442-4111
  Longview *(G-5939)*

SPECIALTY FOOD STORES: Dietetic Foods
- Key Technology Inc .... G 509 529-2161
  Walla Walla *(G-14834)*

SPECIALTY FOOD STORES: Dried Fruit
- Cherry Chukar Company .... E 509 786-2055
  Prosser *(G-8032)*

SPECIALTY FOOD STORES: Food Gift Baskets
- Canter-Berry Farms .... G 253 939-2706
  Auburn *(G-400)*

SPECIALTY FOOD STORES: Health & Dietetic Food
- Barleans Organic Oils LLC .... C 360 384-0485
  Ferndale *(G-3818)*
- Betsy Bells Natyural Solutions .... G 206 933-1889
  Seattle *(G-9518)*
- Penford Products Co .... E 509 375-1261
  Richland *(G-9034)*

SPECIALTY FOOD STORES: Juices, Fruit Or Vegetable
- Emerald City Smoothie .... G 253 564-1966
  Tacoma *(G-13277)*
- Pheasant Brothers LLC .... G 509 539-5899
  Benton City *(G-1623)*

SPECIALTY FOOD STORES: Vitamin

Cascade Intgrtive Medicine LLC............G...... 425 391-5270
  Issaquah *(G-4390)*
Emerald City Smoothie..............................G...... 253 826-6664
  Bonney Lake *(G-1723)*
Terato Products LLC..................................G...... 425 702-6365
  Redmond *(G-8689)*

SPECIALTY SAWMILL PRDTS

Fred Tebb & Sons Inc ....D...... 253 272-4107
  Tacoma *(G-13301)*
Port Blakely Company................................G...... 206 624-5810
  Seattle *(G-10834)*
Precision Beam & Timber Inc ....G...... 509 525-1381
  Walla Walla *(G-14857)*

SPECULATIVE BUILDERS: Single-Family Housing

Riverside Scientific Entps..........................G...... 206 842-7513
  Bainbridge Island *(G-667)*

SPICE & HERB STORES

Bay City Sausage Co Inc............................G...... 360 648-2344
  Aberdeen *(G-4)*
Seasalt Superstore LLC ....E...... 425 249-2331
  Everett *(G-3608)*
Spice Hut Corporation................................F...... 360 671-2800
  Bellingham *(G-1552)*

SPORTING & ATHLETIC GOODS: Balls, Baseball, Football, Etc

Baden Sports Inc ....F...... 253 925-0500
  Renton *(G-8750)*

SPORTING & ATHLETIC GOODS: Boomerangs

Boomerang Boxer LLC................................G...... 206 227-6569
  Seattle *(G-9565)*
Boomerang Express LLC ....G...... 360 449-2173
  Vancouver *(G-14078)*
Boomerang Physical Therapy LLC ....G...... 360 258-1637
  Vancouver *(G-14079)*

SPORTING & ATHLETIC GOODS: Bowling Alleys & Access

Hugos On Hill..G...... 509 822-7149
  Spokane *(G-12299)*

SPORTING & ATHLETIC GOODS: Camping Eqpt & Splys

Badnasty Paintball......................................G...... 509 998-0984
  Moses Lake *(G-6683)*
Cascade Designs Inc ....B...... 206 505-9500
  Seattle *(G-9640)*
Cascade Designs Inc ....G...... 206 505-9500
  Seattle *(G-9641)*
Coaxsher Inc ....E...... 509 663-5148
  Chelan Falls *(G-2571)*
Compass Outdoor Adventures LLC ....G...... 425 281-0267
  Snoqualmie *(G-12007)*
Industrial Revolution Inc ....E...... 425 285-1111
  Tukwila *(G-13752)*
National Banner Supply ....G...... 253 333-7443
  Auburn *(G-504)*
North Face 047 ....G...... 509 747-5389
  Spokane *(G-12407)*
Summit Rescue Inc ....E...... 360 366-0221
  Ferndale *(G-3908)*

SPORTING & ATHLETIC GOODS: Darts & Table Sports Eqpt & Splys

Gt Darts...G...... 206 498-9855
  Shoreline *(G-11777)*

SPORTING & ATHLETIC GOODS: Decoys, Duck & Other Game Birds

Sullivan Manufacturing Inc.........................G...... 509 545-8000
  Pasco *(G-7635)*

SPORTING & ATHLETIC GOODS: Dumbbells & Other Weight Eqpt

Giorgios Fitness Center.............................G...... 509 922-8833
  Spokane Valley *(G-12718)*

SPORTING & ATHLETIC GOODS: Exercising Cycles

Racer Mate Inc...E...... 206 524-7392
  Seattle *(G-10912)*

SPORTING & ATHLETIC GOODS: Fencing Eqpt

Schwalbde North America ....G...... 360 384-6468
  Ferndale *(G-3900)*

SPORTING & ATHLETIC GOODS: Fishing Bait, Artificial

Puget Sound Anglers Educ........................F...... 206 473-1613
  Woodinville *(G-15344)*

SPORTING & ATHLETIC GOODS: Fishing Eqpt

Boggs Manufacturing ....G...... 360 449-3479
  Vancouver *(G-14075)*
Crabhawk..G...... 541 921-3593
  Tokeland *(G-13632)*
Digital Anglers LLC....................................G...... 206 819-7010
  Redmond *(G-8441)*
Freedom Adaptive Systems LLC ....G...... 425 286-9597
  Bothell *(G-1857)*
Golden Creek LLC......................................G...... 425 830-4343
  Issaquah *(G-4423)*
Gsi Outdoors Inc ....E...... 509 928-9611
  Spokane Valley *(G-12725)*
International Longline Supply ....G...... 360 650-0412
  Bellingham *(G-1382)*
Kadco Tackle Manufacturing ....G...... 253 857-5033
  Port Orchard *(G-7822)*
Marco Global Inc..E...... 206 298-4758
  Seattle *(G-10474)*
Marine Cnstr & Design Co........................E...... 206 285-3200
  Seattle *(G-10478)*
Maritime Fabrications Inc........................E...... 360 466-3629
  La Conner *(G-5524)*
North Fork Composites LLC ....F...... 360 225-2211
  Woodland *(G-15450)*
Northwest Hygienetics Inc.........................G...... 253 529-0294
  Auburn *(G-511)*
Petrzelka Bros Inc......................................G...... 360 424-8095
  Mount Vernon *(G-6824)*
Retco Inc...G...... 360 341-1487
  Clinton *(G-2695)*
Sage Manufacturing Corporation..............G...... 206 842-6608
  Bainbridge Island *(G-671)*
What S Next..G...... 425 235-1696
  Renton *(G-8946)*

SPORTING & ATHLETIC GOODS: Fishing Tackle, General

Beau Mac Enterprises ....G...... 253 447-8093
  Sumner *(G-13055)*
Dick Nite Spoons Inc..................................G...... 425 377-8448
  Snohomish *(G-11899)*
Evans Mfg ....G...... 360 332-9505
  Blaine *(G-1669)*
Innovative Outdoor Pdts LLC ....G...... 509 826-0219
  Tonasket *(G-13651)*
Lamiglas Inc ....E...... 360 225-9436
  Woodland *(G-15444)*
Lucky Leaders ....G...... 206 363-2208
  Seattle *(G-10447)*
Macks Lures Manufacturing Co................G...... 509 667-9202
  Wenatchee *(G-15049)*
Point Wilson Co Inc....................................G...... 360 385-7625
  Port Townsend *(G-7907)*
Silver Horde Fishing Supplies ....G...... 425 778-2640
  Lynnwood *(G-6196)*
Yakima Bait Co ....C...... 509 854-1311
  Granger *(G-4264)*

SPORTING & ATHLETIC GOODS: Flies, Fishing, Artificial

Carlson & Fitzwater LLC ....G...... 425 941-4020
  Snohomish *(G-11885)*

SPORTING & ATHLETIC GOODS: Football Eqpt & Splys, NEC

Pee Wee Pros Ltd Liability Co ....G...... 206 276-6707
  Lynnwood *(G-6178)*
Vicis Inc ....E...... 206 456-6680
  Seattle *(G-11414)*

SPORTING & ATHLETIC GOODS: Gymnasium Eqpt

Body Builders Gym Equipment ....G...... 253 631-8274
  Kent *(G-4816)*
New Adventure ....G...... 360 961-4444
  Bellingham *(G-1458)*
R3bar LLC...G...... 647 296-6265
  Redmond *(G-8642)*

SPORTING & ATHLETIC GOODS: Hooks, Fishing

Hook & Line Fish..G...... 360 293-0503
  Anacortes *(G-134)*

SPORTING & ATHLETIC GOODS: Hunting Eqpt

D & L Outdoor Specialties.........................G...... 509 758-5875
  Clarkston *(G-2630)*
Suzabelle ....G...... 206 790-5163
  Seattle *(G-11234)*
Swish...G...... 425 644-3545
  Bellevue *(G-1173)*
World Knives Ltd ....G...... 866 862-5233
  Olympia *(G-7431)*

SPORTING & ATHLETIC GOODS: Masks, Hockey, Baseball, Etc

Bodysense Inc..G...... 206 988-1719
  Seattle *(G-9561)*

SPORTING & ATHLETIC GOODS: Polo Eqpt & Splys, NEC

Phazr LLC...G...... 509 329-8306
  Spokane *(G-12440)*

SPORTING & ATHLETIC GOODS: Pools, Swimming, Exc Plastic

Aqua Rec Inc ....G...... 253 826-2561
  Bonney Lake *(G-1716)*
Aqua Rec Inc ....G...... 253 770-9447
  Puyallup *(G-8123)*

SPORTING & ATHLETIC GOODS: Protective Sporting Eqpt

Bikelid LLC...G...... 206 963-7585
  Medina *(G-6446)*
Makota Co...G...... 206 226-1843
  Edmonds *(G-3132)*

SPORTING & ATHLETIC GOODS: Reels, Fishing

Mako Reels Inc ....G...... 360 757-7328
  Burlington *(G-2170)*

SPORTING & ATHLETIC GOODS: Rods & Rod Parts, Fishing

Emmrod Fishing Gear Inc..........................G...... 509 979-2222
  Spokane Valley *(G-12691)*
Fetha Styx Inc...G...... 360 687-3856
  Battle Ground *(G-701)*
Fetha Styx LLC..G...... 425 242-0014
  Kirkland *(G-5338)*
K&B Custom Rods & Tackle ....G...... 360 354-1945
  Lynden *(G-6028)*
Mustad Longline Inc ....G...... 206 284-4376
  Seattle *(G-10575)*

SPORTING & ATHLETIC GOODS: Rods & Rod Parts, Fishing

R & R Rods .... G 360 423-7935
 Longview (G-5946)
Sage Manufacturing Corporation .... F 800 952-9827
 Bainbridge Island (G-670)
Shoreline Poleholders LLC .... G 360 659-0826
 Arlington (G-328)

SPORTING & ATHLETIC GOODS: Shafts, Golf Club

Angela J Bowen & Assoc LLC .... G 360 252-2440
 Olympia (G-7227)
Harbour Pointe Golf LLC .... G 425 355-6060
 Mukilteo (G-6930)
Mermaid Bay Enterprises LLC .... G 360 312-5522
 Bellingham (G-1433)
Par 4 Golf Services .... G 360 376-4462
 Eastsound (G-3045)
Sturtevants Tennis Shop .... G 425 454-6465
 Bellevue (G-1163)

SPORTING & ATHLETIC GOODS: Shooting Eqpt & Splys, General

Fortis Manufacturing Inc .... G 253 277-3211
 Kent (G-4918)

SPORTING & ATHLETIC GOODS: Skateboards

Amigos Skateboards LLC .... G 901 289-9044
 Seattle (G-9398)
Cloud City Skateboards .... G 206 403-1882
 Seattle (G-9699)
Dashboard Skimboards LLC .... G 253 235-1811
 Fife (G-3948)
Insect Skateboards Inc .... G 206 706-8882
 Seattle (G-10242)
Mervin Manufacturing Inc .... G 206 204-7800
 Seattle (G-10517)
Roeracing Slalom Skateboards .... G 206 371-9710
 Seattle (G-10975)
Sausage Skateboards .... G 206 679-3619
 Seattle (G-11017)
Skate Like A Girl .... G 206 973-8005
 Seattle (G-11125)
Todd M Bearden .... G 509 624-2875
 Spokane (G-12561)
Washington Wind Sports Inc .... G 360 676-1146
 Bellingham (G-1589)

SPORTING & ATHLETIC GOODS: Snow Skiing Eqpt & Sply, Exc Skis

Nwt3k Outerwear .... G 253 318-2371
 Gig Harbor (G-4137)

SPORTING & ATHLETIC GOODS: Snow Skis

Evo .... G 866 386-1590
 Sumner (G-13070)
K2 Sports LLC .... C 206 805-4800
 Seattle (G-10322)
K2 Sports LLC .... G 206 805-4800
 Seattle (G-10323)
Tagline Products LLC .... G 360 927-2719
 Bellingham (G-1566)

SPORTING & ATHLETIC GOODS: Soccer Eqpt & Splys

Seattle Sport Sciences Inc .... F 425 939-0015
 Redmond (G-8659)

SPORTING & ATHLETIC GOODS: Strings, Tennis Racket

Riverside Club .... G 509 967-5756
 Richland (G-9039)

SPORTING & ATHLETIC GOODS: Target Shooting Eqpt

Tight Group Targets LLC .... G 206 227-0201
 Renton (G-8928)

SPORTING & ATHLETIC GOODS: Targets, Archery & Rifle Shooting

Arro Last Target Systems .... G 360 427-9512
 Shelton (G-11680)

Karl Plato .... G 360 875-8289
 South Bend (G-12042)

SPORTING & ATHLETIC GOODS: Team Sports Eqpt

Inventist Inc .... G 360 833-2357
 Camas (G-2258)
Noumena LLC .... G 206 451-3895
 Federal Way (G-3766)
Zooka Sports Corporation .... G 425 861-0111
 Redmond (G-8723)

SPORTING & ATHLETIC GOODS: Track & Field Athletic Eqpt

Vision Leadership Inc .... G 206 418-0808
 Seattle (G-11423)

SPORTING & ATHLETIC GOODS: Trampolines & Eqpt

Westco Engineering .... G 425 481-7271
 Woodinville (G-15403)

SPORTING & ATHLETIC GOODS: Water Skiing Eqpt & Splys

Connelly Skis Inc .... E 425 775-5416
 Lynnwood (G-6098)
Connelly Skis Inc .... G 425 831-1099
 Snoqualmie (G-12008)
Goodmans Ski and Sports Inc .... G 360 733-8937
 Bellingham (G-1358)

SPORTING & ATHLETIC GOODS: Water Skis

Kc Technology Inc .... G 509 933-2312
 Auburn (G-483)
ORyan Marine LLC .... F 425 485-2871
 Redmond (G-8604)

SPORTING & ATHLETIC GOODS: Water Sports Eqpt

Evans Board Shop .... G 360 297-4445
 Poulsbo (G-7962)
H20 Factor .... G 425 868-4017
 Sammamish (G-9212)
Motion Water Sports Inc .... D 800 662-7436
 Snoqualmie (G-12020)
Square One Distribution Inc .... E 425 369-6850
 Snoqualmie (G-12031)

SPORTING & ATHLETIC GOODS: Winter Sports

Pow Inc .... F 206 366-0224
 Seattle (G-10840)

SPORTING & RECREATIONAL GOODS & SPLYS WHOLESALERS

Aro-Tek Ltd .... G 360 754-2770
 Olympia (G-7230)
Gsi Outdoors Inc .... E 509 928-9611
 Spokane Valley (G-12725)
Jonathan Quinn Barnett Ltd .... G 206 322-2152
 Seattle (G-10305)
K Rounds LLC .... G 206 452-0466
 Kent (G-4972)
K2 Sports LLC .... C 206 805-4800
 Seattle (G-10322)
Macks Lures Manufacturing Co .... G 509 667-9202
 Wenatchee (G-15049)
Marine Servicenter Inc .... G 206 323-2405
 Seattle (G-10484)
McNett Corporation .... E 360 671-2227
 Bellingham (G-1431)
Rush Sails Inc .... G 425 827-9648
 Enumclaw (G-3319)
Safs Inc .... G 253 301-0615
 Tacoma (G-13506)
Wind Play Inc .... G 206 784-0414
 Seattle (G-11481)

SPORTING & RECREATIONAL GOODS, WHOL: Sharpeners, Sporting

Design Salt Inc .... G 509 667-1600
 Wenatchee (G-15025)

SPORTING & RECREATIONAL GOODS, WHOLESALE: Bicycle

J & B Importers Inc .... G 253 395-0441
 Sumner (G-13075)

SPORTING & RECREATIONAL GOODS, WHOLESALE: Boat Access & Part

Canvas Man .... G 360 293-2812
 Anacortes (G-108)
Churchill Brothers .... G 360 293-2700
 Everett (G-3417)
Lrt Inc .... G 425 742-0333
 Mill Creek (G-6516)
Railmakers Northwest .... F 425 259-9236
 Everett (G-3594)

SPORTING & RECREATIONAL GOODS, WHOLESALE: Exercise

Racer Mate Inc .... E 206 524-7392
 Seattle (G-10912)
Stl International Incorporated .... E 253 840-5252
 Buckley (G-2076)

SPORTING & RECREATIONAL GOODS, WHOLESALE: Fishing

Beau Mac Enterprises .... G 253 447-8093
 Sumner (G-13055)
Fetha Styx Inc .... G 360 687-3856
 Battle Ground (G-701)
Lfs Inc .... E 360 734-6825
 Bellingham (G-1408)
Lfs Inc .... E 360 734-3336
 Bellingham (G-1409)
Lucky Leaders .... G 206 363-2208
 Seattle (G-10447)
Northwest Hygienetics Inc .... G 253 529-0294
 Auburn (G-511)
Retco Inc .... G 360 341-1487
 Clinton (G-2695)
Trident Seafoods Asia Inc .... F 206 783-3818
 Seattle (G-11334)
Trident Seafoods Corporation .... B 206 783-3818
 Seattle (G-11335)

SPORTING & RECREATIONAL GOODS, WHOLESALE: Fishing Tackle

Dick Nite Spoons Inc .... G 425 377-8448
 Snohomish (G-11899)
Point Wilson Co Inc .... G 360 385-7625
 Port Townsend (G-7907)

SPORTING & RECREATIONAL GOODS, WHOLESALE: Fitness

Jaxjox Inc .... G 425 324-3017
 Vancouver (G-14335)
Mmusa Inc .... G 360 306-5383
 Lynnwood (G-6165)
Totalwave Fitness LLC .... G 509 361-9089
 Moses Lake (G-6754)

SPORTING & RECREATIONAL GOODS, WHOLESALE: Motorboats

Waya Group Inc .... G 877 277-6999
 Everett (G-3653)

SPORTING & RECREATIONAL GOODS, WHOLESALE: Sailboats

Northwest Marine Inds LLC .... G 360 389-5351
 Bellingham (G-1468)

SPORTING & RECREATIONAL GOODS, WHOLESALE: Skiing

Kc Technology Inc .... G 509 933-2312
 Auburn (G-483)

SPORTING & RECREATIONAL GOODS, WHOLESALE: Spa

Distribution Northwest Inc .... G 206 963-6126
 Bothell (G-1846)

PRODUCT SECTION

SPORTING GOODS: Sailboards

Stone Masters Inc .... G 509 667-8833
  Wenatchee *(G-15077)*
Tylohelo Inc .... E 425 951-1120
  Woodinville *(G-15393)*

SPORTING & RECREATIONAL GOODS, WHOLESALE: Surfing

Precision Shapes Nw LLC .... G 206 605-4396
  Seattle *(G-10852)*

SPORTING FIREARMS WHOLESALERS

Bullet Hole LLC .... G 509 868-8884
  Spokane Valley *(G-12646)*

SPORTING GOODS

Alki Sports LLC .... F 206 898-1305
  Redmond *(G-8378)*
Aro-Tek Ltd .... G 360 754-2770
  Olympia *(G-7230)*
B-A-Pro LLC .... G 253 861-3634
  Fife *(G-3936)*
Bowlbys Sporting Goods .... G 509 248-8281
  Yakima *(G-15524)*
Brooks Sports Inc .... G 253 863-4343
  Sumner *(G-13057)*
Buoy Wear LLC .... G 206 899-7926
  Centralia *(G-2386)*
Champion Sports Group .... G 360 258-0546
  Vancouver *(G-14112)*
Chaval Outdoor .... G 206 569-0154
  Bainbridge Island *(G-621)*
Clear Coated .... G 425 495-2369
  Seattle *(G-9693)*
Clear Your Clutter LLC .... G 206 784-1515
  Seattle *(G-9695)*
Clifford W Leeson Inc .... G 509 427-4155
  Stevenson *(G-13010)*
Columbia Cascade Company .... D 360 693-8558
  Vancouver *(G-14129)*
Composite Tooling Innovations .... G 509 637-3836
  Bingen *(G-1635)*
Coppertop Enterprises Inc .... E 360 966-9622
  Everson *(G-3672)*
Cuga Vest .... G 509 834-8378
  Yakima *(G-15544)*
Db Skimboards .... F 253 235-1811
  Fife *(G-3949)*
Diamond Nets Inc .... E 360 354-1319
  Everson *(G-3673)*
Dive Xtras .... G 425 296-6570
  Everett *(G-3443)*
Eastern Washington University .... F 509 359-6047
  Cheney *(G-2584)*
Eccintrixx LLC .... G 360 274-4954
  Castle Rock *(G-2341)*
Eqpd Gear LLC .... G 509 997-2010
  Twisp *(G-13911)*
Evan Martin Lure Inc .... G 425 478-7163
  Kenmore *(G-4572)*
Grassroots Outdoor LLC .... G 425 210-5745
  Everett *(G-3505)*
Hawks Prairie Golf LLC .... G 360 455-8383
  Bellevue *(G-938)*
Hemel Board Company .... G 206 261-2781
  Seattle *(G-10164)*
Homeplate Heroes .... G 360 798-7974
  Vancouver *(G-14301)*
Island Blueback Inc .... G 360 385-0871
  Port Townsend *(G-7892)*
Ixia Sports Inc .... G 425 417-6454
  Issaquah *(G-4432)*
Jig & Lure .... G 360 457-2745
  Port Angeles *(G-7718)*
Jumbo Dti Corporation .... F 253 272-9764
  Fife *(G-3961)*
Kadi Manufacturing .... G 360 668-5633
  Snohomish *(G-11929)*
LP Composites Inc .... F 509 493-4447
  Bingen *(G-1639)*
Maax Hydro Swirl Mfg Co .... D 360 734-0616
  Bellingham *(G-1417)*
Macs Discus .... G 425 483-3729
  Woodinville *(G-15298)*
McKay Shrimp & Crab Gear Inc .... G 360 796-4555
  Brinnon *(G-2025)*
McNett Corporation .... E 360 671-2227
  Bellingham *(G-1431)*
Moore Mfg Co .... G 360 677-2442
  Skykomish *(G-11867)*
Motion Ducks LLC .... G 253 797-0132
  Black Diamond *(G-1651)*
Nimbus Board Sports LLC .... G 360 387-1951
  Camano Island *(G-2219)*
Northwest Sports Products .... G 253 576-5958
  Tacoma *(G-13435)*
Pickle Ball Inc .... G 206 632-0119
  Seattle *(G-10800)*
Play Impossible Corporation .... G 206 852-7015
  Seattle *(G-10821)*
PR Lifting LLC .... G 425 214-4124
  Everett *(G-3581)*
Prism Designs Inc .... G 206 838-8682
  Seattle *(G-10865)*
RDL Enterprises Inc .... F 509 529-5480
  Walla Walla *(G-14859)*
Recluse LLC .... G 253 312-2169
  Gig Harbor *(G-4153)*
Recreational Equipment Inc .... B 206 223-1944
  Seattle *(G-10933)*
Redmond Town Center .... F 425 702-9158
  Redmond *(G-8646)*
Reeves Cricket Ranch Inc .... F 360 966-3300
  Everson *(G-3687)*
Rj Sports Inc .... G 425 227-8777
  Renton *(G-8895)*
Running 26 Inc .... G 425 948-6495
  Mill Creek *(G-6524)*
Seattle Cascades .... G 773 387-0502
  Seattle *(G-11050)*
Seattle Sports Company .... F 206 782-0773
  Seattle *(G-11077)*
Slingshot Sports LLC .... F 509 427-4950
  North Bonneville *(G-7135)*
SMC Gear .... G 360 366-5534
  Ferndale *(G-3905)*
Strike Addiction LLC .... G 206 713-6061
  Yakima *(G-15685)*
Teammates Sports Products LLC .... G 206 780-2037
  Bainbridge Island *(G-676)*
Teamwest Ltd .... G 425 227-8525
  Newcastle *(G-7041)*
Tweet Promotional Impressions .... G 206 660-6074
  Auburn *(G-585)*
United Volleyball Supply LLC .... F 425 576-8835
  Redmond *(G-8698)*
West Coast Athletic LLC .... G 425 413-9200
  Maple Valley *(G-6299)*
Zooka .... G 425 363-3922
  North Bend *(G-7132)*

SPORTING GOODS STORES, NEC

Arro Last Target Systems .... G 360 427-9512
  Shelton *(G-11680)*
Clarks All-Sports Inc .... E 509 684-5069
  Colville *(G-2743)*
Classic Cycle .... F 206 842-9191
  Bainbridge Island *(G-622)*
Darbonnier Tactical Supply LLC .... G 360 672-0216
  Oak Harbor *(G-7146)*
Dayton Traister Co Inc .... G 360 675-3421
  Oak Harbor *(G-7147)*
Hunter Fish Enterprises .... G 253 852-8357
  Renton *(G-8822)*
Moore Mfg Co .... G 360 677-2442
  Skykomish *(G-11867)*
Mvp Athletic Inc .... G 360 915-8715
  Tumwater *(G-13888)*
Recreational Equipment Inc .... B 206 223-1944
  Seattle *(G-10933)*
Redbird Sports Inc .... F 206 725-7872
  Seattle *(G-10939)*
Rj Sports Inc .... G 425 227-8777
  Renton *(G-8895)*
Survival Gear Systems .... F 866 257-2978
  Spokane *(G-12536)*
The McCredy Company .... G 509 773-5340
  Goldendale *(G-4209)*
Trondak Inc .... G 360 794-8250
  Monroe *(G-6634)*
Volcanic Manufacturing LLC .... G 509 427-8623
  North Bonneville *(G-7136)*
Yakima Bait Co .... C 509 854-1311
  Granger *(G-4264)*

SPORTING GOODS STORES: Ammunition

Defense Sales Intl LLC .... G 206 999-8684
  Renton *(G-8782)*

SPORTING GOODS STORES: Bait & Tackle

Beau Mac Enterprises .... G 253 447-8093
  Sumner *(G-13055)*
K&B Custom Rods & Tackle .... G 360 354-1945
  Lynden *(G-6028)*

SPORTING GOODS STORES: Firearms

Aero Precision LLC .... E 253 272-8188
  Tacoma *(G-13158)*
Bowlbys Sporting Goods .... G 509 248-8281
  Yakima *(G-15524)*
Bullet Hole LLC .... G 509 868-8884
  Spokane Valley *(G-12646)*
Hardened Arms LLC .... E 425 530-0837
  Friday Harbor *(G-4050)*
McCann Industries LLC .... G 253 537-6919
  Spanaway *(G-12064)*

SPORTING GOODS STORES: Fishing Eqpt

Lfs Inc .... E 360 734-6825
  Bellingham *(G-1408)*
Lfs Inc .... E 360 734-3336
  Bellingham *(G-1409)*
Petrzelka Bros Inc .... G 360 424-8095
  Mount Vernon *(G-6824)*

SPORTING GOODS STORES: Gymnasium Eqpt, NEC

Body Builders Gym Equipment .... G 253 631-8274
  Kent *(G-4816)*

SPORTING GOODS STORES: Playground Eqpt

Child Inc .... G 425 775-9076
  Edmonds *(G-3100)*

SPORTING GOODS STORES: Soccer Splys

International Athletic .... G 360 384-6868
  Ferndale *(G-3860)*
Jumbo Dti Corporation .... F 253 272-9764
  Fife *(G-3961)*

SPORTING GOODS STORES: Team sports Eqpt

Alki Sports LLC .... F 206 898-1305
  Redmond *(G-8378)*
Edmonds Athletic Supply Co .... G 425 778-7322
  Lynnwood *(G-6111)*

SPORTING GOODS STORES: Water Sport Eqpt

Goodmans Ski and Sports Inc .... G 360 733-8937
  Bellingham *(G-1358)*

SPORTING GOODS: Archery

Clean-Shot Archery Inc .... G 425 242-5970
  Kent *(G-4853)*

SPORTING GOODS: Fishing Nets

3 Lakes Fly Fishing .... G 509 675-4200
  Kettle Falls *(G-5223)*
Diamond Nets Inc .... E 360 354-1319
  Everson *(G-3673)*
Factory Trawler Supply Inc .... G 206 285-6732
  Seattle *(G-9961)*
Lummi Island Wild Co-Op L L C .... G 360 366-8786
  Bellingham *(G-1415)*
Nanook Lodge .... G 206 200-8233
  Seattle *(G-10586)*
Nwfsc .... G 206 860-3415
  Seattle *(G-10676)*
Olympic Fly Fishers .... G 206 546-2677
  Shoreline *(G-11797)*
Research Nets Incorporated .... G 425 821-7345
  Redmond *(G-8649)*
Riptide Charters Inc .... G 360 815-6568
  Blaine *(G-1702)*

SPORTING GOODS: Sailboards

North Sports Inc .... F 509 493-4938
  White Salmon *(G-15124)*

Employee Codes: A=Over 500 employees, B=251-500
C=101-250, D=51-100, E=20-50, F=10-19, G=2-9

SPORTING GOODS: Skin Diving Eqpt

- Carter Lift Bag Inc ....G........ 360 886-2302
  Enumclaw (G-3280)
- Ideations Design Inc ....G........ 206 281-0067
  Seattle (G-10203)
- Seasoft Scuba Inc ....G........ 253 939-5510
  Chehalis (G-2536)

SPORTING GOODS: Sleeping Bags

- Cascade Designs Inc ....E........ 206 505-9500
  Seattle (G-9642)
- Design Salt Inc ....G........ 509 667-1600
  Wenatchee (G-15025)
- Professional Sleep Services ....G........ 253 759-2700
  Tacoma (G-13479)

SPORTING GOODS: Surfboards

- D Crockett Surfboards ....G........ 425 430-9947
  Renton (G-8778)

SPORTING/ATHLETIC GOODS: Gloves, Boxing, Handball, Etc

- Fownes Brothers & Co Inc ....G........ 360 738-3126
  Bellingham (G-1353)

SPORTS APPAREL STORES

- Action Sports & Locks Inc ....G........ 360 435-9505
  Arlington (G-193)
- Alki Sports LLC ....F........ 206 898-1305
  Redmond (G-8378)
- All CS Inc ....G........ 253 474-3434
  Tacoma (G-13163)
- Ascendance Pole & Aerial Arts ....G........ 425 256-2246
  Renton (G-8748)
- Centralia Knitting Mills Inc ....E........ 360 736-3994
  Centralia (G-2390)
- Competitive Edge Athletics ....G........ 206 246-7211
  Burien (G-2098)
- Ers Group Inc ....G........ 360 895-1318
  Port Orchard (G-7808)
- Lady 12 LLC ....G........ 425 218-3080
  Redmond (G-8528)
- Mr TS Trophies ....G........ 360 424-9339
  Mount Vernon (G-6815)
- Mtn Threds and Clothing ....G........ 509 258-4443
  Valley (G-13994)
- Pacific Sportswear LLC ....E........ 253 582-4444
  Tacoma (G-13455)
- U S Practical Shooting Assn ....F........ 360 855-2245
  Burlington (G-2195)
- Wapiti Woolies Inc ....G........ 360 663-2268
  Enumclaw (G-3326)
- Wildrose Ltd ....F........ 509 535-8555
  Spokane (G-12591)

SPRAYING EQPT: Agricultural

- Ag Spray Equipment Inc ....E........ 509 488-6631
  Othello (G-7490)
- H F Hauff Co Inc ....F........ 509 248-0318
  Yakima (G-15578)
- Nozzleworks Inc ....G........ 360 668-2548
  Bothell (G-1881)

SPRINGS: Clock, Precision

- Airborne Ecs LLC ....F........ 319 538-1051
  Port Angeles (G-7679)

SPRINGS: Coiled Flat

- Pohl Spring Works Inc ....F........ 509 466-0904
  Spokane Valley (G-12831)

SPRINGS: Steel

- Sound Spring Inc ....F........ 253 859-9499
  Kent (G-5142)

SPRINGS: Wire

- Sound Spring Inc ....F........ 253 859-9499
  Kent (G-5142)

SPRINKLER SYSTEMS: Field

- Accor Technology Inc ....G........ 425 453-5410
  Kirkland (G-5268)
- Aquatronix LLC ....G........ 425 881-8600
  Redmond (G-8383)
- C & E Sprinkler ....G........ 509 466-2020
  Mead (G-6426)
- Nelson Irrigation Corporation ....C........ 509 525-7660
  Walla Walla (G-14850)

SPRINKLING SYSTEMS: Fire Control

- Security Alarms Plus Inc ....G........ 509 457-8799
  Zillah (G-15758)
- United Association of Journeym ....G........ 206 441-0737
  Seattle (G-11369)

STACKS: Smoke

- Town Smoke Plus ....G........ 360 456-8234
  Olympia (G-7412)

STAGE LIGHTING SYSTEMS

- Pacific Stage Lighting ....G........ 253 248-6344
  Gig Harbor (G-4141)

STAINED GLASS ART SVCS

- Other Worlds ....G........ 360 459-2323
  Olympia (G-7363)

STAINLESS STEEL

- Great Sun Corp ....F........ 206 329-8027
  Seattle (G-10114)
- J and J Stainless Steel Svcs ....G........ 509 952-4568
  Yakima (G-15594)
- Metal Masters Northwest Inc ....G........ 425 775-4481
  Lynnwood (G-6162)
- Poizer Metal Works ....G........ 360 892-2629
  Vancouver (G-14492)
- Source Engineering LLC ....E........ 360 383-5129
  Lynden (G-6053)

STAINLESS STEEL WARE

- Industrial Design & Eqp Inc ....G........ 360 671-9200
  Ferndale (G-3855)
- Mackenzie Spcalty Castings Inc ....E........ 360 435-5539
  Arlington (G-271)
- Rena Ware International Inc ....E........ 425 881-6171
  Bellevue (G-1098)

STAINS: Wood

- Perma-Chink Systems Inc ....F........ 425 885-6050
  Redmond (G-8619)

STAIRCASES & STAIRS, WOOD

- Finishing Touches ....G........ 425 277-6079
  Renton (G-8799)
- Fitts Industries Inc ....G........ 253 474-0376
  Tacoma (G-13297)
- Seattle Stair & Design LLC ....F........ 206 587-5354
  Seattle (G-11078)

STAMPED ART GOODS FOR EMBROIDERING

- Clarks All-Sports Inc ....E........ 509 684-5069
  Colville (G-2743)
- Ideal Commercial Uniforms ....G........ 360 876-1767
  Port Orchard (G-7814)
- Julies Designs ....G........ 206 727-3341
  Issaquah (G-4434)
- Red Creek Embroidery LLC ....G........ 360 956-1792
  Olympia (G-7381)
- Williamson Illustration ....G........ 360 734-5497
  Ferndale (G-3925)

STAMPINGS: Automotive

- Hard Notched Customs LLC ....F........ 360 205-3252
  Vancouver (G-14281)
- Proliance International ....G........ 206 764-7028
  Seattle (G-10875)
- R & A Manufacturing Inc ....G........ 425 228-2109
  Renton (G-8888)

STAMPINGS: Metal

- Buyken Metal Products Inc ....E........ 253 852-0634
  Kent (G-4827)
- Coastal Manufacturing Inc ....E........ 425 407-0624
  Everett (G-3421)
- Foil Graphics ....G........ 360 574-9030
  Vancouver (G-14236)
- Glenns Welding and Mfg Inc ....E........ 425 743-2226
  Lynnwood (G-6131)
- Gompf Brackets Inc ....F........ 425 348-5002
  Mukilteo (G-6929)
- Graphic Impressions Inc ....E........ 253 872-0555
  Kent (G-4925)
- Imaginetics Holdings LLC ....E........ 253 735-0156
  Auburn (G-472)
- Imaginetics LLC ....D........ 253 735-0156
  Auburn (G-473)
- Industrial Revolution Inc ....E........ 425 285-1111
  Tukwila (G-13752)
- Northwest Marine Tech Inc ....E........ 360 468-3375
  Shaw Island (G-11671)
- Northwest Precision Tool Inc ....G........ 509 493-4044
  White Salmon (G-15125)
- Precision Spring Stamping Corp ....E........ 253 852-6911
  Kent (G-5078)
- Whitefab ....G........ 253 277-4047
  Kent (G-5216)

STATIONARY & OFFICE SPLYS, WHOL: Computer/Photocopying Splys

- B G Instruments Inc ....G........ 509 893-9881
  Spokane Valley (G-12635)

STATIONARY & OFFICE SPLYS, WHOLESALE: Blank Books

- Nobelus LLC ....G........ 800 895-2747
  Seattle (G-10614)

STATIONARY & OFFICE SPLYS, WHOLESALE: Laser Printer Splys

- Cartridge Care Inc ....G........ 360 459-8845
  Lacey (G-5540)

STATIONARY & OFFICE SPLYS, WHOLESALE: Manifold Business Form

- Now Impressions Inc ....G........ 425 881-5911
  Redmond (G-8601)

STATIONARY & OFFICE SPLYS, WHOLESALE: Office Filing Splys

- Cartridge World ....G........ 509 469-9711
  Kennewick (G-4643)

STATIONER'S SUNDRIES: Rubber

- Clearsnap Holding Inc ....D........ 360 293-6634
  Burlington (G-2145)

STATIONERY & OFFICE SPLYS WHOLESALERS

- B C T Inc ....E........ 206 343-9355
  Seattle (G-9474)
- Comp U Charge Inc ....F........ 509 484-1918
  Spokane (G-12194)
- JC Global Supply LLC ....G........ 253 275-6093
  Kent (G-4966)
- Lazer Cartridges Plus LLC ....G........ 509 529-0200
  Walla Walla (G-14835)
- Liberty Business Forms Inc ....D........ 509 536-0515
  Spokane (G-12362)

STATIONERY PRDTS

- Bechris Inc ....G........ 253 565-0905
  Tacoma (G-13192)
- Paper Delights ....G........ 206 547-1002
  Seattle (G-10748)
- Ron Hall ....G........ 360 468-2294
  Lopez Island (G-5986)

STATORS REWINDING SVCS

- Overload Electric Winding Svcs ....G........ 253 848-8900
  Puyallup (G-8211)

STATUARY GOODS, EXC RELIGIOUS: Wholesalers

- Nichols Bros Stoneworks Ltd ....E........ 360 668-5434
  Snohomish (G-11951)

T J Pottery .... G 253 946-1974
Kent *(G-5169)*

STEEL & ALLOYS: Tool & Die

Buyken Metal Products Inc .... E 253 852-0634
Kent *(G-4827)*
K B Alloys .... G 360 371-2312
Blaine *(G-1677)*

STEEL FABRICATORS

A B Fabricators .... G 206 763-2600
Auburn *(G-359)*
Aalbu Brothers of Everett Inc .... G 425 252-9751
Everett *(G-3356)*
ABG .... G 253 896-1372
Fife *(G-3927)*
Above & Beyond Unlimited .... G 253 921-3535
Tacoma *(G-13154)*
Abw Technologies Inc .... C 360 618-4400
Arlington *(G-191)*
Acufab Inc .... G 509 525-3833
Walla Walla *(G-14759)*
Addison Construction Sup Inc .... D 253 474-0711
Tacoma *(G-13157)*
Alki Foundry .... G 206 794-4074
Seattle *(G-9377)*
All Fabrication and Supply LLC .... G 509 334-1905
Pullman *(G-8083)*
Allform Welding Inc .... G 360 681-0584
Sequim *(G-11607)*
Allied Steel Fabricators Inc .... E 425 861-9558
Redmond *(G-8380)*
American Structures Design Inc .... G 253 833-4343
Pacific *(G-7522)*
Apex Curb & Turf LLC .... F 509 758-1543
Clarkston *(G-2620)*
Apex Railing Solutions .... G 206 452-3281
Seattle *(G-9409)*
Argo Blower & Mfg Co .... F 206 762-9336
Seattle *(G-9428)*
Artaca Co .... G 425 398-0122
Kenmore *(G-4565)*
ASC Profiles LLC .... E 509 535-0600
Spokane *(G-12120)*
ASC Profiles LLC .... E 253 383-4955
Tacoma *(G-13184)*
Associated Metals Fabrication .... G 360 793-2422
Sultan *(G-13021)*
Atech Services LLC .... C 206 453-3182
Seattle *(G-9450)*
Atkore International Group Inc .... G 253 478-3199
Kent *(G-4796)*
Atwood Fabricating .... G 425 481-5388
Bothell *(G-1826)*
Automatic Products Mfg Co LLC .... G 253 395-7173
Kent *(G-4801)*
Avantech Inc .... D 509 943-6706
Richland *(G-8969)*
Avos Inc .... G 503 713-8404
Vancouver *(G-14049)*
B & B Parrotts Welding Inc .... G 360 825-0565
Enumclaw *(G-3277)*
B&B Custom Metals LLC .... G 425 308-8478
Richland *(G-8970)*
Barreras Precision Fabg LLC .... G 253 850-6227
Kent *(G-4809)*
Barrett Sheet Metal .... G 509 886-8708
East Wenatchee *(G-3008)*
Barrys Steve Pool Service LLC .... G 360 533-0421
Aberdeen *(G-3)*
Bedkers Prtble Wldg Fbrication .... G 253 581-7077
Lakewood *(G-5702)*
Bmt Metal Fabrication Inc .... G 509 244-6107
Airway Heights *(G-49)*
Bowman-Morton Mfg & Mch Inc .... F 206 524-8890
Seattle *(G-9573)*
Bradken Inc .... E 253 475-3464
Tacoma *(G-13208)*
Broomflds Wldg Met Fabrication .... G 206 784-9267
Seattle *(G-9589)*
Brown-Mnnplis Tnk-Nrthwest LLC .... E 360 482-1720
Elma *(G-3243)*
BTS Partners LLC .... G 253 862-4622
Bonney Lake *(G-1718)*
Buyken Metal Products Inc .... E 253 852-0634
Kent *(G-4827)*
C T Specialties .... G 360 786-0274
Tumwater *(G-13854)*
Cameron Steel Fabrication .... F 360 403-9400
Arlington *(G-217)*
Can AM Fabrication Inc .... G 360 653-2245
Marysville *(G-6321)*
Canam Steel Corporation .... C 509 837-7008
Vancouver *(G-14094)*
Centerline Fabrication .... G 509 948-8711
Benton City *(G-1604)*
Centerline Fabricators LLC .... G 253 922-3226
Fife *(G-3941)*
Central Fabricators Inc .... G 509 468-3995
Spokane *(G-12175)*
CH Murphy/Clark-Ullman Inc .... D 253 475-6566
Tacoma *(G-13232)*
Cleveland Enterprises Inc .... G 360 694-0435
Vancouver *(G-14123)*
Columbia Metal Fab Cnstr Inc .... G 360 989-0201
Kalama *(G-4496)*
Columbia Metal Works Inc .... G 360 693-5818
Vancouver *(G-14134)*
Cooper Smithing Co .... G 253 906-0425
Buckley *(G-2054)*
Cr Enterprises Nw LLC .... G 425 290-3800
Mukilteo *(G-6908)*
Craftsmen United Inc .... F 360 379-2500
Port Townsend *(G-7874)*
Crf Metal Works LLC .... F 509 430-7609
Pasco *(G-7571)*
Crown Carriage Works Inc .... G 509 535-4427
Spokane *(G-12210)*
Curfman Custom Fabrication LLC .... G 360 736-7277
Centralia *(G-2396)*
Davids Aquacut & Builders .... G 509 527-8700
Walla Walla *(G-14793)*
Davis & Walker Fabrication .... G 360 944-0057
Vancouver *(G-14167)*
Design Construction Heritg Inc .... G 206 634-1989
Everett *(G-3442)*
Direct Process Metal Fabg .... G 206 276-6014
Seattle *(G-9834)*
Diversifab LLC .... G 253 459-5170
Yelm *(G-15732)*
Doug D Froland .... G 206 932-8433
Seattle *(G-9849)*
Duthie Enterprises Inc .... E 206 767-3314
Seattle *(G-9862)*
Eastside Welding & Fabrication .... G 509 765-6434
Moses Lake *(G-6707)*
Easy Street Custom Metal .... G 509 662-1018
Wenatchee *(G-15028)*
Edco Inc .... E 360 424-6600
Mount Vernon *(G-6792)*
Eridu Designs .... G 360 247-5980
Amboy *(G-93)*
Eugene P Lamm Jr .... G 509 460-1240
Richland *(G-8995)*
Excel Manufacturing Inc .... G 253 939-6446
Auburn *(G-438)*
Expermntal Arcft Met Fbrcation .... G 360 245-3478
Chehalis *(G-2495)*
Fab-Tech Inc .... G 360 755-0215
Burlington *(G-2156)*
Fabricated Products Inc .... C 360 695-5949
Vancouver *(G-14217)*
Fabrication Products Inc .... E 503 283-3218
Vancouver *(G-14219)*
Fabtech Manufacturing LLC .... G 509 488-1950
Othello *(G-7495)*
Faqa .... G 206 362-5916
Seattle *(G-9970)*
Far West Fabricators Inc .... G 509 453-1663
Moxee *(G-6877)*
Farm Built Fab LLC .... G 360 213-8458
La Center *(G-5504)*
Farwest Iron Works Inc .... G 509 662-3546
Wenatchee *(G-15031)*
Farwest Steel Fabrication Co .... D 800 793-1493
Vancouver *(G-14223)*
Fat Daddys Fabrication LLC .... G 253 677-8005
Roy *(G-9159)*
Ferrotek Corporation .... F 360 366-7444
Ferndale *(G-3845)*
Fixture Engineering Inc .... G 360 671-9052
Bellingham *(G-1347)*
Folsom Industries Inc .... F 509 921-6602
Greenacres *(G-4298)*
Frazier Industrial Company .... G 509 698-4100
Selah *(G-11588)*
Frisbee Enterprises LLC .... G 360 991-1662
Vancouver *(G-14240)*
Frys Welding Inc .... G .....
Auburn *(G-445)*
Gepford Welding Inc .... G 509 624-6610
Spokane *(G-12272)*
Gerald McCallum .... G 509 467-8456
Spokane *(G-12273)*
Glenns Welding and Mfg Inc .... E 425 743-2226
Lynnwood *(G-6131)*
Global Incorporated .... F 206 763-4424
Seattle *(G-10084)*
Global Mtal Works Erectors LLC .... E 253 572-5363
Tacoma *(G-13312)*
Global Technical Staffin .... G 512 694-7621
Vancouver *(G-14259)*
Gompf Brackets Inc .... F 425 348-5002
Mukilteo *(G-6929)*
Goodman Custom Fab .... G 253 720-2451
Tacoma *(G-13317)*
Green Mountain Metalworks LLC .... G 360 281-6048
Woodland *(G-15435)*
Greenberry Industrial LLC .... G 360 366-3767
Ferndale *(G-3849)*
Gw 42 Inc .... G 360 862-8319
Snohomish *(G-11918)*
Harris Rebar Seattle Inc .... E 253 847-5001
Tacoma *(G-13332)*
Highlands Welding Repair Inc .... G 206 283-0080
Seattle *(G-10172)*
Hiline Engrg & Fabrication Inc .... E 509 943-9043
Richland *(G-9006)*
Hoffman Manufacturing .... G 509 286-3200
Latah *(G-5791)*
Hydrafab Northwest Inc .... E 509 535-0075
Spokane Valley *(G-12733)*
Illume .... G 206 566-5375
Seattle *(G-10205)*
Imsa Steel Corp .... B 360 673-8200
Kalama *(G-4501)*
Industrial Fabrication Co .... E 360 793-9001
Sultan *(G-13027)*
Industrial Fbrication Tstg Inc .... G 360 345-1400
Chehalis *(G-2505)*
Instafab Company Inc .... E 360 737-8235
Vancouver *(G-14317)*
Integrated Systems Design .... G 360 746-0812
Bellingham *(G-1380)*
Intermountain Fabricators Inc .... F 509 534-1676
Spokane Valley *(G-12746)*
Island Riggers Inc .... G 206 920-3360
Bainbridge Island *(G-642)*
J D Ott Co Inc .... C 206 749-0777
Seattle *(G-10269)*
J L Brooks Welding Inc .... F 360 403-9400
Arlington *(G-259)*
Jabez Marpac Construction Jv1 .... E 253 735-2000
Orting *(G-7483)*
JAS Steel Fabricating .... G 425 424-2107
Woodinville *(G-15273)*
Jesse Engineering Company .... E 253 552-1500
Tacoma *(G-13358)*
Jet City Partners LLC .... G 206 999-0047
Auburn *(G-479)*
Jetco Mch & Fabrication LLC .... F 509 243-8910
Clarkston *(G-2636)*
Jlt Partners Inc .... G 800 325-7513
Kent *(G-4968)*
Johnson Fabrication .... G 360 874-2679
Port Orchard *(G-7821)*
Kalispel Tribe of Indians .... E 509 242-7000
Airway Heights *(G-54)*
Kermit Anderson .... G 509 535-2362
Spokane Valley *(G-12765)*
KY International LLC .... G 253 373-9602
Covington *(G-2831)*
Larry Waits Nemesis .... G 253 863-4444
Lake Tapps *(G-5681)*
Lee Fabricators Inc .... F 360 698-1190
Silverdale *(G-11843)*
Lev Design .... G 425 417-2758
Seattle *(G-10409)*
Lynn L Reynolds Inc .... G 509 536-9396
Spokane Valley *(G-12779)*
M H R A Corp .... G 360 978-6878
Onalaska *(G-7451)*
Machinists Inc .... E 206 763-0840
Seattle *(G-10461)*
Madlyn Metal Fab Llc .... E 360 693-1019
Vancouver *(G-14392)*
Marketech International Inc .... F 360 379-6707
Sequim *(G-11647)*
McVays Mobile Welding LLC .... G 360 657-0360
Marysville *(G-6358)*

Employee Codes: A=Over 500 employees, B=251-500
C=101-250, D=51-100, E=20-50, F=10-19, G=2-9
2019 Washington
Manufacturers Register
1083

Metal Solutions LLC ....D....... 206 767-5587
Seattle *(G-10521)*
Metal Works Inc.......G....... 509 782-8811
Dryden *(G-2953)*
Metal Works Northwest.......G....... 206 624-4766
Seattle *(G-10522)*
Metalfab Inc.......E....... 509 967-2946
West Richland *(G-15098)*
Miller Fabrication Inc.......G....... 253 833-5400
Auburn *(G-498)*
Mohawk Metal Company.......G....... 360 816-0679
Vancouver *(G-14423)*
Monarch Machine and Tl Co Inc.......E....... 509 547-7753
Pasco *(G-7603)*
Morgan Steel & Metal Works.......G....... 360 301-6611
Poulsbo *(G-7986)*
Naimor Inc.......E....... 360 756-9700
Bellingham *(G-1457)*
Newell Corp.......F....... 360 435-8955
Arlington *(G-287)*
Nor-Tech Fabricating LLC.......E....... 360 232-0144
Kelso *(G-4539)*
Northwest Stair and Rail Inc.......G....... 425 348-7880
Everett *(G-3558)*
Nucor Corporation.......C....... 206 933-2222
Seattle *(G-10666)*
Olympic Iron Works.......F....... 360 491-2500
Olympia *(G-7358)*
Omega Industries Inc.......E....... 360 574-9086
Vancouver *(G-14450)*
Omnifab Inc.......E....... 253 931-5151
Auburn *(G-518)*
ONeill Steel Fabrication Inc.......F....... 509 467-5309
Spokane *(G-12421)*
Orbit Industries LLC.......E....... 360 835-8526
Washougal *(G-14976)*
Pacific Fabricating.......G....... 360 588-1078
Anacortes *(G-159)*
Pacific Northwest Iron LLC.......G....... 509 499-0668
Nine Mile Falls *(G-7081)*
Pacific Northwest Mech LLC.......F....... 509 765-9606
Moses Lake *(G-6735)*
Parker Manufacturing LLC.......G....... 509 663-5923
Wenatchee *(G-15060)*
Parkers Truck & Equipment Repr.......G....... 253 833-3696
Pacific *(G-7538)*
Patriot Jabez Construction JV.......G....... 253 293-7100
Auburn *(G-527)*
Pauley Rodine Inc.......G....... 509 773-3200
Goldendale *(G-4205)*
Pederson Bros Inc.......E....... 360 734-9180
Bellingham *(G-1493)*
Pfc Inc.......G....... 360 398-8889
Bellingham *(G-1497)*
Pinnacle Steel Fabricators.......F....... 253 770-1690
Puyallup *(G-8223)*
Precision Iron Works Inc.......E....... 253 887-5555
Pacific *(G-7539)*
Precision Metal Works LLC.......G....... 509 945-8433
Union Gap *(G-13951)*
Precision Rebar & ACC Inc.......F....... 360 574-1022
Vancouver *(G-14501)*
Pro Fab Inc.......G....... 206 762-5149
Seattle *(G-10868)*
Pro Fab Industries Inc.......G....... 360 629-4642
Stanwood *(G-12986)*
Prometco Inc.......F....... 425 486-0759
Bothell *(G-1891)*
Puget Sound Metal Fabrication.......G....... 253 941-7868
Auburn *(G-540)*
Puget Sound Steel Co Inc.......E....... 253 854-3600
Kent *(G-5088)*
Rainier Building Supply LLC.......G....... 206 939-2591
Everett *(G-3595)*
Ramgen Power Systems LLC.......G....... 425 828-4919
Bellevue *(G-1094)*
Ray Fanns Whispering Pines.......G....... 360 384-4750
Custer *(G-2859)*
Red Dog Fabrication LLC.......F....... 360 892-3647
Vancouver *(G-14537)*
Redmond Wlders Fabricators Inc.......E....... 425 222-6330
Issaquah *(G-4465)*
Reinkes Fabrication Inc.......F....... 360 398-2011
Bellingham *(G-1515)*
S & S Welding Inc.......E....... 206 793-9943
Kent *(G-5110)*
Scotts Sheet Metal.......G....... 360 384-3827
Ferndale *(G-3902)*
Sea Cure Technology Inc.......G....... 360 676-1824
Acme *(G-44)*
Sea Pac Transport Services LLC.......E....... 206 763-0339
Seattle *(G-11037)*
Seaview Boat Yard Inc.......F....... 206 783-6550
Seattle *(G-11086)*
Ser Pro Inc.......G....... 206 767-3100
Seattle *(G-11090)*
Skagit Industrial Steel Inc.......E....... 360 854-0074
Sedro Woolley *(G-11567)*
Smileys Inc.......F....... 360 424-7338
Mount Vernon *(G-6843)*
Speedfab.......G....... 360 571-4093
Vancouver *(G-14602)*
Ss Industrial Inc.......G....... 509 427-7836
Stevenson *(G-13020)*
Standard Steel Fabg Co Inc.......G....... 206 767-0499
Seattle *(G-11180)*
Starman Metal Fabrications LLC.......G....... 425 235-1431
Renton *(G-8919)*
Steel Encounters Inc.......F....... 206 281-8500
Seattle *(G-11186)*
Steel Fab Inc.......E....... 425 743-9216
Arlington *(G-333)*
Sunmodo Corporation.......G....... 360 844-0048
Vancouver *(G-14615)*
T Bailey Inc.......C....... 360 293-0682
Anacortes *(G-173)*
T2 Services Inc.......F....... 509 893-3666
Spokane Valley *(G-12899)*
TAC Fab LLC.......G....... 206 755-0519
Woodinville *(G-15385)*
Talco Services LLC.......F....... 425 259-0213
Everett *(G-3626)*
Technifab Inc.......G....... 509 534-1022
Spokane Valley *(G-12903)*
Telegraph Fabrication.......G....... 360 739-8170
Ferndale *(G-3912)*
Teras Construction LLC.......G....... 253 539-2887
Tacoma *(G-13554)*
Three Squared LLC.......G....... 206 708-5918
Bellevue *(G-1187)*
Tl Northwest Corp.......F....... 253 445-4104
Puyallup *(G-8264)*
Transpac Marinas Inc.......G....... 360 293-8888
Anacortes *(G-178)*
Triple C Fabricators LLC.......G....... 360 868-4125
Shelton *(G-11746)*
Triton Holdings Inc.......F....... 360 466-4160
Mount Vernon *(G-6848)*
Trufab LLC.......F....... 360 229-3028
Shelton *(G-11747)*
United Iron Works Inc.......E....... 206 767-3630
Tacoma *(G-13570)*
Universal Stl Fabricators LLC.......F....... 253 891-4224
Tacoma *(G-13572)*
Valleyford Metal Crafters LLC.......E....... 509 448-5583
Spokane *(G-12579)*
Valmont Industries Inc.......G....... 509 921-0290
Spokane Valley *(G-12925)*
Vigor Works LLC.......E....... 360 699-1547
Vancouver *(G-14670)*
Vulcan Products Company Inc.......E....... 425 806-6000
Woodinville *(G-15401)*
Wb Mobile Modular Service.......G....... 253 952-4630
Edgewood *(G-3091)*
Weld-Tech Fabrication Inc.......G....... 425 591-5912
Rochester *(G-9144)*
Wenatchee Qlty Wldg Fbrication.......F....... 509 782-0807
Cashmere *(G-2333)*
West Coast Custom Metal Design.......G....... 360 738-2884
Bellingham *(G-1592)*
Western Metal Products LLC.......G....... 509 962-4895
Ellensburg *(G-3238)*
Whodat Towers.......G....... 360 786-1984
Centralia *(G-2443)*
Wiese and Son Inc.......G....... 509 455-8610
Spokane *(G-12590)*

STEEL MILLS

Advanced All Wheel Drive.......G....... 360 746-8746
Ferndale *(G-3809)*
Ameron International Corp.......D....... 909 944-4100
Vancouver *(G-14029)*
Boutique On Wheels.......G....... 425 369-9324
Sammamish *(G-9192)*
Brooks Steel Fabrication.......G....... 360 403-9400
Arlington *(G-215)*
Centralia Supply & Fabrication.......G....... 360 736-7277
Centralia *(G-2391)*
Cobalt Trailer Sales.......G....... 509 535-2154
Spokane *(G-12186)*
Franks Custom Wheels.......G....... 360 333-6887
Mount Vernon *(G-6798)*
Gundies Inc.......E....... 360 733-5036
Bellingham *(G-1364)*
Intermountain Fabricators Inc.......F....... 509 534-1676
Spokane Valley *(G-12746)*
Northwest Pipe Company.......B....... 303 289-4080
Vancouver *(G-14438)*
Nucor Corporation.......C....... 206 933-2222
Seattle *(G-10666)*
Nucor Steel Seattle Inc.......C....... 206 933-2222
Seattle *(G-10667)*
Pacific Steel Structures LLC.......G....... 509 921-5835
Greenacres *(G-4301)*
Precise Manufacturing & Engrg.......F....... 360 604-8742
Vancouver *(G-14499)*
SIS Northwest Inc.......G....... 360 854-0074
Sedro Woolley *(G-11565)*
Steel Fab Nw Inc.......G....... 360 210-7055
Washougal *(G-14987)*
Steelscape LLC.......C....... 360 673-8200
Kalama *(G-4510)*

STEEL: Cold-Rolled

Puget Sound Steel Co Inc.......E....... 253 854-3600
Kent *(G-5088)*

STENCILS & LETTERING MATERIALS: Die-Cut

Comeau Lettering.......G....... 360 573-2216
Vancouver *(G-14141)*

STILLS: Pressure, Metal Plate

P D M Stilled Service Inc.......E....... 360 225-1133
Woodland *(G-15454)*

STITCHING SVCS

Plastic Sales & Service Inc.......F....... 206 524-8312
Lynnwood *(G-6181)*

STONE: Crushed & Broken, NEC

Kalama River Road Quarry.......G....... 360 673-0795
Kalama *(G-4503)*
Washougal Baselt Rock Qua.......G....... 360 335-0111
Washougal *(G-14998)*

STONE: Dimension, NEC

410 Quarry Dibella Entps Inc.......G....... 360 825-7505
Enumclaw *(G-3273)*
Arris Kollman Trucking Inc.......G....... 360 532-0351
Shelton *(G-11679)*
Arris Kollman Trucking Inc.......E....... 360 532-0351
Aberdeen *(G-2)*
Cadman (rock) Inc.......D....... 425 867-1234
Redmond *(G-8414)*
Lavinal Inc.......G....... 509 857-2224
Cle Elum *(G-2670)*
Wood & Son Earthwork & Utility.......F....... 360 352-1022
Tumwater *(G-13908)*

STONE: Quarrying & Processing, Own Stone Prdts

Kgo Stone.......F....... 360 573-0272
Vancouver *(G-14346)*

STONES, SYNTHETIC: Gem Stone & Indl Use

Nathan Capital LLC.......G....... 360 835-1211
Washougal *(G-14971)*

STONEWARE PRDTS: Pottery

Cascadia Stoneware USA In.......G....... 360 595-1171
Deming *(G-2918)*
Coastal Clayworks.......G....... 315 405-5077
Roy *(G-9158)*
Country Stoneware.......G....... 509 484-6950
Spokane *(G-12203)*

STORE FIXTURES, EXC REFRIGERATED: Wholesalers

Display Manufacturing LLC.......G....... 360 653-0990
Marysville *(G-6330)*
Obcon Inc.......G....... 253 931-0455
Auburn *(G-516)*

PRODUCT SECTION

SVC ESTABLISHMENT EQPT, WHOL: Cleaning & Maint Eqpt & Splys

Spacewall West Inc .... G 253 852-0203
   Kent *(G-5143)*

STORE FIXTURES: Wood

Andrews Fixture Company Inc .... F 253 627-7481
   Tacoma *(G-13172)*
Pacific Coast Showcase Inc .... C 253 445-9000
   Puyallup *(G-8216)*
Silver Star Industies Inc .... D 509 427-8800
   North Bonneville *(G-7133)*
Tc NW Inc .... G 360 683-6655
   Sequim *(G-11664)*

STORES: Auto & Home Supply

Art Morrison Enterprises Inc .... E 253 344-0161
   Fife *(G-3933)*
Drive Line Svc of Bellingham .... G 360 734-7828
   Bellingham *(G-1326)*
Yakima Grinding Co .... F 509 575-1977
   Yakima *(G-15714)*

STORES: Drapery & Upholstery

Shade Sunglo & Drapery Co .... G 206 767-4561
   Seattle *(G-11094)*

STOVES: Wood & Coal Burning

Innovative Hearth Products LLC .... D 253 735-1100
   Auburn *(G-477)*
Travis Industries Inc .... B 425 609-2500
   Mukilteo *(G-6983)*
Wizard Works .... G 509 486-2654
   Tonasket *(G-13662)*

STRADDLE CARRIERS: Mobile

Carrier Transports Inc .... G 509 452-0136
   Yakima *(G-15528)*

STRAPS: Cotton Webbing

Bridport-Air Carrier Inc .... E 253 872-7205
   Kent *(G-4823)*
Pacific Strapping Inc .... F 206 262-9800
   Tukwila *(G-13788)*

STRAW GOODS

Hydrostraw LLC .... E 509 291-6000
   Rockford *(G-9151)*

STRAWS: Drinking, Made From Purchased Materials

Eagle Bev & Accessory Pdts LLC .... D 253 867-6134
   Kent *(G-4881)*

STRINGING BEADS

Crazy J .... G 360 876-6618
   Port Orchard *(G-7800)*
Our Country Beads .... G 509 967-3953
   Richland *(G-9032)*

STRUCTURAL SUPPORT & BUILDING MATERIAL: Concrete

Builders Firstsource Inc .... E 253 847-2900
   Graham *(G-4217)*
Pin Foundations Inc .... G 253 858-3844
   Gig Harbor *(G-4145)*

STUCCO

Master Stucco Hc .... G 425 793-0576
   Renton *(G-8849)*
Perma-Chink Systems Inc .... F 425 885-6050
   Redmond *(G-8619)*

STUDIOS: Artist

Morrison Art Glass Inc .... G 360 714-8732
   Bellingham *(G-1443)*
Pohlman Knowles .... G 206 933-7450
   Seattle *(G-10827)*

STUDIOS: Artist's

Butler Design Inc .... G 360 380-1651
   Ferndale *(G-3819)*
Dick and Janes Spot .... G 509 925-3224
   Ellensburg *(G-3193)*

STUDS & JOISTS: Sheet Metal

Steeler Inc .... D 206 725-8500
   Seattle *(G-11187)*
Steeler Inc .... G 253 572-8200
   Tacoma *(G-13525)*

SUBMARINE BUILDING & REPAIR

Electric Boat Corporation .... E 360 598-5115
   Silverdale *(G-11833)*

SUBSCRIPTION FULFILLMENT SVCS: Magazine, Newspaper, Etc

Karlas Hand Bindery Inc .... E 206 405-3350
   Seattle *(G-10328)*

SUBSTANCE ABUSE COUNSELING

Innovation Resource Center .... G 509 836-2400
   Sunnyside *(G-13127)*

SUGAR SUBSTITUTES: Organic

DFI Mp Eroh LLC .... G 206 499-2687
   Moses Lake *(G-6705)*

SUNDRIES & RELATED PRDTS: Medical & Laboratory, Rubber

Assured Independence LLC .... G 425 516-7400
   Issaquah *(G-4383)*
Entraq Medical .... G 425 495-5143
   Redmond *(G-8450)*
Medilogic Llc .... G 541 991-1006
   Camas *(G-2269)*
Ovalstrapping Incorporated .... E 360 532-9101
   Hoquiam *(G-4352)*
Panther Printing .... G 509 344-4600
   Spokane Valley *(G-12825)*
Rubber & Plastics Inc .... E 503 289-7720
   Vancouver *(G-14560)*
Sterlitech Corporation .... E 253 437-0844
   Kent *(G-5156)*

SUNROOMS: Prefabricated Metal

Awnings & Sunrooms Distinction .... G 360 681-2727
   Sequim *(G-11613)*
Global Solarium Inc .... G 360 695-0313
   Vancouver *(G-14258)*
Northern Lights Sunrm Creatn L .... G 509 747-1110
   Spokane *(G-12409)*

SUPERMARKETS & OTHER GROCERY STORES

Garden Fresh Gourmet Foods Inc .... C 425 407-6400
   Everett *(G-3491)*
Island Enterprises .... G 360 426-4933
   Shelton *(G-11701)*
La Michoacana .... G 360 658-1635
   Marysville *(G-6349)*
Lupitas .... G 253 838-6132
   Federal Way *(G-3754)*
New Continent Food USA Inc .... G 425 644-6448
   Bellevue *(G-1026)*
North Connection Corp .... G 425 637-7787
   Bellevue *(G-1034)*

SURFACERS: Concrete Grinding

Accurate Surface Grinding .... G 206 762-5205
   Seattle *(G-9338)*

SURGICAL APPLIANCES & SPLYS

Pettibon Bio-Mechanics Inst .... G 360 748-4207
   Gig Harbor *(G-4144)*

SURGICAL APPLIANCES & SPLYS

Amfit Inc .... E 360 573-9100
   Vancouver *(G-14032)*
Badger Braces LLC .... G 509 229-3635
   Colton *(G-2732)*
Breast Care Center .... F 360 424-6161
   Sedro Woolley *(G-11534)*
Brooks Tactical Systems .... F 253 549-2703
   Fox Island *(G-4019)*
Coates Innovations LLC .... G 907 617-5801
   Kent *(G-4856)*
Contemporary Design Co .... F 360 599-2833
   Bellingham *(G-1303)*
Cornerstone Attache Group Inc .... G 425 577-2713
   Redmond *(G-8426)*
Hanger Inc .... G 360 423-6049
   Longview *(G-5914)*
Hanger Prosthetics & Ortho W .... G 360 256-0026
   Vancouver *(G-14280)*
Hanger Prsthetcs & Ortho Inc .... G 425 451-8831
   Bellevue *(G-936)*
Hf Acquisition Co LLC .... E 800 331-1984
   Mukilteo *(G-6932)*
Impulse Medical Tech Inc .... F 360 829-0400
   Buckley *(G-2059)*
Intelipedics LLC .... G 509 432-4036
   Pullman *(G-8093)*
Joyson Safety Systems .... C 509 762-5549
   Moses Lake *(G-6718)*
Medical Pdts For Comfort Inc .... G 360 770-2005
   Mount Vernon *(G-6812)*
Medline Industries Inc .... G 360 491-0241
   Lacey *(G-5566)*
Orthocare Innovations LLC .... F 425 771-0797
   Edmonds *(G-3141)*
Preferred Orthotic & Prosthetc .... G 253 838-6726
   Federal Way *(G-3772)*
Puget Sound Innovations Inc .... G 206 575-7500
   Tukwila *(G-13798)*
Repcon NW Inc .... G 800 325-8707
   Brush Prairie *(G-2042)*
Seattle Systems .... G 360 598-8916
   Poulsbo *(G-7998)*
Simulab Corporation .... E 206 297-1260
   Tukwila *(G-13819)*

SURGICAL EQPT: See Also Instruments

Capital Instruments Ltd .... G 425 271-3756
   Bellevue *(G-838)*
Microsurgical Technology Inc .... D 425 861-4002
   Redmond *(G-8586)*
Procedure Products Inc .... G 360 693-1832
   Vancouver *(G-14511)*
Therasigma Inc .... G 800 423-7172
   Washougal *(G-14992)*
Yainax Medical LLC .... G 503 516-7173
   Vancouver *(G-14705)*

SURGICAL IMPLANTS

Progenica Therapeutics LLC .... G 253 347-7018
   Covington *(G-2836)*
Progenica Therapeutics LLC .... G 253 347-7018
   Covington *(G-2837)*
Spinal Specialties .... G 253 861-7329
   Olympia *(G-7400)*

SURGICAL INSTRUMENT REPAIR SVCS

Bens Precision Instrs Inc .... D 253 883-5040
   Fife *(G-3938)*

SURVEYING & MAPPING: Land Parcels

Lanktree Land Surveying Inc .... F 253 653-6423
   Kent *(G-4988)*
Pinnion Inc .... F 206 577-3070
   Kirkland *(G-5434)*

SUSPENSION SYSTEMS: Acoustical, Metal

Acoustical Solutions .... G 253 876-0075
   Auburn *(G-361)*
Architect David Vandervort .... G 206 784-1614
   Seattle *(G-9420)*
Linns Service & Remodel Inc .... G 509 448-2540
   Spokane *(G-12369)*

SVC ESTABLISHMENT EQPT & SPLYS WHOLESALERS

Fleet Feet Sports .... G 509 309-2174
   Spokane Valley *(G-12704)*
Sherwin-Williams Company .... G 425 643-8584
   Bellevue *(G-1129)*

SVC ESTABLISHMENT EQPT, WHOL: Cleaning & Maint Eqpt & Splys

Alpine Products Inc .... G 253 351-9828
   Auburn *(G-373)*

Employee Codes: A=Over 500 employees, B=251-500
C=101-250, D=51-100, E=20-50, F=10-19, G=2-9

SVC ESTABLISHMENT EQPT, WHOL: Cleaning & Maint Eqpt & Splys

Applicator Technology Inc .... G 253 859-9501
  Kent *(G-4786)*

SVC ESTABLISHMENT EQPT, WHOLESALE: Beauty Parlor Eqpt & Sply

Sally Beauty Supply LLC .... G 509 881-2120
  East Wenatchee *(G-3032)*
Sally Beauty Supply LLC .... G 509 783-7292
  Kennewick *(G-4725)*

SVC ESTABLISHMENT EQPT, WHOLESALE: Firefighting Eqpt

Unifire Inc .... F 509 535-7746
  Spokane *(G-12575)*
Western States Fire Equipment .... G 360 723-0032
  Battle Ground *(G-752)*

SVC ESTABLISHMENT EQPT, WHOLESALE: Laundry Eqpt & Splys

SK&y International LLC .... G 253 833-9525
  Auburn *(G-564)*

SVC ESTABLISHMENT EQPT, WHOLESALE: Vacuum Cleaning Systems

Green Label Manufacturing Inc .... G 954 445-0001
  Vancouver *(G-14270)*

SVC ESTABLISHMENT EQPT, WHOLESALE: Voting Machines

Democracy Live Inc .... F 855 655-8683
  Seattle *(G-9819)*

SWEEPING COMPOUNDS

Globek LLC .... G 360 627-9714
  Bremerton *(G-1958)*
United Sorbents Seattle LLC .... E 425 656-4440
  Kent *(G-5197)*

SWIMMING POOL & HOT TUB CLEANING & MAINTENANCE SVCS

Aqua Rec Inc .... G 253 826-2561
  Bonney Lake *(G-1716)*
Aqua Rec Inc .... G 253 770-9447
  Puyallup *(G-8123)*
Aquatic Specialty Services .... G 206 275-0694
  Seattle *(G-9415)*

SWIMMING POOL EQPT: Filters & Water Conditioning Systems

Aquatic Specialty Services .... G 206 275-0694
  Seattle *(G-9415)*

SWITCHES: Electronic

Amx LLC .... C 509 235-1464
  Cheney *(G-2576)*
Black Label Switches .... G 360 607-3559
  Camas *(G-2233)*
Master Switch LLC .... G 206 769-9560
  Seattle *(G-10497)*
Masterpress Inc .... E 206 524-1444
  Seattle *(G-10499)*
Qualitel Corporation .... C 425 423-8388
  Everett *(G-3589)*
Xn Technologies Inc .... D 509 235-2672
  Cheney *(G-2596)*

SWITCHES: Electronic Applications

Travis Pattern & Foundry Inc .... B 509 466-3545
  Spokane *(G-12566)*

SWITCHES: Thermostatic

Index Industries Inc .... D 360 629-5200
  Bellingham *(G-1376)*

SWITCHES: Time, Electrical Switchgear Apparatus

Bluefin Marine LLC .... G 206 276-4087
  Kirkland *(G-5293)*
Timberline Controls & Mar Inc .... F 360 335-8598
  Washougal *(G-14993)*

SWITCHGEAR & SWITCHBOARD APPARATUS

Anderson Electric Controls .... E 206 575-4444
  Kent *(G-4783)*
Eaton Corporation .... F 253 833-5021
  Auburn *(G-431)*
Eldec Corporation .... A 425 743-1313
  Lynnwood *(G-6114)*
G&J Distributors .... G 509 325-2100
  Spokane *(G-12266)*
General Electric Company .... F 253 395-1798
  Kent *(G-4922)*
Ikonika Corp .... G 253 344-1523
  Fife *(G-3960)*
Morpac Industries Inc .... E 253 735-8922
  Pacific *(G-7533)*
Phoenix Power Control Inc .... F 360 794-8550
  Monroe *(G-6606)*
Process Solutions Inc .... E 360 629-0910
  Stanwood *(G-12987)*
Timken Motor & Crane Svcs LLC .... E 509 547-1691
  Pasco *(G-7638)*

SWITCHGEAR & SWITCHGEAR ACCESS, NEC

Superior Custom Control .... F 206 362-8866
  Seattle *(G-11222)*

SYNCHROS

Seattle Synchro .... G 206 856-5239
  Kirkland *(G-5456)*

SYNTHETIC RESIN FINISHED PRDTS, NEC

Cheyenne Livestock & Products .... F 360 256-0293
  Vancouver *(G-14116)*
Composites Consolidation LLC .... G 509 877-2228
  Wapato *(G-14915)*

SYRUPS, DRINK

Eagle Bev & Accessory Pdts LLC .... D 253 867-6134
  Kent *(G-4881)*

SYRUPS, FLAVORING, EXC DRINK

Sunfresh Foods Inc .... G 206 764-0940
  Seattle *(G-11219)*

SYSTEMS ENGINEERING: Computer Related

Leidos Inc .... E 425 267-5600
  Lynnwood *(G-6157)*
Leidos Inc .... G 360 394-8870
  Poulsbo *(G-7975)*
Unix Packages LLC .... G 206 310-4610
  Seattle *(G-11386)*

SYSTEMS INTEGRATION SVCS

5th Wave Mobile Tech Inc .... G 425 898-8161
  Gig Harbor *(G-4070)*
Agjet LLC .... F 509 654-9449
  Yakima *(G-15502)*
Attachmate Corporation .... B 206 217-7100
  Seattle *(G-9458)*
Attachmate Intl Sls Corp .... G 206 217-7500
  Seattle *(G-9459)*
Showalter Systems Inc .... G 206 236-6276
  Mercer Island *(G-6484)*

SYSTEMS INTEGRATION SVCS: Local Area Network

Antipodes Inc .... F 253 444-5555
  Tacoma *(G-13174)*

SYSTEMS SOFTWARE DEVELOPMENT SVCS

Anewin LLC .... G 360 606-5591
  Vancouver *(G-14036)*
Coach Cheetah Inc .... G 206 914-8313
  Seattle *(G-9703)*
Dealer Info Systems Corp .... D 360 733-7610
  Bellingham *(G-1320)*
Ontario Systems LLC .... C 360 256-7358
  Vancouver *(G-14452)*

Plexsys Interface Products Inc .... E 360 838-2500
  Camas *(G-2275)*
Sarangsoft LLC .... G 425 378-3890
  Bellevue *(G-1114)*
Sars Corporation .... F 866 276-7277
  Bellevue *(G-1115)*
Soham Inc .... D 425 445-2125
  Bellevue *(G-1145)*
Zsolutionz LLC .... G 425 502-6970
  Sammamish *(G-9262)*

TABLE OR COUNTERTOPS, PLASTIC LAMINATED

Interior Form Tops Inc .... E 253 927-8171
  Milton *(G-6535)*
Precision Countertops Inc .... E 253 867-5317
  Kent *(G-5076)*
West Coast Laminating LLC .... F 253 395-5225
  Kent *(G-5211)*
Wilsonart LLC 253 833-0551
  Algona *(G-79)*
Windfall Lumber Inc .... E 360 352-2250
  Tumwater *(G-13906)*

TABLECLOTHS & SETTINGS

Anali Incorporated .... F 425 284-1829
  Sammamish *(G-9184)*
Fabrications Inc .... G 888 808-9878
  Mercer Island *(G-6462)*

TABLES: Lift, Hydraulic

Westco Engineering .... G 425 481-7271
  Woodinville *(G-15403)*

TABLETS & PADS

Dannys Electronics Inc .... G 253 314-5056
  Tacoma *(G-13253)*

TABLETS: Bronze Or Other Metal

Creative Motion Control Inc .... E 425 883-0100
  Woodinville *(G-15215)*

TABLEWARE OR KITCHEN ARTICLES: Commercial, Fine Earthenware

Cuttingboard LLC .... G 253 234-7569
  Redmond *(G-8431)*
Food Service Eqp Repr Inc .... G 206 730-2662
  Shoreline *(G-11773)*

TABLEWARE: Household & Commercial, Semivitreous

Crossing Borders .... G 425 466-7680
  Bellevue *(G-870)*

TAGS: Paper, Blank, Made From Purchased Paper

Peacetags .... G 206 932-8247
  Bellevue *(G-1067)*

TALLOW: Animal

Baker Commodities Inc .... E 509 534-2137
  Spokane *(G-12137)*
Baker Commodities Inc .... F 509 837-8686
  Grandview *(G-4245)*
Powder River Drafting .... G 360 679-9859
  Oak Harbor *(G-7161)*

TALLOW: Vegetable

Baker Commodities Inc .... E 509 535-5435
  Spokane *(G-12136)*

TANK COMPONENTS: Military, Specialized

Senior Operations LLC .... D 360 435-1116
  Arlington *(G-324)*

TANK REPAIR & CLEANING SVCS

Praxair Services Inc .... G 360 676-8215
  Bellingham *(G-1501)*

TANKS & OTHER TRACKED VEHICLE CMPNTS

D&Topm Inc .... G 425 334-7667
  Everett *(G-3436)*
Regal Tanks USA Inc .... G 360 707-9948
  Blaine *(G-1701)*
Sound Tanks and Cntrs L L C .... G 425 455-2668
  Bellevue *(G-1149)*
Transmarine Navigation Corp .... F 206 525-2051
  Seattle *(G-11327)*

TANKS: Concrete

Halme Construction Inc .... E 509 725-4200
  Spokane *(G-12287)*

TANKS: Fuel, Including Oil & Gas, Metal Plate

Custom Welding Inc .... G 509 535-0664
  Spokane Valley *(G-12673)*
Ironclad Company .... G 206 588-2272
  Tukwila *(G-13754)*

TANKS: Plastic & Fiberglass

Ershigs Inc .... F 360 733-2620
  Bellingham *(G-1338)*
Fabricated Plastics Limited .... G 360 527-3430
  Bellingham *(G-1340)*

TANKS: Standard Or Custom Fabricated, Metal Plate

Bmt Metal Fabrication Inc .... G 509 244-6107
  Airway Heights *(G-49)*
Brown-Mnnplis Tnk-Nrthwest LLC .... E 360 482-1720
  Elma *(G-3243)*
Greer Steel Inc .... E 253 581-4100
  Lakewood *(G-5727)*
Maintenance Welding Service .... G 360 533-4318
  Hoquiam *(G-4348)*
Psf Industries Inc .... G 800 426-1204
  Seattle *(G-10881)*
Seattle Boiler Works Inc .... E 206 762-0737
  Seattle *(G-11048)*
Specialty Motors Mfg LLC .... G 360 423-9880
  Longview *(G-5956)*
Tech Heavy Industries Inc .... G 509 557-8492
  Riverside *(G-9127)*
Thermal Solar Panels .... G 425 445-0244
  Renton *(G-8927)*

TANKS: Storage, Farm, Metal Plate

Advanced Fuel Systems .... G 425 526-7566
  Fall City *(G-3698)*

TANKS: Water, Metal Plate

Hiline Engrg & Fabrication Inc .... E 509 943-9043
  Richland *(G-9006)*
Northwest Linings & Geo .... E 253 872-0244
  Kent *(G-5033)*
Selg and Associates Inc .... G 425 487-6059
  Woodinville *(G-15359)*

TANNERIES: Leather

Quil Ceda Tanning Co Inc .... G 360 659-1333
  Marysville *(G-6373)*

TAPE DRIVES

Synology America Corp .... F 425 296-3177
  Bellevue *(G-1175)*

TAPE MEASURES

American Mfg & Engin .... F 253 520-5865
  Kent *(G-4777)*

TAPES: Fabric

H A Milton Corp .... G 509 346-1192
  Royal City *(G-9169)*

TAPES: Slide Fastener

Gafftech LLC .... G 844 423-3486
  Sumner *(G-13072)*

TARGET DRONES

Uav Systems Development Corp .... B 803 767-1351
  Moses Lake *(G-6755)*

TARPAULINS

Climacover Inc .... G 360 458-1010
  Eatonville *(G-3052)*
Columbia Tarp Liner & Sup Co .... G 360 577-1834
  Longview *(G-5901)*
George Broom Sons Inc .... G 206 282-0800
  Seattle *(G-10064)*
Nordic Tarps Manufacturing .... G 509 533-1530
  Spokane Valley *(G-12804)*
Seattle Tarp Co Inc .... E 206 285-2819
  Seattle *(G-11080)*

TELECOMMUNICATION EQPT REPAIR SVCS, EXC TELEPHONES

PSI Electronics LLC .... F 253 922-7890
  Fife *(G-3984)*

TELECOMMUNICATION SYSTEMS & EQPT

Avaya Inc .... D 425 454-2715
  Bellevue *(G-803)*
Extreme Networks Inc .... G 408 579-2800
  Snohomish *(G-11907)*
Ict Group Inc .... G 408 907-8000
  Spokane Valley *(G-12737)*
John Deely .... G 206 527-8218
  Seattle *(G-10301)*
Linc Technology Corporation .... E 425 882-2206
  Issaquah *(G-4439)*
Powercom Inc .... D 425 489-8549
  Bothell *(G-1784)*
Rest-A-Phone Corporation .... G 360 750-8686
  Vancouver *(G-14546)*
Ruckus Wireless Inc .... E 425 896-6000
  Kirkland *(G-5453)*
Telecommunication Systems Inc .... C 206 792-2000
  Seattle *(G-11280)*
Xkl LLC .... E 425 869-9050
  Redmond *(G-8720)*

TELECOMMUNICATIONS CARRIERS & SVCS: Wired

Avista Capital Inc .... G 509 489-0500
  Spokane *(G-12133)*

TELEGRAPH STATION EQPT & PARTS: Wire

Choice Wiring LLC .... G 509 588-6185
  Benton City *(G-1606)*

TELEMETERING EQPT

Jeeva Wireless Inc .... G 206 214-6177
  Seattle *(G-10288)*
Westcoast Telemetry Specialist .... G 253 536-1351
  Spanaway *(G-12080)*
Wibotic Inc .... G 503 484-3930
  Seattle *(G-11472)*

TELEPHONE EQPT INSTALLATION

Telco Wiring & Repair Inc .... G 509 547-4300
  Pasco *(G-7637)*

TELEPHONE EQPT: Modems

Electronic Systems Tech Inc .... F 509 735-9092
  Kennewick *(G-4657)*

TELEPHONE EQPT: NEC

Atos It Solutions and Svcs Inc .... G 425 691-3080
  Bellevue *(G-798)*
Dees Communications Corp .... G 425 276-5269
  Newcastle *(G-7027)*
Proctor International LLC .... G 425 881-7000
  Redmond *(G-8633)*
Rest-A-Phone Corporation .... F 503 235-6778
  Vancouver *(G-14545)*
Siemens AG .... G 253 922-4297
  Fife *(G-3992)*
Simpleline Inc .... G 888 743-7903
  Langley *(G-5785)*
Telect Inc .... C 509 926-6000
  Liberty Lake *(G-5863)*
Xeta Technologies Inc .... G 425 653-4500
  Seattle *(G-11504)*
Xeta Technologies Inc .... E 425 316-0721
  Tukwila *(G-13838)*

TELEPHONE SET REPAIR SVCS

Telco Wiring & Repair Inc .... G 509 547-4300
  Pasco *(G-7637)*

TELEPHONE STATION EQPT & PARTS: Wire

New Cingular Wireless Svcs Inc .... F 425 288-3132
  Bothell *(G-1779)*

TELEPHONE SVCS

Choice Wiring LLC .... G 509 588-6185
  Benton City *(G-1606)*

TELEPHONE: Automatic Dialers

Avaya Inc .... C 425 881-7544
  Bellevue *(G-802)*
G-Tech Communications Inc .... F 503 784-1147
  Vancouver *(G-14245)*

TELEPHONE: Fiber Optic Systems

Alaska United Partnership .... G 425 741-3350
  Lynnwood *(G-6068)*
Davan Communications Entp .... G 253 517-9300
  Tacoma *(G-13255)*
Dial One Telecommunications .... G 360 629-2085
  Stanwood *(G-12966)*
Diversified Northwest Inc .... F 425 710-0753
  Everett *(G-3444)*
Green River College .... E 253 856-9595
  Kent *(G-4928)*
Jphotonics Inc .... G 206 397-3702
  Mercer Island *(G-6469)*
P & M Video Lightsource LLC .... G 253 569-0286
  Spanaway *(G-12067)*
Photon Factory .... G 818 795-6957
  Seattle *(G-10797)*
Racal Acoustics Inc .... G 425 297-9700
  Everett *(G-3593)*
Telco Wiring & Repair Inc .... G 509 547-4300
  Pasco *(G-7637)*

TELEPHONE: Headsets

Htc America Innovation Inc .... B 425 679-5318
  Seattle *(G-10192)*
Planet Headset Inc .... G 253 238-0643
  Fox Island *(G-4023)*

TELEVISION BROADCASTING & COMMUNICATIONS EQPT

Fisher Brdcstg - Wash TV LLC .... G 509 575-0029
  Yakima *(G-15571)*

TELEVISION BROADCASTING STATIONS

Casey Communications Inc .... G 206 448-5902
  Seattle *(G-9645)*
Cowles Publishing Company .... B 509 459-5000
  Spokane *(G-12204)*
General Electric Company .... G 253 351-2200
  Auburn *(G-448)*

TELEVISION SETS WHOLESALERS

Xoceco USA .... G 509 808-2480
  Liberty Lake *(G-5869)*

TELEVISION: Cameras

Dannys Electronics Inc .... G 253 314-5056
  Tacoma *(G-13253)*

TELEVISION: Monitors

Elux Inc .... G 360 281-4568
  Vancouver *(G-14200)*

TENT REPAIR SHOP

Everett Tent & Awning Inc .... G 425 252-8213
  Everett *(G-3464)*

TENTS: All Materials

TENTS: All Materials
- Bravo Manufacturing Inc .... G 360 817-9124
  Camas *(G-2235)*
- Hilleberg Inc .... G 425 883-0101
  Redmond *(G-8493)*
- Rainier Industries Ltd .... C 425 251-1800
  Tukwila *(G-13801)*
- Sears Tents & Awning .... G 509 452-8971
  Yakima *(G-15669)*
- Tacoma Tent & Awning Co Inc .... E 253 627-4128
  Tacoma *(G-13549)*
- Yakima Tent & Awning Co Ltd .... F 509 457-6169
  Yakima *(G-15717)*

TEST KITS: Pregnancy
- Heart Hands Pregnacy Care Ctr ...... G 360 532-1104
  Hoquiam *(G-4341)*
- Orchards Pregnancy Resources ...... G 360 567-0285
  Vancouver *(G-14455)*

TESTERS: Environmental
- Aldergrove LLC .... G 360 253-7378
  Vancouver *(G-14018)*
- America West Envmtl Sups .... G 509 547-2240
  Pasco *(G-7551)*
- Viking Industrial Group Inc .... G 360 666-1110
  Battle Ground *(G-750)*

TESTERS: Physical Property
- Gli Interactive LLC .... G 206 201-2708
  Seattle *(G-10082)*
- Olympus Scientific Solutions .... E 509 735-7550
  Kennewick *(G-4704)*

TESTERS: Water, Exc Indl Process
- Evoqua Water Technologies LLC .... G 360 699-7392
  Brush Prairie *(G-2034)*

TESTING SVCS
- All Wave Innovations Inc .... G 509 308-7230
  Benton City *(G-1600)*
- Armour Mfg & Cnstr Inc .... G 253 984-1213
  Tacoma *(G-13180)*

TEXTILE & APPAREL SVCS
- Cory A Stemp .... G 509 491-3847
  Kennewick *(G-4650)*
- Dynamic Specialties .... G 509 447-2755
  Newport *(G-7057)*
- Mid Mountain Materials Inc .... E 360 435-9622
  Arlington *(G-278)*

TEXTILE BAGS WHOLESALERS
- Swivler Inc .... E 360 225-7774
  Woodland *(G-15468)*

TEXTILE FABRICATORS
- Ultimate Sheepskin .... G 253 677-4384
  Graham *(G-4240)*
- Youlookfab LLC .... G 206 709-9541
  Seattle *(G-11513)*

TEXTILE FINISHING: Sponging, Cotton, Broadwoven, Trade
- Blue North Trading Company LLC .. G 206 352-9252
  Seattle *(G-9553)*

TEXTILE MACHINERY ACCESS, HARDWOOD
- Child Inc .... G 425 775-9076
  Edmonds *(G-3100)*

TEXTILE PRDTS: Hand Woven & Crocheted
- Hellroaring Company .... G 509 364-3522
  Glenwood *(G-4184)*
- Knot Your Every Day Crochet .... G 360 791-9154
  Tumwater *(G-13881)*
- Recrochetions .... G 360 450-4757
  Camas *(G-2278)*

TEXTILE: Goods, NEC
- Berg Development Group LLC .... G 509 624-8921
  Spokane *(G-12145)*

- Om LLC Reinstated 2005 .... G 360 821-1802
  Port Townsend *(G-7905)*
- Sonic Patch LLC .... G 425 284-6072
  Seattle *(G-11155)*

TEXTILES: Carbonized Rags
- Chemical Cloth Co .... G 360 582-9684
  Sequim *(G-11617)*

TEXTILES: Crash, Linen
- Line-X Silverdale Inc .... G 360 692-4840
  Silverdale *(G-11844)*

TEXTILES: Fibers, Textile, Rcvrd From Mill Waste/Rags
- Buffalo Industries LLC .... E 206 682-9900
  Kent *(G-4826)*
- Regenerated Textile Inds LLC .... G 206 427-9343
  Seattle *(G-10943)*

TEXTILES: Jute & Flax Prdts
- Garage .... G 425 640-6021
  Lynnwood *(G-6126)*
- Laurelcrest II LLC .... G 206 922-3634
  Seattle *(G-10382)*

THERMOCOUPLES
- Eustis Co Inc .... E 425 423-9996
  Lynnwood *(G-6115)*

THERMOPLASTIC MATERIALS
- High Performance Seals Inc .... G 253 218-0123
  Auburn *(G-466)*
- Zila Works LLC .... G 425 777-6813
  Renton *(G-8954)*

THERMOPLASTICS
- Angeles Composite Tech Inc .... D 360 452-6776
  Port Angeles *(G-7684)*

THIN FILM CIRCUITS
- Applied Multilayers LLC .... G 307 222-0660
  Battle Ground *(G-688)*

THREAD: All Fibers
- Craft International of Wash .... G 360 785-3606
  Winlock *(G-15148)*

THREAD: Embroidery
- Action Sports & Locks Inc .... G 360 435-9505
  Arlington *(G-193)*
- Designs Unlimited .... G 360 792-1372
  Port Orchard *(G-7802)*
- Hope Chest Crafts .... G 509 865-5666
  Toppenish *(G-13670)*
- Orpilla Santiago .... G 360 876-1976
  Port Orchard *(G-7838)*
- Sherri and Brent Wright .... G 360 366-3100
  Ferndale *(G-3904)*

THREAD: Natural Fiber
- CNT Technologies Inc .... G 206 522-2256
  Seattle *(G-9702)*

THREAD: Sewing
- A Good Yarn Shop .... F 360 876-0157
  Port Orchard *(G-7780)*

TIES, FORM: Metal
- Atlas Construction Spc Co Inc .... E 206 283-2000
  Seattle *(G-9455)*

TILE: Brick & Structural, Clay
- Boral Resources LLC .... G 206 394-3734
  Tukwila *(G-13709)*
- L B Foster Company .... G 509 921-8777
  Spokane Valley *(G-12769)*

TILE: Mosaic, Ceramic
- Cultus Bay Tiles Inc .... G 360 579-3079
  Clinton *(G-2687)*

TILE: Precast Terrazzo, Floor
- Alaska Wholesale Hardwoods .... G 360 704-4444
  Tumwater *(G-13850)*

TILE: Wall & Floor, Ceramic
- Dean Thoemke .... G 253 640-2232
  Yakima *(G-15551)*
- Irenes Tiles .... G 206 463-2808
  Vashon *(G-14725)*
- M2 Innovative Concepts Inc .... F 253 383-5659
  Tacoma *(G-13393)*
- Totten Tileworks .... G 360 785-3282
  Winlock *(G-15157)*

TILE: Wall, Ceramic
- Florida Tile Inc .... G 206 767-9819
  Renton *(G-8801)*

TIN
- Jeri -Ohs .... G 206 722-5918
  Seattle *(G-10292)*
- Lilly Tin .... F 509 888-8101
  Chelan *(G-2559)*
- Tin Cup LLC .... G 360 866-1580
  Olympia *(G-7408)*
- Tin Table .... G 206 320-8458
  Seattle *(G-11312)*
- Vietnamese Baptist Church Tin ...... G 360 953-8311
  Vancouver *(G-14669)*

TIN-BASE ALLOYS, PRIMARY
- Modumetal Inc .... E 877 632-4242
  Seattle *(G-10555)*

TINPLATE
- Stephs Custom Sawyering .... G 425 646-8783
  Bellevue *(G-1156)*
- Tinplate Toys & Trains .... G 206 715-8118
  Tacoma *(G-13555)*

TIRE CORD & FABRIC
- Bridport-Air Carrier Inc .... E 253 872-7205
  Kent *(G-4823)*

TIRE DEALERS
- Irenes Tiles .... G 206 463-2808
  Vashon *(G-14725)*
- Kibbey Battery Service Inc .... G 253 845-9155
  Puyallup *(G-8172)*
- Phelps Tire Co Inc .... D 206 447-0169
  Seattle *(G-10793)*

TIRE RECAPPING & RETREADING
- Phelps Tire Co Inc .... D 206 447-0169
  Seattle *(G-10793)*

TIRES & INNER TUBES
- Bentonfranklin Counties Ian BF ...... G 509 783-5284
  Kennewick *(G-4629)*
- BF and BF Co .... G 206 463-2661
  Vashon *(G-14713)*
- Phelps Tire Co Inc .... D 206 447-0169
  Seattle *(G-10793)*

TIRES & TUBES, WHOLESALE: Automotive
- Phelps Tire Co Inc .... D 206 447-0169
  Seattle *(G-10793)*

TIRES: Auto
- Cooper Tire & Rubber Company .... G 253 826-5742
  Sumner *(G-13061)*

TITANIUM MILL PRDTS
- Allied Titanium Inc .... F 302 725-8300
  Sequim *(G-11608)*
- Rk Titanium LLC .... G 253 886-1377
  Kent *(G-5103)*
- Sandvik Special Metals LLC .... C 509 734-4000
  Kennewick *(G-4726)*
- Titanium Industries Inc .... G 425 481-7700
  Woodinville *(G-15390)*

PRODUCT SECTION

TOYS

TOBACCO & PRDTS, WHOLESALE: Smoking

Altria .... G 253 922-4267
   Fife *(G-3929)*
Cigaretto .... G 253 851-2175
   Gig Harbor *(G-4088)*

TOBACCO & TOBACCO PRDTS WHOLESALERS

Cigarland Gig Harbor .... G 253 851-5515
   Gig Harbor *(G-4089)*

TOBACCO STORES & STANDS

Smoke Plus Cigar .... G 425 673-1390
   Lynnwood *(G-6200)*

TOBACCO: Cigarettes

Altria .... G 253 922-4267
   Fife *(G-3929)*
BJ II Inc .... G 253 926-8538
   Fife *(G-3939)*
Cigaretto .... G 253 851-2175
   Gig Harbor *(G-4088)*
Cigarland Gig Harbor .... G 253 851-5515
   Gig Harbor *(G-4089)*
Smoke Plus .... G 206 579-3661
   Kent *(G-5137)*
Tobacco City .... G 425 377-1658
   Lake Stevens *(G-5672)*

TOBACCO: Cigars

Cigarland Gig Harbor .... G 253 851-5515
   Gig Harbor *(G-4089)*

TOBACCO: Smoking

Benson Smoke .... G 253 859-6120
   Kent *(G-4813)*
Piece Mind Tobacco ACC LLC .... G 206 588-0216
   Seattle *(G-10803)*
Smokin Legal Anywhere .... G 509 465-2695
   Spokane *(G-12507)*
Spoony Luv .... G 206 240-8584
   Shoreline *(G-11817)*
Tobacco Station-WA .... G 253 517-5618
   Federal Way *(G-3796)*

TOILET SEATS: Wood

Sittin Pretty Design .... G 206 725-2453
   Seattle *(G-11120)*

TOILETRIES, COSMETICS & PERFUME STORES

Beaming White LLC .... E 360 635-5600
   Vancouver *(G-14058)*

TOILETRIES, WHOLESALE: Razor Blades

Art of Shaving - FI LLC .... G 206 737-8370
   Seattle *(G-9437)*
Art of Shaving - FI LLC .... G 253 777-0993
   Tacoma *(G-13181)*

TOILETRIES, WHOLESALE: Toilet Soap

Eliza K Trowbridge .... G 360 376-5152
   Olga *(G-7214)*
Lch Enterprises .... G 253 313-5665
   Gig Harbor *(G-4129)*

TOOL & DIE STEEL

For-D Inc .... G 425 486-1120
   Woodinville *(G-15246)*
Scott McClure .... G 360 297-7007
   Kingston *(G-5262)*
Ser Pro Inc .... G 206 767-3100
   Seattle *(G-11090)*

TOOLS & EQPT: Used With Sporting Arms

Composite Tooling Innovations ...... G 509 637-3836
   Bingen *(G-1635)*

TOOLS: Carpenters', Including Levels & Chisels, Exc Saws

Uluwatu .... G 206 852-7289
   Seattle *(G-11363)*

TOOLS: Hand

Altos EZ Mat Inc .... G 509 962-9212
   Ellensburg *(G-3181)*
American Craftware LLC .... G 360 606-1827
   Vancouver *(G-14027)*
Cascade Chalet .... E 206 463-4628
   Vashon *(G-14716)*
Dem-Bart Checkering Tools Inc ..... G 360 568-7356
   Snohomish *(G-11897)*
Garden Expressions .... G 360 403-9532
   Arlington *(G-239)*
Industrial Automation Inc .... E 206 763-1025
   Seattle *(G-10229)*
International Carbide Corp .... F 800 422-8665
   Roy *(G-9161)*
Meadow Creature LLC .... G 360 329-2250
   Vashon *(G-14734)*
Pell Industrial LLC .... G 425 222-9672
   Auburn *(G-530)*
Proctor Products Co Inc .... F 425 398-8800
   Woodinville *(G-15341)*
Profiler Inc .... G 360 668-3291
   Snohomish *(G-11962)*
Rulersmith Inc .... E 360 707-2828
   Shoreline *(G-11806)*
Summitview Tooling Inc .... G 509 966-9859
   Yakima *(G-15686)*

TOOLS: Hand, Hammers

Lam-Hammer Inc .... G 509 687-2421
   Chelan *(G-2558)*

TOOLS: Hand, Jewelers'

Gilt LLC .... G 425 468-4458
   Bellevue *(G-925)*
Hihosilver .... G 509 758-8419
   Clarkston *(G-2635)*

TOOLS: Hand, Mechanics

Machstem Inc .... G 801 259-3305
   Nine Mile Falls *(G-7078)*

TOOLS: Hand, Plumbers'

Picote Solutions Inc .... F 425 505-0646
   Sammamish *(G-9241)*

TOOLS: Hand, Power

Apex Tool Group LLC .... C 425 226-4491
   Renton *(G-8745)*
Black & Decker (us) Inc .... G 509 535-9252
   Spokane Valley *(G-12642)*
Black & Decker Corporation .... F 206 624-4228
   Seattle *(G-9536)*
Eaton Electric Holdings LLC .... D 425 271-9237
   Renton *(G-8791)*
Electroimpact Inc .... D 425 348-8090
   Mukilteo *(G-6920)*
Emerald Tool Inc .... G 206 767-5670
   Seattle *(G-9914)*
Global Product Development .... G 509 487-1155
   Spokane Valley *(G-12720)*
Miti LLC .... G 253 833-9119
   Auburn *(G-500)*
Rousseau Company .... E 509 758-3954
   Clarkston *(G-2647)*
Steeler Inc .... G 509 926-7403
   Spokane Valley *(G-12891)*
Universal Repair Shop Inc .... F 206 322-2726
   Seattle *(G-11377)*

TOOTHPASTES, GELS & TOOTHPOWDERS

Soap Aria LLC .... G 206 229-4351
   Tacoma *(G-13516)*

TOPS: Automobile, Stamped Metal

T-Zero Racing Inc .... G 425 222-5800
   Issaquah *(G-4484)*

TOWELETTES: Premoistened

Hydropeptide LLC .... F 425 458-1072
   Issaquah *(G-4427)*

TOWELS: Paper

Envision Inc .... G 509 247-5732
   Fairchild Afb *(G-3695)*

TOWERS, SECTIONS: Transmission, Radio & Television

Harrington Tower Services .... G 206 760-9191
   Seattle *(G-10143)*
Steelhead Communications Inc ..... E 360 829-1330
   Buckley *(G-2073)*

TOWERS: Cooling, Sheet Metal

Mechpro Inc .... G 206 445-5230
   Auburn *(G-496)*

TOWING & TUGBOAT SVC

Foss Marine Holdings Inc .... G 206 381-5800
   Seattle *(G-10014)*

TOWING BARS & SYSTEMS

Pacific Engineering & Mfg Co .... G 360 274-8323
   Castle Rock *(G-2349)*
Zacklift International Inc .... F 509 674-4426
   Cle Elum *(G-2682)*

TOWING SVCS: Marine

Foss Maritime Company Llc .... D 206 281-3800
   Seattle *(G-10015)*

TOYS

Accurate Models .... G 253 630-3126
   Renton *(G-8726)*
Bensussen Deutsch & Assoc LLC .. B 425 492-6111
   Woodinville *(G-15188)*
Boon .... G 360 225-5224
   Woodland *(G-15420)*
Brass Key Inc .... E 866 325-6840
   Maple Valley *(G-6262)*
Bunchgrass Folktoys Inc .... G 509 334-5143
   Pullman *(G-8086)*
Dbcs Innovations .... G 206 919-2249
   Seattle *(G-9806)*
Funko Inc .... F 425 783-3616
   Everett *(G-3488)*
Geospace Products Company Inc . G 206 547-2556
   Seattle *(G-10065)*
Just Think Toys Inc .... G 310 308-5242
   Bainbridge Island *(G-645)*
Kheper Games Inc .... F 206 782-2201
   Seattle *(G-10341)*
LB Games Inc .... G 360 794-7803
   Snohomish *(G-11937)*
Marninsaylor LLC .... G 307 360-6165
   Seattle *(G-10491)*
Michaels Stores Inc .... E 360 892-4494
   Vancouver *(G-14417)*
Nita N Ace LLC .... G 253 209-4413
   Graham *(G-4233)*
Parvia Corp .... F 206 310-2205
   Seattle *(G-10761)*
Play Visions Inc .... E 425 482-2836
   Woodinville *(G-15335)*
Screenlife LLC .... D 206 829-0743
   Seattle *(G-11035)*
Slingshot Sports LLC .... F 509 427-4950
   North Bonneville *(G-7135)*
Tincan Studio LLC .... G 559 906-3521
   Lynnwood *(G-6210)*
Tippecanoe Boats Ltd .... G 360 966-7245
   Everson *(G-3692)*
Tudor Games Inc .... G 800 914-8836
   Kent *(G-5192)*
Wargaming Seattle Inc .... G 425 250-0209
   Bellevue *(G-1224)*
Woodworking Unlimited .... G 425 481-7451
   Bothell *(G-1922)*

TOYS & HOBBY GOODS & SPLYS, WHOL: Toy Novelties & Amusements

LB Games Inc ....G....... 360 794-7803
Snohomish *(G-11937)*

TOYS & HOBBY GOODS & SPLYS, WHOLESALE: Arts/Crafts Eqpt/Sply

Michaels Stores Inc ....E....... 360 892-4494
Vancouver *(G-14417)*
Ridgeline Graphics Inc ....G....... 509 662-6858
Wenatchee *(G-15069)*
Stateside Bead Supply ....G....... 425 644-3448
Bellevue *(G-1155)*

TOYS & HOBBY GOODS & SPLYS, WHOLESALE: Balloons, Novelty

Go Usa Inc ....E....... 509 662-3387
Wenatchee *(G-15034)*

TOYS & HOBBY GOODS & SPLYS, WHOLESALE: Toys & Games

The McCredy Company ....G....... 509 773-5340
Goldendale *(G-4209)*

TOYS & HOBBY GOODS & SPLYS, WHOLESALE: Toys, NEC

OShell Delmont ....G....... 360 427-9600
Shelton *(G-11719)*
Play Visions Inc ....E....... 425 482-2836
Woodinville *(G-15335)*
Tippecanoe Boats Ltd ....G....... 360 966-7245
Everson *(G-3692)*

TOYS, HOBBY GOODS & SPLYS WHOLESALERS

Milestone Products Co ....F....... 425 882-1987
Redmond *(G-8589)*
P F M Industries Inc ....G....... 425 776-3112
Edmonds *(G-3142)*
Simplyfun LLC ....E....... 425 289-0858
Bellevue *(G-1134)*

TOYS: Dolls, Stuffed Animals & Parts

Brass Key Inc ....E....... 866 325-6840
Maple Valley *(G-6262)*
One Atta Time Doll Co ....G....... 360 956-1091
Olympia *(G-7362)*
Trans Pac Enterprises Inc ....F....... 425 688-0037
Bellevue *(G-1198)*

TOYS: Kites

Drachen Design Inc ....G....... 206 282-4349
Seattle *(G-9853)*
Prism Designs Inc ....G....... 206 838-8682
Seattle *(G-10865)*
Touch Sky Kites ....G....... 360 459-2063
Lacey *(G-5596)*
Wind Play Inc ....G....... 206 784-0414
Seattle *(G-11481)*

TOYS: Video Game Machines

Novel Inc ....E....... 425 956-3096
Kirkland *(G-5414)*

TRAFFIC CONTROL FLAGGING SVCS

Highway Specialties LLC ....G....... 360 823-0511
Vancouver *(G-14298)*

TRAILERS & CHASSIS: Camping

Quality Equipment Supply Inc ....G....... 503 544-9779
Vancouver *(G-14518)*

TRAILERS & PARTS: Boat

E Z Loader Adjustable Boat ....C....... 509 489-0181
Spokane *(G-12235)*
E Z Loader Boat Trailers Inc ....C....... 574 266-0092
Spokane *(G-12236)*
Jened Inc ....G....... 509 926-6894
Spokane Valley *(G-12751)*

TRAILERS & PARTS: Truck & Semi's

All Sports School ....G....... 425 747-1511
Issaquah *(G-4379)*
Batp Inc ....G....... 253 677-4706
Edgewood *(G-3072)*
Capital Industrial Supply Inc ....E....... 360 786-1890
Tumwater *(G-13856)*
Ed Ka Manufacturing Inc ....G....... 509 635-1521
Garfield *(G-4068)*
Gibbs Trailer Mfg & Repr ....G....... 509 547-8241
Pasco *(G-7586)*
Helm Manufacturing Co LLC ....G....... 253 537-3382
Tacoma *(G-13334)*
Lincoln Industrial Corp Inc ....G....... 360 681-0584
Sequim *(G-11646)*
Nor E First Response Inc ....G....... 360 738-6467
Bellingham *(G-1461)*
Northwest Services ....G....... 253 922-6475
Puyallup *(G-8208)*
Quality Fuel Trlr & Tank Inc ....G....... 425 526-7566
Monroe *(G-6610)*
Six Robbles ....G....... 360 398-7173
Bellingham *(G-1539)*
Susan Weinhandl ....G....... 509 953-4329
Spokane *(G-12537)*

TRAILERS & TRAILER EQPT

Buzs Equipment Trailers ....G....... 360 694-9116
Vancouver *(G-14088)*
Capital Industrial Inc ....G....... 360 786-1890
Tumwater *(G-13855)*
Erudite Inc ....G....... 253 272-8542
Tacoma *(G-13281)*
Frys Welding Inc ....G.......
Auburn *(G-445)*
Integrated Systems Design ....G....... 360 746-0812
Bellingham *(G-1380)*
Ss Trailer Manufacturing ....G....... 253 750-4724
Bonney Lake *(G-1739)*
Tc Motorsports ....G....... 253 887-0500
Auburn *(G-578)*
Top Notch Trailer Mfg ....F....... 360 273-0468
Rochester *(G-9141)*
Viper Tactical LLC ....G....... 425 341-0529
Salkum *(G-9181)*

TRAILERS OR VANS: Horse Transportation, Fifth-Wheel Type

Marlin Trailers ....G....... 509 345-2316
Marlin *(G-6308)*

TRAILERS: Bodies

Busby International Inc ....E....... 509 765-1313
Moses Lake *(G-6689)*
Manns Welding & Trailer Hitch ....G....... 206 542-7434
Shoreline *(G-11784)*
Micahs Custom Works LLC ....G....... 509 665-9631
Malaga *(G-6232)*

TRAILERS: Bus, Tractor Type

Kic LLC ....E....... 360 823-4440
Vancouver *(G-14348)*

TRAILERS: Demountable Cargo Containers

Integrated Systems Design ....G....... 360 746-0812
Bellingham *(G-1380)*
Ocean Cargo Container Inc ....G....... 253 381-9098
Gig Harbor *(G-4138)*

TRAILERS: House, Exc Permanent Dwellings

J P J 3 LLC ....G....... 360 697-1084
Silverdale *(G-11840)*

TRAILERS: Semitrailers, Truck Tractors

Eagle Systems Inc ....E....... 509 535-8654
Spokane Valley *(G-12685)*
Marquez Mfg Ltd ....E....... 509 837-6230
Sunnyside *(G-13133)*
Star Transport Trailers Inc ....F....... 509 837-3136
Sunnyside *(G-13144)*

TRAILERS: Truck, Chassis

Quality Equipment Supply Inc ....G....... 503 544-9779
Vancouver *(G-14518)*

TRANSFORMERS: Distribution

Jikopower Inc ....F....... 253 678-0074
Auburn *(G-481)*
New Standard Company Limited ....G....... 425 641-5718
Bellevue *(G-1027)*
O-Netics Ltd ....G....... 425 823-2279
Kirkland *(G-5415)*
Power Conversion Inc ....E....... 425 487-1337
Woodinville *(G-15338)*

TRANSFORMERS: Doorbell, Electric

Spore Incorporated ....G....... 206 624-9573
Seattle *(G-11171)*

TRANSFORMERS: Electric

Transformer Diagnostic Testing ......G....... 425 486-4110
Bothell *(G-1803)*

TRANSFORMERS: Meters, Electronic

Electronetics LLC ....D....... 425 355-1855
Everett *(G-3456)*

TRANSFORMERS: Power Related

ABB Inc ....G....... 253 280-9900
Kent *(G-4754)*
Framatome Inc ....F....... 425 250-2775
Redmond *(G-8465)*
Interactive Electronic Systems ....E....... 877 543-8698
Tacoma *(G-13349)*
Maddox Industrial Trans LLC ....G....... 360 512-3355
Battle Ground *(G-718)*
Peoples Solar Inc ....G....... 530 217-6020
Curlew *(G-2846)*
Power and Lighting LLC ....G....... 360 750-0158
Vancouver *(G-14495)*
Roger Habon ....G....... 206 240-0122
Renton *(G-8896)*
True Sol Innovations Inc ....G....... 206 428-7136
Seattle *(G-11343)*

TRANSFORMERS: Specialty

Air Mod Inc ....G....... 360 895-0910
Port Orchard *(G-7784)*

TRANSMISSIONS: Motor Vehicle

Rons Transmission ....G....... 206 772-8200
Seattle *(G-10979)*

TRANSPORTATION EPQT & SPLYS, WHOLESALE: Acft/Space Vehicle

Safran Cabin Bellingham Inc ....C....... 360 738-2005
Bellingham *(G-1521)*

TRANSPORTATION EPQT & SPLYS, WHOLESALE: Marine Crafts/Splys

Ade Holding Inc ....D....... 206 789-3600
Seattle *(G-9350)*
Basta Inc ....E....... 425 641-8911
Bellevue *(G-807)*
Bills Marine Service ....G....... 509 826-5564
OMAK *(G-7435)*
Blue Sea Systems Inc ....E....... 360 738-8230
Bellingham *(G-1278)*
DMC Satellite Systems Inc ....G....... 360 681-4204
Sequim *(G-11627)*
Dungeness Gear Works Inc ....E....... 800 548-9743
Arlington *(G-230)*
Hamiltonjet Inc ....E....... 206 784-8400
Woodinville *(G-15259)*
Koch Machine Inc ....G....... 206 241-7178
Seattle *(G-10350)*
New Found Metals Incorporated .....G....... 360 385-3315
Port Townsend *(G-7899)*
North Island Boat Company Inc ......F....... 360 293-2565
Anacortes *(G-154)*
Northern Lights Inc ....G....... 206 789-3600
Seattle *(G-10632)*
Western Yacht Systems Inc ....G....... 360 384-3648
Ferndale *(G-3924)*

PRODUCT SECTION

TRANSPORTATION EPQT & SPLYS, WHOLESALE: Pulleys
Atkins Machines LLC .... G 253 588-2350
  Lakewood (G-5700)

TRANSPORTATION EPQT & SPLYS, WHOLESALE: Tanks & Tank Compnts
Advanced Fuel Systems .... G 425 526-7566
  Fall City (G-3698)
Quality Fuel Trlr & Tank Inc .... G 425 526-7566
  Monroe (G-6610)

TRANSPORTATION EPQT/SPLYS, WHOL: Marine Propulsn Mach/Eqpt
Marine Engine Repair Co Inc .... E 206 286-1817
  Seattle (G-10480)
North Hbr Diesl Yacht Svc Inc .... E 360 293-5551
  Anacortes (G-153)
Pacific Power Group LLC .... D 360 887-7400
  Vancouver (G-14469)
Systems Engineering Inc .... G 206 633-4972
  Kirkland (G-5473)

TRANSPORTATION EQPT & SPLYS WHOLESALERS, NEC
Advanced Aero Safety Inc .... G 360 387-8472
  Stanwood (G-12952)
Aircraft Propulsion Systems .... G 425 413-4127
  Maple Valley (G-6254)
Forfjord Supply Co .... G 206 784-8171
  Seattle (G-10012)
G B C Enterprises Inc .... G 360 275-3522
  Tahuya (G-13610)
Glasair Aviation Usa LLC .... E 360 435-8533
  Arlington (G-241)
NW Propeller Operations Inc .... G 253 858-5461
  Lakewood (G-5743)

TRANSPORTATION EQUIPMENT, NEC
Green Synergy .... G 206 779-3324
  Ellensburg (G-3206)
Michael M Hennessey .... G 360 471-3313
  Silverdale (G-11850)
Modern Transport Systems Corp ...... G 509 443-5031
  Spokane (G-12397)
Pacific Coast Tools LLC .... G 360 244-5087
  Long Beach (G-5875)
Rum Ruay Inc .... G 206 660-4647
  Seattle (G-10993)

TRANSPORTATION SVCS, AIR, NONSCHEDULED: Air Cargo Carriers
Maren-Go Solutions Corporation ...... G 217 506-2749
  Vancouver (G-14393)

TRANSPORTATION SVCS, WATER: Boat Cleaning
Top To Bottom .... G 206 764-7750
  Seattle (G-11319)
Top To Bottom Inc .... G 360 671-7022
  Bellingham (G-1572)

TRANSPORTATION SVCS, WATER: Log Rafting & Towing
Columbia Navigation Inc .... G 509 684-4335
  Kettle Falls (G-5222)

TRANSPORTATION SVCS, WATER: River, Exc St Lawrence Seaway
Tidewater Holdings Inc .... G 360 693-1491
  Vancouver (G-14635)

TRANSPORTATION SVCS, WATER: Surveyors, Marine
Jr Grennay Co .... G 509 484-5056
  Valleyford (G-13997)

TRANSPORTATION SVCS: Airport
Northwest Smoking & Curing .... G 360 733-3666
  Bellingham (G-1470)

TRANSPORTATION SVCS: Rental, Local
A Millican Crane Service Inc .... G 360 779-6723
  Poulsbo (G-7941)

TRANSPORTATION: Air, Scheduled Passenger
Kenmore Air Harbor Inc .... D 425 486-3224
  Kenmore (G-4587)

TRANSPORTATION: Deep Sea Domestic Freight
Foss Maritime Company Llc .... D 206 281-3800
  Seattle (G-10015)

TRANSPORTATION: Deep Sea Foreign Freight
Foss Maritime Company Llc .... D 206 281-3800
  Seattle (G-10015)
Stabbert & Associates Inc .... C 206 547-6161
  Seattle (G-11174)

TRANSPORTATION: Great Lakes Domestic Freight
Unilode AVI Solution US Inc .... F 206 824-7123
  Auburn (G-587)

TRANSPORTATION: Local Passenger, NEC
Skookum Enterprises LLC .... D 360 475-0756
  Bremerton (G-2001)

TRAPS: Animal & Fish, Wire
McKay Shrimp & Crab Gear Inc .... G 360 796-4555
  Brinnon (G-2025)

TRAPS: Crab, Steel
Dungeness Gear Works Inc .... E 800 548-9743
  Arlington (G-230)

TRAPS: Stem
Paramount Supply Co .... G 360 647-8328
  Bellingham (G-1489)

TRAVEL TRAILERS & CAMPERS
Canopy World Inc .... G 253 531-5192
  Tacoma (G-13219)
Featherlite Trailers .... G 425 334-4045
  Snohomish (G-11909)
Superior Rv Manufacturing .... G 360 693-1398
  Washougal (G-14989)

TRAVELER ACCOMMODATIONS, NEC
Cape Dissapointment State Park .... F 360 642-3078
  Ilwaco (G-4368)

TROPHIES, PLATED, ALL METALS
Bardon Inc .... G 360 455-1790
  Olympia (G-7234)

TROPHIES, WHOLESALE
Athletic Awards Company Inc .... G 206 624-3995
  Seattle (G-9452)

TROPHIES: Metal, Exc Silver
All CS Inc .... G 253 474-3434
  Tacoma (G-13163)

TROPHY & PLAQUE STORES
A & J Graphics & Design .... G 206 439-1766
  Burien (G-2087)
Athletic Awards Company Inc .... G 206 624-3995
  Seattle (G-9452)
Awards Etc .... G 509 758-3537
  Clarkston (G-2621)
Badge Boys Awards & Engraving ..... G 360 876-8414
  Port Orchard (G-7792)
Bay Trophies & Engraving Inc .... G 360 676-0868
  Bellingham (G-1261)
Fine Design Inc .... E 425 271-2866
  Tukwila (G-13735)

TRUCK BODY SHOP

Harrington Trophies .... G 509 943-2593
  Richland (G-9005)
Marysville Awards Inc .... G 360 653-4811
  Marysville (G-6356)
Mr TS Trophies .... G 360 424-9339
  Mount Vernon (G-6815)
Pats Blue Ribbons & Trophies .... F 360 676-8292
  Ferndale (G-3884)
Wildrose Ltd .... F 509 535-8555
  Spokane (G-12591)

TRUCK & BUS BODIES: Automobile Wrecker Truck
Arreolas Auto Wrecking .... G 509 452-0818
  Yakima (G-15513)

TRUCK & BUS BODIES: Car Carrier
Crown Black Car .... G 206 722-7696
  Seattle (G-9757)
DMS Motorsports .... G 360 863-3807
  Monroe (G-6566)

TRUCK & BUS BODIES: Dump Truck
American Pride Corporation .... F 253 850-1212
  Kent (G-4778)

TRUCK & BUS BODIES: Truck Beds
C & V Machinery .... G 509 657-3392
  Endicott (G-3263)
Ute Ltd .... G 206 510-8621
  Burien (G-2135)

TRUCK & BUS BODIES: Truck, Motor Vehicle
Aalbu Brothers of Everett Inc .... G 425 252-9751
  Everett (G-3356)
Fabrication & Truck Eqp Inc .... F 509 535-0363
  Spokane Valley (G-12698)
Northend Truck Equipment LLC .... E 360 653-6066
  Marysville (G-6363)
Star Transport Trailers Inc .... F 509 837-3136
  Sunnyside (G-13144)
Trivan Truck Body LLC .... D 360 380-0773
  Ferndale (G-3917)
Trivan Truck Body Texas LLC .... D 254 799-2360
  Ferndale (G-3918)

TRUCK & BUS BODIES: Utility Truck
BTS Exchange LLC .... G 253 859-5450
  Kent (G-4825)
D & H Enterprises .... G 360 374-9500
  Forks (G-4009)
Dynamic Utility Services .... G 425 742-1670
  Everett (G-3449)

TRUCK & FREIGHT TERMINALS & SUPPORT ACTIVITIES
Conglobal Industries LLC .... E 206 624-8180
  Seattle (G-9727)

TRUCK BODIES: Body Parts
Auto Body Specialties .... G 360 424-1313
  Mount Vernon (G-6772)
Capital Industries Inc .... D 206 762-8585
  Seattle (G-9624)
Dougs Diesel Repair .... G 509 665-7480
  East Wenatchee (G-3010)
Fab Shop LLC .... E 253 568-9124
  Edgewood (G-3077)
Heiser George Body Co Inc .... E 206 622-7985
  Tukwila (G-13748)
Nelson Truck Equipment Co Inc .... F 206 622-3825
  Seattle (G-10598)
Norms Truck & Equipment Inc .... F 253 833-8339
  Pacific (G-7535)
Sign Station .... G 360 379-2954
  Port Hadlock (G-7762)

TRUCK BODY SHOP
Allied Body Works Inc .... F 206 763-7811
  Seattle (G-9381)
C & V Machinery .... G 509 657-3392
  Endicott (G-3263)
Fabrication & Truck Eqp Inc .... F 509 535-0363
  Spokane Valley (G-12698)

TRUCK BODY SHOP

Hunnicutts Truck Shop Inc .... G 360 734-9859
  Bellingham *(G-1375)*

TRUCK GENERAL REPAIR SVC

Aalbu Brothers of Everett Inc .... G 425 252-9751
  Everett *(G-3356)*
Crown Carriage Works Inc .... G 509 535-4427
  Spokane *(G-12210)*
Parkers Truck & Equipment Repr .... G 253 833-3696
  Pacific *(G-7538)*

TRUCK PAINTING & LETTERING SVCS

Norms Truck & Equipment Inc .... F 253 833-8339
  Pacific *(G-7535)*
Sign Up Sign Co Inc .... G 425 488-9247
  Bothell *(G-1792)*

TRUCK PARTS & ACCESSORIES: Wholesalers

Canopy World Inc .... G 253 531-5192
  Tacoma *(G-13219)*
Fabrication & Truck Eqp Inc .... F 509 535-0363
  Spokane Valley *(G-12698)*
Freedom Truck Centers Inc .... E 509 248-9478
  Union Gap *(G-13931)*
Instrument Sales and Svc Inc .... E 253 796-5400
  Kent *(G-4954)*
Nelson Truck Equipment Co Inc ...... E 253 395-3825
  Kent *(G-5018)*

TRUCKING & HAULING SVCS: Animal & Farm Prdt

Hermann Bros Log & Cnstr Inc .... D 360 452-3341
  Port Angeles *(G-7709)*

TRUCKING & HAULING SVCS: Contract Basis

J&N Land Trucking .... G 360 677-2274
  Skykomish *(G-11866)*

TRUCKING & HAULING SVCS: Garbage, Collect/Transport Only

Thurston Co Transfer Station .... E 360 459-1901
  Olympia *(G-7406)*

TRUCKING & HAULING SVCS: Heavy, NEC

A Millican Crane Service Inc .... G 360 779-6723
  Poulsbo *(G-7941)*
Springbrook Nurs & Trckg Inc .... D 360 653-6545
  Arlington *(G-331)*

TRUCKING & HAULING SVCS: Lumber & Log, Local

American Forest Lands .... G 425 432-5004
  Maple Valley *(G-6257)*
Hansen Logging LLC .... E 509 935-4515
  Chewelah *(G-2602)*
Lloyd Remsberg Logging .... G 509 997-7362
  Twisp *(G-13913)*
Mechanical Fuels Treatment LLC .... G 509 486-1438
  Tonasket *(G-13654)*
Paul E Sevier .... G 360 491-1334
  Olympia *(G-7367)*
W-4 Construction Inc .... F 509 529-1603
  Walla Walla *(G-14886)*

TRUCKING & HAULING SVCS: Lumber & Timber

Johnson Forestry Contracting .... G 360 484-3311
  Naselle *(G-7014)*
Mt Adams Lumber Company Inc ..... G 509 395-2131
  Trout Lake *(G-13682)*

TRUCKING & HAULING SVCS: Machinery, Heavy

Neil F Lampson Inc .... C 509 586-0411
  Kennewick *(G-4700)*
Sea Pac Transport Services LLC ..... E 206 763-0339
  Seattle *(G-11037)*

TRUCKING & HAULING SVCS: Steel, Local

PSI Logistics Intl LLC .... G 855 473-5877
  Spokane *(G-12457)*

TRUCKING, DUMP

Bobby Wolford Trucking & Salv ...... E 425 481-1800
  Woodinville *(G-15195)*
Builders Sand and Gravel Inc .... F 425 743-3333
  Snohomish *(G-11884)*
De Rosier Trucking Inc .... E 360 577-1636
  Kelso *(G-4523)*
Taylor Trucking LLC .... F 360 573-2000
  Vancouver *(G-14627)*

TRUCKING: Except Local

Bear Mountin Cutters Inc .... G 360 875-0035
  South Bend *(G-12039)*
De Rosier Trucking Inc .... E 360 577-1636
  Kelso *(G-4523)*
Frank Swiger Trucking Inc .... G 509 258-7226
  Ford *(G-4005)*
Subaru of America Inc .... G 360 737-7630
  Vancouver *(G-14614)*

TRUCKING: Local, With Storage

Kic LLC .... E 360 823-4440
  Vancouver *(G-14348)*
Rainier Ranch Inc .... G 206 243-2044
  Burien *(G-2123)*

TRUCKING: Local, Without Storage

Drolz Log and Rock Inc .... G 360 987-2343
  Hoquiam *(G-4335)*
East Valley Sand and Gravel .... E 360 403-7520
  Arlington *(G-232)*
Edwards Logging Co .... F 360 457-7330
  Port Angeles *(G-7702)*
Fibres International Inc .... D 425 455-9811
  Everett *(G-3471)*
Green Willow Trucking Inc .... F 360 687-7171
  Battle Ground *(G-705)*
Hallmark Refining Corporation .... D 360 428-5880
  Mount Vernon *(G-6803)*
James Smith Trucking .... G 360 423-1027
  Kelso *(G-4531)*
Jensen Barton W Inc .... F 360 825-3750
  Enumclaw *(G-3297)*
Joe Zender & Sons Inc .... G 360 599-2064
  Deming *(G-2920)*
Karvonen Sand & Gravel Inc .... G 360 687-2549
  Battle Ground *(G-712)*
Lloyd Enterprises Inc .... D 253 874-6692
  Federal Way *(G-3753)*
Lloyd Logging Inc .... F 509 997-2441
  Twisp *(G-13912)*
Mitchell Trucking and Paving .... G 509 884-5928
  East Wenatchee *(G-3026)*
Noel Corporation .... C 509 248-4545
  Yakima *(G-15630)*
North Hill Resources Inc .... F 360 757-1866
  Burlington *(G-2173)*
Stanleys Sanitary Service .... G 360 795-3369
  Cathlamet *(G-2376)*
Sterling Breen Crushing Inc .... E 360 736-4240
  Centralia *(G-2436)*
Van Harten .... G 360 868-2011
  Shelton *(G-11749)*

TRUCKS & TRACTORS: Industrial

Atacs Products Inc .... F 206 433-9000
  Seattle *(G-9449)*
Bogden Inc .... G 509 964-2008
  Thorp *(G-13627)*
Conglobal Industries LLC .... D 206 624-8180
  Seattle *(G-9728)*
Fbt .... G 509 457-3484
  Yakima *(G-15568)*
Frys Welding Inc .... G
  Auburn *(G-445)*
General Dynamics Ordna .... D 509 762-5381
  Moses Lake *(G-6710)*
Globe International Inc .... G 253 383-2584
  Tacoma *(G-13313)*
Go Ventures Inc .... G 253 313-4070
  Tacoma *(G-13315)*
Greers Mobile Equipment Repair .... G 360 901-0373
  Woodland *(G-15436)*

Harbor Action Inc .... F 360 417-1316
  Port Angeles *(G-7708)*
Helm Manufacturing Co LLC .... G 253 537-3382
  Tacoma *(G-13334)*
Neil F Lampson Inc .... C 509 586-0411
  Kennewick *(G-4700)*
Nicholson Manufacturing Co .... D 206 682-2752
  Seattle *(G-10607)*
Paccar Inc .... B 425 227-5800
  Renton *(G-8871)*
Paccar Inc .... B 425 468-7400
  Bellevue *(G-1058)*
Portland Plastics .... B 360 887-2230
  Ridgefield *(G-9103)*
Potter-Webster Co .... G 360 577-9632
  Longview *(G-5944)*
Springbrook Nurs & Trckg Inc .... D 360 653-6545
  Arlington *(G-331)*
Terex Corporation .... G 800 536-1800
  Redmond *(G-8690)*

TRUCKS: Forklift

EMC Electro Mechanical Company .. G 206 767-9307
  Seattle *(G-9910)*
Forklift Training Center Inc - .... G 360 515-0696
  Lacey *(G-5550)*
Heavy Duty Transaxle Inc .... G 360 794-2021
  Monroe *(G-6576)*
Jkr Forklift LLC .... G 360 275-4811
  Belfair *(G-766)*
Lynns Forklift Service .... G 206 979-4272
  Bellevue *(G-993)*
Spokane Forklift Cnstr Eqp Inc .... G 509 868-5962
  Spokane *(G-12518)*
US Attachments Inc .... F 360 501-4484
  Kelso *(G-4558)*
Yakima Forklift LLC .... G 509 985-3568
  Toppenish *(G-13675)*

TRUCKS: Indl

Anoxpress LLC .... G 509 220-2741
  Spokane Valley *(G-12619)*
PSI Logistics Intl LLC .... G 855 473-5877
  Spokane *(G-12457)*
Trout-Blue Chelan-Magi Inc .... E 509 689-2511
  Brewster *(G-2017)*
Woodone-US Corp .... G 206 850-0230
  Sammamish *(G-9259)*

TRUNKS

Annies Trunk LLC .... G 509 529-4395
  Walla Walla *(G-14764)*
Trunk Show .... G 253 302-4301
  University Place *(G-13982)*

TRUSSES & FRAMING: Prefabricated Metal

Vanderpol Building Components ..... F 360 354-5883
  Lynden *(G-6058)*

TRUSSES: Wood, Floor

Noble Truss & Lumber Inc .... F 509 662-1877
  Wenatchee *(G-15052)*
Phoenix Truss Corporation .... E 509 925-3135
  Ellensburg *(G-3220)*

TRUSSES: Wood, Roof

A & V Investments Inc .... E 509 276-5088
  Deer Park *(G-2892)*
Ariel Truss Company Inc .... F 360 574-7333
  Vancouver *(G-14041)*
Armstrong Lumber Co Inc .... E 253 833-6666
  Auburn *(G-377)*
BMC West LLC .... D 425 303-0661
  Everett *(G-3393)*
Brooks Manufacturing Co .... E 360 733-1700
  Bellingham *(G-1283)*
Calvert Company Inc .... D 360 693-0971
  Vancouver *(G-14092)*
Calvert Company Inc .... E 360 835-3110
  Washougal *(G-14947)*
Craft Wall of Oregon Inc .... G 509 547-2436
  Pasco *(G-7569)*
Louws Truss Inc .... D 360 384-9000
  Burlington *(G-2169)*
Lumbermens Truss .... E 509 627-0495
  Richland *(G-9023)*

PRODUCT SECTION
UPHOLSTERY MATERIALS, BROADWOVEN

Madera Components LLC ....G...... 800 404-8746
 Monroe *(G-6595)*
Parker Lumber Co Inc..........................E...... 425 806-7253
 Bremerton *(G-1986)*
Parr Lumber Company ....G...... 509 543-7594
 Sunnyside *(G-13137)*
Parr Lumber Company ....G...... 360 750-1470
 Vancouver *(G-14480)*
Peninsula Truss Co..............................G...... 360 297-6026
 Kingston *(G-5261)*
Roof Truss Supply Inc..........................C...... 425 481-0900
 Woodinville *(G-15351)*
Timberline Truss and Sup Inc................F...... 509 226-0100
 Newman Lake *(G-7052)*
Tru-Truss Inc ....E...... 360 491-8024
 Lacey *(G-5597)*
Truss Co..G...... 509 547-2436
 Pasco *(G-7644)*
Truss Company and Bldg Sup Inc.........G...... 509 928-0550
 Spokane Valley *(G-12915)*
Truss Company and Bldg Sup Inc.........D...... 253 863-5555
 Sumner *(G-13107)*
Truss Components of Washington........E...... 360 753-0057
 Tumwater *(G-13900)*
Truss Components of Washington........E...... 360 753-0057
 Tumwater *(G-13901)*
Tvan Inc..D...... 503 285-2615
 Vancouver *(G-14651)*

TRUST MANAGEMENT SVCS: Charitable

First Millennium Bank............................G...... 360 797-5108
 Sequim *(G-11634)*

TUBE & TUBING FABRICATORS

Arrow Manufacturing Inc.......................G...... 253 236-4088
 Auburn *(G-378)*
Off Road Addiction LLC ....G...... 509 999-7824
 Valleyford *(G-13999)*
Stans Headers Inc..................................F...... 253 854-5310
 Auburn *(G-571)*
Triad Products Corporation ....G...... 425 514-8363
 Everett *(G-3636)*

TUBES: Generator, Electron Beam, Beta Ray

Tactical Fabs Inc ....E...... 360 723-5360
 Battle Ground *(G-742)*
Tfi Telemark...D...... 360 723-5360
 Battle Ground *(G-745)*

TUBES: Paper

Caraustar Industrial and Con................D...... 253 627-1197
 Tacoma *(G-13221)*
Nelson-Ball Paper Products..................C...... 360 423-3420
 Longview *(G-5933)*
Olde English Crackers Inc ....G...... 360 715-2972
 Bellingham *(G-1478)*

TUBES: Steel & Iron

Western Sttes Stl Fbrction Inc..............E...... 509 489-8046
 Spokane *(G-12588)*

TUBES: Vacuum

World Tube Company ....G...... 253 756-6489
 Tacoma *(G-13602)*

TUBES: Wrought, Welded Or Lock Joint

Weld-Rite Mfg LLC.................................G...... 509 927-9353
 Spokane Valley *(G-12933)*
Western Pneumatic Tube Co LLC ....E...... 425 822-8271
 Kirkland *(G-5494)*

TUBING: Flexible, Metallic

Lamiglas Inc ....E...... 360 225-9436
 Woodland *(G-15444)*

TUBING: Glass

Area 253 Glassblowing..........................G...... 253 779-0101
 Tacoma *(G-13179)*
Mary Jane Glass Productions...............G...... 360 844-5914
 Washougal *(G-14965)*

TUBING: Plastic

Hancor Inc..E...... 360 943-3313
 Olympia *(G-7302)*

Obcon Inc ....G...... 253 931-0455
 Auburn *(G-516)*
R & R Plastics...G...... 360 694-9573
 Vancouver *(G-14524)*

TUGBOAT SVCS

Western Towboat Company ....C...... 206 789-9000
 Seattle *(G-11456)*

TURBINES & TURBINE GENERATOR SET UNITS, COMPLETE

Supercritical Technologies ....G...... 518 225-3275
 Bremerton *(G-2005)*

TURBINES & TURBINE GENERATOR SETS

Airclean Technologies Inc.....................F...... 206 860-4930
 Seattle *(G-9360)*
Dresser-Rand Company ....F...... 206 762-7660
 Seattle *(G-9855)*
General Electric Company ....G...... 253 351-2200
 Auburn *(G-448)*
Hej LLC ....F...... 425 652-9183
 Seattle *(G-10161)*
Hydrobee Spc...G...... 206 491-0945
 Seattle *(G-10197)*
Opi Wind Technologies Inc ....G...... 206 999-5373
 Seattle *(G-10706)*
Siemens Gmesa Rnwble Enrgy Inc......G...... 509 896-5246
 Roosevelt *(G-9153)*
Teladaq LLC...G...... 661 373-1168
 Everson *(G-3691)*
Windward Ways II LLC..........................G...... 206 364-5236
 Seattle *(G-11483)*

TURBINES & TURBINE GENERATOR SETS & PARTS

Energy Northwest ....G...... 509 585-3677
 Kennewick *(G-4661)*

TURBINES: Hydraulic, Complete

Vestas-American Wind Tech Inc...........F...... 509 382-1800
 Dayton *(G-2889)*

TWINE

Biotwine Manufacturing Company.......E...... 509 865-3340
 Toppenish *(G-13663)*
Fish & Fly Investors...............................G...... 509 865-3340
 Toppenish *(G-13668)*

TYPESETTING SVC

AAA Printing & Graphics Inc ....F...... 425 454-0156
 Bellevue *(G-778)*
Advertising Services Intl LLC...............G...... 206 623-6963
 Seattle *(G-9356)*
Catholic Printery Inc.............................E...... 206 767-0660
 Seattle *(G-9648)*
ESP Printing Inc....................................E...... 425 251-6240
 Seattle *(G-9940)*
Faithlife Corporation.............................C...... 360 685-2300
 Bellingham *(G-1342)*
Fedex Office & Print Svcs Inc...............E...... 206 546-7600
 Shoreline *(G-11771)*
Foster Press ....G...... 425 334-9317
 Everett *(G-3484)*
Graphic Advertising Svcs Inc ....F...... 425 688-9980
 Richland *(G-9003)*
Harold Tymer Co Inc ....F...... 360 573-6053
 Vancouver *(G-14284)*
Hazelwood Farm LLC ....F...... 425 454-5165
 Redmond *(G-8489)*
L G Artworks Inc....................................G...... 425 355-9143
 Everett *(G-3533)*
Marshall Marketing Group Inc.............E...... 253 473-0765
 Tacoma *(G-13400)*
Olympic Graphic Arts Inc.....................G...... 360 374-6020
 Forks *(G-4013)*
Pacific Rim Printing Inc........................G...... 360 676-4606
 Bellingham *(G-1487)*
Plese Printing & Marketing ....F...... 509 534-2355
 Spokane *(G-12448)*
Prestige Copy and Print ....G...... 206 365-5770
 Seattle *(G-10857)*
Prime West of Washington Inc ....E...... 360 424-5783
 Kent *(G-5081)*

Print Services Northwest Inc................G...... 206 763-9230
 Seattle *(G-10860)*
Printgraphics Inc...................................E...... 503 641-8811
 Vancouver *(G-14508)*
Schilling Graphics.................................G...... 253 572-8171
 Tacoma *(G-13507)*
Sudden Printing Inc..............................E...... 206 243-4444
 Seattle *(G-11211)*
Typesetter Corporation.........................F...... 425 455-3055
 Mercer Island *(G-6488)*
V O Printers Inc.....................................G...... 360 577-0038
 Longview *(G-5962)*
Van Quill Larry R...................................G...... 360 736-1776
 Centralia *(G-2441)*
Washington Media Services Inc..........G...... 360 754-4543
 Olympia *(G-7421)*
Wholesale Printers Inc ....E...... 360 687-5500
 Battle Ground *(G-753)*
William Reed & Associates...................G...... 509 534-4727
 Spokane Valley *(G-12938)*

TYPESETTING SVC: Computer

Rapid Print Inc.......................................G...... 360 695-6400
 Vancouver *(G-14532)*
Soulier Southbay LLC ....G...... 360 459-3015
 Lacey *(G-5589)*

TYPESETTING SVC: Linotype Composition, For Printing Trade

Mary Fleming ....G...... 206 246-4871
 Tukwila *(G-13768)*

TYPOGRAPHY

Integrated Composition Systems..........G...... 509 624-5064
 Spokane *(G-12318)*

ULTRASONIC EQPT: Cleaning, Exc Med & Dental

Evelo Inc...F...... 877 991-7272
 Seattle *(G-9945)*

UMBRELLAS & CANES

Parasol Enterprises Inc.........................G...... 360 733-5579
 Bellingham *(G-1490)*

UNDERCOATINGS: Paint

Zirconia Inc..G...... 206 219-9236
 Tukwila *(G-13839)*

UNIFORM STORES

Ideal Commercial Uniforms ....G...... 360 876-1767
 Port Orchard *(G-7814)*
JS Uniform...G...... 509 467-8416
 Spokane *(G-12344)*

UNISEX HAIR SALONS

Stacya Silverman & Associates............G...... 206 270-9465
 Seattle *(G-11177)*

UNIVERSITY

Eastern Washington University............F...... 509 359-6047
 Cheney *(G-2584)*
University of Washington.....................C...... 206 543-5680
 Seattle *(G-11379)*
University of Washington.....................B...... 206 543-2565
 Seattle *(G-11380)*
University of Washington.....................E...... 206 543-4050
 Seattle *(G-11383)*
Washington State University ....F...... 509 335-2947
 Pullman *(G-8111)*
Washington State University ....G...... 509 372-7400
 Richland *(G-9052)*
Washington State University ....C...... 509 335-4573
 Pullman *(G-8114)*
Washington State University ....D...... 509 335-3518
 Pullman *(G-8112)*

UPHOLSTERY MATERIALS, BROADWOVEN

Breezy Upholstery & Canvas.................G...... 206 545-8538
 Seattle *(G-9582)*
K & L Unlimited.....................................G...... 509 965-6451
 Yakima *(G-15604)*
Squalicum Marine Inc...........................G...... 360 733-4353
 Bellingham *(G-1554)*

UPHOLSTERY WORK SVCS
Canvas Man ....G....... 360 293-2812
  Anacortes *(G-108)*
Design Craft Upholstery Inc ....G....... 425 775-7620
  Lynnwood *(G-6107)*

URANIUM ORE MINING, NEC
Silver King Mining & Milling ....G....... 509 445-1406
  Cusick *(G-2852)*

UREA
Micro Ag Inc ....G....... 509 397-4278
  Steptoe *(G-13007)*

URNS: Cut Stone
Savon Caskets and Urns ....G....... 206 390-3797
  Renton *(G-8904)*

USED BOOK STORES
Globe ....G....... 206 527-2480
  Seattle *(G-10086)*

USED CAR DEALERS
Harris-Ford Inc ....C....... 425 678-0391
  Lynnwood *(G-6132)*
Longview Auto Wrecking ....G....... 360 423-9327
  Longview *(G-5929)*

USED MERCHANDISE STORES
Bl Best Inc ....G....... 509 534-0237
  Spokane *(G-12150)*
Rag Man LLC ....G....... 206 653-7125
  Kent *(G-5096)*

USED MERCHANDISE STORES: Computers & Access
Dannys Electronics Inc ....G....... 253 314-5056
  Tacoma *(G-13253)*

UTENSILS: Cast Aluminum, Cooking Or Kitchen
Progressive International Corp ....D....... 253 850-6111
  Kent *(G-5085)*

UTILITY TRAILER DEALERS
Featherlite Trailers ....G....... 425 334-4045
  Snohomish *(G-11909)*
Nor E First Response Inc ....G....... 360 738-6467
  Bellingham *(G-1461)*
Top Notch Trailer Mfg ....F....... 360 273-0468
  Rochester *(G-9141)*
Tuff Trailer Inc ....G....... 360 398-0300
  Ferndale *(G-3920)*

VACUUM CLEANERS: Household
Cleanmaster ....C....... 425 775-7272
  Mukilteo *(G-6903)*
Dyson Inc ....G....... 425 968-2456
  Kirkland *(G-5327)*
Hydramaster ....G....... 425 775-7276
  Lynnwood *(G-6136)*
Whirlpool Corporation ....E....... 253 875-7100
  Spanaway *(G-12081)*

VACUUM CLEANERS: Indl Type
Ausclean Technology Inc ....G....... 360 563-9244
  Kirkland *(G-5285)*
Harolds Power Vac Inc ....G....... 509 529-2088
  Walla Walla *(G-14820)*

VALUE-ADDED RESELLERS: Computer Systems
Armstrong & Associates LLC ....G....... 253 548-6148
  Kennewick *(G-4619)*
Enhanced Software Products Inc ....E....... 509 534-1514
  Spokane Valley *(G-12693)*
Nexus Life Cycle MGT LLC ....G....... 541 400-0765
  Stevenson *(G-13016)*
Pacific Ally LLC ....G....... 360 760-4266
  La Center *(G-5511)*

VALVES
4 Valves LLC ....G....... 360 387-2272
  Camano Island *(G-2205)*
Crown Valve & Fitting LLC ....G....... 360 225-0888
  Woodland *(G-15426)*
Mechpro Inc ....G....... 206 445-5230
  Auburn *(G-496)*
Skoflo Industries Inc ....D....... 425 485-7816
  Woodinville *(G-15365)*
Texas Avenue Associates ....E....... 425 889-9642
  Bellevue *(G-1184)*
Valve Adjusters Co Intl ....G....... 425 322-4241
  Everett *(G-3645)*

VALVES & PIPE FITTINGS
Accor Technology Inc ....E....... 509 662-0608
  East Wenatchee *(G-3006)*
Bridgestone Hosepower LLC ....E....... 206 767-4670
  Seattle *(G-9585)*
Ferguson ....G....... 206 767-7700
  Auburn *(G-440)*
Go Planit LLC ....G....... 206 227-0660
  Mattawa *(G-6407)*
Idex Health & Science LLC ....C....... 360 679-2528
  Oak Harbor *(G-7153)*
Instrument & Valve Services Co ....G....... 360 366-3645
  Ferndale *(G-3858)*
Romac Industries Inc ....D....... 425 951-6200
  Sultan *(G-13034)*
Specified Fittings LLC ....G....... 360 398-7700
  Bellingham *(G-1550)*

VALVES: Aerosol, Metal
Evergreen Mch & Fabrication ....F....... 509 249-1141
  Yakima *(G-15565)*

VALVES: Aircraft
Farwest Aircraft Inc ....E....... 253 568-1707
  Edgewood *(G-3078)*

VALVES: Aircraft, Control, Hydraulic & Pneumatic
Select Fluid Power USA Inc ....G....... 604 343-1111
  Tukwila *(G-13816)*

VALVES: Aircraft, Hydraulic
Northwest Dynamics Inc ....G....... 360 253-3656
  Vancouver *(G-14434)*

VALVES: Control, Automatic
Tri-TEC Manufacturing LLC ....E....... 425 251-8777
  Kent *(G-5190)*

VALVES: Fire Hydrant
Taurman Distributing & Mfg ....G....... 360 330-5886
  Centralia *(G-2437)*

VALVES: Fluid Power, Control, Hydraulic & pneumatic
Hd International Corp ....G....... 503 997-9325
  Vancouver *(G-14290)*

VALVES: Gas Cylinder, Compressed
Joyson Safety Systems ....C....... 509 762-5549
  Moses Lake *(G-6718)*

VALVES: Indl
Accor Technology Inc ....E....... 509 662-0608
  Wenatchee *(G-15007)*
B2r Partners Inc ....E....... 360 225-1230
  Woodland *(G-15419)*
Centurion Process LLC ....G....... 509 759-3001
  Selah *(G-11584)*
Fabricast Valve LLC ....F....... 360 425-0306
  Longview *(G-5910)*
Flow Control Industries Inc ....E....... 425 483-1297
  Woodinville *(G-15243)*
Henry Pratt Company LLC ....G....... 360 225-1230
  Woodland *(G-15440)*
Hilton Acquisition Company LLC ....F....... 425 883-7000
  Redmond *(G-8494)*
Industrial Pipe and Valve ....G....... 360 314-6492
  Vancouver *(G-14313)*
Kilomters To Miles Speedo Exch ....G....... 253 872-3839
  Kent *(G-4976)*
Michael Chapman ....G....... 425 881-0907
  Redmond *(G-8556)*

VALVES: Plumbing & Heating
Accor Technology Inc ....E....... 509 662-0608
  Wenatchee *(G-15007)*

VALVES: Regulating & Control, Automatic
Pegler Automation Inc ....G....... 503 329-5377
  Vancouver *(G-14483)*
Total Home Control ....G....... 509 628-1673
  Richland *(G-9046)*

VALVES: Water Works
Romac Industries Inc ....D....... 425 951-6200
  Sultan *(G-13034)*

VARIETY STORE MERCHANDISE, WHOLESALE
Safs Inc ....G....... 253 301-0615
  Tacoma *(G-13506)*

VARIETY STORES
Hope Chest Crafts ....G....... 509 865-5666
  Toppenish *(G-13670)*
Skyhawk Press LLC ....G....... 360 598-2211
  Poulsbo *(G-8000)*

VASES & URNS: Gypsum & Papier-Mache
Dugger and Associates Inc ....G....... 425 785-6940
  McCleary *(G-6415)*

VASES: Pottery
Alex Daisley ....G....... 206 623-5555
  Seattle *(G-9373)*

VAULTS & SAFES WHOLESALERS
Pell Industrial LLC ....G....... 425 222-9672
  Auburn *(G-530)*

VEHICLES: All Terrain
Blade Cheverlot Rv ....G....... 360 982-2370
  Mount Vernon *(G-6781)*
English Racing ....G....... 360 210-7484
  Camas *(G-2249)*

VEHICLES: Recreational
Alas Rv ....G....... 360 676-1515
  Bellingham *(G-1241)*
Half Moon Bay Bar & Grill ....E....... 360 268-9166
  Westport *(G-15105)*
KMD Invested LLC ....G....... 425 741-9600
  Everett *(G-3531)*
Road-Iq LLC ....F....... 360 733-4151
  Bellingham *(G-1518)*
Roadmaster Inc ....G....... 360 896-0407
  Vancouver *(G-14555)*
Rvs Express LLC ....G....... 253 249-7043
  Auburn *(G-551)*
Skandia Northwest Mfg ....G....... 360 599-2681
  Deming *(G-2923)*
TTI Inc ....G....... 509 998-9456
  Spokane *(G-12572)*

VENDING MACHINES & PARTS
B and P Enterprises ....G....... 509 545-9125
  Burbank *(G-2082)*
Cardlock Vending Inc ....G....... 888 487-5040
  Bothell *(G-1835)*
Cinevend Inc ....G....... 206 388-3784
  Seattle *(G-9684)*
Glacier Water Services Inc ....G....... 360 413-7272
  Lacey *(G-5553)*
K&M Business Systems Inc ....G....... 425 557-7789
  Sammamish *(G-9224)*

VENETIAN BLINDS & SHADES
All Pro Blind Cleaning Repair ....G....... 253 804-9497
  Auburn *(G-371)*
Blue Home Thermal Imaging LLC ....G....... 360 638-0838
  Kingston *(G-5248)*

VENTILATING EQPT: Metal
North Industries Inc .... G 206 940-0842
 Seattle *(G-10624)*

VENTURE CAPITAL COMPANIES
Nova Fisheries Inc .... G 206 781-2000
 Seattle *(G-10658)*
Venspark Inc .... G 206 588-2756
 Seattle *(G-11410)*

VETERANS AFFAIRS ADMINISTRATION SVCS
Transportation Wash State Dept .... G 360 705-7428
 Olympia *(G-7413)*

VETERINARY PHARMACEUTICAL PREPARATIONS
Alcide Corporation .... E 425 882-2555
 Redmond *(G-8377)*
Aquatic Life Sciences Inc .... F 800 283-5292
 Ferndale *(G-3816)*
Cardinal Associates Inc .... E 360 693-1883
 Vancouver *(G-14098)*
Stason Animal Health Inc .... G 360 200-5300
 Vancouver *(G-14609)*
Western Chemical Incorporated .... F 360 384-5898
 Ferndale *(G-3923)*

VIBRATORS, ELECTRIC: Beauty & Barber Shop
Vibratrim LLC .... G 253 238-0675
 Gig Harbor *(G-4171)*

VIDEO & AUDIO EQPT, WHOLESALE
Avitech International Corp .... F 425 885-3863
 Redmond *(G-8395)*
Fusion9 Design LLC .... G 360 831-0899
 Camano Island *(G-2214)*
Intermedianet Inc .... F 425 451-3393
 Bellevue *(G-960)*

VIDEO EQPT
PC Networks Inc .... G 360 362-9684
 Silverdale *(G-11853)*

VIDEO PRODUCTION SVCS
Filmateria Studios Inc .... G 206 938-6791
 Seattle *(G-9992)*
Pattern Integrity LLC .... G 503 752-6018
 Camas *(G-2273)*
Soundings of The Planet Inc .... G 360 738-9368
 Bellingham *(G-1547)*

VIDEO TAPE WHOLESALERS, RECORDED
Shoezandmorecom LLC .... F 216 544-1745
 Renton *(G-8911)*

VIDEO TRIGGERS EXC REMOTE CONTROL TV DEVICES
Evs Manufacturing Inc .... G 360 863-6413
 Monroe *(G-6570)*

VINYL RESINS, NEC
Bioguard Research & Dev .... G 509 628-0170
 Kennewick *(G-4631)*

VISUAL COMMUNICATIONS SYSTEMS
Orca Information Comm Svs .... G 360 588-1633
 Anacortes *(G-158)*

VISUAL EFFECTS PRODUCTION SVCS
Lightspeed Design Inc .... G 425 637-2818
 Bellevue *(G-983)*

VITAMINS: Natural Or Synthetic, Uncompounded, Bulk
Avid Health Inc .... G 360 737-6800
 Vancouver *(G-14048)*

Rmg Nutrition .... G 253 863-7017
 Sumner *(G-13096)*

VITAMINS: Pharmaceutical Preparations
Betsy Bells Natyural Solutions .... G 206 933-1889
 Seattle *(G-9518)*
Performance Packaging Inc .... E 360 737-9966
 Vancouver *(G-14484)*

VOCATIONAL COUNSELING
Bridgeways .... D 425 513-2989
 Everett *(G-3401)*

VOCATIONAL REHABILITATION AGENCY
Bridgeways .... D 425 513-2989
 Everett *(G-3401)*
Lighthouse For The Blind Inc .... B 206 322-4200
 Seattle *(G-10417)*
Nova Services .... E 509 928-1588
 Spokane Valley *(G-12810)*
Pioneer Human Services .... C 206 762-7737
 Seattle *(G-10810)*

VOCATIONAL TRAINING AGENCY
Northwest Center .... C 206 285-9140
 Seattle *(G-10639)*
Northwest Center .... E 425 355-1855
 Everett *(G-3557)*
Orion Industries .... C 253 661-7805
 Auburn *(G-521)*
Orion Industries .... C 425 355-1253
 Mukilteo *(G-6962)*

VOLCANIC ROCK: Crushed & Broken
Beaver Lake Quarry Inc .... G 360 856-5870
 Mount Vernon *(G-6778)*

WALLBOARD: Gypsum
Certainteed Gypsum Inc .... C 206 763-1441
 Seattle *(G-9657)*
Certainteed Gypsum Mfg Inc .... A 949 282-5300
 Seattle *(G-9658)*
Georgia-Pacific LLC .... D 253 627-2100
 Tacoma *(G-13307)*

WALLPAPER & WALL COVERINGS
S J W Studios Inc .... F 206 323-8020
 Seattle *(G-11001)*

WALLPAPER STORE
Sherwin-Williams Company .... G 425 643-8584
 Bellevue *(G-1129)*

WAREHOUSING & STORAGE FACILITIES, NEC
B and D Whirlies .... G 360 887-8471
 Ridgefield *(G-9064)*
K&M Storage .... G 253 862-3515
 Sumner *(G-13076)*

WAREHOUSING & STORAGE, REFRIGERATED: Cold Storage Or Refrig
Allan Bros Inc .... D 509 653-2625
 Naches *(G-6993)*
Dignon Co Inc .... G 206 448-6677
 Lake Forest Park *(G-5612)*
Factory Trawler Supply Inc .... G 206 285-6732
 Seattle *(G-9961)*
Pacific Sea Food Co Inc .... E 360 225-8553
 Woodland *(G-15456)*
R Plum Corporation .... F 509 328-2070
 Spokane *(G-12465)*
Seafreeze Limited Partnership .... D 206 767-7350
 Seattle *(G-11043)*
Trident Seafoods Corporation .... C 360 293-7701
 Anacortes *(G-179)*
Trout-Blue Chelan-Magi Inc .... E 509 689-2511
 Brewster *(G-2017)*

WAREHOUSING & STORAGE, REFRIGERATED: Frozen Or Refrig Goods
North Star Cold Storage Inc .... E 360 629-9591
 Stanwood *(G-12983)*
Twin City Foods Inc .... B 509 786-2700
 Prosser *(G-8071)*

WAREHOUSING & STORAGE: General
Critical Delivery Service LLC .... G 206 724-3653
 Bellevue *(G-868)*
Flexe Inc .... G 855 733-7788
 Seattle *(G-10005)*
George G Sharp Inc .... D 360 476-8896
 Bremerton *(G-1957)*
Gerris Dry Bunk .... G 509 782-2653
 Cashmere *(G-2320)*
Redondo Rv Storage & Service .... G 253 941-3662
 Kent *(G-5101)*
United States Bakery .... G 509 684-6976
 Colville *(G-2778)*

WAREHOUSING & STORAGE: General
Allstar Magnetics LLC .... E 360 693-0213
 Vancouver *(G-14022)*
Noel Corporation .... C 509 248-4545
 Yakima *(G-15630)*
Sea Pac Transport Services LLC .... E 206 763-0339
 Seattle *(G-11037)*

WAREHOUSING & STORAGE: Miniwarehouse
LSI Logistic Svc Solutions LLC .... F 253 872-8970
 Puyallup *(G-8180)*

WAREHOUSING & STORAGE: Refrigerated
Schenk Packing Co Inc .... E 360 336-2128
 Mount Vernon *(G-6834)*

WARM AIR HEAT & AC EQPT & SPLYS, WHOLESALE Fan, Heat & Vent
Nidec America Corporation .... G 360 666-2445
 Battle Ground *(G-724)*

WARM AIR HEATING & AC EQPT & SPLYS, WHOL: Dust Collecting
Woodstock International Inc .... E 360 734-3482
 Bellingham *(G-1596)*

WARM AIR HEATING & AC EQPT & SPLYS, WHOL: Elec Heating Eqpt
Ducoterra LLC .... G 360 788-4200
 Bellingham *(G-1327)*
Heatcon Inc .... D 206 575-0815
 Tukwila *(G-13745)*

WARM AIR HEATING & AC EQPT & SPLYS, WHOLESALE Air Filters
N R G Enterprises Inc .... D 425 556-3993
 Redmond *(G-8592)*

WARM AIR HEATING & AC EQPT & SPLYS, WHOLESALE Condensing
Phazr LLC .... G 509 329-8306
 Spokane *(G-12440)*

WARM AIR HEATING/AC EQPT/SPLYS, WHOL Warm Air Htg Eqpt/Splys
Pacific NW Reps LLC .... G 509 823-7008
 Yakima *(G-15640)*

WASHERS
Karcher North America Inc .... F 360 833-1600
 Camas *(G-2260)*
Marks Keg Washer .... G 503 806-4115
 Vancouver *(G-14397)*

WASHERS: Plastic
Mico Welding & Machining Inc .... G 509 467-5082
 Nine Mile Falls *(G-7079)*

WASTE CLEANING SVCS

Emerald Services Inc .... C 206 430-7795
Seattle (G-9913)

WATCH REPAIR SVCS

DOriginal Jewelers .... G 425 454-5559
Bellevue (G-880)
Kirk Dial of Seattle .... G 253 852-5125
Kent (G-4978)

WATCHCASES

Carlson Brothers Inc .... F 253 472-9232
Tacoma (G-13224)

WATCHES & PARTS, WHOLESALE

Astral Holdings Inc .... G 206 762-4800
Seattle (G-9447)

WATER HEATERS WHOLESALERS EXCEPT ELECTRIC

Torrid Marine LLC .... G 206 920-9002
Bainbridge Island (G-679)

WATER PURIFICATION EQPT: Household

Advanced Water Systems Inc .... G 520 575-6718
Snohomish (G-11871)
Ambient Water Corporation .... G 509 474-9451
Spokane Valley (G-12606)
Pure Drop .... G 425 351-9007
Seattle (G-10888)
Suez Wts Systems Usa Inc .... D 425 828-2400
Bellevue (G-1165)
Waterstation Technology LLC .... G 877 475-7717
Everett (G-3652)

WATER PURIFICATION PRDTS: Chlorination Tablets & Kits

Bayer Hlthcare Phrmcticals LLC .... B 862 404-3000
Seattle (G-9502)
Cascade Designs Inc .... G 206 505-9500
Seattle (G-9641)
Kindex Pharmaceuticals Inc .... G 206 922-2912
Seattle (G-10344)
Shilsholе Bioscience Inc .... G 206 459-8341
Sammamish (G-9247)
Strong Snax Inc .... G 360 953-3753
Ridgefield (G-9114)

WATER SOFTENER SVCS

Connelly Company Inc .... G 509 935-6755
Chewelah (G-2601)

WATER SUPPLY

Fobes District Water & Assn .... G 425 334-3311
Snohomish (G-11910)

WATER TREATMENT EQPT: Indl

Always Pure Water Treatment Sy .... G 253 631-0294
Kent (G-4774)
Basin Nation AG LLC .... G 509 289-9030
Quincy (G-8289)
Bingham Manufacturing Inc .... G 360 863-1170
Monroe (G-6554)
Capital Hope Innovations Inc .... G 360 480-9154
Bellevue (G-837)
Cascade Designs Inc .... G 206 505-9500
Seattle (G-9641)
Ch 2o Inc .... G 360 956-9772
Tumwater (G-13859)
City of Yakima .... G 509 575-6177
Yakima (G-15532)
Endicott Waste Water Treatment .... G 509 657-3407
Endicott (G-3265)
Filtrific Co LLC .... G 425 482-6777
Bellevue (G-910)
Healthier Living Products .... G 509 582-6346
Pasco (G-7589)
Hydroflow Usa LLC .... F 425 497-3900
Redmond (G-8503)
Maury Hill Farm Enterprises .... G 206 463-6193
Vashon (G-14733)
Oiltrap Environmental Pdts Inc .... F 360 943-6495
Olympia (G-7350)

Pace Solutions Inc .... G 604 520-6211
Bellingham (G-1483)
Pacific Fluid Solutions Inc .... G 425 432-6535
Maple Valley (G-6286)
US Water Services Inc .... G 360 695-1270
Vancouver (G-14658)
W Systems .... G 425 616-2512
Seattle (G-11432)
Welwater .... G 360 909-7970
Vancouver (G-14683)
Yakima Water Solutions LLC .... G 509 941-9607
Yakima (G-15720)

WATER: Distilled

Lachselian Distillery .... G 206 743-8070
Seattle (G-10370)

WATER: Mineral, Carbonated, Canned & Bottled, Etc

Talking Rain Beverage Company .... D 425 222-4900
Preston (G-8027)

WATER: Pasteurized & Mineral, Bottled & Canned

Vs Foods LLC .... G 425 279-8089
Bellevue (G-1221)

WATER: Pasteurized, Canned & Bottled, Etc

Connelly Company Inc .... G 509 935-6755
Chewelah (G-2601)
Essentia Water Inc .... E 425 402-9555
Bothell (G-1761)
Glacier Water Company LLC .... G 253 876-6500
Auburn (G-450)
Richardson Bottling Company .... E 253 535-6447
Puyallup (G-8237)

WATERPROOFING COMPOUNDS

Trondak Inc .... G 360 794-8250
Monroe (G-6634)

WAX REMOVERS

Lexys Nails & Spa .... G 360 352-5044
Tumwater (G-13883)

WEATHER RELATED SVCS

Clear Water Compliance LLC .... E 425 412-5700
Everett (G-3419)

WEATHER VANES

B and D Whirlies .... G 360 887-8471
Ridgefield (G-9064)

WEB SEARCH PORTALS: Internet

Hunt Hosted Solutions .... G 425 222-0098
Fall City (G-3702)

WEIGHING MACHINERY & APPARATUS

Avery Weigh-Tronix LLC .... G 800 903-8823
Auburn (G-385)
Lectro Tek Services Inc .... E 509 663-2891
Wenatchee (G-15043)
Pacific Northwest Scale Co .... G 425 259-4720
Snohomish (G-11960)
Rice Lake Weighing Systems Inc .... E 206 433-0199
Kent (G-5102)

WELDING & CUTTING APPARATUS & ACCESS, NEC

Salmon Creek Industries Inc .... G 360 921-5143
La Center (G-5515)
Watts Specialties LLC .... F 253 848-9288
Puyallup (G-8277)

WELDING EQPT

Lincoln Electric Company .... F 360 693-4712
Vancouver (G-14377)
Miller Electric Mfg Co .... C 253 212-5346
Puyallup (G-8194)
Oxarc Inc .... E 509 755-0651
Spokane (G-12425)

Reynold Grey McHining Svcs Inc .... G 360 385-1167
Port Townsend (G-7924)

WELDING EQPT & SPLYS WHOLESALERS

Air Products and Chemicals Inc .... G 253 845-4000
Puyallup (G-8119)
Airgas Usa LLC .... G 360 293-6171
Anacortes (G-97)
Norco Inc .... G 509 764-5032
Moses Lake (G-6731)
Norco Inc .... F 509 535-9808
Spokane Valley (G-12803)
Praxair Distribution Inc .... E 253 620-1620
Tacoma (G-13473)
Qualls Stud Welding Pdts Inc .... G 425 656-9787
Kent (G-5091)

WELDING EQPT & SPLYS: Arc Welders, Transformer-Rectifier

Airborne Ecs LLC .... F 319 538-1051
Port Angeles (G-7679)

WELDING EQPT & SPLYS: Electrodes

Anvil House LLC .... G 406 579-3042
Seattle (G-9407)

WELDING EQPT & SPLYS: Generators, Arc Welding, AC & DC

Risley Sons Wldg Fbrcation LLC .... G 509 427-2206
Carson (G-2306)

WELDING EQPT & SPLYS: Resistance, Electric

Old Iron Classics .... G 360 852-8854
Vancouver (G-14449)
Wilkerson Weld & Fbrcn Inc .... G 509 545-3181
Pasco (G-7654)

WELDING EQPT REPAIR SVCS

Broomflds Wldg Met Fabrication .... G 206 784-9267
Seattle (G-9589)

WELDING REPAIR SVC

A & B Machine & Hydraulics .... F 360 532-2580
Aberdeen (G-1)
A-1 Welding Inc .... F 360 671-9414
Bellingham (G-1237)
AA Welding Inc .... G 360 694-4066
Vancouver (G-14004)
Aalbu Brothers of Everett Inc .... G 425 252-9751
Everett (G-3356)
Above & Beyond Unlimited .... G 253 921-3535
Tacoma (G-13154)
Ace Iron Works .... G 206 903-6161
Redmond (G-8367)
Advance Welding Inc .... F 360 573-1311
Vancouver (G-14009)
Airport Welding & Muffler Inc .... G 360 568-7135
Snohomish (G-11872)
Ajs Welding .... G 253 333-2976
Auburn (G-367)
All Weather Mobile Welding .... G 509 422-3789
Okanogan (G-7194)
Allied Technical Services Corp .... F 206 763-3316
Seattle (G-9382)
Als Wldg Stl Fabrication Inc .... F 360 740-8020
Chehalis (G-2462)
Anvil Alloy .... G 509 891-5914
Spokane Valley (G-12620)
Applied Mfg & Engrg Tech Inc .... F 253 852-5378
Edmonds (G-3095)
Arlington Machine & Welding .... G 360 435-3300
Arlington (G-201)
Armour Mfg & Cnstr Inc .... G 253 984-1213
Tacoma (G-13180)
Assa Abloy AB .... G 253 872-8174
Kent (G-4793)
Auto Spring Service Inc .... G 253 839-3780
Kent (G-4799)
B & B Parrotts Welding Inc .... G 253 862-4955
Buckley (G-2048)
B G Bender Inc .... G 253 848-3742
Puyallup (G-8125)
B K Welding and Fabrication .... G 360 871-0490
Port Orchard (G-7791)

PRODUCT SECTION — WELDING REPAIR SVC

Barnes Welding Inc ..... G 509 745-8588
  Waterville *(G-15005)*
Bills Heli ARC Welding ..... G 509 489-6160
  Spokane *(G-12149)*
Bisson & Associates Inc ..... G 360 856-0434
  Sedro Woolley *(G-11532)*
Blue Star Welding LLC ..... F 360 398-7647
  Bellingham *(G-1279)*
Bobs Welding & Auto Repair ..... G 509 427-5094
  Carson *(G-2303)*
Brad S Welding ..... G 360 668-7135
  Snohomish *(G-11881)*
Bradys Specialties ..... G 253 572-3768
  Tacoma *(G-13209)*
Brite Light Welding Inc ..... E 253 875-6291
  Puyallup *(G-8133)*
Broomflds Wldg Met Fabrication ..... G 206 784-9267
  Seattle *(G-9589)*
Bywater Welding ..... G 360 794-4618
  Monroe *(G-6561)*
C & C Mobile Welding LLC ..... G 360 879-5623
  Graham *(G-4218)*
C & C Welding Inc ..... G 360 966-4772
  Everson *(G-3669)*
C & S Welding Inc ..... G 253 520-2095
  Kent *(G-4828)*
C&T Northwest Services ..... G 509 680-4890
  Colville *(G-2742)*
Cannon Engineering Solutions ..... G 360 840-6731
  Port Townsend *(G-7871)*
Classic Welding ..... G 509 469-8110
  Yakima *(G-15534)*
Cook Welding Services ..... G 425 513-1263
  Everett *(G-3426)*
Corbells Portable Welding ..... G 360 724-4700
  Burlington *(G-2147)*
Crescent Machine Works Inc ..... G 509 328-2820
  Spokane *(G-12208)*
Custom Welding ..... G 206 242-5047
  Burien *(G-2100)*
Custom Welding & Orna Ir LLC ..... G 509 947-8863
  Kennewick *(G-4651)*
Custom Welding Inc ..... G 509 535-0664
  Spokane Valley *(G-12673)*
D S Fabrication & Design Inc ..... G 360 210-7526
  Washougal *(G-14951)*
Daves Mobile Welding LLC ..... G 360 302-0069
  Port Townsend *(G-7877)*
Diversified Welding Works Inc ..... G 360 576-0929
  Vancouver *(G-14183)*
EDS Garage & Welding ..... G 253 845-8741
  Puyallup *(G-8149)*
Extreme Indus Coatings LLC ..... G 509 991-1773
  Airway Heights *(G-51)*
Fabrication Enterprises Inc ..... F 503 240-0878
  Vancouver *(G-14218)*
Fabrication Technologies LLC ..... G 360 293-3707
  Anacortes *(G-127)*
Fall City Welding Inc ..... G 425 222-5105
  Fall City *(G-3701)*
Farrenewelding ..... G 360 941-5571
  Mount Vernon *(G-6796)*
Farwest Operating LLC ..... D 509 453-1663
  Moxee *(G-6878)*
Fithian Wldg & Fabrication LLC ..... G 206 658-3732
  Monroe *(G-6573)*
Flying Wrench Svc ..... F 360 638-0044
  Kingston *(G-5251)*
Frys Welding Inc ..... G .....
  Auburn *(G-445)*
Fuhrers Machine LLC ..... G 360 533-5517
  Hoquiam *(G-4337)*
G E Welding ..... G 253 653-8869
  Algona *(G-68)*
Gem Welding & Fabrication ..... G 360 378-5818
  Friday Harbor *(G-4047)*
Glenns Welding and Mfg Inc ..... E 425 743-2226
  Lynnwood *(G-6131)*
Gorleys Precision Machine ..... F 360 423-4567
  Longview *(G-5912)*
Green River Welding ..... G 253 632-7551
  Ravensdale *(G-8337)*
Gundersons Custom Welding ..... G 360 794-6165
  Snohomish *(G-11917)*
Harbor Machine & Fabricating ..... F 360 533-1188
  Hoquiam *(G-4340)*
Harris Metal Fab & Welding ..... G 360 687-6273
  Battle Ground *(G-707)*
High Desert Maintenance Inc ..... G 509 531-8341
  Kennewick *(G-4670)*

Highlands Welding Repair Inc ..... G 206 283-0080
  Seattle *(G-10172)*
Industrial Iron Works ..... G 509 322-0072
  Okanogan *(G-7197)*
Industrial Welding Co Inc ..... F 509 598-2356
  Spokane *(G-12306)*
Integral Fabrications LLC ..... G 360 831-9353
  Lacey *(G-5560)*
Jack E Brossard ..... G 360 892-7538
  Brush Prairie *(G-2036)*
Jason Dunton ..... G 360 293-7256
  Anacortes *(G-137)*
JC Fabworks LLC ..... G 253 389-5842
  Graham *(G-4228)*
Jobsite Stud Welding Inc ..... G 425 656-9783
  Lake Stevens *(G-5652)*
Joe Constance ..... F 425 347-8920
  Everett *(G-3524)*
Kaisers Welding & Mfg ..... G 509 738-6855
  Kettle Falls *(G-5233)*
Knights Welding ..... G 509 412-1103
  Pasco *(G-7596)*
Larock Enterprises Inc ..... F 509 966-4542
  Union Gap *(G-13938)*
Lc Welding Fabrication LL ..... G 360 359-8853
  Shelton *(G-11708)*
Leo Welding Fabrication ..... G 425 379-5836
  Everett *(G-3536)*
Leos Welding & Gab LLC ..... G 425 343-6920
  Seattle *(G-10405)*
Lincoln Industrial Corp Inc ..... G 360 681-0584
  Sequim *(G-11646)*
Lorenz Welding ..... G 360 384-5258
  Ferndale *(G-3865)*
Lower Valley Machine Shop ..... F 509 882-3881
  Grandview *(G-4251)*
Macklin Welding ..... G 509 926-3597
  Spokane Valley *(G-12781)*
Magaway Fire LLC ..... G 253 394-3255
  Tacoma *(G-13394)*
Magic Metals Inc ..... C 509 453-1690
  Union Gap *(G-13942)*
Maintenance Welding Service ..... G 360 533-4318
  Hoquiam *(G-4348)*
Marine Welding ..... G 360 293-7256
  Anacortes *(G-145)*
Martin Fabrications ..... G 509 457-8309
  Union Gap *(G-13943)*
McVays Mobile Welding LLC ..... G 360 657-0360
  Marysville *(G-6358)*
Metal Tech Metalworks Inc ..... G 253 435-5885
  Puyallup *(G-8189)*
Metal Works Inc ..... G 509 782-8811
  Dryden *(G-2953)*
Metalfab Inc ..... E 509 967-2946
  West Richland *(G-15098)*
Methow Valley Industrial LLC ..... G 509 997-7777
  Twisp *(G-13914)*
Michaels Touch ..... G 509 346-9478
  Royal City *(G-9172)*
Mikes Custom Welding ..... G 360 754-3719
  Tumwater *(G-13887)*
Millers Welding ..... G 360 435-7832
  Arlington *(G-280)*
Ne Welding and Fabrication ..... G 509 549-3982
  Colfax *(G-2718)*
Norco Inc ..... F 509 535-9808
  Spokane Valley *(G-12803)*
North Pacific Crane Fab Hyd ..... G 509 427-4530
  Carson *(G-2305)*
North Winds Welding & Met ..... G 360 379-0487
  Port Townsend *(G-7900)*
Northstar Attachments LLC ..... G 509 452-1651
  Yakima *(G-15632)*
Northwest Welding Academy LLC ..... G 325 574-3212
  Oak Harbor *(G-7160)*
Northwest Wldg Fabrication Inc ..... G 360 338-0923
  Lacey *(G-5568)*
Omega Industries Inc ..... E 360 574-9086
  Vancouver *(G-14450)*
One Time Welding ..... G 360 452-8532
  Port Angeles *(G-7731)*
Osw Equipment & Repair LLC ..... D 425 483-9863
  Snohomish *(G-11959)*
Oszman Service Inc ..... G 360 532-4552
  Hoquiam *(G-4351)*
Pats Welding Service ..... G 360 963-2370
  Sekiu *(G-11583)*
Pearls MBL Wldg & Fabrication ..... G 360 897-9288
  Buckley *(G-2067)*

Pioneer Metal Works Inc ..... G 509 787-4425
  Quincy *(G-8306)*
Plastic Sales & Service Inc ..... F 206 524-8312
  Lynnwood *(G-6181)*
Precise Machining Inc ..... G 360 629-0420
  Stanwood *(G-12985)*
Precision Machine & Tool Inc ..... G 425 745-6229
  Lynnwood *(G-6184)*
Precision Welder and Eng Repr ..... G 206 382-6227
  Seattle *(G-10854)*
Precision Welding ..... G 425 271-7490
  Renton *(G-8884)*
Precision Welding & Boat RES ..... G 360 607-3546
  Vancouver *(G-14503)*
Qualls Stud Welding Pdts Inc ..... G 425 656-9787
  Kent *(G-5091)*
Ranier Welding & Fabrication ..... G 360 829-0445
  Buckley *(G-2068)*
Rathbun Iron Works Inc ..... G 509 865-3717
  Toppenish *(G-13671)*
Rdc Enterprises LLC ..... G 360 265-0723
  Port Orchard *(G-7845)*
Ready Weld ..... F 425 391-4211
  Issaquah *(G-4464)*
Red Dog Fabrication LLC ..... F 360 892-3647
  Vancouver *(G-14537)*
Red Goat Fabrication Inc ..... G 509 240-2896
  Lowden *(G-5991)*
Ron & Leos Welding Svcs Inc ..... G 360 825-1221
  Enumclaw *(G-3318)*
Ronald Johnson ..... G 360 482-4982
  Elma *(G-3256)*
S & S Welding & Repair ..... G 509 657-3340
  Endicott *(G-3266)*
Saitek U S A Inc ..... G 425 672-8748
  Woodway *(G-15480)*
Salish LLC ..... G 206 375-7270
  Seattle *(G-11005)*
Scotts Sheet Metal ..... G 360 384-3827
  Ferndale *(G-3902)*
Seattle Welding Inc ..... G 206 763-0980
  Bonney Lake *(G-1738)*
Service Welding & Machine Co ..... G 206 325-1153
  Seattle *(G-11092)*
Sharps Welding & Muffler Ctr ..... G 509 452-2101
  Moxee *(G-6885)*
Shocker Metalshop LLC Welding ..... G 425 246-5825
  Carnation *(G-2298)*
Site Welding Services Inc ..... E 425 488-2156
  Woodinville *(G-15364)*
Snohomish Iron Works Inc ..... G 360 568-2811
  Snohomish *(G-11982)*
Stach Steel Supply ..... G 509 848-2772
  Harrah *(G-4321)*
Steel Fab Inc ..... E 425 743-9216
  Arlington *(G-333)*
Straight Line Industries Inc ..... G 360 366-0223
  Custer *(G-2861)*
Streich Bros Inc ..... E 253 383-1491
  Tacoma *(G-13527)*
Stromski Repair and Welding ..... G 360 452-1661
  Port Angeles *(G-7747)*
Sue A Priebe ..... G 360 398-7647
  Everson *(G-3690)*
Sunset Company LLC ..... G 425 351-0839
  Renton *(G-8923)*
Superior Industrial Services A ..... E 360 841-8542
  Woodland *(G-15467)*
Superior Sole Wldg Fabrication ..... G 360 653-2565
  Marysville *(G-6393)*
Superior Wldg Fabrication LLC ..... G 360 430-6766
  Kelso *(G-4553)*
Synergy Welding Inc ..... G 360 881-0204
  Kingston *(G-5265)*
Tinsley Welding Incorporated ..... G 509 786-4000
  Prosser *(G-8068)*
Tom Bretz ..... G 509 486-2251
  Tonasket *(G-13661)*
Torch & Regulator Repair Co ..... G 253 272-0467
  Tacoma *(G-13558)*
Torklift Central Wldg Kent Inc ..... G 253 854-1832
  Kent *(G-5183)*
Tramweld LLC ..... G 360 425-1240
  Kelso *(G-4556)*
Van Dam Welding Inc ..... G 360 761-7297
  Buckley *(G-2078)*
Warden Welding Inc ..... G 509 349-2478
  Warden *(G-14937)*
Warren Welding ..... G 425 761-1777
  Marysville *(G-6400)*

WELDING REPAIR SVC

Washington Iron Works Inc .... F 360 679-4868
  Oak Harbor *(G-7167)*
Welding By Craig .... G 253 307-3936
  Edgewood *(G-3092)*
Welding Shop Inc .... G 425 888-0911
  North Bend *(G-7131)*
Western Equipment Repr & Wldg ...... G 253 922-8351
  Fife *(G-3997)*
Westweld Inc .... G 253 862-1107
  Bonney Lake *(G-1743)*
Williamson Brock Wldg Mch Sp .... G 360 321-3227
  Langley *(G-5788)*
Ziglers Welding Shop Inc .... G 360 357-6077
  Olympia *(G-7432)*

WELDING TIPS: Heat Resistant, Metal

Samson Sports LLC .... F 360 833-2507
  Camas *(G-2280)*

WESTERN APPAREL STORES

Clarks All-Sports Inc .... E 509 684-5069
  Colville *(G-2743)*

WET CORN MILLING

Ingredion Incorporated .... G 509 375-1261
  Richland *(G-9009)*

WHEEL BALANCING EQPT: Automotive

Wheel .... G 206 956-0334
  Seattle *(G-11465)*

WHEELCHAIR LIFTS

Balance Construction Inc .... G 206 364-5555
  Lake Forest Park *(G-5605)*
Halls Drug Center Inc .... E 360 736-5000
  Centralia *(G-2405)*
Olympic Home Modification LLC .... G 253 858-9941
  Gig Harbor *(G-4139)*
Paul Parish Limited .... G 509 735-9820
  Kennewick *(G-4705)*
Thyssenkrupp Elevator Corp .... E 425 828-3110
  Kirkland *(G-5482)*

WHEELCHAIRS

AAA Precise Machine Inc .... G 509 375-3268
  Benton City *(G-1599)*
Allnight Wheelchairs .... G 425 774-6814
  Edmonds *(G-3093)*
Cascade Designs Inc .... E 206 505-9500
  Seattle *(G-9642)*
Evergreen Circuits LLC .... G 425 382-8412
  Duvall *(G-2986)*
Evolution Technologies USA .... G 360 392-8600
  Ferndale *(G-3839)*
Exomotion LLC .... G 206 763-0754
  Seattle *(G-9954)*
Seattle Wheelchair Rugby .... G 360 440-2498
  Seattle *(G-11083)*
Tisport LLC .... C 509 416-4245
  Pasco *(G-7639)*
Van Brynns Wheelchair .... G 360 687-8546
  La Center *(G-5518)*
Wheelchair Adl Solutions .... G 509 228-8293
  Liberty Lake *(G-5868)*
Wheelchairs and More LLC .... G 509 926-9357
  Spokane Valley *(G-12935)*
Wheelchairs For Nigeria .... G 206 932-6129
  Seattle *(G-11466)*

WHEELS

2 Wheel Dynoworks .... G 425 398-4335
  Woodinville *(G-15168)*
Auto Wheel Sales .... G 509 483-4251
  Spokane *(G-12129)*
Epic Wheel and Tire Inc .... E 253 691-1785
  Tacoma *(G-13280)*
Global Direct Components LLC .... F 253 661-1100
  Federal Way *(G-3741)*
Mad Fiber .... G 206 402-3925
  Seattle *(G-10463)*
Nails On Wheels .... G 253 839-1123
  Auburn *(G-503)*
Quality Used Tires and Wheels .... G 253 446-6002
  Puyallup *(G-8231)*
Wheels Northwest Inc .... G 206 909-6735
  Snohomish *(G-11999)*

WHEELS & PARTS

Kaper II Inc .... E 360 423-4404
  Kelso *(G-4533)*

WHEELS, GRINDING: Artificial

Blanchard Abrasives .... F 360 653-5273
  Marysville *(G-6317)*

WHEELS: Abrasive

Radiac Abrasives Inc .... D 360 659-6276
  Marysville *(G-6374)*
Radiac Abrasives Inc .... D 360 659-6201
  Marysville *(G-6376)*

WHEELS: Disc, Wheelbarrow, Stroller, Etc, Stamped Metal

Tipke Manufacturing Company .... E 509 534-5336
  Spokane *(G-12559)*

WHISTLES

Clean As A Whistle .... G 425 354-9719
  Kenmore *(G-4569)*
Pign Whistle .... G 206 782-6044
  Seattle *(G-10804)*
Whistle Pig LLC .... G 509 949-1584
  Yakima *(G-15707)*
Whistle Stop Studios LLC .... G 360 652-9728
  Stanwood *(G-12999)*
Whistle Workwear Shoreline LLC ..... G 206 364-2253
  Shoreline *(G-11822)*

WIND TUNNELS

Aeronautical Testing Service .... G 360 363-4276
  Arlington *(G-196)*

WINDMILLS: Electric Power Generation

White Creek Project LLC .... G 360 737-9692
  Vancouver *(G-14689)*

WINDOW & DOOR FRAMES

Atrium Door and Win Co of NW .... G 509 248-4462
  Union Gap *(G-13920)*
Atrium Windows and Door Wash ..... B 509 248-4462
  Union Gap *(G-13921)*
Certainteed Corporation .... B 253 850-9000
  Auburn *(G-404)*
Evergreen Construction Spc Inc .... F 253 288-8455
  Auburn *(G-433)*
Lakewood Holdings Inc .... G 253 284-4897
  Lakewood *(G-5734)*
Novak Windows .... G 253 332-4392
  Edgewood *(G-3088)*
Pacific Coast Marine LLC .... D 425 743-9550
  Lynnwood *(G-6176)*

WINDOW FRAMES & SASHES: Plastic

Milgard Manufacturing Inc .... A 253 922-4341
  Fife *(G-3972)*

WINDOW FRAMES, MOLDING & TRIM: Vinyl

Alpine Industries Inc .... B 425 481-7101
  Bothell *(G-1818)*
American Vinyl Industries Inc .... G 253 473-4731
  Fife *(G-3931)*
Certainteed Corporation .... B 253 850-9000
  Auburn *(G-404)*
Jeld-Wen Holding Inc .... C 509 535-1026
  Spokane *(G-12331)*
Milgard Manufacturing Inc .... C 253 922-6030
  Fife *(G-3971)*
Tal Holdings LLC .... G 509 682-1617
  Chelan *(G-2565)*

WINDOW FURNISHINGS WHOLESALERS

Evergreen Textiles .... G 253 852-6565
  Auburn *(G-434)*
Rodda Paint Co .... G 360 423-4990
  Longview *(G-5948)*
Rodda Paint Co .... G 360 738-6878
  Bellingham *(G-1519)*
Seattle Curtain Mfg Co .... E 206 324-0692
  Mill Creek *(G-6526)*

PRODUCT SECTION

WINDOW SASHES, WOOD

Island Sash & Door Inc .... F 360 331-7752
  Freeland *(G-4031)*

WINDOWS, LOUVER: Metal

Seaclear Industries Mfg Inc .... F 360 659-2700
  Marysville *(G-6383)*

WINDOWS: Frames, Wood

Quantum Windows and Doors Inc .... D 425 259-6650
  Everett *(G-3591)*

WINDOWS: Wood

Draped In Style LLC .... G 425 241-6227
  Snohomish *(G-11900)*

WINDSHIELD WIPER SYSTEMS

Glass Doctor of Wenatchee .... G 509 415-3400
  East Wenatchee *(G-3014)*

WINE & DISTILLED ALCOHOLIC BEVERAGES WHOLESALERS

Corus Estates & Vineyards LLC .... G 206 728-9063
  Seattle *(G-9744)*
Cougar Hills LLC .... F 509 529-5980
  Walla Walla *(G-14791)*
Kiona Vineyards LLC .... F 509 588-6716
  Benton City *(G-1618)*
Mark Anthony Brands Inc .... D 206 267-4444
  Seattle *(G-10486)*

WINE CELLARS, BONDED: Wine, Blended

Arbor Crest Wineries & Nursery ...... F 509 927-9463
  Spokane *(G-12115)*
Arbor Crest Wineries & Nursery ...... G 509 489-0588
  Spokane *(G-12116)*
Bainbrdge Island Wnery Vnyards ..... G 206 842-9463
  Bainbridge Island *(G-612)*
Cellar 55 Inc .... G 360 693-2700
  Vancouver *(G-14110)*
Claar Cellars LLC .... G 509 266-4449
  Pasco *(G-7560)*
DRM Holdings Inc .... G 509 338-4699
  Pullman *(G-8089)*
Horizons Edge Winery .... E 509 829-6401
  Zillah *(G-15755)*
La Toscana Bed Brakfast Winery ..... G 509 548-5448
  Cashmere *(G-2325)*
LDB Beverage Company .... F 509 651-0381
  Stevenson *(G-13015)*
Leaf Cellars LLC .... G 206 860-6888
  Seattle *(G-10393)*
Leonetti Cellar .... F 509 525-1670
  Walla Walla *(G-14837)*
Love That Red Winery .... G 425 463-9014
  Woodinville *(G-15296)*
McCrea Cellars Inc .... G 206 938-8643
  Seattle *(G-10506)*
Mpm Vintners LLC .... E 509 525-2469
  Walla Walla *(G-14847)*
Northwest Cellars LLC .... F 866 421-9463
  Kirkland *(G-5412)*
Oakwood Cellars .... G 509 588-1900
  Benton City *(G-1622)*
Papineau LLC .... G 509 301-9074
  Walla Walla *(G-14854)*
Pomum Cellars LLC .... G 206 362-9203
  Seattle *(G-10829)*
Rain Shadow Cellars LLC .... G 360 320-3115
  Coupeville *(G-2815)*
Rasa Vineyards LLC .... G 509 252-0900
  Walla Walla *(G-14858)*
Schafer Winery LLC .... F 425 985-7000
  Mercer Island *(G-6482)*
Skyline Spirits Wine Works Co .... G 509 967-0781
  West Richland *(G-15100)*
Soaring Suns Properties LLC .... G 509 346-9515
  Royal City *(G-9175)*
Springboard Winery LLC .... G 509 929-4247
  Ellensburg *(G-3227)*
Three Kees Cider LLC .... G 425 238-3470
  Snohomish *(G-11991)*
Tranche Cellars LLC .... G 509 526-3500
  Walla Walla *(G-14870)*
Wagging Tails Vineyard .... G 509 847-5287
  Chattaroy *(G-2454)*

PRODUCT SECTION

WOOD PRDTS: Box Shook

WIRE

Safran Elec & Pwr USA LLC ....D...... 425 407-6700
  Everett *(G-3603)*
Western Wire Works Inc ....E...... 253 964-6201
  Dupont *(G-2977)*

WIRE & CABLE: Aluminum

Mira Technology ....G...... 425 678-0183
  Lynnwood *(G-6164)*

WIRE & CABLE: Nonferrous, Aircraft

Safran Elec & Pwr USA LLC ....D...... 425 407-6700
  Everett *(G-3603)*
United States Dept of Navy ....C...... 360 396-2340
  Keyport *(G-5247)*

WIRE & CABLE: Nonferrous, Automotive, Exc Ignition Sets

Hydra Group LLC ....G...... 503 957-0975
  Washougal *(G-14959)*

WIRE & CABLE: Nonferrous, Building

Ecco Contractors Incorporated ....G...... 425 957-1735
  Bellevue *(G-891)*

WIRE & WIRE PRDTS

Cascade Wire Works LLC ....G...... 360 904-4412
  Vancouver *(G-14107)*
CMC Steel Fabricators Inc ....G...... 253 833-9060
  Auburn *(G-409)*
Columbia Rigging Corporation ....G...... 509 545-4657
  Pasco *(G-7564)*
Cowlitz River Rigging Inc ....F...... 360 425-6720
  Longview *(G-5903)*
Davis Wire Corporation ....F...... 253 872-8910
  Kent *(G-4871)*
Dungeness Gear Works Inc ....E...... 800 548-9743
  Arlington *(G-230)*
Iron Gate Shoppe ....G...... 360 791-3292
  Enumclaw *(G-3294)*
J K Fabrication Inc ....G...... 206 297-7400
  Seattle *(G-10270)*
J N W Inc ....E...... 509 489-9191
  Spokane *(G-12327)*
Majorwire Screen Media ....D...... 253 327-1550
  Fife *(G-3968)*
National Wirecraft Company Inc ....F...... 360 424-1129
  Mount Vernon *(G-6816)*
National Wirecraft Company Inc ....F...... 360 424-1129
  Mount Vernon *(G-6817)*
Neutek Inc ....G...... 206 660-0056
  Lynnwood *(G-6169)*
Quality Fence Builders Inc ....E...... 253 939-8533
  Auburn *(G-541)*
Silicon & Solar Mfg LLC ....F...... 360 703-0701
  Longview *(G-5953)*
Sound Spring Inc ....F...... 253 859-9499
  Kent *(G-5142)*
Sustain Outdoors Inc ....G...... 949 439-4899
  Bellevue *(G-1170)*

WIRE FABRIC: Welded Steel

McBee Metal Fabricators Inc ....G...... 425 486-1410
  Kenmore *(G-4591)*

WIRE MATERIALS: Copper

Aria Trading Inc ....G...... 360 525-0175
  Blaine *(G-1660)*

WIRE MATERIALS: Steel

American Lifting Products Inc ....G...... 253 572-8981
  Tacoma *(G-13168)*
Cablecraft Motion Controls LLC ....D...... 253 475-1080
  Tacoma *(G-13215)*
CMC Steel Fabricators Inc ....G...... 253 833-9060
  Auburn *(G-409)*
Contech Systems Inc ....G...... 360 332-1718
  Tacoma *(G-13240)*
ISS (west) Inc ....G...... 206 470-3754
  Seattle *(G-10261)*
Pacific Wire Group Inc ....F...... 253 249-0249
  Auburn *(G-525)*
Quality Fence Builders Inc ....E...... 253 939-8533
  Auburn *(G-541)*

Seattle Tarp Co Inc ....E...... 206 285-2819
  Seattle *(G-11080)*
Tethers Unlimited Inc ....G...... 425 486-0100
  Bothell *(G-1800)*

WIRE PRDTS: Steel & Iron

Maverick Metalworks LLC ....G...... 253 345-1590
  Spanaway *(G-12063)*

WIRE: Communication

Clear Rf LLC ....F...... 855 321-9527
  Spokane Valley *(G-12658)*

WIRE: Mesh

Twardus Iron & Wire Works Inc ....G...... 206 723-8234
  Seattle *(G-11349)*

WIRE: Nonferrous

Carlisle Interconnect Tech Inc ....G...... 425 656-5235
  Kent *(G-4837)*
Carlisle Interconnect Tech Inc ....B...... 425 291-3991
  Kent *(G-4838)*
Kemcor Inc ....E...... 425 488-7400
  Woodinville *(G-15276)*

WIRE: Steel, Insulated Or Armored

Post Tension Cables Inc ....G...... 425 745-1304
  Everett *(G-3579)*

WIRE: Wire, Ferrous Or Iron

Davis Wire Corporation ....F...... 253 872-8910
  Kent *(G-4871)*

WOMEN'S & CHILDREN'S CLOTHING WHOLESALERS, NEC

Certified Branching Habit ....G...... 206 286-9685
  Seattle *(G-9659)*
Chicago Title Insurance Co ....G...... 509 765-8820
  Moses Lake *(G-6693)*
Contract Sew & Repair Inc ....F...... 253 395-7910
  Kent *(G-4865)*
Kushco ....G...... 206 772-9333
  Seattle *(G-10363)*
Lil Squirtz ....G...... 360 521-9598
  Vancouver *(G-14376)*
Maurices Incorporated ....G...... 253 845-5577
  Puyallup *(G-8184)*

WOMEN'S & GIRLS' SPORTSWEAR WHOLESALERS

Bensussen Deutsch & Assoc LLC ....B...... 425 492-6111
  Woodinville *(G-15188)*
Northwest Designs Ink Inc ....F...... 425 454-0707
  Bellevue *(G-1035)*
Seattle Pacific Industries ....D...... 253 872-8822
  Kent *(G-5123)*
Tuff TS Connection Screen Prtg ....G...... 253 588-8897
  Lakewood *(G-5763)*

WOMEN'S CLOTHING STORES

Garage ....G...... 425 640-6021
  Lynnwood *(G-6126)*
Maurices Incorporated ....G...... 253 845-5577
  Puyallup *(G-8184)*
T Town Apparel ....G...... 253 471-2960
  Tacoma *(G-13539)*
Tik Tik Garment Manufacturing ....F...... 509 624-0806
  Spokane *(G-12557)*

WOMEN'S CLOTHING STORES: Ready-To-Wear

Guess Inc ....E...... 206 682-7005
  Seattle *(G-10131)*
Ideal Commercial Uniforms ....G...... 360 876-1767
  Port Orchard *(G-7814)*
Lady 12 LLC ....F...... 425 218-3080
  Redmond *(G-8528)*
Margaret OLeary Inc ....G...... 206 729-5834
  Seattle *(G-10476)*

WOMEN'S SPECIALTY CLOTHING STORES

Yazdi Corporation ....G...... 425 787-6328
  Seattle *(G-11509)*

WOMEN'S SPORTSWEAR STORES

Derek Andrew Inc ....F...... 425 453-9888
  Bellevue *(G-877)*
Northwest Designs Ink Inc ....F...... 425 454-0707
  Bellevue *(G-1035)*
Swivler Inc ....E...... 360 225-7774
  Woodland *(G-15468)*

WOOD & WOOD BY-PRDTS, WHOLESALE

Grizzly Firestarters North ....G...... 360 659-3948
  Marysville *(G-6341)*
Grizzly Firestarters North ....G...... 360 652-2100
  Mount Vernon *(G-6802)*

WOOD CHIPS, PRODUCED AT THE MILL

Allen Logging Co ....E...... 360 374-6000
  Port Angeles *(G-7683)*
Burke Gibson LLC ....E...... 253 735-4444
  Auburn *(G-398)*
Dapaul Inc ....E...... 360 943-9844
  Tumwater *(G-13869)*
Edman Company ....F...... 253 572-5306
  Tacoma *(G-13272)*
Hermann Bros Log & Cnstr Inc ....D...... 360 452-3341
  Port Angeles *(G-7709)*
Nippon Paper Inds USA Co Ltd ....G...... 360 457-4474
  Longview *(G-5936)*
North Mason Fiber Company ....G...... 360 275-0228
  Belfair *(G-769)*
NW Fibre LLC ....F...... 360 887-8418
  Morton *(G-6671)*
Simmons Densified Fuels Inc ....G...... 509 453-6008
  Naches *(G-7003)*
Sunland Bark and Topsoils Co ....G...... 360 293-7188
  Anacortes *(G-172)*

WOOD EXTRACT PRDTS

RR Products ....G...... 509 773-5227
  Goldendale *(G-4208)*

WOOD PRDTS

De Jong Sawdust & Shavings ....F...... 425 252-1566
  Lake Stevens *(G-5643)*
Fairwood Commerce Center LLP ....G...... 206 903-9200
  Issaquah *(G-4411)*
Greywood Manor LLC ....G...... 206 949-1362
  Seattle *(G-10124)*
Lee Frame Shoppe Inc ....G...... 509 624-2715
  Spokane *(G-12360)*
Little Buddies Shanties ....G...... 360 387-0678
  Camano Island *(G-2216)*
Many Endeavors Incorporated ....G...... 360 652-1854
  Arlington *(G-273)*
Matt Hammar Quality Woodcrafti ....G...... 360 904-9015
  Vancouver *(G-14403)*
Nation To Nation Premium ....G...... 360 731-0330
  Sequim *(G-11650)*
Redwood Subs LLC ....G...... 217 493-9499
  Olympia *(G-7382)*
Rwoodsii LLC ....G...... 206 491-9617
  Auburn *(G-552)*
Sackman Enterprises ....G...... 509 684-5547
  Colville *(G-2774)*

WOOD PRDTS: Applicators

OMAK Wood Products LLC ....E...... 360 432-5048
  OMAK *(G-7441)*

WOOD PRDTS: Barrels & Barrel Parts

Benchmark Barrels LLC ....G...... 360 652-2594
  Arlington *(G-212)*

WOOD PRDTS: Beekeeping Splys

Bees In Burbs ....G...... 425 432-0546
  Kent *(G-4811)*

WOOD PRDTS: Box Shook

Oroville Reman & Reload Inc ....E...... 509 476-2935
  Oroville *(G-7471)*

WOOD PRDTS: Door Trim

Mirror Finish Incorporated .... G 360 384-1710
　Ferndale *(G-3872)*

WOOD PRDTS: Engraved

Eleganza Designs Inc .... G 360 499-2710
　Lacey *(G-5549)*
Forest Concepts LLC .... G 253 333-9663
　Auburn *(G-441)*
Impressions In Wood LLC .... G 425 444-5324
　Snohomish *(G-11926)*
Innovative Manufacturing Inc .... G 360 966-7250
　Bellingham *(G-1379)*
Northwest Wood Products Inc .... G 509 738-6190
　Kettle Falls *(G-5239)*

WOOD PRDTS: Furniture Inlays, Veneers

Dale Butler S Furniture .... G 509 732-4381
　Colville *(G-2750)*

WOOD PRDTS: Jalousies, Glass, Wood Framed

Windorco Supply Inc .... G 206 784-9440
　Seattle *(G-11482)*

WOOD PRDTS: Ladders & Stepladders

One Step Ahead Inc .... G 425 487-1869
　Bothell *(G-1882)*

WOOD PRDTS: Laundry

Grette Custom Woodworking .... G 425 392-8584
　Issaquah *(G-4424)*
Hd Structures LLC .... G 425 327-3931
　Marysville *(G-6343)*
Prewitt Hardwood Floors Inc .... G 360 666-9663
　Brush Prairie *(G-2039)*
Rainier Woodworking Co .... F 253 272-5210
　Tacoma *(G-13491)*
Rawson Woodcraft Llc .... G 503 650-4383
　Vancouver *(G-14535)*

WOOD PRDTS: Logs Of Sawdust & Wood Particles, Pressed

Grizzly Firestarters North .... G 360 659-3948
　Marysville *(G-6341)*
Grizzly Firestarters North .... G 360 652-2100
　Mount Vernon *(G-6802)*

WOOD PRDTS: Mantels

Maizefield Company .... G 360 385-6789
　Port Townsend *(G-7896)*
Pcs Mill Work Inc .... E 425 820-5688
　Kirkland *(G-5431)*

WOOD PRDTS: Moldings, Unfinished & Prefinished

Custom Molding Co Inc .... F 360 830-0108
　Seabeck *(G-9263)*
Fine Woodworking .... G 425 486-3305
　Woodinville *(G-15242)*
Jeld-Wen Inc .... F 206 574-0986
　Tukwila *(G-13755)*
Sauder Mouldings Inc Ferndale .... C 360 384-4774
　Ferndale *(G-3898)*

WOOD PRDTS: Mulch Or Sawdust

Manke Lumber Company Inc .... B 253 572-6252
　Tacoma *(G-13397)*

WOOD PRDTS: Mulch, Wood & Bark

Everett Bark Supply Inc .... G 425 353-9024
　Everett *(G-3463)*
Valon Kone North America .... G 509 434-6436
　Spokane Valley *(G-12926)*

WOOD PRDTS: Novelties, Fiber

American Dream Homes & Cr .... G 360 863-9340
　Monroe *(G-6547)*
Silverfeather Creations .... G 425 771-9389
　Edmonds *(G-3156)*

WOOD PRDTS: Oars & Paddles

Ek Projects LLC .... F 360 757-2300
　Burlington *(G-2155)*

WOOD PRDTS: Outdoor, Structural

Bell Lumber & Pole Company .... G 360 445-5565
　Conway *(G-2796)*

WOOD PRDTS: Panel Work

Northwest Plywood Sales of Ore .... F 360 750-1561
　Vancouver *(G-14439)*

WOOD PRDTS: Poles

Oeser Company .... E 360 734-1480
　Bellingham *(G-1477)*

WOOD PRDTS: Policemen's Clubs

Washington Assn of Sheriffs .... E 360 438-6618
　Lacey *(G-5600)*

WOOD PRDTS: Reed, Rattan, Wicker & Willow ware, Exc Furnitr

Fuze Create LLC .... G 425 212-8807
　Seattle *(G-10043)*

WOOD PRDTS: Sawdust

Rainier Wood Recyclers Inc .... E 425 222-0008
　Fall City *(G-3707)*

WOOD PRDTS: Shoe & Boot Prdts

10-20 Services Inc .... G 253 503-6000
　Lakewood *(G-5692)*

WOOD PRDTS: Signboards

Donnies Peninsula Sign .... G 360 642-4512
　Ocean Park *(G-7180)*
Foley Sign Company Inc .... F 206 324-3040
　Seattle *(G-10011)*
Spectrum Sign Co Inc .... G 253 939-5500
　Auburn *(G-570)*
Vertical Visual Solutions .... G 425 361-1562
　Mountlake Terrace *(G-6873)*

WOOD PRDTS: Stoppers & Plugs

Liteair Aviation Products Inc .... G 360 299-6679
　Anacortes *(G-142)*

WOOD PRDTS: Survey Stakes

D & D Cedar Stake .... G 360 435-2254
　Arlington *(G-226)*
Dahlstrom Lumber Co Inc .... E 360 533-0448
　Hoquiam *(G-4331)*
Lanktree Land Surveying Inc .... F 253 653-6423
　Kent *(G-4988)*

WOOD PRDTS: Trophy Bases

Crown Recognition .... G 509 698-4446
　Selah *(G-11585)*
Dudleys Fine Engraving .... G 360 417-9415
　Port Angeles *(G-7699)*
Etchings Walla Walla .... G 509 301-3300
　Walla Walla *(G-14802)*
Every Occasion Engraving .... G 509 995-9848
　Spokane Valley *(G-12696)*
Military Tails .... G 253 229-2427
　Spanaway *(G-12065)*

WOOD PRDTS: Window Backs, Store Or Lunchroom, Prefabricated

Associated Materials LLC .... G 425 481-7101
　Fife *(G-3935)*

WOOD PRODUCTS: Reconstituted

Columbia Navigation Inc .... G 509 684-4335
　Kettle Falls *(G-5222)*
Eleganza Designs Inc .... G 360 499-2710
　Lacey *(G-5549)*
Glacier Mouldings Ltd .... F 360 629-5313
　Stanwood *(G-12975)*
Marine Lumber Service Inc .... F 206 767-4730
　Seattle *(G-10482)*

Windfall Lumber Inc

Windfall Lumber Inc .... E 360 352-2250
　Tumwater *(G-13906)*

WOOD TREATING: Bridges

McCain Timber & Bridge Inc .... G 360 520-6595
　Napavine *(G-7011)*

WOOD TREATING: Creosoting

John Gibb .... G 360 366-3500
　Bellingham *(G-1388)*
Workbench Productions LLC .... G 206 853-3742
　Seattle *(G-11495)*

WOOD TREATING: Flooring, Block

Panel Artz .... G 253 277-1040
　Kent *(G-5059)*

WOOD TREATING: Structural Lumber & Timber

A-1 Timber Consultants Inc .... F 360 748-8987
　Chehalis *(G-2457)*
Only Solutions Cabinet Install .... G 253 848-8358
　Puyallup *(G-8210)*
Pacific Western Timbers Inc .... F 360 674-2700
　Port Orchard *(G-7841)*
Stampede Forest Products Inc .... F 509 557-3014
　OMAK *(G-7444)*
Trueguard LLC .... G 360 835-8547
　Washougal *(G-14995)*
Virtual Timbers Inc .... G 509 935-4680
　Chewelah *(G-2609)*

WOOD TREATING: Wood Prdts, Creosoted

Conestoga Wood Spc Corp .... G 253 437-1320
　Kent *(G-4863)*

WOODWORK & TRIM: Exterior & Ornamental

CDI Custom Design Inc .... E 360 650-1150
　Bellingham *(G-1294)*
Shellback Ltd .... G 206 463-9054
　Vashon *(G-14742)*

WOODWORK & TRIM: Interior & Ornamental

Anderson Fine Woods .... G 425 422-2753
　Lake Stevens *(G-5631)*
Belina Interiors Inc .... D 253 474-0276
　Tacoma *(G-13193)*
Cams-Usa Inc .... F 253 639-3890
　Kent *(G-4835)*
Pacific Coast Showcase Inc .... C 253 445-9000
　Puyallup *(G-8216)*
Renaissance Fine Woodworking .... G 509 334-7008
　Pullman *(G-8105)*
Woodwork Specialties LLC .... G 360 687-5880
　Battle Ground *(G-754)*

WOODWORK: Carved & Turned

Aprils Indoor Garden Supplies .... G 360 537-6850
　Hoquiam *(G-4328)*
Chips & Del Carvings In Wood .... G 253 858-4751
　Gig Harbor *(G-4086)*
Creative Wood Sculptures .... G 360 825-6069
　Enumclaw *(G-3284)*
George Kenny School Cainsaw .... G 360 275-9570
　Allyn *(G-82)*
Vessels Archtctral Woodturning .... G 509 927-0721
　Spokane Valley *(G-12930)*
Wood Crafts By Pear Company .... G 360 532-6246
　Hoquiam *(G-4363)*

WOODWORK: Interior & Ornamental, NEC

Above and Beyond Cnstr LLC .... G 509 521-8081
　Kennewick *(G-4610)*
Barrys Wood Working .... G 253 312-1585
　University Place *(G-13961)*
Benchmark Woods .... G 360 732-0993
　Chimacum *(G-2611)*
Brian Friesen Fine Woodworking .... G 360 314-6427
　Vancouver *(G-14081)*
Direys .... G 425 788-2026
　Duvall *(G-2983)*
Frank J Madera .... G 253 858-7934
　Gig Harbor *(G-4103)*
Grozdi Inc .... G 253 820-0653
　Tacoma *(G-13327)*

PRODUCT SECTION

ZINC ORE MINING

Hogan Construction Inc .... G 206 290-5553
  Kent *(G-4944)*
Normandie Woodworks .... G 360 446-0352
  Rainier *(G-8319)*
Old School Woodcrafter .... G 509 493-4155
  White Salmon *(G-15126)*
Premier Woodworks LLC .... G 509 591-0839
  Kennewick *(G-4707)*
Red Tail Woodworks .... G 360 852-6883
  Ridgefield *(G-9106)*
Smith & Valley Gallery .... G 360 766-6230
  Bow *(G-1933)*

WOODWORK: Ornamental, Cornices, Mantels, Etc.

Camelot Treasures .... G 360 829-9774
  Buckley *(G-2050)*
Gazebo & Porchworks .... G 253 380-0918
  Puyallup *(G-8155)*
Mark E Padbury .... G 360 376-6200
  Eastsound *(G-3039)*

WOOL PULLING SVC

Belfor USA Group Inc .... E 206 632-0800
  Tukwila *(G-13696)*
Belfor USA Group Inc .... G 509 453-8551
  Yakima *(G-15518)*

WORD PROCESSING SVCS

Laser Writing .... G 253 686-6909
  Tacoma *(G-13383)*

WOVEN WIRE PRDTS, NEC

George Broom Sons Inc .... G 206 282-0800
  Seattle *(G-10064)*

WREATHS: Artificial

Christmas Forest .... E 360 245-3202
  Curtis *(G-2848)*
Unique Wreaths .... G 206 355-2103
  Renton *(G-8937)*
Wreathe Havoc .... G 206 979-6838
  Edmonds *(G-3163)*

WRITING FOR PUBLICATION SVCS

Math Perspectives .... G 360 715-2782
  Bellingham *(G-1426)*

X-RAY EQPT & TUBES

Cgm Imaging Services LLC .... G 509 995-6153
  Spokane *(G-12178)*
Dental X Ray Support Systems .... F 509 279-2061
  Spokane *(G-12224)*
General Electric Company .... C 425 557-3022
  Issaquah *(G-4419)*
Rigaku Americas Corporation .... G 206 780-8927
  Bainbridge Island *(G-666)*

YARN: Knitting, Spun

Emma Knits Inc .... G 509 999-8583
  Spokane *(G-12243)*
Pinchknitter .... G 360 939-0769
  Camano Island *(G-2221)*

YARN: Manmade & Synthetic Fiber, Twisting Or Winding

Evrnu Spc .... G 206 466-5269
  Seattle *(G-9950)*

YARN: Plastic Coated, Made From Purchased Yarn

Fiber Trends Inc .... G 509 884-8631
  East Wenatchee *(G-3013)*

YARNS & ROVING: Coir

Mid Mountain Materials Inc .... E 206 762-7600
  Seattle *(G-10539)*

YOGURT WHOLESALERS

Hain Refrigerated Foods Inc .... F 425 485-2476
  Mountlake Terrace *(G-6862)*
Joe Froyo LLC .... G 909 204-1301
  Tacoma *(G-13361)*

ZINC ORE MINING

Silver King Mining & Milling .... G 509 445-1406
  Cusick *(G-2852)*